THE STAFFORDSHIRE ENCYCLOPAEDIA

A secondary source index on the history of the old county of Stafford,
celebrating its curosities, peculiarities and legends

THE STAFFORDSHIRE ENCYCLOPAEDIA

A secondary source index on the history of the old county of Stafford, celebrating its curosities, peculiarities and legends

TIM COCKIN

Malthouse Press

Publisher's Note

Published by Malthouse Press.
Malthouse Press reserve all rights.
No part of this publication may be reproduced,
stored in a retriveval system,
or transmitted, in any form or by any
means electronic mechanical,
photocopying, recording or otherwise,
without prior permission of the publisher.

First published 2000
Second edition 2006

Printed and bound by
Lightning Source UK Ltd
6 Precedent Drive
Rooksley
Milton Keynes
MK13 8PR

Malthouse Press
Grange Cottage
Malthouse Lane, Barlaston
Stoke-on-Trent ST12 9AQ

Dedicated to

My Mother and Father

who have been so supportive in helping me see
this work to fruition

To elucidate Local History, in the manner in which it ought to be elucidated, is to rescue the worthy from oblivion; to delineate the changes of manners, and the progress of arts; to call back to the fancy, the pomp and splendour of ages that are gone; to restore the ruined castle; to repeople the deserted mansion; and bid, for a moment, the grave render back its inhabitants to the fond eye of regret.

(Censura Literaria. vol 1 p50).

Acknowledgements for the First Edition

I would like to thank especially David Horovitz, author of the History of Brewood (1988. 1992), for his enthusiasm and encouragement shortly after the book was first envisaged, and secondly Dominic Farr, Assistant Librarian at the William Salt Library from May 1995, for his patient, kind and resourceful assistance to me as a researcher in the Library. Further I would like to thank Thea Randall, Head of Staffs Archive Services and William Salt Librarian, Martin Phillips, Keele Information Services, Randle Knight, Dr Anne Andrews, Angus Dunphy and Garry Gatensbury for their additional help in trying to see the Encyclopedia published.

May I also thank John Abberley, Rev Stanley E Ablewhite, Philip C Adams, Ralph Adams, Sharon Aris (The Newsletter), David A Aston, Nancy Lady Bagot, Terry Bailey, Ron Balding, Sister Barbara (St Dominic's Convent, Stone), Alan Barrett, David Bell, JA Bennison. J Blamire-Brown, Thelma Brassington, Kenneth Bowe, Mamie Byrne, David Bywater, Fran Cartwright (Express & Star, Wolverhampton), Cathedral Galley, Lichfield, John Chatwin, Peter Cheeseman and New Victoria Theatre, H Claypole, Bevan Craddock, Olwyn Crane, Caroline Cross (Burton Daily Mail), Rev Robert CW Dampier, Beryl Daniels, Dr Alun Davies, Rev Peter Davies, Roy Davis, Martin Elkes, RF Elton, Michael Fisher, Lynda Fletcher (Uttoxeter Leisure & Development Co. Ltd), Debbie Ford, Dudley Fowkes, Carl Franklin (Walsall Museum), Mrs DC Fry, Geoff Gamble, Ivan Gaskin, Mr & Mrs JG Gatensbury, Derek Godfrey, Lt Col DJK German, Major Edward Green, Michael Greenslade, Mike Griffin, Dave Harper, Helen at News Team, Birmingham, Rudi Herbert, David & Margaret Hewitt, Stan Hill, Lynda Jones (Stone Youth and Community Centre), George Kemp, Geoffrey L King, Rev Stennett Kirby, Chris Latimer,Trevor Law, Fred Leigh, Peter Leslie, Arthur H Little, Sylvia Lloyd, Ken Lovatt, Mr Ludlow (East Staffs Economic Development Service), C Lowndes, Mike Luff, Keith Malkin, Monteney Centre (Sheffield). Rev Stanley J Morris, Harriet Murray, Marguerite Nugent, Derek Owen, Barry Palmer, Mark Pargitter, Roy Parker, Maureen Piper, Peter Robinson, Stewart Robinson (Sentinel Archives), Doc Rowe, Janet Rowley (Handsworth Library), Norman Schofield, MJ Scott-Bolton, Paul Sillitoe, JR Skae, Rev George F Smith, Mark Smith, The staff of London, Staffordshire, Stoke-on-Trent, West Midlands libraries and record offices, and the staff of William Salt Library, Lord Stafford, Richard Sulima, Peter Stockham, Tamworth Borough Council, Neil Taylor, David B Thompson, Philip Thurlow-Craig, Eva Tuff, Lewis Turner, Dan Wade, Alan Wagg, Sir Peter Walker-Okeover, Derek Warrilow, Rev Maxwell W Welsh, Rev Donal R Whiteley, Mark Whittaker. Mike Williams, Phil Williams, Sue Williams, Alan Williamson (of Endon), Alan Williamson (Lichfield Mercury), Peter Wilson and David Wood. I apologise to anyone whose assistance I have received and who I have inadvertently omitted.

Subscribers to the First Edition

Abbotsford Publishing. 2A Brownsfield Road. Lichfield. WS13 6BT.

Dr Anne Andrews. 2 The Hanyards. Tixall. Stafford. ST18 0XY.

Dennis Bell. Hollington Lane. Ednaston. Brailsford. Ashbourne. Derbys. DE6 3AE.

Birmingham City Council Library Services. Bibliographic Services Division. Central Library. Chamberlain Square. Birmingham. B3 3HQ.

Douglas Camm. 59 Merrion Drive. Bradeley. Stoke-on-Trent. ST6 7PH.

Derbyshire Library Service. County Offices. Matlock. Derbys. DE4 3AG.

Dudley Library. St James's Road. Dudley. DY1 1 HR.

Mr A Dunphy. 8 Chestnut Close. Diants Powys. South Glamorgan. CF64 4TJ.

B Edwards. 13 Stencills Road. Walsall. West Midlands. WS4 2HJ.

Mr CJL Elwell. Bottrells Close. Chalfont St Giles. Bucks. HP8 4EH.

Mr RM Haszard. 86 Main Road. Milford. Stafford. ST17 0UJ.

Mr WE James. Askew Green. Witherslack. Cumbria. LA11 6SA.

Mrs EM Johnson. 10 Church Street. Market Drayton. Shrops. TF9 1AD.

University of Keele Library. Keele. Staffs. ST5 5BG.

Randle Knight. Brookside. Milwich. Stafford. ST18 0EG.

Lucinda Lambton. The Old Rectory. Hedgerley. Bucks. SL2 3UY.

Mr ATC Lavender. Staffordshire Parish Register Society. 91 Brenton Road. Penn. Wolverhampton. WV4 5NS.

Leicester University Library. PO Box 248. University Road. Leicester. LE1 9QD.

Dr JP Lester. 24 Belvidere Road. Walsall. WS1 3AW.

Lindsay and Howes. Littlemere. Petworth Road. Wormley. Godalming. Surrey. GU8 STU.

Sylvia Lloyd. 24 Park Road. Werrington. Stoke-on-Trent. Staffs. SJ9 0EB.

John Mitchell. 6 The Chase. Tylers Green. High Wycombe. Bucks. HP10 8BA.

Mr KL Neal. Hon Secretary of the Burton Natural History & Archaeology Society. 53 Belvedere Road. Burton-on-Trent. DE13 0RG.

Miss ES Peers. 23 Westbrook Way. Wombourne. Wolverhampton. WV5 0EA.

Mr MT Sleightholm. 20 The Crescent. Walton-on-the-Hill. Stafford. ST17 0JZ.

Michael Stevens. 2 Place de la Fontaine. 88270 Les Ableuvenettes. France.

Anne M Thompson. 18 Burnaston Road. Hall Green. Birmingham. B28 8DJ.

Mrs NL Wright. 12 Parkway. Trentham. Stoke-on-Trent. ST4 8AG.

Mr FCP Wolferstan. Statfold Hall. Tamworth. B79 0AE.

Yale University Library. New Haven. Conn. USA.

Contents

Commendation
by Rt Hon the Lord Stafford, DL

In September 1999 Tim Cockin brought to my attention his major work 'The Staffordshire Encyclopaedia' which I have looked through and found fascinating. Staffordshire is a county rich in history and in contrasts and which few people outside it's boundaries know much about. Tim has set himself a huge task to piece together the wealth of material which he has done with pains-taking detail and a most readable narrative. I welcome such a work as it has enlightened me in so many aspects of what is in my own back yard. This Staffordshire Encyclopaedia will not only be of interest now, but will be of enormous value to future generations.

Lord Stafford, 2000

Foreword
by The Earl of Lichfield

Staffordshire is one of the lesser known counties of England and is often thought to comprise merely the Black Country and the Potteries. These parts of the County, though rich in many ways, do not give an entirely fair picture of so varied a population and landscape. The point of The Staffordshire Encyclopaedia is to draw together the great wealth of material on Staffordshire from publications and local knowledge, to create a super 'index' on the County for future generations. This Encyclopaedia is a fine attempt to show that Staffordshire is not only rich in history and industry, but also rich in custom, beautiful countryside, innovation, invention and events.

My favourite parts of the County are, of course, those close to my childhood home - Shugborough. I read with interest extracts from the Encyclopaedia about Shugborough Hall being the model for a house in a story by JRR Tolkien; about the pencilled heights of successive generations of Anson children inscribed on the door jambs of the Anson Room in the Hall; about the old yew tree in Shugborough Park grounds, which I remember playing by as a child; and about the wilds of Cannock Chase, which I frequented in my youth.

Many of the publications used by Tim Cockin can be found in the William Salt Library in Stafford. In the late 1860's my great great grandfather, Thomas George Anson, 2nd Earl of Lichfield, was a prime mover in plans to ensure that the collection of William Salt stayed in the county and that a library be found to house it. Apparently, until this happened it was kept in storage in packing cases at Shugborough. In October 1996, following family tradition, I opened the extension of the Staffordshire Record Office: The fact that the Office needed extending only 35 years after being built illustrates the extent of present enthusiasm for local history. With this work Tim Cockin has amply satisfied that appetite. Here is reference after reference and very detailed history on the people, towns, villages and landscapes of our beautiful and varied county.

Lord Lichfield, 2000

Preface

The Encyclopaedia is intended for the enthusiastic local historian, and is not an academic work by a trained historian. It was initially envisaged as a secondary source index of the County's history for my own use, which would bring together light and weightier reading. Since it is a work for myself I have unashamedly allowed my choice of content to be influenced by what has long-held my fascination - the curious, peculiar, and legendary. If there is a theme running through the book then it is an exploration of these three.

Entries are made up of snippets of collected information. Readers are therefore most strongly urged to move on to authoritative works such the Victoria County History, archeological historical transactions, town and parish histories for further reading.

The Encyclopaedia follows a gazetteer format for continuity. In order to create a useful gazetteer I have tried to give individual entries to all named Staffordshire places found in sources consulted. The result is an extremely wide range of coverage, extending from the county's regions and hundreds down to individual homesteads, industrial premises and geographical features. I feel confident that I have included most places from very small hamlets upwards and have included most castles, forests, rivers, hills and houses. Sections on industrial sites, collieries, potteries and public houses can be located in the appendices.

Most entries on large villages and big towns have been separated into time-period or subject paragraphs simply to help break up large amounts of text. Time-period paragraphs appear in chronological sequence, with headings like 'EARLY' (prehistory to the end of the Roman period), '900 to 1500,' and '1500 to PRESENT.' They should not be taken as a complete record of the period in question. Evidence of Saxon and medieval society, for instance in the manor, parish, church, wakes, market, market (butter) cross, fair, gallows, stocks, pound (pinfold), curfew, will appear in the section dated to 1500, even though the evidence may be associated with a date after 1500. Separate headings for a single subject of some importance, on for instance, a person, a family, a custom, or a dispute, may also appear. Generally, subjects within long entries are highlighted. There is sometimes a separate heading 'GROUNDS' to cover the grounds by a house. Garden ornaments and features under this heading are highlighted and usually ordered alphabetically, especially where there are an abundance as at Biddulph Grange, Chillington, Enville, and Shugborough.

With etymology I have given as many possibilities as I could find to show the diversity of thought on the meaning of a name. I appreciate that derivations given by Chetwynd, Wilkes, Shaw and Duignan are now considered somewhat out of date. The remarks 'perhaps' 'probably' 'possibly' etc are the gist of the inferences of the authors themselves. Readers must bear in mind that there are far far more archaic spellings for each place than are listed. A local pronunciation for a place may appear (in italics) after the heading. By and large a reference(s) is given after each piece of information. However, regrettably, there are instances where the reference has slipped below another because an addition (with its reference) has been inserted; looking to the next reference(s) below will reveal the right one.

I appreciate that this work is driven by secondary source material and can only be as good and accurate as the sources from which it has been compiled. I apologise most sincerely for instances where I have been inaccurate; given incorrect references; been naive or have misinterpreted source material. I ask readers to excuse my endeavours and consult the original source. I appreciate that a team of scholar historians would have done a far more objective, balanced and complete work, had they undertaken such a project. Finally, I would like to thank everybody who has helped in any way especially members of my own family.

Tim Cockin, Barlaston, May 2000

I am pleased to reprint The Staffordshire Encyclopaedia rather out of demand. I would especially like to thank David Horovitz and others for their promotion of the book, and kind reviews since 2000. David advised a reprint should not be tampered with in any way. I have striven to do this, but sadly for technical and legal reasons it has not been possible to reproduce illustrations and maps, otherwise the main body of text remains exactly as in the First Edition.

Tim Cockin, Barlaston, April 2006

Introduction

Geography

Staffordshire is a north-west Midland county. Stafford, the county town, lies approximately in the centre. It is north west of London and Birmingham. The former is 125 miles from it; the latter 24.5 miles. One hundred and three miles separate London from Tamworth, the County's nearest town to the capital. The old County was 'more or less lozenge-shaped' (LGS p1). It has been said that North Staffordshire resembles the profile of an old woman in a mop cap, facing west, with the Tyrley quarter of Drayton-in-Hales parish forming the tip of her nose (SHC 1945/ 6 p3) (VCH vol 2 p275). Internally the County is sixty miles long from Orchard Common to Hawkbatch and forty two miles from No Man's Heath to Tyrley Castle, the furthest points east and west. It comprised 1,130 square miles in 1876. In c1886 its acreage was 749,671; in 1965 it was 738,248. In 1974 it was ranked eighteenth largest county in England out of thirty nine including London and Middlesex (NSFCT 1876 p11) (LGS p1) (HOS p55) (SL p251) (OS maps: a concise guide for historians. Richard Oliver. 1993. p163).

Staffordshire, pronounced Staffycher in the Potteries (POP p111), shares boundaries with: Cheshire (NW), Worcestershire (S), Derbyshire (NE and E), a tiny stretch of Leicestershire (E), Warwickshire (SE), and Shropshire (W). Boundary changes are discussed in entries, for instance, Harborne, and in the Beyond Staffordshire section in the appendixes. The County's main river is the Trent which rises in the Northern Upland. Its tributaries are: Blithe, Dove (with tributaries Tean, Churnet (and its tributary Combes Brook) and Manifold (with tributary Hamps)), Fowlea, Lyme, Mease, Sow (with tributaries The Darling, Meece and Penk), and Tame. The Weaver in Cheshire takes in the Dane and Checkley Brook. The Severn in Worcestershire and Shropshire takes in the Stour (with tributary Smestow) and the Tern (with tributary Meese (with tributaries Lonco and Back Brooks)).

The County can be divided into six regions. The northeast or Moorlands - east of the Churnet and north of Leek - is physically an extension of the Derbyshire Peak District. An upland falling away from this is the central north and northwest (Newcastle and Stoke) or Northern Upland. Middle Staffordshire, where the Trent and its tributaries have fallen, is lower pastureland (the east side is the Needwood Forest plateau). Southeast Staffordshire, where the Trent and Tame unite, is an alluvial flood-plain. The central south is upland (Southern Upland). The southwest region is a watershed draining to the Severn on one side and to the Penk on the other. Two regions, the Southern and Northern Uplands, lie on coalfields and geology containing iron ore in the former and clay in the latter. In the Industrial Revolution these minerals were heavily exploited and two memorably-named densely populated conurbations emerged; on the former, the Black Country, and on the latter, the Potteries. After the move to electricity from coal fuel they have ceased to be 'grimy' 'black' and 'smoky' (SL pp30-33) (HOS 1998 p15).

Prehistoric

Evidence of Palaeolithic (300,000-11,000 years ago) activity in Staffordshire has been found in Elderbush, Ossoms, Thor's, and Thor's Fissure Caves in the Manifold Valley; at Drayton Bassett, Shenstone, Essington and Great Wyrley in the Black Brook Valley and headland; and in the upper Trent Valley at Eccleshall Moss. Finds from the Mesolithic (10,000-4,500 BC) Age have been made on the south west watershed at Greensforge, Kinver, Wombourne and Wrottesley Old Park; in the Trent and Tame Valley basins at Lichfield, Greenhill, Bangley, and Branston; on the Northern Upland at Etchinghill, Courtsbank Covert, Bourne Pool and Sandwell; and in the Moorlands at Wetton Mill. Bridestones (Ches) and Devil's Ring and Finger megaliths are probably the remains of Neolithic (4,500-2,400 BC) chambered tombs. Finds of fairly-certain Neolithic origin have also been made in the Upper Trent Valley at Normacot, Northwood Tumulus, Penkhull and Trent Vale. In the Moorlands evidence of this period has been found at Falcon Low Cave (Wetton), Grub Low (Waterfall), and Thor's Cave. Neolithic activity in the Trent and Tame Valleys is represented by evidence of settlement at Fisherwick and Lichfield; an henge at Fatholme; and two large causewayed enclosures at Mavesyn Ridware and Alrewas (HOS 1998 p24). In the south west there have been Neolithic finds made at Kinver and Wrottesley Old Park and there may have been settlement at Lower Penn. On the Southern Upland Neolithic finds have been made at Bourne Pool whilst a flint factory has been discovered at Courtsbank Covert to the south of Cannock Chase. For Bronze (2,400-700 BC) Age or possible Neolithic burial mounds see appendices.

Iron Age

In the far north and Moorlands Iron Age (700 BC-43 AD) artifacts have been found in Thor's Cave and Cheshire Wood Cave; coins have been found at Cheddleton; an enclosure on The Cloud (Cheshire) is said to have been a hillfort. In the Needwood Forest and Trent and Tame basin area gold torcs have been found at Greaves Wood, Alrewas and Glascote, and a bronze necklet discovered at Stretton near Burton upon Trent; there was Iron Age settlement at Fisherwick, and a fort may have stood on the site

of Tutbury Castle. Five definite hillforts lie in the Trent Valley and Northern Upland area: Berry Ring, Bunbury Hill, Bishop's Wood (Fairoak), Bury Hill, and Berth Hill; an enclosure by the latter at Maer Moss may represent a farmstead. Also in this region have been found a spindle whorl in the upper Sow area, a quern at Normacot, and a possible canoe by the River Tern. Of hillforts in the Southern Upland and south west there were: Castle Ring, Castle Old Fort, Kinver Edge, and possibly Church Hill (Wednesbury). Loaches Banks near Bourne Pool may represent an animal grazing enclosure. Iron Age activity has been found at Sandwell. The Cornovii (or Cornabii, or Cornavii - W p30) may have held the west part of Staffordshire from Wall into Cheshire and Shropshire. The Brigantes may have had territory extending into the far north and Moorlands. The Coritani tribe may have held much of East Staffordshire including the Needwood Forest and Trent and Tame basin area (HOS p10. 1998 p25) (Roman site at Wall. DoE Official Guide) (CVH p18). Although, it has been suggested that a minor tribe occupied this area, who had a distinct identity - never lost throughout the Roman period - after the discovery of two similar torcs (from Greaves Wood and Glascote) suggesting the presence of chieftains (SSAHST 1969 p5). It has been suggested that the Cangi tribe or herdsmen, who were themselves controlled by the Cornovii, may have held the Cannock Chase area (W p30). In Pausanias (Paus. Graec. descr. 1. 33. of M.H.B. 4. 2) a tribe known as the Genuini are mentioned. They are thought to have existed in the far north and Moorlands in about 138 AD. 'Genuini' is derived from the Celtic 'gun' signifying 'moorland' (NSFCT 1908 p104). A tribe known as Ceangi, who allegedly gave their name to Congleton, may have had some presence in the far north (SMM pp110,111). Rocester and Chesterton are shown on G Webster's map (in 'The Cornovii' 1975) in Cornovian territory, whilst M Todd (in 'The Coritani' 1973 p19) places them in Coritani territory (NSJFS 1976 p94). Traditional sacred places of the Iron Age (and pagan successors) in the north include: Bawd Stone, Burston, Chebsey, Colton, Egg Well, Fairoak Knoll, Gawton's Stone, Hanchurch, Hangingstone Rock, Load and Cheese Rock, Milwich, Naychurch spring, Penkhull, Shepherd's Cross, Uttoxeter, Thor's Cave, Wicken Stones, Cat Stones (Cheshire). Whilst in the south: Barr Beacon, Cannock Chase, Cuttlestone, Greenhill (Lichfield), Hailstone, Offlow, Penkridge, Sedgley Beacon, Shire Oak, Wednesbury, Wednesfield, and Weeford. Present names of most hills and rivers have a Celtic origin
.

Roman

The Romans did not advance to the Midlands until 48 AD and the area was under their control by 78-79 AD (HOS p10). Their Limes Britannicus of the Notitia, an earthen defence barrier between the Don and the Severn built in about 50 AD to protect Fosse Way, is said to have run through the County. On the later Watling Street were the forts of Letocetum and Pennocrucium. On Icknield Street was Metchley fort which intercepted Letocetum in the north. A road of uncertain course ran from Greensforge fort northwards through Pennocrucium over Richmilde Street (linking forts at Chesterton and Rocester) to Aquae Arnemetiae (Buxton). Another road of uncertain course linked Metchley fort and Chester passing through Pennocrucium. Chesterton, Pennocrucium, Rocester, and Letocetum all evolved into civil centres in the later Roman period; the latter has the most significant surviving remains. In the 3rd Century Staffordshire seems to have been divided between the two provinces of Britain. The E of the county was in the province of Britannia Inferior (capital at York) and the W of the county in the province of Britannia Superior (capital at London). In the early 4th Century, the same E side was in the province of Flavia Caesariensis (capital at Lincoln) and the same W side was in the province of Britannia Prima (capital at Cirencester) (Oxford Illustrated History of Roman Britain. Peter Salway. 1993. p218). White says Staffordshire was in the Roman Consular Province of Maxima Caesariensis and in the Praesidial district of Flavia Caesariensis (W p31 note).
.

Anglian settlers

Anglian invaders appeared in the County possibly from two directions from c570; those out of Leicestershire had arrived at the Wash; those from the Humber estuary came along the Trent (LGS p26) (HOS p11). The population of this part of the country may have been largely British in the early 7th Century (Lucerna. HPR Finberg. pp5,73,75) (VCH vol 3 p1). Earliest Anglian settlers, perhaps members of the Middle Anglian group of people, included: the Hwicce ('salt people') from Gloucestershire, Worcestershire, and West Warwickshire in the Wychnor area; the Bilsætan in the Bilston area; the Tomsætan ('dwellers by the Tame') in the Lichfield-Tamworth area; the Pecsaetan ('Peak dwellers'), possibly Celtic rather than Anglican, in the Moorlands (HOS pp13,54. 1998 pp27,28) (SL pp43,44) (MR p398). To these may be added: the Usmere in the Stourbridge-Clent area; the Pencersætan in the Wolverhampton area (whose royal centre was Penkridge) (SSE 1987 p21); the South Mercians in the Upper Trent-Newcastle-under-Lyme area; the Ridwara ('river people') in the area of the Ridwares (SL p43) (In Search of the Dark Ages. Michael Wood. 1987. pp82-83); the Mierce ('people of the boundary or march between the English and British') lived on the South Upland (SL p43) (BDH pp38,39). The name Mercia derives from the Mierce tribe. The Anglicans met with at least one defeat in the area at Caer Lwytgoed in c655; a place identified with Wall near Lichfield (HOS 1998 p27).

Mercia

Mercia, an area of central, and some of South England, was established in c560 AD under the leadership of Creoda (d593), as a sub-kingdom of Northumbria. Creoda was reputedly descended from Woden, father of Wihtlaeg, father of Wearmund, father of Offa of Angeln, father of Angeltheow, father of Eomaer, father of Icil, father of Creoda (In Search of the Dark Ages. Michael

Wood. 1987). Mercia achieved independence in the 7th Century under king Cearl (d625) (HOS pp13,54). Another account has Creoda being succeeded by Pybba (593-615) who was succeeded by his sons, Penda (632-654 or 655) and Eawa (632-641). Penda is said to have been 80 years old when killed by king Oswy (or Oswiu) of Northumbria at the battle of Winwaed in 655. The kingdom was then subject to Northumberland overlordship (NSFCT 1928 p23) until Penda's son, Wulfhere (king 657-674), reasserted independence. Wulfhere's son Cenred reigned between 704 and 709. Eawa's grandson Aethelbald reigned between 716 and 757, when he was murdered by his bodyguard at Seckington, Warwickshire, near Tamworth. He was succeeded by his cousin's grandson, Offa (757-796), whose palace was at Tamworth. Offa extended the western boundary of the kingdom to the present Welsh border which he defended with a dyke built in the late 780s. From c730 to 821 Mercia ruled all England S of the Humber, with the kings of neighbouring kingdoms paying tribute to Mercian kings. Offa was briefly succeeded by his son, Ecgfrith, who was succeeded in 796 by Offa's distant cousin, Cenwulf I. He was succeeded by his brother Ceolwulf I (821-823), who was succeeded by a distant cousin Beornwulf (823-825). A descendant of Beornwulf, Burghred, brother-in-law of Alfred the Great of Wessex, reigned as the last independent king of Mercia from 852 to 874 when the Mercians submitted to the Danes. The Danes made Ceolwulf II a puppet king of Mercia from 874 to his death in c880. By the Treaty of Wedmore (878) the County north of Watling Street was under Danelaw between 878 and 913. In 910 West Saxons drove the Danes out of South Staffordshire after a battle at Tettenhall or Wednesfield. With the death of Mercian ealdorman Aethelred, his widow Ethelfleda or Aethelflaed, King Alfred's daughter, was given charge of Mercia in 912. In summer 913 she built burhs or forts at Tamworth and Stafford to defend the area against the Danes. In 918 Ethelfleda, who later became known as the 'Lady of the Mercians,' died. Mercia was then annexed by her brother Edward the Elder. From then on it was effectively an earldom, ruled by Saxon ealdormen, who were plagued increasingly by Danish incursions until 1020. Edward the Elder died in 924 and was succeeded by his son Athelstan. After his death in 939 Anlaf (Olaf) Guthfrithsson marched S from York and took Tamworth. The late king's brother and successor, Eadmund or Edmund (939-946), recovered the lost Mercian territory in 940 (SSAHST 1969 p34) (In Search of the Dark Ages. Michael Wood. 1987) (BTIH p13); Lady Wulfrun (or Wulfruna), who founded Wolverhampton (see), may have been his daughter. In 980 Danes ravaged Mercia generally. In 1002 there was, reputedly, a battle at Marchington in which the Danes were defeated. In 1013 the Mercian ealdorman, Eadric allied with Swein, king of Denmark. Swein's son, Canute (1016-1035), now ruler of all England, appointed a Saxon, Leofwine, as Earl of Mercia. He was followed by his son, Leofric (d1057 at King's Bromley). Hughes says Canute appointed Leofric in c1032 (SOSH p71) (In Search of the Dark Ages. Michael Wood. 1987 p197). Alfgar succeeded him, and Edwin succeeded him in 1062. Edwin, last Earl of Mercia, first revolted against the Normans in 1068 and was killed in a revolt against them in 1071 (HOWM p16) (HOS pp14,16) (SSAHST 1969 p33) (SL p49).

Most of the County's place names are of Anglo-Saxon origin, although, Catholme, Croxall, Fatholme, Mytholm, and Thorpe (Constantine), all in the Trent and Tame basin, are of Scandinavian origin. Mercia has always encompassed Staffordshire; the western boundary of the 'core' kingdom was to become, roughly, the County's western boundary (In Search of the Dark Ages. Michael Wood. 1987. p83 see map). (NSFCT 1911 pp49-78).

Founding of the Shire

When Staffordshire was founded is debatable. FM Stenton and others believe it was in the last years of Edward the Elder, sometime between 919-924 (HOS pp16,54. 1998 p30) (WMMA p141) (VCH vol 6 p200); Mrs Dodd thought between 920 and 950 after Edward the Elder had expelled the Danes from Mercia (NSFCT 1945 p96); whilst HPR Finberg thinks, since none of the Mercian shires are mentioned before 1000, the territories may have been formed in 1007 (The Early Charters of the West Midlands. HPR Finberg. 1961. p230); CS Taylor thinks the county was formed in the early 11th Century (SL p50). The County is first mentioned as a shire in 1016, in the Anglo-Saxon Chronicle (TE p490) (SL p58). Staffordshire has five Hundreds: Totmonslow (NE), Pirehill (NW), Offlow (E), Cuttlestone (W), and Seisdon (S): Most other counties have many more. Staffordshire's were, apparently, all named after the meeting-places of the Hundred moots. Wolverhampton and its collegiate estates seem to have operated as a sixth, independent of other Hundred courts (HOWM p5). Dr and Mrs Dodd suggest that portways may have linked some of the sites of the Hundred moots (NSFCT 1976 p44). It has been shown that the normal Hundred in Staffordshire was the 'long hundred' comprising 120 hides, made up of six subdivisions of 20 hides, representing the landed possessions of so many families (SHC 1919 p154) (HOWM p5). As units of local government the Staffordshire Hundreds continued into the 19th Century although their functions had long been dwindling (LGS pp1-2) (HOS p54). Hughes, in earlier 20th Century, says they were still being used for licensing purposes (SOSH p81). Hundreds may be coeval with the creation of counties (HOS p54) (SL pp50,51); they may be of Celtic origin (NSFCT 1908 p119). In the case of Staffordshire, Mrs Dodd thought they were made immediately after the founding of the County. Mander thought hundreding had probably preceded King Æthelred's gift to Lady Wulfrun in 985 (HOWM p17 note).

Castles and forests

CASTLES: Most built in later 11th Century or c1100.

Alton Castle: Perhaps by Bertram de Verdun in later 12th Century and certainly by 1316; de Verduns were succeeded by Furnivalles, Nevilles, and Talbots; perhaps rebuilt in early 15th Century; demolished in Civil War and only some outer walls and a tower survive.

Audley Castle: Held by the Aldithleys (or Audleys); later they resided at their Heighley Castle. Nothing survives but the motte.

Caverswall Castle: Perhaps has Saxon origins; fortified manor house of the Caverswall family of c1270-1320; decayed in Elizabethan period; rebuilt by a merchant in c1615 to designs of John or Robert Smythson; garrisoned in Civil War; continued as a residence and was extended in 1890s.

Chartley Castle: Built by the Earl of Chester and descended by marriage through three families until sold in 1907; only lower stonework of shell-keep and two towers in curtain walling of inner bailey survive.

Dudley Castle: Saxon in origin; from 11th Century until at least 1913 descended with the barony of Dudley in the Ansculf, Paynel, Somery, Sutton families and their descendents, the Dudleys and Wards; hunting grounds of Old Park, Dudley Castle Park and Pensnett Chase; largely demolished in 1647, but domestic apartment blocks of late 17th Century inside survive.

Eccleshall Castle: Bishops of Lichfield fortified their manor house from 1200; they had nearby hunting grounds at Blore and Eccleshall Parks; principal seat of the bishops of Lichfield from mid 16th Century until Civil War when destroyed in a siege; present mansion built on site in 1695; occasional residence of the bishops until 1867.

Heighley Castle: Built by the de Aldithleys (Audley) after 1226. Descended with Lords Audley in the Touchet family; dismantled in the Civil War; only the ditch below the bailey and a fragment of walling of the gatehouse and keep survive; Audley and Heighley Parks were hunting grounds of the Audleys.

Newcastle Castle: Built by 1149 to control major road junction; held by the Crown and later by the Earls and Dukes of Lancaster; a ruin by c1541; site levelled in 1855 and is now part of a town park.

Stafford Castle at Castle Church: Very soon after it was built it was in the possession of the de Staffords and descended with the Stafford barony; demolished in Civil War; rebuilt in the early 19th Century in imitation of the 14th Century rebuild. The early 19th Century castle is now a ruin.

Stafford Castle in Stafford: Very short-lived wooden? castle built by William I in 1070 to suppress local rebellion; alleged later castles in the town have never been conclusively found.

Tamworth Castle: Granted soon after Conquest to the Despencers and descended by marriage through five families until sold to Tamworth in 1897; the 12th Century shell-keep and later insertions and parts of curtain wall surrounding bailey, survive.

Tutbury Castle: Administrative centre of the de Ferrers (Earls of Derby); in 1266 passed to the Crown; stayed in royal family some of whom were Earls of Lancaster; Wychnor held of the Earls on condition a bacon flitch be kept at Wychnor manor house for male tenants who could prove absolute fidelity in marriage for a year and a day; became Crown property in 1377 and has remained so ever since; prison for Mary, Queen of Scots; only partly demolished in Civil War; some earlier work and later apartments survive.

Tyrley Castle: Perhaps Norman; never had any strength or military importance; disused by the later 14th Century?; all trace of it is lost in a farm built on the site.

FORESTS: All had primaeval origins and came under royal control after 1066.

Brewood Forest: Had several possible enclosures, a division, a park belonging to the bishops of Lichfield; disafforested in 1204.

Cannock Forest: Royal hunting lodge at Radmore; Cannock Chase granted to the bishops of Lichfield in 1189; rest survived as a collection of hays until the end of the 16th Century.

Kinver Forest: Had six possible hays and one park; royal hunting lodge at Stourton became the residence known as Stourton Castle; lasted to the mid 16th Century.

Needwood Forest: Soon passed to the de Ferrers and descended with Tutbury Castle; Abbots Bromley horn dance may be connected with the villagers' former rights in it; Barton, Castle Hayes, Highlands, Rolleston and Stockley Parks created in it and perhaps also Chartley Park. Enclosed by 1811.

New Forest: created out of southern extremity of Lyme Forest; disafforested in c1204; Cliff Hay survived for a period after.

Religion

Until the mid 7th Century Mercia was pagan. Conversion took place during and after Wulfhere's reign (657-674); formerly pagan, he sponsored Northumbrian Christian missionaries Wilfrid and Chad, endowed a bishopric of Mercia with lands, and founded Stone Priory, reputedly in remorse at killing his sons Wulfad and Rufin for converting to Christianity; stained glass windows in St Michael's Church, Stone, depict his sons and his daughter, Werburgh; she founded Hanbury Priory and was first prioress of Trentham Priory. Chad became an early bishop of Mercia and had established the See at Lichfield and the foundation for the present cathedral at Lichfield by his death in 672. Perhaps also in the 7th Century an Irish abbess, St Modwen, founded a religious community at Burton upon Trent. The legendary St Bertram may have founded a hermitage at Stafford in the late 7th Century (VCH vol 3 p1) (HOS p13. 1998 p28). These religious establishments were possibly destroyed in the Danish invasions of the later 9th Century. The possible grandniece of Ethelfleda, Lady Wulfrun (or Wulfruna), endowed Wolverhampton Collegiate Church in the 10th Century. The same or another Wulfrun was the mother of Wulfric Spot founder of Burton Abbey in the early 11th Century. According to evidence and tradition there were at least 50 churches in existence in the County prior to the Norman Invasion. There were 84 parishes in 1291 (SL p74); the number had increased to between 125 and 150 by 1520 (SL p251); by 1830 there were approximately 150 ecclesiastical parishes.

Religious houses of the medieval period were all (except Burton and Lapley) founded or refounded after the Norman Conquest. Benedictine monks had: Burton Abbey, Canwell, Lapley, Sandwell and Tutbury Priories. Benedictine nuns: Blackladies, Blithbury, Farewell priories. Cistercian monks: Croxden, Dieulacres, Hulton and Radmore Abbeys. Cluniac order: St James' Priory (Dudley, Worcs). Augustinian canons: Calwich, Ranton, St Thomas Becket, Stone, Trentham Priories, Rocester Abbey. Augustinian friars: St Augustine's Priory (Stafford). Dominican friars: Blackfriars (Newcastle). Franciscan friars: The Friary (Lichfield) and Greyfriars (Stafford). Burton surrendered on Nov 14 1539 and was the last in the County to do so. It was re-established by the king in 1541 as a college of canons. But it, and the County's other collegiate churches - Gnosall, Penkridge, Stafford, Tamworth, Tettenhall Collegiate Churches - were all abolished under an Act of 1545; Wolverhampton Collegiate Church possessed some of its ancient privileges until 1846 (LGS p38) (HOS p28). Keele Preceptory, the Knights Templars' house (later a commandery of the Knights Hospitallers), survived until 1540.

Directly after the Reformation a large majority of the County's population, especially some gentry, clung to Catholicism (LGS p29). In the 18th Century there was more land in Staffordshire held by Catholics than in any other English county (VCH). Those gentry who remained Catholic included: Astons, Biddulphs, Erdeswicks, Fowlers, Giffards, Heveninghams, Ryders (Dunkirk Hall), and Stamfords. Many of their houses, as well as Oscott House, Oulton Old Hall, Pipe Hall and Yieldfields Hall, were illegal Mass centres; Jesuits were active in Wolverhampton in the 1680s. With Catholic emancipation in the 19th Century some country houses, including Oscott House and Aston Hall together with Caverswall Castle and Hawkesyard Priory, were let to religious orders.

John Grace, a hermit and eccentric, if not heterodox, preacher caused some unrest in Coventry and South Staffordshire. He was arrested by order of the Council in c1424 (VCH vol 3 p43). The short-lived Puritan group known as the Feoffees for the Purchase of Impropriations was active in Staffordshire in the late 1620s and the early 1630s (VCH vol 3 p58). The County's earliest recorded instance of Protestant nonconformity is at Checkley in 1632. Baptists were active in the north east of the County in 1644 (HOS 1998 p66). Quakers had a large congregation at Stafford by the early 1650s (HOS 1998 p66). During the Commonwealth there was non-conformist preaching at Stone Park, Stone. The first registration of a dissenter meeting-house in the County was in Newcastle-under-Lyme in 1689. After the failure of the 1715 Jacobite Rebellion non-conformists chapels at Burton, Newcastle, Stafford, Stone and West Bromwich and other places were ransacked in riots. Muggletonians, a sect founded by John Reeve and Lodowick Muggleton (1609-98), have identified their Muggleton with Ilam and Milwich. Edward Elwall (d1744) of Ettingshall, an ardent Unitarian, contemplated forming a sect known as Elwallians. Several later movements in non-conformity had national repercussions. In the early 19th Century Primitive Methodism was born after Hugh Bourne of Bemersley Green and William Clowes of Ball Green (unlocated) quarrelled with Wesleyan Methodists over revivalist camp meetings on Mow Cop. Later, Unitarians all over the country risked losing a number of their chapels when a case in Chancery went against them in favour of Trinitarians to regain their John Street Chapel in Wolverhampton. In the 1860s, the resentment of church rates by non-conformists at Tamworth helped to bring about their abolition. In 1875 the Pleasant Sunday Afternoon, religious light entertainment on Sunday afternoons, was invented by a West Bromwich Congregationalist Minister.

Only seven new Anglican churches were built between the Reformation and 1800. However, the pace of church-building quickened rapidly in the 19th Century to combat the growth of dissension in the growing industrial towns (SL p138). The Staffordshire Historic Churches Trust, formerly The Friends of Ancient Staffordshire Churches, established as a Registered Charity in 1953, with the aim to encourage interest in the heritage of Staffs churches of all denominations, and to raise money for their maintenance (Trust leaflets). By the late 20th Century in urban conurbations, especially in the south, there were places of worship for Pentecostals, Moslems, Sikhs and Hindus.

Civil War

1642: 22 August - War broke out: 2 September - royalists in neighbouring counties tried to obtain support from the King's Commission of Array in Staffordshire; 16-18 September - Charles I and his army marched through County from Nottingham to Shrewsbury, Staffordshire royalist gentry travelled to Aston Hall, Warwickshire, to present themselves to the king: 15 October - Charles I in Wolverhampton: Autumn - Dudley and Tamworth Castles, Lichfield cathedral Close and Stafford garrisoned for the royalists: Mid November - royalist Sir Francis Wortley plundered in the Moorlands: 15 November - sheriff at Stafford called for quiet in the County and produced a scheme to, in effect, raise an independent third force within it - excepting Lincolnshire Staffordshire was the only English county which tried to raise an independent third force. According to Band the Stafford plan was the more consistent of the two: Gentry eventually took sides: An early parliamentarian association covering Staffordshire was the West Midland Association of Warwickshire, Staffordshire and Shropshire led by Lord Brooke.

1643: January - royalist garrison at Biddulph Old Hall besieged: By February Keele Hall royalist garrison had been taken by parliament. February - incited by Wortley's actions the Moorlanders armed themselves and formed what amounted to a dragoon to fight for parliament and marched on royalist Stafford: 5 March - Parliament takes Lichfield Close garrison: 19 March - royalist victorious in Hopton Heath battle: Spring - Rushall Hall parliamentary garrison besieged and taken by the royalists: 20 April - royalists retake Lichfield Close garrison: After winning and retaking Rushall Hall by late April the royalists had squeezed their opponents into the north and east of the County: 16 May - Stafford taken by Parliament: 25 June - Tamworth Castle royalist garrison taken by parliament: Early July - Wootton Lodge royalist garrison taken by parliament: July - Queen Henrietta Maria in Walsall: August 30 - Eccleshall Castle royalist garrison falls after a siege: November - Leek parliamentary garrison fell to royalists: 21 December - Lapley Hall parliamentary garrison taken by royalists:

1644: By March - Leek back in Parliament hands: Spring - Burton fell to Parliament: 22 May - Rushall Hall royalist garrison retaken by Parliament: 12 June - Tipton Green 'battle': 6 July - Parliament raids royalist garrison at Tutbury Castle but does not take it: Late July - Parliament takes Tutbury town: garrisons at Alton Castle, Paynsley Hall, Swynnerton Manor House, Trentham Hall in Parliament hands. 1645: Spring- Caverswall Castle parliament garrison captured by royalists: Mid May - Charles I at Bushbury and Himley Halls. Mid June - Charles I at Lichfield and Wolverhampton. 1646: March - royalist Lichfield city falls to the Parliament: Late April - royalist Tutbury Castle surrenders: 13 May - royalist Dudley Castle capitulates: 10 July - royalist Lichfield cathedral Close surrenders: 16 July - the Close is evacuated. 1650-1651: Major General Harrison sent to Staffordshire and five other counties to quell 'conspiracies to begin new troubles and raise another war.' September 3 1651 - Battle of Worcester: 6-9 September - Charles II in refuge at Boscobel, Moseley and Bentley Halls. 1659: Regicide John Bradshaw of Newcastle dies. 1660: Early May - Regicide Thomas Harrison arrested in Newcastle; executed on 13 Oct. (VCH vol 14 p18) (LGS p30) (TE p491) (NSJFS 1966 pp12-23) (LOU p342) (BFS pp6,8,12) (WAM p81) (SHJ summer 1987 p26) (HOS 1998 pp71-76).

There were, or allegedly were, garrisons, incidents, skirmishes, maraudings, camps, and finds of the Civil War period at: Armshead, Battlefield, Beacon Hill, Blore Ray, Broughton, Bushbury Hill, 'Camp Bank', Camp Hill (Audnam), Cannock, Checkley, Chillington, Cross Guns, Deadman's Green, Dimmings Dale, Dosthill, Doxey, Elford, Gallows Elm Tree, Goldenhill, Great Bridge, Greatgate, Great Haywood, Greene's Museum, Greyfriars, Hangingstone Rock, The Heath (Uttoxeter), Horton, Hostage Lane, Ivy House (Shenstone), Lime Pearl Pool, Madam's Bridge, Milwich, Moorlands, Mottley Pits, Moxley, Newcastle, Oliver's Green, Oulton, Penkridge, Prince Rupert's Mound, Rugeley, St Helen's Well, Sandon, Shire Oak, Shotwood Hill, Smethwick, Stonefield, Swindon, Trentham, Throwley, Tipton Green, Tompkin, Town's End (Eccleshall), Walsall, Warwell, Wednesbury, West Bromwich Common, Whitemoor, Wolseley Bridge, Wolverhampton. And at these halls: Browns Green House, Burgamy House, Freeford Manor, Hall Farm (Bushbury), Hanch, The Hills (Bloxwich), Lea Head Manor, Moseley Old, Okeover, Patshull Old, Pillaton, Pool (Lichfield), Seighford, Shushions, Stone Park, Stourton Castle, Throwley Old, Tixall Old, Toll End, White, Whitmore, Willingsworth, Wrinehill and Wrottesley. And at these inns: Castle, Dog and Doublet, Old Engine, Red Cow, Red Lion Star and Garter, White Hart (Caldmore) and White Hart (Kinver).

Transport

ROADS

MEDIEVAL ROUTES: **London to Carlisle** via: Bassett's Pole, Weeford, Lichfield, Wolseley Bridge, Sandon, Barlaston, Hanford, Newcastle, Dimsdale, Chesterton, Red Street and Talke. **London to Chester** via: Bassett's Pole, Lichfield, Wolseley Bridge, Sandon, Barlaston and Newcastle. **Manchester to Derby** via: Hug Bridge, Leek, Earls Way, Blore Ray, Thorpe, Coldwall Bridge and Ashbourne (turnpiked 1762). **Birmingham to Derby** via Wall, Icknield Street, Burton and Burton Bridge (or to the north Monk's Bridge) (Lichfield-Burton turnpiked from 1729). **Worcester to Carlisle** via: Stourbridge, Wolverhampton, Stafford, Stone, Newcastle and Talke. Newcastle to Derby via: Stoke, Lane End, Blythe Marsh, Checkley, Stramshall and Dove Bridge (turnpiked 1759). **Birmingham to Shrewsbury** via: Smethwick, Oldbury, Tividale, Dudley, Himley and Bridgnorth.

POPULAR 16th AND 17th CENTURY ROUTES: **London to Carlisle** via: Bassett's Pole, Weeford, Lichfield, Wolseley Bridge, Sandon, Darlaston, Strongford Bridge, Hanford, Newcastle, Talke and Carlisle (Coleshill-Lichfield turnpiked 1744; Lichfield-Stone turnpiked 1729; Stone-Strongford Bridge not turnpiked by 1750; Strongford Bridge-Talke turnpiked from 1714; Dimsdale-Talke by-passed from 1827). **London to Chester** via: Bassett's Pole, Weeford, Lichfield, Wolseley Bridge, Sandon, Darlaston, Stableford and Blackbrook (turnpiked from 1729). **Castle Bromwich to Chester** via: Old Chester Road, Brownhills, Watling Street and Newport (Shrops) (turnpiked 1760). **Birmingham to Shrewsbury** via: Smethwick, West Bromwich Common? Wednesbury, Bilston and Wolverhampton (Birmingham-Wednesbury turnpiked from 1726).

SOME ADDITIONAL TURNPIKED ROUTES: Sandon-Hilderstone-Leek-Hug Bridge-Manchester was turnpiked in 1762. These routes were turnpiked sometime after 1763: Uttoxeter-Stafford-Newport (Shrops): Market Drayton-Newcastle-Leek-Buxton: Birmingham-Walsall-Cannock-Stafford: Stafford-Eccleshall-Ashley-Chester.

MOTORWAYS. The **M6** between Junctions 13 and 14 opened on August 2 1962; between Junctions 14 to 15 on December 19 1962; Junctions 15 to 16 on November 15 1963; Junctions 11 to 13 on March 14 1966; Junctions 10 to 11 on September 15 1966; Junctions 9 to 10 on December 20 1968; Junctions 7 to 8 on July 20 1970; Junctions 8 to 9 on May 1 1972; Junctions 5 to 7 on May 24 1972. The **M5** from the M6 to Junction 3 was opened on May 15 1970. The **M54** between Junctions 1 and 3 was opened on November 25 1983 (VCH vol 2 pp275-284) (The Turnpike Road System in England 1663-1840. William Albert. 1972) (OS maps) (Avril McInntyre at Highways Agency).

CANALS

Bentley Canal: Branch: Neachells. Birmingham and Fazeley Canal. Birmingham and Liverpool Junction Canal (alias Shropshire Union Canal). Birmingham Canal with its Old Cut Old Main Line, New Cuts and New Main Lines: Branches: Balls Hill, Bradley, Bradley Loop, Cape Arm, Churchbridge, Dartmouth, Dixon's, Dunkirk, Engine, Gospel Oak, Gower, Houghton, Island Line, Lord Ward's, Ocker Hill, Roway, Soho Loop, Tipton Green, Wednesbury, Wednesbury Oak Loop. Bristol and Hull Canal (never built). Caldon Canal: Branches: Foxley, Leek, Norton Green, Uttoxeter. Cannock Extension Canal: Branches: Norton

Springs. Coventry Canal. Dudley Canal Line One. Dudley Canal Line Two: Branches: Bumble Hole, Netherton Tunnel, Withymoor. Grand Trunk (later Trent and Mersey Canal). Gresley Canal. Lichfield Canal (proposed). Macclesfield Canal. Newcastle-under-Lyme Canal. Newcastle-under-Lyme Junction Canal. Oldbury Loop Canal. Pensnett Canal. Rushall Canal: Branch: Daw End. Shropshire Union Canal: Branch: Newport. Staffordshire and Worcestershire Canal: Branches: Churchbridge, Hatherton, The Narrows, Stafford. Stourbridge Canal: Branch: Fens. Stourbridge Extension Canal: Branches: Bromley, Sandhills. Tame Valley Canal. Titford Canal. Trent and Mersey Canal: Branches: Bond End, Burslem. Two Lock Line. Walsall Canal: Branches: Bilston, Dank's, Haines', Monway, Toll End, Whitehall, Willenhall. Walsall Junction Canal. Wednesbury Canal: Branches: Halford, Izons, Jesson's, Ridgacre. Wolverhampton Canal (later Staffordshire and Worcestershire Canal). Wyrley and Essington Canal: Branches: Birchills, Sandhills, Vernon's, Wyrley Bank. Wyrley and Essington Extension Canal: Branches: Anglesey, Gilpins, Lord Hay's.

RAILWAYS

SOME EARLY, INDUSTRIAL AND MILITARY RAILROADS: **Cotton Plane** (1777). **Gilpin's Basin** mineral railway (c1800). **Stafford to Radford** wharf railroad (1805). **Consall Plateway** (c1815-c1850). **Woodhead Plateway** (c1827-c1890). **Shutt End** mineral railway (1829-). **Pensnett Line** mineral railway (1859-1937). **Firmstone's** mineral railway (Madeley) (1838-c1957). **Sneyd's** mineral railway (Silverdale) (1849-50-1964). **Burton** breweries railways. **Tackeroo Railway** for Brocton Camp (c1915-1918). **Branston** National Machine Gun factory line. **New Haden Colliery** mineral railway.

SOME STAFFORDSHIRE RAILWAY COMPANIES AND LINES: The **Trent Valley Railway**, incorporated in 1845, built the Stafford-Lichfield-Tamworth-Rugby line in 1847. The **North Staffordshire Railway** (NSR), formed by 1846 out of an amalgamation of the Staffordshire Potteries and Churnet Valley Companies, was absorbed by the LMSR in 1923. It was the most independent of all railway companies in its region. It had the nickname 'The Knotty' and was once described as a 'small octopus' for its lines projected out like tentacles from Stoke-upon-Trent. NSR built: Potteries Line (1848-1849); Uttoxeter Branch (Stoke-Uttoxeter) (1848); Churnet Valley Line (North Rode, Cheshire - Uttoxeter) (1849); Market Drayton Branch (Newcastle-Madeley-Market Drayton) (1870-1956). The most famous of the NSR lines was the 'The Loop Line' which linked the pottery towns and collieries. It opened in stages between 1862 and 1875, and ran from Kidsgrove in the N to Etruria passing through Tunstall, Burslem and Hanley. Some of the track bed has been preserved as a part of a reclamation scheme and now forms part of a network of foot and bridle paths known as Greenway. **Potteries, Biddulph & Congleton Railway** (later absorbed by NSR) built the Biddulph Valley Railway or Biddulph Branch line in 1863; it closed in 1927. The **South Staffordshire Railway** (SSR), formed out of an amalgamation in 1846 of two schemes, the South Staffordshire Junction Railway and the Trent Valley, Midlands & Grand Junction Railway. SSR was absorbed by the LNWR in 1867, which in turn became part of the LNER. SSR built: Dudley Port-Wychnor line (1850-); Cannock Branch (Walsall-Cannock) (1858); Norton Canes Branch (Ryder's Hayes-Norton Canes) (1858); Tipton Branch (1863); Darlaston Branch (1863). **Birmingham, Wolverhampton and Stour Valley Railway**, incorporated in 1846, passed to LNWR in 1847, part of LMSR after 1923; opened the Birmingham-Tipton-Wolverhampton line in 1852 (confrontations between LNWR and Shrewsbury & Birmingham Railway over the construction of the line occurred at Wolverhampton). **Oxford, Worcester & Wolverhampton Railway**, incorporated in 1845, opened the Worcester-Dudley-Wolverhampton line in 1854, passed in 1860 to the West Midland Railway (formed 1860), which passed to the GWR in 1863. **Stafford & Uttoxeter Railway** (1867-1957), later a part of GNR (after 1923 LNER). **Birmingham, Wolverhampton and Dudley Railway**, incorporated in 1846, passed to the GWR in 1848, opened the Snow Hill (Birmingham) to Priestfield (Bilston) line in 1854 and a branch from West Bromwich to Dudley in 1866. The **Derbyshire, Staffordshire, Worcestershire Junction Railway**, incorporated in 1847, became the Cannock Mineral Railway in 1855, opened a line from Rugeley to Cannock in 1859. The **Cannock Chase Railway**, incorporated in 1860, opened a line between Hednesford and Heathy Leasows in 1862, and passed to the LNWR in 1863. **Wolverhampton and Walsall Railway**, incorporated in 1865, opened a line between Wolverhampton and Walsall in 1872. In 1876 it passed to the Midland Railway. The **Wolverhampton, Walsall & Midland Junction Railway**, incorporated in 1872, passed to the Midland Railway in 1874, which opened a line between Walsall and Castle Bromwich (Warws) in 1879. **Cheadle Railway** company (1878) built the line from Cresswell to Cheadle opened by 1901; it was taken over by NSR in 1908. **Harborne Railway** (1874-1934 or goods later).

SOME, LIGHT, TOURIST, ENTHUSIAST LINES: **Kinver Light Railway** (Amblecote) (1900-1927). **Manifold Valley Light Railway** (Hulme End) (1904-1934). **Foxfield Light Railway** (Foxfield) (c1967-). **Chasewater Light Railway** (later 20th Century). **Rudyard Lake** light railway (1978). **Churnet Valley Railway** (1996-) (VCH vol 2 pp305-334) (A Regional History of the Railways of Great Britain. vol 7. The West Midlands. Rex Christiansen. 1973. pp24,25,190,274,277) (NSJFS 1964 p87) (IANS pp27,28) (The Local Historian's Encyclopedia. John Richardson. 1993 pp174-185).

AERONAUTICS.

BALLOON INCIDENTS: Millstone Green (1785), Bilston (1816), Gun Hill (1826), Fair Oak (Cannock Chase) (1846), Wolverhampton (1862), Tettenhall Towers (1882), and Longton/ Church Leigh (1908).

AIRPORTS: Stoke-on-Trent, Walsall and Wolverhampton municipal airports opened in the 1930s at Meir, Aldridge Lodge and Pendeford, respectively. All had closed by the early 1970s. The County's only current (2000) commercial airport is that at Halfpenny Green.

UFOS: There were a great many sightings of unidentified flying objects in the County (mainly the Stoke-on-Trent area) from late August to November 1967; individual sightings have been made at these places (see): Bentilee, Berry Hill, Bradwell, Bucknall, Cannock, Cellarhead, Cheddleton Heath, Chesterton, Doley, Flash, Fenton, Hanley, Kidsgrove, Ladderedge, Leek, Light Oaks, Longport, Longton, Meir, Newcastle-under-Lyme, Park Hall Hills, Porthill, Shelton, Smallthorne, Stafford, Trent Vale, Werrington Weston Coyney and Whitehill.

Welfare

The famine which swept Europe from 1315-1317 affected Staffordshire. The Croxden Chronicle describes 1316 as a year 'memorable for dearthness, famine, disease and death' (Abbey of St Mary. Croxden Chronicle. C Lynam pvii) (VCH vol 6 p36). The Black Death had reached the County by spring 1349 (SCSF p133) (HOS p39) (VCH vol 6 p37). According to W Beresford Staffordshire was badly affected in that it 'lost its archdeacon and half the clergy. The Bagots suffered. The whole Forester family at Pillaton Hall was swept away. At Swynnerton both squire and rector died, and Nicholas de Swynnerton, Dean of Stafford, also' (COEA p221). Alrewas and Caverswall also suffered. Many villages, including perhaps Statfold, were possibly depopulated by death and desertion. The second plague outbreak of 1361 left its mark on the County (VCH vol 6 p38); Cannock was affected. Some medieval hospitals: Stafford - Holy Sepulchre (for lepers); St John's; St Leonard's (for lepers). At Penkhull - St Eloy's. Lichfield - Freeford House (for lepers); St John's (for men, later an almshouse); Milley's Hospital (for women). Cannock - St Mary's. Wolverhampton - St Mary's. Tamworth - St James' Hospital. At Wednesbury there is said to have been a Bethlehem hospital. Medieval skin and eye sufferers took the waters of healing wells at Ashenhurst (Egg Well), Bilston (St Crudley's Well), Cannock Wood (Nun's Well), Cheadle, Church Eaton (St Edith's Well), Green Hill (Ashwood), Gunstone (Leper Well), Huntley, Ingestre (St Erasmus's Well), Leek (Lady o' the Dale Well), Lichfield (St Chad' Well), Shenstone (St John's Well), Uttoxeter (Maiden's Well and Pennycroft Well), Wheaton Aston, Wolverhampton (Wulfruna's Well and Spaw Spring) and the spring of Wordsley Brook. From the 17th to the 19th Centuries curative springs at Abnalls (Unite Well), Chapel Ash, Dosthill, Dudley Wood (Saltwell) Worcestershire, Rickerscote, Wheaton Aston, Willenhall, and Willoughbridge Wells became minor spa resorts.

Crosses, troughs and well heads of 17th and 18th Century origin at Basford, Birchall, Mow Cop (Vinegar Well), Oulton Cross, Ranton, Stile House and Stone Cross may have been used in plague times as food-depositing places for infected towns. Plague occurred at Tamworth in 1560-63 and Lichfield in 1564 and 1594-5; Stafford in 1604 and 1610; Dudley, Sedgley and Tipton in 1616; Walsall in 1636; Stafford in 1637 and 1642; Leek, Lichfield (and 1645), Tutbury (the garrison) and Uttoxeter in 1646; Burslem and Stone in 1647; Cheadle, Mow Cop, Rugeley and Wyrley Bank in 1665; Trentham in 1728-9; Bilston in 1734 and 1756. In 1696 there were riots due to the 'condition of the corn' in Staffordshire (LOU p356). The 1832 and 1849 Cholera epidemics swept through the Black Country claiming lives in the parishes of Coseley, Darlaston, Kingswinford, Sedgley, Tipton, Walsall, Wednesbury, Wednesfield, West Bromwich and Bilston, where a special school was opened for the orphans. In 1849 Willenhall had to use land known as Doctor's Piece set aside for a school as an emergency burial ground; whilst Wolverhampton founded an asylum for orphans which became the present Royal Wolverhampton School. An outbreak of mumps in the gypsy community camping at Mumper's Dingle near Willenhall may have given that place its name. There was an outbreak of legionnaires disease at Stafford in April 1985.

For the numerous charities for the poor see the Victoria County History and The Reports of the Commissioners Appointed in Pursuance of various Acts of Parliament to enquire concerning Charities in England and Wales relating to the County of Stafford 1819-1837 (copies in SRO and Keele University Library). Gooding, acts of begging in the community for the poor on St Thomas' day (21 December), occurred at Bobbington, Cheadle, Colton, Eccleshall, Norbury and other places. Some charity dole was distributed on this day at Burton, Church Leigh and other places. Moseley's bread dole funded out of the estate of Thomas Moseley (fl 1452) was distributed on Epiphany eve (5 January) at Walsall; it was long believed there that he had intended his estate to be left to the poor but this was discovered to be not so. There are or have been ALMSHOUSES at these and other places: **Abbots Bromley** Lambert Bagot's (W p408; for six old men date from built after 1702): **Aldridge** (see): **Brereton**; Miss Birch's (W 475) (VCH vol 5 p172; built by Elizabeth Birch and Thomas Birch in 1824): **Brierley Hill** (see The Elms): **Burton**; Dame Paulet's (see entry). **Colton**; 'Ellen Oldham' (CWF p176; built by Ellen's sister Mrs John Harland on land hired for 99 years from the school trustees; Miss Oldham d1883): **Enville**; Lady Dorothy's Cottage (see); **Handsworth** (see): **Hanley**; William Ridgway's (POTP p181; for widows in Northwood; Ridgway died in 1864): **Harborne** (see Bearwood): **Heath Town** (see): **Kinver**; High Street (Kinver a Photographic Record 1890-1930 pl 15; demolished after 1972): **Leek**; Ash (see); Carr's (see); Condlyffe (see): **Lichfield**; Buckeridge's (see entry); Burgamy House (see); Lunn's (see); Newton's College (see); St John's Hospital: **Longdon** (see): **Madeley**; Sir John Offley's (W p395): **Marchington** (see): **Newcastle**; Albemarle (see): **Old Hill**; Lord Ward and John Turton's (W p193; six almshouses; land given 1688): **Penn** (see): **Penkridge**; Hatherton's (PVH p12) (HOP p85; New Road; 1866; given by Dowager Lady Hatherton in memory of Lord Hatherton; five tenements and intended for superannuated labourers on the Teddesley estate): **Rolleston** (see): **Rugeley**; Sarah Hopkins (VCH vol 5 p172; in Church Street; 1826; rebuilt on another site in Church Street c1938) (W p475); HR Sneyd's (VCH vol 5 p172; eight cottages in Fortescue Lane in 1870 for poor aged women and his heirs built further houses); Walter's (VCH vol 5 p172; in Taylors Lane; 1890): **Stafford**; Noel's (see); Palmer's (see); **Tamworth** (see): **Tettenhall**; Cresswell's (see): **Uttoxeter**; Catherine Mastergent's (W p791; in Carter Street; 1646; rebuilt 1815); John Wright's (W p791; in Carter Street founded 1729); Lathropp's (see entry): **Walsall** (see).

From the 18th Century new REGIONAL HOSPITALS arose: **Staffordshire General Infirmary** (1766) at Foregate; **North Staffordshire Infirmary** (1819) first at Etruria and then at Hartshill; **South Staffordshire General Hospital** at Wolverhampton (1848) (HOS 1998 p126). There are currently many more including converted union workhouses, for example, those for: Stoke (later City General Hospital at Hartshill); Stone (Trent House); Burslem and Wolstanton (at Westcliffe); Walsall (Manor Hospital at The Moat Site); and Wolverhampton (New Cross). Some isolation, military, orthopaedic, private, and cottage hospitals have occupied (or the sites of): The Beeches (Penn Hospital), Betley Court, Biddulph Grange, Groundslow Fields, The Hill (Corbett Hospital, Amblecote), Lodge Farm (West Bromwich), Longfield Cottage, Patshull Hall, Pelsall Hall, Prestwood House, Rowley Hall, Sandon Hall, Stallington Hall, and Standon Hall. Some County LUNATIC ASYLUMS: **St George's** at Stafford; **St Margaret's** at Great Barr Hall; **St Matthew's** at Hobstone Hill; **St Edward's** at Cheddleton. Some private and lesser-known asylums: Ashwood House; Barr House at Hamstead; Coton Hill at Stafford; Moat House at Tamworth; Oulton Abbey; Spring Vale at Tittensor; Sandwell Hall.

County newspapers

18th CENTURY. The **Wolverhampton Chronicle** began as the Wolverhampton Chronicle and Staffordshire Advertiser on Sept 2 1789, and is the county's earliest newspaper. It lasted to 1793, when the copyright was for sale. The Staffordshire Advertiser started up on its own from Stafford in 1795. The Chronicle was revived on Jan 9 1811. Often known as 'The Chron' it at some time merged with the Shoppers' Guide (BCM April 1980 pp25-26). In 1930 it was incorporated with the Midland Counties Express, but was revived on May 2 1947 (Wolverhampton & Its Press 1848-1948) (BCM April 1980 pp25-26). The **Staffordshire Advertiser** (SA), was founded by Joshua Drewry on Jan 3 1795. For its first year its full title was Staffordshire Advertiser, and Political, Philanthropic and Commercial Gazette (SHJ spring 1996 p5). In 1953 it merged with the Staffordshire Chronicle to become the **Staffordshire Advertiser and Chronicle**. In 1962 the Advertiser and Chronicle was only the third paper in the country to use a new printing process called web-offset (SN Jan 6 1995 p9); the last issue appeared on Jan 4 1973 (VCH vol 6 pp258-259) (SN Millennium Special Jan 2000 p8p). There are back copies of SA in WSL (H pp88-89) and Keele University library.

EARLY 19th CENTURY. Volume two Nos. 53 (Jan 1 1810) and 60 (Feb 19 1810) of **The Pottery Gazette and Weekly Advertiser for Newcastle-under-Lyme** survive in the WSL (SHJ spring 1996 p10). The **Staffordshire Gazette** was first published in Newcastle from April 6 1813. In 1814 it became the **Staffordshire Gazette and Newcastle and Pottery Advertiser** (SHJ spring 1996 p7). In 1819 this became the **Newcastle and Pottery Gazette and Staffordshire Advertiser**, which had ceased by 1834 (NUL p160). The **Staffordshire Mercury** was printed in Stafford between 1814-15. In July 1815 it moved to Lichfield, becoming eventually the Lichfield Mercury (VCH vol 6 p259) (SHJ spring 1996 p7). The weekly **Staffordshire Mercury, Pottery Gazette and Newcastle Express** was founded on Jan 7 1824 by Thomas Allbut (1777-1857) (OPB p9) (POTP pp18,19). In March 1834 it became the **North Staffordshire Mercury**, but it resumed the title Staffordshire Mercury in April 1845. It appears to have folded in May 1848 (SHJ spring 1996 p8). At some period it was known as The **Pottery Mercury**; WSL has copies of these papers from 1824 to 1831 (SHJ spring 1996 p10). **Drewry's Staffordshire Gazette**, founded by Joshua Drewry, ran for six months in 1827 (VCH vol 6 p259). **The Weekly Register**, founded by Joshua Drewry, ran from Nov 1827 to Dec 1828 (VCH vol 6 p259). The weekly **Staffordshire Gazette**, founded by the same Joshua Drewry, ran from July 1831 to Sept 1832 (VCH vol 6 p259) (SHJ spring 1996 p7).

MID 19th CENTURY. The Potteries-based **Staffordshire Examiner** was founded in 1837 to popularize Liberal ideas. After some early popularity, the rather extreme views of its editor, Cyrus Redding, alienated moderate opinion and by 1841 it had lost most of its circulation (NSJFS 1961 p94). The same or another Staffordshire Examiner, published at Lichfield, ran from at least May 14 1836 to Dec 29 1838 (SHJ spring 1996 p6). The **Staffordshire Gazette**, a Conservative paper, was founded in 1838 (NSJFS 1961 p94), or in Jan 1839 in Rugeley by JT Walters. By the time it closed in March 1842 it had moved to Stafford (VCH vol 6 p259). Its full title appears to have been Staffordshire Gazette, County Standard and General Commercial Advertiser for the Midland Counties (SHJ spring 1996 p7). The weekly Potteries-based **North Staffordshire Independent and Potteries, Newcastle, Congleton Gazette** appears to have run from March 1 to June 7 1851 (SHJ spring 1996 p9). The **Staffordshire Potteries Telegraph**, a Liberal newspaper, existed between 1852-55, and was printed by William Dean (POTP p78) (SHJ spring 1996 p10). The **Potteries Free Press** appears to have run from Feb 12 to April 16 1853 (SHJ spring 1996 p10). The Potteries-based **Staffordshire Sentinel and Commercial and General Advertiser** began on Jan 7 1854 as a 3d weekly; remaining a weekly, it became the **Staffordshire Sentinel, Birmingham, Wolverhampton and Midland Counties Advertiser and Macclesfield, Congleton and Leek Express**, and then the **Staffordshire Sentinel and Midland Counties Advertiser**, and then the **Staffordshire Sentinel** from Dec 1 1860; still a weekly, the paper ran at least until 1954. On April 15 1873 the Sentinel publishers launched the daily **Staffordshire Sentinel**; from Jan 5 1884 this had a Saturday edition. The paper became the **Evening Sentinel** (ES) from 1929, and **The Sentinel** from June 19 1995 and still (1999) runs (H p87) (Rendezvous with the Past. Sentinel Centenary. 1854-1954) (POTP p172) (TSS) (SHJ spring 1996 pp6,8).

LATE 19th CENTURY. The **Staffordshire News and Trade Advertiser** was founded in or after 1874 by Edward Vaughan Hyde Kenealy MP and was launched in opposition to the liberal Staffordshire Sentinel. The first issue contained an attack on the pottery manufacturers Copeland and Minton for burning bones (POTP p134). The **Staffordshire Evening Post** represented the Tory Unionist view and was in opposition to the Liberal Home Rule policy advocated by the Staffordshire Sentinel. The Post became the **Staffordshire Post** from July 1 1894 (SHJ spring 1996 p6) and eventually merged with the Sentinel which compelled the Sentinel editor William Mackie to leave and found the Liberal-orientated Staffordshire Herald (POP p65). The **Staffordshire**

Times, formerly the Newcastle Journal (founded in 1855), took the title of Staffordshire Times in the period 1874-82 (NUL p160). The **Staffordshire Daily Times** has been described as Newcastle-under-Lyme's only daily paper, and lasted for only 10 issues in 1875 (NUL p160) or in early Oct 1874. The **Stoke-on-Trent News Sheet** was produced by Joseph G Fern, printer from c1877. It had a short life (POTP p94). **The Lantern** was published in Wolverhampton from April 2 to Sept 24 1879 (Wolverhampton & Its Press 1848-1948). Volume 1, No. 9 of **Spice**, a short-lived Potteries paper, appeared on Feb 7 1880. **Reporter** was another short-lived Potteries paper, as was the **Potteries Daily Express**, the **Weekly Star**, and the **Staffordshire Courier**, which appeared in 1890 and 1891 (POP p65) (SHJ spring 1996 p6). **The Magpie** was published in Wolverhampton from Oct 7 1882 to Jan 15 1887 (Wolverhampton & Its Press 1848-1948). The Potteries-based weekly **Staffordshire Knot** was founded by Joseph Dawson, William Owen and Enoch Bennett, father of the novelist Arnold in May 1882. Arnold wrote for the paper before moving to London in 1889. The paper became the **Potteries Free Press and Staffordshire Knot** in Nov 1891 (SHJ spring 1996 p7), and it failed in 1892 (H p88) (POP p65) (POTP pp77,165). The daily **Staffordshire Knot** was appearing by mid May 1885. In June 1885 it became the **Staffordshire Morning Knot** but returned to its old title of Staffordshire Knot in Oct 1887 (SHJ spring 1996 p7). The **Staffordshire Chronicle** was founded in 1884 out of the Stafford Chronicle, founded 1877. The Chronicle ran until after 1955 when it was merged with the Staffordshire Advertiser to become the Staffordshire Advertiser and Chronicle (VCH vol 6 p259) (SHJ spring 1996 p5). The daily **Potteries Evening Echo** appears to have run from Nov 29 1886 to Feb 12 1887 (SHJ spring 1996 p10). Volume 1, No. 3 of the Potteries-based **Staffordshire Weekly Press** appeared on March 10 1888 (SHJ spring 1996 p8). The penny weekly the **Staffordshire Herald** or North Staffordshire Herald was founded by William Mackie, a Scots radical. It was Liberal but shortly failed (H p88) (POP p65); copies survive from Nov to Dec 1895 (SHJ spring 1996 p9). The Potteries-based **North Staffordshire Weekly Journal** appears to have run from Sept 15 to Oct 13 1899 (SHJ spring 1996 p10).

20th CENTURY. No. 1001 of the weekly **Staffordshire Times and Echo** appeared on Aug 1 1908; BL have copies up to April 7 1910 (SHJ spring 1996 p8). No. 531 of the **Potteries Advertiser and North Staffordshire Chronicle** appeared on March 14 1908 and copies survive to Aug 1912 (SHJ spring 1996 p10). The **Football** was published in Wolverhampton from Sept 10 to Dec 24 1895 (Wolverhampton & Its Press 1848-1948). The **Staffordshire Herald**, a Wolverhampton-based paper, ran from Nov 16 1907 to Oct 7 1911 when it continued as the **Staffordshire Catholic Herald**. The Catholic Herald continued from Oct 14 to Nov 14 1911 when it closed to allow the **Staffordshire Catholic News** to take over, which was founded on Nov 11 1911 (Wolverhampton & Its Press 1848-1948) (SHJ spring 1996 p38). The **Sporting Star** was published in Wolverhampton from Aug 30 1919 to at least 1948 (Wolverhampton & Its Press 1848-1948). The **Staffordshire Farmer**, founded in 1923, was still running in 1988 (Willings Press Guide. 1988). The Potteries-based **Stoke-on-Trent City Times** seems to have run from Nov 9 1935 to Dec 31 1969 (SHJ spring 1996 pp10-11).

Parliamentary representation

COUNTY SEATS. Staffordshire sent two knights to parliament in 1258, and was sending two knights to parliament by the early years of Elizabeth I's reign. The gentry normally arranged among themselves who should represent the County to avoid expensive contested elections. There was no contest for a hundred years until the election of 1747. A contested election then arose because of Staffordshire Tories' dissatisfaction with Earl John Leveson-Gower (1694-1754) of Trentham Hall, a leading Jacobite in 1715, who had not only gone over to the Hanoverians by joining the Whig government in 1742 but had raised a regiment to fight the Young Pretender in 1745. Two Tories, Sir Walter Wagstaffe Bagot and John Crewe, stood against the two Leveson-Gower nominees, William Leveson-Gower, the earl's brother, and Sir Richard Wrottesley, his son-in-law. There was a hard-fought contest which lasted six days. The result was a draw; Bagot obtained one seat and Leveson-Gower the other (HOS p61). Wrottesley, who was defeated by Bagot, petitioned, but a Tory demonstration against the petition was organised at the Lichfield race meeting on Whittington Heath (LOU p103) on Wednesday Sept 23 1747 (SHC vol 2 1920 and 1922 p253). Sir Watkin Williams Wynn, an important Jacobite of North Wales and a close friend of Walter Bagot, organised a march into Lichfield of Burton Jacobites at the same time as another contingent came in from Birmingham. The event became known as the Elibank Plot (LOU p103). The Duke of Bedford, Gower's son-in-law and leader of a group of Whigs, and Lord Gower were hustled at the race course by the Jacobites, and a dancing master, called Joul, actually struck Bedford. On the same day a Walsall man named Tibbets was arrested for suspected recruiting for the Pretender, but a subsequent investigation found no conclusive evidence to convict him. Those arrested at Stafford and Lichfield were tried before the Assizes at Stafford on Aug 13 1748 (SIOT p53) (LOU p103). (The Lichfield Squabble. An Humorous Poetical Narrative of the Several Transactions at the Elections for the County of Stafford and City of Lichfield. 1747. By Peter Plain-Truth, not Lord Puff) (SHC 1917-18. 1920 and 1922 p253. 1933 (1). 1970 pp115-119) (The Staffordshire County Election 1747. SAH Burne MA. 1967) (VB p15) (SSE 1991 pp21-34). No further election was contested for the County seats before 1832. The Reform Act of 1832 raised the number of County seats from two to four; two in a north division of the County and two in a south division. The Reform Act of 1867 raised the number of County seats to six. The two divisions were abolished and replaced by three divisions - North, West and East - each with two seats (HOS pp61,62. 1998 p82).

OLD BOROUGH SEATS. Together with the two County seats there were from the Elizabethan period until 1832 two seats each for the four medieval boroughs - Lichfield, Newcastle-under-Lyme, Stafford, and Tamworth - bringing the total for the County to ten. The Reform Act of 1832 raised the overall number to seventeen. The Reform Act of 1867 raised the number to nineteen. After an Act of 1885 the County's overall representation was fifteen seats. In medieval times borough representation was sparse and irregular. Borough MPs were at first burgesses, but in the 15th Century an increasing number of gentry were elected (HOS pp61,62. 1998 pp77,78,82). Lichfield first returned to parliament in 1305 (VCH vol 14 pp14,92-95) (W pp487,488; says in 1274). It was deprived of its representation in 1354 and not represented again until 1548. In 1653 it lost one of its two representatives, but regained one in 1659. The Leveson-Gowers of Trentham Hall and the Ansons of Shugborough Hall controlled Lichfield seats in the later 18th Century. By an Act of 1867 it lost a seat and by an Act of 1885 it lost its remaining seat (HOS 1998 p82). Newcastle first returned in 1354 and was fairly regularly represented afterwards. It lost one of its two representatives in 1653, but regained one in 1659 (NM pp92-96) (NTS pp52,151-2) (VCH vol 8 p42). Sir John Davies (1569-1626) poet, philosopher and barrister, was MP for Newcastle in 1614 (VFC p36). In the 1624 election the defeated candidate John Keeling petitioned the House of Commons to have the custom of vesting the right of election in the mayor, two bailiffs, aldermen, and capital burgesses revoked as it was not prescriptive and give the right to the general body of burgesses as had been the case in Edward IV's reign. The commons concluded in favour of the petition and consequently the general body of burgesses had the right to vote unchallenged. It was also established that the freemen residents did not forfeit their title to vote until a year and a day after they had left the town. In the subsequent contests, in 1705 and 1792 the discussion was confined to the question of residence for a year and a day, that they actually ceased to reside in the town, and was decided against their claim (S&W p275) (VCH vol 8 p43). The Leveson-Gower family of Trentham Hall controlled the seats from 1675 to 1820 (VCH vol 8 pp42-44) (NRS pp78-79). By an Act of 1885 Newcastle lost one of its two seats (HOS 1998 p82). Stafford returned two representatives in 1295 and was fairly regularly represented afterwards. It lost one of its two representatives in 1653, but regained one in 1659. The Chetwynd family of Ingestre Hall often held the Stafford seats from the late 15th Century to the late 18th Century; curiously, the antiquarian Walter Chetwynd of that family, MP for Stafford borough on several occasions in the later 17th Century, omitted Stafford from his survey of Pirehill hundred (1679) (SHC 1914 p112). Alexander MacDonald, shoemaker and later MP for Stafford in 1874, was one of the first working class politicians (VCH vol 2 p233). By an Act of 1885 Stafford lost one of its two seats (S&W p279) (HOS p66. 1998 pp77,82). Tamworth first returned in 1275 but did not return again until 1563. From 1653 Tamworth lost its representation but regained two members in 1659. Its seats in the period 1765 to 1832 were controlled by the holders of Tamworth Castle and of Drayton Bassett manor; hence the monopoly was known as 'Castle' and 'Manor.' In the 1818 general election for Tamworth borough the candidate for 'Castle,' the sitting member Lord Charles Townshend, and the candidates for 'Manor,' the sitting member Sir Robert Peel, father of the later PM, and his second son, William Yates Peel hotly campaigned in the contest. Many ridiculing ditties were published and counteracting ditties in reply (THM vol 1 pp77-81). By an Act of 1885 Tamworth lost its two seats (HOS 1998 pp80,82).

In 1832 Wolverhampton was enfranchised with two seats. It gained another in 1885. Walsall was enfranchised in 1832 with one seat. Stoke-upon-Trent was enfranchised in 1832 with two seats. It lost one in 1885. Wednesbury was enfranchised with one seat in 1867. West Bromwich had one seat from 1885 (HOS p62). For the division of the County after 1885 see GLAUE.

In 1965 the County returned eighteen members each representing constituencies called Bilston, Brierley Hill, Burton, Cannock, Leek, Lichfield and Tamworth, Rowley Regis and Tipton, Smethwick, Stafford and Stone, Stoke-on-Trent North, Stoke-on-Trent Central, Stoke-on-Trent South, Walsall North, Walsall South, Wednesbury, West Bromwich, Wolverhampton North East, and Wolverhampton South West (Complete Atlas of the British Isles. The Reader's Digest. 1965).

Some curious, peculiar and legendary personal feats

Whilst the Enville, Kinver and Offley Hay giants are only legendary Staffordshire can claim the human giants Walter Parsons of West Bromwich, William Evans of Hamstall Ridware and the 'Staffordshire Giant,' Mr Bamfield or Bamford of Rugeley. Apparently, there has also been 'Titana - The Staffordshire Giantess' a very large woman who was exhibited at circuses in the late C19 or early C20; her ankle was 14 inches; hips 94 inches; calf 36 inches; thigh 43 inches; waist 62 inches; chest 102 inches. At the age of 26 she was six feet two inches and weighed 36 stone eight pounds (TB Aug 26 1999 p19). George Lovatt, a native of Cheshire but who lived his later life at Round Oak, weighed some 42 stones and was considered 'an unprecedented spectacle' when he died in 1933. But his weight has been surpassed since by that of Muriel Hopkins of Tipton who weighed 47 stone 7lb at her death in 1979. Notable dwarfs include: Isaac Leech of Hanley; Mary Jane Burrows of Halmer End; Jimmy Maddock of Leek and Hannah Bourne of Stoke-upon-Trent. Whilst Dr Thomas Wright of Norton-in-the-Moors who lived in the 19th Century was described by his local community as 'the ugliest man in the world,' the Guiness Book of Records has declared Dorian Yates, a Staffordshire native, the winner of the most consecutive Mr Olympia titles, winning five Mr Olympia contests in a row between 1992 and 1997 (GBR 1998 p110). The same book has declared a lady from Clent the worst singer in Britain or the world. Those who have, or allegedly, lived to great ages include: ancient parish. W Farr of Tamworth 144; James Sands of Harborne 140; Joseph Lees of Totmonslow 127; William Wakeley of Outlands 125; Ann Harvey of Ellastone 120; William Beresford of Park Head 116; Eva Morris of Newcastle 114; Daisy Adams of Burton 112; William Billinge of Fawfieldhead 112; Thomas Burton of Ramshorn 111; Edward Hall of Alrewas 110, Henry Lea of Shenstone 107, and Martha Southall of Sedgley who lived through six reigns from George III to George V.

The achievements of centenarians include: a Seighford man aged 124 who became a father again aged 100; a Wednesfield man, who died aged reputedly 115 having married four times, lastly aged 105; a Longnor man who walked from his own house to Buxton (five miles) within three days of his death aged 105; and a Compton man, the same age, who was backed for 50 L to walk one mile in a race with others so long as they were over 80. For walking endurance there has been Dr Phineas Fowke of Little

Abbey A ward of Sandwell metropolitan borough covering the Warley Park area. The name is from Warley Abbey.

Abbey A ward of Stoke-on-Trent district by 1991 covering the Carmounthead, Milton, and Abbey Hulton areas.

Abbey, The 'The Abbey' is a reference to the remains of a probable pre-Reformation chapel which has long been incorporated into cottages situated close to Abbey Farm in Abbey Road, Gornalwood (AMS p444 p). The Abbey may relate to 'The Abbey' site which has been identified with Ellenvale (see).

Abbey Court Tiny district of south Stone on which Stood Stone Priory (W p359).

Abbey Farm On N side of Birches Head Road at SJ 90244922 about 300 yards W of Hulton Abbey. It was in existence by the early C18 when it was the home of John Bourne, grandfather of the Primitive Methodist leader, Hugh Bourne. The present house, probably built in the early C19, is of brick, but the large stone blocks, some of which are ashlar, in the east-facing gable wall are said to come from Hulton Abbey (VCH vol 8 p248) (SASR 1985 p48).

Abbey Farm Brick house with two gables in Abbey Street, Lower Gornal. Owed its name to the fact that the income from some, or all, of its lands went to a local abbey. In 1842 it was the home of a local doctor, Dr Hicken. The building still stood in 1970 (SDOP p20p).

Abbey Green Hamlet approximately 300 yards WSW of Dieulacres Abbey. Formerly in Leekfrith township in Leek ancient parish (W p728). The 'green' probably originated as open space at the abbey gate (VCH vol 7 p193). Before the later C18 the road between Leek and Buxton passed through Abbey Green (VCH vol 7 p195). Mr Brough drank at the inn at Abbey Green just prior to being murdered by John Naden (OL vol 1 p26). The Young Pretender's army came through Abbey Green on Dec 3 1745 (BPCSM p3). A phantom coach has been sighted in the vicinity of Dieulacres Abbey (DPEM p156).

Abbey House Burton upon Trent Abbey. Supposed to have been the abbot's private residence (W p534).

Abbey Hulton Former manor and township in Burslem and Norton-in-the-Moors chapelries in Stoke-upon-Trent ancient parish. There is a burial mound at SJ 899488, 0.5m NW of Abbey Hulton. It is three feet high and was threatened in 1983 with destruction to make way for a school playground (NSFCT 1983 p12). Hulton manor appears in DB as Heltone. The name Hulton means Hill town or farmstead; the addition 'Abbey' comes from Hulton Abbey (see) erected here in 1223 (DUIGNAN) (SPN pp26,65). The lordship of Abbey Hilton or Hulton (SSE 1994 p73) lay in the vicinity of Hulton Abbey (see) and Abbey Farm. In the C20 a suburb developed to the S which became known as Abbey Hulton (VCH vol 8 p248); this is 3m NE of Stoke-upon-Trent. Abbey Hulton was taken into Stoke-on-Trent county borough in 1922 (VCH vol 8 p260). The modern St John's stands facing Tranter Road on the S side of Greasley Road. Several people in the Tranter Road area saw an UFO in the form of a large, oval-shaped object in July 1980. It was of red or orange colour and could be heard humming (SMM p99).

Abbey Island Tiny island in a small (probably artificial) lake SSW of Batchacre Hall on which was erected the porch or portico to Gerrard's Bromley Hall (NSFCT 1927 p39) (SLM April 1948 p100).

Abbeylands A Jacobean-style mansion opposite Weston-on-Trent church. White says it was lately built by William Moore on land believed to have a bad reputation for a murder may have taken place on it; the house is haunted. In 1851 it was the seat of John Reynolds (W p435) (NSFCT 1900 p142). Pevsner says it was built in 1858 to designs of Gilbert Scott (BOE p305). In 1955 it became the home of Lord Harmer-Nicholls of Darlaston (see) (Offlow hundred).

Abbey Wood Alton Towers. A wood.

Abbey Wood A wood to E of Dieulacres Abbey. The Limes Brittanicus ran through it and the Concangii may have had a camp in it (NSFCT 1946 p152).

Abbot of Burton's Rest House Medieval hostel which housed travellers travelling from Chester to the south and vice versa. It stood on the corner of Stafford Street and Gaolgate Street, Stafford. Here travellers waited for a guide to escort them from the town to Hopwas Bridge near Tamworth. The position of guide was an hereditary one and was originally endowed by the Earls of Chester. The house was described in 1933 as an old building (OSST 1933 p38).

Abbot's Banks By Musden Grange, Calton (NSFCT 1917 p46).

Abbots Bromley Ancient parish, market town and former township nearly 10m ENE of Stafford.

EARLY. The site of an ancient **well** is shown on OS map 1955 at SK 078246, on the S side of Bagot Street.

1000 to 1500. Abbots Bromley **manor** existed in 942 (SSE 1991 pp7,8). A charter was made of its bounds in 993: The charter had not been published by 1975; a C11 copy is at WSL (SL p62). Another charter of 996 (or the same?) grants Abbots Bromley to a thegn (SSE 1996 p8). Abbots Bromley was identified by Dugdale, Shaw and Duignan with the Bromleage mentioned in the will of Wulfric Spot (c1002), founder of Burton Abbey (although Kemble thought, wrongly, it was Bromley in Kent) (SHC 1916 p27) (SSE 1996 p11): The manor, which appears in DB as Brumlege, then belonged to Burton Abbey, who held it until 1545 (AB pp1,6), when it passed to the Pagets. This transition is reflected in the various forms of the town's name: Bromleye Abbatis (1344), Abbotesbromley (1427), Bromley Hurst (1546), Pagettes Bromley (1584), Abbots Bromley (from c1730 to present), and Pagets Bromley (1774) (DUIGNAN) (AB pp15,24,32,33) (VCH vol 3 p297 note) (SSE 1996 p20) (SPN p7). The **name** Bromley, of Anglo-Saxon origin, is from broom, the plant, L Genista, so 'clearing where the broom grows.' Abbots, was added after Wulfric Spot gave Bromley manor to Burton Abbey in 1004 to distinguish it from King's Bromley (DUIGNAN) (SSE 1996 p11) (SPN p7). However, according to the Parliamentary Gazetteer of 1840-43 Abbots was applied from its association with Blithbury Abbey or Priory (AB p26). This error was perpetuated by White (W p407). The prefix Pagets was added after Sir William Paget's purchase of the manor in 1544 (VCH vol 3 p297 note). The **church**, St Nicholas, on the W side of Church Street, dates from shortly after 1002 and was built by c1020: Some Norman work survives in the present church (AB p103). In 1698 the spire and most of the W end of the church collapsed in a storm (NSFCT 1946 p150). The parish was formed before 1086 (SHC 1916 p192). The parish **wake** was on the first Sunday after the 4th September (W p407). Burton Abbey was granted a charter between 1220-1221 to hold a **market** at Abbots Bromley on Tuesdays (NSJFS 1971 p50) (SCSF p95). The charter was confirmed in 1227 (AB p11). There was a market in 1792 (OWEN), but not by 1888 (LHE p264). A **butter cross** covered with stone may have existed in 1339, when described as new (AB p12). There was a cross in 1377 (IVNF). The present butter cross, on the village green, is an hexagonal wooden structure on six posts with a seventh in the centre. It is probably of C17 origin (BOE p51). It has been described as the Town Hall (NSFCT 1886 p22) although 'Town Hall' may refer to what is now the Goat's Head Inn (Shipman p5). In 1932 the Marquess of Anglesey gave it, along with the village green and the pinfold at the corner of Lichfield Road and Ashbrook Lane, to the parish. The market cross was given a new roof when restored in 1935 by the Society for the Preservation of Ancient Monuments at a cost of £200 (CCF pp165,166) (ABMB p40). (HS p200 pl) (AB pp192p,194,195,203) (VESOP 128 pl) (SL p156) (SVB p9). A charter of 1226 granted a **fair** on the vigil, day (Aug 24 or Sept 4 new style), and morrow of St Bartholomew (AB p11). As well as this fair Cooke gives Tuesday before Mid Lent Sunday, and May 23 (SCSF p98). There was a fair in 1792 (OWEN), but not by 1888 (LHE p264). The **curfew bell** formerly tolled from the Monday after old Michaelmas to Shrove Tuesday (GNHSS p17) (SCSF p160). The earliest reference to Abbots Bromley being a **borough** is in 1222 and it had borough status until at least 1606 (NSJFS 1972 p68). There was a common **pound** at Abbots Bromley in the C16 (SHC 1908 p69). An **industry** of the Middle Ages was glass making (NSFCT 1933 pp74-75).

1500 to PRESENT. The free **grammar school** at Abbots Bromley was founded by Richard Clarke in 1606 (ABAB p23). It may have occupied the Goat's Head Inn for a time (OSST 1935 p28). It went into abeyance between 1859 and 1864 and between 1865 and 1867 (LHSB 14 pp12-14). In the C19 it occupied premises in School House Lane. Between 1875 and 1892 the school was absorbed into the Board School of Abbots Bromley (AB pp220-240). For the School of S. Mary and S. Anne, a girls' boarding school at Abbots Bromley see Big House. In 1722 there was a large **fire** at Abbots Bromley (ADD p30). None of the proposals, made in 1862, 1864, and 1896, to link Abbots Bromley with the **railway** system succeeded (S&UR pp6-7) and consequently Abbots Bromley has never expanded beyond being a large predominately C17 and C18 village. In 1868 Abbots Bromley was described by a school commissioner, TH Green as 'a large lifeless village' (LHSB 14 p12). For Abbots Bromley **airfield** see Rugeley Turn. Douglas SE Hayward's **Puppet Theatre Museum**, which closed in 1993 and went to the County Museum at Shugborough, included the unusual triangular punch booth used by Miss Catherine Cockerell from 1922. Richard Bagot has Abbots Bromley as Abbotsbury in his novels (CCF pp187,188) (CCBO p66). **Visitors. Mary, Queen of Scots**, passed through Abbots Bromley on Sept 21 1586 on her way to Fotheringhay (NSFCT 1886 p22) and stayed at Hall Hill Manor (see). In a bid to intercept her descendant Charles Edward Stuart the **Duke of Cumberland**, in the 1745 Jacobite Rebellion, is reputed to have passed through Abbots Bromley on his way to Uttoxeter. The Duke is supposed to have given a shilling to Ann Buxtone alias Nan Brown (HOU pp92-103). **Dr Johnson** of Lichfield (see) may have sold books with his father at Abbots Bromley and he probably passed through the town when travelling between Lichfield and Uttoxeter (AB p195). **Henry Francis Cary** (1772-1844), author, poet, and translator of Dante, was vicar of Abbots Bromley, and spent some of his former years at The Green (see), Cannock. **William Palmer**, the poisoner of Rugeley (see) courted his future wife, Ann Brookes, in Abbots Bromley and married her in the church here on Oct 7 1847 (TPP p12) or at the village hall (SN Feb 10 2000 p18). On May 23 1857 on the road to Lichfield, about a mile from Abbots Bromley, George Jackson, aged 20, and his accomplice Erasmus Brown, aged 21, robbed and murdered a farmer, **William Charlesworth** of Rake End, aged 67, as he returned from the Coach and Horses Inn; Jackson was hung, Brown was reprieved (SA May 30 1857) (TB Feb 1978 pp18-19. July 1993 p19) (RPM pp3-6).

HORN DANCE. Abbots Bromley Horn Dance is a custom with, probably, medieval origins. It is performed in and about Abbots Bromley annually all day on the Monday after the first Sunday following Sept 4. It involves dancing with model deer heads and reindeer antlers. **Origins**. It may have **Pagan** origins: Violet Alford, in 1933, described it as 'the most primitive dance in Europe.' It may have begun in a cult for the forest deity Cernunnos (NSFCT 1908 p111. 1909 pp199-200); or from nature and fertility rituals (FOS p116); or from a winter solstice custom (GLS p9); or from the dance used to entice deer (FOS p116); or from the horns as a sign of prowess (FOS p116); or from the horns as a sign of strength (1 Kings, 22, 11, and Deut. 33, 17); or from the horns as a talisman (FOS p116). It has similarities with pagan customs of North American Indian tribes, Norway and France. Wearing stag horns was regarded as such an evil practice by the latter C7 and St Theodore, Archbishop of Canterbury 668-690 made it prohibitable (History of Witchcraft and Demonology. Summers) (Shipman p8). (ACOB p4). It may have **Danish** origins (Shipman pp6,8) or **celebratory** origins after villagers' obtained hunting rights in Needwood Forest (Shipman p5); a charter of 1125 gave forest hunting rights to some Abbots Bromley villagers (SCSF p5) (COS pp30,31p) (CL Sept 2 1993 p50). Or the dance is of **Christian** origin and began as a pageant to raise funds for the church; collections were made at performances for the church's upkeep and the horns are presently kept in the church (FOS p116). Or it is of **Moorish** origin and a medieval import through Spain (SCSF p5); perhaps via John of Gaunt of Tutbury Castle, seven miles away, who married Constance, daughter of Pedro the Cruel of Castile in 1374 (SCSF p41) (FOS p110). Or it is a **Victorian** invention (R Compton Rose. Birming-

ham Post. 1934). **History**. The dance has evolved to its present form. It is believed that it was performed at the three-day Barthelmy Fair granted to the Abbots of Burton in 1226 celebrating St Bartholomew's day, August 24 (Shipman p3). In medieval times, according to Hackwood, the dance was performed in front of the church on Sundays, a collection was taken by Burton Abbey and distributed to the poor until the Abbey was suppressed in 1540. Plot and Redfern note dancing about this time occurred three times a year (Christmas, New Year and Twelfth Night) and there was a 'pot' preserved by one of four or five persons called the 'Reeves' in which cakes, ale and money were put for repairing the church and relieving the poor. Ladell believes the Horn Dance inspired Scene ii in Act IV of Shakespeare's 'As You Like It' (Shakespeare may have visited Yoxall). Sir Simon Degge, who spent his boyhood 1620-30 in Uttoxeter, reports he often saw the custom and it continued until the Civil War. Plot says the custom was 'within memory' of the people of Abbots Bromley implying that the dance was discontinued during the latter C17 (Shipman p7). The Julian calendar was corrected in 1752 and Barthelmy Fair moved to the beginning of September. In time the three-day fair became one day, to be held on the first Monday after the 4th September (Shipman p3). In 1830 Calvert notes that the custom is discontinued but the horns still hang in the church: Dugdale in 'England and Wales Delineated' (1835) and Harwood in SOS note the same. R Crompton Rhodes in Dancing Times claims the dance was revived later than 1845. In HOU (1860 ed) p335 Redfern says there was attempt in late years to revive the dance; in HOU (1886 ed) p438 he notes the custom had been occurring since c1860. However, other sources imply there was horn dancing by the end of the C18. Rev JM Lowe, vicar of Abbots Bromley in 1844, found the dance in existence in his time and believed it to have been going for ever. Miss Mary Bagot who spent her childhood at Blithfield Hall in the 1790s 'remembers a party from Abbots Bromley who....performed Maid Marion's Dance' ('Links with the Past' Mrs Charles Bagot). William Bentley (b1857) told Marcia Rice in the 1930s he had stories of the dance told to him by his grandfather of when his grandfather was a boy in c1800 (Shipman p9). There was no Horn Dance during WW2 (info a resident in School Lane, Admaston in 1999). In the early 1990s the dancers visited Froggots Farm (unlocated), and Fishers Pit Farm at Bromley Wood. By 1999 there was a Website on the Internet for the Horn Dance (info Doc Rowe). **The dancers**. The number of performers recorded has varied. There have been: 11 (FOS p114), 12 (Shipman p4), and 13 (CL Sept 2 1993 p50). And in 1999 there were 15, including: i) a girl who acted as a relief bowman, ii) an accordion player, iii) a melodeon player, iv) a boy triangle player, v) a boy bowman, vi) Jester (or Fool), vii) Maid Marian, viii) Hobby Horse, ix-xiv) six dancers, xv) an alms collector or relief dancer. By tradition the performers are always male (Shipman p3); but sometimes since the early C20 women have been performers (info Doc Rowe); female guests are regularly invited to participate along with male guests where the dance is given hospitality. Six of the band are the dancers and they hold the horns (FOS p114). In former times dancers were accompanied by Maid Marian, Hobby Horse (STM June 1972 p35p the horse's head image used in 1893), Jester or Fool, a boy carrying a cross-bow (Robin - SMM p147), and a musician who plays an accordion or melodeon (FOS p114), but formerly played a fiddle (Shipman p4) and in more ancient times a drum (SMM p147). Shipman mentions another - one who beats time on a triangle (Shipman p4). The dance has been led by the Bentley and Fowell families for many generations. **The costumes**. The dancers originally wore their own clothes. The first version of the contemporary costumes were made in 1860 (Daily Telegraph Sept? 1991 weekend supplement) or by the vicar's wife in 1880 (GLS p10) or by the daughters of the vicar, Rev JM Lowe, prior to 1887 (Shipman p4). These were replaced and added to in 1904 (Shipman p4). A set of costumes made in the late C19 or early C20 were made out of curtains (local info). In 1915 the men danced in khaki. New costumes provided by Lord and Lady Bagot were made by a London theatrical costumier in 1948 (Shipman p4); these were still being used in the early 1980s (Shipman p4), or had been replaced by new ones made in 1960; these in turn were replaced in 1997 (info Doc Rowe). **The dance**. Douglas Kennedy in English Folk-dancing Today and Yesterday (1964) describes the dance itself, thus: 'The Dance has two parts: one is the winding single file which snakes its way forward making ground gradually as the horn-bearers thread what looks like a figure-of-eight knot .... the second is a stationary dance, formed by the chain winding into a wide circle, then flattening out to make two files facing, and bringing the three white horns opposite the three black, while the Fool and Hobby-horse face (Maid) Marian and Cross-bow. The two lines advance and retire and cross sides, the 'stags' lurching head-on at one another as if butting' (Shipman p4). The leader calls all the instructions in a curious way. 'Oh' means 'Off' and 'Ay' means 'Face.' 'Oo' means 'Through' (SMM p147). Hackwood says the dance is based on the Morris Dance and that it differs from similar local customs of the dance type that it is not merely a May Day revel, but was also performed in mid winter and the steps performed were those of a familiar old country dance called The Hays (SCSF p5).

Dance schedule Sept 6 1999.

7.00am Holy Communion

7.35-7.43 removal of horns from Hurst Chapel

7.45 dancers lined up behind horns in front of altar

8.00 blessing of horns

8.05 dancers assemble outside church

8.08 Jester calls 'fall in,' music starts

8.10 dancing infront of vicarage

8.13 dancing in High Street by Butter Cross

8.15 dancers to Goose Lane

8.20 dancing in front of cottage in Goose Lane

8.22 dancing in Lintake Drive (road of modern houses)

8.27 dancing in front of Shade Elm Cottage, Goose Lane

8.28 dancing and collecting alms in St Nicholas Way

8.40 dancing in Friary Avenue and Preedys Close

8.45 dancing in front of Butt Cottage, Goose Lane

8.50 tea break at Church View Farm, Goose Lane

9.15-9.32 dancing in front of modern houses at Rose Bank, refreshments and guests from the neighbouring houses participating

10.00-10.45 dancing at Yeatsall Farm with refreshments

10.55 dancing at The Granary, Admaston

11.40 dancing in Steenwood Lane, Admaston

11.46-12.05pm dancing in School Lane, Admaston with refreshment at The Smithy

12.28 dancing at Blithfield Hall

1.50 dancing at Little Dunstal Farm

2.27 dancing at Rugeley Turn

2.45 dancing in the Uttoxeter-Abbots Bromley road

2.51 dancing in front of Townend Cottage and at intervals in front of Bankfield (house) and in the road by the entrance to Leafields Farm

3.00-3.25 dancing at Leafields Farm with refreshments

3.45 refreshments at Bromley House, High Street

4.00 dancing in front of the Bagot Arms Inn

4.30 dancing in High Street

4.37 dancing in front of the Royal Oak Inn followed by publican participating in a dance

5.09 dancing in front of Broom and Church Houses

5.10-5.41 dancing in front of The Crofts and the Goats Head Inn followed by the publican and others participating in a dance

5.43-5.47 dancing in front of the Crown Inn

6.33 dancing resumed in front of the Crown Inn

6.36 dancers proceeded up Schoolhouse Lane, whilst a large crowd is left at the Crown Inn to watch morris dancing

6.39 dancing near the Richard Clarke First School by School Cottage

6.41 dancing by The Old School Hall

6.43 dancing in Bagots View (cul-de-sac of modern houses)

6.46 dancing in Swan Lane (road of modern houses)

6.50-6.54 dancing in Clark's Crescent (cul-de-sac of modern houses)

6.55 dancing at No. 9 Swan Lane (home of Mr Fowell, brother of a dancer)

7.11 dancing in Radmore Lane

7.13 dancing in Needwood Grange (cul-de-sac of modern houses)

7.22-7.24 dancing in Lichfield Road by mile post

7.25 dancing at junction of Lichfield Road and Ashbrook Lane and in front of Chapel House

7.28-8.07 dancing in front of the Coach and Horses Inn, Lichfield Road with refreshments

8.10 dancers parade in single file along High Street to village green

8.15 dancers briefly wait at foot of incline to Crown Inn, large crowd (who hitherto had been watching morris dancing) serenade dancers as they climb incline

8.16-8.21 dancing in front of Meadows Newsagents; crowd encircles dancers

8.30 dancing in front of the Crown Inn

8.35 dancers parade to church

8.38 dancers line up behind horns in front of altar

8.40 Lord's Prayer

8.41 horns replaced on wall in Hurst Chapel

9.00 Compline

The dance from a pagan perspective. Pagan interpretations have been read into aspects of the performance: According to Pickford the Maid Marian character is a She-male character. This character is a common folk character who features in many British ceremonies which have pagan origins. When the dancers 'dance' in front of the church and the vicar (or the vicarage?), Maid Marian and the Fool do not dance, because they are pagan characters and unsuitable to dance in front of clergy. The owners of properties visited are always invited to join in a dance, so they can benefit from the fertility and good fortune ritual associated with the custom. The dance is said to have ended with a ceremonial 'killing' of Hobby Horse for the good of the Abbots Bromley community, achieved by the boy bowman shooting at the horse's head; as instantly as Hobby Horse is 'killed' it is revived. But according to Jack Brown, a member of the English Folk Song and Dance Society from Uttoxeter, Hobby Horse formerly lay dead for longer in past years (SMM pp148,149,150). **The horns. Origins.** The horns and the Horn Dance are not necessarily coeval (Shipman p6). It has long been supposed that the horns are deer antlers probably from Needwood Forest (Shipman p5). But Plot in the later C17 and expert opinion in 1892 and 1955 identified them as domestic reindeer; they may have been imported by the Danes (Shipman pp5,6). Dr Wilkes (d1760) of Willenhall Old Hall, mentions 'elk' horns, in his journal, which were brought over by William 6th Baron Paget from Constantinople when he was ambassador there between 1693 and 1703 (CCBO p156). Shipman thinks there was no reason for Wilkes to confuse the two and these may have been an additional set. A replica set was made in 1928 (info Doc Rowe). In 1978 the 'reindeer' horns were proved by carbon dating to be of 1065-80 or 80 years either side of 1065 ('Lore and Language' Magazine. Jan 1980) (SVB p9) (PWIS p106). **Description**. The six horn have a model wooden hobby horse head attachment, and each has a wooden drop handle for the dancers to hold on to; the heads, Ladell says, have C16 characteristics (Shipman p4). In the later C17 Plot noted they had painted on them (or the wooden heads) arms of the families of Paget, Bagot and Wells. Three horns are white-painted. The three 'blue horns' were painted black or brown by at least the 1970s (info Doc Rowe) (FOS p114) (SMM p147) (Daily Telegraph Sept? 1991 weekend supplement). **Weight**. The heaviest of the three white reindeer horns used in the 1990s was about 25 lbs and the lightest about 13 lbs (SMM p147). **Superstitions**. The 'elk' set may have been ones lost in the Trent long ago when the dancers visited Burton upon Trent. In consequence a tradition has arisen of never taking the original set out of the Abbots Bromley area ('Lore and Language' Magazine. Jan 1980) (SVB p9) (PWIS p106). Some have been transfixed by the sight of the horns in the church. Pagans have been stopped from seeing the horns blessed in the church (GLS pp10-11). **Storing**. The horns, the dobby or hobby horse, cross-bow, and wooden spoon for collecting money used to be kept in the church tower and were the responsibility of the vicar (SCSF p6) (CCF p165). However, Pickford says, they used to be kept in the old village hall and then in the Goat Inn, and then in the church belfry (SMM p150). By the 1990s only the horns were kept in Hurst Chapel in the church. In 1981 Abbots Bromley parish council took legal ownership of them (Shipman pp3,9,10). (NSFCT 1886 p22) (SJC p8) (CHMS p15). **Bibliography**. (NHS p434) (SSC p134 in the intro) (SMC p169) (PA pp137,326) (W p408) (GNHSS p17) (HOU p335) (CBD vol 1 p62) (FLJ 1893 p172. 1896 pp382-385 pls x 4, pls iv, vi, vii. 1897 p70. 1910 pp25-30,38-40. 1911 p301. 1913 pp133-134. 1950 p268. 1953 pp364,365. 1955 p414.) (NSFCT 1896 pp123-124. 1908 p111. 1909 pp199-200) (Strand Magazine Nov 1896) (Mrs Berkeley's private notebook 1904) (N&Q vol 1 pp5, 296, 1901-9) (SC pp81-88) (Sword Dances of Northern England. C.Sharp 1911 vol 11 p106 pl1) (LGS pp69,70) (SCSF pp5,6) (Antiquity Magazine 1933) (Dancing Times 1934) (S p49p) (KES p15) (BCC vol 3 pp60-62 pl ii) (CCBO pp154-158 p facing p155) (The Abbots Bromley Horn Dance. Rev AR Ladell. 1932) (AB chapters iv,v,vi pp67-79, pp80-99 ps, one of men in khaki 1915) (Staffordshire Sentinel weekly Sept 16 1950) (NSSG p3) (SJC p8) (BCWJ p7) (SA 6 Sept 6 1956) (HB p122) (FOS pp114-116) (The Hobby Horse and Other Animal Masks. V Alford 1978) (VB pp107, 108) (SJC p8) (STM June 1972 p35 ps of the 1893 dance and the 1927 dance ?) (SGS p45) (WMAG Sept 1979 p31. Oct 1979 p6ps) (The Abbots Bromley Horn Dance. ER Shipman. 1982) (TOS pp108-109) (The Guardian. Sept 12 1989 p3p) (Daily Telegraph Sept? 1991 weekend supplement) (ES Sept 9 1992 p5p).

Abbots Bromley Park A medieval deer park enclosed out of forest held by the abbots of Burton Abbey. Created perhaps in c1222 and in existence by the late C13 (AB pp13,23). It was certainly in existence by 1383 (NSJFS 1962 pp73,75). By the mid C16 it was known as 'the Greate Parke of Bromley' and it has also appeared as Bromley Great Park (AB p35). It can probably be identified with Abbots Park (ABMB). The name is now preserved in the area and house known as Bromley Park (see), 2m ENE of Abbots Bromley.

Abbot's Castle Hill A two mile long escarpment of the Bunter Pebble Beds, rising to over 400 feet, 0.5m SW of Seisdon, in Trysull parish (W p209) (PMPD pp79,81il) (WORF p7p). The northern part of the escarpment forms the county boundary and the ground falls away sharply on the Shrops side (The Staffs Way. Cannock Chase to Kinver Edge. p15). There is evidence here of an ancient British settlement, which would account for the prevalence of Celtic names in the locality - eg - Seisdon, Tresel, Penn, Morfe (SHC 1919 p184). There are or were in a wood on the hill 20 to 30 pit dwellings of ancient British construction, near which have been found human bones. An intermittent ditch extends along the crest of the hill; the county boundary follows it and it may be of Anglo-Saxon or earlier date (VCH vol 1 pp185, 192, 372. vol 20 p185). The name has appeared as Aguardes-Castel (1294), Aquardescastel (1295) (VCH vol 20 p185 note), Apewardes Castle (1300), Apeis Castle (C15), Apeward Castle (C15) (VCH vol 20 p185 note), Apewood Castle (NHS) (SHOS) (W), Abbots Castle (SVS), and as Tinker's Castle. Masefield thought it was originally Ælfwards's Castle (LGS p238). (NHS pp39, 397) (SHOS vol 2 p210) (SVS p327 note) (W p209) (GNHS pp10,66) (WJO May 1908 pp126-127ps) (LGS p238). Aguardes in the Aguardes-castel form may be a corruption Earl Algar of the mid C11; he owned large tracts of the surrounding country, particularly Claverley and Worfield, which this hill immediately dominates (SHC 1919 p184). The connection with an 'Abbot' with the locality can be dismissed. The castle probably refers to the prehistoric earthworks (DUIGNAN) (SPN p146).

Abbots Coachway A strip of ground outside Cheadle Park mentioned in HOC p34 as the Monk's Coach-house Road (ESH p28).

Abbots Hay House marked on 1834 OS map to NW of Hales Hall, Cheadle. Charles John Beech Masefield (1882-1917), poet, novelist and author of LGS, was born at Abbots Haye (PSS pp275-279 p) (VFC p92). He later lived at Hanger Hill, and practiced as a solicitor at Cheadle and Wolverhampton (see), where his cousin, John (1878-1967), later poet laureate, stayed in 1902. In 1917 Charles was awarded the MC. On July 1 1917 he was taken prisoner by the Germans in WW1 and died on July 2 1917 (Preface in 4th ed of LGS); the gate piers at the entrance to Hawksmoor Nature Reserve, Hawksmoor Park, are to his memory.

Abbottsville Council housing estate of the 1920s and 1930s in the NE of Leek, in the Prince Street area (VCH vol 7 p97).

Ablewell Former area of Walsall about present Ablewell Street, NE of the parish church. The name has appeared as Avalwalle (C13) (SNWA p4) and Abelwellsych (1309) (VCH vol 17 pp147,221), Abulwelle Strete (1403) (SNWA p4). It is from a well called Able Well, which was evidently near the junction of Ablewell and Rushall Streets (VCH vol 17 pp147,221). Or 'Aval' is Norman French for 'below, at the bottom of,' and 'walle' is a wall used in connection with a fortification so that the whole word means the street below the fortifications which surrounded the old church (SNWA p4). The old Walsall lock up stood in this street; part of the lock up now forms the cellar of one of the the shops near Warewell Street (SNWA p4).

Ablow Burial mound probably thrown up after the battle of Tettenhall or Wednesfield to a warrior called Ab. It stood on the site now occupied by St Paul's church near Graisley Brook (AOW pp7,10) (WFW p23). In Huntbach's time a bush called Isley Cross stood on it (SHOS vol 2 pp150,172).

Ablow Field Open fields which lay to W of Wolverhampton prior to enclosure. Other Wolverhampton open fields were Broadmeadow, Wind-horn, Windmill, Horseley (SHOS vol 2 p165), and Monmore (HOWM p44). The name which has also appeared as Abley Field, is from Ablow, the burial mound.

Abnalls Tiny hamlet in gentle undulating country near Unite's Well (see), over 1m WNW of Lichfield cathedral. The name has appeared as Abbenhale (C13) (SSE 1996 p10). It is probably of Old English origin and means 'Abba's nook of land' (VCH vol 14 p202). Or 'Æbba's land' (SPN pp78-79). A former interpretation was 'Æbba's or Abba's hall' (DUIGNAN) (SSE 1996 p10). There was a settlement at Abnalls by the later C13, and Abnalls was described as a manor in 1421 (VCH vol 14 pp198,207). At SK 102101 is a moated site which may have been the site for the house of the Abnalls estate or manor (VCH vol 1 p364. vol 14 pp202,208) (SSAHST 1982-3 p44) (CAMS p63 says it is at Maple Hayes). Darwin's Bath and Garden (see) created by Dr Erasmus Darwin lie on the S side of Abnalls Lane.

Abnalls Cottage On N side of Abnalls Lane, Abnalls. The house was rebuilt in 1848. It was the seat of William Gresley, prebendary of Wolvey, in the earlier 1850s. After moving from Wall RC Chawner lived here from the mid 1850s to his death in 1870. His widow and daughter left for Edial House in the mid 1880s. HC Hodson (d1924), diocesan registrar from 1878, lived here from the later 1880s. He became noted for his kennels of pure-bred bloodhounds here. The house was divided into two in 1948 (VCH vol 14 pp207-208).

Above Church House to NW of Ipstones Hall, N of Ipstones church in Ipstones

parish (1834 OS map) (W p779).

Above Park House 2m NNE of Dilhorne, 2m NW of Cheadle. Also a hamlet and one of the four quarters of Cheadle ancient parish (W p753). The name has also appeared as Abovepark and is derived from being a post above the extensive deer park or old hunting park of the Bassets at Parkhall, Cheadle (NSFCT 1913 p145). Little Abovepark is to the W. Lower Above Park is to the ESE.

Ackbury Heath Chillington. Has appeared as Herkebarowe (1199-1209), Erkebarue (1306), Erkebaroheth (1424), Arkeborrowe heath (1587), Arkeborowes (1569), Ackburyes (1724), Hackbury Heath (1834) (SPNO p36) (SSE 1996 p11), and Actbury. Ackbury means 'the burial mound' of someone whose name is represented by 'Ack' or 'Erke' (DUIGNAN), or 'Arncytel.' The first element in Hackbury may be from Old English 'hearg' 'heathen temple or sacred grove' (SSE 1996 p10). The house 'Ackbury Heath' 1m S of Brewood at SJ 878071 is described in 1959 as not ancient. But it is the moated site to the S at the junction of Port Street and Chillington Street at SJ 878067 which may represent the 'manor' house of the ancient small Ackbury estate (VCH vol 5 p36) (SSAHST 1982-3 p37). (OHW pl14).

Acres, The 0.5m ESE of Stanley. Formerly in Stanley township in Leek ancient parish. There was a house here by 1700 (VCH vol 7 p229). A farm at Acre was rented by the Edge family for about 800 years until they left in the C19. Reputedly, they sheltered two retreating soldiers from the Pretender's army in 1745 Jacobite Rebellion, who left a sword and a gun in gratitude (OL vol 1 pp197-198).

Acres Nook Tiny hamlet merging into, and 0.75m SSE of, Kidsgrove.

Acton Small village SW of Butterton (Newcastle-under-Lyme). Former township in Butterton district chapelry in Swynnerton ancient parish (W p425). White wrongly identifies this Acton with the Acton in DB (W) which has been considered to be Acton Trussell (DB. Phillimore. 1976). The village was on the original Shrewsbury-Newcastle road until the present road was built to the N in 1846 (Smith's map) (SVB pp177,178).

Acton Bridge Crossed the Penk between Acton Trussell and Stafford. In the mid C17 its six arches were to be repaired by the various adjoining townships. The first two were to be repaired by Acton Trussell; the fifth by Burton and Rickerscote; the sixth by Dunston and the third and fourth by all the townships, including Bednall, equally. The bridge was rebuilt as a stone cartbridge in 1726 (OSST 1940-44 pp21-22).

Acton Gate Hamlet 1m N of Acton Trussell. There was formerly a toll-gate cottage at Acton Gate, lying in the angle between the main road (A449) and the lane to Acton Trussell (VCH vol 5 p144). The name means 'gap towards Acton Trussell' (SPNO p85).

Acton Hill Small hamlet 1.5m NNE of Acton Trussell. Formerly in Baswich or Berkswich parish. The main house seems to be Acton Hill Farm, which some say was occupied by a shepherd, Richard Burton. He and his wife, Mary, lost five children in 11 days in March 1835; William, aged 15, died on the 8th, Charles, aged five, died on the 11th, Joseph, aged two, died on the 15th, John, aged 17, died on the 17th, Mary, aged seven, died on the 18th. Three more sons died during the next five years; Thomas, aged 22, in Feb 1838, Richard, aged 16, died in Feb 1840 and George, aged 18, on Dec 23 1840. A headstone to their memory lies in Baswich churchyard. The ghosts of the children are said to haunt the house (SKYT p89) (VB p81) (MR p6) (ROT p42). Middlefell says Burton occupied the Shepherd's Cottage (see) to the S at SJ 946193 (BERK2 pp133,135p).

Acton Hill House under 1m SE of Eccleshall. Formerly spelt Hakedon (ECC p18). In 1851 it was the seat of James Hadderton (W p18).

Acton Trussell Large village over 3m SSE of Stafford on a bank by the Penk. Former township with Bednall in Berkswich or Baswich ancient parish. EARLY. A perennial **spring** at Acton Trussell was noted by Plot in the later C17 (NHS p60). There is evidence of **Roman** settlement at Acton Trussell. Fragments of pottery of the C2 and C4 AD have been found in a field N of the church and a second find was made in a field near the Penk in 1980. A Roman villa was discovered to the E of the church using electronic equipment in c1984 and subsequently excavated. 23 coins of the Roman period have been found in the vicinity of the site and two coins of mid C4 origin (depicting Constantine I and his mother Helen) were found in the excavation. 1388 pieces of assorted pottery were found (BDH p25) (BERK2 pp113,115 plan).
1000 to 1500. Dugdale and Shaw suggested that an Acton in Staffs was the Actune mentioned in the will of Wulfric Spot (c1002), founder of Burton Abbey; they probably meant this Acton. GCO Bridgeman thinks it could be an Acton in Shrops (SHC 1916 p25) (SPN p8). The **manor** of Acton appears in DB. It seems to have passed to the Trussells in the C12, and was held by them until 1490 when it passed to the Trussell heir, Elizabeth, who married John de Vere (Earl of Oxford - BERK2 p121); their son, Edward de Vere who

succeeded in 1563 was a poet and playwright, but also a spendthrift. It was probably he who sold the manor to the Ansons, later of Shugborough (OSST 1940-44 pp16-19). A moat NW of the church by Moat House (see) is believed to represent the site of the manor house. The **name** has appeared as Actone (DB), Actona (1167), Aketon (1206), Haketon (1317), Acton Trussell (1481), Acton Tressel (1563) (SPNO p26), and at some time as Actoma Willemi (SPN p8). Acton represents 'oaktown' or the 'farmstead by the oaks.' The Trussells were lords of the manor (DUIGNAN) (OAKDEN) (SPN pp8-9) (CCF p34). The **church**, St James, in an isolated position to the S of Acton Trussell village on the E side of Penkridge Road, has some C13 and C14 work but was largely rebuilt in 1870 (VCH vol 5 p15). The nucleus of the present village is 0.25m to the N of the church; it was moved possibly because of the Black Death or flooding (MR p5). **Stocks** are said to have stood by or on the site of an oak which stood near the Moat House (BERK2 p121). 1500 to PRESENT. In 1671 the township separated and formed a joint ecclesiastical parish with Bednall but remained in Baswich for civil purposes (BERK2 p85). Became a civil parish with Bednall in 1866 (GLAUE p401). **Natives and visitors**. A strong man called **Nicholas Cooper** at Acton Trussell, could lift a sack of wheat of about 240 lbs with his teeth and once lifted three men, one under each arm and the third in his teeth (NHS p293). **Mr Jobber** (his arms appear on Plot's map) could grow fresh and fragrant strawberries in his garden three days before Christmas in the later C17 (NHS p204). In the later C20 **Patrick Fyffe** (or Patrick) alias Dame Hilda Brackett in the comedy duo Hinge and Brackett used to live in the village. They called the village Stackton Tressel in their sketches (One Little Maid: the Memories of Dame Hilda Bracket. Patrick Fyffe. 1980) (MR p6). **Margaret Mayo** (b1936), novelist, was living at Acton Trussell in 1994 (VFC p92).

Adam's Hill Clent. See Clent Hill.

Adams Pond To the E of Old Star, at SK 065454. Named after a local character, Adam Ratcliffe, who, it is believed, lived the life of a hermit at the side of this fish pond in the mid C19. There was a painting of him in the possession of John Harrison of Cotton in 1996 (HAF pp395-396).

Adbaston Ancient parish and village, and former township with Knighton. The village, 10.5m NNW of Stafford, is in an open dale formed by a tributary of the Lonco Brook.
EARLY to 1500. The **Roman** road from Pennocrucium to Whitchurch forms the S boundary of the parish (NSJFS 1964 p13). The **manor** of Edbaldestone appears in DB. The **name** later appears as Adbaldestone (1192. 1224), Eldebaldeston (1224), Alboldestun and Albaldiston (AADB p3) (SPN p9). It means Eadbald's town (DUIGNAN) or tun or settlement (AADB p3) (SSE 1996 p10) or farmstead (SPN p9). The parish probably formed sometime between 1086 and 1291. It was originally a part of Eccleshall parish (SHC 1916 pp192,196,199-200). The parish **church**, St Michael and All Angels, at the NW end of the village, has some work of late C11 or C12 origin. The tower was completed in c1340 (AADB p34). A **medieval village** (deserted between 1379-1524) may lie in the vicinity of the present village (SSAHST 1970 p34). The **prebend** of Adbaston in Lichfield cathedral was founded or refounded by Roger de Clinton and Richard Peche (SSAHST vol 2 1960-61 p42). The parish was a peculiar jurisdiction of the dean until peculiar jurisdictions were abolished in 1846 (VCH vol 3 p93) (AADB p8) (GLAUE p401). The prebend was still attached to the office of dean in the late C20 (LDD). There was a case of **heresy** at Adbaston in 1473-4 (VCH vol 3 p43).
1500 to PRESENT. **Foot-and-mouth disease** broke out in Adbaston parish at Yew Tree Farm, and the Laurels Farm, Tunstall in Dec 1967 (SN Dec 8 1967 p10. Dec 22 1967 p15), and at Adbaston House Farm in Jan 1968 (SN Jan 1 1968 p13) (AADB p62). **Natural history**. In the later C17 Plot noted a birch that grew out of the bole of an oak in a lane leading S from the church. The birch had sent its roots down the trunk of the oak (NHS p213). A giant old yew tree stood near the W end of the church until it was burnt down in 1925. It was then 24 feet 2.5 inches round the trunk at four feet from the ground, and believed to be at least a 1000 years old (AADB p29). Probably this was the yew Garner noted in the mid C19, which had a hollow trunk and a circumference of 20 feet (GNHSS p18). **Charles Bowker Ash**, poet, baptised at Adbaston on April 17 1781, was the son of George Ash of Adbaston Farm. He is said to have travelled widely and lived for a time at Hodnet and Hinstock in Shrops, and at Eccleshall (VFC p5). His 'Hermit of Hawkestone' appeared in 1816. Two volumes of poems by Ash, published in 1831, are said to have pleased Coleridge. The poem for which he is best remembered at Adbaston is his 'Adbaston, or the Days of Youth' which extols the charms of his native village:

'Dear, native Adbaston! - remote from care,
Thy tranquil fields would mitigate despair;

In thy sweet vales a balsam I could find,
When naught on earth could calm my troubled mind'

In the Preface to the poem, written by Coleridge, Coleridge compares it with 'The Deserted Village.' Another poem is based on the battle of Bloreheath (see) (PSS pp138-141) (FLJ Dec 4 1918 p329) (NSFCT 1924 p100. 1927 pp34,35,50) (AADB p57).

Adbaston Hall Stands to W of the site of the Adbaston Manor House, NNW of Adbaston church. Built in 1725 (NSFCT 1927 p26) or completed by 1736 by Col Richard Whitworth II to replace Adbaston Manor House (AADB frontispiece pc p19) (SVB p10). Richard Whitworth III (d1811), who lived here until moving to Batchacre Hall in c1756 (OSST 1931 p29), sold the hall in 1806 to Thomas Palin whose widow sold it in 1825 to John Smith. He sold it to James Howe in 1851, who sold it to Joseph Peake in 1859. The hall later became the property of the Cheswardine estate and had several tenants. It was bought from the estate by William Marsh in 1918. In 1931 it passed from the Marshs to J Somner Billington, author of AADB, still the owner in 1975 (AADB p27b). The stones in the garden wall near the front entrance are of ancient origin and were thought to have been brought here from Ranton Abbey or Haughmond Abbey after the Dissolution. But, since the hall was not built until the C18, the stones are more likely to be from the demolished Gerards Bromley Hall and brought here by Richard Whitworth c1775, at the same time he erected the porch from that hall in the grounds of Batchacre Hall (AADB p27).

Adbaston Heath Houses N of Doley, by Bishop's Wood. Appears on Greenwood's map.

Adbaston Manor House Adbaston manor belonged to the Whitworths by the later C17. Richard Whitworth II, a colonel of the Queen's Dragoons, was the last Whitworth to live here. He had built and moved to Adbaston Hall by 1736. The house was demolished in c1800 (AADB pp19,26).

Adderley Minute hamlet nearly 1m WNW of Cheadle. The chief residence of the Adderley family (SHOS vol 1 p81). The name appears on Yates' map as Adderley Mill.

Adderley Green House 1.5m ESE of Betley. In Audley ancient parish.

Adderley Green House 1.25m S of Flash.

Adderley Green Former hamlet 1m NE of Longton. Now a suburb of Longton. Formerly in Caverswall ancient parish. The Adderley family took their name probably from Adderley Green, not Adderley in Shrops, as thought prior to 1910 (SHC 1910 p263). An Adderley family later resided at Blake Hall (see). The church, St Mary and St Chad, on the corner of Anchor Road and Handsacre Road, was built in 1898 (BOE p261) and rebuilt in 1987 (LDD).

Adders Green House 1.25m S of Flash. Appears in 1564 as Edders Grenehed (SSE 1996 p69).

Adie's Alley An entry leading from Crown Street to High Street, Stone, which ran alongside Adie's book and newspaper shop (MOSP pp14-15).

Admaston Small village 0.5m SE of Blithfield Hall on a ridge above Blithfield Reservoir. Formerly in Blithfield township and ancient parish. The name appears as Ædmundeston in 1176 (SSE 1996 p10) and as Ædmundeston, Edmodeston, Ædmondeston (SPN p20). It means Eadbald's Town (DUIGNAN) or farmstead (SPN p20). Or Chetwynd thought Edmundeston, which it was anciently written (SH p45). Or Eadmund's tun (SSE 1996 p10). The medieval custom Abbots Bromley (see) Horn Dance is performed at Admaston in the middle of the morning on Horn Dance day. Mary Foster of Admaston fell down a well in the C17 and consequently suffered a sleeping disorder giving her the ability to sleep for 14 days and nights without waking. Two years after the accident when living in Uttoxeter she was reported to have slept for three days and nights (NHS p285). The short marriage of William Bagot (d1856) (see Bagot's Bromley) and Emily Fitzroy is recalled in the shield of arms depicting the arms of Bagot quartering royal arms baton sinister (emblem of illegitimacy) on a lodge to Blithfield Hall at Admaston (VB pp104-105).

Adsall Yeatsall Cottages 1m W of Abbots Bromley at SK 064245 in the angle of Yeatsall Lane and the modern road B5013 is now situated on the site. The house, known as Adesole in 1402 and as Adsall in 1682 (Plot's map), was burnt down before 1831 and rebuilt as Yeatsall (ABMB p53).

Afcot House which stood behind Christ Church church, Tettenhall Wood. It was built between 1889 and 1919. The site is now (1990) occupied by a block of flats, but the coach-house still stands in Grove Lane (TCOP p48p).

Agardsley Former manor (W p561) and the original name for Newborough village. The name means the pasture of Edgar or Eadgar (DUIGNAN) (HOPT vol 1 p136) (SHOS vol 1 p92) or Eadgar's woodland clearing (SSE 1996 p10) (SPN p7). Or 'Agath's meadow' (SPN p86; Poulton-Smith is unaware Agardsley was created a new borough). The manor appears in DB as

Edgareslege. The hermitage at Agardsley was given to Tutbury Priory by William, 4th Earl of Derby (1190-1247), of Chartley Castle (see) (VCH vol 3 pp136-137, 332). Robert Ferrers, 6th Earl of Derby, of Tutbury and Chartley Castles, made Agardsley a new borough in 1263 (MR p239). After which it was known as New Borough of Agardsley; later Agardsley was dropped (SVB p129).

Agardsley Park Medieval deer park enclosed out of forest. In existence by 1285 (VCH vol 2 p350) (NSJFS 1962 p75. 1975 p28). Possibly lay in the area of the present house called Agardsley Park (see).

Agardsley Park Residence over 1m N of Newborough.

Agger Hill Hill at 1.5m NE of Madeley (M p21). In Madeley parish.

Albemarle Almshouses The Duke of Albemarle bequeathed £6,000 in 1688 for the erection and maintenance of almshouses in Newcastle-under-Lyme for 20 poor widows. The houses were not built until 1743. It was a pleasant Georgian structure and had to be demolished in 1964 to make way for the inner ring road (NUL pp45-46p). These almshouses are perhaps those in Bridge Street, in existence between 1734 and 1964 (NULOP vol 2 p47p).

Albion A suburb and industrial estate of West Bromwich ancient parish, SE of Greets Green. By the mid C19 brickmaking became important in this area (VCH vol 17 p8). Albion station on the Birmingham, Wolverhampton & Stour Valley Railway was opened at Union Cross (see) in 1853 and closed to passengers in 1960, and to freight in 1964 (VCH vol 17 p14). Several of the early players of West Bromwich Albion Football Club (founded in 1879) were from this area, hence why the name in the club name (VCH vol 17 p74). To SE is Albion Industrial Estate.

Albion Small district by the West Bromwich Albion Football Club ground, The Hawthorns. Formerly in Smethwick township in Harborne ancient parish. Gives its name to a junior school and a council estate, built between WW1 and WW2 (VCH vol 17 p93). The district is possibly so called because of its proximity to the ground of West Bromwich Albion Football Club.

Albion House Old Hall Street, Hanley, formerly considered part of Shelton: Gives its name to Albion Square and Street. Probably built in about the 1830s (VCH vol 8 pp142il). It was the seat of William Parker, Chief Bailey of Hanley, until burnt down in the Chartist riots in 1842; Parker then went to live at Lysways Hall (NSFCT 1925 p89). Parker also owned Rownall Hall (VCH vol 8 p149 note).

Albion Junction Junction of the Birmingham New Cut New Main Line with the Gower Branch Canal (SWY p10).

Albury House Stapenhill. Seat of Sidney Herbert Evershed, Liberal MP for Burton and Uttoxeter (1888-1900) and founder of Evershed's brewery in Bank Square. The house was demolished after WW2 (BTOP p4).

Alder Brook Runs through Rolleston into the Dove (UTR p165) (SVB p142).

Alder Carr By Sher Brook 1m SSW of Shugborough Hall.

Alder Carr N of Loxley Green. Duignan says Carr is Norse and means 'marsh,' 'wet moor' or 'boggy copse' - but Alder Carr is not a wet moor - see Carmountside (NSFCT 1910 p167).

Aldercarr Wood N of Calwich Abbey, S of Ousley Cross.

Alder Coppice W of Ettingshall Park, Sedgley (PHS p2).

Aldergate Street in the N part of Tamworth town (Staffs). Formerly called Ellergate. Gate is of Danish origin meaning 'street' (WMLB pp87 plan,92) (SL p50). The name represents 'street to Ella's farmstead (SPN p125).

Alder Moor Former common land to the N of Anslow, partly enclosed in the later C16. Formerly in Anslow township in Rolleston ancient parish and claimed in the C17 as being in Rolleston township (ANS p104); the present house called Alder Moor on the N side of the common lies in the former Rolleston township. Has appeared as Aldercarre (1597), Aldermore (1597), and Ouldermoor (early C18). The common was enclosed in 1802 (ANS pp57,61,103,126).

Alder Moor Hamlet 0.75m SW of Rolleston.

Alder Lee House under 0.25m W of Meerbrook. The name has appeared as Aldredeslega in 1129 (SSE 1996 p10) and Alderley (DUIGNAN) and means Aldred's pasture-land (DUIGNAN) (SPN p84), or 'Ealdred's wood clearing' (SSE 1996 p10). Possibly the home of Liulf who murdered Gamel at Solomon's Hollow.

Alderley Hall House over 0.5m NE of Great Bridgeford.

Alders Tiny hamlet 1.5m SSW of Denstone.

Alders, The District 1m WNW of Tamworth. Seems to be from Alder Mills on the Tame 0.5m W of Tamworth (W p626).

Alders Brook Runs from Alders near Stubwood to Combridge.

Aldershaw Hamlet 1.5m SSW of Lichfield cathedral on the NW slopes of a slight prominence overlooking Trunkfield or Sandford Brook. Former outtownship of St Michael's parish, Lichfield. The name has appeared as Aldershawe (OS map: 25,000 1976), and is from a plantation of trees, or a

name for many trees planted together, or the shadow of trees (SHOS vol 1 p357). Or means the alder wood (DUIGNAN) (VCH vol 14 p285) (SSE 1996 p10) (SPN p78). Aldershaw was inhabited by the early C13 (VCH vol 14 p285).

Aldershaw Hall Aldershaw. (SHOS vol 1 p358). The Burnes were at first tenants and then owners of a moated mansion known as Motte House at Aldershaw in the earlier C17 (W p518) (VCH vol 14 p288). John Burnes adopted heir of John Floyer of Longdon had added Floyer to his name by the time of his death in 1817. He was succeeded by his nephew Rev Trevor Burnes Jones (d1871) who changed his surname to Floyer (VCH vol 14 p288). The hall was sold in 1893 to WB Harrison, a colliery owner and cricket enthusiast (d1912). He rebuilt the hall in 1896 to the design of S Loxton of Walsall and Cannock (VCH vol 14 pp288-289). On the N and W sides of the hall are pleasure grounds which include pools, grottoes, and plantations probably laid out by Trevor Burnes Floyer. Columns and arches removed from Lichfield cathedral in the C18 were set up in the grounds, and a small brick chapel was built in 1845. WB Harrison laid out a cricket ground N of the house (VCH vol 14 p289). Situated NW of the hall at SK 101075 are a conduit head and well house (DoE II).

Aldersley Suburb of Wolverhampton 0.25m NE of Tettenhall on relatively high ground from which rise springs which feed the rivers Penk and Smestow, the first falls into the North Sea via the Trent, the later via the Severn to the Atlantic Ocean (SHOS vol 1 p357). The old Aldersley estate in Tettenhall Clericorum manor and Tettenhall ancient parish has been described as laying 1m NE of Tettenhall (W p206). Has appeared as Allerley (C13-14), Alderley (1471), Autherley (1588. 1880-6 OS map 2 inch to 1m), and Aldersley (late C18 to the present) (VCH vol 20 p13). In 1613 a windmill stood on the E side of the later Pendeford Avenue S of its junction with Green Lane (VCH vol 20 p34). By the 1930s the area was a growing residential suburb: A rare Edward VIII post box was still standing in Aldersley Road in 1995 (info from Wolverhampton Civic Society). The church, Christ the King, Pendeford Avenue, opened in 1956 (Collegiate Church, Tettenhall. 1989) (LDD). Aldersley Leisure Village, a leisure complex, had opened on the site of the former Aldersley Stadium by 1999 (The News (Wolverhampton) March 4 1999 p8). Edwin T Booth (1833-1893), Shakespearian actor and founder of Booth's Theatre in New York, and his brother John Wilkes Booth (1839-1865), President Abraham Lincoln's assassin, were descended from the Wilkes family of Aldersley (TB Sept 1991 pp16-17. Nov 1993 pp18-19) (WF p45). Jack Hawkins, actor, when making the film 'The Man in the Sky' at Wolverhampton Airport at Pendeford opened Aldersley Stadium on June 9 1956 (TCOP p95) (BUOP p151p).

Aldersley Junction Aldersley. Junction of the Birmingham Canal with the Staffordshire and Worcestershire Canal. The link of the canals was made Sept 21 1772. The builder, James Brindley died a week later (WF p44). The top level of the Birmingham Canal at Aldersley Junction is known by boatmen as 'the twenty one' for it is the last of 21 locks on the ascent from Wolverhampton (The Staffs and Worcs Canal. Alfred E Jenks. 1907 p21).

Aldery Bank Incline 1m SW of Loxley Hall, through which was built a tunnel for the Stafford & Uttoxeter Railway line, and has also been called Tunnel Bank (local info).

Aldridge Ancient parish, former manor and township. The former village of Aldridge lies on high ground 17m SE of Stafford. It has now grown into a town.

EARLY. For **Roman** finds on the parish boundary see under Linley Lodge Industrial Estate. The old village lies remote from a spring (NHS p39); but modern Aldridge embraces Anchor Brook (SNAR p8) a tributary of a head river of the Tame.

1000 to 1500. The original Saxon settlement may have been in the vicinity of Pool Green where a number of roads meet (MOA p129) (SSAHST 1978-79 pp41-49) (SNAR p7). The **name** has appeared as Alrewic (DB), and Alrewyz (C13) (SPN p10), and is supposed to have appeared as Aldrich (THS p1). It is thought to mean 'alder village' (DUIGNAN) or 'village among the alder trees' (SPN p10). The alder trees in question may have stood by the large pool at Pool Green (see) (SNAR p42). It was formerly thought that if it derived from Alrewic or Aldrich then 'ald' represents old and 'wic' or 'rice' represents village or station, so 'ancient station;' a supposed British camp on Druid's Heath lies close by (SHOS vol 1 p10) (THS p1) (HOWW p16). Some have interpreted the second element as a principality, jurisdiction or kingdom and that here was the seat of government of a kingdom whose natural boundaries were the Penk, Sow, Trent and Tame, 26m long, 19m wide and covering 200 square miles (NSFCT 1881 p14). The **manors** of Great Barr and Aldridge are recorded as being held together in DB and were held together in subsequent years. Early lords resided at Great Barr, in a house adjoining a chapel on the site of Chapel Farm, near Great Barr church. The manor was in turn held by

the Mertons, Stapletons (in the C13), Harcourts and or the de Berminghams who were succeeded partly by the Longviles of Wolverton, and partly by the Lords Ferrers; they eventually sold their rights to William Barrol, who sold them to Robert Stamford of London. In 1610 Sir Henry Longvile of Wolverton and Edward Stamford of Perry Hall are described as joint lords of Great Barr manor (MOA pp25,27,39,54,137). The Scotts are said to have either purchased Great Barr manor in 1618 (TBS p9), or a moiety of it after the Civil War (MOA 46). In the early C18 Frances Scott brought the manor to her second husband, John Hoo, who was succeeded by his brother, Thomas (d1791), who was succeeded by Joseph Scott (d1828) (WAM p90) (TBS p12). In the medieval period an inferior manor centred on Aldridge was granted to the de Alrewychs. Later holders of this manor were the Hillarys, Mountforts, Jordans (owners from 1630), and Croxalls. Edward Croxall of Shustoke is described as lord of Aldridge manor in c1800 (MOA pp19,46,60). Aldridge **parish** was formed sometime between 1086 and 1291 out of either Walsall or Lichfield parishes (SHC 1916 p198); the ancient Cannock Forest which covered most of it was disafforested at the end of the C13 (MOA pp13,129). The parish **church**, St Mary the Virgin, on the N side of The Green, has a C14 tower; the rest of the church is mainly of 1852-1853 (BOE p53). There was a Christmas day custom practiced by the rector of Aldridge who used to give to every person of every rank of his parish (Aldridge and Great Barr) who could come to his house, as much bread, beef, mustard and vinegar as they could eat. The origin of the custom is unknown. Some think it dates to before the Reformation. Others, that the parish is large, and people used to receive the sacrament on this day, the Rector would give them dinner to entice them to the divine service in the afternoon and this became an established custom. DrWilkes (d1760) says it had lately been altered into a payment of about 6d a house (SHOS vol 2 p100) (THS) (SCSF p162) (TBS p20). There was **charcoal burning** in Aldridge by the C14 (ADY p4). Aldridge **High Street**, including some medieval cruck cottages near the church, was demolished for the present (1999) shopping redevelopment scheme in 1965; the old street is much lamented by Aldridge inhabitants (local info) (BCP p86p of High Street in 1904) (SNAR p7). There was a **pinfold** near Pinfold Cottage in Erdington Road (SNAR p24).
1500 to PRESENT. The **school**, formerly at the Green, Aldridge, had its origin in 1718 when Rev Thomas Cooper gave the land for the building and John Jordan endowed the trustees with land. New buildings were erected in 1969 (MOA pp134,166il of in 1847) (SNAR pp47il of in 1847,48). An old post **windmill** may have stood on the mound 28 paces in diameter and seven feet high, known as Gossy Knob, N of the church and close to the Rectory at SK 06140101 (NSJFS 1965 p29) (MOA pp15,133). Others have thought it a possible burial mound (Topographical Dictionary of England. S Lewis. vol 1 p32) (HOWB p2). A building known as the Outdoor had been Aldridge cattle **market** (ALOPPR p96p). Aldridge station on a branch of the Midland **Railway** linking Walsall and Castle Bromwich opened in 1879 and closed to passengers in 1930, closing in 1965 (VCH vol 2 p322) (SNAR p45p of Aldridge station). A branch line to Walsall Wood opened in 1884 (ADY p7p). Aldridge station was demolished after 1970 (ALOPPR p124p). The Aldridge Tool and Engineering Co Ltd leaders in the special cutting **industry**, use 'aldridge' as their trade mark (Staffs County Handbook c1958 p59). Swallow Doretti cars were produced at Helliwells Aircraft Company, at Walsall Airport at Aldridge Lodge (see) in 1954 and 1955 (ALOPPR p43). Aldridge **urban district** was formed in 1934 and amalgamated with Brownhills in 1966 and became part of the metropolitan borough of Walsall in 1974 (ALOPP p20). The device of Aldridge urban district consisted of a beacon (CH p337). **Natural history**. A white sparrow which was killed at Aldridge was noted by Plot in the later C17 (NHS p234). **Persons and visitors**. The charity of Mrs **Catherine Walker** helped found almshouses in Erdington Road opposite Portland Road. Mrs Walker lived in Shutt Cross House and died in 1756. The almshouses were built in 1897 and were demolished by 1965 when Hallcroft Way was built on the site (SNAR pp22p,24,27). **Henry Shore** (1911-1977), poet and doctor, who as a refugee from Nazi Germany, lived for a while in Aldridge. His work includes 'The Roundabout' (1972), 'The Nomad and Other Poems' (1973) and 'Apple Harvest' (1974) (VFC p122). **Princess Margaret** and **Princess Diana** visited Aldridge in Nov 1962 and Feb 1986, respectively (ALOPPR p61ps).

Aldridge Lodge 1m SSW of Aldridge, on the S side of Bosty Lane. Built in the late C19, possibly on the site of an older house. John Daniell, who is buried in Lichfield cathedral, lived at Aldridge Lodge between 1783 and 1809. It then passed to his son Thomas, who sold it to Rev Thomas Burrowes Adams of Great Barr in 1821. By 1861 it was occupied by Frederick Furhman Clarke. On his death in 1903 it was sold. In the 1930s it housed Basque refugee children and was demolished in c1958 (SNAR p14). **Walsall Airport**. In April 1930 Walsall council bought Aldridge Lodge and land situated between Bosty Lane and Longwood Lane with a view to establishing an aerodrome. Work began on the site in 1932 and the licence to operate was issued in May 1934. Several well-known fliers appeared at the airfield, including Alan Cobham, Gustav Hamel and Amy Johnson. The runway was extended and a further hanger built in 1936. Helliwells factory opened at the airfield in 1938 and they serviced aircraft in WW2. Aeroplanes were still seen as late as 1953 and the airport closed in 1956. Tube Investments brought their company operations to the airfield in 1960. In 1996 most of the old aerodrome buildings were demolished and a business park established on the site (WMA vol 1 pp75,131-143) (SNAR pp50,51p).

Aldridge Manor House or Old Hall. Originally built in the medieval period on a sandy site near Aldridge church (SSAHST 1978-79 p46).

Aldridge Manor House Built in 1851 by Edward Tongue, last lord of Aldridge manor (WMVB p11). During WW1 it was a convalescent hospital and has twice housed the local doctor. Between 1953 and 1981 it was the public library, and since 1981 has been the Manor Youth Club (WMVB p11) (SNAR p31).

'Alfieri's Academy' One of the brick and stucco villas built by William Ridgway in the early C19 in Birch Street, Northwood, Hanley. Has 'Gothic' features and was once a school (VCH vol 8 p149).

Alfred's Dell By Alfred's Coppice SE of Beaudesert Hall (1834 OS map).

Allen's Rough Modern housing estate in New Invention (Selective Essays on Willenhall. David Potts. 1984. Copy in Willenhall library), 2m NNE of Willenhall. Streets on this estate were named in 1960 (SNW p4). The church at Beacon School, Davis Road, was built in 1984 (LDD).

Alleshurst A gospel place on the perambulation around Tutbury in Rogation week (SHOS vol 1 p57). Has also appeared as Witches Grave.

Allimore Green Hamlet along the lane leading to, and 1m NE of, Church Eaton. Lies partly in Bradley and Haughton parishes. Has also appeared as Aliasmore (1401), Alley-more-greene (1661), Allmoore Green (Morden's map), Allymoor Green (1775) (SPNO p165) (SSE 1996 p10), Almore, and Allemore Green. The name means 'path through marsh' (SPNO p165) (SSE 1996 p10). By 1999 Allimore Green Common, wetland meadow and pasture, was a SSSI nature reserve in the care of the Staffs Wildlife Trust (OSST 1956-59 p12) (Staffs Wildlife Trust leaflet).

All Saints Early planned residential district for the working class in St George Ward, Wolverhampton. The area, centred on Steelhouse Lane and Vicarage Road, was being laid out with houses by 1884, and was developed by 1901 (Mapping the Past Wolverhampton 1577-1986. Mary Mills 1993 pp20,28). Land between Sutherland Place and Gordon Street was the grounds of the former Cleveland House; the first council houses of Wolverhampton stood on the corner of the Cartwright Street and Green Lane, a site which later became the start of the Birmingham New Road (Wolverhampton Chronicle Jan 15 1999 p14).

Allsops Hill Eminence behind Hawes Lane, Rowley Regis. Here was a quarry site for Rowley Rag (VCH vol 2 pp203,204). The hill may have taken its name from the Allsop family who first started quarrying here (HORV p9).

Almington (*Ammington* SHC 1945/ 6 pp19,21). Small village by a tributary of Coal Brook under 1m WNW of Hales. Former manor and township (which appears to have been absorbed into Tyrley township) in Drayton-in-Hales ancient parish in Shrops (W p389). The name has appeared as Almentone (DB), Alkementon (1293), Alkmunton (1327) (SHC 1945/ 6 p19), Alkmonton (c1600) (SOS p104), and Ammington (Plot's map); it means Alchmund's town (DUIGNAN) (SHC 1945/ 6 p19), or Alhmund's tun (SSE 1996 p10). Almington manor was absorbed into that of Tyrley by 1135. Almington settlement has a village street unlike its slightly larger neighbour Hales (SHC 1945/ 6 pp19,21).

Almington Hall Almington. It may stand on or near the site of the manor house of Almington; it was the capital messuage of Almington in the C16, and probably much earlier. The Prestons lived here between c1600 and c1632. It was then occupied by James Higgins, and by the Pitchfords by 1674, and James Creswall by 1705. Edward Sneyd (d1780), related to the Sneyds of Keele, pulled down the old hall after inheriting the Almington estate in 1715 and built a brick house here in which he resided until 1768 when he made over the property to his niece, Frances Horton (d1785). In 1769 it was let to George Parker (d1819), second son of Sir Thomas Parker, lord Chief Baron of the Exchequer; George's son Sir William Parker of Shenstone, the distinguished admiral, was born here. The hall passed to Thomas Dicken in 1786 and then to Thomas Pigott (d1794) of Wollerton in 1792. In 1799 it was bought by Lt Col Robert Dawes, who lived here between 1825 and his death in 1846. The hall burnt down in March 1900. It was rebuilt by 1914 (SHC 1945/ 6 pp21,181,185-187, 213-216, 247, 262-263). Another account says Almington

Hall was built in 1760, and one hall was built by the Broughton/ Adderley family (ALW pl 64 of the hall in c1918).

Almonds Name of field off the Admaston Road in Colton, derived from Almund a freeman who held Colton manor before the Conquest (CWF p3). Or Almar or Aelmar a Saxon who held a separate half hide in Colt. Has also appeared as Alm Holme and Aldwine Holm.

Alrewas (locally *all-roo-as* LGS p71). Ancient parish and large village standing on low-lying land on the S bank of the Trent in the middle Trent Valley 17m ESE of Stafford.

EARLY. An irregular enclosure of **Neolithic** origin has been found at Alrewas (HOS 1998 p24). Neolithic or Bronze Age activity in the vicinity of Alrewas is suggested by the find of a stone axe-hammer at Edwards Farm (unlocated) (NSJFS 1964 p14). Three **Iron Age** gold torcs dating from the C2 to C1 BC were found in Alrewas by a metal detectorist in 1996. They were declared Treasure Trove and had been purchased by the Potteries Museum by Oct 1997. In the later C17 Plot noted a barrel-shaped stone found at Alrewas (NHS p198 fig 22) (SHOS vol 1 pp130-131). At SK 175125 1.75m SSE of Alrewas is a **Romano-British** farmstead complex, revealed by aerial-photography (SSAHST 1973 p32). It was a listed monument by 1994. The circular and rectangular earthworks and enclosures at Alrewas station at SK 177149, SK 178148, SK 177147 are listed monuments.

900 to 1500. There was a parish **church** at the corner of Mill End Lane and Church Road by 822 (some have suggested it was founded by St Chad in the 670s). There is a local tradition that Lady Godiva worshipped at Alrewas' Saxon church, but there is no evidence (SPN p11). The present church, All Saints, is of late C12 origin (History of All Saints Parish Church: Alrewas. Rev John Colston. 1986). The **parish** formed before 1086 (SHC 1916 p194). The parish feast was on the Sunday after All Saints' day in the mid C19 (W p592). The PR dating from 1547 is perhaps the most interesting in the county, telling for instance, of those who drowned in the nearby Trent (SHOS vol 1 pp137-148). In it is recorded the sighting of a blazing star (comet) from Nov 11 1585 for 40 days, a remarkable damask rose tree in the vicarage garden which bore on June 28 1644 two white roses but which had not been grafted, and an earthquake felt on Jan 4 1675 (SHOS vol 1 p139) (W p592) (NSFCT 1879 p23) (OL vol 1 p184). **Beating the bounds**: In 1794 the PR records the boundaries were perambulated not in Rogation week but on Oct 1 (SHOS vol 1 p132) (SCSF pp27,28) (FOS pp116,117). The **prebend** of Alrewas in Lichfield cathedral was instituted in 822 (W p591), but it is said to have been founded by Roger de Clinton in the C12 and was annexed to the Chancellorship. Past holders of the Prebend have been Thomas Wagstaffe, who became a Non-Juror, and Dr Edmund Bateman of Christ Church Oxford: Dr Johnson of Lichfield (see) was unable to attend his lectures and a friend took notes of them for him (SSAHST vol 2 1960-61 p43). The parish was a peculiar jurisdiction of the dean and chapter and certain prebendaries of Lichfield cathedral until peculiar jurisdictions were abolished in 1846 (VCH vol 3 p93). 'Alrewasse,' which can be probably identified with Alrewas, was one of a block of estates granted in a charter of 942 to a thegn (SSE 1991 pp7,8) (BTIH pp13-14). The manor of Alrewas appears in DB. Some have derived the **name** from the British 'ael ir vay,' hill by the water. 'Alder swamp,' from the many alders growing near the Trent (SHOS vol 1 p127) (DUIGNAN) (HOPT vol 1 p136) (SSE 1996 p10) (SPN p10). Gelling thinks 'alluvial land with alders' (NSJFS 1981 p3). The manor formerly consisted of Staffs Edingale, and nearly the whole of Alrewas, Orgreave and Fradley communities. It was situated within the boundaries of Alrewas Hay, which was under the jurisdiction of the steward of the Cannock Forest, but he had no jurisdiction in the manor (SHC 1907 pp249-293). Alrewas manor court rolls are believed to be the oldest in the county. They were found in the parish oak chest in Alrewas church and were described in 1907 as recently discovered. The rolls cover the periods June 11 1259 to May 6 1261, Dec 13 1268 to Aug 24 1269, April 18 1272 to Dec 18 1273, 1328 to 1440 and some of various dates between 1443 to 1551. The church chest has three locks; keys were kept by the churchwardens of Alrewas, Fradley and Orgreave. By 1907 the rolls were being kept at WSL (SHC 1907 pp247-293. 1910 pp89-137) (LGS p72) (HOA pp53-55). The rolls record that Alrewas suffered badly over the summer of 1349 in the Plague (HOS 1998 p88). The custom of **Borough English** prevailed at Alrewas in which land passed to the youngest son, brother, daughter or sister (NHS pp277,278) (SHOS vol 1 p130). According to Plot Alrewas tenants had the right to catch fish a certain number of times a year with a 'unio ingenio' called a 'strike,' a type of stall net, or a net put across the river to stop the fish (SCSF p119). The heading 'Manor of Alrewas' was still being used on property title deeds as late as 1825 (HOA p50). Robert de Somervill was granted a charter on Feb 9 1290 to hold a **market** at Alrewas on Tuesdays. The market had ceased by 1500 (NSJFS 1971 p51). The earliest

reference to Alrewas being a **borough** is in 1328 and the last is in 1369, and then borough status lapsed (NSJFS 1972 p68). The **pinfold** was sited between Gaskell's and Moat Bank House (HOA p33).

1500 to PRESENT. Alrewas had a cottage **industry** in basket making. The willow being grown in osier beds created by regular flooding of the Trent (VB p37). Alrewas is noted for its eels (NSFCT 1879 p23). There were or are many eel and salmon traps at Alrewas (STM Aug 1969 p32p). In 1832 the parishioners erected may poles in the three townships of the parish, with suitable inscriptions to commemorate the passing of the **Reform Bill** and in gratitude to the Earl of Lichfield for his support in getting the Bill passed (W p592). **Newspaper**. The Lichfield Advertiser and Newspaper for Lichfield, Alrewas, Shenstone etc ran from Jan 6 1865 to 1866 (VCH vol 14 p170) (SHJ spring 1996 pp19-20). A quarter of the 200 square mile the **National Forest**, proposed in the late 1980s, covers the E part of Staffs, the southern tip of Derbys and most of NW Leics. A part of the forest, the National Memorial Arboretum, is being sited near Alrewas (SLM July Aug 1996 pp17-19 pcs). The forest is the creation of the National Forest Company, established in 1995; by Aug 1998 there was a sign proclaiming the National Forest at Draycott-in-the-Clay (The National Forest Company Annual Report 1998/1999). The National Memorial Arboretum is planned for a 150 acre site 1m ESE of Alrewas in the triangle formed by the diverging railway from Burton. The site was donated by Redland Aggregates plc. The arboretum will commemorate peace and those who died in wars, and will have a Millennium Chapel (the first to be built for the second millennium). The chapel was to be dedicated in Dec 1999 by c1996, but by Nov 1999 the dedication was put back to April 22 2000 (Daily Telegraph. March 27 1995 p9. April 6 1996. Weekend section p3 plan) (SLM July Aug 1996 pp17-19 pcs. Oct 1996 p12) (E&S Oct 7 1996 p12) (Spotlight. Nov/Dec 1999 p4). Over the door of No. 19 in a street near the church is this **inscription**

> Traveller, as you pass this way,
> A blessing on this house I pray,
> And if you've time (I ask your pardon)
> Spare another for the garden.

(SCSF p168) (SLM Sept 1951 pp19,20p). The **most thundery area** of Britain is considered to be the middle Trent Valley, and one study has claimed that the most thundery place in the country is Alrewas, with an annual average of 24 thunder days (Daily Telegraph May 9 1998 p34). In the later C17 Dr Plot was told about an **unexplained noise** heard at Alrewas (NHS p22). **Natives**. Alrewas PR records that **Robert Nevill** and his son were killed by lightning under an oak in Salterholme field in 1613 (W p592). **Edward Hall** of Alrewas was touched and cured by Charles II for the King's Evil in 1667, aged 110 (NSFCT 1879 p24). **Wyatt Earp** (1848-1929), gambler, lawman, marshall of Tombstone, Arizona, and gunfighter at the OK Corral (1881) is said to have been born in Monmouth, Illinois, USA (Cambridge Biographical Encyclopedia. David Crystal. 1994). However, he may have been born at Alrewas, with the Earp family later moving to Wednesbury (E&S Oct 28 1998 p18).

Alrewas Cottage House 0.75m E of Alrewas, on E side of Icknield Street and W side of the railway. In 1851 it was the seat of John Baggaley (W p18).

Alrewas Hay Former estate which became a hay, or division of Cannock Forest (SL p68). 2m W of Alrewas. The estate was an extra-parochial liberty (APB p6) until entering Alrewas ancient parish in 1885 (GLAUE p401). A spring at Alrewas Hay still assumed locally in the C17 to be bottomless was shown to be 42 feet deep (NHS p60) (SHOS vol 1 p130) (SCSF p143). By this or another spring (that Plot had noted on p51 of NHS) Mr Walter Ashmore of Tamworth observed the fuss ball fungi, which has a texture resembling a sponge. Ashmore had already observed the same near Packington (NHS p200 tab 14 fig 3). About at Alrewas Hayes was found a polished flint axe of the Neolithic or Bronze Age in 1939 (NSJFS 1964 p14). Before the existence of the hay there may have been a Saxon hunting park in the vicinity (MR p10). The hay was in existence by Henry I's reign and is mentioned by name in 1222 (VCH vol 2 p338). It was under the jurisdiction of the steward of the Cannock Forest, and anciently encompassed Alrewas manor (SHC 1907 pp249-293). It was still a constituent element of the forest in the C16. In 1550 the Crown granted it to the Earl of Warwick. His son held the hay in the 1560s (VCH vol 2 p343). In 1567 he sold Alrewas Hay (SHOS vol 1 p132). 346 acres of the hay were enclosed under an Act of 1725 (SHC 1941 p16) (MH 1994 p110). All or further enclosure took place in 1826 (W p598) (NSFCT 1913 p63). Fradley Heath, alias Fradley Common (see), once formed a part of it and it was enclosed in c1805 (W p593). Homeshaw is wrong in identifying Alrewas Hay with Aldridge (SOB p45).

Alrewas Old Manor House Shaw says the remains of Alrewas old half-timbered manor house, which was formerly larger, is situated a little SW of the church near the navigation bridge and the road to Orgreave and King's Bromley. It was occupied by a Mr Fieldhouse by the end of the C18 (SHOS vol 1 p130).

Alsagers Bank (locally *Owgis Bank*, *Odger's Bonk*, *Augers Bonk*). Sprawling miners village on a steep bank on a spur of the Pennine Chain overlooking the Cheshire plain 19m NNW of Stafford. Formerly in Audley and Wolstanton ancient parishes. The views from the village to the W are extraordinary, taking in the Long Mynd, the Welsh Berwyn Mountains and the tower of Liverpool's Anglican cathedral (SVB p13). Alsagers Bank seems to have been entirely in Chesterton district parish after 1846 (W p289). It was created an ecclesiastical parish in 1932 (GLAUE p401). **Stir Pudding Row** is the local name for a row of old, and now demolished, cottages, which stood adjacent to the Methodist chapel (SVB p14). The Anglican **church**, St John, on a hill above High Street, was donated by 1932 by the Heathcote family (SVB p13). **Persons** associated with the village include two gentlemen who seem to have given their names to it: **George Auger** of what is now Church Farm, hired out chain horses to assist horse-drawn carts on the Audley-Newcastle road over the steep hill here. From before 1700 and for a time the bank was called Augers Bank. Auger was followed in this enterprise by **George Alsager** (1738-1805) of Halmer End Farm (now Minnie Farm). When Yates surveyed his map in 1770-75, he used the name Alger Bank, perhaps from confusion between Auger and Alsager, as both names must have been in use then (BOJ Book 3 p8) (SVB p13) (AHJ 1996 p8). **Adolphus Fielding**, a potter aged about 49 of Alsager Bank, who on Nov 12 1845 was murdered by being decapitated with an axe, at a cottage (which probably stood on the site of present 'Farmer's Boy' Inn), where the murderer James Dean, aged 23, was a lodger. Although found guilty of the murder Dean was found to be of unsound mind and not executed but it is not known what happened to him (ILN Nov 22 1845 p327) (AHJ 1997 pp56-67).

Alstone Fragmented minute hamlet 1m NE of Church Eaton, 5.5m SW of Stafford. Formerly partly in Gnosall quarter and ancient parish and partly in Bradley ancient parish. The sub-manor of Aluerdestone appears in DB (SSE 1996 p10). It is commonly accepted that DB Haltone, formerly identified with Alstone, is Haughton (SHC 1923 p44). Later forms are: Aluredestona (1197), Alveston (1280), Alfredeston (C14), Ailston (1518-1529), and Alson (1586) (SPNO pp133-134) (SPN p111). The name is of Anglo-Saxon origin and means Ælfred's tun (SSE 1996 p10), or farmstead (SPNO p134) (SPN p111). A windmill existed at approximately SJ 845186, 0.5m NW of Alston, in 1641 but not by C19 (VCH vol 4 pp84,127) (WBJ p17). By 1958 it lay in Bradley civil parish but in Gnosall ecclesiastical parish (VCH vol 4 p73).

Alstone Hall Alstone. Is referred to as this in the C17 and the C18 and represents the manor-house of Alstone manor (VCH vol 4 p116). There is an Alstone Hall Farm in the centre of Alstone hamlet.

Alstonefield or Alstonfield (spelling is still not standardised). Ancient parish, village and former township. The village lies on a limestone plateau (VCH vol 7 p9) 24m NE of Stafford.
EARLY. A stone hammer of the Neolithic or Bronze Age was found in Alstonefield parish in c1844 (NSJFS 1964 p14). A rude stone hammer was found near Alstonefield in 1686 (WTCEM p11).
900 to 1500. The parish **church**, St Peter, on the N side of Lode Lane, was built by the early C12: But Saxon carvings in the churchyard suggest an earlier building (VCH vol 7 p21). The manor of Ænestanefelt appears in DB. A later form is Alstanesfeld (1178) (SSE 1996 p10). The **name** means 'Ælfstan's field or open land' (OAKDEN) (SSAHST 1967 p32) (NSJFS 1981 p2) (SSE 1996 p10) (SPN p11) and perhaps reflects the geographical situation of Alstonefield village (VCH vol 7 p9). Another interpretation is 'Æne's Stone Field.' Perhaps there was a stone which marked the boundary of Æne's property (DUIGNAN). It may be 'One-Stone Field' - from Steep Low, a sharp summit dome of almost bare rock on the edge of the village (AVH P2). The old extensive **parish** of Alstonefield, which included the present Moorland parishes of Fawfieldhead, Heathylee, Hollinsclough, Longnor, Quarnford, Sheen, and Warslow, was formed out of Ilam parish after 1086 and by 1170 (SHC 1916 p198). By the 1830s a **wake** was held on the Sunday after June 29, the feast of St Peter and St Paul (W p742) (VCH vol 7 p12). There was a one-off perambulation of the parish bounds in 1988. It was an annual custom prior to 1900 (local info). A **market** is recorded at Alstonefield by 1308, although a market charter may never have been granted. The market had ceased by 1500 (SHC New Series vol 11 p257) (NSJFS 1971 pp51,52).
1500 to PRESENT. A **Quaker** burial ground was in use in the C18 at Bowman's Barn on N side of Gipsy Lane at SK 137558, 0.5m E of Alstonefield (SSAHST 1970 pp39-40. 1971 p51). The stone-lined chamber at SK 132553

could be the Vicarage's **ice-house** (IHB p391). The village **pump** on the N side of the village was erected in 1896 and replaced by another in 1928 (AVH pp45il,46) (PWPD p158p) (VCH vol 7 p11). The **workhouse** was haunted (WTCEM p95). The present (2000) Alstonefield Local History Society formed in Nov 1978 (info T Edes). **Natives and visitors**. In 1789 **John Byng**, 5th Viscount Torrington, described Alstonefield village as set 'amidst mountains of height and beauty' (Torrington Diaries vol 2 p58) (VCH vol 7 p12). **John Gould** of Alstonefield, aged 23, was executed in 1811 for the murder of his wife, Elizabeth. It has been said that he was merely trying to abort his wife's second baby, but accidentally killed her (CCSHO pp95-96) (MCS pp29-30). Sir **Henry Ellis** of the BM, visiting Alstonefield and Ilam on Sept 14 1815, noted the paper garlands hanging in the church 'in memory of young females,' although he was told that the custom was dying out (VCH vol 7 p12). **Princess Anne** visited the newly-built homes at Top of Hope in Alstonefield on May 11 1993 (ES May 11 1993 p5).

Alstonefield Hall Manor house to the N of Alstonefield church. Has a date stone with the date 1587 and the initials J.H. for John Harper (d1622), lord of the manor of Alstonefield (NSSG p4) (BOE p55) (MR p10) (VCH vol 7 p15). By 1993 was known as Hall Farm (VCH vol 7 p9), and has also appeared as Alstonefield Manor House.

Alstonefield Hayes Common pasture in the Hayesgate area of Fawfieldhead township, recorded in the later C16 (VCH vol 7 pp28,29).

Alton Ancient parish, large village and former township 15m NE of Stafford. The village lies on a rocky ridge above the Churnet.
EARLY. There have been a few finds of **Neolithic** or **Bronze Age** origin located in the Alton area: A polished stone axe hammer (or celt) was found near the Flag Tower, Alton Towers in 1834 (HAF p28). In 1908 Lynam wrote of 'A fine stone axe hammer found at Alton in possession of Mr Masefield of Cheadle' (NSFCT vol 42 p97) (HAF p28). This may be identified with a stone axe-hammer found at Alton (VCH vol 1 p181) (NSJFS 1964 p14). In 1908 a perforated stone axe hammer was in the possession of a Mr Walker of Alton (VCH vol 1 p180) (HAF p29). A barbed and tangled flint arrowhead of the Early Bronze Age was found on farmland in Alton in 1989. It went to the Potteries Museum (HAF pp29-30). A Late Bronze Age or Saxon leaf shaped bronze sword has been found at Bunbury Hill (see). Three **Roman** gold coins of Vespasian (70-77AD), Titus (71-78AD), and Domitian (81-96AD) were found 900 yards below Alton Castle in 1725 (SHOS vol 2 additions to vol 1 p2) (GNHS p69) (VCH vol 1 p189) (NSJFS 1964 p14) (HAF p33). In 1982 nine Roman bronze coins of c250-275 AD were found in Alton (HAF pp33-34). At the bottom of the garden of Vyse House, High Street, Alton, is a four-feet tall sculpted pillar representing a gruesome pile of bodies stacked on top of each other; long bows and shields mingle with bodies suggesting a battle. The pillar is of marble and of unknown origin, but may be Roman (ES May 20 1999 p15pc).
900 to 1500. The **name** of Alton, probably in existence by 950 (HAF p37), means Ælfa's town or tun (farmstead) (DUIGNAN) (SSE 1996 p10) (SPN pp11-12). Later forms are: Alveton (C13. C17. C18. C19) (SPN p11) and Allerton (1552) (HAF p90) (HOC p254). The present parish **church**, St Peter, at the W end of the High Street, has some C12 work; a church at Alton was in existence by the later 1170s; according to tradition some stones built into the W gable of the N aisle, are of Saxon origin, although some have said they are probably of C14 origin (HAF pp131,132). What was described as an ancient custom in the C19 was the presenting of garlands of flowers by villagers to newly-married couples on their leaving the church (AAD p279). A man has taken a photograph of a misty apparition by the altar in the church (ES March 10 1994 p3p). The **manor** of Alton appears in DB where it is called Elvetone (SSE 1996 p10) and, according to Commander Wedgwood, Halstone; but others have identified Halstone with Horton near Leek (SHC 1916 pp167-168). Alton came into the de Verdun family of Alton Castle (see) in the early C12. By 1299 the lord of Alton had claimed the right of infangetheof, gallows, warren and waif (HAF p56). The **parish**, formed between 1086 and 1291, and probably originally formed a part of Mayfield parish (SHC 1916 pp194,198). The parish **wake** was on the Sunday after St Peter's day in the mid C19 (W p766). Alton was a prescriptive **borough** and does not have a borough charter. The earliest reference to Alton being a borough is in 1239 and the last is in 1705 (NSJFS 1972 p68) (HAF p54p of the seal of the borough). In 1849 the Earl of Shrewsbury erected a police station on the site of the **Moot Hall** (W p766). A **market** is recorded at Alton by 1293, although a market charter may never have been granted. The market had ceased by 1500 (NSJFS 1971 pp51,52). The market was weekly and held on Mondays (HAF p55). Alton's annual **fair** was on the feast of the Exaltation of the Holy Cross (HAF p55). The remains of the Alton **pinfold** could still be seen by the Village Hall in 1996 (HAF p191). The **lock-up**, a round

house with a stone domed roof and cupola, was erected in 1815 (SMOPP vol 1 p108p of c1925) or 1819 (BOE p55). It was renovated in 1977 (ACOPP p71p). (DoE II) (JC p18pl) (PDS&C p46p) (VB p170) (PS pp128,129) (RB vol 3 p80 il by Barbara Jones). **Iron-smelting** was carried on in the parish and neighbouring parishes from the C13.

1500 to PRESENT. **Industry**. There was lead and copper ore mining in the Ribden area by the late C17. Brass wire was manufactured near Alton in the C18. At Alton Thomas Patten began the manufacture of brass wire in 1734. The business transferred to Froghall in 1828 (The Midlands. Past-into-Present series. Clive Gilbert. 1978 p69). A cotton manufactory was established at Alveton in c1780 but it did not prosper. Alton Mill, which had three waterwheels, was converted to paper production in 1847 but the business could not compete with Scandinavian imports and it collapsed in 1867 (The Midlands. Past-into-Present series. Clive Gilbert. 1978 p69) (HAF p301). Limestone, sandstone and sand have been quarried in the parish (SCSF p112) (HAF pp287-325). **Natural phenomena**. On April 20 1805 a shock from an earthquake threw down a number of chimneys in the village (THS p228) (OL vol 1 p184). During a storm on Aug 31 1810 hailstones lay three inches thick upon the ground and some of them measured five inches in circumference (THS p228). On April 30 1849 the shock of an earthquake threw down several village chimneys (W p766). There is a C18 **sundial** on the NW side of the High Street (DoE II). The **village pump** is in Dimble Lane (DoE II). The Uttoxeter Branch of the Caldon **Canal** reached Alton from Froghall in 1809 and had been extended to Uttoxeter by 1811. (STM March 1964 p43p on Alton lock). It closed in 1847 and the Churnet Valley **Railway** used it's bed for a line linking Alton with Macclesfield and Burton opened on July 13 1849. The line closed in 1965 (HAF pp235,238). The pretty Italianate villa-like railway station dates from 1849. In the adjoining three storey tower the Earl of Shrewsbury had his own suite of rooms (IAS p167). It was Landmark Trust property by 1976 (IAS p167). They converted it into a luxury home in the 1990s (SMOPP vol 1 p113p of the station in the flood of July 26/ 27 1927) (SLM Christmas 1995 p29pc). Sandstone from the waiting shelter of the station went to build a house at Oakamoor called 'Railstone' (HAF p399). In the C20 many tourists, and formerly many aristocrats and some royals, including Edward VII, who came through on the morning of Nov 21 1907, have passed through the village en route to nearby Alton Towers (COPP2 p96).

Alton Castle The earliest castle in Alton village was built by a Saxon named Lunan or Juvar (BATR p6). Alton manor came into the de Verdun family in the early C12.

THE VERDUNS, FURNIVALLES, and NEVILLES. Norman de Verdun, son of Bertram de Verdun, lord of Farnham Royal, Bucks, in 1086, was perhaps in possession of Alton manor by 1130. Junior branches of the de Verduns are said to have founded the de Aldithley and Wrottesley families of Heighley Castle (see) and Wrottesley Hall (see), respectively. Norman died in 1153 and was succeeded by his son Bertram de Verdun. He was the founder of Croxden Abbey (see) in 1176, and diplomat with Henry II on his pilgrimage to the shrine of St James at Compestella in c1177. In the 1180s Bertram was custodian of Ranulph 'de Blundeville' (d1232), Earl of Chester, then a minor. According to a tradition Bertram may have brought back with him from a Crusade some Arabs from the Holy Land who founded the race of people in the Biddulph Moor (see) area known as Biddlemoor Men. Bertram died in 1192 whilst on the third Crusade; Benedict of Peterborough records his death as being at Jaffa; whilst the later source - the Croxden Abbey chronicle - records his death as being at Acre; other sources record his death at Joppa and Jeppa. He appears to have been succeeded by his son Thomas de Verdun (d1199) who was succeeded by his brother Nicholas de Verdun (d1231). He was succeeded by his daughter Rohese who married Theobald Butler or le Botiller (d1230). Their successors took the name of Verdun, and they were succeeded by their son John de Verdun (d1274?), who was succeeded by his son Nicholas de Verdun (born before 1248 d1271). He was succeeded by his brother Theobald de Verdun (born c1248). He was summoned to parliament and became Lord Verdun. He died in 1309 and was buried at Croxden Abbey, and was succeeded by his second son Theobald de Verdun (1278). He died at Alton Castle in 1316 and was buried at Croxden Abbey, and was succeeded by his eldest daughter Joan who eventually married Thomas de Furnivalle (or Furnival) (d1339), Lord Furnivalle, and took Alton to the Furnivalles. Their son Thomas de Furnivalle was born at Alton in 1322. On his death in 1395/6 he was succeeded by his brother William (de Fournivalle or Furnivalle) (1326-1383). He was succeeded by his daughter Joan de Furnivalle, who married Thomas de Neville (d1406/7). Their daughter Maud Neville married John Talbot (d1453) in 1406 and Alton passed to the Talbots. For the descent of the Talbots see Alton Towers (The Complete Peerage) (HOS p21) (HAF

pp42,45,49,51).

A castle at Alton in the Castle Hill Road area overlooking the Churnet was built by Bertram de Verdun (d1192) in c1175 and rebuilt or added to with domestic buildings in the early C14 by Theobald de Verdun. A castle which was the residence of the de Verdun family certainly existed by 1316 (LGS p73) (NSJFS 1966 pp42-43) (HOS p21) (CAMS pp14,15p) (MR p13). The de Verduns may have lived on or near the site of Ubberley Hall (see), and or at a later time lived in a house within the moated site at Simfields (see), before settling at Alton Castle (NSFCT 1926 p136). In the Civil War in 1644 the castle was a parliamentary garrison (HOS p35. 1998 p72) (HAF p116) and or a royalist garrison (CAMS p14), with a force of about 40 to 50 men (AAD p278), and thereafter destroyed; the tradition current in the village, was that it was destroyed by firing from the opposite hills (AAD p278); or it was destroyed by order of parliament (NSFCT 1881 p37) (CAMS p14) in c1647. The site was then left neglected for 200 years (NSFCT 1944 p104). Some of the outer walls and a tower survive (DoE I). A bronze sword with seven rivet-holes has been found at Alton Castle (ARCH vol 11 p431) (ABI p282) (VCH vol 1 p180) but is probably the same as a Saxon sword found in 1837 at SK 071432 to E of Bunbury Hill Fort (NSJFS 1964 p22). Deadly Nightshade grew wild among the remains of the castle (W pp765-766). The site is now mainly occupied by Pugin's Alton Castle (see) and St John's Hospital (see) (LGS pp73-74). (NHS p448) (GNHS p95) (JAT p11) (AT pp8-10) (HOC pp199,200) (SK p203) (MOS p facing p32,33,34) (CL Nov 24 1960 p1228p of the fosse and curtain wall) (STM March 1964 pp42,43p) (Norman Castles in Britain. Derek Renn. 1973. p352) (SMOPP vol 1 p106p in c1912). A series of passages under the road below Alton Castle were found in early 1996. The tunnels have been thought to be routes in and out of the castle grounds. Some of the tunnels are thought to be 600 years old. There is a tradition of a tunnel running from the castle to Croxden Abbey (ES June 11 1996 p3p).

Alton Castle Fanciful Gothic house designed by AWN Pugin and built on or near the site of the medieval Alton Castle, perhaps, for the 15th Earl of Shrewsbury's widow, or for the 16th Earl. The inspiration for such a castle high up on the wooded rock must have come from Germany (BOE p59). It is one composition with St John's Hospital (see); the two are linked by a bridge over a moat-ravine (MR p13). The castle was built between 1847 and 1852 (SGS pp50p,51). It is T-shaped with a chapel creating the E arm of the T. It is four-storeys high, with three towers. One of the rooms contained some armorial glass depicting how Alton had passed from the Furnivalle family to John Talbot, 1st Earl of Shrewsbury. There is a tradition that two pieces of armorial glass in the entrance hall came from Croxden Abbey, but they are in fact of a later date (NSFCT 1924 p189). St Aloysius' School for Little Boys (St John's Prep School) moved from St John's Hospital to the castle in 1920. The school closed in 1989 (HAF pp274-286). After the school's closure the castle stood empty until being purchased by Monumental Trust Ltd in 1994. They plan to restore it and turn it into a museum (ES Sept 11 1994 p14p). In 1996 the castle was being used as a Catholic youth centre (HAF p281p) (HOS 1998 p43). Rosa Blake's painting 'Alton Castle' 1925-1938 was on display in Stoke-on-Trent Art Gallery in Feb 1997. (W p766) (CL Nov 24 1960 pp1226-9) (MR p12pc). The chapel is the principle room of the castle (BOE p59). Thorold says the monumental brasses to 16th Earl of Shrewsbury (d1852) and the 17th Earl of Shrewsbury (d1856) are in the castle chapel (SGS p52), whilst Pevsner says they are in the chapel of St John's Hospital (BOE p60). (W p767) (JAT pp15,16) (CL Nov 24 1960 pp1227p,1229).

Alton Common Is marked on current maps 1.25m W of Alton. Freeholders met in 1807 to press for the eviction of squatters on Alton Common. Some or all of the common was enclosed by an Act of 1824 (THS p36) (HAF p192).

Alton Park Medieval deer park enclosed out of forest, held by the de Verduns at Alton. In existence by 1316 (NSJFS 1962 pp73,75). Appears to have formerly stretched over both sides of the Churnet (HAF p126). On the 1834 OS map Alton Park is marked to the E of Alton Towers mansion. AF Bagshaw excavated a chambered long barrow in Alton Park at cSK 083434, 100 yards from Limecroft Farm on Wootton Road between 1952-3. It is 140 feet long and 25 feet across. (NSFCT 1953 pp106-107) (SLM Feb 1953 pp19ps,21). It is in fact a natural feature with traces of recent quarrying (NSJFS 1965 p37). Has also appeared as Alton Old Park (NSFCT 1910 p175).

Alton Park Appears to have been a residence situated where the Alton Towers Hotel and car park now (1996) stand. The Hatfields of Alton Park were bailiffs of the lord of the manor of Alton in the C17 (HAF pp95,128) and the house may be identified with Alton Lodge, the house formerly on the site of Alton Towers mansion.

Alton Towers Huge mansion on a 600 acre estate 15.5m NE of Stafford. Formerly in Farley township in Alton ancient parish. The Alton Towers estate formed part of the Alton Castle estate. The descent of the families - de Verduns, Furnivalles, and Nevilles - who were early holders of that estate can be found under Alton Castle. By the marriage of Maud Neville to John Talbot (d1453) the Alton Castle estate passed to the Talbots.

THE TALBOTS and CHETWYND-TALBOTS. **John Talbot** (d1453) was created Earl of Shrewsbury in 1442. He was succeeded by his son **John Talbot** (c1413-1460), 2nd Earl. He was succeeded by his eldest son **John Talbot** (1448-1473), 3rd Earl, who was succeeded by his elder son **George Talbot** (1468-1538), 4th Earl. He was succeeded by his second son **Francis Talbot** (d1560), 5th Earl. His only son, **George Talbot** (d1590), 6th Earl, had custody of Mary Queen of Scots, and was husband of Bess of Hardwick, Derbys. He was succeeded by his eldest surviving son **Gilbert Talbot** (1552-1616), 7th Earl, who was succeeded by his younger brother **Edward Talbot** (1561-1617), 8th Earl. The title and estates then reverted to the descendents of the 2nd Earl, through his second son Sir Gilbert Talbot of Grafton, Worcs (d1518). He was succeeded by his elder son Sir Gilbert Talbot (d1542), who was succeeded by his half-brother Sir John Talbot of Abingdon. He was succeeded by his son Sir John Talbot of Grafton and Abingdon (d1555), who was succeeded by his son Sir John Talbot of Grafton. Sir John married twice. The earldom of Shrewsbury passed to the children of his first marriage, whilst the children of his second marriage (to Elizabeth, daughter of Walter Wrottesley of Wrottesley Hall) eventually, after a struggle in the C19, succeeded to the title of Earl of Shrewsbury. Sir John Talbot of Salwarp, Worcs (d1581), was the eldest son of this second marriage. He was succeeded by his son Sherrington Talbot of Salwarp and Lacock, Wilts (d1642). He had four sons. The three oldest sons eventually failed in the male line and Sherrington (d1642) was eventually succeeded by his fourth son William Talbot 'of Whittington' (d1686), who resided at Stourton Castle (see). He was succeeded by his son **Rt Rev William Talbot** born at Stourton Castle in c1659. On his death in 1730 he was succeeded by his eldest son Charles Talbot (1685-1736/7), Lord Chancellor of England, and created 1st Baron Talbot in 1733. He was succeeded by his son William Talbot (b1710), 2nd Baron Talbot, who was created an earl in 1761. On his death in 1782 the title of baron passed to **John Chetwynd Talbot** (1749-1793), the son of the 2nd Baron's younger brother, John Talbot and his wife, Catherine Chetwynd (d1785), of Ingestre Hall (see). John became 3rd Baron Talbot. He was created Viscount Ingestre and Earl Talbot in 1784 and added the Chetwynd name to Talbot and assumed the additional arms of Chetwynd. On his death in 1793 he was succeeded by his son Charles Chetwynd Chetwynd-Talbot (1777-1849), 4th Baron Talbot and 2nd Earl Talbot. He was succeeded by his second son **Henry John Chetwynd Chetwynd-Talbot** (1803-1868), 3rd Earl Talbot. Returning to the line who inherited the earldom of Shrewsbury by the first marriage of Sir John Talbot of Grafton (later C16) was **George Talbot**. He became 9th Earl of Shrewsbury and died in 1630 without issue. The earldom then passed through his younger brother, John (d1607), to his son **John Talbot** (d1653/4), 10th Earl. He was succeeded by his second son **Francis Talbot**, 11th Earl, who died in 1667 of a wound received in a duel with the 2nd Duke of Buckingham. His son, **Charles Talbot**, 12th Earl, was one of the signatories of the invitation to William of Orange to take the throne in 1688, and was prominent in the reigns of Anne and George I. He was created Marquis of Alton and Duke of Shrewsbury in 1694. These titles became extinct on his death in 1717/8. The estate and earldom of Shrewsbury then passed to his cousin, **Gilbert Talbot**, 13th Earl, a priest, who died in 1743. He was succeeded by his nephew **George Talbot** (d1787), 14th Earl. (George's sister Barbara married James Aston, 5th Lord Aston, a descendent of the Astons of Haywood Hall (see)). George was succeeded by his nephew **Charles Talbot**, 15th Earl, born in 1753 (The Complete Peerage p117) (Burke's Peerage 1967). In 1812, when nearly 60, Charles took an interest in the Alton estate, one of many estates belonging to him, and began to landscape it, creating the gardens (see below). In 1814 he took over Alveton Lodge as his summer residence to supervise the work. Up to that period the lodge, situated on Bunbury Hill (see), had been the residence of the bailiff or agent of the estate: an Alton Lodge is mentioned in 1644 (HAF p127) and it may be identified with the house, Alton Park (see). During his residency Charles began to enlarge the lodge in the Gothic style and renamed it Alton Abbey (The Shell Guide to England. John Hadfield. 1977), a name it had until at least 1828 (Broughton's Scrapbook p89). There are two listed mile plates inscribed 'Alton Abbey,' one at Threapwood Lodge and one at SK 04254325, both are grade two. Others say work began on the mansion earlier, in 1810 (BOE p56) or in 1812 (NSFCT 1944 p103). Charles was succeeded on his death, in 1827, by his nephew, **John Talbot** (1791-1852), 16th Earl. He continued his uncle's work and took up permanent residency at Alton Abbey in 1831, and renamed it Alton Towers (The Shell Guide to England. John Hadfield. 1977). He was

succeeded by his cousin **Bertram-Arthur Talbot** (b1832), 17th Earl, who died without issue in 1856 (of consumption - GLS pp13-14), and who left the earldom and estates to the Catholic infant son of the Duke of Norfolk. However, their right to the title and estates was contested by the descendents of Sir John Talbot of Grafton (later C16), Barons and Earls Talbot (see above) (HOU 1886 pp134-135) (Burke's Peerage 1967). It was the 3rd Earl Talbot's son, Charles John Chetwynd Chetwynd-Talbot (b1830), Viscount Ingestre, who made the first attempts to claim the title of Earl of Shrewsbury for his father by going to Alton Towers to formally demand possession of the Towers on Aug 18 1856. The Towers were then in the possession of the trustees appointed under the will of the late 17th Earl and the trustees would not let him have access to the estate. Henry, 3rd Earl Talbot, then appealed to the House of Lords to decide the question of the <u>title</u>. The claim was brought before the Lords on May 11 1857. As well as the Duke of Norfolk on behalf of his infant son, there were two other claimants to the title. After a long adjournment the Lords found in favour of the 3rd Earl Talbot on June 1 1858. In Dec 1858 the 3rd Earl, (now also 18th Earl of Shrewsbury), brought a case in the Court of Common Pleas to reclaim Alton Towers <u>estate</u> from the Duke of Norfolk. After a protracted case the court ruled in favour of the 18th Earl of Shrewsbury, and amid much ceremony the 18th Earl took formal possession of the Towers on April 13 1861 (HOU 1886 pp128-150) (HAF pp74-75). Henry, 3rd Earl Talbot and 18th Earl of Shrewsbury, was succeeded by his son, **Charles John Chetwynd Chetwynd-Talbot** (1830-1877), 19th Earl of Shrewsbury and 4th Earl Talbot. He was succeeded by his son **Charles Henry John Chetwynd-Talbot** (1860-1921), 20th Earl of Shrewsbury. He was succeeded by his grandson, **John George Charles Henry Alton Alexander Chetwynd-Talbot** (b1914), 21st Earl of Shrewsbury, son of Charles John Alton Chetwynd-Talbot (d1915). **Charles Henry John Benedict Crofton Chetwynd Chetwynd-Talbot** (b1952), son of John (b1914), is the 22nd and present (1999) Earl of Shrewsbury. By 1985 he was living at Wanfield Hall (see) (Burke's Peerage 1967). Work continued on the building of Alton Towers Mansion until 1852 (BOE p56). The mansion is built of local sandstone (NSFCT 1979 p17). Queen Adelaide, wife of William IV, was a guest in Nov 1839 (R&S p39). She was again at the Towers in July 1840 (R&S p39) (SIOT p74). Thomas Moore, an Irish poet, who formerly lived for a while at Mayfield Cottage (see), was a guest in 1835 (VFC p95). Benjamin Disraeli (1804-1881) used the Towers as the model for Muriel Towers in his novel 'Lothair' (1870) (VFC p39) (Alton Towers: A Gothic Wonderland. Michael Fisher. 1999 p53). Edward VII stayed at Alton Towers in 1907 (RHPS p296). A room known as the Octagon or Sculpture Gallery or sometimes called the 'Saloon' is based to some extent on the chapter house at Wells cathedral (JAT p22) (W p767) (KES p24). In the North West Tower and integral with the Library, was an attractive alcove called Poets Corner (LTD p83). There were about 80 paintings of note at the mansion including some by Holbein, Vandyck, Murillo, Claude Lorrain, Tintoretto and Caravaggio. Whilst at Alton Towers Mr Fradgley painted 500 shields of arms of the Shrewsbury family from the time of the Norman Conquest for Earl John on an immense piece of canvas. It is supposed to be now at Rome (BATR pp10-12). The estate was sold to pay death duties in c1915 (Birmingham Sunday Mercury Jan 8 1995 pp68-69). However, Lady Shrewsbury lived at Alton Towers until 1923 (AUOPP p37). The estate was sold to a limited company in 1924 (HAF p237; or 1923) (HOS 1998 p43). The company appears to have been a consortium led by the local Bagshaw family; it then opened the gardens to the public (NSFCT 1944 p103) (LTD p92). In WW2 the mansion was requisitioned and used by an officer-cadet training unit (The Shell Guide to England. John Hadfield. 1977). In 1948 the Banqueting Hall caught fire and its wooden panelling was destroyed (SMOPP vol 1 pp116p in 1920, 117p of the interior, 118p of the chapel interior). Alton Towers remained military property until 1951 when Mr Bagshaw began restoration of the gardens, and shortly after they were opened to the public (The Shell Guide to England. John Hadfield. 1977) (LTD p92). It was recommended the railway station for Alton Towers be closed in 1963 (ES March 22 1963). Some junior members of the royal family took part in a 'Grand Knockout' tournament at Alton Towers in 1987 (SN June 19 1987 p10). The largest pass the parcel game to ever take place by 1994 was that at Alton Towers on Nov 8 1992. The event was organised by Parcelforce International and involved 3464 people who removed 2000 wrappers in two hours from a parcel measuring 5x3x3 feet. The final present was an electric keyboard won by Sylvia Wilshaw (GBR 1994 p217). The world record for the largest number of firework rockets let off at the same time was set at the Towers on Oct 29 1999 when 48,753 rockets took off, beating the previous record of 39,500 rockets set in Jersey in 1997 (ES Oct 30 1999 p3pc). The mansion and surrounding pleasure grounds had approximately 3,000,000 visitors in 1994, and 2,650,000 visitors in 1999, drawing more visitors than any other admission-charge tourist attraction in Britain (ES Jan 2 1995 p10. April 25 2000 p8). In Oct 1998 the Tussauds leisure division of Pearson Group sold Alton Towers leisure park to Charterhouse Development Capital for £353 million (ES Oct 1998 p2). (AAD pp256-278) (ECFVA) (AT pl pp11,12,18-22) (AWM p5) (JAT pp17,20,21,25,26-28,33,38) (ES May 20 1930 p9 painting of the Towers by RC Haslehurst) (CL June 2 1960 pp1246-1249 ps, il of garden from the S in 1833. June 9 1960 pp1304-1307 ps). **Supernatural**. The ghost of a gipsy woman who foretells the death of the Shrewsbury heir. Dr FA Paley, tutor to the earl's heir, Bertram-Arthur (1832-1856), saw her about a mile from Alton near the canal, in 1847-8 (GLS pp13-14). A gentleman in top hat, black cape and carrying a walking stick, usually accompanied by a large black dog, was seen in c1930 on the steps leading up to the Towers (GOM p22). A wealthy young woman in C19 riding clothes has appeared in various places. She was seen in 1978 and has been seen by the Swiss Cottage and by the moat. According to legend she was prevented from eloping with her lover and incarcerated in a tower from which she jumped to her death in the moat (GLS pp16-17). In 1992 builders making 'The Haunted House' attraction in the Alton Towers leisure park claim they heard a child's ghostly voice. The attraction is based on the local legend of a girl called Emily who lived in Alton village many years ago. She was playing with her cat in the drawing room when a face appeared in the fire (ES Nov 25 1992 p3).

GARDENS. Created by the Earls of Shrewsbury out of a barren warren. Miss Pugh, the daughter probably of a wealthy industrialist from the NE of England, visited in 1825 and saw a plant called 'Cobea' which the guide told her grew an inch in 24 hours, and an ash growing out of an oak (TB May 1993 p20). George Eliot (Mary Evans) visited the gardens in 1840 (NSFCT 1918 p122). The gardens were billed as 'The Fairyland of The British Isles' by a 1930s guide book. The **Alcove** is mentioned on a plan of the grounds, situated at S end of the Grand Conservatory, or below the **Arcaded Wall** (BATR). The **Bath Fountain** is mentioned on the plan of the grounds, situated by the La Refuge (BATR p14). The **Bird Cage**, is a gazebo (DoE II, HBMC I). A seven-arched sham **Bridge**, a dam ending a lake, is probably by Papworth (BOE p58). **Candlestick Fountain** see Corkscrew Fountain. **Canton Pagoda** or Pagoda Fountain or Duck Pagoda (FZ p111) or Duck Tower (F&G p119) (F p319) or Pagoda-in-a-lake. Three-storey Chinese-looking pagoda, completed 1827 (F p319). Influenced by the To-Ho Pagoda in Canton, which was illustrated in Chambers's 'Designs of Chinese Buildings' 1757 (BOE p58) (F p319). Or, and, by one designed by Nash on a bridge in St James's Park lake as part of the victory celebrations in 1814 but not completed until 1831 (CL Jan 29 1959. June 2 1960 pp1248p,1249). It was completed to a simplified design by Robert Abraham and is 44 feet high instead of the intended 88 feet and only three storeys instead of six. In the base was to be a gasholder to illuminate 40 Chinese lanterns suspended from the angles, dragons were to have projected over the angles and to spout water from eyes, nostrils, fins and tails, and a column of water 70 feet high was to spring from the summit (DoE II* HBMC I) (CGE pp42,87 pl 76) (JAT p40) (AT p24) (BATR p14) (KES p23) (SGS p) (IAANS p vi). **Ceres Statue**. Has an uplifted wreath and is by the Bath Fountain (BATR p14). **Chinese Temple** see Prospect Tower. **Choragic Monument** or called Lysicrates Monument (AT p23). Is a replica of the Choragic Monument and commemorates the 15th Earl of Shrewsbury. The original Choragic Monument was found by 'Athenian' Stuart in the early 1750s embedded in the walls of a Capuchin convent between the SE angle of the Acropolis and the Temple of Jupiter, Athens. In the C18 it was commonly called the 'Lanthorn of Demosthenes or Diogenes' and was supposed to have been built by the orator as a place of study and retirement. But Stuart discovered an inscription on the original saying that it was erected by Lysicrates of Kikyana as a memorial to the victory of the tribe of Akamantis in a dramatic contest (SNTG pp25-26). (BATR p13). The Alton one is a facsimile of the original except for the frieze of honeysuckle. It was executed from drawings by Thomas Fradgley, and cast in metal at Derby. The bust is a representation of Charles, 15th Earl of Shrewsbury. The inscription 'He made the desert smile' refers to his transferring the once barren rabbit warren into the gardens. The bust was modelled at Alton by Peter Hollins of Birmingham and sent to Rome to be executed in marble (BATR p13). Shugborough Park also has a replica of the same monument (BOE p58). (DoE II* HBMC I) (W p768) (JAT p37il, 38) (HOC p213) (IAANS p v) (CL June 2 1960 pp1248,1249p). **Cost**. Was being built in 1825. Is 90 yards long, and the estimated cost was £14,000. Has five domes. The centre dome is surmounted by an Earl's coronet (TB May 1993 p20). (JAT pp38,39il). **Conservatory Temple**. Is a temple at the end of the Conservatory terrace and is a circular form, open in front, and filled with seats and central table (JAT p38). **Corkscrew Fountain** or Screw Fountain or Siren Fountain. Or

formerly called Candlestick Fountain. Fountain with five tiers in a pool with aquatic plants (JAT p40), or with four tiers of shelves and short spiral-fluted pillars diminishing in girth (BOE p58). Was divested of its ornaments by 1870 (BATR p14). (DoE II HBMC I) (AT p23) (HOC p213) (CGE p87) (CL June 2 1960 p1249p) (F&G p235) (SGS p50) (F p319) (FZ p111). **Demosthenes Lantern** see Choragic Monument. **Diogenes Lantern** see Choragic Monument. **Dolphin Fountain**. Slightly to N of Canton Pagoda (BATR p14). **Druid's Sideboard** see Stonehenge. **Duck Pagoda** see Canton Pagoda. The **Dutch Garden** appears on the plan of the gardens in BATR S of the Harper's Cottage and slightly W of the Canton Pagoda (BATR p14). It was built by John 16th Earl (The Shell Guide to England. John Hadfield. 1977). The **Flag Tower**, SW of the mansion, is a massive square building with circular turrets at its angles. It was built in c1810-13 and before 1830 (DoE II HBMC I) (JAT p40) (IAANS p vi) (KES pp23,24) (BOE P58) (SMOPP vol 1 p119p c1910) (F p319). A polished stone axe hammer (or celt) was found near the Flag Tower in 1834 (HAF p28). The fountain (HBMC I) could be same as Pagoda-in-a-lake or Dolphin Fountain. **Geometrical Garden** is mentioned on a plan of the grounds in BATR, between the Alcove and the Golden Gate. **Gothic Pavilion** see Prospect Tower. **Gothic Temple** see Prospect Tower. **Gothic Tower** see Prospect Tower. **Harper's Cottage** or Swiss Cottage was designed by Fradgley for an old retainer, some say it was built for a blind Welsh harper, whose harp was to contribute to the visitors' emotions on entering Alton Towers and attune guests to the medieval atmosphere. The Cottage was situated in the valley garden (JAT p38) (AT p23) (IAANS p v) (KES p23) (CL June 2 1960 pp1247p in fig 3 left hand side, 1248. June 9 1960 p1305) (SGS p51). It has two steep bargeboarded gables (BOE p58). **'Her Ladyship's Garden'** built beside the chapel (perhaps the oratory - see below) by John 16th Earl, has been described as 'classically beautiful' (The Shell Guide to England. John Hadfield. 1977) (LTD p84p). **'Her Ladyship's Oratory'** is a little stone chapel with a high-pitched roof with a floriated stone cross on the gable. It was still standing in 1998 in a corner of a walled garden not from the Grand Entrance (Alton Towers: A Gothic Wonderland. Michael Fisher. 1999 p139). **Ingestre Courtyard**. A stable block E of the house. Has a front of two squat towers on the corners and a battlemented wall connecting them, with a fortified entrance in the middle and gives the the impression of a medieval fort. It may date from before 1830; it is a facade only to be seen from across the lake (F pp319-320). **Italianate Lodge** or known locally as the Pink Lodge is at SK 068432, 0.25m W of Alton Towers Mansion. (DoE II) (BOE p59) (SGS p51). **Jacobs Ladder** is mentioned in the Plan of the Grounds situated alongside the Cascade, near the Choragic Monument (BATR). **Lantern of Demosthenes** see Choragic Monument. **La Refuge** or Le Refuge, a recessed alcove with small inner room (JAT p38). May contain columns from the old entrance to Alveton Lodge (Alton Towers: A Gothic Wonderland. Michael Fisher. 1999 p29p). It is mentioned on a plan of the grounds, near the Bath Fountain (BATR). **Lion Fountain** mentioned on the plan of the gardens E of the War Fountain and N of Stonehenge (BATR). **Loggia** is of stone and has nine arches with a top balustrade (DoE II HBMC I) (BOE p58). **Lover's Gate** is between the Dutch Garden and Harper's Cottage (BATR p15). **Lysicrates Monument** see Choragic Monument. **Pagoda** see Prospect Tower. **Pagoda-in-a-lake** see Canton Pagoda. **Pink Lodge** see Italianate Lodge. **Pitt Bust**. Calvert noted a colossal bust of William Pitt, the PM, on a pedestal opposite the Conservatory (SSC p138 in the intro). **Prospect Tower** or formerly called the Pagoda or Gothic Temple, Tower or Pavilion, or wrongly Chinese Temple, stands on 'Thomson's Rock' and was designed by Abraham and is made of cast iron (JAT pp36,38) (HOC p213) (AT p23) (CGE p87) (CL June 2 1960 p1248p) (IAANS p vi) (BOE p58) (F&G p236p) (FZ p111). **Quixhill Lodge** see under Quixhill. **'Rising Sun' Temple** on a rocky base near the Canton Pagoda. Has a coloured glass dome. Noted in 1825 by Miss Pugh (TB May 1993 p20). It is perhaps the same as the Prospect Tower. **Rock Walk**. Leads from the gardens to Ina's Rock over a mile away (HOC p213). Starts at the golden gates by the Gothic Temple in the gardens (BATR p14) (AT p24) (JAT p40). **Rotunda** is of stone and situated at the far end of the Conservatory (BOE p58). **Siren Fountain** see Corkscrew Fountain. **Screw Fountain** see Corkscrew Fountain. The **Scalloped Wall** is mentioned on a plan of the grounds situated directly to left on entrance of the gardens through Grand Entrance: The war Fountain is fixed into it (BATR). **Stonehenge** or Druid's Sideboard (F&G p236) (F p319) is a poor and much abridged replica of Stonehenge, Wilts (BOE p58). (DoE II. HBMC I). It was designed by Mr Fradgley (BATR p14). Each of the stones which comprise it, weigh about nine tons (JAT pp36,40). (HOC p213) (CGE p87) (AT p23) (SGS p50) (FZ p111). **Swiss Cottage** see Harper's Cottage. **Tudor Lodge** is by the Italianate Lodge, and is probably by Pugin (BOE p59). The **War Fountain** is so called because the jets of water dash against each other (BATR p13). **Water Pagoda** see Canton Pagoda.

Alumwell Small district under 1.25m W of Walsall. Named after an alum well, a strong chalybeate spring, situated on the old main road to Wolverhampton (SHOS vol 2 p76). It was a place of much resort but which had fallen into disuse by 1855 (HOWG p5) (VCH vol 17 p222). The area has also been called Moat Hill (VCH vol 17 p222).

Alverton Hall House overlooking a tributary of the Churnet 0.5m NW of Denstone, in Denstone ecclesiastical parish. Occupied by farmers from at least 1876. By 1940 known as Alveton Hall Farm (OS maps).

Alveton Lodge First recorded in 1339. A house which was the residence of the Shrewsbury's agent until it was incorporated into the NW part of Alton Towers Mansion in c1810 (SMOPP vol 1 p114 il 1807). In 1787 Charles Talbot, 15th Earl of Shrewsbury, started to develop the lodge (CAMS p14).

Amblecote Village on a bank above the Stour 0.5m N of Stourbridge, Worcs and 24m S of Stafford. Former hamlet and township in Old Swinford ancient parish, Worcs, Worcester diocese. The manor of Amblecote is recorded in DB where it is written Elmelecote (SVS p578). The name occurs in 1255, 1292, and 1539 (BCM Autumn 1999 p28) and forms have ranged from Emelcote, Amelcot (SSE 1996 p12), and Amblecoat (SVS p105). It means 'Amela's cot' (VCH vol 20 p49) (BCM Autumn 1999 p28). Or 'Hemele's cot' (DUIGNAN). Another explanation is 'The cottage by the river (or sandbank)' (MR p16). Shaw thought Amblecote derived from the British Am bel coit, ad caput sylvae (SHOS vol 2 p236). Scott agreed the ending could have originated from British coed or (p) coit (SVS p103). The original settlement was probably on the high ground at the junction of Hillfields Road and Kirkston Way (VCH vol 20 pp49,62). Coal and fireclay mining was occurring in Amblecote by the late Middle Ages. The best clay in England is said to be found at Amblecote, and it was being used by immigrants from the Lorraine region of France to make glass pots by the 1620s (VCH vol 20 pp58-59), and to make tobacco pipes by the late C17 (NHS p121). Iron working has also taken place in Amblecote (VCH vol 20 p60). An emigrant appears to have taken the name to Canada where there is a house named Amblecote at Duncan, British Columbia (TB June 1986 p6p). The present village is concentrated along the main Stourbridge-Wolverhampton road at Holloway End (see) where the church of The Holy Trinity was built on the E side of the A491 in 1841 (BOE p60) (VCH vol 20 pp49,62). Amblecote remained in Worcester Diocese after becoming a separate ecclesiastical parish in 1842 (LGS p174) (VCH vol 3 p92), or 1844 or 5 (VCH vol 20 p62). The township of Wollaston, Worcs, remained in the new ecclesiastical parish of Amblecote parish (GLAUE pp401,419) until 1860 when the parish was refounded (VCH vol 20 p62). In 1898 Amblecote was made an urban district. The district contained 665 acres (VCH vol 20 p49) and is said to have been the smallest urban district in the country (WMVB p15). The Kinver Light Railway, opened in 1900, ran from The Fish Inn, Amblecote to Kinver. The line closed in 1927 (WMAG Aug 1970 pp22-23. May 1976 p22).

Amblecote Bank Small hamlet in the present Vicarage Road area, 0.75m ENE of Amblecote (1882 OS map). The area was known as such by 1733 (VCH vol 20 p51).

Amblecote Hall There was a hall of the lord of Amblecote manor by the late C13. Two properties close to each other, which became respectively Amblecote Hall and Amblecote Farm (later Amblecote House), were both referred to as 'The Hall' on a map of 1688 (BCM Autumn 1999 p30). Amblecote Hall was leased by 1723 and occupied as a farm by the late C18. It has been said that the hall was demolished in c1820 and rebuilt in 1831 (VCH vol 20 p54). However, Scott in 1832, described the hall as 'the ancient hall.' William King, a coal and clay master, lived at Amblecote Hall from 1838 until 1850. In 1949 both the hall and the neighbouring farmhouse (Amblecote House) were sold to John Hall & Co Ltd for the purpose of fireclay extraction; the hall (perhaps an Elizabethan house and not an early C19 one as alleged by VCH) was demolished in 1952 (BCM Autumn 1999 pp28p,31); or in c1960 (VCH vol 20 p54). The site of Amblecote Hall is now (1999) occupied by the properties of 8-16 Woodcombe Close, whilst the site of Amblecote House is under the properties of 6 and 8 Kirkstone Way, 0.5m ENE of Amblecote (1882 OS map) (BCM Autumn 1999 p31). (E&S Jan 3 1952. Jan 21 1952 p) (SNSV vol 2 p19).

Amblecote Park There may have been a hunting park at Amblecote in the late C13. A park of the lord of Amblecote is mentioned in the earlier 1570s (VCH vol 20 p55).

Amblecote Wood Appears to be an area reclaimed by Dudley Corporation in the area of the railway line E of Coalbournbrook (WFK p39).

Amerton Hamlet by Amerton Brook nearly 1m SE of Gayton, in Stowe parish (W p422). The manor of Mersetone (Amerton) appears in DB. Later forms

are: Aunbriton, Ambrihiton (1230) (SSE 1996 p10), Ambricton (SPN p111) and Ambrighton (SHC 1909 p187 note). The name is Anglo-Saxon origin and means means Eanbriht's town (DUIGNAN) (SPN p111), or Eanbeorht's tun (SSE 1996 p10). Or is from the old Saxon word 'ham' a house, a farm, then corrupted to 'Amer.' Or it may be from the word 'aim' to direct, and 'aimer' which was a word in very common use in these parts to denote a nearer or more direct way - 'It's a much aimer road.' Perhaps the town on the aimest or more direct way to Weston or Stafford (NSFCT 1886 p35). A Wellington bomber which had taken off from Hixon airfield on Oct 31 1942 crashed at Amerton killing two of its occupants, Canadian airman, Flt Sgt DC Hawk air gunner 25, and Sgt RH Woollians navigator 33; they were buried in St Peter's churchyard, Hixon (info Hixon Local History Society). At Amerton Plot noted a whole footed water fowl, locally called French Geese, differing only in the black bill and in the noise it made which was like a Bittern (NHS p229).

Amerton Brook Runs at Weston-on-Trent.

Amerton Heath Former common land to the S of Amerton and to the S of the Stafford-Uttoxeter railway line.

Amington Village by the Anker 23m SE of Stafford, or 23m N of Warwick. The former township of Amington and Stoneydelph, comprising Great and Little Amington and Stoneydelph, lay in Hemlingford hundred, Warws in Tamworth ancient parish. The name has appeared as Alchmunding tuun (889) and Alhmunding tun (889), and Aminton (1150) (Warwickshire. Duignan. 1912) (SSE 1996 p10). It means 'Ealhmund's town' (Warwickshire. Duignan. 1912) or 'the farmstead of Amma's people' (SPN p12). Marks in a field adjacent to Amington Old Hall at SK 232056 which showed up in an aerial photograph taken in summer 1965 probably represent the traces of a lost village deserted in the Middle Ages (SSAHST 1966 p48 pl 1a). Amington was created an ecclesiastical parish in 1864 but reunited with Tamworth parish in the 1870s. It became a separate civil parish in 1866. Parts of the civil parish began to be taken into Tamworth borough from 1932 and the whole civil parish was taken into Tamworth borough and into Staffs in 1965 (GLAUE pp402,425,436). Amington was a ward of Tamworth borough by at least 1993. Both Great and Little Amington feature in a derisory rhyme about Tamworth (see).

Amington Hall Amington. Built in the early C19 and incorporates parts of a much older hall. The hall belonged to the Repington family by at least the later C17: Sebright Repington married a member of the Burdet family; their family tradition was that the sound of a drum foretold a death in their family. A drumming sound was, indeed, heard in a chimney stack, about 8 or 9 o' clock at night for six or eight weeks before her death (NHS p330) (Strange Things Among Us. H Spicer. 1895) (DOG p186). Charles Edward Repington (d1837) was of Amington Hall (mem in St Edith's, Tamworth). In 1904 it was occupied by Sydney Fisher, Chairman of Fisher & Co, paper manufacturers, who was later killed when he fell through the floor at Kettlebrook Paper Mill (TDOPP p78p). (BOE p61).

Amphitheatre An indentation, at SJ 927449, in Park Hall Country Park, possibly man-made, as there was mining and sandstone quarrying in the vicinity (Park Hall Country Park. Staffs County Council Leaflet. Pre-1991).

Amphitheatre, The Rock formation part of Hen Cloud on The Roaches (SGM pp138-139 il).

Anchor Brook Runs through Anchor Meadows on the W side of Aldridge town. The name is preserved in Anchor Road (SNAR p8). It is probably a tributary of a head river of the Tame.

Anchor Brook Rises in the grounds of Park Hall. Runs at Longton where its name changes to Cockster Brook (VCH vol 8 p224).

Anchor Hill Street S of Delph Road, Silver End, in Kingswinford ancient parish.

Anchor House Off Anchor Road, NE of the centre of Longton. Mentioned in 1758. Seat of the potter John Carey by at least 1829. By mid C19 it had been surrounded by a moat, four feet deep, and was known as The Moat or the Moat House. By the late 1870s it was known as the Island House. The moat was drained by the early 1920s. Demolished in c1950 (VCH vol 8 p231) (SHST p595).

Anc's Hill Glacial hillock and highest point of a gravel ridge which runs along the northern side of Aqualate Mere (WSS pp96,97p,99). In Forton parish (W p458). The name is, perhaps, from the burial place of a Roman captain named Ancus (NHS p395) (NSFCT 1902 p119). Or 'the hills of the hermit's well' (SPNO p147). It has appeared as Anxewell hills (1635) (SPNO p147), and Ancks Hill. Here skeletons were found in rows in 1815 (GNHS p69) (W p458) (VCH vol 4 p105). (SLM spring 1956 pp27,28). Nearby is a Roman well.

Andrewshall Prebend of Gnosall. See Chilternhall.

Anglesey Branch of the Wyrley and Essington Extension Canal. Spurs off the

Wyrley and Essington Extension Canal at Ogley Junction and terminates at Chasewater Reservoir (HCMS No. 2). Built in 1850 (VCH vol 2 p296), or opened in 1863 (HCMS No. 2). It was built by the Marquis of Anglesey to serve his coal mines in the Hammerwich area. The canal incorporated the feeder from Norton Pool. The feeder seems to have been built in 1840 (VCH vol 2 p296. vol 14 p215). Closed 1967 (SWY p16).

Anglesey Coppice Former name for Chartley Moss (MR p90). However, the OS map 1834 marks both Chartley Moss and, to the E, Anglesey Coppice.

Anker, River Rises near Bulkington, and falls via Polesworth into the Tame at Tamworth (Warwickshire. Duignan. 1912 p12). Has also appeared as Oncer (c1000-1577), Auncre (1295), and Ancre (1332. c1540) (SPNO p4). It is the 'Silvery Anker' in Michael Drayton's poetry (Staffs County Handbook. c1958. p138). The name is from Anglo-Saxon ancra - a hermit or nun - from the two nunneries on its 20 mile course (DUIGNAN) (SPN p122). Or the first part of the word is probably some corruption of the root 'avon' 'an' (NSFCT 1908 p131). Ekwall suggests it is an old British name. Originally Oncer (RN pp14,15). Prof Kenneth Jackson says it is very speculative (SPNO p4). There was a catastrophic oil spillage into the Anker in 1974 (SLM Oct 1996 p15). It never ran through Staffs before 1910.

Ankerton House 0.5m SE of Slindon. In Three Farms township in the Woodland quarter in Eccleshall ancient parish (W p376). At Cat's Hill is Little Ankerton. At Ankerton or Little Ankerton was possibly a medieval village, probably deserted 1332-1524 (SSAHST 1970 p34).

Annatt's House An old house built in 1686 in Norton chapelry in Stoke-on-Trent ancient parish (ONST 1932 p39). Is probably Annatt's Farm ENE of Norton Green on the N side of High Lane.

Anne's Well Wood Ranton. Small wood 0.5m NE of Ranton Abbey. Could be a corruption of the lost settlement of Frankwell or Frankville, which is reputed to be in this area? Was there a well here called 'Anne's Well'? An Anne Cope was in residence at Ranton Abbey in the later C17.

Ann Roach Ann Roach Farm is over 1m SSW of Flash. For the geology of Ann Roach see NSFCT 1920 p87. The name probably means something like 'one rocher' to which there is an illusion in the medieval epic poem 'Gawain and the Green Knight' (NSJFS 1977 p39). Or it is from Dana or Anu the Earth Mother goddess of the Celts (UHAW p75) (DPMM p108).

Anslow Village on the Needwood Forest plateau at the head of a dale created by Alder Brook 2m N of Tatenhill. Former township in Rolleston ancient parish (W pp576-577).

900 to 1500. There was settlement at Anslow in Anglo-Saxon times. The **name** has appeared as Ansythlege and Eansythelege (later C10) (ANS p8), Ansidelege (1008) (SHC 1916 p123), Ansedlega (1180) (SSE 1996 p10), Ansedelega (C13), Anzedelye (1305), Aunsley (ANS p15) and Annesley (1798) (SHOS vol 1 p34). It is derived from words meaning pastureland (SVB p17). Or means 'St Eanswyth's woodland clearing' (HOPT vol 1 p136) (SPN p27). Or 'hermitage woodland clearing' (SSE 1996 p10) (ANS p8). Anslow became a **manor** in the later C12 with the Toke family holding it from Burton Abbey to c1360 when the lordship was left in dispute (ANS p13). In the early 1540s overlordship passed to Sir William Paget of Beaudesert (SHOS vol 1 p8). A medieval **chapel** at Anslow, St Leonard's, called 'Kinnersley's chantry' in 1546, is not mentioned in the 1563 return (SHC 1915 p216). For the present church see Anslow Gate. There were **curfews** on the nights of Feb 5, St Agatha's day, Midsummer, Twelfth night, Walpurgis Day, and May Day to deter fiends, goblins, witches and warlocks. A field name 'the Bell-grove' at Anslow indicates the site of the curfew bell-tree (UTR p241).

1500 to PRESENT. Anslow was created an ecclesiastical parish in 1861 (ANS p8) and a civil one in 1866 (GLAUE p402). **Persons.** PC **William Price** of Stretton near Burton upon Trent, who on Jan 24 1903 when aged 35 was attacked near Anslow by some gipsy brothers called Sherriff, whilst he was asking the brothers about the theft of some ferrets from a Mr Draper, a local farmer. PC Williams died the next day of his wounds; the brothers were caught and three sentenced to 15 years imprisonment for manslaughter (Staffordshire Police 150th Anniversary Commemorative Issue). **Michael Brassington** (b1942), poet, was living in Anslow in 1994 (VFC p17).

Anslow Common Former common land, later a hamlet 0.75m SSW of Anslow. Formerly in Anslow township in Rolleston ancient parish. There were encroachments on the common forming a sizeable hamlet by 1700. The common was enclosed in 1802 (ANS pp9,100, 126). Has appeared as Anslow Leys (1834 OS map) and Anslow Common (1981 OS map 1:25,000).

Anslow Gate Hamlet 1m W of Anslow. The name is from a former entry into Needwood Forest (ANS p8). Anslow church, built in 1850, is at Anslow Gate, on the S side of Anslow Road. It is now dedicated to Holy Trinity, but was originally known as Needwood Church (ANS p142).

Anslow Park Farm 0.25m NE of Anslow. In existence by 1810 when held by John Hopkins (ANS p130).

Anson Branch Canal of the Bentley Canal (HCMS No. 2), or some say of the Walsall Canal (Birmingham A-Z). Opened in 1830. Closure was sanctioned in 1956 (HCMS No. 2). Diverges from the Bentley Canal at Bentley Mill Bridge and runs to Reedswood Park. There was a proposal in 1893 for an inclined plane from here to join this branch with the Birchills Branch of the Wyrley and Essington Canal to the E (HCMS No. 2).

Anson's Bank 1.75m SSE of Brocton. Anson's Bank was used as a bombing range in WW2 (VCH vol 5 p3). The name is after a member of the Anson family of Shugborough Hall (SPNO p33).

Apedale Dale, or as Ward describes it, a 'glen' (HBST p124), and a hamlet under 1m NE of Alsagers Bank. Apedale lay partly in Audley and Wolstanton ancient parishes until Chesterton district parish was formed in 1846 (W p289). Today Apedale is only accessible by unmade roads. The name appears as Apedal in 1277 (SSE 1996 p10). It is thought to have originated as Apple Dale (NSFCT 1992-93 p48). Or 'Valley of apple trees,' or 'Api's valley' (SSE 1996 p10) (SPN p12). The manor of Apedale was formed out of Audley manor (SHC 1944 pxix). Early lords of Apedale and Heleigh were possessed of the right of holding a Court Leet with the franchises of gallows and tumbril (SCSF p123). Coal and ironstone has been worked in the Apedale area from early times (NSSG p5). At Mr John Middleton's house in Apedale Plot noted in the later C17 white crows had been hatched in the same nest as black ones over a period of three or four years. The white ones were sold as rarities for half a crown a piece (NHS p234).

Apedale Hall House formerly at SJ 813493 at Apedale. The old moated (NSSG p5) hall may have been the ancient seat of the Audley family (TTTD p221) or the Delves family (of whom the Earl of Mulgrave was one): Chetwynd writing in the C17 notes the Delves have a seat 'within Apedale.' In 1646 the Delves' sold the manor of Apedale to William Bowyer of Knypersley, from whom it descended to Sir John Bowyer in 1679 (TTTD p221). When Lord Sheffield was lord of Apedale the old hall was tenanted by Randle Turner. Later, in 1733, it was rented by John Burges (SHC 1944 ppxix-xx, 20). In the mid C18 the Apedale estate passed to Sir John Edensor Heathcote of Longton Hall. His son, Richard Edensor Heathcote (1780-1850) built the hall (which was demolished in the C20), in 1826 or c1832 on the site of a past hall (NSSG p5). This hall was modelled on Heathcote's other property Condover Hall, near Shrewsbury (AHJ 1995 p75); Heathcote's initials appear on the pit chimney of Watermills Colliery, dated 1840. Later, the hall was a Heathcote family summer residence and Capt Edwards Heathcote, MP for NW Staffs 1886-92, lived here (AOPP pl 35p). The hall was occupied at sometime in the early C20 by WE Benton. After Capt Heathcote's death in 1928 it was occupied by Mr Hill, manager of the Midland Coal, Coke and Iron Co Ltd, the new owners of the Apedale estate (TTTD pp222-223). The hall was in decay by 1932. The turreted central part of the front had at the top the demi-dragoon crest of the Bowyers (NSFCT 1932 p122). Since no buyer could be found for it in 1934 it was shortly demolished (NSFCT 1934 p79) on Oct 23 1934 (AHJ 1997 p24) (S&COP pl 34). However, it remained on maps and a medical unit arrived at the hall to requisition it as a hospital during WW2 to find it demolished (NSFCT 1984 pp12p,17. 1992-93 p48). In 1840 a poacher shot dead the parish constable in the hall grounds (CCSHO p15). In 1855 John Edensor Heathcote built a school close to the hall for children of the estate workers. It had a tower over the entrance porch. It probably ceased to be a school in the 1870s and eventually lost its tower. It was used in 1984 as a storage place. The Heathcote crest carved onto a wooden panel is still over the door (NSFCT 1984 pp17-18). (HOE p179). The Drive, perhaps the longest unmade road in the county, runs from Alsagers Bank through Apedale to Chesterton; it led to Apedale Hall (AOPP pl 32).

Apes Tor Tor in Manifold Valley, S of Hulme End. NT property. Apes Tor was a level and shaft of Ecton Copper Mines (EH pp25 pl 6, 81).

Apesford Moorland hamlet 1m SSE of Bradnop, in Bradnop township in Leek ancient parish. There was settlement here by the later C13 (VCH vol 7 pp169-170). A farmer at Apesford hid and cared for a young Highlander who had broken his ankle retreating from Derby in the 1745 Jacobite Rebellion. When it was safe for the Highlander to travel home the farmer put him under the protection of a band of drovers, Apesford being close to a drovers route (PRT pp102-103).

Apeton Hamlet 0.5m NE of Church Eaton, partly in Bradley ancient parish and partly in Gnosall quarter and ancient parish (W p442) (VCH vol 4 p111). Apeton was also a liberty in Gnosall ancient parish (THS pp269-70); the sub-manor of Abetone appears in DB (SSE 1996 p10). Subsequently the name has appeared as Abetone (1203), Apedon (1320), Abbentona (1253), Apen (1609) (SPN p111); it is derived from Abba's tun (SSE 1996 p10) or farmstead (SPNO p134) (SPN p111).

Apeton Brook Flows by Haughton to Allimore Green to Church Eaton Brook.

Appletree Hill On S side of Haughton road from Berry Ring Fort.

Aqualate A hamlet embracing Aqualate Hall, Park, and estate buildings in Forton ancient parish. Near Aqualate House (perhaps the same as Aqualate Hall), was found a melon bead and some perforated stones in a marl pit (NHS pp196,198) (NSFCT 1964 p23). The name occurs in 1129 as Aquila, and subsequently as Aquilade (1227) (SSE 1996 p10), Akilad (1240-70), Aquilot (1327-1526), Akilate (1344), Aquylott (1487), Aculott (1546) and Aquilate (SHC 1923 p304) (SPNO pp146-147). It is thought to derive from Matilda de Aquila, a tenant in capite in Staffordshire in the Middle Ages (DUIGNAN). Mrs John Wollaston Greene believed it was named by the Romans (a Roman road passed to the E of the mere) and was Latin for 'the broad water' (VB p154) (AADB p1) (SSE 1994 p27). It is probably not from the Mere 'aqua late,' but from the Saxon 'ac-gelad' 'the oak stream' (part of the ridge on which it stands is still called 'Oakley Bank') (NSFCT 1937 p64) (SPN p13), Oakden agrees with this (SSAHST 1967 p35). An ancient trackway 'Ac gel ad' ('the oak track'), crossed Mere and Forton manor on the higher ground (SHC 1923 p303) (SSE 1994 p27).

Aqualate Hall House on a ridge called Oakley Bank (NSFCT 1937 p64) over 1.5m SW of Forton. The manor of Mere and Forton was bought by Thomas Skrymsher of Norbury in 1535 (VB p153) or 1547 (SSE 1994 p27) or 1549, because he had been disinherited from the main branch of the family, or because he sought to enlarge the old family estate. After purchasing the manor he built the first hall on a low hill above Aqualate Mere (SSE 1994 p27), or his son Edwin, built the first hall. The first hall was rebuilt in c1600 by Thomas' grandson Sir Thomas (he has an altar tomb in Forton church) (SOS p170) (NSFCT 1937 p64) (VCH vol 4 p104). In the 1680s Plot was impressed with a drainage system to prevent water getting under the door of the hall by use of a groove across the thresh-hold (NHS p360 tab 20). A stone carved head (perhaps from a pier top in the perimeter wall, as seen in the NHS drawing) was on a plinth against the external N facade in 2000 (NSFC visit). In c1687 or in the early C18 the estate was sold to Charles Baldwin or Baldwyn or passed by marriage to him (NSFCT 1937 p64) (SSE 1994 p27). Charles Baldwin built the stables with a clock dated 1730, which still (1937) remains (NSFCT 1937 p64). About 1770 the Baldwins partly remodelled the hall (VCH vol 4 p104). In 1797 they sold it to the trustees of John Fletcher (1784-1823), son of Sir Thomas Fletcher 1st Bt (d1812) of Betley Court (VB p153) (SSE 1994 p27). During the last years of Baldwin ownership and the first of Fenton Boughey the hall was occupied by Baldwin's agent, Francis Wedge (SSE 1994 p29). Probably in late 1805 John Fletcher (who, to inherit a legacy, changed his surname to Fenton Boughey) commissioned John Nash to extend Aqualate Hall in a pseudo-Gothic style (BOE p133) (SSE 1994 p33). The work was completed in 1808, the year Fenton Boughey married (SSE 1994 p33). In early 1810 Fenton Boughey moved from Betley Court to Aqualate Hall (SSE 1994 pp29,35). S Bourne painted a view of the house in 1814. The Bougheys continued as owners of Aqualate Hall. In Nov 1910 Nash's western extension was destroyed in a fire and had to be demolished. In 1927 the house passed to Mrs Ethel Morris eldest daughter of Rev George Boughey, 5th Bt. She had the house restored to its present simplified Jacobean style by WD Caroe in 1929. On her death in 1956 it passed to her sister Mrs John Wollaston Greene, who made a claim that she had foreseen the fire of 1910 in a premonition. On her death in 1973 it passed to her niece, Mrs Celina Juhre. She and her son, Ted, were the owners in 2000 (GNHS p137) (W pp457-458) (VCH vol 4 p106) (VB p154) (BOE p133) (NSFCT 1976 pp18-19) (SSE 1994 p42) (SHJ vol 4 pp40-49 pls) (ASOP p154 p of after the fire) (NSFC visit May 2000). Preserved at the hall is (1948) the sword Richard Skrymsher is supposed to have dropped in a duel after fleeing from the battle of Worcester (1651). It was found near Aqualate Mere (SLM Dec 1948 p187). Drawings of Aqualate Hall reputedly by Repton are still at Aqualate Hall (SSE 1994 p43). A wooden model of the Nash extension was at the hall in 2000.

GROUNDS. In the later C17 Dr Plot noted in Aqualate garden a vine producing grapes of different colours, a phenomenon he thought occurred because of something in the soil here (NHS p207). There is a tradition that Humphrey Repton had a hand in designing the grounds. He did visit in c1812 and make plans of a terrace for the hall, but there is no evidence he designed the grounds (SSE 1994 pp37,38-41). The old Stafford-Newport road, which ran close to the house on the S side, was re-routed further S sometime shortly after 1805 (SSE 1994 p31). In the early C19 Pitt noted Aqualate Park had 'the oldest oaks in the county' (THS) (SSE 1994 p34). Aqualate Castle (1889 OS map 6 inch), a folly in red brick with a castellated tower WSW of the hall was probably the work of John Nash for 2nd Charles Baldwin. It is of three storeys, and possibly an adaptation of an existing building (DoE II) (VCH vol 4 p104)

(SGS p99) (BOE p133) (F p314) (MR p156) (COS p63p) (John Nash: A Complete Catalogue. Michael Mansbridge. 1991). There is an ice-house N of the hall in a wooded mound S of Aqualate Mere at SJ 776198 (IHB p392). The Snake Walk winds like a snake on the S side of the hall and led to a dovecote (1891 OS map 6 inch) (info Ted Juhre). See also the King Oaks.

Aqualate Mere Natural lake 0.75m ESE of Forton. Formed in a glacial hollow created in the Ice Age (SN Feb 14 1997 p16). (GNHS p23). It is fed by three brooks - Wood Brook, Humesford or Guyll Brook and Cowley or Black Brook. At the W end the mere is drained by the Meese (WSS p110). The mere, formerly known as the 'great mere' in consequence of it being the largest of many meres scattered along the Staffs Shrops border, some of which are now lost (SSE 1994 p27), was formerly larger than at present. The 'Mere Eye' was at the mill below Forton church; Mereton then literally stood on its shores (NSFCT 1937 p62). By the mid C18 it had reduced it to its present size; 1840 yards long and 672 yards wide (Bowen's map has floating islands) (SHOS vol 1 part 1 p90) (STM Sept 1966 p38) (SSE 1994 p27; is 220 acres). However, it is said to be still the largest natural lake in private ownership in England (VB p152). N of Aqualate Mere at cSJ 766213 was found a double food vessel of the early Bronze Age, now at Shrewsbury Museum (Antiquaries Journal vol 9 p137) (NSFCT 1964 p23) (WSS p96). Pitt in the early C19 called the mere the finest lake in the county (THS p274). In the C17 local inhabitants were foretelling the weather by noting the direction of the wind over the mere. If the wind was blowing in the opposite direction to the sun it was considered a sign of rain, or if the reverse, it was a sign of good or fair weather (NHS pp25,26,114). It was inhabited by 'vast' carps (NHS p246) but is (2000) no longer. It is the only lake in Staffs where herons nest and has the largest reed bed in Staffs. The area is now (2000) a SSSI and a Ramsar site (NSJFS 1966 p70) (info F Gribble). According to folklore a **mermaid** inhabits the mere. She is said to have some time occupied Vivary Pool until it was destroyed by the building of the Shropshire Union Canal. She was disturbed when the mere was dredged and cleaned and she is said to have cried from the waters -

> If this mere you do let dry
> Newport and Meretown I will destroy.

(NSFCT 1896 p121) (Ghosts and Legends. Roy Christian. 1972 p67). (NSFCT 1896 p121) (SLM Dec 1948 p187) (SW p141). According to Raven she has been seen many times, for instance, before the last two wars. According to tradition whenever she is sighted calamity befalls the world (MR p156).

Aquamoor Tiny hamlet with a number of closely knitted tiny pools in centre of it 1.25m SW of High Onn. The name was pedantically thought up and derives from Latin 'aqua' and 'mor' (SPNO pp142-143).

Arblaster Hays Possible former deer enclosure created by the Arblaster's of Lysways (or Arblaster) Hall in the C14. By the early C17 the name applied to a cottage lying partly in Rugeley and Longdon parishes (SHC part 2 1934 p39). Had appeared as Arblaster Hays by 1798 (SHOS vol 1 p223) and has also appeared as Arblaster Hayes.

Arbor Marked on Smith's map N of Red Street near Talk o' th' Hill.

Arbor Hill Hill under 0.5m SSW of Throwley Hall, 1m NNE of Calton. Has also appeared as Arbour Hill. On it at SK 10815194 is a burial mound. It is EW 25 paces and NS 19 paces in diameter and four feet high. It was excavated by Carrington in 1848 and is a listed monument. Three skeletons, two crouched and one not, were found (TYD pp112-113, 186-187) (VCH vol 1 no 2) (NSJFS 1965 pp54-55). A burial mound 20 paces in diameter and four feet high is 0.75m SSW of Throwley Hall at SK 10705136 (NSJFS 1965 p54). It is a listed monument. To the N is another, 20 paces in diameter and 4.5m feet high, at SK 100805156 (NSJFS 1965 p54). It is a listed monument. Near Throwley Hall is another of about 20 paces in diameter. Carrington excavated it in 1848 but found nothing (TYD p113) (NSJFS 1965 p55).

Arbour Close Low Okeover Hall. Described by Plot in the later C17 as being 'two or three bow shoots NW of Okeover Chapel' (NHS p404) (SSC p137 in the intro) (SCSF p74) (NSJFS 1965 p45).

Arbour Farm 1m WNW of Mucklestone. N of the farm is a rectangular earthwork 900 feet by 700 feet (LGS p190). The Roman station of Mediomanum could have been here (NSFCT 1908 pp114-115).

Arbow Close Low Burial mound on Weaver Hills (NHS p404).

Archberry 0.75m NE of Whiston, Froghall, on the Ashbourne road (1834 OS map) (Dower's map).

Archford Bridge Former bridge which carried a former road from Alstonefield to Hulme End over the Manifold S of Hulme End on the boundary between Alstonefield and Fawfieldhead townships in Alstonefield ancient parish. In existence by 1403. The road over it had ceased to be used by 1820. Archford

Bridge was still used as an address in 1796 (VCH vol 7 p11).

Archford Moor Former extensive waste 0.25m S of Hulme End lying over a northern part of Alstonefield township and a detached portion of Fawfieldhead township (VCH vol 7 p11). Carrington excavated a burial mound on Archford Moor in 1849 (TYD p154) (NSJFS 1965 p31). The burial mound on Archford Moor at SK 10635878 is a listed monument. A ground stone axe of the Neolithic or Bronze Age was found on Archford Moor in c1903 (NSJFS 1964 p14). In the later C17 Plot noted a strange sort of earth here, which glowed at night bright enough for a rider to see by (NHS p115). There was a pinfold at the crossroads near Harecops at SK 115586 in the late 1870s. It still stood in 1901 (VCH vol 7 p20). Has also appeared as Archermoore.

Arkall House 1.5m NE of Tamworth. Formerly Arkhall Farm (1889 OS map) in Wigginton township in Tamworth ancient parish.

Arley Castle Former manor house of Arley on high ground to the E of Arley church (VCHW vol 3 p5). The old house, known as Arley Hall, was apparently built in the latter part of the C16 by the Lyttelton family of Hagley as a dower house and enlarged in James I's reign (VCHW vol 3 p5) or in c1650 (W p168) (AOA p65). In 1844 the house was rebuilt in the Gothic style by George, 2nd Lord Mountnorris, a traveller in Egypt, with the old hall forming the S wing. Lord Mountnorris used several tombstones taken from the churchyard in the building of the cellar. He died in 1844 at Arley Castle without surviving issue and the house and Arley manor passed to his nephew Arthur Lyttelton Annesley (VCHW vol 3 p6). The Annesleys sold the castle in 1852 to R Woodward (AOA p85). By 1913 the external walls of the house had been stuccoed (VCHW vol 3 p5). Lord Dartmouth gave the original painting depicting combats fought at Smithfield and Paris to Arley Castle. It was formerly at Patshull Hall (SLM autumn 1954 p12). Sir Henry Lyttelton cultivated vines from which were produced light wines, thought to be equal to those in France (History of Worcs. Nash vol 2. App 1) (VCHW vol 3 p5). In the courtyard White noted an Egyptian stone coffin, which weighed four tons, 15 cwt, and was seven feet long and three feet high and was presumed to have been a trophy brought back by the travel writer, Lord Valentia (George, 2nd Lord Mountnorris) (W p168).

Arley Street Lost. Marked SE of Over Arley (Upper Arley) on Plot's map. Shaw described Arley Street as one of the five townships of Arley parish (SHOS vol 2 p253).

Arley Wood A wood in the NE of Arley parish, and formerly in Kinver Forest (VCHW vol 3 p5). In it is a burial mound or earthwork (VCHW vol 3 p5). Also an exact square with a double, and at one side a triple, fosse which may be part of a Roman camp; the work of Ostorius Scapulaas as noted by Rev Joseph Chillingworth in the mid C18 (SHOS vol 2 p254) (NSFCT 1902 p121).

Arlington House Ironmarket, Newcastle-under-Lyme, next door to The Steps (see). Built in 1724. Occupied in the C18 by the Ford family. Later, as No. 45 Ironmarket, it was the residence of Ambrose Astle, a surgeon, for a long time. It then passed successively to Arthur Leech, poet, essayist, author of 'The Arlington Lays,' and mayor of Newcastle in 1873 and again in 1875. In the 1870s he renamed the house Arlington House. It then passed to WS Allen MP for Newcastle who sold it to the Corporation in 1887, who had the house demolished for the site of the present Municipal Hall (VCH vol 8 p10) (ES Oct 17 1966 p) (PSS pp465-466) (VFC p84).

Armitage Ancient parish and large village on a bank above the Trent 12m ESE of Stafford. In April 1782 in Armitage parish was found a hoard of two socketed axes and two socketed spearheads of the **Late Bronze Age**. The implements went to Greene's Museum, Lichfield and are now missing (SSAHST 1967 p15). (GM vol 52 pp281,559) (SHOS vol 1 pl a, nos 11, 12 p208) (NSJFS 1964 p14) (CCC p9). A quern was found at Lower Lodge Farm in 1948, and previously an arrow-head had been found in the area (NSFCT 1948 p109). The **name** is from a hermitage established at Armitage by the C12. By probably the mid C13 the hermitage had evolved into a chapel, although the settlement is then still called 'the hermitage of Handsacre.' By 1520 the name Armytage had emerged (SHOS vol 1 pp207,208,209) (DUIGNAN) (SOSH p74) (VCH vol 3 p136) (SSE 1996 p10) (SVB p19) (SPN p13). The hermitage may have stood on or near the site of the present church, St John the Baptist, at the N end of Church Lane. It has a tower of 1632; the rest is of the 1840s (BOE p61) (St John the Baptist Church. May Grimley). On account of Handsacre in Armitage parish being a **prebend** in Lichfield cathedral Armitage parish was a peculiar jurisdiction of the dean and chapter and certain prebendaries of Lichfield cathedral until peculiar jurisdictions were abolished in 1846 (VCH vol 3 p93). **Crosses**. There was a cross at the top of Church Lane where it meets the Rugeley Road about 200 yards from the churchyard. Shaw noted it had gone and a hawthorn was growing over the plinth. There was another cross by the turnpike road on Brereton Hill at the end of a lane leading to Armitage. Here the manors of Armitage, Brereton and Longdon met

(SHOS vol 1 p210). Armitage has been involved in **pottery making** from the C17 when clay was discovered in Stile Cop suitable for tobacco pipes. In the later C20 Armitage Shanks Ltd, sanitary ware manufacturers, had works on the road to Rugeley (SVB p20). The former Armitage **Tunnel** in the Trent and Mersey Canal was the first British canal tunnel to be built with a towpath. It was originally intended to be a tunnel nearly 800 yards long, but due to unstable rock the length was reduced to 139 yards, it was not lined with brickwork (Historic Waterways Scenes Series 'The Trent and Mersey Canal' Peter Lead 1980 pl 53 showing illustration from 1910). The roof of the tunnel was removed in 1971 due to mining subsidence and was replaced by the present road (A513) bridge. All that remains is a short sandstone cutting (BOE p62) (The Way for the Millennium. 2000. p20).

Armitage Tiny hamlet under 1m SW of Denstone.

Armitage Hill Hill 0.75m NNE of Barton-under-Needwood.

Armitage Lodge SW of Armitage church on S side of the Lichfield road. Seat in 1851 of TJ Birch (W p18).

Armitage Park or later Hawkesyard, and recently Spode House. Hall 0.75m W of Armitage. Built by Nathaniel Lister in 1760. In the rock-hewn cellars there is a plaque in elegant C18 writing stating 'These cellars were cut from rock by Richard Benton and Sons AD 1760 for Nathaniel Lister Esq' (LTM Dec 1972 p35). Perhaps visited by Dr Johnson of Lichfield (see) (STMSM Jan 1974 p19). Lister died in 1793 and was succeeded by his son, Thomas Henry Lister (1800-1842), born at Armitage Park. He married, Maria Theresa, daughter of Hon George Villiers, in 1830, and was the author of the novel 'Granby' (1826), 'Arlington' in three vols (1835), and a biography of Lord Clarendon (1838) (BS p284). By 1817 Pitt noted that the house was called Armitage Park, having previously been called Hawksyard Park (THS p78). In 1833 Armitage Park was leased to Sir James Fitzgerald (d1839) (LTM Dec 1972 pp35-36). In 1839 Mrs Mary Spode widow of Josiah Spode III, bought it and it became the seat of the Spodes. (SGS pp52p,55). The top of the house has battlements and pinnacles, but the tall chimneys were removed in 1963 (BOE p62). (SGS pp52p,55). Josiah Spode IV, son of Mary and Josiah Spode III, renamed the house Hawkesyard (see) in 1859 (STMSM Jan 1974 p19).

Armsdale Area S of Fairoak. George Villiers, 2nd Duke of Buckingham, reputedly spent some time a fugitive in the Langot Valley after he was thrown from his horse on Buckerman's Hill (see) having escaped from the battle of Worcester (1651). During his fall he broke his arm and hence the area is called Armsdale (BOV p32).

Armshead Hamlet under 1m N of Werrington. Formerly partly in Bucknall and Bagnall chapelry in Stoke-upon-Trent ancient parish and partly in Cheddleton ancient parish. Great and Little Armshead are mentioned in a perambulation of the boundaries of Bucknall manor in 1803 (WJ p24). EW Bass was told by her aunt that Cromwell came to Armshead and a battle was fought here in the Civil War; there were arms and heads all over the place! (WYV p32).

Arnott's Grave Nearly 1m NW of Cannock in the Shoal Hill area of Cannock Chase. Marked on 1905 OS map. Grave is probably a corruption of Grove (CCBO pp113-115). (BILP2 p63).

Ash, The Principal estate of Eaves township, in the former Bucknall chapelry. Has appeared as Asshe or Aysshe (1327, 1332), and Asche (1433, 1545) (WJ p9). The hamlet of Eaves may have been called Ash in the C16. There is a tradition John Wesley once preached from a doorway of one of the buildings of the Ash Farm (WJ p11). The present Ash Hall (see) was built by Job Meigh owner of the Ash estate (HBST p528). During its construction in 1842 Job Meigh was approached at his temporary residence at The Ash (on the site of the present Ash House) by Chartist rioters from the Potteries. Reputedly he scared them off by making them believe silhouetted clothes horses donned with hats in front of his kitchen fire were armed guards (WJ pp10-11).

Ash Almshouses Corner of Broad Street and Compton, Leek. The almshouses, dated 1696, with eight dwellings for widows or spinsters were founded by Elizabeth Ashe, daughter of William Jolliffe of Leek, and wife of Edward Ashe, a London draper, in 1676 or 1677. Elizabeth bequeathed that her brother Thomas Jolliffe, and his heirs have the right to appoint an almswoman, and her son, William Ashe, have the right to appoint another. The other six were to be appointed by the same or their heirs together with a body comprising Leek parish overseers and others. Half of these six were to come from the rural quarters of Leek ancient parish, Bradnop, Endon, and Leekfrith. In 1727 all the dwellings were appropriated to each patron, to Leek itself and to each rural quarter by putting the name of the patron or place over each door; many of these still (1992) exist (W p725) (VCH vol 7 p166)

Ash Bank Venison Hall is the nickname for a house called Ash Bank in Needwood Forest on account of the number of poached venison carcasses which could be concealed in it (LTD p121).

Ash Bank Hamlet to the W of Werrington. In Caverswall ancient parish. The view from the top of Ash Bank in Werrington includes the Potteries and still further to W the Welsh hills.

Ash Brook Flows from Bagots Park to the Little Blithe (ABMB). The name is from the root 'uisge' see Meece Brook (NSFCT 1908 p130).

Ashcombe Park House 0.75m S of Cheddleton, in Cheddleton parish. The first house on this site was called Botham Hall or Bothams, an Elizabethan stone mansion, which may have been the lodge to the medieval deer park Cheddleton Park, if the park was situated in this area (CVH p160). William Joliffe JP and High Sheriff in 1650 died here in 1669. The Joliffes sold the house in 1765. Ralf Leek was the last resident of Botham Hall (OL vol 2 p105,109). In the later C18 Botham Hall was owned by the Debank family. Jane Debank (d1840) brought the estate to a branch of the Sneyd family when she married, William Sneyd (1767-1851), son of John Sneyd of Belmont Hall (see). After living at Barrow Hill (see) they built a new house on the site of Botham Hall, called Ashcombe Park, completed in c1810 to designs by James Trubshaw Jnr (IHB p392) (BOE p101) (HOC pp237-238) (Cheddleton Remembered. Vera Priestman. 1978 p8p) (SNEDE) (JSD p28p). The house appears to have remained with the descendents of Jane and William until being sold in 1936 (SNEDE). In the grounds is a brick-lined ice-house under the rockery. The entrance was walled up, probably in 1927 (IHB p392). There is a 35 metre tunnel two metres high and two metres wide which connects the house with the stables on the Cheadle Road (DoE II).

Ashenhurst Former estate centred on Ashenhurst Hall (see) and tiny dispersed hamlet approximately 1m SW of Bradnop. Formerly in Bradnop township in Leek ancient parish (W p727) (VCH vol 7 p169). There was settlement here by the later C13 (VCH vol 7 pp169-170). There is a mill, Ashenhurst Mill, under 0.5m to the NW of the hall. At Ashenhurst Plot saw in the later C17 a device which went through a hog nose to stop it rooting, shaped like a two pronged fork (NHS p387 tab 32 fig 8).

Ashenhurst Hall Centre of the Ashenhurst estate. Its predecessor Brew House (see) was the seat of the Ashenhursts and then the Hollinsheads. In 1744 the estate was inherited by William Stanley, who had built Ashenhurst Hall which survived to the mid C20. It was designed by Joseph Sanderson. It remained in the Stanley family until it passed from Frances Stanley, wife of Rev George Salt, to Margaret Leigh, Frances' god-daughter, in 1808. She sold it in 1824 to Richard Badnall, author of 'A Treatise on the Silk Trade,' who reputedly lived here from 1819. In 1828 it was bought by the Phillips family. In that family it remained until the hall was demolished in 1954 (OL vol 1 pp64,65 il,212. vol 2 pp153-154) (SMOPP vol 2 p46) (VCH vol 7 p172 pl 23) (JSD p246il). Frances Stanley or her daughter Lucy, one of whom died of small-pox despite taking every precaution against catching the disease, is said to have escaped to elope with her cousin George Salt through a window of the Brew House or Ashenhurst Hall (NSFCT 1890 p37) (VBB p25il) (SMCC p8). On a stone in the pavement at the rear of the hall were the initials F.A.H. and the date 1675 said relate to the cost of food and fodder during the famine of 1675 (NSFCT 1940 p33) or 1741 (OL vol 1 p64). Ashenhurst Hall Farm was built in 1981 on a site N of the former hall (VCH vol 7 p172).

Ashenough Ashenough Farm is 0.5m SE of Talke. Formerly in Talke township of Audley ancient parish. The small estate of Ashenough was written Ashonhough in 1733 (SHC 1944 p65).

Ashes, The House 0.5m NE of Endon. Formerly in Endon township in Leek ancient parish. The present house was built in the C17 for either John Bellot (d1659) or his son Sir John (d1674) (BOE p129) (VCH vol 7 p177). Thought to have been built on a monastic cell. It has monkish-type vaults in the cellars. A massive stone coffin with Cistercian order type markings lies in the deepest vault (STM Dec 1968 p47p). Busts of Disraeli, an African chieftain, a cobbler and others, which were in the Plough Inn, Endon, until the early C20, were taken to Ashes Farm and now rest against the barn wall there (STM Dec 1968 p52).

Ashes, The House 1.25m WSW of Horton, in Horton ancient parish. There was a house here by 1658 (VCH vol 7 p65).

Ashes, The House N of Easing Farm. Formerly in Tittesworth township in Leek ancient parish. Formerly called Easing. Has a doorhead with the initials ID:ED and a date which is probably 1642 (VCH vol 7 p233).

Ashes, The House 0.75m ESE of Seighford (Dower's map).

Ashfield One of the four medieval common lands comprising the pasturage belonging to the burgesses of Newcastle (W p304) (NUL p107). Roman coins of Marcus Agrippa, Faustina, Antonius Pius, Valens, and Constantine are said to have been found here (Derbys Countryside Oct-Nov 1960) (NSFCT vol 1 p49) (NSJFS 1964 p31). 42 acres of the Burgesses Land at Ashfields still existed by the 1950s (OSST 1956-59 p9).

Ashfield Brook Runs from Chesterton by Holditch into Lyme Brook at Newcastle (NSJFS 1961 p27 see map).

Ashfield Cottage Victorian villa above Sturgess Street, Stoke-upon-Trent. Residence from 1857 of William Henry Goss (1833-1906) pottery manufacturer credited with inventing heraldic porcelain. Owned by Goss from 1870 although he resided elsewhere. He make it his residence again in 1900 (William Henry Goss. Lynda and Nicholas Pine. 1987 pp20,21p,42).

Ashflats 2.25m S of Stafford, in Castle Church parish (W p344). Has also appeared as Ashflatt (W p344) and The Ash Flat (1836) (SPNO p77). Charles Moore, Edward Walsh and Peter Kiran murdered John Blackburn, aged 78, and his wife, Jane, at the farm here on Oct 24 1852 after breaking in to steal Blackburn's savings, which amounted to about five shillings; reputedly he was a miser. The three were tried on April 1 1853. Moore and Walsh were sentenced to hang, but Kiran was found to be innocent and acquitted, whilst Walsh's sentence was commuted to transportation. The case became known as the 'Five Shilling Murder' (MMM 55-58) (MM p93p) (TB Sept 1993 pp18-19) (SAC pp23-25 il of the murder broadsheet) (SMML pp56-59).

Ash Green Former name for an area of Trentham 0.25m E of the Hall, in Trentham parish. The name is preserved in Ash Green Close off Longton Road. Thomas Kirby who made a watercolour of Trentham church (1842) was from here (TTH p54).

Ash Hall At Ash Bank, Werrington. The Elizabethan mansion on the site of the present hall was dismantled in 1841. Soon after this Job Meigh, pottery manufacturer, purchased the Ash estate and built the present hall in the Tudor manorial style (NSFCT 1900 p144) (HBST p528) (WJ p9). Meigh died here in 1862 (POTP p151) (SHST p217). The last owner occupier of the hall was William Meigh (d1922) (WJ p10): Some of the Meigh family appear lightly disguised in several of Vera Brittain's novels; the Meighs being relatives on her father's side (ES Dec 9 1993 p8). About 1924 the Ash Hall estate was sold and broken up and the hall was converted into a hotel and the grounds laid out as a golf club (WJ p10). The hall was modernised to be a country club in 1939, and has a mural painting by L Butler FRSA of Sneyd Green (ES Jan 31 1939 p5). In 1942 the hall was taken over by the Cassel Hospital evacuated from Kent (WJ p10). It became a nursing home for the elderly in 1992 (ES April 18 1997 p70p). The ghost of a former resident at the hall, Godfrey (NSFCT 1900 p143) or Geoffrey Wood, is said to haunt the hall (WJ p10), and the ghost of a lady in white haunts in the vicinity of the hall (WYV p21). Before the present (1946) drive was made, the main approach to the hall was from the top of Brookhouse Lane by a roadway from the verge of Wetley Moor which crossed Ash Clough at the end of Bridle Path (WJ p10).

Ash Hill Hill 2.25m ENE of Colton.

Ash Hill Compton Hall estate nearly stretched to it (VCH vol 20 p10) (TB July 1991 p13). The name is preserved in roads on S side of Compton Road, Wolverhampton.

Ash House Ash Bank on S side of Hanley-Cellarhead road. Was the dowager house of Ash Hall and may stand on the site of a moat (WJ p13).

Ashlands To the E of the railway E of Perrycrofts, Tamworth.

Ashley Ancient parish and large village on high ground on England's main watershed 13m NW of Stafford. Occasionally referred to as Ashley-on-Tern (DUIGNAN).

EARLY. At Ashley Rectory was found a small **Roman** bronze figurine of Hercules, now lost (NSJFS 1964 p14).

1000 to 1500. The **manor** of Esselie appears in DB (SSE 1996 p10). The **name** appears to be of Anglo-Saxon origin and means 'the ash lea or ash tree' (DUIGNAN). Or a clearing (SVB p21) or glade (SPN p13) in the ashwoods. Or 'ash wood' (SSE 1987 p32). Or 'Æsca's ley' (LGS p75). Medieval tenants were obliged to provide bishops of Lichfield with four men and a net whenever one was hunting in nearby Bishop's Wood (SVB p21); visits to Ashley by a bishop of Lichfield are known to have taken place in 1614 and 1633 (NSSG p4) (NSFCT 1917 p139. 1975 p35). There was a parish church at Ashley by 1205. The present **church**, St John the Baptist, at the junction of Charnes and Church Roads, has a tower of C14 origin, but is mainly of the early C17. The rest of the church is of the early 1860s (Church of St John the Baptist, Ashley. Jose Finney. 1987). It has been said that the church was founded by David Kynric (Kenric, Kenrick) between c1350 and 1400 (Annuals of Lichfield) (SHC 1909 p253 note). He has been identified with firstly, Sir David Kenric, husband of the heiress of Ashley, and whose progeny flourished at Woore (Shrops), and secondly, with David ap Kenuric, a Welshman (SHC 1936 pp195-205). But the identification with David ap Kenuric (or ap Kenuric ap Ieuan) has been rejected by a Mr Glenn; he thinks that the Sir David Kenric in question may have been a priest at Ashley (SHC 1938 pp298-317). The tradition is that David Kenric was a soldier under the Black Prince, who, whilst returning home to Flintshire in 1356 after the battle of Poitiers, lost his way in Needwood Forest and emerged out of forest - then stretching across the whole of N Staffs - at Ashley and vowed to rebuild the church here in thanksgiving for his safe delivery (NHS pp295-296) (SHC 1938 p301) (VB p159). A slightly different account says he was a knight who was returning home after the battle of Crecy (1346) (SVB p20). Another story tells he was a native of Ashley and, before leaving home for a war, stuck a spear into the soil where the church now lies and solemnly vowed that should God restore him to his friends after the war he would build a church on the spot (HOMD p102). In the church is a brass to David Kenric with a Latin inscription relating the legend. The brass is believed to have been erected in the mid C17. It was noted by Plot in the later C17 (NHS p329) (SHC 1936 p195). (SD pp73,74) (SOS p115) (GNHS p120) (KES p26). Since there was a church at Ashley by 1205 - King John presented it to the Canons Regular of Motesfunt Abbey, Normandy (VB p160) - some have thought Kenric probably just restored the church out of the spoils of the French wars (SHC 1909 p253 note) (SOSH pp136-138). Phillip de Burewardeslegh was granted a charter between 1219-1290 to hold a **market** at Ashley on Wednesdays. The market had ceased by 1500 (NSJFS 1971 p50). Ashley suffered greatly from the **Black Death** in 1349, land sinking to half its former value (Shropshire. Eyton. vol 2 pp8,9) (SHC 1909 p253). A man-made mound a few yards NW of the church may represent a mass burial ground for victims (MR p22). This may be the same as a mound said to lie NE of the church. It is 84 yards in circumference at the base and 28 yards on top (NSFCT 1923 p123). This in turn may be the mound known locally as Auctioneer's Mound (see). There is another mound at Ashley Dale (see). There were **stocks** in Sovereign Lane (BPS p115). 1500 to PRESENT. For agriculture in Ashley see NSFCT 1975 pp44-45. Ashley **Friendly Societies** processed through the village on Whit-Monday (BPS p114). **Tourists from the Potteries** made Ashley a popular weekend resort from the 1870s. They were encouraged to forego Trentham Gardens in favour of rural Ashley with verses similar to this in the Daily Sentinel:

> How unwise is mankind,
> So strangely inclined
> To go to old places
> With horses and chaises -
> To Trentham so rashley,
> Instead of to Ashley !
> Talk of Trentham,
> Taste the ham of Ashley.

(BPS p110) (SVB p21). On the Newcastle road, Loggerheads, there was an 'AA' or 'RAC' sign which advertised Price's Guest House as 'The Switzerland of England' (ALW). **Natives and visitors. James I** who stayed at Gerard's Bromley Hall for two days in 1617 (NSFCT 1922 p162). His visit to Ashley is recorded in the PR (BPS pp123,124). **Charles I** who with his army marched through Ashley to Stone on May 22 1645 according to PR (NSSG p4) (NSFCT 1917 p139. 1975 p35). **Dr Lightfoot**, the celebrated divine, once held the rectory of Ashley (SCSF p126) and to remove himself from domestic distractions he bought the field adjacent to the church and built himself a little cabin (MR p22). **Ann Scot** of Ashley was living beyond the age of 100 when Dr Plot was in Staffs in the later C17 (NHS p320). In 1796 the first legal Catholic emigre priest to settle in Staffs, **Louis Martin de Laistre**, tutor to the children of the rector of Mucklestone, was appointed priest to an Ashley congregation of Catholics. In 1823 the present RC church of Our Blessed Lady and St John the Baptist was built at the junction of Church Road and Lower Road (VCH vol 3 p112) (BOE p63) (ALW pl 24); Jesuits were active in nearby The Rudge and Gerrards Bromley in the C17 and C18.

Ashley Dale Hamlet in a dale to the W of Ashley. There is a burial mound 10-20 feet high at SJ 754364. It was described as in a very good condition in 1983 (NSFCT 1983 p11).

Ashley Heath Former heath and new residential area 1m WSW Ashley, partly in Ashley and Drayton-in-Hales parishes. Perhaps identifiable with Ashley Common, common land on S side of Ashley village (THS p327). The heath lies on England's main watershed. This tableland is said to be the highest cultivated tableland in England (BPS p109). The New Red Sandstone here is said to be the highest point of the beds in Great Britain (NSFCT 1927 p 171). Ashley Heath is the western outpost of the Bunter Pebble Beds, the most weather-resistant rock of the Triassic system (TTTD p248). It was recommended that Ashley Heath Halt railway station be closed in 1963 (ES March 22 1963). There are long views from the heath; to the W can be seen the Berwyn Mountains in Wales; to the NW, on a clear day, can be seen the docks at Liverpool (NSFCT 1927 p 171); to the ENE Union House in Hanley, and further away, Morridge, Cloud End, Axe Edge (BPS p112).

Ashley House Wood Lane, Handsworth Wood, a little way back from Handsworth Wood Road, where Denewood Avenue now is. Built in 1790.

Has been the seat of John Rawlings, solicitor (1841) and Edwin Hayes, town clerk (1871). Walter Wilkinson lived here at the end of the C19 and John (?) Levick was the last to live here. It is not on maps of 1794 and 1872, but (not named) is on a map of 1879. The house was demolished in c1939 (HPPE pp5,6).

Ashley Park Medieval deer park enclosed out of forest. In existence by 1293 (NSFCT 1910 p175). Was probably the same park as Willoughbridge Park, which it was later called (NSJFS 1962 p75. 1964 p62).

Ashmore Former estate over 1.25m NE of Wednesfield in the foreign of Wolverhampton. A polished flint axe-head was found at Ashmore in the 1880s (HOWM p1). At Ashmore Lodge was found a flint axe in 1943 which went to Wolverhampton Museum. Near the Lodge at cSJ 960018 in c1924 and c1957 three flat pebbles with hour-glass perforations were found (NSJFS 1964 p42). Has appeared as Ashmores (Wednesfield PR 1635) (WFW p82), and Ashmoor. The house of the estate was Ashmore Hall (see).

Ashmore Brook Runs from near Ashmore to Pipe Hall to Bourne Brook? to the Trent. Ashmore Brook has appeared as as Estmorebroc (1242), Estmeresbrok (1254), Asschmorebroke and Ashmeresbroke (C13 and C14) (SPNO p4) (SPN p79). The name means Æscmar's (pronounced Ashmar) brook (DUIGNAN). Or 'east marshland brook' (SPNO pp4-5) (SPN p79).

Ashmore Brook Hamlet 1m ESE of Farewell, 2m NW of Lichfield, formerly in St Michael's parish, Lichfield. There was a settlement at Ashmore Brook by the later C13 (VCH vol 14 p198). The name is from the brook of the same name (SPN p79). The two principle properties which comprise present Ashmore Brook are Ashmore Brook House on S side of Cross in Hand Lane and Ashmore Brook Dairy Farm on the N side. The former has a late medieval central range and was surrounded on three sides by the remains of a moat in the 1840s which are no more. The latter house is said to have been erected in 1795 close to an older house, some of whose moat still survives at SK 096111 (VCH vol 1. vol 14 pp208-209) (SSAHST 1982-3 p42) (CAMS p63). One or both of these houses were at times occupied by members of the Sprott family from the early C16 to 1760 (VCH vol 14 p208). An iris lunaris of a faint white colour was witnessed by Thomas Broughton of Broughton in company with others between Lichfield and Ashmore Brook on Aug 6 1679 (NHS p8).

Ashmore Cottage Stood at the end of a lane off the S side of Blackhalve Lane, on the N side of Kitchen Lane, Ashmore, Wednesfield. The cottage, or cottages, is believed to stand on the site of the ancient house known as 'The Blackhalve' (WFW p70). The recent cottage was a typical miners' cottage, and had been built by a miner (WHTOP p76p).

Ashmore Hall There was a moated hall on the Ashmore estate at Ashmore, Wednesfield, by 1429, when the then Dean of Wolverhampton was termed the 'lord of Ashmore.' Thomas Warynge remitted the rights of the property in 1584 to Thomas Leveson. The estate belonged to the Levesons in Elizabethan times. The house may have been a Jesuit school in the Civil War. Robert Leveson had a hall here in 1666. By the 1800s the hall appears to have disappeared. By 1830 the moat was totally enclosed and was used as an orchard (HOWM p44) (WFW pp65,92) (WHTOP pp77-79) (The News of Wolverhampton. June 18 1998 pp22-23). It measured 270 feet by 210 feet in 1908 (VCH vol 1 p368). A farm, Ashmore Farm (BTW p103p), of more modest proportions, was built nearby to the site of the hall. In 1951 work started on the building of the present **Ashmore Park**, an overspill housing estate for Wolverhampton. The name for it came from the park of the hall. There was very little building at Ashmore before this time (WHTOP pp77-79ps). By the late 1950s a shopping precinct in the present Griffiths Drive at SJ 958018 stood on the site of the hall. The moat which surrounded the hall can still be seen (SSAHST 1982-3 pp54 plans,55) (CAMS p64) (BTW p102p). Erosion from parked vehicles at the shopping precinct was wearing the moat away by 1998 when the site was awarded a lottery grant for its preservation (The News (Wolverhampton) Sept 24 1998 p3. Nov 26 1998 p4). The church, St Alban, Griffiths Drive, was built in 1967 (info Margaret Stevens) (LDD).

Ashmore House House over 1m WSW of Rushtonhall. Formerly in Rushton James township in Leek ancient parish. The present house stands on the site of a house called Ashmoor Hay in 1688 (VCH vol 7 p220).

Ashmore Lake Industrial and residential area N of Willenhall, 1.25m SSE of Ashmore Park. Formerly in Willenhall chapelry in Wolverhampton ancient parish. It was a small mining hamlet in the C19 (WDY p15). Streets on the new Ashmore Lake housing estate were named in Oct 1945 (SNW p5). The name 'Ashmore' is from Ashmore Hall (SNW p5). The 'Lake' part of the name is from land N of Willenhall which was marshy heathland (WDY p15). Or perhaps from a large pool which once lay on the N side of where Pool Hayes Schools stood in 1995; the pool was filled in when development of that area took place during the 1960s (SNW p5).

Ashmore Lodge House 0.25m NW of Ashmore Park.

Ashton Hays House 1.25m ENE of Longdon. Has also appeared as Hayes.

Ashtons, The The Ashtons Farm is 1m S of Slindon.

Ashwood Small dispersed hamlet 1.5m S of Swindon, formerly in Kingswinford parish (W p182). The name is preserved in Ashwood Lodge (NSFCT 1952 p36) and Ashwood House. For the Roman site at Ashwood see Greensforge. Ashwood has been identified with Eswecha, Eswick (WFW p28), Eswich and Ashwick, one of the estates given by Lady Wulfrun to the monastery of Wolverhampton in 994 (SHC 1919 p182) (HOWM p14). It has also been identified with DB Haswic, an estate having been laid waste on account of the creation of Kinver Forest (SHC 1916 pp168-169) (VCH vol 2 p343) (SSAHST 1970 p35). Later forms are: Aswude (1232), Asshewode (SPN p70) (SSE 1996 p10), and Ashwood Lodge (Yates' map). The name means ash wood (DUIGNAN) (NSJFS 1981 p3) (SPN p70) or ash clearing (SSE 1996 p10). Or it could have a Celtic root 'aos' 'os' a forest, giving Aswood (Ashwood did appear in the C13 as Aswode) (NSFCT 1908 p137). There is a canal basin to the side of the Staffs and Worcs Canal called Ashwood Basin. There was a windmill at SO 863884 lying just W of the canal. It was shown on Yates' map (WBJ p28 il v). By 1893 SSWWC had a pumping station at Ashwood (GHC p13p).

Ashwood Hay Formerly one of the hays, or divisions of Kinver Forest (DUIGNAN p6) (NSFCT 1908 p137). Ashwood Hay existed in the Middle Ages (NSJFS 1968 p40 fig 3) (SL p68 see map). The Prestwode family held a house and land at Prestwood by the service of keeping Ashwood Hay from the later C13 to c1500. By the C17 the hay was the property of the Dudley family (VCH vol 2 pp346 note, 348). 1400 acres of Ashwood Hay and Wall Heath were enclosed under an Act of 1776 (SHC 1941 p16). Ridgehill Wood appears on the 1834 OS map as 'Ridge Hill or Ash Wood.'

Ashwood Heath Common land enclosed by 1851, on it are the remains of a Roman Camp (W p182), more usually said to be at Greensforge (see).

Ashwood House Appears to have stood on the E side of Swindon Road, N of Summer Hill, Kingswinford and appears on Greenwood's map and OS map 1834. Built by Lord Dudley. It was occupied by Sir Joseph Scott (1753-1828), created a baronet in 1806 (W p182). By 1801 it was the residence of Hon Washington Shirley, brother of Lord Ferrers (SHOS vol 2 p233), possibly Washington Shirley (1760-1842), whose ancestors were of Chartley Castle (see); later occupied by Edward Dixon (a member of the Dudley family of Dixon's Green), High Sheriff of Worcs in 1815. In the later C19 the house became a private asylum (SNSV vol 1 p95). The manorial courts for Kingswinford manor were at some time held here (BHOP p6).

Ashwood Lodge Ashwood. Lies 0.75m WSW of Ashwood House. In 1801 was occupied by a tenant of Lord Dudley to whom the (Ashwood?) estate belonged (SHOS vol 2 p233). Was a farmhouse for much of the C19 occupied by the Slater family (SNSV vol 1 p207).

Askew Bridge Gornal. There is a tiny street in Gornalwood called Askew Bridge Road. Askew has been identified with Hasco (see) (Himley Hall and Park: A history. David F Radmore. 1996 p10). Duignan mistakenly places Askew Bridge 1.5m W of Himley (DUIGNAN). The name is from 'a skew bridge' (DUIGNAN) (SPN p103). Or there is a forest-root 'sceach' 'sgeach', in Irish 'sce' (NSFCT 1908 p137).

Aspley 1m NE of Coven. In Brewood ancient parish. The name has appeared as Aspelega (1227), Espeleg (1253), and Aspley (1605) (SPNO p36) (SSE 1996 p10). It means 'clearing in the aspen wood' (SSE 1996 p10). Aspley, in the fee of Coven by 1310, was described as a manor in 1507. Aspley Farm seems to incorporate the hall of the manor, which probably dates from the early C16 (VCH vol 5 p27).

Aspley Tiny hamlet 1m NW of Slindon. Former township in the Cotes quarter in Eccleshall ancient parish (W p375). The manor of Haspeleia appears in DB (SSE 1996 p10). A later form is Aspelega (SPN p44). The name means 'the aspen-tree lea' (DUIGNAN), or 'aspen wood' (SSE 1987 p32) or 'clearing in the aspen wood' (SSE 1996 p10) (SPN p44).

Astle's Rock Situated on that side of Kinver Edge known as the 'Compa' and is to the E of Holy Austin Rock. The rock had two cottages set into it in 1831. By 1841 these had been enlarged to three for three tenants. One of the three, Joseph Astle, outlived the others and died aged 87. By 1871 a total of 13 occupied the rock cottages and possibly some ordinary cottages close by. Some were employed at Hyde Ironworks. In early C20 Astle's Rock was owned by Mr Fairbridge who had a museum here, which lasted for over 20 years, after which the caves were left empty (KRH p18p) (VCH vol 20 p122).

Aston Hamlet mainly on the W side of the M6, over 1m from Castle Church. In Seighford ancient parish. The name appears in DB and means 'Eastern tun' (SSE 1996 p10).

Aston (locally *Asson* see rhyme under Betley). Village over 2m SSW of Madeley.

Former township in Mucclestone ancient parish.

Aston Bridge Crosses the Dove into Derbys 1.75m N of Draycott-in-the-Clay.

Aston-by-Stone Village by the Trent 5m N of Stafford. Formerly formed a township with Burston and Little Stoke in Hilderstone quarter in Stone ancient parish (W p362). Aerial photography has shown cropmarks at and near Aston-by-Stone. One may represent a possible **Roman** camp: John Darlington notes a site for a temporary Roman camp on the W bank of the Trent S of Aston-by-Stone (SN Aug 20 1993 p9). Another, by A34, shows a multi-ditch barrow to the right of an undated enclosure (SPJD pp11p,23p). The **manor** of Eastun which appears in a charter of 957 has been identified with an Aston in Staffs, perhaps Little Aston in Shenstone ancient parish (SL p61) (SSE 1991 p8) or this Aston (SSE 1996 p10). The manor of Estone appears in DB. A later form is Little Aston (W p362). The **name** is of Anglo-Saxon origin and means east town (DUIGNAN) (SSE 1996 p10). Or from Anglo-Saxon for 'ashtown' (SVB p22). It may be that 'as' represents the root 'aos' a forest and that the early Angles adopted the word 'as' for a wood as they adopted the word 'bre' for a hill (NSFCT 1908 p137). The main Stafford-Stone road originally came through Aston where a ford or bridge over the Trent existed from the C15. The route was surpassed by the Stafford-Stone turnpike, opened in 1761 (SVB p22). In the later C17 Plot noted a cow of Walter Heveningham of Aston Hall whose teeth were tinged with a golden armature or bass colour, which may have resulted from the cow eating some plants of the Erica kind (NHS p111). The water wheel at Aston Farm still exists but no longer functions (SVB p22). There was a **church** at Aston by 1840 (LDD). The present church, St Saviour, by the Trent to the N of Aston Hall, was built in 1846 (BOE p63). Aston became a separate ecclesiastical parish in 1846 (GLAUE p402).

Aston-by-Stone Old Park A late medieval hunting ground belonging to the Heveninghams (NSFCT 1910 p176).

Aston Cliff House over 1.5m SSW of Madeley.

Aston Hall Aston-by-Stone. The old hall was moated (CAMS p63) and the seat of the Heveninghams in the C17 (GNHS p117) (W p363); one of whom married a Fitzherbert of Swynnerton Hall. It was the Fitzherberts who had the relics of St Chad secreted at the hall. The estate was temporarily taken from the Heveninghams in the Civil War by order of a parliamentary commission in Stafford in 1643 (SIS p42). The estate passed to the Simeons, Catholics, with the marriage of Bridget Heveningham, heiress and daughter of Walter Heveningham, to Sir James Simeon, Bart. Their son Sir Edward Simeon, Bart, succeeded to the estate. With his death in 1767 the estate passed by marriage to the Welds of Lulworth. From c1768 to 1790 the old hall was leased to Frank Sneyd of Keele Hall. By 1790 it had fallen into disrepair and was partly demolished. Subsequently the remaining building was occupied by a series of RC missionaries. Between 1797 and c1815 a refugee-priest from France, Abbe Morais, who had came to serve the Catholic congregation at Aston occupied the hall. It was later occupied by Franciscans (invited by Cardinal Weld) and for a few years by some Brigittine nuns. The last Franciscan was succeeded by Father Ben Hulme who occupied the hall between 1838 and 1842. In 1837 or 1838 St Chad's relics were rediscovered by the missioner when clearing out the chapel. Bishop Wiseman (then co-adjutor in the Midlands) took them to Oscott; they eventually were placed in the new RC cathedral of Birmingham. In Feb 1842 Father Dominic Barberi or Bardi (1792-1849), founder of the English Province of the Congregation of Clerks Regulars of the Passion and Cross of Jesus Christ, or simply known as Passionists, was put in possession of the hall, which he renamed St Michael's Retreat and made the first house of the Passionists. Barberi was beatified in 1963. Cardinal Newman visited him at the hall for a few days in Dec 1846. After the Passionists left, Father Edward Huddlestone (later Canon) (d1871) purchased the hall. In 1855 he rebuilt it in brick. He was succeeded by Canon Bathurst and then by a French priest. In the later C19 the hall was let to non-Catholics. In 1909 it was sold to a non-Catholic solicitor in Stone (RHPS pp310,312) (SCHJ No. 4 winter 1963-4 pp44-46. No. 9 p14) (BSB p209) (VB p24) (SVB p22) (NSFCT 1957 p65) (Aston Hall. Rev Canon FH Drinkwater. 1976). Col Knight of Aston Hall was killed in WW1 (MOSP p6). The hall was owned by the Wengers, Catholics between 1935 and 1959 when it was purchased by Cyril Hartley and given to the Birmingham Diocese for a guest house for retired and convalescent RC priests (Aston Hall. Rev Canon FH Drinkwater. 1976). The hall has a poltergeist (TFTP pp198-201).

GROUNDS. In a walled enclosure to the W is a wooden cross attached to the wall. According to tradition it marks the spot where a monk was struck dead by lightning (SVB p22) or that it marks the spot where Father Dominic Barberi is buried (local info). A mausoleum almost identical to the Jervis Mausoleum in St Michael's churchyard, Stone, but is slightly smaller. It was built by Sir James Simeon in 1757 or c1767 (DoE II). Above the entrance is a worn inscription from the Apocalypse: and translated is 'Blessed are the dead who die in the Lord 1757'. On either side of the interior hallway are four inscribed stones set into the wall. All are of sandstone except Sir Edward Simeon's which is of marble. i) Sir Edward Simeon Bart died Dec 23 1768. ii) Father Jacob Duplangue died Feb 17 1824 OFM. iii) Rev Andrea Turner OFM died Feb 11 1826. iv) Rev Petri Jones OFM died Oct 10 1832. v) Gertrude Allison died June 22 1836. vi) Elizabeth Farnes Abbess? died Feb 18 1837. vii) Rev Edward Canon Huddleston died Dec 14 1871 removed from here in Sept 1882 (SCHJ No. 22 1984 pp24-27).

Aston Hall Aston, between Doxey and Seighford. Grade II. Dates back to the C17. Restored in the C19 and was for sale in March 1996 (SLM March 1996 p6pc). The house had been restored again by 1998 (SN June 25 1998 p22p).

Aston Hay House 1m SE of Handsacre. In King's Bromley ancient parish (W p596). Has also appeared as Aston Hays.

Aston Lodge Aston Lodge Farm is 1.25m E of Stone. The name 'lodge' is from probably a lodge to Stone Park. From the mid 1970s a large area to the WSW of Aston Lodge Farm, known locally as the Ten Fields, was developed with housing and has become known as Aston Lodge Estate (info JG Beecham). In July 1996 Simon Smith of Ashford Grove, Aston Lodge Estate, was sentenced to life imprisonment for the murder of his three children: Eleisha, aged 10 months, and Jamie, aged six months, who were killed in 1989 and 1993 respectively, at different addresses in Stafford; it was originally thought they had died from cot deaths. By another woman Smith had a daughter, Lauren. She was 10 weeks old when he murdered her in Nov 1994 (SN July 5 1996 p1) (ES July 5 1996 p13).

Aston's Fold Former small hamlet 1m E of Amblecote. Appears on 1947 OS map 1:25,000 (sheet 32/98), at SO 916851. The name is preserved in the tiny road Aston's Fold. See also Caledonia.

Atherhurst Former enclosure, enclosed in the medieval period, SW of Pool Green, on the border of Aldridge and Great Barr townships. Here several fields include 'hay' as an element in their names (MOA p137).

Auctioneer's Mound Church Road, NE of Ashley church (NSSG p4). A burial mound a few yards from the churchyard wall and near to a row of cottages at SJ 76533650. Is 21 paces in diameter and six feet high (NSFCT vol 58 p123. 1983 p13) (NSJFS 1965 p32). Is a listed monument. Probably the same as a mound NE of the parish church 84 yards in circumference at the base and 28 yards on top (NSFCT 1923 p123). The mound lies at the junction of several ancient 'ways' linking up trackways from camps of the Late Bronze and Iron Age (DPTB p10). Or it may represent the burial ground of victims of the Black Death in Ashley (see).

Audley (locally *Aidley* see rhyme under Betley BOJ book 2 p95). Village, ancient parish and former township. The village on a small promontory on high ground lies between head streams of the Weaver 19m NNW of Stafford.
1000 to 1500. The manor of Aldidlege appears in DB (SSE 1996 p10). A later form is Aldithelega (1182) (SPN p14). The **name** is probably of Anglo-Saxon origin and means Ealdgyth's lea; Ealdgyth being a female personal name (NSFCT 1984 p11) (SSE 1996 p10); she being a local female warrior chief (SPN p14) and or the holder of land here (SVB p23). Many have thought it takes its name from Harold's Queen, Aldithe, but DUIGNAN found no authority for this theory. Audley **parish** was probably formed out of Wolstanton original parish between c1170 and 1223 (SHC 1916 pp192,195). **Beating the bounds** occurred in Nov 1913 (ES March 27 1993 p15p) (AOPP pls 7,8) (NSFCT 1984 p20). The parish **wake** was on the first Sunday in August (W p428). The parish **church**, St James the Great, on a prominence on the W side of Church Street, was founded by 1223 (A p82). Behind the Town House is evidence of ridge and furrow cultivation (NSFCT 1984 p11). The **curfew** bell tolled at Audley at 8 o' clock every night until 1939 (AHJ 1995 p112). The de Aldithley (or Audley) family, whose original seat was Audley Castle (see) in this village, took their name from Audley; they later built Heighley Castle (see) and Hulton Abbey (see), and became Lords Audley.
1500 to PRESENT. In the **Civil War** there seems to have been a meeting of parliamentary commanders Col Brereton and Col Rugeley at about Audley on May 15 1643 to plan to take the royalist garrison at Stafford, which was taken the next day (BFS p21) (HAF p122). An account of a **flood** at Audley on June 24 1725 is mentioned on an undated slip of paper, which was found amongst the Aqualate Papers in the SRO (A pp36-37). There was a **windmill** at SK 827544 in Butt Lane which had disappeared by 1899 (WBJ p14). The parish **workhouse**, close to the A500, opened in 1734, became a farm known as Old Workhouse Farm, occupied by the Rowley family from c1936 (Weekly Sentinel Dec 19 1980) (SVB p23). In the C18 and C19 the inhabitants were engaged in iron working, nail making, and coal mining; on the back of the latter Audley became a large village (SGS p55) (AHJ 1995 p106). By the 1950s, however, many inhabitants had joined the teaching profession so that the village was then known as 'the village of teachers' (SVB p24). NW of

Audley church in Church Street is a **terrace of three shops** with flats above, an archway, and a house. The terrace was designed by William White. The style is Gothic and the design reduced to the essentials: A precursor of the Art and Crafts Movement in architecture. The windows have pointed arches of various sizes, and no decoration or ornament except a little polychromy (AGT pp50,51il). The terrace is illustrated in The Builder 1855. That illustration (reproduced in BOE pl 90) shows that the pointed windows were intended to be open to the street and create an arcade running underneath the flats above. Dr Muthesius drew Pevsner's attention to the shops and he described them as 'indeed something quite extraordinary' (BOE p64) (AOPP pl 17). However, by the time Pevsner and Malkin were writing, the 1970s, the arcade was lost, and had probably been for many years, if, in reality, it had ever existed. The shops fronts had been brought forward to use the pointed windows and a totally modern shop front had replaced both pointed windows of the middle shop. A **railway** line of the NSR through Audley was completed in 1870. The line ran from a junction on the Silverdale to Market Drayton line at Honeywall to Alsager (East Junction), Ches. It appears at first to have been for goods only (VCH vol 2 p319) (AHJ 1998 pp39-49), but later took passengers until 1931 (NSJFS 1964 p79) (NSFCT 1984 p16). The line finally closed between Audley and Keele in June 1962 and between Audley and Alsager in Jan 1963 (AHJ 1998 pp39-49). A United **Methodist** Free Chapel, which took the name of 'Hilltop,' was built at the highest point of Wood Lane, Audley, in 1872. The building was demolished in the later C20 (AHJ 1997 pp42-43). **Newspaper**. The Newcastle Guardian and Silverdale, Chesterton and Audley Chronicle, found April 23 1881, ran to 1909 (SHJ spring 1996 p21). **Foot-and-mouth disease** broke out in Dec 1967 at Grange Farm, Audley (SN Dec 29 1967 p13). **Friendly societies**. The Audley Court of the Ancient Order of Foresters was founded in 1868. Their parade through Audley on Wakes Monday was led by Robin Hood and his Merry Men mounted on horses loaned by farmers. Children rode while adults walked: The court banner brought up the rear. After a short church service the procession went to wakes field at Castle Hill Farm where there was a fun fair etc. The last procession was in 1928 (NSFCT 1984 p20) (AHJ 1996 pp58-78). The Oddfellows' Friendly Society's parade was on Wakes Saturday (NSFCT 1984 p20) or the Oddfellows' celebrations were on the Tuesday following wakes weekend (AHJ 1996 p111). **Tidy village**. In 1998 Audley won the best urban community award in the Britain in Bloom national competition organised by the Tidy Britain Group (ES Oct 1 1998 p1pc). By 2000 the village had won many Best Kept Village competitions over several years and was claimed to be 'officially the prettiest village in the world' (ES Feb 2 2000 p15). **Audley and District Family History Society**, founded in May 1986, have produced a local history journal, AHJ, since 1995 (info Miss Spode). **Vicars**. Edward Vernon, vicar in 1622, who founded the Grammar School in 1611. It closed in 1900 but an endowment still existed in 1988 to assist scholarship children (NSSG p5) (SVB p23). **William Kelsall**, vicar of Audley, who was turned out of his living on account of his royalist views in the Civil War period. He returned in 1660 (AHJ 1996 p12). **Charles Phillip Wilbraham**, vicar from 1884, turned down a bishopric to stay in Audley; he raised funds for the dependents of the victims of the Talke Colliery disaster (1866) (SVB p24). In Rev **JLD Lewis**, vicar of Audley from 1935 to 1971, Audley had the youngest vicar in England (Weekly Sentinel March 2 1979) (A p91).

Audley Brook Tributary of Checkley Brook which it enters at the S end of Walton's Wood (NSFCT 1919 p22).

Audley Castle Stood in Audley village, N of the church. It may have been the seat of the de Aldithley (or Audley) family, who moved to the Heighley Castle (see) after building that castle in the 1220s (NSFCT 1984 p11). The castle appears to have been not necessarily abandoned thereafter. It is mentioned in a Close Roll 1274-5 (NSSG p5). Its site was excavated in the early C20 and a length of thin walling and a coin of the period 1272-1327 were found (NSFCT 1915 pp92-96) (ESH pp51-52) (CAMS p15). Castle Hill Farm (converted to the headquarters of Audley district council in 1930) on the Newcastle-Nantwich road, at the N end of Church Street, was adjacent to the remains of the castle motte (AOPP pls 20, 21 shows Castle Hill Farm before and after conversion). (STM Feb 1964 pp34p,35) (Newcastle Times April 5 1972).

Audley Old Hall Probably originally just Audley Hall. A timber-framed house on W side of Audley. Was probably built some time in the C14 or the C15 for one of the many yeoman farmers in the area and was at some time the seat of the Vernons. It was the manor house? where Thomas Brown was living when broken into in 1650 and a riot ensued (LOU p78). The entrance porch bore the figures 1230 in the plaster of the gable. In 1927 it was owned by AJ Holding and occupied by several families and in a dilapidated state (NSFCT 1925 p190. 1927 p150). It was demolished in 1932 to make way for two houses (NSFCT 1984 pp14p,15). Now replaced by modern houses (AOPP pls 3,4,6).

Audley Park Medieval deer park in the Audley area enclosed out of forest, held by the de Aldithley (or Audleys) of Heighley Castle (see). In existence by 1283 (NSFCT 1910 pp170,172) (NSJFS 1962 pp73,75). Has also appeared as Audley Old Park.

Audley's Cross Stone cross in a field at SJ 715352, 0.75m N of Hales. It is to the memory of James Touchet, 5th Lord Audley, a descendent of the Audleys of Heighley Castle (see), slain in the battle of Bloreheath (see) (1459) here. There must have been a cross here by 1553 for the adjoining field was known as Barn Cross or Cross field in 1553 (NSFCT 1931 p186) (SHC 1945/ 6 p93 note). The first cross on the site is thought to have been a wooden cross. It was knocked down by a cow rubbing itself against it. The present stone cross was erected in 1765 and is 7.5 feet high and the transverse section of the cross is 20 inches. It was considered in a perilous state of repair and in need of restoration in the early 1920s (NSFCT 1922 p158. 1923 pp123-4). An elder tree was up-rooting the base in 1931 (NSFCT 1931 p186). It was struck by lightning in 1961 (ES Sept 9 1961). The inscription on the N side of the pedestal reads

On this spot
Was fought the battle of
Blore Heath
In 1459.
Lord Audley
Who commanded for the side of Lancaster
Was defeated and slain
To perpetuate the memory
Of action and the place,
This monument
Was repaired in
1765
At the charge of the Lord of the Manor
Charles Boothby Scrymsher

(NHS p449) (SHOS vol 1 part 1 p50) (SOS p115) (SSC p132 in the intro - includes inscription) (GNHS p75) (W pp44,389) (WP pp328,331) (HS p145pl) (PS pp30,39) (MOS p15) (BPS p44) (LGS p190) (KES p102) (SOSH p162p) (SLM Oct 1948 p178ps) (STM April 1966 p30p. July 1971 p24p) (M p11) (VB p159) (IAANS p xvii full inscription) (BOE p138) (TFTP pp208-215) (SGS p128) (MR pp8,167,236) (SVB p85) (SMM p55p).

Audley's Cross Farm Under 0.25m N of Audley's Cross. The house here is thought to have been created after Sir John Chetwode purchased further portions of the former Blore Heath in 1816. It is said its four corner towers were built in imitation of Hougoumont (SHC 1945/ 6 p261).

Audley's Moat Endon. At SJ 931536. Here was found a flint instrument. The so-called moat is about 400 paces round and within the moat or ditch is a raised platform 'in which there is a ring of stonework in the centre' (NSFCT 1931 pp192-193). Is a ring burial mound or circle ? (NSSG p18).

Audmore N tip of Gnosall. In Gnosall parish. May have its origins connected to the Roman Limes Britannicus (NSFCT 1902 p118). The name means 'the old marshland' (SPNO p158) and has appeared as Aldmore (1645), Oldmore (1677), Aulmer (c1680) (SPNO p158).

Audnam District and former hamlet on a bank overlooking a tributary of the Stour 0.75m N of Amblecote. Formerly partly in Amblecote chapelry in Old Swinford ancient parish, Worcs and partly in Kingswinford ancient parish (W p183). Originated as a glasshouse (VCH vol 2 p226). Michael Grazebrook of Audnam had a fossil tree trunk in his garden (SVS p461 note). Formerly Audenham, an Audenham Bank is marked on a Plan of Intended Extension of the Dudley Canal John Snape surveyed 1785 just N of end of Brettell Lane

on Stourbridge-Wolverhampton road.

Audnam Brook Ran through Pensnett Chase (KCPC p12) and alongside Brook Street, Audnam (SNSV vol 2 p12). By the 1990s the brook had been culverted. It has been known locally as Mouse Brook (SNSV vol 1 p235).

Audnam Hill At 175 and 200 feet high it is the lowest hill about Dudley (WMAG Feb 1975 p48).

Auld Farm Former farm on the E side of Walsall. It is reached from Sutton Road and extended to Green Lane (or Gillity Lane as it led to the Gillity Fields, but now lost under housing development). Its acreage was lessened by the construction of the ring road (Broadway) (SNWA p9).

Aust Hill Hill in the Rowley Hills range near Darby's Hill (SVS p438 note).

Austin The house called Austins, built in the later C18 or the early C19, stood in the Camp Lane area of Handsworth (MNB p41). It can perhaps be identified with the house known as 'The Austins' a red-brick Queen Anne-style type house, built by John Whateley, a wealthy gentleman-farmer in the early C18. The present Austin Road, is roughly the site of the carriage way to the house. John Whateley married Mary Pyddoke, and the family name was changed to Pyddoke-Whateley. Before 1892 it was the home of the Hasluck family, and afterwards until 1920, by the Abbott family. Demolished in the early 1930s (HPPE p6). The Austin estate was built on with housing between WW1 and WW2 (HANDR pvii). There were three pools in the grounds of 'The Austins.' One of the Husluck children was drowned in the largest one, and also a gardener who tried to save the child (HPPE p6).

Austin's Cote Farm and Cottage. 1m E of Lichfield cathedral.

Austrells, The Name for an enclosure, enclosed before 1348, standing on high ground in Aldridge (DUIGNAN) (MOA p135). The fields took their name from the conical furnaces for smelting ore (SPN p10).

Autherley District 1.5m NE of Tettenhall, in Bushbury parish. Preserved in Autherley Junction and Sewage Works. May take its name from Autherley Junction.

Autherley Junction Aldersley. Junction of the Staffordshire and Worcestershire Canal with Shropshire Union Canal (WJO Feb 1906 p44p). Takes its name from a past form of Aldersley which appeared from 1588 to the later C17 (VCH vol 20 p13).

Avenues Estate, The Name conceived by Brownhills UDC in 1920-1921 for an housing development N of Lichfield Road and W of Chase Road comprising First, Second, Third, and Fourth Avenues (SNBC p6).

Averhill Side House 1.5m WNW of Warslow. Formerly in Warslow and Elkstones township in Alstonefield ancient parish. There was a house here by the earlier C16 (VCH vol 7 p58). Has also appeared as Avril Side.

Awbridge Bridge Bridge over the Staffs and Worcs Canal 0.5m NE of Trysull. The lock at Awbridge may represent James Brindley's first attempt at combining a lock and a bridge on a public road. The bridge is unusual in having a balustrade of nine brick pillars supporting the sandstone coping (VCH vol 20 p201).

Axe Edge Green Appears on 1834 OS map and 1947 OS map 1:25,000 (sheet 43/ 06), at SK 018672, 0.5m E of Flash.

Axstones Spring House 1m E of Rushton Spencer. The name is said to be from a stone, the Ax Stone, a circular upright shaft, resembling the Cleulow Cross, Ches, and those in West Park, Macclesfield, which stood in this vicinity until being removed to a private garden some miles away. It lay on a powerful ley line with Snowdon and Stonehenge. Prior to 1996 Pickford had mistaken the Ax Stone with another stone, which he had for many years believed was the Ax Stone (DPEM p43) (DPTB pp47-48). There is a spring in the vicinity of the house (DPEM p43).

Aylewardsly Way Ancient path through the centre of Needwood Forest. Used as the boundary to divide Tutbury ward from Yoxall and Barton wards. It ran from Tatenhill Gate in the E to Byrkley Lodge and on to Ravensnest Gate in the W (SHC 4th series vol 4 p79) (VCH vol 2 pp350 see map,352).

B

Babylon Area in the NE corner of Amblecote parish, near Delph. The name for the area was in use in 1774, when there were two houses here; the name was still in use in the earlier C19 (VCH vol 20 p51). The same or another area nearby was known as Ninevah (SNSV vol 1 p55).

Babylon Row of four cottages in Cheddleton standing back from the main road (now - 1978 - used as lock-up garages) (Cheddleton Remembered. Vera Priestman. 1978 pp32,42).

Baby's Well, The Broughton. There was a roadside well on the bank beneath Broughton church in c1890, water was taken from it for christenings. It was possibly still in existence in 1949 (BOV p48). (SJC p10). Perhaps the same as the sulphur well with vitriolic in it in Park Meadow, Broughton (see).

Bacca Terrace Street in West Bromwich, which was perhaps named after the exploits of a Tipton soldier who fought in the Crimean War. While rambling, sightseeing or on reconnaissance with others in the wood at Backal, a village 60 miles or so N of Sebastapol and Balaclava, he surprised and captured a Russian colonel who turned out to be a prince. The prince's family paid an enormous ransom for his return and the soldier's share built Bacca Terrace. Could this soldier be Sgt Tinsley, a survivor of the Charge of the Light Brigade, buried in the churchyard at St Peter's, Greets Green? Demolished in 1979. (BCM Jan 1981 p66).

Bache Pool At Oakley Hall, Mucklestone.

Back Brook Rises near Blymhill forms the Staffs Salop border. Flows into Aqualate Mere.

Back Brook Tributary of Whiston Brook (SPNO p104).

Back Brook Rises 0.25m N of Hen Cloud in Goldsitch trough. Cuts through a gorge in the grit (NSFCT 1868 p22). Joins the Churnet S of Upper Hulme. It has been thought by some to be the true Churnet, but Wardle thinks not (NSFCT 1876 p33). It fed Dains water mill and has appeared as Dain Brook (HOLF p14) and Dane Brook (VCH vol 7 p237 note). Ball Haye Hall, demolished in 1972, was built reputedly of stones from the bed of the brook (HOLF p14) (VCH vol 7 pp191, 236-237).

Back Dane House 0.75m NE of Danebridge.

Back Forest Small forest on a hill to the ENE of Swythamley; Lud's Church Cave is situated on the N side of the hill. Formerly part of Leek or Lac Forest (OL vol 2 p162). Perhaps 'Back' is a corruption of 'Lac.' Has two main rock outcrops called THE MAIN CRAG at SJ 986654 comprising these named crags:- 'Rocking Stone Buttress' 'Broken Nose Buttress' 'Bastion Buttress' 'Bollard Buttress' 'Keep Buttress' 'Holly Tree Buttress' 'The Rostrum': And 1k to the WNW (SGM p122) or 0.25m to the WNW is THE WESTERN OUTCROP. The C17 or C18 bandit or highwayman robber called Black Captain hid in Back Forest to escape his pursuers (LMF p48).

Back Hills Wood To W of Tittesworth Reservoir. The old course of the Churnet passed to the W of it (NSFCT 1928 p93).

Back-of-the-Brook Hamlet N of Waterfall on the N side of Bredon Brook, in Waterfall parish. Has also appeared as Back o' th' Brook. The cross of Waterfall Cross is here used as a footbridge, believed Mr J Clark of Waterhouses (NSFCT 1920 p162); it might be the stone which is the clapper bridge over Bredon Brook (see).

Back of the Cross Area at the W end of Flash village and name for the Quarnford road in Flash village. The cromlech (a megalithic chambered tomb) in Quarnford parish may have been situated in this area. There was a house here by 1750 (UHAW). Has also appeared as The Cross (OS map 1834).

Back-of-the-Street Leek. Former settlement along a track running along the NW side of Leek Town Field. A few houses were built here in c1670. Back-of-the-Street had been renamed Belle Vue by 1841 (VCH vol 7 pp89,92).

Backus End Area on the opposite side of the road to New Cross Hospital, Wednesfield, so called in the 1930s, when it was one of old pit mounds, pools, a canal and general dereliction. In the 1980s and 1990s the area was redeveloped with a supermarket, bingo hall and cinema complex (TB June 1998 p23).

Back Walls Part of the town walls formerly surrounding Stafford.

Baddeley Edge Promontory which rises to 787 feet and is topped by Greenway Hall (ONST 1951 p158). Along the promontory runs the Norton-Bagnall parish boundary. Also a hamlet 0.5m E of Milton, formerly in Norton-in-the-Moors chapelry in Stoke-upon-Trent ancient parish. The early forms Baddilige (1227), Badeleye and Badilegh, deriving from 'Badda's lea' (DUIGNAN) (the addition 'Edge' referring to the edge of the forest - SPN p59), may refer to this Baddeley or Baddeley Green or both (SSE 1996 p10) (SPN p59). There is a well in Spout Lane. In 1996 it was partially hidden by foliage (ES April 13 1996 p21p of c1900).

Baddeley Green Hamlet 0.5m N of Milton. Formerly in Norton-in-the-Moors chapelry in Stoke-upon-Trent ancient parish. The early forms Baddilige (1227), Badeleye and Badilegh, deriving from Badda's leah or wood clearing (SSE 1996 p10), may refer to this Baddeley or Baddeley Edge or both (SSE 1996 p10) (SPN p59). At Baddeley Green an eight year old boy saw two unidentified small men in white suits and crash-helmets fly past his bedroom window in autumn 1976. Bord says, since these type of sightings are rare, this sighting should not be totally dismissed (Northern UFO News 82 pp5-6) (MMSE pp202,287).

Baddeley Hall At Baddeley Green, Milton.

Baden Hall House 1.5m ESE of Slindon. In the Three Farms township in Woodland quarter in Eccleshall parish (W p376). Badehale appears in DB as waste (SSE 1996 p10). Later, the name appears as Badnall (Plot's map), and Badenhall (DUIGNAN); it means Badda's hall (DUIGNAN), or Bada's nook (NSJFS 1981 p2), or Badda's hollow (SSE 1996 p10), or Badda's land (SPN p44).

Badger's Croft House over 1.25m WSW of Hardings Booth, in Heathylee township in Alstonefield ancient parish. There may have been a house here in 1308, when Robert of Bochardescroft was recorded as a tenant of Alstonefield manor. The house was known as Butcher's or Badger's Croft in the C18 (VCH vol 7 p33).

Badger's Folly Bearnett Drive, Wombourne. Roofless Gothic ruined castle folly S of Bearnett House and once stood in the grounds of the house (DoE II) (F p308).

Baggeridge Baggeridge Wood Farm is under 0.25m SW of Gospel End, in Himley parish. There was a chase or wood called Bageridge or rather Baggerugge in 1292 (DUIGNAN) (HC p13); the name means Bacga's ridge (DUIGNAN), or 'ridge where badgers are found' (SPN p144). It lay within the limits of Kinver Forest. Baggeridge Wood straggling the Wombourne Himley parish boundary was mentioned in 1295 (VCH vol 20 p212). In the last 200 years it has given its name to the Baggeridge Colliery and a brick works. Has also appeared as Bageride, and in Ellen Thorneycroft Fowler's novel 'The Farringdons' (1901) as Badgering (PPTP p34). For a rhyme about Baggeridge see Sedgley.

Baggeridge Hay The name occurs for a period from the earlier C13. Has also appeared as Baggerirdge Wood and Baggeridge Chase. Sedgley Hay may be identifiable with Baggeridge Hay (VCH vol 2 p344 note).

Baggeridge Woods Large wood to W of the colliery. Perhaps a remaining part of a Baggeridge Chase which may have existed in the C13. The S part is reclaimed from the colliery and known as Baggeridge Country Park. A cottage in Baggeridge Woods, alias Badgering Woods in Ellen Thorneycroft Fowler's novels (BCM Spring 2000 p47), appears on a Christmas card of 1907 (BCOPP vol 2 pl 52).

Bagnall Tiny hamlet or farm WSW of Alrewas. On land farmed by D Collingwood of Bagnalls Farm is a strange circle which may have been an ancient pen or pound (HOA pp3,4).

Bagnall Hilltop village (SGS p56) between head streams of the Churnet 17m N of Stafford. Former township, and with Bucknall, a chapelry in Stoke-upon-Trent ancient parish.

EARLY. A perforated stone axe-hammer was found at Moor Hall (see) in Bagnall parish in July 1964. Bagnall has a spine cop used since Roman times as a signalling or beacon post (STM July 1970 p27). This feature may be the same as the curious sunken track here, similar to Oliver's Mound at Denstone? (S p97).

1200 to 1500. The **name** appears to be of Anglo-Saxon origin, but forms of it do not appear until 1204. Forms such as Bagenholt, Badegenhall, Baginholt, and Bagenholt occur in the 1270s and 1280s (B pp5,7) (SSE 1996 p10) (SPN p14). Ekwall and others have thought the first element from Old English Bedeca, a personal noun. Since 'holt' and 'hall' endings are equally common forms it is difficult to discover whether the second element is 'holt,' as 'above,' or 'halh' meaning 'a nook, recess, or remote valley' (OAKDEN) (SSAHST 1967 pp34,35) (B p5). Paffard opts for Badeca's halh or hollow (SSE 1996 p10). Duignan opts Bacga's woodland (DUIGNAN). Although Bagnall is not mentioned in DB it was then a part of Endon (B p7). A cobbled path between Bank Farm and Rock Cottage, representing part of a **medieval footpath** linking Hulton Abbey with granges at Bradnop and Onecote, was excavated in autumn 1998 (ES Nov 5 1998 p12p). According to tradition an Hulton Abbey (see) monk called Robert, sought repentance from a hermit at Bagnall (FOS p21). A **church** with a late medieval wooden tower and a stone chancel was superseded in 1834 by the present church, St Chad, in the centre of Bagnall village (B p17). Bagnall celebrates its **wakes** on the Sunday after Oct 11 (B pp137-138). Bagnall had a **market** or butter cross but the village has never appeared on lists of Staffs market towns (SCSF p91). The butter cross stands opposite the old hall. It is probably of C16 origin (DoE II). It is said farmers of the district assembled at the cross to dispose of their produce at the time of the plague 1666. The inscription on its modern base records the planting of five trees on the green to commemorate Queen Victoria's Diamond Jubilee 1887 (ROS vol 1 pp142-143) (SCSF p91) (S p127) (NSFCT 1916 p144) (ES May 23 1933 p9p) (PWNS p115p) (SVB p25). The land in front of the Stafford Arms Inn was known as the **Pound** and was originally a bowling green (B p117). Bagnall bowling green was being restored in c1890 (OL vol 1 p287). Bucknall's **bull ring** was found directly beneath the old cross base at Bagnall (NSFCT 1925 p190) (NSSG p6).

1500 to PRESENT. Bagnall with Bucknall separated to form an ecclesiastical parish in 1716 (GLAUE p405), or 1807 (W p236) (LGS p77). Bagnall separated from Bucknall parish in 1736 but could not sustain its separate ecclesiastical parish identity and 'Bucknall cum Bagnall' ecclesiastical parish was refounded in 1849 (GLAUE pp402,405). **Bagnall School**, demolished by 1990, had a stone lintel over its main door inscribed 'Infants.' This lintel was to be found, in 1990, in the garden of St Chad's Cottage (B p59p). **Bagnall Hospital** opened in 1890. A new hospital was built in 1906 and has a date stone with '1906.' After serving as an isolation hospital, first for smallpox and then for children with Tuberculosis, it became a hospital for the mentally handicapped in 1959. It became known as 'The Highlands' in 1980 and was due to be closed in 1993 (SVB p26) (B pp130-131). **Well-dressing**. The custom of dressing the Bagnall Springs has only been practised once, in 1963. The well is believed to have never gone dry (B p136p) (ES July 23 1994 p25p). The covering of the same or another well is inscribed 'A.D. Public Well S.H.S.H. 1811. Refixed 1891' (DoE II). The annual **Cake Fair** held at Whitsun, became a tradition in the C20 (SVB p26). The first Cake Fair was taking place by the late 1920s (B pp136-137). **Natural history**. In the later C17 Plot noted at Bagnall a mare which gave birth to a colt with a fifth hoof coming out of the fetlock of one of its legs and hanging loose, which in time was thought necessary to shoe (NHS p266). The **Hattons**, an old couple of Bagnall in the C17, both said to be witches, made a cow of Joseph Cope stop giving milk. Confronted with the result of her witchcraft Mrs Hatton revoked the spell and the cow gave milk again (TFTP pp98-99 ils) (GLS pp18-19). **John Ravenscroft**, founder in 1961 of Bridgemere Garden World, Bridgemere, Ches, was born at Bagnall (MIDD vol 5 pp28,29p).

Bagnall Grange 0.75m E of Bagnall. A C18 farmhouse built on or near the site of a grain mill belonging to Hulton Abbey and traditionally connected to the

abbey by trackways (B p61). In the mid C18 the Hulme family lived here (B pp61-62p). Generally, the house seems to have had many occupants in the C19, sometimes the house was split between two families (B pp62-63). It was for a period the residence of Enoch Turner who emigrated to Canada in 1831 and founded the Enoch Turner Schoolhouse in Toronto in 1848 (ES Jan 18 1993 p8p).

Bagnall Hall Situated S of Bagnall church. The house was occupied by John Murrall in 1598. It was the residence of the Murrall (Murhall, Murrell, Merrial) family to the early C19 (B p74). Here lived the infamous William Murrall JP (d1762) who had one of the Scottish stragglers in the 1745 Jacobite Rebellion, who fell into his hands, flayed. Murrall is buried in Endon churchyard (HSP p136) (HOC pp70-71) (NSFCT 1924 p194-5. 1943 p72) (STM April 1964 p35. Dec 1968 p37) (STMSM April 1978 p20) (E p91) (SVB p25) (POTP p12) (SMOPP vol 2 p61) (GLS pp98-99). In the early C19 the hall passed to the Myatt family who lived here until at least 1871. It then had various occupants (B pp73,74p,75,76). The hall appears to have been rebuilt several times and bears the inscription over the doorway 'J.M. (John Murrall) 1603' (B pp73,74) and a datestone with the 1777. It contains a curious cellar the entrance to which is hewn out of solid rock. Tradition says Oliver Cromwell slept here one night and surveyed the country from the roof (NSFCT 1916 p144). A secret tunnel, discovered in 1881, runs from the hall to the church (SLM Sept/ Oct 1995 p11pc). The ghost, who haunted the hall once a year and whose presence racked the owner with aches and pains, had been appeased by the late 1870s (ROS vol 1 pp147-153).

Bagnall Manor House Stone house NE of Bagnall church on the N side of a track leading to Houghwood Farm. The house stands on an old farm site, nothing is known of its occupants prior to 1851 (B pp77,78p).

Bagot's Bromley Hamlet above the valley of Tad Brook (SSAHST 1981-82 p69) nearly 8m ENE of Stafford. Former township in Abbots Bromley ancient parish (W p409). There appears to have been a manor of Bagot's Bromley by 1166, when it was held by William Bagot (SHC 1908) (DB. J Morris. 1976) (SSAHST 1988-89 p53). The Bagots derived their name from Bagod, said to be of Norman extraction and mean the same in Norman that 'scripio' did in old Latin (viz: 'a walking staff'). They resided at Bagot's Hall (see) to c1360 and then at Blithfield Hall (see). The lordship of Bagot's Bromley remained with the Bagots for about a thousand years until sold in London on July 2 1997 (BBC Radio Stoke. Barbara Adams Show. May 27 1997). Some have sought to show that there was a manor of Bagot's Bromley in 1086; Erdeswick tried to identify Bagot's Bromley with DB Branselle (Bramshall) (SHC 1914 p170). Gen Wrottesley tried to identify it with Bradelie, an unidentified DB vill in Pirehill hundred; Bramelie being incorrectly spelt Bradelie (SHC 1908 pp11-13. 1914 p170 note). A possible medieval village of Bagot's Bromley was probably deserted in the C18 (SSAHST 1970 p34). A hamlet of 11 houses at Bagot's Bromley (Bromley Bagot's, Plot's map) was pulled down by Lord Bagot in c1809 (W p408). At Bagot's Mill was a great wych elm (AB p200).

Bagot's Bromley Marsh To E of Bagot's Bromley. Preserved in Marsh Farm. Marked on OS map 1834.

Bagot's Hall Former seat of the Bagots at Bagot's Bromley, at SK 067259.

THE BAGOTS. The Bagots descended from Bagod who held Bramshall from Robert de Stafford at the time of DB. He or possibly his son of the same name was living in 1129. His son, Hervey fitz Bagod succeeded his father in c1130; his son Hervey Bagot married Millicent daughter of his feudal overlord, Robert de Stafford, and heir of her brother, before 1193: Their son, Hervey, assumed the name of Stafford and his descendents of Stafford Castle (see) held the Stafford barony. **William Bagot**, a cadet of the family, is named in a deed 1160, with Henry fitz Bagod (above mentioned). He held two thirds of a knight's fee from Robert de Stafford in 1166, which has been identified as Bagot's Bromley. He was succeeded eventually by **Simon** Bagot, who held Bagot's Bromley in 1198 and died before 1203, and was succeeded eventually by his son **Sir Hugh** knt of Bagot's Bromley, d1256. He was succeeded by his son **Sir Richard** Bagot knt, who died before 1271. He was succeeded by his son **Sir William** knt of Bagot's Bromley, d1290. He was succeeded by his son **John**, died in c1333, who was succeeded by his son **Sir John** knt of Bagot's Bromley. He served at the battles of Crecy (1346) and Calais (1347) and died in 1349. He was succeeded by his son **Ralph**, who by marriage to the heiress of the Blithfield family, Elizabeth, acquired the manors of Blithfield and Littlehay. He died in c1376 and was succeeded by his son **Sir John** knt. He appears to have been the builder of the original part of Blithfield Hall in 1398. For when the Bagots started to reside at Blithfield Hall (see), see below. He served at Agincourt in 1415, and on his death in 1437 he was succeeded by his son **Richard**, High Sheriff of Staffs in 1451-2. He died after 1475 and was succeeded by his son **Richard**, High Sheriff of Staffs in 1478.

He was killed at the battle of Bosworth Field in 1485 and succeeded by his son **John**, MP for Staffs in 1477, who died after 1489 and was succeeded by his son **Sir Lewis** knt. He was present at the Cloth of Gold in 1520, and married five times, dying in 1534. He was succeeded by his eldest son of his third wife, **Thomas** d1541. He was succeeded by his son **Richard** d1596-7, who was succeeded by his eldest son **Walter** (1557-1623), who was succeeded by his eldest surviving son **Sir Hervey** b1590, 1st baronet, High Sheriff in 1626, MP 1628-42. He was created a baronet in 1627 and was a royalist in the Civil War. On his death in 1660 at Field Hall (see) he was succeeded by his eldest son **Sir Edward** (1616-1673), 2nd Bt. His younger brother, Col Richard Bagot (b1618), fourth son of Sir Hervey, was appointed governor of the royalist garrison at Lichfield (see) in the Civil War, and was killed at the battle of Naseby (1645) (History of the family of Bagot. Major General Hon George Wrottesley. 1908). Sir Edward (d1673) was succeeded by his son **Sir Walter** (1644-1704), 3rd Bt. He was succeeded by his eldest surviving son **Sir Edward** (1673-4-1712), 4th Bt, who was succeeded by his only surviving son **Sir Walter Wagstaffe** Bagot (1702-1768), 5th Bt. He married Lady Barbara Legge, eldest daughter of William 1st Earl of Dartmouth of Sandwell Hall (see), and was succeeded by his eldest son **William** (1728-1798). His younger brother, Rt Rev Lewis Bagot (1741-1802), fifth son of Sir Walter, was consecrated bishop of Bristol in 1782, bishop of Norwich in 1783, and bishop of St Asaph in 1790, where he rebuilt the bishop's palace. Some of his verse has been published (DNB) (PSS pp100-101) (VFC p6). The eldest son William who succeeded his father was a created a baron in 1780 and became 1st Baron Bagot. He was succeeded by his eldest son **William** (1773-1856), 2nd Baron Bagot. His younger brother, Richard Bagot DD (1782-1854), sixth son of William 1st Baron, was bishop of Oxford from 1829, and bishop of Bath and Wells from 1845 (DNB). The first wife of William (d1856), Emily Fitzroy, fourth daughter of Charles 1st Lord Southampton, a descendant of Charles II and Barbara Villiers, died in childbirth on June 8 1800, a year after her marriage to William; a shield of arms on the lodge to Blithfield Hall at Admaston (see) represents their brief union (VB p105). William was succeeded by his eldest son **William** (1811-1887), 3rd Baron Bagot, who was succeeded by his eldest son **William** (1857-1932), 4th Baron Bagot. He died without issue and the title passed to **Gerald William** (1866-1946), 5th Baron Bagot, son of Vice-Admiral Henry Bagot (b1810), son of third son of the 1st Baron. Gerald died unmarried and the title passed to his cousin **Sir Caryl Ernest** Bagot (1877-1961), 6th Baron Bagot. His widow, Nancy, continued to reside at Blithfield after her husband's death, whilst his successor, his cousin **Harry Eric** Bagot (b1894), 7th Baron Bagot and 12th Baronet, son of Charles Frederick Heneage Bagot, fourth son of Rev Charles Walter Bagot (b1812), fourth son of the 1st Baron, resided in Australia (The Complete Peerage) (Burke's Peerage) (VB p106). As well as the tradition that the extinction of the white goats in Bagot's Park (see) would lose the Bagot's their title, another old Bagot family tradition was the announcing of meals by the sound of a drum (CCBO pp147-153).

Various dates are given for the departure of the Bagots from Bagot's Hall to Blithfield Hall (see); that they left in Edward II's reign (NSFCT 1948 p121), or after the marriage (before 1357) of Ralph Bagot to Elizabeth, sister of Richard de Blithfield (SHC 1908 p220) (SSAHST 1988-1989 p53), or in 1360 (Blithfield. 1979. Nancy Lady Bagot p11). Bagot's Hall remained to c1811. A drawing made of it when it was being pulled down shows that it possessed an aisled timber hall of great antiquity. The site is now marked by a monument erected by the second Lord Bagot (CL Oct 28 1954) (STMSM April 1973 pp24-25) (BOE p74) (SGS p62) (MR p4). The moat or defensive ditch was excavated in 1981 (SSAHST 1981-82 pp69-78) (NSFCT 1982 p19) (CAMS p63).

Bagot's Park Medieval deer park enclosed out of forest. In existence probably by the late C12, although it is found only documented from 1489 (NSJFS 1962 p75) (ABAB p39). According to the NSFC it was never in Needwood Forest, although many had a notion that it was. It is amongst the Staffs parks distinctly sui generis, lying some 1.5m ENE of Bagot's Hall at Bagot's Bromley (NSFCT 1927 p167). In the later C17 Plot noted hollies and oaks growing from the roots together in Bagot's Park (NHS p213). In the park were a herd of distinctive white **goats** with black necks, Schwarzhals from the Rhone Valley (STMSM April 1973). They may have been brought to England from Normandy at the Norman Conquest (LGS p192), or by the crusaders (STMSM April 1973), or presented to the Bagot family by King John (NSFCT 1896 p123 note) (FLJ 1910 p27) (LGS p192), or by Richard II (LGS p192). There is a tradition that Richard II presented the goats to Sir John Bagot in appreciation for the excellent hunting he had enjoyed in Bagot's Park (TRTC p31). There was a tradition that if the goats die out the peerage of Bagot also dies out (FLJ 1896 p385). By at least the mid C19 there were

keepers for the goats; a post mainly held by members of the Jackson family of Goat Lodge (see). Miss Mary Jackson, the last keeper, who died in the 1950s, described the goats as shy, nervous, but very loyal (TRTC p31) (LTD p128; claims Miss Jackson lived to the 1960s). The herd, which thrived on the estate and numbered 40 in the 1950s (TRTC p32), was sold off in the late 1970s (ESNF p42p) or taken by Lady Bagot to the Rare Breeds Survival Trust in the 1970s (TRTC p33). By 1978 Shugborough Park Farm had examples of the breed (STMSM Nov 1978 p9p) (SN Nov 9 1979 p58). In 1995 the Bagot goat was re-introduced into the area by Nick Phillips, a local farmer, from Abbots Bromley, who hopes to eventually release the goats into Bagot's Wood (TRTC p34). Their image is said to appear in the Bagot crest (LGS p192) and in carvings on the main staircase at Blithfield Hall (SLM May 1953 p22p). Bagot's Park is said to have contained the famous oaks called Beggar's Oak, Squitch Oak, Venison Oak, Cliff Oak, King John's Oak and Walking Stick Oak (LGS pp191-192). Some of the oaks felled in the park in c1933 were used for the panelling of the Queen Mary (SHJ autumn 1993 p21). In WW2 some of the park was converted to agricultural use for the war effort, whilst some was used as a bombing range by the RAF; this later became agricultural land (TRTC p33).

Bagot's Wood In NE part of Bagot's Park. A number of Lorraine glassmakers' furnaces were established in Bagot's Wood by Richard Bagot in the late C16 (NSFCT 1946 p139. 1947 p111). Bagot's Wood, which has also been called Bagot Forest (1981 OS map 1:25,000), is one of the famous covers in the Meynell Hunt (TRTC p34). Holly Covert, near Goat Lodge, is a surviving piece of woodland of the wood. It was purchased by Phil Drabble, the naturalist and broadcaster, in 1963 who maintains it as a wild life haven (TRTC p33).

Bailey's Hill Hill 0.25m NW of Biddulph. In Biddulph ancient parish. The hill was apparently given to some Saracens or Biddlemoor Men brought over by the Biddulphs during the Crusades (FLJ 1896 pp378,379). They were made bailiffs and took the surname Bailey or Bayley. (SVB p33).

Bailey's Pool Lost pool S of Hargreaves Pool, to WNW of Trentham Hall. Probably from a David Bailey mentioned on a C19 estate map. It was still in existence in the 1930s (NSJFS 1974 p117).

Bailey's Warren S of Beaudesert SW of Chorley alias Old Kitchen Warren (AFT p190).

Bailey's Wood Small wood W of Biddulph Grange. At SJ 889595 is an ancient D-shaped earthwork in a strong defensive position at the eastern end of a ridge overlooking Biddulph Brook which could be of Iron Age origin, but is more likely to have been a small defensive site with a bailey made in or before the C12, remade in the C13 and was then occupied by a residence to the C16. In its early existence it was probably kept up for the Biddulph overlords, the de Verduns of Alton Castle, but evidently became de Biddulph family property, and Biddulph Old Hall may have replaced it (NSFCT 1959 p87) (BHS June 1968 pp6-9 plan) (BALH pp22,26 see map). This earthwork, at times called Bailey's Wood Castle and Biddulph Castle, is a listed monument.

Balance Hill Hill and suburb 0.25m S of Uttoxeter. In Uttoxeter ancient parish. According to tradition the hill is so called after sheep, when their fleeces would be weighed on a balance (TSW p43). Another account says Balance is from an old English word meaning beanfield (Official Uttoxeter Town Guide. 1993. p32).

Balds Hill N of The Moat, Walsall (TB 1984 p16 see map). Balds Hill is marked N of The Moat on 1834 OS map. The name is not preserved in any street name nor as the name of the district.

Baldstone Situated near Baldstone Farm behind the Roaches to the W of the Royal Cottage at SK 018640 (Some Random Thoughts on Ancient History of Leek. ND. NA - from vol 10 of local pamphlets in Horace Barks Ref Lib, Hanley) (VCH vol 7 p34). Has also appeared as Bald Stone (1834 OS map). Here midsummer ceremonies of the mistletoe were held (DPMM pp94-95). The name may be from Balder a Norse or Viking god, the son of Odin: Balder was slain by a branch of mistletoe and according to legend he was burnt in a huge fire (DPMM p96). See also Ballstone, and Bawd Stone.

Baldwin's Gate Village under 1m SW of Whitmore. Formerly in Madeley and Maer ancient parishes, and Chorlton chapelry of Eccleshall ancient parish (W pp381,396,398). To the SW at SJ 789397 is a burial mound (NSFCT 1983 p13). The name appears in an account roll for Madeley manor of 1511 (NSFCT 1982 pp10,11), and may be from a medieval park-keeper to Madeley Great Park (MHSP p16) (SL p92). It is mentioned by Chetwynd (1679) and spelt Balding Gate on Smith's map. It is unlikely therefore to be from a toll-gate keeper, on (probably) the Shrewsbury-Newcastle turnpike road (SVB p26); latterly Holt and a friend have pondered on the identity of Mr Baldwin (SFH p50). The village started to expand with the opening of Whitmore (see) railway station here in 1837.

Balk Brook Former name for the lower part of Coksale Brook (HOPT vol 1 p134).

Ballamont Grange 1.25m W of Cauldon. Has appeared as 'Bellyband Grange' (1769) and Ballington Grange (1834 OS map). The property was being used for old cars by 1974 (PRT p71).

Ball Bank Ball Bank House Farm 0.75m SSW of Hollinsclough. Formerly in Heathylee township in Alstonefield ancient parish. There was a house at Ball Bank by 1444 (VCH vol 7 p33).

Ball Edge Hamlet 0.5m S of Brown Edge.

Ballfields House over 1m SSW of Bradnop. Formerly in Bradnop township in Leek ancient parish. Has appeared as Ballfields (1834 OS map) and Sixoaks Farm (1980 OS map 1:25,000). The warden of Combes Valley nature reserve has lived at Sixoaks Farm since 1970 (VCH vol 7 p171).

Ball Green Hamlet 0.5m N of Norton-in-the-Moors. Formerly in Norton-in-the-Moors chapelry in Stoke-upon-Trent ancient parish. At the beginning of the C20 Ball Green was still an entirely separate village from the adjoining villages of Norton Green and Norton with which it now (1958) merges (ONST 1958 p216).

Ball Haye Former hamlet 0.75m ENE of Leek. Now a suburb of Leek. Formerly in Tittesworth township in Leek ancient parish. There was a farm at Ball Haye by 1565 (VCH vol 7 p233). The name is of French origin 'la Belle Haye,' the fair demesne (OL vol 1 p281). Or 'Ball' is a corruption of 'bell,' the general shape of the region (SPN p75). Ball Haye Green is the area to the N in Leek and Lowe township.

Ball Haye Brook Ball Haye (SPN p75). May have formerly been called Church Brook (see), a tributary of the Churnet (VCH vol 7 p84).

Ball Haye Green Former common land and tiny hamlet 0.5m NE of Leek. Formerly in Leek and Lowe township in Leek ancient parish (W p719). The common land was enclosed in 1811 and the area was known as Ball Haye Green by 1820; suburbanisation of it began in 1824 when Leek Building Society started to build 42 houses on the N side of the Haregate road (VCH vol 7 pp92, 235). Ball Haye Green, formerly considered a poor area, has also been called 'Bawly Green' and 'The Island' (HLS p65) (HLSP p147). A house in Ball Haye Road is haunted by a poltergeist (SMM p47).

Ball Haye Hall Stood N of the junction of Park Road and Vicarage Road, Leek (W p721). Formerly in Tittesworth township in Leek ancient parish (VCH vol 7 p234). The Ball Haye estate was granted to Henry Davenport in the mid C16. It remained with the Davenports until 1828, when the estate passed to trustees; a result of a Chancery suit brought by the step-children of James Davenport (b1772) against their step-father in 1814. The trustees, had the power to sell the hall, and after several unsuccessful attempts they sold it in 1853 to Joshua and John Brough and others (OL vol 1 pp281,282,283 il) (Beauties of England and Wales. il by JP Neale). The hall was solely owned by the Broughs by 1862 and it passed to their descendents, one of whom, HH Brindley sold it in 1931 (VCH vol 7 p236). American soldiers were based here in WW2 (ALC p48). After the war it was used as a Polish Club, later being converted into flats. It finally became derelict and was demolished in 1972 (VCH vol 7 p236). The old hall was rebuilt in c1783 (HOLF p14) or in c1790 (HOLF p14) by James Hulme, father of the heir to the estate, James Davenport (b1772), or built at a slightly later date by James Davenport (b1772), reputedly with stones from the bed of Back Brook at Upper Hulme (VCH vol 7 pp235,236il,237). Miller noted that an echo could be heard from the hall when the bells of Leek parish church were rung (OL vol 1 p282). In the rock-pool garden are various sculptured stones including heads of monks, a crocodile and a coiled serpent which were brought here in c1822 from Bridge House on the Churnet - no doubt relics of Dieulacres Abbey (NSFCT 1922 p155).

Ball Haye Wood Wood near Ball Haye Hall. Said to be haunted by the ghost of Ball Haye Jack (HLSP p147).

Ballington Ballington Grange Farm is 1m SE of Leek on Lowe Hill, on the SE edge of Ballington Wood. There was settlement in the area of the present wood by the early C13, when Ralph of Baliden was a tenant in the fee of Leek (VCH vol 7 p85). Ballington Grange Farm existed as Cowhay Farm in 1608 (VCH vol 7 p89).

Ballington House On S side of South Bank Street, Leek. Formerly known as Ballington View, it was known as Ballington House by 1888, and is said to have been built in the later 1870s (VCH vol 7 p96).

Balls Hill There is a Balls Hill street in central Walsall NE from St Matthew's church.

Balls Hill Small district 1m SSE of Wednesbury. Is a corruption of Bald Hill, a hill with no trees on it (WAM p6).

Ball's Mount Small district 1m WSW of Burntwood church marked on OS map 1834.

Ballstone, The A gigantic perched boulder at Ballstone Farm at SK 014658 (SGM p201) (DPMM pp94,97,98p). The name is from Baal's Stan, a site of Beltaine fires (DPMM p94). A hat with a silk tag of a foraging soldier of the 1745 Jacobite Rebellion was found in peat near the Ballstone. It is now (1994) believed to be in the Potteries Museum (UHAW p18). See also Baldstone, and Bawd Stone.

Balterley Small village 20m NW of Stafford. Former township and chapelry of Barthomley ancient parish, Ches, in Chester archdeaconry, and Chester diocese since 1541 (VCH vol 3 p92) (BVC p7). The name, of probably Anglo-Saxon origin, means 'Bealdthryth's lea' (DUIGNAN), or 'Bealdryh's pasture' (SPN p14). Or Baldpryp's leah (or ley) (BVC p34). Or Baldthyth's wood clearing; Baldthyth is a woman's name (SSE 1996 p10) and the original settlement may have been headed by a woman (SPN p14). It has been identified by Dugdale and Duignan with the Baltrytheleage mentioned in the will of Wulfric Spot (c1002), founder of Burton Abbey (SHC 1916 p27) (SSE 1996 p10). The manor of Baltredelege appears in DB. Balterley later appears as Baltrelegh (1289) (SPN p14). Balterley has had associations with the Primitive Methodist movement (NSFCT 1951 p115). The Anglican church (the only one in Staffs in Chester diocese), All Saints, on the N side of Nantwich Road facing Back Lane, was built in 1901 (BOE p65). The vestry was not consecrated along with the rest the building so that the rector could smoke his pipe there (info Beryl Fox).

Balterley Green Hamlet 0.25m N of Balterley. There was no green at Balterley Green in 1856, but there had been a little open green space (BART p164).

Balterley Hall Balterley. Former seat of the Thickens or Thicknesse family (BART p172); their arms appear on Plot's map. Ralph Thickness (of Wigan) sold the hall in 1790 to John Crewe of Bolesworth Castle, Ches, from whom it was purchased by Thomas Twemlow of Hill Top, Sandbach (SHC 1909 p235 note).

Balterley Heath Hamlet over 0.75m W of Balterley on Cheshire border.

Bancroft Tiny hamlet SE of Hamstall Ridware. In Hamstall Ridware parish.

Bandy Woods Area N of the King's Road, Kingstanding, formerly Perry Common. It is said to have received its name from pupils of Oscott College at Old Oscott who used to play hockey, or 'bandy,' here (KPP p15). The area is now covered by housing and the name is preserved in Bandywood Road and Crescent.

Bangley The house Lower Bangley is 1m SE of Hints. The house Great Bangley is 1.25m S of Hints. (SHOS vol 2 p9). Bangley was partly in Fazeley township in Tamworth ancient parish (W p625) and partly in Drayton Bassett ancient parish (SGSAS). Heat-shattered pebbles of a possible former Middle Bronze Age burnt mound was found in Alder Wood at cSK 176013 in 1981. The same field produced worked flint of Mesolithic type, probable Iron Age pottery and Roman and medieval pottery but there was no particular concentration of any of these near the pebbles (SASR 1987 p18).

Bangley Farm 1m E of Hints on S side of Watling Street. It has been noticed that tracks near Bangley Farm are magnetic; they were partly constructed with material taken from slag heaps which contain quantities of iron. Iron being worked at Hints from the late C16 to the middle of the C18 (MR pp185-6).

Bangley Park House over 2m SSW of Bednall.

Bangley Park Medieval deer park perhaps in existence by 1397 and was certainly in existence by 1505. It had been disparked by 1756 (SHOS vol 2 p9). It lay on the W side of the A453 and embraced Great Bangley farm in the S and Lower Bangley in the N, and did not exceed further N than the Bourne Brook (SSAHST 1988-89 pp44-45il). The original lodge, Bangley, which had been converted into a farm by 1756 (SHOS vol 2 p9), may be associated with the present Bangley Farm on Watling Street, N of Bourne Brook.

Bank End Tiny district of Bank End, between Brown Edge and Ball Edge. The small village green at Bank End is common land (OSST 1956-59 p6). The name is probably from a gap in the millstone grit ridge here (ONST 1979 p399) (BEH p31).

Bank End Minute hamlet 0.5m WSW of Longsdon. Formerly in Longsdon township in Leek ancient parish. The Leek road passed this way until being realigned to the N in the 1930s (VCH vol 7 p204).

Bank End Farm Bank End, Brown Edge. Has stone mullion windows. A wooden farm cottage was built on to it in 1742. One of the farm fields is still (1979) known as Buckingham meadow after one of the early lords of Norton manor. Laughing Cottage (see) to the S is a lodge built for this farm (ONST 1979 p398).

Bank Farm On the S side of the Little Lawn Farm road leading out of Bagnall. Bank Farm is a stone building dating from the C16 on which centred a small estate. The estate included Bagnall Bank, a pottery later called Bank House (see), which lies to the E of Bank Farm. At the end of the C18 the estate was owned by John Sparrow of Bishton Hall. Bank Farm was occupied by William Adams between 1794 and 1810. He had a flint mill by Stanley Pool called Stanley Mill and was often visited here by his friend, Josiah Spode, the potter (B pp69,72p,73). The same or an ancestor of William Adams, William Adams, is said to have billeted Prince Charles James Stuart at Bank House (probably Bank Farm is meant) on Dec 7 1745 on his retreat during the 1745 Jacobite Rebellion. The prince is reputed to have drunk from a teapot, later exhibited in Tunstall Museum (NSFCT 1925 p66. 1943 p72).

Bank Fields District 0.25m SE of Lower Gornal.

Bank House On the S side of the Little Lawn Farm road leading out of Bagnall. It was known as Bagnall Bank and was part of the Bank Farm estate until it was divided in 1848. After that date it was a private residence, but prior to that date it may have been a pottery: It is widely believed that Williams Adams, the potter, started his business at Bank House, when he lived next door at Bank Farm, and that somewhere at Bank House there maybe a kiln. Arnold Mountford of the Potteries Museum dated some pieces of pottery found in the garden as being between 1760 and 1850. They were clay pipes and pieces of salt glaze (B pp69,70p,71).

Bank House Swan Bank, Bilston. Home of William Balonger and ancestor of Stanley Baldwin PM. It became the Dudley and West Bromwich Banking Company in 1866. Stood next to the Swan Inn (demolished) (BOP p35).

Bank House A little W of Calton church. Built in 1743 (BOE pp92-93).

Bank House Stands on summit of Endon Bank, in Endon village. Incorporates a house called Endon House, which was standing by 1808. Seat of John Daniel (d1821), one of the owners of the New Hall Pottery works in Shelton. The house was known as Endon Bank in the later C19 (VCH vol 7 p178). In the grounds are the burial places of John Daniel (d1821) and his sister, Alice (d1827) (VCH vol 7 p178).

Bank House House at Etruria Josiah Wedgwood I had built for his partner, Thomas Bentley. It stood to the S of his own Etruria Hall but on the same side of the canal (HOE pp34,48,52 il and p of the site in c1950, p of the original coach house to Bank House, 117,136,372-374p of the well to Bank House rediscovered in 1951. As the site was being cleared for rebuilding it was promptly filled in). It was occupied by Josiah Wedgwood II from 1806 to 1807 before he moved to Maer Hall. VCH implies Josiah II lived at Bank House again between 1812 and 1819 before returning to Maer Hall. It was demolished in 1819 (VCH vol 8 pp150,152).

Bank House House 0.5m E of Newtown. Fawfieldhead township, Alstonefield ancient parish. Appears as Audley Bothesley in the later 1430s (VCH vol 7 p27).

Bank House Hanley. Demolished in c1867 to make way for The Queens Hotel, erected in 1869 (VCH vol 8 p149), which later became the Town Hall (SHST pp582-583 ils).

Bank House There was a house on the E side of High Lane, Smallthorne, by 1619. It was rebuilt on the same site in 1828 by Richard Riley, and was taken over by the Burslem Suburban Club and Institute after WW1. It was still standing in 1960 (VCH vol 8 p116-117).

Bank House, The In Uttoxeter town. So called because Thomas Hart established Uttoxeter's first bank here in the C18. The old safe still exists and another feature is a fine unsupported spiral staircase (ESNF p64p).

Bank House Farmhouse C16 old timber-framed building (NSFCT 1915 p16p) near Uttoxeter. Has also appeared as Bank Farm House.

Banks Farm L-shaped red brick house of c1700 0.75m WSW of Rocester. Appears as a folly or gazebo. Probably an eye-catcher for Woodseat, nearby. At the out angle has a three-storeyed tower (BOE p226) (MR p266p). Has also appeared as Banks Farmhouse.

Bank Top Hamlet 0.5m NNE of Burslem.

Bank Top (1834 OS map). Or Banktop Farm. 0.5m S of Gratwich.

Bank Top In Keele parish (W p394). There is a Bank Top Farm 1m NNW of Keele.

Bank Top House 2m ESE of Werrington, at SJ 970462. Appears on 1834 OS map and current OS maps. In Kingsley parish.

Banktop Tiny hamlet on Blithbury road W of Colton.

Banners Gate Now a large residential suburb 2.25m E of Great Barr. In 1911 Handsworth and Perry Barr were removed to Birmingham in Warws (HOS p55) leaving a narrow strip, protruding into Warws, which included Banners Gate. The name is from a gate to Sutton Park.

Bannut Tree Farm formerly in Arley ancient parish, on the W side of the Severn, 0.75m SW of Upper Arley. Bannut is a dialectic word used in Worcs and some adjoining counties, for walnut (DUIGNAN).

Banqueting Farm House 2m SW of Adbaston.

Banshee House In the area called Islington now a NE suburb of Newport, Shrops

(Yates' map). Removed from Staffs to Shrops in 1965.

Bantock House Built between 1734 and 1788 at Merridale, Wolverhampton. Formerly known as New Merridale Farm, and on the 1889 OS map as Merridale House. It took on its present appearance when a front was built to the house between 1800-1810. The house's present name is from probably the Bantocks; Thomas Bantock (1823-1895), waggon and boat builder, resided here from 1867 (BCM summer 1999 pp25-28). However, Raven thinks the name probably means 'Banna's religious place,' but it could mean 'the murderer's tree' a gallows (Banna is murderer in Old English) (BCTV p92). After the death of Thomas' son Albert Bantock, a councillor and three times mayor of Wolverhampton, in 1938 the house passed to the council. In WW2 it was used by the Home Guard. After the war the council opened the house as a museum in 1948. It was designated as European Small Museum of the Year in 1978. Between 1995 and 1999 the house was restored; the house had reopened to the public by Sept 1999 (BCM summer 1999 p25) (Wolverhampton Chronicle Oct 29 1999 p14p). (WMAG May 1970 front cover pc) (The Story of Bantock House. CA Beardsmore) (BCM Oct 1987 pp16-17il-18) (WOLOP p24p).

Bantock Park Park surrounding Bantock House, Wolverhampton. Now open to the public.

Barbery Gutter Wooded dell on the W side of the road from Alton to Farley. In 1807 the coach road and drainage channels were made through Barbury Gutter (HAF p304). The name has also appeared as Bunbury, Barbary, and Barbara (HAF p304) and Barberry Gutter. A Banbury Wood appears on the 1834 OS map where Abbey Wood is now marked on current OS maps, S of Alton Towers. The name is possibly from the shrub Berberis (Barbary) which was growing in the gutter in the early C20 (HAF p304). The gutter is reputedly haunted by a headless horseman (FLJ 1942 p126); the Chained Oak (see) is here.

Bare Hill Hill in the Rowley Hills range (SVS pp431,433 note). Preserved in Barehill Farm, 1.25m NNW of Rowley Regis.

Bareleg Hill Hill 0.25m ENE of the Royal Cottage Inn, on Morridge. According to tradition the hill was named in consequence of the kilted Scots of the Pretender's army crossing over or close to it in the 1745 Jacobite Rebellion (VB p207) (DPMM p112).

Bargate Bargate Street in the centre of Brewood village is on the N side of the former green. It appears to have been formerly Bargate (W p447).

Bar Green Name for the former village green of Enville. By the later C18 Bar Green had been taken into Enville Hall grounds (VCH vol 20 p91).

Bar Hill Hill over which the Woore-Madeley road runs, over 1m SW from Madeley. In Madeley parish (W p396). Has also appeared as Barr Hill. Perhaps so called from a Bar toll-gate situated on it. There is a possible mound on Bar Hill at SJ 76184433 and another 0.5m to the E at SJ 76884434 (NSFCT 1983 p13). HW Daltry found here a large grey flint, irregularly rectangular. It was thought not to be an implement. It went to the Potteries Museum (NSFCT 1932 p125).

Barlaston Ancient parish and large village 10m NNW of Stafford, situated on a wooded ridge on the E side of the Trent, overlooking the Trent valley (SGS p56). A **Neolithic** or **Bronze Age** stone implement was found at Parkfields (see). A **spring** under the S chancel of church (now the old church) which flooded a grave in the churchyard was noted by Plot in the later C17. The spring remained wet even when a nearby well went dry (NHS p86). A C7 Anglo-Saxon grave was discovered at Upper House (see) in 1850. The **name** is of Anglo-Saxon origin and is derived from Beornwulf's (brave wolf) town (DUIGNAN), or Beornwulf's estate (NSJFS 1981 p2) or farmstead (BAH p7) (SPN p15), or tun (SSE 1996 p10). The village was identified by Dugdale and Shaw with the Beorelfestune mentioned in the will of Wulfric Spot (c1002), founder of Burton Abbey (SHC 1916 p25) (BAH p7) (SSE 1996 p10). The manor of Bernulvestone appears in DB. Barlaston has since appeared as Berleston (1167) (SPN p15). In the C12 Barlaston was covered by or close to the New Forest (see) (BAH p9). There was a **church**, St John the Baptist, NE of Barlaston Hall, in medieval times (a chapel was built at Barlaston in 1225 - TTH p27) and some work of that period remains in the present tower. The rest of the church was rebuilt in c1762 and again in 1855. Owing to mining subsidence this church was abandoned and a new one built and opened in 1984 on the S side of Station Road, 0.75m to the S (St John the Baptist, Barlaston. Rev Godfrey Simpson). The parish feast was on the nearest Sunday to St Peter's day in the mid C19 (W p411). Another account says C19 wakes were held at the feast of the nativity of St John the Baptist (June 24) (BAH p37). Barlaston retains a large picturesque **village green**, a relic of common pasture, in spite of the Inclosure Acts (BAH p9) (LGS p77). The **London-Carlisle road** took a course through Barlaston until c1600 when it was transferred to the higher route through Tittensor (VCH vol 2 p278). The

North Staffs **Railway** line opened southwards from Stoke in April 1848. The station at Barlaston, put up in July 1848 after the villagers petitioned for one (BAH p33), was known as Barlaston and Tittensor Station until renamed Barlaston Station in 1972 (SN June 18 1998 p16p). After its arrival Barlaston developed as a residential area for some pottery manufacturers. A wall post box with 'VR' inscribed on it still (1997) remains by Orsett House, Station Road, by the station. **Newspaper**. The Stone Gazette and Meir, Eccleshall and Barlaston News, founded May 14 1937 ran until at least March 18 1938 (SHJ spring 1996 p25). For a **sampler** made at Barlaston see STM April 1966 p42 il. **Natives and visitors**. A little boy, **John Cheadle**, was killed by a bowling green roller in Barlaston in 1737 (BAH p38). **Francis Wedgwood** of Etruria Hall (see) built Upper House (see) in Barlaston; his grandson, **Josiah Clement Wedgwood**, born at The Lea (see) was created Baron Wedgwood of Barlaston in 1942. **John Masefield** OM (1878-1967), Poet Laureate, is said to have stayed with the Warners at The Mount by the Duke of York Inn (local info).

Barlaston Common Common 2m ENE of Barlaston, comprised 52 acres in 1966 (BAH p21).

Barlaston Hall Situated in a commanding position overlooking the Trent Valley on the SW side of Barlaston old church. Built in 1756-1758 for Thomas Mills (1717-1804), an attorney from Leek, probably to designs by architect Sir Robert Taylor (1714-1788). It is in the Palladian style and has been considered one of the best examples of country villas which Taylor pioneered. It has also been considered one of a group of polygonal houses of the mid C18 in NW Midlands; The Grove, Market Drayton is another. The hall is famous for appearing on Josiah Wedgwood I's Frog dinner service for the Empress Catherine of Russia 1773. The house was stuccoed in the late C18: It is said a Duchess of Sutherland returning to the ducal seat at Trentham then remarked that she thought the house vulgar on account of the red brick being on show. On hearing the story the hall owners duly had it rendered in stucco. The stucco was removed in WW2 because it was felt the house was an eye-catcher to enemy aircraft (OVH pp65,-66). Mills' daughter married Ralph Adderley. On Adderley's death in 1868 it passed to his nephew Ralph Broughton. The hall was leased to a series of tenants, including William Brownfield (1812-1873) pottery manufacturer who lived here from 1869 to his death (POTP p53), and JC Wedgwood (later Lord Wedgwood) (1872-1943). In the 1920s and 1930s it was occupied as the Lichfield Diocesan Retreat House. In 1931 (SN July 1 1994 p13p) or in 1937 (SSBOP p81) (BAH p35) the hall and estate were bought by Josiah Wedgwood & Sons Ltd. In WW2 it was used by the Bank of England (SVB p27) (OVH p69). Wedgwood Memorial College occupied the hall between 1945-49 (BAH p38) before moving to The Limes, Barlaston, in 1950 (see Estoril); thereafter the hall lay derelict. By 1968 it was showing the first signs of neglect and Wedgwood Ltd announced its intention to seek permission to demolish it, for it was considered to have no future on account of subsidence from proposed extensive coal mining. In 1975 a public inquiry led by SAVE Britain's Heritage stopped demolition. After another public inquiry in 1981 it was sold in Sept 1981 to SAVE Britain's Heritage for £1 on condition that the charity restore the building within five years or else Wedgwood's would have it back - for £1 (OVH p62) (ES June 25 1981 p1p) (SN July 1 1994 p13p) (CL July 30 1998 p54). Structural restoration of the hall, including a concrete raft to prevent it from subsiding, had started by at least 1984. By 1992 Barlaston Hall Trust, in which SAVE had vested the house, had run out of funds to restore the interior of the hall, and it was sold to James and Carol Hall; they completed the restoration work and were living at the hall by c1996 (CL July 30 1998 pp52-55pcs) (The Sunday Telegraph Dec 19 1999 Review p17). A replica of the hall in a large dolls house, commissioned by Elizabeth Adams in 1979, completed by Peter Wall in 1981, is on show at the Potteries Museum (ES Jan 1 1994 p24pc). (BAH pp22-24) (CL April 18 1968 pp975-979 ps of hall, and rococo overmantel in N room, chimney piece in the W room) (STMSM Jan 1974 p20p) (SSBOP p81p in 1913) (SHJ vol 1 pp26-41) (CL March 26 1992 p68p) (The Times Dec 16 1995 weekend section p12) (OVH pp62-74 pcs). There is a local tradition that the hall is haunted a C18 old lady who sits by candle light in a window (local info). The park was probably laid out at when the hall was built. Contains a series of pools, the upper two separated by a sham bridge (BAH p24). The house originally had no gates, wall, or fence, and simply a stretch of lawn running back from the road; a rare phenomenon in England for a Palladian house; on the E coast of America it is common (OVH pp64-65).

Barlaston Manor House Formerly situated E of Barlaston old church. From 1086 for 500 years the overlordship of the manor of Barlaston was held by the de Stafford family. In the earlier C14 it was held of the de Staffords by the Corbets. The Bagnall family, yeoman farmers, were tenants of the house from

at least 1433 to the early C17: By the mid C17 it was known as Bagnall's Farm. The Staffords sold the manor to the Cavendish family of Welbeck Abbey (Earls of Newcastle) in 1578. The manor was sold to John Bagnall (a kinsman of the earlier Bagnalls), a draper of London, in 1671. He was the first lord of the manor to reside here. With the marriage of Esther, granddaughter of John Bagnall, to Thomas Mills in 1742 the manor passed to Mills (BAH pp19-21,24). He built Barlaston Hall (see).

Barlaston Park Housing estate of some 200 houses nearly 1m N of Barlaston. Built as a model village for workers at the new Wedgwood (see) factory slightly to the W. The land for both factory and model village was part of the Barlaston Hall estate and had been purchased by Josiah Wedgwood & Sons Ltd in 1937. The model village was laid out to plans of Louis de Soissons, the architect for Welwyn Garden City, Herts, in 1938-39. In its early years the village was known as Wedgwood Garden Village (Staffs County Handbook c1958 p77) (BAH p36) (The Story of Wedgwood. Alison Kelly 1975 p64). Other streets to the E and N were built by the council at a slightly later period, for instance Ivyhouse Drive was built by 1951 (local info).

Barleighford Crossing point over the Dane over 0.75m NW of Heaton, bridged by 1752 (VCH vol 7 p187). Barleighford Farm, to the NNE in Ches, is an ancient homestead with an oak-panelled and curious interior. It became attached to Swythamley in c1700 by an heiress marrying into the Trafford family (OL vol 2 p86). Has also appeared as Barley-ford.

Barley Fields Former hamlet 3.5m SW of Rolleston, formerly in Anslow township in Rolleston ancient parish. There was a hamlet at Barley Fields in medieval times (ANS p9).

Barmore 1m E of Lichfield cathedral.

Barn Farm On W side of Clayton Road, Clayton. Built in 1878 and replaced a house of 1688, which may have been the house called Clayton Hall in 1817, which had been the seat of the Lea family (VCH vol 8 p78 note). To the N, in the 1950s, was a barn with a tablet with the date 1740 and the initials 'S.L.M.' (VCH vol 8 p78). There was an old barn which belonged to Barn Farm, which was said to have been destroyed by fire by 1933. It was, according to a small board which hung in the barn, built in 1656 by Mr Clayton Lea. He was grandfather of Rev Samuel Lea, who purchased it in 1736 (NSFCT 1933 p175).

Barnfields Industrial area SSW of Leek. Barnfields Farm E of the Newcastle road, built on the former common land of Leek Town Field, evidently existed by 1675 (VCH vol 7 p89). The area to the S was developed as an industrial estate from the later 1970s (VCH vol 7 p98).

Barnfields House 1.5m N of Ipstones. On NE side of Combes Valley (TOI p11).

Barnfields Farm Lost farm at Wildwood, at SJ 946207, in Baswich or Berkswich parish. A supermarket for the new suburb of Wildwood was built on the site in the 1970s. The farm was built in the late C18 by a member of the Twigg family and it remained Twigg property until the early C20. It was built near an ancient barn (from probably where comes the name 'Barnfields') with medieval stonework with scratch dials and a possible lepers window in the end wall. This barn may have had a connection with the Holy Sepulchre Hospital (see), a medieval leper hospital at Radford, and may represent the site of the hospital (BERK2 p140p). In 1841 the Twiggs built a game larder at the end of the barn which incorporated a Norman doorway from St Mary's church, Stafford (BERK2 pp139,140p). (Advertiser. Aug 18 1966 p11).

Barngates Former small district of Leek inhabited by 1638 which grew on the former common land of Leek Town Field (VCH vol 7 p89). It was probably in the Barngate Street area 0.25m W of the town centre.

Barnhurst Former estate 1.5m N of Tettenhall, in the Pendeford division of Tettenhall ancient parish (W p207). The name is from the tithe barn of the canons of Tettenhall Collegiate Church sited here (HOPTT pp66,84). Others have interpreted Barnhurst as the 'woodland cleared by burning' (DUIGNAN) (SPN p143), or from Bainhurst, 'hill of the burnt wood,' a prominent burnt tree used as a marker on an ancient trackway (SPN p144). The estate or submanor of Barnhurst was held by the prebend of Bovenhull or Bovenhill and was the residence of its prebendary. It was tenanted by the Barnhurst family (HOPTT p84) by at least 1327 to 1521 when it was sold to James Leveson of Wolverhampton. In the C16 Barnhurst passed from the Levesons to the Cresswells. In c1726 they sold it with the prebends of Bovenhill and Pendeford to Samuel Hellier of the Wodehouse, whose descendents sold it to Wolverhampton Corporation in 1867: The Corporation had built a sewage farm on part of the estate by 1870 (HOPTT pp66,84,85,89) (VCH vol 20 p20-21). (SHOS vol 2 p201). A site at Barnhurst was turned down for an airport in favour of Pendeford as it would have taken too long to drain the ground (BCM 1971). The former rural area about the site of Barnhurst Hall is now (1995) a residential suburb that rarely goes by the name of Barnhurst.

Barnhurst Hall Former Elizabethan hall 1.5m N of Tettenhall. Barnhurst farm can be traced from the later C13 (VCH vol 20 p12). It stood on the E side of Barnhurst Lane S of The Droveway (VCH vol 20 p4 see map). The Barnhurst estate belonged to the Levesons from before Edward VI's reign (HOPTT p85) and the Cresswell family from at least 1540. The Cresswells were 'Merchants of the Staple' or 'woolstaplers' and members of this family seem to have lived here until the 1680s or 1690s (VCH vol 20 p21). (WJO July 1905 pp183,184p). The hall was occupied by the Southwicks from at least the C17, the last member of which died in 1886 (OHW pl13). Barnhurst Farm or Hall, a brick house probably of C18 with a service wing probably encasing a timber framed building, was demolished in 1963 and the present (1980) Barnhurst Farm built on the site (VCH vol 20 p21 p of the old hall c1962 facing p65). A portion of the moat, the square, brick gatehouse with a date stone 1602, and a dovecote survived long after the Elizabethan hall with which they were co-eval (SHOS vol 2 p202) (HOPTT p89 il frontispiece) (LGS p233) (HOWU p11lp in 1961). The gatehouse was demolished in 1961 (VCH vol 20 p21) or in 1963 (TCOP p97p). The dovecote still (1990) remains and has given its name to the 'Dovecotes' area of the new housing estate, built on the site of the former Wolverhampton Airport at Pendeford (TCOP p97). Part of the moat survived until filled in for the new housing estate in the early 1970s (SSAHST 1982-3 p52). Christian open-air services for the residents of the new housing estate were held at the dovecote from 1978 to 1979 (VCH vol 20 p41).

Barns Farm On N side of Barns Lane 1.25m NE of Rushall. Dates back to at least 1742 (SNAR p57).

Barns Lee House 2m NNW of Rudyard, S of Leeside, in Horton ancient parish. The house, which is partly C17 (VCH vol 7 p67), was in existence by 1727. Seat of Mrs Sarah Bostock Haworth before her son, John, built Cliffe Park Hall, to where she and he moved c1811 (RL pp5,13-14). Has also appeared as Barnslea.

Barnswood Former estate and farmhouse 1m SE of Rushton Spencer. Formerly in Rudyard township in Leek ancient parish. The name is from Bernardscroft or Bernardswood, Bernard being probably the Saxon who first claimed the spot. There was also a Bernards Moor (NSFCT 1905 p160). The estate probably originated out of Rudyard manor. It was held by Dieulacres Abbey by 1246 until the Dissolution, thereafter it became a part of Rudyard manor. The present house stands on or near the site of one of the C17 or earlier origin which was demolished possibly when the Leek-Macclesfield road was realigned in 1808 (VCH vol 7 pp216-217,218) (RL p5).

Barr A ward of West Bromwich borough, created in 1928. Encompasses the Hamstead area which was taken into the borough from Perry Barr urban district in 1928 (VCH vol 17 p46).

Barr Beacon Hill nearly 2m NE of Great Barr, 650 feet (TBS p7), or 700 feet (MR p163), or 744 feet (notice on Barr Beacon), or 750 feet (HOWW p16) above sea level. Reputedly Barr Beacon is the highest peak on its longitude before the Urals are reached (info Peter Smith): Shaw claimed the top had a panorama of 15 counties (SHOS vol 2 (2nd) p105). The Malverns (HOWW p2), Birmingham city centre, and the Shropshire Hills can be seen from the summit.
EARLY. Three objects of prehistory origin were found in 'a field near Benbeacon, not far from Sutton Coldfield' in 1877 (PASN series 2 vol 7 pp267-268); Benbeacon can be identified with Barr Beacon (SSAHST vol 32 1990-91 p89). These are mentioned by Gunstone (NSJFS 1964 p24) - one survives and went to the Ashmolean Museum, it is possibly of **Bronze Age** origin and has been described as a macehead (Stone Axe Studies. Research Report 23 pp23-48) (BAST vol 58 p46). (ABI 1897 ed p244). Barr Beacon may have been the site of the archdruid's seat in ancient **British** times (W p552) (HAS pp4,7,8) (RS p9) (SOSH p12) or druids made sacrifices (HOWW p16). There is a Druids' Well in Sutton Coldfield Park. The **name** Barr or Bar is of Celtic origin meaning in Welsh 'the top or point of anything, a summit' (DUIGNAN) (NSFCT 1908 p133) (TBS p7) (LGS p78) (SPN p55). Dr Wilkes says barr may either be derived from the Hebrew 'bara,' a wild uncultivated field, or 'barah' to eat, refresh themselves, or to purify, sacrifices, purifications being made here by the British priesthood (druids); or from the Saxon word 'beapurpe,' or 'bearew,' 'a grove or little wood' (SHOS vol 2 p103) (TBS p7). Flavel Edmunds considered the origin of Barr here to mean 'a bar, fence or gate' (TBS p7). A **Roman** coin has been found on Barr Beacon (SSAHST vol 32 1990-91 p89). Salmon, a C18 writer, tried to show that Barr Beacon was the real site of Letocetum (HOWW p19) (TBS p8), and drew attention to the 'lines' on one side of the hill enclosing a large camp in the form of a half-moon (HPPE p12).
1200 to PRESENT. Barr probably gave its name to the manors of Little and Great Barr. Barr Beacon formed part of Great Barr Common until the com-

mon was enclosed in 1799 (GBP) (ADY p19). As a **vantage point** the hill was used as a beacon for celebrations and to give warnings, probably only from the C16 (MOA p13). A beacon, according to tradition, announced the arrival of the Armada in 1588 (TBS p7) (WMVB p68; in 1988 a beacon celebrated its 400th anniversary); the arrival of Napoleon's troops in this country, if such an event should occur (Lloyds of Birmingham. Samuel Lloyd. 1907) (TBS p7) (WMVB p68); and Queen Victoria's Jubilee 1887 (Birmingham Gazetteer. June 22 1887) (TBS p7) (WMVB p68). C18 crowning features. In c1744 William Scott planted a clump of Scots Pine on the hill top (SNAR p101). The same or another Mr Scott planned to crown the ridge with a lofty gothic beacon of rough massy stone. By c1785 he had a flag flying from the prominence (SHOS vol 2 - 2nd p106) (GBP). In c1799 Sir Joseph Scott planted beech trees on the summit, some were still surviving in 1997 (notice on top of Barr Beacon). On Sept 23 1799 the Colours were presented here to the Walsall Volunteer Association (TBS p8). In 1800 Barr Beacon was occupied for a month by a detachment of Engineers taking the bearings of the different stations as seen from the summit for the Ordnance Survey (TBS p8). In 1897 the SSWWC built a storage **reservoir** on the hill (TBS p38). A rotunda to commemorate those from Staffs and Warws killed in WW1 was built on a piece of land on the summit given by Col J Wilkinson of Sutton Coldfield in 1918 (TBS p8) (ALOPP p7p) (SNAR p84p). By 1997 Barr Beacon had been designated a **Public Open Space**. By this time, however, the area had become a dangerous place to visit after dark and there were local requests for it to be closed at night to deter youths in cars and drug dealers meeting here (BBC 1 Midland Today. May 12 1997). **Visitors**. In the early C19 Sir **Rowland Hill**, founder of the Penny Post, when a teacher in Birmingham, brought a party of boys to the beacon and made them climb a pole here (Scott's flagpole?) in a competition with a rival school so as to avert a possible violent clash between the boys of the two schools (TBS p8). The pole was still standing in 1907 (GBP). The ridge has inspired a poem by **Harold Parry** of Bloxwich (see), entitled 'Beacon Edge.' The first verse goes

> The sunset brims on Beacon Edge,
> And leaves are touched with fire;
> Somewhere beyond that golden rim
> Lies hid our Love's desire

(SOB pp186-188).

Barr House Hamstead area, Great Barr. In the 1860s was a select lunatic asylum (TBS p26). In 1907 one of Dr Garman's children fell down a 50 feet well at Barr House, but was unhurt (TBS p38).

Barr Lea The name in the Middle Ages for the area between Aldridge Road, Streetly, and the village of Great Barr. Together with all the land between Sutton Coldfield it formed part of Sutton Chase (MOA p139) (ADY p19). It was common land by the C13, and is now covered by Pheasey housing estate (MOA p139). It appears to have adjoined, embraced, or become the common land known as Great Barr Common (see).

Barrow Bank Exists in the vicinity of Saxon Lowe (NSFCT 1926 p142).

Barrowhill House 0.75m N of Rocester, in Rocester ancient parish. The present house lies 0.25m N of the site of a Roman Camp at cSK 110400. The Roman camp is nearly seven acres in extent. Masefield, who thought it was the site of Roman Rocester, noted its rectangular lines were still traceable (LGS p203) but its true plan and date remain uncertain (NSJFS 1964 p33). (HOU 1886 p71) (VCH vol 1 pp192,346). Slightly to the N of the camp, or at the NW corner of it, is a mound excavated in 1870 and in 1894; some C1 AD Samian ware was found (HOU 1886 p71) (The Antiquary vol 27 p238) (NSFCT vol 27 p154. 1894 p155. 1912 p196. 1932 pp112-113) (NSJFS 1964 p33); the house is said to take its name from this mound (NSFCT 1932 pp112-113). Barrow is the local dialect for burial mound. Roman coins and pottery were found to the N of the house at approximately SK 110408 in 1872, according to 1882 OS map. The present house, which has also appeared as Barrow Hill, was built in c1780 (AUOPP p66p). It was occupied by William Sneyd (1767-1851), son of John Sneyd of Belmont Hall (see), and his wife Jane, prior to their living in Leek in the early C19 (SNEDE) (JSD p30p). In 1838 it housed some valuable pictures, there was one by Raphael (from the Orleans Gallery) - the dead body of the Saviour reposing on the Virgin's lap, and a van der Neer showing a beautiful landscape in the tints of the evening (AAD p294). It was sometime the seat of Mrs Whyte. By c1910 it was the seat of Capt AF Dawson (b1836), son of Henry Dawson of Barrowhill; the Dawsons were in occupation to least 1940 (SHBP p224) (AUOPP p66). By 1978 the house was the training school and clubhouse for Joseph Cyril Bamford (JCB) Excavators Ltd (BUBA p122). There is an ice-house at SK 110406 on NW edge of the house (IHB p392).

Barrow Hill (locally *Barrer Bonk* TB May 1988 p16). Dolomite mass forming a green boundary between Gornal and Pensnett, 583 feet high. The rock has been covered with layers of subsoil over thousands of years (TB June 1974 p11). It seems to comprise a western and an eastern hill or is one hill. It was anciently a part of Pensnett Chase. In the late C17 Plot, who found transparent stones like crystals on the hill (NHS pp175,180 tab ii fig 8), referred to 'two uniform barrows of rock,' perhaps a reference to burial mounds on the hill or the two hills themselves; the name 'barrow' suggests a burial mound on a hill. A burial mound on it is listed by VCH. (NHS p414) (SHOS vol 2 p233) (NSJFS 1965 p43). The name Barrow Hill appears on A Plan of the intended Extension of the Dudley Canal into the Birmingham Canal by John Snape 1785. The western hill had been much quarried by 1832 (SVS pp134,135). There was a rumour that Barrow Hill contained a burial chamber with hidden treasure which have driven men ill or mad looking for it (TB June 1974 p11). The view from the top includes the Clent Hills, the Clees, the Malverns, the Wrekin, and to the N the Sedgley-Dudley-Rowley Regis escarpment (WFK p37). In 1999 the hill, still of some considerable size, was a public park: Cavities of past quarrying, scarring mainly the W side of the hill, had returned to nature.

Barrow Moor W of Hardings Booth. Formerly in Alstonefield ancient parish.

Barrs Bank (locally *Barrs Bonk*). Pit mound or slag heap thrown up from Haden Hill No 1, Old Lion and Black Waggon Collieries in the late C19. Waterfall Lane Trading Estate now covers this high land mass (OS map Sheet 71.08). Has possibly been called Barracks Bank, a pit mound which was about to be destroyed in c1977 (TB Oct 1977 p1).

Barton Brook Runs on the S side of Main Street, Barton-under-Needwood. Joins the Trent near Tucklesholme (UNT).

Barton Gate Hamlet 1m WNW of Barton-under-Needwood, in Tatenhill ancient parish. The name is from a former entry into Needwood Forest (VCH vol 2 p350 see map), which was situated near the Top Bell Inn (UNT p4).

Barton Green On SW side of Barton-under-Needwood. There was a common of Tatenhill ancient parish here (HOPT vol 1 p135).

Barton Hall Brick house, with 11 bays (SHOS vol 1 p113) (BOE p66) (MR p29p), N of Barton-under-Needwood on the Dunstall Road. The hall was built in 1724 (UNT pp37,117p). From at least the 1830s to c1920 it was owned by the Fowler-Butlers (mems in Barton church) (UNT pp39,113). In 1851 it was the seat of LK Hall (W p18). In 1978 it was modernised by the then owner Stan W Clarke, later of the Knoll (see) (UNT p114). In the grounds is a deer-shelter dated 1724 (BOE p66) (MR p29p).

Barton House House on Station Road, Barton-under-Needwood. Built in c1840. Formerly called Barton Court, and the house is said to have served as a court-house. Occupied in 1881 by the county court Judge, Woodforde F Woodforde. Edward VII was a guest here of the White family in 1902, whilst staying at Rangemore. Occupied by members of the Morris family in the 1950s (UNT pp34,67,70,94,115).

Barton-in-Bradley The two houses - Lower Barton (see) and Upper Barton (see) - are 0.5m W of Bradley. The manor of Bernertone appears in DB and was identified with Barton-in-Bradley by Commander Wedgwood. Barton later appears as Becterton (1242), Bertherton (1305-1423), and Berton (1472) (SHC 1916 p169) (SPNO p134) (SSE 1996 p10). The name is perhaps a compound with the Anglo-Saxon personal name Beorht, meaning bright. The early forms of this Barton are too varied to give 'barley tun,' the usual derivation for a Barton (SPNO p134) (SSE 1996 p20).

Barton Old Manor House Barton-under-Needwood did not have a manor house (UNT p7). But the site of a house known as the Manor House is thought to have been in Hall Orchard, which seems to have been on the E side of Barton (HOPT p134): An early church at Barton is believed to have stood in the Hall Orchard area (UNT p5). The former Hit and Miss Inn in Manor Close off Short Lane, Barton, was formerly known as the Manor House (UNT p52).

Barton Park Medieval deer park, S of Barton Gate, enclosed out of forest, Barton-under-Needwood (UNT p4). It was created by Robert de Ferrers of Tutbury Castle (see), 1st Earl of Derby, d1139 (UTR p36), and was certainly in existence by 1297 (NSJFS 1962 p75) (VCH vol 2 p350). It appears to have descended with Barton manor. George Grenvile, one of the valets of the king's chamber, held the office of park keeper in c1537 (SHOS vol 1 p116). (HOPT vol 1 p134). The name Barton Park is preserved in a house 0.5m W of Barton-under-Needwood.

Barton Turn Hamlet 1m E of Barton-under-Needwood. Ballast pits near the station were excavated in c1851 and a number of urns and two iron knives found (HOBT p189 note) (VCH vol 1 p204) (NSJFS 1964 p15). At first the finds were thought to be of British or Roman origin, but were later considered to be Saxon (BTIH p11). The name, which has also appeared as Barton

Turning (W p605) and Barton Turns (UNT p25), is from the 'turning around' of barges on the Trent and Mersey Canal in a wide, basin-type stretch of the canal after delivering to a wharf here (UNT p25). Or from the turnpike on Icknield Street. The Birmingham & Derby railway line through Barton Turn opened on Aug 5 1839. The first official train on the track was hauled by a locomotive called 'Tamworth' another locomotive used on the line was called 'Barton.' The station at Barton Turn known as Barton and Walton railway station, opened in 1840, closed in 1957 and was demolished some years later (IAS p131) (UNT pp33,88p of the station). The mission chapel, St James, built in 1880 by Lady Hardy of Dunstall Hall, in memory of her son Lieut Henry John Hardy (d1879 in the Zulu War), was being used as a playschool nursery in 2000 (The Way for the Millennium. 2000. pp25-26). For the Anne Statham case see Wychnor Bridges.

Barton-under-Needwood Large village 17m ESE of Stafford, by Barton Brook on slightly rising ground on the western side of the Trent a little over a mile from the river in a level valley (HOPT vol 1 p134) (UNT p1). Former township and chapelry in Tatenhill ancient parish (W p605).

EARLY. An eleven-inch tooth of an **Ice Age** mammoth was discovered in a quarry near Barton-under-Needwood. Some years after this discovery, in 1993, a two-foot tusk section of the same or another Ice Age mammoth was discovered near the same spot as the tooth. Both artifacts went to the Potteries Museum (ES Sept 4 1993 p8p of the tooth). The ashes of 15 people from a **Bronze Age** cemetery were found in cremation pots in summer 1996 (Daily Telegraph Aug 15 1996 p21) at Graycar Business Park, Barton. It is rare to find a flat cemetery of this period, with no mound, outside southern England. Food vessels of C2 AD, suggesting evidence of a **Roman** settlement, have also been found in the area (ES Jan 18 1997 p11). At SK 195176 is an open U-shaped enclosure crossed by irregular ditch lines. S of the village at SK 186176 is a small square enclosure of uncertain date, also two narrow rectangular enclosures at SK 191174 (NSJFS 1964 p15). In 1783 five urns of ancient date were found S of Barton Grammar School at cSK 190182 and later destroyed (SHOS vol 1 p116) (HOPT vol 1 p10) (NSJFS 1964 p15) (UNT p2).

900 to 1500. It is believed the Saxons of a settlement at Catholme, 1.25m away (excavated 1976), migrated northwards and founded Barton (SVB p29). The **name** was formerly just Barton, a Saxon word meaning a fold-yard (SHOS vol 1 p113). Or Barton means 'Barley town or farm or tun' (DUIGNAN) (SVB p31) (SSE 1996 p10) (SPN p15), or a rickyard (DUIGNAN) (LGS p78) or 'outlying grange' (HOPT vol 1 p136) (SL p57) (MR p323) or a fort-settlement (MR p29); the addition of 'under Needwood' is recorded from 1280, being officially adopted in 1377 (UNT p2) (DUIGNAN) (SVB p31) (SSE 1996 p10) (SPN p15). Saxon finds have been made at nearby Barton Turn (see). The **manor** is mentioned in a charter of 942 (SSE 1991 pp7,8. 1996 p10). It later appears in DB. The copyhold manor of Barton in Edward I's reign (then part of the Duchy of Lancaster), was held by certain rents of assize, together with a rent of six hens and one pair of spurs, six dozen arrows and one pound of pepper, and other services (SCSF pp120-121). The manor passed to the Crown in 1399 when Henry Bolingbroke, Earl of Lancaster, succeeded to the throne. In 1629 Charles I sold it to the city of London. Later, it passed to Sir Edward Bromfield, whose son, John Bromfield, succeeded as lord in 1660. In 1733 it passed through marriage to William Busby. In the later C18 it passed to Eusebius Horton of Catton, in whose family it remained for many years (UNT p7). The custom of Amabyr, which gave rise to the consequent custom of Borough English prevailed at Barton (SCSF p121). There was a **church** at Barton by 1157 (HOPT vol 1 pp15,25). The present church, St James, S of Main Road in the centre of the village, was built in 1517-1533 at the expense of Dr John Taylor, chaplain to Henry VIII (BOE p66). The **wakes** at Barton were held on the first Sunday in August (UNT p6). The interest from Henry Leese's charity was distributed at Barton Wake (HOPT vol 1 p155). For **fairs** Cooke gives May 3 (for cattle and sheep), and Nov 28 (if Sunday the Saturday before) (for cows) (SCSF p98) (UNT p6). There was a fair in 1792 (OWEN), but not by 1888 (LHE p264). **Bishop Langton** visited Barton-under-Needwood on Jan 16 1319 (SSE 1994 p4).

1500 to PRESENT. A **grammar school** at Barton was founded by Thomas Russell (c1529-1593) of the Drapers' Company of London in 1593, a probable native of Barton (HOPT vol 1 pp150-151) (UNT pp19-21). The Drapers' Company, in accordance with Russell's wishes, administered the school until shortly after the 1870 Education Act (UNT p20). Until then they were appointing the master, but had entrusted the management of the school to a local committee of 12 (LHSB 14 p18). The old school of C15 origin, which was formerly known as Barton Free School, was replaced by the present building (the present infant school) on N side of Station Road in 1885. Russell's name has been given to Barton Infant and Junior Schools (SVB pp30-

31) (UNT pp20,115). A **sermon in the church** on Good Friday paid for out of the charity of William Key, keeper of Barton Ward of Sherholt Lodge (d1651), still persisted in 1995 (HOPT vol 1 pp152-153) (SVB p30) (UNT p21). Barton was described in 1692 as 'a good country town and hath several gentlemen and freeholders in it...' (ESNF p17). It became a separate ecclesiastical parish in 1796 and a civil parish in 1866 (GLAUE p402). The village **workhouse**, in existence by the early C19, was in Wales Lane. It also housed a lock-up and was demolished in the 1960s to make way for Collinson Road (UNT pp33,60p). For Barton railway station see Barton Turn. The custom of **well-dressing** was observed at Barton (SCSF p30). Barton-under-Needwood is remembered in this rhyme

> Barton under the Needwood,
> Dunstall in the dale,
> Tatenhill for pretty girls,
> and Burton for good ale.

another version is

> The merry Bell of Barton
> and Dunstall in the dale
> the pretty girls of Tatenhill
> and Burton famed for ale.

(HOPT vol 1 p5) (SJC pp2,3) (UNT p8). Barton **Civic Society**, which takes an interest in local history, was founded in 1974 (info Arthur Kennedy). **Natives and visitors. John Taylor.** Some time after 1485 Henry VII, was hunting in Needwood Forest and became separated from his party. At Barton he was shown triplets, the sons of Joan Taylor and her husband William (UNT pp6,15-19), a poor Barton tailor (LGS p78) (SL p87), or a forest game warden (SVB p30). The king was so impressed he paid for their education; triplets were then a rarity and a sign of the Holy Trinity (SVB p30). The boys were born at the family home, which probably lay in area NE of the church, in c1480 (UNT p15). All three became doctors of Canon Law (SVB p30), but the younger two, Rowland and Nathaniel (UNT p15), did not come to such prominence as the eldest, John (d1534). He became an LL.D. at both Cambs and Oxon universities. He was Rector of Sutton-Coldfield in 1516; Archdeacon of Derby and Buckingham; Prolocutor of the House of Convocation in 1515; Master of the Rolls from 1527 to 1534; chaplain to Henry VIII on his visit to the Field of the Cloth of Gold; English ambassador to foreign courts. He is also attributed with building the core of the present Barton church; begun in 1517; his initials and the year 1517 appear on the tower S wall (BOE p66) (SVB p30) (CHMS p18), or restored by Taylor in 1519 (SL p87): And or entirely rebuilt or finished in 1533 for the date 1533 appears in the E window (LGS p78) (SGS p56). A C17 timber-framed cottage on the N side of Main Street near the junction of Dunstall Road is reputed to have been the home of John Taylor (UNT p120). Taylor died in 1534 and although there is a monument to him in St Anthony's church, Threadneedle Street, London, there is no trace of his burial place. Some claim he was murdered, if he fell out of royal favour; and that his will may have been a forgery (UNT p18). A bricked-up arch in the outer S wall of the chancel of Barton church is said to have been intended for Taylor's burial-place (LGS p78), whilst an internal arch presently (1989) containing the organ on the N side is said to have been for his tomb (CHMS p18). Taylor's initials and his coat-of-arms, with three babes' heads and two Tudor roses occur in several places about the church. There is a Latin inscription on four shields above the nave arcades which relates to Taylor. The story of the triplets is depicted in a wood carving on the staircase of Dunstall Hall (IVNF); the present High School in Barton bears John Taylor's name (UNT p18). (NHS p277) (SHOS vol 1 p114) (SMC p166) (HOL p213) (GNHS p146*) (W p605) (NSFCT 1912 p194) (KES p28) (Weekly Sentinel Nov 20 1964) (A Short History of John Taylor. Alison Wood. 1981) (LTD p117). Sir **Walter Walker** lawyer and advocate to Katherine, Queen Consort of Charles II was born at Barton, where it is conjectured, he was interred. His son was created a baronet in 1679, and the title became extinct in 1692 (HOPT vol 1 p157). **Catharine Mewis** of Barton, born on Dec 8 1802, daughter of William and Mary Mewis, was deprived of her eyesight on April 8 1809. Extraordinarily, she regained her eyesight for Sundays. Four surgeons tested her eyes and they verified the claim (SMT Tract 1 pp3-16) (SMC p113). A 16-page pamphlet about her was published by G Wilkins of Derby in 1810 (HOPT vol 1 p147). Wearing a green silk scarf over her eyes Catharine remained a celebrity bringing many visitors to Barton until her death from an unknown cause on May 8 1828 (UNT p32). Henry Whapples of Wales Lane, Barton, is said to have been a survivor of the Titanic, which

sank in 1912 (UNT p67).

Barton Ward One of the five wards of Needwood Forest. First mentioned in c1263. The heirs of the Somerville family were the hereditary foresters of the ward. Barton ward was bounded on the W side by the Lin Brook and on the N by Aylewardsley Way, the other sides formed the SE edges of the forest and comprised six miles and 1,195 acres (HCT p366) (HOPT vol 1 p159. vol 2 p223) (VCH vol 2 pp349,352). William Key, (d1651), keeper of Barton Ward (HOPT vol 1 p152) lived at Sherholt Lodge (SVB p30).

Basford Former hamlet overlooking the Fowlea valley, now a suburb between Newcastle-under-Lyme and Hanley, 0.75m SW of Etruria. Formerly partly in Penkhull-with-Boothen township in Stoke-upon-Trent ancient parish and partly in Wolstanton ancient parish. Poulton-Smith mistakes this Basford for the DB Basford (SPN p15). Ford is possibly from a ford in the Fowlea Brook (SSE 1996 p20). At Basford Bank (SJ 862468) was a turnpike (IANS p19). Between March and June 1888 novelist HG Wells stayed with William Burton (1863-1941), a ceramic chemist and an old college friend, at his terraced house, 18 Victoria Street. Here he is said to have written the short story 'The Cone,' set in Shelton Bar Ironworks. He described his time at Basford in 'How I Died' (1898) and in a letter to AT Simmons, Sept 1889, in the Wells Archive. In his later works 'In The Days of the Comet' and 'The New Machiavelli' Basford Bank is Clayton Crest (Certain Personal Matters. HG Wells 1898 p274) (HOE pp188,189) (Arnold Bennett and HG Wells. Harris Wilson. 1960 p274) (The Wellsian. spring 1980 pp1-5) (ES March 5 1996 p5). By 1985 there was a plaque on 18 Victoria Street telling of Wells' association with the house (POTP p54). Basford is Pireford in Arnold Bennett's novels (Arnold Bennett and Stoke-on-Trent. EJD Warrilow. p122). In 1915 Basford became a separate ecclesiastical parish (GLAUE p402). An housing estate here was bombed in January 1941 (TSS p117p).

Basford Small hamlet overlooking the Churnet valley 1.5m ESE of Cheddleton. Formerly in Cheddleton township and ancient parish (W p763) (CVH p21). The manor appears in DB as Becesword and Bechesword (NSFCT 1906 p168). Basford later appears as Barkeford (1199) (SSE 1996 pp10,20; Pafford seems to have mistaken this Basford for the Potteries Basford), Beresford (late C15 and C16) (NSFCT 1906 p168), and Basford Green. The name appears to be of Anglo-Saxon origin. If from Becesword then 'Bece' is 'beech tree' and 'word' is 'worth, land or farm,' so 'land at the beech tree.' Later 'worth' was changed to 'ford' (NSFCT 1906 p168). It is possible that DB was wrong and 'word' or 'worth' should be 'ford' and that 'ch' should be 'r.' Or it could be that 'ford' was added to Bechesword and contracted to Beresford and then to Basford (CVH p22). Basford means 'birch thicket' (NSFCT 1991 p60). Or possibly 'Beorcol's river crossing' (SSE 1996 p10) (SPN p15). At SJ 989523 1m E of Cheddleton or 0.5m W of Lowerhouse Farm is a cross on three circular steps. Is probably of early C14 origin. The shaft is six feet and 4.5 inches high, and a fragment of the shaft, two feet eight inches long, was lying nearby before the cross was restored. The cross is usually known as the 'Butter Cross.' It is said in the Great Plague butter or other farm produce was placed on its base and money left in vinegar in exchange (NSFCT 1922 pp152-153). Or it is one of three crosses on an ancient road between Dieulacres Abbey to Croxden or Calwich Abbey (NSFCT 1940 p33). It was restored at the expense of Mr William E Challinor of Pickwood Hall in 1926 (CVH p154) or in 1923 (NSFCT 1948 p123). (TOI p173) (PWNS p122p) (ES Dec 9 1989 p22p). It is probably the same as the wayside cross Masefield mentions at Basford Smithy, close to Cheddleton Railway Station (LGS p112). Les Lumsdon's 'Family Walks in the Staffs Peak and Potteries' 1990 shows a cross p44 which may be this or the one on Cheddleton Heath. George Fox, the founder of the Quakers, stayed with Thomas Hammersley of Basford in 1654 (VCH vol 3 p117) and or again in 1667 (SHC 1999 p162). A boggart was seen in Basford Lanes in the late C19 (NSFCT 1900 pp146-147).

Basford Bank Incline at Basford, near Etruria. Is Clayton Crest in the novels of HG Wells based on Staffs (ES March 5 1996 p5).

Basford Brook Tributary of the Churnet.

Basford Hall Basford Green. The Basford Hall estate came to the Debank family in c1809. Jane Debank (d1840) then brought it to a branch of the Sneyd family when she married, William Sneyd (1767-1851), son of John Sneyd of Belmont Hall (see). In the earlier C19 Basford Hall was the seat of their second son, Rev John Sneyd (b1798), and his wife. Their son, John William Sneyd (b1822) was of Basford Hall and the father of Ralph de Tunstall Sneyd of Fair View (see) (County Biographies: Staffordshire. Frederick B Ludlow. 1901) (JSD p63il in c1830). It was occupied by Rev S Bradshaw in 1851 (W p18). In 1926 the hall was inherited by Averil, a descendant of Thomas Sneyd (d1883) of Belmont Hall, younger brother of Rev John. In 1986 the house was owned by her son, Humphrey Scott-Moncrieff (SNEDE). However for some of the C20 the hall appears to have been tenanted; by 1948 it was a school for maladjusted children (NSFCT 1948 p124) (SSE 1997 pp69-79). The earthquake of 3.21pm July 3 1904 was felt at Basford Park (NSFCT 1905 p133).

GROUNDS. The Bathhouse, an elaborate, picturesque sham castle, is 400 metres SE of the hall. Built in 1841 by Rev John Sneyd. It once housed a swimming pool, waterwheel, underground passages, living room and kitchen, and was known by the Sneyds as 'the Castle'(DoE II) (F&G p389) (F pp317-318) (JSD p138p). At SJ 989513 is a domed ice-house cut into the side of the hill. Entry is by an archway at the top. Built by French POWs in c1824. The architect may have been Trubshaw (IHB p392). There is a Quaker burial ground at SJ 988513. Registers record 139 persons buried here including the Welsh Quaker preacher, John ap John, d1697 (TOI p38) (SSAHST 1970 pp40-41) (CVH pp52-53). There is a small stone building between the burial-ground and the farm-house (the old Hall). It is known as 'the old chapel' and was used as a meeting house. It is now a barn (SSAHST 1970 pp40-41).

Basford Hall Basford, near Etruria. It was the seat of Edward Adams (1803-1872) in 1851. He preferred to call this house Basford House, a name it formerly was called. He was succeeded by his eldest son Edward Richard Adams (1835-1895). Later, when the house was occupied by Charles Challinor (b1829), it was known as Basford Hall; Challinor died at Basford Hall in 1890. In WW1 it was used as a childrens home. There is another house called Basford House on the edge of the park (mem in St Margaret's, Wolstanton) (NSF pp42 note, 62) (HOE p136) (SHST pp579,580p) (WWT p of facing p67).

Basfordhurst Over 0.5m NW of Basford Green. House occupied by Mr Rider in 1906 (NSFCT 1906 p177). Has also appeared as Basford Hurst.

Basford Old Hall Basford Green. Is now a farm-house near Basford Hall (SSAHST 1970 p41) called Churnet Grange (see).

Bass Breweries Burton upon Trent. Bass' first brewery began as the adjunct to a town house, 136 High Street, bought in 1777. The Old Brewery as it was still called despite reconstruction in 1884-5, was demolished in 1971 (IAS p154). In the mid C19 Bass began expanding. The Middle Brewery at SK 247232 was built in 1853. The brewhouse was demolished in 1960. New Brewery, now Bass No. 2 Brewery, at SK 246230 on opposite corner of Station Street and Guild Street, started production in 1864 and is now the oldest of Bass's Burton breweries. Bass have more buildings in Wetmore Road, and at Shobnall (IAS pp154-155).

Basset's Heath Presumably waste land. It is said to have covered the W side of Drayton Bassett parish and covered land beyond the parish, as well (SHOS vol 2 p9). Reputedly, a wild boar was slain on Basset's Heath by Ralph Basset (d1390/1) of Drayton Bassett (see), 3rd Lord Basset (HOL p94) (HOWW p74).

Bassets Pole Former high pole on Warws Staffs border at the crossing of the Tamworth-Birmingham and London-Lichfield roads (SHOS vol 2 p9), near Canwell, 4m SW of Tamworth, in Drayton Basset parish. Lord Basset of Drayton Bassett is said to have erected it in 1201 (info from notice on site). The Basset family may have erected it to identify their mansion which was built in the middle of a wood. Or it was erected to mark many boundaries which meet here, for example, the counties of Warws and Staffs, the manors of Sutton Coldfield, Middleton, Canwell, Drayton Bassett, and the ancient limits of Cannock Forest and Sutton Chase (DUIGNAN), or it may also have marked ancient Bassets Heath (SPN p16). A tanner of Tamworth of the famous old ballad may have met and conversed with Edward IV at Bassets Pole (HS p149p). The pole is shown in Ogilby's 'Britannia' (1675) and on Plot's map. F Wolferstan, in a letter, dated 1756, wrote that the pole had been a noted mark and guide for travellers and had stood like a May-pole, 25 or 30 feet high. By the mid C18, he noted, it was worn to a stump, by which time there were plans by the parish or the lord of the manor to renew it (SHOS vol 2 p9). It may have been renewed; Yates' map of Warws (1787), shows a tall pole at that point (DUIGNAN). Currently (1997) the pole site is occupied by a stone or concrete finger post, facing Bassets Pole Inn car park. The post was erected to the memory of Capt JHW Wilkinson and his comrades of the Staffs Regiments who fell in WW1. One of the three signs around the base of the post was stolen in the early 1970s and was replaced by a modern one in Nov 1994. By late Jan 2000 there was a campaign to stop a proposed 175-acre business park being built at Bassetts Pole, for the area by then lay in a protected 'green belt' for Birmingham (Sunday Telegraph Jan 23 2000 p8).

Barnfield Wedgwood's Churchyard Works at Burslem was sited on it; the name still persists (ES Feb 22 1930 p3).

Baswich Ancient parish (sometimes called Berkswich alias Berkswick) (BERK p9) (SKYT p89), village and former township 1m NW of Walton-on-the-Hill. The village, which now forms one conurbation with Walton-on-the-Hill, Weeping Cross etc, lies on a promontory overlooking the confluence of the

Sow and the Penk. In the late C7 or early C8 St Bertelin is said to have had a hermitage on the site of the church at Baswich (BERK pp9,31). The parish was formed before 1086 (SHC 1916 p193). The present parish church, Holy Trinity, on the W side of Baswich Lane S of Dolphin Close, is of C12 origin, but was largely rebuilt in 1740 (VCH vol 5 p7). The manor of Bercheswic appears in DB. Later the name appears as Baswyche (1559), Baswiche (1617), and Baswich (Speed's map) (SPNO p30). The name appears to be a corruption of Berkswich (SKYT p89) which is a derivation of Anglo-Saxon 'Beorcal's dwelling' (MR p296) (SSE 1996 p10) (SPN p111). Near to Baswich House was the gibbet and stocks (SVB p169). Baswich parish council still (c1939) appoint a pinner, the late holder of that office had three cases in 40 years (FSP p52). Near the church salt was worked between 1894-1968 until it was discovered that its extraction was causing subsidence in Stafford (SVB p170) (MR p288) (BERK p42). Berkswich Local History Group, formed in 1992, have published BERK and BERK2. The group became Berkswich History Society in 2000 (info Geoffrey Allen). A woman has had paranormal experience at her home at Baswich; her house was built in the 1960s on farm land (MGH pp61-62).

Baswich Farm S of Baswich church. According to a tradition this house may have been the vicarage before it moved to Walton in 1841 (BERK pp28p,29).

Baswich House Built on the site of Weeping Cross Inn at the junction of the Stafford-Lichfield and Stafford-Cannock roads at Weeping Cross. Probably soon after 1813 the inn was either rebuilt or converted into a private residence, known as the 'White House,' by John Stevenson Salt (1775-1845) of London and Weeping Cross, a member of the firm of Steveson Salt and Sons, bankers in Lombard Street, London.

THE SALTS. John Salt's third son was William Salt (1808-1863), antiquarian, whose collection of Mss on Staffs history forms the basis of the Salt Library (see). John's eldest son, Thomas Salt (1802-1871) pulled down the White House in c1850 and had Baswich House built on or near the site of the White House (VCH vol 5 p4). Thomas' son Sir Thomas Salt MP (d1904), was created a baronet in 1899 and became 1st Baronet Salt of Standon and Weeping Cross. He was succeeded by his son Sir Thomas Anderson Salt (1863-1940), 2nd Bt, who was succeeded by his son, Sir Thomas Henry Salt (1905-1965), 3rd Bt, who in turn was succeeded by his son Sir Thomas Michael John Salt, (b1946), 4th Bt (Debrett's Peerage). On Sir Thomas's death in 1904 Helen, Lady Salt (nee Anderton, niece of Cardinal Manning) left Baswich House and moved to the manor house at Walton, later Walton-on-the-Hill. From 1904 until WW2 Baswich House was used as a boy's preparatory school. In WW2 the house was taken over by Chatham House School from Ramsgate, and used as an ARP post. In 1952 it was acquired by Staffs county council for use as a Police Motor Training Centre (VCH vol 5 p4) (SKYT p80) (BERK pp20-22p).

GROUNDS. In the 1960s the headquarters for **Staffordshire Police** was moved to new premises in the grounds of the house. The county police force was formed in Oct 1842. The South Staffordshire Constabulary had been formed in 1840 to police the area of S Staffs and was amalgamated with the new Force on its formation. Early headquarters were at The Green, Forebridge; later they were at St Martins Place, Stafford; from 1888 at Eastgate House, Eastgate Street, Stafford. The training of recruits was conducted at Forebridge Barracks on a site now occupied by the County Library in Friars Terrace. The Mounted (horse) Branch, formed in 1919, was abolished in early 2000. Women were entered into the force in 1921. The Motor Transport and Patrol Branch was formed in 1930. A Dog Branch was formed in 1955. The Staffs force were in a unique position from the mid 1860s to c1930 in that its police chose to wear a kepi (hat) for day duties and the helmet for night duty, whereas other forces preferred the helmet for all occasions (SVB p169) (STC p42p) (A History of Staffordshire Police. Commemorative Issue 1992). A police cadet hostel in the grounds in the 1960s was reputedly haunted, by, possibly, a man-servant at the house who hanged himself after falling in love with one of the maids; because their romance was forbidden by their employer (GLS pp83-84).

Baswich Priory Not the same as St Thomas' Priory at Baswich, as both are included in 'Medieval Monasteries and Minsters' HE Roberts (1949). This seems to be a reference to a large rectangular stone barn, ornamented in the C19 with a mock-Norman front and situated in a farmyard and used as cowshed. It was probably built with the stones from the old Baswich church (NSFCT 1949 p111).

Batchacre Former monastic estate 1.5m SSW of Adbaston. Some Roman finds have been made at Batchacre (SSC p130 in the intro) (GNHS p70). Batchacre has also appeared as Beacher and Badmak (OSST 1931 p30). It was a grange of Ranton Abbey in the Middle Ages (NSFCT 1927 p22). At the Dissolution Ranton's granges of Ellerton, Knighton and Batchacre with Flashbrook were purchased by Sir John Gifford whose grant is dated 1541. Thomas Roos of Laxton, Notts died in 1578 seized of Ellerton, Knighton, and Batchacre granges. These passed to his grandson, Gilbert, who sold them all in 1626. Batchacre then went to Gerard Fowke of Dunston, who in 1660, sold Batchacre to John Allen of Greys Inn (d1699). Allen's widow sold it to the Baduleys of Ellerton Grange. In 1719 it was sold to Richard Whitworth I of Adbaston Manor House. The occupiers of Batchacre from 1680 to 1683 were the Fletchers; Edward Adderley to 1704; John Spilsbury to 1725; James Bayley to 1730; James Addison to 1737; William Bagshaw (called Bawling Bagshaw because of his powerful voice) to 1754 after which Richard Whitworth III (b1737) took up residence in c1756. After his death in 1811 the estate passed to his cousin's son Lord Charles Whitworth, who resided elsewhere (AADB p26). After the dissolution the estate was considered in Adbaston parish and formed a township with Flashbrook, although some of it is said to have been situated in High Offley parish: It was taken wholly into High Offley civil parish in 1934 (GLAUE p418). By the early C19 it was considered extra-parochial by the owners, on account of it having been monastic property. This entitled them to exemption from payment of poor rates. In 1816 after an expensive law suit, it was declared rateable to the poor of Adbaston (W p382). Somner Billington says the case ran between 1817 to 1819 (AADB pp24-25). Previously, Richard Whitworth III liked to claim Batchacre was either in Staffs or Shrops whichever suited his purpose (NSFCT 1927 p40). The grange farmhouse may have stood on the site of the present Batchacre Hall (see). At Batchacre was a chantry chapel, which was being used as a barn in the C17 (NSFCT 1927 pp36-37). A map of 1775 shows a chapel at Batchacre, but this may have been one of the pseudo-antique monuments built by Richard Whitworth of Batchacre Hall (OSST 1949-50 p14).

Batchacre Hall Hall 1.5m SSW of Adbaston. Built by Admiral Richard Whitworth III (d1811), an eccentric, in c1756. Shortly after it was built Whitworth moved here from Adbaston Hall (OSST 1931 p29). The building incorporates or was built on the site of the grange farmhouse of Ranton Abbey, a house of C16 origin or earlier. Whitworth styled the new house 'Grange' or 'Park.' Among the farm buildings is a block known locally as 'The Barracks' which is probably a survival from monastic occupation (NSFCT 1927 pp15 il of in 1800 facing, 23,26). In 1795 Whitworth III was described as Captain of the Market Drayton troop of Volunteer Cavalry and his troops lodged at 'The Barracks' (AADB p23 p of Batchacre Hall). A Batchacre Troop totalling 40 is mentioned in the Army list in the early C19. It existed for only six years and little is known about it (FSP p63). The solitary ruins of a predecessor mansion to Batchacre Hall remained for Garner to see in the mid C19 (GNHS p547), or was this the porch to Gerrard's Bromley Hall? (SHOS vol 2 pl on p23 at back, excellent engraving showing layout of grounds at its height) (BOE p67).
GROUNDS. To the SSW of the hall Richard Whitworth III built an 80 acre reservoir or lake, by damming the Lonco Brook. It was to serve his proposed Bristol and Hull Canal. The canal was never built and Whitworth used the lake merely for recreational purposes and had a miniature battle fleet floating on it (VB p156). On an island in it, called Abbey Island, he re-erected Gerrard's Bromley Hall porch removed here after the hall was pulled down in 1760 (NSFCT 1947 p175). The porch is dated 1584 and is inscribed with the Gerrard motto 'BONO VINCE MALVM' and the Gerrard arms (SPJD pp64,65pc). It is known locally as 'the Castle' (AADB p27). The Countryman magazine called it 'the old castle' and it was perhaps brought here by Whitworth to help recreate Batchacre's monastic past (NSFCT 1927 pp39-40) (NSSG p3). There was a well, presumably in the lake, perhaps on the island, known as St Anns Well in the Lake or St Augustine Iron Spring (see). To the N by the hall, Whitworth built a look-out tower or obelisk and a mock fort with canons (F pp313,314). The last two have gone and the lake has dried up; Abbey Island is now (1977) represented by a hump in the ground (SGS p47). Raven says the fort was situated on an ornamental island in the lake (MR pp6-7).

Bates' Pool Tiny pool in Bagot's Park over 2m NE of Bagot's Bromley. It was possibly once spelt Betts Pool, after which an oak is named in Bagot's Park. (CCBO p26).

Bath Farm 1.25m SE of Bishop's Wood. Appears as The Bath on the 1834 OS map. A slate bath from this farm is now in the stable yard at Chillington Hall (BDH p228).

Bath Pool Pool 0.75m S of Kidsgrove. Lies on the watershed of England and water formerly drained away to the S to join the Trent and to the N to the join the Weaver. By 1812 it was a reservoir for the upper levels of the Trent and Mersey Canal. In 1889 or 1890 the pool along with the Clough Hall estate was purchased by a Manchester company who turned the hall grounds and pool into a public pleasure attraction: A pagoda was intended for the island in it, but it was never built (NSFCT 1990 p40) (Kidsgrove News April May

1998 pp8-11ps). Jason Skidmore aged 16 drowned in the pool on July 30 1995 (ES Aug 2 1995 p7). See also Clough Hall.

Bathpool Park Small park S of Bath Pool, Kidsgrove.

Bath Pool Valley A pass, a glacial meltwater channel, from the Cheshire Plain to the upper Trent Valley. Bath Pool and Bathpool Park are in it. The valley was called Bath Pool by John Dearden as early as 1962. He thought it may formerly have been called the Clough as Clough was the name given to Clough Hall, which was situated in it (TTTD p 207). Although the valley floor was considered low enough at its highest point for the Trent and Mersey Canal to pass through it, the summit level at 2km in length, was considered not long enough for a rise of eight locks, and tunnels through Harecastle Hill had to be built (NSJFS 1978 p31). For the same reason, and also due to the objections of the Kinnersleys of Clough Hall, the Macclesfield Potteries railway line could not at first be routed through the valley and a tunnel for that had to be built through Harecastle Hill (IAS p173). On Jan 14 1975 Donald Neilson (b1936) a serial killer known as 'the Black Panther' kidnapped Lesley Whittle, a 20-year old heiress of Highley, Shrops, and hid her at the bottom of a shaft in Boathouse Lane, Bath Pool Valley. He intended to ransom her for £50,000, but either by accident or design she died and was found in the shaft in March 1975. Neilson was captured in Mansfield, Notts, in Dec 1975, tried and sentenced in July 1976 (The Capture of the Black Panther: Casebook of a killer. H Hawkes. 1978) (MCGM pp114-115) (ES March 8 1995 pp10-11ps) (KAIW p21).

Bath Wood Wood 0.5m W of Hoar Cross Hall, in which is an alabaster bath (SVB 96).

Batmans Hill Hill and district at Bradley 1.25m SSE of Bilston. Batman's Hill is mentioned in 1655 (HC p48). At the iron works here on Jan 20 1903 there was a boiler explosion which killed four men - Henry Southall, James Warren, Edward Holloway, and Richard Cooper, and injured eleven (TB Feb 1993 p5ps).

Battle Cross Short stone pillar which stands in Paradise Walk on E side of the Manifold, Ilam, in the grounds known as 'The Ley' (STM Sept 1966 p34). The pillar was found in the foundations of a cottage during the rebuilding of Ilam in 1840. It may have some association with the fragment of a cross built into the S chapel of Ilam church. According to tradition Battle Cross (or known as Battle Stone and Cross Stone) is associated with a battle between the Saxons and the Danes (LGS p151) (VB p202) (PDS&C pp58,59p).

Battlefield Area on the Stourbridge road to the E of Wombourne, S of Rushford Bridge (VCH vol 20 p197) (TB Sept 1987 p16 see map). In Wombourne ancient parish. The name, in use by 1841, is probably from Battlefield Hill or Battlestead Hill another name for Soldiers' Hill (see), a burial mound (VCH vol 20 p197). Or it is said to have its name from a conflict in the Civil War (TB Aug 1978 p13), or where one of the forces camped prior to the battle of Tettenhall (SPN p146). George Thomas, one of the boatmen who murdered Christina Collins at Hoo Mill (see) in 1839, was born at Battlefield Terrace, Wombourne, in 1822 (TB July 1998 p25).

Battle Lane Obsolete name. Traditionally the spot where Sir Robert Mavesyn killed Sir William Handsacre, it might be near the High Bridge. It was somewhere in the manor of Hill Ridware.

Battlestead Hill Hill to E of Tatenhill. Perhaps named after the battle of the Standard (1138) to recognise the bravery of local men who fought in it (IVNF p323). Or perhaps between British and the Angles or the Angles and the Danes (MR p323). Here was an airfield in WW2; the planes landing on the grass (WMA p29, vol 1 p149).

Battlesteads Area of Alton. The name is preserved in a street on the W side of Alton village. May have taken its name from a suitor of 1298 called Robert Batayle, who may have lived here (HAF p56).

Bawd Stone A megalithic chambered tomb on the Roaches, at SK 00736205, 0.75m NNW of Upper Hulme (SMM p14 see map). It is near the Blue Hill Pits, a short distance S of Rock Hall, on the western ridge of the Roaches on a part where the range forks into an eastern and western branch (NSFCT 1913 pp161 p facing,162,164 p facing,168). Loxdale and other antiquarians dub it 'an undoubted British altar' (NSFCT 1884 pp21,22,24). The name is a corruption of Balderstone or Baal stone: the stone of the sun-god, Baal (NSFCT 1884 p24). Perhaps 'Bawd' is from 'bawdy' meaning indecent, or perhaps it is a colloquial form of 'bad;' in Christian eyes bawdy or bad (pagan) practices took place at the Bawd Stone. Or the name may be from Balder the Norse or Viking god, the son of Odin (DPMM pp95,96). The irregularly rounded block of gritstone weighing about 20 tons rests or balances upon a short edge of rock and then upon two upright and pointed stone pillars about 18 inches high. Probably was erected by the same peoples who made the Bridestones. In the early C19 the people of the surrounding farms took part in a ceremony at the stone each May Day. At these ceremonies the stone was white-washed with some ritual. There is enough space under the stone for one to crawl underneath (Scientific Rambles Round Macclesfield. Sainter. p42) (NSFCT 1913 p162). (DP p54 top il) (SLM April 1963 p) (VCH vol 7 p34). Bawd Stone perhaps is in astrological alignment with Summer Hill (see) to the NE; Serpent Stone (see); and a man-made cleft on Hen Cloud to the S (SMM p12) (DPEM p56) (DPMM pp92p,104). A few yards or metres S of the rock is a mound 40 or so feet in diameter. Surrounding the mound are two stone circles, one within the other. The circles are oval in shape (SMM p12). In the vicinity of the Bawd Stone was found a gold broach and a couple of sepulchral urns of the Celtic period (Some Random Thoughts etc). See also Baldstone, and Ballstone.

Bayer Hall Stood on the N side of Bayer Street, Roseville in 1904 (OS map sheet 67.08).

Bay Tree House Former C16 timber-framed house on E side of Erdington Road, Aldridge. The house was added to in the C18 and C19. In 1827 it became a school and for many years was run by the Butler family. The school was still running in 1881. The house was demolished in 1973 (SNAR p24), or in the late 1950s and an old people's home built on the site, which has taken the name of Baytree House (ALOPPR p98p).

Baytree House NW of Bloxwich.

Beacon A modern housing estate in New Invention (Selective Essays on Willenhall. David Potts. 1984. Copy in Willenhall library). Probably covers the area of the former Beacon Colliery.

Beacon Gate One of the five gates in Lichfield Town Ditch. In Beacon Street, Lichfield. It is recorded in the mid C13 and has also appeared as Beacon Street Gate. The gate was probably of wood (VCH vol 14 p40).

Beacon Hill Small hill over 0.5m SE of Rolleston.

Beacon Hill Hill 0.5m NE of Sedgley.

Beacon Hill Hill S of Hopton, 2m NE of Stafford. Formerly part of an estate which formerly belonged to the canons of St Thomas Becket Priory and was an extra-parochial liberty (HOT p30), or, and at some other time in the out-township of Hopton and Coton in St Mary's parish, Stafford. In the Civil War the royalists retreated to Beacon Hill after the battle of Hopton Heath and camped here on the night of March 19 1643; a large number of cannon balls from the battle have been found in the vicinity of the hill (SHJ winter 1987 p9). There is a tradition going back to at least the early C19 that the battle took place on the slopes of Beacon Hill on heathland called St Amon's Heath (see) (SHJ winter 1987 p1). White says the hill is distinguished by a vast collection of rocks on its summit, which was formerly crowned by a signal post for communicating alarm to the surrounding country (W p341).

Beacon Hill 0.5m SW of Congreve. At 378 feet high is one of the highest points in the area. An axe-head of Neolithic or Bronze Age was found at Beacon Hill in 1717 (VCH vol 5 p105) (BDH p18). A beacon was lit on the hill in July 19 1588 to warn of the approaching Armada (PVH p60). During the C17 the maintenance of a beacon near Congreve was the responsibility of Cuttlestone hundred (VCH vol 5 p105).

Beacon Park Lichfield's largest park. Situated W of Lichfield cathedral. In 1955 a leaf-shaped arrowhead of the Neolithic or Bronze Age was found in Beacon Park (NSJFS 1964 p28) (SSAHST 1980-81 p21). The park originated in land reclaimed out of Upper Pool, The Moggs, the grounds of Beacon Place, and the gardens formerly known as Museum Grounds and later as Museum Gardens (VCH vol 14 pp70,163). A public garden, the Museum Grounds, came into being with the erection of the library and museum here in 1859. The park was extended in 1891 and 1944 (VCH vol 14 p164). Thomas Rowley gave it a drinking fountain in 1863, JT Law gave it an ornamental fountain in 1871. E of the fountain is a statue of Edward VII, presented in 1908 by Robert Bridgeman. W of the fountain is a seven feet eight inch high statue of Commander Edward John Smith, captain of the Titanic. It is by Lady Kathleen Scott, widow of Capt Robert Falcon Scott, and in bronze. It was unveiled by Smith's daughter Miss Helen Melville Smith, aged 12, on July 29 1914 and stands on a pedestal of Cornish granite. Lichfield was chosen as the site because it is half way between London and Liverpool and would be easily accessible for American visitors, and is in the county of Smith's birth. A petition, signed by 73 Lichfield citizens, objecting to the statue was handed to the city council on June 17 1914 (KES p144) (VB pp27,28) (BOE p192) (MMM pp11-15) (STMSM Nov 1980 pp15-16p) (VCH vol 14 p163) (LAL p19p) (MR pp175,215) (COS p47p). Set against the E wall of the garden are the remains of a large stone carving showing the old seal of the Corporation. This came from the old Guildhall, demolished in 1846 (LAL p20p) (LPL). The Crimean War cannon and WW1 German gun were removed from the grounds for scrap in 1940 (VCH vol 14 pp163-164).

Beacon Place Beacon Street, Lichfield. Built in the late C18 by George Hand, a proctor of the consistory court, who was living in the Close by 1781. From

1827 it was the property of the Hinckleys. Enlarged in c1836. Sometime before 1848 it was renamed Beacon House. The house was sold to the Seckhams of Hanch Hall in 1881. The name was changed back to Beacon Place by 1897 when let to tenants. Used as offices in WW1. Sold by the Seckhams in 1922 to the War Department. Used by the Royal Army Service Corps in WW2. After being bought by the city council was demolished in 1964 (VCH vol 14 p70). At the end of the C19 its grounds had grown to nearly 100 acres (VCH vol 14 pp25,70). An ice-house is marked to the S of Beacon House on 1882 6 inch OS map (VCH vol 14 p26 see map). In the 1960s the grounds were incorporated into Beacon Park (VCH vol 14 p70).

Beaconside Suburb of E Stafford and new housing estate. The name, from Beacon Hill to the NE, appears to have been given to the site for the training college set up by English Electric for its apprentices prior to 1963. In 1963 the College became the Staffordshire College of Technology. In 1965 it started one of the first degrees in Computing Science in the country. In 1970 the College merged with a number of other technical and art colleges in North Staffordshire to form Staffordshire Polytechnic, now Staffordshire University (info Judith Robinson, Staffordshire University). Staffordshire Industrial Archaeology Society was founded by staff or students of the College of Technology in c1970; the society still (2000) has lectures in the Octagon Building of Staffs University at Beaconside (info Dr Anne Andrews). The Business Innovation Centre at Beaconside was the base by 2000 for Staffordshire Environmental Fund founded in 1998 under the Landfill Tax Credit Scheme (SLM April 2000 p56).

Beacon Stoop Highest of the Weaver Hills at 1217 feet (LGS p3), or 1205 feet (NSFCT 1881 p44) at SK 095464. Is incorrectly called The Walk on 1985 OS map 1:25,000; that hill is to the N.

Beakes, The House under 0.75m S of the Old Chapel, Smethwick. The name is perhaps derived from the Teutonic 'Beck' or 'Betch' signifying a brook or rill (STELE June 2 1951). On old maps can be seen a number of trees, which formerly lay on the lines of the county boundaries in this area. They were traceable through 13 fields and finally reached a sharp point of what appears on the maps as a bird's head and beak so that the name may be from the county boundary line here which makes a perfect representation of a bird's head and beak. At the 'mate mark' or extreme point of this 'bird's beak' was a holly bush formerly known as the Three Shires Oak (STELE June 2 1951. July 27 1956). When and by whom Beakes house was erected is not known; in the C17 and C18 it was the seat of the Hinckleys; Henry Hinckley, who came into the manor of Smethwick in c1710, lived here. It remained with the Hinckleys until 1798 when it was sold to Thomas Hanson of Smethwick House (STELE June 9 1951) (SHCB p4).

Beal Hill Rock feature in Churnet Valley in that part which falls away S of the Canton Pagoda in Alton Towers grounds. Here the ancient Britons conducted the worship of Beal or the Sun or Bala Rock; the name could be indicative of the Celtic worship of the Egyptian Toth (BATR).

Beam Hill N of Horninglow (c1887 OS map 6 inch).

Beamhurst Hamlet 1.5m WNW of Stramshall. Formerly in Madeley Holme division of Checkley ancient parish (W p760). On E side of the Tean. For a rhyme about Beamhurst see Checkley.

Beamhurst Hall Beamhurst. In 1851 it was the seat of H Mountford (W p18). (BS; spelt Beamhirst Hall).

Beamhurst Lane Tiny hamlet on W side of the Tean, 0.25m SE of Beamhurst. In Uttoxeter ancient parish.

Bean Farm House on left on the Cannock-Rugeley road from Cannock probably the oldest inhabited farmhouse on the Chase. Originally called Humphrey Moreton's Place. Moreton was a charcoal burner and woodsman in Henry VIII's reign. In 1595 it is recorded that it was occupied by James Brindley, a forest keeper to Thomas Paget. The land above the farm became known as Brindley Coppice, and later the road over the Coppice became known as Brindley Heath (PCC p75). Was Bean Farm on the site now called Bean Court not far from central Cannock?

Bear's Brook A tributary of the Blithe (SPNO p5).

Bearda House over 0.5m WSW of the hall at Swythamley. Formerly in Heaton township in Leek ancient parish. Is partly of C17 origin. In 1666 it was owned by the Tunnicliffe family (VCH vol 7 p186) (MIDD vol 4 p25p). There was a settlement known as Berdeholm in the Bearda area in 1340 (VCH vol 7 p186). This old form of Bearda may derive part of its name from Old Norse 'holmr' meaning raised ground in marsh land (SHC 1999 p7). (VB p213; thought the name was suggestive of Manx). Bearda Hill has a 1: 5.5 gradient (VB p213).

Bear Hill Open space at E end of Uttoxeter Market Place. Scene of bear baiting in Saxon times, later a pillory stood here. (NSFCT 1940 p37). Here was a house in which Dr Johnson of Lichfield (see) lodged; it is believed he made his penance in this area of the Market Place (HOU pp35,113).

Bearnett House House 0.75m WSW of Penn, off Lloyd Hill. Built in c1856 (TB July 1987 p11p). Has an Elizabethan-style facade (PONP p31). The grounds contained a gothic ruin called Badger's Folly (see).

Bear Pits Newcastle-under-Lyme. Permission was given to Thomas Hemmings to extract limestone from the Bear Pits. Bears often appeared at Newcastle fairs, and 'Bear Pits' may indicate where they performed. But there was a bear ring near the Butchery Pump in the Ironmarket (VCH vol 8 p54) (NUL p158).

Bearsbrook Tiny hamlet nearly 2m SSW of Church Leigh.

Bear's Brook Runs from Milwich joins the Blithe at Field.

Bears Hay House S of Hilliard's Cross on E side of Coventry Canal.

Bearstone Rock At Roach End.

Bearwood Hill Former incline and hamlet at the junction of the Birmingham-Dudley road and Bearwood Road, N of Newlands Green. In Smethwick township in Harborne ancient parish. It seems to have been the main centre of population of Smethwick before the C19. It was an inhabited area by 1278, and the name Bearwood Hill was in use by the early C18. At Bearwood Hill stood the Smethwick Cross in the C17 and early C18; it may have been a wayside cross, or just the crossroads here (VCH vol 17 pp88,89). The **name** is perhaps from a bear baiting ground adjoining Harborne almshouses at the rear of the free school. The bear ward or keeper lived on the steep hill, as it was then, near to the Sow and Pigs Inn at Smethwick. Hence the name Bear ward's Hill, since transformed into Bearwood Hill. It has been suggested that Bearwood was a corruption of Berrard or Beddard, a name borne by a family at one time living in the vicinity of Newlands Green. About a mile W of Castle Bromwich, Warws, there used to be a manor house known as Berwood Hall. The Berwood in this name, according to Duignan, means wood-wood (STELE Dec 1 1951). Or the name is from the Bear Inn (see below). The name appears as Berwood's Hill in 1852. From a map of 1859 the road from Cape Hill to Crockett's Lane then bore the name of Bearwood Hill, Crockett's Lane itself was Bearwood Lane (STELE Dec 1 1951). The present residential area (Birmingham A-Z 1995) of Bearwood to the S (0.75m S of Smethwick) is centred on the Bear Inn, at the junction of Three Shires Oak and Bearwood Roads. A Bear Inn has existed on this site since the late C17. In the later C18 this area was still extensive woodland and remained so until the late C19 (VCH vol 17 p96). The **church**, St Mary, on the corner of Bearwood and St Mary's Roads, was consecrated in 1888 (VCH vol 17 p128). On April 3 1822 Samuel Whitehouse, a West Bromwich land-owner, was murdered on the Halesowen turnpike road (Hagley Road?) at Bearwood (TB Nov 1977 pp1-9. Oct 1979 p1) or on the Oldbury-Halesowen turnpike road at Whiteheath Gate (BCWJ pp133-134) (TB Jan 1974 p22. Oct 1984 p27. Feb 1989 p5. March 1989 p5). Whitehouse's body was found on the SE edge of the present Warley Park. Joseph Downing of Rowley Regis was accused and tried for the murder but acquitted after which he is said to have fallen into a quagmire called 'Totnall Bog' with only the daughter of Whitehouse to save him. Some of Downing's children are buried in Rowley Regis churchyard (TB Jan 1974 p22. Nov 1977 pp1-9).

Bearwood Hill Winshill. Until 1837 when the new Ashby Road was cut through Winshill Wood travellers to Ashby used Bearwood Hill (BTOP vol 1 p5p). The name is preserved in Bearwood Hill Road.

Bearwood House In Bearwood Road, Smethwick. By 1951 the house was occupied by British Pens Ltd. The house is said to be haunted by the ghost of a cavalier (STELE July 7 1951).

Beasley Area 0.25m E of Chesterton. (Stoke-on-Trent A-Z).

Beaudesert (*Bo'-des-air* SOSH p11). Hall and estate covering a southern part of Cannock Chase 11m SE from Stafford in Longdon parish (W p566). The name appears as Beaudesert in 1293 (SSE 1996 p10), but has been spelt variously, since. It is from Norman French 'the beautiful, wild place' (DUIGNAN) (SDW p12) (SSE 1996 p10) (SPNO p107). The first house on the site of the most recent hall was built by the medieval bishops of Lichfield. THE PAGETS. In 1546 the house was acquired by **Sir William Paget** (1505-1563), statesman, who built onto, or incorporated, a small part of the bishop's house. There is a tradition that William's father John was born of humble birth (of a family of nailers) in Wednesbury. By the early C16 John was living in London and became a sergeant-at-mace. He prospered sufficiently to send his son to Cambridge. William entered the service of Henry VIII in 1529. He was knighted in 1537 and became principal secretary of state in 1543 and a member of Edward VI's regency council in 1547 (NSFCT 1914 pp175-176) (SGS p125) (BCM Jan 1985 p24) (HOS 1998 p47). **Thomas Tusser** (d1580), musician and agricultural writer (DNB), born in Rivenhall, Essex in c1527 became a retainer of William, 1st Baron Paget, with who he was often at Beaudesert (BS p470). Paget is said to have discovered him when he was a chorister at St Paul's cathedral and brought him to play at

Beaudesert for ten years. He retired to live on a farm in Suffolk. He published 'A Hundred Good Points of Husbandry' (1557) and another edition of this book called 'A Hundred Good Points Married to One Hundred Good Points of House-wifery' (1571), which was followed in 1573 by 'Five Hundred Points of Good Husbandry married to as Many Good Housewifery.' He coined many proverbs which have passed into current speech (CCBO pp37-39; born in 1524). The main building was erected between 1569 and 1574 by **Thomas**, 3rd Baron Paget, second son of Sir William Paget, 1st Baron Paget. When Thomas was suspected of complicity against Elizabeth I in the Throckmorton Plot in Nov 1583 he fled to France and forfeited the estate in 1587. He died in exile in 1590 (VCH vol 2 p111) (SSE 1990 pp51,53). Thomas's son, **William** (later 4th Baron Paget), a Protestant, recovered his father's possessions in 1597 (VCH vol 2 p111) and his title in 1604 (HOS p23) (NSFCT 1976 pp13-14). His son, **William** (1609-1678), 5th Baron Paget, changed his allegiance from parliament to royalist in the Civil War, and his estates were sequestered, but later regained (SHC 1999 pp127-156). He was succeeded by **William** (1637-1713), 6th Baron Paget (HOS p23) (BFS p6) (BPW p39); it was probably this Paget who was the Lord Paget Celia Fiennes visited in c1698 at Beaudesert, which she spelt Boudezworth and Budsworth (Illustrated Journeys of Celia Fiennes edited by Chris Morris. 1984. pp148,229). The 6th Baron was succeeded by **Henry** (d1749), 7th Baron Paget. He was created 1st Earl of Uxbridge in 1714. He outlived his son, Thomas Catesby, (1689-1742), and was succeeded by his grandson, **Henry** (1719-1769), 8th Baron Paget and 2nd Earl of Uxbridge. The 8th Baron died without issue and Beaudesert descended through the descendents of Henry Paget, a younger brother of William, 6th Baron to **Henry Bayley** (Paget) (1744-1812), who became 9th Baron Paget and 1st Earl of Uxbridge (new creation) (BPW p39). He had much renovation carried out and had a highway which ran in front of the house moved to its present position half a mile or more away. Shaw observed in 1798 'The East front was totally disengaged from the gateway walls and other obstructions that encumbered it in the days of Plot.' The 9th Baron was succeeded in 1812 by his son **Henry William** (1768-1854), the 10th Baron Paget and 2nd Earl of Uxbridge (new creation). Before his succession Henry William had eloped with Lady Charlotte Wellesley, wife of the Duke of Wellington's brother, and the divorce proceedings were the sensation of 1809-1810 costing Henry William £20,000: Hon Henry Cadogan (1780-1813), brother of Lady Wellesley fought a duel with Henry William on May 30 1809; pistols were used but neither party was hurt. Henry William went on to be the Duke of Wellington's cavalry commander at the battle of Waterloo (1815). In the battle he lost a leg but received the title of (1st) Marquess of Anglesey (he was then also known as 'Waterloo' Marquess) for his services (HOS p23) (STMSM July 1978 p7. Feb 1979 p32il) (BPW pp18,39). The Prince Regent (later George IV), accompanied by the Duke of Clarence, visited Beaudesert Hall on Nov 6 1815. The next day they were joined by Austrian Archdukes, John and Lewis (W p567) (RVW) (R&S p38) (BPW p11). The Prince was escorted here from Lichfield by the Staffordshire Yeomanry (FSP p64). The 1st Marquess had more work done to the hall including the construction of a great stone staircase, which became known as the 'Waterloo Staircase' (CCBO p81) (NSFCT 1976 pp13-14). The 1st Marquess was succeeded by his son **Henry** (1797-1869), 2nd Marquess (BPW p39). Lady Florence, only daughter of the 2nd Marquess, was known as the 'Pocket Venus' because of her beauty. She eloped with Lord Hastings on the day before her marriage to Henry Chaplin (CCF pp97-98). The 2nd Marquess was succeeded by his son by his first marriage, **Henry** (1821-1880), 3rd Marquess. He died without issue and Beaudesert passed to the 3rd Marquess' eldest step-brother, **Henry** (1835-1898), 4th Marquess. He was succeeded by his son **Henry** (1875-1905), 5th Marquess, who died without issue. Beaudesert then passed to a descendent of a younger brother of the 4th Marquess, **Charles** (b1885), 6th Marquess (BPW p39). He had the house overhauled and replaced some of the C18 additions with work more in the original Tudor style (NSFCT 1976 pp13-14). After a fire in Nov 1909 more restoration was carried out (NSFCT 1914 pp175-176) (Plas Newydd. NT Guide. 1991. p32). On the death of Charles, 6th Marquess in 1947 the title passed to his son **Henry** (b1922), who became 7th Marquess, and he was still living at Plas Newydd in 1992 (BPW pp28,39). (SHOS vol 1 pp221 pl, 222 pl showing NE view) (W p566) (WAM p86il) (CL Nov 22 1919 pp658-665 ps) (KES p100) (SA Nov 10 1928 p2) (ES Aug 21 1931 p8 asks if there was a secret tunnel at Beaudesert).

It has been said that Sir Walter Scott refers to Beaudesert in canto 6 of 'The Lady of the Lake' (BPW pp14-15). A portrait of Beaudesert appears in 'The Great House' a novel written by Stanley Weyman. It is set in the 1840s and has an heroine called Mary Audley (CCF pp185,186).

INTERIOR. In the later C17 Plot noted in the gallery the Paget **coat of arms cut out of cannel coal** dug up from Lord Pagets own coalfields on Cannock

Chase (NHS p126) ('Magna Britannia' 1730) (WAM p77). He also noted some **finger stocks** which were only used at Christmas by the Lord of Misrule for such persons who had committed misdemeanours (NHS p390 tab 32 fig II) (SD p53) ('Magna Britannia' 1730) (WAM p77). By the late C18 the stocks had gone to Greene's Museum in Lichfield (SHOS vol 1 p221) (SLM Sept 1950 p38il). James Wyatt (d1813) of Blackbrook Farm (see) remodelled the interior of the hall in 1771-2 (BPW p19). In the early C19 Pitt noted on a pillar in a corner of the hall a piece of **copper ore of conical shape**, from an Anglesey mine, weighing upwards of 1200 lb (THS p81). The hall contained **portraits** of Lord Paget by Holbein (SSC p120 in the intro) (GNHS p154) (which became a possession of the Duke of Manchester - SG p59); George III by Ramsay; Queen Charlotte by Ramsay; the Earl of Uxbridge by Pocock; Sir Arthur Paget by Hoppner; Henry, Earl of Holland by Vandyck; Henrietta Maria, Queen of Charles I by Vandyck, and some by Reynolds (SSC p120 in the intro) (GNHS p154). (CCBO p138-141). Some **stained glass windows** had the images of Edward IV, Henry VIII, Queen Mary, Elizabeth I and James I (SSC p120 in the intro). During his visit to Beaudesert in 1815 the Prince of Wales gave the Pagets an old **organ** which stood in the gallery. It was removed in the time of the 5th Marquess of Anglesey'. Some of the **tapestries** which were in the Banqueting Hall came from Hampton Court. The bedrooms contained old **Chinese hand painted wall papers** - perhaps one set of only three brought to England in Queen Anne's reign (NSFCT 1914 pp175-176) (BPW p21). The Pagets were lords of Burton upon Trent manor and in the Muniment Room at the hall was the original parchment **will of Wulfric Spot**, founder of Burton Abbey (HOWW p41). At the head of the **Waterloo Staircase** (see above) was placed a portrait of the Marquis of Anglesey by Sir Thomas Lawrence (CCBO p81). A large mahogany desk made in 1809 for Henry William Paget, Earl of Uxbridge, was for sale in July 1993 (ES July 1 1993 p8). The oak beams of Butterhill windmill went to Beaudesert Hall in 1912 (WBJ p18 il vi). In the 1930s Wright noted the hall had a minstrels' gallery (CCBO p37).

SALE AND DEMOLITION. Rising maintenance costs forced the sale of the house (NSFCT 1976 p14). The Pagets moved to Plas Newydd in 1920 (BPW p20) (SGS p125; says 1932). The hall was empty from c1921, for sale from 1924, and striped of its internal fittings by Aug 1931 (NSFCT 1931 p200). The hall was offered to but refused by a number of public bodies. The sale of the estate and hall on Oct 13 1932 took place at the Swan Hotel, Lichfield, but no purchaser was found. A further sale of the fabric of the hall and stables took place on July 18 and 19 1935; this was the auction which Wright probably attended. Shortly after, and probably in 1935, the house was demolished by house breakers for the fittings and fixtures (CCF pp224-227, p of a window of the Banqueting Hall facing p225) (NSFCT 1976 p13; demolished in 1932) (SVB p113; demolished in 1937) (Plas Newydd. NT Guide. 1991. p32) (TB April 1992 pp20-21) (BPW pp22,24,25) (HOS 1998 p48). At the auction in 1935 Sir Edward and Lady Haywood (or Hayward) bought oak panelling, fireplaces, windows and the Waterloo Staircase. The purchases were shipped to Australia and used in a replica Elizabethan manor house they built near Adelaide, completed in 1939. The house was called Carrick Hill. Their daughter was given the house as a wedding present. This house was eventually bequeathed to the people of South Australia (From a note from Ida Wood in CL Nov 22 1919, WSL copy) (BPW p25). Beaudesert's bricks were used to reface St James' Palace in London (The Times 'Magazine' Oct 22 1994 p18 il) or some say they were used in the restoration of Hampton Court Palace and that an oak door went to Churches Mansions in Nantwich, Ches (NSFCT 1976 p14). Some panelling in the Dining Room of the White Hart Hotel, Carter Street, Uttoxeter is from Beaudesert (SGS p173). Some of the massed hydrangeas and camellias which grew in the conservatory went to Plas Newydd, as did the state bed of c1720, damaged in the fire of 1909 (Plas Newydd. NT Guide 1991. pp32,55). An armchair from Beaudesert went to the V&A. The site of the hall was given for the use of scouts and guides and similar organisations (SVB p113). Pevsner records a fragment of a medieval Great Hall with three Late Perpendicular windows still survived in the late 1960s or early 1970s; however, DS Dodd could not locate the site of the house in 1976 (BOE p67) (NSFCT 1976 p14). A photograph of c1992 showing a substantial portion of wall with three windows appears in BPW p27.

GROUNDS. Beaudesert **Golf Club** with a club house at Suker's Lodge was founded by Tom Coulthwaite and others and was visited on several occasions by Edward VIII when Prince of Wales (SSE 1990 p88). **Beaudesert Old Park** (see). In the later C17 Plot noted an **echo** near the house (NHS p29) (SD p53) ('Magna Britannia' 1730) (SHOS vol 1 p221) (WAM p77). For **hills and gutters** lying in Beaudesert Old Park see:- Alfred's Dell; Gadstree; Mutchill's; Piggot's Bottom; Rainbow; Rawnsley; and Russells Bank. There were nine lodges at the entrances to the estate: Park Lodge (sometimes called

Cannock Wood); Suker's Lodge (see); Wandon Lodge at Wandon (see); North Lodge; Hodgkiss's Lodge (sometimes called Horsey Lane); Grand Lodge (see); East Lodge; West Lodge; and Castle Ring Lodge (BPW p24). Marquis' Drive (see). Mutchill's Well in Mutchill's Gutter (see). There were several interesting oaks in Beaudesert Old Park: Beaudesert Oak (see); Gutter Oak (see); Hangman's Oak (see); Magic Oak (see); Mutchill's Oak in Mutchill's Gutter (see); Roan Oak (Rawnpike Oak) (see); Rugeley Oak (see); Seven Oaks (see); Whistle Oak (see). **Regent's Wood** (see). Near the hall's Tudor doorway was a **spring** from Castle Ring which issued out of the mouth of a statue of a lion (CCF p227). **Youth camp**: In 1937 6th Marquess of Anglesey gave 123 acres of land close to Castle Ring in commemoration of George V's reign, to be used by scouts, guides and other youth organisations. The Beaudesert Trust was then set up to administer the land; the campsite was officially opened by the Princess Royal on July 2 1938 (BPW pp28-29).

Beaudesert Barn and Plantation. To NE of Blymhill.

Beaudesert Oak Oak in Beaudesert Park in which Lady Uxbridge sat. By 1844 it had become just a shell (GNHS p409). The same or another was hollow and could shelter eight standing people. Another oak in the park had a girth of 40 feet (HOWW p15) (CCC p64).

Beaudesert Old Park Wooded park which belonged to the Paget family of Beaudesert Hall. But was, perhaps, enclosed earlier than it belonged to them. Appears as Beaudezert Parke in 1584 (SPNO p107). SVB p112 suggests the park was enclosed in the early C19. For features in the park see under Beaudesert Grounds.

Beauty Bank Streets on E side of Halesowen Road, Old Hill. The area or the streets were so called by 1901 (OS map Sheet 71.08).

'Bech' Possible early settlement of Lichfield, SE of Stowe (SHC vol 1 p93) (VCH vol 14 p7).

Beckminster Former estate in the Birches Barn Road area, Penn Fields. In 1659 a farm called Beckmaster was bequeathed by Roger Baker to support 18 poor people (PENOP p7). The present house was built by John William Sparrow in the late 1850s, after first renting Penn Hall - sparrows can be seen in glass panels in the house (PMPD pp44il,45, 47). The area about the house became developed with housing after WW1 (PENOP p9). The bomb dropped on Beckminster Special School on Oct 3 1940 probably was jettisoned to lighten the plane rather than as a deliberate attack (PENOP p72p) (PPTP p26).

Beckminster House Birches Barn Road, Beckminster, Wolverhampton. Built by John William Sparrow in the 1850s. The house having long been the Wolverhampton Teachers' Centre is now the Education Department Professional Development Centre (PENOP p65p).

Becknell Fields Farm 0.5m NNE of Kingswinford church, on S side of Stallings Lane. Becknells Field (1834 OS map). Still standing in c1910 (BHOP2 p103p). Now (1995) the site is partly occupied by a Government Training Centre and Pensnett Trading Estate. The former nearby stone-breaking yard at The Bungalow, Shut End, was known locally as the 'Cracker Hole' (BCM Spring 2000 p64).

Beck's Bridge Carries Pelsall Road over the Wyrley and Essington Canal, over 0.5m W of Brownhills.

Bedbrook Brook which runs eastwards N of Cheadle to join Cecilly Brook (CCT p7).

Bede's Cottage, Adam Upper Ellastone. Said to have been built in 1617 (local info). Home of George and Mary Evans, grandparents of Mary Ann Evans, alias the novelist George Eliot. They were originally of Roston Common, Derbys. Their fourth son, Robert Evans, who was Eliot's father and founder of the building and carpentry business here, was the model for Adam Bede in Eliot's 'Adam Bede' (1859). In the novel her grandparents were the models for Matthias and Lisbeth Bede, and their fifth and youngest son, Samuel, was Seth, and his wife, Elizabeth Tomlinson, was Dinah Morris. Harriet Poynton a domestic servant at Wootton Hall married Robert Evans (Adam Bede). But according to the novel Adam marries Dinah. Robert Evans is reputed to have made the ornate wooden gable fittings (local info). The house had been converted into two cottages and the workshop into a wash-house and cow-shed by 1910. By which time the house had been enlarged and was occupied by a doctor and was known as the Doctor's House (NSFCT 1924 p200). There was a corbel by the sitting room of the cottage said to have been carved by Robert Evans; Bird was shown wood carvings said to be his work. (WTCEM p138) (NSFCT 1894 p154. 1918 pp121-125. 1924 pp200-201) (S p48p) (LGS p132) (KES pp92,177p) (SOSH pp350-351) (SLM Feb 1948 pp78,79. Aug-Sept 1952 pp10,11p,12) (STM July 1965 p40p) (VB p168) (IAANS pp xvi,xvii) (MR p144p) (TB Sept 1994 p20).

Bednall Small village under the NW slope of Cannock Chase (SGS p59) 3.5m SSE of Stafford. Former township with Acton Trussell and chapelry in Baswich or Berkswich ancient parish, but sometimes reputed to have been in Cannock ancient parish. Bedehala occurs as waste in DB (SSE 1996 p10); at some point it became part of the manor of Acton Trussell (VCH vol 5 p14). Later forms are: Bedenhale (1257), Bydenhale (1323), Bednalle (1481), and Bednoll (Speed's map) (SPNO p27). The name is of Anglo-Saxon origin and means Beda's hall, or Beda's meadow or hill (DUIGNAN), or hollow (SSE 1996 p10); Beda being a Saxon chief or thane (BERK2 pp87,100). Beda's nook of land (OAKDEN) (NSJFS 1981 p3) (SPN p16). (CCF p34). The church, All Saints, by the main road and Cock Lane on or near the site of a chapel of C12 origin, was built in 1846 (VCH vol 5 p17). S of Bowling Alley where Bowling Alley forks from Common Lane is the village well, said to be 60 feet deep. A wooden doorway led to it (BERK2 p91). Bednall became a separate ecclesiastical parish with Acton Trussell in 1671 but remained in Baswich for civil purposes until becoming a separate civil parish with Acton Trussell in 1866 (GLAUE p403) (BERK2 p85). Vicars and natives. The will of Rev William Alport, dated 1720, founded a charity for the incumbents of eight Staffs parishes including Bednall, providing that they reside for at least 10 months in the year in their cures and give a sermon at Cannock church on St Barnabas' Day (June 11). It was found that for 34 successive years two former vicars of Acton and Bednall, father and son, received the Alport money, even though they had failed to fulfil the trust conditions (CCF pp32,36) (VCH vol 5 p64). James Richard Alsop, born at Bonehill in 1816, author of 'The Prayer of Ajax and other poems' (1880), was vicar of Acton Trussell-with-Bednall from 1867 until his death on Aug 6 1880 (PSS pp166-169) (ZSB) (VFC p3). His grandson, George Philip Ranulph Alsop, was born at Bednall vicarage, on March 22 1890; he contributed poems, mostly inspired by nature, to several periodicals (PSS pp374-377) (VFC p3).

Bednall Hall To E of Bednall church on E side of Cock Lane, S of Common Lane. Dates from the first half of the C19 (VCH vol 5 p12) (BERK2 pp93-94).

Bednall Head Scattered small hamlet 0.5m E of Bednall (1834 OS map) (CCBO p69). Bednall Head Farm is 1m E of Bednall.

Beech Hamlet nearly 1.5m W of Tittensor. Former township and quarter in Stone ancient parish, and partly in Swynnerton ancient parish (W p362). There is a very large boulder near Beech of andesite granite (NSFCT 1916 p73). The name is from beech (trees) (SSE 1996 p10) and has appeared as Le Bech (1285) (SSE 1996 p10). A hard slate-like marl can be found here (NHS p120). The stone from the old quarry here went to build one of the Trentham Halls, and one of the Madam's Bridges. Not far from Beech the NSFC in the late 1870s observed cottages cut into the rock which were inhabited (NSFCT 1878 p10).

Beech Caves Beech Dale, Tittensor. Originally formed by sandstone quarrying for local building purposes. During WW2 the caves were used to store munitions (TTOPP p82p). A coin of Charles I has been found in the caves (ES Oct 1 1932 p3. Oct 10 1932 p1p of a rally of N Staffs Ramblers' Federation. March 9 1933 p5p). By 1992 the caves formed part of Lord Stafford's estate. Five illicit 'Rave' parties were held in the caves over the summer of 1992 (SN Oct 16 1992 p4). (SLM Dec 1948 p190) (IAANS p xxiii).

Beechcliff Tiny hamlet over 1m WNW of Tittensor. The white post-WW2 cottages lining the heath leading to it can be seen from the M6 north bound.

Beechdale An housing estate built by the council in the early 1950s S of Leamore Lane, Bloxwich. The estate was known at first as the Gipsy Lane estate and was renamed Beechdale estate in 1957 (VCH vol 17 p162 see map, 165) (SNBP p9). The church, St Chad, Edison Road, was built in 1957 (LDD).

Beech Dale Tittensor. E of Beech. Beech Caves are situated at the E end of it. The view from the bridge on the A519 at Beech looking down the dale is not long, but most picturesque.

Beechenhill Hill 318 metres high and a house in Castern township of Ilam parish, over 1m NNE of Ilam. At SK 12675236 is a mound approximately 17 metres by 15 metres and 1.3 metres high with a damaged top. This is possibly the mound that Bateman noted that Carrington had excavated between 'Bitchin Hill and Castern' in 1849 (SASR 1995 no 5 p7). Gunstone lists three burial mounds about Beechenhill. One at SK 12805295 0.25m NNW of the house, is 14 paces in diameter and four feet high. It is a listed monument. Two more, close to one another, are 0.25m NW of the house at SK 12625285 (25 paces in diameter seven feet high) and at SK 12615282 (18 paces in diameter five feet high) (NSJFS 1965 p40). Both are listed monuments. Bateman may have excavated two in 1845; Carrington one in 1850 and another in 1852. But it is uncertain which (TYD pp165-166,185-186) (VAD pp81-82) (BAP vol 1 p158 fig 186) (DAJ vol 75 pp107,110. vol 77 pp26, B2) (NSJFS 1965 p40). The two burial mounds excavated by Bateman in 1845 are called Bitchenhill Harbour (VCH vol 1 p190). In one was found the remains of an urn of coarse pottery with a deposit of burnt bones, and a third brass of Constantine the Great (AD 291-306) (VAD p81). Another burial mound 540 metres NE of

Beechenhill is a listed monument. Excavations on the earthworks immediately to the S of the house have revealed evidence of farming activity from the Romano-British period (SASR 1995 no 5 pp6-8). An area of approximately 100 acres centring on the present Beechenhill farm was an enclosed area by the C16. Excavations in 1983 and 1984 0.25m NE of Beechenhill farm at SK 13055268 revealed farm-buildings of the C16 period. These were deserted by 1700 (SASR 1995 no 5 pp8-20). Beechenhill has appeared as Bychenne Hill (1542) and Bitchin Hill (1861) (SASR 1995 no 5 p8).

Beeches, The House built by 1754 on S side of Penn Road, W of Church Hill, Upper Penn. The house was formerly called Upper Penn Farm (PONP p44), and may have acquired the name Beeches because it contained in its grounds many specimens of copper beech. Francis JJ Gibbons lived here until moving to Penn Hall in 1924. He was succeeded by Harry Evers Palfrey, who lived here to 1935. In 1938 it opened as a hospital and is now Penn Hospital (PAIP pp35-38il).

Beeches Residential area 0.25m to E of the S end of the High Street, West Bromwich. Laid out by GB Nichols, a West Bromwich architect and surveyor. It was considered a well-to-do district when first built in the late 1860s; its large houses were occupied by the West Indian community by the mid 1970s (VCH vol 17 p5).

Beeches, The House 0.75m WSW of Trysull. In Trysull ancient parish. In existence by 1814 (VCH vol 20 p187).

Beech Lanes District over 1m NE of Harborne. The church, St Faith and St Lawrence, at the S end of Balden Road, was begun in 1937 and completed between 1958-1960 (BOEWA p185).

Beehive Cottage Betley, close by Buddleigh. Timberframed (BOE p68) (MR p33).

Beelow Hill Hill 0.5m S of Cotton. Said to have a burial mound on it at SK 06454491 (VCH barrow list). But none can be found (NSJFS 1965 p37). (HAF pp13,27). On the top of the hill is a bronze on sandstone plaque to the memory of Francis Alfred Bolton (1866-1951) (HAF p397).

Beeston Tor Rocky hill on the E side of the Manifold at the confluence of the Manifold and the Hamps 0.5m S from Wetton. Sometimes called Baystun Tor or Jack o' Daws (WTCEM p126) (HLS p52). The tor possesses a cavern (HLS p52). (LGS p183) (PS pp90,91p). The name is perhaps from a corruption of Bertram's Stone, referring to the C8 Mercian hermit prince, or Bel Stone, referring to Bel or Baal, the god of the Sun. Some think 'Bee' is given on account of the many small holes in the rock (WTCEM p6).

Beeston Tor Cave Cave situated in Beeston Tor. Has traces of prehistoric occupation (HOS p9). Between 17 and 29 Sept 1924 a hoard of 49 silver coins, and three gold rings of Ethelwulf, Ethelbert and Alfred the Great and all the C9 kings was found in it by Rev GH Wilson of Chorlton-cum-Hardy, Manchester. The hoard was declared Treasure Trove and went to the BM (eight coins are elsewhere) (TD) (SG p18 on the law case) (NSFCT 1924 pp105-106 ps) (Numismatic Chronicle 1924) (LGS p183) (KES p3) (L p3) (VB p201) (CCOP p85) (NSSG p6) (MR p330) (MIDD vol 2 pp14,15p). Further coins were found by young men from Grindon late one night while the excavation was taking place (DMV p76). Saxons probably hiding from invading Danes in the mid C9 had left it here (NSJFS 1962 p33). Has also appeared as St Bertram's Cave (DMV p76) and Jack o' Daws Cave.

Beffcote Hamlet over 1m NE of Moreton. Formerly in Cowley quarter in Gnosall ancient parish (VCH vol 4 p111). A section of the Roman road from Pennocrucium to Whitchurch to the W of Beffcote was discovered in 1938 (OSST 1938 p29) (NSJFS 1964 p23). The manor of Covelav (Cowley) and Beficote occurs in DB. Later forms are: Befcote (1227), Beofcote (1343), Beffecott (1593), and Bescot (Plot's map) (SPNO p154) (SSE 1996 p10). The name, of Anglo-Saxon origin, means 'Cottage of Beffa' (SSE 1987 p28. 1996 p10), or 'Beffa's cottages' (SPN p112). For Beffcote Mill see Broadhill.

Beffcote Manor House on the S side of the Gnosall road. To the S of the house at SJ 805188 is a rectangular moat (VCH vol 1) (SSAHST 1982-3 p42).

Beggar's Bridge Name used in C19 for an area S of Bush Park, Darlaston (Offlow hundred). The name may be from a bridge over the former Bird Brook (SNDB p16).

Beggar's Bridge Footbridge over the Dove on Derbyshire border N of Longnor.

Beggars Bush Field name near Money Lands or Flats, Wigginton (SHOS vol 1 p432).

Beggars Bush Large hawthorn bush which stood on the boundary of the ancient parishes of Handsworth and Sutton, on the old London to Chester road, 3m SW of Sutton Coldfield (DUIGNAN). According to tradition the bush received its name from the respective parishes placing dead paupers under the bush if the pauper was found dead in their parish so that the parish rate payers from either parish were exempt from payment of burial costs (MNB p55). But Woodall thinks it more likely received its name for marking the spot where vagrants were handed over to adjoining parish authorities to be conducted on to their own parish under the Act of Settlement (TBS p23). There was an illegal prize fight between Birmingham prize fighters near the 'Beggar's Bush' in Nov 1873 which culminated in the arrest of Isaac Bradley, alias 'Boxer' on a charge of prize fighting and of assaulting the police (TBS p31). In 1876 Jemmy Ireland and a man called Parker, undisturbed by police, fought a prize fight in the Beggar's Bush district (Aston Chronicle) (TBS p32). The name is preserved in an inn of this name which is said to stand on or near the site of the bush.

Beggars Bush A Gospel place in the Penkridge perambulation in the E corner of Congreve Field near Cuttlestone Bridge (HOP p30).

Beggar's Bush SE of Wombourne, in Wombourne parish. Marked on 1834 OS map. Preserved in Beggar's Bush Lane (Birmingham A-Z).

Beggar's Hill N end of Cannock Chase S of Weetman's Bridge. Seven Springs are at the foot of this hill.

Beggar's Oak Most famous oak in Bagot's Park. According to the 1834 OS map it stood approximately at SK 098272, 2.25m ENE of Bagot's Bromley. Estimated to be 1200 years old by the early C20 (NSFCT 1915 p160. 1927 p168). The name could be a corruption of Bagot's Oak (NSFCT 1886 p20. 1909 p197). There is a tradition which relates the first Bagot was given as much land as he could walk round in a day by William the Conqueror. At the end of the day, being exhausted, he set his stick in the ground and it grew into this oak. The story could relate to the Walking Stick Oak (ES Dec 29 1932 p4p). Or it was perhaps so named from the fact that gypsies, beggars and other homeless people passing through Needwood Forest from Uttoxeter to Lichfield sheltered under its branches (ABAB p39) (info the Internet - Beggar's Oak Clog site). A popular belief was that the wayfarer had the right to a night's lodging under its boughs, a tradition which probably dated to before the enclosure of the park from Needwood Forest (FLJ 1896 p381). A gardener at Blithfield in the 1930s told Wright the tree was so named because a Bagot of long ago refused to assist a beggar who accosted him beneath the oak, a denial that brought forth the curse of the beggar on the Bagots (CCBO pp25p,26,152). An extension of that story is; the beggar took shelter under Beggar's Oak and was denied alms by Lord Bagot, in retaliation he cursed the Bagots and prayed that when the oak collapsed the Bagot family would die out. It is said that shortly after the wooden props supporting the oak collapsed in the 1930s the Bagot estate was sold off (TRTC p31). A similar story is that two beggars who tried to seek refuge and food at Blithfield Hall were turned away and the next morning were found frozen to death by Beggar's Oak (ABAB p39). Another tradition concerns three beggars; that they asked for shelter from Lord Bagot but were denied. Faint and starving they approached Beggar's Oak and there put a curse on the Bagot family that in every second generation there should be no direct heirs (S. Mary and S. Anne: The Second Fifty Years. Anne Wells and Susan Meads. 1974 p34).

In 1823 the oak contained between 800 and 900 cubic feet of timber and was 60 feet high. Its main butt was 33 feet long, and it had 14 limbs, the largest of which contained upwards of 50 cubic feet. These dimensions were much the same in 1875 (NSFCT 1875 p7. 1900 p of facing p73). The tree is said to have had branches extending 48 feet in every direction and covered an area of quarter of an acre (NSFCT 1901 pp73p,74. 1927 p168). In 1905 it was 26.5 feet in girth four feet from the ground (UTR p107) or 24 feet eight inches (NSFCT 1915 p160). Joseph Palmer timber merchant is said to have done some of his business transactions by it, and his son William 'the Poisoner' of Rugeley (see), is said to have courted his future wife, Anne Brookes Thornton, here. The tree, said to be large enough to shade a troop of cavalry (LTD pp124,126il of in 1826), was often visited for summer outings (ESNF p39p). The Uttoxeter photographer GS McCann had his photograph taken by the oak in the 1920s (LTD p127p), and the tree was visited by pupils of St Mary and St Anne School, Abbots Bromley, in Feb 1932; the tree then was considered the eighth largest oak in England (S. Mary and S. Anne: The Second Fifty Years. Anne Wells and Susan Meads. 1974 p34p of after the oak has collapsed). Mee suggests he is the last to see the oaks on the Bagot estate before they are sold to pay estate duty (KES pp16,161p). The oak, now no longer existing, may have been felled after 1933, in which year many of the finest timbers in Bagot's Park were sold to alleviate death duties (LTD p128). However, a recent account says that the oak was still standing in a very poor state by the late 1940s with many of its wooden props missing and branches broken off; thereafter it declined and died (ESNF p39). At Blithfield Hall by 1973 there were two chests said to have been made out of the last remains of the tree (S. Mary and S. Anne: The Second Fifty Years. Anne Wells and Susan Meads. 1974 p34). In 1983 a morris dance group called the Beggar's Oak Clog formed, taking their name from the oak. The group were still in existence in 1999 (info the Internet). (GNHS p408) (SC p171) (MOS p51p) (S

p15p) (LGS pp191-192) (Abbots Bromley Magazine Sept 1934) (SLM Oct 1947 p35p. Feb 1951 pp18p by GS McCann, possibly taken in 1920s or 30s, 19) (AB p200 il is GG Strutts etching 1824) (STMSM April 1973 p24).

Beggars' Way Former small district of Leek inhabited by 1638 which grew on the former common land of Leek Town Field (VCH vol 7 p89). The Turk's Head Inn was in this area (OL vol 1 p315). The name is presumably preserved in Beggar's Lane at Wallbridge Park (VCH vol 7 p88), 0.75m WSW of the town centre.

Beggar's Well In Beggar's Well Lane, Alton.

Beggar's Well Threapwood. At SK 039429 on 1:25,000 OS map.

Beighterton Small hamlet S of Blymhill. In Blymhill parish. Lower Beighterton is a small hamlet to the NW. A manor of Bertone appears in DB. Later forms are: Becterton (1242), Beyghterton (1392), Beitherton (1534), and Biterton (Plot's map) (SPNO p181) (SSE 1996 p10). The name possibly represents 'Beorhthere's tun or farmstead' (SPNO p181) (SSE 1996 p10).

Belgrave SSW of Amington. In Warws prior to 1910. A district of the large conurbation SE of Tamworth. Belgrave was a ward of Tamworth borough by at least 1993. There is a mission church, St Paul, here (LDD).

Bell Alley Situated next door to the Bell Inn, Willenhall. It is said to be haunted by the ghost of a young girl who had been murdered many years ago. She has been seen on her own and with her mother, who is reputed to have committed suicide upon finding her. She was apparently murdered by one of the mother's men friends (GOM p23 p4 (b) of the Alley).

Bellamour End Colton parish. Presumably is the W part of Colton about Bellamour Hall. Common name for what should be called Town End (CWF p175).

Bellamour Hall House 200 yards W of Colton church. Built by Herbert Aston, second son of Sir Walter Aston (d1639), a descendent of the Astons of Haywood Hall (see), and his wife Catherine in c1639 (SVB p60 says 1635) (CWF ps facing p143). The name for the house came from Herbert Aston who called it Bell amore from the Italian because it was finished by the benevolence or good love of his friends. It is not from Bellamour as if derived from the French, which it became corrupted to (CWF pp143, 175), having in the past appeared as Bellamoore Hall and Bellamore Hall. Because of a lack of direct heirs the hall reverted to the elder branch of the Aston family. It passed out of Aston hands with Mary Aston, daughter and co-heir of James, 5th Lord Aston, of the main line, with her marriage to Sir Walter Blount. About the beginning of the C18 Lady Blount built a larger house here, this too, seems to have taken the name Bellamour Hall. In 1824, her son, Edward Blount sold the Bellamour estate to James Oldham, a retired Indian judge, at whose death in 1857, it was purchased by TB Horsfall, former MP for Liverpool; he made significant additions to the new house. A Mrs Horsfall was living at Bellamour (new) Hall in 1914 (SHC 1914 p156 note). Some ruins of Bellamour (old) Hall remain; these were in a neglected and dangerous condition at the time of the DoE re-survey in c1988 (DoE II). (GNHS p136). On OS map 1955 there is marked the site of a chapel to the S of Bellamour Lodge.

Bellamour Lodge Colton. Built in 1851 by James Oldham of Bellamour Hall for his daughter Miss Ellen Oldham, who enlarged it, and continued to live here until her death when it passed to her sister Mrs J Harland, for life, and then to their nephew, Capt Charles D Oldham, the owner in 1914 (SHC 1914 p156 note). It stands close to the ruins of Bellamour Hall (CWF photograph facing p175).

Bell Bridge Bridge on Ryknild Street over the Coventry Canal 0.5m S of Fradley.

Bell Brook A brook running under the pavement in Bellbrook street in Penkridge (PVH p21).

Bellbrook A street in Penkridge. On W side of Bellbrook is an early C19 lock-up listed Grade II by DoE. Also some stocks, perhaps of C18 origin, listed Grade II.

Bell End Former small hamlet S of Rowley Regis church, in Rowley Regis parish. The name, which appears as Taking Bell End in the 1851 census, is preserved in a street called Bell End between Hawes Lane and Mincing Lane (Birmingham A-Z). Another account says Bell End lay at the bottom of Portway Road (HORV p7) to the N of Rowley Regis church.

Bellman's Cross At Shatterford, in Upper Arley parish.

Bell's Hollow Red Street. Preserved in a road name between A34 and Crackley Bank.

Belmont Chapel House To ENE of Belmont Hall at SK 005498. Built in 1789 (NSFCT 1906 pp168-9) or in 1790 (F p306) as a chapel by John Sneyd of Belmont Hall (1743-1809) after a dispute he had with the patron of the living of Ipstones. The dispute was resolved before the building was finished and it hardly ever, or never, served as a chapel. Fisher Lyttleton, patron of the living of Ipstones had promised John Sneyd's son the living on the death of the incumbent, Parson White. Perhaps, as Raven adds, because Sneyd had paid for Ipstones church. But White outlived the son and at White's death Lyttleton offered it to his nephew Mr Walhouse. This enraged Sneyd and he started to build an alternative chapel. But Walhouse did not want the living, and Lyttleton consented to Sneyd's choice, a Mr Carlisle, his son's tutor (NSFCT 1906 pp168-9. 1916 p136). The residence was restored in the 1980s. (DoE II) (LGS p154) (STM June 1965 p44ps of before restoration. Oct 1966 p31p) (BOE p157) (SMCC p9 il) (MR p196) (NCSS pp213-214). At the second sharp bend past the chapel the grass plot on the left is reputedly haunted by someone murdered there. It is said the only way to get a horse past the spot at night is to put a sack or covering over its eyes (TOI pp44,166).

Belmont Hall Over 1m W of Ipstones, in Ipstones parish. The name means 'a fair mountain' (HLSP p49). Built by John Sneyd (b1743) of Bishton Hall in 1770. He died here in 1809. His grandson, Thomas (d1883), was living at Belmont in the 1840s (SNEDE) and in 1851 (W p18); other accounts, perhaps erroneous, have the hall built by Ralph Sneyd in 1770 (NSJFS 1968 p98), on the site of a house built by John Sneyd of Bishton in the late C15 (NSFCT 1906 p168). The greater part of the hall was demolished in c1806. The beautiful chimney-piece was taken to Ashcombe and placed in the Museum Room there (NSFCT 1906 p167). (TOI pp44,166 p of facing p36) (MR p196p). In 1876 the hall was occupied by Mrs Kinnersley, possibly the same as Mrs Sneyd-Kinnersley who was living at the hall in 1884. The hall remained the property of the Sneyds to at least 1912. It was occupied by Samuel Hall in 1892; unoccupied in 1899; occupied by Mrs Scarratt in 1916; by Miss Slack in 1924 (trade directories). It is reputedly haunted by a young woman. Her appearance to any member of the family who may inhabit the hall is said to presage the death of some member of the family within a year. She is said to be very beautiful, of melancholy mien and quite harmless if people will not cross her path (TOI p166) (OL vol 2 pp300-301) (SMCC p10) (ES Sept 16 1936 p5). There were nine pools in the grounds. Belmont Gardens were in c1806 considered among the seven finest in England. John Sneyd was awarded the gold medal for planting the greatest number of firs in a year (NSFCT 1906 p167) (TOI p10).

Belmont Woods At the entrance to Belmont Woods was a sort of urn monument to the memory of Rev William Sneyd (1794) erected by his cousin (NSFCT 1906 p168). In woods at Belmont a Mr Sneyd found the very rare Lily of the Valley plant or Convallaria Majalis (SHOS vol 1 part 1 p102. vol 1 p66).

Belmot Former hamlet on the edge of Needwood Forest 1.5m SSW of Tutbury. There was a hamlet at Belmot in medieval times (ANS p9). Has appeared as Bellmot (maps of Plot and Bowen), Bellmot Lodge (SHOS vol p94), Belmont (Smith's map) and Belmott Green (OS map 1834). At Belmot Green there were some eight acres of common land, known as Belmot Common, remaining in the 1950s (OSST 1956-59 p15).

Belmot Gate The name, appearing on Bowen's map SW of Belmot in the area of the present Belmot Farm, is from a former entry into Needwood Forest (ANS p8). Has also appeared as Tutbury Gate (VCH vol 2 p350 see map).

Belper Row A row of cottages at Darby End first settled by natives of Belper, Derbys (TB Sept 1974 p19).

Belsize House Corner of Bradford Street and Cross Street (KES p219) (SGS p176) (SNWA p62), or Bradford Place, Walsall. By the late 1850s the house was the residence of Rev Jerome Clapp Jerome, a native of Appledore, Devon, who entertained one Klapka, an exiled Hungarian general, here. Rev Jerome made the name Klapka the middle name of his son, the novelist, Jerome K Jerome, who was born here on May 2 1859. Rev Jerome suffered financial losses in a coal mine disaster at Norton Canes in 1860, thereafter JK Jerome appears to have been brought up in London, but the novelist is generally associated with Walsall (see). Belsize House became a museum to Jerome in 1984 or 1985. In 1989 Walsall borough council refused to hand over to the museum Jerome's writing desk, which it possessed and kept in the mayor's parlour (The Correspondent Oct 15 1989) (MR p358).

Belt View Farm Over 0.5m ENE of Bednall. The name may be from the Beltaine fires of the ancients (SMM p174). See Tar Hill.

Belvide Reservoir Constructed NW of Brewood for the Shropshire Union Canal, built in 1843. Covers some 208 acres. In existence by 1860 (VCH vol 5 p19). Widely recognised as a major nature reserve (SVB p35).

Bemersley Green Small hamlet on a ridge between the head of the Trent and Whitfield Brook valley 2m NNW of Norton-in-the-Moors. Former township in Norton-in-the-Moors chapelry in Stoke-upon-Trent ancient parish (ONST 1926 p8). The name, which appears to be of Anglo-Saxon origin, means 'the trumpeter's leah or wood clearing' (SSE 1996 p10). It is said to appear as Bemersleg in DB (SSE 1996 p10), but is not specifically mentioned in the Phillimore edition of DB (1976). Bemersley or Bemmersley was a member

of Tunstall manor by c1130 (ONST 1976 p374) (SSE 1996 p10). Bemersley Farm (unlocated) was the home of Hugh Bourne (1772-1852), from the age of 16. Bourne, co-founder of Primitive Methodism with William Clowes of Ball Bank, was born at Ford Hayes (see); a class of his at Stanley (see) has been considered the first Primitive Methodist class. At Bemersley Green, Bourne built a printing press and all the organisation of the sect was carried on from the farm until 1842 when it was moved to London. Bourne died unmarried at Bemersley Green and was buried at Englesea Brook, Barthomley, Ches on Oct 11 1852 (MC p60 pl xiv) (LGS p48) (WJ p32) (PSS pp462-463) (NSFCT 1945 p97) (ONST 1952 p166) (ABS No. 5 p10) (STM Jan 1968 p26p. June 1970 pp30-33. May 1972 p25) (NSJFS 1969 p63) (FLJ 1969 p283) (OTP p12) (PPP vol 2 p6p of Bemersley Farm c1900) (PTP pp100-102) (POTP p44) (E pp62-68) (SVB p105) (Hugh Bourne. JT Wilkinson) (VFC p17).

Ben Brook Rises from Goosemoor Green runs by Stoney Well.

Bendey's Green A green which existed in Enville ancient parish in the late C18 (VCH vol 20 p109). It presumably lay in the area near Bendey's Wood 0.75m NNW of Enville.

Bent There is a Bent Farm nearly 1.5m E of Blymhill.

Bent, The Bent Farm is on the W side of the Turnhurst Road at Packmoor. The Bent was the home of the Henshall family; Ann Henshall married James Brindley, canal engineer, in 1765 (SASR 1995 no 6 p11).

Bent Green Settlement S of the main village of Trysull, 0.25m S of the church. Has also appeared as Ben Green and the (Trysull) Green. There was settlement here by 1318 (VCH vol 20 p187). This area is presently called Hunters Green (OS map 1:25,000. 1988).

Bentham House on 1834 OS map and Dower's map. It is now Little Ankerton?

Bent Head House 0.25m E of Bradnop. Formerly in Bradnop township in Leek ancient parish. Has appeared as Bent Head (1690. 1834 OS map) and Brook Farm (1992) (VCH vol 7 p170).

Bentilee House and estate 1.75m ESE of Abbots Bromley. In Abbots Bromley parish. The name occurs between 1280 and 1305 as Le Bentilege (AB p20). It is said to have been in Bromley Hurst manor and to have been its own manor (AB p33). The house belonged to the Pagets from at least 1851 to 1911 (W p408) (AB p39).

Bentilee Near Acton, in Swynnerton parish (W p425).

Bentilee On rising ground by a tributary of the upper Trent 1m SE of Bucknall. Formerly in Bucknall and Bagnall chapelry in Stoke-upon-Trent ancient parish. The name is of Anglo-Saxon origin and means 'rough pasture' (BUB p7). Bentilee, taken into Stoke-on-Trent county borough in 1922 (VCH vol 8 p260), was mainly a rural and agricultural district until the area was developed as a large residential suburb in the 1950s (BUB p5). The new suburb was mainly built between 1952 and 1955 and it was intended that it be self-contained with its own church, health centre, shops and library (NSJFS 1975 p59-76) (TSS p127); it has been said to have once been Europe's largest council housing estate (ES March 10 2000 p15). Between the period 1953 and 1956 over 10,000 people moved to live here (BUB p23). The centre of the estate, and therefore the modern centre of Bentilee, is Devonshire Square or The 'Square' (BUB p27). The Harold Clowes community hall, off Devonshire Square, was opened in stages between 1956 and 1966 (BUB p28). The modern church, St Stephen, stands at the junction of Brassington Way and Dawlish Drive. The RC church, St Maria Goretti (1890-1929), opened in 1960. There is a stained glass window in the church depicting St Maria Goretti (BUB pp7,10-11). Many people on the estate claimed they saw UFOs in late Aug and early Sept 1967, and on Sept 2 1967 at 9.00pm in the vicinity of Wendling Close a brightly glowing object above roof tops was seen by a child, David McCue, and many others (Stoke-on-Trent City Times Nov 1 1967) (FSRP pp8-11,13,34-40) (SMM pp94-95).

Bentilee Park Abbots Bromley. 0.5m SE of Bentilee. There was a park, a hunting ground, called Bentley Parke by the mid C16 (AB p35).

Bentley House and scattered hamlet by Bentley Brook under 1.5m N of Mavesyn Ridware in Mavesyn Ridware ancient parish. The name occurs in Richard I's reign and has appeared as Boneleg and Bonedle (SHOS vol 1 p200). Bentley House (1834 OS map), Bentley Hall Farm (1:50,000 OS map), Bentley Farm (1:25,000 OS map) may have been the seat of William (Moseley) Walsh in 1797 (SHOS vol 1 p200). To the W of this house is Old Bentley (1834 OS map) now called Stone Cottages (OS map 1:25,000).

Bentley Former estate, township and house (Bentley Hall (see)) 1.5m E of Willenhall, in Wolverhampton foreign and ancient parish (W p154) (HOWM p44). The name means 'the lea of the bent' or 'benty grass' (DUIGNAN). Or 'bent grass meadow' (SPN p134). 'Bent' in its Midland sense usually means rough or coarse, so 'area of rough or coarse pasture land' (SNDB p11). Lords of Bentley manor held Bentley Hall (see). To the N of the hall at SO 984994 may have been a medieval village, probably deserted in the C19 (SSAHST

1970 p34). For fairs Cooke gives July 31, and Whit Wednesday (SCSF p98). There was a fair in 1792 (OWEN), but not by 1888 (LHE p264). In the later C19 and earlier C20 Bentley developed as residential and industrial suburb between Willenhall and Walsall. In 1866 it became a separate civil parish in Willenhall. In 1930 some of the civil parish was transferred to Walsall county borough. In 1934 the remaining Bentley civil parish was abolished with part being transferred to Darlaston urban district 'for the purpose of housing development in the 1920s and 1930s' and a part to Short Heath civil parish (in Willenhall urban district) (GLAUE p403) (SNDB introduction). Ecclesiastically, Bentley was severed from Wolverhampton parish to create 'Willenhall St Giles' in 1912. Bentley became a separate ecclesiastical parish in 1958 (GLAUE p403). The church, Emmanuel, Cairn Drive, was built in 1956 (BOE p297). In the later C17 Plot noted the phallus fungi was to be found at Bentley (NHS pp200-201,202 tab 14 fig 4, fig 5). Something invisible bangs on windscreens of moving cars at a certain spot in Bentley Lane, perhaps saving the occupants from being involved in an impending accident further down the road (GPCE pp47-48). In 1973 a young man travelling home in the early hours of the morning found his car grinding to a halt in Bentley Lane with something invisible banging on the windscreen (GOM p26).

Bentley Bank Etruria. Refers to the hall and works built by Josiah Wedgwood I for his partner Bentley. The hall was demolished in 1819 (NSFCT 1945 p100).

Bentley Brook Runs into the Trent at the foot of the High Bridge (SHOS vol 1 p200). The name appears in 1769 (SPNO p5). On the present 1:25000 OS map it joins the Trent at Pipe Ridware.

Bentley Brook Name for the lower part of Sneyd Brook, Walsall. Joins the Bescot Brook at Bentley Mill Lane, which joins the Tame at Bescot (VCH vol 17 p143).

Bentley Canal Runs from the Wyrley and Essington Canal at New Cross or Wednesfield Junction to NW of James Bridge (HCMS No. 2). Is less than four miles long (WHTOP p125p). Completed between 1840-4 (VCH vol 2 p296). Opened in 1843. Closure sanctioned in 1961 (HCMS No. 2). Most of it is now derelict.

Bentley Common Gunstone places this at cSO 984985. To NE of Darlaston Green (Offlow hundred). There was a mound here which may have been a burial mound. It was recorded in 1940 and destroyed during housing estate construction in 1947 (OSST 1949-50 p19) (NSJFS 1965 p19).

Bentley Hall Queen Elizabeth Avenue, Bentley, Willenhall. The manor of Bentley had been granted to one 'Drew' alias 'Gervase' by the service of keeping Bentley Hay. He assumed the name of Bentley in William I's reign. From the Bentleys the estate passed to the Griffiths of Wychnor and from them it passed to the Lanes.
THE LANES. Richard Lane rebuilt the old hall in 1426; the Lanes remained at the hall until at least the mid C18. The original hall may have been moated (WJO Aug 1908 p209) (SSAHST 1982-3 p49). The old hall became famous during the time of Col John Lane when Charles II was concealed in it after the battle of Worcester (1651). Charles left the hall in the early hours of Sept 10 1651, disguised as a servant called William Jackson (the name of the son of a neighbouring tenant), accompanied by Col John's daughter, Jane Lane, riding pillion behind him. The couple are believed to have travelled by West Bromwich old church, by Grigg's Well (see), Hill Top, by Sandwell Mill Wood, and along a narrow lane leading to Handsworth Hill Top, through Aston (Warws), Bromsgrove (Worcs), Stratford-on-Avon (Warws), in order to reach Bristol, where Jane had arranged to visit her cousin (HOS p36) (HPPE pp24,25). Drabble says Jane was the Colonel's wife (PD p59); Harwood says she was Thomas Lane's daughter (SOS 1844 p410); and many have followed Stebbing Shaw's error in alleging she was the Colonel's sister (SHOS vol 2 p95) (THS p150) (GNHS pp82-87) (W pp154) (HOWW p337) (HOWG p81) (LGS pp255-256) (SOSH p217) (KES p229) (VB p83) (SGS pp115,185). In the later Stuart period it was customary for the people of the district to make a pilgrimage to one or all of the houses which had sheltered Charles II (SCSF p18). Jon Raven says they made a pilgrimage to all, starting with Bentley and ending with Boscobel (FOS p99). (NHS pp307-308) (W pp47,499) (WPP p84) (BCM April 1972 pp36-38) (Biography of Charles II. Antonia Fraser. 1979 p121) (TOS pp115-116) (see also the bibliography under Boscobel). Thomas Lane, the owner of the old hall at the time of Plot's book, NHS, died in 1715. In the later C17 Plot noted a measure or hand print of the giant Walter Parsons of West Bromwich (see) upon a piece of wainscot at the hall (NHS p294,308 tab 27) (SHOS vol 1 General History pl. vol 2 pp95,96). Plot also noted at the old hall a raven with a bill which was crooked both ways, the mandibles crossing one another like those of the shell apple or cross bill, the lower chap turning upwards and the upper downwards (NHS p234 tab 22 fig 2) (SHOS vol 2 p95). In 1743 the Wednesbury mob presented

Justice Lane with the Methodist preacher, John Wesley (OWB pl No. 7) (WOPP pl p107).
In 1748 (LGS p256) or 1747 the estate was purchased by the Anson family. About 1811 the old hall was taken down and a number of human bones were supposedly discovered between the joists of a ceiling and the floor above (NSFCT 1976 p13). Yet, Shaw writing in 1801, says the hall had been 'entirely mutilated' since his first volume (1798) and had been converted into a modern farmhouse for a tenant, so that little remained of it except for the stables and a summerhouse in the gardens (SHOS vol 2 pp95,96). The new hall was occupied by Mrs Walker widow of SH Walker in 1908 (WJO Aug 1908 p209p) and demolished in 1927 (LGS p255) or in 1929 (TWDOP p134p of in c1890) or in 1930 (WDY p12p of in 1912). The site was then occupied by Bentley Hall Colliery (LGS p255). A cairn commemorating the hall was erected on the site, presently behind Bentley Branch Library, in 1934 (TB June 1992 pp1,19p). (Willenhall in Old Picture Postcards pl 29) (WROP p118p). The site is allegedly haunted by a spectral cavalier (GOM p16) (GPCE pp15,48).

Bentley Hay Former estate which became a hay, or division of Cannock Forest. The hay was in existence by the reign of Henry I and certainly by 1198 (VCH vol 2 p338). It ran continuously up to Cannock Chase until the C16. The 'great oaks' were felled and the deer destroyed in Edward VI's time (DUIGNAN p13 - papers in Walsall Town Chest) (SL p68). Or in the late 1570s for charcoal for the Walsall iron industry (VCH vol 2 p343).

Bentley Moor Here was a colliery by 1843. Houses were built in this area between WW1 and WW2 (VCH vol 17 p189). The moor appears to have been in the area between Green Lane and Stafford Street, Birchills.

Bents, The Tiny hamlet S of Church Leigh. Has also appeared as The Bent.

Beresford Crossing over the Dove and a district formerly in a detached portion of Fawfieldhead township in Alstonefield township and ancient parish. The name is thought to have been from beavers' ford (TPC p163) (LGS p80), or from bear's ford, in consequence of later spellings of Beresford (Some Random Thoughts on Ancient History of Leek. Author and date unknown. From vol 10 of Local Pamphlets in Horace Barks Ref Lib, Hanley) (VCH vol 7 p11). According to legend the last bear in England was slain here. Has appeared as Beveresford, Berreford, or Barriesford (AAD p138) (VCH vol 7 p11). Gives its name to the Beresford family (VCH vol 7 p11).

Beresford Dale Beautiful dale through which the upper reaches of Dove run. N of Dove Dale. Approximately 26m NE from Stafford. Has sylvan beauty in contrast to the austere beauty of Wolfscote Dale (VB p205). Its most scenic spot is at Pike Pool. A small axe of the Neolithic or Bronze Age was found in Beresford Dale in 1910 (NSJFS 1962 p26. 1964 p14). Izaak Walton of Stafford (see) and his friend Charles Cotton of Beresford Hall fished in the dale in the C17. The dale was probably the property of the Cottons of Beresford Hall. In the mid to late C17 Charles Cotton sold much of his estate to pay off debts. The dale was sold at the Green Man Pub, Ashbourne in 1825, and again at the Green Man in 1932, for £15,500 (ES Nov 10 1932 p1). A bailiff patrolled the dale by the early C20 (DMV p31).

Beresford Hall House at approximately SK 127591 in Beresford Dale.
BERESFORDS and HOPE-BERESFORDS. The hall was the seat of the Beresfords from before the Norman Conquest. The manor or estate of Beresford held by them existed by the C13 (VCH vol 7 p15); the Beresfords were foresters of Malbonck Forest by the early C15. By 1670 there was a tradition that one of the two officers of the forest, a bowbearer, lived at Beresford Hall (VCH vol 7 p6). The estate passed from Edward Beresford to his granddaughter Olive Stanhope in 1623. With the death of her husband, Charles Cotton, in 1658 the estate passed to their son, Charles Cotton (1630-1687), the author, poet and friend of Izaak Walton of Stafford (see) (VCH vol 7 p16). Cotton was the author of a long topographical poem 'The Wonders of the Peake' (1681) and 'Poems on Several Occasions' (1689) (PSS pp30-35) (VFC p32). The hall was forcibly entered in 1643 by 'Club Law' (LOU pp77-78). Charles Cotton, was obliged, in 1681, to dispose of the hall to pay off his debts. It subsequently passed through various owners and lost status, becoming a simple farm-house (Dovedale Guide. Keith Mantell. 1985). It was repaired in the early C19 (W p143). In 1825 it was repurchased by a member of another branch of the Beresford family, William Carr Beresford (b1768), who had been created Viscount Beresford in 1823 (The Complete Peerage). On his death in 1854 the viscounty became extinct and the hall was left to his step-son Alexander James Beresford Hope MP (later Beresford-Hope). He pulled the hall down (NSSG p19) in 1859 (VCH vol 7 p16 pl 22), or in c1860 (LGS pp81-82) or in 1870 (JAT p58) with the intention of rebuilding it. A photograph of it shows a modest, long stone cottage-like house (ES Nov 10 1932 p6p). (A Journey to Beresford Hall, in Derbyshire, the seat of Charles Cotton Esq, the Celebrated Angler. William G Alexander. 1841) (CCR through-

out the book) (AAD pp136,138) (BOB) (DMV p32p of the west wing in ruins c1857). Ownership of the estate passed from the Beresford-Hopes to FW Green in 1901 (VCH vol 7 p16).

A modern tower, the Prospect Tower stands on Castle Rock and was built in 1905, by FW Green, using some of the mullion stones from the hall and has the initials F & W & G (DoE II) (TD p) (TPC pp162,163) (LGS p82) (MR p130) (VCH vol 7 p16); a vault apparently exists at the base (PDS&C p113p). In 1910 a fragment of walling and a doorway of the hall survived (LGS pp81-82) (KES p4).

GROUNDS. To the S of the hall was a tower which Cotton alluded to in an 'Epistle to John Bradshaw Esq,' as his 'Hero's Tow'r' (LPCC p16). The carriage drive, created in 1859 (VCH vol 7 p16), and some stone statues in the vicinity of the Prospect Tower were still remaining in the early 1990s. Near Beresford Hall was found a flint arrowhead of the Neolithic or Bronze Age (NHS p396 tab 33 fig 1) and a small socketed chisel of the Late Bronze Age, but said by Plot to be Roman (NHS p404 tab fig 7) (VCH vol 1 p181) (NSJFS 1964 p14). A selenite or star-shaped and layered crystallised formed stone was found by Charles Cotton in rocks by the Dove (NHS p177 tab 11 fig 2 perhaps illustrates it) (SM il vii on preface page). Near Beresford Hall is a mound excavated by Carrington in 1850. No finds were made (TYD p163) (NSJFS 1965 p32). See also Izaak Walton's Fishing Lodge.

Beresford Manor House 1m SSE of Sheen. In Sheen ancient parish. Is of C17 origin and was extended in the C19. Formerly known as Bank Top House and appears still as Banktop on the 1980 OS map 1:25,000. Prince Serge Obolensky resided here for a few years after 1917 (VCH vol 7 p242).

Beresford Spring Little spring near Beresford House, Beresford Dale. Known locally as Warm Well (GNHSS p4). The spring is dry during the summer. In winter it flows briskly and is tepid and steam rises off it in cold frosty or snowy weather (NHS p92). The explanation may be that the spring is on the same fault line as the Buxton springs (GNHSS p4). (TPC p163).

Berkhamsytch Small moorland hamlet 2m NE of Ipstones, 1.5m S of Onecote. In Ipstones parish, but said to be its own tiny parish, with just 115 inhabitants in 1995 (ES June 10 1995 p3) encompassing Bottom House and Winkhill; it has its own school (TOI pp63,95) and a mission church, St Mary and St John, built on the S side of the Leek-Ashbourne road in 1907 (LDD). White spells it Birkemstich (W p780) and it has been written Bircumsych (NSFCT 1908 p133), see Horesych. There remains Upper and Lower Berkhamsytch either side of the A523.

Berkswich Ancient parish which formerly included the settlements of Acton Trussell, Baswich, Bednall, Brocton, Milford and Walton-on-the-Hill. Is also alias Baswich, but Berkswich is usually used to refer to the parish and Baswich, the village. The name has appeared in many forms such as Bercheswic, Berkeswich, Basswich, Bertleswick, Boswich, Bassewich, Berkleswick, Bassage, Berecleswich, Berkyswiche, Baswicke, Baswich, Barkysweche, Baswych, Baswick, Berkswik, Basswik, Birklewich and Basswige (SKYT p89). It is of Anglo-Saxon origin and means 'Beorcol's village' or 'Beorcol's dwelling' (DUIGNAN) or 'Beorcol's dairy farm' (SSE 1987 p28). Harwood says Berkswich probably takes its name from Bertle or Bertelin, the hermit of Stafford, for perhaps he retired here (SOS p186) (SKYT p89). The prebend of Whittington was founded by Roger de Clinton in the C12 as Berkswich. The prebend did not possess any tithes or land at Whittington. The greater tithes of Radford, Weeping Cross, Walton, Milford and Brocton in Berkswich parish belonged to the prebend. The prebendary has often been termed as of Berkswich and Whittington, or of Whittington and Berkswich (SKYT p88) (SSAHST vol 2 1960-61 p51). The parish was a peculiar jurisdiction of the dean and chapter and certain prebendaries of Lichfield cathedral until peculiar jurisdictions were abolished in 1846 (VCH vol 3 p93).

Berryfields Farm 1.25m WSW of Aldridge, S side of Bosty Lane, W of Walsall Road. There was pasture in this area called Berry by 1586. The farmhouse known as Bury between at least 1834 and 1989, was known as Berryfields Farm by 1995 (OS maps and Birmingham A-Zs). Berryfields road on an housing estate to the N of Bosty Lane was built in 1956 (MOA p135) (SNAR p13).

Berry Hill Hill overlooking the upper Trent, and modern residential suburb 0.5m SSW of Bucknall. In Botteslow township in Stoke-upon-Trent ancient parish (HBST p526) (W p236). Presumably, it was this Berry Hill from where a boulder stone was taken, to outside Newcastle-under-Lyme library. It was presented by Henry Warrington on June 6 1885 (SFH p49). The mound mentioned by Garner at Berry Hill (GNHS p113) was not found by Gunstone (NSJFS 1965 p47; spelt Bury Hill). There was coal mining on the Berry Hill estate before the mid C18 (BUB p32). By 1958 a large residential suburb mainly comprising a post-war housing estate had been constructed at Berry Hill (TSS p127). The Mines Rescue Station (opened in 1911) was based at

Berry Hill from 1962 to the station's closure in Sept 1994 (ES Sept 8 1994 p19). Berryhill Retirement Village was built between 1996 and 1998 in an area off Arbourfield Drive. The village opened with its own shops, inn and library in May 1998. It has 170 houses and was the initiative of Stoke-on-Trent city council, an housing association and a charity. It was inspired by a similar schemes at Bradeley (see) and in Holland. There were plans after the death of Diana, Princess of Wales, in 1997, to name the village the Princess Diana Retirement Village (ES Sept 6 1996 p66. Jan 28 1998 p27. Jan 29 1998 p24. May 5 1998). Berryhill was a ward of Stoke-on-Trent district by 1991. Five people saw what they believed to be a UFO from Berry Hill for about 10 to 15 minutes on Sept 4 1967 at about 9.00pm (FSRP p14).

Berry Hill Hill at N end of Cannock Chase next to Harts Hill.

Berry Hill Hill S of Lichfield, which has also appeared as Bury Hill (HOL p561). Icknield Street passes over it. There was a farmhouse here by the later C18, but Berry Hill had been inhabited in the later C14 (VCH vol 14 p21).

Berry Hill In Kibblestone quarter in Stone ancient parish (W p364). There is a Berry Hill Farm 1m NNE of Moddershall.

Berryhill House N end of London Road, Lichfield. Originated as Berryhill Cottage. Built by 1841 and later enlarged (VCH vol 14 p25).

Berry Ring Hillfort 1.5m ENE of Haughton. In Bradley parish. The fort is of Iron Age origin dating from the C2 to C1 BC (HOS p10). It is of seven acres, defended by a single bank and ditch, with trace of a second on the north. Entrances exist on the E and S sides. Some Roman artifacts were found here (GNHS p70). A flint knife and scraper have been found near the fort but the site has never been excavated (NSFCT 1943 p66). A pottery find has been made on Berry Hill (Staffs Advertiser Sept 18 1969 p8). The name occurs as 'Buryhill' within the lordship of Billington in 1471 (VCH vol 4 p74); it has also appeared as Bury Ring. Plot wondered if a battle between Duke Wada and the rest of the murderers of King Ethelred, and King Eardulf, his successor, was fought here. Matthew of Westminster, Roger Hoveden and Simeon Dunelmensis all agree it was fought at a place called Billingaho or Billingahoth in 798. But Plot considers it unlikely that the King of Northumberland would bring a battle amongst his conspirators so far out of his kingdom (NHS p411). (SD p54) (GNHS p72) (HSS p30-36) (MOS p5) (VCH vol 1 p336) (LGS p145) (SOSH p10) (KES p107) (NSFCT vol 78 p66) (A Guide to Prehistoric England. N Thomas. 1960. p187) (NSJFS 1964 p16) (BOE pp76,77) (SPJD p16p,17).

Berth Hill Hill 0.5m NNW of Maer. There is a spring on the hill which served Maer until the village received a mains supply in 1980 (SVB p119); in the later C17 Plot noted a perennial spring at Berth Hill which was weak or weeping rather than running (NHS p51). A fort of Iron Age origin, dating from the C2 to C1 BC lies on the hill (HOS p10). It is an irregular enclosure of some nine acres, bounded by a single bank, ditch and counterscarp bank. Entrances are on the W and NE sides. The extreme length within the inner vallum is 355 yards and the extreme width is 225 yards (VCH vol 1 p340). It may have been occupied in Roman times; some Roman artifacts were found at Brough near Maer (GNHS p70). The name has also appeared Cop Low? (SOS p114 - mentioned by Harwood), Byrth (LGS p182), Bryth (STM Feb 1964 p31), Bruff and Burgh Hill (VCH vol 1 p340); the latter signifying a Saxon burgh (NHS pp408-409); the fort may have been re-used in Saxon times, when many battles are said to have taken place in the vicinity (see under Maer). Erdeswick noted the fort in the late C16 (SH p29). (NHS pp408-409) (W p397) (SOSH p10) (SMC p163) (NSFCT vol 62 p171. vol 66 p90) (A Guide to Prehistoric England. N Thomas. 1960 p187) (NSJFS 1964 p29). Apparently the W side is haunted by a formless bundle which rolls from the top of the hill and disappears into Meg's Pit on the WSW side. It was seen by a Miss Harrison of Maer Hall at midnight (NSFCT 1931 pp91 plan facing -100).

Bertram's Dingle Beautiful ravine in Needwood Forest near Swilcar Oak, Forest Banks. It was noted by Pitt in the early C19 as 'a singularly romantic valley, which if private property might be made uncommonly beautiful' (THS p55) (NSFCT 1891 p41). So called, according to tradition, because a Bertram or Bartram lived here for some months in a carefully-hidden hut (LGS p191). (SHOS vol 1 p66) (SSC p125).

Berwood Cottage Stood at the junction of Waterloo Road and Birmingham-Dudley road, Smethwick. Residence of William Spurrier (d1848), a Birmingham lawyer. The house has been called Blood Hall on account of Spurrier acting for the Crown in prosecutions for forgery; Spurrier prosecuted the famous coiner, William Booth (STELE Oct 20 1951. Feb 4 1955) (VCH vol 17 p94) (TB Feb 1996 p5). The house is said to have been properly called The Elms (STELE Feb 4 1955).

Bescot Former hamlet in the foreign of Walsall, now a suburb, 1.5m SW of Walsall. At Bescot the two rivers both called Tame converge to form the Tame. The name is of Anglo-Saxon origin and means Beorhtmund's cottage

(DUIGNAN) (SOB p9) (VCH vol 17 p157) (SPN p134). Appears in DB as a carucate of waste land (VCH vol 17 p171). The old tiny hamlet of Bescot was 1m NE of Wednesbury at the N end of the present Pleck Park. (BCM July 1973 p50). The Grand Junction Railway which was built through Bescot in 1837 killed most of Walsall's coaching trade (VCH vol 17 p167). The first station in the Bescot area at Bescot Bridge (see), closed in 1850 when the station moved to its current site 1m ESE of the original Bescot settlement. The ecclesiastical parish of Pleck and Bescot, created in 1860, was called 'Walsall St John' by 1991 (GLAUE p420). In the later C17 Dr Plot noted luminous earth at Bescot. Mr Jones whilst riding at night with Capt Thomas Lane fell into a ditch in Bescott grounds. Helping him up, Capt Lane stirred some mud, which when on their accoutrements shone like a faint flame and continued to glow for a mile's riding (NHS p116) (SHOS vol 2 p82). Plot also noted at Bescot the plant Caryophyllus Hortensis which grew different coloured flowers on the same stalk, which he thought very unusual (NHS p203).

Bescot Bridge Bridge over the Tame carrying the Walsall-Wednesbury road, in Walsall ancient parish near Wednesbury ancient parish boundary. There was a bridge here from c1300 (VCH vol 17 p168). The violent confrontation between Edward Elwell's workers and the builders of the GJR, as the latter tried to gain possession of Elwell's land at Wednesbury Forge in c1834 to construct the line, has been described as the 'Battle of Bescot Bridge' (IE pp73-74). The GJR, which opened on July 4 1837, had a station at Bescot Bridge (IAS p131). It was known locally as Walsall station and closed in 1850 after a new Bescot station was opened at the line's junction with the Walsall branch line (SSR pp7,10). A new station, known as Wood Green, was built on the site at Bescot Bridge in 1881; it closed in 1941 (VCH vol 17 p168).

Bescot Brook Alternative name for the Tame before it reaches James Bridge (SNDB p17).

Bescot Grange Bescot. Demolished in c1930 (HOPL).

Bescot Hall Formerly situated on W side of Bescot Drive, Bescot, NE of Bescot Manor House, its predecessor. Built in brick in the C18 (VCH vol 17 p172 il of c1795 facing p176) (WROP p118p of in c1908). In 1794 Richard Aston, a wealthy coal-mine owner, bought the hall, extending it and laying out gardens. During the C19 the hall was occupied by several owners and tenants. In 1922 it was bought by Pitt Bonarjee for use as a private school. It was later damaged by fire and was demolished in 1929 (SHOS vol 2 p82 pl xii shows two engravings of the hall and ancient moat) (GNHS p550) (WP p97) (WPP p106) (AOBC p17) (HOPL) (VCH vol 17 p159) (SSAHST vol 33 1991-92 p49). The hall is shown on the 1947 OS map 1:25,000 (sheet 32/99). After the house was demolished part of the grounds were built on with houses and part turned into Pleck Park in 1926 and 1938; the moat was filled in about this time (HOPL) (VCH vol 17 p159).

Bescot Manor House Formerly situated in Pleck Park between Pleck Park entrance from Bescot Drive and the M6, at SO 997968. It existed by 1311 when occupied by the Hillarys, lords of the manor of Bescot. In 1345 they were licensed to crenelate it. In at least the later C14 it contained a chapel (VCH vol 17 p172). The house was surrounded by a moat, with an extra ditch on one side (VCH vol 1) (NSFCT 1982 p10) (SSAHST 1982-3 p49). In 1425 the Mountforts became lords of the manor and the manor house was their residence in the C16 and C17; Symon Mountfort had his estate sequestered by parliament in 1646 (WAM pp79,80). The Mountforts were succeeded in 1681 by Thomas Harris, who sold the property to Jonas Slaney in 1725. The house was demolished in 1731 and replaced by Bescot Hall (see) (SSAHST vol 33 1991-92 p49).

Bescot Pool Artificial pool dug in 1804. Its water was used to drive machinery at Wednesbury Forge (IE p72).

Besom Cottage Cottage formed from two C18 cottages, which were originally known as Osborns Barn (1834 OS map) and Osborne's Barns (original OS map 1801). It has been suggested that these cottages were built before the enclosure of Great Barr Common in 1799 and the cottages represent illegal encroachment and that they may have been occupied by besom makers (SLHT p9). Besom House is on the N side of Foley Road West 1.75m NE of Great Barr church.

Betheney Former island on which stood the original settlement of Stafford. The island, created by the twisting Sow, to the N and S, and by a marsh to the N and E, was reputedly first inhabited by the Saxon saint and Mercian prince, Bertram of Stafford (see), according to the Saxon chronicles and Camden. Bertram had his hermitage on Betheney from c705 AD (HOS pp65-66). Later Ethelfleda built her burh on it and founded Stafford (W p321) (SSTY p1). Has also appeared as Bethnei (HOS p65).

Betley Large village on a flat ridge above Mere Gutter over 19m NW of Staf-

ford. Former township and chapelry in Audley ancient parish.

EARLY. The last **Ice Age** had its southern most extent at Betley (BVC p12). An axe-hammer of **Neolithic** or **Bronze Age** was found on the Betley Hall estate in the early C20 (NSFCT 1927 p165) (NSJFS 1964 p16). A Bronze Age axe, which went to the Potteries Museum, was found opposite East Lawns (BVC p33).

1000 to 1500. A **Saxon hearth** was discovered in the central area of the village, near The Black Horse Inn, possibly indicating the site of a nearby settlement (BVC p33). The manor of Betelege appears in DB. Later forms are: Bettelega (C12) (SPN p17), and Beckley (BS p435). The **name**, unique in England, is of Anglo-Saxon origin and represents possibly Beta's lea (DUIGNAN), or 'Betta's woodlands glade or wood clearing.' The personal name refers to a woman (BVC p34) (SSE 1996 p10) (SPN pp17,74). The word 'better' comes from the Saxon 'betan' and Betley may represent 'the better or good meadow' (NSFCT 1886 p58). There was a chapel of ease to Audley at Betley from 1125 and certainly by 1291. The present **church**, St Margaret, at the junction of Church Lane and The Butts, is essentially a timber building of late C15 and early C16 origin (BVC p65) (BOE p68). It was restored in 1842 by Sir Gilbert Scott and was one of the first churches, if not the first, restored by him (NSFCT 1917 p141). Henry de Aldithley or Audley on May 2 1227 was granted a charter to hold a **market** every Thursday (STM June 1964 p30) (NSJFS 1971 p51) (SVB p31). In 1390 the market day was changed from Thursday to Sunday. The market had reverted back to Thursday by 1500 (BVC p36). The market had lapsed by the C19 (SCSF p95) (BVC p210). In the C19 **fairs** were held on the last Tuesday in April, on July 31, and on the last Tuesday in Oct (BVC p210). The original curiously-phrased proclamation, which was read at Betley fairs, is given in NSFCT 1886 pp58-59. The earliest reference to Betley being a **borough** is in 1299 and it was still being styled a borough in 1407 (NSJFS 1972 p68). Betley was styled a Parliamentary Borough in Cal. Inq. 10. Henry IV (NSSG p7). (Oldfield vol vi p309) (SOS p92) (SHC 1909 p214). The allocation of burgage plots may be the reason for the broad high street (NSSG p7); Betley is perhaps the only village in Staffs to have a boulevard (NSFCT 1886 p57). Money was paid for the repair of the **stocks** in 1812 (BVC p130). The earliest recorded fulling mill in the county was at Betley in the 1270s (HOS p42).

1500 to PRESENT. Betley became a separate ecclesiastical parish in 1717 (GLAUE p403). Yet Betley PR dates from 1537 making it one of the oldest in the country (NSFCT 1917 p141). The parish **wake** was on the first Sunday after Oct 6 (W p385), and was established in Henry VII's reign (BVC p65). **Civil War**. The royalist Lord John Byron had his headquarters at Betley at the end of 1643 and in early 1644. From here he besieged the parliamentarian garrison at Nantwich; the Egertons of Betley Old Hall were staunch royalists; Randle Egerton had fought at Edgehill (SHJ summer 1987 pp31-32). Betley was once a **route to Ireland** and apparently the village was renowned for raising the children left on their way by Irish women (info Rose Wheat). Celia Fiennes, traveller and writer, passed through Betley in 1698 noting it in her journal (BVC p8). The natural ruggedness of the road through Betley has evoked this local rhyme

> Aidley, Madeley, Keele and 'Castle,
> Huxon, Muxon, Woore and Asson
> Rainscliffe rugged and Wrinehill's rough
> But Betley's the place where the devil came through

The rhyme implies that if not created by God then the road was made by the devil (NSFCT 1886 p59) (M p29) (NSSG p7) (SCSF p166) (SJC pp2,3) (FOS p34) (SMM p30). It appears that the proposed Liverpool to Hull **Canal**, which was never built, was intended to come through Betley (BVC p170). The nearest station on the Grand Junction **Railway** (opened 1837) to Betley was at Basford, S of Crewe in Ches, three miles away. A station at Betley Road opened on July 1 1875 and closed to passengers on Oct 1 1945 and to goods traffic on March 13 1950 (BVC pp168-169). There was a **well** in Church Lane known as Tommy's Well, which was frequented up to 1935 by coalminers on their way to work (BVC p14). **Betley Ladies' College**, housed in Croft House, was in existence by at least 1870 and closed in 1914 (BVC p184). There were plans for Betley to have its own **Internet** Website for parish information on the computer network as early as Oct 1998 (ES Oct 12 1998 p3). **Betley Show**, an annual produce fair, appears to have been founded in the C19. In the 1960s the show day was changed from the first Wednesday to the first Saturday of Aug (SVB p31). There was an **earthquake** at Betley, presumably related to a movement along the Red Rock Fault or another local fault, at 1.30pm Oct 6 1863 (A History of British Earthquakes. C Davison. 1924) (BVC p9 note). **Natives and visitors**. **William Errington** founded a Catholic school under the direction of Catholic Bishop Richard Challoner, which was opened in Betley in 1762 as a temporary measure before moving to larger premises at Sedgley Park (VCH vol 3 p112). By 1805 **John Fenton Boughey Fletcher** raised and commanded the Betley Volunteers, a volunteer force (BVC p207). On Dec 1 1888 **James Jervis**, aged 34, a pointsman at the signal box at Betley Road Station, killed, in an unaccountable frenzied attack, his wife, Sarah Ann aged 36, and two of his eight children, Harry aged four and Mabel aged 14 months, at his cottage. Having had a mind to take the lives of all his family Jervis died of wounds to the throat he had inflicted upon himself in the attack (DMF pp19-32).

Betley Common To the W of Betley. On the Cheshire border.

Betley Court On W side of Main Road, Betley. Built in 1716 by John Craddock (NSSG p7), who had moved to Betley in 1711 (BVC p116). Jacobean oak panelling on the attic floor is said to come from Shelton Old Hall in Queen Anne's reign; the Craddocks and Fentons of Shelton being cousins (BVC p121). In the later C18 the house was occupied by a daughter of John Craddock who married a Fenton of the Steps, Newcastle-under-Lyme, but formerly of Shelton. Their son John died young without an heir and the estate passed to their eldest daughter Anne who married Sir Thomas Fletcher Bart; he came to live at Betley Court in 1792 (BOE p68) (BVC pp8,121) (SVB p31) (MR pp30p, 32pc). John Nash carried out alterations to the house in c1805 and the house became known as Betley Court in 1807 (BVC p122). With the death of Sir Thomas Fletcher in 1812 the estate passed to his son John (d1823) who took the name of Boughey and was known as Fenton Fletcher-Boughey; he preferred to live at Aqualate Hall, and Betley Court was then occupied by his sister Elizabeth who married Francis Twemlow. They were succeeded by their son, Thomas Fletcher-Twemlow (d1894). Thomas' wife lived at Betley Court until her death in 1911. Successive Fletcher-Twemlows lived at the house until 1940 (BVC pp122-126) (BOPP pls 33,34,35,36), when it was used as a Red Cross hospital. From 1943 it became a rehabilitation centre for patients from Stoke-on-Trent hospitals. For a number of years it remained empty, until in 1977, it was converted into flats (BVC p126). A replica of the famous window once at Betley Old Hall was to be made for the gallery of Betley Court (ES Feb 5 1981 p19p). (ES March 1 1975 p).
GROUNDS. Dovecote (DoE II*). There is an ice-house at SJ 751482 SW of the house between the fishpond and the boathouse (IHB p392). In the garden is a sculpture (1995) by Su Hurrell, incorporating an air raid siren used here (ES Aug 23 1995 p9p). An iron grille fronting the road by Betley Court is inscribed 'J.C. & A.A.' This could refer to craftsman - John Anchors, who has a sword and mace stand in the V&A (BTC p14). The Temple (TOH p117p). The Wilderness is an occasional local name for an avenue in Betley with access to Betley Court, on the main road (BOPP pl 14).

Betley Hall On E side of Main road, at SJ 754491, Betley. Built in 1780 by Charles Tollet at a cost of £3,000 near the site of an older building probably the mill E of the main road. The existing mill pool was enlarged to form a large lake to the N and E of the new hall (BVC p92). The hall was said to have a Staffordshire address, whilst it was actually situated in Cheshire, and its grounds were in Shropshire (BVC p108 pls 7,8). Charles Tollet, who died in 1796, was succeeded by a distant relative, George Embury (d1855), who changed his name to Tollet. Tollet (Embury) was an adviser to Josiah Wedgwood II and Lord Crewe and a correspondent with Charles Darwin; Darwin was a visitor to George (Embury) Tollet's Model Farm near Betley Hall; his daughter Georgina read the MS of 'Origin of Species' before publication (1859) (BOPP) (info David B Thompson). Mrs Gaskell, novelist, was a guest of the Tollets (Emburys) at Betley Hall (BOPP), as was Florence Nightingale, aged nine, who wrote in her diary from Betley Hall in 1829 (BVC pp105-106) (BOPP pl 30). By the 1860s the hall was occupied by the Hope family. Charles Tollet (d1870), son of George Tollet (Embury), took the name of Wicksted in accordance with the wishes of his maternal great-uncle Thomas Wicksted (mem in Betley church). The history of the North Staffordshire Hunt really begins with the mastership of Charles Wicksted of Betley Hall in 1825 (A History of the North Staffordshire Hunt 1825-1902. CJ Blagg. 1902 p4) (VCH vol 2 pp359,362) (MJW p22). Point-to-point horse races, organised by the hunt, took place at Mucklestone and later at Sandon Hall. The widow of his descendant, a George Wicksted, married Col JA Macdonald and they continued to live in Betley Hall until her death in the 1920s. The stained glass window depicting morris dancers which had been in Betley Old Hall (see) was sold at auction in 1922 and went to Leigh manor, Minsterley (BVC p110). The hall had a water softener (SLM April 1988 p30p). WD Caroe designed the portico (TOH p33p). Betley Hall, for sale in 1925, was described as fallen into disrepair, in 1980 (BVC p110), and was demolished in 1984 (BOPP pls 30,31). However, others say it was demolished in c1924 (NSFCT 1956 p115) (STM June 1964 p31). By 1996 the site of the hall was

covered by modern housing (AHJ 1996 p14). Cornelius Varley's painting 'Betley Hall' 1820 was on display in Stoke-on-Trent Art Gallery in Feb 1997. GROUNDS. Clay Pigeon House (TOH p96p). Clock Tower has an inscription with 'T.F.T' (Thomas Fletcher Twemlow) (BTC p21) (VB p185) (DoE II). There was an ice-house near the seven acre lake to the N of the hall. It was built in 1790 with Josiah Wedgwood's involvement as a family friend. It was a bricked, tunnel-shaped construction, about 40 feet long, half above ground. It was demolished several years prior to 1984 (IHB p392). The Foot-bridge (TOH p118).

Betley Mere Small natural lake SW of Betley. (BOPP pl 37) (MR p33p) (WSS p103). Could be the Border Mere, an ornamental lake for Betley Court spanning the border of Staffs and Ches (NSFCT 1886 p58).

Betley Old Hall On W side of Main Road at the N end of Betley. Timber-framed and has a chimneypiece dated 1621 (BOE p68) (LGS p82) (BVC pl 4 il of in 1820). Owned by the Egertons, and when they became lords of Betley in the C15 or C16, Betley Old Hall became the manor house and was extended in the later C16 (BVC pp51-52,54). On one side of a wall in a room wainscoted with dark oak is carved this inscription

Justicia. Sine. Prudentia. Plurimum. Poterit: Sine. Justicia. Nihil. Valebit. Prudentia.

Above are the initials 'RE. FE' and the date 1621. The initials probably refer to Ralph Egerton (d1610) and his wife. On each side of the inscription are two figures, apparently representing Justice (with an unsheathed sword) and Prudence (NSFCT 1917 p141). On one of the bricks is 'R.W. 1626' (DoE II*).
BETLEY WINDOW. A famous stained glass window which portrays 11 dancers of the C16 or C17 period was long housed at Betley Old Hall and then at Betley Hall. It measures 38 inches by 15.5 inches (BVC p112). The dancers are believed to be those from the Betley Morris Dance. It has been known as the Mery Window, Jubilee Window, Tollets Window (RHH pl 28), and the Morris Dancers' Window (BVC p112). Douce has thought the window may date from 1460-1470 on the strength of the pointed shoes worn by the dancers, but is forced to admit that other features suggest a later date or an alteration or insertion of fresh pictures (BVC p113). Hackwood says it dates from early Tudor times, and EJ Nicol thinks it may date to before 1536 and is the design of a C15 Flemish engraver, Israel Van Meckenhem (Journal of the English Folk Dance and Song Society 1953 pp59-67 pc) (SCSF p17). According to Prof Godfrey Brown it may have been a part of a set of 12 windows at Heleigh Castle (see) and looted in or after the Civil War when the castle was destroyed, or that the Earl of Audley gave it to Henry VIII as a wedding present on his marriage to Catherine of Aragon in 1509, and that after his divorce (1533) from her he had it placed in the Tower of London, from where George Tollet took it in 1718 (ES Jan 1 2000 p10). Some, including George Tollet (d1779), have said that it may have been designed for Betley Old Hall in 1621 (FLJ 1968 pp168,169) (RHH pl 28); this date appears over a door in the old hall, and is often taken as the date for the building of the hall. Others say it was designed between 1625-50. Hackwood says it is probably the oldest treatment of the subject of Maypole dancing to be found in England (SCSF p17). The window first came to light because George Tollet (d1779) offered it to illustrate Part I of The History of Henry IV, in Johnson and Steevens' 1778 edition of 'Shakespeare' to which he offered some textual notes about Morris dancing and Mary Games (BVC p112). It awakened the public's interest in the folklore traditions of Morris dancing and the window, itself. Hone, in his Year Book 1832, printed an impression of two of the dancers, one Maid Marian, and the other The Fool (SCSF p17). The window was reproduced in Francis Douce's 'Illustrations of Shakespeare' 1839. And again in Gutch's 'Lytell Geste of Robin Hood' and in colour in Charles Knight's 'Old England' (FLJ 1968 pp168,169), and is written about in Hinchcliffe's 'Barthomley' (BVC p112). In 1886 Mr D'Arcy Ferris revived the 'Shakespearean' Morris Dance at Stratford-upon-Avon decking his dancers out in the garb of that depicted in the window. It could be said that the Morris Dance depicted in the window gave rise to the English Folk Dance revival from the 1905 revival onwards (FLJ 1968 pp168,169). The window, about the size of a fire-screen, bears the legend 'A Mery May.' The hobby horse image 'ridden' by a king (MR p31) is of a continental type almost unknown in England (FLJ 1968 pp168,169). The pole is shown to be planted in a grassy mound and has affixed to it the red cross banner of St George, and a white pennon or streamer emblazoned with a red cross and terminating in two forked points (SCSF p17). In c1924 the window was sold at Sotheby's to Hon Mrs John Bridgeman, whose son had it placed into the main staircase at Leigh Manor near Minsterley, Shrops (NSFCT 1956 p115) (STM June 1964 p31). Another

account says the Hon Mrs John Bridgeman purchased the glass in 1895 so it could be kept at Betley Hall, but in 1922 the Bridgemans sold it at Sotheby's only to repurchase it again some time later at a vastly higher price than they had sold it for (BVC p113). From Leigh Manor the glass went to the V&A Museum in 1976. (BART pp192-202) (HYB) (GNHSS p19) (SHC 1923 pp3-19) (BCWJ p7) (FCRE pp120-122 il on p120) (ES Feb 5 1981) (TOH pp59p,128) (SCM April 1988 pp26,27pc) (MR pp30p,31,32pc). The window appeared on national stamps in May 1981, and a replica of the window was to be made for the gallery of Betley Court (ES Feb 5 1981 p19p).

In 1718 the hall was bought from the Egerton family by George Tollet, Accountant-General of Ireland (1691) and Commissioner of the Navy (1701) (BS p458). It was now known as 'Old Hall Farm' (BVC p87). George Tollet III (1725-1779) was the last Tollet to live at Betley Old Hall, as his brother Charles, who inherited after him, started to build Betley (new) Hall in 1780 (BS p458) (BVC p92). Another account says Betley manor was purchased from the Egertons by John Chetwynd of Maer Hall in 1730 and his second son, William Chetwynd (d1765) was occupying the old hall in the 1750s (COI p241) (NSFCT 1886 p59. 1917 p141) (BOPP pls 20,28,29). The old hall seems to have been repaired in the early C19 (BVC p103). Betley Old Hall may be the Betley Farm House painted by Cornelius Varley in 1820. Three paintings of Betley Farm House were on display in Stoke-on-Trent Art Gallery in Feb 1997.

Betley Old Park Former medieval hunting ground, belonging to the Aldithley or Audley family (NSFCT 1910 p172).

Beverleyhall One of the four prebends of Gnosall Collegiate Church. Its prebendary lived in Beverley Hall; the name appearing in 1366 and as Beverly Hall in 1502 (SPNO p158). It was still standing in 1580, but not by 1677 (VCH vol 4 pp113,115-116). The moated site at Moat Farm on the Stafford Road, not far from the vicarage grounds is the site of Beverley Hall (LGS p263) (VCH vol 4 p115). The name is based on a surname, derived from Beverley, Yorks (SPNO p158).

Bevin's Lane Track to E of Seven Springs (PCC p77), Cannock Chase.

Bexmore Farm 1m E of Lichfield cathedral, at SK 132100. The name is derived from Berkesmoor, meaning birch moor (VCH vol 14 p277). The farm stood in the vicinity of the lost village of Morughale. By 1854 the farmhouse had become the Railway Inn. The inn reverted to a farmhouse in the late 1870s and was demolished when Eastern Avenue was built in 1972 (VCH vol 14 pp278-279).

Bhylls, The Former house at Finchfield, in Penn ancient parish. Appears on 1839 tithe map (ALP p4), but some say the house was built in c1870 for John Clarkson Major (1826-1895), tar distiller and mayor of Wolverhampton 1875-6. The house, later renamed Bellencroft, was demolished in c1950 (WOLOP p25p) to make way for housing (ALP p4) (Wolverhampton Chronicle Oct 15 1999 p20p).

Bickford Small hamlet just W of Whiston. In Penkridge parish. The name, of Anglo-Saxon origin, represents probably Bica's ford, and not from Beckford which usually means 'the ford by the brook' (DUIGNAN) (SSE 1996 p10) (SPN p16). The manor of Bigeford appears in DB (SSE 1996 p10). Later Bickford appears as Bykford (1251), Bigesford (1307), and Byckforde (1547) (SPNO p103). A medieval chapel at Byford, mentioned in April 1553, may be a reference to Bickford (SHC 1915 p206).

Bickford Grange House over 0.5m SW of Whiston. Mostly dates from the C19 when it was enlarged and renamed. The late C18 building which it incorporated was known as the New House. A sundial on the S gable is inscribed with the date 1856 (LCWA p82) (VCH vol 4 p145).

Bickford Green Bickford, Whiston. Appears in 1732. Now obsolete (SPNO p104).

Biddulph (locally *Biddle* TTTD p152). Ancient parish and town in the upper Biddulph Brook valley 22.5m NNE of Stafford.
EARLY. A stone mace head has been found at Biddulph (NSFCT 1908 p194). A **Neolithic** or **Bronze Age** axe-hammer found in the churchyard is in the Potteries Museum (NSFCT vol 43 p144) (NSJFS 1964 p16). A looped palstave of the Bronze Age found in the Biddulph area is in Sheffield Museum (NSJFS 1964 p16). **Roman**. A silver spoon from the C4 was found at Biddulph with other spoons (now lost). It is in the BM and has engraved on it the Christian Chi-rh monogram and alpha and Omega. A boy found four British copies of a Roman coin, a 'third brass' of Tetricus, in c1942, reputedly from Biddulph (NSFCT 1942 p56) (NSJFS 1964 p16).
1000 to 1500. According to tradition there was a **church** at Biddulph on the W side of the present Congleton Road N of the present Biddulph town centre since 999 AD and the stone altar was one of only seven of its kind in England (NSFCT 1938 pp117-118). The present church, built in the C12, is dedicated to St Lawrence. Biddulph has appeared as Bidolf, a manor, in DB, Bydulff

(1382) (BHS p14), Biddle (c1540) (LI appendix p172), and Biddulph (Bowen's map). The **name** of Anglo-Saxon origin means 'by diggings' or 'place by the mine' implying mining here before the Norman Conquest, perhaps iron (SL p78) (SSE 1996 p10) (SPN p17) (HOS 1998 p95). Dr Wilkes in his 'Original Collections for History of Staffs' (1832) asserts it is derived from two words 'Big Delph' meaning a big coal pit, the g being transformed into a d (NSFCT 1888 p69). Coal is found only a few yards from Grange Road and Woodhouse Lane close to the parish church; the nucleus of the original settlement (BHS June 1968 p12). Or the name is of Anglo-Saxon origin and means Beadulf (war wolf). It is a rare instance of a personal name without a suffix (DUIGNAN). Bowers and Clough suggest the war wolf was Wulfhere, king of Mercia (657-74), who may have hid on the moors about Biddulph (RHPS p21). An extensive Biddulph manor was held by Ormus le Guidon, son of Richard the Forester, by 1150. On his death in 1189 the manor was divided between his sons into the manors of Lower Biddulph, Knypersley, Middle Biddulph, and Overton (BALH p21). The de Verduns, the early overlords, held Biddulph Castle in Bailey's Wood (see), and may have returned from a crusade in the Holy Land with **Saracens**, who settled in the Biddulph Moor (see) area. **Knight Templars** may have had a cell at Biddulph. This tradition arises from the belief that the crosses on the grave slabs outside Biddulph church are Templar crosses, and the affinity the Templars had with the Cistercian Order who had several houses in the vicinity (Congleton Chronicle 1992) (SMM pp108-109). Biddulph was created a **parish** after 1086 and before 1291 and must have formed originally out of Wolstanton original parish (SHC 1916 pp192,195). The S part of the parish lies high up on England's main watershed, whilst the N part comprises a valley (BALH p15). There was **mining** in the Biddulph area from the Middle Ages. From the C14 there was **iron working** (BALH p93).
1500 to PRESENT. For the Civil War in the Biddulph area see Biddulph Old Hall. The making of **textiles** in the parish was carried on from at least the C18. Between 1800-1850 cotton spinning was carried on in the northern parts of the parish. Fustian cutting was carried on at Biddulph from c1870 to the 1930s (BALH p93). The hamlet of **Bradley Green** 1m SSW of Biddulph parish church had become the commercial centre of Biddulph parish by at least the 1890s and was to take the name of Biddulph (BHS p12). West Street, a small street on the W side of High Street in Bradley Green, was popularly known as Monkey Row, probably because several properties had a mortgage on them (BHS June 1968 p16). The Biddulph Valley **Railway**, which opened in 1863, and linked Biddulph to the Potteries and Macclesfield, closed to passengers in 1927, but continued to carry coal. The station stood in Station Road to the NNW of High Street. Formerly known as Gillow Heath Station, becoming Biddulph Station in 1897, it closed on Dec 7 1964 and has since been converted into a private residence (NSJFS 1964 pp77,78) (BALH pp107-124). WW1. A Zeppelin was sighted and heard passing over Biddulph in the early hours of Nov 28 1916 moving towards the Kidsgrove-Goldenhill-Tunstall area (TB July 1994 p19). Biddulph **Grammar School**, founded in 1960, later became the state school Woodhouse Middle School (info DJ Wheelhouse). A **well-dressing** ceremony at Biddulph took place on May 21 (ES May 22 1934 p6p). **Newspaper and radio**. The Biddulph Chronicle, appears to have been founded on Jan 1 1959, and is still running (SHJ spring 1996 p11). The BBC radio programme 'Down Your Way' came to Biddulph in Feb 1971 and interviewed Biddulph inhabitants for the programme (BGFB pp100-101). Biddulph **Historical Society**, founded out of Keele University extramural classes, in 1967. It produced transactions, BHS, from the late 1960s. In c1976 the Society folded, but some of its unpublished research was used in BALH (info DJ Wheelhouse). A Mr Farr had a pedigree of the Biddulph family, and a former vicar of Biddulph had a Ms on Biddulph history (NSSG p7)

Biddulph Brook This brook is said to have risen out of New Pool, but it is shown recently (1979 OS map 1:25,000) to rise on the western slope of the Wickenstones. Flows N through Biddulph on through Mossley Gap towards Congleton. Formerly known as the Dane Inshaw, Daningshaw (BALH pp15,16), River Biddle, and Bidle Water (Saxton's map) (SPNO p5).

Biddulph Clough Biddulph. (PS p20p of the waterfall).

Biddulph Common The Bridestones are situated on it (NSFCT 1928 p158). In Biddulph parish.

Biddulph Grange Former marshy moor under 1m NNE of Biddulph town centre. The area is believed to have been a grange of Hulton Abbey from the late C13, although there is no documentary proof (info DJ Wheelhouse) (BALH p23) (BGFB p9). Dame Bowyer of Ye Grange House is recorded in PR in 1668 (BGFB p9). Allegedly, a pool at Biddulph Grange was a ducking place for scolds (TFTP p33). In 1812, when bought by James Bateman of Salford, Lancs, the house was a vicarage known as The Grange. His grandson James

Bateman (1811-1897), son of John Bateman (1782-1858) of Knypersley Hall, moved here in 1842 (BGFB p9). He built a house, and laid out gardens. The estate remained in the Bateman family until it was bought by Robert Heath in 1872. The house was mainly destroyed by fire on Jan 16 1896. Another house was reconstructed on the site incorporating the former portico. It has panels showing Apollo and the Muses, Music and Song Figures, the founding of Troy, and Orpheus taming the Wild Beasts (BGFB p27): arabesque ceramic slabs (BGFB p26). And four circular stained glass windows in the Entrance Hall depicting the mystic elements, earth, air, fire, and water (BGFB p108p) (GS p130) (MR p33p). In early 1923 Robert Heath gave Biddulph Grange to the Potteries and Newcastle Cripples' Guild (or North Staffs Cripples' Aid Society) for a children's orthopaedic hospital. The hospital was officially opened by the Prince of Wales (later Edward VIII) on June 14 1924; taken over by Lancashire county council in 1928; and visited by Princess Margaret in 1972 (BGFB pp51,54,64,100) (TTTD p170) (PWNS p145) (ES Aug 5 1995 p29). Moorlands district council bought the Grange in 1986 for the NT to restore the garden (BGFB p118). The hospital, meanwhile, continued until 1991 when the local health authority vacated the house. The house was then largely unused and fell into disrepair. In 1998 planning permission to convert it into a family home was granted to David Hartley, a Merseyside millionaire, by when it was listed Grade II (BGFB p118) (ES Aug 19 1998 p16).

GARDEN. The garden conceived and designed by James Bateman is perhaps the greatest High Victorian garden in the country, and one of the earliest examples of a compartmented garden - an idea later followed by gardens at Sissinghurst Castle, Kent, and Hidcote Manor, Glous (CL Oct 21 1999 p78). It took 20 years to lay out between c1845-1865 and covers 15-20 acres (Observer Magazine May 27 1979). The first excursion of the NSFC on May 13 1865 was to Biddulph Grange Garden; James Bateman was the first NSFC president (1865-1870) (NSFCT 1917 p142. 1932 p38). The garden was still being maintained when the NSFC visited in 1965 (NSJFS 1966 p67). By the mid 1980s the garden had deteriorated. When the Biddulph Grange estate came up for sale in 1986 (The Times March 31 1986) the Biddulph Grange Garden Appeal was set up (ES Sept 10 1986 p3) to help the NT buy and restore the gardens (NT Magazine autumn 1986). The NT acquired the garden in April 1988 (NT Guide p5) (The Independent Oct 21 1989 p51). Restoration started shortly after and the gardens were opened to the public from May 1 1991 (DVOPP p21). (OVH pp97,100-106pcs). **American Garden** see Rhododendron Ground. **Ape of Thoth** statue is inside the Cheshire House and was probably originally sculpted by Waterhouse Hawkins (GS p131) (NT Guide p14 il). The **Arboretum** is at the beginning of Wellingtonia Avenue (BGFB p45). **Araucaria Parterre** or Monkey Puzzle Tree Parterre is by the Italian garden S of the Mosaic Parterre. Consists of four compartments each containing a Monkey Puzzle Tree ('Araucaria araucana'). This was one of the first parts of the garden to be created (NT Guide p20). Biddulph Grange Garden has perhaps the finest collection of Araucarias in England (BGFB p29) (OVH p103). **Mrs Bateman's Garden** was the private garden of Maria Bateman, wife of James Bateman. It was by the S front of the house: Mrs Bateman's boudoir was in the N wing of the house and it survived the fire of 1896 (BALH p172) (Observer Magazine 27 May 1979). The garden is said to have been destroyed in the late C19 for alterations to take place to the rest of the grounds. The area was enclosed by yew hedges and a mazelike series of borders planted with roses, lilies and many other flowers. The renovation of Mrs Bateman's Garden was completed by end of March 1997 (ES Feb 19 1997 p25pc. March 29 1997 p8). **Boathouse** lies at one end of the Lake and was built in 1903 by Robert Heath. The building was being restored in 2000 (BALH p174) (SLM April 2000 p56pc). **Bowling Green** (BGFB p30) (BALH p173). The **Brahmin Cow** or gilded water buffalo is a principal feature of 'China.' The original sculpture was life-sized and made on site by Waterhouse Hawkins. It was placed in walled portals at the centre of a semi-circle (DoE II). It seems to be replicating the famous bronze ox statue by the lake at the summer palace in Peking (SHJ vol 1 p8 note 14). The **Cherry Orchard** is above the E end of the Dahlia Walk, by the house (NT Guide p19). Near here HRH Princess Alexandra planted a Prunifolia on July 11 1991. The **Cheshire House** or the Cheshire Black and White Cottage is at the rear of the Egypt Garden, a passage through the court leads into it (BGFB p30) (BALH p173). **China** includes a lake, temple (or pavilion), bridge, watch tower, Joss House, Wall of China, Brahmin Cow sculpture and the Golden larch (DoE II) ('Garden Ornament' by Gertrude Jekyll 1918/1982 p450p) (KES p32) (F&G pp118p,119 ils) (BOE p69) (SGS p60,p) (BALH pp172,173) (F p317) (NSFCT 1988 p46) (SMOPP vol 2 p6p c1910). The original temple was destroyed by vandals in 1983 (OVH pp102pc,103). Below the Brahmin Cow there were two serpent forms cut into the lawn (DoE II). The **Dahlia Walk**, on the S side of the house, is a series of beds on a stepped terrace in front of the house. The

beds are divided by yew hedges shaped like buttresses, and within these are planted dahlias. The Walk is also known as the Step Walk, and is terminated by the Shelter House (BGFB pp30,44) (NT Guide p19). The Walk was filled in with a terraced lawn when Biddulph Grange was a hospital (BALH p172). But in 1988 work began on its restoration with the planting of new yew hedges; in 1999 these were clipped for the first time since the restoration (CL Oct 21 1999 p78pc). **Egypt Garden** is a temple made out of yew trees, shut in in a court of yew hedges. The temple and court are guarded with stone sphinxes. The temple entrance has a stone surround in the Egyptian style of architecture. Within the temple is the Ape of Thoth statue. The rear of the temple is the Cheshire House (DoE II*) (Garden Ornament Topiary Work. Gertrude Jekyll 1918/1982 p284p) (KES p32) (BOE p69) (BALH p173) (F&G p119) (SGS p60,p) (F p317) (JC pl.6) (BGFB p29). It has been suggested that the Egypt Garden was the meeting place for 'The Nine,' a secret society in the C19 comprising only of a few dwelling in central England, whose aims were to pass on the secret inner lore taught by Akhenaten and Gwevaraugh. It is believed that James and Maria Bateman were members of 'The Nine' (GS p131). The **Five's Court** (BALH p172) (BGFB p30). **Flower Border** (Garden Ornament. Gertrude Jekyll. 1982/1918. p419p). **Fountain Court** has a fountain with this inscription 'For the refreshment of weary travellers - May God speed them on their way' (BGFB p24). The carving of a frog smiling is on a stone over an entrance to the romantic and twisting tunnel (F&G il of on p118) (Observer 27 May 1979); but could not be found in 2000. The **Geometrical Garden** (BGFB p30). The **Glen** between China and the lake, is filled with exotic species of ferns (BGFB p30) and is perhaps also called the Scottish Glen. The **Golden Larch** tree on the W side of 'China', believed to be the oldest in Britain, brought from China in 1852 (DoE II). There is a sandstone **icehouse** at SJ 892591 50 yards from the Grange built in c1840 concocted out of a lofty mass of rock between the Chinese waters and the larger lake (BALH p172) (IHB p392). **Italian Garden** is near the W corner of the house (BGFB p29) and close to Mrs Bateman's Garden on S side of the house (BALH p172). The **Joss House** situated in a bend in the Wall of China, above 'China,' another name for it is the Prospect Tower (BGFB p107) (DoE II). The original Joss House was in a poor state of repair in 1983 owing to vandalism (OVH p106). A **Lake** constructed by Mr Heath in 1903 for recreational purposes and as a reservoir (BGFB p45). At **Lime Lodge**, which stood at the entrance to Carriage Drive, began **Lime Walk** or Lime Avenue (DoE II) (BGFB pp30,44). The avenue is to the W of the lake and runs parallel to the old turnpike road and leads to the original entrance gates (BALH p172). At the N end of the avenue is an alcove built 1848-60 by Bateman (DoE II). The renovation of the **Mosaic Parterre** by Mrs Bateman's Garden was completed by end of March 1997 (ES March 29 1997 p8. July 21 1997 p7p). The **Music House** (BGFB p30). **Obelisk Walk** see Wellingtonia Avenue. The **Pinetum** is a curved walk and makes the circuit of the gardens, running round the S corner of the gardens (BALH p173) (BGFB p30). The **Prospect Tower** vantage point to view the Chinese Temple to the W (DoE II). The **Quoit Ground** is in the S corner of the gardens (BALH p173) (BGFB p30). The **Rainbow**, a semi-circular bank of rhododendrons and azaleas, at end of the Lime Walk (BGFB p44) was restored in late 1999 and early 2000 (The National Trust Mercia News spring summer 2000). **Rhododendron Ground** is devoted to North American plants, formed in the most luxuriant groups. It is also called 'the American Garden' (BALH p172) (BGFB p30). **Rose Garden** (BGFB p30) or Rose Parterre lies by the house. The **Round Rock** is a bold mass of red sandstone at the end of a walk eventually leading to Biddulph Moor (BGFB p30). The **Scottish Glen** (NSFCT 1988 p46) is perhaps another name for The Glen. **Sphinx Figures** see Egyptian Garden. There are two **spring head basins** in the gardens and another in Overton Road (DoE II). **Step Walk** see Dahlia Walk. The **Strumpery** between 'Egypt' and 'China' is a picturesque assemblage of old roots and stumps of trees with ivies and creepers (BGFB p30) (OVH pp104-105). **'Sugar Dish'** see Wellingtonia Vase. **Tea House** DoE II. A visitor in 1862 noted the original **Upside-down Tree**. A new one, a holly, was transplanted from another part of the garden to the W side of the pool before the house in 1995 (CL Sept 28 1995 p86pc). **Verbena Parterre** is on the S side of the house by the Rose Parterre. **Wall of China** wall forms S and E boundary of 'China' and consists of two walls five metres apart and 2.5 metres high (DoE II). **Watch Tower in China** is on the N side of 'China' and not the same as the Joss House. **Wellingtonia Avenue** was the last and grandest feature created by James Bateman for the garden. It was laid out after 1853 and is a gradual, gravelled ascent of nearly 0.75m broken by several sets of steps. Lining the avenue were Wellingtonia (Giant Redwood) alternated with Deodar Cedars. Bateman left Biddulph before the Wellingtonias matured and his successor Robert Heath felled them. For the restoration of the gardens alternating Wellingtonias and Deodar Cedars were replanted along the avenue in 1996/7. It is envisaged the Wellingtonias will reach early maturity in 2075. (BGFB p45) (KES p32) (BALH p173) (BOE p69) (SGS p60) (BGFB p45) (F p317) (NT Guide p15). The avenue has the appearance of an obelisk if viewed at the foot of the walk, hence an alternative name for it, Obelisk Walk. Half way up is the **Wellington Vase** or 'Sugar Dish' a giant vase which was brought from Knypersley Hall c1861 (DoE II) (BGFB pp22p,45) (BALH p173) at this point the NT property ends but the avenue or walk continues, and was undergoing some restoration in 2000. **Bibliography.** A series of articles about the gardens by E Kemp appeared in the Gardeners Chronicle between 1857-1862 and these appeared in a book by Bradbury and Evans 1862. (CL 1905. Dec 1985) (Garden Ornament. Gertrude Jekyll. 1918, reprinted 1982; mentions a flower border at Biddulph Grange) (The Gardeners Chronicle and Gardening Illustrated 1960) (History of British Gardening. Miles Hadfield) (Oriental Architecture in the West. Patrick Conner) (STM July 1964 p37) (House and Garden April 1972) (Journal of The Royal Horticultural Society May 1977) (BALH pp168-175) (SHJ vol 1 pp16-17 has an excellent bibliography) (SMOPP vol 2 pp4p c1895, 7p c1910) (GS pp129-32,137,142,211).

Biddulph Moor (locally *Biddle Mooer* HLSP p179, BOJ book 2 p53). Moorland village on a high ridge, 1210 feet high (OL vol 1 p156), 22.5m N from Stafford. The W part of the village lay formerly in Middle Biddulph liberty in Biddulph ancient parish, whilst the E part, that E of Hot Lane and New Street, lay in Horton ancient parish. In the Middle Ages the present village area was moorland known as Greenway Moor, appearing as Grenway in 1382 (BHS June 1968 p14) (SVB p32). Some believe druids occupied it (TFTP p169). The present village emerged from an amalgamation of old hamlets, close to one another, and isolated residences in the surrounding moorland. The church, Christ Church, Church Lane, was built in 1863 (BOE p70), and Biddulph Moor became a separate ecclesiastical parish in 1864 (GLAUE p403). By 1934 the village was sufficiently developed to warrant the transfer of the E part of it to Biddulph urban district (VCH vol 7 p65). Biddulph Moor has its own dialect, still in use: It differs from the 'Potteries' dialect, considerably (SVB p32). Part of New Street was formerly Tall Hat Street, so called because the gentry with their C19 tall hats lived there (BHS June 1968 p16). BIDDLEMOOR MEN. This local pronunciation, and another Biddle Muir Men (SMM p106), for Biddulph Moor Men refers to a race of people unlike others in the area who came to the district (or the Norton ridge area - SMM p106), perhaps in the Middle Ages, or earlier. The origin of the Biddlemoor Men, or Biddulphians (OL vol 2 p140), and the reason for their presence in the Biddulph Moor district is unknown. The popular belief is that they were Saracens brought to England during the Crusades by the overlord of Biddulph manor, Bertram de Verdun (d1192) of Alton Castle (see). And that he brought the Arabs from the Holy Land to be servants at his hall (SMM p107) (ES July 18 1978). (OL vol 2 p140). According to Burne their family name became Bayley, derived from their having been appointed bailiffs of the Biddulph estates, or possibly from the Celtic 'baileystyles' denoting those living in new dwellings which later became 'newbold' with the same meaning (SMM pp106-107). Burne attributes the lord of Knypersley Castle with bringing them over. He, she says, also gave them a piece of land - Bailey's Hill - 0.25m NW of Biddulph. Here they lived in tents (FLJ 1896 pp378,379). But the place-name Bailey makes no very early appearance in Biddulph PR (SMM p107). Another tradition is that seven Saracens were brought back, for there are seven grave slabs with Templar crosses outside Biddulph church (English Legends. Henry Bett p23). Another tradition is that the Saracens were employed as stonemasons and they built the first St Chad's at Stafford, a church with carvings in the oriental style (SGS pp60,152). But according to Sleigh and others these servants of the lords of Biddulph went by the name of the 'Paynim' (HOLS) (PS p21). Sleigh was vague as to whether the Paynim were a race, a tribe, or a single person. Sleigh says, Paynim was brought over by a Knight Templar named Ormus de Guidon (the Biddulph tenant of Bertram de Verdun) after a Crusade. He made Paynim bailiff of his Biddulph estates (SMM p107). Or they may have descended from a party of gypsies, who at times are described as Egyptians (SMM p106); or are Phoenicians (SMM p106); or from Palaeolithic or Neolithic or Bronze or Iron Age peoples (NSFCT 1935 p95. 1946 p148) (Congleton Chronicle 1936) (SMM pp105,110). Another tradition is that they were Indian servants brought to the district from India by Col Biddulph of the East India Company (probably in c1698 or 1700); having settled on Biddulph Moor they became a race apart with their own patois, taking to, in the early C19, pot pedlaring and hawking (Staffordshire Pots and Potters. GW & FA Rhead. 1906 pp341-345). Or they are descendents of a few Scottish rebels who stayed on the Moor instead of retreating home during the 1745 Jacobite Rebellion (SMM p107). Whatever their origin the Biddlemoor Men intermarried with the native population and so diluted their original characteristics. This process seems to have taken place gradually and in the vicinity of Bailey's Hill. Bailey's Hill seems to have been their last stronghold and here some were still living up to the 1930s (SGS p60). However, Sleigh says, they were known for their 'nomadic and somewhat bellicose propensities' (SMM p107). CS Burne and her coadjutor Miss Keary visited the Biddlemoor people in 1893 and were told they were more peculiar a generation ago. However, according to Burne, the men were still taller than the average Staffordshire man (FLJ 1896 pp378,379). However, others have always maintained the Biddlemoor Men were smaller than the average native man (SMM p107). Burne goes on to say they wore their hair, which was generally either red or black, cut short in front and hanging long at the back. Their houses consisted of two apartments, one entered through the other. The outer room was the abode of cattle and pigs, the inner of the family. Their dialect included words of Arabic origin and had given the surrounding district some unique expressions which became prevalent. The children's heads were acorn-shaped and very gracefully set on their shoulders, oval faces, brown ruddy complexions, dark eyes and hair in shades of auburn, the colour of autumn leaves (FLJ 1896 pp378,379). (S p49) (ABS No. 5 pp15,16).

Biddulph Old Hall House built by Francis Biddulph in the C16, 2m NNE of Biddulph town centre. A residence which stood on the earthwork in nearby Bailey's Wood (see) may have been the predecessor of this hall. The Biddulphs (or de Biddulphs) were lords of Middle Biddulph (see) manor from the Middle Ages. Their estates were confiscated in the Civil War but restored to them after the Restoration. They were not holding the manor by 1851. A Mr Biddulph of Biddulph claimed to Dr Plot in the later C17 that he had recently 12 tenants all living at a time within Biddulph and Horton parishes whose ages added up to a 1000 years (NHS pp45,329) (SOS 1844 p10 note) (W p386; it was then held by Capt Rowland Mainwaring) (BALH p41). Biddulph Old Hall has the date 1558 on a stone to the right of the entrance (LGS p83). But BOE p69 says this reads 158?. Erdeswick noted the hall in the late C16 (SH p29). It was a royalist garrison in the Civil War, besieged by Capt Ashenhurst in Jan 1643 and destroyed and has remained in a ruinous state ever since. Bullet marks can still be seen in the walls (LGS p83). (NSFCT 1888 p73-75. 1922 pp90-94 ils) (BALH pp37,38-42). A late C17 (BOE p69) or C18 or C19 (NSFCT 1888 pp68-69) farmhouse was built in the middle of the ruins of the old hall (NSFCT 1888 pp68-69). Over its entrance may be seen the inscription:

> Hence Rebel-heart! Nor Deem a Welcome Due,
> From Walls once ruined by a rebel hand;
> 3ce Welcome Those, if Thou indeed be True
> To God and to the Lady of the Land

(NSFCT 1888 pp68-69). Some suggest this inscription is on some entrance of the old hall (PS pp18p,19,20p). One of the properties was the seat of a branch of the Myotts. The deep groove above one of the doors records the height of Richard Myott who was six feet four inches (NSFCT 1932 p33). A Richard Myatt was living at Biddulph Old Hall in 1779 (BIOPP p15p). In 1937 Biddulph urban district council sought to secure it for the NT (ES Aug 3 1933 p6p. Aug 11 1937 p4p) (BALH p231). In 1963 Michael Biddulph, a direct descendant of the Biddulphs, gave up residence in the house next to the old hall and sold the property to the Sangha Association - Order of Ordained Buddist monks (SLM winter 1956 p24p; a Mrs MA Biddulph was preserving a worn cannon ball of the Civil War period in the 'Great Hall' in 1956) (STM July 1964 pp36p, 37). By 1965 it was a Buddhist retreat centre (NSJFS 1966 p67) ceasing to be so in the late 1960s and becoming a private residence (BIOPP p15). The octagonal dome on the roof is known locally as the pepper pot (NSFCT 1922 p93). (GNHS p127 il) (LCAST 1898 p64) (MOS p114) (SOSH p203) (RB vol 3 p68 il by Malvina Cheek) (Reveille. June 30 - July 6 1966 p27) (SLM winter 1956 pp23-25ps) (BHS Dec 1973) (TFTP pp169-173) (SL p97) (SGS p60) (SMOPP vol 2 p1p c1910). GROUNDS. The Box Avenue (PS p20p). There is reputedly a tunnel from the old hall to the church, used in the Civil War (SLM winter 1956 p24) (PS p19) (BALH p40). The tunnel may have been one of the old tunnels driven to work coal (BALH p63). Another tunnel reputedly runs between the old hall and Overton Hall (DPEM p32).

Biddulph Park To E of Biddulph Grange. In Biddulph parish. A medieval deer park enclosed out of forest. In existence by 1383 (BHS June 1972 p29) and still in existence in 1489 (NSJFS 1962 p75. 1964 p64).

Biddulph's Pool (CCF p223). To W of Chase Terrace on N side of A5190. John Biddulph made two pools out of boggy ground at the head of Green Brook Valley sometime between 1734 and 1761 (VCH vol 5 p63).

Bidner Spring Wootton. Was water supply for Wootton Hall and was still serving part of Wootton village in 1988 (SVB p183).

Big Ben Cavern in Castle Hill, Dudley (BCM Oct 1970 p51).

Big Bridge It was whilst crossing the 'Big Bridge' at about 10.00pm on Jan 21 1879 that a labouring man or a waggoner is reputed to have been attacked by a boggart (a man-monkey, or black creature with white eyes - DOG pp34,35) said to be of Norbury. The police thinking it to be a common robbery took a statement from the man (NSFCT 1896 p121). The story of the strange encounter quickly spread and a local man said it was a man-monkey who had regularly been seen on the Big Bridge ever since a man was drowned in the canal cut nearby. The story was taken up by Charlotte Burne and Georgia Jackson and appears in SFL pp106,107. (FLJ 1896 pp366-386) (SCS pp5,6). Big Bridge has been thought by some, including Bruce Braithwaite, to be that which crosses the Shropshire Union Canal, NE of the Norbury at SJ 789242. However, others say the incident took place on a bridge at the S end of the cut at or near Gnosall (VB p149) (MR p160).

Big Crane Brook Runs into Chasewater.

Big Heath Former large heath marked on OS map 1834 (as Big Heath or Kite Post) to NE of Norton Canes. Does not appear on current OS maps. The A5190 runs across it.

Big Hill Alias Hill Street, central Walsall (SNWA p58).

Big House On the N side of High Street, Abbots Bromley. Georgian house built by the 1820s. It was purchased for Rev John Manley Lowe vicar of Abbots Bromley 1844-1888. In 1874 Big House was sold to the Woodard Corporation who considerably extended it to house a **girls' boarding school**, known as St Anne's School, which was formally opened by Dr Mackarness on St Mark's day 1874. Another girls' school in Abbots Bromley, called St Mary's, founded in 1882 provided similar education for lower middle class girls. From 1900 Marcia Alice Rice (d1958), author of AB, was headmistress of St Anne's, and from 1921, after amalgamation, headmistress of both schools until 1931. The united school became the School of S. Mary and S. Anne and still (2000) runs. By 1939 the house and its extensions was known as St Anne's House. **'Jerusalem Heights'**. By at least 1878 a school commemoration festival appears to have been held on St Anne's day (July 26) involving a procession by pupils, dressed in white and wearing white 'chapel' hoods, through Abbots Bromley culminating in a church service. In late July 1885, whilst in procession to the school chapel, pupils sang a hymn. In 1887, whilst in procession, they sang the hymn 'Jerusalem' for the first time. The hymn has been sung at all subsequent festivals and the procession has become known as 'Jerusalem Heights'. In 1927 the Duchess of Atholl attended the festival. On July 1 1933 the Archbishop of Canterbury visited the school. In 1974 the Duchess of Kent visited to open a new wing. The school magazine is known as 'ECCE' from St Mary's motto 'Ecce Ancilla Domini' 'Behold the Hand Maiden of the Lord.' The journal for the Old Girls is called the Guild Leaflet. **Alumni**: Dame Margery Perham, historian and author, authority on African politics; Helen Watts CBE, international contralto; Sue Harmer-Nicholls, actress of Walsall (see); Carole Ashby, actress and model; Dr Philippa Tudor, Librarian, House of Lords; Jennifer Tanfield, Librarian, House of Commons; Joanne Gough, Olympic oarswoman; Wendy Leaversly, BBC children's programme presenter; Alison Gordon, member of the D'Oyly Carte and Royal Opera House, Covent Garden; Pip Moon, artist with Red Door Studio, London; Stephanie Nash, graphic artist, designed commemorative GPO stamp packaging; Alison Nicholas, British Womens Golf champion; Fiona McConnell CBE, UK representative at UN Conference in Rio, Brazil, signatory to the agreement at the 'Earth Summit in 1991; Anna Richardson, television presenter (SA July 25 1885 p5) (info Mrs Mary Steel, Headmistress) (Story of St Anne's Abbots Bromley 1874-1924. Violet Mary Macpherson. 1924) (AB pp225p of St Anne's House facing, 236,237) (The Story of St Mary's Abbots Bromley. Marcia Alice Rice. 1947) (Marcia Alice Rice: The Story of a Great Head Mistress. M Hall and Violet Macpherson. 1961) (S. Mary and S. Anne: The Second Fifty Years. Anne Wells and Susan Meads. 1974).

Big House, The Corner of Wedgwood Street and Moorland Road, Chapel Bank, Burslem. Or called Wedgwood House. Built by the brothers Thomas and John Wedgwood cousins of Josiah Wedgwood I. Inside are their initials dated 1751 (VCH vol 8 pp110,331il) (POP p19 pl 9) (BOE p255) (MR p66p). The Big House was the model for a range of teapots made at the nearby Ivy House Works in the C18 (Channel Four. Time Team. Jan 3 1999). A man was killed outside it during the Chartist Riots in 1842 (SHST p502p). It was the Conservative Club in Arnold Bennett's novel 'Clayhanger' (Arnold Bennett's Bursley Trail leaflet. 1999). It became the Midland Bank in 1922 (VCH vol 8 p117). (POP p88). The walled forecourt and entrance gates were removed in 1956 (VCH vol 8 p110).

Big Lawn Farm Nearly 0.5m SE of Bagnall. Is probably Robert Speake's Lawn Farm, in existence by 1791 (B pp67-68p).

Bignall End Village to E of, and nearly merges with, Audley. Former township in Audley ancient parish (SHC 1944 pxvi). The train from Bignall End to Newcastle every morning during the hunting season was delayed to allow a carriage containing the mount of Reginald N Wood to be attached to the train en route to Keele Hall for a day's hunting (AHJ 1995 p112). Aaron Lockett, cricketer, was born in Bignall End on Dec 1 1892. He played for Oldham from 1929 and for Staffs and the minor counties from 1919 to 1939 (AHJ 1997 pp72-77).

Bignall Hill Tiny hamlet, and former mining hamlet (W p428), to E of Bignall End at the foot of Bignall Hill, in Audley ancient parish. Richard Parrott, who wrote a survey of Audley parish and Talke hamlet in 1733, lived on an estate at Bignall Hill (A pp31-37). Charles Brough murdered George Walker, aged 75, of Bignall Hill Farm about 0.25m from his home on July 27 1864. Brough stole from Walker a chain watch and was identified when he went to pawn it. He was hung on Dec 26 1864 (CCSHO pp15-20) (MCS pp35-37).

Bignall Hill Hill 1.5m E of Audley. Has a panorama which includes the Cheshire Plain, Beeston Castle, the Wrekin, the Denbighshire Hills, Mow Cop, Biddulph Moor, the Roaches, Ramshaw Rocks and Peckforton Hills (NSFCT 1944 p93) (TTTD p220). A bronze ogival dagger of the Early Bronze Age, possibly associated with a burial, was found in 1921 at cSJ 819508 on top of Bignall Hill. It finally went to the NSFC museum (NSFCT 1926 pp144-145 il, 146. vol 64 p172) (NSJFS 1964 p15. 1965 p32). Probably this discovery lead to the belief in the existence of a burial mound mentioned in NSFCT 1944 p93. The name could be a compound of 'Bica' and 'hoh' - 'Bica's hill.' The local surname Bykenou existed in the C14 (AHJ 1995 p44). Or Bignall is a corruption of big knoll - a comparison with the smaller knoll, or hill, at Knowle Bank (AHJ 1997 p98). Gem Edge and Old Hill may be alternative names for the hill. An obelisk crowning the summit commemorates John Wedgwood, colliery owner of Bignall End, who died in Feb 1839. He requested in his will that he 'be interred within my estate at Bignall End, in a vaulted tomb at the summit of a field called Old Hill, and an obelisk or monument be erected' (SVB p34). The obelisk bears the inscription 'John Wedgwood of Bignall End Esquire. Borne February 1760. Died February 6 AD 1839' (AOPP pl 36). But Wedgwood's wish to be buried here was not complied with and he is buried in Audley churchyard (NSFCT 1984 p13). The pinnacle of the memorial was made of Davenport glass (NSFCT 1944 p93). The obelisk was blown down in gales in early Jan 1976 leaving it about a quarter of its original height (S&COP pl 53). Some say it was blown down in 1979 (TTTD p219p of the original obelisk) (SVB p34); but the earlier date is more likely for there were calls in early 1976 for its restoration. There was no money available and the monument was just capped (ES Jan 12 1976. April 2 1976. Nov 19 1976. Dec 22 1976). By 1962 there was a two million gallon underground reservoir under Bignall Hill (TTTD p220). Bignall Hill was the traditional place for those from this area to ascend for Good Friday festivities (AHJ 1995 p111).

Bignall Hill House Bignall Hill. In 1851 it was the seat of NP Wood (W p18).

Big Wood Wood to the W of Chillington Hall in Chillington Park.

Bikersdale 0.5m NE of Dunstall, Tatenhill. Dale which breaks the line of rising banks of Needwood Forest plateau (HOPT vol 1 p134).

Bilbrook District of NE Codsall. Partly in Codsall parish, but mostly in Tettenhall parish (W p206). The name is thought to be Celtic and to mean the brook in which 'billers' (water plants such as watercress) grow (DUIGNAN) (NSJFS 1981 p3) (VCH vol 20 p12) (SSE 1996 p10) (SPN p144). The brook referred to is what is now Moat Brook, the boundary between Codsall and Tettenhall parishes (VCH vol 20 p12). The manor of Bilrebroch appears in DB (SSE 1996 p10). The centre of the former hamlet was where Bilbrook Road turns west towards Codsall: Settlement had extended into Codsall parish by the mid C17 (VCH vol 20 pp12,79). The custom of well dressing was observed at Bilbrook on Ascension Day (Holy Thursday) (NHS p318) (SD pp36,50) (GM 1794) (SHOS vol 2 p293) (BCC vol 1 p140) (AOW p93) (SCSF p29) (FOS p103) (BDH pp276-278) (VCH vol 20 p14). Calvert thought the custom dated back to before the Reformation and was continued by the Giffards of Chillington, who were Catholics (SSC p120 in the intro, 112). Writing in 1908 Hackwood notes the custom continued until recent times (CCC p91). The church, Holy Cross, Bilbrook Road, was built in 1898 (LDD).

Bilbrook House House which stood to the S of Bilbrook Road in Codsall parish. It was built by John Egginton of Oxley, probably in c1805. It was demolished in the late 1960s and an estate built over the grounds (VCH vol 20 p79).

Bilbrook Manor House House which stood on the N side of Bilbrook Road where it turns W. It was probably the 'capital messuage or mansion house' which was the home of John Lowe in the early C18. It was known as Bilbrook Manor House by the 1880s. In 1907 it was occupied by AM Manby (STC p38p) and later by Lt-Col HE Twentyman; the house was demolished after his death in 1945. His son John Anthony became a famous sculptor, and his other son Richard became a famous architect (VCH vol 20 p12) (TCOP p145p).

Bildock's Green A building at Bildock's Green, Rowley Regis, was registered for Protestant dissenters in c1791 (SHC 1960 p131).

Billington Hamlet at the foot of Berry Ring, 1.5m E of Haughton. In Bradley ancient parish. The manor of Bellintone appears in DB. Later forms are: Billinton (1203), Belinton (1285), Belyngton (1304), and Bilyngtone (1453) (SSE 1996 p11). The name, of Anglo-Saxon origin, is from Billing's town (DUIGNAN) or Billa's farmstead (OAKDEN) (SSE 1987 p28) (SPN p112) or tun (SSE 1996 p11). At SJ 897215, 0.75m NE of Billington, on N side of Newport road is a moated site thought to be the site of an early castle of Edward de Stafford, before Stafford Castle was built in c1348 (NSFCT 1943 p65). The note in SOS (Harwood) about a circular entrenchment at Tillington is an error - it is a reference to the circular entrenchment here (SHC 1914 p105 note). St Margaret's chapel at Billington was suppressed in or before 1549, is not mentioned in 1563 or after (SHC 1915 p34). It stood on Billington Bank. The stones were taken to build a wall at Bradley and a C14 stone cross removed to a neighbouring field (NSFCT 1943 p66). This could be the cross close by Billington Hall farm see under Billington Hall.

Billington Hall House 1m E of Haughton, to W of Billington hamlet. Brick farmhouse of c1800. Represents the manor house of Billington manor (VCH vol 4 pp74,79). Close by, Billington Hall farm, are the remains of a medieval wayside cross (LGS p145), which may have a connection with the lost St Margaret's chapel (VCH vol 4 p89-90). This could be the cross removed from St Margaret's chapel. See Billington.

Bill's Rock Rock feature in Cotton Dell. In the C16 a daughter of a local landowner fell in love with a farm worker. But the father disapproved, already having promised her to a neighbouring squire. The lovers were chased by both father and squire with hounds into Cotton Dell and forced to jump off Bill's Rock to their deaths. According to legend the disappointed hounds then turned on the two gentlemen (TFTPM p66). Could be same as Garston Rocks, which lie to the E of the A52 at SK 051476.

Billy's Hill Hill S of Tixall-Stafford road 0.5m WSW of Tixall.

Bilson Brook Tributary of Ashmore Brook. Runs by Farewell and Chorley. Written Bilston Brook on 1834 OS map. Formerly Bourne Brook (VCH vol 14 p195).

Bilston (locally *Bils'on* UBCB p219). Black Country town by Bilston Brook 16m S of Stafford. Former township and chapelry in Wolverhampton ancient parish.
EARLY. The **Roman** forts at Pennocrucium and Metchley were connected by a road, which according to some may have passed through Bilston, with Stone Street (previously Old Street) having formed a part of it (WFW p32). Roman coins of Antoninus and Commodus have been found in the Bilston area (HOWW p25) (NSJFS 1964 p16).
500 to 1500. Bilston lay just within the confines of Cannock Forest according to Lawley (HOBL p10). There is a tradition of a Saxon church at Church Hole (see) between Bilston and Wednesfield being moved by fairies. The **manor** of Bilston was given by Lady Wulfrun to the monastery of Wolverhampton in 994 (HOWM p14) (SL p62). By 1086 Billestune (DB) had passed to the Crown. In the earlier C13 along with neighbouring royal manors it was formed into Stowheath manor (WA vol 2 no 1 p103). In 1265 a manor of Bilston was granted to Walter de Bilston for his valour at the battle of Evesham (1265). In Edward III's reign all Bilston men were certified to be free of toll because the vill had formerly belonged to the Crown (W p138), and for some Bilston inhabitants had apparently fought for Edward III under his standard in France (HOBL p21) (BOP p7). The de Bilstons appear to have continued as lords of Bilston manor until c1458 when by marriage it passed to the Mollesleys, whose residence was the house in Bilston that became the Greyhound Inn (see) (HOBL pp128,131). Later forms are: Billistan (1172-3), Bilestun (Henry III), Billestuna (1190-1), Billestune (Edward III), Byllestone (Henry V), Byllystone (1448), Bylstane, Bylston, and Bilson (HOBL pp4,18-19). Lawley thought 'Belstona,' a misprint of Belstow which appears in HCCW p162 note (but not in the actual text p174), was the correct Latin form of Bilston (HOBL p4): WA vol 2 p85 and Mander disagree and say it is an unidentified place near Trysull called Belstow (HOWM p14 note). The **name** Bilston probably has Anglo-Saxon origins and is derived from a tribe of Angles who settled here in the late C6 - the Bilsaetan (SL p43) or Bilsonii (MR p36). (DUIGNAN) (SPN p17). Oakden thought the first element was difficult to interpret (SSAHST 1967 p35). It was rather foolishly suggested by some in the past that the name derived from 'bill' an agricultural implement, and 'stone' from local stone quarries (HOBL p5). Dr Oliver in HCCW and

Lawley say Bilston is derived from 'Beli,' sun god of the Celts (HOBL pp5-6). **Churches and appointment of the curate**. Bilston's main church between Walsall and Church Streets, was in existence by the late C11 or early C12, or possibly earlier. Some of this was incorporated into a new church, **St Leonard**, of 1726. This church was enlarged in 1825-1826 (HOBL pp12-17,177) (BOE p70) (Looking Round St Leonard's, Bilston. Flora Cope). By ancient custom Bilston inhabitants appointed their own curate with or without the consent of the Dean of Wolverhampton. This occurred until the death of the curate Rev Richard Ames in 1730. Bilston then appointed Rev Richard Ames, Jnr, nephew of the deceased, while the Dean and Chapter, who believed they had the right of nomination, nominated Rev Benjamin Gibbons. This led to a case being drawn up and laid before counsel. At length after great expense the Dean and Chapter abandoned its claim and the Dean reluctantly licensed Rev Ames in 1731. Ames died in 1736. Fierce contests ensued for the curacy in c1736, 1813, 1836, and lastly in 1871. The advowson was sold in 1881, and by 1893 the living had been vested in the hands of five trustees (HOBLL pp88-93). Waking or 'the wakes' was kept at Bilston in the Middle Ages in honour of St Leonard (Nov 6) until the Reformation later moving to the end of July (SCSF p106). In 1930 the Bilston Carnival, held in June, was begun to revive the old wakes custom (WMVB p30) (TB Nov 1975 p30. Nov 12 1998 p6). By 1998 Bilston Carnival was being held in Hickman Park (A Chronicle of Folk Customs. Brian Day. 1998 p104). The custom of decorating the church at Whitsuntide was practised at Bilston and there are records of the church being decorated in the late C17 (SCSF p32). The church, **St Mary**, Oxford Street, was built in 1827 (LDD). Two medieval **crosses** in Bilston may have been market crosses. One was called Nether Cross. It appears to have stood on a site which seems to have been occupied by a dwelling by 1690, but Lawley could not trace its site. The other cross, Overas Cross, according to Lawley, stood near to Swan Bank (SCSF pp91-92). Hackwood deduced from Church records that the Nether Cross was the older, and when it was taken down its materials were used to repair the Overas Cross or Upper Cross. The Overas Cross, which seems to have been a cross house, remained until c1825 (HOBLL pp41-42) (SCSF p92). The former **curfew bell** at St Leonard's church, Bilston, given by Sir Thomas Erdington bore the inscription:

> I am callede ye Curfue Belle
> I ringen at VIII or more
> To send ye alle to Bedde
> And wake ye up at IV

It was taken from the church in the C16 (HOBL pp30-31) (BCM April 1985 pp25-26). **Stocks** were repaired in 1706 and 1710. The Vestry provided for stocks in 1764, and these stood at the entrance to the churchyard. Later, stocks were kept in the Police Station yard. In 1862 they were brought out and used again (SCSF p130). According to Bilston PR a new **cucking stool** was bought for the parish in 1695 (SCSF p126). The old **lock-up** was in Lichfield Street. It later became the tramways waiting room (BOP p46p). There has been **coal mining** at Bilston from the C14 (BOP p7).
1500 to 1830. Bilston seems to have avoided extreme partisanship on either side in the **Civil War** (HOBLL pp53-54). The bells of Bilston church were rung in the C18 and the C19 on May 29 to celebrate Restoration Day 1660 (HOBLL pp54-55,117-118) (SCSF p19). Bilston became a **separate ecclesiastical parish** in 1723 (GLAUE p403) with some rights retained by Wolverhampton. After many disputes Bilston seems to have broken free of Wolverhampton by 1841 (HOBLL pp100-101). **Fire, pestilence and unrest**. In 1722 there was a large fire at Bilston (ADD p30). In 1734 Bilston appears to have been visited by a plague known as the 'bloody flux' (SCSF p139). In Nov 1756 there was a plague in Bilston parish called 'putrid fever' or 'flux of fever' which lasted to June 1757 (SCSF p139). In 1793 there was a large fire at Bilston (ADD p30). Coiners were so active in Bilston at the end of C18 and beginning of the C19 that some detectives were sent down by the Home Office, on several occasions, to capture them (HOBLL p172). Such was the dread of body-snatching in Bilston that the town paid a watchman to guard a new grave for several weeks after burial (SCSF p83). In 1826 a man was whipped at the cart's tail from Sedgley to Bilston for body-snatching (SCSF p129). **Industry**. In the C18 Bilston produced metal-work, buckles, trinkets, boxes and gun-locks (BOP p8) and locks (HOBLL p253). The shoe buckle is said to have been invented by a Bilston locksmith called Thomas Beebee in c1686 (STELE March 29 1956). Bilston started manufacturing enamelled trinkets from 1748 (WMAG April 1966 pp30-31ps). The earliest recorded English enameller was Dovey Hawkesford of Bilston who worked in 1741 (SLM Oct 1996 p28). Hackwood says the enamel ware included snuff-boxes,

patch-boxes, tea-caddies, salt-cellars, brooches, breast pins, links, studs, hussifs, and a variety of other small wares. The trade in trinkets, is described in 1924, as long obsolete. Many of these enamels have been mistaken for 'Battersea Enamels' (SCSF p112). John Wilkinson (b1728), a native of Cumberland, settled at Bradley (see) in Bilston township in the mid C18, and as a great ironmaster made Bilston stand 'unrivalled as an iron making centre' by the time of his death in 1808 (DNB) (HOBLL p245). In 1830 Bilston is said to have made more iron than in the whole kingdom of Sweden - then one of the foremost nations in Europe for iron-making (W p138). Stone for grindstones, whetstones and millstones was quarried at Bilston (W p138). A windmill was built in 1791 on the corner of James Street, Mount Pleasant, at SO 954967. By the 1880s it had become a cement works and in 1902 the machinery and cap were removed (SLM spring 1954 p25) (BOP p55p of in 1954). Demolished in 1970, the site is now Mill House Old People's Home (WBJ p14 il iv) (WIS p24). The **workhouse** in Workhouse Fold was built in 1737 (BOP p18p). For Bilston **trade tokens** see HOBLL pp195-200. For Bilston **toll houses** see BCM July 1984 pp18-22. In 1790 Bilston was described as 'one of the largest villages in England, containing more than 1,000 houses' (HOBLL p170). The **Bilston Troop**, raised in 1798, became a part of the Staffordshire Yeomanry in 1805 (info Yeomanry Museum). **Markets**. In 1824 (W p140) or May 17 1825 (HOBLL p176) Bilston was designated a market town by an Act of parliament. The petitioners had brought it to the attention of parliament that Bilston was then regarded as one of the largest villages in England (HOBLL p176). From 1824 markets were held on Mondays and Saturdays (W p140). The Market Act of 1824 empowered the commissioners to erect a town hall, as soon as the profits of the market were sufficient for that purpose (W p140). The Town Hall designed by George Bidlake was built in 1872 (BOP p36p). Bilston Market Hall opened on Aug 9 1892 and is said to have been the first to be lit electrically in England (BOP p23p). Over Shelley's Chemist, High Street, is a bust of Aesculapius, Roman god of medicine. The shop is no longer a chemists (BOP p17p). **Natives and visitors**. Sir **Richard Pipe**, a native of Bilston, became Lord Mayor of London in 1578 (see Pipe Hall). **William Perry**, alias the 'Boy of Bilston' was a 13 year old boy possessed of the devil, the son of Thomas Perry, a Bilston yeoman. He was believed to have been bewitched by a witch called Joan Cock or Coxe. She was tried on Aug 10 1620 (NHS pp280-284). And, or, he was said to have fallen into the company of an old man, called Thomas, who schooled him in tricks of buffoonery (SHOS vol 2 p171). Fuller's account has the boy practised upon by some Jesuits at Mr Giffard's house; so the Jesuits could take the credit for having driven the devil out of him. Finally, Bishop Morton made him confess to pretending to be possessed of the devil (SMC pp81-87,170). The story was brought out as an eight-page pamphlet by Thomas Wheeler in 1620, and as a boardsheet in 1622, titled 'The Boy of Bilston; or a true discovery ...etc' by a curate of Bilston, named Thomas Baddely (HOBLL pp39-40) (SCHJ No. 11 spring 1970 facsimile). 'The Boy of Bilston' went on to marry a daughter of Walter Foxall (HOBLL p151). (SD pp36) (W p143) (SC pp54-60) (WTCEM p91) (BCWJ p109) (SCHJ No. 11 spring 1970) (TB Sept 1978 p8). For Rev **Thomas Moss**, whose poem 'The Beggar's Petition' became very popular, see under Brierley Hill. **John Wesley** came to Bilston on Oct 2 1745 and March 21 1770. On the second occasion he preached in a house at the S end of Wood Street (HOBLL pp161-162) (SOSH p314). **Adam Round**, aged 13 of Bilston, was prosecuted and nearly hung for burglary in 1798 (TB May 1979 p27). **Frederick Price** (1804-1884), poet, was born in Bilston (PSS pp152-153) (VFC p108). The body of **Abel Hill** who murdered his common law wife Mary (or Maria) Martin and her child in 1820 at Capponfield (see) may have been displayed in public in Bilston by order of the judge. **Seth Boyden**, a native of Bilston, discovered Blackheart malleable iron whilst working in Newark, New Jersey, USA, in 1826. He was a foundryman with his own business in the town and not a scientist. There is a statue to him in Newark, New Jersey (BCM Jan 1969 pp8-10). In c1829 a boy called **Robert Taylor**, a parish apprentice to a Bilston butty collier, was identified by a surgeon as the lost son of the late Lord Kennedy. The surgeon had seen advertisements requesting information on the boy and his whereabouts, for he was heir to a large property near Ashby, Leics, worth at least £60,000 a year. Taylor was confirmed as the heir by the old woman, who had been the nurse in London to the Kennedy baby, before it was stolen by gypsies. In 1838 still a young man Taylor, the new Lord Kennedy, returned to Bilston to find a wife, having squandered the inheritance. In c1839 Taylor was exposed as an impostor, and was arrested in County Durham in 1840 (SA Dec 12 1835. Aug 4 1838) (Newcastle-upon-Tyne Courant May 1840) (Broughton's Scrapbook pp273,274).

1830 to PRESENT. **Cholera and unrest**. The Asiatic Cholera outbreak reached Bilston parish on Aug 3 1832; one in 20 died in seven weeks, a total of 742

(population of Bilston was then 14,492 - SCSF p139), leaving 450 orphans: A special school in Prouds Lane was opened for them in 1833. The school was demolished in the 1960s. The original orphans wore a medal when processing through the town (BOP p77ps of the medals). In 1840 a festival in the market place held by a Conservative Operative Society under Lord Ingestre was broken up by a mob of colliers and puddlers protesting against disenfranchisement. The Conservative gentlemen had to fight their way through the mob to the King's Arms where they sought refuge. Mr Philpotts, son of the bishop of Exeter, narrowly escaped with his life (NSJFS 1961 p95). Another cholera epidemic occurred in 1847 and killed 730 (HOBLL p225; Lawley gives only 1832 and 1849 for the cholera epidemics on p226) and or in 1849 which killed 600. (A Brief Narrative of the events relative to the cholera at Bilston in 1832. Joseph Price. 1840) (HOBLL pp185-194) (W pp139-140) (SOSH pp315,316) (BCM Jan 1989 p59) (TB May 1978 pp20-21. Feb 1998 p17). The **Bilston Riots** on June 21 1919 (BCM April 1970 pp65-67) or July 21 1919 (BOP p53p of the police station) started when two or three men the worse for drink were said to have assaulted two police constables in Church Street and they were joined by some soldiers who were home on leave. The police were forced to walk away towards the Town Hall followed by a crowd of people which became ever larger and more violent. At the refusal to turn out an unpopular police constable from the station the crowd smashed up the building. The next day a crowd again assembled outside the police station. It was successfully pacified when told that the police superintendent, injured the previous day, had lost a son in WW1. The crowd then dispersed (BCM April 1970 pp65-67). A street in Bilston was bombed on Aug 20 1940 destroying one house and blowing one boy onto the roof of his home (BOP p87p). **Industry**. There were 61 collieries in Bilston in the C19 (BOP p7). Ironstone has also been mined at Bilston (W p138). In 1862 there were more blast furnaces in Bilston parish alone than in the whole of Staffordshire in 1800 (HOBLL p247). In the C19, after the decay of the trinket industry, Bilston enamel painters found employment in decorating tea-trays, waiters, breadbaskets, and other articles of Japan ware. For Bilston Enamels see BCM April 1976 pp7-8ps. In the C20 Bilston produced pig-iron, steel bar and strip, galvanised sheets, steel stampings and pressings, boilers, castings, bolts and nuts, tubes, aircraft components, hollow ware (BOP p9), and cars (Thompson Brothers of Bilston produced the TB cycle car between 1919 and 1924 - PVBC p57). The depression of the 1930s in Bilston is illustrated in Fenner Brockway's 'Hungry England' (BOP p9). Bilston Steelworks closed on April 12 1979 after 200 years of production. The last steel cast bit was inscribed 'LAST CAST BILSTON STEEL X21402A W/TON 1520 PM 12 4 79 B FURNACE From 1768' and in 1980 was in the possession Mr Gordon Medley of Keighley, West Yorks (BCM Jan 1980 p23p). The same or another steel works with a blast furnace known as 'Big Lizzy' closed in 1979 and was demolished in 1980 (E&S Oct 21 1999 p9p). In 1866 Bilston became a separate civil parish (GLAUE p403) and in 1933 it was **incorporated** as a municipal borough. Herbert Beach was its first mayor. The arms of Bilston borough, granted in 1933, are: Ermine, a bend sable and thereon a gold fess between two silver martlets, and on the fess a Staffordshire Knot gules. The crest is - On a wreath argent and sable, the rising sun, gold, in front of three oak leaves vert. The supports are: Dexter, Faith represented by a woman proper in a blue robe and bearing a lamb; and sinister, Industry in the guise of Vulcan, also proper, wearing a red tunic and bearing a hammer. The motto is: 'Fidelitate et Industria Stat Bilstonia' (Bilston stands by Faith and Industry) (CH pp332,333il) (BOP p51p). Municipal independence was lost in 1966 when Bilston was amalgamated with Wolverhampton (BOP p8). The bridge on the corner of Church and Walsall Streets opened in Aug 1998 and carries a number of plaques with inscriptions with local sayings (Wolverhampton Chronicle. Jan 14 2000 p5p). The **railway** came to Bilston on Nov 12 1849 (HOBLL p225). Bilston had two railway stations - Bilston West - on the Oxford, Worcester and Wolverhampton Railway opened in 1854, and - Bilston Central - on the GWR connecting Bilston to Tipton, Dudley and Stourbridge built in 1854 by Isambard Kingdom Brunel, closed in 1962 (NSJFS 1964 p79), demolished in 1971 (BOP pp88-89ps). A post box manufactured in 1856 by Messrs Smith & Hawkes of Birmingham was still standing in Oxford Street in 1978 (BCM April 1978 p64p). **Theatre and museum**. The Theatre Royal, Bilston, built in 1902, closed in 1957, was demolished in c1959 (TB Feb 1998 p29). The entertainer, Bruce Forsyth (b1928), first went on the stage here, aged 14 (BBC Radio 4. Desert Island Discs. Dec 1 1996). Brueton House, built by Thomas Brueton, local manufacturer and philanthropist, in c1818 was opened as Bilston Library, Museum and Art Gallery on March 18 1937; the coat of arms of Bilston borough are above the door (BOP pp51p,52p). **References to Bilston**. Bilston is the setting for the novel 'The House of Rimmon' (1885) by Jeanie Gwynne Bettany (VFC p14), and it is Dulston in Francis Brett Young's nov-

els. The heroine in 'A Thousand Witnesses' (1953) a novel by George Beardmore, alias Cedric Stokes, comes from Bilston (VFC p11). 'The Balloon: An Old Bilston Ballad' 1816, concerns a bogus balloon flight engineered by an inn keeper with a view to increasing his custom during the Whitsuntide fair at Bilston: At one time the inhabitants of Bilston were known as 'Bilston Balloons,' a name which probably arose because of this incident (FSBC p61) (UBCB p218). 'The Battle of Bilston' is the title of a ballad from Bilston Almanac 1923. The ballad, written in the early C19, describes a cock fight at the Cock Inn, Swan Bank, Bilston (FSBC p5) (UBCB p199). For some rhymes about Bilston see Sedgley. For Bilston used as a verb see BCM April 1971 p27. **Natives and Visitors. George Price**, a mid C19 poet, was born in Bilston (VFC p108). **Harriet Nokes** (1830-1895), poet, was born in Bilston (PSS pp405-408) (VFC p99). In 1987 a plaque commemorating **John Freeman** (1853-1944), author, was placed on the former town hall at Bilston (Commemorative Plaques by the Wolverhampton Civic Society). **Julia Berrington**, a poet, was born in Bilston in 1851; the work of her younger sister, Emily Edridge, poet and essayist includes 'The Old Homestead' and 'A Lay of Wulfrune's Ham-Tun' (PSS pp422-423,440-443) (VFC pp14,44). Sir **Henry Newbolt**, poet, author and naval historian, was born in St Mary's Vicarage in Bath Street on June 6 1862. Between 1866 and 1869 he lived in Doveridge Place, Walsall, where there is a plaque to his memory. He attended Queen Mary's Grammar School for a short while. His best known work is 'Admirals All' (1897) which contains the poem 'Drake's Drum.' He was knighted in 1915. In WW1 he was controller of telecommunications and an official war historian. He died on April 19 1938 (PSS pp331-341) (VB p56) (BCM Oct 1976 pp24-30 il of. April 1990 p61) (TB June 1986 p14p) (WP p45) (The Cambridge Biographical Encyclopedia. David Crystal. 1994). Another account says Newbolt was born in Baldwin Street, Bradley, near Bilston, and shortly after his birth his family moved to St Mary's Vicarage (VFC pp97-98). In 1862 **Mr Baggot**, a Bilston pawnbroker, was murdered by David Brandrick, and his accomplices, Israel Jones, and others. A ballad entitled 'How Mr Baggot was Banjoed' was written about the case (TB Feb 1978 pp18-19). **Fred R Bartlett**, a late C19 poet was a native of Bilston; his only known work 'Flashes from Forge and Foundry' was published in 1886 (VFC p10). **Charles Frederick Forshaw**, (d1917), poet, biographer and essayist, was born at 149 Oxford Street, Bilston on Jan 23 1863 (PSS pp271-274) (VFC pp49-50). A man called **Edwards**, a murderer from Bilston, was hung at Stafford in May 1865 (TB Jan 1978 p24). **Martha Tupper** celebrated her 103rd birthday on Feb 19 1903 still very active, often walking from her home in Warwick Street, Bilston to Willenhall (TB Feb 1993 p5). In March 1922 **Elijah Pountney** murdered Edmond McCann, a lodger at his inn, the Pheasant Inn, Broad Street, Bilston. He was hung at Winson Green Prison in Aug 1922 (TB Feb 1989 p24). **Hugh Walters** (b1910), a prolific writer of over 20 children's science fiction novels, working between the 1950s and 1980s, lives in Bilston and works under the pseudonym of Walter Hughes. The playwright, **Malcolm Stuart Fellows**, was born in Bilston in 1924 (VFC p47). For Bilston poets see 'Some Bilston Poets' (1951) by GC Daley and F Sherwood. For Bilston authors and pamphleteers see HOBLL pp195-216. NEWSPAPERS. The **Bilston Herald**, founded by late Oct 1871, became the Bilston Weekly Herald on March 18 1882, and the Midland Weekly Herald on Aug 19 1887, and the Midland Herald from July 19 1902, but reverted to the title, Midland Weekly Herald, from May 7 1904. The BL have copies of this to Sept 29 1906 (SHJ spring 1996 p11). The **Bilston Mercury** ran from April 24 1875 to May 12 1877 when it was incorporated with the Bilston Herald (SHJ spring 1996 p11). GT Lawley (d1920), born in Bilston in 1845 and author of HOBLL, was editor of the Bilston Mercury, and a journal 'The Bilston Magazine' printed 1866. He was also a contributor to Midlands Counties Express and Birmingham Post (HOBLL pp213-214) (PSS pp287-289) (VFC pp82-83). The **Bilston Observer**, founded by late Oct 1887, became the Midland Observer from April 10 1888, and the Bilston Observer again from Oct 31 1891. The BL have copies of this to Aug 19 1893 (SHJ spring 1996 p11). The **Bilston Weekly News and Advertiser** seems to have run from March 31 1923 to Feb 18 1938 (SHJ spring 1996 p12). The **South Staffordshire Times**, founded by mid Oct 1919, became the Bilston and Willenhall Times from Sept 20 1924 and that paper ran until at least April 1 1966 (SHJ spring 1996 p12).
CUSTOM, FOLKLORE AND SUPERNATURAL. The custom of lighting a '**boon-fire**' or bonfire on Midsummer night, according to Hackwood, was not unknown in Bilston. It was supposed to be a relic of heathen ritual performed around ancient Baal fires (SCSF p45). The custom of playing **football in the streets** was practised at Bilston (FOS p179). In 1780 the coal miners of Bilston were being terrorised by an evil **spirit haunting a pit**. They consulted a well-known local male white witch, called the White Rab-

bit, who advised them to process down the pit at midnight led by a miner carrying a Bible. The spirit was finally exorcised when the miner held the Bible in his left hand (GLS pp20-21). In the early 1800s, **two witches**, mother and daughter, lived poorly in Walsall Street, and cursed anyone who refused to give them money. Their spell was broken by a woman who inflicted a wound and drew blood from a cat, itself a manifestation of one of the witches (FOS pp39,40) (TB May 1993 p5). Probably in the early C19 some local men were boasting and gossiping in the **Bull's Head Inn**, Bilston. As they boasted about the superiority of the Englishman, mocking the French, German, Scots, Welsh and Irish, an Irish captain with his Irish servant came into the inn. Having acquired rooms the two retired for the night without a word. In the bar the local men decided to make a fool of the captain by sending him a watch so that he could tell the time by an English watch, implying that he had gone to bed too early. At length, despite the servant making it clear that his master was too tired to join them, the captain descended with a tray on which was the watch and pistols. He then proceeded to challenge the men that who ever should claim the watch should fight him in a duel. Needless to say no one admitted to being the watch's owner, and so unclaimed, the watch, was given to the Irish servant and the two left the inn, having made fools of the Englishmen (FTWM pp107-112). For the story of how a **red hot shilling** dropped out of the sky in Bilston and bemused the local people see FTWM pp134-136. Bilston has been haunted by the **ghost of Jimmy**, a butcher occupying an ancient property in Walsall Street. He was an eccentric and dressed peculiarly and was constantly taunted by children and local people; he eventually committed suicide by hanging; his ghost then appeared in his house and field and was seen on one of the butcher's hooks in the passage of the shop. He was finally 'laid' when a railway cutting for the GWR was cut through his house and field. The story was originally told by GT Lawley in the later C19 in local newspapers and unpublished work, now in Bilston Library (WJO Dec 1905 pp322-323) (FOS pp21-22). The **ghost of Edward Gibbons**, who died in an explosion at Queen Street Foundry on Nov 18 1921, has been seen in Bilston (TB Oct 1987 p5).

Bilston Branch of the Walsall Canal. Spurred off the Walsall Canal at SO 964964. Running towards Bilston it seems to have passed under Dale Street, and ran on towards Queen Street. Completed in 1810, closed in 1953 (BCM autumn 1995 p16).

Bilston Brook Rises on high ground in Coseley parish. Runs eastwards to the Tame and flows on the S side of Bilston (TMS p125). A corn mill may have stood on it from the C14 near the present junction of Bankfield Road and Brook Terrace (BCM July 1981 p51). The brook is mentioned at the end of the 12th song of Drayton's Polyolbion (1613) as the little Bourne (HOWM pp4 note, 92). It may have brought the Cholera epidemic of 1832 to Bilston (BCM July 1981 p51). In the 1830s a father and son, who wished to conceal their counterfeiting activities at a derelict house at Bilston Brook, pretended that the house was haunted. People believed that the ghost was an iron puddler, whose head had been blown off in a boiler explosion. Eventually, police heard of the 'ghost' and visited the house and so caught the coiners (FOS p25). The brook was greatly polluted by Stewarts and Lloyds Steel Works (later British Steel) from 1940 onwards (BCM July 1981 p49).

Bilston Folly A stone gothic folly in Bilston. Hidden from public view until a row of shops in Church Street was demolished in 1990. According to local historian, Ron Davies, it was most likely built as 'The Retreat' in the garden of a house which stood at the side of Church Street occupied by John Etheridge, a local worthy, b1772 (TB April 1991 p17p).

Bincliff 1m SSE of Wetton. The mines here were above the Manifold. The burial mound 120 metres NE of the mines at SK 11655407 is 23 paces in diameter two feet high and is a listed monument. The burial mound 70 metres NE of the mines at SK 11635403 is 23 paces in diameter seven feet high and is a listed monument. Carrington excavated a mound in the Bincliff area in 1848 (TYD p117) (NSJFS 1965 p42).

Bingley Hall The main exhibition hall, forming a part of the Staffordshire County Showground, S side of Weston Road, S of Hopton Heath, to the E of Stafford. The showground is the present headquarters of the **Staffordshire Agricultural Society** (SAS). The original society was founded in 1800. The first meeting was at the Swan Hotel (see), Lichfield. The Society ran until 1825 and then lapsed. An new society, known as the North Staffordshire Agricultural Society, formed at The Crown (see), Stone, in 1844. It opened membership to the whole county in 1855 and 'North' in the title was dropped. It was not active between 1914 and 1920, and there were no shows between 1939 and 1946. The last migratory show was held at Walsall in 1957. In 1958 the first show was held on the present permanent showground. In c1974 the Birmingham Agricultural Exhibition Society (BAES) vacated its rented site, Bingley Hall in Birmingham, and in a joint venture with SAS came to share the SAS showground; together the two societies built the present main exhibition hall in the 1970s, and it has taken the name Bingley Hall. From then on Bingley Hall has frequently been used as a function centre by other societies. SAS and BAES amalgamated on Jan 1 1999 to become Staffordshire & Birmingham Agricultural Society (The History of Staffordshire Agricultural Society. Brenda Greysmith. c1978) (info County Showground).

Binns Farm House 0.75m WSW of Elmhurst. Stands on approximate site of an early C18 farmhouse known as Beans Farm. This was in existence in 1848 and had been built on what was once enclosed land, called the Beenes, owned by Lichfield corporation (VCH vol 14 p233).

Birchall Hamlet 1.25m SSE of Leek. There was a burial mound in Birchall Meadows at cSJ 984545 in which workmen discovered a cinerary urn during drainage work in 1859 (SA Nov 26 1859 p5) (TYD p346) (NSJFS 1965 p43) (VCH vol 7 p85). The name is from 'Bircholl' birch knoll, the birch-topped hillock (NSFCT 1905 p160), and has also appeared as Birch Hill. The grange of Dieulacres Abbey, established here by 1246 (NSJFS 1970 p85) (VCH vol 7 p85), and described as the manor of Birchall Grange in 1345, may have been at Great Birchall Farm, mentioned in 1765, possibly the later Big Birchall at the top of Birchall Lane at SJ 989548; a small suburb developed here from the 1920s. Big Birchall farmhouse was demolished some time after 1928 (VCH vol 7 pp97,101). That suburb now merges with the development which grew around the separate settlement of Little Birchall to the N at SJ 986552. There is a plague stone at Little Birchall on the W side of the A520. It formerly stood on the E side and was moved because of road widening in 1927 (NSFCT 1927 p17). Robert Milner thinks it is possible it once formed part of the Cheddleton cross. Tradition has it that here Cheddleton people placed food for Leek townspeople during the bubonic plague in the 1690s (CVH p155) (PDS&C p33p). Or that it served as the place where Market goods were deposited during a plague in Leek 1646-7 (SCSF p91).

Birch Cross To the W of Marchington. In Hanbury ancient parish.

Birchenbooth Abandoned house and mine 1.25m WNW of Flash in the high moorlands, at SK 005677. But appears on some old maps as the most northerly house in Staffs. The name 'booth' is from 'both,' a cowhouse or herdsman's shelter (VCH vol 7 p52). It was possibly the site of a dairy farm in the Middle Ages and there was a house here in 1597 (VCH vol 7 p49). It is mentioned in Camden's 'Britannia' (Gibson's Ed 1695). Has appeared as Birchenbough (Plot, Morden, Bowen maps), Birchen Booth, Birchenbower (map of c1800), Birchenbooth (Yates' map. 1834 OS map) (NSFCT 1932 p58) (1947 OS map 43/06 1:25,000). The house was occupied to at least 1940 but was later abandoned (VCH vol 7 p49) (UHAW p51 il) and now does not appear on OS maps. There was a coal mine at Birchen Booth in the early C19 (SSE 1996 p77). Some of the cottages at Birchenbooth are illustrated in UHAW p51.

Birchen Bower House 1m ENE of Kingstone, 2.25m SSW of Uttoxeter, at SK 079298. Formerly in Woodlands township in Uttoxeter ancient parish (W p798).

Birchendale Near Hollington, Croxden.

Birchenwood Area 1m E of Kidsgrove. Robert Heath built the coke ovens for Birchenwood Coke Works in 1896. The famous Mond Gas burners were installed in 1910. George V and Queen Mary visited the works in April 1913 (KAIW p17).

Birches Between Broughton and Hookgate. Probably represented by the present wood called Broughton Birches. Mr Hulme and two other lay preachers returning together to Hook Gate through the district known as the Birches had three separate versions of the same vision of three spirits at the same time (BOV pp50-51), or Elizabeth Stonemason's ghost appeared to them (STM Dec 1964 p35).

Birches An Upper and Lower Birches SW of Rugeley.

Birches, The Former house and estate partly in Codsall and Tettenhall parishes (W pp174,207), over 1m SE of Codsall. It existed as an estate by 1716 (VCH vol 20 pp81-82). It was some time occupied by the Gaskell family who had business interests in Liverpool and Birmingham (TCOP p134ps). The house was demolished sometime in the late 1960s or early 1970s and an estate of privately built houses laid out over the grounds (VCH vol 20 pp81-82). The road called Meadow Vale is now situated on the site of the house (TCOP p134). The name is preserved in The Birches Primary School.

Birches Barn Former house, in the present Birches Barn Road, and estate in Penn Fields. It is likely that John Stubbs, Gent, of the Birches, lived hereabouts in 1766. At the end of the C19 it was owned by Joseph Rown Cartwright JP. The estate was sold in 1911 and built on with housing by Wolverhampton Corporation between 1919 and 1921 (PAIP p39) (PENOP p9).

Birches Farm To E of Birches Head, but on W side of the Trent. In the late C17 it was the residence of William Sneyd (1642-1708), second son of William

Sneyd of Keele Hall. Later it was occupied by the Primes and the Jenks. The old farmhouse was rebuilt some time after 1926 (VCH vol 8 p249) (SNEDE).

Birches Green At Shelfield on E side of Walsall Road (OS map 1834). Was formerly Shelfield Green, a common. It was an inhabited area by 1763 (VCH vol 17 pp277,279). The name no longer prevails.

Birches Head Suburb of NE Hanley. At No. 6 Cromwell Street, Birches Head, Stan Sheminant, aged 28, murdered the son of his landlady, Harry Berrisford, aged 20, and hid his body in the ground under the floorboards of the house. Sheminant was hanged at Liverpool on Jan 3 1947 (MCS pp45-49). The ecclesiastical parish of Birches Head was created in 1954 (GLAUE p403). The church, St Matthew, on the corner of Birches Head and Barthomley Roads, was built in 1958-1959, replacing an iron church which was dedicated in 1899 (VCH vol 8 p158).

Birches Head Farm Farm on an old site situated on the road between Hanley and Abbey Hulton, approximately at the junction of Birches Head Road and Fairhaven Grove. It was the home of John Adams, youngest son of Thomas Adams of Burslem, by 1611. It remained in the Adams family until 1771 (VCH vol 8 p152). The brick farmhouse standing in c1960 appeared to be of early C19 origin and may have masonry in the walls of C17 origin (VCH vol 8 p152).

Birches Valley Small valley 1m WSW of Slitting Mill, in Cannock Chase. By 1984 there was the Forestry Commission's Forest Centre, later with a deer museum, on the S side of Birches Valley road (CCM) (MR p77pc).

Birchfield Suburb to E of Handsworth and S of Perry Barr. Formerly in Handsworth ancient parish. Recently (1984) a Romano-British kilnsite was found off Wellington Road near Willmore Road (MNB p38). The name is from a medieval field called Birch Field (MNB p38). Or Birch is from the Wyrley-Birch family of Hamstead Hall (HPPE pp12,43). Has also appeared as Birchfield End (HPPE p12). For the windmill at Birchfield see Paper Mill End. Birchfield became a separate ecclesiastical parish in 1865 (GLAUE p403). The church, Holy Trinity, on the corner of Trinity and Birchfield Roads, was built in 1864 (BOEWA p182). The church, St George (Presbyterian in 1966), Heathfield Road was built in 1896 (BOEWA p182). Aston Villa Football Club played their early matches in Aston Park but moved to a site in Wellington Road, Birchfield in Sept 1876. The club moved from there after 1896 (Aston Villa: A Portrait in Old Picture Postcards. Derrick Spinks. 1991 pvi). The most successful club in the team race of the English Cross-Country Championship has been Birchfield Harriers with 27 wins and one tie between 1880 and 1953 (GBR 1965 p270).

Birchfield End Former area or liberty in Handsworth ancient parish (HANDR pviii). Birchfield End occurs in 1815. Birchfield is the present name for the area (HPPE p12).

Birchfield House Birchfield, Handsworth. Built in the later C18 or early C19 (MNB p41).

Birch Hall A 'Swiss' cottage in Ingestre for the Earl of Talbot's land agent (W p393).

Birchills Former hamlet 1.5m NNE of Walsall, in the foreign and ancient parish of Walsall (SHOS vol 2 p73) (W p649). The name has no connection with birch trees. The prefix was originally Anglo-Saxon bryce (pronounced breche) and in time corrupted to birch. Bryce means 'newly enclosed or broken up ground' implying a clearing in the wood (DUIGNAN) (SPN p135). Birchills occurs as an area of wood and waste in the earlier C14 (VCH vol 17 p159). Burch hills (Plot's map). The hamlet, seems to have had its centre at the junction of Birchills, Green Lane and Hospital Street, and was usually poor. In the mid C19 there were large collieries and iron works here; its other industries were similar to those at Walsall (see) (W p649) (VCH vol 17 pp145,160). Birchills Hall Ironworks had a boiler explosion on May 15 (BY p21p) or May 19 (TB Feb 1992 p15) 1880, at which Sister Dora of Walsall (see) attended to the injured; 25 died (TB Feb 1992 p15) or 26 were killed (BY p21p). The church, St Peter, on the corner of Stafford and Hall Streets, was built in 1841 (LDD). The church, St Andrew, in Birchills Street, was built in 1884-1887 (VCH vol 17 p295). Birchills station on the Cannock Branch Railway opened on July 1 1858 (SSR p17). In 1889 Birchills became a ward of Walsall county borough (VCH vol 17 p217). The Zeppelin L19 which made a raid over Walsall on the night of Jan 31 1916 dropped a bomb which damaged St Andrew's church and vicarage in Hollyhedge Lane (BCM autumn 1996 p57). By at least the early 1990s the name Birchills was applied to the area formerly known as Townend Bank (see) (OS map 1:25,000 1993) (Birmingham A-Z 1995).

Birchills Branch of the Wyrley and Essington Canal. Spurs off the Wyrley and Essington Canal at Sneyd Junction and runs to Hospital Street, Birchills. The Wyrley and Essington Extension Canal spurs off it at Birchills Junction. Opened in c1796 (HCMS No. 2). It is often considered a part of the Wyrley and Essington Canal (Birmingham A-Z).

Birchills Hall Stood to the E of Green Lane, Birchills (VCH vol 17 p159) (BAOH p63), in the Newfield Close area (1834 OS map). Built in the C18 (BY p21). Seat of the Whateleys in the late C18, and birthplace of Sir Henry Smith Parkes (d1885) KCB, GCMG on Feb 24 1828, diplomat in China and Japan (S pp123,124) (SOB pp103,214-216) (BY p21) (BCM Jan 1992 pp18-21; date of birth given is Feb 4 1828). By 1850 it was surrounded by pits and ironworks (BAOH p63).

Birchills Junction Junction of the Birchills Branch of the Wyrley and Essington Canal with the Wyrley and Essington Extension Canal (HCMS No. 2).

Birch House Stood on the W side of what is now Swan Square, Burslem. Occupied in 1569. Was still standing in 1838 but no longer exists (VCH vol 8 p117).

Birch House In Mill Meece. Formerly in Cotes division in Eccleshall ancient parish (W p378).

Birch's Green Area just S of where Spring Road crosses the Lichfield Road, Shelfield. Possibly the name is from a former common field (SNBC p22).

Birch Trees Farm 1m N of Horton, in Horton ancient parish. Is probably of the later C18 (VCH vol 7 p67).

Birchwood Park 2m NE of Milwich. Birchwood Old Park was a medieval hunting ground. Shown on Speed's map, it then belonged to the Astons (NSFCT 1910 p176). A house here was the seat of Benjamin Wolfe, master potter; his will is dated 1805 (NSFCT 1923 p35).

Bird Brook Tributary of the Tame, in Darlaston (Offlow hundred), now culverted or incorporated into a canal. Flowed alongside Rough Hay Road (formerly Radley Gutter Lane) through a gutter known as Radley's Gutter. It then flowed S of Darlaston Green (Offlow hundred) and then in an easterly direction to James Bridge (SNDB pp16-17).

Bird End Settlement S of Charleymont Road. Formerly in West Bromwich ancient parish. Bird End is said to have been formerly known locally as Sot's Hole (see) and Sinkhole (TB March 1996 p21), although, a Sinkhole Farm existed in 1886 to the E of a settlement known as Bird End (1886 OS map). Sinkhole seems to have been a term of derision. William Cobbett, writing in 1822, described Haslemere as 'that sink-hole of a borough' (Rural Rides. William Cobbett).

Bird in Hand Place between Stallington and Hilderstone (NSSG p7), where there is an inn of this name formerly run for many years by members of the Shelly family who brewed their own beer (info Michael Cockin).

Birds Grove House at the junction of Birdsgrove Lane and the A52, Mayfield. It was built in c1850 and was the seat of the Greaves family, owners of the Birdsgrove estate; Mrs Sarah Greaves was residing here in 1851 (W p784). It was acquired by the Pharmaceutical Society after WW2 and is now (1993) used by them as a convalescent home (MOM p75p). There is a toll house here which served the Leek-Ashbourne turnpike road, it was rebuilt in 1842. Another toll house, opposite, may have existed (NSFCT 1948 pp33p facing,38,39). Has also appeared as Birdsgrove.

Birdshall Tiny and very obscure manor in Tatenhill ancient parish (SHOS vol 1 p107). It lay between Dunstall village, Fernhill Farm, Rangemore and Highlands Park. The name, which has appeared as Bredsall, Birdshill, Birdshouse, Briddeshall, Briddeshus, Brydehus, Bridshall, Briddeshouse, Brid's hall, Bryddeshale, and Brades-halle (SHOS vol 1 p123) (HOPT vol 1 p136), was preserved in Birdshall Meadow in 1907, which lay near Rangemore Park next to the Dunstall Brook. The name Moats may indicate the site of the original manor house (HOPT vol 1 p132). Sir Philip Somerville held Birdshall manor from John of Gaunt, Duke of Lancaster, in Richard II's reign, by the service of serving the Duke his Christmas dinner at Tutbury and having the Steward of Tutbury serve him his on the Duke's behalf, and leaving on St Stephen's day (Boxing Day) with a ceremonial kiss (NHS pp440-444) (SHOS vol 1 p107) (Dugdale's 'Baronage' vol 2 p107) (SMC p121) (SCSF p119). According to the Rental of Barton (1414-5), Thomas Griffith held Birdshall manor by a similar service (SHOS vol 1 p123) (HOPT vol 1 pp132-133).

Bird Street Lichfield. Anciently known as Brigge or Bridge Street (Shaw called it this), leading as it did to Bishop Langton's narrow bridge over Minster Pool (LAL p42). The George Hotel or Inn is in this street.

Birmingham and Fazeley Canal Built in 1789 (WMLB p53). Runs from Farmer's Bridge Junction, S of Newhall Hill, W of Birmingham, where it diverges from the Birmingham Canal New Cut New Main Line, to Fazeley Junction. The name also is applied to a stretch from Fazeley Junction northward to Whittington Brook at Whittington because the Birmingham & Fazeley Canal Company built it when the route was intended to have been cut by the Coventry Canal Company for the Coventry Canal. They were unable to build this section owing to a lack of money (SWY p11). The curious raised footbridge over the canal, at SK 199008, 0.75m NE of Drayton Bassett, might be coeval

with the canal. It is in a Gothick style with a tower on each side, both 15 feet high. The pedestrian passes up steps in one and down the steps in the other on the other side. David Glower told Jones that the rather Chinese balustrade had been taken away (F&G p389). (BOE p118) (F p318) (TEM autumn 1983 pp70,71) (Canal Companion Warwickshire Ring il) (TDOPP p55p) (BZ p108). On the canal at Fazeley to the N in 1839 the boatmen who murdered Christina Collins at Hoo Mill (see) were caught.

Birmingham and Liverpool Junction Canal Alias Shropshire Union Canal (The Canals of The West Midlands. Charles Hadfield. vol 5 of The Canals of The British Isles. see map on pp66-67).

Birmingham Canal New Cut New Main Line Built by Thomas Telford to provide a shorter and straighter course than Birmingham Canal Old Cut Old Main Line, reducing the distance between Birmingham to Wolverhampton from 22 to 14 miles. Telford surveyed it in 1824 at the instigation of the Birmingham Canal Navigations (VCH vol 2 p294,295) (IAS p202). Others say he was first commissioned to build the line in 1820 (SWY p9). It diverges from the Old Main Line at Factory Junction, Tipton, and joins up with a part of the original Wednesbury Branch Canal. It leaves this when it rejoins the Old Main Line below Spon Lane locks. It then runs through Smethwick in an even deeper cutting passing under the Old Main Line (carried by the Steward Aqueduct (see)). The Old and New Lines rejoin below the three Smethwick Locks. Telford's line then continues E, cutting off several minor loops before entering Birmingham (SWY p9). The canal between Factory Junction and Pudding Green Junction has been called the Island Line (see) and it is supported by two aqueducts; Ryland's Aqueduct (see); and Cooper's Aqueduct, which carries the canal over John's Lane.

Birmingham Canal New Cut Old Main Line A straightening of Brindley's Birmingham Canal Old Cut Old Main Line by Brindley's successor as engineer, Robert Whitworth, and John Smeaton, between 1789 and c1800 in which Brindley's short steep summit level at Smethwick was replaced (SWY p9) and the four mile stretch of the Old Main Line from Bloomfield to Deepfields round Coseley Hill was straightened and reduced to only 1.75m long. This stretch was authorised in 1794 and opened in 1837 with a tunnel through Coseley Hill (VCH vol 2 p292) (HCMS No. 2).

Birmingham Canal Old Cut Old Main Line Built by James Brindley between 1768 and 1772. It was the first branch canal in England (HOS p52). Links Birmingham (at Gas Street Basin), Smethwick, Oldbury, Tipton, Bilston and Wolverhampton with the Staffordshire and Worcestershire Canal (SL p239) at Aldersley Junction. It had a lengthy and winding course on account of it trying to follow the same geographical level to avoid cuts and locks. However, the descent from Aldersley to Broad Street Bridge, Wolverhampton, was only possible by the construction of a great flight of 20 locks; a few years later one more was added at the bottom, making the number 21 (SWY p7). To boatmen these locks became known as the 'Wolverhampton 21' (BCM spring 1994 pp52-59). From 1837 the most winding section of canal round Coseley Hill was superseded by the direct New Cut Old Main Line and its tunnel through Coseley Hill, this winding section then became a mere branch - Wednesbury Oak Loop (VCH vol 2 p292) (HCMS No. 2). At Dudley Port the old canal burst its banks on Sept 9 1899 (TB Nov 1974 p27p. Nov 1983 p14 old postcard shows it) (WBOPP pl 101) (TSSOP p48p). Further on, Brindley took his canal through Tividale and Oldbury, where it swung round the town on the N side; this bit, on being superseded by a straighter stretch S of Oldbury in 1821, became Oldbury Loop Canal (HCMS No. 2). Brindley raised his canal over Smethwick Summit by a series of locks with water being pumped up to them by pumping engines on either side of the Summit at Bridge Street, Smethwick, and at Spon Lane. The engine at Smethwick was constructed by Boulton and Watt in 1779. It was in use until 1891 and removed in 1898 to the Birmingham Canal Navigation Company's depot at Ocker Hill (see) (SMEOP p6p). In 1790 Brindley's Old Summit Level was superseded by a section of the New Cut Old Main Line built close by (HCMS No. 2). Brindley's canal was largely superseded by Birmingham Canal New Cut New Main Line (The Canals of The West Midlands. Charles Hadfield. vol 5 of The Canals of The British Isles. see map on pp66-67) (CL March 22 1990 p197).

Birmingham House Yoxall. Is the formal name for No. 1 King Street, Yoxall. It was the home of George Walton, father of Izaak Walton (YX pp16,17).

Bishop Durdent's Cross A cross which stood by another cross, Bishop Pucelle's Cross, outside Culstrubbe Gate, Lichfield, from the C12 and is named after Bishop Walter Durdent (d1161) (SHC 1924 pp19,52) (VCH vol 14 p10).

Bishop Pucelle's Cross A cross which stood by another cross Bishop Durdent's Cross outside Culstrubbe Gate, Lichfield, from the C12 and is named after Bishop Gerard de Pucelle (d1183) (SHC 1924 pp19,52) (VCH vol 14 p10).

Bishop's Fish Pool A third pool which lay about Lichfield cathedral until beginning of the C18. It lay to W of Beacon Street (WMLB pp86,93 plan shows extent of it). Is also called Swan Moggs (see). The site is now the Museum Gardens.

Bishop's Hill Newborough. See also Mitre Cottage, which sits at the foot of it, which may explain its name.

Bishop's House Is No. 21 Lichfield cathedral Close, situated on S side of the Close between the Rectory and No. 23 the Close. There was a house on this site in 1411 (VCH vol 14 p66). The building was substantially rebuilt in the 1790s. It incorporates the remains of a medieval canonical house. Residence of the bishops of Lichfield since 1953 (GKCLC). (BOE p189).

Bishopshull Prebend in Lichfield cathedral founded by Bishop Clinton in the C12. Takes its name from the estate Bispells (SHOS vol 1 p291) (VCH vol 14 p135). This estate or former hamlet was in Hints parish and is a segment of the original Hints prebend, founded by Roger de Clinton (SSAHST vol 2 1960-61 p43).

Bishop's Lodging A small part of The Friary, Lichfield, which alone remained after it was taken down at its dissolution in 1538. Built of stone, the Bishop's Lodging, was built into Gregory Stonynge's new brick hall in 1545, which was also called The Friary (LAL p17).

Bishop's Offley Small village on a bank above the Sow 2.5m N of High Offley. Former township in Adbaston ancient parish. The village stands high overlooking Adbaston parish and the Shrops Plain to the SW (AADB p31). There is a tradition that Bishop's Offley Pool is the last relic of Noah's Flood (BPS p155) (ROT p18). Roman legionnaires may have excavated the sandstone cutting at SJ 782298 known as The Rock to form a road. It lies slightly to the N of Bishop's Offley on the lane to Offley Brook (STM June 1966 p34p) (EOP p48p). The name has appeared as Offeleia (DB), Offley Cyprian or Cyprian's Offley (Testa de Nevil (c1242 ?) after the Cyprian family who lived in the early C13 (SHC 1914 p81)), Bishopstoffeleg (SPN p44), Bisshopps Offley (1567) (SHC 1938 p106), and Offley Bishops (Plot's map). Offley is from Offa's leah 'woodland cleared by Offa' (ROT p18). 'Bishop's' was added after the bishop of Lichfield who was lord of Eccleshall manor (W p372). Was included in Adbaston prebend (SSAHST vol 2 1960-61 p42). A medieval chapel at Bishop's Offley, certified in 1548, is not mentioned thereafter (SHC 1915 p4). Offley gives its name to the Offley family of Madeley (HOPT vol 1 p79). The Gaywoods, minor gentry, were of Podmore and Bishop's Offley (ECC p41). Bishop's Offley was described by John Dearden in the early 1960s as the nearest approach to a village in the whole of Adbaston parish, having then some 20 houses or farms ranged along the quarter of a mile main street (TTTD p255). The Brown Jug Inn had an amusing sign in 1995. It showed a toby jug with the portrait of a former landlord, smiling, with his customary cigarette alight behind his left ear.

Bishop's Offley Manor John Gerard Heath Lander (1904) was of Bishop's Offley Manor (mem in High Offley church). Manor Farm, Bishop's Offley, is a separate, although adjacent, house (local info).

Bishop's Palace, The Situated in the NE corner of Lichfield cathedral Close. The 'old hall,' presumably part of the bishop's house, stood W of the first palace. The first palace was built in c1304-14 by Bishop Walter de Langton. Its long E side abutted onto the E wall surrounding the Close (VCH vol 14 p58 see map). The palace was said to have been a magnificent structure (W p500) (VCH vol 14 p61) (GKCLC). The great hall, 100 feet by 56 feet, was the fifth or sixth largest in England in the early C14 (VCH vol 14 p61). According to Erdeswick the walls of the great hall were decorated by paintings depicting the coronation, marriages, wars and funeral of Edward I with some explanatory writing; particularly vivid were the array of barons assembled and the scenes of battles against the Welsh and Scots. The paintings were still visible by the 1590s but very poor (SOS p101 1723 edition) (SHOS vol 1 p307) (VCH vol 14 p61). (HOL p288) (Gough's Topography 1768 p485) (Warton's History of Poetry vol 2 p216). The old palace was completely destroyed in the Civil War (SHOS vol 1 pp307-308) (GNHS p158). There is a plan of the Palace in the Bodleian Library (HOL pp287-290) and in VCH vol 14 p63. There are no remains above ground. The only fragment of it which survives above ground is the base of a column found in the early C20 and set up in the garden (VCH vol 14 p61). The present palace was built in 1687 in Bishop Wood's time by the architect Edward Pierce, one of Wren's best masons (BOE p188) (SSAHST 1985-86 pp57-63). It was built slightly to the W of Langton's palace. Pennant and Jackson say the present palace was built by Bishop Hacket. Harwood says he only repaired a prebendal house. After his reinstatement Bishop Wood preferred, as did his successors, to live at Eccleshall Castle (VCH vol 14 p61). In the C18 and C19 it was occupied by various tenants. Lord Stanhope, later Earl of Chesterfield, was a tenant by 1706. Rebecca, widow of Sir Wolstan Dixie, was in occupation in 1727 (VCH vol 14 p22). A production of Farquhar's 'The Recruiting Officer' with 10-

year-old David Garrick making his first stage appearance in the part of Sergeant Kite may have been performed at the Palace in 1727 (VCH vol 14 p165). Gilbert Walmesley (d1751) was the next tenant. He entertained Dr Johnson and David Garrick both of Lichfield (see) here. Canon Thomas Seward resided in the palace from 1754 until his death in 1790 and edited plays of Beaumont and Fletcher here (VCH vol 14 p22). His daughter the poetess Anne Seward (see under Lichfield) continued to live here until her death in 1809. Sir Charles Oakley (d1826), former governor of Madras, and his wife Helena (d1838), followed the Sewards as the next tenants. The last tenant was Rev John Hinckley (d1867) vicar of Sheriffhales and of Woodcote (VCH vol 14 p62). By 1868 Bishop Selwyn was living at the palace. He added a chapel and the two wings (BOE p188). (LGS p174). It was the seat of all successive bishops until 1954. But was occupied by theological college students from 1922 to 1931 during which time Bishop Kempthorne lived in Selwyn House (VCH vol 14 p62 pl 15). George VI and his wife Queen Elizabeth stayed several times at the Bishop's Palace during the episcopate of Bishop Edward Woods (local info). The palace has been occupied by Lichfield Cathedral School since 1954 (VCH vol 14 p62).

Bishop's Park Medieval hunting ground (NSFCT 1910 p175) which lay in the area of the farms called Wood Farm, The Woodend and the Woodcorner 1m NNW of Adbaston (AADB p2). It can probably be identified with Blore Park (see) and Eccleshall Park (see) both of which belonged to the bishops of Lichfield and were carved out of Blore Forest.

Bishop's Stones Heaps of opaque pebbles situated in the hollow way between hills on Weeford Heath in the vicinity of Weeford Park. They were thought to commemorate a murdered bishop of Lichfield and his entourage, killed by thieves and placed exactly where the dead bodies had been found (FOS p30) (MR p363). Sir William Dugdale supplied Plot with the true story. That in c1540 John Vessy, then bishop of Exeter, born at Sutton Coldfield, in trying to benefit his native town by erecting a number of buildings and enlarging the town found the rolling pebbles about Weeford troublesome to travellers in that they tripped up horses and had them moved into heaps and hence they became known as Bishop's Stones. Indeed, this story was the testament of one local woman at a commission of enquiry into the extent of the Common in James I's reign (NHS p157) (SHOS vol 2 pp23-24) (RHS pp39, 40,295) (SH p59).

Bishop's Walk An ancient footpath from Croxden Abbey to Checkley. The name may be recent (STM Feb 1965 p41).

Bishop's Wood Village 10m SW of Stafford. Former common land in Brewood manor, prebend and parish (W p446) (SSAHST vol 2 1960-61 p43). Squatters built cottages on the common and these gave impetus to the expansion of the village, described in c1680 as 'a little vill a little beyond Kiddlemore Green'. The common was enclosed in 1844; the village still retains its fragmented shape (SHC 1919 p241) (VCH vol 5 p18). The church, St John the Evangelist, on N side of Kiddlemoor Green Road SE of the village, was consecrated in 1851 (BOE p71). Bishop's Wood became a separate ecclesiastical parish in 1852 (GLAUE p403). By the late C20 the village, which has also appeared as Bishopswood, was a ward in Brewood civil parish. For Bishop's Wood in a local rhyme see Brewood.

Bishop's Wood The lost wood which gives its name to the village of Bishop's Wood (see above). In 1135 the bishops of Lichfield were given a private hunting reserve here (SVB p34). Parcels of Bishop Wood at Bishop's Wood in the form of copses remain with names like Paradise Wood, and Cream Pots. Has appeared as Bishopes Brewode (1302) and Bishoppe's Wood (1598) (SPNO p39). The bishops had another park 12m to the NNW called Bishop's Park, in the area of Bishop's Wood to the W of Fairoak.

Bishop's Wood Large wood to the SW of Fairoak. It was once known as the 'Forest of Blore' or Blore Forest. Aerial photography has revealed a possible Iron Age hillfort in Bishop's Wood (SPJD p19pc) (HOS 1998 p25). Bishop's Wood belonged to the bishops of Lichfield (BOV p35) and a part of it may have been their Bishop's Park (see). By the wood is a mound where skirmishes are thought to have taken place after the battle of Blore Heath (NSJFS 1968 p99). Bishop Overton brought some glass experts from the Lorraine region of France to Bishop's Wood in 1582 after his appointment to the See of Lichfield. This area was chosen for it abounded in timber needed for the furnaces. By 1615 the glass makers had left the area, for an Act of parliament recently passed forbade them use of wood in glassmaking (ROT pp8-9). Two C15 or C16 glass furnaces were discovered on the E side of the wood in the 1930s (NSFCT 1933 pp92 see map, 105). One of these, known as Glass House (see), is at SJ 759313 or 759312. About this time T Pape was able to identify five glass manufacturing sites in the area (ROT p8). Mr Tom Smith was the discoverer of a glass house in Bishop's Wood (BOV pp36,37). There is a farmhouse called Glass Houses (see), 2m ESE of Hales, where one glass furnace and the site of another have been found (SVB p85). One is also believed to have existed in Glass House Croft (see) at Goldenhill Farm (NSFCT 1919 p33. 1920 p161. 1930 pp51-52). Glass houses have also been discovered at Adbaston in 1933, and at Norbury Manor House in 1951 (VCH vol 2 p225). In 1838 a couple - the woman was called Ann Wycherley - wished to marry. However, his or her child by a former relationship was an obstacle to their plans so they killed the child reputedly at a spot which has become known as Hell Hole and disposed of the body in what was described in the early C20 as 'a gloomy pool on the Cheswardine edge of the woods.' At their trial in 1838 Ann Wycherley was sentenced to death, but the man was released perhaps since he had turned King's evidence or was merely tried as an accessory to the crime (BPS p89) (BOV p37). On Sunday April 2 1843 Charles Higginson murdered his son, aged five, with a blow to the head with a spade in the wood, in the Moss Lane area, supposedly at the spot now known as Hell Hole. In this case also the child appears to have been an obstacle to Higginson's plans for elopement with a woman. Higginson then buried his son in a pit, when not quite dead. He was brought to trial and hanged on Aug 26 1843. The SA described the case as one of the most cold-blooded and heartless murders that had ever occurred in its pages. The 'boy's grave' was subsequently tended, and by the early C20 children of a neighbouring hamlet were still bringing little chaplets of flowers to the grave annually, a custom believed to date from the 1840s (SA May 13 1843) (BPS p89) (BOV p37) (MM pp85-86,87p of his execution ballad) (ROT pp9-10). For names of obscure places in the wood see BOV p37.

Bishton Small village by the Trent over 0.5m ESE of Colwich. Formerly in Colwich ancient parish and Colwich prebend (SSAHST vol 2 1960-61 p44). The circular earthwork 400 yards E of Bishton Hall at SK 028206 is a listed monument. The name Bishton may mean 'the Bishop's tun' (SSE 1996 p11). Perhaps so called for being a residence of one of the Mercian bishops (SHOS vol 1 part 1 p45) (SPN p101), or because the bishop of Chester (and of Lichfield) owned the manor (HCMBOPP p40). But equally could be from the personal name 'Biscop' (DUIGNAN). The manor of Bispestone appears in DB. Later Bishton appears as Bishopston (HAH p44).

Bishton Hall A former house on this site in Bishton was the seat of the de Bishton family, and later the Bowyers and the Sneyds. The hall passed to Ralph Sneyd (b1669), son of William Sneyd of Birches Farm (see), and cousin of Ralph Sneyd (1668-1695) of Keele Hall, with his marriage to Elizabeth Bowyer, heiress. Their grandson, John (1743-1809), built Belmont Hall (see) in 1770 and thereafter resided there (SNEDE). In 1770 or slightly later the hall was bought by John Sparrow, banker, who pulled it down (HCMBOPP p41p). The new hall was the seat of the Sparrow family in the C19 (GNHS p136) (STMSM July 1978 p5) (MR p108p). In c1928 it was occupied by Major Wood (HHHC p27); Charles Edmund Wedgwood Wood of Bishton Hall died in 1945 (mem in Colwich church). The hall has been occupied by the Roman Catholic St Bede's preparatory school since it was founded by Cecil Stafford Northcote in 1936 (SLM Sept 1996 p62). Alumni: Antony Paul Bamford (b1945), director and chairman of JCB from 1975, and his brother Mark Joseph Cyril Bamford (b1951), marine salvager (BUBA pp65,66). There is a Greek temple ornament in the garden (SLM autumn 1953 pp27p,28p) (HCMBOPP p41).

Bispells A 43 acre estate S of the Tamworth road on the boundary with Freeford - place on the perambulation around Lichfield (SHOS vol 1). The prebend of Bishopshull in Lichfield cathedral took its name from this estate. The estate was acquired by the Dyotts in the C19 (VCH vol 14 pp68,135). The former hamlet of Bishopshull (or Bispells) was in Hints parish (SSAHST vol 2 1960-61 p43).

Bitham The name means 'head of a valley' (SPNO p93). 'Bythom,' described as a hamlet within the manor of Penkridge, is mentioned in 1598 (VCH vol 5 p126). Later Bitham has appeared as Betham (1599) and Bitham (Morden's map) (SPNO p93). Bitham Green was a stopping place on the perambulation of Penkridge on the third day (HOP p30) (SCSF p24). Bitham is marked on Plot's map to NE of Otherton, and was preserved in field names in the C19, and in the current tiny Bitham Close on a new housing estate of S Penkridge.

Bithams Former enclosures near Aldridge on Druid's Heath sometime in or prior to the C14. The land helped endow Aldridge Grammar School from 1718 (MOA p134).

Bitterns Dale To N of Middleton Green. Marked on Pigot and Son map (1830). Now Bitternsdale at SE corner of Blithewood Moat.

Bitterscote Hamlet under 0.5m SW of Tamworth. Formerly in Fazeley township in Tamworth ancient parish (W p625). Bitterscote features in a derisory rhyme about Tamworth (see).

Black Bank Also known as Gun Battery Lane, on the W side of Biddulph Moor (BHS June 1968 p16).

Black Bank House 1.5m W of Cheddleton (1834 OS map).

Black Bank 0.5m N of Silverdale. Here was an old colliery shaft (IANS p128 see map), and from 1861 a Primitive Methodist chapel (VCH vol 8 p62). Here is an underground 162 square feet bunker designed to be used in a nuclear war. It was built in the 1950s. With the Cold War over the bunker was sold to a member of the public in Oct 1993 (ES May 21 1993 p12p. Oct 22 1993 p18p).

Blackbank Brook Ipstones. Runs from Ipstones joins the Churnet at Froghall (SPNO p5).

Blackberry Town Former small hamlet in the Blackberry Lane area of Springfield, Rowley Regis. The name appears in the 1851 census.

Black Brook May be the name for the brook which flows W and N from Blackhalve Farm. Forms the new county boundary between Staffs and the West Midlands. Flows S of Moseley Hall through Wobaston to the Penk at Coven Lawn. There is a road called Blackbrook Way at Moseley (Birmingham A-Z).

Black Brook Tributary of the Dane. Rises behind the Roaches. The name is from the colour of the soil or pebbles over which it runs (LMF p26). Raven thinks its valley and the Dane Valley are valleys mentioned in the medieval epic poem 'Gawain and the Green Knight' (MR p316). Was it ever frequented by beavers, since Casters Bridge was spelt Castor and a castor was a beaver? (NSFCT 1932 p57). By 1999 there was a nature reserve to the E of the brook at SK 020645 which was a SSSI in the care of the Staffs Wildlife Trust (Staffs Wildlife Trust leaflet).

Black Brook Tributary of the Hamps. The house called Black Brook, 1.25m S of Upper Elkstone in Warslow and Elkstones township in Alstonefield ancient parish, is situated by a brook. There was a house called Black Brook here by 1444 (VCH vol 7 p58).

Black Brook Rises N of Hammerwich. Formerly Hammerwich Water (VCH vol 14 pp195,196-197 see map). 'Black' refers to the colour of the bed of the stream (SPN p138). At the ford at Hints its name changes to Bourne Brook (see); a tributary of the Tame. (MR p185).

Black Brook Tributary of Smestow Brook. Runs S of Great Moor, Pattingham. In Pattingham parish. For a short distance it is the SW boundary of Wrottesley (VCH vol 20 p1).

Blackbrook Tiny hamlet over 1m SE of Hanbury. No doubt called from the brook which runs through it.

Blackbrook Tiny hamlet 1.75m NE of Foxt, roughly between Bottom House and Winkhill. Has appeared as Blackbrook (OS maps) and Blackbrooke (TOI p41). In Morridge and Foxt liberty in Ipstones parish (W p780). There is a mound or burial mound at SK 049513 on N side of railway line. A stone built cist with paved floor was found by workmen (NSFCT vol 45 p239. 1911 pp135,207) (NSJFS 1965 p42). Here was the home of the Whieldons by the C17, of which potter Thomas Whieldon (1719-1795) was one (TOI p41).

Blackbrook Hamlet nearly 2m WNW of Maer. In Maer parish. There are two mounds surrounded by trees and fences at SJ 773388; one 10 feet high and one five feet high: the northern of the two is slightly elongated southward and with a gap of 20 feet between them. By 1983 it was feared they may be destroyed due to house building (NSFCT 1983 p11).

Blackbrook Farm Red brick house with five bays 0.5m SW of Weeford. In Weeford parish. The house has been described as of C17 origin (James Wyatt. Antony Dale. 1936 p6), or of early Georgian origin.
THE WYATTS. Blackbrook Farm was the residence of **Benjamin Wyatt I** (1709-1772), fifth son of John Wyatt I of Thickbroom Hall (see), by 1737 to, perhaps, at least the late 1760s. Benjamin was a builder and with his sons set up an architectural practice; his works in Staffs include:- Fisherwick Hall (see), Swinfen Hall (see), Soho Manufactory (see), Staffordshire General Infirmary at Foregate (see) and some work at Shugborough. Some of his seven sons became notable, mainly in the fields of invention, building, architecture, and land agency, or they themselves headed dynasties with descendents successful in those fields. Benjamin's eldest son, **William Wyatt II** (b1734), became an architect and designed Soho House (see) and greatly extended Soho Manufactory (see) both for Matthew Boulton. William's eldest son, Charles Wyatt II (1758-1819), was an architect in India. William's third son, Robert Harvey Wyatt (1769-1836), was land agent to Viscount Anson. His son, Harvey Wyatt (d1875), was also land agent to the Ansons; his son, Robert Harvey Wyatt (d1886), too was land agent to the Ansons; his son, Robert Harvey Lyle Wyatt (d1932), was the father of Sir **Woodrow Lyle Wyatt** (1918-1997), journalist and MP, who was created a life peer in 1987, becoming Lord Wyatt of Weeford; his daughter, Petronella (b1968), by his second marriage, is a journalist with the Daily Telegraph. Benjamin Wyatt I's third son, Samuel Wyatt (1737-1807) 'the chip,' born at Blackbrook Farm became a notable architect, designing Heathfield Hall (see); with John Harvey,

the Shire Hall in Stafford; Sandon Home Farm in Sandon Park (see); The Ring at Great Haywood; the interior of Tixall Hall (see); extending Shugborough Hall (see); remodelling Soho House (see); refitting the chancel of Sandon church. Benjamin Wyatt I's fourth son, Joseph (1739-1785/1818), became an architect in Burton upon Trent; in 1769 he worked with his brother Samuel on the construction of the Orangery at Blithfield Hall (see), to designs of 'Athenian' Stuart; this led Samuel to do work for the house itself. A son of Benjamin Wyatt I's fifth son, Benjamin Dean (1745-1818), was Lewis William Wyatt (1777-1853), an architect who supplied designs for Wigginton Lodge (see) and Patshull Hall (see). Benjamin Wyatt I's sixth son, **James Wyatt** (d1813), was perhaps the most famous Wyatt architect. He was born at Blackbrook Farm in 1746: Although the DNB erroneously states he was born at Burton Constable (perpetuated in David Crystal's The Cambridge Biographical Encyclopedia. 1994), an assertion rejected by Antony Dale in his 'James Wyatt' (1936) p7; Burton Constable, is a house in Yorks for which Wyatt designed the drawing room and the lodge. Early in his career Wyatt visited Italy for several years, and achieved fame with his Neo-classical design for the London Pantheon (1772). He became surveyor to the Board of Works (1796), restored several cathedrals, and designed many country houses. His best-known work is the Gothic revival Fonthill Abbey (1796-1807), which largely collapsed in the 1820s. His Staffs work includes: work at Burton upon Trent church, Lichfield Cathedral (and David Garrick's monument there), Beaudesert (see), Canwell Hall (see), Hagley Hall, Little Aston Hall, remodelling Soho House, and he is attributed with remodelling Alton Abbey (later Towers). James' son, Benjamin Dean Wyatt (1775-1855), worked on Stafford House, London seat of the Dukes of Sutherland (BOE p300) (The Wyatts: An Architectural Dynasty. John Martin Robinson. 1979 p20p of Blackbrook Farm) (The Cambridge Biographical Encyclopedia. David Crystal. 1994) (A Biographical Dictionary of British Architects 1600-1840. 3rd ed Howard Colvin. 1995) (Daily Telegraph. Dec 8 1997 p23p).

Black Bull Former industrial settlement at Brindley Ford (OS map 1834) in Norton-in-the-Moors ancient parish. Black Bull Colliery was opened in 1866 (ONST 1967 p280). Biddulph Valley Coal and Iron Works was at Black Bull; it was principally this works which made Bradley Green to the N grow in size (HLS p112). Black Bull station on the Biddulph Valley Railway closed on Jan 6 1964 (BALH p123).

Black Cock Inn, wharf and bridge on the Daw End Branch Canal at Bullings Heath, Walsall Wood (SNBC p39).

Black Country, The Heavily industrialised region mainly covering S Staffs and NE Worcs. It was here the Industrial Revolution reached its zenith. The region stretches from S of Stourbridge and Halesowen in the SW to N of Walsall in the NE, and from NW of Wolverhampton in the NW to S of Oldbury in the SE (MH 1984 p60 see map), and lies on iron ore deposits and two coalfields. Rapid industrialisation occurred after John Wilkinson introduced in 1767 at Bradley (see), Bilston, smelting by using coke in the furnace, not wood-charcoal: Coal which was in abundance in the surrounding coalfields was then exploited to the full leading to the opening of many iron works. The blackness of the coal and that of the basalt found at Rowley Regis and Pouk Hill near Walsall gave the Black Country its name, as did the black smoke which issued from the region's iron works. In the C19 the Black Country was said to be 'black by day and red by night' (BCM Feb 1968 pp11-13). One of the best views of the Black Country was said to be at night and from Dudley Castle keep, as stated in this rhyme

> If thou wouldst view the Black Country aright,
> Go see it from Dudley's Grey Keep at night.

(BCSG vol 5 p64). A perhaps slightly exaggerated scene but one which nonetheless been used on many occasions to illustrate industry in the Black Country at its zenith is that of the 'Fiery Holes area' which appeared in ILN in 1866 (ILN Dec 8 1866 p548il) (BOP p106p).

The boundaries of the Black Country are impossible to define. Prof Beaver says the Black Country could just equate with the exposed coalfield, therefore excludes Walsall, Wolverhampton and West Bromwich (SL p168). TH Gough has the Black Country covering an area from Bloxwich in the N to Stourbridge in the S and from Himley in the W to Soho in the E (BCSG vol 4 p5). Walter Allen defines it as 'never where one lives oneself but begins always at the next town' (SL p168). Few have ever included Birmingham in the Black Country. Robert George Hobbes (1821-1899) describing in the weekly 'The Leisure Hour' in 1872 a tour he had made of the Black Country in 1871 'entered' the Black Country at Soho and regarded himself 'indeed in the Black Country' when he had reached Oldbury (BCM autumn 1993 p54). **Commentators and visitors**. John Wesley (d1790), attracted by the already-large ac-

cumulation of poor in mining and cottage industries suitable for conversion to Methodism, made his first visit to the region in 1738. He frequently returned and by his death had visited Wednesbury, for instance, as many as 33 times. Charles Dickens writing in 1841 referred to 'a black region' (TB Oct 1975 p27). Thomas Tancred in 1843 described the Black Country as '....an endless village intermingled with blazing furnaces, heaps of burning coal, piles of ironstone, forges, pit banks, engine chimneys, countless foundries and factories, an area crisscrossed with canals....' (Cobbs Engine House leaflet. Sandwell Borough Council). Henry Adams, the perceptive American historian, observed the new phenomenon of rapid urbanisation in 'the Black District' in 1858 (The education of Henry Adams: an autobiography. 1918. p72) (NSJFS 1974 p28). Walter White's 'All Round the Wrekin' (1860) contains much information about the Black Country and its industries, and contains perhaps the earliest printed reference to the name Black Country in capitals (TEBC2 p80). Elihu Burritt (1811-1879), USA consul in Birmingham, wrote in BCGB in 1868, that 'Birmingham is the capital, manufacturing centre, and growth of the Black Country' (SL p167). **Unrest and consolidation**. The Staffordshire Yeomanry were sent to suppress riots by South Staffordshire miners in 1822, 1826 and 1855 and the South Staffordshire Union riots of 1831 (info Yeomanry Museum). The Asiatic Cholera swept through the region in 1832 and 1849 and claimed 1,472 lives (TB March 1994 p20). There was a strike by colliers in April 1842 and on July 30 1842 (AOBC p69). A miners strike in the S Staffs coalfields began in June 1884 and lasted 16 weeks. It ended with a defeat for the miners (TEBC). The Black Country Society was founded in 1967 by enthusiasts led by the late Dr John Fletcher who felt that the Black Country did not receive its fair share of recognition for its great contribution to the industrial development of Britain. The Society held its inaugural meeting at Noah's Ark Inn (see), Wood Street, Tipton in 1967. In 1968 it started publishing its own quarterly journal, BCM. The Society and its journal still (1999) continue (TSSOP p41p) (The Black Country Calendar. 1999). The Black Country Living Museum at Tipton, opened in 1978, centres on a recreated Black Country village complete with Broad Street Bridge from Wolverhampton, houses, shops, and an inn brought from Brierley Hill, a Methodist church from Netherton and a school from Dudley (HOS 1998 p135). On July 27 1987 the Black Country Development Corporation was publicly launched. It was a government body set up to manage government funding and entice new investment from the private sector for the region; its headquarters were in the former Accles and Pollock offices in Oldbury. The corporation was wound up on March 31 1998; its main successes were building the Spine Road which runs through Ocker Hill (see), and creating the Black Country Urban Forest (BCM Autumn 1999 pp20,24. Spring 2000 p37).

WILDFIRE. The term Wildfire refers to the subterranean fires which ravage through the coalfields under the Black Country. Wildfire has been called 'Pseudo Volcano' (W p139) (TB Feb 1988 p12) and 'Firing of the Damp' (TB Jan 1992 p16). The fire breaks out spontaneously and can explode at the surface. Clay in the vicinity of the fire hardens and is locally known as Pock Stone. It has been used for surfacing the roads and even for the foundations of a local church (SHOS vol 2 pp85,172). The phenomena was noted by William Camden (d1623), and caused one cluster of cottages to be known for generations as 'The Firestink Housen' (TB Aug/ Sept 1972 p10). In 1622 there was a case in a coal mine between Willingsworth and Wednesbury (HWE vol 2 p323). In the C18 Dr Wilkes noted wildfire in the coal pits in Wednesbury Field (THS p154). In 1851 Bradley Moor was reported to have been burning for upwards of 70 years (TB Feb 1988 p12). In Wednesbury PR - Sept 26 1766 - Thomas Crowder was burnt to death by wildfire in a coal pit in John Wood's field. Others in the PR are recorded as having died in the same way (TB Jan 1992 p16). The fire occurred under King's Hill, Wednesbury, in 1897 where it caused holes in the road, known locally as 'crownings in' (TB Dec 1979 p7p) (TWDOP p135p). (NHS p125) (BCM Oct 1971 pp36-40).

PEOPLE. Black Country people have a distinctive dialect and a peculiar sardonic humour (borne of the district's industrial past) (WMLB p97). They are said to be 'resilient, adaptable. They are able to suffer more and put up with more than other people. The 'little big men' with their thick shoulders, can bend things to their own way. They have literally wrung their living from the available materials, and even their traditional recipes are miracles of economy - tripe and onions, cow-heels, faggots, pork with everything, even with Christmas turkey or fowl, from the pig kept at the bottom of the garden - one or two pigs, one to sell and one for Christmas' (A Journey to the Heart of England. C Hillier. 1978 p86) (MH 1990). The rapidity of industrial expansion, from the C17, resulted in many Black Country towns lacking a definition and central point (VB p41), yet most inhabitants feel strongly they belong to separate communities (SL p168). Much rivalry exists and existed between each com-

munity, their respective trades (for each eventually specialised in a sphere of metal-working) were used by the other to ridicule them, and features of each's town. In the case of Darlaston (Offlow hundred) and Willenhall it was their church weathercocks. Rowley Regis is considered by some the heart of the Black Country and the people there are said to have the purest Black Country accent (BCWJ p14). The Gornal accent preserves the most Old English words in its dialect (TB Sept/ Oct 1973 p14) (BBC Radio 4 John Sparry 9.45am April 14 1994). In some cases nicknames are given by the local inhabitants to streets and areas of their own district and some of these are adopted as the official name: Hell Lane, The Patch, The Island (Mobbs Bank), Blood Hall, Soap Hole, Johnny Cornfield's Backside are examples (BCSG vol 5 p6; gives a list of nicknames). 'Keep out of the hoss road' is the Black Country expression for saying farewell (BBC Radio 4 John Sparry 9.45am April 14 1994). BLACK COUNTY IN FICTION. These novels are set in and around the Black Country - 'Sybil' Benjamin Disraeli (1846), 'Colton Green: A Tale of the Black Country' Rev W Gresley prebendary of Lichfield (1847), 'A Bitter Debt: a tale of the Black Country' (1893) Annie S Swann (VFC p126), 'Capful o' Nails' David Christie Murray, 'The Old Doctor' (1923) and 'Behind the Night Bell' (1938) FG Layton (VFC p83), 'The Village' (1926 or 1931) Rev JR Windsor-Garnett of Lower Gornal (see); 'Dead Man Over All' W Allen (1945-60), 'Dr Bradley Remembers' FB Young (1945-60), 'My Brother Jonathan' FB Young (1945-60), 'Cold Harbour' FB Young (1953-5), 'Rebels' H Treece (1953-5), 'Ruffy and Sons' G Wooden (1953-5), 'The Little Masters' Christian Walford (1970), 'A Black Country Nurse at Large' (1973) Edith Cotterill (VFC p32), 'Ghost in the Water' (1973) Edward Chitham (VFC p26), 'A Corridor of Mirrors' Archie Hill (1975-9), 'Black Cameo' D Baker (1988), 'Crystal' D Baker (1988), 'Striving with Gods' J Bannister (1980-4), and 'Essie' F Pearce (1988), 'Weaver's Daughter' D Baker (1990).
FOLKLORE. For Lent customs in the Black Country see BCM April 1979 pp35-37. It was the custom on old Mothering Sunday in the Black Country for the miningmiddle men, who leased the mine-workings from the owners, and hired the colliers, to give a toast of ale to all the men employed in their pits, and to feast their apprentices with beans and bacon (FOS p88). The most famous Black Country dish on old Mothering Sunday was 'frumity' or 'frumenty' (FOS p86). At Easter in the Black Country it was customary for the schoolchildren of the parish schools to 'clip the church' (FOS p91). Hackwood notes the game of biting an apple prevailed on St Clement's day in the Black Country (SCSF p46). Black Country trains were decorated with oak boughs on Oak Apple Day (May 29). CS Burne saw trains decorated with oak boughs on this day in 1883 (SFL p365) (BCC vol 2 p263) (STMSM Aug 1980 p36). It was the custom to decorate Black Country churches with mistletoe on Christmas Eve, this is considered unusual because mistletoe has pagan associations (BCC vol 3 p224) (FLJ 1987 p195). At Christmas the favourite Wassail drink in the Black Country was mulled elderberry wine (SCSF p49). Hobbes in 'The Leisure Hour' in 1872 noted that the population of Oldbury were addicted to rum, which he described as 'the cream of the Black Country' (BCM autumn 1993 p54). The practice of the 'carol singers' in the Black Country is for them to wait until the bells have ended their midnight peal before they sally forth (FOS p140). For Christmas in the Black Country see BCS pp1-5. For colliers' superstitions see BCSG vol 4 pp67-68, TB April 1976 p15, Nov 1993 p15, WP p57. For Bilston and Wednesbury colliers' superstitions concerning the sound of migrating birds at night see under Wednesbury.
AYNUK AND AYLI. Aynuk and Ayli are invented Black Country characters who embody the Black Country spirit and feature in most local jokes. Many sayings are attributed to them. The characters, colloquial for Enoch and Eli, are folk heroes perhaps invented by the Black Country comedian, Ernie Garner, who died at Bridgnorth, Shrops, on Jan 30 1936 (TB Feb 1975 p17. May 1977 p25). According to Jon Raven their adventures, sayings, tales, jokes, stories and poems reflect the true tenacity, strength of purpose and single-mindedness that marks Black Country people. Much of the humour derives from jokes against themselves. Historically, in the folk poem 'O'd Aynuck,' - FOS gives it - they are in turn nail chainmaker, collier, iron worker. By the 1970s, at least, they were the men who had the answer to everything, whose skills were innumerable, and their lives immortal (FOS pp13,151,152,164-165). Aynuk and Ayli had their own show on Radio WM on Sundays in 1993. There was a Netherton-based comedy duo who played the duo performing on the local comedy circuit in 1996 and called themselves Aynuk & Ayli (TB Sept 1993 p7. Dec 1996 p15). (A Glossary of Black Country Words and Phrases. TV Shaw. 1930) (Aynuk; a collection of over 150 Aynuk Stories. Clement Jones 1950) (BCWJ pp9-13) (BCM Feb 1968 p35. April 1968 p13) (VB p46).

Blackesiche Brook Farewell (SHOS vol p229).

Black Firs Small (about 10 hectares) afforested relict basin mire, situated at Balterley Heath at SJ 748502. By 1999 it was a SSSI woodland nature reserve in the care of the Staffs Wildlife Trust (Staffs Wildlife Trust leaflet). Cultivated cereal pollen of possibly c6000 to 5500 BC has been found in the mire, representing an exceptional early date for cereal cultivation in the British Isles if found to be true (WSS p104).

Blackfords District 0.75m N of Cannock town centre.

Blackfriars Tiny district of Newcastle-under-Lyme in the vicinity of Blackfriars Road SW of the town centre. The name is from St Augustine's Priory of the Dominican order (black friars), which was here by 1277 (HOS p25). (GNHS p129) (NUL pp26,30). They were established some time between 1221 and 1271 (NSJFS 1962 p108). Suppressed at the Reformation on Aug 10 1538 (NSFCT 1935 p79) (NUL p26). The cross in the parish churchyard is from the Friary site (NUL p30p). The foundations were discovered in 1870-1 when the cattle market was being constructed. Further excavations in 1880-1 revealed some skeletons and a large sepulchral slab which were taken to St Giles's churchyard (NM p73) (VCH vol 8 p8) (Newcastle Times March 29 1972). Some masonry, probably from it, was found by workmen in Penkhull Street in 1923 (NSFCT 1923 p133). (NSFCT 1882 p65. 1887 p91) (SOSH p123).

Blackhalve Ancient farm, formerly in Wednesfield chapelry in Wolverhampton ancient parish. The name is from Halve, Haave, Have which are dialectic forms of Haw, applied to either the hawthorn tree or its berries (DUIGNAN), so 'black thorns' (SPN p49). Smallshire interprets the name to mean 'dense growth of hawthorns' (WFW p70); Blackhalve was anciently close to, or in, Cannock Forest. The old house known as 'The Blackhalve,' which was held by the Wakerings in the C17 and appears on Yates' map and in 1840, is the modern site of Ashmore Cottage on the N side of Kitchen Lane. The present farm called Blackhalve on the S side of Blackhalve Lane, over 0.25m to the NW, was built in the later C19, however there was an elongated pool (perhaps part of a moat) and house here in 1840. There is another moat to the NE at Moat House (see) (WFW p70). Shaw noted a very large and entire moat at Blackhalve (SHOS vol 2 p182).

Black Heath Heath 1m NE of Foxt.

Blackheath 0.5m NW of Fradley.

Black Heath Common land N of the Bridestones leading up to the summit of The Cloud (1834 OS map).

Blackheath Large district 0.75m SE of Rowley Regis. Formerly in Rowley Regis parish. Until the C19 there were only three farms on Blackheath or Blake Heath, which was glebe land belonging to Rowley church. The name appears on the Plan of the Mines of Lord Dudley 1812 as Bleak Heath. Some settlement created by nail and chain makers squatting on the common land had taken place by the time the church sold the heath in 1841. Blackheath then rapidly expanded as a commercial and residential district and soon overtook Rowley Village as the parish's main population centre (TB June 1972 p10. May June 1973 pp16-17. June 1998 p21p) (ORR p8). It became a separate ecclesiastical parish in 1869 (GLAUE p403), and is now (1999) a ward of Sandwell metropolitan borough. Joseph Parkes, hymn tune composer, was born in Hackett Street, Blackheath, in c1820. He was the author of the hymn tune 'Rowley Regis.' His other hymn tunes included 'Carr's Lane,' 'Bower Street,' 'Eastern Star,' and 'Diadem.' Mss of his tunes are kept in Rowley Regis library. He is not listed in BS, nor PSS and VFC (BCWJ p132). Rex Williams of Blackheath was All England Boys Billiard Champion in 1948, aged 14. He was later World Professional Championship title holder between 1968 and 1980 and in 1982 and 1983 (ORR p125p).

Blackheath Former heath 1m NW of Tixall. John Sutton thinks it can probably be identified with St Amon's Heath, where some of the royalist forces camped prior to the battle of Hopton Heath (SHJ winter 1987 p7). The name is preserved in Blackheath Lane, and Blackheath Covert, a wood, in which is situated King's Low. In WW2 aircraft engines were tested in a secret factory constructed in Blackheath Covert woods. The original flat-roofed utility building still (1999) survives with numerous additions (info Judith Robinson, Staffordshire University).

Black Hough House 0.25m S of Haughton. In Haughton parish. Has appeared as Hoof, Hoss, Black Hoof, the Blacke Hough, Blakehalghe (C16), and The Black Hough (1834 OS map) (SPNO p165). The house opposite has appeared as Brough (W p442) and The Hough.

Blackladies Former priory and estate 0.25m E of Bishop's Wood, in Brewood ancient parish. Roman fibula brooches, dating from the C1 to C2 AD, have been found near Blackladies (BDH pp28,32).
PRIORY. The priory, of the Benedictine order, was founded by Bishop Clinton in 1130 or c1150 on land taken out of the bishop's manor of Brewood (VCH vol 5 p37). The name, which has also appeared as Black Ladies, is from the

black habit of the nuns; 2m further W in Shrops is White Ladies where the Cistercian nuns dressed in white (DUIGNAN). For the priory seal see BDH p164 il. Blackladies priory is mentioned in a work by Gervase of Canterbury, who was writing in Richard I's reign (WJO Jan 1905 p349p). There were five nuns here at the Dissolution (WJO Jan 1905 p349). It was formerly considered by some that no part of the monastic buildings survived the Dissolution (VCH vol 5 p37). (SHOS vol 2 pp302-303) (W p444) (P p23,24,25). However, David Bywater, the present (1990s) owner of the brick house on the priory site, is of the opinion that the house incorporates much of the priory; a latrine of medieval date has been found in an external wall of the upstairs bathroom, and many interior walls are not at right-angles suggesting major alterations from the original composition (info David Bywater). In the late 1990s Mr Bywater invited the BBC 2 TV programme 'The House Detectives' (BBC 2 Oct 16 1999 7.35pm) to investigate the house's age, and the presenters concluded that the core of it did date from before the Dissolution. During the investigation several skeletons were discovered in shallow graves within a couple of yards of the house; they may be the remains of members of the Giffard family.

AFTER THE DISSOLUTION. Blackladies estate belonged to the Giffard family of Chillington Hall (see) from 1539 to 1919 (VCH vol 5 pp36-37). Much of the present (1959) house was built in the C16 or early C17 (VCH vol 5 p37). Some parliamentary troops may have been stationed at Blackladies in the Civil War (info Mark Whittaker). According to FP Palmer and A Crowquill Blackladies was held against the royalists under Lord Wilmot, for six days in 1644, until they left to raise the siege of Dudley Castle (The Wanderings of a Pen and Pencil. FP Palmer & A Crowquill. 1846) (WJO Jan 1905 p349). Amongst the old pictures at the house was one of Penderell and his family with Charles II in the Royal Oak (SHOS vol 2 pp302-303). A small timber-framed chapel, probably built in the C17, was in existence until c1846 (VCH vol 5 p37 il of in 1837 facing p34) or to 1867 when it was taken down (WJO Jan 1905 p349). Others say a chapel at Blackladies was in use for services until 1944 (SVB p35). The Roman Catholic congregation of the chapel in Chillington Hall started to use the Blackladies chapel when a new Chillington Hall was built by Soane in the C18 (WJO Jan 1905 p349). A little wooden statue of the Virgin and Infant Christ said to have been once at Whiteladies Priory in Shrops and removed to Blackladies chapel, has been claimed to be of medieval origin, but the workmanship is not English. The statue was removed to the lady chapel of St Mary's (RC) at Brewood when Blackladies chapel was demolished (WAS 2nd field study trip pp2,3). Some say the relics of St Chad were kept for a time at Blackladies, in the late C17 and early C18. Whilst here Father Anthony Terill, Rector of Liege, and Father Richard Strange, Rector of Ghent, removed some of the relics to their respective cities (SR p66) (RHPS p258). From the Giffards the house passed to the Vaughans who thoroughly restored it (VCH vol 5 pp36-37). From the Vaughans it passed to the Berrys who occupied it until the 1970s when it was bought and occupied by two families. The Webberleys had the W wing whilst the Bywaters had the E. By the 1990s the Bywaters owned the whole house. The ghost of a nun who was 'walled up' is said to haunt a certain bedroom in the W wing (info David Bywater). The Nun's Walk is a causeway running between a pond and forecourt here (BDH p174).

Black Lake In Forton parish. Noted by Plot in the later C17. Appears in 1527 as Blake Layke (SPNO p148).

Blacklake Farm and plantation. 1m WNW of Fulford.

Black Lake Large pool 1.5m NW of Tittensor. Is slightly smaller than Cop Mere.

Black Lake Is the Swan Lane area of Swan Village, West Bromwich ancient parish. The name is thought to mean 'lake on the plain' (SOWB p23), and was the name of a plot of land by the end of the C14 (when it occurs with 'Whytelake') and the name of a house or cottage by 1502. By 1820 there was a 'continuous settlement along the W side of the main road' at Black Lake (HOWB p50) (HOWBW pp209,210) (VCH vol 17 p7) (WBOPP pl 76).

Blacklands House and estate 1m NW of Bobbington. The estate formerly called Blakeland, existed by the earlier C15 when probably owned by the Brooke family, certainly holders of the estate by the end of the C15. The house was occupied in c1690 by Edward Careswell, a relative of Leigh Brooke. George Brooke sold Blacklands in 1800. By 1828 William Moseley had acquired the estate. The Moseleys sold the estate some time before the break up of their estate in 1916. The house, with a main range of the C18, has a wing of a C17 timber-framed house (VCH vol 20 pp68-69).

Black Lees Ancient estate and brick farmhouse dating from c1800 3m SW of Cannock, in Shareshill parish (SPNO p113). An old enclosure from Cannock Forest (DUIGNAN). The name is from land covered with gorse and heath which was locally called black land, as distinguished from cultivated land

(DUIGNAN). Or 'the dark woodland glades' (SPNO p113) (SPN p30). The estate seems to have been held from the early C14 by the Trumwyns, and by the Swynnertons until probably at least 1525. There after the estate passed through several hands. Mary Sanders lived at Black Lees in 1608. The moat NE of Hollybush Farm, at SJ 965064, 300 yards N of Black Lees Farm, probably represents the site of the homestead (VCH vol 1 p366. vol 5 pp173,177). Has also appeared as Le Blakeleye (1290), Le Blakelie (1380. 1515), the Black Lyese (1526), Black Leys (Yates' map), the Blacklees (1608) (SPNO p113) (SPN p30).

Black Mare (On site of The Leasows ?) Lapley.

Black Patch Former large open space extending over Handsworth ancient parish and Smethwick township of Harborne ancient parish nearly 1.5m NE of Smethwick old church. The space was occupied by gypsies by c1880 and it was given the name Black Patch on account of their presence (STELE Sept 3 1954. Sept 10 1954. Sept 17 1954) (HPPE p11) (HHHW p71p in 1898). The gypsies were evicted in 1904 and Black Patch Park was opened by the city of Birmingham to the public in 1910-11 (VCH vol 17 p94). Another account says the gypsies were evicted in 1909 and the space was purchased by the Open Space Society for £10,000, and it became a park, which had to be enclosed with strong iron railings, as the gypsies tried to retain it (HPPE p12).

Black Planting Wood Wood in which the body of the murdered Thomas Smith of Whiston Farm (see) was found in July 1866. There is a Black Plantation 0.25m ENE of Whiston Eaves.

Blackpool S Burton upon Trent. Former fields belonging to Burton Abbey which were, in the early 1090s, either ravaged in a reprisal by men from Drakelow (see) or where a skirmish took place between abbey servants and men from Drakelow. The name, which has also appeared as Blakepol, is preserved in Blackpool Street (SSE 1996 p33).

Blackroot House Stood on N side of Hall Lane, Hammerwich. Built in the mid 1870s and was then the home of TB Wright, founder of the Hospital Sunday. Formerly called Fair View. The house had been demolished by the 1980s when housing was built on the site (VCH vol 14 p259).

Blackshaw Moor Former moor, and hamlet 1.5m SE of Meerbrook. Formerly stretched into various townships in Leek ancient parish. The N part (containing the present hamlet) lay in a detached portion of Leek and Lowe township, which was removed to Leekfrith township in 1882, whilst the W part had always been in Leekfrith township. The S part lay in Tittesworth township, whilst the E part lay in Heathylee township in Alstonefield ancient parish (VCH vol 7 p234). There is an outlying boulder of andesite granite near Blackshaw Moor (NSFCT 1916 p73). The moor may have been known as 'the moor of Tittesworth' in medieval times and has appeared as Blakeshaw (VCH vol 7 pp233,235). It was an inhabited area by the 1640s (VCH vol 7 p235). A stone causeway was built c1710 by the inhabitants of Tittesworth from Blackshaw Moor to the Mermaid Inn on Morridge for packhorses loaded with salt (VCH vol 2 p279) (DP pp25-26). The moor was enclosed in 1811 (VCH vol 7 p235). Blackshawmoor Reservoir to the E is formed by the damming of the Churnet. A transit camp for anti-aircraft battalions from the USA was based on the E side of the Buxton road (A53), 0.5m NE of Upper Tittesworth, from 1943. In 1946 the camp was taken over by Polish troops. After the war it continued as a Polish re-settlement centre until 1964 when the remaining Polish refugees were rehoused on a new estate 0.5m to the N. In 1983 the camp opened as Anzio Camp a training camp for the regular army, territorials, and scouts (VCH vol 7 pp232-233) (RL p98).

Blackwaters Area on the N side of Croxton Bank (1834 OS map), now the name for a house to the W of Croxtonbank. In the Woodland division in Eccleshall ancient parish (W p380). Here have been found four Roman coins of Carausius (NSJFS 1964 p21). The area was formerly a part of Greatwood Heath (SSE vol 7 1995 p75).

Blackwood Former large plantation, S of Foley Road, Streetly. In existence by 1832. The OS map 1884 shows it as being conifers which would have looked very dark and may be the reason for the name, although it is marked Foley Wood in 1920. The area was beginning to be developed in the 1930s. There was new housing, shops and a library by the early 1960s. Blackwood Park, a public woodland area, was inaugurated in 1973 (SNAR p89p of Blackwood Park).

Blackwood Hall At Blackwood Hill, under 1m WSW of Horton. Seat of the Wedgwoods in the later C15 before they moved to Harracles Hall (VCH vol 7 p67). The Myotts lived here in 1625 and again in 1854 (NSFCT 1932 p32). The old house, which has also appeared as Blackwood House, was incorporated into the present Blackwood Hall in 1885, which was built for John Challenor (VCH vol 7 p67).

Blackwood Hill Hamlet 2m SE of Biddulph Moor, in Horton ancient parish (W p749). The hamlet existed by the late C13 (VCH vol 7 p65).

Blackwood Hill Farm Blackwood Hill. Formerly called Old Hall Farm. Is dated 1698, but retains timber-framing possibly of the C16. Occupied by the Reade family which moved to Fields Farm S of Gratton in the early C18 (VCH vol 7 p67).

Blackwood Old Hall To S of Blackwood Hill Farm, Blackwood Hill. Has a stone with the date 1670 from an earlier house. Occupied by the Reade family which moved to Fields Farm S of Gratton in the early C18 (VCH vol 7 p67). It may have been subsequently called Hodgegreen (The Reades of Blackwood Hill etc. Aleyn Lyell Reade. 1906 ils).

Blake Brook A tributary of the Manifold. Runs through Shawfield to Brund.

Blake Down Moor or heath formerly known as Bleak Down. Hackman's Gate (Hangman's Gate), 0.5m SW of Broome, stood on the edge of it (VCHW vol 3 p33). Gives its name to the Worcs village of Blakedown to the W.

Blake Hall On Delphouse Bank, 0.75m ESE of Dilhorne. Has also appeared as Blackhaugh (SHC 1910 p263) The Adderleys were established at Blake Hall from the C15 and it was the seat of Samuel Adderley (d1716) (SHC 1910 p263). Has also appeared as Blackhaugh (SHC 1910 p263), Blake Hall (Yates' map), and Blackenhaugh (SHOS vol 1 p92). Subsequently the hall came into the hands of the Colcloughs from whom it descended by marriage to the Swinnertons and afterwards to the Pilkingons of Chevet, Yorks. Lately it has been reduced to the status of a farmhouse (NSFCT p176) (mem in Dilhorne church). The farm, sometimes known as Dairy Farm, was sold in 1943 (ACOPP p53p).

Blake Hill Near Great Chatwell, Blymhill.

Blakelands House and estate 1m NE of Bobbington. There was a farmhouse at Blakelands NE of Blacklands by the earlier C17. An estate called Blakelands was occupied by the Corbett family in the earlier C17. A wooden plaque reset in the roof of the house bears the initials 'R.C.' and the date 1638. The initials are probably those of Roger Corbett (d1656). The house remained Corbett property until 1799 when the estate passed to the Beckinghams, who sold it in 1801 to Sherington Sparkes. By 1811 the owner was Thomas Bowen; the Bowens remained owners until at least 1936 (VCH vol 20 pp65,69). On account of some extensions being made to it in the C18 it has been described as a Queen Anne country house by the Morgan family, owners since c1980 (info Heather Morgan) (Staffordshire Millennium Guide 2000 p89).

Blakelands Farm Stood off Aldridge Road N of the Tame Valley Canal, Perry Barr. Formerly known as Lower Moor Farm (MNB pp62,66).

Blakeley House nearly 1m E of Whiston, Froghall, on Blakeley Lane (1834 OS map).

Blakeley Residential area S of Wombourne. The name means 'the black clearing' (BCTV p92). Developed on the edge of Wombourne Common. It was known as Blakeley by the C19 (VCH vol 20 p199). There was a windmill in Blakeley field to the W of Green Hill in the present Uplands Drive area in 1612, it was known as Hills Mill in 1635. It was rebuilt on or near the same site by 1655. It appears to have survived into at least the C18 (VCH vol 20 p213). There was nail-making at Blakeley by 1841 (VCH vol 20 p199). The church, The Venerable Bede, Giggety Lane, dates from c1950 (LDD).

Blakeley Bank Incline E of Dilhorne. Has also appeared as Blakeleybank.

Blakeley Common Former common N of Seisdon. In Trysull ancient parish. It seems to have been called Blackley Heath (VCH vol 20 p191).

Blakeley Green Suburb 1m NE of Tettenhall. Has appeared as Blakeway Green in 1780, when there was a house and cottage here (VCH vol 20 p13) and Blakeley Green (1834 OS map).

Blakeley Hall Lay on the N side of the Birmingham-Dudley road in Smethwick township on the border with Oldbury, and close to the site of Oldbury Manor House (see). The hall was originally a grange which reputedly belonged to Halesowen Abbey (VCH vol 17 p92). It is said to have had a small chapel attached (ORR p25). The old hall, according to W Ellery Jephcott, appears to have been at different times in the C17 occupied by Arthur Robsart, and Charles Cornwallis, lords of Oldbury manor. It was intended that the hall, which has appeared as Blackley Hall (1661. 1713) and Blakesley Hall (1795), be taken down in or after 1795 (STELE Dec 8 1951. Dec 15 1951). Blakeley Hall Farm was demolished shortly after 1934 (ORR p25p).

Blakeley Lane Hamlet on A52 1m S of Consall, 2.25m N of Dilhorne. A Halifax BB 320 crashed at Blakeley Lane on Feb 7 1944. All six crew were killed (MD pp18-19).

Blakeley Pool Trysull. Now just a swampy marsh 1m NW of Seisdon. Situated on the former Blakeley Common.

Blakelow House 1.5m NNE of Garshall Green.

Blakelow Tiny hamlet 1.75m NE of Ipstones (1834 OS map).

Blakelow House 1m E of Swynnerton. Formerly in Swynnerton ancient parish. The name means 'the black low or burial mound' (DUIGNAN). Spelt Blakeley on Plot's map.

Blake Low 0.5m WNW of Stanton.

Blakelow Burial mound on NE side of Warslow at SK 08755885. 22 paces in diameter and two feet high. Excavated by Carrington in 1850. A cremation with a flint arrowhead with scraper was found (TYD p162) (NSJFS 1965 p50). It is of Bronze Age origin and is a listed monument (VCH vol 7 p57). First documented in 1263 (SPN p118). The name means 'black (or dark) burial-mound' (SPN p118).

Blakely Wood Ocker Hill. Formerly in Tipton ancient parish. A 'Thoma de Blakeleye' occurs in 1327 and 1332 (HOTIP p15). The name is preserved in Blakely Wood Road, off Leabrook Road.

Blake Mere (commonly *Mermaid's Pool* SSGLST pp1p-4). Pool over 1.5m NW of Upper Elkstone and 4.5m NE of Leek. Formerly in Heathylee township in Leek ancient parish (NSFCT 1923 pp24-33). A tributary of the Churnet rises out of it. Wardle says some wrongly believe this is the true Churnet (NSFCT 1876 p33). The pool has appeared as Blakemere, Blackmere and Bleak Mere. It has many traditions associated with it. According to one tradition it has no visible inlet or outlet and it is fed by underground sources. That no cattle will drink out of it, no fowl will fly over it and that it is bottomless (SD p106). Yet Plot measured it to be only four yards deep at its deepest and his horse did drink out of it and geese were seen to settle upon it (NHS p44). Some say the pool has had an evil reputation since at least the time of Alexander Neckham (1157-1217) (Albion: A Guide to Legendary Britain. Jennifer Westwood. 1985. p215). Dr Wilkes says the superstitions surrounding it were just trumped up to enhance a private property (SH pp59,92). A **mermaid** is said to live in the mere; she lures men to their deaths at midnight as related in verses on the wall of Blakemere House (see). One tradition alleges the mermaid was a beautiful young woman who drowned here after being accused of witchcraft by a rejected suitor (GLS p96). She may have threatened to destroy all Leek and Leek Frith if her home is disturbed (NSFCT 1896 p121). The mermaid legend probably originated since Plot's visit, since he would have mentioned the story (NSFCT 1923-24 pp24-33). (SC p146) (MOS p2) (Punch Magazine Dec 22 1932) (SLM July 1949 p264. July 1953 p25p) (SJC p5) (STM May 1963 p34) (Ghosts and Legends. Roy Christian. 1972 p71p) (VB p208) (SW p141) (TFTPM pp102,104) (DP p26). Little Van Lake near Brecon, Aqualate Mere, Mermaid Pool on Kinder Scout, NE of Hayfield, Derbys, and a pool at Child's Ercall near Market Drayton, Shrops, have similar traditions (NSFCT 1908 p107) (TFTPM p104). There is a **strange story**, which occurred in 1660 (TFTPM p106), of a woman who was raped by a man by the pool. He returned to murder her and cast her into the mere, but as providence would have it, some men, that night, at the Cock Inn, Leek, had a wager that one of them or a group would defy the terrible weather and go up to the mere and back again, which they did and the man was caught and the woman was saved (NHS p291). Robert Southey (1774-1843) based his poem 'Mary, the Maid of the Inn' (1796) on Plot's story, but substitutes Dieulacres Abbey for Blake Mere, Mary for the man who takes the wager, and Gun Hill for Morridge (UDC Book 1 pp77-81; includes Southey's poem) (TOI pp164-5) (TFTPM pp106-109) (VCH vol 7 p33). **Another story**, which apparently occurred in 1679, with similarities to the other, tells of one Andrew Simpson, a renowned villain who would see his victims come into money and follow them to a secluded place where he would rob them. He followed a lady lace pedlar back from Leek market to Bakewell and strangled her and threw her into the mere. His crime was only discovered because he tried to sell some of the stolen linen and lace to one of the maidservants at a Red Lion Inn in Leek where he had worked as an ostler after leaving his trade as a shoemaker (OL vol 2 pp96-99 copy of the broadside sheet printed in 1679) (TOI pp164-5) (SSGLST pp1-4) (SMML pp27-30). It is said a beautiful young woman drowned in the mere after being accused of witchcraft by a rejected suitor, Joseph Linnett; later Joseph Linnett's body was found floating in the mere with the scratches of sharp talons on his face (VB p208). This gave rise to the belief the mermaid of the mere is the incarnation of the woman (GLS p96). The first verse of a folk song composed by TC Sneyd Kynnersley often sung in Leek, and recited at a meeting of the Staffordshire Agricultural Society at Cheadle in 1848, which laments the end of the wooden plough, went

> Up bey the Bleak Mere o' Morridge not long time ago
> There lived an old chap with an oldwig of tow;
> His name was Tom Morris, and I'll tell you how
> He made up a discourse on the old wooden plough
> Gee-wo Dobbin, gee-up and gee-wo.

(OL vol 1 pp159-161) (Staffordshire Farming. 1700-1840. Staffs. County Council. Local History Source Book. p37).

Blakemere House Inn 0.5m SSW of Blake Mere, 4m NE of Leek, 3m N of

Onecote. Formerly in Onecote township in Leek ancient parish. The house existed by 1638 and possibly stands on the site of a house recorded as at Blakemere in 1348 (VCH vol 7 p212). It was an inn by 1851 and was known as the Mermaid Inn by 1863 owing to its proximity to Blake Mere, which is reputedly inhabited by a mermaid (TFTPM p104 il) (VCH vol 7 p212). The inn is an old drovers one as it lies on a route between Congleton to Nottingham; it is said also to be the third highest inn in England (STM Jan 1969 p31) (PRT p102p) (SSGLST pp3p,4). Verses are carved on the stonework relating to the mermaid of Blake Mere -

> She calls on you to greet her,
> Combing her dripping crown,
> And if you go to meet her,
> She ups and drags you down.

(Ghosts and Legends. Roy Christian. 1972 pp67-68). (COS p3).

Blakemere Pool Pool in a copse by the Shropshire Union Canal, 0.5m NNE of Norbury, formerly in Weston Jones township in Norbury ancient parish (SPNO p174). The pool lay to the E of the former Loynton Moss (see) and formed a part of the moss. Has appeared as Blakemere (1327), Blakemereheth, Blake mere (1668), and Black Meer (1686) (NHS) (VCH vol 4 p155) (SPNO p177). In the later C17 Plot noted its gradual demise by three or four yards every seven years (NHS p114). Blakemere seems to have served as the uppermost of a series of pools that formed part of the watercourse to Norbury Mill, situated in Mill Haft about 1.25m to the SSE (VCH vol 4 pp155-162) (WSS p107). Visited by the NSFC in Aug 1920 who described it as boggy (NSFCT 1920 p160. 1927 p38). It was said to be nearly silted up in the 1950s (VCH vol 4 p155). By the late 1990s the area, sometimes known as Loynton Moss, was a nature reserve under the aegis of the Staffs Wildlife Trust (WSS pp101,103p). To the S of the pool, by the bridge which carries the A519 over the Shropshire Union Canal, is a WW2 re-inforced machine gun emplacement or pillbox (info Bruce Braithwaite). The name is probably preserved in Blakemore House near Oulton.

Blakemore Sixteen acre farm adjoining Pig Lane (now Barrs Road) Cradley Heath (TB Nov/Dec 1973 p16).

Blakemore House 0.5m S of Norbury, formerly in Norbury township and ancient parish. The name, which is probably from Blakemere Pool to the N and its associated moss (SPNO p174), has appeared as Blakemerehouse (1413), Blake Morehouse (1668), and Blakemore House (1725).

Blakenall Heath Former hamlet now a suburb of E Bloxwich, lying between Leamore and Goscote. Formerly in the foreign and parish of Walsall. The name means 'hall of Blac' (DUIGNAN), and has also appeared as Blakenall. It is mentioned in c1300 when it was crossed by the road from Leamore to Goscote, the present Blakenall Lane and Green Rock Lane. It was described as a heath in 1544. By 1763 a settlement of cottages had grown up round the common on the triangle now formed by the streets Blakenall Heath and Ingram Road (VCH vol 17 p163) (BY p22) (SNBP pp10,12). Two post mills in the Blakenall Heath area at SK 000025 and SK 000022 are marked on Plot's map (VCH vol 17 p186) (WBJ p14). By 1693 there was a mill in Chapel field which stood S of Lichfield Road, about 0.25m E of High Street, Bloxwich. It was still in use in 1816 but had disappeared by 1819 (VCH vol 17 p186). The church, Christ Church, Field Road, was consecrated in 1872 (VCH vol 17 p237) (LDD). Blakenall Heath became a separate ecclesiastical parish in 1873 (GLAUE p403).

Blakenhall House, and former manor, 1m WSW of Barton-under-Needwood. In Yoxall ancient parish. The name means 'hall of Blac' (DUIGNAN) or Blake or Black (HOPT vol 1 p136) or Bloc (SOB p9). Or 'Blac's corner of land' (SPN p18). The old hall here was the principle seat of the ancient family of Minors (SHOS vol 1 pp116,117), lords of the manor of Blakenhall, from King John's reign (UNT p5). From the Minors the manor passed to the Chippendales, the Bromfields, Thomas Webb, the Antrobus', Mr Whitaker, and then the Levetts. The moated old manor house, which appears to have been at sometime known as Blakenhall Lodge (UNT p5), was still remaining in 1907 (HOPT vol 1 pp85,93). The NMR has a photograph of a roof here evidently pre-Reformation (BOE p67). To the N of the hall at SK 172182 is a rectangular moat (SSAHST 1982-83 p35) (CAMS p63). There was a park at Blakenhall in the Middle Ages (HOPT vol 1 p134). There is a house called Upper Blakenhall to the NW at Woodhouses.

Blakenhall Former hamlet now a suburb SSW of Wolverhampton. Formerly in Wolverhampton chapelry and parish. The name means 'the hall of Blac' (DUIGNAN). There seems to have been a small settlement at Blakenhall in the Middle Ages (HOWM p6). The hamlet of Blakenhall was centred on Chapel Street and Dudley Street in 1842 (1842 tithe map). Blakenhall be-

came a separate ecclesiastical parish in 1861. The ecclesiastical parish is now (1991) called 'Wolverhampton St Luke' (GLAUE p403). Blakenhall was a ward of Wolverhampton borough by 1982. The church, St Luke, Upper Villiers Street, was built in 1860-1861 (BOE p322). Wolverhampton Wanderers football club was founded out of pupils at Blakenhall St Luke's. They were meeting to play football by 1876. At first the club played on the Windmill 'field' off Goldthorn Hill. In summer 1879 it amalgamated with Blakenhall Wanderers Cricket Club becoming Wolverhampton Wanderers and moved to John Harper's field, situated in Lower Villiers Street, opposite Stoud's Nipon works. It moved to Dudley Road in 1881 and to the Molineux ground in 1889 (The Wolves. Tony Matthews with Les Smith 1989 p7) (The Story of Wolverhampton Wanderers. Tony Matthews with Les Smith 1994 p7). By the early C20 Sunbeam Motor Car Co had opened a factory in Upper Villiers Street (WOLOP p70p). Persons and visitors. A plaque to commemorate Evelyn Underhill (1875-1941), Christian writer, was erected at 'Claremont' 131 Penn Road in 1998 (Commemorative Plaques by the Wolverhampton Civic Society). Sir Keith Joseph MP opened Blakenhall Gardens estate high-rise flats on Dec 19 1967. They were designed by A Chapman, Borough Architect (WOLOP p18p). Horrett Irving Campbell, a paranoid schizophrenic aged 32, of Villiers House, broke into St Luke's Nursery School on the corner of Bromley Street and Upper Villiers Street at 3.15pm in early July 1996 and injured three children and four adults with a machete; Lisa Potts, a teacher at the school, who hid some children under her skirt, was awarded the George Medal for bravery (Daily Telegraph July 9 1996 pp1,3. Sunday Telegraph Dec 5 1999 p11).

Blakenhall Gate Former entry into Needwood Forest. Situated on Bar Lane a short distance S of the Yoxall road, Barton-under-Needwood (UNT p4).

Blake Street In Shenstone parish. The name is from common land which had been referred to as 'black' (SPN p105). It was applied to the old main London road over Cannock Chase running from Brocton Gate to Old Hednesford and on to Coventry (PCC p67) via Watford Gap (DUIGNAN). The name is now obsolete. The track once marked the boundary with Warws (SPN p105).

Blakesuche Moor Name for a moor used earlier than 1719. May have referred to common land E and N of Aqualate Mere (WSS p111).

Blake Water A tributary of the Trent.

Blazebank At Orton, Penn.

Blaze Hill Hill W of Wall Heath. Mentioned in Fowler's Survey of 1840 (SNSV vol 1 p39). Built on with housing by 1997 (TB April 1997 p5). The name is preserved in Blaze Hill Road.

Bleak Hill and Bleak House. Between Cobridge and Burslem (SHST pp358,464). Peter Warburton (1773-1813) built the Bleak Hill Pottery, which was still standing in c1960 between Elder and Waterloo Roads (VCH vol 8 pp107,138). Cobridge in Arnold Bennett's novels is Bleakridge.

Bleak Hills (1834 OS map). It is now Bleak Hill 0.75m SSW of Moreton, Gnosall.

Bleak House Georgian House on E side of Dudley Road, at Moden Hill, Sedgley. After being a doctors clinic and infant welfare centre in the C20 it was demolished in 1968 (TB Jan 21 1999 p19ps).

Bleakmoor House or minute settlement 2.75m WNW of Burntwood.

Blithbury Village over 2m E of Colton. In Mavesyn Ridware parish (W p570); is said to have been anciently in Abbots Bromley parish (AB p26). The name means 'burgh on the Blithe' (DUIGNAN), or 'fortified place on the Blithe' (SSE 1996 p11) (SPN p19). It has appeared as Blidebire (1200) (SSE 1996 p11) and Blithbery, as written by Celia Fiennes who passed through Blithbury on her way to Derby in summer 1698 (Illustrated Journeys of Celia Fiennes edited by Chris Morris. 1984. p149). Erdeswick noted that the ancient seat of the Mavesyns (Kileby Hall) was at Blithbury before they moved to Mavesyn Ridware (SOS p185). Shaw noted at Blithbury a sheep which, after an accident, was opened up and revealed two lambs; one of which had two perfect heads growing from one neck, with mouths, eyes, and ears complete, and clothed with wool. It was stuffed and preserved at Blithbury in a glass case (SHOS vol 1 p204).

Blithbury Cross A public cross at Blithbury. In a court roll of Robert Cawarden 1521 it is ordered that there shall be another gate erected at 'Blythbury Cross.' Shaw supposes it stood at the crossroads at a place anciently called St Giles's Green (SHOS vol 1 p202). The OS map 1955 shows the site of an ancient cross at the crossroads in the centre of Blithbury village.

Blithbury Priory 0.75m NE of Blithbury, on W side of the Blithe at SK 091208. Has also appeared as Blithebury Priory. There was a hermitage here before the religious house (VCH vol 3 p136). A Benedictine nunnery at Blithbury was founded by Hugo Mavesyn (or styled de Rideware), lord of Mavesyn Ridware (see) in c1140 (SOSH p106) (HOS p25). It united with Blackladies in c1300 (GNHS p152). (W p570) (LGS p37) (NSFCT 1922 p129). By 1789 there was a farmhouse on the site of the priory (THS p77). Shaw noted that all that remained of the priory by the end of the C18 was a ruinous building called 'the Chapel' and another building to the W which had become a stable. Both were taken down in 1795, and a fishing lodge, which has gothic windows and fragments of stained glass, was built into the N wall of the latter. The fishing lodge has the Mavesyn arms and Walton's motto 'Piscatoribus Sacrum' (DoE II) (SHOS vol 1 pp202-205) (NSFCT 1923 p129). On Dec 15 1795 after digging about two feet deep within the chapel site, the remains of six or seven bodies were uncovered all lying on the solid marl and covered with light soil, and on Jan 11 three more were found under the floor of the present fishing lodge. In Norman times it was the custom to bury monks in the bare ground (Gough's Sep. Mon. pxxviii) (SHOS vol 1 p204).

Blithe Bridge At The Blythe, Kingstone. In Kingstone parish.

Blithe, River Rises at Withystakes, near Werrington (WJ p23). The name has appeared as bloe, up æfter blipe (996), aqua de Blye (1224), Riva de Blithe (C14), aqua de Blie (1526), and R. Blythe (1559) (SPNO p5). It is of Anglo-Saxon origin from 'blide' or 'blioe' meaning gentle (DUIGNAN) (SPNO p5) (SSAHST 1967 p35) (SPN p19). Or from the Gaelic word 'blaith' meaning 'smooth' or 'soft' (NSFCT 1908 p128). The earliest bridge furthest up stream was probably at Blythe Bridge. Yates' map shows mills on the Blithe at Field, Blythe Bridge Blithfield (now submerged under Blithfield Reservoir), Hamstall Ridware, and Burndhurst - the house there is often flooded when the river rises (TRTC pp68p,69,121). The damming of the river in 1953 1m SSW of Abbots Bromley created Blithfield Reservoir (see). After leaving the reservoir the river divides into the main arm and the Little Blithe, which runs parallel to the main arm on its N side. After 1.5m the two rivers unite; the Little Blithe having been joined by the Par Brook near Hamstall Hall. The united river joins the Trent E of Nethertown. Length 22 miles (Survey Gazetteer of the British Isles. John Bartholomew. 9th ed, post 1951) (VB p109) (TRTC pp119p at Burndhurst, 120). Is famous for its trout (NSFCT 1886 p38). In literature it is the Withy in 'A Creel of Willow' by WH (or WM) Canaway (VB p109) (The Staffordshire Way. Rocester to Cannock Chase. p11) (MR p5).

Blithewood Moat Concentric square moated site over 2m WNW of Church Leigh, at SJ 991365. The upcast which has been built between the ditches is higher than the platform in the middle (NSFCT 1953 p63. 1982 p10). In 1846 the moat was drained and some chain mail and old pointed shoes were found (ESH p59). The house which occupied the site was probably a mid or late medieval manor (NSJFS 1969 p134). (KES p129) (CAMS p63). Has also appeared as Blythewood Moat and Bitternsdale (LGS p164). The Channel Four 'Time Team' programme are scheduled to make an archaeological survey of the moat sometime after 2000.

Blithfield (locally *Bliffield* LGS p84, SHC 1919 p1). Ancient parish, fragmented small hamlet on a low ridge above the Blithe and former township. The village nucleus, Blithfield Hall, is 8m E of Stafford. The name means 'the field on the Blithe' (DUIGNAN), or 'open land by the Blithe' (NSJFS 1981 p3) (SSE 1996 p11). The parish was formed before 1086 (SHC 1916 p192). Blithfield township keeps its wakes early in Sept, whilst Newton township, also in Blithfield parish, is loyal to the dedication of the parish church by keeping theirs in the week in which St Leonard's day (Nov 6) occurs (SHC 1919 p2). There was a church at Blithfield by the late C11. The present parish church, St Leonard, NW of Blithfield Hall dates from the later C13 (Blithfield Church. DS Murray). The manor of Blidervelt appears in DB (SSE 1996 p11). Later forms are: Blithfeud, Bliefeld, Blythefeld, and Blyffeld (comp Elizabeth I). A deserted medieval village is recorded here at SK 040240 or 045240 to the E of the hall or close to it. It was possibly deserted after 1539? (SSAHST 1966 p49. 1970 p34). In the later C17 Plot records an oak tree growing in an hedgerow between Colton and Blithfield which was planted as an acorn by Ralph Bate. It grew very quickly and Ralph Bate saw it in his lifetime bear two feet square of wood at the butt end, where the first 10 feet was sawn into boards it contained nearly a ton of wood (NHS p210).

Blithfield Cross Former tiny hamlet 0.5m SSE of Hamstall Ridware on W side of the Blithe near a footbridge over the Blithe carrying the footpath to Olive Green. Appears as Blithfieldcross on 6 inch OS map 1887. Here Shaw noted the pedestal of an ancient cross, then (1798) called Blythfield Cross, where four ways meet (SHOS vol 1 p151 note). There is a local tradition that the cross was erected as a market cross. The road to Kings Bromley which forded the Trent used to run by this cross. Perhaps, thinks RF Elton, Kings Bromley markets may have been held here when the Trent was too high to cross (HR p11). There were houses here by the late C19.

Blithfield Hall Blithfield. Seat of the de Blithfields for seven generations, until the heiress, Elizabeth, married in 1360 Ralph Bagot of Bagot's Hall (see), lords of Bagot's Bromley manor. It was then the seat of the Bagots (NSFCT 1976 p22) (Blithfield. 1979. Nancy Lady Bagot. p11). Other writers have the

Bagots at Blithfield at an earlier date; from 1087 (SST); from Edward II's reign (NSFCT 1948 p121). The present house is a very ancient one, with later additions. A very early mansion was probably rebuilt by Elizabeth and Ralph's son, Sir John Bagot, in 1398 (Blithfield. 1979. Nancy Lady Bagot. p11) (SSAHST 1988-89 p53). The great hall in the N range is the nucleus of the original moated house. The drawing in NHS tab 17 shows the N front with the great hall with its lantern and three short gabled wings and some prominent groups of chimneys. This front was remodelled in 1740 and now has the appearance of a continuous facade of brick and stucco (NSFCT 1976 pp22-23). The following were lines which appeared among some decorations at Abbots Bromley for the coming-of-age celebrations of Lord Bagot in 1878 -

> May Bagots of Blithfield ever remain,
> Long as the oaks on their domain

(NSFCT 1909 p201). In the 1930s or the 1940s the 5th Lord Bagot sold Blithfield Hall to SSWWC. In 1946 5th Lord Bagot died and the title passed to his cousin, Sir Caryl Ernest (b1877), only son of Rev Lewis Bagot. He became 6th Lord Bagot and re-bought Blithfield Hall, which he opened to the public in 1956. After his death in 1961 his widow, Nancy Lady Bagot, continued to live in the hall, and kept the house open to the public until 1978. In c1982 she had the hall split into apartments which were individually sold off, reserving an apartment for herself. A clause was written into the contract for new owners that they allow the Abbots Bromley (see) Horn Dance to be performed annually on the lawn in front of the hall; the hall being one of the places where the dance has always stopped to perform (NSFCT 1976 pp22-23) (Blithfield. 1979. Nancy Lady Bagot. pp14,16) (The Countryman. Autumn 1983) (Post & Times. Sept 4 1992 p10) (LTD p129).

INTERIOR. The interior of the great hall was refashioned by Bernasconi in 1822 and it is considered to be a masterpiece of the plaster gothic phase (NSFCT 1976 pp22-23). The Paradise Room, the westernmost room in the front range, is so called because it was once the boudoir of a divinely beautiful Miss Bagot (CL Nov 4 1954 pp1578, 1579) (SLM May 1953 p22). The 'Quality Cockloft' refers to the top part of a curious gothic addition in SW corner of the hall above a spacious drawing-room, much higher than the other ground floor rooms, with a bedroom above it lighted by a tripartite lunette and reached by its own staircase. On a C19 plan this was known as 'Quality Bedroom' but it became known as 'Quality Cockloft' (CL Oct 28 1954 p1491). Another room is called the Sun Room (SLM May 1953 p22). On the main staircase are carvings of Bagot goats (SLM May 1953 p22). In the later C19 the hall contained a portrait of Lord Treasurer Burleigh aged 51, dated 1588, and another of Walter Earl of Essex (NSFCT 1886 p21), a miniature portrait of Charles I given to Col Richard Bagot, Charles I's embroidered cap of plum-coloured silk, worked in gold and silver threaded and decorated with tiny sequins, a chest which belonged to Col William Salesbury defender of Denbigh Castle against parliament, in which he kept his body belt full of gold pieces, and some letters from Charles I. It also contains a miniature portrait of Charles I given to Col Richard Bagot, Lely's portrait of Elizabeth Bagot, later Countess of Falmouth, Reynolds's portrait of the first Lord Bagot and his wife, and paintings by Kneller and Opie (CCBO p153) (SLM May 1953 pp11,22p) (CL Nov 11 1954 pp1664,1665p,1667p). The hall contains a dolls house which is the model of a house built in Adelaide, Australia in 1896 (STMSM April 1973 p25). There was a peculiar garden vehicle at the hall with rollers instead of wheels to smooth out the marks of its progress on lawns and gravel and those of the pony's hooves. It was made for the 2nd Baron Bagot and was on loan to Sir Garrand Tyrwhitt-Drake's collection at Maidstone in 1954 (CL Oct 28 1954 p1492p). The Crown jewels were at Blithfield Hall in 1974 (SN April 5 1974. April 19 1974). (SHOS vol 2 plate showing the hall from the SW on p21 at back) (W p412) (CL Oct 28 1954 pp1488-1492. Nov 4 1954 pp1576-1579. Nov 11 1954 pp1664-1667) (CCF pp216-220).

SUPERNATURAL. The hall is haunted by several ghosts. One is referred to as the Grey Lady. She carries a bunch of keys on a leather thong. She may have been a member of the Bagot family, or possibly a housekeeper. Another female ghost disappears whenever anyone approaches. She wears a cape over a long dress. A male ghost in dark clothing was seen by a cleaner and her daughter in the drawing-room in 1973 wearing an unusually shaped ring which he rubbed with the fingers of the other hand. Another ghost is seen and heard in the archery ground. It is of an old man who fell down a well trying to rescue a small child in the C18. The terrified screams echoing up the shaft have been heard at the site of the well. A ghost of uncertain gender manifests itself as the sound of rustling clothing passing along the lower gallery and usually heard in the hour before midnight. It is possibly the swishing of a lady's skirt or priest's robes. One room off the gallery is known as the Priest's Room and is believed to have been used as a sanctuary (RPG pp12-13) (GOT p141) (PL p91) (GLS pp12-13) (The Good Ghost Guide. John Brooks. 1994). GROUNDS. Lord Bagot had an Archery Ground constructed by and on the site of the Rectory for the Needwood Foresters (1822-27), an archery society of which he was a keen supporter. It was some 150 yards in length, and was surrounded by woods and bordered on one side by a Gothic ruin - the remains of the old Rectory (CCHCB pp10-12). The Game Larder with a dovecote in the roof is a short distance from the Orangery and was built in 1895. In the gap between it and the NE block there was a C19 wing containing a dairy, laundry and servants' quarters, described as recently demolished in 1954 (CL Oct 28 1954 p1492) (STM July 1968 p29p) (BOE p73) (Blithfield. 1979. Nancy Lady Bagot. p10pc). Lord Bagot's Sundial has a motto on it said to be Tennyson's favourite 'Non Numero Horas Hisi Serando' 'I count only the serene hours' (SLM spring 1957 pp28,29 il). The Orangery faces S, built by Samuel Wyatt (d1807) (and perhaps his brother Joseph) of Blackbrook Farm (see) from designs and under the direction of 'Athenian' Stuart (CL Oct 28 1954 pp1488-1492p) (STM July 1968 p28p) (BOE p730 (Blithfield. 1979. Nancy Lady Bagot. p10pc). Special beer, which could only be made using local water, was kept at the Park Keeper's Lodge for travellers or visitors. The most famous sampler of the beer was Henry Luttrell poet and author (1765?-1851) in the 1840s (CCF p216) (DNB). A well W of the W range. Square, with open four-centred arches. Pevsner noted it was in a dilapidated state (BOE p74). It is said that HMS Victory was built of oak timber from Blithfield (SST).

Blithfield Reservoir Two-mile long reservoir E of Blithfield; as such is the largest reservoir in the county. Constructed by the SSWWC by damming the Blithe. It was envisaged before WW2 but not built until after WW2; it was opened in Nov 1953 by the Queen Mother (GHC pp22pc aerial view, 24-25p of Queen Mother at opening ceremony). Before the reservoir was built there was a track which ran from Blithfield Hall to the SE of Bagot's Bromley, on the track was situated Blithfield Mill; it and a lodge are submerged under the reservoir. The reservoir covers 790 acres and was built to hold 4,000 gallons of water at a maximum depth of 47 feet. It supplies water to a population of 1.25 million in an area of almost 600 square miles. The dam is 2,810 feet long (OS map 1905) (NSFCT 1954 p93) (MR p5) (SN July 5 1996) (PWIS p107) (TRTC p30). By c1976 the Mercian Yacht Club were using the southern half of the reservoir for sailing; the northern half is reserved for birds; the north-eastern arm of the reservoir, where the Tad Brook flows in, has a scrape for wading birds (SN July 5 1996). In the drought of 1976 the water level fell so much to reveal old river bridges and a mill pool (The Staffordshire Way. Rocester to Cannock Chase. p10) and SSWWC pumped millions of gallons of water from Hampton Loade, Bridgnorth, Shrops, to revive the level (GHC p31). Bill Oddie opened a new environmental centre by the reservoir built by SSWWC in June 1996. By which date the whole reservoir had been designated a site of special scientific interest (SN July 5 1996) (TRTC p30). A lady taxi driver driving across the causeway over the reservoir in the direction of Rugeley noticed the eyes of a man in the rear of her vehicle and felt a chill in her cab which did not leave her until she had passed over the causeway (info Bruce Braithwaite).

Blithford Farm on W side of the Blithe, 1.75m SSE of Abbots Bromley (1905 OS map). The name means 'ford of the Blithe' (SSE 1996 p11).

Blithmoor Moor in the vale of the Blithe (OS map 1955). Now submerged under Blithfield Reservoir.

Blockall Area, and part of the main street between Darlaston town and Darlaston Green (Offlow hundred). The name is from perhaps Middle English 'block-halh' meaning a way obstructed by some physical block; Hackwood in HODW hints that there was in fact a block at this point until some time in the C18; this 'block' would appear to be a pool (SNDB p18). There was a Blockall Field in the C17 (SNDB p18). Here was a warehouse owned by the Rubery family (BCM April 1974 p7).

Bloody Steps Steps leading down to the Trent and Mersey Canal from Brindley Bank, 0.75m NNE of St Augustine's church, Rugeley. So called from Christina Collins' murdered body being taken up them dripping with blood, in June 1839. She was murdered by three boatmen on the Trent and Mersey Canal at Hoo Mill (see). Her ghost was seen on the steps on June 17 1939, the centenary of her death (MMM p30) (MMMR p66). In recent years the steps have been rebuilt in concrete but are still called the Bloody Steps. Local historian John Godwin has doubted whether any of Collins' blood actually dripped onto the steps (John Godwin on 'Open Country' BBC Radio 4 Aug 14 1999).

Bloomfield Suburb, but former village, N of Tipton. In Tipton parish (W p708). A Robert de Blome may have lived at Shrubbery Hall at Bloomfield in medieval times (HOTIP p187). The iron used to make the anchor for the 'Great

Eastern,' considered when made in 1866 to be the largest anchor in the world, was made by Barrows & Sons of Bloomfield (BCM autumn 1996 pp19-22). Lloyd's Proving House was at Bloomfield in the early C20 (OS map Sheet 67.08).

Bloomfield Junction Bloomfield. Junction of the old Birmingham Canal course with the Coseley cut. Now the old course is abandoned (which went via Bradley) and the Coseley cut is the main artery (Canals of the West Midlands. Charles Hadfield. vol 5 of Canals of The British Isles. see map pp66-67).

Bloomsbury House 2m NE of Sheriffhales, in Sheriffhales parish. Written Blomesbury (maps of Plot and Morden). Now in Shropshire.

Bloomsmithy Tipton. Has appeared as Bloom Smythy. The Bloomsmithy Mill estate made by Thomas Fieldhouse in 1761 lay on the N side of Hurst Lane, Tipton (HOTIP p187).

Blore or Blore Ray. Ancient parish and former small hilltop village, now a tiny hamlet, 21m NE of Stafford in the Moorlands. 'Blore Ray' is the usual spelling for ecclesiastical matters, whilst 'Blore' is the usual for civil matters (GLAUE p403). The burial mound 0.25m ESE of Blore Ray at SK 134493 was excavated in 1927 and an axe hammer was found (NSFCT 1927 pp153-155 plan). The burial mound 380 metres SW of the church at SK 13384915 is 14 paces in diameter and 3.5 feet deep and built around a natural rock outcrop. Carrington excavated it in 1849 and found in a cist a cremation with an incense cup inside an cinerary urn, skeletal remains and a iron ring. Pape re-excavated it in 1927. It is a listed monument. (TYD p142) (VCH vol 1 p208) (NSFCT vol 62 p154) (DAJ vol 75 p116) (Proceedings of the Prehistoric Society vol 27 p298 no 194) (Gazetteer of Early Anglo-Saxon Burial Mounds. A. Meaney. 1964. p220) (Medieval Archaeology vol 6-7 p43) (NSJFS 1965 p34). See also Cliff Top, Dun Low, Hazelton Hill, Lady Low, and Top Low. Blore has appeared as Blora, a manor, in DB (SSE 1996 p11), and Bloer (c1540) (LI appendix p171). The name is from possibly Anglo-Saxon 'blew,' a blast, or a roaring wind, but Duignan is unsure (DUIGNAN) (SPN p18). Oakden thinks Duignan's theory is romantic rubbish. He says it is derived from an Old English word 'blor' meaning 'bare hill' (OAKDEN) (SSAHST 1967 p34) (SSE 1996 p20). Blore was never Crown property. So 'ray' could not be derived from 'regis.' It was a manor of the Stafford barony. More probably this word has reference to the physical or geographical surrounding (NSFCT 1925 p199). The parish church, St Bartholomew, in the village centre, was built by 1178. The chancel and tower are C14 (SBB p27) (CHMS2 p23). The chancel arch is unique in the county, the lower portion so narrow that admission is in single file (NSFCT 1925 p198). A deserted medieval village is recorded here at SK 137495 (SSAHST 1966 p49. 1970 p34) (SL p87) and there is evidence in nearby fields of past settlement (SHJ autumn 1992 p3). Parliamentarians in the Civil War are said to be responsible for the removal of the hands of the effigies on the Bassett tomb in Blore church (SBB p190). The Young Pretender's army passed through Blore on Dec 4 1745 in the 1745 Jacobite Rebellion of that year (BPCSM p7). The NSFCT notes that Blore became isolated after 1831 when coaches ceased to use the road to Thorpe over Coldwall Bridge through Blore preferring the longer route via Ashbourne (NSFCT 1925 p195). A servant of the Smith family, who lived on a farm near Blore church, went to the Bassett vault in Blore church and discovered a skull and showed it to his fellow servants. Its removal brought about a change in the medical condition of Mrs Smith who later died and was interred in the church. Just prior to burial the sexton is said to have brought her to life again in trying to cut the rings from her fingers: Revived she was restored to her husband and the coupled lived for many more years (SBB pp187-189).

Blore Hamlet 0.5m NE of Hales. Formerly a township (VCH vol 3 p92) or part of Tyrley township in Drayton-in-Hales ancient parish in Shrops. Formerly in Almington manor (SHC 1945/6 p21). Has appeared as Blore (1239) (SSE 1996 p11), Bluer (1224-1233), Bloower and Bloore (C16, 1773, DUIGNAN) (SHC 1945/6 pp21,32,33), and Blore-in-Tyrley (W p389).

Blore and Swinscoe Park A medieval deer park enclosed out of forest. In existence by 1248 (NSJFS 1962 p76).

Blore Dale Fairoak. (DUIGNAN). To W of Tadgedale.

Blore Farm House 0.5m N of Blore (Hales). Has appeared as Netherblore, a vill and Capital messuage (C14), Hall of Bloore (C16), and Bloore, an estate (1773) (SHC 1945/6 p33). It was granted to the Meverells by 1233. The estate had passed to the Cabots and then to the Hulles or Hills by 1339. It was tenanted by the Bate family from the C16 through to the C18. But ownership passed by marriage from the Hills to the Bulkerleys in the later C16, to the Wilbrahams in 1603, and to the Chetwodes of Oakley Hall in 1624 and it descended with the Oakley Hall estate until at least the end of the C19. The old house was replaced with a new one in the C19 (SHC 1945/6 pp56,118-

120,173-174, 211-212, 261).

Blore Forest Fairoak. Ancient forest of which Bishop's Wood and Burnt Wood are remaining parts (NSFCT 1933 p93). Said to have been given to Devine, bishop of Lichfield, by Penda in 660 and remained the property of the See of Lichfield until 1868 when transferred to the Ecclesiastical Commissioners who were administering it in 1911 (BPS p77).

Blore Hall To the E of the church, Blore (Ray). Late C15 or early C16 house, and the seat of the Bassett family, lords of Blore.

BASSETTS OF BLORE HALL. Blore manor appears to have been held by the Brailsford family by the early C14. By the marriage of Joan Brailsford to John Bassett of Park Hall (see), near Cheadle, Blore passed to a branch of the Bassetts. Their son Sir John Bassett (1345-1411) was of Blore. He was succeeded by his son Edmund Bassett (d1429/30), who was succeeded by his nephew Ralph Bassett (d1455). He was succeeded by his son William Bassett (died in 1456 or lived c1430-1497). His eldest son was Ralph Bassett and Ralph's daughter was Margaret (c1477-c1550), wife of the late Thomas Kebell, a prominent lawyer. On the death of her husband she inherited his substantial estate. On Feb 1 1502 whilst at Blore Hall to celebrate her betrothal to Ralph Egerton of Wrinehill she was abducted by Roger Vernon of Wirksworth. Having taken her back to Derbys Vernon forced her into marriage, which she was unable to have annulled for many years. William (d1456 or d1497) was succeeded by his third son William Bassett (1473-1506). He married Elizabeth daughter of Thomas Meverell, and was succeeded by his son Sir William Bassett (d1553), Knight, MP, Sheriff, and JP, who was born at Blore Hall on July 25 1493. Leland noted him in LI and described him as 'the Kinge of the Morelande.' He was succeeded by his son William Bassett (1507/8-1563), who was succeeded by his son William Bassett (1552-1601). He was succeeded by his daughter and heir Elizabeth, but by her marriages, firstly to Henry Howard, Earl of Suffolk (d1616), and secondly to Sir William Cavendish, Duke of Newcastle (d1676), Blore passed out of Bassett hands. The magnificent tomb of alabaster in Blore church which fills most of the N chapel was erected in c1640-43, possibly by Catherine (or Elizabeth) daughter of Elizabeth Bassett and Henry Howard. The monument contains the effigies of Catherine (or Elizabeth); her mother Elizabeth; her father Henry; her grandfather William Bassett (d1601) and his wife Judith (LI appendix p171) (AAD pp196-197) (GNHS pp98,99) (W p749) (BAST vol 71 pp27-28) (CHMS p20) (SHJ spring 1992 p1. autumn 1992 pp1-2) (SBB). The skull of William (d1601) is said to have been taken from the Bassett vault in the church and taken to Uttoxeter. In 1903 it was reputed to be in the possession of a well-known Ashbourne tradesman (SBB p189).

By at least the early C20 the hall had been reduced in status to a farmhouse (LGS p86) (BOE p74) (SGS p61) (MR p42). The hall had six coat of arms (in glass?) but had none by 1922 (NSFCT 1922 p78). Masefield noted traces of a moat by the hall (LGS p86). Three ghosts are said to haunt in different parts of the hall. There was the ghost of a very pretty young girl who wears a mob cap, and the ghost of young stable hand who was beaten to death by his master; he switches the TV on and off (SBB p190).

Bloreheath Former heath over 0.5m N of Hales. The heath was bounded on the W side by Shifford's Grange; and on the E side by the great woods which extended over all the land to the E of Hales. It was enclosed under an Act of 1773 (SHC 1945/6 pp23,195).

BATTLE OF BLOREHEATH. The second battle of the War of the Roses was fought on the heath on Sunday afternoon Sept 23 1459, St Tecla's day. Richard Neville, Earl of Salisbury, a Yorkist commander, opposed to Henry VI, was marching to join Richard, Duke of York, at Ludlow when taken into combat by Queen Margaret of Anjou (wife of Henry VI) leading the Lancastrian forces. Her chief commander was, James Touchet, 5th Lord Audley, a descendent of the Audleys of Heighley Castle (see). Second-in-command was, John de Sutton (alias Dudley), 1st Baron Dudley, of Dudley Castle (see) (in whose entourage were the Levesons of Wolverhampton). The Lancastrian army's size has been put at between 5000 to 14,000 and the Yorkist's at 500 to 7000 (LGS pp189-190) (NSJFS 1980 p16). Prior to the battle Audley probably had the centre of his operations at Heighley Castle (NSJFS 1980 p11), or camped with the royal forces near Lichfield (HOL p302), but probably did not camp at Audley Brow near Moreton Say, Shrops (SHC 1945/6 p94). Salisbury did not camp the night before the battle at Salisbury Hill, S of Market Drayton (SHC 1945/6 p94), but probably camped in Rowney Wood, choosing for the confrontation the gentle slope down to the small Hemphill Brook or Hempmill Brook (PS pp38,40p), formerly Wemberton Brook. The Yorkists took a stand on the E side of the brook. The Lancastrians took a stand on the W. It seems likely Dudley and Audley made separate and simultaneous attacks (NSJFS 1980 p14). When the Lancastrians attacked Salisbury at first made a show of resistance, and then feigned to retreat, but when

Audley advanced into a gully and was at the bottom of it Salisbury suddenly turned on him and Audley was killed; his death is commemorated by Audley's Cross (see). Dudley at this point probably swung to the centre to prop up Audley and became trapped in the gully himself and was captured; thus a Yorkist victory was secured, with reputedly 2,400 Lancastrians lost and 60 Yorkists lost. Queen Margaret reputedly watched the battle from Mucklestone church tower top and escaped on a horse, whose shoes were reversed to mislead her pursuers by a blacksmith called Skelhorn (NSFCT 1884 pp14-16) (Weekly Sentinel April 9 1965) (SSGLST p26). When she reached Eccleshall she reputedly took refuge in the church there (SOSH ppp161-163). Some say she spent the night at Dimsdale Hall (WWT p80). She laid the blame for the Lancastrian defeat on Thomas, Lord Stanley, who was at Newcastle with a considerable Lancastrian force during the battle, and failed to come in support when asked (LGS p190). Furthermore, it transpired Stanley was able to forewarn Salisbury of Lancastrian movements (NSJFS 1980 p10). Salisbury was less successful at the later battle of Ludford Bridge and by Oct 1459 he, York and Warwick were forced to leave the country (NSJFS 1980 p16). **After the battle** a Burgundian, Jean de Waurin, chronicled the event. He was not an eye-witness and was in many respects inaccurate both with dates and location. Traditionally in Fairoak valley lie ten knights buried in a row with their faces towards a stream. In one of the meadows is a mound known as 'The Old Man's Head' thought to be a burial ground resulting from the battle. Relics such as cannon balls and flints have been found at Greatwood and at Fairoak (BOV p31). A sword found in the C18 was long in the possession of the Goodall family (VBE p36) and was perhaps that in the possession of a John Goodall of Wolstanton in 1932 (NSFCT 1933 p173; his sword may only be a C18 Highland Broadsword). A breast plate with a rose engraved on it belonged to the Butters family of Golden Hill Farm, Fairoak Moss (FLJ 1890 p319) (BOV pp31,34) (SLM Oct 1948 p178ps). An iron spur found on the battlefield was given to the NSFC by Mrs AH John (NSFCT 1953 p107). There is a local tradition that three mermaids appear in Hempmill Brook on the anniversary of the battle; three mermaids appear in the arms of the Warburton family, a member of which fought in the battle (info Bruce Braithwaite). In 1992 and 1993 there was a battle re-enactment in Oakley Hall grounds (ES Sept 22 1992 p7p. Sept 29 1993 p21); and one at Blore Heath Farm on Sept 25-26 1999 (ES Sept 24 1999 p21). The battlefield is haunted (SMM p54) (Bruce Braithwaite). For Chetwynd on the battle see SH p44. The poem 'Zoenlinda' by Charles Bowker Ash of Adbaston (see) is based on the battle (PSS p141). ('Hall's Chronicle' 1548) (SHOS vol 1 part 1 p50) (SMC p164). Rev W Snape's account of the battle in 1812 was copied into Pitt's THS. W Beamont delivered a paper on the battle to the Chester Archaeological Society in 1850, but both Snape's and Beamont's accounts have been discredited by FR Twemlow in SHC 1945/6 p94. (W pp44,389) (WAM p49) (The Battle of Blore Heath. FR Twemlow. 1912. Includes an abridged version of Jean de Waurin's account) (NSFCT 1913 pp206-207) (More Battlefields of England. AH Burne. 1952. pp140-149 il and plan of battlefield) (STM April 1966 p30) (STM July 1971 pp22,23,24p of the battlefield) (England in the Later Middle Ages. MH Keen. 1973. p446) (The Battle of Blore Heath and the Rout at Ludford. RJ Hirons. Unpublished BA dissertation. Keele University. 1973) (NSJFS 1980 pp9-17) (ES Sept 7 1994 p10il) (The Battle of Hopton Heath 1459. Paddy Griffith. 1995).

Blore Park Medieval deer park enclosed out Blore Forest. In existence by 1298. In 1324 the bishop of Coventry and Lichfield threatened trespassers in his park of Blore with excommunication (SHC 1945/6 p2) (NSJFS 1962 pp74,75). Can probably be identified with the medieval deer parks known as Eccleshall Park (see) and Bishop's Park (see), both of which belonged to the bishops of Lichfield and were carved out of Blore Forest (NSJFS 1962 p75. 1964 pp62-63). The name has appeared in old PR entries as 'Blower Parke' leading some to think the name is derived from the glass blowing which was practised along with glass making in this area in the early C17. But the name is really from the hamlet of Blore (NSFCT 1930 p49).

Blorepipe Formerly in Blore Park. In the Woodland quarter in Eccleshall ancient parish. Has also appeared as Blore Pike (W p377). The ghost of George Holland was seen at Upper Blore Pipe Farm in Langot Lane by a local preacher (BOV pp50-51) (STM Dec 1964 p35).

Blore Pipe House Blorepipe. Here George Barlow and his wife gave shelter and refreshment to Col Thomas Blague and the Duke of Buckingham who had escaped from the battle of Worcester 1651. The house was described in 1647 as a 'ffaire Built, well contrived house' (ROT p16). The farmhouse where the Col and the Duke are reputed to have taken refuge was still standing in 1928 (NSFCT 1928 p161). Col Thomas Blague had been entrusted with Charles II's 'Insignia of the Royal George,' the diamond badge of the Order of the Garter. Masefield calls it the 'Lesser George' (LGS p93). With

Cromwell's men hard on Blague's and the Duke's trail, Blague and George Barlow hid the 'George' in the ground. Blague was soon captured and it was left to Barlow to recover the 'George.' Yonge says Barlow contacted a Stafford lawyer, Robert Millard, who contacted Izaak Walton of Stafford (see). Walton secreted the 'George' to Blague, imprisoned in the Tower of London. Blague escaped and took the 'George' to Charles on the Continent. (NHS p311) (BRO p172) (BPS pp26-29) (BOV p31) (ROT pp14-16). See Ashmole's 'History of The Order of the Garter' 1715. Another account says George Barlow was of Broughton Hall and the 'George' was hidden there (TB April 1993 p5).

Blossoms Fold Tiny street located off Darlington Street, Wolverhampton. In the C14 appears as 'Blassom' or 'Blaston.' The original Blossoms Fold would have been used for traders to sort, clear, and sell their flocks (WMAG Nov 1979 p17p).

Blount's Green Hamlet 1m SW of Uttoxeter. Is now (1997) a suburb of Uttoxeter. The wooden posts of the pound or pinfold remain. When T Pape and SAH Burne passed it in 1922 they found the wooden posts were fast falling into decay (NSFCT 1922 pp127-8) (STMSM July 1974 p13. June 1974 p7p). Twelve pound posts made of sandstone and forming a rectangle, were standing in 1998 (TRTC p24). The name is from the Blount family.

Blount's Hall House and manor at Blount's Green, Uttoxeter. In the Woodlands township in Uttoxeter ancient parish (SHOS vol 1 p12) (W p798). Estate and seat of the Blount family in the C16 (TRTC p24). Sir Henry Blount (b1602), famous traveller and author of 'A Voyage to the Levant, with Observations concerning the Modern Condition of the Turks' (c1638), succeeded to the estate in 1638 (The Diary of John Evelyn. Everyman's Library. 1936 vol 1 p337 note). The hall was taken down in 1770, but the moat could still be seen in 1865 (HOU p330). Another account says Blount's Hall Farm now stands on the site of the hall (TRTC p24).

Bloxwich Black Country town 15m SSE of Stafford. Formerly in the foreign and ancient parish of Walsall.
1000 to 1500. The **name** is of Anglo-Saxon origin and means Blocc's (or Blocca's) village (DUIGNAN) (SOB p9) (SPN p18). Blocheswic appears in DB as an area of woodland. Later it appears as Blockswich (SPN p18); Great Bloxwich (the southern settlement) appears in 1300, and Little Bloxwich (the northern settlement) in 1307. Great Bloxwich was the main settlement; here was a chapel of ease by the early C15. The present **church**, All Saints, at the junction of Green Road and High Street, was dedicated to St Thomas the Martyr (or of Canterbury) before 1875. Traditionally an old chapel stood on Church's Lawn next to Yieldfields Hall (SOB p35). The same or another chapel was, unusually, moated; the reason probably being it was formerly close to lawless Cannock Forest (SOB p35); the same or another chapel had its own churchyard, which was unusual since it was a chapel of ease (SOB p35). The present church was mainly rebuilt in 1791-1794 and again in 1875-1877 (VCH vol 17 pp233,235). The church, St James, Old Lane, was built in 1904 (LDD). Bloxwich **wakes** were held on the Sunday nearest to Aug 16 since at least 1769 (BY p20). The original date may have been, Dec 29, being the feast of St Thomas the Martyr (Thomas a Becket) (SOB pp218-224). Bull-baiting took place at Bloxwich wake until banned by law in 1835 (VCH vol 17 p250). There is a ballad describing bull baiting at Bloxwich wake (FSBC pp8-9). There is a well-known C19 broad sheet song called 'Ye Three Tall Men' about a bull bait in Bloxwich (MR p44). For many years the wakes were held behind Lime Tree House (see). The **original centre of Bloxwich** was probably at the southern end of the present High Street in The Pinfold area (VCH vol 17 p161). Little Bloxwich developed 0.75m to the NE around a green (MR p44) (BY p17p of some Little Bloxwich cottages). A **manor** of Bloxwich was mentioned in the later C16, but it was probably an estate with no manorial rights. The manor house of Bloxwich became known as Cowley's Farm (see) (VCH vol 17 p173). The **gallows** of the lord of the manor of Walsall (see) may have been in the Bloxwich area. There were **stocks** apparently near the church at Elmore Green in 1567 (VCH vol 17 p210) (BY p 6). There was a **lock-up** at Bloxwich in 1836 (VCH vol 17 p212). Bloxwich **pound** was built in 1639, probably replacing an older one dating from c1490. The pound still existed in 1849 (BY p5) (SOB p176). It probably stood at the SE end of the village where the street-name Pinfold survives (VCH vol 17 p219) (SNBP pp44-45).
1500 to PRESENT. A **windmill** which passed from the Whitall family to Henry Stone in 1624 may have been at Bloxwich (VCH vol 17 p186) at approximately SJ 997018 (WBJ p15). There were other windmills at Blakenhall Heath (see). Bloxwich's **industries** were making parts for bridles, saddlers' tools, coaches, snaffles and stirrups, cabinet locks, key trunk locks, mattress and padding needles and making awl blades (SOB p149) (SSE 1991 p77). The products of Bloxwich have been referred to as 'Bloxwich

Bitties' (WMVB p32). In Bloxwich Park (see) is a memorial to the metal-working trades - a heap of anvil stones (SOB p160 p facing). Talbot Stead Tube Co Ltd in operation in Green Lane by 1913, supplied boilers and tubes for many famous ships, and were the first to make tubes in 'Staybrite,' a special stainless steel alloy. The firm became part of TI Stainless Tubes Ltd in 1963 and were Sterling Tubes Ltd by 1994 (SNBP p55). The longest needle in the world by 1992 was said to be one six feet one inch long made by George Davies of Thomas Somerfield, Bloxwich, made for stitching on mattress buttons lengthways. One is preserved in the National Needle Museum at Forge Mill, Redditch, Worcs (GBR 1992 p218). Over the centuries Bloxwich has tried to **sever links with Walsall**, its constant rival in parish affairs. It became a separate ecclesiastical parish in 1810 (GLAUE p404). The 1859 general election was about the franchise and aspirations of Bloxwich to form a separate township even a separate borough to Walsall; a satirical broad sheet entitled 'Bagnall's charge to his Bloxwich Committee' dated Saturday 23 April 1859 concerns an incident leading up to the election (SOB p164). In 1889 Bloxwich became a ward of Walsall county borough (VCH vol 17 p217). Homeshaw, writing in the 1950s, says 'The villagers still feel themselves in the Borough but not of it;' hence its need to compete with Walsall and provide the amenities Walsall has (SOB p115). The branch **railway** line running from Ryecroft Junction to Cannock, opened on Feb 1 1858, had a station at Bloxwich. The station closed in 1965 (SSR p17) (VCH vol 17 pp161,168-169). **Aircraft crash**. An aeroplane on a flight to the Isle of Man crashed in Sneyd Lane. **Supernatural**. An old black hearse drawn by jet black horses which shortly vanishes after being seen has been witnessed on at least two occasions, once or both times in the high street. At the bottom of Bloxwich town a telephone box is said to ring at pedestrians as they pass by and to say the name of the pedestrian (GPCE p21). **Natives and visitors**. In June 1629 **Edward Leigh** author of 'Critica Sacra' son and heir of Mr Henry Leigh of Rushall Hall was arrested for illegally playing a game of bowls on the green at Bloxwich by Mr Henry Stone, mayor of the new borough of Walsall, and placed in prison. Edward Leigh protested and sued the mayor but lost the suit at a case heard in Wolverhampton. Afterwards he went to live in Banbury (SOB p71). **William Wollaston** of Shenton, Leics (b1659) author of 'Memoir of William Wollaston' (1709) had descendents from Great Bloxwich and he was brought up here as a child and attended Lichfield Grammar School (Johnsonian Gleanings. AL Reade. Part III. 1922. p135) (SOB pp83-86). **Benjamin Welch** was granted a special licence from the Home Secretary to bury his two children in a Wesleyan chapel built in 1837 at Bloxwich. The chapel became a factory and then a cinema known as 'Wood's Picture Palace.' At length it became redundant and was turned into a garage. The bodies of two children, in a specially-built vault, were discovered and reburied in the cemetery on the hill in Jan 1938 (SOB pp146,148). **Harold Parry**, born, one of twin sons, on Dec 13 1896 at Bloxwich, poet, was killed on May 6 1917 in WW1 (PSS pp280-283 p) (VFC p104). For his poem on Barr Beacon see Barr Beacon (SOB pp186-188). **Maurice Wiggin**, editor of the Birmingham Gazette from 1938 and novelist, was born in Bloxwich in 1912; his 'A Cottage Idyll' (1969) is autobiographical (VFC p142). **Phil Drabble**, naturalist, broadcaster and countryman, was born in Bloxwich on May 14 1914, another account says he was born in 1902 (STMSM March 1980 p22. April 1980 pp32-37). (Book and Magazine Collector. April 1992. No 97). For **Rob Halford** of Bloxwich of the rock music band 'Judas Priest' see Hill Top, West Bromwich.

Bloxwich Hall Station Street, Wall End, Bloxwich. Built in c1830 in the Tudor style probably as a residence for Henry Morson, an ironmaster and leading figure in the community. It later passed to councillor Deeley who was living here in 1881. Mr Deeley is remembered for supplying a feast for the old people of Bloxwich at New Year 1881 (SOB pp156,204) (BY p8p of the coach house c1915). In the 1890s it was the residence of John Smith Foster (glass mem in All Saints, Bloxwich).

Bloxwich Park (Birmingham A-Z 1995). Opened in 1890 on Bloxwich Green, part of the former Short Heath, Bloxwich (VCH vol 17 p163), and called Short Heath Park by Homeshaw (SOB p160). In the park is a heap of anvil stones. It was erected by Walsall corporation by c1915 (SOB p160 p facing) (BY p14p of c1915).

Bluebarn Farm Downsbanks, Barlaston. This, or an older farm on this site or near it was built in the late C18. Hops were grown here for Joule's brewery. The farmhouse was demolished in 1964. Its remains can still be traced in the picnic area (SSBOP p74).

Blue Bottle Cavern A cavern further on than the Seven Sisters Cavern in Wren's Nest. Called Blue Bottle by the author of the BCM article, Joan Cutler (BCM spring 1995 p22).

Blue Cross Farm Derrington. Timber framed. Bares the date 1612 (SVB p66)

(MR p123).

Blue Hills Hills 0.5m N of Upper Hulme. The hills were so called by c1680 (NHS p98) (VCH vol 7 p33). Blue Hill is marked on Bowen's map at approximately SK 018552 to E of Bradnop: but, like the Han Clouds, Bowen has incorrectly placed them. Between Blue Hills and Clusterberry Edge is a stream coming out of an outlet channel containing salt belonging to the coal mine in the Blue Hills which turns the stones and earth a rusty colour and was utilised as a dye for button moulds (NHS p98) (OL vol 2 pp22-23). The hills were apparently so called after the colouring of watercourses by coal deposits, which were mined by the early C15 (VCH vol 7 p33).

Blue House (Farm). Great Barr (Birmingham A-Z).

Blue Stone 0.75m NE of Burslem. The name is preserved in Bluestone Avenue. Here was a tollgate (OTP p101). Perhaps, the turnpike gate in Moorland Road, Burslem at SJ 875500 ?, mentioned by IANS p19. And at Blue Stone Molly Leigh, the witch of Hamel Grange or Jackfield, kept her cows (SSGLST p28).

Blundies Small hamlet over 0.25m NE of Enville. In Enville ancient parish. Has appeared as Blundels (Morden's map) and Blundells (Plot's map). The name is from the Blundel family. The later C13 settlement of Hoo may be identified with Blundies; a Walter Blundel was recorded in the hamlet of 'la Hoo' in 1323. A house called Blundells in c1527 may have been the present Blundies farmhouse, which incorporates one wing of a C16 or C17 timber-framed house. By 1841 there were eight families living at the hamlet of Blundies (VCH vol 20 p93)

Blurton Former village, now a suburb 2.5m E of Trentham, 1.5m SW of Longton, 12m N of Stafford, situated on a shelf above Longton Brook and a tributary of that brook. Former township with Lightwood and chapelry in Trentham ancient parish. The name means 'a village on a hill' (BNDA p3), and has appeared as Blorton (1154. 1195) (Annals of the Diocese of Lichfield Past and Present 1859) (SSE 1996 p11) and Bloreton (Walter Chetwynd in 1680s) (BNDA p22). Blurton has been identified with 'Bloreton' (1535), a minor prebend of Stafford Collegiate Church (BNDA p22). A chapel at Blurton is marked on Saxton's map and was certainly in existence well before 1577, probably as a chapel-of-ease to Trentham Priory. It has been suggested that it was built in the C14 by the de Blorton or Colcough families (BNDA p21). The present church, St Bartholomew, on the W side of Church Road, is of 1626. It was enlarged in 1867 (BOE p266). The discovery of a curious object not unlike a tent-peg made of pure copper together with a much corroded iron chain, both reputedly of medieval origin, was made during road widening at Blurton in 1938 (NSFCT 1942 p54). This could be the same as a flint fabricator found at Blurton in 1938 (STM June 1969 Supplement p12). The small village of Blurton in the earlier C19 centred on St Bartholomew's, as perhaps a settlement had in medieval times (1834 OS map). Penfold Farm, S side of Trentham Road, E of the church, is said to preserve the name of a pinfold in this area (local info). Blurton became a separate ecclesiastical parish in 1721 (GLAUE p404), which was refounded in 1831 (LGS p86) or 1832 (GLAUE p404). It was a ward of Stoke-on-Trent district by 1991 having been taken into Stoke-on-Trent county borough in 1922. By the late 1950s Blurton had greatly expanded with housing on the N side of Trentham Road in the area of Blurton Waste Farm to the W of the village. The church, St Alban, Finstock Avenue, was built for this residential area in 1956 (VCH vol 8 p260) (LDD). In the garden of Sutherland Primary School is a plaque on a stone to the memory of Matthew Thorey who died aged 10 in Aug 1992 whilst crossing the road near the school (ES Jan 9 1993 p3p). A small metal object shaped like an anchor was found near the home of Stephen Morris in 1983. Despite being used as a talisman it brought him nothing but bad luck (GLS pp23-25).

Blurton Grange Farm 1.5m NNE of Barlaston.

Blymhill (locally *Blimmil* SMM p176). Ancient parish, small village, and former manor (SHC 1880 pp290-384. 1881 pp69-147), and township 10m SW of Stafford. The village is situated on a low spur by the upper Dawford Brook. The name means 'hill of the bloomery,' a bloom - a mass of charcoal-smelted iron in Anglo-Saxon (DUIGNAN) (LGS p87). Ekwall, OAKDEN and Gelling suggest - the wild plum-tree hill (NSJFS 1981 p3) (SSE 1996 p11) (SPNO p128) (SPN p19). The manor of Brumhelle appears in DB. Later Blymhill appears as Blumehil (1167) (SSE 1996 p11), Blumenhulle (1218), Blumenhull (1305), Blymylle (1423), Blymehull (1428), Blymmell (1578) (SHC 1880 pp290-384) (SPNO p128), but mainly as Blumonhull (SPN p19). Bridgeman and Commander Wedgwood thought Blymhill ancient parish, formed between 1086 and 1291, formed originally a part of Gnosall parish (SHC 1916 p196). There was a chapel-of-ease to Gnosall Collegiate Church at Blymhill by the C12. The present parish church, Blessed Virgin Mary, in School Lane, Blymhill, may stand on the site of the C12 chapel. It is of mid C14 origin. In c1716 it was altered. The present church is mainly a rebuild of the late 1850s

(BOE p75) (History of Blymhill Church 1200-1990. BDR. 1991). The custom of well dressing was practised in Blymhill (FOS p103).

Blymhill Common Hamlet on the Shrops border 1.5m WNW of Blymhill. Name appears in 1812 (SPNO p130).

Blymhill Grange To SE of Blymhill church. To its NW is a moated site at SJ 811120 (CAMS p63). (SSAHST 1982-3 p35).

Blymhill Lawn Small hamlet 1m SE of Blymhill. In Blymhill parish. Name appears in 1812 (SPNO p130). Formerly Lawn (W p442). For Blymhill Lawn in a local rhyme see Brewood.

Blymhill Marsh Tiny hamlet 0.5m N of Blymhill. Name appears in 1812 (SPNO p130).

Blythe, The Appears to be the collective name for the tiny hamlet of Blythebridge and Blythebridge Hall; In Kingstone ancient parish. 'Blithebridge or The Blythe' appears on a late C19 OS map 6 inch.

Blythe Bridge Former hamlet by the Blithe, now a residential suburb at the tail end of the Potteries, over 3m SW of Longton, to the WNW of Forsbrook, a village it now merges with. Formerly partly in Normacot township in Hilderstone quarter in Stone ancient parish (W p371) and partly in Forsbrook township in Dilhorne ancient parish. Most of the line of the Roman road from Buxton through Leek, Cheddleton, Blythe Bridge, Hilderstone, and Stafford to Pennocrucium (see) on Watling Street has yet to be established (VCH vol 7 p98). Here it crossed Richmilde Street (see), the Roman road between Derby and Chesterton (NSFCT 1982 p23). Blythe Bridge started to expand after the opening of the Stoke-Uttoxeter railway line in 1848 (info D Stoddard). The Cheadle and Tean Times brought out the Blythe and Forsbrook Times in 1992. Blythe Bridge and Forsbrook Historical Society was founded in 1977 (info D Stoddard). For George Wakefield (1828-1888), poet and stationmaster at Blythe Bridge, see Uttoxeter. Sgt Albert Edward Egerton, born in Longton on Nov 10 1897, entered WW1 in the 3rd Batt North Staffs Regt but transferred in 1916 to the 16th Batt Sherwood Foresters. During the battle of Ypres on Sept 20 1917 he gained the VC for launching a brave solo attack on an enemy dug-out. He died at his home in Uttoxeter Road, Blythe Bridge, in 1966 and is buried in Forsbrook churchyard (POTP p87) (ES June 2 2000 p11; refers to him as Ernest Egerton).

Blythebridge Tiny hamlet 1m SW of Kingstone. In Kingstone ancient parish. Has also appeared as Blythe Bridge. The nucleus of the hamlet is a mill on the Blithe called Blythe Bridge Mill; one of a few in the county with architectural pretensions. Above the central first-floor door is a quatrefoil panel within a circle matching the openings on either side. It contains the arms of Robert Shirley of Chartley Castle (see), 7th Earl Ferrers (Ferrers impaling Mundy) and the date 1823 (IAS p174) (TRTC p135p).

Blythebridge Hall House 1.25m SW of Kingstone. In Kingstone ancient parish. Last residence of Sir Simon Degge (1612-1703), historian and antiquarian, son of William Degge of Stramshall; Simon was formerly of Callowhill. Redfern was disappointed not to find his date of christening in Uttoxeter PR (HOU p191). He was the author of 'The Parson's Counsellor,' 'Law of Tithes' and 'Tithing' (SOS pl iv) (W p790) (JAT p68) (HOU pp207-211,244) (LGS p156) (PS p68) (SGS p115) (STMSM Oct 1980 p18) (SH pp72-77,170). Has also appeared as Blythe Bridge Hall and Blithbridge Hall (late C19 OS map 6 inch).

Blythe House 1m WNW of Church Leigh. Has also appeared as Blithe House (1834 OS map).

Blythe House Forsbrook (SMOPP vol 1 p4p).

Blythe Marsh E end of Blythe Bridge. Formerly in Forsbrook township in Dilhorne ancient parish (W p772). A perforated stone axe-hammer head was found here by Mr Day, headmaster of Blythe Marsh School (NSFCT 1953 p105) (NSJFS 1962 p28. 1964 p23).

Boardman's Bank Stretch of road on the W side of Brown Edge village. It takes its name from a William Boardman who was farming in this part of Brown Edge in the early 1800s (ONST 1979 p398).

Boarsgrove House over 2m NNW of Upper Elkstone.

Boat Hill Compton near Tettenhall (WPOPP vol 1 p75p of c1911).

'Boathorse Road' Former 2m bridleway over Harecastle Hill for horses of horse-drawn canal boats which could not go through Harecastle Tunnel (NSJFS 1978 p34) now a lane.

Bobbington Village on a tributary of the Worfe 22m SSW of Stafford. Bobbington has been described as an ancient parish (VCH vol 20 p65). Ecclesiastically, Bobbington was formerly a chapel in Claverley ancient parish, Shrops. The name is of Anglo-Saxon origin and means Bobba's town (DUIGNAN) (SPN p20) or 'the tun of Bubba's people' (VCH vol 20 p65) (SSE 1996 p11). Bobbington was identified by Dugdale and Shaw with the Bubandune mentioned in the will of Wulfric Spot (c1002), founder of Burton Abbey. But it has since been identified with Bupton, Derbys (SHC 1916 pp40-

41). There may have been a church at Bobbington in Anglo-Saxon times. The present church, Holy Trinity, by Glebelands on N side of Six Ashes Road, with some C12 work, may stand on the site of it (Parish Church of the Holy Cross, Bobbington). Sept 27 1813 may have been a wake day (VCH vol 20 p67). The manor of Bubintone appears in DB (SSE 1996 p11). A later form is Bublinton (Blaeu's map). The Bobbinton area anciently lay in Kinver Forest (VCH vol 20 p65). There may have been a hunting lodge for royal use here, as well as one at Stourton Castle. Henry III was at Bobbington in 1238 and 1245. In June 1256 he ordered the sheriff to send wine to Bobbington, to await his arrival en route to Bridgnorth. Royal justices held an assize at Bobbington in 1274 (VCH vol 20 pp67,68). Bobbington remained dependent on Claverley until the Reformation (VCH vol 20 p73), or until it became a separate ecclesiastical parish in 1726 (GLAUE p404). The parish was in Lichfield diocese as part of Bridgnorth peculiar until 1846, when it was transferred with Bridgnorth to Hereford diocese. It was returned to Lichfield diocese in 1905 (VCH vol 3 pp93 note, 95,96. vol 20 p73). The lord of the manor of Bobbington had a windmill in 1686. The same or another windmill stood on Bobbington Common (see) in the later C18 (VCH vol 20 p73). The custom of gooding on St Thomas' day (Dec 21) was practised in Bobbington parish (N&Q Series ii 22 Aug 1857 iv p147) (VCH vol 20 p67). Rev Edward Bradley ('Cuthbert Bede') (1827-1889), author of 'Mr Verdent Green,' was vicar of Bobbington from 1857 to 1859. His romantic novel 'The Curate of Cranston' (1862) is set in Bobbington (VCH vol 20 p67) (VFC pp11-12). The second edition contains much folklore concerning the village (PPTP pp85-94).

Bobbington Common Former common of Bobbington parish to the E of Halfpenny Green and to the N of Manor Farm. A windmill was built on the common N of Manor Farm c1769 (VCH vol 20 p73).

Bobbington Hall Over 0.5m SSW of Bobbington. Tall brick house of c1600 which incorporates a less substantial and possibly earlier timber-framed building (BOE p76) (VCH vol 20 p68). Bobbington Hall and its estate belonged to the Greys, lords of Enville by the late C17. It remained part of the Enville Hall estate until 1864. The estate centred on this hall may have originated in land attached to the capital messuage of Bobbington manor (VCH vol 20 p68).

Bob's Brook Flows by the Crooked House at Himley (VB p48). Or a local pit of this name? (TB Nov 1989 p1).

Bob's Coppice Netherend. On N side of the Stour.

Boden's Cottage There was a dwelling called Boden's Cottage on Great Barr Common by 1611, probably named after a member of the Boden family. The site of the cottage has never been located (SNAR p72), but the name is preserved in Bodens Lane, W of Barr Beacon.

Bodkin Row Terrace of cottages on the N side of Main Road, Little Haywood. It is believed to have been called this on account of the fact that it housed the seamstresses from Shugborough Hall (HHHC pp59,60p).

Bodnets, The Minute hamlet of a couple of properties 1.25m NE of Hints.

Boghay Former place name preserved in the surname Boughey, and in Bowey Lane, which runs from Betley to Knowl Bank, possibly a reference to a bow-shaped enclosure (AHJ 1995 p44).

Bogs, The Area to the SE of Blackbrook, Maer (1834 OS map).

Bold Former place near or by Bull Bridge, Penkridge. Appears as Le Bolde (1327), Le boulde (1598) (SPNO p93). Bold was a prebend in Penkridge Collegiate Church in 1342 (VCH vol 3 p300).

Boldershaw Tiny hamlet to E of Stanton.

Bole Bridge Ancient bridge which crossed the Anker at Tamworth. It was described in the mid C19 as long and narrow, consisting of 12 small arches, with triangular recesses over the piers (SHOS vol 1 p420) (W p616): St Mary Bridge crosses the Tame. The bridge was replaced in 1877 by a cast iron bridge which itself was replaced in 1936 (TDOPP p20). Has also appeared as Bowbridge (c1540) (LI part 5 p105), and Boll Bridge.

Bole Hall In Amington, Bolehall, Tamworth. Early Georgian (BOE p279). Charles Harding (d1868) was of Bole Hall (mem in St Edith's, Tamworth).

Bolehall Hamlet 0.5m ESE of the centre of Tamworth. The former township of Bolehall and Glascote lay in Hemlingford hundred, Warws and in Tamworth ancient parish. Became a separate civil parish in 1866. Parts of the civil parish began to be taken into Tamworth borough from 1894 and the whole civil parish was taken into the borough and into Staffs in 1965 (GLAUE p425). Bolehall was a ward of Tamworth borough by at least 1993. Rev William MacGregor buried two Egyptian mummies on the banks of the Anker behind Bolehall Manor (LTM Oct 1972 pp25-28).

Boley Growing area of Lichfield 1m SE of the cathedral. Bolley (later Boley) field, a former open field, mentioned in the later C13, lay SE of St Michael's churchyard along Boley Lane and Darnford Lane as far as Ryknild Street

(VCH vol 14 p110).In the 1570s it was claimed that Boley and Spearhill alluded to the bows and spears used in the massacre of Christians in the reign of Diocletian. According to Gelling Boley probably means 'wood where logs are obtained' (VCH vol 14 p38 note).

Boley Park Boley, Lichfield. Housing estate begun by the late 1970s and by the mid 1980s was claimed as one of the largest private estates in the country and among the top 10 in Europe (Lichfield Mercury Nov 28 1986 p3) (VCH vol 14 p35). Boley Park is also an industrial estate (VCH vol 14 p129)

Bolland's Hall To the W of Butterton (Moorlands).

Bolton Gate Boltongate Farm is nearly 2m NE of Longton. Is probably from a gate in the perimeter of Weston Coyney Old Park.

Boltstone Former large standing stone which could have been a battlestone, part of a megalithic chambered tomb, or brought here by glacial drift. It stood in a field E of Bannut Tree Lane near Compton (Kinver) (VCH vol 20 p119) (KRC p18). It was, Plot says, two yards and an inch high and nearly four yards about, having two slices in the top of it (NHS pp397-398). Scott visited it in 1818 and noted it was five feet high and three times that depth in the ground (SVS p337). In 1848 the farmer who owned the land on which it stood blew it up with gunpowder (RKE p28). (VCH vol 1 p191; writing as though the stone still (1908) exists) (Trans Worcs Arch Soc new series vol 6 pp143-144). The name, which has also appeared as The Bolt, Baston, Bierstone and Battlestone has been given, or is from, the field name Boston (later Botstone or Boltstone) Field which lay on the E side of Bannut Tree Lane (VCH vol 20 p137). According to an old local tradition the Boltstone or 'The Giant's Thunderbolt' was hurled by the Kinver Giant at the Enville Giant after he found him flirting with his beautiful wife. One day as the Kinver Giant reached a place called Aston (unlocated), after returning from collecting water from a spring on the W side of Kinver Edge, he saw the Enville Giant leaving his wife. In his fury he took a lump of rock - the Boltstone - out of Kinver Edge and hurled it at the departing Enville Giant. The rock travelled for one mile in the air and came to rest in a field near the Comptons. Whether it hit or missed the Enville Giant is not known (WJO July 1903 xxxv). (SD p34) (SVS p337) (GNHS p66) (FOS p42). Near it is a burial mound supposed to be the grave of a Celtic warrior (W p178).

Bond End S end of Yoxall village.

Bond End Area N of Broadway, formerly in Burton Extra township in Burton upon Trent ancient parish. Bond End was an area without Burton Abbey walls occupied by the serfs and bondmen who worked for the abbey (BTOP p16). Has also appeared as Bondend. It consisted of three streets, Fleet Street, Green Street, and Lion and Love Lane (the modern Bond Street) (IHOBT p45). (SHOS vol 1 p8) (1834 OS map) (W p530).

Bond End Branch of the Trent and Mersey Canal. The first section of just over 1m in length, from the Trent at Bond End, was built 1786. In 1796 the branch was extended to link up with the Trent and Mersey Canal at Shobnall. The branch survived until 1870 (SWY p50). (BTOP vol 1 p16). No trace of it is now visible.

Bond House House at Lea Laughton, Horton ancient parish. It was so called by the later C16 (VCH vol 7 p65).

Bonehill Hamlet near Bourne Brook 0.75m WNW of Fazeley. Formerly in Fazeley township in Tamworth ancient parish (W p625). The name is of Anglo-Saxon origin and means 'the hill of the Boll.' In Anglo-Saxon dictionaries bolla is given as a bowl, but it had other meanings, like the bole of a tree trunk, or a bole of cotton, or where lead or other metals were anciently smelted, so could be 'the hill of the bole (or furnace)' (DUIGNAN). Or 'bulls' hill' (SSE 1996 p11). Appears in 1230 as Bolenhull (SSE 1996 p11). To ESE of Bonehill at SK 199021 is Bonehill Mill, of four storeys, used for calico printing, set up by Robert Peel (1750-1830). It was in use until 1965, when it was grinding corn. The iron breastshot wheel is 12 feet in diameter and 14 feet wide, which is unusually wide (IAS pp167-168) (MR p130). Bonehill features in a derisory rhyme about Tamworth (see). Rev James Richard Alsop, poet, who later lived at Bednall (see), was born at Bonehill on March 11 1816 (PSS p166).

Bonehill House Bonehill. Built in the early C19 for Sir Robert Peel's younger brother, Edmund (d1850), who had a calico printing works nearby. In 1851 it was occupied by Mrs Peel, perhaps, Edmund's widow. Lt Col Gerard Chilchester died at Bonehill House in 1906. In 1906 it was owned by NH Everitt (mems in Drayton Bassett and Fazeley churches) (W p19) (BOE p131) (TDOPP p62p).

Bonehill Park To NE of Bonehill, but to the S of the Birmingham and Fazeley Canal.

Boney Hay Suburb of Chasetown, 1.5m WNW of Burntwood church. Appears as 'Burnehew' in 1361. The name is of Anglo-Saxon origin and may mean 'Bondi's island enclosure.' The personal name could have been 'Bundi' or even 'Bola' and island is used in the sense of an isolated area. There was a house at Boney Hay by 1571 and the area became populous in the later C19 (VCH vol 14 p199) (SPN p29). Formerly in an out-township of St Michael's parish, Lichfield.

Bonthorn Area centred on Bonthorn Farm 0.75m NNE of Wychnor 1m SSW of Barton-under-Needwood. Formerly Banethorn, Boghthorn, Bowen thorne and Bonethorn (HOPT vol 1 p136). The circular enclosures 100 yards SW of Bonthorn House, at SK 180170, are a listed monument. The land called Bonthorne which today (1995) funds a sermon at Barton-under-Needwood (see) on Good Friday, initiated by William Key of Sherholt Lodge in 1651, is allotments opposite Bonthorne Farm in Dogshead Lane and the adjacent field known as Bonthorne Common (UNT pp21-23).

Boniface Well Well from which water was sold to c1840. Situated in the Little Hill area of Wednesbury (WAM p6).

Bookland Newcastle-under-Lyme. Land owned by Thomas Wood, mayor of Newcastle between 1656 and 1662, on which Plot noted good earth for brick making (NUL p101).

Booden Farm House 0.5m SSW of Haughton. In Haughton parish. The name has similar origins to Bottom House (see); it has appeared as le Hall of Bolde (1548), Bold Hall alias Bowldhall (1555), Bothall (1579. Speed's map), Boldhall alias Bolden (1624), Booden House (1725. 1880), and Boldon (Yates' map) (SPNO p165). Parts of a wet moat exist around the house at SJ 862198 (VCH vol 1) (SSAHST 1982-3 p43) (CAMS p63). The farm-house is of red-brick and appears to date from the C18 (VCH vol 4 p138).

Boon Hill Hamlet settled by nail makers in the C18 0.5m E of Audley. Formerly in Bignall End township in Audley ancient parish (W p429). The name has its origins in Boundary Hill, as the C16 dividing line between the constablewicks of Audley and Bignall End ran along the centre of the roadway (AHJ 1997 p98). There was an estate of Boond Hill House by the early C17 (SHC 1944 p41). Has also been written Boond Hill (1733) (W p429) (AHJ 1997 p96), Boonhill (BS), and Bound Hill (AOPP pl 25), and is probably the Round Hill on Dower's map.

Boosley Grange House over 0.5m SE of Newtown. Formerly in Fawfieldhead township, in Alstonefield ancient parish. There was a house here by the later C14 when Boosley Grange appears as Boothesley Grange. The present house retains C17 stonework and was probably built for the Wardle family, who were residing here in the 1640s. By 1670 there was a tradition that one of the two officers of Malbonck Forest, a keeper, had lived at Boosley Grange (VCH vol 7 pp6,27). No abbey is known to have owned land in Fawfieldhead township and the name probably refers to buildings used seasonally for dairying (VCH vol 7 p27). A hoard of medieval silver coins were found in Boosley Folly Meadow in 1867 see under Longnor.

Boosmore Brook Crown Bridge used to carry the Cannock road over it to the E of the junction of the present Market Street and Mill Street, Penkridge (VCH vol 5 p105). Is probably the same as, or another form of Boscomoor.

Booth The houses Upper Booth and Lower Booth are 2m N of Blithfield. In Blithfield ancient parish (W p413). The earliest mention of Booth is in 1175-6 and it has appeared as Le Bolde and The Bolde (SHC 1908 p23. 1919 p34), Bold (Plot's map) and Booth Hall (COI p149). The Meverells, a younger branch of those of Throwley, held Bold manor in about Edward I's reign (COI p149). There probably existed here in former times a small hamlet (SHC 1919 p34). On Blaeu's map there is marked a chapel at Bothall which is probably this Booth. The present (1919) farmhouse at Booth, of modern construction and in no part any older than the mid C18, possibly occupies the site of the old manor house (SHC 1919 p41).

Booth Tiny hamlet 1m SW of Ipstones consisting of Booth's Hall (see) and Booth's Farm (see).

Boot Hall C17 house under 0.25m NNW of Horton. Is thought to take its name from the Boot family, which lived in the parish in the early C18 (VCH vol 7 p65). JF Moxon, believing DB Halstone to be Horton near Leek, has identified DB Bughale with Boot Hall (HHHL p99). Others have identified Bughale with Brough Hall (see) near Ranton.

Boothen Suburb nearly 1m SSW of Stoke-upon-Trent. Former township with Penkhull in Stoke-upon-Trent chapelry and ancient parish. The name is usually indicative of the site of the residence of those who acted as cowherds to the cattle agisted in forests - here were the temporary sheds for the shelter of the herdsmen (NSFCT 1910 p176). Boothen, a small hamlet by the Trent by the early C15 centring on Boothen Farm and the Plough Inn, was becoming a suburb of Stoke by the 1870s (VCH vol 8 p176). It is 'Booden' in Arnold Bennett's novels. 'Boothen End' refers to the S end of the old Stoke City's Football Ground, called the Victoria Ground (ES Nov 15 1994 p9). On the E side of London Road is a 12 feet high obelisk raised by public subscription to the memory of Timothy Trow a tram conductor with the N Staffs Tramway

Company who left his tram to try to save four year old Jane Ridgway from drowning in the Newcastle-under-Lyme Canal situated nearby on April 13 1894. Trow was a non-swimmer and two men Henry Lloyd and John Forrester were soon at the scene to rescue both of them. Jane was saved but Trow, aged 21, drowned (SHST pp83-84) (NSJFS 1973 p113) (MMM pp16-18) (ES Nov 22 1976. April 4 1993 p19p) (Weekly Sentinel April 11 1980). A service was held at the obelisk on the 100th anniversary of the incident at which were present the distant descendants of Trow and Ridgway (ES April 1 1994 p3pc. April 22 1994 p12p). The obelisk was damaged when a car collided with it in Oct 1994 (ES Nov 14 1994 p8p).

Boothen Green Common pasture belonging to the tenants of Boothen, Stoke. Name occurs in 1615 (VCH vol 8 p200).

Booth Hall In Kingsley civil parish, 1.5m N of Cheadle, 0.25m to its SE is The Booth Farm. (CCT p12).

Boothlow Area comprising the three farmsteads of Boothlow Hayes, and Lower and Over Boothlow. In Sheen ancient parish. The burial mound at SK 08786314, 0.5m W of Lower Boothlow is 32 paces in diameter and six feet high. It is a listed monument. Another at SK 08926299, to the SE of the former is 24 paces in diameter and 5.5 feet high. It is a listed monument. There is another at SK 09006282 by the house called The Low or Low Farm (see) to the SE of the second. All three were excavated by Bateman in 1848. The first two produced a cremation. (TYD pp35-36). The last is believed to be not a burial mound (NSJFS 1965 p38). A house, Lower Boothlow, 1.5m NW of Sheen, appears as Nether Boothlow in 1573. The present house is of C19 origin. A house, Upper Boothlow, 0.25m to the N, was mentioned in 1611 but there may have been a house on the site in the later C16. The present one is of C19 origin (VCH vol 7 p241).

Booths Farm Lies SE of Booth's Hall, Booth, Ipstones. The 'A.B. 1663' on the front of the house shows when Anthony Brindley at least partly rebuilt the house. 'W.B 1687' on a barn shows when his son William erected a new farm building two years after inheriting the farm (TOI p44) (ref from NSFCT lost).

Booth's Farm Stood at SP 061940 S of Booth's Lane, to the NNW of Perry Beeches Junior School. Formerly in Perry Barr township in Handsworth ancient parish. The farm is said to have been of C16 origin and to have served at one period as a monastery. It was part of the Perry Hall estate. It was certainly in existence by 1794, and in the early C19 it obtained notoriety during the short occupation of the coin forger and villain, **William Booth**, 'King of Coiners,' who rented it from the Goughs of Perry Hall (MNB p62) (HPPE p13). William Booth was born at Ullenhall near Henley-in-Arden, Warws, in 1776. In the early 1800s he had a hand in many illegal ventures in the Birmingham area and became known as 'Birmingham or Brummajum' Booth. As well as forging he sold corpses to Birmingham medics. He was a frequent visitor to the Hare and Hounds Inn (see) at Mayers Green (where he was caught by the authorities on one occasion). He stood trial at Warwick Assizes on April 8 1808 accused of murdering his brother, John, at his father's farm at Wootton Waven, Warws, but he was acquitted; he claimed his brother had been kicked in the head by a horse. Booth was arrested again in 1811 or on March 16 1812 at Booth's Farm and tried at Stafford. According to his gravestone he was hung on Aug 15 1812; according to the church register he was hung on Aug 17 (OWB pp115-116) (TB Sept 1988 pp10-11). According to tradition at his execution the rope broke and he was hung again (Broughton's Scrapbook pp199-200). Some say it took three attempts to hang him (TB Sept 1988 pp10-11). He was buried with a gravestone by his parents or relatives at the entrance to Handsworth old church. The stone was moved when local dignitaries objected to having to pass it on their way to church, but it has since been returned to its original position (TB Oct 1988 p1). After this succession of events it could be said of Booth that he was 'a man twice tried, twice hung, and twice buried' (North Staffordshire Mercury, letter dated Jan 14 1840) (Broughton's Scrapbook pp199-200) (ZSB). At night people in the vicinity of Booth's Farm during pig farrowing have heard strange noise for which there is no explanation (Great Barr and its Haunted Environs. Thomas Wright. 1852) (TB July 1987 p23). The farm was later used for other purposes, including that of a quarry office and store. It was demolished in Feb 1974, owing to encroaching quarrying operations (MNB p62) (HPPE pp13-15).

Booth's Hall Lies NW of Booth's Farm, Booth, Ipstones. There was a farm at Booth by the early C14. It was the seat of the Janneys and subsequently of the Pyotts in the C16 and the C17. Has also appeared as The Booths (SHOS vol 1 p363) (TOI p44). By the late 1930s it had become a farmhouse (TOI p44).

Boothurst 1m SE of Rugeley (1834 OS map). In Armitage parish. Rugeley (see) Power Stations are built on it.

Bore Street Previously known as Boar or Borde Street. This was one of the main thoroughfares of medieval Lichfield (LAL p12).

Borough Hole Name of fields above the Manifold, behind Thor's Cave, 0.75m SW of Wetton on which was discovered a Romano-British pit settlement between 1848 to 1852 (MR p373) or 1845 to 1864 (NSJFS 1964 p43) (BOE pp50,308). (SL p37). It was occupied in the C3 AD (NSJFS 1962 p33). It may have been a settlement for Roman lead miners. In recent centuries local people have taken its stones for building (MR p373). Here were found iron utensils, coins from 253-337 AD, glass, a bronze ring, skeletons and enamelled jewellery (WTCEM p31). (TYD p193) (R vol 5 p217) (VCH vol 1 p196) (LGS p25) (SC p149) (NSJFS 1964 p43). Also within the area of the Roman settlement three burials were found of Anglian origin (VCH vol 1 p208) (DAJ vol 74 p145) (NSJFS 1964 p44. vol 9 1969 pp92-103). Has also appeared as Borough Fields (BOE p308), and has been known as Benebury or Wedin's town, or by the C19 archaeologists, Carrington and Bateman, who rediscovered it, the North Staffordshire Pompeii (WTCEM pp6,8,9). Benebury means the 'good town,' or 'holy burial place' or 'holy borough,' so perhaps corrupted into 'Borough Holy' - 'Borough Hole' (WTCEM pp35,77). Benebury has been confused with Bonebury, which is another name for Bunbury, where there was an Iron Age hillfort and battle between the West Saxons and the Mercians in 716. Roberts, Plot and Abbot Jourval all thought the battle took place near Alstonefield at possibly behind Thor's Cave (WTCEM p35), The Daily Mail (1971) thought it took place at Longnor in 715 (L p2).

Borough Park District 0.75m N of Tamworth. The name was used to describe this area by at least 1971 (OS map 1971).

Borrowcop District of Lichfield around Borrowcop Hill.

Borrowcop Hill Hill under 1m SE of Lichfield cathedral. Most writers have considered it a tumulus (SHOS vol 1 p343). The eminence overlooks the approach from London. There is a tradition that the legendary massacred Christians slain near Lichfield (see) during Diocletian's reign (284-305) are buried at Borrowcop (VCH vol 14 p39). Another tradition says three British kings were killed and buried here in 286 AD (SCSF p74) or c288 (W p490) (HOWW p13). Some versions of the same story say the massacred Christians were in the army of the three kings (VCH vol 14 p39). Bell says there is a tradition of two Mercian kings being killed here and afterwards buried in Lichfield cathedral Close (Bell's 'Lichfield Cathedral' 1908. p35). It was known as Burghwaycop before the C17 (VCH vol 14 p7) and has also appeared as Barrowcop Hill (HOWW p13). Cop means the highest part of a hill. Borrow is probably a corruption of borough, burgh, bury and burh, from Anglo-Saxon for encampment or fort (HOL p561) (VCH vol 14 p7). The hill may have been topped by an Anglo-Saxon fortification (HOWW p13) (VCH vol 14 p7). (STMSM Nov 1972 p41). Commander Wedgwood thought it might be the DB Buruoestone (SHC 1916 p170). Stone was used from a quarry near here to build Lichfield cathedral (Bell's 'Lichfield Cathedral' 1908. p35; although, Bell incorrectly locates Borrowcop to the N of the cathedral). The view over Lichfield is excellent from the summit. The hill was a place for pleasure walks from at least the late C17. A building called the Temple in 1694 probably stood on Borrowcop Hill (VCH vol 14 p163). In the early 1720s there was an arbour on the summit (VCH vol 14 p163). This was apparently replaced with a summerhouse by the corporation in 1750 (VCH vol 14 p163). By 1805 the summerhouse had been replaced by a brick gazebo or observation pavilion with two arches each side and seats around it for shelter for those who climb the hill. The gazebo was restored in the 1980s (F p318) (VCH vol 14 p163). (W p490) (SCSF p74) (BOE p193) (LAL p55p).

Boscomoor 0.5m SSE of Penkridge. In Penkridge ancient parish. The name means probably 'Booth's marshland' (SPNO p93). Has appeared as Bowes More (1598), Boosmore (1681), Boothsmoor (1644-1763) (SPNO p93); there is also a Boosmore Brook (VCH vol 5 pp105,127).

Bose's Well Cannock Wood. S of Castle Ring. A spring which gives rise to a tributary of Radmoor Brook. Heat-shattered pebbles of a possible former Middle Bronze Age burnt mound below the spring were noted in 1916-17 (SASR 1987 p18).

Bosoms End Former hamlet to W of Bearwood Hill, Smethwick. Also called Blossoms End by 1839 (VCH vol 17 p89). By 1953 the area had become known as The Uplands (STELE June 26 1953).

Bosses, The There is a house called Bosses 1m SE of Stonnall. Has been described as an ancient low-lying swampy agricultural region of about 200 acres with Ryknild or Icknield Street running through it (DUIGNAN) (SPN p106). Appears in the C12 as 'in bosco suo de Boshay' (SPN p106). The name is from Old French, bosc meaning a wood. The ending 'hay' in time dropped off (DUIGNAN) (SPN p106). White notes a Little Bossis and Great Bossis in Shenstone ancient parish (W p584).

Bosty Lane Name of road between Daw End and Barr Common, SW of Aldridge. The name appears in 1286 as Boltstile. It is from, perhaps, Anglo-Saxon,

bold, botl meaning a house, and stig meaning a path, road: So, 'the path to the house.' Or perhaps, 'style' may represent Anglo-Saxon stigel, a place of crossing, a stile. Or from a boundary between Cannock Forest and Sutton Chase which also formed part of an ancient cattle road between N Wales and London (DUIGNAN) (SNAR p14).

Botany Bay 1.75m NE of Weeford. Swinfen and Packington civil parish. Hamlet near Packington Hall and Whittington Barracks.

Botany Bay Small hamlet or farm (SNWA p17) to E of The Delves, Walsall. The name, marked on 1834 OS map, is from the penal colony in Australia and was, for derisory purposes, often given to an isolated farm (SNWA p17). There is a Botany Road N of The Delves.

Botany Bay Bridge Bridge on the Caldon Canal, one of the original bridges. It has parapets (The Caldon Canal by The Caldon Canal Society 1994 p6).

Botham Hall Former name for Ashcombe Park (OL vol 2 p105). Has also appeared as Bothams and Bottom Hall (HOC p235). Residence of the Leek family, then demolished and Ashcombe Park built on its site (HOC p235). The hall may have been the keeper's lodge to the medieval deer park Cheddleton Park, if the park was situated in this area (CVH p160).

Botslow Berry Hill, Bucknall.

Botterham In Wombourne ancient parish. Botterham Locks are two locks on the Staffs and Worcs Canal and form an early example of a staircase lock (TB Feb 1976 p1p) (VCH vol 20 p201) and are probably those at the S end of Botterham Lane 1.5m SW of Wombourne.

Botteslow On SE side of Hanley. Preserved in Botteslow Street. Former township in Stoke-upon-Trent chapelry and ancient parish. Lay in Fenton Vivian manor (W p236) (HBST pp467-468) (VCH vol 8 p246) (NSSG p20). (H p5) (BNDA p1). A well here had the reputation for strengthening children. It was an annual custom for children to be ducked in the well during the first nine (H p106) or 10 days (SHST pp214,217-8) of May. Tradition has it that on one occasion a husband was taken and ducked by mistake. The custom continued until c1861 (VCH vol 8 p160) (SHST pp214,217-8).

Bottle Cave Cave in Wren's Nest Hill near Dudley (TTTD p305).

Bottom House Tiny hamlet at crossroads of Leek Ashbourne and Ipstones Onecote roads 1.5m SSW of Onecote. The house which gives it its name dates back to 1680 (TOI p45). It appears to have been formerly Botham House, in Morridge and Foxt liberty in Ipstones ancient parish (W p779), and may be a relic of the Welsh 'bod' a house, with the English meaning affixed, as in Chetwood (NSFCT 1908 p141). A Master W 8840 crashed at Bottom House on Jan 15 1943. The pilot, who was alone, died (MD p54).

Bottom House Inn Former inn at Bottom House. In existence in c1800. A few fields away from this inn, was Gooseneck Farm, where lived the father, brother and sister of the counterfeiters, George and Thomas Fearne. Some say they counterfeited money here, whilst others say the counterfeit notes were made at Flash and taken to Bottom House Inn where the forged money was taken on the turnpike road to Birmingham (OL vol 2 p59). The inn has been identified with the Green Man Inn at the crossroads of Bottom Lane and Ashbourne road (IOM p65) others that it is the Travellers Rest Inn, but Rev Bright thought Upper Berkhamsytch Farm was the probable site of it. The Fearnes gang were all skilfully entrapped by Joseph Nadin, a noted Manchester thief-catcher. George Fearne was hung at Stafford Gaol on Aug 8 1801 for issuing three bills knowing them to be forgeries of the Bank of England. Thomas was not hung (TOI pp166-167) (CCSHO pp69-77) (IOM p65).

Boughey Hall Under 0.25m N of Colton church. Represents the Colton estate of St Thomas' priory, which was formed out of a part of each of the two Colton manors or of their waste. After the dissolution the estate (also comprising the Lount Farm) passed to Bishop Rowland Lee who settled it on his nephew Rowland Fowler, whose son George sold it c1579 to Sampson Boghay (or Boughey). His family gave the hall its name (SHC 1914 pp153 note, 155) (CWF p170). The Boughey Hall estate passed in the late C17 or the early C18 to the Whitgreaves with the marriage of Constance, a co-heiress of Sampson Boughey, to Thomas Whitgreave of Moseley Hall. It was still the property of the Whitgreaves in 1914 (SHC 1914 pp153 note, 156). Immediately behind the hall farmhouse Rev FP Parker noted a remarkable sized oak measuring 26 feet in girth at the lowest point and 21 feet at a height of one yard from the ground. Its age was unknown, but it possibly dated to before the Norman Conquest (CWF pp173-174).

Boulderstone Cannock Chase. (Daywalks Cannock Chase. John Roberts, sketches by Liz Johnson p38 il). Is probably the glacial boulder now on the site of Brocton Army Camp water tower at SJ 980181, N of Womere.

Boulderstone Bridge Crossed the Penk N of Penkridge. It was constructed from glacial boulders deposited at the end of the last Ice Age. In reconquering the area in 910 King Alfred's successors had a skirmish with the Danes near the site of it. The bridge was replaced by the present one called Bull Bridge in c1825 (PVH pp3,20).

Boundary Small village nearly 1m SE of Dilhorne. Partly in Cheadle and Dilhorne parishes. By the early 1990s a young couple called Steve and Sonia had been tragically killed in a car crash in the bend in the Cheadle Road to the N of Newhouse Farm. Their relatives were still laying fresh flowers to their memory by the road where the crash occurred in late Jan 2000.

Bourn Brook Tributary of the Trent. Flows through Stowe to Rugeley.

Bourne Bridge Bridge of the Bourne Brook 1.5m NW of Drayton Bassett.

Bourne Brook Tributary of the Tame. It formed the boundary between Cannock Forest and Sutton Chase. The upstream part of the brook is called Black Brook (see) (which rises E of Stonnall). It changes name to Bourne Brook at the ford at Hints. The lower part of the brook has appeared as la Burne (c1213), aqua de Burne (1235), la Bourne (1286) le Bournebrok (1387), and Borne brooke (1556); whilst the upper part has appeared as Blakewater (c1540), Black brooke (c1600) (Leland) (SOS) (SPNO p6). (MR p185). The name is from Anglo-Saxon 'burn' or Middle English, meaning a stream (DUIGNAN) (SPNO p6) (SPN p20).

Bourne Brook A tributary of the Trent. Flows through Pipe Hall to Orgreave. Appears as Bourne on Saxton's map (SPNO p6).

Bourne Vale Minute hamlet over 2m NE of the church at Great Barr. In Great Barr chapelry in Aldridge ancient parish. Takes its name from the vale through which the Bourne flows. The round hill in Bourne Vale is believed to be natural and not man-made (MOA p15). At the end of the C18 the Bournevale estate, which stretched from Bourn Pool to Foley Road, was home of George Birch who sold his estate and his rights on the nearby enclosed common to Mrs Whitby joint lord of the manor of Great Barr whilst the inclosure Award of 1799 was pending. Bournevale House was occupied by Richard Palmer in 1841. Later in the C19 it was used as a shooting lodge by George Davey Bragg, a wealthy Birmingham brewer. After his death in 1900 his estates passed to his nephew Arthur Turner (d1915). His trustees sold the Streetly estate at public auction to the present tenants and Bournevale was developed with modern housing (SLHT p8).

Bourne Pool Former small lake 3m NE of Great Barr, in Great Barr chapelry in Aldridge ancient parish. The pool is the source of the Bourne Brook (or otherwise Black Brook), which enters the Tame at Tamworth. Flint implements of the Later Mesolithic and post-Mesolithic Ages were found to the W of Bourne Pool at SP 06989978 in 1955. The total collection comprised about 2173 artifacts (BAST vol 74 p53) (NSJFS 1964 p13) (HOS p9) (SSAHST 1972-3 pp6-28 ils) (SL p36) (Guide to Bourne Pool compiled Bryan Balsom, copy in Walsall Local History Centre). The site was excavated in 1958 (SLHT p6). Numerous heat-shattered pebbles of a possible former Middle Bronze Age burnt mound were found at cSP 069998 among a surface scatter of flintwork which was principally Mesolithic in character, with some Neolithic pieces (SASR 1987 p18). To the SW of the pool at SP 073997 were the remains of a rectangular earthwork called Loaches Banks, an area of 80 yards by 25 yards encompassed by a treble ditch. The site has been variously interpreted; in 1783 William Hutton called it a Saxon encampment; in 1798 Shaw thought it was the winter residence of the arch druid (his summer residence was on Druid's Heath); after excavation of parts in 1959 Jim Gould interpreted the earthwork as being associated with medieval charcoal burning; later archaeologists have assigned it to an earlier prehistoric date. In summarising the later evidence Dr MA Hodder in 1990/1 interpreted Loaches Banks as an Iron Age Hill Slope enclosure associated with animal grazing and stock control. The land around is mainly marginal land suitable only for grazing. Since c1800 farming has levelled Loaches Banks so much that it is only clearly seen on aerial photographs (History of Birmingham. W Hutton. 1783. 2nd ed. p321) (SHOS vol 1 p10. vol 2) (HOWW p16) (BAST vol 77 p40) (NSJFS 1964 p13) (SSAHST 1982-83 p34. 1990-91 p90) (MOA p14) (Guide to Bourne Pool. Bryan Balsom). In the C19 Willmore noted S of Bourne Pool two circular mounds, in the hollow of Barr Beacon, in a swampy situation. The larger was 70 feet in diameter and composed of sand. Willmore thought it was built by the Britons since the names 'Bourne' or 'Bowen' are from the Welsh language. Others have thought it to be of Roman origin, and was a summer camp for those stationed at Letocetum (HOWW pp12,13). The 'small clay vases' found near Bourne Pool (Birmingham Weekly Post local notes and queries No. 404. Aug 9 1879) may have been Roman pottery (SSAHST vol 32 1990-91 p89). The pool was created by the Bourne Brook being dammed in the C15 to provide fish, and power for a mill wheel (Guide to Bourne Pool compiled Bryan Balsom, copy in Walsall Local History Centre). At NE edge of Bourn Pool was a mill producing high-quality iron, operating until end of the C15 (SSAHST 1969 pp58-63) (Guide to Bourne Pool compiled Bryan Balsom). In 1834 the pool appears as Bourn Pool, and perhaps it can be identified with Druid's Mere Pool (see). The pool may have been drained to its

present size by the Staffs Water Works by 1902 (DUIGNAN) (SLHT p6). (W p552).

Bovenhill Former prebend of Tettenhall Collegiate Church (HOPTT p84) (VCH vol 20 p19). Bovenhill prebend was known as Tettenhall in 1269; later as Tettenhall and Compton; and as Compton in 1373 and in 1401. The styling of it as Bovenhill had come into being by 1398 (VCH vol 20 p19). It has been considered a former name of Barnhurst with Barnhurst then being considered the same prebend (SHOS vol 2 p201; written Bovenhull) (HOPTT pp66,84,85,89). The prebendal manor of Bovenhill had land at Barnhurst and the two were owned together and descended together from the C16 (VCH vol 20 pp20-21). The name Bovenhull is from Anglo-Saxon 'A'bufan' 'above the hill' (HOPTT pp66,84). It may have taken its name from land at Barnhurst.

Bowen's Bridge Crosses the Stourbridge Canal at Silver End.

Bower End House 0.75m W of Madeley. In Madeley parish (W p396). Has appeared as Bower End (Yates' map). J Phillips & WF Hutchings map of 1831 & 32), and Bowerend (current maps).

Bowers Hamlet 0.25m N of Standon. Former township of Standon ancient parish (HOPS p4) (SHC 1945/ 6 p113 note).

Bowers Bent Tiny hamlet between Bowers and Cranberry. (SVB p154).

Bowgage Farm on high ground near to Chartley Old Park. Has also appeared as Bow Gage and Beau Gage possibly with reference to the beautiful view to be seen from this point, which includes the spires of Lichfield cathedral (NSFCT 1886 p38).

Bowlingalley Brook Tributary of the Churnet. Runs in the Wootton Lodge area (NSJFS 1972 pp126-127).

Bow Moor Little moor on the N side of Shifford's Grange in old Tyrley parish. Has appeared as Bowyer's Moor (1556). It was certainly included in the original grant of Shifford's Grange to Combermere abbey, but how it came to be separated from the grange is not clear. By 1914 it was part of the Oakley estate (SHC 1945/ 6 p84).

Bowsey Wood Small fragmented hamlet to W of Heighley Castle, over 1.25m NNW of Madeley. On the Madeley Betley parish boundary. Has also appeared as Bosey Wood. Here was a mill on Checkley Brook by c1700. It ceased operations in 1939 (AHJ 1996 p15).

Boyles Hall House E of Audley. Was the residence of a William Child, who married Elizabeth Smith - whence comes the surname, Smith-Child (NSFCT 1911 p20); birthplace in 1730 of Admiral Smith-Child (d1813) (AHJ 1997 p101). There was a Boyles Hall shaft in the Diglake Colliery, where 150 men were rescued during the disaster which occurred on Jan 14 1895, (though, 77 men lost their lives elsewhere in the colliery?) (NSSG p5) (IANS pp34,58p).

Boy's Lane In approximate area of Glebe Road, Fenton (1834 OS map).

Bradbury's Farm 1.25m WNW of Enville. Appears on the 1834 as Broadbury.

Braddocks Hay Former hamlet, now a suburb of E Biddulph. Formerly in Middle Biddulph liberty in Biddulph ancient parish. There was settlement at Braddocks Hay by 1500 (BALH). The ancestors of John de Brodock, mentioned in 1427, probably made the hay or enclosure here (BALH p25). In 1947 work started on the construction of the Braddocks Hay housing estate (BALH p234).

Bradeley Hamlet over 1m NE of Burslem. Now part of Burslem's suburbs. Was identified by Commander Wedgwood with the manor of Bradelie in DB (SHC 1916 p169) (DB. Phillimore. 1976) (SSE 1996 p11). The old village comprised South Street (now Brammer Street), Unwin Street, Moorland View (continuation of Chell Heath Road, Hayes Street and Berrisford Street (now Sherratt Street) - the area comprising the last two were known to local people as New Hayes (ONST 1977 p389). With Norton-in-the-Moors formed a ward of Stoke-on-Trent district by 1991. Bradeley Retirement Village in Brammer Street, Stoke-on-Trent's first enclosed housing for the elderly, opened in 1994. The village, with its own shop, laundrette and community centre, was inspired by similar schemes in Holland, and inspired a similar scheme at Berry Hill (see), near Hanley (ES Sept 6 1996 p66) (info Mrs Salih).

Bradenbrook Tributary of the Manifold. Has appeared as Bradenhope (1219-1346) (SPNO p6).

Brades, The Former hamlet in the N of Rowley Regis parish close to the detached portion of Shrops. It developed in c1780 owing to the Iron Works (BCWJ p86) - perhaps, Brades Steel Works in the area of Brades Rise and Brades Road, to the E of Oldbury (OS map 1834). The name The Brades could have been used to refer to Brades Hall.

Brades Hall 2m SE of Tipton Green. In Rowley Regis parish. Brades Hall, perhaps can be identified with the house known as The Brades, occupied by Thomas Y Hunt, in 1851 (W p19).

Bradeshall Junction Junction of the Birmingham Canal Old Cut Old Main Line with the Gower Branch Canal at Brades Village (SWY p10).

Brades Village 1.75m SE of Tipton Green. 0.5m NWW of Oldbury, it was always in Staffs. Also Brades Hill and Bradeshall Farm (O pp18-19). In 1998 work began on a large Hindu temple on a former foundry site on the N side of Dudley Road East to the E of the Gower Branch Canal. The site was chosen due to its close proximity to the motorway network and not because of a large resident Hindu population in the surrounding area; the planning application process was therefore controversial. The temple, in granite stone, is believed to be the first Hindu temple built in the style of architecture of Southern India in Europe (info Doug Parish, Dr VPN Rao, David Mawson and others).

Bradley (*Braidlee* BCTV p8). Former hamlet and estate or manor (HOBLL p155) (BOP p7), now a suburb submerged into the Black Country, 0.75m S of Bilston. The western half of the estate appears to have been called Upper Bradley, whilst the eastern half is still called Lower Bradley. Formerly partly in Bilston township and chapelry in Wolverhampton ancient parish and partly in Sedgley ancient parish. The **name** is from 'broad lea' (DUIGNAN) (TB Sept 1978 p5) (BCTV p8). Or 'Bradda's leah (woodland clearing)' (SPN p18). The **manor** of Bradeleg appears in DB. In the later C15 it was held by the de Bradleys, passing to the Rudgeleys, Husseys, Pipes, Hoos, and Barbors who sold it to John Wilkinson (see below) (HOBL pp158-159). By 1537 some of Bradley settlement stretched into Sedgley manor and parish (HC p19). **Glassware** was manufactured at Bradley in the later C17. Shaw noted that Lord Monboddo had set up a large range of peculiar constructed ovens at Bradley in his time for the extraction of tar from coal but the project had failed (HOBLL pp159-160). Bradley became a separate ecclesiastical parish in 1865 (GLAUE p404). **Churches**. The church, St Martin, on the N side of King Street, was built in 1866-1868 (BOE p322) (CHMS2 p96). Another church, **St Martin**, possibly replacing the earlier church, was built in Slater Street in 1983 (LDD). The old Bradley **Wesleyan Chapel** was struck by lightning in July 1901 and demolished due to being unrepairable (BOP p112p). By 1991 **Easter crosses** were being erected in Wilkinson Avenue, Bradley (BCTV p facing p8). For the Zeppelin bombing of Bradley in **WW1** see Lower Bradley. **Natives and visitors**. Several iron works of **John Wilkinson**, 'father of the South Staffordshire iron trade' were at Bradley. Various aspects about the life and career of Wilkinson remain in doubt. It is mainly accepted he was born at Clifton, Cumberland in 1728 (DNB); however this date has at least once been questioned, for in 1738 he is said to have been working for the Darby family at Coalbrookdale, Shrops (SLM April 1953 p12). Another account says, in 1748 he left his father's employment in Cumberland and came to Wolverhampton (DNB); or that he left for Wolverhampton in 1755 or 56, aged 27 (John Wilkinson. John Hoyland in Institute of Mechanical Engineers, Engineering Heritage vol 2 1966); or that he was an employee of Mr Hoo of Bradley Mines Ltd in 1756 (SOBP p20); or in 1756 he joined his father at his father's works at Bersham near Wrexham (DNB). In 1761-62 Wilkinson was manager at Bersham, and set up a forge at Broseley, near Bridgnorth, Shrops, and commenced the manufacture of wrought iron. It is said that the first engine completed at Soho Manufactory (see) was ordered by Wilkinson to blow the bellows at the Broseley ironworks (DNB). By 1766 Wilkinson had acquired land at Bradley (John Wilkinson. Ron Davies. 1987. Copy in Walsall Local History Centre. p19), perhaps purchasing, Bradley manor, from the Hoo family (or the Barbors or Barbers); the executors of John Wilkinson were lords of Bradley in 1851 (W p138) (HOBL pp148,159). The exact date of the erection of Wilkinson's first furnace at Bradley - the first coke-fired blast furnace in Bilston township and in Staffs (LHSB 23 p8) - is in some doubt. Some say it was erected in or prior to 1757-58 (SR) (SL p180) (WMLB p53). But the date 1767 is the one usually accepted (BP p84) (The Bradley Ironworks of John Wilkinson. GR Morton and WA Smith. reprint from Journal of the Iron and Steel Institute. vol 234. July 1966 p663) (plaque on the memorial). The process of coke instead of wood-charcoal in the furnace was shortly taken up by other local ironmasters preferring coal, an abundant raw material in the South Staffordshire coalfield - smelting by charcoal was obsolete by 1778. This encouraged the growth of iron works in the area and created the Black Country (see) (DNB) (HOWV p130) (WMVB p30). Wilkinson's first furnace was known locally as 'the Mother Furnace' (The Black Country Iron Industry. WKV Gale. 1966 p25) or the Old Furnace. It was situated at Fireholes (see Fiery Holes), Bradley (BP p84) (HOBL p245) (VCH vol 2 p121), where in 1987 by the Travellers Rest Inn on Great Bridge Road near the junction with Leighton Road a concrete pillar was erected on the site with a plaque commemorating the first blast furnace in the Black Country. By 1772 Wilkinson appears to have erected another furnace to the W, at Hallfields, close to the canal in the Upper Bradley area (BP p84) (The Bradley Ironworks of John Wilkinson. GR Morton and WA Smith). By about this time, he had erected streets for his workers at Upper Bradley (see) and is said to have had his own residence in nearby Hall Green, near the Wesleyan Chapel in Hall Green Street (John Wilkinson. Ron Davies. 1987 p20). He gave a chapel to the

Methodists of Bradley, after, so it is said, they prayed for him to do so: Wilkinson was formerly no friend of Methodism. The chapel had metal doors, window frames and other features and became known as the 'Cast Metal Meeting' (HOWV p215) or 'Cast Metal Meeting House' (HOBLL p169) or 'Wilkinson's Cast Iron Chapel' (WMAG May 1968 p27p). The chapel also contained an iron pulpit made at Wilkinson's works. The old chapel was taken down and a new one opened in 1835. The iron pulpit was saved and preserved in the school room of the chapel in 1893 (HOBLL p169) (BOP p108). In c1770s as a result of Wilkinson's collaboration with Boulton and Watt at Soho Manufactory (see), the steam engine was adapted to the forge and rolling-mill (HOBL p245) (VCH vol 2 p121). The first James Watt winding engine or rotative engine erected outside Soho was set up at Bradley by Wilkinson (VCH vol 2 p165). In Jan 1774 Wilkinson took out his famous patent for a new method of boring iron cannon from solid castings by rotating the piece to be bored and keeping the boring bar steady, thus making possible the production of lighter and more accurate weapons (John Wilkinson, ironmaster. WH Chaloner (from History Today May 1951 p65); this gave him a quasi-monopoly of the supply of parts for Boulton and Watt steam engines (The Bradley Ironworks of John Wilkinson. GR Morton and WA Smith). In the 1780s at his new additional works at Bradley Wilkinson cast tubes and iron work. His patent of 1790 (No 1735) for making lead-pipe is of great importance. In experiments at Bradley Wilkinson may have been the inventor of the hot-blast furnace between 1795 and 1799 (DNB). In 1790 Princess Carbristka of Poland with the prince, her son, visited Wilkinson's Bradley works and stayed at Wolverhampton (see) (Wolverhampton Chronicle July 7 1790) (John Wilkinson. Ron Davies. 1987. Copy in Walsall Local History Centre. p18). His sister, Mary, was the wife of Joseph Priestley of Birmingham. In his life Wilkinson had a number of humorous ballads written about him. He died on July 14 1808 (DNB). According to the GM 1808 ii p662, DNB and a biography by HW Dickenson of Coalbrookdale he died at Bradley; to John Randall of Madeley in his 'Life of Wilkinson' he died at Hadley, Shrops; to Edward Vale in his book on Shrops and to Underhill in AMS he died at Castle Head (SOBP p19). He was buried in an iron coffin (according to tradition to deter body-snatchers) near his seat Castle Head, at Lindale near Grange-over-the-Sands, Lancs (from where his remains have been removed three times) (DNB) (TOS pp75-78) (TB Feb 1988 p12). The site of the grave at Lindale church was lost after the church was rebuilt in 1828 (SOBP p19). There is a portrait of him in Wolverhampton Town Hall (DNB) and in Bilston Art Gallery, where it is stated he died at Bradley (SOBP p19) (SLM April 1953 p12il). In subsequent years Wilkinson became something of a folk-hero and on July 14 1815 (John Wilkinson, ironmaster. WH Chaloner (from History Today May 1951 p69) several thousand people assembled on Monmore Green 'expecting his ghost to make an appearance, riding his grey horse' (SFL p137) (VCH vol 2 p122) (STMSM Jan 1973 p34. July 1980 p32). (SHOS vol 2 p172) (SOSH p298) (VCH vol 2 pp74,121,122,124,165, p facing p231) (WF p45). Two furnaces formerly belonging to Wilkinson called the Bradley furnaces still existed in 1836, but had by then probably ceased production (The Bradley Ironworks of John Wilkinson. GR Morton and WA Smith). During land levelling in 1946 on the site of Wilkinson's first furnace an old engine believed to have been used by him was discovered (SOBP p20). Ironworks, containing the furnace called the Hallfield's furnace, was still in full working order in 1836 (The Bradley Ironworks of John Wilkinson. GR Morton and WA Smith). In 1836 a painting by Robert Noyes of one of the former Wilkinson works, with the canal and the spire of Wednesbury church in the background, was made. The works depicted have crenellated walls, said to have been a recent addition in a comical attempt to add architectural character (SL pp180-181, 184 pl 31). For the murder committed by **Abel Hill** in 1820 see Capponfield. The body of **Eliza Cartwright**, brickmaker, aged 21, of Chell Street, Bradley, was found near Deepfields Cement Works on Jan 7 1884. Her murderer has never been found (TB Jan 1985 p15). The Prince of Wales (later **Edward VIII**) visited Salop Street in 1927 to open the Birmingham New Road (BOP p114p).

Bradley (locally with a long 'a'). Ancient parish and village on a hill (400 feet above sea level - ACOB p3) overlooking tributaries of Church Eaton Brook, over 4m SW of Stafford. For glacial boulders in the vicinity see Webb Stone. The manor of Bradelia appears in DB. Later Bradley appears as Bradel (1150-1159), Bradelega (1161-1180. 1221), Bradele (1206), Bradeleya (1221), Bradley-juxta-Stafford (W p442), and Bradeley (W p442) (SPNO p133) (SSE 1996 p11). The name is of Anglo-Saxon origin and means 'broad lea' (DUIGNAN) (LGS p88). Or 'the broad glade in the wood' (SPNO p133) (SSE 1987 p30) (SSE 1996 p11) (SPN p20). The extensive Bradley manor (ACOB pp6-7 see map) and the manors of Stafford and Madeley were held by Edmund Lord Stafford of the king by barony on condition he find three armed men with three horses and equipment for war whenever there was war between England and Wales, or Scotland (temp. Edward II) (SMC p122) (SCSF p117) (NSFCT 1943 p66). The Bradley PR for 1635 mentions a heriot was taken for the death of Thomas Steee (SCSF p120). The parish formed between 1086 and 1291 out of either Church Eaton or Stafford parishes (SHC 1916 pp192,196). The parish church, All Saints, on the S side of Church Lane, has C12, C13, C14 and C16 work (VCH vol 4 p87). The pillars between the nave and the N aisle are from Saint Augustine's Priory, Stafford. The church was the setting for a TV programme 'Wedding of the Year' 1987 (MR p46). At Bradley was a strange custom for the upkeep of the churchyard whereby all the parishioners repaired sections of the churchyard wall (or fence) and grounds in proportion to the land they occupied in the parish, owing to the church being originally built by the whole community (GM 1798) (SL p53) (ACOB p3). The churchyard cross of C13 origin was a focus of medieval life (ACOB p8pc). Wakes appear to have occurred on All Saints day (Nov 1) (ACOB p5). At approximately SJ 879180 was a windmill recorded in 1337 (WBJ p15). There was another windmill at Woollaston (see). A school at Bradley, said to have its origins in an endowment of Humphrey de Hastang in 1344, was in existence by 1546. It was the Free School or Church of England or National school of the later C19 and became the Bradley Endowed Voluntary Primary School in 1928. It closed with 12 pupils in 1988 (VCH vol 4 p90) (LHSB 14 pp18-19) (ACOB pp18-23). The school building, built in 1850 on the bend of Church Lane, was then turned into the village hall. Princess Anne reopened the village hall in 1993 (Staffs Village Halls Directory. Susan Miles. 1994).

Bradley Branch of the Birmingham Canal Old Cut Old Main Line or of the Walsall Canal. Spurred off the Walsall Canal at Moorcroft Junction and ran to the Old Cut at SO 959944 (HCMS No. 2). Had nine locks. The branch was started in 1796 but did not link with the Old Main Line until 1849. It was abandoned in 1961 but its remnants were still visible until the 1970s. The last half a mile at the E end was still intact in 1994 (BCM autumn 1995 pp16,18).

Bradley Elms Minute hamlet nearly 1.5m NW of Bradley-in-the-Moors.

Bradley Green The central shopping area of Biddulph, under 1m SSW of Biddulph. Formerly in Knypersley liberty in Biddulph ancient parish. The name Bradley is of Anglo-Saxon origin and represents 'broad lea' (BHS p12) (BALH pp185,186,210). There was settlement at Bradley Green by 1383 (BHS June 1972 p29). The name occurs as Bradlegreen in 1577 (BALH p185). By the later C18 Bradley Green was a small village. With the opening of coals mines in the Biddulph area from 1800 Bradley Green grew to a large village by the 1840s and became the commercial centre of Biddulph between the period 1897 and 1913; Biddulph Valley Coal and Iron Works at Black Bull helped Bradley Green swell in size (HLS p112).

Bradley Hall Stood near Wednesbury Oak Furnaces (AMS p471) in the area of the present St Martins C of E Junior School. The ancient house on or near this site is said to have been called The Hoo, and gave its name to the Hoo family, lords of Bradley, and early occupants (WA vol 2 p90). On June 5 1635 it was the birthplace of Nathaniel Bisby (or Bisbie) son of Rev John Bisbie, vicar of Tipton, and Margaret, daughter of Anthony Hoo of Bradley Hall. He was the author of 'The Modern Pharisees,' 'Persecution no Persecution,' 'Mischiefs of Anarchy,' 'Korah and his Company proved to be the Seminary and Seedplot of Sedition and Rebellion' (HOTIP p195). By the late C18 the hall had become a farmhouse (SHOS vol 2 p172) (HOBLL p50). The same or another Bradley Hall was built or rebuilt after the mid C18. The house, occupied by a Mr Nailer in 1824, belonged to the early Coseley ironmasters. It is at present (1952) owned by Charles Udall (HC p80). Bradley Hall may have given its name to Hall Green and Hallfields.

Bradley Hall House on Mitton road, 0.75m S of Bradley, near Stafford. Represents the manor house of Bradley manor. NE of the house, part of a moat remains. The old house, of c1688, an L-shaped gabled structure was pulled down and rebuilt in 1939. The new house incorporates the original staircase and a stone fireplace lintel inscribed 'W. 1688' (VCH vol 4 pp75-76,90 il facing of the old hall) (SSAHST 1982-3 p36).

Bradley Hall Formerly at Towns End, S of the High Street on the Bromley Road, Kingswinford, in Kingswinford ancient parish. Dated 1596, timberframed (LGS p157). Shaw says part of the house was used as a RC chapel. It was the property of the Homfray family but tenanted (WJO Dec 1909 p323p). It was sometime a butcher's shop and also a farm of 15 acres run by a Mr Webb (TB July 1996 p5p). It was dismantled and re-erected in Tiddlington Road, Stratford-upon-Avon in 1924-5, where it is known as Bradley Lodge (BHOP2 p93p). (SHOS vol 2 p233) (SVS p132) (GNHS p181) (W pp181-182) (BCM April 1976 pp12-16. Jan 1991 pp20-22 ils) (TB Oct 1983 p15p of it being dismantled).

Bradley Howel House 1.5m SW of Flash (Dower's map). It was the home of

John Bradley in 1825 (VCH vol 7 p51) (UHAW p49).

Bradley-in-the-Moors Tiny hamlet 14m NE of Stafford. Former chapelry in Rocester parish. The name means 'Wood where boards were got' (SSE 1996 p11). The manor of Bretlei appears in DB (SSE 1996 p11). Later Bradley appears as Bradley Le Moors. There appears to have been a church at Bradley by the C12 (LDD). The present church, St Leonard, at the NW end of the hamlet, was built in 1750 and has not been altered since, which is rare (BOE p77). Became a separate ecclesiastical parish in 1744 (GLAUE p404). For the letters from two soldiers, the sons of a Bradley-in-the-Moors farmer, written between 1837 and 1848 which leave valuable portraits of life in Ireland, in the Aegean, and in India during that period see SHJ vol 1 pp42-45.

Bradley Loop Canal Small loop canal, S of Bradley, Bilston. Spurred off the Birmingham Canal Old Cut Old Main Line Canal to E of Weddell Wynd road and followed that road, then turned S and followed Batmanshill Road, then turned E and followed Turton Road to rejoin the Old Main Line at the end of that road (BCM autumn 1995 p16).

Bradmore Former hamlet (PENOP p7), now a suburb of Wolverhampton, 1m N of Penn. In Penn ancient parish. Bradmore had been identified as 'the plain' in the charter of King Ethelred 985. Later here were the Penn manor open fields (HOWM p10 note). In 1659 a farm called Bradmore was bequeathed by Roger Baker to support 18 poor people (PENOP p7). Bradmore was once famous for making gun locks. The pistol which William Howe shot dead Benjamin Robbins at Dunsley Hall (see) in 1812 was made at Bradmore by Obediah Wellins. The industry, which continued in a small way up to the 1950s, is remembered by the inn Gunmakers Arms in Trysull Road (PAIP pp76,77) (PENOP p8). The former No. 61 Victoria Road (E side) was a cottage whose second floor consisted entirely of an old railway carriage (broad gauge). The cottage, which may have been erected in the 1890s, appears on a postcard (Wulfrun Series GE Lee of Wolverhampton c1910). It had electricity and water, and two rooms upstairs and two downstairs. Between approximately 1948-1952 it was occupied by Mr and Mrs Jones; Mr Jones, who smoked, liked to smoke in the Non-smoking compartment upstairs. The cottage was demolished in c1960 when Lutley Close was built on the site (BCM Jan 1975 p30p) (TB Sept 1985 p4p. Jan 14 1999 p15p) (WPOPP vol 2 p63p) (PONP p91 il) (PENOP p63p) (PPTP p80).

Bradnop Small village on a high west-facing slope by the upper reaches of tributaries of Leekbrook 21m NNE of Stafford. Former township (with Cawdry) and quarter in Leek ancient parish. The quarter comprised Bradnop and Onecote townships (VCH vol 7 p82). The name appears in 1197 (VCH vol 7 p169), and in 1219 as Bradenhop (SSE 1996 p11). Plot calls it Nether Bradnop on his map (1682) to define it from Upper (or Over) Bradnop, 0.75m to the N. Confusingly, the 1834 OS map calls Bradnop Over Bradnop. 'Brad' represents Old English bradan meaning broad, and 'nop' represents Old English hop, so the 'broad enclosed valley' (OAKDEN) (SSAHST 1967 p34), alluding to the broad enclosed valley which opens to Cheddleton in the area from Ashenhurst to Apesford (VCH vol 7 p169) (NSJFS 1980 p2) (SSE 1996 p11). A former interpretation from Hackwood is that nop was from hupp, a sloping plain, which Brada conquered from the ancient Britons, this Brada being the later St Brades in the Oldbury legend (O p19). The manor was held by Hulton Abbey from 1223 to 1538; between 1547 and 1770 it was held by the Astons of Tixall Hall and later Ashcombe Hall (SSE 1994 p73) (VCH vol 7 pp171-172). By the mid C14 Hulton Abbey had a grange at Upper Bradnop (VCH vol 7 p171). The line of the medieval Earl's Way (see) passed through the village (VCH vol 7 p170). In 1973 two medieval or packhorse horseshoes were found at Sytch Farm (NSJFS 1974 pp139-140).

1500 to PRESENT. The Young Pretender's army came through Bradnop on Dec 4 1745 in the Jacobite Rebellion of that year (BPCSM p7). Bradnop was formed into a separate ecclesiastical parish with Onecote in 1862 (LGS pp196-197) (GLAUE p404). The school in the village centre served as a mission church from 1862 until 1990 when services moved to the neighbouring Methodist chapel (VCH vol 7 p175; the school closed in 1978) (LDD). The station on the Leekbrook to Waterhouses railway line to the SW of Bradnop village opened in 1905. It closed in 1935 (VCH vol 7 p171). The Bradnop ghost was said to be laid in the shape of a bird in a cupboard at Leek. The cupboard was then nailed up (NSFCT 1900 p145) (FOS p24). An Anson K 6283 aircraft crashed at Bradnop on Feb 17 1941. Two of the three crew survived (MD p51). The success of Jim Shaw of Bradnop in the battle of Waterloo was, according to the third verse of a ballad written by Joseph Allen of Onecote, due to his having been brought up on the Moorland dish lumpty-tums

That Bradnop man, Jim Shaw, who slew
Ten valiant French at Waterloo;

His nervous arm dealt them their dooms,
'Cause he was reared o' lumpty-tums.

(FSBC p45). Thomas Bond, prior to murdering Frederick and George Bakewell at Orgreave on May 31 1895, stole a colt and three heifers at Bradnop. He was executed for the murders on Aug 20 1895 (CCSHO pp53-68).

Bradshaw House 1.5m SW of Hollinsclough. Formerly in Heathylee township. There was a house here by 1429. The place name 'shaw' means a copse (VCH vol 7 p33).

Bradshaw Bradshaw Farm is 1m NNE of Ipstones. There was a farm at Bradshaw by the early C14 (NSFCT 1977 p11). The name may be from the Bradshawe family who were living at Ipstones Hall in medieval times (TOI p37). Fairies are reputed to exist at Bradshaw Farm (FOS pp45,46).

Bradshaw Hamlet 1m NW of Longsdon. Formerly in Longsdon township in Leek ancient parish. An estate centred on Bradshaw Farm existed by 1371, by when there was probably a property on the site of the farm. It was held by the Rode family and their relations from the later C15 to the early C19 (VCH vol 7 pp203,206).

Bradshaws, The Wrottesley. House 0.5m SW of Wrottesley Hall.

Bradwell House 0.5m S of Biddulph Moor (1834 OS map). Does not appear on current maps.

Bradwell Former hamlet now a suburb 1m NNW of Wolstanton, in Wolstanton ancient parish. Has appeared as Bradewull (1227) (SSE 1996 p11), and Brodewal (c1540) (LI appendix p172). The name means the 'broad spring or stream' (SSE 1996 p11). By Henry III's reign a manor of Bradwell belonged to the Aldithley or Audley family (HBST p125) of Heighley Castle (see). Henry de Audley held the vill of Bradwell and four other vills within Newcastle manor by the sergeanty of serving on foot with a bow and arrow at Newcastle Castle for eight days in war time (SCSF pp116-117). From the Audleys the manor passed to the Touchets who in 1401 granted it to Richard Sneyd and it was then held for many years by the Sneyds (HBST p125) (SNEDE). A Lanthorn fly or flying glow worm was spotted by Ralph Sneyd in 1678 at Bradwell. The first official noting of a Lanthorn fly was in mid-summer 1680 and the first official noting by a member of the Royal Society was in 1684 (NHS p236). The streets of a mid C20 housing estate to the NE all have names that have appeared in Arnold Bennett novels. At the junction of Cauldon and Oldcastle Avenues, stands the modern church, St Barnabas. From Knype Way two bright red cigar-shaped objects, one larger than the other, were seen on Aug 29 1967 at approximately 10.10pm onwards (FSRP p7).

Bradwell Hall Hall to W of Bradwell, Wolstanton. A hall here was standing in the C12 (NSFCT 1941 p39). The Sneyds appear to have had a hall at Bradwell after becoming lords of Bradwell manor in the early C15. In 1526 Sir William Sneyd (d1573), mayor of Chester in 1543 and 1566, moved back to Bradwell and enlarged the hall and created the first of the Sneyd gardens; he purchased Keele manor in 1544 which led to the Sneyds moving to Keele in the later C16 (SNEDE). For the Elers brothers activities at Bradwell Hall see Dimsdale Hall. The hall had been rebuilt by 1843, probably in Georgian times, and incorporates the medieval core of the former hall. It was occupied by William Sneyd until his death in 1836; his nephew was the owner in 1843 (HBST p125). It was bought by a Mr Twigg in 1951, and was in a derelict state by 1978 when still owned by the Twiggs (ES June 20 1978 p). There may have been a tunnel from the hall to Dimsdale Hall (see). (HOE p7 il of painting by Stubbs of Wedgwood family shows the hall through the trees on the extreme right).

Bradwell Old Park A medieval hunting ground of the Aldithley or Audley family of Heighley Castle (see) which stretched away in the direction of Chatterley along high ground. Bradwell Wood was probably inside it and Bradwell Hall just outside the southern fence. It had been recently disparked in 1686 and was then Sneyd property. Perhaps in existence as early as 1327, and is shown on Morden's map. The name Parkhouse, as in Parkhouse Colliery, suggests that its western boundary would have come up close to Chesterton village (NSFCT 1910 p172).

Brakenhurst Farm over 1m SE of Newborough.

Bramford Former name for hamlet to N of Mons Hill. Coseley. There is a windmill in Oak Street directly W of St Chad's church at SO 938932. The mill first appears on Yates' map. The machinery was removed in 1895. Was a private residence by 1974. (WBJ p18) (WIS pp9p,17) (STMSM June 1980 p40p) (BOE p108) (TB April 1983 p15p) (MR p112).

Bramhouse Over 1.5m SW of Cheddleton (1834 OS map).

Brampton, The Residential suburb 0.5m NE of Newcastle-under-Lyme. Formerly in Newcastle chapelry in Stoke-upon-Trent ancient parish. A Neolithic

or Bronze Age stone implement has been found at the Brampton (NSFCT vol 70 p85) (NSJFS 1964 p30). The name was used to describe a common field here in 1763 (SHC 1934 p69). Houses in Gower Street S of The Firs were bombed in June 1940 and a boy was killed (TSS p117p).

Brampton House Brampton House Academy attended by the novelist, Dinah Maria Mulock of Longfield Cottage (see), stood nearly opposite St George's church in Queen Street, Newcastle-under-Lyme (NSFCT 1925 p86). Brampton House was the birthplace in 1878 of Oliver WF Lodge (d1955), poet, playwright and son of Sir Oliver Lodge (PSS p342) (VFC p86).

Bramshall Ancient parish, manor (HOU p332) and village on a high shelf of land overlooking Dagdale Brook valley, 11.5m NE of Stafford. The name is probably Anglo-Saxon in origin and means 'Brum's shelf' (DUIGNAN). Or 'broom shelf' (NSJFS 1981 p2). Or '(place at) the broom-covered slope' (SPN p21). Or 'broomy shelf of land' (SSE 1996 p11). The manor of Branselle is in DB. Later forms are: Brumeshel (1195), Bromsholf (1272), Bromschulf (1327) (SSE 1996 p11) (SPN p21), Bromsull (SHC 1908) and Bromshall (mid C19) (W p770). The parish church, St Lawrence, in Church Croft, was built in 1835 and was preceded by a church of Edward III's reign (HOU p435) (BOE p77). The parish wake was on the first Sunday in Aug in the mid C19 (W p771). The (ecclesiastical?) parish was united with Uttoxeter in 1920 (TRTC p75). Capt Daniel Astle (1743-1826), an associate of Dr Johnson of Lichfield (see), veteran of the battle of Bunker's Hill and author of 'A Prospect from Barrow Hill' June 25 1777, was vicar of Bramshall. Mary Howitt, novelist, wrote about him (Life of Johnson. Boswell. 1860. p767) (BS p27) (SHJ spring 1992 p22). There was a station on the Stoke-Uttoxeter railway line, opened by 1849, at SK 055332. The Stafford & Uttoxeter Railway line, opened in 1867, had a station 0.5m to the SE at Bromshall Junction (IAS pp131,136). The civil parish was abolished in 1934 with parts being transferred to Uttoxeter rural and urban districts (GLAUE p404). For a rhyme about Bramshall see Checkley.

Bramshall Manor House Bramshall manor has been held by the Erdeswicks, Willoughby de Brooke, and Sir Faulke Greville. In 1865 the manor house was occupied by Dr Lassitter. It was previously in the family of Roger Warner for about 400 years (HOU p332).

Bramshall Park Medieval deer park enclosed out of forest. It was existence by 1413 (NSJFS 1962 p75). Many places with 'Park' in the name survive to the E and N of Bramshall. A house at SK 067335 on the N side of the Uttoxeter road is called Bramshall Park (1887 OS map 6 inch).

Brancot House 1.25m WSW of Tixall. In Tixall parish. The name means 'the cottage on the heath:' The heath being Tixall Heath (DUIGNAN). Or 'broom-cottage' (SSE 1996 p11), or 'the cottages near the broom trees' (SPN p128). In the C16 appears as Bromcote (SSE 1996 p11). There is also a Brancot Gorse (DUIGNAN). For Brancot's involvement in the Popish Plot see Tixall Old Hall. There was a terrible fire at Brancot farm in c1865 (OSST 1932 p47).

Brandon-on-the-Moor Small colliery situated between Albion gas works at West Bromwich and Bromford Lane, Oldbury and adjoining the hollow ware works of Izons & Co. Brandon probably had some association with the neighbouring Bromford which at one period was known as Brand Ford, but traces of the moor have long since disappeared. The colliery was in existence in 1883 (STELE March 11 1955).

Brandy Lea House 0.5m NW of Heaton. Formerly in Heaton township in Leek ancient parish. The name means 'a place in woodland cleared by burning' (NSFCT 1932 p53) (VCH vol 7 p186). Brandy Lea was an occupied site by the earlier C16 (VCH vol 7 p186), and has also appeared as Brandlee.

Brankley Tiny hamlet consisting of about three houses over 1.5m NE of Yoxall.

Brann Farm Between Offleymarsh and Lea Knowl (1834 OS map) (Dower's map).

Branston Village by the Trent 1m SE of Tatenhill. Former township in Burton ancient parish.

EARLY. A wooden (alder) spear has been found at Branston at SK 215215 (info KL Neal). In 1943 a human skull and bones of a near complete female skeleton of the period c7000 BC (**Mesolithic** period) were found in lagoons 800 metres SW of Gallows Bridge, Branston at SK 212202. In 1946 and 1948 excavations at the same site revealed the remains of ancient huts of the same period. The site was identified as a Mesolithic settlement, and as such was proclaimed by AL Armstrong to be the oldest known settlement of its kind in Britain (NSFCT 1953 p104) (NSJFS 1964 p16) (IVNF) (BTIH p9). In 1960 the tooth of a mammoth was found in a gravel pit at SK 215205 (info KL Neal, who was in possession of the tooth in 1999). Branston has been identified with the **Roman** settlement of Ad Trivonam (see). In 1942 a fragment of Red Roman pottery (Roman Tazza with finger-marked frill) was found in the Trent at Branston (info KL Neal); Roman mortar has been found at Lawns Farm (see) (NSJFS 1964 p17). At Branston Cottage was found an iron key and a mortarium fragment of Roman origin (HOBT p22) (NSJFS 1964 p18). Near Lawns Farm (see) there is a roughly rectangular enclosure with pits within and a ditch attached. Also a small irregular rounded enclosure with irregular ditches approaching it, and possibly a larger rounded enclosure attached (NSJFS 1964 p17). In 1868 in Lichfield Road was found an iron spearhead and fragments of pottery, together with a lead weight marked with an 'S' (?Roman) of Anglian origin (NSJFS 1964 p17).

700 to 1600. The **name** has appeared as Brentiston (771) (DUIGNAN), Brontiston (942) (SSE 1991 pp7,8. 1996 p11) (BTIH pp13-14), Brantestun (956) (SHC 1916 p97), Braunston (Plot's map 1682), Branstestun, Braunteston, Braneston (SHOS vol 1 p21), Brontiston and Brantestone (SPN p26). It is of Anglo-Saxon origin and means 'Brand's town' (DUIGNAN), or 'Brant's farmstead' (SSE 1996 p11) (SPN p26) or tun (SSE 1996 p11). There is a Anglo-Saxon burial site at Branston (HOS p13). An iron key, a mortuary vessel, an iron spearhead of 23 centimetres and fragments of brown pottery found close to the Leicester branch of the railway in Broadway Closes between Burton and Branston in c1860, were at first thought to be of Roman origin, but later stated to be of Saxon origin (BTIH pp10,11). The manor of Brantestone appears in DB. In the early 1540s overlordship passed to Sir William Paget of Beaudesert (SHOS vol 1 p8).

1600 to PRESENT. In 1870 Branston became a separate parish known as Branstone (W p540) (IVNF), but this was renamed Branston in 1958 (GLAUE p404). The **church**, St Saviour, Main Street, was built in 1864 (LDD). The original recipe of **Branston Pickle** is said to come from the experimenting of Mrs Graham and her two daughters Miss Evelyn and Miss Ermentrude at Branstone Lodge. Miss Evelyn did research work for Edinburgh University in cancer. She kept poultry in the orchard for the eggs she needed for her research, feeding them on cod liver oil and mash. The younger daughter, Ermentrude, did translation work for the BM (IRB p42) (SVB p40). In 1915 Thomas Lowe and Sons built at Branston the **National Machine Gun factory** for the Enfield Armament Company, which had an internal railway system; the company also built the houses nearby known as Wayside (see); and German POWs built the wall along Burton Road. In 1921 the factory was taken over by Messrs Crosse and Blackwell, who produced Branston Pickle. In 1927 the factory was taken over by Mr Harmon's Artificial Silk Company. That company used the Viscose process which used Carbon Disulphide, and this required the building of a 360-feet high chimney to carry the fumes away. In 1937 the chimney was demolished as it was considered too noticeable in the event of war. That year the War Department took over the factory as an Ordnance Depot. It was used for storing clothing and other equipment until it was slowly run down after 1962. It closed in 1964 (SVB p41) (ABTOP p73p) (info KL Neal); Martin Coles Harmon, a chairman of Branston Artificial Silk Company, was at one time 'king' of Lundy Island and introduced his own coinage to the island (IRB pp37-38).

Branston Hall Formerly situated on Main Street, Branston. The Sanders family are shown at Branston on Plot's map. Branston Hall, a neo-classical residence, was demolished in the 1960s when the houses and bungalows of Leamington Road were built (SVB p41).

Branston Hill Eminence also known as Kingstanding Beacon and Brunston Hill 475 feet high, situated in the Landswood Close area of Old Oscott (MNB p55).

Branston Houses Branston. In 1851 it was the seat of H Mason (W p19).

Branston Moor Branston. The name appears in 1499 (ANS p58).

Branston Pool Situated parallel with the canal at Branston (SVB p41).

Brantley Brook Forms county border W of Bobbington.

Branton Hill Hill N of Bourne Pool, 1m ESE of Aldridge. It gave its name to, or is from, a medieval open field of Aldridge called Brampthull, or Brantial (Guide to Bourne Pool compiled by Bryan Balsom, copy in Walsall Local History Centre). The hill has been quarried for sand and gravel since 1932 (SNAR p15).

Brass Hall Mentioned in the Hearth Tax roll of 1674. It has been identified with the later Cold Comfort (see), 1.25m ENE Hales (SHC 1945/ 6 p156 note).

Brassworks Farm 1m SE of Stone by the Trent & Mersey Canal at Little Stoke. The name is from a brassworks which stood here. It was a brass and copper wire and sheet manufactory begun by Vernon and Keys in 1794, who took some of their materials from the works at Oakamoor and Ecton. The works ceased in the 1830s (SIT). The farmhouse still (1999) exists but the farm closed in c1970s, later much of the farmland in the surrounding area was developed with housing.

Bratch, The Hamlet 1m ESE of Trysull, in Wombourne ancient parish. Name implies 'a clearing in the wood' (DUIGNAN p15). Or 'newly enclosed land' (SPN p146). The hamlet developed on the northern part of Wombourne Com-

mon. It was in existence by 1775 (Yates' map) (VCH vol 20 p200). The three locks at Bratch on the Staffs and Worcs Canal are unique in being an embryo form of staircase (IAS p205). There was originally a two-lock staircase where the bottom gates of one lock created the top gates of the next lock down. But they wasted so much water they were altered in the 1840s to make a unique system of three separate locks. The locks were restored in 1994 and re-opened by Sir Patrick Cormack, MP for South Staffs (VCH vol 20 p201) (Wolverhampton Chronicle Nov 27 1998 p16ps). Such a complex and unusual series of locks needed a lock-keeper and the lock keeper's cottage is by the top lock (IAS p205). Between this lock and the middle lock is the much-photographed octagonal tollhouse or office or look-out, described by the DoE as by Bumble Hole Lock (IAS p205). It is of c1800 with later alterations (DoE II). (BOE p327) (SGS p173p) (MR p392p) (F p308) (WWW p90p) (COS p66p). Nearby, at SO 868937, is a pumping station for Bilston Water Works and to supply water to Bilston. The building is dated 1895. It first supplied water in 1896 and was officially opened by RA Harper in 1897 (VCH vol 20 p217) (TB Nov 1984 p4p). Wolverhampton corporation took it over in 1959, and later Severn Trent Water took possession. The pumping station was made redundant in 1986 (BOP p93p), and has since been restored (info Michael Cockin). The building is in the Venetian Gothic style (DoE II) or in the Graeco-Roman Modern style (Staffs and Worcs Canal Conservation Area Booklet) or Scottish baronial (IAS pp205-206). Inside are or were two redundant steam engines of the triple expansion type, installed 1897 (DoE II); they were named Victoria and Alexandra when the works was officially opened on Aug 12 1897 (VCH vol 20 p217) (TB Nov 1984 p4p). (BOE p327) (BCM July 1980 pp20-25. Oct 1980 pp38-44) (MR pp392p,393) (WWW p91p) (COS p67p).

Bratch Common Former common in Orton township in Wombourne ancient parish. An area of waste was called The Bratches in 1644. Much of the common was enclosed in 1825; it was then known as Bratch Heath (VCH vol 20 p210).

Brazenhill Tiny hamlet 0.5m N of Haughton. In Haughton parish. The name has appeared as Brussenhull (1238), Brasvill (1575), Brazenhill (1657-1758) (SSE 1996 p11) and Brasnill (maps of Plot, Morden, Bowen, Yates), and Brizehill (1726) (SPNO p165). It may mean '?pers n + hill' (SPNO p165) (SSE 1996 p11). SAH Burne asks why it is given much precedence on C17 maps (ESH p31).

Breach Hall In Waterfall village. It appears to be the same as Breech Hall (KD 1888) and Breach Hall Farm. Breach House stands in the Breech Close area on the W side of Waterfall Lane (WOY2 p102).

Breadmarket Street Runs on the W side of the Market Place in Lichfield before Dr Johnson's House. Formerly known as Women's Cheaping until the early C19. Women's Cheaping means women's market (VCH vol 14 p41). This short thoroughfare was distinguished in past times by the title of 'Via Processionalis.' Along the street the clergy and lay members of the Guild of St Mary would move regularly in procession from the Church to the Guildhall where they administered the affairs of the city (LAL p10).

Breadham Oak Lost oak formerly on the Longnor-Ipstones road. Approximately at The Holmes on Yates' map (1775). Or now Broadham on the Reaps Moor road.

Breakback Hill The steep part of Darlaston Road at King's Hill, Wednesbury. The road was created across open land by a Turnpike Act of 1787 but was unpopular with local carriers because it was so steep (1834 OS map) (SNDB p44).

Bredon Brook Runs from Felthouse SE passed Back-of-the-Brook to the Hamps (WOY pl 6, pl 7 shows the stepping stones where Bredon Brook crosses the road) (WOY2 p43). Has also appeared as River Bredon (SPNO p6). A long stone over Bredon Brook creating a clapper bridge (WOY2 p10p), may be the cross of Waterfall Cross used as a footbridge at Back-of-the-Brook (NSFCT 1920 p162).

Brerehurst A member of Tunstall manor by c1130 (ONST 1976 p374). It has been identified with Brieryhurst (see) N of Kidsgrove, a township in Wolstanton ancient parish (W p289); others have located it to the Bull Lane area between Brindley Ford and Packmoor (ONST 1976 p374).

Brereton (locally *Bre-ten*). Village on a small hill by Red Brook on the edge of Cannock Chase, 9m SE of Stafford, but now considered a suburb of S Rugeley. Formerly lay in the parishes of Armitage, Longdon and Rugeley. Brereton has appeared as Breredon (1279) (SSE 1996 p11), Brereton (1412), Bruerton (Saxton's map) (SPNO p106). The name is from Anglo-Saxon, 'brier,' 'a bramble,' and 'don,' 'a hill' - so 'the bramble-hill' (DUIGNAN) (LGS p89) (SSE 1996 p11) (SPN p21). Mining occurred in the area from at least the early C19 (VCH vol 5 p149). With an expansion in population the village became a separate ecclesiastical parish in 1838 (GLAUE p404) and a district chapelry in 1843 (VCH vol 5 p166). The church, St Michael, on the W side of

Brereton Main Road, was built in 1837 (VCH vol 5 p166). In the later C17 Dr Plot noted at the Red Lion Inn a curious instrument like a mechanical hoe for rooting out gorse and furze out of sandy land, and on the Handsacre-Brereton road a holly tree growing out of the bole of an oak tree (NHS pp213, 344 tab 32 fig 2) (SD p20) (SHOS vol 1 p227). The most famous visitor to Brereton has been Dr Livingstone, the explorer, who came to lecture at Redbrook Lane School in 1857 and left his display map, as a memento; it now hangs in the church.

Brereton Cross Tiny hamlet over 1m SE of Brereton on Chester-Lichfield road, a medieval thoroughfare. Here was a cross at the start of a lane to Armitage. Here the manors of Armitage, Brereton and Longdon met (SHOS vol 1 p210).

Brereton Hall Brereton. A house which forms one range with another house known as Lanes End. A ground room at the S end of Brereton Hall had in the mid 1950s moulded oak beams, probably of C17 date. The general structure and layout suggest that a C17 house had a long mill or other early industrial building of slightly later date adjoining it (VCH vol 5 pp153-154). The hall was occupied by G Cockin in 1925 (SOSH pviii); probably GM Cockin, co-author of Neolithic Flints from a Chipping-floor at Cannock Wood (1917).

Brereton House Late C18 house at Brereton (BOE p77). The property was owned and occupied by Elizabeth Birch in c1842 (VCH vol 5 p153).

Breretonhill Hamlet following a lane running parallel to the Chester-Lichfield road SE of Brereton. Was this lane the old Chester-Lichfield road? Has also appeared as Brereton Hill (W p568).

Brettel Ancient former house 0.5m N of Amblecote gives its name to Brettell Lane district. The name is from a personal name, probably of Anglo-Saxon origin, 'Brihtelm' (DUIGNAN). Or the name is a corruption of Bredhulle - a reference to the ridge or hill which Brettell Lane follows (SNSV vol 1 pp45-46). Or the name, which first appears in 1614, is from the Brettel family, who lived in this area until the early C20; they lived in a large house at the top of Brettell Lane, which is now (1999) demolished (BCM autumn 1999 p59). Their name is possibly of Saxon origin, derived from Brithtelm (SPN p70).

Brettell Lane Former liberty in Kingswinford ancient parish (BHOP p5) and long village which evolved along a ridge lane, which took its name from a house known as Brettel (see) near Silver End; the lane forms the boundary between Kingswinford and Amblecote parishes. A bamboo fossil was found during the building of a railway near Brettell Lane and went to the garden of SVS author, William Scott (SVS p379 note). In medieval times the area lay in, or was close to, Kinver Forest (see); the horn blown by the ghost of a lesser lord caught poaching in the forest could still be heard in Brettell Lane long after his execution by flaying. A small village of Brettell Lane may have existed by the C16, and the name, which has appeared as Bredhull, was in use for the area by 1727 (BCWJ p106) (VCH vol 20 p51) (BHOP p5). On Aug 23 1858 there was a disaster on the OW & WR, at Brettell Lane, 14 people died and 50 were badly injured. Some say 220 were severely injured. A coupling snapped and certain carriages slipped back down the hill from Round Oak to collide with the rest of the train which it had previously been connected to. The carriages were very overloaded and it was surprising not more were killed (BCM July 1971 pp60-61. autumn 1999 pp71-72) (TB Nov/Dec 1972 p9; 40 died and 80 were injured) (TTTD p303). (Red for Danger. LTC Rolt). (Stanzas, written on the late Railway Accident near Dudley on August 23 1858. We all do fade as a leaf. Published by WG Proverbs, Britannia Printing Office, Princes End, runs to 22 verses). It has been described as the worst train accident that had ever happened in Britain to that date (TB Oct 1980 p15). The anchors for the Canberra (1961) were made at Samuel Taylor & Sons of Brettell Lane (BHOP p24p). By 1992 the longest stuffed toy that had ever been made was that of a snake measuring 274 feet and weighing 154.3 lb made in 60 hours by members of Brettell Lane Day Centre in Feb 1990 (GBR 1992 p218).

Brew House Stands or stood in the vicinity, or on the site, of Ashenhurst Hall. Seat of the Ashenhurst family from the C13 to C17. From 1667 it belonged to the Hollinsheads. In 1744 the Ashenhurst estate was inherited by William Stanley, who had Ashenhurst Hall (see) built.

Brewhouse Bank District of, and 1m NW of, Kidsgrove.

Brewood (locally *Brood*). Ancient parish and small town 10m SSW of Stafford. By the late C20 was a ward in Brewood civil parish.

EARLY. An axe-head of **Neolithic** or **Bronze Age** was found at St Dominic's School in 1985. It is kept by the Headmistress (BDH pp18,21). An axe-head of Neolithic or Bronze Age was found in the Engleton Lane Watling Street area (BDH p19il). A hoard of **Roman** coins was found at or near Brewood (GNHS p70). A Roman bronze statuette of a female has been found between the Penk and Engleton Lane on the E side of Brewood (BDH p32).

600 to 1500. The name has appeared Breude (1086), Breoda (1139), Breode (1151), Broude (c1150), Brewuda (1188), Brehude (1290), Breuwode (1306),

Brude (1462), Brerewood (c1540), Breewoode als Braywoode (1571) (LI appendix p170) (SPNO p35) (SPN p21). The first syllable of the **name** is of Celtic origin and means 'a hill' (SHOS vol 2 p293) (LGS p89). The ending is Anglo-Saxon 'a wood.' So 'a hill wood' (DUIGNAN), or 'the wood on the hill' (SSE 1987 p28. 1996 p11) (SPN pp21-22). Gelling thinks 'wood by hill called Bre' (NSJFS 1981 p3). Brewood can be seen to be situated in a high position if viewed from Watling Street (NSFCT 1908 p133). **Church** field, between High Green and Hockerhill, may represent the site of a Saxon church, or just a field which belonged to the later church (BDH pp52,58). St Chad reputedly preached at Brewood in c670 on a spot now occupied by the present parish church, SS Mary and Chad, at the corner of Church Road and Dean Street; it has some work of c1250 (The Parish Church of Brewood). The **parish** formed before 1086 and probably originally contained Weston-under-Lizard ancient parish (SHC 1916 p193). **Beating the bounds** was practiced in the parish (SCSF pp26-27) (BDH pp285-287). At the **wake** held on the Sunday following the September fair horse-racing was substituted for bull-baiting after 1835. The wake seems to have lapsed after 1918 (VCH vol 5 p20). Bishops of Lichfield have held Brewood **manor** since at least the later C11; the manor is recorded in DB. In the Middle Ages the tenants had to pay a pecuniary fine called Stuck on the feast of St Michael to keep the flood-gates in the brooks maintained (SCSF p119). Brewood remained with the bishops until 1852 when it passed to the Ecclesiastical Commissioners (VCH vol 5 p25). Brewood was a prebend in Lichfield cathedral for some time before c1176 (SSAHST vol 2 1960-61 p43) (VCH vol 5 pp35,40). In the later C12 an estate at Brewood including the prebend was given to the dean of Lichfield (so that every dean of Lichfield is Prebend of Brewood). The dean's manor house of his prebendal estate, or Deanery manor, was Dean's Hall (see). Although the dean lost his peculiar jurisdiction over the parish in 1846 the tithes of Brewood were still attached to the office in 1975 (WMAG Sept 1975 p19) (VCH vol 3 p93. vol 5 p35) (GLAUE). **Visits by bishops and kings**. Bishops of Lichfield appear to have had a manor house at Brewood in medieval times. It was known locally as 'the Bishop's Palace.' It is not known quite where it stood or what it looked like but it is believed to have occupied the E side of the Market Place, near Church Road (BDH p56) (W p444). The manor house had been leased out to the Vicar of Brewood by 1473 and no house is recorded by 1538 (VCH vol 5 p26). Glenhouse, formerly incorrectly called The Manor House, stands on the S side of Market Place (BDH 1992 p189). Bishop Roger de Weseham was at Brewood in 1253 and 1254 and retired here in 1256 and died the next year (VCH vol 5 p25). The importance of Brewood in medieval times is shown by the visits to Brewood of medieval kings travelling through their kingdom. The historian Gough described Brewood as that 'great old city (of Brewood) King John kept his court,' the description 'city' here is no more than literary licence (BDH p54). King John was in Brewood in April 1200, Jan 1206 (VCH vol 5 p21), and on Aug 18 1207 (SMC p170) (NSFCT 1909 p183) (R&S p8) (VCH vol 5 p21). Henry II was at Brewood in 1165 when he granted a charter to Newport (Shrops) (SOSH pp113-115) (VCH vol 5 p21). Edward I visited Brewood in Oct 1278 (R&S p10) (VCH vol 5 p21). It is fanciful but possible that a papal bulla of Pope Innocent III (1179-80), found on the NE outskirts of Brewood in c1985, had been attached to a document relating to a dispute between King John and that Pope as to the Archbishopric of Canterbury (BDH pp57il,56). As lord of Brewood the bishop of Coventry and Lichfield was granted a charter on July 28 1221 to hold a **market** for Brewood on Fridays. In 1259 the bishop was granted a market to be held in his manor each Monday. It was confirmed by Richard II some time between 1387 and 1390 (W p443) (VCH vol 5 p25) (NSJFS 1971 p50). The Monday market had been discontinued by 1680, but by 1747 a Tuesday market was being held. The Friday market was revived in Nov 1833 but been discontinued by 1851 (VCH vol 5 p25). Hackwood says Friday continued to be the market day until the market ceased at the end of the C18 (SCSF pp90,95). There was a very old **market cross** in Brewood until it was replaced by a market cross building in the later C17. This fell down in 1810. It was used by the lords of the manor for the Court Leet held at the annual fair in Sept. After the building was destroyed the Court transferred to the Swan Inn (SCSF p90) (HOB p5) (VCH vol 5 p25). In 1259 a bishop of Lichfield was granted an annual **fair** for Brewood on the vigil, feast and morrow of the Nativity of the Virgin (Sept 7-9). The grant was confirmed some time between 1387 and 1390 (VCH vol 5 p25). Moved to Sept 19 after 1752 (Whitaker's Almanac) (COOKE) (SCSF p98). In the mid C19 there was a second fair, free of tolls, held on the second Tuesday in May. The Sept fair seems to have lapsed after 1918 (VCH vol 5 pp20,25). The earliest reference to Brewood being a borough is in c1280 and the last in 1315-16 and then at some time borough status lapsed (NSJFS 1972 p68). The local **street names** Bargate, Broadgate and Westgate do not refer to gates in a town wall.

They may have referred to gates where market tolls were collected (BDH 1992 p250), or were the sites of tollgates (SPN p23), or the 'gate' part of the name means road or street (LGS p89). The two centre cottages of the Old Smithy Cottages in the lower end of Dean Street retain evidence of a single-story hall of c1350 (VCH vol 5 pp21,22 dias). There was a plaque on one cottage, but it was removed as it was deemed unsafe (COS p7p). Customs such as the ringing of the **curfew bell** at 8.00pm from All Hallowtide to Candlemas for 15 minutes had discontinued by the end of 1872. The ringing of the **'Pudding Bell'** in the church at the end of Sunday's midday service, and the ringing of the **'Pancake Bell'** for a quarter of an hour before 11.00am on Shrove Tuesday had discontinued by 1874 (HOB pp10-11) (VCH vol 5 p20) (SCSF p160) (WJO Aug 1907 p211). A meadow by Brewood Park Farm said to have been known as Hangman's field may represent the site of **gallows** (BDH pp74,75). There was a **pinfold** at High Green in 1680 (BDH p224). There was a **forge** in Brewood by 1485 (VCH vol 5 p20). A writer in GM in 1794 mentions **well-dressing** was observed at Brewood and at Bilbrook on Ascension Day (Holy Thursday) (SCSF p29) (FOS p103).

1500 to PRESENT. Brewood **Grammar School** was endowed or some say founded by Sir John Giffard (d1556), his son and heir Sir Thomas (d1560) and Dr Matthew Knightley (d1561) in c1550, the initiative coming from latter (VCH vol 6 pp149-152). It is described in a bill of complaint in Chancery in 1628 (LHSB 14) or in 1629 (W p445). Dr Johnson of Lichfield (see) applied and was rejected for the post of usher in 1736 (VB p78). The school was on the SW side of School Road in the C16 and C17 and disappeared in a reconstruction of 1856 (VCH vol 5 p23). Closed 1975 and the buildings used for Brewood Church of England Middle School from 1977 (VCH vol 6 pp149-152) (SHJ autumn 1989 pp35-38). **Alumni**: Richard Hurd DD (1720-1808), bishop of Lichfield and Coventry (mem in St Peter's, Wolverhampton); James Amphlett (1775-1860), editor of SA, Lichfield Mercury and Shrewsbury Journal, and poet, born near Stafford (PSS p461) (VFC p3); Rev Henry Higginson (1805/6-1871), the 'Roving Ranter' born at Pendeford Mill (see); James Hicks Smith (1822-1881), author of HOB (SH p133); Alfred Hayes (1857-1936), poet, born at Chapel Ash (see), taught at the school (VFC p63). C18 **trades** included timber and tanning. Agricultural machinery was manufactured in Brewood in the early C19. Some say Brewood was a lockmaking centre in early times but lost out to Willenhall and Wolverhampton by the C18 (SVB p42). Others say there was some lockmaking in Brewood in the C19 but it had declined by 1874 (HOB pp35,86) (VCH vol 5 p20). There was a **windmill** between Hyde Mill and the Kiddemore Green Road (BDH pp214,215), this could be Kent's Mill (see) at Hockerhill Farm. There was another windmill near Long Birch (see). The Shropshire Union **Canal**, built in 1835, passes on the W side of the town. Brewood and Coven (see) are mentioned in a ballad sung by boatmen. The **workhouse** was formerly in the lane leading to Kiddemore between Churchfields and Hockerhill. Between 1795 and 1811 it moved to Bargate. In 1837 it became the workhouse for Penkridge Union (VCH vol 5 p19). On Nos. 14 and 16 Shop Lane appear the inscription 'DVFAL BARA/ LLE/ 1873' (BDH p188). **Newspapers**. Nos. 2686 to 7655 of the Brewood Courier, an edition of the Cannock Chase Courier, appeared between April 7 1955 and April 9 1964. Nos. 4717 to 4995 of the Brewood Advertiser, an edition of the Cannock Advertiser, appeared between Feb 27 1969 and June 27 1974 (SHJ spring 1996 p12). The Staffordshire Newsletter brought out a South Staffs edition to cover the Brewood area in 1996 (Willings Press Guide 1997). **Natural phenomena**. In 1665 Brewood had a serious fire (ADD p22). In 1678 an earthquake shock was felt in the area (OL vol 1 p184). **Folklore**. The location of cottages known as Hell Cottages is uncertain, but they may have been those on the corner of Ivy House Lane and the Horsebrook lane at Cobblers Bank (BDH 1992 p333). Further allusions to the devil and hell in local field names may have given rise to this rhyme from Brewood:

> Blymhill Lawn where the devil was born
> Wheaton Aston where he was Christened
> Weston where he learned his lesson
> Church Eaton where he was beaten
> Watling Street Road where he took up abode
> Ivetsey Bank where he drank
> Bishops Wood where he stood
> Boscobell where he fell
> Gailey Pool where he was called a fool
> Langley where he was angry
> Pearce Hay where he was sent away
> Kiddemore Green where he was seen
> Hungry Hill where he took the pill

> Bargate where he ate
> Brewood where he was shoed
> Giffard's Cross where he lost his horse
> Horsebrook where he lost his pluck
> Tong where he was hung
> Coven where he was put in the oven
> Stretton where he was eaten
> Chillington Hall where he was finished off bones and all
> Boscobell where he was sent to hell.

(ABW p65) (BDH 1992 p333). Hackwood and Jon Raven given slightly different abridged versions (SCSF p166) (FOS p34). The Devil at Brewood and Kiddemore Green in legend was the subject of a lecture given to the OSS by FJ Cope on Nov 4 1927 (OSST 1928 p20). **Natives and visitors**. For **Col William Careless** see Broom Hall. **George Burder** (1752-1832), Congregationalist preacher, encountered a missile-throwing mob at Brewood in 1777 (VCH vol 4 p133. vol 5 p45) (SSAHST 1971 p52). Major **John Edmonstone Monckton**, 2nd Madras Light Cavalry, died at Bargate on Aug 2 1891; a horse-trough in Stafford Street is to his memory (VB p78). **Thomas Andrew Walker**, engineer, was born in 1828 at Broadgate House on S side of Market Place, Brewood. In 1879 he took charge of the building of the railway tunnel under the Severn, begun in 1873. Construction was constantly hampered by repeated floodings and the first passenger train ran through it until 1886. (plaque on Walker's birthplace) (NSFCT 1976 p54) (BDH 1992 p189). **A Bill**, author of 'Wrath of the Ice Sorcerer' (1988), and **Jimmy Lea**, bass guitarist with the 'Glam' rock group, Slade, were living in Brewood in 1989 and 2000, respectively (Stafford Post June 1 1989) (BBC 1 Midlands Today Feb 14 2000).

Brewood Forest Ancient lost forest created or enlarged by William I. In 1200 King John, after his visit to Brewood, gave the bishop of Lichfield licence to enclose a park - Brewood Park. Brewood Forest was disafforested in 1204 (SHC 1923 p300) (VCH vol 2 p337. vol 5 p26). Some think it stretched from Chillington and Brewood in the E to the Shrops border; others that it touched the bounds of Cannock Forest in the E. It stretched from Weston and Bishop's Wood in the N to Tong and Albrighton in the S (SL pp67,68). It contained one hay or division in 1139 (NSJFS 1968 pp40,48 fig 3). Enclosures which have been identified are Cowhay, Harriot's Hay(es), Pearse Hay (Farm), Wet Hay (Wood).

Brewood Hall Lies on the eastern outskirts of Brewood. Brewood Hall is said to have been the seat of William son of Roger Fowke in Edward IV's reign. It then descended with the Fowkes and from 1785 with the Moncktons to 1930 when Major FRP Monckton sold it to Mr CO Langley. The house in 1959 was built late in the C17 on a medieval plan (VCH vol 5 p37) (LGS p91). In the Victorian period its windows were replaced with ill fitting ones with cement quoins (BDH p97p of in c1900). In the later C17 Plot noted Ferrers Fowk, had created fantastic topiary in his garden to form several animals, castles etc, and a wrens nest in the Hortyard, all cut out of whitethorn (NHS pp380-381). There was a yew tree in the grounds wide enough for a spacious arbor (SD pp49,50).

Brewood Hall Brook Runs near Brewood (VCH vol 5 p19).

Brewood Park Park enclosed out of Brewood Forest in 1200 when, King John, after his visit to Brewood, gave the bishop of Lichfield licence to enclose a park two leagues in circumference within the woodland of the manor (VCH vol 2 p337). Permission to make a deer-leap in Brewood Park on the boundary of Cannock Forest was granted in 1206 (VCH vol 2 pp342-343). The park seems to have lain on the western side of the Penk opposite Coven. Park Lodge 150 yards E of Chillington Wharf perpetuates the name (VCH vol 5 pp24,26).

Brewood Water Erdeswick was mistaken in thinking this brook rose from Sheriff Hales and joined the Penk at Engleton, says Shaw (SHOS vol 2 p304). Has also appeared as Brewood Brook.

Brickbridge Area SW of Wombourne. An extensive housing estate has been built up here (VCH vol 20 p199).

Brick Hill In Hanbury parish (SGSAS). There is a Brickhill Farm 0.5m E of Newborough and the small hamlet of Newborough Brick Hill 1m SE of Newborough.

Brick House On E side of what became St John's Square, Burslem. Built by the potter, John Adams, in the early C17. It was the first brick house to be built in Burslem (VCH vol 8 p117). Now (1977) demolished (SL p100). It was the residence of Josiah Wedgwood I, born at Churchyard House (see), Burslem. Here he first received his future wife, Sarah, and entertained guests, such as the Duke of Marlborough, Lord Gower, and Lord Spencer in 1765 (ES Feb 15 1930 p3. Feb 22 1930 p3). Gave name to the pottery known as the

Brickhouse Works.

Brickhouse Farm Stood on the site of Rowley Regis manor house and near Rowley church, and may have incorporated parts of the original manor house. It seems probable that a de Somery of Dudley Castle (see) first built a 'brickhouse' here in the Middle Ages constituting a manor house for his Rowley Somery estates. Being of brick it was a sign of great wealth and was known as 'Ye Brickhouse' in the C16 and C17 when it was a rambling building of five bedrooms. Demolished after WW1 and an housing estate built on the site (BCWJ p37) (TB Oct 1975 p27). Whether the same as Brickhouse Barn? Or whether the Barn was the last remnant of the Farm? The Barn was sketched by Mr Wilson before it was taken down to make way for the construction of lock-up garages in c1950 (BCWJ pp54,58il of Brickhouse Barn) (BCM Jan 1979 il on front cover of Brickhouse Barn, p17).

Brickhouse Green Area of Rowley Regis. The name is now preserved in Brickhouse Road. Rowley Regis's Manor Green at Cock's Green was known in the C17 as Ye Brickhouse Green (BCWJ p54).

Brickhouse Street Quaint alleyway through which can be seen the clock tower on Burslem Town Hall surmounted by an angel (PPP p14p).

Brickkiln Tettenhall Wood. Long Lake Cottages were situated in an area known as Brickkiln (TCOP p43p).

Brick Kiln Wood A small copse on the Charnes to Whittington Road (BOV p86).

Bridestones A Neolithic burial chamber (NSJFS 1965 p33), on the Ches Staffs border, 1.5m W of Rushton Spencer. That part in Staffs lies partly in Biddulph ancient parish; Biddulph Common once stretched as far as the Bridestones before it was enclosed; and partly in Rushton Spencer township in Leek ancient parish. By 1936 the Bridestones were said to lie entirely in Buglawton parish, Ches (DPTB p3). (W p387) (SL p36). **Origins.** The monument has been assigned to the Early Bronze Age period (NSFCT 1943 pp64-65. 1946 p148), but recent opinion favours a date nearer to 2500 BC. It has been thought to be the burial place of either scores of people or just one chieftain (BHS June 1968 p11). The original grave was in the shape of a ship and it has been suggested that it was positioned high up looking over the Cheshire Plain to the Irish Sea so that the deceased could 'sail' away into the next world (The Remarkable History of Congleton. J Colin Jones 1983). The chamber is unlikely to have had anything to do with the hillfort, 0.75m to the NW on the Cloud, which, if it was a hillfort, has been assigned to the Iron Age (DPTB p9). The **original form** of the Bridestones is believed to be that of a thin lizard-shaped mound, 360 feet long by 36 feet wide, narrowing at the E end. Within the mound were several chambers. At the W end stood a rectangular chamber (the galley), 18 feet by 7 feet, divided by a slab with a porthole. One compartment was set aside for some ruling chief, in the other were placed his personal possessions, with food in pottery vessels. A pear-shaped chamber, 30 feet by 45 feet, to the E was supported by at least 13 pillars, some 12 feet high, which, interspaced with stones as walls, was roofed with slabs. Evidence of burning in the centre of this chamber suggests it was used for fire rituals. Two pillars stood in a line running away to the E of the pear-shaped chamber (DPTB pp4-5,7). The **name** may be from the Saxons (E p7), or possibly from the Vikings who called it the Breitha Stones, meaning Broad Stones (BHS June 1968 p11). Or it was named on account of a legend that a young newly-married bride of a general, who accompanied her husband to wars was killed in battle near the spot and this is her burial place (NSFCT 1896 p122). Or the name is from St Bride, a Christianised form of pagan, Brigit, the fertility goddess of the Brigantes, a tribe of the area north of the Mersey (DP p77) (SMM pp9,113) (PNPD). Perhaps from Brython stones, in consideration that the Brython people (Ancient Britons) built the Bridestones. But the Brythons did not arrive until some 1,800 years after the building of the mound (DPTB p9). The Bridestones may have been called Mystylowe (see) in the early C17. Rev JE Gordon Cartlidge, vicar of Astbury, Ches, thought the mound had been called The Bridestones prior to 1764 (DPTB pp31,33). It is sometimes now called Bridlestones (DP p77). The Bridestones was **rediscovered** in 1750 (NSFCT 1943 pp64-65). Rev Thomas Malbon of Congleton noted in Rowland's 'Mona Antiqua Restaureta' (1766) the mound was still more or less complete (DPTB p5). In 1764 it was destroyed, with much of the stone taken away for the turnpike road 60 yards to the S (NSJFS 1965 p33). The Bridestones were further mutilated when stone was taken in 1825 for the building of a cottage nearby (demolished in 1914), and the erection of Bridestones House to the N in c1866; the garden and drive of which cut through the site with some stones being used as garden features (SMM p8) (DPTB pp41,46). Some stones found their way to Tunstall Park (see), where some still remain (DPTB pp19,20-21ps). The leaning stone about 20 feet distant, to the NE, bears the same relation to the 'blocking stone' or sighting-stone at the E end of the chamber or gallery, to that of the 'Friar's

Heel' to the altar stone at Stonehenge, ie: it stands along the line of sunrise at the summer solstice. This suggests the Bridestones may have been built for astronomical use (NSFCT 1911 pp155-161ps. 1925 pp186-188 plan). In 1936 Prof Fleure and a party from Manchester University excavated the site in an attempt to determine the original formation of the stones, discovering that the gallery had been constructed with a paved court. During this year and in 1937 Margaret Dunlop restored the gallery and re-erected one of the two eight-feet high stones which stand on the E side of it (NSFCT 1937 p114) (LCAST vol 53 (1938) pp14-31) (NSJFS 1965 p33) (DPTB pp19,41). There was perhaps another investigation in c1939 (ES May 15 1939 p7) (NSFCT 1943 pp64-65). Today only the restored gallery survives with the two eight-feet tall stones at the eastern end of it; these stones make the Bridestones the tallest surviving single stone prehistoric monument in the Peak District (PDS&C p119p). Two man-made rock-lined caverns have been found in the garden of the nearby house. These certainly have some association with the stones. If they are not the second and third cistvaens referred to in accounts of 1766 and 1854, lying about 60 yards from the main cistvaen, then they probably contain stone which formerly formed a part of the mound (DPTB pp23-27ps). The Bridestones form a corner of a triangle formed by lay lines which connect Cleulow Cross, Ches, to Roche Grange to the Bridestones to Cleulow Cross (DPTB pp47-49). The ghost of a female draped in white has been seen in the vicinity of the stones (DPTB p46). On June 16 1991 a businessman claimed he was abducted by a UFO after he had stopped his car by the Bridestones (DPEM p45) (DPTB pp43-45). **Bibliography.** (Mona Antiqua Restaurata. H Rowlands. 2nd ed. 1766 pp319-320 plan) (SMC p169) (SOS p7; noted by Harwood) (SSC p130 in the intro) (GNHS p65) (Scientific Ramblings around Macclesfield. Dr JD Sainter. 1878) (ROS vol 2 p140) (WP p351) (SK pp182-185) (SC p147) (LGS p84) (S p70) (SOSH pp9p,10) (NSFCT 1928 p158) (OS Megalithic Survey. CW Phillips. 1934. vol 4 pp11-13,21) (LCAST vol 10 (1892) pp202-212) (Prehistoric Chamber Tombs of England and Wales. GE Daniel. 1950. p181) (STM July 1964 p37p) (SMCC p5) (SL p36) (CDPOPP p64p in 1907) (SMOPP vol 2 p21) (DP pp77,78 ils from Sainter).

Bridge One of three wards of Walsall municipal borough (W p639), and a ward of Walsall county borough from 1889 (VCH vol 17 p217). Probably takes its name from The Bridge (Bridge Street).

Bridgecroft House 0.75m SE of Bishop's Wood (1834 OS map). Not on current maps.

Bridge Cross 0.5m N of Chasetown. 'Byrdes Crosse' which appears in 1578 is probably an early form of Bridge Cross (VCH vol 14 p201).

Bridge End Hamlet nearly 1.25m NW of Leek at an ancient crossing of the Churnet. Formerly in Leekfrith township in Leek ancient parish. Appears as Bridge End in 1641. The hamlet developed in the earlier C19 after the opening of a dyeworks by 1824 (NSFCT 1885 p54) (VCH vol 7 p195).

Bridge End House 0.75m Sheen. In Sheen ancient parish. Close to Derbys border. There was a house here by 1772. The present house dates from c1800 (VCH vol 7 p242).

Bridge End Tiny district of Wednesbury (WAM p53). Hackwood suggests that the name Bridge End was in use in the medieval period (WAM p53), but Ede rejects this (HOWV p108).

Bridgewood Place near the original site of Red Cross, Knypersley. The name appears in 1327 as Brugge-Wode (BHS June 1972 p28).

Bridgtown Suburb of, and 1m S of Cannock, in an area contained within a triangle between Watling Street and Walsall Road. The area was developed throughout the C19 (VCH vol 5 p49). The church, St Paul, replaced an iron church which was becoming dilapidated in 1899 (VCH vol 5 p67). An old milestone made of a large block of red sandstone was found when widening Watling Street near Bridgtown. It read 'John Chester 53' which at first was thought to be a gravestone, but turned out to be 'From Chester 53' and was estimated to date between c1500 and c1700 and is interesting in that it gives the distance from Chester not to it (CCBO p48).

Brierley Former fragmented hamlet 2.25m ENE of Sedgley (W p198) (DUIGNAN), and liberty in the Lower Side division in Sedgley ancient parish (W p195) (HC p42). The name means 'Bramble lea or thorny meadows' (AMS p440), and has appeared as Bruer (1221), Brerley (1332) and Bryerley (1632) (HC pp10,14). The 'wood of Brierley' was held by Wolverhampton church in the C13 (HC p6). The name is preserved in Brierley Lane off Daisy Street, Hall Green.

Brierley Hill Large town in the Black Country 22.5m S of Stafford. Former liberty (BHOP p5) and chapelry in Kingswinford ancient parish.
1000 to 1500. The **name** means 'rough lea (pasture)' (DUIGNAN). Brer or Brere in Anglo-Saxon or Middle English means a briar, thorn, or bramble, so was, the thorny pasture (SR p3). Or 'glade of briers.' 'Hill' is a comparatively

recent addition (SPN p24).

1500 to PRESENT. The present town lies over a hill covered by Pensnett Chase in the Middle Ages (BHOP p5), and over the most westerly coal basin of the Black Country; here the coal was accessible at the surface; mining started at an early date (WMLB pp118,124) giving impetus to the development of a village. Brierley Hill, probably a small village by the C16 (BHOP 5), is first recorded as an inhabited place in 1619 (WMLB p126). The town grew in the C18 as a settlement of squatters where the lane from Dudley to Stourbridge crossed over common land (SPN p24). The squatter settlement occupied the steep flank of the Coalbournbrook to the S of St Michael's church (WMLB p126). The brick **church**, St Michael, in a commanding position between Bell Street South and Church Hill, was built in 1765 (BOE p80). Brierley Hill developed its own **wakes** festival when it was taken out of Kingswinford ancient parish. Its wakes were then held at Michaelmas, its church being dedicated to St Michael (Sept 23) (SCSF p106). Brierley Hill's **industries** were in iron, glass, and firebricks (LGS p92). Later industries included tin plating and galvanizing, holloware production and heavy steam engineering (MR p53). It is also known for its ornamental iron work, knit-wear, and ham and bacon curing (WMVB p37). The flames from the fur-naces and steel mills that used to light the sky over Brierley Hill gave rise to the saying

When Satan stood on Brierley Hill and far around him gazed,
He said: 'I never shall feel at Hell's fierce flames amazed.'

(KCPC p32) (BCSG vol 5 p64) (O p248) (SCSF p166) (FOS p35) (Sunday Telegraph Nov 13 1994 p19). The Brierley Hill company of Roberts and Cooper made a **steam ship** called 'Brierley' (TB Feb 1998 p6). In 1854 24 miners and their families emigrated from Brierley Hill to **Nanaimo**, Vancou-ver Island, British Columbia, on Hudson's Bay Company contracts. In 1954 contact with Brierley Hill by the descendants of the emigrants was re-estab-lished for their centenary celebrations (BHOP2 p59). Brierley Hill became a separate ecclesiastical parish in 1842 (GLAUE p404) or in 1848 (W p183). That part of Brierley Hill N of the church, continuing on the summit ridge, was developed in the last quarter of the C19 (WMLB p126). Brierley Hill **urban district** was created in 1894 (GLAUE p404) and enlarged in 1934 on amalgamation with Quarry Bank urban and Kingswinford rural districts to form Brierley Hill urban district (BHOP p5). This was abolished in 1966 with parts going to the county boroughs of Stourbridge, Dudley, and Warley, and the ancient parishes of Himley and Kinver (GLAUE p404). The arms of Brierley Hill urban district, granted in 1942, are: Or, a pale gules between two beacons sable in flames proper, and on the pale two roundels barry wavy argent and azure, on a chief gules two gold boars' heads and between them a golden roundel charged with a red rose with stalks and leaves proper. The crest is: On a wreath gold and gules, an anchor sable within and pendent from a circular chain also sable, and about the stock of the anchor a gold Stafford Knot. The motto is: 'Sine labore nihil floret' (Nothing prospers without in-dustry) (CH p338il). Brierley Hill station on the Oxford, Worcester and Wol-verhampton **Railway** line opened in 1858 and passenger services ceased on July 30 1962. The station was demolished in 1968. The road facing the line is West End, now Bradleymore Road (BHOP2 p65p). **Newspapers**. The Brierley Hill Advertiser, founded in 1853, became the Advertiser from Jan 2 1858. Between 1860 and 1870 it was edited by the short story writer, John Addison (d1911). From Sept 7 1907 the paper became the County Advertiser for Staf-fordshire and Worcestershire, and then the County Advertiser and Herald for Staffordshire and Worcestershire from March 14 1925. This paper ran until 1967 (TEBC2 p68) (SHJ spring 1996 pp12-13) (VFC p1). The County Ex-press; Brierley Hill, Stourbridge, Kidderminster and Dudley News seems to have run from Jan 5 1867 to Nov 21 1885 (SHJ spring 1996 p13). **Riots** occurred in the Dudley constituency at the general election on Feb 4 1874. Mobs assembled and outbreaks of violence occurred at Brierley Hill and other places (BCM summer 1995 pp69-73). Nine **high-rised blocks of flats** were erected in Chapel Street in 1965 in the area of the original squatter settlement S of St Michael's church (BHOP p17p) (BHOP2 pp16p,17p). A **panorama** from the church, clear in the 1930s (KES p48), is somewhat spoilt today by these flats which block the view to the Clent Hills; to the E, however, can still be seen the Bull Ring at Birmingham; Dudley to the N; the Wrekin and the Clees to the W. **Aircraft crash**. On March 16 1944 a damaged Halifax MK 3 bomber No LW413 crashed in Adelaide Street at 3.30am returning from a bombing raid in Germany. Mrs Bessie Rowbottom, aged 32, staying the night at her parents house, was killed; about 60 houses in the street were damaged or destroyed (BHOP p53p) (BHOP2 p53ps). The **ghost** of a grey-haired man in a grey suit has been seen in a new (1978) semi detached house in Brierley

Hill (MS&S p33). For Brierley Hill as a verb see BCM April 1971 p27. **Per-sons**. For **'Poor Old Cookey'** born in Brierley Hill, who allegedly lived to at least the age of 112 see Wordsley. Rev **Thomas Moss**, a poet whose poem 'The Beggar's Petition,' became very popular, was born in c1740 according to Lawley and others probably at Bilston (HOBL pp201-202) (BCSG p45) (VFC pp95-96); some say he was born in Wolverhampton (SVS pp155,156). He attended Wolverhampton Grammar School and became the first incum-bent of Brierley Hill church, erected in 1767, and was curate of Trentham in 1793. He is believed to have written the popular poem 'The Beggar's Peti-tion' which begins

'Pity the sorrows of a poor old man,
Whose trembling limbs have borne him to your door,'

in 1769, aged 23, but the work is not dated. However GM vol lxix p1014 claims that Dr Joshua Webster is the author of the poem, and in a subsequent volume of GM, a clergyman named Garret is presumed to have been the author. Moss stipulated that his name should not be affixed to more than 20 copies. He died in Stourbridge on Dec 7 1808. A second edition of Moss's poems was published in 1827 by B Guy Phillips (SVS pp155,156) (HOBL pp201-202). (GM vol lxix p1014. lxx p41) (SHOS vol 2 pp237-238 gives full poem and woodcut done by a boy of 10) (W p183) (BS p318) (CR p31) (PSS pp86-89 gives full poem) (SWH pp95-98) (O p247-48) (PSS pp86-89 gives full poem) (KES p48) (HOTC p38) (MR p53). For a time **Noah Cooke** (1831-1919), poet, born in Kidderminster, known as the 'weaver poet,' worked in the clay works at Brierley Hill (VFC p30). For **George Lovatt**, the 'Fat Man' of Brierley Hill, see Round Oak. **Joseph Lewis**, Musical Director with the BBC in Birmingham from 1923 and later in London, was born in Brierley Hill in 1878 (TB Sept 1997 p13p). A man called **Maughan** of Brierley Hill, known as Miser Maughan, a merciless rent collector, was murdered. The murderer was never identified (TB June 1984 p29). **Billy Hill**, a notorious bully, was murdered by Tom Millward, a former miner who Hill had been intimidating. The murder by a blow with an axe took place in Bull Street on July 16 1931, and was said to be in revenge for Hill had shamed Millward's sister-in-law's honour, or had courted her. Millward was charged with mur-der and would have been sentenced to death but the jury asked for mercy (TB April 1988 pp1,10-11. May 1988 pp10-11). **Ray Westwood** (d1982), foot-baller, was born at Brierley Hill in 1912. He played for England in 1934, and in 15 representative matches. At the end of his career he bought a newsa-gent's shop in Fenton Street (BHOP2 p76). **Robert Henry Wood**, a child-ren's writer, was born in Brierley Hill in 1923, and was living at Kingswinford by 1994 (VFC p145). **Archie Hill**, a late C20 novelist, radio playwright and broadcaster, was born at Brierley Hill. His autobiography 'A Cage of Shad-ows' describes his childhood in the slums of the Black Country (VFC p65). **Tim Longville** (b1940), poet, was born in Staffs, and was living in Brierley Hill in 1994 (VFC p87). **Paul Darby** (b1949), poet, songwriter and broad-caster on BBC Radio WM, was teaching in Brierley Hill in 1994 (VFC pp34-35).

Brierly Brook Area N of Bignall End, Audley. (Stoke-on-Trent A-Z).

Briery Coppice Former wood N of the Stour, at the SE end of Coppice Road, Hayseech. The name is preserved in Briery Close (SNSV vol 2 p21).

Brieryhurst Minute hamlet 1.5m NNE of Kidsgrove. (AGT p63). Brieryhurst is said to have been formerly Brerehurst, a member of Tunstall manor by c1130 (ONST 1976 p374), and later a township in Wolstanton ancient parish (W p289); others have located Brerehurst in the Bull Lane area between Brindley Ford and Packmoor (ONST 1976 p374). There is a spring well at Brieryhurst Farm, dated 1850 (WMC).

Brimstone Alehouse Codsall. Here ale was made out of the water from the Leper Well which was served in the later C17 (NHS pp101-102). This Brimstone Ale-house replaced the Leper House (AOW p94).

Brindleford Hall Stood near Prince's Road (BTRA p25p) at Tividale Hall, 1.5m SE of Tipton Green. Seat of the Sheldon family from the reign of Edward III. Lady Elizabeth Monnins was the first resident in the hall rebuilt in 1703 (TB Aug 1977 p27p). This or an earlier hall had an even more interesting con-struction than Haden Hall. It was honeycombed, according to legend with secret passages, some leading to Dudley Castle and others to Wren's Nest (BCWJ pp66,104-105). The ruins of the hall revealed to the Birmingham Historical Society in 1766 a secret passage with a skeleton of a horse and two human skeletons in a secret chamber, thought to be those of 'Rowley Jack' of Rowley Regis (see) and his accomplice, Rebecca Fox, who had disappeared in 1754; their exit must have caved in (TB March 1978 pp18-19). The hall, haunted by the sound of footsteps (TB Aug 1977 p27), was demolished in 1927. It appears to have had many names including Brinfield Hall, Brindfield

Hall, Pemberton Hall, Bradley Hall, or Bradley's Hall (TB March 1990 p20p) and Tividale Hall; the last giving its name to the current area of Tividale Hall.

Brindley Bank Etruria. Named after James Brindley, engineer and canal builder?

Brindley Bank On W bank of the Trent 0.75m NNE of St Augustine's, Rugeley. Here are some steps, called the Bloody Steps, leading down to the Trent and Mersey Canal up which Christina Collins's murdered body was taken dripping with blood, hence the name the Bloody Steps.

Brindley Coppice Wood which appears to have crowned the summit of Brindley Heath, a high point on Cannock Chase (1834 OS map). From Brinsy Coppice in summer 1698 Celia Fiennes said she could see towards Shrewsbury, the Wrekin and on a clear day, something of Chester (Illustrated Journeys of Celia Fiennes edited by Chris Morris. 1984. p148). For the origin of the name Brindley see Brindley Heath.

Brindley Ford Hamlet E of Newchapel. In Wolstanton ancient parish. Brindley Ford takes its name from James Brindley, engineer. There used to be a ford close to the Board School, which has now been culverted over (NSFCT 1938 p67).

Brindley Heath (locally *Brin'ley* BILP2 p14). Heath and road to the NE of Pye Green, Cannock Chase. All the Cannock Chase area Brindley names are from a forest keeper to Thomas Paget named Brindley who was living in 1595 (PCC p75). The road, Brindley Heath, was formerly called Ridgley Road and linked up Cannock, Hednesford and Rugeley. It was an old coach road which ran over Brindley Coppice and fell into disuse in the mid C19 when the railway was taken through from Walsall to Rugeley (PCC p75). The civil parish of Brindley Heath was created in 1934 (GLAUE p404). RAF Hednesford lay on the S side of Marquis Drive. It was operational in WW2 but had no airfield. A grid of regular tracks which linked the units of the base remain and represent the site (info Ron Balding) (1989 OS map 1:25,000). The story of it is told in 'Kitbag Hill' by Jake and Gale Whitehouse (SLM Oct 1996 p13). The base was taken over in 1956 as a camp for Hungarian refugees (VCH vol 5 p152). By 1984 part of it was Cannock Chase Visitors Centre with exhibitions focusing on the environment and natural history of the chase (CCM).

Brindley's Bath Pseudo Roman bath at Crompton, to W of Kinver. Presumably built by the family of John or Joseph Brindley of Union Hall. It is sited adjacent to a woodland stream. And there is a passage cut into the rock behind it (TB Sept 1989 p29il. May 1994 p15p).

Brindley's Heath N of Kinver.

Brindley's Mill Water-powered corn mill on the Churnet in Mill Street, Leek. The mill has long been popularly linked with James Brindley, the engineer, and stands, perhaps on the site of an earlier mill. The arches and keystones of the windows and doors are of a design associated with Brindley, and the building bears, on the first floor, the inscription 'TI(J) 1752 JB,' suggesting a possible connection between him and a local landowner, Thomas Jolliffe (EL pp14-15ps) (IANS pp83p,153) (BOE p172 note) (WTMS p146) (PDS&C p84p). Brindley lived in Leek from 1726 (SOSH p345) or from 1742 to 1765 (OL vol 1 pp157-158). He set up as a millwright in Mill Street in 1742 (VCH vol 7 p104). The mill was abandoned in 1940, or in the 1940s. The part containing Brindley's workshop was demolished in 1948 for road-widening. The building was restored and opened as a working mill and a museum by the Brindley Mill Preservation Trust in 1974 and received an award from the Royal Institute of Chartered Surveyors in 1978 (WTMS p146) (VCH vol 7 p104). (STMSM Oct 1980 pp10-13 p of Theodolite preserved in the mill) (ES April 26 2000 p9p).

Brindley's Row Row of cottages at Cross Heath, Newcastle-under-Lyme. Supposedly named after engineer, James Brindley (NSFCT 1938 p67).

Brindley Valley 'Deep' valley lying on the E side of Brindley Heath. Appears in 1735 as Brindley Slade. For the origin of Brindley in the name see Brindley Heath. Here was forge and a furnace in the earlier C18 (WMLB p81). The pools in the valley: Upper and Lower Brindley Pools and Furnace Pool (1834 OS map) and? Brindley Pool (1708) (SPNO p106), appear to have been made for the iron industry here.

Brindley Village Name for a lost settlement on Brindley Heath at SJ 993150, 3m NNE of Cannock, to E of Broadhurst Green. Sometimes called Tackeroo. The settlement began with the building of a military hospital, Cannock Military Hospital, with 12 wards in WW1. The hospital closed in 1920 and became a Ministry of Pensions hospital specialising in the treatment of shell shock patients (SLM Oct 1996 p13). In 1924 the hospital is said to have been taken over by West Cannock Colliery who housed the miners and their families of its No. 5 Pit in the redundant wards, so creating a village community. But to outsiders Brindley Village had a reputation for being the home of tough and unruly characters. By 1926 a club and school had been installed, and the hospital chapel re-dedicated as St Mary's church (probably the church, St Mary, at Brindley Heath which was dismantled in 1954 - VCH vol 5 p67).

Later, the inhabitants were re-housed on a new housing estate, the Brindley Heath Estate. By the late 1950s the buildings of Brindley Village had been demolished. Remains of the buildings could still be traced in the undergrowth in the 1990s (PCC p77) (Discover Cannock Chase: Brindley Heath Trails. Staffs County Council) (Discover Cannock Chase: Follow the Great War Motor and Foot Trail. Staffs County Council).

Brineton Large hamlet to the W of Dawford Brook 1m N of Blymhill. Former township in Blymhill ancient parish. The manor of Brunitone appears in DB (SSE 1996 p11). Later forms are: Brintona (1116), Brininton (1211), Brumton (1225), Brunton (1223), Broynton (1364), Brineton (Yates' map) (SPNO p129). The name is of Anglo-Saxon and means 'Bryni's tun' (SSE 1996 p11) (SPN p19), or 'Brown's town' (DUIGNAN). The house of 1678 in Blymhill parish, which Palliser thought was perhaps one of the first to be built in brick in the W of the county, is perhaps Laurels Farm (see). Dr Plot noted Sarah Wood of Brineton who was born in 1670 with two teeth which traditionally was supposed to be bad luck for life (NHS p271). Shaw noted at Brineton an alder tree standing in a meadow of rich soil by the side of a fountain. At one foot from the ground it was four yards round, at 25 feet it was two yards one foot one inch round and was 50 feet high altogether (SHOS vol 1 part 1 p100).

Brineton House Dates from the C17. The top story is described in 1958 as recently removed and the roof reconstructed (VCH vol 4 p64).

Brinsford Tiny hamlet 1.25m W of Featherstone. Formerly in Bushbury ancient parish (Seisdon hundred) but was transferred to Brewood parish (Cuttlestone hundred) in 1934 (VCH vol 5 p18). The name appears in 996 as Brunesford (SSE 1996 p11). It is of Anglo-Saxon origin and means 'Brun's river crossing' (SSE 1996 p11) (SPN p144). Or 'Brown's ford' (DUIGNAN). John Huntbach had a house here in which Lord Wilmot took refuge after the battle of Worcester (1651) (SHOS vol 1 p79 of the General History. vol 2 p184) (SMC p170), or Wilmot went to Northicote Farm (info Mark Whittaker). By the late C20 Brinsford was a ward in Featherstone civil parish.

Brisley Hill Penkhull. Appears as Bear's Hill in 1842. The Croft led to it. It was flattened or demolished in 1964 (PRA pp15,63,64p, 111). Is now Trent Valley Road (VCH vol 8 p178).

Bristle Hall Coley Lane, Little Haywood, and close to the Old Manor House. Built by Squire J Bristowe in 1540. The name, from a corruption of Bristowe Hall, has also appeared as The Old Hall (HAH p37il). Now lost.

Bristnels End Former hamlet which lay at the junction of Walsall Road, Wellington Road and Aston Lane, nearly 1m ESE of Handsworth, in Handsworth ancient parish. In existence by the C16 (MNB p40). Has also appeared as Bristnolds End, Bristnells End and Bristnall End (1759). In 1757 or from 1759 a windmill for paper making was erected at SP 067895, between Lozells and Birchills to the N of St James' church, on former Handsworth Heath, waste land belonging to Mr Wyrley, for William Hutton (or Hulton), the Birmingham printer and Birmingham's first historian. But his operation was unsuccessful, failing in c1761; the mill was sold in 1762. It was used for a while to grind corn and polish brass nails, and pulled down in 1794. Later, the mill house was converted to a small farmstead and run by a dairy farmer into the later C19. It was probably demolished before 1830 for building development (WBJ p26) (Birmingham and Warws Arch Society Trans. vol 88 (1976-7) pp136-138) (WIS p24) (HPPE p63) (MNB p43).

Bristol and Hull Canal Canal proposed by Richard Whitworth of Batchacre Hall to link the Severn at Ternbridge with the proposed Liverpool to Hull Canal near Shallowford. The canal, which would have passed along the valleys of the Tern and Strine to Newport, Shrops, would have continued on to Batchacre, Garmelow, and Eccleshall. It was never built but part of the course appears on the maps of Yates, Smith, Pitt (1817), and Cary (1787-1831) (NSFCT 1927 pp32-34).

Britannia Park Rowley Regis. Also a high school called Britannia near Blackheath.

Britch There was an area E of Compton, in Kinver ancient parish, called Britch by the early C19 (VCH vol 20 p122).

British Oak Inn Stallings Lane, Wall Heath. Built in 1684 as a solitary farm known as Duncalf's Barn after John Duncalf, because it was built on site of the barn where Duncalf reputedly died in 1677 (TB March 1974 p25p. May 1993 p7). John Duncalf, born in c1655, stole a bible from Humphrey Babb of the Grangemill at Kingswinford in or shortly prior to 1677. He promptly sold it to a maid living near Heath Forge, not far from Grangemill. Mr Babb soon came to hear of the maid's bible and Duncalf was shortly accused. He vehemently denied taking it, stating that if he was lying his hands would rot off. After working for a joiner at Dudley for two weeks his wrists went black and his hands started to rot. He then went to recuperate in a barn at Perton where his condition deteriorated. He was then committed by the Justices of the Peace to the care of John Bennet of Wall Heath in his native Kingswinford parish, who put him up in his barn. On June 21 1677 he died with both hands and legs rotted and dried hard (A Just Narrative or Account of the Man whose Hands and Legs rotted off: In the parish of Kingswinford in Staffordshire where he died June 21 1677. Rev JA Illingworth 1678) (NHS pp304-305) (SHOS vol 2 pp230-231*) (BCM Oct 1988 p34) (TB July 1978 p10. Nov 1982 p23. March 1987 pp10-11. Feb 1993 p15p facsimile of title page of the Illingworth Narrative).

Brizlincote Valley Estate Staffordshire. A modern housing estate 0.75m SE of Winshill, 0.25m N of Brizlincote Hall.

Broad Eye Former virtual island created by the twisting Sow and Doxey marshes, less than 0.25m WNW of St Mary's church, Stafford. The 'Eye' part may come from an Old English word meaning an island, although the meaning 'hill jutting out into flat land,' may be more accurate in this context (Place-names in the landscape. Margaret Gelling. 1984. pp34-40) (WSS p113). Another explanation is that the name is from some rampart or outwork that anciently commanded the passage of the Sow (W p319). It was first inhabited by St Bertelin according to the Saxon chronicles and Camden, and this has led it to be referred to as Betheney and Bethnei. Ethelfleda built her burh on it (W p321) (SSTY p217). The Stafford castle of 1070 was probably built at Broad Eye (VCH vol 6 p189): The 1900 large scale edition of the OS map of Stafford marks a castle site here. Broad Eye was recorded by name in 1290 (VCH vol 6 p189). A **windmill**, still standing, was erected at Broad Eye in 1796. It is sometimes referred to as Castle Hill Mill, Broad Eye Mill and Stafford Mill. There is a tradition it occupies the site of the fort of Ethefleda's burh (DoE II) (SSTY p217) and may even incorporate in the lower portions some masonry from one of the ancient castles on this site (OSST 1933 p38). It was built by John Wright, a banker, and Francis Brookes, who signed a 500 year lease for the land in 1795. They built it using stone from the old Shire Hall of 1586; the stone was advertised in SA on April 11 1795. On the windmill is a circular iron plate bearing the date 1796 and the initials 'J.W.' or 'I.W.' (SKYT p3). The royal coat of arms from the Shire Hall was set over the doorway although this was later removed to the Wragge Museum (see); no record of it now exists. The Wright family were still working the mill in c1818 (VCH vol 6 pp212-213). An engraving of 1830 shows a staging around the mill which would be necessary to reach the common sails but there are no holes in the stonework for timber supports. An apocryphal story is told of the miller and his boy: The miller judged there to be a wind at night if he heard the sound of an inn sign in the neighbourhood sqeaking as it swung and by this he would rouse his son to assist in mill work. Soon the boy grew tired of this and gained some extra sleep by oiling the inn sign until his ploy was discovered (WIS pp13p,22,36-37 il x). Steam power was introduced to the mill in 1847. The mill remained in use until the early 1880s. It was used as a grain store sometime after this (VCH vol 6 pp212-213) and the wheels ceased to grind in the 1920s. The ground floor opened as a shop in 1925 and closed in early 1930s. The mill remained unused and in a dilapidated state (SKYT p3p) until bought by Stafford borough council in 1993 (ES June 21 1993 p4p. Nov 24 1993 p5). The Friends of Broad Eye Windmill, formed in the early 1990s, then aimed to renovate the mill and set up an industrial heritage centre here. By 1997 they had re-roofed the building and had inserted glass into the windows. It opened to the public on May 11 1997 (ES May 10 1997 p3p). (SSC Etching by F Calvert c1830) (STM spring 1954 p24) (BOE p246) (IAS p188) (STMSM Aug 1978 p26p) (ASOP p20) (SOPP pl 29p) (SAIW pl 21p) (ROT pp36-37p) (SN Jan 25 1991 p12p. Aug 26 1994 p9p). William Fleetwood Gallaway was born at Broad Eye (The Life of WF Callaway. Eric A Lawrence. 1890).

Broadfield W of Hoar Cross Hall. Presumably lies beside the Pur Brook. (NHS p105).

Broadfield House N end of Barnett Lane, Kingswinford. Originally built in the later C18 on former medieval open field called Broadfield, hence the name. The house appears to have been rebuilt or remodelled in a Regency style by c1850 and was occupied from the 1840s to the early C20 by a family called Dudley. From 1949 to 1980 it was a local authority home for unmarried mothers and later a home and catering centre for the elderly. By 1980 the house had transferred to Dudley borough council leisure department who had the Duchess of Kent open it on April 2 1980 as a museum for the glass collections of Stourbridge, Dudley and Brierley Hill. The museum was refurnished in 1993, and the front of the house was returned to the Barnett Lane side where a structure wholly of glass - said to be the largest in the world - was erected for an entrance foyer (info John Smith caretaker in 2000 and notes by John Hemingway 1995) (DoE II).

Broadfields House 0.25m S of Chetwynd's Bridge. Elford.

Broadfields Farm On the N side of Edingale village. In Croxall parish formerly in Derbys, now in Staffs. Has also appeared as Broadfield.

Broadgate Hall 1.25m WSW of Croxden. Has also appeared as Broad Gate Hall.

Broadgatehall Brook and Drumble. The brook flows from Broadgate Hall to Fole where it joins the Tean.

Broad Hay Now Broad Haye N of Cheadle.

Broad Heath Hamlet 1.75m SE of Ellenhall. In Ellenhall parish. 800 acres of Broad Heath in Ellenhall, Seighford, and Ranton parishes were enclosed under an Act of 1720 (SHC 1941 p16). Rev John Nash vicar of Ranton witnessed a meteor of fire here which appeared like a globular and made short rests. It was seen at other distant places as well, on the same evening, Sept 20 1676 (NHS p20). Plot noted at Broad Heath a mare that gave birth to a deformed colt with only two hind legs (NHS p266).

Broadhill Hill, small common (THS p270) and tiny district 2m SW of Gnosall. In Gnosall ancient parish. The name Broadhill Common appears in 1839 (SPNO p159) and there were 43 acres of common land here by the 1950s (OSST 1956-59 p12). In an article about Gnosall reference is made to a hollow ledge in a sandstone ridge on Broadhill where Charles I fed his horse whilst marching with his troops from Stafford to Wellington in 1642 (STM Feb 1966 p25); this may relate to the Cavalier's Stable. At SJ 80331960 is a windmill, called Broadhill Mill and originally called Beffcote Mill. The mill had a very short working life and was used as a dwelling before becoming derelict in c1900 (VCH vol 4 p127) (EOP p87p of c1910). It was incorporated into a house called the 'Coffee Pot' in c1975 (DoE II) (STMSM Aug 1978 p26p) (WBJ p16 il xxvii in 1963 and il xxviii in 1979). It has been claimed that Snowdon mountain, 100 miles distant, can be seen from Broadhill (SPN p55).

Broad Holme Island in the Trent, N of the Isle of Andressey at Burton upon Trent. Trent Bridge currently crosses over it. But the old Burton Bridge crossed the Trent just to the N of it. Broadholm is said to be a corruption of Beresfordesholme (HOBTU p9).

Broadhurst Green Cannock Chase. Minute hamlet at crossroads half a mile NNW of Pye Green.

Broad Lane Hamlet in 1851 2m NNE of Sedgley, 0.5m SW of Bilston. In Sedgley parish. It adjoined the hamlet of Lady Moor (W p198). Has also appeared as Broad Lanes (SGSAS).

Broad Lane Mock Begger Hall stood in Broad Lane. By the late C20 Broad Lane was a ward of Essington civil parish.

Broadmans Bank House at Brown Edge, probably occupied in the early 1700s by Henry Hargreaves who died in 1738. He left his property to his eldest son, Francis Hargreaves, who appears to have rebuilt the house. There is an inscription 'F and A.H. 1742' over the E door. In 1851 William Broadman was living in the house. According to Hugh Bourne's journal he was one of the early non-conformists, being a member of the Wesleyan Methodist Society in Sandy Lane (BEH p13p). There is a street, Broadmans Bank, in the N end of Brown Edge.

Broad Meadow Area over 1.5m WNW of Chesterton.

Broad Meadow An island S of Lichfield Road, Tamworth, created by the Tame on N side and a relief channel on the S side.

Broadmeadow Field Open field which lay to the W of Wolverhampton prior to enclosure (SHOS vol 2 p165). There seems to have been a small settlement at Broadmeadow in the Middle Ages (HOWM p6). Later Broadmeadow Field was a venue for pugilist fights. In 1825 a race course was established here. It was laid out on land leased from Lord Darlington and later from the Duke of Cleveland. In 1878 the lease expired and Wolverhampton town bought it from the duke for West Park (see), with the race course moving to Dunstall Park (see). Has also appeared as Broadmeadow Fields and Broad Meadows (WP p19) (Black Country Calendar 2000).

Broadmeadow Hall C17 house over 1m N of Sheen, close to the Derbys border. In Sheen ancient parish. There was a house on this site by the later C16. The house was the Sheen manor house when the Sleighs were lords of Sheen in the later C17 to 1709; they having probably owned the house from the later C16. In 1825 the hall was offered for sale with Sheen manor. It was restored in the earlier 1990s after it had stood empty for some years (VCH vol 7 pl 32, 241, 244).

Broadmeadows House 1.5m NW of Horton, situated on former Horton Hay. May have been created when Horton Hay was divided into farms in the later C17. It existed by 1805 (VCH vol 7 p72). Seat of the Myotts (NSFCT 1932 p33).

Broadmore, The Minute hamlet 0.5m SE of Stowe-by-Chartley. Seems to have been formerly Broad Moor. In Stowe parish (W p423). The S&UR planned a short railway branch line to Broadmoor from a junction near Chartley, but it was never built (S&UR p7).

Broadmore Area about Hill Top, Warley (STELE May 24 1957) (ORR p64). The name is preserved in Broadmoor Avenue.

Broadoak 2m E of Withington, Church Leigh.

Broad Oak House 1.75m WNW of Kingsley. In Kingsley ancient parish.

Broad Ridding Farm Formerly stood in Nabb Lane, Alton, over 0.5m S of Alton. The Wilson family are recorded at Broad Ridding in 1705. The last Wilson to live here died in 1904. It was sold in 1918 by the Earl of Shrewsbury and became part of Newhouse Farm; this farm appears on the 1985 OS map 1:25,000 close to the site of Broad Ridding Farm, 'a few humps in the field' by 1996 (HAF p200p).

Broadstone Formerly lay to the E of Birchills, in Walsall foreign and ancient parish (SOB pp107,161 see map facing).

Broadwaters Near Moxley. Formerly in Wednesbury liberty. Ede has identified it with the coal pits 'near Bradeswalle' mentioned in a document of 1315; the second element representing a well or spring. However, Hackwood thought 'Bradeswalle' referred to the outer Saxon fortifications of Wednesbury burh (HOWV p106). Has also appeared as Broad-waters. Shaw and Pitt noted it was in a coal mine here that one of the first constructed Newcomen engines developed by Thomas Newcomen (1663-1729) and Thomas Savery (c1650-1715), for the extraction of water out of collieries, was tested. But the water here was too powerful for the machinery (SHOS vol 2 p120) (THS p154). Although in 1965 JS Allen identified the site to be at or near Lady Meadow, a part of the Conygree Colliery (SL p207).

Broadwaters Marsh Lay about Bilston and Wednesbury (AMS p3).

Broadway A ward and suburb S of Uxbridge in the Bond End area of Burton upon Trent. The Trent forms the E boundary of the ward.

Broc Hill Hill 500 feet high (OSST 1954-56 p17) on the edge of Cannock Chase to the E of Brocton Lodge. Perhaps, once topped with Scots pines, reputedly, planted by Thomas Anson to commemorate his brother's World circumnavigation in 'Centurion' 1740-44 (CCM), or planted in 1780 to add variety to the open heath country, which was within view of Shugborough (WMLB p77) (CCAP p39p of the Scots pines in 1950). In The Hole (see) on the NW side of Broc Hill were dwellings made into the hollow side. The name appears in 1836 and means 'hill frequented by the badger' (SPNO p31).

'Broc Hill' House on Brocton Road, between Milford and Brocton. Built in the C19 and described as a 'Superior Gentlemen's Residence, with enclosed meadow land, gardens and pleasure grounds' (BERK2 p53).

Brockholes Well 0.5m NE of Garshall Green. A well at SJ 975347.

Brockhurst Tiny hamlet on a hill by Lincoln Brook and another tributary of Mottymeadows Brook, 1m ESE of Blymhill, in Blymhill parish. Brockhurst is also the name of a rivulet. White says the rivulet gave its name to Brockhurst (W p441). There is a Lower Brockhurst to the N of it. Brockhurst was identified with DB Ruscote by Rev Ernest Bridgeman and his identification was accepted by Col Wedgwood in SHC 1916 p170 (SHC 1923 pp31-32), then appears as Brokhurst (1349) (SSE 1996 p11) and Brockhurste (1533) (SPNO p129). Parts of two moats remain S of the farm at SJ 824118 (VCH vol 4 p64p of on facing page of Brockhurst Farm) (CAMS p63) (SSAHST 1982-3 p35). The name Brockhurst means 'badger wood' (SSE 1996 p11). Ruscote is said to derive from 'rush cottage' (SSE 1987 p28).

Brockley Moor House 1.5m SW of Hales, SW of Old Springs Hall. Formerly in Drayton-in-Hales parish, Shrops (W p389). The name is from land here called Brockley Moor (SHC 1945/ 6 see map facing p82).

Brockmoor Village and district 0.5m NNW of Brierley Hill, in Kingswinford ancient parish (W p183). The name has appeared as Brockmeer (Plot's map) and erroneously Brockworth (Birmingham A-Z 1975 copy in WSL). The Brockmoor of the earlier C19 lay to the N of where it appears to have been centred (junction of High Street with Cressett Lane) by the later C19 (1887 OS map) (WFK p25). There was a Brockmoor Village (perhaps that to the N) and Brockmoor New Town in the 1851 census. The latter probably centred on the street called New Town just to the E of St John's church, N of High Street, built in 1844-1845 (BOE p80). This area appears to be now modern Brockmoor with 'Brockmoor Village' having now become Pensnett. In 1842 Brockmoor became a part of the new Brierley Hill ecclesiastical parish; it became a separate ecclesiastical parish in 1844 (GLAUE p405). Riots occurred in the Dudley constituency at the general election on Feb 4 1874. Mobs assembled and outbreaks of violence occurred at Brockmoor and other places (BCM summer 1995 pp69-73). There was a boiler explosion at the ironworks of Messrs Brown and Freers on Oct 11 1887, which claimed the lives of seven of its workers (TB April 1977 p25. May 1984 p14). There was an explosion at the Brockmoor House inn on May 26 1900 which killed the publican John Jackson aged 47 (TB March 1983 p5). The Duke of Gloucester officially opened Brockmoor Primary School on Nov 17 1994 (BCM spring 1995 p34). Brockmoor was considered a rough place in the earlier C19; yet

in the eyes of some it could be commended: A man named Webb, of Quarry Bank, in c1800 sings its praises in verse

> Where beautiful females step swift to the wheel,
> While others sit down and count knocks on the reel;
> If any young bachelor would alter his life,
> He must go to Brockmoor to choose him a wife,
> For they are modest and prudent, and never too bold,
> And there's no wife in Brockmoor knows how to scold.

(Old Brierley Hill. Dudley Teachers' Education and Development Centre. 1986 (originally published in 'The Advertiser' March 6 1887).

Brockmoor Junction Junction of the Fens Branch of the Stourbridge Canal with the Stourbridge Extension Canal (HCMS No. 2).

Brockton Hamlet 0.5m SW of Slindon. In Three Farms township in the Woodland quarter in Eccleshall ancient parish (W p376). The name means 'Brook town, or farmstead on a brook (the Sow)' (DUIGNAN). Or brook settlement (NSJFS 1980 p2). Broctone appears in DB as waste. A later form of the name is Brocton (DUIGNAN).

Brockton Brook Seems to rise in woods NW of Charnes flows to join the Sow NW of Eccleshall Castle.

Brockton Hall Brockton, Slindon. In the later C20 was the residence of the Hobson family, farmers (local info).

Brocton Large village in ravines and on the slopes of hills at the N end of Cannock Chase by Oldacre Burn (Brook), 4m SE of Stafford.

1000 to 1500. The name means 'Brook town, or farmstead on a brook (DUIGNAN) (SSE 1987 p28) (SPN p111). Or brook settlement (NSJFS 1981 p2). Or 'the settlement by the brook, or by the badger's den' (MR p56). For the use of Broc in place-names see JEPS No. 23 p27-47. Broctone appears as waste in DB (SSE 1996 p11). Later the name appears as Broctuna (1167), Brocton (1199), Brocton sur le Kannok (1327), Brocton sub Canoc (1342), Brocton juxta Bastwyche (1545), Brokton in Barkeswiche (1549), and Brockton on Cannock (1574) (SPNO p33). There was a medieval chapel, perhaps situated in Chappel Leasowes bounded by Nun's Lane or Nannas Lane which used to run off Walton Lane and ended in the vicinity of Milford (NSFCT 1923 p143) (BERK2 p66). Brocton chapel, certified in 1549, is not mentioned thereafter (SHC 1915 p25). A cross stood in front of the park in the road and was pulled down in 1780 and the stones were used to build the park wall (NSFCT 1923 p144) (BERK2 p63). There has been a manor of Brocton, known as Sowe and Brocton, and Brocton was a township in Baswich or Berkswich ancient parish (W p439) (VCH vol 5 p5). The pound stood opposite the post office and it was rather neatly constructed with stone coping and a stone gateway (NSFCT 1923 p144) (BERK2 p67). To the E side of the post office or pound were the village stocks (NSFCT 1923 p144) (BERK2 p67).

1500 to PRESENT. There was a windmill at approximately SJ 978205, to the NE about Oat Hill, which was not shown on maps later than 1749 (WBJ p16). There was a windmill by the pool on Bank Farm until at least 1820 (NSFCT 1923 p144) (BERK2 p73). Brocton became a separate civil parish in 1866 (GLAUE p405). The present church, built as a mission church in 1890, at The Green in the centre of Brocton village, was dedicated to All Saints in 1950 (VCH vol 5 pp7,10). Brocton Camp was built on Cannock Chase above the village for training troops in WW1. The camp was marked out in Jan 1915 and the first huts were erected in summer 1915. The camp arose on either side of Chase Road (built in 1915) which starts in Brocton and runs to SJ 977173 (HCMBOPP p84p). The camp was also served by a railway which ran from Tackeroo (see). The first troops to arrive were from the RASC to organise supplies for the troops which followed. The camp was mainly a training camp for Reserve Battalions of the British Infantry Regiments until the recruits of 'Kitchener's Army' arrived. New Zealander forces later used the camp, and part of the camp was used to accommodate German prisoners, many of whom died in a flu epidemic in 1918 and were buried in the German Cemetery on Cannock Chase (see) (BERK2 p82). In Aug 1923 a NSFC excursion visited the site of the dismantled camp and saw paintings which had been executed by German POWs (NSFCT 1923 p142). The Messines Model or Village of Messines was a concrete scaled model of the village and ridge of Messines, France. It was built during WW1 by camp occupants near the camp billets at approximately SJ 9780190 (Discover Cannock Chase: Follow the Great War Motor and Foot Trail. Staffs County Council), opposite the head of Hollywood Slade (RRCC p4). The model was 150 yards by 50 yards. A misconception has arisen that it was built so that units in training at the camp could familiarise themselves with the layout of Messines prior to the battle of the Messines Ridge in 1917. But it appears to be only a copy of a larger scale model built in Flanders for that purpose. The New Zealanders who built that model seem to have been later based at the camp and recreated the model whilst here. When they left the camp in 1919 they left the model to the town of Stafford (TFW) (BERK2 pp82p,83) (SLM Oct 1996 p13). Some say it was constructed by German POWs under the direction of New Zealanders (Cannock Chase: The Second Selection. June Pickerill. 1997. p123p). Others say it was built by Canadians (RRCC p4). At length it became overgrown and a local man took it upon himself to clear the undergrowth. But he died and the task was never completed, the concrete was left disrupted (RRCC p4). In Feb 1932 a local resident was removing overgrowth from the model or renovating it (ES Feb 10 1932 p4). By 1957 it had become completely overgrown again (PCC p21). It is rumoured that a man charged people admission to see the model (info Ron Balding) (CCBO) (CCF p229). An unidentified entity - a small body with a large head enclosed in a bowl - pushed a car, weighing a ton, up hill at Brocton, with ease in winter 1959-60 (FR vol 13 No. 3 p19) (MMSE pp199,287).

Brocton Coppice Wood with many old oaks to ENE of Brocton (SN May 1987 p14p of an gnarled oak) (MR p57pc). The oaks here have been thought by many to be the last surviving relic of the ancient oak woodland that once covered Cannock Chase, but others have said they were planted in 1760 (PCC p19). Evidence that a few of the trees were once coppiced has been noted since 1994 (WMARCH 1995 p66).

Brocton Field Seems to be a bare heath SSE of Brocton.

Brocton Grange Farm 4.5m SE of Newport in Sheriff Hales parish (W p480). But it remained in Staffs after Sheriff Hales was transferred to Shrops.

Brocton Green Small nucleus of timber-framed houses dating from the C16 and early C17 situated in the vicinity of Oldacre Lane and Chase Road (VCH vol 5 p4).

Brocton Hall Brocton. Replaces an earlier house, Brocton Manor House (see), which may have stood on the site of the present red brick hall or nearby. Built in 1760 (BERK2 p62p), or in c1760 by Walter Chetwynd, Inspector of Stage Plays from 1737 to his death in 1778 (COI p172) (NSFCT 1923 p144). Others say the hall was built in 1801 for Sir George Chetwynd Bt (F p313), or in the early C19 (BOE p80). Others say the present hall may incorporate a C18 house but dates largely from c1815 (VCH vol 5 p3). Middlefell says the hall was added to in 1815 (BERK2 p62). The hall has a semi circular colonnade to the bowed entrance front and the stone pillars are thought to have formed the entrance to the Chapter House of St Thomas' Priory, when it ceased to function as a Catholic centre in 1730 (BERK p60) (BERK2 p62). On the colonnade there was a meteorite which fell in a field near the old bailiff's house in 1850 and was found by a son of William Chetwynd (NSFCT 1923 p144) (BERK2 p62). The hall was the seat of WF Chetwynd in 1851 (W p19). When the Prince of Wales (George IV) was entertained at the hall by Sir George Chetwynd he slept in a room called 'The Eagle Room' (BERK2 p62). The hall belonged to the Chetwynds until 1922 when Mary Chetwynd sold it and 120 acres to Brocton Hall Golf Club, who were established here by 1923 (NSJFS 1971 p18) (HCMBOPP p76p). The top storey was destroyed in a fire on Oct 4 1939 and removed (BOE p80) (MR p58p) (HCMBOPP p76) (BERK2 p65). The house and or grounds are reputedly haunted by a grey lady (SVB p43). (SHOS vol 2 p325).
GROUNDS. To the S, by the approach from Brocton, is an octagonal brick dovecote, made Gothick by pointed and quatrefoil windows (DoE II) (VCH vol 5 p3) (SN Nov 9 1957 p14) (BOE p80) (MR p58) (F p313). The dovecote dates from the late C18 or early C19 and may stand on the site of an earlier dovecote (BERK2 p63p). Some gargoyles at Brocton Hall may be from St Thomas' Priory, Baswich (NSFCT 1934 pp72-73). Some ruins between the kitchen garden and a pond to the N of the hall, consist of two medieval arches which may be from St Thomas' Priory, Baswich (DoE II) (NSFCT 1934 pp72-73) (BOE p81). The base is of a different stonework and may be from an earlier Brocton Hall (F p313) or was part of the old bailiff's house and is probably of C17 origin (BERK2 p63p). There are two isolated walls with fireplaces at some distance from the house which Rev RG Jones thought were part of the old bailiff's house and probably of the early C17 (NSFCT 1923 p144). These may be the chimneys of Brocton Manor House (see) or Brocton Farm.

Brocton Hill Sometime after 1762 Lord Anson of Shugborough erected a wooden obelisk on top of Brocton Hill as an eyecatcher for Shugborough Hall. The obelisk had fallen down by 1817 and no longer exists; it had stood within Haywood Park (HOT p63) (SNTG p74) (F p313). Shaw mentions an obelisk on Lord Uxbridge's property, but erected by Lord Anson (SHOS vol 2 p325). It appears in Nicholas Dall's painting 'An extensive View of the Park and Monuments' (SNTG p74).

Brocton Lodge White stucco house at N end of Brocton. Built in the early

1800s. It was at first occupied by Henry, youngest son of the first Sir George Chetwynd, whilst William Fawkener Chetwynd occupied Brocton Hall (BERK2 p58p). However, Pitt says, in c1817 it was the residence of George Chetwynd, son of Sir George Chetwynd (THS p266). In 1851, when the house was called Brocton Villa, it was the residence of Henry Chetwynd (W pp19,440). The use of the Villa by the Chetwynds appears to have ended by 1861, from then on the house had a succession of different occupants. It became known as Brocton Lodge in c1916 (BERK2 p58).

Brocton Manor House Is the early Brocton Hall, which was built on or near the site of the present Brocton Hall (VCH vol 5) (BERK2 p61). There was a picture of it at Milford Hall. The last resident was Walter Chetwynd who came from Rugeley. His son built the present Brocton Hall in c1760 (NSFCT 1923 p144). A capital messuage in Brocton called Brocton Hall is mentioned in 1611 when the Craddocks were lords of Brocton manor. It may have been situated about 200 yards from the present Brocton Hall, where stone chimneys remained standing until the mid C20. But these ruins may represent the remains of another timber-framed building, Brocton Farm (BERK2 p61il of Brocton Farm).

Bromford Hamlet of West Bromwich. The name is an abbreviation of Bromwich-Ford, the Tame being forded here (SOWB p24). It has also appeared as Brand Ford (STELE March 11 1955), and is preserved in Bromford Lane and Road. (A History of Bromford 1780-1880. WKV Gale. 1980).

Bromford Junction Junction NE of Oldbury of the Birmingham Canal New Main Line with the initial section of the Wednesbury Old Canal and the Parker Branch (HCMS No. 2). Here was a tiny island in the canal for collecting tolls known as Bromford Stop Toll Island (Galton Valley. A Walkers Guide. Sandwell Metropolitan Borough Council. 1993).

Bromhall Grange 1.5m WNW of Hales.

Bromley Bromley Farm is 0.5m NW of Arley.

Bromley District and former liberty in Kingswinford ancient parish (BHOP p5) 1.25m ESE of Kingswinford. Plot noted a salt spring 0.5m E of Bromley (NHS p99). There is a mission church, St Holy Trinity, at Bromley (LDD).

Bromley Branch of the Stourbridge Extension Canal. Spurred off the Stourbridge Extension Canal S of Bromley Lane, Bromley and more or less followed the S side of Nanaimo Way (HCMS No. 2).

Bromley Brook It rises near Hookgate below the road from Broughton to Ashley Heath and strikes for Bromley Pool. Some have called this the Sow. Flows NW of Chatcull and Bromley Pool at Bromley Mill Farm to Chatcull Brook. Has also appeared as Chatkill and Standon Brook (NSFCT 1916 p58).

Bromley Green House or Farm 1.75m N of Whitmore. In Whitmore parish.

Bromley Hall Bromley, Kingswinford. It was in a ruinous state in the early C19 (SVS p134).

Bromley House Penn Road, Penn. Home of Vernon Lee Walker, trader in the New Herbrides who was murdered by natives on Pentecost Island on Dec 21 1887. There are two tinted glass windows to his memory in St Phillip's church, Pennfields (POAP pp38,39il) (PONP pp119-121).

Bromley Hurst Very fragmented hamlet by and to the N of the confluence of the Blithe and Ash Brook, former manor and township approximately 1.5m SSE of Abbots Bromley, in Abbots Bromley ancient parish (W p408). Here was possibly a medieval village, probably deserted in the C18 (SSAHST 1970 p34). For a time in the mid C16 Abbots Bromley was known as Bromley Hurst (AB p33). The manor was in the possession of the Pagets from 1545 to 1911 (AB pp33,39). A trial of witchcraft took place at the 1857 spring assize at Stafford. The accused was a 69 year-old publican from Thorney Lane, Abbots Bromley, who was accused of placing a spell on a farming family from Bromley Hurst. The family had been beset by family squabbles over the previous two years between the wife and the mother-in-law as well as cattle running dry, milk not cheesing and the dairy maid becoming ill. The old innkeeper was asked to remove the curse. But he only made matters worse; the farmer's child died and there were spectral visits from a phantom dog. Much money was also extorted from the family. This publican was sentenced to 12 months hard labour (STM July 1969 p27) (FOS p38) (SSE 1987 pp179-193).

Bromley Lane Tiny settlement on King's Bromley Lane. In Armitage ancient parish. Bromley Lane Farm is 1.5m ENE of Armitage.

Bromley Marsh Abbots Bromley ancient parish (W p409). Bagot's Bromley Marsh appears on 1834 OS map to E of Bagot's Bromley at the present site of Marsh Farm.

Bromley Park House 1.75m ENE of Abbots Bromley. Preserves the name of Abbots Park or Abbots Bromley Park (see), a medieval deer park formerly belonging to the abbot of Burton. By the mid C19, when it was enclosed, it contained about 1000 acres. It then belonged to the Earl of Dartmouth (W p408).

Bromley Pool Pool with Bromley Mill at E end of it, 0.75m N of Charnes.

Bromley Wood Collection of farms creating a fragmented hamlet 1.5m E of Abbots Bromley. In Abbots Bromley parish. Plot's map splits up Bromley Wood into two parts - Bromley Nether Wood (south) and Bromley Over Wood (north), which was in the approximate position of present Bromley Wood.

Bromshall Variant spelling of Bramshall (W p770). The S side of Bramshall village was known as Little Bromshall (W p771). At SK 064326 was Bromshall Junction, the junction of the Stafford & Uttoxeter Railway ('Clog & Knocker'), opened in 1867, with the Stoke-Derby line, opened by 1849. (VB p138). Bromshall Station was the name for the station on the Stafford & Uttoxeter Railway. (IAS pp131,136). The station on the Stoke-Derby line 0.5m to the NW at SK 055332 may have been known as Bramshall Station. Bromshall Tunnel was a single bore tunnel 321 yards long, on the Stafford-Uttoxeter railway line, at SK 050314. Formerly called the Loxley Tunnel (S&UR p30 p). The S entrance is near Aldery Bank Farm. (VB p138) (IAS p136).

Bromstead Hamlet ESE of Moreton. Formerly in Moreton quarter in Gnosall ancient parish (W p460). Has also appeared as Bromstead (1815. 1880) Bramstead (1834 OS map). Foot-and-mouth disease broke out at Bromstead in Nov 1967 (SN Dec 8 1967 p10).

Bromstead Common Hamlet 0.25m N of Bromstead Heath, Moreton (1972 OS map 1:25,000). This area also appears as Bramstead Heath on the 1834 OS map.

Bromstead Heath Former common land and tiny hamlet N of Bromstead, Moreton (1972 OS map 1:25,000). Has appeared as Bramston Heath (1674. 1749), Bromstead Heath (1793), Bramstead Heath (1834 OS map) (SPNO p159). At a farm-house here the Congregationalist preacher, George Burder (1752-1832), gave his first sermon in 1776 (VCH vol 4 p133) (SSAHST 1971 p52). Midway between Bromstead Heath and Orslow a 'Mill Hills' is recorded on 1817/ 1833 OS maps at SJ 800159, suggesting here was a windmill (WBJ p16).

Broncote Former estate lying on the Heathylee township side of Upper Hulme hamlet (W p743). The name is derived from words meaning broom cottage (VCH vol 7 p32). The estate existed by 1299 (VCH vol 7 p32). The house Bramcott appears on 1834 OS map. It currently lies within an 'island' formed between the old and the re-aligned Leek-Buxton roads. William, son of Baron Malbonc (who was given Malbonck Forest), lived at Broncote in Upper Hulme. There is still a cottage called Broncott in Upper Hulme in the C20 (HOLF p14) (UHAW p51 il).

Brookend Minute hamlet 1.5m NE of Stramshall. (Plot's map). In Uttoxeter parish.

Brook End The N end of Longdon village. Seems to have appeared as Brock End in the mid C19 (W p568) (1887 OS map 6 inch).

Brook Hall Sandon Road, Stafford.

Brookhay Tiny hamlet 1.5m S of Fradley. In Whittington parish.

Brook House House by corner of Biddulph Road and Peck Mill Lane, S of Brindley Ford (1834 OS map) (Stoke-on-Trent A-Z 1995).

Brookhouse The Brookhouse area appears to have been both in Botteslow township (HBST p526) (OS map 1834) and in Bucknall township in Stoke-upon-Trent ancient parish. It appears to have stretched from Brookhouse Farm in the W by Fenton Road by Ash Brook to the hamlet of Brookhouse Green (see) further E, in Bucknall township; to Big Brookhouse (also known as Brook House - see below) and Little Brookhouse, which lie still further E on the S side of Werrington Road; to Brookhouse Wood to the N of them (OS map 1834). The name 'Brookhouse' was used for a ward of Stoke-on-Trent district by 1991 covering the Bucknall, Bentilee and Ubberley areas, and appears to be from a house known as Brook House (see).

Brook House Black and white timbered house which stood at the bottom of Brookhouse Lane on S side of Werrington Road, to the E of Bucknall. It is said that it was so called because a stream actually ran through the kitchen; in the kitchen was a brick cistern into which used to flow a continual supply of water piped from a spring in a nearby field. Johnstone thinks it was probably named owing to its proximity to a brook; there was a disused bricked well in the cellars (WJ p14). It has also appeared as Brooke House and Brook House Farm (NSFCT 1940 ps of on origin site facing pA91 - original ps in Warrillow Collection), and can be identified with Big Brookhouse (1834 OS map); the house was known as Brookhouse by 1924. On the front porch of the house was the date 1636. It may have stood on the site of a much earlier house; there is a reference to a Brookhouse in 1589. It was then the seat of the Allen (or Alleyn) family; they remained at Brook House to at least c1710. The Allens were succeeded by the Ford family. In the mid 1970s the owner was Mr Mellor, who proposed demolishing the house and building a new one. In 1974 he sold the house to Ian Bailey for £2 so that it could be re-erected elsewhere and preserved. After a period of about four years Mr Bailey gained

permission to rebuild the house by a disused railway line in Smithy Lane, Knighton, near Mucclestone. Those stones lining the original cellar (thought to be from Hulton Abbey) still carrying mason's marks were also brought to the new site and used to line the new cellar. At 12 feet square the original hood over the fireplace is believed to be the largest in Staffs. Mr Bailey and his family were still living at Brook House in 1999 (WJ p14) (NSFCT 1988 p45) (info Ian Bailey and Norma Fradley).

Brook House Tiny hamlet or house 1m SW of Cheddleton. In Cheddleton parish.

Brook House Farmhouse on S side of Doxey Road, Doxey, occupied in 1921 by David Davies, aged 44, farm bailiff of Charles Richard Hambleton, aged 62, of Doxey House Farm, 200 yards to the E of Brook House; Hambleton owned both farms. In a mad frenzy Hambleton shot Davies dead in the foldyard of Brook House on Sept 22 1921. Hambleton was found guilty of murder, but insane (SA Nov 19 1921 pp10-11) (SN Oct 1 1921 p3. Oct 8 1921 p4).

Brook House House at Lea Laughton, Horton ancient parish, on W side of Horton Brook. It was so called by the later C16 (VCH vol 7 p65).

Brook House House SE of Lysways Hall, E of Longdon Green. In existence by 1887 (1887 OS map 6 inch).

Brook House Eccleshall Road, Stafford. Built in 1783, demolished in c1969. Appears to have stood to the N of the present (1999) Bristol Street Ford garage in Tillington (Old OS maps: Stafford 1900).

Brook House 0.25m SE of Uttoxeter.

Brook House 1m S of Wetley Rocks.

Brookhouse Green Small hamlet in the earlier C20 in the Twigg Street, Malthouse Road, and Wooliscroft Road area of S Bucknall, formerly in Bucknall parish.

Brook Houses 0.25m SSE of Uttoxeter. Appears on the 1834 OS map, and has appeared as Brook House (W p792).

Brook Houses Former hamlet N of Bramford and between Woodsetton and Swan Village, in the Roseville area. Marked on 1834 OS map.

Brookhouses Large hamlet 1m W of Cheadle. In Cheadle parish. Here is an old brass foundry. Copper and brass were smelted here and some walls in the district are made out of blocks of copper slag (NSFCT 1948 p122). Has also appeared as Brockhouse (NSFCT 1948 p122).

Brook Houses Small hamlet 1.5m W of Marchington. Appears on 1834 OS map. Formerly in Marchington Woodlands township in Hanbury ancient parish (W p561).

Brooklands A Kingswinford rural district council housing estate at Audnam. Developed in c1926 on fields between Audnam Brook and the rear gardens of houses in Alwen Street (SNSV vol 1 p53).

Brooklands, The House at Longdon Green, Longdon. Appears on six inch OS maps 1903 and 1924. Capt HS Stokes MC of the Welsh Guards designed the garden. He thought up the designs whilst in the trenches at Ypres in WW1 and he brought back with him from the Western Front a souvenir of a bush rose rescued from the garden of a smashed-up cottage in No-man's land, near Ypres. It was said to be one of 'The Seven Sisters.' At Brooklands it flourished vigorously, producing a mass of white roses touched with pink. A sundial commemorates that H.S.S. won the Military Cross in France on Sept 25 1915. In the shadow of a tree was a stone inscribed 'Herbert 1917 to 1920,' this being the Captain's memorial to a favourite tucan (CCF pp139-142). (SLM Aug 1948 p145p of the summerhouse).

Brook Leasow Brook which raises S of Whittington Barracks and runs in a ENE direction to the Tame E of Hademore. For the Iron Age settlements at its confluence with the Tame see under Fisherwick.

Brookleys Lake Small lake 1.5m SW of Wootton.

Brooklyn Farm Stood at the junction of Beeches and Aldridge Roads, Old Oscott. Formerly known as Upper Moor Farm. Brooklyn Technical College, opened in 1953, now (1983) stands on the site (MNB pp62,66,73).

Brooks, The According to Scott, the Mr Levington, an antiquarian and collector of coins and minerals, noted by Shaw (SHOS vol 2 p277), lived at the Brooks (SVS p184) near Blakelands, Bobbington.

Broome Small village, parish and manor nearly 2m WSW of Clent (VCHW vol 3 p33) at the SW foot of the Clent Hills, formerly in an enclave of Staffs in Worcs.

EARLY. There was probably a Roman road in the vicinity of Broome (Trans of the Worcs Arch Soc vol 39 (1962) p49). The field name, Castle Hedge, suggests according to an ancient tradition that there was a Roman station near Broome (Antiquities and Folk-lore in Worcestershire. Jabez Allies. chapter 4) (Broome: A Worcestershire Village. Geoffrey Parkes. 1978. p5).

1000 to 1500. Broome was part of neighbouring Clent manor and came to be annexed to Staffs with that manor. The two as separate parishes continued to form a curious detached portion of Staffs in Worcs until annexed to Worcs for parliamentary purposes in 1832 and removed to Worcs for all purposes in 1844 and put into the Worcs hundred of Halfshire (VCHW vol 3 p50) (SL p29). The present church, St Peter, in a triangle of land surrounded by lanes in the centre of the village, may have its origins in a church reputedly built by the first lord of Broome in the mid C12 (Broome: A Worcestershire Village. Geoffrey Parks. 1978). Broome was in Clent manor until Henry II granted it to Maurice de Ombersley in 1154. According to tradition he chose Broome because its descriptive name recalled the bright gold of the broom in his ancestral Anjou. Broome manor belonged to Black Ladies Priory from 1199 to 1539 (Broome: A Worcestershire Village. Geoffrey Parkes. 1978. pp5,7,9). The field name Hangman's Croft probably preserves the site of the manorial gallows tree (SCSF p123).

1500 to PRESENT. There seems to have never been any large house of any importance in Broom expect the rectory and a C18 house called Broom House (VCHW vol 3 p33). Noake, writing in 1868, noted that Broom parish had 'no manufactures or public works, no local squire, no mansion, no Dissenter's chapel, no church-rate disturbances, no Fenianium or agitation of any sort' (Guide to Worcs. Noake 1868. p78) (VCHW vol 3 p33). Thomas Dolman (d1745), Rector of Broome in 1709, was the guardian of the poet and landscape artist William Shenstone (1714-63). The village is celebrated by Shenstone in lines addressed to his first cousin Miss Dolman, beginning

> In Brome so neat, in Brome so clean,
> In Brome all on the green:
> Oh there did I see as bright a lass,
> As bright as ever was seen.

(GNHS p184).

Broome House House S of Broome church. A short time before 1780 the house was used as a scythe mill, with water power, and probably it was altered and extended about this period. Thomas Hill lived here between 1780 and 1820 (Broome: A Worcestershire Village. Geoffrey Parkes. 1978. pp8il,11il,13 note). In 1851 Broome House was the seat of Mrs Addenbrooke (W p19). (BOEW).

Broomfield Or now Broomfields Farm, Kingstone. In Abbots Bromley parish (W p409).

Broomfield Former rural area now covered by the Manor Road and Warley Road, West Smethwick. The name, which has also appeared as Bloomfield, is from two pastures known as Broom Close (STELE Oct 20 1951. Sept 26 1952 il of the area c1850).

Broomfield Hall Stood on the E side of Wellhead Lane, Handsworth. Built in the later C18 or early C19 (MNB p41).

Broom Hall House and estate 1m NNW of Brewood, in Brewood ancient parish. The name means probably from brom-halh 'the nook or corner where the broom grows' (SHJ spring 1997 p19). It has appeared as Bromehale (1150-2), Brumhale (1306), Bromhalle (1593), Brumhall (1664) (SPNO p36) and Bromwall (SHJ Spring 1997 p2). Broom Hall formed part of the bishop of Lichfield's manor until granted in c1155-1159 to the dean and chapter of Lichfield (SSAHST 1982-3 p37). Has been described as a manor since the C14. Later partly held by both the Giffards of Chillington Hall and the Lanes of Brewood of the bishops of Lichfield (as overlord); the Giffards held Broom Hall house until the early C20 (VCH vol 5 pp27-28) (SHJ spring 1997 p2). The Careless' were tenants of Giffard lands in Broom Hall from at least the mid C16. John Careless was tenant in 1656. In 1651 his brother Col William Careless (or Carlos) (d May 28 1689) was with Charles II at Boscobel (VCH vol 5 p28). There is a tradition that Col Careless was born at Broom Hall (NHS p274) (WJO Jan 1905 p350) (SHJ spring 1997 p2) or lived here (LGS p90). It has been asserted that the hall was demolished in c1884 (The Flight of the King. Alan Fea. 1908) and then rebuilt (LGS p90). But, according to Horovitz, this may be a reference to the demolition of a cottage on the Broom Hall estate, which may have been known locally as Carlos's birthplace, the birthplace of Col Careless (or Carlos). An alleged rebuild of this cottage in c1884 could not be found in 1997 (SHJ Spring 1997 p20). In 1959 the hall was described as a much-altered brick building of late C17 origin (quintessentially a late C18 building - SHJ spring 1997), which may have been surrounded by a moat (VCH vol 5 p28) (SSAHST 1982-3 p37). There is a modern memorial to Col William Careless in Brewood church and his grave (nameless) is said to lie in the churchyard (SM p523) (LGS p90) (SOSH pp213-214) (VB p78) (SGS p66) (BDH p144) (SPN p21).

Broomhall Grange 1.5m WNW of Hales. A bronze axe head, or celt, was dug up in the Tern Valley near Broomhall Grange c1910 (SHC 1945/ 6 p11). There was a grange here from the C12 to the Reformation belonging to Combermere abbey. The property was acquired by Sir Rowland Hill at the time of the dissolution of the monasteries. There appears to have been no

house here in the C16 nor between 1600 and 1700, but there was by 1726. On the death of Sir Rowland in 1561 the estate seems to have passed by marriage to the Corbets. It passed to another branch of the Corbets in 1823 and passed out of Corbets hands in the later C19 (SHC 1945/6 pp12,104,122-123, 209-210,260).

Broomhill (locally *Broom'ill* BILP1 p51). Now a suburb of Cannock 1m N of Cannock. In Cannock old parish. J Eric Roberts (d1991), author of 'Bilberry Pie' (1963) (BILP1) and 'More Bilberry Pie' (1966) (BILP2), both written in local dialect, was born and brought up in Broomhill (VFC pp113-114). There is also a Broomhill Common (locally Broom'ill Common) (BILP1 p51).

Broom Hill Obsolete name for the area at Lea Heath Farm, Lea Heath, near Drointon (1834 OS map) (Dower's map).

Broom Hill Eminence at Newton, Perry Barr (MNB p57). The name is preserved in Broom Hill Close S of Newton Road.

Brooms, The Former private house S of Stone. Formerly in the Beech quarter in Stone ancient parish. From Brooms Meadow, a field name in medieval times (SIS p25 see map). The house dating from at least the late C18 was later the seat of WB Taylor in 1851 (W pp19,362), and at sometime that of Clarke McIlroy JP (MOSP p30) (SSBOP p47). Thomas Godwin (d1857) was of Broome Villa, Stone (mem in Norton-in-the-Moors church). In the C20 it became The Brooms Hotel and was renamed Stone House Hotel in 1984 (SSBOP p47).

Broomy Leasow To the E of Kingstone, seemingly inaccessible by road or track. Has also appeared as Broomleasow.

Broomyshaw Hamlet to WNW of Cauldon. In Cauldon parish (W p751).

Brough Hall 0.5m SW of Ranton, in Ranton parish (W p402). Brough has been identified with the Veterum alias Veneris of the Notitia, a Roman station on the Limes Britannicus (see) of the Notitia (NSFCT 1902 p119). However, Veterum alias Veneris has been identified with another place in the north of England (VCH vol 1 p186). Brough has been identified by Erdeswick, Charles GO Bridgeman, and Gerald P Mander as the virgate in DB Bughale (unlocated) and is probably a mistake for Burghale (SHC 1919 pp157,158) (VCH vol 4 p125) (SPNO p155). Later forms are: Burgh (1283), Overborough (1392), Burrowehall (1537), Brough Hall (1547-1551), Broughhall (1601), Borrough Hall (1616), Bruff (1686), (NHS) (SPNO p155). The name means 'fort nook' but Gelling is unsure (NSJFS 1981 p2). Or 'manor halh (hollow)' (SSE 1996 p11). Burgh Hall is known to have existed and to have been in the possession of the Stafford family as far back as 1180 and even earlier (SHC 1919 p158). The present rectangular brick farmhouse dates from the late C17. The large rectangular moat surrounding the hall and stockyard was filled in c1950 (ESH p58) (VCH vol 4 p126).

Brough Park Public park to the N of St Edward's churchyard, Leek. The original part was given by William Spooner Brough (1840-1917), county councillor, alderman, and NSFC President (1878) (LR p33), out of his Ball Haye Hall estate in 1913. It was added to in 1921 and officially opened in 1924 (VCH vol 7 p148). The army of the Young Pretender reputedly camped in this area when in Leek in Dec 1745 in the Jacobite Rebellion of that year (ES Nov 28 1995 p8). The park is reputedly haunted by the ghost of a Roman soldier and the ghost of a man with a dog (GLS pp63-64).

Broughton Minute village on high undulating land above the head of the Sow, 12.5m NW of Stafford. Former township and chapelry in the Woodland quarter in Eccleshall ancient parish (W p376).

EARLY. Ward identified Broughton with the Roman camp, Rutunium (HBST pp6,15) (GNHS p118) (NSJFS 1961 p26).

1000 to 1500. Broughton is said to appear in the will of Wulfric Spot c1004 (BH p7). Hereborgestone (Broughton) appears as waste in DB (DUIGNAN). Later forms are: Borgheston, and Burghton (1281) (SHC 1914 p29) (SSE 1996 p11). The **name** is perplexing: It may be from the chief deity of the ancient British 'Ebor;' the place becoming 'Eboriton' corrupted to Eboroughton (BH p7). If of an Anglo-Saxon origin it may represent Hereburh's house (LGS p92), or 'fort settlement' (NSJFS 1981 p2), or 'fort tun' (SSE 1996 p11) (MR p60) (SPN p24). 'Here' in the DB form does not represent Anglo-Saxon 'army' (as in Hereford which means 'where the army went over') (BPS p53): the derivation 'army' in Broughton's name has been used to support the theory of it being the site of Rutunium. A possible medieval chapel at Broughton was replaced by the present **church**, St Peter, built in 1634. It stands on the S side of the Ashley-Eccleshall road and may stand on the site of an earlier chapel (The windows of St Peter's Church, Broughton. Brian T Swinnerton. 1976). The lord of Charnes manor had the right of hawking once a year through Broughton Grounds, or Gardens (BPS p128). At Broughton was possibly a **medieval village**, it was probably deserted between 1327 and 1524 (SSAHST 1970 p34), and lay adjacent to Broughton Hall; there were eight inhabitants to tax at Broughton by the C14, yet by 1524, there was only one (SPJD p67).

1500 to PRESENT. In the **Civil War** marauding parliamentarian troops are said to have damaged Broughton church windows (The windows of St Peter's Church, Broughton. Brian T Swinnerton. 1976). A hard slate-like marl had been located at Broughton by the late C17 (NHS p120). There was a sulphur well with vitriol in it in Park Meadow under Broughton Park Pale in the later C17 (NHS p105); it was a holy well (OSST 1944-1945) and may be the same as the Baby's Well (see). The church was a private chapel of the Broughtons of Broughton Hall (see) until they ceased to be lords of the manor in 1711 (ROT p7). The village became a separate ecclesiastical parish in 1787 (GLAUE p405). **Supernatural.** Local ghost stories include: i) local preacher who was scared of a black calf boggart under a holly tree between Dark Lane and Broughton which followed him (BOV pp50-51): ii) the ghost of George Holland seen at Upper Blore Pipe Farm in Langot Lane witnessed by the same preacher as above (BOV pp50-51) (STM Dec 1964 p35): iii) Mr Hulme and two other lay preachers returning together to Hook Gate through the district known as the Birches had three separate versions of the same vision of three spirits at the same time (BOV pp50-51), or Elizabeth Stonemason's ghost appeared to them (STM Dec 1964 p35): iv) Mr Oakley witnessed a flame and clouds of smoke floating across the sky coming from the direction of Charnes, at the same time a woman in Charnes Farmhouse called Mrs Cooper had hung herself (BOV pp50-51) (STM Dec 1964 p35): v) the spirit of a mother transmuted into the form of her little daughter appeared to a preacher as he was returning home to the 'Lees' from taking the Sunday School at Fairoak at a gateway leading into Bishop's Wood just below the Park House at the same time as her mother's death (the writer's mother) (BOV pp50-51): vi) a figure crossing the Eccleshall-Ashley road slightly S of Broughton church (info Bruce Braithwaite): vii). in 1892 turf sank on a murderer's grave in Broughton churchyard (FLJ 1909 p220). Miss **Rhoda Broughton**, novelist, spent her childhood at Broughton Hall (see). Sir **John Betjeman** (1906-1984), Poet Laureate, visited the village and described Broughton church as 'a small, late Gothic gem' (The windows of St Peter's Church, Broughton. Brian T Swinnerton. 1976).

Broughton Folly Farm WNW of the church at Broughton. The Sow rises just S of it.

Broughton Hall Ancient timber-framed house at Broughton. It has been described as 'the most spectacular piece of black and white in the county' (BOE p81). The present timber-framed house is built onto or over the original manor house possibly built by Roger de Broughton in the early C14 (BH p7). A descendant, Thomas Broughton, in 1637, altered and extended it, using great oaks from his estate to build a substantial four storey building. The initials 'T.B' and the date 1637 appear above the front door on the S front (LGS p262), a hole in the door is said to be a bullet hole (BOV pp3-4). Charles I is said to have stayed at the hall (BH p15). During the Civil War Thomas Broughton, a royalist, was heavily fined and the hall was requisitioned. After the war Thomas had to buy the hall back for £3,500, but died shortly after, in 1648 (BH p8). His son, Brian (made a baronet in 1661 as a reward for his father's loyalty) completed the building. Sometime between 1686 and 1760 the hall was faced in stucco (BH p16) (SPJD p67p) (ALW pl 57 in c1906). Sir Brian Broughton, 1st Bt, died in 1708 and his son, Sir Thomas Broughton, 2nd Bt, died in 1710. His son, Sir Brian Broughton, 3rd Bt, married Elizabeth, daughter of the last male of the Delves family of Doddington, Ches (but anciently of Delves Hall (see) Uttoxeter), and their son, Sir Brian Broughton, inherited both estates in 1727, and the family then moved to Doddington, Ches, or perhaps made Doddington their permanent residence from 1776 (ROT p7). Broughton Hall then descended with Doddington. Sir Brian Broughton (d1724), 3rd Bt, was succeeded by his son Sir Brian Broughton-Delves (d1744), 4th Bt, who was succeeded by his son Sir Brian Broughton-Delves (d1766), 5th Bt. He was succeeded by his brother Sir Thomas Broughton (d1813), 6th Bt, who was succeeded by his son Sir John Delves Broughton (d1847), 7th Bt. He was succeeded by his brother Sir Henry Delves Broughton (d1851), 8th Bt. His second son, Rev Delves Broughton (1812-1863) married Jane Bennett and their daughter, **Rhoda Broughton** (d1920), was a novelist. She was born near Denbigh on Nov 29 1840 and spent her childhood at Broughton Hall on account of her father having the living at Broughton. Broughton Hall forms the background for her first story. Her work includes 'Cometh Up as a Flower' (1867), 'Not Wisely but too Well' (1867), 'Goodbye, Sweetheart' (1872), 'Nancy' (1873), 'Joan' (1876), 'Belinda' (1883), 'Doctor Cupid' (1886), 'Alas!' (1899), 'A Beginner' (1899), 'Foes-in-Law' (1900), 'A Waif's Progress' (1905) (DNB 1912-1921) (Records of an Old Cheshire Family. Sir Delves L Broughton Bt. 1908) (Burke's Peerage 1967); she is said to have written parts of 'Cometh up as a Flower' in Broughton churchyard (STM Aug 1964 p33). Sir Henry Broughton (d1851) was suc-

ceeded by his son Sir Henry Broughton (d1899) (Records of an Old Cheshire Family. Sir Delves L Broughton Bt. 1908). The Broughton family sold the hall to John Hall in 1914 (BH p16) (SSGLST pp32-34) (ROT pp6-7), or in 1917. John Hall restored the hall and doubled it in size between 1926 and 1939 (LGS pp261-262) (BOE p81) (EOP p54 in c1908). Some say the hall was rendered of its stucco by Mr Hall in 1926 (BH p18) (ALW pl 57). Vernon-Yonge says it lost its stucco in 1917 and in the process some important finds were made including four sacred pictures, old slippers, a wine bottle with the Broughton crest, old letters and papers from Cromwell's period, all went to the WSL (BPS p174). The hall was let out to tenants and in the early C20 it was an hotel. Mr Hall suddenly died in 1930 and his son, John Hall died accidentally when he fell from a London building on June 9 1934, aged 22. There is a window to his memory in the Great Hall (BH p19) (SSGLST pp32-34). Between 1926 and 1939 a N wing in the same Tudor style was constructed (SPJD p68pc). From 1940 to 1951 the hall was used by The Grange Prep School, Stevenage (BH p19). Another school was also evacuated here during WW2. The two headmasters, Mr Park and Mr Thompson did not get on. Mr Park and his pupils returned in the summer term of 1943 to find their belongings out in the drive. A court case ensued which Mr Thompson won partly due to the testimony of the 10 year-old pupil, Michael Heseltine, later MP (BOV p86). Julian Critchley may have been a pupil at the other school, and here the two future politicians first met. The hall was donated by Hall's widow to the Franciscan Missionaries of St Joseph in Nov 1952 and it became their Mother House (BH p19) (NSFCT 1976 p25) (ROT p7). The Missionaries put the hall up for sale in 1993 and it was bought by Stoke-on-Trent businessman John Cauldwell by 1994 (ES Nov 19 1992 p13. Jan 26 1993 p15p) (CL Jan 6 1994 p63p). (SFH p40) (MR pp59p,60p from the rear). The author Frederick Forsyth attended a Stone Conservative Association event here in late 1997 (SLM Jan Feb 1998 p14). **The hall interior**. The Long Gallery, 58 feet by 17 feet, has a frieze with stories, beasts and monsters (STM May 1952 pp13-15,25. Aug 1964 p32p) (BOE p81) and an 18 feet refectory table which must have been built in the house as there is no passage or doorway large enough for it to go through (BH pp15,16). There is a tradition that during the Civil War some marauding parliamentarians shot dead the young heir to the hall who had leaned out of the Long Gallery window to shout at them as they approached. He is said to have cried 'I am for the King.' His blood, long stained the Long Gallery floor, and his ghost called **'Redstockings,'** after the red socks worn by it, haunted the hall in the C19 (BH p10) (SMM pp52-53). Blood-stained floor boards were replaced during the reconstructions in 1926 (BEV p39). The story may be a Victorian invention to explain sightings of the ghost of a boy in blood-stained stockings (ROT p7) (Braithwaite lecture at Barlaston 1996). (BPS pp57-58) (Secret Chambers and Hiding Places. Allan Fea) (BOV pp4,6-7) (RPG pp11,12) (SLM May 1952 pp13-155) (STM Aug 1964 p32) (VB pp156,157) (STMSM March 1973 p30 p of the Long Gallery. Jan 1977 p15) (SN Dec 20 1974 p6. Jan 11 1980 p3) (MMM pp90-92) (MR p60) (SVB p45) (Stafford Post Oct 6 1988 p4) (SN Oct 29 1993 p8) (The Good Ghost Guide. John Brooks. 1994) (GLS pp107-109). Above the Long Gallery, in the rafters, is a hiding place. It is called the 'King's Hole' from a mistaken tradition that Charles II once took refuge there. It was probably a priest's hole (BH pp15,16). During the restoration in the late 1920s ornate and unusual woodwork from Sizergh Castle, Westmorland, was used in panelling one of the upper rooms - now called the Sizergh Room (BH pp18p,19). Some C17 glass wine bottles were found in the hall in the 1920s (NSFCT 1932 pp120-122). In the Dining Room is a painting of Italian peasants 12 feet by nine feet (BPS p57). In the cellars are gravestones with the inscriptions still legible (NSFCT 1922 p131). A bay window in the hall has fragments of ancient glass in the top lights, one of them has the date 1651, it, or another, or all of them, are Flemish (CL July 23 1910 pp126-133 many ps). For armorial glass at the hall see NSFCT 1926-27 vol 61 pp65-71 il. A small cell leading off one of the cellars is known as the dungeon (BPS p59). The hall has an impressive staircase (ALW pl 57).

GROUNDS. The moat was dredged in 1922 and many finds were made (NSFCT 1922 p131). There was an old oak which lined the avenue to Broughton Hall, which, when in the saw mill was found to contain a Cromwellian leaden bullet (STM Aug 1964 p32). An ice-house is somewhere in the grounds and may have given rise to the story of a secret passage from the hall to Broughton church (BOV p4).

Broughton Hall Situated about one furlong NE of the turnpike road at Longdon Green near to Lysways Hall (SHOS vol 1 p226). Has also appeared as Brocton Hall. The possible moat to the E of Moat House (see), 0.25m WSW of Longdon, possibly represents the site of the hall, if the hall was moated (SSAHST 1982-3 p44). There was a hall here by Henry III's reign. A later hall was long in the possession of the Broughton family, and was sold by them to Simon Walton, whose great grandson, Thomas Walton, a member of the Corporation of Lichfield, was the owner in 1819 (SOS pp182,183). It was the residence of Misses Wakefield in 1872 (KD 1872).

Broughton Pool Sugnall Park, Croxton.

Brow Hill Hill on which Leek is built. On Dec 3 1745 in the Jacobite Rebellion the Young Pretender's army passed up the hill on the N side (BPCSM p3).

Brown Bank Farm 2m NW of Croxden. Formerly in Croxden parish. Transferred to Checkley ancient parish in 1934 (GLAUE p408). There was a farm at Brown Bank by 1722 (CDS p19).

Brown Brook Tributary of the Dove. The name is from Old English brun, 'dark in colour' (SPNO p6).

Brown Edge Large village and promontory of the south western Pennine Chain (SVB p45) 800 feet high (ONST 1951 p158) 19m N of Stafford. In Norton-in-the-Moors chapelry in Stoke-upon-Trent ancient parish until Norton-in-the-Moors parish was formed (W p400). It is thought that 'Brown' refers to the poor, uncultivated land of the edge and was inserted before 'Edge' to define it from the many other nearby edges (ONST 1960 pp229-230) (SVB p45) (BEH p5). The name was in use by 1599 (BEH p5), by then probably an inhabited area; some of the oldest properties date back to the early C17 (ONST 1960 pp229-230). The village mainly expanded on account of the many squatters coming to this area in search of work in the local coal mines and occupying the waste of Norton manor. In time these encroachments reached such proportions that the squatters were compelled by the manor court to pay a small annual rent (SHJ spring 1992 p15). At least one stone-built squatters' cottage, built before 1840, had survived through to 1979 (ONST 1979 p399). There is a pair of working men's clogs from Brown Edge at the County Museum, Shugborough. The village had grown sufficiently to warrant an Anglian church by the early 1840s (SHJ spring 1992 p15). The church, St Anne, School Bank, was consecrated on May 28 1844 (BEH p26) (LDD). Brown Edge became a separate ecclesiastical parish in 1844 (ONST 1964 p251) (GLAUE p405), or 1845 (LGS p93). There is a bell ringing custom at Brown Edge. On Christmas Day bells are rung at 6.00am, 6.30am, 7.30am, 10.30am. Previously, on Christmas Eve the bell ringers tour the village with hand bells and enter several houses where one takes off his coat and places it on a table. As the changes are rung, the bells are shifted from one hand to the next, then laid on the overcoat to be picked up by the next man. When the bells have come into rounds the leader calls stand. Then out comes the music, suitable Christmas hymns and carols are rung on the bells (SLM winter 1955 p25). The custom of souling and guising on All Soul's day was still in evidence at Brown Edge in the 1960s. To some extent Brown Edge inhabitants still (2000) use family nicknames, principally but not exclusively, to differentiate between different branches of families of the same name (info Peter & Janet Turner). Spout Well in Sandy Lane was dressed with flowers in June from at least 1921 until the late 1940s. It was originally staged jointly with Brown Edge's Hospital Saturday (ES April 25 1998 p19p). Dressing Spout Well and another well, Sytch Trough in Sytch Road, is to be revived in July 2000 (ES Feb 21 2000 p7). A Liberator B24 aircraft crashed at Brown Edge in WW2. All the crew survived including an American army nurse (MD p54).

Brown Edge Common Occupied some of the Marshes Hill area (BEH p28).

Brown Fields House which occurs on the 1834 OS map approximately at the corner of Ubberley Road and Beverley Drive, Ubberley.

Brownfields Works Pottery works at the junction of Waterloo Road and Elder Road, Cobridge. Messrs Myott's factory went on to occupy part of the site. Founded by the Brownfield family. Brownfields made a vase for Gladstone which was presented to him when on a visit to the Potteries (ES Sept 13 1930 p3p). Edward Arthur Brownfield (1853-1939) and Ludwig Jahn, Brownfields' artistic director, created the largest single piece of china ever made. The 11 feet high, six feet in diameter vase was known as 'The Brownfields Vase.' It was fashioned in the Louis XV style and the modelling was completed by French sculptor Monsieur Carrier. It never reached the great Paris Exhibition of 1878, for which it was made. However it was exhibited at Crystal Palace in 1879 and in 1884, and at Paris in 1889. It was destroyed in a fire at the works in 1894 (SLM April 1948 p95p) (POTP p52).

Brown Heath Common land at Acton, near Butterton (Newcastle). Enclosed in 1796 (SHC 1933 part 33 p99).

Brownhill Former name of Warslow Hall (OL vol 1 p199), 0.5m NNE of Warslow. There was a house at Brownhill by 1515. Upper Brownhill Farm 0.25m W of Warslow Hall is part C17 in origin (VCH vol 7 p57).

Brownhills Area N of Burslem. Formerly in Burslem chapelry in Stoke-upon-Trent ancient parish (W p269). Is the area which lies to the N of the road from Longport to Tunstall. Brownhills was the name of a plot of pasture owned by the Burslem family at the end of the C16, and was inhabited by the mid C18 (VCH vol 8 p106). For William Littler (1724-1784) of Brownhills, soft-paste

porcelain manufacturer see Longton Hall Works. At Brownhills was cut the first sod of the Trent and Mersey Canal by Josiah Wedgwood I, with Brindley present, on July 26 1766 (NSFCT 1938 p60). There was a toll house at Brownhills on the turnpike road (UDC vol 2 pp12 il facing, 15) (ES June 7 1932 p5 il), now demolished (TFTP pp106-107) (SHST p23p in 1871).

Brownhills Late C19 town on high former boggy common land near the source of Ford Brook 14m SSE of Stafford. Formerly partly in Norton Canes ancient parish (W p573) and partly in the extra parochial liberty of Ogley Hay. No town of Brownhills existed prior to the mid C19. The **name**, the earliest reference to which is said to be on Plot's map where it is located between present day Clayhanger and Birch Coppice (BLHT), originally appears to have been applied to hills here (SPN p25). **Highwaymen** operated on the main highway from London to Holyhead which ran through Brownhills until 1752, when it was re-routed via Birmingham and Wolverhampton (WAM p35) (QVTM p70). Dick Turpin on 'Black Bess' is said to have jumped the toll bar on the old Chester turnpike road at Brownhills to avoid paying the fee (BWWOPP p3p of the old Toll House at Anchor Bridge, Brownhills c1910). **Growth of the town from the C19**. In 1837 most of Ogley Hay liberty was purchased by Charles Foster Cotterill who over the next ten years set about developing it with industry and housing for new collieries, and in doing so had some of the streets of the future town of Brownhills built (MH 1994 p121) (SNBC p6). Brownhills and Ogley Hay were formed into a joint ecclesiastical parish in 1852 (GLAUE p418), or 1853 (BLHT) or 1854 (LGS p195). Brownhills urban district was created in 1894 (BLHT) and Brownhills was described as a town at the beginning of the C20 (LGS p195). The council amalgamated with Aldridge urban district in 1966 (ALOPP p20). The amalgamation came to an end in 1974. The **church**, St James, on the N side of Church Road, was built in 1851 (BOE p82). The South Staffs **Railway** opened a line through Brownhills on April 9 1849 which ran from Walsall to Lichfield. Brownhills station closed in 1965 (BLHT) (SSR p10). **Newspapers**. Brownhills and Chasetown Post seems to have run from Feb 11 1888 to Sept 12 1890 (SHJ spring 1996 p13). Brownhills & District Weekly Reporter seems to have run from Sept 3 1904 to May 1 1909 (SHJ spring 1996 p13). The Lichfield, Rugeley & Brownhills Post was founded in 1983 (Willings Press Guide. 1988). A bolt of **lightning** struck near Brownhills on June 24 1994 and killed a 16-year old girl (Sunday Telegraph June 26 1994 p2). A young female **ghost** haunts the open market area (GOM p29) (GPCE p24). Brownhills and Walsall Wood Local **History Society** was founded in 1991 (info W Mayo). **Persons. Jacob Birch** murdered his sister at their parents house in Lindon Road, almost opposite the Wheel Inn. The murder took place in the backyard before Birch went to work in c1919 (TB Nov 1982 p11). On March 11 1982 **Reg Morris** (alias Sam's Son) of Brownhills (or of Walsall see) extinguished 7225 torches of flame successively in his mouth in two hours at the Railway Tavern, Brownhills (GBR 1983 p24). On Nov 5 1983 he blew a flame from his mouth to a distance of 27 feet igniting a bonfire at The Castle Working Men's Club, Brownhills (GBR 1988 p20). On Dec 5 1983 he extinguished 8393 torches of flame successively in his mouth in two hours at the Wheel Inn, Brownhills (GBR 1985 p19). On July 23 1988 he walked 31.5 miles continuously balancing a full pint milk bottle on his head, the furthest ever walked by anyone in this state (GBR 1989 p312). Four members of the **Brownhills Majorettes** of Walsall twirled batons for 78 hours two minutes on July 20-23 1981 (GBR 1983 p182).

Brownhills Common Unenclosed common land 0.75m WNW of St James' church at Brownhills (MH 1994 p108).

Brownhills Hall N of Burslem. It was built by John Wood son of Ralph Wood the famous potter in c1782 with a pottery attached. John Wood was murdered in 1797 by Dr John Oliver, the disappointed suitor of John's daughter Maria (UDC vol 3 pp47-68). Brownhills Pottery nearby was demolished when the house was improved in 1830 (VCH vol 8 pp118,137). Demolished in 1964 (HBST pp151pl, 152) (SHST pp45,594p,595). A girls' high school was built in its grounds and incorporated a part of the house (VCH vol 8 pp106,113). Has also appeared as Brownhills House.

Brownhills Common Unenclosed common land 0.75m WNW of St James' church at Brownhills (MH 1994 p108).

Brownhills Hall N of Burslem. It was built by John Wood son of Ralph Wood the famous potter in c1782 with a pottery attached. John Wood was murdered in 1797 by Dr John Oliver, the disappointed suitor of John's daughter Maria (UDC vol 3 pp47-68). Brownhills Pottery nearby was demolished when the house was improved in 1830 (VCH vol 8 pp118,137). Demolished in 1964 (HBST pp151pl, 152) (SHST pp45,594p,595). A girls' high school was built in its grounds and incorporated a part of the house (VCH vol 8 pp106,113). Has also appeared as Brownhills House.

Brownhills West A suburb 1m NW of St James' church at Brownhills, S of

Chasewater. Built on former Norton Common.

Browning's Well Newcastle-under-Lyme. The spring from Browning's Well supplied Newcastle with its first piped water (W p302). In the mid C19 the water from the well was pumped to two reservoirs in Merrial Street (PWW p9).

Brown Knoll Knoll over 1.5m ESE Warslow.

Brown Lees Suburb 0.25m SW of Knypersley.

Brownlow House 0.75m SW of Warslow. Formerly in Warslow township in Alstonefield ancient parish. Built in 1854 (VCH vol 7 p57). To the N of Brownslow is a burial mound at SK 07655812. It is 28 paces in diameter and five feet high and a listed monument. Excavated by Manclarke in 1848. Human bones were found (TYD p245) (NSJFS 1965 p50). It is of Bronze Age origin (VCH vol 7 p57). Also Little Brownlow and Brownlow Bridge.

Brown's Bridge Tiny hamlet NNE of Slindon on the lane to Walford.

Brownsett House 0.25m N of Roche Grange, below the Roaches. Appears in Leek PR in the C17 as Brownsword, Braunsott, Brounsote, Brownsort, and Brownsword (SSE 1997 pp91-92).

Brownsfields Farm just under 1m NW of Streethay. Brownsfields is said to have taken its name from the Brown family of Lichfield. John Brown of Lichfield owned an estate here in 1440 (VCH vol 14 p278). Brick house which may have been built or rebuilt in the earlier C17 (VCH vol 14 p275) or the earlier C18 (VCH vol 14 p278) and may incorporate an older core (VCH vol 14 p278).

Brown's Island An island in the Trent S of Chetwynd Bridge.

Browns Green There was probably settlement at Browns Green, Handsworth, at the junction of Friary Road and Handsworth Wood Road, by the end of the C13. The name occurs in 1538 as a croft held by Roger Browne; by the C16 there was probably a small hamlet here (MNB p39) (HPPE p16). Is marked on Morden's map and has appeared as Brown's Green.

Browns Green House The original house of the settlement known as Browns Green, Handsworth, was perhaps the croft of Roger Browne in the early C16. Oliver Cromwell is said to have occupied the old Browns Green house and stables on his way to besiege Dudley Castle in the Civil War. The cellars of the old house were numerous, and there were reported to be two secret passages running from them. One is said to have run to a clump of rhododendrons some distance from the house, and the other was said to have come out near the Lodge. A later house was built by Nathanial Clarke KC near the end of the C18, situated well to the rear of what is now a triangle with Handsworth Wood Road and Englestede Close. It was the seat of Nathaniel Gooding Clarke KC (d1833), Crown Counsel in the 'Mary Ashford Murder Case' (1828), the last case of 'Trial by Battle.' He was succeeded by his son, who was succeeded by his son, Registrar Clarke (HPPE p16); Rev HJ Clarke was born at Browns Green in 1823 according to Simms (BS p107). The Chinese Ambassador is said to have stayed at the house. It was tenanted in 1861 by Sir James Timmings Chance, the Smethwick glass manufacturer. It was later occupied by Mr Lancaster, and later still by a Mr Lister and a Mr Wilson. After their brief stay it was taken over by TC Lowe in the late C19, as Hamstead Hill School. Shortly after serving briefly as a school, the house appears to have been demolished (HPPE pp16-17).
GROUNDS. An ice house stood in a corner of land between Elmwood and the Cherry Orchard fields (HPPE p17). A lodge, built in 1810, was still standing in 1984 (HPPE p17). Mr Lancaster laid out a series of seven pools fed by a stream in the grounds (HPPE p17).

Browns Lake Lost lake 0.5m NE of Enville, situated on the E side of Blundies Lane. By the 1950s the lake had been drained and 12 council houses were then built here (VCH vol 20 p93).

Brownslow Burial mound. Said to be near Castern. Excavated by Carrington in 1850. Two cremations were found with cinerary urns, a beaker fragment and the burial of an alleged suicide (TYD pp168-169) (DAJ vol 75 p116) (NSJFS 1965 p41).

Brownspit House nearly 1m SSW of Longnor. Formerly in Fawfieldhead township in Alstonefield ancient parish (W p746). There was a house at Brownspit by 1594 (VCH vol 7 p28).

Brownswall Farm Gospel End Road, Gospel End. Similar building to High Arcal Farm. It stood in the early 1960s. Hamilton Close is now (1997) built on the site (SDSSOP p24 il).

Brund 0.75m SSW of Cheddleton. Appears as Upper Brund on the 1834 OS map.

Brund Hamlet 0.75m WSW of Sheen, on the E side of the Manifold. In Sheen ancient parish. For burial mounds near Brund see Brund Low and Rye Low. There may have been a mill here on the Manifold by the mid C13 and there was a house at Brund by the early C16 (VCH vol 7 p242) (DMV p53p of the present mill). There is a bargain stone now used as a gate post at 0.5m SSW

of Brund at SK 097604 (PDS&C p73p).

Brund Hill Hill over 4m NNW of Upper Elkstone. The A53 passes over it.

Brund Low Burial mound at SK 10256182, 0.5m N of Brund, Sheen. It is 38 paces in diameter and a listed monument. A bronze weapon had been found from it prior to Carrington's excavation in 1851. A cremation and two sandstone fragments with cup marks were found. Sheldon in 1894 found some burnt bone (TYD p177) (Proceedings of the Society of Antiquaries of London series 2 vol 15 pp428-429) (NSJFS 1965 p46).

Brund Mill Bridge Sheen. Presumably crosses the Manifold. According to Mr JP Sheldon, replaced in 1890 by a pack-saddle bridge carrying a mule track across the moors from the salt springs of Nantwich and Chesterfield (ESH p16).

Brunswick Tiny wealthy area of Newcastle-under-Lyme now just a street name (NUL p63). Most of the housing dates from the early C19. Marsh Parade in it was known as 'Nobs Row' (Newcastle-under-Lyme. A Town Portrait. Newcastle Civic Society. 1984. p57).

Brunswick Park Public park on the E side of Wednesbury. Formerly opened to commemorate Queen Victoria's Golden Jubilee in 1887 (WAM p122) (TWDOP p117p). Created by Messrs Baron and Son of Derby on 28 acres of waste land purchased from the Patent Shaft and Axletree Co. Has a walk called Invalids' Walk because of its gentle climb with plenty of seating, and a gun from the Crimean War captured in 1854 (WDOP pp49p,51p).

Brush Ride A 'ride' through Swynnerton Old Park (NSFCT 1917 p152).

Bryan's Hay House 0.5m WSW of Longsdon, on the S side of the Leek road. There was a cottage here in 1611. The present farmhouse here is partly of the C17 (VCH vol 7 p203). Was a meeting house for early Methodists prior to 1754 (HLSP p176).

Bryan's Well Formerly in Bryan's Wood in c1835, now Bryan Street, Hanley (H p106) (VCH vol 8 p160) (SHST pp214,217).

Bryan's Wood Lost wood in the vicinity of Bryan Street, Hanley (OPT p54). Formerly in Stoke-upon-Trent chapelry in Stoke-upon-Trent ancient parish.

Bryn Hill Near Madeley Manor, Middle Madeley, and on it may have been a hill fort (M p21).

Buckeridge's Almshouses Lower Sandford Street, Lichfield. Cottages in Lower Sandford Street were given as parish almshouses by Rev George Buckeridge (d1863). The cottages had become uninhabitable in 1908 and were sold (VCH vol 14 p185).

Buckerman's Hill A knoll in the Armsdale (see) area on the E side of the Langot Valley, Fairoak. It is said to be named after George Villiers', 2nd Duke of Buckingham, fall from his horse here, after arriving in this area having escaped from the battle of Worcester (1651) (BPS pp26,28,29) (BOV p32) (NSFCT 1928 p161). A cottage off Langot Lane is known as the Duke of Buckingham's Cottage (NSFCT 1932 p122).

Buckingham's Cave Cave in Outlands, Adbaston parish. Situated below New Inn Bank, behind the home of 'Old' Matthews (BOV p32). Reputedly George Villiers 2nd Duke of Buckingham hid in this cave for three days whilst a fugitive in the Langot Valley having escaped from the battle of Worcester (1651). He was led to it by an ancestor of 'Old' Matthews called Nick Matthews, a carpenter. (George Villiers 2nd Duke of Buckingham. 1628-1687. 2 vols. Lady Winifred Burghclere. 1903) (BPS p150) (SOSH p219) (George Villiers; A study of George Villiers 2nd Duke of Buckingham. 1628-1687. Hester W. Chapman. 1949) (STM April 1966 p31) (ROT p16) (MR p18).

Buckley's Drumble 0.25m NNE of Mucklestone.

Buckmoor Hill W of Tamworth. Marked on J Cary's map (1805).

Bucknall Village on a gentle eminence near the Trent (HBST p527), and parish, now a suburb of Stoke-on-Trent, 16m N of Stafford. Former township, and with Bagnall a chapelry in Stoke-upon-Trent ancient parish.
EARLY. **Roman** pottery of the C2 was found in the bank of a stream between Berry Hill and Bucknall at SJ 900469. No evidence of Roman occupation was discovered (NSJFS 1964 p36. 1965 p120).
900 to 1500. The Badecanwell mentioned in a charter of 949 was identified by Birch in his Cartularium Saxonicum with Bucknall. But CGO Bridgeman suggests Bakewell, Derbys (SHC 1916 p87). The manor of Bucenhole appears in DB (SSE 1996 p11), Bucenhale (1227), Buccenhal (1230). Later Bucknall appears as Bukenhal (1272) (SPN p14) and Buckenhall? The **name** appears to be of Anglo-Saxon origin and means 'Bucca's nook' (NSJFS 1981 p2), or 'Bucca's halh (hollow)' (SSE 1996 p11). Duignan, who was unsure about the right suffix, thought 'Buca's hollow or hall' (DUIGNAN); Poulton-Smith gives 'corner of land' (SPN p14). Ward thought 'Bucen-knoll' from the eminence on which Bucknall sits which had been covered with beech trees (HBST p527). Bucknall Eaves may have been a manor distinct from Bucknall or Great Bucknall or Bucknall-cum-Bagnall (SHC 1885 p71 note.

1909 p64). A medieval or late medieval **church** built of wood, may have preceded a church at Bucknall built in 1718; which, according to tradition, was built with stones procured from the ruined Hulton Abbey. The present church, St Mary, on the E side of Marychurch Road, was built in 1854-1856 (BOE p266) may stand on its site (HBST p527). Bucknall **wakes** were held in a field near Lime Kiln Bank and known locally as Pickled Onion Wakes as local publicans put out pickle onions and cheese on plates for those attending the wakes (FWMBS p27). The bull ring is fastened into a huge stone at Bucknall. It used to be in a butcher's yard. It was found directly beneath the base of the old cross base at Bagnall (NSFCT 1925 p190). An old mill on the Trent situated by Bucknall railway station was a ruin by 1922 (NSFCT 1922 p154).

1500 to PRESENT. Bucknall was formed into separate a parish with Bagnall in 1736 (GLAUE p405), or 1807 (LGS p93). Refounded as Bucknall cum Bagnall in 1849 (GLAUE p405). Bucknall was taken into Stoke-on-Trent county borough in 1922 (VCH vol 8 p260). The Biddulph Valley **Railway** opened a line from Stoke to Biddulph through Bucknall in 1863. A line from Bucknall to Normacot opened in 1875 (VCH vol 2 p309). In Bucknall New Road is a double-layered **trough**. Horses drank at the top and dogs at the bottom. It was donated by the Wedgwood family in the C19 and bears this inscription

'To Man, Beast and All Akin. G. Wedgwood 1879'

It was presented to the Borough of Hanley in 1879 (COS p21p) (ES Aug 5 1995 p29). The first **'silent peal'** rung in Britain was accomplished at St Mary's April 6 1897. The six bell ringers rang in silence without a caller counting on the ropes (Plaque inside the church tower) (TWWW April 1997 p2). **UFO** sightings were made from Ubberley Road on Aug 30 1967 and on Sept 1 1967 (FSRP pp9,10). **Natives and visitors** (and a dog). For body snatchers at work in Bucknall churchyard who were frightened off by the pot pedlar, **Ned Saunterer**, see Hanley. **Mrs Mellard**, grandmother of the novelist Dinah Maria Mulock, lived in the 'Big House' in Bucknall from 1825 to her death in 1839 (NSFCT 1925 p83). **Angela Smith**, squash player, was born and brought up in Bucknall. In 1989 she won 35 titles including the hat-trick of the British Open, the British Closed and the World Championship (FWNS pp81-83ps). **Peter Whelan**, playwright, was born in Bucknall in c1932. He attended Hanley High School and Keele University (ES Feb 29 2000 p13). The smallest dog in Britain in Jan 1971 was a full-grown poodle named **'Giles'** owned by Mrs Sylvia Wyse of Bucknall. It stood 4.5 inch at the shoulder and weighed 13 oz. Shortly afterwards he was exported to Canada (GBR 1973 p41).

Bucknall Eaves May have been a manor distinct from Bucknall or Great Bucknall or Bucknall-cum-Bagnall (SHC 1885 p71 note. 1909 p64).

Bucknall Hall Bucknall. A Bucknall Hall was the seat of the Adams family, potters, in the early C17 (mem in St Margaret's, Wolstanton), and that of William Adams in the C18 (NSF p49). The Bucknall Hall to which Dinah Mullock (Mrs Craik) came to visit her grandmother, Jane Mellard (d1839), as a child stood at the top of Marychurch Road (SHST p597), close to the church, and appears to have also been called the Big House (PSS p401).

Bucknall Sands Area of S Bucknall by the brook which flows from Wash Well (FWMBS p4).

Buckpool Area 1.25m NNW of Amblecote. In Kingswinford ancient parish. Has often been referred to as Bug Pool (Pigot's Atlas 1840) (SNSV vol 1 p161); the pool was a ducking pool for witches (TB Sept 1990 p5).

Buckstew Field name in Newbold grounds, 1m E of Dunstall, Tatenhill. In the later C17 Plot noted if cattle grazed on the grass or hay of it, their coats would turn a different colour for up to two to three years, perhaps, owing to the salt wells hereabouts (NHS p111).

Buddileigh Tiny hamlet or locality (BART p202) 0.5m NW of, and nearly merged with, Betley. Has appeared as Bodiley, Bud-Heighley (1679) (SHC 1909 p212), Buddy Lees (Plot's map), Buddilee (1856) (BART p202), and Buddleigh. Here was the site of a mill in the C13 (BVC p34). One of its timberframed cottages is called Buddleigh, dated 1622 (BOE p68). It was the ancient freehold property of Mr Steele (BART p202). It was for sale in Aug 1993 (ES 12 Aug 1993 p of in the property pages). Buddileigh Farm, a house said to have been rebuilt in c1906 incorporating some timbers from a C17 predecessor, was for sale in Aug 1999 (ES Aug 5 1999 property supplement). Another cottage is called The Beehive (see).

Buffalo Bill's Railway Carriage Ashley. Perhaps once the dwelling of a woodman or recluse made out of a wooden railway carriage. Appears to be used as a shed in Raven's photograph (MR p22p).

Bughole Area situated on the boundary of Darlaston ancient parish and Willenhall township. The name is of ancient, but unknown, origin (HOWI p188), but may be from a hollow haunted by an evil spirit (SNDB p21). It is preserved in Bughole Bridge which crosses the Walsall Canal N of Darlaston Green (Offlow hundred).

Bug Hole The name Bugpole appears in the Pensnett area in 1785 on A Plan of the intended Extension of the Dudley Canal into the Birmingham Canal by John Snape 1785. The carriage of coals by packhorse and ass and panniers persisted to some extent on Pensnett Chase until c1900 when Sally Smith of Moor Lane carried coals on her donkey and

When the donkey died, old Sally cried,
Whatever shall I do
To carry coal from old Bug Hole
To the folks in Tackeroo?

(KCPC p16).

Bull and Spectacles Inn Blithbury, Colton. The inn sign shows a bull wearing spectacles. There are three explanations for the name: that a Blithbury man gave spectacles to the bull (the inn was formerly the Bull's Head), because its eyes looked weak; or more likely that the sign painter put the spectacles on the bull's nose to win a bet (and ever since it has been known as the Bull and Spectacles) (QML pp130,131p-134); or that the name is a corruption of 'B. Hullen Esquire - Specabilis' (because the inn is built on the site of Kileby Hall built by Robert Hullen) (TB Oct 1994 p18p). Yet another explanation may be that it is from 'Bullen Spectabilis,' a corruption of (Anne) Boleyn the notable; bull being an old symbol of condemnation to death (VB p109). (LGS p260) (SJC p5).

Bull Bridge About 0.5m down stream on the Penk from Cuttlestone Bridge, built in c1825 (W p466). It now carries the A449. Built on the site of a clapper bridge called Boulderstone Bridge (PVH p20). According to tradition their was a skirmish between some Danes retreating from the battle of Tettenhall and some Saxons at Bull Bridge in c910 (St Michael and All Angels, Penkridge: Royal Collegiate Parish Church. R Cheadle). Has appeared as le Bolde brugge (1375), and the Bouldbridge (1587) (VCH vol 5 p105) (SPNO p93). When the A449 road was widened and the bridge reconstructed in 1963 a stone macehead was found (SSAHST 1971 pp46,47il). David Horovitz found a mace head at Bull Bridge in 1963 (BDH p297). Since the bridge carried the main road from the south to Stafford the people of South Staffs had an expression to go 'over Bull Bridge,' which meant to go for trial or imprisonment at Stafford (HOP p88). The early forms of the name indicate some association with the nearby place called Bold (see). See Rodbaston for Bull Bridge's relevance in a curious lease.

Bull Clough Near Ford, Grindon. Has also appeared as Bullclough.

Bullfield Farm Formerly at Springfield, presumably near Bullfields Close, Rowley Regis. Home of the White family and then the Darby family for almost 300 years. When Christopher White was the resident in 1605, Stephen Lyttleton and Robert Winter, the Gunpowder Plotters, took refuge here. White was pursued and burnt to death in this house. A fire burnt down the next house built on the site in the 1960s (TB Oct 1988 p16p). The house is reputedly haunted by phantom footsteps (TB Feb 1975 pp14-15p). Others say Christopher White was of Rowley Hall (see) and sheltered the Gunpowder plotters there.

Bull Gap Farm 1.25m N of Stanton (NSJFS 1972 p122).

Bull Hill Stafford. The name occurs in 1631 and it has been suggested that Boley, Bullie and Bully are derived from the bailey of an early castle in Stafford town. But more likely the land took its name from the messuage called the Bull which stood in the area in the C16 (VCH vol 6 p200). Bully Hill, or Bully Hill, is just slightly NE of Broad Eye. Ethelfleda reputedly built the first castle at Stafford, on the N bank of the Sow (GNHS p103). Although White and others say Ethelfleda built her burh at Broad Eye (W p321). Some say Bull Hill was the site for the castle erected by the Normans in 1070 (SSTY p5). Roxburgh in 1928 says Bull Hill is the alley leading from Gaol Square to the Broad Eye. At No. 1 Bull Hill, in 1925, a well was discovered 21 feet deep and 4.5 feet wide. It was bricked up (SKYT pp49,51).

Bullings Heath Former common and hamlet at junction of Green Lane and Hall Lane. Formerly in a detached portion of the foreign of Walsall ancient parish. There was settlement here by 1763. There was a pound here in the earlier 1840s (VCH vol 17 pp278,281). Has also appeared as Bullens Heath (SNBC p35).

Bull Moors (SHOS vol 2 p56). There is a Bullmore Lane running between Chesterfield (Lichfield) and Wall Butts (1888 OS map 6 inch).

Bullockcroft Brook Rises S of Whitgreave and joins the Sow at Creswell.

Bullock's End Tiny hamlet under 0.5m NE of Drayton Bassett, on the Fazeley road. The name appears on the 1884 OS map 6 inch.

Bull Ring Central area of Sedgley (MR p276) (Staffs County Handbook c1958 p121p). Name is from bull baiting which was carried on here. Here stood the manorial stocks (SDOP p8p).

Bullstake, The Situated at the junction of Pinfold Street, Darlaston and Walsall Roads and St Lawrence Way in the town centre part of Darlaston. In 1965 this area, which had stood partly in Darlaston and Wednesbury ancient parishes, was wholly taken into Darlaston (BCS p88) (SNDB p22). It is implied in an old ballad, 'The Darlaston Dog Fight,' probably of the early C19, that the bull stake was removed from The Bullstake to Darlaston Green when The Bullstake became too built-up (SNDB p23). A ballad entitled 'The Darlaston Dog Fight' has recently been written down by Tom Langley, a retired policeman (UBCB p129) (MR p122); perhaps the same as Tom Langley of Chasetown (see). Bullstake derives from the fact that bulls - and occasionally bears - were baited here (SNDB p22). (WDY p27p) (BCM Jan 1982 p12. Jan 1983 p34).

Bully Thrumble Formerly situated on the crest of the Cloud. Odd-shaped rock feature jutting out of that part of The Cloud situated in Rushton Spencer parish (TSW p86). It had been quarried and destroyed by 1884. It strongly resembled a gigantic cork-screw and was 60 or 70 feet high (Leek Times, week ending July 18 1884) (MC p30) (DP p76) (DPEM p138).

Bumble Hole The Trysull lock keeper's cottage on the Staffs and Worcs is described by the DoE as by Bumble Hole Lock. They are at The Bratch.

Bumfrey Castle Name given to an old thatched cottage built in a circular shape in Northfield Road, Harborne. It stood at the junction with the path through a field leading to Welsh House Farm, just opposite Tibbett's Lane. After a severe outbreak of an epidemic it was destroyed by fire (HOHH p59).

Bunbury Hill Hill on which Alton Towers mansion stands (AT pp11,12), and is the E bank of Slain Hollow. Has also appeared as Bonebury. A hillfort on Bunbury Hill is of Iron Age origin and dates from the C2 to the C1 BC (HOS p10). Plot said the camp covered 100 acres and was defended by double or triple banks (NHS p410). Possible Roman finds have been made at Bunbury Hill (STM March 1964 p42). The fort was re-occupied in Saxon times by Ceolred, king of Mercia, as a defence against Wessex or the West Saxons in 715. The two sides fought a battle known as the battle of Bunbury or Bonebury in nearby Slain Hollow in 716 in which the West Saxons were led by their king, Ina or Ine. The West Saxons lost. Ina was killed, or as Plot says, retreated, and is remembered in nearby Ina's Rock. Some believe Bunbury or Bonebury is Benebury or Borough Hole (see) at Wetton, and that the battle took place there. A leaf-shaped bronze sword of Late Bronze Age was found in the earthwork of Bunbury Fort before 1794 (ARCH vol 11 (1794) pp431,432 pl 19 fig 9) (ABI p282) (NSJFS 1964 p22) (HAF p29 il). A Saxon sword and celt are recorded at SK 071432 to E of Bunbury Hill Fort on the OS six inch map (SK 04 SE) as found in 1837 (VCH vol 1 p212). This may be the same as the Late Bronze Age sword (NSJFS 1964 p22). Most of the camp was destroyed by the construction of Alton Towers and its gardens. Only a short length of rampart existed by the 1960s. The site was excavated in 1961 (NSJFS 1964 p22). (GNHS pp70,73) (SMC p163) (HOU 1865 ed pp345-346) (WTCEM pp32,33) (LGS p31) (NSFCT 1924 p189. 1944 p104) (IAANS p vi) (MR p14).

Bunker's Hill Former hamlet 0.5m NE of Bilston in Bilston parish, centred on the present Bunkers Hill Lane and Portway Road. The name appears on the OS map 1885 OS map 6 inch. A toll house formerly stood at the corner of Willenhall Road and Bunkers Hill Lane (BOP p92p). The church, St Chad, Connaught Road, was built in 1955 (LDD).

Bunker's Hill Toll house which stood in Tipton Street at the entrance to the present Richmond Road, Sedgley. It was demolished in 1933 (SDOP p94p).

Bunker's Hill Hill 2.5m SE of Stourton Hall, Stourton.

Bunker's Hill Hill at Talke.

Bunster Hill Hill 1079 feet high NE of Ilam with an extremely steep S face. (W p52 note). Topped with a burial mound, at SK 14195166, 14 paces in diameter and three feet high. Excavated by Carrington in 1849. A crouched skeleton was found (TYD pp143-144). It is a listed monument. Another on the upper slopes at SK 14025169 excavated by Carrington in 1852 (TYD p186) is natural (NSJFS 1965 p40). At the bottom of the hill is St Bertram's Well. The name means perhaps 'hill cleared of scrub by burning' (PNPD).

Burchen Lesow A wood in Bushbury parish near Bushbury Low (NHS p403).

Burgamy House Almshouse founded in 1504 in Bacon or Beacon Street, Lichfield. The houses in this street were mostly burnt down in the Civil War (SHOS vol 1 p319).

Burgesses, The Area of Kinver about the southern end of the High Street (VCH vol 20 p119). It was also the name of a massive brick building in High Street of the Jacobean period, demolished in 1963 (George R Humpreyes 1973 p2

il) (KEOP p27ps). The name is preserved in a tiny street on the S side of the High Street.

Burgess Hall Former old timbered building in St Matthew's churchyard, Walsall. Has also appeared as St John's Hall, from having belonged to the Guild of St John. It was an early residence for Walsall Grammar School (SNWA p30).

Burgh Hill Gnosall. Hackwood describes it as the manor house of Gnosall. The name is from Adam de Burgh, to whom it once belonged. It descended from Adam de Burgh to Knightley of Knightley, one of whose family demised it to Robert Harcoate. Hackwood vaguely implies that the Gnosall Jury (see under Gnosall) was selected or convened at Burgh Hill (SCSF p161).

Burleyfields House 0.5m N of Stafford Castle. Foot-and-mouth disease broke out at Burley Fields Farm in early 1968 (SN Jan 26 1968 p13).

Burlington Hamlet over 1m ESE of Sheriff Hales. Has also appeared as Burlauton (Plot's map).

Burned Heath Area of ground bounded by Lordswood Road, Court Oak Road and Wood Lane, Harborne. Perhaps so called because of the destruction by fire of a part of the woods which covered the land from Court Oak Road to Beech Lanes and were called Lord's Woods (STELE June 26 1953) (HOHH p58).

Burnet's Low A burial mound said to be near Deepdale. 17 paces in diameter. It was excavated by Carrington in 1848. A crouched skeleton in a deep rock-cut grave with a small round heeled bronze dagger near the shoulder was found (TYD p115) (VCH vol 1 no 4) (DAJ vol 75 p111) (NSJFS 1965 p38).

Burnhill Green Hamlet 1m WSW of Patshull. In Patshull ancient parish. There was settlement here by the mid C13. Burnhill Green was known simply as Burnhill until the later C16 (VCH vol 20 p162), and has also appeared as Burnell Green. There is a small damaged moat behind a row of cottages at SJ 787008 (VCH vol 1 p365. vol 20 p162) (SSAHST 1982-3 p45) (CAMS p63). A pound for Patshull parish was situated near the Dartmouth Arms Inn in Burnhill Green in the early 1880s (VCH vol 20 p169).

Burnsfield Farm Lost house which stood 2.75m WSW of Horton, N of Brown Edge. In Horton ancient parish. There was a house here by 1474 (VCH vol 7 p67).

Burnt Hill An housing estate 0.25m SW of Rugeley town centre. Built before WW2 on N side of road to Hednesford (VCH vol 5 p149).

Burntoak Hollins House 0.75m W of Meerbrook. Formerly in Leekfrith township in Leek ancient parish. A house on this site was in existence by the earlier C16; it stands on a packhorse way (VCH vol 7 p193). The name Burntoak may be from an ancient boundary tree, and the house lies on a ley line between Lud Church, Knight's Low, and Dieulacres Abbey, Lady Dale (SMM p132 see map).

Burnt Tree Former village and a ward of Tipton borough, now an industrial area 1m SSE of Tipton. In Tipton parish. By 1849 there was considerable development along Burnt Tree to Dudley Port (BTRA p6). The name is from the 'Burnt Tree' which stood at the junction of Tividale Road and the road known as Burnt Tree (BTRA p6).

Burntwood Large village near the head of Bilson Brook at the SW foot of Hobstone Hill 12.5m SE of Stafford. Former township in St Michael's parish, Lichfield.

1200 to 1500. The area was anciently waste of Longdon manor (VCH vol 14 p205) and covered by Cannock Forest. The name implies settlement created out of woodland cleared by fire (NSFCT 1933 p93) (SL p67) (NSJFS 1980 p3) (SSE 1996 p11) (SPN p25). Proceedings against Hammerwich vill for deliberately causing a fire in Cannock Forest were brought before the forest courts in 1262. This fire is believed to have cleared the land on which Burntwood grew and gave it its name. The name 'Brendewode' (Burntwood) was in use by 1298 (DUIGNAN) (VCH vol 14 p198). The original settlement, which existed by 1570, was probably centred on the green at the junction of Norton Lane and Cannock Road at SK 068087, the present Burntwood Green (VCH vol 14 p198). Burntwood was a peculiar jurisdiction of the dean of Lichfield cathedral (GLAUE). Burntwood wakes were held on the Sunday after Michaelmas in the Middle Ages (VCH vol 14 p203).

1500 to PRESENT. There were various forms of iron-working in the Burntwood area from the early C17. Some brick-making, using local clay, and stone quarrying have been carried on since the C18. Nailing and coalmining had become important in the area by the mid C19 (VCH vol 14 pp199,216). The **church**, Christ Church, at the junction of Church Road and Farewell Lane, was built in 1819-1820 (BOE p83). Burntwood became a separate ecclesiastical parish in 1821. It became a civil parish, known as 'Burntwood, Edial, and Woodhouses,' in 1866. This was changed to simply 'Burntwood' in 1929 (GLAUE p405) (SVB p48) (VCH vol 14 pp195,201,218). There was a racecourse in the Spring Hill and Ball's Mount area between c1835 and c1854 (VCH vol 14 p203). Common land at

Burntwood, a remnant of Cannock Forest, was enclosed in 1861 and or 1863 (PCC p16) (MH 1994 p108). For the county lunatic asylum opened at Burntwood in 1864 see Hobstone Hill. Between 1961 and 1971 the population nearly doubled as Burntwood became an overspill area for people from Birmingham and the Black Country. In 1974 the civil parish was designated an urban parish (in Lichfield District). The urban parish council is styled a town council, and its offices are at Sankey's Corner (see) (SVB p48) (VCH vol 14 pp195,201,218). **Persons and visitors**. In 1531 **Robert Talbot**, antiquary, was teaching at a school at 'Borned Wodde' (DNB), identified with Burntwood; but Greenslade thinks it more likely to have been Brentwood, Essex (VCH vol 14 p227). **George Hitchinson** of Burntwood sold his wife, Elizabeth, at Walsall market in 1837 (SCSF p71). **Dave Wilkins** of Burntwood single-handedly pulled a BAC 1-11 aeroplane over 75 feet at Birmingham Airport on May 25 1986 (GBR 1989 p179). **Reg Morris** set a world record for fastest frankfurter eater when he ate 30 frankfurters in 64 seconds at Burntwood in Dec 1986 (GBR 1999 p60).

Burnt Wood A wood near Hales, Drayton-in-Hales; part of Bishop's Wood. Formerly called Rowney Wood, then Rounhay, then Brand (NSFCT 1933 p93) (SHC 1945/ 6 p52). There is a legend that the last wolf in England was killed in Burnt Wood (NSFCT 1930 p163). It derives its name from charcoal burners at work here (SHC 1945/6 p156). By 1999 the oak woodland within plantation at SJ 738354 was a SSSI nature reserve in the care of the Staffs Wildlife Trust (Staffs Wildlife Trust leaflet).

Burntwood Green Area SSW of Christ Church church, Burntwood. This is the original settlement of Burntwood. It was known as Hanley Green in the later C17 but was called Burntwood Green by 1724 (VCH vol 14 p198).

Burnwood There is a Burnwood Nursery and County High School and Burnwood Place at Chell Heath (Stoke-on-Trent A-Z).

Burslem (locally *Boszlum* POP p34). Parish and Potteries town on a south-facing slope of a escarpment between Whitfield Brook and Fowlea Brook valleys, 17m NNW of Stafford. Former township and chapelry in Stoke-upon-Trent ancient parish. It can be looked down upon from Mow Cop hill as alluded to in the poem 'Mow Cop' composed by David Oakes:

> He shewed the stranger Sandbach town,
> He showed him Burslem too.
> The stranger asked, "What's your employ?"
> Said he, "I've plenty of work to do."

(KBT vol 2 pp38-40).
EARLY to 1700. The **manor** of Barcardeslim appears in DB. A later form is Borewardeslyme (1242) (SSE 1996 p11). The **name** is of Anglo-Saxon origin and means Burhweard's stream (a reference to Lyme Brook) (DUIGNAN). Or the ending is taken from the Forest of Lyme (SOSH p281) (POP p13). (HSP p26): A corruption of Burgheard's Lyme, meaning either Burgheard's woods, or Burgheard's clearing in Lyme Forest (MR p65) (SSE 1996 p11) (SPN pp25-26). Gelling thinks 'fort-guardian's estate in Lyme' (NSJFS 1981 p2). (NSFCT 1943 pp16-39). In the early C19 Simeon Shaw thought the name originated from 'bull ward' or 'dog ward,' whilst some of his contemporaries thought it originated from 'Boar's Lane' (HSP p26). Tunstall courts sat at Burslem when not at Tunstall (NSFCT 1943 p18). The **church**, St John the Baptist, S of the town centre at Cross Hill, has a tower of c1536 and a chancel of 1788; the rest is of 1717 (VCH vol 8 p122) (BOE p254). The **wakes** were held in the week following 24 June, the feast of St John the Baptist to whom the old church is dedicated (VCH vol 8 p141). In a bid to bring the wakes of the pottery towns into unison with Stoke's in August, it was banned in 1879, but resumed the following year after protests (HOS p63). A custom of decorating the church with branches of trees and shrubs on Wakes Sunday survived until c1700 (HBST pp269-270) (VCH vol 8 p141). The **stocks** formerly stood in the Market Place somewhere near the maypole. It is known that they were in existence before 1680. They were removed to the Town Yard in c1820? A post of it was in the possession of HJ Steele (NSFC President) in 1944 (NSFCT 1943 pp37-38). Burslem had some **parochial rights** from the C16 and separate civil identity at an early period (GLAUE p406). It became a separate parish in 1807 (W pp222,270) or 1849 (GLAUE p406). An **infection**, perhaps, brought from Italy by the governess to the Biddulph family caused a plaque at Burslem in 1647 (SOSH pp203-204). The dead were buried in pits near Rushton Grange. The plague is not mentioned in PR (NSFCT 1921 p27). The tomb of **Elizabeth de Aldithley** (d1400), wife of Nicholas de Aldithley, 5th Lord Audley, originally at Hulton Abbey (see) where she was buried has been identified with the stone coffin, hewn in the shape of a figure, presently in St John's churchyard, Burslem (Complete Peerage) (AGT p82) (SASR 1985 p78). **Dr Plot** visited Burslem

sometime between 1675-7 (NSFCT 1943 p20). Whilst here he was misled into thinking a spring at Burslem was purely vitriolic, but after testing it with galls he proved it not to be (NHS p105).

POTTERIES. **Early pottery-making**. Clay was abundant in the Burslem area and the Romans may have had a kiln at Burslem (The Wedgewoods. LL Jewitt. 1865 p13 note) (NSJFS 1964 p36). Hulton Abbey and Burslem formerly lay in the same township and the monks of Hulton Abbey are said to have initiated potting at Burslem (OTP p110). Two kilns dating from the C13 and pottery fragments of the C13 have been found at Sneyd Green (see). Fragments of pottery of the same period have been unearthed to the NW of the junction of Sneyd Street and Crossway Road (VCH vol 8 p132). An old kiln and very coarse saggars were found in a field near the Hamil in the early C18 (HSP p7). The Adams family were involved in pottery in the Burslem area by the mid C15. It has been asserted by Adams in 'Adams Family' p15 that the monks produced pottery and their works was taken over by the Adams family at the Dissolution, but there is no evidence they did (VCH vol 8 p132 note 13). All sorts of pots including butter pots for the butter market at Uttoxeter were made at Burslem in the C17. In 1662 an Act of Parliament called upon the butter-pot makers of Burslem to restrict the weight of their pots to about six pounds, so that a 20 pound load could contain a stone of butter, so no one could deceive the purchaser (POP p14). According to Plot by the later C17 Burslem was the greatest pottery centre in the county (NHS p422). The different sorts of local clays he noticed which were used for unglazed pots of that time were later abandoned in favour of imported clay from Dorset, Devon and Cornwall which could withstand the high temperatures needed for salt glazing (POP p18). When several air-raid shelters were being sunk in WW2 at Massey Square and ground previously occupied by the old police station and adjoining the meat market, pottery of the C17 and C18 was found (NSFCT 1939 pp65-69 map of Burslem showing potteries in c1720, 70). In consequence of Burslem's early involvement with pottery it is often known as the 'Mother of the Potteries,' a phrase coined by 1817 (THS p395) (POP p10).

1700 to 1840. A **windmill** was erected in c1750 on the Jenkins (see). There was an open air **market** in the area of the town hall by c1761 (HBST pp235-236) (NSJFS 1962 p112) (VCH vol 8 p141). Open air markets continued to c1835 when the market moved to a covered market house (demolished in 1957). In 1878-9 a market hall opened between Market Place and Queen Street; it was still existing in 1963 (VCH vol 8 pp130-131). Hackwood notes Burslem's markets are held on Mondays, Wednesdays, and Saturdays (SCSF p95). The first of three **town halls** was erected in the centre of the market place in c1761. It also, for a time, served as the lock-up. The second town hall was built on the site of the first in 1854-7. In 1911 the third and present town hall was built on the E side of the market-place (VCH vol 8 pp112-113) (AGT p77il) (BOE p254). (ILN May 1 1869 p445il). It has been called Malkin's Folly after councillor and alderman Sydney Malkin (1865-1953) who promoted its building. According to the poem 'Mow Cop' composed by David Oakes the ashlar stone for Burslem market hall was hewn at Mow Cop (KBT vol 2 pp38-40). The 'gilded angel' surmounting the town hall was made famous by being alluded to in the novels of Arnold Bennett (SHST p285). It stood precariously on a golden orb (AGT p77). By 2000 the angel had been taken down for repairs (ES Feb 8 2000 p7p). Some figures from the building went to EJD Warrillow's garden (LLST p48p). A naive nativity painting was in the town hall (STMSM Sept 1976 p9p). There was no **fair** in 1792 (OWEN), but there was in 1888 (LHE p264). Hackwood says it is difficult to say when Burslem's fairs originated, which were held on Saturday before Easter, Whitsunday, and Christmas, but they probably came about as pleasure fairs for the growing populace (Whitaker's Almanac) (SCSF pp98,104). For Burslem Sunday School see Hill Top, Burslem. For a sampler made at Burslem see STM April 1966 p42 il. **Natives and visitors**. **Josiah Wedgwood I**, the great potter, was born at Churchyard House (see), Burslem, in 1730. **John Wesley** visited Burslem in 1760 (SOSH p284). **Abraham Lindop** (1738-1832) of Burslem, was a disciple of Wesley; he may have heard Wesley preach at Burslem or at some other place. Lindop became a preacher himself, claiming in his sermons that his religion or faith was tested in a vision in which he was commanded to preach to a congregation of devils which he did until they faded away (TFTP pp24-27). Dr **Thomas Milward Oliver** (1769/70-97) shot dead John Wood at his house on Jan 27 1797 in reprisal for Wood's attempt to terminate the relationship between Oliver and Wood's daughter, Maria. Oliver had come to Burslem in c1792 to be partner to Dr Hickman and after being prevented from seeing Maria had gone to her house intending to commit suicide with a gun but instead shot Wood. Oliver was hung on Aug 28 1797 (UDC book 3 pp47-68) (STM March 1971 p29) (STMSM Oct 1974 p8) (MMM pp61-64) (POTP p164) (TFTP pp19-23ils) (TB March 1993 p5) (SMML pp75-78). **James Holland** RWS (d1870), was born in Burslem on

Oct 18 1799 (POTP pp122-123) (ES April 8 2000 p2) or 1800 (STMSM June 1973 pp30,31il). He became successful enough to give drawing lessons to Queen Victoria. There is a portrait of him by WH Hunt in the V&A, and a copy in Hanley Art Gallery (POTP pp122-123). In 2000 two of his watercolours fetched nearly twice the expected price at auction (ES April 8 2000 p2). (STMSM July 1973 pp32-33. Aug 1973 pp22-23. Sept 1973 pp24-25. Oct 1973 pp24-25. Nov 1973 pp30-31. Dec 1973 p28). For **John Davenport**, poet, born in Burslem in 1799 see Westwood Hall, Leek. **Mrs Brettell** (nee Wood) was born in Burslem; her works include 'Meriden: or, The Memoirs of Matilda' (1819), and 'Susan Ashfield and Other Poems' (1820) (PSS p463) (VFC p18). Rev **Thomas Baker**, poet, was born in Burslem in 1804. His 'Leisure Hours' was published in 1837 (PSS p461) (VFC p7).

1840 to 1900. **Chartist unrest**. The battle of Burslem refers to events which occurred on Aug 16 1842 at the height of the Chartist riots in the Potteries (TB Nov 1994 p19). Several marches from out-lying Pottery villages converged on Burslem on this day. In the chaos which ensued the George Inn was attacked and the Riot Act read. When a contingent of soldiers from Leek arrived, the magistrate, Capt Powys, gave the order to fire and one man died and others were seriously wounded and the crowd dispersed, pursued by soldiers (LOU pp243-249) (The Crisis of 1842: Chartism, the colliers' strike and the outbreak in the Potteries in The Charter Experience. J Epstein & D Thompson pp194-200. Robert Fyson) (AGT p84). **Further unrest and natural phenomena**. Burslem experienced some rioting in c1874. All the windows of the 'old' Town Hall were smashed in. Henry Cartledge JP, the Mayor, had to read the Riot Act (OTP p132). The epicentre of a mini earthquake which measured 2.8 on the Richter Scale, which occurred at 4.50am May 6 1996, was at Burslem (ES May 7 1996 p7). **Growth from the mid C19**. The Wedgwood Institute (see) was built in 1863. Burslem was connected to Kidsgrove and Hanley with the Potteries Loop railway line between 1873 and 1875 (VCH vol 2 p319). It was recommended Burslem railway station be closed in 1963 (ES March 22 1963). Burslem was made a borough in 1871 (POP p74), or in 1878 (OTP p133). It's arms were granted in 1878 and according to Scott-Giles they are: Gold and red quarters with two vertical and two horizontal stripes interlaced and counter-changed; in the first and fourth quarters a Portland vase, in the second a scythe, and in the third a silver fret. The crest is: A red fleur-de-lis in front of a gold wheatsheaf between two branches of laurel in proper colours. The motto is: 'Ready' (CH p330). Warrilow has an illustration of the civic arms (SHST pp277, 280il). The old drinking fountain which formerly stood at the top of Newcastle Street, now in St John Square, was given by the Maddock family in 1881 (JC 34 il). The town was one of the Six Towns which federated in 1910 to form Stoke-on-Trent. **Persons and visitors**. **Ellis Roberts**, artist who was visited in his studio in 1902 by the Prince of Wales, was born in Burslem on Oct 27 1860. After studying at Minton's Art School (1874-1882) he followed a scholarship to South Kensington Art Training School. He painted the portraits of many society beauties and members of the aristocracy including Millicent Duchess of Sutherland and Sir Henry Doulton (Art Journal 1899) (ES Oct 13 1960) (POTP p182). **John Lockwood Kipling** (1837-1911), an architectural sculptor and illustrator came to work for Pinder Bournes of Burslem designing dinner plates by 1863. He reputedly became engaged to his future wife at Rudyard Lake (see) and the couple left for Bombay, India, in 1865, where their son Rudyard Kipling, the novelist, was born (POTP pp135-136). For **Arnold Bennett** (1867-1931), novelist, whose childhood home was Burslem, see below. **Charlotte Rhead** (d1947), ceramic artist, was born in Burslem on Oct 19 1885. For decorating earthenware she specialised in the 'tube lining' technique and worked at Wood and Sons, Crown Pottery, Ellgreave Pottery, Burgess and Leigh all in Burslem, and at AG Richardson's Gordon Pottery, Tunstall, where she produced her prestigious Crown Ducal Ware (POTP p176) (FWNS p60). **Princess Louise** visited Burslem in c1890 (photograph in the Warrillow Collection, Keele University).

1900 to PRESENT. Burslem **School of Art** in Queen Street was built in 1905-7 to designs of AR Wood (BOE p255). Susie Cooper (1903-1995) of Stanfield (see), ceramic designer, was a student here by 1921 (FWNS p49). By the early 1970s the school accommodated the painting section of the Fine Art department of the Faculty of Art and Design of the North Staffordshire Polytechnic (AGT pp80il,81). **Persons and visitors**. **Frederick Harper**, novelist, was born in Gordon Street, Burslem, in 1901. He later lived in several different houses in Stoke-on-Trent. His 'Tilewright's Acre' (1959), a story about the potters of Staffs, was intended to be the first in a trilogy; his novel 'Joseph Capper' (1962) is also set in the Potteries (VFC p60). **A Bernard Hollowood**, novelist and cartoonist, was born in Burslem in 1910. His works include 'Hawksmoor Scandals' (1951) and 'Story of Morrho Velho' (1954) (VFC p67). For Lance-sergeant **JD Baskeyfield** VC, see Stanfield. **Philip**

Oakes, poet, scriptwriter and novelist, was born in Burslem in 1928. His work includes a collection of poems entitled 'Unlucky Jonah' (1954) and the novels 'In the Affirmative' (1969), 'Experiment at Proto' (1973) and 'Shopping for Women' (1994) (VFC pp99-100). **Gracie Fields**, singer and comedian, performed at Queen's Hall, Burslem to 1,200 pottery workers in 1947 for a broadcast concert (ES Nov 7 1998 p19). The family of the sisters **Lorna and Jill Washington**, singers, originate from Burslem. Lorna, born in 1953, and Jill, born in 1955, are sopranos who have sung in light and grand operas, nationally and internationally (FWNS pp72-76ps). The record score for a single game of ten pin bowling is 300 by **Albert Kirkham**, aged 34, of Burslem, set on Dec 5 1965 (GBR 1970 p241. 1981 p248). The biggest football pools win by 1986 was one of £937,807 for a 36p stake on Littlewoods Pools won by **Dennis Turner** of Burslem on April 13 1985. His cheque was the largest ever paid by one company (GBR 1986 p258). Rev **Robert Johnson**, Rector of Burslem, introduced a drinks bar into his church to increase attendance in 1998 (New Statesman. Oct 2 1998 p27 cartoon).

ARNOLD BENNETT. **Early Years**. Arnold Bennett, eldest child of Enoch and Sarah Bennett, was born on May 27 1867 over the pawnshop or draper's shop kept by his father at Nos. 90-92 Hope Street, Hanley. Bennett lived at Nos. 90-92 Hope Street until the age of five. The Bennetts lived at various addresses during his later childhood on account of his father studying to be a solicitor. They are said to have moved to Burslem in 1875, first to Dane Street, and then to No. 175 Newport Lane (the house that Hilda Lessways lived in), Middleport (see). He spent much time in the draper's shop of his maternal grandparents in St John's Square, Burslem. In 1878 or 1879 the Bennetts moved to No. 198 Waterloo Road, Cobridge, after Bennett's father had qualified as a solicitor. In 1881, when Bennett was 14, they moved into the house newly erected by his father, No. 205 Waterloo Road, Cobridge. In 1953, Stoke-on-Trent city council purchased No. 205 Waterloo Road for a museum to Bennett's memory; his fob watch was presented to the museum by his widow Madame Marguerite Bennett in 1954. In 1960 the museum was officially opened to the public by Richard Bennett, his nephew, but it had closed by the mid 1990s (SLM winter 1954 p11p) (AGT pp88il,89) (ES April 22 1981 p5p). By 1999 No. 205 Waterloo Road was split into flats (ES Jan 19 1999 p11). From 1875-6 Bennett was attended Wesleyan Infants School. In 1877 he went to Burslem Endowed School in the Wedgwood Institute. From the autumn term 1880 the school was based at Longport Hall. Here too Harold Hales (his Edward Henry Machin in The Card) was a pupil. From May 1882 Bennett attended Orme Middle School (see Newcastle High School, Newcastle). In Dec 1882 he passed Cambridge Junior Local Examination but did not transfer to Newcastle High School which the pass had qualified him for. Instead, in 1883 he entered his father's office in Piccadilly, Hanley. He was a contributor to the 'Staffordshire Knot' (Arnold Bennett and Stoke-on-Trent. EJD Warrilow. 1966 pp18-23). **Visits from London, and Burslem in his novels**. After failing to pass his law exams Bennett moved to London in March 1889 to work as a shorthand clerk. He returned to the Potteries at Christmas 1899? 1903, and 1907. He passed through the area in a train in 1927. He died at Chiltern Court, Baker Street, London, on March 27 1931 and his ashes were buried in his mother's grave in Burslem Cemetery in July 1931. Burslem is one of Bennett's five towns of the Potteries and as 'Bursley' the setting for his: 'Anna of the Five Towns' (1902), 'The Old Wives' Tale' (1908), 'Clayhanger' (1910), 'Helen with the High Hand' (1910), 'Hilda Lessways' (1911), 'The Card' (1911), 'These Twain' (1916). No. 1 and 1a Queen Street were the basis for Bennett's Clayhanger's Steam Printing Works in 'Clayhanger' (DoE II) (VCH vol 8 p112). In his novels these 1993 Burslem places are:- Queen's Theatre (Snagge Theatre); Leopard Hotel (the Tiger); Swan Inn (the Duck); Bournes Sports (Daniel Povey's confectionery shop); Woolworths (Critchlow's chemists' shop), Provincial Racing (Baines' shop), Best Wishes Cards and Kismet Restaurant (printing works) (ES June 16 1993 p8). In Wedgwood Street to the E of the Town Hall stood the Shambles referred to in 'The Old Wives' Tale' as 'a majestic edifice....for the sale of dead animals.' The Big House (see) is the Conservative Club in 'Clayhanger.' The Wedgwood Institute (see) is the Bursley Endowed School in 'The Old Wives' Tale' and 'The Card.' In Bennett's novels Swan Bank (or Square) is the fictional Duck Bank; Newcastle Street is Oldcastle Street; Westport Road is Sytch Bank; New Street is Buck Row; St John's Square is St Lukes Square; Brickhouse Street is Cock Yard; Clayhanger Street is Bugg's Gutter; Queen Street is Wedgwood Street; Nile Street is Aboukir Street; Chapel Lane is Chapel Alley; Moorland Road is Moorthorne Road; and Hamil Road is Bycars Lane. The present George Hotel between Nile Street and Chapel Lane is the Dragon Inn in 'Clayhanger.' The fictional Duck Bank Chapel and Sunday School in 'Anna of the Five Towns,' 'Clayhanger' and 'The Old Wives' Tale' was a building partly on the site of the present Central Methodist Church in

Chapel Lane (Arnold Bennett's Bursley Trail leaflet. 1999). **After Bennett's death**. On May 10 1932 a bronze plaque to Bennett's memory designed by Gordon M Forsyth was officially unveiled on the wall of his birthplace. By 1972 the birthplace had been demolished and the plaque transferred to the present building built on the site. In 1960 Stoke-on-Trent city council and Civil Trust redeveloped 'The Shambles,' Burslem, as a garden with a pedestal on which is a portrait plaque to Bennett made by Wedgwood's (VB pp189-190). An Arnold Bennett Society may have formed in 1954. It was reactivated by Councillor Horace Barks in May 1978 and called the Arnold Bennett Literary Society. The society reverted to the title Arnold Bennett Society in c1997 (info Jean Potter) (Biography of Horace Barks 1986). His grave was visited by the writer, Beryl Bainbridge, in the early 1980s. The first Bennett memorial lecture was delivered in 1990 by the writer, John Wain. Annual dinners to Bennett's memory were being held at the Prince's Hall, Burslem, by 1993 (ES March 28 1931 pp1p,3. May 26 1931 p5. April 11 1931 p3. July 22 1931 p1ps. Sept 1 1931 p1p. Nov 3 1931 p6. May 7 1932 p3p. May 10 1932. March 19 1993 p8) (STM Dec 1963 p63p. March 1964 p53. May 1967 p22) (SHST p372) (Arnold Bennett. Margaret Drabble. 1974) (POTP p33) (VB p189) (English Journey Beryl Bainbridge. 1983. p79) (TOS pp89-92) (GMS pp104-139) (TWWW Feb 27 1999 p2).

Burslem Branch of the Trent and Mersey Canal. Spurs off the Trent and Mersey Canal at Newport and terminated at the end of Navigation Road, where a tramroad, authorised in 1802, carried traffic up into Burslem (HCMS No. 5). The branch opened in 1805 (VCH vol 8 p110), and closure was sanctioned in 1962 (HCMS No. 5).

Burslem Grange A ward of Stoke-on-Trent district by 1991 embracing S Burslem, Cobridge, Middleport areas. The Grange part of the name is perhaps from the former Rushton Grange.

Burslem Park Opened in 1894 (PPP vol 2 p17p). Was laid out on 22 acres of waste land between Hamil Road and Moorland Road, Burslem. The lake disappeared in 1921 when the covering of an old colliery shaft beneath the water collapsed (VCH vol 8 p107 note).

Burston Small village near the confluence of Jolpool Brook and the Trent 1m NW of Sandon. Formerly formed a township with Aston-by-Stone and Little Stoke in Hilderstone quarter in Stone ancient parish (W p362). A tiny hoard of bronze Roman coins was found in Jolpool Brook below Beck House in the village in 1979; in 1999 they were kept by Robert Selby (BBH p4) (info Robert Selby). A former chapel at Burston is said, by tradition, to have been built on the spot where Mercian King Wulfhere murdered his second son, Rufin, for converting to Christianity (SMC p170) (SIS p7) and was built by Rufin's mother Queen Ermenilda, daughter of Egbert, King of Kent (NSSG p12). Another tradition has Rufin and his brother Wulfad being slain by their father in Eccleshall church (W p373). Bowers and Clough say a chapel stood at Burston in 1580 (RHPS p79); Erdeswick saw it. It stood at SJ 94603000 (LGS p95) (NSSG p12). Cox, writing in the early C18, notes its remains were still standing until recently (SD p79). Garner and White writing in the mid C19 noted that its door had been used in a barn in the village (W p363), and the capital of a column of it had recently been dug up (GNHS p546). Bowers and Clough say the door of Burston Lodge is said to be from the ancient chapel (RHPS p80). A curious stone sign inscribed 'WT AI 67 688' now high up on the exterior W wall of the present chapel, approximately 100 yards away, is believed to come from the old chapel (RHPS p79il). Chetwynd says the chapel was much visited by pilgrims, which has led a later writer to suggest that the great road from London formerly passed through Burston village, not to the E of it as at present (OSST 1949-50 p13). The present mission chapel, St Rufin, at the W end of the village was built in 1859 (LDD). The name. Burston has been identified by Duignan and others with Burweston which has been identified with DB Burouestone (SSE 1996 p11). Others imply Burston was both DB Burouestone (Burweston) and DB parua Sandone (Little Sandon) (BBH p6). The name is from Anglo-Saxon Bura's (BBH p5), Burgwine's or Burgwulf's or Burgstan's town or farm or tun (DUIGNAN) (SSE 1996 p11) (SPN p118). Burston may be derived from 'burial stone' after the tradition of Rufin being buried here (SMM p21). A Lancaster bomber crashed in a field on the hill between Burston and Sandon on April 30 1945, the crew of seven, one British and six Canadian, all died. On Aug 28 1999 a square stone was set up to their memory on the W side of the Stone-Lichfield road, S of Burston (ES April 20 1999 p13. Aug 12 1999 p15p. Aug 30 1999 p2) (SLM Oct 1999 p20pcs).

Burston Hall Burston, Sandon. Sometime seat of Henry Fourdrinier, inventor of a paper-making machine. In 1840 he celebrated his golden wedding here, but died at Mavesyn Ridware in 1854 (RHPS pp159,160) (SIS p100).

Burton Former manor and township in Castle Church ancient parish (W p343). The name means farmstead by a fortified manor (SPNO p75). The sub-manor

of Burtons appears in DB. Later, Burton appears as Burton (1276), and Burton-juxta-Stafford (1295) (SPNO p75). Burton Hall (see) was the manor house.

Burton Abbey Former Benedictine abbey in the centre of Burton upon Trent, and the most important monastery in Staffs in the Middle Ages. The date 1002 is always given as the year of the foundation (HS p51). It was founded by Wulfric Spot, Earl of Mercia, perhaps in that year because he had taken part with other Saxons in the treacherous massacre of Danes at Marchington and was in remorse (HS p51). He founded it at Burton because a religious house established by a C7 Irish woman, Modwen, had existed here and her shrine was here. In 1004 he obtained a charter of confirmation from the king (HS p50). The name 'Spot' or 'Spott' appears only in a reference in the abbey Annals of the C13 and in a passage in a history of Abington abbey, Limerick. Its meaning is obscure unless it refers to the place Spot Acre (see), or to Spotland, Lancs (IHOBT p5). Wulfric is thought to have granted 48 estates to the abbey and in subsequent years it acquired many others in E Staffs. It acquired Wetmore, which included Horninglow and Anslow in 1012; Stapenhill by 1050, and Branston after 1066 and before 1086. The abbot was lord of Burton manor until the Dissolution (IHOBT p5). William I visited the shrine of St Modwen here during his reign (HOS p26). For a long time after its foundation it was the only Anglian monastery N of the Trent (even if only six feet N of the Trent) (SSE 1996 p24). In 1214, Nicholas, the Pope's legate came from Rome to remove the Interdict. At the Pope's bidding he went through England filling up all vacant livings. Whilst at Burton Abbey Langton, Archbishop of Canterbury, wrote to him forbidding him to interfere with English livings (SOSH pp110,118). King John is said to have stayed at Burton Abbey (R&S p8). With its 35 professed monks in 1295 Burton Abbey had the largest community in the county of any period and was the most wealthy (HOS p26). The abbey was the only one in Staffs which came within the category of the greater houses (except perhaps Tutbury) (LGS p96). However, in 1310 the monks complained that they were the poorest of all Benedictine monks in England. Bishop Langton stayed the night of Jan 15 1319 at the abbey (SSE 1994 p4). In the rebellion of Thomas, Earl of Lancaster, against Edward II, in 1322, the earl stored his treasure in the abbey. When he retreated after failing to hold Burton Bridge, the abbey suffered at the rebels' hands and the abbot was accused of retaining the earl's treasure and had difficulty clearing himself (HOS p26). Henry V stayed at Burton Abbey in 1414 and oversaw the proceedings of the King's Bench which were occurring at Lichfield (Henry V. GL Harriss. pp65-66) (VCH vol 14 p12). Edward IV visited the abbey in 1473 (HOS p26). It surrendered on Nov 14 1539; the last in the county to do so. But Burton was re-established by the king in 1541 as a college of canons (HOS p28). It was abolished with the other Staffs collegiate churches (except for Wolverhampton) under an Act of 1545 (HOS p28). In 1546 Sir William Paget acquired the lands of the abbey (HOS p23). In 1549 he acquired the property and possessions of the abbey (LGS p96).

AFTER THE DISSOLUTION. At some time after the Dissolution the abbey's Annals, a major source for the political history of England in the C13, went to the BM (HOS p26) (SH pp3,8,9) (SK p202 No. 120, also in the BM is a copy of the will of Wilfrid Spot). The abbey church continued as the parish church; by the later C16, Erdeswick noted, a wall had been built to shut off the church from the rest of the abbey ruins. By that date the E end of the church was in ruins (SH pp2,4,33) (info KL Neal). The old church, incorporating parts of the abbey church, was found to be unsafe in 1718 and was demolished in 1719-26. It was replaced by the present church built nearby by 1728. The font and some alabaster slabs from the old church survive in the S porch of the present church (LGS p96). An etching, an ink drawing, and two plans said for several centuries to represent the old church do not agree, and have been shown recently to contain some inaccuracies or to relate to other churches. The etching by Wenceslaus Hollar c1660 showing the church from the S appears in Monasticon Anglicanum by William Dugdale (1661), and may be of the church with some inaccuracies. An ink drawing in WSL signed 'WH 1643' purporting to be by Wenceslaus Hollar and entitled 'A Picture of the Abbey Church of Burton on Trent' has seduced many but it is a forgery by Peter Thompson (c1800-1874). It is an almost direct copy of an engraving of Hereford cathedral after the collapse of its W tower in 1786, and was erroneously used by Henry Rye to reconstruct the abbey's ground plan in the late C19 and has been used since: in work published in 1929 and the 1950s. A plan found among papers once belonging to Browne Willis, an historian, in the Bodleian Library, Oxford shows the church at the time of its demolition in the earlier C18, but it does not agree with Hollar's etching in Monasticon Anglicanum; another plan which was found in the Paget papers at Beaudesert Hall (see) and published by Shaw in his SHOS vol 1 pl III, is definitely not of Burton Abbey church (info KL Neal) (SSE vol 5 1993 pp35-70) (SSAHST vol 37 1995-96 pp105-118). A remnant of the wall of the E range of the cloisters could still be seen in the late C20 in poor condition behind the Market Hall (info KL Neal); the same or another wall retains masonry from the abbey (STMSM Sept 1973 p27), and perhaps either can be identified with the buttressed walling (formerly part of the abbey) in the alley known in the late C19 as Friars' Walk (see) (HS p facing p47); a rescued figurehead from the abbey has been inserted into the same or another wall (STMSM Aug 1976 p23p of). Built over the infirmary, S of the former abbey church, is a Victorian mansion called Burton Abbey (see). A part of the infirmary site was excavated in 1975 (SSAHST 1977-78 pp11-31). The abbey's enclosing wall had three gateways. The gateway known as the Abbey Gate, with its porter's lodge, which stood in High Street opposite New Street until 1927 when Lichfield Street was widened, has been partly rebuilt at Newton Park, Newton Solney, Derbys (HS p52p of porter's lodge) (STMSM Sept 1973 p27) (ABTOP p142) (info KL Neal). (GNHSS p22) (W pp533-535) (NSFCT 1883 pp82-86 ils, plan. 1922 pp134-5) (BTNHAST 1897; readers are warned to be wary of Henry Rye's work in this volume, according to KL Neal (1999) his research was done in too much hurry and was badly reported. 1903) (SSE 1993 pp35-70 ils).

Burton Abbey Victorian gabled house by the Trent S of Burton upon Trent Market Hall. The house was built into and over the infirmary of the monastery, Burton Abbey (see above) (HS p51p) (BOE p85) (SGS p73). In the chimney stack above the entrance is a carving of the C13 seal of Burton Abbey. This depicts the Virgin Mary seated on a lean-to roof of a church. Many people in the past have thought this church was a representation of Burton Abbey, and the lean-to structure as a Galilee porch, but there is no proof of this (info KL Neal). The house has been a club and was an inn known as Abbey Inn by 1999. The arch in the grounds is not a genuine remnant of Burton Abbey left in situ, but may contain abbey masonry. Sculptured figures from Burton Abbey can be seen in niches in the wall surrounding the car park (info KL Neal).

Burton Bache Field name in Tutbury derived from the Burton family who were resident here, a descendent of which resided at Fauld Hall (see) (SHOS vol 1 p56).

Burton Bridge Ancient bridge which crossed the Trent at Burton upon Trent. It ran in a sweep from the old Ashby road on the Derbys side N of Broad Holme to cross over the southern tip of Burton Meadow to join Bridge Street in Burton. On account of its length it was considered the most famous bridge in the county until it was demolished. The bridge was first mentioned soon after 1100 (HOS p48) or in the early C12 (SHC 1916 pp242,243) (VCH vol 2 p280). Shaw thought it had been built before the Norman Conquest and probably at about the same time of the founding of Burton Abbey (1004) (SHOS vol 1 p6 note, pp14-17 pl 1) (W pp532-533) (IHOBT p17). Others say it was built in c1174, or in 1175 (SOS) (SOSH p357) (W pp532-533) by Abbot Bernard of Burton Abbey (d1175) (NHS p372) for in 1175 William de la Warde gave land for the benefit of the Bridge of Burton (SOS) (ABMEE p5). (BTNHAST vol 5). The bridge was originally 515 yards long and 15 feet wide. It was widened to 26 feet in 1831 from the Winshill end to the Trundle Hole, the beginning of the third arm of the river, later silted up (IHOBT p17). The number of arches noted has varied from 33 in the later C16 to 37 in the mid C19 (NHS p372) (ABMEE p5) (SGS p73) (IHOBT p17). The monks of Burton were responsible for its upkeep, although gifts were also made (HOS p48). An abbey rental of 1319 includes a reference to a keeper of the bridge. By 1441 the keeper was a layman (IHOBT p17).

In an attempt by Edward II to crush his powerful cousin, Thomas, Earl of Lancaster of Tutbury Castle (see) a skirmish was fought over Burton Bridge on March 10 1322. The skirmish has became known as the **battle** of Burton Bridge. The Earl had the bridge - the only crossing on the Trent for many miles - defended against Edward II. But a tenant of the abbot of Burton, who had suffered at Lancaster's hands, advised the king's forces to cross a ford at Walton which might be passable. The Earls of Richmond and Pembroke were sent to secure it, followed by the king and the main army. They passed safely and approached Burton via Branston. Meanwhile a sham attack by some of the king's forces at the E end of the bridge lead by Robert Waters, kept Lancaster's forces occupied. Finding himself trapped and without his Scots allies, who had failed to arrive, and Robert de Holland, who had deserted to the king, Lancaster retreated to Tutbury Castle to secure a treasure chest containing money to pay the Scots levies. In his escape north to Pontefract Castle, Yorks, the chest fell into the Trent near Tutbury Castle and was lost for the next 500 years (UTR pp49,50) (W p535) (SHJ vol 9 p95) (LGS p239). 'Tales of the Midlands' by Kathleen Fidler pp150-161 is an account of the battle in novel form.

The bridge had a **chapel** at the town end. Mass was frequently celebrated in it and the donations went to the bridge's upkeep. The chapel was dedicated to St James, and by 1465 there was a bridge guild with its own priest (SHC vol 1 p249) (BTNHAST vol 5 part 1 pp8-9) (VCH vol 2 p280 note). It was demolished in c1777 (HOBT) (SHC 1934 p26) and a warehouse occupied the site by the mid C19 (W pp532-533). According to tradition the chapel was erected by Edward II after the battle of Burton Bridge as a thanks-giving for his victory (W 1834 ed), but this appears to be not the case (VCH vol 2 p280 note); an abbey rental of 1319 shows that the chapel existed before that year (IHOBT p17).

On the grant of Burton Abbey property to Sir William Paget at the Dissolution, liability for the bridge's upkeep passed to him and his successors (VCH vol 2 p280). The bridge was noted in the C16 by Leland (LI vol 5 p19) and Erdeswick (SH p31). For the bridge in the Civil War see under Burton upon Trent. The Paget estate papers record expenditure on repairs in 1636, 1684, 1716, 1718, 1747, and 1781 (IHOBT p17). In the mid C18 the leading horses pulling a carriage over the bridge which contained a lady of note jumped over the parapet, and in order to save the coach and its occupant the traces of the leading horses were cut, and they fell into the Trent and were drowned (GM vol 21 1751 p296) (SHC 1934 p26). The route over the bridge was turnpiked in 1753; a proportion of the tolls going to Lord Paget (VCH vol 2 p280). The third arch from the western end fell during the flood of 1795 and was rebuilt in 1796 at a cost of £200 (ABMEE p5). The bridge was always barely wide enough for one carriage and was demolished in 1864 (VCH vol 2 p280) (STMSM Sept 1973 p27) (SGS p73) or in 1876 (BTOP vol 1 p1 il drawing assigned to WF Francis) (IHOBT p17). A far shorter and wider bridge called Trent Bridge (see), built slightly further down stream, was opened in 1864. Traces of the old bridge remain under a house in Meadow Lane and one arch was rebuilt in the rock garden at Newton Park, Newton Solney, Derbys. Other stones were used to build a grotto at the bridge end of the Stapenhill Recreation Grounds (BTOP vol 1 p1). (Wyatt's map 1757) (GM 1751? vol xxi p296 pl) (The plate of the bridge in Shaw is an engraving taken from a drawing in the possession of Miss Greattorix of Leicester) (HS p47 il) (ABTOP p142).

Burton Castle Burton upon Trent. Based on the Burtone (see) entry in DB some have concluded that there was a castle at Burton in the later C11. A license to crenellate Burton Abbey was granted to Lord Paget when he came into possession of it at its dissolution in 1540. Among the Paget papers is a drawing of the abbey with Tudor artillery bastions sketched in. However, the bastions may never have been built (CAMS p16). (NSJFS 1966 p43).

Burtone Is recorded twice in DB as land belonging to Henry de Ferrers. Its identity has long been disputed, and whether two separate places are being alluded to. At the first recorded Burtone Henry de Ferrers has half a hide, 'in which his castle stands.' Traditionally this entry had been explained as a scribal error for Tutbury or as an attempt at Burgtone, the tun of the borough of Tutbury. According to Dr Philip Morgan the two entries probably relate to the same holding. Dr Morgan thinks there is little reason to doubt that Henry de Ferrers had a castle at a place called Burtone. The theory that Henry de Ferrers held a second castle at a place called Burtone (his first being at Tutbury) has been preferred by most writers; they have assigned this second castle to Burton upon Trent, which has helped to prove that Burton upon Trent is mentioned in DB. But Dr Morgan says there is no later evidence of a Ferrers' interest in Burton. Dr Morgan prefers the theory that Burtone relates to the later castle and borough of Tutbury; that Burtone (the 'tun of the fort') was the settlement named as a result of its proximity to Tutbury and was ultimately displaced by the expansion of the borough in the later C12. Nearby Burton upon Trent, as Margaret Gelling suggests, would therefore have been a 'burhtun' (a 'fort settlement'), perhaps established in the centuries before the Danish wars of the late C9, quite independent of Tutbury: A rentpayer called Asketill of the Castle at Stretton, near Burton, is mentioned in an early C12 survey of the Burton abbey estate (SHJ summer 1987 p46). (VCH vol 4) (SHCST 1971-3 pp11-12) (DB edited by John Morris. Phillimore. 1976. Notes).

Burton-Extra Former township in Burton upon Trent ancient parish, outside the Burton township boundaries. Became a separate civil parish in 1866 (GLAUE p406). Bond End was in this township (IHOBT p45).

Burton Hall or Manor House. House over 1.5m SSW of Stafford, at the S end of Burton Manor Road. The old hall, the manor house of Burton manor, was surrounded by a moat (ESH p58). It was owned by the le Tayeurs in the C13. By 1247 the manor was jointly held with William le Palmer and later it was held solely by this family. They held it to 1444 when it passed to the Whitgreaves, who held it until George II's reign (HOSCC p94) (SAC p36). It was some time their seat except in the C17 when the hall was tenanted by the Riley or Ryley family (VCH vol 5 p89). The old hall with turrets was haunted by Sir Thomas Whitgreave's ghost (FSP p10). Sometime in the C17 or C18 a farm seems to have been built on the site. After George II's reign the manor passed through several hands until, Francis, a member of another branch of the Whitgreave family, purchased the farm a short time before 1851 (VCH vol 5 p89). Francis Whitgreave had built on the moated site the present brick house designed by EW Pugin. It was completed in 1855, with blue and yellow brick embellishments (VCH vol 5 p89) (BOE p250) (MR p294) (SN July 5 1958 p5p. July 15 1994 p12ps) (SAC p37p). The hall became a social club for the workers at British Reinforced Concrete Engineering Co Ltd in the mid 1920s (VCH vol 6 p196). It became Stafford Grammar School (new creation) in 1982 (SN July 15 1994 p12).

Burton Hall House in Tutbury and seat of the Burton family, a descendent of which resided at Fauld Hall (see) (SHOS vol 1 p56).

Burton Holmes Field name in Tutbury derived from the Burton family who were resident here, a descendent of which resided at Fauld Hall (see) (SHOS vol 1 p56).

Burton House Appears to have stood on N side of Burton Bank Lane, Moss Pit, Stafford. It may have been a house known as Moss Pit Bank, occupied by William Keen in 1811. Burton House was occupied by John Morgan, solicitor in 1860, and in 1882 by another solicitor, Charles Hand. After WW2 it became a hospital. In c1970 it was demolished and the area became an housing estate (SAC pp22,23il of gardens).

Burton Manor Suburb of S Stafford, 1m NE of Coppenhall. The name is from Burton Hall or Manor House.

Burton Meadow Name for a large island in the Trent at Burton upon Trent N of Broad Holme.

Burton Moors To W of Burton upon Trent (HOBTU p3).

Burton Turnings Name for the old junction of Burton Old Road and Ryknild Street which stood in the vicinity of Cappers Lane roundabout, 1.25m E of Lichfield cathedral. A cross, recorded in the mid C13, may have stood at this junction. The name Burton Turnings was prevalent in the mid C19 (VCH vol 14 p276).

Burton upon Trent Ancient parish and large town 21m E of Stafford on the W bank of the Trent.
EARLY. In Brighton Museum is a small axe said to have been found at Burton (NSJFS 1962 p30). A small stone axe of? jadeite of the **Neolithic** or **Bronze Age** has been found in the Burton area (NSJFS 1964 p18). Burton's etymology has suggested to some a settlement of **Roman** or earlier origin; it has been identified with the Roman settlement of Ad Trivonam (see). Stukeley supposed that a Roman station was situated at Burton, but no Roman finds had been made at Burton by c1900, except the somewhat indefinite statement that in pulling down Burton Bridge in 1876 a buttress of what was said to be of Roman origin was discovered (THS p41) (BTNHAST vol 5 part 1 p4) (VCH vol 1 p189). A native imitation of a coin of Emperor Claudius (41-54 AD) was found in Grange Street in 1948 (BTIH p10). Icknield Street passed in a direct line through Burton parish, entering it at a point known as Gallows Bridge above Branston, across the Butts and through the wood where the remains of it can be plainly seen near the cottage of the gamekeeper on the Anglesey estate leaving Staffs at Monk's Bridge (STMSM Sept 1973 p26). See also Shobnall.
600 to 1000. According to aural tradition an Irish missionary **Modwen** (or Modwena, Modwenna, Monennae, Modwenna, Mowenna, Mudwin, Modwenn, Monenna) is said to have founded a religious community on the Island of Andressey in the Trent at Burton probably in the C7, although some say it was found in c900 (LGS p95). Her community was probably sacked by the Danes in the 870s. Bones purporting to be hers were enshrined in Burton Abbey when it was founded in 1002 or 1003 (LGS p95) (SL p54). She has been identified with the Monennae in a work titled 'Vita Sanctae Monennae' written by Conchubranus, an Irish monk, probably between 1000 and 1050. The essential details of her life are that, many years after founding a convent at Faugha, County Lough, Ireland, in c630 AD she spent some time at Whitby Abbey under the protection of King Aldfrith of Northumbria. Later, in c685, on her way to Rome, she established a small community of nuns on the Island of Andressey (see) (BTIH p11). In the early C12 she was identified by Geoffrey (abbot of Burton 1114-1151) in his 'Sanctae Modwennae Vita et Tractatus de Miraculis ejus' with St Monenna, an early Irish royal abbess saint, who founded the monastery of Killevy in south Armagh, Ireland, and died in 517. However, it has been discovered St Monenna never left Ireland (SSE 1996 pp24-28) (BTIH p11). St Modwen gives her name to a spring on Andressy Island and another at Canwell and she is depicted on glass in churches at Burton (St Paul), Pillaton Hall and Stapenhill. (SHOS vol 1 pp1-2) (GNHS p139) (W p533) (SOSH pp355-356) (STMSM Sept 1973 p26) (BSB p509) (SH pp2-3) (ODS p304) (SSGLST pp39-40). Burton may have developed as an armoury town in the reign of King Offa (757-796) (IHOBT

p5). The **name** is of Anglo-Saxon origin from Burhton, 'an enclosed or fortified place' (DUIGNAN). Or 'fort settlement' (NSJFS 1981 p3) or 'tun of the fort' (SSE 1996 p11). It has long been identified with the Byrtune mentioned in the will of Wulfric Spot (c1002), founder of Burton Abbey (SHC 1916 p31) (SSE 1996 p11); Dugdale also thought the Burhtun mentioned in the same will to be Burton; but others have identified this with Burton Hastings, Warws (SHC 1916 p38). On account of Burton's identification with Byreton (or Byrtune), a word which is synonymous with Bureton, a word used by people in the Middle Ages to denote a place of Roman or British origin it was assumed Burton possessd a bury or fort of a British chief or Roman general (W p531). Burton makes an appearance by name as Birtuna in the C12 (SHC 1916 p135). Today it is properly written Burton upon Trent, however it has appeared as Burton-upon-Trent and Burton-on-Trent (info KL Neal).
1000 to 1500. Burton may have been an original parish from which Tatenhill broke away or Tatenhill was the original parish from which Burton broke away (SHC 1916 p197). Burton **manor**, held by the abbot of Burton Abbey in 1086, does not appear in DB, although it was then extensive having many estates in Staffs, Derbys and Warws. Some think Burton manor was intended to be in the survey: The Register of Burton Abbey gives a copy of the original Return, and it appears that the two teamlands (1.5 hides) which Burton Abbey was supposed to hold in Stafford town were really in 'Staffordsire.' The copying clerks, in entering up Domesday, had missed out the 'sire,' and entered the land under Stafford instead of under Burton upon Trent (SHC 1916 p170). Or Burton may have appeared in DB as Burtone (see). It may have been omitted because there were Domesday commissioners for each county and the Staffs commissioners thought the Derbys commissioners had recorded the town and vice versa so no report was made, or perhaps, the reports were lost or suppressed (NSFCT 1952 p35). Of the different tenants, and by what services they held their land see Shaw (SHOS vol 1) and Hackwood (SCSF p118). Widows, at the end of the C13, customarily held onto their husbands property on Burton Abbey manors until their heir came of age, although usually widows held their dead husbands' tenements for life (VCH vol 6 p35). The court of record at Burton held every Friday in the later C18 was known as Jenter's Court (SHOS vol 1 p11), or Genters Court (W p531). A town of Burton grew at the gates of Burton Abbey. It was increased in size by the abbots in the late C13 who created the gridiron pattern of the streets still surviving (HOS p56). The earliest reference to Burton being a **borough** is in 1203-04. By the early C18, or earlier, borough status had lapsed, although in 1798 it was still nominally a borough, and became a true borough when incorporated in 1878 (NSJFS 1972 p68). Shaw noted Burton retained the name of Borough, merely with reference to the translation of it as Burgos, a town (W p531). Burton inhabitants enjoyed the privilege of unknown origin of being excused from jury service at the county court (SHOS vol 1 p11). There were **gallows** at Branston at Gallows Bridge (see), at Derby Turn (see), and near Winshill at Hanging Hill (see) (IHOBT pp16,21). The **curfew bell** was tolled each evening from 7.45pm from Michaelmas Day to Lady Day at Burton (SCSF p160). There was a **pinfold** in the C18 in Horninglow Street (IHOBT p35). There were four **religious guilds** in Burton in the Middle Ages (NSJFS 1979 p15). The custom of **well dressing** was observed at Burton (FOS p103). Burton suffered **natural disasters** when the Trent overflowed in Nov 1254 and flooded the town, and in 1255 when most of the town was destroyed by fire (SOSH p356) (SHOS vol 1 p17) (W p535). On Dec 16 1292 a boy called William Bond fell through Burton parish church roof whilst working on it as a carpenter. He landed in front of the altar during Vespers and died (VB p100).
Royal visits. Edward I visited Burton in 1275 and 1284 (R&S p10). In 1322 during the rebellion of Thomas, **Earl of Lancaster**, against his cousin Edward II, the earl occupied Burton Bridge (see) to stop royal troops crossing the Trent. He then retreated and set fire to the town (HOS p26). **Henry V** stayed at Burton Abbey in 1414. **Edward IV** was at Burton Abbey in 1473 (R&S p16) (HOS p26).
MARKETS AND FAIRS. A **market** to be held on Thursdays was granted to Burton Abbey by King John on April 2 1200 (HOS p56) (NSJFS 1971 p50); King John is commemorated by a sculpture in the top pediment over the main entrance to the present market hall (VB p101) (IHOBT p20). The charter was confirmed by Henry III (THS) (SCSF p94). The old **market cross** stood in front of the Almshouses in the Swine Market, on a site which in 1869 was occupied by the Old White Lion Inn (HOBT) (SCSF p89). The first recorded market house was built in the market place by Abbot Thomas Field (1472-1493). This was pulled down in 1772. The old Town Hall, with a market arcade below, was erected by the Earl of Uxbridge in its place. This in turn was demolished to make way for the present market hall, which was opened on Oct 23 1893. St Paul's Institute at the other end of the town became the new Town Hall (IHOBT p20). Some say the old Town Hall was

demolished in 1883, and the market hall opened that year (BTOP vol 1 p15). There were **fairs** on: **Candlemas day** (Feb 2) (W p531) (IRB pp32-33) (Whitaker's Almanac) (COOKE gives Feb 5), it was toll free (THS p45) (SCSF p102). April 5 (W p531) (IRB pp32-33) (Whitaker's Almanac) (COOKE) (THS p45) (SCSF p102). **Holy Thursday** (Ascension Day) (W p531) (IRB pp32-33) (Whitaker's Almanac) (COOKE) (THS p45) (SCSF p102). Cooke gives **July 16** and describes it as 'of no note' (SCSF p98). Vigil, feast, and morrow of St Modwen (**Oct 29**) granted by King John in 1200 (W p531) (IRB pp32-33) (IHOBT p20). According to Pitt this fair was granted by Henry III; it was Burton's principle fair; and a fair, lasting five days, preceded it during which 'more fine horses, particularly of the black breed, are usually exposed to sale than at any other fair in the kingdom' (Whitaker's Almanac gives 28 Oct) (COOKE) (THS p45) (SCSF pp98,102). There was a fair in 1792 (OWEN), and there still was in 1888 (LHE p264).

BREWING. Brewing, which is Burton's chief industry, was started by the monks of Burton Abbey in the C11. They discovered that the geology of the area, comprising gypsum beds, produced the hard water containing magnesium and calcium sulphates excellent for beer making (NSFCT 1974 p80). After the dissolution of the abbey in 1540, brewing continued in the former abbey premises and in numerous inns throughout the town. By the early C17 there were almost 50 licensed victuallers in the town of a population of 1,500. Surplus beer was sold in London under the name of 'Darbie Ale' (NSJFS 1974 p80). It has been suggested that Burton beer was known in London as early as 1625, when sold in the Peacock Inn in Gray's Inn Road, but there is no convincing evidence for this. The first certain reference to Burton beer in London appeared in the Spectator of May 26 1712 (IHOBT p36). The victuallers personally sold to the public. Professional brewers who sold to merchants and innkeepers began to appear at the beginning of the C18. Benjamin Printon (d1728/9), the first common brewer of Burton, established a small brewery at the western end of the Trent Bridge in 1708 (SHOS vol 1 p13) (VCH vol 2 p243) (NSJFS 1974 p80) (IHOBT p36); out of this developed the Musgrave Brewery which grew to be one of Burton's largest after 1750 (NSJFS 1974 p89). Beer was transported on the Trent to the Baltic and Russia. The Wilson-Allsopp Brewery was founded in 1736 by Benjamin Wilson I (d1800) (VCH vol 2 p245) (NSJFS 1974 p81). The Sketchley Brewery founded by Samuel Sketchley was established in 1741 (NSJFS 1974 p88). The Worthington Brewery was founded in the High Street in 1760 by William Worthington I (NSJFS 1974 p89). The Bass Brewery was founded by William Bass in 1777 (NSJFS 1974 p89). Between 1740 and 1777 the number of brewers in the town increased to 15 (IHOBT p36). These were some of the 13 breweries in Burton by 1780 (NSJFS 1974 p90). Increased strife in the Baltic countries and the war with France in the 1790s damaged the ale trade. The Baltic trade suddenly and totally collapsed in 1807, as a result of the Berlin and Milan Decrees. By 1822, of the 13 breweries of 1780, five survived. In 1826 prohibitive tariffs effectively terminated trade with Sweden and Russia (The Times. Weekend Section. Nov 9 1991 p10). For the rest of the C19 beer was sold almost entirely to the home market (IAS p83). India Pale Ale was conceived in London but perfected by Burton's water. Two thirds of the ale exported to India was supplied by Burton brewers (The Times. Weekend Section. Nov 9 1991 p10). These brewers moved to Burton in the later C19: Ind Coope from Romford (1856), Charrington (1872), Truman Hanbury Buxton (1874), Mann Crossman Paulin (1875), AB Walker from Liverpool (1879), Thomas Syand James Parker (1879), Peter Walker from Warrington (1880), and Everards from Leicester (1892). In 1869 there were 26 breweries in Burton, in the 1880s there were 31: Two, Bass and Allsopp, were then the biggest in the world (The Times. Weekend Section. Nov 9 1991 p10) (IAS p83). The malting season in the winter began with a 'Statutes Fair' in Oct, when extra labourers (known as 'Norkies') needed for turning the grain in the malthouses came from Norfolk and Suffolk. The trains bringing them to Burton also brought the grain (The Bass Museum guide). In 1921 the private railway which linked the central breweries with the suburban malthouses gave rise to 32 level crossings in the town and 87 miles of track (The Times. Weekend Section. Nov 9 1991 p10) and totalled 50 miles when closed in 1967 (IAS p83) (SL p162). Concentration of ownership of the breweries led to there being only four breweries remaining in 1976 (IAS p83).

OTHER INDUSTRIES. Besides brewing another industry based on the local geology, which Burton had taken to by the Tudor period, was ornamental work in alabaster, a chief exponent in this art was Joseph Hollemans (see below). The working of alabaster at Burton was noted by Leland, Camden and Plot (NSFCT 1979 p21). Woollen cloth-making was carried on at Burton in the C16 (IHOBT p28). In the C17 a chief trade of Burton was again in clothing and woollen cloths, with specialties known as 'kersies' and 'tammies' (SCSF p112). In 1780 Robert 'Parsley' Peel, grandfather of the famous Prime

Minister, moved his cotton textile mill from near Accrington, Lancs to Burton. Eventually, there were five Peel mills at Burton, one near the old corn mill, two at Bond End, a fourth at the Upper Weir and the fifth at Forge Mill. By 1841 all the mills had closed (IHOBT p39). Ryknield Engine Co Ltd in Wellington Road produced cars, buses and lorries before going into liquidation in 1910 (BCFF p158). A windmill was in existence by 1818 at approximately SK 241234 to NW of the railway station, in the yard of the Railway Hotel, at the end of Derby Lane (later Derby Street). It was sold off in 1844 (WBJ p17). It was demolished in 1891 when owned by George Read & Son (ABTOP p17il). Job thinks, 'Read's Mill' which appeared in CL July 31 1969 at Burton upon Trent, could be the windmill at Hartshill, Stoke-on-Trent (WBJ p17).

GRAMMAR SCHOOL. There was a school at Burton by 1453. Burton Grammar School was founded or endowed by Abbot William Beyne, Bene, Bean or Beare sometime between 1502 to 1530. The school was functioning in 1531. Beyne erected the school house on ground belonging to the Abbey in Friars' Walk (see). A school house in the churchyard is mentioned in 1549, it was extended in 1568 and rebuilt in 1834. It moved to Bond Street in 1877. The headmaster's house there was damaged in the 1916 air raid and subsequently adapted for school use. When the school moved to Winshill in 1957 the vacant buildings (gone by the late 1990s) were used by the technical college. The grammar school became the comprehensive, co-educational Abbot Beyne School in 1975 (VCH vol 6 pp154-156) (ABTOP p27p). (W p537) (SOSH p125) (A History of the Burton upon Trent Grammar School. GE Radford. 1973) (Grammar Schools in Staffs. Staffs Study Book 14. p25il). **Alumni**: Earl St Vincent; a resident of the town remembered a school desk having the name John Jervis carved upon it in schoolboy fashion (NSFCT 1923 p134); Major John Coleman-Cooke (alias Langridge Ford) (b1915), editor, scriptwriter and critic; his film 'The Harvest That Kills' appeared in 1967 (VFC p29).

1500 to 1642. After the Dissolution Burton manor became the possession of Sir William Paget of Beaudesert, in whose family it remained until at least the end of the C18 (SHOS vol 1 p8). Burton Abbey **church** continued as the parish church. During the Civil War it was wrecked by a gunpowder explosion. This church was demolished in 1719-26 and the present one, St Modwen, E of the Market Place, built on or near the site (LGS p96) (BOE p83). There was no **wake** in the later C18 (SHOS vol 1 p13). Burton had a parish feast on the nearest Sunday to Oct 29 in the mid C19 (W p531). The **administration of the town** was the responsibility of the Town Masters, two officials appointed by the trustees of the lands owned by the town. The Town Masters also had to maintain the market cross, a gate in Derby Street (the modern Waterloo Street) and the school house. Two charities were honoured on St Thomas' Day (Dec 21); one known as the 'Widows Groats,' and the other was a distribution of the rents collected from a benefaction property by the 'two Town Masters' (SCSF p47) (FOS p132). In 1775 an Act of parliament appointed 75 town commissioners with powers to levy a rate to pave, repair, cleanse and light the town (IHOBT p35). A big **flood** occurred in 1514 (LGS p96). On the nights of Nov 15 and 16 1574 an aurora borealis or northern lights was seen from Burton (W p535). **Persons and Visitors**. For the case of a boy said to be possessed of the devil, similar to the Boy of Bilston, see under Stapenhill. For **Dame Paulet**, who endowed an almshouse in 1593, see Dame Paulet's Almshouse. Mrs **Ellen Parker** endowed in 1634 an almshouse for six poor women on the E side of High Street. Shaw in the late C18 described it as 'lately new-fronted' (SHOS vol 1 p12). A lecture funded out of a gift given by **Thomas Boilston**, a citizen and cloth-worker of London, who left 800L in trust to the Company of Cloth workers to pay the lecturer's salary. The lecture was given in the parish church every Thursday morning. The lecturer was appointed by the bailiff or chief officers in Burton and five or six inhabitants with the advice and approbation of three ministers. In the late C18 there was a board in the church about the lecture. No date is given (SHOS vol 1 p17). **Robert Sutton**, the son of a carpenter, was in born in Burton in the early 1540s. He studied at Douai College and was ordained a Catholic priest. Under the Act of 1585 which made it treason for any priest ordained aboard to enter England Sutton was arrested in Stafford in 1587 after being caught saying Mass in the town gaol and executed at Forebridge (see) in 1588. Some of his relics were at several Benedictine convents on the continent; at St Edward's church, Sutton Park, Surrey; and at the Poor Clares' Convent, Arundel, West Sussex (formerly at the Franciscan Convent, Taunton) (HOS p30. 1998 p62; says he was caught saying Mass in the house of Erasmus Wolseley in Stafford) (SSTY p142) (SCHJ No. 23 1988 pp1-13) (SIOT p2). **Mary, Queen of Scots**, is reputed to have passed through Burton on her way from Chartley Old Hall to Fotheringay in Sept 1586 (SHOS vol 1 p17). **Joseph Hollemans**, one of the greatest known alabaster sculptors from Holland had settled in Burton by 1599. Nine monuments in Staffs are attributed to him or by those working under him (BAST vol 71 p1) (VCH vol 2 p202).

CIVIL WAR. In the Civil War with Tutbury and Ashby de la Zouch castles garrisoned for the king, and Derby garrisoned for parliament by Sir John Gell from Oct 1642 control of Burton Bridge became very important. This resulted in the town changing hands no less than eight times in two and half years during the Civil War. In 1642 there were probably more parliamentary supporters than royalists in Burton. But the Earl of Chesterfield who supported the king fortified his house at Bretby, Derbys, and took control of the town. He was supported by the lord of Burton manor, Lord Paget, who shifted his initial allegiance from parliament to the royalist cause. In Dec 1642 the royalist garrison at Bretby was taken by parliament. A small parliament guard at Burton Bridge was defeated by royalists in Jan 1643. The bridge was retaken by parliament in April 1643, but retaken by royalist troops escorting Queen Henrietta Maria in July 1643 when she was on her way to Oxford with arms and money for Charles I. This last engagement was commemorated in July 1993 when members of the English Civil War Society in period costume marched along High Street to Burton Bridge, where a plaque was unveiled to commemorate the retaking of the bridge. In spring 1644 the town as captured by Parliament and two barrels of gunpowder stored in the parish church exploded, blowing off the roof and bursting all the windows (CHMS2 p28) (HOS 1998 p74) (IHOBT pp31,32). In 1644 the Earl of Essex, the parliamentary commander-in-chief, commented on the poverty of the town, and reported that if the town was garrisoned it would be impoverished. On more than one occasion the parliamentary committee at Stafford excused Burton from the weekly levies which maintain local forces (IHOBT p28). Burton was captured by the royalists in the spring of 1645 (HOS p36). (SCSF p127).

1660 to 1800. In 1715 there were riots against **Protestant dissenters**, which included a violent incident in the town. According to a despatch from Burton in the 'The Flying Post or Post Master' dated July 30 1715 rioters caught a young bull, cut off its ears and tail, pointed fireworks at it, and tried to drive it through the Congregationalists meeting house in High Street. The bull broke free, dashed up the street, turned into the parish church and killed and injured a number of worshippers (HOBTU 1976 p128) (IHOBT p55). Methodism reached Burton in 1754 when Thomas Hanby, one of John Wesley's itinerant preachers, passing through the town was seized by 'a desire to preach.' By 1765 a meeting house was registered. John Wesley was in Burton on March 20 1766. The first Methodist chapel in Burton was the 'new house' of Edwin Slater in Horninglow Street, on or near the site now occupied by the magistrates' court (IHOBT p31). **Badging the poor**. In the C18 recipients of Poor Relief were required to wear a badge on the upper sleeve with the letters 'BP' for Burton Pauper (IHOBT p29). **Natural phenomena**. The Trent burst its banks and flooded Burton in 1771, 1792, 1795, and 1798 (THS p46). An earthquake running on a NE to SW axis was felt in the town on Nov 18 1795 (SHOS vol 1 p19). **Drawing**. In 1731 Samuel Buck drew 'The East Prospect of Burton upon Trent in the County of Stafford.' It appears in 'Buck's Antiquities or the Remains of over 400 Castles etc in England and Wales' (1774) (IHOBT p41il). **Persons and visitors. Isaac Hawkins Browne**, the elder, poet, was born at Burton on Jan 21 1705; his father, William, was vicar of Burton. He was educated at Lichfield. Later, he settled at Badger Hall, Shrops, and was elected MP for Much Wenlock in 1744 and 1747. Dr Johnson of Lichfield (see), talking to Boswell and Bennet Langton, said of Browne 'We must not estimate a man's powers by his being able to deliver sentiments in public; Isaac Hawkins Browne, one of the first wits of this country, got into Parliament and never opened his mouth.' His 'Design and Beauty' (1734) and 'A Pipe of Tobacco' (1736) brought him literary renown, but his best-known work is 'De Animi Immortalite' (1754). In 1768 his collected poems, under the title of 'Poems Upon Various Subjects; Latin and English' were published by his son, the essayist Isaac Hawkins Browne (1745-1818). Isaac, the elder, died in London on Feb 14 1760 (DNB) (HOL p232) (GNHS p139) (PSS pp47-51) (KES p56) (VFC p20). **George Stayley** (d1779), poet, playwright, actor and elocutionist, was born in Burton in 1727. His work includes 'The Life and Opinions of an Actor' (1762) and the comedies 'The Rival Theatres (1759) and 'The Chocolate Makers' (VFC p125). In c1736 **Nathaniel Johnson**, Dr Johnson's brother, moved to Burton to take charge of a branch of the family's bookshop. He left, in 1736, after a very short time for Frome, Somerset, and died at Lichfield on March 5 1737 (Young Samuel Johnson. James L Clifford. 1955 1962ed. p159). **Thomas Chamberlain**, an industrious breeches-maker near Burton Bridge, had eight children, most of whom were musical. Rev Stebbing Shaw, author of SHOS, paid for the youngest son to be musically educated in London. The boy became somewhat of a success (GM vol 71 pp113,232) (SHOSA vol 2 p1). **John Stokes** of Burton and his wife had seven children, five of whom were born dumb; two of these

had died by 1801 (SHOSA vol 2 p1). **Thomas Hollier**, farmer, was murdered in Lichfield Lane, Burton, in July 1828 (Broughton's Scrapbook pp256-257).

1800 to PRESENT. Of new **churches** built in the C19 and C20 to cater for the growth in population there was Trinity church (1824-1880); a pinnacle from which went to Newton Park, Newton Solney, Derbys (ABTOP p142). The Commissioners' church, **Christ Church**, in Uxbridge Street, was built in 1843-1844 (BOE p84) in the district which became known as Uxbridge. **St Paul**, ENE of the town centre near the Town Hall in St Paul's Square, was built in 1874 (BOE p86). **All Saints**, SW of the town centre in Branston Road, was built in 1903-1905 (BOE p87). **St Chad**, N of the town centre in Hunter Street, was designed in 1903 and completed in 1910 (BOE p87). It was designed by GF Bodley and is probably one of his last buildings: Pevsner states it is by far the best building in Burton. It was financed by Lord Burton. Both he and Bodley died before it was completed; Cecil Hare, one of Bodley's pupils supervised its completion (info KL Neal). The Birmingham & Derby Junction **Railway** line which opened on Aug 5 1839 had a station at Burton (IAS p131) (VCH vol 2 p307). A line to Stoke-on-Trent via Tutbury opened in 1848. A branch line to Horninglow was opened in 1868 (VCH vol 2 pp309,320). The second WH Smith bookstall at a railway station was at Burton (BTOP vol 1 p25). The 'Tutbury Jenny' a famous steam train made its last run from Burton on June 11 1960 at 8.12pm (ABTOP p101p). Burton was **incorporated** in 1878 when created a municipal borough. William Henry Worthington (1826-1894) head of the brewing firm, chairman of the Town Commissioners in 1878, served as the first mayor of Burton between 1878-9 (ABTOP p67p). Burton became a county borough in 1901 (HOS p58). The borough **arms** include the spread eagle from the Mosley family arms (UTR p171). The Burton upon Trent county borough arms, granted in 1928, as given by Scott-Giles are: Barry wavy of six pieces argent and azure; a chief gules charged with a silver eagle displayed between two gold fleurs-de-lis. The crest is: Out of a gold mural crown, a right hand proper grasping a lozenge azure charged with a silver saltire. The motto is: 'Honor alit artes' (Honour fosters the arts) (CH p329il). Burton **Cricket Club** was founded by 1830. Abraham Bass is likely to have been a founder. He has been referred to as 'the father of Midland cricket' (VCH vol 2 p368) (BTIH p115) (MR p71; the club is said to be the first recorded cricket club in the county). Burton upon Trent **Aviation Week**, one of the earliest events of its kind in Britain, was held at Bass' Meadow, Meadow Road, between Sept 26 and Oct 1 1910 with a team of French aviators (EAS pp34-35) (BTOP vol 1 p64p) (ABTOP p104p). Another aviation meeting was held at Burton in 1913 (EAS pp34-35). In **WW1** there was a Zeppelin raid on Burton on Jan 31 1916 at 8.30pm. A cluster of bombs was dropped. One bomb fell on a mission house, where the clergyman's wife was holding a service; three of the congregation were killed and a fourth fatally injured (TB July 1994 p19). Shobnall Street was hit by a bomb and 15 were killed (IRB p49) (BTOP vol 1 p68p). The original Christ Church vicarage was not used after this raid, when the parish room was hit and six people died (ABTOP p12). A tank inscribed 'Burtonia' was presented to the town in 1919 and was positioned at the town end of the Trent Bridge (ABTOP p115). In **WW2** a bomb fell on Wood Street and Edward Street in Aug 1940 killing five people. In Jan 1941 a bomb injured four in Calais Road (BTOP vol 1 p68). The Burton upon Trent **Natural History and Archaeological Society** (BTNHAS) was founded by Sir Oswald Mosley, 2nd Bart, of Rolleston Hall (see), in 1842. It is one of the oldest societies of its kind in the country and still flourishes today (1999). It has published BTNHAST from 1889 to 1933, and at one point had a museum in High Street, Burton, which contained the natural history collection of Mrs Abney of Stapenhill (see) (info KL Neal). An annual **regatta** on the Trent at Burton was started in or by 1848 by local rowing clubs. It was still being held in 1999 when it was held in July (BTIH pp116,117,137; formerly thought to have been founded in 1865) (SLM Oct 1999 p23). The **Art Gallery & Museum**, opened in 1914, lay in Guild Street (Staffs County Handbook c1958 p106) (BOE p84). Burton **Operatic Society** formed in 1886. Burton Opera House opened on the corner of George and Guild Streets in 1887. In 1932 it was converted into the Ritz Cinema (BTOP p46p) (BTIH p121). The first **barrel-rolling** competition at Burton was staged in May 1933 and took place from the junction of High Street and Station Street to King Edward Place. A cup, presented by the Burton Chamber of Trade, was won by James Rose of Eadie & Co (BTIH pp157,160p of in 1944). The event lapsed in c1945, but was revived in 1973 (Burton Daily Mail June 26 1978 p2ps), or in 1975 (G June 28 1976 p4) (STMSM Aug 1976 pp3,19ps) (Burton Observer & Chronicle July 1 1977 p12ps. June 30 1978 p12ps) (FOS p168). In 1999 barrel-rolling took place at the Burton Festival Sept 16-26 1999. **Records**. The Burton upon Trent Youth Choir sang accompanied for 25 hours 30 minutes on April 18-19 1974 breaking the world record for marathon accompanied singing by a group (GBR 1974 p230).

Burton Albion achieved the shortest time ever for a semi-professional football team to score three goals from the start of the match when they scored three goals in 122 seconds against Redditch United in a Beazer Homes League Premier Division on Jan 2 1989 (GBR 1996 p256). The most press-ups (push-ups) ever achieved in 30 minutes by 1981 was 1845 by Noel Barry Mason at Burton Sporting Club on Nov 16 1979 (GBR 1981 p285). The youngest ever table tennis player to play for England was Nicola Deaton (b Oct 29 1976) aged 13 years 336 days when England played against Sweden at Burton upon Trent on Sept 30 1990 (GBR 1995 p296). At the inaugural Ind Coope British Beer Mat-flipping Championships at Brewery Vaults, Burton on May 31 1985 Darren Ault, 18, flipped and caught a record pile of 67 mats through 180 degrees (GBR 1987 p164). In 1967 Burton was the first town in Britain to convert to North Sea Gas ('The Rock and Roll Years' BBC 1 July 9 1993). BCM July 1970 p35 claims the Black Country was the first district. The pipe line could and probably did go through Burton first. **Floods**. Many streets in Burton flooded in July and Oct 1875 when the Trent burst its banks (BTOP vol 1 p27). Two men drowned in the streets in the floods of 1875 (LGS p97). **Persons and visitors** (and a dog). **Michael Arthur Bass**, 1st Lord Burton, was born at the Bass town house, 136 High Street, Burton in 1837 (BTOP vol 1 p43p). Bass died in 1909. A statue to him sculpted by FW Pomeroy ARA and paid for by public subscription, was unveiled in King Edward Place by the Earl of Dartmouth, Lord Lieutenant of Staffs, on May 13 1911 (ABTOP p51p) (BOE p86). **Edward VII** visited Burton on Feb 22 1902 before going on to stay with Lord Burton at Rangemore Hall (BTOP vol 1 p41). On this visit the king brewed a special ale known as 'King's Ale' at Bass brewery (The Bass Museum guide). In Shobnall school yard 2,000 school children sung the National Anthem as the king drove past (ABTOP p32p). In consequence of the King's visit King Edward Place was laid out in front of the present Town Hall (built 1878-1894) and named in 1906. **SH Evershed** built one of the earliest aeroplanes to fly in the country, in the malt house of his family's brewery - Evershed's in Bank Square - from Nov 1909 to May 1910. It flew for only a 30 yards in summer 1910 (EAS p15). The Prince of Wales (later **Edward VIII**) arrived by aeroplane at Bass's Meadow to visit Burton on July 23 1929 (ABTOP p52p). On this visit the prince brewed a special ale known as 'Prince's Ale' at Bass brewery (The Bass Museum guide). **Layton George Joseph Layberry**, novelist, was born in Burton in 1914. He attended Rolleston village school. After employment as a farmer in Derbys, Sussex, and Kent, Layberry became an Inland Revenue employee due to ill-health and started writing a family saga based on a farm called Oakleigh in South Derbys. The saga begins in 1911 in the first novel 'Hayseed' (1980) and runs for at least another six novels to 'As Long as Fields are Green' (1987). Burton and other Staffs places briefly occur in the novels. **Dorothea Waddingham**, nurse, who served her apprenticeship in Burton workhouse, was hung at Winson Green prison on April 16 1936 for poisoning patients in her care (TB Dec 24 1998 p11p) (TB Annual 1999 pp85-86). **Elizabeth II** and the Duke of Edinburgh, visited Burton on March 28 1957, arriving from Tutbury (R&S p47). Their daughter, **Princess Anne**, visited Burton in 1978 and whilst in the town brewed a special ale at Bass brewery (The Bass Museum guide). The highest football pools win by 1981 was that won by **David Preston**, 47, of Burton on Feb 23 1980, when he won £953,874.10 (£804,573.35 from Littlewoods, and £149,300.75 from Vernons) (GBR 1981 p277). Sir **Ivan Laurence** Conservative MP for Burton made the longest ever back-bench speech in parliament, under present standing orders, whilst opposing the Water (Fluoridation) Bill on March 6 1985 which lasted four hours 23 minutes (GBR 1996 p183). Mrs **Daisy Adams** of Burton, aged 112, was believed to be the oldest person in Britain according to GBR after the death of Charlotte Hughes of Cleveland, aged 115, in 1993 (Daily Telegraph March 18 1993 p7). **Miss Price** was murdered at some time by George Caddell in the vicinity of the 'Nag's Head' on a road leading to Burton. Caddell strangled Price perhaps in order to see another woman (MCGM pp112-113). **Watchman** (1949-1959), a bull terrier and from 1958 the regimental mascot of the 6th Battalion, the North Staffs Regiment has a memorial situated in the low retaining wall on the S side of King Edward Place (Historic Burton. The Borough Trail notice board in King Edward Place).

NEWSPAPERS. The **Burton upon Trent Times and General Advertiser**, founded on June 23 1855, became the Burton upon Trent Times and Tamworth Weekly News from May 6 1865; this paper ran until at least Dec 14 1874 (SHJ spring 1996 p15). The **Burton Weekly News and General Advertiser**, founded on Jan 25 1856, became the Burton upon Trent Weekly News and General Advertiser from Nov 3 1865 and the Burton News and Standard and General Advertiser from Jan 5 1888; this paper continued until at least March 1890 (SHJ spring 1996 p15). The **Burton Weekly News and General Advertiser** was founded on Jan 25 1856. The **Burton Chronicle** founded Oct

18 1860 ran to June 20 1957 (SHJ spring 1996 p14). The **Burton upon Trent Express**, founded on June 11 1874, became the Burton upon Trent Express and County Advertiser from Jan 21 1875; this paper run until at least Dec 1879 (SHJ spring 1996 p15). The **Burton and Derby Gazette**, founded by June 1 1881 ran until at least July 13 1887 (SHJ spring 1996 p13). The **Burton Evening Gazette**, founded by July 15 1887, ran until at least 1931 (SHJ spring 1996 p14). The **Burton Independent** seems to have run from April 15 to July 29 1893 (SHJ spring 1996 p14). The **Burton Guardian**, founded on Feb 24 1894, continued until Dec 7 1895 when it became the Burton, Ashby and Coalville Guardian; this paper ran until at least Dec 26 1914 (SHJ spring 1996 p14). The **Burton Observer**, founded by May 5 1898, became the Burton Observer and South Derbyshire Weekly Mail from Oct 19 1916, and the Burton Observer and Chronicle from June 20 1957; this paper continued until at least 1979 (SHJ spring 1996 p15). The **Burton Mail**, founded by Jan 2 1899, became the Burton Daily Mail from May 2 1907. It reverted to its former title, Burton Mail, on March 23 1981 and continues as such (SHJ spring 1996 p14).

REFERENCES TO BURTON. The abbey's involvement in brewing is commemorated in this rhyme

> The Abbot of Burton brewed good ale,
> on Fridays when they fasted -
> But the Abbot of Burton never tasted his own
> As long as his neighbour's lasted.

(OSST 1933 p38) (IADC p41) (SJC pp2,3). For a rhyme briefly celebrating Burton ale see Barton-under-Needwood. Bass bottles are shown in the Impressionist painting 'A Bar at the Folies-Bergere' (1881-2) by Edouard Manet (The Bass Museum guide). 'Going for a Burton' is an advertising slogan to promote Burton beer. AE Housman in 'A Shropshire Lad' 1887 canto lxii asked:

> Say for what were hop-yards meant,
> Or why was Burton built on Trent?

(VB p89). The Hartlebury-on-Dane in the novel 'The Mount' (1909) by CF Keary (d1917) may loosely refer to Burton upon Trent or Cheadle; Rosemary Toeman, who states the author is believed to have lived in or near Walsall, has identified Hartlebury with Hartwell, Staffs (VFC p77). The novel 'Tales of the Midlands' by Kathleen Fidler contains an account of the battle Burton Bridge.

Burton upon Trent Manor House Gabled house next to, and to the S of, the Victorian Market Hall in the Market Place. A possible 'Noble' coin of Edward III's reign was found in the foundations of the Manor House in 1836 (SA June 18 1836) (Broughton's Scrapbook p257). A building called the Manor House existed within the abbey precincts in 1514 and William Paget planned to extend this into a grand mansion; a plan of 1562 shows the house was to be three stories high, with a long galley; the old abbey buildings were to be reused in its construction. It is not certain how much of this house was actually built. William Paget's death in 1563, and the death of his eldest son, Henry, a few years later, delayed further building, and Thomas, 3rd baron, William's second son, was engaged in building Beaudesert Hall. In 1583 the family estates were confiscated and the title lost because of Thomas' complicity in the Throckmorton Plot. William, 4th baron Paget was restored to his estates in 1597 and to his title in 1603. By this time many of the former abbey buildings were in ruinous condition and in 1621 the Manor House was leased to Richard Almond. The lease stated that Almond would not be charged if he allowed certain abbey buildings to decay (IHOBT pp22-23). Some of the present house appears to be of C17 origin (SGS p73). It is mainly of brick but was formerly of stone, and timber-framed. There were major alterations to the house in the C18, C19 and C20. The early C19 range probably occupies the site of the medieval open hall (IHOBT pp22-23,26p). It was used as the estate office for the Pagets (SGS p73).

Bury, The A 'cup' or 'saucer' shaped burial mound on top of Spring Hill at N end of Cannock Chase, N of Pudding Hill, over 1.75m NNE of Brocton or 0.5m SE of Milford, at SJ 976207. It is near the entrance to Sherbrook valley on the Milford side of the old Roman cart track (HSS p28). The 'saucer' burial mound is one of only 60 in the country and perhaps the only one in Staffs. 'Saucer' burial mounds date from 1800-1200 BC (SPJD pp9p,12pc). The Bury was excavated by W Molyneux in the 1860s. It is a mound of Bunter pebbles with three layers of burnt bones and fragments of coarse brown British pottery at its base (HOBT p12) (NSFCT 1926 pp141-142; probably a reference to this mound) (CCC p5) (OSST 1949/ 50 p20) (NSJFS 1965 p32).

Perhaps these remains may be the sacrificial victims of the fires of Baal (SMM p173). Has also appeared as Milford 'Bury.' According to tradition it is perhaps the grave of three kings slain in a battle on this spot (HSS p28) (SCSF p74) (SMM p17). In 1996 its inner perimeter measured approximately 200 feet and its outer perimeter measured approximately 300 feet; the E side of the hill was badly eroded and consequently so was the E side of the 'saucer' burial mound (visit in 1996).

Bury Bank Hill 492 feet high nearly 2m NW of Stone. In Beech quarter in Stone ancient parish (W p362). It has appeared as Le buri in Wulpherceastre in the C13 (SSE 1996 p11) and is often formerly written Berry Bank. It has been suggested that the hill was dedicated to the god Ebor or Ebori, hence its former appellation of 'Le Bori' (STM May 1964 p32). Burial mounds of Bronze Age origin (there are two or three in the vicinity) lie in or by the hillfort covering the summit (SPJD p15). Two were excavated in 1859 and one contained charcoal and human bones (HOTM p8) (GNHSS p5*) (LGS p222) (SIS p3) (NSFCT vol 72 p158) (NSJFS 1965 p48). The one in the southern part of the fort enclosure, at SJ 883358, was in good condition in 1983 (NSFCT 1983 p13). According to legend this one or another contains the Mercian King Wulfhere (657-674) (NHS pp406-407) who made the hillfort his palace. A burial mound on Bury Bank is said to be the grave of a giant (SCSF p74), and this tradition probably arose out of the belief that a 'giant' among men - a warrior leader - was buried here (SMM p17). Bury Bank lies on a ley line between Stone church and Grounds Lowe (SMM p23 see map). Foot-and-mouth disease broke out at Berry Bank Farm in late 1967 (SN Dec 22 1967 p15).
HILLFORT. A hillfort of Iron Age (C2 to C1 BC) origin on Bury Bank encloses 3.5 acres of the summit of the hill. To the NW there is a well-defined entrance and some indications exist of a similar entrance in the opposite quarter (SIS pp1,2 il). It is possibly of Roman origin (SHC vol 6 part 1 p9) (HOPS p2). In the C7 it may have been occupied by Wulfhere, king of Mercia (657-74) and the hill has been identified with the settlement known as Wulfherecester (see) (RHPS pp21-26) (HOS p13) (SL p49) or Ulf Ulfacaster (NSFCT 1936 p79): A tradition states that the C7 settlement on Bury Hill migrated to found the village of Swynnerton (Bowen's map) (ESH p31) (SAS p8). However, there is no historical or archaeological proof that Wulfhere occupied the hill (NSFCT 1936 p79) (SPJD pp14pc,15pc,17). In the C16 Leland noted great dykes and squared stones on Bury Hill. In 1879 William Molyneux noted the tradition that a portion of an old farmhouse at the foot of Bury Hill contained timber and stones from the ruins of a castle on the hill top (SIS p7). The British Archaeological Society made a visit to it during their 52nd Congress at Stoke in Aug 1895 (SK p193). (SD p80) (SHOS vol 1 General Intro p36) (SOS pp33,35; Harwood's notes on it) (GNHS p133) (W p359) (HOTC pp8-9) (NSFCT 1892 pp136-138. 1914 pp110-111) (VCH vol 1 pp192,341-343) (MOS pp5,106-110) (SCSF p74) (SOSH p10) (Stone Guardian Aug 29 1959 pl 2) (A Guide to Prehistoric England. N Thomas. 1960 p187) (HOS p10) (BOE p269) (MR p303) (SMM p21p).

Bury Brook Waterhead brook which appears to run from Essington westwards N of Blackhalve Lane, through Westcroft, Moseley, Fordhouses to Pendeford where it joins the Penk. Appears in 1240 as Biribrok. The hundreds of Seisdon, Offlow and Cuttleston meet at Bury Brook at the junction of Old Hampton Lane and Wood Hayes Road (HOWM p29) (WFW pp30,32).

Bury Hill Hill in Moreton on which the manor house of Forton and Mere stood before the Skrymshers made Aqualate Hall the manor house. The name had completely dropped out of use by 1937 (NSFCT 1937 p62).

Busford Pool Small pool at end of the Long Walk S of Loxley Hall.

Bush Bank Alias Gospel End Street, Sedgley. So called because of the inn called the Bush or Bush Bank (SDOP p51p).

Bushbury (locally *Bishbiri* DUIGNAN, SPN p145). Former township, ancient parish and village on the W side of Bushbury Hill 13m S of Stafford.
EARLY. Boulders of the glacial drift abounded at Bushbury, near the church, and especially on the NW flank of Bushbury Hill in 1909 (WJO Nov 1909 p293). For a **Bronze Age** palstave found in Bushbury parish see Bushbury Low.
1000 to 1500. The **name** means 'Bishop's fortified place.' There is no evidence of a bishop residing here. But Biscop was a personal name in the Middle Ages. Perhaps, a bishop preached from the Saxon cross in the churchyard. A pre-Norman Conquest **church** may have preceded the present church, said to have been founded in c1350. It is dedicated to Assumption of the Blessed Virgin, and lies on the E side of Bushbury Lane at the foot of Bushbury Hill (A Guide to Bushbury Church). In it is a memorial known as the **Friar's Stone**, or possibly what Dr Plot refers to as the Friars Tomb. He notes that when the tomb was opened a localised earthquake occurred which made the pewter clatter in peoples houses and the cauldron at Bushbury Hall leap from

the ground (NHS p143). **Parish and manor**. The parish may have originally formed a part of Wolverhampton original parish and was perhaps founded a little before 1291 (SHC 1916 p197). The two townships of the parish lay in separate hundreds - Bushbury in Seisdon and Essington in Cuttlestone (W p170) (HOWM p17 note). Two estates in Biscopesberie are recorded in DB; one held by the Canons of Wolverhampton; another by William, son of Ansculf. Seven manors - Bushbury, Moseley, Oxley, Elston, Showell, Wobaston and Essington - evolved in the parish, so that Bushbury was never a nucleated village with most of its population living in a single community around a church. Each manor had its own centre with a small community living around the principal house (BUOP p6). About 60 yards W of the church lay a large moat, the remains of which still existed in the late C18, but are no longer visible (SHOS vol 2 p182) (SSAHST 1982-3 p56). Another moat about 0.5m NW of the church was also in existence then but had been destroyed by housing development by 1954 (SHOS vol 2 p182) (OHW pl12) (SSAHST 1982-3 p52). There is a photograph of the 'Old Moat' opposite Fir Coppice in WJO Nov 1909 p294. There are also moats at Westcroft Farm and Blackhalve.
1500 to PRESENT. For a skirmish in the **Civil War** in Bushbury parish see under Bushbury Hill. The Grand Junction Railway opened in 1837 through Bushbury parish, from Showell in the S to Brinsford in the N. The Stour Valley Junction **Railway** commenced at a junction with the GJR at Bushbury taking passengers on to central Wolverhampton (WF p44). The Shrewsbury and Birmingham Railway (later GWR) crossed the Birmingham Canal on Gorsebrook viaduct. Bushbury station opened in 1851 and closed in the 1960s (Wolverhampton Chronicle Oct 25 1996 p18) (BUOP p8). From the mid C19, owing to the proximity of many railway lines belonging to various companies, railway companies built locomotive construction works and shunting yards in the parish. From 1890 Electric Construction Corporation (later the Electric Construction Company) manufactured electric rotary parts such as motors, dynamos and switchgear at their plant at the junction of the old drive to Showell Manor and Stafford Road. For much of the C20 the whole parish has been residential and industrial suburb of N Wolverhampton. For Goodyear Tyre and Rubber Company see Oxley. Bushbury was a ward of Wolverhampton borough by 1982. The **'ringing himself in' custom** involving the new clergyman vigorously tolling the bells of the church he has just taken over, occurred at Bushbury in 1883 after Rev Frederick Aston had been formally inducted by the Rev JT Jeffcock of Wolverhampton with the usual presentation of the church key (SCSF p121). **Natural history**. In the late C18 Stebbing Shaw noted the Bird-Cherry or Prunus Padus seemed to be growing indigenously here, appearing in the fences near the hall and on the adjacent enclosures (SHOS vol 2 p181). On very high ground near the top of Bushbury Great Field, Shaw also noted, a well which in the very dry summer of 1785 strangely regained its normal level seemingly by the action of heavy clouds over head which did not rain and this happened another time in the same year (SHOS vol 2 p182). **Bowling record**. The highest score in 24 hours of bowling by 1994 was 212692 achieved by a team of six at Strykers Pleasure Bowl, Bushbury on June 20-21 1992 (GBR 1994 p244). St Mary's has been identified as the church **George Borrow**, as a gypsy, went to for Sunday service on July 24 1825 and alluded to in his 'The Romany Rye' (chapter 8). The chancel door is known as 'Borrow Door' (NSFCT 1950 p22).

Bushbury Hall NE of Bushbury church. Charles I stayed here on May 1 1644 (SHOS vol 2 p182). Others say he stayed here as the guest of Walter Grosvenor on May 16 1645 (W p65) (BUOP p7) (HOS 1998 p74). Between at least the later C18 and at least 1817 the chair in which the king had sat, known as the king's Chair, was preserved at the hall, but the chamber in which he had slept had been renovated by c1800. In 1770 some workmen discovered several spoons of solid gold, which they spirited away. The few that remained went to the lord of the manor. There was no way of identifying to whom they had belonged, although they were probably owned by the Bushburys of Bushbury (SHOS vol 2 p182) (THS p181; says it is a chair Charles II sat in). (WJO Nov 1909 p294p). The W front of the hall still standing in c1920 was built in c1730 when Bushbury manor belonged to Edward Chandler, bishop of Lichfield (BUOP p11p of c1920).

Bushbury Hall Farm Stood adjacent to St Mary's church, Bushbury. A tunnel is said to lead from it to Moseley Old Hall (TB Nov 1981 p27).

Bushbury Hill Hill, 590 feet high (HOWM p6), to the E of Bushbury church, and former small hamlet (BUOP p6). There were boulders of the glacial drift on the NW flank of Bushbury Hill in 1909 (WJO Nov 1909 p293). A skirmish on the morning of Friday May 21 1645 took place within two miles of Charles I's quarters at Bushbury Hall when a parliamentary squadron attacked a detachment of royalist horse, killing 16 men and capturing 26 horses. Charles I is reputed to have watched the encounter from the top of Bushbury Hill (BUOP p7). According to tradition some of the dead are buried in a raised piece of ground N of Bushbury church tower (BUOP p10p). A bonfire was erected on the summit to celebrate Queen Victoria's Diamond Jubilee in 1897 (BUOP 88p). Most of the trees which formerly stood on the hill were vandalised in the 1940s. In the C20 a reservoir was built on top of the hill (BUOP pp14-15ps).

Bushbury Hill Farm Stood on the corner of Old Fallings Lane and the path leading over Bushbury Hill, Bushbury. Built in the 1780s for Richard Phillips (1755-1833) and faced S. Richard's son, Escrike (1787-1871), was involved in horse bloodstock breeding and the farm was known as 'Bushbury Paddocks.' During the residency of E Phillips in 1851 the house was known as Bushbury House. The land belonging to the farm was mainly on the eastern flank of Bushbury Hill, where Bushbury Hill School now stands. On the death of Richard's son, Henry, in 1876 the estate passed to his son Escrite Henry. The Phillips family appear to have left the area and the farm passed to William Hordern Clifft, who emigrated to New Zealand in 1913. Afterwards it belonged to the Jeavons family. The house was demolished in the 1940s (W p19) (BUOP p13p) (Wolverhampton Chronicle Oct 25 1996 p18p).

Bushbury Low Burial mound, presumably in the vicinity of Low Hill, Bushbury. (SD p37). Huntbach says it was very visible in his day. Only faint traces were discernible in May 1794. A few old yew trees identified the place in the late C18 (SHOS vol 2 p187). A celt or palstave in a wood called Birchen Leasow in the later C17 and Gun Birch in the late C18 was supposedly found in the Bushbury Low area. Plot supposed it to be a brass head of a bolt of a catapulta and Shaw thought it was probably a weapon used in the battle of Tettenhall or called Wednesfield (SHOS vol 2 p181). (HOWM p1). It has, later, been thought to be of Bronze Age origin (ABI p86) (NSJFS 1964 p44).

Bushton Former hamlet (ANS p9) 1.5m SSW of Tutbury. In Tutbury ancient parish. Has appeared as Bussones (1300), Busshumes (1305) (ANS p30), and Bushens (1682). Bushton Farm remained with the Mainwaring family, lords of Anslow, until 1738, when it passed with the manor to the Davenports. Under the Mainwarings it was tenanted by the Ford family, under the Davenports it was leased to the Strettons (ANS p109).

Bush Park Appears to be a small public park to the E of Bush Street and S of Owen Street, Darlaston (Offlow hundred) (SNDB p16).

Butcroft Area 0.5m SE of Darlaston. In Wednesbury ancient parish until 1965 when transferred to Darlaston ancient parish (SNDB). The area is of indeterminate extent including the Walsall Road from the Bullstake to about Birmingham Street and then from some distance S of that (SNDB pp25,27). According to a local tradition the name is from the site of butts where archery was practiced in the Middle Ages. A more likely explanation is that 'butt' derives from land in the old open field system abutting at right angles to the main strips (SNDB p27). Has also appeared as Burcroft, Butscroft, Buttcroft, and Buttscroft (SNDB p27). A large old house which backed onto Birmingham Street, was haunted by a poltergeist according to some childhood memories of Ray Askey (TB March 1994 p5).

Butler's Coppice Wood on the E side of Handsworth Wood Road. Was a remaining part of the former Handsworth Wood and was still existence in the later C19 (MNB p47). The name is preserved in Butler's Road.

Butter Bank Minute hamlet and bridge over 1m S of Seighford.

Butterbank Brook Joins Doxey Brook at Coton Clanford then joins the Sow. The name is from probably a field name and means 'the bank which yielded good butter from cows grazing there' (SPNO p6).

Butter Hill Hill 503 feet high nearly 1m WSW of Coppenhall. The name means Butter meadow or meadows (DUIGNAN) (SPN pp37-38). Or 'butter halh (hollow)' (SSE 1996 p11).

Butterhill Tiny hamlet on E side of Butter Hill, Coppenhall. In Penkridge ancient parish. Has appeared as Buterales (c1160), and Butterall (1558) (VCH vol 5 p138) (SSE 1996 p11). Butterhill was a small hamlet by 1680 (SAC p30). There is a disused windmill at SJ 898191, over 0.5m WNW of Coppenhall. It dates from c1800, although there was a mill on the site, previously from about the C16 (WBJ p18). (IAS p161). A deed of 1607 remitted rights of Coppenhall windmill to John Giffard for £41 (SLM spring 1954 p23p). This may relate to another windmill said to be in Chaseview Lane, Coppenhall (see). The Butterhill Mill was said locally to have been the only six-sail mill in the county and was in use by 1820 (VCH vol 5 p141) (SVB p62p,63). It seems to have gone out of use between 1872 and 1876 (VCH vol 5 p141). Its oak beams went to Beaudesert Hall in 1912 and one pair of stones went to Great Haywood watermill and the other pair to France (WBJ p18 il vi). The brickwork is 'English garden wall bond' (DoE II). (STMSM Aug 1978 p26p) (WIS pp9p,16) (ASOP p87p of c1891) (MR p112).

Butterhill Bank Incline NW of Burston. Appears as Buttershill on 1834 OS map and Dower's map.

Butterhill House Butterhill. Owned by Edward Moore and occupied by Rich-

ard Wright by 1849 (SAC p31p).

Butterlands House over 1m NNE of Biddulph Moor. Occurs on 1834 OS map.

Butterley Bank Farm House 0.5m S of Croxden, in Croxden parish. Fields at Butterley Bank Farm show clearly the ridges of former open fields (CDS p18). There was a farm at Butterley Bank by 1722 (CDS p19).

Buttermilk Hill Hill in the escarpment of the Needwood Forest plateau over 3m NE of Bagot's Bromley. Appears on Plot's map. Marks the boundary of Bagots Park and Needwood Forest (LTD p124). The road up it is narrow, steep and uneven, and it is claimed that milk turned into butter when taken on the road (LTD p124).

Buttersbank Tiny hamlet 0.25m SW of Wetwood. On the Wetwood-Croxton road is a roadside trough supplied by a spring from nearby Buttersbank. It had never been known to go dry even during droughts (BOV p48).

Butters Green E end of Bignall End 1m E of Audley. In Audley parish.

Butterton Moorland village lining the steep valley of Hoo Brook 23m NE of Stafford. Former out-township in Mayfield ancient parish (AAD p210) (W p784). To E of the village is a burial mound at SK 08445651 called Town Low and is tree covered and 26 paces in diameter and three feet high (NSJFS 1965 p35). It is a listed monument. Butterton has appeared as Buterdon (1200), Butterton (1223), Boterdon (1236) (SSE 1996 p11) (SPN p28). It means either Butter town (DUIGNAN), or 'the butter hill' (SSAHST 1967 p32) (SSE 1996 p11) (SPN p28). Or equally may be derived from Old Norse 'budar' or 'buttr' - the latter being a nickname implying shortness of stature. There is evidence that in certain cases the prefix 'butter' represents contracted Anglo-Saxon forms meaning boat reach - an explanation which might be applicable to the Butterton (Newcastle) a small stream flows at the base of the hill on which it stands (NSFCT 1916 p79). The church, St Bartholomew, at the N end of the village, S of Wetton Road, appears to have been founded by 1254 (LDD), but most of the present church is of 1871-1873 (BOE p92). In the later C17 Dr Plot noted, beside How Brook a sulphur spring which was like the Baths of Banca in Hungary in that it tinged silver a blackish colour in an hour's time. If disturbed, when raining for instance, it bubbles? (NHS p105) (GNHS pp25,26) (W p784). Butterton became a separate ecclesiastical parish in 1775, and a separate civil parish in 1866 (GLAUE p407). Moses Smith, a clock cleaner of Butterton who lived in c1800, has returned as a ghost (WTCEM p93). Poltergeist activity at a C17 cottage in the S of the village about Back Lane in July 1834 turned out to be a hoax (OL vol 2 pp26-27).

Butterton Former township and small village on rising ground above and at some distance from Meece Brook, 13.5m NNW of Stafford. Butterton has appeared as Butereton (1182) and Botertun (1208) (SSE 1996 p11) (SPN p28). The name means either 'Butter hill' (DUIGNAN) or 'the butter tun or town' (SSAHST 1967 p32) (SSE 1996 p11) (SPN p28). See also Butterton (Moorlands). Whilst the name Butterton has been used for the old hall and hall, the village was formerly called Millstone Green (see). As well as being in Newcastle manor, Butterton lay partly in Butterton township in Trentham ancient parish and partly in Swynnerton ancient parish (W p433) (SHC 1900 p89). That part in Swynnerton was still in Swynnerton civil parish by 1914. Became a separate ecclesiastical parish (or Butterton district chapelry) in 1845 (LGS p100), which was abolished and amalgamated with Newcastle-under-Lyme in 1940 (GLAUE p407). The church, St Thomas, in an isolated position SE side of the village, was built in 1844 (BOE p91).

BUTTERTON DYKE. A geological fault, a trap dyke, known as the 'Butterton Dyke,' or sometimes referred to as the Butterton-Swynnerton Dyke or Swynnerton Dyke was formed by an up-thrust of volcanic lava squeezing into the overlying sandstone leaving molten matter a few feet wide in places intruding above the surface. It is believed to exist, in a narrow line, between Butterton and Norton Bridge. The process took place millions of years ago. The dyke was first located by the natural historian, Charles Darwin, when on visits to his uncle, Josiah Wedgwood II at Maer Hall, Maer (see) between 1842-44. Darwin had been prompted to locate the dyke by an ill-founded theory of Sir Roderick Murchison of Shropshire conveyed by Josiah Wedgwood II and Wedgwood's physician, Robert Garner, author of GNHS. They had asked him to look out for the presence of igneous dykes in North Staffs, using his considerable experience of seeing dykes in Chile and Argentina. Darwin located the Butterton-Swynnerton dyke swarm at two localities: in the Hanchurch Hills (SJ 841400) and where it cropped out of a shallow road-cutting near Butterton Lodge gates, just to the N of Butterton village (SJ 830428). His findings were reported to Robert Garner; hence the dyke was marked on Garner's map (NSFCT 1944 p99) (info David B Thompson). Subsequently, and largely through the work of James Kirkby, a local amateur geologist, the dyke was traced for a distance of about eight miles. In 1928 McLintock and Phemister showed the existence of the dyke under tracts of ground where there were not drift-deposits, and filled in gaps in its line about

Yarnfield. It exposes itself in an old quarry 330 yards SSE of Butterton church (NSFCT 1894 pp129-140 plan. 1919 pp36-43. 1922 p159. 1944 p99. 1953 p120. 1979 pp23-24) (NSJFS 1966 pp25-37) (STM May 1966 p33). A piece of Dolerite rock from the dyke, measuring about half an inch by three quarters of an inch, which has been given the title 'The Millennium Rock,' was flown to the MIR space station. The rock was in space for 380 days from Aug 13 1998 to Aug 28 1999 and made about 6,080 orbits of the Earth and covered over 257 million kilometres. A card now attached to the rock was signed by the three cosmonauts on board the station - Avdeyev, Haignere and Afanasyev. Displayed in a frame with the cosmonauts signatures the rock was on show in the Potteries Museum in Hanley in Nov 1999.

Butterton Grange Red-brick farmhouse 1m ESE of Butterton (Newcastle). Designed by Sir John Soane in 1816-17 (BOE p92) (ES Aug 25 1982 il). David Watkin says in CL 'he (Soane) gave much to this stripped-down essay in trabeation, which recalls the work of KF Schinkel, his opposite number in Germany. It is an idiosyncratic design with the curious splayed angles of the piers at the ends of the facade and of the entrance bay. The roof, with its broad Tuscan eaves, has a stone chimney-stack capped by a small sarcophagus' (CL Sept 2 1999 pp60pc, 63). Appears on 1882 6 inch OS map as Butterton New Farm.

Butterton Hall Butterton (Newcastle). Built in c1847, demolished in 1924 (NSFCT 1944 p99) (SVB p48; built in 1850, demolished in 1921). In 1851 it was the seat of Lady Pilkington (W p19). There is an illustration of it in WSL. Some of the stone was re-used in the Newcastle Golf Club club house (SVB p48).

Butterton Moor Moor and fragmented hamlet 1m W of Butterton (Moorlands). Between Butterton Moor and the Warslow Brook is a boulder of probably Pendle Grit (NSFCT 1916 p74). The headless horseman of the Moorlands has been seen on Butterton Moor. An organised ghost-hunt for this spectre took place on Butterton Moor on the night of May 7 and 8 1933. In the crowd anticipating it was Ralph de Tunstall Sneyd of Fair View (see) (FLJ 1942 p126) (DPMM p117).

Butterton Moor End House N of Onecote (IANS p18).

Butterton Old Hall Butterton (Newcastle). Built in 1540. It was replaced by Butterton Hall. A part of the Old Hall still remains (SVB p48). Built in either the late C16 or early C17 by William Swynnerton. It was still standing in 1844. There were only scanty remains left in 1944 (NSFCT 1944 pp98,99). (SHOS vol 2 pls on p30 at back). Has also appeared as Butterton Manor. For Holt describing sketching the ruins of Butterton Manor see SFH p44.

Butterwomen's Causeway Name for the former site of the butter and poultry market which was held outside Burton upon Trent in times of plaque (SPN p27), and in 1665 (SCSF p139).

Butt Lane Area 1m W of Kidsgrove. Formerly in Talke township and chapelry in Audley ancient parish (W p430). Written But Lane and Butte Lane in 1733 (SHC 1944 p67). **Reginald Mitchell**, Spitfire designer, was born at 115 Congleton Road, Butt Lane on May 20 1895. He spent his childhood in Normacot (see) where he became a pupil at Queensbury Road Junior School, and later at Hanley High School. He received training in engineering skills at the firm of Kerr, Stuart and Co, Fenton. He was a director at the Supermarine Aviation Works, Southampton between 1928 and his death in 1937. His high speed seaplanes were successful in the Schneider Trophy races between 1922 and 1931. For many years a 1944 Spitfire R.W. 388 Mk. LF 16e, acquired by the City of Stoke-on-Trent was on permanent display in Lichfield Road until being housed in the new City (later Potteries) Museum (AGT pp58il,59). In 1943 an appeal to raise funds for a memorial to Mitchell was launched. The fund provided for the present youth theatre, known as the Mitchell Memorial Theatre, in Broad Street, Hanley, opened in 1957. A statue of Mitchell was erected in front of the Potteries Museum in 1995 (ES May 22 1995 p5p of statue). (plaque on the house) (POP pp147-148) (STMSM Sept 1980 pp22-24) (TTTD p216) (ES Feb 21 1994 p10p) (TB Sept 1993 pp1p,20-21p. Oct 1993 p11p) (info Mitchell Memorial Theatre).

Buttons Farm Stood in the area of the present Buttons Farm Road, S of the Penn Road, near where it turns into Stourbridge Road, Upper Penn. The farm

was named after the Button family, who were living in this area at the end of the C16 (PAIP p79).

Butts Area in the vicinity of Butts Road 0.5m N of Walsall. Formerly in Rushall ancient parish. Some have thought the name derived from an area where archery was practiced. But the name 'Butts' usually was used for the triangular areas that did not fit easily into the ploughing schemes of medieval open fields (SNWA p24). The church, St Mark, in Butts Road, was built in 1871 (BOE p295). Butts was added to Walsall borough in 1876 (VCH vol 17 p151). For its industry see Walsall.

Buxton Brow House 2m N of Meerbrook. Formerly in Leekfrith township in Leek ancient parish. Appears as Buckstone Brow in 1640 (VCH vol 7 p194).

Buxton Villa Mansion at junction of Buxton Road and Abbots Road, Leek. Built by Joshua Brough, silk manufacturer, in 1837 (VCH vol 7 p94).

Byanna House 0.75m N of Eccleshall. After Eccleshall Castle had been destroyed in the Civil War the bishops of Lichfield made it their residence. In 1695 they moved back to the castle site, into a new mansion just completed by Bishop Lloyd (SHOS vol 2 pl on p24 at back) (EOP p21) (ROT p24). Seat of the Bosville family by the later C17 and in the C18, when it appears as Biana (Plot's map). It was encased in brick in c1830 (info Mrs Bell).

Bycars Park To NNE of Burslem. The name preserves the old name Bicars which may preserve the kernel of the name Burslem of which the earliest spelling is Barcardeslim (NSFCT 1922 p155). Small estate consisting of two properties in the C18. Bycars gives its name to a tiny district, colliery and flint mill (VCH vol 8 p118).

Byrkley Lodge Former lodge of Tutbury Ward of Needwood Forest 1m WNW of Rangemore. In Yoxall ancient parish. Formerly Brickley, and Berkley Lodge. The name is from probably Birk- (birch) ley (HOPT vol 1 p136). Or it took its name from Thomas de Berkeley, Baron of Berkeley, Gloucestershire, keeper of Needwood Forest in Henry II's time (IVNF) or of Henry III's time and who married Joan Ferrers (HOPT vol 1 p136). In the C13 the lodge was used by him (The History of Byrkley Park. Gaye King. post 1986) (IVNF) (HOPT vol 1 p136). In medieval times the lodge alternated with Tutbury Castle as the place for Needwood Forest court; in 1561 a verdict was given at Byrkley Lodge about Sir Henry Paget Knt and Walter Grytteth etc hunting and killing bucks (SHOS vol 1 pp64, 66 il facing). For hunting in Needwood Forest James I was often a visitor at the lodge (The History of Byrkley Park. Gaye King. post 1986. p2). In the C18 Daniel Astle was keeper of Byrkley Lodge. His older son was the antiquary Thomas Astle FRS FSA (1735-1803), whilst the younger son was Capt Daniel Astle (1743-1826) who was the author of a little local book entitled 'A Prospect from Barrow Hill' (1777). He served in the army under General Howe, and was at the attack of the American forces at Bunker's Hill. He subsequently became a clergyman and is said to have been a friend of Dr Johnson of Lichfield (see) and to have made the pen and ink sketch on p119 of HOU (HOU pp228-229). In 1754 Lord Townshend acquired the leasehold of Byrkley Lodge as his hunting seat. He rebuilt the house in a more elegant style. From Townshend the lodge passed to the Marquis of Donegal. From him it was purchased by Edward Sneyd (d1832) in 1795. In 1850 Michael Bass became tenant of Emma Sneyd at the lodge. It was later the seat of the Bass family (Lords Burton). Between 1887 and 1891 Hamar Bass (brother of Lord Burton) rebuilt the house (mem in Newchurch church) (SL p258) (The History of Byrkley Park. Gaye King. post 1986. pp4,9). Hamar's son, WAH Bass, inherited the house in 1898 and after Boer War service married Lady Noreen, a daughter of the Earl of Huntingdon in 1903 (ABTOP p130p). The house was demolished in 1952 (SL p258) (SVB p96) (ESNF p23p) or 1953 (ABTOP p130p) or 1954 (LTD p119p). In 1986 the site of the house became a garden centre called Byrkley Park. A miniature replica of Byrkley Lodge is in the foyer of the garden centre (IVNF) (The History of Byrkley Park. Gaye King. post 1986). The Lodge is depicted in stained glass in Newchurch church (MR p244). (GNHS p145). The grounds appear to have been landscaped in the later C18 by the Marquis of Donegal; a cascade in the garden in 1786 is depicted in a Staffs View in the WSL collection (The History of Byrkley Park. Gaye King. post 1986. pp7-8il,9).

C

Cabbage Hall House 1.5m NNW of Cotton College.

Cadbury Hall Knighton, Adbaston. Built in 1936 for factory staff at the Cadbury Bros milk processing factory on its recreation grounds in Knighton. The hall, officially opened by Mrs LJ Cadbury on Dec 3 1936, is sometimes used as a village hall by Adbaston inhabitants (AADB p65) (SVB p11).

Caddick House Formerly Rose Villa, which had been built probably before 1834, and was approached via Church Street, Clayhanger near Brownhills. By 1902 it was called Caddick House; a John Caddick is mentioned in the 1841 census as a mine agent. The house was demolished in the 1960s (SNBC p19).

Cadlow On the northern boundary of Foxt (FX p5).

Caer Lwytgoed A settlement existing in the early or mid C7, identified with the Letocetum-Lichfield area (SSAHST vol 33 1991-92 pp7-10). The Welsh poem 'Marwnad Cynddylan,' or 'Elegy for Cynddylan' printed in the Myvyrian Archaeology relates the story of Cynddylan, a C7 prince of Powys, who allied with a prince, Morfael of Luitcoet (MR p211). Together they defeated the Angles (DUIGNAN p92), or Oswy's Northumbrian forces in c655 (SSAHST 1972 p30), at Caer Lwytgoed. Shortly after, according to Raven, Cynddylan was killed, Morfael fled to Somerset and the Angles took Caer Lwytgoed, having become Christian in the meantime (MR p211). (Earliest Welsh Poetry. JP Clancy. p 89) (Wales in the Early Middle Ages. W Davies. pp99-101) (Mercian Studies. pp36-39) (VCH vol 14 p4). The **name** means 'town of the grey wood.' Llwyd goed is the modern Welsh of early Welsh 'luitcoet,' meaning 'grey wood.' 'Luitcoet' itself evolved from an earlier Celtic form 'Letoceton,' the native name of the Roman settlement at Wall (VCH vol 14 pp4,37). 'Caer' implies a fortified place (The Roman Site at Wall. DoE Official Handbook), or 'town' (VCH vol 14 p4). (JEPS No. 8 p56). Has also appeared as Caer Lwydgoed. **Caer Lwytgoed's identification with the Lichfield area.** In the 1880s Henry Bradley suggested that Bede's 'Lyccid' (Lichfield) was an Anglicization of the early Welsh 'luitcoit' and that 'luitcoit' itself had evolved from an earlier Celtic form of Letocetum (Letocaiton). Then he identified 'luitcoit' with 'Cair Luitcoit' (see), and 'Cair Luitcoit' with the 'Caer Lwytgoed' of the Welsh poem 'Marwnad Cynddylan' (VCH vol 14 pp4,37). The poem says 1,500 cattle were captured as booty by the Welsh. This suggests the Welsh raided a place with a large tract of pasture. The 'feld' in Lichfield perhaps meant 'common pasture' in the C7 (VCH vol 14 p37). Mr McClure in his notes on 'British Place Names' in the Dawn of Day volume for 1907 p238 says that Bede gives the shortened form 'Lyccid' in his Lyccidfelth, and refers to an original charter in the BM of 803, in which the name is written Liccidfeld. Harold Peake identifies Lichfield with the Caelichyth of the Mercian Councils of 799-802 and the Celchyth of 788 (NSFCT 1908 p122). If Caer Lwytgoed was at Lichfield or Letocetum then as a place of local power it was replaced by Saxon Tamworth (SSAHST vol 33 1991-92 p10). The **site of Caer Lwytgoed**, according to Greenslade, has never been traced. There is no archaeological evidence to prove it was on the site of the present cathedral. There is no evidence that Wall was inhabited later than the C5 (VCH vol 14 p4). Duignan is sure Cynddylan's battle took place in Wales, and there were no Welsh in the Lichfield area in the C7 (DUIGNAN).

Cage Hill Hill 360 feet high NE of Stowe-by-Chartley. There is a mound on top of it, at SK 006280 (NSFCT 1886 p35) (MOS p193). Is said, by Gunstone, to be a natural rock outcrop (NSJFS 1965 p48). Cage Hill House must stand near the site where hunting birds were housed (SVB p158).

Cair Luitcoit Is included in a catalogue of 28 British towns compiled by Nennius (fl 769) from Wales (VCH vol 14 p37). Bradley in the 1880s identified it with the C7 settlement Caer Lwytgoed (see), which is thought to have been in the Lichfield area. Has also appeared as Luitcoith and Luitcoyt.

Calais Hill At Horninglow (IRB p42).

Calcot Hill Hill in the Clent Hills range, 800 feet 1m SE of Clent. The name means 'cold cottage' (TB Jan 1974 p13). The Calcot estate seems to have formed the main part or nucleus of the manor of Church Clent (also styled King's Holt) and Church Clent manor court was held at Calcot Hill House in the C17 (VCHW vol 3 p52 note). (SHOS vol 2 p247). There was also a common called Calcot Hill (VCHW vol 3 p50).

Calcutt Manor Calcot, Clent.

Calderfields Farm Under 1m NE of Walsall. Here is a circular moated site of Caldewelle Hall (see).

Caldewall A spring in Barlaston ancient parish. Recorded in 1501 (BAH p17).

Caldewelle Former manor in the lordship of Rushall, centred on Caldewelle Hall. Has also appeared as Calewenhull (in the Cartulary of Waleshale), Caudy Fields (1834 OS map), Calder Fields (1892), Caulder Fields (1892) (ROR pp16,17), and Calderfields Farm. The name is perhaps from a cold well (SNWA p24).

Caldewelle Hall 1.25m ENE of Walsall, at SP 035991. The surviving circular earthwork may date from the turn of the C13 and C14, when Sir Hugh de Boweles, lord of Rushall manor, gave 'Caldewelle' to his son, William, on the occasion of his marriage; Sir Hugh then built and repaired the mansion at Caldewelle and made the moat about the house. A circular moat at Calderfields Farm still remains (ROR p17) (VCH vol 1 p368) (NSFCT 1982 p9) (SSAHST 1982-3 p49) (SSAHST 1982 p49) (CAMS p60).

Caldmore (locally *Karmer* Murder on the A34. Harry Hawkes. 1970). Former hamlet 0.5m SW of Walsall, lying between the old roads to West Bromwich and Wednesbury. In the foreign of Walsall ancient parish. In Anglo-Saxon 'cald mor' would mean cold waste land (SNWA p26). Although mainly arable, Caldmore was an inhabited area by the early C14. The main settlement was round Caldmore Green, where several old ways meet (VCH vol 17 p155). For its industry see Walsall. For the windmill here see Highgate. Caldmore became a separate ecclesiastical parish in 1872. The church, St Michael and All Angels, on the corner of Bath Road and St Michael Street, was built in 1870-1871 (VCH vol 17 p238) (LDD). The parish is now (1991) known as 'Walsall St Michael' (GLAUE p407). Caldmore became a ward of Walsall county borough in 1889 (VCH vol 17 p217). Lord Francis Tombes of Brailes, Warws, was born at Caldmore on May 17 1924. He attended St Mary's Junior School, Walsall and Elmore Green High School, Bloxwich. He was chairman of the Electricity Council for England and Wales 1977-1980. He was knighted in 1978 and made director of Rolls-Royce in 1982 and chairman in 1985. He sits in the House of Lords as an independent (BCM July 1990 pp10-12 p).

Caldmore Green Tiny green in Caldmore, Walsall. Caldmore's main settlement was at Caldmore Green. On the W side of it is the White Hart Inn.

Caldmore Hall Has been described as lying near Hawe Hall (alias White Hart Inn - see) in Caldmore, Walsall. Caldmore Hall may have been a large house which stood in open ground between Victor Street and Rutter Street. In the 1850s it was occupied by a Mr Woodward, railway contractor engaged in the construction of the SSR (SNWA p26).

Caldon Canal Built to transport limestone from Caldon Low to the Potteries. Has also been called Caldon Branch (HCMS No. 5). Considered in 1769 (NSFCT 1991 p41). James Brindley was taken ill whilst surveying it and died on Sept 27 1772 (IANS p24). Authorised in 1776. Is 17 miles long.

Some say it spurs off the Trent and Mersey Canal at Summit Lock, Shelton. Whilst others say it is the Shelton Branch which spurs off at Summit Lock and the Caldon Canal spurs off this at Etruria Vale Road (HCMS No. 5). The canal opened in 1777 (MR p110). It was never formally opened when it came into operation at Christmas 1778 (The Caldon Canal. Caldon Canal Society). The canal terminates at Froghall. It never reached its proposed destination, Caldon Low. Due to a steep gradient of 700 feet in four miles, the canal had to end at Froghall and a plateway, Cotton Plane (see), covered the rest of the distance (IAS pp173-174). By the C20 many parts of the canal had fallen into decay. Part of the canal had closed by 1947 (SL p257). The canal at Cheddleton burst its banks not far from the old flint mill on July 10 1927 (Cheddleton Remembered. Vera Priestman. 1978 p37). The British Waterways Board in conjunction with Staffs county council, Stoke-on-Trent council, and the Caldon Canal Society carried out restoration work for over two and half years. The canal was formally re-opened in Sept 1974 (The Trent and Mersey Canal, in the Historic Waterways Scenes Series. Peter Lead 1980 pl 98). The lock keeper's cottage at Stanley, Bagnall, and the canal tunnel entrance at Longsdon are both DoE II. At Consallforge is the last milepost on the canal to survive in anything like its original condition. It dates from shortly after the opening of the canal in 1778. The '3' records the distance in miles to Froghall Wharf and the '14' to Etruria (The Trent & Mersey Canal in the Historic Waterways Scenes Series. 1980. Peter Lead. pl 101). (CVH pp134-143).

Caldon Grange House 0.5m SE of Cauldon. Formerly a grange of Buildwas Abbey, Shrops, until being exchanged for Adeney, Shrops with Croxden Abbey in 1287 (NSFCT 1952 pB62) (VCH vol 3 p226) (CDS p7).

Caldon Low Hill in the Moorlands S of Cauldon at SK 080487 about 1017 feet high.
EARLY. The bones of fox, bear, woolly rhinoceros, bison and deer of the period 8000-4000 BC were found 'under the floor' of caves of Caldon Low by Barke in 1906 (HAF p25). A perforated stone axe-hammer, a flint spearhead and flint arrowheads have been found on Caldon Low (Barrows and Bone Caves in Derbys. R Pennington 1877. p63) (NSFCT vol 83 p110). In the BM is a natural pebble with an hour-glass perforation from Caldon Low (NSJFS 1964 p42). A **burial mound excavated by Carrington** in 1849 can no longer be found. It was seven paces in diameter and revealed fragments of an ornamental urn (TYD p150) (VCH vol 1 no 29) (NSJFS 1965 p51). A **burial mound near or at the bottom of Caldon Low** of 22 paces in diameter was excavated by Carrington in 1849. Only a few bones and pottery fragments were found (TYD p132) (NSJFS 1965 p51). A **burial mound 'at a lower situation' on Caldon Hill** of 18 paces in diameter and three feet high was excavated by Carrington in 1849. A rock-cut grave was found, a skeleton and pieces of a bottle-shaped vase of C7 date (TYD p153) (DAJ vol 74 p147) (Gazetteer of Early Anglo-Saxon Burial Mounds. A Meaney. 1964. p221) (Medieval Archaeology vol 6/ 7 p44 fig 13a) (NSJFS 1965 p51). A **burial mound on Caldon Low** marked on the 1882 OS map at approximately SK 076487 was excavated in 1857 and human remains were found. A **burial mound near or at the bottom of Caldon Low** was excavated by T Redfern of Leek in 1871. Human bones and pottery were found (NSFCT 1875 pp52-53) (JBAA series 2 vol 2 1896 p14) (NSJFS 1965 p51). A **burial mound on Caldon Low** at SK 07794880 has been obliterated by quarrying (OS map 6 inch 1894 ed) (NSJFS 1965 p52). **Big Low** was probably in Big Low field in which cinerary urns have been found (KD 1896) (NSSG p13) (MR p84). If at SK 07964851 (NSJFS 1965 p51) then this has been destroyed by quarrying. **Crow Low** (see) at SK 083487, excavated in 1868, may be the same as one at SK 08264872, which has been destroyed by quarrying (VCH barrow list) (OS map 6 inch 1924) (NSJFS 1965 p52). At Earle Cement Works was found some Roman pottery of the C3 and a pottery crucible (NSJFS 1964 p42).
1300 to PRESENT. The name has also appeared as Caldelowe (1339), Cauldon Hill (1686) (NHS p404) (SPNO p24), and Cauldon Low(e). 'Lowe' refers to one, possibly the Big Low (MR p84), or many burial mounds once on the hill, now (1980s) mostly obliterated by quarrying (MR p84). In the later C17 Plot noted two subterraneous passages under Cauldon Low but he did not know whether water passed along them (NHS p89). **Limestone quarries.** Since at least the early C19 Caldon Lowe has been extensively quarried for limestone for the pottery industry. The limestone was taken on one of the Cotton Plane (see) plateways, collectively known as Caldon Low Tramways, to Froghall. At Froghall and Consallforge it was broken down and taken on the Caldon Canal, or on the Woodhead Plateway, or on the Consall Plateway, to be used in pottery making in the Potteries. A blast, known as the Coronation Blast, brought down tons of limestone in 1902 and was attended by an O-4-O saddle tank engine 'Toad' with a NSR official party. Another blast at Caldon Low on July 12 1938, detonated by electricity from Euston Station,

London, brought down about 1,000,000 tons of limestone (The Trent and Mersey Canal in the Historic Waterways Scenes Series. Peter Lead. 1980 pl 125). After the opening of the Waterhouses branch railway the Caldon Low quarries became a tourist attraction boasting a cave system lit by electricity which illuminated stalactites and stalagmites. It had been discovered by quarrymen and became known as the Fairy Cave. The cave had to close in 1908 due to its proximity with encroaching quarry workings (PSM pl 77) (The Trent and Mersey Canal, in the Historic Waterways Scenes Series. Peter Lead. 1980. pl 125). The same or another cave which appears on an NSR postcard of c1910 was 30 feet wide and 100 feet high and penetrated about 140 feet into the hill (SMOPP vol 2 p80p c1910) (HLSP p145). There has long existed in the Moorlands and Peak District **folklore** that fairies inhabit burial mounds. A ballad by Mary Howitt, who spent some of her childhood at Uttoxeter (see), titled 'The Fairies of The Cauldon Lowe' (1847) is based on an old legend that the hill is inhabited by a race of fairies. The ballad tells how the girl Mary spends midsummer night on the hill observing 100 fairies dancing to the music of nine harpists. The rest of the fairies' night is spent doing good deeds for the neighbourhood.

> And where have you been, my Mary?,
> And where have you been from me?'
> 'I've been to the top of Cauldon Lowe
> The midsummer night to see.

(NSFCT 1896 p147) (FLJ 1942 p127) (FPSB p162) (VB pp199-200) (GLS pp31-32). Mee gives three other verses (KES p223).

Caldonlow (OS map 1:25,000) or Cauldon Lowe (OS map 1:50,000). Small fragmented hamlet 0.75m S of Cauldon. A newly-built house in West Fields is reputedly haunted; figures appearing at a bedside in 1989 (GLS pp32-33). A Hughes 500 helicopter crashed near the hamlet on Oct 19 1996 killing the pilot (ES Oct 21 1996 p4p).

Caldrey Hayes Former small enclosure of about seven acres 0.75m E of Market Drayton in Tyrley parish. The name, which has appeared as Caldey Hay (1524) and Caldrey Hayes (1669), may be from causeway or the old Shrops surname Caldey or Calder (SHC 1945/ 6 pp83-84).

Caledonia Former cluster of cottages noted by Scott in the early 1830s (SVS p140). Towards the end to the C19 the name applied to a road running E from where Bagleys Road continues as Woods Lane from the old settlement of Aston's Fold to Thorns Road, Quarry Bank (SNSV vol 1 p55).

Calf Heath Hamlet and former common nearly 1.5m SE of Gailey. The W half was in Water Eaton liberty in Penkridge parish whilst the E half was in the detached township of Hatherton in Wolverhampton ancient parish (W pp154,469). There were two burial mounds of possible Roman origin near the road side from Somerford to Four Crosses at cSJ 917081 in the later C17 (NHS p403) (WSAS 1938 p297) (NSJFS 1965 p35). The mounds could not be found by Thomas HF Whitgreave and others in 1781, nor could they be found in the 1930s (SHC 1938 p297). Hackwood mentions one on Calf Heath, which he says is of British origin (SCSF p74). The name has appeared as Calfre heie (994), Calonheth (1286), Caleshuve (c1290), Calwehet (1311), Caulfesheath (1612), Calves Heath (DUIGNAN p30) (SPNO p88). It means 'hedge of the calves' (SPN p60) or 'enclosure of the calves' (SPNO p88). Or is from the root 'calb,' Gaelic 'calbh' signifies a slope (NSFCT 1908 p141). For most of its history Calf Heath has been a vast moor (DUIGNAN). It is said to have been a hay of Cannock Forest (NSFCT 1908 p141), but it may just have been a part of Gailey Hay. Under an Act of 1799 550 acres of Calf Heath in Water Eaton manor were enclosed (SHC 1941 p17) in 1813 (VCH vol 5 p127) (MH 1994 p108). Under an Act of 1856 315 acres of Calf Heath in Hatherton township were enclosed (SHC 1941 p19) in 1859 (MH 1994 p108) (PCC p16).

Calf Heath Reservoir Reservoir built to supply the Staffs and Worcs Canal, appears on Greenwood's map. Is to the S of, and earlier than, Gailey Reservoirs (NSJFS 1967 p53).

California House or tiny hamlet on N side of the Foxt to Winkhill road.

California Lock An abandoned lock on the Uttoxeter Branch Canal of the Caldon Canal at East Wall. Built in c1811. Has also appeared as Morris's Lock (VB p174). (IANS pp53,24,159) (The Trent and Mersey Canal in the Historic Waterways Scenes Series. Peter Lead. 1980. pl 130 shows it in a derelict state).

Callingwood Hamlet in Needwood Forest above the upper reaches of a tributary of the Trent 1.5m NW of Tatenhill. Partly in Tatenhill and Rolleston ancient parishes. In 1793 a hoard of 32 Roman gold coins was found at Callingwood, at SK 195235, dating from 20 BC to 96 AD. Coins of Augustus, Nero, Galba, Vespasian, and Domitian were in it (GM 1796 p983) (SHOS vol 1 General Intro pp18,109) (SSC p123) (GNHS p70) (NSJFS 1964 p38) (STMSM Sept 1973 p26) (BTIH p10) (info KL Neal). Bluish-brown Roman pottery fragments have been found at Callingwood (HOPT vol 1 p10) (BTIH p10). The name has been written Boscum Calumpriatum, Boschalenge, Le Chaleng (1247), or Chalengwode, now corrupted to Callingwood (SHOS vol 1 pp106,109) (HCT pp7-8) (GNHS p147) (HOPT vol 2 p221) (SHC 1937 pp83,113) (VCH vol 2 p349) (SPN p125). According to tradition Callingwood received its name from the offer made by Robert de Ferrers 1 (1st Earl of Derby d1139 - UTR p36) of a wood in Needwood Chase (Needwood Forest) as the prize to the bravest in his army at the battle of the Standard (1138) (HOPT vol 1 p109), or the battle of Northallerton (1138) (VCH vol 2 p349) or it arose from some dispute about the wood (HOPT vol 1 p136) (Discovering Parish Boundaries. Angus Winchester. 1990. p38) (SSE 1996 p11). Duignan interprets the word, but does not relate the story (DUIGNAN). Callingwood Gate Farm at Callingwood implies there was a gate here to Needwood Forest.

Callingwood Dingle NE of Dunstall, Tatenhill. Dingle which breaks the line of rising banks of Needwood Forest plateau (HOPT vol 1 p134).

Callingwood Gate House 1m SW of Anslow Gate. The name is from a former entry into Needwood Forest (ANS p8).

Callingwood Hall Callingwood (IVNF photograph) (ESNF p20p of in the early C20). To W of Callingwood Hall a burial mound was noted in the later C17 (NHS p414) which could not be located in the 1960s (NSJFS 1965 p49).

Callis, The Minute hamlet, now part of Tamworth suburbs, 2.5m SE of Tamworth town centre, 1.5m S of Amington. Formerly in Ammington and Stoneydelph township. In existence in 1888 (1888 OS map 6 inch).

Callowhill House S of Dilhorne. In Dilhorne parish.

Callowhill House (BOE p74) on a spur of land by the Blithe (0.75m to N is the house Upper Callowhill), 2m SSW of Kingstone, in Kingstone parish. Southern-most place in Totmonslow hundred, and is surrounded, except on the N side, by Pirehill hundred. The name is from Anglo-Saxon 'calu-hyll' meaning the bold, or bare, hill (DUIGNAN) (SPN p20). Has also appeared as Callow Hill. As a young man Sir Simon Degge (1613-1703), antiquarian and historian, seems to have lived the life of a country gentleman at Callowhill, still living here in 1649. He was knighted in 1670 (SH p73).

Calthorpe Cottages Stand on the N side of Wood Lane, Handsworth. Built in the 1840s the cottages were still standing in 1983. The name is from Lord Calthorpe, lord of Perry Barr (MNB p53).

Calton Tiny moorland village on high ground above the Hamps 20.5m NE of Stafford. The parochial chapelry of Calton formerly lay in the parishes of Blore (Ray), Croxden, Mayfield and Waterfall. On the E of Calton and 160 metres N of Lower Green House at SK 10815027 is an unusual type of burial mound with a level raised centre platform surrounded by a bank, 18 paces in diameter and 1.5 feet high. Carrington excavated it in 1849 and found a crouched and a child's skeleton and evidence of an Anglian intrusive burial with thickbacked knife (TYD pp128-129) (VCH vol 1 no 14. p208) (Gazetteer of Early Anglo-Saxon Burial Mounds. A Meaney. 1964 p221) (Medieval Archaeology. vol 6/ 7 p45 fig 13b) (NSJFS 1965 pp53-54). It is a listed monument. Another burial mound at Calton, unlocated, revealed burnt human bones (NSJFS 1965 p54). Near Calton, is another, unlocated. Carrington excavated it in 1849. A crouched skeleton of a boy was found (TYD pp129-130) (R vol 3) (VCH vol 1 no 15) (NSJFS 1965 p54). Pevsner mentions four round cairns covering Bronze Age burials 0.5m to the E of Calton on Marsden Low (probably Musden Low (see) is meant) (BOE p93). Calton, along with Ilam and Castern, was mentioned as part of a bequest to Burton Abbey in 1002 (SASR 1995 no 5 p37). It is not in DB, but has since appeared as Calton (1238) (SSE 1996 p11), Cawlton (1631), and Caulton (1710) (SASR 1995 no 5 pp38,41). The name is of Anglo-Saxon origin and means 'the enclosure or tun where calves were reared' (OAKDEN) (SSAHST 1967 p34) (SSE 1996 p11) (SPN p28). The village seems to have started as a planned settlement created in or by the C13 by the lords of Blore, Mayfield, and Waterfall. They would have populated it with people from these villages. The site was chosen because of its isolated situation, far from an existing village from which there would be competition. With the E end of the village spilling over into the adjoining estate - Musden in Croxden parish - this would explain why Calton was divided between four parishes or chapelries (SASR 1995 no 5 pp37,40). There was a church at Calton in the C16 (LDD). The present church, St Mary, on the N side of Back Lane, was rebuilt in 1762 and restored in 1875 (CHMS2 p31) or built in 1839 (BOE p92). Calton became a separate civil parish in 1866 (GLAUE p407) and a separate ecclesiastical parish in 1902 (LGS p100). For a rhyme about Calton see Cauldon.

Calton Buds Over 0.25m WSW of Calton. There was a toll-house of this name on the Ashbourne-Leek turnpike road. Tolls ceased to be collected in 1855.

The cottage still existed in 1948. 'Buds' is the name still used by the older people of the district for the steep rising above the right bank of the nearby Hamps (NSFCT 1948 p44). Has also appeared as The Budds.

Calton Green Tiny hamlet at the E end of Calton village. Formed part of the Musden Grange estate, in Croxden parish. Entries in the PR for Calton Green occur regularly from the late C16 to the C18 (SASR 1995 no 5 p36).

Calton Moor Former common stretching S from Calton village to Dale Tor. Written Cawlton Moore in 1631 by which time some enclosure had taken place. The rest of the common seems to have been enclosed by agreement, gradually (SASR 1995 no 5 p38,40). The Young Pretender's army passed through Caltonmoor on Dec 4 1745 in the Jacobite Rebellion of that year (BPCSM p7).

Caltonmoor House 1.25m SE of Calton. To the W of the house at SK 11094867 is a burial mound, 22 paces in diameter and three, excavated by Carrington in 1851. A cremation was found. An old driveway had cut through it and damaged it (TYD p176) (NSJFS 1965 p52). For a burial mound 0.5m N of Caltonmoor House see Thorncliff Low. The house is the 'Red Lion Inn' on Yates' map. It still preserves the wine cellars with their external entrance (NSFCT 1948 p42). In 1844 an exhausted stranger, dressed as a gentleman, was discovered at Blore Lime Kiln and taken to Caltonmoor House. At length a doctor was called to see the stranger and he pronounced that the person was a woman. Shortly before the woman's death she claimed to Rev Day, private tutor to the sons of John Russell of Ilam Hall, that she was of noble birth. Her death is recorded in Blore PR as 'Ellen H_____ of C_____ Aged 21 buried 10th March 1844 Frederick Day, Officiating Minister. This young woman had wandered about in the disguise of a man's clothing for several years, through England, Wales, and Ireland and died at Calton Moor House.' She has since been revealed as Ellen Hatfield (alias Hadfield) of Chapel-en-le-Frith. A few days after her burial her grave sank and it was assumed her body had been stolen (SBB pp189-190).

Calvan's Hill Between Blackfords and Cannock (CCF p71). Part of Cannock High School playing field? Has appeared as Calughull (1304), Calughhullefeld (1341-1370), Caloughehyll-filde als Calfe hylles fylde (1580) (SPNO p58) and presently as Calving Hill.

Calwich Fragmented hamlet covering the steep W side of the upper Dove valley; Calwich Home Farm is 1.25m E of Ellastone. Former tithe-free township in Ellastone ancient parish (W p775). According to OS map 1:25,000 (1985) there are three burial mounds on the N of the Ellastone-Mayfield road on the former Calwich Common. The westernmost one, known as Calwich Low, at SK 12914376, is 38 paces in diameter and 2.5 feet high, and a listed monument (is possibly Plot's burial mound 'without name' - NHS p404) (VCH barrow list) (NSJFS 1965 p37); the middle one, at SK 1317438, is 32 paces in diameter and 4.5 feet high, and a listed monument (NSJFS 1965 p37); the easternmost mound, at SK 13854417, is Plot's Rowlow (see). The name has appeared as Calewich (1197) (SPN p28) and Calowic (1314) (SSE 1996 p11). Many say it has the same origins as Colwich. The first element, Saxon 'calf,' the second element, Saxon 'wic' could be 'dwelling,' 'village,' 'hamlet,' 'town,' 'farm,' so 'calf tun' (SSE 1996 p11) (SPN p28). There was possibly a medieval village in the vicinity of Calwich Abbey (SSAHST 1970 p34), later depopulated. Calwich became a separate civil parish in 1866 (GLAUE p407).

Calwich Common Calwich, Ellastone. Plot noted two burial mounds on 'Colwich Common' near Mayfield (NHS p404) (AAD p207) (SCSF p74).

Calwich Low Burial mound 0.25m N of Calwich Abbey, see under Calwich.

Calwich Park To W of Calwich Abbey, by the Dove.

Calwich Priory Priory 0.5m E of Ellastone. Often referred to as an abbey. There was a hermitage here before the religious house (VCH vol 3 p136).

PRIORY. The priory originated as a cell of Kenilworth Abbey. The date of the foundation was after c1125, and often said to be before 1148. It is mentioned in 1130. Given to Kenilworth by Nicholas de Gresley alias FitzNigel (or Fitz-Nigel) and his wife Margery, the latter was the ward of Geoffrey de Clinton, founder of Kenilworth. Dedicated to St Margaret (VCH vol 3 pp237-239). For Augustinian Canons (LGS p135) (SOSH p109) (NSSG p12) (HOS p25. 1998 p56). Or a convent of Black Canons (Carthusians) a branch of the Benedictines (AAD p238). Towards the end of C15 the priory had a community of only one or two monks. A single canon was left when the prior died in 1530. The patron, Sir Ralph Longford, then had the property secularized, anticipating its suppression. It was suppressed with his agreement in 1532. Henry VIII granted it to Merton Priory in exchange for the manor of East Molesey, Surrey, which itself was suppressed in 1538. Longford continued as leaseholder but fell into debt and the property was sold to John Fleetwood in 1543 (VCH vol 3 p239). (W p775) (LGS p135) (HOCA).

AFTER THE DISSOLUTION. In 1544 the Fleetwoods secured the site and made the abbey their home by turning the chancel of the church into a parlour, the nave into a hall, and the tower into a kitchen (HOS p28). The Mason's Arms, now private houses, in Gallowstree Lane, Mayfield incorporates stones from the abbey; a ghost of a monk has been seen in one (GLS pp73-75). The Mayfield house was derelict by 1993 (MOM p49ps). In the early C18 Fleetwood's house was rebuilt (ESNF p110), during this period the abbey estate passed to Bernard Granville. Here he entertained many celebrities of the C18, including Mrs Delaney (his sister), Rousseau, Erasmus Darwin, Anna Seward, and Rev John Gisborne, whose poem 'Vales of Wever' (1796), describes Calwich. Handel was a frequent visitor and left many of his manuscripts to the Granvilles, which remained at the house until they went to the BM. He reputedly wrote his 'Water Music' here (AAD p241) (LGS p135) (STM July 1965 p41) (TFTP p183) (MR p144), and or a portion of his 'Messiah' (NSFCT 1877 p6 note. 1908 p190). During his stay at Wootton Hall 1766-67 Rousseau is said to have met here Lady Andover, Lady Cowper, the Russian Count Orloff, probably Brooke Boothby of Ashbourne Hall, and the Duchess of Portland. Whilst here he is said to have taken an interest in Granville's 20-year old niece Mary Dewes (Jean-Jacque Rousseau in Staffordshire 1766-1767. JH Broome. 1966. p11), who he called 'Little Shepherdess of Calwich' (LTD p67). The house contained a landscape by Rembrandt and other paintings and drawings (AAD pp240,242-243 il facing p239 when the seat of Court Dewes Granville). In 1849-50 William Burn rebuilt the house for Rev A Duncombe (W pp19,775) (SVB p73) (ESNF p110p). This house was demolished in 1927 (SVB p73) or largely demolished in 1928 (ESNF p110). (SGS p97). One of Calwich Priory houses may have been the model for Donnithorne Chase in George Eliot's novel 'Adam Bede' (1859), but the model is more likely to have been Wootton Hall (LGS p132) (LTD p64). (GNHS p93) (GNHSS p10) (LGS p37,135) (MR p143). GROUNDS. An ornamental nine-acre lake (MR p144) with Portobello Bridge at the W end of it and a temple at the E end. The fishing temple has a portico of detached columns and a copper domed roof and bears the date 1797 (BOE p128) (SVB p73). Is also known as Handel's Temple (SLM Feb 1959 p17il). Gisborne says a number of skulls and human bones were frequently discovered in the grounds, probably the remains of those buried at the abbey (AAD p240).

Camomile Green Former area beyond Hart's Green, Harborne (VCHWA vol 7 p23), at the junction of Tennal Road and Queen's Park Road (GMH pp18-19). A small community of nailmakers lived here (HA pp45,50). (OHOPP p29p of Camomile Cottages c1900). Francis W Aston (1877-1945) was born in a house here long since demolished. He was the inventor of the mass spectrograph (GMH pp18-19), and winner of the Nobel Prize award for Chemistry in 1922 (HOHE p29).

'Camp Bank' Near Edith Street and Chapman Street, West Bromwich. Thrown up by parliamentarians in 1644 in the Civil War to raise a cannon to shoot at Dudley Castle. But it was found the distance was too great. A few years before 1924, it was destroyed (OWB p73) (TB May 1995 p16).

Camp Farm 0.75m SE of Ellerton Grange. In Adbaston parish. Situated on the highest point of the Roman road from Stretton (Penkridge) to Ternhill, Shrops. An article once printed in the local press alleged that Roman remains were once found here and that other finds included bronze spears and swords but there is no evidence that any of these items ever existed (AADB p2). Has also appeared as Camp.

Camp Farm 2m NE of Enville, in Morfe manor and Enville ancient parish. Built by 1744 on former heath or waste land, enclosed in 1683 (VCH vol 20 pp93-94). To the E of the farmhouse at the top of 'Camp Bank' at SO 851890 is an ancient yew tree which had a girth of 16 feet 11 inches in 1998/9. It is believed locally to be the largest hedgerow yew in Staffs and Shrops (BCM spring 1999 pp71p,72).

Campfield Coppice at Hollywood near Hilderstone at junction of Whitesytch Lane and Wolliscroft Lane, in which is an earthwork, thought to be of Roman origin (NSFCT 1902 p117. 1941 pp35-36) (SIS p3).

Camp Hall Slymansdale, Maer. Marked on current OS map 1:25,000. N of Camp Hill. Same as Camp Hill Hall? (see).

Camp Hill Sandstone hill and cut in that hill for a stretch of the Stourbridge-Wolverhampton road at Audnam. There is a local tradition that it was the site where troops in the Civil War camped. The name appears on the 1921 OS map. Camp Hill House (or Camp House) stood on Camp Hill. It was occupied by Frederick Englebert Knt, glass engraver of Bohemia (SNSV vol 1 p56).

Camp Hill Highest point of the Maer Hills at 708 feet, 1m NNW of Maer. There are two mounds which may be burial mounds on it. One at SJ 78083975 (about 15 paces in diameter and four feet high) and another at SJ 78104011 (about 15 paces in diameter and three feet high). Both have been excavated and no finds made (GM vol 82 part 2 1812 p603) (NSFCT vol 66 p99. vol 63

p114) (NSJFS 1965 p44). These, or others, were opened by Mr Tollet of Betley in c1830 (NSFCT 1931 p99). At the S foot is a large elongated burial mound of the inverted dish form thought to be of the Late Bronze Age (NSFCT 1931 p99). In the 1860s pugilist combats were fought here after the sport was made illegal; the spectators and participants arriving by train at Whitmore station (TSS pp46-47). Has also appeared as Camphills.

Camp Hill Hall 'Camphill' on Maer Heath in Maer parish was built for Sarah Wedgwood (1776-1856), daughter of Josiah Wedgwood I, in 1827 (WCW p194). Residence of William Davenport, lord of the manor of Maer in the mid C19. It had formerly been called Slimersdale (W p397). Both Slymansdale and Camp Hall were just outside Madeley Great Park pale.

Campions Woodland area in Norbury parish (VCH vol 4 p155).

Campville House At the end of Coppice Lane, 1m SSE of Clifton Campville.

Camrose Hall Rudyard. Built in 1891 by Hugh Sleigh. Formerly known as Holly Bank. It incorporated two shops at road level and offered extensive accommodation facilities (RL pp28,124p).

Canada Lake Small lake 0.25m N of Wootton Lodge, Wootton.

Candle House Eaves Lane, Bucknall. Residence of the Bentley family, candle makers (FWMBS front and back covers)

Cank Thorn Thorn tree at Broadhurst Green on Cannock Chase. Marks the boundary of Teddesley, Baswich and Cannock parishes, and was used as marker for the old salt-carrying roads of Old Camp Road and Penkridge Road (WMAG Dec 1979 p17). The tree is mentioned in the C13 and C14 and was reported to be buckthorn (NSFCT 1908 p120. 1948 p126) (SLM Feb 1951 p19) (CCF p135). In the C13 it was written Haughmarethorn (? Haugh-mare-thorn). Dugdale in Mon. vol 6 p1253 notes it. By the early C18 the ancient thorn had decayed and a new tree was planted on the site. This was still living in 1902 (DUIGNAN). Another account says the ancient thorn was replaced by a blackthorn in the C18 (SPN p29). Wright visited the tree in the 1930s when James Fisher, one in a succession of a line of keepers of the Cank Thorn, lived in a nearby lodge. Wright noted soldiers from Brocton Army Camp had damaged it in WW1 (CCBO pp71-73). ES Edees visited the tree in the 1940s and in consultation with the BM concluded that it was a cockspur thorn, a species of hawthorn of North American origin (NSFCT 1948 p126. 1949 p119) (PCC p13). The tree standing in 1959 was considered then to be probably of not more than 100 years old (VCH vol 5 p2 note). In 1971 the tree was accidentally broken off at ground level, but fortunately a rooted sucker had previously been taken from the old stock and had thrived. This was planted with due ceremony on the original site, and was then maintained by Staffs county council (The Staffordshire Way. Rocester to Cannock Chase. p17). Planting took place in March 1972 (SN March 10 1972 p10) (VB p114). (WMAG Dec 1979 p17p). Spurs or cuttings have been taken from the tree but will not take at all in other parts of the Chase (info wildlife warden 1993). The tree growing by the roadside opposite the Commonwealth Cemetery is probably the same as the one Prince mentions at SJ 983155 (COS p57p).

Can Lane Former hamlet adjoining Sodom, straggling along a lane, formerly known as Can Lane, 1m ENE of Sedgley, in Sedgley ancient parish (W p200). The name is from perhaps Thomas Cann a prize fighter of some repute in the Cann Lane area (SR). The Canns are believed to have originated from Devon, and the name may be from Abraham Cann (b1794) of Devon, inventor of 'Stay-lace,' a wrestling hold, when on a visit to relations at Tipton (TB Oct 1995 pp30-31). Has appeared as Cann Lane and is marked on the 1834 OS map. The name no longer prevails and the lane is now called Hurst Road (CWBT p24). Lawley, writing in 1893, notes Can Lane has become Hurst Hill (HOBLL p175). (BCM Oct 1990 p61). Can Lane was renowned for being frequented by criminals (TB Nov 1976 p24). For John Cornfield, poet, see Hurst Hill.

Cann Hill In the Orton area, Wombourne (PONP p140).

Cannock Old parish and former township. The present large town of Cannock by Ridings Brook lies on former heathland anciently covered by Cannock Forest, now on the southern edge of Cannock Chase, 9m SSE of Stafford. EARLY. The Cannock Stone was a large stone which Erdeswick and Cox say was in a field S of the church (SD p56) (CCC p4); its origin remains lost in obscurity (HOWW p14). It was perhaps an example of a particular type of iron ore called Cannock Stone, or Cannotstone. Dud Dudley of Dudley Castle (see) noted it in his Metallum Martis (1665). He thought it was so sulphurous and terrestrial it was not fit to make iron. Whilst, White in the mid C19, thought it must be capable of much useful application for it oxygenates so rapidly (W p450). (NHS p397). A barbed and tangled arrowhead of the **Bronze Age** was found at 176 Stafford Road (NSJFS 1964 p18).
1000 to 1500. One of the two manors called Chenet, which appear in DB, belonged to the Crown. Later Cannock appears as Cannoc (c1135-40), Cancia (1155), Chenot (1162), Chnot (1170), Kanot (1187), Canet (1203), Gannok

vel kannok (1221), Kankbury (1352), le Canke (1403), Cannock als Canck (1493) (SPNO p56) (SPN p28), and Cannoll (c1642) (Staffordshire and the Great Rebellion. DA Johnson & DG Vaisey. 1964. p69). The **name** is of perhaps Old English origin and means 'cnocc' meaning a 'hill' or 'hillock' (SPNO p56). Others have thought Cannock is from a Saxon term meaning 'a great oak forest' (NSFCT 1881 p14). Shaw thought it was from the ancient British word Cannoc (SHOS vol 1 part 1 p10, vol 2 p312 and the 2nd p312*) (SDW p9). It may be from various Celtic forms 'chnoc' 'cnoc' 'cnwc' 'cunaco' meaning a hill or high place (SOS p191) (DUIGNAN) (NSFCT 1908 p134) (WMLB p76) (SSE 1996 p11) (SPNO p56) (SPN p28). Some say it derived from the Cangi tribe (W p450) (NSFCT 1908 p120): Others from the Danish King Canute (W p450) (HOWW p9). The erroneous identification of Clent with Chenet in the C16 enabled the Clent inhabitants to claim confirmation of their rights as dwelling on ancient demesne of the Crown, and obtain a charter giving them exemption from toll, stallage, passage, portage, etc, from contributing to the expenses of sending knights to parliament, and from serving on juries except those in their own parish (VCHW vol 3 p51). Henry I was probably at Cannock. It was at Cannock he granted a charter of free warren to the son and heir of Marmion (RVW p9). Richard I sold the manor in 1189 to the bishop of Coventry and Lichfield. The bishop was granted a charter on June 2 1259 to hold a **market** here on Tuesdays (NSJFS 1971 p51). The market seems to have declined by the C19 (SCSF p95). There was no market in 1792 (OWEN), but there was in 1888 (LHE p264). The charter of 1259 also granted an annual **fair** on the vigil, feast and morrow of St Michael in Monte Tumba (Oct 15-17). The right was confirmed between 1387 and 1390. By 1747 fairs were being held on April 20, Aug 20, and second Monday after Michaelmas (VCH vol 5 pp61-62). White, Owen and Cooke give May 8 (for horses and pedlary), and Oct 18 (for horses, cattle and sheep) (W p449) (SCSF p98). White adds Aug 24 (W p449). There was a fair in 1792 (OWEN), and there was in 1888 (LHE p264). The parish **church**, St Luke, by Market Place and Mill Street, has some late C12 or early C13 work (BOE p93). **Ecclesiastical dispute**. Cannock church, probably founded as a dependency of Penkridge Collegiate Church, was attached to a prebend of Penkridge Collegiate Church by the later C12. However, in 1189 along with Cannock manor the king granted to the bishop of Coventry and Lichfield Cannock church and rectory, who in turn granted them to the canons of Lichfield cathedral. Subsequently such issues as the holding of the rectory estate, the right to appoint a chaplain, and the right to burials and mortuaries were constantly disputed between the canons of Penkridge, and those of Lichfield. In the early C13 some concessions were made on either side; that Penkridge keep the right of mortuaries and Lichfield keep the right of appointing the chaplain. But the two sides vehemently disputed over rights in the later C13 and in the earlier C14: The dean and chapter of Lichfield even tried to overturn the Penkridge canons' right to burials and mortuaries by having the bishop of St Asaph secretly consecrate a graveyard at Cannock in 1330. From the mid C14 Lichfield seems to have claimed all rights in Cannock. Cannock parish remained a peculiar jurisdiction of the dean and chapter of Lichfield cathedral until peculiar jurisdictions were abolished in 1846 (VCH vol 3 pp93,300. vol 5 p58) (GLAUE p407). Cannock was certainly a separate parish from the Dissolution (GLAUE p407). **Wakes** were on the Sunday after the fair on Oct 18 in the C19 (W p449). Cannock was slightly affected by a **plague** in 1361 (SCSF p133). In the Dorchester Road and Wellington Drive area at SJ 968097 was a **moated site**, built over in 1975 (SSAHST 1982-3 p37).

1500 to 1830. In the **Civil War** the royalist commanders the Earl of Northampton and Col Hastings were in Cannock on March 17 1643, prior to the battle of Hopton Heath; here they learnt of the Moorlanders encamped at the Haywoods (HAF p121). The Earl of Denbigh (a parliamentarian) died of wounds at Cannock on the Saturday following his defeat by Prince Rupert in a skirmish at Camp Hill, Birmingham (sometimes called the battle of Birmingham) in April 1643 (OWB p71) (WAM p81). Col John Lane of Rushall Hall attacked the baggage train of Sir William Brereton at Cannock and seized 'a pretty good store of powder and match' (SOB p75). In 1646 a parliamentarian horse troop repulsed a royalist force from Lichfield at Cannock (VCH vol 5 p52). Cannock **Grammar School** was founded by John Wood of London in 1680. It was endowed in 1752 and 1761 by John Biddulph (W p451). A new Grammar School opened in 1956 (Staffs County Handbook c1958. p107). The **Cannock Conduit Trust** was founded in 1736. That year the trust erected the stone conduit head building W of the Bowling Green at High Green. The building, hexagonal and with a pyramidal roof, still exists. The water came from Stringer's Meadow, Rumer Hill, Leacroft and was given by Dr William Byrrche of Leacroft Hall. The undertaking was endowed by lord of the manor, the Earl of Uxbridge, the Bishop of Worcester, Sir Robert Fisher

and others. The Trust became a registered charity and served the township of Cannock for over 200 years until mining subsidence damaged the pipework in 1942. After 1954 the trust's income was used to purchase facilities and amenities beneficial to Cannock (DoE II) (W p451) (WJO July 1906 p184p) (CCBO pp99-101) (VCH vol 5 p52) (BOE p93) (Plaque on the Conduit Head) (STMSM Aug 1979 p27p). The **Bowling Green**, forming an island site at High Green in the centre of town, existed in 1753 when a brick wall was built around it. After a long dispute over the ownership of this small piece of land, the Green was vested in trustees in 1896. They leased the Green to the Bowling Club at a pepper-corn rent. The Trust still existed in 1956 (VCH vol 5 p52). For the Cannock Troop of the Staffordshire Yeomanry see Teddesley Hall. **Persons and visitors**. In the C17 a **Mr Coleman** of Cannock, spent all his money on making a waggon to go by itself. The 1st Lord Aston took up the idea or encouraged it, but it was criticised for when it had strength it wanted speed and when it had speed it wanted strength (SHOS vol 2 p316). For **Nathaniel**, who committed patricide and matricide in c1674 see Cheslyn Hay. Rev **William Alport**'s will, dated 1720, founded a charity for the incumbents of eight Staffs parishes - Bednall, Brewood, Colwich, Lapley, Abbots Bromley, Penkridge, Shareshill, and Weston-on-Trent, providing that they reside for at least 10 months in the year in their cures and give a sermon at Cannock church on St Barnabas' day (June 11). The incumbents of the last four parishes together with those of Bloxwich, Bradley, Castle Church, and Coppenhall received further charity under the same conditions from the will of Miss Eleanor Alport, sister of William, dated 1727. Alport sermons were still being given by the 12 incumbents in rotation at a service at Cannock church in 1956 (VCH vol 5 p64). **Anne Craycroft** (1766-1843), wife of Moreton Walhouse (1761-1821) of Hatherton Hall (see), in c1805 had a portion of an arch in the church cut away by a mason so she could pass through the arch in her capacious coal-skuttle C18 bonnet. The niche remained until 1925 when the arch was restored to its former state (CCBO pp96-98). For Rev **Henry Francis Cary** (1772-1844), author, poet and translator of Dante, see The Green. Rev Thomas Cotterill (d1824), hymn writer, was born in Cannock on Dec 1 1779 (PSS p129) (VFC p32). **Matthias Willington**, a labourer in the kitchen of the Crown Inn, Cannock, shot in the head and murdered, James Hawkins, an under game-keeper of the Earl of Lichfield, in Oct 1836 (SA Oct 22 1836).

1830 to PRESENT. Cannock was described as 'a little town' in 1836 (SA Oct 22 1836). A windmill probably stood on Windmill Bank at SJ 990102 to NE of Cannock watermill (WBJ p17). Coal mining has been Cannock's chief industry; the town grew significantly in the last quarter of the C19 (SL p117). Cannock Branch **railway** from Cannock to Walsall opened on Feb 1 1858 (VCH vol 2 p317) (SSR p17) (ESSN p52) (NSJFS 1964 p86; says 1850); the Cannock Mineral Line from Cannock to Rugeley opened in 1859 (VCH vol 5 pp51,151). It was recommended the railway station at Cannock be closed in 1963 (ES March 22 1963). The **arms** of Cannock urban district, granted in 1951, are: Barry of eight pieces vert and sable, a gand antlers between in chief an ancient crown of fleurs-de-lis, also gold, and in base a silver cross potent quadrate. The crest is: Rising from a circlet vert with flames proper issuing therefrom an oaktree bearing acorns also proper with a gold Stafford Knot about the trunk. The motto is: 'Labor in venatu' (Exertion in the hunt) (CH pp338,339il). The **County Mining College** was opened in Cannock in 1928 (VCH vol 5 p63) (CCAP p11p of in 1951). The Benton Memorial Clock turret in Market Square was erected in 1935 (VCH vol 5 p53). There is a Bakelite Bush **television** set from Cannock in the County Museum, Shugborough. For Cannock as a verb see BCM April 1971 p27. A family from Bevan Lee Road saw a **UFO** on Sept 18 1967 (FSRP p15). There have been sightings of the **ghost** of a former patient at New Cannock Hospital (info Bruce Braithwaite). **Persons and visitors**. **William Henry Robinson** (1847-1926), poet, novelist printer, journalist and astronomer, was born at Cannock; his father later founded the Walsall Advertiser. His 'Collected Poems' appeared in 1900, and he also published two novels 'Kathleen O'Leovan' (1896) and 'Till the Sun Grows Cold' (1904) (PSS pp261-263) (VFC p114). **Leonard Galletley**, poet, was born in Cannock on Jan 6 1872. His work includes 'The Call of the Miles' (1916), 'Inishtor and Other Poems' (1925), 'Evening on the Morddach Estuary' (1929), and 'An English Village' (1933). He lived most of his life in Shrops (PSS pp361-366 p) (VFC p52). At the beginning of the C20 Dr **John Kerr Butter**, born at Farfar in 1856, moved to Cannock to be Medical Officer to Staffs Constabulary and Surgeon Capt in the S Staffs Regt (Volunteers) after practising medicine in Middlesborough. Kerr was a noted character with a passion for exotic animals. He had a stuffed gorilla in his hall, and would harness zebras to his carriage; he was engaged to the daughter of the owner of Bostock and Wombwell's Travelling Circus. He is remembered in Cannock as 'a huge giant of a man who shouted a great

deal' (info notice board at County Museum, Shugborough). **George VI** visited Cannock in July 1934 (R&S p46). **Jennie Lee** (1904-1988), Britain's first Arts Minister (1964) and wife of Aneurin Bevan, was Labour MP for Cannock and Rugeley from 1945 to 1970, when she was created Baroness Lee of Asheridge. When in Cannock she stayed with Millie Rowley, a district nurse and labour councillor (VB p118) (The Cambridge Biographical Encyclopedia. David Crystal. 1994) (Jennie Lee: A Life. Patricia Hollis. 1997). **Bruce Beddow** (1897-1976), novelist and short story writer, lived in Cannock. Most of his work, including 'The Golden Milestone' (1925), 'A Man of the Midlands' (1928), 'The Coal Merchant' (1929), and 'Coals from Newcastle' (1929), are set in Staffs (VFC p11). **Keith Alldritt**, author of 'The Visual Imagination of DH Lawrence' (1971), 'The Good Pit Man' (1976), 'The Lover Next Door' (1977), and 'Elgar on the Journey to Hanley' (1979), is a native of Staffs and lives in Cannock.
NEWSPAPERS. No. 55 of the **Cannock Chase Examiner** appeared on Jan 2 1875, and the paper ran until at least Oct 5 1877 (SHJ spring 1996 p16). The **Cannock and Hednesford Mercury** ran from April 21 1883 to Sept 12 1890 (SHJ spring 1996 p16). The **Cannock Chase News**, founded in May 1889, became the Cannock Chase Courier and Pelsall News from June 25 1889. From Dec 21 1889 it became the Cannock Chase Courier, and from July 6 1901 it became the Cannock Chase Courier and West Staffordshire Counsellor; this paper seems to have run to April 1964 (SHJ spring 1996 p17). The **Cannock Chase Mercury** seems to have run from Sept 19 1890 to Feb 1905, with a two-year break between 1896 and 1898 (SHJ spring 1996 p16). No. 17 of the **Cannock Chase Herald** appeared on Oct 29 1892, and the paper ran until at least Aug 14 1897 (SHJ spring 1996 p16). The **Cannock Advertiser**, founded by mid Aug 1893, became the Cannock Advertiser and Courier from April 17 1964, but reverted to its former title, Cannock Advertiser, from July 25 1974 and continued as such until at least Aug 1 1985 (SHJ spring 1997 p16). **Cannock Chase News and Weekly Advertiser** ran from Sept 4 1953 to July 29 1955 (SHJ spring 1996 p17).
Cannock Bog Seems to be the areas now called Chadsmoor and West Chadsmoor, NE of Cannock (OS map 1834).
Cannockbury One of the main manors belonging to the bishop of Lichfield in medieval times (NSJFS 1970 p5). Cannockbury may be identified with the manor of Cannock and Rugeley.
Cannock Castle In existence to Elizabeth I's reign - existed on Castle Ring (SMC p170). (SC p109) (CCC p129). Has also appeared as Cannock Chase Castle. This is probably a reference to foundations found within the Castle Ring complex which may be the base of a medieval hunting lodge.
Cannock Chase Large chase six miles across at its widest point and stretching for six miles in a SE direction from Milford Common, 4m ESE of Stafford. EARLY to 1546. For the glacial boulder at SJ 980181 see Spring Hill. A little spring in Cank Wood which ran or did not run regardless of the weather was noted by Plot in the later C17 (NHS p49). The chase was created out of the royal manors of Rugeley and Cannock, which lay in the N part of Cannock Forest, when the bishop of Coventry and Lichfield, Hugh de Novant, bought them from Richard I in 1189; confirmation of purchase came in 1230 (VCH vol 5 p58) (NSJFS 1968 p44). (SOSH p334; in 1190) (WMLB p76; in 1290) (SL p67) (CCM). The bishop's new territory, comprising Rugeley Hay (VCH vol 2 p338), was known as the Bishop's Chase within the Forest of Cannock or Bishop's Chase of Cannock; it was spelt by Celia Fiennes, who crossed the chase in summer 1698, Kanck-wood, Kankwood, Kank Wood, Kankewood, and Kank forrest (The Illustrated Journeys of Celia Fiennes. Christopher Morris. 1984. pp147,148,188,229; misleadingly identifies the various forms with Cannock Wood); by the Cliffords in 1817 as Cank Wood and Cank Heath (HOT p47); and by Wright in the 1930s as Cankwood (CCF p47). The bishops were not granted the right to turn their new property into a private forest until 1290. In the intervening time much disagreement occurred between the bishop and forest officials. In 1286 the bishop was accused of creating leaps to allow deer to roam into his Haywood Park and Brewood Forest (SHC 1924 p285) (NSJFS 1968 p48). After the grant of free chase bounds were established of which Chad's Dyke is a part (NSJFS 1968 pp48-49). The king's forest officials were dispensed with, and Bishop Meuland appointed the Astons of Haywood Hall (see) hereditary wardens of the chase. The feud between Sir Walter Devereux of Chartley Castle (see), 3rd Lord Ferrers, and Edward Aston (1533), carried before the 'Star Chamber' proved a constant subject of difference (SHC 1914 p131 note). The Astons were frequently in dispute with the Pagets, the new owners of the Chase after 1546, over possession of game - the Astons evoking their ancient rights - until a compromise was arrived at in 1712 (VCH vol 5 pp59,60) (SHC 1999 pp97-126). The Earl of Richmond (Henry VII) is said to have met with Lord Stanley on Cannock Chase (STMSM Nov 1972 p41) in Aug 1485 before the battle of Bosworth

Field, having travelled from Milford Haven. (Lord Stanley changed his allegiance from Richard III to the Earl during the battle). Others say that they met at Stafford Castle (SSTY p10), or at Lord Stanley's seat, Elford Old Manor House (R&S p18) (HOL pp302,303).
1546 to PRESENT. In 1546 ownership of the chase passed to Sir William Paget (his descendants becoming Earls of Uxbridge and Marquises of Anglesey) who started the iron industry on the chase. A few years after 1589 Sir Fulke Greville took the lease of the ironworks and much woodland was destroyed for charcoal. Chase oak and chestnut bark was used in Walsall's tanning industry (VB p59). Heather was used for packing pots in the Potteries. (The Industrial History of Cannock Chase. Francis Roger. 1987). The 'woods of o'grown oaks,' complained Michael Drayton in 'Polyolbion', 'are by vile gain devoured' (NSJFS 1974 p26). Soon after Paget's purchase of the chase he introduced rabbits and sheep, which intruded on commoners' land, and whose grazing produced heathland. Amid protests, the rights of the copyholders were defined by Chancery in 1605 and remain today as commoners' rights (CCM). In 1690 there was a protest over the landlord's attempts to increase revenue and let the chase to a rabbit warrener (LOU p354). Piecemeal enclosure of the chase mainly by private agreement continued, with periods of aggravation. In 1710 Lord Paget tried to establish a rabbit warren at Haywood Warren and the lodge was attacked by commoners (LOU p72). In the mid C18 the commoners' petitioned the Earl of Uxbridge for him to remove his warrens from their common land. But these were ignored and riots, known as the **Rabbit Riots**, ensued. There were disturbances just before Christmas 1751. The leaders were arrested and the rest of the commoners waited for the results of the legal action against them. In 1753 a number of court actions were heard at the Stafford Assizes. The most significant of which was the failure of the commoners' claim to right of common on the chase. This incited even worse riots which occurred two days after Christmas 1753. The main assault took place on Dec 28. Two hundred are said to have taken part; 60 coming from Walsall. Most others came from Rugeley, Longdon, Hammerwich and two came from Cannock; many were colliers. The leaders were men called the Avarnes of Rugeley, Thomas Birch of Brereton and Charles Marshall of Longdon. Five or six warrens in all were destroyed, including one NW of Boney Hay, which may have been Coney Warren (see), and another, Lamb's Warren (see), W of Hammerwich (AFT pp190,229-230,235) (VCH vol 14 pp214,267). One warren was left alone, which the men considered rightfully Uxbridge's. A protest-march past Beaudesert occurred and songs with Jacobite sympathies sung. Although it appeared that the commoners had been successful the Earl had the final legal victory. Marshall and his diggers were sued and many of Uxbridge's tenants, who had taken part, were evicted (LOU pp108,173-176). (Atlas of Rural Protest in Britain 1548-1900. A Charlesworth. p42). **Enclosure and public space**. The unenclosed land remaining in Cannock parish, now containing the suburbs of Blackfords, Broomhall, Chadsmoor, Green Heath, High Town, Oldfallow, Pye Green, West Chadsmoor, and West Hill, was enclosed in 1868 (PCC pp16,17). Enclosure culminated in an award of 1885 which enclosed 4,780 acres W of Rugeley either side of the Rugeley-Cannock road N of Hednesford and E of the Sherbrook Valley, where a curious iron fence that follows every twist and turn of the brook was probably placed to mark the limit of the enclosure. But most of this land consisted of poor upland ground and was generally not divided into plots. It then remained in a wild state until the Forestry Commission secured the lease of several thousand acres in the 1920s (PCC pp17,18) (CCM) and the area has become known as Cannock Forest (see). The land at the N end of the chase was never enclosed. In 1893 the Marquess of Anglesey conveyed 1,784 acres of it comprising Satnall Hills, Milford Common, Spring Hill, Oat Hill, Broc Hill, Brocton Coppice, Coppice Hill, Hollywood Slade, Sherbrook Banks, Dry Pits, Tar Hill, Old Acre Valley, Sye Hill, Brocton Field and Anson's Bank to Lord Lichfield. In 1930 a Regulation Scheme was drawn up by which control of this part of the chase would have passed to Stafford rural district, by then lying in their jurisdiction, but local residents seem to have opposed the measure and it never came to fruition. In 1934 a pitched battle was fought on the chase to prevent South Staffordshire and North Worcestershire Joint Town Planning Committee gaining control over this part (SN Aug 6 1998 p6). An association of friends of the chase formed but disbanded before WW2 (SN May 1997 p8); perhaps the group had come about as part of the movement for public access. In 1934 about 230 acres on Hednesford Hills was given by the Marquis of Anglesey for the benefit of the people of Cannock and Hednesford, the trustees being Cannock urban district (PCC p19). In the late 1940s the MOD attempted to turn the Milford Hills area into a training ground. They were blocked by a protest rally of 2000 people and a petition with 13,000 signatures in 1948 (SN Aug 6 1998 p6). In 1947, and possibly as a result of this, the pre-WW2

association of friends reformed as the Association of Friends of Cannock Chase under the direction of Dr Peter Jennings of Brocton (SN May 1997 p8); the association have produced GCC (1951) and PCC (1957). In 1952 200 acres comprising the unenclosed Gentleshaw Common, together with two smaller commons further south, were purchased by Lichfield rural district council for public recreation (PCC p19). In 1955 or 1956 Lord Lichfield conveyed his land at the N end of the chase to Staffs county council and it now forms part of Cannock Chase Country Park (see) (VCH vol 5 p5) (PCC pp18,19). Apparently, to commemorate this event a glacial boulder was moved from Pudding Hill to Spring Hill (see) (WMAG Feb 1968 p15p). In 1958 the chase was designated an AONB by the National Parks Commission (now Countryside Commission) and, at 26 square miles, is the smallest AONB in mainland Britain (SL p261) (CCM). By 1997 the chase was semi-protected as a SSSI (SN May 30 1997 p8). **Wild life.** Plot's noting of the **chalice moss** or scarlet headed cup (Muscus Multiformiter Pyxidates, Capitbus five apicibus coccineis) on the chase in the later C17, may be the first documentation of it anywhere. It is the size of, and sometimes the shape of, a clove and the flower is an ash colour. It grew on the hills in Cank Wood, Wildmoore Hollies, Fairoak and Wolseley Park. Plot was told about it by Edward Brych of Leacroft (NHS p199 tab 14, fig 1). **Cank Thorn** (see). The **Cannock Chase Berry** is the common name for the Hybrid Bilberry (Vaccinium x intermedium Rultie) a rare hybrid between the common bilberry and cowberry. It was first recognised as a distinct species in 1826 in Germany and was first discovered in Britain, in the Maer Woods, in 1870. It seems to be restricted to less than 25 localities in the three counties of Yorks, Derbys, and Staffs. Cannock Chase is the plant's main stronghold and it grows more abundantly here than anywhere else in the country (The Natural History of Cannock Chase. WEA. Harry Goode. 1973. pp50-52) (AA p255). The **red grouse** has its southernmost nesting haunt on Cannock Chase (Staffs County Handbook c1958 p21). The **bog brush cricket** - mainly confined to southern England - can be found on the heathlands, although it is rare (CCM). In April 1949 an adder was found on the chase (SN 23 April 1949 p4). An escaped baboon was captured on the chase in July 1969 (SN July 18 1969 p1. July 24 1969 p3). The chase has been hit by **fires** in 1649, 1709, '55, '56, '62,'72, '74, '79, March 1938, early June '39, early April '46, March '48, Aug '52, May '54, June '55, April '74, Aug '76 (PCC p72) (AFT p253). The chase had to close to the public for a period from Aug 2 1995 due to fire risk because of the dryness of heathland (SN Aug 4 1995 p7). **Accidents and crime.** An accident occurred on the chase in 1788 when two men who were riding across it fell into a deep pit hidden by snow. They were not discovered for two days and were dead when taken out (SOSH p336). In 1944 two boys were injured in an explosion on the chase (SN June 3 1944 p4). In Jan 1966 the bodies of two young girls were found in a ditch on the western edge of the chase at Mansty (see). The body of Christine Ann Darby, aged seven, of Camden Street, Walsall, was found on Cannock Chase, in Plantation 110 on Aug 22 1967. She had been abducted in Corporation Street, Walsall, by Raymond Leslie Morris, aged 39, whilst showing him the way to Caldmore Green on Aug 19 1967. Morris of Walsall was discovered as he tried to abduct another child in Walsall. He was tried in Feb 1969 and sentenced to life imprisonment (Murder on the A34. Harry Hawkes. 1970) (MCS pp96-110). From Aug 18 1873 **army manoeuvres** took place on the NW side of the chase for one month (PCC p73) (Army Quarterly vol 68 pp248-256) (NSJFS 1971 p15). **Cannock Chase Golf Club,** which stretched from Mere Valley in the S to Milford Common in the N, opened in 1894 and moved to Brocton Hall in 1922 (BERK2 pp33-35 plan); the Golf House was built in 1898 (BERK2 p36p). The course was laid out over part of the chase which was leased from Lord Lichfield at the annual rent of one shilling (HCMBOPP p74p). For **Brocton Camp** see Brocton. The **German Military Cemetery** at SJ 985155, at Broadhurst Green, was consecrated in 1917 on land given by the Earl of Lichfield (VCH vol 5 p3). (CCM). The cemetery is the only German military cemetery in Great Britain. After the conclusion of the German-British War Graves Treaty Oct 1956 most of the German war dead in Britain were transferred to this cemetery. The cemetery was publicly inaugurated on June 10 1967. The crews of four Zeppelins (shot down Sept 3 1916, Sept 24 1916, Oct 2 1916, and June 17 1917) have been brought here from their original resting places at - Potters Bar, Great Burstead, and Theberton. In 1996 the cemetery contained 2,143 German soldiers who died on British soil in WW1, and 2,797 German soldiers who died in WW2 (info at the cemetery). Five German women - Sophie Sowa (d1943), Gerda Maiwald (d1942), Margaret Kircheiss (d1941), Mathilde Grassner (d1941), and Anna Rathman (d1941) - are also buried here (SLM Oct 1996 p13). The entrance enclosure was designed by Diez Brandi (BOE p94) and may date from 1962. (VB p113) (STMSM Nov 1978 p15) (SN Jan 11 1980 p2) (COS p56p). The **Commonwealth Cemetery** at SJ 983154, to the SW of

the German Cemetery, by the road to Pye Green, contains the dead of WW1, including Commonwealth and Polish soldiers (CCM). Wright in the 1930s writes of 220 graves to Germans, 73 to New Zealanders (who died in the Spanish influenza epidemic at Brocton Camp in Nov 1918), and the rest to the British (CCBO pp113-115). An ANZAC service is held here each April (CCM). One year it appears to have been attended by the Maori Queen. (STMSM Nov 1978 p15). There were 408 headstones in 1996. The **Katyn Memorial**, at SJ 984165 according to CCM, is to commemorate the massacre of 14,000 members of the Polish Armed Forces and professional classes in Katyn Forest, Poland in 1940 (CCM). (MR p79p). A Wellington bomber leaving Hixon airfield on Sept 18? 1942 was unable to deliver its attack and jettisoned its bomb load over Cannock Chase (info Hixon Local History Society). **Museums.** By 2000 there were three visitor centres on the chase: the Cannock Chase Visitors Centre at Brindley Heath (see); the Forest Centre in Birches Valley (see); the Museum of Cannock Chase in Hednesford Hills (see). **Arts and literature.** Mr Masters in his Iter Boreale 1675 describes his journey over the chase. It is in Latin and Shaw gives an extract with a translation (SHOS vol 1 part 1 p91). John Frederick Herring, Snr's painting of horsemen on Cannock Chase, commissioned by William Taylor Copeland (1797-1868), titled 'Scene on Cannock Chase,' dated 1842, long in the possession of the Copeland family, was for sale in July 1996 (CL June 27 1996 pc). The novel 'Facing Death, or the Hero of Vaughan Pit' (1882) by GA Henty (1832-1902) about coalmining is partly set in Birmingham and on Cannock Chase (VFC p64). The poem 'Cannock Chase' by Cecil James Croydon Tildesley of Penkridge (see) begins

> Oh! have you seen, on Cannock Chase,
> The birches, queens of silver grace,
> When Autumn's magic hand hath set,
> On each a golden coronet.

(PSS p369) (TRBI p154) (VFC p130) (TB April 1996 p11). For the poem 'Cannock Chase' by Marjorie Crosbie of Penn Fields (see) see PSS p439. For the 'King of Cannock Chase' (Patsy Kilgariff) see Chasetown. **Supernatural.** For the ghost of a young monk who haunts the woods by Castle Ring see Castle Ring. A tall cowled figure has been seen by the roadside near the Commonwealth Cemetery (info Bruce Braithwaite). A man in a broad-brimmed hat and old-fashioned clothes carrying a stave which he bangs on the ground to attract the attention of passersby has been seen near a fishing pool halfway between Cannock and Rugeley (GPCE p25). A moving ball of light was seen and heard above Cannock Chase in winter 1990 (ES Sept 21 1998 p8). A case of witchcraft on Cannock Chase was reported to Cannock police station in 1936 (TB May 1988 p21).

Cannock Chase Country Park A 4.5 square mile (3,000 acres) part of NW Cannock Chase open to the public. Given to Staffs county council in 1956 by the 4th Earl of Lichfield of Shugborough Hall (see). Stretches from Milford Common in N to the Commonwealth Cemetery in S, and from Brocton Gate in W to Hangman's Oak in E (VCH vol 5 p5) (CCM).

Cannock Extension Canal Spurs off the Wyrley and Essington Extension Canal at Pelsall Junction (HCMS No. 2). Had been constructed as far as Churchbridge by 1844 and to its termination in Hednesford by 1858 (VCH vol 5 p51). The canal was closed and dewatered N of the A5 in 1963 and the Churchbridge locks on the link to Hatherton were abandoned eight years earlier (SWY p16). The canal is known locally as the 'Curliewurlie' (BBC Radio 4. Word of Mouth. Jan 7 1999).

Cannock Forest Former huge primeval forest and one of the 68 ancient forests of England (SHOS vol 1 p131); the remaining fragment of it is now called Cannock Chase (see). For the glacial boulder at SJ 980181 see Spring Hill. A prehistoric trackway between Stafford and Streetly, where it joins the Icknield Street, passed over Cannock Forest, through Brocton Field, Pye Green, Norton Canes, and Druid's Heath. Another prehistoric trackway passed from Cannock northwards via Pye Green, Sow Street across the Trent at the old ford at Colwich, through Swansmoor and Chartley (OSST 1949-50 p17). Druidism may have been practised in the forest in ancient British times (HOWW p16). Hackwood identifies Castle Ring as a druidical site (SC pp144-145). Before the Norman Conquest the forest stretched to the Forest of Arden, Warws, and covered all the land between the Penk, Sow, Trent, and Tame, covering an area of some 230 square miles (SSAHST 1965 pp21-39) (NSJFS 1968 p44). It is referred to as 'great Arden's eldest child' by Michael Drayton in 'Polyolbion' (VCH vol 2 p338). The ancient forest is said to have been a favourite hunting ground of Mercian (W p450) and Anglo-Saxon kings who may have granted bishops of Lichfield hunting privileges in it. After the Norman Conquest it was made a royal forest and was known as the King's Forest of Cannock (CCM). It was a hunting ground of William II, Henry I, and Henry II (R&S pp4,6) (HOP p83) (SSAHST 1965 p26) (VCH vol 2 p341). The first reduction of the forest's extent occurred in 1125 when Sutton Chase was granted to the Earl of Warwick as a free chase (NSJFS 1968 p44). The earliest known reference to the forest by name is in the 1140s (VCH vol 2 p338). In 1153 and 1155 1,500 acres about Lichfield were granted to the bishop of Lichfield (NSJFS 1968 p44). By 1166 the boundaries of the forest were the Penk on the W, the Sow and the Trent on the N, and the Tame on the E. The southern boundary ran from the Penk at Coven to the centre of Wolverhampton and then along the Wednesbury road to the bridge over the Tame on the S side of Wednesbury; there it turned NE to run through Walsall and S of Aldridge and Stonnall to the Bourne Brook which it followed to the Fazeley area (VCH vol 2 p338). (WAM p31) (SHC 1923 pp294-295) (HOWV p103). In 1189, Richard I sold a central part of it - Rugeley Hay - to Bishop Hugh de Novant (this became Cannock Chase) to raise money for the third Crusade (SOSH p334; in 1190) (R&S p7) (WMLB p76; in 1290) (SL p67) (CCM). Perambulations of the forest were made to record its bounds in 1286 and 1300 (WAM p33) (NSJFS 1968 p44). William I made the first-known appointment of a **chief forester**. He was Richard Chenven, supposedly the son of a Saxon thegn. The foresteship remained with his descendants - the de Crocs, the de Brocs or the de Broks (by 1175 to 1195), then the de Loges (1195 to c1246) (DUIGNAN) (VCH vol 5 pp79-80) - until c1246 when Hugh de Loges was deprived of the position for poaching. (The foresteship was in the sheriff's hands from at least 1164 to 1174 - VCH vol 2 p338 note). The foresteship or stewardship passed in c1246 to Geoffrey fitz Warin. By 1255 it was held by Ralph de Coven. Thomas de Weseham was steward from 1255 to 1272. William Trumwym was steward in 1272. Trumwyn and de Weseham are found to be holding the position alternatively until Weseham secured permanent re-appointment in c1280. The stewardship was conveyed to Philip de Montgomery in 1284; to Ralph Bassett of Drayton Bassett in 1293. By the marriage of Bassett's daughter in 1306 it passed into the Swynnerton family in whose family the stewardship remained until the C17 (VCH vol 2 pp338-339). (Harl M.S.S. temp Henry VII No. 5174 p20) (SMC p121). Since before the Conquest to c1246 land in Rodbaston and Great Wyrley (see) seems to have been attached to the office of chief forester (VCH vol 2 p339). Hugh de Loges held five tenements in Sow, Warws, of the Earl of Chester by the service of conducting his lord, the Earl, to the king's court, through the midst of Cannock Forest, meeting him at Radford Bridge, upon notice of his coming, and at Hopwas Bridge upon his return. The Earl had liberty to kill a deer as he went, and another as he returned giving Hugh de Loges, each time he had attended him, a barbed arrow (SHOS vol 2 p313) (Dugdale? Warws. pp212,470). Wolves still roamed the forest in the 1280s (HOS 1998 p34). Edward II passed through the forest in or just before 1324 (VCH vol 2 p342). **Hays**. After the granting of Rugeley Hay to the bishop of Lichfield seven hays remained: Alrewas, Bentley, Cheslyn, Gailey, Hopwas, Ogley, and Teddesley (NSJFS 1968 p46) (CCF p24) (SSAHST 1963 p27) (VCH vol 2 p338) (Staffs County Handbook. c1958. p120) (BERK2 p103). Calf Heath has been identified as another hay (NSFCT 1908 p141), but it may just have been a part of Gailey Hay. Most of the hays had a head forester with walking foresters under them (VCH vol 2 p340). With many settlements within the forest claiming, and being granted, disafforestation Cannock Forest by 1350 became only a remnant of its former considerable extent (NSJFS 1968 p46) (CCF p24). By the earlier C16 the forest merely comprised the seven hays: Leland in c1540 referred to it as the Forest of the Seven Hays. The hays were a source of royal revenue until Elizabeth I's time, chiefly through deer and timber sales (SL p67); over 15,000 oaks are said to have been blown down during one storm in her reign (NSFCT 1881 p15). In 1550 all the hays except Hopwas were granted by the Crown to the Earl of Warwick (VCH vol 2 p343). For the subsequent history of the hays see individual entries. Remaining common land of the former forest seems to have become known as Cannock Heath (see).

Cannock Forest Cannock Forest is the current name for that part of Cannock Chase (20 square miles on the E and S sides) which was formerly the enclosed land of the Rugeley Award 1885. Being poor upland ground it was never properly enclosed and in the 1920s the Forestry Commission secured the lease of it (PCC p18); they currently own and manage it, having an office in Birches Valley (CCM). This forest was one of the first to be formed under the 1919 Act (NSJFS 1961 pp137-138). (VCH vol 2 p343. vol 5 pp58-60).

Cannock Heath Common land which emerged after the remaining Cannock Forest was disforested. In the late C18 Pitt estimated that the heath was about 40 square miles (SHOS vol 2 p315). In 1817 the heath was described as 'bleak and dreary waste' (THS p264). It is said to have covered the ground now occupied by Hednesford village (VCH vol 5 p49), come within a mile of

Rugeley on its S side, taking in Stile Cop (THS p265), and may have stretched S to the Chasetown area (VCH vol 14 p266). Norton Canes is said to have been situated on the S side of it (THS p165). Cannock Heath was the name for a ram and ewe indigenous to Cannock Forest or Chase; a breed without horns, with grey faces and legs and close and compact fleeces, but lacking in weight in proportion to their length (AOS p13) (SHOS vol 2 p315) (SG p109). The terms Cank Heath and Cannock Heath were used in the early C19 to refer to the present Cannock Chase (HOT pp47,49). The name also appears to have been given to an area of some couple of square miles of heathland to the E of Cannock (SHC 1999 p104 see map).

Cannock Manor House High Green, Cannock. Demolished in 1936. Modern buildings, including a cinema, occupy the site (VCH vol 5 p53).

Cannock Wood Village on a high spur of land above Radmoor Brook on the southern fringe of Cannock Chase 10.5m SE of Stafford. Former township of Cannock old parish, extending from two to four miles NE of Cannock town which included parts of Beaudesert Park and Radmore (W p452). Cannock Wood is described as a hamlet in the C17 and in the mid 1950s (VCH vol 5 pp49,51). The colliers of Cannock Wood assembled in riotous manner in Jan 1741 and seized several waggons of corn going to market (LOU pp124-125). The founder of Primitive Methodism, Hugh Bourne (1772-1852), visited Cannock Wood in 1810 (ESSN p67). The Kanck-wood, and Kank or Cank Wood referred to between the C17 and the early C19 appear to be references to the woodland of present Cannock Chase (HOT p47) (The Illustrated Journeys of Celia Fiennes. Christopher Morris. 1984. p147) (SHC 1999 p104 see map).

Cantrell's House At Back of Ecton S of Ecton. The name Cantrell appears on a charity board in Butterton (Moorlands) church, and there are Cantrell headstones in its churchyard (VB p197).

Canwell Tiny and fragmented village on high ground overlooking the Trent Vale to the N, 20m SE of Stafford. Former extra parochial estate (W p556). Canwell has appeared as Canewelle (1209) (SSE 1996 p11), Canewell, Ceneswell (SPN p30), Canol (c1540) (LI part 5 p103), Cannal (Bowen's map). The name may be of Anglo-Saxon origin and derive from 'canne' meaning any vessel or receptacle holding water or other liquid; perhaps a reference to St Modwen's well (DUIGNAN). Or is from 'Cana's well' (SSE 1996 p11) (SPN p30). Or is said to receive its name from 'Well of Power' (SMM p80). Or is from Gaelic 'gennos,' Irish 'cenn' as in Caen Hill (Lincs), and Kenwood near London (NSFCT 1922 p170). There was possibly a medieval village at Canwell (SSAHST 1970 p34), now depopulated and lost. For a fight at Canwell between Lord Lisle and Henry Willoughby in the C15 see Weeford. A charcoal-burning hearth, 18 feet in diameter, was found at SK 152005 in 1972 (SSAHST 1973-74 p40). Became a separate civil parish in 1858 and a separate ecclesiastical one in 1927 (GLAUE p407). The church, St Mary, St Giles, and All Saints, on the S side of Brick Kiln Lane, was built in 1911 (BOE p94).

Canwell Gate Hamlet on Lichfield Birmingham road S of Canwell, N of Bassets Pole.

Canwell Hall Canwell. A later hall was built for Sir Robert Lawley Bart, Lord Wenlock, by James Wyatt at a cost of £60,000 (W p557). Soho House dining room vaulted plaster ceiling and its columns are a reduced version of Wyatt's design for Canwell Hall (CL Feb 27 1997 p42). Shaw writes about a sad accident in this hall: In Dec 1800 two of Sir Robert's men servants sleeping with a pan of charcoal in their bedroom were found suffocated one morning. One was revived the other died (SHOS vol 2 p22). The grandson of Sir Robert, Rt Hon Paul Beilby Lawley Thompson, was created Lord Wenlock in 1839 and occasionally lived at the hall (W p557). In c1865 the hall was occupied by Lord Newport, and by 1868 to 1872 by Col Ferrars Loftus. In 1872 Lord Wenlock sold the hall to Abraham Briggs Foster. Foster was succeeded by his son Philip of gentlemen's outfitting fame; probably the Philip Staveley Foster who was occupying the hall by 1907 to at least 1916 (post office directories) (DM p53) (STC p16p) (mems in Canwell and Weeford churches). The hall was a children's hospital after WW2 (DM2 p125), and was mainly demolished in 1958 (SVB p50). Only one wing was surviving in the early 1970s (BOE p94). In the later C17 Plot noted that the grounds of the old hall contained a fine display of topiary (NHS p381). In the grounds is or was an icehouse.

Canwell Priory Canwell. Founded by Geve illegitimate daughter of Hugh 'd' Avranches, Earl of Chester (see under Chartley Castle), and widow of Geoffrey Ridell, a justice under Henry I who was drowned in 1120 in the wreck of the White Ship. Founded in c1140 (VCH vol 3 pp213-214) or in 1142 (SVB p49). Masefield says her husband, Geoffrey Ridell, was the founder (LGS pp37,105). A Benedictine house for monks, dedicated to St Giles (VCH vol 3 pp213-214). Some have said it was a Cluniac priory (SOSH p108). It was not, although some of its community were Cluniacs (VCH vol 3 p215). In 1272 a monk of Canwell, William de Sutton, killed a man, fled and was outlawed (VCH vol 3 p215). At length the priory became a cell for a solitary monk (HOL p406). Bishop Langton visited the priory on Jan 12 1319 (SSE 1994 p2). It was suppressed in 1525 and secured to benefit Wolsey's new college at Oxford, the present Christ Church (VCH vol 3 p216) (SL p95) (HOS 1998 p58). In the later C18 the new stables of Canwell Hall were erected on what was said to be the site of the priory using the remaining ruins. There was a spring near the site of the priory known in later times as St Modwen's Well (VCH vol 3 p216). (SHOS vol 2 p22 both p22s) (SMC p170) (W pp556-557) (HOS p27).

Cape Arm Tiny canal. Spurred off the Birmingham Canal Old Cut Old Main Line at Soho E of Smethwick. Ran to Grove Lane (HCMS No. 2).

Cape Hill District of ESE Smethwick close to the Warws border. The name is from an inn called Cape of Good Hope which stood by 1814 at the junction of Grove Lane and the Birmingham-Dudley road. The inn was rebuilt in 1925 (STELE July 18 1952 il of the old inn c1827) (VCH vol 17 p94) (SMEOP p109p). At approximately SP 027876 in Cape Road was a windmill in 1836 (WBJ p36) (VCH vol 17 p109), and there was another windmill in Windmill Lane, Smethwick (see). There was an annual fair at Smethwick known as the Cape Fair by the 1860s. It was held on the first or second Monday in September (VCH vol 17 p134) and was presumably held at Cape Hill.

Capethorn House of c1800 which stood in the Capethorn Road area, 0.25m ESE of Smethwick Old Church. Demolished in 1908 (VCH vol 17 p89).

Capponfield Area in Sedgley ancient parish. It may appear as Capons in the late C16 (HC p37). Cappon Field appears on 1834 OS map on the W side of Dudley Street, N of Hall Green. Highfields Road was formerly Capponfield Road (SDSSOP p43). According to Underhill the name is said to have been a favourite title given to newly-built houses about the time they were built. It had, however, to do with the estate upon which the houses were built. And in this case, seems to go back to the time when the property was reserved to the grantor, and the reservation took the form of a capon, that is, a fat, cock chicken. In some cases it took the form of gloves, spurs etc (AMS p448). On Feb 23 1820 Abel Hill murdered his common law wife, Mary (or Maria) Martin, and their 16-month old son, Thomas. He either drowned them in the canal at Glasshouse Bridge (TB Jan 1978 p25), or, and near the Seven Stars Inn, close by Capponfield and Highfield furnaces near Moses Hill, or disposed of their bodies in the canal at this spot. Hill was hung on July 27 1820. He may have shown no remorse at his execution and his body may have been displayed in public in Bilston (Wolverhampton Chronicle. Aug 2 1820) (HOBLL p176) (TB March 1981 p5. June 1992 p16. Dec 3 1998 p5) (MMBCC p80). The noose was later worn at Bradley, Bilston, as a charm to prevent bewitching (SR p107) (TB April 1988 p5), whilst his skeleton was kept by Dr Tom Dickenson of High Street, Bilston (TB March 1981).

Capponfield West Bromwich. From Capponfield furnaces at Golds Hill (BCM Oct 1982 p37).

Capponfield House Bilston (BCM Jan 1987 pp29il,30-31).

Captain's Barn House nearly 1.5m SE of Werrington.

Captain's Cottage At Compton Hall, Tettenhall. Here supposedly a Captain Rainsford, returned from the Seven Years War without warning, to find his wife cohabiting with his friend. In his rage he killed his friend and wife. The Compton estate was very large and stretched from Finchfield Hill to Ash Hill. The Captain's Cottage was situated just inside the entrance to the woods and is now built over by an housing estate. The cottage was reputedly haunted (TB July 1991 p13).

Carabbee Island Former area of very dense housing centred on the E side of Stafford Street and to the N of Lichfield Street, Wolverhampton. The area has also appeared as Caribee Islands (1842 tithe map) and Caribee Island. Crab Tree Lane appears in this area on Isaac Taylor's Map of Wolverhampton (1750), and the name is probably a corruption of this. Its population swelled with the influx of a large number of Irish migrants fleeing from the Irish Potato famine (1845-6) who came to the area to work in the collieries (HOWU p108). Carabbee Island was described in 1849 as a 'collection of the most squalid looking houses on the north side of Stafford Street.' The area was cleared under the Artisans Dwelling Act of 1875 (Mapping the Past Wolverhampton 1577-1986. Mary Mills 1993 p18) (MH 1984 p88) (WOLOP p50p).

Carder Green Longnor town, in Alstonefield ancient parish. Here was Longnor's lock-up (L p27). The W side of Longnor market place was known as Carder Green by the mid C19 (VCH vol 7 p42) (DMV p47p).

Carder Well Spring that is said to never dry up, situated about 0.5m from Mow Cop. Has also appeared as Corda Well (TTTD p174). Its streams flow in the pool at Rode Hall, Ches, and the mill pool at Moreton Hall mill (MC p26).

Careley Green A green which existed in Enville ancient parish in the late C18,

N of Mere Mill over a mile N of Enville (VCH vol 20 p109).

Carmounthead Residential area 0.75m E of Milton. The name occurs in a deed temp Henry III as Caer Muned, this suggests the Welsh Caer Mynydd. The elements 'car' in this case seems to be a corruption of 'caer' a stronghold (NSFCT 1908 p134). Ward thinks it may be of Roman origin 'Caver Mont' 'a caverned hill' and the name, as Kenermont (see), was a hay or park in medieval times (HBST p289 note).

Carmounthead Farm Carmounthead. The old farmhouse, which may have dated from the C17, was rebuilt in the C19; there is a barn dated 1836. The C19 house still stood in the 1950s (VCH vol 8 p250).

Carmounthead Old Park In the Carmounthead area. A very short-lived medieval hunting ground given to the monks of Hulton Abbey by Henry de Aldithley or Audley of Heighley Castle (see) in 1223 (NSFCT 1910 p173).

Carmountside S of Milton, a cemetery is here. It is the area in which Hulton Abbey stood (VCH vol 8 p248).

Carmountside Farm Occupied in the early C18 by the Heaths, and in the early C19 by the Worthingtons. In 1856 it was rebuilt on a site farther W (VCH vol 8 p250). In 1883 (LGS p188) or 1884 (VCH vol 8 p250) this new house was found to have been built over the site of the chancel of Hulton Abbey. The farmhouse still existed in 1930, but was probably demolished for the building of Carmountside Secondary Modern School in 1938 (VCH vol 8 p250). Masefield called this farmhouse Abbey Farm (LGS p188), whilst Sleigh calls it Carmount Farm and says it was being built in 1848 (HOLS (1862) p52) (SSE 1994 p96).

Carr, The An estate in Audley township. It belonged for many generations prior to 1733 to the Smith family (SHC 1944 p4).

Carr House House 1m ESE of Aston-by-Stone. In Hilderstone quarter in Stone ancient parish (W p370). The name is from the Norse word 'car' or 'carr' meaning marsh (SIS p9) (Duignan thought that the name only existed in the Moorlands area - DUIGNAN). Here may have been settlement dating from the Danish occupation of Mercia: Carr is a very common word in the Lindsey division of Lincs, where it is applied to low-lying land subject to flood (NSFCT 1916 p79). Or is a Celtic word meaning 'rock' (SPN p30). At Carr House was an important coaching inn (NSFCT 1921 p51).

Carroway Head Tiny hamlet on undulating heathland 1m SE of Canwell. F Wolferstan in a letter to Dr Wilkes (1756) thought it ought to be Carriageway Head (SHOS vol 2 p9). Legend says it was once called Gallows Way Head, where stood a gibbet (SVB p50). Indeed, Hill and Dent call it Garroway Head. According to the famous old ballad 'The Tanner of Tamworth' the tanner suggested to Edward IV he go through Carroway Head to travel between Bassets Pole and Drayton Basset (HS p150).

Carr's Almshouses E end of Fountain Street, Leek. Founded by Isabella Carr (d1899), daughter of Thomas Carr, a Leek silk manufacturer, in 1893 to the memory of her sisters Ellen and Rosanna Carr. Comprises three dwellings (VCH vol 7 p167).

Carry Lane Bramshall. A two mile track from Aldery Bank Farm to Painleyhill. Also nearby a Carry Coppice.

Carter's Green Area around Dudley Street and Bilhay Lane, West Bromwich (BCM Jan 1981 p65). In West Bromwich ancient parish. The name was in use by 1764 (VCH vol 17 p7). Hackwood suggests that the name is from John Carter, High Constable of the Offley hundred in 1647, who was appointed to conduct the inquiry into the seizure of goods during the Civil War (SOWB pp24-25). In 1768 Edward Lane, a native of West Bromwich, committed suicide. His body was buried in the middle of a crossways at Carters Green, with a stake thrust through it. The bones were taken up in 1835 when road alterations were made (OWB p101). A skeleton with a stake through it, probably a suicide case, was found in a chapel at Carters Green in 1874-5 (WMAG Dec 1979 p17). The clock tower at Carter's Green was erected in memory of Alderman Reuben Farley JP (1826-1899) in 1897. It was designed by Edward Pincher. The clock cost £185 and the total cost was £800. The total height is 65 feet. On three sides of the tower are engravings of the West Bromwich Town Hall, the Oak House and the head and shoulder of (presumably) Rueben Farley, all signed by A Hopkins, 1897 (BCM April 1986 pp7p,10) (WBOPP pls 80,81) (TB June 1991 p6p). For Sharratt motor cycles and Jensen cars see West Bromwich. The church, St Andrew, at the roundabout, Carters Green, was rebuilt in 1940 (LDD).

Carters Heath Former heathland to SE of Godstone, marked on a map of the early C19.

Cartledge Brook Runs westwards from Colts Moor (VCH vol 7 p169). Joins the Churnet near Leekbrook station. At Birchall is joined by Fulhe Brook. Fisher suggested that in medieval times it was called Faling Brook or anciently Falingbroke (DA - Michael Fisher's MA Thesis 1969) (NSJFS 1970 p85). It was recorded as Easing Brook in 1223 (VCH vol 7 p232). The name

Cartledge means 'boggy stream in stony ground' (SPNO p6).

Cart Low Hill and burial mound 0.25 N of Calton. The hill is 1145 feet high. The burial mound, at SK 10435100, is on top of it. Is NS 28 paces, EW 19 paces in diameter and four feet high. Carrington excavated it in 1849. A small bronze pin and an incense cup and four cremations were found (TYD p130) (R vol 5 pp171-174) (VCH vol 1 no 16) (BAP vol 2 pp30,119 fig 263) (NSJFS 1965 p54). It is a listed monument.

Cartwright's Drumble Drumble N of Dilhorne.

Casey Bank Land on Ipstones Edge. Purchased by Staffs Wildlife Trust by Jan 2000. It is considered one of the finest examples of lowland wet grassland in Staffs, and is a Site of Biological Importance (SBI) (Staffs Wildlife Jan 2000 p17).

Cash In Horsley division in Eccleshall ancient parish (W p380) (1834 OS map) (Dower's map). There is a Cash Farm 1.75m SSW of Eccleshall in Cash Lane which runs from Whitley Heath to Kempsage.

Cashheath Minute hamlet N of Forsbrook. Formerly in Forsbrook township in Dilhorne ancient parish (W p773).

Castern Minute hamlet over 1.25m NNW of Ilam. Township of Ilam ancient parish (SASR 1995 no 5 p1). For Castern Springs see SCSF p142. A stone Neolithic or Bronze Age axe has been found at Castern (DAJ vol 1 p99) (NSJFS 1964 p26). A bronze armilla, made from flat ribbon metal, half inch wide, and ornamental outside with a neatly engraved lozengy pattern was found at Castern (ABI p385) (TYD p167). A burial mound at Castern excavated by Carrington in 1848 revealed a Roman fibula and pottery fragment (TYD pp116-117) (VCH vol 1 no 6) (NSJFS 1965 p41). Between Bitchinhill (Beechinhill) and Castern is a burial mound excavated by Carrington in 1849, 18 paces in diameter and 1.5 feet high. A crouched skeleton and skeletal remains were found (TYD pp152-153) (VCH vol 1 no 32) (NSJFS 1965 p41). The burial mound by the Manifold 0.5m SW of Castern at SK 11755209 is a listed monument. For another in the Castern area see Brownslow. A burial mound at Castern has revealed burials of Beaker people (NSJFS 1962 p33). Castern was identified by Dugdale, Shaw and Duignan as the Caetesthyrne mentioned in the will of Wulfric Spot (c1002), founder of Burton Abbey (SHC 1916 p36) (SPN p67) (SSE 1996 p11). The name means 'Coet's thorn' (DUIGNAN), or 'Caet's thorn' (PNPD), or 'Catt's thorn' (SSE 1996 p11) (SPN p67). At Castern was possibly a medieval village (SSAHST 1970 p34), since depopulated and lost. By 1999 Castern Wood, at SK 119537, was a SSSI nature reserve in the care of the Staffs Wildlife Trust (Staffs Wildlife Trust leaflet).

Castern Hall Hall S of Castern, Ilam. The manor of 'Over and Nether Casterne' originally belonged to Burton Abbey. It was purchased by Nicholas Hurt in 1617. The Hurts (of Alderwasley, Derbys - SPN p67) had been at Castern since the early C16, perhaps as leaseholders. Some of the present house, which has a combination of Baroque and Palladian motifs in the manner of Gibbs, could date from the 1730s and 1740s and be the work of the Smiths of Warwick. There was some restoration in 1830. Castern Hall was let to tenants throughout the C19. The Hurts sold the hall in 1929 to the White family who had long been tenants. Another member of the Hurt family, Michael Hurt, purchased the house in 1953 and did necessary restoration (CL Feb 1 1979 pp274ps,275-277 ps of interior). (NSFCT 1922 p157).

Caster's Bridge Crosses the Black Brook about 20 yards upstream from the junction of the Dane with Black Brook near Swythamley. Partly from natural decay and partly from undulation of the stream the bridge fell in c1840 uprooting two old trees of beech and sycamore which stood near it. It consisted of a single arch, with battlements. A temporary wooden bridge with rails is now thrown over the place where it stood (LMF pp26-36) (DP pp51-52p) (HOLF pp41,49p). In the C18 or the C19 the inhabitants of a house or houses near the bridge had a sinister reputation for robbing and murdering every stranger who came by, for the gold they had. And being cannibals they ate their victims, too. A pedlar once hid from them under Caster's Bridge. Having escaped he informed the militia in Leek who came and arrested them and burnt down their house or houses. Ever since, by tradition, gold has been found from time to time in the burnt-out ruins. Has also appeared as Casters' and Smelters' Bridge (NSFCT 1947 p169). (OL vol 2 p85). Casters Bridge was spelt Castor and a castor was a beaver. Since there was forge here it is more likely to have been Smelters' Bridge (NSFCT 1932 p57).

Castle A ward of Tamworth borough by at least 1993, covering the area of central Tamworth, Kettlebrook and The Leys.

Castle, The House 0.75m NNE of Shenstone. S of Watling Street.

Castle, The House on Church Hill, Upper Penn. In the C19 it was the home of James Lakin; he gave the house its castellated appearance (PENOP p16p).

Castle Church Village at the SE foot of Stafford Castle hill, now residential suburb 1.25m WSW of Stafford town. Formerly a chapelry in Stafford Colle-

giate Church. Over 1,000 shards of Roman pottery, dating from C3 and C4 AD have been found by Stafford Castle. This is evidence for a possible Roman farmstead or small villa at Castle Church (SN Aug 20 1993 p9) (SPJD p23). A church at Castle Church was built possibly in the late C11. One is specifically mentioned in 1252 and a tower from this period survives in the present church. This church, St Mary ('in Castre'), on the N side of Newport Road, SE of Stafford Castle, was built mostly in 1845 (VCH vol 5 pp95-96) (SIOT p133) (SKYT p35). The early church may have served the medieval village of Monetville (see). It had all rights except burial and that right was gained in 1573, thereafter the parish was completely independent (VCH vol 5 p95) (GLAUE p407). The parish was a peculiar jurisdiction of Stafford Collegiate Church, until the college was dissolved (VCH vol 3 p93). Has appeared as Villa Castri Stafford (1293), Castel (1332), le Castel parke (1439), Castel juxta Stafford (1424), Le Marshe juxta Stafford (1462), Chastel chuerche (1562-6) (SSE 1996 p11), Castle Church (Yates' map) (SPNO p75), and Castle Church on the Sow (NSSG p12). For a moated site at Castle Church see ESH p58. There is a very ancient oak in St Mary's churchyard close to Thomas Mulock's grave which Mee noted had a circumference of 25 feet (KES p39).

Castle Cliff Cliff Vale, Stoke-upon-Trent. Another name for Cliff Hay or Hay of Clive, a hay of the lost New Forest and belonged to Newcastle-under-Lyme Castle (hence the application of 'Castle'?). The name still prevailed in 1677 (VCH vol 8 p201 note).

Castle Cliff An old rock buttress in Beresford Dale (ES Nov 10 1932 p6).

Castle Cliff Rocks Rocks 1m NE of Swythamley, between Hangingstone Rock and Lud Church. Has also appeared as Castle Rocks (SMCC p4) and Castle Cliff (PS p145p). Is called the Western Outcrop by climbers (SGM p122). Some believe these are the 'rughe, knokled knarres with korned stones' mentioned in the medieval epic poem 'Gawain and the Green Knight' (NSJFS 1977 p29) (MR p316).

Castle Clump Stowe-by-Chartley. At SK 009304. Was in the centre of Chartley Park.

Castle Croft Former seat 0.5m S of Cheadle or E of Huntley. Marked on Plot's map.

Castle Croft Name of field by Colton church (CWF p7). It represents the site of an early manor house, which may have been crenellated (LTM Oct 1971 p35).

Castlecroft Suburb of Wolverhampton 1.25m N of Lower Penn. Later in Tettenhall Wood ecclesiastical parish. Is said to take its name from a farm in the valley here (BCTV p84) (PAIP p48 il of Castlecroft Farm). Has also appeared as Castle Croft. Plot, in the late C17, noted stones found here (NHS p156). The church, the Good Shepherd, adjacent to the windmill, Windmill Lane, was built in 1954 (LDD).

Castle-Croft Field name at SK 101065 in the SE corner of the village of Wall, between the Trooper Inn and Manor Farm. An early fort of Letocetum was sited on it (W p517). The last surviving walls of Letocetum visible above ground, seen by C18 antiquarians and referred to by them as 'the castle,' were at Castle Croft (SSAHST 1963).

Castlecroft House 1m N of Lower Penn, S of Castlecroft Road. Built probably by Joseph Tarratt in the late C18. It was later the seat of the Twentyman family (PENOP p86). By 1988 it was an hotel (1988 OS map).

Castle Ditch A stretch of Lichfield Town Ditch (see) between Tamworth Street and St John Street (VCH vol 14 pp39-40). The eastern part had become a lane by the earlier 1340s, and was lined by houses by 1781 (VCH vol 14 p40). (John Snape's map of Lichfield 1781) (W p490). Castle Ditch probably received the appellation 'Castle' in consequence of its proximity to an Anglo-Saxon fort on Borrowcop Hill (VCH vol 14 p7). But others have identified it with the site of Lichfield Castle (see).

Castle Dyke Remnant of Lichfield's old defensive moat found in Wade Street by the Civic Hall (LAL p53). Whether the same as Castle Ditch?

Castlefield Promontory near the Severn, on the W side, in the vicinity of Arley. It may have been named in consequence of a Roman camp having been here, but no ruins nor any Roman finds had been made here by the late C18 (SHOS vol 2 pp253,254).

Castlefields Castle Church. Former race horse training ground (info Bruce Braithwaite). Has also appeared as Newtown (Stafford Post 12 May 1988 p12). Newtown may have once referred to Castletown. Castlefields seems to be now a residential development to W of Castletown. It was planned to build 9,000 new houses here by 2000 in 1992 (SN May 22 1992 p9).

Castleforebridge In Bradley manor (VCH vol 4 p77). Forebridge, formerly in Castle Church parish, appears as Castelforbrugg in 1372.

Castle Garden Fairoak. Name for a garden at the foot of a small hill, now occupied by a house at Fairoak Bank. The name 'Castle' suggests the hill had been the site for a fort (BOV p27).

Castle Hayes Park Former hunting or deer park in Tutbury ancient parish created by Robert de Ferrers (d1139), 1st Earl of Derby (UTR p36). The park is mentioned in 1261 (VCH vol 2 p350), and in 1303 (NSJFS 1962 p76. 1964 p63). It was disparked in 1549 (VCH vol 2 p355) (ANS p52). Castle Hayes Park Farm is 1.25m SW of Tutbury. Lower Castle Hayes Park Farm is further S. John of Gaunt's supply of alabaster came from the gypsum deposits here. Possibly some if not all went into making his wife's tomb in St Paul's cathedral (no longer existing, but noted by William Burton, 1622) (SHOS vol 1 pp58,61) (VCH vol 2 p198). War horses bred at a stud in the park were used for John of Gaunt's invasion of Scotland. The stud became a royal one when the Duchy of Lancaster passed to the Crown. The stud and or that at Hanbury Park was disbanded in 1650. Near Lower Castle Hays Farm in the area of the former park was seen the ghost of a 12 year old girl dressed in fine clothes of the late C15 period (LTD pp161-162). Has also appeared as the Hay of the Earl (UTR p36) and Castlehay Park.

Castle Hill Over 0.5m NE of Arley church (marked on OS map 1:25,000).

Castle Hill Wooded hillock 0.5m NNE of Ashley, between Rock and Wharmadine Lanes, at SJ 765375. It may be a natural mound once utilised as a Norman motte (CAMS p15).

Castle Hill End of Church Street, N end of Audley. Site for Audley Castle (see). The Roman pottery and coins from here exhibited at a meeting of the NSFC were in fact of medieval date (NSFCT vol 48 p233. vol 49 p92. 1911 p206. 1914 pp92-96) (NSJFS 1964 p15) (ESH pp51-52).

Castle Hill Limestone hill on which Dudley Castle is situated. Is similar in structure and stratigraphy to the Wren's Nest Hill, and formerly mined in the same way (WNNNR pp4,22-23); the limestone quarried caverns in it are: Big Ben, Dark Cavern, Hurst's Cavern, Little Tess Cavern, and Singing Cavern (Dudley Canal Tunnel leaflet). Has also appeared as Dudley Castle Hill.

Castle Hill Tutbury Castle is sited on it. It was most likely a defensive position long before the Norman period, perhaps a Saxon stronghold, if not of earlier date (NSFCT 1912 p189).

Castle House N side of Station Road, Barton-under-Needwood. Built in 1730. Formerly was known as The Grove. Residence of Miss Mary Holland, who was a suffragette in the early 1900s (UNT p115).

Castle House Impressive red brick mansion in Castle Bank, Stafford. Built in 1840 (SAC p93p).

Castle Liberty Former township in two parts; the township has also appeared as Tamworth Castle Liberty. The main portion extended for over 1m in a narrow strip from Kettlebrook in the N to Dosthill House in the S. A detached portion of the township to the N stretched S from Tamworth Castle. The township was in Wilnecote chapelry in Tamworth ancient parish but in Hemlingford hundred, Warws. Castle Liberty seems to have also formed a township with Wilnecote and this became a separate civil parish in 1866. Parts of the civil parish were taken into Tamworth borough and into Staffs in 1932 and 1965 (GLAUE p425). (W p627).

Castle Mill Basin Part underground and part exposed canal basin and wharf at the junction of three tunnels; viz - Dudley Tunnel, Tipton Tunnel, and Wrens Nest Tunnel (IAS p164) (HCMS No. 2) 0.5m N of Dudley Castle. It is 34 yards long and was formerly a large round limestone quarry at the end of Tipton Tunnel (IAS p164) (info Dudley Canal Trust). Contains a fossilised coral roof (VB p45).

Castle Old Fort Iron Age hillfort on Castle Hill (NSFCT 1881 p44; height is 783 feet), 0.75m W of the church at Stonnall, or 0.5m ENE of Holly Bush. Dates from the C2 to C1 BC. Height is 500 feet, extreme inner length is about 171 yards, width is 138 yards (VCH vol 1 p373). The N part has been built on, and the interior converted into a garden (VCH vol 1 p341 dia) (NSJFS 1964 p34) (HOS p10). Spearheads and other warlike instruments, all of iron, have been found here (NHS p396) (W p583). It is believed by some to be of Roman origin (MR p308). Some Roman pottery has been found here and coins of Otho, Domitian and Nero (HOWW or ROR p25) (SOB p7). Or it was a Saxon fort (SVB p156). (SD p24) (SHOS vol 2 p53) (GNHS pp65,70) (HOWW p11) (WJO May 1908 p129) (CCC p5) (LGS p31) (SOB p7) (OSST 1949-50 p18) (STMSM Nov 1972 p41). Has also appeared as Old Castle Fort (NSJFS 1964 p34).

Castle Park Former medieval deer park enclosed out of forest, situated by Tutbury Castle. In existence by 1329 (VCH vol 2 p350) or 1374 (NSJFS 1962 p76). The park, formerly known as Tutbury Park (VCH vol 2 p350), had a circuit of one mile and contained 40 acres (EDP p175). (HTC p75).

Castle Ridge Estate At Castle Church, Stafford.

Castle Ring Iron Age hillfort 0.75m WSW of Beaudesert Hall, in Longdon parish; a stretch of rampart forms the boundary between Offlow and Cuttlestone hundreds (W p566). The fort, on Castle Hill (W p566), is 671.2

feet or 801 feet high above sea level and the highest point of Cannock Chase. Similar hillforts, at Brownhills, Staffs, and on the Wrekin, Shrops, could be seen from the fort (Notice board at site. Feb 2000). Covers 8.5 acres and is one of the most complete encampments in the county (NSFCT 1950 p101). The extreme length within ramparts is 267 yards and width within is 203 yards. The rampart is four metres high in places (VCH vol 1 pp336,337 plan. vol 5 p52,62p) (Notice board at site. Feb 2000). Dates from the C2 to C1 BC (HOS p10 pl 1 - aerial view 1948). Within the Ring was a small settled community; and the fort may have been a focal point for people in the area. There are presently entrances in the SW and NE sides (VCH vol 1 p337 see plan). Originally there was only one entrance. The second entrance was cut in the C19 to take a carriageway to Beaudesert Hall. The Ring was occupied until c50 AD. Exactly why the site ceased to be used is not known (Notice board at site. Feb 2000). On the N side, where the land falls away steeply, it is fortified by two earthen walls and ditches and towards the S side by five similar walls (NSFCT 1950 p101). A gold coin was found on the Ring which the BM declared to be Greek and from the period of the Roman occupation (CCBO pp27-29). In 1826 a flint 'strike-a-light' was found on the Ring and in 1908 a flint scraper of unusual formation was found and thought to be coeval with the date of the Ring (CCF p85). In summer 1932 a flint instrument 'a thumb-scraper' was found at Castle Rings (NSFCT 1931 p192). Hackwood identifies Castle Ring as a druidical site (SC pp144-145). (NHS pp39,418) (SD pp53,56) (SHOS vol 1 p221) (GNHS p72) (W p450) (NSFCT vol 49 p177. vol 66 p192) (OSST 1949-50 p18) (WJO May 1908 p129) (HS p143 pl) (CCC pp4,5,6,13,15,22,128.129) (MOS p5) (LGS pp32,105) (SOSH pp10-12) (OSST 1949-50) (A Guide to Prehistoric England. N Thomas. 1960. p187) (NSJFS 1964 p18) (STMSM Nov 1972 p41) (VB p120) (BOE p93) (SOP p15) (SGS p101) (SL p37) (MR pp80,81) (COS p58p). Inside the encampment, in the NW corner, are the foundations of a stone building of late C14 origin, 65 feet by 37 feet, which on excavation was found to have consisted of two rooms with a roof supported by eight pillars. It was perhaps a hunting lodge, or a monastery (NSFCT 1891 p47. 1892 p139. 1950 p101) and, or, is believed to have been built by an early bishop of Lichfield (LGS p105). This building may give the fort its present name (NSFCT 1892 p139; Castle Ring appears on Yates' map. Other forms are Old Castle Hill and Castle Rings (DUIGNAN). Wakes were held here in the summer and a dance of the Lichfield Morris called 'Castlering' may have evolved at these wakes (LTM Nov 1971 pp10-11). Castle Ring became the property of Cannock urban district council in 1932 (SVB p113). The ghosts of a young monk, who possibly served at Radmore Priory, and a young girl who sits weeping have both been seen in the vicinity of the ring (RRCC p8) (info Bruce Braithwaite) (GPCE p25). From Castle Ring a view extends over nine counties, viz: Stafford, Derby, Leicester, Worcester, Warwick, Shrops, Chester, Montgomery, and Flint ('Magna Britannia' 1730) (HOWW p12) (WAM p77).

Castle Rock Precipice on which Alton Castle, Alton stands (HAF pp11,13).

Castle Rock Precipice on which Beresford Hall's Prospect Tower stands (PDS&C p113).

Castles and Shire Oaks Hill, The The village of Stonnall stands on this hill. From it can be seen seven counties including Staffs (SHOS vol 2 p53).

Castletown Suburb 0.25 W of Stafford town centre, close to Stafford windmill. Formerly in Castle Church parish. Developed as a village for workers on the GJR (opened in 1837) and at a railway maintenance depot situated here (MR p295). Was called Newtown (VCH vol 6 p195), but was known as Castletown by the 1860s (SAC p71). In 1844 it was transferred to Forebridge ecclesiastical parish. The church, St Thomas, was built in 1866 close to the railway station. It was known as the railwaymen's church and served until 1972 and was then demolished (VCH vol 6 pp248,249) (SOPP pl 78p). Castletown became a separate ecclesiastical parish in 1867. The parish is now (1991) known as 'Stafford St Thomas' (GLAUE p407).

Castleway Baulk A ridge in Shobnall (IVNF).

Castle Well Former public well in Wednesbury at the back of St Bartholomew's church (HOWY p227).

Castle Whitworth At Green Gate, Stafford. A lost folly, which looked like a Martello Tower and came complete with a cannon, built by the eccentric Richard Whitworth of Batchacre Hall in 1803 at the outbreak of the war with France. He built it to circumvent a covenant in his deeds regarding his property at Green Bridge over the Sow, although he claimed it was to protect the town against a Napoleonic invasion, citing Ethelfreda's work of fortifying the town in the C10 as his inspiration. Some pictures of this fort can be seen on the details of his labour bills used in the action the Corporation brought against him for failure to observe his covenant. Whitworth liked to call it his 'Castle Whitworth' (OP p15-16) (ROT p41) (SAC p112). Built between 1804-1807 (VCH vol 6 p199).

Castlow Cross A burial mound in the Weaver Hills (NHS p404). The name means 'a burial mound with a heap of stones' (SPNO p24). Is probably the same as Hackwood's Astlow Cross (SCSF p74).

Catchems Corner Former small hamlet 1.5m SE of Wolverhampton (Yates' map) (1834 OS map). Formerly partly in Bilston and Wolverhampton townships in Wolverhampton ancient parish (W p144). It was situated S of present day Millfields Road within a bend in the Birmingham Main Line Canal. Hell Lane ran through or by it. This area is the present Upper Ettingshall. Formerly frequented by criminals (TB Nov 1976 p24). The name is said to allude to the evilness of the place and perhaps paganism (BCM Oct 1993 p56). Or so called from those placed here to catch prisoners who had escaped from Priestfield (the field where prisoners from the north of England were rested overnight and consoled by a priest, en route to Birmingham or London). Or more likely from the toll gate house here which had a reputation to catch travellers who had eluded previous toll bars (TB Jan 1987 p5. Aug 1997 p3). Or from the highwayman Jack Ketchum, who was reputedly hung here. There was a tree to hang criminals on in this area. Another suggestion is that the name is from a public executioner called Jack Ketch (d1682), whose name passed into common use as a nickname for hangmen (TB Oct 15 1998 p16). Or from the hamlet being on the parish boundary; here vagrants and criminals could evade parish authorities (TB Nov 5 1998 p10). Ettingshall Road and Bilston LMSR Goods station was formerly Catchems Corner Goods station and was known throughout the railway system as 'Ketchum' (TB May 1997 p3). The name no longer prevails.

Catchem's End Over 0.5m E of Brewood at SJ 894089 (1834 OS map). (VCH vol 5 p40). The name is of C19 origin (SPN p23).

Catherine's Cross District just W of central Darlaston (Offlow hundred) (CCBO p172). The earliest documentary reference to this locality is in 1750 when, on a mining map, it is designated 'Mr Offley's Waste,' Mr Offley being then lord of the manor. Has also appeared as Catton's Cross (1837), but has never appeared as St Catherine's Cross, despite Ede in HOWY referring to it as this (SNDB p29). The name is said to be from a wayside cross which stood in a widening of the road where the highway from Walsall cuts into the main road between Wednesbury and Wolverhampton. Hackwood says the cross has vanished; perhaps it was a shrine dedicated to St Catherine (SCSF p88). Or probably from a crossroads; Catton may have been a property owner in the vicinity (SNDB p29). Catherine's Cross was the severest hit area of Darlaston in the Asiatic Cholera outbreak of Oct 1848 (WAM p114).

Catholes Wood On W side of Ellishill Brook, 0.5m NE of Stanton.

Cat Holme Island in the Trent near Wychnor (HOA p18). The first part of the name 'Cat' is from Katti. 'Holme' is Norse and means island, so 'Katti's island' (HOBTU p9). Excavations between 1973 and 1976 revealed a Saxon settlement, occupied between the period 450 and 950, on the Trent gravel terrace at Cat Holme. It is believed the community migrated northwards and developed Barton-under-Needwood, 1.25m away (SVB p29) (UNT pp2,3). The early prehistoric ceremonial monument at SK 196166, and the circular enclosure and pit alignment 300 yards SE of Catholme Bridge, at SK 195167, are listed monuments. There is a farmhouse called Catholme NW of the island. At the confluence of the Trent and Tame at SK 192153 are three WW2 pillboxes, two are hexagonal (WMARCH 1993 p35). Has also appeared as Catholm and Catholme.

Cats Edge Small hamlet on an edge 1.5m W of Cheddleton.

Cat's Hill Hill to the N of Cat's Hill Cross, Slindon.

Cats Hill Burial mound at cSK 052048, about mid way between Shire Oak and Frog Hall (NHS p403) (SHOS vol 1 General Intro p32. vol 2 p56) (SSC p129 in the intro). In Shenstone ancient parish. Is possibly of Roman origin (SD pp14,99). It was cut in two when the canal was built (CCC p5). Gould says that two burial mounds were damaged when the canal was built (MOA p114) (NSJFS 1965 p46). Has appeared as Canute's Hill, Catts Hill, Catshill, Cats Hall, Catishall, Cattes Lowe alias Cattes Hill (1576) (VCH vol 17 p278 note), and Cutteslowe. The name is from the burial mound, which was the grave of Cutha, the great warrior brother of Ceawlin, the founder of Wednesbury and conqueror of Mercia (SCSF p74) (SMM p19). Or the name is from the mound which probably belonged to, or was near to, the property of an Anglo-Saxon called Catt (DUIGNAN) (CCC p5). Or is from Canute's Hill (W p583). Or 'Cat' signifies the site of an ancient battle (SMM p19). There was settlement at Catshill on N side of Walsall Wood Common (formerly in a detached portion of the foreign of Walsall ancient parish) by 1763 (VCH vol 17 p278). The Cat's Hill area was enclosed in 1812 (W p583).

Cat's Hill Cross Tiny settlement nearly 1m SSE of Slindon at a cross roads; lies at the foot of Cat's Hill.

Catshill Junction Brownhills. Junction of the Wyrley and Essington Extension Canal with the Daw End Branch of Rushall Canal (HCMS No. 2).

Cat's Wall Between Wall Grange and Caverswall. Possibly same as Cats Edge. 'Wall' is from an ancient line earthwork called The Mark (see) (OL vol 2 p15).

Cat Tor Bank A hill on the Leek side of the A53 out of the valley of the Churnet below Upper Hulme (SMCC p2). Here, beyond the outcrop known as Rock Bar, stands Cat Tor House (UHAW p51). Takes its name from Cat Tor, a rock feature, by the A53 SE of Naychurch.

Cauldon Moorland village above a tributary of the Hamps on the N side of Caldon Low 19m NE of Stafford. Former chapelry in Ilam ancient parish. A stone axe and an axe-hammer found (1864) in Cauldon went to the Potteries Museum (NSJFS 1964 p41). Land at Caldone is recorded as waste in DB (SSE 1996 p11). Later forms are: Caluedon (1196) and Calfdon (1200) (SPN p30). The name is Anglo-Saxon celfdun and means 'calf hill' (DUIGNAN) (NSJFS 1981 p3) (SSAHST 1967 p34) (SPN p31). Cauldon was identified by Shaw, Wolferstan, Duignan as the Celfdum mentioned in the will of Wulfric Spot (c1002), founder of Burton Abbey (SHC 1916 p36). There was a church at Cauldon in the C12 (LDD). The present church, St Mary and St Lawrence, on the N side of Church Lane, was built in 1781-1784 (BOE p94) on the site of a medieval church (CHMS2 p32). The parish wake is on the nearest Sunday to Aug 20 (W p751). Cauldon had separate civil identity early and obtained separate ecclesiastical status in 1748 (GLAUE p407). Cauldon Mill was a possession of Croxden Abbey (NSSG p13). There has been a large cement works in Cauldon since the late 1950s (SVB p172). The village is currently spelt with a 'u,' but spelt without on the 1834 OS map. Caldon place names have never been standardised, even sign posts have spelt the village differently (STMSM April 1979 p41 ps of sign posts). The canal has rarely if ever been spelt with a 'u.' Caldon Low, a hill, 0.5m SE of Cauldon and its nearby limestone quarry, seem to have been spelt without a 'u.' A fragmented hamlet 0.75m S of Cauldon spelt Caldonlow on the 1:25,000 OS map is Cauldon Lowe on the 1:50,000 OS map. George Fox, the founder of the Quakers, preached at Cauldon in 1651 or 1652 (VCH vol 3 p117. vol 7 p140). The custom of dressing the village well was revived by 1988 (SVB p172). Cauldon is mentioned in this rhyme:

> Caldon, Calton, Waterfall, and Grin,
> Four of the foulest towns ever man was in.

(FOS p149). Hackwood gives a different version:-

> Callow, Cauldon, Waterfall and Grin,
> Are the four foulest places I was ever in.

(SCSF p167).

Cauldon A ward of Hanley from 1895 (VCH vol 8 p158).

Cauldon House Used in connection with air raid precautions during WW2 and then demolished (SHST p220). Could be Cauldon Place House (see).

Cauldon Place House Shelton, Hanley. Built by Job Ridgeway (OTP p145). Cauldon Place, John Ridgway's 'elegant modern mansion' attached to his pottery works was changed out of all recognition by c1960 (VCH vol 8 p150). Built prior to, or during, or after, Ridgeway built the works?

Cavalier's Stable A hollow below a piece of rock, a couple of miles NE of Aqualate Mere where Charles II's horse is reputed to have hidden after the battle of Worcester and Charles' arrival at Boscobel in 1651. The 'great grey horse' was brought here by Richard Skrymsher, who may have dropped his sword in a duel; it was found near the mere and is at Aqualate Hall (SLM Dec 1948 p187). In another article, about Gnosall, reference is made to a hollow ledge in a sandstone height on Broadhill where Charles I fed his horse whilst marching with his troops from Stafford to Wellington in 1642; this may relate to the same (STM Feb 1966 p25).

Cave, The 174A Lichfield Road, Stone. An individual-architect designed house, which was for sale in Sept 1994. Has a curious summerhouse raised on a post and approached by a raised gantry (ES Sept 8 1994 property pages).

Caverswall (perhaps proverbially *Carsa*, see below). Ancient parish and village on raised ground on the E side of the upper Blithe valley 12.5m NNE of Stafford.

EARLY. A glacial boulder in the High Street and another at the corner with the Red House and High Street by the square existed in 1979 (STP pp4p,7p). A stone hammer head and a stone macehead have been found at Caverswall (NSFCT 1908 p194. vol 42 p97. vol 43 p144) (AJ vol 21 p337) (NSJFS 1964 p19). A mound, although not a burial mound, lies NW of Caverswall at SJ 94214303 (NSJFS 1965 p35). There is a burial mound 50 feet in diameter 0.5m NE of Caverswall at SJ 95484338 (WJ p29) (NSJFS 1965 p35). There is a **legend of King Arthur** having kept court at Caverswall (SLM July 1949 p260). The tradition of King Arthur at Caverswall was still persistent in 1937. The writer of 'The County of Stafford and its Family Records' 1897 reports there was a 'Lady of Caverswall upon whose shoulders the magic kirtle of chastity did not not wither but retained its pristine freshness.' There is a version that states the lady of the castle was rescued by King Arthur from some danger (NSFCT 1937 p60).

1000 to 1500. The manor of Cavreswelle appears in DB (SSE 1996 p11). Later forms are: Cauereswell (1167), Chauereswella (1185), Cavereswall (1242) (SPN p31), and Careswell (HOC p257). The **name** is from perhaps Caversmound or Carmount (NSFCT 1908 p125). Or perhaps from the hillroot cabar, the 'b' passing into 'f.' This may be the first element in Charnes, as well (NSFCT 1910 p162). Duignan suggests the terminal is from Anglo-Saxon 'wiell,' meaning a spring, and the prefix from cafer, meaning a hall, court, or mansion. Johnstone thinks 'wall' is from the Lime Brittanicus, the Roman fosse from the Don to the Severn, a later boundary for the Saxons of Mercia (WJC p8) or the same earthwork but called 'The Mark' (see) (OL vol 2 p15). Others think it is named after the original inhabitant Cafhere, who founded a spring here, so 'Cafhere's walle or spring' (STP p vii) (SVB p51). 'Wall' is a West Midland dialectal form of the word 'well' meaning spring (SSAHST 1967 p35). Or 'Cafhere's stream or spring' (SSE 1996 p11) (SPN p31). The parish **church**, St Peter, S of Caverswall Castle, dates from the late C12 (BOE p95) (CHMS2 p32). The parish was formed after 1086 and probably before c1270 and certainly by 1291 out of Cheadle parish (SHC 1916 p199). The **wake** was on the nearest Sunday to St Peter's day in the C19 (W p752). Caverswall was one of the last places in the country to give up bull baiting (IOM p67). Wakes known as 'Carsa wakes' took place in the C20 (The Spirit of the Place. MJW Rogers. 2000). The **stocks** in the village square are beneath a tree planted on March 9 1935 which replaced the old Constablewick Tree, planted in c1670. At the same time the stocks were replaced (ES March 27 1935 p21p). (ROS vol 3 p31) (SLM Dec 1952 p21p) (JC pl 23). These were replaced by new stocks by Sept 1996. To the S of Caverswall beyond Dove House Farm is evidence of the ancient **field system** (STP p44p). The **Plague** of 1349 visited Caverswall. A woman called Agnes, who had been labelled a witch, survived it and was killed by villagers who blamed her for starting it (STP pp60,62). **King John** was reputedly at Caverswall for a hunting expedition - there is a carved overmantel depicting the king in pursuit of the wild boar (STP p35), possibly a reference to the tympanum in the church.

1500 to PRESENT. For Caverswall **windmill** see WIS pp9p,16. For a sampler made at Caverswall see STM April 1966 p42 il. 'Rum Tum Tardy um' are words of a well-known old song, thought to have started life as a marching song for the **Caverswall volunteers** during the Napoleonic Wars. They are written in the sign of The Red House Inn (SVB p52). In the mid C19 Caverswall was a great place for pugilist fights (IOM p67). There was **fair** at Caverswall in 1888 (LHE p265). **Folklore and the supernatural**. Some of Caverswall thought the 'blue moon' effect over the sun on June 20 1783 an evil curse brought upon them by the dead mistress of Caverswall Castle, Lady Vane, when in reality it was the effect of the Icelandic volcano eruption of Laki (STP p166). A St Mark's eve superstition prevailed at Caverswall. It was believed a maiden would see her future husband if she hung a freshly washed chemise over the back of a chair on St Mark's eve (April 24) or if she hung it from a peg and woke up at the stroke of midnight she would see the image of her future husband coming to reverse it. Also if a girl slept with a yarrow taken from the grave of a young man or plucked from Salters Lane underneath her pillow (STP p129). A child in a white night dress running across the Blythe Bridge Road, possibly a ghost, was seen by a man. A ghost-like tiny figure appeared on a wedding photograph taken at Caverswall church in the early 1950s. It was sent to the News of The World who were unable to prove it was false. A large orange-coloured shape roughly 16 feet by 8 feet has been seen in a field where the public footpath crosses to Blythe Bridge (D Peake in The Advertiser. Jan 1993). **Persons and visitors**. Some have been mistaken in thinking **James I** stayed at Caverswall. The mistake could have arisen from the statement that the castle was built in James I's reign (S p129). **Robert William Buchanan**, dramatist and publisher, was born in Caverswall on Aug 18 1841. Soon after Buchanan's birth his family moved to London. He was the author of 'Idylls and legends of Inverburn' (1865), 'David Gray, and other essays chiefly on poetry' (1868), 'The book of Orm; a prelude to the epic' (1870), 'The Martyrdom of Madeline' (1882), 'Lady Kilpatrick' (1895), and 'The Wandering Jew' (1890). He died on June 10 1901 (Who Was Who 1897-1915) (PSS pp236-247 p) (VFC p21).

Caverswall Hamlet 1m E of Gratwich. In Uttoxeter ancient parish. Has also appeared as Caveswall (W p797).

Caverswall Castle In Caverswall village. A peculiarly-shaped axe found at

Caverswall Castle was in the collection of Lady Forester of Meaford Hall, near Stone (NSFCT 1883 p51). (DoE II). The castle is thought by some to have Saxon origins (SVB p51). It was thought by Plot, Calvert, Garner, Plant and Masefield to have been first built in c1320 (NSFCT 1937 pp49-61). But was shown by Col Wedgwood to have been built in c1270 (MOS p36). Sir William de Caverswall (Sheriff of Staffs. 1260-69 d1292) was licensed to crenellate in 1275; the deep and wide moat, now filled in, and the lower parts of the outer walls probably date from this period (CAMS p17). Lynam said that fragments of the lower part of the tower date from the first quarter of C14 (NSFCT 1937 pp49-61). The castle mound is about 150 square feet (NSFCT 1937 pp49-61). The enclosure is roughly oblong. There are at each corner of the enclosure four polygonal angle towers (BOE p95). The Caverswalls lived at High Ercall Hall, Shrops, in the C14. Their line came to an end with the death of Sir Peter Caverswall in 1398. According to Col Wedgwood Caverswall had passed to the Marchingtons, through Sir Peter's daughter Petronella, in 1346, and not to the Montgomeries as Leland and others say. It passed to the Giffards in c1515 and they moved to Chillington in 1555, perhaps renting it to a religious order for a time after which it was finally vacated (NSFCT 1937 pp49-61). In the C16 Leland called the castle a 'pretty pile.' In the Elizabethan period it was allowed to decay under the tenancy of a farmer called Browne. In the early C17 it was bought by the wealthy wool merchant Matthew Craddock who built a house in the N part of the court in 1614 or c1615. As to who was architect: Pevsner favours John Smythson (who designed Bolsover Castle, Derbys) (BOE p95), whilst Girouard favours Robert Smythson (Robert Smythson and the Elizabethan Country House. M Girouard. pp181-182). During this period the medieval towers were terminated by balustrading (BOE p95). In the Civil War it was held by parliamentary troops, and captured by the royalists in the spring of 1645 (GNHS p77) (HOS p36). In 1655 there were three co-heiresses and they sold the castle to William Joliffe, to whom the engraving of the castle in Plot is dedicated (NHS p448 tab 37) (NSFCT 1976 pp24-25). Later owners included Viscount Vane of Ireland, Capt Packer (1730), and the Hon Booth Grey (NSFCT 1937 pp49-61). A print dated April 11 1785 of the castle was made by S Hooper. From 1811-50 Mr Brett leased it to a community of Benedictine nuns from Ghent (NSFCT 1976 p25), who conducted a girls' school here; they were the first to re-establish a Catholic order in Staffs after the Dissolution (HOS p28). The novelist, Mary Howitt (1799-1888), visited the hall before and during its time as a nunnery (SHJ spring 1992 p26). The nuns left in 1853 destroying their chapel and sisters' memorials (SVB p51). In 1817 JA Blackwell of Cobridge made a drawing of the castle. A subsequent owner was Sir Percival Radcliffe; in autumn 1878 the castle was leased to Godfrey Wedgwood, later of Idlerocks (see). In 1890 William E Bowers bought it and made improvements. He employed Charles Lynam of Colwich to build a new wing connecting the house with the turret flanking the northern side of the gate (STP p220) (STC p15p) (WCW p312). He also built lodges and the two gates and brought some beautiful woodwork for the interior of the new part of the house from Fauld Hall near Tutbury (NSFCT 1937 pp49-61 pls facing 49,52). Another owner was WA Bowers, whose wife sold it in June 1933 to the Sisters of the Holy Ghost who sold in 1965 to another community of nuns, Daughters of the Heart of Mary, who moved to the castle in Sept 1965 (ES June 21 1965). In 1977 (NSFCT 1949 p121) (STP p238), the castle was sold in various lots (SVB p51). Since then, a businessman, has undertaken some restoration on it. It was again for sale in c1988 (MR pp85p,86). (Magna Britannia. Cox) (SD p99) (GNHS pp96il,97) (W p751) (ROS vol 3 pp1-40il) (HOC pp238-241) (NSFCT 1888 pp59-61) (LGS p106p) (CL 1911 pp886-895 ps) (KES pp59p,60) (ES Aug 19 1931. Nov 4 1931 p6) (NSFCT 1937-8 pp49-61) (STM Sept 1964 pp44-45) (NSJFS 1966 p43) (SGS p79) (STP pp69,96p,105-111) (CAMS p16 plan) (SMOPP vol 1 pp10,11p of interior and drawing by Harriet Blagg).

GROUNDS. The Italian Gardens (STP p221p). The Moat bridge is of C17 origin and has 'M.C. 1625' stamped on it (pp95,96). There is a sundial 20 metres S of the entrance, probably of c1890, is of redstone and the top and dial have been replaced (DoE II). The nuns' small burial ground near the castle was visited by the strange phenomenon of flickering lights of an unexplained nature in 1876. These were known locally as 'Corpse Candles' (NSFCT 1901 p135). There is a tradition of an underground passage from Caverswall Castle to a farm SW of the castle. The railway company purchased the farm and bricked up the passage (NSFCT 1937 pp49-61).

Caverswall Common Dispersed hamlet over 1m NNW of Caverswall.

Caverswall Park A medieval deer park at or near Caverswall enclosed out of forest. In existence by 1293 (NSJFS 1962 p76).

Caverswall Park House nearly 1.5m WNW of Forsbrook or 0.5m SW of Caverswall.

Caverswall Wood Residential area over 1.5m WNW Forsbrook.

Cawarden Springs House 1.5m SE of Colton. In Mavesyn Ridware parish (W p570). Has also appeared as Carden-Spring; the name is from the Cawarden family, lords of Mavesyn Ridware (SHOS vol 1 pp187,200). Here was a sulphur holy well (OSST 1944-1945).

Cawbrook Tributary of the Manifold. Is perhaps derived from a dialectal version of cold (SPNO p6).

Cawdry Formerly in Bradnop township in Leek ancient parish (W p727). Benedict de Cawdry occurs from 1230 to 1256 (SHC 1910 p423).

Cawdry House Cawdry. St Luke's church, Leek, is close to the site. Once the home of Mrs Whillock and others of the Sleigh family, including John Sleigh author of HOLS. In 1815 it was the property of Miss Davenport - one of the Davenports of Ball Haye (OL vol 2 p50).

Cecilly Brook Tributary of the Tean. Flows near Cheadle; Cecilly Bridge is near Cheadle (NSFCT 1900 p100). Is probably the brook which rises in the Kingsley area and flows on the E side of Cheadle and joins the Tean at Mobberley.

Cedar Bridge Between Tibbington and Bloomfield.

Cedar Court House on E side of Walsall Wood Road, Aldridge. Built by William Allport in the late C18, who with his wife ran a school here. It has C19 additions (SNAR p52). Some time after the occupation of the Allports it was the home of the Tibbits family. It was converted into luxury apartments in the 1980s (ALOPPR p117p).

Cedar Garden At the back of Sandon Hall.

Cedar Hill Hill S of Toot Hill on W side of Alton (HAF p217 see map).

Cedars, The Former substantial house on the E side of the Old Walsall Road, Hamstead, just before new Walsall Road is reached. It was long occupied by James Bissell and may have been built by him. By 1899 Jim Kaye of Messrs EC & J Kaye Ltd lived here. During WW2 the house was owned by Jack White and used by officials of the Coal Programming Authority. The house was falling into a ruin by 1951. The grounds contained cedar trees (HPPE pp21-22).

Cedars, The Former late C19 house in the Cedars Avenue area of Wordsley. Occupied by Thomas W Robinson (d1912), ironmaster. Later occupied by Henry Edward Richardson (1870-1955), after whose death the property was sold and demolished. The grounds contained cedar trees (SNSV vol 1 p60).

Cellarhead Village E of Werrington on a high ridge; now merges with Werrington. Partly in Caverswall and Cheddleton ancient parishes. The meaning of the name was unknown to Johnstone. Some have said it is connected with a huge cellar attached to the Hope and Anchor Inn in Cellarhead. Others attribute it to a miserly old woman whose husband used to say of her that she would 'sell 'er yed' if it were loose! (WJ p24). There was a Hugh the Cellarer, a servant of the prior of Trentham in c1330 (BNDA pp14,15). According to Whitaker's Almanac Cellarhead had two annual fairs, one on May 17, and one on the first Thursday in Nov (W p752) (SCSF p98) (WJ p25). There was no fair in 1792 (OWEN), but there was in 1888 (LHE p265). The fair occurred at the crossroads (FWMBS p5). The bull tether found in a field next to the Hope and Anchor Inn (NSFCT 1925 p190) (Staffs Weekly Sentinel Feb 13 1926) (WJ p27) eventually went to the County Museum at Shugborough (MR p364p). A Wellington 1C aircraft crashed at Cellarhead on Jan 30 1943 killing two of its five crew (MD p32). Four or five people together at Cellarhead saw unusual lights in the north sky in the early morning sometime between Oct 19 and 25 Oct 1967; it was possibly a UFO (FSRP p17). The longest recorded game of Snakes and Ladders has been one of 121 hours by a team of six (four always in play) from Moorside High School, Cellarhead Road on Feb 10-15 1975 (GBR 1975 p279). 'Old' Gervase Forester of Cellarhead turned to ballad making after he had failed in business as a maltster, his bankruptcy occurring in 1838. He wrote a ballad entitled 'The Rival Railway Bubbles; or, Which is the most Feasible Line? A New Song to the old tune of the Cork Leg' a year after the NSR formed in 1845 (HOC p173) (WJ p27). Edward Hassall (Neddy Asser) of Cellarhead claimed he was the strongest man in Staffs. He could lift 90lb weights above his head and knock them together 14 times. He could carry a stone gate post under each arm (WJ pp25-26).

Central Forest Park Public park N of Hanley constructed in 1971 (POP p63) (MR p177) on reclaimed land of Hanley Deep Pit (closed 1961). Elizabeth II opened the park in 1973 (ES Jan 17 1995 p10) (PCCSC p243). Two grassed-over slag heaps, the spoils of Hanley Deep Pit (VB p190), are the main features of it, there were three, and they were called the 'Three Ugly Sisters.' Has appeared as 'Hanley Alps.' Only two heaps existed by 1974 (NSJFS 1974 p128). The park has also been called Hanley Forest Park and Forest Park.

Chad Brook Formed the county boundary between Staffs and Warws at Harborne (VCHWA vol 7 p22). Named after St Chad for it also marked the boundary of

the diocese of Lichfield and Chad may have perambulated the boundary (HOHE p2).

Chad's Dyke Fosse which formed the boundary of Cannock Chase. It was made by 1290, probably by the bishops of Lichfield (Lichfield cathedral is dedicated to St Chad), who were granted 'free chase' within Cannock Forest in 1290. Unlike medieval parks chases were not usually bounded by ditches (NSJFS 1968 p49). Has appeared as 'the dike of St Chad' (1290), 'the diche of St Chadde' (1300) (SPNO p121), and 'the fosse of the Blessed St Chad' (DUIGNAN p35). Traces of the bank and ditch remained long after the chase passed into secular hands. In the C20 it has been located about a mile N of Huntington, between Pye Green and Pottal Pool, where the ditch is about four feet high and eight feet wide (DUIGNAN) (CCF p222) (SSAHST 1965 p36) (NSJFS 1968 p49) (PCC p77).

Chad's Gate W of Pye Green (DUIGNAN) (PCC p77). The name is probably from an entrance through the medieval Chad's Dyke (see).

Chadsmoor (locally *Chadsmer* BILP1 p17). Originally a moor, probably called Cannock Bog, now a NE suburb of Cannock 2m from Cannock. In Cannock parish. The estate appears to have been given the name after St Chad, in, or slightly before, the C19 (SPNO p58). The church, St Chad, was built in 1891 replacing a school-church of 1874 (VCH vol 5 p67). Gustav Hamel landed in a plane at the Central Athletics Ground at Chadsmoor in 1913 (EAS p20) (TB March 1994 p18p). Sydney Francis Barnes (b1873) the famous cricket bowler died at Chadsmoor on Dec 26 1967 (TB Aug 1997 p10).

Chadstow Stowe at Lichfield could have been called this (SHOS vol 1 p231).

Chadwell Hamlet over 2m NE of Sheriff Hales. In Sheriff Hales parish, formerly in Staffs. Has appeared as Lytel Chatwalle (1472), Little Chetwall (1546) (SPNO p155), Little Chatwell (1834 OS map), and Chadwell (1980 OS map). The name is from a spring here called Chad's Well, probably dedicated to the patron saint of Lichfield cathedral (DUIGNAN). There was a St Chadd's Well at Little Chadwell in 1834 (OS map 1834).

Chained Oak Old oak with great roots which wind round a big stone in Barbary Gutter, the former main drive to Alton Towers (SLM July 1951 p31 il by Elliot Green) and whose branches are bound by iron chains. Has also appeared as Druid's Oak (SLM July 1951 p31 il) and Earl's Oak, and is believed to be about 900 years old (NSFCT 1945 p93). The story explaining the chains is that a poor old conjurer who had been refused employment by the Talbots at Alton Towers put a curse on the family whereby if a branch of the oak fell off a Talbot would die, so that, at length the head of the family ordered the tree to be chained up (local info) (GLS pp14-15). Or that a murderer was caught and tried by the local people and condemned to death. With nobody prepared to carry out the execution he was chained to the oak and left to die; his ghost still haunts the gutter (local info). The excessive use of chains makes this story seem unlikely. (HAF p402).

Chambley Green W side of Coven. Is a three-sided court of 14 terrace houses built by Cannock rural district council in 1955 (VCH vol 5 p24) (OS map 1:25,000).

Chancellor's House The back drawing room of the Chancellor's House in Lichfield cathedral Close was haunted (RSL pp11-12). The Chancellor of Lichfield cathedral occupied No. 12 The Close up to 1942 (VCH vol 14 p64), or 1941 as St Chad's School (Lichfield Cathedral School) opened there (School House) in Jan 1942 (info Michael Cockin).

Chandlers Green Small housing estate which was being built on the W side of the railway line in Baldwin's Gate in summer 1999.

Chantry, The Brick house in Dean Street, Brewood, of 1712. Probably so called after a chantry chapel or priest in Brewood. Adjoining this house on its E side is a brick house called 'West Gate,' dated 1723. A grotesque mask of a woman's face with the tongue sticking out protrudes from the ornate doorcase over the entrance of 'West Gate.' The mask is said to be grimacing at The Chantry; two jealous or rivalling sisters are said to have lived in these two houses (VCH vol 5 pp23,41) (VB p78; erroneously calls West Gate The Deanery) (COS p70p) (BDH p190. 1992 p202).

Chapel Ash Former hamlet, now a suburb 0.25m of E Wolverhampton, in Wolverhampton township, chapelry and ancient parish (W p95). In 1844 part of a possible moat remained in the Paget Road area at SO 895990 in a field called Moat Leasow, later occupied by (land of?) Chapel Ash Farm, a farm on which the Oxneford estate centred, and Wulfrun College (HOWM p44) (SSAHST 1982-3 p57). (VCH vol 2 p144). At Chapel Ash was founded the medicinal Wolverhampton Spa (SHOS vol 2 p163) as noted by Dr Wilkes (W p76). (SD p32) (SCSF p140) (SMM pp75p of c1904, 76). With the passing of the Town Act of 1777 bull baiting moved out of central Wolverhampton to places like Chapel Ash (HOWM p164). The Commissioners' church, St Mark, on S side of Chapel Ash road, was built in 1848-49 (BOE p325). By the early 1990s the building had been converted into architects' offices (info John Garside). Its probable replacement, St Mark, in St Mark's Road, was built in 1953 (LDD). Alfred Hayes (d1936), poet, was born at Chapel Ash in 1858 (PSS pp299-306 p) (VFC p63). Alfred Noyes (d1958), poet, essayist, and playwright was born at Chapel Ash in 1880. He left Staffs when very young. 'The Highwayman,' perhaps his best-known poem, was made into a film. His novels include 'Walking Shadows' (1918) and 'The Hidden Player' (1924) (PSS pp343-353 p) (VB p 56) (VFC p99).

Chapel Ash House Chapel Ash. Occupied in 1851 by Mrs Thorneycroft (W p19).

Chapel Chorlton Small village on SE facing slopes of a high promontory overlooking the upper Meece valley 12m NW of Stafford. Former township and detached chapelry of Eccleshall ancient parish. Cerletone is recorded as waste in DB (SSE 1996 p12). Later forms are: Cherleton (1267) (SPN p32), Chorlton Devisover (ESH p31), and Chapel Norton (later C18) (SHC 1934 p98). The name is from Anglo-Saxon 'ceorlestun,' meaning the churl's town, a churl being a free husbandman (DUIGNAN) (NSFCT 1922 p169), or 'churls' tun' (SSE 1996 p12). Chapel is an addition to distinguish it from Hill Chorlton and Chorlton Moss. The first part of Chorlton may represent 'ceorl' or a personal name related to English Charles and German Karl (SPN p32). The church, St Lawrence, in the village centre, appears to have been founded by the C12 (LDD). Most of the church was rebuilt in 1826-1827 (BOE p96) (CHMS2 p32). Chapel Chorlton has a large triangular village green with a pinfold on one side (SVB p52). The separate ecclesiastical parish of Chapel Chorlton created in 1743 (GLAUE p407) had a detached portion in Maer (NSFCT 1913 p60). Chapel Chorlton became a separate civil parish with Hill Chorlton in 1866 (GLAUE p407).

Chapel Farm Stands on or near the site of a chapel built before 1257, to the N of Great Barr church. Adjoining the chapel was the original manor house of Great Barr manor (MOA p137).

Chapel Green Name for a central district of Willenhall. A Primitive Methodist chapel stood on the Green in the early C19 until it was replaced by a larger building in Russell Street, opened in 1850 (SNW p15).

Chapel House Tettenhall Road, Chapel Ash, Wolverhampton. Seat of GB Thorneycroft and his wife Eleanor. The house was later divided into two to form 'Granville House' and 'Salisbury House' (WMAG July 1963 pp16p,17). GB Thorneycroft built Summerfield (see) in the grounds of Chapel House as a home for his daughter, Mary, on the occasion of her marriage to Charles Corser (WMAG July 1963 p17. Sept 1963 p19p).

Chapel House Farm At the S end of Redhill Lane, S Tutbury. Stands on or near the site of a lost wayside chapel set up and maintained by Tutbury Priory, for the use of travellers on the way to Needwood Forest (LTD p178).

Chapel Wood Close to Charnes Hall, Charnes. Represents the site of a chapel which may have existed up to the C17 (BPS pp136-137).

Chapel Yard Field name in Colton. In c1830s workmen digging the gravel on a small rising ground then known as Chapel Hill situated on the S side of Bellamour House discovered some foundations of an ancient chapel, from which the field derives its name Chapel Yard. A carved corbel of a man's head was found and many small and very narrow bricks from an inch and a half to two inches thick (CWF pp176-177).

Charlemagne Pool The N pool in the Park, Chillington.

Charlemont Area 1.75m NNE of West Bromwich High Street. The area seems to have been formerly called Crumpall Green (VCH vol 17 p20), Crump's, Grumpy's and Grompe's Ground. Charley Mount (SHOS vol 2 p128) was just the name for a local hill (WBOPP pl 68), and in 1758, the house of Jesson Lowe alias Charlemont Hall. The area was becoming known as Charlemont by 1723. With the division of Lyndon ward Charlemont became a ward of West Bromwich borough in 1952 (VCH vol 17 pp20-21,46). The church, St Mary Magdalene, Beacon View Road, was built in 1964 (LDD). By 1999 Charlemont was a ward of Sandwell metropolitan borough.

Charlemont Hall Stood on the W side of Charlemont Crescent, Charlemont. The origin house known as Crump Hall (WB p50) (VCH vol 17 p20) was built by a member of the Lowe family - probably John Lowe of Lyndon in c1656. The hall burnt down in c1755 (SHWB 8p). According to tradition the hall burnt down on this or another occasion as the then occupant of the hall, Jesson Lowe, left a candle burning after retiring to bed, and the candle soon set fire to some papers and burnt the house down (SNWA p29). Soon after the destruction of the house by fire in c1755 Jesson Lowe built a new house which he referred to in his will of 1758 as 'Charley Mount.' The last Lowe died here in 1793 and left the hall to her cousin, the Rev John Hallam, Dean of Bristol, who left the estate to his son Henry Hallam, the famous historian, author of 'Middle Ages' and 'Constitutional History of England' (SHWB 8p). Henry married the daughter of Rev Sir Abraham Elton, vicar of West Bromwich 1782-1790, and their son was the 'A.H.H.' of Tennyson's 'In

Memoriam' (VB p63). In 1813 Thomas Jesson purchased Charlemont Hall and after that it had many owners including Col John Nock Bagnall of Bagnall's Ironworks. The last owner was Madam Jones, the Belgium widow of Thomas Jones, Town Clerk of Wednesbury (SHWB 8p). It was sometime the residence of Joseph Halford (SNWA p29). Demolished in 1948 and the site has since been covered by a housing estate (VCH vol 17 p21) (TB Jan 1995 p25p). Madam Jones claims she saw the ghost of a woman dressed in white which was a portent of the death of her sister in Belgium a few days later (TB Nov 1994 p13). The hall had a large cellar with a long passage way leading off it that may have led to a further passage that went as far as Lime Pearl Pool (see) (TB Feb 1997 p29).

Charleymount To the W of Wolverhampton (1834 OS map).

Charnes Tiny village on high ground near the head of a tributary of Brockton Brook, over 11m NW of Stafford. Former township in the Woodland quarter in Eccleshall ancient parish (W p376). Ceruernest is recorded as waste in DB (SSE 1996 p12). The **name** is from Anglo-Saxon 'ceafer' meaning a beetle or chafer a cock. The terminal is nest meaning in Anglo-Saxon a promontory headland, cave, or an abyss (DUIGNAN) (SSE 1996 p12). (BOV p9), hence 'beatle ness' (NSJFS 1981 p3). Or perhaps from the hill-root cabar, the 'b' passing into 'f.' This may be the first element in Caverswall, as well (NSFCT 1910 p162). Its etymology must be considered unsettled (NSFCT 1908 p141). A chapel, of perhaps medieval origin, stood in Chapel Wood opposite the gateway of Charnes Hall (SSGLST p31). It was probably a private chapel in origin. The building is marked on a map of 1775 and it is believed to have disappeared between 1750 and 1800. Foundations were still visible in 1814 (OSST 1949-50 p14). In the later C17 a hard slate-like marl could be found at Charnes (NHS p120). **Folklore**. In the Fairoak Broughton area Mr Oakley witnessed a flame and clouds of smoke floating across the sky coming from the direction of Charnes, at the same time a woman in Charnes Farmhouse called Mrs Cooper had hung herself (BOV pp50-51) (STM Dec 1964 p35). A curious custom took place at Charnes Farm House at Halloween known as the 'roasting competition.' It involved two sporting lads who offered themselves to be tied to two enormous spits and lowered down over a fire. The lad who shouted 'cut me down' first was the loser, while the winner's reply to the cry of surrender was 'baste me, baste me' (BOV p14). A phantom coach haunts the Charnes area (FLJ 1942 p126). The same or another reputedly drives along Dark Lane travelling to Charnes Hall where it disappears (info Bruce Braithwaite).

Charnes Bridge Weston E Vernon Yonge traced a deed which gave the lord of Charnes the right of stopping the mill at Gerrard's Bromley and fishing down the brook as far as Charnes Bridge (BPS p128).

Charnes Hall Forms the nucleus of the hamlet of Charnes and has appeared as Charnes New Hall. The Yonges are said to have established themselves at Charnes in the Middle Ages when John le Yonge married the orphan daughter of William of Charnes (BPS additional note at rear of book). The Yonges had a hall at Charnes, perhaps in the Middle Ages. The present hall was built in c1680 according to Dr Gomme (BOE p82 note), with additions of 1720 and 1800 (BOV p10,64-65il). The hall is reputedly haunted by the wife of a Yonge, who is said to have lived in the later C17 and who, when young, was thought to have died after an illness. Shortly after the funeral her grave in Chapel Wood, opposite the hall entrance, was robbed and a ring taken from her finger. She had in fact been buried alive and was revived when her finger was cut off. After death in old age she returned as a ghost to look for the ring. The rustling and sight of her silk shroud in the hall and grounds is why the ghost is called 'Silkie.' Rev WE Vernon Yonge was told that the thief was the family coachman. (BPS pp136-137) (BOV pp14-15) (STM Dec 1964 p35) (BEV pp39-40) (VB p157) (STMSM Jan 1977 p15) (MR p120) (TB April 1993 pp5) (SSGLST pp30-31) (GLS pp109-110) (SMM p53). However, the story was only orally passed through generations of Yonges (STMSM Jan 1977 p15) and may have different versions and not even be true. A slightly different version is that the story occurred in c1711 and the wife was only laid out for burial in Charnes chapel near the hall and here the coachman stole the ring from her. Shortly after her husband noticed her at the window calling to him 'I am so cold husband let me in' (info Bruce Braithwaite). In c1810 the hall was let to a retired colonel, to whose young bride a tragic event occurred. She was brought back to Charnes from the wedding. At Eccleshall her horse bolted and she fell. Her foot caught in the stirrup and she was dragged behind it all the way to Pershall Bank and arrived at Charnes a corpse (BPS pp137-138). Her ghost reputedly haunts the area of Eccleshall where she fell, known as Washpit (info Bruce Braithwaite); Edward Drakeford (d1814) was of Charnes Hall (mem in St Mary's church, Stafford). The Yonges were succeeded by relations known as the Vernon-Yonges. In 1898 a flag flying at the hall to celebrate the golden wedding anniversary of the parents of Rev WE Vernon-Yonge, author of BPS (mem in Madeley church) (EOP p56p) (MR p120p), sunk to half-mast for no clear reason. Later it was revealed their son had been accidentally killed in Durban, S Africa at that very time (BPS p136). Rev WE Vernon-Yonge also noted on a document at the hall the seal of Edward I, in dark green wax (BPS p126). In 1916 the hall was bought by the Hall family who were still living there in 1987. It was a girls' boarding school for some of WW2 (EOP p56). In the walled garden is an old summer house in which many a play was acted (BOV p10). A noble yew tree which was the meeting place of several pairs of lovers between 1840-48 (BOV p10).

Charnes Old Hall Is 0.25m E of Charnes. The old hall, surrounded by a moat (CAMS p63), was pulled down in c1890 when reputed to be over 500 years old (BOV pp9,10 il). The present house is on or near the site.

Charnes Park Park S of Charnes.

Charnes Well Charnes. Vernon Yonge says it was timed to be running two and a half gallons per minute during the late drought. Last February (1910?) it was running five gallons (BPS p149 note).

Charnwood At Netherstowe, Lichfield.

Chartley Former manor and extremely dispersed hamlet in undulating country on Amerton Brook N and NE of Stowe-by-Chartley. In Stowe ancient parish. The manor of Certelie is recorded as held by the king in DB (SSE 1996 p12). Later forms are: Certelea (1192), and Cerdel (1199) (SPN p32). The name appears to be of Anglo-Saxon origin and means 'Ceort's lea' (DUIGNAN). Or 'rough pasture land' (SSE 1996 p12) (SPN p32). Or perhaps represents the forest-root 'ceirt' (NSFCT 1908 p139). The manor had passed to the Earl of Chester by the late C11. An Earl of Chester built Chartley Castle (see) and obtained a charter on Sept 26 1221 to hold a market at Chartley on Thursdays. The market had ceased by 1500 (NSJFS 1971 p50). In the lord's park, Chartley Park (see), roamed the famous Chartley Wild Cattle. There was a medieval village at SK 006285, to the WNW of Chartley Castle (SSAHST 1966 p49. 1970 p34), or to the E of the castle's outer bailey, where earthworks have been found (SN Aug 9 1991 p9). It was deserted between 1524-1666 (SSAHST 1966 p49. 1970 p34). There was a station at Chartley on the Stafford & Uttoxeter Railway line. A train carrying huntsmen, horses, and hounds of the Meynell Hunt from Derby to Ingestre and Weston derailed at Chartley on March 30 1882 killing some horses (S&UR pp15,16-17). Chartley station closed to passengers in 1939. A platform shelter was still remaining in situ in 1993 (info Hixon Local History Society). In Broad Leasows near Chartley an oak and an ash grew intertwined in the later C17 (NHS p213).

Chartley Castle On Castle Hill, 1m NNE of Stowe-by-Chartley, formerly in Chartley Holme. Possibly built on the site of a Bronze Age settlement for two stone axe-hammers, a stone axe, a Bronze palstave and a mace head have been found in the vicinity (NSFCT 1959 p86). Chartley belonged to the Earls of Chester by the end of the C11 (CAMS p17), and the castle was built by Ranulph 'de Blundeville' (d1232), Earl of Chester in the c1220s.

THE D' AVRANCHES, DE BLUNDEVILLES, FERRERS. **Hugh 'd' Avranches'** (d1101), was created Earl of Chester of the County Palatine of Chester, and acquired Leek manor in the later C11; his illegitimate daughter, Geve, founded Canwell Priory (see). He was succeeded by his son **Richard 'd' Avranches'** (d1120), Earl of Chester. The title then passed through his aunt, Margaret, to her son **Ranulph 'le Meschin'** (died c1129), Earl of Chester. He was succeeded by his son **Ranulph 'De Gernon'** (d1153/4), Earl of Chester, probable refounder of Trentham Priory (see), and possible builder of Newcastle-under-Lyme Castle (see). He was succeeded by his son **Hugh 'of Kevelioc'** (b1147), who died in 1180-1 at Leek, or perhaps more precisely at the Earl's hunting-lodge at Swythamley (see). He was succeeded by his son **Ranulph (or Randolf or Randall) 'de Blundeville,'** (or 'the Good' - SCSF p123) (born c1172), Earl of Chester, and founder of Dieulacres Abbey (see). On Ranulph's death in 1232 the earldom of Chester lapsed to the Crown. It was recreated for Ranulph's nephew **John 'le Scot'** (born c1207), Earl of Huntingdon and Cambridge. On his death in 1237 the earldom of Chester was annexed to the Crown. The Earls' Staffs estates had covered a vast area of NE Staffs. They had used Earls Way (see), a route through the Moorlands, to travel between their estates in Ches and Derbys, and they may have also used another route over Gun Hill known as Trussway (see); they may have also had constructed Turner's Pool (see) near Swythamley. Chartley Castle and other estates passed on the death of Ranulph (d1232) to his sister Agnes, who married **William de Ferrers** (d1247), 4th Earl of Derby. For the ancestors of the 4th Earl see Tutbury Castle. The 4th Earl was succeeded by his son **William de Ferrers** (d1254), 5th Earl of Derby, who was succeeded by his son **Robert de Ferrers** (c1239-c1279), 6th Earl of Derby, who founded Newborough (see), and fought against the king in the Barons' Wars. He was captured at the battle of Chesterfield (1266) (DNB), taken prisoner, forfeited

his title, and, for a while, Chartley Castle, and other lands including Needwood Forest (see). He was succeeded by his son Sir **John Ferrers** (1271-1312), who was created baron by writ in 1299, becoming 1st Lord Ferrers. He was succeeded by his son **John de Ferrers** (d1324), 2nd Lord Ferrers, who was succeeded by his brother Sir **Robert de Ferrers** (1309-1350), 3rd Lord Ferrers. He was succeeded by his son Sir **John de Ferrers**, 4th Lord Ferrers, who was slain at the battle of Najera in 1367. He was succeeded by his son Sir **Robert de Ferrers** (d1412/3), 5th Lord Ferrers, who was succeeded by his son Sir **Edmund de Ferrers** (d1435), 6th Lord Ferrers, who was succeeded by his son Sir **William de Ferrers** (d1450), 7th Lord Ferrers. He was succeeded by his daughter **Anne** (c1438-1468/9), Lady of Chartley, who married **Walter Devereux** in 1446. Walter was created Lord Ferrers in 1461 and slain at the battle of Bosworth Field in 1485. He was succeeded by his son **John Devereux** (d1501), 2nd Lord Ferrers, who was succeeded by his son **Walter Devereux**, 3rd Lord Ferrers, who feuded with Edward Aston of Haywood Hall (see), and died at Chartley in 1558 and was buried at Stowe-by-Chartley. He was succeeded by his grandson, **Walter Devereux**, 4th Lord Ferrers, son of Sir Richard Devereux (d1547). The 4th Lord was created Earl of Essex in 1572. He died in Dublin in 1576, reputedly poisoned by Robert (Dudley), Earl of Leicester, with whom his wife, Lettice (nee) Knollys, was allegedly having an affair; however, others think he died of dysentery. Lettice, who married the Earl of Leicester in 1578, was 'the little western flower' on whom 'the bolt of cupid fell' in Shakespeare's 'Midsummer Night's Dream;' she died at Drayton Bassett Manor House (see) in 1634 (The Complete Peerage). The 1st Earl of Essex was succeeded by his son **Robert Devereux** (b1566), 2nd Earl of Essex and 5th Lord Ferrers. He appears to have resided at Chartley Old Hall with his mother until the age of ten (DNB). He became the celebrated favourite of Elizabeth I and was beheaded and attainted in 1600/1. He was succeeded by his son **Robert Devereux**, 6th Lord Ferrers, who was styled Viscount Hereford until 1604 when he was restored to the titles of Earl of Essex (1572) (becoming 3rd Earl of Essex), Viscount Hereford (1550), Lord Ferrers (1299), and Lord Bourchier (1348). He was a parliament general in the Civil War and died without issue in 1646 (HOS p20) or in 1647 (SHOS vol 2 p8). He was succeeded by his youngest sister **Dorothy**, sometime resident at Weston Hall (see), Weston-on-Trent. By her marriage to Sir Henry Shirley, 2th Bt, of Staunton Harold, Leics, in 1615, she took Chartley to the Shirleys. Staunton Harold and Chartley descended through her eldest son Sir **Charles Shirley**, 3rd Bt, who died unmarried in 1646, to her second son Sir **Robert Shirley** (d1656), 4th Bt. His eldest son Sir Seymour Shirley (d1667), 5th Bt, succeeded to Staunton Harold, whilst Chartley passed to the second son, Sir **Robert Shirley** (1650-1717), 7th Bt. Sir Robert (d1717) was probably the Shirley who exploited the salt reserves at Shirleywich (see). He was created Lord Ferrers in 1677 and 1st Earl Ferrers in 1711. It is said he has been the most prolific peer of all time. By his first wife, Elizabeth (nee Washington) (d1693), he had 17 children (10 sons and seven daughters), and by his second wife Selina (nee Finch) (d1762) he had 10 children (five sons and five daughter), making a total of 27 legitimate children. In addition he fathered 30 illegitimate children (GBR 1970 p181). The son of Sir Seymour (d1667), 5th Bt, Sir Robert Shirley (d1668/9), 6th Bt, was the father of Hon Robert Shirley (d1699). By his marriage to Anne Ferrers of Tamworth Castle (see), the junior line of the Ferrers of Groby, and Tamworth Castle were united with the representatives of the senior line of the Ferrers of Chartley. Their descendents succeeded to the barony of Ferrers, whilst Chartley and the earldom of Ferrers passed to the younger son of Sir Robert (d1717) by his first marriage, **Washington Shirley** (1677-1729), who became 2nd Earl Ferrers. He was succeeded by his brother, **Henry Shirley** (1691-1745), 3rd Earl, who was succeeded by his nephew **Laurence Shirley** (b1720), 4th Earl, son of Laurence, fourth son of Sir Robert (d1717). The 4th Earl was executed in 1760 for the murder of his steward, a man named Johnson. He was succeeded by his brother **Washington Shirley** (1722-1778), 5th Earl, who was succeeded by his brother **Robert Shirley** (1723-1786), 6th Earl, who was succeeded by his son **Robert Shirley** (1756-1827), 7th Earl. He is said to have purchased Mount Pavilion (see) near Colwich, and was succeeded by his brother **Washington Shirley** (1760-1842), 8th Earl. His son Robert William Shirley, Viscount Tamworth, died in 1830 leaving a son **Washington Sewallis Shirley** (1822-1859), who on the death of his grandfather became 9th Earl (The Complete Peerage) (Burke's Peerage). Whilst under a private tutor at Austrey, Warws, Washington Sewallis, aged 17, is alleged to have formed a relationship with a girl called Mary Elizabeth Smith, aged 14, whose family lived at Austrey. On Jan 1 1844 the Earl is supposed to have promised to marry Mary. In 1845 she instituted a suit for breach of promise against him. At the hearing lasting four days in Feb 1846 at Westminster Hall the Solicitor-General produced on her behalf a series of ardent love-letters purporting to be by him. The judge found the letters to be fabrications, possibly written by Mary Smith herself, and dismissed the case (SA Feb 21 1846 pp2,4) (Proceedings upon the Trial of the Action Brought by Mary Elizabeth Smith Against The Right Hon Washington Sewallis Shirley Earl Ferrers etc 1846 - copy in WSL). According to Masefield, who describes the case as one of the most extraordinary legal actions on record, the case cost the Earl nearly £5000 (LGS p108). From her residence at Syerscote Manor (see) Mary published in 1846 a pamphlet defending her actions. Washington Sewallis was succeeded in 1859 by his son **Sewallis Edward Shirley** (1847-1912), 10th Earl, who sold Chartley to Sir William Congreve in 1907. Sir Geoffrey Congreve, Bt sold Chartley Hall in 1939 to Alfred G Johnson, of the pottery manufacturing family (ES March 10 1939 p1p). AH Johnson was the owner of Chartley Hall in 1965 (HOS p21) (CAMS p19).

THE CASTLE. The earthworks of the present castle probably date back to the 1090s (CAMS p17). In 1191-2 the castle was repaired and garrisoned by the Crown. The bulk of the present (ruined) castle - the stone keep and bailey curtain walls and towers - were built in c1220 by Ranulph 'de Blundeville' (d1232) (NHS p447) (NSFCT 1886 p36. 1905 pp143-149 pl v shows plan) (HOS p20) (CAMS p17). The builder of the castle is said to have put the cross in the masonry in the first turret E of the keep to show it was the work of a Crusader (LGS p107) (SOSH pp96,97 plan,98). During the Barons' Wars, in 1263, forces under William la Zouche, Justiciar of Chester, and David, brother of Llewelyn, Prince of Wales captured the castle (SIS p22). On the defeat of Robert de Ferrers at the battle of Chesterfield in 1266 Henry III gave the castle to his younger son Edmund, but Robert seized it back at night and held it until dispossessed by the king's forces. Edward I returned the castle to Robert in 1274 (CAMS p17). It became Devereux property in 1461; by which time it had been abandoned in favour of the moated mansion immediately to the W (HOS p20). In 1515 or 1545 Leland visited the castle, by which time it was a ruin (CAMS pp17p,18 plan,19). In the early C19 Pitt visited it and thought the ruins would remind the reflecting observer of the description of the Hall of Ossian (THS p309). It was visited by the British Archaeological Society on the fifth day of their 52nd Congress which met in N Staffs in Aug 1895 (SK pp202-203). (DoE II*. AM). (SD p29) (SOS p56) (SSC p134 in the intro) (GNHS p113) (HOU pp333-334) (HS pp94,95 pl) (Chartley Earthworks and Castle. Alex Scrivener. 1895) (SHC 1909 pp181-183 note) (SC p29) (S p85p) (MOS p179) (SHC vol 12 New Series 1909 pp176-183) (S pp85p,86) (ES June 12 1935 p6p) (STM Oct 1964 pp40p,41. May 1971 pp26,27ps) (NSJFS 1966 p43) (VB p137) (BOE p96) (SGS p79p) (MR pp88ps,89) (SN Aug 9 1991 p9p. May 28 1993 p12) (SLM May June 1992 p19) (SPJD pp28pc,29il,30p,31p).

Chartley Hall Ancient seat of the Devereux family, formerly in Chartley Holme. Supersedes Chartley Castle (see) and has descended with the owners of Chartley Castle. The first hall was embattled and probably built in the mid C15 (CAMS p17). In summer 1575 Elizabeth I was entertained here, by her cousin Lettice (nee) Knolly, wife of the 1st Earl of Essex (SMC p164) (LGS p107) (R&S pp23-24) (Stafford Post June 8 1989 p4). **Mary, Queen of Scots** (1542-1587), brought from Tutbury Castle (see), was confined here from Dec 1585 to Sept 1586 when she was transferred to Fotheringhay (SOSH p186) (CAMS p19); although some imply she was held prisoner in the castle (VB p137). The owner of the hall at the time was Robert Devereux (b1566), 2nd Earl of Essex and 5th Lord Ferrers. He was not consulted about, nor consented to, Mary's imprisonment at the hall, and her imprisonment here annoyed him (DNB). Once at the hall Mary began to receive letters from her supporters and was able to reply to them via the French embassy in London; some from the Pope (SMC p170). The letters were smuggled in and out in beer casks through a brewer from Burton upon Trent. Unbeknown to Mary her correspondence was being intercepted by agents, one of whom was Gilbert Giffard of Chillington Hall (see), of Sir Francis Walsingham, working for Elizabeth I. During her time at Chartley Mary received correspondence from Anthony Babington (1561-1586), a Derbys squire with Catholic sympathies (and is said to have married a Draycott of Paynsley Hall), who had fallen under Mary's influence while a page in the household of Lord Shrewsbury at Sheffield, about a plot to murder Elizabeth I and rescue her. Her positive reply was evidence Walsingham needed to incriminate her in Elizabeth I's eyes (UTR pp95-98) (ROT pp55-56). Towards the end of her time at Chartley Mary spent the period between Aug 8 and 28 1586 at Tixall Old Hall (NSFCT 1886 p35), so her apartments could be searched to implicate her in what has become known as the Babington Plot (SPJD pp32-33il). In order to lure her away from the hall so neither she nor her servants would suspect anything, Sir Amyas Paulet, her custodian, is said to have invited her to hunt in Chartley Park. In the park a force to escort her to Tixall appeared to her in surprise at the Queen's Oak (see) (info Tim Moss of Hixon Local His-

tory Society). Mainly on the evidence of copies of these letters, Mary was brought to trial in 1586. Babington was executed for treason. The story of her imprisonment is told in Charlotte Yonge's novel 'Unknown to History' (SOSH p186 note) and in a play 'The Axe Must Fall' (c1994) by Harry Wilson, first staged by Stafford Players at the Gatehouse, Stafford in April 1998 (info Harry Wilson). (SHOS vol 1 part 1 p51) (SOS p55) (TOS p53) (GNHS p142) (LGS pp107-108,126,235) (KES pp63-64) (VCH vol 2 p243) (CE pp55-56 note 2) (Reign of Elizabeth. JB Black. pp328-329). A chair cover and curtains said to have been embroidered by Mary were at the hall in the mid C19. Also at the hall were one of the patten horse shoes supposed to have been worn by the horse which conveyed her in one of her attempts to escape, for the purpose of misleading her pursuers (W p422). Robert Devereux, 3rd Earl of Essex, was the parliamentary commander-in-chief for some of the **Civil War**. Immediately after losing the battle of Hopton Heath the parliamentarian commanders Sir John Gell and Sir William Brereton retired to Chartley Hall where, next day, they entered into negotiations with the royalists. Gell and Brereton sought captured cannon and ammunition in return for the Earl of Northampton's body, but no exchange took place (BFS pp7,18). In c1680 Plot noted a wooden shuffleboard table at the hall which was 10 yards one foot and one inch long and compiled of 260 pieces (NHS p383) (SD pp55,56). The hall was accidentally destroyed by fire in 1781 (SOS p56) (HOU pp333-334) (CAMS p19) or 1782 (NSFCT 1886 p35). A drawing was made of it in 1837 (NSFCT 1976 p20). The next house on the site was destroyed by fire in 1847 (W p422). An early Victorian country house, which still stands, was built on W side of the moated platform (CAMS p19) (Stafford Post June 8 1989 p4p). Its cellars are said to be part of the dungeons of the original C15 manor house (NSFCT 1976 p20). (ESH p58) (AWM p13 - could relate to Chartley Manor).

GROUNDS. A curious fountain is depicted in front of the hall that is depicted in NHS p338 tab 5. The 90 metre square moat surrounding the first hall survives and the present hall stands in the SW corner, 0.25m NE, at Daffodil Wood, is a second moat which is smaller (CAMS pp19,63). It possibly surrounded the residence of a younger son, steward or park-keeper (SPJD p32). A looped bronze palstave was found in a stream bank to the S of Chartley Hall in the C19 (NSJFS 1962 p30. 1964 p37). In the later C17 Plot noted an oak and an ash intertwined in Broad Leasow near Chartley (NHS p213).

Chartley Holme Former extra-parochial liberty (W p422) owing to its wild, physical aspect - no village community ever sought to bring it within its boundaries (NSFCT 1913 p62). It roughly coincided with the bounds of 'old' Chartley Park (SL p121) and contained Chartley Castle and Hall. It was a separate civil parish between 1858 and 1934 when it entered Stowe ancient parish (GLAUE p407).

Chartley Manor S side of Stafford-Uttoxeter road, 1.25m NE of Stowe-by-Chartley. Built in the C17 and formed a part of the Chartley Hall estate until sold in 1904. Thomas Armett is recorded as living here in 1912 and 1940 (KD 1912. 1940). In 1997 the house belonged to Mr and Mrs Jeremy Allen (TRTC p206p). (MR pp89p,90) (AWM p13 - could relate to Chartley Hall). Has also appeared as Chartley Manor House or Manor Farm. A large prehistoric axe-hammer was found near the house in 1851, and possibly another has been found here, both went to the Potteries Museum (Leics Arch Soc Trans vol 1 p134) (Proceedings of the Prehistoric Society vol 25 p139) (NSJFS 1962 p28. 1964 p36).

Chartley Moss Large bog nearly 1.5m ENE of Stowe-by-Chartley. To the W of Anglesey Coppice (6 inch OS map 1884). Covers 104 acres (SMM p51). Formed in a glacial hollow created in the Ice Age (SN Feb 14 1997 p16). The moss is claimed to be Britain's largest Schwingmoor bog (Geographical Magazine. 65 (4) April 1993 pp17-19) and one of only two of its type in Britain (ES July 14 1995) (TRTC p188). In it is a pool 70 feet deep with floating layers of peat and moss three metres thick (SMM p51). Any tree which grows here becomes unstable after reaching a certain height and collapses. The moss is shown on Yates' map. The earlier less reliable Bowen's map suggests the moss lay within the park of Chartley Castle (WSS p112). In WW2 a German bomber dropped an incendiary bomb on the Moss and set a part of it on fire for three weeks (TRTC p20). The moss became a Nature Reserve of the Nature Conservancy Council in 1963 (MR pp90,91 ps) (TRTC pp185,186-187) and is a Ramsar site (SN Feb 14 1997 p16) (WSS p98). (NSFCT 1886 p38). In late Feb 1994 a light aircraft carrying mail from Edinburgh to Coventry crashed in woodland near Stowe-by-Chartley killing the pilot, Beau Winter-Myers, but not the co-pilot, Raymond Cole, who planned in June 1994 to plant a tree and erect a memorial plaque at the site of the crash (ES Feb 26 1994 pp3p. June 30 1994 p16. May 18 1996) (Uttoxeter Post and Times. March 4 1994) (SN March 4 1994. Dec 30 1994 p10p) (TRTC p191). A ghostly apparition of a huntsman with a pack of hounds has often been seen riding over the moss. Over the centuries many people have been lost in the moss. A bulldozer and a railway engine are believed to have sunk into the moss (SMM p51) (TRTC p201).

Chartley Out-woods Neighbouring forest or and park to Chartley Moss.

Chartley Park Old deer park enclosed in c1248 out of Needwood Forest (NSFCT 1886) and certainly in existence by 1279 (NSJFS 1962 p76. 1964 p63). It appears to have been the hunting ground of the de Ferrers and their successors at Chartley Castle and Hall. It was circular in shape and stretched to within 0.5m E of Gayton and 0.5m W of Gratwich and 1m N of, and from, Chartley Castle. In the C16 Leland noted 'the Mighty large park' of Chartley, and Erdeswick observed it. The W and S parts were disparked in the late C17 or C18 (SL p121). (SHC 1909 p183 note). The park remaining is marked on OS map 1834. Its extent in 1867 was about 900 acres (EDP p177). There may have been a Bronze Age settlement in the park or in its vicinity (NSFCT vol 94 p85), but there is no evidence for this (NSJFS 1964 p37). Two magnificent axes (of prehistoric origin?) were found in the park in the mid C19 (NSFCT 1950 p86). A large stone axe of Neolithic or Bronze Age was found in Oak Wood NW of Chartley Park at SK 006316 in Sept 1956 (NSJFS 1962 p26. 1964 p23). A flat, medium sized macehead was found at Masons Farm near Chartley Park in c1918 (NSJFS 1962 p31. 1964 p37). Redfern records a Roman camp and pottery from the park (HOU 1886 p437), but no confirmation of this can now be made (NSJFS 1964 p37). Queen's Oak (see) in the N of the park may have had some association with Mary, Queen of Scots. In the later C17 Plot noted deformed red deer in Chartley Park, some having no heads at all, others being unicorns, and some of them only having one horn which was dwarfed. He thought their deformities arose from something in the soil (NHS pp259-260).

CHARTLEY WILD CATTLE. A rare breed of cattle, descendants of indigenous cattle, formerly lived in the park. They were noted for their all-white hides, black ears, muzzles and hoofs, and long horizontal horns, tipped with black, and bent upwards; slightly different in type from the kindred herds of Craven, Chillingham, Northumbria, Lyme Park, Cheshire and Cadzow, Lanarkshire (LGS p9). Berwick in his 'Quadrupeds' says the whole ear and about one third of the outside, from the tip downwards is red (HHFT p401). The Chartley herd, possibly descendants of prehistoric British aurochs, were perhaps driven from Needwood Forest into Chartley Park by one of the Earls of Derbys in the C13 (MR p90) (VB p138) (HOS 1998 p94). Some say they were introduced to the forest or park from the Continent by the Romans (LGS p10), or were introduced by the Anglo-Saxons in the C6 (SOSH pp118,199p). Scarratt noted there were about 30 in the herd in c1870. The herd numbered 53 in 1898 (LGS p9). The herd were hit by tuberculosis in c1900. The eight survivors were bought by the Duke of Bedford and taken to Woburn Abbey, Beds, in 1905 (S p37) (LGS p10) and had to be crossed with the domestic Longhorn (SL p70) in order for the breed to continue. There is a stuffed Chartley bull at the Ferrers present seat, Ditchingham Hall, Norfolk; it was for many years at their old seat at Staunton Harold, Leics (Bricks and Flowers. Katherine Everitt. c1950). In 1994 Earl Ferrers was supplying the breed's beef to the Savoy Hotel, London (CL March 3 1994 pp36-37). Recently (1999), the owners of Chartley have restored some of the breed to Chartley Park (LTD p124). (SHOS vol 1 part 1 p92) (GNHS pp113, 241) (W p422) (NHT) (BCGB p366) (EDP p177) (NSFCT 1886 pp32-34, 36-37. 1896 pp44-46) (MOS pp186-190p) (OTP pp27,31) (LGS pp9, 10p) (SPP p33p) (KES pp64, 65) (SLM Oct 1952 pp18,19p from 1891) (VB p138) (HB p123) (SL p70) (AR p24p in 1923) (MR p90). **Beliefs.** The long-held belief in the families that have held Chartley Castle (see) is that a black calf born in the herd portends a death in the family (FLJ 1896 p385) or, and, some disaster will befall them. A black calf was born prior to: i) Robert de Ferrers' defeat at the battle of Chesterfield in 1266: ii) the decease of Robert Shirley, 7th Earl Ferrers, in 1827, and of his Countess - perhaps his first wife Elizabeth Prentise d1799, or his second wife Elizabeth Mundy: iii) the decease of his son, Robert Sewallis Shirley, Viscount Tamworth (d1824): iv) the decease of the 7th Earl's daughter, Mrs William Joliffe, perhaps Julia-Anne, died Nov 23 1825: v) the decease of the 8th Earl's son and heir, Washington Sewallis Shirley, died March 13 1859: vi) the decease of the 8th Earl's daughter, Lady Frances Shirley (d1834): vii) the decease of the 8th Earl's second wife, Sarah Davy, in spring 1835 (Staffordshire Chronicle July 1835, 1842) (HHFT pp401,402) (FG pp25-27) (HE p161) (FSP p94) (STM May 1971 pp26,27) (FOS p72).

Chase Ward in Huntington civil parish.

Chaseley Large stucco house, on N side of Chaseley Road, Etching Hill, 1m WSW of Rugeley. It was still standing in its own grounds in the 1950s. The house formerly had a symmetrical late-Georgian front. The house under another name was the Rugeley parish workhouse until 1841 (VCH vol 5 p151). The name means 'the wood of (Cannock) Chase' (SPNO p107).

Chasepool Chasepool today is represented by the pool of Swindon and by Chasepool Farm (formerly Chasepool Lodge (see)) at SO 855898 0.75m NW of Greensforge (NSFCT 1952 p36). In Wombourne ancient parish. At Chasepool Farm has been found pottery of the late C2 (West Midlands Arch News Sheet vol 15 p18) (VCH vol 20 p197). The name means probably 'Catt's pool or Catte's pool' (DUIGNAN) (SSE 1996 p12) (SPN p70). Chasepool has been identified with the waste known as Catspelle or Capspelle (unlocated) recorded in DB. At Chasepool was possibly a medieval village, probably deserted sometime after 1086 (SSAHST 1970 p34).

Chasepool Common Seems to have been synonymous with Chasepool Hay and lay W of Smestow Brook. On the common is the site of a Roman marching camp; it is different to that at Greensforge (Salop Arch Soc Trans vol 56 p237) (VCH vol 20 p197). Enclosure of the common took place from 1624, but most of it was enclosed by an Act in 1796 and the final bit was enclosed in 1825 (VCH vol 20 p210).

Chasepool Hay Swindon. Formerly one of the hays, or divisions or deer enclosures of Kinver Forest (NSJFS 1968 p40 fig 3) (SL p68). The custody of the hay became hereditary in the Dudley family from the later C15 (VCH vol 2 p346). The area seems to have become the later Chasepool Common.

Chasepool Lodge Chasepool. Called Chasepool Farm by 1980 (OS map 1:50,000). It was occupied by a Mr Parker, who was poisoned to death with White Mercury on April 6 1808 by his coachman William Hawkeswood (TB Feb 1975 pp4-5. Dec 1981 p23. Sept 1998 p25).

Chase Terrace Large village over 1.25m WNW of Burntwood. The area anciently lay in Cannock Forest and later was farm and common land. Chase Terrace a hamlet in the out-township of St Michael's parish, Lichfield, had come into existence by 1870 to house miners and continued to expand (VCH vol 14 p201). The church, St John, High Street, was rebuilt in 1997 (LDD). A house in Stamford Road was once haunted by three ghosts, one a young lady, and the others, a young couple (GOM p28).

Chasetown Large village over 1.5m WSW of Burntwood. The area anciently lay in Cannock Forest and later was farm and common land until the mid C19. A map of 1820 shows that much of the land was owned by the Marquess of Anglesey. There were no houses in the area except one called Lamb Lodge. The beginnings of Chasetown began six months after a coal mine was opened near Chasewater in 1849 with the manager of the pit a Mr Landor recommending the construction of houses for the overlooker and underlooker and a few miners cottages, which appear to have been built in the Church Street area. By 1855 the present 'Bleak House,' a house for the manager had also been built. By 1861 there were houses at the Triangle and Paviers Row (demolished by 1980) (LGS p109) (VCH vol 14 p199) (SL p118) (LHSB 38. p58) (MR p91); that year land at Chasetown was enclosed (PCC p16). At first the village, then in Burntwood out-township of St Michael's parish, Lichfield, was known as the village of Cannock Chase but by 1867 it was known as Chasetown (VCH vol 14 p199). That year the village became a separate ecclesiastical parish (GLAUE p407). The **name** was thought of between c1849 and 1867 and literally means 'the town on the chase' (SPN p32). It was reputedly devised by George Poole, vicar of Burntwood and his wife. It has been said that Elijah Wills, master of the boys' department at the school from 1863, was the first to describe the area as Chasetown (Found Ready. Mason p48) (LHSB 38. p58) (BCM vol 9 No. 2 p26) (VCH vol 14 p199). The **church**, St Anne, Church Street, was built in 1865 (BOE p96). It claims to be the first church in the country to be lit by electricity. Electricity was supplied from The Fly pit (see) in 1883. The device installed in 1938 to make the church bell ring electrically is also claimed to be the first in the country (Lichfield Mercury Oct 15 1886 p5) (BCM vol 9 No. 3 pp5-57) (VCH vol 14 p222). The **'Chase Wakes'** originated in the wakes at Chasetown held to celebrate the opening of St Anne's church in September 1865. By 1883 the wakes had been changed to a date in August. The wakes ceased in 1959 and were revived in 1970 and were still continuing in the mid 1980s (VCH vol 14 p203). For a fire breathing world record set at Chasetown see the Miner's Rest Inn. **Persons. Patsy Kilgariff**, coal miner, workers political activist at the end of the C19 and a character known as the 'King of Cannock Chase' was a large man of Chasetown of Irish origin. He was a heckler and verbally abused Joseph Chamberlain at an election rally. At political meeting and elections he would hold aloft a silken banner inscribed with the names of GLADSTONE. SWINBURNE. FULFORD. WARNER. KILGARIFF (CCF pp129-134). In 1902 a clock was erected at the junction of High Street and Queen Street as a memorial to those killed in the Boer War. It was knocked down in 1967, and was replaced by a new clock in 1969. This was damaged in 1979, and there was no clock here in the mid 1980s (VCH vol 14 p201). **Tom Langley**, author of many books on pugilist fighters including the Tipton Slasher (1970), educated at Lichfield Grammar School, was born in Chasetown in 1907 (BCM

Jan 1974 p25). He notes his native town has a ghost (BCM April 1986 p42), and he may have been the author of 'The Darlaston Dog-fight,' see under Darlaston (Offlow hundred). **Gladys Edwards** (b1896) of Chasetown was still living in Dec 1999 (BBC 1 Midlands Today Dec 20 1999).

Chasewater Reservoir 1.25m E of Norton Canes. It was formerly a part of the extensive Norton Bog. Mining operations caused land to sink and a pool called Norton Pool was formed (SNBC p11) (PCC p67) (CCBO p69) (CCAP p36p) (BWWOPP p16ps). Or the pool was formed, probably by the damming of Crane Brook, as a canal reservoir in c1798 (VCH vol 14 p258), or made in 1800 by the Birmingham Canal Company (BHT). It was enlarged on various occasions up to 1905 (HCMS No. 2). Covers 260 acres (LHSB No. 38 p26). The pool has appeared as Cannock Chase Reservoir (English Reservoirs. Bill Howes. 1967 p56) and Cannock Reservoir (HCMS No. 2). Rev Charles Lewton Brain (1863-1919) wrote his 'Elegy on Norton Pool' whilst vicar of Chasetown, a post he held from 1897 (PSS p477). Leslie Thompson, aged 19, Edward Swindells, aged 8, Samuel Booth and his son, Roy, aged 5, all drowned after a boat capsized in Norton Pool in 1939 (ES Aug 8 1939 p1). In 1956 the pool, having been taken over by Brownhills urban district council, was renamed Chasewater and opened to the public (VCH vol 14 p204). Chasewater Light Railway runs from Chasetown over the N end of Chasewater to Brownhills West. The Society which runs it was founded in 1959 and is the third oldest preservation group in Britain (STMSM Sept 1980 p43ps). The British record for harness racing against time (trotting in one mile) was set at Chasewater on June 21 1975 when Ted Trot driven by John Blisset achieved 2 minutes 06.8 seconds. The British record for harness racing against time (pacing in one mile) was set at Chasewater on July 7 1975 when Bomber driven by Thomas Brown achieved 2 minutes 04.3 seconds (GBR 1981 p286).

Chatcull Tiny village on a shelf of land between Bromley Brook and a tributary of Brockton Brook 1.25m ENE of Charnes. Former township in Cotes quarter in Eccleshall ancient parish. Ceterville is recorded as waste in DB. Later Chatcull appears as Chatculne (1199) (SSE 1996 p12), Chatulum (1344), Chatkyll (1490) (RHPS p128), often Chatkill up to the C20 (NSFCT 1916 p58), and Chat-kilne (SHC 1914 p22). After the name appears as Ceterville (from Old French) in DB Chatcull seems to have reverted back to its Anglo-Saxon name. Chat representing the personal name Ceadd or Ceadda. And for the ending, Anglo-Saxon 'cyln' or Middle English 'culne' meaning a kiln, so 'Chad's kiln,' perhaps a lime-kiln (DUIGNAN), or 'Ceatta's kiln,' a kiln probably for smelting iron (SSE 1996 p12) (SPN p44). Or the prefix represents the old forest-root 'coid,' 'coed,' the Welsh 'gwydd,' the Latin 'cetum' as in the words Etocetum and Letocetum (NSFCT 1908 pp138-139). John de Harcourt held Chatcull and over 1000 acres in Podmore, Mill Meece, Great and Little Bridgeford and Seighford by service of bringing four men from Chatcull and Podmore to act as beaters to the bishop's hunt (ECC p13). These lands probably comprised the manor of Gerrard's Bromley, and its tenure custom was that the lord had to find four men three times a year to accompany the bishop when he hunted in Eccleshall Park (HOG p194). On Chatcull Green within the memory of those living in 1911 stood the parish stocks (BPS p147) (BOV p17). For Chatcull characters see BOV p17.

Chatcull (New) Hall Chatcull. Admiral John Jervis of Meaford Hall (see) stayed many times at the new Chatcull Hall, and the lamp he had on his flag ship was in the house in the early C20 (BOV p16).

Chatcull Old Hall Chatcull. Reputedly built in the mid C12 (BOV pp16-17) (BPS p147). The Jervis (formerly Gervie, Gervoyse, Jervys and other variants) family were established at Chatcull by the mid C14 (RHPS pp128,140). John Jarvys of Chatcull was succeeded by his daughter Elizabeth who married John Jervis (d1670) of Meaford and took Chatcull to the Jervis' of Meaford Hall (see) (Burke's Peerage 1879, 1967) (Accessions 8144-77/45 in WSL). The old hall is said to have been a resting place of Margaret of Anjou on her return from the battle of Blore Heath (1459) (BOV pp16-17) and Elizabeth I stayed here (BPS p147). Some of the doorways of Chatcull Old Hall are only four feet to five feet high (BOV pp16-17). There is an old print of the hall in WSL (BPS p147). The chapel in the grounds had long been taken down by 1949; but its foundations could still be seen by then. Some of the stones were reused to make a wall around the house (BOV pp16-17).

Chatterley Small hamlet in the upper Fowlea Brook valley 0.75m W of Tunstall. Former township in Wolstanton ancient parish (W p289). Chatterley was a member of Tunstall manor by c1130 (ONST 1976 p374). The name appears in 1212 as Chaderleg (SSE 1996 p12). The prefix in the name represents the Anglo-Saxon personal name Ceadd or Ceadda. Either Chad's lea or Chad's dell (dale) (DUIGNAN). Gelling gives 'wood by the hill called Cader' (SSE 1996 p20). Or 'meadow by the hill-fort' (SSE 1996 p12) (SPN p88). In the earlier C13 the tenant held the manor of Chatterley of the king for a fee and by the service of performing guard duties at Newcastle Castle (SCSF pp116-

117) (VCH vol 8 p13). The hamlet of Chatterley amounted to no more than two farms in 1843 (HBST p125).

Chatterley Hall Common name for Shelton Hall (see) built in 1782, demolished in 1959. Name is from the builders, the Chatterley brothers, Charles and Ephraim (H p136) (POTP p60). Has also appeared as Chatterley House (OTP p145).

Cheadle (locally *Chea-dal*). Ancient parish, quarter, and town 14m NNE of Stafford. The town lies at the foot of the SE side of Cheadle Park hill, a hill encircled on the W, S and E sides by several brooks and the Tean. An excellent view looking down on the town can be had from Ipstones Edge.

EARLY. A **Neolithic** or **Bronze Age** celt was found in a peat bog in Cheadle ancient parish (VCH vol 1 p181) (NSJFS 1964 p19). In the churchyard was found a fragment of decorated Samian ware of the Roman period (GM 1832 part 1. p414). Cheadle may have been on a long-distance saltway, from Nantwich to, perhaps, Derby (SL p111); malt being sent the other way (MR p93).

1000 to 1500. There was a **church** at Cheadle by 1086 (SHC 1916 p173) and certainly by the late C12. Old Cheadle church was taken down in 1837 and a new church, St Giles the Abbot, built further up the hill on the W side of Church Street (NSFCT 1933 pp68-73 ps) (The Story of Cheadle Church. WG Short. 1970). The **parish**, formed by 1086, probably originally contained the ancient parishes of Kingsley, Dilhorne, and Caverswall (SHC 1916 p194). **Beating the bounds** occurred on June 18 1763 (HOC pp52-53). By the mid C19 the parish **wake** was on the first Sunday after Sept 1 (St Giles' day) (W p754) (HOC p18). There was bull baiting at Cheadle wake in c1815 (HOC p19). Waste land belonging to the king called Cedla, and a **manor** called Cella, in DB, have been identified with Cheadle (another Cedla mentioned in DB has been identified with Checkley) (DB. Phillimore ed. John Morris. 1976). This follows CGO Bridgeman who took Celle and one of the two DB Cedlas as representing the two C13 manors of Cheadle (viz - Cheadle Bassetts and Cheadle Grange) (the other DB Cedla he identified with Checkley) (SHC 1923 pp35-40). Cheadle was identified with DB Cedla by Erdeswick and Shaw. Eyton identified Cheadle with DB Celle. Commander Wedgwood dubiously follows Eyton in identifying Celle with Cheadle, although he thinks it could be Chell, but suggests that Cheadle is not mentioned in DB, although it existed then with a church and parson. He says Cheadle parish included the manor of Kingsley (described as very large in DB) and the manor of Cheadle (if it was a manor), and that when Cheadle parish church was built a virgate was cut out of Kingsley and called Cheadle (SHC 1916 p173). Later Cheadle appears as Chelda (1166) (SHC 1923 p41), Chedele (1197) (SSE 1996 p12) and as Chedlhe Basset (SPN p33). The **name** is of Celtic origin (SL p44 note) from 'ceto' meaning woodland, with the Saxons adding 'leah' giving 'woodland clearing' (SSE 1996 p12) (SPN p33). Another possibiltiy is that it is from the personal name Ceadel (DUIGNAN). Another suggestion has been that Cheadle took its name from Cecily Brook on the E side of the town (The Story of St Giles' Parish Church. WG Short. 1970. p5). Since early forms have been Celle and Chella, another suggestion is that it shares the same forest-root as Chell, from Celtic 'coll' (NSFCT 1908 p138). It is more probably derived from the root 'coed' or 'coid' (NSFCT 1910 p162). Bassett was added in the Middle Ages in recognition of the Bassetts lords of Cheadle (NSFCT 1913 p143). Lord of Cheadle, Ralph Basset was granted a charter to hold a **market** here on Thursdays sometime between 1216-1272 (NSJFS 1971 p50). The market day was changed from Thursday to Friday in 1652 (HOC pp47,48il,49,50) (SCSF p91). By the C19 the market is recorded as occurring on Friday and sometimes on Saturday. Hackwood thinks there is probably no charter right for the Saturday market (SCSF p95). There was a market in 1792 (OWEN), and there was one in 1888 (LHE p265). Plant says the butter cross or **market cross** in the High Street is not very ancient and was probably erected when market day was changed from Thursday to Friday (HOC pp47,48il,49,50). Hackwood thinks this would be unlikely since the erection of a cross during the Commonwealth period would probably not have been allowed (SCSF p91). The cross is said to mark the division of the old or pre-C17 part of the High Street from the later development (NSFCT 1991 p53). The cross, now in its former state, was painted and being used as a lamp post by 1910 (PS p61) (LGS p109) (BOE p98) (PSM pl 95 of c1870) (SL p156). The renowned pot seller and hawker, Ned Saunterer, who lived in the C18, sold his pottery at Cheadle market (TOS pp111-113). There were **fairs** on: Jan 6 (W p754) (the 'Gayboys' or 'Gawboys' wake, a labour-hiring fair, was held on the first Friday of Jan - SJC p7), March 25 (W p754), perhaps the same as that March 28 (COOKE), Holy Thursday (COOKE) (W p754), July 5 (W p754), Aug 21 (COOKE) (W p754) or otherwise known as the 'Mellow Pear' fair (HOC p18), and Oct 18 (COOKE) (W p754). There was a fair in 1792 (OWEN), and there was one in 1888 (LHE p265). Plant noted that as well as the 'Mellow Pear' fair there were five other fairs in Cheadle (HOC p18). Close to the market cross were the **stocks** (HOC p50) (SCSF p129). There has been **coal mining** since the C12 and Cheadle gives its name to the surrounding coalfield.

1500 to PRESENT. A hoard of silver coins, chiefly of Elizabeth I's reign, were discovered in 1834, in premises in the High Street. The hoard consisted of 595 shillings and 298 sixpences, some of which were of Edward VI's reign. The find was declared treasure trove. Some of the coins went to the Potteries Museum (NSFCT 1934 p72). Items, including a shoe, clay pipes, and an unbroken egg, of C17 origin were found at 77 High Street in 1907. This house was next door to CG Sleigh's shop (SLM Oct 1947 p29p). The plague of 1665 visited Cheadle (SCSF p139). A **grammar school** was set up when Henry Stubbs of Kingsley endowed the Monkhouse School in 1685. The school was situated behind the church and Market Place (CCT pp54,177). A new building housing a school called Cheadle Grammar School opened in 1962 and closed in 1975. By 1999 the building was Moorlands Sixth Form Centre (COPP2 p20). **Societies.** Cheadle was never an incorporated town but by the late C17 it had a mock corporation (HOC p62) (N&Q April 1878) and a mock mayor (NSSG p13). The original minute book of Cheadle's mock corporation turned up in 1929 and covers the years 1699-1729. During this period the leading inhabitants chose annually a mayor who gave a dinner to the self-elected burgesses when he went out of office. It was probably formed as a Jacobite sympathisers club. After the 1715 Jacobite Rebellion the county settled down and the Cheadle corporation waned and the society became defunct (NSFCT 1929 pp52-88) (NRS p47). St Thomas' Club was a social club at Cheadle, the membership of which were confined to persons whose Christian names were Thomas. One member, Thomas Bakewell (d1835), born in Cheadle in 1761, was notable. He founded a lunatic asylum at Spring Vale (see) and wrote a poem in his collection entitled 'The Moorland Bard; or, Poetical Recollections of a Weaver in the Moorlands of Staffordshire' called 'The Oyster Eaters Disappointed' which describes how club members were disappointed to find a tub of oysters they had brought to dine on was empty (HOC p63) (PSS p113) (VFC p7). Cheadle formed its own agricultural society in 1857 after disappointment that the County Show of the SAS was not to be held at Cheadle (The History of Staffordshire Agricultural Society. Brenda Greysmith. c1978). Cheadle and District Historical Society was founded in 1951 (info Mrs Johnson). Copper working is another old **industry** of Cheadle; the copper coming from Ecton. This industry was at length transferred to Oakamoor and Froghall (NSFCT 1948 p122). Since the late C18 there has been a textile industry at Cheadle (MR p92). The **work house** in Watt Place was built in 1775 (BOE p98) (COPP2 p123p). **Roads and railway.** To the W of the town there is a toll-house on the Blythe Marsh-Calton Moor road, at Rosehill, at SK 002430. It was built by 1833 (IAS pp156-157). A toll-house at the N end of the town at the corner of Froghall Road and Leek Road, built in 1835, was demolished in March 1963 (ACOPP p108p). Authorisation for a railway to Cheadle was granted by 1878. The first sod of the line was cut on March 22 1888 (CCT pp116,118). Cheadle was finally connected to the railway system in 1901 (VCH vol 2 p319) by Cheadle Railway Company, who were taken over by NSR in 1908. The last freight train on the Cheadle branch line ran on Nov 16 1984 (COPP2 p30p of Cheadle station,33p). The station was in Station Road, S of the town centre. Augustus Welby Pugin was invited by the 16th Earl of Shrewsbury to design Cheadle's **Roman Catholic church**, St Giles, in 1837. It was built between 1841 and 1846 (Pugin's Gem. Church Guide. WG Short 1981). Pugin was free of financial stringency (BOE p97) - the building cost £40,000 (ES June 23 1994 p14) - and the result is a church with a gorgeously rich interior, with colour on every possible surface (SL p139). (W pp754-755) (HOC pp117-137 ils) (STMSM Oct 1979 pp56,57ps). Pugin described the church as 'a perfect revival of an English parish church of the time of Edward I.' Pevsner describes the W steeple as 'one of the most perfect pieces of the C19 Gothic Revival anywhere, especially the sharp spire with two sets of pinnacles' (BOE p97). The church stands in a complex comprising a school, Convent of St Joseph, and Presbytery (BOE pp97-98). **Cheadle Well** or drinking fountain bears the inscription 'The Gift of Sarah Bourne John Colclough Bourne A.D. 1879.' (DoE II) (HOC p141) (STM Nov 1964 p42p). The **pumping station** of Cheadle Water Works Company has the unique status of not being part of a surrounding Severn-Trent complex (NSFCT 1991 p53). The **earthquake** of 3.21pm July 3 1904 was felt at Cheadle (NSFCT 1905 p133). **'The Spirit of Cheadle,'** a Spitfire MK2 R7211 donated to the RAF by the people of Cheadle, came into operation on March 27 1942 but was written off following an accident on April 27 1942 (MD p78). **References to Cheadle.** Cheadle is 'Cradleby' in the fictional essay 'Gilbert Hermer' (1908) by Charles Masefield of Abbots Hay (NSFCT 1917 p107) (PSS p276). The Hartlebury-on-Dane in the novel 'The Mount' 1909

by CF Keary (d1917) may loosely refer to Burton upon Trent or to Cheadle. For a rhyme from Cheadle see FSBC p56. **Outer Cheadle.** In the later C17 Plot noted an inhabited conical house made of turf situated between Cheadle and Oakamoor (NHS p358). A little out of the town is a C17 farmhouse called the Mill House and another called Long Croft (LGS p109). The lodge to The Croft or Croft House (see) is often referred to as a roundhouse (STM May 1972 p35p) (STMSM Sept 1975 p6p. Sept 1976 p3p) (JC 21 il). **Customs and folklore.** Gooding was a St Thomas' day (Dec 21) custom at Cheadle (BCC vol 3 p205); those who made private donations to this day were thanked generally with a sprig of mistletoe (FOS p132). The custom of playing football in the main street of Cheadle was practised on Shrove Tuesday; shopkeepers put up their shutters on this day (HOC p19) (SCSF p11) (FOS p84). There was a woman of Cheadle who went to fetch some flour. On her return she was harangued by a witch who changed the flour into manure and then back to flour after she had deposited the manure in a pig-sty (FOS p38) (STMSM July 1980 p33). The custom of the Procession of Witness, involving people from the main churches of Cheadle processing through the town behind an eight-foot high cross on Good Friday, began in c1983 (ES March 31 1998 p1). A phantom coach travelling to Hales Hall has been seen in the lanes about Cheadle (TFTPM p66). **Natives and residents. John Wesley** visited Cheadle (HOC p139). **Joseph Banks** (1743-1820), naturalist and fellow voyager with Capt Cook, had property at Cheadle and once resided here. He made a voyage to Newfoundland and Labrador collecting plants. From 1768 to 1771 he sailed with Cook around the world. In 1772 he visited the Hebrides and Iceland. In 1777 he was elected President of the Royal Society and remained so to near his death. The colony of Botany Bay owes its origins mainly to Banks (HOC pp153-154). **Charles Askin**, born in Cheadle in 1788, was a self-taught metallurgist, who developed a nickel necessary for the process of electric-plating. He died and was buried on Aug 25 1847 in an extraordinary way. Whilst staying with a friend in Norway at a pastor's house when a man from the firm playfully suggested that he and his friend should stand back-to-back to see which was taller. As they stood up Mr Askin died and fell to the floor. He was buried in the village where he died. However, his friends desired that he be buried in England. The body was brought to Christiania, Norway, where it was again buried due to the on coming of winter postponing the voyage. In the spring it was again exhumed, but owing to the superstition of the sailors, who refused to sail on a vessel containing a corpse, there was considerable difficulty. At length this was overcome by extra payment. On the voyage there was storm and the ship had to be abandoned; it was brought to Yarmouth a wreck. Eventually Askin's body was buried in Edgbaston churchyard (HOC pp163-169). **Ann Spilsbury** of Cheadle (d1825) lived to the aged of 104 (HOC p171). The father of **Dr Lowe**, the celebrated physician who attended the Prince of Wales (later Edward VII) in his severe attack of typhoid fever, was a native of Cheadle and practised as a physician in the town. Dr Lowe Snr, was satirised by Thomas Bakewell, the 'Moorland Poet,' of Hall Gate Farm (see), and had died by 1881 (HOC pp169,170 il of his house). For the poet, **Samuel J Looker**, who resided at Cheadle, see Oakamoor. **Alan Keates** of Cheadle broke the record for brick lifting when he lifted 26 8.5 inch bricks of 5 lb weight horizontally in Cheadle on May 15 1984. The span was 66.5 inches and weighed 130 lb (GBR 1987 p165). Strongman **Fred Burton** of Cheadle broke the world record for step-ups doing 2,469 in 60 minutes on July 8 1995, and broke the world record for bricklifting carrying 200lb 8 oz between his outstretched arms in July 1995 (ES July 25 1995 p3p) (GBR). He broke this record on June 5 1998 when he picked up 20, weighing more than 226lb (ES June 6 1998 p1pc).

NEWSPAPERS. Cheadle's first newspaper was the **Cheadle Herald** published by Mr Machin from Sept 6 1877 (HOC p144) or Sept 8 1877 (COPP2 p112). It ran until Dec 28 1895 and then continued as the Cheadle Herald, Tean News and General Advertiser; this seems to have run until at least Dec 26 1924 (SHJ spring 1996 p17). The weekly **Cheadle and Tean Times** was founded in 1896 and still continues (SHJ spring 1996 p17). The weekly **Cheadle Post and Times** was brought out by the Leek and Post Times in 1991. Some Leek (see) and Stone (see) newspapers have Cheadle in their title.

Cheadle Brook A tributary of the Tean (SPNO p7).

Cheadle Common Former common land 1.5m SE of Cheadle, in Cheadle ancient parish. Since at least the 1950s gravel has been excavated in the Bunter Pebble Beds on the former common (CDS p72).

Cheadle Eaves Appears on the maps of Plot and Bowen to the SE of the Cheadle. In Cheadle ancient parish. Is now probably submerged into the town.

Cheadle Grange Former manor and quarter in Cheadle ancient parish which extended in a north-easterly direction from Cheadle town between the water of Bedbrook and Cecilly Brook over High Shutt as far as the Churnet (NSFCT

1913 pp142,145,146). At an early date it passed to the bishop of Lichfield but by 1245, or perhaps earlier, it came into the ownership of the Cistercian monks of Croxden Abbey (SHC 1947 p50), or it passed to the abbey in c1290 (CCT pp7-8) and was a grange of Croxden Abbey from the late C12 (VCH vol 3 p226). Has appeared as Cedla (DB), Dogge-Chedle (1275), Hundchedial (C16) (SHC 1947 p50), Hound's Cheadle, and Cheadle Grange (Plot's map): The prefix Dog or Hounds is unique in Staffs and may be in England. The Levesons acquired Cheadle Grange at the Reformation. The grange buildings were for some years in the C17 tenanted by the Crompton family until they themselves leased them in the late C17. The manor passed to the Countess of Kent, daughter of Gilbert 7th Earl of Shrewsbury, then to her legal adviser, Seldon, the antiquary, who left, in 1653, the estate to four of his friends of the Inner Temple - Edward Heyward, John Vaughan, Rowland Jewkes and Matthew Hale. The estate was officially divided into quarters in 1694. The NE quarter with its land running down to the Churnet went to John Vaughan, another quarter went to Chief Justice Hales on whose quarter Hales Hall (see) was built in the early C18 (CCT pp12,19). The approximate site of the grange may be represented by the present Lower Grange Farm, 1m to E of Cheadle.

Cheadlemoor Over 0.5m E of Cheadle parish church.

Cheadle Park Medieval deer park enclosed out of forest, 0.25m N of Cheadle parish church. In existence by 1369 (NSJFS 1962 p76). The park was 3m in circumference. By 1817 it contained 33 inclosures. From it the spires of Lichfield cathedral can be seen on a clear day, 27 miles away (THS p229) (NSFCT 1915 p161).

Cheadle Park Victorian mansion in Mill Road (unlocated), Cheadle. Built by Robert Plant, author of HOC (d1902), in c1870, behind Ebenezer Cottage. Was approached from the Tean road. Demolished in 1980/1. The mansion had also been called The Mansion (CCT pp112,120il), and there is a Mansion Close off Rakeway Road, S of the town centre.

Cheapside Central area of Willenhall. Originally formed a part of Cross Street. The name came into use in the mid C19 (SNW p16).

Cheat Hall This name once applied to a house named Spring Hill House, in Jesson Road, Walsall, when it was occupied by a lawyer. There were some who looked dubiously upon lawyers and considered them cheats (SNWA p29).

Chebsey Ancient parish and former township. The small village of Chebsey lies on low ground on E side of the Sow 5.25m NW of Stafford. According to local tradition the present church stands on the burial ground of early Christian converts, and possibly formerly a pagan burial site of the Ancient Britons. An Anglo-Saxon cross shaft with knot-work still stands in the highest point of the churchyard. The cross is said to be of C8 origin or earlier. The precincts of the present church are bounded by the Sow, and early inhabitants, in order to make the site more secure, are said to have constructed a cut or canal to create the loop into an island (Chebsey Website 2000). Early Christian missionaries are believed to have taken a thoroughfare running N to S across the swampy Sow valley at Chebsey to the preaching station (NSFCT 1919 p118): St Chad is reputed to have preached at the Saxon cross at Chebsey (NSJFS 1973 p118). A church may have been built in the Anglo-Saxon period. The present parish church, All Saints, on the W side of the road to Stafford, has work dating from between 1070 and 1170. A curious fact is that up to 1220 the Priory of St Oswald's, York, claimed rights in Chebsey church and other churches in the diocese of Canterbury (NSFCT 1908 p171). Chebsey parish formed before 1086 (SHC 1916 p195). At some time it was appropriated to the dean and chapter and certain prebendaries of Lichfield cathedral but did not come under their peculiar jurisdiction (VCH vol 3 p94 note). The manor of Cebbesio appears in DB (SSE 1996 p12). Later forms are: Chebbesee (C13), Chebbeshey (C13) (SPN p34). It has also appeared as Chebseya, Cebbesia, Chebborseye, Chebbeseye, Jebbesia, and Jeheborsey (Chebsey Website 2000). The name is from Anglo-Saxon and means 'Ceob's Island or place near water' (DUIGNAN) or 'Cebbi's island' (NSJFS 1981 p3) (SSE 1987 p32. 1996 p12), or 'Ceob's river island' (SPN p34). Another suggestion is that the original form was Jeheborsey, a compound of a personal and physical appellation, derived from Jah-Ebor, the chief deity of the Ebor-attens (Britons), and the Anglo-Saxon 'eye' meaning island, hence 'Jah-Ebor's-eye' (Chebsey Website 2000). (STM Jan 1965 pp40-41). A very heavy hail storm occurred on the Sunday before St James tide 1659 at Chebsey. The hail stones were as big as pullet eggs and brought down young apples and tore cabbage leaves from stalks so they appeared naked (NHS p23) (SD p79). The Lawrence Panting School, built in 1886, closed in 1981, has subsequently become a village community centre (Chebsey Website 2000). Thomas (Patrick) Anson (b1939) of Shugborough Hall (see), 5th Earl of Lichfield, has lived in Chebsey (Chebsey Website 2000).

Chebsey Park A medieval deer park enclosed out of forest at Chebsey. Was about 5m NW of Stafford. In existence by 1388 (NSJFS 1964 p63).

Checkhill Checkhill Farm is 3m N of Kinver, in the N of Kinver ancient parish. Marked on Morden's map. The Forest of Schecheel (see) which appears on the Staffs Pipe Roll from 1190-1 until at least the reign of Edward I has been identified with Checkhill (SHC 1925 p244) (VCH vol 2 p335 note). For the windmill at Checkhill see Spittlebrook Mill.

Checkhill Common Former waste area N of Stourton. By the C17 it was shared between the inhabitants of Stourton, and Enville and Morfe manors. All the common was enclosed by 1804. It lay in the area now covered by the wood, The Million (VCH vol 20 pp123,138).

Checkley (perhaps locally *Chetley*, see below) Ancient parish and village on a bank on the E side of the Tean 12m NE of Stafford, formerly in Tean division of the ancient parish.

EARLY. An irregular discoidal macehead was found in c1909 during the construction of a barn at Checkley and kept for many years by a shop keeper in Uttoxeter. After his death his wife sold it to an unknown person and all trace of it has now been lost (NSJFS 1962 p31. 1964 p19).

600 to 1500. There is a tradition that St Bertram preached at Checkley (STM Feb 1965 p40). Dr Whitaker in his 'History of Whalley' (p35) contends that Checkley is the place where the Calclinth, a council under the control of Offa, was held, and not at Culcheth an obscure place near Manchester, as hitherto believed: For why should Offa hold his council so near the Northumbrian border which Culcheth then was (HOU p350). There are three **cross-shaft fragments** in the churchyard, about 25 feet from the S porch of the church (BOE p100). They are usually assigned to the Saxon period, however, some say they are of Danish origin. The cross furthest from the church is carved on most of its faces, whilst the cross nearest the church has no carvings. On one face is three human figures side by side and on another a series of three human figures side by side (LGS p110). According to a local tradition, related to Plot in the later C17, the three crosses commemorate the three bishops killed in a battle between the Danes and the Saxons at nearby Deadman's Green (see) (NHS p432) (An Account of the Three Ancient Cross Shafts etc. Bishop Browne. 1888. p17) (HOU p351; Dr Whitaker used this tradition to support his theory that Calclinth is Checkley). Some say it is the carvings of three figures on the cross furthest from the church which commemorate the three bishops (THS part 1 p221) (GNHS p92) (HOC pp187-190) (STM Feb 1965 p41) (IAANS p xiii) (CHMS p24) (CJF p2p) (COS p29) (CHMS2 pp34,35p). Redfern thought the crosses were really fragments of one broken cross; if so this would dispel the tradition of the three bishops (HOU 1865 pp349 il. 1886 p451). The parish was formed between 1086 and 1291 probably out of Uttoxeter parish and may at first have formed a joint parish with Leigh, with a church at Leigh; Checkley perhaps becoming a separate parish in the early C13 (SHC 1916 pp194,199). There may have been a **church** at Checkley in Saxons times (LGS p110), and by the C11 (LDD). The parish church, St Mary and All Saints, on the E side of Church Lane, has late C12 work (CHMS2 p34) and was consecrated in 1196 (COPP2 p74). Grooves on a buttress outside the church are supposed to have been caused by medieval bowman sharpening their arrow heads (CJF p5p). The identification made between Checkley and the DB manor of Cedla by Eyton has been adopted since (SHC 1923 pp35-41). Later forms are: Checkelega (1196), Checklee (1196) (SSE 1996 p12), Chekkesleye (1227), Checkele (1227) (DUIGNAN), and Chekeleg (SPN p33). The **name** appears to be from Anglo-Saxon and means 'Cecce's lea' (DUIGNAN) or 'Ceacca's clearing' (SSE 1996 p12) (SPN p33). Some have said it is from the 'check,' either the Danes or Saxons (whoever lost), received in a battle reputedly fought between them at Deadman's Green (see) near Checkley (see below) (HOC pp188,189-190, 251).

1500 to PRESENT. The earliest recorded instance of **Protestant nonconformity** in the county concerned the Puritan Thomas Wood of Checkley who confessed to 'absenting himself from church......and using and frequenting disordered and unlawful conventicles and assemblies under pretence and colour of exercise of religion' in 1632 (VCH vol 3 p116). There was a cannon ball, perhaps of the **Civil War** period, in Checkley school. The ball was believed to account for one of the plain windows in the church and one of its odd pillars. The ball disappeared when the school house was pulled down in c1980 (CJF p104). Rev Dr Langley wrote an account of Checkley which passed to Stebbing Shaw who died before he was able to make any use of it for a volume of SHOS (HOU p351). Checkley is mentioned in this rhyme:

> Stramshall and Bramshall,
> Beamhurst and Fold,
> Leachurch and Parkhurst,
> And Chetley i' th' hole.

(FOS p148). Jim Foley gives a different version:-

Upper Tean, Lower Tean,
Beamhurst and Fole,
Leigh Church and Park Hall,
And Checkley i' th' Hole.

He says it was recited by local children in the early C20 (CJF). **Persons. Thomas Chawney**, last abbot of Croxden Abbey, is buried in the church next to that of the abbey's purchaser. It has been suggested Chawney finds his company uncongenial and Chawney's ghost - the figure resembling a robed monk with a cowl - haunts the churchyard (GLS pp36-37). Rev **Samuel Langley** who died on Sunday Feb 10 1838 (SMASCC p23p or 123p; says he died 1839) and his successor, Rev **W Hutchinson** who died on Sunday Feb 10 1879 are remembered for sharing the same hour, day of the week, day in the month, and month, for their deaths 41 years apart: Each died shortly after burying a corpse (HOC p185). Hutchinson's wife (d1895) was very unpopular in the village; her ghost has been seen with a dog (info Bruce Braithwaite). She may be identifiable with the ghost of an old lady dressed in a bonnet and a black cloak with a white lace collar who haunts the churchyard (CJF p78) (The Good Ghost Guide. John Brooks. 1994). The ghost of a little white dog which passes through walls has been seen around the rectory (GLS p37).

Checkley Brook Rises below Heighley Castle in Walton's Wood. Leaves Staffs at Wrinehill to join the Weaver in Cheshire. Dodgson in the Place-Names of Cheshire part 1 p18 has shown that the Lea was the old name for Checkley Brook (SPNO p12) (SPN p74). An early name for it may have been Saxon 'wrigian' 'go forward, bend (in the sense meander)' and this gave its name to Wrinehill (SPN p148).

Checkley Fields 0.25m N of Checkley. Has also appeared as Checkleyfields.

Cheddleton Parish and former township. The large village of Cheddleton lies on the top of the steep W side of the upper Churnet valley 18.5m NNE of Stafford.
EARLY. Three curious worked stones ovoid in form which appear to be of **Neolithic** or **Early Bronze Age** found in the Cheddleton area were brought to the attention of the NSFC by Mr A Milner (NSFCT 1953 p105-106). A polished stone axe of Neolithic or Bronze Age was found at Ashcombe at about SJ 976513 (JBAA series 2 vol 2 pp7,85) (CVH p20). A basalt axe-hammer has been found in Cheddleton parish (NSJFS 1964 p19) (CVH p20). A perforated axe-hammer now in the Potteries Museum was said to have been found in Cheddleton parish (CVH p20). A leaf-shaped arrowhead found by M Miner at Windy Arbour in 1936 (SK? 968508) went to the Potteries Museum (CVH p20). A barbed and tangled arrowhead of the Neolithic or Bronze Age was found in Basford Bridge Lane in 1961 (CVH p20) and an arrowhead of the Neolithic or Bronze Age has been found in Cheddleton parish (NSJFS 1964 p20). The same or another arrowhead in the Potteries Museum was found in Cheddleton parish (NSFCT vol 70 p85) (CVH p20). Two coins of **Iron Age** date are said to have been found in the district: one of Central Gaulish type; the other of doubtful type (Problems of the Iron Age in Southern Britain. S Frere. ND. pp279,284) (NSJFS 1964 p20) (CVH p20). Most of the line of the Roman road from Buxton through Leek, Cheddleton, Blythe Bridge, Hilderstone, and Stafford to Pennocrucium (see) on Watling Street has yet to be established (VCH vol 7 p98).
1000 to 1500. Commander Wedgwood considered Cheddleton an ancient **parish** from the late C13; it having been carved out of Leek original parish (SHC 1916 p199). It seems to have reverted to being a chapel in Leek by 1535. Had separate civil identity early and became a separate ecclesiastical parish in 1721 (GLAUE p408). The **church**, Edward the Confessor, on the N side of Hollow Lane, has some C14 work (Cheddleton & District Official Guide). Cheddleton had a wakes weekend in Oct 1890 and on Oct 22 1893 (Cheddleton Remembered. Vera Priestman. 1978 p10). The manor of Celtetone appears in DB. Later forms are: Chetilton (1201) (SSE 1996 p12), and Cheteltun (SPN p34). **Beating the bounds** occurred to c1970; at Wetley Rocks the boundary (of Cheddleton township) passed through the centre of the Plough Inn, and participants were known to climb over its roof in order to follow it. Participants were also known to wade through the canal at Consallforge (SVB p174) (info Arnold Cordon). The **name** appears to be of Anglo-Saxon origin and means 'Ceadwal's town' (DUIGNAN). Or 'cietel (narrow valley) town' (OAKDEN) (SSAHST 1967 p34) (SPN p34). (STM March 1965 p18). Barns thinks it has the same etymology as Cheadle (NSFCT 1910 p163). Pickford thinks it is from 'Chad's town' (SMM p21). Erdeswick probably wished to associate the name with the Celts, this has usually been read as Celte tone, but could easily be Cet le tone (CVH p22), or 'the town of the Celt' (OL vol 2 p13) (TOI p9). The lord of Cheddleton **manor** owed the lord of Leek a

special hunting service at Hollinghay in the early C13 (SSE 1993 p6). By the early C18 the manor boundary was marked with stones, possibly erected by Thomas Joliffe who in 1698 paid off the debts of Edmund Arbaster and acquired a share in the lordship of Cheddleton manor. Some of these stones remain and are inscribed 'PD' (Philip Draycott) on one side and 'TI(J):EA' (Thomas Joliffe: Edmund Arblaster) on the other (CVH p155). Dieulacres Abbey had a grange at Cheddleton (VCH vol 3 p233). For the crosses E of Cheddleton see under Basford Green and Cheddleton Heath. Some cast iron **stocks** are by the E wall of churchyard opposite the Black Lion Inn (LGS p112) (CVH p151) (SVB p54). Porter says they were damaged between the taking of her photograph and the publication of her book 1988 (PDS&C p40p). 1500 to PRESENT. The Young Pretender's army in the 1745 **Jacobite Rebellion** marched through Cheddleton parish in Dec 1745. Cheddleton PR records that some Scots soldiers remained in the district; that Alexander Barr from Glasgow was buried here on May 5 1750 and on May 7 1757 Angus MacBean, a native of Scotland, married Mary Lovat of Shaffalong here (CVH p19). There are **two water mills** to the NE of Cheddleton between the Churnet and the Caldon Canal. A mill may have stood on this site since the C13 (WTMS p145). The present N mill dating from 1756-65 ground flint; its powder being used in ceramic ware. It is possible James Brindley constructed or adapted the N mill (NSJFS 1969 pp53-59 ps). The S mill is older. It first ground corn and then drove machinery to make paper. The Cheddleton Flint Mill Preservation Trust was formed in 1967 to restore the mills (NSJFS 1969 p136). They opened to the public in 1969 (BOE p101) (IAS p157) (SVB p54). In 1980 the Churnet was lowered, and water now passes under the wheels, converting the mills to undershot from the original low breastshot (WTMS p145). (STM June 1969 pp26-27) (CVH pp86-89,87,88) (SMOPP vol 2 p65p) (AA p255) (HLSP p62). The station opened on the Churnet Valley **railway** to passengers in 1849. It was designed by AWN Pugin in the neo-Jacobean style; closure of the station was recommended in 1963. Later it was saved from destruction due to the intervention of the Poet Laureate Sir John Betjeman with the station gaining Grade II listing. By 1983 it had become a museum, cafeteria shop and office (ES March 22 1963) (SVB p55) (CVH p134). The line from Milton to Cheddleton Junction, authorised on July 13 1863, opened to passengers on Nov 1 1867 (CVH p128). The Churnet Valley railway line has a tunnel at Cheddleton. Its entrances are intended to resemble a natural cavern in the rock (NSJFS 1962 p103). **St Edward's Hospital** was built on the Bank Farm estate, 0.75m NNE of Cheddleton, between 1895 and 1900 as an additional lunatic asylum for the county. The foundation stone was laid by Lord Wrottesley, the chairman of the County Lunacy Committee, on Oct 31 1895. Construction was slow and hampered by a fire in July 1897 which destroyed the newly-built dining hall and theatre. The building was completed in Feb 1900. The name of the hospital seems to have been at first Cheddleton Asylum, then Cheddleton Mental Hospital, and is currently St Edward's Hospital (SA Nov 2 1895. Nov 6 1897. Feb 3 1900) (CVH pp185-187) (A History of Psychiatry in North Staffordshire. Dr Edward D Myers. 1997). Cheddleton **Historical Society** was founded by Arnold Cordon and others in 1976 (info Mr Cordon). Crooney Bank is the incline on the Cheadle Road near Ashcombe Park. The name is preserved in Crony Close (NSSG p15) (info Arnold Cordon). **Persons. Isaac Findler**, artist, was born in Cheddleton in 1809 of parents of Scottish origin. Amongst his best works were: 'The Tight Shoe,' 'Daniel in the Lion's Den,' 'Rebecca at the Well,' 'Cheddleton,' 'Captives at Babylon.' Findler painted the inn sign of the Red Lion Hotel, Leek. He died on May 26 1888 (OL vol 2 pp28-29). **Arthur Brittain**, father of Vera Brittain, writer born in Newcastle-under-Lyme (see), was a director of Brittain's paper mills at Cheddleton (FWNS p35). Mrs **Sybil Leek**, author on witchcraft, was born in 1917 as Sybil Fawcett in Railway Cottages, Station Road. Mrs Leek, a distant relative of Gertie Gitana of Hanley (see), died at Melbourne, Florida, USA, in 1982 (CVH p177).

Cheddleton Grange At SJ 973522 under 0.25m SE of Cheddleton (1834 OS map). Seems to have been once the property of Dieulacres Abbey (CVH p160).

Cheddleton Hall Possible Saxon long house in Hollow Lane, Cheddleton, by the church. Also known as Hall House (OL vol 1 p257) (info Arnold Cordon).

Cheddleton Heath Former common land now a hamlet 0.5m NE of Cheddleton, on the E side of the Churnet. At SJ 987533 on private land and difficult to find is a cross, at the point where the old Fynney Lane, now known as Cheddleton Heath Road crosses through Basford Lane. It has a stump rising over 50 cms out of a solid base stone (CVH p154) (NSFCT 1948 p123). Les Lumsdon's 'Family Walks in the Staffs Peak and Potteries' 1990 shows a cross on p44 which may be this or the one at Basford Green. A Mosquito KB 206 aircraft crashed on Cheddleton Heath on March 2 1945. The crew of two died (MD pp26-27). A very bright silvery-white oval shaped object was seen from Cheddleton Heath on Oct 11 1967 at 9.57am (FSRP p17).

Cheddleton Park A medieval deer park enclosed out of forest. In existence by 1379 (NSJFS 1962 p76). Owned by John de Haukestone and seems to have descended with successive lords of the manor of Cheddleton. There are three possible sites for the park - i) Ashcombe Park, or ii) in the Park Lane area between Cheddleton Park and Cumberledge Park, or iii) in the vicinity of Wetley Abbey and land to the E of. Perhaps parks existed in all these areas; this would explain the abundance of 'park' names in the Cheddleton area. Perhaps the lords of Cheddleton moved the park from the Park Lane area to the Ashcombe Park area in the later Middle Ages, creating an Old Park and a New Park (CVH pp160-161). There was another park, Hanley Park (see), lying in the SE corner of Endon township, which stretched into Cheddleton parish (VCH vol 7 p182).

Cheddleton Park House under 1m NNW of Cheddleton. May preserve the name of the medieval deer park, Cheddleton Park, which may have been in this area.

Cheeseyard Area of Longnor. Ghostly apparitions have been reported in the area (L p49).

Chell Former township in Wolstanton ancient parish. Formerly thought to be DB Celle by Erdeswick, Shaw and Commander Wedgwood; but this has been identified with Cheadle (SHC 1916 p173. 1923 pp35-41). The manor was a member of Tunstall manor by c1130 (ONST 1976 p374). The name appears in 1227 as Chelle (SSE 1996 p12), and in 1313 as Ceolegh (NSFCT 1908 p138). It is of Anglo-Saxon origin and means 'Ceol's lea' (DUIGNAN), or 'Ceol's or Ceola's woodland glade' (SSE 1996 p12) (SPN p26). Ekwall suggests the first element Old English 'ceole' may be interpreted as throat for some topographical sense (SSE 1996 p20). Or it may be traced to the forest-root 'coill' or 'coll' (NSFCT 1908 p138). The township divided into Great Chell and Little Chell possibly as a result of the division of the manor of Chell in the early C13 (VCH vol 8 p83). For the workhouse at Great Chell known as the Bastille see Westcliffe. Prince Charles opened Claybourne Residential Home at Chell on March 3 1998 (ES March 3 1998 p13p). Created a civil parish in 1894 (GLAUE p408). Chell was a ward of Stoke-on-Trent district by 1991. For the church see Great Chell.

Chell Green Small settlement by 1834 on S side of Biddulph Road and to the E of High Lane to the E of Great Chell (1834 OS map). The name is preserved in residential street names.

Chell Heath Probably former common lane on the boundary of Chell and Norton-in-the-Moors townships. Now a suburban area 1.5m NNE of Burslem. Birthplace of Abraham Lindup (d1832), in 1738 (PTP pp39-46). The church, Church of the Saviour, stands at the corner of Whitehead and Spring Bank Roads. Chell Heath was taken into Stoke-on-Trent county borough in 1922 (VCH vol 8 p260).

Chell House Former residence at Great Chell of John Henry Clive, nephew of Clive of India, later of Clanway Hall (see). By 1985 the house was the Victory Club (POTP p63).

Chell Lodge On S side of Little Chell Lane, Tunstall. Built by Thomas Cartlich in the late 1830s and was his home until he moved to Woore Manor, Shrops, in c1860. Appears as Little Chell Hall in the mid C19. The site is now occupied by a post WW2 housing estate (VCH vol 8 pp89-90).

Cherry Eye Bridge Bridge over the Caldon Canal between Consall Forge and Froghall at SK 014483 on OS map 1:25000. Iron ore from one of Britain's richest mines was loaded here. The dust reddened the eyes of the workmen, hence the name (SMCC p10il). However, Raven says it is so called after Cherry Eye Mine (MR p111). It has also appeared as Cherryeye Bridge. (The Caldon Canal by The Caldon Canal Society 1994).

Cherryfields Modern housing estate at Walton, Stone between A34 and the Trent.

Cherry Hole A limestone cavern at the SW end of Wren's Nest Hill, near Dudley (BCM Oct 1970 p51). It is a 'crown-hole' formed as a result of underground mining having collapsed (WNNNR p22).

Cherry Orchard Former farm and estate now a suburban area 0.75m N of St Mary's church, Handsworth. There was a farm at Cherry Orchard possibly in 1327 when it was the residence of Atte-le-Berg (otherwise Atterbury) (HPPE p20), or by the late C18 (MNB p45). The Cherry Orchard estate was owned by the Geaste-Dugdale family, related to the Dugdales of Blythe Hall, Coleshill and Merivale Atherstone and was mostly sold in 1812; the Dugdales sold the last small portion of the former estate just before WW1. The old farmhouse, known as the Homestall, and tenanted by the Hales family from at least 1841 to c1900, was demolished in 1930 (HPPE p21). The Cherry Orchard estate was built on with housing between WW1 and WW2 (HANDR pvii).

Cherry Orchard Road, and possibly area, 0.5m SE of Lichfield cathedral. The name is from an orchard on W side of Sturgeon's Hill called Cherry Garden

in the earlier C18, but by 1781 had become Cherry Orchard (J Snape's Plan of Lichfield 1781) (VCH vol 14 p163).

Cherry Orchard Euphemistic name for a small dreary area of Newcastle-under-Lyme, on the N side of Nelson Place. It was in existence by the early C19 and situated close to the Ebenezer Chapel. It consisted of rows of cramped workers cottages. The area is now a car park (NULOP vol 1 p45p of in c1928).

Cherry Orchard To E of Old Hill and W of Waterfall Lane Colliery (TB Aug 1989 p5 see map), in Rowley Regis parish. There is an Enilless (or Endless) Orchard on 1834 OS map in approximately this area. The ghost of a Scotsman, one McBane, who allegedly murdered for gold is seen in this vicinity. He walks the area close to the Waterfall Lane in C17 dress with a pouch holding his gold attached to his wrist (BCWJ p105) (TB June/ July 1973 p28. Aug 1982 p24. Aug 1989 p5) (GOM p26) (GPCE p37).

Cheshire House N end of Waterhouses.

Cheshire Wood Wood on W bank of the Manifold, Calton.

Cheshire Wood Cave Is 0.25m E of the summit of Old Park Hill at SK 116536. Originally had a stream running through it with a pool at the entrance. Excavated in 1959. Evidence of Neolithic, Iron Age and Romano-British occupation was found (NSJFS 1962 pp33-35. 1964 p42). (HOS p9) (MR p330).

Cheslyn Common Part of it belonged from time immemorial to the freeholders and copyholders of Great Wyrley. In 1668 some of it was enclosed by agreement, the rest was enclosed by statute in 1797. By at least the late C17 the common was squatted. The settlement was known as Wyrley Bank but later took the name Cheslyn Hay (VCH vol 5 pp78,100) (PCC p16).

Cheslyn Hay Former estate which became a hay, or division of Cannock Forest (DUIGNAN), later and presently a large village 0.5m WSW of Great Wyrley. There is a local legend of a Saxon cemetery at Cheslyn Hay (SPN p29). The name has appeared as Haya de Chistlin (1236) (SSE 1996 p12), Haya de Chiste, Chysteling (1252), haya de Chestling (1308), Chesling Hay (1644), Cheslinhay (1695) (SPNO p67) (SPN p29), and Chesland Hay (1817) (THS p263). It is from Anglo-Saxon, 'the hay of the little chest' (a stone sepulchre) (DUIGNAN) (SPN p29). Or 'coffin-ridge + hay (enclosure)' (SSE 1996 p12). Or is from the Irish 'caisel,' a stone fort. There is a prominent hill near Cheslyn Hay Farm (NSFCT 1908 p142). The hay, which was situated to the N of the settlement of Wyrley Bank (1834 OS map), was held by the Trumwyn family in the 1230s and may have been held by them since 1066 (VCH vol 2 p338). Except for a short period in the C13 it was held by the king until 1550, and was a constituent element of the forest until then. In 1342 it was stated that Great Wyrley manor was held by the petty serjeanty of giving the king a barbed arrow when ever he came to hunt in the hay. In 1550 the Crown granted it to the Earl of Warwick. His son held the hay in the 1560s (VCH vol 2 p342. vol 5 p101). It contained some 500 acres and was surrounded by a hedge and ditch in the 1530s (SL p102). The tenants of Great and Little Saredon who had common rights on the hay are said to have clashed with John Leveson the owner of the hay when he tried to enclose it in Henry VIII's reign (VCH vol 5 p178). But the Levesons do not appear to be holders of the hay until the end of the C16 (VCH vol 5 p101). Nathaniel (surname unknown), who murdered his parents, or some say his parents-in-law, and wife to gain control of their small estate, was often seen at Cheslyn Hay. He was charged in March 1674-5 and refused to plead. He was executed by being pressed to death by heavy weights, a form of punishment abolished in 1772 (SMT tract 2) (SMC pp105-107,209,210 il) (SM p555) (CCSHO p97). Because of the hay's wild and uninviting physical aspect no village community ever sort to bring Cheslyn Hay within their boundary (NSFCT 1913 p62). After the demise of the hay the estate obtained extra-parochial liberty status. The Lanes of King's Bromley were owners in the C19, and owners of Lodge Farm (VCH vol 5 p101). In the C19 the name 'Cheslyn Hay' was applied to the former squatter settlement of Wyrley Bank (see). By 1817 Cheslyn Hay had been annexed to Cannock as a township. The township obtained civil parish status in 1858 (THS p263) (GLAUE p408). (W p455) (APB p6). The mission chapel in Pinfold Lane, Cheslyn Hay, dedicated to St Peter, opened in c1950 (VCH vol 5 p102). The severed head of a Kuwaiti businessman was found in a shallow pit in a field near Cheslyn Hay High School? Primary School about late Jan 1994. His body was found in Manchester (ES April 20 1994 p1).

Cheslyn Wood Appears in 1300 as Chistlyn Wode (SPNO p67).

Chestall Area centred on the present Chestall Farm which is 0.5m E of Castle Ring. In Longdon parish. The name is of Anglo-Saxon origin and means 'the hill of the little chest' (a stone sepulchre) (SPN p80). Or it is from the root 'caisel,' a stone fort (NSFCT 1908 p141); nearby is Castle Ring Fort. The Rugeleys of Hawkesyard had a residence at Chestall from the C14 to the C16, after which it was held by the Husseys, and the Wrights until c1600 (VCH vol 5 p57). About this time Sir Edward Littleton also had a house here (SHOS vol 1 p211) (VCH vol 5 p57). The name Chestall Hall appears for one of these houses c1640. By the end of the C18 there was no mansion here only a C18 farmhouse, bearing the name of Chestall. It was then the property of the Earl of Uxbridge (SHOS vol 1 p222). This house, which still existed in the 1950s, was occupied by the Darling family throughout most of the C19, during which time they much enlarged it (VCH vol 5 pp57-58). The house has also appeared as Cheshall and Chestalls.

Chester Lane A Roman way on which Kinver is situated, runs from Chester to Worcester and Bath (KMC p3).

Chesterfield Hamlet over 0.5m S of Wall. In Shenstone ancient parish. A broken pillar of Roman origin was discovered here (NHS p404 tab 33 fig 4) (SD p15). The name is of Anglo-Saxon origin and means 'Cestre,' a fortress, castle (DUIGNAN). (SHOS vol 2 p55). Or open land by a Roman settlement (NSJFS 1981 p3) (SSE 1996 p12) (SPN p106). Has appeared as Cestrefeld Alani (C12) (SPN p106), and Chestrefeud (1262) (SSE 1996 p12).

Chesterton Large village 17.5m NNW of Stafford built on a Roman site. Former township in Wolstanton ancient parish.

EARLY. Traces of a **Roman** fort have long been evident in the Mount Pleasant and lower Castle Street area and at the Hollows (see) but have been mistaken for buildings of the medieval period by many writers over the centuries. Erdeswick and Camden mistook the Roman remains for a Norman castle (NSFCT 1912 pp144-150). Erdeswick, in the late C16, noted the 'ruins of a very ancient town...' here (SOS Harwood ed (1844) p22) (SH pp29,30). Camden, writing then, who drew on Erdeswick, elevated the remains to castle status, saying Newcastle is named in consequence of an 'old' castle at Chesterton (some have thought that the house of Walter de Waleton at Chesterton, where Henry II stayed, according to the Roll of 1199, was the castle (NSJFS 1961 p26 note 2)). Chetwynd thought the settlement was of Saxon origin (SH p45). Plot saw no Roman remains (NHS pp434-435). Miss Meteyard said that Josiah Wedgwood found traces of a potworks here (OTP pp60,63). Shaw reports nothing of Roman origin had been found (SHOS vol 1 General Intro pp15,34). A bronze fibula possibly of Roman origin exhibited at a meeting in 1853 was said to come from Chesterton (Hist Soc of Lancs and Ches vol 5 p99). Excavations in 1892, 1905, and 1925 or 6 revealed nothing (NSFCT vol 26 p139. vol 60 p184). In 1895-6, some undated masonry was found (JBAA series 2 vol 2 p121). By 1895 the N vallum and fosse were exposed and a few traces of the E and W defences, and in Farm Walls were some worked stones of Roman character (SK p200). (WWT p5) (ESH pp52-55). In 1932/3 some Roman pottery in the NE corner of the fort was found by T Pape (AJ vol 14 p183) (NSFCT (1933) vol 68 pp159-162). A housing estate was built over part of the site in c1955 (NSFCT 1954 p88). In 1956 some Roman pottery of the late C1 and early C2 AD was uncovered, and near Old Hall Farm, during the building of Chesterton County High School, a pipe-clay figurine and Roman pottery were uncovered (NSJFS 1961 p28. 1964 p30) (NSFCT vol 91 p96). In 1969 the southeastern ramparts were revealed and the exact position and dimensions of the fort could be plotted (NSJFS 1976 pp1-15 dia ps). Richmilde Street (see), a Roman road from Derby, led to Chesterton. The settlement at Chesterton has been identified with Veratinum (NSJFS 1976 p94) and Mediolanum of the 10th Itinerary of Antoninus ('Magna Britannia' vol 2 part 2. 1806-22. p433. D&S Lysons) (GNHS p68) (HBST pp6,15) (AJ vol 30 (1873) p159) (NSFCT 1886 pp53-54. 1892 pp139-140. 1911 pp142-143. 1912 p142) (LGS p113) (OTP pp60,63) (E p8) (S p72) (WWT pp4,5) (Roman Roads in Britain. ID Margary. vol 2 1957 pp249,251,254). South of Chesterton fort a rectangular enclosure of 2.5 acres straddling Loomer Road was discovered between 1959-60. This may have been a camp for troop reinforcements or a labour camp for the construction of Chesterton fort (NSJFS 1962 pp53-58). In 1957 the site of a Roman settlement was discovered at Holditch, 0.75m to the SSE.

1100 to PRESENT. Henry II stayed at the house of Walter de Waleton at Chesterton, according to the Roll of 1199, in either 1155 or 1157 on his way to or from Ireland - suggesting to some there was no Norman castle at Chesterton for him to stay at (NSFCT 1912 p147) (SOSH pp113-115) (R&S p6) (NSJFS 1961 p26 note 2). The **name**, which means '(Roman) fort tun' (SSE 1996 p12), appears in 1214 as Cestreton (SSE 1996 p12). Camden called Chesterton Chesterton-under-Lyme. **William Maxfield** of Chesterton was martyred at Tyburn in 1616 (SCHJ No. 23 1988 pp1-8). Chesterton became a separate ecclesiastical parish in 1846 (GLAUE p408). The **church**, Holy Trinity, on the S side of Church Street, was built in 1851-1852 (BOE p101). The stone to build it was reputedly given on the understanding that it rained on a certain day. It did rain on that day, and the church was completed in 1852 (SVB p55). **Newspaper**. The Newcastle Guardian and Silverdale, Chesterton and Audley Chronicle, found April 23 1881, ran to 1909 (SHJ spring 1996 p21). Chesterton became a separate civil parish in 1894 (GLAUE p408) and became a part of Newcastle borough in 1932 (ES April 17 1970). A lone

bombing raid was made on Chesterton in **WW2** on Dec 16 1940. But owing to the censorship of the time, the ES could only report that a 'Midland town' was hit (Newcastle Times March 11 1970) (ES Feb 18 1977) (TSS p125). It was recommended that Chesterton Lane Halt **railway** station be closed in 1963 (ES March 22 1963). **UFO**. Two people saw a red roundish object, elongated in shape, and as large as sixpence held at arm's length, from Chesterton on Sept 1 1967 at about 10.45pm (FSRP p11).

Chesterton Hall Chesterton. Seat of the Macclesfield family by the later C17 (Plot's map) (NSFCT 1886 pp53,55) (NSSG p14). The hall is said to have been the residence of Thomas Maxfield, a Roman Catholic martyr, who was born in Staffs in 1590. He was executed at Tyburn in 1616 for refusing to renounce his Roman Catholic beliefs. There is a biography of Maxfield written in Latin in the WSL. By late 1966 the former St Patrick's high school in Ashfields New Road, Newcastle-under-Lyme, had been renamed Blessed Thomas Maxfield to his memory and a motif portraying his image was erected on the wall of the school chapel (ES Nov 22 1966). This school became St John Fisher High School when it amalgamated with St Dominic's school, Hartshill, in 1980 (info Mrs Woodcock). In the C18 it was a Catholic worship centre (VCH vol 8 p54) (NUL p68). It was situated on a circular site perhaps of great antiquity, perhaps of Roman origin (NSFCT 1908 pp105-106). Excavations in front of the hall in 1925 revealed nothing (NSFCT 1925 p185). (S&COP p on back cover of what is called Chesterton, Old Hall). An icehouse belonging to it still survives in the public park called Chesterton Park in the centre of Chesterton. There may have been a secret tunnel to Dimsdale Hall (see).

Chetwynd Bridge Crosses the Tame between Alrewas and Elford 1.5m SE of Alrewas. Originally built for the old saltway from Shirleywich and Weston-on-Trent to the E (DUIGNAN p130). Formerly called Salter's Bridge. It was repaired and widened by two feet in 1601 at a cost of £200 (SHOS vol 1 p138) (ESH p16). It survived the great frost of the winter of 1794/95 (SHOS vol 1 p141). Many people drowned in this stretch of water according to PR. The present bridge was rebuilt by the County Surveyor in 1824 and has three arches. It is constructed of iron made at Coalbrookdale, Shrops (BOE ppp53-54) (IAS pp149-150) (BZ p108). The county authorities then changed its name to Chetwynd, after the Chairman of the Quarter Sessions of the time (DUIGNAN p130) (NSJFS 1962 p97 pl vi).

Chetwynd House Greengate Street, Stafford. Built in 1745 (LGS pp217-218) or soon after (SIOT p148) in 1746. It was built by William Chetwynd (1684-1770), Lord of the Admiralty under Walpole and Working Master of the Mint, third son of John Chetwynd of Ingestre Hall (COI pp245,246il of in 1887) (ES June 2 1934 p3) (SKYT p32p) (SSTY p214). However, the house looks of the Queen Anne style (BOE p245). The Duke of Cumberland probably stayed here in 1746 (SKYT p34). There is a tradition that he partook of the first meal eaten here (SIOT p148). On Aug 13 1748 during the general election a riot occurred at Stafford in which Chetwynd House was broken into (SIOT p53). Richard Brinsley Sheridan is said to have occupied the house (FSP pp13-19), and to have written 'The School for Scandal' here, in 'Sheridan's Room' (SKYT p33p of as a private residence), and may have been first introduced to the actress Harriot Mellon at the house (OSST 1934 pp18-19). Others say Sheridan merely socialised here as the guest of the resident, William Horton, shoe manufacturer (SKYT p33) (SSTY pp202,214). And that in the dining room Sheridan made his great speech against Warren Hastings (SKYT p33). The house is presently (1999) a post office; it opened as such in 1914 (ES June 2 1934 p3). It is said to be haunted by the Duke of Cumberland, who may have been entertained here on the way to suppress the 1745 Jacobite Rebellion, and Lord George Gower, lord lieutenant of Staffs (FSP pp11-13), and the ghost of Richard Brinsley Sheridan (FSP pp13-19).

Childerend Pipe Area in the late C13 around Spade Green. Known as Childerhay End in the later C16 (VCH vol 14 p198).

Childerhay Area in the NE part of Burntwood township, and W of Spade Green. The name occurs in the late C13 (VCH vol 14 p198).

Childerplay Near Brindley Ford, Knypersley. In Biddulph parish. The name occurs in 1334 (BHS June 1972 p28). Childerplay Colliery was in existence in the C19 (BALH p66).

Children's Bridge, The Coven. Small footbridge to enable children to pass over a brook to school and to join two large areas of new housing estate. The bridge was the idea of Major RFP Monckton of Stretton Hall, Stretton (Penkridge). The Major paid for it and attended its opening in May 1968 (WMAG June 1968 p15p).

Child's Oak Field name in Colton Parish (CWF). Probably from an oak of this name? The field is situated 0.5km N of Hamley House.

Chillington Former liberty of Brewood town (W p446) (VCH vol 5) and fragmented hamlet in the vicinity of Chillington Hall, which lies on a small plateau to the E of Moat Brook, 12m SSW of Stafford. The manor of Cillentone appears under Warws in DB (NSFCT 1952 p34) (SSE 1996 p12). Later Chillington appears as Cildentona (1130), Chylinton (1175-82), Chillyngton (1236) (SPNO) (SPN p23). The name appears to be of Anglo-Saxon origin and means 'Cille's Cilla's town or farm or tun' (DUIGNAN) (SOSH p76) (SSE 1996 p12) (SPN p23). Chillington manor has descended with the Giffard family since sometime between 1175 and 1182 to the present (VCH vol 5 p28). A village of medieval origin stood at SK 865068 to the E of the hall (SSAHST 1966 p49. 1970 p34). Because it obstructed views from Chillington Hall it was cleared by Thomas Giffard in the 1760s to complete the beautification the park (VCH vol 5 p18) (SL p136). Chillington was included in Brewood prebend (SSAHST vol 2 1960-61 p43). In March 1624 John Brent of Chillington, an ardent papist of 40 years' standing, was prosecuted by the mayor of Evesham, and taken to Oxford, charged with making scandalous speeches against Queen Elizabeth and the Church of England (HOWM p65). For Chillington in a local rhyme see Brewood.

Chillington Brook Runs presumably from The Park to Brewood.

Chillington Farm 0.25m NNW of Chillington Hall. A fragment of water and a field named Moat Meadow near the farm at SJ 860074 may preserve the memory of a moated site; perhaps the site of a former Chillington Hall (SSAHST 1982-3 p37).

Chillington Hall Chillington, 2m WSW of Brewood. The Chillington estate was purchased by the Giffard (pronounced Jifford) family in 1178 and the family have kept it ever since. The family is said to be descended from Avelina, younger sister of Gunnara, a pre-Norman Conquest Duchess of Normandy (NSFCT 1956 p113), or descended from William de Longueville, who was standard bearer to William the Conqueror at the battle of Hastings (1066). He was one of the four Norman knights who killed King Harold, according to the chronicler William of Poitiers (Daily Telegraph July 29 1998 p29). The family history was written up in 1905 by Major Gen George Wrottesley, but his research was lost when a fire at the hall destroyed the archive (CL Sept 30 1999 p81). On the death of his father in 1971 Peter Giffard (1921-1998) became the 28th of his family to possess the estate (Daily Telegraph July 29 1998 p29p). The **Norman manor house**, which had the appearance of a castle, was replaced in c1547. A small corner of the Norman manor house is said to remain in the cellars of the present hall (Chillington Hall Guide). However, a curved stretch of water near the present hall at SJ 864068 which survived in 1756 was probably part of a moat, which may have surrounded the original hall. A possible moat at Chillington Farm (see) may also have surrounded the original hall (SSAHST 1982-3 p37). A new house was built by Sir John Giffard in 1547. His arms and that date were over the principal entrance (of a later hall) (SHOS vol 2 p302). He was Henry VII's standard bearer (NSFCT 1956 p113). The **Tudor hall** was of quadrangular form (Chillington Hall Guide); its former courtyard can still be distinguished (BOE p102). There was a chapel and gatehouse (Chillington Hall Guide). Elizabeth I visited the hall on Aug 11 1575, travelling from Stafford Castle (SMC p164) (SSC p120 in the intro) (R&S pp23-24) (VCH vol 5 p21). In a bizarre move she had Giffard (Catholics until 1861) senior members arrested for not attending Anglican services only shortly after her departure (NSFCT 1975 p38) (HOS 1998 p63). Chillington was considered as a place of confinement for Mary, Queen of Scots, in 1585. Her custodian, Sir Amyas Paulet, visited the hall but rejected it because the garden wall was too low and the brewhouse too small to supply all Mary's retainers, and the neighbourhood too sympathetic to Catholics (VCH vol 5 p21) (Chillington Hall Guide). Gilbert Giffard (b1561), after having been expelled from the English College at Rome for deceit he returned to England and became a confidant of Mary, Queen of Scots, in her confinement at Chartley Old Hall. In the Babington Plot (1586) he acted as a double agent for Sir Francis Walsingham and betrayed her. Persecution from Roman Catholics forced him to flee to Paris where he was arrested in 1588; he died in prison in 1590 (LGS p52) (S pp112,113) (Biography of Charles II. Antonia Fraser. 1979 p114 notes). In the C16 Erdeswick thought the hall 'remarkable for the various forms of its windows and chimneys' (SOS p159) (VCH vol 5 p29). In the 1780s Sir John Soane, the architect of the present hall, made a plan of the old hall. A plan by Soane of an old house believed to be of Chillington Hall was bought by the Canadian Centre for Architecture in Montreal. However, it has since been shown to be of Hinton St George, Somerset, whilst the real plan of Chillington old hall had been miscatalogued in Soane's other Hinton St George drawings at the Soane Museum, London (CL Sept 30 1999 p81). The hall, garrisoned for the king in the **Civil War**, was taken by parliament after a two-day siege on Aug 11 1643. Parliamentarians described it as 'one of the strongest places in that county, exceeding well provided of all necessaries and manned with such a company of obstinate papists and resolute thieves as the like were hardly to

be found in the whole kingdom' (VCH vol 3 p105 note). The royalists under Col Leveson regained the hall in Sept 1643 (HOWM p87). Charles Giffard, owner of the Boscobel estate in the early 1650s, recommended Charles II hide at Whiteladies, Shrops after the battle of Worcester (1651). At the Restoration it was his name who Charles II forgot but wished to reward (Biography of Charles II. Antonia Fraser. 1979 pp114,121,128). In the later C17 Plot noted the Tudor hall had no less than **eight tunnels** to one hearth in the chimneys and the fretwork of the tunnels was also very varied and not two were the same (NHS p359) (SHOS vol 2 p302). The Tudor hall had been demolished by 1724. Some Elizabethan or Jacobean panelling went into the present hall in the bedrooms of the S wing, and a few linenfold panels have been worked into a chimney-piece in the billiard room, built in 1911 at the W end of the wing (CL Feb 20 1948 pp378-381). The **present hall** is almost entirely Georgian. The S side, of c1724, built by Peter Giffard is from this period; the heads of the lead rainwater pipes bear his initials P.G.B. and those of his wife Barbara Throckmorton, and the date 1724. His architect may have been Francis Smith of Warwick (VCH vol 5 p29) (BOE p102). The rest, including the main facade or E facade, was designed by Sir John Soane for Thomas Giffard in 1786-9 (LGS p91) (BOE p102) (NSFCT 1975 p38). The E facade has the portico whose columns are composed of Tunstall stone and the Ionic capitals are designed after the Temple of Fortune at Rome (Chillington Hall Guide). Inside, the **main staircase**, in a block attached to the S range, is early Georgian. The nosing of each tread is continued below the stair above to form brackets, in each of which is carved a panther (Chillington Hall Guide). In the window above the main staircase is **armorial glass** from the oriel window of the Great Hall of the Tudor hall but mostly dates from early C19 and some is by John Freeth of Birmingham in c1830 (BOE p102). The **Saloon** is built on the site of the Great Hall of the Tudor hall (Chillington Hall Guide) but Pevsner says it covers the site of the original courtyard. The chimneypiece depicts the story of the shooting of the panther, commemorated by Giffard's Cross (see) in the grounds (BOE p103). (CL Feb 13 1948 pp326-329 ps. Feb 20 1948 pp378-381. Feb 27 1948 pp426-429 ps. Sept 30 1999 pp80-87pc) (AWM p15). The **chapel** at Chillington was regularly in use from at least 1721. It was demolished in c1786 while the hall was being enlarged (VCH vol 5 p44).

GROUNDS. The **Bowling Green Arch** of c1730 is W of the SW corner of the grounds. It is the screen to the former bowling green, the modern iron gates bear the initials of Peter Giffard (DoE II) (CL Feb 13 1948 p329p) (BOE p103) (Chillington Hall Guide pc). **Brown's Bridge**. There is said to have been a bridge by 'Capability' Brown at the farther end of the ornamental canal (VCH vol 5 p29). **Cowper's Acorn**. An ornament in the shape of an acorn in an iron cage named after the poet William Cowper (1731-1800) (SLM Dec 1991 p23 pc). By the stables is a **Dovecote** of c1730 and swagger and octagonal (DoE II) (BOE p103). **Giffard's Cross** (see). The **Gothic Temple** was on the W side of The Pool, near the beginning of the dam, and had polygonal turrets left and right. In the centre was a Gothick window, but the rooms were in the classical style of c1770. It was described as 'half ruined' in 1948 and in 1959, and as being a 'sad sight' in the early 1970s (CL Feb 13 1948 p329) (VCH vol 5 p29) (BOE p103) (SN July 4 1975 p9p) and in ruins in 1984 (DoE II). The building was demolished in the mid 1980s because of a falling tree (BDH p155). A watercolour made of it in 1975 by John Piper is at the foot of the main staircase in the hall. (F p307). The **Grecian Temple**, according to the OS map 1:25,000, is on the S side of the Pool, close to the drive, at SJ 854053. The photograph of it in the Chillington Hall Guide shows it has Ionic columns. However, Pevsner says, its columns are in the Roman Doric style. He also says, the temple is unkept, situated in a wood near the Sham Bridge and difficult to reach (BOE p103). Pevsner seems to have details for the Ionic Temple and the Grecian Temple mixed up. His description of the Ionic Temple - that it was built probably in 1771, is Adamish in style, has five bays, and a dome - seems to apply to the Grecian Temple. The Grecian Temple has been referred to as the Garden Temple (DoE I). (BDH p155). There is an **ice-house** at SP 863069, 0.25m N of the hall. It is an igloo-style structure partly below and partly above ground, and approached by an eight feet long tunnel (DoE II) (IHB p393). The **Ionic Temple** is unkempt, situated in a wood and difficult to reach. It is situated on the E side of The Pool, at approximately SJ 855059. Neo-classical temple with four Roman Doric columns with pediment (DoE II), an Ionic portico and a low dome above an attic storey which has pedestals for four statues (Chillington Hall Guide). The temple masks a gamekeeper's cottage and has a little bronze cannon standing between two columns, beautifully ornamented with the Giffard crest and arms and the inscription: 'W&F Kinman fecere 1786.' Doubtless the cannon was fired on festive occasions or when water parties were held. The temple is more likely to have been designed by Soane than by Paine or Brown (CL Feb

13 1948 pp328p,329) (VCH vol 5 p29) in the 1780s (F pp307-308). The temple seems to have been in an unkempt state in 1974 (BOE p103) and derelict in April 1984 (DoE II). (BDH p155). Pevsner seems to have details for the Grecian Temple and the Ionic Temple mixed up (BOE p103). The **Long Avenue** of c1725 lined with oaks is the ornamental approach to the hall from the E in two sections. The Upper Avenue is about 1m long, and the (abandoned) Lower Avenue is about 1.25m. The latter is intersected by the Shropshire Union Canal. A classical-style bridge by Telford of 1826 carries the avenue over the canal (BOE p102). **Paine's Bridge** is a stone bridge in the classical style with one arch designed by James Paine where the Pool and Ornamental Canal join (BOE p103) (Chillington Hall Guide p). Built some time between 1756 and 1776 (VCH vol 5 p29). A plate of it is included in the 2nd volume of James Paine's 'Designs of Noblemen's and Gentlemen's Residences' (1783) where it is shown with urns in the niches and a stone balustrade with sphinxes in the place of the iron railways (CL Feb 13 1948 p328). (DoE II*) (BDH p155). There is a **panther statue** in the Dairy Courtyard at the hall carved out of Ancaster stone by JA Twentyman of Claverley (Chillington Hall Guide). The **Pool** or Lake, an ornamental lake 0.75m SW of the hall, is upwards of 60 acres and was formed by 'Capability' Brown who constructed a dam and amalgamated three smaller pools. James Paine described it as 'one of the finest pieces of water, within an inclosure, that this Kingdom produces: the verges of which are bounded by fine plantations, intermixed with groves of venerable stately oaks' (SHOS vol 1 part 1 p90) (CL Feb 13 1948 p329p) (Chillington Hall Guide). **Ornamental Canal.** There is a canal or 'private navigation' used for the transport of fuel and building materials. It leads from the SE corner of the Pool towards the house (VCH vol 5 p29). The **Sham Bridge** is at the N end of the Pool and is by 'Capability' Brown. It has five arches (BOE p103) (Chillington Hall Guide) and has details similar to Paine's Bridge (VCH vol 5 p29). (DoE II*). **Sluice House** is on the canal at Chillington Hall probably once a boat house for start of journey to lake (DoE II). There is an eight feet deep **sulphur well** (ABW pp51-52) (VCH vol 5 p20) (BDH p276). **White House** (see).

Chillington Park Late medieval hunting park, which existed into the C17 and C18 (EDP p180). A part of it close to the house was occupied by the tiny Chillington village. Was landscaped by Lancelot 'Capability' Brown and James Paine between 1756 and 1777 (NSJFS 1975 pp37,38 map, 39) (SL p133).

Chilternhall One of the four prebends of Gnosall Collegiate Church. Formerly known as Andrewshall. Its prebendary lived in Chiltern Hall, a house, which may have adjoined the churchyard in Gnosall, and which appears as Chilternehall (1395), and Chyltenehall (1447) (SPNO p158). It was still standing in the C18 (VCH vol 4 pp113,115-116). The name is from the Chiltern Hills (SPNO p158).

Chistals Brook Farewell (SHOS vol p229).

Chitlings Brook Tributary to the Trent. Runs by Sideway to Stoke. This is perhaps onomatopoeic for a bubbling stream (SPNO p7).

Chitta, River Small stream flowing from Grindon to the Manifold (WTCEM) (SPNO p7). Has also appeared as River Chilta.

Cholpesdale Dieulacres Abbey is situated in it (W p720) (NSFCT 1889 p72). Or former site for Dieulacres Abbey after its move from Poulton and before moving to N of Leek. Pickford thinks Cholpesdale is possibly Lady Dale (see). Has also appeared as Cholpes Dale and Sudden Dale?

Chopesdale Dale in Langot Valley area. Fairoak Knoll is in it (info Bruce Braithwaite). Has also appeared as Clopesdale.

Choristers' House The house stood on N side of Lichfield cathedral Close. It was built in c1527 for the residence of the cathedral choristers and their master. By the 1580s the choristers were no longer living in common, and the house was let. In front of this house stood an impressive **gateway** erected in 1531 at the expense of Bishop Blithe and Dean Denton. Shaw thought Denton paid the whole expense; his arms and rebus were engraved over the archway. The gateway was demolished in 1772, in which year the old house, by now probably divided into its present two halves (now represented by the houses Nos. 13 and 14) was remodelled to its present appearance by John Daniel (GM Nov 22 1782) (SHOS vol 1 pp308-309 pl xxviii is from GM) (In 'Lichfield' in Bell's Cathedral Series on p17 there is a copy from a print, dated 1773, showing the gateway) (NSFCT 1924 p88 il) (VCH vol 3 pp189, 197. vol 14 pp64, 65 pl 9) (GKCLC) (MCC). By 1942 No. 13 was the residence of the chancellor (info Michael Cockin). In 1924 the **Dean Savage Library**, a library to house the collection of Dean Savage, was opened in No. 14. It was moved to the back of the house in 1975 when the dean and chapter's office was established in the front. By 1999 the front of No. 14 was private accommodation, whilst the Library had been moved to a separate building to the rear of No. 14; this building was known as 'The Song School' in 1942 when it was used as a school room by Lichfield Cathedral School (St

Chad's) (info Michael Cockin) (VCH vol 14 pp59, 65).

Chorley Small village on Shute Hill above Maple and Bilson Brooks 1.5m ESE of Cannock Wood. In Farewell parish. The name has appeared as Cerlec (1231) (SSE 1996 p12) and Charley (SHOS vol 1 p230). It is of Anglo-Saxon origin and means 'the churl's (free peasant) lea' (SSE 1996 p12), or 'Ceorl's lea' (DUIGNAN) (SPN p79). The very productive ducks belonging to Mr Noble of Chorley in the C17 could lay nine or ten or even 12 eggs in a night (NHS pp234-236). A calf with two heads was taken to Stafford from Mr Saunders' of Chorley in March 1763. Both heads bleated and it had eight legs and two tails. It was intended to send the calf up to the Royal Society. Shaw found this noted in Dr Wilkes' grangerised edition of Erdeswick (SHOS vol 1 p230).

Chorley Hall Former ancient mansion on W side of Farewell parish, NW of Chorley on the N side of the road to Goosemoor Green. Occupied by the Noble family, perhaps in the later C17 (Plot's map), and certainly in the mid C18. It was the seat in 1834 of William Adey (W 1834 p55). It was described in the mid C19 as having been taken down some years prior to 1851 and replaced by a farmhouse (mem in Farewell church) (W p577). The farmhouse, predominately occupied by farmers, was demolished in 1998 by the retiring farmer Mr Walker, whose family had lived at Chorley Hall Farm since at least 1940 (info Mr and Mrs Walker).

Chorlton Moss Small hamlet 1.5m NW of Chapel Chorlton. In the detached chapelry of Chapel Chorlton in Eccleshall ancient parish.

Christchurch The Guns Village area of West Bromwich (1834 OS map). Possibly the parish name for this district of West Bromwich.

Christ Church Name for the area S of Beacon Park, WSW of Lichfield cathedral (1976 OS map 1:25,000). The name is from probably Christ Church, Christchurch Lane, Leamonsley.

Christchurch-on-Needwood Is Needwood (APB p45). But rather it is the former name for Newchurch (see). Or rather Christchurch-on-Needwood was a parish created in 1804 at the time of the disafforestation of Needwood Forest (LGS p192) and what came to be known as Newchurch was where the parish church, dedicated to Christ, was placed.

Christian Field Land near Stichbrook or Stychbrook, Lichfield at cSK 115113. Has appeared as Cadaverum Corpus (HOL pp2,515). From the 1680s, on account of the name of the land, Christian Field has been identified with the place of massacre and burial of the legendary massacred Christians slain during Diocletian's reign (284-305), see under Lichfield (VCH vol 14 pp38-39). Quantities of human bones and pottery of different periods are believed to have been found here (A Short Account of the City and Close of Lichfield. JC Woodhouse. 1819 p4), although they are now lost (NSJFS 1964 p28).

Chuckery, The Residential suburb 0.5m of E Walsall. The name may be derived from Churchgreave, the name of one of the common fields of Walsall (VCH vol 17 pp153,180). Or is a corruption of Church grove field; before the suppression of the monasteries the fields belonged to one of the guilds attached to Walsall parish church (DUIGNAN) (SPN p135). A ridiculous suggestion given by some local inhabitants is that the name arose from the 'chuck, chuck, chuck' of a farmer beckoning his fowl home to roost (SNWA p29). There is a legend that Walsall parish church was begun in the Chuckery area but removed to its present site by witches in the shape of white pigs (N&Q 4th series vol 12 p245) (VCH vol 17 p153 note). Has also appeared as Chuckery Fields (DUIGNAN). The church at The Chuckery, St Luke, in Selborne Street, was built in 1879, rebuilt in 1934 and again in 1989 (LDD). In 1994 an unexplainable presence in the form of a twisted skein of something bluey white and misty was caught on a photograph taken of the stair lobby of a terraced house in the Chuckery (MS&S pp35-36p).

Churchbridge Area centred around the junction of the A34 with A5, 1.25m S of Cannock. In Great Wyrley township in Cannock parish. The name is from the bridge carrying Watling Street over Wash Brook (VCH vol 5 p77). Yet there was no church here, anciently. Land adjoining the bridge belonged to a Lichfield guild, afterwards suppressed, and it is not unlikely the guild built or rebuilt this bridge (DUIGNAN). Has appeared as Chyrche Brugge (1385), Chirche Bridge (1538), Churchbridge (1834 OS map) (SPNO p71) (SSE 1996 p12). The edge-tool factory built by W Gilpin (d1834) at Churchbridge housed a James Watt steam-engine, until removed c1953 (Cannock Chase Courier Jan 23 1953) (VCH vol 5 p78). Churchbridge was linked to the railway system on Feb 1 1858 (SSR p17).

Churchbridge Branch of Staffs and Worcs Canal. Built in 1860 to link the Hatherton Branch of the Staffs and Worcs Canal at Churchbridge Junction to the Cannock Extension Canal at Rumer Hill Junction (HCMS No. 2). Or possibly also called Churchbridge Extension of the Hatherton Branch: Abandoned by 1957 when part of the E end was destroyed for open-cast mining (VCH vol 5 p51). Churchbridge Branch was 0.5m long and had 13 locks; these were destroyed in the later C20. This small branch is beyond restoration and the Lichfield and Hatherton Canals Restoration Trust, formed in 1988, have to by-pass it by building a new section of canal in order to link the Hatherton Branch of the Staffs and Worcs Canal with the Cannock Extension Canal (Trust leaflet).

Church Brook Appears in 1281 as Kyrke-broke and in 1569 as a tributary of the Churnet. The name may be an early form of Ball Haye Brook (see) (VCH vol 7 p84).

Church Clent A separate manor to that of DB Clent (otherwise Lower or Nether Clent, a manor of the de Somery family of Dudley Castle). At the time of the dissolution of the monasteries the manor belonged to Halesowen Abbey. It seems to have belonged to the Crown until 1633 when Charles I sold it and a house called Calcot Hill. In 1660 the manor and Calcot Hill House belonged to the Underhill family and manor courts were held at Calcot Hill House in the C17. Bishop Lyttelton gives a list of some of the customs of the manor of Church Clent in the C16 from a manuscript formerly in the possession of a Mr Tyrer, steward of the court (VCHW vol 3 p52). (SHOS vol 2 p247). Has also appeared as Upper Clent and King's Holt.

Church Croft Nearly two acres of land about 200 yards N of the Old Hall, Handsacre. It has revealed no site of an ancient church, but Mill Croft adjoining Church Croft did reveal the foundation of a building about 18 yards long by 10 or 11 wide pointing E and W which stood directly opposite to the N front of the hall and about 120 yards from the moat bridge. Shaw is convinced it was a chapel and he employed a man to dig here who discovered pieces of glass and lead suggesting stained church glass. Church Croft probably received its name not because it belonged to the church, but because it adjoined the churchyard, therefore called churchyard-croft, or church croft (SHOS vol 1 p207).

Church Croft House Station Road, Rugeley, near the Old Chancel of the former parish church. Birthplace on Oct 21 1824 of William Palmer (d1856), the poisoner. Built in c1800, has six bedrooms (TPP p5) (SN Sept 30 1994 p5p).

Church Eaton Ancient parish, township, manor and village in pastoral country by the confluence of Apeton and Church Eaton Brooks 6m SW of Stafford. Charters of 940 and 949 which may not be authentic may refer to Church Eaton (SHC 1916 pp88-89) (SSE 1991 pp7,8). The manor of Eitone appears in DB. Later Church Eaton appears as Eiton (1200), Chirche Eyton (1261), Eytona (1298), and Chirche Eton (1481), Churcheton (1570), and Eyton-juxta-Gnoweshalle (SHC 1883 p14) (SPNO p140) (SSE 1996 p13). The **name** 'Eaton' appears to be of Anglo-Saxon origin and means 'the dwelling or town on the stream' (DUIGNAN) (LGS p113) (SPN p35). Or 'the farmstead in land partly surrounded by water' (OAKDEN), hence 'an island settlement' (NSJFS 1981 p3) or 'island farm' (SSE 1987 p28). Church is a medieval addition to distinguish it from Water Eaton and Wood Eaton. The site of the manor-house of Church Eaton manor remains unlocated (VCH vol 4 p94). There was formerly a moated site in Alleys Lane about 300 yards N of the Royal Oak Inn, on the N side of Church Eaton, at SJ 844177. It was filled in at the end of the C19 (VCH vol 4 pp91-92) (CAMS p63) (SSAHST 1982-3 p38). For a moated site at Church Eaton see ESH p58. There is a legend that a local witch, Joan Eaton, prevented a **church** being built at Little Onn by repeatedly removing the stones to Church Eaton where it was eventually built (OSST 1931 p18). In a local rhyme (see Brewood) the devil is said to have been beaten at Church Eaton. The parish church, St Editha, at the E end of High Street, is of C12 origin with later additions (VCH vol 4 p99). There is a tradition that the E window is from old St Paul's cathedral, London (NSFCT 1946 p146). The **parish** formed before 1086 and probably originally contained the ancient parishes of Haughton, Bradley and Lapley (SHC 1916 pp192,193).

ADVOWSON CASE. The possession of the church advowson or living at Church Eaton was the centre of a very complicated dispute in the Middle Ages, in which nearly all the leading families in the middle and north of the county took part on one side or the other. It was claimed by the abbey of Polesworth, Warws, that Robert de Stafford had given them the advowson, when his kinswoman, Edelina, was about to become a nun there, in the early C12. But it was also claimed by the family of Robert de Brinton (or Brumpton), heir of Edelina, that the advowson was theirs. The advowson was then constantly contested over the next two centuries between the abbess and the descendants of Edelina, all court cases going in favour of the abbess, until Thomas de Brinton, a descendant of Edelina, had been instituted to the living in the early C14 and held it until ejected by force by William de Ipstones. The party of William de Ipstones also besieged Brinton's mother's manor house. Then Thomas de Brinton and his kinsmen came and ejected Ipstones. Ipstones with his kinsmen then attacked Stafford, held by the king, in reprisal. In 1325-6 a special commission was sent into Staffordshire which this case was presented before. It was heard before Edward II at Tamworth 1326. The out-

come is unknown. The Pope attempted, without success, in 1327 to induce the bishop of Hereford to arbitrate (VCH vol 4 pp98-99). Perhaps the two parties came to a compromise; the presentation being made by the abbess with the consultation of the Brintons, who would make a nomination. The matter was settled when the abbey of Polesworth surrendered to the Crown in 1539. In 1553 Edward VI gave the advowson to Thomas Lord Darcy of Chiche, after which it was frequently sold off. (SHC 1883 part 2 p4) (COI pp62-64) (NSFCT 1911 pp224-225) (CE pp28-32) (TOI pp27-30).

Adam de Brinton was granted a charter on Jan 28 1251 to hold a **market** here on Mondays. And also granted an annual fair on the vigil and feast of St Edith (16 and 17 Sept) (VCH vol 4 pp93-94). The market had ceased by 1500 (NSJFS 1971 p51). The earliest reference to Church Eaton being a **borough** is in 1275. Burgage tenure existed at least until 1505 and the offices of borough bailiffs until 1599 (NSJFS 1972 p68). The foundation date or date of endowment of the **grammar school** at Church Eaton is unknown. A school, presumably, the grammar school, was in existence in 1620. It stood in the churchyard until 1857. Church Eaton schools including the grammar school were amalgamated in 1897 and the grammar school building was demolished soon after WW1 (VCH vol 4 pp101-102). In the later C17 Plot noted at Church Eaton an **hour glass**, shown to him by Walter Jennings, rector, which stopped if coal was put into it (NHS p333).

Church Eaton Brook Tributary to the Penk. Could rise at Gnosall or farther N at Knightley. Passes to the E of Church Eaton.

Church Eaton Common Minute hamlet on the Bradley road over 0.5m SE of Church Eaton. One acre of common land at Church Eaton Common still survived in the 1950s (OSST 1956-59 p12).

Church Eaton Green Minute hamlet on the Bradley road under 0.5m SSE of Church Eaton. In Church Eaton ancient parish.

Church End Former area of Handsworth ancient parish (HANDR pviii).

Church Farm To E of Bishop's Wood village. Originally called Church Stud Farm and Livery Stable. Now has an arena which is on the National Show Jumping Circuit and frequently sees top international riders including The Princess Royal (SVB p35).

Church Fenton S of City Road and W of Glebedale Road, Fenton. Formerly the area known as Lower Lane (see). The name came into being after the building of Christ Church in 1838-9 (VCH vol 8 p207).

Church Field Between Chesterton and Dimsdale (Stoke-on-Trent A-Z). In Wolstanton ancient parish.

Churchfield District 1m NNE of the High Street, West Bromwich. In West Bromwich ancient parish. The name is from probably West Bromwich's parish church, All Saints (C14), being just N of here. A 'Churchfield,' in the Wednesbury area, which may be this Churchfield is mentioned in 1315 (HOWV p108).

Churchfield House West Bromwich. Built in c1758 by Earl of Dartmouth of Sandwell Hall (see) for the incumbent of All Saints. It was twice altered and modernised. Had become derelict by 1945 (WBOP p101).

Church Fields 0.75m SE of Chesterton (1882 OS map 6 inch): slightly to the E, in the Sheldon Grove area, is Dunkirk.

Church Green A green in Enville parish. Mentioned in 1342. It presumably lay near Enville church (VCH vol 20 p108).

Church Hill A spot in the old part of Anslow, where stood 'Kynnersley's Chantry' chapel dedicated to St Leonard (UTR p236).

Church Hill In Handsworth parish. Church Hill Road runs eastwards from Handsworth parish church.

Church Hill (locally *Church'ill* BILP2 p52). Hill on which St Peter's, Hednesford is situated. In Cannock ancient parish.

Church Hill Hill on which the churches, St Bartholomew and St Mary, stand, at Wednesbury, in Wednesbury ancient parish. Is strategically placed between the headstreams of the Tame (WMLB p98). Reputedly there was an Iron Age fort on the hill (MR p360). In 916 Ethelfleda built a graff on it against the Danes. At approximately SO 992954 and SO 990954 to the E of St Bartholomew's were two windmills. Two mills are shown on Plot's map. There may have been three for Plot writes that two of the three windmills in the town echo the five church bells (NHS p28). Two mills appear on all the later maps. They would have both, undoubtedly, been post mills. One of the mills was sketched by Barber in 1811 (Birmingham Art Gallery). One of the mills, probably the western one, was at some stage replaced by a tower mill. Both mills had disappeared by 1889 (WBJ p42 il II). Hackwood says there were windmills in Windmill Lane, which is on the E side of Church Hill, and Reservoir Terrace (unlocated) as well as one at King's Hill (WAM p54). The hill is very prominent from the M6 travelling S and has also been called Wednesbury Hill, and locally Bull Hole since it was a place of bull baiting (Wednesbury Notes & Queries vol 1 Hackwood. No. 10 - copy in Smethwick ref library).

Church Hill House House at Church Hill, Brierley Hill. Stands below and adjoining a house called Fairview. It was the seat at the end of the C19 or early C20 of members of the Cooper family of the local industrial company Roberts and Cooper. The house, a Victorian-looking villa, still (1998) stands (TB Feb 1998 p6).

Church Hill House A C16 house, presumably on or near Church Hill Road, Handsworth, was perhaps the Church Hill Farm occupied by Joseph Wadhams in the C18. The C16 house was rebuilt in 1820 and subsequently was perhaps occupied by Miss Emma Lewis (1854) and Henry Elwell (1816-1872), son of John Elwell of Heath House, Wombourne, who appears to have been living here in 1861. It was the seat of Philip Muntz MP and Philip Henry Muntz in 1889, and Tom Smith from 1903. It later became a private hotel called Hill House Hotel. In the 1930s it became known by its present (1984) name Endwood Hotel (IE p120) (HPPE p22).

Church Hill House House on Church Hill, Wednesbury. Former residence of George Silas Guy JP. Was St Mary's Convent by 1953. Nos 56-74 Church Hill now (1994) occupy the site (WDOP p86p).

Church House Old timber-framed building at Abbots Bromley. Built in 1619 restored in 1967. Was being used as a parish room in 1972 (LTM Oct 1972 p7).

Church Leigh (locally just *Leigh*, and pronounced locally *Lay*). Small village on a slight incline on the E side of the Blithe 10m NE of Stafford in Leigh township and ancient parish. A bronze spearhead was found E of Dairy House Farm at SK 000364 in 1894/ 5 (NSFCT vol 39 p141. 1908 p194) (VCH vol 1 181) (NSJFS 1964 p28). A Neolithic or Bronze Age stone axe has been found in Leigh parish (HOU 1886 p43). A perforated, naturally-shaped stone, which went to the Potteries Museum, has also been found near or at Church Leigh (NSFCT vol 88 p105) (NSJFS 1964 p28). The manor of Lege appears in DB. The name Leigh is from Anglo-Saxon and means 'pasture' (SPN p35). Church was added from some time from the Middle Ages to define it from Upper, Lower and Dod's Leigh. Leigh parish church, All Saints, W of the Withington road in the village centre, was founded in or by the C12, and was restored in 1845 (HOU p435). Some tiles in the church are the earliest Minton work in an ecclesiastical building (NSFCT 1923 pp151,152). The church had a curfew bell which was financed with money left to the parish by a traveller who became lost on a foggy night on the Church Moors and was finally guided by the church bell. The curfew bell rang at dusk every night until the 1940s (SVB p111). St Thomas' Dole was still being distributed at Church Leigh on Dec 21 (St Thomas' Day) and Good Friday in 1988. By 1988 the Spencer Trust still had land and monies left in trust, to accrue interest to be used to assist local students during further education (SVB pp110-111). For a rhyme about Church Leigh see Checkley. On June 9 1908 two lady parachutists, Miss Dolly Shepherd (1886-1983) and Miss Louie May, landed at Church Leigh after what is believed to have been the first mid-air parachute rescue (GBR 1996 p132); Louie's parachute having failed. They had ascended in a balloon from Longton fete to 11,000 feet (3350 metres). Dolly was nursed at Field Farm (EAS pp11-12). Rev David Neaum was vicar of Church Leigh to 1952 when he left to be a priest on the isolated South Atlantic island of Tristan da Cunha (VB p104).

Church Mayfield The southernmost hamlet of Mayfield, which contains Mayfield's church, St John the Baptist, 0.75m SSW of Hanging Bridge.

Church Rocks Rock feature or features 0.25m N of Jacobs Ladder on the Staffs side of Dove Dale (Dovedale Guide. Keith Mantell. 1984. see centrefold map). It can possibly be identified with Dove Dale Church (see).

Church Style Former estate in Audley township. One part of it belonged to the Vernon family by at least the early C16 until at least 1733 (SHC 1944 p1).

Church Vale Suburb of West Bromwich, now part of Church Field N of the town centre. In West Bromwich parish. Formerly Sot's Hole (VCH vol 17 p4).

Churchyard House Stood close by or occupied by the Churchyard Works, Burslem. The Wedgwoods originate from Wedgwood (see) in Wolstanton ancient parish, branches of which lived at Blackwood Hall (see) and Harracles Hall (see). Gilbert Wedgwood (1588-1678) came to live in Burslem after his marriage to Margaret Burslem, and through her inherited an estate of about 200 acres. His second son Thomas (1617-1679), is said to have built the Churchyard Works (see). He was succeeded by his son Thomas (1660-1716), who was succeeded by his son Thomas (1687-1739). He married Mary Stringer and they had 13 children; the eldest son Thomas succeeded as 'master' of the Churchyard Works. Their youngest child Josiah Wedgwood I was born at Churchyard House in July 1730 (The Story of Wedgwood. Alison Kelly. 1962 p70. 1975 pp10-11). Churchyard House was probably demolished after Josiah Wedgwood I's death when the estate was sold to Thomas Green and the works

extended. However, according to Jewitt the house may have still existed in 1883 as the Mitre Hotel (Ceramic Art. Ll Jewitt p439) (Life of Josiah Wedgwood. Eliza Meteyard. vol 1 pp188il,200-222) (VCH vol 8 p118).

JOSIAH WEDGWOOD I. Josiah Wedgwood I vastly improved pottery ware by industrialising the pottery industry and has been called 'father of the Potteries.' From 1751 or 1752 he worked at Upper Cliff Bank Works (see). In c1754 Wedgwood left that works to be a partner with Thomas Whieldon at his works at Fenton Low and Fenton Hall (see). From 1759 he rented the Ivy House Works (see). In 1762, on being appointed potter to Queen Charlotte, he took additional premises at the Brickhouse Works (see), where he introduced an engine-turned lathe in 1763. During which time he resided at Brick House (see) where he first received his future wife, Sarah, who he married in 1764. In March 1765, possibly at the Leopard Hotel (see) in Burslem, he met with the engineer, James Brindley, to discuss the possibility of the building of the Trent and Mersey Canal (see) for the easier transportation of his wares. On July 26 1766 he cut the first sod for this canal at Brownhills (see), Tunstall. In 1768 on medical grounds Wedgwood's right leg had to be amputated. On June 13 1769 having out-grown Brickhouse Works (see) he opened the new Etruria Works (see) at Etruria, a new district, which he named himself, on the former Ridge House (see) estate. By 1770 he had built Etruria Hall (see) for himself and his family in the vicinity of the works. For Thomas Bentley (1730-1780), a Liverpool merchant and his partner since 1768, he built Bentley House (see), and a pottery works known as Bentley Bank (see). To beautify the area close to the works he may have had planted a grove of trees known as Etruria Grove (see). In Wedgwood's later years the company increased in notoriety after being commissioned in 1773 by the Empress Catherine II of Russia to make a dinner and dessert service of nearly a thousand pieces, and by employing artists such as John Flaxman, George Stubbs, and John Bacon, to design models for the bas-relief on ware. As a member of the Lunar Society Wedgwood was entertained at Great Barr Hall (see). As a Unitarian he may have attended services at the Old Meeting House in Newcastle-under-Lyme (see). He died on Jan 3 1795 and despite being a Unitarian was buried in the Anglican churchyard of St Peter's, Stoke-upon-Trent. For his descendants see Etruria Hall. His widow, Sarah, resided at Parkfields Cottage (see) from 1805 until her death in 1815. A statue of him was erected in Winton Square (see), Stoke-upon-Trent, in 1863. In 1957 a second bronze statue of him was made from the old cast and erected by the Wedgwood company offices at Barlaston. It was moved to the new visitor centre there in 2000 (ES March 8 2000 p8p). In 1869 the Wedgwood Institute (see) was opened in Burslem to his memory. There is a statue of Wedgwood by AH Hodge on the facade of the V&A in London. Great celebrations to commemorate the Bicentenary of Wedgwood took place in the Potteries in 1930, the principal attraction being an historical pageant between May 19 and May 24. The firm of Josiah Wedgwood and Sons continued at Etruria Works until moving to Barlaston in 1939, occupying a previously undeveloped site in an area which has since become known as Wedgwood (see) (SMC p166) (ILN March 7 1863 p249) (HSP pp180,182,183,184) (SSW pp62-83) (Life of Wedgwood. Miss Meteyard) (Josiah Wedgwood. Prof AH Church. 1903) (H pp49-52,148,149) (S pp120,121) (SOSH pp262,264,265-269) (ES Feb 22 1930 p3 il of Churchyard House. May 13 1930 p4. May 8 1995 p8) (HOE pp27,284-302,309,326) (NSFCT 1956 pp18-46) (STMSM Oct 1980 pp24-26) (POTP pp224-225) (TOS pp23-28) (The Story of Wedgwood. A Kelly) (Life of Wedgwood. John Leslie) (Life of Wedgwood. R Nicholls) (Life of Wedgwood. Llewellyn Jewitt).

Churchyard Works The Churchyard estate was SE of St John's church, Burslem. The pottery is said to have been built by Thomas Wedgwood (1617-1679) of Churchyard House (see) (The Story of Wedgwood. Alison Kelly. 1975 p11). It was inherited by Thomas Wedgwood (d1739) father of Josiah Wedgwood I. Here Josiah Wedgwood I served his apprenticeship (OTP p143). The pottery was bought by Josiah Wedgwood I in 1780; he installed his nephew, Thomas, here, leasing it on Thomas's death to a relative, Joseph Wedgwood, in 1788 (POP p22). It had passed out of Wedgwood hands by 1811 and had been demolished by 1896 when St John's School was rebuilt on the site (VCH vol 8 p133). Has also appeared as Churchyard Bank (OTP p143).

Churnet, River One of the principle rivers in Staffs. The site of its source and upper reaches has long been in dispute. Speed's map shows it rising near Hardings Booth and flowing E of Meerbrook. Garner has it running at Rushton. In fact the old course ran to the S of Rudyard and through Horton Gap (NSFCT 1928 pp96-97): Meer Brook is said to have joined the Churnet at New Grange (SSE 1993 p4). The source is about 300 yards S of the Royal Cottage Inn at a place christened by the NSFC in the C19 'Churnet Well' (NSFCT 1876 pp10,33-36. 1880 pp26-27) (OL vol 1 pp47-51. vol 2 p290), by a small farm called White Middle Hills (HOLF p14). 'Old Nanny Moberley' lived near the source of the Churnet (HOLF p55). Blackshawmoor Reservoir is formed by its damming. It runs through Thorncliffe and Solomon's Hollow. It has been described as fast flowing (HAF p295) and the mills at Upper Hulme, Leek (Brindley's Mill), Leek, Leekbrook, Cheddleton (the flint mills), Froghall, Oakamoor, Alton, and Rocester were powered by it (HAF p295). Thomas Wardle (1831-1909), a leading figure in the Leek silk-dyeing industry, claimed that the water of the Churnet and its tributaries was among the best dyeing water in Europe. It was much utilized for this purpose in Leek and produced the unique raven-black dye for which Leek was celebrated (SOSH p346) (VCH vol 7 p109). The river is navigable from Froghall to its confluence with the Trent, S of Rocester. In c1900 a horse and trap, with its driver plunged over a cliff in Cotton Dell and into the river, but remarkably they survived, all three landing up-right (TFTPM pp67-68). The level of the river was lowered in 1980 (WTMS p145). (GNHS p22*). Has appeared as Chirnet (1240-1318), Chernett (1272), Chirnete (1284), Chyrnet (1318), Churnett (1540), and Churne (1586) (SPN p35), and incorrectly as the Hamps on T Hutchinson's map 1798 (NSFCT 1925 p79). Sleigh thought the name was from the Gaelic 'Car' 'turn or bend' (OL p51). Possibly from Anglo-Saxon meaning little churn, but possibly pre-Roman or Welsh? Celtic (DUIGNAN). Ekwall, Prof Jackson, and Oakden have come to the conclusion that the origin is pre-English and unknown (SPNO p7). Means the river of many windings from 'car;' the Gaelic for 'turn' or 'bend;' the Celtic equivalent of Manifold, both rivers pursuing a winding course (NSFCT 1876 p36. 1908 p128. 1946 p159). Is of Celtic origin (SDW p9) (SL p44 note), and means 'river' (SPN p35).

Churnet Grange 0.75m NW of Basford Green. Formerly Basford Old Hall. Bears the date 1662 (NSFCT 1906 171).

Churnet Hall, The Cheddleton. The upper storey was used as a clubroom for boys prior to the cinema; the basement was used as a malthouse for the Cheddleton Brewery (Cheddleton Remembered. Vera Priestman. 1978 p40).

Churnet Valley Valley of the Churnet. Picturesque pre-Triassic gorge (NSFCT 1928 p93). Stretches from Cheddleton and reaches its zenith and end about Alton, where it is likened to the Rhineland (F p497). The valley has been referred to as the 'Hidden Valley' and the 'Secret Valley' (HLSP p58). The Duke of Cumberland in pursuit of the Young Pretender in the 1745 Jacobean Rebellion described the upper Churnet valley as viewed from Blackshaw Moor as 'the finest valley he had ever seen' (NSFCT 1884 p21). A stone axe possibly of Neolithic or Bronze Age found in the Churnet Valley is in the Potteries Museum (NSJFS 1964 p27). At Consall Forge and Froghall the scenery is considered blighted by old mills and kilns, which supplied the Potteries with lime and flint. The Caldon Canal was built to transport, mainly, lime and flint, as was, the Churnet Valley Railway. The line closed in 1965 with a part between Oakamoor to Leekbrook remaining open for freight. When the last freight train ran in Aug 1988 a campaign was started for a light railway on the line; in the 1970s preservationists had established a railway centre by the line at Cheddleton. Churnet Valley Railway PLC, obtained the track and started running stream trains on the Leekbrook-Cheddleton stretch from Aug 1996, and on to Consall from 1998; an extension to Froghall is due to open in 2000 (SL p257) (info Churnet Valley Railway). For Churnet Valley Ironstone see Froghall.

Churnet Way Recent walkway devised to run from Denstone to Oakamoor along the Churnet (VB p179).

Churnet Well Near the source of the Churnet (OL vol 2 p290).

Cinder Hill Hamlet, now suburb, 0.75m ENE of Sedgley. In Sedgley ancient parish. There was a small mining settlement here by 1600 (HC p24). The name appears on the Plan of the Mines of Lord Dudley 1812.

Cinder Hill Is a hill adjacent to Saxon's Low on the former Tittensor Common. The name may be from Cendred, brother of St Werburgh, who succeeded his uncle Ethelred to the Mercian throne (Annals of the Diocese of Lichfield Past and Present 1859).

Cinderhill House Colliery managers house. SE of Longton. Known locally as Cinderhill Hall (SHST pp529,533).

Cinders District S of Lower Gornal.

Circuit Brook Seems to raise to N of Cross in the Hand. Runs N of Lichfield in an easterly direction. Joins Curborough Brook at Nether Stowe, which flows to the Trent. The brook, whose name is self-explanatory (SPNO p7), may have been called Stychbrook.

Clamgoose Lane Field name derived from an animal name (APB p48) near Cheadle. There is a Clamgoose Lane marked on 1834 OS map N of Harewood Hall.

Clanbrook S end of Enville Common. In Kinver parish. The Fox Inn stood here on the Stourbridge-Bridgnorth road by 1850 (VCH vol 20 p121). Has also appeared as Clambrooks (SGSAS).

Clanford Tiny hamlet 0.5m SW of Seighford. The name is from Anglo-Saxon 'claene,' 'clane' meaning clean, pure; so, 'the clean ford' (DUIGNAN p45) (SPN p72).

Clanford Brook Joins Doxey Brook which flows to the Sow.

Clanford Grange Grange of Ranton Priory (VCH vol 3 p254).

Clanford Hall House 0.75m SW of Seighford. In Seighford parish. Occupied by Antony Titley (d1845) (mem in Seighford church).

Clan Park House 1.25m SW of Trysull. In Trysull ancient parish. In existence by 1814 (VCH vol 20 p187).

Clanway Small settlement in the area of the present Clanway Sports Stadium, N of Hoskins Road (1834 OS map) (Stoke-on-Trent A-Z), and the name is preserved in Clanway Street off Furlong Road, Tunstall.

Clanway Hall Seat of a branch of the Bourne family from before 1575 until the early C17. In 1829 it was owned by Thomas Wedgwood. Philip Egerton Wedgwood leased it to John Henry Clive (1781-1853), pottery manufacturer and nephew of Clive of India, who was occupying the hall in 1851. In childhood Clive lived with the Heathcotes at Longton Hall. When working at Newfield Pottery he lived at Newfield Hall, later he was a resident at Chell House; one of his life achievements was to develop a system of shorthand, part of which was adopted by Pitman. His grandson William Clive was living at Clanway Hall later in the C19. The C19 farmhouse was still standing adjacent to the Clanway Brickworks in 1958 (VCH vol 8 p90) (POTP pp62,63).

Clapgate Small area 1m SE of Trysull. Formerly in the extra parochial district of Woodford Grange. It was an inhabited place by 1666 and it may have also been called Woodford Gate (VCH vol 20 p225).

Claregate District 0.75m N of Tettenhall. It was probably an inhabited area by 1327 when Nicholas le Clare was a tenant here (VCH vol 20 p7). However, Raven thinks the name may be from Welsh 'claear' 'bright,' or Middle Welsh 'clayer' 'gentle' as in a slope, or from Anglo-Saxon 'claefren' 'clover' or a corruption of clay (BCTV p18).

Clare Hays Former common shared between the commoners of Lutley and Mere in Enville ancient parish. The common appears to have remained open until 1746 when it was enclosed by agreement despite attempts by the lord of Lutley to enclose it early in the C16 (VCH vol 20 p108). The name may be preserved in a property called Claire Hayes on the E side of Gospel Ash Road in Bobbington parish.

Clarke's Haye In Armitage parish (W p556). Occurs as Clark's Hay in 1834 (W 1834 p306). The house Clark's Hays to the SE of Handsacre Hall on the E side of Lichfield Road appears on maps between 1887 and 1938. The site of the house had been developed with housing by the 1990s.

Clark Well Stood near the National Schools, Mow Cop. Built by a man named Clarke. It claimed the life of a girl who tried to jump over the stones placed over the well, she tripped and later died (MC p26). The stones have been rebuilt in a garden in Congleton Road (WMC). Has also appeared as Clarke's Well.

Clasp Hill A hill at one end of Abbot's Castle, Trysull (SVS p327).

Clatterbatch Deep ravine descending to Clent from St Kenelm's cemetery (SVS pp226, 289 note). The name is from 'noisy valley.' The noise having been caused by stones clattering down the stream (A Short History of Clent. John Amphlett) (TB Jan 1974 p13). Said to have been where the Britons massacred the Romans in c416 AD in a battle on Clent Heath (TB Aug 1975 p9. Sept 1975 p5). Appears to have been formerly written Combach, Cowbach, Cowbatch, Cowdale (NHS p412) (maps of Plot and Bowen) (SVS) (CR p19) and Clatterbach. Clatterbatch Road runs down from St Kenelm's to Clent.

Clatterbatch District N of the Stour just in Staffs. 0.75m ESE of Amblecote. Clatterback Forge on the banks of the Stour was in existence by 1832 (BCWJ p85).

Clattershall District 0.75m WSW of Brierley Hill.

Clayers Pool In a corner of Enville Park (NHS p91).

Clay Gates Small hamlet to E of Engleton, 1.25m NE of Brewood. Clay Gates has been known as Hell Gates (BDH 1992 p333). 'Pepperpots' is the local name for two single-story square brick cottages here. They were built by Mrs Monckton of Stretton in the mid C19 and their design is said to have been suggested by workers' dwellings in Scotland (VCH vol 5 p24).

Clayhanger Former small hamlet, now a large village, 4m N of Walsall. Formerly in a detached portion of the foreign of Walsall ancient parish. The name is of Anglo-Saxon origin and means 'the clayey hanging wood.' There is a great deposit of red marls, and a sloping bank, still sparsely timbered (DUIGNAN) (SPN p35). The name occurs as arable, pasture, and woodland in the later C14 and early C15, and appears in a Court Roll of 1617. By 1763 there was settlement here on the W side of Clayhanger Common. There was a small village of Clayhanger by the earlier C19 (VCH vol 17 p278) (SNBC p17). An old iron chapel, Holy Trinity, in Church Street, was demolished by c1980. In c1999 work began on a new multi-purpose church building on the former site. The new church is to be dedicated to Holy Trinity (info Mike Branscombe). The ghost of a scout in old scout uniform has been seen (1991) by Clayhanger Lane Bridge, at SK 044048. It was assumed that the scout had fallen from the bridge here in WW1 despite efforts to save him (MGM (lost source info) or MCGM or MGH pp44-45p).

Clayhanger Common Former common situated over the E part of the present village of Clayhanger and further to the E. It once formed a single continuous waste with Walsall Wood Common. Any remaining common was enclosed in c1876 (VCH vol 17 p278).

Clay Hills W area of Tunstall. At Clay Hills was a windmill built in c1813, which stood in Windmill Street now renamed Holland Street, at SJ 857515, between America Street and Goodfellow Street. (WWT p86 il of facing) (TFTP pp54,55 il). It was demolished in 1855 (SLM Spring 1954 p24) (VCH vol 8 p98) (WBJ p40), or in 1860 and Windmill Inn built near the site (OTP pp10,29 il of by Scarratt). The materials were reused for buildings in Windmill Street and adjoining Peel Street, renamed Robert Street (WBJ p40). George Smith (d1895), social reformer, later of Reaps Moor (see), and Coalville, Leics, was born here in 1831 (OL vol 1 pp103-108il) (WIWC pp3,4,132) (SOSH p346; says Claymills) (POTP p169).

Clay Lake Farm and lane W of Endon Bank, in the Woodhouse Green area. Formerly in Endon township in Leek ancient parish. Clay Lake Farm was so called in 1678 (VCH vol 7 p177) (BEH p5).

Clay Mills 0.5m NE of Stretton (Burton). In Burton upon Trent ancient parish. In 1943 the skull of Bos longifrons of C1 BC was found at SK 271262 (info KL Neal). A bronze beaded torque 105 millimetres in length was found in 1944 at a depth of two metres in gravel at Clay Mills, only a short distance from the line of Icknield Street. It is of Romano-British origin (Brigantian) dating from c130 AD (BTIH p10). In 1943 oak piles and a millstone grit milestone was found a few yards W of the line of Icknield Street in a gravel pit by Fleam Mill at SK 261270 (info KL Neal). The name is thought to be a corruption of Cliff Mill (LTD p214). References to a mill on the Dove at Stretton occur from the late C12. Appears as Clyffe Mulne in 1398, and as Cleymill in 1597 (SHJ autumn 1991 p8). There is a pumping station at Clay Mills, at SK 262258, to pump away all the discharge from the Burton breweries. Its four steam engines of 1885 in operation to 1971 were the largest of their kind in the county (IAS p196).

Clayton Former village, now a large suburb, 1.5m S of Newcastle-under-Lyme. Former township in Stoke-upon-Trent chapelry and ancient parish (W p236). The name means 'clay town or tun' (DUIGNAN) (SSE 1996 p12). Or 'farm on the clay' (SPN p88). The manor of Claitone appears in DB (SSE 1996 p12). It was known as Clayton Culvert or Great Clayton in the Middle Ages to distinguish it from Clayton Griffith (see) manor (SL p71). There may have been a chapel at Clayton in Henry III's reign (HBST p522) (TTH p27). Limestone used to be mined here (VCH vol 2 p193). In 1828 14 people were involved an attempt to rescue John Highfield from the custody of a special constable at Clayton. During the course of the rescue, they apparently set a dog on the constables (LOU p234). The civil parish of Clayton, created in 1896, was abolished in 1932 when it entered into Newcastle-under-Lyme parish. The ecclesiastical parish of Clayton was created in 1969 (GLAUE p408). The church, St James the Great, at the junction of Clayton Lane and Clayton Road, was built in c1963 (ES May 30 1969) (info Rev Roger Legg). The (Staffordshire) Post House, Clayton Road, was unique when built in 1967 in that it was the first motor hotel to be built in a designated green belt area. The hotel was officially opened on Oct 2 1967 (Newcastle Times Sept 27 1967) (ES). A direct descendant of the Albanian national hero Alexander George Castriot, also known as Skanderbeg, who rescued his country from the Turks in the early C15, Charles Castriot de Renzi, was living in Beresford Crescent, Clayton in 1992 (MIDD vol 5 pp32-35p). Another descendant of this family was appointed vicar of St Mary's, Tunstall (see) in 1898. The ghost of a cowled figure haunts Clayton Lane and Springfields and has been seen by every member of a certain family (SFH pp19,21). In 1992 a couple saw a UFO in the form of a huge light descend onto the middle of the road at Clayton (SMM p96).

Clayton Griffith Former township and manor separate to Clayton (Great Clayton) (W p236). Formerly in a detached portion of Trentham ancient parish in Stoke-upon-Trent ancient parish (later Newcastle-under-Lyme parish) until removed to Newcastle-under-Lyme parish in 1894 (GLAUE p426). The Griffith or Griffyn or Griffen family were lords of it in the C13 (SPN p88). (SDW p12). It was probably founded after 1086 since it is not mentioned in DB. In the late C17 it was centred on the estate and house called Hill Farm in the area now occupied by Westlands housing estate (VCH vol 8 p76). Has also appeared as Little Clayton (VCH vol 8 p77).

Clayton Hall Clayton. On E side of Clayton Road, near the junction with Clayton Lane, before the lane was diverted to the N. The old hall, a low gabled building of probably C16 or early C17 date (HBST p521 il facing), was rebuilt on a site farther E in the 1840s on a larger scale in the classical style with Italian features. Perhaps the Lovatt family had had a house here from their arrival in Clayton in the early C15 (NSF p44). The last male Lovatt died at the old hall in 1803. It then passed in the female line to the Booths and then to the Wises, who left in 1916. Seat of John Ayshford Wise MP, who died here in 1870 (POTP p232) and Sir James Heath, MP for the old NW Staffs constituency. Until 1940 the hall was owned by the Johnsons, pottery manufacturers, when it was requisitioned by the Admiralty and in WW2 served as a training centre for the Fleet Air Arm, during which time it was known as HMS Daedalus (ES Oct 26 1992 p8p). Sept 12 1996 p8il of the hall camouflaged in WW2). In 1948 the hall became a girl's grammar school (VCH vol 8 p78) (NUL p155).

Clayton's Folly Stood on a slight eminence on the corner of Dudley Street and Billhay Lane, Carters Green, West Bromwich. Built by John Clayton (d1887) who worked for Walkers Bros of Gospel Oak, Tipton, makers of cannon and cannon shot. Clayton was an inventor and designer of smelting furnaces and invented a method of heating cannon shot red hot, a devastating innovation against wooden ships or wooden buildings. He went to the Crimea to build suitable furnaces in the war with Russia and came back with a small fortune. With it he built a flamboyant 20-roomed house in the Empire-rococo, French and Italian style, complete with large couchant lions on the cap-stones of the garden pillars. Soon after he had spent his money the government rescinded his pension and he was unable to maintain it in a manner to which he had hoped, and so it became known as the folly - Clayton's Folly (BCM Jan 1981 pp65-66il on p65) (TB June 1989 p3). Clayton is said to have used his past employers' house, Walker Hall (see), as the model for his house (HOTIP p188).

Cleat Hill Hill 374 feet high over which the A51 runs 1m SE of Longdon.

Clementson's Pool Lost. It existed in what is now Broad Street, Hanley. The pool where the ducking stool was used (SHST p488).

Clent Ancient parish and village lying on the southern slopes of the Clent Hills 28m S of Stafford, 17m NNE of Worcester.
EARLY to 1086. By the roadside just beyond Clent in c1952 there was an Ice Age granite boulder (STELE Feb 29 1952). The **name** is from perhaps a corruption of the British 'glenn,' the Cornish 'glyn,' the Irish 'gleaun' or Saxon 'glenn' denoting a narrow valley or dingle encompassed with wood (SHOS vol 2 p241). Or is possibly a form of the Danish 'Clint,' meaning hard or projecting crag or rock (A Short History of Clent. John Amphlett). Or is from Middle English 'hard flinty rock' (TB Jan 1974 p12). Clent was anciently in the Forest of Feckenham. Reputedly, there was a royal palace and shooting lodge of the Mercian kings at Clent (The Worcs Village Book. Women's Institute. 1988 p49). According to legend Prince **Kenelm**, the son of Kenulf or Cenwulf, king of Mercia, was murdered in Clent parish in the C9. According to the legend when Kenulf died, his son Kenelm, then aged seven or eight, was proclaimed king, but his sister, Quendreda, wishing to be queen persuaded her lover Ascobert to take the child into the woods and kill him. This supposedly took place in a furrow - St Kenelm's Furrow (see) - on Knoll Hill near Clent. Ascobert buried the body at the scene of the murder or close by. The burial place was discovered on account of a dove rising from the severed head of Kenelm and travelling to Rome where it dropped a scroll on the high altar of St Peter's or some say at the Pope's feet bearing the words

> In Clentho vaccae valli Kenelmus regius natus,
> Jacet sub spino, capite truncatus.

One translation is

> In Clent Cow-pasture under a thorn
> Of head bereft lies Kenelm, King born.

(SW p124). Messengers were then sent to England to locate the body at Clent. It was found on the boundary of Clent and Romsley parishes, 1.25m NE of Clent. As soon as the body was found a nearby spring - St Kenelm's Well (see) - is said to have burst open. Kenelm's body was taken for burial to Winchcombe Abbey, Glous, which Kenulf is believed to have founded. When the foundations of the abbey church were excavated in 1815, two stone coffins were found, one containing a man and the other a child, which may possibly have been the remains of Kenulf and Kenelm. Leland had recorded that they were buried together in the church (ESS pp69-71,156,157) (SW p124). The Anglo-Saxon Chronicle says Kenulf died in 819 (VCHW vol 3 p50), or in c821 (NSFCT 1928 p31), a modern account says he reigned from 796 to 821 (In Search of the Dark Ages. Michael Wood. 1981 p10). Kenelm seems to have reigned for little or no time and Kenulf's brother Ceolwulf or Cedwulf is usually given as succeeding Kenulf. A Saxon chapel, dedicated to St Kenelm, was built near the site where Kenelm was found buried in c890 (BCWJ). A long lost settlement in the vicinity of St Kenelm's chapel, called Kenelmstowe (see), grew up in the Middle Ages. The legend of St Kenelm, as he became, was first written down in the C11, by which time many miracles had been recorded at the saint's shrine at Winchcombe. The outline of the legend has been traced back to Florence of Worcester who was living in 1118. Matthew of Paris, Leland, Erdeswick and Plot all record the legend (NHS pp411-413) (VCHW vol 3 p50 note) (SH p31). The feast of St Kenelm has been given as July 17 (SHOS vol 2 p243) (The Worcs Village Book. Women's Institute. 1988 p50) or July 28 (CR pp65-75). (SVS pp290-294) (GNHS p183) (Short History of Clent. Amphlett. App A) (St Kenelm Church Guide. 1976 pp1-2) (TB Jan/ Feb 1973 p17. March/ April 1973 p21). **Removed to Staffs**. Clent, formerly a large manor including Broome, came to be in Staffs for it was bought by a courtier called Æthelsige, Dean of Worcester, from King Ethelred. Æthelsige intended to grant it to Worcester cathedral but on Æthelsige's death in c1016 the sheriff of Staffordshire seized it and is thought to have transferred it to his own county for administrative convenience (VCHW vol 3 p51) (SL p29) (Broome: A Worcestershire Village. Geoffrey Parks. 1978 p7).

1086 to 1600. Ecclesiastically Clent parish, formed before 1086, has always been in Worcester diocese (SHC 1916 p193) (VCH vol 3 p92). The parish **church**, St Leonard, of c1170 origin with many later additions, possibly stands on the site of a former church (The Parish Church of St Leonard, Clent). The living was, and still (1988) is, in the ecclesiastical patronage of the Lord Chancellor (The Worcs Village Book. Women's Institute. 1988 p49). The wake of Kenelmstowe or St Kenelm's Wake or the Crab Wake seems to have been the same as St Kenelm's fair (see below). The **manor** (including Broome), appears in DB under Worcs as a possession of the king (VCHW vol 3 p51). Broome was severed from Clent in 1154 when Henry II granted it to Maurice de Ombersley (Broome: A Worcestershire Village. Geoffrey Parks. 1978 pp5,7). Clent manor remained with the Crown until King John exchanged it, together with Mere and Kingswinford, with Ralph de Somery, of Dudley Castle (see), for Wolverhampton (SHOS vol 2 p226). In Henry VIII's reign the inhabitants of Clent petitioned for a confirmation of their rights as dwelling on ancient demesne of the Crown and obtained a charter in 1566 (VCHW vol 3 p51) or 1567 (W p181), which was confirmed in 1625 (VCHW vol 3 p51) or 1630 (W p181). (The Worcs Village Book. Women's Institute. 1988 p49). The charter gave them exemption from toll, stallage, passage, portage, etc, from contributing to the expenses of sending knights to parliament, and from serving on juries except those in their own parish (W p181) (VCHW vol 3 p51). The charter was granted on the strength of an erroneous identification. When search was made for Clent in DB, the fact that it had been originally in Worcs was overlooked, and it was identified with Chenet (Cannock) in Staffs, the only place in the county to which its name bore any resemblance (VCHW vol 3 p51). By at least the C18 the manor had been divided into two, Upper or Church Clent, and Lower or Nether Clent (Plot's map) (SHOS vol 2 p241). In 1253 Roger de Somery of Dudley Castle (see), lord of the manor, was granted a **fair** to be held on the eve and day of St Kenelm's feast (July 17) and two days following. The fair, held in St Kenelm's churchyard just within Romsley parish (SHOS vol 2 p243) (VCHW vol 3 p51), seems to have been also known as the wake of Kenelmstowe or St Kenelm's Wake or the Crab Wake. By at least the late C18 the unique custom of the inhabitants pelting each other with crab apples was practised at the fair or wake. It was of unknown origin and commonly known as Crabbing the Parson, for rarely did the clergyman escape being hit by crab apples as he went to and from chapel. Hackwood in SG suggests Rev John Todd (curate of St Kenelm's 1801-1833) may have been the last parson to be 'crabbed' for people were beginning to throw more than just apples by the period of his curacy. The fair or wake continued until the middle of the C19 (Short History of Clent. Amphlett. pp26-27) (VCHW vol 3 p51). (GM 1797 vol 67 p738) (SHOS vol 2 p243) (NSFCT 1912 p216) (St Kenelm Church Guide. 1976. pp6-7). In 1868 Clent had a cattle and a cheese fair 'at which the inhabitants are allowed by an old charter to sell beer without licence' (CR). The fair had been discontinued by 1913 (VCHW vol 3 p52). Hackwood noted Clent had a fair for cheese on July 29 (SCSF p106). The field names or topographical features Hanging Close and Hanging Hill at Clent probably preserve the site of the manorial **gallows** tree (SCSF p123).

1600 to PRESENT. Although agriculture has always been the main occupation of Clent inhabitants, in the C16 and the C17 some were employed in the scythe-making trade, which was followed by nail-making which died out in the late C19 (VCHW vol 3 p50). **Oak Apple day** (May 29), which commemorates the restoration of Charles II, seems to have been commemorated in Clent by the hanging of oak branches from the top of the church tower. The custom was believed to have not been performed for hundreds of years by the late C20, when there were some in the village who wished for its revival (info Carole Hodgson) (The Worcs Village Book. Women's Institute. 1988 p50). **Returned to Worcs**. The curious detached portion of Staffs in Worcs formed by Clent and Broom parishes was annexed to Worcs for parliamentary purposes in 1832, and removed to Halfshire hundred, Worcs, for all purposes in 1844 (VCHW vol 3 p50) (SL p29). The 150th anniversary of the final removal was celebrated at The Woodman Inn, Clent, in 1994 by **Clent History Society**, formed in Sept 1985; since 1997 the society has produced an occasional journal called 'Clent Clarion' (info Carole Hodgson). The name 'Clent' has given its name to a hundred of Worcs. After the opening of a railway station at Hagley Clent and the Clent Hills became a popular destination with **excursionists** from the Black Country (SNSV vol 2 p83). The parish council is the only one in the country to have its own coat of **arms** (BCM summer 2000 p78). In the novels of Francis Brett Young Clent is Wychbury (BCM autumn 1989 p58). On a road leading towards Clent a **UFO** was seen on Oct 15 1978 (TB April 1979 p4). **Persons**. **Nathan Withy** alias 'The Blind Bard of Clent' wrote poetry in the style of the poet, William Shenstone (1714-1763). He had a daughter who he referred to as the 'Shepherdess of the Clent Alps' (Guide to the Clent Hills. William Timings. 1835) (TB Oct 28 1999 p6). Between at least 1981 and 1986 Mrs **Hazel Saunders** of Clent was considered the worst singer in Britain or the world (GBR 1981 p102. 1986 p95).

Clent Grove Thomas Liell (d1807) was of Clent Grove. In 1851 the house was occupied by Misses Liell (W p19). The house was later occupied by George F Chance (d1933), High Sheriff of Worcs in 1910 (mems in Clent church), and at another time by Richard Stuart Todd, a partner in a flour milling business in Birmingham. In the early 1930s the house became the Sunfield Home for mentally handicapped children (SNSV vol 2 p83).

Clent Hall Clent. Occupied in 1851 by Mrs Durant (W p19).

Clent Heath Clent Heath has been identified with Lower Clent Common in the Thicknall Farm area (SNSV vol 2 p76). A battle between the Britons and the Romans is said to have been fought on Clent Heath in 416 AD; prior to the battle the Britons camped on Walton Hill, Rumbow, and Calcot, whilst the Romans camped on Wychbury Hill. The Romans were massacred at Clatterbach (TB Aug 1975 p9. Sept 1975 p5). In 1781 five burial mounds remained on Clent Heath, which may have had some association with this battle. Dr Nash had one opened in the C18 and then Bishop Lyttelton had some opened, one of which was found to contain a considerable quantity of burnt wood and ashes at a depth of 14 feet. Another contained small human bones. In another was discovered an urn, filled with small human bones, which Dr Nash thought belonged to a Roman general. During the enclosure of Clent Heath in 1785 most of these burial mounds were carted away and used as manure. In the process many bones were discovered. By 1845 only two mounds remained and they were covered by fir and beech trees (History of Worcestershire. Dr Nash. pp485-486) (SHOS vol 2 p241) (CR pp57,60-62) (VCHW vol 3 p50).

Clent Hill Hill in the Clent Hills, 1013 feet high, 0.5m NNE of Clent. Has the best panorama in the county. The hill, locally known as Adam's Hill (info Margaret Handford), is perhaps the same as Plot's Knoll Hill (see). It is Pen Beacon in the novels of Francis Young (History Around Us. Halesowen. John Billingham). On a ridge to the W, at 997 feet, is a mock druidical temple, called the Druids Temple, consisting of four upright stones. They were erected as an eye-catcher for Hagley Hall by George, 1st Lord Lyttelton sometime between 1686 and 1773. But his successor Lord Lyttelton claimed they were of ancient origin; they are sometimes considered of Druidical origin and have been called in relation to a tradition 'Ossian's Grave.' The stones are believed to have come out of a quarry in Hagley Park (VCHW vol 3 p50) (STELE Feb 24 1955. March 2 1956) (CR p50). The origin of the stones was the subject of debate in N&Q in 1865 and 1885 (N&Q series 3 vol vii pp323, 365, 389, 507; vol viii p18. series 6 vol viii pp247,349). In 1995 the upright stones were situated by a triangulation pillar and were defaced with graffiti.

Clent Hills Small range of hills in Clent parish to the N and E of Clent. The hills rise to 1035 feet (BOEW p121). The main peaks seem to be Clent Hill (alias Adam's Hill) (1013 feet), Walton Hill (1033 feet), Calcot Hill (787 feet) and Romsley Hill (CR pp17,52) (info Margaret Handford). The highest hills have superb views and Clent Hill provides an excellent panorama. The first glacier intrusion into the Midlands in the Ice Age left boulders of volcanic ash and felsite from the Arenig Mountains in North Wales on the top of the Clent Hills (WJO Nov 1909 p295). The ancient Britons are said to have camped on

Walton Hill, Rumbow, and Calcot, prior to a battle fought against the Romans on Clent Heath (see). Leland referred to the hills as the Blake hills (LI part v p96). The hills and the surrounding views are described in Drayton's 'Polyolbion' (song 7) (VCHW vol 3 p50). The owners of certain land in Clent still had the rights of common on the Clent Hills in 1913 (VCHW vol 3 p50).

Clent House Red brick and stone house 0.5m WNW of Clent. The older portion of the house dated from the early C18, but the main part of the house dated from the late C18. In 1851 the house was occupied by Henry Bradley. John Amphlett was the owner of the house in 1913 (W p19) (VCHW vol 3 p50). The house was demolished in 1936. The remaining stable block, dating from 1709, remained and was converted, after WW2, into residential accommodation for Tony Norris, son of the former vicar of Cradley, who became a specialist plant breeder (BOEW p121) (SNSV vol 2 p83). The stable block is of brick and consists of eleven bays, with a three-bay centre, stressed by a steep pediment and a cupola (BOEW p121).

Clerk's Pool Small medieval fishpool formerly situated 0.5m E of Tyrley Castle on Clerk's Pool Brook. Having been remade in c1770 it was drained in 1881 (SHC 1945/ 6 pp7-8). Has also appeared as Clark's Pool.

Clerk's Pool Brook Rises on Brockley Moor and flows northwards on the W side of Peatswood to the Coalbrook. At the time of DB it formed the boundary between Tyrley and Almington manors and later formed the boundary between Tyrley and Almington townships (SHC 1945/ 6 p7 note).

Cleveland House Stood in the area of Sutherland Place and Gordon Street, All Saints (see), Wolverhampton. Occupied in 1851 by John Barker, High Sheriff of Staffs, it was still standing in c1900 (W p19) (Wolverhampton Chronicle Jan 15 1999 p14).

Clewley Coppice 2m SSW of Coven.

Cliff Or Cliffe (1834 OS map) is a house 1m S of Swythamley.

Cliff Bank Hill leading up to Hartshill from Stoke-upon-Trent (POP p74). The name is from probably Cliff Hay, a derivation of Clive Hay (see). Cliff Bank Pottery was at the junction of Shelton Old Road with Hartshill Road, and appears to have been occupied in 1740 by Daniel Bird, who was known as 'the flint potter' as a result of his having discovered the right proportion of flint and clay needed to prevent the ware from cracking in the oven; it was pulled down in 1914 (VCH vol 8 p202). On the opposite side of the road from Cliff Bank Pottery stood Upper Cliff Bank Works (see) where Josiah Wedgwood I was a partner with Thomas Alders. Newcastle-Uttoxeter turnpike road joined the one to Burslem and Lawton at Cliff Bank. In 1842 the whole length of Honeywall, Penkhull, was divided into four different names; the bottom division was known as Cliff Bank or previously Castle Cliff (PRA p74).

Cliff Bank House Stoke-upon-Trent. The seat of William Adams between 1811 and 1819 before removing to Fenton Hall (NSF pl facing p16).

Cliffe Park Hall Gothic castellated mansion 1.25m NNW of Rudyard, on W side of Rudyard Lake. In Horton ancient parish. Built by John Haworth of Reacliffe in 1811 (RL p12) or by 1818 (VCH vol 7 p70), or in c1830 (DoE II) (BOE p227). Some say it was built for a member of the Wedgwood family (DoE II) (BOE p227). After Haworth's death in 1831, the property was left to his first cousin, Fanny Bostock. She fought and won a five year long High Court action against the NSR between 1851-56 to stop the railway company taking commercial advantage of Rudyard Lake. She died unmarried in 1875. In 1885 Rev Edward Duncan Boothman, husband of Fanny Bostock's niece Georgina, bought the estate. He sold it in 1903 to the NSR. From 1908 to 1926 it was the Club House of the Rudyard Lake Golf Club. The mansion was let to the Leigh family from 1926 to 1933. In 1933 it was sold to the Youth Hostel Association who used it as a hostel until 1969 (VCH vol 7 p70 pl 34) (RL pp12p,13-14,20,45,96,98). By 1871 Cliffe Park Cottage had been built as a lodge to the hall (RL p27). On May 27 1944 a Stirling Bomber on a RAF training flight, en route to the Menai Straits, crashed 100 yards to the S of the hall; four of the crew were killed (RL p98), but four parachuted to safety (MD pp23-24).

Cliff Hall William Gordon Bagnall, railway engine manufacturer at Stafford, was born at Cliff Hall, Tamworth, in 1852 (SAC p73).

Cliff Oak Ancient oak which stood in Bagot's Park (LGS p192), and could have been near Cliff Farm 4.5m NE of Bagot's Bromley? There is also a Woodroffe's Cliff Farm and Cliff House Farm 3.5m NE of Bagot's Bromley. The tree has also appeared as Cliffe Oak, King Oak, and King's Oak; it may be identifiable with King John's Oak (see). In 1812 contained 428 cubic feet in the butt and 103 feet in the limbs (NSFCT 1875 p7). After felling it was used in the Cunard Liner, the Queen Mary (SLM Oct 1947 p35. Feb 1951 p19 - gives the impression it is different from the Cliff Oak). (CCBO p26) (STMSM April 1973 p24).

Clifford's Wood Area of Swynnerton (W p425). In Swynnerton parish.

Cliffs, The Great Haywood. Chambers cut into sandstone rock (AR p22p of in 1863).

Clifft Common Former common which lay between Great Moor and Dadnal Hill on the eastern boundary of Pattingham ancient parish (VCH vol 20 p177).

Cliff Top Hill 1036 feet high 0.25m SE of Swinscoe. The burial mound 150 metres S of the hill at SK 13654807 is a listed monument. It is 15 paces in diameter and 2.5 feet high and was excavated by Carrington in 1849. A skeleton and Samian pottery was found (TYD pp151-152) (NSJFS 1965 p34).

Cliff Vale Area of low ground 1m NNW of Stoke-upon-Trent, along the Fowlea Brook between Shelton Old Road and Etruria Road (VCH vol 8 p177). In Stoke-upon-Trent chapelry in Stoke-upon-Trent parish. The name is from probably Cliff Hay, a derivation of Clive Hay (see). The mission church, St Stephen, lies on Garner Street (LDD). Cliff Vale only began to become urbanised towards the end of the C19 (VCH vol 8 p177).

Cliffville A fine old Georgian house at Hartshill, which has also appeared as Cliffeville. Built in 1810 by John Tomlinson, solicitor (SHST pp383,601 il of in 1831). Occupied in 1851 by FW Tomlinson (W p19). It was the Stoke rectory from 1864 to 1889 (CAST p34). Since the 1920s it has been occupied as a girls' school (VCH vol 8 pp176,183,186) (POTP p208) (SOTB p68p).

Clifton Campville Ancient parish and former township with Haunton. The small village of Clifton Campville lies at the N end of a shelf of land by the Mease 22.5m ESE of Stafford.

EARLY A stone axe of the **Neolithic** or **Bronze Age** found in Clifton Campville parish is in Birmingham Museum (NSJFS 1964 p20).

900 to 1500. The manor of 'Clyfton,' which may be identifiable with this Clifton, is mentioned in 942 (SSE 1991 pp7,8. 1996 p12). The parish, formed before 1086, may have originally contained the ancient parish of Elford (SHC 1916 p194). The present parish **church**, St Andrew, at the S end of Church Street, was built largely in c1300-1350 (BOE p105). Clifton Campville parish feast was on Advent Sunday in the mid C19 (W p596). The manor of Clistone appears in DB. Later Clifton Campville appears as Clifton Caunvil (1242) (SDW p12) (SPN pp35-36). The **name** is from its situation, on a bank with the Mease to the NE; cliffe, or clive in Anglo-Saxon signifies not only a rocky bank but any shelving ground (SHOS vol 1 p393) (SSE 1996 p12). The **de Caunvil** (or Camvill, Canville, Camville) family were lords from 1200 to 1315 (SOS p464 note) (DUIGNAN); they take their name from Canappeville (Dept d L' Eure, Normandy) (DUIGNAN). The second son of Geoffrey de Canville of Clifton (dead in 1219), William, was in a long dispute about the manor with his half brother Richard; William was eventually successful in claiming the manor. His son, Geoffrey was of age by 1272 and attended parliament as Lord Canville or Camville in 1295. He died shortly before 1308 and was succeeded by his son William de Camville, who was succeeded on his death in 1338 by his five daughters. The barony then fell into abeyance (The Complete Peerage). There was a dispute between Geoffrey de Campville and the men of Newton Solney, Derbys, concerning assarting or land being taken into cultivation. It was claimed in 1284 that men came with many beasts and trampled down oaks. The dispute flared up again in 1300. In 1306 after two later episodes, Geoffrey alleged that £300 worth of damage had been done to his wheat, rye and oats (VCH vol 6 p7). From William Camville the manor appears to have passed to one of his daughters, Maud, and through her it passed to her second husband Sir Richard Stafford of Pipe Ridware (d1381), second son of Edmund Baron Stafford (d1308), younger brother of Ralph (d1371), Lord Stafford of Stafford (see). Sir Richard's grandson, **Edmund de Stafford** (1344-1419), prebendary of Ufton (see) in 1369 and prebendary of Weeford (see) in 1377, was appointed to the See of Exeter in 1394-5. He was Lord Chancellor of England in 1369-1399, and in 1400-1402/3. He was a great benefactor to Exeter College, Oxford (DNB) (NHS p272) (SMC p166). In 1629 Sir Walter Heveningham knt sold the manors of Clifton Campville and Haunton to the lord keeper Coventry; it was sold by them, in c1700, to Sir Charles Pye. It remained with the Pyes until 1774, when it descended through the female Pyes to the Severnes and then to the Watkins; on the death of the widow of Richard Watkins (d1813) the manor reverted to the Pyes; TH Pye was lord in 1844 (SOS p464 note). **Plough Monday** was held for the last time in Clifton Campville in 1890 (LTM Jan Feb 1973 p15). **Bishop Langton** stayed the night at Clifton Campville on Jan 14 1319 (SSE 1994 p4).

1500 to PRESENT. The Lichfield diocesan archives, or called the Chronicle of Lichfield, dating from the C14, were saved by Bishop Wright at the outbreak of the Civil War. He had them concealed in the thatch of a house at Clifton Campville. Here they remained until the house was demolished in 1684. The volume passed to the Cottonian Collection and the BM (HOL p26 note) (OP p19). A mock sun was witnessed by Francis Wolferstan of Statfold at Clifton Campville on Dec 4 1680 at noon (NHS pp3,4,5,6,7 tab 1 fig 2,3).

Clifton Hall Hall 0.75m E of Clifton Campville. Built in the C18 by Sir Charles Pye, who apparently ran out of money half way through its construction and the main range was never built. The architect was Francis Smith. The Pye family lived in the two wings, which were built, for the next 200 years (SGS pp86,88p). Sir Charles Pye cut a little verse on the glass of a window, which is still visible in the N wing, and indicates that he was certainly then actuated by religious feelings (SCC pp139,142). Henry James Pye was Poet Laureate between 1790 and 1813, but did not live at Clifton (LTM Jan Feb 1973 p15). A descendant of Sir John Pye, Capt Charles Severne Watkins (1783-1813), left his estate to his widow, Sarah Bickerton (1787-1823), a former dairy maid of Doveridge, Derbys. After the death of Capt Watkins she married the son of the vicar of Doveridge, Mr Stokes (SCC pp154-158). There is a tradition that bricks intended for the unbuilt centre part of the hall were used for the wall around Fisherwick Hall park (SGS p183) (MR pp101,379).

Clifton House House close to the Leics border, 1.5m ESE of Clifton Campville, in Clifton Campville ancient parish. The house appears as such on the 1884 OS map 6 inch.

Clifton Lodge House 1m ESE of Clifton Campville, on the N side of the road to No Man's Heath. A house called Clifton Lodge on or near the site of the present house is described as 'ready to fall' in 1677. The lodge was purchased by Dame Rebecca and Sir Charles Pye Bt in 1701 (SHJ autumn 1989 pp21,26). In the late C18 Shaw noted the lodge had two pieces of glass fixed in the windows which came from a large old mansion from the Chilcote area, which had just been demolished. One bore the arms of Milward, the other of the family of Palmer (SHOS vol 1 p403). The name lodge may be from a lodge to a medieval deer park belonging to the manor of Clifton Campville (SHJ autumn 1989 pp21,26).

Clive, The House nearly 1m S of Pattingham, 5.5m W of Wolverhampton. In Pattingham ancient parish. The name is from Anglo-Saxon 'clive' and means a cliff (P p160). The Clive was an inhabited place by 1312 (VCH vol 20 p173).

Clive Common Former common on the southern boundary of Pattingham ancient parish (VCH vol 20 p177).

Clive Garden, Dorothy Modern woodland and spring garden 2.5m NE of Mucklestone, 1.5m W of the junction of A51 with A53. The garden, also known as Willoughbridge Gardens, was created by Col Harry Clive in a disused gravel pit NE of his home for his wife Dorothy, suffering from Parkinson's disease (CL May 15 1997 pp98-104pcs). Work began in 1939 (SST) or 1940 (Dorothy Clive Garden Guide). When Dorothy died in 1942 Col Clive continued the garden to her memory. In 1958 the Willoughbridge Garden Trust was formed to safeguard the future of the garden (SST) with Col Clive continuing as curator until his death in 1963 (CL May 15 1997 p100). It contains azaleas and rare rhododendrons. The garden was described in 1983 as being recently extended to include a scree rockery and a pool, a heather garden and a camellia trial garden (NSFCT 1983 p33).

Clive Hay A division or deer enclosure of New Forest in the Newcastle, Penkhull, Hartshill area. Whereas the forest was disafforested in the early C13 the hay survived for some time after (NSJFS 1968 p48). William Murrell held a quantity of land (15 to 40 acres) in Shelton in the reign of Edward II by the sergeanty of keeping Clive Hay (SCSF p116) (NSSG p5). Park Lane which climbs up the hill from Honeywall probably had some association with it (NSFCT 1910 pp173-174). Has also appeared as Castle Cliff (see), the King's Cliff (SK p93), King's Park, Cliff Hay (VCH vol 8 p201), and Hay of Clive (CAST p18). The name is from Anglo-Saxon 'clive' and means a cliff.

Clockfields New housing estate on land reclaimed from mining and industry on S side of Brettell Lane to E of Dennis Hall Road, Amblecote. Built since 1990. The name, preserved in Clockfields Drive, is from an area here formerly known as Clock Fields, which took its name from the clock in the tollhouse on Brettell Lane a few yards E of Dennis Hall Road (SNSV vol 2 pp7,18-19).

Clock Mill Area to the WNW of Pelsall church. The name is from the common name for an old corn mill. The right form is 'clack,' ie; the clapper, which by striking the hopper caused the corn to be shaken into the millstones (DUIGNAN) (SPN p91). Or it may have reference to the noise made by the machinery or to the shape of the mill sails (SNBP p70).

Clock Mill Brook At Goscote it formed part of the NE boundary of old Walsall borough. Along with Ford Brook (which it joins S of Station Road, Rushall) was called Walsall Water by Erdeswick and Willmore (VCH vol 17 p143 note); Willmore says Walsall Water rises at a spring near the two Wyrleys (HOWW p6). The 'Peol's ford' mentioned in a charter of Pelsall's bounds in 994 probably was the Wolverhampton Road crossing over the brook (PTYV p4). Has also appeared as Clockmill Brook and Clockmill Stream (SHOP p2). (DUIGNAN).

Clod Hall In Pinfold Lane, 1.25m WNW of Hales. The Clod Hall of 1914 was an old thatched cottage of perhaps C17 date with later additions (DoE II) (SHC 1945/ 6 p176). (MR p24p).

Clothiers Farm and house which stood at the junction of Dingle Lane and Wellington Place, Willenhall. From a very early date this farm was freehold. The name may be from the Merchant Tailors' Company, often referred to as the Clothiers, who owned the farm. By 1951 the farm had been demolished and the Clothier Street Housing Estate built on the site. Its associations with a City of London company may have given the nearby district of Little London its name (HOWI p186).

Clots, The Field name in Newbold grounds, 1m E of Dunstall. In the later C17 Plot noted that if cattle grazed in this field their coats would turn to a whitish colour, for the length of the summer (NHS p111).

Cloud House House 1.75m NW of Rushton Spencer church. Formerly in Rushton Spencer township in Leek ancient parish. The present house is dated 1612 but there was a house on the site by 1596 and by perhaps 1451 (VCH vol 7 p223).

Cloud Side Straggling tiny hamlet on the lane leading up to The Cloud, Ches, on the Staffs side, 1.5m WNW of Rushton Spencer church. Formerly in Rushton Spencer township in Leek ancient parish. In existence by the later C18 (VCH vol 7 p224).

Clough Hall Formerly in Talke township in Audley ancient parish. The name may be from 'Clough,' a former name for Bath Pool Valley (TTTD p207). Clough is probably of Norse origin. It means a ravine or narrow valley, with steep sides, usually forming the bed of a stream. The old pronunciation was as in bough, but is now become cluff (DUIGNAN). It has been believed that a house stood on or near the site of the later Clough Hall by the late 1300s. In 1583 Thomas Unwyn (or Unwin) said his house here had been built by an ancestor. This house was replaced by another built by John Unwyn some time before his death in 1641. Clough Hall remained with the Unwyns up to about the mid C18 (KAIW p3). The old house was replaced by a house built by 1800 by either by John Gilbert, canal engineer (SHC 1944 p66) (KBT vol 2 pp41p-42) or by his son, John of White Hall, Kidsgrove (KAIW p6). After the death of the younger John Gilbert in 1811 or 1812 the hall was bought by Thomas Kinnersley (d1819) or his son Thomas (d1855), bankers and iron merchants in Newcastle-under-Lyme. Thomas, junior, built Kidsgrove church in 1837. After Thomas junior's death his widow continued to live at Clough Hall until her death in 1877. The hall then belonged to Georgiana Attwood, a niece of the Kinnersley's. On her death in 1879 Edward Williamson became owner (KAIW pp7,10). During his period the hall is said to have been left empty and the grounds neglected. In 1890 the estate was sold with 126 acres of grounds and lake to a Manchester company which developed the hall as an entertainment centre and the grounds as a pleasure garden. Charles Blondin (1824-1897), tightrope-walker, was a leading attraction on the opening day in 1891. The gardens closed in the 1920s. The hall may have been purchased in c1912 by the Johnny Walker Brewery who turned some or all the house into an inn. JT Johnson was owner of the Clough Hall Park Hotel in 1912. The hall was an hotel during WW1 and at one time housed Belgian refugees. It was used by a local football team as a changing room in the early 1920s (KAIW p15). Kidsgrove urban district demolished the hall in May 1927. The 1947 OS map 1 inch marks the site of the gardens as 'Church Hall Park' although the correct title should have been 'Clough Hall Park.' Some of the garden features still existed in 1962 (TTTD p209-212) (MR p198) (ES May 28 1927) (KBT vol 2 p41) (Kidsgrove, Talke and Mow Cop. Postcards from the Past. Roger Simmons 1998 p73p).

GROUNDS. After the grounds had been developed as a pleasure garden it contained aviaries, a fountain, a Swiss chalet for children, a maze, a switchback railway, and a monkey house (TTTD p209-212). A pagoda to rival that at Alton Towers intended for the island in Bath Pool was never built (KAIW pp3,6,11,21p of the hall c1910). The South Lodge on Newcastle Road remains. It was built in the neo-classical style sometime between 1823-37. The lodge was restored between 1995 and 1997 (ES Dec 21 1995 p3p. ES Jan 7 1997 p5ps). William Smith of Heathcote Street who was attending a demonstration organised by the North Staffs Miners Federation in the grounds was murdered on the main drive leading to the Avenue near the park gates on June 9 1902, whilst walking Bertha Peters of Hanley, an acrobat's wife, to the railway station. According to her evidence she fainted as three men attacked Smith. The case, which remains unsolved, tarnished the reputation of Clough Hall as a place for functions and entertainment (KAIW p14). A freak whirlwind occurred at Clough Hall on Aug 5 1911 (KTM p74p). By the late C19 the ghost of a white rabbit had been seen crossing the avenue leading to the hall: It is said to predict a death in the family of the one seeing it (NSFCT 1900 p144). (KNS pp158, 165, 166, 167).

Clough Hall Housing estate 0.5m SW of Kidsgrove built in the grounds of Clough Hall.

Cloughhead House 0.75m SSE of Ipstones.

Clough Head House 2m N of Meerbrook. Formerly in Leekfrith township in Leek ancient parish. There was a house here by 1640 (VCH vol 7 p194).

Clough House 0.5m SSE of Onecote. Formerly in Onecote township in Leek ancient parish. There was a house here by 1663 (VCH vol 7 p211).

Clough House 0.5m E of Stanley. Formerly in Stanley township in Leek ancient parish. The house here was so called by 1602 (VCH vol 7 p229).

Cloughs, The House and estate partly in Clayton Griffith township (W p236) to the W of Newcastle-under-Lyme, S of Keele Road. It appears as Clough Hall on Greenwood's map and as The Cloughs on Teesdale's map. It was the seat of Rev John Basnet in 1843 (HBST p525). In the C19 it was noted for the monkeys kept by the owners. Later the house was rented by Adeline Goss (d1916), daughter of the pottery manufacturer William Henry Goss (William Henry Goss. Lynda and Nicholas Pine. 1987 pp120p,121).

Coach and Horses Plantation S of Weeford (1834 OS map and current OS map 1:25,000).

Coalbournbrook District N of Amblecote, N of Holloway End, formerly a hamlet in Old Swinford parish (Worcs), then in Amblecote parish, lying around the junction of the Stourbridge-Wolverhampton road and the road to Wollaston. The name is from the brook Coalbourn or Colbourne Brook and was in use for this district by the late C17. There may have been a windmill at Coalbournbrook in medieval times since there was some land E of the Stourbridge-Wolverhampton road called Windmill Hill in 1466 (VCH vol 20 p55). There were glass houses at Coalbournbrook by the late C17 (VCH vol 20 p49).

Coalbournehill Area of SW Coalbournbrook, Amblecote. The name was in use by the late C18 (VCH vol 2 p228. vol 20 p51). Has also appeared as Coalbournhill.

Coal Brook Tributary to the Tern. Forms the Shrops Staffs boundary. A looped palstave was found in the brook in 1960 at SJ 70493348 (NSJFS 1962 p30). The name may be a corruption from the root 'gil' 'giol' 'cuil' (NSFCT 1908 p133). Means 'cold' (SPNO p7).

Coalheath A former common in the Shelfield area. May have formerly been Colliers Ford Heath (VCH vol 17 p279). There is a Coalheath Lane running off the W side of Lichfield Road, Shelfield (Birmingham A-Z).

Coal Hill A hill near Christchurch-on-Needwood (Newchurch) (NSFCT 1875 p34). Has also appeared as Coalhill.

Coal Pit Hill District 1.25m WSW of Kidsgrove. Formerly in Audley ancient parish. Leese thinks that the Talk o' th' Hill wagon explosion of 1781 took place on Coalpit Hill (KBT vol 2 pp21-22). By 1924 Coalpit Hill was a small village centred on Thomas Street and Swan Bank (1924 OS map).

Coalpool A small settlement at junction of Harden, Goscote and Coalpool lanes 1.5m N of Walsall, in the foreign of Walsall. Existed by the mid C16. The place name implies early mining activity (BY p24p) (VCH vol 17 p164) (SNBP pp18-19) and has also appeared as Coal Pool. By the early C20 there was an Irish settlement in Coal Pool (PBH p42) (VCH vol 17 p145).

Coalville Coalville Estate is a housing estate on the E side of the Weston Road, Weston Coyney, embracing Dimmelow Street (formerly Raglan Street). From his house in this street David Rayner witnessed UFO activity in Sept 1966 (Out There. No 1. July 1999. produced by RG Bennett of Westonfields, Longton).

Coalway Lane Part of a former well-known coal route from collieries at Rough Hills, Parkfields and Bilston to the Staffs and Worcs Canal at Dimmingsdale wharf. Many have thought the name is from it having been a coal route, but Dunphy thinks the name may be from Celtic 'coel' or variants 'cold,' 'col,' 'cole,' 'coal,' referring to a magical place, an omen, a belief, and that Coalway represents an ancient trackway between Bilston and the Wrekin. To support this theory the crossroads where Coalway Road meets Goldthorn Hill was known as Cold Lanes, another derivation of coel (PPTP p36). The name occurs on Pigot & Son map (1830) between Upper Penn and Wolverhampton and is currently preserved in Coalway Road running from Penn Fields to Merry Hill.

Coatestown House SW of Hollinsclough on the edge of Hollinsclough Moor. Formerly in Hollinsclough township, in Alstonefield ancient parish. It was possibly the home of Isaac Coates, a chapman, in the later C18 (VCH vol 7 p38). Towards Hollinsclough at SK 06336631 is a burial mound 13 paces in diameter and two feet high. A bronze brooch and some burnt bones have been found in it (R vol 3 p162) (Ancient Remains near Buxton. W Turner. p2) (NSJFS 1965 p39). It is of Bronze Age origin (VCH vol 7 p37).

Coatfield Minute hamlet over 0.5m W of Hamstall Ridware.

Cobb Moor In Wolstanton ancient parish (SGSAS). There is a Cob Moor Road and a Cobmoor Cottage to the W of Brieryhurst.

Cobbs Engine House Brick engine house 0.75m E of Netherton, in Rowley Regis parish. Situated near to the entrance to the Netherton Tunnel in the present Warrens Hall Park. It was built in c1831 and was the earliest engine house of its type. Its engine pumped water out of Pit No. 3 of Windmill End Colliery (OS map Sheet 71.04). From 1877 the engine house was officially known as Windmill End Pumping Station. Pumping ceased in 1928. It stood abandoned until 1974 when it was repaired (BTBC p38). It is one of only a few which survive in the region and has often been photographed with the slag heaps from Warrens Hall Colliery in the background in the area called Sledmere (TB Jan 1976 p of when in working order with pithead gear, p11) (BCM Jan 1978 pp67-74 ps) (Portrait of the Black Country. Harold Parsons. 1986. cover picture) (MR p238p). The engine house, listed grade II in 1972 and as an Ancient Monument in 1975, was so called apparently after a farmer who owned land in the district before the engine house was built (OS map Sheet 71.04) (Cobbs Engine House, Windmill End. GLA Price. 1971) (Cobbs Engine House Leaflet. Sandwell Borough Council). A winding engine housed in an adjacent building was purchased by Henry Ford and shipped to a museum at Dearborn, Michigan, USA (Portrait of the Black Country. Harold Parsons. 1986. p61).

Cobblers Bank House 0.75m NNE of Brewood, where a road to Horsebrook diverges from the Brewood-Congreve road (1884 OS map 6 inch). Here may have stood Hell Cottages, see Brewood.

Cob Hall Stood N of Knightley Grange, Knightley. Cob Hall farm existed in 1834 (1834 OS map). Knightley Grange was built near it and some of the farm was incorporated into Knightley Grange outbuildings (VCH vol 4 p120). The name means 'dwelling on a round lump' (SPNO p159).

Coblers Park A tiny croft of less than an acre in High Offley parish (ESH p20).

Cobridge Former hamlet crowning a ridge to the E of Fowlea Brook. Formerly in Stoke-upon-Trent and Burslem chapelries in Stoke-upon-Trent ancient parish, nearly 1m SSE of Burslem. The district was formerly the vill of Rushton Grange (VCH vol 8 p107). Cobridge Gate on the hill-top to the E of Rushton Grange farm was an inhabited area by the mid C17. The name gate is from a gate across the road (VCH vol 8 p107). 'Cob' means, anciently, anything big (HBST p273 note). It has also appeared as Coe Bridge and Cow Bridge. Simeon Shaw suggests there was once a windmill at Cobridge (HSP pp42,43). The Old School House in Elder Road, built in 1766, was demolished in 1897. A square plinth commemorating the school has been placed on the site (ES April 7 1986 p). The church, Christ Church, was built in 1839-1841 in Church Terrace as a chapel of ease to St John's, Burslem (VCH vol 8 p124). Cobridge became a separate ecclesiastical parish in 1845 (GLAUE p408). It was considered a wealthy area in the C19: 'The Cob of Cobridge' was a local saying in Ward's day to give to principle residents (HBST p273 note). In 1878 or 1879 Arnold Bennett and his family moved from Burslem (see) to Cobridge. In Bennett's novels Cobridge is Bleakridge; Bleak Hill is the hill between Burslem and Cobridge and there was a Bleak Inn (TWWW Feb 16 1991 p13p). Anna Tellwright the heroine in Bennett's Anna of the Five Towns (1902) was from Cobridge. The suburb of Cobridge had a railway station on the Potteries Loop line; it was recommended that it be closed in 1963 (ES March 22 1963). In the later C20 and for much of the C20 Cobridge has been the red light district of the Potteries.

Cobridge Gate Cobridge (HBST p273). On the hill-top to E of Rushton Grange farm. At junction of Waterloo Road, Elder Road and Cobridge Road. So called from a gate across the road (VCH vol 8 p107).

Cobridge Hall Burslem. Built in c1780 by William Adams (1748-1831) upon the site of Cobridge Gate House. The rear of the hall faced Sneyd Street. The drive to it began in what is now Vale Place. It survived until after WW2. (POTP p12) (SHST pp578il -579). But Greenslade says the hall was being demolished in 1913 (VCH vol 8 p119).

Cobridge House Cobridge Road area, Cobridge. Seat of the Hales family from the late C17 to the late C19. It was replaced by St Augustine's Home in the early C20 (VCH vol 8 p145).

Cobridge Park Cobridge. Public park alongside Elder Road. Opened in 1911 (VCH vol 8 p107).

Cocket Knob 2m ENE of Cheddleton (1834 OS map) (Dower's map).

Cocket Knowl Gradbach (NSFCT 1947 p169); can possibly be identified with the Cocker Knowl on the 1834 OS map on the S side of Turn Edge.

Cock Green District at foot of Hailstone Hill 1.5m E of Netherton. In Rowley Regis parish. Appears on 1947 OS map 1:25,000 (sheet 32/98) at SO 964879. The name is said to be from the Cock Inn (SNSV vol 2 p23).

Cock Heath Former hamlet at SO 972958, to E of Moxley (OS map 1882) (TB April 1978 p17 see map. Jan 1983 p9). In Darlaston ancient parish. In the early C15 Cockheath is named as the scene of coal workings (HOWV p120).

Cocking House 0.75m N of Caverswall, in Caverswall ancient parish (1834 OS map).

Cockintake House 1.25m NNE of Foxt. Perhaps land taken into cultivation by one Cock.

Cock Low Burial mound which stood SW of Leek town centre between Waterloo Road (Street?) and Spring Gardens (VCH vol 7 p85). Pickford says houses of the present Westwood Road and Spring Gardens were built on the site (SMM p16). However, Hackwood says it was situated a few miles to the NE of Leek (SCSF p74). It has appeared as Catteslowe (later C16), Cock Lowe (1723), Great Lowe (1723) (NSFCT 1923 p81) (VCH vol 7 p85) and is probably the 'mound near the town' mentioned in NSFCT 1906 p145. In 1851, when it was described as 40 yards in diameter and 18 feet high, an excavation uncovered flint implement and fragments of an urn and of human bone (TYD pp183-185) (VCH vol 7 p85). Rev W Beresford and others give varying dimensions for the mound (MOS pp269-271) (NSJFS 1965 p43) (SCSF p74). Rev W Beresford excavated it prior to its demolition in 1907 (NSFCT 1908 p193) (VCH vol 7 p85), perhaps in 1905, when it was said to have been practically obliterated (NSFCT 1915 p186). Beresford found a cremation burial in a collared urn, an iron ring of prehistoric times and sundry stone implements including a heart-shaped carved stone (VCH vol 7 p85): A fund, to try and save the mound, had failed to raise the necessary amount - £600 or £700 (NSFCT 1908 p193). It was said to have been demolished to make way for a new road (SCSF p74), and some stone cottages were then built on the site (NSFCT 1915 p186). (NHS p404) (TYD pp183-185) (SCSF pp74,75) (R 1909 p154) (S p69) (Treasure Trove in Law and Practice. Hill. 1936. pp254,255). Pickford says there were two mounds known as Cock Low, one near Leek and one at Warslow (SMM pp15-16). But since he attributes facts about the Leek Cock Low to the Warslow one, and a Cock Low at Warslow is not mentioned in VCH vol 7, he is possibly mistaken: the heart-shaped carved stone found in the Leek Cock Low is said by him to have been found in the Warslow one, along with child bones, a factor used by him to explain the presence of a young boy ghost seen on the road by the site of the mound (SMM p16). A phantom coach has been seen in the area of Cock Low (FPSB p163).

Cocknage Hamlet on hills (perhaps the Lightwood Hills) 1.25 ENE of Barlaston. In Barlaston ancient parish (W p411). The name, perhaps of Anglo-Saxon origin, means Cok's oak (DUIGNAN). Or 'Cocca's gate (or entrance to an enclosure)' (SSE 1996 p12) (SPN p130) (BNDA p3). Cocknage has appeared as Cokenache (1195) (SSE 1996 p12), Cokenegge (C13) (COI p24), and Cocknidge. In the later C17 Plot relates William Leveson-Gower's claim that the ages of four of his tenants here added up to 360 years, a marvel in the C17 (NHS pp45,329).

Cockoo Cage Near Tatenhill. Field name derived from an animal name (APB p49).

Cockoo Cliff Side of Ellishill Brook under 1m NNE of Stanton.

Cockoo's Nest In Standon parish. Field name derived from an animal name (APB p49).

Cockpit Hill At Cross Keys, Cannock (CCBO p84; it really did form a natural dip). Is in Hednesford Hills at SK 007124.

Cocksfold Farm In the Pinfold Lane area of Great Barr. In existence by 1685 (SNAR p80).

Cocksheds Lezzers Place on the Halesowen Blackheath border (TB Oct 1981 p5. Nov 1984 p7). Here Stafford hangman Jethro Homer was murdered by hanging in the late C18; a great elm in his garden became known as 'the hanging tree' (TB June/ July 1972 p10). The name is preserved in Cockshed Lane S of Blackheath. Lezzers may be from the local pronunciation of leasowes.

Cockshoot Hill Hill SE of Swindon. A windmill called Kems Mill stood on it or near it in the early C18; this mill may be identifiable with Kenes Mill, which existed in 1458 (VCH vol 20 p213).

Cockshutts Former small mining hamlet 1.5m SSE of Wolverhampton (MH 1984 p81). The name, which has also appeared as Cockshut, may be from a large net suspended between two poles employed to catch and shut in woodcocks (NSFCT 1910 pp176-177). It is preserved in Cockshutt Lane off Thompson Ave.

Cockster Brook Joins Chitlings Brook which is a tributary of the Trent. It flowed passed Longton Hall (SHST p551). Starts as Anchor Brook, which rises in Park Hall grounds (VCH vol 8 p224).

Codsall Large village 13m SSW of Stafford on a hill above Moat Brook. Church Hill (453 or 442 feet) is said to be the highest point until Russia is reached (St Nicholas' Church, Codsall: A Brief History) (SVB p57). The tall gas Round Lamp, which stood at High Green in the centre of Wolverhampton between 1821 and 1842, could be seen from as far away as Codsall (WJO Dec 1903

lxi).
EARLY. The last Ice Age reached its maximum southern extent about Wolverhampton and glacial boulders lie about Codsall (WJO Nov 1909 p293). At White Cottage was found 1942/3 a Neolithic or Bronze Age flint scraper (NSJFS 1964 p20).
800 to 1800. The Codeswelle mentioned in a charter of 855 AD was identified by Birch in his Cartularium Saxonicum with Codsall. But CGO Bridgeman identifies it with Cutsdean on the Cotswold Hills (SHC 1916 p76). The manor of Codeshale appears in DB (SSE 1996 p12). Later forms are: Coddeshal and Codeshall (SPN p36). The **name** appears to be of Anglo-Saxon origin and means 'Code's hall' (DUIGNAN). Or 'Cod's nook or corner of land' (NSJFS 1981 p3) (SSE 1996 p12) (SPN p36). The **church**, St Nicholas, on Church Hill, has some C13 work in the W tower (St Nicholas' Church, Codsall: A Brief History) (SVB p57). Codsall was anciently a chapel and prebend in Tettenhall Collegiate Church and Tettenhall ancient parish although it had obtained most of the rights of a mother church by 1550. It became a separate ecclesiastical parish in 1756. However, this remained within the peculiar jurisdiction of Tettenhall until 1846. There was a **wake** held at Codsall on May 6 1821 and on May 5-6 1823. **Beating the bounds** has taken place at Codsall (SCSF pp26-27) (HOPTT p67) (WMAG July 1968 p28) (VCH vol 3 pp93 note, 319, 320. vol 20 pp19,80,86) (GLAUE p408). The early settlement at Codsall probably lay near the church. The open space on the S side of the churchyard may be the remains of a green (VCH vol 20 pp76-77). Part of Codsall lay in the Wolverhampton (see) Deanery manor (HOWM p26). Teesdale's Map of Staffordshire 1832 records at least one moat at Codsall (NSFCT 1982 p17). There was a **pound** in 1596 and one stood against the S wall of the churchyard in 1850. In the earlier 1880s the pound stood NW of the churchyard; it had been removed by 1900 (VCH vol 20 p86). For Codsall Well see the Leper Well. To NE of Codsall church was a **windmill**. It was built before 1775. It was still working in 1850, but was converted into a house in the later C19. It is now called Millfield House (WBJ p17 ils xx, xxv) (WIS pp9p,16) (STMSM June 1980 p40p) (VCH vol 20 p85).
1800 to PRESENT. From the 1840s Codsall village became a residential area favoured by people working in Wolverhampton. By the earlier 1880s Codsall had become a popular resort for day excursionists, especially from Wolverhampton (TCOP p8) (VCH vol 20 pp77,80). A station on the Wolverhampton-Shrewsbury **railway** line S of the village was opened in c1850. It closed to goods in 1964 but was still open to passengers in 1983 (VCH vol 20 p80). Baker's Nurseries formerly situated in Church Lane were nationally noted for their landscaping and the creation of the multi-coloured Russell lupins in 1935, and the Bishop delphinium (SVB p57). They were established between 1900 and 1904 and closed in the late 1960s (TCOP p115p). **Persons**. Sir **Charles Wheeler**, sculptor and president of the Royal Academy 1956-1966 (d1974), was born at No. 12 Church Road, Codsall. His bronze sculpture, 'The Lone Singer,' was presented to Codsall by his daughter in 1974. The following year it was erected in a public garden S of Bakers Way (SLM autumn 1954 pp24-25) (High Relief: the autobiography Sir Charles Wheeler. 1968) (E&S Dec 12 1974) (VCH vol 20 p81) (CPP p11p of 'The Lone Singer') (WF p45). His statue of St Wulfrun was erected by St Peter's church, Wolverhampton (see) in 1974. **Audrey Erskine Lindop**, novelist and playwright, came to live in Codsall when aged 16. At the beginning of WW2 she wrote children's articles for E&S. Her novels include 'In Me My Enemy' (1948), 'The Tall Headlines' (1950), and 'The Singer not the Song' (1953). Some of her work is set in Staffs and Shrops (VFC p85). For the assassination of **Rex Farran** at Codsall in 1948 see The Myron.

Codsall Coppice Small area of woodland on a steep slope, now surrounded by residential development, on N side of Barrs Road, 0.5m SE of Cradley Heath (SNSV vol 2 p21). It was one of three coppices in the area which were exploited to provide wood for charcoal-making, for use in iron-smelting. Earthworks in the western part of the coppice are a rare survival surface coal-mining, once prevalent in the Black Country (WMARCH 1993 p106).

Codsall Hall Stood on the N side of Bakers Way, Codsall. There was a house on this site by 1659 known as New Hall or Upper House. By 1758 the hall had replaced Codsall House as the capital messuage of Codsall manor. A nursery was established at Codsall Hall Farm by Baker's of Wolverhampton between 1900 and 1904; it closed in the later 1960s. The hall appears to have been demolished by 1983 (VCH vol 20 pp81,85).

Codsall House House on the W side of Station Road, Codsall. The house stands on the site of Codsall manor house, called Hall House in the early C17 and Old Hall or Lower House in the late 1650s. By 1758 the house had been replaced as the capital messuage of Codsall manor by Codsall Hall. The house was rebuilt in the late C18 and was called Codsall House by the early C19. It was a private school from 1815 until at least 1851. From 1972 until at least

1983 the house was an office of Staffs county council social services department (VCH vol 20 pp77,81).

Codsall Lanes Area to W of the original settlement of Codsall centred on Moatbrook Lane in the C18 (Yates' map) (VCH vol 20 p77).

Codsall Wood Small village 2m NW of Codsall. In Codsall parish. There may have been settlement on the common at Codsall Wood by the early C14. The name Codsall Wood was being used to describe the area by the C17 (VCH vol 20 p79) (Wolverhampton Chronicle May 23 1997 p32). In the late C17 the dean of Wolverhampton turned part of his property at Codsall Wood into a park (VCH vol 20 p85). The common was enclosed by an act of parliament in 1824 (SVB p58). The church, St Peter, Church Road, was built in c1885 (LDD). Eight of the village wells were found to be polluted in 1927 and the village was then linked up to the Wolverhampton Waterworks Company supply (Wolverhampton Chronicle May 23 1997 p32). For the sulphur spring by the Newport road see under Pendrell Hall. The village is renowned throughout the Black Country as an ideal setting for a day trip and is famed for its annual flower show. There were tea rooms at Codsall Wood by the early 1900s (TCOP p7) (Wolverhampton Chronicle May 23 1997 p32).

Coffin Well One of the wells in the vicinity of Wash Well, Washerwall Lane, Washerwall (WYV p60il) (FWMBS p40).

Coksale Brook Descends from Knightley Park and runs below Callingwood by Cuckoocage Plantation. The name for the lower part was Balk Brook (HOPT vol 1 p134).

Colbourne Brook Runs from off Pensnett Chase. Joins the Stour at Stourbridge (TB Nov Dec 1973 p17 see map). Has also appeared as Coalbourne Brook. See Coalbournebrook.

Colclough (as in *bough* NSFCT 1908 p134). There is a place called Colclough in Staffs (DUIGNAN p42). There is a Colclough Lane, between Goldenhill and Newchapel, and a Colclough Farm to E of Goldenhill. Perhaps Colclough Lane is the name for an ancient path linking the Colclough estates with Hanley (OTP pp53-54).

Colclough Hall The Colclough family, extensive landowners in N Staffs, had a hall in Hall Fields by the Hanley windmill. They left Staffs in c1600 to live at Tintern Abbey, County Wexford, Ireland (OTP p54).

Colclough House Colclough Lane, Goldenhill. Dates from the late C18 or the early C19. Its frontage was altered in the early C20 when converted into two dwellings (VCH vol 8 p90).

Cold Comfort House 1.25m ENE of Hales. It may have formerly been called Brass Hall (see) It was called Cold Comfort by 1833 and was still known as this in 1914 (W p389) (OS map 1834) (SHC 1945/ 6 p156). It was called Parkhill Farm by 1981 (1981 OS map 1; 25,000).

Coldham Tiny hamlet 1m SE of Bishop's Wood. From a house known as 'Coldhome' in 1660 (VCH vol 5 p38). Oakden found earlier references; such as Coldhome (1581), and Colldome (1626). The name perhaps means the cold dwelling (SPNO p40).

Cold Harbour Near Madeley. Is a variant form of Windy Harbour. The word 'harbour' has been derived in these cases from the Celtic root 'coll,' this would give the meaning forest fortress (NSFCT 1908 p138).

Cold Lane Hamlet or house in the vicinity of what is now Willenhall Road, NE of Bilston (TB March 1987 p17). Has also appeared as Cold Lanes (OS map 1834). Duignan identified 'Cold Lanes' near Bunkers Hill, Bilston, with White Sike (see), a name occurring in Lady Wulfrun's charter of 994 (WFW p30).

Coldmeece Hamlet on the E side of Meece Brook 1.75m S of Swynnerton. Former township in Cotes quarter of Eccleshall ancient parish. The name means 'Cold marsh' (SSE 1996 p12). Coldmeece has been identified with the waste in DB called Mess (SSE 1996 p12). One of the busiest railway stations in WW2 was at Coldmeece to serve the ammunitions base at Swynnerton. Owing to the secret nature of the operations at Swynnerton the station never appeared on railway timetables (local info).

Coldmoor Brook Runs from Lawn Farm in Botteslow township northwards to Brook House Green and Ash Brook (OS map 1890). The name may be from the house, Colamoor.

Cold Norton Small hamlet on a small watershed between the Trent and Meece Brook 2.5m NE of Chebsey. Former township in Chebsey ancient parish. There is a Norton Farm 0.5m S, where there was found in c1950 a stone axe-hammer of a coarse felspathic grit of the Neolithic or Bronze Age (NSFCT 1950 p85) (NSJFS 1964 p19). Near the farm was found a perforated mace-head (NSJFS 1964 p19). The name appears as Calde Norton in 1227 (SSE 1996 p16). Erdeswick thought Norton derived from being the north town of Chebsey (SOS p102). Was Coldmorton in the C13; the m became n; the meaning of the form is 'Cold moor town' (DUIGNAN p108). Or 'cold' is a corruption of coal, giving 'the northern farmstead on coal' (SPN p118). A reputed manor (SHC 1914 p64). It was considered a sizeable village in the Middle

Ages after which it was deserted for some reason. Walter Chetwynd in 1679 was the first to identify a settlement here from, probably, earthworks (SL p82), it was either at Cold Norton Farm or Norton Farm and probably deserted between 1334-1539 (SSAHST 1970 p34). The moated site at Cold Norton Farm was being excavated in 1982 (NSFCT 1982 p19). Cold Norton had separate civil parish status between 1866 and 1932, it was then incorporated back into Chebsey (GLAUE p408).

Cold Riding Minute hamlet in the countryside, 1.75m SSE of Longton. Has also appeared as Coldriding. Is derived from 'cow ridding' (BNDA p17).

Coldshaw Former house 2.75m W of Longnor, in Heathylee township. There was a house here by 1429 (VCH vol 7 p33). The place name 'shaw' means a copse (VCH vol 7 p33).

Coldwall Minute hamlet nearly 0.5m E of Blore. 'Wall' is a West Midland dialectal form of the word 'well' meaning spring (NSFCT 1917 p27) (SSAHST 1967 p35).

Coldwall Bridge Over 0.25m NE of Coldwall, crosses over the Dove. Was nine feet wide when built in 1726, but it has since been widened; it replaced a wooden bridge. It is now abandoned (PDS&C pp66-67p).

Cold Well To W of Gentleshaw.

Colehill Street in central Tamworth, to NE of Tamworth Castle. It was the dividing line between Warws and Staffs counties. In medieval times Colehill was known as Cross Street: At its northern junction with Butcher Street (later Church Street) stood the Staffs market cross (Around Tamworth in Old Photographs. Richard Sulima. 1994 p47).

Colepool Brook Tributary of the Tame. The name which appears in 1768, means 'the cool stream' (SPNO p7).

Coles Lane Hill Top, West Bromwich. Named after Daniel Cole who lived at the Ridge-Acres in c1750 (SOWB p23).

Coley Small settlement 1.5m NNW of Moreton. Formerly in Moreton quarter in Gnosall ancient parish (VCH vol 4 p111). Coley Mill, appearing as Colyemill in 1656, lies by Back Brook (SPNO p159).

Coley Dispersed tiny hamlet 1.25m E of Great Haywood. In Colwich ancient parish. Commander Wedgwood identified DB Scoteslei with Coley (SHC 1916 p168) (SSE 1996 p12).

Coley Brook Runs from Coley Mill to Moreton.

Coley Hall 1.5m NNW of Moreton. Formerly in Moreton quarter in Gnosall ancient parish. A hall of this name was inhabited by a yeoman in 1540. The hall which lay on the S side of the Stafford-Newport road (A518) had been demolished by 1955 (VCH vol 4 p127).

College Farm Formerly Bobbington Farm. 1m SW of Bobbington. The estate centred on this farm was one Edward Careswell of Blacklands (d1691) endowed exhibitions at Christ Church, Oxford. The farmhouse was rebuilt in 1841, and the name was changed to College Farm about then (VCH vol 20 p69).

Colleswayne's Lake Large vanished lake close to another expanse of water called The Marsh, also vanished, which lay under the area of Nelson Place, Newcastle-under-Lyme (NM p157) (VCH vol 8 p3) (NUL p158).

Collets Brook Forms boundary between Staffs and Warws. Runs S from Canwell.

Collins Brook At Trentham. Mentioned in John Ogilby's 'Britania' road atlas.

Collyhole House WNW of Coltstone, Ipstones (TOI p11). Has also appeared as Collymoor (1834 OS map), and Colley Hole.

Collyhole Brook Rises N of Ipstones. A tributary of the Churnet.

Colomoor House in Botteslow township (HBST p526), which stood to the S of Berry Hill County High School. Occurs on the 1834, 1890, 1879-1937 OS maps and has appeared as Colamoor.

Colshaw Small dispersed hamlet on high ground above the upper of Dove 1.25m ENE of Flash. In Hollinsclough township in Alstonefield ancient parish. The family of John Lomas (1747-1823), a pedlar and wholesale dealer, who argued successfully against a proposal to abolish licensed hawkers and pedlars in the House of Commons in 1785, were living in Colshaw in the later 1740s. In 1785 John Lomas moved to Hollinsclough village (VCH vol 7 p38) (MH 1996 pp156-165), where he had built a Methodist chapel (L pp19,20). Mary Brunt of Colshaw died in 1782 aged 104 (W p744). Has also appeared as Calshaw (W p744).

Colt Is a DB berewick (SSAHST 1970 p34). It is present day Littlehay 0.5m N of Colton. Referred to as Coltune in CWF. Erdeswick and Chetwynd failed to recognise it (CWF p3). Here was possibly a lost village (SSAHST 1970 p34).

Coltham Area 1.5m NNE of Willenhall, in the area between Straight Road and the Wyrley and Essington Canal, and stretched from Lane Head to Coppice Lane (SNW p19). The name Coltham or Cotham Bush appears in the court rolls in the C18. The name is preserved in Coltham Road (HOWI p187).

Colton Ancient parish and village on Moreton Brook not far from the Trent 8.5m ESE of Stafford.

EARLY. The four large Ice Age boulders in Colton may be by Brook Bridge (ES Dec 4 1993 p21).

600 to 1600. The parish **church**, Blessed Virgin Mary, S of Bellamour Way, was established before 1086. Some portions of the present church date from the early C13 (A Brief History of Colton Church). The parish is not listed in the Papal Return of 1291 but was almost certainly in existence by then (SHC 1916 p200). The parish wake was on the nearest Sunday to 19 Sept in the mid C19 (W p413). Chetwynd following Erdeswick failed to notice that Colton is entered twice in DB; the two writers only mentioning the manor (Coltune) held by Geoffrey (the Wasteney's ancestor) of Robert de Stafford, which became known as the de Colton, or Church estate and subsequently the 'Mareshall and Griffin' manor (CWF p3). The other manor (Coltone) was held by Azeline (or Ansell) de Mavesyn of Earl Roger de Montgomery; of which the small estate of Colt (Little Hay) formed a separate part (SHC 1914 p153 note). The **name** has also appeared as Colastun (SPN p36), and Colton (1698) (Illustrated Journeys of Celia Fiennes edited by Chris Morris. 1984. p149). It is of Anglo-Saxon origin and means 'the charcoal town' (DUIGNAN) because of its proximity to Cannock Chase, where the wood came from to make it. Or is 'Cola's farmstead' (SSE 1996 p12) (SPN p36). Or 'colt tun' (SSE 1996 p12). Erdeswick and others have thought perhaps from Celtic 'col,' meaning holy (SOS p52) here druids worshipped (LTM Oct 1971 p34). Or is from the forest-root 'coll' (NSFCT 1908 p138). No doubt that col in Colwich and Colton are the same. Rev FP Parker also believes that the explanation is either col, a Saxon thane, or hill inclosure or farm. 'Ascending the coll' is an expression used in West Dorset. It is said to be derived from an old British word having its synonym in the Latin collis a hill, a Norse word is colla. Whence Col-Kirk is to 'the church-on-the-hill. Colwich lies below Haywood Hill and Colton lies below Martlin's Hill (CWF p204). William de Wasteneys was granted a charter on May 1 1241 to hold a **market** here on Fridays. The market had ceased by 1500 (NSJFS 1971 p51). The earliest reference to Colton as a **borough** is in 1275 and the last in 1361-2 and then borough status lapsed (NSJFS 1972 p68) (SL p147). The **stocks** stood at the NE corner of Colton Hall garden wall. The stone foundation of the stocks could still be seen in c1897 (CWF p183). The **pound** adjoined the entrance of the field path to Rugeley and was still known as the 'pinfold' in c1897 (CWF p183). There was possibly a windmill at SK 041207 on the evidence that to the W of the village was a field called 'Windmill Field' on the 1834 OS map (CWF p153) (WBJ P18).

1600 to PRESENT. **Customs**. Until the end of the C19 it was the custom in Colton for the women to rise early on St Thomas' Day (Dec 21) and go round the parish to receive at each farmhouse a pint to three pints of corn, which they exchanged for flour at the mill. The custom ceased when the mill became a 'plaster' mill. Brand notices the practice in Warws as called 'corning' (CWF p183). Rev FP Parker wrote in 1897 that within the last 20 years some of the inhabitants used to put flowers on the doorstep of their houses on May Day (CWF p183). In the later C17 Dr Plot noted an **oak** tree growing in an hedgerow between Colton and Blithfield which was planted as an acorn by Ralph Bate. It grew very quickly and Ralph Bate saw it in his lifetime bear two feet square of wood at the butt end. Where the first 10 feet was sawn into boards it contained nearly a ton of wood (NHS p210). **Persons and visitors**. Erdeswick or Harwood say Colton was the birthplace of the distinguished philosopher, **William Wollaston** (SOS p53), whilst others say he was born in Coton Clanford (see) on March 26 1650 (GNHS p110) (W p406), or 1659 (SHOS vol 1 p430). **Robert Eyres Landor** (1781-1869), poet and playwright, was curate of Colton (VFC p81). The death of **John Landor**, the seven year old son of the rector of Colton, in March 1782 may have been foretold by an ominous encounter by the canal bridge on the road between Colton and Rugeley. The boy was ill at Rugeley Grammar School. On their way from Colton to Rugeley to care for him a nurse accompanied by the family groom met with a woman, carrying a dead child in a bundle, which was shaped like a coffin. The woman, who wore a brown cloak, knew them but she was unknown to them. She asked to see the rector so that he could bury her child. The woman then disappeared and subsequently did not see the rector about burying her child. The next night John Landor died (GLS pp78-79). For the case of **Mary Peate** of Eccleshall, who fell ill in Colton parish and was taken to Colwich parish where she died and her burial became chargeable to Colwich ratepayers, see Colwich.

Colton Hall S of Colton. Built in c1730 (BOE p107), and is believed to occupy the site of Colton Old Hall (see). In 1777 it belonged to William Piggot; Lady Blount also lived here at one time and in 1795 it was owned by the sheriff of Staffs. Later still it became a boys school (LTM Oct 1971 p35). Frederick Bonney nephew of Charles Bonney lived at Colton Hall (AR p63p). Has also appeared as Colton House. An old dovecote, belonging to the manor, stood

c1897, nearly opposite to Colton Hall close to the wall of the present school yard (CWF p175).

Colton Old Hall Colton. May have stood on the site or incorporated the original Saxon timber-built manor house (not Colt Manor House alias Littlehay) (LTM Oct 1971 p35) (TSW p48) (SVB p59). There was a murder at Colton manor house in 1271. A priest named John, chaplain of Colton (perhaps serving the chapel on the site of Bellamour Lodge), is alleged to have killed Christina, wife of Nicholas de Colton, while interposing in a quarrel between her and a stranger residing at the house. It is not known whether the lady was killed accidentally or not, but John fled from the scene and went uncaptured and was outlawed (CWF pp39-40) (SHC vol 4 p211) (HOA p186) (CCBO p66). For several centuries Colton Old Hall was the Staffs seat of the Gresleys of Drakelow, Derbys. The lower half of the hall was constructed of masonry whilst the upper part was of timber. It is said the hall had 80 rooms, of which 52 were bedrooms. It was sold by Sir G Gresley to Sir Walter Aston in James I's reign. Here the younger members of the Aston family resided during their father's second embassy in Spain. Sir Walter himself resided here in 1628; some of his letters to Lord Conway are dated from Colton Old Hall. The hall burnt down in Charles I's reign through the carelessness of a servant. From the Astons William Chetwynd purchased the site in 1658 (COI p170). A new house, Colton Hall (see), appears to have been built on the site in c1730.

Colton Hills Small range of hills rising to 608.1 feet high (HOWM p6). In Penn ancient parish. The name is preserved in Colton Hills Special School which is nearly 1.25m ENE of St Bartholomew's at Penn. Mander, who could only find the name occurring in recent times, has a theory about how the area was named (WA vol 2 no 1 p36). However, 'Col' in Welsh means hill or ridge (PPTP p37).

Colton Old Park A medieval deer park enclosed out of forest, 1m NE of Colton. The park pale is still evident. In existence by 1349 (NSJFS 1962 p76). Rev Parker refers to a park enclosed by the De Wasteneys in or by Henry III's time. From the De Wasteneys it passed to the Gresleys and from them to Sir Walter Aston in 1610 and was conveyed by Walter Aston 2nd Lord Aston to Sir Harvey Bagot (CWF p164). Shirley notes one deer park at Colton (EDP p179).

Colton Park A medieval deer park enclosed out of forest, 1m S of Colton. In existence by 1359 (NSJFS 1962 p76). Shirley notes one deer park at Colton (EDP p179).

Colts Moor Area which seems to have been held by Hulton Abbey as part of their grange at Upper Bradnop in medieval times (VCH vol 7 p171). Coltsmoor Farm is 1.25m N of Bradnop and is built on former waste land, enclosed in the later C18 (VCH vol 7 p171). Formerly in Bradnop township in Leek ancient parish.

Coltsmoor Former house under 0.25m W of Stanley. Formerly in Stanley township in Leek ancient parish. There was a house called Coltsmoor here by 1750. It still existed in c1830 (VCH vol 7 p230). A Cotslow appears in this area on the 1834 OS map.

Coltstone Small hamlet 0.5m NW of Ipstones. For the ghost of a black dog in this area see Inde Font Well.

Colwich (locally *Col-ledge*). Ancient parish and village on a slight bluff by the Trent 6.5m ESE of Stafford.

EARLY to 1400. The first part of the **name** 'col' is a reference to men who burned charcoal from timber felled in Cannock Forest, the second part 'wich' is a reference to village (CCBO p164) (SSE 1996 p12) (SPN p37). Alternatively the name may be derived from the Celtic river-root 'gil,' 'giol,' Gaelic 'cuil' and 'uig,' an enclosure (NSFCT 1908 pp114,133). The parish was formed before 1086 (SHC 1916 p192), and was curiously intertangled with that of Stowe-by-Chartley (NSFCT 1913 p60). There was a **church** at Colwich in the C11 (LDD). The present parish church, St Michael and All Angels, between the Trent and the main road, has some C13 work, but it was rebuilt mainly in the 1850s (CHMS2 p38). 'The church of Hewode' has been identified with Colwich church (HAHS p7). Colwich is not in DB but is reputed to have been a manor since (SHC 1914 p135). It has appeared as Colewich (1240), Colewyz (1247) and Colwich (1247) (SSE 1996 p12) (SPN p37). The moated site 160 metres SW of St Michael and All Angles' church at SK 00882103 is a listed monument. The prebend of Colwich in Lichfield cathedral was founded by Bishop Hugh de Patteshull in 1241 (SHOS vol 1 p292) (SSAHST vol 2 1960-61 p44). For a dispute concerning Colwich between the Pope and the king in the early C14 see VCH vol 3 p143.

1400 to PRESENT. By the early C16 Shugborough was a much larger place than Colwich as the muster rolls of Henry VIII prove, having double the population (SHC 1914 p131 note). Colwich **railway** station was known as Haywood Junction when built in c1845 (HAHS p54). On Sept 19 1986 an Inter City train travelling from London to Manchester collided at Colwich with an Inter City train journeying from Liverpool to London; nine coaches were seriously damaged, 74 people were injured, and the train driver lost his life (ADD pp177,179p) (ES March 9 1996 p4). **Persons.** The most famous prebendary of Colwich was **Thomas Bourchier** (c1404-1486), great-grandson of Edward III, appointed in 1424. He was appointed bishop of Worcester (1434), bishop of Ely (1444), archbishop of Canterbury (1454) and crowned Edward IV, Richard III, and Henry VII (HOL p221) (Cambridge Biographical Encyclopedia. David Crystal. 1994). For **Dr Johnson** of Lichfield (see) at Colwich church see The Old Manor House, Little Haywood. Colwich PR records under Nov 6 1755: 'Buried a poor women belonging to Eccleshall.' The poor woman was **Mary Peate** of Eccleshall who was travelling home to her native village on foot and fell in Colton parish on the boundary with Colwich, two men and a boy assisted her to Bishton to Mr Pegge's house, where she died, so laying the cost of her burial at the expense of the Colwich ratepayer, Sir William Wolseley objected and brought a case against the two men - William Emery, Josiah Beardmore and the boy, John Styche (OPM pp20-24). Capt **Michael Clements**, son of Rev Clements of Colwich, distinguished himself when he commanded the Pallas, at the defeat of Thurot in 1776 and subsequently in the Mediterranean. He died a superannuated Rear-Admiral in 1796 (THS p313). The children of the village school are given a half holiday on the birthday of the school founder, philanthropist and sister of Lady Chetwynd, **Charlotte Sparrow** of Bishton Hall (1784-1874), May 13. The annual ceremony at her grave in Colwich churchyard on this day still (1997) continues. In the service flowers are placed on her grave by children of the school, who also sing her favourite hymn. Her grave is situated close to the wall on the W side of the graveyard. The first reference to this ceremony is in 1879 (W p289) (SLM Aug-Sept 1952 pp15,16) (STMSM July 1978 p5) (SVB p84) (AR p75ps from 1950s) (HHHC pp29-30,35p) (HCMBOPP p41). **Charles Lynam** architect was born at Colwich on Feb 9 1829. In 1850 he joined his father's architectural practice in Glebe Street, Stoke-upon-Trent. Early in his career he is said to have designed the garden suburb of Stokeville (see), but later mainly worked on churches in the middle and north of the county. With his wife Lucy Emma, the daughter of Robert Garner of Foley House (see), Fenton, he lived at The Quarry (see), Hartshill. He was a founder member of the NSFC and set up the archaeology section for the club. He undertook excavations on Croxden and Hulton Abbeys and was a major contributor to NSFCT. He died in 1921. His son Charles Cotterill Lynam (1858-1939), headmaster, appears in 'DNB Missing Persons' (BOE) (SH p150) (POTP pp143p,144). The lock on the Trent and Mersey Canal at Colwich has been claimed as the scene of the murder of **Christina Collins** in 1839 (HCMBOPP p39p). **Samuel John Stone** (1839-1900), poet and hymn writer, born at Whitmore (see) spent some of his childhood at Colwich (PSS p229) (VFC p126).

Comber District of SW Kinver on the NE slopes of Kinver Edge, to NW of Kinver church. In Kinver parish. Has been identified with DB Cippemore (see) (SHC 1919 p164). Some villa's and artisans' houses were built here in the mid C19 (VCH vol 20 p121).

Comberford Small hamlet by the Tame, which was considered much larger in the Middle Ages 1.25m WNW of Wigginton. The name is from Anglo-Saxon 'cumb,' a valley, and ford - 'the ford of the valley.' There are two valleys combe is a common word in S of England but rare in the Midlands (DUIGNAN). Or 'Britons' ford' (SSE 1996 p12). The name appears in 1187 as Cumbreford (SSE 1996 p12). Some traces of a moat remain by E of a house at SK 192073 (CAMS p63). The former manor of Comberford belonging to the Comberford family of Comberford Hall (see), lay partly in Elford and Tamworth ancient parishes. A mission chapel, St Mary and St George, in Manor Lane, was founded by Hon Mary Howard. The building is unconsecrated although it has been granted a licence for celebration of divines services and offices (local info) (LDD). A message in a bottle was found in the Tame at Comberford on Oct 30 1862 by Capt Levett. The message was to the effect that the author had drowned himself because his lover had eloped with another and he was distraught. It was thought to be a hoax since a similar message was found in the Anker in the summer (THM vol 2 p39). Comberford features in a derisory rhyme about Tamworth (see). A WW2 pillbox is situated on the E of the Tame at SK 185067. It was made to look like a railway shed (WMARCH 1993 p35).

Comberford Hall 0.5m S of Comberford. Formerly in Wigginton township in Tamworth ancient parish. Seat of the Comberford (or Cumberford) family from soon after the Norman Conquest. The last male Comberford, Robert, died in 1671 (SHOS vol 1 p432). In the later C17 Plot noted the life-size drawing kept at the hall of a burbot. It had been caught in the Tame at Fazeley Bridge in Aug 1654 and presented to Col Comberford. The burbot was considered a great rarity in the C17, only four had been found in the county

within living memory (NHS pp240-241 tab 22 fig 4) (SHOS vol 1 part 1 p96). Here members of the family of the house were warned of an imminent death to one of them if one or more of them heard three knocks (NHS p329) (SD p15) (SC pp42,43) (WP p56) (FOS pp22,23). In 1844 the old house was described as long destroyed. After the Comberfords the manor passed through several families until being purchased by the 1st Marquess of Donegal, and was sold by his son Spencer. In 1844 it was the property of the daughter of the late Richard Howard (SOS 1844 p444). By the early C19 a house called Comberford Hall was occupied by the Pagets (mem in St Edith's, Tamworth). That house may be the Comberford House which appears on Greenwood's map. According to trade directories a Comberford Hall was occupied by William Tongue between 1834 and 1851; Charles Haywood, farmer, in 1872; John Wilson in 1884; Sydney Fisher in 1888 and 1892; Frederick Arthur Morris in 1896; William Felton Peel in 1900 and 1904; Christopher Askew Chandos-Pole in 1912; Charles Frederick Palmer in 1916; Percival Allen Warden in 1924 and 1932; Charles Pickin in 1940. The hall had been converted into luxury flats by 1988 (SVB p60).

Comberford Lodge House slightly N of Comberford, in Elford ancient parish (1884 OS map 6 inch).

Comberford Lodge Bridge Street, Wednesbury. Frederick William Hackwood, author of many works about the Black Country, born in Wednesbury in 1851, lived his later years here. He died at Balham, London in 1926. The house was named after the Comberford family (BCM spring 1993 pp16-21. July 1993 pp16-21 il of on p18) (SH p135 il of on p facing p137).

Combes Brook Rises on Blakelow near Bottom House. The head water has been called Lemon Brook on some C18 maps, and the brook has appeared as Cowms Brook (1686), Cooms Brook (1810), and Coombes Brook (NHS p43) (SPNO p8) (VCH vol 7 p171). Forms the border of the ancient parishes of Leek and Ipstones. At Apesford it enters Combes Valley. At the S end of the valley, S of Basford Hall, it joins the Churnet. The name means 'the brook that runs through a hollow' (SPNO p8).

Combes Valley Valley through which Combes Brook runs 1.75m NW of Ipstones. Brighton says the W bank has a defensive earthwork from the Saxon period (TOI p174). It was envisaged that the Consall Plateway be continued to Mixon Hay on the E side of the Churnet. The line was started but never completed. In several places in Combes Valley can be seen the even level track and sleepers (CVH pp126-127). Ralph de Tunstall Sneyd of Fair View (see) in the early C20 wrote

> In the fair valley of the Coomb
> The fox and magpie find a home
> The lapwing to his mate does call
> When the high sun shines on Sharpcliffe Hall
> But the Devil's Hole is a place of fear,
> A spirit wild is prisoned here.

(SMM pp41-42). Part of Combes Valley became a nature reserve in 1961, which was enlarged in 1962 (VCH vol 7 p171). The valley has also appeared as Coombes Valley (CVH p126) and a part of it is sometimes called 'Hell Hole' or Devil's Hole (see).

Combridge Hamlet near the confluence of Nothill and Alders Brooks 1.5m NE of Stramshall. In Rocester ancient parish. The name means 'Coomb bridge' (NSJFS 1980 p2). Or 'the ridge with a crest' (SSE 1996 p12) (SPN p133). Has appeared as Kanbrugge (1246) and Combrugge (SPN p133) (SSE 1996 p12). Poulton-Smith erroneously spells it Cowbridge (SPN p99). In the later C17 Plot found the Elder Sambucus fructu albo growing plentifully in hedges near Combridge. It is similar to the Elder in most respects except in the colour of the fruit and rind. It was first found by Tragus in the woods of Germany. Plot had only heard of it growing in one other place in this country; near Maidstone, Kent (NHS p206).

Commonend Farm Swinscoe. To the N of the farmbuildings is a round burial mound of the Bronze Age called 'Swinscoe Barrow.' It was excavated in 1929 and some skeletal finds were made. It was not mentioned by Bateman and is not Top Low. Unlocated (NSFCT 1929 pp89 plan facing, 90,95-96).

Commonside Area over 1.5m E of Kingswinford. In Pensnett parish district in Kingswinford ancient parish (W p184). The name appears in the 1851 census, and the area is now called Pensnett. In 1958 Wesley Churchman of Commonside murdered his brother by stabbing him 124 times. He was released from a life sentence in 1964. In 1972 he befriended an elderly man, Alfred Martin, whilst in hospital. On invitation Churchman went to Martin's house in Smethwick and murdered him (MM pp49-58).

Commonside There is a road called Commonside running S from Gentleshaw.

Common Side 1m ESE of Norton Canes. Probably takes its name from Norton

Common which formerly lay here.

Commonside Road to SE of Pelsall church.

Commonside Road at Shire Oak, Walsall Wood. Took its name from, perhaps, Walsall Wood Common (SNBC p38).

Compton Large rural area 1.5m W and NW of Kinver church (SVS p172). Former township in Kinver ancient parish (VCH vol 20 p149). The name means 'the farmstead in the narrow valley' (SPN p72). Compton was mentioned in 1167 as belonging to the lord of Kinver manor. By 1293 the main settlement probably centred on a green in the bend of Herons Gate Road 2m WNW of Kinver church; this is the Lower Compton on the maps of Plot and Yates. The green at Compton was mentioned in 1353 and probably extended W from Pigeonhouse Farm as far as Herons Gate Road. It had all been enclosed by 1856. Upper Compton was the area to the S round the Lydiates (VCH vol 20 pp122,139). What may have been the spectre of a red Triumph motorcycle passed a lorry in Compton. The lorry driver was sure he heard it crash in a bend further on the road but found nothing there (GPCE pp32-33). In the vicinity of Compton is Brindley's Bath (see).

Compton Area and name of a street connecting St Edward Street and Cheddleton Road, Leek. The name is from camp town (NSFCT 1905 p159) (HLS p13). The church, All Saints, Southbank Street, was built in 1887 (LDD).

Compton Former village situated by Smestow Brook, now a district of Wolverhampton 1m SSW of Tettenhall. In Tettenhall ancient parish. The area anciently stood in Kinver Forest (VCH vol 20 p9). The name is probably of British origin from 'cum' to mean a narrow and deep valley or in Saxon 'comb' or 'comp' (SHOS vol 2 p200) (HOPTT p50) (NSJFS 1981 p10) (SSE 1996 p12) (SPN p145). (SVS p172). Has appeared as Contone (DB) (SSE 1996 p12) and Cumpton (1291) (HOWM p8). Tettenhall prebend was later known as Tettenhall and Compton; and as Compton in 1373 and in 1401. Bovenhill (or Bovenhull) became the styling of the prebend thereafter (VCH vol 12 p19). Compton was an inhabited area by the later C13. It was described as a hamlet in 1539. By the early C17 the centre of the settlement was mainly at the junction of Compton Road West and Finchfield Hill (VCH vol 20 p9). The Staffs and Worcs Canal passes through Compton. It was here that the first part of it was begun in 1766; the first stretch opened was that between the Severn and Compton. It opened in 1770 (VCH vol 2 p288. vol 20 p9). Others say James Brindley cut the first turfs for the canal in a field at Compton on Sept 1 1776 (WF p15). Compton Top Lock was Brindley's first lock on the canal (WMAG April 1971 front cover pc). Until the rest of the canal was complete in 1772 the wharf at Compton was the terminus for Wolverhampton goods (WF p44). A man named Moore of Compton, aged 105, was backed for 50 L to walk one mile in a race with another, or others, so long as they were over 80 years old (Bells Messenger June 18 1837) (Broughton's Scrapbook p460). Compton is Crompton in the novels of Ellen Thorneycroft Fowler of Woodthorne (see) (Wolverhampton Chronicle April 30 1999 p31).

Compton Court Farm On N side of Sheepwalks Lane, Compton, in Kinver ancient parish. Is probably of C17 origin, being once timber-framed. The external walls were rebuilt in brick perhaps in the later C18. Further additions were made in the C19 (VCH vol 20 p122).

Compton Hall Compton Road West, Compton, Wolverhampton. Thomas Elwell, a prosperous hardware merchant, owned buildings, possibly a farm, on the site of Compton Hall, in 1827 or 1828. He probably built the hall between 1840 and 1850. The architect was Edwin Banks. It was later the seat of Sir John Morris famous locally as the mayor who was knighted in Queen Square by Queen Victoria on the occasion of the inauguration of the Prince Consort's statue. During the residency of Laurence Hodson, a connoisseur and a director of the Springfield Brewery Company Ltd, between the mid 1890s and c1906 important pieces of Arts and Craft Movement work were commissioned for the hall. These include the last wallpapers to be designed by William Morris, which are called 'Compton' (1895-6), fireplaces with tiles by Sir Edward Burne-Jones, and three tapestries by Burne Jones woven to hang in the Billiard Room where the ceiling was decorated to a design by either Morris or his assistant JM Dearle; the tapestries went to Birmingham Museum and Art Gallery. After WW2 the hall became a nurses' home and it opened as a hospice in 1982 (VCH vol 20 p9) (Compton Hospice: The First Ten Years. 1992) (BOE p326) (TCOP p59p).

Compton Hall Over 2m WNW of Kinver church, in Kinver ancient parish. Is mentioned in 1538 when it was the manor house of Horewood manor (or Compton Hallows manor). It was the seat of the lord of the manor, Thomas Whorwood, until he moved to Stourton Castle, which he had done by 1605. The hall was let after 1651 and it was rebuilt in the earlier C18. In the early C19 it was sold as a farmhouse and it is now (1982) know as Compton Hall Farm (VCH vol 20 pp133-134).

Compton House House at the N end of Bannut Tree Road at its junction with Compton Road, over 1.75m NW of Kinver church. It was known as Compton House by 1836 and it was enlarged in stages during the C19 (VCH vol 20 p123).

Compton Park Former medieval deer park which lay in the present Roughpark Wood area, 2.25m WNW of Kinver. It seems to have centred on Horewood Wood and license to enclose the wood was granted in 1269. The same park, extended to the S, or a new park, existed by the earlier C16 (VCH vol 20 p141), and Compton Park is marked on Saxton's map. In the late C16 Erdeswick noted 'The Fair Park' at Compton. Greyfield Gate, mentioned in 1616, was a gate into it on its SE side. It appears to have been without deer by the Civil War period (EDP p180) and was enclosed in the 1650s (VCH vol 20 p141). The name is preserved in Compton Park Farm, 2.5m W of Kinver, a farm created by 1672 out of the enclosed park; the farmhouse stands on the moated site of the manor house of Horewood manor (SSAHST 1982-3 p43) (VCH vol 20 p133). (CAMS p63).

Condlyffe Almshouses Condlyffe Road, Leek. Almshouses with eight dwellings founded by Elizabeth Condlyffe (d1878) and built in 1882 in the Arts and Crafts style (VCH vol 7 p167).

Coneydale 1.5m NW of Croxden. Has also appeared as Coney Dale.

Coneygreave Minute hamlet 1m NE of Draycott-in-the-Moors. At Coneygreaves Farm was found a quartzite axe-hammer Neolithic or Bronze Age (NSFCT vol 78 p62) (NSJFS 1964 p21).

Coney Greave Minute hamlet 0.75m WSW of Whitmore.

Coneygreave Farm 1m NNW of Horton, in Horton ancient parish, on NW side of Horton Hay. The farm may stand on the site of a rabbit warren (VCH vol 7 p72).

Coneygreave Pool Pool which lay on the E side of Shropshire Union Canal 0.5m E of Norbury. It was Skrymsher property and in 1775 contained 'with bogs' 25 acres (NSFCT 1927 p38). Known as Coney Grove Pool in 1781 it still existed at the time of the 1834 OS map and the Norbury tithe map of 1835 but had been drained by 1889 (1889 OS map 6 inch) (WSS p108).

Coneygree District 0.75m ENE of Dudley, in Tipton parish. Iron-mining at Coneygree is recorded from 1291 (VCH vol 2 p120) (SL p207). Le Conyngre Park or Le Conigree Park (see), a hunting ground, occurs in documents of the C16 and C17 (VCHW vol 3 p90).

Coneygrey Small area of central Bloxwich consisting of Marlborough, New and Clarendon Streets which were laid out in 1875 by John Farrington Crump on land behind the farmhouse of Thomas Arch in an area formerly known colloquially as the Cunneries, a corruption of Coneygree, meaning rabbit warren (SNBP p40).

Coney Warren and Lodge. Coney Lodge Farm is 1.5m NW of Chasetown. Coney Lodge, a lodge attached to a rabbit warren, was in existence by the C17. It may have been the lodge, NW of Boney Hay, which was destroyed in the Rabbit Riots on Cannock Chase (see) 1753-54 (VCH vol 14 pp199,214).

Congleton Edge On Staffs Ches border 1m WNW of Biddulph. Partly in Biddulph and Congleton parishes.

Congreve Hamlet by the Penk 1m SE of Whiston. In Penkridge ancient parish. An axe-head of Neolithic or Bronze Age was found at Congreve in the early C18 (SHOS vol 1 p31) (BDH p18). Has appeared as Comegrave (DB) (SSE 1996 p12), Cungrave (1203), Congreve (1215), Cungreyve (1321), Congreyve (1543), Coungreve (1554) (SPNO p88). Congreve was a prebend of Penkridge Collegiate Church (VCH vol 3 p300. vol 5 p113). The name means 'the grove in the valley,' but the forms are all in conflict, thinks DUIGNAN (SSE 1996 p12) (SPN p93). Or 'comb grove' (NSJFS 1981 p3). Persons. Congreve is said to have been the birthplace of the poet, William Congreve (1670-1729) (THS p257), but he was born in Bardsey, West Yorkshire (Cambridge Biographical Encyclopedia), and is merely of the family who were anciently of Congreve (W p468). Richard Hurd, bishop of Lichfield (1774-1781) and bishop of Worcester (1781-1808), was born at Congreve in 1720. He was educated at Brewood and Rugeley Grammar Schools. He was tutor to George IV and to Sir Edward Littleton of Teddesley Hall; to Littleton, Hurd dedicated one of his works. He was editor of the poems of Abraham Cowley and Joseph Addison, and died at Hartlebury Palace in 1808. Sir Edward Littleton visited him in his last years at Hartlebury and as he was leaving Hurd is said to have asked of him 'is the old house at Congreve, where I was born, yet standing!' By some he was known irreverently as 'the Beauty of Holiness' for his moderate and orthodox beliefs and being suspicious of religious enthusiasm. He was offered and refused the archbishopric of Canterbury in 1783. In one instance Shaw says he was born at Pendeford, Staffs, in another he says he was born at Congreve and shortly after his birth his family moved to Pendeford where they resided for several years (SHOS vol 1 pp274,280. SHOSA. vol 2 p8) (THS pp257-258) (HOL p158) (W p467) (BS p240) (PSS pp73-75) (CCBO pp173-175) (VCH vol 3 p68) (HOP p87). Miss Barker author of 'A Welsh Story' was born at Congreve. In that novel she introduces the character of Sir Edward Littleton, her patron, under the name of Sir Edwin (THS pp257-258) (W pp467-468).

Congreve House 250 yards NE of Congreve Manor House, Congreve. A red-brick house dating from c1800. Sold by the 3rd Lord Hatherton in 1919. May have been prebendal property (VCH vol 5 p113). Occurs as Congreve House in 1959. Appears as Congreve Farm on 1:25,000 OS map.

Congreve House Timber-framed and brick house in the old part of Walton-on-the-Hill village (VCH vol 5 p3). Formerly Manor Farm (BERK p69). Built in c1736 by a Thomas Congreve, a farmer. In 1742 he had a son named William (later Sir William, Bart), who entered the army and became Superintendent of Military Machines. Sir William had a son Sir William (1772-1828), Comptroller of the Royal Laboratory, Woolwich (1814-1828), inventor of the Congreve rocket and brimstone matches (VCH vol 5 p4) (SVB p169). The Congreves were succeeded by the Kents, the Evans and the Burtons. Middlefell thinks the Evans applied the name 'Congreve House' (BERK pp69,84p). The house is named after Thomas Congreve, grandfather of the inventor of the Congreve rocket (SVB p169).

Congreve Manor House Red brick building standing above the W side of the road at Congreve (PVH p61 il). Incorporates an early C18 farmhouse. The manor of Congreve was held from the C14 by the Congreve family. They may have lived at Congreve before the C17, at a hall on the site of Congreve Manor House, or at a hall on the site of Manor Farm, a late C17 or early C18 farmhouse on E side of the road (VCH vol 5 pp112-113).

Conigree Lodge Seat of the Willets, in Tipton or Dudley parishes. Has appeared as Conneygree Lodge (1664), Cunigree (1671). It may have been the residence known as Coneygree Hall, or it may have been only a lodge at the entrance to the grounds (HOTIP pp180,181), or a lodge to the former Conigree Park.

Conigree Park, Le Hunting ground said to have lain in Dudley parish. It occurs in documents from 1553 when the custody of it was granted to John Lyttelton, and has appeared as Le Conyngre Park. In 1554 it was granted to Edward Lord Dudley, and it then contained a house or lodge called the Wrennesnest. A park in the same district, mentioned in an inquisition of 1592, called Quingedde, may be the same park (VCHW vol 3 pp90,100). It may have been known at some time as Tipton Park, mentioned in 1638 (HOTIP pp91). It probably gives its name to Conygree or Coneygree Colliery.

Conqueror's Farm Brick house with cornices in Catholic Lane, Lower Gornal. Occupied at the beginning of the C20 by the Caswell family. Demolished in 1962 (SDOP p19p).

Consall Small village at the top of a dale which descends to the Churnet 16.5m NNE of Stafford. Former township in Cheddleton ancient parish. A spring at Consall has been found to be sulphurous (NHS p101) (NSFCT 1944 p40). The name means 'Cuna's hall' (DUIGNAN) (SSE 1996 p12). OAKDEN says the first element is from 'kuning' - Danish for king. (SSAHST 1967 p34). Gelling says it is partly unexplained (NSJFS 1981 p2). 'Cuna's corner of land' (SSE 1996 p12) (SPN p77). Or 'corner in a deep valley' (PNPD). Waste held by the king known as Cuneshala is recorded in DB. Consall later formed one of the four divisions of Cheddleton manor (CVH p21). Written Cunsall until the C20. The Draycott family who owned Consall from the C13 may have had a deer park in the Folly Lane area (CVH pp160,161). On the road to Consall New Hall is an old chapel erected for the miners working the local shafts (NSFCT 1945 p87). Consall became a separate civil parish in 1866 (GLAUE p408). Consall railway station, recommended for closure in 1963 (ES March 22 1963), was cantilevered out over the Caldon Canal (PDS&C p82).

Consallforge Hamlet in the upper Churnet Valley by the Churnet and Caldon Canal 1.25m ENE of Consall. In Cheddleton ancient parish. Has also appeared as Consall Forge. Iron was worked at Consallforge between at least 1688 and 1750, and probably later. The Foley family refined pig iron here from their furnace at Meir Heath (MR p109). From the end of the C18 limestone from Caldon Low was broken down at Consallforge for the pottery industry and taken to the Potteries on the Caldon Canal or the Consall Plateway, which terminated at Consallforge. The kilns date from the early C19 (DoE II). The kilns probably ceased production in c1855 (NSFCT 1945 p87). Raven says the huge kilns in the S bank of the Churnet, owned by the NSR, reputedly worked to 1921 (MR p109p). The Consall kilns have a mason's mark (+) incised on several of the stones, similar to the tunnel under the road from Wetley Rocks to Cheadle (WJ p36). For a canal milepost at Consallforge see Caldon Canal. Rupert Simms (d1937), bookseller, antiquarian and author of BS, was born at Consallforge on July 31 1853. In 1862 he lost his arm in an industrial accident in Longton (see). In 1883 he became a second-hand book

dealer in Friar Street, Newcastle-under-Lyme (BS ppviii-xi, 404) (SA May 14 1921. Aug 7 1937) (SHST p446) (STM Jan 1971 p25p) (BCM July 1975 pp52-56) (POTP p192) (SH p152 p).

Consall New Hall 0.25m SE of Consall Old Hall, Consall. Built in c1810 (BOE p108). Mary Leigh (d1833) was of Consall New Hall (mem in Cheddleton church). It was sometime the seat of the ironmaster 'Ironstone' Smith. By the mid C20 Consall New Hall estate belonged to William and Alberta Podmore, who both died at the hall on Oct 31 1958 from carbon-monoxide poisoning leaking from a new central heating system put in by Mr Podmore. Their descendant, Mr Podmore, an industrialist, was the owner in 1988 (mem in Wetley Rocks church) (MR pp108-109). In the grounds is Rousseau's Grotto (see).

Consall Old Hall 0.5m ENE of Consall. Built in the late C17 (BOE p108) (CVH pl 14). Henry Harris (d1756) was of Consall Old Hall (mem in Cheddleton church).

Consall Plateway Railroad laid in c1815-20 to transport lime from the lime kilns at Consallforge to Longton, via Consall, Knowlbank, Tunnel Farm, and Rangemoor, across the Hanley-Cheadle road at Lime Wharf terminating at Stormy Hill, S of Moorville Hall. Consall Plateway was the second railway to be opened in N Staffs after the Cotton Plane. It was envisaged that the plateway run to Mixon Hay on the E side of the Churnet, but that extension was never completed (WJ pp35-41) (CVH p126 pl 30). Ceased working in the early 1850s (NSFCT 1944 p106. 1945 pp86-7). Total length was more than six miles (IAS pp122,161) (RM Jan-Feb 1949 p15).

Consall Wood Large wood 0.5m SE of Consall on W side of the Churnet. Thomas Brown of Broad Oak Farm discovered a small hoard of 48 coins - shillings, sixpences and groats - in a pasture field adjoining Consall Wood, early in 1941; all the coins were of Elizabeth I's reign with the exception of three belonging to the reign of Philip and Mary (NSFCT 1942 p55).

Cooknall In Kingswinford ancient parish. 'Cooknall Piece' and 'Little Cooknall' appear on Fowler's map of 1822, S of Stream Road, Wordsley (WFK p24 see map). Cooknall may be the Cooken Hill mentioned by Scott in 1832 (SVS p130). A Cooknell Wood appears on the 1834 OS map to the NE of Wordsley in the area of the present Ridge Hill Hospital. There is no longer an area of Cooknall (WFK p11).

Cooksgate House 1m E of Betley. Formerly in Knowl End township in Audley ancient parish. The name Cook may be from a man named Cooke who tenanted a house here in the C17 called Cooks Gate (SHC 1944 p34). Gate may be from a gate to Heighley Park, a medieval deer park (BVC p35). (NSFCT 1919 p23).

Cookshill Large hamlet 0.5m NW of, and almost merging with, Caverswall. In Caverswall parish. There is an earthwork 0.25m SW of Cookshill known as Swan Bank (WJ p28).

Cook's Hollow About at Gorstead Mill (NSFCT 1948 p51).

Cooksland Tiny hamlet 0.25m N of Seighford. The name means 'Cuc's land' (DUIGNAN) (SPN p104). Or 'Cucu's newly-cultivated land' (NSJFS 1981 p3) (SSE 1996 p12). The manor of Cucheslund appears in DB (SSE 1996 p12).

Coombesdale Minute hamlet 0.75m NW of Chapel Chorlton.

Cooper's Bank Hamlet 0.75m SSW of Lower Gornal. In Sedgley ancient parish. Geologically, the hamlet lies on a dolerite intrusion (PAIP p102). The name appears in the 1851 census and has appeared as Coopers Bank.

Coopers Green Former estate in Audley township. It belonged for many generations up to 1733 to the Smyth or Smith family (SHC 1944 p3).

Cooper's Lodge House to the WNW of Prospect Village (1834 OS map). To here Cannock Chase Railway opened a line in 1862 from Hednesford (VCH vol 2 p318). The name is preserved in Cooper's Cottages (OS map 1:25,000).

Cooper's Well Mitton, Whiston. A gospel-reading place on the Penkridge perambulation. Recorded in the PR 1732. Spelt Coopre's (HOP p30).

Copeland House Mid-Victorian house in Copeland Street, Stoke-upon-Trent. Built by the Copeland firm for their factory manager, demolished in c1976 (AGT pp156,157il).

Copeland Wharf Former warehouse on the Trent and Mersey Canal and the Newcastle Branch Canal. It stood behind Copeland House, Copeland Street, Stoke-upon-Trent. Demolished when the southern section of the A500 was built (AGT p156).

Cop Hall Stood in the angle formed by the junction of Whitehall Road and Sheepwash Lane, S of Great Bridge (SHWB 13), West Bromwich. Existed by the early C17 and was the seat of John Turton in 1685 (HOWBW p172) (VCH vol 17 p8). The Cophall council estate W of Whitehall Road was begun in 1959 (VCH vol 17 p9).

Copley Farm SW of Pattingham on the border with Shrops. In Pattingham ancient parish. Copley was an inhabited place by 1312 (VCH vol 20 p173).

Cop Mere A pool covering 40 (NSSG p18) or 50 acres 2.5m NE of High Offley.

Formed in a glacial hollow created in the Ice Age (SN Feb 14 1997 p16). (ES Aug 5 1989 p20p). It has appeared as Coke Mere (1298) (ECC p14). The name means Coppa's lake (MR p247). Or Cop is quite likely from Cob, meaning, anciently, anything big (HBST p273 note). The bishop of Lichfield held the fishing rights, but Weston E Vernon Yonge traced a deed which gave the lord of Charnes manor the right of fishing once a year in the pool 'as far as a man could throw a two penny hatchet.' In the C19 the custom of a large man throwing a hammer into the pool to determine the extent of the lord's fishing area, was still occasionally practised (BPS p129) (NSFCT 1910 pp198-199) (ROT p21). The original boathouse, by the mere, dated from 1735, was reconstructed in the early C19 (DoE II). On the N side of the mere is an old folly, which was presumably a fishing lodge (ES Aug 5 1989 p20).

Copmere End Hamlet 2.5m NE of High Offley on S side of Cop Mere. In Horsley quarter in Eccleshall ancient parish. A perforated axe-hammer of the Neolithic or Bronze Age was found at Copmere in 1948 (NSJFS 1964 p21) (WSS p95). Has also appeared as Cockmeer (NHS p43).

Coppenhall Village 2.75m SSW of Stafford. Former township and chapelry in Penkridge ancient parish. Has appeared as Copehale (DB), Coppenhale (1166), Kopenhale (1236), Coppnall (1564), Coppinghall (1613) (SPNO p82) (SPN p37). The name is of Anglo-Saxon origin and means 'the meadow-land of Coppa' (DUIGNAN). Or 'Coppa's nook of land' (SPNO p82) (NSJFS 1981 p3), or 'Coppa's land' (SSE 1996 p12) (SPN p37). A church at Coppenhall may have had its origins in a cell of the monks of Stone Priory; they built the present church, St Lawrence, on the W side of the village soon after they obtained possession of the manor in the late C12 (NSFCT 1911 p222) (VCH vol 3 pp242,243. vol 5 p142). Pevsner describes the church as 'a perfect C13 village church, small but of great dignity' (BOE p108). Coppenhall was a prebend of Penkridge Collegiate Church. The vicarage of Coppenhall was another prebend of the collegiate church (VCH vol 3 p300. vol 5 p140). A windmill may have stood in The Windmill Field in Chaseview Lane. A deed of 1607 remitting rights of Coppenhall windmill to John Giffard for £41 (SLM spring 1954 p23p) may relate to this windmill or a predecessor to Butterhill windmill at Butterhill (see). Henry Cholmeley and his wife Francis conveyed a windmill and half an acre of land in Coppenhall to John Giffard (or Halfepenye) in 1616. This may have stood in the Windmill Field 'adjoining Hyde Lea' mentioned in 1661, but by the mid C19 the field name alone survived (VCH vol 5 p141). Coppenhall became a separate ecclesiastical parish in 1744 and a separate civil parish in 1866 (GLAUE p408).

Coppenhall Gorse Large moat enclosing about 100 yards in diameter and approximately oval at Coppenhall. It probably represents the site of an important dwelling occupied in the early C14. The site was excavated in 1951 (OSST 1951-51 pp15-23) (VCH vol 5 p138). Nancy Linley thinks the moat forms one large complex with the moat called Hyde Lea Mottes, and this is a moated site with an associated mill and mill works. The VCH lists Coppenhall Gorse and the Hydes Lea as two separate moats (NSFCT 1982 p21).

Coppenhall Hall Coppenhall. Timber-framed and brick house dating from the C16 or earlier (VCH vol 5 p139). May have been occupied by the Cholmeley (or Chumley or Chomley) family as tenants since the early C15. The hall was bought and occupied after WW1 by James Holt, farmer (VCH vol 5 p140) (SAC p27). Depressions to the N and W of the house may represent the remains of a moat (VCH vol 5 p139) which Nancy Linley thinks is one and the same as the moat of Coppenhall Farm (NSFCT 1982 p21).

Coppenhall House Coppenhall. Occupied by Parker Williams, a wheelwright, in 1700. Thought to have been haunted for centuries. A ghost is said to have appeared at the side of the four-poster bed at the house. After the death of Cynthia Sukiennik in 1981 the house was sold at auction (SVB p61) (SAC p27).

Coppice, The District 1m WSW of Wednesbury. Appears on 1947 OS map 1:25,000 (sheet 32/99) at SO 972943.

Coppice, The Large mansion situated half way down Cape Hill opposite what is now (1952) Mitchells and Butlers brewery, Smethwick. Here lived Elizabeth Reynolds, an artist who recorded many local scenes, in the mid C19 (STELE Oct 31 1952) (SHCB p4).

Coppice Farm A modern housing estate in New Invention (Selective Essays on Willenhall. David Potts. 1984. Copy in Willenhall library). There is a Coppice Farm Way on N side of Lichfield Road, W of Essington Road (Birmingham A-Z).

Coppice Hill Hill under 1m ESE of Brocton, 602 feet high. Has a fine view of the Wrekin to the WSW in Shrops (GCC p31). Devil's Drumble (see) and Freda's Grave (see) are on or near it.

Coppice Hills Inclines and wood directly N of the site of Beaudesert Hall.

Coppice Village District on E side of Turls Hill, 0.75m E of Sedgley. The original settlement centred on the junction of King Street and Bond Street. The

Coppice had become a small centre of industry by the beginning of the C19 (HC p62). It is now (1994) a tiny area of Hurst Hill (TB May 1994 pp12-13). Has also appeared as The Coppice (W p200) (IE p20).

Coppin Hall Aldridge. Home of Rev Joseph Shutt (BS between pp244-249?). Probably same as Coppy Hall.

Coppy Hall Former medieval house on Druid's Heath, Aldridge, at SK 05790230. The house, built in an enclosure on Druid's Heath, was held by the Gorwey (or Gorway) family in the C14. That family and the Wolrich family are associated with the hall in the C17. In the later C18 Coppy Hall was a school. It later passed to Rev Daniels and was demolished in the C20. There were two groups of buildings, the hall and the farm; various members of the Partridge family lived at one of the properties until the mid 1960s. Has also appeared as Copy Hall, and could be the same as Coppin Hall. The name is preserved in the street Coppy Hall Grove, built in 1957, on the N side of Lazy Hill Road (W p551) (MOA pp105, 134) (SNAR p20p). At Coppy Hall was found a charcoal-burning hearth (SSAHST 1973 p40 note). The Aldridge gravel pit was in front of Coppy Hall, where there was a pool by the 1980s (MOA p105).

Coppy Nook 0.75m NW of Hammerwich. Was an inhabited area by 1783 (VCH vol 14 p259).

Corbyn's Hall Stood beyond Lenches Bridge at Pensnett to the right of Male's Transport garage and back from the road, in Kingswinford ancient parish (BCM autumn 1999 p60). There may have been a house on the site of Corbyn's Hall by the early C14; the hall was surrounded by a moat (TB Sept 1977 p13p. Nov 1980 p4p). A later hall was built in the C16 by the Corbyn family, Pensnett gentry; they gave their name to it (W p182) (BHOP2 p103p), and it has appeared as Corbins Hall. George Corbin (d1636) and son Thomas (d1638) were of Corbin's Hall (mem in Kingswinford church). The oak table nearly a yard wide and 25 yards three inches long from Dudley Castle had been bought to Corbyn's Hall by the 1680s. In order to get it into the hall it had had to be cut down by seven yards nine inches (NHS p211) (SVS p133). Thomas Corbyn of Hall End, Warws, last male heir, sold the hall and estate to John Hodgetts. It was later sold to the the Gibbons family, iron masters and coal producers (BHOP2 p103) (SNSV vol 1 p82); John Gibbons of Corbyn's Hall designed and built the first 'round hearth' furnace which immediately increased the tonnage of iron produced by 25 per cent (TB Sept 1977 p13). The hall was occupied in 1851 by William Matthews (W p19). The manorial courts for Kingswinford manor were at some time held here (BHOP p6). The hall was demolished in 1910 (SNSV vol 1 p332) (TB) or in 1916 owing to mining subsidence (BHOP2 p103). For the mizen mast of the Three Sisters erected near the hall see Kingswinford. (SVS p133) (SHOS vol 2 p228 but nothing really about the hall).

Corney Hill Rowley Regis. Hill in the Rowley range (SHOS vol 2 p240).

Corngreaves Small district on N side of the Stour 0.5m S of Cradley Heath. In Rowley Regis parish. Corngreaves Works. A witch of Cradley is said to have caused a large boiler to burst at the British Company's Ironworks at Corngreaves, forcing the local people to evacuate the district (Wolverhampton Chronicle. July 26 1848) (BCM Jan 1982 p59). At the New British Iron Company works there was an explosion on July 2 1887 which killed two men; William Thomas Kilvert, aged 38 and Benjamin Hodgetts, aged 44. Thomas Hill was seriously injured. They were engaged at a blast furnace when a tuyere suddenly exploded and workmen were hurled in all directions (BCM April 1985 pp36-39). The works were demolished in 1927 and the site had become the Corngreaves Trading Estate by 1991 (ORR p110).

Corngreaves Castle It stood on the site of the present Congreaves Hall. Seat of the Attwood family or a connecting family from the time of the Norman Conquest. Some stones may have gone into the building of old Hawne House and or one of the slitting mills of the Stour (TB April 1972 p7). Skeletons are said to have been found in a cupboard at the house (TB Jan 1978 p30). It was said to be haunted by the ghost of a monk (probably that of Haden Old Hall). The two daughters of the owner of the castle drowned after seeing the ghost whilst fleeing from it (TB Dec 1979 p5).

Corngreaves Hall Near Haden Hill Park. It replaced an old castle, and was built by James Attwood (b1744) in the 1780s (BCWJ pp54,66), or 1808 (AOBC p53). Attwood's brother was, Matthias Attwood (1746-1836), iron manufacturer, owner of Hawne House, the Leasowes and other estates, and the father of Thomas Attwood, the celebrated political reformer (BCWJ pp54,66). The hall was known as Corngreaves House for much of the C19 (AOBC p66p).

RHINOCEROS CASE. On the death of James Attwood in 1821 the estate passed to his son John who, in 1825, sold it as an investment to James Shears, Robert Small and John Taylor, directors of the British Iron Company as the estate contained many mines and ironworks. A condition of the sale was that payment was to be made in instalments. After the first instalment had been made the British Iron Company fell into financial difficulties and the directors refused to pay the second instalment, demanding a reduction in the price: The company nevertheless took possession of the property. The directors then claimed that Attwood had mislead them about the value of the property and the company wished to rescind the contract. The trials over the estate's ownership began in June 1826 and after a succession of 14 trials, the House of Lords ruled in Attwood's favour on March 22 1838. The case was called the 'Rhinoceros Case' by Lord Brougham who sat in judgment over it. One late Victorian writer called it 'one of the most extraordinary civil cases ever tried before any tribunal whatever' (AOBC pp53-67) (SNSV vol 2 pp2-3).

Benjamin Best, a principal witness for the British Iron Company, lived at Corngreaves House until he died in 1852. He was succeeded by his son George Alfred Best (1839-1921) who adopted the name Haden, and built for himself Haden Hill House (see) in 1878. John Attwood died in 1865 (AOBC p57). Sandwell council were hoping to restore the house for use possibly as a community centre between c1976 and 1989, and it was being considered for demolition in the early 1980s (BCM July 1981 pp53p-54. April 1989 p33ps) (AOBC p67) (TB Feb 18 1999 p1p of New British Iron Co Works). Two skeletons have been discovered behind panelling both had died a violent death each holding a dagger up to the other. The dagger was kept at the hall as a memento and the skeletons given a burial (TB June 1983 p5). (TB April 1972 p7p) (ORR p112p). Corngreaves Hall is Mawne Hall in Francis Brett Young's novels (BCM autumn 1989 p58).

Corn Hill Leek cemetery is here on the S side of Leek. The cross (tomb?) in Leek churchyard with '1180 H.Q.C.C.' is described as the Cornhill Cross (NSFCT 1882 p23). A murder was committed in the Corn Hill area and the spectre which haunts this area is known as the Cornhill Ghost (NSFCT 1900 p147) (FOS p18). Has also appeared as Cornhill and the name is preserved in Cornhill Gardens on the W side of Cheddleton Road.

Cornhill Small district N of Norton-le-Moors.

Cornpark Over 1.5m NW of the church at Church Mayfield, Mayfield.

Coseley Former Black Country hamlet lying near the foot of the Sedgley-Dudley watershed, now a town 17.5m S of Stafford. Former liberty in the Lower Side division in Sedgley ancient parish (W p195) (HC p71).

900 to 1800. Coseley is said to have been mentioned in Lady Wulfruna's charter in 994 (WMVB p49). Lady Wulfruna's spring at Coseley, noted by a C16 writer (WMVB p49), is possibly a reference to the well at Spring Vale (see). Hollywell at Hurst Hill (see) has also been identified with Wulfruna's spring at Coseley. The earliest mention of Coseley was thought to be in 1357 until a reference showing Coseley as Colseleye in 1292 was discovered in the mid C20. Later Coseley appears as Coulssley (1555) (HC pp13,36) (CWBT). The **name** probably of Anglo-Saxon origin has been considered to derive from 'Cole's lea' (SR p4) (AMS p440). Or 'Cossa's lea' (MR p112). Or from Anglo-Saxon 'colere-leah' 'the charcoal burner's glade' (SPN p38), or 'the charcoal burners' wood' (WMVB p49). From the early Middle Ages there was a fragmented village of Colseley or Coseley which extended from the borders of Woodsetton to what is now Highfields and Broad Lanes and comprised many hamlets for instance Hurst Hill, Deepfields, Woodsetton and Lanesfield, many were built on former manorial wasteland (HC). There was a bull ring for bull baiting at Coseley (BHOP2 p8). For windmills see Bramford and Roseville.

1800 to PRESENT. In the C19 a village with a nucleus called Coseley grew up at the junction of Church and Gough Roads, and Legge and Yewtree Lanes (HOS p44). The **church**, Christ Church, on the W side of Church Road, was consecrated on Aug 27 1830 (A History of Christ Church. John Roper. 1980). It was formed into an ecclesiastical parish in 1832 (LGS p117). Coseley's chief **industries** were coal mining, nailing and tin-plating. Cannon Industries founded in 1826 is probably the best known firm in Coseley. Their electric cookers and 'Gas Miser' fires are leading brand names (MR p112). A great number of miners gathered at Coseley on the afternoon of Nov 14 1815, the day after miners had rioted in Wolverhampton. Two troops of the Staffordshire Yeomanry came to Coseley after suppressing the riots in Wolverhampton to prevent the Coseley gathering from becoming riotous (HOWM p151). The tunnel in the Birmingham Canal New Cut Old Main Line at Coseley, built in 1837 by Thomas Telford (BCM autumn 1995 p15), is 360 yards long (OS map for canal navigations 1977) (HCMS No. 2) (SWY p8p). In 1849 **cholera** returned to Coseley and claimed the lives of 86 in over two months (TEBC2 p61). In 1867 Lower Side division became Lower Sedgley civil parish or later Coseley **urban district** - then the second largest urban district in the country (CWBT p21). Coseley became a separate civil parish in 1903. This was abolished and split up between the county boroughs of Dudley, Walsall, Wolverhampton, and West Bromwich in 1966 (GLAUE p409). The

arms of Coseley urban district, granted in 1951, are: Checky gold and azure, a chevron gules charged with a Stafford Knot or; on a chief sable three gold cressets with flames proper. The crest is: Within a gold palisado crown a mount vert, and thereon a representation of Sedgley beacon-tower proper. The motto is: 'Fellowship is life' (CH p339il). In 1968 the council house of the urban district, which stood on the corner opposite Roseville chapel at the junction of School Street East and Green Street, was demolished (CWBT p21p). For the Tipton & Coseley Building Society see Tipton. **Newspaper**. The Tipton and Coseley Times and South Staffordshire Advertiser, founded Dec 1 1928, ran until at least Dec 27 1930 (SHJ spring 1996 p28). A house in Minith Road was bombed in 1940 (TB Feb 1996 p3). **Supernatural**. Two ghosts are said to haunt the Old Meeting Road area, Coseley, one is of an old miner, perhaps on his way to some lost mine (GOM p16) (GPCE p16). The other is the ghost of the former caretaker of Coseley Youth Centre. The centre was built in the 1960s on the site of railway worker dwellings. In one a station master threw himself in front of a train at Coseley railway station (GOM p21 p4(d)) (GOD pp28-29). In 1974 a ghost, reputedly that of a past caretaker, was seen at Coseley swimming baths in Peartree Lane. The staff called him 'Old Sid' (GOD p29). **Persons**. For the murder of **Eliza Silleto**, aged 6, in 1864 see Daisy Bank. **Harry Eccleston** OBE, photographer, was born on Jan 21 1923 at Coseley (BCM Jan 1994 pp38-43). For the 'Coseley Poet' **John Cornfield** see Hurst Hill.

Coseley Hall Avenue Road, Coseley. Parts of the hall date from c1800 (HC pp62,80). Built by the Sheldon family, founders of the Cannon firm in 1826, makers of holloware pots, gas stoves and fires. The company moved to Stoke-on-Trent in 1992 (OS map Sheet 67.04). Former home of the Clayton family (CWBT p24p). Residence in 1907 of Richard Clayton JP (STC p22p).

Coseley Moor Former moor in the Swan Village area which stretched as far S as the Tipton Sedgley road. Coseley Moor appears in 1537 with out-lying districts known as Crowesbridge and Andersley, and there were local law suits about the moor in the early C17 (HC pp21,25). Some houses were built here during 1989-90 (CWBT p69p).

Cotehill Werrington. Cotehill Road runs off Washerwall Lane, on the E side, N of Ash Bank Road.

Cotes Hamlet 0.75m SW of Swynnerton. Former township and quarter in Eccleshall ancient parish (W p375). The name is from Anglo-Saxon and means 'cot,' a cottage (DUIGNAN) (SSE 1996 p12) (SPN p38). The waste known as Cota appears in DB. Became an ecclesiastical parish in 1844 (LGS p117) (GLAUE p409).

Cotes Hall N side of the Cotes-Standon road, Cotes Heath. The house, a stuccoed Georgian villa built in 1796, may have been a Sneyd seat. It was was occupied by JJ Matthews between at least 1851 and 1880. Dr William Whiston ran a private boarding school - Cotes Hall College - at the hall between at least 1884 and 1896. Later occupants have included Mrs William in 1904 and 1916; Bartholomew Snowball in 1924; Sidney James Kemp in 1928; Miss Timmis in 1932; Arthur Clyde Deane Prall in 1940. It had many owners in the later C20, including, apparently, a pop music star, and was for sale in Feb 1999 (W p376) (KD 1880 etc) (DoE II) (W p19) (CL Feb 11 1999 pc) (ES Feb 18 1999 property pages pc) (local info).

Cotes Heath Small village by the Meece and bigger than Cotes 1.25m WSW of Swynnerton. In Eccleshall ancient parish. Formerly known as Moorfield Green (SVB p153). The church, St James, on the W side of the Newcastle-Eccleshall road, was built in 1837 (BOE p109). The station at Cotes Heath on the GJR, known as Standon Bridge station, opened on July 4 1837, closed many years ago (info Michael Cockin in 1999) (IAS p131). Foot-and-mouth disease broke out in late 1967 in Cotes Heath at these farms - Cotes Lodge Farm, Hulton Heath Farm, and The Hollies (SN Dec 22 1967 p15. Dec 29 1967 p13). Great rivalry once existed between Cotes Heath and Standon, giving rise to this rhyme -

Standon men, like bulls in a pen
Hemmed in by Cotes Heath men.

(SVB p153).

Coton Hamlet 1.25m WSW of Gnosall. Formerly in Cowley quarter in Gnosall ancient parish (VCH vol 4 p111). Has appeared as Coton (c1260), Coten (1329), Coton juxta Gnoushale (1346), and Cotton (1616) (SPNO p155) (SSE 1996 p12). It is from Anglo-Saxon, cot, a cottage, so; cottages (DUIGNAN) (SSE 1996 p12).

Coton (*Coat-town*). Small hamlet 0.5m E of Milwich. In Milwich parish. Appears in DB as Cote. The name means 'cottage' (SSE 1996 p12). Coton was considered a sizeable village in the Middle Ages after which it was deserted for some reason. Walter Chetwynd in 1679 was the first to identify a settlement here from, probably, earthworks (SL p82). The other Cotons to the E of Coton - Coton Green, Coton Hill, Coton Hayes - now more or less merge with each other.

Coton Former manor and hamlet by Marston Brook now a suburb of Stafford, 0.75m ENE and NE from the town centre. Coton with Hopton was an out-township in St Mary's parish, Stafford (W p341). The manor of Coltone appears in DB. The name is of Anglo-Saxon origin and means 'farmstead of cottages' (SPN p112). By Hopton Pools, SE of Hopton at SJ 950255, or in the vicinity of Prospect Road at SJ 930240, was possibly a medieval village, probably deserted in the C16 (SSAHST 1970 p34). Coton was a prebend of Stafford Collegiate Church (SHC 1914 p116) (VCH vol 3 p305). Corporation Street running from Weston Road to Sandon Road dates from the mid 1890s (VCH vol 6 p193). It was known locally as 'Clembelly Avenue' because those who bought houses here had to go without other things, and tightened their belts (SPN p109).

COTON FIELD DISPUTE. The manor of Coton, before the Reformation, belonged to the Prior and Convent of St Thomas and consisted of three large fields - Pool Field, Broad Field, and Kingstone Hill Field, all of which were unenclosed. It was then the custom for two of the fields to be ploughed every year and the third to be left fallow; the latter was common to the burgesses at all times in the year. Differences between the owners of Coton manor, at first the priors of St Thomas and then the Fowlers, and the burgesses raged for upwards of 250 years and were only temporarily settled by intervention from the manorial overlord and the issuing of a series of leases to the burgesses, the first of which, lasting 99 years, was issued in 1455 and the next in 1554. After a series of trials-at-law it was decreed in Nov 1699 that the mayor and burgesses enjoy their right of common in the three fields. In 1705 the corporation gave up the common of pasture over Broad Field and Kingstone Hill Field and shortly after the corporation obtained a licence from the Crown to take a grant of Coton Field in mortmain. By 1808 Coton Field consisted of 195 acres (OSST 1931 pp48-51) (SIOT pp49-50, 62). In the C19 the possession of any plots seemed to have been entirely at the discretion of the mayor. The petition to obtain a new charter in 1827 insisted upon the distribution of plots to benefit all freemen and not just members of the Common Council (OSST 1931 pp48-51) (SIOT p62). In 1836, the Corporation, as trustees, passed a rule to allot only to poor burgesses, but this definition was too freely interpreted and led to the former abuse. The abuse appears to have continued until 1880 when limited rights of Common exercised by burgesses and householders were removed and the land was reduced to 71 acres and divided into 401 allotments (OSST 1934 pp25-27. 1956-59 p11). Later only 22 acres remained in the form of allotments off Prospect Road (SSTY p3). These allotments have lately (1994) been the centre of a dispute. The allotment trustees sold them for £2000 to a property developer. A writ was served by the freemen of the town backed by the borough council contesting the legality of the sale (SN 25 March 1994 p8).

Coton Hamlet on low ground by the Tame nearly 1.75m WNW of Tamworth; was by the late C20 nearly merged with Tamworth. Formerly in Wigginton township in Tamworth ancient parish. The name means 'at the cottages' (SSE 1996 p12). It appears in 1313 as Coton (SSE 1996 p12). Was a prebend of Tamworth Collegiate Church (VCH vol 3 p310). Coton features in a derisory rhyme about Tamworth (see).

Coton Clanford Small hamlet on low ground near the confluence of Presford and Butterbank Brooks 1m SSW of Seighford. In Seighford ancient parish. Has appeared as Cote (DB), and Cotun (C13) (SPN p112). The name is of Anglo-Saxon origin and means 'the farmstead cottages at the clean ford (ie not muddy)' (SSE 1996 p12) (SPN p112). Clanford is from a neighbouring hamlet (DUIGNAN). So is a collective name for these two tiny hamlets? Or a hamlet lying between the two tiny hamlets? Or was a part of Clanford hamlet belonging to Coton? Here was possibly a medieval village (SSAHST 1970 p34), since depopulated and lost. The distinguished philosopher, William Wollaston, was born in Coton Clanford on March 26 1650 (GNHS p110) (W p406), or 1659 (SHOS vol 1 p430). Erdeswick or Harwood say Colton was his birthplace (SOS p53). Shortly after his birth his family moved to Shenstone (SHOS vol 1 p430). His principle treatise was 'The Religion of Nature Delineated:' Upwards of 10,000 copies were sold in a few years. He died in London in 1724 (W p406) and is buried at Great Finsborough, Suffolk (SOS p53).

Coton End Tiny hamlet 1.5m SW of Gnosall, 0.5m S of Coton. Has appeared as Cotonend (1573), Cootenende (1619), Cottonend (1636), Coton End (Plot's map). Means the end quarter of Coton (SPNO p156).

Coton Green Small settlement 0.5m E of Milwich.

Coton Hall To W of Coton-in-the-Clay, Draycott-in-the-Clay. John Bott (d1863) was occupying Coton Hall in 1851 (W p19). Later the hall was owned by

Hubert John Broughton-Adderley from at least 1896 to at least 1912. It was tenanted by Capt Dugdale (1900) and Major James Towers-Clark (1904). It was unoccupied in 1912. From at least 1916 it was occupied by Annie Isobel Brace (d1944), to at least 1940 (trade directories) (mems in Hanbury church) (LTD p137).

Coton Hall House 1.5m WSW of Wigginton. Formerly in Wigginton township in Tamworth ancient parish. Appears as Coton Hall in 1890 (1890 OS map 6 inch). Was called Coton Hall Farm by 1976 (1976 OS map 1:25,000).

Coton Hayes Small hamlet 1.25m ENE of Milwich. In Milwich parish. The name means 'the cottage enclosures' (DUIGNAN). Or 'the farmstead cottage of the enclosure' (SPN p84).

Coton Hill Small hamlet 1m E of Milwich. In Milwich parish. Sophia Caroline Viscountess Tamworth lived at Coton Hill House in the 1840s (NSFCT 1992 vol 18 p12).

Coton Hill In Hopton and Coton out-township of St Mary's parish, Stafford. Situated on the N side of Weston Road, the Uttoxeter-Stafford road. Has also appeared as Cotonhill. A mental hospital for private patients opened here in 1854 (KD 1904 p340) (BOE p248). (SKYT pp72p,73,74). There were plans to demolish the old asylum in the mid 1970s (SN June 23 1972 p5. Sept 26 1975 p6. March 5 1976 p3). A new hospital, Stafford District General Hospital, was opened to the E of the old asylum by the Duchess of Kent on June 15 1984 (local info), and the old asylum became the Mid Staffs Post-graduate Medical Centre. The ghost known as the Little Grey Lady is said to have flitted from the old asylum to the hospital (SN Jan 25 1985 p1. Feb 8 1985 p7). For the outbreak of Legionnaires disease at the hospital in April 1985 see Stafford. Sidney Clews, aged 100, and Damian Peake, aged 24 days, who both received 'keyhole' surgery at the hospital in 1994, were thought to be the oldest and youngest recipients of this new type of surgery in the country (ES Aug 3 1994 p3p). Terry Waite, former emissary of the Archbishop of Canterbury and hostage in Beirut, visited the hospital in April 1996 (SN April 26 1996 p3).

Coton House House 1.5m SW of Seighford.

Coton-in-the-Clay Small village by the Dove under Row Hill and the northern escarpment of the Needwood Forest plateau 1m NE of Draycott-in-the-Clay, 1m NW of Hanbury. Formerly in Hanbury township and ancient parish. Has appeared as Coton (Plot's map) and Coton-under-Needwood (W p560).

Coton-in-the-Clay Hall Draycott-in-the-Clay. The old manor house was of plaster and timber with large gable ends. In a pane of one of the Elizabethan windows was cut the name of Prince Rupert, who was probably here during the Civil Wars. The old hall was pulled down in c1787. In the late C18 Shaw said some years prior to his writing Messrs Adderley and Scott lived here together as hospitable bachelors. They pitched a tent on the round hill above Coton from where they used to fly a flag as a signal to their friends that they were in. The flag pole was removed in 1796. FNC Mundy in his poem 'Needwood Forest' alludes to it (SHOS vol 1 p82). The new hall was built in 1790 (W p560) (BOE p109).

Cotonwood Hamlet over 1.5m W of Gnosall. In Gnosall parish.

Cotterills Farm Stood on the site now occupied by the park keeper's house in Jubilee Park, near to the junction of Cotterills Road and Powis Avenue, Ocker Hill, Tipton. A base of a chimney piece was dated 1538. Over the porch were the initials 'C.W.M.' and the date 1695. During the demolition of the farm in the 1920s a priest's hole was discovered (TB Jan 1977 p5il from 1911). It was occupied at some former time by the O'kell family (OH p55). Cotterill's Farm may have been Mr Jeaven's farm mentioned in a survey of 1690 (HOTIP pp25, 188-189 pl vi c1700).

Cotton Small village on the edge of a dale in the Moorlands, 17m NE of Stafford. Former township in Alton ancient parish containing the hamlets of Upper and Lower Cotton. Cottonplain, a meeting point of many tracks, is 1.5m N of Cotton. The church, St John the Baptist, near Cotton College N of Cotton, was built in 1795 (BOE p109). Became a separate ecclesiastical parish in 1796. But its separate status was not sustained and it reverted back to Alton parish. Became a civil parish in 1866. Became a separate ecclesiastical parish with Oakamoor in 1932 (GLAUE p409). The Faber Primary School at Cotton has its origins in a school founded by Father FW Faber during his time at Cotton Hall (see) between 1846 and 1849. There is a tradition in Cotton village that the school room was built, unusually, before Pugin's Cotton RC chapel of the same period. In 1944, in accordance with the 1944 Education Act, schools were obliged to state their status or become part of the local education authority. In the case of the Faber Primary School the local priest failed to send in the necessary form ensuring that the school stay in the control of the RC Midland diocese. By default it then transferred to Staffs Local Education Authority, who, unusually, allowed it to maintain its RC ethos and have RC head teachers. On Sept 1 1999 the school took the first opportunity to leave local authority control and revert back to voluntary-aided status with the RC Midland diocese. During the period 1944 and 1999 it was considered the only RC local authority controlled school in the country (ES Sept 14 1999 p15) (info Silvia Alcock and Francesca Devine).

Cotton Dell Dell W of the Cotton College, N of Star Wood. It is said that Father FW Faber of Cotton Hall (see) was inspired to write the hymn 'Hark, hark my soul' whilst walking near Cotton Dell hearing the bells ring out from Kingsley church (SVB p105). Rev J Ogmore Morgan, one time minister of the Memorial Free Church, wrote of the Dell as 'Enchanting beyond compare' (TFTPM p66). At the N end of the dell is Bill's Rock (see). An area of 160 acres of Cotton Dell had been purchased by Staffs Wildlife Trust by Jan 2000 (Staffs Wildlife Jan 2000).

Cotton Hall 0.5m N of Cotton village, by the Anglican church. The Gilberts may have had a hall at Cotton by the early C17 (COPP2 p91). The present hall was built by the Gilberts in the C18 (CCT p26). Richard Badnall author of 'A Treatise on the Silk Trade' died here in 1839 (OL vol 2 pp153-154). In 1844 T Gilbert sold it to Earl of Shrewsbury (the earl originally bought it for his nephew) (BOE p109). The Shrewsburys converted it into a monastery for monks of the Order of Passion. Connected with it is the chapel of St Wilfred erected by the earl in 1846 (W p768). In 1846 the earl gave it to Father FW Faber and his Brothers of the Will of God. They amalgamated with the Oratorians of Birmingham, but left in 1849. In 1850 the Passionists took over the property, but they shortly left. Cotton Hall was used as an occasional holiday retreat for pupils at Sedgley Park School. From 1868 it became a preparatory school for Sedgley Park. From 1873 the senior school transferred here from Sedgley Park (see) (VCH vol 6 pp156-157) (MR pp112-113) becoming known as **Cotton College** or St Wilfrid's College. There were extensions to the house in 1874-5, 1886-7 and 1931-2 (BOE p109) (COPP2 p93). Cotton College magazine 'The Cottonian' was founded in 1911 (VCH vol 6 p157) (MR pp112-113). The college closed in 1986 (ES May 29 1999 p1) or in July 1987 (COPP2 p93) or in 1988 and the buildings left derelict. On May 29 1999 some of the derelict school buildings were gutted in a fire (ES Nov 25 1998 p18ps. May 29 1999 p1pc). For alumni see Sedgley Park. (Sedgley Park. Canon FC Husenbeth. 1856) (Sedgley Park and Cotton College. Canon Willibrord Buscot. 1940) (SPCC). **Father Faber's Retreat**, a hut shelter erected in 1848 by Father Faber in a dell in the hall grounds, is a shrine dedicated to 'Our Lady of Lasalette.' It was repainted and refurnished in 1956 by a master of Cotton College. In about the 1970s the shrine was vandalised (COPP2 p92p).

Cottonmill Farm 0.75m N of Uttoxeter, by the Tean.

Cottonplain 1m N of Cotton. The plateway, Cotton Plane, ran here. Possibly the name is from the plateway.

Cotton Plane Old railroad built to transport limestone from Caldon Low quarries to the Caldon Canal at Froghall for the Potteries. Built by the owners of the Trent & Mersey Canal. It was the first railway to be opened in N Staffs and was the second railway to obtain parliamentary consent in England, after the Middleton Colliery Railway near Leeds (CVH p126). The plateway was built because the Caldon Canal (completed 1777) could not be built to the quarries for the gradient of 700 feet in four miles was considered too steep. The first plateway, one of about four, all collectively known as Caldon Low Tramways, opened through Shirley Hollow, with horse-drawn carts, in the late 1770s (IAS pp173-174) (CVH p126) (HCMS No. 5). A line spurring off this running slightly to the S, through Whiston Common and past Garston House, was built in 1785 (HCMS No. 5). A further line, to the S, through Whistonbrook, Whiston, Whiston Common, Upper Cotton, Cottonplain and Hoften's Cross was built in 1804 (1834 OS map) (VCH vol 2 p306) (HCMS No. 5). A further line, to the N, taking a straight course along Shirley Brook and by Oldridge opened in 1847 and was cable mechanically driven, with a 475 yard long tunnel at Cottonplain (HCMS No. 5) (IAS pp173-174), and was dismantled by 1983. Apart from the Caldon Canal, other plateways - Woodhead Plateway (see) and Consall Plateway (see) - W of the Churnet also carried the lime to the Potteries.

Cotton's Fishing Lodge, Charles Stone fishing lodge built in the Artisan Mannerist style by Charles Cotton in 1674, situated in a bend of the Dove on the W side of Beresford Dale, N of Beresford Hall, at SK 127593. It is surrounded by the Dove on three sides and was built partly as a tribute to Cotton's friend and fishing companion Izaak Walton, hence its occasional name, Izaak Walton's Fishing Lodge. It has also appeared as Fishing Temple, Fishing Lodge, and Charles Cotton's Fishing House (PDS&C p114p) (DMV p30p). Walton mentioned it briefly in a letter to Cotton dated April 29 1676 (LPCC p52). It is square with a pyramid roof, although the roof was not complete in Cotton's time (KES pp4,5p,21). The stone floor is composed of blocks 15 inch square (ES April 25 1930 p6p). The front has two windows to the left

and right of a round-headed doorway with flanking Tuscan pilasters (BOE p68). Over the door are two plaques, one inscribed "Piscatoribus Sacrum. 1674," (Sacred to Fishermen) and the other bearing the intertwined initials of Izaak Walton and Charles Cotton. It was falling into decay by 1784 (VCH vol 7 p17). Its state of disrepair in the early C19 called for restoration in c1830s (AAD p137) (W p743) (LGS p81). The lodge was scheduled as an Ancient Monument in Nov 1931 (NSFCT 1931 p196). It was included in the sale with Beresford Dale in 1932 (ES Oct 26 1932 photograph of), and was being restored in 1935 (NSFCT 1935 p87). There used to be a bowling green in front of it - all traces of this have gone (PDS&C p114p). Several tall irregular pine trees stand guard over the Fishing Lodge, apparently planted by Cotton himself, who was a well-known arboriculturist (ES April 25 1930 p6p). There are also stone benches 15 yards S of the lodge which are listed by DoE. The original sundial was found in the grounds in c1935 and placed back on the lodge (NSFCT 1931 p196). (PS p106p) (CCR - throughout the book) (JAT p55 with il of the Cotton/ Walton insignia) (WTCEM p61) (GNHS p19) (TPC pp160-162) (POD p311) (HS p327 pl) (S p191) (All Over Britain. JHB Peel) (MR p128p).

Cotton's Hole or Cave. Beresford Dale. The cave or small cleft in which Charles Cotton hid from his creditors. It is on the W side (the Staffs side) of the Dove below the 'modern' tower (which marks the approximate site of Beresford Hall). Cotton apostrophizes about it in his poem 'The Retirement' (LPCC p16). (CCR p2) (AAD pp137-138) (ES April 25 1930 p6p. Nov 10 1932 p6).

Cotton's Well Cracow Moss, Betley. A well in existence in c1880 (BVC p192).

Cotwall End District 0.5m SSW of Sedgley town and former liberty in the Upper Side division in Sedgley ancient parish (W p195). A Thoma de Cutwall is mentioned in 1327. The place later appears as Cattewall, Cotewall, Cotwellend (1632) (AMS p446) (HC p39), and Cattern's End (TB Nov 1981 p5). There is a valley at Cotwallend (PAIP p92).

Cotwall End House Stood in Catholic Lane (formerly Downing's Lane), Cotwall End. The present house bearing the date 1685, stands on the site of a former house (AMS p446 p). Seat of the Turtons in the C17 and C18. Occupied by the Downings in the early C19. Demolished in 1961. Now occupied by Cotwall End nature reserve, a public park (SDOP p16p) (BCM spring 1999 p43il).

Cotwalton Tiny hamlet above a gulley high above and overlooking the Trent valley 1.25m W of Hilderstone. In Kibblestone township and quarter in Stone ancient parish. Was identified by Shaw as the Cotewaltune mentioned in the will of Wulfric Spot (c1002), founder of Burton Abbey (SHC 1916 p35). Appears in DB as Cotewoldestune and Codewalle (SHC 1916 p35) (SSE 1996 p12). 'The cottages of the woodland farmstead' (SPN p118). It is possible that the first element is from the Celtic root 'coed' (NSFCT 1908 p139) or from the Anglo-Saxon personal name Cotta - so possibly 'Cotta's tun at the wood or stream (wald or waella)' (SSE 1996 p12). By 1872 Cotwalton was in Moddershall township (KD 1872).

Cotwalton Drumble Pretty wooded gulley, formed by the brook known as Hilderstone Brook? Here are the Petrifactions (see) (SSBOP p60).

Coulter Hill House over 2m NW of Rangemore. The Wilkinson family have been at Coulter Hill Farm since 1953. In c1990 they started producing ice cream. Their ice cream sold in 2000 was known as 'Needwood' (info Mrs Wilkinson 2000).

Counslow Counslow Cottage and Plantation are 1.75m ESE of Cheadle. In Cheadle ancient parish. Rev J Mould was born here in 1655 (BS p319). Has appeared as Counslow (Plot's map), Cunslow (Smith's map), and Cownslow.

County Building Offices for Staffs county council in Martin Street, Stafford. The building was built in 1895 (seven years after the creation of the county council) and designed by HT Hare in a Baroque style (VCH vol 6 p202) (BOE p244). On Nov 2 1955 Elizabeth II and the Duke of Edinburgh attended an evening reception here (R&S p47) (SSTY p16). Princess Anne, the Princess Royal, visited Stafford on June 10 1991 and re-opened, after a restoration, County Buildings (plaque in lobby of County Buildings). In the Brenham Room, County Building, in 1997 was the banner (made in 1914) of the Staffordshire Society. The Society was founded in London in 1905 by prominent natives residing in London (SLM May June 1996 p15) as a men-only group meeting mainly for visits to smoking concerts and the music hall. Membership later broadened to include Staffs men and women everywhere. It was still active in 1997 (info Mark Pargitter) (ES Jan 28 1993 p8 p of the society banner). The Staffordshire Record Office (SRO), founded in 1947, originally centred on the collection of county archives kept in the attic in the County Building. A purpose-built record office was opened behind WSL in 1961. It has been extended on several occasions since (HOS 1998 p134).

County Stone 1.5m NE of Upper Arley, by the Bridgnorth-Kidderminster road (1834 OS map).

Court Oak Small district of NW Harborne. There is a tradition that here was an oak under whose boughs courting couples met in the C17 and C18. By 1951 the three-dimensional sign of the Court Oak Inn showed a man and a woman in C18 dress on either side of an oak (IOM p165p). The name appears as Courl Oak on Yates' map and is preserved in Court Oak Road. Court Oak House in Queen's Park was built in the Victorian era. By the late 1970s the house had become redundant but was eventually saved and restored (HOPP pl 29). The oak may have had its name from the meeting place of a manor court.

Court Oak A tree which stood at the top of the Holloway, Tettenhall Wood in the early C17. It may have been a meeting place for Kingsley manor court (VCH vol 20 p36).

Courtsbank Covert Small wood to the E of Red Moor at SK 042116, Cannock Wood (MR p81). Earthworks in Courts Bank Covert reveal evidences of a moated site, but very few stones remain (CCBO pp30-32). In 1910 a Neolithic flint factory was discovered at SK 04091169 by TC Cantrill - the only one of its kind in the county. The finds - leaf-shaped arrowheads, trimmed points, scrapers, flakes and cores - are of the Mesolithic and Neolithic Age (The Antiquary 1911 p229) (NSFCT (1916) vol 51 pp85-97. vol 65 p143) (The Mesolithic Age in Britain. JGD Clark. 1932. p109) (CCF p84) (NSJFS 1964 p18). Hackwood thought the 'Court' part of the name was possibly derived from some manorial court which was held here (CCC p22). Here, Wright noted, was the Pillar Box Oak and Elephant Oak. Other oaks he noted here were one with a girth of 22 feet which came to an end in the main trunk then thrust out for another 80 feet. An oak whose main trunk rose for 25 feet then branched out. The oak which had lumps of smelting-furnace slag wedged into folds of its stanchion and a rhinoceros surface - evidence that it had existed perhaps when there had been iron-smelters on the Cannock Chase in the later C16. An oak which was hollow for the first 20 feet of its rise then grew another 40 feet. A derelict oak which had a pose reminding Wright of Eros Statue. And an oak whose main trunk was 30 feet then branched out for 60 feet at 45 degrees angle (CCF pp82-86).

Coven (*Covan*). Large village on a low shelf by the Penk and a tributary 10.5m S of Stafford. Former liberty of Brewood town in Brewood ancient parish. The manor of Cove appears in DB (NSFCT 1910 p162). Later Coven appears as Covena (1116), Koven (1236), Covun (1342), Couon (1413), Coven (1434), Covon (1482) (SHC 1910 pp151, 202-203) (SPNO p37) (SPN p38). The name is from Anglo-Saxon 'cofa' which represents cave, repository, inner room, chamber. Possibly a charcoal-burner's hut in the woods (DUIGNAN) (SSE 1996 p12), or 'the forge of a smith' (SPN p38) or 'at the huts' (SSE 1996 p12). Perhaps from the hill-root 'ceap,' 'ceip,' 'cap' (NSFCT 1910 p162). Oakden gives the meaning as 'a recess in the steep side of a hill.' To which Paffard notes that there is no obvious feature of this kind at Coven (SPNO p37) (SSE 1996 p21). Coven was included in Brewood prebend (SSAHST vol 2 1960-61 p43). The brick house in the village of 1679, is perhaps one of the first to be built in the W of the county (SL p100). In the later C18 and early C19 a canal was built either side of Coven: on the W side the Shropshire Union Canal (1835), and on the E side the Staffs and Worcs Canal (1772). Printed in a Wolverhampton paper the following ballad shows that perhaps boatmen on that canal were not 'what they should be.' Chorus of boatmen:

> Gaily the fire in our cabooss is crackling,
> Where many a rabbit and hare has been stewed,
> And many a hen has stopt in her cackling,
> That wakened the echoes at Coven and Brewood.

(WMAG Sept 1975 p21). The **church**, St Paul, on the N side of Church Lane, was built in 1857 (BOE p110). Coven became a separate ecclesiastical parish in 1858 (GLAUE p409). By the late C20 Coven was a ward in Brewood civil parish. **Folklore**. There is a local belief that Coven is named after a coven of witches. For Coven in a local rhyme see Brewood. The ghost of a little white-haired old lady was seen in the vicinity of a modern cottage in Lawn Lane. It was believed to have been that of a Mrs Lawrence, former owner of the cottage; the ghost disappeared after her identity was discovered and her soul prayed for (GLS pp39-40). **Persons**. **John Smith** of Coven (1827-1879), began to make colliery engines at his village foundry and thereafter became well known as a supplier of narrow-gauge locomotives to local manufacturers and colliery owners (Newcomen Society vol 26 pp164-166) (VCH vol 2 p163). PC **Henry William Brown** was killed at Coven on Aug 6 1887. He was knocked unconscious and then drowned (TB Feb 1985 p5. May 1993 p22).

Coven Hall The Coven family were occupying a hall at Coven at some time shortly after 1331. In 1738 the hall was tenanted by William Jellicoe. No

house known as Coven Hall existed by 1959 (VCH vol 5 p31).

Coven Heath Former common land, now a hamlet 1.25m S of Coven. Formerly in Bushbury parish (Seisdon hundred) (W p170). Has appeared as Covenheythe (1348) and the heathe (1574) (SPNO p40). A windmill appears on Yates' map at approximately SJ 910048, 1m S of Coven to W of the canal. Job believes the mill had gone by 1790 (WBJ p19). 55 acres of Coven Heath and Slade Heath were enclosed under an Act of 1850 (SHC 1941 p19). The mission church on the N side of Ball Lane dates from about the end of the C19 (info Rev Neil Hogg). In 1934 Coven Heath was transferred to Brewood parish (Cuttlestone hundred) (VCH vol 5 p18). By the late C20 it was a ward in Brewood civil parish.

Coven Lawn Minute hamlet 0.75m SSE of Coven. The name appears on the 1834 OS map (SPNO p40). At Coven Lawn are the anti-aircraft guns to protect the former aerodrome at Pendeford (BCTV p18) (MR p114p).

Coventry Canal Built in 1790 (SSAHST 1969 p2 note). Envisaged as a link in the Grand Cross, to link the Trent with the Thames. The Coventry Canal Company obtained an act of parliament to build it in 1768 and the company had completed the section from Longford N of Coventry, where it leaves the Oxford Canal, to Atherstone by 1772 (SWY p25). The Company then ran out of money, which was a matter of concern to the neighbouring canal companies anticipating links with it. In 1785 the Trent & Mersey Canal Company decided to build the 5.5m N end of the canal, from its own canal at Fradley Junction to Whittington Brook; this was completed by 1787 (IAS pp118,119). At the same time the Birmingham & Fazeley Canal decided to build the missing section from Whittington Brook to Fazeley. The canal, now owned by various companies, was completed in July 1790. Length is 32.5m (IAS pp118,119). Shortly after the completion of the canal the Coventry Canal Company were able to purchase the northern section, but were never able to buy the Whittington Brook to Fazeley stretch and so this section keeps the name of the Birmingham & Fazeley Canal, although, since nationalisation, the whole length has been regarded as Coventry Canal (SWY p25).

Cowall House over 1.5m SSW of Biddulph Moor. In Horton ancient parish. There was a house here by 1308 (VCH vol 7 p67).

Cowall Moor Moor to ENE of Cowall, in Horton ancient parish.

Cowhay Former hay, otherwise moor, in Brewood Forest at Kiddemore Green (BDH p72).

Cowhay Head This could be the Cow hamlet in Butterton (Moorlands) township mentioned in White's directory (W p784).

Cow Hey Wood Wood in Weston Park, Weston-under-Lizard. Has appeared as the Nether Cowhey (1530), the Upper and Lower Cowhey (1666), Cow Hey (1834 OS map) (SPNO p181).

Cowley Hamlet near Doley Brook and a tributary, 1m SSW of Gnosall. Comprises Upper Cowley (E side of Shropshire Union Canal) and Lower Cowley (W side). Former township (THS pp269-70) and quarter in Gnosall ancient parish (VCH vol 4 p111). Has appeared as Covelau (DB), Culeg (1215), Couveley (1280), Coweley (1413), Cowley (1535) (SPNO p156) and Colweley (BS). Early forms show the name means 'Cufa's woodland glade' (SPNO p156) (SSE 1996 p12) (SPN p55). Possibly the affix is from Old Norse 'kur' 'rounded top' or 'cufe' 'log' (SSE 1996 p21). Another interpretation is 'cow lea' (DUIGNAN). To W of Cowley House Farm was possibly a medieval village, probably deserted in the C18 (SSAHST 1970 p34). There was a windmill at approximately SJ 830198. It was in existence by 1587, but not later than 1775 (VCH vol 4 p128) (WBJ p19). The Shropshire Union Canal tunnel at Cowley is 81 yards long and cut through solid sandstone. A 720 metre tunnel was planned but the rock proved too unstable; the remainder was excavated as a cutting (SPJD p88p) (SWY p32p,33).

Cowley Hill House 0.25m S of Hamstall Ridware on a hill called Cowley Hill. In Hamstall Ridware parish. Shaw identified this Cowley with the manor of Cowley named in the bacon flitch tenure of Wychnor (see) manor (SHOS vol 1 p152).

Cowlow House 1m ENE of Warslow. Formerly in Warslow township in Alstonefield ancient parish. There was a cottage by 1600 at Cowlow. The present farmhouse dates from 1860 (VCH vol 7 p57). Cowlow Lane was formerly Cawlow Lane (HLS p53).

Coxen Green Minute settlement which is at the southern tip of Butterton (Moorlands). In Grindon parish. Has also appeared as Coxon Green.

Coxgreen Minute hamlet 1.25m W of Enville. In Enville ancient parish. Coxgreen Farm was inhabited by the late C16, and probably earlier (VCH vol 20 p94). The name Cox is from the Cox family, members of which held land in Enville parish by the C15 (VCH vol 20 p106).

Cox's Bridge Former bridge carrying the Wednesbury Oak Road over the Wednesbury Oak Loop Canal or Birmingham Canal Old Cut Old Main Line. The bridge is known locally as Murder Bridge after the body of Mrs Eliza

Jane Worton (alias Jinny), aged 25 of Phoenix Street, West Bromwich, was found in the frozen canal by it on Feb 15 1936; Mrs Worton having been murdered the night before. William (or Frederick - MCGM pp161-162) Oakley, a lorry driver and a friend of Mrs Worton, was charged with her murder, but acquitted at his trial. The case remains unsolved (TB April 1995 pp30-31ps) (MMMR pp106-110) (BCM summer 1999 p66). A few days after the discovery of Mrs Worton's body, the body of William Haynes of Tipton was found in the canal about 1.5m to the S at Eagle Lane, Great Bridge (TB April 1995 pp30-31ps) (MMMR pp106-110). An elderly man in the 1990s remembered the bridge being in existence in his childhood (BCM autumn 1995 p17).

Cox's Rough Near Darby's Hill, Tipton. Could the area have been around Ash Terrace near Tividale Hall? (SVS p432). One of the eight Rowley Hills (TB Jan 1983 p13). Is the oldest quarry in the Rowley Rag (NSFCT 1876 p9). Has also appeared Coxes Rough and Ash Rough.

Crabbery Hall Crabbery Street, Stafford; perhaps on the site of the present Booklands bookshop and Princess Street (info Mr Pitt). Has also appeared as Cranberry Hall. In existence by Sept 1883 when the Gladstone Club moved here (SA Sept 15 1883 p4 col 7) (info Mr Pitt). By 1933 the building had undergone many changes. It was for many years, sometime prior to 1933, the residence of the Whalleys, a well-known family of lawyers in Stafford. In 1933 the building was said to have been never really completed and to have always been considered something of a white elephant. The oak entrance door and supports, carved all over with quaint figures of men and women in the style of the early C14, had been removed at some time to Pillaton Hall, from where they reputedly had originated (OSST 1933 p36). Some armorial bearings carved in oak discovered here went to the chapel at Pillaton Hall (NSFCT 1891 p47).

Crabtree Bank Handsworth. Land leased by John Wyrley in 1757 to Matthew Bolton which he purchased and built the Soho works on in 1762 (SHOS vol 2 p117).

Crabtree Field Etruria. Here Charles Shaw and others murdered John Holdcroft on Aug 4 1833 (HOE p61) (TOS p94).

Crabtree Crabtree Village, in existence in 1775, lay WNW of Biddulph Grange (BGFB p7 see map) to the N of Biddulph (BALH p49). Biddulph's school was at Crabtree Green in the early C19 (W p387). Crab Tree Farm stood on the site of the present Grangefields in 1842 (BALH p65).

Crackley District NNW of Chesterton. In Wolstanton ancient parish.

Crackley Gates Junction of Crackley Lane and Scot Hay Road, S of Scot Hay. Crackley lies to the W (IANS p129) (Stoke-on-Trent A-Z).

Cracow Moss Small hamlet between Wrinehill and Ravenshall on main road to Betley and slightly to W of the main road. In Betley parish. Former marshy moss, which was being drained in by the C18. The small hamlet had 16 houses in 1845 (BVC p192). Further to the W, by the county border, is the moss, Cracow Moss.

Craddocks Moss Large raised mire or moss (WSS p95) 1.5m E of Betley. Formerly in Halmer End township in Audley parish. The moss lies on a flat-bottomed valley 600-700 yards wide, 360 feet above sea level (NSFCT 1919 p23). A mound of possible man-made or natural origin is situated on the northern fringes of Craddocks Moss. Immediately to the S of Craddocks Moss Farm and W of the M6 a number of cropmarks have been identified. These include an enclosure, two linear features, and two small ring ditches (WSS pp95-96,103). The name appears to be from the Cradocke family who built the Moss House here in c1730 (SHC 1944 p27).

Cradley Forge District of Cradley Heath 2.5m SW of Rowley Regis. The name is from a C17 forge which stood on the N bank of the Stour near the bridge and ford at the S end of Quarry Bank High Street, just in Staffs (SNSV vol 1 p86). At the beginning of the C17 Dud Dudley, illegitimate son of Edward Sutton, 5th Baron Dudley of Dudley Castle (see), managed a forge here for his father and is said to have discovered or practised smelting iron with coal instead of charcoal here (WMLB p122) and or on Pensnett Chase (see) (VCHW vol 3 p100). Cradley Forge has also been called 'Hell Hole' (TB Feb 1998 p6). In 1849 the forge was closed for a week, on account say some, of mischief caused by a witch called 'Ode Magic' of Blue Ball Lane, Cradley (TB July 1977 p4).

Cradley Heath Black Country town on a promontory between the Stour and Mousesweet Brook over 1.5m SW of Rowley Regis. Formerly in Rowley Regis parish. The settlement was founded by nail and chain makers squatting on common land (SL p190) (SGS p88), which appears to have belonged to Cradley, a former village, to the S in Worcs. The heath was enclosed under an Act of 1799? In the period between at least 1820 and 1840 the area was deemed very poor (BCWJ pp86,99). The **church**, St Luke, junction of Upper High Street and Corngreaves Road, was built between 1843 and 1847, and

restored in 1874-5 (BCWJ p101). In 1844 the separate ecclesiastical parish of Reddal Hill (later or sometimes known as Cradley Heath) was created out of Rowley Regis parish, and it covered the Cradley Heath area (GLAUE p420). Cradley Heath's chief industries have been nail and chain making. Prior to 1922 Cradley Heath **market** had been held in the High Street. A market hall was opened in 1928. A new market hall was opened in 1969 (ORR p106). Riots occurred in the Dudley constituency at the general election on Feb 4 1874. Mobs assembled and outbreaks of violence occurred at Cradley Heath and other places (BCM summer 1995 pp69-73). The High Street caved in due to **mining subsidence** on Feb 19 1914. The subsidence was caused by the extensive workings of Stour Colliery or Rattle Chain Pit (TB March April 1973 p15p. Aug 1978 p15). The Majestic cinema at Cradley Heath opened on March 27 1933 with a **Christie console organ**, said to have been the first in England with an all-electric action and the largest of its kind produced up to that date (TB Nov 1997 p16). **New British** produced cars between 1920-23 from Colonial Works in Overend Road (BCFF p200). Cradley Heath had won the British National **Speedway** Knock-out Cup (started in 1965) eight times (including joint holders in 1986) by 1992, and have twice been Provincial league winners in 1961 and 1963 (GBR 1990 p283. 1992 297). Cradley Heath now (1999) forms a ward with Old Hill of Sandwell metropolitan borough. **Natives and visitors**. For nail manufacturer, **Eliza Tinsley**, see Old Hill. **Mary Macartu(e)r**, liberator of Cradley women from poor conditions in the chain-making industry, first visited Cradley Heath in 1907 (TB Jan 1979 p29p). **Florence Alice Clee**, poet, was born in Cradley Heath in the later C19 or early C20 (PSS pp427-429 p) (VFC p27). The funeral in 1951 of **John Tom**, a vagrant at Cradley Heath, was paid for by public subscription (MMBCC p92p). **Richard Billington**, photographer, born in 1971, is a native of Cradley Heath (Daily Telegraph June 3 2000 pA7).

STAFFORDSHIRE BULL TERRIERS. The breed of dog known as the Staffordshire Bull Terrier was developed gradually by the county's coal and iron workers by crossing working bulldogs of those times with various types of local terrier (usually old English) for fighting and baiting bulls at wakes and fairs from at least the C18. Formerly each part of Staffs tended to favour a colour of coat, a breeding line or a particular style of build, the Walsall type for example being lithe and 'reachy.' The characteristics of the new breed are gameness, staunchness, equable temperament and loyalty. The new breed has evolved as a 28 lb dog, about 15 inches at the shoulder; the coat, is either red, fawn, white, black or blue or brindle of any shade but never black and tan or liver. The 'Dudley' or flesh-coloured nose, formerly encouraged, was discouraged by the late 1990s (SHJ vol 2 pp7-10). It has been said the breed was first reared at Cradley Heath (SGS p90), possibly because the Staffordshire Bull Terrier Club was founded in 1935 at Cradley Heath by Joe Dunn, Jack Dunn and Joe Mallen, and the club was instrumental in having the breed accepted by the Kennel Club in May 1935. It held its first show in 1935, at Cradley Heath. Joe Mallen, born in Cradley Heath in 1890, former chainmaker and smith at William Griffin's Triton Works, landlord of the Cross Guns Inn (see), Cradley Heath, became the most prominent proponent of the breed. He retired to Kinver and died in 1975. The most famous 'Stafford' terrier and progenitor of the breed was Mallen's own dog, called Champion Gentleman Jim, champion of many battles; on the dog's death in 1947 Cradley Heath went into deep mourning (The Staffordshire Bull Terrier Handbook. John F Gordon. 1951) (The Staffordshire Bull Terrier Owner's Encyclopaedia. John F Gordon. 1968) (BCM April 1969 p65. July 1971 p55. Oct 1971 p34p. Jan 1983 p46) (TB Nov/ Dec 1972 p14. Feb/ March 1973 p11. June/ July 1973 p13. Jan 1976 p18. Feb 1979 p5. Jan 1994 pp30-31. Jan 28 1999 pp1,34) (The Staffordshire Bull Terrier. John F Gordon. 1975) (The Staffordshire Bull Terrier. WM Morley. 1982) (All About the Staffordshire Bull Terrier. John F Gordon. 1984) (The Staffordshire Bull Terrier. AK Nicholas. 1989) (TEBC) (MR p114) (TOS pp16-17).

Cradley Pool Former large pool at Mushroom Green, close to Saltwells Inn. Created by the damming of the Mousesweet, slightly S of its confluence with Black Brook, in the mid C18 to power Cradley Forge. Has appeared as Cradley New Pool (map of 1812) and New Pool (SVS p139) (SNSV vol 1 p87). The pool burst its banks in 1799 and flooded the surrounding low lying area (BCWJ p112). At 'Goppy wakes' and on the first Sunday in May Cradley Pool was crowded with visitors. The pool was drained in 1878 (NEE p34) (TB Dec 3 1998 p4).

Craigside Housing estate off Station Road, Biddulph. Built in the 1920s. Named after Dr Craig, GP and Medical Officer of Health to Biddulph (BALH p222).

Crakelow House 0.75m SSE of Sheen. Has also appeared as Crateley (W p787).

Crakemarsh Hamlet in the middle Dove valley 1m NE of Stramshall. Former constablewick in Uttoxeter ancient parish (W p789). The name may be of Anglo-Saxon origin and mean 'the quaking marsh.' Or in Norse, crake means a crow or raven. Crake in a name is unique S of Yorkshire. The whole name is said to be unique (DUIGNAN). A low place, or land overflown by a river or pool, or ditch (HOU p38). 'Water-crane marsh' (NSJFS 1981 p2) (SSE 1996 p12) (SPN p120). The medieval chapel at Crakemarsh is not mentioned in the returns of 1533 or after (SHC 1915 p295). Mary Blood of Spath (see) is said to have been the last person to be baptised in Crakemarsh church. She died a few years prior to 1865, aged 106 (HOU p244). Redfern knew of it from an old inhabitant who recollected both the building and the gravestones standing about it (OSST 1949-50 p14). The manor of Crachemers appears in DB. Later Crakemarsh appears as Crakemers (SPN p133). An early example of violent action to protect common rights against inclosure by the lord of the manor was the throwing down of hedges on Crakemarsh by Uttoxeter inhabitants. The inclosures had been made by Sir John Delves at the beginning of Edward IV's reign (VCH vol 6 p52). Croxden Abbey is said to have had a grange at Crakemarsh (CDS pp7,16); this may have stood on the site of Crakemarsh Hall (see). A grange of Croxden Abbey called the Grange of the Leys is said by some to have been at Crakemarsh (see) (VCH vol 3 p226). But this may have been a grange at Nothill Farm, formerly known as Lees Grange (see).

Crakemarsh Hall The hall in Crakemarsh hamlet may stand on the site of a grange of Croxden Abbey (certainly there are Norman foundations in the cellars). It belonged to the Cotton family in the C18 and passed to the Sheppards by marriage. It was rebuilt in c1815 (SGS pp164-165) (or c1820 - BOE p291) around a staircase of Charles II's reign (later removed in the 1970s) of the former house. The staircase is reminiscent of the beautiful one at Sudbury Hall, Derbys (COS p40). In 1851 the hall was the residence of Lady Sheppard (W p19) (JSD p27p). Later, it was the seat of a branch of the great Cavendish family who went down on the Titanic in 1912 (COS p40p) (LTD p102p). Charles Tyrell Cavendish (d1933) was of Crakemarsh Hall (mem in St Mary's, Uttoxeter). In WW2 it was used by American troops (LTD p102). The hall remained deserted after the Cavendish family left except for a portrait in the entrance hall which had a curse upon it. It was of a member of the Cavendish family who had particularly loved Crakemarsh. The curse was that ill-luck would befall whoever removed it. At length it was cut from its frame and stolen (COS p40). In the early 1970s the house was bought by the excavator manufacturing firm JCB Ltd for residential accommodation for their nearby factory. Sir Anthony Bamford later chose the house for his family home. However, after the death of his wife in a car accident and the discovery of dry rot in the house it was abandoned (LTD p103). The hall was mostly demolished in 1980 (IHB p393). The last remains were demolished in 1998 after which date it was proposed that superior houses be built in the grounds (SLM Oct 1999 p17) (LTD p103). (AAD pp300-301, il facing p301). Situated SW of the hall is an ice-house (1924 OS map) (IHB p393). From c1947 the excavator firm of Joseph Cyril Bamford (JCB) occupied part of the old stables and coach house. After producing the 'Major Loader' in 1949 for fitting to Fordson E27N and Nuffield Universal tractors - the first industrial hydraulic front-end loader in Europe - the company left for bigger premises at Rocester in 1950 (TRTC p16). The works here were known as the Lakeside Works (BUBA pp114-115).

Cramp Hill Small street in Darlaston (Offlow hundred). Now lies to the E of St Lawrence Way. Until the mid C19 Cramp Hill was known as Cromp Hill Bank. Cromp is a dialect word meaning bent or crooked (SNDB p38).

Cranberry Small village on a bank on the E side of the Meece 0.75m NE of Standon. In Standon ancient parish. In the 1800s it was known locally as Baggum from an argumentative villager who was bagged in a sack and dropped into a well, but survived (SVB p153). A hermit with a long white beard and miser tendencies occupied a cottage opposite the village shop (SVB p153).

Crane Brook Runs from Biddulph's Pool when it is called Big Crane Brook. In Shenstone parish. Passes through Chasewater Reservoir to Black Brook at Shenstone. The name is from the bird, the crane (APB p48), or the heron (NSFCT 1908 p133) (SPN p106). In the Midlands a crane has always meant a raven, and in any case cranes rarely ventured to the Midland counties (DUIGNAN). Crane Brook is mentioned in 1300 (VCH vol 14 p258).

Crank Hill 2m E of Wednesbury. Crank is a Middle English word of doubtful origin meaning bent, crooked, twisted. Perhaps, a crooked hill (DUIGNAN). Or 'crank' is the Celtic word for 'hill' (WAM p77). Perhaps from 'garann,' 'crann' forest, and 'uig,' 'wig' Old Celtic 'viko-s,' Latin 'vicus,' house or enclosure, hence 'forest-house.' This would be corrupted to crank or cronk (NSFCT 1908 p142). Has also appeared as Cronk Hill. Sandwell Priory had a grange on Crank Hill (DUIGNAN p63). Crank Hill Lane is perhaps the same as Crankhall Lane in the present Birmingham A-Z.

Crankhall The hall was 1.25m ESE of Wednesbury.

Cranmoor 0.5m S of Wrottesley. It was a park of the Wrottesley family by

1382. It became effectively disparked in the C17 (VCH vol 20 p33). Has also appeared as Cronemoor (HOPTT p195).

Crateford Hamlet 1.5m of Brewood. In Brewood ancient parish. Has appeared as Crakeford (1327), Crackford (1660) (SPNO p37), Crakeford (Plot's map).

Crawley Brook Tributary of the Trent. The name means 'the glade where crows nested' (SPNO p8).

Craythorne Once Great Thorne, preserved in Craythorne Farm to E of Rolleston (UTR p167). In Rolleston ancient parish. Has also appeared as Craythorn.

Craythorne Hall Craythorne. A Miss Thornewill was occupying Craythorne House in 1851 (W p19). In 1901 Craythorne Hall was the seat of Robert Thornewill JP (CBHBT p27).

Cream Pots A copse. Remaining part of the lost Bishop's Wood SE of Bishop's Wood village (SVB p34). The name is a result of Victorian whimsy (SPN p23), appearing in 1842 Tithe Award as 'Far Green Pot' (SPNO p40).

Creighton Small hamlet 0.5m NE of Stramshall. Former constablewick with Stramshall in Uttoxeter ancient parish (W p789). Has appeared as Crectone (1166) (SSE 1996 p12), Cracton, and Creiton (SPN p133). The name may be from Anglo-Saxon craet, crat meaning a cart; so, cart-house (DUIGNAN). The prefix is of Celtic origin (HOS p13). Perhaps from Gaelic 'crott' the Old Irish 'crode,' 'cruaid' a stronghold (NSFCT 1908 p142). Gelling gives 'settlement by the rock called Creik' (SSE 1996 p21). Or from Old Welsh 'creic' 'the settlement near the rock' (SSE 1996 p12) (SPN p133).

Creighton Park The name is preserved in Creighton Park Farm 0.75m NW of Stramshall.

Cress Brook Flows to a brook which feds Rudyard Lake. Forms the northern boundary of Rushton James township (VCH vol 7 p219). So called by the early C14 (VCH vol 7 p223).

Cressel Pool and Wood. The pool is in the middle of the wood, both are 0.5m SE of Walton-on-the-Hill.

Cresswell Village by the Blithe 10.5m NE of Stafford. In Draycott-in-the-Moors ancient parish. The 'well' in the name is from the 'Wall' an ancient line earthwork called The Mark (see) (OL vol 2 p15). The medieval vestments in the RC church here were seen by NSFC and reported to be in a remarkable state of preservation, having formerly been lost for 80 years. The registers are said to be the earliest of any post-Reformation Catholic church in England (NSFCT 1956 p112).

Cresswellford Minute hamlet over 0.5m E of Caverswall.

Cresswell's Almshouses Tettenhall. Six almshouses and gardens founded by Richard Cresswell in 1707 (HOPTT p300). By 1990 they were replaced by Lower Green Health Centre.

Crestwood, The and Crestwood Park, Kingswinford.

Creswell Ancient parish and hamlet by the Sow on E side of the M6, 1.5m SE of Great Bridgeford on NW fringe of the Stafford suburbs. A medium polished prehistoric axe was found in 1960 in the garden of The Mount (NSJFS 1962 p29. 1964 p20). Near Bridgeford chapel (Creswell chapel ruins?) was found a stone implement of the Neolithic or Bronze Age (Staffs Chronicle April 22 1905) (NSJFS 1964 p20). The manor of Cressvale appears in DB. Later Creswell appears as Cressewella (C12) (SPN p39), and Cresswell. The **name** means 'watercress well' (DUIGNAN), or 'spring where watercress grows' (SPN p39), or 'the stream where watercress grew' (Oxford Dictionary of Place Names) (ROT pp30-31) (SSE 1996 p12). Chetwynd and Ekwall says an old form of Creswell, Crassevale, is from 'crass a valle,' from the rich and fertile vale that surrounds it (NSFCT 1884 p28) (SHC 1914 p109) (SH p45). Or 'well' is from the 'Wall' an ancient line earthwork called The Mark (see) (OL vol 2 p15). A mill at Creswell is recorded in DB. A large mound of earth, was noted by Garner in the early 1840s, not far from Creswell, on the banks of the Sow; he thought it was perhaps artificial in construction (GNHS p110). The remains of a **chapel** of at least C15 origin, still (late C20) stand at SJ 895210, isolated in a field (LGS p118). Some say no service has been held in it since the Reformation, except when the new rector reads himself in (NSSG p15). Or that an annual open-air service is held here (SN July 13 1907 p2. Sept 1 1928 p2). It was noted by Chetwynd in the C17 (SH p46), and excavated in the 1870s and or 1880s when a skeleton was found under stonework, which was believed to be that of the founder (NSFCT 1883). In the early 1970s Pevsner noted that two walls of the chancel survived; the N wall was fairly intact, with two lancet windows, and the E wall with the outline of the E window (BOE p110). (GNHS p110) (VED pp137,138) (NSFCT 1884 p28) (KES p74) (CHMS p27) (MR pp116p,118) (ROT pp30,31p,32). Creswell was a prebend in Stafford Collegiate Church (SHC 1914 p111) (NSSG p15). In the vicinity of the chapel was a **medieval village**. It is mentioned in 1316 and was deserted for some reason between 1334 and 1539 (SSAHST 1970 p34). Walter Chetwynd in 1679 was the first to identify a settlement here and noted that all that remained was the manor house (SHC 1914 p109) (SL p82).

By at least 1633 Creswell had become an extra parochial liberty (W p389) (GLAUE p409). The liberty was taken into Seighford with Derrington and Creswell ecclesiastical parish in 1930. Creswell became a separate civil parish in 1858 (GLAUE p409). A campaign by villagers to have the speed limit lowered on the Eccleshall Road through Creswell, begun in c1970, was still being waged in 2000 despite many accidents (BBC 1 Midlands Today April 27 2000).

Creswell Green Hamlet S of Chorley, 2m SE of Cannock Wood. Has also appeared as Cresswell Green (1834 OS map).

Creswell Hall Creswell, Great Bridgeford. In 1811 Capt Whitby of the hall presented to the borough of Stafford the Colours of the ship 'Le Caronne' which he captured from the French and Italians in the Adriatic (ROT p32). The hall was the seat of Rev Edward Whitby in 1851 (W p19). In 1897 GE and AW Meakin of the hall presented two oxen for Queen Victoria's Jubilee to be roasted in Market Square, Stafford (SOPP pl 4). There was a fire at the hall in Dec 1914 (SN Dec 5 1914 p2) (STC p34p).

Crick Farm Handsworth. Farmhouse built in c1709. Said to take its name from a track from Grove Lane to St Mary's church with an arm going off somewhere near Philip Victor and Hinstock Roads (HPPE p23).

Crockington The Cocretone and Cocortone (alias Corcortone) which appear in DB have been considered a pair of vills or the same vill. It was still inhabited by the late C13 but was subsequently abandoned (SHC 1911 p194) (SSAHST 1970 p34) (VCH vol 20 p185). Shaw spelt it as Colverton (SHOS vol 2 p208). Scott wondered where it was in the earlier C19 (SVS p578) and Eyton left it unidentified. Commander Wedgwood identified it with Crockington (formerly Cockerton) Lane running from Seisdon to the southern end of Trysull village in the area of The Beeches 1m WSW of Trysull, in Trysull ancient parish, where land called Cockerton survived (SHC 1916 p170) (NSFCT 1952 p36) (DB edited by John Morris. Phillimore. 1976. Notes) (VCH vol 20 pp185,187) (SPN p130). The name means 'Coca's farmstead' (SPN p130).

Croft, The Red brick tall late Georgian house at Trysull. Built 1808 by 'Gentleman Perry' (SGS p172) (MR p339).

Croft House Circular toll house at Cheadle was a lodge to it. The house was demolished by 1992 (MIDD vol 4 p23p).

Croftshead To NW of Waterfall (W p787).

Cromer Hill Hill 0.5m SW of Milwich. According to local tradition the name is a corruption of Cromwell Hill on account of a belief that Cromwell's army passed over it on the way to the battle of Hopton Heath (1643) (local info).

Cromsley Place near Tad Brook, NW of Heatley in Abbots Bromley parish. Has appears as Cromberle (early C13) and Cromsley (by 1774). The name means 'crooked barley' (ABMB p53).

Cromwell House Stood by the Roundabout House near the SE side of Cannock churchyard. A corruption of Cronwell House (CCF pp123-124).

Cromwell's Rock In Dimmingsdale. It commands a striking view of Alton and the Churnet Valley (NSFCT 1921 p138).

Cronehills, The District on E side of the High Street, West Bromwich. Formerly on edge of West Bromwich Common. In Mill Street at approximately SP 002918 on N side of what is now Tantany Lane was a windmill. It was first shown on a plan of 1837. It still existed in 1842 (WBJ p45). Bell relates a story concerning the widow of a clock enthusiast here whose husband's clocks re-wound themselves without explanation and gave the right time (GLS pp106-107). A colliery called The Cronehills was developed by the 4th Earl of Dartmouth (VB p62).

Cronkhall Former hamlet on the present Windermere Road between Barnhurst Lane and Codsall Road, 1m N of Tettenhall (VCH vol 20 p12). In the Pendeford division in Tettenhall parish (W p207). Has appeared as Cronewall (Plot's map), and Cronkwall (DUIGNAN). Its etymology is the same as crank (DUIGNAN). It was an inhabited area by the 1220s (VCH vol 20 p12). (NSFCT 1908 p142).

Crook House House 0.5m NE of St Margaret's church, Great Barr. A bedroom has a blood-stained floor. A supernatural force occurring when St Margaret's church bells strike 'chilled' a passerby and halted horses near the house in the later C19 (TB July 1987 p23). (Great Barr and its Haunted Environs. Thomas Wright. 1852. A sheep of Crook Farm was maliciously wounded in 1908 mimicking animal maiming occurring at the time in the Great Wyrley district (TBS p29).

Cross Ash 1.25m NW of Farewell. In Longdon parish. Crossroads very close to Gorton Lodge. It was a hamlet in the mid C19 (W p568).

Cross Conduit A conduit in the market place, Lichfield. Mentioned in the 1540s and has appeared as Market Cross Conduit. It was removed in 1803 (VCH vol 14 pp96,97).

Crossfields Victorian house on the Cannock Road, near Weeping Cross. Built by the Twigg family in the mid C19, a short distance from their home at

Weeping Cross House (BERK2 p141p).

Crossgate Small hamlet 0.75m SW of Fulford. In Hilderstone quarter in Stone ancient parish.

Cross Green Hamlet 0.5m SE of Coven. In Brewood ancient parish. The name appears in 1806 (BUOP p68).

Cross Guns West Bromwich. Thought to be so called after the deserter who was executed here during the Civil War (SOWB p25). May take its name from the Cross Guns Inn on Bromwich Heath.

Cross Guns Inn Near Five Ways church, Cradley Heath. Joe Mallen (1890-1975) of Cradley Heath (see), proponent of the Staffordshire Bull Terrier, was manager of this inn (TB Nov/ Dec 1972 p9. May 1974 p1), consequently it was a popular haunt for Staffordshire Bull Terrier breeders; here puppies were sold and purchased. According to tradition HRH Prince of Wales (Edward VIII) visited the inn in disguise to buy a 'Stafford' pup with the Earl of Dudley, when a guest at Himley Hall, or that the earl went alone, or that the earl just sent an agent (TB Feb 1979 p5. March 1979 p30). Possibly in error, Raven asserts that Joe Mallen was landlord of the Cross Keys Inn, Cradley Heath (MIDD vol 4 p6).

Cross Hayes House 0.75m S of Hoar Cross Hall, Hoar Cross. Appears as Crosshayes Hall in 1887 (OS map 1887 6 inch) and Cross Hayes House in 1981 (OS map 1981 1:50,000). Whilst Hoar Cross Hall was being built (completed in c1871) Cross Hayes was the temporary seat of Hugo and Emily Meynell Ingram, the builders of the hall, after their marriage in 1863; in 1870 Hugo died in an hunting accident before Hoar Cross Hall was completed (A Vision of Splendour: Gothic Revival in Staffordshire 1840-1890. Michael Fisher. 1995. p127).

Cross Heath District 1m NW of Newcastle-under-Lyme, between Knutton and Milehouse. Formerly partly in Newcastle-under-Lyme chapelry in Stoke-upon-Trent ancient parish, and partly in Wolstanton ancient parish (SGSAS). It has been said that here was a Saxon or earlier stone cross (boundary marker) (SPN p86). In 1797 Richard Thompson built a cotton mill in Liverpool Road at Cross Heath. It was unusual for being built so far from Manchester. It carried out spinning and weaving. In 1864 James Evans bought the business, and in 1896 A & S Murray operated the works. It was a cotton-doubling mill by 1934. In the 1960s the firm of A & S Murray stopped operating. Royal Doulton retail sales division took over a part of the building (built later then 1797) and renamed it Swift House (NSFCT 1947 p164) (NSJFS 1965 p91 pl VIa) (NULOP vol 2 p37p). Cottages were erected by Richard Thompson in 1797-8 for his millworkers at Cross Heath (NULOP vol 2 p46p). Cross Heath became a separate ecclesiastical parish in 1952 (GLAUE p409). That year a church, St Michael and All Angels, was built in Linden Grove (LDD). The church is said to be haunted; the figure of a lady in white was caught in a photograph taken inside (ES Feb 18 1980).

Crosshill St John's, Burslem, stands on this hill (SSGLST p27). The lane passing Josiah Wedgwood I's birthplace went to Crosshill (ES Feb 22 1930 p3). Has also appeared as Cross Hill.

Cross in Hand Lane Leads to St Bartholomew's church, Farewell. It is believed that travellers seeking sanctuary would take this lane, bearing a cross (SVB p56). Or rather this was a lane taken by parish processions making their way to take offerings to Lichfield cathedral at Whitsuntide; each procession was preceded by someone bearing a cross (MCC).

Cross in the Hand Near end of Beacon Street, 0.5m NW of Lichfield cathedral. The name is said to be from 'the cross with the hand' mentioned in the later C15 and early C16, evidently a direction post. A post stood here in 1675, but it had gone by 1728 when it fell upon highway surveyors to erect a hand to direct travellers here (VCH vol 14 p203). Has also appeared as Cross o' the Hand (SHOS vol 1), and Cross and Hand (HOL p356). A hamlet evolved at the fork in the London-Chester road where a road diverges to Ashmore Brook and was in existence by the later C17 (VCH vol 14 pp21,203). Here the perambulation of Lichfield begins and ends. Here was an ancient cross (HOL p511).

Cross Keys Inn Coaching inn on Birmingham to Stafford route at Old Hednesford, Cannock (VCH vol 5 pp51,53). Originally Cross Keys farm of C16 origin (SPNO p58). The present house was built in 1746 (date is carved on the front of house). In the mid C18 Wesley reputedly passed the inn (CCBO p103). (BOE p145) (MR p180). Parts of it may be older and it may be the oldest surviving inn in the area (CCAP p29p). Was the scene of a strange event which remains a mystery. A big burly navvy who had made a nuisance of himself in the inn was punched unconscious by Bob Brettle a prize fighter of Birmingham. The navvy was laid out in the stables. Several checks throughout the night found him still unconscious. In the morning his body was gone. Brettle's backers were Dr William Palmer of Rugeley (see) and Joseph Cook. It has been suggested that the navvy never came round and Palmer had him removed (CCF pp150-152,192-196). The landlord, John Wilkins, trained the 1861 Grand National winner 'Jealously' here (SSE 1990 p87). A cockfight is recorded here after WW1, despite the sport having been banned in 1835 (HOS p63). It could also be close to Cockpit Hill. Cross keys is the symbol of St Peter (SPN p61).

Crossley Stone House or street or square in central Rugeley. VCH vol 5 p153 implies that it is a property.

Cross of the Hand Crossroads at Bromley Hurst nearly 1.5m SSE of Abbots Bromley.

Crossplain Poultry farm 1.5m NW of Rangemore. The nearby airfield is called Tatenhill (see) airfield.

Crowesbridge Land near to the top of Upper Ettingshall Road and Coppice Road, Coppice Village. The name has appeared Crows Britch, Croksbridge, Croksbritches, for example, Croks Britch, is a form which was still used in the early C20 (HC p26).

Crowesbridge House Coppice Road, Coppice Village. Is of mid C18 origin (HC p79).

Crowborough Area 2.25m WSW of Horton, in Horton ancient parish. The second element of the name 'boorugh' is derived from an Old English word 'bearu,' meaning a wood or grove (VCH vol 7 p67). 'The hill or wood where crows predominate' (SSE 1996 p13) (SPN p77), but also quite likely to be 'a rookery.' Rooks often being called crows (DUIGNAN). Has appeared as Crowbarwe (C13) (SSE 1996 p12) and Cranborough (Smith's map). The oldest house in the area appears to be Crowborough Farm to the E of the Trent, and probably stands on the site of a house held in 1299 by John of Crowborough (VCH vol 7 p67).

Crowgutter House at Ipstones Green on S side of Park Lane, Ipstones. In this vicinity was the former Ipstones Manor House (see).

Crowgutter Wood Ipstones. Wood on E side of the Churnet. In it are the Devil's Staircase and Price's Cave.

Crowhalt To SE of Finney Lane (PWNS p112).

Crow Low Burial mound on Caldon Low at SK 083487, to W of Caldon Grange. Here human teeth remains and flints were found in 1868 (1882 OS map 6 inch). Has been probably lost owing to quarrying.

Crown Inn Old coaching inn and hotel in High Street, Stone. First recorded in 1575 when the landlord was also postmaster (IOM p62); it is said to have existed before this, taking its name to show its allegiance to Henry VIII in his conflict with Rome (SPN p117). Richard Vaughan, a prominent Catholic and strong Jacobite, one of the Young Pretender's staff in the 1745 Jacobite Rebellion, captured at Darlaston (Pirehill hundred) was briefly held prisoner at the Crown (NSFCT vol 43 1908-9 p137) (SIS p58). The first meeting of the committee to promote the Trent & Mersey Canal met at the Crown on June 10 1766 (SIS p63). The present premises was built in 1779 as a coaching inn, made to accommodate Royal Mail coaches; the architect was Henry Holland (SIT). John Byng, 5th Viscount Torrington, diarist and author, stayed a night at the Crown in 1792 (SIS p68). It has been used as a post office, excise office, lock-up, court house for petty and licensing sessions, and for RC services before a Catholic church was built in Stone. The court of Pyepowder (or pie powder or dusty foot court) associated with Stone fair was held at the Crown in 1810 (SIS p85). The first meeting of the North Staffordshire Agricultural Society (later SAS) was held at the Crown in 1844 (The History of Staffordshire Agricultural Society. Brenda Greysmith. c1978). The custom of ale-tasting which took place here had ceased by 1951 (IOM p62). In the Jervis Bar is a mural by Eric Tunstall of Sir Francis Drake at bowls (SLM summer 1955 p18p). Six wall murals in panels were discovered underneath wallpaper in the ballroom in late 1999 or early 2000 (ES Jan 13 2000 p16pc). The Soviet leaders Kruschev and Bulganin were entertained at the Crown in the 1950s (ES Sept 27 1997 p21). Sir Harry Secombe stayed at the hotel and happened to stop a pig, which had escaped from the market, entering the hotel (COS p53). In 1999 Bass Breweries sold the Crown to the Hall family of Barlaston Hall (see).

Crown Bank Former estate in Talke township in Audley ancient parish, S of Talke village. It came to be known as such after Richard Stonier of Bignall End kept an inn by the sign of the Crown on this estate which was by the old post road to the north in c1600 (SHC 1944 p60). A main street in Talke is still called Crown Bank.

Crown Lands House 5m SW by S of Burton upon Trent. Seat of George Birch in 1851 (W p19).

Crownpoint House under 1m NW of Cheddleton standing on a hill which commands fine views (Cheddleton Remembered. Vera Priestman. 1978 p42).

Crow's Castle 0.75m WSW of Hints. Probably the mound at SK 14890248 thought to have been a burial mound (NSFCT vol 36 p157) (VCH barrow list) but found to be natural (NSJFS 1965 p39).

Crowtrees House 0.75m N of Oakamoor. Field name derived from an animal name (APB p48).

Crowtrees House(s) under 0.25m NW of Waterhouses.

Croxall Ancient parish and former township (UCC). The tiny village of Croxall on low ground by the Mease and SE of Trent confluences with the Tame and Mease is 18m ESE of Stafford or 17m SW of Derby.
EARLY. A burial mound lay to the SE of Croxall church and just outside the churchyard at SK 19791362. In c1800 Thomas Prinsep tried to have it removed but stopped when human bones were found in it (UCC p19) (VCH barrow list). Two urns containing cremations and a British cup have been found in the mound (Minutes of the Tamworth Natural History Geological and Archaeology Society May 26 1873) (NSJFS 1965 p36). Civil War armoury once in Croxall Hall was not found in the mound, as formerly believed by local inhabitants (UCC p19). In 1881 the mound was 12 feet high and 40 feet in circumference (UCC p19). In 1965 the mound was some 34 paces in diameter and seven feet high and badly mutilated (NSJFS 1965 p36). By 1966 it was considered to have been a motte (SSAHST 1966 p46). In the later C17 Plot noted about a mile ENE of Edingale a part of a Roman raised way pointing towards Lullington - which he thought might lead to Repton (NHS p402) (SHOS General History p35. vol 1 p391). Ussher traced it running in a westerly direction, passing Croxall to the Tamworth-Burton road a little N of the bridge over the Mease (UCC p18).
500 to PRESENT. The Crokeshalle mentioned in a charter of 942 has been identified with Croxall (SHC 1916 pp86,87). The manor of Crocheshalle appears in DB. Later Croxall appears as Croxhale (1208), Crokeshale (1239), Crosal (1275), Crocsal (1275), Crouxhale (1317), Croxhalle (1330), Croxhall (1450), Croksalle (1490), Croxsall (1509), Croxal (1605), Croxall (1639) (UCC p10) (SPN p39). Ussher thought the prefix of the name derived from Celtic 'cnoc' a hill, so 'hall of, or at the hill' (UCC p3). But Duignan rejected Ussher's interpretation, favouring an Anglo-Saxon personal name for the prefix, so 'Croc's hall': A family of Croc (descended from Richard the Forester) were hereditary foresters of Cannock Forest, until 1167 (DUIGNAN). Some have thought it of Scandinavian origin (SDW p11) (SL p49). Or that the suffix has another derivation 'Krokr's or Croc's nook, valley or hollow' (NSJFS 1981 p3) (SSE 1996 p12) (SPN pp39,133). The parish church, St John the Baptist, S of Croxall Road, dates from c1200 (BOE p110). Aerial photography reveals the pattern of a deserted village to the SE of the church (SSAHST 1966 p46. 1970 p35). The present village and Croxall township lay in Repton and Gresley hundred, Derbys, until transferred to Staffs in 1894 (SL p29) or 1895 (GLAUE p409): Oakley township in Croxall ancient parish has always been in Staffs. The parish formerly lay in the archdeaconry of Derbys in Lichfield diocese, but was transferred with Derbys to Southwell diocese after 1881 (UCC pp12-13).

Croxall Hall House in Croxall village centre. Is on the site of an earlier and larger hall, which was the seat of the Curzons from Henry I's reign. The present hall has been described as Elizabethan (CL July 31 1997 property pages pc). Joyce Lewis, the daughter of Sir Thomas Curzon, was burnt for heresy in the Market Place, Lichfield on Dec 18 1557 (UCC pp6-7) (VCH vol 3 p46). In Charles I's reign the Curzon heiress, Mary, daughter of Sir George Curzon (d1622) brought the estate to Sir Edward Sackville, later Earl of Dorset, by marriage. Mary was sometime governess to the children of Charles I; Henrietta Maria, queen of Charles I, stayed here on July 7/8 1643 on her journey from the north to join the king at Edgehill; the next day she travelled to Walsall. Mary died in 1645 and was honoured by parliament with a public funeral - the only woman ever to be so honoured (UCC pl 5). John Dryden (1631-1700), poet and dramatist, friend of the Earl of Dorset, may have been a visitor to the hall in the 1680s. Lionel Cranfield Sackville (b1687/8), 7th Earl and 1st Duke of Dorset, Lord Lieutenant in Ireland from 1730, died in 1765 and was succeeded by his son, Charles, 2nd Duke of Dorset, who died unmarried in 1769. He was succeeded by his nephew John Frederick Sackville (d1799), 3rd Duke of Dorset, who sold the estate in 1779 to Thomas Prinsep, well-known as an agriculturalist and breeder of long-horn cattle. Croxall was famous towards the end of the C18 for its herd of long-horn cattle; paintings of the best in the herd were at Croxall Hall in 1881. Prinsep reputedly had the largest farm in Derbys at Croxall (AOS) (UCC p11) (SSAHST 1966 p46). Prinsep was succeeded by his son, Thomas, who died without issue. The estate then passed to the second son of Prinsep Snr's sister, Mary, wife of Theophilus Levett of Wychnor Hall, called Thomas. He was owner by 1817, and assumed the arms and name of Prinsep in 1835. His son, Thomas Levett-Prinsep was the owner in 1881 (Magna Britannia. vol 5. Rev Daniel Lysons. 1817. pp92-93) (UCC p10). The hall appears to have been let for a while; John Lager (d1852) lived at Croxall Hall (mem in Croxall church). The hall was occupied by Thomas Levett-Prinsep JP between at least 1907 and 1916. Between at least 1924 and 1932 it was occupied by Thomas Jenkins. In 1940 it was occupied by Capt Geoffrey Nicholas Charlton JP (Magna Britannia. vol 5. Rev Daniel Lysons. 1817. pp92-93) (STC p41ps) (KD 1916 etc) (SSAHST 1966 p46) (MR pp117pc,119). The hall, occupied by James Rose by at least the time of his death in 1976, was for sale in July 1997 (mems in Croxall church) (CL July 31 1997). Civil War armoury once at Croxall Hall was not found in the mound SE of Croxall church, as formerly believed by local inhabitants, but was brought to the hall probably by a Sackville who was active in the Civil War (UCC p19). There is a dovecote to the W of the hall. It is a square and in brick and has a cupola (BOE p111) (CL July 27 1989 p175). Dryden's Walk, named after John Dryden (d1700), is a walk running NE from Croxall Hall (SSAHST 1966 p46).

Croxden Tiny village 14m NE of Stafford by Croxden Brook. Its mother church is uncertain (SHC 1915 pxxxi). The manor of Crochesdene appears in DB, and it may have formed part of Alton manor prior to 1176 (CDS p30). Later Croxden appears as Crokedene (SPN p133). The name is of Anglo-Saxon origin and means 'Croc's valley' (DUIGNAN) (NSJFS 1981 p2) (CDS p15). Or 'Krokr's or bent valley' (SSE 1996 p12). Or is of Scandinavian origin (SDW p11). In the village centre is Croxden Abbey. A grange of Croxden Abbey (VCH vol 3 p226) (CDS pp7,16) may have been Lees Grange in Croxden parish. The abbey chapel, which stood to the E of the abbey gatehouse, slightly to the S of the present church, served the separate parish of Croxden after the Dissolution. The present church, St Giles, on the N side of the village was built in 1884-1885 (VCH vol 3 pp229-230) (GLAUE p409). The parish has had detached portions at Doglane, near Calton and at The Grit near C0mbridge (CDS p4). In 1934 a part of Alton parish was added to the N side of the parish, and parts of Uttoxeter and Checkley parishes were added to the S side (CDS 4). Fields at Brook Farm show clearly the ridges of former open fields (CDS p18). Stone has been quarried in Croxden for hundreds of years (CDS p70). Guisers or mummers from Uttoxeter formerly performed at Croxden on Christmas morning (CDS p89). Foot-and-mouth disease broke out at a farm at Croxden Abbey in Dec 1967 (SN Dec 29 1967 p13).

Croxden Abbey Former Cistercian abbey at Croxden. Founded by Bertram de Verdun (d1192) of Alton Castle (see), in 1176. Many of Bertram's descendents were buried in the abbey (NSSG p16). Bertram at first granted land for the abbey at Chotes, a place of doubtful identity (LGS p119), but thought by Sister M Laurence and others to be Cotton (Staffs). The abbey moved to Croxden in 1179. The new site was not dedicated until 1181. The dedication is to St Mary. The abbey was known as the Abbey of the Vale of St Mary. It was given to the Savignac branch of the Cistercian order and was a late foundation for this order (HAF p46). The mother house was L' Aunay, Normandy (VCH vol 3 pp226-230). Received its foundation charter on Aug 5 1190 and a charter of confirmation from Henry II. Its charters are in the BM (SK p204). The original seal is in the BM (AAD pp286-287) (S p facing p90) (VCH vol 3 p230) (SLM Feb/March 1988 p16p). The first abbot, Richard de Schepshead, compiled a chronicle which was continued for 200 years and is presently in the BM (HOU p347) (NSSG p16). (GNHSS p11; says the chronicle was compiled by Abbot Thomas Shepsher(v)ed) (AAD pp283-286 - extracts from it) (LGS p119) (KES p77) (SLM Feb/March 1988 p16p?) (MR p119).

KING JOHN'S HEART. It is a long-held belief that King John's heart was buried at the abbey. The king was a benefactor to the abbey to the amount of £10 a year, and he received the abbot of Croxden on his death bed at Newark-upon-Trent and the abbot administered the last rites to him. As he died on Oct 18 1216 his last words were 'I commit my soul to God, and my body to St Wulstan' so his heart was buried at Croxden and his body in Worcester cathedral (that cathedral being dedicated to St Wulstan) (AAD pp287,288); his bowels were buried at Croxton, Leics (W p771). Bird lightly suggests that it could have been the monks of Croxton, Leics, that attended him on his death bed (VB pp170,171). Another account has King John dying at Swinshead Abbey, Lincs, with his body being interred at Worcester; bowels at Croxton Abbey church, Leics; and heart at Croxden (Broughton's Scrapbook appendix p6). (SMC p171) (SSC p139 in the intro) (GNHS p94) (HOU p347) (KES pp77,78) (NSSG p16) (MR p119).

The abbey had granges at Caldon Grange (see), Cheadle Grange (see), Crakemarsh (see), Croxden (see), Musden Grange (see), and Oaken (see). Other granges, known as Lees Grange and Grange of the Leys, may be identified with those at Croxden and Crakemarsh, respectively, or may have been the same grange. The first two hundred years were prosperous based on a trade in wool, timber and charcoal. When, however, the male Verdun line died out and the patronage passed to Thomas de Furnivalle, many demands were made on the monks and economic decline began. The community in 1405 was very poor, with only six monks and the abbot. There were 13 mem-

bers at the Dissolution (NSFCT 1991 p60).

AFTER THE DISSOLUTION. The abbey surrendered in 1538. The last monk died as vicar of Alton in 1569 (NSFCT 1991 p60). Geoffrey Foljambe obtained most of the property at the dissolution. It probably passed to his son Godfrey Foljambe (alias Brownlowe) for a Godfrey Foljambe sold it in 1595 to Edward Bellingham. He sold it in 1606 and it passed through several hands until it came by marriage to the Pierrepoints in 1637. It passed through several branches of that family until Evelyn Pierrepoint, Duke of Kingston, sold the manor to Henry Walker in 1723. Probably the Walkers were agents of the Earl of Macclesfield, who henceforward appears in documents as lord of the manor. It remained with the Macclesfields until the estate was broken up and sold in 1913. The ruins of the abbey were then purchased by Col Richard Verdin. It was bought by WG Vickers in 1938. When Vickers died in 1945 the property was sold to Martin Bolton (CDS pp12,30). Another account has a Sergeant Harris at sometime owning the property, probably shortly after the dissolution (NSFCT 1953 pB 89). Changes to the abbey site have included the building during the lifetime of 1st Earl of Macclesfield the 'convenient house within the ruin'; an estate map of 1722 shows this house built in the SW corner of the cloister court and the road going round the N side of the abbey church (CDS p12). The abbey gatehouse, to the NW of the church, was said to be 'almost entire' in 1719. The chapel, built in the mid C13 to the E of the gatehouse, survived as Croxden parish church until 1886, when it was replaced by the present church, built slightly further N (VCH vol 3 pp229-230); a human skull, in a vault below the S transept in the old chapel, could still be seen in the earlier C19, as could the kitchen fireplace, near the abbey gatehouse (GNHS p545). The abbey site was excavated by Charles Lynam of Colwich in 1911 (NSFCT 1991 p60). By 1913 the road to Greatgate passed directly through the ruins of the abbey church (CDS p12). By the late 1930s the ruins had become dangerous and an arrangement was made between WG Vickers and the HM Office of Works for their repair (ES Nov 23 1937 p1p) (CDS p12). Excavations on the abbey complex took place in 1956-57 (in the E end of the abbey church and a building to the SE of the abbey complex) and in 1975-77 (on the latrine block and by the novice's room and dormitory over it, and the area towards the infirmary) (SSAHST 1994-95 pp29-51 plans). In 1958, the building considered by Lynam to be the chamber (the abbot's lodging) built by Abbot Richard of Shepshed in 1335-36, was excavated (NSFCT 1959 p88). In 1968 further work to expose the foundations of the abbot's lodging was in progress. By 1970 the W front of the abbey church survived as did the S transept and E range of the cloister and walls around the chapter house, but no remains of the cloister arcade were left standing. Some of the stone wall around the 70 acre precinct (finished by 1274-1284) was still in evidence (VCH vol 3 pp229-230). An effigy of a de Vernon knight, which may have been the founder of the abbey, may have existed long after the abbey's suppression (MOS pp23, 38-42) (NSSG p16). A crucifix, with an image of the Saviour, was found, broken, amongst the ruins, by Mr Carrington, who had it repaired. A curious carved oak panel of Jesus and the 12 apostles, discussed at an antiquarians meeting at Manchester, was found in the vicinity of Croxden Abbey (HOU p347). Some early English C13 floor tiles from the abbey are in Buxton Museum, Derbys. The two pieces of armorial glass in the entrance hall of Alton Castle or St John's Hospital, Alton, came from Croxden Abbey according to tradition, but are in fact of a later date (NSFCT 1924 p189). There is a tradition of a tunnel running from Alton Castle to Croxden Abbey (ES June 11 1996 p3p). Holt admits to having taken a fragment of masonry for his rockery (SFH p14). (SD pp100, 101) (SMC il of facing, p97 1731, pp101-102) (SSC p138 in the intro pp86,88 il) (SM pp24,67) (AAD pp280-283) (GNHS pp93,94ils) (W p771) (HOC pp259-276 il Appendix ppxiv-xvi - deed of surrender) (NSFCT 1868. 1874 plan pp29-35. 1913 pp129-141) (SK pp203-204) (HS pp106,109pl) (IAANS p xv) (PS p126) (LGS pp37,118-120 plan) (S pp94p,96) (KES pp10,77,78) (SOSH pp110,168p) (HOS p27 plan) (STM March 1966 p38ps. Aug 1968 pp24-25p of the master masons trade marks) (BOE pp111-112 pl 11) (SL pp72,73, pl 10) (TB Jan 1977 p8 postcard from 1888 showing ruins. Feb 1977 p8p of stone coffins) (SGS p90) (CDS pp5-14) (SLM Feb/March 1988 pp16,17) (MR p119p).

Croxden Brook Common and present name for the Peake Rivulet; so named from the Peakstones (see) in Alton parish (SPNO p15). Greatgate and Croxden are situated on it and it is a tributary of the Churnet (W p771) (NSFCT 1950 pB24) (CDS p42).

Croxden Common Common land which lay on high ground adjoining Cheadle Common in the N of Croxden parish. The common, known as Great Yate Common in 1722, was enclosed by the Earl of Macclesfield in 1814. The area was transferred to Checkley parish in 1934 (CDS pp3,4,27,89). Since at least the 1950s gravel has been excavated in the Bunter Pebble Beds on the former common (CDS p72).

Croxden Park Medieval deer park. Is marked on Saxton's map (EDP p177).

Croxton Small village on high ground overlooking the Fairoak valley, 10.5m NW of Stafford. Former township in the Woodland quarter in Eccleshall ancient parish. The manor of Crochestone, a member of Eccleshall manor, appears in DB. The name is of Scandinavian origin (SDW p11). It represents 'Krokr's tun or tun in a bend' (SSE 1996 p12). Or is 'Croc's farmstead' (SPN p39). Or it is from the town or place of the Cross, there was probably a gospel or preaching cross at Croxton (BPS p143). According to tradition an Armada beacon (DoE II) (BPS p149) was on a hill, from which can be seen Worcestershire Beacon on the Malvern Hills (BOV pp22-23), at SJ 782318, 0.25m W of Croxton. In 1777 a windmill, built by Samuel Barlow of Greatwood Lodge, was built on the hill. It was for sale in 1840 at which time it lost its cap in a violent storm (WBJ p19 il xiv). Or built in c1800 and worked until c1870 (EOP p60p c1906). The inside gear was removed in 1891. By 1930 the tower was being used to hold rubbish. The Home Guard used the windmill in WW2 as an observation post (WBJ p19 il xiv). (WIS p9p) (STMSM Aug 1978 p26p) (MR p120). The church, St Paul, Church Lane, was built in 1853-1854 (BOE p113). For the murder of John Poole of Croxton in 1866 see Offleybrook. Croxton became a separate ecclesiastical parish in 1857 (GLAUE p409). Foot-and-mouth disease broke out at Greatwood Lodge Farm, Croxton in early 1968 (SN Jan 5 1968 p13). The oldest cat living in Britain in 1989 was believed to be a female black moggy named 'Kitty' owned by George Johnston of Croxton. She was discovered as a stray (with four kittens) in Nov 1951, and was considered the oldest feline mother in the world when she had two kittens in May 1987. She celebrated her 31st birthday in 1988 (GBR 1989 p30. 1998 p242).

Croxtonbank Tiny hamlet 0.5m NW of Croxton. Croxton's church is here. Croxtonbank formerly lay by Greatwood Heath (SSE vol 7 1995 p75).

Croxton Cross Croxton. It is the crossroads leading to four manors (BOV p18). Possibly was the site of an ancient cross, if a cross existed.

Crucifix Conduit A public conduit in Bird Street, Lichfield, S of the Friary gate. (HOL p484,489-491 pl facing p483) (VCH vol 3 p268. vol 14 pl 27). It became known as Crucifix Conduit from the crucifix which surmounted it. Enlarged and decorated in 1708. Rebuilt in the late 1750s. Crucifix Conduit was the only Lichfield conduit standing in 1806. In 1827 the trustees ordered the rebuilding of its dome. In 1863 it was adapted as the base of a clock tower designed in a Romanesque style by Joseph Potter the younger, but the conduit continued in use. In 1927 the tower was sold to Lichfield corporation who, in 1928, re-erected it several hundred yards away at the W end of the new road across the Friary (VCH vol 14 pp32,96,97). (LPL p) (LAL p18p) (STMSM July 1980 p17p) (BOE p192).

Cruck House, The House in Stowe Street, Lichfield. There were plans to turn it into a modern meeting place for the district's pensioners (STMSM Aug 1974 p21p).

Crumpall Green Former hamlet in the Charlemont area, West Bromwich. Here was Crump Hall (later Charlemont Hall) (VCH vol 17 p20).

Crumpwood Alton. Crumpwood Farm and weir are 1.25m E of Alton. On S side of the Churnet.

Crumwithies 1m ENE of Ipstones. Appears as Cromwithys on the 1834 OS map.

Cuckold's Corner May be the former name for the Oak Hill area of Finchfield. In 1780 there were two houses here (VCH vol 20 p9).

Cuckoostones House 1.5m NNW of Warslow. Has also appeared as Cuckoo Stone (1834 OS map).

Cuddeston Pool Lay about where Cherry Orchard Primary School is situated in Cherry Orchard Road, Handsworth. It may have evolved as a gravel pit (HPPE p21).

Cullamoor Small dispersed hamlet. Formerly in Kibblestone township and quarter in Stone ancient parish. By 1872 was in Oulton-with-Meaford township (Post Office Dir for Staffs 1872). Big Cullamoor is 0.5m S of Middle Cullamoor, which in turn is 0.25m E of Lower Cullamoor, which in turn is 0.75m ESE of Barlaston. Has also appeared as Cullamore.

Culstrubbe Lost marsh in Lichfield that was situated near Culstrubbe Gate. The name is derived from Middle English words 'collen,' to pull, and 'stubbe,' a tree-stump (VCH vol 14 p42). Gave its name to Culstrubbe Gate, Hall, and Street, all of which later were replaced by the appellation St John after St John's Hospital (VCH vol 14 p40).

Culstrubbe Gate or Bar. One of the five gates in Lichfield Town Ditch. Former name of St John Street gate. Recorded as Culstrubbe Gate in 1208 (VCH vol 14 p40). It was situated in St John's Street. St John's Hospital lay without it. The main London road went through it. Beyond it was a drawbridge (LAL pp14,15). Name is from the nearby marsh Culstrubbe (see) (VCH vol 14

p40). Bishop Durdent's Cross and Bishop Pucelle's Cross stood outside the gate (VCH vol 14 p10).

Culstrubbe Hall Stood opposite St John's Hospital, Lichfield. Mentioned in 1577. Seat of physician Sir John Floyer in the late C17. Demolished before 1732 and St John's House, later Yeomanry House (see), built on the site (VCH vol 14 p21).

Culvert's Low Former burial mound at Fenton, in the area of Brookside Drive. Appears on Hargreave's map (1832), and has appeared as Mole Cop or Cop Low (NSSG p19). It possibly gives its name to the manor of Fenton Culvert (FF p15). The name is derived from the cry 'craven,' craven meaning cowardly. The low or burial mound is thought to be where the vanquished Aelfric, a Saxon who held lands here on fee, lies buried. He was killed in a dispute over ownership of the land (FF p15). (HBST p544) (NSFCT vol 61 p136) (VCH vol 8 p205).

Culwell Spring formerly to be seen at the junction of Wednesfield Road and Bridge Street (unlocated) (WHTOP p129), Springfield, Wolverhampton. Shaw noted that the Cullwell Well was a very clear and powerful spring, and one of the sources of the Smestow (SHOS vol 2 p165) (W p76) (HOWW) (SCSF p140). It was never known to go dry and local people made offerings of money and statues to it (SMM p76). The name is preserved in Culwell Street off Wednesfield Road and a Culwell Works off Woden Road, and Culwell Tavern (WHTOP p129p).

Cumberland House W of the High Street on the S side of The Terrace, Cheadle. Built in 1745 (COPP2 p120p). In the 1745 Jacobite Rebellion the Duke of Cumberland reputedly hid in the house from the Young Pretender, or stayed here on the night of Dec 9 1745 (NSFCT 1925 p68). Refurnished in 1994 (ES Jan 2 1995 p5p). Plant says the Duke stayed one night in Cheadle sleeping in a house opposite the churchyard. The house was demolished shortly before 1881 and a new one built on the site (HOC pp66-67,70,71,72,149 il - is behind the tomb of the Grosvenor family).

Cumberland House On the W side of High Street, Stone. In the 1745 Jacobite Rebellion the Duke of Cumberland stayed here in 1745 whilst his army encamped on Stonefield (VB pp140-141). Others say he came to Stone on Dec 2 1745, but returned to his quarters at Stafford for dinner (NSFCT 1925 pp58,60). Cope says he arrived in Stone from Stafford at 11.00pm on Dec 2 and laid on straw at Mr Hinckley's house, which was No. 8 High Street, which was later renamed Cumberland House. He did not accept the bed John Jervis offered him at Meaford Hall. The Duke left Stone on Dec 4 (SIS pp56,57il,58). (The Yeoman Adventurer. Gough) (Midwinter. Buchan) (A Compleat History of the Rebellion. James Ray. 1757) (The Gazette. Nov 1987 p14p) (MOSP p16).

Cumberledge Park House 1m NW of Cheddleton. Overlooks Deep Hayes Reservoir. Seat of the Cumberledge family in the C17. The medieval deer park, Cheddleton Park, may have been in this area (CVH p160). Marked on 1834 OS map.

Cumbersome Hill Groundslow, Tittensor (VCH vol 6 p100 see map).

Cumber Stone To the W of Saxon's Lowe (SMM p23 see map).

Cumbwell Brook Tributary of the Smestow. The name means 'the broke of Cumbwell' (SPNO p8).

Cundesfen Mentioned in a charter of 951. Has been identified as the low-lying area just S of Smallwood Manor which floods regularly every winter and obstinately resists all attempts to drain it effectively (SMSE p3).

Curborough Small dispersed hamlet on the gentle S slopes of Trent Vale 1.75m NE of Lichfield consisting of about three houses. Curborough and Elmhurst formed an out-township in St Chad's parish, Lichfield (SHOS vol 1 p291) (VCH vol 14 p229). Has appeared as Corrun (1291) (SSE 1996 p13), Curborud, Curburg, Curburgh, Corbrun, and Corburn (SPN p78). The name derives from Old English words 'cweorn burna' meaning 'mill stream' evidently a reference to Curborough Brook (VCH vol 14 p229) (SSE 1996 p13), or if the first element is from a personal name then 'Creoda's mill stream' (SPN p78). It was formerly believed that the first part of the name was a remnant of some name like Curda or Creoda whilst the second part was believed to have derived from bury, a walled or defended enclosure (DUIGNAN). The first element may be traced to the root 'caor' brook - the reference being to a walled enclosure on the Curborough Brook (NSFCT 1908 p142). By 1970 it was believed that there was a medieval village at either 0.5m ENE Curborough Hall Farm, or at Curborough Farm, or at Curborough House (SSAHST 1970 p35). By 1990 two lost settlements - Great Curborough, which lay about Curborough Hall Farm, and Little Curborough, which lay about Curborough House - had been identified (VCH vol 14 p229). Curborough is a prebend in Lichfield cathedral. The estate which formed the endowment has been called Curborough Turvile (see). Curborough became a separate civil parish in 1866 (GLAUE p409).

Curborough Hall Farm Curborough, at SK 125120. Built in 1871 (VCH vol 14 p229).

Curborough House 0.5m ESE of Curborough Hall Farm. Formerly in Streethay township. In the late C13 an estate here was held by John de Somerville, lord of Wychnor. He or his family gave his name to the surrounding township, formerly known as Little Curborough. It was known as Curborough Somerville by 1327 (VCH vol 14 p282). The Langtons, who had acquired the estate from the Somervilles by 1497, held it to at least the early C17. The present house dates from the C18 with later alterations, but stands on a site occupied since the late C13 (VCH vol 14 p278). In the mid 1980s the remains of a dovecote stood on the E side of the house (VCH vol 14 p278).

Curborough New Hall Stood in the vicinity of, or on site of, the present Curborough Hall Farm. Built by 1780 it was described as ruinous and was demolished presumably soon afterwards (VCH vol 14 p233).

Curborough Old Hall Stood to the N of Curborough Hall Farm. Dr Zachary Babington, prebendary of Curborough from 1584, had a house known as Curborough Hall at Curborough by 1613. The hall passed by marriage from the Babingtons to the Levetts in 1745. It was demolished by 1848. A tablet bearing the Babington arms and the initials 'Z.B.' and 'W.B.' went to Field House, a house slightly to the E of Curborough Hall Farm (VCH vol 14 p229). (W p514).

Curborough Somerville Former township for the area around Curborough House, formerly known as Little Curborough. It was called Curborough Somerville by 1327, after John de Somerville, lord of Wychnor, who held an estate in Little Curborough by the end of the C13 (VCH vol 14 pp278,282). (HOL p357).

Curborough Turvile Name of the prebendal estate of Curborough, founded by Roger de Clinton in the C12 (SSAHST vol 2 1960-61 p44). The estate was known as this by 1415. The name is probably from Philip de Turvile, prebendary of Curborough 1307-37. By the early C17 the name had been corrupted to Darvell or Darvile. The estate centred on a moated site which existed to the N of Field House at SK 126120 (VCH vol 3 p141. vol 14 p233). Thomas Alstree who is said to have composed 500 sermons and preached over 5,000 times during his ministry was a Prebendary of Curborough (SSAHST vol 2 1960-61 p45).

Cutler's End Former name for the area now called Lambert's End (see), West Bromwich. Marked on Charles Henry Blood's Map of Birmingham and Its Environs 1857. A wake called the Gooseberry Wake was held at Cutler's End on the first Sunday in August in the early C19 (West Bromwich and Oldbury Chronicle. May 10 1901) (VCH vol 17 p71).

Cuttlestone There was a place called Cuttlestone in the C14. It appears to have been situated near Cuttlestone Bridge (VCH vol 4 p61). This may be the place that was remembered by local people from at least the later C18 as once a town or settlement of considerable magnitude and note (SHOS vol 2 p291) (DUIGNAN p48). It may have given its name to Cuttlestone Bridge.

Cuttlestone Former administrative division (hundred) of Staffs, covering the centre west part of the county. Has appeared as Colvestan (DB), Cudolvestan (DB), Culvestan (DB), Cudulvestan (DB), Cudeluestan (1130), Cuthulvestan (1203), Cothelstone (1280), Coutleston (1306), Cuttleston (1567) (SPNO p24) (SPN p94), Cuddlestone, and Cutteslowe. The name is of Anglo-Saxon origin and means 'Cuthwulf's stone' (DUIGNAN) (SPN p94), or possibly 'King Ceolwulf's stone' (SHC 1919 p155). (WMMA p144). It is perhaps a reference to a megalithic chambered tomb (SL p51) (SOSH p80), or Druidic stone circle (SOP p27), which may have stood in the area of Cuttlestone Bridge; at this stone the hundred court may have met in late Anglo-Saxon times. With the passing of Cannock Forest into royal hands after the Norman Conquest some of Offlow hundred is said to have been transferred to Cuttlestone (GWY p13). The hundred was divided into two divisions - East Cuttlestone and West Cuttlestone - between 1604-1611. The hundred courts were being held in Penkridge by the C17. In name at least the hundred court survived until about the mid C18 (VCH vol 4 pp61-63). (GNHS p74) (NSFCT 1908 p119) (ESH pp45-50) (SLM April 1959 pp16,17). Parishes, townships and extra-parochial liberties in the **East Division** were: Acton Trussell, Baswich or Berkswich, Bednall, Brewood, Brocton, Cannock, Castle Church, Cheslyn Hay (extra-parochial), Coppenhall, Dunston, Essington, Featherstone (township in Wolverhampton parish), Great Wyrley, Hatherton (township in Wolverhampton parish), Hilton (township in Wolverhampton parish), Huntington, Kinvaston (township in Wolverhampton parish), Penkridge, Rugeley, Saredon, Shareshill, Teddesley Hay (extra-parochial) (W p438) (S&W p381). In the **West Division** were: Blymhill, Bradley, Church Eaton, Forton, Gnosall, Haughton, Lapley, Norbury, Sheriff Hales (the Staffs part of), Stretton, Weston-under-Lizard (W p438) (S&W p381).

Cuttlestone Bridge Bridge at an ancient crossing over the Penk 1.5m ESE of Whiston or 0.5m SW of Penkridge. It has appeared as Pons de Cuthulueston (1225-59), Cothelstonebrugge (1307) and Cuddlestone Bridge (Yates' map). It carried the ancient thoroughfare called King Street (see), and appears to have been situated near a place called Cuttlestone (see) (DUIGNAN p48) (NSFCT 1908 p119). The present bridge is mainly of late C17 to early C18 origin; it has subsequently been widened. At the E end is a cast iron notice for owners, drivers of locomotive traction engines warning them not to cross the bridge for it is not strong enough to carry such vehicles (NSJFS 1967 p48).

D

Dab Green Minute hamlet under 1m NW of Whitmore.

Dacey's Hill To W of Bromley, Kingswinford (TB March 1983 p34 see map). At SO 902882.

Dadnal Hill Partly in Pattingham and Tettenhall ancient parishes, to the E of Nurton. It may have had its origins in the place called The Hill, mentioned in 1392, which was a settlement by 1428. The name Dadnal Hill was in use by the mid C17 (VCH vol 20 pp11,173) and has appeared as Dadenhill. It appears as a small hamlet on the maps of Yates and Smith but not on current maps.

Daffodil Dell A dell formed by part of Sweltenham Brook near Newcastle-under-Lyme, there is a mill nearby and a small stone from Appian's Way, Italy, reputed to be the original stone from which St Paul preached his sermons (STM June 1971 p23p).

Daffodil Farm House and estate at Wood End, 1.75m E of Walsall. In the foreign of Walsall. Stood S of Sutton Road near the present Fallowfield Road. The estate centring on this farm seems to have belonged to the Hurst family in the C14. By the mid C16 the house was moated, and by 1816 it was known as Daffodilly House; it was known as Daffydowndilly House in 1843, and as Daffodil Farm from c1900. The estate was broken up from 1957. The house had been rebuilt by 1885 and demolished by 1959 (VCH vol 17 p175) (SSAHST 1982-3 p50).

Dagdale Small hamlet on the E side of Dagdale Brook 0.5m NW of Bramshall. In Bramshall parish. The name is from perhaps the Irish Dagda, the good god. Nearby is Nobut - holy grave (NSFCT 1908 p145). There was a rail accident at Dagdale in the 1960s when a tractor crossing the line in fog was hit by a train and a farmer and his young daughter were killed (TRTC p116).

Dagdale Brook Runs from Dagdale N of Bramshall to join Picknal Brook at Loxley to the Dove.

Dager House House formerly situated at the junction of Dagger Lane and Salter's Lane, Mayers Green, West Bromwich. Is recorded by 1667 when it was owned by William Turton of the Oak House. It was still owned by the Turtons of the Oak House in 1725, but had become a part of the estate of Lord Dartmouth of Sandwell Hall (see) by 1845. In the C19 it was occupied by the Hall family. It was demolished in 1894-95 (VCH vol 17 pp4,21) (TB Nov 1997 p15). Has also appeared as Dagger Hall (TB Nov 1997 p15).

Dairyfields Area of superior housing to the W of A34, S of Whitmore Road, directly N of Trentham, built on a part of the Trentham Hall estate which had been sold in 1919. Some of the housing here dates from the 1920s (TTH p127); the name is probably from the Dairy Fields of Trentham Hall and the Sutherland's Dairy House which stood in this area.

Dairy House 1m SSW of Hales (Drayton-in-Hales) (1834 OS map).

Dairy House House 0.75m NNW of Horton, in Horton ancient parish. Dairy House Farm was built in the earlier C17 and was so called by 1645 (LGS p151) (VCH vol 7 pp67,72). A fine Stuart farmhouse of red stone, it was a dairy farm to Horton Hall, and outbuildings which once connected the two have long been pulled down (NSFCT 1885 p55).

Dairy House Farm 2m WNW of Church Leigh. A prehistoric axehead implement was found in fields to the E of the house at the W side of a peculiar rounded eminence in c1895 (NSFCT 1905 p141). The earthworks near Dairy House Farm form an excellent specimen of a double moat with a third ditch on one of its sides. C Lynam said that the late Dean Lane considered it a Roman camp - but Lynam thought a Roman camp could not have fitted within the square although it might have been a station where a few men were quartered (NSFCT 1913 p198). (NSSG p17).

Daisy Bank SE of Calton (1834 OS map).

Daisy Bank House at Cheadle (JSD p203p).

Daisy Bank Former hamlet SE of Ladymoor, Coseley (BCM April 1981 p17). In Sedgley ancient parish. It was a district of Coseley by 1832 (HC p63). Had a railway station (BOP p116 p). Richard Hale of Sedgley murdered his illegitimate daughter, Eliza Silleto, aged 6, on July 20 1864 in a cornfield in the vicinity of Daisy Bank. He was hung on Dec 26 1864. Cecila Baker was thought to be his accomplice (CCSHO pp21-30) (TB July 1993 p19).

Daisy Bank Tiny area of Longton, E of Edensor, centred on Spring Garden Road. A pottery works established here in the late 1770s. Some houses were built here by 1820 (VCH vol 8 pp227,240). Rupert Simms (1853-1937), author of BS, lost his left arm and right hand in perforating machinery at Daisy Bank Brickworks as a young man (SH p152). The dismembered parts of his body were buried by the wall of Longton church (SHST p446).

Daisy Bank House 1.75m SSE of Marchington Woodlands. Appears as Daisey Bank on 1834 OS map.

Daisy Bank At the crossroads linking the Mayfields (1834 OS map). This area has since become known as Mayfield and has grown to be the largest hamlet in Mayfield (OS map 1:25,000).

Daisy Bank Area of extreme E Walsall, S of the Sutton Road. The church, St Martin, Sutton Road, was built in 1960 (LDD). This area appears as Daffodilly on OS map 1834.

Daisy Lake Bloreheath, 1m NNW of Hales. A pool recorded from 1669 and probably dates from the C17. It lies on Wemberton or Hempmill Brook (SHC 1945/6 pp7-8). A house was built here by Stafford Huntbach using stone from the part of Maer Hall demolished in the 1960s or 1970s (local info).

Dale Small area 0.5m E of Warslow in Warslow and Elkstones township in Alstonefield ancient parish. Dale tollgate, in existence by 1781, stood at the junction of the old road to Hulme End and the road to Ecton (VCH vol 7 p58). The name is preserved in Dale Cottage and Dale Bridge over the Manifold.

Dale, The Deserted? (OS Street Atlas: Staffs. 1995) hamlet in a narrow isolated dale 1.5m ESE of Cauldon, 2m NW of Stanton. Has appeared as Pantons-in-the-Dale (1682-1801) (maps of Plot, Morden, Bowen, Smith), Pontons of the Dale (Yates map; showing two properties here), The Dale (Dower's map) and Stanton Dale. The Panton family were Barons of Wem, Shrops in the C13 (SHC 1910 p417); they may have given their name to this area. There are several slightly raised platforms of regular shape in the ground by the convergence of several lanes lined with crumbling stone walls (now trackways) (visit in April 2000). To the SE is a rock outcrop known as Dale Tor, appearing as Torr Dale in 1631 (SASR 1995 no 5 p38). Further to the SE was Stanton tollhouse at SK 109477 on the Stoke-Ashbourne turnpike road. The building was called Y-Bwthyn by 1976. Although dated '1845' on the E gable, its site was not conveyed to the trustees until 1847 (IAS p189).

Dale, The House 1m NNW of Statfold. Appears on the 1834 OS map and Dower's map.

Dale Abbey Farm The Dale. Here are two burial mounds. One at SK 10724812 is 16 paces in diameter and 1.5 feet high another excavated by Carrington in 1848 at SK 10774808 is 15 paces in diameter. Two skeletons laid head to foot were found. Skull fragments suggest a third burial (TYD p125) (VCH vol 1 no 11) (NSJFS 1965 p47). Both mounds are listed monuments.

Dale Common Common land in Haughton parish, 0.75m NE of Haughton. Has also appeared as The Dale (1725) (SPNO p165), and Haughtondale (OSST 1956-59 p12).

Dale End Small street in two halves in Darlaston (Offlow hundred) to the E of St Lawrence Way. The area was formerly known as Dale End, which comprised a triangular area containing the brewery and malthouse of the former Bell Inn and a row of small houses. The name fell from use, but by the later C20 had been revived. Timmins thinks that Dale End may be the original area of settlement of Darlaston (SNDB pp41,43).

Dalehall Middleport, Burslem. Formerly in Burslem chapelry in Stoke-upon-Trent ancient parish. (SHST p129). The Dale Hall estate formed a part of the Overhouse estate which belonged to the Burslem family by the end of the C16 (NSSG p9) (SHJ winter 1987 pp25-26). The house, Dale Hall, was still occupied in c1880 (photograph in the Warrillow Collection, Keele University). The site is thought to be in the built-up area SE of St Paul's churchyard (VCH vol 8 p120). Spencer Rogers had a pottery here and later in the same building James Edwards had a pottery (OTP p95 il). The church, St Paul, Church Square, built in 1828-1831 as a chapel of ease to St John's Burslem, was due to be demolished in 1974 (VCH vol 8 p123) (BOE p254) (OTP p76).

Dale House 0.75m SSE of Bagnall. Occurs on 1834 OS map and Dower's map.

Dale House Willenhall. Built in the mid C18. Thought to have been the seat of the Hincks family (WMAG Sept 1968 p27p).

Dalesgap NE of Barrowhill in Rocester ancient parish. For Roman coins and pottery found near Dalesgap in 1872 see under Barrowhill.

Dales Green Hamlet 0.75m SW of Mow Cop. In Wolstanton ancient parish. There is a well at 12 East View, and another at 25 Dales Green, Rookery, from which rises a tributary of the Weaver? (WMC).

Dallow Tiny area of Burton upon Trent. There is a Dallow lock on Trent & Mersey Canal. Nearby Dallow Bridge takes Dallow Street over the old LNWR line, by which stood in 1900 Dallow Chemical Works (OS map 1900 Burton (North)).

Dame Oliver's Infant School School kept by Anne Oliver, wife of Peter Oliver, on the corner of Quonian's Lane and Dam Street, Lichfield. Here Dr Samuel Johnson (b1709) of Lichfield (see) was taught to read and write as a young boy (CL Oct 3 1957 p662) (VB p16) (LAL p pp38,49,51). The only anecdote concerning Johnson here is, one day on his way home from the school Dame Oliver went out to keep a protective eye on the visually disabled boy. Sensing he was being followed Johnson turned and attacked her. Johnson had left the school by 1716 to be taught by Tom Brown. He remained deeply touched throughout his life by a visit from Dame Oliver shortly before he left for Oxford. She brought him gingerbread and told him that he was the best scholar she had ever had (Young Samuel Johnson. James L Clifford. 1955 1962 ed. pp23,42,107). The cottage which was pointed out as Dame Oliver's in c1800 was, in the mid 1980s, a structure of the early C19 incorporating parts of an earlier timber-framed structure (VCH vol 14 p171).

Dame Paulet's Almshouse Formerly stood in Bank Square, on the W side of the Market Place, Burton upon Trent. In 1593 Dame Elizabeth Pawlett (or Paulet) endowed an almshouse for five poor women. By at least the mid 1990s the almshouse had been demolished except for the door arch which has been built into the present wall of Littlewood's Store. The inscription on the door arch is erroneous. The first two letter of Anno Domini having worn off, a local mason, not knowing Latin, engraved it symmetrically as NO DOMI NI (SHOS vol 1 pp12,16) (ABTOP p18p).

Damgate 1m N of Ilam. In Ilam parish. The burial mound 260 metres N of Damgate at SK 12805367 (EW 16 paces and NS 11 paces in diameter and 2.5 feet high) was excavated by Carrington in 1850 (TYD p174) (NSJFS 1965 p41). It is a listed monument. Carrington excavated two others to the N of this at SK 12855380 (20 paces in diameter and three feet high) and at SK 12835385 (21 paces in diameter and three feet high) in 1850 but found nothing (TYD pp173,174) (NSJFS 1965 pp41,42). Both are listed monuments. Has also appeared as Dam Gate (Smith's map).

Dam Mill Small district 1.75m SE of the church at Codsall. In Codsall parish. Takes its name from a mill on the Penk originally owned by the dean of Wolverhampton, and in existence by 1341. The area remained inhabited after the mill was first demolished in the C17 (VCH vol 20 pp77,79,85).

Dams, The 0.75m WNW of Caverswall. Here is a burial mound at SJ 941431. It was described in 1983 as somewhat dilapidated and 10 feet high (NSFCT 1983 p12).

Damslane C17 house 0.25m NNW of Gratton hamlet, in Horton ancient parish (VCH vol 7 p65). May be from the land called Damsgate, mentioned in 1445: Damsgate suggests the presence of a deer enclosure (VCH vol 7 p72).

Dam Street Street running SW from Lichfield cathedral Close between Minster Pool and Stowe Pool. William de Lichfield Knt had houses in this street. George Stanley held the corner house in Quonian's Lane (HOL p503). Parliamentary leader, Lord Brooke, was shot dead in front of Brook House in the Civil War. Dame Oliver's school, attended by the young Dr Johnson of

Lichfield (see), was in this street (LAL p49). (W p488) (SOSH p198- in Civil War) (COS p46p).

Dane, River Rises on Featherbed Moss, a desolate stretch of Axe Edge Moor, Derbys at SK 029705, near the source of the river Goyt (DPMM p73). After one mile it forms the Ches Derbys border. (Bowen's map and maps prior to it suggest the Staffs border followed the Dane to its head, almost). The Ches Derbys Staffs borders converge at it, at Three Shire Heads, 1.5m further down stream. It continues to form the Ches Staffs border for the next 12m until it runs into Cheshire one mile N of The Cloud. After much meandering it joins the Weaver at Northwich. (GNHS p23) (BALH p16). Has appeared as Davene (C13), Daven (1343), Daan (1416), and Dane (c1540. 1577) (SPNO p8). The name is from 'deann' of Celtic origin meaning impetuous, swift (DUIGNAN). Ekwall compares it with Welsh 'a drop,' dafn, suggesting a slow, trickling stream (RN p112) (SPN p39). This is not at all comparable with the river, thinks Oakden, unless it was used in a figurative sense or even ironic sense, which was unlikely (SPNO p8). Some have said it is from Dana or Anu the earth mother goddess of the Celts (DP pp47-48) (DPMM p73) (UHAW p75). The Dane represents the root 'don' probably the Goidelic 'tain' water (NSFCT 1908 p126). Or a shortened form of 'daven.' Perhaps 'daven' contains a primitive river or water name 'aven' with a Celtic locative dative preposition 'di.' 'Avon' is a Celtic word meaning 'river' (NSFCT 1932 p51). Fish Ladder Falls is a weir in the Dane Valley at or near Swythamley (PS p142p). Devil's Elbow is a picturesque spot in the Dane Valley (ES Aug 2 1930 p4p).

Danebridge Hamlet in the steep-sided valley of Dane (MIDD vol 4 p24), on the S side, 1.75m NE of Heaton. Formerly partly in Heaton township in Leek ancient parish and partly in Prestbury (Ches) parish. The hamlet grew up in the C18 on account of a corn and later cotton mill at a medieval river crossing (VCH vol 7 pp187,190). The crossing was known as Scliderford (meaning 'slippery ford') in c1190. It was bridged by 1357. In 1545 the bridge here was known as Sliderford Bridge. The single-arched bridge of 1632, replaced a newly-built bridge which was washed away by a flood in 1631. Described as picturesque, but very narrow, the 1632 bridge was replaced by the present bridge in 1869 (NSFCT 1931 p184) (VCH vol 7 p187) (PRT p57).

Dane Brook Passes S of Miles Green, through Mill Dale, S of Crewe enters the Weaver at Rookery Hall. Its upper reaches are called Win Brook (NSFCT 1919 p22).

Danes Court House 0.75m WNW of Tettenhall. Gothic-style villa with a four-storey tower built by Edward Perry, a Wolverhampton japanner, in 1864. It was owned by an ironmaster and then by an industrialist in the early part of the C20. In 1941 it was occupied by troops and then by the territorial army. It was demolished in 1958 (TCOP p34p) (VCH vol 20 p8). To the NW is a modern cemetery (Birmingham A-Z). The name may allude to the battle of Tettenhall in c910 (St Michael and All Angels, Penkridge: Royal Collegiate Parish Church. R Cheadle p3).

Danescourt Farm Stockwell Road, Tettenhall. Has a datestone with the date '1520,' but it was considerably altered in the C19 (Tettenhall Village Trail. History Dept, Regis School, Tettenhall).

Dank's Branch of the Walsall Canal. Spurs off the Walsall Canal at Great Bridge and joins the Tame Valley Canal at Golds Hill (BCM autumn 1995 p19). It was built, apparently under the Act of 1783. Abandoned in stages between 1954 and 1960 (VCH vol 17 p14).

Dapple Heath Small hamlet NE of Newton. In Blithbury parish.

Darby Hill House Darby's Hill. Occupied in 1851 by William Bennett (W p19).

Darby's Hill Hill in the Rowley Regis range 1.25m ESE of Dudley. In Rowley Regis parish. The view from the top includes the Post Office tower at Pye Green on Cannock Chase and Barr Beacon, both to the N and NE. Has also appeared as Derby Hill (1834 OS map). The hill was owned by the Darby family (TB Feb 1975 p14).

Darfur Bridge Bridge over the Manifold? Or under the old Manifold Valley Railway track? S of Wettonmill. 'Darfur' is perhaps a corruption of 'deerfold' (NSFCT 1894 p156).

Darfur Crags Rock feature in Manifold Valley presumably near Darfur Bridge. Is 615 feet high. Behind Darfur Crags is Redhurst Gorge and Redhurst Cave (see), once occupied by Old Anna (WTCEM p94). The Manifold sinks into its subterranean course at Drafur Crags (KES p3) (LGS p185) (SGS p111). Has also appeared as Darfur Bridge Rock (WTCEM p94).

Dark Cavern Former limestone quarry under Castle Hill, adjoining and on the S side of Dudley Tunnel. The canal leading to the quarry was roofed-over in 1797 to stop rocks falling into it. The huge groined vault soon became known locally as 'Cathedral Arch' and is an early example of 'cut and cover' method of tunnelling. The cavern was used as a ballroom and was lit by gas. Access was by way of the '144 Steps.' Little Tess Cavern was an off-shoot of Dark Cavern. They were linked by a new canal tunnel to Dudley Tunnel in 1989.

That year a former rock tunnel was re-opened to the adjacent Singing Cavern. The caverns are now a tourist attraction for boat parties from the Black Country Museum at Tipton (Dudley Canal Tunnel leaflet) (VB p45).

Darkhouse Lane Former hamlet in the C19 situated along Darkhouse Lane, 0.25m NW Coseley. In Sedgley ancient parish. A community of Baptists from Brettel Lane came to Coseley in c1776 and used a farmhouse for their meetings. The house had a large number of trees surrounding it which obscured the light from reaching the interior. It had become known as the Darkhouse by 1783 (AMS p364) (HC p60). (BCM Oct 1990 p61).

Dark Lane and Darkhouse Farm. 1m SW of Longdon.

Dark Pool Small pool NE of Clent marked on 1:25,000 OS map. It is one of four shown.

Darlaston (locally *Darlas'on* UBCB p219). Black Country town on the South Staffs plateau between two major headstreams of the Tame, 16.5m SSE of Stafford, in Offlow hundred.
EARLY. A fossil tree 50 feet long in a prostrate position has been found at Darlaston (AMS p11).
900 to 1500. Darlaston has often been confounded with Darlaston in Stone parish (HODW p1) so that it is sometimes wrongly considered the Darlaston that appears in 956 (SL p61 see index) and the Darlaston which appears in DB (MR p121). Hackwood could find no certain reference to this Darlaston in documents of the C12 and early C13 (HODW pp15-18). An early form is Deorlavestun (SPN p41). The **name** is perhaps of Anglo-Saxon origin and means 'Deorlaf's town' (SOB p9), as in Darlaston in Stone parish (DUIGNAN) (SOSH p76) (SPN p40). Smallshire says it takes its name from Deorlaf, bishop of Hereford in the late C9 (WFW p18). It could be that the lord of the manor of the Stone Darlaston held land here and named it after his manor (SHOS vol 2) (HODW), but this is unlikely (BCM Oct 1982 p23) (Darlaston Community History Project. 1984. p2. Copy in Willenhall library). The two places have a link in St George. Black Country Darlaston's parish church is dedicated to St George. Stone Darlaston has a pub with the sign of St George (RHPS p21). Darlaston may mean the 'place by the greywater' (WMVB p53). Darlaston appears to have formed a separate manor by some time in the C12 (SNDB p30), with the lord owing suit and service to Sedgley court leet, incidentally in Seisdon hundred (WAM p98), despite Darlaston lying in Offlow hundred. However, Erdeswick found no mention of the manor before Henry III's reign (SOS p412) (SHOS vol 2 p89). The manor house is said to have been near the present Campbell Place (WDY p18). Darlaston is said to have been a township and ancient parish (GLAUE p409). Originally it appears to have been a chapel of Sedgley ancient parish (SHOS) (WMVB p53) (Darlaston Community History Project. 1984. p5. Copy in Willenhall library) (SNDB p30). **Church**. A chapel may have preceded one said to have been built at Darlaston in the C12; there was a priest at Darlaston by 1310. The present parish church, St Lawrence, on the corner of Church and New Streets, which was built in 1871-1872, may stand on the site of the medieval church (HODW p55) (LDD) (BOE p296) (SNDB p30). Darlaston held its **wake** on St Lawrence's day (Aug 10) (SCSF p106). There is a ballad entitled 'Darlaston Wake Bull-baiting' (Broughton's Scrapbook appendix p10). Bull baiting charges occasioned riots in Darlaston on Aug 28 1815 and Sept 21 1815 (LOU p239). There was a **pinfold** in Pinfold Street (SNDB p78). A contingent from Darlaston seems to have fought for Henry VI at the battle of Northampton (1460) under the leadership of Humphrey Earl of Stafford (SOSH p317).
1500 to PRESENT. The bells of Darlaston church were rung in the C18 and C19 on May 29 to celebrate Restoration Day (1660) (SCSF p20) (FOS p99). Tobacco pipe clay could be found at Darlaston (NHS p121). In the C18 Darlaston's chief industries were the production of locks for guns (MR p121); since 1805 it has been nuts and bolts. There was a **windmill**, at approximately SO 974969, 0.5m W of the church. It was probably built after 1775 and by 1818. It was for sale in 1795 and disused by 1886. It is not shown on maps after 1902 (WBJ p20). The mill house was still in Dorsett Road in 1979 (WIS p24). There was a **workhouse** in Pardoes Lane (WDY p21p) (SNDB p76p). **Methodism**. There was an anti-Methodist riot at Darlaston in early 1742 (LOU p114). John Wesley visited Darlaston on April 2 1751. After this occasion or another he called the place 'the lion's den' after his poor reception here (SA Jan 17 1885 p6) (BCM July 1980 pp32-35) (SNDB p15). At Easter 1762 a Methodist preaching house called the New Room was erected in Bilston Street (known as Meeting Street in the later C18). As far as it is known this was the first purpose-built Methodist meeting place in the Black Country, although meetings had been held in private houses since 1742. The meeting house, later known as the Old Stone House, became a school room and later a private dwelling until being demolished in a slum clearance programme in 1958; in 1981 the site, near Bilston Street Clinic, was part of St Lawrence's Way (WDY p22p of the house in c1880) (SNDB pp15-16). The

cholera epidemic of 1832 reached Darlaston parish on Aug 13 and claimed 68 lives in the parish (TB May 1978 pp20-21. Feb 1998 p17). White described Darlaston in the mid C19 as 'one of the largest villages in Staffordshire' (W p598). All Saints' church, Walsall Road, built in 1872 as a memorial to Samuel Mills by his widow and children, was demolished by a German bomb in a raid on July 31 1942; the bomb made a crater in the ground 50 feet deep and 40 feet across. A new church dedicated to All Saints opened in 1952 (SNDB pp6p,7p) and or in 1962 in Walsall Road (LDD). Darlaston was linked to the railway system from Sept 14 1863 (WAM p112) (SSR p25). **Newspapers**. The Darlaston Weekly Times, Fallings Heath and Kings Hill Advertiser was founded on March 25 1882 and ran until at least July 29 1887 (SHJ spring 1996 p17-18). The Darlaston Herald, a Darlaston edition of the Wednesbury Herald, was founded in 1891 (TEBC2 p133). The Darlaston Leader was first published in 1897 (TEBC). Many Wednesbury (see) papers had Darlaston in their title. Darlaston is Dulston in Francis Brett Young's novels (BCM April 1980 pp10-15). Darlaston urban district, created in the 1880s, was abolished in 1966. The area was then taken into Walsall county borough (GLAUE p409). The device of the district consisted of a shield bearing a bend between two Stafford Knots, and on the bend a lion passant guardant (CH p340). The Bullstake (see) area which lay partly in Darlaston and Wednesbury ancient parishes was then taken into Walsall County Borough and now forms Darlaston's town centre (SNDB p22). **Folklore**. The story of how a pocket watch dropped by a traveller in a field near Darlaston frightened the local people - for they did not known what it was - has been passed down in Darlaston folklore. Those that heard the watch ticking thought it was a demon grasshopper and that judgment day had come (FTWM pp116-120). The ghost of a young girl with long blonde hair, dressed in a white, flowing dress is said to haunt the area close to the entrance of the old Rubery Owen factory in Owen Road (GPCE p27). 'Darlaston Geese' was the nickname for those who tried to remove the weathercock off the church steeple (APB p50) (AOW pp104-105). For a rhyme about Darlaston see Walsall. For Darlaston as a verb see BCM April 1971 p27. **Persons**. **Thomas Oliver**, a Darlaston man, invented the first machine for forging nuts and bolts (Staffs County Handbook c1958 p56). **John Duffield** of Darlaston, coiner and counterfeiter, was executed at Stafford on Aug 21 1819 (TB Feb 1981 p5). **Thomas Rubery**, manufacturer of chains for stage coaches in Darlaston, was killed in an accident on Feb 1 1833 on a railway trip on one of the first lines to be opened between Manchester and Liverpool. He is buried in Cheetham Hill Cemetery, Manchester (BCM April 1974 p9). Rev **George Fisk** (d1872), poet, was rector of Darlaston between 1835 and 1837, and then vicar of Walsall. From 1843 he was a prebendary of Lichfield cathedral (VFC p49). Mrs **Henry Wood**, novelist, wrote some of 'East Lynne' (1861) at Darlaston whilst staying with relatives at Poplar House (see). Lord **Harmer-Nicholls**, former MP for Peterborough, father of Sue Nicholls, the actress (born in Walsall), was born in Darlaston on Nov 1 1912. From 1955 Harmer Nicholls resided at Abbeylands (see). He returned to the town in July 1971 to open St Lawrence Way, and was created a life peer in 1974 (MR p368p) (BCM Dec 1997 pp10-12) (MIDD vol 2 p21p) (SNDB p85). **Alan Cash** (1916-1989) crossword compiler, was born in Darlaston (BCM Oct 1990 p72).

Darlaston Small fragmented hamlet on a bank by the Trent, approximately 1m W of Stone, in Pirehill hundred. Former township in Beech quarter in Stone ancient parish. A prehistoric antler-pick was found in the Trent in Aug 1959 as an additional bridge was being built for the A34 (NSFCT 1959 p86) (SIS p2 il). Darlaston is the Deorlavestun mentioned in a charter of 956 (SHC 1916 pp96-97) (SSE 1991 p8). It was identified by Dugdale, Shaw, Kemble and Duignan as the Deorlafestun mentioned in the will of Wulfric Spot (c1002), founder of Burton Abbey (SHC 1916 p35) (SSE 1996 p13). The manor of Derlavestone appears in DB as a possession of Burton Abbey. The name is of Anglo-Saxon origin and means 'Deorlaf's town' (DUIGNAN) (SOSH p76) (SSE 1996 p13). Or 'Deorlaf's estate' (NSJFS 1981 p2). Smallshire says it takes its name from Deorlaf, bishop of Hereford in the late C9 (WFW p18). In Edward I's reign spelt 'Dereleston.' This could be a corruption of 'De La Eston.' It could have belonged to an East Town. It was the property of Burton Abbey, away to the E (RHPS p21). Hackwood shows instances where this Darlaston has been confounded with Darlaston in Offlow hundred (HODW p2). London-Chester-Holyhead road continued N to Newcastle at Darlaston until the 1570s after which it swung W to take a route via Woore and Nantwich (VCH vol 2 p277). The bridge at Darlaston was only a horse bridge until 1663 (SHC 1934 p23) (VCH vol 2 p279). The first Turnpike Act in North Staffs passed in 1714 was for the route between Darlaston and Talke on the London-Carlisle road (IANS p16). There was a turnpike at SJ 885355 (IANS p19). The compact little hamlet at the foot of Bury Bank, formerly called Darlaston (1834 OS map), was called Meaford by 1963 (1963 OS map 1 inch).

Darlaston Brook Formed the boundary between the Darlaston ancient parish and Willenhall township. Appears to have been incorporated into Walsall Canal (SNDB pp16-17).

Darlaston Grange House 1.25m W of Stone.

Darlaston Green District 0.5m NNE of central Darlaston (Offlow hundred). Common land from which 'Green' is derived embraced a large area, nearly as far as Willenhall township boundary (SNDB pp55-56). The area has also appeared as The Green and on the 1834 OS map it is split into Lower Green (north) and Upper Green (south). There was a Darlaston Green Colliery to the N. At the Green, according to tradition, the controversial Rev Moreton would baptise a child in the pool here, if importuned to do so, when passing through (WAM p123). The church, St George, E of Bush Street, was built in 1852 and demolished in March 1975 (BOE p297) (SNDB pp84,85). A poem has been written alleging that The vicarage at Darlaston Green was haunted by a former vicar according to a poem (TB March 1998 p9). In March 1869 the 'Darlaston Ripper' raped Ann Proctor, aged 27, and Sarah Mullet, and murdered Elizabeth Bowen, all of Darlaston Green. The assailant in all cases was never found (TB May 1978 p17). There is a statue at the N end of The Green of St George, titled St George and The Dragon sculpted by Thomas Wright in 1958 (SGS frontispiece) or in 1959 (BOE p297).

Darlaston Green Former tiny hamlet on W side of the Trent at Stone. Appears on Yates' map at the present site of the junction of Yarnfield Lane with the A34 and where the Walton Inn (formerly The Filley Brooks, then (prior to 1997) The Wayfayer Inn) stands (SIS p72 see map).

Darlaston Hall Stood to the W of the Trent, between Filleybrooks and Darlaston, Stone (SSBOP p75p). The hall could be reached by a long drive from the lodge at Yarnfield Lane behind the Wayfarer Hotel (later Walton Inn) (MOSP p17) or by a shorter route from Darlaston. The poet, Richard Barnfield, baptised in Norbury (see) church, lived at the old hall from 1599, and died at the hall in 1627; his will is dated Feb 27 1627 (NSFCT 1888 p65) (RHPS pp155-158) (SIS pp38,118il) - this would doubtless be an earlier hall to the one depicted in Cope, and Clough and Bowers. Darlaston Hall was the seat of the Colliers, lords of Stone manor, in the C17. The estate was taken from them in the Civil War by order of a parliamentary commission in Stafford in 1643 (SIS p42). In 1653 (RHPS p128) or in 1655 it was sold to William Jervis, a member of the Jervis family of Meaford Hall (see). The estate remained in the Jervis family until they sold it to James Meakin, a pottery manufacturer in 1880; he or his descendants were still the owners in 1910. In 1924 the estate was sold and the hall was subsequently demolished and a superior bungalow built on the site (SSBOP p75) (SDOPP p60p of the hall in 1910), known as Springfields, occupied by Miss Ethel Parker-Jervis (formerly of Meaford Hall (see)) and Mrs Meakin (info Michael Cockin). Mrs James Meakin was of the Flat, Darlaston Hall in 1948, but had moved to Lea Hall, Eccleshall, by 1951 (SHC 1947. 1950/1 List of Members). (RHPS il. No. 18, p155).

Darlaston House Stood near the post office in Rectory Avenue, Darlaston (Offlow hundred). The dovecote or columbarium and stables remained after the main house was demolished in c1900 (Darlaston Community History Project. 1984. p9. Copy in Willenhall library) (SNDB p83).

Darlaston Manor House Darlaston (Offlow hundred). Seat of the de Darlastons, lords of Darlaston to 1434. Its site has never been located, but it may have stood near the present Campbell Place, perhaps where the United Methodist church stood until it was demolished in 1984 (Darlaston Community History Project. 1984. p9. Copy in Willenhall library) (SNDB p54).

Darley Oaks House 2.5m NNE of Yoxall.

Darleyshire Minute hamlet or area (ES Nov 9 1999 p16) 0.5m SSW of Wetley Rocks. The name is from the medieval Darley -said to be a clearing where deer graze (ES Nov 9 1999 p16).

Darling, The A river which flows by Great Bridgeford and joins the Sow just above Broad Eye Bridge (SKYT p102) in Doxey Marshes (WSS p113). The name was presumably a pet-name for a favourite stream (SPNO p8).

Darnelhursts Field name in Shenstone parish (SHOS vol 2 p46). Has also appeared as Durnhursts.

Darnford Tiny hamlet on low ground by a tributary of Fisherwick Brook 1.5m W of Whittington. In Streethay out-township of St Michael's parish, Lichfield. The name means 'the hidden or secret ford,' in contrast to the ford of Freeford that was open or accessible, further up stream (VCH vol 14 pp253,275-276). It appears to be a later spelling of Dornford, a place on the route of the beating of bounds around Lichfield (SHOS vol 1). It may also have been written Durnford (see James Bell, the younger BS p52). And some appear to have confused Darnford with the Lichfield cathedral prebend Dernford (Warws) (SHOS vol 1 p291) (W p517).

Dartmouth Branch of the Birmingham Canal. Ran from the Ridgacre Branch

of the Wednesbury Branch of the Birmingham Canal at Hateley Heath, terminated at Hall Green. Opened 1828. Largely abandoned in 1947 (VCH vol 2 p297 see map. vol 17 p14). The course of the canal has been lost.

Dartmouth Park Sandwell. Leased to the borough by Earl of Dartmouth in 1877. In 1919 he presented the freehold to West Bromwich in recognition of its men killed in WW1 (SHWB 13) (VCH vol 17 p5). Named after the Earl of Dartmouth whose residence was at Sandwell Hall (see).

Darwin's Bath and Darwin's Garden. A rectangular bath house built over a spring called Unite's Well situated in a hollow at the head of a stream at SK 096099, N of Maple Hayes, S of Abnalls Lane, by Home Farm, Maple Hayes. The spring was first brought to the public's attention by Sir John Floyer in Charles II's reign as a fine spot for cold bathing. He called it Unite Well (see) (HOL pp562-563) (NSFCT 1934 pp74-75) and built a bath house here with two baths in c1700. A surviving bath (VCH vol 14 pl 42 shows the bath house in 1770) was bought by Dr Erasmus Darwin (1731-1802) and his son, Erasmus Darwin, in 1780 (or 1779) from Sir Thomas Weld of Lulworth Castle, Dorset, lord of Pipe manor. Harwood says Darwin bought the land in 1777 and started to erect his garden by it (HOL pp562-563). The garden, about 7.5 acres in extent, was noted by poetess Anna Seward (VCH vol 14 p202), and Stebbing Shaw (SHOS vol 1 p347). Darwin left Lichfield in 1781, and William Jackson, a fellow member of the Lichfield Botanical Society then looked after the garden until his death in 1798. Darwin's daughter-in-law conveyed the lease to John Atkinson in 1804. The site was for sale in 1823 (VCH vol 14 pp202-203). In 1890 the bath house was restored, using the original materials, by Albert Octavius Worthington (info from the plaque erected by the bathhouse). In the mid 1980s there was evidence of terraces and low banks, perhaps the remains of former garden features (VCH vol 14 p203). (SHOSA vol 2 p9) (CCBO p124) (VCH vol 14 p107) (TB Oct 1993 p22).

Darwin's House Georgian house in Beacon Street, Lichfield (CCHCA p33). In 1758 Erasmus Darwin (1731-1802), see under Lichfield, physician and botanist, converted a timber-framed house on the W side of the lower courtyard of Lichfield cathedral Close into the present large brick house with a front facing Beacon Street and its S side is close to the corner of The Close lane (VCH vol 14 pp43,64 pl 20 in probably c1800). He occupied the house between 1756 to 1781 (plaque on house) or to 1780 (BOE pp192-193) (LAL p22) (TB Oct 1993 p22p). The house was being restored in 1998 to be used as an exhibition and education centre for the work of Erasmus Darwin (Friends of Lichfield Cathedral 1998 pp47-49).

David's Rock Tinker's Borough Cave at Salt is in it.

Daw End District above Ford Brook 0.75m NNE of Rushall church. In Rushall ancient parish. The limestone foundations of the bath-house at Letocetum (see) may have been quarried at Daw End (VCH vol 2 pp189,192-193. vol 14 pl 55). Duignan found no forms of Daw End earlier than the C17. The name is perhaps from 'David's End.' Daw was a pet form of 'David' in medieval times (DUIGNAN). Or 'David's place' (ADY p22) (SPN p134). Or is probably from Old English 'dael' or 'denu,' both mean 'valley.' Daw End is more or less at the end of a shallow valley, the broad green lowland followed by the Rushall Canal (BCTV p54).

Daw End Branch of the Rushall Canal. Built in 1800 (SWY p16), opened in c1802 (HCMS No. 2). The Daw End Branch runs from Longwood Junction to the Wyrley and Essington Extension Canal at Catshill Junction.

Dawford Brook From Great Chatwell it joins the Lynn Brook in Shrops. Near Windford Mill (SHOS vol 1 part 1 p106).

Dawley Brook Runs to Wall Heath then to Smestow Brook. Ran through Pensnett Chase (KCPC p12). In Kingswinford ancient parish.

Dayhills Small hamlet 1.25m SE of Hilderstone. In Milwich parish (W p420).

Dead Knave Area or house marked on Yates' map and as 'The dead Knave' on 1834 OS map in the area of the present Long Meadow Drive to the W of Sedgley.

Dead Lads Grave This name applied to an area at the southern corner of Bantock Park, Wolverhampton. It appears on census returns until 1841 and on maps until at least 1919. It is probably the same as the Dead Lad's Grave Piece, a field name or close at Penn, noted by White in the mid C19. The revenue from it provided money for a poor dole (W p191). Perhaps it can be identified with the burial mound Shaw noted in the Penn Fields area (SHOS vol 2 p165).

Deadman's Dale Now submerged under Blithfield Reservoir. Has also appeared as Dimsdale (1834 OS map), a name which persists in the name of a house on the W side of the E arm of the reservoir.

Deadman's Grave Stone at the end of Old Draw Well Lane, between Armshead and Werrington, Wetley Rocks, at SJ 939479. There is a big stone dividing the gardens where someone died and was buried. The name appears in 1689 and 1803 (NSFCT 1924 p187) (WJ p24). According to legend a poor man died and the local inhabitants could not decide which parish to bury him in;

whether he was from Caverswall parish or Cheddleton. Hence he was buried on the boundary - which is marked with a big stone (WYV p32). Here it is said a man was killed. When children inquire as to the identity of the man buried here, they are told it is the grave of the first man who ever lived (WJ p24). The stone is positioned at the meeting point of three parishes - Stoke-upon-Trent, Cheddleton, and Caverswall. It is said to be a corruption of Denman Grave, after a man named Denman who was travelling this way, died and was buried here (NSFCT 1924 p187). (STP p74p of Wetley Moor, Deadman's Grave is mentioned in the caption).

Deadman's Green Hamlet on E side of the Tean 0.5m ESE of Checkley. Formerly in Madeley Holme division in Checkley ancient parish (W p760). Has also appeared as Tetterton Green (Checkley PR) (HOU p348). The field called Naked Fields, at SK 035380 (OS map 1887 6 inch), at Deadman's Green is the supposed site of a battlefield (STM Feb 1965 p41), perhaps where the Danes fought the Saxons (LGS p11). The name Naked Field, according to tradition, is from three bishops slain in the battle who were left naked on the battlefield (NHS p432) (OL vol 2 p22). The three crosses of Saxon or Danish origin in Checkley churchyard are said to commemorate these bishops (COS p29). There may have been a skirmish in the vicinity of Deadman's Green in the Civil War; Oliver Cromwell is said to have watched a battle at Deadman's Green from a tower at Rectory Farm, but there is no proof for this legend, and, according to Jim Foley, the church tower would have been a more suitable site for a view (CJF pp2,81). Totmonslow (see) signifies Deadman's Grave (HOC p4). (COS p29 - Top Naked Field).

Deadman's Heath It lay across the main highway from Wolverhampton to Lichfield in the Foreign of Walsall ancient parish (SOB pp107,118).

Deadman's Lane Birchills, Walsall. Existed by 1545. Renamed Hospital Street in c1872 (VCH vol 17 p159) (BAOH p63). Probably here was the smallpox hospital which Sister Dora of Walsall (see) took charge of in 1875 (TB Oct 1978 p1).

Deadman's Lane Hamlet in Handsworth parish (W p698). Now lost or name changed.

Deadman's Lane A narrow road leading from Barr Common to Aldridge along which all corpses were carried from Great Barr to be buried at the mother church at Aldridge (SHOS vol 2 p100).

Deadman's Lane Perhaps preserves the tradition of the old route to an ancient burying place at Wolstanton (NSFCT 1915 p82). Has also appeared as Does Dead Lane.

Deadman's Walk A track which connected the Brindley Military Hospital with the Commonwealth Cemetery during WW1 (CCM) (Cannock Chase Country Park Notice Board at Cank Thorn) (HSS p27 - a Deadman's Grave. See also Hangman's Oak which has same reasons for existing).

Dead Woman's Burial Lane Name for a tree (HOWW pp184,245) and or lane at Tamebridge. It is mentioned in a deed concerning the upkeep of a bridge at Friars Park (WAM p77) (IE p43). Mentioned in 1606 and is thought to have been the cemetery of the monks of Friars Park, which belonged to Sandwell Priory (HOWW pp184,245).

Deadwoman's Grave Field name in the N corner of the junction of Shutt Green Lane and the track to Birk's Barn Farm, NW of Brewood. The name is possibly from a burial place of a woman vagrant, or 'grave' may be from Old English 'græfe' meaning copse or thicket (BDH 1992 p98).

Deadwoman's Grave A stone slab which rests in the grass verge at the end of Husphins Lane, near Little Harriot's Hayes Farm, Codsall Wood, at SJ 841044. The slab has been in this position for the past 200 years. Supposedly marks the site or grave of a murdered woman whose ghost is supposed to haunt the locality. Near by was a cottage called Dead Woman's Grave (OS map 1834) (VCH vol 20 p79) (TB Feb 1989 pp1p,5). (SVB p58).

Deadwoman's Grave Field name at SJ 863016. NW corner of the cross roads of the Perton-Codsall road with the Wolverhampton-Newport road. Marked on a title deed. There is a tradition that suicides were buried at crossroads (info J Blamire-Brown).

Dean Brook Flows NW of Halmer End. A tributary of the Weaver in Cheshire. The name means 'the small stream in a valley' (SPNO p8).

Deanery, The House of the dean of Lichfield, W of the Bishop's Palace, Lichfield cathedral Close. The medieval deanery was destroyed in the Civil War. The present house which was built on the site of it stands to the W of the Bishop's Palace. William III stayed a night at the 'old' Deanery in June 1690 when Lancelot Addison was dean (HOL p309) (Bell's 'Lichfield Cathedral' p134). It was rebuilt by Dean Binckes in 1707 (GKCLC). The entrance door, originally in the centre of the front, was moved to the E side in 1807-8 (GKCLC). (HOL pp290-291) (VCH vol 3 p189. vol 14 p62 pl 10). In the late 1940s and early 1950s, during the time of Dean FA Iremonger, the Deanery was used as part of Lichfield Cathedral School (info Michael Cockin). Has also appeared

as The Deanery House.

Deanery, The House of the dean of Stafford Collegiate Church. The dean had a residence close to the college by 1295. In 1550 the Crown sold the Deanery with the rest of the deanery estate to Lord Stafford (VCH vol 6 p206). It is said to have fronted St Mary's Square (now Victoria Square) and Earl Street, and in 1817 passed to Stafford corporation (SKYT p96).

Deanery, The House of the dean of Tamworth Collegiate Church. It was situated on the E side of the churchyard NE of the church, in Mould's Yard. Its walls were noted by Shaw (HS p176). Masefield noted only a single wall remained (LGS p230). Only fragments of wall remained in 1970 (DoE II). The vicar's house, stood S of the church, on the site of the present College Lane School (VCH vol 3 pp309-325).

Deanery, The House for the dean of Wolverhampton Collegiate Church. Formerly stood close to St Peter's church, Wolverhampton, on the opposite side of the Horse Fair (TB Aug 1986 p4p), perhaps on the site of earlier Wolverhampton deaneries which may date back to the C12 (OHW pl1) (SHOS vol 2 p162). The deanery was rebuilt in 1655 (WF p12). Or built of brick in 1684 (LGS p259). Built by Richard Best, first a stationer in London, and after a farmer of the excise to the parliamentarians (SHOS vol 2 p162). At the Restoration the Deanery Hall was occupied by Sir Clement Throckmorton, the young MP for Warwick (1660), who died here on Nov 11 1663 (HOWM p96). The deanery contained a splendid oak staircase. Between 1692-1713 it was the residence of William Wood (1671-1730) of the famous 'Wood's Halfpence' case; a scheme to supply Ireland with copper coins. The project is discussed in the Drapier's letters by Dean Swift, Archbishop of Dublin. Wood's son Charles, the ironmaster, was born here in 1702 (SHOS vol 2 p163) (KES pp238-239) (HOWM p116) (WMAG July 1965 pp20-21p) (Commemorative plaque erected by the Wolverhampton Civic Society in 1987). Later the house was the seat of the deans of Wolverhampton, whose office remained until 1846 (LGS p259). Charles Dickens stayed here (TB Aug 1986 p4p). There was said to be a secret passage from the Deanery to some old religious houses which formerly stood upon the site of Messrs Warner's shop in Queen Square. But it could not be found when sewer drains were being laid. No doubt the existence of a deep well in the basement of the house gave rise to this tradition (OHW pl1). In 1912 the Deanery was purchased to be either used as a technical college or its site used for that purpose. After a protracted fight for its retention it was demolished in 1921 (WAIW vol 1) (MR p385) (University of Wolverhampton Web Page. 1998) or in 1925 (TB Aug 1986 p4p) (Mapping the Past Wolverhampton 1577-1986. Mary Mills 1993 p6), and by the 1930 edition of Masefield (LGS p259). From 1926 part of the Wolverhampton and Staffordshire Technical College (later the University of Wolverhampton (see)), Wulfruna Street, was built on the site of the Deanery (BOE p317) (MR p385) (University of Wolverhampton Web Page. 1998). Part of the C17 carved panelling from the Deanery went to the principal's room in the college (WAIW vol 1).

Deanery Farm 1m WNW of Dunstall, in Barton-under-Needwood parish. Formerly belonged to the Dean of Lichfield as rector of Tatenhill. Had been taken into the Rangemore Hall (Needwood School) estate by 1907 (HOPT vol 1 p114).

Deanery Hall The house of the resident canons of Penkridge Collegiate Church appears to have survived until at least the late C16. It can perhaps be identified with Deanery Hall which stood on the N side of Church Lane (former lane leading to Penkridge church, off present Clay Street). This house was for a long time the seat of the Chambley family. In the earlier C19 it formed part of a row of buildings and was an demolished in 1850. Another house, the house known as the Old Deanery, N of the church, was built after the dissolution of the college and does not appear to have had any association with the college, nor did another house called Deanery Farm, demolished in 1937 (W pp466-467) (VCH vol 5 p111) (BOE p221).

Dean's End Obsolete name for the S part of Brewood village. Appears in 1430 as le Denesend and was noted in c1680 by Gregory King. The name is from the Deanery manor, so called as it was held by the dean of Lichfield; the manor house was Dean's Hall (see). The manor covered this part of the village. Dean's End became, from about the end of the C19, the present Dean Street. In this street are or were town houses called The Chantry (see), West Gate, Dean's End, The Old Deanery (c1810), Dean Cottage, Dean House (formerly The Den c1800), Dean Street House (1792) (SHOS vol 2 p293) (VCH vol 5 p36) (BDH p223. 1992 pp202,203,288, 350). Deansfield, the ground of Brewood Cricket Club in 1974 (VB p78), Deansfield Close, Dean's Gate, and Dean's Croft, all take their name from the Deanery manor. There was, apparently, another house called Dean's End on the E side of the junction of Newport Street and School Road, Brewood (BDH 1992 p68).

Dean's Farm Newport Road, Stafford. The farm anciently belonged to Stafford

Collegiate Church, and was occupied between 1831 and 1845 by the Painter family, celebrated race-horse breeders and trainers. John Painter was a close friend of the poisoner, William Palmer of Rugeley, who was a visitor here (SIOT) (CC p41) (OSST 1928 p39il. 1929 p18. 1933 p49) (SAC p98) (Bruce Braithwaite has an illustration of this farm).

Deansfield E of Wolverhampton.

Dean's Hall House in Coven Road, S of Brewood. The manor house of the Deanery manor of Brewood. Leased to the Tomkys in 1628; the Whitwicks by the end of the C17; the Calmels to 1780; and the Moncktons of Somerford from 1780. It can be identified presumably the 'Dean's Hill in Dean's End' noted by Gregory King in c1680. As Dean's Hall Farm it was bought in 1927 by TAW Giffard who sold it to S Robinson in 1950. The house in 1959 dated largely from c1700 (VCH vol 5 p36). There is a dovecote, built in 1700, to the SE of the house (DoE II) (VCH vol 5 p36).

Dean's Hall Bridge Bridge over the Shropshire Union Canal S of Brewood.

Dean's Hall Brook Runs near Brewood (VCH vol 5 p19).

Deanshill N of the Newport Road, near Stafford Castle (W p343). In Castle Church parish. In 1871 it belonged to Alfred Williams. It was occupied in the late C19 and early C20 by the Benhams (SAC p96il). Has also appeared as Deans Hill; it seems to have taken its name from a field name on the Dean's Farm (see) estate.

Deans Slade Farm S of Leamonsley, on the boundary of Lichfield City (HOL p358). By 1176, and apparently before 1135, the dean of Lichfield cathedral had an estate at Deanslade. There was a house here by 1560. By the late 1980s most of the estate was part of the Aldershawe Hall estate (VCH vol 14 p68).

Dean's Walk Walk on N side of Lichfield cathedral Close (SOSH p227) (LPL p) (KES p139). The walk may have been created by Dean Binckes when he planted lime-trees along the N and E sides of the Close in early C18 (VCH vol 3 p189). Farquhar described it in 'The Beaux Stratagem' as 'leading to the house of Lady Bountiful, and in which Aimwell pretends to faint...' Dean's Walk was much loved by Dr Johnson (Dr Johnson and his Birthplace. A Retrospective and Guide. Johnson Birthplace Committee. 1933 p42).

Dearnsdale House 1.25m ENE of Haughton. In Bradley parish. The name is from perhaps Anglo-Saxon 'dierne-dale,' 'the hidden (or secluded) dale' (SPN p40). Has appeared as Dearnesdale (1551-1616), and Dernsdale (1605) (SPNO p135). The house is gabled red-brick, and probably of c1616 (VCH vol 4 p84).

Dearndales, The House 1.25m SW of Uttoxeter, on N side Stafford Road. Former dowager house (TRTC p52). Sold in 1945 (SVB p40).

Dee Bank Farm Mount Road, Leek (VCH vol 7 p103).

Deepdale Dale rising out of W side of the Hamps, S of Grindon. In Grindon parish. The closest burial mound to the road at SK 08265317 is 14 paces in diameter and two feet high (NSJFS 1965 p38). Another (unlocated) was excavated by Bateman in 1846 and by Carrington in 1848 revealed a young man's skeleton, beaker fragments and a child's skeleton (VAD p85) (TYD p154) (VCH vol 1 no 33) (DAJ vol 75 p104) (NSJFS 1965 p38). Another at SK 08735335, on the N side of the dale, is 14 paces in diameter and 1.5 feet high (NSJFS 1965 p38). Close by is another at SK 08775340, 16 paces in diameter and 1.5 feet high (NSJFS 1965 p38). A burial mound in Deepdale revealed remains of Beaker people (NSJFS 1962 p33). See also Burnet's Low, The Lows, Mouse Low, Oldfield Farm, Round Low, and Top Field Low.

Deepfields Hamlet, now submerged into the Black Country conurbation, 0.5m NW of Coseley. In Sedgley ancient parish. The name was perhaps Dip Field, with reference to a healing well (SR p107) (SMM p76). Or a field in the hollow (AMS p442). In 1718 one of the largest coke furnaces in the Midlands was set up at Deepfields by the Penn brothers (HC p53 il of Deepfields). Deepfield was identified by R Meade in his 'Coal and Iron Industries of the United Kingdom' (1882) p523 with the 'Duffield' where H Scrivenor in his 'History of the Iron Trade' 1854 places two blast furnaces said to have been in existence by the end of the C18 (The Black Country Iron Industry. WKV Gale. 1966. p34). The name appears as Deepfield on the Plan of the Mines of Lord Dudley 1812.

Deepfields Junction Deepfields. Junction of the former Birmingham Canal Old Main Line, now the Wednesbury Oak Loop, with the Coseley cut of the Birmingham Canal New Main Line (Canals of the West Midlands. Charles Hadfield. vol 5 of Canals of The British Isles. see map pp66-67) (SWY p9).

Deep Hayes Reservoir Former impounding reservoir 0.75m WNW of Cheddleton, in Deep Hayes Valley. Built by SPWWC to compensate the Churnet for the abstraction of water from tributary springs, one being St Caena's Well (see). The first turf was cut in a ceremony by William Davenport, chairman of SPWWC, on Aug 31 1847. The spade used in the ceremony was kept by the Davenports until 1915. By 1999 it was on show at Millmeece

(see) pumping station museum (PWW p12) (info Millmeece Pumping Station Preservation Trust). Problems with the reservoir occurred in 1979 and Severn Trent Water Authority abandoned it. In collaboration with several local authorities they then reconstructed the reservoir and created three pools out of it - Cumberledge Pool (the N pool), Park Pool (the middle pool), and Hayes Pool (the S pool); the surrounding area was then made into a public country park, known as Deep Hayes Country Park (SMOPP vol 2) (Deep Hayes Country Park. A Staffs County Planning & Development Dept Production).

Deepmoor Former enclosure created by the C14 NW of Aldridge (MOA p135).

Deepmore A bridge and farm 2m SE of Gailey. In Shareshill parish. The name means 'the deep boggy marshland' (SPNO p114). Has appeared as Deepemore (1604) (SPNO p114), and Deepmoor (W p480).

Deggs Leasow House 1.25m WSW of Stramshall.

De Grey Cottage Stands in Oxley Moor Road, Oxley. It was the seat of HJ Winstone, agent to Henry Staveley-Hill of Oxley Manor. The house was named after Henry's wife, Eileen De Grey Darcy (BUOP p43p).

Delbert S end of Wootton (near Ellastone).

Delph Small district 0.25m SSE of Brierley Hill by the Nine Locks or Delph Locks on the Dudley Canal. In Kingswinford ancient parish. Has also appeared as Black Delf (1774) (SNSV vol 1 p97) (Baugh's map 1808), and Black Delph (A Plan of the intended Extension of the Dudley Canal into the Birmingham Canal by John Snape 1785) (1834 OS map) (W p184). Here was an ironstone deposit site (VCH vol 2 p120). The hamlet of Black Delph, created by squatting coal miners, was demolished in the 1960s for open cast mining, and by the 1970s for fireclay mining. The land has been recently reclaimed for an housing estate called Withymoor Village (SL p189) (SNSV vol 1 p97). An area called Lower Delph occurs on Fowler's map of 1822 at the junction of Delph Road, Church Street and Brettell Lane (now present Silver End) (WFK p17).

Delph Brook Ran through Pensnett Chase (KCPC p12).

Delph Junction Junction of the Stourbridge Canal with the Dudley Canal Line One (HCMS No. 2).

Delph Locks A staircase of nine locks on the Dudley Canal Line One. In 1858 (SWY p12) or 1857 (MR p56) (BHOP p66ps) the staircase was rebuilt on the N side. The middle seven locks were replaced by six in a straight line, making, now, eight. The old line can still be followed. The Delph Locks are said to be the most beautiful urban flight in the country (SWY p13) and have been known as Nine Locks (1861 census), the 'Delph Nine' (BCM July 1977 p65 p on p66), and affectionately known by boatmen as 'the nine.'

Delves, The Hamlet with iron-ore workings (WMLB p101), 1.5m SSE of Walsall. Formerly in Wednesbury ancient parish. The name is from Anglo-Saxon 'daelf' 'delf' to dig; so, the Diggings. There were measures of ironstone close to the surface on Delves Common (DUIGNAN) (SPN p137) (SNWA p36). Some have thought that old iron workings at the Delves, known as Dane shafts, were of Roman, and or of Danish origin, but these suppositions have been discredited (OW p22) (WAM p19) (OCHW p7) (Birmingham and Its Regional Setting. H Thorpe. 1950 pp99-100) (HOWV pp4-5,11). The name has sometimes formerly appeared as Walstede Delves, from an old family named Walstead who lived at Walstead Hall (DUIGNAN). The Delves was transferred to Walsall borough in 1931 (VCH vol 17 p155). Acorns Children's Hospice in Walstead Road has the only wing for adolescents in Europe (BBC 1 Midlands Today June 21 1999) (info Jessia Foster). At Delves occurred the murder of a miser Matthew Adams who occupied a cottage on the W side of the road towards Fullbrook. A gang of four, Tom Boswell, George Giles, James Wilkes, and his 17 year-old brother, Joseph Wilkes, broke into his cottage in a robbery on Nov 30 1841. The first three were transported, but Joseph, who had struck the fatal blow, was hung. This caused a considerable outrage because of his youth (The Delves. Henry E Green. 1983) (TB Oct 1983 p4).

Delves Common The Delves. May once have been the 'Tower Hill' of Wednesbury. Arose in Saxon times as a place of public execution (WP pp2,9-13). The common has appeared as Delves Green Common and Delves Green (VCH vol 17 p155).

Delves Green Former common land and hamlet slightly S of The Delves. In Wednesbury ancient parish. Transferred to Walsall borough in 1931 (VCH vol 17 p155).

Delves Hall Apedale. Seat of the Delves of Delves Hall, Uttoxeter. Henry Delves obtained a licence from the bishop for an oratory in his house at Apedale in 1379 (SHC 1909 p45). The hall has been demolished.

Delves Hall On W side of West Bromwich Road, adjacent to Bell Lane, 1.5m S of Walsall. Formerly owned by the Earl of Dartmouth (TB Oct 1983 p4). About 1928 it was bought by West Bromwich corporation and in 1931 it was included in the area transferred to Walsall corporation. Delves Hall Farm was still standing in 1968 (The Delves. Henry E Green. 1983 pp12,13p).

Delves Hall Former hall near Uttoxeter. It was the seat of the Delves family. John de Delves was living at Delves Hall in 1303. He was succeeded by Richard de Delves (d1339). His successor Henry de Delves was of Delves Hall and Dodynton (or Doddington), and his successors resided at Doddington, Ches (Records of an Old Cheshire Family. Sir Delves L Broughton Bt. 1908 p2). The same or another branch of the Delves family resided at Delves Hall, Apedale, according to Harwood (SHC 1909 p45 note). The name is probably preserved in Delves Hall Meadow, near Bridge Street (HOU p359).

Denbigh Hall Between Near Sheepwash Lane, New Town at Horseley Heath (HOTIP pp27,188) (STELE Aug 22 1952 il of c1850). The Hills, relations of Sir Rowland Hill, promoter of the Penny Post (1836), resided here in the late C19 (mem in St Martin's, Tipton). Denbigh Hall Colliery was on the Haines' Branch of the Walsall Canal (BCM autumn 1995 p20). There is a Denbigh Road running off the S side of Horseley Heath road.

Denford Small hamlet over 0.5m SSW of the church at Longsdon. Formerly in Longsdon township in Leek ancient parish. The name is from an ancient crossing over Endon Brook and means a hidden or secret ford, presumably in contrast to a more open or accessible ford nearby. It appears as Derneford in 1341 (VCH vol 7 p203).

Denms Brierley Hill, N of Stourbridge.

Dennis Area on S side of Brettell Lane. Formerly in Amblecote chapelry in Old Swinford parish, Worcs. Takes its name from land here which was called Dennis by the 1380s. The name is from the Denis family of Amblecote who were living in the C12 (VCH vol 20 p51).

Dennis House which stood in the present Dennis Hall Road area on S side of Brettell Lane. Some time residence of Henry Hall (SNSV vol 1 p98). Occasionally called Dennis House to distinguish it from Dennis Hall (SNSV vol 2 p19).

Dennis Hall S of Brettell Lane, near its junction with the Stourbridge-Wolverhampton road. It was built by Thomas Hill in the 1760s (VCH vol 20 p51). A Thomas Hill, ironmaster, glass manufacturer and banker, was of Dennis Hall in 1815 (SNSV vol 1 p296). It was later the seat of WS Wheeley, ironmaster. By 1845 he had sold the estate to William Blow Collis and others (SVS pp105,108) (SNSV vol 1 p98). The house was tenanted by Rev John Crier in 1851 (SNSV vol 1 p98). In 1981 the house survived as part of the glassworks built in the earlier 1850s (VCH vol 20 p51). Formerly Dennis House. The grounds were built over in the mid C19 (VCH vol 20 p51).

Dennis Park Former estate covering the area S of Brettell Lane at Coalbournbrook. It included Dennis Hall.

Densley Lodge Draycott Mill. Takes its name from Dene's Brook, mentioned in a charter of 951 (SMSE p3).

Denstone Village on a bank on the W side of the Churnet, 15.5m NE of Stafford. Former township in Alton ancient parish. Denstone has appeared as Denestun (1008) and Denestone (DB) (SPN p40). The name means 'Dene's town' (DUIGNAN) or farmstead (SPN p40) or tun (SSE 1996 p13). A place at Denstone is called Cromwell's Green (HOU p359). Denstone railway station on the Churnet Valley line opened in 1849 (AUOPP p56p). It was recommended that it be closed in 1963 (ES March 22 1963). In 1860 the ecclesiastical parish of Denstone was formed out of the parishes of Alton, Rocester and Ellastone. The church, All Saints, on the W side of the Rocester road was built between 1860 and 1862. Denstone became a separate civil parish in 1866 (GLAUE p409). The village, which was the winner of the first Staffs Best Kept Village competition (Melting Pot. Spring 1997 p9), was renowned in the early C20 for its damson fruit. Some supplied local markets and others the dye works of Lancashire. Damsons are still (1993) grown around the village (SVB p64) (TSW p37). The earthquake of 3.21pm July 3 1904 was felt at Denstone Vicarage (NSFCT 1905 p133). The largest litter of domestic ferret in the UK by 1995 was 15 to a ferret owned by J Cliff of Denstone in 1981 (GBR 1995 p32).

Denstone College 0.75m SW of Denstone on Moss Moor (HOC p197). Was the first Woodard School in the Midlands. Designed in a Gothic style by William Slater and RH Carpenter in an H pattern (VCH vol 6 pp158-159). The foundation stone for the college was meant to be laid by the Marquis of Salisbury on Oct 22 1868 but in his absence it was laid by Rev Canon Lonsdale, son of the late bishop of Lichfield. But the brass plaque with Latin inscription on the stone makes no mention of this (HOC p198) (COPP2 p97p). The school, built on a site given by Sir Thomas Percival Heywood, was finished in 1872 and opened in 1873 as St Chad's College (ESNF pp104-105il) (COPP2 p97). The chapel was dedicated by Bishop Selwyn on July 27 1887 (COPP2 p97p). The school was partly destroyed by fire on May 25 1894. The roof of the centre and right of the main building was destroyed (ACOPP p35p) (AUOPP

pp58ps,59ps). The world record for Eskimo Rolls in canoeing was set by Robert A Hignell in a Merano Kayak in the college swimming pool on March 2 1971 when he achieved 325 in 22 minutes 44 seconds (GBR 1971 p244). For its collection of coal fossils see S p33ps.

Denstone Hall On E side of road to Rocester at Denstone, SE of the church. Built on the site of an ancient seat of the Okeover family and was the scene of a murder in 1293. Thomas Chawner was living at Denstone Hall in the 1830s and 1840s. Ancient timbers and a mud and wattle wall remain in the present house, which was re-fronted and partly rebuilt in 1853 (mem in Hanbury church) (SVB p65). The hall appears on OS maps of 1887, 1900, and 1924.

Derby Turn Name for the junction of Icknield Street (A38) with the Burton-Tutbury road at Little Burton. The name occurs on a plan of Burton dated 1865. Here was a horse trough (CBHBT pp11,82). There were gallows here in medieval times (IHOBT pp16,21).

Derrington Village near Doxey Brook 2m WSW of Stafford. Formerly in Seighford ancient parish. The manor of Dodintone appears in DB. Later forms are: Dodinton and Dudingtun (SPN p41). Herrington on Smith's map is probably Derrington. The name, which appears to be of Anglo-Saxon origin, is from 'Dodd's or Dodda's town or tun' (DUIGNAN) (SSE 1996 p13), or 'the farmstead of Dudda's people' (SSE 1996 p13) (SPN p41). The medieval chapel at Derrington is not mentioned in 1563 or after (SHC 1915 p227), although reference is made to it in a C17 manuscript (NSFCT 1922 p162). Loxdale noted that the chapel had been removed from the chapel yard and turned into a barn. The present chapel field is near Lane End Farm at Derrington. It was never a chapel of ease but was provided by the Stafford Barony for the ease of their tenants (OSST 1949-50 p14). The present church, St Matthew, NE of St Matthew's Drive, was completed in 1847 (BOE p116). In the 1800s Derrington had a cobbler, reputed to have made shoes for the royal family (SVB p66). Derrington became a separate ecclesiastical parish in 1847 (GLAUE p409). The Lord Lieutenant of Staffs officially opened The Way for the Millennium footpath at the Red Lion Inn, Derrington, on April 7 2000. The footpath, 40 miles long, stretching from Newport, Shrops, in the W to Burton upon Trent in the E, uses the old Stafford-Newport railway line and canal towpaths (The Way for the Millennium guide book. 2000) (Stafford Chronicle. April 21 2000 p8p).

Derrington Old Hall Derrington. Built in c1708. A stone covers a well in the garden bearing the initials 'S.D.' and 1606 (SVB p66).

Derry The name Derry appears in the 1841 census in Brierley Hill parish. There is a Derry Street and a Lower Derry Street S of Church Street, Brierley Hill.

Devil's Bridge Local name for the C18 high arched footbridge on the E side of Somerford Mill, near Brewood (BDH 1992 p333).

Devil's Den A dell or an inlet cut on the E side of the Staffs and Worcs Canal at SO 863856. It is of natural origin or may have been made for the canal or the Smestow Brook since both run parallel here. It was, perhaps, once a boathouse, or a dwelling for the navvies who built the canal or something more sinister (SWY p46). (S&WC p) (Staffs and Worcs Canal Conservation Area Booklet) (KRH p28). (JEPS No. 9 p23 The Devil in field names: Devil's Den is common).

Devil's Dressing Room, The Old quarry in a copse from which the stone to build Tamworth church was hewn (VB p33) (MR p186), 1m SSW of Hopwas (1834 OS map two inch to 1m).

Devil's Drumble A spur near Coppice Hill (GCC p31) in Sherbrook Valley, Cannock Chase. To W of Dick Slee's Cave. Appears as this on 1834 OS map.

Devil's Elbow, The On the Staffs and Worcs Canal N of Laches Bridge. So called from the difficulty experienced in steering barges round it (The Staffs and Worcs Canal. Alfred E Jenks. 1907 p21).

Devil's Elbow Bridge Over the Wyrley and Essington Canal NE of Wednesfield (Birmingham A-Z) in Devil's Elbow Lane. In the 1960s the residents campaigned to have the name of the lane changed to Kennedy Avenue after US President JF Kennedy. Part of the road was actually renamed Whitehouse Avenue, after a large house in the neighbourhood, but the section closest to the canal remains Devil's Elbow Lane (WHTOP p73p).

Devil's Entry At Goldthorn Hill (TB Oct 1986 p15).

Devil's Hole In Combes Valley, Ipstones. Here was the site for a battle between the Celts and the Saxons (TOI pp9,11) (Some Random Thoughts on Ancient History of Leek. From vol 10 of local pamphlets in Horace Barks Ref Lib author and date unknown) (SVB p101). For a rhyme about Devil's Hole see Combes Valley. The spot was overgrown and hidden in 1994. The name is from earth worship not Devil worship (SMM p39). Has also appeared as Devil Hole, Clough Meadows, Devil's Nook (IAANS p xiii), and Hell Hole.

Devil's Horn, The Name for a field adjoining the S side of the stream between Kiddlemore Green and The Whitemoor, in Brewood parish. The name may be a reference to its poor soil or shape (BDH 1992 p333).

Devil's Mouth Cave The most fascinating cavern (of Wren's Nest Hill?) was the infamous 'Devil's Mouth' (TB March 1990 p5).

Devil's Ring and Finger Two standing stones which rest against each other side by side, 1.25m WNW of Mucklestone, at SJ 707377, probably of Neolithic origin (SL p36) and may represent the remnants of a megalithic chambered tomb. They are so called because, in their present position, they look like a huge finger and ring. The western stone has a hole in the centre and represents the 'ring'; it is 1.8 metres from side to side and 1.2 metres tall (about six feet), and its porthole cut is some 20 inches in diameter. The 'finger' stone is also 1.2 metres high, and 0.9 metres wide (SMM p34). Grooves caused by water erosion indicate that the stones are not in their original position (NSJFS 1965 p44). The hole in the 'ring' stone may have been used at the end of a burial chamber for the ghost of the occupant to escape through. Or it may have formed part of an henge and was used for the alignment of some celestial object, or in a fertility rite; local tradition persists that if a woman passes through the 'ring' she becomes pregnant. Later, it may have been used to put a head through to cure a sore throat, or to pass a child through suffering from rickets to effect a cure, or as a bargain stone (SLM autumn 1955 pp22ps,23) (SMM pp34,35) (info Mr Lovatt of Forge Farm). The 'finger' stone probably formed part of the same chambered tomb, or was the alignment stone in a henge for the 'ringed' stone (SMM p34). The stone may have been erected later or re-used later: If Market Drayton was an ancient British city as Ussher thought then it may have had some connection with that (NSFCT 1922 p170). The stones are on the Roman road Leominche Street and may have formed part of the Roman or Romano-British city of Little Manchester, otherwise Mediomanum (NSFCT 1937 p118). Mucklestone may take its name from the stones (SLM autumn 1955 pp22ps,23), or from the chambered tomb or henge the stones were once a part of. (NSFCT vol 43 pp133,195-196. 1911 frontispiece) (Antiquity vol 1 pp229-230) (LGS p190) (SOSH p10) (KES pp8,155) (Prehistoric Chamber Tombs of England and Wales. GE Daniel. 1950. p184) (NSJFS 1965 p44) (HOS p9) (STM Oct 1967 p31p) (VB p159) (BOE p215) (SL p36) (FPSB p163) (Prehistoric England and Wales. James Dyer. 1981) (MR pp236,237p) (SVB p128) (SMM pp10-11,33p). A disc burial mound of the central monolith type was discovered recently (1938) on the banks of the Tern in proximity to Devil's Ring and Finger (NSFCT 1938 p112). Pickford thinks the stone circle was slightly to the W of the Devil's Ring and Finger (SMM p35 see map). Bradley Stone to the W in Norton-in-Hales, Shrops, may have been part of the same megalithic chambered tomb (KESH p163) (NSFCT 1946 p153).

Devil's Staircase Long irregular stone steps set at some remote period (HLSP p127) on an incline on the E side of the Churnet, 20 yards or so below Price's Cave, Ipstones. It was called as such by the early C20 (HLS p14) (NSFCT 1906 p167). Raven calls it Devil's Causeway (MR p110). Poole counted at least 204 steps (HLSP p129). Another Devil's Staircase climbs out of the valley at Consall Forge, leading up to Consall (HLS p58) (SMCC p9).

Devil's Staircase, The A brook or stream known as The Devil's Staircase in the Burntwood Bishop's Wood area at Fairoak (BOV p27).

Devil's Well Appears to be a spring between Audley and Heighley Castle (BOJ book 2 p59).

Dial Lane Lane leading to the Bridestones, Rushton Spencer. The name is derived from Gaelic 'deiseil' or 'deasil' which means the sunwise direction used in rituals, or south and to the right (DP p77) (SMM p10).

Dibdale Bank Former small hamlet 0.5m S of Upper Gornal, over 0.25m E of Lower Gornal. In Sedgley ancient parish (W p200). The name means 'a field in the hollow' (AMS p442). It has appeared as Deepdale Bank (1851 census) and Dipdale Bank (OS map 1834), and is preserved in Dibdale Road.

Dibdale House Dibdale. 1m NW of Dudley.

Dickie's Gutter Ancient cobbled footpath which runs steeply downhill from St Edward's church, Leek, and the Garden of Remembrance towards Brough Park. Shaded by overhanging trees and is close to the area called Petit France. Reputedly haunted by the ghost of a fascinating-looking, gipsy-like girl, who Roger Turner claims to have seen in June 1993 (GLS p64), and a Cavalier with a flowing black wig and rapier sword (SMM pp47-48).

Dick's Hill Colley Gate, Cradley, Rowley Regis. An old pathway running from near the bus stop in Windmill Hill to Two Gates Lane (TB Oct 1981 p17).

Dick Slee's Cave Former hermit's dwelling, which was at approximately SJ 993197 on the N side of Haywood Slade in Cannock Chase. The dwelling, a rustic hut in a hollow in Sherbrook Valley, was made by Dick Slee or Sleigh in c1770. Lord Bagot told Miss Levett in 1845 that he recollected driving Mrs Bagot (Miss Levett's grandmother) to see the hermit 50 or 60 years before. An old cutting from 'The Mail' (presumably the Birmingham Mail) with the heading 'Quaint Place Names' says Slee was a servant of the Ansons at Shugborough Hall and there he fell in love with a maid. But on being

rebuffed by her he left his post to become a hermit. An account by Alfred Camden Pratt in Midland Counties Express Dec 22 1883 tells the story slightly differently; that the hermit was called Reynold Rudock (or Raddock). He was a young man from Cannock, who took refuge on the chase after being spurned in love by his cousin, Bertha Wheatwell, and after injuring his spine by a fall on ice. Alone, he befriended a hare which he called Bess who was his sole companion. Bertha, meanwhile, went to London in search of her lover, but the lover once having made her pregnant, spurned her. She returned to Cannock and ended her days in Cannock workhouse. With the death of Raddock's pet hare Raddock became distort and was taken to Rugeley workhouse where he died (TB Oct 1997 p10) (John Godwin on 'Open Country' BBC Radio 4 Aug 14 1999). The hut is said to have been built of turf and contained two rooms with a brick vault underneath in which Slee wished to be buried. After his removal to the workhouse relic hunters made havoc with his hut and garden. Before long only a few bricks remained to show where he had lived. In the later C19 the hermit's cave was called 'Abdullam's Cave' on OS maps and 'Adulalhs Cave' on the 18346:12 pm OS map (HOSCC p107). A curious sort of small pit in the ground was noticed by NSFC excursionists in 1922, and slight traces of the cave were said to be visible in 1951 (GCC p24). By at least 1980 not a trace of it could be found, nor the exact site be easily located. OS maps continue to mark it. (Old Dick Sleigh's Cave. Miss Susanna Trubshaw. 1867) (SA Sept 1 1923) (NSFCT 1923 p142) (RRCC pp7-8) (CCBO pp110-112) (PCC pp21-22) (SN Sept 9 1949 p9) (FOS pp31-32) (MR p80) (BERK2 p52).

Dick's Well Approximately 1m NE of Upper Tean. At SK 024401 on 1:25,000 OS map.

Dieulacres Abbey (locally *Delacres* S&W p295). Ruined Cistercian abbey 0.75m N of Leek.

EARLY. In a field near the abbey site are signs of a rectangular Roman camp. Striking northwards is a mound - part of the 'Mark' or border of Mercia (NSSG p16). There may have been a hermitage near the abbey site before the abbey was founded (VCH vol 3 p136). A cave in a rock cliff on the left as the abbey site is approached may have been a hermit's dwelling before the mid C12; Byrne suggests St Chad took sanctuary here (TFTP pp24-25,74). The cave may have been the chapel of the Virgin by where Earl Randulph was instructed to build Dieulacres Abbey in a vision (see below) (OL vol 1 pp150-152 il). The cave appears to have been a dwelling in more recent times; a building once projected from it (DP pp86,88,89il), and it has traces of a fireplace, roof-plates, and door-jams (KES p126). Rev W Beresford and Rev JF Phelps thought the opening in the rock was a kiln but later came to the conclusion it was an anchorite's cell of C14 or C15 origin (MOS p267). In the cave are unexplained markings resembling the Evil Eye, or a serpent symbol. A similar marking can be found carved in a rock on the summit of the Cloud (DP p90il,94p). (LGS p163).

ABBEY. In 1155 Robert, hereditary butler of the Earls of Chester, founded at Pulton in Cheshire a daughter-house of Combermere Abbey (itself a daughter of Savigny). The Pulton site proved a poor choice suffering from Welsh incursions. It was refounded by Ran(d)ulph 'de Blundeville,' Earl of Chester (d1232), whose pedigree can be found under Chartley Castle (see), on the Earl's lands to the N of Leek in 1214; the Combermere connection remained (VCH vol 3 p136). The name has appeared as Dieu l'ocreisse ('may God give increase it') (SPN p41), Dieu Le Cross (Speed) (NSJFS 1962 p78), De La Cres (Plot's map), Dieu-la-Cross (SK p196), Dieu Encres, Dieulacres, Dieulacresse, Dieulaucres, Deleucres, Deulacres, Delacres, Dulacres, Delacrees, Dieulecres, Deulacresse, Deulecresse (1214), Deuleencress, Dieuleucress, Dewenlecres, and Delyencrise (NSJFS 1962 p85 note). The traditional story which explains how the abbey received its name is in the abbey chronicle, or a chronicle by Henry of Lincoln. Earl Ranulph saw in a dream his grandfather Ranulph, who told him 'Go to Cholesdale in the territory of Leek, and in that place where there was formerly a chapel to the blessed Virgin, you shall found an abbey of white monks.' After relating this to his second wife, a French lady called Clemence de Fengares, she said to him 'Deuxencres' (May God grant it increase) and the Earl pleased with her remark, exclaimed 'Then the name of the place shall be Deulacres' (NSJFS 1962 pp78,85 note) (SPN p41) (HOS 1998 p57). (SCC pp25-26) (LGS pp162,163) (HOS p27) (SLM Nov 1984 p14). The name was perhaps not from 'God prosper it' but from a play on the original name of the land, which may have been similar to Celtic 'tulach,' 'a hill' (as in Talk o' th' Hill). The second element is the forest root roed, rud, rus - hence 'hill wood.' The moor above is still called Hillswood (NSFCT 1910 p163). When the founder, Randulph, died in 1232 his heart was buried at Dieulacres; his widow was buried here in 1253. The only miracle recorded at the abbey was said to be the return of the sight of a blind monk over the tomb of the founder's wife

(DA pp37,208). The abbey had granges at Nether Hulme (New Grange), Swythamley, Roche (SVB p123), and Fairboroughs (SSE 1993 p5). Apart from Burton, Dieulacres Abbey was the richest of the Staffs monasteries (NSJFS 1962 p84. 1970 pp83-101). Monks are said to have used the Earl's Way and a packhorse way over Gun Hill (see) to transport wool from their estates to Ches. There was a long-standing quarrel in which the abbot and the lord of Alton manor on the one side were ranged against the combined gentry of the hills on the other, which lasted about 50 years from 1275. The abbot seems to have taken an illegal toll of persons passing through his lands, offending the Rudyerds, Beresfords, Meverells, Okeovers and Cheddletons (OL vol 1 p255) (HOLF p11). In 1351 the Black Prince visited the abbey (VCH vol 3 p234).

AFTER THE DISSOLUTION. The abbey surrendered on Oct 20 1538 and was dissolved in 1539. The Earl of Derby was put in possession of the abbey. In 1552 the estate passed to Sir Ralph Bagnall. In 1597 the abbey site and manor of Leek and Frith were sold to the Rudyards (NSJFS 1962 p84). The Rudyards built Dieulacres Abbey Farm in 1612. This building incorporates many remains from the abbey (NSSG p16) (VCH vol 7 pl 27). They sold the estate in 1723. Sleigh lists all its subsequent owners (NSJFS 1962 p87). In the first edition of Dugdale the abbey was placed in Cheshire, but a correction was made in the C19 revision. Further abbey remains were uncovered in 1818 and many were used in the erection of outbuildings for the farm (W p720) (VCH vol 3 pp230-234). According to tradition the roof of the N aisle of Astbury church, Ches, came from Dieulacres (NSJFS 1962 p87). Some masonry in the grounds of Ball Haye Hall is said to come from the abbey (NSFCT 1922 p156). The chalice in St Edward's church, Leek, is said to come from the abbey (STM Feb 1967 p32p). Rev W Beresford noted an old coffin lid lying a little NE of the ruins; also an old rock fortress at Abbey Green where the monks stayed whilst the abbey was being built (MOS pp266-268p of the cell floor with tiles bearing the cognizance of the Earls of Warwick). In 1904 a C17 copy of the cartulary of the abbey became available (NSFCT 1905 pp157-163) (SHC 1906 pp293-366) (SH pp6,7) (SLM Nov 1984 p14). For the seal see TFTP p134il, SLM Nov 1984 p14il, SK p196. Buxton Museum has some C13 or C14 Early English glazed floor tiles from the abbey. Miller notes near to the ruins a bowling green believed to have been made by the monks, since it is lined by ancient yews (OL vol 1 p286). The abbey site was surveyed by archaeologists in summer 1995 (WMARCH 1995 pp66-72 plans ils). (NHS p447) (SD p101) (SM p289) (SSC p137 in the intro) (GNHS pp89 il facing,102) (OL vol 1 pp150,258-261 ils of some remains) (UDC vol 3 pp1-14) (NSFCT 1878 pp29-31. 1889 pp71-74) (Some Random Thoughts on Ancient History History of Leek. No author or date. vol 10 of local pamphlets in Horace Barks Ref Lib) (HS p78 pl) (LGS pp37,163) (SOSH p110) (ES Jan 10 1934 p6p) (SLM winter 1954 pp23p,25,26) (STM May 1969 p28) (BOE pp172-173) (SGS p117) (TFTP pp132,133) (MR pp208,209) (DP pp86il-88). A poem by Elisha Walton (1843-1914) describing the abbey appears in his 'The Romance of the Hills - Tales of the Staffordshire Moorlands' (VFC p138).

Digbeth Centre area of Walsall, at the foot of High Street. The name is from perhaps dyke-path (SNWA p37). So named by 1583 (VCH vol 17 p146).

Diglake In Bignall End township of Audley ancient parish. Small estate which by the end of the C17 had belonged for many generations to the Parkers of Town House, Audley (SHC 1944 p39).

Dilhorne (*Dillon* SGS p93). Ancient parish and former township. The village of Dilhorne lies on the slopes of a hill overlooking the head of a tributary of the Tean, 13.5m NNE of Stafford. To the SE of the church at SJ 97354321 is a mound 11 paces diameter and three feet high. It was excavated by Stoke-on-Trent Museum Archaeology Society (NSJFS 1965 p36). The manor of Dulverne appears in DB. Later Dilhorne appears as Duluerne (SPN p41), Dulvorne, Dillon, Delvern (HOC pp243,257), and Dilhorn. The **name** is from Anglo-Saxon 'dulf,' the plural form of 'delf,' a delving or digging; so, here was probably some quarrying thinks DUIGNAN (JC 22) (SSE 1996 p13) (SPN p41). Or named after a family who once resided here (NSFCT 1940 p29). The parish was formed after 1086, but probably by 1166 and certainly by 1291, out of Cheadle parish (SHC 1916 p199). There was a **church** at Dilhorne in the C12 (LDD). The present parish church, All Saints, on the E side of New Road, N of Caverswall Road, has some early C13 in its tower (CHMS2 p40) - one of the few octagonal W towers in the country (BOE p116). Dilhorne parish was appropriated to the dean and chapter and certain prebendaries of Lichfield cathedral but did not come under their peculiar jurisdiction (VCH vol 3 p94 note). In the churchyard was found a magnificent C13 to C14 jug which was deposited at the Potteries Museum; it was probably made at Audlem, Ches (NSFCT 1950 p83). Dilhorne **Grammar School**, a free grammar school, was endowed according to tradition by an

Earl of Huntingdon in Henry VIII's reign. However from an indenture dated 1606 it appears that Rev John Whitacres and others conveyed lands for the erection and establishment of the school in 1532. The school still existed in 1852 (THS p231) (LHSB 14 pp30il,31-33). Red ochre at Dilhorne was noted in the later C17 (NHS p124). A **windmill** is shown on Yates' map N of the village at approximately SJ 974436. It is not shown on a map of 1900 (WBJ p20). A Whitley LA 765 **aircraft** crashed at Dilhorne on Jan 31 1944 killing all five crew except the rear gunner F/ SGT Weightman who went to the local colliery to get help (MD pp35-36). **Strange phenomena**. In Sept 1978 a couple claimed a UFO flew over their car as they travelled through Dilhorne and fired a blinding beam of light at the car (SMM p98). On March 22 1983 an unexplainable 'rain of tiny shells' showered over the village (MMSE p288). **Persons and visitors**. **Charles Wesley** preached at Dilhorne (HOC p139). **Admiral Leveson-Gower** (1740-92) alluding to the poor state of Staffordshire roads, of which Moorland ones were thought the poorest, declared that he 'would rather be in the Bay of Biscay in a storm than on one of Dilhorne roads in a carriage' (SL p231). **Thomas James** of Forsbrook was accused of bestiality which allegedly took place with a she-ass on Good Friday 1811 in a field near the Stone House, Dilhorne. He was convicted and executed on the evidence of just one man, Thomas Inskip (CCSHO pp41-45). For the murder of **Sarah Anne Burndred** by her husband John see Newclosefield. **Susie Cooper** (1903-1995) of Stanfield (see), ceramic designer, lived at the Old Parsonage, Dilhorne until 1987 when she moved to the Isle of Man (ES Sept 11 1996 p34) (FWNS p53). **Eddie Heath** was building models of famous buildings and objects for Nov 5 bonfire parties behind the Royal Oak Inn, Dilhorne from the early 1990s; he made a 20-foot high replica of the Houses of Parliament and 'Big Ben' for the 1996 bonfire, and a 120-foot long 40-foot high 'Dracula's Castle' for the 1998 bonfire (ES Oct 29 1996 p3pc. Oct 30 1998 p5p).

Dilhorne Brook Tributary of the Tean. Appears in 1272 as aqua de Dylun in 1272 (SPNO p8).

Dilhorne Common Former common land now a tiny hamlet E of Dilhorne, on high ground. Perhaps can be identified with the Dilhorne Heath mentioned in VCH vol 1 p294.

Dilhorne Hall Stood NE of Dilhorne church. Copwoods, who bore arms in the later C17, are placed on Plot's map by Dilhorne. Copwood Hollins (d1705) was of Dilhorne Hall (mem in Dilhorne church) (HOC p245). Later in the C18 it was the residence of John Holliday, who in 1792 was awarded a gold medal by the Society for the Encouragement of Arts and Manufacture for having planted 118,000 mixed timber trees (HOC p30) (S&W p308). It has also been the residence of the Bullers family, and Sir Edward Manningham-Buller Bart (in the C19), and Lord Dilhorne a former Lord Chancellor who took his name from the village (MR p125). The hall was demolished in the 1930s (SPN p41). By at least the early 1980s Dilhorne Recreation Centre had been built on the site. In the centre are photographs of the hall. In the former grounds the gatehouse still stands. (STM April 1965 p43p of the gatehouse) (SMOPP vol 1 p14p of the hall) (HOC p246) (JSD p31p of the hall). The NSFC inspected the ice-house set into the solid sandstone of the hillside in June 1985 (NSFCT 1985 p46).

Dilloways Slang Small area of W Willenhall. The name, and that of Dilloways Piece occurring on the 1841 tithe map, is preserved in Dilloways Lane, S of the new The Keyway ringroad (SNW p22).

Dimmings Dale Very picturesque valley 1m S of Oakamoor. In Cheadle ancient parish. A gorge about 1.5m long (NSFCT 1922 p32). The name has appeared as Demon's Dale (J Carter in The Magazine of Natural History. 1839), Dimsdale (NSFCT 1947 p108), and Dimminsdale. It is derived from 'dead man's dale,' for here was a skirmish between the parliamentarians and royalists in the Civil War (IAANS p vi). There is a small brick and stone lodge to Alton Towers built by Earl of Shrewsbury at SK 049434 in the upper reaches of the dale called the Round House or Round House Farm. It is curious for being triangular in shape. The corner facing out over the dale is circular. (SLM Oct/Nov 1991 p22p of the Round House). It was situated on the Earls' private drive leading from Cheadle to Alton Towers, called Serpentine Drive, which runs through the dale. A wreath with a card with this inscription: 'RSM Tom Beardmore, Number 9, Commando Unit, killed in action at Anzio, February 2nd or 3rd 1943. He loved this place but like so many others he didn't make it home. Always remembered. The Family' first appeared, pinned against a tree along the public path in the dale, in c1993 (ES May 6 1994 p3p. May 11 1994 p21pc). It was still there in 1995 (PWIS p93). 500 yards S of the youth hostel, called Little Ranger, on a footpath by a stile is a steel plaque with this inscription 'To the Memory of Paul Rey 1925-1977 - A Rambler and World Traveller who inspired so many with his love of the Countryside' (COS p4p) (PWIS p93). There is another to Rey on Morridge.

Dimminsdale Former area of Willenhall (W p161) (SNW p22). The name is of ancient but unknown origin (HOWI p188). The name is now just a tiny street off Railway Lane off New Road.

Dimmingsdale Over 0.5m W of Lower Penn. A wharf with a substantial basin was built at Dimmingsdale at about the time of the construction of the Staffs and Worcs Canal. It has long been abandoned. Dr J Langford wondered why such a substantial basin had been built so remote from industry. It could have been constructed for the transport of Lower Keuper Sandstone, quarried locally, or for the transport of coal or lime, or for iron from Trescott forge (S&WC p114). The area was bored for water in c1900. The present pumping station was built by 1932 (PAIP pp56,58il). Dimmingsdale Reservoir, on W side of the Staffs and Worcs Canal, covers five acres (LHSB No. 6 p26) (Wolverhampton Chronicle Oct 15 1999 p20p). For the fish in it see English Reservoirs. Bill Howes. 1967 p56.

Dimple House In NW corner of Lichfield cathedral Close. It was probably built in the later C18 (VCH vol 14 pp58 see map, 67).

Dimsdale District 1m WNW of Wolstanton. Formerly in Chatterley liberty in Wolstanton ancient parish. There is a tradition St Wolstan was born at Dimsdale. According to medieval writers who may be unreliable a Wolstan of Dymsdale filled successively the episcopal throne of Worcester, and the archiepiscopal chair of York in the C10. His grandson, also a Wolstan of Dymsdale, is said to been bishop of Worcester, and he is said to have been the father of St Wolstan who died in 1095 (NSFCT 1886 p53). The manor of Dulmesdene appears in DB. Later forms are: Dimesdal (1242), and Dymmesdale (1281) (SPN p42). The second part of the name 'dene' is Anglo-Saxon for a dell or little valley. 'Dulmes' is unexplainable - perhaps the name of a former owner (NSFCT 1886 p51). Perhaps, the real original now unknown form became Middle English 'dimple,' 'a small depression' (SPN p42). At Dimsdale Plot in the later C17 saw the oddest carriage for transporting hay he had ever seen. It was made only of two strong pieces of timber dragging on the ground and a triple behind (NHS p354).

Dimsdale Hall Dimsdale, Wolstanton. The estate was held by the Knutton family in 1211. An early hall may have been moated. Queen Margaret is reputed to have stayed a night here on the way back from the battle of Blore Heath (1459) (WWT pp77,78,79,80). The estate appears to have been the property of the Bretts by the C16. Thomas Brett may have built the hall before Oct 1589 (NSFCT 1918 p11), or it may have been built or encased by the family in c1600 (NSFCT 1953 p57). The Bretts were living here in 1608 (HBST p117 il of facing). In the Civil War there was a skirmish in the vicinity of the hall between royalists and parliamentarians which resulted in bullet marks on some of its out-buildings (WWT pp77,78,79,80).

THE ELERS. The Elers brothers of Nuremburg, John Philip Elers, godson of the Elector of Mentz, and David Elers, probably came to England with the Prince of Orange (William III). They may have occupied Dimsdale Hall in the late C17, but probably did not have a pottery at Dimsdale Hall as suggested by Simeon Shaw, but used the hall as a residence and warehouse. They were attracted to the area by the local clay beds. In 1699 JP Elers married a Miss Banks and thus became connected by marriage with the Vernon family. At Dimsdale they would have been tenants of the Sneyds. Several traditions are associated with their occupation - that unsaleable pieces of ware were smashed into small fragments and buried in secret places; that they only employed imbeciles who would not betray Elers' pottery secrets; that a man named Twyford (identified by Morland as Joshua Twyford) and another named Astbury (identified by Morland as John Astbury, father of Thomas Astbury of Ashworth's Works (see)), spied on them; that they may have introduced a method of salt glazing into Staffs; that they had a mysterious means of communication between Dimsdale Hall and their pottery consisting of speaking tubes; in c1900 W Wall discovered pottery tubes, thought to be the Elers speaking-tubes. The Elers may have had a pottery on the site of Bradwell House or Bradwell Hall Farm, where a search was made in 1920 for the site of their oven, but nothing was found (HSP pp111,118,119) (H p34) (NSFCT 1920 p156) (POP pp69-70) (HBST p125). The Elers left Staffs in 1710 (Staffordshire Pots and Potters. GW & FA Rhead. 1906 pp138-165ils) (WWT pp77,78,79,80) (NSFCT 1945 p83). Another account says a family called Ears, stone producers, occupied the hall between 1693 and 1700 (Newcastle Times Nov 4 1970).

The Bennetts were occupying the hall possibly by late C18 and certainly by the later C19 (mems in St Margaret's, Wolstanton) (NSFCT 1953 p57). The hall was gutted by fire in 1895 (NSFCT 1941 p39), and it seems to have remained in a ruined state (inspected by the NSFC in 1918) and very little of it was left standing when the estate was sold in c1925 and that which was was restored (NSFCT 1918 p110. 1925 p190. 1926 p147). When the hall was demolished in 1940 it was a building with Dutch gables and a half-timbered

back. The owners, the Bennetts, then moved to a more recent farm building (NSFCT 1953 p57) (Newcastle Times Nov 4 1970). (NSFCT 1886 p53) (SLM March 1949 p213p of the ruins of the back of Dimsdale Hall in 1940) (NOPP pl 86 shows the hall c1916). The name, which has also appeared as Dimsdale Old Hall, is preserved in Dimsdale Hall Farm and is surrounded by Wolstanton Golf Course.

GROUNDS. There is a moat lying immediately N of the site of the hall, which may have been the site of an early Dimsdale Hall, later it was thought it was for a pond of C18 origin (NSFCT 1957 pp39-45 plans). A stone barn connected with the hall, generally known as the 'Old Barn,' stands on a filled-in section of the S side of the alleged moat. It is said to be of the C13 and could have been built using stones of the medieval manor house, but the mullions suggest a date in the C17 (NSFCT 1953 pp56-69 plan. 1982 p19). It was still standing next to the golf club house in 1970 (Newcastle Times Nov 4 1970 p). The grounds now form part of Wolstanton Golf Course and a mound on it has been the subject of much speculation as to its origin (NSFCT 1983 p13). There are other earthworks, too, of what is thought to have been a cock fighting pit, and a tunnel or two tunnels (one to Chesterton Old Hall and one to Bradwell Hall) (Staffordshire Pots and Potters. GW & FA Rhead. 1906. p156) (NSFCT 1941 p39) (Newcastle Times Nov 4 1970).

Dingle, The Stapenhill. Narrow pathway beside a stream running down to the Trent. The path led to the Ferry Bridge. The Dingle was frequented in Victorian times as a beauty spot (ABTOP p4p).

Dingle Brook Rises E of Newtown. Flows through the centre of the former Rushton James township. By its damming Rudyard Lake or Reservoir was formed. W of Leek it flows into the Churnet (SVB p144) (SHC 1999 p7; it is identifiable with the brook called Fulhe in the early C13). The name means 'a narrow valley' (SPNO p8).

Dippons 1.25m WSW of Tettenhall. It was in the Wrottesley Prebend of Tettenhall Collegiate Church (SHOS vol 2 p198). By the late C20 was a ward in Perton civil parish. Has appeared as Dippins (Yates' map), Dipen (OS map 1834 2 inch to 1m), and Diptons. Dippons Farm, in Tettenhall Regis manor, was built in the early C18 (VCH vol 20 pp8, 17). There is a Lower Dippons marked to the N of Dippons Farm (1:25,000 OS map 1988). With the construction of the new Perton housing estate in the area of Dippons Farm in 1974, it was proposed that the farm be converted into three homes (E&S June 12 1974) (WMA vol 1 p230), but it was in fact demolished that year (VCH vol 20 pp8, 17).

Dirty Gutter House nearly 0.5m NW of Bottom House. It may be identified with Green Gutter; the Young Pretender's army passed Green Gutter on Dec 4 1745 in the Jacobite Rebellion (BPCSM p7).

Dividy Lane Former small hamlet 1.25m NNE of Longton. In Caverswall ancient parish. Preserved in Dividy Road.

Dividy Lane Brook Runs from Brownfields northwards to Coldmoor Brook (OS map 1890).

Dixon's Branch of the Birmingham Canal. Ran from the Birmingham New Cut New Main Line (or Island Line) in a ENE direction to Clarkes Grove, Horseley Heath. Opened in 1828. Closure was sanctioned for the N end in 1954 and for the S end in 1965 (HCMS No. 2). A section adjacent to the now (1995) deserted St Martin's Cemetery had disappeared by 1995 (BCM autumn 1995 p19).

Dob Hill In the area of the present Swiss Drive, on N side of Brierley Hill Road, Buckpool, in Kingswinford ancient parish. The name occurs on Fowler's map of 1822 (WFK p24 see map). Has also appeared as Dobb Hill (SVS p130).

Doctor's Corner Buried in the NE corner of the churchyard of Leek's St Edward the Confessor church are eight doctors - Isaac Cope d1801, Eli Cope d1812, Peter Walthall Davenport d1813, Charles Chadwick d1836, Joseph Brindley d1841, James Davenport Hulme d1848, Charles Flint d1864, Richard Cooper d1872. Miller seems to be the first to call this corner of the churchyard Doctor's Corner (OL vol 1 pp144-149). From here is the best place to see the sun setting twice behind the Cloud at mid summer (GLS p63). However, it is believed no one has seen the double sunset from here between 1958 and at least 1999 on account of foliage blocking the view (local info).

Doctor's Piece Former land of Dr Richard Wilkes (d1760) of Willenhall Old Hall. It eventually passed into the ownership of the chapel of ease estate. In 1840s it was proposed that the land be used for a National School but following the 1849 cholera epidemic it was used as an overspill burial ground for victims (WDY p4p in c1948) (SNW p23). It is now (1988) a memorial garden (MR p381). By 1951 the name had also been given to a street lying near to this land (HOWI ps facing p124, p187).

Doctor's Trees A little hut, a few hundred yards up the road from Dunbrook, Longnor, formerly used by a man who doctored animals. It is haunted by a big black dog, which appears harmless (although a true Barghest, or dog-like goblin, is said to portend death) (L pp48,49).

Doddeslow Rolleston. A Doddeslow Field is on the southern slopes of Beacon Hill (UTR pp166,179).

Doddlespool Minute hamlet 0.75m N of Betley. Thought to be derived from Toad's Pool (MR p33).

Doddlespool Hall 1m SW of Balterley (W p384). Formerly in Balterley chapelry in Barthomley ancient parish, Ches. Built in 1605. Additions were made in blue and red brick in c1700. Purchased by John Hodgson in 1763 from Thomas Rowlison. In 1783 Robert Hodgson bought the hall and estate from John Hodgson. When R Hodgson died in 1816 he left the property to his nephew Thomas Hodgson and in default of issue to the present (1856) Lieut Col Tomkinson. The hall was lately (1856) the residence of Dorning Rasbotham (BART p203); a Col Tomkinson of Willington Hall was a member of the Wilbraham family (BVC p126). Rebuilt in the C19 (SGS p59). Between 1873 and 1879 it was the home of Francis Cradock Twemlow. In 1903 it was sold to Eliza Ann Twemlow and became part of the estate of Betley Court. Charles Fletcher-Twemlow (d1976) seems to have moved here after leaving Betley Court in 1940 (SGS p59) (BVC p126). The hall was known locally as Toad's-pool Hall (BART p203). 'F.R.T.' is carved on Doddlespool Hall Farm. This refers to Col Francis Randall Twemlow of Peatswood (BTC p31).

Dods Leigh Hamlet 1m SW of Church Leigh. Formerly in Leigh township and ancient parish. The name appears in 1167 as Dedeslega. It means possibly 'Dæddi's wood clearing' (SSE 1996 p13). Has appeared as Dods Leigh (Yates' map) and Dodsley (J Phillips & WF Wutchings map 1832).

Dodsley House 0.25m WS of Dods Leigh. There was a house here by at least 1887. It appears as Dodsley Farm in 1928 and Dodsley Cottage Farm in 1987 (OS maps). The name is perhaps a corruption of Dods Leigh.

Doe Bank Farm to E of Pheasey on N side of Doe Bank Lane, Kingstanding, in existence by 1841. The name, preserved in Doe Bank Lane, schools, and wood, may be from a bank and ditch in Great Barr Park to contain deer (SNAR pp75-76).

Doe Bank Former district N of Ocker Hill, at 975940. Appears on 1947 OS map 1:25,000 (sheet 32/99). The name is preserved in Doe Bank Road off Leabrook Road.

Doe Bank Hall The house of Coppice farm at Lea Brook, Ocker Hill. In existence by 1690. Doe Bank House was later divided into tenements and one part of the house was used as an inn called Doe Bank Inn. The house was dismantled by 1946, and the farmland had completely disappeared by then when it was covered by pit banks, large pools and some new housing estates (OH pp59-60).

Dog and Doublet Inn Former inn on the main road farther N than the present inn (built in 1905) in Sandon. The old inn, reputedly, received its name after a dog brought a blooded doublet of a murdered man to the pub and so alerted the neighbourhood to the murder (IOM p63) (SSBOP p55) (SPN p103). There is a tradition that in the Civil War the parliamentarians drank all the inn's ale vats dry as they went to the battle of Hopton Heath (SIS p42) (BFS p15). Sandon was on the main London-Holyhead(-Carlisle) route from the Middle Ages. In 1830 the host, James Ballantine, had a name for hospitality. There was a verse scratched onto a window at the 'old' inn saying

'Most travellers to whom these roads are known,
Would rather stay at Sandon than at Stone:
Good chaises, horses, treatment, and good wines
They always meet with at James Ballantine's.'

(IOM p63) (VB p134). James Ballantine's daughter made a runaway match with a young man, of whom her father disapproved. One night, he broke into the inn to get some property belonging to his wife. His father-in-law handed him over to the police. Though it was a minor theft, he was found guilty and hanged. On the night of the execution a crowd of villagers congregated outside the inn to chant the 69th Psalm, coupled with curses for James Ballantine (IOM pp63-64).

Dog Croft On the lane to Chell Heath, Burslem.

Doggingtree 2.25m N of Cannock. Has appeared as Doggintree (1843) (SPNO p68). There is a small new housing estate here.

Dog Hole Wetton. Cave or fissure about or near Thor's Cave (WTCEM pp128-132).

Dog-Kennel Pool At or near Bentley Hall, Willenhall (NHS p155).

Dogkennel Pool Weston Park, Weston-under-Lizard.

Doglands House 0.5m SSW of Fradswell. Appears on 1834 OS map.

Doglane House and area (W p750) 0.25m E of Calton. Formerly part of Musden Grange estate, a grange of Croxden Abbey. After the Dissolution Doglane remained in Croxden parish, as a detached portion, until removed to Calton

civil parish in 1886 (GLAUE p407). Dog Lane appears as early as 1421 and may have been a small hamlet in the C16 and the C17 (SASR 1995 no 5 p36).

Dolefoot Farm House 1m SSE of Newborough. The name may be from Dolsfore Gate (see).

Doley Small hamlet over 1.5m NW of Adbaston. In Adbaston parish. Has also appeared as Dowley (W p382). Two people saw an unusual object, possibly a UFO, for about one minute from a house at Doley on Sept 6 1967 at about 8.30pm (FSRP p14). At about 10.00pm on the same day a very bright red round object with three bright red lights spaced evenly and horizontally across the centre of the object was seen from Doley (FSRP p15).

Doley Brook Rises to NW of Gnosall joins Church Eaton Brook at Reule.

Doley Common Former common land about 1m NW of Gnosall. The name is from possibly 'dor' in the sense of 'a narrowing valley' and 'leah' a wood (SPNO p159). Has appeared as Dorley (1586), Doreley Common (1686), Dawley Moor (1817), Dauley Common (NHS) (THS p270) (SPNO p159).

Doleygate Former extensive reclaimed fen lying in a linear glacial hollow (WSS pp100,101p), now a tiny hamlet 0.75m WNW of Gnosall. In Gnosall parish. To the N is Doley Common.

Dollymakers Hill Near Grand Lodge, Beaudesert (Cannock Chase by Car. Staffs Nature Conservation Trust Ltd. ND, but between 1971 and 1974 p8).

Dolsfore Gate Former entry into Needwood Forest (VCH vol 2 p350 see map) near Dolefoot Farm, 1m SSE of Newborough.

Domvilles House 1.25m NE of Balterley. Occurs as Dumvells on Dower's map.

Donegal House Bore Street, Lichfield. Built in 1730 for James Robinson, mercer, probably to the designs of Francis Smith of Warwick (VCH vol 14 p43). (BOE p194 pl 42) (LAL p11p). Adjoins the Guildhall.

Donkey Hole A cave near Thor's Cave, Wetton. It is good for hiding in (WTCEM pp71,128-132).

Donnithorne Chase Bungalow on the corner of Waterfall Lane and Ashbourne road at Waterhouses. Built by Sam Green between 1937 and 1945 using stone from the demolished Wootton Hall, Wootton near Ellastone. The house had been long derelict by 2000 when it was restored to be let (local info).

Dormston House Formerly Sedgley Villa on the E side of Sedgley town. It was the residence of FA Homer, founder of the temperance movement in Sedgley in 1859 - his temperance army was known locally as 'Homer's Army' (SDOP p73). The last Homer to occupy the house was John Twigg Homer (d1934). The house then lay empty until WW2 when it was taken over by the Home Guard. After the war it was purchased by JR Hickling, a local businessman (SDSSOP p36p).

Dorrington Modern housing estate and industrial park, 0.75m N of Stafford. Named after John Dorrington, builder of the High House, Stafford (SPN p111).

Dorslow Former village in the vicinity of Croxton. Has appeared as Dorueslau (DB), Doreslowe when an endowment belonging to Stone Priory (VCH vol 3 p246), Derueslowe (1199), Derneslowe (1272), Dorslow (1284-5), Dawslow (1510), Durslow (1511), Doreslow (1553), Doresley (1584), Dosley in field names on a C19 tithe map (ECC p21), The Dawsley, a field name on a C19 tithe map (ECC p21), and Dervislouwe (SHC 1923 p34). The DB name suggests it was a 'leah' or 'clearing in the woods' (ECC p21). If Dordsley, then 'Daeddi's woodland glade' (SPN p42). Even in the time of DB it was not much of a settlement. It was still a township in 1298 although by then it was held with Little Sugnall (SSAHST 1970 p35). In the C16 Erdeswick (SOS) thought it was near Little Sugnall; in the late C18 Shaw proposed to identify it with Dodsley, Church Leigh; in the early C19 Harwood (SOS) identified it with Horseley (SHC 1923 pp32-35). Commander Wedgwood identified it with a place in or near Sugnall (SHC 1916 p168). PV Bate and DM Palliser placed it 0.75m SSE of Chatcull, 1m NE of Croxtonbank, a little N of Little Sugnall, at SJ 800333 (SSAHST 1970 p35). John Morris placed it near Sugnall (DB edited by John Morris. Phillimore. 1976. Notes).

Dosthill Small village on a bank near the Tame, 21.5m NNW of Warwick and 23m SE of Stafford. Formerly in Kingsbury township and ancient parish, Warws. The name has appeared as Dercelai or Dershull (DB), Dertehulla (C12), Derchethull (C12), Dertsechul (1236), Dercetehill (1242), Dersthull (1316), Dersthulle (1327), Dorsthull (C14) (DUIGNAN. Warwickshire. 1912) (SSE 1996 p13) (SPN p42). It represents 'the hill where deer are found' (SSE 1996 p13) (SPN p42). An old chapel on the W side of Church Road is of Norman origin (THM vol 4 p91ps,118). It is oblong in shape (BOE p117). In 1912 it was being used for Sunday school and as a parish room (THM vol 5 p37). It was being used as a parish hall in 1988 (MR p125). A new church, St Paul, was built to the SW in 1870-1872 (BOE p117) (CHMS2 p40). There is a moated site at SP 211000, slightly NNW of the church (SSAHST 1982-3 pp47-48) (CAMS p63). Turkish oaks at Dosthill, which were described in 1972 as recently cut down, are said to have been planted by Crusaders on their return from the Holy Land (LTM Sept 1972 p11). The old barn with impressive cruck-trusses N of the old Norman chapel, may be of C15 origin, or earlier (BOE p117). There is a legend Oliver Cromwell in the Civil War once fired cannon at Tamworth Castle from Dosthill. But the story is only supported by the 'huge cannonball' which was once used as a doorstop at Dosthill Lodge (LTM Sept 1972 p11). Dosthill Spa, to the N of Dosthill near Dosthill House, in Wilnecote manor and township was a famous purging water. Near the spa, in the same field (Water Linch) was a chalybeate spring, which according to Shaw, was said to be inferior to none in England (SHOS vol 1 p433). A George IV four shilling piece and a medallion commemorating Admiral Vernon's victory at Portobello 1739 was found in the Old Cottage on Wigford Road (LTM Sept 1972 p11). Dosthill was transferred to Tamworth municipal borough, Staffs, in 1965 (GLAUE p425).

Dosthill House Near Dosthill Spa. Formerly in Wilnecote township in Tamworth ancient parish. Built in 1830, with a nice porch (BOE p117). White noted it was unoccupied in the mid C19 (W p627).

Dosthill Lodge Dosthill, formerly in Warws. Occupied in 1851 by Mrs B Peel (W p19).

Dosthill Old Manor House Dosthill (LTM Sept 1972 p11p).

'Double Lock House' Wordsley, Kingswinford. Lock keepers cottage, stands on Stourbridge Canal. Dates from the C18 (TB Oct 1979 p7il).

Dove, River (upstream as in love, downstream as in stove LTD p9). River more or less forming the boundary between Staffs and Derbys. Its source, a spring in Axe Edge, is known as Dove Head (S p19p). It is 1m NE of Flash at SK 032685, below Dove Head Farm on the Leek-Buxton road. At Newton Solney, Derbys, after 57 miles, the river flows into the Trent. For the first part of its journey it travels through some named dales in the Peak District, viz: Beresford, Wolfscote, Mill, and Dove. After leaving the dales, passing out between Bunster Hill and Thorp Cloud, it creates what is generally known as the Dove Valley, which has for centuries been considered some of the richest pastureland in England. Leland in the early C16 remarked 'there be wonderful pastures upon the Dove' (SL p94). This richness was due to the river flooding and overflowing in spring time. In these lower reaches the inhabitants had a saying which showed their appreciation for spring floods:

> In April Dove's flood
> Is worth a King's good.

(Britannia. William Camden. 1586) (NHS p108) (HWE vol 2 p303) (Nightingale) (History of Lancs Cheshire and Derbys. Leigh) (HOU p11) (SCSF p165). Because its flooding made adjacent lands fertile Plot and FNC Mundy likened it to the Nile. The latter described the Dove as 'the British Nile' in his poem 'Needwood Forest' - 'Down you mid dale the British Nile' (HOU p10). There was a serious flood in autumn 1903 at Uttoxeter (AUOPP p54p). The river was also peculiar in that it used to rise extremely within 12 hours, but within 12 hours return again to its banks (SMC p119). Shaw described the river as rapid (SHOS vol 1 p90). However, it froze between Tutbury and Rocester for 16 weeks in 1894, the ice was thick enough for some to skate between the two towns (VB p96) (ESNF p101) (SK p167 photograph of facing p160) (BTOP vol 1 p12). The river may have formed a boundary between Celtic kingdoms: David Ford considers it a disputed boundary between two such kingdoms, and that Iron Age promontory forts in Needwood Forest and at Tutbury were set up to defend the territory of one kingdom (LTD p169). Dove appears in several Anglo-Saxon charters as Dufan (SHC 1916 pp90,123). It has appeared as an, and long dufan (951), of, on dufan (1008), Dove (1200-1225. c1540), Douve (1235), Duve (1305), and Dowve (1475) (SPNO pp8-9). The **name** appears to be Celtic in origin, from perhaps, the British word 'dubo,' or Primitive Welsh 'duB,' or Welsh 'du,' or Gaelic 'dhu' all meaning 'black' or 'dark' (SSAHST 1967 p35) (HOA p10) (SPNO p9) (LTD p9). (NSFCT 1908 p126) (SDW p9). Or from the Celtic word dwfr (stream) or dawfre (water) (LGS p122) (NSFCT 1919 p53). It was formerly thought to derive from the bird, dove, to which it seemed, in many respects to bear a likeness, for instance in colour, in its rapidity, and in its cooing noise near the source (SHOS vol 1 pp89-90). Or perhaps from the diver, from Anglo-Saxon. Although it does not dive like some of its tributaries, like the Manifold, do (DUIGNAN). Successive generations have delighted in the beauty of stretches of the river, especially in Dove Dale (see), where limestone protrusions contrast with wooded dale sides. The poet Charles Cotton (d1687) of Beresford Hall by the river in Beresford Dale, was a keen angler in the upper reaches, and the beauty of it there inspired some of his poetry, such as this verse

> The silver Dove (how pleasant is that name!)
> Runs thro' a vale, high crested cliffs o'ershade,
> By her fair progress only pleasant made

> But with so swift a torrent in her course,
> As shews the nymph flyes from her native source,
> To seek what's there deny'd, the sun's warm beams,
> And to embrace Trent's prouder swelling streams.

(SHOS vol 1 p90). Also Cotton wrote

> O my beloved Nympha! fair Dove -
> Princess of rivers! how I love
> Upon thy flowing banks to lie,
> And view thy silver stream....'

(S&W p284) (NSFCT 1886 p93). Subsequently, others have been inspired by the Dove: Edwards' poem 'The Tour of the Dove' is given in AAD p130; 'The River Dove and Human Life Compared' (1856) by George Wakefield of Uttoxeter (see) is a long rural poem; 'Dove Valley Rhymes' (1875) is by Francis Redfern (VFC p112). Cotton and his friend and fellow angler Izaak Walton of Stafford (see) visited the source, where Cotton claimed he could cover the spring with his hat. The spring head, which has since been occasionally called Izaak Walton's and Charles Cotton's Well, has their initials in a monogram inscribed onto the cap stone. This monogram is believed to have been made by them. The cap stone cracked during the severe frost of 1903 (LTD p12) (WTCEM p61) (HLS p8) (CCR pp1,165) (LTD p5p) (SMCC p2). In 1936 a log of black bog oak computed to be 6,000 years old was found when searching for the body of a child, Leonard Goodall, who was believed drowned in the river. Leonard's parents gave it to Tutbury church. It was made into a lectern to Leonard's memory in 1939 and is still (c1992) used in the church (SLM autumn 1958 p27) (Tutbury Church Guide) (LTD p152). (GNHS pp18,19,20,21,22) (DAJ vol 42). On Oct 5 1998 salmon was re-introduced into the Dove near Eaton Dovedale, 2m S of Rocester, in Derbys. Salmon was last recorded in the Dove in 1926 (ES Oct 6 1998 p1) (LTD p101).

Dove Bank District of Kidsgrove, 0.5m NNE of Kidsgrove.

Dove Bridge Now two bridges over the Dove 1m NE of Uttoxeter. The old disused bridge said to be of C14 origin (LTD p147) was rebuilt or repaired in 1691 (NSFCT 1980 p47) just crossed over the Dove. Michael Sadler, social reformer and MP, is said to have been held over the side of the bridge by religious fanatics when a boy in the late C18. The bridge was widened in 1915 (LTD p147). In 1987 a hoard of silver coins from Edward I and II's reigns was found near the bridge (LTD p147). The new bridge, slightly further down stream carrying the A50 dual carriageway, crosses over both the Dove and the Tean, which join here.

Dove Bridge Tiny hamlet on both sides of the Dove, in Uttoxeter ancient parish in Staffs, and in Derbys. A house or the houses on the Staffs side seem to go by the name of Noah's Ark.

Dovecliff House 0.75m N of Rocester. In Rocester ancient parish.

Dove Cliff Brick late Georgian house (LTD p213) 0.75m N of Stretton (Burton upon Trent). The Thornewill family, iron masters, bought Dove Cliff from the Earl of Uxbridge in the late C18 and built the present house here (SHOS vol 1 p27) (LTD p214). Birthplace of Harriet Georgina, Lady Burton in 1841. She was the fourth daughter of Edward Thornewill (BTOP p44p), who was occupying the hall in 1851 (W p19). Harriet Georgina was a renowned hostess, especially to Edward VII when staying at Rangemore Hall (LTD p214).

Dove Dale An extremely narrow steep wooded gorge through which the Dove flows in its upper reaches. Perhaps, the most beautiful dale in England. It is 1.75m long. It starts at about Dove Holes or about 15 miles downstream from the Dove's source on Axe Edge Moor. It ends at the Stepping Stones over the Dove, which is about 22.25m NE of Stafford. Some use the term Dove Dale to refer to a far longer stretch of land either side of the Dove, from its source, even, until the valley floor widens after Ellastone. The county border between Staffs and Derbys follows the Dove and consequently only half the dale is in Staffs. The public footpath is on the Derbys side. There are many limestone rock-pinnacles jutting out from the sides of the gorge, and many have names, some of which allude to their shape. On the Staffs side there is (see): Church Rocks, Dove Dale Castle (or Dove Dale Church), Ilam Rock, Jacob's Ladder, Raven's Tor, Shepherd Abbey Rocks, Twelve Apostles. On the Derbys side there is (see): Dove Holes, Grey Mare's Stable Cave, Lion's Head Rock, Lover's Leap (or Sharplow Point), Reynard's Cave and Kitchen, Three Sisters, Tissington Spires, Watch Box (above Lion's Head Rock). Several Roman coins including one of Constantine and one of Maximinian were found in c1910 and in c1914 in Dove Dale (NSFCT vol 49 p185) (NSJFS 1964 p14). Has appeared as Duuedale (1296) (SSE 1996 p13) and Dovedale. Michael Drayton alluded to the dale in his poem 'Polyolbion' (1613). Izaak

Walton, author of Stafford (see) and Charles Cotton poet of Beresford Hall (see) were anglers in the dale in the C17. Subsequent visitors include: Dr Johnson of Lichfield (see), Rousseau of Wootton Hall (see), Wordsworth (LTD p35), Tennyson and Ruskin (Dovedale Guide. Keith Mantell. 1985; the latter described the dale as 'An alluring first lesson in all that is beautiful' (LTD p35). The upper reaches by the Nabbs was frequently visited by Tom Moore, Lord Byron, and Nat Gould, the Derbyshire novelist (NSFCT 1936 p30). It is Eagledale in George Elliot's 'Adam Bede.' Sir Walter Scott wrote about Dove Dale in his poem 'Rokeby' canto ii (JAT p52). A good deal of the dale was presented to the NT in 1933 (NSFCT 1936 p30). It is reputedly haunted by the Dovedale 'Deadhead,' a legendary highwayman who robbed journeymen and merchants who used the packhorse way through the dale (Peak District Monsters. Alan Smith. 1994 pp39-41).

Dove Dale Castle Rock feature on Staffs side of the Dove above the Stepping Stones. It bears a strong resemblance to a rustic church, but is called the 'castle' (DDI p16) (PS p122) (JAT p52) (DMV pp9p,10p). Has also appeared as Dovedale Church (according to the turn, secular or ecclesiastical, of one's architectural fancy - Dovedale Guide. Keith Mantell. 1984. p6).

Dovedale Church Rock feature in Dove Dale on Staffs side resembling a church with a round turret. Is situated opposite the pump house near to Tissington Spires (DMV p11p) and may be identified with Mantell's Church Rocks (see). But Mantell identifies Dove Dale Church with Dove Dale Castle (see) (Dovedale Guide. Keith Mantell. 1984. p6).

Dove Fields House 1.75m N of Draycott-in the-Clay.

Doveflats House 0.5m N of Rocester.

Dove Head Farm House 0.75m NNE of Flash, just in Staffs on Leek-Buxton road. 20 yards S of it is the source of the Dove.

Doveridge At or near Caldmore, Walsall, there was a hamlet of this name in mid C19; part of the area, known as Doveridge Fold became known as Little London (see), and only the tiny Doveridge Place seems to survive. (W p649).

Dove Street (1834 OS map). Appears to be the present Lower Ellastone.

Dowdswell Brook which joins the Sow just above Broad Eye Bridge, Stafford (SKYT p102).

Dower House Dunstall Road, Barton-under-Needwood. Built in the early C19 (BOE p66). Residence for the dowagers of the Gresley family of Drakelow Hall, Derbys (UNT p77).

Dower House House in Hollybush Lane, Oaken. It dates from the later C18 (VCH vol 20 p79).

Dowles Brook Tributary of the Severn. Forms the southernmost boundary of Arley ancient parish, and was the southernmost boundary of Staffs until Arley was removed to Worcs in 1894-5.

Downfield Hamlet 0.5m W of Milton. Downfield Side S of Norton-in-the-Moors, with Downfield to its S, with Downfield Bank to its S all appear on OS map 1834. The name is preserved in Downfield Place.

Down House Moated farmhouse 1.5m SE of Bradley (VCH vol 4 p84). In Bradley ancient parish. Has appeared as la Duoune (1289), la Doune (1293), le Doune (1401), le Downes (1548), The Downe or Downs (SPNO p138). Sir Edward Littleton owned in 1614 an estate called The Downs, with a moated house of that name (SSAHST 1982-3 p36).

Downs Banks Braken-covered heathland between Oulton and Barlaston. Probably created due to glacial action rather than river erosion (NSFCT 1940 p31). It is crossed by a trackway, traditionally regarded as part of the ancient packhorse route from Chester to the East Midlands. The name Downs Banks occurs in the journal of Admiral John Jervis of Meaford Hall for Sept 22 1765 (SIS p63). The area has also been called, commonly, Barlaston Downs and the Downs. The Downs was common land in Meaford township in Kibblestone quarter in Stone ancient parish (W p364) until the end of C18 when it was enclosed with hedged fields, and a farm (Bluebarn Farm) built. Probably the higher ground was never cultivated, and left for grazing. Hops were grown on the low land for Joule's Brewery. In 1946 John Joule and Sons Ltd purchased the land from Viscount Sidmouth to prevent it being taken over by the Electricity Board (SSBOP p74p). The Downs was presented by Joules to the NT on July 22 1950 as a thank offering for victory in WW2 (public notice board on the Downs) (SN May 16 1980 p1) (Stafford Gazette May 1988 p8). The Downs were frequented by people from the Potteries for walks and picnics in Wakes Week, the first week in Aug (Memories of the Downs Banks. Kathleen Day. c1999 p10). In the mid 1990s a baboon-like creature was spotted roaming the Downs (ES Sept 23 1996 p4). By 1997 the Downs consisted of 166 acres. In May 1997 the NT appointed the first warden of the Downs (SN May 30 1997 p5). By Dec 1999 Stone Rural and Barlaston parish councils had had erected a circular pillar on a vantage point at SJ 902370 to commemorate the Millennium.

Downsdale Near Hardings Booth (W p743). Formerly in Heathylee township

in Alstonefield ancient parish (W p743) (NSSG p17). The Downside which appears on 1834 OS and Dower's maps 1m S of Flash is now Downsdale.

Dowrey Appears by Kingstone Wood on Yates' map. Now lost.

Doxey Village near the confluence of the Sow and Doxey Brook 1.5m WNW of Stafford; Doxey now more or less merges with Stafford. In Seighford ancient parish. The name appears in DB as Dochesig. It is from Anglo-Saxon 'docce' meaning duck, and 'ig' meaning island applied to a marsh (Stafford Post May 5 1988 p4 May 12 1988 p12). Duignan accepts it may be 'Duck's island' or 'Duck's marsh,' but could be 'Docca's island' (DUIGNAN). Gelling thinks 'Docc's island' (NSJFS 1981 p3) (SSE 1996 p13). Poulton-Smith thinks it may not be from a personal name (SPN p112). Mr EA Mercer of Doxey found a cannon ball in an old marl pit near his home. It was probably used in the Civil War when nearby Stafford Castle was under attack (SLM summer 1956 pp18,19p). A mission church, St Andrew, in Doxey Road, was built in 1914. A new church in Doxey Road, dedicated to St Thomas and St Andrew, opened in 1975 (VCH vol 6 p249).

Doxey Brook Created out of Presford Brook and Butterbank Brook E of Coton Clanford joins the Sow N of Doxey.

Doxey Fields W side of Doxey.

Doxey House Doxey. Listed house of C17 origin. Restored by Stafford borough council (SVB p67). (Stafford Post May 5 1988 p4). The garden contains, according to Roxburgh, built into an arch, parts of the old priest's door of the S transept of the Anglo-Norman church of St Mary's, Stafford (SKYT p92) (OSST 1929 pp38ils,39).

Doxey Marsh Marshes at Doxey through which the little River Darling runs. An attempt to drain the marshes was made in the late C19 after the Tillington Drainage Act of 1875. But drainage schemes failed and the area was still flooding in the 1970s (WSS pp112-113). An area of marsh of 360 acres situated mainly between the railway line and the Sow, became an SSSI in 1983, protecting over 130 species of plant and bird life (ROT p34), and was by 1999 in the care of the Staffs Wildlife Trust (Staffs Wildlife Trust leaflet). A pyramid obelisk was unveiled at the site to the memory of Henry Attwood at the opening of the nature reserve in Oct 1983 (E&S Oct 14 1983 p). Has also appeared as Doxey Marshes (WSS pp112-113).

Doxey Pool Small pool on the E side of the Roaches, at about 1547 feet above sea level (NSFCT 1942 p62). Situated on the nearly topmost ridge of the Roaches at SK 004628. The pool, which has also appeared as Doxy's Pool (SGM p20), is lozenge-shaped and is 30 yards long and 15-20 yards wide and about 45 yards in circumference (NSFCT 1944 pp27-28) (TTTD p108) (MIDD vol 1 p32p). The depth of the pool is about three feet (TTTD pp108,118p). The water is said to be always cold and of a brown shade (OL vol 2 pp120,121 il by James McAldowie) and remains at the same level each year (NSFCT 1942 p62). The pool, lying on England's main watershed, may be one of the oldest lakes in Britain and is certainly the oldest in the county and may have been created by erosion (NSFCT 1922 pp48-57 figs 1-3 show the pool in 1878 and 1922. 1937 p119). It is never known to go dry and is 100 feet above any other known spring in the district (SSGLST p22). The name is probably from Anglo-Saxon 'ox' and 'pol' - the 'ox's drinking place' (NSFCT 1922 pp48-57). Or the Doxey family of Pheasants Clough in the C17 probably gave their name to it (OL vol 2 p145) (HOLF pp12-13il). According to legend the pool was named after a daughter of Bess of Rock Hall (see); perhaps Hannah (b1825) who disappeared in c1845 (SGM pp19-20) (DPEM pp51,52). (SK il of facing p64). An 'evil looking hag' has been seen in its waters, and a mermaid reputedly inhabits it (SMM p16il) (DPEM p52).

Doxey Wood Appears to have been a wide stretch of woodland in the Doxey and Doxeywood Farm areas. The name which appears in 1616 and 1836 (SPNO p77) has also appeared as Doxey Woods. The High House, Stafford, is supposed to have been constructed with timber from these woods (Stafford Post May 5 1988 p4).

Doxey Wood Cottage Opposite Doxeywood Farm 2m NE of Bradley or 2.25m S of Doxey in Thorneyfields Lane. Perhaps the smallest and quaintest cruck-framed cottage in the county (MR p46p), some of the framing dates from the late C16 or early C17 (VCH vol 5 p139).

Drake Hall A hostel 1m SE of Slindon built in c1938 for workers, relocated from Woolwich Arsenal, at the new Royal Ordnance Factory at Swynnerton. It housed ammunitions workers in WW2 (SN April 7 1995 p9). Named after Sir Francis Drake (SSE 1996 p2). It now houses what has been described as the biggest women's prison in Britain (ES Nov 7 1997 p2).

Drakelow Covert S of Great Bridgeford.

Draw Well Draw Well Lane, Werrington. In which it is said a young woman tried to commit suicide but her crinoline saved her (WYV pp56, 60il).

Draycott Cross Small hamlet 1m NNE of Draycott-in-the-Moors. In the later C17 Plot noted about midway between Cheadle and Draycott rocks containing pebbles; evidence that the pebbles are far older than the rock (NHS p171).

Draycott Cross Drayton Manor, Dunston. A lost cross and gospel place on the Penkridge perambulation. It stood on the N bank of the Four Lanes' Ends at the upper end of Drayton hamlet. The parishioners stopped at it on the first day of the perambulation. Recorded in PR 1732 (HOP p29).

Draycott-in-the-Clay Village and township in Hanbury ancient parish, 15m ENE of Stafford. The village lies in a tiny dale created by Salt Brook in the northern incline to the Needwood Forest plateau. The manor of Draicote appears in DB. Draycott later appears as Draykote, Draycot sub Nedwode, Draycott-under-Needwood, Draycot in the Clay (1798) (SHOS vol 1 p82) (W p560). The name appears to be of Anglo-Saxon origin and means 'cottage of the drag (net),' a dragnet being an agricultural implement (DUIGNAN). Or is from Anglo-Saxon 'droeg,' 'a portage,' referring to a site where boats had to be dragged across a narrow strip of land or river obstruction in order to continue their journey (SSE 1996 p13) (SPN p33). The manor was held of the overlord at Tutbury in the Middle Ages by the tenant performing some service (SHOS vol 1 p82) (SMC p123) (Baronage vol 2 p108). An alum spring at Draycott-in-the-Clay became a holy well (NHS p105) (HOU p15) (OSST 1944-1945) (SJC p10). A saline spring near Draycott Mill, 1m NNE of Draycott village, proved salt for the nuns of Hanbury Priory (HOU p15). Draycott became a separate civil parish in 1866 (GLAUE p409). The church, St Augustine, on the corner of Draycott Cliff and Greaves Lane at the S end of the village, was built in c1924 (LDD).

Draycott-in-the-Moors Ancient parish and village on a bank above the Blithe 11.25m NNE of Stafford. A perforated stone axe-hammer has been found in Draycott-in-the-Moors parish (Society of Antiquaries Ms. 'Primaeval Antiquities' vol 1 p43) (NSJFS 1964 p21). Less than 0.5m from the church at SJ 981397 by Manor Farm is a burial mound. By 1983 it was nearly ploughed out and was three feet high (NSFCT 1983 p12). Richmilde Street (see), the **Roman** road between Derby and Chesterton, passed through Draycott. The Romans had a legionary outpost here. The rock face at the back of the post office was perhaps carved into by them to make shelving to hold implements for their cobblers and chariot repairers (SVB p67). Probably this is the ancient smithy the NSFC saw in 1956 (NSFCT 1956 p112). Draycott-in-the-Moors is not in DB (NSFCT 1888 p58), but may have been surveyed under Niwetone alias Newton 1m to the SSE (NSFCT 1915 p90). It has appeared as Draicot (1251) (SSE 1996 p13) and Draycott-le-Moors (NSFCT 1909 p170). The **name** means the 'cottage of the drag (net)' (DUIGNAN). Or it is perhaps from the forest-root 'droigheann,' Welsh 'draen' with other forms 'draigen' 'dragino' (NSFCT 1908 p139). The terminal 'in-the-Moors' was not only descriptive of the physical conditions of the settlement but its omission from a writ - served in an action for the recovery of land in 1342 - lost the plaintiff her case, and simply raised the technical objection that there was no such place as 'Draycott' and obtained judgment (NSFCT 1915 p156). The parish **church**, St Margaret, Church Lane, has some late C13 work (BOE p117) and is said to have been built and consecrated in 1286 (COPP2 p68p). Draycott parish formed between 1086 and 1291 probably out of Stone original parish (SHC 1916 p195). Richard de Draycote was granted a charter March 20 1297 to hold a **market** at one of the Staffs 'Draycotts' on Thursdays. The market had ceased by 1500 (NSJFS 1971 p51). The making of tape was carried on at Draycott (SCSF p112). The old cock pit referred to at Draycott-in-the-Moors (NSFCT 1956 p112) (STM May 1965 p43p) is probably that at SJ 984399. The special dish to celebrate mid-Lent 'Mothering Sunday' in Draycott-in-the-Moors parish was a fig pie, made of dry figs, sugar, and treacle. This fourth Sunday in Lent was known in the C19 in Draycott-in-the-Moors as Fig Pie Wake. Any visitor expected and received a piece of fig pie (SCSF p12) (FOS p86). There is a legend concerning a particular spot at Draycott where the last dragon was slain (NSFCT 1908 p107). By Nov 1998 there were two small worn wooden crosses attached to a signpost at the junction of Uttoxeter Road and Cresswell Lane, probably commemorating victims of a road accident.

Drayton Bassett Ancient parish and village near the Tame between two of its tributaries 22.25m SE of Stafford. Some of the parish was formerly in Hemlingford hundred, Warws (GLAUE p409). At Drayton Bassett and at Shenstone were found a hand axe from the **Upper Palaeolithic** (pre-Ice Age) period; the earliest evidence of man in the county when found in 1971. It was found during a potato harvest between Drayton Bassett and Bullock's End Farm (SSAHST 1972-3 pp1,3,4 fig 3) (NSJFS vol 12. 1972. pp1-20) (SL p35). A polished flint axe of **Neolithic** or **Bronze Age** was found in Drayton Bassett parish in c1927 (NSJFS 1964 p21). The manor of Draitone appears in DB. The **name** is from perhaps a brook that flowed from Bourne Pool by the village, and had a Celtic or Anglo-Saxon name, similar to Drave, Drai or Dray. Or Drayton may be from Celtic words signifying a town lying on a

straight road (SHOS vol 2 p1 note). Or it may derive from an Anglo-Saxon word for a place where boats and timber are beached from a river (DUIGNAN) (DM p4), and hence 'the settlement by a portage' (SPN p43). Drayton might be from a derivation from 'whitley stakes' 'urkeltisher sprachschatz' 'drai' (Irish) meaning druid and it could be that Draytons and Draycotes might be settlements of the druids still lingering on into Christian times (NSFCT 1922 p170). See also the NSFCT 1908 p139 explanation for Drayton-in-the-Moor. By the early C12 the manor was held by the Ridells; Geoffrey Ridell, a justice under Henry I was drowned in 1120 in the wreck of the White Ship, his widow Geve founded Canwell Priory (see). By the mid C12 it had passed by marriage to the Bassets; 'Basset' is found attached to the place name in 1301 (SSE 1996 p13).

THE BASSETS OF DRAYTON BASSETT. The descent of the Bassets in Shaw and in The Complete Peerage do not agree. Shaw's Ralph Basset of Colston and Drayton, Chief Justice of England in Henry I's reign, who was buried at Abingdon, was the father of Richard Basset the Justiciar (d1144) who married Maud Ridel (SHOS vol 2 p12). The Complete Peerage says Richard Basset the Justiciar (d1144) inherited Drayton through his marriage with Maud Ridell. He was succeeded by his son Richard Basset (d1160). He was succeeded by his son Richard Basset (d1211), who was succeeded by his son Ralph Basset (d1254-1261). He was succeeded by his son Ralph Basset, who married Margaret daughter of Roger de Somery of Dudley Castle (see), and was summoned to parliament in 1264. He was slain at the battle of Evesham in 1265 and succeeded by his son Ralph Basset who served in the French and Scottish wars. He was created Lord Basset of Drayton in 1295. On his death in 1299 he was succeeded by his son Ralph Basset (d1342/3), 2nd Lord Basset, who was succeeded by his grandson Ralph Basset (d1390), 3rd Lord Basset, son of Ralph Basset (d1335) and his wife Alice daughter of Nicholas, 3rd Lord Audley. On the death of the 3rd Lord Basset the barony fell into abeyance. A magnificent tomb to the memory of 3rd Lord with an effigy of the 3rd Lord was erected between the choir and St Mary's chapel in Lichfield cathedral; the feet of the effigy rest on a wild boar; 3rd Lord Basset reputedly killed a wild boar on Basset's Heath in his life. The monument was desecrated and lost in the Civil War (SHOS vol 1 p248. vol 2 il of monument facing p6) (HOL p94) (W p498) (GNHS p164) (The Complete Peerage) (DM p6) (SPN p43). From Richard Basset the Justiciar (d1144) descend the Bassets of Sapcote, Park Hall (see) near Cheadle, Blore Hall (see), Hints, and Weldon (NSFCT 1922 p79) (Swinscoe, Blore, and the Bassett. David & Martine Swinscoe. 1998).

A boundary stone erected by the early C13 by a Basset, lord of Drayton, may have stood where the war memorial was situated in the 1930s (KES p79). The parish **church**, St Peter, S of Heathley Lane on the W side of the main road, existed by 1327. The church was rebuilt in 1794 (LDD). According to the famous old ballad 'The Tanner of Tamworth' Edward IV inquired of the tanner the way to Drayton Basset (HS p150). Evidence of former charcoal burning hearths of perhaps C15 to C18 date were found in a field centred on SK 176017 in 1972 (SSAHST 1973-74 p40). The descent of the manor after the Bassets is uncertain. In the C16 it was left to Walter Devereux (d1576), 4th Lord Ferrers owner of Chartley Castle (see), who left it to his wife, Lettice (nee) Knollys. She died at Drayton Bassett Manor House in 1634. The manor subsequently passed through many families and was sold in c1790 to Robert Peel and others (SHOS vol 2 p8). The Peels of Drayton Manor (see) were benefactors in the village in the C19; the village school founded by Sir Robert Peel II in 1862, with ornate blue patterns in the brick work, was in ruins by the late 1970s (DM p49).

Drayton Bassett Manor House Stood to the N of Drayton Bassett village. Drayton Bassett manor was held by Lettice (nee) Knollys (b1539/40) by the late 1570s. In 1578 she married secondly Robert (Dudley), Earl of Leicester. The Earl of Leicester and her son the 2nd Earl of Essex (celebrated favourite of Elizabeth I) frequently resided here; over the chimney piece in one of the large bedrooms hung a portrait of a lady believed to be Elizabeth I (SHOS vol 2 pp6,9,10). Lettice died at Drayton Bassett in 1634 (The Complete Peerage). Later in the C17 it passed to the Thynnes, later Viscounts Weymouth, who sold it in 1790 to Robert Peel, father of Sir Robert Peel PM, who had demolished all of it and built a new house on or near the site by 1801 (SHOS vol 2 pp8-10) (HOS 1998 p80). (LTM Dec 1972 p40p). That house was rebuilt from c1820 and became the house known as Drayton Manor (see below).

Drayton Bassett Park Medieval deer park created in Sutton Chase by the Bassetts in c1200 (SOS p565) (NSJFS 1968 p50). The park covered 692 acres and lay E of the A453 and on both sides of Bourne Brook nearly up to Watling Street; Shirral Park lay on the S side (SSAHST 1988-89 pp40-44 ils plans). For a fight at Canwell in the C15 between Lord Lisle and Henry

Willoughby arising out of an alleged breach of this park see Weeford. Noted by Saxton in 1577. It was disparked at the end of the C18 (EDP p180). (SHOS vol 2 p9). A burnt mound was noted near Alder Wood in the area of the former park and a Roman coin has been found at cSK 173015 (SSAHST 1988-89 pp40-44).

Drayton-in-Hales Drayton-in-Hales appears to have been part of, or an, ancient parish, in the archdeaconry of Salop (VCH vol 3 p92). It appears to have been either that part of Market Drayton (Shrops) ancient parish lying in Staffs (W p389) (a territory comprising one township of Tyrley, or three townships of Almington, Blore-in-Tyrley, and Hales - W p389), or another name for Market Drayton ancient parish and covering Market Drayton as well as the Staffs territory. An ecclesiastical parish of Hales, comprising Tyrley township? appears to have formed in 1856 (LGS p142). Tyrley township became a separate civil parish from Drayton-in-Hales ancient parish in 1866. In 1965 the area comprising Tyrley Castle Farm and land W of the Shrops Union Canal was removed to Sutton upon Tern civil parish in Shrops (GLAUE p427).

Drayton Manor and Drayton Manor House and Lower Drayton, 1m N of Penkridge. In Penkridge parish (W p466). Draitone, a member of Penkridge manor, is recorded as waste in DB. Later the name appears as Draitun (1194), Draiton (1236), Dreyton (1633) (SPNO p89). The name is from Anglo-Saxon and means 'the farmstead by a portage' (SSE 1996 p13) (SPN p93). Or 'farmstead where drays for portage were used' (SPNO p89). The farmhouse known as Drayton Manor dates from the early C19, and the site is not ancient (VCH vol 5 p113).

Drayton Manor and Park. To N of Drayton Bassett village. A mansion was built by Robert Peel, father of Sir Robert Peel PM, by 1801 on or near the site of Drayton Bassett Manor House, and this appears to have been rebuilt by him in c1820-35. The house of the 1820s was designed by Sir Robert Smirke in the Jacobean style at a cost of £100,000. In 1844-45 it was enlarged by the erection of a picture gallery (W p579) (BOE p118). Whilst, and after being, the seat of Sir Robert Peel PM, it received many famous visitors; Gladstone in 1835, Queen Adelaide widow of William IV in Nov 1839 (R&S p39), Duke of Wellington (he sat here for his portrait by Lawrence (DM p18)), Czar Alexander of Russia, Grand Duke Constantine (STC p30p), King Louis Philippe of France, Wordsworth, and again Gladstone in 1895, accompanied this time by the Archbishop of Canterbury (RVW p15) (DM pp36,39,39) (TB March 1993 p3p of the hall). Sir Walter Scott was another visitor (DM p17). The miniature silver barrow and spade presented to Sir Robert Peel when he cut the first sod of the Trent Valley Railway on Nov 13 1845 was kept at Drayton Manor (TB March 1993 p3). The 4th Robert Peel was an habitual gambler and spent the family fortune (TDOPP p56p of the house in 1912); goods were sold from the house in 1910 (DM p57). He was forced to sell the house in 1925. It failed to find a buyer and was eventually demolished for building materials (TDOPP p56). There is a tradition that some of the front brickwork went to Connecticut, USA. The stuffed wild life went to Tamworth Castle museum (DM p66). William Tolson of Tolson's Mills purchased two white marble life-sized busts of Alexander the Great and the Italian poet Branarotti. They were sold in 1972 when the last Tolson, living at Dosthill Hall, died (TB March 1993 p3). In 1949 the site of the house was 'a derelict rubbish dump' when bought by GHH Bryant who developed it as a zoo and pleasure park (TDOPP p56). The first Golden pythons to be hatched in Britain were hatched at Drayton Manor Park in 1991 (The Independent May 11 1991 p1p) and four rare fishing cats, indigenous to south-east Asia, were born at the zoo in June 1999 (Daily Telegraph. Aug 17 1999 p7p). The house and grounds had been haunted by several ghosts, including allegedly that of a favourite horse of Sir Robert Peel; the horse was believed to have been buried beneath a chestnut tree somewhere along the avenue from Swiss Lodge to Park Farm (THM vol 4 p93) (DM p35).

GROUNDS. Plot noted a thorn which passed through an oak in the walk before the manor at Drayton Bassett, although, thought Plot, it was more likely that the oak grew through the thorn it being an older tree (NHS p213) (SHOS vol 2 p9). Gilpin laid out the garden (W p579) (BOE p118). American Garden may have contained Californian Redwoods, The 'Araucaria Avenue'; the American Pool, to the NE of the house and to the N of the American Garden, was fed by natural streams (DM pp45,52 see map) (STMSM Nov 1978 p26 ps, and p of the American Pool). (SHOS vol 2 engraving of the manor facing p1, and on p1, pp9-10 description of the manor house). The banqueting house, or detached building in the garden represented in plate, was pulled down by Mr Fisher, soon after the drawings were made. The clock tower (SLM April 1953 p9p). There were two ice-houses in the grounds (DM p66). The Swiss Lodge, a lodge in the Swiss style at the Fazeley entrance, was built in c1900 by the 4th Robert Peel to remind his wife, Mercedes, daughter of Baron de Grafferied, of her home country. It was pulled down

after WW2 (DM pp54,66) (TDOPP p58p). Some of the garden urns were later purchased by a Solihull businessman and are still in his garden (1978) (DM p59).

Dresden Suburb of Longton, 0.75m S of Longton. Formerly partly in Normacot township in Stone ancient parish (W p363) and partly in Blurton township in Trentham ancient parish. Dresden, sometimes (formerly?) called Redbank (GLAUE p410), or Red Bank (TTH p68), started as a development of one of the Longton Freehold Land Societies. They had acquired 30 acres of land by 1851 (W p363). Building was under way in 1854 (SL p229) and by the late 1870s (VCH vol 8 p227). The name is from perhaps Dresden, Germany (POP p145). Became a separate ecclesiastical parish in 1853 when the church, The Resurrection, in Chaplin Road, was built as a chapel of ease to Blurton church. Dresden was added to Longton borough in 1884 (VCH vol 8 pp227,235,253) (TTH p68). **Natives**. **William Havergal Brian**, composer of over 30 symphonies, was born at 35 Ricardo Street on Jan 29 1876. He married in Stoke-upon-Trent (see) church in 1899 and later lived in that town, after living at Hartshill (see), and then at Trentham (see). His Symphony No. 2 (the Gothic), the longest symphony ever written, was performed at the Victoria Hall (see), Hanley. After living for many years in London he died in Shoreham-on-Sea on Nov 28 1972. He has been the subject of a play, 'Awkward Cuss' produced in the Victoria Theatre, Basford, and there is a Havergal Brian Society (Havergal Brian, the man and his music. R Nettel) (Havergal Brian, the making of a composer. K Easthaugh. 1976) (Havergal Brian and the performance of his orchestral music. RLE Foreman) (The Symphonies of Havergal Brian (3 vols). M MacDonald) (The Faraway Years. H Brian) (STMSM Jan 1973 p31) (POTP p47) (TSS p134p). A collection of poems 'Hours of Meditation' by **Edith Morris**, who was born in Dresden, appeared in 1890 (VFC p95). **Francis (Freddie) Charles Jones**, actor, born on Sept 12 1927, attended Longton High School, is said to be a native of Dresden or spent some of his childhood here (local info) (People of Today 1997. Debrett's). **Thomas Smith** (b1960) of Fairfield Avenue, known as 'The Tank,' won the title of Britain's Strongest Man in Oct 1994. In Nov 1994, on a specially converted bench, he lifted 18 pupils of Edensor High School, his old school, and pulled the school minibus with 12 pupils inside (ES Oct 19 1994 p3p. Nov 10 1994 p1pc).

Drointon Hamlet on a small hill on the E side of Bourn Brook, 1.25m NW of Newton. Formerly mostly in Stowe ancient parish but partly in Colwich ancient parish (W p416). Drointon was in Colwich prebend (SSAHST vol 2 1960-61 p44). The manor of Dregetone appears in DB (the identification was made by Eyton - SHC 1909 p186 note). Later Drointon appears as Drengeton (1199) (SSE 1996 p13). The name is from Anglo-Saxon and means 'the town of the warrior, or soldier,' or 'Dreng's town' (DUIGNAN). Probably from the Old Norse personal name Dreng; the word when used as a common noun, also meant a serving man (NSFCT 1916 p80). A dreng was a free Saxon tenant who retained the privileges he held before the Conquest, so 'tun of the free tenants' (SSE 1996 p13) (SPN p8). Perhaps from Welsh 'draen' 'a ticket' (NSFCT 1908 p139). At Drointon are several square moats (now dry), one of them probably surrounded 'The Moated Grange' from which was found an old oak beam which formed part of the drawbridge. In 1886 Dr ET Tylecote said that this drawbridge had been re-utilized in a nearby farm building (NSFCT 1886 pp38,39. 1982 p15).

Druid's Heath Former common land, now a minute hamlet 1m NE of Aldridge. In Aldridge ancient parish. It has been thought the arch druid had his summer residence in this area in ancient times (having a winter camp near Bourne Pool) (SHOS vol 1 p10. vol 2 p103 and second p105) (HOWW p16) (SSC p128 in the intro) (GNHS pp64,65) (CCC p6) (GATD p13). The Wolverhampton Journal loosely mentions a British camp, an oval enclosure of 500 or 600 yards round, on Druid's Heath, which may have been used by druids (WJO June 1904 p156p). The name was formerly said to be from these druids (SHOS vol 2 p103 and second p105). Or it is a corruption of the root 'doire' 'duire' 'deru' a forest and particularly oak-forest (NSFCT 1908 p139). Or is a corruption of Dru or Drew wood, from the Norman family of Dru, deriving their name from Dreux (Dept of Eure-et-Loir, Normandy) who were medieval lords of Aldridge (DUIGNAN) (SPN p10). Gould says Dru is a shortened form of the Christian name Drogo, a person called Drogo was living in this area in 1201 when he was fined for committing an offence in Cannock Forest. Drewed, was the name for one of the open fields of Aldridge (MOA p13) (SLHT p7) (SNAR p23). The common, which has appeared as Druwode (1343), Druywode (1343), Aldridge Common and Aldridge Heath (MOA pp13,156), was enclosed in 1799 (MH 1994 p108). John or Charles Wesley inquired the way to Stafford from a cottager on Aldridge Heath (CCBO pp102-103). The church, St Thomas, St Thomas' Close, was built in 1969 (LDD).

Druid's Heath Farm To S of Stonnall Road, Aldridge. Perhaps the same as

Druid's Heath House (see). Described as the most supernaturally disturbed house in the county by Thomas Wight in 'Great Barr and its Haunted Environs' (1852) when it was occupied by Edward Arblaster (TB July 1987 p23).

Druid's Heath House Stonnall Road, Aldridge. Perhaps the same as Druid's Heath Farm (see). Was originally a school. By the 1940s it was being used as an annex for a Dr Barnardos' home. By 1984 it was known as Richard House and was being used as an old people's home (ALOPP p22p) (ALOPPR p114p).

Druid's Mere Pool Former pool in Aldridge ancient parish, on the E side of Druid's Heath (SD p11) (HOWW p16). Has also appeared as Drudemeer (SD p11), and perhaps can be identified with Bourne Pool (see). It lay by the old drovers way (Old Chester Road) and was a watering spot for the cattle (MOA p135). In the later C17 it was believed that if the pool overflowed it was a sign of harvest shortage, and if the pool was shallow it was a sign of plentiful harvest (NHS 46) (SHOS vol 2 p40) (FOS p168).

Druids Place Old house on Druids Heath (W p551).

Druid's Well In a field on Mr Chawner's farm at Burston. Some people say it is St Rufin's Well as it was near the old chapel, which was standing in 1580 (RHPS p79).

Drumbus House 0.5m SSW of Sheen. In Sheen ancient parish. There was a house at Drumbus by 1785 (VCH vol 7 p241).

Drummer's Knob Copse on a small knoll close to the Congleton road, directly E of the Bridestones, at SJ 909621 (DPTB p15). It is much frequented by picnickers. So called from a drummer boy in the army of the Young Pretender in the 1745 Jacobite Rebellion who was shot dead when he stopped to rest here as the army was retreating to Scotland (BPCSM p13) or marching on London (DP p76). He was shot by a marksman of the Duke of Cumberland's army (BPCSM p13). According to local tradition the knob is haunted by the ghost of the drummer boy (DP p76). (An Account of the Ancient Chapel of Rushton. Rev TW Norwood MA. 1856) (GNHSS p14) (MC p29).

Drybrook Runs W of Brewood near Kiddlemore Green.

Drybrook Tributary of the Pipe. Forms a part of the northern boundary of Burntwood civil parish, joins Redmoor Brook. Has appeared as Driebrouk (1286) and Bye Brook (C19) (SPNO p9) (VCH vol 14 p195). The name possibly arose as the brook was apt to run dry in the summer (SPNO p9).

Drystone Edge Former common land on an edge 1m N of Flash (SLM April 1996 p16). Has also appeared as Dry Stone Edge (1834 OS map), and Drystones (UHAW p51 il).

Duckhole Former group of houses at the back of Pelsall Ironworks which were completely hidden from view at one time by pit mounds from Plant Colliery. By 1981 the houses had long since been demolished and the area levelled and returned to common (SHOP p11). Also known as Queen Street (SNBP p71).

Dudley Canal Line One Runs from Park Head Junction, below the S entrance of Dudley Tunnel, westwards to join the Stourbridge Canal at Delph Junction at the bottom of Delph Locks. Built between 1776 and 1798 (WMLB p53). Some of it may have been open by 1779 (BCM summer 1994 p47. winter 1996/7 pp20-23). The canal was realigned between Level Street and Mill Street in 1977 (BCM June 1998 pp54-56).

Dudley Canal Line Two Runs from Park Head Junction below the S entrance of Dudley Tunnel. Runs for 10 miles and seven furlongs. Travels through the Brewins (removed), Gorsty Hill, and Lapal Tunnels and ends at Selly Oak where it joins the Worcester and Birmingham Canal. Constructed in 1792-98 (The Dudley No. 2 Canal Guide. The Lapal Canal Trust) (SWY p14). Owen says Line Two branches off Line One at Windmill End Junction (SWY p14). In 1924 two boys drowned in the canal at Old Hill (see). By the mid 1990s it was in water for only roughly half its original length; from Parkhead to Hawne Basin. The Lapal Canal Trust (formed in 1990) were then hoping to restore the other half (BCM winter 1996/7 pp20-23).

Dudley Castle Over 0.25m NNE of St Edmund's church, Dudley, on Dudley Castle Hill, an extra-parochial liberty (W p580). Formerly lay in Offlow hundred (W pp580-581) in Staffs; Dudley town lay in Halfshire hundred, Worcs. A fort on the promontory on which lies Dudley is said to have been founded by a Saxon, Dudo, Dud, or Dodo in c700 (Britannia. Camden) (NHS p408) (SHOS vol 1 part 1 p36. vol 2 pp138,141) (W p580). From the C11 until at least 1913 the ownership of the castle has mainly descended with the barony of Dudley, and later the viscounty of Dudley and Ward and earldom of Dudley, in the Ansculf, Paynel, Somery, Sutton families and their descendents, the Dudley and Ward families.

THE DUDLEYS AND WARDS AND THEIR ANCESTORS. Dudley, like Stafford, was one of the great baronies held direct from the king as lord paramount, by a tenant-in-chief or tenant in capite (SCSF p117). The DB estates of William Fitz Ansculf and his successors, which included the Dudley manor and land held in chief in the counties of Stafford, Warwick, Worcester, Surrey, Berkshire, Northampton, Buckingham, Rutland, Oxford, Middlesex and Huntingdon, later became known as the barony and honour of Dudley, with Dudley Castle as the head of the honour (VCHW vol 3 p90). Dudley Castle, barony and manor supposedly passed from William Fitz Ansculf to his daughter Beatrice and to her husband Fulk Paynel. It then passed to their son **Gervase Paynel**, founder of St James' Priory, Dudley, sometime before 1160. He was succeeded by his daughter, Hawise, who married John de Somery. On his death in 1194 the castle, barony and manor passed to his son Ralph de Somery (died c1210). **Roger de Somery** (fl 1229), builder of an early castle at Dudley, died in or before 1273. He was succeeded by his son Roger de Somery (1255-c1291), who was succeeded by his son John de Somery (b1279/80-1322). He was created baron Lord Somery by writ in 1307/8. During this period the castle was said to be held by barony of the king in chief by the service of three knights in the time of war in Wales for forty days. The barony stayed with the de Somerys until John died without issue in 1322 and the barony then became extinct. John's estates became divided amongst the families of his surviving sisters. The manor and castle passing to his eldest sister, Margaret, wife of John de Sutton. Margaret was the ancestor of **John de Sutton** (or Dudley) (1400-1487). He was created 1st Baron Dudley by writ of summons to parliament in 1440. He fought at the battle of Blore Heath (see), in 1459, and he and his widow were buried in St James' Priory, Dudley, but he was later removed to St Edmund's church, Dudley. He was succeeded by his grandson **Edward Dudley** (or de Sutton) (c1459-1531/2), 2nd Baron Dudley, son of Sir Edmund Dudley (or de Sutton) (d c1483). The 2nd Baron was made a KB at the coronation of Elizabeth, Queen Consort, and was succeeded by his son John (1495-1553), 3rd Baron. He was succeeded by his son Edward (d1586), 4th Baron, who was succeeded by his son Edward (1567-1643), 5th Baron. **Dud Dudley** (b1599), the 5th Baron's fourth natural son by Elizabeth Tomlinson, daughter of William Tomlinson of Dudley, was a notable and innovative ironmaster. He managed and opened forges at Himley, Hasco-Bridge (see) (or Askew Bridge), Cradley Forge (see), on Pensnett Chase (see), and perhaps at Swindon (see). He is said to have been granted Himley Hall (see) in 1622, but from the early 1620s he resided at his house, Greens Lodge (see), and he perhaps either owned or occupied for a time Tibbington Hall (see). In 1665 he published 'Metallum Martis, or Iron made with Pit-coale, Sea-coale etc and with the same fuell to melt and fine imperfect Metals, and refine perfect Metals.' He died in 1684 and is buried at St Helen's church, Worcester (DNB). The 5th Baron was succeeded by his granddaughter Frances (b1611), suo jure Baroness Dudley (6th Baron) daughter of the 5th Baron's son Sir Ferdinando Sutton (1588-1621). In 1628 Frances married **Humble Ward**, who was created Baron Ward of Birmingham. Their son Edward Ward succeeded his mother to the Dudley barony in 1697, becoming 7th Baron Dudley, and he succeeded his father in the manor, castle and borough of Dudley and Ward barony in 1670, becoming 2nd Baron Ward. Edward Ward died in 1701 and was succeeded by his grandson Edward Ward (1683-1704), 8th Baron Dudley and 3rd Baron Ward. He was succeeded by his son Edward (1704-1731), 9th Baron Dudley and 4th Baron Ward, who was succeeded by his uncle William Ward (d1740), 10th Baron Dudley and 5th Baron Ward. On his death in 1740 the Dudley barony was inherited by his nephew Ferdinando Dudley Lea, 11th Baron Dudley. He died without issue in 1757 and the Dudley barony then fell into abeyance, although his sister Anne styled herself as Baroness Dudley. On the death of William in 1740 the Ward barony, Dudley Castle and estates passed to William's cousin John Ward of Sedgley Park (1700-1774) who became 6th Baron Ward. In 1763 he was created Viscount Dudley and Ward of Dudley. He was succeeded by his son John (1724-5-1788), 7th Baron Ward and 2nd Viscount Dudley and Ward, who was succeeded by his brother, William (1750-1823), 8th Baron Ward and 3rd Viscount Dudley and Ward. He was succeeded by his son John William Ward (b1781), 9th Baron Ward and 4th Viscount Dudley and Ward. He was created Earl of Dudley and Viscount Ednam of Ednam in County Roxburgh, Scotland, in 1827. In 1833 he died unmarried and the earldom of Dudley became extinct. The Ward barony then devolved on his second cousin Rev William Humble (1781-1835), 10th Baron Ward. His son William (1817-1885), 11th Baron Ward was created Earl of Dudley (second creation) in 1860. He married Georgina (has mem in Memory Garden at Himley Hall), and was succeeded by his son William Humble (1867-1932), 2nd Earl of Dudley and 12th Baron Ward. Both the 2nd Earl and his second wife, Gertrude Millar, have memorials in the Memory Garden at Himley Hall (see). The 2nd Earl was succeeded by his son William Humble Eric Ward (b1894), 3rd Earl of Dudley and 13th Baron Ward. His wife, Lady Rosemary Leveson-Gower, daughter of the 4th Duke of Sutherland of Trentham Hall (see), was killed in a plane crash in 1930 and she has a memorial in the Memory Garden at Himley Hall. The 3rd Earl's son and heir in 1967 was William Humble David Ward (b1920). The 2nd Earl of Dudley was lord of the manor of Dudley and the castle in 1913 (VCHW vol 3 pp90-94) (The Complete Peerage) (Debrett's Peerage 1967) (NSFCT 1976 p16).

1100 to 1650. The castle was held for Empress Maud in 1138 and consequently attacked by King Stephen (VCHW vol 3 p90). Gervase Paganel aided Prince Henry in his rebellion against Henry II 1173-4 and consequently the castle was demolished (SMC p163) (VCHW vol 3 p90). A new castle, for which there was no license, was begun by Roger de Somery (fl 1229) out of his manor house in 1261-2. In 1263/4 Roger obtained a license to crenellate the house. By 1273, it is described as 'newly commenced' and was still unfinished in 1310 (The Complete Peerage) (D pp12-56) (NSJFS 1966 p43). It was completed in 1321 (NSFCT 1976 p16); local limestone was used in its construction (VCH vol 2 p193). The new castle was apparently not built on the same site as the former one, as it was situated in Sedgley manor in Staffs (SHC 1888 part 2 p1). This probably explains why Dudley Castle Hill was extra-parochial (VCHW vol 3 p91 note). The castle was raided in 1321 (VCHW vol 3 p92). In 1330 it was besieged by a number of local notables. In c1340-60 the Suttons built a new hall and the block containing the principal private apartments and chapel (CAMS p50). John Dudley, later Duke of Northumberland, took possession of the castle in c1533 and remodelled the hall and built a new set of apartments to the north of it; and probably also built the outer bailey walls (CAMS p51). Northumberland was executed for high treason in 1553 by Queen Mary after he made an abortive attempt to have Lady Jane Grey made Queen. In 1554 the castle was granted to the Suttons who entertained Elizabeth I here in 1575 (MR p131). Dudley Castle was considered as a place of confinement for Mary, Queen of Scots, in 1585 (VCHW vol 3 p93). In 1642 during the **Civil War** parliamentarians took the castle with the help of nailers and colliers (VCH vol 2 p239). It was a royalist garrison in 1643 under Col Thomas Leveson and withstood a siege by the Earl of Denbigh in 1644 (LOU p33) owing to royalist reinforcements being brought in from Worcester. The castle was besieged in 1646 by parliamentarian garrisons from Wrottesley House and Edgbaston. The former took up a position on the Staffs side whilst the latter took up a position on the Worcs side. On May 10 the governor, Sir Thomas Leveson, surrendered the castle to the parliamentarian Sir William Brereton. The castle was largely demolished by order of Parliament in 1647 (VCHW vol 3 pp93-94) (CAMS p51) (OWB p73) (HOS 1998 p75; the castle capitulated on May 13 1646). Lord Ward and his family seem to have occupied the castle during the period of the royalist garrison at the castle and the siege of 1646, but he is said to have taken no active part in the Civil War (VCHW vol 3 p94). In c1985 fragments of ten individual animal-membrane condoms dating to 1647 were found by archaeologists in the latrine of the keep garderobe. The condoms are believed to be the earliest definite physical evidence for the use of animal-membrane condoms in post-medieval Europe (info Debbie Ford, Potteries Museum) (Post-Medieval Archaeology. vol 30 1996 pp129-142 ils).

1650 to PRESENT. The castle's residential portions were left untouched after the order to demolish in 1647. A new block of apartments between the keep and gatehouse were built in the 1690s (CAMS p51). In the later C17 Plot noted white buck kept by the Wards at the castle which every year grew deformed antlers topped only by balls or knobs (NHS p39 tab 3 shows the castle, pp260-261 tab 22 fig 12) (SHOS vol 2 p143). By the 1680s an oak table nearly a yard wide and 25 yards three inches long made of one entire plank from the new park at Dudley (perhaps Dudley Castle Park (see)) that had been in the Great Hall had been removed to Corbyn's Hall (NHS p211) (SHOS vol 2 p142) (SVS p133). In 1712 Thomas Newcomen's first steam engine, known as 'Dudley Castle' (perhaps the first steam engine to be erected in England), was set up to drain water out of the coal mines of Lord Dudley and Ward. A near-contemporary source placed it 'at Dudley Castle in Staffordshire' and for many years it was believed to have been situated in the grounds of Dudley Castle, but in 1965 was located at Lady Meadow (see) at Coneygree (SL p207). The castle was drawn by Samuel Buck and engraved by Nathaniel Buck in 1731; a copy is in the Staffordshire Collection in WSL (NSFCT 1976 p16). In 1750 the castle served as a retreat to a gang of coiners, who having set fire to the buildings were consequently discovered and driven out (W pp580-581). Another account says the origins of the fire, which occurred between 24 to 26 July 1750, are a mystery (OWB pp99-100) (NSFCT 1976 p17). The fire continued for so long because no one tried to put it out for fear gun powder was stored in the castle and might explode at anytime (OWB p99). The fire turned the limestone walls to powder, and when rain came the liquid lime ran into the town (OWB pp99-100). The Wards then went to live at Himley Hall (see) and each successive Lord Dudley allowed the castle grounds to be used for fetes and festivals. Later, Dudley corporation became the owners for a peppercorn rent (NSFCT 1976 p17) (BCM spring 1994 pp14-18). On Bowen's map it is stated there is a prospect from the castle of five

counties and a great part of Wales. One of the best views of the Black Country is said to be from the keep, as stated in this rhyme

If thou wouldst view the Black Country aright,
Go see it from Dudley's Grey Keep at night.

(BCSG vol 5 p64). The castle was used by Yates as a triangulation point for his map (1775), and by the surveyors for the first OS map (SHC 4th series vol 12 1984 vii). William Ward, Viscount Dudley and Ward, rebuilt the keep in 1779 (OWB pp99-100). There is a painting of the castle by R Paddy and an engraving by F Jukes of 1793 in the BM (BCM July 1969 pp51-57). At the end of the C18 Shaw noted Deadly Nightshade growing wild amongst the remains (SHOS vol 2 p143). Turner painted Dudley Castle and the canal below. His painting is referred to in 'Lectures on Landscape' reproduced by Photogravure in Turner and Ruskin Vol II p324 and in colours in 'The Works of Ruskin' (O pp245-247). William (d1823), 8th Baron Ward, restored the ruins and laid out the grounds. Elihu Burritt began his tour of the Black Country with a view of it by moonlight from the keep. Robert George Hobbes (1821-1899), a correspondent for the weekly 'The Leisure Hour' in the 1870s also surveyed the Black Country from the keep at night (BCM autumn 1993 pp53,55). A pageant was held at the castle in 1908 (TB Feb/ March 1973 pp14-15ps). The **zoo** which surrounds the castle opened in 1937 (WMAG Sept 1976 p34) (BCM winter 1994/ 95 p54). In June 1937 a bear escaped from it. It was recaptured in a garden in Birmingham Road, Burnt Tree (TB July 1996 p17). Britain's largest captive gorilla (Western Lowland gorilla) named 'Bukhama' (b1960) at Dudley Zoo was reportedly 500 lb in 1969, but has not been weighed since (GBR 1993 p27). By the mid C20 the castle remains consisted of work from the de Somery rebuilding between 1272 and 1322, the keep, some curtain walling and the gatehouse. There is also a barbican on the outer defence to the Great Gate from c1340 and various later additions (D pp12-56) (NSJFS 1966 p43). (SHOS vol 2 pp139 pl showing principal entrance to the castle, pl xx, 141-142, 144-146) (GNHS p179) (WJO June 1905 pp153-155ps) (SOSH pp333p,334) (VCHW vol 3 pp94-98) (SLM spring 1957 pp20-21,29ps) (SHJ vol 5 pp45-48) (TB March 1986 p9) (WMARCH 1994 pp105-108).

LEGEND AND THE SUPERNATURAL. An old woman lived in the keep tower - one story tells that she hung herself off the battlements on All Hallows Eve and her black cat was found dead beneath her swinging body, another story says that youths threw the cat and old woman off the battlements. The old woman was buried just outside the walls of St Edmund's churchyard, near the former estate offices of the Earl of Dudley (MGH p35). The ghost of a small **dog** has been seen standing on one of the ruined towers of the Keep, howling mournfully. In 1994 the skeleton of a small dog was found buried on the lower slopes of the Castle Motte on which the Keep has stood for centuries. Some have thought it is the ghost of the Grey Lady's dog (BCM winter 1994/ 95 p55). **Figures walking around a fire** (including one wearing a goats head) have been seen between the cannons by the castle; later five animal skulls were unearthed by the cannons, each had a pentagram carved on it (GOD pp3-5). **Dudley Zoo aquarium** in the ancient crypt of the castle has attracted six teams of psychic investigators trying to solve poltergeist activity reported from the 1960s (GOD pp3-5) (Ghosts Among Us. Harry Ludlam. 1994 p25) (BCM winter 1994/ 95 p55). **Footsteps** have been heard by 200 staff in the offices which are in a C17 stone house, once the estate offices of the Earl of Dudley, and on the site of the old St Edmund's churchyard. There is a **ghost** who plays the piano and changes place settings at Fellows Club restaurant which is built over the old St Edmund's churchyard (MGH p35). A **ghostly couple** are said to stroll the grounds of the zoo (GOM pl 5 (d). The same or another couple in clothing of the early 1930s period are said to walk the grounds of the zoo (GPCE p28). The same or another couple in C17 and C18 costume were sighted in the late 1930s (GOD pp3-5). The **Grey Lady** was last seen by zoo staff in the chapel window in the 1970s. During the 1960s she appeared to two keepers in the old aquarium. The Grey Lady could be Mrs Dorothy Beaumont wife of the royalist second in command when the castle was besieged in May 1646 by parliamentary forces. She died of natural causes, perhaps in childbirth. The parliamentary commander allowed her funeral cortege to leave the castle for the church, but her husband was not allowed to leave the castle (MGH p38) (BCM winter 1994/ 95 pp54-55) (GPCE p28). An **elderly woman** in a sackcloth shift and grey shawl has only appeared to zoo staff once when she won a fancy dress competition in 1983 (MGH p39). The sound of **horses' hooves** along the wall passage that leads to the 'cellar of death' has been heard on numerous occasions and the sound of horses' neighing are said to echo throughout the castle (BCM winter 1994/ 95 p55). An **incredible cold** was suddenly felt by the assistant manager as he left for home in 1992. A **skeletal figure** in monk's black habit has been seen at the bottom of a stairway carrying a white crucifix (BCM winter 1994/ 95 pp55,56) (GPCE p28). Staff at Dudley Zoo have seen the ghost of a monk in a black habit on three occasions; once at the entrance to the keep and twice in the window of the castle's chapel. The Benedictine Monks of St James' Priory, Dudley, wore black habits (MGH p38). In May 1978 three MEB workmen saw several hooded figures (GOD pp3-5). The **skeleton of a woman** (aged 40) was found in 1961 in a nearby limestone cave quarry, nothing about her could be found out. The **sound of a pickaxe** on rock can sometimes be heard; nearby a miner was buried alive under a rockfall.

Dudley Castle Hill A ridge in Sedgley manor, Staffs. Extra-parochial place to 1858 when formed into a separate civil parish. Seems to have been in Dudley metropolitan borough (Worcs) between 1865 and 1889, thereafter in Staffs. In 1929 it re-entered Worcs into Dudley county borough. It was removed with the county borough back into Staffs in 1966 (GLAUE p410). Protrudes like a peninsular into the Dudley enclave of Worcs. Dudley Castle stands at the S end of it, and its presence may account for the hill having been extra-parochial (VCHW vol 3 p91 note). The neck of the peninsular, at Kettle's Hill, is only about 100 feet wide. There are limestone caverns under Dudley Castle and this hill. Some could be reached via the Dudley Canal Tunnel (built 1786). The caverns were visited by the British Association in 1849 and 1865. On the last occasion the main cavern was lit up for them by thousands of candles and coloured lamps. Robert George Hobbes (1821-1899), a writer in the weekly 'The Leisure Hour' in the 1870s, visited the caverns sometime in the later C19 (BCM autumn 1993 pp54-56il).

Dudley Castle Park A deer park of the Ward family, and was by Dudley Castle (EDP p180). The park of Dudley Castle is said to have 'extended as far as Eve Lane, Upper Gornal, including Park Farm, the Wren's Nest and the Old Park between Tipton and the Wren's Nest' lying mainly in Sedgley parish (SR p13) (SNSV vol 2 p97). Dudley Castle Park may have been the 'new park' from which came the single oak strip which made the long table in Corbyn's Hall, formerly in Dudley Castle (NHS p211). The tree out of which it came was said to have contained upwards of 100 tons of timber (SHOS vol 2 p142).

Dudley Fields District at N end of Brierley Hill.

Dudley Fields District in the suburbs of Bloxwich, in the Foreign of Walsall. 0.75m WNW of Bloxwich, approximately S of Central Drive, E of Heather Road and N of Willenhall Lane. By the early 1970s it contained an housing estate built since WW2 and an industrial estate of the later 1960s (VCH vol 17 p163). The name is from Walter Dudley who owned several of the fields on this estate in the 1840s (SNBP p23).

Dudley Port Industrial area situated between the Birmingham Canal and the Birmingham Canal New Cut 1m SE of Tipton. In Tipton ancient parish. The settlement grew up as a port by the Birmingham Canal Old Cut to serve Dudley before the Dudley Canal Tunnel was built, so was active between 1777 and 1792 (OH p62) (MR p332). It was so named by 1834 (W 1834). The first train ran between Dudley Port and Walsall on May 1 1850 (BCM April 1976 pp53-57). On July 29 1853 a goods train from Great Bridge went into the back of a passenger train waiting at Dudley Port Low Level station (SSR p21). Dudley Port (low level) station was closed to passengers in 1964 (BTRA p18). The Birmingham Canal Old Cut (see) burst its banks at Dudley Port on Sept 9 1899. In Horseley Road Cemetery, Horseley Heath is a white obelisk memorial to 19 girls who died in a explosion at Knowle's factory in Groveland Road, Dudley Port, whilst breaking up miniature rifle cartridges on March 6 1922 (TB May 1977 p24p. Jan 14 1999 pp18-19ps) (BCM Oct 1975 pp44-45p, 46) (Wolverhampton Chronicle Oct 1 1993 p7).

Dudley Port Junction Junction of the Birmingham Canal New Cut New Main Line with the Netherton Tunnel Branch Canal (SWY p10).

Dudley Tunnel Constructed between 1785 and 1792 to join together Dudley Canal Lines One and Two and the Birmingham Canal Old Cut Old Main Line via a stretch of Lord Ward's Canal (incorporating Tipton Tunnel) and was the second longest canal tunnel in the country when complete. The tunnel has its N entrance in Castle Mill Basin (see) (HCMS No. 2) (The Dudley No. 2 Canal Guide. The Lapal Canal Trust) (BCM summer 1994 p48). The S entrance, at SO 932892, is on the Thornleigh Trading Estate at Parkhead. It is 2,942 yards long (HCMS No. 2), but combined with Tipton Tunnel it is 3,154 yards (info Dudley Canal Trust). By the mid C19 the tunnel could not cope with increased traffic and Netherton Tunnel was opened to relieve it in 1858. During 1884 the Parkhead end of Dudley Tunnel was affected by mining subsidence and rebuilt; however one section, known as 'The Gaol,' remained problematic. Owing to a significant decline in traffic the tunnel closed in 1962 (HCMS No. 2) (info Dudley Canal Trust); some say it closed in the

early 1950s (BCM summer 1995 pp25-27) (DOG p17). In 1963 it was proposed to infill the Tipton end. In 1964 local enthusiasts formed the Dudley Canal Tunnel Preservation Society (Dudley Canal Trust from 1969) to campaign for its preservation. The tunnel, known locally as 'Legging Tunnel,' reopened at Easter 1973 (info Dudley Canal Trust) (DOG p17). By 1976 it was the fifth longest canal tunnel in England (IAS p163). In 1981 it closed owing to the failure of brick lining near Parkhead. It was re-opened in June 1992 (info Dudley Canal Trust). By 1995 it was the longest open canal tunnel in the UK (GBR 1995 p99). The longest recorded underground swim is one of 3,402 yards in 87 minutes by David Stanley Gale through the Dudley Old Canal Tunnel in August 1967 (GBR 1969 p359. 1977 p323). (SVS p356) (W p581) (BCM July 1973 pp36-42) (BCOPP vol 2 pl 74 shows the canal tunnel entrance at Dudley in 1908).

Dugdale House and wood 0.75m SE of Hednesford.

Dug-out, The Stoke-upon-Trent. There is a plaque on a rock off Hartshill Road and Honeywall - 'On this site in a small room known as the Dug-out, scouting in the Potteries and Newcastle was re-organised and co-ordinated in 1926. Through the vision and generosity of Ronald Copeland Esq C.B.E. D.L. J.P.' The rock is one of three rocks. Local tradition believes it is a meteorite which landed on the spot (info an NSFC member).

Duke Bank Hamlet on road between Norton-in-the-Moors to Norton Green.

Duke's New Road Road between Butterton (Moorlands) to Grindonmoor built by the Duke of Devonshire for better communication for the packhorses taking copper ore from his Ecton mines to Whiston copper smelting works. The road is now called Pothooks Lane (PRT p71).

Dumble Derry There is a Dumblederry Farm 1m WNW of Aldridge. Appears as Dumble Dairy on 1834 OS map. (VB p44).

Dunbrook Tributary of the Dove. Means, perhaps, 'the dark brown stream' (SPNO p9).

Duncan Hall Hostel 2.25m SSE of Swynnerton. Built in c1938 for workers, relocated from Woolwich Arsenal, at the new Royal Ordnance Factory at Swynnerton. Named after Admiral Duncan. The hall was never used by them, instead they preferred to live in the Potteries. The hall was occupied by the US Air Force in WW2 (MOSP p28). In 1981 it was used as a GPO training centre (MOSP p28). Demolished in c1987 (MR p399). The site is now an housing estate in Yarnfield.

Duncan's Hill Littleworth, Hednesford.

Dun Cow's Grove House 1.25m W of Hollinsclough. Formerly in Hollinsclough township in Alstonefield ancient parish. Is recorded as Duncote Greave in 1600 (VCH vol 7 p38).

Dunge Near Drabber Tor, Wolfscote Dale.

Dungeon Well said to have existed near the lane later known as Strangeman's Walk, Leek, noted in 1837 (VCH vol 7 p128).

Dungeon Appears on Yates' map between Hateley Heath and All Saint's church, West Bromwich, close to the present junction of Marsh Lane with Clarke's Lane. Here was an incarceration place for parish prisoners. Not far away is believed to have stood the gallows for West Bromwich parish (TB Aug 1995 p6ps).

Dunkesford Crosses the Sow E of Eccleshall at Hilcote or Byanna? (ROT p25). Not on OS maps. Has also appeared as Dungsford. Means Dunks Ford (ECC p47).

Dunkirk Former estate in West Bromwich ancient parish (W p686), centred on Dunkirk Hall (see). The estate was the home of the Rider family by the C16. In 1703 the estate consisted of a brick house, gardens, a windmill and a watermill on the Tame (later known as Gutteridge's Mill). The name Dunkirk, in use by 1748 (VCH vol 17 p21,22), is preserved in Dunkirk Avenue.

Dunkirk Hamlet 1.5m NE of Audley. See Dunkirk, Chesterton for a tradition which may apply to this Dunkirk.

Dunkirk 0.75m SE of Chesterton in the Sheldon Grove area of present Church Fields (1882 OS map 6 inch). Has a tradition of seven churches. There is no parallel tradition in the organisation of the English Church. It is probably on the analogy of the evidence of Church history in Gaul, that at one or other of these sites (the other is at Dunkirk, near Audley) there was a college of the clergy of St Martin of Tours and that the Martinmas traditions in Stoke derive their origin from an early Christian centre at Dunkirk, Chesterton (NSFCT 1908 p106).

Dunkirk Branch of the Birmingham Canal New Cut New Main Line. Spurred N of the Island Line at Albion Junction. Opened in 1850 (HCMS No. 2). Abandoned in 1953 (VCH vol 17 p13).

Dunkirk Hall Whitehall Road, Dunkirk, Greets Green. Seat of the Ryders (or Rider), Roman Catholics, by the late C16 (VCH vol 17 p8). Simon Ryder (d1638 or 40), miller, born in 1558, was a member of this family - in the WSL is an old document called the 'Hypomnemia sive Commentarium' (1580) of

Simon Ryder (OWB p61) (TMS p154) (SH p19). The Ryders remained here until 1703 (SHWB 8) or 1708 (HPPE p25) (TB Sept 1995 p11p). There is a tradition that an upper room at the back of the hall was used by Catholics as a chapel during the Ryder period, and what is said to have been a priest's hole was probably a space made for a stairway (WB pp49-50) (VCH vol 17 p60). In the C18 the house was occupied by the Gutteridge family (SHWB 8) (VCH vol 17 p22). The front part was rebuilt in c1690 and the rear was pulled down in c1900 (OWB p61). Became an inn in the mid C19 and was demolished in the 1970s: it was still standing in 1976 (VCH vol 17 p22). It may have been haunted by William Norgrove, the first licensee of the inn. Some claim there was a tunnel from the hall to Dudley Castle (TB Sept 1995 p11).

Dunlea Farm Nearly 2m NW of Onecote. Formerly in Onecote township in Leek ancient parish. There was a house on this site by 1510 (VCH vol 7 p211).

Dun Low Mound 2m W of Blore, 1.25m SE of Calton at SK 11944940. Is 26 paces in diameter and five feet high. Carrington excavated it in 1849 and found nothing. Planted with trees and is a listed monument (TYD p151) (NSJFS 1965 p33). It may be identifiable with Dan Low, a possible burial mound in Blore and Swinscoe parish (SHC 1916 p207).

Dunn's Bank Small district 1.25m SE of Brierley Hill and road linking Park road and Cradley Mill with an arm to Lawnsdown Road, Quarry Bank. Formerly in Kingswinford ancient parish. The name, which appears in the 1851 census, is from a family called Dunn (SNSV vol 1 p107).

Dunnimere Ancient farm (SHOS vol 1 p402) 1m SSE of Harlaston. Has also appeared as Dunimeer, and Donimere.

Dunns Cross Here was the Tutbury Elm (see), which was probably the same as the 'Great Elm' marked on 1834 OS map at SK 211281, just over 0.5m S of Tutbury. Has also appeared as Duns Cross. The name is from a gospel tree, here, on the Tutbury perambulation, which stood midway between the Park house and Tutbury (SHOS vol 1 p57).

Dun's Field House 1.5m S of Marchington Woodlands. Appears as Dun Field on 1834 OS map.

Dunsley Large hamlet on a high escarpment above the Stour and Staffs & Worcs Canal, 1.25m SW of Stourton, E of Kinver. Former township in Kinver ancient parish. The name is from 'Dane's lea' which suggests Danish occupation in the area (WMAG March 1976 p22). Poulton-Smith is unsure of the personal name in the first element. The suffix is from Anglo-Saxon 'leah,' 'a woodland clearing' (SPN p72). Dunsley was an inhabited area by c1200 when it was a part of Kinver manor. But it later became a sub-manor with Dunsley Hall as its manor house (VCH vol 20 p124). A green at Dunsley, on the Dunsley Road 0.25m SW of Dunsley Hall, was mentioned in 1780 and had been enclosed by 1830 (VCH vol 2 p139). There was or is a windmill on the S side of Mill Lane at approximately SO 856842 on high ground to W of Wolverhampton-Kidderminster road, shown only on Yates' map (WBJ p28) (DoE II) (VCH vol 20 p144). There is a 25 yard long tunnel here for Staffs and Worcs Canal called Dunsley Tunnel. Dunsley formed a township with Halfcot from 1830 to the mid C19 (VCH vol 20 p149). By the late C20 was a ward in Kinver civil parish.

Dunsley Common Common at Dunsley, Kinver. All the common was enclosed by 1780 (VCH vol 20 p138).

Dunsley Dell The bridle path from Dunsley to The Hyde, Kinver runs through it. The path is possibly an ancient pack-horse trail (KEOP p14p of in c1906).

Dunsley Bank Heath S of Stourton. In Dunsley Bank were some sandstone caves which were once inhabited (RKE p20). 0.5m SE of Dunsley Bank is Gibbet Wood (see) where William Howe was gibbeted.

Dunsley Hall Situated on a rocky outcrop overlooking the Stour Valley commanding excellent views 0.75m SW of Stourton. Became the manor house of the sub-manor of Dunsley (VCH vol 20 p124) and as such was occupied by Gilbert le Dunsley in 1316 (KEOP p59p of the present house). The present house dates from the later C16 but has many additions. From the early C18 the hall was regularly let. The Robins family were in residence for much of the C19 (VCH vol 20 pp134-135). In 1812 Benjamin Robins was murdered here by William Howe (SPN p71) (BCM winter 1999/2000 p28p) with a pistol made at Bradmore (see). The same or another Mr Robins, a farmer, was murdered by a highwayman (RKE p19) (KRC p26). As part of the Prestwood estate the hall was for sale in 1913 (TB June 1998 p6p).

Dunsley Hill A villa at Dunsley, NE of Kinver. It may be the 'The Hill,' the seat of the Hillman family in the C17 and until 1775. It was advertised for letting in the 1820s (VCH vol 20 p124).

Dunsley House 0.5m NE of Kinver church. Dates from the early C19. As Dunsley Villa it was the home of the Hancox family until the mid 1860s. By 1912 it was occupied as a home of rest by the Girls' Friendly Society, which used it until the later 1930s (VCH vol 20 p124) (KEOP p61p).

Dunsley Manor 0.75m NE of Kinver church. Has a timber-framed range dating back to the late C16. The range had been encased in brick by the early C19 (VCH vol 20 p124).

Dunsmore Brook Tributary of the Churnet. Has appeared as Dunnismour (1278), Dunsmore (Speed's map), and River Dunsmore (1689) (SPNO p9). Formerly dammed at the end of the C18 to create Rudyard Lake (RL p5). There is a Dunsmoore Brook which is a tributary of the Trent (NHS p42).

Dunstal Small hamlet 0.75m E of Bagot's Bromley. In Abbots Bromley parish. To the E of it is a small pool called Dunstal Pool. Has appeared as Dunstal (1402) and Dunstall, and means 'homestead' (ABMB p53). Dunstal Hall is a Georgian-style building of rendered brick (ABAB p39).

Dunstal Brook Flows in Bagot Forest N of Abbot's Bromley to Ash Brook.

Dunstall Tiny hamlet and wharf on Coventry Canal 0.5m S of Fradley. In Alrewas ancient parish (W p593).

Dunstall Dunstall Farm is 1.25m W of Tamworth. Formerly in Fazeley township in Tamworth ancient parish (W p625). Formerly Tunstall (DUIGNAN).

Dunstall Small village in a fairly narrow dale (HOPT vol 1 p134) in the southern incline to the Needwood Forest plateau, 17m ESE of Stafford. Former township and manor in Tatenhill ancient parish. The name Tunstall, which Dunstall appears as in the C13, means 'an enclosed farmstead' (DUIGNAN), or 'homestead' (SPN p43), or 'farmstead' (SSE 1996 p13). Another form of Dunstall is Donestal (SPN p43). In 1323 Philip de Somerville granted to Hugh Newbold some land in Dunstall if he rendered to him at Wychnor four loaves of bread, corn and bacon to give to the poor, annually on Holy Thursday. But if Philip or his heirs should convert the bread etc to any other use than distributing it to the poor, then the annual payment was to be abolished. Also the Newbolds were to give eight hens on Christmas Day and one chaplet or nosegay of white or red roses annually on the feast of St John the Baptist for all services except the king's foreign service and two appearances at the two great courts of Wychnor (HOPT vol 1 p117). There was possibly a medieval village by Dunstall Old Hall; or by the church; or by Dunstall Hall. It was probably deserted in the C18 (SSAHST 1970 p35). There was a chapel at Dunstall by 1553 (HOPT vol 1 pp22,23). The present church, St Mary, on the N side of the main road facing the lane to Smith Hills Cottages, was built in 1852-1853 (BOE p123). Dunstall became a separate ecclesiastical parish in 1852, and a separate civil parish in 1866 (GLAUE p410). At Dunstall John Bott witnessed a hail storm so strong that it cut the stalks off wheat and barley, the stones were nearly four inches in circumference. It occurred only in the vicinity of the village (NHS p23) (SHOS vol 1 p112). The well in Dunstall has a drinking fountain which issues water from the mouth of a white lion (IVNF p1). For a rhyme about Dunstall see Barton-under-Needwood.

Dunstall Former hamlet by the Smestow, now large suburb 1m N of Wolverhampton. Formerly in Wolverhampton township, chapelry and ancient parish (W p95). There seems to have been a small settlement at Dunstall in the Middle Ages (HOWM p6). Prior to the C19 the name appears as Tunstall, meaning 'farmstead' or 'the outlying farmstead' (SPN p144). A peculiar sighting of the moon was witnessed by Mr Franc and Mr Joseph Wightwick at Dunstall in Oct 1678 (NHS p8). Dunstall Halt railway station opened by Oxley Viaduct, close to Dunstall Park (Wolverhampton race course), in 1896 (Black Country Calendar 2000). Courtauld's moved its rayon-producing operations to Dunstall in 1925. Prince Philip visited the factory in 1948, and the Duchess of Kent visited the factory in 1968 (BUOP p94p). For rioting at Dunstall on July 10 1981 see Wolverhampton.

Dunstall Cross Tiny hamlet 0.75m WNW of Dunstall.

Dunstall Gate 0.5m NW of Dunstall, Tatenhill. There was settlement here in the C19 (1834 OS map). The name, no longer prevailing, is from a former entry into Needwood Forest (VCH vol 2 p350 see map).

Dunstall Hall Dunstall, formerly in Tatenhill ancient parish. The hall seems to have represented the capital messuage of the manor of Dunstall. Since the C14 the owners of the manor seem to have been the Newbolds, Griffiths, Boyntons, Turtons (from 1660), Agards, Meeks, and Charles Arkwright (d1850): he enlarged the present (1907) house. The house was called Dunstall Lodge before 1850. In 1851 it appears to have been sold by Mrs Mary Arkwright (perhaps widow of Charles Arkwright (d1850)) to John Hardy MP and barrister (d1855), who is described in the poem 'The Bar' (1825). The estate continued to be held by the Hardys for the rest of the C19 (W p20) (HOPT vol 1 pp129,131) (EDP p177): Sir Reginald Hardy (b1848) author of HOPT occupied the hall until at least 1938 (SHC 1938 List of Members). In c1953 the hall belonged to Sir Robert Douglas. Dunstall Hall, DoE II, and the Dunstall Hall estate were for sale in May 1997 (CL May 15 1997 property pages pc) and purchased by the entrepreneur Stan Clarke in June 1997 (ES June 28 1997 p11p). The house has a porte-cochere in the Ionic style with parapet fretted. In the central hall there is a genuine Roman floor mosaic

(Cerberus is represented in the centre) said to come from Tivoli. The staircase was carved by Edward Griffiths in c1900 with lush foliage and all kinds of zoo animals. In 1898 Griffiths carved into the front door a landscape with galloping horsemen, trees, a castle, and many humans and beasts (BOE p124). WH Bullock says he saw the staircase and it depicted the story of John Taylor of Barton-under-Needwood (IVNF photographs of the hall). In 1912 a short pillar of dark-green marble was described as the oldest art treasure in the house. It apparently came off an Egyptian temple. There was mosaic in the flooring of the hall, and a mosaic table, with designs taken from the Vatican. There were also figures of lions which are supposed to represent some of the oldest statuary in the world -believed to be sculpted at Athens 400 to 500 BC. There were also pictures by Belloni, Murillo, Greuze, Claude, Morland, Leighton, and a portrait of Lady Hamilton by Romney (NSFCT 1912 p193).

Dunstall Hall Dunstall, Wolverhampton. The estate and the ancient moated hall, in the foreign of Wolverhampton, belonged to the de Hampton family by Henry II's reign to 1580 when it passed to the Moseley family. They rebuilt the house in the Elizabethan style and built a gatehouse (HOWM p44). The hall and estate were purchased by the Wightwicks in 1675. The grandfather of Rt Hon William Huskisson, Secretary of State, held the hall in c1753. It passed to James Hordern in 1793 (OHW pl16) (SSAHST 1982-3 p57) or 1818 (WAIW vol 2 p) and from him it passed to his son Alexander Hordern (OHW pl16). Shaw noted over the entrance between the two lower windows a painting of a female figure representing Truth, followed by the motto VIGET VIRET VINCIT VERITAS, between the two upper windows was a shield with a horse's head cabossed on a wreath argent and sable; underneath which was inscribed VITA PERIIT MORTIS GLORIA NON MORTITUR under one of the windows, on the E side, was another shield charged with the arms of Wightwick (SHOS vol 2 p175 pl on p173). The old castellated mansion was enlarged to be a hall in c1830 (W p95). In 1851 it was the seat of Capt Annesley (W p20), at another time in the C19 it was the seat of the banker, Henry Hordern (BUOP p57p). By 1889 the hall was the property of Alexander Staveley Hill QC and MP but untenanted and surrounded by railways and modern housing (OHW pl16). The hall was demolished in 1916 (TB Oct 1980 p5). The gatehouse and moat were demolished in 1925 and Courtaulds' factory was built on the site (SSAHST 1982-3 p57) (WA vol 1 no 9 p257) (BUOP p57). (GM 1794) (NSFCT 1982 p13).

Dunstall Hill Hill, 472 feet high (HOWM p6), and district in Dunstall 0.75m N of Wolverhampton.

Dunstall Hill House Dunstall, Wolverhampton. Built in the C19 and stood to the E of Dunstal Hall. At one time it was the seat of Thomas William Shaw, son of John Shaw the Wolverhampton industrialist. A lodge to the house still stands in Dunstall Lane (BUOP p57p).

Dunstall House Wolverhampton. Birthplace on April 17 1888 of Dame Maggie Teyte (d1976), one of the greatest British operatic sopranos: She lived in Wolverhampton until the age of 13 (TEBC) (TEBC2 p128). By the mid 1990s there was a plaque which commemorated the birthplace of Maggie Teyte in Exchange Street, at the rear of the National Westminster Bank in Queen Square, Wolverhampton. Maggie was the daughter of the landlord of the Old Still Inn in King Street, Wolverhampton. She went to the Royal College of Music and later to Paris to study under Jean de Reszke. In 1908 she was selected to sing the title role Melisande at the Opera de Commique in Paris starting her Opera career. She died in poverty (WF p48) (MR p391).

Dunstall Old Hall House 0.25m W of Dunstall, in Tatenhill ancient parish.

Dunstall Park Dunstall, in Tatenhill ancient parish. A small deer park at Dunstall had been enclosed shortly before 1867 (EDP p177).

Dunstall Park 1m NNW of Wolverhampton. It appears to have been the grounds of Dunstall Hall (see). In the late 1880s Alexander Staveley Hill, owner of the Dunstall Hall estate, sold part of the grounds to be used for Wolverhampton's race course, formerly at Broadmeadow Field (see). The first race meeting held here was in 1886. In 1894 Lillie Langtry (Edward VII's mistress) won the Dudley Plate here with Montpensier, when she was still racing as 'Mr Jersey.' In 1895 the course became the only one to stage flat racing in Staffs after the closure of the course on Whittington Heath (see). In 1962 the course was Britain's first to stage Saturday night race meetings (One Hundred Years of Racing at Dunstall Park 1887-1987. Richard Onslow p4) (WF pp22,54) (Black Country Calendar 2000). The best performance by a British correspondent in horse race tipping is seven out of seven winners for a meet-

ing at Wolverhampton on March 22 1982 by Bob Butchers of the Daily Mirror (GBR 1994 p262). Wulfruna's Stone, near Wulfruna's Well (see), is a memorial to Lady Wulfrun, and was presented by Alexander Staveley Hill of Oxley Manor in 1901. The well and stone lie just S of Gorsebrook Road (SLM Feb 1959 p26p) (WMAG Aug 1969 p25p) (TB July 1988 p6p). Mander says the stone fountain head presented by A Staveley Hill was erected in 1895 (HOWM p4 note). Midland Aero Club held Wolverhampton's first aviation meeting here between 27 June and 2 July 1910 with SF Cody, C Grahame-White, Hon CS Rolls, AV Roe and others taking part (info Ron Balding) (EAS p33) (TB Dec 1993 p17) (WMA vol 1 p15). In 1988 Richardson brothers' proposals to redevelop Dunstall Park as a giant shopping centre were voted out (HOWU p165).

Dunstall Wharf Wharf and hamlet S of Fradley on the canal (W p593).

Dunston Small village on a low ridge between Pothooks Brook and the Penk, 3.5m S of Stafford. Former hamlet, township and chapelry in Penkridge ancient parish (W p468). In c1986 an axe-hammer of Early Bronze Age origin was found in a field near junction 13 of the M6 (ES July 31 1996 p1p). The manor of Dunestone appears in DB. Later forms are: Duneston (1201), Doneston (1201), Doneston (1242), Dunstone (1281), Dunstane (1367), Dunson (1552) (SPNO p84) (SPN p43). The name means 'Dun(n)'s town' (DUIGNAN) (SSE 1996 p13) (SPN p43). The church, St Leonard, on the W side of the A449, appears to have its origins in a chapel which existed by 1445. That church was rebuilt, except the tower, in the C18. A new church was built in 1876-1878 (VCH vol 5 p148). The prebend of Dunston in Penkridge Collegiate Church existed by 1261 (VCH vol 3 p300. vol 5 p147). William Anson, a lawyer, who bought Shugborough in 1624, was from Dunston (VB p117) (SNTG p18). In the later C17 Plot was told of an echo in a field W of the chapel (NHS p29). Dunston became a separate ecclesiastic parish in 1824 (refounded? in 1844 - LGS p128) and a separate civil parish in 1866 (GLAUE p410). There was an outbreak of foot and mouth disease at Dunston in March 1961 (SN March 4 1961 p8). In 1967 and 1968 large scale outbreaks occurred in the mid county area.

Dunston Hall Dunston. Rebuilt on the site of an older house by Frederick C Perry in c1870. It is a large stuccoed mansion bearing his monogram (VCH vol 5 p143). The older house may have been the seat of the Ansons from 1607 to the time they moved to Shugborough in 1624. William Critchley was living at the old hall some time in the first half of the C19. Frederick C Perry was living here by 1852. The new hall passed to George Benjamin Thorneycroft in c1901. His grandson, Rt Hon GEP Thorneycroft, sold the hall in 1951. It was sold to the English Electric Company in 1956 (VCH vol 5 p147). Lord Thorneycroft, who was Chancellor of the Exchequer, was born here (MR p137). (WMAG Sept 1963 p19p). Depressions in the NE corner of the garden may indicate the presence of a former moat (VCH vol 5 p143) (SSAHST 1982-3 p39).

Dunston Heath Dispersed hamlet 1m W of Dunston, on former common land. Has appeared as Dunston Heth (1460) and Dunston Heath (Yates' map) (SPNO p85). One hundred acres of common on Dunston Heath were enclosed in 1827 (VCH vol 5 p127). 'Rodney' Hall of Dunston Heath sold his wife at Penkridge in 1832 (SCSF p71).

Dunwood Fragmented hamlet on S-facing slopes rising above Endon Brook 0.75m W and NW of Longsdon. Formerly in Longsdon township in Leek ancient parish. The manor of Nether Longsdon, in existence by 1278, may have centred on the area of old Dunwood, 0.75m NW of Longsdon, and the settlement Nether Longsdon, recorded in 1278, also may have been in this area (VCH vol 7 pp203, 205). By the early C17 this area was known as Dunwood, the name of a nearby wood. The oldest surviving house at old Dunwood is Dunwood House Farm, dated 1678 (VCH vol 7 pp203,208).

Dunwood Hall Dunwood, over 0.5m WSW of Longsdon. Built by Thomas Hulme, formerly of nearby Dunwood Lodge Farm, in 1871. The central hall is paved with Minton tiles (VCH vol 7 p203). Hulme was elected first mayor of Burslem in 1878 (SHST p275).

Dunwood House Dunwood, 0.75m W of Longsdon. Known as New House in 1736. It was rebuilt in the mid C19 (VCH vol 7 p203).

Dustystile House? 2m S of Foxt.

Dutton's Brook Joins Fradswell Brook at Fradswell.

Dydon House over 1m W of Mayfield.

Dydon Wood Dydon, Mayfield. Described as famous in NSFCT 1909 p173.

E

Eagle House Cross Butts, Eccleshall. Built in 1810. Until the 1830s it was the Eccleshall Poor House (VE 92). At some time it is said to have been a young ladies finishing school. For sale in 2000 (DoE II) (SLM April 2000 pp9,14pc).

Eardleyend Common name for Eardley (SHC 1909 p24). Minute hamlet if not a single house 1.25m N of Audley. Former manor (SHC 1909 p24) and township in Audley ancient parish (W p428) (NSJFS 1971 p66). Has appeared as Erdeleye (1327), Yeardley End (1512), Yardley End (1621) (AHJ 1995 p46. 1997 p7). The name may be from Old English 'ear' meaning gravel - hence 'clearing noted for its stoney or gravelly soil' (AHJ 1997 p7. 1998 p7).

Eardley Hall 1.25m NNE of Audley. The original hall is believed to have been built by the Eardley family who gave their name to it (SHC 1944 p54). The old hall, which resembled Audley Old Hall, was built by 1585. The male line of the Eardleys of Eardley Hall failed in 1656 and the estate passed by marriage to the Wilmot family, later to be referred to as the Eardley-Wilmots; they sold the estate in 1823 to Sir John Fenton Boughey (AHJ 1998 pp7-23).

Earl's Drive A drive to approach Alton Towers mansion built by the 15th Earl of Shrewsbury in 1810 for his exclusive use. Runs through the entire length of Dimmingsdale, passes over the Churnet on Lord's Bridge and up Barbary Gutter (JAT p36) (SMOPP vol 1 p120p c1920). A lodge along the drive, designed by AW Pugin, has been restored and is called the 'Ramblers Retreat,' a tearoom for ramblers (JC 17 il).

Earl's Rock Rock feature at SK 055435 between Ousal and Dimmings Dales, S of Oakamoor.

Earls Way Long distance route thought to have been created in the C12 and linking lands in the North Midlands which belonged to the Earls of Chester (see under Chartley Castle) (SL p81 map). A recent suggestion is that the route may pre-date this period and take its name from the pre-Conquest Earls of Mercia (SHC 1999 p11). (PRT pp54-56 il) (DP p22). It entered Staffs by The Cloud and ran through Rushtonhall, Abbey Green, Leek, Bradnop, Lower Lady Meadows, and Waterhouses, and left for Ashbourne (VCH vol 7 pp98,219) (HOLF p4). Yearlsway (Ye Earlsway, Yarlsway) referred to that part from Cauldon to the Crown Inn at Waterhouses (VCH vol 2 p279) (DP p22) (MR p84). At Caldon it was known as the 'via comitis' in c1200 (VCH vol 2 p279). Has also appeared as Earlsway.

Earlsway House House on the Earls Way, under 1m WNW of Rushtonhall. Formerly in Rushton James township in Leek ancient parish. The present house stands on a site occupied by 1350 (VCH vol 7 p219) (DP p22).

Earlswood House at Penn built probably by Thomas Moss Phillips, a Wolverhampton solicitor, in the early 1860s. His wife Ellen Persehouse Phillips was tragically killed here in 1863 when her dress caught fire and she was badly burned. Following his death in 1877 the estate was sold to the industrialist George Benjamin Wright and has passed through a number of owners since. It is now (1990) used by the 2nd Penn Scouts (PENOP p34p).

Easing Scattered settlement to NE of Leek; Easing Villa (of the later C19) is 1.25m ENE of Leek and Easing Farm (possibly of the C17) is 2m ENE of Leek. Formerly in Tittesworth township in Leek ancient parish. The prefix 'Es' may represent god, suggesting Easing was a pagan worship site (DPMM p116). Easing was an inhabited area by the early 1230s (VCH vol 7 p233), appearing in the C13 as Esynge and Hesinge (DPMM p115). The house called The Ashes (see) to the N of Easing Farm was formerly called Easing (VCH vol 7 p233).

East Bank Burton upon Trent. Residence in 1907 of TE Lowe (STC p45p).

East Ecton Ecton. A 'Bradder Beaver,' a hard hat for miners, in this case at the Ecton Copper Mine, survived at a farmhouse here. It went, along with a kibble or tub (used for raising ore and rock up a mine shaft), to the Peak District Mining Museum at Matlock Bath, Derbys (PDS&C p107p).

East Gate Medieval gateway in the wall surrounding Stafford, on the E side. Is recorded from the later C12 (VCH vol 6 pp188,199). It stood at the end of Eastgate Street between Backwalls North and Backwalls South (SIOT p90). It guarded the London Road and was not needed to be as strongly fortified as the North Gate, since, before it, lay marshy land (SSTY p2). A mill built outside the East Gate in the mid C14 was driven by water from the King's Pool for about 200 years (SSTY p3). Elizabeth I arriving in Stafford from Chartley was met by the town's bailiffs and councillors at Eastgate mill dam in 1575 (VCH vol 6 p197). The arch above the gate was standing as late as 1800. It was taken down in c1800; Roxburgh says it was standing until 1799 (SKYT p49). The N side of the gate, containing a portion of the portcullis, was left standing in situ until C20. In 1939 it was moved due to road widening and set against the end wall of a cottage further along North Walls. When the cottage was demolished in 1964 it was left freestanding (VCH vol 6 p200). (W p325) (LGS p213) (SOSH p148) (SN Dec 1 1972 p9p).

East Park Ward of Wolverhampton borough by 1982, and an area and public park 1.25m ESE of Wolverhampton. The park opened on Sept 21 1896, on former barren waste of Stowheath and Chillington collieries given by Sir Alfred Hickman MP and the Duke of Sutherland. In 1909 it contained an Ice Age glacial boulder found at Cornhill, Horseley Fields, in 1904 (WJO). The lake had drained away by 1906 and the site of it was redeveloped as a playground and paddling pool in 1951 (WJO Nov 1903 lix. Nov 1909 p293) (TEBC) (WF p24) (Mapping the Past Wolverhampton 1577-1986. Mary Mills 1993 p24). The church, St Matthew, East Park Way, was built in 1849 and rebuilt in 1969 (LDD).

East Vale Area lying N of the railway line and E of the Adderley Green road, centred on Goddard and Ford Streets, Longton. The area was built up in the late 1870s and added to the borough of Longton, from Caverswall parish, in 1883 (VCH vol 8 pp224, 227,253). Or created a civil parish from the part of Caverswall ancient parish in Longton municipal borough in 1894. This was abolished in 1896 when it joined Longton civil parish (GLAUE p427).

East Valley A ward of Stoke-on-Trent district by 1991 covering the Baddeley Green, Smallthorne, and Sneyd Green areas.

East Wall Farm over 1m W of Oakamoor. Has appeared as Heystiswell (C12). An iron slag found under the farmyard is evidence of past iron smelting here (VB p174).

Eastwood District of Hanley, as opposed to Northwood (H p106). Also was a ward of Hanley from 1895 (VCH vol 8 p158). The Cauldon Canal runs by it (Trent & Mersey Canal. Peter Lead 1980. pl 80).

Eaton Brook Tributary of the Penk (SPNO p9). Is it the brook that runs from S of Gailey to join the Penk N of Water Eaton?

Eaton House 0.25m W of Gailey on S side of Watling Street (1834 OS map).

Eaton Lodge Large house in its own grounds on N side of Wolseley Road, Rugeley. Probably built in c1830 by Capt George Hamilton. It had become the home of the Sneyd family by 1854. By the mid 1950s was Eaton Lodge Hotel and Country Club (VCH vol 5 p153).

Eaton Park Modern housing estate at Berry Hill, S of Bucknall.

Eaves Hamlet on the slopes of a hill above a tributary of the Trent and former township in Bucknall and Bagnall chapelry in Stoke-upon-Trent ancient parish. It was united with Bucknall for civil purposes by 1843. The hamlet of Eaves may have been called Ash (as in Ash Hall) in the C16 (HBST p528). There is a small moated site opposite the farm of Little Eaves (NSFCT 1926 p136). William Willet, who died on Sept 8 1827 aged 105, was from Little Eaves (W p57) or of Endon (MMM p59). Willet claimed he and others danced at Endon for 11 days continuously from the evening of Sept 2 or 3 to the morning of Sept 14 1752; neglecting to mention that these 11 days were lost with Britain's move over from the Julian to the Gregorian calendar. Willet is buried in St Luke's churchyard, Endon (HSP pp136,137) (W pp57,237) (KES p95) (STM Dec 1968 p38) (VB p191) (MR p239; he danced at Newborough). There is a house and lane called Little Eaves. There is an Eaves Farm E of Abbey Hulton between Great Eaves and Little Eaves.

Eaves, The House 1m SSE of Cheadle.

Eavesford House nearly 1.5m SSW of Foxt.

Ebstree Ebstree Bridge over the Staffs and Worcs Canal is 0.75m NE of Trysull.

Eccleshall (a native is an Ecclian). Ancient parish and township. The small town of Eccleshall on the S side of the Sow backed by the Sow valley S bank, is 7m NW of Stafford.

EARLY. A glacial boulder, with grooves, lies just inside the churchyard. It was dug up from beneath the roadway and now bears the date 1909 in Roman numerals (STM June 1965 p41). An unusually small mire lies immediately N of Eccleshall at SJ 825295 possibly created in the early Flandian or possibly even the late Devensian period (WSS p101p). This is perhaps the 'moorish' ground near Eccleshall Castle Plot refers to with bottomless springs (NHS p59). Portions of quern stones, and a wooden paddle have been found in a moss in Eccleshall parish (GNHS 1860 ed p5) (NSJFS 1964 p21). See also under Eccleshall Moss. There may have been a settlement at Eccleshall in Celtic times. The first part 'eccles' being the Celtic word for church (SPJD p38). The Romans may have founded Eccleshall. A correspondent of William Pitt thought the town was founded in 60 AD when Vespasian built a fort or town here (W p373). The **Romans** are attributed with building a temple to Jove here (W p373) which may have been on the site of the present church (NSFCT 1944 p92). Another argument in support of a Roman founding is that DB lists so many settlements in the vicinity of Eccleshall all held by the bishop of Chester (of which the diocese of Lichfield then formed a part) that they constitute a unitary estate. And that this estate was created in pre-Norman Conquest times, and could be of Anglian or Romano-British origin (SL p45).

600 to 1086. A large **estate** centred on Eccleshall may have been granted by King Penda of Mercia (d655) to the first bishop of Lichfield, Dwina (or Diuna), on his appointment to the See in 655 (BPS pp92-93). Or King Wulfhere of Mercia (d674) granted it to his bishop of Lichfield, Chad, later in the C7. Perhaps it was among the endowments showered on the See by King Offa when he had the See temporarily raised to an archbishopric in the late C8, or perhaps it came to the bishops by purchase or gift at two different times (ECC p9) (SSE 1987 p30). According to Malmesbury the **prebend** of Eccleshall was founded in 822 and is considered to have been part of the original endowment of the See of Lichfield (HOL p227). Certainly portions of the manor had become a prebend in Lichfield cathedral by the end of the C12. In 1332 the prebend was styled Eccleshall and Offley, and sometimes Johnson (SHOS vol 1 pp291-292) (SSAHST vol 2 1960-61 p45) (VCH vol 3 pp140,141,144). Eccleshall parish was a peculiar jurisdiction of the dean and chapter and certain prebendaries of Lichfield cathedral until peculiar jurisdictions were abolished in 1846 (VCH vol 3 p93). **Church.** A supposed Roman temple at Eccleshall is said to have been rebuilt for Christian worship in 661. According to tradition Chad instructed Rufin and Wulfad, the sons of King Wulfhere, a pagan, in it; in fury at their conversion to Christianity, Wulfhere went to Eccleshall and slew his sons in the church and destroyed it in 670 (W p373). There is another tradition of the princes being slain at Stone or at Burston. It is known that a restoration of a church was in progress in 1019 (NSFCT 1944 p92). White says the church lay in ruins until being restored by Elias de Jantonice, prebendary of Eccleshall in 1090 (W p373). The present church, Holy Trinity, on the N side of Church Street, has its origins in a church built in 1190 (Holy Trinity Church, Eccleshall. Malcolm Gray and Kenneth Bowe. 1990) (Holy Trinity Church: A Brief History. Rev Stephen Cooke). In all to date there are said to have been six churches on the site of the present church (NSFCT 1944 p92). The ancient parish, formed before 1086, probably originally contained the ancient parishes of Cheswardine, and Adbaston (or High Offley) (SHC 1916 p192). The parish church is one of the few to have a bishop's throne (STM June 1965 p40p), probably on account of Eccleshall being an estate held by the bishops of Lichfield from the C7 and their formerly residing at Eccleshall. The parish feast or **wake** was on Trinity Sunday in the mid C19 (W p373). An Anglo-Saxon settlement at Eccleshall is said to have been laid waste by the Danes in 1010 (W p373).

1086 to 1500. The manor of Ecleshelle, held by the bishop of Chester (Lichfield), appears in DB. Later forms are: Eccleshale (1227) (SSE 1996

p13), Ecclyshale (SPN p43), and Eccleshaul (c1540) (LI appendix p170). Eccleshall has not been considered the Eccleshale in the will of Wulfric Spot (c1002), founder of Burton Abbey, by most antiquarians (SHC 1916 pp39-40). The first part of the **name** 'Eccles' is the Celtic word for church (SL p45) (VB p161). 'Hall' is from 'halh,' Old English 'nook, corner of land' so giving 'land of the church by the river or hollow' (ECC p8) (SPJD p38), or from 'halgh,' Anglo-Saxon 'meadow or pasture' so giving 'meadow of the church' (BPS p98 note). But 'eccles' could mean a British Christian community without a church, so giving 'Nook at a Celtic Christian centre' (NSJFS 1981 p3), or 'ecles in a hollow or corner of land' (SSE 1987 p30). Other derivations have been 'Ecclesiae Aula,' or the 'hall or palace of the church' (BPS p92) (NSFCT 1908 p124), or 'Æcle's hall' (DUIGNAN) (SPN p43), or 'Eagle's Hall,' from a Roman standard flying from the Roman fort here (W p373). In 1153 Bishop Walter Durdent obtained a royal charter for a weekly market at Eccleshall (ECC pp11,12). The bishop of Lichfield was granted a charter sometime between 1149-1154 to hold a **market** at Eccleshall on Sundays (NSJFS 1971 p50). Another account says the bishop established Eccleshall's market for Fridays in 1161 (THS) (SCSF p95). There was no market in 1792 (OWEN), and 1888 (LHE p265). There were proposals to close the cattle market in Oct 1975 (SN Oct 10 1975 p1). The site of the former cattle market was developed with housing and a street called Marketfields by the mid 1990s. The earliest reference to Eccleshall being a **borough** is in 1199. Borough tenure continued until at least in 1697 (NSJFS 1972 p68) (BOE p126 note). Another account says the charter granting Eccleshall a borough does not survive, but must have been granted before 1240, possibly as early as 1199 (ECC pp11,12). In 1259 Bishop Roger Meuland or Longespee obtained a royal charter for an annual **fair** on Ascension eve, day, and morrow (ECC pp11,12). Cooke gives Thursday before Mid Lent Thursday, Holy Thursday, August 16, first Friday in Nov (for cattle, sheep, and saddle horses). Hackwood is doubtful of the accuracy of Cooke's list and he gives Mid Lent Thursday, Holy Thursday, Aug 5, and the first Friday in Nov (SCSF p98,99). There was a fair in 1792 (OWEN), but not in 1888 (LHE p265). A riot occurred subsequent to a bull bait in Eccleshall on Feb 11 1823 (LOU p239). There was a street with houses called Usulwall Street N of and parallel to the High Street (MR p140 - says it was S of the High Street), this together with some settlement on the N side of the Sow was abandoned by the late Middle Ages (SL p85). There was bull baiting in Eccleshall until about the mid C19 (BPS p104). Hackwood says the **curfew bell** at Eccleshall was heard in quite recent years (SCSF p161). **Royal visitors.** Edward I was at Eccleshall in July 1277 staying at Eccleshall Castle. **Queen Margaret of Anjou**, wife of Henry VI, may have stayed the night at the Royal Oak Inn, High Street, before the battle of Bloreheath in 1459, with her young son Edward (VE p135). She is said to have sought shelter in Eccleshall church after the battle (NSFCT 1886 p62). (ES July 14 1986 p7).

1500 to PRESENT. In the **Civil War** Eccleshall Castle (see) was a royalist garrison. The parliamentarian, Henry Stone, is said to have taken a force through Eccleshall to take the royalist garrison at Stafford (SHJ summer 1987 p35). **Coaching station.** After the road from Stafford through Ashley to the Nantwich road was turnpiked in 1763 Eccleshall became a posting station on an alternative route for Chester; inhabitants were employed in inn-keeping and at stables; the town still retains the appearance of a typical elongated coaching town (NSFCT 1925 p203) (VE p14). In 1807 a driverless coach pulled up at T Bagnall's house in Eccleshall. The driver had fallen off, asleep, at Sugnall, three miles away. The passengers, who were asleep, did not notice. The horses proceeded to the house, instinctively. The driver was later found dead by the roadside at Sugnall (GM 1807) (PWNS p30). Eccleshall **Grammar School** is mentioned in a 1834 directory as being rebuilt in c1760 (W p374). But it is not clear whether this was a continuation of the charity school, a survival of the C17 grammar school, or a fresh beginning. It decayed in the second half of the C19 and had closed by the end of the C19. In 1900 the school building became the church room (ECC pp59,60). **Work.** The Eccleshall area has long been agricultural, and has produced over the centuries glass, ironwork, quarried stone (ECC pp22-30), shoes, leather work, and timber (ECC pp53-55). There was a **windmill** at Eccleshall (WIS p17). There was an **anti-enclosure riot** in Eccleshall on Oct 4 1796; 25 fences were torn down (LOU pp178,375). For the **Stone and Eccleshall Troop** see Stone. No **canal** (see Bristol and Hull Canal) nor **railway** has come through Eccleshall to supplant road transport. In the early 1830s GJR envisaged a line through the town but instead laid it through Norton Bridge. An anticipated Stafford to Whitchurch, Shrops, line through the town in the 1860s was never built, although The Railway Inn on the corner of Newport Road and Green Lane was named in anticipation of its arrival. In consequence of no railway Eccleshall is said to have remained as small as it has (VE pp16,17,141). There was a **lock-up** in front of the Eagle Inn in Horsefair (VE p141). **Survey of Eccleshall**. A census of the inhabitants of Eccleshall parish in the late C17 with some curious incidental notes about certain persons was compiled by William Lloyd, bishop of Lichfield. It is known as the 'Survey of the Parish of Eccleshall 1693-1698.' Lloyd's Ms, written in tachygraphy, the same short-hand used by Samuel Pepys, is in Lichfield Record Office. WSL has a transcript made by Norman Tildesley prior to 1970. Lately, **Eccleshall Historical Society**, founded Sept 19 1991, have acquired a copy of the Tildesley transcript (info Jan Baker and Lichfield Record Office catalogue) (SSE vol 7 1995). **Newspapers**. The Eccleshall Reminder, founded on Nov 15 1923 ran until at least Dec 12 1940 (SHJ spring 1996 p18). Many Stone (see) newspapers have Eccleshall in their title. **Outer Eccleshall**. Between High Offley and Eccleshall, Garner noted, built into a bridge over a stream, a tombstone with the figure of an ecclesiastic and escutcheons (GNHS p547). A stinking sulphur well in a watery lane not far from Eccleshall was noted by Plot in the later C17 (NHS p105). The rustic wooden tree house near Eccleshall by lanes leading to Shropshire noted by AE Dodd in SLM winter 1956 p22p may be a reference to the tree house at Wood Farm near Adbaston. Foot-and-mouth disease broke out in Eccleshall parish at Bromley Hall Farm, Gerrard's Bromley (see) in late Nov 1967, and at Wood End Cottage in Dec 1967 (SN Dec 8 1967 p10. Dec 29 1967 p13). For the case of Mary Peate of Eccleshall, who fell ill in Colton parish and was taken to Colwich parish where she died and her burial became chargeable to Colwich ratepayers, see Colwich. **Cuisine, superstition and the supernatural**. The special dish to celebrate mid-Lent 'Mothering Sunday' in Eccleshall parish was a roast veal and custard, eaten at mid-day. This occurred on the fourth Sunday in Lent (FOS p86). In the C20 a butcher created the 'Eccleshall Pie' still on sale in the town (PWNS p28). An 'Eccleshall Pie' is featured on the wall of the Pie Factory Inn of Mad O' Rourke's Little Pub chain in Tipton. There is a superstition concerning the churchyard gate that two persons passing through it at the same time is unlucky and good luck comes to those who pass through one at a time (SFL p276). It was the custom on May Day for mayflowers to be placed on the doorstep of the Crown Inn. The custom was still being practised in 1878 when CS Burne witnessed it (SFL p356) (BCC vol 2 p212). The custom of gooding on St Thomas' Day (Dec 21) at Eccleshall was kept up into the C19 (SFL p392). About 1810 a retired colonel brought his young bride back to live at Charnes Hall. At Eccleshall her horse bolted and she fell and died (BPS pp137-138). Her ghost reputedly haunts the area of Eccleshall where she fell, known as Washpit (info Bruce Braithwaite). Eccleshall churchyard is haunted. A ghost reputedly haunts an upstairs room of the Ye Olde London House, dated 1717, on N side of the high street (info Bruce Braithwaite). Ghost Mile is the local name for a road about Eccleshall where there have been sightings of a gentleman dressed in Tudor clothes (EGH p121) (GOS p31). There was a man, long ago, who returned as a ghost at night after he had hanged himself in the corner of a waste ground field at Eccleshall, on the property of CS Burne (STMSM July 1980 p32); she resided at Pyebirch Manor in the later C19. Whether this relates to Ghost Mile?

Eccleshall Castle Mansion on site of a castle 0.25m NNE of Holy Trinity church, Eccleshall. The present mansion was preceded by castles built by the bishops of Lichfield, lords of Eccleshall. A licence to fortify a castle here was granted in 1200 (BOE p126) (CAMS p20). The castle was rebuilt by Bishop Walter de Langton in the late C13 for an episcopal residence for the bishops of Lichfield. Edward I was at Eccleshall Castle on July 12 1277 (NSFCT 1882 p65) (VCH vol 3 p272). In 1322 Sir Roger de Swynnerton had custody of Eccleshall Castle (SHC 1914 p3 note). Queen Margaret of Anjou fleeing from the battle of Bloreheath (1459) took refuge here by the direction of Bishop Hales (John Hulse), according to Leland (NHS pp447,449). Bishop Richard Sampson (1543-54) is believed to be the first bishop to make Eccleshall Castle the principal seat of the bishops of Lichfield, perhaps as a result of losing his estates at Beaudesert and Shugborough in 1546 (ECC pp36-37). The royalist garrison in the Civil War at the castle was taken after an eight week siege, which ended on Aug 30 1643. During the siege the 83-year-old Bishop Wright, then in residence, died. The castle then appears to have been a parliamentary garrison (HSS pp98-103) (ES summer number 1907) (HOS p36. 1998 pp72,74) (ES July 14 1986 p7) (MR p138) (SPJD p41). (HOS 1998 p72). Loxdale says some stones went to build the bridge at Great Bridgeford (SH p78); whether after the Civil War or at another time? In the Bodleian Library is a sketch of the ruined building and a measured plan, together with an estimate of the cost of repair. A quaint and somewhat fanciful painting preserved in Eccleshall church may well represent the castle. It is believed that the footings are still to be seen (OP pp18-19). The castle layout was probably with four angle towers a la Bolton, or Bodiam (BOE p126). The present remains of Eccleshall Castle are the C14 bridge over the moat and the

NE tower. The base of a second tower has, in last half of the C20, been found by archaeologists. Charles I (perhaps accompanied by his eldest son Charles) is said to have stayed at the castle (info Jan Baker). Erdeswick and Chetwynd noted the castle; the latter had more to say about it (SH p46). MANSION. In 1695 Bishop Lloyd built the present mansion on the site of the castle. In the intervening years the bishops had resided at nearby Byanna. Bishop Cornwallis (1781-1824) entertained Sir Walter Scott here (ES July 14 1986 p7). It was he who insisted on driving through Eccleshall in his four-horse carriage to the church for services, despite the fact that the churchyard adjoined the house. He also desired that no one leave the church before him after services (Friends of Lichfield Cathedral 1998 p25). The last bishop to live here was Bishop Lonsdale, in residence by at least 1851, who died in its parlour in Oct 1867 (W p20) (The Church Guide 1990 p11) (MR p138; died in 1864). Afterwards the bishops lived in the Bishop's Palace in Lichfield. (RSL pp15-16 life at the castle in the C19). The house was purchased in 1908 by George Carter, a brewing and shipping magnate from Yorks (Daily Telegraph. Weekend Section. April 25 1987 pvi). The Carter family still (1997) live here. (DoE II*) (SSC pp106, 132 in the intro) (HOL p11) (GNHS p117) (BPS pp93-98) (LGS p129) (S p86) (HOG p194) (STM June 1965 p41p) (NSJFS 1966 pp43-44) (VB p161) (SGS pp95,96; there is an oil painting of the castle in the church) (EOP p24p of c1910) (ROT pp23-24) (SPJD pp38,39pc,40ps,41) (AA p255).

GROUNDS. In the later C17 Plot noted some **springs** in 'moorish' ground near Eccleshall Castle, which the locals told him were bottomless, because they were never failing, and yet never running over (NHS p59). The **Dungeon** is in the entrance into the lower part of the NE tower. Presumably it served as a dungeon at some time (EOP p25p). A **font-bowl** was still (1954) to be seen in the grounds of Eccleshall Castle (NSFCT 1954 p89). The nine-sided NE **tower of the old castle** - originally one of four at each corner of the castle joined by curtain walls - remains. It dates from the early C14 (EOP p24p). It was recently revealed that the tower housed a medieval chapel of Our Lady; on hearing this Sister Mary Barbara Pearce of St Dominic's, Stone, presented a statue of the Virgin Mary, which the Carters installed in it (SCHJ No. 24 1990 p32). The twin-arch bridge over the moat had a **gatehouse** which was taken down by Bishop Cornwallis because his coach could not pass through safely (ES July 14 1986 p7). Shaw noted **The Grove**, which according to tradition had been planted by Bishop Hough (b1657), and possibly personally planted by him: By the end of the C18 it had been turned into a shrubbery (SHOS vol 1 p281) (HOL p123). The castle grounds are said to be haunted by the **ghosts** of a grey lady, a white lady, a spectral cavalier and a black dog (GPCE p43).

Eccleshall Moss An oak paddle from the Early Stone Age (Palaeolithic?) has been found in Eccleshall Moss (OSST 1949-50 p16). The moss can be possibly identified with Eccleshall Water (see).

Eccleshall Park A medieval deer park enclosed out of forest belonging to the bishops of Lichfield. In existence by 1307. It can probably be identified with Blore Park (see) and Bishop's Park (see), both of which belonged to the bishops of Lichfield, and both were carved out of Blore Forest (NSJFS 1962 p76. 1964 pp62-63).

Eccleshall Water Former lake which formed the main part of Eccleshall Castle defences. Eccleshall Water is Erdeswick's River Sow and tributaries of (SOS pp104,106). Plot, who according to Eccleshall Church Guide p9 claimed that Eccleshall Water was the second largest stretch of water in the county (this is erroneous; Ladford Pool (see) was meant), writes of Eccleshall Castle Pooles (NHS p43). It was drained in 1820 to provide meadow land (Eccleshall Castle Guide p9). Eccleshall Water may have been the area called Eccleshall Moss (see), where may have been the small mire at SJ 825295. It can probably be identified with the castle mere nature reserve adjoining Eccleshall churchyard leased to the Staffordshire Wildlife Trust (Holy Trinity Church, Eccleshall in the Diocese of Lichfield 1190-1990. Malcolm Gray and Kenneth Bowe 1990 p18).

Echills House 1m WSW of King's Bromley. Formerly Eachills and Each Hills (1834 OS map). In King's Bromley parish. At Echills farm were several pieces of heraldic glass, including the Lane coat of arms. In 1927 there was a storm which damaged the glass, and it went to London (NSFCT 1923 p133. 1927 p159).

Ecton Dispersed hamlet in the Moorlands, situated around Ecton Hill 0.75m ESE of Warslow. In Wetton parish. To the SE of Ecton is Back of Ecton; to the E of Ecton is East Ecton; to the SW of Ecton is Ecton Bridge; to the S of Ecton is Top of Ecton. The personal name cannot be decided on, but may be 'Ecca's farmstead' (SPN p45). The mining of copper out of Ecton Hill is believed to pre-date copper mining in Cornwall, and therefore could be the first copper mining in Britain. There may have been copper mines here prior to the mid C16 when the area was part of an estate held by Tutbury Priory. At the Dissolution the estate passed to the Cavendish family (WTCEM) (LTD pp43-44). There was certainly mines at Ecton by at least 1640. In addition to copper; lead, zinc and silver have been mined out of the hill. Here was used gunpowder for blasting the rock, for the first time in England, an innovation introduced by German miners brought over by Prince Rupert in 1632 (WTCEM pp8,20,78,79). In 1660 the Cavendish family, Dukes of Devonshire, started mining copper out of Ecton Hill, and began or deepened a perpendicular mine which appears to have been referred to as Ecton Pipe, and later Ecton Deep Adit (see). In 1767 Sir Joseph Banks, scientist, visited this mine. By 1795 it had reached a depth of 1,300 feet. It closed in 1825 (LTD p44), perhaps when at a depth of 1,650 feet. Copper mining in Ecton Hill finally ended in 1889 and Ecton village then depopulated (The Midlands. Past-into-Present series. Clive Gilbert. 1978 p70). The same or another shaft appears to have been called Dutchman's Level (see). **Samples from mines.** Walter Chetwynd was sent an example of a lead ore made up of eight solid triangles found in Ecton Hill in the C17 (NHS p188 tab 12 fig 2). There were ore samples from the mines in the school of mining in Jermyn Street, London in 1925 (SG p17). (NHS p165) (W p788) (LGS pp185-186) (EH many refs) (SM il on preface page viii) shows lead ore of an eight-sided form found near Ecton Hill) (MR p141). The engine house, at SK 098583 below the massive spoil-heap that covers the entrance to Dutchman Mine, is a two-storey stone and tiled building. It contained a Boulton and Watt steam engine of 1788: The site of a gin-race lies to the N (IAS p203) (MR p141). At Ecton Lea (or now The Lee?) there was a **refreshment room** for the Leek and Manifold Valley Railway (SMOPP vol 2).

Ecton Cavern Cavern at Ecton created by copper mining in the late C18. When the mine was abandoned it became a tourist attraction (MR p140).

Ecton Hill Hill 1210 feet high, 0.75m SE of Warslow. Contains many disused copper mines, see under Ecton. On the summit at SK 09985800 is a damaged possible burial mound under the trigonometrical point (NSJFS 1965 p57). The burial mound 200 metres SW of Ecton Hill at SK 09825787 is a listed monument. The low spread mound at SK 09675736, 0.5m SW of Ecton Hill, is a listed monument (NSJFS 1965 p57). It is 15 paces in diameter and two feet high. Three other burial mounds, unlocated by Gunstone, are about Ecton Hill. There is a burial mound at Hanging Bank (see). Bateman excavated one in 1848 in which he found a child's skeleton and a cremation with a bone pin and a flint arrowhead (TYD p34) (NSJFS 1965 p57). Carrington excavated another, in 1850, and found eight burials, seven crouched inhumations and a cremation (TYD pp164,165) (NSJFS 1965 p57). He excavated another in 1851, 16 paces in diameter, and found a cremation on the natural surface (TYD p176) (NSJFS 1965 p57).

Ecton Low Whether at SK 097577 or SK 097574? Has also appeared as Ecton Hill Low. The second map reference may be a reference to a burial mound situated on a hill called Summer Hill, from Summerhill Farm.

Ecton Park Former medieval deer park enclosed out of forest near Warslow. In existence by c1220 when owned by the prior of Tutbury (NSJFS 1964 p63).

Edensor Area of SW Longton. Formerly in Stoke-upon-Trent chapelry in Stoke-upon-Trent ancient parish. Did Sir John Edensor Heathcote, who received a knighthood in 1784, and died at Longton Hall, give his middle name to this district or did it give it to him? (SHST p547). Edensor became a separate ecclesiastical parish in 1846 (CAST p57) (GLAUE p410). The church, St Paul, in Edensor Road, was opened in 1854, but was replaced by a new church on another site on the S side of Longton Hall Road in 1940 (VCH vol 8 pp234-235). There is a mission church, St Mark, at Edensor (LDD).

Edge End House over 1m WSW of Thorncliffe. Formerly in Tittesworth township in Leek ancient parish. Former timber-framed house remodelled in stone in the C17 (VCH vol 7 p233).

Edgehill A ward of Burton upon Trent in the south Stapenhill area. Forms a boundary with Waterside ward.

Edge Hill Lower Penn. One of the Orton Hills (PPTP p58). Is not named on the 1834 OS map and takes its name from the field it is situated in (ALP p12). The hill is 402 feet high and may once have been fortified (IP). Frank Noble visited the hill in 1970 and thought it had qualities suitable as the site for a fort, but found no evidence for it ever having been one (ALP p16).

Edgelands Farm SW of Longnor, Lapley. Represents an ancient estate, in existence by the end of the C13 (VCH vol 4 p148). The name means 'Hiddi's land' or less likely 'a hide of land' (SPNO p168). Has appeared as Hydesland (1263), Hyddeslande (1428), Heddeslandes (1548), Hyddeslande (1576), Higdland (1604), and Edgeland (1834 OS map) (SPNO p168).

Edge Top Farm House 1m S of Hollinsclough. Formerly in Hollinsclough township in Alstonefield ancient parish. The present house is dated 1787 and was built for Micah Mellor, a hawker (VCH vol 7 p38).

Edge Top Farm House 0.75m ESE of Longnor. Formerly in Longnor township in Alstonefield ancient parish. There was a house called Edge Top by 1785 and there may have been a house here in 1600 called Edge Houses (VCH vol 7 p38).

Edial Tiny hamlet 2.5m WSW of Lichfield cathedral. Formerly in Burntwood out-township of St Michael's parish, Lichfield. There was a settlement at Edial probably by the later C13 (VCH vol 14 p198). Has also appeared as Edjal (Young Samuel Johnson. James L Clifford. 1955 1962 ed. p153), Edgehill (W p514) and Edjiall. The name means 'Eadgeat's hall,' then corrupted to Edgale (DUIGNAN). Or 'Eddi's corner of land' (SPN p57). A very productive hen in the C17 belonging to Ann Biddulph of Edial normally laid three eggs in a day or 24 hours (NHS pp234-236).

Edial Hall 2.5m WSW of Lichfield cathedral. The hall demolished in 1809 was probably built some time from the late C17 (VCH vol 14 p202) and resembled the first brick house of the governor of Maryland at St Marys City, Maryland, USA (Time Team. Channel 4. Jan 5 1997). The hall was owned by the Hammonds by at least 1680 to 1716 when it passed to the Fettiplaces from whom Samuel Johnson of Lichfield (see) rented the property for his academy (VCH vol 14 p209).

JOHNSON'S ACADEMY. Samuel Johnson had opened an academy at Edial Hall by spring 1736. Its only pupils were David Garrick, Garrick's younger brother George, and Lawrence Offley. The advertisement for the academy appears in June and July 1736 issue of GM. The academy lasted a very short time and was closed by Feb 1737. Johnson and his wife Tetty continued to live here for a short while after the academy's closure. Johnson's 'Irene' was begun here and some of his activity as a school master appears in this play (NSFCT 1931 pp84-90). An appeal to find Charles Bird, a servant at Edial Hall during Johnson's tenancy, appeared in GM in 1800. He died aged 81 in 1801 (CCBO pp192-193). (SHOS vol 1 p355) (HOL p564 il of facing p564) (LGS p94) (CCBO pp189-193, p of the hall facing p189) (SMC p171).

In 1750 the hall was advertised for letting. The Fern family acquired the hall in 1779 (VCH vol 14 p209). C Pye made a drawing of the hall, published by Cadell and Davis in 1805 (Young Samuel Johnson. James L Clifford. 1955 1962 ed. pp145-165 il). Richard Greenhough acquired the hall in 1806 and for a time a school was run here in 1807. The hall was demolished in 1809 (VCH vol 14 pp202,209). The Styche family acquired the site in 1811. (W p514). According to their own family tradition in early C20 the Styches lived in a remaining farmhouse which had adjoined the old hall (NSFCT 1931 pp84-90). This farmhouse was later known as Edial Hall Farm and had become known as Edial Hall by at least the mid 1980s (VCH vol 14 p209 pl 49 shows the hall in 1824). An oak settle from Edial Hall, belonging to Samuel Johnson, went to the Johnson Birthplace museum in Lichfield.

Edingale Parish and village on a bank between the Mease and Pessall Brook, 19.5m ESE of Stafford; the E part of the village lay in Derbys, whilst W part is in Staffs. Plot noted a Roman burial mound at Edingale (NHS p402 (SD p16). There is a mound 14 paces in diameter and four feet high at SK 21571216 in the centre of Edingale, and it may be the mound noted by Plot (NSJFS 1965 p37). For the possible Roman road which passes near Edingale see Croxall. The name means possibly 'the hall of the descendants of Eada,' or 'the hall of Eada' (DUIGNAN), or 'nook of Eden's or Eadin's people' (NSJFS 1981 p3) (SSE 1996 p13), or 'the corner of land of the people of Eadwine' (SPN p45). The old church had some Saxon work; some stones of a small Saxon window are preserved in the present church (LGS p130). A church of 1735-36 (LGS p130) was struck by lightning and destroyed by fire in the later C19 (PWIS p128). It was replaced by the present church, Holy Trinity, at the W end of Church Lane (then in Staffs), built in 1880-1881 (BOE p127). Edingale parish feast was on the first Sunday in June in the mid C19 (W p602). Erdeswick identified DB Etinghale with Edingale but that has since been identified with Ettingshall. Edingale manor appears in the DB Derbys survey (SHOS vol 1 p391) (DB. Phillimore. 1976). It has been implied that Edingale grew as an out-settlement of Croxall where the manor house and church were (SVB p72). The Derbys part remained in Croxall manor and ancient parish (W p602) until the whole of Croxall was removed to Staffs in 1895. The Staffs part was a part of Alrewas manor (SHC 1907 pp249-293), but had separate civil identity early. With its church it became a chapelry in Alrewas ancient parish (GLAUE p410). The chapelry became a separate ecclesiastical parish in 1824 (GLAUE p410). It was a part of Alrewas prebend by 1259 (SSAHST vol 2 1960-61 p43) (VCH vol 3 p93) (GLAUE p410). A solar rainbow was witnessed by Francis Wolferstan at Edingale on May 17 1681 at noon (NHS pp3,4,5,6,7 tab 1 fig 4) (SHOS vol 1 p414). Rev Theophilus Buckeridge, correspondent on antiquarian matters to GM, Master of St John's Hospital, Lichfield, and curate of Edingale in the C18, resided at Edingale (SHOS vol 1 p392). The village has a pump (MR p142). 'Edingale Mascot' has been described as the most famous Shire horse champion that has been bred by Mr Holland (d1986) of Edingale House Farm (SVB p72).

Edingale Field Farm House 1.25m ENE of Edingale.

Edstree 1m N of (is it same as Ebstree?), Trysull.

Edward's Bridge Over the Wyrley and Essington Canal SW of Bloxwich (marked on 1:25,000 OS map).

Efflinch Tiny hamlet formed by encroachment on former common land 1m S of Barton-under-Needwood, in Tatenhill ancient parish (HOPT vol 1 p135) (ESNF p18p). The earthworks 320 yards NW of the Junction Inn at SK 187175 are a listed monument. The enclosures and cursus 300 yards SE of Efflinch at SK 194171 are a listed monument. The name is from Anglo-Saxon 'haiflinch' meaning heather on marsh land (HOPT vol 1 p136) (UNT p36).

Egg Well Spring 0.75m SSW of Bradnop, SE of Ashenhurst Hall and has been called Ashenhurst Well (OL vol 1 p64). It is of unknown age. Miller considered it of Roman origin (OL vol 1 p64) (NSFCT 1890 p37). Sometime between 1744 and 1752 William Stanley of Ashenhurst Hall covered the spring with an oval stone surround bearing his initials and a Latin inscription (VCH vol 7 p171). The Latin inscription advises that its waters are the cure for most ailments known to man (SMCC p8). The inscription can be translated in many ways. Miller gives four different translations. In the C19 the well was covered by a square shelter built of stone (VBB p22) (SMM pp70,72ps) (VCH vol 7 p171). It was probably so called on account of the oval shape of the surround. However, Pickford says Druidic lore often refers to eggs in connection with healing rites (DP p19). Perhaps Stanley made the surround oval in consideration of this.

Eherryholm By the Trent at or near Alrewas (HOA p18).

Eid Low Large symmetrical mound on the end of a spur over 1m WSW of Wootton, SK 09104456. Could be a burial mound (VCH barrow list as Gid Low) (NSJFS 1965 pp45-46).

Eight Locks Ryders Green (WBOP p151).

Eland Brook Tributary of the Swarbourn. Runs through Needwood Forest (SHOS vol 1 p66). The name is from Gaelic 'all,' white, and 'afon' and 'avon,' water (NSFCT 1908 p129). Or 'land by a river' (SPNO p9). Has appeared as Ealands Brook (1650), and Ealand (1798) (SHOS) (SPNO p9).

Eland Lodge House 1.25m NE of Newborough. The lodge was the residence of the keepers of Marchington ward of Needwood Forest (ESNF p8). (W p571). Shaw thought Sir William Fitzherbert of Tissington was born here. In the later C18 Francis Noel Clarke Mundy (d1815), the poet, rented the property. He was of Markeaton, Derbys, and a distant relative of the Mundys of Alstonefield. The first edition of his poem 'Needwood Forest' written in 1776 and published in 1811 is very rare as there were only a few copies printed for his friends. His 'The Fall of Needwood' was published in 1808 (SHOS vol 1 pp67-68) (GNHS p145) (W p572) (JAT p70) (BS p321) (APB p43) (YX p21) (LTD p130). Has also appeared as Ealand Lodge (W p571).

Elderbush Cave Near Thor's Cave, Manifold Valley, at SK 098549. Is situated a little above the 900 feet contour line. When discovered the entrance was masked by a sturdy elder shrub whose roots went deeply into the floor (NSJFS 1964 pp46-59). Excavated by Peakland Archaeology Society from 1935. Some finds of the Palaeolithic, the Neolithic or Bronze Age and the Romano-British period have been found in it (PASN vols 1,2,3,4,8) (Trans Cave Research Group vol 1 No 4,47) (British Caving p275) (NSJFS 1964 p43) (HOS p9).

Elder Well Blymhill. Its waters were believed to be a cure for the eyes, but did not show to contain any minerals in experiments in the C17 (NHS p106). (SCSF p143). Is probably the St Chad's Well of Chadwell and the Brineton mentioned by Plot (OSST 1944-1945). Has also appeared as St Mary's Well and Wise Well (SMM p80).

Elephant Oak Court Bank Covert, Cannock Wood. So called because it looked like an elephant. Wright suggested it was 1000 years old. It had died by the 1930s. It was black, dwarfed and bulky. One gaunt branch was pushed upward, 'just as Jumbo would strive with his trunk to reach something overhead' (CCF p84).

Elephant's Clump A group of fir and birch trees crowning a hill N of Black Lake on footpath from Trentham Hall to Beech. It is mentioned on a walk through Trentham Woods, after Kingswood Bank is passed. Has also appeared as Elephant Trees (NSJFS 1962 p147. 1974 pp114 see map,115).

Eleven Lane Ends Here eleven lanes meet (HLSP p41). Presumably the crossroads at SJ 962617 on W side of Gun Hill.

Elford Ancient parish and village on a slight bank above a bend in the Tame 18.75m SE of Stafford. For the Romano-British farmstead discovered 0.25m W of Elford see Fisherwick. The **name** is derived presumably from the great number of eels formerly taken in the Tame (SHOS vol 1 p380). Duignan accepts Shaw's interpretation that it could be 'Eel ford,' but opts for 'The ford of Elle' (DUIGNAN). Or 'elder ford' (SSE 1996 p13), or 'Ella's ford'

(SSE 1996 p13) (SPN p45). Elford was identified by Dugdale, Shaw and Duignan with the manor of Elleforda bequeathed in the will of Wulfric Spot (c1002) ultimately to Burton Abbey (SHOS vol 1 p380) (SHC 1916 p27). The manor of Eleford appears in DB (in which survey the name is unique - SPN p46). The parish, formed after 1086 and before the end of the C12, out of Clifton Campville parish (SHC 1916 p198). There was a **church** at Elford in the C13 (LDD). The present parish church, St Peter (but formerly St Swithun - LGS p130), at the W end of the village, E of Old Hall Drive, has some C14 work in the chancel. It was rebuilt (except for the tower of 1598) in 1848-1849 (BOE p127) (CHMS2 p44). Wakelin de Ardern was granted a charter March 22 1254 to hold a **market** at Elford on Fridays. The market had ceased by 1500 (NSJFS 1971 p51). In the **Civil War** the villagers are said to have buried their church memorial effigies to save them from being desecrated by parliamentarian troops (Birmingham Post Weekend Section Oct 21 1995 p25). **Trees.** In the later C17 Plot noted an ash tree in the churchyard that had grown to an exceptional size in a short period of time. It was valued at £30 and had a body of seven or eight feet in diameter and a girth of seven or eight yards. It was only planted in c1590 and cut down in c1670 (NHS p210) (SHOS vol 1 p382). The huge weeping beech tree in the churchyard still standing in 1997 is reputed to be one of the largest in the country (E&S Nov 1 1997 p10p) or the 'third best weeping beech in the United Kingdom' (Birmingham Post Weekend Section Oct 21 1995 p25). The village **friendly society** had a custom of carrying strange poles during their parades (VESOP pl 135). In **WW2** two German bombs landed on village fields in quick succession; the first on June 5 1941 at 1.17am landed near Model Farm (Birmingham Post Weekend Section Oct 21 1995 p25). A high accident rate on the A513 at the notorious lettucefields bends near Elford led to a 30 year campaign by villagers to have it straightened; work totalling £700,000 to straighten part of it had been completed by 1997 (E&S Nov 1 1997 p10). **Persons. Robert Bage**, born at Derby, author of 'Mount Kenneth,' 'Barham Downs,' 'The Fair Syrians,' 'James Wallace,' and 'Harmspring: or Man as He is Not, and Man as He is,' owned a paper mill near to the Tame Bridge at Elford. His son, John (d1785), is buried in Elford (SHOS vol 1 p383) (History of Derby. Hutton. p296) (S&W pp142-143) (THM vol 1 pp17 note, 21). Rev **Francis Edward Paget** (1806-1882), children's writer, was rector of Elford from 1835 to his death. His 'The Hope of the Katzekoffs' (1844) has been described as the first English fairytale (VFC p102). Some years prior to 1877 Rev Francis Paget at the Rectory saw a ghost made up of mist which resembled his close friend. It transpired that Paget's friend had died at the same time as Paget saw his apparition (GLS pp40-41).

Elford Hall The hall near Elford church was begun by Henry Bowes Howard (1688-1757), 4th Earl of Berkshire and 11th Earl of Suffolk, and lord of Elford manor. He intended to reside here but died in 1757 before it was completed. The hall was finished by his son William Howard, Viscount Andover (SHOS vol 1 p381) (W p603) (SGS p96). The same or another son, William, born at Elford in 1714, died in a coach accident near (Elford Hall?) lodge gate on July 15 1756 (BS p74). The former manor house may have stood on the moated site by the house called Elford Park to the N (SHOS vol 1 p382). By marriage the manor passed from the Howards to Richard Bagot, fifth son of Sir Walter Wagstaff Bagot of Blithfield Hall, in 1783; he then assumed the name of Howard (SHOS vol 2 p381). A drawing of the hall in 1835 was made into a lithograph by Edward Lear (Birmingham Post Weekend Section Oct 21 1995 p25il). In 1851 the hall was the residence of Hon Mrs Mary Howard (W p20). Later, it appears to have passed by marriage to the Pagets; Howard Paget was the owner in the early C20. In 1936 his son, Francis Paget, donated the Elford Hall estate of 650 acres and Elford manor to Birmingham corporation, in response to a request by Stanley Baldwin PM for landowners to give their estates to the people as a token of their gratitude for the reign of George V. The estate had until then always descended by inheritance from Anglo-Saxon times, and was remarkable on this account; although outlying portions had been sold from time to time. The transfer of 1936 initiated a peculiar custom applicable only when Elford estate is transferred to another who has not inherited it (STC p29p) (Birmingham Post Weekend Section Oct 21 1995 p25). The custom stipulates that the owner of the estate take a sword and with his own hand cut a turf from the estate which is handed over to the new owner in a casket as a symbol to represent the property. The casket at the 1936 presentation bore the arms of the Pagets and of the Howards and of Birmingham and was designed by SH Meteyard and was placed in Birmingham Art Gallery and Museum (Evening Dispatch Nov 5 1936) (THM vol 6 pp22,23). Another account says the hall, which had Saxon origins, had only descended by descent since the time of Richard I (NSFCT 1938 pp121,122). In 1938 the hall housed Basque refugee children (NSFCT 1938 pp121,122). In WW2 it housed for safe-keeping art treasures from Birmingham museums

(Birmingham Post Weekend Section Oct 21 1995 p25il). It was demolished in 1964 (SL p268) or 1966 (GLS p40) having deteriorated due to neglect, and by 1995 had been built over with new housing, whilst the stable block had been converted into housing (Birmingham Post Weekend Section Oct 21 1995 p25). The hall has also appeared as Elford Old Hall (MR p142).

Elford Heath Heath on WSW side of Eccleshall. In Eccleshall ancient parish. Half an acre of common land still remained by the 1950s (OSST 1956-59 p13). Elford Hill is in Horsley division in Eccleshall ancient parish (W p379).

Elford House Elford. Occupied in 1851 by Theophilus Levett (W p20).

Elford Low Mound at SK 19390924 at Elfordlow Farm. Is 16 paces NS and 19 paces EW and eight feet high. Plot thought it was of Roman origin and may have been a burial place or erected for a watch tower. He excavated it in 1680. Traces of a cremation were found. Plot considered that if it had been made by the Saxons it was probably erected for the dead of the battle fought in 755 at Seckington, Warws, S of Thorpe Constantine. The battle was fought between Aethelbald, king of Mercia (712-757), and Cuthred, king of the West Saxons (NHS p405). By the mid C18 the mound was considered one of the Robin Hood Shooting Butts, the other being called Robin Hood's Butt (see) (SHOS vol 2 p381) (W p603). Pennant and Shaw thought the mound was of Saxon origin (SHOS vol 1 part 1 p33). The mound has also been called The Low. The three skeletons, Shaw notes, found in a gravel pit at Elfordlow Farm, near the mound, are said by Gunstone to come from another nearby mound (NHS p405) (SHOS vol 1 General Intro pp33,37. p381) (GNHS p66) (W p603) (HOWW p14) (NSJFS 1965 p37) (MR p142). By the late C18 Elford Low had a single large oak tree growing on its summit (SHOS vol 1 p381); Slang Oak (see) is said to have stood on Elford Low (NSJFS 1962 p148). Some think Elford Low is the burial place of Ella (NSFCT 1938 pp121,122).

Elfordlow Farm House 1m SSE of Elford.

Elford Old Manor House May have stood on the moated site by the house known as Elford Park, and is said to have been surrounded by a medieval deer park known as Elford Park (SHOS vol 1 p382) (HS p159 note) (VB p34). The house was the seat of the Stanleys, lords of Elford, in the C15 and C16; Lord Stanley changed his allegiance from Richard III to the Earl of Richmond (Henry Tudor, Henry VII) during the battle of Bosworth Field in 1485. Some have alleged the Earl of Richmond stayed with Lord Stanley, during the two days (Aug 16 to 18) in his progress to the battle, between Lichfield and Tamworth, which cannot be accounted for (STMSM Sept 1980 p21). Although, the official line was he and his retinue had lost their way (R&S p18) (HOL pp302,303). Others say Richmond met with Stanley at Stafford Castle (SSTY p10), or possibly on Cannock Chase (STMSM Nov 1972 p41). After the reign of Henry VIII the status of the house fell to that of a farmhouse (HS p159 note). When Richard Huddlestone, lord of Elford manor, died in c1556 the manor passed by marriage partly to the Bowes' and later wholly to them. By marriage it passed from the Bowes' to Hon Craven Howard (d1700) in 1683. In the earlier C18 Craven Howard's eldest son Henry Bowes Howard (1688-1757), 4th Earl of Berkshire and 11th Earl of Suffolk, began to build Elford Hall (see) near Elford church to the S, but died before it was complete (SHOS vol 1 p381) (BS p74) (SGS p96).

Elford Park Former medieval deer park belonging to the lords of Elford manor 1m N of Elford, in the area of the house called Elford Park. In the later C18 Pennant noted seven burial mounds 0.25m NE of Elford Park at cSK 193126. According to Shaw Pennant had mistaken these for the seven near Lichfield, Hants. Those here were noted by Dr Wilkes, who records that during their removal in the C18 the largest mound revealed a piece of bayonet, some brass, a wooden bowl and other things (Journey from Chester to London. T Pennant. 1782 p119) (SHOS vol 1 pp381-382) (NSJFS 1965 p37). Slang Oak (see) is said to have stood in Elford Park. To the N of the Elford Park house at SK 190123 lies a moated site. Part of the drawbridge over the moat was dug up in the late C18 (SHOS vol 1 p382) (SSAHST 1982-3 p41) (CAMS p63). According to Shaw this moat may represent the site of Elford Old Manor House (SHOS vol 1 p382). Elford Park house dates from the 1760s (CAMS p63) and was occupied by the Allen family in the early to mid C19 (mems in Croxall church).

Elkstones Moorland chapelry and collective name for Upper and Lower Elkstone, the former is 24m NE of Stafford. Formerly formed a township with Warslow in Alstonefield ancient parish (W p742). Became a separate ecclesiastical parish in 1785 and a joint ecclesiastical parish with Warslow in 1902. Became a separate civil parish with Warslow in 1866 (GLAUE pp410,427). The older of the two Elkstones seems to be Upper Elkstone (VCH vol 7 p57).

Elkstone Park Elkstone. A medieval deer park enclosed out of forest. In existence by c1210 (NSJFS 1962 p76).

Ellastone Ancient parish and former township. The village Ellastone lies on a hill above the confluence of Tit and Sandford Brooks on the western slopes of the Dove valley, 16.5m NE of Stafford.

EARLY. In the Dove Valley near Ellastone was found a **Neolithic** or **Bronze Age** stone axe. Capt Duncombe of Calwich Abbey had it in his possession (HOU p42) (NSJFS 1964 p21). There is a bowl burial mound in Marlpit Lane at SK 11074304, 1m WSW of Ellastone. It is listed monument.

1000 to 1500. The two manors of Ellastone recorded in DB are written Edelachestone (held by the bishop of Chester) and Elachestone (held by Robert of Stafford). The **name** is of Anglo-Saxon origin and means 'Æthelac's town' (DUIGNAN), or 'Eadlac's tun' (SSE 1996 p13) or farmstead (SPN p47). Ellastone later appears as Elaston (Speed's map 1627), and may have appeared as Glaxton in 1496 (OSST 1935 p42). The parish, probably dating from after the founding of Calwich Priory, probably originally formed a part of Mayfield parish (SHC 1916 p199). There was a **church** at Ellastone in the C13 (LDD). The present parish church, St Peter, on the N side of Church Lane, was built in the later 1580s. The nave was rebuilt in 1830 (BOE p128). The parish wake was on the Sunday after St John's day in the mid C19 (W p775). On the strength of a house named 'Bloomsmithy' recorded in 1433, it has been assumed that **iron** was worked here during the C15 (MR p144).

1500 to PRESENT. A hard slate-like marl can be found at Ellastone (NHS p120). The NW end of the village is known as Upper Ellastone; the middle, Ellastone; the SE end, by the Dove, Lower Ellastone. The film 'Blanche Fury' was shot at Ellastone (MR p144). **Persons**. According to Ellastone PR **Thomas Burton** died aged 111 and was buried on Feb 5 1654 (NSJFS 1972 pp127-128). Some time prior to the later C17 **Ann Harvey** of Oakamoor, born at Ellastone, reputedly lived to the aged of 120 (NHS p321) (SD p107). **Lord Loughborough** of London (d1805), married Charlotte Courtnay by special licence at Ellastone church on Sept 12 1782. As Alexander Wedderburn he became Lord Chief Justice and was created Lord Loughborough in 1780 and appointed Lord Chancellor in 1793 and created Earl of Rosslyn in 1801. This was Lord Loughborough's second marriage but it is unknown why Ellastone was chosen (NSJFS 1972 p121). **George Eliot**, novelist, came to Ellastone in 1826, aged seven, and in 1840 to visit her relations (NSFCT 1918 p122); the home of her paternal grandparents, George and Mary Evans, at Upper Ellastone still stands, although much rebuilt, and has long been called Adam Bede's Cottage (see). She set her novel 'Adam Bede,' (1859), at Ellastone, calling the village Hayslope. The fictitious Donnithorne Arms is the Bromley Davenport Arms (LGS p132) (TB Sept 1994 p20), although Channer says it is the Duncombe Arms (PWIS p87).

Ellastone Old Hall A late C17 house on the main road in Ellastone (BOE p128) (SVB p73). It became the Bromley Davenport Arms Inn or the Bromley Arms Inn. Between at least 1977 and 1988 it was an antiques shop (SGS p97p) (SVB p73). The house is said to have been the model for George Eliot's Donnithorne Arms in her novel 'Adam Bede' (1859) (LGS p132) (ESNF p109p).

Ell End It seems to have been a short cul-de-sac leading off St George's Street, Darlaston (Offlow hundred). The name appears in mid C19 census returns. An ell was an old measure of length which varied between 18 and 47 inches, so it could be a derisory name for a short thoroughfare, or a nickname for a piece of land (SNDB p48).

Ellenhall Ancient parish and village on Gamesley Brook or a tributary of that brook, 5.5m NW of Stafford. The parish church, St Mary, at the N end of the village on the W side of the Eccleshall road, was rebuilt in 1757 but has some Norman work (BOE pp128-129). The name has appeared as Linehalle (DB), Ælinhale (c1200) (SSE 1996 p13), Elinhale (1242) (SPN p47), Elnehaul (c1540) (LI appendix p169), and apparently Henleight (SH pp78-79). It means 'the hall of Elle' (DUIGNAN). 'Flax nook by a river' but Gelling is unsure (NSJFS 1981 p2). If from Linehalle, then from Saxon 'lin halh' 'corner of land where flax grows,' if from Elinhale then 'the wet corner of land where flax grows' (SPN p47), or 'the corner of land by a river where flax is grown' (SSE 1996 p13). Or 'flax nook' (SSE 1987 p32). There is a rectangular moat with a house on site at Ellenhall (ESH p58). The antiquary, Rev Thomas Loxdale (1675-1742), was curate of Ellenhall from 1717 until at least 1720 but not later than 1723 (SH p77) (SHJ spring 1991 p7). Foot and Mouth disease broke out at Ellenhall in 1924 (AADB p62).

Ellenhall Old Hall Formerly the manor house. Ellenhall, previously a member of Eccleshall manor, became a distinct manor (SHC 1914 p83). From the Noels it passed by marriage to the Harcourts in the early C13. They sold Ellenhall, Seighford and Ranton to William Willaston in 1617. Later in the C17 Ellenhall passed to the Copes who held Ranton and Ellenhall until c1790, when Ellenhall manor was sold to the Ansons. The house had been tenanted by the Whittinghams for several centuries by the late C19 (SA June 13 1885 p6) (NSSG p18).

Ellenhall Park A medieval deer park enclosed out of forest at Ellenhall. In existence by 1293 (NSJFS 1962 p76). Noticed by Saxton in the later C16 (EDP p179). In the later C17 Plot noted an extremely wide girthed tree near the Lodge House in Ellenhall Park which was so thick he and his man could not hold themselves around it, even standing on horseback (NHS p210).

Ellenvale In the vicinity of Ellowes Road, Ellowes Hall and Ellowes Row, Ruiton. 'The moor of Ellenvale' and 'the house and garden of Ellenvale' are mentioned as portions of Sedgley manor in 1272. Ellenvale means the vale of Elle or Aella. CJL Elwell believes his ancestors inherited their name from Ellenvale (DUIGNAN) (IE pp18,19).

Ellerton Grange House 2.5m SW of Adbaston. In Adbaston parish. The village of Ellerton is over the border in Shrops and has appeared as Adhelardeston (C13), Adhelartone, Athelartone, Ethelartone, and Ellerton (AADB p11). In the Middle Ages Ranton Abbey created a grange here (NSFCT 1927 p22) (VCH vol 3 pp253,254). At the Dissolution Ranton's granges of Ellerton, Knighton, and Batchacre were purchased by Sir John Gifford whose grant is dated 1541. Thomas Roos of Laxton, Notts died in 1578 seized of Ellerton, Knighton, and Batchacre granges. These passed to his grandson, Gilbert, who sold them all in 1626. Ellerton Grange then went to the Baduleys until John Baduley died in 1717. It then passed to Richard Whitworth I. The Vickers family moved to Ellerton Grange in 1830 and left for Offley Grove in 1860. The first wife of Valentine Vickers (d1867), Anne, was thrown from her horse and killed when it bolted on a journey she was making from Newport, Shrops to Ellerton on Aug 18 1846 (AADB pp19,26,60). The present (1975) house was built alongside the old Tudor house in c1930 by George Dodd. After the new house was completed George Dodd demolished the old house in 1933. By 1982 Ellerton Grange was famous for its champion Ayrshire cattle kept by George Dodd (AADB p32).

Ellfield House and Lodge. On the S side of Whittington Common Road, to the W of Whittington (near Lichfield).

Elliot Stone Stone on Axe Edge End. It was used as a marker from 1673 to define the border in a settlement which established the long-disputed boundary here (UHAW p11).

Ellishill Brook Rises on Stanton Moor. Runs to Ordley Brook, which is a tributary of the Dove via Northwood Brook and Tit Brook (SPNO p9). Named from Ellis Hill, Blore (Ray), which was named after Richard Elly (SPNO p10).

Ellowes, The Gornal. Whether The Ellowes and Ellowes Hall are the same? The name is from 'Ella's vale,' later Ellenvale, then corrupted to Ellowes (DUIGNAN) (AMS p442).

Ellowes Hall 0.5m NNW of Lower Gornal, at SO 913923 (1947 OS map 1:25,000 (sheet 32/99)). In Sedgley ancient parish. 'The house and garden of Ellenvale' are mentioned as a portion of Sedgley manor in 1272 (DUIGNAN). Persons with the surname Elwall and Ellow are recorded in Sedgley parish from the C14 (IE p19) (SNSV vol 2 p27). In the early C19 there was a cottage on the estate of Samuel Fereday, ironmaster, of Over Gornal, known as 'Ellors, Fereday's Cottage.' In c1820 his nephew, John Turton Fereday of Ettingshall Hall (possibly Ettingshall Park) (d1849), built a new hall on or near the site of the cottage. This hall was then called Ellers Hall, and locally The Ellers. It contained the fine oak staircase removed from Horseley Hall, demolished at this time. Subsequently, in 1854, William Baldwin resided here, and later Sir Horace St Paul (HOTIP p185) (BCM Dec 1997 p42il) (SDOP p41p) (SNSV vol 2 pp26-27). Ellowes Hall appears in Ellen Thorneycroft Fowler's novel 'The Farringdons' (1901) as The Willows, the seat of the Farringdons (PPTP p34), and as Maltings Hall in Rev JR Windsor-Garnett's 'The Village' (1926) (TB Sept 1986 p14). Ellowes Comprehensive School preserves the name of Ellowes Hall, which was demolished in 1964 (MR p162) (PPTP p34). In the orchard were five inter-connecting man-made caves. Some of the older people of Ruiton refer to them as Hermit's Caves, this may be linked with a lane nearby called Hermits Row (PHS p22). The hall had an ice-house.

Ell Park Former stretch of open land which once stood between Stringes Lane and Clarke's Lane, Willenhall. The name became Elm Park after the opening of the nearby Elm Park Tavern, a name preserved in Elm Street. By the 1990s the site of the park was completely built on (SNW p24).

Elmerson House 0.75m NNE of Whitgreave. Appears in 1252 as Elmershull (SPN p113). The name means 'Ælfmaer's (later Elmer's) hill' (DUIGNAN) (SPN p113).

Elmhurst House 0.75m NE of Biddulph. Built in c1840 for Rev William Henry Holt (vicar of Biddulph 1831-1873) who was James Bateman's uncle. William vacated the old Grange House (at times referred to as the vicarage) when James moved from his father's house at Knypersley Hall to live there with his wife and two children (BIOPP p14p). Elmhurst pumping station was

opened in 1929 at Biddulph Park (BALH p225). After the station's demolition, in or prior to 1992, the commemorative block laid at the opening of the station by Thomas Walley went to Geoffrey Goodier, his grandson (ES Nov 5 1992 p4p).

Elmhurst Hamlet on the gentle S slopes of Trent Vale 1.5m N of Lichfield cathedral. Elmhurst and Curborough formed a township in St Chad's parish, Lichfield (SHOS vol 1 p291) (VCH vol 14 p229). Appears in the C13 as Elinghurst (SSE 1996 p13): Duignan finds it first recorded in Kirkby's Quest c1275 and it has been written Helmhurst (HOL p514). The name is of Anglo-Saxon origin and means either, 'elm wood' (VCH vol 14 p229) (SPN p79), or 'Elle's wood' (DUIGNAN) (SSE 1996 p13). Elmhurst developed on the road from Lichfield to King's Bromley. There was a green at Elmhurst in c1300, probably at SK 113119, where there was a pinfold in the early C19 (VCH vol 14 p229).

Elmhurst Hall The Elmhurst Hall estate, at Elmhurst near Curborough, which had in the earlier part of the C16 belonged to the Clerksons, passed to the Biddulphs by 1571. Michael Biddulph (d1658), who received a coat of arms in 1635 and was MP for Lichfield in 1646 and 1648, was probably the first Biddulph to live at the hall (VCH vol 14 p231 pl 43 il is from NHS). In DS Dodd's opinion the view of the hall in Plot is the least imposing of all the houses depicted in NHS. The hall seems to have been altered some time before 1754, when it was sold by Sir Theophilus Biddulph to Samuel Swinfen. In 1790 Major Francis Perceval Eliot, writer and a skilled agriculturist, moved in as tenant; Swinfen shortly sold the house to him. Shaw, writing in the late C18, said it was one of the strongest-built houses in the kingdom. The house was demolished in 1804 and the estate was sold in 1808 to John Smith. He built a new hall, in the Elizabeth style, at Elmhurst and died there in 1840. From then on the new hall had several owners. In 1894 it was let to the Duke and Duchess of Sutherland so that they could entertain the Prince of Wales here on his visit to Lichfield for the centenary of the Staffordshire Yeomanry. It was demolished in 1921 (SHOS vol 1 p351) (NSFCT 1976 p15) (VCH vol 14 p232 pl 44 shows the hall in 1874) (SHJ autumn 1993 p23). DS Dodd searched for the house in 1976 but was only able to find a walled garden and several small houses (NSFCT 1976 p15). In the later C17 Plot noted an echo on the terraces in the garden behind the house, and another echo in a meadow SE of the house (NHS pp29,30 tab 2 il of the hall) (SHOS vol 1 p351).

Elmore Green Area containing Bloxwich's church, Great Bloxwich. For many centuries it was known as Chapel Green (SOB pp156,167). Bloxwich's stocks were at Elmore Green. By the C18 Elmore Green was the focal point of Bloxwich life (BY p 6). Mrs Sarah Ann Walker, a widow of Elmore Green Road, was murdered on June 9 or 10 1900. Jabez Pugh, a miner, was arrested and charged but was not found guilty (TB Aug 1979 p5). The name perhaps represents 'alder-more,' 'more' representing unused, poor quality land (SNBP p23).

Elmore House Elmore Green, Bloxwich (SOB p178).

Elms, The Aldridge. House in existence in the C17 and still stood in the C19 (MOA p133). There was The Elms Inn, a timber-framed gabled-building in the High Street, Aldridge. It was demolished in 1954 (BCP p86p). An ornamental summer house, made from old timbers, stone, and bricks from a demolished farmhouse, was built in 1951 in the Memorial Gardens next to the Elms Hotel (ALOPPR p21p).

Elms, The Early Victorian-looking villa which was situated at the junction of High and Bank Streets, Brierley Hill. On the death of the owners, the Misses Harris, whose family had owned firebrick works and had donated the almshouses in Seagers Lane, the property was acquired and demolished by Brierley Hill urban district council, and the Civil Centre developed on the site (BHOP p38p) (BHOP2 p38p) (Staffs County Handbook c1958 p101p of the Civil Centre).

Elms, The Former house in Pattingham village. Demolished by 1997 to make way for an housing estate (TPOP p116p).

Elms, The Worcester Road, Wolverhampton. Pitt described it as an elegant villa (THS). The house had been demolished by 1951 (HOWM p158).

Elmsdale Hall Stood at the top of Wightwick bank, with a lodge on the Bridgenorth Road, Tettenhall Wood. Built in the 1860s. In 1914 it was bought by Jesse Varley, Clerk to the Education Authority, with some of the £84,335 4s 7d he embezzled from Wolverhampton council between 1905 and 1917, when he was discovered, arrested and sentenced to five years in prison; Varley later repeated his crime in another local authority. The house was occupied by Miss Swift in 1919 and she changed the name to Viewlands. It was converted into an elderly persons home some time prior to 1990. In 1990 it was being converted to flats known as Elmsdale (TCOP p75p).

Elmstone Near the summit of Pire Hill, Stone. This is its former name. May be derived from a megalithic chambered tomb and Celtic sanctuary (NSFCT

1908 p119).

Elmwood House at Hamstead Hill. The original owner of Elmwood was Joseph Henry Wilkinson (1845-1931) who had the house built in c1873. From JH Wilkinson the house passed to Arthur Rabone, who lived here, and his son, Col Rabone, until the 1930s. It was later acquired by the Congregationalist Church (later the United Reform Church) who made it into a religious centre. During repairs and alterations to the house in 1983 the monogram 'J.H.W.' (JH Wilkinson) was uncovered in the outside brickwork at the rear of the house (HPPE p28).

Elston Former manor and hamlet over 0.25m SW of Bushbury in Bushbury ancient parish (BUOP p6).

Elston Hall Situated on the S side of Elston Hall Lane, Bushbury. Seat of the Purcells until Edward II's reign when the heiress Amicia married first Sir Richard Bishbury then after his death Richard de Hugford but she had children by neither and settled the estate on Ralph, Earl of Stafford, who shortly passed it to the Stanway or Stanley family who owned it in Henry VI's reign. After John Stanley's death in 1516 it was left to his daughters Elizabeth and Isabell who left it to William Smith, bishop of Coventry and Lichfield, afterwards bishop of Lincoln, who gave it to the rector and fellows of Lincoln College, Oxford, who were owners of it in the later C18 (SHOS vol 2 p182). The hall, which has also appeared as Ailston Hall and Alleston Hall, was then a small old half-timbered house inhabited by a tenant farmer, and seems to have been moated. It was pulled down in c1879 and a new house built on the site (OHW pl12) (SSAHST 1982-3 pp52-53 plans). Private housing was built on the estate before WW2 (BUOP p8).

Elwell's Pool By Wednesbury Forge, Wood Green. Artificial pool built to feed Wednesbury Forge (IE p77). On June 9 1859 an engine off the SSR line plunged into Elwells Mill Pond which was to the rear of the former Bescot steam depot (SSR p22).

Endless Orchard Hamlet in the early C19 in the Cox's Lane area of Rowley Regis (BCWJ p107) (TB Aug 1982 p11). Could it be same as Cherry Orchard?

Endon (locally *Yen* OL vol 1 p90). Large straggling village covering N side of Endon Brook valley, 19m N of Stafford. Former manor, chapelry, quarter, and township in Leek ancient parish. The quarter comprised the townships of Endon, Longsdon, and Stanley (VCH vol 7 p82).

1000 to 1500. The second element of the **name** is from probably 'dun,' a hill, although some have thought it may be from the Welsh 'din' and 'dinas,' a hill fort (NSFCT 1908 p134). The hill from which Endon takes its name is presumably Endon Bank (VCH vol 7 p177). The first element has been thought to represent the woman's personal name Æne meaning once or one (DUIGNAN), or the personal name Eana (NSJFS 1981 p2) (MR p145) (SSE 1996 p13) (SPN p47). Oakden says the first element is from 'ean' a lamb (SSAHST 1967 p34) (SSE 1996 p13). Or the place name is derived from Enandon or Eanandon, meaning 'a high hill or down' (E p10). The manor of Enedun appears in DB. Other forms have been: Enedon, and Eanandun (SPN p47). The infamous heriot was enforced in Endon manor (NSJFS vol 10 1970 pl) (E p13). From 1411 the manor amalgamated into Horton manor (W p727) (VCH vol 7 p181). The moated site 0.25m SE of Endon church, crossed by Park Lane, may represent the site of the manor house, in existence in 1246 (VCH vol 7 p181). There was a chapel at Endon by 1246. The present **church**, St Luke, at the N end of Church Lane by High View Road, was built in 1719-1721, but was mostly rebuilt in the 1870s (VCH vol 7 pp183-184). **Beating of the bounds** took place in the week prior to the well dressing in 1934 (ES May 11 1934 p5).

1500 to PRESENT. Several stone houses at Endon are of at least C17 origin; a stone above the fireplace at Gate House Farm is dated '1660' (E p96). Endon became a separate ecclesiastical parish in 1720 (GLAUE p410) or 1737 (LGS p135). There were at least two **tanyards** in Endon township. One stood to the S of Park Farm 1m SE of Endon. There was another in the village in Hallwater Lane. Both were operational probably in the C18 and earlier C19. The warehouse of the latter survived in 1991 as Hallwater Cottages (VCH vol 7 p182). There is a tradition that the skin of a 15 year old drummer boy, called Tam, in the Jacobite army which passed through the area in Dec 1745, was flayed and tanned at the Hallwater Lane tannery by the local squire, Murhall, in revenge for Highlander atrocities. Some accounts say the skin proved impossible to tan and was buried in a field at Tompkin (see) whilst others say it was made into a drum which hung for many years in Endon church (STMSM April 1978 p20) (EFS p26). The fact that this tannery was owned by John Sutton in 1740 (VCH vol 7 p182) may have misled some into identifying the tannery with Sutton House (see) (STM Dec 1968 p37p) (E pp93,94,95). **Chartist rioters** marched through Endon for Burslem along the Leek Potteries turnpike road in the 1840s (NSJFS 1965 p114). Endon became a separate civil

parish with Longsdon and Stanley in 1866 (GLAUE p410). The **railway** from Stoke to Leekbrook opened in 1867 and there was a station 0.5m S of Endon church; it closed in 1960 (VCH vol 7 p180). A fountain **well** was erected in 1898 at the top of Leek Road to commemorate Queen Victoria's Diamond Jubilee (VCH vol 7 p179) (E pl facing p145); there was a fountain at the cross roads of Clay Lane, Station Road and Leek Road on the site of a tollhouse (NSJFS 1965 p112). Some say the fountain was moved from Leek Road in c1934 due to road-widening (ES Dec 7 1934 p9p). Others that it was mostly demolished in the 1930s except for an inscribed stone which survives as the base of a seat (VCH vol 7 p179). Endon Brook flooded the village in 1914 and in 1927 (SMOPP vol 2 pp55p,59p) (E p193p facing). The **Endonian Society**, founded in 1961, takes an interest in all local social and historical matters (info Alan Williamson). **Legend and custom**. An Endon witch in c1880 caused the cattle and pigs of a farmer at Upper Hulme to pine and die, even though the farmer and his wife had protected themselves by carrying witch-elm, such was the Endon witch's curse the farmer had to move to Swythamley (FLJ 1942 p127). The custom of 'bumping' the chairman of the parish council occurred in Endon in 1932, when the chairman was a JP Ledgar (ES May 21 1932 p1ps). **Natives and visitors**. For **William Willet** dancing at Endon over the period Sept 3 to Sept 14 1752 see under Eaves. John Wesley visited Endon on Aug 11 1772 and in 1788, perhaps during his visit to Leek on April 5 1788 (E p57). **John Daniel** (d1821), china manufacturer of Hanley, and his sister, are buried in the churchyard; their ghosts are said to wander down hand in hand the narrow lane which skirts the churchyard with their dog, Nell (EFS p27). **Thomas Turnlock**, aged 34, broke into Thomas Bosson's house at Endon on Aug 5 1831 and stole a pair of breeches and some money. He was sentenced to death (OL vol 2 p235). The mother of Sir **Oliver Lodge** was a member of the Heath family of Endon, and is buried in the churchyard (EFS p26). **Charles Perkin** (d1969), the village blacksmith in the earlier C20, won the title of champion farrier of England at the Royal Show, when held at Wolverhampton in 1937. Perkin had a smithy in Brook Lane until moving to new premises in Endon in 1947 (SVB p75) (ES March 13 1999 p21p).

WELL DRESSING. At Endon is held the most famous well-dressing ceremony in the county. The ceremony has occurred every year since the erection of a stone well head over the spring known as Sinner's Well (perhaps from Maecenas or the French 'Sainte Cene' (the Lord's Supper)) given to the village by local landowner, Thomas Heaton, in 1845. The well head stands in the old part of the village known as 'the village.' Water issues from the mouth of a small bearded man. It is believed before 1845 the villagers adorned a spring with flowers in the field above (E p206) (EFS p48). Bell says the ceremony was revived in 1845. A spring on site, or nearby, is said to have continued to flow during a great drought in early C19 (ES May 14 1932 p1p. May 24 1932 p7p. May 14 1937 p9p. May 25 1937 p13). Endon's well dressing was unique in Staffs (SGS p97) until the custom was revived in Newborough. Well dressing always occurred on May 29, apparently, to commemorate the Restoration (S p133) (VCH vol 7 p180). According to 'The Book of Endon Village' compiled by a committee of Endon WI, the well dressing was begun on Royal Oak day 1845 by Philip and Hannah Rogers, the shoemaker and his wife, who adorned the new well head with oak boughs they had collected. With the encouragement of the village the event thrived and attracted visitors from other places. Nearby Jawbone field (named after a whale's jawbone which formed an archway over the entrance to it) was hired to provide visitors' teas. In 1872 the church service, crowning of a May queen, and maypole dancing was introduced by the vicar; crowning of a May queen being introduced in 1868 (Well-dressing Guide 1996). In 1906 it was decided to hold the events over a weekend, beginning on the Saturday nearest May 29 and ending on the Monday. In 1916 the events were changed to Whit weekend (VCH vol 7 p180). The well was being dressed in mid May in the mid 1930s. In 1949 the ceremony took place on June 4. In the early 1990s the events were taking place on the spring bank holiday and the weekend proceeding, with a church service on Saturday afternoon. The well is then blessed by the priest. The first well water is given to the well-dressing queen. She is crowned twice on Saturday and twice the following Monday. The Monday festival includes a fair including a competition of Tossing the Hay (GLS p42) or Tossing the Sheaf (FOS pp103,104). (W p728) (SA May 29 1853) (Leek Post and Times June 6 1889) (SCSF p30) (ALC p69p of in 1928) (ES May 27 1939 p1p) (STM July 1963 p on front cover) (VB p191) (STMSM July 1977 p13ps) (E pp205-214) (SW p77) (SOTOPP pl 140) (SVB p75) (MR p146) (GLS pp42-43).

Endon Bank Promontory overlooking Endon Valley. Endon church and Bank House (formerly Endon House) stand on the summit and it may be the hill from which Endon partly takes it's name (VCH vol 7 pp176,177).

Endon Brook Flows eastwards from Endon to the Churnet. Appears as Yendon River on Saxton's map (SPNO p10).

Endon Edge Promontory 1m SW of Endon; Moss Hill and Clay Lake Farm stand on it.

Endon Hall Mid-C19 house which stood on W side of Leek Road, 0.5m SW of Endon church (VCH vol 7 p179 pl 36). During the 1930s the owners, Mr and Mrs Andrew McClelland, said that the hall was built with stone taken from the site of Hulton Abbey they also claimed that seven stone heads in a retaining wall in the grounds were from Hulton Abbey. In 1955 the hall was demolished by Mr Kent, a Hanley builder. The site is now (1985) covered by the modern housing in St George's Avenue, and Kent Drive (SASR 1985 p77) (VCH vol 7 pl 36).

Endon House House 2.5 NNW of Alstonefield, on Archford Moor. Formerly in the detached portion of Fawfieldhead township in Alstonefield township. Existed by 1839 (VCH vol 7 p11).

Endon Lodge House at junction of Leek Road and Hillside Avenue, Endon. Built for William Orford (d1897) by 1868 (VCH vol 7 p179).

Endon Park Medieval deer park enclosed out of forest, held by the de Audleys, lords of Endon. In existence by 1273 (NSFCT 1910 pp170,172) (NSJFS 1962 pp73,76), when it appears as the Chase of Horton. Later it appears as the Old Park (1308) (VCH vol 7 p181 note). It stretched across the whole of Endon township and had been disparked by the mid C16. By the C14 there was a new park stretching into the SE corner of Endon township called Hanley Park (VCH vol 7 pp181-182).

Endon Valley (B pp15,16). Is the valley created by Endon Brook (VCH vol 7 p176).

End Stone Bank S end of Foxt village (1834 OS map).

Endwood Court Former gothic villa in its own grounds on the corner of Church Lane and Handsworth Wood Road, Handsworth. Erected in 1838 or 1839 by James Russell of Wednesbury for his own occupation, and bears his arms. William Sharp was described as of Endwood Court in 1854. It was purchased by JB Clarke JP in 1882. It has at some time been occupied by the Woodall family. It was much altered and reduced in size in the 1930s. In 1962 the site was purchased by Dares Estates Ltd and the present (1984) block of flats were erected (HANDR p5p) (MNB p50) (HPPE pp26-27).

Engine Arm Canal Known as Engine Branch or Birmingham Feeder Arm. Diverges from Birmingham Old Main Line at Rolfe Street, Smethwick. Is very short. The canal's main purpose was as a feeder from Rotton Park Reservoir. It was made navigable so coal could be brought to the Smethwick Engine Site at Bridge Street. It is carried over the Birmingham New Main Line by Engine Arm Aqueduct built by Telford in 1825; restored in 1985. (Galton Valley. A Walkers Guide. Sandwell Metropolitan Borough Council. 1993).

England's Hall Cottage at Ranton Green, Ranton. It was built on common land by one England probably in the later C18. A later owner left its rent to charity (W p402) (1834 OS map). An inn is now (1995) marked on the site.

Engleton 1.25m SSE of Stretton (Penkridge) near the Penk. Former manor (VCH vol 5 p31) and liberty of Brewood town in Brewood ancient parish. For the Roman villa at Engleton see Pennocrucium. The name means 'English town' (DUIGNAN), or 'tun of the Anglians' (SSE 1996 p13). Appears in 1242 as Engleton (SSE 1996 p13). Here was possibly a medieval village, probably deserted between 1327 and 1539 (SSAHST 1970 p35). Formerly included in Brewood prebend (SSAHST vol 2 1960-61 p43).

Engleton Hall Engleton, Stretton (Penkridge). The old hall was the seat of the Moretons. The hall of 1959 was probably built in 1810, a date which appears on the brickwork (VCH vol 5 p32). Seems to be the only property in Engleton. A Roman pillar said to come from Engleton Roman villa has been utilised as the shaft of a sundial in the grounds of Engleton Hall Farm (BDH pp26,27). Ponds and depressions by the hall may represent a moat which surrounded a former hall (SSAHST 1982-3 p37).

Enson Hamlet by the Trent 1m NW of Salt. Former out-township with Salt of St Mary's parish, Stafford. The name, probably of Anglo-Saxon origin, means 'Eansige's tun' (SSE 1996 p13), or 'Eana's farmstead' (SPN p112). The manor of Hentone appears in DB. Later forms are: Enstone, and Eneston (SPN p112). Here was possibly a medieval village, probably deserted between 1377 and 1524 (SSAHST 1970 p35). Enson medieval chapel, certified in 1563 as a chapel with a cure, is only mentioned in the returns of 1533 and 1563 and was annexed to that of Salt early in Elizabeth I's reign (SHC 1915 p98). In the later C17 Plot noted a weak salt brine spring at Enson (NHS p97). (SOS p48).

Enville Ancient parish and village near the head of a tributary of a Spittle Brook, 24m SSW of Stafford.
  EARLY. The last Ice Age reached its maximum southern extent about Wol-

verhampton and glacial boulders lie about Enville (WJO Nov 1909 p293). A socketed spear-head was found by the plough on a pasture of Grove Farm at cSO 80558835 in June 1966 (SSAHST 1971 p50).
  1000 to 1500. There was a church at Enville in Saxon times. The present parish **church**, St Mary the Virgin (St Lawrence in the C16), on the S side Bridgnorth Road, has C12 work (Enville: St Mary the Virgin Church Guide. Geoffrey Smith). The manor of Efnefeld appears in DB. Later forms are: Euenfeld (1183), Evenefeud (1240) (SPN p48), Envill (Saxton's map); forms such as Enfeld, Enfield, Enveld, and other variants remained in use until the late C18 (VCH vol 20 p91). The **name** means 'the even (level or smooth) field or plain' (DUIGNAN) (SSE 1996 p13) (SPN p48), or 'level open ground' (NSJFS 1981 p3), presumably a reference to the flat ground in the E of Enville parish (VCH vol 20 p91). At the time of the Norman Conquest, a Gilbert was in occupation of Enfield. He may have adopted the surname of Enfield, and this Enville estate was for a long period in possession of persons of that name: they may have given their name to the place (RKE p26). In medieval times Enville village and parish lay in Kinver Forest (VCH vol 20 p91). The parish formed between 1086 and the early C13, having probably originally formed a part of Kinver parish (SHC 1916 p197). In 1254 the lord of Enville, William of Birmingham, was granted a **fair** in his manor on the eve, feast, and morrow of the finding of the Holy Cross (May 2-4) (NSJFS 1971 p58) (VCH vol 20 p111). A **pound** in Enville parish is mentioned in 1612 and 1615 (VCH vol 20 p112). There were **stocks** in Enville parish in 1827 (VCH vol 20 p112). There were stocks at Enville crossroads. A vagrant Billy Pitt and his mongrel dog were put in them on a cold night. Pitt died of exposure and his ghost and the dog are said to haunt Enville Heath (TB March 1979 p5).
  1500 to PRESENT. There was a **windmill** beyond Little Morfe at SO 837884 marked on early C19 maps (WBJ pp21,22) (VCH vol 20 p112). (WIS pp10,17). See Spittlebrook Mill and Grove Farm, for windmills in Enville parish. The variety of black cherry which possess a peculiar vinous flavour for which Enville was noted had given rise by the early C19 to what were called the **Cherry Wakes**, held on the first, second and third Sundays in August (W pp50,175), or on three consecutive Sundays in late July and early August (VCH vol 20 p95). Burritt refers to Enville Wakes (BCGB p306). Drabble implies 'Enville Wakes' and a 'Cherry Fair' were the same, whereas Bird implies they were different. The Cherry Fair, attended by the Black Country populace, was notorious as 'a boisterous, roistering, ring-fighting and cockfighting holiday with the usual amount of drunkenness and demoralisation' (BC p149) (VB p65). Owing to the general riotousness of the wakes they were shortened to a single Monday by the mid 1840s (VCH vol 20 p95). The **Enville Troop** of the Staffordshire Yeomanry was raised in 1819 (info Yeomanry Museum). In July 1821 a disturbance was caused at George IV's coronation celebrations at Enville by men from Wordsley who were supporters of his estranged wife, Queen Caroline (VCH vol 20 p95). **Cricket festivals**, featuring teams styling themselves as All England and United England, were held at Enville during Lord Stamford's term as President of the M.C.C. in the 1850s. In 1872 a county team played the M.C.C. at Enville. The cricket ground at Enville was exceptionally smooth and was considered superior to that at Lord's. The ground lay immediately E of Enville Hall and had been taken into the hall grounds by c1880 (ILN Aug 1 1857 p116il) (VCH vol 20 p95) (PPTP pp95-96). **Custom and legend**. The children of Enville school who went clementing at Enville Hall (see) may have been the same children who went clementing at Mere Farm (see). In or near the village was an oak with branches that formed the shape of England (BCGB p305). There have been reports of the ghosts of a former lord and his lady of the manor of Enville seen walking in the Enville area (GOM p26). The rector of Enville in 1875 is said to have special powers which revived only those dying in his parish. He cured one woman, who seemed to be possessed by some evil spirit which was draining her blood away and reducing her to a skeleton, by every few days supplying her with port wine and soup until she recovered (STMSM July 1980 pp32,33). Luxury flats standing on the site of the Rectory are believed to have been haunted (GOM pl 3(a), pl 10 (b)). According to an old local tradition there was a giant, the **Enville giant**, who lived in Samson's Cave (see). Meanwhile there lived another giant at Kinver - the Kinver Giant - who lived with a beautiful wife in a rock dwelling in Holy Austin Rock (see). He would go to a certain spring, 'the Giant's Spring,' on the W side of Kinver Edge to collect water in a trough, 'the Giant's Water Trough,' for water was scarce at Holy Austin Rock. One day, whilst the Enville Giant was out collecting water, the Enville Giant strode across to his neighbour's dwelling and flirted with his wife. The Kinver Giant returned to find the Enville Giant leaving his wife. He was furious and hurled a very large stone, the Boltstone (see), at the departing Enville Giant and it landed in a field near Compton (WJO July 1903 xxxv). (SVS p337) (FOS p42).

Enville Common To W of Enville. A wood which is the size of a small forest called The Million covers it. The common may be identifiable with Enville Heath. The ghost of Billy Pitt and his mongrel dog Jim are said to haunt Enville Heath. Billy had been put in Enville stocks on a cold night and died of exposure (TB March 1979 p5).

Enville Hall In Enville village. Sir Edward Grey (d1529) bought Enville manor in 1528. His son Thomas Grey (d1559) had built the brick hall, which succeeded the medieval manor house, by 1548 (VCH vol 20 pp96-97).
THE GREYS. **Thomas Grey** (d1559) was succeeded by his son, John, who died childless in 1594 and the hall passed to his widow, who in c1605 granted the hall in accordance with her late husband's wishes to his distant cousin, **Ambrose Grey** (d1636), a younger son of Sir Henry Grey 1st Lord Grey of Groby (d1614) of Pyrgo, Haveringham-atte-Bower, Essex (he was a nephew of Henry Grey, 3rd Marquess of Dorset and Duke of Suffolk, whose eldest daughter, **Lady Jane Grey** (b1537), was queen of England for nine days in July 1553, and executed in 1554; reputedly, she stayed at the house which became the Whittington Inn (see), near Stourton). Ambrose Grey was succeeded by his son, **Henry Grey** (d1687). He devised his estates to his relation, **John Grey** (d1709), the great grandson of Sir Henry Grey (d1614), 1st Lord Grey of Groby. John Grey (d1709) was succeeded by his son, **Harry Grey** (d1739), who inherited the earldom of Stamford in 1720 and became 3rd Earl of Stamford. He was succeeded by his son Harry (d1768), 4th Earl. He was succeeded by his son, George Harry (d1819), 5th Earl (and of Warrington from 1796). He was succeeded by his son George Harry (1765-1845), 6th Earl. He was succeeded by his grandson, George Harry (1827-1883), 7th Earl, who left the Enville Hall estate to his wife. On her death in 1905 she left it to her grandniece, Catherine, whose husband Sir Henry Foley Lambert, Bt, then took the name of Grey. In 1938 the estate passed to Sir Henry's granddaughter, Eileen (VCH vol 20 pp96-97). Another account says Eileen inherited the hall in 1945. In 1942 she married firstly the 11th Earl of Harrington. In 1947 she married secondly Capt Jack Bissill. In 1999 Eileen (Mrs Bissill) died and was succeeded at Enville by her daughter Mrs Diana Williams; Eileen's son by her first marriage, Viscount Petersham, has a daughter, Serena, who married Lord Linley, Elizabeth II's nephew, in 1993 (E&S Sept 4 1999 p7).
THE HALL. The Tudor hall which Plot saw in the later C17 faced S; the only one, apart from Ingestre, in the county to do so at the time. It contained a water wheel in the kitchens which turned the spit (NHS p40 tab 32 fig 1 of the water wheel, tab 7 of the hall). The hall was enlarged and remodelled in the later C18 by the 5th Earl. The older central part was gothicised, although the two towers, depicted in Plot, can still be traced (NSFCT 1976 p23) (BOE p130) (VCH vol 20 p97). A view of the improved hall appears on the Wedgwood dinner service made for Catherine II of Russia in 1773-4 (VCH vol 20 p98). Shaw gives a poem on Enville, by Anthony Pasquin, which he composed whilst staying at the hall? (SHOS vol 2 pp270,272). Scott noted the hall had a menagerie (SVS pp275,276,278). In 1856 Lord Stamford staged a three-day fete in connection with a cricket festival. It was attended by between 60,000 and 80,000 people (VCH vol 20 p95). The hall, partly remodelled in the 1870s, was badly damaged in a fire on Nov 25 1904, which led to the porte-cochere being replaced and the interior being rebuilt (NSFCT 1976 p23) (BCM Oct 1979 pp44-50) (VCH vol 20 p98) (MR p146) (KEOP p118ps) (ADD p39p of fire). The children of Enville school annually clemented at Enville Hall on Nov 23. They were met by the butler at the main entrance. After singing the usual doggerel the butler regaled them with cake, apples and new hot pennies from a shovel. Afterwards they were granted a half holiday (KMC pp18-19,34). The hall and a part of the grounds were requisitioned by the army in WW2 (VCH vol 20 p100). (GNHS p182) (SMC p171) (CL March 16 1901 pp336-342 ps, p of the conservatory).
GROUNDS. In the later C17 Plot noted a woodbine shrub in the garden that grew six or seven feet high, having several substantial branches devoid of any support. There was also a black cherry tree growing in the courtyard which grew very ripe and tasty in only a particular type of soil (NHS pp206,208). The first planned landscaping of the grounds was undertaken in the early C18 (VCH vol 20 p99). In 1853 Lord Stamford opened the gardens to the public for two days a week between May and Sept (VCH vol 20 p95). The **Billiard Room** is under 0.25m NW of the hall at SO 823863. It is the most impressive building in the grounds with a facade with ogival arches and three rose windows. Essentially Gothick in style but has all kinds of not quite archaeologically correct motifs and is therefore particularly attractive (BOE p130 pl 55). The Greenhouse, designed by Sanderson Miller in 1750, and mentioned in William Shenstone's letters, has been identified with the Billiard Room (BOE p130); Roger White believes Miller's design was altered in execution by TF Pritchard of Shrewsbury (F p322). But Timothy Mowl has

argued that the Greenhouse was short-lived and that the Gothicist, Henry Keene built the Billiard Room (Journal of Garden History. 1983) (VCH vol 20 p99 note). Heely in 1777 noted it housed a billiard table, an organ, and the busts of Homer and Cicero and apparently it could only be seen from the Gothic Gateway (LHEL vol 2 pp82,83). Perhaps it is the Gothic Summerhouse mentioned in Sanderson Miller's letters. It was known as the Billiard Room in the 1770s; as the Museum in the C19; and as the Gothic Summerhouse by the 1980s (VCH vol 20 p99 note); it has also been called the Greek Summerhouse (FZ p111). The roof had collapsed by c1986 and it was in a poor state of repair. At this period it was said to have been the most important unrestored building in Britain. It was restored in 1988-90 at a cost of £130,000 (local info). (CGE p42 pl 27 A) (F&G p388) (F pp322-323). **Boathouses**. One was noted by Heely in the 1770s (CL Aug 1 1996 p42). This may be the classical boat house built in the later C18 in the SE corner of Temple Pool, which was demolished after WW2 (VCH vol 20 p99). Shaw noted the best view of the Cascade was from the room above the boathouse (SHOS vol 2 p271). There is a boathouse on the N side of Jordan Pool. The **Cascade** was created out of pools on the stream running down from Shenstone's Chapel passing Lyndon to Temple Pool. Shaw, who says it was best viewed from the room above the boathouse, attributes it to William Shenstone (SHOS vol 2 p271) (SVS pp275,277) (VCH vol 20 p99). Heely and Siren mention it (LHEL vol 2 pp29,30) (F&G p388). Pevsner says it is still going strong (BOE p130). (Marshall's 'Planting and Rural Ornaments' vol 1 p329). **Chinese Pavilion** or House. At SO 818862, over 0.25m W of the hall. But the DoE think it is of early to mid C19 origin (DoE II). Siren missed it (F p322). Jones saw it and noted its cruciform shape and dimensions; about 60 feet by 20 feet by 25 feet high. Over the crossing is a lantern with more frosted glass. Ogival arches mark the nave and choir. It is made of wood and was once painted red (F&G pp388p,389). Some have called it a Pagoda in the wood (BOE p130) (MR p146). Vaguely resembling a Russian summer residence it was in a very ruinous state in 1989 (visit to hall). The **Chinese Temple** was erected on an island in Temple Pool between 1747 and 1750. It was one of the earliest recorded chinoiserie garden buildings in England (VCH vol 20 p99). It is probably the Chinese House noted by Sanderson Miller on a visit he made to the gardens on June 13 1750; it was taken down in the late C18 when Temple Pool was reshaped. A **conservatory** in the neo-Indian style, considered one of the most fanciful in England. It was built at SO 823864 under 0.25m NNW of the hall to designs of Gray & Ormson of London in 1855. It was demolished in 1927 (TB May 1989 p27p - excellent photograph of the conservatory) (SGS p99) or partly demolished c1928 and demolished in 1938 (VCH vol 20 p100 p facing p96). The **Cottage** is mentioned by Heely and Scott. Heely describes it as 'this humble thatched cot, its little circular sloping lawn in front, and the graceful clustering trees, that verge the area, and form a perfect canopy over the building...' (LHEL vol 3 pp71,72,73) (SVS p278). It is perhaps identifiable with the Hermitage. **Dolphin Fountain** incorporates shells, mermaids etc (CL March 16 1901 p340p). The **Doric Seat** according to Headley and Meulenkamp had gone by 1986 (F p322). Barbara Jones mentions a Doric summer-house with square rusticated columns (F&G p388). The **Eyecatcher**, or called Gothic Gate(way) (BOE p130) (VCH vol 20 p101 see map), is an assemblage of three Gothick arches, the central one with a portcullis (F p322). It is situated 0.25m WSW of the hall, at SO 821859 (VCH vol 20 p101). It was designed by Sanderson Miller, in the mid to late C18 (DoE II). The gateway probably marked the passage from the grounds to the wood, and the high-lying Sheepwalks (BOE p130). Jones says the Eyecatcher is probably the Gothic Summerhouse mentioned in Sanderson Miller's letters (F&G p388il), but that has been identified with the Billiard Room. (LHEL vol 2 p32) (SHOS vol 2 p271) (CGE p42) (SGS p98) (BOE p103) (FZ p111). The **Gothic boat-house** lay by Jordan's Pool and was designed by Sanderson Miller. It was noted by Heely as an octagonal structure with a curious sliding window adorned with painted glass depicting whimsical groups of grotesque figures (F p322). It was rather rustic with a thatched roof and was situated over a stone arch which provided the boathouse (CL March 16 1901 p339p. Aug 1 1996 p42). Pevsner implies it was still standing, although, in a ruinous state, when he toured the grounds, in the late 1960s or early 1970s (BOE p130). By c1986 the octagonal Gothic boat-house had gone, crushed by a falling tree some years ago (F p322). The **Gothic Gateway** see Eyecatcher. The Gothic Summerhouse see Billiard Room. The **Greenhouse** designed by Sanderson Miller in 1750 has long been identified with the Billiard Room (see). But T Mowl has suggested the Greenhouse was short-lived and different to the Billiard Room (VCH vol 20 p99 note). The **Grotto** decorated with ivy and grassy cinders is only mentioned by Heely (1777) (LHEL vol 2 p44). **Haha Pool** is a small pool under 0.25m WNW of the hall. In it is the Triton fountain; the pool is sometimes called the Sea Horse Pool (KEOP p120p in c1905). The **Hermitage** or Hermit's House. Heely noted a thatched cottage (F&G p388). Siren noted a little octagonal bark summer-house or hermitage (CGE p42 pl 27B) (F&G p388). Pevsner says the Hermit's House once had a thatched roof and was very ruinous in c1974 (BOE p130). Headley and Meulenkamp in c1986 say it has stained glass windows (F p322). A ruinous brick cottage perhaps identifiable with the Hermitage lay at the W end of Jordan's Pool in marshy bracken surroundings in 1989 (visit to hall). **Hermit's House** see The Hermitage. There is an **ice-house** at SO 82908541, 0.5m SSE of the hall. A domed chambered structure excavated out of the natural sandstone and partly lined with brick, with a square headed doorway. Is probably of C18 origin with C19 repairs (DoE II). It is possible that the ice-house is the same as Sampson's Cave and or Shenstone's Chapel. **Jordan's Pool** is the large pool to the W of Haha Pool and 0.25m W of the hall. The **Museum** see Billiard Room. **Pagoda** see Chinese Pavilion. **Ralph's Bastion** is at SO 822856, over 0.25m SSW of the hall. A big yew tree growing on a semicircular bastion with a stone retaining wall. One huge branch is sawn off and

TRAF'S
ASTION
1753

is cut on the end of it (F&G p388) (F p322). **Rotunda.** Noted by Heely (F p322). Or called the Round Temple (CGE p42). (SHOS vol 2 p271) (SVS p276). A Rotunda is marked at SO 817853, over 0.5m SW of the hall on a map on p101 of VCH vol 20. **Round Temple** see Rotunda. **Sampson's Cave** is a rock-cut cottage at SO 828852, over 0.5m SSE of Enville Hall. According to Barbara Jones Shenstone's Chapel is known locally as Sampson's Cave (see) or Samson's Cave (F&G p388). Headley and Meulenkamp suggest she is mistaken (F p322). The **Seat** was mentioned by Heely (LHEL vol 2 p39). Sheepwalks (see). The **Shell Fountain** has a side bowl shape concertinaed and riveted like a shell pattern (CL March 16 1910 pp340-341p). **Shenstone's Chapel,** at SO 818852 over 0.5m SSW of the hall on the N side of Priest Wood, is to the memory of William Shenstone (b1714), poet, who is said to have died at Enville Hall on Feb 11 1763 (TB Sept 1989 p29il by Ron Davies). Shaw says it was designed by Shenstone (SHOS vol 2 p271); but Heely says not (Description of Hagley, Envil and the Leasows. J Heely. ND but earlier than 1777) (VCH vol 20 p99). Shenstone's Chapel is described as in thick and gloomy umbrage in 'The Beauties of England and Wales.' Pevsner says it is still in dense woods and near the Cascade and describes it as with a round tower with conical roof (BOE p130). It seems that Barbara Jones mistook it for Sampson's Cave (see) (F&G p388) (F p322). (LHEL vol II pp49,50) (SVS p275) (SSC p137 in the intro) (W p175) (CGE p42) (F p322). The **Shepherd's Lodge** is a Gothick structure noted by Heely (LHEL vol II pp59,60) (F&G p388) (F p322), but has never been identified since. An illustration of it appeared on a dessert plate of the Wedgwood dinner service made for Catherine II of Russia 1773-4 (ES June 29 1996 p4p of reproduction plate). (SHOS vol 2 p271). Heely noted that one room contained profiles of friends and family of the then owner, the Earl of Stamford, and that the other room was decorated with simple illustrations, maps and music sheets written by the inhabitant a shepherd called Swain (LHEL vol II pp59,60). Scott writing in the early 1830s described it as a truly elegant gothic cottage strictly in unison with its surroundings, with its rooms and the staircase covered with ballads, carols, and similar congenial embellishments (SVS p280). A recent account states the lodge still (1989) stands beyond Shenstone's Chapel on the summit of the Sheepwalks (see), and that it was built in c1623 and is also called Warrener's Lodge (TB Sept 1989 p29 il by Ron Davis); the warrener's lodge, known as Enville Lodge by 1623, on the Sheepwalks was gothicised in the C18, perhaps by Sanderson Miller; the ruins of a C17 building stood there in 1982 (VCH vol 20 pp99,111). (CGE p42). The **Summer House** may be another name for The Temple (see) and The Museum (see). However, in 1989 Mr F Scott Bolton at the Enville estate office marked 'Summer House' at SO 818858, 0.5m SW of the hall. Here stood a ruinous, roofless, brick and stone structure which once had a beautiful pediment. It was in a classical style and commanded fine views. Mr Scott Boulton was not confusing this with The Museum which he also marked (visit to hall). The **Temple** in a valley towards the Sheepwalks. Has four alternately blocked front columns (BOE p130). **Temple Pool.** Pool 0.25m S of the hall. Created as a rectangular ornamental lake on the site of the old stables in the mid C18. It was made into an irregular shape in the late C18 (VCH vol 20 p99). The **Triton Fountain** in Haha Lake is a fountain with a statue of Triton blowing a shell trumpet surrounded by four sea-horses with fish tails. (DoE II) (CL March 16 1901 pp338p,340) (CGE p42 pl 26) (F&G p388) (BOE p130) (SGS p98) (MR

p146) (KEOP p120p). In 1989 Triton was in a kneeling position and had lost his arms whilst one horse had completely disappeared and another had lost its head. **Walls, The** (see). **Warrener's Lodge** see Shepherd's Lodge.

Enville Park There was a deer park within a pale at Enville in 1548. It covered a large part of the present grounds of Enville Hall (VCH vol 20 p98). It belonged to the Greys (Saxton's map) (EDP p180).

Eskew Bridge 0.75m N of Brewood on the Shropshire Union Canal.

Essex Bridge Best-preserved packhorse bridge in the county 0.25m ENE of Shugborough Hall. An antler tool, pierced with a small rectangular hole, of Iron Age or Roman origin, was found here four feet six inches below the Trent bed in 1961 (NSJFS 1964 p20). The bridge crosses the Trent, only yards downstream from it's confluence with the Sow. According to tradition the bridge was built by Robert Devereux, Earl of Essex, favourite of Elizabeth I (SOSH p188), to carry his hounds from Chartley to Cannock Chase (ESH p16), or reputedly for Elizabeth I (HAH pp62-64) (SVB p84). It was formerly called Shugborough Bridge (SHC 1934 p24) (HAH pp62-64) and is locally known as Haywood Bridge (HHHC p72); the name Essex Bridge seems to have been a C19 renaming based on the legend that the Earl of Essex had built the bridge (HAHS p54) (SHC 1970 p90 note). In the Birmingham Art Gallery is an oil painting of it dated c1830 showing three of the old arches. The artist calls it 'Queen's Bridge, Shugborough,' having probably heard that Elizabeth I passed over it (HAH pp62-64). Many authors have mentioned it including Camden, Chetwynd, Plot, Cox (who called it the Horse Bridge), Defoe, Bowen, Loxdale, and Pennant, although not Erdeswick who said little about the bishop's palace (near the site of Shugborough Hall) to which it led. From the various and varying accounts it can be deduced that: It was formerly a very long wooden bridge of at least C16 origin with between 39 to 46 arches and may have formed a causeway over surrounding boggy ground as well as over the Trent. The bridge was repaired in 1633. The central part over the river may have been replaced with a stone bridge of 16 arches in 1649 or in 1679. Certainly some of the bridge was of stone by 1729-33. Repairs to the bridge occurred in 1818 and or in 1833 (NHS p372) (SD p89) (Bowen's map) (S&W p257) (W p416) (SHC 1934 p24) (SHJ spring 1991 p13) (CCF pp106-111) (SH p46) (BERK2 p45) (BOE p144) (Shire County Guide. Peter Heaton. 1986. p40) (MR pp163-164,165p) (SHC 1934 p24) (BZ p108) (HAH pp62-64) (ABMEE p2) (DoE I) (SOS p72 - noted by Harwood) (LGS p141p) (KES pp7,101) (S p97p) (SLM winter 1953 p14p) (PS p60p) (SGS p105) (COS p60p) (HCMBOPP pp8 il,9p). By at least 1932 it has had 14 arches (ABMEE p2) (SHJ spring 1991 p13). By 1934 it was known as the Essex Bridge (SHC 1934 p24). Its weight is 4000 tons (STM June 1969 p32p), and it is only four feet wide and 100 yards long (SL p110). It was alleged to be the longest packhorse bridge in England in the mid C18 and in the 1980s (Bowen's map) (ROT pp59p,60).

Essex Wood Large wood to W of Enville Hall. This area of woodland was known as Evezetowode in the early C14, a name of Old English origin (VCH vol 20 p109).

Essington Large village on a hill above the source of a brook that may be called Black or Wybaston Brook which flows westwards through Moseley, 17.75m SSE of Stafford. Former manor and township in Bushbury ancient parish, Seisdon hundred, and yet is in Cuttlestone hundred (VCH vol 4 p61).

EARLY. The last Ice Age reached its maximum southern extent about Wolverhampton and glacial boulders lie about Essington (WJO Nov 1909 p293). A stone vessel found in an ancient lake bed at Rosemary Tileries at SJ 968042, 0.75m NE of Essington, which may be of **Palaeolithic** origin (Walsall Times and S Staffs Advertiser 1931) (ESSN p9).

700 to 1500. Formerly identified with DB Estendone by Erdeswick (SOS p552) and Shaw (SHOS vol 1 p*xi), and with DB Ogintune (or Hocintune?) by Shaw (ESSN p8) - since identified with Ogley Hay (DB. Phillimore. 1976) - Essington's current accepted DB identification is with Eseningetone, that made by Scott in the early C19 (SVS p578) (SHC 1923 pp24-31). Has also appeared as Esingetun (996) (SSE 1996 p13), Eseninton (1227), Eseuinton (1285), Eseningtun (1270-5), Esnynton (1293) (SPNO pp49-50) (SPN p48). The **name** means 'tun or town of Esne's people,' or 'the tun or town belonging to Esne' (DUIGNAN) (SSE 1996 p13) (SPN p48). Esne, an Anglo-Saxon common name, means servant, although it was taken by men of rank (ESSN p7). According to Smallshire Essington was named after Esne termed 'Princep Ealdorman' and Comus Praefectus' in charters of the period 781-799 (WFW p18). In Norman times Essington manor was held as part of the barony of Dudley, but, later in the Middle Ages it was held by a peculiar feudal service of the lord of Hilton manor. By the term of his charter the tenant of Essington had to take to Hilton Manor House a goose every New Year's Day. For further details of this service see Hilton Park Hall. The service ceased when the Vernons, lords of Hilton manor, became owners of Essington (BCC vol 2

pp37,38) (ESSN pp17-18 il).

1500 to PRESENT. At Essington is the only surviving **post mill** in the county, at SJ 943036, over 1m W of the village. It stands in the grounds of Windmill Farm. Built by 1681, perhaps even by 1641. Used by the Home Guard in WW2. In 1959 it was badly vandalised, but had been in a reasonable condition until then (WBJ p22 il II). (WIS pp10p,18 - showing John Simkin with the millstone, and beam dated 1681) (KES p178 writes of a windmill at Shareshill, which may be this) (LGS p211 refers to an old mill bearing the date 1681 and the initials H. V. (Henry Vernon)) (SLM spring 1954 p24p) (IAS pp166-167) (STMSM June 1980 p40p) (ESSN pp26-27p of in 1900). Hugh Bourne (1772-1852), founder of Primitive Methodism, visited Essington in 1810 (ESSN p67). Essington then centred on a hamlet by Essington Hall. By at least the mid C19 there were several collieries in the area and a village (the present village) for miners emerged 0.75m to the E of the hamlet. A **chapel** for the inhabitants in the present village was built of iron in 1859 at the corner of Hobnock and Bognop Roads. It was known as the 'Iron Church.' It was replaced by St John's, dedicated on Dec 9 1933, on the W side of Wolverhampton Road (The Beloved Disciple: The Story of St John's Church Essington. Ralph Tomkinson. 1992). Separate civil parish status for Essington came in 1866 (GLAUE p410). There was a mineral **railway** line from Essington Wood Colliery to the Wyrley & Essington Canal at Sneyd (VCH vol 2 p323). In c1880 a railway was made from this line to the Cannock-Walsall railway at Springhill between Long Lane and Broad Lane (VCH vol 2 p323). The most unusual overhanging signal box where this railway crossed the Bursnip Road (ESSN pp52,53p) was restored and incorporated into a new house, built by 1993 (E&S July 28 1993 p8p) (BCM spring 1999 p39il). Nearby Hilton Main Colliery, opened in 1924, brought further expansion to present Essington, and a railway from the Cannock-Walsall line opened in 1924 to the colliery (VCH vol 2 p326). Essington became a separate ecclesiastical parish in 1934 (GLAUE p410). In 1963 Beacon Estate, Crab Lane, and part of Sneyd Lane were removed from the parish and in 1978 Kitchen Lane and Ashmore Park were taken out of the parish (The Beloved Disciple: The Story of St John's Church Essington. Ralph Tomkinson. 1992). A badge of the Ancient Order of Foresters was found by W Guest of 2 Hawthorne Road (ES July 24 1969 p6p) in the vicinity of Essington. The hamlet by Essington Hall has remained a hamlet.

Essington Hall 0.75m W of Essington. Essington village centred on Essington Hall in the C19. At Essington Hall Farm, at SJ 951035, is a moat (SSAHST 1982-3 p39) (CAMS p63). The house is listed Grade II by DoE.

Essington Wood Wood 1m to NE of Essington, marked on OS map 1834. Here is or was an earthwork. William Pitt wrote of it in a letter to Shaw (19 May 1794). It was probably built for military purposes in the C18. It is on rising ground about 400 or 500 yards W of the Lodge House (SHOS vol 2 p312). Essington Wood was enclosed in 1815 (MH 1994 p108). A Spanish agent, Emilio Ripoll, working for revolutionary forces, trying to eject the Spanish from Cuba, came to England in c1900 to procure arms. Before being captured by the pursuing counter forces he hid the money (French Francs, Spanish Pesetas and French gold coins - Louisdors) in the vicinity of Essington Wood. Ripoll could not precisely remember where he had hid the money and from prison he wrote to Thomas Cope, landlord of the Old Mitre Inn (see) to ask his assistance in locating it. Cope eventually declined to help although the family kept the correspondence. The buried treasure, if it really does exist, has never been found (TB March 1993 p17ps of the pub and letter).

Essington Wood Brook Forms the northern boundary of Walsall ancient parish by Yieldfields Hall (VCH vol 17 p143).

Esta Mora Some land on the S side of the Sow facing St Thomas Becket Priory. It was given to that priory some time after its foundation (BERK pp44 map,47; spelt Estmora).

Estoril Early C20 house in Station Road, Barlaston. It was the residence of Cuthbert Wilshaw, governing director of Wilshaw and Robinson pottery manufacturers in the mid C20. His wife, Maud Alice, was battered to death here on July 16 1952, by the family's chauffeur and handyman, Lesley Green, in an attempt to steal £3,500 worth of jewellery. He was convicted of murder in Nov that year and hung at Winson Green Prison, Birmingham, on Dec 23 1952. The Wilshaws appear to have named the house Estoril after travelling in Spain (STM July 1963 p39) (MCGM pp110-112) (ES April 4 1993 p7p. April 13 1993 p3. April 14 1993 p9p. April 15 1993 p12) (MCS pp70-79). The ghost of what may have been Maud Alice Wilshaw was seen in Station Road in the 1970s (info Bruce Braithwaite). **Wedgwood Memorial College** was founded in 1945 by a Joint Advisory Committee comprising representatives of Oxford University, and Stoke and Staffs Education Committees. It was the first residential college to be established under the Education Act of 1944 (NSJFS 1961 p104). Between 1945 and 1949 the college occupied

Barlaston Hall (see); Francis Donald Klingender's classic 'Art and the Industrial Revolution' (1947, revised 1968 and 1972) is said to have come about after he tutored there (POP p142). The college then moved to The Limes, a house dating from 1893 in Station Road, below Estoril. In 1953 it purchased Estoril; the college still (1999) owns both properties (SSBOP p85). In late 1999 the college was preparing to build accommodation in the grounds at Estoril for the National Esperanto Centre (info Derek Tatton, Wedgwood Memorial College).

Etching Hill (*Hitchin Hill* LTM Nov 1972 p9). Hill 454 feet high, over 1m W of Rugeley. In Rugeley ancient parish. The hill, with a sandstone escarpment on its summit (GCC p9p), looks like a mini Table Mountain (CCBO p68). It has an artificial amphitheatre on its eastern side which contains a high rock cut from the solid rock of which the hill is comprised. DHT Smith thought that as the amphitheatre lies directly E of Etching Hill and is open on the E side it was constructed for some prehistoric religious significance (OSST 1949-50 p19). A mound on the hill at SK 027187 has been thought to be a burial mound (VCH barrow list. vol 5 p149) but is not (NSJFS 1965 p46). The same or another mound, used as a view point, can be seen from a distance (STMSM Nov 1972 p41). In early autumn 1991 a man found pieces of bead-like glass near the Wolseley sand and gravel quarry on Etching Hill and after an archaeological excavation a medieval glass works was found. It may be identifiable with the 'le glashoushay' at Wolseley mentioned in 1452 (MIDD vol 2 pp42p-43p). Etching Hill has appeared as Eychilhill (1504), Ichinhill (1584), Eaching Hill (1798), Hitching Hill (1834 OS map) (VCH vol 5 p149) (SPNO p106). Celia Fiennes, who visited the hill in summer 1698, spelt it Itching Hill (Illustrated Journeys of Celia Fiennes edited by Chris Morris. 1984. p148). The name 'Echeles' seems to mean 'land added to an estate by reclamation' (NSJFS 1974 p31). There was foot-racing on a three mile course at Etching Hill by 1678. Horse racing became popular here in C19 on a one and a half mile course (VCH vol 5 p152) (LTM Nov 1972 p9). The commander of the Cannock Chase manoeuvres of 1873 set up his flag on Etching Hill (Army Quarterly. vol 68 No. 2 pp248-256) (VCH vol 5 p152) and a flag pole was still positioned on the summit in 1951 (GCC p9p).

Etchinghill Village now merged into the suburbs of Rugeley, surrounding Etching Hill. SVB p75 makes no distinction in spelling, between the hill and the village, both go by the spelling of Etching Hill. The three burial mounds noticed at Bower Lane in 1947 (OSST 1949-50 p19) turned out to be natural features (NSJFS 1965 p46). A sandstone cave over 1m NW of Rugeley 0.25m N of Bower Farm at SK 03051950, discovered by children in 1978, revealed flints of the Mesolithic period. The cave is small and quite regular being approximately 2.5 metres at its deepest, and rarely more than one metre high (SASR 1986 pp1- 12 plans ils) (HOS 1998 p23). There was a 'tin tabernacle' church in Church Lane. It was built in the 1930s, but was replaced by the church, Holy Spirit, on the corner of Mount Road and Whitworth Lane in the mid 1960s. This church was rebuilt in c1991 (info Rev MJ Newman).

Etheridge House Church Street, Bilston. House in which the philanthropist and Japan ware artist John Etheridge (1772-1856) was born and died. The house was called Etheridge House by 1893 (HOBLL pp226-227).

Eton A ward of Burton upon Trent in the E Horninglow area.

Etruria Former industrial hamlet 15.5m NNW of Stafford. Formerly in Shelton township in Stoke-upon-Trent chapelry and parish.

EARLY. Various mammal bone finds have been found in the Etruria area. Josiah Wedgwood found the skeletal vertebra of a massive fish (HOE p63). An ox (Bos Primigenius) skull and horns was found at a depth of 14 feet during the construction of the Hanley-Etruria railway in 1863 (HOE p71). In 1877 the skull of a forest ox was discovered in the silt on the side of the Fowlea Brook near Etruria Station (NSFCT 1878 p32. 1896 p108 pl) (NSSG p18) (STM April 1963 p28). The two ox skull finds may be the same.

1750 to 1800. The area received its name from Josiah Wedgwood I's Etruria Works (see) opened by 1769. Formerly the area had been open country in Fowlea Brook valley. The works together with the purpose-built workers hamlet, from which the urban area of Etruria has evolved, was one of the earliest small self-contained industrial communities of the Industrial Revolution (NSJFS 1965 p82), and described in GM 1794 as 'a colony newly raised where clay-built man subsists on clay' (POP p39). Wedgwood's Trent and Mersey Canal, which he had built by 1777 for the better transportation of his pottery and which ran passed the works played a central part in an incident of the 'Bread Riots' which occurred at Etruria on March 7 1783. There was a national dearth after the American War of Independence and prices were low. Owners of a barge bringing flour and cheese to Etruria decided to go on and sell it in Manchester, where prices were higher. An incensed mob from Hanley and Etruria went after it and captured it at Longport. The barge was brought back to Etruria in triumph and the contents sold in the locality on March 8 at bargain prices. The over-jubilant mob then took to rioting in Etruria and were suppressed by the Staffs Militia under Major Sneyd. The ring leaders, Stephen Barlow and Joseph Boulton, were executed on March 17 1783 (H pp94-95) (The Rise of the Staffordshire Potteries. John Thomas. pp181-182) (HOE pp260-262) (HBST pp445-446) (LOU pp146-148) (POP p50) (CCSHO pp35-40). Samuel Pattison, poet, fl 1792, appears to have been born near Etruria, for in his 'Original Poems Moral and Satirical' there are lines to Josiah Wedgwood I which include

'Nor should a bard from near Etruria rise,
Without enthroning Wedgwood in the skies,'

(PSS p161) (VFC p104).
1800 to PRESENT. The North Staffordshire Infirmary at Hartshill has it origins in a 'house of recovery' for the poor. It appears to have been established in 1802 and built in 1804 at Etruria Vale; The North Staffordshire Infirmary was built nearby in 1819 (said to be in an area called Wood Hills, see). Four years before the hospital moved to Hartshill (1869) (VCH vol 8 p197) (HOS 1998 p126) on April 18 1865 Dr William Dunnett Spanton convened a meeting at the hospital which resulted in the founding of the North Staffordshire Naturalists Field Club; this was one of the earliest local scientific and learned societies to be formed in Great Britain as a whole. Its first transactions (NSFCT) were published in 1866. The club became the North Staffordshire Naturalists' Field Club and Archaeological Society from 1877; **North Staffordshire Field Club** from 1896 to the present. The Spanton Medal, instituted in 1925, is given in recognition of original work on the natural history of Staffs, and is not restricted to club members. Robert Garner (d1890) of Foley House, author of GNHS, was a founder member, and the Garner Medal for services by club members to the club was instituted in 1893. The club library was named The Daltry Memorial Library in 1905 after Rev TW Daltry, vicar of Madeley, an official of the club (info Randle Knight). Further industrialisation of the Etruria area occurred between 1824-26 with the building of the gas works in Etruria Vale. There was a race course in Etruria Vale between 1823 and 1859 (NSFCT 1945 p100). The Commissioners' **church**, St Matthew, on the corner of Etruria and Belmont Roads was built in 1848-1849 (BOE p258), and demolished some time after 1976 (AGT pp96il,97), because of mining subsidence. Etruria became a separate ecclesiastical parish in 1844 (GLAUE p411), and was a ward of Hanley from 1895 (VCH vol 8 p158). The area is now (1990) practically merged with Hanley. In **WW2** the Germans made a bombing raid in the area and four gasholders of the Etruria Gas Works were set afire and 'lit up the valley between Stoke and Longport' (TSS p125). **Persons.** Rev **Robert Topham**, vicar of Etruria, who retired in 1890 had eccentric tendencies (perhaps brought about from sunstroke as an army chaplain in India). He was noted for marrying anyone for a shilling and flinging open the vicarage windows to announce the wedding banns to anyone who might be passing. Boatman passing on the Trent and Mersey Canal gave him quite a bit of trade in marriages. As well as marriages he undertook many funerals burying some 900 bodies in St Matthew's tiny churchyard; it was found that some coffins were not buried less than six inches deep (HOE pp263,265-269) (AGT p97). **Edward Smith**, captain of SS Titanic, born in Hanley (see), attended Etruria British School, later Etruria Middle School, where (from 1961) there has been a tablet to his memory (MMM pp11-13). **Ernest JD Warrilow** MBE, documentary photographer in the Potteries, author of 'Arnold Bennett and Stoke-on-Trent' (1966), SHST, HOE, and LLST, was born in Etruria in 1910. Many of his photographs comprise the Warrilow Collection in Keele University Library, where there is a room named after him. He died in Horton, Staffs, on Jan 12 2000 (ES Jan 15 2000 p3p).
Etruria Grove Grove of trees in Etruria, said to have been planted by Josiah Wedgwod I (VCH vol 8 p145) and considered very pretty. Destroyed by c1850 due to increased urbanisation. Or because of sulphur from the blast furnaces, in the area from the late 1830s, gradually destroying the vegetation. The last of the grove of trees had disappeared by 1873 (NSFCT 1945 p100). The grove was approximately in an area between Etruria Park and Hanley. It would be somewhere by the present (1950) Grove Garage (HOE p134). The name has also been used for the model 'garden village' built by Josiah Wedgwood for his workers (NSJFS 1963 p9). A piercing scream and the spectre of a **white rabbit** haunted the grove. They are supposed to be the representation and voice of John Holdcroft, murdered by his companion, Charles Shaw, whilst playing pitch and toss. Shaw was aged 16 and Holdcroft aged 14. The murder took place in Crabtree Field somewhere on the Etruria side of Macaloni Bridge in the vicinity of Etruria Grove on Aug 4 1833. Shaw strangled Holdcroft for cheating and then hung him from a tree to make it appear he had committed suicide. He later confessed and was convicted of murder at

Burslem in March 1834 and sentenced to death. This was later commuted to transportation (ROS vol 1 pp45-50) (HOE pp49,134-135) (EGH pp202-203) (PTP pp21-24) (TOS pp93-95) (GOM p20) (TFTP pp28-31) (GLS pp38-39) (SMML pp106-108).
Etruria Hall Lay to the NE of Etruria Works. Designed by Joseph Pickford of Derby for Josiah Wedgwood I, born at Churchyard House (see), Burslem. Completed in 1770 (VCH vol 8 p150) (BOE p259). The artist George Stubbs stayed at the hall for three weeks in Aug 1780 and here met Dr Erasmus Darwin. Stubbs' painting of the Wedgwood family is at Weston Park (HOE p47,67il) or it was for a time at Wood House (see) near Cheadle, or in the Wedgwood Museum at the Barlaston factory (SHJ vol 3 p51). Whilst at Etruria Stubbs developed acute toothache (SHJ vol 3 p51). After Josiah Wedgwood I's death the hall stood unoccupied for a while. In 1803 it was occupied by Thomas Byerley (d1810), Josiah II's cousin and partner in the pottery firm; between 1812 and 1819 occupied by Josiah Wedgwood II; from the mid 1820s used as a boarding school; unoccupied in c1829; by 1834 occupied by Francis Wedgwood, a younger son of Josiah II; in c1848 sold to the Duchy of Lancaster; in 1851 occupied Edward Kinnersley, possibly as a tenant; by 1854 let to John Lancaster; by 1860 sold to Earl Granville who, in 1858 established a new branch of the Shelton Works on a site to the W of the hall; between at least 1868 and 1872 the hall was the seat of Col William Roden, mayor of Hanley; in 1876 it was unoccupied, but let in tenements by 1880. From at least 1892 it was used as offices by the Shelton Iron, Steel and Coal Company. The hall was extended in 1916. The Shelton Iron, Steel and Coal Company bought the hall from the Duchy in 1930 (HSP p50) (W p20) (VCH vol 8 p152). A secret passage about six feet high reputedly led out from one of the cellars to the works beyond the canal. The hall caretaker told Warrilow in the 1950s that he had walked down the passage for about 60 feet, but, finding nothing, went no further. It was bricked up in 1920 (HOE pp33,54,56,72p). Morland says there is no truth in the story of a secret passage. It was probably just an underground compartment for Wedgwood's laboratory and workshop (POP p42). (SHST pp558-561 p of an Adam fireplace in the hall). (HOE pp120,182,183, 219, 220, 271, 284, 295, 306, 307, 329, 349, 380- Etruria Hall Lake) (SSW pp74,75). In the 1990s a distant American cousin of Josiah Wedgwood I, Harry 'Chips' Wedgwood, wanted to remove the hall and Round House to the USA; he bases his claim on a deed dated April 1 1829 (ES April 1 1995 p8). The first registered car in the Potteries, with a number plate 'EH 1' was privately owned at Etruria Hall in 1903 (SHST p103).
DESCENDANTS OF JOSIAH WEDGWOOD I. JOSIAH I's CHILDREN. **John** (1766-1844) left the Wedgwood firm in 1793 for banking and horticulture, becoming a founder member of the Royal Horticultural Society in 1809. Richard (1767-1768). **Josiah II** (1769-1843), inherited the firm and lived at Bank House from 1792-1799 and later resided at Maer Hall (see). Thomas (1771-1805), was a partner in the firm from 1790. He contributed especially in the field of ceramic chemistry and physics. He left the firm in 1793. His experiments in chemistry led him into experiments with photography. There was a memorial to him in Etruria Park. Susannah (1765-1817) married Robert Darwin. She then became the daughter-in-law of Erasmus Darwin and was to become the mother of Charles Darwin. Catherine (1774-1823). Sarah (1776-1856). Mary Ann (1778-1786). JOHN's CHILDREN. John Allen (1796-1882) rector of Maer (Wedgwood vols I & II Robin Reilly. 1989), and fought at Waterloo. He was later a member of the Tenby, Pembrokeshire, Bench (NSFCT 1933 pp33-44). Col Thomas Josiah (1797-1860). Lieut Charles (1800-c1820). Robert (1806-1880) rector of Dumbleton. There were three daughters. JOSIAH II's CHILDREN. **Josiah III** (1795-1880) resided at Leith Hill, Surrey, and became a partner in the firm in 1823. **Henry Allen** (1799-1885) barrister-at-law, and contributor of stories on the Potteries to the Staffordshire Times and Staffordshire Sentinel; some were then republished in ROS, UDC and PTP (PTP Introduction by John Thomas). **Francis** (1800-1888), became a partner in 1827 and built Upper House (see) in Barlaston in 1849 (buried Barlaston cemetery). **Hensleigh** (1803-1891) barrister-at-law and achieved fame as an etymologist (WCW). There were five daughters; the youngest Emma (1808-1896) married Charles Darwin at Maer (see). JOSIAH III's DESCENDANTS. Josiah III married his cousin Caroline Darwin, daughter of Robert and Susannah Darwin. They had four daughters. The third, Margaret Susan, was the mother of Dr Ralph Vaughan Williams OM, the distinguished composer. HENRY ALLEN's CHILDREN. John Darwin (1840-1870). Arthur (1843-1900). Rowland Henry of Slindon, Sussex (b1847). There were three daughters. FRANCIS' CHILDREN. **Godfrey** (1833-1905) became a partner in 1859, but withdrew in 1891. Later resided at Idlerocks (see). **Clement Francis** (1840-1889) was made a partner and made his seat at The Lea (see), Barlaston (buried Barlaston cemetery). **Lawrence** (1844-1913) was made a partner and made his seat Upper House, Barlaston (buried Barlaston cemetery). There

were four daughters. HENSLEIGH's DESCENDANTS. Hensleigh's children include: Frances Julia (or Julia Frances) 'Snow' (1833-1913), novelist. James Mackintosh (1834-1864). Ernest Hensleigh (1837-1895). Alfred Allen (1842-1892), who had a son Bertram Hensleigh (b1876); his son Hensleigh Cecil (b1908) joined the firm in 1927 and was associated with Josiah Wedgwood & Sons Inc of America. GODFREY's DESCENDANTS. Godfrey's son Major Cecil (b1863), DSO, was the first mayor of Stoke-on-Trent. He appears to have been resident of a house at Leadendale (see) and Wood House near Cheadle; he was killed in action at La Boiselle during the battle of the Somme in 1916. Cecil's second daughter Doris Audrey (1894-1970) joined the firm in 1915 and retired as company secretary in 1928. CLEMENT FRANCIS' CHILDREN. **Frank** (Francis Hamilton) (1867-1930) (mem Barlaston church). Clement Henry (1870-1871). **Josiah** Clement IV (1872-1943), built Moddershall Oaks (see), and was created 1st Baron Wedgwood of Barlaston in 1942. He appears to have been born at The Lea (see), Barlaston (mem Barlaston church and buried Barlaston cemetery). **Ralph Lewis** (1874-1956), 1st Baron Wedgwood of Etruria (mem Barlaston church). Arthur Felix (b1877) killed in action attacking Bucquoy Bapaume Ridge in 1917 (mem Barlaston church). Cisely (or Cecily) Frances (1876-1904) (mem Barlaston church and buried Barlaston cemetery). LAWRENCE's DESCENDANTS. Lawrence's children include: Kennard Lawrence (1873-1950) became a partner in the firm, and in 1906 left for the US to represent the firm's interests there. Mary Francis (b1874). Capt Gilbert (b1876). John (b1877), who had a son Godfrey Josiah (b1907). Geoffrey (1879-1897). FRANK's DESCENDANTS. Frank's children include: Frances Dorothea Joy (b1903). Cecily Stella 'Star' (1904-1995) ceramic designer with the firm (mem Barlaston church). **Clement Tom** (1907-1960) retired from the firm and emigrated to Rhodesia in 1951 (mem in Barlaston church). Clement Tom's son Francis Alan (b1937) joined the firm in 1966. JOSIAH CLEMENT IV's DESCENDANTS. Josiah Clement IV's children include: Helen Bowen (b1895). Rosamund (b1896). Francis Charles Bowen (1898-1959), 2nd Baron Wedgwood of Barlaston, artist (mem Barlaston church). Francis' son appears to have been Hugh Everard (1921-1970), 3rd Baron Wedgwood (mem Barlaston church). **Josiah V** (1899-1968) joined the firm in 1927/8, and served as managing director (1930-1960) and chairman from 1947, from about the 1930s to at least the later 1940s residing at Stoke Grange (see), Stone. He is buried in old Barlaston churchyard. Josiah V's children are John (b1919), Ralph Josiah (b1924), and Jenny (b1927). Camilla Hildegarde (1902-1955), anthropologist (mem in Barlaston church). Elizabeth Julia (b1907). SIR RALPH LEWIS' DESCENDANTS. Sir Ralph Lewis' children include: **Sir John Hamilton** (1907-1989), joined the firm in 1930, deputy chairman from 1955, became 2nd Baron Wedgwood of Etruria in 1956, and retired in 1966. Sir John married Diana Hawkshaw and their children include: H Martin (b1933) who joined the firm in 1947. J Julian (b1936). Oliver (b1940). Germaine Olivia (b1944). Adrian CH (b1948), who drowned at sea in a storm off Sydney Harbour, Australia, in 1974 (mem Barlaston church). Sir John appears to have later married the art historian Pamela Tudor-Craig. Cicely Veronica (1910-1997), biographer and writer, created Dame in 1968 (FWNS pp46-48p). (HOE) (The Story of Wedgwood. Alison Wedgwood. 1962 and 1975) (BAH) (A Personal Life of the Fifth Josiah Wedgwood 1899-1968. John Wedgwood) (Wedgwood. Geoffrey Wills. 1989) (Wedgwood. A Collector's Guide. Peter Williams 1992) (Wedgwood: The New Illustrated Dictionary. Robin Reilly 1995).

Etruria Park Public park at Etruria, opened in 1904 and contains 11 acres (VCH vol 8 p145). The park was presented with a drinking fountain cut in grey stone by Alderman Jesse Shirley. It was first intended that it should be placed in the centre of Howard Place, Shelton. In the rear of the fountain is fixed a thermometer and barometer. Panels made of Wedgwood blue jasper on a background of black basalt are placed either side of the fountain. Whilst the Portland Vase is represented on the fourth side panel. Warrilow writes it was sadly in need of restoration (HOE pp143p,146) (H pp86,87) (PPP p47p).

Etruria Vale Valley of the Fowlea Brook. Etruria village and the North Staffs Infirmary were situated in it.

Etruria Works Former famous pottery works of Josiah Wedgwood I, born at Churchyard House (see). Built because he had outgrown his Burslem factory, the Bell House or Brickhouse Works. Probably it was the first pottery to be anything other than entirely functional in appearance. The original settlement consisting of works (often called Wedgwood Works) and neighbouring purpose-built workers hamlet was complete by 1769 (NSJFS 1965 pp82-84). It was called Etruria, a name thought of by Josiah Wedgwood I after the classical vases, of C8 BC origin, which he so admired from Etruria, an ancient region of Italy, roughly modern Tuscany (SPN p49). In fact, these vases mostly came from Calabria (LGS p137): A Mr Gibson wished he had chosen the name 'Attica' so that Stoke-on-Trent could have been known as 'the Ath-

ens of Great Britain'! (NSFCT 1991 p61). In time the name was also applied to the whole urban area in the vicinity of the original Etruria settlement. The works were built on the Ridge House estate, in Shelton township, which Wedgwood bought in 1766 for £3,000 (NSFCT 1945 p100) or in 1767 (VCH vol 8 p152) (POP p39). A bell to call the workers to work, an innovation from Brickhouse Works, hung above the centre of the pediment on the factory facade, above the clock, and lasted until 1923, when a replica one was made to hang in its place. Previously a horn had been used for the purpose. The original bell is preserved at the new works at the new factory at Wedgwood (see) (HOE pp26,308p of the bell cupola). A windmill for grinding materials had been built at Etruria by 1779 by Erasmus Darwin, who liked to spell Etruria Hetruria, the classical way of spelling the place. A watercolour of the windmill by Stebbing Shaw from 1794 shows a six-sided tower standing behind the range of buildings which fronted onto the canal (HOE p17) (VCH vol 8 p166 il facing) (WBJ pp22-23). The Wedgwoods owned the company well into the C20; by 1900 no potting firm, except theirs, had survived to the third generation (The Journals. Arnold Bennett. May 26 1901). In 1906 a Wedgwood Museum opened at Etruria Works (Wedgwood. Geoffrey Wills. 1989 p112). George VI, when Duke of York, visited the works on May 22 1924 (R&S p46). The firm Josiah Wedgwood & Sons Ltd moved to a new factory at Barlaston in 1939, in an area now (1999) known as Wedgwood (see). The Etruria factory continued in use until June 1950 (The Story of Wedgwood. Alison Kelly 1962 p64), but was sold to the Shelton Iron and Steel Company in 1943. In 1951 the buildings were leased to Dunlop Rubber Company. The Shelton Iron and Steel Company demolished the buildings in 1966 (Wedgwood. Geoffrey Wills. 1989 p113) or 1968 (IAS p190) (MR p176), save for a curious brick round house, which is prominent in a 1794 drawing. Its function has yet to be discovered. Some think it may have been used to grind corn in, the corn being used for packing wares, and that it was made circular as a counter-balance with a bottle oven situated at the other end of the work's main range (IAS p190). It is listed by DoE II* (ROS vol 3 see chapter headed 'The Old Soldier of Etruria') (HOE p24il from a drawing by FW Hulme c1845) (AGT p93il) (BOE p259) (IANS p72p of the Etruria roundhouse) (LLST p166p). Sentinel House, the head office and printing works of ES, was officially opened on the site of the former Etruria Works on Nov 25 1987 by Princess Margaret.

Ettingshall Former village lying near the foot of the Sedgley-Dudley watershed, and liberty 2.5m SSE of Wolverhampton, in the Lower Side division of Sedgley ancient parish (W p195) (HC p42). The manor of Etinghale appears in DB. Later forms are: Etyngh (1291) and Etensall (1555) (SVS p578) (HC pp12,36). The name means 'the hall of the descendants of Eatta' (DUIGNAN) (AMS p440), or 'the corner of land of Etti's people' (SPN p145). Or is from an old English family 'Ettings' who once held the manor of Stow Heath (S&W p332) (HOBLL p2). Partly unexplained (NSJFS 1981 p3). The northern extremities of the old village extended to the Parkfield-Millfields road in the N to the Coppice and Woodsetton in the S, and formerly centred on Lanesfield (HC p2) (LAIW p1). **Edward Elwall** or Elwell, was born at Ettingshall in 1676, the son of a yeoman and nailer Thomas Elwall. He moved to Wolverhampton in his early twenties and became an iron manufacturer. He was a Unitarian by strong conviction and issued religious tracts opposing the Trinitarian doctrine of the Anglican and Roman Catholic churches. He is said to have tried to form his own sect called 'Elwallians.' He was prosecuted for heresy and blasphemy at the Stafford Assizes in 1726 before Judge Denton, but conducted his own defence so well that he was acquitted. He later moved to Stafford and then to London, where he died in 1744. Dr Johnson of Lichfield (see) had a low opinion of him; he told Boswell 'My countryman, Elwal, Sir, should have been put in the stocks: a proper pulpit for him; and he'd have had a numerous audience. A man who preaches in the stocks will always have hearers enough' (SR pp73,74) (AMS pp339-341) (SIOT pp33-38) (TTTD p298) (IE pp23-27). **New Village**. White notes that the Wesleyan chapel and some buildings of the old village were brought down by mining subsidence and this instigated the building of the modern suburb known as Ettingshall New Village (see) 1m to the N (HC p2) (LAIW p1). Ettingshall was formed into an ecclesiastical parish in 1837 (GLAUE p411), or in 1841 (LGS p137). It was a ward of Wolverhampton borough by 1982.

Ettingshall Hall Ettingshall. The gambling of Daniel Fellows earned this house, which he either owned or occupied, the name of Hell Hall (PSS p19). It can be perhaps identified with the house Ettingshall Park.

Ettingshall House House with a Georgian style frontage in Highfields Road (formerly Capponfield Road), Ettingshall. It was still standing in c1958 (SDSSOP p43p).

Ettingshall Lane Hamlet in the form of a long street partly in Wolverhampton and Bilston townships in Wolverhampton parish and partly in Sedgley parish. Ettingshall Lane may have been Ettingshall Road, otherwise Hell Lane.

Ettingshall Manor House Lanesfield. Manor Road may have led to it and there is a strong tradition that it was on the site of the 44 Club in Lanesfield. 44 Club has appeared on documents as Rookery Hall (see) and on the 1834 OS map as 'Lane's Hall,' although on the Tithe Survey of 1844 Rookery Hall refers to a large house built just W of Rookery Road. It is likely that Manor Road did lead to the manor house and that it was on a site behind Wood Street (LAIW p1).

Ettingshall New Village Industrial area 1.5m SE of Wolverhampton. Formerly in the manor of Stow Heath, in Bilston chapelry in Wolverhampton ancient parish. Built sometime shortly before the mid C19 in the area around George Street, John Street, and Frost Street (LAIW p1) owing to the old village of Ettingshall having been affected by mining subsidence (W p199). Ettingshall New Village, or known as Ettingshall New Town, extended no further S than the railway bridge on Manor Road (LAIW p1). Ettingshall Road station on the LNW Railway line was opened in 1852 and closed to passengers in 1964 (Wolverhampton Chronicle. Nov 12 1999 p15). The heaviest load carried by British Rail was a 122-foot-long boiler drum, weighing 240 tons, for generating electricity, which was carried from Ettingshall Road to Eggborough, Yorks on June 5 1965 (GBR p137). The church, St Martin, Dixon Street, was built in 1938-1939 (BOE p322).

Ettingshall Park Former medieval deer park in the Ettingshall Park Farm area. Is mentioned in 1291 (HC p12). There was a Thomas Smith of Ettingshall Park in 1575 (HC p38). In the mid C19 Rev JL Petit had a large estate at Ettingshall, which was anciently a park (W p199). The area is now a residential suburb. The church, Holy Trinity, Farrington Road, was built in 1961 (info Rev Alan Jones); an earlier church (of wood?) dedicated to Holy Trinity at Ettingshall was drawn in 1841 by TP Wood (TP Wood's Staffordshire. 1990).

Ettingshall Park House 1m NNE of Sedgley, in Sedgley ancient parish. An earlier house dated back to at least 1552. It was the ancestral home of the Gibbons family and was rebuilt in 1682 by Thomas Gibbons. In the C18 a farmhouse by the name of Ettingshall Park Farm was built on or near the site of the Gibbons' house (HC p79). It was later the seat of the Feredays, ironmasters. On Thanksgiving day (July 7 1814) to celebrate the defeat and exile of Napoleon Mr Fereday and his partners entertained their workforce of some 5,000, with a feast at 100 tables in a field in front of the house at Ettingshall Park at which was consumed 100 barrels of 'Stout Staffordshire Ale,' after having made them first attend church (HOWM p150). The Feredays are said to have been the model for the Farringdons in the novel 'The Farringdons' (1900) by Ellen Thorneycroft Fowler of Woodthorne (see) (PPTP p34). John Turton Fereday (c1785-1849) of Ettingshall Hall (possibly Ettingshall Park) had Ellowes Hall built in 1821 (SNSV vol 2 p27). The farmhouse was still standing in 1956 but was demolished shortly after (SDSSOP p27p).

Extons or Hextons (Farm). House 1.25m NNW of Arley.

Eyeswell Former estate in Eccleshall town. Eyeswell has appeared as Usulwall (1298), Uselwall, Uireswell, Isewall, Isehaul (c1540), Isewell, Iselewall, and Iselwall, and Eyeswell (1900). In 1900 the estate was reduced to a field of four acres (SHC 1900 p82) (LI appendix p172). The name appears to have arisen from a little perennial spring traditionally said to be good for sore eyes. The spring still existed in 1900, and it fed the moat of the old house of Isewall (SHC 1900 p82). The ancient mansion, Isewell Manor, was one of the three burgages in Eccleshall belonging to Roger de Waure in 1225. By marriage Isewell passed from the Waures to a branch of the Swynnertons of Swynnerton in the later C13. It remained with various branches of the Swynnertons up to the C20 (SHC 1900 p82). When it was the seat of Edward Swynnerton ('Wild Swynnerton') in c1590 it was a fortified and moated Tudor house. Iselball, the house of the Swynnertons, was noted by Chetwynd in the C17 (SHC 1914 p57). It was dismantled in c1800 (SAS p15). In the late C19 HE Chetwynd Stapylton wrongly identified Iselwall with Biana (COI p38). Its moated site off Churchfield Road at SJ 82932901 was excavated between 1981 and 1983 (NSFCT 1982 p19) (SASR 1984 pp7-39 plans ils). The same or another house, Eyeswell House (SAS p15), was in this area and the name was preserved in the former Usulwall Street which crossed over the site (ECC pp48-49).

F

Factory Area of Tipton, centred on Factory Road. The name Factory (1851 census) is from the soap factory of Capt James Keir of Hill Top which was situated here. It was founded in 1790 and produced Alkali Soap, Whitelead, Redlead and metal sashes for windows (OH p69) (OS map sheet 67.08). In 1825 Telford rebuilt Factory Bridge carrying the Tipton-Wednesbury road over Brindley's canal. The bridge was removed to the Black Country Museum in 1970 (IAS p203) (TSSOP p56p).

Factory Junction Here Telford's 'New Cut' Birmingham Canal diverges from Brindley's 'Old Cut' Birmingham Canal, N of Tipton Green (MR p331p). It may also go by the name of Old Turn Junction (plaque in photo in Black Country Breaks. Black Country Tourism brochure 2000).

Fairboroughs Farm 1m SSE of Heaton. Formerly in Heaton township in Leek ancient parish. The name means 'fair hills' and was perhaps so called by the monks of Dieulacres Abbey. By 1291 the abbey had a grange here. After the Dissolution the grange estate passed to the Crown and then into secular hands (VCH vol 7 p187).

Fairfields In the approximate position of Newton to the E of Threapwood, Alton (1834 OS map).

Fairoak Small village formerly on the edge or partly in Blore Forest 11.75m NW of Stafford. In the Woodland quarter in Eccleshall parish (W p377). The N end of the village is called Fairoak Green, which is 0.5 acres of common land (OSST 1956-59 p13), another part is called Fairoak Bank (BOV p27). At Greatwood Lodge Farm, Langot Lane, at SJ 765327 is a burial mound, described in 1983 as in good condition and 8-10 feet high (NSFCT 1983 p12). A coffin-shaped Neolithic or Bronze Age axe-hammer was found in a gravel pit near Fairoak (NSJFS 1962 p28. 1964 p21; Gunstone gives the ref SJ 75913881, which is 1.5m NNW of Ashley). Perhaps the same as the Early Bronze Age axe head, Raven says, was found at Fairoak, which went to the Potteries Museum (MR p18). As well as the possible hillfort in nearby Bishop's Wood (see). There may have been a fort on or in the vicinity of Mr RJ Smith's house at Fair Oak Bank. A garden below this is still known as Castle Garden (BOV p27). Fairoak formerly lay in Greatwood Heath (SSE vol 7 1995 p75). A UFO has been sited in the locality (UFO Study p30).

Fair Oak Old oak at approximately SJ 995163 (1834 OS map), 1m W of Fairoak Lodge, Cannock Chase. In the later C17 Plot noted it had a girth of 9.5 yards (NHS p210), so did Willmore (HOWW p15). The tree was the first target at the trials for a new experimental bomb discharger from an air balloon on Nov 28 1846. Mr Warner was the inventor of this offensive flying machine. The Board of Ordnance had given him a grant of £1,300 for trials which were carried out on Cannock Chase. They were carried out in secret in the presence of the Marquis of Anglesey (minus one leg), a Col Chalmer, a Capt Chads, and Lord Ingestre. The tree must have survived, for in the 1930s, Wright noted it had a girth of 30 feet (CCC p64). The tree gives its name to this area of Cannock Chase. A hollow here is the remains of Sir William Paget's iron workings in the C16 (SL p105).

Fairoak Grange House 1m NW of Fairoak. To the N of it is the source of the Sow.

Fairoak House House 1.75m SW of Rugeley. In 1952 at SK 039167 near Fair Oak House was found a stone axe of rock of the Neolithic or Bronze Age (BAST vol 73 p118) (NSJFS 1964 p17). Sarah Hopkins moved from Fair Oak House (then 'The Forge') to Stone House in 1808 (VCH vol 5 p158).

Fairoak Knoll Small hill behind the terraced houses in Fairoak village centre, at SJ 764326. The top has been quarried. Druids reputedly were active on the summit in ancient times and the 'sort of tablerock' on the summit has been considered a druid's altar (BPS p79) (BOV pp27,33il of Fairoak Lowe) (MR pp17-18,20p) (ROT p11p) (SMM p161p). Has also appeared as Fairoak Lowe.

Fairoak Lodge House 2.75m WSW of Rugeley, on Cannock Chase. The name is from the tree called Fair Oak? (CCBO pp42,69).

Fairoak Rivulet Rises W of Broughton church and runs to Fairoak where it falls underground (the only stream or river in the county to do so, apart from the Hamps and Manifold, to Plot's knowledge). It is visible under a flat stone at Blore Pipe, but unlike the other two rivers it will never travel above ground again (NHS p89).

Fairview House at Church Hill, Brierley Hill. Stands above and adjoining a house called Church Hill House. Here Caleb William Roberts Jnr, second son of Caleb William Roberts of the local industrial company Roberts and Cooper, died in 1923. The house, a Victorian-looking villa, still (1998) stands (TB Feb 1998 p6).

Fair View House nearly 1.5m S of Onecote. Formerly in Onecote township in Leek ancient parish. So called by 1873. By 1901 it was the residence of Ralph de Tunstall Sneyd (1867-1947), only son and heir of John William Sneyd (b1822) of Basford Hall (see) and of Park House, Consall (County Biographies: Staffordshire. Frederick B Ludlow. 1901; Ralph was born in 1862) (VCH vol 7 p212). Tunstall Sneyd was a poet and eccentric, and after being disinherited for marrying against his father's wishes he and his wife came to live here (SVB pp133-134). From at least the 1930s Tunstall Sneyd became interested in druidism and was a seeker of the Holy Grail (SMM p40p). He took part in religious ceremonies in Thor's Cave (see) and in a ghost hunt on Butterton Moor (see). He had in his collection at Fair View certainly by the 1930s the mummies of Egyptian pharaoh Ptolemy II Philadelphus (ruled 285-246 BC) and Syrian King Antiochus II. They were kept in a chapel at the back of the house (ES April 29 2000 p3p of Tunstall Sneyd). According to Tom Henshall (owner of Fair View since Ralph's son's departure in 1977) Ralph is buried in the new Onecote Cemetery: He had wanted to be buried at Fair View, no doubt, in some strange splendour. The perimeter wall round the grounds of the house, with towers and battlements, was built by Tunstall Sneyd as protection against expected enemy attack during WW1. In the 1930s? (info Tom Henshall) he built a Druid temple in a roofless stone outhouse to the N of the house consisting of an altar and circular dais in the centre, and created a megalithic chambered tomb in the garden W of the house. The latter is 20 feet long. Long six-sided raised rods are enclosed on the long sides by bollards, probably these were used once as corn sack props. The ends are circular stone walls (VCH vol 7 p212).

Fair View Horton Bank, N of Rudyard, on W side of Rudyard Lake. House built by John Munro of Tain, near Inverness 1879/80 (RL p27). It became a home for the mentally ill in 1988 and was enlarged in 1991 (VCH vol 7 p68).

Fairyland Cave At Cotwalton. Perhaps in Cotwalton Drumble.

Falconer's Bath Two bath-houses on N side of Stowe Pool, Lichfield, at SK 119310077. Built by Canon James Falconer (1737-1809) in about the 1780s (VCH vol 14 p107). The water would have been less frigid than the baths at Unite Well (see) at Abnalls. It was out of fashion by the mid C19. The foot-path 'Stowe Pool Walk' now crosses the site (SSAHST 1970 p51) (Lichfield Mercury Feb 17 1826).

Falcon Farm On the E side of the Kinver Road, 1m SSE of Enville, in Enville ancient parish. Or Upper Falcon Farm and had been built by 1688 (VCH vol 20 p93).

Falcon Low Wetton. Burial mound at SK 104532, on summit of Old Park Hill.

Falcon Low Cave Falcon Low. Wetton. Excavated in 1958, which disclosed a sepulchral cave probably of Neolithic origin containing skeletons of six people and animals (NSJFS 1962 p33) thought to be of Neolithic origin (British Caving. CHD Cullingford. 1962 p320) (NSJFS 1964 p41) (WOY p1). The cave had been blocked with boulders and covered with earth (MR p330).

Faling Brook Rises E of Leek. Runs past Lowe Hill. Fisher suggested that it was the medieval name for Cartledge Brook (DA - Michael Fisher's MA Thesis 1969) (NSJFS 1970 p85).

Fall, The House 1m WSW of Biddulph parish church. Formerly in Lower Biddulph liberty in Biddulph ancient parish. The Cotton family were at The Fall by 1500 (BALH p25). Falls Colliery in the Akesmoor Lane area of Gillow Heath, Biddulph (ONST 1975 p365), may have been in existence by 1808 and certainly by 1834 (BALH pp66,67).

Fallings Heath Suburb 0.75m E of Darlaston, covering the area of Walsall Road between Butcroft and James Bridge (SNDB p48). In Wednesbury ancient parish. The name means 'the dwelling of the heathen descendants of Farl, outside the later fortified and Christianised Wednesbury' (WAM p9). Or a name indicating the felling of trees (TWDOP p139) and representing the edge of Cannock Forest (SNDB p48).

Faln Gate Until the late C18 this was that part of the Walsall Road, Darlaston (Offlow hundred), on either side of its junction with Heath Road and Sparrows Forge Lane (now Park Lane, Wednesbury). Faln is a medieval word relating to the felling of trees and 'gate' in this instance is from Middle English 'gata' meaning street, giving 'street made by the felling of trees' (SNDB pp49-50).

Fanlizard Lane Runs W from the Manorhouse Farm at Cowley, near Gnosall. The name is a curiosity. The lizard has reference to some old fort on the high ground stretching S to High Onn. (See Lizard Hill). The word 'fan' slope, declivity, occurs in an Irish hymn in praise of St Brigit. The name refers to the slope leading up to some old fortified enclosure on these hills (NSFCT 1908 p142). Or the name may be from some spread-out shape reminiscent of a lizard (SPNO pp159-160).

Far Brook Tributary of the Dane. The name is self-explanatory (SPNO p10).

Farcroft Large, white Regency-style house on Sandwell Road, Handsworth. The house is shown on a map of 1922. It eventually became the site of Farcroft Housing Estate, built by Birmingham Corporation (HPPE pp29-30). The name is preserved in Farcroft Road and Grange.

Farewell Ancient parish and tiny village on upland above Bilson Brook 12.5m SE of Stafford. The name means 'the fair, or clear spring' (DUIGNAN). Or '(place at) the beautiful or pleasant stream' (SSE 1996 p13) (SPN p49). There is a strong spring on the W side of the church, said to have been opened or utilised in c800 (info from a local farmer). The parish church, St Bartholomew, SE of Farewell Hall, was formerly Farewell Priory church, and retains a fragment of mid C12 work, but was mainly rebuilt in 1745 (BOE p131) (CHMS2 p46). Has appeared as Fagerwell (1200), Faierwell (1200), Faurewell (1251) (SPN p49) (SSE 1996 p13), Fairweld, Faurwell, Fagrowell, and Fagereswell (HOL p283 note). It is more correctly spelt 'Fairwell' (CCBO p58). In fact, says Masefield, the spelling 'Farewell' is fatuous (LGS p137). At Farewell was possibly a medieval village, since depopulated and lost (SSAHST 1970 p35). Farewell parish was, from 1527, a peculiar jurisdiction of the dean and chapter of Lichfield cathedral until peculiar jurisdictions were abolished in 1846 (VCH vol 3 p93) (GLAUE p411). In the late C18 Shaw noted there was a couple of Farewell who lived to the age of 170. Whether he meant they had each arrived at that age, or together their ages computed to 170? (SHOS vol 1 p230).

Farewell Hall Late C17 house overlooking Farewell church (BOE p131). In one of the parlour windows is cut with a diamond, 'Humphrey Wightwick at New Romney in Kent, 5 August 1749' (SHOS vol 1 p230).

Farewell Priory Former priory in Farewell village. There was a hermitage here before the religious house, probably associated with a spring (VCH vol 3 p136). A Benedictine nunnery founded by Bishop Roger de Clinton in c1140 (CHMS p31). Dedicated to St Mary. The nuns received a charter from Henry II probably in 1155 (VCH vol 3 pp222-225). In the 1527 Wolsey suppressed the priory and the property was given to the choristers of Lichfield cathedral (SOSH p172) (LGS p138) (VCH vol 3 pp222-225) (SL p95) (HOS 1998 p58). During its total demolition in 1747 (CCBO p58) a number of curious earthen vessels were found in the S wall. They were six feet below ground and several feet from each other. They were in three ranges, and were in varying sizes. The vessels were laid on their sides, the mouth towards the inside of the church, and were sealed with a thin coat of plaster. One of the vessels went to Greene's Museum in Lichfield (GM 1771 see pl A fig 14) (SHOS vol 1 pp230,231) (CCBO pp30,31, 32,58). The chancel of c1300 origin (BOE p131), now used as part of the parish church, is all that is left of the priory. (GNHS p153) (GNHSS p25) (ES Aug 21 1931 p8 about an NSFC field trip made to the priory and church).

Fargelow House 0.75m ESE of Alton.

Far Green Old tiny hamlet of Hanley (OTP p138). The name is preserved in Far Green Industrial Estate. This area on the 1834 OS map is Upper Green. So was probably another name for Upper Green.

Far Hoarcross Small hamlet 0.5m S of Hoar Cross or 0.5m SE of Hoar Cross Hall. Appears as Hoar Cross Gate on 1834 OS map.

Far House House 0.75m NW of Upper Hulme, S of Windygates. Formerly in Leekfrith township in Leek ancient parish. There may have been a house on the site of the present C17 house by the earlier C16 (VCH vol 7 p194).

Farley Small village on high ground with a deep ravine to the N formed by a Hole Brook tributary and the Churnet Valley to the S, 1.5m SSE of Cotton. Former township in Alton ancient parish. The name means 'the fern or ferny, lea' (DUIGNAN), or 'glade where ferns are found' (SSE 1996 p13) (SPN p34). Farley was probably a named place by 950 AD (HAF p37). Waste at Fernelege appears in DB. Farley appears to have held separate wakes to Alton (HAF p304). Farley became a separate civil parish in 1866 (GLAUE p411). For Prince Charles at Farley see Wootton, Ellastone.

Farley Tiny hamlet about the A51, 0.75m S of Hixon. In Colwich parish. Mary, Queen of Scots, is said to have travelled from Chartley to Tixall via Farley (HV p10).

Farley Hall Farley near Cotton. The Farley estate passed to Richard Bill of Norbury, Derbys by marriage in 1607. The original hall was built in c1609. Extensive alterations were made to the hall in 1784. The large semi-circular glasshouse with a domed-roof was added to the hall in the mid C19 (ACOPP p68p). The Bills lived here to 1957 (HAF p81). It was at some time a youth hostel (NSFCT 1945 p93). It was the residence of Anthony Bamford, Managing Director of JCB in 1988 (MR p149p).

Farley Park Public park in Whitehall Road, New Town, West Bromwich, presented by Alderman Farley in 1890 (SHWB 13) (WBOPP pl 86) or in 1891, and extended in 1955 (VCH vol 17 p9).

Far Low Mound or burial mound at Waterfall. It has been investigated (WOY p1). Presumably on or near Far Hill. Is 21 paces in diameter. Excavated by Carrington in 1849. A young person's skeleton was found in the framework, an ox rib bone, a skeleton with a food vessel and nine flint implements (TYD pp132-133) (VCH vol 1 no 19) (BAP vol 1 p158 fig 175) (DAJ vol 75 pp108,110. vol 77 p26, B3) (NSJFS 1965 p52). Food vessels of the Beaker people, of the Yorkshire type, have been found in it (NSJFS 1962 p33).

Farmer's Fold Tiny street between John's Lane and Victoria Street, Wolverhampton (WAIW vol 3 p). Remnant of Wolverhampton's involvement in the wool trade.

Farmoor 1m WNW of Butterton (Moorlands). Appears to have been formerly known as Foxholes (1834 OS map).

Farthing Hall Prouds Lane, Bilston (TB Oct 7 1999 p27).

Far Things Is a house 1.25m N of Arley. Marked on OS map 1:25,000. Near the Shropshire border.

Fastings (Dower's map). Fastings Coppice is 1m W of Upper Arley.

Fatherless Barn Former farm at Colley Gate, Cradley. Now the name for an housing estate (BTBC p41p of the farm). Fatherless Barn Colliery stands on a prominent ridge N of Wassel Grove (the locale of Cold Harbour in Francis Young's novels) (BCWJ p11) (History Around Us. Halesowen. John Billingham).

Fatholme House 1.75m NE of Wychnor. There was a Neolithic circular wooden henge at Fatholme consisting of a number of concentric circles of large upright timbers (NSJFS 1964 p15) (HOS 1998 p24). A Saxon settlement was found at nearby Cat Holme. The name is from, probably, an island here created by the Trent and one of its cuts; holme being the Norse word for island.

Fauld (*Fold*). Small village on the northern incline to the Needwood Forest plateau, 0.75m NE of Hanbury. Formerly in Hanbury township and ancient parish. The name means 'a fold, farm-yard' (DUIGNAN) (SSE 1996 p13) (SPN p57). The manor of Felede appears in DB. Later Fauld appears as Faulde and Felde (W p560). Fauld once had a church (HOU p340). Fauld is one of

the few places in the country where alabaster and gypsum could be extracted (NSFCT 1892 pp112-114).

Fauld Crater Man-made crater, 0.5m S of Fauld created by the largest single explosion of WW2, before atom bombs (GLS p45), the UK's worst explosion disaster by 1965 (GBR 1965 p236), and the world's biggest non-nuclear explosion (LTD p159). In 1938 the RAF opened an underground gypsum mine in Stonepits Hills for ammunition storage (the later RAF Maintenance Unit No. 21). At 11.10am on Monday 27 Nov 1944 a technician accidentally set some 3000 to 4000 tons of ammunition off using a hammer of brass or copper (SSE 1988 p58) (LTD p158) (NSFCT 1991 p54) (GLS p45). The subsequent explosion killed some 70-81 people; 62 are said to have been from Hanbury (GBR 1965 p236) (MR p173) (SSE 1988 p58) (GLS p45). It obliterated one farmhouse (Upper Castle Hayes Farm) and damaged another (Hanbury Fields Farm), so that it had to be demolished. It wrecked the Cock Inn, Hanbury, and Hanbury village hall, and made the spire of Christ Church, Burton upon Trent, so unsafe it had to be taken down. It destroyed much of Brown's Coppice and Queen's Purse Wood along the bluff of Stonepits Hill (SSE 1988 pp58-59) (ESNF p53p of the old Cock Inn, or also known as the Fighting Cock). It was heard at many places throughout England (including Sheffield, the Humber, the Wash, and London), and the seismic waves transmitted through the upper portions of the earth's crust were detected at West Bromwich, Kew, Stoneyhurst and Oxford. On the Continent the explosion was recorded at Puy de Dome Observatory, France, in Switzerland, Belgium, Geneva and Rome (GLS p45). It has created the present 800-1000 feet long, 300 feet wide, and 100-150 feet deep (SSE 1988 p58) (GLS p45) (SVB p88). Hanbury people have long wished the area an official war grave, since some bodies have never been recovered; more than 10 weeks passed before the body search was abandoned. The dead are remembered in Memorial Hall, Hanbury, where they are listed within an alabaster frame (SVB p89) (NSFCT 1991 p54), by an Italian granite memorial erected at the edge of the crater in 1990 (COS pp36,37p), and by two makeshift crosses created out of alabaster rubble at the bottom of the crater (SSE 1988 p57 fig 7); only one could be seen in 1995. (UTR pp136-9) (MMM pp65-68) (VB pp96,97) (STMSM Jan 1975 p18 p of) (SL p260, pl 42) (SSE 1988 pp54-76 ils ps) (The Guardian. Weekend Section. March 11 1989 pp2-3) (TB Aug 1994 p19p) (SN Nov 25 1994 p9p of a good aerial view) (Sunday Telegraph. Nov 27 1994. Review Section p1p of a good aerial view) (Saga Magazine. Jan 1995 pp43-45 ps and aerial view in 1950).

Fauld Gate Former entry into Needwood Forest approximately 0.75m NNW of Hadley End (VCH vol 2 p350 see map). The name no longer prevails.

Fauld Hall House 0.5m NE of the British Gypsum mine at Fauld. The same or an earlier Fauld Hall was the seat of William Burton (d1645), author of History of Leicestershire, and elder brother of the famous Robert Burton, author of the 'Anatomy of Melancholy' since 1604. Some have asserted that Robert was born at Fauld (Plot was shown the house where he was reputedly born). But it has been asserted that the Burton brothers were born at Lindly, Leics (NHS p276) (SHOS vol 1 pp78,79) (SOS p xliv il) (GNHS p146) (HOU p340) (BS p91) (LGS p143) (SH p16). Some beautiful woodwork for the interior of the new part of Caverswall Castle was taken from Fauld Hall after 1890 (NSFCT 1937 pp49-61). A house known as Fauld Hall was occupied by Sir Ian and Lady Ley in 1999 (Daily Telegraph. July 24 1999. p24 see weddings).

Fauld Manor Known locally as The Manor, situated at the entrance to the British Gypsum mine. Built in 1903. Some of the roof timbers are of 1680, but where they came from is not known (MR p174p).

Favourite House Name for the commercial premises of Robert Smith (d1956), born in Great Bridge in 1869, a Darlaston (Offlow hundred) shop keeper, philanthropist and character, known for his catchword 'favourite' which he applied to his many ventures and multitude of goods. In the 1890s he moved to James Bridge, probably to 39 Station Street, where he was a hairdresser by 1904. That year he is said to have built Favourite House in Church Street, Darlaston, and by 1908 he had moved to the Favourite House. Here he stayed until at least 1940, employed as a hairdresser, picture framer and general dealer; his Favourite Motor Trip Club ran trips to Brewood, Kinver, Bridgnorth and Bewdley. Favourite House was converted into flats in 1990 (trade directories) (VB pp50-51) (TB March 1982 p17p. Jan 1986 p4) (MMBCC pp96p-101) (SNDB pp33-34).

Fawfieldhead Tiny hamlet on moorland hills to the S of Oakenclough Brook 1.25m WSW of Longnor. Formerly in Longton chapelry and a township in Alstonefield ancient parish (W p743) (LGS p138). The township was covered by Malbonck Forest in medieval times (VCH vol 7 p5). The first part of the name 'Faw' is probably Old English 'fah' meaning 'variegated' (SSAHST 1967 p34). A house at Fawfieldhead in the early C15 presumably stood in the present hamlet. In the earlier 1630s the hamlet was also known as Fawfieldgreen (VCH vol 7 p28). Often known since 1679 as 'Fairfieldhead' (Plot's map) but has now reverted to its oldest known form (SSAHST 1967 p34). Fawfieldhead was the largest township in Alstonefield and included Fawfieldhead, Hulme End, Newtown, Reaps Moor, Wigginstall (W p743), and Beresford in a detached portion in Alstonefield township which was transferred to Alstonefield civil parish in 1934 (VCH vol 7 p27). Fawfieldhead became a separate civic parish in 1866 (GLAUE p411). There is a church at Newtown (see). In Longnor churchyard is a stone to the memory of William Billinge, born in 1679, who fought at the capture of Gibraltar in 1704, at Ramillies in 1706, and in the rebellions of 1715 and 1745. He died in 1791 aged 112 (LGS p180). He was allegedly born in a cornfield near Fawfieldhead and died within 150 yards of the same spot (W p744). He is reputed to have been the last surviving private who fought under the Duke of Marlborough, and is said with others to have saved the Duke's life at Ramillies (NSFCT 1908 p195. 1949 p118). A new stone was made for his grave in 1903 (VB pp206-207). (SMC p172) (GNHS p101) (WTCEM p76) (L pp8p,16,56) (STM April 1967 pp30p,31) (MMM pp39-41) (MR p217) (PDS&C p52p) SMOPP vol 2 p103) (COS pp5p,6p) (SMML pp79-82).

Fawley 0.75m S of Rowley (Hamstall Ridware). Marked on 1905 OS map.

Fawside Tiny hamlet, if not a single house, 0.75m W of Longnor. Formerly in Heathylee township in Alstonefield ancient parish. There were houses here by c1420 (VCH vol 7 p33).

Fawside Edge Minute hamlet 1.5m W of Longnor, or 0.75m S of Hollinsclough. In Alstonefield ancient parish. An Oxford V 3626 aircraft crashed at Fawside Edge on Nov 16 1941. The pilot, who was alone, was killed (MD p44).

Fazeley Large village 22.25m SE of Stafford, by the Tame, on Watling Street. Former township in Tamworth ancient parish (W p625). The **name** has appeared as Faresleia (c1142), Farisleia (C12), and Faresleye (1335) (SHOS vol 1 p433) (SSE 1996 p13) (SPN p49). It is from Anglo-Saxon 'fearr' meaning a bull, ox. So 'the bull's (or ox) pasture' (DUIGNAN) (SSE 1996 p13) (SPN pp49-50). Shaw thought it might be from the fair meadow; Fazeley is situated in what may be described as a fair meadow (SHOS vol 1 p433). Ralph Basset of Drayton was granted a charter on Aug 5 1335 to hold a **market** here on Mondays. The market had probably lapsed by 1387 (NSJFS 1971 pp51,53). There was no market in 1792 (OWEN), but there was one in 1888 (LHE p265). Fazeley was once noted for its **fairs**. The charter of 1335 granted a fair (NSJFS 1971 pp51,53). The 'Goose' Fair was held for four days from the Feast of St Michael (Oct 10). Three other fairs were established in 1795, one being on April 1 (for cattle) (SHOS vol 1 pp421, 433). Owen and Whitaker's Almanac gives the Monday after Oct 10 (for cattle) as one of the fairs. Owen lists March 21 (for Cattle), second Monday in Feb, last Monday in June (for wool), and second Monday in Dec as the other fairs (SCSF pp98,99). There was a fair in 1792 (OWEN), and there was one in 1888 (LHE p265). Fazeley formed into an ecclesiastical parish in 1813 (GLAUE p411), refounded in 1842 (LGS p138). **From 1790** Fazeley became a junction of The Birmingham and Fazeley and Coventry Canals and on this account Sir Robert Peel (1750-1830) built the largest of his cotton mills here in the late C18 (BOE p132) (SL p116) (MR p149); producing ribbon? (VB p29). One, at the end of Mill Lane by the canal, known as the Old Mill from 1851, survives. It is now owned by William Tolson Ltd (IAS p168) (MR p130). Peel expanded the then hamlet of Fazeley with model housing for his workers and there was a significant growth in population for Shaw to note it at the end of the C18. A terrace of houses, of costly design, in Mill Lane was fireproof by the use of brick roof-vaults and floors. It is probably the first fireproof housing in the country (SHOS vol 1 p433) (Post-Medieval Archaeology vol 6. 1972. pp191-197) (SL p116). The last of these houses was demolished in 1972 (IAS p168). Subsequently, Peel took an interest in affairs of the village. In 1825 a child fell from a window at a Fazeley inn and was miraculously unharmed. Sir Robert Peel related the story to his wife in a letter (KES p97). In 1839 boatmen who had murdered Christina Collins at Hoo Mill (see) were captured on the canal at Fazeley by police (MMM p30) (MMMR p65). The **church**, St Paul, on the W side of Coleshill Street, was built in 1853-1855 (BOE p131). The wake was on the first Sunday after old Michaelmas day in the C19 (W p625) (THM vol 6 p31). Fazeley became a separate civil parish in 1866 (GLAUE p411). A **WW2** concrete pillbox is situated on the edge of the Coventry Canal near the aqueduct over the Tame at SK 209022. It was made to be disguised as a canal shed (WMARCH 1993 p35). Fazeley features in a derisory rhyme about Tamworth (see).

Featherstone Large modern village on the slopes of a low hill overlooking a tributary of Saredon Brook 11.5m S of Stafford. Former out-township in Wolverhampton ancient parish, Seisdon hundred, and yet is in Cuttlestone

hundred (VCH vol 4 p61).
900 to 1800. A charter was made of the bounds of Hilton and Featherstone (SL p62), when the estate was given by Lady Wulfrun to the monastery of Wolverhampton in 994 (HOWM p14). Appears in the C10 as Feorther(e)stan (SSE 1996 p13). Later appears as Federestan (1186), Fetherstan (1280-90), Fetherstone (1294) (SPNO pp122-3). The name means 'feader's stone,' 'feader' being Anglo-Saxon for father, although it was also a somewhat common personal name (DUIGNAN). Or from a four-stone monolith or tetralith, 'feoder-stan' (OAKDEN) (SSE 1996 p13). Featherstone was one of the seven prebends of Wolverhampton Collegiate Church (W p82); it was first named as such in 1291 (VCH vol 3 p324). In his flight after the battle of Worcester (1651) Charles II is said to have walked alone from Featherstone to Moseley Old Hall after being escorted so far by the Penderells as it was considered safer for him to travel the last stretch alone (info Mark Whittaker). Others say he made the journey to Moseley on foot from Pendeford Mill (Moseley Old Hall. National Trust Guide. RA Chand. 1993). At Featherstone were found some transparent stones like crystals (NHS p175).
1800 to PRESENT. Featherstone became a separate civil parish in 1866 (GLAUE p411). The small hamlet, centred on the junction of Featherstone Lane and the present New Road, expanded to a large village, from the mid 1920s after the opening of Hilton Main Colliery; thereafter there was expansion eastwards from the old centre to the Cannock Road (Wolverhampton Chronicle. June 4 1999 p21. Dec 31 1999 p29). In 1940 the Royal Ordnance built a factory on a site at Featherstone partly occupied by Courtaulds. The factory was still producing weapons in the early 1980s (Nostalgic Wolverhampton. 1999). By the late C20 Featherstone was a ward in Featherstone civil parish. **Persons.** In 1982 **Anne Kelsall**, whilst in a car on New Road, 500 yards from HM Prison Featherstone, was helped to see her way through a wall of fog by powerful lights on a vehicle behind her; mysteriously, this vehicle did not emerge from the fog (MS&S pp63-64). **Jack Atherton** achieved 1052 repetitions of his bodyweight (133.4 lb) in one hour by bench press-ups on April 1 1988 at HM Prison Featherstone (GBR 1989 p307). Twin sisters, **Jayne and Jodie Scrivens**, aged 12, On Sept 11 1998 were tragically killed in a collision with a car in Brookhouse Lane. The girls were cycling home to Bushbury after visiting a friend in Featherstone. In late Jan 2000 there were wreaths and a memorial to their memory by the site of the accident placed by relatives and friends (The News (Wolverhampton) March 4 1999 p7).

Fegg Hayes Small district over 2m NNE of Burslem. In Wolstanton ancient parish.

Feiashill Feiashill Farm Cottages are 0.5m SSW of Trysull. In Trysull parish. Fiershill Farm, in existence by 1722 (Yates' map) (VCH vol 20 p 187), is to the S of the cottages. Has appeared as Feirshill (1834 OS map), and Fearshill (SGSAS).

Fell Brook Runs from Townsend, Bucknall to the Trent near the present of Howard Crescent (OS map 1890).

Fellows' Farm Stood at the bottom of Rough Lane (unlocated), Woodsetton. It has also been called Fosters' Farm. It still stood in the 1960s but had been demolished by 1997 (SDSSOP p25p).

Fellows Park Name of Walsall Football Club ground, on the E side of Hillary Street, Pleck. The park was the ground of Walsall FC from 1896 to 1990. It has been known as Fellows Park since at least 1931. The name is from HL Fellows, chairman of the club in 1931 (VCH vol 17 p253) (local info).

Felthouse 2m SW of Grindon.

Felthouse Common and Wood. 1.25m S of Cheddleton. There is a medieval cross at SJ 976504 (NSFCT 1982 p23) or at SJ 977505 (CVH p154) at the point where the old road from Folly Lane to the Boat Inn crosses the old road known as Felthouse Lane which ran over the Common from the main road near Prospect House towards Consall village. Its height above ground is 35 cm. The general shape is of a lozenge with major axis approximately 150 cm. It was probably erected by the monks of Dieulacres Abbey and served as a landmark for travellers. It may be on an old way, that may follow the Roman road from Blythe Bridge to Buxton (NSFCT 1982 pp23-24) or at SJ 977505 (CVH p154) (HOLS p210).

Feltysitch House 3m N of Onecote, to the E of the source of the Hamps (NSFCT 1908 p133. 1927 pp101-102). Formerly in Onecote township in Leek ancient parish. The house is probably of the earlier C19 (VCH vol 7 p212). See Horesych.

Fens, The A low-lying area NW of the ridge that carries the main road from Brierley Hill to Dudley. Appears on Yates' map (SNSV vol 1 p117). The area appears to have covered a part of the boundary of Dudley and Kingswinford ancient parishes.

Fens Branch of the Stourbridge Canal. Spurs off the Stourbridge Canal at Leys

Junction. Ran to Fens Crescent. Sanction of closure was given to the N end in 1935 and to the S end in 1960 (HCMS No. 2).

Fens Pool Canal feeder (BHOP2 p106), 1m N of Brierley Hill. Fens Reservoirs appears on A Plan of the intended Extension of the Dudley Canal into the Birmingham Canal by John Snape 1785. The pool has one of the largest populations of Great Crested Newt in the UK and because of this it has been designated a SSSI (The Countryside in Dudley. Dudley Planning & Leisure).

Fenton Potteries town on a bank above a tributary of Cockster Brook, in the federated city of Stoke-on-Trent, 13.25m N of Stafford. Formerly in Stoke-upon-Trent chapelry and ancient parish. In 1900 a part of a **tusk of a mammoth** found in a Fenton marl pit (STM April 1963 p28). In Brighton Museum is a polished **prehistoric axe**, perhaps found on a footpath called 'Ritings' or 'Rytens' through Fenton Glebe Colliery (NSJFS 1962 p30. 1964 p34). The battle of Fethanleag 584 AD in which the British were defeated by the Angles may have taken place at Fenton Culvert in the vicinity of the field called Groaning Meadows. Tradition says the dying lay here groaning for days and nights after the battle (RHPS pp21-22). The **name** means 'the settlement by the marsh' (DUIGNAN) (POP p101) (MR p149). Or 'tun or farmstead by a fen' (SSE 1996 p13) (SPN p116) (BNDA p3). Or is a Norman corruption of the Celtic 'Fethan-leag,' forest (RHPS p21). The manor of Fentone (later Fenton Vivian) is recorded in DB. In the earlier C13 the tenant held the manor of the king on condition he pay a fee and perform guard duties at Newcastle Castle. The manor had many successive tenants but from at least the earlier C13 until at least 1650 overlordship descended with Newcastle manor (VCH vol 8 p211) (SCSF p116). By the C18 Fenton was a collection of separate villages - Great Fenton, Little Fenton, Lane Delph, Lower Lane (later known as Church Fenton), The Foley, and Whieldon's Grove (VCH vol 8 p207) employed in making pottery. The **church**, Christ Church, Albert Square, was dedicated on Jan 11 1839 (Christ Church, Fenton. Rev AH Yates. 1988), and was rebuilt or altered in 1891 (LDD). Fenton became an ecclesiastical parish in 1841 (W p236) (LGS p138) (GLAUE p411), or in 1860 (CAST p57) (VCH vol 8 p188). Perhaps in protest at not receiving incorporation Fenton adopted an **unofficial arms** in c1840. The arms - A device containing inter alia two vases (CH p330) - are not recognised by the College of Arms (SHST pp277,280il). Fenton was created an urban district in 1894. It was one of the Six Towns which federated in 1910 to form Stoke-on-Trent. Arnold Bennett, the novelist, neglects to mention it in any of his novels, which upset the inhabitants. An **amusing incident** occurred in Aug 1936 when a cow came to the Sunday morning service at the Temple Street Methodist Church and preened itself in front of a mirror in the vestry before being driven out (ES Aug 25 1936 p9). There is an **underground passage** connecting two old inns. It leads from Park Street to the main Fenton-Longton road. It is about 30 yards long (ES Feb 8 1938 p1 ps). A **UFO** was seen in the day from Fenton on June 19 1967 (FSRP p5). **Persons.** The 'Great Bazaar' at Fenton in 1897 was attended by the Prince and Princess of Wales (Christ Church, Fenton. Rev AH Yates. 1988). **Frank Bough**, television sports presenter, was born in Tirley Street on Jan 15 1933 (Cue Frank. Frank Bough. 1980) (ES Aug 24 1994 p20p). **Reginald Mitchell**, Spitfire designer, born Butt Lane (see), served his apprenticeship with Kerr-Stewart, locomotive builders, at Fenton (info Ron Balding). **Michael Bettaney** (b1950), spy, was brought up in Wileman Street. He attended Chell Junior High School, Longton High School 1961-1968, and joined MI5 in 1974. He was jailed for 23 years for spying for the KGB in 1984 and released in May 1998 (ES May 13 1998 p1. May 14 1998 p19).

Fenton Culvert The southern and later manor of Fenton as opposed to Fenton Vivian. Fenton Culvert manor may have been in existence by the late C12 (VCH vol 8 p212) (MR p149). Former township in Stoke-upon-Trent chapelry and ancient parish (W p236) and has also appeared as Great Fenton (HBST p535). The name Culvert means Coward (NSFCT 1888 p70). (FF p14). The name referred to an area mainly S of City Road and included the present town including the church and Town Hall, with Heron Cross, Great Fenton, Lane Delph and Mount Pleasant (NSFCT 1986 p12) (NSSG p19). Fenton Culvert and Vivian manors were made into one in 1839 (SOSH p292).

Fenton Green A ward of Stoke-on-Trent district by 1991 covering the Fenton Park, Fenton Low and Adderley Green areas.

Fenton Hall Lay to W of Fenton Manor, to the N of City Road, Fenton, in extensive grounds. A house on or near the site, known as Fenton Hall, was owned by Simon Degge in 1719. In the C18 and C19 it had these owners or tenants: William Cotton of Crakemarsh (1734-35); Thomas Braode (1735-42); John Peate (1742-48); Thomas Whieldon (1748-1810); Robert Hamilton (1810-17); William Adams, potter, (1824-27); Lewis Adams (1834-); Michael Daintry Hollins (1846-) (VCH vol 8 pp207,209,213). During Whieldon's occupancy the hall became known as Whieldon's Hall (FF p53);

by 1810 it was known as Little Fenton Hall (VCH vol 8 p213); when tenanted by the potter William Adams (1772-1829), who may have been in occupation after moving from Cliff Bank House, Stoke-upon-Trent, in 1819, it was known as Fenton House (NSF). The hall was demolished in 1847 when the railway was being built (F p70) (VCH vol 8 pp207,209). Morland suggests the Sixth Form College was built on the site of Fenton Hall (POP pp103-104), but according to Talbot and others it was built on the site of Fenton Manor.

FENTON HALL WORKS. As well as pottery works at Fenton Low, Thomas Whieldon, the occupant of the hall between 1748 and 1810, also had from 1748 works in part of, or by, the hall, hence the Fenton Hall Works (NSFCT 1968 p118) (MR p149). From 1754 to 1759 he was in partnership with Josiah Wedgwood I. The site of the works was excavated in 1969 by Stoke-on-Trent Museum Archaeological Society and a biscuit butter tub surmounted by a cow was found (HSP pp29,67,156) (SSW p67) (H p50) (HOE pp58,111,291,293) (S p120) (SOSH p264) (ES May 19 1930 pp8-9) (TOI pp41-44) (NSJFS 1968 p118) (STM Jan 1970 p35) (VCH vol 8 p218) (FF pp53,54) (POTP p228).

Fenton Hall Just W of present Heron Cross (1834 OS map). This was Great Fenton Hall (see).

Fenton House Approached from Glebedale Road, S of Victoria Place, Fenton. Probably built in c1800. Once belonged to the partners and brothers-in-laws Ralph Bourne and William Baker. Used by William Meath Baker at least until 1896. It became Christ Church vicarage in the 1920s and in the 1960s was converted into a china factory (VCH vol 8 p210).

Fenton Low 0.5m N of Victoria Place, Fenton in the area of the junction of Victoria and Dewsbury Roads. The name suggests a primitive burial-place (VCH vol 8 p205). Perhaps thrown up over the dead after the battle of Fethanleag 584 AD, in which the British were defeated by the Angles, and thought by Clough and Bowers to have taken place at Fenton Culvert (RHPS pp21,22). Fenton Low is in Fenton Vivian manor (NSSG p19). The mound mentioned by Garner at cSJ 891453 (GNHS pp113,133) was not found by Gunstone (NSJFS 1965 p47). Perhaps, the Victoria Road (A50), built in the C19, obliterated it. Thomas Whieldon had works here before moving to Fenton Hall, see Fenton Low Pottery.

Fenton Low A modern industrial and residential district at Fenton built around and over the lost Fenton Low (FF p16).

Fenton Manor Represents the site of a later manor house of Fenton Vivian manor. The house has also appeared as Fenton Manor House, and Little Fenton Manor House, and The Manor (NSF p42 note). The older part of the house may have dated from c1800 and it was said to have been much improved in the early 1840s. From the mid C19 it was occupied by Philip Barnes Broade (1851); Edward Challinor (c1868-c1884); Henry Warrington (c1892-c1912). The house was partly derelict in 1960 (VCH vol 8 pp207,209,212). It was demolished in the 1960s and the Sixth Form College built on its site (FF pp11,68): Morland says Fenton Hall stood on the site of the Sixth Form College. The name of the manor was perpetuated in the name of the railway station 'Fenton Manor' (SOSH p290), off Manor Street, and in 'Fenton Manor Quarry' on the site of Fenton Hall. Local children of the 1920s and the 1930s had a saying:

> Why was the Heron Cross?
> Because of the Fenton Manor !

(info Mary Blakeman).

Fenton Manor Farm Stood near to and to the NE of Fenton Manor. In 1960 it was owned by the National Coal Board (VCH vol 8 p212).

Fenton Old Park Old park stretching from Fenton Low to Adderley Green, Fenton. SAH Burne found Richard the parker of Fenton mentioned in Edward I's reign (NSFCT 1910 p174). Includes the hill, 662 feet high, topped with a radio mast.

Fenton Park Estate and property in Fenton Vivian, perhaps taking its name from the former Fenton Old Park, and situated in the area of that park. From the mid C18 the estate descended in the Fenton family, subsequently the Fenton Fletcher Boughey family, and was held in c1840 by representatives of the elder line of the Fenton family. The estate was mined from the C18 (HBST p422) (VCH vol 8 p213). Fenton Park farm (VCH vol 8 p213) appears to have been the birthplace of George Heming Mason (1818-1872), the painter (STM Oct 1971 p24).

Fenton Park Public park in the area of Fenton Low, Fenton. Opened in 1924 over the site of old coal shafts (VCH vol 8 p208).

Fenton Vivian The northern manor of Fenton as opposed to Fenton Culvert, the southern manor. Former township in Stoke-upon-Trent chapelry and ancient parish (W p236). The name is from Vivian de Stoke, lord of the manor in the 1240s (FF p11) (MR p149). Its boundary with Fenton Culvert is discussed in FF p11. Fenton Vivian was the (Fentone) Fenton (see) mentioned in DB. It contained Fenton Low and Botteslow (NSSG p19). The site of the old Fenton Vivian manor house may have been at Lawn Farm, where there is a moat (HBST p526) (VCH vol 1 p366. vol 8 pp205,207). The later manor house was Fenton Manor (see). Morland suggests the manor house was on the site of the Sixth Form College (POP p104). Brindley erected a steam engine at Fenton Vivian to pump water out of the Thomas Broad's Mines in 1756-8 (VCH vol 2 p165).

Fenton Vivian Park Fenton. A medieval deer park enclosed out of forest. In existence by 1310 (NSJFS 1962 p76).

Fernhill House 1m NNE of Forton. In Forton parish. Has appeared as Fernyhale (1229-1272. 1344). The name means 'the fern covered nook of land' (SPNO p148).

Fernhill Farm 0.75m NW of Dunstall, Tatenhill. Formerly Merry's Green (HOPT vol 1 p132).

Fernyford Over 1m SSE of Newtown. Formerly in Fawfieldhead township in Alstonefield ancient parish. Little Fernyford lies on the N side of Blake Brook, whilst Big Fernyford lies on the S side. There was a house at one of the Fernyfords by 1327 (VCH vol 7 p27). Thomas and Ralph Ashenhurst were charged with the murder of John Bull at his house at Fernyford on June 10 1590 (VBB p24).

Ferny Hill There is an Upper Fernyhill Farm NE of Basford Green. Here is a wayside cross, see under Basford Green.

Fernyknowle N of Sheen Hill, 1.75m SE of Longnor. A former property here was built in a day in order to claim Squatters' Rights (DP p56).

Ferry Bridge Crosses over the Trent at Burton upon Trent. Built in 1899. It was the gift of the 1st Baron Burton (STMSM Aug 1976 p20p) (BTOP vol 2 p19 p of). It is said to be unique of its type in Europe (SLM Oct 1999 p22pc).

Ffirestone Brook Rises on Orchard Common, N of Flash. Runs S of Orchard Farm. To S of Blackclough (Derbys) starts to form the Staffs Derbys border until it joins the Dane at Three Shire Heads. Has also appeared as Raddlerake Brook (SSE 1996 p69, 70).

Fibbersley The road 'Fibbersley' is NNW of Little London, Willenhall. Believed to have been a part of Wednesfield parish until 1895 when it became part of Short Heath civil parish (SNW p25). Near the junction of Fibbersley and Broad Lanes stood an erratic boulder, known as the Hoar Stone; it marked the boundary between Willenhall and Wednesfield. It was lost by 1995 (SNW p25). The name is said to be from fibbing, the practice of ducking and weaving in bare knuckle fights (TB June 1983 p25). Horace Davis says he knew of no origin for the name, other than it was of great antiquity (SNW p25).

Fiddler's Bank Stretch of road to E of Brown Edge village approximately 900 feet high. It is said to be so called after a man named Sheldon, who lived here, who travelled the district playing a fiddle in public houses to keep himself after an accident in the local mines had disabled him (ONST 1979 p399). (BEH p31).

Field Tiny hamlet at the confluence of Bear's Brook with the Blithe, 1.5m S of Church Leigh. Former township in Leigh ancient parish. The name means 'open land' (NSJFS 1981 p2) (SSE 1996 p13), within a forested region (SPN p50). Appears in 1130 as Felda (SSE 1996 p13). The medieval chapel at Field, may have been at Painleyhill (see). Here was a witch elm 120 feet long. When it was felled in 1680 it took two able men five days to stock it. Its girth in the middle was 25 feet six inches and 17 yards in circumference. There were 61 loads of firewood on it or 96 tons of timber (NHS pp210-211) (SD p102) (SHOS vol p58) (W p782) (HOU p333). Field became a separate civil parish in 1866 (GLAUE p411). In 1908 a lady parachutist, Dolly Shepherd (1886-1983), was nursed at Field Farm by the Hollins family after landing poorly at Church Leigh on June 9 after a parachute descent in which she had had to rescue her partner, Miss Louie May, in what is believed to have been the first mid-air rescue. The Hollins family planted an ash tree at the spot where Dolly landed and this became known as Dolly's Ash (EAS p12) (ES July 23 1994) (TRTC p146).

Field Hall Field. This was the preferred residence of Sir Hervey Bagot, descendent of the Bagots of Bagot's Hall (see), who gave up living at Blithfield Hall, which he left to his eldest son Sir Edward who was living there by 1642. Sir Hervey died here on Dec 27 1660, aged 70 (SHC 1908 p102) (CL Nov 4 1954 p1578). By 1851 its status had been reduced to a farmhouse (W p782).

Fieldhead House to S of Doglane. Formed part of Musden Grange estate, in Croxden parish. The name first appears in 1766. The present farmhouse was probably not built until the mid C18 (SASR 1995 no 5 p36).

Field Head Farm 1.75m SW of Rocester.

Field House C18 house on E side of Stafford Road, Wallington Heath, Bloxwich. Former seat of Richard Thomas, local industrialist. Became the club house for Bloxwich Golf Club (SNBP p53).

Field House Harborne Park Road, Harborne. The present house was probably built in the late C18 but around the core of an earlier timber-framed building (OHOPP p25p of c1890). In the drive is a well, perhaps of Roman origin (OHOPP p25).

Field House 2m SW of Dudley. Occupied in 1851 by Charles Woodcock (W p20).

Field House Georgian-style house 1.25m W of Clent. It was probably the site of a small settlement near medieval open fields or common fields in Lower Clent manor. Built by the later C18 (Yates' map) probably by a member of the Waldron family; Thomas Waldron of Field House established a Sunday school at Clent in 1799. From the Waldrons the house passed to the Dudleys - probably the Tipton and Kingswinford family, members of whom became rectors of Broome or married Amphletts. Later the house was occupied by Henry Addenbrook. Occupied in 1851 by Charles Roberts (1801-1868) (mem in Clent church). He was succeeded here by his sons. Following Alfred Roberts' death in 1901 the house was taken over by AC Kenrick for a few years. A subsequent owner was Ernest Vaughan. After WW2 the house was acquired by Birmingham Corporation as a home for young children in need of care and later it housed delinquent girls. In the 1980s it became a private residential home for the elderly (SVS p588) (W p20) (Short History of Clent. John Amphlett. 1908. p165) (SNSV vol 2 pp28-29). Ernest Vaughan laid out a cricket ground between Broome Lane and Field House (SNSV vol 2 p29).

Field House (1834 OS map) (Dower's map). Fieldhouse Farm is 1.25m E of Eccleshall.

Fields, The House over 1m WSW of Maer (1834 OS map) (Dower's map).

Fields Farm 0.5m S of Gratton, in Horton ancient parish. It was called Fields in 1588. The Reades came from Blackwood Old Hall in 1702 (NSFCT 1932 p30) (ils of in The Reades of Blackwood Hill etc. Aleyn Lyell Reade. 1906). The present house was built in the early C18 and a N wing was added later in the C18 (VCH vol 7 p67).

Fiery Holes Former small hamlet in the present Belmont Gardens area on W side of Great Bridge Road, 1m SE of Bilston. The name, in existence by 1882, was still current in 1947 (OS maps). Has also appeared as Fireholes. In 1767 ironmaster John Wilkinson of Bradley (see), Bilston, built here the first coke-fired blast furnace in Bilston township and in Staffs; a memorial to him was erected on the site of a toll houses in Bradley Lane in the 1950s (BOP p114p). (BOP p106il from ILN Dec 8 1866 p548 of a Black Country Scene about the Fiery Holes area) (TB May 1983 p11).

Fighting Cocks Farm 0.5m N of Stonnall. The farm was so called by 1887 (1887 OS map 6 inch).

Filley Brook Tributary of the Trent. Runs at Darlaston, Stone. The name appears as fulcan broc in a charter of the bounds of Darlaston dated 956 (SPNO p16). Filleybrooks is the name for the area by The Walton Inn (formerly The Wayfarer) on the A34 near Stone. For etymology see NSFCT 1908 p132.

Fimbley 1m due S of Lichfield. Land at Femley Pits was granted to Lichfield cathedral's common fund, by Ernulf, a canon, in the early C13 (VCH vol 14 p68). Affords numerous varieties of gravel substances (SVS pp486 note, 491). The Lichfield pit produced a small specimen of quartz embedding a cluster of shells (SVS p519 note).

Finchfield Former hamlet (PENOP p7), on a piece of upland above the Smestow and its tributaries, 1.5m NNW of Upper Penn. Now a suburb of Wolverhampton, but formerly lay partly in Penn and Tettenhall parishes. A Bronze Age palstave with a broken loop of 600 BC has been found in a Finchfield garden (HOWM p1) (AJ vol 20 p64) (NSJFS 1964 p44). The name means 'the field of Finch,' Finch by the Middle Ages being a personal name (DUIGNAN). Or 'finches open land' (NSJFS 1981 p3). There was a moated site at SO 883971; excavated in 1983 prior to being built on (SSAHST 1982-3 p57) (CAMS p61). Winifred Mantle (1911-1983), novelist and children's writer, lived with her two sisters in Finchfield. Her first book, a romance entitled 'Happy in the House,' was published in 1951. She wrote under the pseudonyms Frances Lang, Jane Langford and Anne Fellows (VFC p90). White Oak Drive, off Finchfield Hill, was chosen as the location for a TV washing powder advert of the 1960s (WOLOP p25p). There is a mission church, St Thomas, at Finchfield (LDD).

Finchpath Former hamlet about which differences of opinion have occurred as to its exact location. There are numerous references to Finchpath or variant spellings in West Bromwich manorial court rolls (TMS p103). It has appeared as Wynchespath (C13) and Fynchespath. A hamlet of Finchpath is recorded in the 1420s (HOWV p108) (VCH vol 17 p6). At Finchpath Alice, wife of Roger le Cok, was murdered by Roger de Borleye in 1337 (WAM p52). At

Finchpath is said to have been a lodging for the monk of Sandwell Priory who took the services at West Bromwich church. The lodge was at Wallface, Hill Top (see) (OWB p36). In the 1780s a district still known as Finchpath was populous. By the mid C18 the area at the top of Holloway Bank (or Finchpath Hill) was becoming known as Hill Top (see) (VCH vol 17 pp6-7). The many former references to Finchpath can all be located to cover an area from the foot of Holloway Bank to S of Black Lake (Nether Finchpath); to as far E as Hill Top and to as far W as Harvills Hawthorn; however, nowhere is Hateley Heath referred to as being in Finchpath (TMS p103) (HOWBW p216) (HOWB p50) (SHC vol 13 p294) (VCH vol 17 p6). Hackwood thought the site of the hamlet was the present Bridge Street crossing the Tame or that of the Hyde's Lane crossing (WAM pp33-34,36), and that Finchpath gave its name to a bridge in Hydes Road, and a mill on the Tame, but not on the site of Wednesbury mill (WAM p52). But Dilworth states that there is strong evidence that Finchpath never extended to the Hydes Road area and that Finchpath Bridge was situated on the site of the present Wednesbury Bridge (TMS p104). The name is preserved in a tiny road at Blacklake.

Finchpath Hall Hill Top. Now known as 71 and 73 Hill Top opposite Hawkes Lane. Seat of Capt James Keir from c1770 (OWB pp101-102) or 1791 (AOBC p8), a 'mighty chemist' friend of Matthew Boulton, James Watt, Joseph Priestley, Dr Erasmus Darwin and others of the Lunar Society: It was one of their meeting places. Whilst Keir was staying with his partner it burnt down in 1807. Keir rebuilt the house (OWB p102).

Fingery Hole A row of cottages near the top of Turners Hill. So called as someone, reputedly a robber, put his finger through one of the cottages' front door drop latch holes and it was swiftly cut off by the old lady occupant with a hatchet (BCWJ p115) (TB Jan 1983 p13). Has also appeared as Finger o' the' Hole Cottage.

Finney Green Small hamlet 1.75m NE of Madeley. In Keele parish. Has also appeared as Finny Green.

Finneylane 2m NE of Cheddleton. A farm here (whether called Fynney Lane Farm?) has inscription in gable end; 'W.F.- A.F. 1610.' It was the home of the Fynney family, descendants from the Norman, Baron de Fenis, or Fiennes (there is a Fynney mem in Cheddleton church). Fielding Best Fynney found a treasure of gold Roman coins in one of the fields about Finneylane? or Friar Moor (see) in 1776 (VBB p24 il of the inscription on the gable end of the farm). Has also appeared as Fynney Lane.

Fireman's Rest A house on Leek Road, 1m E of Werrington. A former venue of cockfighting (WJ p26).

Firs Farm On the E side of Moat Lane WNW of Audley. A reverse horse-shoe was found in a gravel pit on the farm in 1932 (NSFCT 1932 p125) (SSGLST p26).

Fir Tree Farm An old house at Ball Green, 0.75m NNW of Norton-in-the-Moors. Formerly in Norton chapelry in Stoke-on-Trent ancient parish (ONST 1932 p39).

Fir Tree Hill Could be now Round Hill, Stourton? Here William Howe murdered Ben Robins (TB Feb 1993 p22) and here William Howe's dead body was displayed after he was hung for the murder. Appeared as Gibbet Lane in the C19 (TB Oct 1975 pp18-19), and generally the surrounding area became known as Gibbet Wood (see).

Fir Tree House 0.75m SE of Himley (1834 OS map). Is not marked on current maps.

Fish and Chip Hole Cavern in the Wren's Nest Hill (BCM Oct 1970 p51).

Fisher's Hall Greets Green (SHWB 13) (SOWB p24).

Fisherwick Tiny hamlet on low ground to the W of the Tame 1.5m E of Whittington. Former township with Tymmor in St Michael's parish, Lichfield, by the late C13 (VCH vol 14 pp239,252).
EARLY. There was a **Neolithic** settlement in c1900 BC on the W bank of the Tame 0.25m W of Elford at SK 184103 (SSAHST 1968-69 pp1-22 ils plans) (VCH vol 14 p239). Crop-marks at SK 178082, S of the Fisherwick-Hademore road, 1m SSE of Fisherwick Hall Farm, revealed by aerial photography and excavations, are ice-wedge casts formed during periglacial activity during the Late Devensian phase of the Pleistocene period and the post-hole structure of a **Middle Bronze Age** settlement (SSAHST 1974-75 pp1-17 p and plans). A looped socketed axe of the **Late Bronze Age** was found at Fisherwick Park Farm in 1945 (NSJFS 1964 p23). There may have been two other prehistoric settlements near the Tame in the SE of Fisherwick township (SSAHST vol 20 map 6) (VCH vol 14 p239). There may have been an **Iron Age** settlement W of Fisherwick Park Farm in c1000 BC (SSAHST vol 16 p8) (VCH vol 14 p239). An Iron Age site on a terrace by the Tame N of Brook Leasow seems to have been occupied in the C3 and C2 BC; it is possible that its occupation began in the C4 BC and continued into the C1 AD. There was another Iron Age settlement to the S on the opposite side of Brook Leasow

(Fisherwick. C Smith) (VCH vol 14 p239). A **Romano-British** farmstead, occupied in the C2 and C3 AD, which specialised in stock-rearing was discovered by aerial photography in the 1960s on W bank of the Tame 0.25m W of Elford at SK 184103 (SSAHST 1968-69 pp1-22 ils plans) (VCH vol 14 p239).
1100 to PRESENT. The **name** Fisherwick means 'the dwelling of the fisherman' (SHOS vol 1 p363) (VCH vol 14 p239). Fisherwick does not appear in DB, but was the name of a manor by 1167 (VCH vol 14 pp239,252) (SSE 1996 p13). There was a **medieval settlement** of Fisherwick by the manor house. The settlement, still in existence by the late C17, was swept away probably in the extension of Fisherwick Park in the late 1750s (VCH vol 14 p239). Some place a lost settlement at SK 180100 (SSAHST 1966 p49. 1970 p35). Fisherwick was a peculiar jurisdiction of the dean of Lichfield cathedral (GLAUE). The **pinfold** of Fisherwick is mentioned several times in the C16 (VCH vol 14 p252). In the later C17 Plot cites **William Francis** of Fisherwick being melancholy mad and having fasted for 14 days together (NHS p286). The massive ox, known as the **'Fisherwick Ox,'** which existed until Nov 1788 was famous in its day. The dimensions of the beast were from the back of the horns to the rump 10 feet; the girth was 11 feet; and the height at the shoulders 16 hands one inch. Round the legs, below the knee he was 10.25 inches. His weight, when living, was 3017 lb. The carcass weighted 2006 lb. His chine, when severed, was 10.75 inches thick of solid fat. A picture of him hung over the chimney piece in the steward's room at Fisherwick Hall in the late C18 (SHOS vol 1 p369). Fisherwick Lodge, Doagh, County Antrim, Northern Ireland, is called after this Fisherwick, being built by the 2nd Marquis of Donegal, the same family owning the Staffordshire Fisherwick Hall (CL July 28 1983 pp250-251 p of Fisherwick Lodge). Fisherwick became a separate civil parish in 1866 and was transferred to Whittington ecclesiastical parish in 1967 (GLAUE p411) (VCH vol 14 pp239,252).

Fisherwick Brook Runs from of Whittington flows past Fisherwick Hall.

Fisherwick Hall House which lay 1.5m NE of Whittington, in the vicinity of Fisherwick Hall Farm, a farm which incorporates the outbuildings of the second hall.
FIRST HALL. The Skeffingtons acquired Fisherwick manor in 1521. In the later C16 John Skeffington (d1604) built 'a very proper brick house' at Fisherwick (VCH vol 14 p241 pl 45 is from NHS). The old manor house was a magnificent example of the Elizabethan style (NSFCT 1976 p15). Sir William Skeffington was created Viscount Massereene in 1660. In the later C17 Plot saw this mansion (and gardens) and had it illustrated in NHS (NHS p209 tab 15). (EDP p180). The estate was sold in 1756 to Samuel Swinfen, who had only just bought the nearby Elmhurst Hall. He shortly sold Fisherwick Hall, re-bought it, and sold it again in 1758 to Arthur Chichester, 5th Earl and then 1st Marquess of Donegal (1739-99); there is portrait of him by Gainsborough (NSFCT 1976 p15). Work was carried out on the house in 1757 and 1758 by Samuel Hill, Samuel Egerton, Benjamin Wyatt of Weeford and his son William (VCH vol 14 p243). In 1766 the Marquess had the hall demolished and proceeded to build a second hall (NSFCT 1976 p15). There was an etching of the first hall on show in Donegal House, Lichfield.
SECOND HALL. For the second hall and its grounds the Marquess employed Lancelot 'Capability' Brown as his architect; the hall was finished by 1774 (SHOS vol 1 p369) (VCH vol 14 p243 pls 46,47). Shaw noted in this hall: the head and horns of a stag killed by Prince Charles (later Charles I) when hunting in the park, with the inscription within the garter 'C.P. 1621;' a ceiling by Monsieur Rigaud, in the centre of which appeared Apollo in his meridian course conducted by the rosy hours; in the servants hall a large elk's horn dug out of a bog in Ireland (SHOS vol 1 p369,370). I Spyers, in 1786, painted a series of views of this house (NSFCT 1976 pp15-16) (SHOS vol 1 pp368-370* pl xxxv, and a catalogue of its curious antiquities (GNHS p166) (CL July 1983 pp250-251 il by John Spyers 1786, and Shaw's engraving 1798). The estate and hall were sold to RB Howard of Ashtead Park (Surrey), lord of Elford, in 1808. Howard had the hall pulled down before he died in 1818; making the second hall the shortest lived (c1779-1818) of any major country house ever built in the county. The portico went to the George Hotel in Walsall (VCH vol 14 p244. vol 17 p167). (SGS p183).
GROUNDS. Brown started landscaping Fisherwick Park (see) from 1766. In 1779 the Marquess received a medal for planting 10,000 trees at Fisherwick that year (VCH vol 14 p244). For the **Chinese Pavilion** see a 'Ladies' botanical garden.' A **haha** ran N to the orangery and S to the area by the house. A remaining part of the haha by the hall was once mistaken for a moated site (VCH vol 1 p363. vol 14 p244 note). The **icehouse**, formerly at SK 169095, 0.25m WSW of the hall, was demolished in c1980 (VCH vol 14 pp244-245). Beaman and Roaf say three icehouses were unearthed here in c1980 (IHB p393). A **'ladies' botanical garden'** with a Chinese pavilion were erected on

the N side of the lake N of the hall in the later C18 (VCH vol 14 p244). **Moated site** see haha. An **orangery** was built on high ground above the Tame at SK 172102 in the later C18 (VCH vol 14 p244). It was intended to build a **wall** surrounding the whole park, but only a mile of it, on the SE, was built (VCH vol 14 p244). The large gate piers and a lodge house remain. There is a tradition that the bricks used were originally intended for the unbuilt centre part of Clifton Hall, Clifton Campville (SGS p183) (MR pp378-379). A collection of curiosities of the Marquess, kept by the gardener in a small house in the garden, included: a unique brass figure of Antioch, around the inside of his hat was this inscription 'ANTIOXEON. T N. EIII'; a i vory staff head of Henry III; and a small miniature of Mary Queen of Scots, painted from life, for a gold locket (SHOS vol 1 p370).

Fisherwick Park There was a deer park, enclosed with a pale, at Fisherwick by the late C16. It was disparked and divided into farms in the earlier C19 (EDP pp180-181) (VCH vol 14 p244). A stretch of the pale at SK 175098 at Fisherwick Park Farm, was formerly mistaken for a moat (SSAHST 1982-3 p59).

Fishley Tiny hamlet on fairly high ground near the source of a head stream of the Tame 1.5m NNE of Bloxwich. In Walsall ancient parish. There is a granite Ice Age boulder here (SOB p2); perhaps that which is known as 'Fishley Church' (see). In a charter of Pelsall's bounds of 994 the Fishley area is described as 'the great moor' (SNBP p73). The name has nothing to do with fish, but means 'the thistley lea' (DUIGNAN). The main road from Walsall to Stafford is said to have passed through Fishley, but it may have gone via Yieldfields (SOB p139) (VCH vol 17 p166). At Poplar Farm, Fishley Lane, short lengths of bank and ditch of a moat remained in 1908 (VCH vol 1), but had been obliterated by the early 1980s (SSAHST 1982-3 p49).

Fishley Charity Farm 0.75m NNE of Fishley. Represents the farm on land belonging to the Fishley Charity. The charity was founded in 1616 by William Parker, a London merchant and a native of Bloxwich. In 1657 his endowment was invested in land at Fishley. Under the management of various bodies the charity has been put to several local educational uses for poor children (W p646) (VCH vol 17 p269), and was still continuing in 1982 (BY p16). The farm was called Fishley Charity Farm by at least 1887 (OS map 6 inch).

'Fishley Church' Boulder at SK 012048, on Pelsall North Common by Fishley Lane. Said to mark the meeting point of five parish boundaries (SNBP p73p). So called as John Wesley is said to have stood on it to preach. The boulder was damaged and broken in half during the building of a new sewer in 1987 (SNBP p73). Recently (1997) some earth covering it has been removed, and a 'blue plaque' on a timber post relating the history of the boulder erected by it (Forest of Mercia News. No. 4) (info David Grundy). There is a tradition that the Keay family, who lived at the N end of Fishley Lane, used to conduct an orchestral concert on summer Sunday evenings at this large boulder (SOB p168).

Fishpool Walk Hanley. It formed part of Northwood Park opened in 1907. The pool in the park is the old fish pool, which gave its name to the walk, which was the forerunner of Eastwood Road (H p87). In medieval times formed a stretch of Lady's Walk (NSFCT 1989 p36).

Five Clouds Stretch of rock outcrops WSW of The Roaches and often, but wrongly, considered part of The Roaches. Have also appeared as The Five Clouds. They are NW of Hen Cloud, Upper Hulme and consist of five clouds or craggy hillocks or buttresses called:- The First Cloud, whose crags all remain unnamed: The Second Cloud: The Third Cloud, considered the 'big brother' of The Clouds (SGM pp106-107 il): The Fourth Cloud, whose face is bordered on the right by a rounded proboscis (SGM p109): The Fifth Cloud, a large angular block with a smooth face (SGM p112). There was a family living in the Five Clouds area in 1681 (VCH vol 7 p194).

Five Lane Ends Common land opposite Woodmill Farm, Woodmill, N of Yoxall. There were some three acres of common land here in the 1950s (OSST 1956-59 p15).

Five Lanes End Junction of five lanes 1m SE of Ellenhall. The fifth lane that ran directly to Seighford was lost in the 1940s when Seighford airfield was built (info Bruce Braithwaite).

Five Oak Hill On W edge of Cannock Chase. Five Oak Hill Plantation 1.5m SE of Bednall.

Five Ways Is now the village of Heath Hayes. In Cannock parish. Takes its name from the five roads which met at the junction of the Cannock-Lichfield road with the Walsall-Hednesford road. It grew rapidly in the 1870s with the opening of coal mines in the area (LHSB 50 pp4,6), but developed largely in the period 1890 to 1910 (VCH vol 5 p51). Soon after 1900 the Post Office is said to have asked the post mistress at Five Ways to suggest another name for the village on account of there being too many places called Five Ways. She is said to have suggested the village call itself after the farm to the N called

Heathy Hayes (LHSB 50 p6).

Five Ways Road junction in High Street, Brierley Hill, so called by 1901 (OS map Sheet 71.07).

Five Ways At Cradley Heath, Rowley Regis. A ghost has been seen in this area (TB Oct 1982 p24). The Cross Guns Inn, here, was run by Joe Mallen from 1921 and was soon recognised as the headquarters of the Staffordshire Bull Terrier fanciers (TB Jan 1976 p19).

Five Ways Appears as Four Ways in Rev JR Windsor-Garnett's 'The Village' (1926) (TB Sept 1986 p14). There is a Five Ways at Lower Gornal in Sedgley parish, an area, possibly, formerly known as Gornal Green.

Five Ways Approximately 1m SE of Walsall on the old road to Birmingham. Was an occupied area by the earlier C17 when known as Five Lanes End. Five Lane End Farm, mentioned in 1696, was known as Sergeant's Coppice Farm in the earlier C19 (VCH vol 17 p154). Fiveways Bridge carries Park Hall Road over the Rushall Canal (Birmingham A-Z 1995).

Five Ways Road junction in the Stafford Road at Dunstall Hill, Bushbury. So called by 1901, when, in fact, six ways met here (OS map Wolverhampton (NW) 1901 62.06) (BUOP p55).

Five Ways House Villa in Swan Village at junction of Swan Lane and Blacklake, where five roads converge. Residence of Edward Elwell in the C19 (IE p47).

Flash Tiny moorland village high on a slope immediately S of Axe Edge 28.25m NNE of Stafford. Formerly in Quarnford township and chapelry in Alstonefield ancient parish (W p744).

EARLY. In Buxton Museum is a stone axe hammer found at Flash. The megalithic chambered tomb said to contain the remains of a woman (UHAW), said to be between Flash and Quarnford (GNHS pp66il,416) (WTCEM p10) (SC p147), is perhaps that in the Back of the Cross area (UHAW).

1000 to 1700. Flash appears in the C16 as Flashe (SSE 1996 p13). The **name** is from possibly Anglo-Saxon, 'plesc,' pronounced plash, the word was applied to wet flat land where water lies after rain and gradually disappears (DUIGNAN) (NSFCT 1932 p58) (SSE 1996 p21) (PNPD). In the martyrology of Oengus there is mention of a river Flesc with a legendary derivation. There is also a word 'fliuchaime' wet land (NSFCT 1908 p143). The name Flash is common in N Lincs and denotes wet, spongy land frequently enclosing a pool. Madsen 'Archaeological Journal of Scandinavia' 1863 p203 says that in Denmark Flaske means in a local sense a small creek surrounded by meadows, and hence the word may colloquially be interpreted as 'bottled up' (NSFCT 1916 p80). The name may be from the Celt's rural chief - the Flaith (UHAW p75). Poulton-Smith suggests that Flashbrook inhabitants moved to Flash in the C16 (when Flashbrook was vacated and Flash first recorded) and took the name with them, but there is absolutely no evidence for this, and it is pure speculation (SPN pp50,51). The name has even been thought to derive from 'flash' in the sense of showy, from coins and trinkets produced here (VB p210). Raven believes Flash is 'the flosche' in the medieval epic poem 'Gawain and the Green Knight' (MR p316).

1700 to PRESENT. The **church** of 1744 in the centre of the village was replaced by the present church, St Paul, in 1901 (VCH vol 7 p54). Joseph Brunt of Flash died in 1782 aged 104 (W p57). The **Flash Loyal Union Society**, a local form of health insurance, was established in c1790 (DP p58) or on July 27 1846 (SVB p77) (VCH vol 7 p51). The subscription money was kept in a teapot. By 1906 the society was known as the 'Teapot Club' (VCH vol 7 p51). It has been said the name may be a corruption of the Irish 'taoiseach' meaning leader or chief, and that the society had a Celtic origin (DPEM pp54-55). The 'Club Feast' and 'Club Parade' used to be held on the third Monday in June, but by 1988 they were being held on the Saturday nearest the third Monday (SVB p77). The club parade took a route from the old Methodist chapel to the Travellers Rest Inn (see). By 1992 it was starting from the village hall (DP pp56,58, 59ps,60). The Society closed in the early 1990s (DPEM p54) (VCH vol 7 p51). There was no **fair** in 1792 (OWEN). In 1851 there were fairs at Flash on the Saturdays before Easter and Whit Sunday, at Michaelmas (Sept 29), and on the Saturday before the fair at Rugeley on the second Tuesday in December (W pp472, 744) (VCH vol 7 p52). There was a fair in 1888 (LHE p265). The Michaelmas fair may have continued beyond the others; it is described as the Flash Fair by SVB p77. There is a cockpit site at Saltwell (see) at the E end of Flash village. **Trades**. Button-making was formerly the main occupation in Flash. John Gaunt, a button merchant in the 1760s and 1770s, was known locally as 'the king of the Flash' (VCH vol 7 p39). Pedlars did occupy the Flash area by the later C18; one is found described as 'a Flash man' in a law case in 1766 (VCH vol 7 p52). Pedlars (known locally as Fudge-mounters - HOLF p50) (PRT p77) are said to have established dwellings on common land in the Flash area in the C18 (DP p56). It is said Flash pedlars gave the English language the word 'flash' in the sense of criminal, showy, and ostentatious, hence 'Flash Harry,' and 'flashy'

(NSFCT 1952 p101) (ZSB), or those that took to the alleged money forging (see below) did (DP p56) (SG p18) (MR p154) (A Portrait of Macclesfield. Doug Pickford). Flash lies near the summit of the main watershed of England (TTTD p98p) and is noted for being the **highest village in England** at 1,518 feet (GBR 1965 p87 pl 30. 1979 p177p) or 1,526 feet above sea level (VCH vol 7 p1). As a consequence of its height Quarnford post office, at Flash, in existence by 1904 (VCH vol 7 p51) and run from a terraced cottage on the N side of the Quarnford road (Back of the Cross) in July 1999 is the highest in England (GBR 1996 p169): the New Inn is regarded as the fourth highest in England; the village has only had national grid electricity from 1962 (before which the village school derived its from wind power), and mains water from March 1984, after a reservoir was built on Oliver Hill (VCH vol 7 p51) (TTTD p100) (SVB p77) (DP p56): (TTTD p100). A Thunderbolt P47 **aircraft** crashed at Flash on Jan 3 1945. The American pilot was killed (MD p67). A UFO was seen from Flash on Oct 22 1967 (FSRP p17). A **headless horseman** is said to haunt the roads between Longnor (see) and Flash.

TRADITION OF COINERS. There is no evidence for coining or the forging of notes at Flash other than the first reference to it in a local history by Aitken (1795) and perpetuated ever since (NSFCT 1952 p107). For instance by an early C19 magistrate who wrote to N&Q (N&Q 5th series vol x p521) (OL vol 2 pp59-60), and by Hon Judge Alfred Ruegg KC, a native of the locality (later of Highfields Hall) in his novel 'Flash' (1928) (ES Sept 23 1931 p4p) (SMOPP vol 2 p109) (VCH vol 7 p51). The tradition rests on: Flash's close proximity to several county borders, excellent for quickly crossing into another county to evade authorities; that many local pedlars were involved in coining (DP p56); or that coiners masqueraded as button makers and struck their coins on button presses at certain locations, for instance, Pastures Farm (see) (VB p210), and Wolfe Edge (SVB p77); that two coining machines were found in a well in the yard of a house sometime prior to 1874, photographs of which were at Swythamley Hall (NSFCT 1931 p184); that a pedlar known as Ward-of-the-Brook travelling via Danebridge took refuge under Caister's Bridge after being pursued by counterfeiters (SSGLST pp16-18); that a crack set of law enforcement officers were sent into the area to deal with coiners (Family Walks in the Staffs Peak and Potteries. Les Lumsdon. 1990. p69); that coiners from Flash were executed at Chester (NSFCT 1931 p184); that 'Bowyer of the Rocks' of Rock Hall perhaps had some affiliation with coiners (DPEM p51); and that George and Thomas Fearne, brother coiners of Bottom House Inn (see), may have operated at Flash (OL vol 2 p59).

Flash, The S of Tunstall on the Burslem road. Seems to have been a hamlet or district in c1829 (HSP p19).

Flash Bar A toll bar on the Leek turnpike road (DP p58), NE of Flash, at a place called Flash Head. Built in 1771 (VCH vol 7 p51) (UHAW p49). Here is the Travellers Rest Inn (TTTD p97).

Flash Bottom House 0.5m SSW of Flash. Is near the source of the Dane (NSFCT 1908 p143). There was a house here by 1750 (UHAW) (Yates' map).

Flash Brook Tiny brook that flows into Lonco Brook. Gives its name to Flashbrook hamlet. Duignan thinks the prefix could be a personal name. So perhaps, Flode's brook, or Flote's brook (DUIGNAN). It is partly unexplained (NSJFS 1981 p3). Both first and second elements are Anglo-Saxon and both mean 'stream' (SSE 1996 p13) (SPN p51).

Flashbrook Small hamlet of scattered properties comprising Flashbrook Common, Grange and Manor. Former township with Batchacre in Adbaston ancient parish (W p382). Has appeared as Flotesbroc (DB), and Flassenbroke (1679) (SHC 1914 p72). Chetwynd thought it took its name from 'that shallow flashy brook that passeth by it' (SHC 1914 p72). See Flash Brook.

Flashbrook Common Near Flashbrook Grange. The meres on the common were frequented by the superstitious pewits from 1770 to 1794 (NSFCT p38).

Flashbrook Grange House over 0.5m SSW of Flashbrook Manor. Ranton Abbey had a grange here in the Middle Ages (NSFCT 1927 p22). At the Dissolution Ranton's granges of Ellerton, Knighton and Batchacre with Flashbrook were purchased by Sir John Gifford whose grant is dated 1541. Richard Whitworth I of Adbaston Manor purchased Flashbrook Grange from the Baduleys in 1719. The present house was built later than the C17 (AADB pp26,32). Here or at Flashbrook Manor was possibly a medieval village (SSAHST 1970 p35).

Flashbrook Heath Former common land S of Flashbrook Grange, mainly in Shrops. The Shrops Staffs boundary runs through it. But it formerly contained so much unenclosed land that the county boundary may have been a little uncertain (NSFCT 1927 p40). After the heath was enclosed it became part of Whitworth's Batchacre estate (AADB p32). The name Flashbrook Heath appears on the 1834 OS map, but appears as Puleston Common on the present OS map.

Flashbrook Manor House 2m SW of Adbaston. Has also appeared as Flach-

brook Manor (NSFCT 1908 p143). The Jordans held the Flashbrook Manor estate in 1404. Before 1443 it passed by marriage to John Barbour of Stafford. In 1566 his grandson built the house which was demolished in the C20 (NSFCT 1927 p24) (AADB p32). Richard Whitworth I of Adbaston Manor purchased Flashbrook Manor from the Barbours in 1728 (AADB p19). About 1954 Frank Dodd demolished the C16 house and replaced it with a new house (AADB p32). Here or at Flashbrook Grange was possibly a village in medieval times (SSAHST 1970 p35).

Flashbrook Wood A coppice NW of Flashbrook Grange.

Flashcroft Former house on S side of the Dane 0.75m NNW of Heaton. Formerly in Heaton township in Leek ancient parish. There was a house here by the earlier C16 (VCH vol 7 p186).

Flash Gate Former toll gate at Travellers Rest Inn, Flash. Also called Flash Bar.

Flash Head Presumably from some hill or rock 0.25m E of Flash. Is near the source of the Manifold (NSFCT 1908 p143). An Order was made in 1714 for stocks to be set up on a green at 'Flashhead' (VCH vol 7 p53). Here the toll bar was situated on the Leek turnpike road (DP p58). A house at Flash Head has a datestone with the date 1783 (UHAW p51).

Flashside Gate House near Oxensitch, NE of Flash, in existence in 1780 (UHAW p49).

Flatheridge Bridge Crosses over a canal. Whether Coventry, or Staffs & Worcs? (BZ p108). Could be Flotheridge see Flotheridge Wharf.

Flatts, The SE area of Darlaston Green, Darlaston (Offlow hundred). The name is from one of Darlaston's open fields. There are references to the area, presumably after it had been enclosed, as Godden's Flatts. In the earlier C19 it was known as Golden Flatts (SNDB p50).

Flaxhall Former name in the C17 for High Arcal Farm, Woodsetton (TB April 1983 p15) and before that for land about that farm. It may be the Flaxhale mentioned in 1272 (HC p11). The name is preserved in a primary school at Upper Gornal on Eve Hill.

Flaxhill Near Perry Crofts N Tamworth.

Flaxley Green Area of Cannock Chase 0.75m S of Slitting Mill. Appears in 1834 as Flaxley Green (SPNO p108) (CCBO p69). The name means 'woodland clearing where flax was grown' (SPNO p108). Tom Coulthwaite moved his horse training business from Hazelslade to Flaxley Green after 1908 (SSE 1990 p88). At the former and or the latter he trained three Grand National Winners: Eremon (1907), Jenkinstown (1910), and Grakle (1931) (SSE 1990 pp87-100). In Feb 1928 Edward VIII, then Prince of Wales, visited Coulthwaite twice in one week and spent several hours riding over his 74 jump course (R &S p45).

Fleetgreen Burton upon Trent. Promontory on the Derbys side of the Trent S of Annsley (Andressey?) Island.

Fleetgreen The oldest of the three properties called Fleetgreen in the former Fawfieldhead township in Alstonefield ancient parish is at Lower Fleetgreen, 1.25m SSW of Newtown; it probably stands on or near a house called Fleetgreen in 1514 (VCH vol 7 p27). The other two Fleetgreens, which lie to the N, are called Fleetgreen and Upper Fleetgreen. The name is from Old Norse 'fliot' a small river or channel (NSFCT 1916 p80). A Hurricane V 6793 aircraft crashed at Fleetgreen on July 27 1944. The pilot, who was alone, was killed (MD pp42-43).

Flewells Sandon.

Flooded Mine Cave in Castle Hill, Dudley (BCM Oct 1970 p51).

Florence S suburb of Longton developed by the 3rd Duke of Sutherland of Trentham Hall from the 1860s. In Stoke-upon-Trent chapelry and ancient parish. Became a separate civil parish in 1894 and entered Longton civic parish in 1896 (GLAUE p411). The duke gave it the name of his eldest daughter, Florence (d1881), who married Sir Henry Chaplin in Trentham church in Nov 1876 (ILN Jan 23 1875) (VCH vol 8 p227 note) (SL pp228-229) (TTH p89). It was added to the borough of Longton in 1884 (VCH vol 8 p253).

Flotheridge Wharf Near Green's Forge, Swindon (SVS p124). A Flotheridge Basin appears on 1834 OS and Dower's maps.

Foker Area centring on the house, Upper Foker, 1.25m NNW of Leek. Formerly in Leekfrith township in Leek ancient parish. There is said to have been a Roman road 'above' Foker (HLS p116). The name means 'foul marsh' (VCH vol 7 p194) and is recorded in the 1330s. Dieulacres Abbey had a grange at Foker by the Dissolution, probably on the site of Upper Foker (NSJFS 1970 p85) (VCH vol 7 p194). The house called Foker Grange, 1m WSW of Upper Foker, was called Lower Fowker in 1770 and had taken its present name by the late 1890s (VCH vol 7 p194). There is presently another house called Lower Foker under 0.5m W of Upper Foker.

Folds End Farm House on E side of Longnor town, in Alstonefield ancient parish. The site of the house was occupied by 1505. The earliest part of the present house is probably of the C18, and there is a barn dated 1829 (VCH vol 7 p42).

Fole The small village of Fole, on the N side of the Tean, is over 1m ESE of Checkley. It was formerly in Madeley Holme division in Checkley ancient parish (W p760); it has formerly appeared as Nether Fold (Plot's map), Nether Fo, and the Tole (S&W p311). Overfole, a house 2m SE of Checkley, lies on the S side of the Tean, in Church Leigh and Leigh ancient parishes; it has formerly appeared as Over Fold (Plot's map) and Over Folde. Fole has appeared as Falled (1593-1603) (SOS p380), and perhaps erroneously Tole (S&W p311). In 1316 Nether Fold was held by Hericus St Maure (SOS p380). For a rhyme about Fole see Checkley.

Fole Hall House nearly 0.5m S of Fole, in Leigh ancient parish. The Taylor family are marked here on Plot's map. There is a coat of arms of the Vincent family in a window of the hall (STM March 1967 p30p of the arms). There are memorials to the Brown family of Fole Hall in Church Leigh churchyard. The hall once belonged to the Vincents of Pecleton, Leics (NSFCT 1922 p80). Also some time it was the seat of the Woods (NSFCT 1923 p151).

Foley, The Tiny district of Fenton off King Street, wholly in Fenton Culvert manor. In Stoke-upon-Trent chapelry and ancient parish. The name is from perhaps the Foley family of Birmingham, lords of Longton manor from 1651 (POP p131) (SASR 1987 p100). Perhaps from the Foley Pottery. Or from a curious piece of architecture considered a folly (HBST p553) (POP p119). John Wesley preached in the yard of a house with a potworks at the E end of the Foley, in 1790 (VCH vol 8 p219); Simeon Shaw says Wesley preached at the southern extremity of the Foley (HSP p72), whilst others say he preached at the Old Foley Pottery (see). (MR p151p of the Foley Arms in Foley Place).

Foley House House situated just in Fenton urban district, S of the railway and N of the Anchor Brook. Birthplace in 1808 of Robert Garner (d1890), doctor, poet, founder of a natural history museum in Stoke-upon-Trent, author of GNHS and gives his name to the NSFC's Garner Medal; he was educated at Aston Hall, Warws, and Sedgley Park (PSS pp156-159) (SH p127) (POTP p100) (VFC p52) (William Henry Goss. Lynda and Nicholas Pine. 1987 p37p). The house still existed as a farm in the early 1950s (VCH vol 8 p214).

Foley Wood Appears as a plantation on the 1832 OS map and covering about 73 acres in the area of Foley Road (made between 1965 and 1968), Streetly (SNAR p93).

Folly Hall 0.5m to E of Newborough.

Folly Hall S of Borrowcop Hill the property of John Levett (SHOS vol 1 p343).

Folly House Folly House Lane to E of Maw Green, Walsall. Existed by the early C19. Described in 1855 as an ancient habitation; later known as Rock's Cottage, it was demolished in 1931 (HOWG p32 note) (VCH vol 17 p155). It appears to have given the 'Folly' part of its name to 'Taylor's Folly' alias The Hawthorns (see).

Folly Wood A wood 1m SW of Mucklestone. Described as a modern plantation on former heathland in 1914 (SHC 1945/ 6 p5). Has also appeared as The Folly, and was saved from being felled for a gravel quarry by a very public campaign in c1995. The name is from probably the 'Oakley Folly,' a mock chapel at the N edge of the wood.

Foomes Between Bitham Green and Rodbaston. A gospel place on the perambulation of Penkridge parish (SCSF p26) (HOP p30).

Footherley Hamlet on fairly low ground near Footherley Brook, 1m SW of Shenstone. In Shenstone ancient parish. At Forge Mill at SK 09070187 a Roman coin, an aureus of Claudius, was found in 1925 (BAST vol 53 p205. vol 86 p86) (Roman Imperial Coinage. H Mattingly and EA Sydenham. 1923-51. i-v, ix) (NSJFS 1964 p34). Has appeared as Fulwardlee (C12) (SSE 1996 p13), Fulverle (C13), Fulfordleigh (C14), Foterley (Plot's map), and Fotherley (SPN p52). The name is from perhaps 'Folcweard's lea' (DUIGNAN) (SSE 1996 p13). Or '(place at) the clearing by the dirty ford,' 'dirty' is used in the sense of 'muddy' or 'clogged (with mud or water plants)' (SPN p52).

Footherley Brook Runs from Mill Pond, Little Aston to Crane Brook at Shenstone which runs to the Black Brook.

Footherley Hall 0.75m WSW of Shenstone. In Elizabeth I's reign Francis Floyer, a younger son of the Hintz family was settled here. From him it passed to the Dolphins. The house and estate belonged to Mr Cooper of Shenstone Court at some time in the later C19 (ASE p8). By 1993 the hall was a nursing home for the elderly run by Spanish nuns (St John the Baptist, Shenstone. Dick & Audrey Davies. 1993. p11).

Ford Hamlet 1.5m WSW of Grindon. The original settlement lies on the E bank of the Hamps in Grindon parish. By the mid C17 there was settlement on the W bank in Onecote township in Leek ancient parish (VCH vol 7 p211). Birthplace at the end of the C18 of the antiquary and collector, Thomas Mycock (OL vol 2 p174).

Ford Brook Tributary of the Trent. Appears in 1571 as ffordebrooke (1571) (SPNO p10).

Ford Brook Ford Brook with Clock Mill Brook (which joins it S of Station Road, Rushall) was called Walsall Water by Erdeswick and Willmore (VCH vol 17 p143 note). It has been considered one of the three Tame head rivers and is called the Tame by Dilworth in TMS. Rises at Clayhanger, or further N on Brownhills Common. Flows between Pelsall and High Heath to Walsall where under the site between Lichfield and Darwall Streets occupied by Walsall central library and the Gala Baths it is joined by The Holbrook. The united brook then continues as Walsall Brook under Walsall and joins the Tame (or Bescot Brook) close to its confluence with the main Tame (VCH vol 17 p143). The name may be from a family named 'de Ordeseye' who were living on or near the stream in the C13 and C14. So; 'Ord's brook' (DUIGNAN) (SPN p91).

Ford Green Tiny hamlet in the vicinity of Ford Green Hall. In Norton-in-the-Moors chapelry in Stoke-upon-Trent. Is the small district to the SSW of it, called New Ford; there is a primary school called New Ford.

Ford Green Hall Timber-framed hall 1.5m ENE of Burslem. Built in Elizabeth I's reign, or in 1624 (WMARCH 1995 p76) (ES July 31 1997 p16). The N wing was rebuilt in 1734. Seat of the Ford family for more than 200 years before passing in the early C19 to the Warburtons, potters (NSFCT 1955 p76). There is an inscription in a window pane in the lattice of the front bedroom casement which reads - 'James Oakes from Macclesfield and Hezechich Harrison from Stanley repaired these windows July 9 1790' (SFH p9) (STM Sept 1964 p32p. Feb 1970 pp26-29. March 1970 p22p). The hall, surrounded by floods in 1946, was sold to Stoke-on-Trent corporation in 1951, and was restored and made into a folk museum in 1952 (SHST pp230p of it surrounded by water, 562,563p). Some of the artifacts are a C14 dole cupboard with a carving of an abbot, a 'Peter's pence' money box, a scold's bridle and a C18 Soho Tapestry (STM March 1969 p31ps) (STM 1964 p32). The hall is said to be haunted (ES Dec 9 1977). (SLM autumn 1955 pp18-20ps) (STM Sept 1964 pp32-33). Eliot Green's painting 'View of Ford Green Hall' (1952) was on display in the Potteries Museum in Feb 1997. In the garden is a brick dovecote. Excavations in to the rear of the hall between 1995 in and 1997 showed evidence of an earlier house on the site (WMARCH 1995 p76) (ES July 31 1997 p16). At the rear of the hall in 1985 were worked stones from a farmhouse in Birches Head Lane, demolished in 1956. The stones are thought to have originally come from Hulton Abbey (SASR 1985 p31). In the garden is a finial from reputedly Turnhurst Hall gateway (SASR 1995 no 6 p25).

Ford Hayes House 1.5m SE of Bucknall. Formerly in Caverswall ancient parish. Hugh Bourne (d1852), founder of Primitive Methodism, was born at Ford Hayes farm on April 3 1772. In later childhood Bourne moved to Bemersley Green (see).

Ford Houses Former hamlet now a suburb of Wolverhampton 1m WNW of Bushbury. In Bushbury ancient parish. Takes its name from a hamlet which emerged on the old road between Wolverhampton and Stafford, near the ford across Wybaston Brook (SHOS vol 2 p184) (SPN p145). Persons living here in the C14 are described in documents as 'atte forde' (DUIGNAN). Fordhouses is said to be the birthplace of William Pitt (1749-1823), agriculturist and author of AOS and THS. A plane crashed at Ford Houses in April 1970. Three people were killed when the 12-seater executive aircraft almost demolished a house in Redhurst Drive. The victims were Mrs Nellie Hilton, who lived in the house, the pilot and co-pilot. The plane, belonging to Dowty-Boulton Paul, had been trying to land at Wolverhampton Airport (BUOP p90p). The church, St James, Taunton Avenue, was built in 1967 (LDD).

Fordhouses Mill Farm Stood in the area of the present Cricket Meadow, Fordhouses. Formerly owned by Lincoln College, Oxford. The house had been rebuilt by 1846 and was demolished in c1960, when the houses were built in Cricket Meadow (BUOP p24ps).

Ford Wetley Fragmented settlement to the W of Ford, Grindon. Formerly in Onecote township in Leek ancient parish. Of the three surviving houses which form the settlement, the one called Ford Wetley over 0.5m WSW of Ford is of the late C19 but stands on the site occupied by a house in 1666; the other two are probably of the C18 (VCH vol 7 p212). Wetley Ford may be another (erroneous) way of referring to Ford Wetley.

Forebridge Suburb and former manor (VCH vol 6 p228) and township in Castle Church ancient parish. The name has appeared as For(e)brigge (1221) (SSE 1996 p13), Forbrige (1291), Castelforbrugg (1372), Fforbryge (1439), Forde Bridge als Stafford Grene (Leland c1540) (SPNO p76). It means 'Bridge before (the town)' (SSE 1996 p13). Forebridge suburb evolved in the Middle Ages outside Stafford town walls in fields by the South (or Green) Gate, and centred on The Green (SSTY p3) (VCH vol 6 p194). Stafford burgesses had the right of cultivation in Green Field (between the Wolverhampton and Lichfield Roads), their rights were lost at the time of the enclosures in the

C19 (SSTY p3). The Manor of Castre (see) (or manor of Stafford) started to hold its courts in Forebridge from at least the C16 (VCH vol 5 p88) and the court house may have been built on the site of Saint John's Hospital (see). The manor may have had its gallows N of Lichfield Road at Queensville (near the site of the present cricket grounds at the Hough) where there were field names such as Gallows Flat and Gallows Leasow (VCH vol 6 p228). Reputedly there the Catholic recusant, Father Robert Sutton of Burton upon Trent (see), was executed for his faith July 27 1588 (SSTY p142) (SCHJ No. 23 1988 pp1-8). One of Stafford's two pairs of stocks was on the Green opposite the Ivy House (SCSF p130) (VCH vol 6 p228). The lock-up next to the White Lion Inn, Lichfield Road (DoE II) (SSTY pp119,120p) (BOE p248) (MR p293) (SAC pp131p,132) dates from the early part of the C18. It then served Castle Church parish and later the whole of Stafford. Its stone is said to come from the ancient St John's Hospital at Forebridge. Sidney Horne has said that the white sandstone blocks came from the quarries at Tixall and the red ones from quarries at Kingston Hill. The interior, curiously, has a massive brick-built arch roof and it has been suggested that the lock-up was customised to serve as an ice-house (SKYT pp58,59ps). In the late C18 Shaw noted the very rare Wild Licorice or Astragalus Glycyhyllus growing on a ditch bank in the road leading from Stafford to Penkridge, nearly opposite the RC chapel (SHOS vol 1 part 1 p99), presumably that of St Austin in Forebridge. Forebridge was transferred to Stafford Borough in 1835 (W p320) (VCH vol 6 p194). A church, St Paul, was built at some distance SE of the Green in Lichfield Road. It was consecrated in 1844 (VCH vol 6 p248). The name Forebridge appears applied to an emerging settlement by St Paul's in the later C19 (1834 OS map). The separate ecclesiastical parish of Forebridge created in 1844 is now (1991) called 'Stafford St Paul' (GLAUE p411). For the ghost of Garden Street see Stafford.

Forebridge Hall On N side of the Lichfield Road, Forebridge, Stafford. In 1452 a hall here belonged to John Barbour and it remained in his family until 1600 when sold to the Leighs from London, who sold it in c1615 to the Drakefords. Gregory King records in c1680 that shields of arms of the Drakefords and others were set in the windows of Green Hall. The Drakefords were still the owners in the early C19 (SAC p133); Richard Drakeford of Forebridge Hall was a member of two very early Stafford clubs for gentlemen (OP p8). In 1825 the present hall with an impressive stucco facade was built. By 1831 the Forebridge Hall estate belonged to CH Webb (SAC p133). The hall was occupied by Edwin Bostock, mayor of Stafford, between 1842 and 1892. During his occupancy a tenant at the hall, Miss RL Weston, claimed it was haunted (SAC p133p). He was succeeded by Capt Hon George Augustus Anson (SAC p107). WE Pickering sold the hall to Staffs county council in 1922. Thereafter it was used as the prep school for the Girls' High School and took the name of Green Hall, probably from its proximity to The Green or Stafford Green. From 1949 to at least the late 1950s it was occupied by the Architect's Department of the County Council Education Committee (VCH vol 5 p91). There was an ice-house to the NE of the house (OS Map of Stafford 1900).

Forebridge House Lichfield Road, Stafford. Built in c1760. Owned by William Perkins (d1774), who was both a farmer and schoolmaster. He ran a small charity school from here. As an inventive mathematician he was the first person known to have drawn longitudinal lines on an atlas globe for the guidance of ships at sea. The house appears to have continued as a school to the mid C19 and thereafter became a private residence. In the early C20 it was used as a private hospital (SAC pp123p,124).

Forebridge Villa Lichfield Road, Stafford. Built by Benjamin Rogers in 1809. Since 1907 the villa has been St Joseph's Convent (VCH vol 5 p91) (BOE p248) (SAC pp135-136p of rear).

Foregate Suburb which grew up outside the town walls of Stafford in the Middle Ages in fields by the North Gate or Gaol Gate. In St Mary's parish, Stafford. Foregate is recorded as early as 1170 (SSTY p3). Formerly anciently part of Marston manor but had enjoyed the privileges of Stafford borough from 1206 (VCH vol 6 p222). The name is now applied to the larger district or suburb in the same area. Here was a Franciscan friary (see Grey Friars) and Stafford's pinfold. In 1585 in Foregate Field was a **windmill** (VCH vol 6 pp212-213) (WIS pp13p,22,36-37 il x). **Quakers** were in Stafford in c1650 (SKYT p38p of the meeting house). In 1674 they established themselves at Foregate. They built a meeting house on the E side of Foregate Street in 1730. The meeting house was still being used in 1948 and was still standing in 1996 (DoE II) (HOS p66) (BOE p246). The approach to the meeting-house was a Quaker burial ground (SSAHST 1970 p44). (SKYT pp37-41). **Staffordshire General Infirmary** was built on the W side of Foregate Street in 1769-72 to designs of Benjamin Wyatt of Blackbrook Farm (see) (BOE p246) (VCH vol 6 pp234-235). The hospital appears to have also been referred to as Stafford General Infirmary, here William Withering MD FRS (1741-1799),

physician, botanist, mineralogist, and discoverer of the use of digitalis in certain forms of heart failure, made his early pharmacological studies. He was in practice at the hospital from 1767 to 1775 and was sole physician at it when it opened in 1766; a copy of his 'A Systematic Arrangement of British Plants, with an easy Introduction to the Study of Botany' (5th ed 1812) is in the Daltry (NSFC) Library in Hanley Library (DNB) (VCH vol 6 p187) (SKYT p65) (NSFCT 1998-99 pp8-9). Dr Erasmus Darwin of Lichfield (see) was surgeon-extraordinary here from 1783 to 1801. The hospital has also appeared as Stafford Infirmary, here Francis Barber, former servant to Dr Johnson of Lichfield (see), died in 1801 (The Life of Johnson. James Boswell. 1791. Penguin ed 1984 p356). In 1909 Thomas Gainsborough's portrait of Mr Eld of Seighford Hall, founder of the hospital, was discovered at the hospital. It was said to have been painted in Bath in c1783 (Staffs Sentinel June 2 1909) (SN June 5 1909 p3), but another account says it was commissioned in 1774; it was sold in 1912 to the Museum of Fine Arts, Boston, USA (SHJ spring 1994 p22). The hospital, taken over by the National Health Service in 1948, has been superseded by Stafford District General Hospital at Coton Hill (see). By 1997 the old hospital was closed and becoming derelict. (SIOT pp27-28) (SKYT pp62-65) (SHJ spring 1989 pp1-6). A union **workhouse** was built in Marston Road in 1838 (HOS p68), by the early 1970s it was Fernleigh Hospital (BOE p246). A plaque from it is now in the reserve collection of the County Museum, Shugborough. Sometimes Foregate refers to the gate called North Gate (SOSH p148). **Forehead** was the name of wakes in the N end of Stafford. Held in October, they had lapsed by end of the C19 (VCH vol 6 p256) (HOS p69).

Foregate Field One of the open fields of Stafford. Stafford burgesses had the right of cultivation in Foregate Field, their rights were lost at the time of its enclosure in 1807 and most of it was built on by boot and shoe factories (HOS p69) (NSJFS 1975 p30). But part of the field survives as Stafford Common (see) in Stone Road (SSTY p3).

Foreign, The Some large parishes and manors were divided into two districts - the town or borough, and the territory left outside the town or borough, known as the foreign. Borough and foreign districts evolved in the parishes of Dudley (see), Walsall (see) and Wolverhampton (see).

Foreign One of three wards of Walsall municipal borough (W p639) (VCH vol 17 p217).

Forest, The District E of Birchills (DUIGNAN pp16,74). The name The Forest appears on the tithe map of 1843. This lay between the present Forest Lane and Hawbush Road. Gives its name to Forest Colliery (SNBP p27).

Forest Banks Watershed escarpment (LTD p115) to the SW of Marchington, and a remaining part of Needwood Forest that was surviving anything like the former state of the forest by the early C20 (LGS p191). A Neolithic axe and a Bronze Age palstave have been found on Forest Banks (LTD p115).

Forest Gate A modern housing estate in New Invention (Selective Essays on Willenhall. David Potts. 1984. Copy in Willenhall library). There is a Forest Gate on S side of Lichfield Road (Birmingham A-Z).

Forest of Blore Fairoak. Known as Bishop's Wood because it belonged to the bishops of Lichfield (BOV p35). Has also been known as Blore Park.

Forest of Leek Medieval palatinate forest centred on Leek and belonging to the Earls of Chester (see under Chartley Castle). It was in existence by c1170 to the C16. It covered Leekfrith township (VCH vol 7 p197), Rushton Spencer, and Hollinhay Wood (SSE 1993 p5).

Forest of Mercia New fragmented forest. One of 12 in the country developed by the Countryside Commission and Forestry Commission and five local authorities since 1989. The forest stretches from Bednall in the N to Great Barr in the S and from Coven in the W to Lichfield in the E. Woodland is planned for only one third of this area, and the urban conurbations of Cannock, Brownhills, Aldridge and Burntwood are merely to be surrounded by woodland (The Forest of Mercia Forest Plan. Oct 1993) (David Grundy) (HOS 1998 p34).

Forest of Schecheel From 1190-1 until at least Edward I's reign a payment of 9 shillings 'in wasto forestae de Schecheel' appears on the Staffs Pipe Roll as part of the sheriff's farm. Appears as Schehulle from 1201. It has been identified with Checkhill (SHC 1925 p244) (VCH vol 2 p335 note).

Forest Side Tiny hamlet 1m NNE of Yoxall. In Yoxall parish (1834 OS map). The name is preserved in Forest Side Farm.

Forge At Cradley (Plot's map). It probably just refers to a forge. But an area here did become Cradley Forge, and there is a Forge Lane.

Forge Farm At N end of Sandwell Valley, 2m N of Sandwell. (WBOPP pl 36). The oldest dog to have lived in the United Kingdom by 1998 was a Welsh Collie, named Taffy, owned by Evelyn Brown of Forge Farm, West Bromwich. He was whelped on April 2 1952 and died on Feb 9 1980, aged 27 and 313 days (GBR 1995 p31. 1998 p240).

Forge Farm Near Rolling Mill and Slitting Mill (SOSH p337). Perhaps it is the 'Forge' marked N of Stilecop on Plot's map. 'The Forge,' residence of Sarah Hopkins to 1808, later became Fair Oak House (VCH vol 5 p158).

Forge Houses Marked on Plot's map on the opposite side of the Penk to Somerford Hall. It probably just referred to some houses by a forge here.

Forge Mill Farm Sandwell. New and modern dairy farm by the Old Forge site, where Francis Asbury was apprenticed to the blacksmith, Mr Foxall (250th Anniversary of the birth of Bishop Francis Asbury. Aug 1995).

Forsbrook Large village on a tributary of the Blithe 13m NNE of Stafford. Former township in Dilhorne ancient parish (W p772) (HOC pp243-257). A one metre high Ice Age boulder of 200 weight, dating back 475 million years, was found by grave diggers in Forsbrook cemetery in Oct 1994 (ES Oct 14 1994 p69). Forsbrook may have been on the Roman Limes Britannicus, and it was under a mile from Richmilde Street (see), the Roman road between Derby and Chesterton. At Forsbrook a labourer who was levelling a hedge bank found in or c1879 a coin pendant containing a solidus of Valentinian I (375-392 AD), made in the Anglo-Saxon period (VCH vol 1 p212) (The Arts in Early England. G Baldwin Brown. vol 4 p539) (Early Anglo-Saxon Art and Archaeology. ET Leeds. 1936. p107) (NSJFS 1964 p23) (HAF p35) (SASR 1987 pp12-14 ils) (MIDD vol 5 p42p). The Potteries Museum had a replica made of it in 1977; the original was purchased by the BM in 1879 (SASR 1987 p12). The name has appeared as Fotesbroc (DB) (NSFCT 1915 p90), Fotesbrock (SPN p51), and Fosbroke (NSFCT 1902 p117). It means 'Fot's brook' (NSJFS 1981 p2), or 'Fotr's brook' (SSE 1996 p13); there is some doubt as to the personal name (SPN p51). There appears to have been a tollgate house called Tollgate House at Forsbrook on the Cheadle turnpike road. It was erected in 1838 and demolished in the 1960s (SMOPP vol 1 p16p). The church, St Peter, on the E side of Cheadle Road, slightly N of Uttoxeter Road, was built in 1848-1849 (BOE p132). Forsbrook became an ecclesiastical parish in 1849 (LGS p138) and a separate civil parish in 1896 (GLAUE p411). The Cheadle and Tean Times brought out the Blythe and Forsbrook Times in 1992. For Thomas James of Forsbrook who committed bestiality in 1811 see Dilhorne.

Forton Ancient parish and small village on a shelf of land above the Meese 11.5m WSW of Stafford. A flint arrowhead of the Neolithic or Bronze Age was found at Forton Rectory c1906 (NSFCT 1964 p23). The name has appeared as Forton (1198), Fortone (1292), and Fauton (Speed's map) (SPNO p146) (SSE 1996 p13). It is from perhaps 'the tun or town of the ford' or 'the hill of the ford' (DUIGNAN) (SSE 1996 p13). From a ford over the Meese forded by a Roman road (NSFCT 1937 p63). The parish was formed out of Norbury parish between 1086 and 1291: Commander Wedgwood could see no obvious reason why a church should have been founded at Forton and hence why it became a parish (SHC 1916 pp192,196). The church, All Saints, on the E side of the Meretown road, dates from c1200 with later additions (VCH vol 4 p108). The descent of the copyhold manor of Mere, in which is Forton, was governed by the custom of Borough English (VCH vol 4 p106). The parish is generally called, in legal documents, 'Forton and Meer' (W p457). The now-abandoned Newport branch of the Shropshire Union Canal, opened to the S of the village in the 1830s, brought no expansion to Forton. Its only interest here is in a bridge which carries both the Meretown road and the canal in one combined structure, a quite curious, if not rare piece of engineering (COS p62p). The view from the bank on which Forton Monument stands is extensive on a clear day. It includes Cannock Chase to the ESE; Broad Hill, Aqualate Mere and Hall, Newport and Lilleshall Hall in the S to W. In the distance can be seen Brown Clee, Wenlock Edge, Wrekin, Caer Caradoc, Long Mynd, Stiperstones, Long Mountain, Breiddens and the Berwyns to the vale of Llangollen (NSFCT 1937 p63). In the later C17 Brian Careswell of Forton parish had an eating disorder and would choose to gnaw and eat linen, wool, ropes, blankets, sheets and even his nightshirt when he was asleep (NHS p301). The antiquary, Rev Thomas Loxdale (d1742), was curate of Forton between 1698 and 1703 (SHJ spring 1991 p7).

Forton Hall Lies just W of Forton church. Built in 1665 by Gerard Skrymsher and his second wife Anne, possibly as a dower house. The first tenant was his cousin, Richard, a strong royalist (NSFCT 1937 p64). The porch is dated 1665 and the initials G.A.S. are above the door (VB p153), which stand for Gerard and Anne Skrymsher (VCH vol 4 pp104,109p facing). The hall is built of brick and is, perhaps, one of the first to be built of brick in the W of the county (SL p100). (BOE p133). Richard Skrymsher, who is said to have conducted Lord Derby to Boscobel in 1651, lived here from 1670 to 1704 (VCH vol 4 p104).

Forton House Forton. Probably built for Jeffrey Pigot in the first half of the C17. But was much altered in c1860. A brick wing of the early C19 accommodates oak panelling of c1700 from Newport, Shrops (VCH vol 4 pp104-105).

Forton House House adjoining Forebridge House, Lichfield Road, Forebridge, Stafford. Built in the later C19 as a boot and shoe factory belonging to Edwin Bostock. Between 1903 and 1905 it was occupied by French nuns, sisters of St Joseph of Cluny, who moved to Forebridge Villa in 1905 (SAC pp123p,124) or in 1907 (VCH vol 5 p91).

Forton Monument Dilapidated red sandstone conical tower over 0.25m NE of Forton church, at SJ 759217, which started life as a windmill. Formerly 30 feet high (BEV p182). Has also appeared as Forton Folly, and The Folly, and The Monument. There is a legend that on a nearby stream was a watermill, and when the stream failed the landowner built a windmill for the miller on this site (VB p155) (MR p154). A mill on this hill is recorded in 1573. In 1780 the windmill was converted into an eye-catcher for Aqualate Hall by Charles Baldwin III (NSFCT 1937 p63). It was surmounted by a ball finial in 1838 (IAS p169), which fell down in c1910 and lay beside a gatepost at a nearby farm in 1962 (BEV p182). The top of the tower started to fall in in the 1960s. It has graffiti inside, for example; '1775 FORTON,' and 'WOL 1777' (WBJ p24 il xi in 1961 with top part). (Staffordshire Views viii p8 in WSL) (VCH vol 4 p105 see plate of it in 1838 facing p166) (NSFCT vol 72 p63) (NSJFS 1966 p70) (STMSM Aug 1978 p26p). Plans in 1993 for the monument to be restored on condition that it be incorporated into a new house to be built nearby (ES Feb 23 1993 p5p) were not carried out and by early Feb 1999 the neck of the tower had collapsed. For the view from it see Forton.

Fort St George Scaled-down imitation of Fort St George, Madras, India, built of brick at SJ 878126, near Lapley. It was built by Col George Singleton Tudor of Park House, Lapley, and some of the Wolverhampton Troop of Yeomanry (to which he belonged) in 1858. It was gradually added to until 1870. When finished it consisted of earthworks, faced with stone, with deep ditches, and stone and brick buildings (WJO July 1903 xxxv). Col Tudor was a keen supporter of the 1st Lapley Rifle Volunteers and this was the Volunteer's headquarters. During the 1860s, and until 1874, the Wolverhampton Companies had training camps here over Whitsuntide and the fort was attacked and defended in mock battles. In 1903 it was said to be in ruins (WJO July 1903 xxxv). By 1955 it was derelict. The fort still stood in the early 1980s but by 1987 it and the surrounding moat had been demolished and the site reclaimed for farming. It was architecturally rather poor and was never listed by the DoE. (LCWA p79) (VCH vol 4 p145) (BOE p168) (WAAIW p13p).

Fosseway Court House at Pipehill. Built probably in the early C19 by Samuel Hamson, otherwise Bradburne, of Pipe Hill House; either the house itself or a garden feature here was known as Bradburne's Folly in 1836. Major JM Browne, hunt master of the S Staffs Hunt, was of Fosseway Court. Between 1873 and 1885 the hunt's were kept here (VCH vol 2 p363. vol 14 p286). To the E of Fosseway Court is Foss Way level crossing at SK 100079 on the SSR on the boundary of Lichfield city and Wall parish. An accident here caused a legal debate. The gatekeeper was struck by an engine and killed. This occurred within the jurisdiction of the Lichfield City coroner but since the gatekeeper's body was taken to a public house outside Lichfield city the case was dealt with by the county coroner (SSR p22).

Fould House 1.25m N of Leek. Formerly in Leekfrith township in Leek ancient parish. There was a house here by the earlier C16. It was at first called Sheephouse but had been renamed Fould Farm by 1673 (VCH vol 7 p194) and it appears as Fold on Plot's map.

Foulsitch A tract of arable land on E side of Rolleston takes its name from the little stream which drains the upper reaches of Craythorne Field (UTR p216).

Foulwell Near Aldershawe. Here was a spring which was piped to the Friary in Lichfield, half a mile away, from the early C14. The spring was granted to Lichfield corporation in 1550 (VCH vol 3 p268. vol 14 p96).

Four Alls Small hamlet at the junction of lanes with the Market Drayton-Newport road S of Pellwall (Yates' map), formerly in Drayton-in-Hales ancient parish. Now The Fouralls or The Four Alls. The Four Alls public house had a sign with a king, a parson, soldier and John Bull painted on it. The king says 'I govern all,' the parson says 'I pray for all,' the soldier says 'I fight for all,' and John Bull says 'I pay for all' (NSFCT 1913 p207).

Four Ashes Small hamlet 1.5m WNW of Enville, in Lutley manor, in Enville ancient parish. For the windmill at Four Ashes see Grove Farm. The point where Mere Lane crosses the Stourbridge-Bridgnorth road was marked by four ash trees, mentioned in 1496. There were still four trees standing there in 1817 (VCH vol 20 p94).

Four Ashes Hamlet on low ground to the N of Saredon Brook 1.5m S of Gailey. In Brewood parish. So named from an inn which had four ash trees (Saxton's map) (SPNO p41). The present inn, the Four Ashes, has a sign showing four ashes by a lane. The hamlet existed by 1775 (VCH vol 5 p18). It has been made quite large by a modern chemical works. Here was a station on the former Grand Junction Railway, opened on July 4 1837, the station closed on June 15 1959 (IAS p131) (Railways In and Around Stafford. Edward Talbot. 1994 p4).

Four Ashes Hall At SO 800877, on the W side of the Enville-Six Ashes road, Enville. It was standing by 1680 and was the seat of the Amphlett family from 1725 until at least 1982 (VCH vol 20 pp94,104).

Four Crosses Hamlet on Watling Street above Saredon Brook 1.75m WSW of Cannock. Formerly in Hatherton out-township in Wolverhampton ancient parish. Pottery was anciently made here. Roman tiles have repeatedly been found here (HOOP p63). The name appears to be from the Four Crosses Inn, which had the sign depicting the arms of the See of Lichfield, which has four forme crosses in each corner (CCBO). Has appeared as 4 Crosses (NHS p400) and Fower Crosses (Morden's map).

Four Crosses Inn An old coaching inn on Watling Street at Four Crosses. On a beam in the front of the house is or was carved '1638 I.N.E.' (WJO Nov 1904 pp295-296) (CCBO) or '1636 N' (DoE) and accompanied by a Latin inscription:

Fleves, si scires unum tua tempora mensem;
Rides, cum non sit, forsitan, una dies

(SHOS vol 2 p172) (SCSF p168). One translation is:

You would weep if you knew you had but one month to live,
You laugh, when perchance you have not one day

This is thought to be the work of Sir Thomas More (CCBO). Another translation is:

You'd weep, if doom'd but for a month to stay;
Yet laugh, uncertain of a single day

(SHOS vol 2 p172). Another translation is:

You'd weep and cry
If sure to die
Before one month were past:
And yet you play
And sport away
This one poor day,
Though it may prove your last.

(WJO Nov 1904 pp295-296) (SCSF p168). JR Veall gives a slightly different translation again (OHW pl 20). Dean Swift is recorded as having always stayed here on his way between London and Ireland. By the 1930s the couplet he is reputed to have written on a window pane -

Thou fool! to hang four crosses at thy door; Hang up
thy wife, there needs not any more.

(SSC p121 in the intro) (IADC p220) - had gone. A member of the Lovatt family, whose family had kept the inn for more than a couple of centuries, told Wright in the 1930s she had seen the window with the inscription when she was a little girl in the 1840s. In the late C18 it was the property of Mr Fowler, attorney of Burton (SHOS vol 2 p172). (WJO Nov 1904 pp295-296) (NSFCT 1924 p198) (CCBO pp49 p facing,50-52) (CCC p93) (IADC p220) (KES p58) (IOI p16 no mention of Swift). There used to be a Four Crosses Inn at Offley Brook in the late C19 (EOP p49) (ROT p20).

Fourlane Ends Southern tip of Outlands? Here the Eccleshall-Cheswardine road crosses the Fairoak-Adbaston road.

Four Lanes End Local name for the junction of the Church Eaton-Bromstead and Goosemoor-Brineton roads (info Ron Balding).

Four Lanes End To S of Ladfordfield.

Four Lanes End To E of Haughton.

Four Lanes End Highwood, 1m SSE of Uttoxeter. According to tradition here was Uttoxeter's gibbet (HOU p268). Has also appeared as Four Lane Ends.

Four-Trees Minute hamlet 0.25m SE of Lower Tean.

Fowlchurch House 0.5m NE of Leek. Formerly in Tittesworth township in Leek ancient parish. Has appeared as Fowker (1246), Fowcher Grange (1552) Foucher House (1648), Foulchurch (1677), and Fowlchurch (Later 1630s. 1834 OS map) (VCH vol 7 p237). Dieulacres Abbey had a grange here by 1246 (VCH vol 7 p233). Since the Dissolution the Fowlchurch estate has had many owners. It was occupied by Hugh Washington at the end of the C16.

The present house appears to date from c1700. It was bought by William Challinor in 1799 and sold by his son, William, to Mr Brough; he re-fronted it in 1849 (OL vol 2 pp196-197il) (VCH vol 7 p237).

Fowlea Brook Rises N of Ravendale, Tunstall. It was anciently forded at Longbridge or now called Longport (SHST p11). Runs by Etruria railway station (HOE p26). Joins the Trent at Stoke-upon-Trent (CAST p7). Has also appeared as aqua de Foulehee (1414), Fowley brooke (1538), ffowley broke (1533-1539), the fowle lea (1635), ffouley brooke (1648) (SPNO p10), The Fowley, Fowl Lea, Foulea (H p20), Fowlhay (CAST p7) and Fowl Haye (SK p32). The name is from 'Fugle ea' bird (frequented) water rather than 'fule ea,' foul or dirty water. 'Fugle' became contracted to 'fule' (NSFCT 1946 p160) (SPNO p10).

Fowlea Valley Valley of the Fowlea Brook (POP p18).

Fowl Hay Etruria. Former enclosure in the vicinity of Fowlea Brook? On the 1834 OS map Foul Hay is a tiny hamlet at the bottom of Basford Bank. Has also appeared as Fowl Hey (POP p19) and may be another form of Fowlea.

Fox Earth House and tiny district over 0.75m E of Moddershall. Formerly Fox Holes in Kibblestone quarter in Stone ancient parish (W p371) (OS map 1834) (local info).

Fox Earth There is a house called this 1m SE of Werrington. Formerly in Weston Coney township of Caverswall ancient parish (W p753). Has also appeared as Foxearth.

Foxfield Over 0.5m N of Dilhorne, at Godleybrook. The Foxfield Stream Railway Society was formed in 1967 (STMSM June 1978 p13ps). They run the Foxfield Light Railway an enthusiasts line on the former line between Foxfield Colliery and the Uttoxeter-Stoke line (BCM July 1976 pp10-11) (IANS pp28-29) (A Foxfield Album. John K Williams. 1978) (The Cheadle Railway. Allan C Baker. 1979) (ES May 10 1999 p5).

Foxhills Orton Hills (PMPD p77il). A former quarry site (POAP p12 il facing). Foxhills, the house in Orton Lane, was built in 1932 (PAIP p67).

Fox Holes Former estate 0.5m NW of Talke. Formerly in Talke township in Audley ancient parish. It belonged to the Unwins of Clough Hall for many years prior to 1733 (SHC 1944 p70). Foxholes Farm still formed part of the Clough Hall estate in 1811 (KAIW p6).

Fox Holes Draycott-in-the-Clay. Has also appeared as Foxholes.

Foxley Hamlet in Cotes division in Eccleshall ancient parish (W p379). 1m SW of Standon.

Foxley House 1.5m N of Audley. In Audley ancient parish. There is a house called Lower Foxley further N.

Foxley Branch of the Caldon Canal. Spurred off the Caldon Canal at Foxley Lane and ran to Daisy Bank Bridge on the New Road. Opened in c1820 (HCMS No. 5).

Foxley Bridge Hamlet 0.5m W of Milton. Formerly partly in Burslem and Norton-in-the-Moors chapelries in Stoke-upon-Trent ancient parish (1834 OS map). The name is preserved in Foxley Lane.

Foxlowe C18 house in Market Place, Leek. Once the seat of the Cruso family (NSFCT 1990 p39). William Cumberlidge was killed at Fox Low in 1854 (OL vol 1 p330). Overlooking Foxlowe were a clump of twelve trees on high ground known as the 'Twelve Apostles' (OL vol 1 p282). There were plans to turn the early C19 building called Foxlowe into a hotel in 1996 (ES Jan 12 1996 p9).

Foxlow Hollow The Trent flows through it at Crowborough.

Fox's Wood Farm 1m S of Milwich. Appears as Foxes Wood on 1834 OS map and Dower's map.

Foxt Moorland village on a high promontory above Shirley Brook 17.5m NE of Stafford. The village formerly lay partly in an out-township of Checkley ancient parish, which was removed to Ipstones civil parish in 1893, and partly in Morredge-with-Foxt township in Ipstones ancient parish. The name has appeared as Foxwiss (1176) (SSE 1996 p13) (SPN p52) (NSFCT 1977 p43), Foxwyst (1311. 1333) (FX p6), Foxewist (1333), Foxeweist (1610) (FX p6). The first element in old forms of the name may be from Anglo-Saxon 'fox' meaning 'fox,' or Fox, a post-Conquest personal name (DUIGNAN) (FX p5). The second element 'yate' or 'gate' in old forms may be from an early Norse word meaning 'road' (NSFCT 1977 p43). The compound has lead Dr and Mrs AE Dodd to think Foxt lay on a medieval trackway then known as the Fox's road (NSFCT 1977 p43). Or is 'place by the foxes burrows' (SSE 1996 p13) (SPN p52). Or is perhaps from 'uais' lofty, or from Irish 'uchd,' or Welsh 'uchedd' meaning a height (NSFCT 1910 p161). The church, St Mark the Evangelist, on the corner of the main road and Shay Road, was built in 1838 (LDD) (BOE p133). Foxt with Whiston ecclesiastical parish was formed in 1897 out of Checkley and Kingstone ancient parishes, and Ipstones ecclesiastical parish (TOI p12) (GLAUE p411) or in 1898 (LGS p138). The Causeway a road leading up to Foxt from Froghall on which are many houses is in local dialect The Casey (PRT pp71-72) (NSFCT 1977 p43) (SVB p78). A UFO was seen over Foxt by Mrs Mylan of Woodcutters View, Foxt, at the end of July and the beginning of Aug 1967 (FSRP pp5,22-23).

Foxyards An area and ironstone deposit site in Sedgley ancient parish (VCH vol 2 p120) to the S of Sedgley Road West and to the W of Dudley Road, Tipton (CWBT p72). Foxyards Colliery was in operation in the early C19 to at least the early C20 (Plan of the Mines of Lord Dudley 1812) (OS map Sheet 67.08) (TB Dec 1994 p10).

Fradley Village on a gentle incline on the S side of Trent Valley, 16.25m SE of Stafford. Former township in Alrewas parish (W p592). Appears in 1262 as Fodreslege (SSE 1996 p13). The name is from perhaps 'feader' meaning father. So, 'Feader's lea' or it may be 'Frod - Frod's lea' (see Fradswell) (DUIGNAN) (SSE 1996 p13) (SPN p52). Fradley was in Alrewas prebend (SSAHST vol 2 1960-61 p43). Became a separate civil parish in 1866 (GLAUE p411). The church, St Stephen, on the corner of Church Lane and Old Hall Lane, was built in 1861 (BOE p133). In the later C17 Plot was told about shrieks heard here which sounded like someone about to be murdered (NHS p22), and it was at Fradley he noted a deformed cow which was in effect two calves joined together (NHS p262).

Fradley Common SW of Fradley. Formed part of the extensive waste of Alrewas Hay (W p593). Has also appeared as Fradley Heath and Alrewas Common (SHOS vol 1 p131). Lichfield races were held here from the early 1680s until 1701, when they were transferred to Whittington Heath, where they were held in 1702 (VB p14) (VCH vol 14 pp22,161). The Staffordshire Volunteer Cavalry (later Staffordshire Yeomanry) trained on the common in 1794 (Alrewas PR) (FSP p61). The common was enclosed in c1805 (W p593). In 1920 point-to-point races were held here. The RAF built an **airfield** on Fradley Common in 1939 and it was known as RAF Station Lichfield. It is said that Amy Johnson was the first pilot to touch down on the airfield (1940) (WMA vol 1 pp190-208). After 1941 the airfield came under the control of No. 6 Group Bomber Command who introduced the Wellington Bomber (SVB p79). During the Battle of Britain Day Air Display at the station in 1947 station test pilot, Flight Lieut Hadley, and his passenger, Squadron Leader Shaw, the Station stores officer, died in a crash as a result of a high speed stall during a low level aerobatic display. After the RAF left in 1957 or 1958 and the station closed in 1962 (WMA vol 1 pp190-208) the land returned to agriculture (SVB p79). At about the time of the airfield's closure, or shortly after, sightings were made of lights flickering on and off in the control tower, then mainly disused. Also, and perhaps in connection with this, was seen the ghost of a headless officer walking towards the control tower. The ghost was believed to be a pilot killed in a Wellington Bomber which crashed here in WW2 (Ghosts Among Us. Harry Ludlam. 1994 p26) (WMA vol 1 p198) (MS&S pp60-61). A large WW2 pillbox, 18 feet long, with walls three feet six inches thick is situated at SK 150122 (WMARCH 1993 p35).

Fradley Hall The remains of an old half-timber-framed house, called Fradley Hall, could be seen in Fradley village in the later C18 (SHOS vol 1 pp131,135). The house had belonged to the family of Gilbert of Woodford, Essex, in the C17 (SHOS vol 1 p131) and passed by the marriage of Sarah Gilbert in 1672 to William Goring of Kingstone, Staffs, a descendant of the Gorings of Sussex, whose arms he bore, as in Plot's map (SOS (1844) p317). The coat of arms of the Goring family still remained over the front door by the late C18 when the hall was occupied by a farmer (SHOS vol 1 p131). A moat used to surround the hall until its stagnant waters were reputed to have caused the owner's daughters to catch scarlet fever and it was filled in (SVB p79). Has also appeared as Fradley Old Hall, or Old Hall Farm? (SSAHST 1982-3 p34).

Fradley Junction Junction of the Coventry Canal and the Trent and Mersey Canal 1.25m WNW of Fradley. Formerly in the extra-parochial liberty of Alrewas Hay. When completed this junction and the Great Haywood Junction were the crossing points which achieved Brindley's plan for a 'Grand Cross' of canals linking together the estuaries of Mersey, Trent, Thames and Severn (SL pp236,237).

Fradswell Small fragmented village on the side of a small valley created by Fradswell Brook, 10.25m NNE of Stafford. Former chapelry and out-township of Colwich ancient parish (NSFCT 1913 p60). The manor of Frodeswelle appears in DB as a member of Great Haywood manor (HAHS p17). The name is from Anglo-Saxon 'Frod's well or spring' (SSE 1996 p13), or 'Frod's stream' (SPN p52). Frod means 'wise' (DUIGNAN). (STM Sept 1965 p36). The church, St James the Less, SE of Fradswell Hall, has work of c1200 (BOE p134), but was mainly rebuilt in 1764 and enlarged in 1852 (LGS p139). The wake was on the first Sunday in August in the C19 (W p416). There was possibly a medieval village, now lost, at Fradswell or 0.5m ENE of the church at SJ 998315 (SSAHST 1970 p35). Fradswell was in Colwich prebend

(SSAHST vol 2 1960-61 p44). It became a separate ecclesiastical parish in 1851 (W p416) and a separate civil parish in 1866 (GLAUE p411).

Fradswell Brook Rises N of Coton Hayes joins Dutton's Brook at Fradswell.

Fradswell Hall In Fradswell village. The first Fradswell Hall was built by Thomas Lord Cromwell 1st Earl of Ardglass in the C17 (NSFCT 1924 p112). The hall was the residence of Edmund John Birch (d1829); later of John Smith (Joule?) (d1865); later of Josiah Dimmock (d1892); later of Judge Sir John Ashworth (d1975), appointed to the Queen's Bench Division of the High Court in 1954 (mems in Fradswell church) (SSTY p131). (Staffs Illustrated Jan 1968 pp8-9). In 1622 William Burton noted gypsum near the hall which he hoped to exploit commercially, but he thought there was not enough (although there was some) (NHS pp173-174) (VCH vol 2 p198).

Fradswell Heath Former common land on which there are a few houses making a tiny hamlet 1.25m NE of Fradswell. Formerly partly in Fradswell township in Colwich ancient parish and partly in Stowe ancient parish. 39 acres of Fradswell Heath in Colwich parish were enclosed under an Act of 1852 (SHC 1941 p19). About this time a notice in SA described the inhabitants of Fradswell, and especially those of the 'barren' Heath, as an immoral, superstitious lot, who totally disregard the Sabbath, because they are without a resident clergyman (SA Sept 1850 - an appeal for a Rectory at Fradswell) (NSFCT New Series vol 18 1993 p13).

Frameyard, The Name of field which is within five yards of the SW corner of Rocester church. Here in 1932 the foundations of the house built by the Trenthams after the demolition of Rocester Abbey could plainly be seen (NSFCT 1932 p113). Has also appeared as Frame Yard.

Frank i' th' Rocks Cave Manifold Valley. Is probably the 'Frank's Hole' in WTCEM. If it is, this was a workshop for the cobbler, Frank Marsh or Beresford, and in it he reared his family (WTCEM p145).

Franklins House 0.75m SW of Meerbrook. Formerly in Leekfrith township in Leek ancient parish (NSFCT 1905 p162). Has also appeared as Franklyns.

Frankville Former Norman settlement between Ranton and Ellenhall at SJ 844253. In the vicinity of Frankville has been found a Pre-historic quern and a Stone Age (Palaeolithic-Neolithic) axe (NSFCT 1908 p176. 1928 p165) (STM Aug 1965 p31). According to Hadfield the vill of Frankwell was given by John de Frankville to the prior of Ranton (SHC 1914 p83 note). It has appeared as Frankwell and Frankwell Orchard. The depopulated medieval village, noted by Loxdale (NSFCT 1908 p176), was probably deserted in the C16 (SSAHST 1970 p35). Foundations have been excavated; one spot in the ploughland was known locally as the 'market place' and a kind of cobbled pavement was exposed with a plough. This was thought, in 1902, to have been of Roman origin: The vallum of the Roman Limes Britannicus (see) passed this way (NSFCT 1902 p118). The remains of an old wooden drain system, 20 yards long and 1.5 feet wide, have also been found. This was perhaps the remains of a fulling mill. Local tradition suggests that a row of cottages stood in the middle of a field to almost within living memory (1964). The existence of such a village would account for the enormous bulge in the parish boundary (SN July 17 1964 p5). Could the nearby Anne's Well (Anne's Well Wood), be a corruption of Frankwell?

Freda's Grave Gravestone commemorating the dog who was the mascot of the New Zealand Rifle Brigade (VB p113). On Coppice Hill 0.75m ESE of Brocton, on E side of Camp Road, at approximately SJ 978188 (BERK2 p80 see map) on Cannock Chase. Freda was a Dalmation (Discover Cannock Chase: Follow the Great War Motor and Foot Trail. Staffs County Council). The grave is cared for by The Friends of Cannock Chase (STMSM Nov 1978 p15p). (SA Oct 1 1964 p10. Oct 8 1964 p1p) (Cannock Chase Country Park Notice Board) (Before the Houses Come: The Story of a Farming Family in the Rural Parish of Berkswich. Marjorie Knight. 1992 pp10p,11).

Freeford There seems to have been two small hamlets of Freeford, one over 1.25m SE of Lichfield cathedral centred on Freeford House, and another centred on Freeford Manor, 0.5m to the SSE. Former township in St Michael's parish, Lichfield (VCH vol 14 p253). The manor of Fraiforde appears in DB. Later forms are: Freford (SPN p78), and Friesforde (C16) (DUIGNAN). The name is from a ford on the Lichfield-Tamworth road over Darnford Brook. The 'Friesforde' form points to a heath, Friesland being always 'heath-land,' from Anglo-Saxon 'fyrs,' Middle English 'firse,' and a great heath, called Whittington Heath, did commence here; so perhaps, 'the heath ford' (DUIGNAN). 'Or the ford with no toll' (SSE 1996 p14) (SPN p78). Or rather 'free' in the sense that it was open or accessible, presumably in contrast to Darnford, the hidden or secret ford, further down stream (VCH vol 14 p253). Freeford is a prebend in Lichfield cathedral founded by Bishop Clinton in c1140 (SHOS vol 1 p292) (VCH vol 3 p141) and was one of the earliest foundations. It included St John's Hospital, Lichfield; by Bishop William Smith's Statutes of 1495 the prebendary of Freeford had the right to appoint one of the 13 almsmen at the hospital (SSAHST vol 2 1960-61 p46). There was a deserted medieval village in the vicinity of Freeford Manor, at SK 135075 (SSAHST 1966 p49. 1970 p35). St Leonard's Hospital, a medieval leper house, was at Freeford House (see). Once St Leonard's hospital was no longer a leper house its chapel was used by local people (VCH vol 14 p258). Edward II stopped at Freeford in 1326 before entering Lichfield city (VCH vol 14 p253). Freeford had extra-parochial status by the late 1790s to 1858 when it was created a civil parish. The civil parish was abolished in 1934 and it then entered Swinfen and Packington civil parish (VCH vol 14 pp253, 258) (GLAUE p411). When Lichfield council took an electricity supply from Walsall in 1926, it supplied Freeford free of charge because the cable ran over the Dyott estate (VCH vol 14 p253).

Freeford House 0.5m NNW of Freeford Manor at SK 132084, on W side of A38 and S side of A51. Formed the centre of a small hamlet of Freeford. Here was a green, mentioned in 1327 (VCH vol 14 p253). Freeford House stands on the site of the medieval leper house, St Leonard's Hospital established by the mid C13 (VCH vol 14 p253). Some say the leper house was at Freeford Manor (WAM pp33,39) (SVB p179). It may have been founded by a prebendary of Freeford; the patronage was certainly held by the prebendary in the late C15 (HOL p548). The hospital, which had a chapel, appears to have ceased functioning by the later C14, and in 1496 its estate was added to that of the almshouse of St John the Baptist, Lichfield. The present house is of the early C18 (VCH vol 14 p256). The chapel burial ground was discovered in 1917-18 (NSFCT vol 52 p135) (SA Feb 16 1918) (A Sentimental Journey in and about the Ancient and Loyal City of Lichfield. 1925. AD Parker. p53) (VCH vol 3 pp274-275).

Freeford Manor 1.75m SE of Lichfield cathedral. Known as Freeford Hall until the 1930s (VCH vol 14 p255). It may stand on or near the site of a medieval house (VCH vol 14 p255); probably the manor house of Freeford. Some say the hall was once the medieval leper house of St Leonard's Hospital, but this has been identified with the site of Freeford House (see). The manor passed from the Freefords to the Dyotts in the C16. Anthony Dyott was succeeded by Sir Richard Dyott (d1659-60). The Dyotts were ardent royalists in the Civil War. Richard's son or nephew, John 'Dumb' Dyott, a mute, obtained fame in Dyott family history by shooting dead the parliamentarian leader, Lord Brooke, in Dam Street, Lichfield, on 2 March 1643 during the first siege of the Lichfield (see) garrison. The gun he used was kept at the hall until at least the mid C19 (GNHS p76) (W pp488,515-516). The right for the family of **night burial** is said to have been granted to him and his descendants by Charles I in recognition of his shooting Lord Brooke. Thereafter night burial was regularly observed by the Dyotts, and although it was practised amongst other notable families, with them it became a tradition. Deceased family members were carried from Freeford Hall in procession at night to the family vault at St Mary's church, Lichfield. The cortege was lit by torchlight. General William Dyott (d1847) was buried in this way. It was also a tradition that no relative be present (FLJ 1896 p385). Col Richard Dyott, whose funeral took place on Feb 19 1891 at 9.00pm, was the last Dyott to be buried at night. There were many scenes of drunken disorder during the funeral, which was accompanied by 50 torchbearers, and the Dyotts decided to end the tradition. Richard Dyott, was also the last Dyott to be buried in the family vault in St Mary's, Lichfield, thereafter, the Dyotts were buried at Whittington (SCSF p77) (LPL) (KES p140) (SLM Sept 1950 p16) (RSL p91) (VB p15) (CCHCB pp157-159) (MR p157) (VCH vol 14 p258). A silver tankard with the figure of a Roundhead, pointing at a knat and swallowing a camel, kept at the hall illustrates Dyott family loyalty to the royalist cause. On the lid was this inscription: -

> The tankard says to Presbiter'an Jack,
> Th' art lyer lusty; in deceit no quack;
> Yett sipp, hay drinke, none sees or heares,
> Come we'll agree like savage beares;

Crest, underneath, on a wreath two wolves rampant reguled or. Underneath the man is the following:

> No ignoramus Hypocrites drink here:
> Ye lips of saints with hands of hell forbeare,
> Profane not (Regicides!) our loyall bowles,
> Sacred to Charles his heath, and all true souls.

Arms, or a tiger passant sable. Crest, the same collared and chained. (SHOS vol 1 p361). Sir Richard (d1659-60) was succeeded by his son Richard (d1677), who was succeeded by Richard (1667-1719). He was succeeded by his son

Richard (b1687) (SHOS vol 1 p362) (SHC vol 1 New Series 1898). In the C17 the Dyotts preferred to live in Lichfield. Richard Dyott (d1769) built a brick house at Freeford in the 1730s for himself. This possibly incorporated the manor house. Over the main doorway was the following inscription 'Nil Nisi Bonum, Portus amicis' (SHOS vol 1 p361, pl xxxiv of the hall). Richard Dyott of Freeford, agriculturalist, was promoter and first president of the original SAS, founded in 1800 (The History of Staffordshire Agricultural Society. Brenda Greysmith. c1978. chapter one). It was probably his pig which was the **'Spherical Pig'** which was painted by an unknown artist in 1794. It had a live weight of about 800 lbs (NSFCT 1991 p15p). The hall was altered in c1826 to designs of Joseph Potter, and altered again in 1848-9, 1851-2, and in the C20 (VCH vol 14 p255 pl 48 shows the hall in the 1790s). Pevsner attributes the whole hall to the early C19 (BOE p272). A travelling coach and a Baroche (type of Landau) made for the Dyott family in 1865 are now at the County Museum, Shugborough. To the S of the hall in a wood, at SK 136073 is an icehouse, built in 1842 (VCH vol 14 p255) (IHB p393).

Freehay Small village 1.5m SE of Cheadle. In Cheadle parish until becoming an ecclesiastical parish in 1847 (LGS p139) (GLAUE p411). The church, St Chad, on Church Bank in the village centre, was built in 1842-3 and was the first church built to the designs of (Sir) Gilbert Scott (St Chad's Church, Freehay. JDS).

Freeth Bridge Brick arched bridge which carries a road at Tower Hill over the Tame Valley Canal. Named after John Freeth, a clerk of the Birmingham Canal Navigation Company (MNB p70).

Freezeland Former hamlet E of Bilston, at the bottom of Wolverhampton Street, near its junction with the Wolverhampton Road (HOBLL p220). In Bilston chapelry in Wolverhampton ancient parish. The name is from perhaps Frieslanders who had come over to England with the Saxons (HOBLL p220). Or it is represents 'heath land,' from Anglo-Saxon 'fyrs,' Middle English 'firse' or 'furze' (same as Friezeland) (DUIGNAN). The name is preserved in Freezeland Street off Hall Park Street off Wellington Road. Has also appeared as Friezeland. Is there also a Friezeland in the Tipton area, or are they the same? Freezeland is clearly marked on the present 1:25,000 OS map.

French Croft Farm 1.25m SSE of Stonnall.

Frenchmans Street Place which occurs in a deed of C16 relating to Upper Arley (VCHW vol 3 p5). Has appeared as Frenchman Street and appears on Bowen's map, but not on recent OS maps. It was about at Shatterford. Shaw said it was one of the five townships of Arley parish (SHOS vol 2 p253).

Frenchman's Walk Walkway behind the railway station in Lichfield.

French Walls The farm French Walls was situated on the E side of Rabone Lane, Smethwick, between the railway and the canal, nearly 1m NE of Smethwick Old Church. It belonged to the Piddock family in the mid C17 and until 1661 when sold to John Pearsall. The estate became built on with factories after the building of the Birmingham Canal (1769), and may have been broken up in c1815. By this time there was some workers' housing on the estate. George Frederick Muntz (1794-1857), the political reformer and MP for Birmingham from 1840 to 1857 produced 'Muntz metal' at French Walls from 1842. By 1953 the French Walls district was the district around Smethwick Goods Station (STELE Sept 19 1952 il of the farm c1850. June 26 1953. Dec 23 1955) (VCH vol 17 pp88,100-101) (SHCB p7).

Friar Park Former estate by the Tame and now a suburb 1.25m ESE of Wednesbury, in West Bromwich ancient parish. Friars Park appears to have been an estate belonging to Halesowen Abbey in the Middle Ages. At Halesowen's suppression the estate passed to the Dudleys, Earls of Warwick. In 1614 it was acquired by Sir William Whorwood and thereafter formed part of the Sandwell estate (VCH vol 17 pp6,22). However, according to tradition the name arose because the area originally belonged to Sandwell Priory. A grange of that priory, of which the park was a part, was in a place called Moat Meadow (see) or on Crank or Cronk Hill (DUIGNAN) (WAM p54) (SPN p137). It was demolished in 1536, but parts of the moat were still visible in 1836 (SOWB p23). Ede, who could find the name in no medieval document nor in any connection with Sandwell Priory, thought the name may be from a surname (HOWV p109). Has appeared as Friar Park (by 1590) (VCH vol 17 p22), Fryars Park (1608) (HOWV p109), and as a 400 acre wood known as Friars Park Wood in 1834 (1834 OS map) and in 1887 (OS map 6 inch); this area is now (1980) known as The Woods (see) (1980 OS map 1:50,000). With the division of Lyndon ward Friar Park became a ward of West Bromwich borough in 1952 (VCH vol 17 p46). By 1999 Friar Park was a ward of Sandwell metropolitan borough. The church, St Francis of Assisi, Freeman Road, was licensed in 1931 (VCH vol 17 p59) (LDD). The Friar Park area was bombed with dozens of small incendiary bombs in a WW2 raid (TB Jan 1996 p3).

Friar Park House Friar Park. In existence between at least 1634 and the mid C19. May earlier have been the seat of the Middlemores, who were living at

Friar Park between at least 1602 and 1627 (VCH vol 17 p22).

Friars' Walk A pedestrian way in central Burton upon Trent, running N from the W front of the parish church, along the W side of the old parish churchyard (now Garden of Remembrance). On the W side of the path stood the old Grammar School. Walling along the path incorporates masonry from Burton Abbey (see) (info KL Neal).

Friary Small district of Lichfield in which stood The Friary.

Friary, The Former Franciscan friary founded in c1229 (SHOS vol 1 pp320-322), or c1230 (HOS p25), or c1237 (BOE p191) (VCH vol 3 pp268-270. vol 14 p70) by Bishop Stavenby (W p489) (LAL p17), and was Lichfield's most important religious foundation outside the cathedral Close (LAL p17) and sole religious house (NSJFS 1979 p4). It was erected on free burgages (HOL pp480-488, plan facing p483) on the W side of Bird Street and St John Street in the later 1230s (VCH vol 14 p10). It burnt down in 1291 (VCH vol 14 p11), and rebuilt. Was subject to the dean and chapter of Lichfield cathedral to 1531 (NSJFS 1979 p4). Dissolved on Aug 7 1538 (SHOS vol 1 p321) (BAST vol 55 pp53-55).

REMAINS. What is thought to have been the tombstone of Sir **Roger Hillary** and his wife Margaret, sister and coheir of Nicholas, Lord Audley, d1410-11, was seen by Dugdale during his Staffs Visitation of 1663 and 1664. It shows a man in a surcoat knelling before Christ and St Francis. Over the man is written 'Orate pro animabus mri Fogeri' 'Jll ari, dominae mar_____' (SHOS vol 1 pp320-322) (VCH vol 3 p269). The tombstone of **Richard the Merchant** was found by workmen in the foundation of an old wall and gateway on N side of the Friary on Oct 14 1746 (GM vol 16 pp465,546) (SHOS vol 1 p321* pl xxxi of the tomb; Shaw has a translation of the Latin verse) (HOL pp487-488) (GNHSS p26*) (W pp489-490; gives the verse inscription in Old English characters). It was built into the S wall of the Friary School in 1928 (LGS p264) (VCH vol 3 p269) (LTM Sept 1971 pp16-17 il). The foundations of the Friary church were excavated in 1933 (VCH vol 14 p33) and are exposed in the Friary Gardens on the corner of the street called The Friary, and Bird Street. Shaw says in levelling the ground on the N side of the Friary site, in 1783, many human skeletons were found suggesting this had been the area of the Friary cemetery (GNHS p26*) (LGS p264) (CL Oct 3 1957 p660) (STMSM July 1980 p19 p of the signboard and plan on the old Friary site p on p19) (DoE II*). The northern end of the W range of domestic buildings was demolished in the later 1920s when a new road was cut across the site (VCH vol 14 pp70-71). Friary Road follows the line of the S wall of the cloister (VCH vol 3 p270).

AFTER THE DISSOLUTION. The site of the friary was granted to Gregory Stonyng in 1544 (VCH vol 14 p70). The church, cloisters, refectory, and most of the domestic buildings were destroyed. Part of the site was described as 'wasteland where building stood' in 1552 (NSJFS 1979 p4). The W range of domestic buildings and a house, presumably 'the inn called le Bishop's Lodging or le Great Chamber' survived (VCH vol 14 p71). The **Bishop's Lodging**, built of sandstone in the early C16, was used by the friars as a guest house. It was remodelled by Stonyng and further improved by William Inge in the late C18 (VCH vol 3 p270. vol 14 p71) (LAL p17). Several arms and figures were in the windows. Michael Rawlins (d1754) was a tenant (SHOS vol 1 pp320-322 pl xxxi) (HOL pp480-488). The Duke of Cumberland had his headquarters here when the king's army was stationed at Lichfield in the 1745 Jacobite Rebellion (HOL p310). Thomas Cobb, political agent for Lord Anson and Lord Gower, was a tenant from 1754 (VCH vol 14 p70). In 1779 the residents were Mrs (Moll) Cobb and Miss Adey, who were visited by Dr Johnson and Boswell during a visit to Lichfield (W p489). Another tenant was William Inge of Thorpe Constantine (d1785), a magistrate (VCH vol 14 p70). One of its former occupants was William Loge whose abilities as a JP gained him the applause of Lord Mansfield (W p489). From c1898 the Staffordshire Yeomanry, formerly at Yeomanry House (see), had their headquarters here. In 1907 The Friary belonged to Col HD Williams (STC p43p). In 1920 the 11.5 acre Friary estate was presented to the city by Sir Richard Cooper, Bt (VCH vol 14 p32). In 1921 the house was taken over by the girls' high school. In 1928 new buildings for the school incorporated the house (VCH vol 14 p71). A Tudor fireplace from the old house and the 'Richard the Merchant' tomb were preserved (LGS p176) (LAL p17). The girls' high school was founded in 1892 and amalgamated in 1972 (LTM Sept 1971 pp16-17 il of the old Friary). The Friary School is now (1990s) the city library. The Friary was extra-parochial (W p489) until 1857 or 1858 when it became a separate civil parish, but was taken into the civil parish of Lichfield St Michael in 1934 (VCH vol 14 p87) (GLAUE p416).

Friary House Stood on the N Side of Friary Road, Handsworth, opposite Handsworth Theological College. Has also appeared as The Friary. According to tradition and Hackwood the house was built on the site of a Friars

house belonging to Sandwell Priory to which an underground passage was supposed to run. Hall does not believe the tradition of the tunnel owing to the distance to Sandwell Priory; the level of the land between, and that Sandwell was a poor priory. The house was built in 1658 as a medium-sized farmhouse, and extended into a gentlemen's residence in c1700. Alterations were made to it in c1780, when the owners were the Freer family. The property was later bought by the Earl of Dartmouth of Sandwell Hall (see), who let it in turn to Mr Birch, and Mr Frederick Arthur Walton. It was later purchased by Walter G Griffith, who lived here until it was sold and demolished in 1937, as part of the Grestone Estate (see) (HPPE pp30-31). Another account says the house was built in the later C18 or early C19, and the name bears no relation to a former religious house or site here (MNB p41).

Friezeland Walsall Wood. Brownhills. (HOBLL p220). The name represents 'heath land,' from Anglo-Saxon 'fyrs,' Middle English 'firse' or 'furze' (DUIGNAN) (SPN p91).

Frith Bottom House 0.5m NE of Meerbrook, at the bottom of Meer Brook Valley. Formerly in Leekfrith township in Leek ancient parish. Is first recorded in 1695 (VCH vol 7 p194).

Frobisher Hall Hostel built to house workers at the Royal Ordnance factory at Swynnerton in c1938. Was situated on the SW outskirts of Swynnerton village. The site became an housing estate (SN April 7 1995 p9).

Froghall Small hamlet 0.75m E of Kingsley in a hollow where the Churnet is joined by several tributaries which have fallen from Ipstones Edge. Partly in the former Morredge-with-Foxt township in Ipstones ancient parish and partly in the former Whiston township in Kingsley ancient parish. The name appears in the C15 as Frogholle (SSE 1996 p14) and has appeared as Frog Hall. It is of Middle English origin (DUIGNAN) and means 'frog hollow or valley' (SSE 1996 p14). It may be from the river-root 'bier,' 'feor' of rushing water, with the root 'uig,' 'wig' Latin 'vicus,' a strong place. 'Feor-uig' would easily pass into frog (NSFCT 1910 p161). Froghall was a natural pass into the Moorlands and must have long been a pack-saddle centre for Ipstones, Foxt, Whiston, Kingsley, and Cheadle (NSFCT 1910 p161). The Caldon Canal, constructed in 1777, culminating at Froghall but extended to Uttoxeter in 1811, and a plateway, Cotton Plane (see), transporting limestone from Caldon Low to Froghall (and on, via canal, to the Potteries), brought expansion to Froghall in the C19. Limestone was broken down in kilns at Froghall and at Consallforge; some kilns in both places still remain (DoE II) (PDS&C p106p). Patten's brass wire works, begun in Alton in 1734, was transferred to Froghall in 1828 (The Midlands. Past-into-Present series. Clive Gilbert. 1978 p69) (SL pp118-119). A colony of Welsh quarrymen settled at Froghall (ES March 2 1939 p9). In consequence of Froghall's industrial nature by the end of the C19 it was known locally as Smokeamoor (HLS p61). In 1840 a Cornish miner named Bishop discovered a band of valuable iron ore near Consall Forge, commonly known as **'Froghall Ironstone.'** It had, however long been used by the farmers of the district as 'raddle' and Plot in the later C17 noticed its use. There does not appear to be another example in the county of a deposit of this character. About the period 1860-1870 most of the iron ore had been worked out (TOI pp17-18). Another account says it was called Churnet Valley Ironstone and was found on the Belmont estate (NSFCT 1916 pp135-136). Froghall tollgate house on the road leading to Whiston closed in 1878 (COPP2 p87p). There was a train crash at Thomas Bolton's works in Froghall in 1944 (COPP2 p109p).

Froghall Area of Newcastle-under-Lyme lying between Holborn and Bridge Street. Was a housing blackspot (NULOP vol 2 p50p in 1935). Has now been developed with the ring road and car parks.

Froghall Approximately on site of Moss Farm, N of Watling Street and S of Norton Canes. Now lost. Possibly submerged beneath Chasewater? Has appeared as Frog Homer and appears on Plot's map.

Frog Hall House 1.5m SE of Stourton. Not found on current OS maps.

Froghall Canal Tunnel Kingsley. It was not a part of the original canal as opened in 1778, but formed a section of a 540 yards extension constructed between 1783-5. It is 76 yards long. There was no tow path, so boats had to be legged through. (The Trent and Mersey Canal in the Historic Waterways Scenes Series. Peter Lead. 1980. pls 113, 114).

Frog Hole House 1.5m N of Brund.

Froghole A school built by the Jervis family near Stone was called this. It was in existence by at least the mid C18 and later removed to Darlaston, near Stone (W p361).

Fryerstone Rock Between Orchard Common Colliery and Blackclough in Quarnford parish (UHAW p46). The name may be from Ffirestoen Brook.

Fulbrook Farm 0.5m S of Barton-under-Needwood. Takes its name from the Full Brook which runs close by (HOPT vol 1 p134).

Fule Brook It was said to form the boundary of Birchall Farm. It starts at

Meerbrook and descends to Tittesworth and so down to the Churnet. Has appeared as Fulhee (C13), and Fulhe (1330) (SPNO p10). It appears to be identifiable with Dingle Brook (see).

Fulfen Fulfen Farm is 1.5m E of Lichfield. Former township in St Michael's parish, Lichfield. The name means foul marshland (VCH vol 14 p275) (DUIGNAN). Fulfen hamlet was mentioned in the mid C12. A green, to E of Fulfen Farm at SK 143093, is recorded in 1435 (VCH vol 14 p275). An estate at Fulfen, known as the manor of Fulfen in 1453, seems to have centred on Fulfen Farm. Fulfen was claimed as extra-parochial in 1825, probably because it was by then owned by the Dyotts of Freeford, itself extra-parochial (VCH vol 14 pp279,282). It was created a separate civil parish in 1858. Fulfen civil parish was abolished in 1934 and it then entered Streethay civil parish and Whittington parish (GLAUE p411).

Fulfen Burntwood. 3m W of Lichfield. The name means possibly 'foul fen' (SSE 1996 p14). Appears in the C14 as Fulfon (SSE 1996 p14). Fulfen Way is mentioned in 1446; Fulfen was an inhabited area by the 1530s (VCH vol 14 p199). Fulfen Middle School is on the E side of Rugeley Road.

Fulfin House Slightly N of Fulfen Middle School, Fulfen, Burntwood (VCH vol 14 p210). Dates from the C16. Originally timber-framed. In, or later than, the C18 the house was encased in brick. The house has been thought to be too small to have been the seat of the Cotton family, who owned the Fulfen estate in the C16 and C17, and it may have been a hunting lodge or a standing from which spectators could watch the hunting on Cannock Chase (VCH vol 14 p210). Has also appeared as Fulfen House.

Fulford Small village situated in a healthy position on high ground above the Blithe Valley (Stone Rural District. The Official Guide. 3rd ed. ND. Late 1940s?), 10m NNE of Stafford. Former township and chapelry in Hilderstone quarter in Stone ancient parish (W p370) (LGS p139). Has appeared as Fuleford (DB) and Fulford-in-Stone. The name may represent either 'foul ford,' or 'full ford' (DUIGNAN). Is 'the full ford' (SPN p53). Or 'foul (muddy) ford' (SSE 1996 p14). The name perpetuates a ford across the village street which became unduly swollen in wet weather, but now (1917) a culvert carries off the excessive rains (NSFCT 1908 p132. 1917 p145). An old church stood on the site of the present, St Nicholas (1825), in the N end of the village, NW of Fulford Hall (LGS p139) (BOE p134). There was a wake on the Sunday after All Saints' day in the C19 (W p363). Fulford reputedly was the 'Gretna Green' of N Staffs, allowing runaway marriages; a claim also held by Norton-in-the-Moors (TOS p63). The PR shows no less than 84 marriages taking place in 1828 (NSFCT 1956 p112) (STM Nov 1965 p39). Couples mainly came from Longton (SVB p81). In 1916 a pair came and approached the vicar asking for an instant ceremony (NSFCT 1917 p145). Fulford became a separate ecclesiastical parish in 1774 and a separate civil parish in 1897 (GLAUE p411). In the late C19 Fulford was described as a large village (Stone Rural District. Late 1940s?). Foot-and-mouth disease broke out at Telford Hall Farm, Fulford in Dec 1967 (SN Dec 22 1967 p15). Rev Stebbing Shaw (d1802), author of SHOS, was born in Fulford in 1762 (STM Nov 1965 p39). Others say he was born in Stone (BS p397), or in or near Stone; his father was Rev Stebbing Shaw, son of John Stebbing Shaw of Stone (SH pp98-113). (SOS pplxv, lxvi il) (GNHS p57) (SLM Oct 1952 p24il). Edward VIII, probably whilst Prince of Wales, crash landed his aircraft near here in fog, trying, no doubt, to make for Meir Aerodrome, on a visit to the Potteries in the 1930s. He was uninjured (ref lost).

Fulford Dale Small dale 0.5m W of Fulford.

Fulford Green Common land in Fulford parish. There was three quarters of an acre remaining in the 1950s (OSST 1956-59 p13).

Fulford Hall Fulford. A seat at Fulford was held by the Fodon family in the later C17 (Plot's map). Has some good panelling (NSFCT 1956 p112). Has a pretty brick summerhouse with a pyramid roof in the garden wall (BOE p134).

Fulhe Brook Lies between Morridge and the Churnet (NSJFS 1970 p85). Probably rises S of Bradnop and runs to Faling Brook or Cartledge Brook.

Full Brook Forms S boundary of Walsall ancient parish (VCH vol 17 p143). Tributary of the Tame (SPNO p10). For etymology see NSFCT 1908 p132.

Full Brook Tributary of the Trent. Has also appeared as Filley (see) and Philley

Brook (SPNO p11).

Fullbrook Suburb 1m S of Walsall. In the foreign of Walsall. The name may mean a full brook or a muddy brook (SNWA p45). There was settlement at Fullbrook by the C18 where the West Bromwich road crosses the former southern boundary of Walsall (VCH vol 17 p155). Has also appeared as Fullbrooke (W p649). For the murder of Mathew Adams near Fullbrook in 1841 see Tame Bridge. The church, St Gabriel, in Walstead Road, was built in 1938 (VCH vol 17 p239).

Fullbrook Farm 2.5m ESE of Longdon. Built in c1835. Was the centre of an estate belonging to Lichfield corporation which had been devised by Richard Walker (d1547) master of Lichfield Grammar School to provide an income for the grammar school (VCH vol 14 pp233-234).

Fullbrook House Captain's Lane, Barton-under-Needwood. The house, which appears as Foo Brook in 1834, was described as a handsome Gothic building in the modern style in 1863. It was occupied in 1851 by Capt William Arden and in 1863 it was occupied by Mrs Arden (W p20) (KD 1863) (UNT pp37,122). From the Ardens it passed to Mr Davenport, who sold it in 1933 to the Hoults who lived here to 1963 (UNT p51).

Fullmoor A wood and a lodge over 2m ENE of Gailey. A place about 1m from The Four Crosses Inn. Has also appeared as Foulmire (DUIGNAN p66) and Fulmer. Here the aromatic shrub of the myrtle kind grows spontaneously, it is called gale or sweet gale and gives its name to the hamlet, Gailey (GM 1786 part i, 408).

Fullwoods End Former hamlet in the Ivy House Lane and Gough Road area, over 0.25m W of Coseley church, in Sedgley ancient parish (W p200) (BCM autumn 1989 p45). Has also appeared as Fullers End (1834 OS map), and Fullards End (SGSAS). The name is from the Fullwood family, who occupied Furlongs House, Dudley Road, Upper Gornal in the C19 (SDOP p44p). The Coseley canal tunnel passes under this area. The name is still preserved in the street, Fullwoods End, a shopping area of Coseley (CWBT p29). There is a poem entitled 'Fullwoods End' by the poet Michael W Thomas in which it is described as

> A pale place, linking Bilston's wasted grime
> to tailbacks on the Birmingham New Road

Thomas was born in 1954 in Willenhall Road, Bilston and attended High Arcal School (then High Arcal Grammar) in Sedgley. The poem was 'Recommended' in the 1996 Housman Society Poetry Competition 'Remembered Places' (BCM winter 1996/7 p71).

Furlong House House which stood in the Furlong Lane area of Burslem. Built by John Ward, a Burslem solicitor and author of HBST before 1834. Ward was living here in the early 1840s (HBST p267) (VCH vol 8 p112).

Furnace Brook Rises from several springs in Normacot. Joins Cockster Brook. At one time formed some ornamental pools for Longton Hall (VCH vol 8 p224) (POP p128).

Furnace Coppice Cannock Chase. To the SW of Furnace Coppice is the site of one of Paget's early charcoal fired iron smelting works, and first blast furnace in the Midlands to use the Indirect Process (CCM). Celia Fiennes noted Furnes Coppice as 'a fine covert of tall trees on a hill' when she was here in summer 1698 (The Illustrated Journeys of Celia Fiennes. Edited by Christopher Morris. 1984. p148). Appears in 1821 as Furnace Coppy (SPNO p108).

Furnace Grange House by the Smestow, 1.5m NNW of Trysull. Formerly in Lower Penn township in Penn ancient parish. Richard Foley had a furnace for smelting iron at Furnace Grange by 1636. Has appeared as 'ye furnace' (1641) (Penn PR) and 'the Grange Furnace' (1677) (ALP p27). The bellows of the charcoal furnace were driven by the Smestow. It was occupied by the Jordens from the mid C18 (POAP p30 il facing p31) (PENOP p8p) (PAIP p52).

Further Hill Lichfield Road, Stafford. Possibly a private house.

Furzebank The Furzebank Worship Centre, built in 1985, is in Stroud Avenue, Lane Head, Willenhall (LDD); Furzebank Way is a modern circular road on the E side of Stroud Avenue.

G

Gables, The House in Wood Road, Tettenhall. At one time the seat of John Marston, founder of the Sunbeam Motor Car Company (TPOP p45p).

Gadstree Hill To W of Mutchill's Gutter (PCC p77). Beaudesert Old Park.

Gaia A prebend in Lichfield cathedral. It was split into Gaia Major and Gaia Minor before 1279 (VCH vol 3 p144).

Gaia Lane Lane leading to the land which is called in the vernacular 'Gayfields' (NSFCT 1908 p140), running SW to NE, N of Lichfield cathedral. Has also appeared as Gay (HOL p25). A Neolithic or Bronze Age flint axe has been found here (SHC 1950/ 1 p144) (NSJFS 1964 p28). In the Appendix to Nennius the last fight of Penda was at Gayfield (NSFCT 1908 p140). The name Gaia is a medieval Latin name for a jay, and French gai, gay (g soft) has the same meaning. It is rare to find a Latin word surviving in a place name, and its exact form preserved (DUIGNAN). Or it can be traced to the Welsh 'cae' enclosure, and corresponds to the Anglo-Saxon forest ward hay (NSFCT 1908 p140).

Gaia Major Prebend in Lichfield cathedral, lying in St Chad's parish and not in Hints parish as Willis says (SHOS vol 1 p292). Willis' confusion may have arisen from the fact that the Gaia prebends were sub-divisions of Bishopshull prebend; based on the estate or former hamlet of Bishopshull (or Bispells), said to be in Hints parish (SSAHST vol 2 1960-61 pp43,46-47). Before 1279 the prebend of Gaia was divided into two - Gaia Major and Gaia Minor (VCH vol 14 p68). The father of the poet and author Izaak Hawkins Browne, William Browne, was prebendary of Gaia Major in the earlier C18 (HOL p232).

Gaia Minor Prebend in Lichfield cathedral, lying in St Chad's parish (SHOS vol 1 p292). For the origin of Gaia Minor see Gaia Major.

Gailey Hamlet on upland heath near the Penk 8m S of Stafford. Former manor (W p468) in Penkridge ancient parish. Mr Codrington and CGO Bridgeman thought the site of Roman Pennocrucium to be at or near the old Spread Eagle Inn, Gailey (Roman Roads in Britain. Codrington. p79) (SHC 1916 p321), but it has since been shown to be further W, astride Watling Street. Gailey was identified by Shaw and Duignan with the Gageleage mentioned in the will of Wulfric Spot (c1002), founder of Burton Abbey (SHC 1916 p31); later appears as Gragelie (DB), Gaeleg (1200), Gaghley (1252), Gaeleg (1267) (SPNO p89) (SSE 1996 p14) (SPN p53), Gaull (later C16) (SHC 1938 p81), Galey (Yates' map) and Gayley (W p468). The name is from the shrub 'Myrica Gale' which is known by many names, such as bog-myrtle, gale, gaul bushes, gaul, moor myrtle (English Plant Names. EDS Britten and Holland) (DUIGNAN) (SSE 1996 p14) (SPN p53). At Fullmoor the aromatic shrub of the myrtle kind grows spontaneously, it is called gale or sweet gale and gives its name to the hamlet, Gailey (GM 1786 pt. i, 408). Was the gagol-leah or meadow choked by bog myrtle (Along the Roman Roads of Britain. JHB Peel. 1971. p45). Or it can be traced to the Welsh 'cae' enclosure, and corresponds to the Anglo-Saxon forest ward hay (NSFCT 1908 p140). The present centre of Gailey (junction of A5 and A34) was called Spread Eagle until c1834 (VCH vol 5 p104). Here was a station on the GJR which opened on July 4 1837 (IAS p131). Gailey and Hatherton were formed into a joint ecclesiastical parish known as 'Gailey cum Hatherton' in 1869 (LGS p139) (GLAUE p412). By the late C20 was a ward in Penkridge civil parish. The church, Christ Church, at the junction of Watling Street and the A449, was built in 1850 (VCH vol 5 p134). The church was converted into a pottery studio in c1981, and was still being used as such in 1999 (local info). For Gailey in a local rhyme see Brewood.

Gailey Common 600 or so acres of common land on the N side of Watling Street and to SE of Rodbaston within the manor or lordship of Gailey were enclosed in 1775 (VCH vol 5 p127).

Gailey Hay Former estate which became a hay, or division of Cannock Forest (NSFCT 1908 p140) (SL p68), 2.5m S of Penkridge. The estate became a possession of the Crown in Henry II's reign and there was a hay of Gailey by 1235 (VCH vol 2 p338. vol 5 p104). The name is commonly found in Forest records as the 'Hay of Gauley' (DUIGNAN p65). It was still a constituent element of the forest in the C16. In 1550 the Crown granted it to the Earl of Warwick. His son held the hay in the 1560s (VCH vol 2 p343). Gailey Hay was enclosed in 1774 under an Act of 1773 (MH 1994 p110).

Gailey Pools or Reservoirs. Two reservoirs built to supply the Staffs and Worcs Canal in c1840 (NSFCT 1924 p198) (NSJFS 1967 p53). There is a causeway separating the two reservoirs. Calf Heath Reservoir is another.

Gailey Wharf On the Staffordshire and Worcestershire Canal 0.5m ESE of Gailey church. Here a Georgian 'Gothick' house and a brick, circular, battlemented tower face each other across the canal. These were the offices and toll house of the wharf, and or lock keepers cottage (DoE II) (The Staffs and Worcs Canal. Alfred E Jenks. 1907 p28p) (BOE p134) (SL p239) (Stafford Advertiser Jan 21 1965 p8p) (TEM autumn 1983 pp70,71) (F p308) (MR pp158,159p) (Amenities Guide Staffs & Worcs Canal).

Gains Brook Flows from Norton Canes to Wyrley Brook.

Gainsborough Hill Farm 0.75m SSE of Stonnall, 2.25m SW of Shenstone. Formerly Greensborough Farm or represents the approximate site of Greensborough Farm (SSAHST 1967 p7). Here was a burial mound opened in 1824 and in a rock-cut grave were found fragments of human bone and wood and a few inches away, on the W side, was found a hoard of bronze implements considered the most important Late Bronze Age artifacts found in the county. The whereabouts of the implements is unknown (SSAHST 1967 pp1-15). (HOWW p14) (SC p148) (Proceedings of the Prehistoric Society vol 28 p93) (ARCH vol 21 p548) (Hist of the Forest and Chase of Sutton Coldfield. L Bracken. 1860 p2) (ABI pp285, 465 no. 40) (VCH vol 1 pp178-9,181) (LGS p25) (AJ vol 120 p261) (NSJFS 1964 p34).

Gales Cottage Priory Lane, Sedgley town. The building was still standing in 1997 (SDSSOP p35p).

Gallows Bridge 0.75m SSW of Branston. Probably indicates the site of a manorial gallows (HOPT vol 1 p139) (SCSF p123) (IHOBT pp16,21). Has also appeared as Gallow Bridge.

Gallows Brook Clent (SCSF p123).

Gallows Brook Tributary of the Tame. Runs at Drayton Bassett.

Gallows Elm Tree Lost elm tree used as gallows, after, reputedly, a Cavalier was hung from it in the Civil War (1651). The tree is supposed to have been situated at SO 842853, opposite where the Elm Tree Inn now stands, on the crest of the hill above Potters Cross. A human bone of a victim of the gallows was found in 1975, although it is unlikely that it belongs to the Cavalier (TB Aug 1983 p23p. July 1984 p17. Feb 1990 p12 p of the bone). Capt Kidson in 'Bladys of The Stewponey,' based on highwayman, George Baxter, was hung on it. The tree may have been the gallows of Kinver manor, but that may have stood W of Potter's Cross to the S, where a hill, Gallowstree Hill, was mentioned in 1650 (VCH vol 20 p150).

Gallows Field Medieval field boundary of Newcastle-under-Lyme where there was probably a gallows (NUL pp107,123). Gallows Tree was probably in it. In C17 was found a human skull complete with teeth. Mr Weaver an alderman owned another or the same skull (NHS p171).

Gallows Flat and Gallows Lane. In the locality of Wetmoor, Burton upon Trent. Or Wetmoor was known as this (HOBT) (DUIGNAN p170) (SCSF p123).

Gallows Green Tiny district of Alton. 0.5m SSW of the church. In Alton parish.

Gallows Hill Gallowes Hill is mentioned in a plan of the boundary of the manor of Handsworth (SHOS vol 2 p108).

Gallows Knoll Noted by Plot as Gallows Knowl on the Weaver Hills (NHS p404) (SPNO p24). (SCSF p74).

Gallows Lane Former name of a by-road which preserves the site of Wolverhampton's public execution place. Stood off the highway to Willenhall (SCSF p123).

Gallows Tree Bank A low hillock near what was originally the intersection of two roads at Baldwin's Gate (NSFCT 1935 p70).

Gallowstree Elm Area over 1m NNW of Kinver church. It may take its name from the legendary Gallows Elm Tree (see) or from the Kinver manor gallows, if different, which may have stood on Gallowstree Hill, a hill W of Potter's Cross, mentioned in 1650. The name Gallowstree Elm was used for land N of Potter's Cross and had given its name to that area by the mid C19; the area had many houses by 1851 (VCH vol 20 pp121,150).

Gallowstree Hill There is a Gallowstree Lane in Mayfield (see Calwich Abbey).

Gallows Wharf Situated at four cross roads where the Tamworth and Wall roads cross the London Road, Lichfield. In 1650 there was a gallows on the W side of the London road near its junction with Shortbutts Lane. The gallows here fell down in c1700, its foundations were undermined by people digging for sand, but it was re-erected (SHC 4th series vol 6 pl facing p118). It was used, apparently, for the last time in 1810 when forgers were hanged (SA June 2 1810) (VCH vol 1 p85). About 1875, writes Hackwood, a decayed oak stump stood two feet out of the ground, and was said to be the remains of the ancient gallows tree (SCSF p123).

Galton Bridge A magnificent iron bridge at Smethwick built by Thomas Telford in 1826 and made by the Horseley Works, Tipton (TB Feb 1993 p21 il). Others say its date is 1829. It carried Roebuck Lane over Telford's New Main Line of the Birmingham Canal and is 50 feet above the navigation (SWY p11). Summit Bridge carried Roebuck Lane over the Old Main Line. The name is from Galton House (see). Has a single span of 150 feet and is 71 feet above the canal at its deepest part of the cutting. Was considered the longest single span bridge in the world over what was claimed to be the largest earthwork in the world. Superseded by Telford Way in 1974 and now carries a footpath (SL p242). Telford Way spoils the view of the bridge (SWY p11).

Galton House House on E side of Roebuck Lane between the Birmingham Canal Old Cut Old Main Line and the New Cut New Main Line, Smethwick (VCH vol 17 p93). Built sometime between 1767 and 1771, perhaps on the site of Holt Hall; Holt Hall is shown on the canal survey in 1767 (STELE Nov 4 1955). In the later C18 it was the seat of Samuel Galton (1753-1832), gunmaker and banker. Galton gave his name to the house (Galton Valley. A Walkers Guide. Sandwell Metropolitan Borough Council), which was known as Galton Hall by 1790; later it was known as Galton Bridge House (STELE Nov 4 1955). The Lunar Society met at Samuel Galton's house at Great Barr (CCBO p122). The house was owned by the Birmingham Canal Navigations company by 1842, and was occupied by their agent for some years. Alderman William Elwell, twice mayor of Dudley, was resident from c1886 to c1905. It was demolished in c1916 (STELE Nov 4 1955) (VCH vol 17 p93). (W p704) (RS p125) (E&S Nov 6 1999 p8).

Galton Tunnel On the Birmingham Canal Old Cut or New Cuts at Smethwick. Is 122 yards long (OS map for canal navigations 1977).

Galton Valley (Galton Valley. A Walkers Guide. Sandwell Metropolitan Borough Council).

Galton Village Area between Birmingham Canal New Main Line (Birmingham Level). (Galton Valley. A Walkers Guide. Sandwell Metropolitan Borough Council).

Gamballs Green House 0.75m ENE of Flash. Formerly in Hollinsclough township in Alstonefield ancient parish. Slightly to the N is Lower Gamballs. It takes its name from a green called Gamon Green in 1564, Gambushe Green in 1600, and Gambles Green in 1720 (VCH vol 7 p38).

Gamesley Brook Tributary of the Sow. Runs at Ellenhall to Doxey in the Seighford area.

Gamton Green Perhaps now Gorton Lodge, Farewell (Yates' map).

Gander Well Ramshorn. A well at SK 083452 on 1:25,000 OS map. Has also appeared as Ganderwell (HAF p17).

Gaolbutts Street running SW out of Eccleshall town from Horse Fair towards Johnson Hall (SGSAS).

Garmelow Hamlet 1.5m NE of High Offley. In Horsley quarter in Eccleshall ancient parish. The name is from Anglo-Saxon Garma's grave (MR p247). Or means 'shallow valley' (TTTD p257). Here was possibly a lost village (SSAHST 1970 p35).

Garrick's House, David Beacon Street, Lichfield. House of Capt Garrick father of David Garrick (1716-1779), actor. David Garrick spent the first 20 years of his life in this house, but he was born in Hereford (LAL p21p of plaque). It was pulled down in 1856 (plaque on house) and the probate court built on the site (SOSH p240).

Garshall Green Hamlet on high ground above Wheatlow Brook 7.75m NE of Stafford. In Milwich ancient parish and manor. The name has appeared as Garnonshale (1310) (SSE 1996 p14), Geringeshalgh (C14) (DUIGNAN), Gerynshale, Grendonshale, and Milwich Garingshall (SHC 1909 pp156-157). The terminal 'halgh' in the Geringeshalgh form is seldom found in the Midlands in so perfect a form; in the N it is common. It means meadow-land, Garinge is an Anglo-Saxon personal name; so 'Garinge's meadow-land' (DUIGNAN). Or 'Garnon's halh or corner' (SSE 1996 p14); the surname is from Old French meaning 'moustache' (SPN p84). For Garshall Castle see under Milwich. There was a windmill known as Milwich Mill which stood S of the chapel at SJ 969340. Documented briefly in the early C19 (WBJ p24). The Snape family ran a pottery at Garshall Green from c1860 to 1940 (NSFCT 1977 p41-42).

Garston In approximate position of Moneystone (Plot's map). The name is preserved in Garston House 1.25m NW of Cotton.

Garston Rocks Rocks S of Garston House, 1.25 NNW of Cotton, at SK 051476. Lies to the E of the A52. Appears from the A52 as two buttresses (SGM pp218-220). Could be same as Bill's Rock (see).

Garth, The Site of the Austin Friars (St Augustine's Priory), or Stafford Green, Stafford (Leland c1540) (SPNO p77).

Gartmore House on N side of Hall Lane, Hammerwich. Faces the vicarage. Built in the later 1890s by WG Leckie, a Walsall saddlery and harness manufacturer (VCH vol 14 p259).

Gastilea A house marked on Plot's map in approximate position of Shortwood, S of Maer.

Gas Yard Small area of Moxley. Name is of unknown origin (TB Jan 21 1999 p3).

Gateham Two houses 1m NW of Alstonefield. Formerly in Alstonefield township in Alstonefield ancient parish (W p742). Two mounds at Gateham were excavated by Carrington in 1849. The one which had the legend of dead men being buried under it revealed nothing, the other contained a cremation under an inverted cinerary urn (TYD pp141,149) (NSJFS 1965 p32). They may be the burial mounds on Wetton Hill (see) to the W. Gateham has appeared as Gauntham (AVH p57) and Gatam (W p742). Appears to have been a grange of Combermere Abbey by 1134 (AVH p57). Gateham may have been large enough to be considered a hamlet in the C19. Its decline may have been brought on by the closure of Ecton Mines (AVH p57).

Gateham Grange One of the two houses of Gateham. Has medieval cellars. Formerly occupied by the Yates family (NSJFS 1965 p112). Supposedly haunted by a ghost in the C19 which played the piano, but the ghost was believed to be nothing more than a mouse or a cat running across the piano (WTCEM p94).

Gate House House under 0.5m NNE of Endon. Formerly in Endon township in Leek ancient parish. Is partly the C17 (VCH vol 7 p177).

Gatherwynd House in Blymhill parish, over 0.5m WNW of Blymhill. Appears as Ryecorn Hill or Gatherwind on the 1834 OS map. Means 'a hill exposed to the winds' (SPNO p130).

Gauledge House to W of Longnor. May have appeared as the land called Gorlage in 1415. There was house called Gauledge in 1608 (VCH vol 7 p42). Ghostly apparitions, including a small phantom dog, have been reported in the area of Gauledge Lane (L p49).

Gaw Brook Flows in a westerly direction towards the Trent, S of Hixon. After the building of the Trent & Mersey Canal it flowed into the canal (HV pp1,2).

Gawton's Cave Cave in Knypersley Park. According to Plot this is the cavity under Gawton's Stone and it was occupied by a hermit called Gawton (NSFCT 1945 p92. 1954 p94. 1991 p61).

Gawton's Stone Huge peculiarly-shaped and poised sandstone in Greenway Bank Country Park nearly 1.5m SE of Knypersley. Weighs some 60 tons (NSFCT 1906 p156) (STM July 1964 p37). Is perched on three stones; so, situated like a cap stone (SMCC p6). Originally thought to have been a megalithic chambered tomb (SMCC p6), and used by druids, but by at least 1888, was considered to have been not druidical (NSFCT 1888 p68. 1913 p230). Is now considered to have got here naturally (LGS p84) by falling from the cliff above (NSFCT 1991 p61). May be the very large andesite granite boulder by Knypersley Pool mentioned in NSFCT 1916 p73. (NHS p106) (HBST p181) (GNHS pp66, 417) (ES Plus Section 10 June 1989) (SCSF p143) (Biddulph Grange Friends Books p31) (SMM pp116,119ils,120). Has also appeared as Cawton's Stone (SMCC p6), Gorton and Gawstone (NSFCT 1906 p156).

The name is from German 'gau,' a spring in a hollow or furrow, and 'stan' a stone (NSFCT 1906 p156). According to Plot it was named after a hermit called Gawton who lived under it and never cut his hair or finger nails (NSFCT 1945 p92. 1954 p94. 1991 p61). Gawton was originally of Knypersley Hall (Greenway Bank Country Park. Staffs County Council Leaflet).

Gawton's Well Spring situated by Gawton's Stone in Yew Tree Grove (BGFB p31), Knypersley. It had the reputation for curing the king's evil (Bowen's map), and the hermit named Gawton may have bathed in it in C17 to cure himself of the plaque (Greenway Bank Country Park. Staffs County Council Leaflet). But Plot in the later C17 could not find any of the minerals which would help it (NHS p106). (SD p85) (HBST p182) (GNHS il pp26,417) (OSST 1944-1945) (SLM Oct 1951 p20) (STM July 1964 p37) (ES Plus Section 10 June 1989) (SCSF p143) (NSFCT 1991 p61) (SMM p118p).

Gayfield District? The name is preserved in Gayfield Avenue between Holloway End and Withymoor Village.

Gaythorne Created out of the Lloyd estate, Penn, when sold in 1901 (PONP p31).

Gayton Ancient parish and small village on low land in Trent Valley by Gayton Brook 5.25m NE of Stafford. Between Sandon and Gayton Plot noted a sulphur spring which showed evidence of petrifying the fibres of moss? In the later C17 Dr Plot found a stalagmite at Gayton (NHS p99 tab 12 fig 6 may illustrate the stalagmite). For fossils in the rock at Gayton see SN Nov 17 1978 p3. The name has appeared as Gaitone, a manor, in DB; later as Gaytone (1227), and Gaytun (1272) (SPN p54). SAH Burne described Gayton as 'one of the most typical feudal villages in the county' demonstrated by remains of the field system (NSFCT 1976 p52). The **name** is from Anglo-Saxon 'gate town' (DUIGNAN), or 'gate-way,' used in the sense of allowing access to an enclosure (SPN p54). Or it can be traced to the Welsh 'cae' enclosure, and corresponds to the Anglo-Saxon forest ward hay (NSFCT 1908 p140. 1910 p161). Or 'Gaega's tun,' but most Gaytons are 'goat farm' (SSE 1996 pp14,21). The parish **church**, St Peter, on the S side of Church Lane, has some C12 work (LDD). The tower is of 1732, but most of the church is of 1870 (BOE p135). The wake was on the nearest Sunday to St Peter's day in the C19 (W p420). Reputedly, Samuel Wright (d1849), in the early C19, conceived the idea of manufacturing encaustic tiles from studying the examples in the church. The idea was patented in 1830 and the patent later sold to Herbert Minton who made this type of tile famous and such tiles became known as 'Minton tiles' (mem in Acton Trussell church) (NSFCT 1933 p182) (STM Dec 1965 pp42,43) (BOE p52) (NSFCT 1976 p52). For the curious system of moats at Gayton see Moat House Farm. **Nuclear war bunker.** At Gayton is an underground 162 square feet bunker designed to be used in a nuclear war. It was built in the 1950s. With the Cold War over the bunker was sold to a member of the public in Oct 1993 (ES May 21 1993 p12p. Oct 22 1993 p18).

Gayton Brook Runs at Fradswell to past Gayton to join the Trent at Weston-on-Trent.

Gayton Manor House At the N end of Gayton. It does not appear to be moated (NSFCT 1912 p186).

Gaywode Hall Ancient house in Stretton, Penkridge. Is mentioned in the C14 (VCH vol 4 p167).

General's Farm, The By Keeper's Pool on N side of A518 to E of Chartley Castle. Occupied by the Christy family up to the mid 1950s (TRTC p45).

Gentleman's Rock Oakamoor. At SK 053430.

Gentleshaw Village on a hill above Redmoor Brook over 0.25m ESE of Cannock Wood. In Longdon ancient parish. The name appears in 1505 as Gentylshawe (SSE 1996 p14). By the late C18 Gentleshaw was the name for a coppice (SHOS vol 2 p315). The name was originally applied to a grove of ancient oaks on a high part of Cannock Chase. Shaw is Middle English for a grove. In 1341 a John Gentyl was sued by Simon de Ruggeley for cutting down his trees in Longdon (DUIGNAN), so 'Gentil's grove of trees or wood' (SSE 1996 p14) (SPN p54). A rather foolish suggestion has been that here was a gentle chap called Shaw! (CCF pp221,222). A Quaker burial ground in use in the C18 was at SK 05451175 (SSAHST 1970 pp41-42). A windmill stands at SK 051119. Job noted the tower still bore the legend in peeling paintwork 'Bass Worthington Windmill Inn.' Built before 1820; disused by 1902. In 1912 a boy fell off the sails and broke his leg whilst looking for birds' eggs. As a consequence the sails were removed (WBJ p24 il ix) (STMSM Aug 1978 p26p). There was another windmill at Windmill Bank (see). The church, Christ Church, on the corner of Chapel and School Lanes and Commonside, was built in the period c1837-1845 (BOE p135). Became a separate ecclesiastical parish in 1840 (GLAUE p412). Mrs Nip of Gentle Shaw, who lived probably in the C17, reputedly lived to the age of 109 or older (NHS p320) (SHOS vol 1 p227) (W pp57,565). Betsy Parker is a variety of apple indigenous to the Gentleshaw area (ZSB).

Gentleshaw Hill Hill 676 feet high S of Gentleshaw on Gentleshaw Common.

George Hotel Waterloo Road, Burslem. Formerly George Inn. Probably built in c1815 for it had buried under it horse shoes and nails from the battle of Waterloo (TFTP p61). The old inn suffered greatly in the Chartist riots in Burslem on Aug 16 1842. The publican from c1866 to 1871 was William Frederick Horry (1843-1872) of Boston, Lincs. On Jan 15 1872 he shot dead his wife at Boston and was executed at Lincoln Castle on April 2 1872. The people of Burslem however, had the highest regard for him and he was thought of as a martyr. His friends erected a memorial to him and his wife in St John's churchyard, Burslem (Staffs Sentinel Jan 20, Apr 6, Apr 13, Apr 20, May 6 1872) (MMM pp76-78) (POTP p126) (SMML pp18-20). The inn is 'The Dragon' of Arnold Bennett's novels. Rebuilt and enlarged in 1928-9 (VCH vol 8 p112) (POP p36). Known as the George Hotel by the 1970s (AGT pp84,85il).

George Hotel or Inn. Bird Street, Lichfield. A coaching inn named after the dragon-slaying saint and not a Hanoverian king. George Farquhar (1678-1707), playwright, was billeted at the George when quartered at Lichfield as a recruiting officer in 1704 (LAL p43); a plaque on the outside of the present building says Farquhar stayed here in 1705. Farquhar made the George the scene of his comedy 'The Beaux' Stratagem' (1707), which, reputedly he partly wrote at Castle Inn (see). Some say he based the character of 'Boniface' on the landlord of the George, one Harrison, and the character of 'Cherry' on Harrison's daughter, and Lady Bountiful on Lady Biddulph, then staying at the Bishop's Palace (HOL p501) (CL Oct 3 1957 p661) (LAL p43). (SHOS vol 1 p322 note 2) (CCHCA p21) (VFC pp46-47). The ballroom at the George had a carved frieze, fluted pillars, sphinxes and amorini above the doors. It accommodated 233 people for a race dinner in 1743 (CL Oct 3 1957 p661). Here the 1st Marquis of Anglesey lay in state in 1854 (CCBO p82). In April 1910 Claude Graham-White and Louis Paulhan, participants in the Daily Mail's London to Manchester Air Race, stayed here to rest during the competition (EAS pp25,29). It is now (1997) part of a chain of inns run by John Jarvis and is now called the Jarvis George Hotel (Daily Express Magazine. Oct 25 1997 p13).

George Rose Park Public park to the W of Darlaston (Offlow hundred). Opened in 1924. Named after John George Rose (1867-1924), a local nut and bolt manufacturer (Staffs County Handbook c1958 p111p) (WDY p16p) (WMVB p53) (BCM Oct 1992 pp34,35-37 p) (SNDB p52).

Gerrard's Bromley Tiny hamlet overlooking Bromley Brook over 0.5m NNW of Charnes consisting of a few dispersed houses. Former township in the Woodland quarter in Eccleshall ancient parish. Bromley has appeared as Bramelie, a manor, held of the bishop of Chester (Lichfield) in DB (SSE 1996 p11); later forms are: Bromley-in-Halys (or Hales) (C15) (DUIGNAN p26), Bromley Gerrards' (Plot's map), Garrerd's Bromley (Greenwood's map), and Gerard's Bromley. Bromley is from 'leah where broom grows' (SSE 1987 p32. 1996 p11). Gerrards was applied when the manor passed by marriage from the Bromleys to Sir William Stanley of Hooton, whose daughter, Margaret, married Peter Gerrard (COI p220). The manor was held from at least King John's reign by the de Bromley family. Sir Walter de Burwardsley (or de Bromley as he called himself after he married the Bromley heiress) held Bromley in 1272 from his overlord the bishop of Coventry and Lichfield by attending his lord with four of his men three times a year when the bishop hunted in Eccleshall Park (COI p220) (HOG p194). At Gerrard's Bromley was possibly a medieval village, probably deserted between 1332 and 1666 (SSAHST 1970 p34). There was a windmill at approximately SJ 779349. It was recorded in 1564, a later mill was recorded on this site on maps of 1818 and 1831 but not after (WBJ p25). Jesuits are recorded as being active in the Rudge during the C17, and afterwards at Gerrards Bromley (ALW pl 24). For the Dog-kennel path at Gerrard's Bromley see BOV p108 see map. Foot-and mouth disease broke out at Bromley Hall Farm in late Nov 1967 (SN Dec 1967 p10).

Gerrard's Bromley Hall The manor of Bromley (Gerrard's Bromley) was sold by William Gerrard of Etwall, Derbys, to Sir Gilbert Gerrard, Elizabeth I's Attorney-General (COI p220). He built the hall shortly after his appointment as Master of the Rolls in 1581 (NSFCT 1924 pp94p facing,100). It has been said he built it in expectation of entertaining Elizabeth I, although, Shaw could find no record of her ever having stayed here (SHOS vol 1 part 1 p51). On the death of Sir Gilbert in 1593 the hall passed to his eldest son Thomas, 1st Baron Gerard. It then passed down in the male line to Digby Gerard, 5th Baron, whose daughter married the Duke of Hamilton. It then passed to Digby's cousins Charles, 6th Baron, and Phillip, 7th and last Baron Gerard d1733; it was the Gerard seat until 1707. Charles Fleetwood, their sister's son, next inherited the hall but lost it through gambling. Its next owner, Hugo Meynell of Bradley, Derbys, had no use for it and it stood empty and neglected for some time before being demolished (SHC 1909 p257 note) (NSJFS 1970 p117) (AADB p27) in c1740, or 1750 (LGS p263) (NSFCT 1976 p16) (SPJD p61), or 1760 (NSFCT 1947 p175). James I, a keen huntsman, paid a two-day visit to Gerrard's Bromley in 1617 (NSFCT 1922 p162). Between the end of 1669 and 1672 the herald Gregory King of Lichfield (see) served as steward, auditor and secretary to the Dowager Lady Jane, Lady Gerard, Baroness Gerard of Gerrard's Bromley Hall, widow of Charles and mother of Digby, lord Gerard; however, King resided with the lady's father, George Digby (d1675) at Sandon Old Hall (see), during his term of office (DNB). In the later C17 Plot described the hall as 'the most magnificent structure of all this county' (NHS tab 6 shows the hall). Its appearance was not unlike the late C16 Hardwick Hall, Derbys (SPJD p60il). Plot also noted that at the hall was a convex portrait on a board of Henry the Great of France and his queen. If one looked directly at the portrait one saw both king and queen together; if one looked from one side the king alone could be seen and from the other the queen only (NHS p391). Dowager Lady Jane, Lady Gerard, Baroness Gerard was living at Sandon Old Hall in the 1680s. **Remains**. Some of the stones from the hall may have been used to build Bromley Mill by Bromley Pool (NSFCT 1933 p174). Hugo Meynell, who demolished the hall, was a fellow MP and friend of Richard Whitworth (1737-1811) and gave him the porch or portico which Whitworth re-erected at his seat Batchacre Hall (SLM April 1948 p100) (MR p7p). He may also have given him stones from the hall, which Whitworth made into a garden wall at Adbaston Hall (AADB p27). By the later C19 a few cellars underground alone survived to show where the house had stood (COI p187). The present farmhouse is believed to have been the servants wing. The Elizabethan barns are still standing. In one of them is a Tudor hunting frieze clearly showing a huntsman and three hounds chasing a fox (BOV pp39-40,108 il of all that is left of the stalls in the hunting stables with the pineapple emblem carved in oak). (SS 1922). Foot-and mouth disease broke out at Bromley Hall Farm in late Nov 1967 (SN Dec 1967 p10). GROUNDS. There was or is a dovecote to the N of the hall (BOV pp39-40,108). The gardens were surveyed in 1985 by the Royal Commission on Ancient Monuments who identified walkways and garden courts, probably constructed during the Tudor period. The gardens may have been adapted by the famous C17 florist and gardener, and writer on these subjects, John Rea (SPJD pp63-64).

Gerrard's Bromley Park A deer park noted by Plot on his map. It belonged to Lord Gerrard (EDP p179).

Gerrard's Valley Pretty valley S of Tittensor lined by a series of pools - there were once six - which fed a mill, formerly on E side of A34. Named after the Gerrard family. An alternative name for the valley, Orme's Valley, is from the Orme family. Both families were of Tittensor Old Manor House (NSFCT 1940 p35).

Gettliffe's Yard Off Derby Street, Leek. Here the Oat Cake Witch of Leek lived.

Giant's Well Well which supplied water to Kinver for many centuries. It stood near the junction of Compton Road and Stone Lane in 1982. It was so named by 1774 (VCH vol 20 pp151-152). The Giant's Well may be the same as the Giant's Spring, a spring the Kinver Giant reputedly collected water from, or by the Giant's Water Trough, which may have been situated over, or by, the Giant's Spring. By 1903 the stream arising from the spring had been diverted and the water trough had been moved to the wayside and was overgrown with nettles (WJO July 1903 xxxv).

Gibbet Gate (or Gibbet Lane) Priestfield, Wolverhampton. Reputedly the street in which the Tipton Slasher died (TB Oct 1986 p7).

Gibbethill Hill 1m NW of Seisdon.

Gibbet Wood Wood 0.5m S of Stewponey, Stourton. The wood, covering a part of Whittington Common, seems to have been named after the gibbeting here of William Howe (alias John Wood) (VCH vol 20 p125) (RKE p20; gives erroneous date of 1805) or 1813 (VCH vol 20 p125) (TB Feb 1993 p22). He was a native of Stourbridge, a travelling carpenter (SCK p8), and a notorious footpad (GLS pp61-62). He shot Benjamin Robins, a farmer of Dunsley Hall (see), at Fir Tree Hill (see) in Gibbet Wood with a pistol in a highway robbery on Dec 18 1812; Robins died of his wounds on Dec 28 1812 and is buried at the eastern end of Enville churchyard (TB Feb 1993 p22) (BCM winter 1999/2000 pp29,30). He was arrested in London (VCH vol 20 p125) on Jan 13 1813 (BCM winter 1999/2000 p29) or at the Whittington Inn, near Kinver (The Manor House of the de Whittingtons), and tried at Stafford on March 16 (TB Feb 1993 p22) (BCM winter 1999/2000 p29) or March 20 1813 (BCWJ pp105-106) and hung at Stafford, being one of the first men to be hung using the new 'trapdoor' system (SCK p8) (VCH vol 20 p125) (BCM winter 1999/2000 p29). After the execution Robins' family and the Stourbridge magistrates had Howe's body taken back to the scene of the murder and placed in

an iron cage (BCM winter 1999/2000 p28) (BCWJ pp105-106) or in chains, viewed by huge crowds. Here it remained for 12 months until it fell to pieces (VCH vol 20 p125). Estimates vary that from 20,000 and 100,000 people came to visit Howe's body in the gibbet (BCM winter 1999/2000 p30). Some imply his execution took place in the iron cage in Gibbet Wood (BCWJ pp105-106). The site of the gibbet was marked by a young oak and a stout post. Campbell, writing in 1979, says that a few years ago the old oak was inadvertently hewn down (SCK p8). Many say Howe was the last man in England (HOWM p155) (RKE p20), or the last in the Midlands (SCK p8), to be gibbeted. But a man in Leics was gibbeted in 1832 (Hist of Eng Criminal Law from 1750. L Radzinowicz. vol 1 p218 note, 219) (VCH vol 20 p125). (SA Dec 26 1812. Jan 2 1813. March 20 1813) (KRC p26) (RPM pp20-21). There are many stories concerning Howe's corpse, the gibbet, and sightings of his ghost thereafter. **Howe's corpse** was reputedly asked by a drunken passerby, or one of three youths; - "Will Howe, how bist thee?" To which the corpse answered;- "cold and clammy!" The three youths were then scared off (BCWJ pp105-106). Concerning the removal of Howe's body there is the story that a Dr Downing illegally removed it for dissection. While doing this he was alarmed by a person approaching and slipped. Howe's body then fell on top of him and there he had to lie under it until the person had passed. Downing later exhibited the skeleton at his residence (SCK p8). It is also said that Downing left the decayed and dried flesh under a bush and that it was discovered by a pack of hunting dogs (BCM winter 1999/2000 p30). Apparently, a Dr Robins, legally removed the skeleton for his surgery (SCK p8). In 1903 a skeleton, staked through the heart with a rusted dagger and thought to be that of William Howe, was found unearthed at the nearby cross roads (BCWJ pp105-106) (TB Oct 1975 pp18-19. Jan 1976 p15) (GLS p62). **Howe's gibbet** was made into a stile and used in a nearby field and was said to be in good preservation in 1979 (SCK p8) (RKE p20). Another account states that it was allegedly made into stile posts for Prestwood Hall (BCM winter 1999/2000 p30). **Howe's ghost** may have been the ghost which was seen crossing Whittington Common at night in 1872. The person who saw the ghost was returning from a fair at Kinver and wrote about the experience in the Brierley Hill and Stourbridge Advertiser in Dec 1872, under the pseudonym 'ET.' The person claimed he struck the tall lanky spectre with his stick twice. The first time the spectre laughed, the second time it paralysed him to the spot until daybreak. The spectre also did not move. After the spell was broken the person went on his way (DG p115). (MS&S pp29-32). A Mrs Whitworth who lived near the gibbet site saw a man swiftly overtake her. When he reached Gibbet Wood he disappeared (BCWJ pp105-106). A ghost was spotted in Gibbet Lane in the 1940s (TB Feb 1993 p22). Betty Lloyd saw a ghost in Feb 1957, and reported that he wore a tricorn hat and carried a brace of long-barrelled pistols. The same spectre was seen by a policeman in 1972 (GLS p61). The ghost that haunts the area in the vicinity of the Stewponey Hotel is said to be that of William Howe (GLS p61). Supposedly at the identical spot where 'ET' saw the spectre, at Whittington Crossroads, Lynne Williams saw a ghost on March 13 1990 (TB May 1990 p5). (TB Jan/ Feb 1973 p21. Oct 1975 pp18-19. Jan 1976 p15. July 1977 p25 ballad concerning Howe) (GPCE p32). By at least 1950 the area of the murder scene, which appears as Little Dunsley Bank and Gorse Cover on 1834 OS map, had become known as Gibbet Wood (BCWJ pp105-106). A doctor, also appears to have been placed in an iron cage in Gibbet Wood; his crime was stealing a dead body (RKE p20).

Gibbon's Hill Sedgley (PHS p5). Possibly from John Lloyd Gibbons who owned an estate in Sedgley parish (PHS p18).

Gibbs Leasow Farm 0.75m ESE of Loxley Hall. Appears as Gibleasow on 1834 OS map.

Gibraltar Bluff SE of Knightley Grange, Knightley. The area was given this nickname on account of its remoteness, lying on the boundary (SPNO p160).

Gibraltar By 1780 the area on the E side of the Staffs and Worcs Canal S of Dunsley House, Kinver, was known as Gibraltar. By 1830 there were 12 rock houses in the sandstone rocky hillside here, known as Gibraltar Rock, and there were 17 households in the rock houses in 1851, many of whom were labourers at the nearby wharf. The dwellings had been condemned by the 1880s, and in the C20 they were considered too unsafe to be visited; they had nearly disintegrated by the later C20 (RKE p20) (KRH pp21,22p) (VCH vol 20 pp124-125). The Wesleyans are said to have held services in a 'rock house' here in 1846, prior to which they had been holding meetings in the Lock Inn. It is debatable how Gibraltar received its name (KEOP p18ps in 1908).

Gibridding Wood Small wood to W of East Wall Farm, on the NW borders of Hawksmoor Park. The Woodhead Plateway passed through the wood and a part of it may still be traced (IAS p157). There is a small monument to Major General W Reid Martin of Tissington Hall, Derbys, on a sunken footpath at the SE corner of the wood about 100 yards from the SW corner of East Wall Farm pond at SK 043447. It is a 28 inch high stone block with a cruciform top and is placed on the spot where he was accidentally shot dead when out with a shooting party from Farley Hall on Dec 31 1892 (NSFCT 1986 pp29-30).

Gib Torr House 1.5m SSW of Flash. Formerly in Heathylee township in Alstonefield ancient parish. For the geology of Gib Torr see NSFCT 1920 pp79,81,82. Gib Torr Rocks, in Quarnford township, are 0.25m WSW of Gib Torr house. May have appeared as Gylfields (1481) (VCH vol 7 p33), but has certainly appeared as Gybter (1564), Gvblor (Smith's map 1801), Gyblor (J Cary map 1805), and Gibtor. The name means gibbet rocky hill. There is still evidence of where the gibbet used to be on top of the highest rock (DPMM p111). Worship or sacrifices to Wotan, the Celtic gibbet god, may have taken place on the hill (UHAW p75). Gib Tor house was once the show farm of the Harpur Crewe estate. It was claimed by the public health department of the old Leek urban district council to have the 'sweetest tasting water in England,' which came from a stream rising half a mile to the N, and flowing to the Dane (DPMM pp111-112). At Gib Torr there was a tollgate from c1775 to 1825 when it was moved to Hazel Barrow (UHAW p49).

Giddy Well Small hamlet 0.5m NW of Longdon. Has also appeared as Giddywell.

Giffard House North Street, Wolverhampton. Built by Henry Arundel of the family of Arundel of Wardour Castle and later passed to the Giffards (W p67). Dated 1728. It was the residence of the vicar apostolic or Roman Catholic bishop of the Midland District from 1804 to 1841, when he moved to Birmingham (VCH vol 3 p110). In 1841 the house became a convent of the Sisters of Mercy (W p67). By the end of the C20 the house was the presbytery of the adjoining church of St Peter and St Paul (RC), built in 1825-7 (BOE p316) (HOS 1998 p63). (SHOS vol 2 p162) (GNHS p177) (WMAG April 1964 p38. Sept 1965 p16p).

Giffard's Cross A wooden cross at SJ 881075, 1.25m ENE of Chillington Hall, by a lodge to Chillington Hall at the junction of Upper Avenue and Port Lane, in Brewood ancient parish. **Legend of the cross**. It is said to have been set up to mark the spot where Sir John Giffard shot dead a panther. The panther, given to the Giffards or brought to this country by them, had been kept in a menagerie. One day it escaped and ran wild in nearby Brewood Forest. Giffard, accompanied by his young son, Thomas, went in search of it. The two discovered it just in time to save a woman with a baby in her arms onto whom it was about to pounce. As Sir John shot the beast dead with his bow and arrow his son reputedly cried 'Prenez haleine, tirez fort' (take breath, pull hard). The event became Giffard family legend and Giffard's Cross was set up to commemorate the site where the event took place (WMAG April 1964 p42. March 1968 p28p) (LGS pp91-92) (Chillington Hall Guide p). Accounts of the incident in the early part of the C20 claim Giffard shot the panther while standing at Chillington Hall door (SHJ autumn 1995 p18). The tradition is supported by the Giffard crest, an archer shooting at a panther's head, and the motto 'Prenez haleine, tirez forte.' **The legend discounted**. There is significant evidence to discount the legend. A cross on the site may long pre-date the period in which the incident is said to have occurred; there was a Johannes Atte Crosse, living within Brewood parish in 1380, and places in Brewood parish with 'cross' names occur throughout the C14 and C15. Also the original crest, granted in 1513, only showed a panther's head, and the first part of the motto. Another crest showing an archer with the second part of the motto, granted 1523, may really commemorate Richard fitz Gilbert, Earl of Clare, popularly known as Strongbow, conqueror of Ireland in 1169 and patron of Peter, first Giffard of Chillington. Although Gyffarde's Crosse is mentioned in 1569 there is no written evidence of the legend until the 1840s. Plot, writing in c1680, does not mention it nor the cross. A Chillington estate map c1727 suggests that it formerly stood in the centre of Port Lane, although it is possible that Port Lane was subsequently re-aligned and the cross left in place. It was probably Giffard's Cross that Hon John Byng (in the Torrington Diaries. 1936 ed pp142-144) saw on July 1 1792 and noted as 'the first I ever saw, or heard of, in this country.' Shaw, who tells nothing of the story, noted the cross was similar to those seen in Catholic countries (SHOS vol 2 p302). The cross was in existence by 1838 (DoE II). Garner in c1840 says it was moss-clad (GNHS p134). Aurally the panther story may date back to c1800 (SHJ autumn 1995 p23 note), but it was only first recorded in the 1840s (Abbeys, Castles & Ancient Halls of England & Wales. Their Legendary Lore and Popular History. John Timbs & Alexander Gunn. 2nd ed vol 2 p554) (Wanderings with a Pen and Pencil. FP Palmer. 1846) (St James Magazine. Sept 1849) (SHJ autumn 1995 pp21,23 note). The story was then perpetuated by W Harrison Ainsworth in his historical novel 'Boscobel, or the Royal Oak: A Tale of the year 1651' (1872) (FSBC p23p). Ainsworth may have

been told it by William Parke, author of NCB, and or James Hicks Smith, author of HOB (SHJ autumn 1995 pp21-22); Ainsworth's book may have led some to think the original cross was erected in 1651 (FOS p30). The legend was roundly refuted by Somerset Herald, JR Panche in Archaeologia 1873 pp66-67. **Present state of the cross**. In 1959 the cross, standing in its present position, was described as 'ancient' and six feet high with much decayed arms; the arms formerly terminated in trefoils (VCH vol 5 p30 il of in 1838 facing p35). This cross had become so worn that it was replaced by a full-size replica in 1984 (SN Sept 7 1984 p4) (SHJ autumn 1995 p19). The old one was then kept indoors at the hall (John Timpson's England. 1987 p234 pc). In the Dairy Courtyard at the hall is a modern statue of a panther carved out of Ancaster stone by JA Twentyman of Claverley (Chillington Hall Guide). (WJO April 1905 pp101,105) (KES pp43, 46) (CL Feb 20 1948 p378) (VB pp74,77) (SGS p66) (FOS pp29,30) (TB April 1981 pp18-19) (Albion: A Guide to Legendary Britain. Jennifer Westwood. 1985) (COS p68p) (BDH p156) (MR pp50p,51,52) (FTWM pp125-129) (SHJ autumn 1995 pp18-23). For Giffard's Cross in a local rhyme see Brewood. Giffard's Cross has also been called Panther Cross.

Giggetty Area SW of Wombourne. In Wombourne parish. Developed on the edge of Wombourne Common. It was at first known as Giggatree, but by the C19 was known as Giggetty. Became a industrialised area from the 1950s (VCH vol 20 p199).

Gig Hall 1m W of Swythamley, at SJ 956642. According to records there was never a hall here. The name, which has also appeared as Gighall, is probably derived from a corruption of Middle English 'hole' and 'hale' allied words denoting a hollow or a nook. One kind of gig was a machine for teazling or fulling cloth and a gigmill was a fulling-mill. By the 1930s no one could remember a mill having existed here, although some said Brindley had a fulling mill here (NSFCT 1932 p54). Here is born the Dane feeder that supplies Rudyard Lake and the Caldon Canal.

Gighall Bridge A narrow wooden bridge over the Dane at the fishladder and weir near the Gighall Farm (NSFCT 1932 p54).

Gilbert Bridge Former name of a bridge which crosses the Hamps at Waterhouses. Here was a toll-house on the Leek-Ashbourne turnpike road known as Waterfall Gate (NSFCT 1948 p45).

Gilbert's Cross A couple of houses at a crossroads 0.75m W of Enville, in Enville ancient parish. The cross, which possibly took its name from the terre tenant of Enville in 1086 called Gilbert, may have served as a boundary mark between Enville and Morfe manors. The area was inhabited by the C17 (VCH vol 20 p94). (SPN p48).

Gill Bank Tiny area 0.5m E of the church at Kidsgrove, marked on the OS map 1:25,000, but not an area on the Stoke-on-Trent A-Z. There was a house called this in the C18 (VCH vol 8 p90).

Gilleon's Hall House (or minute hamlet consisting of about two houses) over 2m SE of Abbots Bromley.

Gillotty Greaves House and old estate 1.5m ESE of Walsall. The house stood at the S end of the present Allington Close. The name has appeared as 'le greve' (in deeds of C14 and C15) (DUIGNAN), Gyllot in greves (1525) (VCH vol 17 p175), Gillott o' th' Greaves, and Gillitty Greaves (SNWA p47). If from 'le greve' then is Middle English for a grove or wood (DUIGNAN). Gyllot may be a personal name or may mean 'hussy' (VCH vol 17 p175 note) (SNWA p47). The house was occupied until at least 1939 and then demolished. By the early 1970s its site was an open space and playground for the housing which had been built in the area (VCH vol 17 p176).

Gillow Heath Hamlet now a suburb of Biddulph. 0.5m SW of Biddulph church. In Biddulph ancient parish. There was settlement at Gillow Heath by 1383 (BHS June 1972 p29). The name occurs as Gylloowe Hetht in 1427 (BALH p27). It may mean 'Gil's Hill Heath;' Gil being once a popular Norwegian name; the Norwegians were prevalent the area in the C10 (BHS June 1968 p13). The mission church in Well Lane was built in 1900 (LDD). In 1979 here was the only mine in England which quarried a type of silica rock known as Whetstone (NSFCT 1979 p18).

Gillowshaw Brook Runs from Gillow Heath to Buglawton in Congleton, Ches. Another name for the brook is River Bug (BHS June 1968 p12).

Gillway Residential area 1m N of Tamworth. The name occurs on a map of the late C19 for the present Gillway Lane and for the name for the area on the 1971 OS map 1:25,000. By 1995 the name Perry Crofts was used to describe the same area (Birmingham A-Z 1995).

Gilpins Arm of the Wyrley and Essington Extension Canal. Spurred off the Wyrley and Essington Extension Canal 0.75m NNE of Pelsall at SK 026043. Ran to a basin on Pelsall Common near Pelsall Colliery. It was authorised in 1794 (HCMS No. 2). Named after William Gilpin, an edge-tool manufacturer from Wedges Mills. It was built in c1800 to transport coal, iron and limestone to work Gilpin's mill. The canal was almost derelict by 1840, and most of it was filled in and built over with an housing estate in the 1970s (SNBP p74p).

Gilpin's Basin W of Upper Landywood, at SJ 977057. Here the mineral railway of c1800 built by William Gilpin (d1835) joined the Wyrley Bank Branch of the Wyrley & Essington Canal. It had run from William Gilpin's edge tool works at Churchbridge (CCBO pp107-109) (VCH vol 2 pp259,260,261) (GWY pp32-33).

Gingerbread House Blurton. A toll-gate cottage which stood opposite another toll-gate cottage (which existed in the C18) at the junction of the road to Barlaston with the Longton Road. It is highly probable that two gates were erected; one across each road. Legend has it that an old lady used to bake gingerbread 'snap' to sell at the longer surviving toll-gate cottage (BNDA p40).

Gipsy Bank On Staffs side of Mill Dale at SK 143565. Or called Gypsy Banks, once a rendezvous for Romanies (PRT p73).

Gipsy Green Tiny hamlet 0.5m S of Bednall. The buildings at Gipsy Green are mostly Teddesley estate cottages of the mid C19 (VCH vol 5 p12). The name appears in a 1953 sale catalogue and means 'a green open space favoured by gypsies' (SPNO p121).

Gipsy Lane Road in central Willenhall. Runs from Walsall Street to Shepwell Green. A house in it is said to be haunted by the ghost of a miner (GOM pp4p,17).

Girthing Bank Half way along Congleton Edge from Nick o' th' Hill to Whitemoor Corner (SMM p123).

Gladstone Pottery Pottery works on corner of Uttoxeter Road and Chadwick Street, Longton. Adjacent to Park Place Works. The site had formed part of a potworks held by the Shelleys before 1789. It then passed to William Ward who split the Shelley site up; a part becoming this works and a part becoming Park Place Works (POP p132) (AGT p166). A plan of the works in 1857 appears in IAS p40. The kilns were fired for the last time in 1960. Bought in 1971 by H and R Johnson and turned into a museum, opened in 1975, to show a working pottery and the pottery trade (MR p219) (HOS 1998 p135). In 1976 it won the Museum of the Year award (POP p131). Some of the exhibits include examples of Minton encaustic monastic tiles; a Marshall single-crank tandem compound steam engine of the 1890s donated by Harrison Mayer; a lavatory suite made by Johnson Brothers, 1895, for the billiard room at Oulton Grange, printed decoration painted over the glaze, donated by DP Shelley; a Cardinal Patent hand basin installed in 1900 at Moor House, Biddulph, home of Thomas Twyford, inventor of the one-piece ceramic water closet. The pottery is haunted: The sounds of smashing china in a former warehouse building have been heard, as have the sounds of shovelling from one of the bottle ovens which so unnerved a former employee that he had to leave the premises (BBC Radio 2. Jimmy Young Show. 1978) (MMSE p288) (GOT p142) (ES Oct 24 1996 p5).

Glascote Former village on ground above Kettle Brook centred on New Street and Glascote Road 1m SW of Ammington. The former township of Bolehall and Glascote lay in Hemlingford hundred, Warws and in Tamworth ancient parish. It is now a suburb of Tamworth. A gold alloy torc was found in c1943 by men working in a boat-yard by the Coventry Canal between Glascote and Amington. When coiled it is seven inches at its greatest diameter. It is of C1 BC to C1 AD origin, and is similar to one found in Needwood Forest. It was declared treasure trove in 1970 (SSAHST 1969 pp1-6 p). Appears in the C12 as Glascote (SSE 1996 p14). Perhaps 'glass-worker's cottage(s)' suggesting that the place was where glass was made (NSFCT 1933 p74) (SSE 1996 p14) (SPN p54). Became a separate civil parish in 1866. Parts of the civil parish began to be taken into Tamworth borough from 1894 and the whole of Glascote civil parish was taken into the borough and into Staffs in 1965 (GLAUE p425). Glascote was a ward of Tamworth borough by at least 1993. The church, St George, Bamford Street, was built in 1880 (BOE p135) (CHMS2 p97). Glascote features in a derisory rhyme about Tamworth (see).

Glascote Heath Former common land nearly 1m ESE of Glascote. There was a small hamlet on Glascote Heath by 1888 (1888 OS map 6 inch). The area is now covered by housing estates (OS Street Atlas: Staffs 1995). There is a church, St Peter, at Glascote Heath (LDD).

Glazleyfield House over 1m NE of Barlaston station. In Barlaston parish and appears in the mid C19 as Glazeley Fields (W p411).

Glebedale Park To W of Victoria Place Link, Fenton. Created out of reclaimed land on site of Glebe Colliery, which had become known as 'Fenton Tip.' The official inauguration of the clearing of the site was performed by by Rt Hon Edward Heath PM on Oct 1 1971 and the park was officially opened on May 2 1973 (plaques on memorial rail wagon at S end of Glebedale Road) (SOTB p114).

Glebe House Thorpe Constantine. Large Victorian house. For sale at £450,000 in May 1997 (CL May 15 1997 pc property pages).

Glebeville Council housing estate of 1925 in the S of Leek, in the Sandon Street area (VCH vol 7 p97).

Gledelowe Possible burial mound on the western boundary of Rushton James township (VCH vol 7 p219).

Glossom's Fold Field name in Wolverhampton. Remnant of the towns involvement in the wool trade (SOSH p308).

Glovers Farm House in Botteslow township (HBST p526), which stood to the W of Hall Hill. Occurs on the 1834 and 1890 OS maps.

Glover's Hill Former hamlet (VCH vol 5 p149), now small suburb of Rugeley, N of the church at Brereton. Name is from a hill called Glover's Hill? In Rugeley parish.

Glynne Arms Former miners' inn and house 1m ESE of Himley. Lies in an isolated position facing E. The building, lying at an angle of 15 degrees, slopes dramatically due to mining subsidence being on the Himley coalfield; the S side being lower than the N (SVB p94). The effect is accentuated by the lintels being levelled. According to Bird the building was originally called Oak Farm Mill (VB pp48,49). Raven says Oak Farm Mill was the manor house, a different building, where the Glynne family resided, and is now (1988) demolished (MR p162p). Glynne Arms first appears as the Crooked House in KD 1898, by which time it also went by the name of its sign, Glynne Arms. That name was taken from Sir Stephen Glynne, brother-in-law of the Prime Minister WE Gladstone, who owned the estate on which it was situated. It has also appeared as Glyn Arms (SVB p94) and is known to those at Gornal as Siden House, the sunken house (VB pp48,49) (PONP pp148-152). Since being crooked the inn has been a national curiosity appearing on postcards and song sheets, as well as a destination for tourists (BCP p21p). Bank's brewery saved the building from falling down in about the mid C20. The same brewery modernised the inn in 1987 (PONP pp148-152). (Picture Postcards No. 315) (Inns, Ales, Drinking Customs of Old England. FW Hackwood. 1909. p222) (Staffs Sketches. FW Hackwood. p142) (NSFCT 1909 p182) (LGS p147) (KES pp107,108) (IOM pp74p,138) (BCM Jan 1977 pp22,23 ps of interior, 24. Oct 1977 pp71-72 - the Glynne and Gladstone connection, July 1983 pp18-28 - the Glynne and Gladstone connection) (TB June July 1973 p15ps. Nov 1979 p9p of. Dec 1979 p7. Oct 1982 p9p. Dec 1985 p15 il - the cover of the 'Siden House' song sheet. July 1998 p11ps) (BCOPP vol 1 pl 80, pl 81).

Glynwood Ipstones. Formerly called Pettyfields, now (1937) a farmhouse belonging to the Scarratt family (TOI p45).

Gnosall (locally *Nawzell, Nozall* SWY p33, SGS p101). Ancient parish and large village on a gentle slope rising above Doley Brook 6m WSW of Stafford. Gnosall was noted anciently for sheep with four horns, which also occurred at Knightley, Blore and Ingestre parks, and formerly at Loxley (John Johnston's Natural History de Quadruped. tab 27) (NHS p257) (SD p58). The **Roman** road from Stretton on Watling Street to Chester passes through Gnosall parish. A section of it was excavated SE of Aqualate Mere at SJ 790200 in 1938 (OSST 1936 pp30-38. 1938 pp28-36 maps plans). A Roman coin, a sestertius of Hadrian, was found 1948/9 to W of Gnosall at SJ 82912100 (NSJFS 1964 p23). The **name** has appeared as Geneshale, a manor, in DB, Gnowesala (1140), Gnoweshale (c1149), Cnoushale (1223), Gnousal (c1255), Gnousale (1291), Knowesalle (1296), Gnosall (Speed's map 1610), Nosall (1643), Knossall (1562-1566) (SPNO p153) (SSE 1996 p14) (SPN p54). Perhaps, Cnofwealh's hall (DUIGNAN). Oakden and others have found the first element very difficult to interpret (SSAHST 1967 p33) (SPNO p154) (NSJFS 1981 p3) (SSE 1996 p14). Ekwall thinks the origin form to be Saxon 'gneap,' meaning 'niggardly' and given as a nickname to the original owner, hence, 'the corner of land of the stingy one' (SPN p54). SAH Burne notes a rectangular moat with a house on site at Gnosall (ESH p58). The parish **church**, St Lawrence, on the S side of Sellman Street, has some noteworthy C12 work, but probably has origins in a church founded in the C10 or C11 (HOS 1998 p30). The church has been described as 'one of the finest in the county' (VCH vol 4 p129). The parish was formed before 1086 and probably originally contained Blymhill ancient parish (SHC 1916 pp192,193). Gnosall parish was said, in 1816, to have been a peculiar jurisdiction of the bishop of Lichfield and Coventry and may have been a probate jurisdiction of the lord of the manor. All peculiars were abolished in 1846 (VCH vol 3 p94 note). Gnosall parish **wake** was on second Sunday in August in the C19 (W p459). The village had a curious **ecclesiastical jury** comprising 12 or more men chosen by the minister and churchwardens. They joined with them and the sidesmen in making the presentations to the official (the church being a peculiar, anciently exempt from jurisdiction to all power except that of the Pope). The jury were impanelled and brought in their verdict in all ecclesiastical causes.

In the later C17 Plot was aware of no other instance where a civil law judge determined according to the verdict of a jury (NHS p313). Hackwood vaguely implies that the jury was selected or convened in Burgh Hill manor house (SCSF p161). (SD p58) (SOS p174 - noted by Harwood) (S & W vol 1 p6). Gnosall formerly formed a quarter in Gnosall parish. The quarter was also known as the Holding quarter (VCH vol 4 p111). There was no **fair** in 1792 (OWEN), but there was one in 1888 (LHE p265). In 1829 a riot occurred in Gnosall over the ownership of property. It was caused by Barber and Scott (LOU pp167,294). The Women's Institute attempted to save Gnosall **pound** in 1965 (Stafford Advertiser Jan 17 1965 p8 il). There is a small square **lock-up** at the side of the A518 on the N side. It formerly stood elsewhere and was nearly demolished to make way for road widening (SN Nov 8 1968 p25. Jan 14 1972 p3p). Some say it is probably of C18 origin (DoE II), others that it dates from 1830 (VCH vol 4 p112) (TTTD p258). It is known locally as the 'Round House.' No food or drink could be passed to the prisoner in it and the sole keyholder, had to ride out from Stafford to release him or bring him his provisions (SVB p82). (SHC 1936 vol 93 p135) (SLM Dec 1949 p67p of the time when it stood in its original position) (STM Feb 1966 p24p when the roof was covered by ivy and grass). Gnosall had a **windmill** at SJ 829209, to the W of the church. An inn stands on its site. It dated from 1815; appears on a map of 1831, but not after (WBJ p25). Between 1830 and 1835 the population of Gnosall swelled dramatically with navvies building the new Shropshire Union **Canal** to the W of Gnosall Heath; thereafter the population fell to levels lower than before 1830 suggesting that many had married canal workers and had moved away (SPJD p88). For the labouring man who was attacked by a boggart on the canal bridge known as Big Bridge in the Gnosall area see Big Bridge. There was a **railway** station at Gnosall on the Shropshire Union Railway (Stafford to Wellington, Shrops) opened on June 1 1849, closed on Aug 6 1966 (W p459) (Railways In and Around Stafford. Edward Talbot. 1994 p4). The two red brick semi-detached **villas** known as 'London Villas' on the Newport Road built in the style of 1898-1904 contain fittings brought from demolished London houses (TTTD pp262-263). There was a **well** in a garden with a wooden water drawing apparatus above it (SLM autumn 1957 p27p). For two **ash trees** which Plot noted growing together between Gnosall and Walton Grange see under Walton Grange. **Persons and visitors. Elizabeth Payne** of Gnosall, was 105 years old, when Plot was in Staffs in 1680 (NHS p320). The Congregationalist preacher **George Burder** (1752-1832) incited a 'formidable riot' at Gnosall in 1778 (VCH vol 4 p133) (SSAHST 1971 p52). Gnosall **Handbell Ringers** are internationally famous (SVB p83). 'Country' singers, **Mike Beer**, and **Phil Silver**, residents of Gnosall, produced the record album 'Spring Again' (Kaleidoscope. BBC Radio 4, week 4 -10 Oct 1993).

Gnosall Collegiate Church There is a tradition that the church at Gnosall was founded by King Wulfhere and his Queen Ermenilda, and that it was made a Royal Free Chapel (or Royal Peculiar) by Ethelfleda, daughter of King Alfred (TTTD p261). Gnosall had an establishment of a dean and four prebends - Beverleyhall, Chilternhall, Moorhall, Sukarshall (LGS pp140,163). But the college developed on different lines from other collegiate churches in the county. It never became collegiate in the strict sense, since its prebendaries were not a corporate body with a common fund and a common seal, under a dean or other head. Yet the bishop was named in 1535 as nominal dean (SHC 1927 pp80-116) (VCH vol 4 pp128-129).

Gnosall Heath Former heath and now a large hamlet 0.75m SW of the church at Gnosall, now practically merged with Gnosall. The name appears on Yates' map (SPNO p160). The settlement here expanded greatly as a hamlet after the Shropshire Union Canal opened in 1835. The canal crosses the heath (TTTD p262).

Goat Lodge At Dunstal, on the E side of lane leading to Bagot's Park. Built to designs of James Trubshaw the younger for Lord Bagot in 1839 (ABAB p39), or in 1835 (ESNF p90p) for his woodman (TRTC p32). The lodge appears to have been occupied by members of the Jackson family, keepers of the Bagot Goats in Bagot's Park (see), from the mid C19 to the death of Miss Mary Jackson in the 1950s (TRTC pp31,32). Has barge-boarded gables decorated with a profusion of carved goats' heads (ABAB pp39,40il). The lodge was described as 'picturesque' in 1901 (NSFCT 1901 p188) and in 1982 as 'a piece of over-decorated Victoriana' (ABAB p39). It was called the goat house in 1946 (NSFCT 1946 p149) (ESNF p90). In 1963 the lodge was purchased by Phil Drabble, naturalist, writer and broadcaster, for his residence (STM Feb 1965 pp20-21) (COS p32p) (TRTC p33).

Goblins Pit Former hamlet near Green Lane, Walsall Wood. Formerly in a detached portion of the foreign of Walsall ancient parish. There was settlement here by 1763 (VCH vol 17 p278). Goblinspit Farm and Wood (possibly a remnant of Cannock Forest) appear on maps between 1834 and 1969. The

pit referred to is a limestone pit (SNBC p39). (TB Feb 1993 p25).

Godley Brook Tributary of the Tean. Has appeared as Godley Brook (1837 OS map). Perhaps means 'Goda's brook' (SPNO p11).

Godleybrook Tiny hamlet N of Dilhorne, now merges with Dilhorne. In Dilhorne parish.

Godstone Tiny hamlet 0.5m SSE of Dod's Leigh, Church Leigh. In Leigh parish.

Gog and **Magog** Former ancient oaks which stood near Mavesyn Ridware. According to tradition it was by these oaks Sir Robert Mavesyn (born c1360), lord of Mavesyn Ridware (see), and Sir William Handsacre, lord of Handsacre, fought a small battle as they left to fight on opposite sides in the battle of Shrewsbury on July 22 1403. The two neighbouring lords and their tenants had long been in dispute. The two had argued over fishing rights in the Trent, which formed the boundary between the two manors, since the later C14; in 1399 Mavesyn's followers burnt and destroyed the mill at the centre of the dispute and one of Sir William's men was killed. In the small battle Sir Robert (supporter of Henry IV) slew Sir William (supporter of Hotspur), only to be slain himself in the battle of Shrewsbury (LGS p203) (St Nicholas Church, Mavesyn Ridware guide). The Mavesyn and Handsacre families were shortly united in marriage, when Margaret, younger daughter of Sir Robert Mavesyn, married Sir William Handsacre, son of Sir William Handsacre (St Nicholas Church, Mavesyn Ridware guide). The oaks probably stood between Mavesyn Ridware and the High Bridge (LGS p203). They were cut down in the 1880s. A photograph taken of their vast trunks was shot by the Walsall Photographic Society. Rev GS Hewins was in possessions of a print (SLM Oct 1947 p37). (CCC p64) (HS p133) (KES p151) (MR p263). A fragment of one of the trees - the one under which Sir William is reputed to have been slain - is preserved in a locked safe in the vestry of Mavesyn Ridware church. The battle between Handsacre and Mavesyn is described in Shakespeare's 'Henry IV' Part II Act V Sc 3 (SHOS vol 1 p180 note 4). Gog and Magog feature in George Griffith's tragedy 'The Two Houses' 1866. Griffith, writing in 1866, says the oaks are believed to be 900 years.

Golden Hill Hill on Butterton Moor in the moorlands over 1.5m W of Butterton. The name may have arisen out of an association the hill had with spirits of ancient times (DPMM p117).

Golden Hill Farm 1m W of Fairoak, at SJ 748329. In the Woodland quarter in Eccleshall ancient parish. The farm is said to have been tenanted by the same family since the battle of Blore Heath (NSFCT 1930 pp51,163). On the farm is Glass House Croft (see); the name preserves the site of a glass house (NSFCT 1919 p33. 1920 p161. 1930 pp51-52).

Golden Hill Tiny district of Longton, about Golden Hill Road. Formerly in Stoke-upon-Trent chapelry in Stoke-upon-Trent ancient parish.

Goldenhill Large village on high ground above Bath Pool valley nearly 1.5m N of Tunstall. Formerly in Oldcott township in Wolstanton ancient parish. In c1810 (NSJFS 1964 p36; possibly a typing error and c1910 is meant) or in c1909 (NSFCT 1959 p84) in the garden of Goldenhill Rectory was found a Romano-British bronze figurine of Hercule. It was returned to the county in 1959 (NSFCT 1959 p84) and went to the Potteries Museum, Hanley. A leather purse tied with rush containing silver coins (mostly of Elizabeth I's reign) and gold coins of the reigns of Charles II and James II was discovered by workmen in the tiering of the roof of a thatched house in March 1832 (HBST p128) (SHST p646). A settlement was in existence at Goldenhill by 1670 (VCH vol 8 p83). Ward is at a loss to find an explanation for the **name** Goldenhill. But a hoard of gold is said to have been hidden here in the Civil Wars (HBST pp122,128). Part of which may have been the hoard found at Goldenhill in 1832, see above. Pickford thinks Goldenhill denotes the Shining One, the god of the ancients who lived on top of a hill; there is a Shining Tor to the N that has the same derivation (SMM p128). The **church**, St John the Evangelist, at the corner of High Street and Elgood Lane, was built in 1841 (VCH vol 8 p94) (BOE p265). Became a separate ecclesiastical parish in 1842 and a separate civil parish in 1894 (GLAUE p412). Is now increasingly becoming just a suburb between Tunstall and Kidsgrove. For Goldenhill **railway** station see Newchapel. Three young children died in a **fire** at Goldenhill just before Christmas 1955 (ADD p152). **Persons and visitors. James Nixon**, one of the earliest Primitive Methodist preachers, was born in Goldenhill in 1785. A close disciple of Hugh Bourne he was expelled from the Wesleyan Connection in 1811 (BS p330) (OTP p12). It is said that the fanatical preacher, James Nixon, wore out the knees of his trousers praying in Leek market place. His commitment was exemplified by the fact that despite fruit and vegetables being thrown at him and water poured over him he carried on praying (DP p68). Rev **Osmond Dobree** formerly curate at Knypersley church was appointed vicar at Goldenhill in 1873. His appointment caused considerable controversy for his connections with the Oxford

Movement, also known as the Catholic Revival. Opposition to his appointment broke out even before he arrived at Goldenhill with the parishioners petitioning the bishop of Lichfield to change his mind. But the then bishop, GA Selwyn, who was also a supporter of the Oxford Movement, refused to meet with a parishioners' delegation who went to see him at Lichfield (TTTD pp193-194). Dobree was vicar at Colwich from 1890 until his death in 1929 (HHHC p27). **Tony Walker** (b1942) of Goldenhill, cross-country running champion, won the national junior title at West Bromwich in 1960 and was chosen three times to run for the English Cross-Country Union (TWWW Feb 27 1999 p24).

Goldhayfields N of Hunger Hill. There was a Gouldhay Farm in Pipe Ridware parish in the mid C19 (W p575).

Goldhurst House 1m E of Upper Tean (1834 OS map).

Goldie Brook There is a bridge of this name at Saredon. Has appeared as Goldybridge (Bowen's map), Goodybridge (early C18) (SPNO p114). The name means 'island of land where marsh marigolds grow' (SPNO p114).

Gold's Clump Large mound at Hints S of Watling Street, at SK 15680328. In the later C17 Plot thought the mound was a burial mound and of Roman construction (NHS p414). White notes others have thought it to be of Roman construction (W p564). (SHOS vol 2 p19). Gunstone says it is natural (NSJFS 1965 p39). In 1902 it was noted that the summit was flat, and round the foot of the hill was a ring of stones (NSFCT 1902 p158). Raven says it is 60 yards in diameter and is a prehistoric burial mound (MR p186).

Golds Green Small industrial district by Golds Hill, West Bromwich. In West Bromwich ancient parish. May take its name from the Golde family, who were living in the Finchpath area in 1332. Mining was taking place here by the 1760s (VCH vol 17 pp6,7). Has also appeared as Gold's Green.

Golds Hill Hill 2m NW of the centre of West Bromwich. To W of Gold's Green. The church, St Paul, Bagnall Street, was built in 1881-1882 (VCH vol 17 pp56,57). Bagnall's Church refers to the new church at Golds Hill, built by a Mr Bagnall, a churchwarden at St Mark's church, Tipton (OH p11).

Goldsitch Brook Sends its arms within a few yards of the source of Dane Brook. Takes a westerly course. Flows through a deep ravine at Gradbach Wood. Joins the Dane at the foot of Back Forest (NSFCT 1868 p22).

Goldsitch Moss Moss 2m SSW of Flash. In Alstonefield ancient parish. The name appears as Goodsich in 1564 (SSE 1996 p69), and is probably from marigolds growing by Black Brook (VCH vol 7 p50). There was probably a house on the site of the present Goldsitch House, which is C17 in origin, by 1634. The house lies on the southern edge of the moss (VCH vol 7 p50) (UHAW p51 il). Goldsitch Moss is the name for a coalfield in this area, but is really the southerly tip of the Cheshire coalfield (SSE 1996 p66). Coal has been mined in this area from at least 1401 to the mid C20 (IANS p35) (SSE 1996 pp66-95). Its extent is shown on a map in IANS p32 (VCH vol 2 p70).

Goldthorn Hill Hill, 610.4 feet high (HOWM p6), and suburb of Wolverhampton 1.5m SSW of St Peter's church (SHOS vol 2 p165). Formerly partly in Wolverhampton township, borough and ancient parish and partly in Sedgley and Penn parishes. In the mid C19 White noted the view from the summit was magnificent, with the Malvern Hills, Bredon Hills, the three Clee Hills and the Wrekin discernible on the horizon (W p67). The name may be from the Goldhoard mentioned in Lady Wulfrun's charter 994 (PENOP p7), or from Goldhord mentioned in the later C13 and refers to a place where treasure (from a burial mound?) has been found (WA vol 2 no 1 pp41-42), or from a corruption of Coldthorne; the element 'cold' being from Celtic 'coel' or variants, referring to a magical place, an omen, a belief; Coalway Lane (see), similarly derived, passed over Goldthorn Hill (PPTP p37). Later, Goldthorn appears as Goldhord (1261.1291) (WA vol 2 no 1 pp41-42) (HOWM p8), Gawthorne (1647), Gowthorne (1647) (PPTP p37), and Goldthorne (Plot's map 1682) (Bowen's map). There was a windmill at SO 909969 to E of Goldthorn Road or at SO 907969 (WIS p25). It is shown on Greenwood's map. It was disused by 1902. A photograph of it in 1905 shows a derelict brick tower with sloping sides and a cylindrical upper section (WBJ p47) (TB Oct 1986 p15). Wolverhampton Wanderers were at first known as Goldthorn Football Club and played on the Windmill 'field' off Goldthorn Hill between 1877 and 1879 (The Story of Wolverhampton Wanderers. Tony Matthews with Les Smith 1994 p7) (WF p61). In 1997 a plaque was erected on the house at No. 123 Goldthorn Hill to commemorate Gwen Berryman (1906-1983), who played Doris in the radio soap opera 'The Archers' between 1951 and 1980 (Commemorative Plaques by the Wolverhampton Civic Society).

Goldthorn Park Suburb of Wolverhampton 1.5m S of St Peter's church.

Golling Gate Near Tenterhill, Hollinsclough. Has also appeared as Gollingate (W p747).

Gonder Hall An old house at Fairoak. Here the Home Guard met every night in

WW2. The last occupants were the late Joe Wenlock and family. The ruins still remain in Frank and John Palm's fields (BOV pp86,88).

Goodall's Farm House in Ellastone. It could have been the model for 'Hall Farm' in George Eliot's novel, 'Adam Bede,' which she set in Ellastone (SVB p73).

Goodfellow Bank An incline at Leek. Said to be inhabited by fairies. Flattened by 1942 (FLJ 1942 p126) (DPEM p100).

Good's Green Nearly 1.5m ENE of Arley, marked on OS map 1:25,000.

Goodwins House which stood in approximate position of Brackendale Drive, Yew Tree (Dower's map).

Goodwin's Hole Former row of old houses below the level of the present Church Street, Stone, on the same side as the Robin Hood Inn. Also known as Goblin's Hole. The houses were described by a Local Government Board medical officer in 1874, as one of the worst places he had seen in all his experience (SIS pp124,126 note).

Goosemoor Central Burton upon Trent (1834 OS map). Moor Street probably preserves the name.

Goosemoor Dispersed minute hamlet over 1.5m W of Church Eaton. In Church Eaton ancient parish. Has appeared as Gosemere (1331), Gosemer sych (1349), and Goosemoor Sitch (1838) (SPNO p143). The name means 'a lake for geese' (SPNO p143).

Goosemoor Common Former common land in Church Eaton parish in the area between the Brineton road to the Shropshire Union Canal. Has appeared Gorsemoor Heath (Yates' map) (OS map 1834) (SPNO p143).

Goosemoor Green Tiny hamlet over 1m ESE of Cannock Wood. In Longdon ancient parish. Appears as Gosmore Green in 1820 (SHC 1960 p50).

Gooseneck Farm House 2m SE of Bradnop. Formerly in Bradnop township in Leek ancient parish. Built on former waste land and is partly of C18 origin (VCH vol 7 p171). It has been said that here lived the father, brother and sister of the counterfeiters, George and Thomas Fearne in c1800 (OL vol 2 p59). Probably takes its name from a field name which in turn is derived from an animal name (APB p48).

Goosey Green Former hamlet in the Eve Lane area of Upper Gornal. The name appears in the 1851 and 1861 census.

Gorge, The Gorge just W of the limestone ridge at Hurst Hill (SDSSOP p31p).

Gornal Collective name for the Black Country villages, Lower Gornal (see), Upper Gornal (see) and Gornalwood (see); they lie on interweaving ridges on the crest of England's main watershed. In Sedgley ancient parish. Lower Gornal has always been the largest and is 20.5m S of Stafford. The name has appeared as Gornhal, Goronhale, Gwarnell (SPN p103), and Guarnell (C15) (SR p4). It was thought that the previous name for Gornal was 'Sheepcote Wall' (PHS p24). If from Guarnell then perhaps from gwarn and guarn representing Anglo-Saxon 'cweorn,' Middle English 'quern,' 'cwerne,' a mill. The suffix 'al' was derived from 'hale,' a meadow giving 'mill meadow' (SR p4) (DUIGNAN). Or possibly from 'caor' Breton 'goer' a stream with the diminutive 'in' may be the source of the first part of Gornal (NSFCT 1908 p143). Or 'mill nook' (NSJFS 1981 p3) (SPN p103). Some have suggested 'Gor-on-al' or 'sun worship,' or from 'gorn' or 'gwan,' a small round tub with handles which was used to carry wort during the brewing of beer; beer has been brewed in the area of the Gornals for many generations (AMS p446) (WMVB p156). For Gornal windmills see under Rewardine, The Round House, Ruiton, and Sandyfields. 'Gornal' ecclesiastical parish was formed in 1824. It is now called Lower Gornal (GLAUE p412). JB Priestley refers to one of the Gornals in 'English Journey' (1933). He writes 'I remember arriving at the very end of the earth, where the land appeared to have been uprooted by a pig and where there were cottages so small and odd that they must have been built for gnomes, and this end of the earth was called Gornal, and there the women, returning home from the brickworks, wore caps and shawls. The shawls were like those that the weavers used to wear in my own town, but our women had worn their shawls over their heads. Here, however, they wore caps as well, and looked as outlandish as the place they lived in.' For Gornal as a verb see BCM April 1971 p27.

Gornal Green Has been identified with the Five Ways area of Lower Gornal (TB Aug 1982 pp1,14).

Gornalwood Small village or suburb of Lower Gornal, 0.5m SW of Lower Gornal. The name Gornal Wood appears in the 1851 census.

Gorsebrook Brook which runs S of Dunstall Park and joins the Smestow.

Gorsebrook Former hamlet (SHOS vol 2 p186) and mill on the Wolverhampton-Stafford road, 1.25m SW of Bushbury, 1m N of Wolverhampton. In Bushbury parish. The name appears in the charter of King Ethelred (985), and has appeared as Gosebrok (1300), Goose Brook, and Gosbrook. It is from the brook Gorsebrook (SVS p373 note). Or from goose, but the word included, and includes, many varieties of wild aquatic birds, as well as the tame species (DUIGNAN) (SPN p145). The hamlet was in existence by the Middle Ages (HOWM p6).

Gorsebrook House Stood with its side towards the Stafford Road, on the bend opposite to Gorsebrook Road, Dunstall Hill, Bushbury, close to the canal. Built probably in the 1770s or 1780s. In the early C19 it was the seat of John Corser, a Wolverhampton solicitor, and later John Gough. By the early C20 its land had been sold to the Electric Construction Company who built its works in the gardens. The house then became the home of Mr Jones, the first works manager. It was demolished in the 1980s following the closure of the works (BUOP p56).

Gorse Cottage At Essington on Wolverhampton-Cannock turnpike road. On Dec 22 1824 Ann Spencer was murdered in the cottage by Thomas Powell, a thief (TB Sept 1981 pp1,10-11).

Gorse Hall N of Barton Turn. Under 1.5m SW of Branston (1905 OS map). Formerly called Goss Hall (OS map 1884 6 inch).

Gorsty Bank Steep area at the E end of High Street, Brockmoor, where it joins Bank Street, Brierley Hill (SNSV vol 1 p144). The name is preserved in Gorsty Avenue.

Gorsty Bank Minute hamlet 0.25m N of Silverdale. Gorsty was the name of an old colliery shaft (IANS p128 see map).

Gorstybirch House 1.5m WNW of Cresswell. Also slightly to the S a house called Lower Gorsty Birch.

Gorsty Hall Gorstyhill, near Balterley. In Ches, but was in Staffs. Situated on the current Staffs border. Closed as an hotel, which it had been since c1976, in 1996 (ES Aug 9 1996 p72p).

Gorsty Hayes In Haywood Drive, Tettenhall. Timber-framed house dating from the C16 or C17 and is believed to have been a forester's lodge. According to local tradition Henry II once spent some days hunting in this area (BTW p76p). Belonged to Col Thorneycroft in 1894 (HOPTT p4). The building was bought by the RC church in 1962 for use as a presbytery for the adjacent church of St Thomas of Canterbury (BTW p76).

Gorsty Hill Small hamlet 2.5m SW of Marchington. Formerly in Marchington Woodlands township in Hanbury ancient parish. There is a square wet moated site at SK 109289. The platform is tree-covered (CAMS p63).

Gorstyhill Tiny hamlet 2m WNW of Balterley. Was in Staffs before 1834, is now in Cheshire.

Gorstyhill Small hamlet 1m NE of Upper Tean. In Checkley ancient parish. Also a hill Gorsty Hill on the very top of which is the burial mound 'Wentlow' (NSFCT 1983 p12).

Gorsty Hill Tunnel Gorsty Hill, Rowley Regis. Carries the Dudley Canal Line Two. Was 648 yards long, but has been reduced to 557 yards (HCMS No. 2).

Gorsybank Appears to be an incline 1m NW of Standon. Does not appear on current OS map 1:25,000, but a house? called Gorse View does.

Gorton Green House E of Gorton Lodge. In Longdon parish. May appear as Gamton Green on Yates' map.

Gorton Lodge Minute hamlet 1m NW of Farewell. Hamlet in mid C19 (W p568). Presumably here was a lodge to Beaudesert Park?

Gorway The Gorway area of SE Walsall, containing Gorway House, takes its name from the Gorway family, residents of Walsall by the mid C16 (SNWA p50).

Gorway House 0.75m SSE of Walsall. Built by Peter Porter, land agent to the Earl of Bradford in the later 1820s. The house was demolished by West Midlands College of Education in c1966 to make way for extensions to their college building, built in 1963 (VCH vol 17 pp154-155). (W p649) (WROP p116p of in 1948).

Goscote District, former hamlet and manor 1m ENE of Bloxwich. In the foreign of Walsall. Goscote has also appeared as Gorsticote (BY p25). The name means 'the cottage in the gorse' or 'on the heath.' The locality was formerly within the limits of Cannock Forest (DUIGNAN) (VCH vol 17 p164) (SPN p134) (BY p25) (SNBP p28). Goscote existed by the end of the C13 and apparently lay towards the N end of Goscote Lane. By the later C18 this area is referred to as Old Goscote and by the same period the area round Goscote Hall is referred to as New Goscote (Yates' map) (VCH vol 17 p164). Goscote manor was subject to the overlordship of the manor of Walsall (BY p25). (BCM July 1973 p50). There was a windmill in Goscote field between 1735 and 1744; it still stood in 1786. The same or another windmill, about 100 yards W of Goscote Lane, is shown on Yates' maps of 1775 and 1799; it had disappeared by 1816 (VCH vol 17 p186).

Goscote Hall Formerly situated on the corner of Slacky and Goscote Lanes. Formed part of an estate owned by the Price family in the mid C18 (VCH vol 17 p176). The hall was built by the mid C18 (BY p25) and had been demolished by 1966 (VCH vol 17 p176).

Goscote Manor House Goscote Lane, Goscote. The lord of Goscote manor

held a house and garden in Goscote by 1649. The house which was destroyed and replaced by the present Barley Mow Inn was a C17 building (BY p25) (VCH vol 17 p174). The inn incorporates remains of an earlier building (VCH vol 17 p174).

Gospel Ash S of Halfpenny Green, Bobbington. Formerly in Bobbington chapelry in Claverley ancient parish, Shrops.

Gospel End Tiny hamlet 1.25m W of Sedgley. (BCOPP vol 1 p59 pl). Formerly in the Upper Side division of Sedgley ancient parish (W p195). Erdeswicke followed by Shaw and Eyton erroneously identified Gospel End with the DB manor of Capspelle (see) (SNSV vol 2 p33). Appears in 1632 as Gosple end (HC p39). The name means gospel border or place (AMS p441). There is a mission church, St Barnabas, at Gospel End (LDD).

Gospel End Farm Stood opposite the entrance to Southerndown Road, Gospel End. It was demolished in 1966 in error; the demolition contractors having reportedly mistaken it for Sedgley Hall. It was at one time called Morgan's Farm and was a brick building with a stone facade. It was Georgian in appearance (SDOP p42p).

Gospel Oak Here the ancient parishes of Wednesbury, Sedgley, and Tipton met (SCSF p21). The hamlet of Gospel Oak lay partly in Sedgley parish (W p200) and Tipton parish (SGSAS). The name is literally from a gospel oak tree (SR p4) (SCSF p21). Gospel Oak, Gospel Tree, and Gospel End are common place names on parish boundaries (DUIGNAN) (SPN p137). The name is preserved in Gospel Oak Road, which is 1.5m NE of High Street, Tipton.

Gospel Oak Branch of the Birmingham Canal. Runs from the Birmingham Canal Old Cut (Wednesbury Canal Loop) at Wednesbury Oak to the Walsall Canal at The Patent Shaft Steel Works. Constructed in 1800. Officially closed in 1966. The W end is abandoned (BCM autumn 1995 p18).

Goss, The Small area of land at the Delph, Brierley Hill, W of Mill Street and S of the Nine Locks on the Stourbridge Canal. Does not appear in Fowler's 1840 survey. The name, thought to be from the presence of gorse bushes, is preserved in a cul-de-sac (SNSV vol 2 p33).

Gosse, The Narrow field. A remnant of a pre-enclosure plot in Hazel Lane, Landywood (GWY pp21p facing,31).

Gothersley Tiny fragmented dispersed hamlet 2.75m NNE of Kinver on Smestow Brook. In Kinver parish. Gothersley may have been the site of the hermitage of Gutheresburn in Kinver Forest, mentioned in 1248 (VCH vol 20 p123). The name means Godric's lea (DUIGNAN). There was a blade mill on Smestow Brook at Gothersley by 1685, possibly built by Philip Foley in early 1670s (VCH vol 20 pp123,147). Gothersley Mill, to which an industrial hamlet was attached, closed in the early 1890s (VCH vol 20 p123). Gothersley Round House, a ruined castellated tower on the W bank of the Staffs and Worcs Canal, was part of a wharfhouse serving some ironworks. It was built about 1805 and adjoined a small cottage now demolished (S&WC p) (TB Feb 1985 p4 ps. March 1985 p29 p of it in 1926 when it adjoined the cottage. June 1989 p11p) (BCM April 1991 pp39,40il) (RKE p18) (Staffs and Worcs Canal Conservation Area Booklet). Rev John Hodgson, local historian, was born here in 1828 (BS).

Gower Branch Canal of the Birmingham Canal. Links the Toll End Branch with the main branch of the Birmingham Canal (Birmingham A-Z).

Grace Mary Estate To E of Darby's Hill, Rowley Regis.

Gradbach Isolated tiny hamlet in the Moorlands on the steep northern slopes of Gradbach Hill overlooking the Dane, 1.75m NE of Swythamley. It was formerly a small industrial community consisting of a mill, two factories and about 50 houses (HOLF p46). There was a house at Gradbach possibly by 1374, when there was mention of Henry Gratebache (VCH vol 7 p49). The place appears as Gratbache in 1564 (SSE 1996 p69). The name means 'grassy stream' from Old English 'baec' brook and 'graede' grassy (NSFCT 1932 p57). Pickford suggests that it is from Gradbach Hill, which at one time was known as the Great Bitch, a reference to the Earth goddess; out of this hill flows a stream of red that may well have given the illusion or suggestion of menstruation (DPMM p81). There was a corn mill at Gradbach in 1640. This or a later mill burnt down in 1785 (VCH vol 7 p52). Breeze and others have confused this mill with the late C18 silk mill of the Dakeyne family (IANS p45) (HOLF p44), of whom Miss J Dakeyne, poet and folklorist, author of LMF, was one (PSS p464) (VFC p34). In the early 1790s a mill was built by the Dane to spin wool, cotton, or silk. In the late 1790s the Dakeynes, cotton spinners of Darley, Derbys, took over the lease of the mill and converted it to flax spinning. The Dakeynes continued as lessees until 1864. The mill had closed by 1868 (VCH vol 7 p53). About 1885 Sir J Harpur-Crewe acquired it and used it as a saw mill and joiners' shop for the estate. During his time it is said to have had the largest pocket water wheel in England. The wheel had a diameter of 38 feet and around it were 96 water pockets, each with a capacity of 35 gallons. It was sold for scrap in the 1950s. The mill was purchased by the YHA in 1977 (HOLF p44p) or 1978, who opened it as a youth hostel in 1984 (VCH vol 7 pp50,53). Gradbach methodist chapel opened in 1849 and services were still being held here in 1994 (UHAW p35). A stone trough with a seat either side is at Gradbach (PDS&C p28p).

Gradbach Hill Hill to S of Gradbach. On the hill is a rock feature known as the Yawning Rock.

Gradbach Old Hall Mainly C19 house with C17 stonework at Gradbach (VCH vol 7 p49). A room in the hall is said to be haunted by the ghost of a young boy, the son of an early owner, Lady Sarah Downes. She and her husband had a beautiful daughter and heir, who married a gentleman of high breeding from a foreign land. They settled at the hall, but then, very late in life the daughter's parents produced a son, to whom the daughter lost her inheritance. After her parents died the young boy was left in her care. Through her severe ill-treatment he shortly died (UHAW p77). An identical story is told by Breeze (although the ghost she sights is that of the cruel elder sister) but she is vague as to the location of the house suggesting it might be one at White Middle Hills or Upper Hulme (HOLF pp14-15). In 1951 the hall was bought by the Buxton and District Scout Association, which uses its fields as a camping ground (VCH vol 7 p49) (UHAW p51 il).

Graingers Hall Farm of 22 acres in the heart of the valley 'of lodge' in the environs of Lodge Forge, near Cradley Heath (TB Nov Dec 1973 p16). The farmhouse or hall appears to have been taken down with the construction of the Stourbridge Extension Railway (1866). It stood about 100 yards away from the land between the Old Chapel (Cradley Heath) and the Jolly Collier Inn; there still exists a Graingers Lane (BCWJ pp67,99,100).

Graisbrook Hall The hall formerly stood behind the present Oddfellows Hall in Shenstone. In 1204 Bartholomew de Gresebroke acquired the manor-house of Shenstone from Robert de Gredon - this was afterwards called Gresbrok Hall (SSAHST 1970 p25). It continued as the seat of the Grazebrook or Graisbrook family, and has also appeared as Grazebrook Hall and Greisbrook Hall. Having become a dilapidated cottage it was demolished in c1855 to make way for the railway, when it passed into the possession of Chancellor Law (ASE p8) (SVB p151) (BCM Jan 1988 pp30-31il).

Graiseley Former estate and tiny hamlet, now a suburb 1m SSW of Wolverhampton (W p95). Formerly Grazeley or Graseley in Wolverhampton township, chapelry and ancient parish. The church, St Chad, Lime Street, was built in c1908 (LDD). There seems to have been a small settlement at Graiseley in the Middle Ages (HOWM p6). The name means the grassy lea (DUIGNAN) (SPN p144). Was a ward of Wolverhampton borough by 1982.

Graiseley Brook Runs through Merridale. GP Mander identified this brook with the River Bourn, Beadgyth's Bourn.

Graiseley House At Graiseley Hill, Graiseley. Once the residence of the Stevens family of AJS motor cycles. Had a lodge resembling a temple (PENOP p42).

Graiseley Old Hall Claremont Road, Wolverhampton. Formed the nucleus of an ancient estate, in the foreign of Wolverhampton (HOWM p44). The date generally given for the building of the hall is 1485. However there is a plaque dated 1377 in the exposed wattle and daub wall and it is certain that there was a house here at least 50 years prior to that because it is recorded that Geoffrey de Graisley had to pay a subsidy to Edward II towards his Scots war (AWM p21). The hall passed from the Graisleys to the Ridleys (Nicholas Ridley who died c1524 was a merchant of the staple - WAIW vol 3 p of in 1913). With the death John Ridley in 1608 the hall passed to his daughter, Rachel who married John Rotton of Moseley, Birmingham. The wild life of their son Walter ended this line (SHOS vol 2 *p172) (HOWM p61). The hall passed to the Normansells, of whom William was Oliver Cromwell's JP while Charles II was in flight after the battle of Worcester (1651), to the Jessons, who were responsible for encasing the hall in brick during Queen Anne's reign. From the Jessons it passed to James Perry in the early C19 (WAIW vol 3). By the mid C19 the hall belonged to Moses Ironmonger, mayor of Wolverhampton, and a friend of Alexander Graham Bell (WF p45). The first telephone in Wolverhampton is believed to have linked the hall with Ironmongers' rope factory in Salop Street. George Green carried out major restoration to the hall in c1911 bringing to it timber from the belfry of St Peter's church, Wolverhampton. The poet Annie Hilda Green (1882-1926), probably a relation of George, lived at Graiseley Old Hall. Flora Forster was a later occupant and entertained Dorothy Sayers, Margaret Kennedy and Vera Britain here (WMAG July 1976 p5il) (Wolverhampton AdNews June 16 1994 p8) (Graseley Old Hall Leaflet by Sue and Paul Williams) (E&S Oct 8 1996 p15p) (Our House. Central Television. Oct 13 1996). The hall was bought in 1930 by The Royal Wolverhampton School who built a junior school in its grounds, which opened in 1932 (VCH vol 6 p181). In 1957 Enoch Powell MP for Wolverhampton South East obtained Grade II* listing for the hall. The school used the hall as an office and after their departure it was long on the market before being

bought by Sue Williams and her brother Paul in 1991 (info Sue Williams) (Wolverhampton Chronicle Aug 7 1998 p13ps) (BCM June 1997 pp68p-69). There may have been a moat surrounding the property, but no traces of it survived by the early 1980s (SSAHST 1982-3 p58). There is an octagonal ice-house in Penn Road at SO 907974, which probably had associations with the hall, although, Beaman and Roaf make no connection (IHB pp444-445) (WMAT No. 24 1981 pp131-132).

Grand Lodge One of nine lodges to Beaudesert Hall, situated on the circumference of Beaudesert Old Park, at the top of Borough Lane, 1m SW of Longdon. Said to be built in 1814 (BPW p24) or in 1815 for the home coming of the Marquis of Anglesey after the battle of Waterloo (SLM Aug/ Sept 1986 p9). The design has been attributed to John Shaw (1776-1832) (BOE p67) (BPW p24). It was the ceremonial gateway to the hall (SVB p112) and over the central part was a small bell tower; the bell could be heard from the hall and warned of the approach of a Marquis of Anglesey or of visitors (BPW p24). (MR p216).

Grange A council housing estate in the Grange Road area of Tettenhall. Built in the mid 1950s (BTW p69).

Grange, The Rakeway Road, Cheadle. Built in 1493 and was demolished in 1966 (COPP2 p128p).

Grange, The Just off the Wergs Road, Tettenhall. Not to be confused with the house of the same name in Grange Road, Tettenhall; this house overlooks Wrottesley Park. Built in 1863 (BTW p79p).

Gratton Hamlet on a hill above Horton Brook 2m SE of Biddulph Moor. It was also a manor in Horton ancient parish. The last element in the name 'ton' is probably from Old English tun, meaning settlement (VCH vol 7 p65). Has been thought to mean 'Great farm' (PNPD). There was a hamlet at Gratton by the earlier C12 (VCH vol 7 p65). George Heath (1844-1869), the Moorland Poet, was born at Hall Gate Farm (see) at Gratton.

Gratton Hall To E of Gratton hamlet. The site was probably occupied by the late C12 (VCH vol 7 p65). Thomas Ernest Hulme (1883-1917), philosopher, was born at Gratton Hall Farm (VCH vol 7 p68) (VFC p70). Has also appeared as Gratton Hall Farm.

Gratton Hill Hill in the Moorlands, over 1m N of Alstonefield. There is a burial mound at the SE end of summit of the hill at SK 13195715. It is nine feet in diameter and two feet high and was excavated by Bateman in 1845. A crouched skeleton and the skeleton of a woman with food vessels, of the Irish type, of the Beaker people were found in it (VAD pp78-79) (DAJ vol 77 p26 C4) (NSJFS 1962 p33. 1965 p31). Another burial mound at the NW end of the summit at SK 13135720 is 12 paces in diameter and four feet high. It was excavated by Bateman in 1845 and revealed a rock-cut grave containing a skeleton and a decorated urn (VAD pp77-78) (NSJFS 1965 p31). There is another burial mound at the NW end of the hill at SK 13095719. All the above burial mounds are listed monuments.

Gratwich Ancient parish and former manor (HOU p332). The remote minute village of Gratwich by the Blithe is 2.25m E of Fradswell. Has appeared as Crotewiche, a manor, in DB, Crotewich (C11), Grotewic (1176), Grotrewis (C13), and Gretewyz (C13) (SSE 1996 p14) (SPN p55). The name means the 'great village' (DUIGNAN). Barns thinks its position on the Blythe suggests the same origin as Great Bridge (see) in (NSFCT 1910 p162). Or from Saxon 'greot wic,' 'the gravelly place' (SSE 1996 p14) (SPN p55). There was a church at Gratwich in the C13 (LDD). The parish church, St Mary the Virgin, in the village centre, may be of early C17 origin. The church was rebuilt in 1775 (BOE p137). The civil parish of Gratwich was abolished in 1934 and civilly it then entered Kingstone parish (GLAUE p412). For Rev John R Palmer (b1858), poet and novelist, rector of Gratwich from 1905, see Kingstone. Wilmot Martin, the 'Staffordshire Harry Lauder' (1875-1963) farmed at Gratwich in c1900, moving to Hixon (see) with his wife Edith in 1906 (ESNF p94p).

Gratwichwood Farm 0.75m SE of Gratwich. Appears on 1834 OS map as Woodhouse Farm.

Gravel Bank Former piece of Northfield Road extending from the almshouses to what was known as Home Farm, which is now (1953) on the Harborne golf course, in Harborne parish (STELE June 26 1953). The name is preserved in a road called Gravel Bank 1.5m WSW of Harborne over the Lapal Tunnel (Birmingham A-Z).

Gravelly Bank Incline 0.5m W of Grindley, Stowe-by-Chartley. On Gravelly Bank at SK 037298 on the N side of the Stafford-Uttoxeter road two home-made wooden crosses were erected in Dec 1987 to the memory of Elizabeth Meddings, aged 9, and her cousin Christopher Burnett, aged 6. The children were knocked down and killed by a car which careered onto the grass verge here on Dec 13 1986. The two, and Elizabeth's brother, David, aged 8, were taking a birthday card to their aunt in the nearby garage. David survived the crash (ES Dec 4 1987) (MIDD vol 2 pp22,23p) (TRTC pp183-184).

Gravelly Bank Between Meir and Meir Heath (a bus stop).

Gravelly Bank Bank 1m NW of Pye Green.

Gravelly Way Tiny hamlet 0.75m SSE of Gailey. In Brewood parish.

Greasleyside The house, Greasley Side (1834 OS map), stood at the junction of Holehouse and Greasley Roads, Abbey Hulton.

Greasleyside Brook Runs from Greasleyside to the Hole House Brook.

Great Bangley Great Bangley Farm is over 1.25m S of Hints. There are signs of former charcoal-burning hearths at SK 165012, SK 177013 and SK 177014, which may indicate the presence of an iron industry in the area operating between the C15 and the C18 (SSAHST 1973-74 p40).

Great Barr Large village on the SW slopes of Barr Beacon 18.75m SSE of Stafford. Former township and chapelry in Aldridge ancient parish (W p552). Great Barr's Anglo-Saxon charter of bounds dating from 957 was mistakenly printed as an Hants charter by W de G Birch in 'Cartularium Saxonicum' (3 vols, 1885-93), but E Ekwall in 'Selected Papers' pp38,39 identified it as a Staffordshire charter (SL p61 note). The **name** has appeared as Bearre (957), Barra (DB), and Great Barre (1322); Little Barre appears in 1208 (SPN p55). 'Barr' may be from the Barr Beacon (TBS p7) (LGS p78) (SPN p55). 'Great' was probably applied to define it from the manor of Little Barr. Great Barr was formerly covered by Cannock Forest and was disafforested in 1125 and had been taken into Sutton Chase by 1153 (MOA pp20,129) (GBP). For Great Barr manor see under Aldridge. Field names Great Moat Piece and Little Moat Piece and depressions in the ground in the Wilderness Lane area of Great Barr at SP 041953 may indicate the site of a moat (SSAHST 1982-3 p51). There had been a chapel of ease to Aldridge church on the site of the present **church**, St Margaret, on the S side of Chapel Lane, since the C12 (SNAR p 72). The present church was built in 1860 (LGS p77). The Rector of Aldridge (see) practiced the custom of giving charity to every person of every rank in his parish (including the chapelry of Great Barr) on Christmas day (SHOS vol 2 p100) (THS) (SCSF p162) (TBS p20). Became a separate ecclesiastical parish in 1849 and a civil one in 1866 (GLAUE p402). In 1931 Great Barr parish was reduced in size with some land being transferred to Walsall, Sutton Coldfield and West Bromwich (Grove Vale and Red House) boroughs and ancient parishes (TBS pp34-35) (GLAUE p402). By 1999 the ward called Great Barr in Sandwell metropolitan borough covered that area formerly in West Bromwich. There was a **pinfold** midway between Cocksfold Farm and Great Barr Old Hall. The name is preserved in Pinfold Lane (SNAR p80). There was a **fire** at Great Barr in 1726 according to Bilston PR (TBS p21). Great Barr **Association for the Prosecution of Felons** was founded in 1824 and continued into the C20 as a social club with annual dinners held at the Scott Arms (TBS p16). The station on the Grand Junction **Railway**, known as 'Great Barr Station,' was more correctly situated in Hamstead (ADY p7) and opened by the LNWR on Oct 1 1862 (TBS p31). A collision between a shunting train and a special coal train from Hednesford occurred at Great Barr in Dec 1874 (TBS p29). Great Barr station won a first prize in the London Midland Region 'Best Kept Stations' competition in 1950 (TBS p31). The largest **'human centipede'** to move 98 feet five inches (with ankles firmly tied together) consisted of 1004 people. Not one single person fell over in the course of the walk, which took place on May 18 1990 at Great Barr School (GBR 1991 p179). **Spectral horses** and alarming noises are reputed to have been heard on the corner of Chapel Lane and Crook Lane (GOM p22) (GPCE p17). **Persons and visitors. John Wesley** travelled through Great Barr in Feb 1746 as he went from Birmingham to Stafford as the rain turned to snow (TBS p22). **William Hardwicke** (1772-1843), the famous Shropshire genealogist and Bridgnorth solicitor, was educated by Isaac Dixon at Great Barr (TBS p25). **Stephanie Slater**, an estate agent, was kidnapped and ransomed for £175,000 by Michael Sams whilst showing him round a house in Turnberry Road on Jan 22 1992 (Daily Telegraph June 10 1993 p3).

Great Barr Common Remnant of Sutton Chase and former extensive common comprising Barr Beacon and land about the beacon stretching towards Aldridge. It appears to have adjoined or embraced the common land known as Barr Lea (see). Aldridge tenants had common rights on Great Barr Common. The common has also been called The Colefield (from 1304) (MOA pp60,136,138) (SSAHST vol 32 1990-91 pp87-95) and Barr Common. The latter is presently used for the name of a growing suburb 1m S of Aldridge. The Colefield or Coldfield was an even wider expanse of land than the common and stretched across to Little Aston and Sutton Coldfield (MOA p138). Cold in Coldfield is said to be from either Celtic 'coel' or variants 'cold,' 'col,' 'cole,' 'coal,' referring to a magical place, an omen, a belief, or 'co,l' a sharp hill (HPPE p12). Colefield was used to describe an area to the S and SW of Aldridge, where many nefarious activities, including murder, were enacted, particularly in medieval times. In the earlier C19 an illegal prize

fight took place here and was reported in a broadsheet. It lasted for 213 rounds and attracted a rabble of pickpockets. The gravel pits where events of this nature took place still existed in the earlier C20 (WMVB p10). There was a dwelling on the common (Boden's Cottage) by 1611 (SNAR p72). The common was enclosed in 1799 (ADY p19).

Great Barr Hall At the end of an avenue off Queslett Road, Great Barr. The Scotts of Great Barr Old Hall (see) acquired Great Barr manor in the earlier C17 (TBS p9). The original Great Barr Hall was built by Richard Scott probably in c1650 (GBP) and certainly by 1675 (MOA p139). Another account says that 'the present hall was built in about 1629, and later extended and altered in Gothic style about 1760 - 1780, with Nether Hall or Little Barr Hall 1730 adjoining' (HPPE P35). Great Barr Hall has appeared as Nether House (Pigot & Son map. 1830) (W p552), Nether-house farm, 'The Hall' (GBP), Lower Hall, and Barr Hall (TBS p11). In the early C18 Frances Scott brought Great Barr manor to her second husband, John Hoo (TBS p12), who resided at Great Barr Old Hall (see). In 1777 Sir Joseph Scott, a relation of the Scotts, former lords of Great Barr manor, is found fronting the facade of Nether House (Great Barr Hall) in the 'Strawberry' gothic style (GBP). Sir Joseph was reputed to be an admirer of Charles James Fox, Whig politician and statesman (TBS p13), and Fox may have visited the hall in 1784 or 1785 (GBP). Sir Joseph wrote six lines of poetry to accompany the piece of shilling which his uncle had given to him; both were on show in the library. The lines went

> Behold me, sole fruit of all the care
> An honour'd uncle gave his heir
> Yet judge not harshly, think him not unkind.
> Good and indulgent yet, like Isaac blind,
> Deluded by Jacob's happier star,
> He gave to Shustoke what was due to Barr.

(TBS p13). In 1786 Great Barr Hall was let to Samuel Galton Jnr, a banker and industrialist from Birmingham who was a member of the Lunar Society. Here Galton entertained fellow Lunar members, Joseph Priestley, Matthew Bolton, Samuel Parr, Josiah Wedgwood, 'Warwickshire' Dr Johnson, LR Edgeworth, Thomas Day, James Watt, and Dr Withering (TBS p13) (ADY p13) (MOA p77) (GBP). On the death of Thomas Hoo, younger brother of John Hoo, in 1791, Sir Joseph Scott, inherited Great Barr manor (MOA p64), and he moved back to the hall in 1797 (GBP). The hall is described as 'the hospitable mansion of Sir Joseph Scott Bart' in Cooke's Warwickshire (1800) (MOA pp76-77). Leigh in 1820 called the hall 'one of the finest and most delightful mansions in this part of the country....It stands in a beautiful vale ornamented with trees of good variety and abundance.' (BOE p137). John Glover, John Allport, and John Rider all made paintings of the park in the earlier C19 (GBP). Sir Walter Scott visited the hall and is said to have modelled Abbotsford on what he saw here (TBS p11); or he modelled his estate at Abbotsford on Great Barr Hall's gardens (SNAR p69). In the mid C19 it was the seat of Sir Edward Dolman Scott (W p552). When Sir Edward Scott was lord of a manor and in residence he kept a flag flying from the top of the hall to show constables and others, who had manorial and magisterial business with him, that he was in (WAM p94). Lydia Robinson, the second wife of the second baronet (Sir Joseph's son), is remembered for being accused by Mrs Gaskell in her biography of Charlotte Bronte of being romantically involved with Bramwell Bronte, the ailing brother of the Bronte sisters. The accusation outraged the Scott family so much they threatened libel and Mrs Gaskell was forced to apologise in a letter to The Times (WMVB p67). Sir Francis Edward Scott (b1824), the third baronet, also resided at the hall in the C19. After his death in 1863 his widow Lady Mildred Anne Scott continued to live at the hall. In 1868 she married Edward Pakenham Alderson, who was brother of the Marquess of Salisbury, and in the 1880s and the 1890s Lord Salisbury PM visited the hall (TBS pp11,13,14). Lady Mildred Anne Scott lived at the hall until her death in the early C20 (TBS p13). (ADY p of the dinning room 1897). In 1907 a Unionist rally was held in the grounds. Mrs RH Berkley, Lady Mayoress of Birmingham, and her daughter were injured in a coach accident in Barr Hall grounds in 1907 (TBS p11). The hall was sold by the Scotts to Walsall and West Bromwich Union in 1911 (GBP) who converted it into a mental hospital called St Margaret's Hospital. A large complex of buildings was built in a semi-circle in front of the hall in 1914-16 (BOE p137). (WOPP pl 139 of it in 1911). An oval quartzite pebble with an hourglass perforation of the Neolithic or Bronze Age was found at St Margaret's Hospital at SO 056953 (BAST vol 77 p3) (NSJFS 1964 p42).

GROUNDS. The grounds were landscaped in three major phases. Firstly, according to tradition, by the poet William Shenstone in the mid C18, then by

Repton and Nash in the 1790s (SHOS vol 2 pp105-106 pl xv) (GBP), then by Sir Gilbert Scott in the mid C19 (GBP). Shaw noted a moss-clad **alcove** (SHOS vol 2 p105). The **Big Pool** was created shortly before 1744. The present **cascade** was put in c1799 (GBP). (SHOS vol 2 p105). **Fox's Plantation**, which ran along a walk, planted in 1784 or 1785, may have been put in by Charles James Fox, politician and statesman (GBP). The **French Garden** was by the summerhouse (GBP). The **ice-house** was built probably before 1797 (GBP). The maze was planted in c1862 (GBP). The **pets cemetery** was established shortly before 1863 (GBP). At least one **seat** with a thatched crowned roof with a verse inscription, similar to those at Enville and the Leasowes was noted by Shaw (SHOS vol 2 p105). The **summerhouse**, near the French Garden, may have been rebuilt in c1863, and was converted in 1914 (GBP). In the garden of the Scott's C17 house at Great Barr Plot noted a piece of **topiary**, a yew tree cut conically like a spire eight or nine yards high (NHS p381) (TBS p12). About 1799 the **upper lake** was built (GBP). Shaw noted, to NE of the flower garden, an **urn** of statuary marble, fluted, with a medallion of Miss Dolman in the centre. Miss Dolman was second cousin to Mrs Scott and first cousin to the poet Shenstone (SHOS vol 2 p105) (GBP p of in 1907).

Great Barr Old Hall A medieval or C16 timber-framed house 0.5m ENE of Great Barr church. It has appeared as High House (MOA p136), Over Hall and later as the Dower House (TBS p10), Old Hall (1834 OS map), 'the Old House at Barr' (HPPE p35), The Old Hall (Birmingham A-Z 1989) and Old Hall Farm (1996) (SNAR pp80,82p; perhaps erroneously referred to as Nether House). Elizabeth I may have visited Over Hall in her progress around the county in 1575, because her 'favourite,' the Earl of Essex, owned the estate, or a neighbouring estate (HPPE p35) (TBS p10). The house was owned by the Scott family by the later C16, and became in effect the manor house of Great Barr manor after the Scotts acquired the manor in the earlier C17 (MOA p139). NHS has a plate of an old half-timbered hall at Barr. In the early C18 Frances Scott brought the house to her second husband John Hoo, and he became lord of Great Barr manor; during his time manorial business of Barr and Wednesbury was conducted at the Scott Arms (HPPE p35). He was succeeded by his brother, Thomas, a bachelor, who also took up residence here. He was High Sheriff of Staffs in 1772 (MOA pp55,169il). With his death in 1791 the manor passed to Sir Joseph Scott (d1828), who chose to reside at Great Barr Hall (see) (WAM p90) (TBS p12).

Great Barr Park A deer park had been established at Great Barr by 1335 (GBP). It lay to the N of Chapel Lane, Great Barr, in the area now covered by Great Barr Golf Course. By the mid C16 the park had been divided into six enclosed fields and perhaps subdivided further (MOA p137). Doe Bank (see) to the E of Pheasey may represent part of the enclosure, and Heygate on the N side may have been an entrance into the park.

Great Bridge Bridge over the river Tame (which divides the ancient parishes of West Bromwich and Tipton): the Tame in this area was called 'Grete Brook' until the late C17 (TB May 1995 p16) and the bridge was called Grete Bridge. It was becoming known as Great Bridge by the end of the C17 (VCH vol 17 p8). The first 'Grete Bridge' existed by 1550. Appears on Plot's map as Gritbridg. The parliamentarians in the Civil War are supposed to have crossed it going to besiege Dudley Castle in 1644 (TB March 1996 p4). Some say Oliver Cromwell or Lord Denbigh named the bridge 'Great Bridge' in appreciation of being able to use it to cross the Tame in the Civil War (TB May 1995 p16). But the accepted view is that Great is derived from Grete and its associated forms. The various early forms of Grete in Grete Bridge, Brook, End, Green are perhaps of Celtic origin (DUIGNAN) (NSFCT 1910 pp161-162), and derive from a British word for 'murmuring' (SPN pp137-138), or are from the grit found in this area (BCM Oct 1990 p61) (TB May 1995 p27), or from the gravel of the area (English Place Name Elements. vol 1 p209) (VCH vol 17 p8). A new bridge was completed by 1706. This forms the northern part of the present bridge, built in 1780 (VCH vol 17 p12 p facing p33). Some have thought Fisher Bridge, built in c1832, the bridge (TB May 1995 p16). The bridge gives its name to the settlement which grew about it.

Great Bridge Small industrial district 2m NW of High Street, West Bromwich. Partly in West Bromwich and Tipton ancient parishes (W p681). The name is from the bridge, Great Bridge (see). A commemorative plaque recording that John Wilkinson erected the first Black Country blast furnace in nearby Bradley was erected at Great Bridge playing fields by Bilston Historical Society on Nov 24 1956 (BOP p18p) (WMVB p30). An accident occurred at Mr Morris's Colliery at Great Bridge on June 16 (TEBC2 p61) or 26 1849 killing 14 miners (TB May 1995 p16). There was a railway station at Great Bridge on the Dudley-Walsall line which opened on May 1 1850 (SSR p11). A branch line linking Swan Village with the SSR at Great Bridge, opened in 1866, closed in 1964 (VCH vol 17 p14). The Tipton and Great Bridge Times, was published in 1889 (SHJ spring 1996 p28). Some Wednesbury (see) papers

had Great Bridge in their title. By 1999 Great Bridge was a ward of Sandwell metropolitan borough.

Great Bridgeford Hamlet on the Sow over 3m NW of Stafford. In Seighford ancient parish. Little Bridgeford is 0.25m to the NW. Loxdale says it was so named from a bridge over Eccleshall Water (the Sow?), which was built of stone and which was brought from the ruins of Eccleshall Castle in the time of the Civil Wars (SH p78) (BL, Stowe MS 878ff. 6,19,22). Possibly a 'ford with a footbridge' (SSE 1996 pp11,20). Possibly the bridge was an insubstantial one and could only carry travellers on foot, or became unusable and the river had to be forded (SPN p24). Brigeford manor held by the bishop of Chester (Lichfield) is recorded in DB (SSE 1996 p11). John de Harcourt held Chatcull and over 1000 acres in Podmore, Mill Meece, Great and Little Bridgeford and Seighford by service of bringing four men of Chatcull and Podmore to act as beaters to the bishop's hunt (ECC p13). A dispute in 1534 occurred between inhabitants of Great Bridgeford and Whitgreave over intercommoning rights and led to accusations and counter-accusations of enclosure going back to the end of the C15 (SHC 1912 pp69-70) (VCH vol 6 p52). In the later C17 Plot noted a pigeon with two heads at Great Bridgeford (NHS p234). Richard Whitworth had proposals in 1765 to build a canal to link the Severn with the Weaver and the Trent. The canal, which was never built, would have had a junction at Great Bridgeford, where arms from the Trent and the Weaver would have met (BVC p170). The GJR line was built through Great Bridgeford in the 1830s. There was a railway accident at Great Bridgeford in June 1932 when the Rhyl to Birmingham train jumped the points and derailed (EOP p78p). Great Bridgeford railway station closed in 1959 (Railways In and Around Stafford. Edward Talbot. 1994 p4).

Great Chatwell Small hamlet above the tiny ravine containing Dawford Brook nearly 2m NW of Blymhill. Formerly in Moreton quarter in Gnosall ancient parish (W p460) (VCH vol 4 p111) until transferred in 1934 to Blymhill. Great Chatwell has appeared as Chattewell (1203), Chattwelle (1315), Chatwel (1454), Much Chatwall (early C16), Gt Chatwall (1604) (SPNO p155) (SSE 1996 p12). The name is derived probably from St Chad's Well (at Chadwell - see), which was formerly in some repute (W p460). Or from Saxon 'Ceatta's spring' (SSE 1996 p12) (SPNO p155) (SPN p33). A chapel at Great Chatwell was certified in 1548, but is not mentioned thereafter (SHC 1915 p107). It was disused by 1680 (VCH vol 4 p132). In 1922 a barn in the hamlet was believed to have been the chapel (NSFCT 1922 p162). By 1958 a remaining wall of what was believed to have been the chapel may have been incorporated into modern outhouses of a cluster of cottages called the Bull Ring. Remains of an ancient stone cross existed in c1839, but had disappeared by 1958 (VCH vol 4 p132). A moated site at Great Chatwell was identified in 1908 (VCH vol 1 p364) (SSAHST 1982-3 p35). The Little Chatwell on Plot's map is probably Chatwell, once in Staffs, now in Shrops.

Great Chell Former vill of Chell township in Wolstanton ancient parish, slightly over 1m NE of Tunstall. Great Chell was a village by the late C18 (VCH vol 8 p83) and in 1843 it was considered larger in size than Little Chell (HBST p126). Now a suburb 2m N of Burslem. The church, St Michael and All Angels, on the N side of St Michael's Road near the N end of High Lane, was built in 1894 (VCH vol 8 p94).

Great Clayton Former manor which has appeared as Clayton Culvert and covered the present area of Clayton. 'Great' was added to distinguish it from the manor of Clayton Griffith, held by the Griffith family (SL p71).

Great Curborough The principle former settlement of Curborough. It lay below Curborough Hall Farm in the Middle Ages and was later depopulated. A Little Curborough lay about Curborough House (VCH vol 14 p229).

Great Eaves Tiny district 1m NE of Bucknall.

Great Fenton Is the area of Fenton now called Mount Pleasant, to the WNW of Heron Cross. It was in Fenton Culvert manor (NSSG p19). The name was used for a ward of Stoke-on-Trent district covering this area by 1991. Rev William Ferneyhough, poet, was born in Great Fenton in 1754. His work includes the poem 'Trentham Park' (1789), and 'Poems on Several Occasions' (1814) (BS p167) (PSS pp104-108) (POTP p95) (VFC p48).

Great Fenton Hall Formerly situated on N side of Grove Road, to the E of Great Fenton House, Fenton. Represented the manor house of Fenton Culvert. Seat of the Fenton family in the later C17. From 1715 it was owned by the Smith family (VCH vol 8 pp210,213); the Smiths eventually moved to Elmhurst near Lichfield (NSF p42p). Erroneously, appears as Fenton Hall on the 1834 OS map. May have been tenanted by Joseph Gimson in 1881 (POTP p102). Demolished in c1900 (VCH vol 8 pp210,213).

Great Fenton Hall House situated on S side of Grove Road, Fenton. The hall was formerly known as something else and acquired the name of Great Fenton Hall in the C20. Seat of the Fentons in the C17. About 1840 it was the residence of the widow of John Bourne, potter. May have been tenanted by Joseph

Gimson in 1881 (POTP p102). Used by the Stafford Coal and Iron Company as offices in the C20. Demolished in c1955 and the site then used for a garage for the colliery. Great Fenton Hall or Great Fenton House may have occupied an ancient fortified site (VCH vol 8 pp210,213).

Great Fenton House Formerly situated on S side of Grove Road, to the W of Great Fenton Hall, Fenton. Great Fenton House or Great Fenton Hall (S of Grove Road) may have occupied an ancient fortified site. Owned by the Allens from the late C17 to the early C20. Tenanted by Edward Challinor from 1855. Was used by the Home Guard in WW2. Demolished in c1948 (VCH vol 8 pp210,214).

Greatgate Small hamlet at the foot of the steep slopes of Croxden Brook valley, 0.75m WNW of Croxden. In Croxden parish. Has appeared as Greth (c1176) (CDS p15), Gretyatt (1532-3), Greetyate (1595) (CDS pp30,50), Grityate (Plot's map), Greetyatswood (1692) (HAF p201), Great Yate (W p771), and Great Gate (LTD p100). Greatgate first appears in the Croxden Abbey chronicle in 1373 and may not have been a settlement until then (CDS p15). Garner suggests the name is from the great gate to Croxden Abbey (GNHS p545), or otherwise called the gatehouse. Others believe Greatgate is too remote to have been the site for a gate to Croxden Abbey. In Old English 'gate' also meant a valley. So that the name may simply imply 'the gate into the wood called the Greet' (NSFCT 1917 p150). The hamlet came to the relief of those suffering in a plague in Stafford in 1642 (SCSF p136). A Civil War cannon ball 8cm in diameter and 2.27 kg in weight was found at SK 050402 on the road to Threapwood in 1972. It had perhaps dropped out of a parliamentary baggage train (NSJFS 1974 p139). A pound, stocks and a whipping post, a sandstone pillar four feet high with iron clamps on either side, still (1999) survive in Greatgate (LTD p100).

Great Hall Situated in Old Hall Street in SE part of Wolverhampton. Built for the Leveson family, by Thomas or his brother, John Leveson, and therefore before 1575 (HOWM pp43, facing 53il of from Bilston Street in 1835). Built in c1555 (WF p8), or and probably at the same period as Taylor's Plan (SHOS vol 2 p163). The Levesons, prominent Wolverhampton wool merchants, continued to live here until the reign of James II (WF p8). Formerly had a large moat around it (SSAHST 1982-3 pp56-57). The house is said to have been taken by parliament with the rest of Wolverhampton in May 1643 (HOWM p84). Great Hall was sold to the Earl of Bradford in 1684 and then descended to the Pultney family. Joseph Turton (1671-1729) or his father purchased the Great Hall at the end of C17 and restored it (HOWM p115). The upper storey was taken off in the early C18, by Joseph Turton, then tenant (SHOS vol 2 p163). The hall was licensed for Protestant dissenters in 1715 (SHC 1960 p118). The hall has also appeared as Old Hall and Turton's Hall; the earliest document recording it as 'Turton's Hall' is the Constables' Accounts for 1718 (HOWM p115). Another account says the hall was let to ironmaster, John Turton, who gave it the name 'Turton's Hall' (WF p8). John Turton (1735-1806), Physician in Ordinary to the King and Prince of Wales was born here (HOWM p115). Later it was occupied by a tin and japan-ware manufactory and was then known as the Old Hall Works. Elihu Burritt visited it in 1860. (GNHS p177) (VCH vol 2 p180) (SL pp183,184). The hall was demolished in 1883 (WAIW vol 2 ps of the hall being pulled down) and a pupil-teacher centre built on the site in 1899 (Wolverhampton AdNews Aug 22 1996 p10il). It is now (1999) used as an adult education centre.

Great Haywood Large village on the W side of the Trent, 5m ESE of Stafford. Formerly partly in the ancient parishes of Colwich (W p416) and Stowe (SGSAS).

EARLY to 1750. The **name** is from Anglo-Saxon haga, an enclosure, the meaning is 'the fenced or enclosed wood.' Haywood abuts on the ancient bounds of Cannock Forest (the Trent). Haywood Park was within the forest, and was enclosed by the bishops of Lichfield. 'Great' was a late Middle English addition to define the village from Little Haywood. The villages are said to have their additions appellations on account of their proximity to woods in Haywood Park or Cannock Forest known as Great Wood and Little Wood, a small and thinner wood (HAHS p7). (DUIGNAN) (SHC 1914 p130) (NSJFS 1981 p3) (SSE 1996 p14) (SPN p60). Haiwode a manor held by the bishop of Chester (Lichfield) in DB is considered by the Phillimore edition of Staffordshire DB (1976) to be Great Haywood. Others say the present villages of Great Haywood and Little Haywood were not in the original manor of Haywood; its eastern boundary stretched only as far as the Trent (BERK2 p38). The bishops of Lichfield had Haywood manor seized from them at the Reformation (SL p105). 'The church of Hewode' has been identified with Colwich church (HAHS p7). The bishop of Lichfield and the Earl of Derby were granted a charter Dec 14 1251 to hold a **market** at one of the 'Haywoods' on Thursdays. The market had ceased by 1500 (NSJFS 1971 p51). Fairs. Under the heading Hayward Heath, which Hackwood suspects stands for

Great Haywood, Cooke lists a fair on Nov 17 for pedlary and cattle (SCSF p99). Owen says 'Hayward Heath' had a fair in 1792 (OWEN), but there was not one in 1888 (LHE p265). Was in Colwich prebend (SSAHST vol 2 1960-61 p44). The church, St Stephen, on the W side of the Little Haywood road, was built in 1840 (BOE p144). Created an ecclesiastical parish in 1854 (GLAUE p413). In the garden at Wharf College? there are some interesting remains of ecclesiastical stonework probably from the former Haywood Chapel adjoining Astons house at Tixall (STM March 1966 p24). In 1938 the remains of an ancient bridge were discovered between Great Haywood and Tixall (SN July 2 1938 p5). One pair of stones from Butterhill windmill went to Great Haywood watermill (WBJ p18 il vi). During a visit made by Dr Plot he found along the Trent at Great Haywood a red sort of marl with blue veins (NHS p119), and a hard slate-like marl can be found here (NHS p120). Plot also noted an extraordinary rennet (local dialect runnet) at Great Haywood (NHS p388). **Persons and visitors.** Like Stone and Lichfield, Great Haywood was on the Great North West Road and we find **Edward II** visited Haywood on July 4 1309 whilst going from Chester to Coventry, and **Richard II** was at Haywood on Feb 21 1399 (SHC 1914 p131 note). Some 200 **Moorland Dragoons** camping at 'Heywoods' were captured by royalists on March 17 1643 (BFS p15), and the **Duke of Bedford's Regiment** seems to have been in Great Haywood on Dec 2 1745 to support the Duke of Cumberland in the Jacobite Rebellion at Stone (NSFCT 1925 p55 note). **Dr Johnson** of Lichfield (see) was a tutor to the five children of Thomas Whitby of Great Haywood for less than two months in May and June 1735 (Young Samuel Johnson. James L Clifford. 1955 1962 ed. p152).

1750 to PRESENT. Trent Lane leading to Essex Bridge is lined by terraced cottages built to house the occupants from the last depopulated village of Shugborough in the early C19 (SL p136). Lord Lichfield gave permission for the Trent Valley **railway** line (1848) to run through the Shugborough estate on condition a station was built at Great Haywood, which would be easily accessible for him. The station closed in the 1960s (HCMBOPP p7p). The **Haywood Society**, an amenity and historical society covering the Haywoods and Colwich, formed in c1975 (info Geraldine Carter). For the painting of a Gloucester Old Spot pig at Great Haywood see under Little Haywood. **Persons and visitors.** For Dr Johnson of Lichfield who was tutor to the children of the Whitby family of Great Haywood, see Colwich. The highwayman **Robert Lander** alias Bradbury was born near one of the Haywoods. He was found guilty of highway robbery upon 'Cannock Wood' or near Teddesley Park and hung at Stafford on Aug 25 1798 (Berkswich PR) (BERK2 p46) (CCSHO pp31-32). The artist **Thomas Peploe Wood** (1817-1845) was the son of a shoemaker who kept a toll gate on the main London to Liverpool road at Great Haywood. His talent for drawing was admired even as a boy and his work was sold to coach passengers at his father's toll bar. His career was furthered by Thomas Trubshaw. The WSL has over 300 of his pictures (TP Wood's Staffordshire. 1990) (BCM Oct 1991 p75). There is a cross to his memory in Colwich churchyard. **William Palmer** (1824-1856), the poisoner, served an apprenticeship to Edward Tylecote, a surgeon of Great Haywood (SHCST 1971-73 p22), who lived at the house called Hazeldene (see) (HHHC p69). There was a motor car accident at Great Haywood mill by a sharp S bend in the Trent on March 9 1905. The passengers seem to have included **Mrs Challenor**, wife of Hanley Town Clerk, her niece, and the chauffeur. One account implies that only the niece was killed and her body was not found until three weeks after the accident when it was found half a mile away downstream in the Trent (HCMBOPP pp12p,13p). Another account says the two women died (AR p94p). Several different postcards depicting the scene of the accident were made. The author **JRR Tolkien** (1892-1973) is said to have stayed at The Presbytery in Little Haywood in 1914 (SN Oct 28 1999 p23). In March 1916 he lived in Great Haywood for a few months after his honeymoon in Somerset. He and his wife, Edith, and her cousin were established in 'good lodgings,' thought to be the Clifford Arms. In June 1916 Tolkien left for France to fight in WW1 leaving his wife in Great Haywood. In 1917 he convalesced with his wife at Great Haywood. He is said to have had his ideas for 'The Lost Tales' whilst staying here. 'The Cottage of Lost Play' was transcribed by Edith in a notebook dated Feb 12 1917; the opening scene of which is about a traveller arriving at a village; most probably this was inspired by the walk over the hill from Little Haywood to Great Haywood. It has also been suggested that the House of Many Chimneys was inspired by Shugborough Hall (see), although differing drafts give room for conjecture (HHHC p94). For the ghost of **Reggie Smith** see Coach and Horses Inn.

Great Haywood Junction Junction of the Staffs and Worcs Canal and the Trent and Mersey Canal. When completed this junction and the Fradley Junction were the crossing points which achieved Brindley's plan for a 'Grand Cross' of canals linking together the estuaries of Mersey, Trent, Thames and Severn

(SL pp236,237) (SPJD p86pc aerial view). The aqueduct here is by Brindley (SL p244).

Great Holney Was near Lower Reule. The name has disappeared (VCH vol 4 p84).

Great Longsdon House over 0.5m N of Longsdon. Formerly in Longsdon township in Leek ancient parish. Stands on top of a long ridge, which may be the long hill which gives Longsdon its name (VCH vol 7 p203). See also Little Longsdon.

Great Moor Tiny hamlet on Nurton Brook over 1m ESE of Pattingham. In Pattingham ancient parish. Has been identified with DB Cippemore (see) (SHC 1919 p164). It was probably the place called Moor in 1229, which was a settled area by 1312. Great Moor was so called by 1514 (VCH vol 20 p173).

Greatoak Tiny hamlet under 1m NE of Audley. Appears as Great Oake in 1733 (SHC 1944 p48).

Great Sandon Former and long depopulated village which lay at the foot of Sandon church on the E side. The manor of Scandone appears in DB (SSE 1996 p17) (DB Phillimore 1976). It is possible that the village was destroyed for emparking in the C15 or C16 (SL pp89,90,96) (STM July 1969 p33p. Aug 1969 p27). Excavations between 1968-9 failed to locate medieval housing (SL p83). Aerial photographs show it, clearly, and according to Darling the 1960s excavations revealed walls, cobbled floors and pottery (SPJD pp47pc,48).

Great Saredon Hamlet on a conspicuous hill above Saredon Brook 1.25m NNE of Shareshill or 0.75m NNE of Little Saredon. Formerly formed a township with Little Saredon, known as Saredon (see), in Shareshill ancient parish. Hackwood notes a burial mound on enclosed ground E of Great Saredon (SCSF p74). The name has appeared as Sardone (DB), Seresdone (DB) (SSE 1996 p17), Magna Saredon (1242), Beresardon (1279) - 'Bere' from the le Bere or le Boer family, lords of the manor, Magna Saredoun (1413), and Great Saredon (Yates' map) (DUIGNAN p131) (VCH vol 5 p176) (SPNO p113) (SPN p104). Saredon means Sear's burgh. A yeoman family of 'Sayer,' perhaps the descendants of the original 'Sear,' were living in the area at the turn of the century (DUIGNAN p131). Oakden suggests 'Saeru's hill' (SSE 1996 p17). 'Don' represents 'dun,' a hill of moderate height (NSJFS 1981 p11). Or from Saxon 'sear dun,' 'the dry (or barren) hill' (SSE 1987 p28) (SPN p104) (SSE 1996 p17). Great Saredon lay in Cannock Forest between at least 1167 and 1301 (VCH vol 5 p178). It was a separate manor to Little Saredon (DUIGNAN p131). The tenants of the Saredons who had common rights on Cheslyn Hay clashed with John Leveson the owner of the hay when he tried to enclose it in Henry VIII's reign (VCH vol 5 p178).

Great Saredon Hall Brick house at Great Saredon, the oldest part of which appears to date from c1700. A brick outbuilding with stone dressings is c1600 or earlier (VCH vol 5 p174).

Great Saredon Low To E of Great Saredon; probably of Roman origin (NHS p403) (NSJFS 1965 p46).

Great Stone Rock feature on Staffs Derbys border, 1.25m N of Flash. It was used as a marker from 1673 to define the border in a settlement which established the long-disputed boundary here (UHAW p11). The name appearing on the 1834 OS map also appears on the 1947 OS map 1:25,000 (sheet 43/06), at SK 02696919.

Greatwood Tiny settlement comprising Greatwood Lodge (see); 0.75m to the SSE is Greatwood Farm; under 0.25m to its S is Greatwood House. The area was formerly a part of Greatwood Heath (SSE vol 7 1995 p75). Has appeared as Gratwood (maps of Plot and Bowen). A saddle quern of quartzose sandstone 41cm long and 28cm wide and approximately 6cm thick was found in the garden of an old farmhouse in 1972 (NSJFS 1974 p139). A hermit, Joe Wilson, lived in a cave near the marlpits on Greatwood Farm from 1899 until 1905, when, aged 80, he was taken off to the poor law institution against his will (BOV pp43-44).

Greatwood Heath Extensive common land in Eccleshall ancient parish (SGSAS). It covered an area of approximately four square miles from the Broughton road in the N to Offley Hay in the S, and from Croxtonbank in the E to Fairoak in the W (SSE vol 7 1995 p75). A thousand acres of Greatwood Heath were enclosed under an act of 1719 (SHC 1941 p16). Has also appeared as Gratwood Heath and Gratewood Heath.

Greatwood Lodge Very ancient farmhouse 0.75m SE of Fairoak. It was once the hunting lodge of the bishops of Lichfield, who came from Eccleshall Castle to hunt in Blore Park. It has been added to and utterly altered on many occasions and struck by lightning and survived. The house is built so close to the hillside that as one comes down Lodge Lane towards Offley Brook one can see its chimneys before the rest of the house is seen (BOV pp42-43). There is a mound at SJ 77083216, SW of the house (NSJFS 1965 p36). Foot-and-mouth disease broke out at Greatwood Lodge Farm in early 1968 (SN

Jan 5 1968 p13).

Great Wyrley Former village now a town on a ridge overlooking Wash Brook, 11m SSE of Stafford. Former township in Cannock old parish. Some remarkable marked stones of possible Palaeolithic origin were found at Great Wyrley before 1929. The finds consisted of ironstone nodules which had been thrown out of a the shaft as a coal-mine was being sunk. They depict carved human figures, animals, and various primitive objects. However, members of the BAS doubted they were of such ancient origin (BAST 1929-30 vol 54 pp69-70 ils). The Wyrley (see) in DB is probably a reference to Little Wyrley, not Great Wyrley. The **name** is said to have appeared as Wirlega (1170), Wyrleg (1198), Great Wyrleg (1222), Wirlege (1231-4), Werleg (1262), Great Worley (1418), Mochyll Wirley (1463), Worley (1561), Great Wurley (1555) (SPNO p71), and Great Worley (Plot's map). Wyrley means 'the lea of the myrtle' (DUIGNAN p177). Since before the Norman Conquest land in Great Wyrley was attached to the office of keeper of Cannock Forest (VCH vol 5 p79) (GWY p13); in 1337 a barb arrow was stated to be due to the king from the lord of Great Wyrley manor whenever the king passed through Great Wyrley on his way to hunt in Wales. In 1342 the manor was held by John de Loges or de Warrewyk by the petty serjeanty of giving the king a barbed arrow when ever he came to hunt in Cheslyn Hay (VCH vol 2 p342 note. vol 5 p80). The **church**, St Mark, S of Station Road, was built in 1845 (VCH vol 5 p81). On the 1834 OS map there are two settlements called Great Wyrley; one at the junction of present Walsall Road with Norton Lane, and another at the junction of Landywood Lane with Hilton Lane. Later growth has merged the two settlements. Great Wyrley is often mistaken for being the modern Wyrley Bank (currently called Cheslyn Hay; Wyrley Bank was over 1m to the W). Great Wyrley became a separate ecclesiastical parish in 1845, refounded in 1846, and a separate civil parish in 1866 (GLAUE p430). The custom of lighting a **'boon-fire'** or bonfire on Midsummer night, according to Hackwood, lingered longest at Wyrley. It was supposed to be a relic of heathen ritual performed around ancient Baal fires (SCSF p45). In the Staffordshire Police Museum at Staffs Police headquarters at Baswich House, Stafford, is a **footprint** taken from a field at Great Wyrley in early Sept 1897. Great Wyrley has **'Jellyman'** as the hero of a peculiar brand of stories, as the Black Country has Aynuk and Ayli; there was still a family by the name of Jellyman living in the Great Wyrley area by the early 1970s (VB p123).

WYRLEY GANG. A gang of unknown number who claimed to carry out the mutilation of farm animals, principally horses, in the Great Wyrley district between 1903 and 1915. The gang's true identity remains a mystery, and the series of animal mutilations it purported to be responsible for remains the most perplexing case the Staffs Police has ever tried to solve. Rev Shapurji Edalji, a Parsee converted to Christianity was married to an English wife and succeeded her uncle to the living of Great Wyrley. Between **1888** and **1892** his family were plagued with anonymous letters, and later from ill-natured hoaxes, meanwhile the son, George Ernest Thompson Edalji, studied and became a successful lawyer in Birmingham. On Feb 1 **1903** a horse was killed at Cheslyn Hay. On Feb 10 another horse was found killed. On April 16 a horse belonging to E Thomas was killed. On May 2 a cow belonging to Mrs Bungay was maimed. On May 4 a horse of Mr Badger and sheep belonging to Thomas Green were killed. On June 6 two cows of Brownhills Colliery Company were killed. On June 29 a horse was killed and another mutilated at Quinton Colliery. On June 30 the first anonymous letter claiming to have carried out the atrocities was received by Staffs Police. On Aug 18 a pony was found mutilated at Great Wyrley Colliery. George Edalji was then arrested. Edalji accounted for his movements during the evening and night of the atrocity, and corroborative evidence came from a vet. Even so, Staffs Police called in a handwriting expert who said that the writing in letters signed by 'G.H. Darby, Captain of the Wyrley Gang' threatening more killings was the 'ill-disguised' writing of George Edalji (TB Oct 1974 pp18-19) (VB p124). Another account says the first 'G.H. Darby' letter was sent on Oct 25, after Edalji was convicted. During Edalji's remand, on Sept 21 a horse of John Henry 'Harry' Green's was killed at High House Farm. This was merely considered the work of Edalji's accomplices (VB p124). On Sept 29 Harry Green confessed to the killing. Green made his second confession on Oct 5, and on Oct 14 claimed his confession was not made voluntarily. (Another pretender in the case was Thomas Farrington, a collier who had spent his youth in a slaughter house. For his drunken boast that he was the Wyrley ripper at the Star Inn, Great Wyrley, he received a three year prison service - TB May 1993 p18). The trial of Edalji took place between 20 to 23 Oct at Stafford Quarter Sessions. Edalji was found guilty and sentenced to seven years imprisonment. The press was unhappy about the case and mounted a campaign, which after three years, secured Edalji's release. On Nov 2 one horse was killed and another maimed at Landywood Farm. In Dec RD Yelverton appealed to the Home Secretary. In March **1904** two sheep and a lamb were mutilated. Thomas Farrington was arrested. On Aug 27 an article about the Edalji case appeared in the Daily Telegraph (GWY pp39-41). In Oct **1906** Edalji was released. In Dec Arthur Conan Doyle, creator of Sherlock Holmes, was in Stafford (see) taking up Edalji's case. Doyle believed the real perpetrator was one Royden Sharp, a Cannock man. In Jan **1907** Conan Doyle tried to prove Edalji's innocence in the Daily Telegraph. In March the Home Secretary set up a committee to review the Edalji case. They reported on it in April. In May the Home Secretary granted Edalji a free pardon. In Aug a horse was killed and one was mutilated in Great Wyrley. In Sept a horse was wounded in Brewood and another maimed in Huntington. In July **1912** a horse was maimed in Darlaston (Offlow hundred). In Aug a horse was maimed in Walsall. In Oct a horse was maimed in Wednesbury. In Aug **1913** a pony was maimed in Darlaston (Offlow hundred) and a horse was maimed in Wednesbury. In Sept two horses were maimed in Bradley, Bilston, and a horse was maimed in Walsall. In Sept **1915** a horse was maimed in Darlaston (Offlow hundred) and two horses were maimed in Bradley, Bilston. In Oct **1934** Enoch Knowles was captured and convicted. In June **1953** George Edalji died. (G.H. Darby, Captain of the Wyrley Gang. GA Atkinson. 1914. a booklet) (E&S Nov 7 1934) (QMMH pp28-34) (MMBC pp142-157 map) (BCM Feb 1968 pp38-40) (SHJ vol 2 pp36-40) (TB Sept 1981 p5. May 1993 pp18-19. June 1993 p15ps) (The Uncollected Sherlock Holmes. Richard Lancelyn Green. 1983) (The Case of George Edalji. Staffs County Council Education Dept History Unit 5. 1987) (TOS pp69-74) (ACOP p112p) (MR p165) (SMML pp43-47). In the Staffordshire Police Museum at Staffs Police HQ at Weeping Cross, Stafford, is a case of George Edalji memorabilia, including the shaving knife used to maim horses presented as evidence at Edalji's trial.

Greaves Tiny hamlet to SE of Draycott-in-the-Clay (W p562).

Greaves Wood Large wood to SW of Greaves, Draycott-in-the-Clay; part of Needwood Forest. Here a large C2 BC Iron Age gold torc, similar to the one that was to be found at Glascote, was discovered by Queen Victoria's ranger, Thomas Hollis, in 1848. It was turned up by a badger or by foxes. Hollis afterwards forwarded it to the Queen. Edward VIII lent it to the BM who permanently borrow it. It weighs 15.25 ounces and consists of eight twisted wires and rods, each itself formed of three other wires and having two solid chased perforated ends (GNHSS p5) (HOU il of facing p339) (ARCH vol 33 pp175-176) (AJ vol 7 p467) (BM Quarterly vol 11 pp3-4) (NSJFS 1964 p25) (SSAHST 1969 pp3-6 p) (BTIH pp9-10) (LTD p115). Another account has a gold torc of Belgae origin (C4 to C1 BC) being found by a saw mill slightly the W of Greaves Wood at SK 152276 in 1935/7; this torc went to the BM (info KL Neal).

Greek Temple, The Massive limestone formation structured like great terraces (NSFCT 1936 p30). The formation is on the upper northern slope of Hall Dale on the Staffs side of Dovedale. Or the name refers to the whole upper northern slope of Hall Dale. It is comparatively bare, not densely wooded (Dovedale Guide. Keith Mantell. 1985 p15) (MR p128).

Green, The Oldest building in Cannock, dating from the C16. Sir Robert Fisher lived here until 1735. Another resident was Capt William Cary, his son Henry Francis Cary (born Gibralter 1772) spent some of his childhood here; he attracted the poetess Anna Seward, the Swan of Lichfield (see). It was in one of the rooms of 'The Green' that Henry Cary later commenced his translation of Dante's 'Divine Comedy.' He is also well-known for his additions to Dr Johnson's 'Lives of the Poets.' He was vicar of Abbots Bromley between 1796 to his death in 1844 (BS p97) (NSFCT 1909 p198) (CCBO pp89,90) (KES p58) (AB pp141-153) (VB p122; the date of 1872 given for his birth is inaccurate) (MR p74) (VFC p25). In later years Francis Gilpin a leading citizen of Cannock lived at 'The Green.' Also Charles Henry Cope, who took immense pride in the 45 different varieties of apple and pear he grew in his orchard at 'The Green.' From 1927 it was the offices of Cannock urban district council (CCBO pp89-90) (VCH vol 5 p53).

Green, The Tiny district S of Stafford town centre and S of the Sow. The area covering the triangle now formed by the Lichfield and Wolverhampton roads and White Lion Street was built up on all sides and in the centre in c1840 (VCH vol 5 p83). It has also been called Stafford Green (see). With the expansion of the town the Green is now considered part of the town centre. Gives its name to Green Gate or South Gate, and Green Hall. In 1220 there took place on the Green a trial by duel (SIOT p110) (SAC p52). There was a pinfold at the top of the Green in c1540 (SAC p52). The house at Grapes Corner, the Green, was occupied by the 'Staffordshire Chronicle' when founded in 1877. The paper moved to No. 19 Greengate Street in Oct 1894. The old house (SKYT p104p of in 1910) was knocked down and Stafford Borough Library built on the site in 1914-15 (SKYT p105p) (BOE p249). An annual festival known as the Green Wakes was held on the Green in Forebridge

on two days following the second Sunday in Aug (probably relates to the feast of the Assumption of the Virgin). The Green was enclosed in 1878 (VCH vol 6 p256).

Greenbank Former tiny settlement on High Lane over 0.75m E of Tunstall (1834 OS map). The area could now be said to be roughly either Bank Top or Stanfield. The name is preserved in Greenbank Road, in which road stands the childhood home of Robbie Williams, pop singer, born on Feb 13 1974. By 1992 Williams was in the pop group known as Take That, formed in Manchester. They produced the album 'Take That And Party' in 1992. In 1997 Williams produced the solo album 'Life Thru A Lens.' Roguish and handsome, in 2000 he was voted the world's sexiest man for the second year running in a women's magazine readers' poll (info Hanley Library) (The Encyclopaedia of Popular Music. Colin Larkin. 1998) (ES May 31 2000 p4p).

Green Baulk Alias Margaret Street, Stone. Since it was on the edge of the old Stone Field (SIS p5).

Green Birch Green Birch Farm is 1m SW of Tittensor, 3m NW of Stone. In Beech quarter in Stone parish (W p369).

Green Bridge Bridge over the Sow in Stafford. It is the original crossing point which led to the ancient settlement of Stafford from the south (ROT pp40,41). The bridge here was probably the 'great bridge' recorded in c1200, and the 'bridge of Stafford' recorded in 1285. Greengate Street passed over it. William Worswick, in his notebook (in WSL) says, that in 1583 the middle arches were rebuilt in stone. According to an old map of the town 1593-1611 it was a five-span stone bridge (NSFCT 1923 pp56-57). The name Green Bridge was in use by the 1590s (VCH vol 6 p197). At some time, probably in 1660, a single-span narrow stone bridge was built (SKYT p101). The bridge was rebuilt in 1781-2 as a single span bridge. Widened in 1860 (VCH vol 6 p197) or 1866 (SKYT p102). Has also been called Greengate Bridge (SN July 22 1961 p9 il). (OSST 1934 pp19-20) (SKYT pp98p,99il,101) (SAC pp109-112ps).

Green Common The Green, Stafford. Five acres of land on Lichfield Road, Stafford, were allotted to the parishioners of Castle Church. Used as allotments from 1917 until English Electric Co Ltd bought the land in 1957 (VCH vol 6 p210).

Greendale House and Lane. 1m WSW of Oakamoor. In Alton parish.

Greendock Area SW of Longton. Was already developing in c1820. Centres on Heathcote and Edensor Roads and Greendock Street (POP p129). John Turner (1738-87) potter utilised a peculiar peacock marl found at Greendock from c1780, to make stoneware (Staffordshire Chimney Ornaments. Reginald G Haggar. 1955 p52) (VCH vol 8 pp227,239) (POTP p210).

Green End House Stafford library was built on the site of this house in 1914 (VCH vol 6 p195) (SAC p54p).

Greene's Museum A museum established by Richard Greene or Green (1716-1793), an apothecary, at his house on the S side of Market Street (known in his time as Sadler Street), Lichfield (VCH vol 14 p22-23) (SCSF p125) (SSAHST 1988-89 p64). Greene arrived in Lichfield in 1741 or 1742 and started making his collection shortly after his arrival. The museum must have been in existence by 1748 for it is mentioned in the Universal Magazine of that year. Greene printed a catalogue of exhibits in 1773 (VCH vol 14 p168). Dr Johnson of Lichfield (see) (who was a relative of Greene's - The Reades of Blackwood Hill with a Full Account of Dr Johnson's Ancestry, Aleyn Lyell Reade, 1906 p145. LAL p46) and the Thrales visited the museum in July 1774 (DJL pp225,226,227). Johnson is said to have said to Greene 'Sir, I should as soon have thought of building a man of war, as of collecting such a museum' (LAL p46). Greene died in 1793 and the collection was sold for £1,000 (SHOSA vol 2 p9) (SSAHST 1976-77 pp79-82). Some of the collection was bought by Greene's grandson, Richard Wright. Between 1803 and 1806 Wright put the remaining collection on display at No. 20 the Close, and then at premises next to his house at the N end of Dam Street. It remained here until his death in 1821 (VCH vol 14 pp66,168-169). The items were then sold, although some remained in Lichfield, forming part of the collections shown at Donegal House and St Mary's Centre. The musical altar clock displayed in the Victoria Art Gallery, Bath, is said to have come from Greene's Museum and is now known as the Lichfield Clock (SSAHST 1976-77 pp73-78 ils p).

EXHIBITS. Shaw (SHOS vol 1 pp331-332) noted these relating to Staffordshire: A **model of Lichfield cathedral** in tobacco-pipe clay. Ancient **wooden chair** thought to have come from Lichfield cathedral. A curious reticulated slate, found over the bed of coal at Brown Hill's works, Staffs. The **stone-carved head of a mitred bishop** taken from Lichfield cathedral in the Civil War. An ancient **iron mace**, probably carried before the master of a Lichfield guild. A scold's bridle (SMC pp200-202). A **Roman urn**, one of 40, found in Yoxall parish a few years before 1797. **Sepulchral relics** in a small leaden box; and two pewter chalices, with some gold lace; found in stone coffins in Lichfield cathedral. A **carved-stone head**, and a **brass key** from Ranton Priory. An **earthen vessel** found when the old church at Farewell was taken down in 1748. Part of the **porch under which Lord Brooke stood** when shot in Dam Street by 'Dumb' Dyott from Lichfield cathedral. **Finger stocks** from Beaudesert Hall. A **pig of lead** from Hints Common found in 1772. A **piece of rudely carved wood** taken from the roof of Stone old church. A **piece of ancient English fowling equipment** thought to have belonged to the Skeffingtons of Fisherwick Hall. **Painted glass** from Yoxall church. A curious **altar piece** with painted panels from Longcroft Hall (SHOS vol 1 p102). The **runic almanac**, dried **foetus of a calf**, and a bony substance like a **tooth from the ear of mare** from Thorpe Constantine all noted by Plot in NHS. **Models of gravestones** of Hugo de Mavesyn and Sir Henry de Mavesyn. **Artifacts found in a coffin** on one side of the choir of Lichfield cathedral in 1787. The **head of a pike** (which had weighed 40 lbs) caught at Burton upon Trent; this was exhibited on the ceiling of the museum. A **human female foetus** taken from a 17-year-old girl of Stafford in 1772, preserved in a jar. These other Staffs artifacts were also in the museum: A **Roman vessel** found in 1788 at Uttoxeter High Wood. A hoard of two socketed **axes** and two socketed **spearheads** of the Late Bronze Age found in Armitage parish in 1782. An **iron mace**, probably of C17 origin, belonging to the Guild of St Mary, Lichfield. In the 1980s and 1990s this mace was on show at St Mary's Centre, Lichfield (SAL). The **penknife** given to a Lichfield family by Elizabeth I during her visit to Lichfield 1575. A **painting of St Francis** showing signs of stigmata from an altar piece once in the possession of the Arden family of Yoxall (SHOS vol 1 p253 note 6 pl xxxii). **Gothic sculptures** of a king etc from St Mary's chapel Lichfield cathedral (SHOS vol 1 p254). A **bullet** which had been lodged in the old pulpit of St Chad's church, Lichfield, and thought to be from the Civil War period (HOL p429 note).

Green Farm On the W side of Fairoak village. Here Mr Henry Palmer found a stone hammer head which was sent away to be exhibited (BOV p36).

Greenfield Former hamlet in the area of Furlong Road 0.5m NNE of Tunstall, formerly known as Smithfield. In Wolstanton ancient parish. The hamlet was created by Theophilus Smith in the early 1790s near his hall, Greenfield Hall, and pottery works. Smith was declared bankrupt in 1800. Either in June or July 1800 he attempted to murder his friend, John Wainwright, a Liverpool merchant, whom he suspected of having an affair with his wife. Smith fled to London and was arrested in Pall Mall and committed to Bridewell Prison. While in Stafford Gaol hospital he shot and wounded his wife and then shot himself dead; his wife later died (W p288) (ROS vol 1 pp1-10) (SHST pp555-557) (POTP p196). The hamlet, like the estate, was re-named Greenfield by the new owner John Breeze after Smith's attempt at murder, and his subsequent suicide (VCH vol 8 p83).

Greenfield Farm Hales Lane, Smethwick. Farmed by members of the Holloway family. It was still standing in 1932 (SMEOP p124p).

Greenfield House Greenfield Road, Harborne. Occupied by David Cox (1783-1859), artist, between 1841-1859 (VCHWA vol 7 p50). He was born at Deritend, Birmingham. The much altered house still remains. It was restored in 1984 (GMH pp21-22) (HOHE p22; saying Cox died in 1858) (OHOPP p27il from a heliotype of 1842) (TB April 1986 p27).

Greenfields A C17 farmhouse 2.5m W of Wetley Rocks (WJ p15) in Bagnall parish. It was the seat of the Steele family in the late C17 and possibly into the C18. The Unwins have lived at Greenfields from at least 1892 to at least 1990 (B pp81-83p).

Greenfields Hall Stood 400 yards E of Christ Church, Tunstall (SHST pp555,556 il,557). Built in 1791 by Theophilus Smith. Extended in 1842. At first called Smithfield Hall and has also appeared as Greenfield Hall. The hall, like the estate, was re-named Greenfield by the new owner John Breeze after Smith's attempt to murder, and his subsequent suicide in Stafford Gaol. Shortly before 1908 the hall was demolished to make way for further coal mining. Greenfield housing estate now occupies the site (VCH vol 8 pp83,91).

Greenford Drayton Bassett. Small islands in the Tame on NW side of Drayton Manor (SHOS vol 2 p9). Shaw may be mistaken and he means Bourne Brook. But there are islands in the Tame to N and NE of Drayton Manor.

Greengates Furlong Road area of Tunstall (HBST p103). 0.5m from Sandyford on way to Tunstall. At sometime up to the mid C19 also called Botany Bay. House and pot works of William Adams (OTP p43). The name, which appears as Greenway on Dower's map, is preserved in Greengates Street.

Greengates House Opposite the later Christ Church, Tunstall. Built in 1787 by William Adams, who founded the Greengates Pottery (OTP p5 il of the house) (POTP p11). Was the seat of the Meirs in the C19. Became part of the Adams' factory in 1896. It was demolished between 1922 to 1925 (VCH vol 8 p91), or in the C19 (TFTP pp7-10).

Green Gutter Head Rock feature which also gives name to a minute hamlet consisting of a couple of houses? 1m SW of Flash.

Greenhead Area N of Burslem centre, preserved in Greenhead Street. (OTP p130).

Greenhead Tiny hamlet 1.75m W of Kingsley in Kingsley parish.

Green Heath Suburb of Cannock over 2m NNE of Cannock centre. In Cannock parish. The church, St Saviour, High Mount Street, was dedicated in 1888 (VCH vol 5 p67) (BOE p138) (LDD).

Green Hill One of the finest residences in Cheadle (HOC pp159,160). The name may be from a hill called Green Hill (NSFCT 1907 p80). Green Hill is marked on 1834 OS map 0.25m NE of Cheadle parish church at SK 008437. Seat in 1902 of Charles J Blagg, author of 'A History of North Staffordshire Hounds and Country 1825 to 1902' (1902).

Greenhill Blakeley, Wombourne. In Wombourne ancient parish. At Greenhill Nurseries a Neolithic or Bronze Age axe was found (NSJFS 1964 p44) (VCH vol 20 p197). Greenhill House was built in c1830 (VCH vol 20 p199).

Greenhill Area 0.5m ESE of Lichfield cathedral. Takes its name from a triangular green which still survives and a high sandstone bluff. St. Michael's church is situated E of the 'green.' Fragments of **Mesolithic** flints have high ground occupied by St Michael's churchyard and they may indicate a flint industry site (SSAHST vol 22 pp2,70,72) (VCH vol 14 p4). **Early religious site**. St Michael's churchyard consisting of seven acres was considered exceptionally large and to have been the cemetery of pagans (SMM p157); or, after the discovery of a crouched burial, of early Christians (SSAHST vol 16 pp58-61. vol 22 p71); the burial place of the legendary massacred Christians slain during Diocletian's reign (284-305) (VCH vol 14 pp39,135); and a Mercian tribal necropolis (Church Heritage of Lichfield. HE Savage. 1914 pp7-9) (VCH vol 14 p135). St Michael's may have replaced a pagan sanctuary, and or arose as the chapel for the cemetery; it occupies a prominent hilltop site within view of Ryknild Street. It is first recorded in c1190 (VCH vol 14 pp4,135). At Greenhill, possibly, was one of three pre and post Norman Conquest settlements which comprised Lichfield before a new town was built in the 1140s (SSAHST 1968 p49). It has been suggested that Chad's 'more retired dwelling place' was on or near the site of the church of St Michael at Greenhill and that Stowe church stands on the site of Chad's cathedral (hitherto identified as close to the present cathedral). But there is, however, no evidence Chad was the object of any special cult at St Michael's (VCH vol 14 p135) (SSAHST 1972 p31 note). Greenhill **wakes** were mentioned in 1828, when they were held on Monday and Tuesday, 20 and 21 October (VCH vol 14 p160). This old ballad about bear and bull baiting which begins

> Success unto yo' Wedgbury lads
> whereever yo' may be,
> Who took a bull to Greenhill Wake
> to stir up mirth and glee!

may relate to the Greenhill wakes or the Greenhill Bower (SCSF p36). Greenhill may have been the traditional site for Lichfield's bear baiting from earliest times (VCH vol 14 p161). Lichfield's **maypole** was at Greenhill, and there was one here in 1674. A new pole was set up at Greenhill in the early C18 (VCH vol 14 p160).

GREENHILL BOWER. Popular name for a festival anciently centred on Greenhill, occurring on Whit Monday. The festival is also known as the Lichfield Greenhill or Whitsun Bower or Greenbower Day or Greenbower Gala. **Origins**. It became the custom in the Middle Ages to erect at the Whitsun fair at Greenhill booths or bowers for the bishop's steward (VCH vol 14 p159), or for the exhibition of the city's products in craftsmanship, where cakes (Greenhill Bower Cakes) and ale were distributed, followed by sports and merry-makings (SCSF p34). More anciently the Bower may derive from a flower festival (FOS p102) or from Prehistoric heathen worshipping (HOA p7). **The changing festival**. The Bower was noted by Celia Fiennes in 1698 and Dr Wilkes, the antiquary, in the 1730s or 1740s (VCH vol 14 p160). Dr Johnson of Lichfield (see) attended the Bower in his youth. He attended it again in 1779 with a Mrs Cobb and reported to Mrs Thrale in a letter that 'It is much degenerated. Everything grows old' (Young Samuel Johnson. James L Clifford. 1955 1962 ed. p27). Stebbing Shaw wrote a detailed description of the festivities in the 1790s which appears in SHOS vol 1 pp316-317. Anna Seward noted with disapproval how vulgar the festivities had become in 1795. In c1800 Thomas Harwood, author of HOL, wrote of how the ceremony had become just a spectacle for children (VCH vol 14 p160 fig 16 show the Bower Procession in the later C18). The Bower seems to have lapsed in the early years of the C19. It is said to have been revived by 1811 (VCH vol 14 p160) or for the Whit Monday fair 1816 (June 3) (SCSF p34). William Pitt, author of THS (1817), noted the Bower (SCSF p34). The Lichfield Mercury of May 8 1818 recalls that the festival was lasting three days at this time. There is an account of the festival of 1825 in Hone's Everyday Book vol II p334. Rail transport brought large crowds from the Black Country, the Potteries, and the East Midlands from the mid C19 (ILN May 25 1850 p364ils) (VCH vol 14 p160). The Bower stopped in 1939 and was not resumed until 1947. (W pp492-493) (SC pp118-124) (LGS p178) (SCSF pp34-36) (BCC vol p166) (Lichfield Mercury May 28 1926 p5ps. June 9 1933 p5ps. May 30 1947 p7ps. May 22 1959 p1ps) (VESOP pl 134) (SMM pp158-159). **Additional attractions.** The Bower has long had associations with the **Court of Array** (see under Lichfield), an inspection of military equipment. The Court's proceedings also occurred on Whit Monday and anciently met at the Guild Hall. According to Rev Dr Falconer the old Guild Hall became too small for the Court and a growing number of officers and the Court decided to meet on the more spacious Greenhill (SCSF p35). This may explain the Array's association with the Bower. The Court continued to assemble at the Guild Hall and then process to Greenhill, where the Court officials partook of the refreshments at the booths or bowers. By probably the C20, the now much reduced Court, a mere piece of theatre, returned to be held in the Guild Hall. Today (1995) when the Court closes at noon it has little to do with the Bower of the afternoon, except for the Mayor and other Court officials going on to join the Bower procession. The **Bower procession** may be a relic of the Court's procession to Greenhill, or, the marching of the Constables and men-at-arms to fetch and bring the dozeners (tithingmen) of each ward to Greenhill in the Array, or as Hackwood suggests, the processioning of the City Corporation and Trade Guilds (SCSF p34). A Maid Marian character was added to the procession in the early C19; a knight character in c1850; Tableaux were introduced in the 1870s; pageants were still carried in the 1880s; a bower queen, who accompanies the floats, was first crowned in 1929 (VCH vol 14 p160). The Lichfield Morris dancers (see under Lichfield) played a part in the procession until 1884 when their participation lapsed. After one or two abortive revivals the dance was a feature, again, by at least 1978 (FOS pp102-103). By the 1990s the procession had become a float and carnival affair. It starts between 12.30 and 1.00pm from Cherry Orchard (see). The procession does a circuit of the city, taking in Greenhill and the Market Place and returns to Cherry Orchard, where it disperses. Traditionally the streets were garlanded with ribbons, boughs and flags (FOS p102). The **afternoon celebrations** of sports, food, drink and entertainments formerly took place at Greenhill. There was formerly morris dancing. Theatrical performances, menageries and circuses were added to the festivities in the early C19, and in 1827 there was a fireworks display (VCH vol 14 p160). By at least 1978, the afternoon celebrations were taking place at Beacon Park (FOS p103).

Green Hill At Ashwood, Stourton. At the foot of it is a spring once celebrated for the cure of various diseases (RKE p18). Plot mentions it (SVS p124).

Green Hill House Wombourne. Seat of ironmaster, George Addenbrook in the late C19 (Wolverhampton Chronicle Jan 29 1999 p24p).

Greenhills Large house 1.25m SSW of Codsall, and to W of Heath House. It was built in the later 1850s for Thomas Boulton, a Wolverhampton lawyer (VCH vol 20 p80).

Greenhills Small Moorland district 1.25m ENE of Ipstones. Two farmhouses appear on 1834 OS map as Green Hill. The Moorlands Farm Park, a rare breeds animal farm aimed primarily at children, at Upper Greenhills Farm was founded in c1985. It contains examples of the Tamworth Pig, and has been continued by the Byatt family from 1987 (info P Byatt).

Green House, The Tipton Green, on borders of Tipton and Sedgley parishes, near St Matthew's church. Seat of a branch of the Dudley family who later moved to Shutt End. It was the residence of Thomas Dudley, who married Katherine, the daughter of 'stud' Sutton and his 'concubine' Elizabeth Tomlinson (TB June 1977 p5 il in 1612). Edward Dudley of Greenhouse was a parliamentarian in the Civil War (WAM p80). By the end of the C18 the old house had been taken down and rebuilt with the same materials and then extended. In 1825 it belonged to Sir Horace St Paul and was occupied by Richard Bradley. The last occupant was EJ Morris, who held an academy here in 1868. The hall has appeared as The Greenhouse, Green Hall, and de la Greenhouse (HOTIP pp87,186).

Green Lane By Hanging Bridge, Mayfield. Here was a toll-house on the Leek-Ashbourne turnpike road. In 1765 an order was made allowing a local resident, Mrs Boothby to 'pay nothing at the Gate at Green Lane for going to take the benefit of the air but to pay upon journies further than Hanging Bridge' (NSFCT 1948 p35).

Green Lane House 0.75m NNE of Meerbrook. Formerly in Leekfrith township in Leek ancient parish. Is first recorded in 1675 (VCH vol 7 p194) and has appeared as Greenland Farm. It was left to Anna Hulme (nee Doxey) (d1702)

by her son Doxey Hulme (OL vol 2 p145).

Green Lanes District by Priestfield, over 0.5m NW of Bilston. In Bilston chapelry of Wolverhampton ancient parish. Appears as a small hamlet on 1947 OS map 1:25,000 (sheet 32/99).

Green Lea A school named this near Milwich.

Greenleighs Former small hamlet, now a residential district over 0.75m N of Sedgley. Appears on 1947 OS map 1:25,000 (sheet 32/99), at SO 917950. But is only a street on Birmingham A-Z.

Green Low Small burial mound in Castern hamlet. It was excavated in 1860. Several articles of different periods were found; a green hone celt, a round-ended flint, a piece of coarse pottery, and a very perfect harp-shaped bronze fibula, said to be of Roman type. All the articles appeared to be independent of each other or of any interment. In another cutting the skeleton of a child with a flint arrow point was discovered, and in a third trench another child skeleton. Pieces of stags' horns, animals' teeth, rats' bones, numerous pebbles and flints were also found (TYD p116) (VCH vol 1 p190).

Greenlow Head Is a house over 0.25m W of Butterton (Moorlands) and no doubt here was or is a rock feature or burial mound.

Green Man Farm Farmstead built between 1722 and 1802 in Croxden parish (CDS p23). The name may be from the inn known as the Green Man, now known as The Highwayman, a short distance away in Alton parish.

Green Rock Area 0.75m E of Bloxwich. The area was Goscote on the 1834 OS map. The name is from Green Rock House, built by 1870 from a greenish rock obtained from Goscote Colliery. The house, said to be haunted and containing a external bell in the chimney stack which would sometimes ring unexpectedly in the night, was pulled down and an housing estate, known as Green Rock, built on the site near Green Rock Lane (BY p22) (SNBP p30).

Greensforge Tiny hamlet on the Smestow 1.25m S of Swindon. Formerly partly in Kingswinford and Wombourne ancient parishes. Post-Mesolithic flint artifacts have been found at Greensforge Farm (VCH vol 20 p197). It has long been believed there was a Roman settlement at Greensforge. Often writers, misleadingly, say it is at Ashwood. Plot said it was called 'Wolverhampton Churchyard.' He thought it was a Roman cemetery (NHS p406). Cox referred to the earthworks as burial mounds (SD p46). The local people, who called it 'The Churchyard,' had a tradition that Kingswinford church was built here but was spirited to its present site one night (SHOS vol 2 p233) (HOWM p22). The local people may, unbeknown to them, have had good reason to call the site 'Wolverhampton Churchyard,' for nearby Ashwood, formerly Haswic, belonged to the monastery of Wolverhampton in the C11 (HOWM p22). It has probably been called 'Walls:' 'Walls' giving its name to Wall Heath. Its Roman name is unknown (SL p41). Dr Wilkes noted an entrenchment here, which he thought was Roman and possibly one of their winter stations because of its low situation. Some suggest the site is really a Saxon village (WAS First Field Trip p11). In C18 a large brass of Nero was found here (SHOS vol 1 General Intro p31. vol 2 p233) (SVS pp124,333-334) (NSJFS 1964 p27). In c1860 numerous pottery fragments of Roman origin and a coin of Vespasian were found (SHC 1927 p185. 1928 p271). Excavations in 1928 (LGS p265) or 1929 in the SE corner revealed traces of a turf rampart, quantities of burnt wattle and daub and C1 AD pottery. Air photographs, from after WW2 (SL p41), show a complex site. There is a four-sided fort of Roman origin of 6.25 acres at SO 863887 and a larger fort of Roman origin defended by a single ditch to the S at SO 863885 (NSJFS 1964 p27). (VCH vol 1 pp190,344) (LGS p223) (S p74) (BAST vol 80 1962) (HOS p10) (Antiquity vol XL 1966) (BOE p166) (MR p203) (BCM June 1997 pp60-63). The name is from perhaps Thomas Green who occupied Greens Lodge (see) at Greensforge, and which he also seems to have given his name to; there was a forge here by 1602 (VCH vol 20 pp208,213). Or from a former blacksmith by the name of Green, or a forge sited on (or near) the village green (SPN p71).

Greensitch House at Gradbach, Flash. Greensitch is equal to Green-gutter sich and means dry (water course) (NSFCT 1932 p58).

Greens Lodge Former lodge, perhaps for Chasepool Hay, at Greensforge, Swindon. It was occupied by Thomas Green in 1600, and the name Greens Lodge was used for the house in the C17 and the early C18. It was also called Swin Lodge in the early C18. In 1612 Edward Sutton, 5th Baron Dudley of Dudley Castle (see), gave the house to his illegitimate son, the ironmaster, Dud Dudley (1599-1684). Dud Dudley was probably living here in the early 1620s, and he was still living here in 1674, when he was working the nearby forge. The house probably stood on the site of Greensforge House, later known as Bank Farm, a brick building dating from the late C19 (VCH vol 20 p209) (SVS p125). Dud Dudley claimed that the first use of pit coal in the making of glass was in the 1620s near Greens Lodge (Mettallum Martis. Dud Dudley. 1665. p35) (From Broad-glass to Cut Crystal. DR Guttery. p5) (VCH vol 2 p225.

vol 20 p215).

Greenway Former name for an area about the junction of Furlong Road and Little Chell Lane to the S of Clanway, 0.5m NE of Tunstall (1834 OS map). The footpath along the trackbed of the former Potteries (or North Staffs) Loop line was known Greenway by 1989 (1989 Stoke-on-Trent A-Z), and since the line ran through Greenway it may take its name from this Greenway, or it may be named because it is a 'green way.'

Greenway Bank Country Park 1.25m SE of Knypersley. Created after Staffs county council purchased the Greenway Bank estate in 1973 and more or less completed by May 1990. Contains: Gawton's Stone (see), Gawton's Well (see), parts of Greenway Wood, Hollins Wood and Knypersley Wood, the Jubilee Arboretum, situated at the W end of the park, has 79 species of native trees (NSFCT 1991 p61), Knypersley Pool (see), The Serpentine (see), and Warder's Tower (see). (MR p35 - misspelt Greenbank) (Greenway Bank Country Park. Staffs County Council Leaflet).

Greenway Bank House Over 1m SSE of Knypersley. Has also been written Greenaway Bank (POTP p231 see HH Williamson). The Greenway Bank estate was purchased by Hugh Henshall, successor and brother-in-law of James Brindley in 1778. Between 1800 and 1820 (BEH p29) Henshall built a house at SJ 889551 on the N side of Greenway Bank lane. With Henshall's death in 1817 the house passed to his nephew Hugh Henshall Williamson (d1867) (ONST 1975 pp364-365) who had rebuilt the house by 1828 (BIOPP p19). The fob watch of the man killed when his wagon of gunpowder blew up at Talke o' th' Hill in 1781 came into Williamson's possession. The watch had been reduced to a solid mass of metal in the explosion. To pay off Williamson's debts the estate was sold to Robert Heath in 1871. Heath bought it for his son, William, who died at Greenway Bank in 1872 (ONST 1975 p364-365). Members of the Heath family continued to live here until 1971 (BIOPP p19p) (BEH p29p). Staffs county council bought the 121 acre estate in 1973 and demolished the house shortly after but retained some of its outbuildings (ES June 10 1989 p22). By May 1990 the council had turned the estate into Greenway Bank Country Park (AGT pp56-57) (Greenway Bank Country Park. Staffs County Council Leaflet).
GROUNDS. The grounds appear to have covered the former Knypersley Park (BIOPP p19). To the N of the house is a grotto, and an ornamental shrubbery. On the old boundary of the estate with the Knypersley Hall estate between Knypersley Reservoir and The Serpentine is a boundary stone with the initials 'H.H.W.' (Hugh Henshall Williamson) (Greenway Bank Country Park. Staffs County Council Leaflet), Knypersley Pool (see), The Serpentine (see), and Warder's Tower (see).

Greenway Hall Stood near the Biddulph Arms Inn (Greenway Bank Country Park. Staffs County Council Leaflet), S of Biddulph Grange. Formerly in Middle Biddulph liberty in Biddulph ancient parish (BALH). The home of the Greenway family to 1427 (the Greenway coat of arms was for more than a century adopted by the Biddulphs) (BALH p25).

Greenway Hall Situated at the highest point on Baddeley Edge (W p401) (ONST 1951 p158) in Bagnall parish. Formerly Greenwood Hall and sometimes confusingly Greenaway. The first occupant was Roger Bradshaw who was named as one of the appraisers of the Inventory of William Adams in 1577. Bradshaws are found living at the hall at various intervals throughout the C17 (B pp80-81) and many have associated the hall with the regicide republican John Bradshaw, one time recorder of Newcastle-under-Lyme (see), who became prominent in the Civil War as the President of the High Court of Justice, the court which condemned Charles I to death. It is often said Bradshaw died at Greenway Hall in indigence and left his wife to become a pauper (GNHSS p11) (ONST 1929 p25) (TFTPM p120). But Speake does not allude to him in relation to living here. It is also said the original death warrant of Charles I was kept here when in the hands of John Bradshaw: he appears third on the list of witnesses to the warrant. The warrant eventually fell into the hands of Rev Daniel Turner of Norton-in-the-Moors (SMC pp172,181). Ward says when Greenway Hall was pulled down in c1820 none of Bradshaw's 'blood money' was found (HBST p531). Nicholls says although a Bradshaw did live at a hall here it was not the regicide (NSSG p6). Speake says the house was occupied by many different families in the C18 and C19 (B p81). Broughton writing in 1823-25 says a Ralph Stevenson of Cobridge had brought the property and the warrant and rebuilt the hall. Ward, writing in the early 1840s, notes the hall had been rebuilt using the materials from the former hall (HBST p532). The Hand family were living here in 1851 (B p81). Garner says the hall was in ruins by 1860 (GNHSS p11). A family called Tring were here in 1861 and a farmer called Stoddard was here in 1873 and his relations the Baileys were still here in the 1880s (B p81). In 1924 Greenway Hall Farm is described as 'a modern brick building reputed to be on the site of the stone-built house belonging to Judge Bradshaw' (NSFCT 1924 p194). Probably

this building was the one said, in 1970, to have been specially built to stand up to the strong winds on the ridge. It has no windows on one face (STM July 1970 p26). According to Byrne, the Greenway Hall occupied by the regicide John Bradshaw is now (1986) demolished (TFTPM p120). At this or the Greenway Hall at Biddulph a Thunderbolt P47 aircraft crashed in 1943. The American pilot died shortly after landing, having baled out (MD p67). A nine-hole golf course called Stockton Brook Golf Club was established on land belonging to and lying to the N of Greenway Hall Farm in 1909. In 1924 it was extended to 18 holes and in 1929 it was renamed Greenway Hall Golf Club (B p135).

Greenway Moor It appears to be another way of referring to the extensive former common land of Biddulph Moor that lay in Middle Biddulph manor. The name, probably from the Greenway family of Greenway Hall, is said to have been the early name for Biddulph Moor village (SVB p32).

Green Wood Wood 0.75m NNW of Canwell. The wood was made a protest camp by late 1997 by ecology demonstrators protesting against the Birmingham Northern Relief Road, due to be built through the wood; the protesters were still occupying the wood in Dec 1998 (BBC Radio 4. PM programme. Sept 15 1998) (BBC Midlands Today. Dec 21 1998).

Greet The name Greet has been used for many centuries for the area along Greet Brook (a head river of the Tame) between Bromford and Great Bridge (TMS p162).

Greet Brook Former name for the Tame in the area of Great Bridge and Greets Green (TB May 1995 p16). The brook divides the ancient parishes of West Bromwich and Tipton. Has also appeared as Grete Brook.

Greets End Near the bridge, Great Bridge. The name occurs in 1713 (VCH vol 17 p8).

Greets Green Suburb hamlet over 1.25m W of West Bromwich. In West Bromwich ancient parish. A mill at 'Grete' existed by the late C12. 'Grete' persisted as the name of that part of the parish for at least another 400 years. There was some settlement on the West Bromwich side of the Tame, by the mid C16, and Greets Green, the area around the junction of the roads from the bridge called Great Bridge (see) and Swan Village, is mentioned then. In 1777 there was still a common or waste commonly called Greets Green. By the mid C19 brickmaking became important in this area (HOWBW p170) (VCH vol 17 p8). Some have thought Greets is a corruption of great (SOWB p24). Others think it is derived from Grete and its associated forms, see Great Bridge. Greets Green became a ward of West Bromwich borough, when created in 1882 (VCH vol 17 p45). The church, St Peter, Whitehall Road, was consecrated in 1858 (VCH vol 17 p57). By 1999 Greets Green formed a ward with Lyng in Sandwell metropolitan borough.

'Gregory' Remote oval flat-topped motte at SJ 76772427, in Gregory Lane 1.25m NW of Norbury. For a long time of uncertain origin. Thought to have been a burial mound (VCH barrow list). It is 180 feet by 150 feet and 8 feet high (MR p245). More recently thought to have been a motte-and-bailey built by a Norman lesser lord in the C12 (VCH vol 4 p155) (NSJFS 1965 p44) (SL p65).

Gregorys Green Another name for Lower Green, a NW part of Coven, or became Lower Green (1834 OS map).

Gresley Canal Newcastle-under-Lyme. Authorised in 1775 (IANS p21) (SWY p28). Opened in the late 1770s. Built by Sir Nigel Gresley and his son Nigel Bowyer Gresley to bring coal from his mines at Apedale to Newcastle, where it terminated beside the present Liverpool Road. It was two miles long. It was connected to the Newcastle-under-Lyme Canal (see) in 1799 by the very short Newcastle-under-Lyme Junction Canal (see) (IANS p23) (Nicholson's Guide to the Waterways No. 5 'Midlands' pp46-47) and in time to the railway at the West Brampton (NSFCT 1947 p164). Or sometimes called Heathcote's Canal for ownership of the canal passed from the Gresley family to Robert Heathcote in 1827. Was discontinued in 1856, the coal was then transported by rail (NSJFS 1973 p107) (S&COP pl 35).

Greyfriars A Franciscan friary outside Stafford town walls, at North Gate or Goal Gate in Foregate (LGS p217). The Friary lay on the E side of the main Stafford-Stone road N of what is now the junction with Browning Street. It was founded by one of the Staffords of Sandon (VCH vol 3 pp270-271). Erdeswick says it was founded by Sir James Stafford (SOS pp144 note,153-5). VCH says Erdeswick is wrong to opt for Sir James since he was not born until c1300. It was a house of the Franciscan or Grey Friars (SIOT p90), or the Friars Minor. They were settled in Stafford by 1274. The Friary was suppressed on Aug 9 1538 and granted to James Leveson (SOS pp153,154) (W p326) (VCH vol 3 pp270-271) (HOS p25). The Friary is shown on an old plan of Stafford c1600 as a single ruined building (this map is not Speed's map) (NSFCT 1923 p56). It was demolished in 1644 by order of a parliamentary committee to facilitate the defence of the town in the Civil War (VCH vol 3 pp270-271). When the site was being developed in the C20 several coffins (including two of stone) were found, and a cross in one of the cellars (SSTY p140). In the 1970s the skeletons of 30 friars were found in the Greyfriars area by archeologists from Keele University. The majority of skeletons were kept by Selwyn Davis at Werrington until 1997 when they were given to Stafford borough council (ES March 1 1997 p3p). Very occasionally, and not in recent times, 'Greyfriars' was probably used to describe this area of Stafford. For the seal of the Friary see OSST 1929 pp41il,42.

Greyfields Court House 2m WSW of Kinver. Greyfield Gate, in the SE corner of Compton Park, was mentioned in 1616. There was a farmhouse on the site of Greyfields Court in 1775, prior to the building of the present house (VCH vol 20 pp122,141). The name means 'clearing where badgers are found' (SPN p71).

Greyhound Inn High Street, Bilston. Said to be Bilston's oldest building (BCOPP p23pl). It appears to have been the manor house built by the Mollesleys shortly before or after their succession to the lordship of Bilston manor, formerly a part of Stowheath manor. The Greyhound is timber-framed and cut into one of the beams in one of the bedrooms was found, in 1820, 'John Mollesley 1438' (TB March 1978 p10p. April 1978 p17p) (BCOPP p23; the house dates back to 1458) (MR pp36p,39). By marriage the Mollesleys succeeded the de Bilstons as lords of Stowheath manor (or the Bilston part of Stowheath manor?) by 1458. In the Civil War the house was sold to John Green. The Greens were here until at least 1715 (HOBL p128) (HOBLL pp49,131) (BOP p12p). The house became an inn in 1820 and was some time subsequently known as the Greyhound and Punchbowl Inn. After a period of deterioration it was renovated in 1936 (BOP pp12p,13p of interior, 14p of in 1950) (Wolverhampton AdNews March 30 1995 p12p c1904 from the rear). Said to be haunted by several ghosts (HIE p170) (GOM pl 8/a) (MS&S pp28-29). (IOM pp65-66, 70,71 ps) (BCP p30p).

Greyhound Inn Very old building at Penkhull. It was originally a lock-up adjoining the old court house of the manor of Newcastle-under-Lyme (The Greyhound Inn was still being called 'Penkhull Lock-up' up to the middle of the C19). Talbot has proved beyond doubt that up to 1828 the building was all one. The old court house serving as Ellis' Oakcake Shop in the 1920s, was demolished in 1936. (VCH vol 8 p182). There is a legend that Charles II stayed here. It was said he was caught dallying in the upstairs room by an irate husband, a scuffle ensued and swords were drawn. The fight continued on the staircase and it was a sword thrust missed which made the scar on the woodwork (PRA pp33,34ps of the manor courthouse in 1936 before it was demolished and of the Inn c1940,35,36). (POP p89) (STM Nov 1963 p48ps in 1936 when being reconstructed and in 1963) (AGT p27).

'Grey Lady' Tree Old limbless hollow tree, 20 feet tall, which was shaped like a hooded man carrying something in his arms. It stood about 0.5m from Sinai House, Sinai Park. The tree was removed between June 1993 and March 1994. There is a legend that a young peasant girl murdered by a monk from Sinai House in the Middle Ages is buried under it; her ghost is known as the 'Grey Lady' (GLS pp8-9).

Grey Mare's Stable Cave Cave in Dovedale, possibly on the Derbys side, and possibly that slightly to the N of Lion's Head Rock, which it is said, by PS, to be near, but PS also says it is close to Ilam Rock. An old woman is said to have resided in it a few years prior to 1908 (PS p122). The centrefold map in the Dovedale Guide by Keith Mantell 1984 features an unnamed cave slightly to the N of Lion's Head Rock.

Greystones House on N side of Stockwell Street, Leek. Dates from the 1680s. Stands to the S and in front of the Nicholson Institute. The house is said to have faced demolition when the Institute was built in 1884, but the Arts and Crafts designer, William Morris, led a campaign to save it (VCH vol 7 p96) (ES Feb 10 1998 p7). In Feb 1998 a specially commissioned wrought iron gate in the Arts and Crafts style to William Morris's memory was erected in the entrance way. It was designed by Edmund Sveikutis (ES Feb 10 1998 p7p).

Grigg's Well Trotter's Lane, Hill Top, West Bromwich. Supplied the cottages and neighbourhood with water. Believed to be the well where Charles II in disguise as William Jackson, with Jane Lane halted in his escape from the battle of Worcester (1651). They then either went up Trotter's Lane or Cole's Lane, along the main road to Black Lake, down Swan Lane on to Halesowen (OWB p76).

Griffyn's Island Island in the Trent. Is it the island by Rugeley railway station? Named after the Griffyn family, lords of Colton manor in the C13 and C14 (CWF p174).

Grimblebrook Pretty timber-framed cottage on N outskirts of Milwich. Perhaps the oldest building in the village. There is no Grimble Brook in the vicinity.

'Grimsdyke' Appears on 1834 OS map by Crowgutter on Ipstones Edge as Grimditch (NSFCT 1920 p161).

Grindlestone Edge A ridge running N to S, N of Horton village, about 0.25m E of Horton church (NHS p105) (VCH vol 7 pp65,66 see map).

Grindlestone Ford Ford in the Trent near Branston. Lends weight, like Millstone Ford, to Erdeswicke's assertion that the area was once renowned for grinding stones (SHOS vol 1 p142).

Grindley House or minute hamlet marked on 1834 OS map to the W of Blythe Bridge. Formerly in Normacot township in Hilderstone quarter in Stone ancient parish (W p371). The name is preserved in Grindley Lane.

Grindley Tiny hamlet in a short dale near the confluence of Stoney Brook and the Blithe, 4m SW of Uttoxeter. In Stowe parish. Appears in 1251 as Grenleg (SSE 1996 p14). The name is from Anglo-Saxon and Middle English the 'green lea' (DUIGNAN). Or 'the green glade' (SSE 1996 p14) (SPN p131). Salter gives a plan of a square moat at Grindley but no information about it (CAMS p10 plan). There is a moated site 0.5m NNE of Grindley at SK 041296. At Grindley was a station on the Stafford & Uttoxeter Railway.

Grindley Hill Site of N Staffs Royal Infirmary, Penkhull. Name appears in 1651 (VCH vol 8 p187).

Grindon (locally *Grin* NSJFS 1972 p127). Ancient parish and small moorland village on high ground above the confluence of the Manifold and Hamps, 22m NE of Stafford. **Burial mounds**. There is a burial mound at Grindon 18 paces in diameter and two feet high. Excavated by Carrington in 1848 (TYD p118) (NSJFS 1965 p39). There is a burial mound near Weag's Barn at SK 09705387, 0.75m ESE of Grindon, 14 paces in diameter and four feet high was excavated by Carrington 1849 and fragments of bone found (TYD p133) (NSJFS 1965 p39). It is a listed monument. A burial mound here revealed the burial remains of Beaker people (NSJFS 1962 p33). The **name** has appeared as Grendone, waste, in DB, and Gredon (SHC 1916 p198). From Anglo-Saxon 'green hill' (DUIGNAN) (PNPD). Oakden and Gelling agree (SSAHST 1967 p34) (NSJFS 1981 p2) (SSE 1996 p14). Poulton-Smith offers 'the great hill (or slope)' (SPN p67). There was a **church** at Grindon in the C12 (LDD). The present parish church, All Saints, on the N side of Church Avenue, was rebuilt in 1845 (BOE p138). The church spire is very prominent over the Moorland landscape and the church has been referred to as the 'cathedral of the moors' (LGS p142) (PWIS p77). Commander Wedgwood notes that according to the Burton Cartulary the parish was formed out of Ilam parish. It was formed between 1086 and 1291 (SHC 1916 p198). Grindon parish **wake** was on the nearest Sunday to All Saints' day in the C19 (W p777). There was no fair in 1792 (OWEN), but there was one in 1888 (LHE p265). There is said to have been a pinfold in the village centre from c1800. Having fallen into decay in the earlier C20 it was rebuilt in 2000 for historical purposes and to celebrate the millennium (ES May 26 2000 p16). A stone pillar (resembling an obelisk mem) stands near the church gate with the inscription 'The Lord of the Manor of Grindon established his right to this rindle (brook) at the Stafford Assizes, March 17, 1862' (VB p198) (DoE II). **Aircraft crashes**. A Wellington 2 1566 aircraft crashed at Grindon on May 22 1942. The crew of nine all died except for F/ SGT Chappell (MD pp28-29). Grindon was thought to have been cut-off in the great blizzard of early 1947. A Halifax RT 922 aircraft was dispatched on Feb 13 from RAF Fairfield to drop necessary supplies. But it crashed on Grindon Moor near Sheldon Farm killing all eight occupants - Squadron Leader Donald McIntyre, Flight Lieutenant Ernest Smith, Warrant Officer Richard Sydney Kearno, Warrant Officer Gordon Victor Chapmen, Flight Sergeant Kenneth Charles Pettitt, Sergeant William Sherry, Joseph Gordon Rearden, and David William Savill (MMM p22). Bird says six died (VB pp195-196). The official inquiry revealed that the village had never solicited a mercy flight, nor were Grindon villagers particularly short of food (MMM pp19-23). (MR p166) (COS p9) (ES Feb 12 1994 p23p) (MD pp79-80) (TWWW Feb 1997 p14ps) (SMML pp31-34). Shortly after the disaster a memorial was erected in Grindon church to the memory of those killed. In 1987 a further plaque was erected. There is also a tapestry of Christ on the Cross embroidered by Andrew Barlow of Leek to the memory of the dead airmen. A memorial erected at the scene of the crash was requested in Feb 1997, and a six-foot high cairn was officially unveiled at the site on Sept 28 1999 (ES Feb 21 1997 p15. Sept 23 1999 p5p. Sept 29 1999 p5p). For a rhyme about Grindon see Cauldon. **Persons and visitors**. **Thomas Tetlow** of Chapel-en-le-Frith, Derbys, was accused of stealing a bay nag at Grindon in 1607 (NSJFS 1969 p10). In c1923 **Rev Smith** of Grindon killed his maid and then committed suicide (VB p199).

Grindon Moor A house called Grindonmoor Gate is 0.75m WNW of Grindon, the moor extends from here in a north westerly direction. There are two burial mounds 1m NW of Grindon: one at SK 07075518, 14 paces in diameter and eight feet high and close by at SK 07055529 another 23 paces in diameter and six feet high (NSJFS 1965 p39). There is another on Grindon Moor which Carrington excavated in 1848. An arrowhead and a quernstone were found in it (TYD pp117-118,126-127) (NSJFS 1965 p39).

Grit, The Former detached portion of Croxden parish consisting of 22 acres of meadow land 2m E of Croxden parish at the confluence of the Churnet and the Dove (CDS p4). Removed to Doveridge ancient parish, Derbys, in 1883 (GLAUE p409).

Groundslow Small hamlet over 0.5m SW of Tittensor. Formerly in Beech quarter in Stone ancient parish (W p369). In 1877 it was noted by NSFC excursionists that in a field of Groundslow Farm there was a block of igneous rock, reputed to be the largest boulder in the neighbourhood. NSFC members doubted whether it was a boulder, and thought it rather a portion of the greenstone (sandstone) left 'in situ' (NSFCT 1878 p10). There is a burial mound at SJ 867375 situated on top of an eminence opposite the Groundslow Hospital gates. In 1983 it had five trees on the top. It had been dug into on one side to allow a feed reservoir to be inserted (NSFCT 1915 p154. 1983 p11). The OS map marks another burial mound at SJ 867373, 0.25m SE of Groundslow. Grounds Lowe, one of these mounds, lies at the N end of a ley line stretching from Stone church and running through Bury Bank and Saxon's Lowe (SMM p23 see map). Aerial photography has shown cropmarks at Groundslow Grange showing an oval enclosure, which was used probably for penning cattle (SPJD p13p,15).

Groundslow Fields This appears to be the name for the principal estate at Groundslow, centred on a brick villa (S side) and a house (N side), on the W side of Winghouse Lane, Mrs Elizabeth Unitt (d1749) was of Groundslow Fields (SIS p60). In the earlier C19 it belonged to the Duke of Sutherland of Trentham Hall (see); he built one of the properties at Groundslow Fields (that which was called Groundslow House) in 1832 (TTOPP p81); that house was probably the one William Lewis, agent of the Sutherlands, occupied between at least 1834 and 1851 (W 1834 p56) (W p369) (VCH vol 6 p102). The Earl of Huntingdon was another occupant of either house. The villa was occupied by Frank T Rigby between at least 1907 and 1912 (STC p23p) (KD 1912). Later, by 1916 to at least 1940, the villa or the house was occupied by members of the Copeland family (trade directories). In the 1920s the villa was extended and made an annex of Staffordshire General Infirmary, Foregate, Stafford, for tuberculosis patients (local info). It became known as Groundslow Hospital. By 1965, and probably by the early 1950s, the hospital had become a maternity hospital. It had a salmonella outbreak in February 1975 (SN Feb 14 1975 p1), and closed in 1982. In 1984 Groundslow Hospital was purchased and divided into two: Groundslow Hospital, forming one part, opened as an old people's home called Camelot Court in 1986 (TTOPP p81): A modern building which formed the nurses' hall for the hospital, forming the other part, became Groundslow Grange Residential Home for the elderly. In May 1999 Camelot Court was still a residential home for the elderly. By late 1998 Groundslow Grange had closed as a home for the elderly, and there were then plans to turn it into an hotel (ES Oct 13 1998 p9p. Aug 3 1999 p13) (local info).

Groundwyns House on the Bobbington Enville parish boundary N of Grove Farm. It existed by 1391. There was still a farmhouse here by 1770, when it was also known as Greenage (VCH vol 20 p94).

Grove, The House which stood in what is now Grove Park, Harborne. The house, originally a farmhouse, was owned by Thomas Green, lord of Harborne manor, in the late C18 (HOHE p10). It was occupied by Madam Carless prior to 1806 in which year her daughter, Elizabeth, married Thomas Attwood (1783-1856), political reformer and Birmingham's first MP. Attwood lived here with his wife from 1811 to 1845 (HOHE p16). The DNB says he lived at The Larches, Sparkbrook, Birmingham, from 1806 to 1811, and then at The Crescent, Birmingham (GMH pp3-4). A later house on the site of The Grove was occupied by the Kendrick family, and the complete panelling and contents of one room of this, designed by the architect of Harborne Hall, John Henry Chamberlain in 1876, was on display as 'The Harborne Room' in the V&A, London, in 1989. The grounds of the Grove were given to Birmingham city council to become Grove Park (HOHE p16).

Grove, The House in Wood Road, Tettenhall Wood. Before WW2 it was the residence of HT Fullwood (TCOP p46p of the old house). In WW2 it occupied by the Pratt family, and received a direct hit by a German bomb. Rebuilding could not take place until after WW2 and the family moved elsewhere. The property was sold to Harold Fullwood who had the house rebuilt and moved in in c1946. This house was in turn demolished and is now the site of Maythorn Gardens, a residential development (BTW p78p of the new house) (TCOP p47p of the rebuilt house) (PPTP p26).

Grove Brook Rises in the Ox Hill area of Handsworth. Runs in a NE direction to the Tame (MNB p35).

Grove Farm 1.5m NW of Enville, in Enville ancient parish. There was a house here by the late C14. The present farmhouse dates from the early C18 (VCH vol 20 p94). At Grove Farm, S of Mere Lane and E of Four Ashes, there was a windmill. It is shown on maps of the early C19 (VCH vol 20 p112) (WBJ pp21,22).

Grove Hill Incline 1m NE of Druid's Heath to the W of Stonnall church. It is probably a prehistoric earthwork and may have been a sighting mound (OSST 1949-50 p19).

Grove House Stood in the SW corner of Handsworth Park. Built in the later C18 or early C19 and survived until after WW2 (MNB pp41,46).

Grove House Junction of Snow Hill and Bedford Road, Shelton, Hanley. Home of Charles Meigh, who altered and enlarged it in c1840 (VCH vol 8 pp144,149-150). The house was celebrated for its huge library of some 4,000 books and art collection (HBST pp384 il facing, 385-386) (SHST p590 il from c1840).

Grove House Birmingham Street, Walsall. Stands on a part of the estate of Capt Henry Stone, active in the Civil War. The old mansion became known as the 'Wheatsheaf.' For a time it or the later house was the residence of Rev Thomas Grove (d1817) (hence the name) minister of Bridge Street Congregational church. The old mansion was purchased by Joseph Cowley in 1813, and dismantled. Some of the old materials were reused in a new house built by Cowley. At one time it was occupied by Misses Harrison as a school which was moved to Melrose House, King Street (Birmingham Road). Later occupants have included James Symons in c1892, and George Thompson (SNWA p52). The foundations of Capt Stone's residence were found in the garden (SNWA p52). The old mansion had a bowling green and spacious garden (SNWA p52).

Grove Park Public park SE of St Peter's, Harborne. Formerly the grounds of The Grove. There are traces of what appear to be medieval ridge and furrow ploughing in Grove Park (HOHE p3).

Grove Pool Former canal feeder reservoir on Pensnett Chase now part of a recreational area (BHOP2 p106).

Grove Vale Residential district over 1.25m SW of Great Barr. Formerly in Great Barr township in Aldridge ancient parish. The name occurs as Grove Vale on Greenwood's map; a Groves Holes appears on the 1834 OS map in the Grove Vale area. For Bishop Asbury's Cottage see Newton.

Grub Low Burial mound over 0.5m N of Waterfall at SK 08045254. It was excavated by Carrington in 1849 and is a listed monument. It revealed the remains of two burials; one a contracted inhumation, the other a cremation (TYD pp147-148) (VCH vol 1 p181) (NSJFS 1965 p52) (WOY p1). Is of Neolithic origin (HAF p26).

Grub Street Small hamlet over 1m N of Norbury, formerly in Weston Jones township, in Norbury ancient parish. Straddles both sides of the Shropshire Union Canal. Appears on 1834 OS map (SPNO p177). The Grub Street cutting for the canal posed great problems for its builders as did the Shelmore Great Bank to the S. Here the Lower Keuper Sandstone frequently collapsed into the cutting. The engineer, Thomas Telford, struggled with the problems from 1829 to 1834 when a 10,000 cubic yards of rock collapsed near Blakemere and buried 60 yards of cutting (Thomas Telford. LTC Rolt. 1958 pp173-186) (WSS pp107-108).

Grubbers Ash Between Apedale and Knutton. Here was a windmill (Plot's map). This may have been Sneyd's Mill, which in 1684 was bought for £12 and taken down and re-erected at Whitmore (WBJ p32). Tobacco pipe clay could be found here (NHS p121). To the SW is Grubbers Hill.

Grubbers Hill Silverdale. Here is an old colliery shaft (IANS p128 map).

Gruel Spout A well at Biddulph. The dressing of which had been revived by 1994 (SMM p74).

Guild of Monks House over 2m ESE of Forton. In Forton ancient parish. The name has appeared as Gyle de la Monks (1487) and Gill a Monks (1606), Gild of Monkes (1693) (SPNO p148) (SHC 1923 p305). A hermit's habitation in woods here was given to Shrewsbury Abbey in the mid C12; later the abbey established a grange here (VCH vol 4 p107). The house was described as modern in the 1950s. A building known as Old Guild formerly stood about 300 yards to the W of the house and was built on by cottages in C19 (VCH vol 4 p107). Believed to have a secret tunnel which runs to Forton church (VB p155) (Shropshire Star? late 1970s). See also New Guild.

Gun Cross A cross in the vicinity of Gun Hill. An ancient meeting place for the parishioners of Leekfrith quarter in Leek parish (OL vol 1 p190).

Gun End Tiny hamlet under 1m NNW of Gun Hill, or 1m SSW of Swythamley. A stone trough, believed to be 200 years old in 1998 when vandalised, is situated opposite Gun End Farm (ES Sept 25 1998 p5p).

Gungate A solitary spot on the W side of Gun Hill, almost opposite Lockgate (OL vol 1 p217). There was once a farm here. Here and at Lockgate there is supposed to be a fortification where the Ancient British took their stand (HOLF p7). Local inhabitants were judged responsible for the upkeep of the road from the end of the 'Surrey Pavement to Gun Gate' at the Quarter Sessions in 1724. AE and EM Dodd identify it with the Trusseway, a deep hollow way climbing over Gun, which starts at Fould (PRT p56).

Gungate Upper and Lower Gungate street running northwards out of Tamworth town (Staffs) was formerly called Gumpigate. Gate is of Danish origin meaning 'street' (WMLB pp87 plan,92) (SL p50; spelt Gumpegate). The name represents 'street to Gumpi's farmstead' (SPN p125). (SA May 23 1885 p6).

Gun Hill Hill over 3m NNW of Leek, and 1.75m S of Swythamley. The height of the hill is 1200 feet (NSFCT 1874 p8), or 1210 feet (OL vol 1 p156), or 1263 feet (VCH vol 7 p191), or 1264 feet (HOLF p5) (PRT p56). It has fine views of the Welsh mountains, the Wrekin and Peckforton Hills (NSFCT 1921 p140. 1943 p70).

EARLY to 1700. Here was possibly fought a great **battle** between the Romans and the Britons in c22 BC. There is an earthwork running down the side of the hill; Hostage Lane, Wall Hill, Wall Grange, Wallbridge all suggest a stockade or wall (OL vol 1 pp216-218). There is a statement in Pausania (Paus. Graec. descr. 1. 33. of M.H.B. 4. 2) which may have reference to Gun Hill: 'Antoninus Pius deprived the Brigantes of a great position of their land (possibly a reference to Gun Hill), because with arms they had begun to overrun the territory of the Genuini, who were tributary of the Romans.' The name 'Genuini' does not occur elsewhere. The Genuini must have dwelt S of the Brigantes. 'Genuini' is derived from the Celtic 'gun' signifying 'moorland.' This raid took place about 138 AD (NSFCT 1908 p104). Pickford says a tribe known as the Ceangi had a camp on Gun Hill. The camp or fort was close to the Limes Britannica (SMM pp110,111). There is said to have been a conflict between the Saxons and the Britons on Gun Hill (SK p196). The burial place of Thoni, mentioned in the bounds of the estate granted to Dieulacres Abbey in c1220 and lying at the S end of Gun, may have been a **burial mound** (VCH vol 7 p193). Gun was covered by woodland in medieval times (VCH vol 7 p197). For a packhorse way which appears to have passed over Gun Hill see Trussway. The **name** has appeared as Dun (1593-1603) (SOS p366), Dun Mountain (Bowen's map). It is from gieth or gunth, the great hill to the north? (SK p196). Gun may be a corruption of Dun, which in turn is from 'don' meaning 'hill' (PNPD). In Cornish the word 'gun' is equivalent to 'heath' or 'moorland' (NSFCT 1908 p134). There is local tradition that it was from Gun Hill Oliver Cromwell's troops fired a cannon at St Edward's church at Leek. The cannon ball hit the tower of the church. A clock was later installed in the hole left by the cannon (this explains why the clock is not in a central position on the tower). This is sometimes put forward, quite wrongly, as the reason why the area is known as Gun (HLS p71) (DP pp79-80).

1700 to PRESENT. The body of **John Naden** was rehung from a 21 feet high gibbet on the top Gun Hill on Aug 30 1731. Nadin, an employee at the farm at Whitelee (see), had murdered his master Robert Brough at the farm. Nadin's chains were made so that they kept his body together until his bones turned to powder. The gibbet is said to have remained on the top of the hill until 1875, but there were no traces of it in 1943 (NSFCT 1943 p70) (VCH vol 7 p195). Pickford says the execution took place on Aug 31 1731 (DP p80). In time the gibbet post was made into two gate posts and a stop post, which were partly burnt in the great fire on Gun in 1855-6 (OL vol 1 pp25,27). The Young Pretender's army, perhaps using an old packhorse way between Leek and Macclesfield (HOLF p5), passed over Gun Hill on Dec 3 1745 in the **Jacobite Rebellion** (BPCSM p3). A leather wallet left by the army was found on the hill (HOLF p2). In Nov 1763 Mrs **Ann Hulme** of Wetwood was dragged to her death from her horse by her dress getting caught on a gate on Gun (OL vol 1 p315). A **balloon** which had ascended from Beverley, Yorks in early June 1826 and deposited its pilot, a Mr Brown, on Thorne Moor, near Doncaster, continued in flight and came down on Gun Hill to the consternation of the native inhabitants (Pottery Gazette June 10 1826) (Broughton's Scrapbook p257). Other accounts say the balloon descended on May 25 1826 and that it had on board a bottle of wine, a few biscuits and a compass (OL vol 1 p328) (HOLF p6).

Gunside House 0.75m SW of Meerbrook, or 1.25m SE of Gun Hill (HOLF p7). Formerly in Leekfrith township of Leek ancient parish (W p728).

Gunstone Tiny dispersed hamlet on rising ground above Moat Brook, 0.75m NNE of Codsall church. Former liberty with the Hattons of Brewood town in Brewood ancient parish. There is a sulphur well in a field at Gunstone near the Water Splash (ABW pp51-52) (VCH vol 5 p20). The name has appeared as Gonestone (c1176-84), Gunston (1227), Gunestone (1240), Gunniston (c1260), Gunstone (1341-1482) (SSE 1996 p14) (SPNO p37), Guston (Blaeu's map), and Gunston. It is from perhaps the personal name Gunnr, which was an Old Norse word; so Gunnr's town (DUIGNAN). Or 'Gunni's tun' (SSE 1996 p14). Or has same derivation as Gun Hill (see) (NSFCT 1908 p134).

Gunstone Hall Gunstone. The old hall was held by the Fowkes in the C17. The hall in 1959 was a gabled stucco farmhouse of c1840 (VCH vol 5 p32). Gunstone Hall in Virginia, USA, is said to take its name from this Gunstone, having been built by a Roger Fowke, an active royalist, who settled in Virginia with his friend Col Mason in the mid C17 (HOB pp39,87) (VCH vol 5 p32 note) (SLM March 1952 p20p; misspelt Gunstall Hall).

Guns Village Suburb of and 0.5m NW of the High Street, West Bromwich. In West Bromwich ancient parish. The area N of Dartmouth Street had some building by the 1830s and was extensively built up by the 1880s (VCH vol 17 p9).

Gutter Oak An oak in a ravine in Beaudesert Park (GNHS p409) (SG p109). No doubt the tree died long ago.

Hackman's Gate Hamlet 0.75m SW of Broome, over 2.25m WSW of Clent. In Broome parish, now in Worcs. Formerly the Hangman's Gate, situated on the edge of the Blake Down (VCHW vol 3 p33) (SNSV vol 2 p47).

Hadden Minute hamlet 0.75m W of Meerbrook. Consists of a Lower and Upper Hadden.

Hadderidge Field name in central Burslem in the C18, to SW of the present Market Place. Lower, and Upper Hadderidge appear on a plan of the town of c1750 (SL p213 see plan). Gives the name to a house which stands at the junction of Wycliffe Street and Lower Hadderidge. It was built after the mid C18 (VCH vol 8 pp112,119). A street called Lower Hadderidge preserves the name.

Hademore Small hamlet near the source of Fisherwick Brook, 1m ESE of Whittington. Formerly in Fisherwick out-township of St Michael's parish, Lichfield. It was an estate belonging to Sir Robert Peel in the mid C19 (W p515). On April 21 1910 Claude Graham-White, a participant in the Daily Mail's London to Manchester Air Race, landed his plane at Hademore level crossing. The wind prevented him from taking off again and he returned to London and attempted the challenge again on April 27. But hearing his only challenger, Paulhan, had reached Manchester before him, Graham-White gave up and landed his plane again at Hademore crossing (Lichfield Mercury April 29 1910 p8. May 6 1910 p7. April 26 1985 pp32,49) (EAS pp25,29) (VCH vol 14 p240).

Haden Area in Rowley Regis parish embracing Haden Cross, Old Hall, Hill, and Park. The name was in existence in medieval times, occurring as a surname for William atte Hauedene, Stephanus de la Haueden (1299), Richard Hadene (1388), Richard at Hadene of Rowley (1399) and Henry atte Hadene (1403). The ending is from denn an Anglo-Saxon word for a valley, den being a wooded valley and a dene a dell (SNSV vol 2 p41).

Haden Cross Ancient cross which stood at the junction of the two roads at the top of Haden Cross Hill at the foot of the High Haden upon a strip of common which formed part of Hayseech Common (BCWJ p64), or a few yards NW of Haden Old Hall (Haden Hill House and Park Guide). In Rowley Regis parish. Appears as Heydon Cross on Plot's map and appears on OS map 1834. The name Haden is from the Haden family, living in Rowley Regis in 1417, and probably long before (DUIGNAN). Inhabitants from Haden Cross were referred to in medieval records as 'Atte Haudene,' 'of the wooded rise' (TB April 1972 p7). The cross was one of four wayside crosses marking the boundary of Halesowen Abbey lands: The others were at Holy Cross, Lye Cross and Rood End. The name Haden was given to New Haden Colliery, W of Cheadle, by its owners, the Bassano brothers of Haden Cross, one brother being AH Bassano, when it opened in c1906. The district covered by the colliery has, since the closure of the colliery, adopted the name, New Haden (CCT p152).

Haden Hall Haden Hill House, Haden Hall and Haden Old Hall are often confused with each other. The two properties - Haden Old Hall (C17), and Haden Hill House (1878) - stand side by side on Haden Hill.

Haden Hill Is also called Haden Cross Hill? But J Wilson-Jones stresses Haden Cross is different to Haden Hill, and Haden Hall, or rather the houses Haden Hill House and Haden Old Hall are built on it (BCWJ p57). (TB March 1976 p11p of Haden Hill in 1910).

Haden Hill House Situated on W side of Halesowen Road, to the immediate W of Haden Old Hall. In Rowley Regis parish. Built in 1878 by George Alfred Haden Haden-Best (1839-1921) next to Haden Old Hall after his purchase of the Haden Old Hall estate in 1877. He considered the old hall 'insufficient

for a Gentleman' and contemplated demolishing it but instead built a house next to it and landscaped the surrounding 60 acres into what has become Haden Hill Park (see) (TB Jan 1986 p11) (MGH p46) (ORR p97ps). Here he lived with his two adopted daughters, Emily Bryant, and Alice Cockin. After his death in 1921 the whole estate was sold to Robert Fellows who re-sold it to Rowley Regis urban district council in 1922. The house was used in a variety of ways until at least the end of WW2. In 1983 work on restoring it began. It is now (1997) open to the public and contains furniture and fittings of the Victorian period and artifacts once belonging to the Barrs and Haden-Best families (Haden Hill House Guide). Pevsner and Palliser appear to have mistaken this house for Haden Old Hall (see) (BOEW p90) (SL p100). The house is said to be haunted by the ghost of a lady who appears on the stairs in a white mist and of a man in black of Victorian appearance and dress, carrying a stick (GPCE p37).

Haden Hill Park Public park between Halesowen Road and Barrs Road in Hill (MGH p46), 1.5m SW of Rowley Regis. It was the grounds of Haden Old Hall. George Alfred Haden Haden-Best's landscaped the grounds after his purchase of the Haden Old Hall estate in 1877; there is a date stone ESE of Haden Hill House stating the grounds were landscaped in 1878. The park was increased in size in 1903. There are two gravestones to pets of Haden-Best S of Haden Hill House. One is to 'Floss' dated 1898, and the other has no inscription (Haden Hill House and Park Guide). The park was presumably opened to the public after Rowley Regis urban district council's purchase of Haden Old Hall and Haden Hill House in 1922. There is also a brick dovecote (BOEW p90).

Haden Old Hall Old brick hall situated on the W side of Halesowen Road to the immediate E of Haden Hill House, 1.5m SW of Rowley Regis. There are various dates for its construction. Some say the hall was built in medieval times, and rebuilt or built in c1500 (TB Jan 1986 p11p. Feb 1992 p12), or that it dates from 1531 (BCWJ p57), or that it was built in the early C17 (BOEW p90). The house looks the same period as the Brick House, Burslem which is of early C17 date (SL p100 - calls it Haden Hill House) (ORR p96p). The hall was the seat of the Hadens until 1801 when by marriage it passed to Rev George Barrs (1771-1840), curate of Rowley Regis (see). His grandson, George Alfred Haden Haden-Best (1839-1921), chose not to live here after he acquired the estate in 1877, and built the adjoining Haden Hill House for his residence. Both houses were acquired by Rowley Regis urban district council in 1922 (TB April 1974 pp1p,18-19ps. May 1974 pp16-17. Feb 1977 p23p. Jan 1986 p11p. Feb 1986 pp30-31ps. Oct 1993 p20. Nov 1993 p20. Dec 10 1998 p21. Dec 24 1998 p19ps). In 1934 Haden Old Hall was considered dangerous and demolition was proposed. But it was saved; the chief campaigners to save the building were Joseph Perry, the 'Chainmaker Poet,' and his brother, Rev Lyttleton Perry. There were plans to turn it into a museum. The building was being restored in 1997. There is a tradition of a secret tunnel running to Halesowen Abbey from it, but it is probably nothing more than a priest hole (BCWJ pp58il,63,64,65). (BCM April 1974 pp20p,21-23. Jan 1982 pp33-37). Supernatural. Haden Old Hall is haunted by Elaine and her lover, a monk, who were bricked up and died in the cellars or in one of the tunnels of the medieval Haden Old Hall (TB April 1974 pp18-19p of the tunnel they are said to have died in). Elaine or Eleanor of the Hayseech Mill fell in love with a young priest of Halesowen Abbey. The abbot was informed of them and partly went in search of them. They are said to have hidden in one of the secret passages between the abbey and Haden Old Hall and were bricked up in it. Ever since, the monk's ghost is often seen walking and praying, whilst Elaine's ghost is seen crying and with wringing hands. The story was told by William Green (1834-1924) whose father had been a gardener on the Haden Hall estate (BCWJ p104) (FOS pp20-21) (GOM p24). A ghost of a lady in white, seen on the stairs of the house and drifting across the surface of a pond in the S part of Haden Hill Park, has been identified with Elaine (MGH p46) (TB April 1974 p19. Feb 1992 p12) (MS&S p112). The ghost of Miss Eliza Haden (1790-1876) has been seen through a window of Haden Old Hall (TB Jan 1977 p1).

Hadley To the W of Six Roads End, Newborough.

Hadley End Hamlet 1m NW of Yoxall. Partly in Yoxall and Hamstall Ridware parishes.

Hadleygate House 1.5m E of Colton. Appears as Hadley Gate on 1834 OS map and Dower's map.

Hadleys Pool An old pool in Hanley which was in the market place. The old Town Hall was built on it (SHST p646).

Hag Cottage Near Swythamley; perhaps the same as the house Old Hag (see). Said to be named after its inhabitant, an hag or old witch who could transform herself into an hare (DPEM p61).

Hagley Former manor 0.5m SW of St Augustine church, Rugeley, centred on Hagley Hall. In Rugeley ancient parish. Has appeared as Hageleia (1130), Hagelega (1169), Haggele (1242), and Hageley (1570) (SPNO p106) (SPN p56). The name is from Anglo-Saxon 'hacga-leah,' 'the clearing where haws are found' (SPN p56).

Hagley Hall Hagley, Rugeley. The first and second manor houses of Hagley manor probably stood to W of Crossley Stone (300 yards E of the present hall, but since 1957 cut off by Western Springs Road) surrounded by a large moat which still existed in the mid 1950s. The first hall burnt down some time prior to c1388 (VCH vol 5 p156) (SSAHST 1982-3 p46). These old halls were probably occupied by the lords of Hagley manor - the de Puys, de Thomenhorns (Tamhorns), Muttons, and Westons (probably of Weston-un-der-Lizard). Sir Richard Weston (d1658), who rebuilt the hall in 1620, became a Papist. By 1725 the manor was held by Warin Faulkner (d1748) whose Jacobite sympathies seem to have led to the plundering of the hall in 1745 (VCH vol 5 p156). Assheton Curzon (Baron Curzon of Penn in 1794, Viscount Curzon in 1802) (d1820) had acquired the property by 1752 (VCH vol 5 p156) or some say in 1748 (SLM May 1950 p116). James Wyatt (1746-1813), architect of Blackbrook Farm, is said to have worked on the house (Biographical Dictionary of British Architects 1600-1840. Howard Colvin. 3rd ed 1995): Towards the end of the C18 Assheton Curzon had the house remodelled and greatly extended. The E side was altered in the early C19 (VCH vol 5 p156 il of in 1814 facing p52). It was known as Hagley Farm in the late C18 (SHOS vol 2 pl of Hagley Farm), and has also been called Bank Top (SHOS vol 2 p322) (VCH vol 5 p156). In 1851 the hall was owned or occupied by Hon Robert Curzon (d1863), son of Assheton Curzon, and the Baroness Zouche (W p20). In 1864 Hagley Hall was sold to William Harrison, local colliery owner. He sold it to the 3rd Marquess of Anglesey in 1878 or 1879. The 6th Marquess sold it to Cumberland Brown in 1927, who sold it to the SSWWC in or soon after 1931. (VCH vol 5 pp156,157). (W p475) (LGS p104) (CCF pp208-211) (VCH vol 5 il of in 1814 facing p52). Mr CJ Whieldon who had bought the hall in 1941 or 1942 was still living here in 1957 (VCH vol 5 p156). By 1971 the hall was being used as Rugeley Arts Centre (LTM Nov 1971 p9).

GROUNDS. Assheton Curzon improved the grounds towards the end of the C18 (VCH vol 5 p156). A small late C18 bridge spans Rising Brook. It is of vermiculated masonry and a wrought-iron balustrade with circular piers surmounted by vases (VCH vol 5 p157). In the cliff below the hall are a series of rock-cut chambers which may represent a C18 garden feature or grotto (VCH vol 5 p157). These are probably the same as the fantastic underground caverns in the grounds described by another writer. They are said to have been made by some eccentric squire in the C18. Or were used for some pagan or cult purpose: There is evidence of an altar in the central hall and there was a leaden statue of a river god known as the 'River God of Cannock Chase' (SLM May 1950 p116ps). Or it has been suggested that the caves were cut by colliery owner William Harrison to provide work for his unemployed miners (VCH vol 5 p157). The largest of the chambers has a barrel ceiling and two flanking aisles, the arcades supported on square-cut piers. A niche and pedestal at one end has prompted the suggestion that the room contained an altar and was used as a chapel (VCH vol 5 p157), leading some to think the chambers were built in the C17 for Roman Catholics to worship or hide in (SLM May 1950 p11). In the 1980s the cavern was uncovered as a small housing estate, known as The Coppice, was being built (source lost). There is an ice-house to the W of the hall, at SK 040180, sunk in the hillside consisting of a circular domed brick chamber approached by a narrow passage (BAST vol

72 pp22-23 pl 10) (VCH vol 5 p157). By 1990 it was in the garden of the caretaker's house (IHB p393). (GNHS p136).

Hailstone, The Former colossal and very curious rock out-crop formation embedded some 50 or 60 feet up on the W slopes of Turner's Hill (BCWJ p84) (TB Nov Dec 1972 p21. April May 1973 pp16-17ps. Jan 1983 p13). The outcrop, which stood eight or nine feet out of the hill, comprised dolerite (TB Sept 1998 p13il in 1845), or commonly called Rowley Rag stone (THS p35). It was often wrongly attributed to be a meteorite (BCWJ p84), firstly by Plot who doubted it was a work of nature (NHS p175) (O p223). A local tradition prevailing in the C19 was that it had been an ancient Druid shrine and the top slab used for sacrificial purposes, hence the slab was given the name of Altar Rock (TB Sept 1998 p13). The Hailstone, or Rowley Hailstone (THS p35), could be seen plainly from Clent Hill in 1831. It was described by Rev George Barrs in 1840 as 'rearing up in disarranged splendour and as a well known landmark were all climbed upon and worked smooth.' It looked almost like a piece of castellated masonry (O p223, il No. 9 facing p208 from 1845). The body of Matilda Stringer, a maidservant of Rowley Regis, was found at the foot of the Hailstone rock. She had been murdered. The case was known as 'The Hailstone Murder.' To discover the identity of her murderers the authorities reputedly used an ancient custom, known locally as 'Tutchen the Jed' or 'Bleeding the Corpse.' This involved contact between the suspects and the body of the victim, which it was believed would give a sign or signs if in the presence of the murderer (TB Nov/ Dec 1972 p21. March 1993 p15). The Hailstone was blown up by Thomas Redfern and Thomas Masters for road building material in c1879. During its demolition two of the dynamiters are said to have died in the blast, so bearing out an old Druid curse, to some, that if ever the Hailstone was destroyed, Saxon blood would stain the hillside (TB Jan 1983 p13. Sept 1998 p13). The name is preserved in a nearby inn called The Hailstone, owned at one time by the Danks family (TB Sept 1998 p13). (W p192). The name might have been coined due to the peculiar balls of rock in the Hailstone consisting of numerous onion-skin like formations with a hard core. Possibly they reminded someone in the distant past of hailstones (TB Jan 1983 p13).

Hailstone Farm Was demolished in 1972 (TB April May 1973 p17). Presumably stood near the Hailstone.

Hailstone Hill Over 0.5m NW of Rowley Regis. (SVS p437). Whether another name for 'The Hailstone' or a hill called Hailstone Hill on which was 'The Hailstone'? When 'The Hailstone' is described as being some 50 or 60 feet up Turner's Hill then this respects the fact that Hailstone Hill, if a hill, was connected to Turner's Hill on that hill's south westerly side. If a hill, then this was one in the Rowley Hills range. At any rate it has long been ravaged and obliterated by quarrying. It was so called probably from the curious rock formation on the hill known as 'The Hailstone'. See Hailstone, The.

Haines' Branch of the Walsall Canal. Spurred off the Walsall Canal at Great Bridge. Once reached the Pumphouse Brickworks, Sheepwash Forge and Denbigh Hall Colliery (BCM autumn 1995 pp19-20). Opened in 1833 (VCH vol 17 p14), now (1994) closed (HCMS No. 2).

Hakeston Hall At Park End near Audley, had become Brook(e) House by 1733, by which year it belonged to the lords of Audley manor (SHC 1944 p18) (A p31).

Hales Hamlet high on a slope above Coal Brook valley, 14.75m NW of Stafford. Formerly in Tyrley township in Staffs, although in Drayton-in-Hales ancient parish in Shrops. An ecclesiastical parish of Hales appears to have formed in 1856 (LGS p142), whilst Tyrley township became a separate civil parish from Drayton-in-Hales in 1866 (GLAUE p427). A Roman Villa of probable C2 date was discovered and excavated in 1926-8 by T Pape to the E of the village at SJ 72173370. A late C1 bronze fibula was found and Samian ware said to be of C2 (LGS p190) (Staffs Weekly Sentinel Dec 10 1927. April 28 1928. Nov 24 1928) (NSFCT 1928 pp98 plan, 99 p facing shows the E end of S wall -103 il of bronze fibula - 110. 1938 p113) (KES p101) (NSJFS 1964 p39. 1969 pp104-117 ps ils) (STM April 1966 p30) (BOE pp138,139) (SL p39) (MR p167). Excavated again in 1966 and a bath house was discovered, and again 1970-72. The site was under more or less constant occupation from at least a late Bronze Age date until mid C4 AD (NSJFS 1968 p100. 1974 pp1-20). Is perhaps the Roman station of Mediolanum (NSFCT 1928 p110). The villa lay off the Pennocrucium Whitchurch road (HOS p12). Hales, transferred to Staffs from Shrops in the C12, has appeared as Hales (1291) (SSE 1996 p14), and Halys (SHC 1945/ 6 p21). The name means 'meadow or pasture land' (DUIGNAN) (SPN p56). Hales was anciently in Almington manor (later absorbed into Tyrley manor) and had no village street like Almington (SHC 1945/ 6 p21). The private oratory of the lord of the manor of Tyrley (see) of the late C14 has been found at Hales. The church, St Mary, on the corner of Almington road and Blore Road, was built in 1856 (BOE p138).

Hales Green Hales. Has thought to be near the back gate of Hales Hall, where the two lanes form an angle. There were some cottages here by the later C16 (SHC 1945/ 6 p161 note).

Hales Hall Over 1m NE of Cheadle. In Cheadle ancient parish. A quantity of arrowheads was found in the vicinity of Hales Hall in 1831 (GM 1832 part 1 p414) and subsequently destroyed (SCSF p75). The estate of Hales Hall arose out of a division of the Cheadle Grange estate which was granted by the Countess of Kent to her legal advisor Seldon. In 1653 he bequeathed it to four of his friends of the Inner Temple, of whom Chief Justice Sir Matthew Hale was one. Hales Hall is built on Hale's quarter of Cheadle Grange estate and the hall is named after him. The house was built in 1712 by Archibald Grosvenor, in honour of his wife, granddaughter of Sir Matthew Hale (NSFCT 1906 p165) (CCT pp12,19) and is dated 1712 (BOE pp98-99 pl 41). (HOC pp148-151.il-153). Mrs Grosvenor outlived her husband and died in 1736. The estate then passed to her brother-in-law Edward Mountford of Walsall and his male heirs, upon condition that they assumed the name of Grosvenor. The Mountfords as Grosvenors remained at the hall until the death of Edward Smith G Grosvenor in 1830. The estate was then sold and broken up. It was occupied by Edward Whieldon (1787-1859), rector of Burslem (TOI p43) (SSAHST 1982-3 p91). The hall belonged to the Air Ministry in 1947 (SHC 1947 p54). The panelling in the dining room is by Robert Evans ('Adam Bede') (STM Nov 1964 p48). The hall is 'Adams Hall' in the essay 'Gilbert Hermer' a fiction (1908) by Capt Charles JB Masefield of Abbots Hay (NSFCT 1917 p107) (PSS p276). A phantom coach seen in the lanes about Cheadle is travelling to Hales Hall where it disappears as soon as it reaches the front door. It has been claimed that a former owner of Hales Hall had been attacked and killed by a highwayman during which the horses bolted and, with the coach, returned to the hall (TFTPM p66).

Hales Hall Hales. Built in 1806 (SVB p85). Had a wing added to it in Victorian times. Seat of Rev AH Buchannan in 1851 (W p20) and remained the seat of the Buchannans in the later C19 and the early C20. From 1915 it was the seat of Ernest Hall who made alterations to the front of the house. He was one of the pioneers who imported the first Friesian cattle from Holland into this country, and was a founder of the British Friesian Society. Ernest Byfield Hall of Hales Hall died in 1955 (mems in Hales church) (ALW pl 62 in c1909). On the Hales Hall estate one field is known as the Chapel Field and represents, according to tradition the site of a chapel (NSFCT 1927 pp149-150).

Hales View Farm At SK 021437 on B5417, ENE of Cheadle. Farmhouse converted into a very large and garish warehouse, for storage, and exhibiting for sale reclaimed architectural ornaments, by the eccentric Les Oakes (COS pp14p,15ps of interior and Les Oakes' collection of memorabilia) (ES June 18 1997 p10), hence the farm has also been called Fool's Paradise Hall. Here is the ornate stone doorway from the Mansion House, Cheadle. In 1997 the facade of the old Alhambra cinema, Normacot was being stored here (ES June 21 1997 p6p).

Halfcot Area and former township covering the NE part of Kinver ancient parish; formed a township with Dunsley from 1830 to the mid C19. Halfcot Farm is 0.5m NNE of Stourton. It was an occupied area by 1293 (VCH vol 20 pp123,149). Here was possibly a medieval village (SSAHST 1970 p35). The name means 'the cottage(s) at the nook of land' (SPN p72).

Halfcot Common Common which extended S from Stapenhill across the Stourbridge road and beyond Gibbet Lane. All the common was enclosed by 1780 (VCH vol 20 p138).

Halfhead Farm Famous timber-framed cottage which once belonged to Izaak Walton, author of Stafford (see), at Shallowford, 1m ENE of Chebsey. In Chebsey ancient parish. Now known as Izaak Walton's Cottage. At first rented by Izaak Walton, then subsequently bought by him, probably in c1654. Walton occasionally resided here to fish until his death in 1683. Walton left the cottage in his will to his son, Izaak Walton jnr, on certain conditions he was unable to fulfil and so it and a parcel of land devolved to Stafford corporation on Dec 29 1719. Izaak Walton's will directed that the annual rents from the cottage estate should be used to educate two poor boys, and provide a marriage-portion for a maid servant, and buy coal for the poor (LGS p210) (SN Millennium Special Jan 2000 p3). The Stafford Charity Trustees administered it until 1920 when it passed at their request to Staffs county council. Halfhead Farm cottage was sold, but bought by the Izaak Walton Cottage Trust in 1923. They restored it and opened it as a Walton museum in May 1924 (Staffs Chronicle spring 1924) (LGS p265). Sparks from the nearby railway ignited its thatched roof and the property was destroyed by fire in 1927 (SOPP pl 108p) (ASOP p91) and in May 1938 (ES May 11 1938 plps). Restored the following year. DoE II (SSW p2) (S p115) (KES p177p on facing p) (SOSH pp204,205,206) (STM Sept 1963 p49. Nov 1968 pp34-35)

(VB p57p) (AGT p10il) (MR pp95ps,96) (EOP p75p) (AA p257) (COS p61p). The name is a corruption of 'half hide' (VB p139) as it was anciently rated at half an hide of land (SHC 1914 p63). It has been suggested that 'Half' in Half Street, former name of Lichfield Street, Burton upon Trent, is from an Old Norse word indicating its use as a place for drying fishing nets (SPN p27).

Halford Is probably now Halfcot, Stourton. House 2m NW of Stourbridge (DUIGNAN). Appears in the C14 as Oldeford (SPN p119). The Stour was forded here by the ancient road leading from Shropshire to the S (DUIGNAN) (SPN p119).

Halford Branch of the Ridgacre Branch Canal. Spurred off the Ridgacre Branch near its end. Ran southwards to Gladstone Street and then tailed northwards for a short stretch ending at Vicarage Road, Hall End (BCM autumn 1995 p20). Opened in 1828 and largely abandoned in 1947 (VCH vol 17 p14).

Halfpenny Green Hamlet 1.5m NE of Bobbington. Formerly in Bobbington chapelry in Claverley ancient parish, Shrops. VCH implies that the name Halfpenny was in use by 1448: there was a cottage here by 1662, evidently the result of encroachment on Bobbington Common. There was a small hamlet here by 1775 (VCH vol 20 p65). There was a well in the centre of the green for which withdrawers of water were expected to pay half a penny (N&Q Series ii 22 Aug 1857 iv p147). Others say the name is derived from rents (VCH vol 20 p65). An airfield was opened here by the Air Ministry in 1939 (SVB p37). The airfield was originally named Bobbington but was changed to prevent confusion with Bovington airfield, because U.S.A.A.F. B17's frequently landed here by mistake. The airfield's worst disaster occurred on Aug 28 1972 in the 1972 Goodyear International Trophy Race when a plane crashed in Six Ashes Road killing Prince William of Gloucester (WMA vol 1 pp152-174a) (VCH vol 20 p67). Probably it was here where Dave Gauder, aged 30, frustrated the take-off of two Piper Cherokees by holding two tow ropes despite a pull of 1349 lb on July 16 1985 (GBR 1989 p179). In early 2000 Jim Dexter and Mike Kendrick broke the world airship speed record over the airfield reaching a speed of 94.7km per hour (Wolverhampton Chronicle March 10 2000 p15). The airfield, sometimes known as the 'Black Country Airport,' was renamed Birmingham Business Airport in 2000 to attract business traffic (BBC 1 Midlands Today. March 28 2000) (A Personal History of Halfpenny Green Airport. Cyril Harper) (BCM Spring 2000 p82). For Halfpenny Green vineyard see Upper Whittimere.

Halfway House House at SJ 829331, between Slindon and Millmeece (info Michael Cockin).

Halfway House Bentley (W p154). There is a Halfway House marked between Walsall and Red House on 1834 OS map.

Halfway House House 1.75m NW of Horton, situated on former Horton Hay, in Horton ancient parish. May have been created when Horton Hay was divided into farms in the later C17. It existed by 1805 (VCH vol 7 p72).

Halfway House Farm which stood on the W side of Kingstanding Road at its junction with Blenheim Way, Kingstanding. Formerly in Perry Barr township in Handsworth ancient parish. There may have been settlement here in Roman times; the site is half way between the Roman stage posts and camps of Wall and Metchley. By 1983 the site was occupied by Nixdorf House (MNB pp62,64) (KPP p12p).

Halfway House To the E of Rushall (1834 OS map).

Halingdene House off the Cannock Road, Penkridge. Built in 1840, for a retired colonial bishop, in the style of a colonial governor's residency (PVH p24). Rt Rev Sir Lovelace Tomlinson Stamer (b1829), formerly of Stoke Hall (see), Stoke-upon-Trent, died here in 1908 (POTP p199). In 1959 it was the offices of Cannock rural district council (VCH vol 5 p108). It is now Penkridge Community Centre. There is a small arboretum in the grounds (PVH pp24p,38,39il of the rear). Has also appeared as Haling Dene and Haling Grove (VCH vol 5 p108).

Hall Name for one of the Whitgreave prebends of Stafford Collegiate Church, united with Marston prebend from the C13 (VCH vol 3 p305).

Hall, The College Road area, Tettenhall. A mid C18 house which housed what became Tettenhall College (see Tettenhall Towers) from 1863 (VCH vol 20 p8).

Hall Bridge Yoxall. The bridge that crosses the Swarbourn to Woodhouses? (W p612).

Hall Court House which stood by Walsall Road, Cannock. Appears on the 1889 OS map 6 inch. The name is preserved in Hallcourt Crescent.

Hall Court Brook Runs past Simfield on the N side to Brook House Green and Ash Brook.

Hall Dale Near Dove Dale, but not a dale through which the Dove flows. Stanshope is at the head of it. It opens out into Dove Dale S of Dove Holes. Formerly called Stanshope Dale (VCH vol 7 p8). The N side of the dale rises to 1,027 feet (VCH vol 7 p9). The most notable rock feature in it is the Greek

Temple (see). Hall Dale was given to the NT in 1933 (NSFCT 1933 p187).

Halle Moor Barren area to W of Lichfield near the upper reaches of Trunkfield Brook. Appears in 1283 (VCH vol 14 p111).

Hall End Tiny area of Pattingham village, S of High Street. Pattingham manor house, mentioned by 1336, was probably at Hall End. It had a gate, probably a gatehouse, by 1405. Pattingham Hall (see) stood at Hall End, and may have been a rebuilding of the manor house (VCH vol 20 pp173,176). The name Hall End is preserved in Hall End Lane and Close.

Hall End Is present Peal Street, central Walsall. This street appears as Hole End in 1380 and Newgate Street in 1385-6; both names were in use in the C16 and C17, with Hall End as another variant (VCH vol 17 p147) (SNWA p60).

Hall End Tiny district of Wednesbury, at junction of Manor House Road and St Mary's Road, to NW of the church (WAM pp7 see map, 53). The name is not found in the medieval documents (HOWV p108). Was it this Hall End where Cecil Warburton lived in the early C17 (BS p492)?

Hall End A small district 2m SE of Wednesbury, near Churchfield, in West Bromwich ancient parish, in the vicinity of Vowles Brothers Foundry (SOWB p25). Was an inhabited area by the end of the C16 (VCH vol 17 p4). Walter Parsons, the giant, is said to have been born in the Hall End area of West Bromwich (see) in c1580.

Hall Farm Bushbury. About 1770 Thomas Bolton, the then tenant of Hall Farm, found a skeleton in a complete suit of armour in a pit. It was conjectured that the person might have been a straggling cuirasseur in the Civil Wars, as it was similar to that found near Shushions. The artifact was later thrown into a lumber room and lost (SHOS vol 2 p182).

Hall Farm Fulford. Red brick house dating from the early C18, but, according to NSFCT, obviously on the site of a much earlier house of stone (NSFCT 1917 p145).

Hallfields Northwood, Hanley (SHST p480).

Hallfields At Upper Bradley, Bilston (W p79). A furnace and ironworks of John Wilkinson (1728-1808), ironmaster, was at Hallfields (The Bradley Ironworks of John Wilkinson. GR Morton and WA Smith. reprint from Journal of the Iron and Steel Institute. vol 234. July 1966). By 1901 Hallfields was a small hamlet centred on the present Jordan Place (OS map 1901 sheet 67.04). Hallfields and the nearby Hall Green in Sedgley ancient parish may be named after Bradley Hall.

Hall Gate Farm C17 house on E side of Gratton village. Birthplace on March 9 1844 of George Heath, builder's apprentice and poet, who has become known as the Moorland Poet. When aged 15 he joined the Wesleyan Society at Gratton. His work includes 'Simple Poems' (1865), 'Heartstrings' (1866), and 'Tired Out' (1869). He died of consumption in 1869 aged 25. There is a runic cross designed by his friend Herbert Wilson Foster to his memory in Horton churchyard. A collection of his poems were published posthumously by Rev James Badnall and illustrated by Herbert Wilson Foster in 1870. The work contains a 'memoir' by Francis Redfern, author of HOU (NSFCT 1885 p56) (BS p218) (LGS pp150-151) (PSS pp254-260 il) (KES p113) (STM Aug 1966 p35p) (STMSM Feb 1974 p20 ils) (VB p214) (SVB p144) (E pp59,129) (SMOPP vol 2 p19) (VCH vol 7 p68) (HLSP pp181-185) (VFC p63). George Heath's old cottage at Gratton, with its gables showing the oak 'crucks' belonging to a former timbered structure was seen by the NSFC in May 1965 (NSJFS 1966 p69). The house was added to in 1991 (VCH vol 7 p65).

Hall Green Minute hamlet or single house half way between Upper and Lower Tean.

Hall Green Former hamlet 1.5m NE of Sedgley. In Sedgley ancient parish (W p200). Hall Green appears as Hall Greene in 1655 (HC p48). John Wilkinson (1728-1808), ironmaster at Bradley, Bilston, is believed to have lived at Hall Green (John Wilkinson. Ron Davies. 1987. Copy in Walsall Local History Centre. p20). Hall Green and the nearby Hallfields in Bilston township may be named after Bradley Hall.

Hall Green District over 2m N of West Bromwich. In West Bromwich parish. Here the West Bromwich Manor House is situated (WBOP p152p). On S side of Hydes Road at approximately SP 003941 stood a postmill which was in existence in 1616 when it was in the hands of the Lord of West Bromwich. In the early C18 it passed to Peter Giffard of Stafford and from him to Robert Throckmorton. Then to Sir John Throckmorton, Baronet of Berkshire. It still existed in 1822 but had certainly disappeared by the 1840s (WBJ p45).

Hall Hill The Audley end of New Road was formerly called Hall Hill (AHJ 1997 p99).

Hall Hill House in Botteslow township (HBST p526). Occurs on the 1834 and 1890 OS maps. The site is preserved in the present Hall Hill Drive on the S side of Dividy Road.

Hallhill House 0.75m E of Newtown. Formerly in Fawfieldhead township in Alstonefield ancient parish. Existed by 1406 (VCH vol 7 p27).

Hall Hill Manor Farm The manor house of Abbots Bromley (NSFCT 1926 p138). It stands above Abbots Bromley village, looking down on the main street and the parish church (AB p27). Said to have been originally a 'cella' of Burton Abbey, inhabited by the monks of that abbey when the abbey held Abbots Bromley manor (AB p27). Has appeared as Hall Hill House, the Manor House (1939), and the Manor Farm (1939). The house is erroneously called Hill Hall in 'Mary Queen of Scots' vol II p415 Agnes Strickland 1888, and Hill Hall Castle in 'Tragedy of Fotheringhay founded on the journal of D Bourgoing' Hon Mrs Maxwell Scott p22 1905 (AB pp1,11,60). After the dissolution, the Pagets purchased Abbots Bromley manor and came into possession of Hall Hill. Sir William Paget may have lived at Hall Hill during the period he was deprived of his estates in the mid 1550s. In the later C17 the property passed by inheritance from the Pagets to the Sanders or Saunders. In the 1860s the house passed from Joseph Sanders to his niece and her husband Mr Cox who sold it in 1883 to Mr Massey. It was sold in 1891 and has had several owners since; in 1939 it belonged to Staffs county council (AB pp35,39,48). Stebbing Shaw claimed that the seal he found at Hall Hill bore the coat of arms of Wulfric Spot (SHOS vol 2 p12). This is described as an absurd assumption by a contributor to NSFCT 1922 p76. There is a tradition of a passage running from Hall Hill to Abbot's Bromley church (AB p27). The house still (1998) stands (TRTC p28p). It is believed Mary, Queen of Scots, stayed one night here on Sept 21 1586 en route between Chartley and Tutbury. Whilst here she is believed to have written on a diamond-shaped piece of stained glass, 4.5 inches long, this inscription: 'Maria Regina Scotiae quondam transibat istam Villam 21 Sept 1586 usque Burton.' Shaw noted this glass in a window in the parlour of the house in the later C18; others have said it was in an upstairs bedroom, others reported it to be over the front door. However, in c1927 it was proved that the inscription was not written by the queen, but possibly by Willoughby, brother-in-law of the then Lord Paget, to commemorate her visit. It is possible that she only spent a few hours here and not one night (SHOS vol 1 part 1 p51) (AB pp43,44,63-64). Heraldic glass. In the late C18 Shaw noted in a fan light over the front door of the house coloured glass depicting a warrior in armour riding a richly-caparisoned horse, and having a coat of arms in the left-hand corner. The warrior depicted is thought to have been an abbot of Burton Abbey or the founder of the abbey, Earl Wulfric of Mercia, whilst the arms are said to be those of Wulfric's and or an abbot's. Pape in the Staffordshire Weekly Sentinel July 1927 thought the glass had later origins and the warrior depicted was of the late C15 or early C16 and the coat of arms were those of Burton collegiate church 1515-17 (AB pp27,32 note, 43). This panel along with that believed to be have an inscription written by Mary, Queen of Scots, and four others, all lozenge-shaped, disappeared when Hall Hill was sold in 1891. The glass appears to have been with a Mr Lawrence Chew, a Manchester solicitor, until 1914, thereafter it was sold to a London dealer. In 1927 it was brought to the attention of interested parties in Staffs and passed to the Trustees of the WSL for safe-keeping; the library still (1998) keeps it. By 1927 all the glass had been fitted into the present rectangular window-light measuring 37 inches by 18 inches; although it may always have been fitted into this window-light. The window-light has variously been known as the 'Mary Pane,' 'The Mounted Warrior Glass,' and 'Heraldic Glass.' The other lozenge-shaped panels bear; the Scriptural monogram 'I.H.S;' the coat of arms of Thomas, third Lord Paget; the Paget crest of an heraldic tiger tufted and chained, and dated below 1599; and a less interesting broken design showing some foliage. Some of these panels may have adorned the chapel or oratory of the cell of the monks who formerly occupied the site at Hall Hill (NSFCT 1909 p198) (The Connoisseur Dec 1927) (NSFCT 1927 p158. 1929 p177) (AB pp27,42-66 il) (SVB p9). The house had an ancient tapestry or tapestries depicting 'Potiphar's wife sewing Joseph's coat,' 'The Cup is found in Benjamin's Sack,' 'Joseph interpreting Pharaoh's Dream' (AB pp42-66il). The tapestry was sold when Hall Hill was sold in 1891 (NSFCT 1928 p156) (NSSG p3), others say that it was sold in 1901 (NSFCT 1909 p198). It was said to have been kept at Holyrood, Edinburgh, in 1909. But was found to have never been there. It was in fact kept with the heraldic glass from Hall Hill by a Mr Lawrence Chew, a Manchester solicitor, until 1914. The tapestry was then sold to a Mr Simmonds, a London dealer. Its whereabouts in 1939 was unknown (AB pp42-66il).

Hall House Cheddleton. The capital messuage of Cheddleton manor. It stood or stands in the area of the house, Cheddleton Park and Cumberledge Park (CVH p160).

Hall House Tunstall. In existence by 1829. Seat of Ralph Hall owner of the Swan Works until the 1860s. The house was demolished in the early C20 and the site has been built on. Its lodges of the 1830s were still in Copes Avenue in c1960 (VCH vol 8 p85).

Hall House Farm House to N of Rushton Spencer church, so called in 1600. Formerly in Rushton Spencer township in Leek ancient parish (VCH vol 7 p223).

Hall-in-the-Hole Nickname for a farmhouse on the outskirts of Hill Ridware to the NE. It may be a corruption of Alwynehul, Aylwynehul (1340), and as Ailewynehul (1397), an unlocated place in Mavesyn Ridware parish (SHOS vol 1 pp199-200).

Hall Orchard A house close to Cheadle church, which may represent the site of the original Cheadle manor house (NSFCT 1913 p143).

Hall o' th' Wood Timber-framed hall 0.5m E of Balterley, formerly in Barthomley ancient parish, Cheshire. Said by Lysons in his History of Cheshire p501 to have been built by Thomas Wood, Lord Chief Justice of the Common Pleas, but he is incorrect (BART p166). It was built by George Wood a judge of Chester in 1557. He possessed Balterley manor by purchase probably from the Blounts; but if so not before 1580 (SHC 1909 p234 note). Pevsner, who described the hall as 'one of the most delightful black and white houses in the county,' thought it was built later than 1557 (BOE p65). From George Wood the estate passed to his daughter who married William Lawton in 1560. The estate, Lysons says, passed to one of the family of Kelsall by marriage. Parrot in 1733 implies it belonged to a Kelsall in the early C17 and was owned by them in 1733. Hincliffe thinks it was purchased by Richard Kelsall in the earlier C17. The Kelsall family became extinct when William Kelsall died in 1802. The estate was then inherited by the Tait family from whom Samuel Peake of Silverdale purchased it. In the earlier C19 his son sold it to Mr Goodfellow of Tunstall (BART pp165-172) (SHC 1944 pxvi). In 1921 it was described as recently restored (NSFCT 1921 p141) (NSSG p5) (MR p27p). Has also appeared as Hall o' Wood and Hall a Wood (Plot's map).

Hallriddings Under 1.5m WNW of Rocester, to SW of Stubwood.

Hallsteds Barrow 0.5m SSW of Okeover Hall. Is part of a dry moat which surrounded the old hall, said by tradition to have belonged to the Cockain family (NHS p449), and, or either, the ancient lords of Okeover (AAD p200). Has also appeared as Hallsteads Barrow.

Hallwater Farm In Endon village on S side of Hallwater Lane. Is of the C17. Hallwater Lane was so called in 1495 (VCH vol 7 p177).

Halmer End (locally 'Ommerend BOJ book 2 p66). Village on high ground overlooking the Cheshire Plain over 0.5m NW of Alsager Bank. Now merges with Alsagers Bank. Former township in Audley ancient parish (SHC 1944 pxvi). Has also appeared as Hammerend (Bowen's map), and Halmor End (c1875) (Charities of Staffordshire further report p254). For Halmerend Groats see Hayes Wood. For the murder of William Cooper in 1844 see The Hays. Mary Jane Burrows, a dwarf born in Halmerend in 1869, joined Wall's (or Well's) Ghost Show at Tunstall in c1896, and became something of a celebrity. She was only 42 inches high and 48 lb in weight. She was travelling with the show in Dublin in 1916 during the Easter Rising. She was advertised as 'Princess Tiny, the renowned lady midget.' Known in the Halmerend district as 'Little Polly' and in the Potteries as 'Dot,' Mary Burrows died in 1917 (Weekly Sentinel. March 3 1918) (AHJ 1998 p90). Sarah Hammond of Halmer End died at Bradwell Hall Nursing Home aged 104 (ES Oct 27 1993 p7p. April 20 1994 p13p).

Halmerend Hall Hall 0.75m NW of Halmer End (AOPP pl 28).

Hamel Former hamlet 0.75m NE of Burslem; the homestead of Sneyd (NSSG p10). Or, by the C18, an alternative name for the whole of Sneyd township (VCH vol 8 p106). Formerly in Burslem chapelry in Stoke-upon-Trent ancient parish. Now submerged into Burslem. It had its own small church, St Werburgh (OTP p134). Has also appeared as Hamill (W p269). A pottery here was referred to by Scarratt as the old Hamil, although, mainly demolished, a part had been turned into a private residence.

Hamel Grange Former cottage which appears to have been formerly known as Jackfield (MMM p69), the seat of the Leighs since the early C17. The cottage, later known as Hamel or Hamil Grange, stood on land opposite the present Port Vale FC ground in Hamil Road. The most famous member of the Leigh family was the Burslem witch, Margaret or **Molly Leigh**, born here in c1685 (SLM Dec 1947 p50ps) (STM July 1970 p31p) (MMM p69) (ES May 8 1995 p8p). She was probably the daughter of William and Margaret Leigh of Burslem and niece of Thomas Leigh of the Hamil, the father of Mrs Thomas Wedgwood of the Churchyard House, the grandmother of Josiah Wedgwood I (NSF pp33-36) (ES May 8 1995 p8). Molly Leigh had a smallholding with a herd of cows in the Blue Stone area and sold milk and butter. She was ridiculed for being very ugly and consequently did not attend church. Probably on account of these factors she was labelled a witch, and consequently was made an outcast. It was at Jackfield she died in 1748 (reputedly on April 1) (VCH vol 8 p120 note 57) (SSGLST p28) (COS p25). After she was bur-

ied in St John's churchyard, Burslem, there were sightings of her ghost in the churchyard and at her cottage where her ghost was found knitting by the fire mumbling to herself

'Weight and measure sold I never,
Milk and water sold I ever.'

To lay the ghost, Burslem vicar, Rev Thomas Spencer, embarked on an elaborate exorcism service involving her re-interment in the churchyard by the S side of the church on a north south axis at right angles to the other graves and the placing of a caged blackbird in her coffin. However, her ghost has been frequently seen since in the churchyard area, for instance on July 17 1967 by Mr and Mrs Boland (MMM p71) (PL pp88-89), and knowledge of the ghost frightened Mrs Eaton when a child in the 1920s. The ghost still haunted the churchyard in the 1990s (GLS pp28,29). The present heavy chest tomb over her grave, visited by the folklorist Miss Jackson in the late C19, may have come from Hulton Abbey (SFL pp120,121) (MR p66p of her grave; she is erroneously called Peggy Lee). In 1998 prostitutes soliciting in the vicinity of the tomb were becoming troublesome (ES April 20 1998 p7). There are several traditions associated with her and her tomb; that she was the great-aunt of Josiah Wedgwood I (see above); that Burslem children have challenged each other for centuries to chant the jingle

'Molly Leigh, follow me
Molly Leigh, follow me'

whilst walking around her tomb, but few have accepted the challenge (MMM p71) (TFTP pp14-18 il); that Burslem people piled extra stones on her tomb to keep her spirit in (GLS p28). By the late 1990s the public mood was more enlightened towards Molly Leigh and there was a campaign to rid her of the label of witch (ES Oct 16 1998 p87. Nov 27 1998 p84. Jan 1 1999 p11). (Staffs Mercury Dec 25 1830) (Broughton's Scrapbook p448) (ROS vol 1 pp17-19) (NSFCT 1896 pp118-119) (FLJ 1941 p237) (STM Oct 1971 p23p of her grave) (FOS p22) (AGT p82) (POP p32) (LLST p5) (STMSM March 1975 pp24,25. July 1980 p32) (TFTP pp14-18 il) (SCS p10) (EGH pp40-42) (Library of the Unexplained - Great Mysteries. Robert Jackson. 1992 p54) (TB May 1993 p5) (SMML pp13-17). By 1760 Jackfield was held by another family and subsequently became known as Hamel Grange. A low thatched building known as Molly Leigh's cottage was still standing in 1900 (HBST p223) (SLM Dec 1947 p50p) (VCH vol 8 p120 note 57) (SSGLST p27). Scarratt went round the cottage many times. He noted the well was still in the buttery where it was said Molly adulterated her milk. The cottage garden was close to the footpath going up the Hamil towards Blue Stone Tollgate. Her garden was about 200 yards square (OTP p101).

Hamley House Colton. Has also appeared as Homeley (CWF p178).

Hamley Heath Hamlet N of Colton. Has also appeared as Hanby Heath (mid C19) (W p414). In Colton parish.

Hamley Park Wood 0.75m SW of Pattingham on Shrops Staffs border. In Pattingham ancient parish. Former medieval park which was considerably larger than the existing wood. Known as Armeley Park by 1452 still known as this in 1841. It was later called Hamley Park (VCH vol 20 p272).

Hammer Bank Former small hamlet on a steep slope at Quarry Bank, Brierley Hill. It extended from the junction of Evers Street, Quarry Bank, High Street and Forge Lane. The area contained a few scattered houses until well after WW2. The name is presumably after the hammering of iron at the nearby forge. It may have erroneously appeared as 'Homer Bank' or 'Homer Hill,' a hamlet on the other side of the Stour in Cradley, Worcs (SNSV vol 1 p156). There was a Hammer Inn on the N side of High Street here in 1822 (WFK p18).

Hammer Houses Marked on Pigot & son map (1830) N of Shallowford. In Chebsey parish (W p388). The timber-framed Hammer House at Norton Bridge was a farm in 1920 but was not a farm by 1989 (EOP p76p).

Hammerwich Village on a hill above Crane Brook 13.5m SE of Stafford. Former out-township in the SW corner of St Michael's parish, Lichfield (VCH vol 14 p258), anciently in Cannock Forest. Two 'Hammerwich' settlements are mentioned in DB (SL p46) (VCH vol 14 p259), where it is written Humeruuich. It appears in the C13 as Hamerwic (SPN p57). The **name** is from Anglo-Saxon 'hamor,' 'hill,' 'the village by a hill' (VCH vol 14 p259) (SPN p57). Or 'smithy wic' (SSE 1996 p14). 'Hammer village' is a very unsatisfactory interpretation, it is probably 'Homa or Hama's village' (DUIGNAN). A chapel, possibly on the site of the later **church**, may have had C12 origins. The church, St John the Baptist, on the E side of Church Lane, on an elevated site with a view to the W, was rebuilt in 1872 (VCH vol 14 pp269,271). Hammerwich was a peculiar jurisdiction of the dean of Lichfield cathedral (GLAUE). **Medieval development**. By the C14 there were three Hammerwich centres - Middleton, Netherton, and Overton, each with its own green, giving each the appellation 'Green.' Middleton Green seems to have been the open space in the village centre now known as the village green. Netherton Green lay around the junction of Hall Lane and Coppice Lane, to the ESE of Middleton Green. Overton Green lay along Overton Lane between its junction with Pingle Lane and Coppy Nook Lane (LTM Jan Feb 1972 p18) (VCH vol 14 p259). Proceedings against the Hammerwich vill for deliberately causing a fire in Cannock Forest were brought before the forest courts in 1262. This fire is reputed to have cleared the land on which Burntwood grew and gave Burntwood its name (DUIGNAN) (VCH vol 14 p198). One of the seven dances of the Lichfield Morris is called 'The Vandalls of Hammerwich.' This is believed to refer to an incident in Norman times when some of the villeins of Hammerwich set fire to the woods in Cannock Forest (LTM Nov 1971 pp10-11) (MR p170). There was a **windmill** at Hammerwich in 1300. It is the earliest windmill in Staffs, although one in Blymhill parish may be older (VCH vol 14 p267). There was a windmill in Chapel field in 1574 (VCH vol 14 p267). The windmill tower of Speedwell Mill still stands at SK 067073. The windmill recorded in 1300 may have stood on this site (BEV p180). The present windmill was built in 1779 by Henry Middleton. It is reputed to be one of the last working mills in the county (BEV p180) and was converted to a house in 1908 (VCH vol 14 p267) or 1909 (WBJ p25) when the tower gained a castellated top. The house lost this in 1976 when a fourth storey was added with a fibre glass top (WBJ p25 il xxix in 1973 and xxx in 1984). (LTM Jan Feb 1972 p19) (WIS pp11,19). Hammerwich became a **separate ecclesiastical parish** in 1737 and a separate civil parish in 1866. Civilly it entered Brownhills urban district when it was formed in 1894, but was removed to Lichfield rural district in 1896 (GLAUE p412). Common land at Hammerwich, a remnant of Cannock Forest, was enclosed in 1856 (PCC p16) and or 1857 (MH 1994 p108). Hammerwich **railway** station on the Lichfield-Walsall line opened at Netherton on April 9 1849 (SSR p10). Hammerwich **cottage hospital** in Hospital Road, 1m NW of Hammerwich, opened in 1882. It is named after Thomas Barber Wright, the Birmingham manufacturer, and founder of Hospital Sunday in 1859, who lived at Quarry House (see), Hamstead, and later at Blackroot House (see), Hammerwich (MR p170) (VCH vol 14 p269). In the later C17 Dr Plot noted the **strange noises** heard by Francis Aldridge in 1668 at Hammerwich. The noises, heard at 2.00 am, sounded like a sort of whistling in the air, a melodious tune coming from some winged creatures. Perhaps it was from the wild geese that the colliers of Wednesbury mistook for Gabriels hounds (NHS p22).

Hammerwich Hall Formerly Hammerwich House. N of Hammerwich village centre, at SK 068077. There had been a farmhouse on the site since at least 1824. The farmhouse was rebuilt in c1870 and was known as Hammerwich House by 1868. From 1941 it became a hospital annex and was converted into a girls' remand home in 1946, later becoming a children's home. In 1985 it became a residential home for the elderly and about this time the name was changed to Hammerwich Hall (VCH vol 14 p263).

Hammerwich Hall Farm Formerly Hammerwich Hall. To the ESE of Hammerwich, close to the Hammerwich settlement of Netherton, at SK 075073. Inhabited by 1645 and was known as Hammerwich Hall by 1741. The old timber-framed range was demolished in 1960 and a new house built in its place (VCH vol 14 pp262-263).

Hammerwich House Farm To NW of Hammerwich church at SK 068074. Brick farmhouse, which was described in 1833 as newly built (VCH vol 14 p263-264).

Hammerwich Park Farewell Priory had a park at Hammerwich in the late 1370s (VCH vol 14 p267).

Hammerwich Square Tiny hamlet W of Hammerwich. Existed by 1871 when several mines were working here (VCH vol 14 p259).

Hamps, River According to OS maps the source is at SK 033598 on the top of Morridge, 0.25m SSW of the Mermaid Inn. Others say it is SE of Feltysitch (NSFCT 1927 pp101-102). (GNHS p21). The river is approximately 14.5m in length. It joins the Manifold opposite Beeston Tor. Up stream at a little below, or at (NSFCT 1917 p27), Waterhouses the river sinks into the ground and follows a subterranean channel like the Manifold (see). The Hamps joins the Manifold at Beeston Tor; below ground in summer; above and below ground in winter; or there is another subterranean channel for the Hamps which takes a short cut under the hills, and joins the Manifold at Hamps Spring? (NHS pp88-89) (Bowen's map) (OL vol 2 pp287-289) (LGS p248) (PDS&C p8). The Hamps and the Manifold have been compared to the Alpheus and Arethusa famed in Greek mythology for their underground united courses (NSFCT 1878 p34). Has appeared as Hanespe (c1200), Honsp (1223. 1227),

Hans (1577. 1686), Hanse (c1600), Hunsye (Speed's map), Hamps Fall (1751), Churnet (T Hutchinson's map 1798), and Hamps (1820) (NHS) (SOS) (NSFCT 1925 p79) (SPNO p11) (SPN p57). The name means 'the small river' (NSFCT 1908 p127). Or perhaps from Middle English 'hampre' 'hampres' or modern 'hamper' some of the meanings of which are 'to entangle, restrain, clog, hold back, fetter, shackle' some of which allude to the eccentricity of the river (DUIGNAN). Is from Old Welsh and appropriately means 'dry in summer' (NSFCT 1946 p159) (SPNO p11) (SPN p57). Is of Celtic origin (HOS p13).

Hamps Spring Calton. Spring marked on OS map 1:25,000 at SK 127507, by the Manifold 0.25m SSE of Musden Grange. Is this where the Hamps re-emerges, and joins the Manifold, after taking a short-cut subterranean channel under the hills instead of joining the Manifold at Beeston Tor? Porter says the Hamps reappears a few feet from the Manifold at Ilam (PDS&C p8).

Hamps Valley Valley of the River Hamps. Mainly considered to be that stretch of the Hamps from Waterhouses to Beeston Tor. A large part of the valley became NT property in 1936 (NSFCT 1936 p31).

Hampton Former hamlet in Newton township in Blithfield ancient parish. Belonged to Burton Abbey at time of DB. The de Hamptons were often in conflict with the Bagots in the C14. Hampton seems to have been held by Geoffrey de Hampton of John Bagot in 1402. Its population was absorbed by Newton. Hampton Wood, Hampton Hayes and Hampton Dale are all to be found in a survey of 1677. Hampton is described as a small farm in 1679. The name of Hampton is preserved in the two fields, Big and Little Hampton, in the Rectory farm (SHC 1908 pp34,44. 1914 pp167-168. 1919 p32) (SVB p36).

Hampton Hill Central Wolverhampton. Hill and incline on which St Peter's church is situated.

Hampton Lodge Over 1.25m N of Kinver, W of Stourton Hall, in Kinver ancient parish. Built by Jane Mary Davenport in 1846. Formerly Hampton House (VCH vol 20 p123).

Hampton Valley 1.5m SE of Enville. Valley on E side of Enville Common.

Hamstall Hall Brick hall with stone dressings (BOE p140) of early C17 origin, in Hamstall Ridware village, has long been mostly demolished, with some parts remaining and built onto. The estate was owned by a branch of the Fitzherbert family. It was sold to Sir Thomas Leigh in 1601 and the hall may date from the early C17 (SSAHST 1984-85 p49). It was occupied by the Leighs only to c1666 (SSAHST 1984-85 p49), and was omitted from Plot's map (SH p58). The hall, remaining with the Leighs, was mainly tenanted from the late C17. It has been argued that between 1708 and 1753 the great hall was partly demolished or partly destroyed by fire. Some demolition and rebuilding was taking place in the 1780s. Large scale demolition and renovation again took place in 1821 (SSAHST 1984-85 pp52,71,73,75). In the late C18 Shaw saw in the hall a leather pistol proof coat of mail, musquet, and broad sword with pistols and holster cases, and all other accoutrements for a horseman, which the lord of this manor provided for Charles I in the Civil War (W p558). He was also shown a scold's bridle (SHOS vol 1 p157). Some panelling from the old hall was in the dining room and some linenfold panelling was in the bedroom; the date for this is probably c1530-40 (NMR) (W p558). William Jaggard (d1869) was of Hamstall Hall (chest tomb in Hamstall Ridware churchyard). The Leighs sold the estate in 1920 (HR). Lieut Col Sir Ian Walker Bart DSO sold the estate in 1946 (HR). The hall was damaged by fire in 1964 (SSAHST 1984-85 p54). The present (late C20) fifty foot **Tower** or Watch Tower (SHOS vol 1 p157 pl vii facing p157), ivy-clad when Masefield saw it in the early C20 (LGS p201), formed a part of the hall complex, as did the present **Loggia** or Porch, called in the sales particulars (1946) the Stone Columned and Balconied Baldachin (HR).

GROUNDS. There was a large **courtyard** and a second one to the W of it with outbuildings (BOE p140). The smaller quadrangular building has recently (c1995) been converted into an arts centre. The brick and stone **Gatehouse** with two polygonal turrets is said to date from the period c1820 (SSAHST 1984-85 p71), but was seen by Shaw at the end of the C18 (SHOS vol 1 pl vii facing p157). In the C20 it was used as a dovecote (LGS p201) (NSFCT 1924 pp87-88il) (SLM Summer 1958 pp34-35,37 p of). There is or was an Elizabethan **Yew Walk** stretching throughout the whole width at the N end of the walled-in garden (HR many notes and ils).

Hamstall Ridware Ancient parish and village at the foot of a promontory by the Blithe 12m ESE of Stafford. A perforated stone axe-hammer of Neolithic or Bronze Age has been found in Hamstall Ridware parish (SHOS vol 1 intro to the General History p12) (NSFCT 1878 p21. vol 48 p212) (NSJFS 1964 p24). A stone hammer head was at new Hamstall Ridware Hall in 1877 (NSFCT 1913 pp211,212). The **name** has appeared as Rideware (1004), Rideware (DB), Ridvare (DB), Hamstede Ridewale, Hamstal Media Ridewar (SPN p98), and Hamstal Ridewar (1242) (SSE 1996 p17). 'Ridware' is from rhyd and wara (or waru) (HOA p10): Rhyd from Celtic meaning a river ford, and wara from Anglo-Saxon meaning inhabitants: so together, Ridware has been taken to mean 'ford dwellers' (SHOS vol 1 p150) (SL p56) (NSJFS 1981 p3). Another explanation is that the root Gaelic 'rea' rapid or the Welsh 'rhe' swift ('rhe' is one of the five primary river roots) occur in 'Ridware' (NSFCT 1908 p131). 'Hamstall' is of Saxon derivation meaning homestall or homestead, the place of the house (SHOS vol 1 p152) (SPN p98) and was adopted to designate this Ridware the original settlement (SL p57) (SPN p98) (SL p56). Hamstall Ridware is probably the earliest Ridware settlement (SL p57); it has always been the largest. Early lords of the **manor**, the de Ridewares may have had a seat at Moat Close (see), S of Hamstall Ridware village near the Blithe. The Rydeware Chartulary is a quarto volume containing 66 folios of parchment which are filled on both sides with handwriting of the early part of the C14. It contains information on the manors of Hamstall Ridware, Boylestone (Derbys), Draycott-under-Needwood, Callingwood. It was probably compiled by monks of Merivale and had become attached to the Gresley papers by the C19 (SHC 1895 pp229-302). The parish **church**, St Michael and All Angels, on the E side of Blithbury Road through a field, was built in c1130 (The Church of St Michael and All Angels, Hamstall Ridware. RF Elton. 1985). The parish was originally a part of Needwood Forest and as such formed a nominal part of Hanbury parish. It came into being between 1086 and 1291 (SHC 1916 pp197-198). The parish feast was on the nearest Sunday to old Michaelmas day in the C19 (W p558). A perambulation of the bounds of Hamstall Ridware parish is recorded in 1285 (SHOS vol 1 p152). Two **hermits** are recorded living in the wood of Hamstall Ridware in the Middle Ages (VCH vol 3 p136). A **silver medieval seal matrix** displaying the arms of Walter de Thornton was found in Hamstall Ridware parish in June 1998. It went to the Potteries Museum (info Debbie Ford, Potteries Museum). There was a **scold's bridle** (SHOS vol 1 p157) or gagging cage (S&W p96) kept at old Hamstall Hall. The bridle continued to be preserved at the Hamstall Hall house after the old hall was pulled down. It was there in 1877 when the NSFC visited (NSFCT 1913 pp211,212). But by 1910 it had been taken to Stoneleigh Abbey, Warws (LGS p201) (SCSF p123) (HR pp41-42). **Natural History.** At the house of Jane Arnold at Hamstall Ridware, Dr Plot noted, a pear tree which bore fruit twice in a year; in June and at Michaelmas 1680 (NHS p226) (SD p21). **Ridware History Society**, covering the Ridwares, was formed in 1990 (info Peter Clarke). **Persons and visitors. William Evans** who lived in the early C19 was known locally as the 'Hamstall Giant' for his great strength; he made some body-snatchers take a body back to the churchyard (HR pp10-11). **Jane Austen** reputedly stayed with her cousin, Rev Edward Cooper (b1770), in the old Rectory, at Hamstall Ridware, and may have written some of her work here. Donald Greene in the English Department at the University of Southern California has confirmed the tradition of her stay; she stayed here with her mother and sister Casandra in 1806. Reputedly, Austen found her cousin, rector of Hamstall Ridware to his death in 1833, rather boring (SVB p88) (HR pp33-35). The same Rectory or a more recent one was said to be haunted by a poltergeist in the 1930s (POE pp303-306 pl - an account by Rev GS Hewins from Aug 1938). Bill Sherratt one of the oldest villagers alive in 1988 remembered stories of a ginger-haired ghost. The Rectory has four or more attics. In the Coussmakes time the girls here frequently complained of noises and ghost appearances (HR p56). **Francis G Cholmondeley**, poet, was born in Hamstall Ridware on March 23 1850; his father was Hon and Rev Henry Pitt Cholmondeley. In 1872 he won the Newdigate Prize for his poem, 'The Burning of Paris' (PSS pp295-297) (VFC p27).

Hamstall Ridware Manor House Perhaps stood on or near the site of the present Hamstall Hall (SSAHST 1984-85 p47).

Hamstall Ridware Park Medieval deer park at Hamstall Ridware taken out of Needwood Forest (EDP p176).

Hamstead Former village by the Tame and now a suburb of Birmingham over 1.25m S of Great Barr. In Handsworth ancient parish. Hamstead may have appeared in DB under Oxfordshire as Hunesworde (MNB p32). The name first appears in a recognizable form in 1213 (MNB p32). It appears as Hampsted in 1564 (SHC 1938 p185), and later as Hampstead (W p695) (OS map 1834). It is from Anglo-Saxon 'ham-stede' meaning 'home stead' (DUIGNAN). The original settlement was probably N of the Tame in Perry Barr township, but Hamstead old and new halls lay on the S side of the Tame in Handsworth township (VCHWA vol 7 p24) (MNB p54). The **railway** station on the GJR at Hamstead was known as 'Great Barr Station' (ADY p7). The mining village of Hamstead which grew rapidly after the opening of Hamstead Colliery in 1875 had been demolished by 1983 (WMVB p75) (MNB pp60,69). The **church**, St Paul, Walsall Road, was built in 1892 (BOEWA p181). Became a separate ecclesiastical parish in 1894 (GLAUE p412). Hamstead was removed to Birmingham diocese in 1905 (VCH vol 17 p60).

In 1911 Hamstead was removed to Birmingham, Warws. The post-WW2 housing estate to the S and SE of Hamstead New Hall (Hamstead Hall Secondary School) is sometimes known as the Grestone Estate, after the builders - Greaves and Johnstone (WMVB p76). Bishop **Francis Asbury**, founder of the Methodist Episcopal Church and first bishop of the American Methodist Church (1785), was born on Aug 20 or 21 1745 in a simple cottage at the foot of old Tame Bridge, later known as Hamstead Bridge. The cottage was demolished in the C19 for the railway and was near to the present Hamstead railway station. When still a baby his parents moved to Newton Road, Newton (see). Asbury was apprenticed to an ironmaster in West Bromwich. When aged 15 Asbury held Methodist meetings in his father's house, and locally at Wednesbury, Bromwich Heath, and Sutton Coldfield. He entered the Methodist ministry in Beds in 1767, and became known as a leader in Methodist locally. He was sent by John Wesley as the first Methodist bishop of America. In 1773 he attended his first American Methodist Conference. During his career he is said to have travelled 150,000 miles, mostly on horseback, across the USA; preached 18,000 sermons; took the chair at 270 conferences, and ordained 3000 ministers. He died in Fredericksburg, Virginia, on March 31 1816. The Asbury Memorial Chapel, Holyhead Road, Handsworth, was named after him, and opened on Good Friday 1873. A statue was erected to his memory in Washington, USA, in 1918 (HPPE pp7,8) (TBS p22) (BCM summer 1995 p45) (250th Anniversary of the birth of Francis Asbury. Aug 1995).

Hamstead Bridge Hamstead. Bishop Francis Asbury was born at the foot of it; his parents removed to Newton Road, Great Barr, shortly after his birth (OWB p92).

Hamstead End Former area or liberty in Handsworth ancient parish (HANDR pviii).

Hamstead Hall Park Medieval deer park belonging to the Wyrleys of Hamstead Old Hall. In 1538 it covered 300 acres and lay in the area of the present Handsworth Golf Course and residence area W of Hamstead Hill (MNB p40).

Hamstead Hill Hill S of Hamstead Hall. HH Horsley, an octogenarian, writing in 1890, claimed that in his youth a descendant of Sir Christopher Wren lived at the bottom of Hamstead Hill (TBS p26).

Hamstead House Stood back from Tan House Lane, now known as Hamstead Road, Hamstead. The house was built after the Napoleonic Wars. Seat of Hamstead Colliery manager, Isaac Meacham, to c1902 (VH pp4p,il,5,6).

Hamstead New Hall Hamstead. The new hall was built 0.25m to the W of the old hall by Sir John Wyrley in 1690. It was enlarged in 1735 (WMVB p74). (SHOS vol 2 p111 pl xvi of the hall). Sir John Wyrley was succeeded by his nephew, Humphrey Wyrley. Humphrey's daughter and heir, Sybil, married Dr Peter Birch of Harborne. Their two sons adopted the surname Wyrley-Birch. Both died without issue and the estate passed to a relative George Birch of Harborne, who married Anne Lane, granddaughter of Mary Wyrley (THS p157) (HPPE p43). George Wyrley-Birch left the hall in 1813 (HPPE p43), and sold it and much of the estate to the Earl of Dartmouth of Sandwell Hall (see) in 1819. The hall was never again owner-occupied. At first it was used as a dower house to Sandwell Hall, followed by short leases (WMVB p75). The Moilliets of Smethwick Grove (see) moved to Hamstead Hall in 1826 (STELE March 20 1953 p) (VCH vol 17 p105) and were still there in 1841. It was the seat of William Bagnall, coal and ironmaster, in 1851 and 1861. From 1886 to 1890 the hall was leased to George Kynoch, the Witton industrialist. Another tenant was Mr Kirkham, a herbalist of Smallbrook Street, who opened the grounds as an 'Entertainment Garden.' During WW1 the hall was used as a hostel (W p20) (WMVB p75). The hall was pulled down in c1935 (VCHWA vol 7 p69) or 1936 (WMVB p76). (VH pp55p,59). Hamstead Secondary School, nearly 1m SSW of St Paul's church, Walsall Road, now stands on the site.

GROUNDS. A hermit was employed at weekends to occupy the natural cave by the banks of the Tame for guests in the late C19 (TBS p31) (VH p60). The cave was a hole in the sandstone bank. It was identifiable though destroyed by 1983 (MNB p41). The ice-house at SP 043926, said to have been built in c1775, was circular and partly below ground and topped with a dome (Birmingham Weekly Post April 17 1936) (N&Q March 29 1941) (TBS p31) (IHB p442). Some circular brick courses of the ice-house remained among tall trees in 1983 (MNB p41). Shaw noted a witch-lime which stood in the grounds upon a rocky eminence over the Tame some of its roots perforating through the rock into an excavated hermitage below. It was 70 feet high, 20 feet in girth at three feet in height and had three noble arms each about six feet in girth. The extensive branches covered a shadow of 180 feet (SHOS vol 2 p112).

Hamstead Old Hall There was an homestead near Hamstead Hill which was the residence of 'Guy of Hamstead' in 1290; a chapel for the homestead was licensed in 1360 (HPPE p41). A new hall - Hamstead Old Hall - was built on the S side of the Tame near Hamstead Mill, Hamstead (VCHWA vol 7 p69), reputedly in c1450 (WMVB p74). It was the seat of William Wyrley in 1538, and thereafter the seat of subsequent Wyrleys (HPPE p42), hence it has been occasionally referred to as Wyrley's Hall. In 1680 Sir John Wyrley Knt bought the manorial rights of Handsworth from Richard Best, and became the lord of Handsworth and Hamstead. In 1690 he began building Hamstead New Hall (see) on a site 0.25m to the W (HPPE p43). Some say sometime before 1690 the old hall was destroyed by fire (WMVB p74) or it was pulled down by George Birch (MNB p41). Bishop Francis Asbury's father was a servant at Hamstead Old Hall (250th Anniversary of the birth of Francis Asbury. Aug 1995). In the later C17 Plot noted an echo in a field SE of the hall (NHS p29), and a vitriol well (NHS p105).

Hanbury Former township and extensive ancient parish. The village of Hanbury lies high on an escarpment (formed by Hanbury Hill and Stonepit Hills) on the northern edge of the Needwood Forest plateau, 15m ENE of Stafford. Despite Plot's assertion that Hanbury is unusually remote from a natural spring (NHS p39), a purely vitriolic spring exists on Needwood Forest, near Hanbury (HOU p15) and there is Pilgrim's Well (see) behind the church. For a gold torc found in Hanbury parish see under Greaves Wood. A hoard of Roman coins has been found at Hanbury (GNHS p70). Shaw and others thought DB had mistakenly called Hanbury Fauld, so leading us to think Hanbury does not appear in DB (SHOS vol 1 pp71,72) (THS p56). Has appeared as Hambury (c1185) (SSE 1996 p14), Hanbyri (c1540) (LI appendix p172), Handbury (Bowen's map), and Hanbury (Smith's map). The name is from probably its lofty position. Hean or hen signifying 'high' in Saxon (SHOS vol 1 p71) (DUIGNAN) (SPN p57). 'High (or chief) fort' (SSE 1996 p14). The parish church, St Werburgh, on the N side of Church Lane, was begun in c1100 and in the early C14 was almost rebuilt. The prospect from the church tower top northwards includes the Weaver Hills and the Pennines; eastwards it includes the castles at Nottingham and Belvoir (SHOS vol 1 p77) (St Werburgh's Church, Hanbury) (LTD p152). The parish formed before 1086 and may have originally contained the ancient parishes of Yoxall and Hamstall Ridware (SHC 1916 pp197-198). The medieval parish of Hanbury had a detached portion separated by Tutbury parish (SL p55). Hanbury parish feast was on the Sunday before Midsummer day in the C19 (W p559). The manor of Hanbury and Houndhill was called Knight's Fields (NHS p39?). Notice of two ancient deeds relating to Hanbury appear in DAJ vol 15. A silver groat of Edward III's reign was found in the alterations to the church (GNHS p146). There was a pound at Hanbury in the later C15 (UTR p81). The name of the hills to the E of Hanbury - Stonepit Hills - implies quarrying (probably alabaster) (The Guardian. Weekend Section. March 11 1989 pp2-3). Hanbury had a windmill of uncertain location which existed in 1567 (WBJ p26). A slight shock of an earthquake was felt at Hanbury in 1777 (SMC p171).

Hanbury Fields Farm This farm was buried under the debris from the Fauld explosion (GLS p45). The other farm lost in the explosion was Upper Hayes Farm.

Hanbury Grange House 1m WSW of Hanbury. Is called Hanbury Cottage on the 1834 OS map?

Hanbury Hall The old hall which represented the manor house stood a little to the NE of Hanbury church. In the C14 the lords of Hanbury were the Hanbury family. In Edward III's reign the manor passed by marriage from them to the Boweles. From them it passed through several families to the Leighs, who were holding the manor in the earlier C16. From them it passed to the bishops of Lichfield, under whom the Villiers held it until at least the late C18; the bishops are said to have frequently stayed here. The old hall was demolished in c1757 and replaced by a new house built further E (SHOS vol 1 p72) (SOS 1844 p518). (IVNF p of). The new hall was tenanted by Mr Hunt in the later C18 and he was still the tenant in 1817 (THS p56). It appears to have been known as the Manor House when occupied by Miss Smith in 1834 (W 1834). In 1851 it was the seat of Richard Greene (W p20). By at least 1863 it was owned by Capt Reginald Peel, lord of the manor. By at least 1868 it was occupied by Misses Bott, who were still the occupants in the early C20 (trade directories).

Hanbury Hill Just N of Hanbury village 440 feet high. Former common land of which some 5.75 acres remained in the 1950s (OSST 1956-59 p14). Mary, Queen of Scots, when in captivity at Tutbury Castle is said to have hawked on Hanbury Hill (LTD p185).

Hanbury Park Former medieval deer park enclosed out of forest, 1.25m S of Hanbury. In existence by 1265 (VCH vol 2 p350) (NSJFS 1962 p76. 1964 p63) and was disparked in 1549. Hanbury Park lay between Marchington Ward of Needwood Forest, on the W side, and Castle Hay Park, on the E side (VCH vol 2 pp350 map, 355) (ANS p52). Contains in compass 2.5m (EDP pp175-176).

Hanbury Park House 1.25m S of Hanbury.

Hanbury Park Gate House over 1.5m S of Hanbury

Hanbury Priory A nunnery was founded at Hanbury by King Ethelfred (LGS p37), who appointed as prioress his niece, the future St Werburgh of Trentham (see), daughter of King Wulfhere (SGS p102). Some claim Werburgh founded the priory. She died at Trentham Priory (see) in c700 and her body was brought to Hanbury Priory for burial (SVB p88) (FWNS p9). Hanbury Priory did not survive the Danish Invasion of 875 (SGS p103). To avoid falling into Danish hands St Werburgh's relics were removed by the Anglians from Hanbury Priory to Trentham and later to Chester for safe-keeping. Shaw found no remains of the priory, which he thought had stood a little E of the present church; human bones had been frequently dug up there in Mr Hunt's garden and in the pit below (SHOS vol 1 p71).

Hanbury Woodend Hamlet 1m SSW of Hanbury. In Hanbury township and ancient parish. Two Hanbury Woodends are marked on the 1834 OS map. The W one is still called Hanbury Woodend, whereas the E one appears to be now just called Woodend. Earthworks reputedly marking the boundary of Forest Law in Needwood Forest can still (1999) be seen at Hanbury Woodend (LTD p117). Woodend as an addition usually implies a settlement found in a clearance, made by men from the place whose name it succeeds, in this case Hanbury, out of Needwood Forest (SL p71).

Hanch Hall House 1.25m ESE of Longdon. The name is from Old French 'hanche,' an occasional field name, arising from the shape of an enclosure (DUIGNAN) (SSE 1996 p21). The earliest hall on the site was built in Edward I's reign by one of the Astons of Haywood and was the residence of his successors for several generations. From Astons it passed to the Ormes in Elizabeth I's reign (SOS p182). The first of whom, William Orme (d1623), married Grace daughter of Nicholas Hurt of Castern, Staffs (THS p87). The present hall has C15 origins, a Queen Anne front of seven bays, and 1880s improvements (CL July 24 1997 p70pc). In the Civil War William Orme, son of William (d1623), was taken by parliamentarians from his bed when sick and imprisoned at Stafford for giving financial support to Charles I. The hall passed from the Ormes to the Parkhursts. Dormer Parkhurst voted at the contested election for the county in 1747. It was afterwards repaired and inhabited for a short time by Thomas Fowler of Pendeford, Staffs (THS p88). From the Parkhursts it passed by marriage to George Bird; then by purchase to the Riders; then to Francis Cobb; then to James Patton; then by 1819 to the Breyntons (SOS p182); John Breynton was in residence in 1834 (mems in Longsdon church) (W 1834 p363). In 1843 the hall was purchased by John Forster (b1786), brother of Charles Smith Forster of Lysways Hall (see). John appears to have been the owner until his death in 1860, after which the hall was occupied for a while by his nephew, Sir Charles Forster of Lysways Hall (W p568) (SNWA p44). Cuthbert Thorne Seckham (d1871) was of Hanch Hall (mem in Longsdon church). In the mid C19 there was an armorial window depicting the arms of Orme, Parkhurst, and Forster in the tower staircase (W p568) (Country Houses Open to the Public). For other antiquities of the hall see STMSM July 1978 pp14ps,15. The story of Noah's Ark is depicted on two panels in the servants wing (DoE II*). The hall contains the four-poster bed of Percy Bysshe Shelly (Country Houses Open to the Public) (MR p216p). Colin Lee, assistant manager for Wolverhampton Wanders FC and ex-footballer for Chelsea and Spurs football clubs, bought the hall, DoE II, in late 1995 to restore it. It was for sale in June 1997 (CL June 26 1997 property pages pcs) (The Times. Weekend Section. probably June 1997 p7pc). Mr Lee and his wife claim to have seen several ghosts at the hall; one of them is an elegant lady, another is a pretty serving girl. Also strange perfumes abound (GPCE p33). (SHOS vol 1 pp226-227) (BOE p197). Has appeared as Haunch Hall (SOS p182).

GROUNDS. In the earlier C19 Garner noted a chestnut tree here (GNHS p411). In 1997 the grounds consisted of 20.29 acres, a lake, and a 40 feet-high model of Lichfield cathedral, which was constructed by past owners of the hall. This was situated in a copse in the grounds by the mid 1980s (Country Houses Open to the Public) (CL July 24 1997 p70) (The Times. Weekend. p7pc).

Hanch Reservoir Reservoir S of Hanch Hall built by the SSWWC, opened in 1880 (GHC p12).

Hanchurch Small village on high ground between two tributaries of the Trent one being Park Brook, over 1m WNW of Trentham. Former township in Trentham ancient parish.

EARLY. A stone hammer head has been found here (NSFCT 1908 p194). The house called Hanchurch Yews, on the W side of Peacock Lane, lies in the middle of an enclosure about 200 feet square. The enclosure is still (2000) lined by ancient yew trees. By the mid C19 there were 27 yews remaining; the greater number then stood on the S side of the enclosure. By the early

1930s the yews were estimated to be about 900 years old. The girth of the largest was then no more than 17 feet five feet from the ground (Annals of the Diocese of Lichfield Past and Present. 1859) (NSFCT 1932 pp126-127. 1944 p100) (Hanchurch Conservation Area booklet) (info Harry Davis). However the enclosure may have been occupied much earlier with a Bronze or Iron Age camp (NSFCT 1944 pp99-100). A stone or a bronze implement of Neolithic or Bronze Age was found at Hanchurch in c1875 (HOTM p13) (NSFCT 1934 p29) (NSJFS 1964 p38). Earthworks of Iron Age type N of the yews on the hills to the W, were described in 1937, as recently discovered (NSFCT 1937 p116). The yew tree plot could have been a Celtic pagan site (NSFCT 1932 pp126-127). Supporting this theory is the fact that Hanchurch wakes began on the first Sunday after old All Saints day (the Saxon church was possibly dedicated to All Saints) a day coinciding with the Celtic New Year (NSFCT 1908 p112. 1944 pp99-100), and the yew tree site was still known as the 'Pleasure Ground' in 1934, suggestive of a wakes site (NSFCT 1934 p29). The yew tree plot could have been occupied by a Roman camp (HOTC p17) (TTH p15). Some Roman remains were found in a plot of land surrounded by yew trees. A fragment of what may be Roman pottery was found at Hanchurch in 1860 (HOTM p14) (NSFCT 1934 p29) (NSJFS 1964 p37).

600 to PRESENT. In the early Anglo-Saxon period the yew tree plot could have been the site for a church, or small **cell of Trentham Priory**, which was possibly here until c675 or 680, or the Danish invasion in the C9, or the C12, when it was transferred to Trentham (NSFCT 1908 p112. 1932 pp126-127. 1934 p29. 1944 pp99-100). A persistent local tradition, presupposing that there was a church at Hanchurch in or before the C12, relates that Hanchurch church was removed to Trentham by four white swans, or white oxen or mice. This may symbolise the removal of the holy vessels when taken to Trentham in procession by four white surpliced priests (NSFCT 1934 p29). The fact that Trentham church has the double dedication of St Mary and All Saints supports the tradition that Hanchurch church was removed to Trentham, when it is remembered that Hanchurch wakes began on the first Sunday after old All Saints day (NSFCT 1908 p112. 1944 pp99-100). (Notes Illustrative of the History of the Church in Trentham. Rev FJ Edwards. 1859). Swan myths often have an association with the story of the transformation of the Children of Lir into swans (NSFCT 1908 p112). In the enclosure where a church is believed to have existed bones have turned up and pieces of gravestone by the plough in the C18 (NSFCT 1934 p29), or in the C19 (HOTC p17) (TTH p15). The **manor** of Hancese appears in DB. Erdeswick mistakenly identified Hanchurch with DB Haswic, which has since been shown to be present Ashwood (SHC 1916 p168). Hanchurch appears in 1212 as Hanchurche (SSE 1996 p14). If from Hancese then 'cese' may represent Anglo-Saxon 'church.' 'Han' may be 'high' or may represent the Welsh 'hen,' meaning 'old' (SVB p89). Shaw points out hean or hen signifies 'high' in Saxon with reference to Hanbury (SHOS vol 1 p71). 'High church' (DUIGNAN) (SSE 1996 p14) (SPN p57). (STM May 1966 p32). The 'High road from Stafford to Cestre (Chester)' mentioned in a deed of 1280 in the cartulary of Trentham Priory may have passed through Hanchurch (NSFCT 1957 p64). A **Mr Doody** of Hanchurch was a grandfather and a grandchild at the same time, there being five generations living together in the C17 (NHS p328). There was a **chapel** of ease to Trentham in a barn in the garden of Chapel House, on the E side of Peacock Lane, by 1841 (TTH p69). The present brick chapel to the rear of Chapel House was built in 1888 (LDD). **Retreat for poor children**. In 1898 a holiday home for poor Potteries children was founded on the N side of Hanchurch Lane, W side of the village, by Millicent, Duchess of Sutherland (d1955) of Trentham Hall (see). In 1911 a convalescent home for patients of the Potteries and Newcastle Cripples' Guild (or Cripples' Aid Society), a society which was also the inspiration of the Duchess, was built adjoining the holiday home. Later the convalescent home moved to the Church Institute, Stoke-upon-Trent, and then to Woodhouse Street, and in 1918 it moved to Longfield Cottage (see) becoming the Hartshill Orthopaedic Hospital. The convalescent home building at Hanchurch, known as Hanchurch Holiday Home in 1900, Hanchurch Residential School in 1925. In 1929 City of Stoke-on-Trent took over the Home and it became the Hanchurch Residential Open Air School for delicate children. The building was still standing in 1991 (OS maps 6 inch 1900, 1925) (VCH vol 8 p197) (The Crusade against Crippledom: The Story of Millicent Duchess of Sutherland and the North Staffordshire Cripples Aid Society. Tony Carter. 1991. pp7,12,18,25) (TTH p122). In c1992 the building was demolished and the present (2000) Hanchurch Christian Centre, a range of buildings vaguely resembling the former school, built on the site by the United Christian Broadcasters.

Hanchurch Hall Hanchurch. There are ruins of Hanchurch Hall next to the

new hall (STM May 1966 p32p of the ruins).

Hanchurch Heath Former common said to be contiguous to the common known as Millstone Green (THS p385). 1m SW of Hanchurch (1834 OS map).

Hanchurch Hills Small range of hills in size and area 3m N of Swynnerton. A fragment of a polished quartzite macehead with a cylindrical perforation, of Neolithic or Bronze Age, was found in the Hanchurch Hills in 1894 which went to the Potteries Museum (NSFCT vol 32 p154. vol 41 p169) (AJ vol 21 p337) (NSJFS 1964 p37).

Hanchurch Manor House lying to the S of Hanchurch village, S of Ridding Bank. Whether the same as Hanchurch Hall? Has or had in the Rook Room a mural by Boulliemier dated 1880, depicting a scene showing life after a day's rook shooting. The fountain in the garden came originally from Sutton Place, near Guildford, it was formerly owned by the Dukes of Sutherland and recently by the late Paul Getty (SLM July 1984 p7p of the fountain). A secret passage believed to exist between Hanchurch Manor and Trentham church and discovered when the M6 was first built turned out to be an ice-house, probably for Trentham Hall (TTH p143).

Hancock's Cross Ancient name for High Bullen, Wednesbury. Former possible wayside shrine erected by the wealthy Hancock family (WAM pp51,53). Has also appeared as Hancox Green (WAM p100). Now vanished (SCSF p88).

Handford Brook Runs S off Weaver Hills into Bowlingalley Brook in Wootton Park.

Handford Brook Runs from the Weaver Hills to Wootton Park.

Handfords, The Dispersed small hamlet nearly 2m SSW of Seighford.

Hand Leasow Wood Wood 2.5m ESE of Fradswell.

Handley House To the W of Longdon (old) Hall, Longdon.

Handsacre Former manor in Armitage ancient parish. The village of Handsacre lies on a low promontory near the Trent and one of its tributaries, 11.75m ESE of Stafford. The name has appeared as Hadesacre, a manor, in DB, Hendesacra (1167), Hundesacra (1176), Handesacra (1196), and Hondesacre (1242) (SSE 1996 p14). It is from hund, hunda meaning 'hound' which was also an Anglo-Saxon personal name, so 'Hund's field' (or farm)' (DUIGNAN), or 'Hand's newly-cultivated land' (NSJFS 1981 p3), or 'arable field of Hand' (SSE 1996 p14). The suffix is Saxon 'acra,' not a measure but simply '(the total) ploughed land.' The first element may be 'Hound' (a nickname), 'Hand' (nickname suggesting 'manipulator'), or 'Hana' (a personal name) (SPN p58). The hermitage at Armitage, in the mid C13, still an unnamed settlement, was still being referred to as 'the hermitage of Handsacre' (SHOS vol 1 pp207,208,209). Handsacre is a prebend in Lichfield cathedral, spelt Hansacre (SHOS vol 1 p292) (VCH vol 3 p141), founded by Roger de Clinton in the C12. The prebendary has on occasion been termed the prebendary of Armitage and Hansacre (SSAHST vol 2 1960-61 p47). There is a mission church, St Luke, in Hall Road (LDD). About 0.25m N of the High Bridge was the Handsacre Toll House built in c1831, possibly the last toll house to be built in England (STM June 1969 p32p). Otter hunting along the Trent, revived in the 1920s and early 1930s, started at Handsacre. The Staffordshire pack lasted only a few years and were sold up in 1935-6 (TOS p18) (info County Museum, Shugborough). On the Handsacre-Brereton road Plot found a holly tree growing out of an oak tree (NHS p213) (SD p20) (SHOS vol 1 p227). D Collingwood of Bagnalls Farm, Alrewas, was told of strange circles existing at Handsacre similar to the one on land farmed by him near Alrewas. These circles may have been ancient pens or pounds (HOA pp3,4). For the small battle in 1403 between Sir William Handsacre, lord of Handsacre, and Sir Robert Mavesyn, in which the former lost his life, see Gog. James Broughton, author of historical notes in the early C19 Staffs press was of Handsacre. His notes appear in the Pottery Gazette (1823-1825), and in 'Notices of Staffordshire' in the Lichfield Mercury; these appear in compilations abbreviated for this encyclopaedia as SMT, SMC, SM. Broughton styled himself as the 'Hermit of Hanley' when replying to correspondence (OPB p9) (SH pp112,113,121,123-126,136,160,185).

Handsacre Cross Handsacre (SHOS). Formerly stood at the junction of three roads in the centre of the village, and not far from the church. It had disappeared by the C18 (SCSF p87).

Handsacre Hall It was near the turnpike, a little S of Handsacre. Dated from c1320 (SL p268) (AR p36p in c1903). The moat dates from the C12 (SSAHST 1982-83 p35) (SVB p19) and the site within is 60 yards from E to W and 54 yards from N to S (NSFCT 1982 p13). In the late C18 Shaw noted what was in the chapel or oratory (a separate building close by?); it had been altered somewhat, from its original state. On a beam he saw a plaster shield with an emblem embedded in it resembling a hart's head, although most likely a horse's head, with a dagger through the neck with two sprigs, or ears of corn in its mouth, which he surmised was the coat of arms of Hawksyard quartered with Handsacre (SHOS vol 1 pp210-211 pl on p211). Shaw went on to mention the heraldic glass in the hall. White, in the mid C19, noted some remains of the ancient manor house surrounded by a moat, the part remaining was occupied by a farmer (W p556). The central section was largely pulled down by vandals in 1972 (SSAHST 1973-74 p50 il of in 1818 from a grangerized copy of HOL in the Bodleian Library) (SL p268). In 1973 the best sections went to the Avoncroft Museum, Bromsgrove, Worcs (VB p110). In 1986 the remains were examined by archaeologists (SVB p19). (GNHS p152) (LGS p75) (BOE p141) (MR p17). Is featured in and illustrated in George Griffith's tragedy 'The Two Houses' 1866.

Handsacre Park Was a farm by 1817 (THS p78). Former enclosure?

Handsworth Ancient parish, former manor and township with Soho. The former village of Handsworth, in a low valley formed by a tributary of the Tame, is now a large suburb of Birmingham, 22.5m SSE of Stafford, or 2.5m NNW of Birmingham.
EARLY to 1850. A brass head of a bolt of a **Roman** catapulta although this one was without an eye which confused the people who found it as to what it could be (NHS p403 tab 33 fig 5) (SHOS vol 2 p117) (GNHS p70). The **name** has appeared as Hundeworde or Hunesworth (912) (HANDR pvi), Honesworde, a manor, in DB (SVS p578), Hansworth (1564), and Hownesworth (1566) (SHC 1938 pp77,185). It is from probably 'Hun(e)'s property' (or farm) (DUIGNAN) (A History of Greater Birmingham down to 1830. Victor Skipp. 1980. p14). Or 'the Worth or estate of Hondes' (WAM p9). The parish formed before 1086 and may have originally contained West Bromwich ancient parish (SHC 1916 p198). The parish church, **St Mary**, on the W side of Hamstead Road facing Church Hill, has late C12 or early C13 work in the lower parts of the tower. There were major alterations to it in 1820 and it was enlarged in 1876-1880 (BOEWA p179). Elihu Burritt, American author and diplomat, who lived in Harborne (see) from 1865, described the church as 'a kind of Westminster Abbey to Birmingham, consecrated to the memory of its dead, whose names have won illustrious fame' (Old and New Birmingham. Robert K Dent. 1879 p618). Handsworth **wakes** were normally held on the first Monday in Oct on a piece of waste ground known as Bricknell, near Baker Street (HPPE p127). There was bull baiting in the Handsworth district at the end of Queens Head Lane and at the bridge at Niveveh (just in Warws) (HPPE p11). The Easter Monday custom of 'clipping the church' or 'watching' was practised at Handsworth (HPPE p25). In a plan of the boundary of the manor of Handsworth **Gallowes** Hill is mentioned, also a mear stone, and Sir Robert Holt's Conduit (SHOS vol 2 p108). There was a **pound** near St Mary's church and the National School. The building was removed in 1908, but the site was still clearly defined in 1962 (HPPE pp56,98). The bells of Handsworth church were rung in the C18 and C19 on May 29 to celebrate **Restoration Day** (SCSF p20). **Suppression of local alehouses**. There was a disturbance at Handsworth in which the effigy of the vicar of Handsworth, Rev Thomas Lane, (a meeting of his was attended by Boulton and Watt in 1791), was hung in the village in 1796. Rev Thomas Lane was a local justice and had tried to suppress local ale houses. The effigy was placarded as 'the Devil or the fiddler's son.' As a consequence of the disturbance Lane prosecuted for libel six of Gough's tenants who had been involved in the incident (LOU pp374, 185-186). The **Handsworth Volunteer Cavalry**, raised in 1798, was independent of the Staffordshire Yeomanry for the whole of its 30 year's existence (FSP p62) (info Yeomanry Museum). There was a **windmill** at SP 065905 (Bothan's map 1794) on 'Windmill Piece,' off modern Livingstone Road. There was another windmill for Hutton's Paper Mill at Bristnels End (see). Handsworth **Grammar School** has its origins in a National School opened near St Mary's church in 1812 by the trustees of the Bridge Trust with surplus income from trust funds. A new school, the Bridge Trust School, was opened by the Trust in Grove Lane in 1862. In 1890 the name was changed to Handsworth Grammar School (HPPE p15). Between Handsworth church and Handsworth Heath Rev Ange noted a **mysterious circle** which was four yards in diameter but when Plot noted it had increased to nearly 40 yards in diameter. It was locally believed that the circle had been made by witches (NHS pp9,10,17). An **earthquake** was distinctly felt at Handsworth in April 1805 (Broughton's Scrapbook p81). In Handsworth the **New Year custom** was for gangs of boys to parade the streets from midnight to breakfast time chanting 'New Year in!' (SCSF p3). **Persons and visitors**. For **William Wyrley** (1565-1618), antiquarian, see Little Wyrley. For **Andrew Bromwich** (c1652-1702), Roman Catholic priest condemned to die in the Popish Plot in 1679, see Old Oscott. **John Boulton**, coiner and counterfeiter in the early 1800s, had a movable mint in the Birmingham and Handsworth areas. He was eager to form a partnership with the notorious coiner William Booth of Booth's Farm (see), but informed on him when his proposition was turned down (TB Sept 1988 p10).
1850 to PRESENT. What constituted Handsworth parish in 1911 was then

removed to Birmingham, Warws (SL p169). Handsworth Council House was built between 1878-79 in Soho Road (BOOP p25). The **Rhodes Almshouses** on Soho Road, built in 1874, were still standing in 1983 (MNB pp46,53). **Handsworth Museum** has a note in David Murray's 'Museums' 1904 vol 2 p279. **Bridge fall**. In Aug 1854 a tubular bridge between Soho and Handsworth designed by John Robinson Maclean collapsed and fell into the road during the construction of the Birmingham, Wolverhampton and Dudley Railway line (SSR p14). A **highway robbery** of an alarming nature for the time occurred at Handsworth in 1888 and was reported by the Police News. A young man named George Henry Jackson and a young lady, Miss Watts, were robbed at gun-point in Camp Lane near its junction with New Inns Road. After shooting Mr Jackson in the shoulder, for he had risen his walking stick to hit the robber, the robber made off (TB Nov 1997 p20). **Social change and unrest**. From about the 1950s West Indian and Asian immigrants have settled in Handsworth. In a protest by the youth of the local West Indian community against insensitive policing and social deprivation riots, said to have been a copy of earlier ones at Brixton, London, took place in Handsworth in the evening of July 10 1981. Handsworth's took place in Lozells and Villa Roads, Grove Lane, and in Soho Road, where police had to retreat so strong and violent was the crowd. About 800 people rioted and looted at Handsworth, and there were 68 arrests. A further riot occurred in the evening of Sept 9 1985 centred on the disused Villa Cross Bingo Hall and Social Club in Lozells Road. The rioting occurred after a period of insensitive policing of the local West Indian community, with the police making raids and arrests on suspected drug dealers. Two brothers, Asian shopkeepers, Kassamali Moledina, 38, and Amirali Moledina, 44, were burnt to death in their store and post office in Lozells Road during the riot; Mark Barratt, 21, and Samuel Murrain, 17, were charged with manslaughter. Another riot occurred in the area in the evening of Sept 10 1985. In an attempt to calm the area and bring hope to it Prince Charles visited Handsworth's new St Paul and St Silas church centre on June 25 1986 (Birmingham Post July 11 & 13 1981. Sept 9 & 11 1985) (The Times Sept 11 1985) (Birmingham Mail July 11 1981. June 12 & 25 1986) (E&S Sept 10 1985. July 18 1986). The **Handsworth Carnival**, a street carnival, started up after the riots, displays the current multi-cultural nature of the local community. **Supernatural**. A couple walking in Grove Lane on Oct 24 1968 saw a bearded policeman carrying a lantern who faded out of sight until only his trousers could be seen (MMSE p292). There was an outbreak of unexplained poltergeist activity in the area in late 1976 to early 1977, at a private house or houses; furniture moved, lights went on and off (MMSE p292). **Persons and visitors**. **Rosa Ayscoughe Hayden** (1855-1922), poet, was born and brought up in Handsworth (PSS pp412-415) (VFC pp62-63). The minor poet and novelist **Samuel Tomkins**, born in Handsworth in the C19, later resided in Wombourne and or Trysull (PSS pp150-151) (VFC p131). Thomas Boulton murdered his niece Elizabeth Bunting, aged 15 or 16, at Crick Lane, Handsworth, on April 20 1885. He was arrested in Bilston (DOB p155) (TB Feb 1982 pp1,5). **Wallace B Nichols**, poet, playwright and novelist, was born in Handsworth, on March 2 1888. His work includes the epic poem 'The Song of Sharruk' (1916), the narrative poems, 'The Saga of Judas' (1949), and 'Jericho Street, Selected Poems' (1921), a trilogy of historical plays entitled 'Earl Simon' (1922), a one-act play in blank verse, 'The Glory of the World' (1924), and a novel called 'Secret Market' (1928) (PSS pp370-371 p) (VFC p98). **Bill Morris**, born in Jamaica in 1938, General Secretary of the Transport and General Workers Union from 1992 to at least 1999, came to live with his mother in the Birchfield Road and Heathfield Road area of Handsworth after 1953 (Desert Island Discs. BBC Radio 4. Nov 22 1998). **Frederick Walter Jeffs**, aged 37, was murdered on April 19 1957 at his tobacconists in Stanley Road and his body was found in Park Lane ('Lovers Lane'), Handsworth. The murder was witnessed by his black poodle, Perro, and a woman may have also been a witness, but she was never found (MM pp14-20).

Handsworth Hall Rather flat red brick building, with a low-pitched slate roof of the late Georgian period situated in the area now (1984) covered by Villa Road, Rose Hill, Crick Lane and Broughton Road, Handsworth. Its actual site was at the point of the sharp northward bend of Hall Road, which takes its name from the hall. In the C18 it was occupied by Anna Maria Sacheverell and Jane Gough, both of whom were heiresses (mem in St Mary's church, Handsworth) (HPPE p55). It was later occupied by Joseph Grice JP (d1833) (mem in St Mary's, Handsworth) and his descendants to 1852 when the hall passed to Joseph Barrow. In 1874 the area about the hall was developed with housing (HPPE p55), and the hall was then demolished?

Handsworth Heath Residential suburb 1.25m W of Handsworth. The former common land stretched from Great Hampton Street on the border with Birmingham to the West Bromwich boundary, and from Handsworth Wood to the Dudley Road area of Smethwick (STELE March 9 1956). Handsworth's common was said to be 'one of the most barren in England' (MNB p35). Development in this area started when the Birmingham to Wednesbury road was turnpiked in 1727 (HANDR pvi). Further development took place with the enclosure of the heath after an award of 1793 (WMLB p52). Still further development occurred when Thomas Telford raised the status of the turnpike road to form a part of the Holyhead post road (HANDR pvi). To serve this emerging residential area several new churches were built from the 1830s. In the W part of Handsworth parish there is St James' on the corner of Crocketts and St James' Roads. It was built in 1838-1840, and another church, built in 1894-1895, was added onto it (BOEWA p181). Serving the NW part of the parish on the corner of Oxhill Road and Slack Lane is St Andrew. It is essentially of 1907 (BOEWA p180). St Peter, Grove Lane, was consecrated in 1907, and was still a church in 1966 (BOEWA p182).

Handsworth Hill Marked on OS map 1:25,000 at SP 045910, S side of Friary Road, 0.75m NW of Handsworth. Now part of a college complex?

Handsworth Manor House Stood on Shirle Hill about 500 yards from St Mary's church, Handsworth. Built by Peter de Parles in c1160-1180. Seat of the de Parles to Sir William de Parles, who went on the Seventh Crusade, upon returning from which he was later charged with felony, and tried and hung in 1277. The house had fallen into decay by 1300. A heather garden in Handsworth Park possibly hid some foundations in 1984 (HPPE p55).

Handsworth Park Large public park to W of St Mary's church, Handsworth. Bounded by Grove Lane, Holly and Hamstead Roads. The park was formerly the land of The Grove, and was purchased by the urban district council and officially opened as a park in 1887 by the Earl of Dartmouth; the Dartmouths were formerly of Sandwell Hall (see). It was at first called Victoria Park. The park was enlarged in 1890, 1895 (HPPE pp57,58), 1898 (HANDR p83p), and 1901 (HPPE p57). (The Founding of Handsworth Park 1882-1898. Simon Baddeley. 1997).

Handsworth Wood Residential district of Handsworth under 0.5m NW of St Mary's church, created from the mid C19 (VCHWA vol 7 p24). The name is from a wood which existed for centuries on the E side of Handsworth Wood Road, some of it remained as Butler's Coppice until the later C19 (MNB p47). A railway station at Handsworth Wood opened in 1896 and closed on May 5 1941 (HPPE p40p).

Hanford Former manor (SHC 1909 p71) and township in Trentham ancient parish (W p431). The village of Hanford now a suburb of the Potteries, 1.25m NNE of Trentham, lies on a hill by the Trent. A Roman road ran from Stone through Hanford to Chesterton (TTH p15). There may have been a Roman fort on the high ground guarding the Trent at Hanford, abandoned at the time of Boudicca's revolt (HOS p12). In 1957 a stone Roman lamp dish was found at Hanford (photograph in the Warrillow Collection, Keele University). The name has appeared as Heneford (DB), Honeford (1212) (SSE 1996 p14), Hondford (SPN p131), and Handford (1827) (Potteries Gazette Sept 1 1827). It is from probably Anglo-Saxon 'heanford' meaning 'high ford.' The village stands on a hill, at the foot of which the Trent is crossed by the great North West Road (DUIGNAN) (SPN p130). Mills thinks the first element may represent 'hana' 'cock of wild bird' or 'han' 'stone/ hone' so 'cock's or stone ford' (SSE 1996 pp14,21). Or is derived from Hana's ford - Hana's village by the crossing (BNDA p3). The church, St Matthias, in a high position on the N side of Church Lane, was built in 1827 and reopened after repairs and extensions in the 1860s (TTH p73). Hanford became a separate ecclesiastical parish in 1828 which was refounded in 1832 (LGS p143) (GLAUE p412). A chapel, which may have been a Primitive Methodist Chapel, was built at Hanford in 1818 (TTH p73). Hanford was described as a populous village in 1827 when a new church was being built here (Potteries Gazette Sept 1 1827) (Broughton's Scrapbook p325). Hanford was taken into Stoke-on-Trent county borough in 1922 (VCH vol 8 p260). A house here, built in the 1920s is believed, by its present owners, to be haunted. Instances of the paranormal have been experienced (GLS pp46-47). For a rhyme from Hanford see FSBC p55.

Hanger Hill Cheadle. Residence of Capt Charles JB Masefield (d1917), born at Abbots Hay (see). Hanger Hill was close to his parents residence at Rosehill (see) (NSFCT 1917 p107).

Hanging Bank 0.25m WSW of Ecton Hill. The burial mound at SK 09685778 is a listed monument. It is 18 paces in diameter and five feet high. Carrington excavated it in 1848. It had previously been disturbed. A cremation, worked flints, two skeletons; one disturbed and a decorated urn were found. This is possibly the same burial mound Plot mentions on Ecton Hill containing 'mens bones.... of extraordinary size' (NHS p330) (NSJFS 1965 p57). (TYD pp111,147) (VCH vol 1 nos 1, 27).

Hanging Bridge Bridge carrying the Manchester to Derby road over the Dove at Mayfield on the border with Derbys. An earlier bridge at this site could

have been a packhorse bridge (ESH p17). (PS p124). Believed to be so called because this was where the Staffs (or Derbys?) authorities hung convicted villains to warn others from the other county of their fate if they broke the law in that county (local info). Another tradition is that many of the Scottish rebels in the 1745 Jacobite Rebellion were hung from gibbets on the bridge (MOM p3). The W half was the responsibility of Staffs, the E of Derbys until 1717, after which maintenance was carried out jointly (NSFCT 1948 p36). Its repair was requested in 1617 (VCH vol 2 p279). It was repaired in 1682. The Staffs side was repaired in 1711. The bridge may have been widened in 1766 (NSFCT 1948 pp35-7). The Young Pretender's army passed over Hanging Bridge on Dec 4 1745 in the Jacobite Rebellion (BPCSM p7). When in retreat from Derby the army reputedly shot dead the innkeeper at Hanging Bridge, Humphrey Brown, after he had refused to hand over his horse to them (NSFCT 1948 p29) (MOM p3). Coaches on the Ashbourne-Leek route used the bridge from 1831, hitherto they had gone via Coldwall Bridge (NSFCT 1948 p41). On New Year's day 1830 a coachman accidentally fell off the box and pulled a passenger with him on the Telegraph coach from Manchester on the hill leading down to Hanging Bridge. The horses of the Telegraph proceeded over the narrow Hanging Bridge but then collided with the corner of the public house and the toll gate, losing a wheel and overturning; the coachman and guard were believed to be drunk (SA Jan 9 1830) (NSFCT 1921 pp56-57). A new bridge was reconstructed over the old arches in 1937 (NSFCT 1948 pp35-7) (MOM pp10-11ps,18-21), using some masonry from the demolished Wootton Hall (see). According to White Hanging Bridge is a hamlet in Mayfield township (W p784). There is a hamlet on the Derbys side close to the bridge called Hanging Bridge. For Rock Houses near the bridge see Mayfield.

Hangingstone Rock Rock feature over 0.5m N of Swythamley Hall (MIDD vol 4 p29p). Rev Thomas Loxdale visited the rock in 1708 and concluded in an elaborate argument that the rock must be man-made and have been used as a pagan altar (SH p78). (SHOS Additions and Corrections to General History in vol 1 pp1-2). It is called a cromlech (a megalithic chambered tomb) in MC p30, a similar feature has been reported in the Trentine Alps. In the early 1800s the GM alleged the rock was the scene of sacrifices. In 1834 a forester called Hughes discovered gold, silver and copper coins from the Civil War period at the base of the rock (NSJFS 1977 p39) (DP pp36-37p). (STMSM July 1980 p24) (HOLF p41 il). On the W side of the rock is a plaque to a dog of Sir Philip Brocklehurst, called 'Burke' buried here Aug 1 1874

> A noble mastiff, black and tan,
> Faithful as woman, braver than man:
> A gun and a ramble his heart's desire,
> With the friend of his life, the Swythamley squire.

(OL vol 2 p85) (NSFCT 1905 pp168-169) (TTTD p114) (STMSM July 1980 p24) (PS p144p) (DP pp37-39). In 1949 a bronze plate with an inscription to the memory of Lt Col Henry Courtney Brocklehurst (b1888), Game Warden of the Sudan, killed on Active Service in Burma on Commando, June 1942, was erected on the S side of the rock. In the 1930s Brocklehurst kept a zoo at Roaches House (see) (TTTD p115) (DP p38). The Hanging Stone may have been an observatory from where the lunar rise and fall could be witnessed (DPEM pp140il,144). Hangingstone Farm, 0.25m SW, is of the C17 (VCH vol 7 p187). (Photographs in the Warrillow Collection, Keele University).

Hanging Wicket Farm 2.25m WSW of Marchington at Scounslow Green. Redfern found Roman pottery in what he describes as a Roman camp near Hanging Wicket House in 1872 (HOU 1886 p73) (NSJFS 1964 p40).

Hangman's Hall Local name for George Smith's cottage in Oakham Road, Rowley Regis. Smith, born at Turner's Hill in 1805, was the county hangman in the C19 (TB Oct 1984 p27) (ORR p116p) (MMBCC pp8p-34). A tree called Hangman's Tree (see) stood in front of the cottage.

Hangman's Oak Tree in Cannock Chase (CCF p222). Near the head of Sherbrook Valley on the E side of the brook (1905 OS map). Appears as Hangemanstrete (1570) and Hangman's Oak (1834) (SPNO p108). The tree is a remnant of turbulent times between local feuding families with country seats (HSS pp26,27). So called after a sheep stealer Humphrey Haycock hung himself in the tree after being chased by the Sheriff's men; he had never been caught before (RRCC pp5,6,7). Oakden places it in Beaudesert Old Park (SPNO p108).

Hangman's Oak Between Rugeley and Brereton on E side of the road. Marked in John Ogilby's 'Britannia.' Possibly on Glover's Hill or at Mossley.

Hangman's Tree Tree which stood in front of George Smith's cottage in Oakham Road, Rowley Regis (O p226) (ORR p116p). On or near the site is now an inn called The Hangman's Tree. It was built in the late 1950s (TB May 1975 pp28-29. Jan 1997 p5). (The Common Hangman. James Bland. 1984. pp152-158). See Hangman's Hall.

Hankerchief Barn S of Whittington Hall, Kinver.

Hankerses Well Greenhead, Burslem. The brothers W and John Taylor had a pottery works here in the C18 (HSP p181).

Hanley (locally *'Anley*). Former collection of hamlets on a high ridge astriding the Trent and Fowlea valleys. It became the largest of the pottery towns in the Potteries. Now a large town in the City of Stoke-on-Trent 15.5m N of Stafford. Former township in Stoke-upon-Trent chapelry and ancient parish (LGS p143).

EARLY. A medium size perforated prehistoric axe was found before 1900 while constructing a timber yard at the top of Charles Street (NSJFS 1962 p28. 1964 p35).

1000 to 1800. The **name** has appeared as Henle (1212), Hanlih (1227) (SSE 1996 p14) (SPN p59). It is from 'hean lea' meaning 'high meadow' or 'at the high leah (wood clearing)' (DUIGNAN) (SOSH p278) (MR p174) (SSE 1996 p14) (SPN p59). There was a manor of Hanley by the early C13; Hanley Hall is said to have been the manor house (see). Hanley was anciently made up of the old vill 'Hanley' and two hamlets, Upper Green and Lower Green, 0.5m apart; together they were known as Hanley Green (POP p38). The present town centre developed on the common land on the boundary between Lower Green and Shelton (SASR 1987 p101). Hanley Green was an alternative name for Hanley by the end of the C16; its use lingered on up to the mid C19 (VCH vol 8 p142) and it was used by the later C20 for the ward of Stoke-on-Trent district covering Hanley. Hanley and Shelton appear bracketed together as early as 1714. Some say Hanley became a separate ecclesiastical parish in 1740 (GLAUE p412), shortly after the building of its church St John (1737), whilst others say it did not become a separate ecclesiastical parish until 1891 (CAST p57) (VCH vol 8 p188). The present **church**, St John the Evangelist, on the corner of Town and Quadrant Roads, dates from 1788-1790. There may have been a chapel in what is now Town Road, built in 1738 (VCH vol 8 p154). Being within Stoke parish Hanley took part in Stoke wakes (VCH vol 8 p171). The **market** was apparently established in 1776 (VCH vol 8 p158). Between at least 1834 and 1850 fairs were held on Feb 16, April 6 and May 25 (VCH vol 8 p163). The **Ancient Corporation of Hanley** is a current society of leading pottery manufacturers, professional and business people in the Potteries. It has its origins in a self-appointed corporation for Hanley in the later C18, when it was felt the town ought to have a royal charter of corporation and some self-government. The inaugural feast was held on Sept 18 1783. The ceremony next took place on Sept 30 1784. The corporation has its own mock Mayor, Aldermen, Councillors, Cup-bearers and Recorder. The feasts at which inauguration takes place have become known as the Mayor's Feast (W p230) or **Venison Feast**, on account of in the past the Marquis of Stafford annually presenting a fat buck, from either his seat, Trentham Hall (see), or his seat at Dunrobin in Scotland. The feast of 1783 took place at the Swan Inn, Hanley. It took place there in 1826 and for some years subsequently, later moving to the Albion Hotel and Saracen's Head Hotel. In the C20 it has taken place mainly at the North Stafford Hotel, Stoke-upon-Trent, and sometimes at the Grand Hotel, Hanley and Hanley Town Hall. The feast did not take place in the Napoleonic and WW1 wars, nor in 1939. A Junior Corporation was founded in 1857. Qualification for membership of the corporation was being able to drink a yard glass of ale at a draught. Arnold Bennett described the feast as 'a piece of elaborate machinery for dinner-eating.' The feast still continues and took place on Dec 5 1996, and in early Dec 1999 at the Moat House Hotel, Etruria. The records of the corporation from 1783 to 1900 by WD Spanton (1901), 1901 to 1958 by George Eyre Stringer (1960), and 1959 to 1983 by John Francis Moxon (1984) are in the WSL (W p230) (HSP pp137,138) (SA Oct 14 1860) (H pp98,99) (SCSF p163) (NSFCT 1929 pp68-69) (ES Oct 14 1939 p3. Dec 6 1996. Dec 4 1999 p15p) (SLM 1949) (VCH vol 8 p173) (SHST p259) (FOS p123) (SLM March 1996 p22ps). A **hoard of coins** dated 1773-1852 and stone were found on the site of the Old Saracens Head in Stafford Street (ES Nov 5 1937 p1). **Persons and visitors**. In 1752 the charge of sedition was brought against **Joseph Straphan**, a printer from Hanley, for publishing part II of Paine's 'The Rights of Man' and the 'Letter addressed to the address on the late proclamation' (LOU pp159-160). **John Voyez** (born c1735), of French extraction, has been described as the most interesting ceramic modeller of the C18. He worked in London before being employed by Josiah Wedgwood in 1768. Whilst in his employment Wedgwood caught him in a state of inebriation modelling from life a semi-nude girl and a confrontation between him and Wedgwood ensued. Voyez was imprisoned for three months and whipped. By 1769 he was working for Wedgwood's rival, Humphrey Palmer of Hanley. Later, whilst in residence at Hanley, for others and on his own he made imitation Wedgwood

ware and passed it off as the real thing. He appears to have had a factory at Cobridge in 1772. He left for London in March 1776 and reappeared in the Potteries briefly in 1788. Some of his work is in the BM (Staffordshire Chimney Ornaments. Reginald G Haggar. 1955 pp41-49). **Simeon Shaw**, author of HSP, was born in Salford, Lancs in 1785 (SH p124 il) (POTP p190); Simms and Huntbach say he was born in Hanley (BS p397) (H p145). He came to the Potteries to work as a printer and compositor for the Pottery Gazette and Newcastle-under-Lyme Advertiser, but had taken to school teaching by 1822. He died in the County Asylum in 1859 and is buried in Bethesda churchyard, Hanley (OTP p79) (STM March 1972 p31. April 1972 pp32-33). **Ned Saunterer**, was a pot pedlar who lived in a thatched hovel in Saggar Row (now Parliament Row) in the 1790s. Formerly, he was an employee of the pottery manufacturer, Mr Toft, but proving to be unreliable Toft suggested he became a pot seller and hawker. He did so well at this he had to buy a donkey which he dressed with horns, flickering candles, and chains to represent a demon to ward off footpads. He and his donkey presented such a supernatural sight that they scared off body snatchers at work in Bucknall churchyard in 1797. Saunterer became so successful he was able to eventually buy his own pottery factory (ROS vol 1 pp53-62) (PTP pp30-35) (MMM p82-84) (TFTP pp11-13) (TOS pp111-113) (SSGLST pp45-46) (SMML pp24-26, 86-88). **John Wesley** came to Hanley on March 30 1784, and preached at the new Methodist chapel which stood near St John's church (SOSH p281) (H p66). **Alexander Kilham**, founder of the Methodist New Connexion, visited Hanley after his expulsion by the 1796 Methodist Conference (VCH vol 3 p126).

PUNISHMENTS. The **ducking stool** for women and compulsory church attendance for men was introduced into Hanley by Rev John Middleton in mid C18 for those who misbehaved (H p94). The town had double **stocks** on the site of Lloyd's Bank. They were once on show in the Potteries Museum (ES June 12 1931 p6). Warrilow writes of a set of cast iron stocks in the Potteries Museum. Some stocks also stood in front of Hanley parish church and later on the NE side of the Old Market Hall, other stocks were said to have existed at Brookley's Square (SHST p488). Stocks stood outside the market hall of 1819 (VCH vol 8 p159). A **lock-up** was established in 1790 and adjoined the market hall of 1819 (VCH vol 8 p159 note).

INDUSTRY. Hanley industries have been pottery, coal and ironstone mining (but to a lesser extent than in the northern Pottery towns), bricks, paper, silk and brewing (VCH vol 8 p170). In the later C17 Plot noted that peacock coal was mined at Hanley (NHS p126). Unusually, a colliery engine house, far from a colliery, is in the yard of an old pottery works in Warner Street. Thompson asks what is it doing there (IANS p60p). The Patent Balance Hanson Cab was invented at the firm of AT Poole of Foundry Street. The hansom cab had usually two wheels; another variety, having four was known as a 'Growler' (SHST p51). From 1858-1888 the Patent Balance Hansom Cab was made at the Foundry Street works (Arnold Bennett and Stoke-on-Trent. EJD Warrilow. 1966. p110). There was a windmill at SJ 888478, S end of St John Street (SHST p520), dating from c1795 which stood close to the Bucknall Old Road. By 1850 it had been converted into William Dodd's Hallfield Observatory. It was last recorded in 1857 (VCH vol 8 p163). It was eventually demolished and the Observatory Inn built on the site. A paper bag from Moses Mollatt, a grocer, of 13 Hill Street, illustrates the mill (WBJ pp26,27). (A Short History of the Old Windmill which was situated on the site of the present Observatory Inn. FW Dale 1912).

1800 to 1850. Authorisation for the Hanley Tramroad to link the town with the Caldon Canal at Etruria Vale Road was given in 1802 (HCMS No. 5). In 1813 an Act of parliament formed Shelton and Hanley into a market town (H p18). By the 1830s Hanley was considered a 'large modern town' (VCH vol 8 p143). **Lawlessness**. The Rough Fleet gang terrorised Hanley in the earlier C19. They operated in the Town Road area and their ringleader was one Jack Wilson, the son of an earthenware manufacturer in the firm 'Neale and Wilson,' who lived in c1817. Some of his exploits are told by Henry Wedgwood in PTP pp65-72. His last exploit was to accidentally kill his brother with a cannon ball (see below) (SHST p489). In early Feb 1820 five young men, Daniel Collier, William Toft, William Walklate, Cooper and Holford, mainly all potters, were accused of raping Hannah Bowers, aged 18, near the Lamb Inn, Bryant Street, Hanley. All five were sentenced to hang at Stafford, but the last two were eventually reprieved. After the executions on April 15 1820 the bodies of the men were transported in a waggon back to Hanley. At a toll house in Stone it was noticed Collier breathed and twitched, but he died further on on the road (PTP pp47-52) (STMSM July 1974 p19) (MMM pp44-47) (ES Sept 28 1994 p19) (SMML pp21-23). References in QMMH pp22-27 and SLM April 1983 p26 to a murderer called William Collier may relate to a William Collier of Whiston Farm (see). Thomas Cooper, the Chartist leader, addressed a crowd of 10,000 in front of the Crown Inn at Crown Bank, Hanley, on Aug 14 1842: the Chartist riots in the Potteries ensued over the next week. Cooper was the inspiration for Alton Locke the protagonist of Charles Kingsley's novel 'Alton Locke, Tailor and Poet' (1851) (TB Nov 1994 p19). The Chartists rioted in Hanley in 1842 (ILN Oct 15 1842 p1il). **Persons and visitors.** On Aug 1 1807 an accident happened at Hanley when **Mr Wilson,** a pottery manufacturer, had a son and grandson of his killed by a cannon which accidentally set off two others in front of the one where the father was standing holding his child. Their remains were buried in Hanley churchyard (Hanley churchyard was cleared Aug 1974 and the remains interred at Hartshill cemetery) (SHST p631). Novelists, **William and Mary Howitt,** lived in Hanley for a short while after their marriage in 1821. Here William owned a chemist's shop (NSSG p47) (SHJ spring 1992 p20). **James Broughton** of Handsacre (see), author of historical notes in the early C19 Staffs press, styled himself as the 'Hermit of Hanley' when replying to correspondence. **Bernard Batigan** (d1908), poet, critic and elocutionist, was born in Hanley on Feb 13 1832. Some of his work includes 'Pen Pictures of Great Actors' and 'Pen Portraits of Famous People' (PSS pp207-208) (VFC p10). Isaac Leech, a dwarf of Hanley, who was involved in many fights with bulldogs was known as the 'Hanley Dwarf' (TB Nov 1993 p31). **Edward John Smith** (d1912), captain of SS Titanic, was born in Well Street, Hanley, on Jan 27 1850. Smith was educated at Etruria (see) British School. On leaving school Smith worked at Etruria Forge. In 1871 he went to Liverpool to become a seaman. A tablet to his memory in Hanley Town Hall was unveiled on April 16 1913 by the Lord Mayor. In 1961 during alterations the tablet was moved to Smith's old school, now (1979) Etruria Middle School (HOE pp101,235,253p,262,263) (STM Feb 1964 p36p) (SHST p566) (Staffs Sentinel April 24 1973) (The Loss of the SS Titanic. L Beesley. revised ed 1973) (STMSM April 1974 p13. April 1980 p13. Nov 1980 pp15-16) (MMM pp11-13) (POTP p194) (TB Jan 1986 p5) (The Town That Has Forgot Its Past. Fred Leigh. c1998/9 p63).

THE POTTERIES MUSEUM AND CITY CENTRAL LIBRARY. The present Potteries Museum and adjoining City Central Library in Bethesda Street have their origins in the Mechanics' Institution, founded in 1826. They had their first building in **Gitana Street,** formerly Frederick Street. By 1850, a museum, known as the North Staffordshire Museum, had been added. In 1861 the Institution and its museum moved to new premises in Pall Mall. The **Pall Mall** premises were enlarged with a second storey in 1880 (VCH vol 8 p171). In 1887 most of the Pall Mall building was acquired by Hanley borough council for its Free Library. This occupied the ground floor and the Mechanics' Institution museum occupied the upper floor. In 1890 the North Staffordshire Technical and Art Museum founded by the Chamber of Commerce in 1890 was added to the Mechanics' Institution museum. In 1891 Hanley borough council took over the Mechanics' Institution museum, and the museum became the Hanley Borough Museum. The Hanley Borough Museum was added to by the North Staffordshire Natural History Museum (established by the NSFC), in 1908, and by the Russell art collection, in 1926; the year it was given to the City. By this time Hanley Borough Museum had become the City Museum and Art Gallery. On the corner of **Broad Street** and Bethesda Street a new building for a City Museum and Art Gallery was opened on Oct 13 1956 by Alderman Horace Barks. It was designed by JR Piggott, built on the site of the former Bell Pottery, and was the first new museum opened in England since WW2. Here other collections from Burslem, Stoke-upon-Trent, and Tunstall were added to the existing collection. This building which had only a life of some 25 years was demolished and the present larger building opened on the site by the Prince of Wales on June 3 1981. The name changed from City Museum and Art Gallery to The Potteries Museum in April 1998. The library, now City Library, remained at Pall Mall until the present building, S of the City Museum and Art Gallery, was opened by Rt Hon Baroness Lee of Asheridge on Dec 10 1970. It is now known as City Central Library (VCH vol 8 pp170,171,270p facing of the 1956 Broad Street museum) (AGT pp120-121) (ES April 17 1998 p12). Arnold Mountford, director of the City Museum, was a prime-mover in founding in 1959 the present (2000) Stoke-on-Trent Museum Archaeological Society (info Helen Outram).

1850 to 1900. The **'Woodisun'** was a local name for a tiny area of Hanley about Marsh Street before c1900 (OTP p147). **Penny Readings,** which reached their height in the 1860s, are thought to have originated at Hanley in public readings from the war correspondence in 'The Times' read from the Market Terrace. The promoter was S Taylor formerly identified with 'The Sentinel' as part proprietor (OTP pp126,155) (ES Dec 4 1930 p11). A **newspaper** known as The Lever was founded in Hanley in Jan 1851 by Robert Hopkinson. It maintained a radical, temperance, and anti-clerical stance, but failed in Oct 1851 through lack of support (POTP p126). **Lightning** killed a man in a

violent storm in Hanley in July 1852 (SHST p630). A temporary structure erected on the top of Hanley church by a party of soldiers carrying out a **survey for the Board of Ordnance** late in 1850 was wrongly assumed, by some elderly ladies, to be a defence against the 'papal aggression' prevalent at the time (SA Dec 21 1850) (VCH vol 3 p114). **Hanley Economic Building Society,** founded on Oct 21 1854, is still (1998) active (Building Societies Yearbook 1998-99: Official Handbook of the Building Society Association). Hanley with Shelton became a **borough** on May 22 1857 (SOSH p280) (VCH vol 8 p158). The first town hall, as distinct from the market halls, was opened in 1845 in Fountain Square, on the site of the old butter market. In the mid 1880s the council moved to the Queen's Hotel in Albion Street. The old town hall was demolished in or by 1936 (VCH vol 8 p158). Hanley became a county borough in 1889, but in doing so, a blow was dealt to current plans for the federation of the Potteries (VCH vol 8 p254). Scott-Giles describes Hanley's **arms** thus: The shield was parted chevronwise, and the chief palewise; the first compartment was barry of six pieces gold and ermine with three blue jugs; the second was ermine with a black cross in outline between four blazing towers (perhaps furnaces); the base was red with four silver stars from the arms of the Wedgwood family. The crest is: A kneeling camel charge on the body with a silver shield bearing a red cross (CH p330) (SHST p280il). **Theatres.** The Grand Theatre of Varieties at the junction of of Trinity Street and Upper Foundry Street was opened in 1898 and appears to have closed in 1932 because of a large fire at the theatre (VCH vol 8 p172) (ADD p108). The Theatre Royal, Pall Mall, opened in 1871, burnt down on June 2 1949 and was reopened in 1951 (VCH vol 8 p172) (ADD p146) (ES Aug 24 1996 p21ps). **Persons and visitors. Jenny Lind** sang in Hanley in 1854. She appeared in the covered market in the absence of a more suitable hall (TSS p134). For **Arnold Bennett,** born in Hope Street in 1867, see Burslem; Hanley is Hanbridge in his novels. **Alfred Huntbach** (1866-1950), author of H and sometime chairman of NSFC (NSFCT 1949 p62p facing; born May 25 1867) (SLM vol 1 no. 3) (POTP p128). **George Stanton** was squashed to death against a wall by an elephant in Messrs Bostock and Wombwell's Menagerie in the vicinity of the Angel Inn in April 1872 (The Police Illustrated News) (TB Feb 1993 p3). The **wife of General Booth** (1829-1912), founder of the Salvation Army, preached in Hanley in 1883 (TSS p49). **Mrs Wood,** wife of bookseller William Wood, is mentioned in 'A Mummer's Wife' a novel by George Moore (1885) set in a Hanley draper's shop (POTP p235). **Gertie Gitana** (1888-1957), music hall artist, moved with her family from Longport to Frederick Street, Hanley, when aged three. Frederick Street was renamed Gitana Street in her memory in 1957 (PPP p46p). **Edward Luke Roberts** shot himself to death after attempting to murder his lover, Mrs Jane Lindop, at No. 55 Bucknall New Road on Feb 22 1891 (DMF pp93-108). For another murder case in the Bucknall New Road area in 1904 see The Rocks.

1900 to PRESENT. **Hanley Swifts** were a football team and had a football ground at Northwood in c1910 (H p101) (VCH vol 8 p171). In 1910 the six towns of the Potteries including Hanley were federated to form Stoke-on-Trent. In **WW2** the Germans bombed Hanley on June 26 1940 at 1.42am (ES Feb 4 1977). **Records.** At the Finney Gardens Hotel, Hanley, on Dec 27-28 1980 the highest table skittle score in 24 hours, 90,446 skittles by 12 players, as achieved (GBR 1989 p287). 'The Place' night club in Bryan Street is believed to have been the first or one of the first disco night clubs in Britain, when it opened in the 1970s. The club re-opened in Nov 1994 (ES Oct 29 1994 p3). The first wedding to take place in a night club in Britain took place at Valentino's night club, Etruria Road, on June 12 1999. The marriage was between Jenny Shaw, aged 19, and Paul Edwards, aged 45 (ES June 14 1999 p1). **'Hanley Castle'** and 'Faulty Towers' are derogatory references to the Hanley office block Union (or Unity - ES Jan 6 1997 p1) House, built in 1973 (POP p38) (ES Oct 21 1996 p11p). Plans in Jan 1997 to turn the block into an hotel had not materialised by Nov 1999, when there were plans to demolish it so the site could be redeveloped (ES Jan 6 1997 p1p. Nov 24 1999 p11p); it can be seen from Ashley Heath, 11m to the WSW. In Adventure Place was a large house, over the uppermost window was a quaint inscription carved in stone

> Thease bricks were but claei
> On ye first of Maie.

(OTP p161). **Strange sights.** Prof Baker had visions of a future Windmill Street when aged seven in 1896, and in 1917; the street was not built until 1950s? (The Unexplained. Orbis Publishing 1980/3) (MGH pp64-65). The ghost in St John's which once scared the bellringer of that church turned out to be nothing more than a pet monkey (TFTP pp196-198). In 1950 a 40-foot whale called 'Jonah' was displayed to the public on a trailer by the Bryan

Street entrance to the old Port Vale football ground in Hanley (ES Nov 16 1996 p21p. May 29 1999 p21p). A UFO was seen from Ogden Road in February 1967; from Howard Place on Aug 24 1967; from Timmis Street on Aug 29 1967; from Dresden Street by two girls, Barbara Hemmings and Kathleen Price, on Aug 30 1967; from Whatmore Street on Aug 30 1967 (FSRP pp12,29,32). Two strange dark grey objects shaped like child's bootees, moving backwards and forwards in front of a parked car, all surrounded by orange and yellow halo, was seen from Nelson Place on Sept 2 1967 at about 1.30am (FSRP p11). There was a sighting of a UFO over Hanley in Feb 1996 (ES May 7 1996 p9). **Persons and visitors. Thomas Holland** of Northwood, having stepped on the joint in the paving stones in St John Street to avoid some horse manure, fell down a hole in the pavement on Dec 3 1903. He was never found and a funeral service was said over the hole on Dec 5 when all hope of his re-emerging had gone (SHST pp631-633) (POP p67) (TSS p76). The widow, **Mary Elizabeth Gilbert**, aged 48, was murdered by her jealous lover Henry Jones, a Hanley collier, aged 50, in the Rocks area (the Bucknall New Road area) at her house, 14 Back West Street (lost street name), late on Jan 28 or early on Jan 29 1904 (DMF pp1-18). For **Anna Pavlova** (1881-1931), Russian ballerina, in Hanley see ES Jan 22 1981 p16p. Sir Henry Irving died on tour 1905 a week before he was due in Hanley (TSS p140). Many famous performers who appeared at the Theatre Royal stayed at the nearby Capesthorne Hotel (see). **Norman Wright**, swimmer, was born in Hanley in 1914. He represented Great Britain at swimming at the 1932 and 1936 Olympics and was the swimming captain at the 1948 Olympics. Dr **Hilda Hulme** was born in Hanley on June 13 1914. She became a nationally recognised authority on the works of William Shakespeare and died on March 16 1983; the Hilda Hulme Memorial Prizes are awarded annually for Scholarship in English at the Sixth Form College, Fenton, where a photograph of her hangs in the library. Sir **Stanley Matthews** CBE, footballer, was born on Feb 1 1915 in Seymour Street, Hanley, the third of four sons of Jack Matthews, a barber. He learnt his football on 'Meakin's Square,' a rough piece of ground alongside a local pottery. He attended Wellington School, Hanley. For Stoke City and Blackpool he was a brilliant outside-right and was the first footballer to be knighted (1965) whilst still a player. He became known as 'the wizard of dribble.' The FA Cup Final of 1953 became known as the Matthews Final owing to Matthews turning the game around for Blackpool. He was Footballer of the Year in 1948, 1956 and 1963, and European Footballer of the Year in 1957. He was capped 54 times in his career. In 1964 he was the oldest player to score in the FA Cup, aged 49. He retired as an active football player in 1965. In 1987 he received an honorary degree from Keele University and on Oct 21 1987 a statue of him by Colin Melbourne was unveiled in Market Square, Hanley. In June 1994 a play about his life opened at the New Victoria Theatre at Stoneyfields (see). He lived his final years in Penkhull and died at Nuffield Hospital in Clayton, Newcastle-under-Lyme on Feb 23 2000 (Stanley Matthews. David Miller. 1989) (HOS 1998 ed p22) (Daily Telegraph Feb 24 2000 pp1p,4) (ES Feb 24 2000 Sentinel Tribute). **Geoffrey Marks**, England Golf Captain (non-playing) 1990-1993, was born in The Parkway, Hanley, in 1938 (info Geoff Marks). **Les West**, champion cyclist, was born in Hanley in 1943. In 1964 he set the record for achieving over 26 miles in an hour at Lyme Valley, Newcastle-under-Lyme. He won the 1965 and 1967 Milk Races and broke the record for London to Brighton and back in 1970. **Paul Robeson**, singer, visited Hanley on March 19 1930 and on Feb 23 1939 (ES March 10 1930 p5. Feb 17 1939 p6). **Stanley Sherminant** murdered the son of his landlady, Harry Berrisford. The body was discovered by Harry's mother, Mrs Berrisford, under the floor boards of her house in Cromwell Street. The murder occurred on July 19 1946 or the body was discovered on that day, having lain under the floor boards for over a year. The case became known as the 'Floor Boards' murder case (STM July 1963 p39). **Prince Charles** was in Hanley on June 3 1981 to open the new City Museum and Art Galley (later Potteries Museum) (ES June 3 1981 p1p). Three siblings of the **Lee family** of Stoke-on-Trent (Hanley?) were all living at great ages in Feb 2000; Bill Lee, aged 108, then the second oldest man in Britain, his sister, Elsie Callcott, aged 99, had a attended a school in York Street, Hanley, and his brother, Tom Lee, aged 97 (ES Feb 4 2000 p3ps).

Hanley Cottage Roadside cottage on Butterhill Bank, Burston, on E side of the road. The cottage was inhabited by the 1970s by Mrs Frances Palmer and her son Dennis Palmer. He worked for a builders merchants and made painted concrete figures which decorated the garden. There were many figures and the garden became quite a curiosity; the large full-length 'Aunt Sally' being the most memorable. (STMSM April 1976 p of on front cover). The figures started to decay after Mr Palmer ceased to make them in 1975. They were in a poor state when the cottage and garden were demolished in 1992 or 1993. A new house was then built on the site.

Hanley Hall Said to have been the manor-house of Hanley manor. It stood near the junction of Hall Street and Bucknall New Road and was the home of the Smith family in the C17 and the C18. The Old Hall Pottery stood on or near the site (VCH vol 8 p152) (SASR 1987 p103). Bradley says Hanley old manor house still (1911) exists as Old Hall, near the Bucknall Road (SPP p47). In 1212 William of Hanley held the vill of Hanley of the king on condition he pay a fee and perform guard duties at Newcastle Castle. The manor had many successive tenants but from at least the early C13 until at least 1650 overlordship descended with Newcastle manor (VCH vol 8 p151).

Hanley Hayes House or minute hamlet 0.75m NW of Werrington. Also Hanley or Handley Ease or Eaves. Here was a colliery called Handley Hays Colliery (NSFCT 1914 p65), mentioned in 1772 (WJ p19).

Hanley Hills Was a district round about Cannon Street, Hanley, now back of the Central Library (H p107).

Hanley Old Hall It was situated approximately E of Albion Square, demolished in 1804 (SHST p566). Perhaps synonymous with Hanley Hall (see).

Hanley Park Nearly 1m S of Hanley. Laid out in 1892-7 on some 63 acres of Stoke Fields, a tract of waste ground (VCH vol 8 p144) (POP p57). Occupies the site of part of Shelton Hall estate. The bandstand (1896) commemorates George Howson. Opened in 1897 (POP p57) (AGT p135). Or opened in 1894. It was the first public park designed by TH Mawson (BOE p258). A Wright Monoplane was on display at Hanley Park fete held on July 6-7 1910 (EAS p35).

Hanley Park Medieval deer park to the E of Endon. Formerly in Endon township in Leek ancient parish. In existence by 1341. It lay between Park Lane and Endon Brook and extended into Cheddleton parish. It had been disparked by the mid C16 (VCH vol 7 p182).

Hannah's Well Seabridge, Newcastle-under-Lyme. Marked on OS map 1:25,000 series.

Hannel Farm House 1m NNE of Heaton. Formerly in Heaton township in Leek ancient parish (VCH vol 7 p189). The site of Hannel Farm was occupied by 1617 (VCH vol 7 p186).

Hannocks Moor Name for a field S of Vicarage Road, Upper Penn. The name occurs in the C14 and has appeared as Hannokes. At one time this field formed a part of the Penn Moor estate (PONP p36).

Hansley Cross Small hamlet 1m W of Alton. Here is a possible burial mound in a field called Round Knowl (see). Has also appeared as Hawsley Cross (HAF p30).

Hanyards Consists of two houses - Lower Hanyards and Upper Hanyards over 1m NW of Tixall. In Tixall ancient parish. The name has appeared as Hagonegate (1227) (SSE 1996 p14), Haveneyate (1305) (A History of Tixall. volume 1: Tixall's Churches. Anne Andrews. 1995 p7) and Hagenyate (SPN p128). It is from Anglo-Saxon 'han,' high and 'yate,' gate or road (perhaps from a road called Wilson's Lane, which in 1817 was a little-used track from Hanyard farmhouse to Hopton Heath) (HOT p84). Or from 'Haguna's gate,' which may have been an entrance to Tixall Park, an ancient enclosure (DUIGNAN) (SSE 1996 p14). Or 'Hagga's gate' (SPN p128). In the early C19 the Cliffords noted the fine view from Hanyard, which, looking W on a very clear day, included the steeples of Wolverhampton, the Malverns, the Wrekin, the Clees, Beacon Hill, and Sugnall Hall (HOT p84).

Harborne Ancient parish and former village on a slight slope above Bourne Brook. Harborne is now a suburb of Birmingham, over 3m to the SW of Birmingham, and 25.5m SSE of Stafford.
EARLY. There was an Ice Age boulder stone, weighing five or six tons, opposite Tennel Road and another opposite Camomile Cottages in Tennel Road, so large that it was impossible to move it and a sewer had to be diverted around it. For others in Harborne parish see under Harts Green (STELE Feb 29 1952). There was a **Roman** camp at Metchley in c48 AD (HOHE p1). A Roman well, described as recently discovered by Hackwood in 1896, was found in Park Road. It stood lined with blocks of sandstone from Warley quarry. Park Road was a portion of the old road from Smethwick to King's Norton (now obsolete). It lies 0.75m W of Icknield Street (RS p9).
600 to 1800. The manor of Horeborne (Harborne) is recorded as being held by the bishop of Chester (Lichfield) in DB. Later forms are: Horeburn (1255), Horeborn (1291) (HOHH p2), Horborn (1576), Horbourne (1618) (STELE Sept 29 1951. Dec 22 1951. Some have thought the first part of the **name** 'Har' represents 'chief,' or 'principal,' or 'high,' or 'grey,' or 'old' (HOHH p2) or 'fair' or 'pleasant' (RS p8) or 'boundary' (DUIGNAN) or 'dirt' (NSJFS 1981 p3). Some have thought 'borne' represents 'boundary,' or 'hill,' or 'brow,' or 'brook' (HOHH p2). Bourn Brook to the S is thought to have been the boundary between the Tomsaetan from the N and the Hwicce from the S, and long formed the old boundary between Worcs and Staffs (HOHE pp1-2). A large stone was found under the floor of St Peter's church, Harborne, during

excavations in 1983. It was thought at first to have been used as the foundation of the medieval S door, but has also been thought to be the base of a cross at which St Chad preached when at Harborne in the C7 (HOHE p2p). The parish **church**, St Peter, on the corner of Old Church and Vicarage Roads, has a C15 tower which is the only remains of the the original medieval parish church; the rest of the church dates from the rebuilding in 1867 (BOEWA p185). The parish was probably founded by the late C13, although it is not in the Papal Returns of 1291. It probably originated as a chapel of Walsall parish (SHC 1916 p200). Most of the ancient parish (excluding Smethwick urban district) was removed to Birmingham county borough and Warws in 1891 (GLAUE p413) (TB April 1986 p27). The ancient parish included the chapelry of Edgbaston, Warws, which became a parish no later than 1658 (GLAUE p413). Harborne was made a prebend in Lichfield cathedral in c1165, assigned to the common fund in 1279 (VCH vol 3 pp141,144). The parish was a peculiar jurisdiction of the dean and chapter of Lichfield cathedral until peculiar jurisdictions were abolished in 1846 (VCH vol 3 pp93-94) (GLAUE). For the descent of the **manor** see Smethwick. During the **Commonwealth period** marriage banns could not be read in the market place at Harborne, for Harborne did not have a market place, and the banns had to be read in the church (SCSF p65). In John Sanders of Harborne, the nailers of the area found a champion during the Commonwealth. He was a Fifth Monarchy man and formerly an ironmonger, who wrote 'An Iron Rod for the Naylors and Tradesmen near Birmingham' (1655), urging the nailers to strike for better prices for their nails and to petition the Lord Protector for a 'Corporation' (VCH vol 2 p239). **Parish administration.** From the later C17 Harborne ancient parish was reduced to an 'hour-glass' shape with Smethwick forming the northern 'side,' and Harborne forming the south. By at least the beginning of the C18 it was usual to appoint one or more officers for each 'side' of the parish. Eventually, in alternate years each 'side' was able to appoint a constable for the whole parish (SHCB p9). For **pounds** in Harborne parish see Smethwick. It is said the village of Harborne received the title **'Healthy Harborne'** and hence ironically 'Hungry Harborne' for being situated 585 feet above sea level and because it receives pure, warm SW prevailing winds from the Bristol Channel making it a healthy place to live. It is said that the Bristol Channel can be seen from the top of the church tower (S&W p152) (HOHH pp7,67). The women who lived in the Moor Pool area of Harborne who did the washing for the wealthy of Edgbaston in the soft water of the Moor Pool may have given rise to this jingle

> Hungry Harborne proud and poor,
> A washerwoman at every door.

(WMVB p77). Perhaps the first **Penny Club** (a subscription of one penny per week given by poor children, the interest from which goes to provide clothes for them) on record was established at Harborne. This was done by a man named Green in 1799 (Aris's Birmingham Gazette. April 27 1801) (S&W pp153-154) (Century of Birmingham Life. Langford. vol 2 pp109-110) (HOHH p9). For Harborne and Smethwick **charities** see RS pp63-66. **Natural History.** During his visit to Harborne in the later C17 Dr Plot saw the people make an odd sort of manure by planting vetches and letting them die in the ground and ploughing them back into the soil; also he noted lupins and beans are ploughed into the earth (NHS p346). **Persons and visitors. James Sands** lived to the age of 140, outliving five leases of 21 years each. His wife is believed to have lived to the age of at least 120 years. According to Plot he died on Dec 6 1588; according to Fuller he died in 1625 (Harborne PR) (HWE vol 2 p312) (NHS pp326,327) (SHOS vol 2 p124) (SMC p171) (Encyclopaedia Britannica. 3rd ed (1788-1797). **Thomas Attwood** (1783-1856), political reformer and Birmingham's first MP, lived for some time at The Grove (see), Harborne.

BLUE COAT SCHOOL. In Nov 1722 a body of commissioners formed to found a school in Harborne which opened on Aug 9 1724 for boys and girls. The old school entrance was in Colmore Row (with original statues of a boy and girl in the school uniform). The school at the junction of Harborne Hill and Metchley Lane and extending along Somerset Road opened on Oct 29 1930 (BOEWA p186). A small plaque on the side of Colmore Road now (1972) marks the original site. In 1951 some land at the rear of the school was sold to Birmingham Education Committee as a site for a new secondary Modern School, now known as Harborne Hill. Prince William of Gloucester visited the school on July 17 1972 (he died in an aeroplane accident at Bobbington in Aug 1972) (The Blue Coat School, Birmingham. 250th Anniversary 1722-1972. VDB Still. 1972). The original statues of a boy and a girl wearing the school uniform are now inside the school. Those set in niches above the porch outside are copies. The originals are by Edward and Samuel

Grubb (BOEWA p186).
1800 to PRESENT. **Harborne annexed to Warwickshire.** Sir Henry Wiggin of Metchley Grange, MP for Handsworth between 1885 and 1893, opposed Harborne's transfer to Birmingham. In 1885 he said in parliament after the Third Reform Act that Harborne was, as Elihu Burritt had described it, part of the 'green borderlands of the Black Country,' and that Liberals and Conservatives alike objected to its inclusion in Birmingham. Sir Charles Wentworth Dilke defending the Liberal Government said of Harborne that 'like a rich jewel in an Ethiop's ear, it hung like a pendant to the county (of Staffs) by a narrow thread' and he held up a map to prove it (GMH p15): The first person to have likened Harborne to 'a rich jewel in an Ethiop's ear' (Romeo and Juliet) is believed to have been Edward Capern (GMH p28). In 1888, and again in 1889, Harborne residents voted to oppose the Greater Birmingham Scheme, which would have annexed Harborne to Birmingham, mainly because Harborne rates were lower than those of Birmingham. By 1890, however, Harborne's rates were higher than Birmingham's, and the residents agreed to the annexation. **Chad Valley Toys**, one of the best known British toy manufacturers which operated from 1897 to 1972, had a factory in Rose Road (HOHE p31p). Harborne **Railway**, linking Harborne with Birmingham, opened on Aug 10 1874. The service became affectionately known as 'The Harborne Express or Flier,' a misnomer as the journey took 22 minutes going into Birmingham (WMVB p78). The line closed to passengers in 1934, and to goods in Nov 1963. The line ended at Station Road, Harborne. The railbed is now Harborne walkway. Frensham Way is now (1996) on the site of the station (VCHWA vol 7 p41 see map) (HOHE pp27-28) (OHOPP p44p of Harborne station) (HOPP pl 4). The **Little Sisters of the Poor** moved to Queen's Park Road, Harborne in 1874 and were still ministering to elderly residents and local people in 1989. They had begun work in the centre of Birmingham in 1864 (BOOP 16) (HOHE p28). The world's **first Girl Guides** originated out of a group of about six girls from Harborne formed by Miss GN Commander, aged 15, their patrol was called the Ravens. In 1909 they went to a scout rally in Warley Woods attended by Lord Baden Powell who, on seeing them, suggested to his wife that she form a separate movement (HOHE p32). By 1900 the Harborne **gooseberry society**, founded in 1815 by Mr Simcox, was considered one of the longest running gooseberry societies in the country. The society had a reputation for its giant gooseberries. The annual show took place at the Sportsman Inn in Metchley Lane; another venue for it was at the Green Man Inn, Harborne, where it was held in 1900. The show came to an end in c1902, but the grower's society may have been in existence as late as 1913 (STELE May 11 1956). In **WW2** Harborne Young Mens Bible Association Hall in High Street was bombed (OHOPP p127). In 1941 a German bomb destroyed St John's church, Harborne Heath (HOHE p34). There was a great **storm** at Harborne and Quinton on Sunday Sept 15 1875 (HOHH p28). **Persons and visitors.** Rev **James Thomas Law** (1790-1876), eldest son of the bishop of Bath and Wells, Chancellor of the Diocese of Lichfield from 1821, author of numerous works on church law, was vicar of St Peter's, Harborne, from 1825 to 1845, when he was succeeded by his nephew William Towry Law (1809-1886). It is said that the people of the parish chalked 'No Popery!' on walls because he introduced a surpliced choir. He remained vicar until 1851 (GMH pp7-10) (HOHE pp13,19). **David Cox**, artist, lived at Greenfield House (see), Harborne between 1841-1859 (VCHWA vol 7 p50). **Elihu Burritt**, American Consul in Birmingham and author of BCGB, lived at 11 Victoria Road, Harborne from 1865. By 1989 the house was known as Burritt's House (GMH pp24,25,28) (HOHE p24) (TB April 1986 p27. Jan 1987 p14p). **Charles Leaver** (fl 1867-1883), painter, was based at Harborne and frequently exhibited at the Royal Birmingham Society of Arts. He painted landscapes and rural subjects in a whimsical style and specialised in atmospheric 'church in snow' scenes (CL Sept 23 1993 p53). **Charles Badham** DD (1813-1884) clergyman and classical scholar lived in Harborne until 1867 (GMH p26). **Edward Capern** (1819-1894), the 'singing postman poet' of national renown, friend of Elihu Burritt, came to live in Harborne from his native Bideford, Devon, in 1866. At first he lived in Moor Pool Lane (Ravenhurst Road), but in 1868 moved to Heath Road (High Street); that building was still standing in 1933, although it was then part of a row of shops. His last book 'Sungleams and Shadows' includes many poems with a local theme. He returned to Devon in 1884; his name is commemorated in Capern Grove (Birmingham Post Feb 18 1933) (GMH p27) (TB April 1986 p27) (HOHE p28) (OHOPP p126). Sir **Henry Rushbury** RA was born in Harborne on Oct 28 1889. He later became distinguished for his paintings and etchings, and was elected a member of the Royal Academy (HOHE p30). **Thomas Hodgson**, who accompanied Robert Falcon Scott on his first voyage to the Antarctic in 1901, was born in Harborne (HOHE p32). **WH Auden** (1907-1973), poet, lived with his family at 42 Lordswood Road (demolished

1979) from some time after WW1 to 1940 when his family moved to 13 Court Oak Road. His father, Dr GA Auden, was Birmingham's first school medical officer. The first poem that appears in all his collected works 'The Watershed' was written in Harborne (GMH pp5-7) (HOHE p33). The Prince of Wales, later **Edward VIII**, stayed at Bishop's Croft (formerly Harborne House see) for three days in 1923 (HOHE p33).

Harborne Hall On S side of Church Road, Harborne. An old house on the site was tenanted by a branch of the Birch family: George Birch became lord of Harborne manor in 1710 (HOHE p7). The hall was built in the 1790s (HOPP pl 5), and rebuilt by Dr Capt Charles J Hart (OHOPP p26p of in 1922). He was occupying the house by 1868, and married one of the daughters of Joseph Chamberlain the statesman. He had John Henry Chamberlain (1831-1883), the Birmingham architect, add Gothic extensions to the hall which overpower the original Regency building (HOHE p26). The hall was later the seat of Walter Chamberlain (1884-1901). It was a VAD Auxiliary Hospital from 1916 to 1918 (HOPP pl 5), and was a prep school between 1919 and 1924, and later a convent and multi-faith centre (HOHE p26) (OHOPP pp26,109p of in 1921). (The History of Harborne Hall. Frances Wilmot. 1991).

Harborne Heath District 0.75m NE of Harborne church. Harborne Heath, formerly heathland then a small hamlet centred on the Green Man Inn (HOHH p92), had become the centre of Harborne village by the mid C19 (HOHE p23). The name 'Heath' is still retained in Heath House in St John's Road (HOHH p56). The church, St John the Baptist, towards the W end of the High Street, built in 1858 was rebuilt in 1959-1960 (BOEWA p185). Harborne St John the Baptist was refounded as Harborne Heath ecclesiastical parish in 1859 (GLAUE p413).

Harborne House Old Church Road, Harborne. Thought to have built by Thomas Green, lord of Harborne manor, in 1790 (OHOPP p28p of c1960); the central part of the C17 remains (HOHE p10). Since c1911 it has been used as a residence for the bishops of Birmingham diocese and is now known as Bishop's Croft (VCHWA vol 7 p72). It was purchased by the Church Commissioners in 1921 for the official residence of the bishop and it was still the residence of the bishop of Birmingham in 1998 (Birmingham Diocesan Directory. 1998/9) (OHOPP p28). The Prince of Wales, later Edward VIII, stayed here for three days in 1923 (HOHE p33). Has also appeared as Manor House and Bishop's Croft. (VCHWA vol 7 p23).

Harborne Reservoir Created by the damming of the Bourn Brook. Marked on Kelly's Directory Map of Birmingham.

Harden Former village on slight rising ground on the W side of Ford Brook, now a suburb of Walsall over 1.25m SW of All Saints church, Bloxwich. Lay in the foreign of Walsall. It was anciently an enclosure in Cannock Forest (DUIGNAN). Existed as a hamlet by the late C13 (VCH vol 17 p164) (BY p26), centred on the junction of Harden Road and Well Lane (SNBP p31). Has appeared as Harding, Harder, Hawarden, and Harping. The name means 'the high farm or estate' (DUIGNAN). (NHS p188). On p75 of SHOS vol 2 Shaw notes an Arden a mile from Walsall where there was an inn called the Valiant Trooper in 1800, although Shaw may have called this place Harding on a previous page. Cromwell Cottage is one of the oldest buildings in Harden area. In c1800 it was a shop and was later converted into a Roman Catholic chapel. No Oliver Cromwell associations have been found to explain its name (BY p26) (SNBP p31). Harden became a ward of Walsall county borough in 1931 (VCH vol 17 p217).

Hardings Booth Minute hamlet 1.25m S of Hollinsclough. Formerly in Heathylee township of Alstonefield ancient parish, at the confluence of the Manifold and Oakenclough Brook. There was a settlement here by 1327 (VCH vol 7 p33).

Hardingswood District of Kidsgrove, and 0.5m NW of St Thomas church, Kidsgrove. Formerly in Talk o' th' Hill township in Audley ancient parish (W p430). Created a civil parish in 1894 (GLAUE p413). Has appeared as Hardings Wood, and Hardingwood (HSP p19). In the later C17 Plot noted the coal here and it was at Hardingswood he went down Mr Poole's mine (NHS pp130-131, 147-148). Simeon Shaw noted that The House at Hardingwood, was in a peculiar situation. That whenever its inhabitants go to church (that of Lawton, Ches) they pass, out of the province of Canterbury into that of York; out of Staffs into Ches; out of Lichfield and Coventry diocese into Chester diocese; out of Pirehill hundred (Staffs) into that of Nantwich (Ches); being successively in three constablewicks - Tunstall, Chell, and Lawton; and in three parishes, Wolstanton, Audley, and Lawton (HSP p19).

Hardiwick House 1m NNE of Caverswall. Here, at SJ 956444, in 1962 JD Wilcock and J Gee excavated a section of road and deduced that it was Roman and formed part of the Roman Road from Buxton to Blythe Bridge (Report City of Stoke-on-Trent Museum Arch Soc. vol 1 1965 p10) (NSFCT 1982 p23).

Hardiwick Tiny hamlet above the Trent Valley on a ridge between two tributaries of the Trent 2m SSW of Hilderstone. In Sandon parish. The name has appeared as Hardywicke (W p404) or Hardewick (SGSAS). The first element is the Celtic 'ard,' 'ardd,' a height (NSFCT 1910 p163). Plot noted Mary Woodward of Hardiwick who had lost her hearing aged six but could lip read perfectly and could lip read in the dark by putting her hand to lips (NHS p288) (SD pp41, 82).

Hardwick Former hamlet at the junction of Hardwick Road and Old Chester Road (W p552) on NE slopes of Barr Beacon 2.5m NE of Great Barr. Formerly in Great Barr township and chapelry in Aldridge ancient parish. At Hardwick Farm at the N end of Great Barr Common at SP 07259965 a small bronze disc ornamented with classical figures was found. It was thought by Garner to be the umbo of a Roman shield (GNHS p543) (HOWW p25) (VCH vol 1 p190) (CCC p9) (MOA p15), but is too small for this (NSJFS 1964 p24). The earliest reference to Hardwick is in a document in the C15 (ADY p15) (SNAR p94). It first appears on maps on the 1832 OS map. The first houses of the present large residential suburb of Hardwick were built in the early 1920s (SNAR p94). Gould thought the name could have been brought from Hardwick in Derbys; the Countess of Shrewsbury, who held nearby Drayton Bassett and Hardwick, may have introduced the name here (MOA p138). Or it may be of Anglo-Saxon origin meaning a sheepfold (ADY p17).

Hardwick Former farm and settlement 1m WNW of Pattingham. It was a place name by the mid C12 and a settlement by 1311. Hardwick Farm disappeared in c1820 (VCH vol 20 p173).

Hardwick Covert Lodge Great Barr (Birmingham A-Z).

Hardwick Lodge House nearly 1m SSW of Little Aston.

Harecastle Former hamlet centring on the present Harecastle Farm, a stone-built Jacobean hall on a hillock above Bathpool Valley, 0.75m SE of Talke. Formerly in Talke township of Audley ancient parish. There is a tradition that Harecastle Farm was once moated, but no map shows it as such (KAIW p3). There was an estate at Harecastle, with Hare Castle House later forming a part, by the late C16 (SHC 1944 p59). There was a station on the North Staffs railway line known as Harecastle at the N end of the Harecastle tunnels (IAS p131). (BOE p274) (MR pp318,319p of Harecastle Farm).

Harecastle Hill 700 feet high hill at Harecastle. It is faintly possible that the bank and ditch crowning the hill is a prehistoric earthwork (KAIW p2). The hill has appeared on a map as 'Harecastle Clump,' suggesting that a clump of trees stood on the summit (TTTD p214). Harecastle tunnels run through it (NSFCT 1938 p61).

Harecastle Tunnels Two canal tunnels, one railway tunnel, and some minor railways tunnels which pass through Harecastle Hill. Formerly in Wolstanton ancient parish. The first two were built to take the Trent and Mersey Canal through the hill, they are approximately just over 1.5m in length. Simeon Shaw probably saw them (HSP pp23,24,25). (ES Sept 5 1934 p8 ps) (STM July 1963 p33p of the air vent Kidsgrove to one of the tunnels, Oct 1963 p65p) (SGS p114) (AGT p66il) (The Trent and Mersey Canal. Peter Lead. 1980. pls 26,27,29,30) (KNS chapter vii) (KTM p58).

BRINDLEY'S TUNNEL. Surveyed by James Brindley in 1758. Work started on the tunnel on July 27 1766 (IAS p171) and it was opened in 1777. It was probably the largest civil engineering project ever carried out in Britain up to that time (IANS pp20-21); the world's first straight and level transport canal of more than 2600 meters (NSJFS 1978 p33); the first transport tunnel in England and in its day the longest (IAS p171): It took all of the 11 years it took to build the whole canal, to build. Brindley died in 1772 and it was completed by his brother-in-law Hugh Henshall in 1775 (NSFCT 1990 p40). Viewed at the S entrance it is the tunnel on the left. It is 2,880 yards (IAS p171) (SL p236) (IANS p20) (MR p198) or 2897 yards (NSFCT 1938 p61) (SHST p112) long and 8 feet 6 inches wide. It was built with no towpath and could only carry a barge in one direction at a time. It was dug out of 32 faces simultaneously by sinking 15 shafts along the line and working outwards from each shaft as well as inwards from the two ends (NSFCT 1990 p40). The labourers building the tunnel found a prolific seam of coal which gave the major impetus to start up the North Staffordshire coalfield (VB p186). A contemporary of Brindley called it 'our Eighth Wonder of the world - the subterraneous Navigation which is cutting by the great Mr Brindley who handles Rocks as easily as you would Plum Pies' (SL p236). Brindley's tunnel was used up to the beginning of the C20. Mining subsidence reduced the headroom and the tunnel became unusable in 1914 and was abandoned in 1918 (The Trent and Mersey Canal. Peter Lead. 1980. pl 24 shows a romantic interpretation of the engineers feat of tunnelling through the hill, it was published in 1785) and has remained derelict ever since; continued subsidence and a fall near the S end has made Brindley's tunnel quite unusable (SWY p61). In 1979 two canoeists travelled through the tunnel (ES Dec 20 1979).

(KAIW pp4,5) (COS p24p).

TELFORD'S TUNNEL. Built by Thomas Telford. Started in summer 1824 (NSFCT 1938 p61) (IAS p171). Opened on April 30 1827 (SHST p113). It was built to accommodate the overwhelming traffic using Brindley's Tunnel. They were used together, one for each direction (SL p243). It runs parallel to Brindley's Tunnel (Pottery Gazette April 10 1824. Feb 26 1825. July 23 1827) (Broughton's Scrapbook p125) (NSFCT 1938 p61). It is 2920 yards long (MR p198) (IANS p21; 2926 yards), 14 feet wide, 16 feet high, and an esti-mated 8,814,000 Newcastle blue bricks were used in its construction. The tunnel was electrified in Nov 1914. A ventilation engine house was built at the Chatterley end in 1954. Mining subsidence has caused a reduction in the headroom (SWY p62). In 1963 British Waterways Board started removing the sunken towpath, which was four feet nine inches wide (SWY p62p of the two tunnel entrances at N end). Two roof-falls caused by subsidence forced its closure on Sept 10 1973. It was repaired and reopened in 1977 (ES Nov 3 1975). To travel through Telford's Tunnel now takes approximately 40 min-utes (Trent and Mersey Canal Society). (HOE pp59,60) (NSJFS 1978 pp31-41). A spot at the north end of one of the tunnels is believed to have been where Christina Collins was murdered by bargees and gives rise to stories of a headless ghost at Kidsgrove. But she was, in fact, murdered near Rugeley (NSFCT 1990 p41). The same or another lady ghost called Kit Crewbucket haunts Telford's Tunnel; the name may be just a play on the old pronuncia-tion of Kidsgrove (ES Dec 20 1982. Sept 16 1994 p10) (The Good Ghost Guide. John Brooks. 1994).

RAILWAY TUNNELS. The old railway tunnel mostly runs between the two canal tunnels, but slightly higher, the floor of the rails being 18 feet above the water level (IAS p172). Built for the NSR Macclesfield-Potteries line. Took two years to build, opened on Oct 9 1848 (IAS p173). Is 1768 yards long and is Staffordshire's longest railway tunnel (NSJFS 1962 p103) (IAS p172). When electrified in the 1960s the line was re-routed overland via Bathpool Park and the tunnel closed (SL p246). This line, too, has a tunnel which is 183 yards long. Further along is a 150 yard cutting, which being alongside Kidsgrove church, has been covered so the congregation cannot hear the passing trains (NSJFS 1962 p103). There was a tradition that the air in the railway tunnel (and or canal tunnels?) was good for whooping cough. It was observed by Mr Andrew Roberts in the C19 that a lady pulled down a carriage window to take the air for this reason (STMSM July 1980 p33). (A History of the Rail-ways of Great Britain. vol 7 The West Midlands. Rex Christiansen. 1973 p192).

Harecops House 2m NNE of Alstonefield, on Archford Moor. Formerly in the detached portion of Fawfieldhead township in Alstonefield township. Ex-isted by 1839 (VCH vol 7 p11).

Haregate District of Leek, 1m NE Leek, on a NW-facing slope S of the upper Churnet. Formerly in Tittesworth township in Leek ancient parish (W p730). There was a farm here by the Dissolution (VCH vol 7 p233). 'Echeles' ap-pears in the earlier form 'Harecheles.' 'Echeles' seems to mean 'land added to an estate by reclamation' (NSJFS 1974 pp22,31). The church, St Paul, Novi Lane, was built in 1968 (LDD).

Haregate Hall Haregate Road, Leek. Formerly in Tittesworth township in Leek ancient parish. The Haregate estate belonged to Dieulacres Abbey until the Dissolution and passed to Sir Ralph Bagnall in 1552. He sold it to Thomas Wardle in 1565. In 1620 the Wardles sold it to the Baylys. In 1679 they sold it to the Samuel Bromley, who sold it in 1720 to Joshua Toft, a button mer-chant and Quaker. On Joshua's death in 1769 the estate passed to his daugh-ter Mary, widow of Charles Chorley. On her death in 1821 the estate was divided between various members of the Chorley family (VCH vol 7 p237). Some say the hall belonged to Joshua Chorley from 1764 to his death in 1817 (NSFCT 1870 p37) (SASR 1984 p87); a Joshua Chorley (d1837), grandchild of Mary Chorley, did inherit a share of the estate (VCH vol 7 p237). The hall and estate seem to have then descended with the Chorley heirs, and their heirs by marriage, the Atkinsons and the Argles, until at least 1923 and possi-bly 1948 when it was acquired by Leek urban district council (VCH vol 7 pp237-238). The hall was tenanted in the later C19; Ernest Andrew Worthing JP of Ball Haye Hall lived here from the early 1880s to his death in 1896 (VCH vol 7 p238) (ALC p53p). The main range of the house dates from the C17 or earlier (NSFCT 1882 p23) (BOE p172) (VCH vol 7 p238). Officers of the Young Pretender's army in the Jacobite Rebellion were lodged at the hall when they marched through on Dec 3 1745 (VCH vol 7 p237) (BPCSM p6).

Hare Hayes Farm Stood in the Hawthorne Terrace area of Leek. Formerly in Tittesworth township in Leek ancient parish. Existed by 1811 and was called Ball Haye Cottage in 1838 (VCH vol 7 p234).

Hare Hills Hills 0.5m NNW of Beaudesert Hall.

Hare House 1m N of Bradnop. Formerly in Bradnop township in Leek ancient parish. The S front of the house retains a C17 doorhead. The house may stand on the site of a house called Field House in 1342. This area was known as Upper Bradnop (VCH vol 7 p170).

Harehurst Hill Hill 1.5m S of Lichfield cathedral (VCH vol 14 p1).

Harewood A hay in Perton manor, mentioned in 1258. It was apparently waste later in the C13 (VCH vol 20 p29).

Harewood Hall The name is preserved in Harewood Hall Farm NW of Harewood Park.

Harewood Park Hall in Leek Road, 0.5m N of Cheadle. In Cheadle ancient parish. It was built in the 1860s by WE Bowers as a gentleman's residence (COPP2 p81p of in 1906). In the garden is a summerhouse with communion rails from Cheadle old parish church; a flower vase in the garden may also have come from the church (NSFCT 1908 p96 pl iv) (HOC p75) (SLM Oct 1952 p12).

Harford Park Pool King's Hill, N of Wednesbury. Existed in 1798 (WMLB p101)

Harlaston Village by the Mease 20m SE of Stafford. Former township and chapelry in Clifton Campville ancient parish (W p597). Harlaston was iden-tified by Dugdale as the Heorlfestun mentioned in the will of Wulfric Spot (c1002), founder of Burton Abbey (SHC 1916 p25) (SSE 1996 p14); later appears as Hernulveston, a manor, in DB (SHOS vol 1 p399), Horulvestone, and Herlaueston (SPN p59). The name means 'Heorlulf's town' (DUIGNAN) (SSE 1996 p14) (SPN p59). The church, St Matthew, on the N side of Main Road in the village centre, may, according to local tradition have origins in a Saxon church of the C9 (SVB p90). The present church has an early C13 tower, but the rest of it was built in 1882-1883 (BOE p142). Harlaston seems to have shared its feast with Haselour at Harlaston (W p564). Harlaston had a fair but not a market in medieval times (NSJFS 1971 p58). Became a sepa-rate parish in 1845 (LGS p144), 1846 (GLAUE p413) or 1850 (W p597). Became a separate civil parish in 1866 (GLAUE p413). Bishop Langton vis-ited Harlaston on Jan 14 1319 (SSE 1994 p2). For Samuel Johnson, a native of Harlaston, who murdered his own child, see Smethwick. At Grange Farm, 0.75m to the NW, French aviator Paul de Lesseps (son of the Suez Canal builder) landed his plane after losing his bearings during Burton Aviation Week between Sept 26 and Oct 1 1910. Although some said it was a publicity stunt (EAS p34).

Harlaston Hall Shaw in the late C18 refers to a Harlaston Hall which he says is only a very ordinary farm house (SHOS vol 1 p402).

Harlaston Manor Farm Lies on the western edge of Harlaston, at SK 214110, adjacent to St Matthew's parish church. A late C16 or early C17 timber-framed house (BOE p142). It dates to 1540 and has recently been restored and listed Grade II by DoE (SVB p90). There is a moated site to the N of the church, which was possibly surrounded on only three sides by water. During excava-tions at the moated site between 1991 and 1994 fragments of structures which appear to date from the C13 and C14 were found (SSAHST 1982-3 p42. 1994-95 pp21-28 plans) (CAMS p63) (WMARCH 1995 p73). Has also ap-peared as Manor Farm and Harlaston Manor House.

Harlestones Field At Coalbournbrook, Amblecote.

Harley Thorns Wood to W of Harley Farm (1834 OS map) (later Harley Thorn Farm), which is on the W side of Harley Thorn Lane, NNW of Beech.

Harlow Harlow Greave, probably in the vicinity of Harlow Farm over 1m NW of Mayfield, it is a possible Roman burial mound (NHS p404) (AAD p207 note). It is mentioned in the VCH barrow list with dimensions of 107 feet by 78 feet and three feet high. In recent years has been bulldozed flat. In 1961 traces of an excavation by unknown persons could still be seen (NSJFS 1965 p44). Has also appeared as Hardlow and may be connected to Ousley Cross (see) (NSFCT 1918 p117).

Harper's Gate Former hamlet lining a ridge by Dunsmore Brook (later dammed to create Rudyard Lake). In the C19 Harper's Gate became the present vil-lage of Rudyard (HHHL p100); Rudyard was still called Harper's Gate in 1775 (Yates' map) (VCH vol 7 p67). A small district at the S end of Rudyard village is still called Harper's Gate. In Horton ancient parish. Harper's Yate is described as eight acres of land in 1568 (SHC 1938 p154).

Harpfield Area between Penkhull and North Staffs Royal Infirmary. The name is preserved in Harpfield Road and a primary school on S side of Hartshill Road.

Harplow Perhaps a tiny hamlet or house 2m NW of Upper Tean. Perhaps was once a burial mound called Harp.

Harracles Hall C18 brick hall under 1m ESE of Horton. In Longsdon township in Leek ancient parish. Harracles appears as Harecheles in the C13 (SSE 1996 p14). The name means 'an addition of land added to an estate' (VCH vol 7 p203) (SSE 1996 p21). Or if 'har' is boundary, and 'echeles' a ladder or staircase as in Nechells, so 'the two-storied house on the boundary' (DUIGNAN). By the mid C13 Harracles was an estate held by Henry de Audley (d1276), lord of Horton. By 1477 the estate had passed to the Wedgwoods of Blackwood by the marriage of Margaret Shaw to John Wedgwood. The Wedgwoods held it until the death of the last surviving daughter of John Wedgwood (d1757), Susannah, wife of John Fenton, in 1790. The estate then passed to a distant relative who sold the hall in 1791 to Thomas Mills, a Leek solicitor. The Mills family sold the hall to John Davenport of Westwood Hall in 1827. It passed to the Robinsons in 1868. In the C20 the Woolliscroft family acquired the hall, having been tenants since the early C19; they were still the owners in 1991 (VCH vol 7 pp206-207). There has been a house on this site since 1470 (SVB p114). Some say the Daniel family succeeded the Wedgwoods (SVB p114). It was rumoured that one of the owners pulled down a portion of the hall saying he would make it unfit for any gentleman to live in. The Wedgwood arms appear in the central pediment of the N front (VCH vol 7 p207), or on the W side where the main entrance had been. By 1885 the old main entrance had been blocked up (NSFCT 1885 p57) (VCH vol 7 pl 31).

Harriot's Hayes The name is said to be from a former hay in Brewood Forest (BDH p72).

Harris Close House 0.5m NNE of Sheen. In Sheen ancient parish. The present house is dated 1842 (VCH vol 7 p241).

Harriseahead Large hamlet under 1m S of Mow Cop and stretching for over 0.5m along the road N leading up to Mow Cop. Formerly in Thursfield township and Newchapel chapelry in Wolstanton ancient parish (W p299). In 1801 Hugh Bourne of Bemersley Green (see) had erected a Wesleyan Methodist chapel in the backyard of Dan Shubottam's house at Harriseahead (info John Anderson) (MC p22 pl xx).

Harry Mitchell Park N of Parkes Street, Bosoms End, Smethwick. The land for it was conveyed to Smethwick corporation by Henry Mitchell in 1899 in memory of his son Harry (VCH vol 17 p89).

Harston Rock and Wood. Kingsley. The railroad from Froghall to Caldon passes it (Trent and Mersey Canal. Peter Lead. pls 119,120). The rock acts like a giant sentinel (SMCC p12p).

Hartley Green Tiny hamlet on a gentle S-facing slope between Stocking and Gayton Brooks 0.75m NNW of Gayton. In Gayton parish. In the late C17 Plot noted a sulphurous spring here (NHS p105), a holy well (OSST 1944-1945) (SJC p10). It is not to be confused with the one Plot mentions between Sandon and Gayton. A selenite was found here, a rare occurrence (NHS p176). Foot-and-mouth disease broke out at Hartley Green Farm in early 1968 (SN Jan 5 1968 p13).

Harts Green Tiny district of Harborne, slightly to the W of St Peter's church. In Harborne ancient parish. For many years there were two Ice Age boulders on the grassy verge outside Hart's Green Farm (STELE Feb 29 1952) (HOHH p2). The name occurs on Yates' map and is from the Hart family (HOHE p26). By 1952 Harts Green Farm was known as Six Ways (STELE Feb 29 1952).

Hartshill Former hamlet on high ground between the Lyme and Fowlea valleys over 0.5m N of Penkhull. Formerly in Penkhull-with-Boothen township in Stoke-upon-Trent chapelry and ancient parish. There was Clive Hay, a deer enclosure, of the forest called New Forest, in the vicinity of Hartshill in medieval times. Hartshill occurs as a name attached to land in Stoke parish in c1600 and was an inhabited area by 1738. In 1775 the hamlet centred on the junction of the present Hartshill Road and Stoke Old Road, W of the later church (VCH vol 8 p176). There was a **windmill** at Hartshill built in 1780. It was demolished prior to 1830 (AGT p34), or in the late 1830s (VCH vol 8 p202), or in 1842 (WBJ p27), and Holy Trinity church built on the site in 1842; the millfield becoming the burial ground. Wolley's Almanac, 1891 gives a sketch of it (WBJ p27). (SHST p522il). Job thinks, 'Read's Mill' which appeared in CL July 31 1969 at Burton upon Trent, could be the windmill at Hartshill, Stoke-on-Trent (WBJ p17). The **church**, Holy Trinity, Hartshill Road, was built in 1842 (BOE p264). By at least the mid C20 Hartshill was a built-up residential area; by 1991 it a ward of Stoke-on-Trent district. In **WW2** the Germans bombed Quarry Road, Hartshill, on June 30 1940 (ES Feb 11 1977). For the **Victoria Theatre** see Stoneyfields. The oppressive system for controlling disruptive children in care known as **Pindown** was practiced at the care home at 245 Hartshill Road between Nov 1983 and Oct 1989. The Pindown regime, one in which children were kept in solitary confinement and deprived of basic privileges until they respected discipline, was brought to national attention and condemned in summer 1990. Granada Television's 'World in Action' programme entitled 'Pindown' was screened nationally on June 25 1990. On June 29 1990 Allan Levy QC and Barbara Kahan were appointed by Staffs county council to conduct an independent inquiry into

the system, which was published in 1991. The name is said to have derived from a statement made by Tony Latham, a senior member of the Social Services department of Staffs county council and an exponent of Pindown, when he talked of pinning down the problem of disruptive children in care. There were various types of Pindown ranging from 'Total Pindown' to 'Sympathetic Pindown' and also adjectives to describe the venue of the Pindown, whilst children who experienced it, spoke of 'being in Pindown.' About 132 children were given Pindown at four care homes - 245 Hartshill Road, Hartshill; the Birches, Newcastle-under-Lyme; the Alders, Tamworth and Heron Cross House, Heron Cross (The Pindown Experience and the Protection of Children: The Report of the Staffordshire Child Care Inquiry 1990. Staffs County Council. 1991) (The Times May 31 1991 pp4-5) (MIDD vol 1 pp54-56). **Supernatural**. A shop at Hartshill is haunted by a poltergeist (RPG pp3-5) (GLS pp47-49). A strange flying spherical object was seen floating around 120 feet above Harthill Park, in North Street, in Sept 1995 (ES Sept 21 1998 p8). **Persons and visitors**. Almshouses at Hartshill were built by Evans of Ellastone (see), who might have been **Robert Evans** (the Adam Bede of the novel of that name by George Eliot) (NSFCT 1924 p201). The composer, **Havergal Brian**, born in Dresden (see), lived for a short while at 11 Gordon Street (now Dominic Street) in the early C20 (POTP p47). The Prince of Wales, later **Edward VIII**, stopped his car in Hartshill in 1924 after opening Biddulph Grange Hospital (ES Aug 5 1995 p29); he came again to Hartshill to open the extension to the orthopaedic hospital at Longfield Cottage (see) in 1931.

NORTH STAFFORDSHIRE HOSPITAL. The North Staffordshire Hospital has its origins in a 'house of recovery' (1804) near the junction of the Trent & Mersey and Caldon Canals at Etruria. In 1819 it was superseded by the **North Staffordshire Infirmary** built near the present Festival Park area in Etruria. In 1869 the hospital moved to Hartshill having purchased a portion of The Mount (see) estate (info Dr Alun Davies) (HOS 1998 p126). The Prince of Wales laid the foundation stone for the new hospital buildings in 1866. It is said Sir Oliver Lodge first demonstrated electric light in North Staffs to a select audience at the infirmary in 1868 (TSS pp48,79ps aerial views). The infirmary was one of the first civil hospitals in the kingdom to be built on the pavilion system -plans and advice were received from Florence Nightingale (Governor's minutes SRO) (VCH vol 8 p197). The name was changed in 1890 to the North Staffs Infirmary and Eye Hospital, and in 1925 to the North Staffs Royal Infirmary (VCH vol 8 p197). In WW2 a German bomb hit the new nurses home of the North Staffs Royal Infirmary on June 26 1940 at 1.42am (ES Feb 4 1977). The **City General Hospital**, on the E side of London Road and to the W of the North Staffs Royal Infirmary, had its origins in Stoke parish workhouse, built in 1832-3 (later (1836) Stoke Union Workhouse and later (1922) Stoke and Wolstanton Union Workhouse). The workhouse hospital building survives and has inscribed above its main entrance 'Stoke-upon-Trent Parish Hospital 1842' (VCH vol 8 p200). By the 1890s the workhouse hospital had become a large institution, caring for the mentally ill, the elderly, maternity and medical cases, especially those of longer duration, and also acted as a large 'orphanage,' until the opening of the Penkhull Children's Homes in St Christopher Ave between 1900 and 1902 (info Dr Alun Davies) (VCH vol 8 p200). By the late C19 or the early C20 the hospital was known as the London Road Hospital. In 1929 it passed to City of Stoke-on-Trent and became known as the City General Hospital. As part of the nationalisation of health services in 1948 many North Staffs hospitals, including the North Staffs Royal Infirmary, **Hartshill Orthopaedic Hospital** (which occupied Longfield Cottage -see), and the City General Hospital, came under the Stoke-on-Trent Hospital Management Committee. From 1948 the Hospitals developed a full range of services, and gradually these became integrated, and this was recognised by the name North Staffordshire Hospital Centre. In the reorganisation of 1992, two NHS trusts were formed; the North Staffordshire Combined Healthcare Trust, based at Bucknall Hospital, with responsibility for community, geriatric and mental healthcare; and the North Staffordshire Hospitals Trust providing acute services at the City General and North Staffordshire Royal Infirmary sites, and based at the City General Hospital (info Dr Alun Davies). A visit to the Chemotherapy Unit of the North Staffordshire Hospital was made by Prince Charles on March 3 1998 (ES March 3 1998 p13p).

Hart's Hill Hamlet in the mid C19 in Kingswinford ancient parish (W p184). There is a tiny hamlet called Hart's Hill in the area of The Crestwood School and Landrake Road 0.75m SSE of Kingswinford on the 1834 OS map.

Harts Hill Cannock Chase. Perhaps, once topped with Scots pines, reputedly, planted by Thomas Anson to commemorate his brother's World circumnavigation in 'Centurion' 1740-44 (CCM), or planted in 1780 to add variety to the open heath country, which was within view of Shugborough (WMLB p77).

Hartshill Hall On the N side of Prince's Road, Hartshill, Penkhull. Completed in 1881 by Thomas Aidney, colour manufacturer (POTP p15). Occupied by Robert Nicholls, author of 'The Boulton Family of Madeley,' 'History of Stoke Church,' 'Life of Josiah Wedgwood,' 'History of Penkhull cum Boothen' (1929) NSSG, HOSC, SGNS, and M, who was born in Penkhull in 1864. He had hoped to marry the widow, Frances Aidney, from whom he had purchased the hall, but she refused him. In consequence of this he built a high wall to hide the grounds from her view, as she had merely removed to a house behind the hall (SS Sept 21 1907) (PRA pp89-91 p) (POTP p163).

Hartsmere House 0.25m NW of Hamstall Ridware, at SK 102197. Appears on 1834 OS map. In Hamstall Ridware parish. Richard Fitzherbert of the Fitzherberts of Swynnerton was from Hartsmere.

Hartwell Fragmented hamlet near the source of the Scotch Brook or a tributary of that brook, 1.5m ENE of Barlaston, comprising Lower Hartwell Farm, Little Hartwell, Great Hartwell Farm, Hartwell Hall and a few other houses. Former manor in Barlaston ancient parish.Has appeared as Hertwall (1346) (SHC 1908 p26) and Hertwalle (1361) (SSE 1996 p14). The name means 'the hart's spring' (DUIGNAN), or 'stag's stream' (SSE 1996 p14) (SPN pp59,118). The spring called Hartwell was still appearing in the manor court rolls in the early C16 (BAH p13). Great Hartwell Farm, at SJ 917390, is built on part of a moated site (NSFCT 1953 p64) (CAMS p63). The farm was held by the Chetwynds of Kibblestone in the 1280s. Permission was granted to Adam de Chetwynd for a chapel at the farm in 1282 (VCH vol 3 p257) (BAH pp13-14). The Hartwell which Rosemary Toeman has identified with the fictional place Hartlebury in CF Keary's novel 'The Mount' (1909) (VFC p77) may be this Hartwell, but Hartlebury may be Burton upon Trent (see).

Hartwell Hall Hartwell, Barlaston. Built by the Paddock family, solicitors of Hanley, in the 1860s (BAH p35). The Paddock family were still resident at Hartwell Hall in 1996 (local info).

Hartwell Hills Hills to the E of Hartwell. According to 1834, 1851, 1912 and 1932 directories the name also applies to a small hamlet 0.5m E of Hartwell, in Barlaston parish (W 1834) (W p411) (KD 1912. 1932) (gravestone in Barlaston old churchyard to Martha Edgerton (d1844) of Hartwell Hills).

Harvey Gate Farm 1.5m NW of Onecote. Formerly in Onecote township in Leek ancient parish. The present house is of the C19, but there was a house here by 1710 (VCH vol 7 p211).

Harvills Hawthorn Now (1976) a residential area, over 1.25m S of Wednesbury. In West Bromwich ancient parish. Formerly Harvills Oak (still current in the 1820s), probably from the tree called 'Harvyls Oke' which occurs in 1531. Harvyls is said to be from the Heronvilles family, lords of Wednesbury from 1182 (WAM p23) (SOWB p24) (VCH vol 17 p7 note). The area, on slight upland to the S and E of the Tame, was becoming known as Harvills Hawthorn by 1816 (VCH vol 17 p7).

Hasco-Bridge Here Dud Dudley, illegitimate son of the 5th Baron Dudley of Dudley Castle (see), experimented with smelting coal (SVS p126) (VCH vol p114). Here was a colliery. Hasco or Hascod or Horsecroft has been identified with Askew Bridge, which lay just to the E of Himley on the Dudley Road (Himley Hall and Park: A history. David F Radmore. 1996 p10).

Haseley Mentioned in the late C13 (VCH vol 5 pp3,6). Reputed to have been a former manor. In 1732 Haseley Manor or farm, S of Radford Bank, 0.5m SSW of Baswich church was owned by Richard Drakeford. A C18 brick barn still (1959) stands near the site of Haseley manor-house (VCH vol 5 pp3,6) (BERK p13 see map) (BERK2 p141) (SAC p16).

Haselour Minute hamlet between the Tame and the Mease 0.5m W of Harlaston. The hamlet seems to only contain about two houses - Haselour Hall and Haselour House. The name has appeared as Haselovre (1242) (SSE 1996 p14), and Haselouere (SPN p124). It is from the quantity of hazels, or nut trees formerly growing here (SHOS vol 1 p388). So 'hazel bank, ridge, slope' (DUIGNAN) (NSJFS 1981 p3) (SPN p124) (SSE 1996 p14). The medieval chapel of C13 or c1370 (BOE p142) attached to Haselour Hall was later used as a pigsty. It was described by Pennant in the C19 (OSST 1949-50 p14). By 1910 it was used for RC worship (LGS p144). The chapel was a prebend in Lichfield cathedral (W p564). Haselour parish was a peculiar jurisdiction of the dean and chapter and certain prebendaries of Lichfield cathedral until peculiar jurisdictions were abolished in 1846 (VCH vol 3 pp93-94). The wake was on the same day as that at Harlaston (W p564). A deserted medieval village is recorded at SK 205108 to the NW of the hall, probably deserted between 1377 and 1524 (SSAHST 1966 p49. 1970 p35). Haselour was claimed to be a member of an out-township of St Michael's parish, Lichfield, until 1832 when those who held the manor obtained extra-parochial status for the estate after long and expensive litigation (W p564). Haselour ceased to have separate ecclesiastical status in 1968. Some of the territory went to Harlaston

ecclesiastical parish and some went to Elford ancient parish. Haselour became a separate civil parish in 1858 (GLAUE p413). A mock sun was witnessed by Fisher Dilke at or near Haselour on Aug 28 1679 (NHS pp3,4,5,6,7) (SHOS vol 1 p390).

Haselour Hall Old hall 0.5m W of Harlaston. An old hall here was moated; a field named Moat Yard exists and there was still a fragment of water in the vicinity of the present house in 1845 (SSAHST 1982-3 p42). The core of the present timber-framed house is perhaps of the Tudor period, whilst most of the exterior is of 1885 (BOE p142). Has been the seat of Selvein in the early C12 to 1337, when it passed to the de Timmors, then it passed to Ardernes, the Stanleys, and the Brookes. The hall was sold to Samuel Dilke in 1672. In subsequent years Thomas Neville carried out a great deal of restoration on it; a J Neville was occupying the hall in 1851 (W p20); John Neville JP (d1892) is described as of Haselour Hall (mem in Harlaston church). In 1885 it was bought by Augustus de Trafford (LTM Jan Feb 1973 pp25-28) and largely restored (BOE p142). The hall has a priests hiding-place and an oak chimney piece with carvings of performing bears, boar hunts and battle of Hastings scenes (KES p106). Attached to the house is a chapel see Haselour. A drawing of the hall made by Edward Ould appears in the second volume of John Douglas's Abbey Square Sketch Book. The dovecote at Haselour Hall, probably of c1600 origin encased in brick in the C18, was protected from demolition being listed Grade II. In 1981 it was in a dilapidated state as it was gradually being uprooted by a nearby copper beech tree which itself was protected by a Tree Preservation order. In 1985 the dilemma was solved by having the dovecote re-erected at Avoncroft Museum of Buildings at Bromsgrove, Worcs (SHOS vol 1 p388 engraving of the hall and chapel) (AMSN Winter 1958) (SGS p104p) (SSAHST 1986-87 pp44-50ps).

Haselour House Close to, and to the W of, Haselour Hall, near Harlaston. Haselour House Farm, a brick Georgian house of c1742, was for sale in 2000 (DoE II) (SLM April 2000 p9pc).

Haskell Grange Former house slightly N of Fullbrook, Walsall. The name is preserved in Grange Street and Haskell Street (SNWA p50).

Hatchetts Close Well A well situated on land of Mr and Mrs F Chaddock of Wood Farm, Wood Street, Mow Cop (WMC).

Hatchley House 1.5m NNE of Dilhorne. Here was an open cast mine (CCT p166 see map).

Hateley Heath Former hamlet above Greet Brook now a district 1.5m N of the High Street, West Bromwich. In West Bromwich ancient parish. The name occurs from the later C15 as a piece of common land within the triangle formed by the present Wyntor, Allerton, and Jowett's Lanes; a cottage here was mentioned at the end of the C16 (VCH vol 17 p7). Has appeared as Hakle-Heath and Hately Heath (SOWB pp23-24) (TMS p103). It is thought that previously the area was known as Longnor (SOWB pp23-24). Most probably Hateley Heath took its name from the Hateley (or Haickley) family (SOWB p24): There has been a family of Hateley or Hayteley here recorded from 1403. A Hateley was living at Mayrick House (see) in the early C19 (SHWB 8). With the division of Lyndon ward Hateley Heath became a ward of West Bromwich borough in 1952 (VCH vol 17 p46). By 1999 was a ward in Sandwell metropolitan borough.

Hatherton Small hamlet by a brook at the foot of Shoal Hill 1.5m W of Cannock. Former out-township in Wolverhampton ancient parish, Seisdon hundred, and yet is in Cuttlestone hundred (VCH vol 4 p61). A charter was made of the bounds of Hagerthorndun (Hatherton) (SSE 1996 p14) in 994 (SL p62) or 996 (DUIGNAN) when the estate was given by Lady Wulfrun to the monastery of Wolverhampton (HOWM p14). The original text is printed in Dugdale's 'Monasticon,' and translated in CGO Bridgeman's 'Staffordshire Preconquest Charters' (SL p62). The manor of Hargedone is recorded as being held by the canons of Wolverhampton in DB. Later forms are: Hatherdon (1203-1307), Hatherton (1227), Hatherdon (1307), Hathurdon (1365) (SPNO p124) (SPN p59). The name means 'the hill of the hawthorn' (DUIGNAN) (NSJFS 1981 p3) (SPNO p124) (SPN p59). Hatherton's St Mary's chantry was one of the seven prebends of Wolverhampton Collegiate Church, until abolished in 1846 (W p82) (VCH vol 3 p324 note). The medieval chapel at Hatherton is not mentioned in the returns of 1546, 1563 or after (SHC 1915 p336). The present church, St Saviour, Church Lane, N of Four Crosses, was built in 1876 (LDD). Became a separate civil parish in 1866 (GLAUE p413). Gailey and Hatherton were formed into a joint parish in 1869 (LGS p139). Despite its proximity to mining Hatherton remains on the edge of Cannock Chase. Bird says, Hatherton has a haunting quality, which is captured in a poem by Cannock writer, Diana Hallchurch, of which these are the first two lines

Hatherton whispers of dangling woodsmoke
tangling into acid black trees.

(VB p80).

Hatherton District of Walsall (SSE 1991 p77), and from 1889, a ward of Walsall county borough (VCH vol 17 p217). For its industry see Walsall. Possibly centred on Hatherton Road and Street between Walsall town centre and Butts, or possibly centred on Hatherton Furnaces at Leamore.

Hatherton Branch of the Staffordshire and Worcestershire Canal. Opened in 1841. It ran from the Staffs and Worcs Canal at Calf Heath or Hatherton Junction (see) and joined the Churchbridge Branch Canal at Churchbridge Junction, Churchbridge. This in turn joined up with the Cannock Extension Canal (HCMS No. 2). Closed in 1949 or 1951 and now derelict (Nicholson's Guide to the Waterways No. 5 'Midlands' p48). The Lichfield and Hatherton Canals Restoration Trust, formed in 1988, seek to restore the canal and build a new section linking this branch with the Cannock Extension Canal at Grove Basins by-passing the destroyed Churchbridge Branch locks (Trust leaflet).

Hatherton Hall Under 0.5m N of Hatherton, Cannock. Built on the site of the Norman manor house (SPN p59) occupied by the de Hatherstones; the ghost of Sir Hugh de Hatherstone haunted the C19 hall. His skeleton was unearthed some years before the mid C19 on a spot where a private chapel had stood. Since the head had become separated from the body, the then Lord Hatherton made it into a goblet and lined it with silver. Whilst a dinner party was taking place, at which the goblet containing wine was passed around, the headless figure of Sir Hugh in armour appeared and snatched the goblet away. The next day, a silver ball was found in the grounds and it was presumed Sir Hugh had only need for his head back and not the silver lining (CCF pp79-81) (GLS pp50-51). (SHOS vol 2 p320). (CCF pp61-65p). The Walhouse family owned lands in Hatherton manor in the C16. Walter Walhouse, who succeeded his father in 1615 appears to have been resident at Hatherton Hall. His son, John, was a parliamentarian in the Civil War (Burke's Peerage. 1931). Walter Walhouse (c1651-1735) was succeeded by his son John Walhouse (d1738), who was succeeded by his son Moreton Walhouse (b c1730). He married Frances Littleton, daughter of Fisher Littleton of Pipe Ridware. Their son Moreton Walhouse (1761-1821) succeeded; his wife Anne Craycroft had a portion of an arch in Cannock (see) church cut so she could pass through the arch in her capacious bonnet. Moreton (d1821) was succeeded by his son Edward John Walhouse (b1791), who, in 1812, succeeded to the Littleton estates and Teddesley Hall with the death of his childless great uncle Sir Edward Littleton in 1812. Edward then took the name of Littleton and took up residence at Teddesley Hall (see). He was created 1st Baron Hatherton (CCBO pp74,96-98) in 1835 (Burke's Peerage 1879). He was succeeded by his son Edward Littleton (1815-1888), 2nd Baron Hatherton, who was succeeded by his son Edward George Percy Littleton (1842-1930), 3rd Baron Hatherton. He was succeeded by his son Edward Charles Rowley Littleton (1868-1944), 4th Baron Hatherton. He was succeeded by his son Edward Thomas Walhouse Littleton (1900-1969), 5th Baron Hatherton. His younger brother, John Walter Stuart Littleton (1906-1973), succeeded as 6th Baron Hatherton. He was succeeded by his younger brother Thomas Charles Tasman Littleton (b1907) as 7th Baron Hatherton (Burke's Peerage 1980). Hatherton Hall was rebuilt in 1817 in the Tudor-Gothic style (CCAP p43p). The hall was occupied by Mrs Walhouse in 1835. With the Lords Hatherton residing at Teddesley Hall from 1812 Hatherton Hall was tenanted by a succession of professionals and gentlemen: Thomas Entwistle (c1851); Joseph Loxdale Warren JP (c1861); Capt RP Dawson (c1863); Sir Charles Clifford (c1876-c1888); Francis Simpson (c1892-1896); unoccupied (c1900); George William Rogers (c1904); Col George Fleming Alexander Hughes Le Fleming (c1912); and Hon Edward Charles Littleton DL JP (possibly the later 4th Baron) (c1916). After the death of the 3rd Baron Hatherton in 1930 the Littletons left Teddesley Hall (see) and came to Hatherton Hall; the hall was occupied by 4th Lord Hatherton to at least 1940 (trade directories) (SOP p186). Edward, 5th Baron Hatherton was living at Hatherton Hall prior to his death in 1969 (Burke's Peerage 1980). In the 1930s W Byford-Jones 'Quaestor' stayed one night at the hall to investigate the strange sounds and a cold chill feeling reported to have been experienced here (QMMH pp55-61p). Earthworks S of the hall at SJ 958104 shown on a tithe map (1841) may represent a former moat (SSAHST 1982-3 p43).

Hatherton Furnaces Appears to have stood in the vicinity of the junction of Fryer's Road and Leamore Lane, SW of Bloxwich. Two blast furnaces were built in the early 1850s and later a forge and rolling mill were added. The furnaces were the last in Walsall to operate and were blown out in 1948, but refining of iron was continued until c1965. The area occupied by the furnaces is almost certainly that immortalised in John Petty's 'Five Fags a Day' (SNBP p27p).

Hatherton Junction At Calf Heath. The junction of the Staffs and Worcs Canal

with the Hatherton Branch Canal.

Hatherton Lake In Walsall Arboretum park. 0.5m NNE of St Matthew's church.

Hatherton's Oak, Lord Teddesley Park. Grown from an acorn which was dropped into the ground by the third Lord Hatherton on the day he was baptised in 1842; it was still growing in c1933 (CCBO p26).

Hatton Former township in Swynnerton ancient parish. Fragmented hamlet in and above the Meece Brook valley, containing the smaller hamlets of Lower Hatton (see) and Upper Hatton (see), Hatton Pumping Station (see), and to the W of the pumping station Hatton Mill, by and on the E side of Meece Brook. Has been identified by Commander Wedgwood and others as the Hetone in DB (SHC 1916 p168). Appears as Hatton in 1205 (SSE 1996 p14). The names Hatton and The Hattons are common in the Midlands; the places usually started as single homesteads or hamlets between the C12 and the C14, but if of Anglo-Saxon origin then corrupted from 'haethtun' meaning 'heath town' (DUIGNAN) (SSE 1996 p14) (SPN p23).

Hatton Pumping Station Austere late-C19 Italianate-style buildings 1.75m NW of Swynnerton, built after 1888 (SHST p225) for SPWWC to pump water to an underground reservoir (Hanchurch Reservoir) in the Hanchurch Hills for the Potteries. It was built on land belonging to the Fitzherberts of Swynnerton Hall. However, the Fitzherberts agreed to the works on condition that the Company also provide water for Swynnerton Hall and village. To this end it built the present 50-foot high brick water tower to the N of the village, at SJ 852359, in 1891. By the early 1980s water having been brought to Swynnerton by more modern means the tower was redundant and Severn Trent Water Authority sought to sell it. It was converted into a house between 1988 and 1998 by Frank Wilson and his family (PWW p16) (ES Oct 17 1986 p28p. July 11 1998 p14pc. Aug 6 1998 p17p). (SHST p225) (MR p313p). Hatton Pumping Station, opened in 1893 (IAS p199), but it was not complete until 1907. It had four pumping engines and the water was drawn from a bore hole 1,240 feet down (ES Jan 30 1933 p6ps of the interior) (PWW p16p). By 1999 the station was still in use although water was pumped electronically, making the large engine house redundant (info Millmeece Pumping Station Preservation Trust). Another tower to receive water for Hanchurch Reservoir stands by the reservoir at SJ 839397. It is architecturally identical to Hatton Pumping Station and the tower at Swynnerton; it was probably this tower which Holt remembers as the one camouflaged with brushwood in WW2 (SFH p7). The reservoir built in 1891 holds 2,866,000 gallons of water. Another underground reservoir in Hanchurch Woods, holding six million gallons, was built by 1927 (PWW pp17,18) (ES April 1987 p8p). (BOE p273). As an addition to Hatton SPWWC built another pumping station, 2m to the S at Millmeece (see) in 1914.

Hattons, The Collection of three farmhouses by the Penk 1.5m ENE of Codsall. Former liberty with Gunstone of Brewood town in Brewood ancient parish and was included in Brewood prebend (SSAHST vol 2 1960-61 p43). The oldest, The Old Hattons (see), is the most northerly (VCH vol 5 p33). 200 yards to the S is The Middle Hattons (see). To the SW of this farm, at SJ 888047, was possibly a medieval village, probably deserted between 1524 and 1666 (SSAHST 1970 p35). Has appeared as Hatton (1199-1396), Hadton (1227), le netherhatton (Lower Hatton) (1556), The Hattons (1723 to 1800) (SPNO p38). The third and most southerly farm is The Hattons (see).

Hattons, The A C18 brick house with later additions. The third and most southerly farm of The Hattons, 1.5m ENE of Codsall. The farmhouse was described as Lower Hattons in c1841 and as the Upper Hattons in 1959. On current OS map 1:25,000 it is referred to as The Hattons.

Hattvoll House May be the house which lay N of Rudge Manor, formerly in the manor of Rudge in Standon ancient parish. In 1885 it was a ruined skeleton of a timber building (COI pp219-220). The property had vanished by 1981 (OS map 1:25,000 1981).

Haughton Ancient parish and village on a low watershed near the sources of Butterbank and Allimore Brooks, 4m SW of Stafford. The **name** has appeared as Haltone, a manor, in DB, Halstone (DB), Haleton (1201), Halghton (1205), Halughton (c1291), Halyton (1486-1515), and Haughton (1559) (SPNO p164); Haltone (DB) has also been identified with Alstone (SHC 1923 p44). It means 'the farmstead by the nook of land' (SPNO p164), or 'nook or hollow tun or settlement' (NSJFS 1981 p3) (SSE 1996 p14), or 'farmstead of the meadows' (SPN p60), or 'a town in the meadows' (DUIGNAN) (SVB p92), or is an original English settlement; the spot where a group of invaders (Anglians?) determined to cry 'halt' and where they created a settlement or town (ESH p61). The parish **church**, St Giles, near the village centre on the N side of the Newport-Stafford road, is possibly of pre-C12 origin, but was largely rebuilt in 1887 (VCH vol 4 p140). The parish formed between 1086 and 1291 out of Church Eaton parish (SHC 1916 pp192,196). SAH Burne noted a moated site at Haughton and that there are a disproportionate amount of moats in the

Haughton area (ESH pp58,60); for the original Haughton Manor House three moated sites have been considered: Booden Farm (unlikely); Moat House (likely); Woodhouse Farm (manorial from c1563) (SSAHST 1982-3 p43). Records show a **windmill** with a cottage leased out from the manor to Ralph Sneyd in 1576, which was sited at SJ 874192. And in 1638 William Bassett, miller, was buried at Haughton (WBJ p27). Two fields, each named Windmill Piece, may have been the sites of two mills (VCH vol 4 p139). There was a **railway** station at Haughton on the Shropshire Union Railway (Stafford Wellington, Shrops), opened on June 1 1849, closed on Aug 6 1966 (Railways In and Around Stafford. Edward Talbot. 1994 p4). By 2000 it had become a car park (The Way for the Millennium. 2000. p1). A photograph of Fieldside Cottage c1937 is in ASOP p88. **The Darwells.** Rev John Darwell, hymn composer, was born in Haughton in 1731 the eldest of four children of Rev Randle Darwell, rector of Haughton. Darwell was curate successively at Haughton, Bushbury and Trysull before his appointment as curate to St Matthew's, Walsall, in 1761. He is famous for composing 'Darwell's 148th' the tune for psalm 148 first published in 1770, which starts 'Ye Holy Angels Bright.' He died in Walsall in 1789. His wife, alias Mary Whateley (b1761), was a poet and published 'Poems on Several Occasions' and 'The Triumph of Liberal Sentiment' (BS pp131-132) (PSS p464) (BCM April 1992 pp42-45) (VFC p35), and some were on the beauties of Hockley Abbey (see). The book 'The Storm and Other Poems' (1810) by their daughter, Mary (1779-1851), is dedicated to the Prince of Wales (PSS p464) (VFC p35).

Haughtondale Minute hamlet 0.75m NE of Haughton.

Haughton Hall To the W of Haughton church. Built in the late C16 (BOE p143). It was in a dilapidated condition in 1889 (NSFCT 1915 pp172-173). It was restored in 1889, but was little altered (VCH vol 4 pp138,139 p facing). Its barn, now converted to a cottage, has within it reclaimed timber thought to have come from sailing ships (SVB p92). Has also appeared as Haughton Old Hall and the Manor House.

Haughton Motte Haughton. In the rectory garden, at SJ 865204, there are slight remains of an earthwork to W of the church which may have been a small Norman motte (VCH vol 4 p136) (CAMS p21).

Haughton Parks Haughton. In 1340 Thomas de Haughton had licence to empark his wood of 'Oldhaye.' Field names suggest this was in the neighbourhood of Woodhouse Farm. There are indications that there was another park called Haughton Park to the S near Booden Farm moat. It was enclosed sometime before 1668 (EDP p179) (VCH vol 4 p136) (SL pp107,108). There is a deer leap fence at Haughton (NSFCT 1910 p170).

Haughtons Bank N of Onneley, on the Ches Staffs border. Occurs on Dower's map.

Haunton Small village by the Mease 1m W of Clifton Campville. Former township with Clifton Campville (W p596) and chapelry in Clifton Campville ancient parish (GLAUE p408). Has appeared as Hagnatun (942) (DUIGNAN) (SSE 1991 pp7,8. 1996 p14), Hagheneton (C13), Hauneton (C13) (SPN p60), and Hanton (Plot's map). The name means 'Hagene's town' (DUIGNAN), or 'Hageta's tun' (SSE 1996 p14), or 'Hagona's farmstead' (SPN p60).

Haunton Hall Haunton. Georgian in style (SGS p86). Has a chapel built by Charles Hansom in c1848 (BOE p143). Was the Convent of St John of Bordeaux by the 1970s (BOE p143) (SGS p86); a school by 1988 (MR p101); a retirement home by 1995 (SPN p60).

Hawbush There was a Hawbush Farm on the N side of Brettell Lane by the junction with Hawbush Road by 1822 (WFK p20 see map), just in Kingswinford ancient parish. The area to the N is now known as Hawbush. At Hawbush was a glasshouse. On the Hawbush estate since 1990 a woman and her family claim to have heard strange noises and be plagued by the ghost of perhaps the grandmother of the former occupants of the house. They call her Mrs Popoff (MGH pp39-43).

Hawcroft Grange Hood Lane, Longdon. It contains an arch and door from St Andrew's church, Derby (VB p120).

Hawes An area of Rowley Regis. The name now only persists in Hawes Lane. (As opposed to Hawne N of Halesowen).

Hawes Hill Hill slightly SE of Hailstone in the Rowley Regis range. In 1932 120 Roman coins and a medallion bearing the words OB cives servatos were found near the Hawes Hill Spring (BCWJ p15). Rowley Regis church stands on Hawes Hill. Hawes Hill Spring was still being frequented by people up to c1875, some carried its water back to Cherry Orchard (BCWJ p69). On the hill was a windmill called, by Barry Job, Hailstone or Hawes Hill Mill (see). Wilson-Jones noted a quaint country lane overhung with trees on Hawes Hill which he and others claim they had walked along but were unable to relocate on subsequent visits. Wilson-Jones believed that he had been transported back in time to an age when the lane existed. The lane, as those remember it, leads past an old tithe farmhouse, from which issued sounds of life and industry.

There may have been a lane which led from Hawes Hill near the quarries into Rowley (BCWJ p106).

Hawkbatch House in the mid C18 (SHOS vol 2 p254), and settlement on W side of the Severn over 1.25m S of Arley in Arley ancient parish. Formerly in Staffs and the most southerly point of the county, but transferred to Worcs in 1895. A bronze axe-head of c1400 BC origin was found in the Severn at Waterworks Bridge, Hawkbach, some years prior to 1914 (AOA p92). Shaw noted that there was formerly a town and bridge at Hawkbach before Bewdley was built: White ascribes this to being Roman: some watermen had assured Rev Joseph Chillingworth that at low water they had been able to discover the ruins of the bridge. Some Roman coins of gold were dug up near the bridge, one of Tiberius (SHOS vol 2 pp253,254) (W p168) (SC p148). Has also appeared as Achebache and Hawkbach (AOA p11); Hawkbatch Valleys, a wood, is marked on the present OS map 1:50,000. The name means 'hawk valley' (DUIGNAN). The HED recognises 'bache' as 'the vale of a stream or rivulet.' There is a Hawkbach in the Madeley charter of bounds (975), which Palliser implies is derived from 'hawk's stream' (SL p61 note).

Hawkes Hill In Marchington Woodlands township in Hanbury ancient parish (W p563). There is a Hawkshill Farm 1m W of Marchington Woodlands near Scounslow Green.

Hawkesyard Formerly Armitage Park (see). In 1839 Mrs Spode, widow of Josiah Spode III, the potter, bought Armitage Park, and moved here with her son Josiah Spode IV, an antiquarian. In 1859 on discovering the Rugeley family had a seat called Hawkesyard Hall in the vicinity (0.25m to the SW) Josiah IV had the place renamed Hawkesyard after their hall (STMSM Jan 1974 pp18-19) (SGS p52). Josiah IV had no children, and after his wife's death his niece Helen Gulson came to live with him. Both were converted to Catholicism. Josiah IV left the house to the Dominican Order after his death in 1893. Hawkesyard was renamed Spode House (see) sometime after WW2.

Hawkesyard Hall Former medieval hall which stood about 860 yards W of Armitage church, 0.25m NE of Hawkesyard Priory, on W side of Hawkesyard Lane. It was the seat of the de Ruggeleyes or Rugeleys. Spelt 'Hawkeserde' by Erdeswick (STMSM Jan 1974 pp18-19). Possibly the name is from horse yard, a horses head appears in the arms of the Rugeley family (SHOS vol 1 p211). The house was surrounded by a moat which was, in 1798, choked with reeds and rushes (SHOS vol 1 p214). The moat was mostly virtually ploughed out by 1958, and was totally destroyed by 1974 (SSAHST 1982-83 p35). Until 1963 a hewn stone believed to be from the hall appeared in some places in field walls in the area (STMSM Jan 1974 p18). Since about this time, and after 1955 (LTM Dec 1972 p34), the site has been covered by a stretch of water owned by Rugeley power station (SVB p19). There is an illustration of Hawkesyard Hall in George Griffith's tragedy 'The Two Houses' 1866. Josiah Spode IV, an antiquarian of Armitage Park, on discovering this hall had existed in the vicinity of his own house (0.25m to the SW) renamed it Hawkesyard after this Hawkesyard Hall (SGS p52) in 1859 (STMSM Jan 1974 pp18-19).

Hawkesyard Priory 0.75m W of Armitage. Dominican priory in the grounds of Armitage Park or later called Hawkesyard and now called Spode House; the seat of the Priory's founder, Josiah Spode IV. He had converted to Catholicism with his niece Helen Gulson, who had come to Hawkesyard to care for him after the death of his wife. They had friends among the Dominicans and Josiah left it to the Order on his death in 1893 (SGS pp53,55). The Dominican friars came in 1894 (VCH vol 3 p115). The Dominicans built a house for themselves between 1896-1914 to designs by Edward Goldie (BOE p62) above Hawkesyard. In 1915 the priory had a school and college with the power to confer university degrees in philosophy and technology by order of the Pope (S p127). At first the whole of the training for the priesthood was undertaken at Hawkesyard. However, when Father Bede Jarrett OP opened the Dominican House of Studies at Blackfriars, Oxford, in 1929 all theological students departed for Oxford. The priory was used for the training house for young Dominicans until 1967 (LTM Dec 1972 p36). (Guide and History of Hawkesyard Priory and Spode House. OP Columba Ryan. 1962). By 1974 both Spode House and Hawkesyard Priory were a single conference centre which closed in 1987 (STMSM Jan 1974 pp18-19ps) (HOS 1998 p60). **Priory Chapel.** Dedicated to St Thomas. Has an organ by Hill which was originally from the hall in Spode House. The casing is by William Bird - one of Wren's carvers - and was made 1700-1 (BOE p62). It comes from Eton College chapel. Mr Hill found it in a builders yard when the college had installed a new one. It bears the royal arms of William III and the arms of Eton (bottom left) and King's College, Cambridge (bottom right) (STMSM Jan 1974 p9. May 1980 p23). (DoE II) (KES p26) (SGS p55) (MR p17).

Hawk Hills A hill 2.5m N of Yoxall.

Hawk's Green Former small hamlet 0.75m NE of Cannock. The name, which appears on the 6 inch OS map 1889, is preserved in Hawk's Green Lane, and Industrial Estate. There have been several reports of the sound of phantom horses hooves and of riders shouting to one another, sometimes in the vicinity of Hawk's Green Lane and in fields nearby (GOM p30) (GPCE p24).

Hawkshutts, The House 1.25m NW of Bishop's Wood.

Hawksley House 0.5m ENE of Heaton. Formerly in Heaton township in Leek ancient parish. Is partly of C17 origin (VCH vol 7 p187). On the track between Hawksley and Hollinhall en route to Whitelee John Naden murdered Robert Brough (TFTPM p56). Has also appeared as Hawkesley.

Hawksmoor Park Nature reserve 0.5m W of Oakamoor opened by Lord Grey of Fallodon on May 7 1927 (ACOPP p64p). It consists of 214 acres (LGS p263) and is owned by the NT. There are gate piers at the entrance to Hawksmoor Nature Reserve on the Oakamoor road to the memory of Charles JB Masefield (d1917), author of LGS, of Abbots Hay and Hanger Hill (SMOPP vol 1 p82), who campaigned for the reserve. John Masefield, his cousin and Poet Laureate of the day, officiated at the opening ceremony of the gates on Oct 21 1933 (ES Oct 20 1933 p1p. Oct 23 1933 p of the Poet Laureate signing autographs at the gates) (NSFCT 1933 pp55-59). Has also appeared as Hawksmoor Nature Reserve.

Hawk's Nest House 1m WNW of Flash. Soon after the 1745 Jacobite Rebellion James Shatwell, a rebel of the Scottish army, or a native of Hollinsclough, lived in a hut called Hawk's Nest (UHAW p18).

Hawk's Well In High Park, Patshull (Marked on 1:25,000 OS map).

Hawk's Yard House to E of Newtown, 2m SW of Longnor. Formerly in Fawfieldhead township in Alstonefield ancient parish (W p746). There seems to have been a house here by the later C14 (VCH vol 7 p27).

Hawthorn Former hamlet 3m SE of Great Barr, close to the Warws border. The name is preserved in Hawthorn Junior School and Hawthorn Road.

Hawthorn Brook Runs northwards across Handsworth Golf Course to the Tame (MNB p35).

Hawthornden Manor Late Victorian mansion on the Bramshall Road, Uttoxeter. Built by Samuel Bamford (1845-1932) after his marriage to Dorothy Bond Hawthorn in 1875. By 1978 the house had been converted into flats (BUBA pp26p,27,29,69) (UOPP pl 59).

Hawthornes House? just N of Keele.

Hawthorn Hill House built in the later C18 or early C19. Stood in the area of Hawthorn Park on the W side of Hamstead Hill (MNB p41).

Hawthorn House Situated off Hamstead Hall Road, Handsworth. Built in the late C18. Mr Villiers is named as owner in c1801 (SHOS vol 2) and in 1821. In 1841 it passed into the possession of Edwin L Bullock. It remained with the Bullocks until at least 1886. In 1891 it was owned by FA Walton who let it in turn to Mrs J Butler and William W Davis (1896). In 1896 it was sold to Dr WE Parkes. In the C20 it was bought by Birmingham Corporation for a children's home and was being used as such in 1981 (HPPE pp60-61).

Hawthorns, The Highgate Road, Walsall. Built by Henry Taylor. It was generally called 'Taylor's Folly;' the name 'Folly' seeming to come from an already existing house in the neighbourhood called Folly House (see) later 'Rock's Cottage.' The Hawthorns was sold to James Trees (SNWA p43). The effigies of a school boy and girl of the Walsall Blue Coat School were brought to the garden by Henry Taylor and used as ornaments; they are now (1992) lost (SNWA p19).

Hawthorns, The New name for an area containing West Bromwich Albion football ground, and the Hawthorns Industrial Estate. Appears on Birmingham A-Z (1995). The name is from a house, the Hawthorns, built on the site of Street House (see). The house became the Hawthorns Hotel in 1903 to serve the patrons of West Bromwich Albion football club whose ground was on the opposite side of Halford Lane from 1900 (VCH vol 17 p10). Hawthorns Hotel and the football ground were in West Bromwich ancient parish, but the Hawthorns Industrial Estate area was in Handsworth ancient parish.

Hay There was settlement at Hay by the earlier C14, probably at the present Hay Farm (VCH vol 20 p65), which is 1.25m S of Bobbington. Some of the present Hay Farm (1981) may date from the early C17 (VCH vol 20 p69).

Hay, The An island or marsh between Burton Abbey and Broad Holme and Island of Annesley.

Hay Brook Flows eastwards from E of Newtown to fed Rudyard Lake. Forms the southern boundary of Rushton James township (VCH vol 7 p219).

Hayden Cross At Cradley. Derived from Haden as in Haden Hall.

Hayend House 0.75m NW of Hamstall Ridware. In Hamstall Ridware ancient parish.

Hayes, The Georgian house 0.25m SE of Oulton. Henry Taylor (d1840) was of The Hayes, near Stone (mem in Whitgreave church). The house, which has also appeared as Hayes House, was enlarged in the late 1870s by James Meakin, master potter. The Meakins were succeeded by the Tams; a John

Tams was living here by 1896. The Tams were succeeded in c1900 by the Hollins of Minton Hollins, the pottery family. It was bought by the Hand family in 1972 (SOK p74) (ES June 15 1991 p26ps). The property was for sale in Oct 1999 (SLM Oct 1999 pc). (SVB p134) (MR p234p).

Hayesgate NW of Hulme End. Formerly in Fawfieldhead township in Alstonefield ancient parish. A cottage at Hayesgate in 1597 seems to have been kept as an alehouse in the early C17. At Hayesgate the Alstonefield manor court was held by 1697 and it was still held here when last recorded in 1853 (VCH vol 7 pp6,28).

Hayes Mill Corner of Nicholls Lane and Longton Road, 0.25m S of Oulton. One of the last bone mills in N Staffs (DoE II). In the early C19 it ground flint - was one of the flint-grinding mills of Moddershall Valley (IAS pp43,195) - converted to grind calcined bone in 1910, working to some degree until c1970 (SDOPP p72p) (SPJD p83p). Name is perhaps from The Hayes (see). Has also appeared as Oulton Mill (SIT).

Hayes Wood Wood 1.5m SSW of Audley. Formerly in Halmer End township in Audley ancient parish. It may be identified with Hase or Hease Wood, an estate divided into two in the C17. John Sherratt of Redstreet (d c1683) built a house on his half into which he had some Yorkshire men install an organ, but in the locality the men were suspected of participating in the production of Halmerend Groats, counterfeit tin coins, which were then being made and were still being made in the Halmer End district in 1733 (SHC 1944 pp27-28). By throwing herself down an old pit shaft in the wood Maria Smith, aged 13, is said to have taken her own life in mid May 1881. She is believed to have committed suicide after suffering extreme cruelty at the hands of her step mother (The Times. July 30 1881) (AHJ 1996 pp88-91).

Hayfield Hill Hill and small district S of Cannock Wood.

Hay Hall Farm Ipstones. Dated 1625 (NSJFS 1968 p98). There is a Hay House 0.5m W of Ipstones at Noonsun Common.

Hayhead House under 0.5m NE of Cotton. Formerly in Cotton township in Alton ancient parish (W p769).

Hay Head Farm 0.75m NE of Kidsgrove, on White Hill. Formed a part of the Clough Hall estate in 1811 (KAIW p6). The name is preserved in Hayhead Close off Whitehill Road.

Hay Head Farm and bridge 1.75m E of Walsall. In the foreign of Walsall (W p649). Has been described as a manor (VCH vol 17 p174). Hayhead Farm was surrounded by a moat (SSAHST 1982-83 p33). Here was mined grey limestone in the mid C19 said to be surpassed by none in the kingdom for its extraordinary adhesive qualities, strength and durability (W p637) (DUIGNAN p67).

Hay Hill House 1m NW of Knypersley. Formerly in Lower Biddulph liberty in Biddulph ancient parish. There was settlement at Hay Hill by 1500 (BALH).

Hay House House 0.75m ESE of Ipstones. There was a farm at Hay House by the early C14; a Henry de Hay is mentioned in 1333 (TOI p44). The datestone 1625 on the cross wing of the house points to new building (NSFCT 1977 pp11,14). Here was a pottery and a jenny site in an outhouse (NSFCT 1941 p41. 1942 p59).

Hay House Near Dunston Heath, over 0.5m ENE of Levedale. Has also appeared as Heyhouse. On account of the moat, which surrounded the house and was filled in in 1956, there may have been a house here in medieval times. The moat was a listed monument in 1994. Lands called 'le Heywood' were possessions of Penkridge Collegiate Church. There was a house here by 1680 and the present (1959) house was reconstructed on the site in the early C19 (VCH vol 5 p124) (SSAHST 1982-3 p39).

Haying Wood and Haying Pit. 1m W of Silverdale (IANS pp128 see map, 129) (MIDD vol 1 p12p view from).

Hayley Green Rowley Regis. On Haden estate (BCWJ p15).

Hays, The A house, area and wood SW of Minnie Pit, near Pheasant Hall. William Cooper, the son of one of the gamekeepers Sir TFF Boughey, Bart, aged 23, was shot dead in the doorway or threshold of the house called The Hays, by Paul Downing, a miner aged about 20, and his cousin Charles Powys, aged 17, in Aug 1844. The evidence against Downing and Powys was that the prints on their boots matched those found in mud leading up to the house. Added to this Downing had just completed a two month prison sentence for poaching on the evidence of the deceased's father. Despite the fact that the two maintained their innocence they were convicted of murder and hung in early 1845 (ILN Aug 17 1844 p99) (TB Sept 1980 p11; the victim is called John Cooper) (CCSHO p15) (RPM pp11-14) (MCS pp30-31) (SMML pp9-12).

Hays House 0.75m SW of Rushtonhall. Formerly in Rushton James township in Leek ancient parish. There was a farmhouse here in 1756 (VCH vol 7 p220).

Hayseech Former small hamlet by the Stour 1.5m SSW of Rowley Regis. In

Rowley Regis parish (W p194). The name appears on the Plan of the Mines of Lord Dudley 1812 as Haysitch. The hamlet enlarged around the Gunbarrel Forge here (BCWJ p86).

Hayseech Brook Bird gives one verse from an irreverent song which contains the name

John Wesley had a bony 'oss
As Lean as ever was seen,
We took him down to Hayseech Brook
And shoved him yed fust in.

(VB p53).

Hayseech Common Rowley Regis (BCWJ p15). Preserved in Hayseech Road which crossed the Worcs and Staffs border S of Haden Hill.

Hay Walk Path along the W side of the Trent from the Abbey Inn to Trent Bridge. Burton upon Trent.

Haywood There is a Haywood High School at Stanfield, Burslem.

Haywood Grange House 1.5m NNW of Dilhorne (1834 OS map).

Haywood Hall Ancient seat of the Astons at Great Haywood. It is believed to have stood W of the railway and 200 feet N of the railway bridge in Great Haywood (OS map 1924 38 SW) at approximately SJ 997228.
THE ASTONS. The site of the house was given by Bishop Meuland (or Morlend or Mulend) to Roger de Aston in Henry III's reign; during Meuland's episcopacy Meuland granted the office of hereditary wardens of Cannock Chase (see) to the Astons. The office remained with them even when the chase passed from the bishops to the Pagets. From another Roger Aston the estate and office passed to his son Sir Robert Aston, and from him it passed to his son John Aston (d1483-4). From John it passed to his son **Sir John Aston** (d1523-4). By his marriage to Joan Littleton, Sir John inherited Tixall (A History of Tixall. Anne Andrews. 1995. p8). Sir John was succeeded by his son Sir Edward Aston (d1567-8): He and his successors resided at Tixall Old Hall. He was succeeded by Sir Walter Aston (d1589), son by his second wife. He was succeeded by Sir Edward Aston (d1597). He was succeeded by **Sir Walter Aston** (1584-1639). Sir Walter was created a baronet in 1611 and served as Ambassador to Spain (1620-1625). He was created Lord Aston of Forfar in 1627. His second son Herbert was the builder of Bellamour Hall (see), Colton. His eldest son, **Walter Aston** (1609-1678), 2nd Lord Aston, was his successor. He was a royalist in the Civil War and patron of Izaak Walton of Stafford (see), author. He was succeeded by his son **Walter Aston** (1633-1720), 3rd Lord Aston. He was charged and imprisoned in the Popish or Titus Oates Plot, and succeeded by his son **Walter Aston** (1660-1748), 4th Lord Aston. In 1712 the 4th Lord Aston was prepared to relinquish the office of warden of Cannock Chase on the recommendation of the Court of Chancery on condition that every year four bucks from the chase should be delivered to him (then at Tixall), without fee or reward, by the keeper of Cannock Chase (CCF p47). Walton (d1748) was succeeded by his son **James Aston** (b1723), 5th Lord Aston. He married Barbara, sister of George, 14th Earl of of Shrewsbury of Alton Towers (see). He died of small pox in 1751 whilst in the process of building Tixall Hall (see). The baronetcy then became extinct, but the barony passed to another branch of the Aston family. James was succeeded by his second daughter Barbara. She married Hon Henry Thomas Clifford and Tixall passed to the Cliffords. She was succeeded by her son Sir Thomas Hugh Clifford, who was created a baronet in 1815 (Complete Peerage).
THE HALL. Haywood Hall continued as the seat of the Astons until they built and moved to Tixall Old Hall in the C16 (SHC 1914 p134 note) (HCMBOPP p3p). The Astons abandoned Haywood Hall in c1500 (HHHC p68) and the hall began to be ruinous by 1700 when it was known as 'The Manor House.' Its remains are believed to be represented by two upright stones in a gateway opposite the RC chapel and four more close to the arch of the railway bridge; a curiously carved cross, part of a circular stone, and two rams' heads in the old grounds. There are said to be two subterranean passages running from the hall; one runs near to Tixall Old Hall. By the later C19 the Clifford Arms Hotel stood in front of the site and some remains were incorporated into an old malthouse in the angle enclosed between the canal and the railway (HOSCC p99): Whilst the hotel is believed to incorporate the gatehouse (HCMBOPP p3p). Stones from the chapel were in a garden near the Old Mill, Great Haywood, in 1930 (HAHS il facing frontispiece). The present **Abbey House** (HAH pp51,52il,53,54il), or Heywood Abbey (GNHS p116) at the corner of Mill Lane and Great Haywood main street was built in 1830-32 on the ruins of the chapel of Haywood Hall. In the earlier C20 Abbey House has been occupied by the Dukes; then by Mrs Blackham; then by the Moreton-Thomas' (HAHS p54) (HHHC p68). In the earlier 1960s it was

occupied by Capt Haywood. In 1967 it was for sale (Stafford Advertiser July 6 1967 p1). By 1997 it had become a private nursing home. (HAH pp51,52il, 53,54il).

Haywood House Stands to S of Haywood Manor House, Great Haywood. Formerly a farmhouse. It was used for a time after WW1 to house Belgian refugees (HHHC p69).

Haywood Manor House On the opposite side of the road from Abbey House, Great Haywood. Built for the manager of Haywood Brewery (HHHC pp68,89). The house has also appeared as the Manor House.

Haywood Park Former medieval deer park 1m S of Shugborough, on N side of Cannock Chase. The bishop of Lichfield had a park with two deer leaps at Haywood by 1286. According to Harwood Leland may have confused it with Beaudesert Old Park (EDP p179) (VCH vol 2 pp342-343). Miss Susanna Trubshawe (b1810) always maintained that the hewn walls in Haywood Park were a quarry where the stone was taken for the first Shugborough Manor House (HAHS p8). The park may have been separated into a Great Wood and a Little Wood - 'Great' and 'Little' being applied to the villages of Haywood, giving Great Haywood and Little Haywood (WFW p7). The park, though leased by the Ansons of Shugborough for a time in the C18, was not bought by Lord Lichfield until c1890 (SHC 1970 facing p110); in the later C18 Lord Anson erected an obelisk on Brocton Hill (see) in Haywood Park as an eyecatcher for Shugborough Hall.

Haywood Park Hall Stone house of considerable size by Haywood Park, near Shugborough. There was a house in Haywood Park, called Heywood Park, by at least the 1660s. Thomas Chetwynd, fifth son of Thomas Chetwynd of Rugeley was of Heywood Park; his son, William, was living at Heywood Park in 1664 (COI p174) (Plot's map) (Haywood Parke has several entries (1662 & 1672) in Colwich PR). Celia Fiennes visited her cousin and her husband Mr Wedgewood at Heywood Parke in summer 1698 (Illustrated Journeys of Celia Fiennes edited by Chris Morris. 1984. p148). Colwich PR Nov 3 1715 states William Wedgwood, son of John Wedgwood of Haywood Park Hall and Susannah his wife were buried there. The field called 'The Hall Croft' has been identified as the site of the hall (SHC 1914 p134 note). Haywood Park House was situated at SJ 986211 until the early C19 (SHC 1970 facing p110).

Haywood Warren 2m E of Brocton on Cannock Chase. In 1710 Lord Paget tried to establish a rabbit warren on this hitherto common land and the lodge was attacked by commoners (LOU p72). (AFT p190).

Hazel Barrow House over 1.5m NNE of Upper Hulme. Formerly in Heathylee township in Alstonefield ancient parish. There was a house here by 1719 (VCH vol 7 p33). The tollgate at Gib Torr was moved to Hazel Barrow in 1825 (UHAW p49). Has also appeared as Hazlebarrow (W p746), and Hazelbarrow.

Hazel Brook A small stream draining the land around the former Keele railway station (NSFCT 1919 p22). A tributary of Checkley Brook?

Hazeldene House now occupied by the surgery in Main Street, Great Haywood. Residence of the doctors of Great Haywood, including Dr Edward Tylecote, who Dr William Palmer (the poisoner), was apprenticed to. By the late 1930s the doctors had moved to High Meadows (HHHC pp69,76ps,98).

Hazeley Brook Madeley.

Hazelhurst House over 1.5m E of Endon. The name is of Anglo-Saxon origin and means 'wooded hill' (SPN p48).

Hazelhurst Aqueduct Aqueduct, at SJ 954536, under 0.25m N of Hazelhurst. Allows the Leek Branch Canal to pass over the Caldon Canal. Built in 1841 to relieve congestion on three locks leading up to Hazelhurst 'old' Junction used by traffic of both Leek Canal and Caldon Canal. Is a whitewashed brick and stone structure (IAS p166).

Hazelhurst Brook A tributary of the Churnet (SPNO p11).

Hazelhurst Junction Junction of the Caldon Canal and the Leek Canal. The 'old' junction, abandoned in 1841, was at SJ 954536, the 'new' junction is 700 yards to the W. Here is Hazelhurst Bridge, made of cast iron in 1842, which takes the towpath over to the Leek Canal (MR p146). Beyond stands a lock keeper's cottage by the Caldon Canal (The Trent & Mersey Canal in the Historic Waterways Scenes Series. Peter Lead 1980. pl 86).

Hazelslade Large village on Bentley Brook 1.5m ENE of Hednesford. The name is found in 1682 as Hazell Slade (SPNO p107). It means 'the valley where hazel trees grow' (SPN p30). The village was non-existent until the middle of the second half of the C19 when pits near Cannock Wood were opened. It was described as a hamlet in the 1950s (VCH vol 5 p149). Hazelslade was transferred from Rugeley to Cannock ancient parish in 1934 (VCH vol 5 p149). Thomas Coulthwaite (1861-1948) of Manchester came to Hazelslade to train horses in 1899 (SSE 1990 p87). Hazelslade was reputedly chosen by him on account of its central position in the country and the springy turf in the area (TWWW April 1997 p23p). Coulthwaite was at Hazelslade until at least 1908 before moving the business to Flaxley Green (SSE 1990 p88). At Hazelslade or Flaxley Green he trained three Grand National Winners: Eremon (1907), Jenkinstown (1910), and Grakle (1931) (SSE 1990 pp87-100). (MR p181). The church, All Saints, was built in 1884 (VCH vol 5 p67).

Hazelton Hill Hill 0.75m WNW of Blore (Ray). The burial mound topping the hill at SK 12504985 is 18 paces in diameter and 2.5 feet high and a listed monument. It was excavated by Carrington in 1849. Contains a rock-cut grave, cremations, two thumb scrapers and an inverted food vessel (TYD pp140-141) (VCH vol 1 no 22) (DAJ vol 75 pp93,117. vol 77 p26 B4) (NSJFS 1965 p33).

Hazelwood House 1.75m N of Meerbrook (HOLF p22). Formerly in Leekfrith township in Leek ancient parish (W p728). There was a house at Hazelwood, which has also appeared as Hazlewood, by 1635 (VCH vol 7 p194). The name represents the shrub hazel which grows in abundance here (NSJFS 1977 p36). John Plant of Hazzlewood Farm, aged 65 in 1851, kept a diary between 1849 and 1853 (SHJ vol 8 pp22-29).

Hazlecross Small hamlet high above the Churnet Valley 0.5m N of Kingsley. In Kingsley parish. Has also appeared as Hazlescross and Hazelcross.

Hazlehurst Brook Runs from Farley to Wootton Park where it joins Hole Brook which runs to the Churnet.

Hazlestrine S of Wildwood, Walton-on-the-Hill. In Baswich parish. Middlefell places the small Hazelstrine district in Acton Hill hamlet. At Hazlestrine was a brick works and quarry in the C19 (BERK2 p138). Has also appeared as Hazel Strine (Yates' map) (SPNO p5), and Hazelstrine.

Hazles Tiny hamlet over 0.5m NW of Kingsley.

Headlands Over 1m SE of Church Leigh (1834 OS map).

Head o' th' Lane Appears as a tiny hamlet on the 1834 OS map in the area of Woodstock Street and Rodgers Street, 0.25m N of Goldenhill. The name possibly related to the long lane which ran through the Potteries. The name no longer prevails.

Heakley Near Baddeley Green, Norton-in-the-Moors. Barely a minute hamlet centred around Heakley Hall Farm.

Heakley Hall Now Heakley Hall Farm? Nearly 0.75m E of Norton-in-the-Moors, in Norton chapelry in Stoke-on-Trent ancient parish (ONST 1932 p39). Nancy Linley in her researches into moated sites in the 1970s and early 1980s discovered a moat at Heakley Hall Farm (NSFCT 1982 p22).

Heamies Very fragmented minute hamlet on a hill on the E side of Meece Brook, 1.5m N of Chebsey. In Chebsey parish. No road links the principle properties of Upper Heamies and Lower Heamies which are only accessible off different roads. The estate of Heamies Farm was taken from Peter Giffard in the Civil War by order of a parliamentary commission in Stafford in 1643 (SIS pp42,43). There was a windmill at Heamies at approximately SJ 860315, which was in the possession of John Robinson, who in 1824 was advertising for a journey-man miller. The mill was not recorded again (WBJ p48).

Heath Hamlet in the mid C19, 0.5m NE of Darlaston (Offlow hundred). Partly in Darlaston and Wednesbury parishes (W pp599,675). The name is preserved in Heath Road, now a suburb of Darlaston.

Heath, The Amblecote. Here was a glasshouse.

Heath, The Local name for Clifton and Newton Common, former wasteland to the ESE of Clifton Campville, stretching towards No Man's Heath, Warws. The rights to graze livestock on the common were only held by the inhabitants of Chilcote, a township of Clifton Campville in Derbys, as they had paid a rent for this privilege (SHJ autumn 1989 p19).

Heath, The Residential district of N Uttoxeter. Former wasteland called Uttoxeter Heath (HOU p236). In Uttoxeter ancient parish. Redfern records a Roman coin was found here and a quadrangular Roman camp near the Three Tuns at cSK 086344, and claims to have Roman pottery from it (HOU 1886 pp74,76). Gunstone thought the site was a moat (NSJFS 1964 p39). Detachments of the parliamentary army were encamped here in the Civil War (Official Uttoxeter Town Guide. 1993. p16). Alice Key, a widow of Uttoxeter Heath, was a victim of the enclosure movement in c1787. Enclosure claimed all her land but the house in which she lived a bit of adjoining land. Legally a squatter on the rest of the land she had owned, she was taken to court and because she could not pay the court costs was sentenced to indefinite imprisonment. She was secured release by the attorney for the enclosure trustees only on condition that she surrender everything she owned for the sum of five shillings for her discharge (OP pp30-31). Here at SK 085340 was a windmill, described as 'newly erected' in 1809. The tower was reputedly demolished in 1919 when the stones were used in the construction of a house in Holly Road (SLM spring 1954 p25) (WBJ p40) (WIS p25). The mission church, Holly Road, was built in c1880 (LDD).

Heathbrook Area near Swindon Road, Wallheath, through which runs Dawley

Brook. Heath Brook Piece appears in 1840. The name is preserved in Heathbrook Avenue (SNSV vol 1 p168).

Heath End In the late C16 and early C17 a John Smith had a forge at Heath End in Keele parish (Newcastle Times Dec 29 1971). 'Heath' may be from Knutton Heath.

Heath End Small district of Pelsall, and 0.25m SSE of Pelsall church. Formerly partly in a detached portion of Wolverhampton chapelry in Wolverhampton ancient parish and partly in Rushall ancient parish. The name is derived from the end of Pelsall Heath (later Pelsall Common) (SNBP p79). The area was inhabited by at least 1779 when a non-conformist place of worship here was registered; the first to be registered in Pelsall township (SNBP p79). Heath End had a poor reputation as a 'rough area' with the more respectable aspiring middle-class villagers in Pelsall (SNBP p79). Flora Pearce, novelist, was born in Heath End. The village is the setting for her novel 'Essie' (1988). In her first novel, 'No Work Today,' a semi-biographical work, she uses the area's nickname of 'Cod End' to refer to Heath End (SNBP p79).

Heath End West Bromwich ancient parish. The area called Heath End SE of the junction of the roads from Tipton and Wednesbury existed by 1723 when the Cross Guns Inn is mentioned here (VCH vol 17 p4).

Heath End Common Heath End, Pelsall (ADY p24p).

Heather Hills Hills between Norton Green and Endon Edge (SVB p155). There is a lane called Heather Hills to W of Moss Hall.

Heathfield Former hamlet in Handsworth ancient parish, now merged into the suburbs of N Birmingham. The name, preserved in Heathfield Road 0.5m SE of St Mary's church, Handsworth, is from a medieval field called Heath Field (MNB p38).

Heathfield Bridge Over Walsall Canal, at Loxdale (OS map 1:25,000).

Heathfield Brook Rises in the Oxhill area of Handsworth and runs eastward to the Tame (MNB p35).

Heathfield Common Former common bounded by Heathfield, Church Hill, Gibson and Hamstead Roads. Enclosed in c1794 (MNB p45).

Heathfield Hall Former mansion which bore a similarity to Doddington Hall, Ches. It lay within the triangle bounded by Hamstead Road, Church Hill Road, and Heathfield Road, Handsworth. It was built by Samuel Wyatt (1737-1807) of Blackbrook Farm (see) between 1787 and 1790 for James Watt, the famous engineer (James Wyatt. Antony Dale. 1936. p6) (The Wyatts: An Architectural Dynasty. John Martin Robinson. 1979 p21) (A Biographical Dictionary of British Architects 1600-1840. 3rd ed Howard Colvin. 1995) (HPPE pp58-59). James Watt was born at Greenock, Scotland, in 1736. In 1768 he was introduced by Dr Small to Matthew Boulton of the Soho Manufactory (see) and later Soho Foundry (see). Shortly after, he became Boulton's partner in the business there. Watt died at Heathfield House on Aug 25 1819 and was buried in a chapel adjoining Handsworth church, where there is a huge statue of Watt to his memory sculpted by Sir Francis Chantrey (DNB) (ILN Sept 9 1865 p248il of the chapel) (SOSH pp302,303p of the statue). After Wyatt's death the house was occupied by members of his family, two of whom were James Gibson Watt and Agnes Gibson (1841). Thomas Pemberton, brassfounder, was a tenant in 1861. In the later C19 the house was occupied by Richard Tangye, and by William Tangye in 1899. Also known as Heathfield House, it was demolished in 1927 or 1928 for housing development (VCHWA vol 7 p51) (MNB pp41,45,47) (HPPE pp58-59) (HHHW p28p in 1901).

Heath Forge Stood at the confluence of Wom and Smestow Brooks in Wombourne. It was a hammer mill in the C17. Sir Walter Wrottesley owned it in 1650 when it was in the tenure of Thomas Foley. It passed to Philip Foley (VCH vol 20 pp212-213). The Heath forge which is alleged to have been mentioned in 'Metallum Martis' (1665) by Dud Dudley of Dudley Castle (see) may be a reference to Wallheath, but more probably the Heath forge on Smestow Brook (SNSV vol 1 p123).

Heath Green Residential area off Old Park Road adjoining Upper Gornal and the A459 Dudley-Wolverhampton road. Here is the Hare and Hounds Inn which stands on or near the site of Old Lodge Farm, birthplace in 1678 of Abraham Darby (d1717) (BCTV p36).

Heath Hayes Large village on high ground by Watling Street 1.25m SSE Hednesford. In Cannock ancient parish. A palstave of the Bronze Age was found at No. 103 Gorsemoor Road in 1943 (NSJFS 1964 p18). The present large village was called Five Ways (see) prior to c1900 (PCC p67) (LHSB 50 p6). The present name is from the farm to the N now (1978) called Farm Grange (St John's Heath Hayes 75th Anniversary. JC Oakes. 1978 p5) on the S side of Hednesford Road, which was known as Heathy Hayes by 1882 (1882 OS map); this area or farm being known as Hethhey in 1570 (SSE 1996 p14). The name is from Anglo-Saxon 'haeth' an area of unmanaged or untilled pasture, and 'geahaeg' (or 'hay') (SSE 1996 p14) (SPN p61). The church, St John the Evangelist, on the E side of Hednesford Road, facing

Lyndhurst Road, was built in 1902-1903 (VCH vol 5 p67) (BOE p144). Tom Lunn of Stafford Street, Heath Hayes, was goal keeper for the Wolverhampton Wanders team who beat Newcastle United in an FA Cup final (St John's Heath Hayes 75th Anniversary. JC Oakes. 1978 p11). Teddy Buckley of Bank Street carved with his penknife from an 11 foot plank of wood an unbroken chain with over a thousand links, two swivels and two hooks. It was being kept in Lichfield Museum in 1978 (St John's Heath Hayes 75th Anniversary. JC Oakes. 1978 p11).

Heath Hill Hamlet nearly 1.5m NNE of Sheriffhales. (W p480). Edward Ingram, the very capable blind man, noted by Plot in the later C17, was from Heath Hill (NHS p300).

Heath House 0.75m SSE of Cheddleton. Ralph Leek, and Katherine Winifred Ridgeway (d1892) were of Heath House (mems in Cheddleton church).

Heath House House on the E side of Heath House Lane 1.25m S of Codsall, in Codsall parish. A former house on the site may have existed by the earlier C17. The present farmhouse dates from the C19 (VCH vol 20 p79).

Heath House 0.5m NNE of Horton on top of Grindlestone Edge. Existed by 1446 (VCH vol 7 p65). Seat of the Heaths (NSFCT 1932 p33).

Heath House House 0.5m WSW of Longnor. Formerly in Heathylee township in Alstonefield ancient parish. There was a house here by 1406 (VCH vol 7 p33). Moses Charlesworth (d1881) was of Heath House (mem in Longnor church). The sound of a phantom horse and rider is said to leave Longnor taking the direction of the Heath House (L p49).

Heath House House 1m ESE of Upper Tean. Built on or near the site of a former house built in 1690 (ACOPP p58). The present house was built by John Burton Philips, owner of the Tean Hall Mills, in 1836 to the design of Thomas Johnson of Lichfield (BOE p280). There is a Philips family tree in the house (CJF p66) and portraits of John Burton Philips by George Richmond, and Joanna Philips by Jackson (CL Jan 10 1963 pp62-65). (SMOPP vol 1 pp35 il drawing by Sarah Pease 1824,36) (SLM July 1950 p168p). And Johnson's designs for the house were still kept at the house in 1985 (DoE). The house was Baskerville Hall in the TV dramatisation of Sir Arthur Conan Doyle's 'Hound of the Baskervilles' c1987 (info Mark Smith) and has been used for filming Agatha Christie's 'They do it with Mirrors' a Miss Marple detective story (MIDD vol 2 p12) (ES June 19 1993 p24). In the garden there is an orangery 200 yards NE of the house. It was designed by Thomas Trubshaw in 1831. (CL Jan 3 1963 pp18-21 ps, 10 Jan 1963 pp62-65 ps mainly of interior fig 10 of the orangery). There are two planting troughs 200 yards NE of the house designed by Thomas Trubshaw in c1830 (DoE II). 0.5m NE is a temple, a prospect for the house. Built in the 1850s using eight unfluted Ionic columns of the veranda of the old house of the 1820s (DoE II) (BOE p281) (ES June 19 1993 p24p) (ACOPP p58p).

Heath House Three-storey brick house of the early C18 (VCH vol 20 p199). Situated in the vicinity of Heath House Drive, 1.25m WSW of Wombourne. Has an ice-house. Appears to still stand in 1988 (OS map 1:25,000. 1988), but to have been demolished for an housing estate by 1995 (OS Street Atlas; Staffordshire 1995). It appears to have been occupied by John Elwell (1785-1859), ironmaster, in c1810 whilst he was working the Heath Mill (IE p116).

Heath Town Former hamlet on a SW-facing incline near the source of the Smestow, now a Black Country town 1m WSW of Wednesfield. Formerly in Wednesfield township and chapelry in Wolverhampton ancient parish. Duignan says here was fought the battle often called the battle of Tettenhall in 910 or 911 AD. The nucleus of the original settlement centred on the junction of Deans Road and Old Heath Road. The Pitt family, of whom Thomas Pitt (b1619) was one, may have had a farm on the site of the Jolly Collier Inn at Heath Town; Thomas Pitt may have been the Pitt or Pytt who was used to try to bribe into surrender the commander of the garrison of Rushall Hall (see) in the Civil War (WFW pp71,90-92) (TB Nov 1985 p13). Heath Town was formerly called Heath Houses (maps of Morden, Plot, and Bowen), The Heath (OS map 1834) and Wednesfield Heath (W p96) (DUIGNAN p97). In 1764 a **tollhouse** was situated on the main Wolverhampton-Wednesfield road at Heath Town by when fields in the area were enclosed (WFW p71). There was a **windmill** at approximately SO 932999 lying to NE of the double railway bridge over the canal. It appeared in an advertisement in 1824. The mill was sold at auction in 1849 and does not appear on the 1886 OS map (WBJ p42). The Grand Junction **Railway** opened a station at Wednesfield Heath on July 4 1837 (WF p20). The Shrewsbury and Birmingham Railway opened a temporary station at Wednesbury Heath in Nov 1849 (WF p44). Heath Town station closed in 1910 but still (1985) stands in a timber yard off Station Road near Heath Town baths and library (WP&P p5). The line between Wolverhampton and Walsall passing through Heath Town continued to be used until 1965 (WHTOP p126p). The **church**, Holy Trinity, to the W of Church Street, was built in 1850-1852 (BOE p321). Became a separate ecclesiastical parish,

known as Wednesfield Heath, in 1852, refounded 1853. Created a separate township in 1866 (Mapping the Past Wolverhampton 1577-1986. Mary Mills 1993 p22) and a separate civil parish in 1894 known as 'Heath Town' later known as 'Heathtown.' The civil parish was abolished in 1927 when it entered Wolverhampton county borough (GLAUE pp413,428). Was a ward of Wolverhampton borough by 1982. Sometime after the mid C19 six **almshouses** for 12 widows were erected near Holy Trinity church. The benefactor was Henry Rogers. The almshouses were derelict for many years but had been restored by the late 1990s (WPOPP vol 2 p78p of c1910) (Wolverhampton Chronicle Nov 19 1999 p24). Heath Town grew rapidly in the period c1891 (Mapping the Past Wolverhampton 1577-1986. Mary Mills 1993 p22). In the early C20 Heath Town manufactured safes, pumps, locks, hinges, and other iron goods (LGS p145). Viking Cycles established in Heath Town in 1908. The firm moved to Wolverhampton in 1928 (WOLOP 72). By the later C20 Heath Town was in the middle of the conurbation stretching all the way from Wolverhampton to Wednesfield. Princess Margaret visited Heath Town on April 1 1969 (WHTOP p119p). By June 1969 the old Wednesfield Road containing terraces and shops had been demolished and was replaced by the present stretch of dual carriageway and the vast housing estate, including three tower blocks, which line its route (Wolverhampton Chronicle Nov 19 1999 p24p).

Heath Town Park Public park on N side of the Wolverhampton Road, Heath Town. The land, previously probably rough colliery ground, was leased for a park by the Heath Town urban district council from the Ecclesiastical Commissioners in 1917. The council bought it in 1920 (WHTOP p109p).

Heathyards Farm Nearly 1m ENE of Hopton, on Hopton Heath. The 'walled-close' containing parliamentarian musquettiers at the battle of Hopton Heath in 1643 was identified with this farm by Lt Col Alfred H Burne in OSST 1995--51-52 pp24-29 (SHJ winter 1987 p2). The enclosure appears on Yates' map.

Heathy Leasows The name occurs on the 1834 OS map due S of Scout House Reservoir. To here Cannock Chase Railway opened a line in 1862 from Hednesford; here it connected with the Littleworth tramway (VCH vol 2 p318).

Heathylee Former moorland township in Alstonefield ancient parish includes Broncott, Downsdale, Hardings Booth, Barrow Moor, Longnor Mill, Middle Hills and Morridge Top (W p743). Partly in the chapelries of Longnor and Quarnford (GLAUE p413). The township was covered by Malbonck Forest in medieval times. By the C15 there were farms in the township (VCH vol 7 pp1,5). A house called Heathylee was recorded in 1406. It may have been NW of Hardings Booth where there were two houses called Heathylee in 1571 (VCH vol 7 p33). The name is self-explanatory and fairly modern (SSAHST 1967 p34). The 1834 OS map shows a Heathylee House under 1m SW of Hollinsclough at SK 055656. Heathylee became a separate civil parish in 1866 (GLAUE p413).

Heathy Roods House 0.75m NNE of Butterton (Moorlands).

Heatley Fragmented hamlet on a W-facing incline above Tad Brook 0.75m N of Bagot's Bromley. In Abbots Bromley ancient parish. A star-shaped and layered crystallised stone has been found in a field called Willmon between Heatley and Bagot's Bromley (NHS p177 tab ii fig 3 could illustrate it). According to their own family tradition the Brown family had been on the Bagot estate at Heatley for six centuries up to the 1930s. Their ancestors had come from Wales to Staffs with members of the Bagot family, who had estates in Wales (CCF pp163-164).

Heatley Green Heatley Green Farm to the W of Heatley dates from the C17. It is the oldest surviving building in Heatley and may be the original settlement (ABAB p39).

Heaton Fragmented hamlet above a narrow high valley 0.75m E of Rushton Spencer lying on high ground to the W of Gun Hill. Former manor and township in Leek ancient parish. An old stone used to stand at Heaton (DPEM p70). Part of an Anglo-Saxon circular cross shaft stands in a field NE of Heaton hamlet (NSJFS vol 6 p10 note) (VCH vol 7 p186); perhaps the same as the cross found at Heatonlow (see). The name Heaton is an Old English one meaning a high settlement (VCH vol 7 p186). The manor, probably originally carved out of that of Leek, belonged to Dieulacres Abbey until the Dissolution, when it fragmented. It was not reunited until the end of the C18 after which it descended with the Swythamley estate (VCH vol 7 p187). Heaton was in Rushton Spencer ecclesiastical parish after 1726. In 1866 it became a separate civil parish (GLAUE p413).

Heaton Hall Under 0.25m W of Heaton. The site of the house was occupied by 1775, and the house was called Heaton Hall by 1851. It was rebuilt in the 1860s (VCH vol 7 p186). Has also appeared as Heaton Hall Farm.

Heatonlow House under 0.5m NNE of Heaton. Formerly in Heaton township in Leek ancient parish. A Saxon cross with tracery was discovered here sometime before 1951 and had been used as a gate post (NSFCT 1951 pp112-113). There was a house on the site of Heatonlow by the earlier C16. The porch of the present house carries the date 1651 and the initials of William Nabs, joint lord of Heaton manor in 1654 (VCH vol 7 p186). Has also appeared as Heaton Low and Heaton Lowe (VCH vol 7 p186).

Hednesford (alternatively *Hedgford*, *Edgeford* Pigot & Sons' map 1830, locally *Hensford* CCBO pp70,74, or *Hedgefud* BILP1, a native is a Hedgefudian BILP1 p8). Former mining town overlooking Ridings Brook, 8.5m SE of Stafford. Formerly in Cannock township and old parish (VCH vol 5 p49). At the Hednesford end of the Rawnsley Road an axe-hammer was found in 1969 (SSAHST 1971 pp46,47il). The name has appeared as Edenesford (SPN p61), Hedesdene (Cart. Sax. 544), Hedenedford (sic) (c1153) (SPNO p57), Hedenesford (C13) (SSE 1996 p14) Heddenesford (1307), Hednesford(e) (1362) (SPNO p57). If from Hedesdene then the name means Heoden's valley. The 'ford' part is probably referring to a stream that the ancient British London to Chester trackway had to ford at Old Hednesford (DUIGNAN). Is 'Heddin's ford' or possibly 'Hedda's ford' (SSE 1996 p14) (SPN p61), or 'Haden's ford' (SOB p117), or is of Celtic origin (HOWW p8). The original Hednesford, now known as Old Hednesford (see), was superseded in the later C19 by a town for miners built to the NW on common land known as Cannock Heath (VCH vol 5 p49). Present Hednesford dates almost entirely from between 1860 and 1880, and is centred on Hednesford Lodge. It expanded after the opening of the Uxbridge Colliery (VCH vol 5 p49). The **church**, St Peter, Church Hill to the NE of the old settlement, was built in 1868 and rebuilt in 1987 (VCH vol 5 p66) (LDD). Hednesford became a separate ecclesiastical parish in 1870 (LGS p145) (GLAUE p413). **Hednesford Town FC** attracted national notoriety by winning their way to the fourth round of the FA Cup in which they were only narrowly beaten 2-3 by far superior Middlesborough on Jan 25 1997 (The Times Jan 25 1997 p59) (Daily Telegraph Jan 25 1997 p18) (Sunday Telegraph Jan 26 1997 pS3). For **RAF Hednesford** see Brindley Heath. **Persons and visitors**. The self-styled **'King of Hednesford'** was a character known as 'Old Jacky Wright' who lived in Hednesford or Old Hednesford in the mid C19. One of his eccentric forays was to lie in a specially-made coffin suited to his dimensions at the head of festival processions and be carried along by bearers who placed him down on the lawn in front of the Anglesey Hotel, from which he would spring and make a characteristically funny speech to the crowd (CCF pp77,78). **Thomas Thomas**, poet and miner of Hednesford, gained local fame. He was the author of ballads which were designed to win public sympathy and support for the striking miners in the 'Great Federation Lock-out' of 1893 (CCC p133) (VCH vol 5 p62) (Cannock Chase District Guide 1987). **George VI** visited Hednesford in July 1934 (R&S p46). For the murder of **Elizabeth Gaskin** see Hednesford Pool. **Bruce Beddow**, author of 'The Wine of Illusion,' was a native of Hednesford. The heroine of the novel is Madeline Lucian, a beautiful gipsy girl (CCF p188). **Nancy Foster** (b1913) of Market Street, poet and West Cannock Colliery office telephone operator, took her own life in the East Cannock Canal basin on Oct 28 1933. 'The Collected Poems of Nancy Foster,' including two poems 'The Miner' and 'Market Street, Hednesford, on Saturday Night,' appeared in 1934 (TB March 1986 p17) (VFC p50).
NEWSPAPERS. The **Cannock and Hednesford Mercury** ran from April 21 1883 to Sept 12 1890 (SHJ spring 1996 p16). The **Hednesford Advertiser**, a Hednesford edition of the Cannock Advertiser, seems to have appeared over the period 1884 to 1973 (SHJ spring 1996 p18). No. 2686 of the **Hednesford Courier** appeared on April 7 1955 and the paper ran at least until April 9 1964 (SHJ spring 1996 p18). The **Cannock Chase News and Weekly Advertiser**, which ran from Sept 4 1953 to July 29 1955, was published at Hednesford (SHJ spring 1996 p17). Many of the newspapers of Cannock (see) and Lichfield (see) covered Hednesford.

Hednesford Hills Hills to the E of Hednesford. There was a race-horse track in the hills; many early C20 Grand National winners were trained here (CCBO pp60-64), and at Cockpit Hill (see), and at Rawnsley Reservoir (see). In 1887 a bust main pipe from Scout House Reservoir (see) caused a chain reaction, and 43 million tonnes of water cascaded through the hills (Cannock Chase: The Second Selection. June Pickerill. 1997. p8). Hednesford Hills were given to the public by Marquis of Anglesey in 1934 (PCC p19) (Cannock Chase by Car. Staffs Nature Conservation Trust Ltd. ND, but between 1971 and 1974 p10). The Museum of Cannock Chase opened in Valley Road in 1989 on the site of the former Valley Colliery on the W side of the hills. It focuses on the history of the chase (info Glen Small).

Hednesford Pool Formerly comprised two pools lying between the railway and Rugeley Road at Hednesford. Hednesford Lodge was built beside it in 1831. It covered about 27 acres in 1834 and was reduced to 23 acres in 1851

(W p452) (VCH vol 2 p111. vol 5 p52). On Feb 19 1919 Henry Thomas Gaskin, aged 25, former miner at West Cannock Colliery and Royal Engineer, murdered his estranged wife Elizabeth Gaskin (nee Talbot), aged 23, in a copse (now known as Gaskin's Wood) by the pool. She had been unfaithful to him whilst he was serving in WW1 and had had two children by another man. After a meeting in the copse by the pool which ended in an argument Gaskin stabbed her then cut off her head and dismembered her body. At length with ingenuity he placed the body in the moat surrounding a gasometer in Victoria Road. Soon Gaskin confessed and was found guilty of murder after a trial starting at Stafford on July 11 1919. Despite a large petition signed by 6000 supporters, who thought he should have been shown leniency as he had fought for his country and had been wronged by a promiscuous wife, Gaskin was hung at Winson Green Prison, Birmingham, on Aug 8 1919 (MM pp21-28) (TB Nov 1984 p5. April 1993 p22) (ACOP p111p) (MMMR pp20-25) (MCS pp38-41). By 1989 the area was called Hednesford Park (Birmingham A-Z 1989).

Heighley (locally *Yelly* BOJ book 2 p59). Fragmented small hamlet on a bluff above Checkley Brook, 1.5m N of Madeley. In Audley ancient parish. There is a local tradition that a Roman road passed Bower End and Heighley Castle to the Wrekin (M p21). Heighley appears in 975 (BVC p34), and has appeared as Heolla (DB), Heyley (maps of Plot and Bowen), Heeley (W p427), Heleigh (LGS p145) (SL p94) (NSJFS 1962 p76), Healey (STM May 1967 p27p), and Heley (BVC p34) (NSFCT new series vol 19 1994). If from Heolla then 'Heol-y-gwint' is the Milky Way in Welsh. The road in question could be an ancient salt way from the SE to Nantwich (DUIGNAN). Heighley is a Celtic name meaning 'a road' (M p21). Or is 'the high glade' (SPN p88), or 'high leah (wood clearing)' (BVC p34) (SSE 1996 p14). Krausse shows how the aspirate corruption of 'coill' 'coll' produces in this district 'holle' (NSFCT 1908 p140). There was possibly a medieval village to the N or to the S of the castle (SSAHST 1970 p35). The ancient lords of Apedale and Heleigh had the right of holding a court leet with the franchises of gallows and tumbril (SCSF p123).

Heighley Castle A Saxon castle at Heighley had probably existed on the site prior to the medieval castle (NSFCT 1949 p120). The site for the castle on a bluff above Checkley Brook was given by an heir of William de Bettelih or Betley to Henry de Aldithley (or Audley) in 1226 not by Harvey de Stafford as Camden and Dr Fuller say (SD pp63,103).
THE AUDLEYS. The Audleys or Aldithleys seem to have been a cadet branch of the de Verduns of Alton Castle (see) (NSFCT 1993-94 p13). **Henry de Aldithley**, second son of Adam of Audley (died between 1203-1211), built Heighley Castle, Redcastle (Shrops), and Hulton Abbey (see). He died in 1246 and was succeeded by his son **James de Aldithley**, keeper of Newcastle-under-Lyme Castle and royalist in the Barons' Wars (1264). On his death in 1272 he was succeeded by his son James de Aldithley (1250-1273). The succession then passed through his brothers, Henry (1251-1276), William (1253-1282), and Nicholas (d1299) to Nicholas's son Thomas. Thomas was slain at the battle of Bannockburn in 1314. He was succeeded by his brother **Nicholas de Aldithley** (1289-1316), who by a writ of summons to parliament in 1312 became 1st Lord Audley. He was succeeded by his son **James de Aldithley** (1312/3-1386), 2nd Lord Audley. He has been identified erroneously as the James de Audley who fought at Poitiers (1356), and was identified as such by Dugdale in 'Baronage' (1675); Ashmole in 1693; Ormerod in his 'Cheshire;' Ward in HBST; Burke in his 'Peerage and Landed Gentry;' Harwood in SOS; and Eyton in his 'Antiquities of Salop.' However, GF Beltz, Lancaster Herald, was the first to show in his 'Memorials of the Order of the Garter' (1841) that Sir James de Audley KG and hero of Poitiers was not the same as James 2nd Lord Aldithley (d1386) and of Redcastle (Shrops) but Sir James de Audley (c1322-1369) son of James de Audley of Stretton. James de Audley, lord of Heighley (d1386), did fight at Crecy as did the other James de Audley (SHC 1906 pp245-268). James (d1386) was succeeded by his son **Nicholas de Aldithley** (1328-1391), 3rd Lord Audley. His widow, Elizabeth (d1400), was buried at Hulton Abbey and her tomb may have been taken from there to St John's churchyard, Burslem. Nicholas, whose daughter Alice married Ralph Basset of Drayton Bassett (see), was succeeded by his nephew, **John Touchet** (b1371), 4th Lord Audley, son of Joan, sister of Nicholas (d1391), and wife of Sir John Touchet (or Tuchet). John, who fought against Glendower in Wales, was succeeded by his son **James Touchet** (1398-1459), 5th Lord Audley. He lead the Lancastrians at the battle of Bloreheath (see) in 1459 and was slain during the battle; Audley's Cross (see) there commemorates him. He was succeeded by his son **John Touchet** (d1490), 6th Lord Audley, Lord Treasurer 1484. He was succeeded by his son **James**, 7th Lord Audley, who joined the Cornish insurrection and was beheaded in 1497. His son **John**, 8th Lord Audley, was restored to the title in 1512. He was suc-

ceeded on his death in 1557/8 by his son **George** (d1560), 9th Lord Audley, who was succeeded by his son **Henry Touchet** (d1563), 10th Lord Audley, who married Elizabeth daughter of Sir William Sneyd, ancestor of the Sneyds of Keele Hall (see). Henry was succeeded by his son **George** (d1617), 11th Lord Audley, created Baron Audley of Orier in 1616. He was succeeded by his son **Mervin Touchet**, 12th Lord Audley, who was attainted of felony and beheaded in 1631. In the later C18 the male Touchet line came to an end and the family married into the Thicknesse family of Fathinghoe, Northants; the Thicknesse-Touchets held the title of Lord Audley to at least the later C19 (The Complete Peerage).

THE CASTLE. In 1354 there was a murder committed in the kitchen castle (BVC p45) (NSFCT 1994 p14). In 1534 the castle was used as a prison (CAMS p21). In 1538 the Audleys complained they had 'no house but an old ruinous castle' (SL p94). In 1578 the castle was bought by the Gerards (LGS p146). It remained intact until 1644 (NSFCT 1942 p63) (BOPP pls 75,76) or 1645 (LGS p146) when the parliamentary committee at Stafford sent three masons to take it down; only the ditch below the bailey and a fragment of walling of the gatehouse and keep remained by the later C20 (M pp10,11p). The hill on which it stands is named locally Mahull (NHS pp44,205,445). On the hill in the later C17 Plot noted buck wheat growing which mixed with barley will make bread? Celia Fiennes passed the castle in 1698 on her way to Chester and noted it in her journal spelling the place Healy; she noted it was 'ruinated' but the walls still remained (The Illustrated Journeys of Celia Fiennes c1682-c1712. Christopher Morris. 1984 p156) (BVC p8). In the late C18 Shaw noted the very rare Common Navel Wort (Cotyledon Umbilicus) growing in rocks under Heighley Castle Bank (SHOS vol 1 part i p102). Excavations in c1830 uncovered two pieces of wall on the motte, the well and a small portion of Early English arcading with the springers for a groin roof (M pp10,11p). As a precautionary measure the castle was further demolished in 1845 (NSFCT 1949 p120) (NSJFS 1969 p133). The tradition of parishioners from Audley, Betley, Madeley and other neighbouring parishes picnicking at the castle on Good Friday came to an end in or shortly after WW2; Wilf Bloor, author of BOJ books, attended picnics here in his youth (BOJ book 2 p59) (info Les Bradshaw and Tom Houghton). DoE II scheduled AM (SD pp63,85,103) (SSC p130 in the intro) (GNHS p124) (SK p200) (IAANS p ix) (VCH vol I pp351,352 dia) (MOS p34) (LGS pp145,146) (KES pp148,149) (BOE p145) (M pp10,11) (STM Feb 1964 pp34,35) (A pl 2 - painting of 1840) (SL p94) (TFTP pp146-148) (NSJFS 1966 p44) (SGS p126) (BTC p32) (MR p221). The view from the hill takes in the Wrekin, Church Stretton Hills, Caradoc, Breidden Hills, Peckforton Hills, Beeston Castle and Delamere Forest in Cheshire and Mow Cop (NSFCT 1880 pp35,36-45). At the foot of the hill on which the castle stands was a pool with clear water which revives horses in hunts and deer so that they appear totally rested. The story of this pool comes from Camden. Plot identified it as the one at the foot of the castle (NHS p44) (SD p85). The castle ruins were visited by the NSFC in 1885 after which occasion a club member wrote a little verse which goes

Whoever would visit Heleigh aright,
Should visit it by the pale moonlight.

(NSFCT 1886 p66. 1917 p140).

Heighley Park A medieval deer park by Heighley Castle enclosed out of forest, held by the de Aldithleys (or Audleys): It was their home park and was constructed in 1222 (NSFCT 1910 pp171,172. 1993-94 p14). In existence by 1227 (NSJFS 1962 pp73,76). Had gates at Cooksgate and Redgate (BVC p35). Has also appeared as Heighley Old Park.

Hell Clough To E of Park Hall, Church Leigh.

Hell Entry Off Church Street, Bilston. Hell Entry led to the house of the Pipe family. The name is perhaps a corruption of Hall Entry (BOP p32).

Hell Floor Coppice at middle of, and N of, Upper Avenue to Chillington Hall. Local tradition says here ghosts have been seen. The name is recorded in 1867 and although there is a legend of the Devil at Brewood (see) the name may allude to something of antiquity, perhaps of Roman origin, perhaps Watling Street (BDH 1992 p333).

Hell Hole Sometime alternative name for Cradley Forge (see).

Hell Hole Hell Hole is a brook or stream, like The Devil's Staircase, in the Burntwood Bishop's Wood area at Fairoak (BOV p27). For the two child murders which took place in the Hell Hole area see under Bishop's Wood.

Hell Hole Tiny run-down area of S Burslem. Near the junction of Waterloo Road and Nile Street demolished between 1890 and 1900 (When I was Child. C Shaw pp121-2) (VCH vol 8 p114) (POP pp35-36).

Hell Hole Above the Hamps below Soles Hill, Calton (HLS p45).

Hell Hole Mire situated in a hollow possibly created in the Ice Age NW of Gnosall and to the NW of Doleygate (WSS pp101,102p).

Hell Hole To NE of Norbury Park, Norbury.

Hell Hole Covert Over 0.25m WSW of Blithfield, at SK 038212.

Hell Lane Alias the hamlet Ettingshall Lane (Bowen's map) which lay in the present Monmore Park Industrial Estate area of Ettingshall Road, 1.5m SE of Wolverhampton, near the Birmingham Canal Old Cut Old Main Line (Yates' maps 1775 and 1799, Smith's map (which marks both Ettingshall and Hell Lanes), and later maps of Cary) (W pp95,144). It also appears to have been the name for settlement continuing S on Ettingshall Lane, a road that ran all the way from the present day Bilston Road through Catchem Corner to Sodom (present Hurst Hill). The road currently goes by other names in parts such as Manor Road, Spring Road, and Rookery Road. Hell Lane was considered the most unruly place in the Black Country from at least the C18 up to the early C20. To quote John Freeman writing about Bilston Methodism in 1923 'Hell Lane was a nesting spot of sheep stealers and highwaymen, who have been known to stop coaches, relieving travellers of their valuables and hold up menageries while they selected and led away some of their best horses.' The people of Coseley had a saying that 'Sodom begins where Hell ends' (BCM Oct 1990 p61) (TB Nov 1976 p24. June 1994 p29). Attempts by Methodist missionaries to convert the local inhabitants came to some success in the period 1802 to 1806 when a small chapel was erected in Hell Lane, said to have been near Ruffian Lane, leading to Dark Lane and Sodom (HOBL pp167-168). According to Robert George Hobbes (1821-1899), a correspondent for the weekly 'The Leisure Hour' in the 1870s, Gideon Ouseley made Hell Lane the centre of a mission, and according to John Freeman in Black Country Stories and Sketches Ouseley often preached in Hell Lane. Neither Underhill nor Hackwood mention him. He is said to have paid only three visits to England, but may have preached in Hell Lane in 1818 when on a visit to Wolverhampton (BCM autumn 1993 pp56-57). Hell Lane, the name is said to allude to the evilness of the place and perhaps paganism (BCM Oct 1993 p56), was no longer known as Hell Lane by 1873 (Samuel Griffiths' Guide to the Iron Trade of Great Britain. 1873. New ed by WKV Gale. 1967. p87). It is in Benjamin Disraeli's Hell House Yards in his novel 'Sybil' (1846) (AOW p167). VILLAINS, CHARACTERS AND GHOSTS. The **Bratts** were infamous in Hell Lane in c1800 (SCSF p128). The **British Queen Inn** in or near Meadow Lane, Hell Lane, was an inn of ill repute (HC p54). Hell Lane was home to **Devil Lees**, a notorious highwayman, and his gang. It was their ways which were probably responsible for the name Hell Lane (BCM Oct 1990 p62). **Hell House** in Hell Lane was the residence of Dick Evans, a great fighter (TB April 1994 p13). Another gang, known as the Hell-Lane Gang, were led by **Billy Moore**. The gang frequented Hell Lane in the 1920s and 1930s and frequented the Duke of York (TB April 1980 p10 - on Hell Lane characters). The Hell-Lane Gang are said to be responsible for the murder of a woman who has reappeared as a ghost without a head (TB April 1994 p13). **Kat Rhodes** of Hell Lane had the reputation of being something of a wizard. His attire, always of red and yellow, was similar to the modern Rastafarian. His long hair was worn in pig tails (TB April 1994 p13). The White Rabbit Witch, called **Nell Nicholls** (or Nelly Nichols), haunted in the area of Hell Lane. She lived in an old cottage which stood close to the spot where a crude wooden bridge spanned a black stream near Hell Lane, and not far from the residence of Billy Moore. She had the ability to turn herself into a white rabbit and in that form pry about the neighbourhood listening to conversations. If anyone spoke ill of the witch she could ensure that the offender met with some ill-luck (SR p107) (FLJ 1942 p127) (TB April 1988 p5. Oct 1989 p29. April 1994 p13). A large **black dog spectre** has also been spotted in Hell Lane. It followed a man to his home and just as the man reached the threshold of his house the spectre dog gave a long-drawn howl. Just as he did so the house collapsed and the man died in the ruins (SR p107) (TB April 1988 p5) (GOM pl 8 (d)). The ghost of a **headless woman**, supposedly murdered by the Hell-Lane Gang, was seen in Hell Lane by Dick Ormes. Some time later she was seen to go into Dick Ormes's Cottage. Ormes was later found dead in his cottage with a pipe in his mouth, and his livestock consisting of a dog, pig and cow gone (TB April 1994 p13).

Hell's Hole A yard in Walsall with several cottages in Peal Street near the top of Dudley Street and approached by a very sloping passage. It communicated with Gameson's Yard, Dudley Street. The houses were occupied by notorious characters of the lowest class, hence the name. Has also appeared as Hell Fold (1773. 1785) (SNWA p57).

Hembs The former farm of this name stood in the Hembs Crescent area of Newton. A library now (1983) stands close to the site of Hembs Cottages. Formerly in Perry Barr township. Hembs is a corruption of Hams, and may refer to the Tame loop nearby rather than to the estate of Hamstead (MNB pp62,66).

Hem Heath Tiny hamlet on ground rising above Longton Brook 0.75m WSW of Blurton. In Trentham parish. A house at Hem Heath was registered for Protestant Dissenters in 1828 (SHC 1960 p72). Now part of the conurbation stretching from Trentham to Longton.

Hemlock Presumably in the vicinity of Hemlock Bridge and Hemlock Way 1m NE of Cannock.

Hemmings Low To W of Cauldon Low, Cauldon.

Hemp Butts To the NE of Stone Priory, Stone (SIS p18 see map). Has also appeared as Hempbutts.

Hemp Holm Marshy land on S side of the Trent by Rugeley Power Station. (VCH vol 5 p158 note).

Hemphill Brook Brook over which the battle of Blore Heath was fought (LGS p190). Masefield spells it 'Hemphill' and it is spelt 'Hempmill' by SVB p85. Has also appeared as Wambrimebrok (C13), Wemberton Brook (late C15, C16), and Wembleton Brook (1713) (SHC 1945/ 6 p7) (NSJFS 1980 p13). It has also been variously called Stow, Sow, and Tern Brook (NSFCT 1884 p15). It is a tributary of Bloredale Brook (SHC 1945/ 6 p7).

Hempstalls The name is preserved in Hempstalls County Primary School. 1m N of Newcastle-under-Lyme. Scarratt thinks Hempstalls is literally from a place with stalls where people sold hemp, and probably flax, too (OTP p59).

Hen Cloud The most southerly pinnacle of the Roaches Range, isolated from the Roaches to the NW and the Ramshaw Rocks to the NE. Under 0.5m N of Upper Hulme. Topped with a fortress-like rock formation rising to 1345 feet high. Known locally as the Cloud and was at some period the site for an open-air zoo (SGM pp22,124-125 for a minutely detailed description of the rock formation). Two vessels of apparently Bronze Age origin have been found near Hen Cloud (NSJFS vol 4 p28. vol 8 pp70-72) (VCH vol 7 p193). Has also appeared as End Cloud and Hern's Cloud (DPMM p102). The name is from Old English 'hean' or 'henge' and 'clud,' together meaning 'high rocky hill' (NSJFS 1977 p39) (VCH vol 7 p191) (PNPD). Or derives its name from it resembling an hen sitting on her clicks (ie: the crags below or by it) (DPMM p92). For a Celtic interment found on the slopes of Hen Cloud and Brocklehursts' private zoo said to have been covered Hen Cloud see Roaches House. A Wellington III aircraft crashed at Hen Cloud on Nov 22 1942. The crew of six all died except F/ SGT Cheek (MD pp30-31). (NHS p171) (HS p10p) (BOE pl 1 view of the pinnacle from the N).

Henhurst Wood Former wood belonging to Burton Abbey to W of Shobnall, Burton upon Trent. Prior to 1499 was known as the Abbot's Wood (ANS p59).

Henridding Henridding Farm is 0.75m W of Endon. Formerly in Endon township in Leek ancient parish. A Bronze Age flat axe-head, incised and decorated with zig-zag lines and rows of dots on one side, was found at Henridding in 1916. The length is 128mm, width 65mm, thickness 9mm, weight 508gn (NSFCT 1926 p143. 1931 pp190-1p. 1940 p37. 1953 p105) (NSJFS 1964 p22) (VCH vol 7 p177). Has also appeared as Henrhydding and Penrhydding.

Henwood Farm Lay next to Henwood Lane, Compton, Tettenhall (TPOP p77p).

Herbage House N of Upper Elkstone. In Alstonefield ancient parish in Fawfieldhead township until 1934 when transferred to Warslow and Elkstone civil parish (VCH vol 7 p27 note). Has appeared as Harebache (1439) (VCH vol 7 p27 note) and Hairbage (Bowen's map).

Herbert Park Former name for The George Rose Park near Wolverhampton Street, Willenhall. It was probably a hunting enclosure in Middle Ages (WDY p16). During the C18 and C19 Herbert Park was the scene of intensive coal mining. Has also appeared as Herberts Park (SNDB p58).

Hermitage House under 0.25m N of Froghall, Kingsley. A newspaper cutting dated 1916 notes a 300 year old haunted farmhouse in Ipstones called the Hermitage (GLS p59) (SMM p49): The house had been frequently haunted by poltergeists and the paranormal, reported the newspaper? According to local legend sometime ago an old miser resided at the Hermitage, who hoarded his wealth and whose little bent figure in a tall hat was known far and near. His ghost or presence reputedly haunts the place as witnessed by the occupant (in 1916?) and prosperous agriculturist, Bennett Fallowes. The Hermitage was owned by Col Beech of Shaw Hall (TOI pp175-176). A black dog or padfoot reputedly haunts the area of Hermitage (FLJ 1942 p126) (GLS p59) (DPEM p110). It has been implied that Hermitage is an area and that Moosey Moor Wood Valley is in it (NSFCT 1926 pp116-117). The name is from the miser who lived here and who hoarded his wealth (SMM p49).

Hermitage, The House near Mayfield Hall, Middle Mayfield (W p784). An inscription on a door lintel reads 'William Bolt, in his old age, built himself a Hermitage. 1749.' The Regency-style addition is probably of the early C19. It was occupied in the mid C19 by the Greaves family (MOM p56p).

Heron Court Albion Street, Rugeley. A large mansion in the 'Tudor' style built in 1851 by Joseph Whitgreave (W p472). Had become St Anthony's Convent by the mid 1950s (VCH vol 5 p153) (MR p268).

Heron Cottage Former curious small mansion (HSP p19) (HBST p554) at the SE corner of the crossroads at Great Fenton (the area is now called Heron's Cross), recorded in 1829. Residence of Charles J Mason, third son of Miles Mason, until he was made bankrupt in 1848 (VCH vol 8 p210). It was firebombed by the Chartist rioters in 1842. Charles ran the Minerva Works, Fenton, from 1813 and was the patentee of Mason's Ironstone China (POTP p147) (MR p151). The site had been built on by the 1920s (VCH vol 8 p210).

Heron Cross Former hamlet above Cockster Brook, now a district of Fenton, under 0.5m SSE of Fenton. For a rhyme about Heron Cross see Fenton Manor. The name may be from Heron Cottage (see).

Herons Gate Former entry into the ancient royal Coton estate in Shropshire, on Staffs Shrops border (Coton Hall near Quatt) (KRC p13). Has also appeared as Herring's Gate.

Hethcote Grange A grange, formerly probably in the neighbourhood of the modern Grange Farm in NW Seighford parish (VCH vol 3 p254 note). Has also appeared as Heythehouse Grange.

Hextall House 0.5m NNE of Ranton. In Ranton ancient parish. Has appeared as Hegstal (1176) (SSE 1996 p14), Hecstall (C13) (SPN p97), Extalls, and Extolls. The name is from Anglo-Saxon 'haecce-sall,' 'place with a hatch' (SPN p97). Perhaps 'hedged place' (SSE 1996 p14). To the S of the house is the remains of a rectangular moat (ESH p58).

Hextall Brook Flows N of Lawnhead joins Coton Clanford Brook to E of Ranton.

Hextons Hextons Farm is 1m NNW Upper Arley. Former small estate and manor held of Arley manor from the early C13 (SHOS vol 2 p258) (VCHW vol 3 p7) (DUIGNAN). Has also appeared as Extons. The name represents 'the hatch stone;' since Hexton is close to the Severn, hatch in this case may mean an instrument for catching fish (DUIGNAN). There is said to have been a chapel at Hextons called Hextan's Chapel; the name 'Chapel Leasowe' is a field adjoining the farmyard. The Crusader's Tomb (now in Upper Arley church) is said to have been placed in this chapel (AOA p29). The disused quarries to the S of Hextons Farm once probably produced the freestone, first found in c1680, which was considered excellent for making grindlestones and which proved a great benefit to the country (according to Bishop Lyttelton of Carlisle) about the mid C18 (History of Worcs. Nash. vol 2 App. 1) (DUIGNAN) (VCHW vol 3 p7).

Heybridge, The Lower Tean in Checkley parish. Built in 1813 as a family home for a branch of the Philips family. Demolished in the 1950s (SMOPP vol 1 p27p) (ACOPP p56p) (COPP2 p73p). At Heybridge Farm, Uttoxeter Road, there is a dovecote with the initials 'J.W.P' (DoE II).

Heyfields Tiny hamlet by the Trent under 1.5m WSW of Barlaston. In Barlaston ancient parish (W p411). The hamlet developed in the C17 or C18, and a road to the N running between Barlaston and Tittensor via Madam's Bridge appears to have been re-routed S through Parkfields and Heyfields (its present route) about this time. There was a bridge across to Tittensor at Heyfields by 1729 (BAH p15).

Heygate The moat of Heygate still remained in the early 1980s, at Moat Farm on S side of Walsall-Streetly road (Sutton Road), 1.5m N of Great Barr at SP 054981. The name, perhaps from an entrance in Great Barr Park (SSAHST 1982-83 p33), has appeared as Moat How (Yates' map) and Hayehead (1801) (SHOS vol 2 p98). Shaw claimed that one lord of Aldridge and Great Barr manor, Sir Robert Stapleton, lived at the moated site at Heygate (SHOS vol 2 p98) (MOA pp39,40,137).

Heynes Well A well in Walsall, mentioned in the C17. Can be probably identified with Haynes's soft-water pump which stood at the S end of Ablewell Street in 1782 (VCH vol 17 p221).

Hey Sprink Wood 2m NW of Whitmore.

Heywood Grange House 1.5m NW of Dilhorne. Dated 1672 (NSFCT 1924 p187) (BOE pp28,116).

Hickbury House 0.75m W of Hamstall Ridware (1834 OS map) (Dower's map). Not marked on current maps.

Hickman Park Public park to W of Bilston. Opened in 1911 on land donated by the Hickman family (BOP p98p).

Hickman's Farm Pensnett. Now (1972) demolished (TB Sept/Oct 1972 p19p).

Hickmerelands Farm Sedgley. Highmere is the origin of the name. The farmhouse was built by 1834 and was still standing in 1975 (SDSSOP p28p). It presumably stands in or near Hickmereland Lane on the W side of Sedgley.

Higgar's Hill Cheddleton parish. The name has been current since the C18, but by 1983 had given way to being called 'Basford View' (CVH p174).

Higgs's Lezzards Area of Cherry Orchard, Old Hill. The name is from the Higgs family (TB April 1983 p5). A black dog ghost was anciently seen in this area (TB Sept 1983 p23).

High Acres 0.75m NW of Longnor (1834 OS map).

Higham Hill Lost hill in the Rowley Regis range N of Powke Lane.

High Arcal Former house 0.75m ESE of Sedgley, S of Tipton Road, in Sedgley ancient parish. The area is now merged into Woodsetton. The house, in cruciform shape, was built in the early C17. It was built entirely of local stone and some of the walls were over four feet thick. It was known as the Flaxhall probably up to the early C19, taking its name from land here, which may be the Flaxhale which appears in 1272 (HC pp11,77-78 il). Reputedly, the house was occupied by Cromwell's soldiers, who used it as a look-out, during the attack on Dudley Castle in 1646. Roper thinks this is not an improbable tale (HC pp77-78) (AWM p23). The house was deserted by the 1950s and was demolished sometime after (SDSSOP p24p) (SDOP p20p). The name is preserved in High Arcal School, High Arcal Drive, and Higharcal Wood 2m to the SW.

Higharcal Wood Wood 0.75m ENE of Himley. Close by is a house called Higharcal House. 2m to the NE is High Arcal hamlet.

Highash House 0.25m SSW of Abbots Bromley. Appears as High Ash on 1834 OS map and Dower's map.

High Bent House 1m NE of Biddulph Moor. At High Bent Farm, Thomas Bough, was murdered by his brother, John, in 1845. The house has also been called New House and Brough's Farm (CCSHO pp1-13). George Beardmore (alias Cedric Stokes) mentions in his novel 'The Staffordshire Assassins' pp14,15,118 High Bent, High Bent House and a High Bent Abbey.

High Bridge Crosses the Trent 0.5m N of Handsacre. Formerly called High Bridges on account of there having been two wooden bridges here consisting of two arches apiece. They were in danger of being lost on account of floods in 1626 and were rebuilt in stone in 1665 (SHC 1934 p25). Another account says the old bridge, anciently called Ridware Bridge or Great Ridware Bridge, stood a few 100 yards down stream from the present bridge and was 74 yards long and about 11 feet wide between the parapets, the middle part of it stood on an island or eyot in the Trent. It had seven pointed arches with angular recesses over the piers and a very low parapet. It was rebuilt 1622/23 and repaired 1674/75. The N and S arches of the bridge were widened about 1784 (SHOS vol 1 p187). The old stone bridge was replaced by the present 140 feet iron bridge built up stream, made at Coalbrookdale erected in 1829 and opened in 1832. (ABMEE p3). It is said to contain 500 tons of metal (NSJFS 1962 p97 pl vi). The old stone bridge was taken down to make way for the railway bridge (W p555).

Highbridge Area and bridge over the Wyrley and Essington Canal where Lichfield Road turns into Pelsall Road, Pelsall. Has also appeared as Highbridges. There was a row of 32 houses here called Highbridge Row by 1884; the row was demolished in 1964 (SNBP pp81,82). For a German bomb which landed here in 1940 see Pelsall.

High Bullen A street in central Wednesbury. Formerly an open space and known as Hancock's Cross, a name perhaps dating from the C14 or C15, when the Hancock family were prominent in Wednesbury. The cross may have been a wayside shrine erected by them (WAM p53), or a market cross (HOWV p109). According to Hackwood the 'Spital,' a manorial hospital, and a Bethlehem hospital were situated at High Bullen in medieval times (WAM p53). In Jan 1743 Charles Wesley spoke in High Bullen whilst his brother John preached in the Town Hall. John Wesley is said to have preached from a horse block or steps giving access to a malthouse along High Bullen on his visit to Wednesbury on Oct 20 1743 (TWDOP p112p). The steps became known as John Wesley's horse block (SOB p141). The block was removed in 1891 and now (1994) stands beside the Central Mission in Spring Head, Wednesbury (WDOP p89p). The pinfold was situated in High Bullen opposite the road to Dudley in 1828 (WAM p100) (HOWV p109).

High Carr Minute hamlet on high ground overlooking the Upper Fowlea valley, 1.75m W of Tunstall. In Chatterley liberty in Wolstanton ancient parish (W p289). Also in the Carbrook Plantation, Car Meadow, and Big Car (NSFCT 1910 p167).

Highdown Kinver. Southern extremity of Iverley (SVS p184).

High Elms House 0.5m NE of Hilderstone (1834 OS map).

High Ercal Small district of Brierley Hill, 0.5m SW of Brierley Hill.

Higherland Tiny area, now just a street name to W of Blackfriars, Newcastle-under-Lyme. Newcastle workhouse was here in the C18, and from 1802 a prison was attached to the workhouse. In taking prisoners to it the borough constables were presented with a problem, that of having to cross a detached portion of Stoke parish where they had no jurisdiction, and where, consequently, rescue attempts were made (VCH vol 8 p41). The Union Building Society of Newcastle-under-Lyme had built 42 houses around Union Street (unlocated) at Higherland by 1816 (SSE 1993 p108). The Orme School was here in the C19. Sometimes Higherland has been commonly called Ireland (VCH vol 8 p33).

Highfield Grove Former estate with a hall in S Stafford, which appears to have been created in the mid C19. In 1891 the hall was occupied by Robert Griffiths, architect and surveyor. The name is preserved in the road Highfield Grove, Highfields, Stafford. (SAC p38).

Highfield Hall Between Bridge End and Pool End near Leek (NSFCT 1885). Formerly in Leekfrith township in Leek ancient parish. Built by Richard Badnall, Leek silk dyer, in 1819 (OL vol 1 p328). It was the seat of the Fowler family, Leek bankers, from 1827 to 1870, when it passed to the Glovers. In 1885 they sold it to Sir Arthur Nicholson, a noted breeder of horses. George V and Queen Mary visited the hall in 1911 (VCH vol 7 p196) and or when they visited Leek on 23 April 1913 (ALC p55p). The hall was demolished in 1940 or 1941 (VCH vol 7 p196). The grounds were opened as a public park for the people of Leek between 1867 and 1870 (VCH vol 7 p148).

Highfields Small district of Chasetown 1.75m SW of Burntwood.

Highfields Former hamlet 0.75m N of Coseley in Sedgley ancient parish. Highfields was in existence by 1832 (HC p63). Site of the C19 engineering works of William Thompson in c1840, which gave the name to the works (VCH vol 2 p137). 'The World's Charity and Other Poems' a collection of poems by George AH Eades of Highfields appeared in 1858 (VFC p43). Highfields was made a ward of Coseley urban district in 1912 (HC p71).

Highfields District of SW Stafford, 1.25m from the town centre. In Castle Church parish. Comprises two estates built in two stages, one in the 1950s and another in the 1960s. Two blocks of flats were completed in 1967 (VCH vol 6 p196). The name may be from Highfields Farm; High Fields occurs on Yates' map (SPNO p77).

Highfields House 1m W of Thorpe Constantine. Appears on 1834 OS map as Highfield Farm.

Highfields Hall Highfields, Bradley, Bilston. The house was standing in 1901 on the S side of Highfields Road (OS map 1901 sheet 67.04).

Highfields Hall House near Blount's Green, 1.25m SW of Uttoxeter. In Loxley district in Uttoxeter ancient parish. Seat of Mrs Kynnersley in 1851 (W pp20,797). It was the seat of Mrs Sneyd-Kynnersley, widow of Clement Sneyd-Kynnersley d1909 or of Gerald Sneyd-Kynnersley d1912, after leaving Loxley Hall in the late 1910s (TRTC p36) (JSD p48p). It was the seat of Judge Alfred Ruegg KC (d1941), the novelist and Staffs county court judge between 1907 and 1939 (VFC p116), in the 1920s. Here he may have written 'John Clutterbuck,' 'A Staffordshire Knot' (1926), 'Flash: A Moorland Mystery,' and 'David Betterton' (1931) (ESNF pp74,92), many of his novels are set in the Flash (see) area. The hall was sold in 1945 (SVB p40). It appears to have been purchased by a Capt Ridout, who, having terminal cancer, committed suicide by running onto his sword. The hall continued to be occupied by his widow, who at length was joined by her sister Mrs Bates. The old hall was demolished in c1986 and was replaced by a purpose-built nursing home for the elderly (MIDD vol 2 p19), still serving as such in 1998 (TRTC pp36,37p,43).

Highfields Manor Newport Road, Stafford. Built by David Hollin (d1916), shoe manufacturer, in 1888. His widow lived at the house until her death in 1926. In c1960 the house was demolished and the area developed as the housing estate called High Park (VCH vol 6 p195) (SAIW pls 40,41 pls 42-45 interior scenes) (SAC pp94p,95p) (Stafford Past: An Illustrated History. Roy Lewis. 1997 p77).

Highfields Mine Disused mine 0.5m SE of Bincliff Mine on E bank of Manifold Valley, 0.5m E of Castern. The burial mound at SK 12025355 is 32 paces in diameter and five feet high excavated by Bateman in 1845 and Carrington in 1850 revealed the skeletons of a crouched female, a child and one with a decorated bronze bracelet of the Early Bronze Age (Proceedings of the Prehistoric Society vol 30 pp427-148) (VAD pp73-74) (TYD pp166-167) (DAJ vol 74 pp142-143) (Gazetteer of Early Anglo-Saxon Burial Mounds. A Meaney. 1964. p221) (Medieval Archaeology vol 6/ 7 p50) (NSJFS 1965 p41). It is a listed monument. The burial mound at SK 12415327 is 12 paces NS and 21 EW in diameter and six feet high. It was excavated by Bateman in 1845 and two crouched skeletons were found (VAD pp87-88) (BAP vol 1 p88 fig 55) (DAJ vol 75 pp104,120) (NSJFS 1965 p41). It is a listed monument. The burial mound 350 metres SE of the mine at SK 12075331 is a listed monument.

High Forest House 2.5m N of Meerbrook. Formerly in Leekfrith township in Leek ancient parish. There was a house here by 1640 (VCH vol 7 p194).

High Frith A district of Alstonefield ancient parish identified for taxing and rating purposes. In existence by 1403. It covered the townships of Fawfieldhead, Heathylee, Hollinsclough, and Quarnford. By 1611 Fawfieldhead was removed to form Low Frith. All of which had become separate townships by 1733 (VCH vol 7 p7).

Highgate S of Tunstall on the Burslem road. Seems to have been a hamlet or district in the early C19 (HSP p19). Presumably gives name to Highgate Pottery.

Highgate Area of Walsall, 1m to S of St Matthew's church (VCH vol 17 p154). A windmill was still standing off Highgate Road, formerly Windmill Lane in 1973. It dates from the beginning of the C19 and is probably on the site of Persehouse's Mill (see) or Blackham's Mill (see). It was probably disused between 1864-8. In 1916 it was struck by lightning causing a piece of parapet to fall. The men that came to mend it only made off with the roof lead and were never seen again. In the later 1920s it was converted into an observatory. It is of five storeys and reaches a height of some 50 feet, and has a crenellated top (BCM July 1968 p44p) (VCH vol 17 p186) (WBJ p41 il xiii).

Highgate Common Low-lying barren common 1.25m WSW of Swindon, mostly lying in Enville ancient parish. The common was enclosed in 1746 but remained uncultivated (VCH vol 20 p94). Bought by Staffs county council in c1956 to be open to the public (SL p261). The name is from reputedly one of the gateways in the fence which once surrounded the royal Coton estate in Shropshire.

Highgate Farm Farmhouse with origins dating back to at least 1677, or on the site of a house dating back to that period. Stands in the area of the old Rudyard hamlet in Rudyard township in Leek ancient parish, over 0.75m ENE of modern Rudyard village (VCH vol 7 p216) (RL p5).

Highgate Farm House 2m WSW of Swindon on the edge of Highgate Common, in Enville ancient parish. Inhabited by 1693 (VCH vol 20 p94). The Sweet Chestnut (BCM spring 1999 p72) or Spanish Chestnut tree in the garden by the house is reputedly the largest in England with a girth of 26 feet (LGS p137) (KES p96). A fat branch, which was supported by a pole, protruded so far into the lane it was obstructing passing buses and had to be cut off in c1992 (local info). In 1998/9 John Sparry noted it had a girth of 27 feet 10 inches (BCM spring 1999 pp71p,72).

High Green Street leading to Kiddemore Green Road, Brewood. An extension of Brewood's The Green which lay to the E between Bargate Newport Streets.

High Green Name of road on SW side of The Green and the house known as The Green (see), in Cannock town centre (MR p74) (Birmingham A-Z 1995).

High Green SE of Lambert's End, West Bromwich (1834 OS map).

High Green Central Wolverhampton, is now Queen Square. Here was the market place, the Shambles, Roundabout pump and the Town Hall (SSAHST 1967 p47). High Green was the site of Wolverhampton market place until 1853 (WPOPP vol 1 p3). (WJO Jan 1904 p14p of in 1860. March 1907 pp69-71) (HOWM p134). Wolverhampton's maypole dancing on May Day took place here (SCSF p16). For John Wesley preaching in High Green see under Wolverhampton. The painting by JMW Turner (1775-1851) of High Green painted in 1795 was in Wolverhampton Museum and Art Gallery in 1999 (info Marguerite Nugent). **Cope's Wine Lodge**, a fine mansion, on the N side of High Green was built by a member of the Persehouse family, perhaps William Persehouse. It bore the date 1726. An extension of the premises was carried out in 1755 and this date was also recorded on the spouting. The building became known as Cope's Wine Lodge (HOWM p134). The **Round Lamp** was a 45 feet high round iron column fixed onto a square substantial base which had steps inside to enable a man to ascend to light the gas lantern which surmounted the column. It was erected in 1821 for the double purpose of commemorating the establishment of gasworks in the town in 1821 and lighting the market place. The light could be seen as far away as Kingswood Common and Codsall. The colliers from Willenhall and Bilston dubbed it the 'Big Candlestick' and idlers and 'loafers' of the town frequented it. The column was taken down in 1842 (WJO Dec 1903 lxi ils) (WMAG Aug 1969 p21). After the Crimean War the site of the Round Lamp was occupied by a **Russian gun** captured in that conflict (WJO Dec 1903 lxi) which faced Darlington Street (WP&P p13p). Queen Victoria, during her visit to Wolverhampton in 1866, unveiled the present nine-feet high **statue of Prince Albert** on the site of the Russian gun. The statue, designed by Thomas Thorneycroft and costing £1,150, was made by Elkington & Co of Birmingham. The prince wears the uniform of a Field Marshal (WMAG Aug 1969 p21. Sept 1979 p44p) (RVW pp16,17,18-21). A local tradition says the sculptor committed suicide because he supposedly got the sequence of the horse's legs wrong (Wolverhampton AdNews. March 23 1995 p12). After Queen Victoria's visit to High Green the area was renamed Queen Square.

High Grove Farm 0.5m SSE of Kinver church. It probably represents the Heygrewe, Heygreve, Haygreve, High Greaves, mentioned in c1200, 1262, 1387, and 1683, respectively. The name High Grove, had come into being by 1796 (VCH vol 20 p136).

High Haden Area which appears on 1834 OS map to E of Haden Hill, and may be heathland. In Rowley Regis parish (BCWJ p15) (SNSV vol 2 p41).

High Hades One of the riverside meadows in Penkridge is called High Hades -

the vicarage stands on it (VB p80).

High Hall To SE of Blymhill. On this site was supposed to have been the residence of William Bagot the lord of Blymhill in Henry II's reign (W p441). The present house dates from the mid C17 and is built of brick (VCH vol 4 p64). Appeared as Hall Hill in 1583 (SPNO p130).

High Hall Former three-storey block of buildings of the early Tudor period which stood at High Green, Wolverhampton. Seat of James Leveson, merchant of the staple of Calais, owner of Stowheath manor in the early C16. High Hall was demolished in 1841 (HOWM pp45, 79, facing 101 il of from the S side) (WAIW vol 1 p). It seems to have been the seat of Mrs Anne Normansell, widow (d1691) (SHC 1923 p47p).

High-Hall-Hill Mansion House 0.75m ESE of Yoxall, near Woodhouses. It was the seat of Mr Swinnerton a descendent of the Swinnertons of Butterton (SHOS vol 1 p101). A small tape factory was established in it in 1817 (MR p399). Formerly called High-Wall-Hill Mansion.

High Harcourt Farm Clent. The name is from Hawker's Cottage (TB Jan 1974 p12).

High Heath Former common now a district of Shelfield 0.75m ESE of Pelsall. Formerly in a detached portion of the foreign of Walsall ancient parish. There was settlement here by 1576 (VCH vol 17 p277). A postmill was situated at SP 034027, and is shown on Plot's map (WBJ p35). The heath when common land may have been frequented by highwaymen; Mob Lane in the locality may have been so called in consequence of a mob of men bent on lawlessness (SNBC pp25,27).

High House Most impressive timber-framed mansion in Stafford and said to be the largest timber-framed town house in England (Staffordshire Millennium Guide 2000 p89). It is situated on the W side of Greengate Street, with four storeys on an E-shape plan. No comprehensive history of it seems to have been written. A sketch of its history is this: It was built in 1595 by the Dorrington family (VCH vol 6 p190) (BOE p245). Oak for it is said to have come from Doxey Wood; a youth is said to have served his apprenticeship during its building making only pegs (SKYT p6,7p). By 1642 Capt Richard Sneyd RN owned the house, in which year Charles I and Prince Rupert stayed here from Sept 17 to 19. The king then left for Wellington, Shrops. According to tradition in the garden Prince Rupert took potshots at the weathercock on top of St Mary's church tower with a horse or rifled-barrelled breech-loading pistol and hit the tail of it twice (NHS p336) (SHOS vol 1 p82. vol 2 pl) (LGS p217) (FSP p22) (SIOT p65) (SKYT p6) (BFS p7); bullet holes were still there for Plot to see in the early 1680s (NHS p336). After the battle of Hopton Heath (1643) and the fall of Stafford to the parliamentarians the house was used as a place of custody for high ranking royalist prisoners (SKYT p6). From the Sneyds it passed to Edward Wettenhall MD of Cork (identifiable with Bishop Edward Wetenhall born in Lichfield in 1636?), who bequeathed it to his daughter who became the second wife of Dr William Hawkins, the son-in-law of Izaak Walton of Stafford (see); Walton is said to have resided here (SKYT p6). Another account implies that the Sneyds never owned the house and that the Dorrington heiress Dorothy (d1672) married Sir Richard Dyott, and that the Dyotts were in occupation until the early C18 (Ancient High House etc. FWB Charles. 1975. duplicated booklet in WSL). The house was for many years the residence of visiting circuit judges until official judge's lodgings were built (SIOT p140) (SKYT p6). In 1792 the house was sold (W p323). In c1818 it was owned by a Mrs Fielden who resided in a part, whilst a part was occupied as a boarding school for young ladies (SKYT p6). Between 1823 and 1826 the house was leased to Capt Ferneyhough, later to become one of William Salt's transcribers; he made one of the earliest-known (1823) drawings of it. Shortly after 1824 it became the property of John Marson. He converted the ground floor into shops. During the conversion a piece of wood with 'Richard Dorrington made this house, 1555' cut into it, was found; this has led some to believe the house was built in 1555 (LGS p217) (Ancient High House etc. FWB Charles. 1975) (SGS p156p showing the arms of Sneyd and the date 1555 above the entrance). Later in the C19, and perhaps by 1885 when renovation was taking place to the shop fronts, the house passed to William Albert Marson (d1918?), perhaps a relation of John Marson. By 1894 Marson appears to have had a curiosity shop 'Ye Olde Curiositie Shoppe' at the rear of the house. His scrap book containing much valuable information about Stafford is in WSL. Up to 1946 the house was owned by Alderman RJ Young of Rowley Park and in 1948 was owned by his daughter, Mrs WJ Dean (Views of Stafford. WA Marson. 1894) (SKYT p6) (SPP p27p of Marson's curiosity shop at rear of High House). In the 1970s the upper rooms were apparently used for lodging students (info Bruce Braithwaite). The completion of major restoration work on the house by Stafford borough council between 1976 and 1986 was commemorated by a visit by the Duke of Gloucester on Nov 24 1987. In 1983 there were plans to turn the house into a museum (SN July 1 1983 p7) and sometime after restoration it was turned into the present (2000) museum. The Staffordshire Yeomanry museum formed and opened here in 1992 (ES Nov 27 1992 p4). It was still occupying an upper floor in 2000. Presently (2000) a painted wooden coat of arms of Charles II presented to the town of Stafford by Mayor William Feake in 1677 hangs in an upstairs room. (SLM May June 1995 p53 il) (ASOP p14 shows an aerial view of the back of the High House). The Friends of the Ancient High House formed in 1986 (info Den Delves). A figure in white has been seen, as well as the figures of small children. One room in particular is thought to be haunted (info Bruce Braithwaite).

Highlands Park Former hay (HOPT vol 1 p159), and medieval deer park enclosed out of Needwood Forest, 1m W of Tatenhill. Formerly in Tatenhill township and ancient parish (W p605). The park was created by Robert de Ferrers, 1st Earl of Derby, d1139 (UTR p36) and was certainly in existence by 1263 (VCH vol 2 p350) or 1379 (NSJFS 1962 p76). Has appeared as Le Heylondes (1341) (ANS p33), Heye-lindes (HOPT vol 1 p136) and Heylins Park (Plot's map). The name means 'the hay of the lime trees' (HOPT vol 1 p136). The park was purchased in the Commonwealth period by Gregory Walklett, who destroyed the deer, felled the timber and ploughed up the soil. However, Highlands or Heylins, belonging to John Turton 'was stored with deer' in 1735 (SHOS vol 1 pxxiv) (EDP p176) (HOPT vol 1 p159). A coarse gypsum was anciently mined here according to William Burton in 1622 (NHS pp173-174) (VCH vol 2 p198). (APB p44). The house now known as Highlands Park lies 1m W of Tatenhill.

High Lane Small hamlet in the mid C19, 1m NE of Norton-in-the-Moors. In Norton-in-the-Moors chapelry in Stoke-upon-Trent ancient parish. Appears on the 1834 OS map. The name is preserved in High Lane on which road the hamlet was situated.

Highlanes Tiny hamlet 0.75m ENE of Croxton.

Highlows, The House and site of a burial mound 0.75m N of Yarnfield (SIS p2 see map) (Dower's map).

High Oak Cannock Chase. At approximately SK 006169 (1834 OS map).

High Oak Short street running off High Street (A4140) to Commonside, in Kingswinford ancient parish (WFK p11); 'High Oak' is a hanging tree which gave its name to a small area on Pensnett Chase. William Harrison and John Allen were hanged here for robbery and violence (TB Aug Sept 1972 p10).

High Offley Ancient parish and former township (THS p319). The small village of High Offley lies on a hill with a plateau top overlooking Lonco Brook 9m WNW of Stafford. On the hillside S of the churchyard was found a hoard of Roman coins, flat bricks, armour and pottery. On the strength of these discoveries Pitt considered High Offley to be the site of the Roman settlement of Mediolanum (THS p319) (GNHS p118) (W p390). No confirmation of these finds can be obtained (NSJFS 1964 p25). Raven thought a Roman villa or small settlement had stood on the site (MR p247). Romano-British skeletons and a bronze spear were found during draining in the winter of 1862-3 on land of Mr Furber, junior, of High Offley. Also on the edge of Lonco Brook was found a Romano-British bronze spear 5.5 inches long and in fine preservation (Shrewsbury Chronicle Nov 28 1884) (NSFCT 1926 pp142-143). The manor of Offelie is recorded as being held of Robert de Stafford in DB. The name means 'Offa's lea' (DUIGNAN) or 'Offa's wood' (SSE 1987 p30). All the Offley's are from King Offa's lands (SOSH p59). Or perhaps from a Celtic deity? - probably 'Uffa' also called 'Wffa' and 'Hwffa' thinks Harnaman (STM June 1966 p34). The church, St Mary, on an eminence in the village centre commanding views of the Wrekin, Brown Clee, Caradoc, Long Mynd, Bredons, Grinshill, and Hawkestone (NSFCT 1888 p63. 1910 p200), may have been founded in the C11 (LDD). It has some work of c1200 (BOE p145). The parish probably formed sometime between 1086 and 1291, although it is not listed in the Papal Return of 1291. It was originally a part of Eccleshall parish (SHC 1916 pp192,196,199-200). The prebend of Eccleshall in Lichfield cathedral was turned into the prebend of Eccleshall and Offley by 1332 (VCH vol 3 p144). Others write of Eccleshall and Offley as two separate prebends; Offley, including Shebdon and Woodseaves, being founded by Roger de Clinton in the C12. Offley prebend was annexed to the Fifth Residentiarship, but when the Treasurership was restored without its former annexed stall of Sawley the holding of Offley prebend was combined with the office of Treasurer in the cathedral (SSAHST vol 2 1960-61 p47). High Offley or Otley was a prebend in Lichfield cathedral until 1846 (GLAUE p418). The parish was a peculiar jurisdiction of the dean and chapter and certain prebendaries of Lichfield cathedral until peculiar jurisdictions were abolished in 1846 (VCH vol 3 pp93-94). By the late C20 the prebendary of Offley held the office of Treasurer in the cathedral (LDD). (SHOS vol 1 p292). Garner noted a tombstone with the figure of an ecclesiastic and escutcheons built into a bridge over a stream between High

Offley and Eccleshall (GNHS p547). There is a curious oval-shaped chest tomb to the Lander family of High Offley Manor in High Offley churchyard. Thomas de Halghton was granted a charter on June 17 1327 to hold a market at one of the 'Offleys' on Tuesdays. The market had ceased by 1500 (NSJFS 1971 p51). Offley gives its name to the family of Offley of Madeley (HOPT vol 1 p79). A couple called Mary and Joseph of High Offley, were paid tribute to by children with whooping cough in the hope of receiving gifts like bread and butter which it was believed if neither asked for nor thanked for would effect a cure (STMSM Sept 1980 p56).

High Offley New Park Medieval deer park, probably in existence by 1463. Partitioned by agreement in 1479. It almost certainly lay to the E of Garmelow in the area of 'Park Hall' (NSJFS 1962 p77. 1964 p63).

High Offley Old Park Medieval deer park, probably in existence by 1283. Probably lay near the modern hamlets of Tunstall and the Lea, to W of Garmelow (NSJFS 1962 p77. 1964 p63).

High Onn Small hamlet on a hill 425 feet high (TTTD p266) to the N of Marston Brook, 6.5m SW of Stafford. Former township in Church Eaton ancient parish. The Devil's Highway is the local name for the Roman road W of High Onn. It runs from Watling Street at Stretton (Penkridge) to W of Market Drayton, and it is often lost. The name has appeared as Otne (DB), and Onna (c1130), Othna (c1130), Magna Oune (c1255), Magna Onne (1327), Hyghon (1577), Highone (1612), and Great Onn (SPNO p141) (SHC 1883 part 2 p52). In Welsh 'onn' (plural) is ash-trees, hence 'high ashes' though 'high' is probably a Middle English addition (DUIGNAN). Oakden agrees with Duignan on origin but not on meaning (SSAHST 1967 p33). Ekwall tentatively suggested that onn may be from the Welsh 'odyn' 'kiln' from older Primitive Welsh 'otn.' Oakden finding Ekwall to be wrong thinks 'river on whose banks ashes grew' (SSE 1996 p22) (SPNO pp141-142). Onn represents the Celtic root, 'onn,' 'unn' rock or hill (M p4) or mountain (NSFCT 1908 p136). Perhaps High Onn was a larger settlement in comparison with Little Onn in the Middle Ages; now deserted, may have stood near High Onn Manor (see). By at least the later C19 it was noted Little Onn was the larger of the two (SHC 1883 part 2 p52 note). At High Onn in the later C17 Dr Plot saw the farmers add to their ashes at stubble burning time all the bushes, furze, broom and fern and other rubbish, so helping to fertilize the earth (NHS p334). A field called 'Windmill Field' suggests there was a windmill of the late medieval period at approximately SJ 827162 (WBJ p17).

High Onn Manor House on the lane leading due W out of High Onn. There was an High Onn manor by 1230 when it was held by the priory of Ware, Herts. In 1414 possessions of Ware passed to the new priory of Sheen, Surrey. After the Dissolution overlordship remained with the Crown until at least 1633. The manor was sold in 1540 to Sir John Giffard of Chillington whose family held it until 1863. High Onn House or Hall went to James Wyrley. The Wyrleys still held the house in 1954. The old manor house had a moat, the W side of which is still (1959) in existence. The house was demolished in the early C19 and rebuilt, but some masonry, possibly the base of a chimney, has been left standing near the entrance gates (VCH vol 4 pp91 il facing,92,94,95) (TTTD p266). Has appeared as Highonn Manor (1884) and High Onn Manor (1903) (OS maps). The moat may represent a sunken road of a deserted village (SSAHST 1982-3 p59).

High Onn Wood Wood to W of High Onn.

High Park House over 1.75m NNE of Milwich. Appears on 1834 OS map, and as High on Dower's map.

High Park Park to E of Patshull Hall,Patshull.

Highridges House Farm 1.75m WSW of Croxden. See also Rectory Farm Checkley.

High Roach, The The Roaches. Cannot be identified from the photograph in HS p5p. Perhaps the highest pinnacle of the Five Clouds? Has also appeared as The High Roche.

High Sheen House beneath Sheen Hill 0.5m N of Sheen. In Sheen ancient parish. Seat of the Mort family by 1620. Rebuilt by Thomas Mort in 1663 (VCH vol 7 p241).

Highshut 1.5m WSW of Oakamoor. The name 'High Shut' has been used to refer to an elevated piece of barren common land (THS p36); there is also a farm called this on it. It has also appeared as High Shutt. Here stood an isolated dark fir tree which could be seen from Cheadle, Kingsley, Ipstones, and Foxt churches, and from Alton Towers. Tradition says not many generations ago the people in the neighbourhood heard strange sounds if they walked round the tree a given number of times. Even in 1881 local people were still trying to avoid the footpath running close to the tree and firmly believed a walk around the tree nine times would lead to the sound of bells summoning them to prepare for the next world (HOC pp147,148il) (SMML pp50-51;

story of Josiah Alcock found dead at the tree in 1806). This tree has the added fact of being the meeting point from c1810 for three young gentlemen who later became MPs for N Staffs, N Lancs, and S Devon, and two became peers in the House of Lords. Lord Winmarleigh (formerly Col Wilson Patten) owner of Lightoaks was one; he could not say when the tree was planted but a mound was made around it to protect it as a memorial of these meetings (NSFCT 1885 p63). In 1922 the view from it included the peak of Shutlingslow due N, Cheadle and Werrington and the smoke from the Potteries (NSFCT 1922 p30).

High Shutt A farm in Hilderstone ancient parish. The name means 'high forest.' See also Shuttgreen (NSFCT 1908 p146).

High Town (locally *'Ightown* BILP2 p35). Small suburb on high ground above Pyegreen Valley 1.5m NNE of Cannock. In Cannock ancient parish.

High Town Small area of Cracow Moss hamlet (BVC p193).

High Trees Hamlet in Abbots Bromley ancient parish (W p409). There is a High Trees Farm on the northern edge of Bagot Forest, 2.5m N of Abbots Bromley.

Hightrees Farm 2.75m W of Kinver, in Arley parish. Appears as High Trees on 1834 OS map.

Highwood Fragmented hamlet on high ground above the Dove Valley 1.25m SSE of Uttoxeter, formerly in Uttoxeter Ward of Needwood Forest. A quern stone of uncertain date was found whilst land was being enclosed 1881-2 (HOU 1886 p74) (NSJFS 1964 p40). Hackwood notes a burial mound at Highwood (SC p148). On High Wood a Roman vessel was found in 1788, which perhaps went to Greene's Museum in Lichfield (GM) (HOU p323il). Levies assembled at Uttoxeter on July 1 1640 to suppress the rebellion in Scotland rioted at Uttoxeter High Wood (BFS p4) tearing down the fences of enclosure. Further enclosure at Highwood took place under an act passed in 1787 (W p789). Enclosure was occurring in 1881-2 (HOU 1886 p74) (NSJFS 1964 p40). Uttoxeter gibbet was situated in the Highwood area (LTD p113).

Highwood, The Victorian villa at Highwood, S of Uttoxeter, the last house on the right on the Highwood Hill, on the Marchington road. A house called Highwood was occupied in 1851 by Willoughby Wood (W p20), who was at Holly Bank, Barton-under-Needwood, by 1863 (KD 1863). It was sometime seat of Henry Bernard Bamford (1876-1955) (BUBA pp43,45p).

Hilcote Tiny hamlet on a slope overlooking the Sow, 1.25m ENE of Eccleshall. In Chebsey parish (W p388). Has appeared as Helcote (DB), and Hillcourte (c1540) (LI appendix p172). The bridge over the Sow at Hilcote was formerly called Dunforde Bridge (SHC 1934 p29).

Hilcote Hall Hilcote. Seat of the Noel family by c1600 (SOS p112); Sir William Dugdale made his visitation to the Noels here in April 1663 (COI p200). The Noels remained at Hilcote until 1759. The Anson family held the estate from 1772 until at least 1851. The present Hilcote Hall was probably built in the early C19 and incorporates parts of an older building. By 1851 the hall was occupied by WS Dixon (W pp21,388). By 1960 it was owned by the 1st Lord Nelson of Stafford, George Horatio Nelson (1887-1962), Managing Director of English Electric (1930-1956). After his death his son 2nd Lord Nelson of Stafford, Sir Henry George Nelson (b1917), Chairman of English Electric (1962-1968), appears to have lived here (Burke's Peerage 1970). The hall was sold in May 1971 (SN May 7 1971 p6). About 1987 it was converted into a nursing home (EOP p30p).

Hildersheaves House to the S of Old Lea (1834 OS map) (Dower's map; Hildersheayes). It could now be the present Oldershaws, High Offley.

Hildersholme Formerly Hildebaldesholme. Shaw says it was formerly surrounded by two arms of the Trent but the S arm being diverted, this holm now lies S of the river, cut off from the rest of Mavesyn Ridware manor to which it once belonged, though it continued to pay its dues to the rector of Mavesyn Ridware (SHOS vol 1 p170 note 19).

Hilderstone Village in and backed by hills beyond the Trent Valley near the source of the head brook of Gayton Brook (Stone Rural District. The Official Guide. 3rd ed. ND. Late 1940s?), 7.5m NNE of Stafford. Former township and quarter in Stone ancient parish. There is a very dilapidated **burial mound** on the W side of Hilderstone at SJ 947347 (NSFCT 1983 p13). Most of the line of the **Roman** road from Buxton through Leek, Cheddleton, Blythe Bridge, Hilderstone, and Stafford to Pennocrucium (see) on Watling Street has yet to be established (VCH vol 7 p98). A small Roman coin was found in the garden of the vicarage in c1896. The vicarage was built on the old village green and this may explain how a Roman coin came to be in the vicarage garden (NSFCT 1908 p165). John Hobson, the schoolmaster, had in his possession an old sword which had been found on land near Hilderstone found by a group of school boys. The sword was originally thought to be Roman but it may be a copy. The emblem on the pommel might be the French cockerel holding an orb and can be dated to c1833. The find may have been made

in c1900 (PHH p6il). Comprises two manors in DB: a fact neglected by Chetwynd (SHC 1909 pp151,154 note). The manor owned by the king is Hidulvestune, that held by Robert de Stafford is Helduluestone. Eyton thinks that the smaller manor of Hildulvestune was annexed to Robert de Stafford's larger manor soon after 1086 (SHC 1909 pp151,154 note). The **name** appears in the C13 as Hildulveston (SPN p61). The prefix is derived from an Anglo-Saxon personal name - Hildewulf, meaning 'warrior wolf' (DUIGNAN) (SVB p93). 'Hildwulf's or Hildufr's tun or farmstead' (SSE 1996 p14) (SPN p61). Or the 'village of Heldulva' (BNDA p3). Some say the vicarage was built on the old village green (NSFCT 1908 p165). Winifred Bossen places it at the field called 'Green Field' on Home Farm (PHH p10). Just S of Hilderstone Hall, at SJ 957347, by a wood with two small pools, is a moated site. It is rectangular, 400 feet by 320 feet with an extra bank on the N side and altered on the S side (MR p181) (CAMS p63). Opposite Hilderstone Hall gates there is a spinney - completely waste ground. According to the Staffordshire Sentinel there was once a manor house standing on this spot. A chimney still stood here in 1986. The water close by is called Chimney Pool and is reputed to be haunted at night by a lady in white. Miss Bossen is sceptical of the ghost story (PHH pp16-17). Garner was shown by Mr Molineux a **medieval bronze key** found at Hilderstone (GNHSS p9). The old three **field strip system** operated in some parts of the village until the C19 (MR p183pc). They were known as the Hilderstone Doles the freehold strips of which were individually owned although all in one tenancy. The deeds showing them were kept at Walters and Welch solicitors, Stone, until at least the 1980s (info Michael Cockin). Bearstakes, a field name, at the top of the village suggests bear baiting took place in Hilderstone (PHH p9). A **windmill** existed by 1798 and in 1816. It was still in existence in 1855, sited at SJ 949345 (WBJ p27) (SLM Spring 1954 p25). Seaby and Smith place it S of the church at SJ 948343 (WIS p24). Miss Bossen, who places it at Mill Farm, says it was in existence by at least 1818 and burnt down in a gale in 1837 (PHH pp84-85). The **church**, Christ Church, on the Cresswell road, NE of the village, was built in 1827-1829 (BOE p146). Hilderstone became a separate ecclesiastical parish in 1833 (GLAUE p413) or 1840 (LGS p147). It became a separate civil parish from Stone Rural civil parish in 1897 (GLAUE p413). Foot-and-mouth disease broke out in Hilderstone parish in early 1968 at Spot Grange Farm (SN Jan 26 1968 p13). **Ghosts**. A phantom white cow is said to haunt Milwich Lane (NSFCT 1900 p146). A phantom dog is said to haunt Garshall Lane (NSFCT 1900 p146). A figure in white with black hair was seen in the village (probably in the Hall Wood area) in about the 1830s by Mrs Hazelhurst of Hilderstone which forewarned her of her sister's death (NSFCT 1900 pp145-146) (PHH pp16-17). **Natives. William Meath Baker** (d1935), son of Rev Ralph Bourne Baker, was born at Hilderstone on Nov 1 1857. He later moved to Hasfield Court, Glous, where he became friendly with a then unknown piano teacher, Sir Edward Elgar. Mr Baker is said to have inspired the Fourth Movement of Elgar's Enigma Variations (POTP p28) (SVB p93). Hilderstone village school, opened in 1819, closed at Easter 1981 with one pupil, **Sharon Fairbanks** (ES Jan 14 1981 p1p) (PHH p36) (SSBOP p59; says school closed in 1980 with one pupil and two teachers, becoming in 1982 a private residence).

Hilderstone Brook Perhaps can be identified with the brook which rises in the Moss Lane area and flows on the NW side of Hilderstone village, N of Wooliscroft, forms Cotwalton Drumble, to join the Scotch Brook in Moddershall Valley. There is an earthwork with double fosse near this brook (SIS p3). Raven says the outer one forms a rectangle 200 yards long in which a Roman coin was found (MR p308).

Hilderstone Hall Hilderstone. The Hilderstone estate from 1674 to 1904 passed through these families - Gerard, Berrington, Fleetwood, Meynell, Fitzherbert and Beresford, Vernon, and Bourne (PHH pp20ps,61). Cope mentions an Hilderstone Old Hall; the artist Peter de Wint, when young, made a watercolour of it (SIS p77) (The Gazette. 1988). The new hall was built by Ralph Bourne, pottery manufacturer, in c1750, on the site of a former house. The Bournes left the hall in 1950 (PHH p61) in which year it was sold (SLM Oct 1950 p33). Hilderstone Hall has been a residential home for the retired since 1987 (SSBOP p58p in 1914) (SDOPP p75p in 1907). (W p363). A ghost of a man under the stairs was seen by a maid (NSFCT 1900 p146). In its grounds remain an 800 year old cedar of Lebanon tree possibly brought back from the Crusades (SSBOP p58).

Hilderstone Green and Green Farm. Field name at Hilderstone - Tells of a sad story of enclosure (NSFCT 1910 p165).

Hilderstone Manor House House 0.75m NE of Hilderstone. Is a comparatively new house to the hall (PHH p18). Reputedly haunted by a poltergeist (NSFCT 1900 p146) (PHH p18) (FOS p24).

Hill, The On E side of Wolverhampton-Stourbridge road, Amblecote. It was the seat of a John Grove in 1724. Later it was the seat of Thomas Rogers, who owned the Holloway End glasshouse and grandfather of the poet Samuel Rogers. From 1893 the house has been known as Corbett Hospital (VCH vol 20 p51) (BCM summer 1994 p14).

Hill, The House over 0.75m NW of Butterton (Moorlands) (1834 OS map).

Hill, The There was a place called The Hill in Pattingham ancient parish in 1392. It was a settlement by 1428. It may have become the later Nurton Hill (see) or Dadnal Hill (see) (VCH vol 20 p173). The Hill is marked on Plot's map NE of Pattingham.

Hill, The Stood 0.25m WSW of Stramshall (1834 OS map).

Hill Chorlton Hilltop hamlet overlooking the Whitmore gap 1.5m NW of Chapel Chorlton. Former township in the detached chapelry of Chapel Chorlton in Eccleshall ancient parish. To the S of the hamlet at SJ 800394 is a burial mound 15 feet high, thought by Richards to be an outliner of the Whitmore Baldwins Gate group (NSFCT 1983 p12). Hill Chorlton has appeared as Cerueledone (DB), and Hylle (1194) (SSE 1996 p12); Chorton as an addition appears at the end of the C14 (SPN p62); Chawton on the Hill (Plot's map). At SJ 814391 is a watermill of stone, three storeys high. Has a keystone over the first-floor door inscribed 'REBUILT 1848.' The owner was the Duke of Sutherland (IAS pp158,159il). The mill became derelict in about the 1950s. In 1987 it was bought by businessman Derek Smith who had plans to restore the building (ES Nov 10 1987 p5p). Became a separate ecclesiastical parish with Chapel Chorlton in 1743 and a separate civil parish with Chapel Chorlton in 1866 (GLAUE p407).

Hillcrest Modern house facing Airdale Road on S side of Longton Road, Stone. It is believed to have been designed by the architect, Sir Edward Lutyens (1869-1944)(ES July 8 1999 property pages).

Hillcroft Park Small residential suburb of Walton-on-the-Hill or a park? Bounded by Old Croft Road and Selworthey Drive (SN Guide 1999).

Hill End Former small hamlet at the top of the present Knights Hill, S of Aldridge. The name appears on Yates' map, the 1834 OS map and the 1918 Electoral Register. By 1925 the name had changed to Knights Hill, probably from the Knight family (SNAR p33).

Hill Farm Former house and estate of a former detached portion of Trentham ancient parish in Stoke-upon-Trent ancient parish, over 0.5m S of Newcastle-under-Lyme (1834 OS map). The estate has become part of the Westlands (see).

Hill Farm House 1m ESE of Slindon. In Three Farms township in the Woodland quarter in Eccleshall ancient parish (W p376).

Hill Farm 1.5m WSW of Warslow. Formerly in Warslow and Elkstone township in Alstonefield ancient parish. Existed by the mid C17 (VCH vol 7 p58).

Hill Hall 1.5m W of High Offley. In High Offley ancient parish. In 1851, when occupied by Henry Cartwright, it was considered a large, handsome mansion (W pp21,391). Formerly the 'Hulle' and Hill House (see). In 1858 the Cartwrights sold it to Valentine Vickers (d1867) who made extensive alterations to it. In 1860 he moved here and renamed the house Offley Grove (see) (NSFCT 1927 p30) (AADB p60).

Hill Hall Over 0.5m WNW of Swinfen Hall, formerly in Weeford parish, now in Swinfen and Packington civil parish. Hill Hall or Hill Hall Farm was in existence by the late C18 (SHOS vol 2 p30) (1834 OS map), but may stand on or near the site of the moated Weeford Hall (see). By the mid C19 it was a farmhouse owned by Rev Trevor Owen Burns Floyer (W p610); later still it was known as Hill Farm (SSAHST 1982-3 p60). By 1976 the house was called Whitehouse Farm (OS map 1976).

Hill Hook Former small hamlet now a suburb N of Four Oaks on the Staffs border, in Warws, over 0.5m E of Little Aston. There was a plaque on Hill Hook Farm, on the S side of Clarence road near Blake Street on the Sutton Coldfield-Little Aston boundary to the memory of John Bickley who was struck dead by lightning in Aug 1797. The farm was pulled down in 1907 and the tablet subsequently erected on a block of flats on the site of the farm (GATD p80p of Hill Hook Farm in 1907).

Hill House House between Knighton and Adbaston (Plot's map). Seat of a branch of the Skrymsher family in the later C17. Became Hill Hall (see) and later Offley Grove (see). Shrops Union Canal intersected its park. The two of three remaining pools are called Horobin's and Wharf Pool (NSFCT 1927 pp35-36).

Hill House House 0.25m SSW of Upper Elkstone. Formerly in Warslow and Elkstones township in Alstonefield ancient parish. The site was occupied probably by 1521 and certainly by 1660 (VCH vol 7 p57).

Hill House 0.5m S of Farewell. The house was known as Hill House or Hill Farm by the later C18. Later as Hill Farm (1834 OS map), later as The Hill Farm (1:25,000 OS map). The house dates from the C18 (VCH vol 14 pp210-211).

Hill House W of the Hill House, Stramshall, are the Hill House Terraces, rectangular earthworks some 420 feet long (SHC 1916 p207) (MR p310).

Hill House N end of Dagger Lane, West Bromwich. (BOE p302). Built in the earlier C16 (VCH vol 17 p23). Once the seat of the Grove family, relations of the Turtons of the Oak House. Also the home by at least 1839 of Capt James Eaton RN who served with Nelson at the battles of Nile, Copenhagen, and Trafalgar. He died here in 1857 (SHWB 8) (VCH vol 17 pp4, 22-23). Charles Dickens stayed here when writing 'The Old Curiosity Shop' (SHWB 8). Later, the house was bought by West Bromwich corporation (VCH vol 17 pp22-23 plan) and it is still (1997) standing (TB Nov 1997 p15). It is said to be haunted by a servant girl who had become trapped in a secret room and had died there of either starvation or suffocation (Old Midland Manor-houses. Alan Fea; incorrectly stating this is Dagger Hall) (TB Oct 1997 p25. Nov 1997 p15).

Hilliard's Cross House on the E side of Ryknild Street, 1m SSW of Fradley. It was originally a shooting lodge and was known as Eaglestone House; so called when an eagle was seen to land on the chimney during its building. Since becoming a farm Hilliards Cross has remained in the same family (SVB p79). Has also appeared as Hilliards Cross.

Hillocks, The Unusual private house at Ecton built in 1933 by Arthur Ratcliffe, Conservative MP for Leek, noted for his lack of attendance at the House of Commons. It replaced a single storey cottage with a thatched roof. The copper spire apparently came from a demolished chapel. Has also appeared as 'Castle Folly.' (WTCEM pp106-109) (MOS p241) (EH p7) (BOE pp126,127) (SGS p96) (F p317) (MR p142) (PDS&C p117p).

Hill of the Lloyd The name, Hill of the Lloyd, occurring in the C14 may have been the bank rising up to Earlswood and Bradney Wood, Upper Penn (PONP p36).

Hill Ridware Village on a bank above Bentley Brook near the Trent 10.25m ESE of Stafford. In Mavesyn Ridware ancient parish. Appears in the C13 as le Hulle. 'Hull' is Middle English 'hill' (DUIGNAN p127). In the village street where three roads met Shaw noted the village stocks and whipping post (SCSF p130). It was at Hill Ridware he thought the cross called 'Le Hyll Cross,' named in 1530, stood (SHOS vol 1 p200). A maypole was erected at the S end of the village by the cockpit when George I was crowned (SHOS vol 1 p200) (THS p77). In the later C17 Dr Plot noted a white popinjay at Hill Ridware (NHS p233).

Hills, The A house on Bealeys Lane, off Bell Lane, Bloxwich, which was the centre of an estate dating from the early C17 (VCH vol 17 p176). The old house of C17 origin or earlier, was the seat of the Cowleys to the late C17 (SOB p108) (SNBP p7). There is a tradition that it was used as a billet for parliament troops on their way to attack Rushall Hall in the Civil War (SNBP p7); another tradition was Oliver Cromwell staying here in May 1644 (SOB p76). Has also appeared as the Narr (C17), Further Hills (C17), Hills Farm (SNBP p7), Hill House Farm. The house, known as Hills farm by 1766, was the seat of the Bealey family by 1781 to 1889. The present (1974) house is a three-storeyed brick building of c1800 with mid C19 extensions (SOB p131) (VCH vol 17 p176) (BY p8). By the early C20 the house was occupied by the Arch family. By 1994 it was derelict (SNBP p7). It is reputedly haunted by loud noises heard in the bedroom by a Mrs Roe, which sound like nuts being cracked (GOHK pp288-9) (SMM p53).

Hillsdale Tiny moorland hamlet 0.75m NW of Grindon, one of its few houses is called Big Hillsdale another is called Hillsdale Green. In Grindon parish. Has also appeared as Hilldale.

Hillsdale Hall Hillsdale. At SK 079554. Bears the date 1620 (PRT pp70-71).

Hillswood Former wood covering ground some 850 feet high, 1.25m N of Leek. Formerly in Leekfrith township in Leek ancient parish. Appears as Hellis Wood in 1340 (VCH vol 7 p197). Is featured on the C17 maps of Speed, Blaeu, Blome and Moll. Had become known as Abbey Wood, after nearby Dieulacres Abbey, by the late C19. A fragment of the original wood remains. On the top of the high ground is a burial mound (NSFCT 1921 p140). Could be the mount 'bi a mounte' in the medieval epic poem 'Sir Gawain and the Green Knight' (NSJFS 1977 p36). Prior to 1953 the high ground was crowned by a clump of trees known as the Nine Pins (NSFCT 1978 p37). North Hillswood, a farm W of Tittesworth Reservoir, was in existence by 1870 (VCH vol 7 p197); the farm called South Hillswood is S of the reservoir (NSFCT 1905 p161).

Hill Top House or tiny hamlet over 0.25m ESE of Brewood. In Brewood ancient parish.

Hill Top Primarily a name for tiny area of Burslem (NSFCT 1943 p32) in the Fountain Place and Westport Road area (Enoch Wood's Plan of Burslem in c1750). Hill Top Chapel, Arnold Bennett's Sytch Chapel in his 'The Dog' (Arnold Bennett and Stoke-on-Trent. 1966. EJD Warrilow. p131) can probably be identified with the Burslem Sunday School, built as Hilltop Methodist Chapel in 1836-7 (BOE p255) (AGT p73il) (DoE II). Facing this chapel on the other side of Westport Road (formerly Liverpool Road) was Royal Pottery, alias Hill Top Works and Hill Pottery, see under Potteries.

Hill Top Appears on 1947 OS map 1:25,000 (sheet 43/22) on N side of Burton Ashby-de-la-Zouch road at SK 275227, 0.5m ESE of Winshill.

Hill Top Hamlet to NE of Brown Edge, 1.25m WNW of Endon. Formerly in Endon township in Leek ancient parish. In existence by the later C18. In the earlier C19 it was occupied mainly by miners who worked in Brown Edge (VCH vol 7 p179). In 1832 Hugh Bourne opened a chapel at Hill Top, which occupied the N end of a low stone building. Bourne was himself a member of the congregation. In 1880 the congregation moved to a chapel over the boundary in Norton-in-the-Moors parish and it has become known as Hill Top Methodist church (SHJ spring 1992 p15) (VCH vol 7 p184). The name, taken from being the highest point of Brown Edge (BEH p31), is preserved in the street called Hill Top Close.

Hill Top Old Hednesford or the original hamlet of Hednesford is situated on it (VCH vol 5 p49). In Cannock ancient parish.

Hilltop Hill 500 feet high 1.5m NW of Handsworth. The hill may now be known as Battery Hill. There was settlement at Hilltop by the end of the C13 (MNB pp35,38).

Hill Top Minute hamlet 0.5m E of Longdon. In Longdon ancient parish (W p568).

Hill Top Farm on Tittensor Chase, to NW of Bury Bank on 1834 OS map. In Beech quarter in Stone ancient parish. Had some C17 plaster work. Above were the initials 'G.M.V.' (and perhaps 'I') with the date 1662 (NSFCT 1927 p158). At end of the C19 or beginning of the C20 some student farmers taken on here took to cockfighting for recreation, long after its abolition. One day the police made a raid. This was the last prosecution of cockfighting heard at Stone. Masefield's father was one of the magistrates who tried the case (NSFCT 1915 p156).

Hill Top Central area of Walsall. Famous 'trouble spot' and was rarely policed in the C18. The 'Hilltop Mob' became almost legendary (LOU p293). A riot occurred here on May 19 1751 when a Non-conformist chapel being built was pulled down (VCH vol 17 p248) (LOU p107) (SSAHST 1983-84 pp50-71). Hill Top may be a variant form of Holtshill (see), which had a variant form in Holtshill Top in 1512.

Hill Top Hamlet and district 1.5m NNW of the High Street, West Bromwich. In West Bromwich ancient parish. By the mid C18 the area at the top of Holloway Bank (or Finchpath Hill) was becoming known as Hill Top (HOWB p50). By the end of the C18 it consisted of 'a large street' of small houses and also 'several good gentlemen's houses' - including Finchpath Hall (see) and Mayrick House (see) (SHOS vol 2 p134) (VCH vol 17 p7). Hill Top was the centre of West Bromwich until c1830 when the present centre of West Bromwich with its nucleus around the High Street superseded it. The church, St James, Hill Top on A41, was consecrated in 1844 (VCH vol 17 p56), when Hill Top was formed into a separate ecclesiastical parish (GLAUE p413). St James on the A41, a later church, dates from 1995 (LDD). Hill Top became a ward of West Bromwich borough, when created in 1882 (VCH vol 17 p45). The Brockhouse engineering firm were to be based at Hill Top (VCH vol 2 p134). William Henley, dubbed the 'English Paganini,' in his day, was born at Hill Top in 1874. He was considered to be the only English violinist who possessed 'the fire and brilliancy' to match foreign artistes (WBOP p154p). JJ Shaw, seismologist, had a pawn shop at 166 Hill Top in c1905 (BCM spring 1995 p52). Ken Downing, a member of the rock music band 'Judas Priest' was born at Hill Top in 1951. Other local members of the band are Ian Hill, from West Bromwich, and Rob Halford from Bloxwich (BCM Jan 1993 pp10-14).

Hill Top Farm Nearly 1.5m NNW of Wall, N of Pipe Grange, not marked on 1:25,000 OS map. An estate was centred on this brick farmhouse, of c1800 date, by 1720. Between 1808 and 1986 it formed a part of Maple Hayes estate (VCH vol 14 p289).

Hill Top Park Hill Top, West Bromwich. Formerly the grounds of Mayrick House (VCH vol 17 p7). Purchased by West Bromwich Corporation in 1896 (SHWB 13). Extended in 1960 (VCH vol 17 p7).

Hillyfields, The Harborne. Lover's Walk ran from St Peter's church to Weymoor Farm (Whitehouse Farm) via The Hillyfields (OHOPP p11). (HOPP pl 16p of before the land was sold off for development). Has also appeared as The Hilly Fields.

Hillylees House nearly 1.75m NE of Heaton. Formerly in Heaton township in Leek ancient parish. There was a house on the site of Hillylees by the earlier C16 (VCH vol 7 p187).

Hilton Fragmented hamlet on high ground near the source of a tributary of Saredon Brook, in the vicinity of Hilton Hall (11.75m S of Stafford) and the estate or Hilton Park. Former out-township in Wolverhampton chapelry and ancient parish (Seisdon hundred), and yet is in Cuttlestone hundred (VCH vol 4 p61). This may explain the anomaly that a Hilton in Seisdon hundred is described as being possibly the site for a medieval village (SSAHST 1970 p35), yet this Hilton is in Cuttlestone. A charter was made of the bounds of Hilton and Featherstone (SL p62), when the estate was given by Lady Wulfrun to the monastery of Wolverhampton in 994 (HOWM p14). Eyton thought DB Iltone was this Hilton. But Bridgeman and others have identified this Hilton with DB Haltone, a manor belonging to the canons of Wolverhampton (SHC 1916 p169) (DB. Phillimore. 1976). The name means 'hill town or settlement' (DUIGNAN) (NSJFS 1981 p3). Hilton later became a prebend of Wolverhampton Collegiate Church (W p82) (VCH vol 3 p324). Hilton became a separate civil parish in 1866 (GLAUE p414).

Hilton Tiny hamlet by Crane Brook 1.5m SE of Hammerwich. (SHOS vol 2 p56). In Shenstone ancient parish (W p583). A rectangular crop-mark was found by air-photography at SK 084051. It was at first thought to be the site for a Roman marching camp but was then thought to have been used by the Romano-British community for farming purposes (SSAHST 1972-73 p29 p). A charter was made of its bounds (SL p62), when the estate was given by Lady Wulfrun to the monastery of Wolverhampton in 994 (HOWM p14). DB Iltone, a manor belonging to the canons of Wolverhampton, has been identified with this Hilton; Eyton thought DB Iltone was the Hilton near Featherstone (SHC 1916 p169. 1919 p157) (DB. Phillimore. 1976). Later forms of this Hilton are: Hylton, and Hultone (SPN p106). The name means 'hill tun or town' (DUIGNAN) (SSE 1996 p14) (SPN p106).

Hilton Minute hamlet on the southern flank of a promontory, 0.75m NNE of Sheriffhales.

Hilton Hall Hall at Hilton 11.75m S of Stafford. There was at least one former hall on or near the site of the present hall, one of which was surrounded by a moat at SJ 952052 (VCH vol 1) (SSAHST 1982-3 p43) (CAMS p63). The lords of Hilton manor in medieval times were the Swynnertons. By the marriage in 1547 of Margaret, daughter and co-heir with her sister Elizabeth, of Humphrey Swynnerton of Swynnerton and Hilton, to Sir Henry Vernon of Sudbury, Derbys, Hilton passed to the Vernons. Sir Henry Vernon (d1569) was succeeded by his eldest son John (d1600), who having died without issue was succeeded by his niece, Margaret, who kept Hilton in the Vernon family by marrying her cousin Sir Edward Vernon (b1584) in 1613 (Sir Edward was grandson of Thomas Vernon, second son of Humphrey Vernon (d1542) himself third son of Sir Henry Vernon, Lord of Haddon (d1511)). Sir Edward (d1657) was succeeded by his eldest son Sir Henry of Houndhill, Staffs (1615-1658), who was succeeded at Sudbury by his eldest son, George, and at Hilton, by his second son, Henry (b1636/7). He was succeeded by his eldest son Henry (1663-1732), who built the present hall in the early C18 (BOE p146). Two of Henry's sons were notable; his fourth son was Sir Edward Vernon (1721/3-1794), the admiral, whilst his fifth son was Richard Vernon (1726-1800), who became known as the 'Father of the Turf' for furthering horse-racing and was an original founder the Jockey Club. In 1787 he succeeded in winning the Oaks with Annette (by Eclipse) (DNB) (CCBO pp186-188) (HHH pp21,22). The first Derby winner, Diomed, in 1780, was trained at Hilton Park (VB p126). Henry (d1732) was succeeded by his eldest son Henry (b1718), who was succeeded by his eldest son Henry (1748-1814), who was succeeded by his eldest son Major General Henry Charles Edward Vernon (1779-1861) (Burke's Landed Gentry) who altered the hall in 1829 with an additional third storey (ESSN p57p). He was succeeded by his son Henry Charles Vernon (1805-1886), who was succeeded by his third son Augustus Leveson Vernon (1836-1925), who was succeeded by his second son Walter Bertie William Vernon (1871-1948). He was resident at Hilton Hall in 1940 and was succeeded by his son Richard Leveson Vernon (Burke's Landed Gentry) (KD 1940). The Vernons sold the hall in c1951 and moved to Keevil Manor, Wilts. For a time Mr Pickard of Pelsall owned the hall. He sold it to an order of nuns, the Sisters of Joseph of Bordeaux who ran it as a guest house for the elderly (ESSN p57). The hall was occupied by a Catholic Order in 1978 and used as an old people's home (FOS p78). The hall was for sale in 1981. Tarmac PLC, who purchased it as their group head office in 1985 and refurbished it in 1986, were selling the hall in 1999 (HHH) (ESSN p57) (Black Country Business Journal May 6-13 1999 p4). (AWM p26 of Hilton Park) (MR p182p). John Wesley was at the hall in 1782 (SA Jan 31 1885 p6), 1785 and 1787 (ESSN p66). In the 1930s Wright saw in glass cases in the entrance hall brushes made out of fox tails caught hunting and a treasured souvenir - the leather pouch for the huntmaster's horn used by WP Giffard when he was master of the Albrighton in the 1840s. Other possessions of Augustus Leveson Vernon, shown to Wright were a large painting hanging on the Grand Staircase of Henry Vernon (b1748) who found a fox at Boscobel on 14 Feb 1770 and ran six hours 10 minutes before the fox was killed in a field near Buildwas church. Also a portrait of Penelope Vernon daughter and co-heir of Arthur Graham of Hockley Lodge, County Armagh, who married Henry Vernon in 1775 d1782 (CCBO pp180-185,186) (VCH vol 2 p359; gives a history of the Albrighton Hunt). For the grounds see Hilton Park.

JACK OF HILTON. The 'Jack of Hilton' was a small brass figure used in a strange jocular tenure service custom at Hilton manor house. The custom was perhaps the strangest of its kind in the county or in the country (SCSF p5). In Norman times the manor of Essington was held as part of the barony of Dudley, but, later in the Middle Ages it was held by a peculiar feudal service of the lord of Hilton manor. By the term of his charter the tenant of Essington had to take to Hilton manor house a goose every New Year's Day. Dr Plot, perhaps the first to note the custom, says 'Yet there are many old Customs in use within memory, of whose originals I could find no tolerable account, that possibly might commence as high as these times; such as the service due from the Lord of Essington in this County to the Lord of Hilton, about a mile distant, viz. that the Lord of the Manor of Essington (now one St Johns Esq; late Sir Gilbert Wakering) shall bring a goose every New years day, and drive it round the fire in the Hall at Hilton, at lest 3 times (which he is bound to doe as mean Lord) whil'st Jack of Hilton is blowing the fire. Now Jack of Hilton, is a little hollow Image of brass of about 12 Inches high, kneeling upon his left knee, and holding his right hand upon his head, and his left upon Pego or his veretrum erected......; having a little hole in the place of the mouth, about the bigness of a great pins head, and another in the back about two thirds of an inch diameter, at which last hole it is fill'd with water, it holding about 4 pints and a quarter, which, when set to a strong fire, evaporates after the same manner as in an Æolipile, and vents it self at the smaller hole at the mouth in a constant blast, blowing the fire so strongly that it is very audible, and makes a sensible impression in that part of the fire where the blast lights, as I found by experience May the 26. 1680. After the Lord of Essington, or his Deputy or Bailiff, has driven the goose round the fire (at lest 3 times) whilst this Image blows it, he carrys it into the Kitchen of Hilton-Hall, and delivers it to the Cook, who having dressed it, the Lord of Essington or his Bayliff, by way of further service, brings it to the Table of the Lord paramount of Hilton and Essington, and receives a dish of meat, from the said Lord of Hiltons table, for his own Mess. Which service was performed about 50 years since, by James Wilkinson then Bayliff of Sir Gilbert Wakering, the Lady Townsend being Lady of the Manor of Hilton, Tho. a Stokes and John a Stokes brothers, both living An. 1680, then being present' (NHS pp433-434 tab 33 fig 12). Broughton says Harwood was incorrect in SOS in saying the figure leans upon his left knee and has his right hand placed upon his breast (SMC p121). The custom is said to have lasted for 140 years (S&W p379) (SCSF p5) (FOS p78). It ceased when the Vernons, lords of Hilton manor, became owners of Essington (BCC vol 2 pp37,38). Origins for this service and the Jack's involvement are unknown. The figure is thought to have had something to do with phallic worship and to have come from some eastern country (SCSF p5), or is a fertility symbol of Etruscan origin, brought to Britain by the Romans (FOS p78) (TB Feb 1993 p25), or it was brought to this country by a member of the Swynnerton family (who held Hilton manor) from the Holyland on a Crusade - perhaps, he who has the tomb in Swynnerton church (SAS p15). Wright was shown the Jack on a visit he made to the hall in the 1930s; it was then kept in its own green bag (CCF pp153-158). The Jack was still at Hilton in 1951 (SLM March 1951 p11). The figure was located to a private house in Wiltshire in Nov 1971 (FOS p78). The Jack was said to be with a senior member of the Vernon family in a village near Kington, Heres in 1988 (MR p182). (SD pp57,58) (Archeologic vol 1) (SHOS vol 2 p312) (SM p561) (W p155) (N&Q iii 4 1863 p461) (RS p17) (SC pp99-102) (SSHL pp99-102) (LGS p211) (KES p178) (VB p126) (Beauties of England) (HHH pp8,27) (ESSN pp17-18 il).

Hilton Park The estate or park of Hilton Hall. Four pit dwellings of ancient British origin were discovered in Hilton Park some years prior to 1908 by WH Duignan (WJO May 1908 p128). The Vernons had deer in the park in the C17 and C18 (EDP p180), during which time the park was landscaped. **Hilton Park Stand** was used by Yates as a triangulation point for his map, and by the surveyors for the first OS map (SHC 4th series vol 12 1984 vii). The **Portobello Tower** is a brick, hexagonal, embattled tower built to commemorate Admiral Vernon's capture of Portobello in 1739. It was perhaps designed by Richard Trubshaw of Haywood and erected between 1739 and 1765 and is over 0.25m SSW of the hall (DoE II) (LGS p211) (BOE p147) (F&G p390) (SGS p107) (SHJ vol 4 p62 p on p63) (F pp308,309) (HHH p23) (ESSN p20p). A walk in the park is called **Cat Walk**. The park is surrounded on one side by a mile long wall. By it LB Jackson in c1979 saw at night the ghost of a young woman with long, tangled raven hair wearing a white robe held at

the waist by a thin dark cord, her pale arms were bare, and so were her feet (TB Feb 1993 p25).

Himley Ancient parish and village on a tributary of Smestow Brook on the lower slopes of England's main watershed, 20.25m SSW of Stafford. Appears in DB as Himelei, a manor (SVS p578). The name may mean 'Hemele's Patureland' (SR p4). Or 'the leah (wood clearing) of the hop (plant)' (DUIGNAN) (SSE 1996 p14). Poulton-Smith opts for Duignan's definition but is unsure (SPN p62). In 1273 it was recorded that Roger de Somery of Dudley Castle (see), received one pound of cumin as rent for Himley (Himley Hall and Park: A history. David F Radmore. 1996 pp8-9). The present church, St Michael and All Angels, at the junction of the Stourbridge and Dudley Roads, consecrated in 1764, replaced a private chapel attached to Himley Hall (The Parish Church of St Michael and All Angels, Himley. RD Payne). In the later C17 Plot found under a rock near the springs near Himley Hall a red chalk, as good as any imported from France at the time (NHS p124). There was a windmill 0.5m W of the church and S of the Bridgnorth road at SO 874913 built between 1818-31, not recorded after 1881 (WBJ p27). The Himley Troop of the Staffordshire Yeomanry was raised in 1819 and were stoned by colliers in riots at West Bromwich in 1826. A Staffordshire Yeomanry troop were sent to quell the Himley Miners' riot of 1831 (info Yeomanry Museum). For a case of rick burning in 1831 near Himley see Swindon. There was a station at Himley on the Wolverhampton & Kingswinford Railway (1925-1932). The Pensnett mineral railway is said to have ran from Himley to The Wallows (TB March 1975 p28). For the Phantom Horsemen of Himley see under Himley Plantation.

Himley Hall There may have been a hall at Himley, a manor held of the de Somerys of Dudley Castle (see), in 1326 when there is mention of a 'certain chief messuage' there. An old hall was leased to Edward Stone and William Leighton in 1601. It was granted to Dud Dudley, illegitimate son of 5th Baron Dudley of Dudley Castle (see), in 1622, but later became the property of Humble Ward (d1670), 1st Baron Ward, of Dudley Castle (see). Henceforth to 1947, Himley Hall descended with the Wards (Himley Hall and Park: A history. David F Radmore. 1996 pp8-9). Charles I stayed at the old hall on May 14 (HOWM p90) or May 15 (Himley Hall and Park: A history. David F Radmore. 1996 p10) 1645 (HOS 1998 p74). In the later C17 the house was occupied by Lady Dudley (Plot's map). The old hall was rebuilt in c1720 (SL p183) - the present W front is from this period (SGS p107). Others say the central block of the present hall which faces W dates to 1740-50 and was built by John Ward, 6th Baron Ward. The Wards had their main seat at Dudley Castle until it was destroyed by fire in 1750. Later, the central block was extended by two pavilions. John Ward (d1833), 9th Baron Ward, employed William Atkinson to add the present S front and portico to the hall in 1824-7. In 1824 the external walls were rendered in 'Roman Cement' to represent stone work (SHOS vol 2 pl xxxii - SW view, p224 facing - engraving from the S) (SGS p107) (BOE P147) (BCM spring 1997 pp48-51). Scott says the hall was extended between 1828 and 1830 (SVS p286). The hall is said to have been 'rendered uninhabitable' by 1836 owing to fumes issuing from Oak Farm Ironworks (MR pp183pc,184). Lord Ward or Dudley left Himley for Witley Court, Worcs, having bought that hall in 1845 (SL pp182,195). Some internal changes were made to Himley Hall in the 1920s and the 1930s creating a swimming pool, squash court and cinema (BCM spring 1997 pp48-51). Himley Hall is, with Hagley Hall, Worcs, the basis for the great country house in Francis Brett Young's novel 'Wistanslow' (1956 - but written earlier) (BCM autumn 1989 p58) (Francis Brett Young leaflet in Dudley resource centre, Coseley). The Prince of Wales, later Edward VIII, was the only user of a temporary airfield which existed to the right of the lodges at the entrance to the grounds on visits to his friend, William Humble Eric Ward, 3rd Earl of Dudley (WMA vol 1 p176). In April 1936 Edward VIII planted a Cedar of Lebanon tree in the grounds and a commemorative plaque is still to be seen by it; his later wife, the Duchess of Windsor, visited the hall in 1975; other visitors have included the late Duke of Marlborough, Stanley Baldwin, and Alec Guinness (The Parish Church of St Michael and All Angels, Himley. RD Payne). George VI stayed a night at Himley Hall in July 1934 (R&S p46). The Duke of Kent and Princess Marina spent the first part of their honeymoon here between Nov 29 and Dec 12 1934 (1937 - MR p184 - Raven is wrong) (ES Nov 13 1934 p6) (The Parish Church of St Michael and All Angels, Himley. RD Payne). In 1939 Queen Mary visited the hall and in 1942 a large Red Cross Garden party was organised in the grounds, opened by the then Mrs Winston Churchill (The Parish Church of St Michael and All Angels, Himley. RD Payne). In 1947 the Wards sold the hall to the National Coal Board (NCB) and whilst it was being adapted for their use (as a regional office) a fire started one night in the S wing and within a few hours the wing was gutted. It has been said that with no real feeling the NCB rebuilt it in the

1950s style - complete with a concrete roof. In summer 1966 the hall was purchased from the NCB by the county boroughs of Dudley and Wolverhampton and then opened to the public. Wolverhampton council used the accommodation as part of its polytechnic. At some time after, Dudley council became the sole owner. In 1988 and for five years the hall was used by various departments, and public events were held in the grounds. A National Glass Museum envisaged in the mid 1990s to be opened at Himley Hall housing the glass collection from Broadfield House (see) has not materialised (WMAG Sept 1967 p22) (AWM p27) (VB p facing p7) (BCM Oct 1977 pp44-45. Jan 1993 pp16-17) (Himley Hall and Park; a brief history. David F Radmore. 1982) (TB May 1988 p13 il in 1735) (MR p184) (BCM spring 1997 pp48-51) (info John Smith at Broadfield House 2000).

GROUNDS. A **moat** at approximately SO 889916, presumably to a former Himley Hall, contained a huge eel, a yard and a quarter long, in the late C17 (NHS p246) (SSAHST 1982-3 p43). The moat could have been filled in for the present hall to be built on in c1720. In the later C18 Shaw noted that a coat of arms of some of the Dudley family, cut in stone, probably from the old hall, was fixed over the garden door near the Porter's Lodge, and a rapacious pike had destroyed a whole brood of young ducks in the length of a day in the moat (NHS p245) (SHOS vol 2 pl xxxi of the old hall, pp223,224) (NSFCT 1982 p12). John, son of John 6th Viscount Ward, employed 'Capability' Brown to landscape the grounds (often known as Himley Park (see)) (BCM spring 1997 pp48-51). The **Great Lake** (possibly alias Great Pool) at Himley Hall is said to be haunted by the ghost of a Lady Dudley of the Civil War period who drowned herself in the Great Lake (GOM pl 2(c)) (GOD pp26-27). George III's escape from assassination in 1786 along with naval victories was celebrated with a fireworks display at Himley Hall (W p177), presumably in 1786. After a visit to the hall Dr Booker wrote this poem titled 'Himley'

> If rais'd the eye above the Elysian-bound,
> What grandeur marks the wide horizon 'round,'
> Yonder, where Phoebus seeks his golden bed,
> Old Wrekin rears his cloud-encompass'd head.
> Next Clee's twin-mountains, tow 'ring, meet the skies,
> And far-fam'd Enville's beauteous woods arise.
> Hagley, as emulous - not so in vain -
> The palm of rural loveliness to gain,
> Lifts her green hills, her columns, and her groves,
> Where many a faunic dryad-spirit roves;
> Where many a son of sweetest rhyme has stray 'd.
> And none more sweet than he those scenes who made. (Lord George Lyttleton).
> Like clustering clouds, irregularly-grand,
> Soft welling from whose verdant sides, where flow
> Waters divide, (The Holy Well - St Anne's Well) to solace human woe.
> Still more remote, suffus 'd with living light,
> Cambria's unnumber'd hills arrest the sight;
> Which seen a mass of undulating waves,
> Rais 'd to the clouds when mighty Boreas raves.

(SVS p288). The **Great Pool** lies W and SW of the hall. The **Rock Pool** lies NE of the hall. The **Island Pool** lies NE of Rock Pool. The hall has two icehouses: The **first ice-house**, egg-shaped, half below and half above ground, 0.25m from the hall, is situated in a field of the neighbouring farm. It has a circular walkway around the interior (IHB p443). A correspondent to The Bugle, Mr AG Oakley, who was stationed at Himley Hall during WW2, was totally baffled as to its identity (TB July 1990 p5 dia). The **second ice-house** is smaller and cut into the stone near the hall (TB Aug 1990 p5p). A romantic spot in the park, planted by Lady Burgoyne, was known as **'Robin's Dell'** in the late C18. Dr Booker wrote a poem about this dell (SVS pp287,288). In the late C18 a **yew tree** in the grounds had this poem by WT Fitzgerald attached to it for ornamental purposes

> This stately Yew, which has for ages stood.
> The gloomy monarch of its nature wood;
> Perhaps some Norman baron planted here,
> Who liv'd by rapine, and who rul'd by fear.
> The tree a symbol of its master's mind.
> Emblem of death, and fatal to mankind!
> Beneath its boughs no verdant plants are seen,
> Its baneful branches poison ev'ry green.

> And thus the feudal tyrant's hated reign,
> Oppress'd the village, and made waste the plain.
> To these dire scenes a happier age succeeds,
> No despot threatens, and no vassal bleeds.
> At Himley, now the poor man finds relief,
> Forgets his poverty, and checks his grief;
> Raises his languid eyes, and drooping head,
> To bless the lib'ral hand that gives him bread;
> While in the mansion mirth and song attend,
> To cheer the stranger, and delight the friend.
> But still the Yew, though hastening to decay,
> Retains the venom of its pristine day;
> Its branches still their gloomy nature shew,
> And frown upon the cheerful scene below.

(SHOS vol 2 p224) (SVS p287). The **Memory Garden** is an enclosure including a temple S of the Great Pool near the church. The garden is to the memory of John Jeremy Ward killed in a car accident on the Embankment in London on Dec 9 1929. He has a gravestone designed by the sculptor Eric Gill. Gill also designed the gravestones here for the graves of Georgina, Countess of Dudley, wife of the 1st Earl of Dudley; William Humble Ward, 2nd Earl of Dudley, and Rosemary, wife of Viscount Ednam (later 3rd Earl of Dudley) and daughter of the 4th Duke of Sutherland of Trentham Hall (see), killed in a plane crash in Kent in July 1930 (the extension to the orthopaedic hospital at Longfield Cottage (see) is to her memory). The garden is also the burial place of Gertrude Millar, second wife of the 2nd Earl of Dudley (BOE p147) (The Parish Church of St Michael and All Angels, Himley. RD Payne).

Himley Park Medieval deer park created by the lords of Dudley. It centred on the Park Farm area (Himley Hall and Park: A history. David F Radmore. 1996 p8). It still existed in 1735 (EDP p180). In the C18 it was landscaped by Lancelot 'Capability' Brown (SL p133) (SVB p93) and the area is roughly the present Himley Hall grounds.

Himley Plantation 50 acre wood 1.5m W of Himley. Up to at least 1987 there was a boggy area of about half an acre within the woodland known locally as 'The Swamp.' It was said to be haunted by a phantom horseman who is thought to be the ghost of Gideon Grove, a groom of Stephen Lyttleton, Gun Powder plotter, escaping from Holbeche House on the night of Nov 7 1605. In the early 1990s a metal detector found lead musket balls and a pewter button of the period 1605. By 1997 the woodland was owned and managed by the Woodland Trust (TB Sept/ Oct 1972 p17. Aug/ Sept 1973 pp28-29. Sept/ Oct 1973 p1. Oct 1980 p12. Feb 1981 p16. Feb 1992 pp1,6. Nov 1997 p6p. Oct 22 1998 pp18-19) (Black Country Ghosts and Mysteries. Aristotle Tump. 1987) (GOD pp24-26).

Hind Brook Stream which runs eastward through Stowheath to Willenhall (HOBLL p3). It is presumably the Hindebrook which occurs in Lady Wulfrun's charter of 994. The name 'Hinde' means female stag (WFW p29). Has also appeared as Stag River. Hackwood identified Hindebroc with Back Brook (HODW p18).

Hind's Clough On W side of Tittesworth Reservoir 0.75m ENE of Dieulacres Abbey. Formerly a part of a small hunting ground. Held by William Davenport of Sheephouse bailiff of Leek and steward of the manor in 1543. A prehistoric implement, formerly in the possession of Rev W Beresford, was found here (HOLF pp7,8).

Hinksford Tiny hamlet at the confluence of Holbeche and Smestow Brooks over 1.5m NW of Kingswinford on E side of Staffs and Worcs Canal. Partly in Wombourne and Kingswinford parishes. Two fragments of antler, believed to post date 7000 BC and perhaps used in the Roman period, were found at Hinksford in 1969 (SSAHST 1975-76 pp85-87). Has also appeared as Hincksford. The name means 'Hengest's ford' (DUIGNAN). SSWWC built a pumping station at Hinksford in 1900 (GHC p15p). John Dutton, born in 1820 at Stone Lane, Kinver, landlord of the Old Bush Inn, Hinksford, was given the title of 'England's Oldest Licensee.' He died on Aug 20 1910. His father Joseph (Carver) Dutton had made the headstone for Benjamin Robins, victim of William Howe (TB May 1982 p27).

Hints Ancient parish, former manor, and small village on an incline above Bourne Brook (or Black Brook), 19.5m SW of Stafford. Plot and Cox noted an unnatural hillock at Hints, which they thought may have been a Roman burial mound. By the late C17 it appeared like a rock of stone and had possibly been a heap of earth solidified (NHS p402) (SD p20). It could be now what is known as 'Gold's Clump' (see) on the S side of Watling Street, and possibly a spoil heap from the building of that road? Or possibly the spoils of medieval iron workings? Pitt noted a large burial mound on Watling Street near Hints which he describes in 1817 as 'a ruck of stones.' Hackwood assigns it to the British period (SCSF p74). The mounds 0.75m WSW of Hints at SK 14890248 (probably Crow's Castle) and SK 14790270 are natural and not burial mounds (NSFCT vol 36 p157) (VCH barrow list) (NSJFS 1965 p39). Plot and Shaw noted a spring at Hints which never froze, nor did the pool it fed (NHS p91) (SHOS vol 2 p19). Plot was told of another spring by Matthew Floyer noted for being warm in winter in the vicinity of Hints (NHS pp92,93). Appears in DB as Hintes, a manor belonging to the bishop of Chester (Lichfield). The name is from Celtic 'hynt' meaning a road (DUIGNAN) (SL p44 note) (SPN p62), so '(place on) the roads or paths' (SSE 1996 p14). (SHOS vol 2 p14) (HOWW p8). The Meynells held the manor from the C12 to the C14 when it passed by the marriage of Thomasia, daughter of Sir Hugh Meynell of Meynell Langley, to Reginald Dethick. By the marriage of their daughter Margaret Dethick to Raufe Bassett of Blore (Ray) in the 1400s Hints passed to the Bassetts (Swinscoe, Blore, and the Bassetts. David and Martine Swinscoe. 1998). There was a church at Hints in the C14 (LDD). The present parish church, St Bartholomew, on the W side of School Lane, was rebuilt in 1882-1883 (LGS p148). A prebend in Lichfield cathedral based on Bishopshull in Hints parish was founded by Roger de Clinton. It was later divided and split into the prebends of Gaia Minor, Gaia Major, and Bishopshull. Shaw says the prebend was divided into six, but it seems that he mistook the Roman figure III for VI (SSAHST vol 2 1960-61 p43). Hints parish was a peculiar jurisdiction of the dean and chapter and certain prebendaries of Lichfield cathedral until abolished in 1846 (VCH vol 3 pp93-94). Hanging Wood, a wood near Devil's Dressing Room, may represent the site of the manorial gallows. For the nine Limousin cattle which escaped from a farm at Hints in summer 1999 see Hopwas Hays.

Hints Common Hints Common is not marked on the OS map 1:25,000. 'Common Barn' and 'Common Plantation' situated approximately 0.75m NNE of Hints preserve the name 'Common.' A Roman lead pig ingot was found here in 1692 (HOWW p25) (CCC p9; information from Garner?), or in 1792 (W p564), or in 1771. The inscription on the top is IMP VESP VII T IMP V COS, and on the side DECEA(N)G(L). It weights 150lbs (HOWW p25), or 152 lbs or 71 kg and is 22.5 inches long and went to the BM (GM vol 42 1772 p558. vol 43 p61) (Corpus Inscriptionum Latinarum vol 7 p1205) (SHOS vol 2 pp17-19; weights 150 lbs) (VCH vol 1 p190) (Flint Hist Soc Publication vol 13 1 no. p22) (NSJFS 1964 p25). The inscription on the top tells it was made in 76 AD when Vespasian and Titus were consuls, the first the seventh, and the other the fifth time (W p558) and the side inscription refers to the source of the metal which was from the territory of the Deceangli tribe, Flintshire (BM PRB 1856 6-21.1). Another Roman pig of lead weighing 150l lbs with a similar inscription was found in the same area in 1833 or 1838 and went to Tamworth Museum (TCN p5) (Flint Hist Soc Publication vol 13 1 no. p22) (Ephemeris Epigraphica vol 9 no. 1264) (NSJFS 1964 p25).

Hints Hall Hints. Former seat of the Floyer family; Ralph Floyer (d1643), lord of Hints, appears to have been followed by his son Richard Floyer (d1679), who was followed by his son Matthew Floyer (d1716). He appears to have been followed by his son Major Scott Floyer (d1762) (SHOS vol 2 pp19-20). In 1851 it was the seat of Samuel Pole Shawe. It was later the residence of James Chadwick, who rebuilt Hints church in 1883 (mems in Hints church) (W p21). Demolished after WW2 (SGS p108) and replaced by a more modest modern villa (MR p185). Raven suggests it stood by the Black Brook (or Bourne Brook) to the SW of the church. Plot's map shows it S of the church. (SHOS vol 2 p17 pl facing p17).

Hints Hill Hill and minute hamlet 0.5m NE of Hints.

Histons Hill SE of Codsall church (Birmingham A-Z). Houses were built in the Histons Hill area from the 1970s, some of them in the grounds of former villas (VCH vol 20 p77). The South Staffs district council offices were built at Histons Hill in 1975; the buildings were disliked at first and given the name 'Colditz' (Wolverhampton Chronicle. Aug 20 1999 p17). Although not associated with the council Staffordshire Gardens and Parks Trust meets here. The trust, formed in 1992, seeks to safe-guard Staffs historical landscapes by evaluating planning proposals and keeping a register of parks and gardens (info Jim Earle). For the assassination of Rex Farran in 1948 see The Myron.

Hixon Large village pleasantly situated on the sloping hillside on the NE bank of the Trent (HV p1) 5.25m ENE of Stafford. Formerly partly in the ancient parishes of Colwich and Stowe. In 1917 Rev WH Briddon noted 24 **Ice Age** boulders in Hixon, some of which lay by the road side from the old Hixon station to the top of Egg Lane (HV pp5-6). The **name** has appeared as Hustedone (DB), and Huchteshona (1130) (SSE 1996 p14). The terminal is clearly from Anglo-Saxon dun 'a hill.' The prefix is perhaps from the personal name Hengestes (DUIGNAN) or Hyht (NSJFS 1981 p2), or Hyth (SSE 1996 p14). Or from Old Scandinavian hus (house), giving 'houses on the hill' (SPN p63). From the later C11 Hixon lay in two manors: most of the village

lay within Great Haywood manor held by the bishop of Lichfield, with a small part, laying in Chartley manor. It has been thought that the moat which remained opposite Bank House in Hixon in the earlier C20 anciently surrounded the house of the Wasteney or Wastineys family, gentry tenants of the Gresleys, lords of Chartley manor in the C13. The site was sold among Lord Ferrers' property to a Mr Johnson in c1914 (SHC 1914 p148 note) (HV p8). Hixon had a **pillory**, which Langford says, remained until recently (W p423) (S&W p270) (SCSF p127). A **windmill** built in 1801 which was probably a postmill stood at SK 002257. It was last recorded in 1841 when it was to be let (WBJ pp27,28). The **church**, St Peter, on the W side of Church Lane at the S end of the village, was consecrated in 1848 (BOE p148); that year Hixon became a separate ecclesiastical parish (LGS p148) (GLAUE p414), but it remains in Stowe civil parish (HV p1). Hixon was in Colwich prebend (SSAHST vol 2 1960-61 p44). Hixon station on the North Staffs **Railway** opened in 1849 and closed on Jan 6 1947. A train crashed at Hixon on Boxing Day 1860. It happened as the evening local train from Colwich reached Hixon. A nine year old girl was killed and eight other passengers were slightly hurt (info Hixon Local History Society). Edward VII arrived at Hixon railway station for a five day visit to Needwood Forest and Ingestre on Nov 18 1907 (HCMBOPP p59). There was an horrific accident at Hixon Level at 12.26pm on Saturday Jan 6 1968 when the Manchester to Euston Express train collided with a heavy road transporter carrying a 120 ton transformer over the automatic crossing. The train driver, the second man, a spare driver and eight passengers were killed. An independent inquiry was held which was the first of its kind since the Tay Bridge disaster of 1879. (Report of the Public Inquiry) (Catastrophic Failures. Victor Bignell. 1977) (Historic Railway Disasters. OS Nook. 1987 4th ed) (SN Jan 8 1993 p16ps) (Railways In and Around Stafford. Edward Talbot. 1994 p4). Hixon **airfield** opened in May 1942 and was used until 1962 (WMA pp178-180) (Military airfields of Wales and the North West. DJ Smith. 1990 2nd ed) (SN May 1 1992 p9). No. 30 Operational Training Unit flew Vickers Wellington III bombers from Hixon between May 1942 and Feb 1945; the 'Thousand Bomber Raids' originated here (SHJ autumn 1989 pp63, 64). For the fate of some of these bombers see Amerton and Cannock Chase. The **horse trough** which now (1998) stands on the triangle of land at the end of Egg Lane had previously lain buried and forgotten opposite the Green Man Inn for nearly 80 years. It was rediscovered in 1994. To commemorate **Hixon Millennium Green** a four-ton granite block inscribed 'Hixon Millennium Green January 1st 2000' was unveiled in Hixon on Jan 1 2000 (SN Jan 6 2000 p18p). Hixon was flooded in April 1993; info from **Hixon Local History Society**, founded in 1990 (info Malcolm Garner). **Persons and visitors. Mary, Queen of Scots**, is said to have travelled from Chartley to Tixall via Egg Lane and turned off on the high ground for Farley. A sixpence or shilling of Elizabeth I was found in a field on this route in 1912 (HV p10). **Thomas Bond**, who murdered Frederick and George Bakewell at Orgreave (see) on May 31 1895, when aged 30, was born at Hixon, the son of a labourer (CCSHO pp53-68). **Wilmot Martin**, the 'Staffordshire Harry Lauder,' was born at Worston Mill House, Worston in 1874 (SOPP pl 98p) or 1875. In 1899 he married Edith Kennedy of Chorley near Lichfield and they moved to Grange Farm, Hixon in 1906, having farmed at Gratwich in c1900. He became nationally famous as an impersonator of the famous Scots comedian and singer Sir Harry Lauder, and obtained an MBE in 1949. He was very active in Hixon affairs being a founder member of the 1st Hixon Scout Troop, formed in 1914, and was a parish councillor for 30 years. He died on Jan 16 1963 and is buried at the rear of St Peter's, Hixon. In May 1998 his Harry Lauder costume and stick were displayed at Hixon Memorial Hall (A Minstrel in Staffordshire. Wilmot Martin. 1923) (HR p13) (ESNF p94p) (info Hixon Local History Society).

Hixon Heath Former common land to the W and NW of Hixon. The buildings for Hixon airfield were built here.

Hixon Moss Hixon. Lost by the later C17 (NHS p114).

Hoar Cross Small fragmented village by and on slopes above the Swarbourn, 13m E of Stafford. Formerly partly in the ancient parishes of Abbots Bromley (GLAUE p414), Hamstall Ridware, Hanbury and Yoxall (W p562). The **name** has appeared as Horcros (1230) (SSE 1996 p14), Horecros, and Harecros (SPN p63). 'Hoar' may represent 'grey' (SSE 1996 p14), or is thought to represent boundary; Hoar Cross being situated on the old parish boundaries of Yoxall and Hanbury (DUIGNAN) (SL p57) (SPN p63). Hackwood says the cross was a landmark where the four wards of Needwood Forest came together (SCSF p99). Or the cross could have been one of the four crosses which marked the bounds of Burton Abbey. However, by 1988 village inhabitants knew of no meaning for the name (SVB p95). The settlement known Hoar Cross at SK 134233 to the E of Hoar Cross Hall might be the original settlement? Hackwood thinks the two **fairs** (second Wednesday in April and

Sept) Cooke gives under the heading Holy Cross may be a reference to Hoar Cross (SCSF p99). He seems to be unaware of the Holy Cross near Clent. There was a chapel in Hoar Cross Manor House (see). The present **church**, The Holy Angels, by Hoar Cross Hall (see) in Maker Lane, was built between 1872 and 1877 by Emily Charlotte Meynell-Ingram of Hoar Cross Hall (see) to the memory of her husband, Hugo, killed in 1871 in a hunting accident. The church was designed in the Gothic style by George Frederick Bodley (1827-1907); the interior is perhaps Bodley's most lavish church interior; Sir John Betjeman (1906-1984), Poet Laureate, described the interior as 'a perfect church interior of late Victorian vigour and hope.' David Peace described the church as 'a perfect association of splendour and intimacy architecturally expressed' (The Church of The Holy Angels: Hoar Cross. p5). Henry Thorold described the church in the 1970s as 'one of the most beautiful 19c churches in England, and Bodley's masterpiece' ... 'There is a sense in which Bodley put all of himself into Hoar Cross' (BOE pp148-149) (SGS p108). Hoar Cross became a separate ecclesiastical parish in 1874. There was an **airfield** at Hoar Cross (Military airfields of Wales and the North West. DJ Smith. 1990 2nd ed). In 1972 there was an **Oberammergau cross** nailed to a tree in the garden of the vicarage (VB p88). On Nov 23 1874 **Robert Taylor**, a vagabond, aged 21, cut the throat of Mary Kidd, a labourer's wife, in a frenzied attack on a road near her home at Hoar Cross as she was returning from shopping in Yoxall. The simple reason for the murder was Mary had been unable to give Taylor, a stranger she met by the road, a crown coin he asked for. After the murder on hearing approaching wheels Taylor fled, and Sarah Ann Hollis, the daughter of a neighbour of Mary Kidd, aged eight, accompanying her, escaped being attacked. Taylor was found guilty of murder and hung (RPM pp9-11).

Hoar Cross Gate Appears on OS map 1834 at what is now called Far Hoar Cross, over 0.5m ESE of Hoar Cross church (OS map 1:25,000).

Hoar Cross Hall Hall at Upper Hoar Cross, 0.5m W of Hoar Cross. (SGS p108). The new Hoar Cross Hall was begun by Hugo Meynell-Ingram just before his marriage in 1863 to Emily Charlotte, daughter of Sir Charles Wood Bart, later 1st Viscount Halifax, to designs by Henry Clutton, and completed in 1871. It is partly modelled on Temple Newsam, Yorks. The oriel windows are of Runcorn stone. The portico has the Meynell motto 'Ung Dieu, Ung Roi' (One God, One King) (LTM Dec 1971 pp8-9,11). The hall has a chapel decorated by Bodley (BOE p150). In the hall or in the church was, or is, a chest and cabinet from Florence dated 1648 and a painting by Delacroix depicting a flight for a ladies hand (STM May 1972 pp26p,27,28). (CL May 10 1902 pp592-599ps). On May 26 1871 having just completed the hall Hugo was killed in a hunting accident. His widow overcome by grief had Hoar Cross church built beside the hall to his memory. The last Meynell to live at the hall was Col Hugo Meynell who moved to Newborough in 1952. For a time it was tenanted, and for seven years it stood empty. (AWM p30). The hall was for sale from June 1968 (Staffs Illustrated June 1968 advert), and in 1970 it was bought by William Bickerton Jones, an alabaster sculptor and Formula II motor racing team manager, and his wife, Gwynth (LTM Dec 1971 pp8-9,11). Or some say they bought the property in 1973 (PL p87) (Hello Magazine No. 300 April 16 1994). The Bickerton Jones' claimed to have seen the ghost of a young lady dressed in Victorian custom in one of the upper rooms which at first they thought was one of their three daughters and called her but the figure vanished before their eyes (PL p87) (GOT p142). Hoar Cross Hall became a health spar resort in April 1991 (MIDD vol 5 pp8,9p), probably that founded by Steve Jones, a millionaire from Walsall, who was running a health farm at the hall which he owned in 1994 (Hello Magazine No. 300 April 16 1994).

GROUNDS. In the 1930s there was a Pleached Walk, an arcade created by the branches and trunks of trees or shrubs, and a Yew Tree Walk, an avenue lined by yew trees and one of the finest examples of this type of topiary in England (KES ps facing p97) (CL May 10 1902 pp594p, 598p of an Italian well-head on a circular border of plants).

Hoar Cross Manor House 0.25m NW of Hoar Cross Hall, at Upper Hoar Cross. Large house erected in 1421-71 with additions over the years; at one point the hall bore this inscription on its front: 'William Yates made this House MDLV' (COI p188). It stood on a hill with a moat and drawbridge. There was a small chapel in the house dedicated to Our Lady in the mid C15 (The Church of the Holy Angels: Hoar Cross. p4). In the C16 the house was the seat of the Wells, Willes, Weld or Welles family. Has also appeared as the Manor of the Cross. The manor passed from them to Winifred Cassey in James I's reign (SHOS vol 1 pp103,104) (GNHS p204 note) (W p612) (Hoar Cross Hall. Gareth Evans. 1986). From Tixall Old Hall James I proceeded to Hoar Cross Manor House and stayed here from Aug 30 until leaving on Sept 1 1617 for Ashby-de-la-Zouch (Alrewas PR) (SHOS vol 1 p47) (SIOT p73). The manor

passed to the Howard family when Winifred Cassey married Sir Robert Howard, Knight of the Bath, younger son of Thomas Howard, Earl of Suffolk (GNHS p204 note). In the early 1700s the occupant was Mrs Mary Ann Howard, a widow (Hoar Cross Hall. Gareth Evans. 1986 p22). Sir Robert's daughter and heir, Winifred, married Peter Giffard of Chillington. Having no children the manor passed to their heirs, the Earls of Bristol and Lord Griffin of Braybrook who sold it in c1734, to Mr Webb who in 1748 sold it to Hon Charles Talbot (d1766) (GNHS p204 note). In 1740 the old manor house was demolished and a new one built. This in turn was demolished in 1794 and superseded by Hoar Cross Old Hall (see). Traces of the old manor house are said to have been observable in the 1890s (Hoar Cross Hall. Gareth Evans. 1986). In the garden was a summer-house of two storeys, taken down in c1748 (SHOS vol 1 p104) (COI p188).

Hoar Cross Old Hall 0.25m NW of Hoar Cross Hall at Upper Hoar Cross. Superseded the second Hoar Cross Manor House (see). In 1793 Charles, son of Hon Charles Talbot (d1766), and subsequently Earl of Shrewsbury, sold Hoar Cross manor to Hugo Meynell of Bradley, Derbys, who has been described as the son of the celebrated sportsman, Hugo Meynell of Quorndon, founder of the Quorn Hunt in 1750. In 1794 Hugo Meynell demolished Hoar Cross Manor House and built this house as an occasional hunting lodge (SHOS vol 1 p103) (LTM Dec 1971 pp8-9,11) (Hoar Cross Hall. Gareth Evans. 1986. pp27,28ps,66ps). White says it was built or rebuilt by Lord Scarsdale, who occupied it as a hunting lodge (W p612). The manor remained with the Meynells passing to Hugo Charles Meynell (d1869) who was obliged to assume the name Ingram in 1841, becoming Meynell-Ingram (W p612). He was succeeded by his son Hugo Charles Meynell-Ingram (d1871), who built Hoar Cross Hall (see) between 1862 and 1871. In 1888, Hugo's widow, Emily, founded the Home of the Good Shepherd, an orphanage for young boys at Hoar Cross Old Hall. With the diminution of the Orphanage Fund, the Home was subsequently taken over by the Church of England's Children's Society in the early 1920s. It was renamed St Michael's House and became mixed-sex. It closed in 1986 and re-opened as a residential nursing home for the elderly. Has been called sometimes Hoar Cross Hall (Hoar Cross Hall. Gareth Evans. 1986. pp65,67ps,70) (IVNF photograph of).

Hoar Cross Park A medieval deer park enclosed out of Needwood Forest. In existence by 1494 (NSJFS 1962 p76). Erdeswick noted it still existed in the late C16, and it appears in Saxton's Survey 1577 (EDP p176). Seems to have been S of Hoar Cross Gate (1834 and 1887 6 inch OS maps) in Hamstall Ridware parish (W p557).

Hoarstones House 1m ESE of Upper Elkstone.

Hobbergate House on high ground above Scotch Brook 1.25m N of Oulton. Formerly in Kibblestone township and quarter in Stone ancient parish. By 1872 Hobbergate was in Moddershall township (KD 1872). The ending of the name 'gate' is from perhaps a gate in Kibblestone Park (SOK p15), or a toll gate here on the Cheadle (turnpike) Road. (SIS p68).

Hobbhill To E of Painleyhill, Church Leigh.

Hobble End Minute hamlet near Wash Brook 1.75m SSE of Great Wyrley. In Cannock ancient parish. However, Oakden places Hobble End in Essington township, Bushbury ancient parish (SPNO p51). There is a granite Ice Age boulder here (SOB p2). Has appeared as the Obbleyes (1302, 1548 to 1617), Hobbley End (KD 1880) (SPNO p51) and possibly Hobbling Corner. Obbleyes means 'woodland pasture and tussocks' (SPNO p51).

Hobgoblin Gate Most northerly tip of Swynnerton Old Park. A gate of the old forest park, suggestive of medieval superstitions and days of the woodman (NSFCT 1917 p152).

Hob Hay House 0.25m NW of Upper Elkstone. The word 'Hob' implies boggart or ghost (DPMM pp114-115).

Hobhill Hill? nearly 1m NE of Bucknall (1834 OS map) (Dower's map).

Hob Hill Upper Hulme. On E side of A53.

Hob Hill Small hill 2.75m SW of Ellenhall topped by an earthwork? Close by was a farm called Cob Hall.

Hobholme Ancient boundary point of Tutbury, near the Dove (SHOS vol p56). Perhaps once Hobba's Holme (UTR p26).

Hob House Upper Hulme.

Hobnail Brook Served the Halls mill at Hateley Heath (VCH vol 17 p31); the pool of which gave its name to the area Millpool. Also known as Hobbin's Brook, Hob's Brook (TMS p119) and Devil's Brook (TB Aug 1995 p6). Hobnail Valley seems to be W of All Saint's church, West Bromwich (VCH vol 17 p27).

Hob's Gate Hart Road, Wednesfield, was driven through land known as Hob's Gate. Possibly so named in ancient times by some superstitious people since this area lay at the edge of marsh land (the later March End). The present (1978) Hope's Gate Works is adjacent and its name may be derived from this

(WFW p68).

Hob's Hill Place on the route of the beating of bounds around Lichfield (SHOS vol 1).

Hobs Hole Aldridge. The name is preserved in Hobs Hole Lane which runs ENE of Aldridge to Mill Green. 'Hob' is Middle English word for a sprite, an elf, a hobgoblin. 'Hole' in Middle English means a hollow, dingle, or small valley (DUIGNAN) (SPN p10). (NSFCT 1908 p136).

Hobs Hole Near Willenhall (DUIGNAN). There is a Hob's Hole near Portobello (HOBLL p61 note).

Hobs Hole In Wednesbury parish. (DUIGNAN). There is a Hobs Hole Iron Mines N of Wednesbury on 1834 OS map. There was a conduit called 'Quaker's Gutter' (see) from Hobs Hole Colliery to the canal at Willingsworth (HOWV p151). The name, which has also appeared as Hobbs Hole, is preserved in Hobs Road.

Hobstone Hill Hill to NW of Woodhouses, Burntwood. Rises to 489 feet (VCH vol 14 p198). The name is preserved in Hobstone Hill Lane. A lunatic asylum, designed by WL Moffatt, was built on Hobstone Hill in 1864, and has been frequently extended since. It was built to cater for the insane of the south of the county. In WW2 it became an emergency hospital and took in some rescued from the Dunkirk evacuation. In 1947 the name St Matthew's Hospital was adopted (SKYT p73) (VCH vol 14 pp202,219). The hospital is reputedly haunted. The great aunt of Tom Langley who was a nurse here had seen ghosts. She reported that after laying out a dead man his relatives appeared by his bedside (BCM April 1986 p42). On the road from Woodhouses to Burntwood, close to the hospital, have been more sightings of ghosts. A very tall man walking a dog have been seen (GLS pp25-26). (History of St Matthew's Hospital. D Budden. private print 1989) (St Matthew's Hospital, Burntwood 1864-1964. Copy in WSL).

Hockerhill Farm House 0.25m W of Brewood. Here was a windmill known as Kent's Mill (see). The name means 'the rounded hill' (SPN p23).

Hockley Former hamlet, now a suburb of Tamworth, 2.75m SSW of Ammington, 2.5m SE of Tamworth. In Tamworth ancient parish. Transferred to Staffs from Warws in 1910. The church in Gorsey Bank Road is dedicated to St Matthew (LDD).

Hockley Former small hamlet 0.25m S of Uttoxeter. In Uttoxeter ancient parish (W p792).

Hockley Abbey Folly-house built in the Gothic style by Richard Ford (d1806) in c1770 or c1779 on Handsworth Heath, between the head of Soho Pool and Icknield Terrace. It was also known as Cinder House as it was partly built of cinder slag. It was built in a pseudo-medieval style and resembled a monastery, hence its name; the 'phoney' date 1473 was shown in small white pebbles and a cross in similar material near or over the entrance. For a number of years Ford occupied it himself before retiring to Newtown, Montgomeryshire (STELE March 9 1956) (HPPE p59). Henry Elwell (1816-1872), son of John Elwell of Heath House, Wombourne, lived here for a time in the earlier C19 (IE p118). Edward Elwell, merchant, lived here in 1851. The building was in a state of disuse after 1860 and later demolished (HPPE p59) (HHHW p46p). Mary Whateley (see Haughton) wrote several poems celebrating the beauties of the grounds (IE p118 note).

Hockley Brook The ancient corn mill of Uttoxeter stood by it (HOU p285).

Hockley Brook Divides Warws from Staffs in Handsworth parish (SHOS vol 2 p117). Runs eastward to the Tame.

Hockley Hall Whateley Lane, Hockley (Tamworth). Formerly just in Kingsbury township and ancient parish in Warws. In existence in 1884 (1884 OS map 6 inch).

Hockley Hill To SE of Soho Hill. Could have been just in Warws. Duignan implies it was in Handsworth parish. The root of the name may be Welsh 'ochr,' 'ochren,' a side, a shelving locality. Hockley, is a somewhat common name, always in relation to a hill or hill-side (DUIGNAN p109). Thomas Barns thinks perhaps from 'aighe' 'ag' a height - which would easily produce Hockley by means of an aspirate (NSFCT 1908 p136).

Hodgefield 0.5m N of Brown Edge. In Horton parish. Has also appeared as Hodgfield.

Hoften's Cross Tiny hamlet 1m SSW of Cauldon. Formerly Houghton Cross, which was in Cauldon parish (W p751), or in Alton parish (SGSAS). There is a cross on a green facing The Crosses Inn. It is a rough hewn rock jutting out of the ground, not very firmly implanted. This may be the way-mark stone on Ipstones Edge (see) noted by Porter (PDS&C p77p). It was probably a medieval direction post (NSFCT 1920 p162). At SK 07064717 0.25m SW of Hoften's Cross is a mound (NSJFS 1965 p35).

Hoggs Hall 1m S of Harlaston. The name is preserved probably in Hogs Hill.

Hogley Lodge Brownhills. Now lost.

Hogshead Bishop's Wood. W tip of Belvide Reservoir on site of The Hawkshutts.

Hogs Hill Harlaston. Ancient farm (SHOS vol 1 p402) and a hill. Has also appeared as Hogshill.

Holbeche House House 1m NNW of Kingswinford. In Kingswinford ancient parish. The earliest recording of Holbeche Duignan found was in 1300. The house was built of brick in the early C17. It presently looks as though it dates from the C19. There are two priest holes (BOE p164). Has also appeared as Holbatch (earlier C19) (WFK p37), and Holbeache House. The name means 'the hollow or deep valley' (DUIGNAN) (SPN p62). **Gunpowder Plot conspirators at the house.** The house is famed for being the final hide-out of most of the Gunpowder Plot conspirators who tried to blow up the Houses of Parliament on Nov 5 1605. The conspirators who came here were: Stephen Lyttleton, Sir Everard Digby, the brothers John and Robert Winter, Robert Catesby, Henry Morgan, Grant, Percy (or Piercy), Rockwood (or Rookwood), Bates, and the two Wright brothers; Fawkes had already been arrested. The conspirators arrived here on Nov 6 1605 from Huddington Court (BCWJ pp70-71), or on Nov 7 (NSFCT 1909 p182) and the night of Nov 7 (WJO Dec 1904 pp321-323). On the way to Holbeche the conspirators had to ford the Stour in flood and in doing so wetted their gunpowder. Whilst it was being dried in the house it went off, badly injuring Catesby, Grant, and Rockwood (NSFCT 1909 p182). Digby, who was the eldest son of Mary Digby, second wife of Sampson Erdeswick (d1603) of Sandon Old Hall (see) (SH p24), seems to have never taken shelter in the house and took to the woods at once (NSFCT 1909 p182). The authorities led by Sir R Walsh, the sheriff, arrived and besieged the house on Nov 7 (SGS p109) or on the morning of Nov 8 (WJO Dec 1904 pp321-323). Those that remained entered into a brief skirmish with the authorities; Catesby, Percy, and the Wright brothers were shot, whilst Rockwood, Grant, Thomas Winter, and Morgan were captured inside Holbeche House (NSFCT 1909 p182) and taken to London for trial. Stephen Lyttleton and Robert Winter were not caught and remained at large on Pensnett Chase, in the Rowley Hills, at Bullfield Farm (see), and or Rowley Hall (see), and finally under the protection of 'Red' Humphrey Littleton at Hagley House or Hall, Worcs, where they were betrayed by Mrs Littleton's cook, John Fynes, alias Jobber. They were caught on Jan 9 1606 (HOWM p64). Robert Winter and Stephen Lyttleton were executed at St Paul's, London on Jan 27 1606. 'Red' Humphrey Littleton was tried and executed at Worcester. The Rowley Regis men (Thomas Smart and Henry Holyhead) who sheltered Winter and Lyttleton whilst they were at large were tried and executed on High Green, Wolverhampton (TB Nov 1987 pp1,5. Jan 1988 p17) (BCM Sept 1997 pp13-17. Dec 1997 p37). (SHOS vol 1 part 1 p51) (SMC p206) (GNHS pp87,88) (W p182) (LGS pp147,148) (KES p108) (S p135) (SOSH pp192,194,195p) (SLM autumn 1955 pp24,25) (STM Nov 1963 p33p) (WMAG Nov 1963 pp18-19. Nov 1979 p30p) (TB Oct/ Nov 1972 pp12-13. Oct 1976 p16. Oct 1994 pp20-22) (BOE p164) (SGS p108) (SOP p130) (MR p185) (SVB pp94,169) (GS pp32,36,50; the belief that the Gunpowder plotters were really descendants of the Megalithic Order or Order of Meonia). The ghost of either Robert Winter or Stephen Lyttleton may haunt the Barnett Lane district of Kingswinford (TB Nov 1987 pp1,5. Jan 1988 p17). Lyttleton's groom, Gideon Grove, escaped on horseback but was pursued and shot down in a swamp in an area currently called Himley Plantation (see); his ghost, a phantom horseman, is said to haunt that area. Holbeche House subsequently belonged to the Bendys of Shut End (SVS p134). It was for auction in 1947 (BHOP2 p98p) and is now (1985) a residential home. The house and surrounding area has many ghosts (GOM pl 3(b)).

Holbeach Millstream Ran through Pensnett Chase (KCPC p12).

Holbrook House on Saltersford Lane, 0.75m ESE of Alton, 1.25 WNW of Denstone. Has appeared as Holbrook (KD 1863 p469) (1887), Holebrook (1900. 1924), and Holbrook Farm (1985) (OS maps).

Holbrook, The A brook which formed the pre-1890 boundary between Walsall and Rushall ancient parishes in the present Walsall Arboretum area. It joins Ford Brook under the site between Lichfield and Darwall Streets occupied by Walsall central library and the Gala Baths. Ford Brook then continues as Walsall Brook under Walsall (VCH vol 17 p143). Also said to have appeared as Hore Brook, River Or, Hor, and Hoar (SNWA p24).

Holbrook Brook which separated Perry from Barr. It rises at Great Barr and flows S to join the Tame W of Perry Bridge. It is visible in Booths Farm recreation ground and in Perry Park. The brook has also been called Barr Brook and Perry Stream. Sutton Chase stretched as far as W as Holbrook (MNB p55).

Holclowe Possible burial mound on the northern boundary of Rushton James township (VCH vol 7 p219).

Holden Name for a lane, school and viaduct at Sneyd Green, Hanley. At SJ 885497 at Holden Bridge was a turnpike (IANS p19). The viaduct is dated 1844 (IANS p18).

Holden Farm N of the road from Sneyd Green to Milton. Has its origins in the C17, if not before. The house had been abandoned by 1957 when it was occupied as a temporary Methodist church (VCH vol 8 p250).

Holdiford Bridge Bridge S? of Tixall. Is probably of c1805 origin (BOE p283).

Holditch Colliery site and industrial area in the upper Lyme valley 1m SSE of Chesterton. Formerly in Chatterley liberty in Wolstanton ancient parish (W pp289,297). At Holditch was a large Roman settlement, probably a vicus, a civilian supply and habitation centre, occupied from c70 AD to the C3. The settlement covered an area of 450 yards by 250 yards and was occupied by Roman and non-Roman people (HOL p12). Roman pottery was discovered when a factory was being built on the site of Holditch Farm, demolished in 1956 (NSJFS 1961 pp28-50). Revealed 1957 (NSFCT 1957 p69). The site was excavated between 1960-61 (ES Aug 6 1960. Aug 12 1960) (NSJFS 1962 pp60-71. 1964 pp30-31) and in 1994 (WMARCH 1994 pp61-63). Hitherto writers had thought Chesterton was the Mediolanum in Antonine's Itinerary, but after the discovery of the Holditch site, it was thought it might be Mediolanum. (IANS p89). To the N at Mount Pleasant (see) was a Roman fort of the C1 AD on the site of an Iron Age settlement (MR p242). A site at Lymedale Employment Park, off Holditch Road (the former car park for Holditch Colliery) excavated in 1998 revealed a large Roman public building, which may have been a temple, or forum, or basilica, suggesting an extensive Roman settlement (ES Aug 28 1998 pp24-25pcs) (Staffs County News. Staffs County Council. Oct 1998 p4pc). Today (1995) there is an industrial estate and a colliery at Holditch. It was a hamlet in the C19 spelt Hol-ditch on OS map 1834. The name means 'the gulley in the hollow' (SPN p86). Or perhaps a corruption of 'old ditch'.

Hole, The A hollow with dips and undulations on the NW side of Broc Hill, over 0.5m S of Milford. By the beginning of the C19 quaint hermit-like dwellings had been made by squatters in the dips and burrows of the hollow and in the sandstone rock faces. These dwellings or cottages had gardens (BERK2 p53). Wright in the 1930s noted the rock cottages that were here. One of the remaining cottages, 'Rock Cottage,' was occupied by Miss Mary (Polly) Evans who had in her possession a silver cup, which belonged to a young professor at Owen's College in Manchester, who was killed whilst mountaineering on Scafell (CCF pp66-67). 'Rock Cottage' was condemned after Miss Evans' death and demolished after WW2 (BERK2 p55). The Hole has also appeared as The Hollow and seems to be the same as Sleepy Hollow (BERK2 p53).

Hole Farm 0.75m SSE of Upper Elkstone. Formerly in Warslow and Elkstone township in Alstonefield ancient parish. The site was occupied probably by 1608 and certainly by 1738 (VCH vol 7 p58).

Hole, The Area S of Ball Haye. Formerly in Tittesworth township in Leek ancient parish. Occupied by the later 1730s. It was called the Hole, probably because of its proximity to the steep banks of Ball Haye Brook here (VCH vol 7 pp233-234).

Hole, The West Bromwich. Appears in 1380. May refer to Sink Hole, or Sot's Hole or even to the Hollow (Holloway).

Hole Brook Runs from Wootton Park to the Churnet (SPNO p11).

Hole Brook Tributary of the Tame. Appears in 1286 as 'the brook of Holebrook' (SPNO p11).

Hole Carr House 1.25m SW of Hollinsclough. Formerly in Heathylee township in Alstonefield ancient parish. Appears as Holehouse in 1414 and Hole Carr in 1568 (VCH vol 7 p33).

Hole End (1834 OS map). Hole End Cottage is NE of Hulme End.

Holehouse C19 house to S of Holehouse Lane 0.5m NNW of Endon. Formerly in Endon township in Leek ancient parish. There was a house on the site of Hole House by 1561 (VCH vol 7 p177).

Hole House Brook Appears to rise in the Kerry Hill area and runs westwards to the Trent.

Hole-in-the-Wall A spot at E end of Silver Street, Uttoxeter, from which the Alwynehall may possibly be traced implying that one Alwyne, a Saxon thane, had his residence here (HOU p36).

Holford Former hamlet on the Tame 1.75m ENE of Handsworth. Formerly in Handsworth ancient parish. Transferred to Birmingham with Handsworth in 1911. There was settlement at Holford by the end of the C13. Holford Mill was granted to Roger of Wyrley in 1358 (MNB pp32,38). The name may have appeared as Hurstford in the C16 (VCHWA vol 7 p24) (MNB p40). It is from 'old ford,' a ford over the Tame on the Roman road Icknield Street (MNB p37). A new estate was developed on the site of Holford Farm after the 1960s (MNB p44). The name is preserved in Holford Drive and Holford Mills.

Holgates, The It took the name of Bobbington, a neighbouring parish (SVS p162).

Holland House Stood on Station Road, Barton-under-Needwood. Takes its name from the Holland family, residents at Barton from c1330. Once visited by the famous cricketer, WG Grace, who came to have tea with the Holland family. William Richard Holland, author of 'Some records of the Holland Family' (1929), was one of the last, or the last Holland, to live at Holland House. By 1995 the site was occupied by Meadow Rise housing development. The name is preserved in Holland Park, a housing development opposite the site of Holland House (UNT pp14-15,37,116).

GROUNDS. In the late C18 Shaw noted a large model of the church or temple of Christ Sepulchre at the house of Mr Jolland (or Holland?). The model was of perhaps fine shittim wood. The wood was curiously inlaid with ivory and mother of pearl. The church was about 100 paces long and 60 paces wide. It is said Empress Helena finding the cross at Jerusalem built the original church over the holy sepulchre. Shaw found no details concerning the model's past beyond that it had been purchased by Charles Jolland (or Holland?) at Mr Smith's repository in the old play-house, in Lincoln's Inn Fields, London, in 1764 (SHOS vol 1 p116).

Holland Park Park S of Watling Street by Brownhills Comprehensive School, Brownhills. Named after Councillor Hyla John Holland (SNBC p10).

Hollands, The Fragmented tiny hamlet 1m NNE of Biddulph Moor.

Holland's Well Well said to have existed on W side of Spout Street, Leek, in 1789 (VCH vol 7 p128).

Hollens, The An estate in Halmer End township of Audley parish. It belonged to a Mr Bloor in the early C16 (SHC 1944 p22). It may be identified with Hollins Farm on N side of Station Road, Halmer End.

Hollies,The House 1m S of Codsall church, on the W side of Hawthorne Lane. Built in c1870 apparently for Henry Anslow, a Wolverhampton grocer (VCH vol 20 p80).

Hollies, The Area near the source of Sneyd Brook 1.5m SW of Enville, in Morfe manor, and Enville ancient parish. It was an inhabited area by the C16. The area then consisted of two estates centred on two properties; in the later C17 one was held by the Dyson family, whilst the other was held by the Hale family; their houses and arms are shown on Plot's map. The two houses came to be solely owned in 1802 and now form one farm called The Hollies (VCH vol 20 pp94,107).

Hollies, The Common (called Hollies Common in 1839) and fragmented small hamlet 1m NW of Gnosall. In Gnosall ancient parish. Has appeared as le holyes (1327. 1331), Holys (1451), and lez hollies (1585-1834) (SPNO p160). At the NW end of the Hollies a field name preserves the memory of a moat which may indicate the site of a medieval house (VCH vol 4 p127). There were 11 acres of common land at The Hollies by the 1950s (OSST 1956-59 p12).

Hollies, The House? at Nurton, Wrottesley.

Hollies, The House in Newport Road, Stafford, facing Rowley Avenue. Built in the mid C19 for the Staffs County Police. The Chief Constable, Capt William Congreve, was in residence in 1870. It was much later taken over by Stafford rural district council (SAC p104p).

Hollies Brook Rises at Knightley joins Doley Brook at Gnosall which in turn joins Church Eaton Brook at Reule.

Hollies Common Minute hamlet to W of The Hollies, Gnosall.

Hollies Farm Stood on a site now (1995) occupied by Russell's Hall Hospital, near Springs Mire (TB Nov 5 1998 p10).

Hollingbury Hall Former hall which stood on the S side of Uttoxeter (Plot's map) (OS map 1834) overlooking Dove Valley in Toothill Lane (SMSE p8). In Uttoxeter ancient parish. Its site was at the highest part of the field at Bull's Bank opposite the Alleyne's grammar school. Seat of the Mynors and previously the Woods. A Mr Wood was in residence when Charles I stayed here in 1642. There are many secret places at a chimney back and elsewhere, and in one Charles I reputedly hid. The building had many strange ghost stories associated with it. Inscribed upon one of the old green glass windows was this inscription:

> 'I bleeding at your feet do lie
> And unless you yield; or else I die,
> Harmless Anne Wood.
> Soul and body murdered here,
> I shall never rest till I see my dear'

A most improbable tradition was that there was a secret tunnel from here to Tutbury Castle (HOU pp73,74,234-235,250-251). In the later C17 Dr Plot noted a partridge-scull-shaped stone, which he calls a perdicites, found in the horseway near the hall (NHS pp179-180 tab ii fig 6).

Hollinghay Wood Small wood 0.75m SE of Longsdon. It is a remnant of the Forest of Leek and a chase of that forest, belonging in the early C13, to the

Earl of Chester (VCH vol 7 p208). The lord of Cheddleton owed the lord of Leek a special hunting service at Hollinghay in the early C13 (SSE 1993 p6).

Hollington Small village on high ground near the source of Nothill Brook overlooking Croxden Brook 0.75m SSW of Croxden. Formerly in Madeley Holme division (W p760) and a chapelry in Checkley ancient parish (LGS p149). A damaged Bronze Age palstave was found near Hollington (NSFCT vol 42 p97) (NSJFS 1964 p19). Richmilde Street (see), the Roman road between Derby and Chesterton, passed through Hollington. In 1960 a section of it was cut across (NSJFS 1964 p19). The name appears in the C13 as Holyngton (SSE 1996 p14). It means 'the town or tun in the hollies' (DUIGNAN) (SSE 1996 p14). Croxden Abbey and many of the county's churches (W p760) (LGS p149) as well as the present Coventry cathedral were built using the excellent pink sandstone found here (HOS p8) (SL p33) (CDS p70). This stone is known as 'Red Hollington' stone (NSFCT 1906 p146) (ESNF p102p). A C16 seven-feet high stone cross - which could have been in Hollington churchyard - was found in Messrs Steventon & Son's Quarry, Hollington, in c1900 (NSFCT 1906 pp146,147 p facing p146). Hollington had a bull ring. It used to exist c1865 and is now (1925) unlocated (NSFCT 1925 p190) (Staffs Weekly Sentinel Feb 13 1926). The church, St John the Evangelist, in the village centre, was built in 1859-1861 (BOE p150).

Hollinhall House 0.75m NNE of Heaton. Formerly in Heaton township in Leek ancient parish. There was a house on the site of Hollinhall by the earlier C16 (VCH vol 7 p186). Seat of the Davenports (NSFCT 1932 p33). Near Hollin Hall John Naden murdered Robert Brough (OL vol 1 p26). The house was largely rebuilt in 1896 (VCH vol 7 p186).

Hollin House Former estate, in existence in the 1830s, centred on Hollin House Farm 0.75m SSE of Mow Cop (BALH p69). Formerly in Thursfield township and Newchapel chapelry in Wolstanton ancient parish.

Hollin House C17 house to S of Holehouse Lane 0.75m NW of Endon. Formerly in Endon township in Leek ancient parish. There was a house on the site of Hollin House by the later C17 (VCH vol 7 p177).

Hollinhurst House on a hill over 1.25m ESE of Endon. Formerly in Endon township in Leek ancient parish. The area was covered by the deer park called Endon Park in medieval times (VCH vol 7 p181). The site was occupied by 1574 and the present house retains a date stone of 1656 (VCH vol 7 p177). To the W is a house called Little Hollinhurst.

Hollins House 1.25m SE of Consall (1834 OS map).

Hollins District of Kidsgrove, 0.5m SW of Kidsgrove. In Talke township and chapelry in Audley ancient parish (W p430). Formerly Hollen Wood (1733) and Hollins Wood (1834 OS map) (Dower's map), an estate belonging for many generations prior to 1733 to the Tayler family. By 1733 there was a Hollenwood House (SHC 1944 pp65-66).

Hollins S of Tyrley Heath. Marked on Pigot & Son map 1830. The estate was created in the early C17 by John Tryner (SHC 1945/6 p188). Is now (1981) The Hollings, 1.5m SSE of Tyrley Castle.

Hollinsclough Tiny moorland village at the mouth of a narrow short ravine by the upper reaches of the Dove, 29.25m NNE of Stafford. Former township in Alstonefield ancient parish. The burial mound at SK 06336631 0.25m SW of Hollinsclough is a listed monument. The township was covered by Malbonck Forest in medieval times (VCH Vol 7 p5). The name has appeared as Howelsclough (late 1390s) (VCH vol 7 p37), Howellescloughe (C16), Hol(l)escloughe (C16) (SSAHST 1967 p34), and Holes Clough (maps of Plot and Morden). The form Hollinsclough, used occasionally by the later C18, became standard in the early C19 (VCH vol 7 p37). The village takes it name from its position at the mouth of a short ravine formed by a stream which flows N into the Dove (VCH vol 7 p37). The first part of the name is possibly derived from Old English 'hol' a hollow (SSAHST 1967 p34) (VCH vol 7 p37). 'Clough' is considered by Duignan to be of Norse origin. Some have thought it is from a Celtic root word and means a stone or crag (NSFCT 1908 p134). Another interpretation is 'the farmstead where holly grows' (SPN p34). Ecclesiastically Hollinsclough was partly in the chapelries of Longnor and Quarnford (GLAUE p414). The church, St Agnes, is a short way from the village centre on the Nabend lane. It was built in 1840 and is attached to a house (BOE p151) (MR p188) (PDS&C p26p). It was described by the Edwardian traveller JB Firth as 'the baldest structure wherein a dull sermon was ever preached.' By 1999 the building was an educational residential centre (LTD p13). Hollinsclough became a separate civil parish in 1866 (GLAUE p414). Hollinsclough was the setting for the A.T.V. film 'Murrain.' A pupil in the village school was recruited as an actor (L p54). John Lomas, the famous pedlar who spoke in the House of Commons in 1785, lived in Hollinsclough from 1785. In 1801 (DMV p47p) (PDS&C p64p) or 1804 (LTD p14) he built the present Methodist chapel in his garden, see also Colshaw.

Hollinsclough Moor Common land covering 386 acres in the late C18 to the

SW of Hollinsclough. It seems to have been enclosed mostly privately (VCH vol 7 p38).

Hollow Audley area; became Dean's Hollow in the C20 (AHJ 1997 p96).

Hollow Way An old road from Alton to Oakamoor. It passes the Ramblers' Retreat at Dimmingsdale. Children of the 1930s called it 'The Stret,' which has suggested to some it may be of Roman origin (HAF p34).

Holloway, The NW of Compton, 1m SSW of Tettenhall. By 1586 there was settlement in the Holloway, then known as Compton Holloways; this was the origin of the village of Tettenhall Wood (VCH vol 20 p8). (WPOPP vol 2 p58p of Compton Holloway c1925).

Holloway Bank Cut through an incline between Wednesbury Bridge and Hill Top, West Bromwich. According to local tradition 'the Holloway' was cut to facilitate the transport of coal by packhorse to Aston furnaces, near Birmingham (HOWBA p97) (HOWV p117). It was anciently known as Finchespath (see Finchpath), the road to Finch's house (DUIGNAN p60), and has also appeared as Wednesbury Holloway (HOWV p151).

Holloway End Former hamlet in Amblecote parish on the Stourbridge-Wolverhampton road by the Stour. Has also appeared as Holloway Head and Hollow's End (SVS p107). It was inhabited area by 1540 (VCH vol 20 p49). Derived from Hooe the name may commemorate the de Houx family (VCH vol 2 p226). One of the first glasshouses in Amblecote was built at Holloway End in the earlier C17 (VCH vol 20 p49). It had become the centre of Amblecote by the mid C19; the church of The Holy Trinity was built here in 1841 (VCH vol 20 p62). The Holloway, a cul-de-sac off High Street, occupies the site of an old house occupied for a short period towards the end of the C18 by the famous industrial chemist James Keir when he was partner in a glass works at Holloway End; the road is misnamed for it is not a hollow way (SNSV vol 1 p184). In the later C17 Plot noted some rock houses at Holloway End which were inhabited by poor people (NHS p172).

Holloway Lane There is a Holloway Lane and a Holloway Lane Farm and Holloway Farm 2.25m NW of Maer. In Maer parish (W p398).

Hollows, The Said to be part of an old fosse, part of the Roman settlement Chesterton near Mount Pleasant. The enclosure contains some 20 acres, part of the moat is still (1944) visible on the N side and the site of the praetorium can still be traced (NSFCT 1944 p93). The former Hollows Farm stood just off Castle Street (S&COP pl 37).

Holly Bank In Armitage parish (W p556). There is a Holly Bank 0.5m WNW of Armitage church on OS map 1834.

Holly Bank Hilton. Holly Bank Farm is 1.25m ESE of Hilton Park Hall.

Holly Bank Holly Bank Farm is nearly 1.5m WNW of Barton-under-Needwood. Willoughby Wood, formerly of The Highwood was Holly Bank by 1863 (KD 1863).

Holly Bank In Madeley parish (W p396). There is a Holly Wood and Hollywood Lane 2m NE of Madeley. Or is the same as the Holly Bank in Maer parish.

Holly Bank Tiny hamlet by the Tern 2.75m WNW of Maer. In Maer parish (W p398).

Holly Bank Common Part of Walsall Wood Common S of Lichfield Road was known as Holly Bank Common by 1805 (VCH vol 17 p280). Holly Bank appears as an area, 0.5m SE of Walsall Wood church, on OS map 1:25,000 (1976), but is not marked on the Birmingham A-Z. (MR p308).

Holly Bank House House over 0.5m ESE of Essington. Near the house at SJ 969028 was a J-shaped moat, filled in in 1896 (VCH vol 1) (SSAHST 1982-3 p41).

Hollybush Suburb of Fenton. S of Heron Cross.

Holly Bush House over 0.5m N of Newborough. In Hanbury ancient parish. It was noted by Shaw at the end of the C18 when it appears as Holly Bush Lodge (SHOS p94) and it has also appeared as Hollybush Hall. By 1832 it was 'an elegant, comfortable residence,' but earlier FNC Mundy of Markeaton had rented it as a hunting lodge (ESNF p89p). John Gisborne, poet (1770-1851) lived here for a while (NSFCT 1947 p100). It was the seat of Thomas Kirkpatrick Hall in 1851 and remained with the Hall family to c1913 (mem in Newborough church) (W p561). Was for sale in 1995 (SLM Christmas 1995 p15pc).

Holly Bush Former notable landmark on the perambulation route of Harborne parish. Situated near the Beakes, Smethwick (STELE July 27 1956).

Holly Bush Farm House 1m WSW of Cheslyn Hay, in Saredon township in Shareshill ancient parish. Is probably Hollybush Hall mentioned in VCH vol 5 p174 which describes it as a timber-framed house of the early or mid C17. The moat to the NE at SJ 965064 (VCH vol 1) (SSAHST 1982-3 p46) (CAMS p63) probably represents the homestead moat of the ancient Black Lees (see) estate.

Holly Greave Lost. Marked on Smith's map 1801. SE of Bucknall.

Holly Grove Formerly in Fawfieldhead township of Alstonefield ancient parish (W p746). There is a Holly Grove Farm 0.25m NE of Newtown, 2m WSW of Longnor.

Holly Hill Eminence just 450 feet high in the Warren Hill Road area of Perry Barr. Holly Farm near here, an encroachment on Perry Barr Common, was in existence by 1794 (MNB pp55,66,67).

Holly Lodge Former estate and house situated between Holly Lane and West Park Road, Smethwick. The house and estate were purchased by Smethwick corporation for housing development in 1920. The house was used as a school to 1932 and then as an orthopaedic clinic until at least 1971 (VCH vol 17 p101). Julie Walters, actress, born in Smethwick in 1950, attended Holly Lodge Girls' Grammar School (BCM April 1990 pp10-12).

Hollyoak Farm Stoney Lane, Lyndon, West Bromwich. It was a Tudor farmhouse. Demolished in c1945 (WBOP p110p).

Holly Park Just N of Holly Bush house, Newborough. Has an ice-house.

Holly Tree Well Well by the road by Beelow Hill. It was opened with great ceremony on Nov 21 1868 to supply Farley village with water (HAF p397).

Holly Wall Tiny hamlet on Harecastle Hill above Fowlea valley, S of Goldenhill. In Wolstanton ancient parish. There was a chapel at 'Halywalle' which appears in the court leet records 1366 (NSFCT 1924 p36). 'The hermitage of the well of Dunstall' and land there cultivated by Walter the Hermit, mentioned as being a possession of Trentham Priory in 1162, may have been here (VCH vol 8 p93). Yet in a later VCH it was thought to have been close to the priory (VCH vol 3 p136 note). Here was a house of the lord of Tunstall by the end of the C14 (VCH vol 8 p87).

Hollywood Minute hamlet 1.25m SW of Hilderstone. The earthwork here in Campfield Coppice is thought to be of Roman origin (SIS p3) (MR P308) (SN Aug 20 1993 p9). It is a Roman camp on the Roman road from the Blythe Bridge to Stafford (SPJD p24pc).

Hollywood Slade 0.5m E of Brocton.

Holmcroft Suburb of Stafford by Sandyford Brook, 1.5m NNW of Stafford. Privately-built housing estate dating from the mid 1930s, W of Stone Road. The council built houses at Holmcroft in the late 1940s (VCH vol 6 p193). The church, St Bertelin, Holmcroft Road, was built in 1956 (LDD).

Holme, The House W of Maer (1834 OS map) (Dower's map).

Holme Farm At Reapsmoor, Longnor, a German bomb fell near here in 1941 (L p53).

Holme Farm By Mayfield Hall, Middle Mayfield. L-shaped house which dates from 1440 and is built of locally quarried pink sandstone. It is believed to be one of the oldest surviving houses in Mayfield, and is said to have replaced a timber-framed wattle and daub building (MOM p55p).

Holmhaye Park Probably in the vicinity of Cheadle. A medieval deer park enclosed out of forest. In existence by 1227 (NSJFS 1962 pp75,77).

Holten End N of Lyndon, West Bromwich. Marked on Charles Henry Blood's Map of Birmingham and Its Environs.1857. Name now no longer prevails.

Holt Hall 1.5m NW of Newborough. (SOS p97?). It was the seat of Willoughly Manly, his father Edward Manly having purchased it from William Patrich (SHOS vol 1 p94).

Holt Hill Near Holt Hall, 1m NW of Newborough. Holt appears in 1247 as Hout (SSE 1996 p14). The name may be from Saxon 'holt' (otter). But in a topographical sense probably represents 'copse' or 'wood' rather than the home of an otter (SSE 1996 p14) (SPN p64).

Holt Hill Farm which covered 79 acres in the Roebuck Lane area of Smethwick in 1780. It was the seat the Birch family in the earlier C18 (VCH vol 17 p92).

Holtshill Area of 0.25m NE of Walsall. It was called Holt in the C14; Holtshill was in use by 1440, and Holtshill Top occurs in 1512 (VCH vol 17 p151) (SNWA p61). Hill Top (see) in Walsall may be another derivation.

Holy Austin Rock Huge sandstone rock 0.5m WNW of Kinver at the N end of Kinver Edge. According to tradition the rock was the home of the Kinver Giant (see under Kinver) and his beautiful wife in ancient times (WJO July 1903 xxxv). The name 'Holy Austin' first appears in the C16 (info board on site in 1997). 'Holy Austin Rock' had appeared by 1801 (VCH vol 20 p122). It is from perhaps a priest of the Augustine Order who occupied a cave in it in pre-Reformation times. There is also a belief that a Kinver school master lived in a cave here and he was given the name Holy Austin (RKE pp27-28). The rock, comprising malleable sandstone, may have had a cave which was occupied by a recluse in the Middle Ages (Hermits and Anchorites of England. Rotha M Clay. p48) (VCH vol 3 p136). The rock probably had some dwellings carved into it by 1774, and certainly by 1801; by 1830 it had seven dwellings (VCH vol 20 p122); by the 1850s it housed 12 families (info board on site in 1997); by the second half of the C19 it contained about 10 dwellings, each with two or three stories (RKE pp27-28). The cave dwellings started to be evacuated with the closure of the local iron works, some were still

inhabited up to the 1940s; a number of people who were living in them were attending Brierley Hill Institute of Education in the early 1940s (TB Feb 1994 p34. Jan 1997 p30). One rock house was inhabited up to 1948 (NSFCT 1981 p48). Several occupants provided teas to tourists and the last cafe in a cave dwelling closed in 1967 (info board on site in 1997). The lower rock houses along with some 200 acres of Kinver Edge were presented to the NT by the Lee family in 1917 (info board on site in 1997). Unattended, the caves deteriorated, mainly through vandalism. In 1992 and 1993 the caves on the S side were renovated and re-fronted for the habitation of NT wardens, Judith and Julian Thompson, so they could reside in the vicinity to deter further vandalism. (SVS pp165-166,167) (GNHS il p333) (HS p262) (LGS p158) (LHM vol 50? Sept) (QBSS pp183-186) (KES p121) (TB June/ July 1973 p13) (BOE p164) (SL p101) (SGS p115) (MR pp199pc,202) (SVB p107) (KRH pp6-15ps & dias) ('Womans Hour' BBC Radio 4. 20 Oct 1993) (photograph c1895 when occupied - in The Glebe Pub, Stoke-upon-Trent).

Holy Cross Large hamlet at the foot of the Clent Hills 0.25m SW of Clent. In Clent parish. Here was one of four wayside crosses marking the boundary of Halesowen Abbey lands. The others were at Haden Cross, Lye Cross and Rood End (BCWJ p64). Holy Cross had two cheese fairs by 1818 (VCH vol 6 p113) - second Wednesday in April and first Wednesbury in Sept (for cheese, linen cloth, and cattle) (History of Worcs. Nash. vol 2 App p14). There was a fair in 1792 (OWEN), but not one in 1888 (LHE p265). The fair had been discontinued by 1913 (VCHW vol 3 p52) (SCSF p99).

Holy Cross Green Old hamlet a short distance from the main Hagley-Bromsgrove road, near Clent (SNSV vol 2 p47).

Holyoak Farm Lyndon, West Bromwich. (OWB p53 pl No. 13 shows its barns and stables).

Holy Sepulchre Hospital Radford, 0.25m SE of Stafford. A medieval leper house (SSTY p140), the exact site of which has never been located. A barn with medieval and ecclesiastical features at Barnfields Farm (see), Wildwood, is thought to have had connections with the hospital and may represent the site (BERK2 p140). The hospital, a leper hospital, was in existence by the mid C13. It was probably founded by a member of the Stafford family. Patronage lay in the hands of a member of the Stafford family by the end of the C13. The hospital existed into the early C14 and may have been refounded in the mid C14 on a new site with a new dedication (VCH vol 3 pp289-290), as, perhaps, St Leonard's Hospital at Forebridge (SSTY p140). Has also appeared as Hospital of St Lazarus of the Holy Sepulchre (BERK2 p140).

Holy Well Well in Sandwell Park where there was a hermitage in the Middle Ages which developed into Sandwell Priory (VCH vol 3 p136). When the priory site was occupied by Sandwell Hall it stood on the front lawn on S side and was at one time protected by iron palisades as Shaw's illustration shows (SSC p130 in the intro, p66). (GNHS p173) (SCSF p141). Lawley says the well was dressed with garlands every year to the accompaniment of music and dancing in honour of its patron - St Augustine (OWB p45).

Home Farm Landywood. Charles Wesley preached here in 1754 (GWY p26).

Home Farm Near Lowe Hill, to S of Leek. Has a date stone with the date 1628, but a part of the house may be a little earlier (VCH vol 7 p89).

'Home of the Martyrs' An early C17 building, SE of Amington church (VCHWA vol 4 p246). Has also appeared Fir Tree House.

Homestead, The Harlaston. Built in 1773 by a collar and harness maker. Perhaps, had been the inn, The Whip and Saddle, at some time (SVB p90).

Honest Munchins Cottage Former cottage in a row of cottages at Holloway Bank, near Fountain Inn, off Bridge Street, Wednesbury. It was the home of George Clifton (1704-1789) alias 'Honest Munchin,' a converted prize fighter and ruffian, who rescued John Wesley from the mob in Wednesbury riots of 1743. The cottage was demolished in 1934 (HOWV p208 note) (WBOPP pl 137) (WDOP p89p). Others say the cottage survived into the 1980s (BTBC p27p) (OWB pl No. 16) (BCOPP vol 2 pl 44).

Honeywall Former small hamlet (VCH vol 8 p182), now a district between Penkhull and Stoke-upon-Trent. The unusual interpretation of the name is 'on-nig' meaning a hill fortress or fortified place. Talbot has seriously heard it mentioned that the name means 'hole in the wall' implying Honeywall was a hole in the defensive wall around Penkhull - but there never was one. HV Thompson thinks 'Honey' is an Old English 'hunnig,' and wella is a Welsh word for well or spring - so could be 'the well where the bees lived.' Rev Aston thought 'wall' may have been connected with a holy well, and SAH Burne thought it was from a wall around the Lyme Forest (PRA pp20,74), whilst others have thought 'wall' was from a wall surrounding the old park of Cliff Hay (NSFCT 1910 p174). Others have thought that 'wall' referred to the paved way to the early site at Penkhull. There was in 1910 a record in the offices of the Stoke Surveyor of a cobbled pavement found beneath Honeywall. This pavement was considered similar to that found in the Roman road in

Stoke-upon-Trent (NSFCT 1910 p163).

Honeywall Former hamlet on high ground above Hazeley Brook to W of Keele; the name is preserved in Honeywall Farm (W p394). In Keele ancient parish. It is on the Pepper Street. The name may be derived from the root 'onn, unn,' a rock or hill, in other words - 'the hill way' (NSFCT 1910 p163).

Hoo Hoo Farm with a brick front of the C19 is by Sneyd Brook, 0.75m NE Enville and incorporates one wing of a C16 or C17 timber-framed house. There was a settlement called Hoo in the later C13. This settlement may be identified with Blundies 0.5m NE of Enville; a Walter Blundel was recorded in the hamlet of 'la Hoo' in 1323 (VCH vol 20 p93). The houses to the S of the road to Hoo Farm in the late C18 may have made up the subsidiary settlement of Over Hoo; an Over Hoo was mentioned in 1313 (VCH vol 20 p93). Plot marks Nether Hoo on his map. Shaw spells it Hoo Hough (SHOS vol 2 p105). The name is from Middle English 'hoo,' a hill (DUIGNAN). Or from Anglo-Saxon 'hoh' (or hoe) meaning a 'spur of land' (SPN p48).

Hoo, The Former principal house of the Hoo family (who took their name from this house) at Bradley, Bilston. Their house was called Bradley Hall or their house on another site was later called Bradley Hall. The name Hoo is derived from hoh, meaning a spur of land, or steep ridge (WA vol 2 p90).

Hoo Brook Runs from Butterton Moor to Butterton. Joins the Manifold at Wetton Mill (PRT p70 see map). Has also appeared as Harbrocke (1434), Howbrook or Holebrook (1586), le holbroke (1593), and How Brook (1686) (NHS p105) (SPNO p11). Perhaps is from hol, meaning a ravine, which is topographically appropriate (SPNO p11).

Hookgate Fragmented hamlet on high ground near the source of Bromley Brook 1.25m WSW of Ashley. Partly in Ashley and Eccleshall parishes. Has also appeared as Hook Gate. Mr Hulme and two other lay preachers returning together to Hook Gate from the Broughton Fairoak area through the district known as the Birches had three separate versions of the same vision of three spirits at the same time (BOV pp50-51), or Elizabeth Stonemason's ghost appeared to them (STM Dec 1964 p35). The name is from perhaps a gate in Blore Park.

Hooks Green Area on the northern edge of Downs Banks 1m SE of Barlaston (W p371). In Kibblestone township and quarter in Stone ancient parish. By 1872 Hooks Green was in Moddershall township (KD 1872). Has also appeared as Hook's Green.

Hoo Marsh A piece of bog land N of Wednesbury: the town end of Wednesbury (WAM pp6,7,109). John Wesley described it as a quagmire. The Hoos, lords of Bradley manor (HOBLL p221) or Wednesbury in the early C18 (WAM p89), gave their name to the marsh (HOBLL pp137,221) or took their name from it (WAM p89).

Hoo Mill On a brook very close to the Trent 1.25m SE of Ingestre (W p393). In Ingestre parish. Appears in 1311 as Howe Mulne Green (COI p62). **Christina Collins**, aged 37, the daughter of a middle class Nottingham inventor, was murdered at Hoo Mill Locks in 1839 by three boatmen (James Owen, William Ellis and George Thomas, alias 'Dobell' of Wombourne) who were conveying her on the Trent and Mersey Canal from Liverpool to London; they were captured at Fazeley (see). Her body was found near steps by the canal at Rugeley, which have become known as the Bloody Steps (see); the case is sometimes referred to as the 'Rugeley Murder' (TB Oct 1977 pp26-27). There is a tradition she was murdered at the N end of one of the Harecastle Canal tunnels giving rise to the story of the headless ghost at Kidsgrove (MM p94p of her murderers execution notice) (MMM pp28-30) (SN April 28 1978 p6) (Canal Town: Stone. John M Bolton. 1981 reprint 1989 p33; reference to her in Stone) (NSFCT 1990 p41) (TB Jan 1992 pp10p-11p of her grave in Rugeley cemetery. March 1993 p18. Feb 1994 p19. June 1998 p16. July 1998 p25) (SMML pp48-49). The story was the model for Colin Dexter's story 'The Wench is Dead' (set in 1858) for the TV Inspector Morse series televised from Nov 11 1998 (MMMR pp63-66) (The News (Wolverhampton) Nov 5 1998 p27).

Hooters Hall Farm 0.75m NW of Knutton (Stoke-on-Trent A-Z 1992) (ES March 2000 p13).

Hop and Barleycorn Inn Mason Street, West Coseley (BCP p126p). Joseph Nicholds (or Nicholas or Nicholls), composer, born near Birmingham in c1784 was landlord of this inn. It was here that his 'Babylon' was first rendered in preparation for its publication. About 1812 he published 'The Monmouthshire Melodist,' a collection of hymn tunes. He died in on Feb 18 1860 in Dudley workhouse and is buried in the Old Vicar Street cemetery, Sedgley. In 1871 a memorial to him was erected over his grave (by 1985 broken in three parts and lying on the ground). The original memorial before it was bulldozed was between 12 and 14 feet high (BS) (AMS) (HC pp92-93) (TB Nov 1976 p24. April 1978 p10p of his tomb in Sedgley churchyard. May 1979 p5. Dec 1984 p7. Jan 1986 p3) (BCM April 1985 pp51-52. Oct 1993 p57). The inn was

demolished in 1957 (SDSSOP p76p).

Hope Small moorland hamlet at the head of a narrow dale running down to the Dove 0.5m SW of Alstonefield. In Alstonefield ancient parish. Was an inhabited place by the 1320s (VCH vol 7 p9). There was common land at Hope Dale, Hope Heath, and Hope Marsh (VCH vol 7 p19). The name means 'valley' (NSJFS 1981 p2). A small land-locked bay was termed in Old Norse 'hop' but when applied to inland places denoted a sheltered sloping hollow between two hills and is used in this sense in northern counties of Scotland (NSFCT 1916 p81). This is probably a reference to the steep-sided dale which runs from Hopedale E to the hamlet of Milldale (VCH vol 7 p9).

Hope Ecclesiastical parish created in 1845 out of Shelton parish (W p231) (GLAUE p414). Formerly in Stoke-upon-Trent chapelry in Stoke-upon-Trent ancient parish. The parish presumably lay about the present Hope Street. Hope was also a ward of Hanley from 1895 (VCH vol 8 p158).

Hopedale Tiny hamlet SW of Hope. It was apparently an occupied site by 1657 when there was a house of that name (VCH vol 7 p9).

Hopestone Rock feature over 0.5m N of Foxt in or near the former Ipstones Park. This natural rock outcrop, vaguely resembling the head of a man, may be the 'upper stone' or 'yppe,' which is referred to in the origin of the name Ipstones (TOI p9). Made to look more curious since the erection of a farmhouse, called Hopestone Farm, against it (MR pp156,157p). Has also appeared as Hope Stones and Hopestones Head.

Hopes Valley In the Orton area, Wombourne (PONP p140).

Hopley Lakes Area to the S and SW of Anslow. In existence in 1300 (ANS pp7,24).

Hopleys Former hamlet in Amington township in Tamworth ancient parish, situated to W of Shepcote Lane at SK 227039. In existence in 1888 (1888 OS map 6 inch). The name no longer persists on current maps.

Hopper Fort An embankment creating an enclosure, at SJ 926447, in Park Hall Country Park, possibly man-made, as there was mining and sandstone quarrying in the vicinity (Park Hall Country Park. Staffs County Council Leaflet. Pre-1991).

Hopton Village on high ground above a brook which joins the Penk near its confluence with the Sow, 0.75m SW of Salt. A Neolithic or Bronze Age axe-hammer was found in Hopton in 1829 (Proceedings of the Prehistoric Society vol 25 p139) (NSJFS 1964 p26). A fractured polished blade of a medium stone Neolithic or Bronze Age axe was ploughed up near Pool Farm in Dec 1951 (NSJFS 1962 p29. 1964 p26). Near Pool Farm at SJ 957258 was found in 1956 a leaf-shaped arrowhead of Neolithic origin (NSJFS 1964 p26). In 1792 an iron spearhead was found during road repairs in Hopton parish (VAD p10) (NSJFS 1964 p26). The name has appeared as Hotone, a manor in DB, Hoptuna (1167), Hopton (c1200) (SSE 1996 p14) (SPN p65). It means 'enclosure settlement' (NSJFS 1981 p2), or 'enclosed tun' (SSE 1996 p14). Is 'farmstead in or of the valley' (SPN p64). Ecclesiastically, Hopton was a chapel of St Mary's parish, Stafford. But it may have had status equivalent to a separate parish by the late C13 (SHC 1916 p199). Civilly, it formed an out-township in St Mary's parish, Stafford, with Coton (W p341). The chapel of Hopton was called a prebend of Stafford Collegiate Church in 1535 (VCH vol 3 p307). The mission church, St Peter, at the junction of Hopton, Hoptonhall, and Wilmorehill Lanes, was built in 1876 (LGS p149) (LDD). Hopton became a separate civil parish in 1866 (GLAUE p414). There were plans in the mid 1970s to mine coal in the Hopton area. Two married women Margaret Annie Humphreys, aged 20, and Sarah Florence Woolley, aged 23, tragically drowned in Hopton Pools on July 5 1932, despite attempts by Richard Banks to try to save them (SN July 9 1932 p4).

Hopton Heath Former common land to the E of Hopton and 2.5m NE of Stafford, mostly enclosed by 1910 (LGS p149). A mock sun was witnessed by Walter Chetwynd and Fisher Dilke on Hopton Heath on July 12 1678; the same day others saw it at or near Lower Gornal (NHS pp3,4,5,6,7) (SHOS vol 1 p390). Two small worn wooden crosses on the N side of Weston Road at Within Lane junction in 1999 commemorate the deaths of 'Kevin and Clare' in a road accident.

BATTLE OF HOPTON HEATH. The battle of Hopton Heath, the only Civil War battle fought in the county, was fought on Sunday March 19 1643. The battle came about as the parliamentarians under Sir John Gell and Sir William Brereton were intending to capture Stafford, a royalist garrison, when in a bid to seize the initiative, a royalist force under the Earl of Northampton, Commander-in-Chief of forces in Northants and Warws, with the commander of Leics, Col General Hastings, confronted them. The result was a royalist victory. The exact **site of the battlefield** has been disputed. The site has long been marked on OS maps at SJ 951262, where an RAF supply depot is situated (MR p189). However, sometime probably in or from the 1960s, John Sutton proved that the true site was slightly farther N at SJ 953266 (info

Mark Smith). There is a tradition going back to at least the early C19 that the battle took place to the S on the slopes of Beacon Hill on heathland called St Amon's Heath (see) (SHJ winter 1987 p1). The **parliamentarian force** consisted of 1,850 - 1,200 foot, 400 horse and about 250 dragoons (BFS p16) (SHJ winter 1987 p2). Of the foot there were 300 Moorlanders. The parliamentary cavalry regiments were led by Lord Brooke, Col Simon Rugeley and Sir George Gresley. Some of Sir William Brereton's contingent including the Staffordshire foot under Capt John Bowyer's command did not arrive until the battle had finished (BFS p16). The combined **royalist force** amounted to about 1,200 - 800 cavalry, 300 dragoons, and 100 foot. Of the two royalist cavalry regiments brought from Bambury one was commanded by Lord Compton the son of Earl of Northampton, and the other - the Prince of Wales' - by Sir Thomas Byron. The contingent of Col General Hastings contributed two regiments - his own, and that of Col Ferdinando Stanhope. A third element comprised the troops of Capt Francis Biddulph and John Lane from the Stafford garrison, those of Richard Bagot and his brother Hervey, and the remnants of the Lichfield garrison. The royalists also employed the cannon known as Roaring Meg (BFS p16) (SN April 1953 p8). The cannon ball found on the heath in 1940, which went to the officers mess at RAF Stafford, is believed to have been fired by Roaring Meg (NSFCT 1888 pp74-75. 1940 p26). **The battle** was fought between 3.00pm and sunset (BFS p15) (ROT p48). Both sides were hindered by many rabbit holes in the ground which made horses trip (HWE vol 2 p322). The Earl of Northampton was killed and his body taken to the Crown Inn, Uttoxeter, by Gell (HAF p121). Despite the loss of the earl the superior royalist cavalry caused the parliamentary force to retire. Parliament may have lost up to 100 killed and wounded, the royalists half that number (BFS p18). John Sutton in SHJ winter 1987 pp1-10 gives a good account of the battle. Sandon and Weston-on-Trent PRs record the burials of some of the dead. **After the battle** the royalists marched to Tamworth and Ashby-de-la-Zouch, taking with them some captured ammunition, powder and carriages (BFS p18). Gell and Brereton retired to Chartley Hall. The next day, Lord Compton, dispatched a trumpeter to Chartley to request the return of his father's body for burial (BFS pp7,18). Gell and Brereton offered to surrender it in return for their captured soldiers and ordnance (VB p133). But no exchange took place (BFS p18); because Lord Compton refused the offer (info Mark Smith). (HOS p35). On May 16 1643 the parliamentarians obtained their objective; the capture of Stafford. Chetwynd does not mention the battle in his history of Pirehill hundred (1679) (SHC p141 note). An inn at Salt has a notice on the wall in its bar which bore these lines written by T Ward of Tinkerborough

> And now we come to Hopton Heath,
> Where many poor warriors lie beneath,
> On the 19th March, 1643
> The men fought hard for liberty.

A further verse claimed the landlord would let visitors see the battle relics the inn possessed (FSP p25). A cannon ball was found in c1858 (Stafford Advertiser April 30 1964 p5). In 1923 a 15-inch long silver sword of the Civil War period was found in the thatched roof of the Holly Bush Inn, Salt (SN Oct 29 1993 p8). During excavations for the present RAF supply depot near Hopton village in 1940 an iron cannon ball weighing 29 pounds and five inches in diameter was found and went to the RAF officers' mess at Stafford. It was found close to Square Covert (NSFCT 1940 p25). A cannon ball was found at Beacon Farm, Hopton in 1945 (Stafford Advertiser April 30 1964 p5p) (SHJ winter 1987 p9). A cannon ball was found during the demolition of a stone wall (in which it was encased) at Brickhouse Farm in 1963 (SHJ winter 1987 p9) and another at the same farm in June 1964 (SN June 26 1964 p1). About a hundred 28 pounders have been found at 16 M.U. (RAF Stafford). To mark the 350th anniversary of the battle a memorial plaque was erected in Hopton village hall (ES March 22 1993 p4p). The **ghosts** of some of the dead, including a man on horseback in Civil War costume seen riding up Salt Lane (SN Oct 29 1993 p8), and battle sounds, have been seen and heard by some of the inhabitants of Salt (info Bruce Braithwaite). (SHOS vol 1 part 1 pp53-54) (SOS p64) (ROS vol 3 pp60-69) (HSS pp90-97) (MOS p25) (LGS pp30,149,150) (KES pp112,113) (SOSH pp201-203) (SHC 1936 pp181-184) (OSST 1951-52 pp24-29) (FSP pp25-32) (NSJFS 1966 p20) (NUL p58) (SGS p109) (A Battle Atlas of the English Civil War. A Baker. 1986) (BDH p106).

Hopwas Village on a shelf of land rising out of the Tame 19.5m SE of Stafford. Formerly in Wigginton township in Tamworth ancient parish. Has appeared as Opewas, a manor, in DB, Hopwas (1166), Hopewas (C13) (SPN p64), Hopper (c1540), Hopwais (later C16?), Hopweys (later C16?) (LI part 5 p103), and Hoppas (maps of Bowen and Smith). The name means 'the marshy val-

ley' (DUIGNAN), or 'alluvial land near an enclosure' (NSJFS 1981 p3) (SPN p64), or 'enclosed watermeadow' (SSE 1996 p14). There is a tradition that the Earl of Richmond (Henry VII) camped with his army of 5,000 men at Hopwas on Aug 18 (R&S p18) prior to the battle of Bosworth Field (1485), having travelled from Milford Haven by way of Shrewsbury, Stafford and Lichfield. The title of Act 5 Scene 2 of Shakespeare's Richard III is 'The camp near Tamworth' (SHOS vol 1 part 1 p50) (HOL pp302,303) (LGS p227) (SOSH p163) (RVW p10). An abandoned baby found at night in the village at the end of the C17 was adopted and brought up by the village. The village named him Thomas Barnes, after the barn he was found in. He became a prosperous merchant in London and in 1717 endowed Hopwas with a school. The original school was replaced in 1909, and named after its benefactor (SVB p98). The church, St Chad, at the N end of Church Drive, was built in 1881 (BOE p151). Hopwas wake was on the Sunday after Lammas day in the C19 (W p626). Hopwas features in a derisory rhyme about Tamworth (see).

Hopwas Hay Former estate which became a hay or division of Cannock Forest, 3m WNW of Tamworth. The hay, which has also appeared as Hopwas Hayes, was in existence by 1222. It remained with the Crown until at least 1550 (VCH vol 2 pp338,343). By the mid C19 it was a wood of 373 acres with extra-parochial status (W p565) (APB p6). In 1857, with the introduction of the Poor Relief Act, Hopwas Hay became a parish for poor relief purposes and was attached to Tamworth Union. The rate was duly levied, and the Hopwas overseer in due course demanded payment from a gentleman who probably owned the whole parish. But the overseer did not publish the rate (as required by law) on the church door, as Hopwas Hayes had no church. The owner refused to pay and was upheld in his decision by the judges of the High Court. This shortly necessitated the passing of a Short Act stating that the rate could be published in some public and conspicuous place (NSFCT 1913 p63). Hopwas Hay lost its separate civil status in 1934 when it entered Wigginton civil parish, and its separate ecclesiastical status in 1967 when it entered Whittington parish (GLAUE p414). In July 1999 about three quarters of the wood, by then known as Hopwas Wood, was sold to Nash Rocks Ltd, who, despite protests from local inhabitants, planned to mine some of the eight million tonnes of high quality sand and gravel under the wood (TH Oct 15 1999 p3). In July 1999 nine Limousin cattle escaped from a farm at Hints and were soon in Hopwas Wood. In Oct 1999 began an operation, known as 'Rawhide,' comprising a squad of 100 soldiers from Whittington Barracks, together with NFU representatives, expert marksmen and mounted police, which tried to catch the so-called 'Tamworth Nine' cattle. By Dec 22 1999 four cattle had been shot dead. The remaining five became something of a cause celebre with campaigners seeking that they be spared from slaughter when caught. On Feb 7 2000 the remaining cattle were caught and taken to Hillside Animal Sanctuary, Notts (Evening Mail Oct 20 1999 p1) (TH Oct 22 1999 p6) (The Times Weekend Section. Nov 6 1999 p7) (BBC Midlands Today. Dec 22 1999. Feb 7 2000).

Hopwas House Farm House SW of Hopwas.

Hopyard Former area centred on Siddons Road, Coseley. The Hopyard Colliery was disused by 1887, when the Hopyard Foundry was still producing iron (OS maps).

Hore Sitch Boundary brook at Hilderstone. Alternatively Horesych and pronounced locally The Ostriches; Sytch is a name frequently applied in Staffs to a more or less dry watercourse (NSFCT 1908 p132. 1922 p169).

Horewood There was a wood called Horewood in the W of Kinver parish by 1269. A manor of Horewood, eventually covering the whole of the Compton area, existed by 1292. The manor seems to have always been a sub-manor of Kinver manor, and in the early C19 it became united with Kinver. In 1294 Edward I was at Horewood on his way to Wales. The manor was known as Haulowe and Halowes in Compton in the later C14, probably after the Haudlo family, its lords in the early C14. It was later held by the Horewood family, whose name was spelt Whorwood by 1527. In the C15 the lord moved from the moated manor house at Horewood, which probably stood on the moated site where Compton Park Farm now stands, to Compton Hall (see). By the later C16 the manor was called Compton Hallowes, and it was also called Whorwood and Compton Whorwood in the C17 and C18 (VCH vol 20 pp122,126,132,133).

Horn End Tiny area of SE Hixon, where Egg Lane turns a forty-five degree angle at Grange Farm (HV p10).

Horninglow Former village in the Trent Valley at the foot of the incline rising to the Needwood Forest plateau, now a suburb 1.25m NNW of Burton upon Trent. Former township in Burton upon Trent ancient parish. A looped palstave of the Bronze Age was found at Horninglow station at SK 251248 (NSJFS 1964 p18) (BTIH p9p). It was at the Bass Museum, Burton upon Trent by the 1990s (info KL Keal). The name occurs in the early C12. Shaw thought

'Horning' was derived from the place's situation. 'Horn' signifying a corner, and it is situated on an angular hill projecting into meadows cornered by the union of the rivers Trent and Dove, 'ing' signifying a meadow (SHOS vol 1 p24). Or represents 'Horning's burial-mound,' though not necessarily the place where a man called Horning was buried, but could be a burial-mound belonging to Horning (DUIGNAN). Or 'the people of the horn-shaped hill' (SPN p26). In the early 1540s overlordship of Horninglow manor passed with other Burton Abbey estates to Sir William Paget of Beaudesert (SHOS vol 1 p8). Ecclesiastically severed to help create Burton upon Trent Christ Church ecclesiastical parish in 1821. The church, St John the Divine, on the corner of Horninglow and Rolleston Roads, was built in 1864-1866. Became a separate ecclesiastical parish in 1867, and a separate civil parish in 1866 (BOE p88) (LDD) (GLAUE p414). A branch railway line from Burton to Horninglow was opened in 1868 (VCH vol 2 p320). Horninglow station opened in 1883 and closed in 1940 (LTD p199) or on Jan 1 1949 (ABTOP p131). For Horninglow characters see IRB pp42-43.

Horninglow Cross Rolleston. There was an ancient boundary cross on the Stretton boundary. An old Horninglow man (b1810) remembered having seen at Horninglow Cross a square stone platform with a hole in the centre. He thought Sir Oswald Mosley had removed the stone or stones to a rockery at Rolleston Hall (UTR p167). Dr Auden thinks the cross is the one now in the churchyard at Rolleston (NSFCT 1946 p45).

Horn's Pool At Slitting Mill, Rugeley. Created in the late C18 as a header pool to provide a fall of water capable of driving a millwheel (SVB p152). There is a pub at Slitting Mill called The Horns.

Hornton Manor Little Aston. Just in Staffs SE of the church.

Horse Bridge Small hamlet by Endon Brook 0.5m S of Longsdon. Formerly in Longsdon township in Leek ancient parish. The bridge over Endon Brook from which Horse Bridge takes its name existed by 1603 and may have replaced a ford called Keghton Ford, mentioned in 1438 (VCH vol 7 p203). For water works at Horse Bridge see Wall Grange.

Horse Brook Flows from Stretton to Horsebrook to the Penk. The name means 'the brook frequented by horses' (SPNO p38).

Horsebrook Small hamlet by Horse Brook 0.75m S of Stretton (Penkridge). Former liberty of Brewood town in Brewood ancient parish and was included in Brewood prebend (SSAHST vol 2 1960-61 p43). Has appeared as Horsebroc (1262-72), Hossebroke (1478) (SPNO p38). In the later C17 Plot noted a sulphur well which stank, at the crossroads on Watling Street (NHS p104) (SOS p166 note). It was an holy well, and it may have been the custom to dress it with flowers in an annual ceremony (OSST 1944-1945). Two entirely white chimney swallows (Hirundo Rustica) were bred at Horsebrook in 1796 (SHOS vol 1 part 1 p94). For Horsebrook in a local rhyme see Brewood.

Horsebrook Hall S side of A5 (Watling Street). Near by was a Roman camp (NSFCT 1908 p116).

Horsecroft Farm House 0.75m NE of Leek. Formerly in Tittesworth township in Leek ancient parish. May have appeared as Horsecroft Gate in 1639. The present C19 building stands on earlier foundations (VCH vol 7 p233).

Horse Fair A street in Eccleshall.

Horse Fair Former small district of Penkridge where nationally renowned horse fairs took place from the C13. Marshbrook First School and nearby recreation grounds stand on the site where the fair was held. (VCH vol 5 p129). Horse Fair Cottages were inns serving the Horse Fair. In the garden of one of them was the site of a Lollard pulpit (PVH p21).

Horse Fair The main street in Rugeley.

Horsefair Open space in Eastgate Street, Stafford, in the C17. The space later became known as Pitcher Bank from the crockery market here in the C19 (VCH vol 6 p188).

Horsehills Farmhouse at Merridale, Wolverhampton, where Sir Rowland Hill spent his youth in 1800-3. The site is now occupied by flats in Horsehills Drive (TB July 1993 p4).

Horse Holme Island in the Trent at the southern end of the Isle of Andressey, opposite Stapenhill gardens (HOBTU p9). Formerly in Stapenhill township in Burton ancient parish. The name means 'Horsa's holm (island)' (1884 OS map 6 inch) (HOBTU p9).

Horseley Field Open field which lay to the E of Wolverhampton prior to enclosure (SHOS vol 2 p165) (HOWM p44). An Ice Age glacial boulder found at Cornhill, Horseley Fields, in 1904 went to East Park (WJO Nov 1909 p293). The name is a corruption of Horse Low (see) (SHOS vol 2 p150).

Horseley Field Industrial suburb of Wolverhampton 0.75m ESE of St Peter's church. The name is from the open field called Horseley Field which formerly lay in this area (WOLOP p14). The lock-making firm of Chubb opened a factory in the old workhouse at Horseley Field in 1841. The workhouse had been built in 1700 (WOLOP pp68,122). The area about Commercial Road

and Walsall Street had become a red light district for Wolverhampton by the 1990s.

Horseley Fields Junction Horseley Field, Wolverhampton. Junction of the Birmingham Main Line Canal with the Wyrley & Essington Canal (Canals of the West Midlands. Charles Hadfield. vol 5 of Canals of The British Isles. see map pp66-67) (SWY p9).

Horseley Hall A hall at Tipton on the site of Horseley Hall was standing in the C16. Here Joseph Amphlett reputedly died on Jan 1 1801 of fright after seeing a ghost on the staircase. It was also the seat of John Turton Fereday, who has this old rhyme associated with him - 'Fereday was not long there, could not abide the haunted stair.....' The hall was demolished in c1820 due to mining subsidence and its fine staircase conveyed to Ellowes Hall. A remnant of the drive was still to be seen facing Tipton Cemetery. Has also appeared as Dixon's Hall (HOTIP p185) (TB Oct 1986 p5). The hall can probably be identified with Horseley House; there is a memorial to Joseph Amphlett (d1801) and other Amphletts of Horseley House between the late C18 and the later C19 in St Edmund's church, Dudley.

Horseley Heath (locally 'Osley BCM Spring 2000 p71). Black Country district 1m E of West Street, Tipton, and a ward of Tipton borough. In Tipton ancient parish (W p708). A 'Ph'o de Horseleye' occurs in 1327 and 1332 (HOTIP p15). Has appeared as Horseley (Plot's map). Had deposits of potter's clay which was extracted for common ware (OH p68). Ben Boucher 'The Dudley Poet and Rhymist' was born at Horseley Heath in 1769. Formerly a miner, he moved to Dudley and resided there maintaining himself by selling his own poems at one penny each. Of him it was written

'Oh rare Ben Boucher - Boucher Ben
The best of Poets - the worst of men.'

(TB June 1978 p18il). He died in Dudley workhouse in 1851 (HOTIP p195) (PSS pp115-118) (VFC p16).

Horse Low Horseley Field, Wolverhampton. A burial mound supposedly containing a dead warrior or warriors of the battle of Wednesbury in 592, which resulted in the driving out of Ceawlin (king of Wessex), or the battle of Wednesbury 715 between the kings of Wessex and Mercia, or the battle of Wednesfield or Tettenhall in 910. The name was gradually corrupted from Horslowe Field to Horsehull Field to now Horseley Field (WFW p23). Shaw says that he could not see the burial mound owing to coal works being on the site (SHOS vol 2 p150). (SVS p332) (AOW pp7,10; Huntbach and Duignan mention it).

Horse Well A well for horses in Wolverhampton which arose from a spring at the back of Cock Inn in Townwell Fold. All the wells here, including the Meat Well for washing meat and the Washing Well for washing, were later collectively called the Town Well's (W p76).

Horsey Lane In Longdon parish (W p568). Horsey Lane Farm is 1.25m WSW of Longdon.

Horsley Fragmented tiny hamlet on ground rising out of the Sow valley, one house is called Little Horsley, another Horsley Farm 1m SW of Eccleshall. Former township and quarter in Eccleshall ancient parish (W p379). The name means Horsa's farm (MR p247). According to Chetwynd Horsley belonged to Peshall (Pershall) prebend, a prebend in Lichfield cathedral (SHC 1914 p51). At Horsley Hall was possibly a medieval village (SSAHST 1970 p35). Harwood (SOS p101) identified Horsley with DB Dorslow (see) (SHC 1923 pp32-35).

Horsley Hall Hall 1m SW of Eccleshall. Built in 1883. It is not on the site of the old hall, which was where Horsley Farm now stands (EOP p40p). In 1895 Horsley Hall belonged to Rev John Clegg (SHC 1914 p51 note). During WW2 the hall was used by the RAF (EOP p40). Subsequently it became a boarding school; the headmaster achieved national notoriety in the 1940s and 1950s (local info).

Horsley Old Hall Stood where Horsley Farm now stands, 0.5m WSW of Horsley Hall. The hall, which had been built by the end of the C15, was the seat of a cadet branch of the Peshall or Pershall family of Weston-in-the-Hedge. In 1611 Sir Thomas Peshall replaced the hall after it had been destroyed by fire with Sugnall Old Hall (see) (COI p39) (ROT p21).

Horsley Park A deer park belonging to the Pershalls in the mid C17 (EDP p179).

Horsley's Stone A boulder by Combes Brook and Buttermilk Spring in Combes Valley. The name means probably either 'old stone in the clearing' or 'boundary stone in the clearing.' However, according to tradition, brothers, one a lawyer and one a doctor, fell in love with their young housekeeper and one called Horsley or Hawkesley killed his brother by this stone in a jealous rage (SMM pp40,42). Some say the lawyer poisoned his brother the doctor (SMCC p8), and to hide his crime he threw down a stone to conceal him. Others say the stone was just used to execute captives of war on (TOI pp163-164). The valley is haunted by one of the brothers (the lawyer - VBB p23 il), his ghost is called 'Horsley's Ghost' and emanates from the stone in the form of a bird which sings melancholy songs. To lay the ghost a clergyman held the stone on end and then let it fall on the ghost when the service was finished. As the stone seems to be 10 or 15 tons, wrote Rev Bright, it seems improbable that one man could hold it on end. Prior to the 1930s some masons refused to cut up the stone, further than taking a piece off the top, for a landowner in the district, because either the stone was too hard to cut, or on superstitious grounds (TOI pp163-164). (FLJ 1941 p237) (GLS pp19-20). By 1994 the stone had been broken in two; a large section remained on the N bank of Combes Brook, whilst a small section lay in the brook (SMM p39p).

Horton Small village on the 'heel' of a narrow hill-spur (SSE 1996 p21) above Horton Brook, 21.75m N of Stafford. About 0.25m E of the church is a sulphur **well** mixed with vitriol (NHS p105). The type derived from the **Cro-Magnons**, who originated in N Africa and came to live in the Cloud area prior to 2000 BC, are said to still persist in the Horton district (NSFCT 1946 p148). Erdeswick thought Horton appeared in DB as Hortbury, but this was a misreading for Nortberie (SOS p367 note); others have thought it appears in DB as Halstone (SHC 1916 p167-168) (HHHL p97), but that place has been identified with Haughton. The 'Hortone' that does appear in DB is Horton near Tamhorn. Horton near Leek has appeared as Horton (1239), and Horton (1252) (SPN p65) (SSE 1996 p14). The **name** means 'the dirty enclosure' (SSAHST 1967 p34). Or 'farmstead on muddy ground' (SPN p65). Or possibly 'muddy tun' (SSE 1996 p14). Horton was a manor by the mid C12. In the C13 the manor included Bagnall, Endon, Horton, Longsdon, Stanley and Rushton James (VCH vol 7 pp70,80). Horton was perhaps a separate ancient parish, but was probably at an early period a chapel in Leek ancient parish. It became a separate civil parish early, and had become a separate ecclesiastical parish by at least 1745 (GLAUE p414). The **church**, St Michael, on the E side of Tollgate Road in the village centre, probably stands on the site of a chapel which was at Horton by the 1220s (VCH vol 7 p75). After the change of calendar in 1752 Horton parish wake took place on the nearest Sunday to Old Michaelmas day (W p748). It was still held in the early C20 (VCH vol 7 p68). In 1484 there was a dispute among the parishioners about seating arrangements in the church, so much so that Hugh Egerton of Wall Grange assembled the parishioners to prove by ancient custom where each person ought to sit for the messuage he occupied and with the joint consent of the parishioners at that time assembled, nominated, and appointed nine persons to settle the seats (NSFCT 1932 pp34-35). There is a legend, still (1997) current in the village, that the font in Horton church was damaged by parliament soldiers during the Civil War; an old repair to it may give some validity to the story (HHHL p22). A stone enclosure which stood E of Horton church in 1991 was probably once used as a pinfold (VCH vol 7 p74). **Persons and visitors. John Best** of Horton parish lived to at least the age of 104 when he married a woman of 56 and had a son by her (NHS pp269,324). **James Heath** (1757-1834), historical engraver from 1794 to George III and his successors, was born in Horton parish (VCH vol 7 p68). **James Bostock** of Horton joined Wombwell's Circus when it visited Leek in 1839. He married George Wombwell's niece and managed the company from 1867, and was succeeded by his son Edward, who became known as 'the British Barnum' (VCH vol 7 p149). **Samuel Broster** was the author of 'The life and adventures of Samuel Broster, a native of Horton, Staffs' 1825.

Horton Appears in DB as Hortone. From Old English, meaning a settlement on muddy ground (VCH vol 14 p240). Horton formed a township with Tamhorn in St Michael's parish, Lichfield by the late C13. Horton village was depopulated in or shortly after the medieval period. Its site was believed to be 'near Tamhorn, perhaps in Fisherwick' but it has been located to not far away in the present Hademore area, at SK 174081 (SSAHST 1970 p35) (DB Notes) (VCH vol 14 p240).

Horton Brook Runs to Endon Brook, which is a tributary of the Churnet. Some believed the lower reaches of it were part of the old course of the Churnet (NSFCT 1928 pp90-97). Appears as Horton Brook on 1837 OS map (SPNO p11).

Horton Gap A dry valley running near the S end of Rudyard Reservoir to a point S of Horton. Many believe that the old course of the Churnet passed through it (Geology of the North Staffordshire Coalfield 1905 p7) (NSFCT 1928 pp90,93).

Horton Hall Stands NW of Horton church (W p748). The former hall on the site of the present appears to have been owned by the Edge (or del Each or del Egge) family from 1338 (HHHL p17). According to the manuscript 'Family

of Edge with notes' in WSL the present stone hall was built by an Edge descendent, Richard Edge (d1592) or by his grandson Richard (d1647) (NSFCT 1932 p33) (RL pp5,10p c1925) (HHHL p17). The hall was owned by the Edge family to 1720 when it was sold to John Alsop (HHHL p17). He left it to John Hough, who left it to his daughter, Elizabeth (HOLS), the niece of John Alsop's wife: some believe it passed directly from Alsop to Elizabeth (HHHL) (VCH vol 7 p71). By Elizabeth's marriage to Henry Fowler it passed to the Fowlers until the death of John Fowler in 1827. It then passed to his only child, Phoebe Elizabeth Hough Fowler, and through her marriage to FitzJames Watt it passed to the Watt family. During the C19 and in the early C20 it had many tenants. In 1917 after the death of Arthur Fowler Watt in 1915 the Horton Hall estate was sold. In 1918 it was purchased by Robert Hall. In 1948 his widow sold it to George Methuen Greaves who sold it in 1951 to JF Moxon (d1987), author of HHHL (VCH vol 7 p71 pl 26 view of from the SE in 1844) (HHHL pp82-87) (info Michael Cockin). In 1991 Moxon's widow sold the hall jointly to Ernest Warrillow, author of HOE and SHST, and his daughter, Christine, and her husband, Philip Cooklin (ES Jan 3 1995 p8p) (VCH vol 7 p71). Another account says the hall was some time the seat of the Condlyffes, Debanks, and Devilles (NSFCT 1870 p37). A datestone or lintel in the garden wall suggests the hall was rebuilt in the C17 (DoE). There is a stone gate with a lintel inscribed with the date '1668' (HHHL p16p).

Horton Hay or Common. Former woodland pasture said to have covered the NW quarter of Horton parish, and covered the Shirkley Hall and Broadmeadows area. The hay was enclosed by a fence in the early C15. The fence gives its name to Rails Farm (see) on the W side (VCH vol 7 p67). The hay was an estate owned in the C16 and C17 by the Biddulphs of Biddulph and later by the Kynnersleys, and the chief house of it at that time was the Dairy House (see) (Plot's map) (Bowen's map) (VCH vol 7 pp66 see map, 67, 71). Horton Hay had a reputation for longevity in the later C17. Plot noted four generations of the Stanton family living together here; four generations alive at the same time was a rare occurrence in the C17. There were four buried here (perhaps Horton is meant) whose ages computed to 320 years (NHS p329). The hay was divided into farms in the later C17 (VCH vol 7 pp67,72), or was enclosed in c1815 (W p748). With Horton village the hay formed one of the two townships in Horton parish by 1803 (W p748) (VCH vol 7 p74).

Horton Head Farm On S side of Horton village, in Horton ancient parish. Is of C18 origin (VCH vol 7 p65).

Horton Lodge N of Rudyard village. Built by Stephen Chesters-Thompson, a Manchester businessman, in 1890. Purchased by William Anthony Marsden Tellwright of Wolstanton, owner of the Sneyd collieries, in 1894. Was the North Staffs Collieries Owners' Association convalescent home from 1925 to 1948 (VCH vol 7 p68) (RL pp43,51p,95).

Horton Manor House Horton ancient parish. Medieval manor house of Horton manor. It was probably occupied in 1308 by a tenant named Adam de la Halle (VCH vol 7 p70).

Horton Park A medieval deer park at Horton enclosed out of forest. In existence by 1411 (NSJFS 1962 p76).

Hostage Lane In the vicinity of Gun Hill, Leek. The name suggests a battle took place in the vicinity whether between the Saxons and the Britons, or a skirmish in the Civil Wars, or the Jacobite Rebellion of 1745? (SK p196).

Hothill The name is preserved in Hothill Lane and Hothill Farm which lies 1m S of Church Leigh.

Hot Lane Former 'cottage settlement' 0.5m SE of the centre of Burslem. Formerly in Burslem chapelry in Stoke-upon-Trent ancient parish. Appears as Whatt Lane in 1631 (SASR 1987 p104). The name is a corruption of Hut Lane or Out Lane (NSSG p10). By the late 1990s there was an industrial estate in Hot Lane (Business Directory. City of Stoke-on-Trent. 1997/8).

Hot Lane Brook Runs at junction of Elder Road and Hot Lane, Burslem (VCH vol 8 p109).

Hough House (Farm) 0.25m S of Haughton. Brough (W p442). A house opposite is called The Black Hough.

Hough, The Just S of Pershall, Eccleshall. In Eccleshall ancient parish. It was a farm anciently belonging to the bishop of Lichfield, but which for centuries has been held on permanent lease by the family of Blest, or had belonged to the Blests of Pershall (see) and came into the hands of the Blests of the Hough in the late C17 (ECC p44). At the head of whose lease or indenture is the following couplet:

> While the ivy is green and the holly is rough
> This is a lease for the Blest of the Hough.

(W p374) (HOP p13) (SCSF p167). Or the last line could read:

There always shall be a Blest of the Hough.

(BPS p108 note). (S&W p567) (NSFCT 1916 p57). A photograph of the rushlight stand and fire-screen at the Hough was shown to a meeting of the Folklore Society on March 16 1904 by W Wells Bladen (FLJ 1904 p130).

Hough, The Former hamlet on the Lichfield Road, S of Forebridge Villa, Stafford, in Castle Church ancient parish. Has appeared as Le haugh (1358), le halgh (1401), the Houghes (1643) (SPNO p77). In a cottage here, William Horton (d1832), boot and shoe manufacturing pioneer, was born in 1750 (SAC pp141 plan of Hough area,142). St Paul's church in Lichfield Road was opened in 1844 and 'the little suburb of the Hough' grew up along the road about then (HOSCC p94) (VCH vol 6 p194).

Hough House Two-storey, stucco villa at The Hough, Stafford. Occupied by JH Webb from 1841 and continued as a Webb residence until being sold to Siemens Bros, the electrical company, who built a factory on the site, opened in 1903 (SAC pp142p,143-145).

Hough Brook To E of Alton. Marked on Pigot & Son map 1830.

Hough Hill Road that runs northwards to Hill Top and Lask Edge from the old Newcastle-Leek turnpike road. The road reaches a gradient of one in nine. It probably takes its name from the old farmhouse named Fernyhough which is situated at the top of the hill (BEH p31).

Hough Wall Between Audley and Miles Green. The name is preserved in Hougher Wall Road. Parrott used the word 'wall' in 1733 when he called it Haughawall. Has also appeared as Haugher Wall and became Hougher (AHJ 1997 p96). A 'hough' is a knoll or hill. 'Wall' is a corruption of well (AOPP pl 24).

Houghwood, Bottom, House, Top To NW of Bagnall. Bagnall villagers have reputedly seen a funeral procession at night go through the wood. The mourners were said to be famine-stricken Scotchmen of the Pretender's army in the 1745 Jacobite Rebellion (ROS vol 1 pp147-153).

Hound Hill Hill 321 feet high, and former estate 0.25m SSE of Marchington church. Formerly in Marchington township and chapelry in Hanbury ancient parish (W p561). A tiny seam of gypsum outcrop has been found here (VCH vol 2 pp197,198). According to Hollinshead a battle took place here on the day of St Ryce (or Brice?) (Nov 13) 1002 (1012 - HOU pp337-338) between the Saxons and the Danes, the Danes were massacred. Some say the battle was carried out in secret. Some say it took place at Wellowyn, Hertfordshire. (UTR p26) (SOSH p70) (KNS p117) (STM Nov 1966 p30p) (HOA p18). The name has appeared as Hunhyle (C13) (SSE 1996 p14), Hownehill, Hogenhull, Howenhull, and Hounhill (SHOS vol 1 p46). The name represents 'Hund's hill,' or 'Hoga's hill;' 'Hoga' means 'the prudent' (DUIGNAN) (SSE 1996 p14). Possibly from Anglo-Saxon 'hund' (a hound) used as a nickname for a man (SPN p83) (SSE 1996 p14). Or from the old hill root 'onn' (NSFCT 1922 p171). The manor was held by the Houndhill family from the 1230s to the 1330s when it fragmented; subsequently parts were held by the de Hanburys, Shailes, and Hills. The whole manor appears to have been held by the Vernons from 1514 to at least the late C18 (SHOS vol 1 pp85-88). An ancient bronze key was found here (HOU pp337-338). There is a rhyme which is a play on the place names Marchington and Hound Hill:-

Don't let us lie like hounds upon a hill,
But march into town.

(LTD pp150-151).

Hound Hill Manor House On the E side of Hound Hill. Has fine views of Tutbury Castle to the E. The moat of a probable former manor house of Hound Hill manor was evident in fields adjoining Hound Hill Manor House in the late C18. In 1635 Sir Edward Vernon, lord of Hound Hill, purchased from Matthew Craddock of Caverswall Castle, the manor house, then commonly known as Houndhill Old Hall. By marriage the same Sir Edward Vernon reunited the Vernon families of Sudbury Hall (Derbys) and Hilton Hall (Staffs). The Vernons were still lords of Hound Hill at the end of the C18, by when Hound Hill Manor House had been modernised and added to (SHOS vol 1 p88). Another account has the manor house being largely rebuilt in c1680 so that Lord Vernon could reside here while extensive rebuilding was going on at his main residence, Sudbury Hall, Derbys. It has been said the house was sold by the Vernons after WW1 to repay gambling debts (AUOPP p79p).

House-in-the-Rocks Rock by the A53 NE of Blue Hills. By this house is carved on a stone the Grindley family tree (UHAW p51 il).

'House that Jack Built' Compton Road, Tettenhall. Seat of Samuel Loveridge, ironfounder. It is believed one owner of the house fired cannons off the roof

during the Napoleonic wars (Wolverhampton Chronicle Nov 7 1997 p18).

Howard Hall A residence at Yarnfield built in c1938 for workers, relocated from Woolwich Arsenal, at the new Royal Ordnance factory at Swynnerton, under 2m SSE of Swynnerton. The hall was never used by them, instead they preferred to live in the Potteries. The hall was occupied by the US Air Force in WW2 (MOSP p28). Named after Admiral Howard. In the 1980s the site was a BT training centre and an housing estate.

Howitt Place Balance Street, Uttoxeter. Childhood home of author Mary Howitt (Official Uttoxeter Town Guide. 1993. p32).

Huddale House and a small dale on SE side of Milk Hill, E of Cauldon. An early deviation of the Leek Ashbourne turnpike road passed this way (NSFCT 1948 p42). The Young Pretender's army passed through Huddale on Dec 4 1745 in the Jacobite Rebellion (BPCSM p7).

Huddlesford Tiny hamlet 0.75m NNW of Whittington. In Whittington ancient parish.

Huddocks Moor House and boggy upland, NW of Pelsall Wood, E of Fishley Charity Farm. Here is the source of Wash Brook. The charter of Pelsall's bounds of 994 describes the great 'mor' or marsh on the north western corner of the township (SNBP p84). Not marked on OS map 1834. Appears in the 1843 tithe apportionment, fields in this area are named 'The Hullocks' and 'Little Hullocks.' 'Hurrock's Moor' appears in the 1891 census (SNBP p84).

Hug Bridge Carries the Leek Macclesfield road (A523) over the Dane, 1m N of Rushton Spencer church. The bridge was known as Hug Bridge by the early C13 (NSFCT 1932 pp51-52) (VCH vol 7 p224) when it gave its name to the manor, later known as Rushton Spencer (SSE 1993 p2) (VCH vol 7 p224). Hug is derived from Hugh Despencer, so originally - Hugh's Bridge (DP pp8-9p). Or probably from Hugo de Mara and named following the Norman conquest (DVOPP p12p). The bridge was wooden in 1620 when it was destroyed by a flood. It was rebuilt in stone in 1622, although the Staffordshire side remained in wood and was not as extensively rebuilt as the Cheshire part (DP pp8-9p). In 1624 Rushton Spencer township appealed for a grant from the Staffs justices to have their side of the bridge built in stone (VCH vol 2 p280). The present bridge is of the C18 and the early C19 (VCH vol 7 p224). (MR p272).

Hulland Former district at SO 910874, in the Pheasant Street area. In Kingswinford ancient parish (BCM spring 1995 p27). The name appears as Holland on Fowler's map (1822) (1834, 1887 OS maps) (SNSV vol 1 p259) and as Hulland on the 1947 OS map 1:25,000 (sheet 32/98). There is no longer an area of Hulland and this area is now known as Brockmoor (WFK pp11,25).

Hullock's Pool House and former estate under 1m NNE of Audley in Eardley End township of Audley ancient parish. Appears as Whillocks Pooll in 1733 (SHC 1944 p51).

Hulme, The Is a small area 0.5m WNW of Alton, centred on Holme Cottage. Here is Holm Farm and Holm Road and Hulme Springs. 'Holm' is of Danish origin and it is likely that the Danes or Norsemen settled here (HAF p38).

Hulme Small village on the northern flank of the Park Hall Hills under 1m SSW of Werrington. In Caverswall ancient parish, formed a manor with Weston Coyney (W p752). Has appeared as Hulme (1227), Hulm or Holm sub Kevermund (see Kenermont Hay) (after 1227) (SPN p65), and Nether Holme and Over Holme (Plot's map). Hulme is of Scandinavian origin (SDW p11). In Old Danish 'hulm' means 'piece of land by a stream' (SPN p65).

Hulmedale Farm over 0.5m SSE of Werrington. In Caverswall ancient parish. George Brandreth, champion pugilist fighter of the Potteries, was born at Hulme Dale (WJ p26).

Hulme End Small moorland hamlet by the Manifold over 1m ENE of Warslow. The original settlement, in existence by 1775, lay in Sheen ancient parish but had spread over the Manifold into Fawfieldhead township in Alstonefield ancient parish by the early C19 (W pp743,787) (VCH vol 7 pp28, 242). There was a mound at Hulme End excavated by Carrington in 1849 and built over with a cottage (TYD p150) (NSJFS 1965 p32). Near Hulme End at SK 10635878 is an irregular mound. Its diameter in paces is NS 17 and EW 13 (NSJFS 1965 p32). A Roman coin of Severus, said to be part of a hoard, was found at SK 10415934 c1919 (Leek Post and Times Feb 2 1961) (NSFCT 1964 p22). Appears in 1246 as Hulme (SSE 1996 p15). A slight mound in a an enclosure beneath a yew tree near the junction of the Sheen and Hartington roads at SJ 108593 is said to be the burial place of John Bonsall who died in c1770, and who wished to be buried on his own land (VB p205) (HLSP p85). The Warslow-Hartington road was turnpiked in 1770 and realigned to pass to the N through Hulme End (VCH vol 7 p242). Here was the northern end of the line of the Manifold Valley Light Railway, which opened in 1904 and closed in 1934. The booking office and engine shed still remain (PDS&C p90p pl 154) (ES Oct 5 1992 p8p).

Hulton Abbey The abbey stood on a shelf of land above the upper Trent over 0.5m SSE of Milton, off Woodhead Road and by Carmountside County Primary School.

ABBEY. It was a Cistercian house founded by Henry de Aldithley (or Audley), builder of Heighley Castle (see). A charter, with the seal of Henry de Audithley attached and dated 1223 (VCH vol 3 pp235-237), at Trentham Hall in the C17 and early C18, purported to be the original foundation charter, but may have been a C16 forgery: Walter Chetwynd, Sir William Dugdale and Rev Thomas Loxdale saw and made copies of it (SSE 1994 pp75-84). An abbreviated version appeared in Bishop Thomas Tanner's 'Notitia Monastica' (1744) p501 (SH p81) (SSE 1994 p75). A two volume cartulary purporting to be the cartulary of Hulton Abbey, or a part of it, was said to be in existence in the later C19. It has come to be known as the Hulton Abbey Ms. Members of the Sneyd family had seen it. It was claimed that the cartulary had been plundered from Keele Hall by Capt Barbour in the Civil War and kept in his family until the C19 when it was shown to the Sneyds. Apart from photographic snippets no other person saw the cartulary and it probably never existed (SSE 1994 pp84-99). Hulton Abbey was the poorest of the three Staffs Cistercian houses. The abbey surrendered on Sept 18 1538 (VCH vol 3 pp235-237). Has also appeared as Hilton Abbey (SMC pp194-200).

AFTER THE DISSOLUTION. The abbey lands were granted to Sir Edward Aston of Tixall (HSP p135). In 1611 Aston, who had run into debt, sold the abbey estate to Ralph Sneyd of Keele (SASR 1985 p69) (SSE 1994 pp85,89,91). By 1610 maps of the area show a large house on or near the abbey site (SASR 1985 p69). Carmountside Farm (see) or Carmount Farm was built over the site of the E end of the conventual church in 1848 (SSE 1994 p96) or in 1856 (VCH vol 8 p250), during the construction of which bodies of several monks were discovered (SSE 1994 p96). During the following years there was probably considerable utilisation of the stonework of the abbey buildings. According to tradition some stones were used in **Abbey Farm** (see). An ivory crucifix in the RC church at **Abbey Hulton** is said to come from the abbey (SASR 1985 p78 pl 46). Stones from the abbey may have lined the original cellar of **Brookhouse**, a Tudor timber framed house formerly at Bucknall now at Knighton (NSFCT 1988 p45). Some stones are said to have been used in the building of **Bucknall** church (1718. Rebuilt 1841) and Church Farm, situated below Bucknall church; it was demolished in 1935 (Staffordshire Sentinel summer number 1910 pp5-7) (LGS p188) (SASR 1985 p77). Five 'millstone grit' carvings in the garden of a house in High Street, Bucknall were thought to have come from the abbey (ES Oct 1931), but are believed to date from the C19 (SASR 1985 p77). A coffin to the S of St John's church, **Burslem**, traditionally associated with Elizabeth (d1400), wife of Nicholas, 3rd Lord Audley, is said to have come from the abbey church (Complete Peerage) (AGT p82) (SASR 1985 p78). A stone found during excavations on the site of Swan Bank Methodist Church in Burslem in 1970 is thought to have come from the abbey (SASR 1985 p32). Some stones reputedly were used in the building of **Caldon Canal** and **Endon Hall** (see). By tradition **Wetley Abbey** (see) incorporates masonry from the abbey. Yet by the C18 there were still ruins of the abbey to be seen above ground on the site (UDC vol 1 p69).

EXCAVATIONS AT THE ABBEY SITE. An excavation of the abbey site occurred in 1884, as a result of the accidental discovery of the ruined buildings by workmen improving the land drainage at Carmountside Farm (SASR 1985 p1). The excavation was led by Charles Lynam of Colwich. In 1884 the landowner, Rev Walter Sneyd, took a great number of incised coffin lids and other relics to Keele Hall. At Keele he constructed an ornamental amphitheatre out of some of them, but these were returned to the abbey site in c1950 (NSFCT 1885 pp29-30, 98-102. 1887 pp39-40) (HOL pp96,97p) (NSFCT 1950 p85) (SASR 1985 p31). The coffin lids were not in their origin positions, but were forming the bottom of a drain (LGS p188). The abbey site was visited by the British Archaeology Society during their meeting in Stoke for their 52nd Congress Aug 1895 (SK pp194-195). A second excavation occurred in the early 1930s. On Oct 14 1930 a small hollowed tree trunk thought to have been a log boat was found by men laying a sewer in the meadows behind the Sneyd Arms Inn (ES June 12 1931 p6p) (NSFCT vol 65 p156. vol 66 p190. 1930 pp156-7) (AJ vol 11 p162) (NSJFS 1964 p36) (SASR 1985 p54). It was probably used by the monks for fishing (ES July 28 1930 p4. Oct 14 1930 p1p. Oct 16 1930 p6p. Jan 9 p7p). It is now in the Potteries Museum (STM April 1963 p29p). Alterations to nearby Carmountside school in 1959 allowed for excavation of the abbey's domestic buildings (NSFCT 1959 p88). (DoE II - the Abbey Farmhouse) (SOS p16 noted by Harwood) (GNHSS p19) (UDC Book I. pp63-72) (NSFCT 1885 pp29,30. 1950-51 pp84,85. 1959-60 pp84-90) (R vol 25 pp113-116) (SS summer number June 1905 p46) (MOS pp110,111) (LGS pp37,155) (KES p10) (SOSH pp111,281-

282) (KNS pp131,132) (The Weekly Sentinel April 5 1930) (NSFCT 1930 pp149-156. 1931 p190) (Stoke-on-Trent Bi-Monthly Review May 1952) (ES 27 Sept 1968 p15p) (HBST pp288-296) (BOE p266) (SL pp72,73,95) (BALH p23) (WYV pp12,13 Plan of the abbey site, showing the secret passage the authoress says she went through as a child) (ES July 17 1992 p8). Scheduled as an Ancient Monument in 1963. From 1959 to 1964 the E end of the abbey church was excavated (NSJFS 1968 p117). Excavations in 1964 were made on the site of the southern range of domestic buildings (NSJFS 1965 p121). In 1967 the N chapel altar of the S transept (NSJFS 1968 p117). A new series of excavations were conducted in the abbey church between 1972 and 1983 during which 22 skeletons, a C13 gold and sapphire ring (now in the Potteries Museum), and a papal bulla of Innocent VI, were found (1352-62) (NSFCT 1975 p34) (SASR 1985 p1).

TRADITIONS ASSOCIATED WITH THE ABBEY. Hulton Vale is said to be haunted by the ghost of a monk called Robert of Hulton Abbey who made a pact with the devil in return for power and fame. Shortly after this pact was made Robert heard that he had been appointed abbot. He was then so filled with remorse for his thoughts that he went to a hermit at Bagnall for repentance. The hermit admonished him and advised him to return to the abbey to resume his duties; by properly performing them and leading a sinless life he would finally escape the influence of the devil; however, his ghost was condemned to wander the vale for a thousand years before he could enter heaven (SS summer number 1910 pp11-12) (FOS p21) (SASR 1985 p78). There is a tradition of a tunnel from Ubberley Hall to Hulton Abbey (BUB p3).

Hulton Abbey Park Between Bucknall and Bucknall Hospital. Opened in 1956 (TSS p130).

Hulton Manor House Abbey Hulton. Presumably where the lord of Hulton manor, Ralph Sneyd, was living in 1615 when he was described as of Hulton. The house, which evidently stood near the site of Hulton Abbey, was of some size in 1682; it appears on the maps of Plot and Morden. It was still in existence in the mid C18 ((VCH vol 8 p249).

Hulton Vale Appears to be that part of the upper Trent valley near Hulton Abbey (see) (SS summer number 1910 pp11-12).

Humesford Brook From Coton Wood, near Gnosall, runs into Aqualate Mere then to the Meece.

Hundred Acre Wood Former wood to the W of the Chester Road, Streetly, Great Barr, planted by local land owners on the former Great Barr Common after the Enclosure Acts. In 1884 the Birmingham Small Arms Company bought the area for a factory for making weapons and ammunition and an area for a firing range. A few houses on Aldridge Road at 07599680 were built for the factory workers, they are called Ammunition Cottages and still (1996) exist. The small church-like building on the opposite side of the road at SP 07429685 may be the iron chapel that is referred to as being built in 1892. It subsequently became a school for factory workers' children. It is still often referred to as the 'tin tabernacle.' It has for many years been used a small printing works. The rest of Hundred Acre Wood became an housing estate after being purchased in 1959 (SNAR pp87,88p of the 'tin tabernacle',96).

Hungary Hill Farm nearly 1.5m SE of Bishop's Wood, in Brewood ancient parish. The name means 'hill with poor soil' (SPN p23). For Hungary Hill in a local rhyme see Brewood.

Hungerford House Farm to E of Madeley. Probably Hungerford from the Hungerford family who married into the Crewe family. The Hon Miss Annabel Hungerford Crewe was resident at Madeley Manor in the mid C19 (W p396).

Hunger Heath The name appears on the 1834 OS map. Hungerheath Farm is 1.25m N of Ashley.

Hunger Hill Small hill 315 feet high over 0.5m SW of Hamstall Ridware. In Hamstall Ridware parish.

Hunger Hill Gate Junction of Eaves Lane and Greasley Road, Abbey Hulton (OS map 1834). The name is not preserved.

Hunger Moor Slade Whittington, near Lichfield. In the church field not far from the Whittington well, noted Plot in the late C17, in a piece of ground called Hunger Moore Slade, is a spring that only flows in times of great dearth (NHS p47) (SHOS vol 1 p377).

Hungershutt Common in Ashley ancient parish which was being enclosed in 1817 (THS p327), and by 1851 was a hamlet (W p384). It probably can be identified with Hunger Heath (see).

Hunger Wall A spring which Plot was shown by Rev John Paston of Himley near Ashwood Bridge, Kingswinford situated by a small lake. It foretold a dearth in corn if it ran, and when it ran it made a noise which frightened people, once scaring off some rabbit poachers (NHS pp47-48) (SHOS vol 2 p233) (SMC p141).

Hungryhill On the W side of the Severn. Over 0.5m W of Arley. The name is preserved in Hungryhill Cottage. Marked on OS map 1:25,000.

Hungry Leas Former barren land in part of outer Wolverhampton, but once having been put to cultivation, says Shaw, became Upper and Lower Broadmeadows and Whitmore-ends (SHOS vol 2 p165).

Hungry Pool A small marshy pool at Billingham near Stafford, situated below Berry Ring. It predicted, noted Plot in the late C17, a scarcity of corn, if it rose there was going to be a drought if it did not there had been heavy rain. The local people had set up sticks in the pool which helped them judge the rise and fall of corn in the markets (NHS pp46-47). Has also appeared as Hungry Pit.

Huntbach Former hamlet, manor or house in the Eccleshall area. Lay between Acton Hill and Walton (ECC p18). Appears in medieval times as Huntenebache, Huntebache (SSE 1997 p91), and Humpage Green (ECC p18). The name means 'the valley or stream of the huntsmen' (SSE 1997 p91). It was the origin of the Huntbach family of Featherstone and later The Showells (SHOS vol 2 p187) (NSFCT 1949 p62).

Hunters Green Minute hamlet S of and merging with Trysull. Seems to have been formerly Bent Green (see).

Hunter's Lane In Handsworth parish (W p698). There is a Hunter's Road to E of Soho Hill (Birmingham A-Z).

Hunt House Farmhouse 1m N of modern Rudyard village on E side of Rudyard Lake. Formerly in Rudyard township in Leek ancient parish and stands in the area of old Rudyard hamlet. Has origins dating back to at least 1636, or is on the site of a house dating back to that period (VCH vol 7 p216) (RL p5). Appears as Hunts House on 1834 OS map.

Huntington Village on W-facing slopes running up to the Cannock Chase plateau, 1.75m NNW of Cannock. Former township in Cannock old parish. Huntington has been identified with DB Estendone. Later forms are: Huntendon (1167) (1198), Huntedon (1247), Huntindon (c1255,1272-1322), Huntingdon (1262), Hontindon (1271), Huntydon (1395), Huntyngton (1444), Huntigeton (1623) (SPNO p68) (SPN p66) (SSE 1996 p15). Has its name probably from being frequented formerly by hunters of the forest (SHOS vol 2 p320) (DUIGNAN) (NSJFS 1981 p3). 'The huntsmen's hill' (SSE 1987 p28. 1996 p15) or 'hill of the huntsman' (SPN p66): The village originally grew round a hunting lodge (SVB p99). If from 'Estendone' then may be derived from 'stand-tun' representing the king's stand or standing place when the deer were driven past him in the chase. It may be derived from Eastandun (east down or hill) or from East-end-tun (east end town or homestead) (SHC 1923 pp24-31). Huntington manor was anciently held by the service of keeping the hay of Teddesley in Cannock Forest for the king (VCH vol 5 p76) (M.S. Mus. Brit. temp. Hen. 7) (SMC p122) (SCSF p117). By 1548 there was a chapel dedicated to St Margaret in Cannock parish. It was possibly at Huntington. The site of a former chapel existed W of Huntington Farm but has been obliterated by colliery workings (SHC 1915 p49) (VCH vol 5 pp64,76,77); and is preserved by the field name Chapel Field? (DUIGNAN p82). The village grew in the C19 and C20 on the back of coal mining and is now (1988) overshadowed by the Littleton Colliery winding gear and slag heaps (MR p191p shows a typical drab view). In 1880 SSWWC opened a pumping station at Huntington (GHC p12p). Huntington became a separate civil parish in 1866 (GLAUE p414). The mission church, St Thomas, on the E side of the Stafford Road, was built in 1872.

Huntley Small hamlet in a short dale at the confluence of two brooks which make the Tean 1m NNW of Upper Tean. Former quarter in Cheadle ancient parish. There was a healing well at Huntley similar to that at Rockcliffe, Cheadle (SMM p79). The Rocks is a road cut through rock at Huntley. It was made in 1818 to conform with the Turnpike Act (ACOPP p59p). Huntley Toll Gate House was built then and sold into private hands in 1878 (COPP2 p78p).

Huntley Hall Upper Tean. An earlier hall was the residence of John Bulkeley (d1802) (mem in St Edward the Confessor's church, Leek). A later hall was built for Rear Admiral Clement Sneyd (d1851 or 1854), younger brother of William Sneyd (b1767) of Ashcombe Park (see) in the 1820s (SMOPP vol 1 p44p) (SNEDE) (COPP2 p79p). The Huntley Hall estate was for sale in 1927. The central part of the hall was demolished in 1929 (COPP2 p79) (SMOPP vol 1 p44). The stable block survives and there were plans in 1996 for its conversion into homes (ES March 14 1996 property pages p3p). On the highest point in the grounds was discovered an earthwork in the early C20, perhaps of artificial origin since no stones had been found on the site (NSFCT 1915 pp158-159).

Huntley House Huntley. (Whether the same as Huntley Hall?). The residence of the eccentric Mr Gibbons, who, on seeing a dog run through the churchyard at Cheadle with a bone in its mouth believed it had been taken from a grave and to prevent the same fate happening to his own bones, directed his body to be buried in his own orchard. The property passed to a Mr Holmes of Teanford (HOC p171).

Huntley Wood Wood to W of Huntley. There was a sighting of a UFO in this wood in the week April 29 to May 5 1996 (ES May 7 1996 p9).

Hunt's Farm 0.75m NW of Elmhurst. Dates from early C19, probably on the site of an earlier farm dating from the mid C17. Formed part of the endowment to Dr Milley's Hospital, Lichfield (VCH vol 14 p234).

Hunts Green There was probably settlement at Hunts Green, Handsworth, at the junction of Handsworth Wood Road and Church Lane, by the end of the C13. By the C16 there was probably a small hamlet here (MNB p39). It is marked on maps as late as 1797 (HPPE pp37,62).

Hunt's Mill Gornal. Huntsmill Farm is very ancient (TB Oct Nov 1972 p22p) (TB June 1985 p17).

Hurden Hall On the N side of the Meir Heath-Barlaston road at Hartwell.

Hurdlow House 0.5m E of Upper Hulme. Lay in a detached portion of Bradnop township in Leek ancient parish. Was transferred to Heathylee civil parish in 1934 (VCH vol 7 p31). Hurdlow Farm belonged to Dieulacres Abbey at the end of the Middle Ages (VCH vol 7 p33). Hurd is from Old English 'hord,' treasure, and low from 'hlaw,' a hill or possibly a barrow (burial mound) (VCH vol 7 p33) (PNPD).

Hurst Small hamlet over 1.5m NE of Biddulph town centre.

Hurst There is a Lower Hurst Farm and an Upper Hurst 0.75m ESE of Hulme End.

Hurst Ancient small settlement in Tipton. A 'De Petro atte hurst' appears in 1327 and 1332 (HOTIP p15). The settlement, known as The Hurst in c1815, was on the former Horseley Heath in the present Hurst Lane area (HOTIP p190).

Hurst, The There was a hamlet known as The Hurst in the mid C19 on N side of The Two Lock Canal Line. To the SE on S side of the Two Lock Canal Line was a smaller hamlet known as Lower Hurst (BCM summer 1995 pp26,27 see map).

Hurstfield In Sedgley parish and manor. Plot said the best sort of lime could be found here (SHOS vol 2 p221). Could be in the vicinity of Hurst Hill?

Hurst Hill Hill 705 feet high over 0.5m ENE of Sedgley, in the area of Hursthill Wood. Has the same limestone geology as Wren's Nest Hill to the S (WNNNR p4). A head river of the Tame rises near Hurst Hill (AMS p2).

Hurst Hill Former hamlet situated on Hurst Hill, now a residential district. Hollywell in Hollywell Street at Hurst Hill has been identified with Wulfruna's spring at Coseley (AMS p445) (HC p3). Has appeared as Hurstemore (1272), and Hurst' Hyll (1537) (HC p11). If from Hurstmore, then 'the woody moor' (AMS p441). The **church**, St Mary, N side of Gorge Road, was built in 1872 (BOE p108). By the late C19 the hamlet of Can Lane, nearly 0.5m to the E, had become known as Hurst Hill (HOBLL p175); this is the present residential district of Hurst Hill. The present Hurst Hill also covers the former hamlet of Upper Ettingshall, still a separate hamlet in 1901 (OS map Sheet 67.03). Hurst Hill was made a ward of Coseley urban district in 1912 (HC p71). **Johnny Cornfield's Backside** is the local name for a district just off Hurst Road and Hollywell Street. It is from John Cornfield, 'Coseley's Poet,' see below (TB May 1994 p12). **Persons and visitors. John Wesley** preached at Hurst Hill after 1761 at a house owned by the Harper family which stood on the site of 'Holly Cottage' (HC p59) (AMS p389). **Joseph Darby**, born at Hurst Hill in April 1825, became the village schoolmaster, and was looked upon as the 'Coseley Poet' and composed a poem entitled 'The Primitive Fire' at the camp meetings for Primitive and Wesleyan Methodists that were held in the Coseley area in the C19 (BCM Jan 1985 pp51-52). **John Cornfield** Jnr, born on Oct 1 1820 or in 1827, 'Coseley's Poet,' was for sometime engaged in the brickmaking trade and later became a pawnbroker in the Hurst Hill district. He was active as a radical in local politics, his 'A Round Unvarnished Tale of the Exploits of the Vicar of Sedgley' appeared in 1862 and he was involved in a dispute about tithes with Rev William Lewis, vicar of Sedgley. Cornfield made his name as a poet in the 1870s. His long narrative poem 'Allan Chace and other poems' (1877) is believed to be his best known work. He was found drowned in a pond on his Coseley estate on Dec 6 1890 (BS p121) (HC p91) (PSS pp186-189) (VFC p31) (TB May 1994 p12). The monument at the corner of George Road, Hall Lane, and Hurst Hill is to the memory of Dr **James Baker** (d1913), a benevolent local doctor. It was unveiled in 1914 (TB May 1984 p17p. Nov 1984 p22p) (SDOP p118p).

Hurst Hill Wood On N side of Turls Hill, to the E of Sedgley. Roman coins have been found at Hurst Hill at cSO 933941 (AMS p17) (NSJFS 1964 p20). The quarry here is reputedly haunted by two brothers who shot themselves in it at different times in the late C19 (TB June 1985 pp10-11). Has also appeared as Turls Hill Wood.

Hurst's Cavern Former limestone quarry under Castle Hill, adjoining and on the N side of Dudley Tunnel (Dudley Canal Tunnel leaflet).

Hurt's Wood Became NT property in 1933. It is nearly 50 acres in extent. Perhaps, so called from a Derbys family called Hurt (NSFCT 1933 p187. 1936 p29). The name appears on the 1834 OS map facing Dove Holes in Dove Dale on the Staffs side.

Husphins 0.75m S of Codsall Wood, Codsall. Husphins Farm on the S side of Husphins Lane was inhabited by the earlier C18 (VCH vol 20 p79).

Hussey Hall Very ancient hall, the seat of William Hussey d1230 (HOP p12), near Penkridge. Formerly moated. A house known as Hussey's Hall existed throughout the C16 (VCH vol 5 pp125-126). A depression in a ploughed field about 300 yards S of the old road from Penkridge to Pillaton Green may mark the site (VCH vol 5 p108).

Hyde Former manor probably centred on a manor house at Hyde Lea Mottes (see). About 1140 the manor passed to the Bagots, a junior branch of the House of Stafford (OSST 1951-52 p15). The manor is said to be recorded in DB as The Hyde (NSJFS 1964 p18), but is not identified as a DB entry by John Morris in the Phillimore DB edition 1976. According to Mazzinghi and James Simpson Hyde manor is the anonymous entry in DB listed as the two hides held of Robert de Stafford by Urfer between entries relating to Ridware and Haughton; others have identified the same anonymous entry with a manor at Weston Jones (OSST 1951-52 p16). The manor house at the Hyde is mentioned in 1372. By the beginning of the C16 Hyde manor or estate appears to have lost its separate entity and become a part of Hyde-Coppenhall manor (OSST 1951-52 pp15-16).

Hyde, The Small hamlet 0.5m NNE of Kinver on W side of the Stour. Former township in Kinver ancient parish from 1806; formed a township with Stourton from 1830 (VCH vol 20 p149). Has appeared as Hyde (1199) (SSE 1996 p15) and Hide (SHOS vol 2 p265); and was an inhabited area by 1293 (VCH vol 20 p123). The name means 'hide' or 'estate' or 'farm' (SSE 1996 p15). In c1590 a fulling mill was erected at The Hyde. In 1628 it was taken over by Richard Foley (1580-1657) and rebuilt by him as a slitting mill to serve his ironworks elsewhere. The mill appears to then have contained a mechanical process, first introduced into England by Foley, in which rollers and circular cutter plates driven by water-power converted the bar into rod (VCH vol 2 pp114,115. vol 20 p146). Some have said Foley stole the process from Holland by pretending to be a simpleminded itinerant beggar in order to gain access to mills. Hence he has become known as 'Fiddler Foley,' first appearing as such in Playfair's 'British Family Antiquities' (1809). But there is no evidence that he ever stole his information (BCM April 1988 pp29,53. July 1988 p10) (RKE p31). By the late 1630s the Hyde Mill was worked by Foley's brother-in-law George Brindley of the nearby Hyde House (see). His great grandson, John Brindley, was working the mill in the early C18, when Dr Wilkes noted that at The Hyde was the first mill for rolling and slitting iron erected in England (SHOS vol 2 p265) (VCH vol 20 p146). Some have confused the 'one Brindley' referred to by Dr Wilkes in SHOS vol 2 with 'Fiddler Foley' and his supposed espionage in Holland (W pp177-178). (WJO July 1903 p153). Raven says Walke Mill Ironworks is on the site of it (MR p203) (MIDD vol 2 p41p). Regarding the slitting mill Poulton-Smith mistakes this Hyde for the Brewood Hyde (SPN p22). A late C18 lock-keeper's cottage is still (1982) occupied. In the hillside E of the cottage was a rock house in 1830 (VCH vol 20 p123).

Hyde Farm House 1.75m SW of Brewood. In Brewood ancient parish. Has appeared as la Hide, Hyde (1199), Hyd(a) (1228), Hyde juxta Brewode (1295) (SPNO p38). 'Hide' in Anglo-Saxon means an estate or farm; originally 'as much land as would support one family' necessarily a flexible quantity (DUIGNAN) (SPN pp22,66). The estate and house, anciently The

Hyde, belonged, from the C15, to the Lanes of Bentley (DUIGNAN p82) and later to others and then the Giffards who were holding it in 1956 (VCH vol 5 p34). The farmhouse in 1959 was brick and built in the early C18. A ground-floor room contained reset panelling which incorporates carved medallion heads of the mid C16 and shields bearing the arms of Lane and of Lane impaling Bagot (VCH vol 5 p34). The Hyde was surrounded by a moat (VCH vol 1. vol 5 p34) (CAMS p63) (SSAHST 1982-3 p37). There is a hexagonal red brick late C18 dovecote with a hipped plain tile roof with central louvre, listed grade 2 by DoE.

Hyde House The Hyde, Kinver. An old house on or near this site called Hyde House was occupied by George Brindley, who was working the slitting mill at The Hyde in the later 1630s. The C17 (KEOP p66) or C18 house (VCH vol 20 pp123,146) was renamed 'Bethany' and opened as a home for crippled children by Rev EG Hexall in 1906. The home closed in 1918 and the house was demolished in the 1920s. No trace of it now (1996) remains (VCH vol 20 pp123,146) (KEOP p66ps). A C18 octagonal pigeon house and C18 garden walls from the old house survive (VCH vol 20 p123).

Hyde Lea Small village above the upper reaches of Rising Brook 0.75m N of Coppenhall. In Castle Church parish. Near Hyde Lea was found a Roman coin of Trajan (NSJFS 1964 p18). For the manor of Hyde and its possible appearance in DB see under Hyde. Has appeared as Hida (1224) (SSE 1996 15), Hide (c1255. 1725. 1327), Hyde Lee (1448), Hydecopynhall (1503), manor of Hyde or Hyde-Coppenhall (1628), Hyde ley (Yates' map), Hide ley (1836) (SPNO p75) (SPN p66). Means 'the hide of land, the amount of land for the support of one free family and its dependents (SPNO p75). According to 1834 OS map there is an ancient camp in the centre of Hyde Lea. The village seems to have grown out of squatters encroaching on common land. 'Hyde Lea Common was ringed by small encroachments by 1788' (VCH vol 5 p84).

Hyde Lea Mottes Two moat-like earthworks lying side by side 0.25m NW of the village of Hyde Lea, at SJ 906203 at the confluence of Rising Brook and a lesser stream. The earthworks, which have been called The Hollies, The Mottes, Hyde Lea Moat, and The Moat, are said to have surrounded the manor house of Hyde manor, and have formed fish ponds (ESH pp27,58) (SAC p35 plan). In the early C18 Rev Loxdale referred to the 'ruins of an ancient place called the Hyde, of which nothing is now remaining save the pools and the moat' (NSFCT 1928 p164). Nancy Linley thought the earthworks represented a moated site with an associated mill and mill works and they form one large complex with the moated site called Coppenhall Gorse. The VCH lists Coppenhall Gorse and the Hyde Lea as two separate moats (NSFCT 1982 p21). The two sites - Coppenhall Gorse and Hyde Lea Mottes - have been identified with a residence of a branch of the Bagots, who by marriage, held the Stafford barony from 1194 and assumed the name of Stafford. The last Bagot baron died in 1339. The Bagot name is perpetuated in two fields, near earthworks, called Upper and Lower Bagot's Oak (NSFCT 1944 p94) (HOS p22). It has been said that a Lord Stafford (Ralph, 2nd Lord Stafford, d1372) lived at Hyde manor house during the rebuilding of Stafford Castle at Castle Church in the mid C14 (SVB p100) (SAC p35). These moats were the ones excavated by boys from King Edward VI School, Stafford in the early 1950s (OSST 1951-52 pp15-23) (NSFCT 1982 p19). According to 1834 OS map there is an ancient camp in the centre of Hyde Lea. There is another moated site at SJ 897215, 1.25m NW of Hyde Lea, near Billington (see), and this is thought to have been the site of an early castle of Edward de Stafford (NSFCT 1943 p65).

Hye Moor Barren area to SW of Lichfield W of the London Road, near Longbridge Brook. Recorded as pasture in 1298 (VCH vol 14 p111).

I

Icknield Street There were formerly four Roman roads called this in Britain. The one that relates to Staffs ran N to S through the counties of Gloucester, Worcester, Warwick, Stafford, and Derby. It has appeared as Hickenels Street (1686), Hykenalde Stret (1243), Ikenhildestrete, Ickenell, Ikenild, Ricnelde, Ricnild, Ricning, Rikelinge, Ricknell (1597), Rychnield, Rycknield, Rykenild, Ryknild, Ykenhilde, and Ykenild (SHOS vol 1 General History pp16 note,17) (VCH vol 2 p275) (BTIH p10) (SPN p66) (HOBTU pp2,3). Leland, in c1540, thought it was formerly called Akeman Street, because it led to Bath, which the Saxons called Akemancester, or the 'city of the sick people' (SHOS vol 1 p17 note). Shaw, who noted that neither Ikenild or Rykenild is necessarily the correct spelling, thought that the road may have been made by Oftorius, when he left this part of the country with a guard sufficient to secure it against the enemy, whilst he went to attack the Brigantes (SHOS vol 1 General History pp16,17). Duignan considered Riknield or Ryknild a corruption of Icknield. But Ryknild is used on current OS maps (DUIGNAN pp82-83) (SPN p66). Ickneild Way, Norfolk, and Ikenild Way, Oxon, are thought to be derived from the Iceni tribe, but the tribe had no influence in Staffs (SPN p66). The road entered Staffs in the Handsworth area and crossed the Tame at Holford. It ran through Kings Standing and Sutton Park. It is visible in Little Aston, and is traceable in the Bosses area. It passed close to the Roman station, Letocetum, and SE of Lichfield. The course N from Shenstone follows mainly the later highway. It leaves the county E of Stretton (Burton upon Trent) (VCH vol 14 pp44,276). Locally, the road has appeared as le Stanway (literally 'the stone way'). About Lichfield it was known as Ryknild Street in the mid 1270s and in 1442, but in the C14 and early C15 was called Stony Street, and was called Broadway in the earlier C13 at Streethay (VCH vol 14 pp44,276). Henry III passed along it in 1235 on his way from Burton to Lichfield. The road appears on the Gough Map of c1360 (VCH vol 2 p275 note). A stone marked the supposed site of the intersection of Ryknild Street and Watling Street in 1888 (1888 OS map 6 inch). In 1928 the exact site of the cross roads was discovered (NSFCT 1928 pp147-148) (BAST vol 60 p53) (NSJFS 1964 p34). An examination of the Ryknild Street from Wall to Streethay was made in the 1970s (SSAHST 1977-78 pp1-4). In the museum at Wall there is a fragment of a cylindrical milestone, made of local sandstone, found at Wall. It has been ascribed to the period of Claudius II (268-270). It may have stood on Ryknild Street but there is no proof. In the southern hedge of a field at SK 1060630 is a fragment of another milestone made of local sandstone. It was originally at SK 10590627 and is so marked in large scale OS maps (SSAHST 1977-78 p4). (HOWW p23-24) (SSAHST 1966 pp39-41) (PRT pp29-30).

Idlerocks Minute hamlet 0.5m NE of Moddershall. Formerly Sale Rocks, after Sale Brook. The first two letters had become metamorphosed into 'Id,' as was attested by deeds of various dates (NSFCT 1917 p146). The mansion of this name here was built by Godfrey Wedgwood, a descendant of Josiah Wedgwood I of Etruria Hall (see), in 1888 (WCW p) (SVB p126). Foot-and-mouth disease broke out at Idlerocks Farm, Hilderstone Road, in Dec 1967 (SN Dec 8 1967 p10).

Ilam (*Eye-lam* PNPD). Ancient parish and former township (SASR 1995 no 5 p1). The tiny village of Ilam lies backed by hills on all sides at the entrances to Manifold Valley and Dove Dale, 22m NE of Stafford: An attractive view of the village as it nestles at the foot of Bunster Hill can be seen from the road leading down to it from Blore.
EARLY to 1500. A large bronze spearhead with loops at the base was found in Ilam parish before 1848 (VAD p10) (NSJFS 1964 p26). Garner mentions the discovery of Roman finds at Ilam (GNHS p70). Ilam was identified by Dugdale and Shaw as the Hilum mentioned in the will of Wulfric Spot (c1002), founder of Burton Abbey (SHC 1916 p36) (SSE 1996 p15). Ilam does not appear in DB, yet parts of the church fabric can be dated to before the Norman Conquest (SL p52). The **name** has also appeared as Hilum and Ylum (SPN p67). It is a stream-name of British origin and may be a former name of the Manifold (SSAHST 1967 p34) (NSJFS 1981 p2), and mean something like 'trickling stream' (SPN p67). It may be the 'ham' on the Hyle, the old name of the Manifold (NSJFS 1961 p137). It could derive from the plural of Old Norse 'hylr' meaning 'pool' (Lund Studies in English. vol 65 (1983), p34) (NSJFS 1981 p19). Mills gives 'at the pools' (SSE 1996 p15). It may be from Hylum 'at the hills' (dative plural of hyl) (LGS p151) (DUIGNAN). It could be from 'Ilium,' as its situation reminded its first settlers - sun-worshipping people from the Eastern Mediterranean - of the 'City of the Sun' mentioned in Homer's 'Iliad,' the sacred city of Troy (STM Sept 1966 pp34-35). The **church**, Holy Cross, to the E of Ilam Hall, is of Saxon origin; a 20 feet section of the S wall of the nave is of Saxon origin and there are two crosses of Saxon origin in the churchyard (ARCHJ vol 120 (1963) p283) (NSJFS 1966 p9) (BOE p153); there are also Norman, Early English and later additions to the church. According to tradition Ilam is the resting place of St Bertram, patron of Stafford (see), and the church contains a stone chest believed to be the shrine of St Bertram (NHS p410) (SMC p171) (W p778) (APB p31) (AAD p187) (GNHSS p11) (WTCEM p40) (CHMS p35il) (PS p118) (STM Sept 1966 p34. Nov 1968 pp38-39). The **parish**, formed before 1086, may originally have contained the ancient parishes of Grindon and Alstonefield (SHC 1916 p194). It also contained the chapelry of Cauldon until 1748 and probably formerly the chapelries of Okeover and Sheen. In 1946 the ancient parish was abolished and 'Ilam with Blore Ray and Okeover' ecclesiastical parish was created (GLAUE p414). The **wake** may have anciently fallen on Holy Cross Day (Sept 14). Removal of the feast by the mid C19 to the Sunday after Sept 20 (W p778) may have occurred at the time of the change over to the Gregorian calendar (1752). More anciently, Ilam church may have been dedicated to St Bertoline supporting the tradition of St Berteline or Bertram at Ilam, with the parish festival held on St Bertoline's Day (Sept 9) which is only less than a week before Holy Cross Day (OSST 1953-54 p9 note).
1500 to PRESENT. The old village was swept away by Jesse Watts Russell, owner of Ilam Hall, after he had rebuilt the hall. He replaced it with a 'model' village built at the hall gates in the 1840s and 1850s. The model village consists of about ten cottages and a school with stone ground-floors, tile-hung upper floors and gables with barge boards grouped irregularly round a memorial cross to the first Mrs Watts Russell, inspired by the Eleanor Crosses of the 1290s (SL p140). Another account says the cross, built in 1840, commemorates Mary Watts Russell, the daughter of David Pike Watts. The top of the cross came away in a gale in 1962 (DMV p87p). Ilam has been identified with **Muggleton** (ZSB) - where, Muggletonians (a sect founded by John Reeve and Lodowick Muggleton (1609-98)) said God made his last revelation to man; Thomas Tomkinson (1631-1710), poet, of nearby Slade House was a member of this sect (PSS p472) (LTD p40); the village of Milwich also has been claimed to be Muggleton (ESH p31). **Dr Johnson** of Lichfield (see) and James Boswell visited Ilam or Islam (as Boswell writes it) on 22 September 1777 (Hopkin says Johnson was here on July 11 1777 - DJL p185) and a gardener at Ilam Hall assured them that Plot's story of the Manifold re-emerging here from a subterranean channel was true (NSFCT 1926 p119); he had

tested it out with corks; but still Johnson would not believe it. They were also told of a particular recess under a projection of rocks where William Congreve (1670-1729) wrote the 'Old Bachelor' (Boswell's Life of Johnson). Boswell does not mention whether Johnson wrote his 'Rasselas, Prince of Abyssinia' whilst staying here (written January 1759; within the evenings of one week) as JAT p64 and MR p193 claim. Some say the stretch of the Manifold here (which is known as Paradise) was the inspiration for 'Happy Valley' mentioned in the novel (GNHS p100) (VB p202) (SMM p64) (HLSP p171). However, Roberts thinks 'Happy Valley' was based on Milldale (WTCEM p63). **Customs and the supernatural.** The custom of decorating the village well with flowers was observed at Ilam on Midsummer's Day (SCSF p29). An authority on the village in the late 1980s had never heard of such a custom (local info). The custom of placing bridle garlands, white gloves and garlands, on the coffin of a maiden in the church was practised at Ilam: Sir Henry Ellis of the BM, visiting Alstonefield and Ilam on Sept 14 1815, noted the paper garlands hanging in the church 'in memory of young females,' although he was told that the custom was dying out (VCH vol 7 p12). At least one set of paper garlands and gloves, and possibly two, have hung in the church from the arch between the chapel to St Bertram and the nave since at least 1910 (LGS p152) (VB pp201-202) (LTD p38); two sets were there in the late 1980s (PDS&C p53p). In the last 200 years the only case in which the custom may have been practised was in the case of Hannah Ditling (local info). FLJ 1911 p322 noted a wooden crown with paper rosettes was hung in the church on the death of a betrothed person. A phantom coach has been seen above the Manifold ravine between Ilam to Throwley (FLJ 1942 p126).

Ilam Hall Ilam. The old hall was the seat of the Ports by 1556 to at least the 1680s (Plot's map) (SOS 1844 p483). William Congreve (1670-1729), playwright, is said to have visited his friend Robert Port here; in Congreve's Grotto (see below) he is said to have written some of his work. The old hall was taken down by Jesse Watts Russell and a new one erected on the site between 1821-26 to designs by the elder John Shaw (BOE p152) in the gothic battlemented and picturesque style (SL p259) (W p777) (AAD p175 facing il of the hall, pp175-183 on the interior and paintings in the hall). Sir Humphrey Davy (1778-1829), chemist, visited Ilam (AAD pp173,174 described by Mr Rhodes in Peak Scenery). In 1875 Jesse Watts-Russelll died and the hall passed to the Hanbury family. In c1910 it was the seat of Mrs Ellen Bowring-Hanbury, widow of Rt Hon Robert William Hanbury, late MP for N Staffs. Ellen married secondly in 1904 Victor Bowring-Hanbury. In 1927 it was sold to a restaurateur, who after financial difficulties, sold it to a demolition contractor. It was three-quarters demolished when Sir Robert McDougall of Manchester bought it (SHBP pp231-233) (MR p192) (DMV pp78-83ps). Sir Robert gave the property to Stoke-on-Trent city council in June 1934 (ES June 22 1934 p1p). Other accounts suggest much of the hall was taken down after it became council property in 1934 (SMOPP vol 2 p117p in 1934, before it was mostly demolished), the remaining part opened as a youth hostel in 1935. The hall was still a youth hostel in the mid 1990s.

GROUNDS. **Battle Cross** (see). **Congreve's Grotto** is a rocky recess at SK 130505, in which is situated a stone desk and seat. Here playwright William Congreve (1670-1729) is reputed to have written some of his work. His 'The Old Bachelor' (first draft said to have been made under Congreve's Oak at Stretton Hall (see); the play was produced in 1693), and part of his 'The Mourning Bride' (1697) are said to have been written at Ilam Hall (AAD p183) (NSFCT 1936 p29) (HLSP p170) (VFC p30). (SMC p171) (GNHS p100) (DDI p20) (JAT p64) (LGS p153) (KES p116) (CCOP p93) (STM Sept 1966 p34) (MR p193) (SMM p64). W p468, AAD p183, NSFCT 1936 p29, HOP p87 refer to Congreve but not the Grotto. The hall has or had an **icehouse**. There is an octagonal tower, possibly a former dovecote, near the entrance. It was probably built by James Trubshawe and has a Caernarvon arch head over the door (DoE II). It is called the **pepper pot** (MR p192). **St Bertram's Bridge** (see).

Ilam Moor Upland 1m N of Ilam. On the moor are round cairns of the Bronze Age. Some were excavated in the C19 and found to cover inhumation burials accompanied by Beaker and Food Vessel pottery (BOE p154). Is Ilamtops Low the round cairns referred to? When the common was cultivated disputes arose in 1542 and 1551 (VCH vol 6 p52).

Ilam Rock A tall shaft of limestone sometimes known as 'Nature's Leaning Tower of Pisa' situated on the Staffs side of the Dove at the N end of Dove Dale in Hunts Wood facing a similar shaft of limestone known as Pickering Tor on the Derbys side. The two are perhaps, the tallest free-standing pillars in the Peak District (PDS&C pp10,11p). In c1900 there was a refreshment room by the rock (DMV pp20-21p,26p). (LGS p123) (ES Dec 7 1933 p10ps) (TD ps) (PS p122) (EF pp73,75). It is said to be called Ilam Rock as it was a boundary marker for Ilam parish (PNPD).

Ilam Tops House and small area 1m NNE of Ilam. Ilam Tops is also known as Dove Dale Church or the 'Abbey' (POD pp304,305). Yet the rock feature known as Dove Dale Church is 0.5m to SE on W bank of the Dove. Near Ilam Tops Low is another burial mound which Bateman excavated in 1845. A crouched male skeleton was found (VAD p83) (NSJFS 1965 p40).

Ilamtops Low 1.25m N of Ilam. Burial mound 2m NNE of Ilam at SK 13585269. It is 24 paces in diameter and seven feet high and was excavated by Bateman in 1845. In a square rock-cut grave were the skulls of a child and a bull, an adult's bones, beaker fragments and a bronze awl (VAD pp82-83) (DAJ vol 75 pp74,105) (NSJFS 1965 p40). It is a listed monument. In 1914 someone noted that Ilamtops Low was, or near Ilamtops Low was, the only case of a stone alignment in the neighbourhood - that here was a little bit of stone and further on in a straight line two bigger stones. And that further up the hill still in a straight line with the summit were three stones close together, one fallen. And that the first six stones were thought to have been placed here in prehistoric times. And that higher up there were two more in the same line, but these might have come naturally. And that if the line continued it would pass through the Great Low and Ilam Tops (NSFCT 1914 p186). Is Ilamtops Low Pevsner's round cairns on Ilam Moor?

Ina's Rock A natural rock feature in grounds of Alton Towers at SK 087428, 1m ESE of Alton Towers Mansion and is arrived at at the end of a walk known as 'Rock Walk' (JAT p40) (HOC p213). Reputedly here King Ina (Ine) of the West Saxons sheltered before a battle which took place in Slain Hollow (see). Has also appeared as King Ina's Rock (MR p14). (WTCEM p35) (IAANS p vi) (STM March 1964 p42). An ancient British sword was found here. It was given to Sir Joseph Banks (BATR p6).

Inde Font Well An old well at the bottom of the hill between Ipstones church and Whitehough, probably at The Clough, Coltstone. Famous for its pure water but by the 1930s was disused, covered with brambles and almost out of sight (TOI p161). It was anciently haunted by the kirkgram and padfoot or phantom black dog (OL vol 2 p301) (FLJ 1942 p126) (The Good Ghost Guide. John Brooks. 1994) (GLS pp57-58). Has also appeared as Indefont Well.

India Hills Small ranges of hills 0.5m SW of Brereton church.

Ingestre Fragmented small hamlet on E-facing slopes overlooking the Trent 3m ENE of Stafford. Aerial photography has shown cropmarks at Ingestre showing a double-ditch barrow (SPJD p11p). The **name** has appeared as Gestreon (DB), Ingestrent (1242) (SSE 1996 p15), Higgistrent (COI p42) and Inglestre (c1540) (LI appendix p171). Walter Chetwynd, the antiquary of Ingestre Hall, in the later C17 thought the name derived from the Greek for 'near,' and the river Trent (COI p42). Later it was thought the first element was from Ings meaning flat meadows (COI p42) or from Ing or Inga, an Anglo-Saxon personal name, giving possibly Inge's strand, Inge's Trent, and Inge's tree (COI p42) (DUIGNAN). Oakden thinks Ingestre is difficult to interpret (SSAHST 1967 p35). Ekwall suggests from Old English 'gestreon' 'gain, prosperity' (SSE 1996 p21), or 'acquired property' (SPN p67). The original Ingestre settlement may have been at Little Ingestre to the E (COI p42). There was a church at Ingestre in the C13 (LDD). As a separate parish Ingestre is not listed in the Papal Return of 1291 but it probably had separate ecclesiastical identity by then, perhaps even by 1248. It remained a peculiar jurisdiction of Stafford Collegiate Church, until the college was dissolved in the C16 and was then a royal free chapel of St Mary's until 1846 (SHC 1916 p199) (VCH vol 3 p93) (GLAUE p414). The present **church**, St Mary the Virgin, to the E of Ingestre Hall, reputedly was designed by Sir Christopher Wren (1632-1723). The old church had fallen into disrepair after the Civil War. The church built by Walter Chetwynd III (d1692), the antiquary, was dedicated in 1676. Chetwynd was a member of the Royal Society as was Wren and they are believed to have been friends. When the church was restored in the 1960s two names were found inscribed in the plaster: 'Gilbert' and 'S. Hand.' Members of a Hand family are known to have been in charge of quarrying the stone for St Paul's cathedral. One of the the carved faces in the ceiling looks uncannily like Wren, whilst the other bears a resemblance to Walter Chetwynd. The oak cover of the marble font bears a knob which is formed in the shape of Wren's favourite pine-cone. There exists a drawing by Wren annotated 'Mr Chetwynd's Tower.' Members of the Wren Society (defunct), Sir John Summerson in a note hung in the church dated May 7 1960, Pevsner in BOE pp28,155, Derry Brabbs in 'English Country Churches,' Marcus Whiffen in 'Stuart and Georgian Churches' all take the claim, seriously. However, there is no documentary evidence to support the claim. Plot, who mentions the church, makes no identification, despite the fact that Plot was a friend of Wren (ES 1932. April 9 1987 p14p); some have suggested Plot's account of the church may have come from Wren himself (VB p136). Ingestre is mentioned (as a town) in a rare example of early C16 **English courtly love lyric** verse kept in the manuscript MS Rawlinson C813 in the

Bodleian Library, Oxford (Summary Catalogue 12653) (The Review of English Studies. Feb 1990 pp12-44). Whilst at Ingestre in the later C17 **Dr Plot** noted: in a ground called the Marsh a weak brine spring (NHS pp97-98) (SCSF p143; whether the same?); in the salt marshes near Ingestre the Sea Starwort of Germany, which normally grows along the sea coast (NHS pp202-203); along the Trent a red sort of marl with blue veins (NHS p119); a buck which grew brow antlers but no back ones (NHS pp260-261 tab 22 fig 11) (SHOS vol 2 p143). At Salt there is an **engine house** with a classical facade dated 1823 in Brick Kiln Lane at SJ 960267. The coal-fired engine drove a water pump and supplied water to the whole of Ingestre estate (MR pp195,273p,368) (DoE listed grade 2).

Ingestre Hall There was probably a manor house when Ingestre manor was held by the Marescallus family in 1166. Later in the C12 the manor was held by the de Muttons and passed from them to the Chetwynds in 1260 with the marriage of Isabella de Mutton, heiress, to Philip Chetwynd (d1286) (COI pp42,43,51).

THE CHETWYNDS. Sir Philip Chetwynd, a direct descendent of Philip Chetwynd (d1286), died in 1444 without issue and was succeeded by his uncle John Chetwynd of Alspath (or Meriden), Warws. He was succeeded by his son Thomas (d1451), who was succeeded by his son **Sir William Chetwynd** of Alspath and Ingestre. He was murdered on Tixall Heath (see) in 1492 or 1494 by Sir Humphrey Stanley of Pipe, Lichfield, who was jealous of his progress at court. Sir William was succeeded by his son Sir William Chetwynd of Alspath and Ingestre (d1546/7). His younger son Anthony Chetwynd headed the Chetwynd branch at Rudge who eventually succeeded to the title of Viscount Chetwynd (see below). However, Sir William was succeeded at Ingestre by his son Thomas Chetwynd (d1555). He was succeeded by his son John Chetwynd of Ingestre and Grendon (d1592), who was succeeded by his son Sir William Chetwynd (d1612). He was succeeded by his brother Sir Walter Chetwynd (d1638), who was succeeded by his son Walter Chetwynd (d1670). He was succeeded by his son **Sir Walter Chetwynd** (d1692/3), the antiquary and friend of Dr Robert Plot (author of NHS), who wrote a history of Pirehill hundred, which appears in SHC vol XII (1909) New Series. He died childless and Ingestre passed to his cousin, John Chetwynd (d1702) of Maer and Rudge (COI p219). He was succeeded by his eldest son William (created Viscount Chetwynd in 1717, d1735) who was succeeded by his brother John (2nd Viscount Chetwynd, d1767), who appears to have left his Ingestre estate to his daughter Catherine (d1785). In 1748 she married John Talbot, younger brother of William, 2nd Baron Talbot, a relation of the Talbots of Alton Towers, and Ingestre passed to the Talbots in 1767 and descended with Alton Towers (see); John and Catherine's son, John, added the Chetwynd name to Talbot, and inherited the barony from his uncle in 1782 and was created 1st Earl Talbot (new creation) in 1784 (COI p241) (NSFCT 1976 p24); 3rd Earl Talbot succeeded to the title of Earl of Shrewsbury in 1858.

THE HALL. A manor house is said to have been built sometime between 1327 and 1377 and another is said to have been built at the end of the C15 or during Henry VIII's reign. These may have stood on the higher ground in the park or down by the Trent (COI p95). The present one at SJ 976246 was built by Sir Walter Chetwynd (d1638) between 1613 and 1615 (NSFCT 1950 p101. 1976 p24) (HCMBOPP p58). The front of the hall faces S, a position it only shared in the county with the old hall at Enville (NHS pp40,41 tab 26 of Ingestre Hall). The N side may incorporate the outer walls and foundations of an earlier manor house. Sir Walter Chetwynd (d1692/3) repaired and considerably altered the interior in 1675 and 1676. Dr Plot used the hall as his working centre when in Staffs in the 1680s (NSFCT 1976 p24). The N and W facades were Georgianized in the C18, but re-Jacobeanized in 1808-10 for the 2nd Earl Talbot by John Nash (BOE p156). Ingestre Hall was enlarged in 1870 (NSFCT 1950 p101). In 1873 Prince and Princess Christian visited Ingestre (SIOT p74). A fire on Oct 12 1882 gutted the interior of the house (ILN Oct 21 1882 p425 il) (ASOP p154). Reconstruction was completed in 1885 (NSFCT 1976 p24). Queen Mary visited Ingestre Hall on July 28 1939 (ES July 29 1939). By 1950 Ingestre Hall was the only property owned by the Earls of Shrewsbury (NSFCT 1950 p101). In 1953 there appeared in SHC a catalogue of the pictures at the hall including one of Walter Chetwynd (d1693) and one of James Butler, first Duke and 12th Earl of Ormonde both by Sir Peter Lely, one of Charles Talbot, 1st Baron Talbot, Baron of Hensol (d1737) by John Vanderbank, one of William III by the school of Kneller, and one of Sarah Elizabeth, Countess of Shrewsbury (d1884) by Sir Thomas Lawrence (SHC 1950/1 pp55-105). In the mid 1960s the 21st Earl of Shrewsbury sold the hall to West Bromwich corporation as an arts centre for its schoolchildren (Stafford Advertiser Oct 29 1964 p8) (VB p136). (SHOS vol 2 pl on p15 at back) (W pp391-2) (S p89p) (The Country Seat Studies in the

History of the British Country House presented to Sir John Summerson on his 60th birthday pp55-57) (CL Oct 1957 pp17,24,31,772-775 figs 8 and 9 amateur artists' impressions of the S front before and after the fire of 1882. Oct 24 pp874-877 p of the orangery. Oct 31 pp924-927 ps of interior and paintings). The old stables were built in 1782, the new in 1885 (NSFCT 1950 p101). The Lion Gates are the iron ornate gates to a courtyard containing the stables (SGS p113p) (MR p195). For the park ornaments see Ingestre Park.

Ingestre Old Hall Has also appeared as Ingestre Manor and Ingestre Castle (HAH p84 il from an old engraving).

Ingestre Park A medieval deer park at Ingestre enclosed out of forest. In existence by 1417 (NSJFS 1962 p77).

Ingestre Park Park to Ingestre Hall, and probably occupies the area of the medieval deer park. In the early C18 Defoe praised Ingestre as 'the finest park and gardens that are in this part of England' (SL p133). Later in the C18 it was landscaped by Lancelot 'Capability' Brown (SL p133). At the Mount in the grounds of Ingestre is a **cedar of Lebanon tree** planted by Edward VII on Nov 21 1907 (HCMBOPP p59p). A square stone **deer shelter** of C17 origin still stands in the bound wall of Ingestre Hall deer park at SJ 962264 (MIDD vol 2 p31p). There was a **gothic tower** on higher ground to the W (marked on Brown's map at (i)), which may have been designed by Brown; its ruined foundations were still visible in 1957. On Brown's plan dated 1756 there was a broad east-west ride interrupted by an **obelisk** in a pool on the axis of the house, the obelisk has been removed (it now stands on a green at Tixall?). There is a **pavilion** in the Ionic Order at SJ 972247 NW of the hall. Built in c1752 (BOE p156). It may pre-date Brown's improvements to the park and may have been designed by Charles Trubshaw (CL Oct 1957 p875p). The original grand building behind seems to have been demolished by 1802 (SLM Christmas 1995 p31). For a long time in the C20 it was in a ruinous state but was restored by the Landmark Trust in 1992 (SLM May/June 1992 p18p. Christmas 1995 p31pcs) (ES Aug 3 1992 p4p). There was a temple or **rotunda** (marked on Brown's Map at (vi)). The rotunda of the mid C18 is octagonal and has Tuscan columns in the Doric Order and a dome roof. In 1960 it was moved to the centre of Tixall village (CL Oct 1957 p875p at Ingestre) (BOE p283) (SGS p171) (DoE II). Also there was a **sham bridge** (marked on Brown's map at (xi)) and a **triumphal arch** (marked at (xv)) (CL Oct 1957 pp875p,876).

Ingle Hill Weeford, S of Freeford Manor.

Inland Pool Pool 0.25m E of Wrottesley Hall, Wrottesley.

Intack Calton. If 'Intake' then this is not an uncommon name in the Moorlands. Probably from Danish 'indtag,' land taken from a common, or the sea (NSFCT 1916 p81).

Intake House 0.5m W of Ipstones. Intakes (1834 OS map). Perhaps identifiable with Twist Intake or Twistintake (TOI p117).

Intakes House 1m ESE of Rushton Spencer church.

Ipstones (locally endearingly '*Appy Ippy*' HLSP p50). Moorland village crowning high ground at the head of tributary of the Churnet, 18.25m NNE of Stafford. Former chapel with cure of souls in Leek ancient parish.
EARLY to PRESENT. A fragment of a Neolithic or Bronze Age quartzite axe-hammer has been found in Ipstones parish (NSFCT vol 42 p92. vol 80 p82) (NSJFS 1964 p26). The **name** has appeared as Yppestan (1195), Ipestanes (1206), Ipstone (1220), and Ippestanes (1244) (SPN p67). There has been little doubt that the second element 'stanes' represents 'stones.' 'Yppe' may be either Norse or Anglo-Saxon for a raised or look-out place (DUIGNAN) (NSFCT 1916 p81), giving 'up stones,' which should be interpreted as 'stony hill' or 'raised ground where stones are found' (SPN p67). Perhaps from Epiakon, 'a town of the Brigantes,' a British tribe occupying the district before the Romans. Perhaps from Yppa or Eoppa an Anglo-Saxon person; the 'stones' part may refer to his burial chamber near here (TOI p9). Oakden thinks the personal name is not 'Yppe' but 'Ippe' (SSAHST 1967 p34), giving 'Ippa or Ippe's stone(s)' (SPN p67). The stones in question, or rocks, could be Sharpcliffe Rocks which may have been an ancient encampment for the Celts (TOI p9), or perhaps the standing stones known as the Sun Stone (see) on Ipstones Edge (DPEM p74). There was a **church** at Ipstones possibly in the Saxon period (TOI p45), and certainly in the C14 (LDD). The present church, St Leonard, was rebuilt in 1790; there is a Norman tympanum in the church (LGS p154). Became a separate ecclesiastical parish in 1720 (GLAUE p414). The **manor** was held by the de Vernons in the early C12 and passed to the de Ipstones in Henry III's reign. By the marriage of Sir Ranulph de Brereton to Alice, heiress of William de Ipstones, the manor passed to the Breretons in the early C15. By the marriage of the Brereton heiress, Mary, to Sir Richard Egerton the manor passed to the Egertons in the early C17. Their son Richard Egerton sold it in 1633 to Matthew Craddock of Caverswall Castle. His son George sold it in 1639 to William Fowler and

John Hollins of Moseley as trustees. In 1649 the trust sold the manor to the freeholders of Ipstones. Much of the land of the manor but not the manor itself was purchased by John Sneyd the builder of Belmont Hall in 1770 (TOI pp21-35). Early in the C14 the villagers beat and wounded a village authority called Mr Farrow. The Abbot of Dieulacres, lord of Leek manor, and others took revenge by murdering the one who they supposed had wounded Mr Farrow. The widow protested to the king for redress and never got it (OL vol 2 p159). Ipstones had separate civil status early (GLAUE p414) and was a township in Ipstones parish. The village is somewhat fragmented with three nuclei - Stocks Green (NW end; where the church stands); Ipstones Green (NE end: where the manor house stood); Schoolhouse Green (S end; commercial area and where the village school stood) (1900 OS map 6 inch). The village **stocks** at one time were on the Stocks Green at the bottom of the Vicarage Drive. Later they were removed to the Policeman's Cottage in Upper High Street. The framework of the stocks were in the garden of this house up to the 1930s but then disappeared (TOI p170). There is still in the village a cast **iron hand pump** 20 metres S of Hawes Farmhouse with this inscription: 'This small plot of land was given by T Brandon, Rochdale, March 1 1876' (DoE II). There was no **fair** in 1792 (OWEN). White notes Ipstones has two annual fairs on March 24 and Nov 9 (W p779). There was at least one fair in 1888 (LHE p265). **Trades**. Dr Plot noted a red ochre could be found here (NHS p124). The site of the little known Ipstones pottery was seen by NSFC in April 1967 (NSJFS 1968 p98). Grit for grindstones has been quarried here (NSJFS 1961 p78) and at nearby Black Bank (W p779) although Ipstones has been a predominantly agricultural village. There was some coal mining by the early C20 (HLSP p50). The first evidence of **Baptist activity** in the county comes from Ipstones, where in 1644 a Capt and a James Cokayne were preaching Baptist philosophies (VCH vol 3 p116). For Ipstones **charities** see TOI pp117-142. At the top end of the village is a toll house, at SK 024502, where the road to Butterton Moor End joins that to Foxt, erected in 1837 (IAS p170) (IANS pp19,49p). **Persons and visitors**. A remarkable instance of longevity is the case of **George Clowes** and his wife of Colts-stone Heath (or Ipstones), her brother (the best man), and his sister (the bridesmaid), who all lived long enough to celebrate the Clowes' 60th wedding anniversary in 1885. Their united ages amounted to 326 years. During the marriage, which had taken place at Alton church on Feb 7 1825, boys entered the church and irreverently snow-balled the wedding party (OL vol 2 p43) (TOI p168). **Elijah Cope** (d1917), poet and author of 'The Moorlands in Winter' was born in Ipstones on Sept 18 1842. His Elegy on George Heath was praised in a letter from Tennyson (KES p119) (TOI pp165,173) (PSS pp248-249) (VFC p31).
SUPERNATURAL. **Fairies** are believed to exist at Bradshaw (see) and Lady Meadows (see) and in the Ipstones area (TOI p172). There were numerous traditions that the Ipstones area was inhabited by a race of **giants**. Plot mentions that there were found in a burrow at Ipstones men's bones of an extraordinary size, which were preserved by a Mr Hamilton, vicar of Alstonefield (TOI p9). There are **secret passages** from farm houses to the church (SVB p101). A strange **unexplainable force** was experienced by a man returning home to Clerk's Bank, according to the Rev Bright, from a church social evening at the schools he found his way barred round the corner of the churchyard by an invisible barrier. He turned round and tried again but at the same spot he was stopped again - there was no pressure or touch he simply could not obey his will to go forward. The man went home a different way (TOI p177) (SMM p49). For the story of the **Wandering Jew** see the Moorlands. A couple driving from Werrington claim they were abducted by **aliens** and taken by them in an unconscious state from Werrington to outside Ipstones (SMM p93).
Ipstones Booth (W p779). Presumably is the district encompassing Booth's Hall and Booth's Wood.
Ipstones Edge Ridge 1m NNE of Ipstones with superb views especially to the W and S taking in Cheadle, the Potteries, Wrekin, Cannock Chase and the Trent Valley as far as Tamworth. Brighton noted a market cross on Ipstones Edge (TOI p173). At the SE end of the edge, at SK 058490, at Windywaycross (see), is a cross. Further to the SE, at SK 065483, is another cross known as Hoften's Cross (see). Not far from the Red Lion Inn on Ipstones Edge on the road to Bottom House, Brighton noted a spinney which was haunted by the ghost of a young woman murdered and buried at the spinney. Her mother was led to the site where her daughter's body was buried through a vision. Another supernatural incident also occurs near the spinney. Four different people are said to have seen what appeared to be three persons standing over a bicycle who all disappeared into thin air as the people approached (TOI p176).
Ipstones Green NE part of Ipstones village on the Onecote road (1834 OS map).

Ipstones Hall Stood by the church on the site of the Hall Farm, near the vicarage. Some stones from the former Old Hall may have been incorporated into the present (1937) farmhouse. It is sometimes thought that the hall was used as a residence for the lords of Ipstones more than the manor house, which later was used as a place of the manor court. A John de Bradshawe was living at Ipstones Hall in 1333. The Bradshaws were still living here in the later C16. In the early C17 it was occupied by Sylvester Plunkett second husband of Mary, whose first husband was Richard Brereton, joint lord of Ipstones. In 1835 the Hall Farm was held by J Birch. The Birch family were believed to be still the owners in the 1930s (TOI p37). But the house was occupied by Thomas Silitoe, farmer, in 1863, and by Joseph Southall, farmer, in 1876 (KD 1863. 1876). There is a tradition of a underground passage from Ipstones Hall to the church (TOI p37).
Ipstones Manor House A very ancient residence and former seat of the lords of Ipstones at Ipstones Green on the edge of a little stream in the vicinity of the present Crowgutter Farm. Later it was a farmhouse and became ruinous and was pulled down. A house called The Manor House (see) by 1900 was built on the other side of the road (TOI p36, facing p36p).
Ipstones Park A medieval deer park at Ipstones enclosed out of forest. In existence by 1283 (NSJFS 1962 p76. 1977 p11) (FX p10). It was still existing as a deer park in 1867 and belonged to the Earl of Shrewsbury and formerly belonged to the Chetwynds (EDP p179). Has also appeared as Ipstones Old Park. It stood over 1m E of Ipstones in the area of the house Ipstones Park. Scattered houses to the E - Parknook, Lower Parkhead and Higher Parkhead, and Parkgate preserve the name of the park, as does the lane Park Lane.
Ipstones Park House over 1m E of Ipstones. The name is from a medieval deer park, see above.
Ipstones The Hall Ipstones. Was on the site of the Hall Farm near the Vicarage and the Vicarage is in one of the Hall fields (TOI p36).
Ireland Green Former hamlet in West Bromwich ancient parish. Lay in the Gads Lane area of Guns Village. Takes its name from a person named Ireland who lived in the area in 1750 (SOWB p24). There was some settlement here by the later C18 (VCH vol 17 p9). There is a tradition that John Wesley preached in the open at Ireland Green during a visit to the Oak House (West Bromwich, Oldbury and Smethwick Midland Chronicle and Free Press. Aug 4 1944), but Wesley makes no mention of the event in his journal (VCH vol 17 p64 note). Ireland Green appears on Charles Henry Blood's 1857 Map of Birmingham and its environs and on the 1947 OS 1:25,000 (sheet 32/99).
Irondish Former district which was to the ENE of Shelfield. There was settlement here by 1763 (VCH vol 17 p277). It was swallowed up by Shelfield as Shelfield expanded in the C18. It was near the junction of New Street and Walsall Road (ADY p25). The name occurs on the 1883 OS map (SNBC p25).
Ironmonger Pool Pool in existence by 1754 to the E of Pillaton Hall (VCH vol 5 p106).
Ironstone Road Road that runs from Prospect Village to Chase Terrace (OS Street Atlas Staffs 1995) (MR p82). Built after 1834 (1834 OS map) and it seems some time before 1925 (SOSH p338).
Isabella's Well, Lady Well on the Boscobel-Bishop's Wood road (BDH pp277,278).
Island, The Flat ground N of Smethwick through which Telford made a new cut for his Birmingham Canal New Cut New Main Line (VCH vol 2 p294).
Island House Stood within the triangle formed by Austin, Island and Holyhead Roads, Handsworth. Built by 1794, but was no longer standing by 1862 (MNB pp41,45,47).
Island Line The Island Line is the straight part of Telford's stretch of the Birmingham Canal New Cut New Main Line between Factory Junction, Tipton, and Pudding Green Junction, at Oldbury Road (BCM autumn 1995 pp16 see map). Opened in various stages between 1828 and 1838 (HCMS No. 2). The cutting for it when complete was said to have been the largest man-made cutting in the world (Black Country Breaks. Black Country Tourism brochure 2000).
Island of Andressey An island in the Trent opposite Burton parish church. According to legend St Modwen made it her last home and erected a chapel to St Andrew on it (W p533) (SL p144) (MR p69) and founded another church on the E side of Trent (VCH vol 3 p199). She returned to Ireland, leaving one of her companions at Andressey as abbess. Modwen reputedly died in Scotland and was buried at Andressey; her bones were later translated to a shrine in Burton Abbey (VCH vol 3 p199). Her chapel was probably destroyed by the Danes in the 870s. However, Andressey remained sacred to the memory of St Modwen, and early in the C13 a chapel on Andressey, endowed by Abbot Melburne of Burton Abbey, which had its own keeper, was dedicated to St Andrew. The chapel was known as the chapel of St Modwen after being

rebuilt by Abbot Feld (1473-93). The statue of St Modwen, a woman holding a shaft with a red cow, was probably kept in the chapel. It was removed in 1538 (VCH vol 3 p212). Up to the Reformation St Modwen's chapel attracted many pilgrims (VCH vol 3 p204). Reputedly, the site of Modwen's chapel is currently (1997) represented by the cherry orchard and yew trees situated across the Trent from the rear of Burton parish church (Notice Board). Appears anciently Modwenstow. Andressey is from 'Andrew's eye' (SPN p26) (IHOBT p45).

Island Pool Pendeford, Coven.

Isley Cross Wolverhampton. A bush? which stood on Ablow in Huntbach's time (SHOS vol 2 pp150,172). Huntbach noted it stood in a field called Ablow field, which covered 40 acres of unenclosed land near Graiseley Brook. Abblow itself once occupied the site now covered by St Paul's church (AOW p7).

Islington Former hamlet NE of Newport, 0.5m SW of Forton. Formerly in Forton parish in Staffs until transferred to Newport urban district in Shrops in 1965 (GLAUE p411). Islington, described as a residential outskirt of Newport in 1958 (VCH vol 4 p105), is not signposted today (1999), and the name is only preserved in a modern street, Islington Close.

Iverley Fragmented small hamlet 2m SSE Stourton. On its range of hills see SVS pp77,183.

Iverley Hay Formerly one of the hays or divisions or deer enclosures of Kinver Forest (NSJFS 1968 p40 fig 3) (SL p68) (VCH vol 20 p126). Later the area was known as Iverley Wood and Iverley Common, and rights of common in it were held by villagers on all sides of the hay in both Staffs and Worcs. The common was enclosed from the 1630s and farms were created in the area from the late C17 (W p178) (VCH vol 2 pp346, 348. vol 20 pp126,138) (RKE p21) (HOS p40).

Iverley House Farm 2m SE of Kinver. The old house stood on the S side of Sugar Loaf Lane until the mid C18 when it was rebuilt on the N side of the lane. This house was rebuilt sometime in the C19. It was known as Bum Hall in the 1850s and had become Iverley House Farm again by the 1880s (VCH vol 20 p126).

Ivetsey Hamlet 0.5m N of Bishop's Wood on N side of Watling Street. Ivetsey in Lapley and Blymhill parishes (Ivetsey Bank lies in Lapley, whilst Ivetsey Farm or Ivetsey Bank Farm lies in Blymhill). Has also appeared as Uvetshay

(C13), Oveyhotes (C13), Ovyhetteshay (C14), Evotteshayes (1473), Yvetts hay (1585), Evetts heyes alias Ovetts heyes (1613), Ivetsey (Plot's map), Ivetsey (Morden's map), and Ivetsey Bank (OS map 1834) (SPNO pp168,170). The ending hay means a hedge, enclosure (of Brewood Forest?). The prefix represents the Anglo-Saxon personal name Ufegeat, so Ufegeat's Hay. 'Bank' was a later addition (DUIGNAN) (SPN p23). A gamekeeper of the Earl of Bradford, Richard Gripton, was murdered with a shot through the chest at Brockhurst Coppice near Ivetsey Bank (SA Nov 16 1833) (Broughton's Scrapbook p464). For Ivetsey Bank in a local rhyme see Brewood.

Ivy House Abbey Street, Burton upon Trent. Former residence of Charrington's head brewer. In 1930 it became the vicarage for Christ Church. The original Christ Church vicarage was not used after the Zeppelin raid of Jan 31 1916, when six people died in the parish room (ABTOP p12il).

Ivy House Church Lane, Penkridge. It is dated 1741. It was occupied by the vicar before 1832 and was a boarding school in 1834. Later in the C19 it became the doctor's house (HOP p38) (VCH vol 5 p107 note).

Ivy House Corner of Lichfield and Wolverhampton Roads, Forebridge, Stafford. Built in the late C18. A pair of stocks which were used until 1866 stood by this house. The house was demolished in the 1970s for the present new road layout (SAC pp125p,126).

Ivy House Shenstone. Has been described as a very old building and has the reputation for having hidden Charles I when the parliament side were in the ascendancy in the Civil War. It was also for some years the residence of Rev George Dawson MA of Birmingham (STC p28p).

Ivy House Farm House on E side of School Lane, under 0.25m S of Warslow. Is dated 1742 (VCH vol 7 p57).

Ivy House Hall Formerly Ivy House. S of Bucknall Road, Hanley. Owned by the Vyse family in the early C18, later by the Baddeleys. It was known as Ivy House Hall in 1872 and was still standing in 1911 but not by 1960 (VCH vol 8 pp152-153).

Izons Former tiny branch canal N of Pudding Lane Junction, and an old canal turn (closed in 1954) S of Pudding Lane Junction (VCH vol 17 p14) (HCMS No. 2). Also an industrial estate N of West Bromwich Street and S of the Island Line (Birmingham A-Z). The name is from Izons Works on Oldbury Road, started by John Izons in 1782 (STELE March 11 1955).

J

Jackfield 'Jacparok' the name of arable land in Tunstall manor in 1408 has been identified as Jackfield (VCH vol 8 p119 note 54). A house, Jackfield, was occupied by the Leighs since the early C17 and was the home of Margaret Leigh 'the Burslem witch' (d1748). By 1760 it was held by another family and was later known as Hamel Grange (see).

Jackfield Tiny district adjacent to Hamil (POP p32). Probably named from the house.

Jack Hayes Minute hamlet 2.5m W of Wetley Rocks. The principle property is Jack Hayes Farm or Jackhayes Farm, in existence by 1652. For the rest of the C17 and it seems most of the C18 it was owned and sometimes occupied by the Cliffe family. Above the door at the back of the house are the initials 'T.C. 1675' (B pp84,85p-95).

Jackson's Bridge Over the Penk at Lower Green, Coven. So called from a man named Jackson who hung himself beneath it with a chain (VB p73) (SVB p63). Formerly Kings Bridge (OS map 1834), was Jackson's Bridge by 1959

(VCH vol 5 p19).

Jack Stones Settlement 1m W of Cotton, just N of Crowtrees. Appears on Yates' map as Jack Elms. Is said to have become Jack Stones by 1825. The settlement disappeared under the upper British Industrial Sand quarry which had opened in c1970 (CCT p41).

Jacob's Hall 0.75m ESE of Great Wyrley. Residence of John Benton in 1834 (1834 OS map) (SPNO p71).

Jacob's Ladder A flight of worn steps off Sandy Lane, Brewood, which lead to the back of the churchyard and straight through to Dean Street (SVB p42).

Jacob's Ladder A former stile at NE corner of Cop Mere leading from the road to a footpath in the field. The stile was very high and tradition has it that a gamekeeper once hanged himself from the top of it; his ghost is said to haunt the spot (SVB p132).

Jacob's Ladder Rock feature on Staffs side of Dove Dale, 0.25m N of Twelve Apostles and 0.25m S of Church Rocks (Dovedale Guide. Keith Mantell.

1985). (PS p120).

Jacob's Ladder The northern part of a tree-lined footpath which runs from Orton Lane alongside the barn wall of Orton House (New Farm in the C18) in the direction of Lower Penn (POAP p13).

Jamage Hamlet in former Talke township in Audley ancient parish, nearly 1m S of Talke. Has appeared as Gemetts (1479) and Jamitch (1733). An estate at Jamage existed by the early C17 (SHC 1944 p57). Jamage Industrial Estate on the W side of Jamage Road, 0.25m S of Talke, was in existence by 1992 (Stoke-on-Trent A-Z 1992). In March 1999 the shopping centre, Freeport Outlet Mall, opened on a part of the industrial estate.

James Bridge Bridge and hamlet 1m ENE of Darlaston (Offlow hundred). In Walsall ancient parish. There was a bridge here carrying the Walsall-Darlaston road over the Tame by the 1330s (VCH vol 17 p168). James Bridge is mentioned in 1576 and in 1608 (SOB p118) (SNWA p62). The bridge was built of stone by 1625. It was a county bridge by 1825 (VCH vol 17 p168). Here was a station on the GJR which opened on July 4 1837 (IAS p131). The unpretentious brick toll house by the bridge was demolished in 1963 (SSAHST 1966 p48 pl 1b). The James Bridge area was still considered an industrial area in the early 1970s (VCH vol 17 p158). On Sept 23 1998 on the M6 at James Bridge a truck spilt much of its load of cow's blood being transported from Exeter to Widness. Great care was taken in its removal for it was from cows of over 36 months old, some of whom could have had the disease known as BSE.

Jeffreymeadow Farm in Alton ancient parish, 1m S of Alton. The farm was owned by the Boswell family from at least 1655 and remained with the family until becoming a part of the Shrewsbury estate in 1849 (HAF pp195,198).

Jeffrons Hays House and former estate 1.5m WSW of Audley. Formerly in Knowl End township in Audley ancient parish. Has appeared as Gefrons Hase (1733). It belonged for many generations up to 1733 to the Smith family (SHC 1944 pp36-37).

Jenkins, The Field name in central Burslem in the C18, to NE of the present Market Place. Appears on a plan of the town in c1750 (SL p213 see plan). Jenkins Street off Wedgwood Street preserves the name. Thomas John Wedgwood had James Brindley construct a windmill at The Jenkins in c1750. It wet ground flint and worked until 1832. By 1860 only the derelict base remained (HSP p160) (WBJ p16) (MR p65).

Jervis Wood Lies to the S of Trentham Lake. Is Great Shendon Wood in Arnold Bennett's novel The Card.

Jesson's Branch of the Halford Branch Canal. Hall End, West Bromwich. Spurred off the Halford Branch at Gladstone Street and ran southwards for a very short stretch. Constructed in 1831, closed in 1954 (VCH vol 17 p14) (BCM autumn 1995 p20).

Jigs Nook Former area of Walsall Wood. The name only occurs in the 1841 census. The area may have been near Goblins Pit (SNBC p41).

Joan Eaton's Cross Small triangular green at the fork of two lanes 0.5m SW of Church Eaton at SJ 839171. The local tradition is that Joan or June Eaton was a witch, who objected to the erection of a church at Little Onn and by her incantations caused the stones laid during the day to be transported by night to the site of the existing church at Church Eaton. She continued to do this, until the builders gave up and built the church there. She is also attributed with milking the Dun Cow of Red House Farm dry and putting the cow and calf footprints on the stone by Red House Farm. At length Joan Eaton was condemned and burnt at the stake here (OSST 1931 pp18-19) (MR p100). Another legend tells that Joan Eaton was such a pattern of purity and good living, that when she died, quite young, she was buried at these crossroads because she had been loved by everyone who knew her. A cross was then erected, and she was known as a saint. It is supposed that her grave was visited by pilgrims from all over the country (OSST 1931 p20). Another theory is that the place was named by someone in the earlier C19 wishing to account for the fork in the road here and who was unacquainted with the legend (OSST 1931 p19). Yates' map shows there were crossroads here in the late C18 (info Bruce Braithwaite). The small pits, known locally as Black Pits, by the lane from Joan Eaton's Cross to Turnover canal bridge have a tradition of being witches' ducking pools (info Ron Balding). (VB p150) (SN March 11 1988).

Joan's Well Gives rise to Withymere Brook which flows down to Withymere House (1927) on Lloyd Hill, Penn (POAP p8).

Job's Hill A hill at Hints.

Job's Pool Tiny pool 0.25m SE of Brown Edge. Is thought to have been named after Job Bailey who built a squatter's cottage, named Apple Tree farm (BEH p31), on unenclosed land near a stream which he dammed to make a pool to water his cattle. The cottage or pool or both appear on a tithe map of 1843 (ONST 1979 p398).

Job Willis Rock Gritstone outcrop of rock 0.5m NNW of Biddulph Moor church

(TTTD p158).

Jockey Hill Hill 640 feet high, 2.75m SW of Rugeley on Cannock Chase.

Johnson Hall Neo-Tudor mansion 0.5m SSW of Eccleshall. In Horsley quarter in Eccleshall ancient parish. Appears as Johannestun (1227) (SSE 1996 p15) and Johnson Hall (Plot's map). There is some doubt as to how the name originated (EOP p34). The original owner or manager may have been one John or Johann (SPN p68). Ekwall gives 'John's tun' (SSE 1996 p15). Johnson, alias Eccleshall, was a prebend in Lichfield cathedral, and here was a prebend house from c1100; it was rebuilt in c1500 (SHC 1938 p5) (EOP p34p). It was the seat of a branch of the Skrymsher family in the C16 (ECC p41) and a branch of that family is marked there on Plot's map. In the mid C19 it was owned by HS Hartshorne and lived in by Robert Hargreaves (W p376). Restored in 1883. Mrs Moat occupied the hall between at least 1935 and 1941 (SHC 1934. 1941 List of Members). There was a fire at the hall in 1947 (SN Oct 4 1947 p5). It was occupied by Mr Rawlins, arms dealer, in 1992 (MIDD vol 2 p51p).

Johnson's Birthplace House on the corner of Breadmarket Street and Market Street, fronting Market Place, Lichfield. Here Dr Samuel Johnson of Lichfield (see) was born in 1709. The house was built in 1707 by Johnson's father, Michael Johnson, partly on the site of a house he had lived in and purchased from Nathaniell Barton in 1707. The corporation issued him a 40 years' lease in 1708. This lease, said to have been recently found in 1933, is preserved in the Birthplace Museum (Dr Johnson and his Birthplace. A Retrospective and Guide. Johnson Birthplace Committee. 1933 p13il). Dr Samuel Johnson was born in the house on Wednesday Sept 7 (18 new style) 1709, his brother Nathaniel was born in it in 1712. It remained Johnson's property after the deaths of all his family members. In 1767 the corporation renewed the lease on a term of 99 years, at the old rent, which was five shillings (Boswell's Life of Johnson). In 1776 Johnson took Boswell round it. After Johnson's death in Dec 1784 in accordance with his will it was sold. It sold at auction at The Swan Hotel for £235 (STMSM May 1979 p39). Another lease was granted in 1866 for 31 years to the then owner at a yearly rent of two shillings. The house was sold at the Three Crowns on Oct 20 1887 to James Henry Johnson of Southport (Dr Johnson and his Birthplace. A Retrospective and Guide. Johnson Birthplace Committee. 1933 p16). Mr Johnson had the intention of preserving the house because of its historical associations. Under his will the house was sold to the city in 1900 (VCH vol 14 p169). It opened as a public museum on Whit Monday May 27 1901 (STMSM May 1979 p39). The museum was founded by Col John Gilbert in 1900 (SSW p52). The birthplace as a **museum** contains portraits of Lord Chesterfield, Joshua Reynolds, Michael Johnson and copies of Johnson's friends (SSW pp51,52), Johnson's wedding ring, shoe buckles, walking stick, teapots, and cups and saucers, Johnson's oak settle from Edial Hall, Boswell's bureau from Auchinleck, and a silver pen which Edmund Burke gave to Johnson to celebrate the completion of his Dictionary (KES p142) (VB p16). (GM Feb 1785 engraving of the house) (HOL p503) (SHOS vol 1 p323 pl) (LGS pp175,176 p of on facing page) (CL Oct 3 1957 pp662-663). The collection of 1000 books of Rev Dr Peter Hay Hunter was given to the museum in 1911 (VCH vol 14 p169). For Johnson's associations with Lichfield see under Lichfield.

Johnson's Willow Willow tree supposed to have been planted by Dr Samuel Johnson of Lichfield (see) or his father, Michael. Johnson Snr had a parchment manufactory adjoining the garden where this tree stood on the N side of Minster Pool, Lichfield. Johnson Jnr would visit the willow first on one of his return visits to the city. It was the delight of his 'early and waning life' and still more of Miss Seward's: It was the ornament of Stowe Valley - the subject of every writer - the gratification of every naturalist and admiration of every traveller (SMC pp172,210il of) (SM p559). Some boys tried to burn the tree down in 1824 (Pottery Gazette Nov 13 1824). The greater part of it was blown down in 1815 (W p503) or on April 28 1829 (Lichfield Mercury May 1 1829) (Broughton's Scrapbook pp80,81) (VCH vol 14 p163) or in 1830 (Dr Johnson and his Birthplace. A Retrospective and Guide. Johnson Birthplace Committee. 1933 p46) and the tree in 1851 was a shoot from the old one (W p503). This second tree was blown down in 1881. A third tree was planted from it but was felled in 1956 because it was unsafe. A fourth tree, planted from it in 1957, was surviving in the late 1980s (VCH vol 14 p163). (GM June 1785 vol 55 pp496, 640 drawing) (SHOS vol 1 part 1 pp345-346) (GNHS pp412*,413) (SG p110) (KES p139) (SLM Feb 1951 pp18 il,19 has coloured engraving which appeared in GM June 1785). Wilkinson implies that Johnson's Willow is an unusual species of willow, rather than just the name for this willow (LAL p35p). There was some information about the tree on the second floor of Johnson's Birthplace in the 1980s. There was a small circular box carved from a Johnson willow on display in the Donegal House, Lichfield.

Johnson's Wood Wood 1m S of Hales, lying partly in Staffs and partly in Shrops. Takes its name from a family called Johnson (SHC 1945/ 6 p183). Has also appeared as Johnson Wood (W p389), and gives its name to the two farms called Johnson's Wood Farm. Here John Highfield of Millmeece, forger, was arrested in 1828. He later escaped (CCSHO p79).

Joiner's Square District nearly 1m SSE of Hanley. Formerly a chapelry in Stoke-upon-Trent chapelry in Stoke-upon-Trent ancient parish. A fossil tree was found in a marl pit at Joiner's Square (NSFCT 1870 pp22-27,28-32. 1880 pp84-85il-90). The district known as Joiner's Square existed by 1829; it probably developed because of its proximity to the Caldon Canal (VCH vol 8 p143). Scarratt remembered Joiner's Square from a walk he made through it in 1859. It comprised an irregular group of cottages, almost all of the houses having their own plots. The church, All Saints, Leek Road, was built in 1913 (LDD). By the late 1990s there was an industrial estate at Joiner's Square (Business Directory. City of Stoke-on-Trent. 1997/8).

Jol Pool (locally *Jelpel*). Tiny pool under a mile NNE of Burston. Probably can be traced to the Celtic adjective 'gel' bright, white. The element 'pel' is the river-root 'bial' 'bual' (NSFCT 1908 p143). Robert Selby, an authority on Burston, has been unable to find out the meaning of the name.

Jolpool Brook Runs from S of Hilderstone to join the Trent at Burston.

Jongham's Cottage 2m NW of Colton.

Jordan's Grave New Oscott, Great Barr. Lost. It was on the border with Warws.

Jubilee Park Public park at Ocker Hill, Tipton. Officially opened on April 13 1935 by Councillor AF Welch chairman of Tipton urban district council to commemorate the jubilee of George V. The park covers 25 acres (TSSOP p72). The Jubilee Park area was the customary site for huge bonfires for the people of Tipton, West Bromwich and Wednesbury, to celebrate such events as all coronations from Elizabeth I, Waterloo, and Sevastopol (BCM July 1979 pp8,9p of a bonfire for George V's coronation (1911), it was 65 feet high and estimated at 265 tons) (TB June 1979 p1; the coronation bonfire 1911).

Jug Bank Small hamlet 0.5m SW of Ashley, on Ashley Heath. In Ashley ancient parish. Has also appeared as Jugbank. Vernon Yonge had not come across an origin for the name (BPS p111). It is perhaps from the root 'sceach' bush or forest under the influence of Slavonic sibilation. Under a similar sibilation the word may have become corrupted into Jug (NSFCT 1908 pp43-44).

Judgefields House nearly 0.75m NNW of Brown Edge.

Junction House At Wordsley Junction by the canal. Demolished sometime since the 1950s (TB Dec 3 1998 p25p).

Kate's Hole A burial pit behind Biddulph Old Hall. The name is from the Italian lady who came to be governess to the Biddulph family in 1647 and was known as 'Singing Kate' because of her exceptionally beautiful and powerful voice. She died of bubonic plague, which either started an outbreak in the Rushton Grange area of Burslem, or which she received from an outbreak there. Some years later the burial pit containing the Biddulph household of the C17 period was discovered at the back of Biddulph Old Hall and was christened Kate's Hole (TOS pp19-21) (SMML pp103-105).

Keele (locally *Keyle* BOJ Book 3 p4). Former chapelry in Wolstanton ancient parish. The village of Keele lies on high ground near the source of Park Brook 15.5m NNW of Stafford. **Keele Series** refers to the red sandstone outcrop in the Keele area (VCH vol 2 p187). The village is on the watershed of England: A stream that rises in the parish runs E to the North Sea via the Trent, while another, Hazeley Brook, runs W to the Irish Sea via the Weaver and Mersey (SSE 1996 p2). Keele, on a commanding hill, may have been an occupied position for the **Romans** in the early advance N and then inhabited the site for centuries. During the building of the University College of N Staffs (Keele University) in c1952 two Roman coins were discovered. The first a sestertius of Faustina II struck 146 AD, the second a follis of Justinian I, curious for he came to the throne after the Romans had left Britain in 527. The coin, if not brought to Keele when current, may have been brought by the Knight Templars or Knights Hospitallers from the C12 (NSFCT 1953 pp23-31ps) (Numismatic Chronicle series 6 vol 13 p144) (NSJFS 1964 p26). Keele does not appear in DB. It has appeared as Kiel (1169), Kyle (C13), Kel (C13) (SPN p68) (SSE 1996 p15), and Keel in the C18 and C19 (maps of Morden and Bowen) (1834 OS map). The **name** is from Welsh 'cell' meaning a cell belonging to a hermit or monastery, or small church (DUIGNAN) (SPN p68). In Iceland and Norway the term kjolr, a keel, is used in the sense of hill ridge from the supposed resemblance to an up-turned boat; Keele suits this situation very well (NSFCT 1916 p81): This derivation was supported by Prof SH Beaver of Keele University (1950-1974) (SSE 1996 p2). Gelling gives 'cow's hill' (NSJFS 1981 p2). Mills gives 'cattle hill' (SSE 1996 p15). The old **church**, St John the Baptist, on an eminence known as Keele Hill, N of Keele Road, was built in the 1780s and replaced probably a late C12 or early C13 Templar chapel (HOK pp13,14) (LDD). Became a separate ecclesiastical parish in 1774 (GLAUE p414). The present church on or near the same site was built in 1868-1870 (BOE p158). Became a separate civil parish early and a separate ecclesiastical parish in 1774 (GLAUE p414). **'New village'**. The Sneyd family, who owned the entire village, more or less swept away the old village between 1828-30 and 1869 and erected a 'model' village. W Rothwell, an agricultural commentator, noted in 1856 that 'there is no village in England where the cottages are more comfortable, more convenient, more substantial or in better taste than in the village of Keele' (NSJFS 1982/5 p104). In the later C17 Plot noted flat **iron plates** (frying-pans) were made at Newcastle-under-Lyme by John Holland (one of only two in the country involved in this trade, the other was at Wansworth, Surrey - POP p159). Greenslade and Stuart say Holland was actually at Keele (HOS p43). The **railway** line from Keele to Leycett, Halmer End and Audley closed to passengers in 1931 (NSJFS 1964 p79). The **motorway service station** opened on the M6 0.75m S of Keele had the first restaurant which was built over a motorway (ES Sept 18 1962) (Weekly Sentinel Aug 2 1963). The service station is reputed to be haunted by a Puritan-looking gentleman who frequents the toilets. He was seen by Geoffrey White in Jan 1974 and the same ghost was seen by him at his home in Colchester; his home facing the Siege House (one of the last strongholds of supporters of Charles I) (EGH pp148-149). Keele community magazine, published by 2000, known as The Yew Tree, may take its name from a **yew tree** growing since c1700 at the junction of Keele and Whitmore Roads on a 'green' island in the roadway. By early 2000 the tree was said to be dying because of neglect (ES April 10 2000 p3pc). Keele is mentioned in a local rhyme, see under Betley.

Keele Hall Principal seat of the senior branch of the Sneyd family from c1580 to c1900, 0.75m ESE of Keele village. The first Keele Hall was built for

Ralph Sneyd in c1580 (NHS tab 28 il of the hall) (NSFCT 1887 pp40-41). The **Sneyd family** originally from Sneyd (see) arose as a branch of the de Aldithley family, later Lords Audley of Heighley Hall (see) in the early C13. In the later C14 they were granted land in Bradwell and in the early C15 the manor of Bradwell (see). In 1544 Sir William Sneyd of Bradwell, mayor of Chester in 1543 and 1566, purchased Keele manor, the former estate of the Knights Hospitallers of Keele (see). He is perhaps the same Sir William Sneyd of Bradwell who married Henry Touchet (d1563), 10th Lord Audley, a descendent of the Audleys of Heighley Castle. When the lease of Keele manor granted to Henry Delves by the Knights Hospitallers expired in 1580, Sir William's son, Ralph (d1614/5) built the first hall on the present site of the hall, a mile away in parkland, after, probably finding the hospitallers' old house in Keele village unsuitable as a residence (SL p96). According to Erdeswicke in the late C16 the new hall was 'a very proper and fine house of stone' (SL p96). Ralph was succeeded by his younger son, Ralph (1543-1643), who was succeeded by his eldest son, Col Ralph (c1612-1650), who was succeeded by his brother William (1613-1695) (The Sneyds of Keele Hall. JM Kolbert. 1967). The hall was garrisoned by the Sneyds on behalf of the royalists in the **Civil War** but had fallen to parliament by Feb 1643. On Feb 29 1644 an order was given to demolish it by the parliamentary committee at Stafford. But the parliamentarians under Capt Barbour only plundered it. Cartulary documents purporting to relate to Hulton Abbey in the Barbour family's possession in the latter C19 are said to have been part of the plunder (SOS (1884) p44) (SSE 1994 pp86-89) (GNHS pp77,123) (NSJFS 1966 p16) (NUL pp53 il of the hall,58) (HOS p35. 1998 p72). (Staffordshire Gazette end of 1839 - description of the hall) (W p393) (Agricultural Gazette 1856). William was succeeded by his son, Ralph (c1641-1703). He married Frances Dryden (cousin of the poet) (SLM winter 1955 p19); Dryden, the poet, visited the hall in the 1680s (SSAHST 1966 p46). Ralph's brother, William (1642-1708), founded the branch of the family who lived at Birches Farm (see), Bishton Hall (see), Belmont Hall (see), Basford Hall (see), Barrow Hill (see), Ashcombe Hall (see), Huntley Hall (see), Loxley Hall (see), and Fair View (see). Ralph (d1703) was succeeded by his grandson, Ralph (1692-1733), who was succeeded by his youngest son, Ralph (1723-1793). He was responsible for altering and partly rebuilding the hall sometime between 1741 and 1791. He was succeeded by his son Col Walter (1752-1829), who was succeeded by his son Ralph (1793-1870). He had the present hall built between 1856 and 1861, by the architect Anthony Salvin. He was succeeded by his brother Rev Walter (1809-1888), who was succeeded by his son Col Ralph (1863-1949). Col Ralph as DAPM in Paris during WW1 arrested the female spy, Mari Hari. From 1926 he resided in Wilts, and in 1947 entered into negotiations to sell the estate to Stoke-on-Trent corporation who were looking for a site for the University College of North Staffordshire. The corporation purchased the estate in 1949 and conveyed it to the University College in 1950 (STC p13p) (SLM Dec 1948 p204) (The Sneyds of Keele Hall. JM Kolbert. 1967) (BOE p158) (NSFCT 1976 p21) (NSJFS 1962 p25 note. 1982/5 p67) (HOK pp67,70,71 plan of the grounds, 78il,79il,87,90p,97,98) (KH - p1 il of the hall from NHS, and whole book) (MR p197). In 1901 **Grand Duke Michael of Russia** purchased the lease of the hall for 10 years. Edward VII visited the Grand Duke here in July 1901 (STMSM June 1975 p30p); the Rajah of Putacota, and Lady Randolph Churchill and her son, Winston Churchill were other visitors (SLM Oct/ Nov 1987 p53). Whilst at Keele the Grand Duke unveiled the statue to Queen Victoria in Newcastle-under-Lyme to celebrate the coronation of Edward VII. The Grand Duke, who is said to have regarded Keele with much affection describing it as the 'Switzerland of England,' left the hall on March 1 1906 (SHST pp389-92) (SLM Oct/ Nov 1987 pp52-53). But many accounts say he stayed until 1910 (SVB p102). The hall was empty in the mid 1930s (KES p119), and was badly damaged in a fire in 1941 (photograph in the Warrillow Collection, Keele University). The **library** contained some first edition proof sheets of Dr Johnson's Dictionary (1755) which were sold at Sotheby's on Nov 30 1927. The corrections and additions on 1630 slips are believed to have been partly written by Johnson (NSFCT 1927 p164) (HOK pp125,130). A view of the hall appears on three pieces of the Wedgwood Green Frog service for Catherine the Great 1774 (NSJFS 1982/ 5 pp72,73p of it on dish cover). The hall has also appeared as Sneyd House (SVB p102).

UNIVERSITY OF KEELE AT KEELE HALL. The university was the result of a long-envisaged college for adult education in North Staffordshire. The prime mover in realising the university was Alexander D Lindsay (b1879), 1st Baron Lindsay of Birker, educationalist and former fellow of Balliol College, Oxford, who chaired a committee set up after WW2 to find a way to found the university. The university received its charter in Aug 1949 (VCH vol 6 pp182-183). For the university arms see The Sneyds of Keele Hall by

JM Kolbert (1967). The university was formally opened by Queen Elizabeth (wife of George VI), on April 17 1951 (ES Sept 4 1993 p25p). In 1961 it became the University of Keele (TSS pp128ps,129). Many of the unique academic ideas of the university belonged to Lord Lindsay, the founder and first principal. He believed that it was not so much what was taught or at what level but whether it was taught in such a way as to bring out the interconnectedness of all branches of learning. The curriculum marked a decisive break with tradition. Work for the first degree would last for four years, the first of which was spent on foundation studies, and there was to be innovation in the make-up of courses. Educational experts from around the world came to Keele to observe the academic system, and Keele University was once titled 'The Dream on the Hill' in a TV feature with reference to the educational innovations of Lord Lindsay. Lord Lindsay died at his Keele residence, the Clock House (see below), on March 18 1952 (DNB 1951-60) (NSJFS 1961 pp101-114) (HOK p162) (ES Sept 9 1977. Oct 28 1977). The university covers the hall grounds and is the UK's largest integrated green campus university (ES Oct 27 1999 p18). The hall was used as the university **library** up to 1966 (VCH vol 6 pp182-183) and has since been used for a faculty. The library then moved to the present new building on the campus built to designs of Sir Howard Robertson in 1960-1 (BOE p160). By 1988 it contained the Tamworth Court Rolls; manuscripts relating to Arnold Bennett; to the families of Wedgwood, Spode, Sneyd, and Chetwode. It also contained the collection of Thomas Pape of Newcastle-under-Lyme (SSE 1988 pp77-92) (DRBSC pp476,477): It was to house the Havergal Brian Archive in Nov 1996 (ES Nov 21 1996 p23). In summer 1998 the university sold for £1 million to a private collector the collection of old and 'sometimes' rare mathematics books bequeathed to it by Charles Turner. The sale of the collection, which included one edition of Newton's 'Principia,' eight books from Newton's library, some annotated by him, including one he used in his first studies of mathematics, caused some national controversy as it was considered a loss to the nation. The University responded to the controversy by pledging to ringfence the monies raised to improve the conservation and listing of existing collections (info Martin Phillips) (Daily Telegraph Dec 22 1998 pp1,2). The **chapel** on the campus, opened in Dec 1965, was one of the first multi-denominational chapels in the country. It was built by GG Pace in Staffordshire blue brick and is noted for its pioneering spirit. In 1998 it was listed Grade Two by English Heritage (BOE p161) (ES Sept 28 1998 p8p). In 1956 Princess Margaret became President of the university and in 1962 she became Chancellor of it, serving until 1986 (ES Oct 27 1999 p18). However, another account says, still as Chancellor she visited Keele on Nov 25 1987 to officially open the new Science Park (SLM Oct/ Nov 1987 p53; says she became Chancellor in 1957). In 1962 Princess Margaret was awarded an honorary degree by the university; in 1965 Queen Elizabeth (wife of George VI), was awarded an Honorary Doctor of Letters Degree by the university (ES Oct 27 1999 p18). In 1968 the students protested to improve their rights at the university. At one demonstration outside the Chancellor's Building the students hummed for a long period of time and tried to make the clock tower levitate 250 feet. A recording of this is kept by Radio Stoke (BBC Radio 4 Dec 31 1993 'PM Programme') (TWWW July 1998 p9p). The student's radio station, Kube Radio, was on air by May 1999 (ES May 8 1999 p7). Elizabeth II visited the university on Oct 28 1999 to celebrate its 50th anniversary (ES Oct 27 1999 pp18-19). **Alumni:** Roy Fisher (b1930), poet and lecturer in American Literature at Keele (VFC p49); Philip Higson (alias Philip John Willoughby-Higson) (b1933), poet (VFC p65); John I Jones (b1938), poet and short story writer (VFC p76); Clare Short, politician; Michael Mansfield QC, barrister; Lord John Taylor, barrister; Tony Elliot, magazine publisher; Marina Oliver (born Walsall), historical novelist, Chairman of the Romantic Novelists' Association 1991-93; David Pownell, playwright; Peter Whelan, playwright; Paul Clarke, MP for Gillingham (info Brian Rawlins); Keith Butler, who decried Bob Dylan a 'Judas' at a rock concert in Manchester in 1966, when Dylan played the electric guitar (BBC 2. Newsnight. Jan 29 1999). GROUNDS. Were laid out by William Gilpin? (HOK pp71,72,81,86,89 plan, 91p). The two-storeyed hexagonal **pavilion** on the highest point of the estate, where the observatory now stands, was built in 1723, 500 yards NNE of the hall. It was also called the Summer House, and was demolished sometime after 1823 (NSJFS 1982/5 pp67-68) (HOK pp67,99 note 24). It was used by Yates as a triangulation point for his map (1775), and by the surveyors for the first OS map (SHC 1984 vii). To the NE of the hall are the **Clock House**, built in the 1830s by Edward Blore, it was the former stables (BOE p160). It was converted into living quarters for Col Sneyd in the 1920s and used as a residence for the first principal of the university, Lord Lindsay (HOK p62) (VCH vol 6 pp182-183). In the grounds are or were a **stone viaduct** (HOK pp83,84,93p), a **fountain**, which was restored in c1987 at a cost of £10,000 because shells covering the fountain had been completely broken (SLM Oct/Nov 1987 p53). The **amphitheatre quarry** contained follies built by Rev Walter Sneyd in 1884 using stone from the ruins of Hulton Abbey. About this time it was turned into a fernery. By 1998 the amphitheatre had become very overgrown and work then started on clearing it (ES April 5 1940) (SASR 1985 p31) (SSE 1994 pp94,95ps) (NSFCT 1998-99 p22). It was reached by a 16 metre tunnel possibly built by William Andrews Nesfield 1860-80 with an arched viaduct, and a dog-leg turn in the middle (SFH p29). The Hulton Abbey stones were returned to the abbey site in c1950 (NSFCT 1950 p85). Also a C19-looking **summerhouse** (HOK pp92,94p,95) (NSJFS 1982/5 p94p). Mee noted in the 1930s at Keele Hall an **avenue of deodars** and a wonderful **holly hedge**, a centenarian 600 feet long and over 20 feet high (KES p119). Also a **racecourse** (HOK p98) opened in May 1895. It was served by Keele Park railway station. Closed in c1905; the grandstand was moved to Uttoxeter race course in c1911. Racecourse Farm over 1m SW of the hall preserves the name. The M6 covers part of the track (NSJFS 1982/5 pp87,98). A **sculpture** by Dame Elizabeth Frink is at Keele.

Keele Old Hall Manor house of Keele manor, may have been the residence of Knights Templars and Hospitallers of Keele in medieval times. Could it be the 'Old Hall' farm marked on an estate map of 1829, situated a little SE of Keele church (NSJFS 1982/5 p80 see map). Has also appeared as Keele Old Manor.

Keele Park A deer park at Keele was created in the C16 (HOK p14), probably by the Sneyds after their removal to Keele from Bradwell. Keele had long been disparked by 1867 (EDP p178).

Keele Preceptory The Knights Templars had an estate at Keele from 1168-9 to sometime in the C13 when it became a preceptory. The preceptory was retained by the Crown from 1308 to 1314, when it was secured by Thomas, Earl of Lancaster, evidently as lord of Newcastle-under-Lyme. On his execution in 1322 the preceptory passed to the Crown and in 1324 it passed to the Knights Hospitallers, who, instead of establishing a new preceptory here made it part of their commandery of Halston, Shrops (VCH vol 3 pp267-268). Anticipating their suppression, which occurred in 1544, the knights leased Keele manor to Henry Delves in 1540 in an attempt to avoid takeover by the Crown (NSJFS 1982/5 pp7-21) (SNEDE). Chetwynd in the later C17 noted at least one of the Orders (SH p44). (IAANS p xx) (S p137) (LGS p37) (SLM winter 1955 p20) (HOK pp6-21) (Keele Church Guide. Christopher Harrison. 1988. p3) (SVB p102) (MR p197) (SSE 1996 pp36-49).

Keeper's Brook In the Colton area (CWF p136 in the index, but could not be found on p136).

Keeper's Pools In Teddesley Park to the E of Teddesley Hall. There is another Keeper's Pool to the E of Chartley Castle and nearby is Keeper's Cottage Farm.

Kelson Just N of Forsbrook and Cheadle (Pigot and Son map 1830) (1834 OS map).

Kempsage Lane A lane or and very fragmented minute hamlet by Garmelow, High Offley.

Kempsey Manor or Kemsey (W p391). House near Weston Jones 1.75m NW of Norbury. In High Offley parish.

Kempson's Hag 1m SE of Hilton Park, at approximately SJ 9650040 (1834 OS map).

Kenermont Hay Former hay, park or enclosure of the abbots of Hulton Abbey; an abbot was holding it in 1288 (SSE 1994 p82). Has also appeared as Cavermont Hay, Kevermunt and Kevermund Hay, and Kenermont Park. Weston Coyney and Norton-in-the-Moors have appeared as Weston sub Keveremont (1242) and Norton sub Keuremunt (SPN pp32,77) and Hay or Small Park of Cavermont (HBST p136). The name now (1843) adheres to two farms taken out of the ancient park called Carmont, or Carmont Side (Carmountside Farm) (HBST p289 note). Ward thinks it may be of Roman origin Caver Mont 'a caverned hill' (HBST p289 note). Or from the French name Chevremont (or Quevremont); the word is usually given to a field or moor. Chevremont and Quevremont mean 'hill where goats are kept' (SPN pp31-32).

Kenrick Park Public park 0.25m S of the S end of the High Street, West Bromwich. Originated in a gift of 19 acres presented to West Bromwich borough by Messrs JA and WK Kenrick in 1895 (VCH vol 17 p10). Opened 1897 (TEBC) (SHWB 13).

Kenrick's Village Built to the N of the Kenrick foundries, to the E of Spon Lane (see), West Bromwich ancient parish. (Kenrick's in Hardware. RA Church. 1969). The village, centred on Glover Street and completed by 1837 (VCH vol 17 p10), is marked on Charles Henry Blood's 1857 Map of Birmingham and its environs. Monkey Green is the local name for an area around Glover Street. It was developed by a building society and it has been sug-

gested that the name may be from the expression 'a monkey on the house' meaning a mortgage (VCH vol 17 p10).

Kent Hills Small hills in the Audley area (BOPP pl 2). There is a Kent Hill Farm 0.5m W of Audley.

Kerry Hill Minute hamlet 2.5m W of Wetley Rocks, Wetley. There is a good viewpoint about Kerry Hill Farm (NSJFS 1963 p84).

Ketley Ketley Farm 0.75m W of Kingswinford had two secret tunnels one which led to the old Summer House and another under Bell Inn in High Street, Kingswinford (TB Feb 1983 p9p). The name Ketley Works appears in the 1851 census.

Ketley Hills Behind Ketley Farm? Kingswinford.

Kettlebrook Former hamlet now a suburb of Tamworth, 0.5m S of Tamworth. Formerly in Bolehall and Glascote township in Tamworth ancient parish, Warws. The railway viaduct of 19 arches over the Anker, built in 1851 to carry the Birmingham and Derby Railway was the most expensive engineering work on the line (MR p322). Pevsner says it was built in 1837-9 (BOE p279). Kettlebrook was transferred to Staffs in either 1894 or 1932 (GLAUE p425). The church, St Andrew, at Kettlebrook, was built in 1896 (LDD). The car works of Reliant Engineering Co of Two Gates (see), operating by the 1970s, were occupied by Metrocab, taxi car manufacturers, after Metrocab formed in 1989 (BCFF p161).

Kettle Brook Runs from Warwickshire and joins the Tame S of Tamworth. The name appears in 1845 (SPNO p12). The name is from Old Norse 'ketill' probably replacing Old English 'cetel,' meaning 'a bubbling spring' (SPNO p12).

Kettle Hill Northern tip of the Dudley Castle escarpment (BCM April 1980 p29). Just outside the Dudley enclave (Worcs), and has always been in Staffs. Has also appeared as Kettle's Hill. On Saturday May 12 1934, Frederick Lester of Netherton, aged 14, plunged down a 150 feet chasm into flooded limestone workings at Kettle Hill. His body was never recovered and the funeral on June 2 had to be held at the site of the shaft (Dudley Herald May 19 1934) (BCM April 1980 pp28-34).

Kettlehouse Farm Stood on W side of Kingstanding Road near its junction with King's Road. In existence by 1884. There was a farm here, an encroachment on Perry Barr Common, by 1794 (MNB pp66,67). In 1936 Birmingham Corporation developed the Kettlehouse estate with housing. Kingstanding Library was built on the site of the farm (MNB pp62,75).

Kewell Green Land, also known as Keywall Green, at Mixon, the rent from which helped to keep the Ash Almshouses, Leek (W p725) (OL vol 1 p36). Is in the vicinity of, or became, Lower Green Farm, N of Mixon.

Khyber Pass A knoll, at SJ 927449, in Park Hall Country Park, possibly manmade, as there was mining and sandstone quarrying in the vicinity (Park Hall Country Park. Staffs County Council Leaflet. Pre-1991).

Khyber Pass Former gap in an embankment once bridged by a small mineral tramway which ran along the embankment between coal pits at Rough Hay, Darlaston (Offlow hundred) and the Walsall Canal. The embankment was demolished for the construction of Rough Hay council housing estate built in the late 1920s and early 1930s. The name Khyber was preserved in one of the streets of the estate, Khyber Close (SNDB p64p).

Kibblestone Very fragmented minute hamlet on high ground above Scotch Brook NNE and NE of Oulton. Former township and quarter in Stone ancient parish (W p364). Between 1851 and 1872 Kibblestone township seems to have been divided into the townships of Oulton-with-Meaford, and Moddershall (W) (KD 1872). Kibblestone is believed to have been formerly Cublesdon or Cublestone (COI p21) (NSFCT 1913 p156). Cantor's 'Cublesdon,' which he places N of Stone, probably represents Kibblestone. The manor of Kibblestone or Cublesdon probably dates from the beginning of the C12 (SOK pp13-14). In the Quest of 1284, Roesia Trussell holds Kibblestone from the Barony of Wem, on condition she find one soldier equipped with bow and arrows, to serve for eight days in the year at Tyrley Castle (SOK p15). In the vicinity of Kibblestone Camp, N side of Kibblestone Road, was possibly a medieval village, probably deserted in the C18 (SSAHST 1970 p35) (SOK p17). Garner was shown by Mr Molineux a medieval bronze key found at Cubblestone (Kibblestone) (GNHSS p9). For Kibblestone Mill see Wetmore Mill.

Kibblestone Hall Kibblestone, 0.5m NE of Oulton. A house on the site was in existence by 1831 and is shown as being owned by Edward Barlow in 1844. When Barlow died in 1876 the house at Kibblestone passed to Richard Pirie Copeland of the prominent potting family. The Kibblestone estate remained with the Copelands until 1960 when it became the property of the Scouts of the City of Stoke-on-Trent District (SOK pp77p,78,79) (SVB p134). In WW2 the Dalcroze School of Eurythmic Dancing were evacuated to here from London. Other tenants before 1950 used the hall as a junior residential house for a private school. By 1950 the hall was empty and unusable and was demolished in 1954; the site is now occupied by the Ronald Copeland Training Centre (SOK pp78-79). The first scouts to camp on the Kibblestone estate, in Beech Field, were five scout leaders from Longton at Easter 1927 (SOK p78) (ES March 29 1997 p21p). Lord Baden-Powell visited the camp in 1936 (TWWW pp6-7pcs). The Devil's Ledge is a ledge halfway up some sandstone cliffs in the hall grounds. In recent years it has been utilised by Kibblestone camp scouts as a swing platform (TWWW p7p).

Kibblestone Manor House Kibblestone. Seat of the Trussell family in the C13 (COI p22). The site of the house has never been located (SOK p14). It may have stood at the bottom of the valley opposite Kibblestone Hall, perhaps by Mosty Lee Farm (COI pp22-23). Its ruins are believed to have been seen by Erdeswick. Some stone from it may have gone into building Oulton Old Hall (SOK p18).

Kibblestone Park Medieval deer park enclosed out of forest. In existence by 1311 (NSJFS 1962 p76) (SOK p15). Owned by William Trussell. It was raided by the parson of Swynnerton the same day he raided Fenton Old Park (NSFCT 1910 pp174,176). The park, also known as Kibblestone Old Park, may have occupied the area subsequently called Oulton Heath, whose southern boundary followed the present Kibblestone Road, and whose northern edge was the Downs Banks (SOK p15).

Kiddemore Green Small hamlet stretching for a long way along the lane between Brewood and Bishop's Wood, 1.25m ESE of Bishop's Wood. Former township in Brewood ancient parish (THS p255). An axe-head of Neolithic or Bronze Age was found at Kiddemore Cottage in 1983. It is kept by David Horovitz (BDH p18). Has appeared as Kudimor (1308), Kyrremore (1383. 1723), Kerrymore Green (1611), The Kerrimores (1661), Kidimoor Green (Yates' map) and Kiddermore Green (SPNO p38) (SPN p23) (SHC part 2 1934 p39). The name is a corruption of Kerri-moor (W p447). 'Marshland where brushwood grows' (SPN p23). Kiddemore Green was included in Brewood prebend (SSAHST vol 2 1960-61 p43). For Kiddemore Green in a local rhyme see Brewood.

Kidsgrove Former mining hamlet at the mouth of the Bath Pool valley, now a town 20m NNE of Stafford. The present town covers an area which lay partly in Ravenscliffe, Brerehurst and Oldcott townships in Wolstanton ancient parish (W p290). The trunk of a large **fossilized plant** was discovered in the 1920s on The Avenue (KAIW p18). The bridle path which diverges from Clough Hall drive by the Leg O' Mutton pool, climbing towards the Lodge Cafe on the A34, has been considered locally to be of Roman origin (KAIW p2). The **name** means 'Cyda's grove' (SPN pp68-69). Kidsgrove has appeared as Kid Crew, Kidgrew, Killegrew (1763) (SHC 1934 p69), and Kidcrew (1843) (HBST p128). The place was still a **tiny hamlet** in 1775 (Yates' map) but had grown through coal mining and being a thoroughfare to the size of a small town by 1837. The turnpike road from Burslem to Red Bull was built through Kidsgrove in 1765, and the Trent and Mersey Canal was constructed through Kidsgrove in the late 1770s (Tithe maps of 1837-9) (KAIW p4). The **church**, St Thomas, The Avenue, was built in 1837 (BOE p162) by Thomas Kinnersley (d1855) of Clough Hall, in just six weeks (TTTD p209-212), but said to have been designed by Mrs Kinnersley of Clough Hall (BOE p162). In c1914 the church had a reputation as a bargees runaways church because marriages could be performed (according to one witness, without banns being called) after only a short residence (KAIW p17). The tower at Kidsgrove on a hill at Long Row on the E side of the railway W of Ravenscliffe Road was a **windmill** probably built in 1812 at the instigation of the owner of Clough Hall on whose land it was situated. By 1897 it was described as the old windmill. It is reminiscent of Chesterton Windmill in Warws. Undoubtedly the parapet was a later addition, although the owner was keen to have it in the appearance of a non-mill. Job does not think the doorway is Norman as C Lynam does in NSFCT 1916 (WBJ p28 il xii). It stands on a hill 669 feet above sea level and it has been claimed that whatever the purpose of the building it was never finished (NSFCT 1916 pp49-53). The windmill was repaired in 1980 (ES Sept 28 1981). DoE II (BOE p163) (WIS pp11p,19) (SLM June/July 1987 p15) (MR p198) (F p317) (KNS pp137,138). Its **industry** in the C18 to the early C20 was coal mining. It has been said Kidsgrove was one of the first local authorities to lay out an industrial site. The site laid out in 1958 is situated on the Cheshire side of Butt Lane and Talke (Kidsgrove Town Guide 1962) (KAIW p19). **Railways.** It was recommended that Kidsgrove station (Liverpool Road) be closed in 1963 (ES March 22 1963). A collision occurred at Kidsgrove station on April 27 1973. Kidsgrove became a **separate ecclesiastical parish** in 1853 (LGS p155). The urban district of Kidsgrove appears to have been formed in 1894 and was abolished in 1974 (GLAUE p414). The device of the urban district consists of kids gambolling in a grove (CH p340). **Newspaper.** The Kidsgrove Times, founded by late May 1954, ran until at least Oct 1972 (SHJ spring 1996 p18). There is a **black dog ghost**

or boggart at Kidsgrove which foretells a mining disaster (FLJ 1941 p237. 1958 p185). (NSFCT 1900 p144) (FOS p17) (The Kidsgrove Boggart and The Black Dog. Philip R Leese. 1989). Malkin and Raven say the boggart is the apparition of a woman murdered in one of the Harecastle Tunnels by the narrow-boat man with whom she was travelling. She returns as either a white horse (AGT p60) or a headless figure (MR p198) and her appearance foretells a disaster. A **UFO** was seen over Kidsgrove by Mr and Mrs Turner and Mr and Mrs Brogan on Aug 4 1967 at about 11.00pm (FSRP pp24-26). **Natives and visitors.** 'Leisure Moments; or, The Breathings of a Poetic Spirit' by **Elizabeth A Needham**, born in Kidsgrove in 1868, was published in 1889 (VFC p97). On Oct 2 1911 **Karl Kramer**, aged 28, a German fitter, employed to install the Mond Gas burners at Birchenwood Coke Works broke into his employer's lodgings, Avenue Villa in St John's Wood Road, to steal a cash box belonging to his employer. During the burglary he murdered Mrs Mary Weir, the landlady who was a widow, and her four year old daughter, Margaret, and their maid. At his trial Kramer was found to be insane (KAIW p17) (Kidsgrove, Talke and Mow Cop. Postcards from the Past. Roger Simmons. 1998 p69) (info Kidsgrove Library).

Kids Wood Small wood on E side of railway, Kidsgrove.

Kileby Hall Blithbury, Colton. It has been considered the seat of the Mavesyns, lords of Mavesyn Ridware, before they moved before the mid C12 to Mavesyn Ridware Old Hall. The house was then granted to a Mavesyn daughter who married Sir William Kileby who made it his seat (SHOS vol 1 p201) (SOS pp184-185). Has appeared as Kilbynshall (1307), Kilby Hall en Blithbury (1332), Kylby Hall Fyldes (1407); the name, which also appears in Kileby Holmes, was lost by 1798 (SHOS vol 1 p201). It has been said that a rebuilder of the hall or a later occupier was Robert Hullen, and the hall was demolished and the Bull and Spectacles Inn built on the site (TB Oct 1994 p18p).

King Charles' Oak Roughcote, Caverswall. An ancient oak in a field. Topped at some period; according to GJV Bemrose this was a customary sign of mourning in Tudor times (NSFCT 1946 p145).

King Charles's Lane Patshull. A byway or hollow road dividing Wrottesley and Patshull estates, down which Charles Stuart fled after the battle of Worcester according to Rev F Wrottesley (MOS p195 notes).

King Clump Local name for a burial mound 0.25m SW of Swynnerton at SJ 84743510 of about 24 paces in diameter and four feet high (NSFCT vol 75 p25) or 10 feet high and was surrounded by 14 large trees evenly spaced with a fifteenth inside the circle in 1983 (NSFCT 1983 p11). It is of the Bronze Age origin and is now covered by trees. It was probably excavated in 1836 and was excavated by WP Richards in 1967 (SPJD p9p,10). The mound had been broken into by 1983. Later a rescue dig was undertaken but nothing was found except a hammer stone. There are stories of seven kings being buried here (NSFCT 1983 p11). Has also appeared as King's Clump.

King Dick's Entrenchment Small square or rectangular entrenchment in Teddesley Park. A short iron sword or dagger, thought to be Roman, was found in the fosse in 1780 (SHOS vol 2 Additions p2) (SSC p121 in the intro) (SOS p182) (GNHS p70) (VCH vol 1 p193. vol 5 p182) (NSFCT 1926 p151) (BERK2 p103). Or it is possibly of Saxon origin (NSJFS 1964 p38).

King George V Park Public park on the S side of Lawnswood Road and on the W side of Bells Lane, Wordsley.

King Hayes Walsall Wood. S of Vigo, at SK 05320271 was found a charcoal-burning hearth (SSAHST 1973 p40).

King John's Oak Bagot's Park. Said to be even impressive when reduced to a stump (NSFCT 1927 p167). It may be identifiable with Cliff Oak (see).

King Oaks Aqualate Hall, Forton. Oaks with wide girths. It is a mystery why these trees are so called (SLM Dec 1948 p187).

King of Oaks A tree from the Gnosall area. Felled and bought for £20 by John Palmer in c1892 and taken to Fairoak to make seats and panelling for the methodist chapel there (BOV p28). Whether the same as King Oaks?

King's Bank At SJ 78163956 in the Maer Hills. Has a burial mound at its apex and another burial mound a few yards to the S on another hillock (NSFCT 1931 p100). One is called Coplow, the other Sandylow, or one is called both Coplow and Sandylow. Sandylow is alone mentioned in NSFCT 1927 p172. Henry of Huntingdon and other early historians asserted that Oswy (or Oswald) Christian King of Northumbria was slain in a battle at Mere probably by Kenred king of Mercia in 642 AD (NSFCT 1931 p92) (STM June 1967 p27p), or in c705. Plot and others believed Mere referred to Maer, Staffs, and identified one of these mounds, or the only one, which was of conical shape (VCH barrow list), to be Oswy's resting place (NHS pp408,409) (SHOS vol 1 p36) (GNHS p74). In the C20 it has been asserted that the mound is, or may be, natural (NSFCT 1931 p92. 1983 p13) (NSJFS 1965 p44).

King's Bridge References to this bridge figure many times in the records of the Staffordshire Quarter Sessions of the early C18 and may be a reference to

Yoxall Bridge (ABMEE pp3-4). However, King's Bridge has been shown to be the Wychnor Bridges Bridge (see) (SHC 1934 pp25-26).

King's Bromley Ancient parish and village on rising land above the Trent (SVB p103), 13m ESE of Stafford.
EARLY. There is a small irregular rounded enclosure, and at the end of an elongated rectangular one 1m E of King's Bromley at SK 140171 (MOT p55) (NSJFS 1964 p26). At SK 115157, 1m SW of the village, is an open-ended U-shaped enclosure, with small circles nearby (MOT p55) (NSJFS 1964 p26). At SK 116162, 0.5m SW of the village, are two ditch lines crossing obliquely; pits and a circle (MOT p55) (NSJFS 1964 p27). These could be the same as three small oval enclosures of a probable Romano-British site at SK 116165, 700 yards SW of the village, which were partly excavated in 1969. Two enclosures were found and a pit containing part of a mortarium of 100 AD (SSAHST 1968 p71. 1973 pp29-32). At SK 110169, 0.75m W of the village, is part of a rectangular enclosure, small irregular circle, pits, and a short length of ditch (MOT p55) (NSJFS 1964 p27).
900 to PRESENT. The name occurs in a charter of 942 (DUIGNAN) (SSE 1991 pp7,8). Leofric, Earl of Mercia, died at King's Bromley on Aug 31 1057 (NSFCT 1896 p124 note) (WAM p21) (HOS p16). The parish **church**, All Saints, on the N side of Church Lane by Yoxall Road, may stand on the site of a wooden Saxon church. The present nave has some Norman work (All Saint's Church - a church guide) (BOE p163). King's Bromley may have been a chapelry in Alrewas ancient parish, for Archbishop Boniface, in 1259, says chapel Bromley was in Alrewas prebend (SSAHST vol 2 1960-61 p43). The parish was a peculiar jurisdiction of the dean and chapter and certain prebendaries of Lichfield cathedral until peculiar jurisdictions were abolished in 1846 (VCH vol 3 pp93-94). The **name** has appeared as Bromelei (DB), Bromleage (NHS p433), kynges bromley (1308), and Bromley Regis (SHOS vol 1 p143). It is from 'Broom leah' wood clearing (SHOS vol 1 p143) (SSE 1996 p11). King's was added when Bromley became a royal possession with the marriage of Harold I to Algitha or to Eadgifn (NSFCT 1896 p124 note) (SOSH pp71-72). Or it was added after the Norman Conquest, when the land was held by the Crown (SVB p103) (info Mrs D Fox). DB states it belonged to Harold T.R.E; his sole possession in Staffs. It passed to the Crown probably through his marriage to Algitha (granddaughter of Leofric, Earl of Mercia) (SOSH pp71-72), or Eadgifn (sister of Edwine and Morkere) (NSFCT 1896 p124 note). Harold and Algitha or Eadgifn are said to have married in Bromley church (SOSH pp71-72). King's Bromley **parish feast** was on the nearest Sunday to All Saints' day in the C19 (W p595). According to RF Elton King's Bromley had a **market**; when the Trent swelled and a ford across it was impassable those from the N side of the river may have had a market at Blithfield Cross (HR p11). The village suffered floods in 1935, 1947 and 1955. The custom of an **annual duck race** on New Year's day with hundreds of sponsored plastic ducks raced down the Trent ending at Yoxall Bridge? organised by the local PTA was occurring by at least the early 1990s (info Mrs D Fox) (TB Feb 1994 p18). The local history society, **King's Bromley Historians**, was founded in 1979 to help a boy of the village with a history project (info Mrs D Fox). **Natives and Visitors**. The Staffordshire Plea Rolls for 1292 or 1293 relate there was a law suit concerning eleven acres of land here, which was claimed by one Thomas Corbet (the plaintiff). The jury was told that when **Henry I** was hunting in Cannock Forest he breakfasted with Thomas's ancestor at King's Bromley and that the ancestor persuaded the king to give him a certain piece of land (about eight acres) out of the king's hay. And together with three acres without the king's hay, he claimed eleven acres (DUIGNAN pp26-27) (SSAHST 1965 p26) (HOS 1998 p34). **Mary Cooper** of King's Bromley claimed notoriety in the C17 for being a 'beldam,' the eldest of six living generations. She is noted in the PR (NHS p322) (SHOS vol 1 p148) (SSC p122 in the intro) (S&W vol 1 p8) (STMSM Nov 1973 p27) (HOA p187).

King's Bromley Hays Extra-parochial liberty. Became a separate civil parish in 1858. Incorporated into King's Bromley civil parish in 1922 (GLAUE p405).

King's Bromley Manor The earliest manor house of King's Bromley dates from c1227. In Henry III's reign the manor had passed to the Corbets. In the 1460s it passed from them to the Praers, followed by the Patrichs, and others (SHOS vol 1143-146). The same or a later house was the residence of Thomas Fleetwood, a Catholic, in 1708, when an anti-Catholic riot occurred here (LOU p57). In 1794 the estate passed by marriage to the Lane family of Bentley Hall. Jane Lane who aided Charles II whilst a fugitive was one of the most famous of the family. Her portrait by Sir Peter Lely once hung in the hall and a letter from the king to her was shown in a glass case. The house also contained a portrait of Charles II by Lely (STMSM Nov 1973 p27). (SHOS vol 1 pls of the hall pl VII and facing p147). For the armorial glass at

the hall see NSFCT 1927 p159. The Lane family left the Manor House in 1921 and the house was demolished in 1928 (Melting Pot summer 1996 p12) or some say in 1927. Only the water tower has been left standing. (HS p113 pl). Has also been called King' Bromley Hill (NSFCT 1900 p142). An ice-house lies 300 yards from the house at SK 119711. Built in 1753. Originally built of brick, covered with earth and planted with trees. Had collapsed by 1990 (IHB p394). Dovecote (BOE p163) (DoE II). When the house was demolished the entrance gates with the letter 'L' for Lane went to Milford Hall (BERK2 p13).

King's Bromley Park A fairly modern (1867) deer park enclosed by Mr Newton Lane of King's Bromley Manor (EDP p181).

King's Bromley Wharf Wharf on the Trent and Mersey Canal 1.5m SSW of King's Bromley (W p595). Has also appeared as Bromley Wharf (W p595).

King's Ditch Built by King Offa as a defence to Tamworth, also known as 'Offa's Dyke' or 'King's Dyke' (GNHS p169) (SOSH p351). Was constructed between 755 and 796. The dyke is about 470 to 500 yards long - the rivers Tame and Anker forming the defence on the S side (NSFCT 1910 p215). References to the 'King's Ditch' frequently appear in documents dating from the C13. It was 45 feet wide, with a raised bank and palisades. Traces were found in excavations in 1908, 1957 and 1960 (STMSM Sept 1980 p19).

Kings Field Medieval field boundary of Newcastle-under-Lyme (NUL p107).

Kings Hayes Former enclosure made out of Druid's Heath by the C14 (MOA p134). The name was preserved in Kingshayes Farm, situated a little to the N near Walsall Wood, and is preserved in Kingshayes Road, built in 1965, on the housing estate on former Druid's Heath (SNAR p33).

King's Head Inn Small old coaching inn in Bird Street, Lichfield. It preserves the archway giving access to the courtyard behind. Col Luke Lillington raised a regiment of foot at the King's Head on 25th March 1705. From this regiment has evolved the present (1999) Staffordshire Regiment. The inn is said to be haunted by three ghosts. The 'Laughing Cavalier' ghost is said to be the ghost of a Cavalier who was murdered and his body dumped in the inn's cellars (RSL pp10-11) (GOM p29) (GLS pp68-69) (GPCE p33). The ghost of 'George,' a former licensee, appears in the cellar where he died (GLS pp68-69). There have also been sightings of the ghost of a young girl who died in a fire; this fire occurred here, according to the landlord, Sid Farmer, in c1690 (GOM p29) (GLS pp68-69).

King's Hill Area N of Wednesbury, in Wednesbury parish. Some have thought that some shallow bell-shaped pits at King's Hill, which were reopened at the end of the C19 for coal extraction, were of Roman origin, but this supposition has been discredited (OCHW p7) (Birmingham and Its Regional Setting. H Thorpe. 1950 pp99-100) (HOWV pp4-5). According to local tradition at King's Hill, was fought one of the battles said to have been fought at Wednesbury (see) in 592 or 715 (WAM pp17-18). The name King's Hill appears in 1315 (HOWV p108). It is probably not from a Saxon king or battle, but may be from manorial demesne when the king held the manor or it may indicate a part of Wednesbury, a royal manor, as opposed to Darlaston (Offlow hundred) (HOWV p108). There was a post mill at approximately SO 981965 shown first on Plot's map over a mile NW of the church at Wednesbury. The OS map of 1886 describes the mill as disused (WAM p54) (WBJ p42). Subterranean fires in the coal seams under King's Hill in 1897 caused holes in the road. These were known as 'crownings in' (TWDOP p135p). The church, St Andrew, Darlaston Road, was built in 1893 (HOWY p314) (LDD). Ghosts. There have been numerous reports of a ghostly brown dog that roams the King's Hill area and usually brings a warning to those who see it (GOM p29) (GPCE p57). A large old house which backed onto Birmingham Street, was haunted by a poltergeist according to some childhood memories of Ray Askey (TB March 1994 p5).

King's Hill Park King's Hill, Wednesbury. Public park which opened on what had been a colliery mound in 1900 (WDOP p53p).

Kingsland Kingstanding, Great Barr. Name for a school in Kingsland Road, opened in 1935 (KPP p19).

Kingsley Ancient parish and former township. The village of Kingsley lies on an E-facing slope high above the Churnet Valley, 16m NNE of Stafford. The manors of Chingeslei and Chingesleia appear in DB; the later was then held of the king (SPN p69) (SSE 1996 p15). The 'King's lea'; probably because the manor, or part of it, belonged at some time to the Crown (DUIGNAN) (LGS p156). 'The king's woodland clearing' (SPN p69) (SSE 1996 p15). There is a moated site at SK 007471 (CAMS p63), which seems to have been the site of the manor house (CCT p57). There was a church at Kingsley in the C12 (LDD). The present parish **church**, St Werburgh, N of Church Street on the E side of the village, has C13 work in the tower (BOE p163). The parish formed between 1086 and 1291 out of Cheadle parish. Kingsley township lies in South Totmonslow hundred division whilst Whiston township lies in

North Totmonslow hundred division (THS p233) (SHC 1916 p194) (GLAUE p415). The parish **wake** fell on the first Sunday after midsummer day (W p781) - an unusual date, and gives rise to the old couplet

> Let mid summer day be early or late,
> the Sunday after is Kingsley wake.

(STM Dec 1966 p32). The village had combined **stocks** and **whipping post** beside the churchyard wall (KES p120) (LGS p156) (NSFCT 1925 p189) (STM Dec 1966 p32p) (SLM May 1984 p9). The village was noted for its wickedness and immorality in the locality (SVB p104). There was a bull-tether or **bear-ring** beside the churchyard wall (KES p120) (LGS p156) (STM Dec 1966 p32p) (SLM May 1984 p9). The bear-ring was described as 'recently discovered' in 1925 when the new road was being made by the church through glebe lands (NSFCT 1925 p189) (Staffs Weekly Sentinel Feb 13 1926). Once a bear became loose at a Kingsley fair (HOC p156). The **making of tape** was carried on at Kingsley (SCSF p112). It was recommended that Kingsley and Froghall railway station be closed in 1963 (ES March 22 1963). **Persons and visitors**. It is said that the bells from Kingsley church which Father **FW Faber** could hear whilst walking near Cotton Dell inspired him to write the hymn 'Hark, hark my soul' (SLM Sept 1950 p29il) (SVB p105). **Abraham K Mosley**, one of the unsung poets of the Staffs Moorlands, wrote this poem about Kingsley church in 1920

> For o'er five hundred years and more,
> Has Kingsley's tower crowned Kingsley Banks,
> Embattled, moss-grown, grim and gray,
> A landmark score o'mile away;
> Guiding errant wanderers to their homes
> And worshippers to Church.
> For centuries bronze bells have pealed
> On Yuletide morn and New Year's Eve,
> Ringing in joyous mirth the call -
> Peace and Goodwill and Joy to all.
>
> The Parish Church o' Kingsley's Tower,
> A beacon fired with mother's love e'er watches o'er
> Whiston, Holt Cross and th' Moors
> To Morridge snows and Cauldon's Lowe,
> O'er Churnet's Vale from Consall Wood
> To Oakamoor and Alton;
> Ne'er idling lazily, but creaking,
> Racking, straining beam and stone
> Its bells waft hallowed peals abroad;
> And betimes speak a parting knell,
> 'Mid sighs and tears for loved ones gone before.

(HLSP p59).

Kingsley Tettenhall. Former manor which extended SW from Old Hill to Mill Lane, Wightwick Bank, and Smestow Brook between Wightwick and Compton. The area included Kingsley Wood a detached portion of Kinver Forest, and the manor seems to have originated as an outlying part of Kinver manor (VCH vol 20 p21); it descended with Kinver manor until at least the end of the C19 (SVS p161 note) (HOPTT pp28,268). Tettenhall Towers (see) stands on land which was within Kingsley manor (VCH vol 20 p21).

Kingsleybanks 0.5m E of Kingsley, on the E side of the Churnet.

Kingsley Hay Is mentioned in 1358. Sometimes considered a hay of Kinver Forest. Was presumably Kingsley Wood in Tettenhall, now Tettenhall Wood (VCH vol 2 pp343, 344 note).

Kingsley Holt Village high above the Churnet Valley 0.75m SE of Kingsley. In Kingsley parish. A curious stone carving semi-circular in shape on a flat base was found here in May 1945. It was of, perhaps, C16 or C17 origin, and may have formed part of a column, possibly the capital of an old house in the area (NSFCT 1945 p82). The Blacksmiths Arms Inn has or had above its door a quotation from Dr Johnson of Lichfield (see) expounding on the happiness provided by a good inn (VB p176). Has also appeared as Kingsley Halt (NSFCT 1945 p82).

Kingsley Moor Small hamlet 1.25m WSW of Kingsley.

King's Low 1.5m WNW of Tixall. Burial mound at SJ 955237 in Blackheath Covert. 28 paces in diameter and four feet high. There is a burial mound called Queen's Low at SJ 964239, 0.5m to the E. Their origin is unknown although two urns were found near them at the beginning of the C18 (W p426). (HOT pp86-87) (SOS p70) (NSFCT 1881 p14) (SC p148) (KES p207)

(NSJFS 1965 p49). Was excavated in 1986-1992 and a Bronze Age cremation urn and barbed and tangled flint arrowheads were found. Discovery of bones indicated a secondary cremation dating to 1600 BC (SPJD p9ps,11-12). Just E of King's Low was a cross, which marked the site of Sir William Chetwynd's assassination (1905 OS map). The cross is now in Tixall church.

Kingsmead Name for an area? of Stafford about Kingsmead Hospital, which opened in 1974 on the S side of Corporation Street on the E side of Stafford (VCH vol 6 p235). The name is from King's Poole Meeds.

King's Pool King's Pool is marked on an old map of Stafford, covering an area without the town walls between East and North Gates in Stafford. Has also appeared as King's Pools. Evidence of human activity of c6000 BC has been discovered in the marshes. A flint scatter of supposed late Neolithic or early Bronze Age origin was located about 1km N of King's Pool (WSS pp97,98). In medieval times the pool or pools formed an integral part of Stafford's NE defences and may have even stretched to the Norman castle in Stafford town (SHC 1887 p9) (SHCST 1971-73 p10). The pools were formed by glacial action during the last Ice Age. They were in places more than 21 metres deep (SN June 23 1995 p9). In medieval times the pools were owned by the Crown and contained the royal fish and were let to a tenant on condition that he provide fish for the royal household; according to some authorities the Wymer family were tenants in King John's reign (OSST 1933 pp30-32). Ralph de Waymer is said to have held King's Pool of the king in fee and inheritance on condition he allowed the king to keep all the pike and bream the king could catch there, whilst he and his heirs could have the other fish and eels if he gave half a mark at the feast of St Michael (SMC p123) (SCSF p119) (FSP p52). It is said that Edward I is said to have used fish from the pool (R&S p10). The pool appears in 1345 as 'he Kingespol' (OSST 1933 pp30-32). A mill built outside the East Gate in the mid C14 was driven by water from the King's Pool for about 200 years (SSTY p3). By 1600 the pools had become meadowland (HOS p67). It is now part nature reserve, car park, and Stafford's inner by-pass, Queensway.

Kings Poole Meeds Stafford. Could be same as the King's Pool.

King's Rise Kingstanding, Great Barr. Name for schools in Peckham Road (KPP p19).

Kings Standing Mound shown on OS 6 inch maps at SK 12081386, 0.5m SE of King's Bromley Wharf. It was flattened by ploughing and was about 35 paces in diameter. There is nothing more known about it (NSJFS 1965 p43).

Kings Standing House 1.5m NW of Rangemore. In Tutbury parish. The name is possibly from Henry VII's visit to Burton and his hunting in Needwood Forest. It is alluded to in FNC Mundy's poem 'Needwood Forest' (SHOS vol 1 p66). Or it is named after a favourite resting-place of James I during the hunt; he came to Needwood Forest in 1619, 1621, and 1624 (HCT pp88,207-8,219) (VCH vol 2 p356) (ESNF p25p) (LTD p117).

King's Standing Kingstanding, Great Barr. A mound 20 feet in diameter and five feet high on former Perry Barr Common. So called as it was from here Charles I reviewed his troops brought up by the Staffordshire gentry on Oct 16 or 18 1642 on his way to Edgehill, Warws, and in 1643. The present mound, which lies on the W side of Kingstanding Road, may not be the mound on which the king stood. The original mound, which may have been a burial mound of ancient origin (although Plot thought it was not of Roman origin), is thought to have stood at a little distance from the present mound. The old one is said to have been destroyed when plundered by labourers for its treasure of silver chains at the beginning of the C19. The tenant on hearing of the relevance of the old mound then built a new one by the Kingstanding Road to commemorate Charles I's visit. He then surrounded the mound with a fence, which was dilapidated and broken by 1930 (NHS p403) (SHOS vol 1 p17) (SVS p379) (DUIGNAN - info from The Forest and Chase of Sutton Coldfield p117) (THM vol 4 p55) (BAST vol 32 1906 pp41-61) (Birmingham Post March 11 1930) (CCC p5) (TBS p10) (KPP pp6-7) (MNB p64) (SSAHST vol 32 1990-91 p90).

Kingstanding Former hamlet now a large residential suburb 2m E of Great Barr. Formerly in Perry Barr township in Handsworth ancient parish. The name is from the burial mound called King's Standing (see). The Roman road Icknield Street, now Chester Road, passes along the E side of the area. Roman coins of Domitian, Trajan, Hadrian, Antoninus Pius, Marcus Aurelius, Lucius Verus, Faustina and Faustina junior, possibly part of a hoard, were found before 1884 in Roman Field, at the junction of Dunenin and Templeton Roads, where the pumping station now stands (Antiquities. C Chattock. 1884 p236) (SSAHST vol 32 1990-91 p89) (KPP p6). A Roman coin was found on the E side of the Kingstanding Road near George Frederick Road, and another or others on the W side of College Road near the junction of Brackenbury Road and Dulwich Road (SSAHST vol 32 1990-91 p89). The original hamlet, centred on the Hare and Hound Inn (see), was surrounded by common land known as Perry Barr Common. After the sale of the Perry Hall estate in 1928 Kingstanding was developed with housing. Local residents have called Kingstanding 'Little Roosha,' possibly on account of its proximity to Rushall or because it was reputed to be very cold in Kingstanding village on account of its exposed situation which reminded local inhabitants of Russia (KPP pp5,9,14). Kingstanding was in Perry Barr ecclesiastical parish from 1862 until becoming a separate ecclesiastical parish in 1933. In 1967 Old Oscott broke away from Kingstanding (GLAUE pp415,419). The church, St Luke, on the corner of Caversham and Peckham Roads off Haringay Road, was built in 1937 (BOEWA p196) (BDD). The church, St Columba, on the corner of Banner's Gate Road and Chester Road North, was built in 1957-1960 (BOEWA p196) (BDD). In 1791 a pugilist called Henry Smith died in a battle which local gentry had tried to stop in the Kingstanding district (TBS p31).

Kingstanding Warren The name for that half of Perry manor which was granted to George Birch, joint lord with George Birch of Perry manor by 1779 (KPP p8).

Kingsthorne Kingstanding, Great Barr. Name for a school in Cranbourne Road, opened in 1931. Built on or near the site of Pool Farm, an encroachment on Perry Barr Common, in existence by 1794; the name Pool may be from the nearby Lodge Pool (KPP p19) (MNB p62).

Kingstone Ancient parish and former manor (HOU p332). The village Kingstone lies in a dale on the upper reaches of Tad Brook (SVB p106), 10m ENE of Stafford. Kingstone was the usual ecclesiastical spelling whilst Kingston (LGS p156) was the usual civil spelling (GLAUE p415). The name appears in 1166 as Kingeston (SPN p70) (SSE 1996 p15). It means 'the king's farmstead or tun' (SPN p70) (SSE 1996 p15). It is possible that the first settlement was known by another name (SPN p70). (JEPS No. 20 pp13-37). There was a church at Kingstone in the C12 (LDD). The present parish church, St John the Baptist, on a slight hill (SVB p106) on the W side of Church Lane in the village centre, about 100 feet from the old church (OS map 1925 sheet 32), was built in 1860-1861 (BOE p163); the old church was taken down as it was said to be beyond repair (SVB p106). The manor of Kingstone anciently belonged to the Gresley family. In the C16 Sir John Gresley sold it to Sir Edward Aston. In 1865 it belonged to the Earl of Shrewsbury and Talbot (HOU (1865) p331). Rev John R Palmer (b1858), poet and novelist, was vicar of Kingstone and rector of Gratwich from 1905. His work includes 'Lines of Poetry' (1876), Burden-Bearing' (1884), 'A Hero in Strife, Sunbeam's Influence' and 'From Darkness to Light' (VFC p103).

Kingstone Hall Timber house covered with plaster near Kingstone old church (HOU p431). It appears to have been the seat William Goring in 1672, who is described as of Kingstone in SOS (1844) p317; the arms of Goring or Goreing appear on Plot's map at Kingstone. Sometime seat of John Stonier (ESNF p43p).

Kingstone Manor House Kingstone. The many old yew trees near to the site of the old churchyard indicate the site of the ancient residence and grounds, the moat of which remains (HOU pp330-331).

Kingstone Wood Wood over 0.5m S of Kingstone.

Kingston Hill Hill and modern suburb 1.25m E of Stafford. In St Mary's parish, Stafford. A Neolithic or Bronze Age flint scraper was found at Kingston Hill in 1929 (NSJFS 1964 p34). In the later C17 at Kingston Hill Plot noted a blue marl which he likened to Fullers earth (NHS p119). From Kingston Hill was possibly hewn the sandstones of the Bunter Pebble Beds to build the walls around Stafford and later for the town hall which in turn were reused in building the windmill at Broadeye (VCH vol 2 p190). Plot wrote about two floating islands about 20 feet broad by 30 feet or 40 feet long on Kingston Mill Pool, which in March 1680, began to move from under the hill on NW side of the pool and come together first to the SW corner where they continued for about three weeks, and then in May, when Plot was there, to the SE corner, lying just in the passage of the water out of the pool toward the mill (NHS p114).

King Street Ancient thoroughfare leading from Penkridge to the W (Newport, Shrewsbury, and Chester). It is mentioned in old deeds (DUIGNAN p117) (NSFCT 1908 p119; called Kings Street). A part of it ran by the Webb Stone at Bradley and in the High and Little Onn areas.

Kingstreet Grange House 1m ENE of Sheriffhales (1834 OS map).

Kings Vale Name for two settlements, encroachments on Perry Barr Common, in existence by 1794. Kings Vale Farm was situated near the junction of King's Road and Carshalton Road (MNB pp66,67). The name was given to the original village school for Kingstanding in Kingstanding Road, opened in 1914 (KPP p19).

Kingswell Preserved in Kingswell Cottages 2m SW of Adbaston. In Adbaston parish.

Kingswinford Ancient parish and large village on the upper reaches of Dawley Brook at the foot of the Pensnett Chase escarpment, 21.75m SSW of Stafford.

EARLY to 1700. Hackwood notes two burial mounds at Kingswinford (SCSF p74). These are probably the mounds at Barrow Hill (see), which are, in fact, natural. Mr Fletcher of Dudley showed Garner a Roman bottle of porous red pitcher found near Kingswinford (GNHS p543). Kingswinford lies on one of the **saltways** radiating out from Droitwich (WMVB p38). The Swinford mentioned in a charter of perhaps the period 946-955 AD may be identified with Kingswinford or Old Swinford (SHC 1916 pp92-93). The **name** has appeared as Svinesford (DB), Kyngesswynford (SPN p70), and Swinford Regis (W p181). It is said to be from Sweyn, first Danish king who conquered the Saxons in 1010 (W p181) (STM Nov 1966 p30), either his ford, or because he forded the river here (TB Aug 1982 p16). 'Swinford' was recorded before the Danish personal name Sweyn was introduced into the country, so it cannot have influenced this name, this supports Duignan's belief it must be 'swine's ford;' the manor laying on the borders of Kinver Forest, where the pasturage of swine was of importance (DUIGNAN) (SPN p70). (SVS p119 and 120). Kings was added to distinguish it from Old Swinford, the next parish to it in Worcs (SHOS vol 2 p226). The manor was held by the king by 1086 and remained with the Crown until King John exchanged it, together with Mere and Clent, with Ralph de Somery of Dudley Castle (see), for Wolverhampton. With the de Somerys the manor remained until at least the end of the C18 (SHOS vol 2 p226). By a **charter** granted by Elizabeth I in 1567 and confirmed by Charles I in 1630 the inhabitants of the parishes of Kingswinford and Clent enjoyed several valuable privileges as tenants of ancient demesnes of the Crown. The principal of these was their exemption from toll and stallage at markets and fairs throughout the country (W p181). For the customs of the manor see SHOS vol 2 p226. The local people had a tradition that Kingswinford **church** was built on the Roman site at Greensforge, which they called 'The Churchyard,' (or Wolverhampton Churchyard (see)) but was spirited to its present site at The Village one night (SHOS vol 2 p233). The present parish church, St Mary, is of C11 (BHOP p87) or C12 origin (LDD); the tympanum in the church above the door in the Vicar's vestry, shows St Michael killing the dragon, and has been dated to 1120 (BCM autumn 1999 p60). The church remained the parish church until it was threatened by mining activities in the earlier C19, and Holy Trinity, Wordsley, built in 1831, was built to replace it. St Mary's reopened in 1846 to cater for a smaller parish (BHOP p87). The church-school, founded in 1857 in Cot Lane, was the Glynne School (BHOP p91). The ancient **parish** had formed after 1086 and probably by the later C11 and certainly by 1291, probably out of Sedgley parish (SHC 1916 p197). Kingswinford **wake** was on the first Sunday after Sept 19 (W p181) or in the third week in Sept (KCPC p19). The old **parsonage** at the E end of Kingswinford at SO 893894 was formerly moated (SHOS vol 2 p233) (SSAHST 1982-3 p39).

1700 to PRESENT. There was a hunger riot in Kingswinford in 1766 (MH autumn 1976 p262). On July 29 1789 there was a small anti-enclosure riot at Kingswinford involving nailers (LOU p178). The **cholera epidemic** of 1832 reached Kingswinford parish on June 30 and claimed 87 lives in the parish (TB Feb 1998 p17). There is a **windmill** at SO 874895, which was covered in ivy in 1985. Reputedly built in 1818, the mill was disused in 1886. The cap has been replaced by a flat roof surmounted by a weather vane from Northampton church (WBJ p28 il v). (WIS pp11p,20) (SVB p168). **Westfield Sports Cars** Ltd, car manufacturers, have occupied several industrial estate sites in Kingswinford since the company was founded in 1985 (BCFF p201). The **mizen mast of the Three Sisters** merchant ship had been erected near Corbyn's Hall to commemorate the men who lost their lives in it against a much larger French frigate of 20 guns and 40 men sometime before 1821. A brass plate with an inscription was attached to the mast but no date accompanied the inscription. In time the mast was used as an artillery target and because of this came to be reduced to a stump. It may have disappeared by 1850 (GM 1820 and or March 1821) (SVS p133) (SMC p141). For a **ghost** that may haunt the Barnett Lane district of Kingswinford see Holbeche House. **Persons and visitors**. Kingswinford was the name for a parliamentary division between 1885 and 1948 (GLAUE p415) or 1950. **Charles Henry Sitch** (1887-1960), Labour, represented it between 1918 and 1931 when he was convicted of embezzling the funds of the chainmakers' trade union and imprisoned. **Alan LS Todd**, Conservative, served the division between 1931 and 1935. He was defeated by **Arthur Henderson** (b1893), Labour, who served the division between 1935 and 1950; Henderson then served the new Rowley Regis and Tipton constituency to 1964. In 1966 he was created a life peer, becoming Lord Henderson of Rowley (the title being taken from Rowley Regis) (Whitaker's Almanack 1968. 1969) (SNSV vol 2 p83). **Charles Hatton**

(1905-1977), novelist, journalist and media writer, was born at Kingswinford. In the later 1920s he lived in Brierley Hill, moving to Worcester in 1942 (VFC pp61-62).

Kingswinford Cross Formerly Townsend, or Towns End, Kingswinford. Here Bradley Hall was situated until it was removed in 1924 (BCM Oct 1989 p68. March 1998 p21). Townsend Place, at the crossing of Market Street with Moss Grove, preserves the name.

Kingswood Small village 2m WSW of Codsall. Formerly partly in Codsall and Tettenhall parishes. Was a ward with Trescott in Perton civil parish by the late C20. It anciently lay probably in Brewood Forest, and after the forest's disafforestion became common land. The area was called Kingswood by 1403. There was encroachment on the Tettenhall side of the common by the early C17 and some families may have been living on the Codsall side in the C17 (VCH vol 20 pp11-12,80,84). At Kingswood Pool in the later C17 Plot noted quantities of red ochre. There was some enclosure of the common in 1707, and 1824 (NHS p124) (VCH vol 20 pp11-12,80,84). By 1990 the common was considered a place which had been used for a long time by Wolverhampton people for recreation and picnicking (TCOP pp7,157p). By the late C20 there was settlement on the W side of County Lane in Shrops. Some years prior to 1998 the local historian Alec Brew, lived on the Shrops side of County Lane, but parked his car on the E side in Staffs, when it was stolen one night the Staffs police force claimed they could do nothing about the matter because Mr Brew lived in Shrops, whilst the Shrops force felt they could do nothing for the car was stolen in Staffs (Wolverhampton Chronicle Sept 11 1998 p14). Has also appeared as King's Wood.

Kings Wood Churchbridge. Farm N of Watling Street, 1.75m SE of Cannock.

King's Wood, The and Kingswood Bank (W p434). Forms the backdrop to Trentham Park Lake as would have been seen from Trentham Hall. It still incorporates traces of the formal rides visible on a map of Trentham estate of 1727 (CL May 9 1996 p69). The name preserves the fact that the Mercian kings held Trentham (SHC 1909 p74 note).

Kingswood Bank Wrottesley. Kingswood. S of Kingswood Common.

Kingswood Common Hamlet 1.75m SW of Codsall. The tall gas Round Lamp, which stood at High Green (Queen's Square) in the centre of Wolverhampton between 1821 and 1842, could be seen from as far away as Kingswood Common (WJO Dec 1903 lxi). Illegal pugilist fights were fought at Kingswood Common due to the closeness of Shrops which could be easily entered to evade the Staffs authorities (Wolverhampton Chronicle Sept 11 1998 p14).

King Tree Tree over 0.5m S of Gorsty Hill, Marchington Woodlands. Appears on OS map 1925 sheet 32. Slightly to the NE of it is Queen Tree.

Kinsell Hill Hill N of Sedgley town (SDSSOP p124).

Kinvaston Former prebendal estate by the Penk centring on Kinvaston Hall Farm, 1.5m ENE of Stretton (Penkridge), 7.5m N of Wolverhampton. Former out-township in St Peter's parish, Wolverhampton, Seisdon hundred, and yet is in Cuttlestone hundred (VCH vol 4 p61). For the Roman fort S of Kinvaston see Pennocrucium. A charter was made of its bounds (SL p62), when the estate was given by Lady Wulfrun to the monastery of Wolverhampton in 994 (HOWM p14). The name has appeared as Kinwaldestun (996), and Chenwardestone, a manor held by the canons of Wolverhampton, in DB, Kinaldeston (1203), Kinwaston (1307), Kynnaston (1479. 1610), and Kynerston (1604) (SPNO p127). It means 'Cynewald's farmstead or tun' (Speed's map) (SPNO p127) (SPN p94) (SSE 1996 p15). At Kinvaston was possibly a medieval village (SSAHST 1970 p35), since depopulated and lost. Kinvaston was a prebend of Wolverhampton Collegiate Church, abolished in 1846 (W p82) (VCH vol 3 p324). Became a separate civil parish in 1866 (GLAUE p415).

Kinvaston Hall Stretton (Penkridge). Whether now Kinvaston Hall Farm (see)? which is 1.5m ENE of Stretton (Penkridge).

Kinver Ancient parish (VCH vol 20 p149) and former township. The small town of Kinver lies at the foot of a promontory by a bend in the Stour 25.5m SSE of Stafford.

EARLY to 1500. Mesolithic and Neolithic flints have been found in various parts of the parish (Worcs Arch Newsletter vol 4 p2) (W Midlands Arch News Sheet vol 17 pp20-21. vol 20 pp31-32. vol 22 pp39-41) (VCH vol 20 p118). Has appeared as 'the wood called Cynibre' a document from (736) (DUIGNAN), Cynefare (964), Chenevare (DB), Kenefare (C12), Kinver (Saxton's map), Kinfare (1682. C19); Kinver was considered a common form in the C19 (Plot's map) (W p177). The **name** may be derived from the Celtic words 'keun' and 'vaur' meaning a large or high hill or mountain (SHOS vol 2 pp262,263). Or from Anglo-Saxon words 'cyne, chine, chene' meaning royal or great, and 'fare,' a road, giving great or royal road (the Roman road from Chester to Bath which passes near Kinver, or a road to the King's House or hunting lodge, near Wolverley) (SHOS vol p262) (DUIGNAN) (KMC

p3). The origin is sometimes taken from the form 'Cynibre' (736) which has been translated as 'royal hill' (DUIGNAN) (SPN p71); the element 'bre' a hill is frequent on the Welsh border (NSFCT 1908 p134). In the later C17 Plot interpreted the Saxon word 'fare' to mean death so that it could be deduced the name was from a king who had died and was buried here (NHS p413); but Shaw found no Saxon word of 'fare' to mean death, other than the Saxon verb 'faran,' which sometimes signifies 'to die' (SHOS vol 2 pp262,263 note). Scott put forward the theory that Kinver may be from Earl Cynebert who was given the estate by Ethelbald (Aethelbald, king of Mercia 716-757?), and founded a monastery at Usmere, bordering Kinver wood, a wood near Kidderminster anciently called Cymbre, or Kynber (SVS p162) (RKE p7). From cefn-mawr (BCWJ p65). (SDW p9). The present parish **church**, St Peter, on Church Hill, probably stands on the site of a former church, in existence by the late C11. The present church has some mid C12 work (St Peter's, Kinver. Rev MF Walker. 1992) (BOE p164). The parish formed by 1086 and may have originally contained the ancient parishes of Enville and Upper Arley (SHC 1916 p193). In 1719 Kinver **wake** was held on Monday and Tuesday, 14 and 15 Sept (VCH vol 20 p127). A **wayside cross** in Mill Lane, a road leading to Dunsley, is mentioned in 1440 (VCH vol 20 p121). The **curfew bell** formerly tolled at Kinver (RKE p32). The **day bell** rang every morning at Kinver at 4 o' clock. It was discontinued in 1750. The **plum pudding bell** was rung a month before Christmas (KMC p17). The earliest and only reference to Kinver being a **borough** is a C13 charter John fitz John fitz Philip granted to his burgesses (NSJFS 1972 p68). The area without the borough but still in Kinver manor has been described as the foreign (VCH vol 20 pp143,149-150). On display in the church is the Kinver Charter granted in 1629 (LGS p157). The lord of Kinver claimed **gallows**, pillory and infangetheof in 1293. Gallows probably stood on Gallowstree Hill W of Potter's Cross (VCH vol 20 p150). **Persons and visitors**. The royal hunting lodge, recorded at Kinver at the end of the C12, was probably at Stourton, where a royal hunting lodge was in 1207 (VCH vol 2 p347. vol 20 p123). **William II** was at Kinver on at least one occasion; Henry II may have been in 1176 and 1186; **King John** was here on April 5 1200, Jan 24 to 27 1206, and Aug 18 1207 (NSFCT 1909 p183) (VCH vol 2 p346) (R&S p8).

MARKETS AND FAIRS. John son of Philip was granted a charter on July 3 1221 to hold a **market** here on Tuesdays. This appears to have not been renewed in 1227 when the grant lapsed. In 1257 John's son John was granted a market for Wednesdays. The market was still held in the mid C15 but nothing more is known of it (NSJFS 1971 p50) (VCH vol 20 p143). In 1544 a Tuesday market was granted to the lord of the manor. The market was mentioned in 1717, but had been discontinued by the mid C18 (VCH vol 20 p143). The **market hall** or town hall, built in High Street S of Vicarage Drive in 1619 (VCH vol 20 p149), once contained some ancient pieces of armour (SHOS vol 2 p263). It was taken down in c1825 and its timber frame work had been re-erected near Barratt's Coppice S of the Stourbridge road (SVS p170) (SCSF p95) (VCH vol 20 pp149-150). A **fair** in Kinver manor on the vigil, feast, and morrow of St Peter and St Paul (June 28-30) was granted in 1257. Nothing more is known of it after 1293. In 1544 two fairs were granted to Kinver, on May 1 and Dec 8, with a court of Pyepowder. The Dec fair was held on Dec 14 by the late 1750s (VCH vol 20 p143); Shaw records it as taking place on Dec 5 (SHOS vol 2 p263). There was no fair in 1792 (OWEN). By 1851 the three new fairs, mainly for the sale of swine, were on the first Tuesday in Feb, the second Tuesday in May, and the first Tuesday in Dec (W p177). All were held until the late 1880s (VCH vol 20 p143), but there was one in 1888 (LHE p265).

GRAMMAR SCHOOL. The founder or original endower is unknown. The earliest document relating to the school is a lease dated Oct 22 1571. William Vinsent made a grant to the school in 1592 and Roger Jesten made a grant to the school in 1605 (LHSB 14 pp35il-37) (VCH vol 20 pp157-158). A school house was built at the junction of Church Hill and Dark Lane in the C16. In 1820-1 a new school was built to the NE of the C16 building. Thereafter the C16 building became the master's house. It was known for a time as Clifford Cottage (WMAG March 1976 p22p). In 1982 it became a private house known as the Old Grammar School House. The school closed in 1916 and the C19 school building was demolished in c1965 (A House in the High Street. George R Humpreyes. 1973 p11il) (VCH vol 20 pp121,158-159) (KEOP p65p).

1500 to PRESENT. Kinver was noted some time before the mid C19 as a place for the manufacture of coarse and fine narrow woollen cloth and later for the manufacture of iron (W p177). A company of **rifle volunteers** for Kinver was formed in 1860. It had ceased to exist by 1871 (Hist of Volunteer Force of Staffs (1859-1908) pp6,14-15) (VCH vol 20 p128). Kinver and Kinver Edge were resorts for visitors from the Black Country from the early C19 and by the early C20 there was a tramway called the **Kinver Light Railway** to transport them from the Black Country to Kinver. It opened on April 4 (Good Friday) in 1900 or 1901. It was 4.2 miles long and ran from The Fish Inn, Coalbournbrook, followed roads through Wollaston, Worcs, ascended Ridge Top and descended to Stewponey before entering Kinver and terminating at Mill Lane. The line closed in 1927 (WMAG Aug 1970 pp22-23. May 1976 p22) or in 1930 (VCH vol 20 p127). (BCM July 1974 pp10-12) (TEBC) (RKE) (KRC) (KMC) (PWIS p10) (By Tram to Kinver (1901-1930). DM Bills and E & WR Griffiths). The 'Illustrated Guide to Kinver' (Birmingham and Midland Tramways. 1904) referred to Kinver as 'the Switzerland of the Midlands' (VCH vol 20 p118) (PWIS p8). John Adlard (1929-1993) wrote a poem titled 'The Last Tram From Kinver' describing the journey on a tram returning from Kinver to the Black Country

> The subject of a comic picture-card,
> The last tram from Kinver, green and cream,
> Everyone's final hope of reaching home
> In Stourbridge, Lye, Dudley or Dudley Port,
> Moves into the dark water-meadows. All
> Her cross-benches are packed, and hanging from
> Her canopies, her roof, her window-frames,
> Dashes and fenders are some dozen more
> Clinging for dear life, laughing fit to burst.
>
> Over the Hyde they go, bridging its streams
> And restless tributaries, pause at a halt
> And then at an iron depot. The boughs dance,
> The moon ignores the owls. In Dunsley Meadows
> Glow the invisible flowers. Stourton Castle
> Presides above the woods. Three times the Stour
> Pours beneath, and finally the car
> Swings to the right, crosses the high-road, slows,
> Labouring to reach the lights of the Ridge Top.

(BCM summer 1993 pp48-49). In woods somewhere between Kinver and Enville is an **icehouse** (TB May 1994 p15p). Kinver won the **first Best Kept Village competition** for Staffordshire in 1978 (STMSM). **Webbs' use of the name Kinver**. The 'Kinver Chevalier' was a barley variety developed by Webbs of Wordsley, and mentioned in their catalogues as late as 1941; they were awarded a gold medal for it. 'Kinver Gem' was a variety of pea developed by Webbs, acknowledged for its blue hue and earliness, while the 'Kinver Globe' was a variety of Savoy cabbage developed by them, the 'Kinver Monarch' was a variety of seed potato which was first offered in their 1889 catalogue (BCM July 1971 pp8,10). The present (2000) **Kinver Historical Society** formed in 1955 (info DM Bills). **Persons and visitors**. **Richard Moreton** (1637-1698) was curate of Kinver from 1659 until his ejection in 1662; he then turned to medicine, eventually becoming a physician in ordinary to William III (VCH vol 20 p155). **Robert Parr**, the great grandson of the celebrity Thomas Parr who lived to the age 152, resided at Kinver until his death at the age of 124 in 1757 (SVS p171) (GM 1821). For **John Dutton**, 'England's Oldest Licensee', born in 1820 at Stone Lane, Kinver see under Hinksford. Rev **Sabine Baring-Gould** (1834-1924), folklorist, author, and hymn writer, visited Kinver in the late C19. Here he wrote the hymn 'Now the day is over.' In his 'Bladys of the Stewponey' (1897), much of which is set in Kinver parish, he says of Kinver 'if we call it a town we flatter it, if we speak of it as a village we insult it.' His 'Guavas the Tinner' (1897) and 'Perpetua' (1897) are said to be set in the Kinver area. A film of the novel was mainly shot in Kinver in 1919 (VCH vol 20 pp118,126) (VFC p9). **Nancy Price** (d1970), stage and film actress and novelist, was born at Rockmount (see), Kinver in 1880. Her autobiography 'Into an Hour-glass' (1953) records her early life in Kinver (VCH vol 20 p126) (BCM spring 1997 p15). **Harold Parsons** (1919-1992) of Dudley, short story writer and editor of BCM, moved to Kinver in 1965 (VFC p104). **Kenneth Wrigley** bequeathed most of his £2 million to Kinver in June 1995 (Daily Telegraph Aug 7 1995 p3).

TRADITIONS AND CUSTOMS. According to an old local tradition there was the **Kinver Giant** who had a beautiful wife and both lived in a rock dwelling in Holy Austin Rock (see). Meanwhile there lived another giant at Enville - the Enville Giant - in Samson's Cave. Water being scare at Holy Austin Rock the Kinver Giant would go to a spring, 'the Giant's Spring,' on the W side of Kinver Edge to collect water in a trough, 'the Giant's Water Trough.' One day, whilst the Kinver Giant was out collecting water, the Enville Giant strode across to his neighbour's dwelling and flirted with his wife. The Kinver Giant returned to find the Enville Giant leaving his wife. He was furious and hurled a very large stone, the Boltstone (see), at the departing

Enville Giant and it landed in a field near Compton (WJO July 1903 xxxv) (FOS p42). It is said that a **secret passage** led up to the church from the vicarage (RKE p31). The **Whit Sunday** custom of throwing bread and cheese to be scrambled for once prevailed in the Kinver Forest district, and at Kinver, where villagers used to save up their cheese for weeks to honour this tradition (KMC p34). Kinver had a custom which involved **children tying the church gates** at weddings and refusing to untie the gates until the bridegroom had thrown coins at them (KMC p34). The custom of **thatch-wetting**, a blessing for new houses to preserve them from evil spirits, anciently prevailed at Kinver. The ceremony which involved blessing the house by a clergyman, the wetting of the thatch with water, coins being thrown from an upstairs window and an assembly of local people singing 'Bless This House,' was last practised or revived for a special occasion on June 8 1963 at the newly built cottage of Miss Timmings at Hydeaway, Hyde Lane (Ancient Kinver Custom. Miss Mable Timmings. 1963) (KMC p35).

Kinver Edge Ridge running NNE to SSW from Kinver to Blakeshall Common in Worcs. From the top of the ridge, its highest point is 538 feet, is a remarkable view which includes the Clent Hills, the Cotswolds, the Malverns, the Habberleys and the Clees (LGS p158). The edge was so named by the later C17 (VCH vol 20 p122). In 1798 William Hodgetts of Union Hall, Compton, fell off his horse on Kinver Edge and died (VCH vol 20 p123). Some 200 acres of the edge were presented to the NT by the Lee family in 1917 (info board on site in 1997), or in 1918 (LGS p158 note). The **Boltstone** (see), 1m to the NW of the edge, was said by White, to be near a **burial mound** which was on the E side of the edge. The burial mound was destroyed in the C19 and had been surrounded by a narrow ditch and was supposed to cover the ashes of a Celtic warrior (SHOS vol 2 p263) (W p178) (Hodgeson MS in WSL) (NSJFS 1965 p43) (VCH vol 20 pp118-119). There was another burial mound on the E side of the edge between Dunsley and Whittington where the name Low Hill appears (VCH vol 20 p119 note). Pickford says there is evidence of **pre-Christian worship** on Kinver Edge (SMM p172). **Kinver Edge Fort** (see), an Iron Age hillfort, lies on the E side, and that side of the edge is known as '**Compa**' or 'The Compa' (KRH p18). The same or another area has been called **Kamchatka**; whilst another area has been called Moscow (SNSV vol 1 p55). The **Holy Austin Rock** (see), a huge sandstone rock with rooms carved into it, is at the N end of the edge. '**The Battle of Kinver Edge**' was a pugilist fight between Jem Hall of Gornal and Charley Hedge (or Edge) 'The Brierley Hill Pet' on the edge in a memorial tournament on Nov 22 1836: Jem Hall won. The fight epitomised the rivalry between various Black Country townships and was fought on the edge due to the closeness of Shrops and Worcs which could be easily entered to evade Staffs authorities (TB March 1979 pp18-19. Jan 1997 pp30-31). The site of a **sham ruin**, occupied by 1832 by a clump of trees, was situated at the foot of the southern end of the edge. The sham ruin or lodge was built as an eye-catcher by Mr Brindley, who had died by 1832 (SVS p165) - it may have been just in Worcs. The '**Eleven Apostles**' is a clump of trees on the edge, existing in c1920 (KEOP p86p). The same or another group has been called the '**Twelve Apostles;**' it is a line of trees on the brow of Kinver Edge (RKE p29). **Supernatural**. A ghost known as 'Old Joe,' a former land worker, has been seen in the 'Compa' area. He was so frequently seen that a local couple set a place for him at their table (GOM p25 p 2(a)) (GPCE p32). The ghosts of a former lord and his lady of Enville manor may walk the edge (GOM p26).

Kinver Edge Fort Roughly rectangular hillfort on the E side of Kinver Edge, at the N end. It is of Iron Age origin and dates from the C2 to the C1 BC (NSFCT 1892 p139) (HOS p10) (NSJFS 1964 p27). Is at SO 835833. It comprises seven acres (LGS p158 - 7.5 acres) (SL p37. pl 3) (MR p202). A single bank and ditch on the S side is the only artificial projection. No entrance is visible (NSJFS 1964 p27). Plot notes it was the tradition of the town in the later C17 that the fort was of Danish origin, but he favoured the notion it was of Saxon origin (NHS p413). (Magna Britannia. T Cox. vol 5 p33) (SVS pp336-337) (SHOS vol 1 General Intro pp22,37. vol 2 p263) (VCH vol 1 p338) (GPE p188) (SOSH p10).

Kinver Forest Royal forest which was probably in existence by 1086 and lasted to the mid C16 (NSJFS 1968 p46) (SL pp67,68 see map) and had come to be called Kinver Forest by 1168 (VCH vol 2 p343). Has also appeared as Forest of Kinver. It stretched from Seisdon and Lower Penn in the N to Kinver Edge and Kidderminster in the S. Its hays were Ashwood, Chasepool, and Iverley (VCH vol 2 p344), and others add Sedgley, Kingsley (at Tettenhall Wood) (VCH vol 2 p344 note), and Prestwood. Stourton Park seems to have been the only deer park in it (NSJFS 1968 pp40,47 map). William II hunted in the forest on at least one occasion; Henry II may have done in 1176 and 1186; King John did in 1200, 1206, 1207, 1215 (R&S p4) (VCH vol 2 pp346-347): Henry III was at Bobbington in 1238, 1245 and possibly 1256 (VCH vol 20 p67). A medieval royal hunting lodge at Stourton became the later Stourton Castle, and there may have been a hunting lodge at Bobbington (VCH vol 20 p67). The hermitage of 'Gutheresburn' in Kinver Forest, which has been identified with Gothersley (see), was granted by Henry III in 1248 to Brother Walerand of Kidderminster, but this hermitage may have been in the Worcs part of the forest (VCH vol 3 p137. vol 20 p123). In 1286 Roger de Somery of Dudley Castle (see) was fined 100 marks because his men had, in the excitement of the chase, killed a stag 100 yards within Kinver Forest (LGS p157). A perambulation of the forest was made in 1300 (HOPTT pp28-30) (WAM p33). After the final acceptance in 1327 of the 1300 perambulation Kinver Forest shrank to an area roughly between Smestow on the N and the county boundary on the S, with Kingsley Wood - Tettenhall Wood - forming a detached portion further N (VCH vol 2 p343). In March 1358 the rider of the forest and other foresters were attacked by armed men from Wolverhampton, Willenhall, Wednesfield, Codsall, and Bilston, near Wolverhampton (VCH vol 2 p346). In 1360 the prior of Saint James' Priory, Dudley, was held at Stourton Castle for an offence against the forest laws (CAMS p29). A lesser noble was caught poaching deer in Kinver Forest in medieval times and was punished by being flayed to death, and his skin left exposed upon the site of Potter's Cross (see). He is believed to retaliate by blowing a nightly blast upon a hunting horn. It is said that on a clear night the horn can be heard from the Hayes, Brettell Lane, and Stourbridge (BCWJ p106). Kinver Forest had a keeper or chief forester from at least the reign of Henry II, a rider from the mid C14, and a ranger for the hays by the end of the C14: VCH vol 2 pp344-345 lists them. Kinver Forest survived nominally into the C17, but by the reign of Elizabeth I only Iverley Hay was in the hands of the Crown. The remaining forest - the hays of Ashwood and Chasepool (owned by C17 by the Dudley family) - was then considered merely an extension of Pensnett Chase (VCH vol 2 p348).

Kinver Heath It was probably the area of common land later known as Kinver Common which lay N and W of Kinver and extended into Compton (VCH vol 20 p138). On the heath between Kinver Edge and The Comptons are a number of burial mounds, thought by Plot to be probably of Saxon origin (NHS pp413-414) (NSJFS 1965 p43). Charles II and his party escaping after the battle of Worcester lost themselves on Kinver Heath as night fell on Sept 3 1651 (SCSF p18) (Boscobel House and White Ladies Priory. English Heritage. 1987. p7). The common was enclosed in 1774 (VCH vol 20 p138).

Kirksteads Near the Manifold, Butterton (Moorlands), between Butterton and Wetton Mill stations. The prefix is from Old Norse and means a church, the suffix is from Old Norse 'stadr,' a place, or Danish 'sted,' a place (NSFCT 1916 p81).

Kitchen Brook A tributary of the Dove. Has also appeared as Monastery Kitchen Brook. The name is probably from a field name in allusion to the land for the maintenance of a monastic kitchen (SPNO p12).

Kitling Brook A brook in the Victoria Park area of Stafford (SKYT p96).

Knappers Gate Former name for an area about the junction of Newcastle Lane with the London Road (A34). Hereabouts was the Hospital of St Loys (SHST p450).

Knaves Castle A mound of unknown origin which was encompassed by three ditches which stood, according to the 1834 OS map, just S of Watling Street at SK 04950643, 0.5m N of Brownhills. Formerly in Ogley Hay extra-parochial liberty (W p574). Was 18 paces in diameter and 2.5 feet high (NSJFS 1965 p45). It was possibly a burial mound (NHS pp399,403,448) (THS p6) (SOS p302) (VCH vol 1 pp192,345-246) (SOB p50) (MOA p14). It is believed to be of Bronze Age origin, but has never been excavated (SNBC p2). White says it was a Roman encampment. Others say it was erected by the authorities to catch highwaymen; a promontory being needed to rise above the wooded landscape. Alternatively, the highwaymen could have erected it themselves for their use (NHS pp399-400,448). Even if the mound was of an earlier date the name Knaves Castle was perhaps applied in medieval times (CCC pp4,5). Enclosure swept all traces of it away (W p574). Duignan says it was very clear in c1840 but by 1902 was almost obliterated and enclosed in a garden (DUIGNAN). In the later C17 Plot noted some 16 pits (man-made?) beside Watling Street between Knaves Castle and Froghall one was noted for never filling with water after rain, whereas the others filled to the brim. Plot thought it may be comprised of gravel so letting water seep through (NHS pp112-113). The name, which has also appeared as Knaves' Castle, is preserved in Knaves Castle Avenue, Castle Close, and Old Castle Grove on the N side of Watling Street (SNBC pp2,9,10). Duignan thought it was from Hnaef, a famous Danish sea king (HOWW pp11-12). Later he thought Knave was from Anglo-Saxon cnafa, or Middle English cnave, a boy or servant; so 'the burial-mound of the boy' (or 'servant') (DUIGNAN).

Knenhall Minute hamlet on high ground above Scotch Brook 0.5m NNW of Moddershall. Formerly in Kibblestone township and quarter in Stone ancient parish. By 1872 was in Moddershall township (KD 1872).

Knightley Fragmented hamlet in a wide dale on the upper reaches of Hollies Brook 1.75m SW of Ellenhall. Former township (THS pp269-70) and quarter in Gnosall ancient parish. Has appeared as Chenistelei, a manor, in DB, Knicteslega (1199), Cnitteley (1203), Knittele (1207), Knihtele (1227), Knychtheleye (1332), and Knightley (1498) (SPNO p156) (SSE 1996 p15). The name means the 'knight's lea,' remembering that 'knight' meant a boy or servant prior to its present meaning of man-at-arms or man of gentle birth (DUIGNAN) (SPN pp72-73) (SPNO p156) (SSE 1987 p30). Knightley manorhouse may have been at Knightley Dale (VCH vol 4 p111). Knightley was included in Adbaston prebend (SSAHST vol 2 1960-61 p42). A chapel at Knightley was in existence by 1395. It is not mentioned in or after 1563. Its site may be SW of Knightley Dale where a field name preserves the memory of a chapel (SHC 1914 p107) (OSST 1949-50 p12) (VCH vol 4 p132). The present mission church, Christ Church, on the N side of the Woodseaves-Great Bridgeford road near its junction with the Whitley Heath road was built in 1840 (VCH vol 4 p132) (LDD).

Knightley Common Former common land at Knightley, in Gnosall parish. Over part of it was a pool frequented by the pewits noted by Plot at Offley Moss. Enclosed by an Act of 1806 (WSS p110). The name appears in 1811 (SPNO p160), and may be synonymous with Knightley Hay (see), and Knightley Heath (see).

Knightley Dale Area under 1m SSE of Knightley, Ellenhall. There is a moat situated in a field known as 'moat meadow' (VCH vol 4 p120) (CAMS p63). This may represent the site of Knightley manor-house. SW of Knightley Dale a field name preserves the memory of a chapel. The chapel was in existence by 1395 (VCH vol 4 pp111,132).

Knightley Eaves House 1m E of High Offley (gravestone in High Offley churchyard).

Knightley Gorse House N of Knightley (1834 OS map).

Knightley Grange House 0.75m SSW of Knightley, by a farm called Cob Hall, of which parts were incorporated into outbuildings. Built in the Tudor style 1860-8 by Major Robert Halstead Hargreaves; his daughter Ruth married William Ralph Joseph Wolseley second son of Sir Charles Wolseley, 9th Baronet, of Wolseley Hall (VCH vol 4 p120) (Burke's Peerage 1967) (BOE p167). Or built in c1850. Has been reduced in size (EOP p85p). To the S of the house is a pyramid obelisk monument to 'Lincoln' a horse. An inscription on a tiny brass on the E side of the base reads 'In memory of a very favourite horse called Lincoln shot 29 May 1865 aged 22. This monument was erected by its owner Rob Hargreaves AD 1866.' Bruce Braithwaite visited the monument whilst compiling ROT. Five dogs' gravestones are situated at the foot of the obelisk. The inscriptions on two graves are worn away. The other three read: 'Soot 1905,' 'Joe 1905,' and 'Flush d1909.'

Knightley Green House at Lower Knightley.

Knightley Hall SW of Knightley Dale. Dates from early C19, but there are signs that the W end may be part of a C17 structure (VCH vol 4 p120). Has an enormous chimney stack (MR p204).

Knightley Hay Former common land in Gnosall parish (VCH vol 4 p113. vol 6 p52). May be synonymous with Knightley Common (see), and Knightley Heath (Yates' map) (SPNO p160).

Knightley Moss House 0.25m N of Knightley. The name appears in KD 1880 (SPNO p160).

Knightley Park Knightley, Eccleshall. A medieval deer park enclosed out of forest. In existence by 1308 (NSJFS 1962 p76. 1964 p63). The park belonging to the manor of Knightley was decayed by 1610 but was then restocked (VCH vol 4 p120). Marked on Saxton's map (EDP p179) and Plot's map to SW of Knightley. Knightley Park Farm, NNW of Hob Hill, appears in 1847 (SPNO p160).

Knightley Park Wood 0.75m ENE of Rangemore. Near Knightley Park a fragment of pottery of uncertain date was found (HOBT p18) (HOPT vol 1 p10) (NSJFS 1964 p38). Knightley Park preserves the name of the Knightleye family holders of the lost manor of Rudlow or Rudlowe in the C13 and C14 (HOPT vol 1 p113).

Knighton Small village on ground rising out of Lonco Brook 1m SW of Adbaston. Former manor, and a township with Adbaston in Adbaston ancient parish. Has appears as Chnitestone, a manor held of the bishop of Chester (Lichfield) in DB, Chenistetone, Knichton (SPN p45) (SSE 1996 p15), and possibly Knighton-in-the-Hales (C14) (DUIGNAN). The name means perhaps, 'the boy's (or servant's) town' or 'the soldier's town.' If the name is of Anglo-Saxon origin then the latter meaning must be excluded, since 'knight' only had the meaning boy or servant then (DUIGNAN) (SPN p45). The grange of Knighton once belonged to Ranton Abbey, or Knighton was a grange of that abbey (NSFCT 1927 p22) (VCH vol 3 pp253,254).

KNIGHTON EXEMPT FROM TAX. In the C17 Knighton township was bought by William Adams of Newport, Shrops, citizen and haberdasher of London, formerly of Newport, Shrops. In 1656 he gave certain lands in Knighton manor, together with the lordship of the manor to the Haberdashers' Company. The gift was used for the foundation and maintenance of four alms houses and a free grammar school (later Adams' Grammar School) in Newport, Shrops. In 1660 Adams died. By an Act of parliament of 1660 the charity for the maintenance and governance of Adams' gifts was established. By this Act, Knighton manor and Knighton Woods and the land upon which the school stood were exempted from the payment of all taxes, assessments or charges, civil or military. From then on Knighton inhabitants living on the charity lands were exempt from tax on their property (info John Cope, Archivist to the Haberdashers' Company). Parliament had passed the Act in recognition of the fact that Adams had lent Charles II £1000 at a time when the king was in need of finance (Daily Express April 8 1975 p3il of Adams). There is a tradition that Knighton was free from rates and taxes because the villagers helped Charles II to escape after the battle of Worcester (1651). By the mid C19 the Haberdashers' estate consisted of 1000 acres and was an extra parochial liberty (W p382). The exemption from taxation made the income from Knighton manor more valuable (MR p7) (SVB pp10-11). Cadbury Bros of Bourneville built their milk processing factory at Knighton in 1911 partly on account of Knighton's exemption from rates and taxes (AADB pp32,64). By 1975 Knighton residents were still exempt from rates. However, the local authorities did not then supply refuse removal or street lighting, but did provide a free mobile library service and free schooling (Daily Express April 8 1975 p3). Despite protests from Knighton inhabitants and the matter being taken up by the local MP the new Community Charge (and subsequently the present Council Tax), which replaced rates from April 1 1990, was levied on Knighton residents. By the late C20 the Stubbs family had been at Knighton Hall Farm, which forms part of the estate, for many years. In 1999 Peter Stubbs of that farm recollected that Knighton residents had always paid income tax in his lifetime (info Paul Kelly at Stafford Borough Council, and Peter Stubbs).

Knighton Small village by a tributary of the Tern 1.5m N of Mucklestone. Former township in Mucklestone ancient parish. Has appeared as Chenistetone, a manor, in DB, and possibly Knighton-in-the-Hales (C14) (DUIGNAN). The village hall also serves as a mission church (LDD).

Knighton Grange Knighton, Adbaston. It was said in 1975 to be a very old farmhouse, probably of C16 origin (AADB p32). So called after having been a grange of Ranton Abbey.

Knighton Hall Knighton, Adbaston. The house in 1975 was one which had replaced an earlier house, which may have been the first habitation at Knighton (AADB p32).

Knighton Reservoir Reservoir 1.5m WNW of Adbaston. The Staffs Shrops border runs through it. For the fish in it see English Reservoirs. Bill Howes. 1967 p56.

Knight's Fields To E of Hanbury Woodend, Hanbury. Is it an ancient manor of Hanbury and Houndhill? (SHOS vol 1 p72).

Knightsfield Farm 1.25m S of Uttoxeter.

Knightsland Farm 0.5m S of Knightsfield Farm, 3m W of Marchington.

Knight's Low Name T Pape gives to the burial mound in Swythamley Park from which is an excellent panoramic southward view (NSFCT vol 80 p37) (NSJFS 1977 p35). Had a stone column or cross standing on it, exactly the same as the one nearby at Cleulow Cross, Ches. Pickford notes, at one period in its history it was removed and replaced a few metres or so away and, perhaps at the same time, it was found necessary to place a stone cross on its top: The shaft is identical to at least six others in the area (SMM pp32p,131). Pickford believes Knight's Low is the site for 'Bercilak's Castle' in the poem Gawain and the Green Knight. Here Gawain relaxed before fighting the Green Knight at the Green Chapel (Lud Church) (SMM p131). Knight's Low is on a ley line between Lud Church, Burntoak, Dieulacres Abbey and Lady Dale (SMM p132).

Knights Mill House Former estate in Knowl End township of Audley ancient parish. Prior to 1733 it belonged to a man named Knight. Prior to the Knights it belonged to the Henshalls (SHC 1944 p38).

Knights Wood To the W of Butterton Grange Farm (1834 OS map) (Dower's map).

Kniveden House high on a hillside above Kniveden Brook, 1.5m E of Leek. Formerly in Leek and Lowe township in Leek ancient parish. There was a farm at Kniveden by 1535, when it was held of Dieulacres Abbey by Thomas Smith. The Smiths bought it in 1562 and remained here until the 1840s (VCH vol 7 pp87-88). The Derbys Kniveden means 'Cengifu's farm' (PNPD).

Kniveden Brook Brook rising on Leek Moor and flowing on the E side of Leek. Joins Leek Brook to E of Leekbrook (VCH vol 7 p87 see map).

Kniveden Hall Large house in Mount Road, 1.5m E of Leek. Is dated 1901 (VCH vol 7 p97). FG Johnson lived at Kniveden Hall in 1948 (SHC 1947).

Knob, The A knoll on the Lichfield Plain or Greenhill, Lichfield (LPL p of St Michael's).

Knoll, The House off Upper Main Street, Barton-under-Needwood. An early house on the site is said to have been built as a hunting lodge. The same or another building was built by Sir Robert Peel. The present house was built in 1884 by John Reid Walker, JP, of whisky fame, and he was the occupier in 1896. The rear part of the house was rebuilt after a fire in 1894. It was occupied by a Major Lamin in 1915. In the 1960s it was owned by the Roman Catholic church who used it as a training school for priests (UNT pp37,39,56,121). By 1997 it was the home of Stan Clarke, head of St Modwen property group, and owner of the Grand National winner Lord Gyllene, formerly of Barton Hall (see). On Dec 10 1997 masked raiders burgled the house; the men were believed to be the notorious Quality Street Gang, who target the rich and famous (ES Dec 12 1997 p3) (Daily Telegraph Dec 12 1997 p3p).

Knoll, The Former house and a road from Oakfield Avenue extending E to Standhills Road, Kingswinford. The Knoll was developed with housing in the 1950s (SNSV vol 1 p199).

Knoll Hill 0.5m NNE of Clent, in Staffs; St Kenelm's Furrow, where according to legend Kenelm was murdered, is on its slopes (NHS pp411-413). Is possibly the same as Clent Hill.

Knoll Wood Wood 3m S of Tyrley Castle. In it was the oak connected to the curious Tyrley (see) manorial custom.

Knotbury Minute moorland hamlet on a plateau hill under the shadow of Oliver Hill 0.75m NW of Flash. Is quite possibly an ancient settlement site (MR p316). Raven believes it is the 'a knot' in the medieval epic poem 'Gawain and the Green Knight'; 'a knot,' a rare word meaning 'a rocky formation' (NSJFS 1977 p39) (MR p316). A coal-mining area from the C18 to the earlier part of the C20 (VCH vol 7 p52).

Knotbury Common A plateau 1m NNW of Flash. The hamlet of Knotbury lies in a semi-circular layout along a track on the S flank of the common (MR p316).

Knowl and Knowl Wood. In Drayton-in-Hales parish (W p389). The house, Knowleswood, is 1.5m ESE of Hales.

Knowl Bank Incline (SHC 1909 p231 note) and fragmented minute hamlet 1.5m E of Betley. Formerly in Knowl End township in Audley ancient parish. The Peter de Knoll, who existed in the C14, may relate to Knowl Bank or Knowl End (AHJ 1995 p47).

Knowlbank House 0.25m NW of Consall. The Consall Plateway passed it.

Knowle, The Former hamlet now a suburb 0.75m NW of Rowley Regis. In Rowley Regis parish. Seems to have been originally The Knoll (W p194), a sacred hillock; the name is possibly of Saxon origin? (BCWJ p100). Or from Middle English 'knol' meaning the top or crown of a hill, generally a gently rounded hill or mount (DUIGNAN).

Knowle Brook Emerges from the Level Wood which lay between Merry Hill and the Nine Locks area (SNSV vol 1 p87). Ran through Pensnett Chase (KCPC p12) and just W of the Tipsyford Bridge joins Black Brook (SNSV vol 1 p87).

Knowle Farm House on Watling Street 1.5m S of Lichfield cathedral. Formerly in an out-township of St Michael's parish, Lichfield. There was a farmhouse here by the later C18 (VCH vol 14 p21). Has also appeared as Knowle Hill Farm and The Knowle. Takes its name from a nearby knoll (VCH vol 14 p21).

Knowle Hurst House to S of Knowle Lodge, Lichfield. Was known as Belle Colline by 1881 (VCH vol 14 p25).

Knowle Lodge At N end of Knowle Lane, Lichfield. Had been built by 1861 (VCH vol 14 p25).

Knowlend Behind the Roaches a hundred yards up the field from Whetstone Hole (NSFCT 1920 p87; geology of) (UHAW p51). Appears on the 1834 OS map as Knowl End.

Knowl End House above Englesea Brook 0.75m NE of Balterley. Former township in Audley parish (W p428) (NSJFS 1971 p66). The Peter de Knoll, who existed in the C14, may relate to Knowl Bank or Knowl End (AHJ 1995 p47).

Knowles House in the Moorlands 0.5m NE of Upper Hulme. Formerly in Heathylee township in Alstonefield ancient parish. There was a house on the site of Knowles Farm probably by 1308, and certainly by 1476 (VCH vol 7 p33).

Knowles Farm C19 house to N of Holehouse Lane nearly 0.75m N of Endon.

Formerly in Endon township in Leek ancient parish. There was a house on the site of Knowles Farm by 1607 (VCH vol 7 p177). Appears as The Knowls on 1834 OS map.

Knowles Hill Rolleston. Formerly Cross Field Lane it lead to the upper reaches of Dodslow Field, derived not from Anglo-Saxon 'cnoll' but from a former resident GT Knowles, a former agent to the Mosley estate (UTR p212).

Knowle Style Formerly a farm now a district between Knypersley and Biddulph shopping centre. The name is from the style next to the knoll or hillock (BHS June 1968 p15).

Knowsley Cross House on a high ridge above the upper Dove 1.75m NNW of Sheen. In Sheen ancient parish. There was a house at Knowsley by 1733 (VCH vol 7 p242). The present house has a dovecote in one of its gable ends (PDS&C p37p) and takes its name from a C15 cross (DoE II), which stands nearby by the Longnor-Sheen road. The cross was re-erected near its former site in 1897 (VCH vol 7 p242) or restored in 1899 (NSFCT 1927 p151) (PDS&C p78p); the restorer was Mark Taylor, whose name appears on the base. It was a tradition in the 1830s that the cross had formerly had 'a dial for the country people to mark the hour' (VCH vol 7 p242). Also on the same road, nearby, is a horse trough.

Knowl Wall Minute hamlet on a bank above a ravine 1.5m NW of Tittensor. Seems to have been at the meeting point of Stone, Swynnerton and Trentham parishes (W p434). The tollhouse at Knowl Wall on the Newcastle-Eccleshall turnpike road, set up under an Act of 1823, was built in c1825 (IAS pp197,198il,199)

Knowl Wood A wood which existed in the C15, S of Burnt Wood (NSFCT 1933 p93). Robert Percival was at Knowlwood in 1684 (SHC 1945/6 p190). The house called Knowleswood is 1.5m ESE of Hales.

Knox Grave At cross roads SW of Botany Bay, 1.5m NE of Weeford (1834 OS map).

Knutton Former hamlet on a bank above Lyme Brook, now a suburb 1m NW of Newcastle-under-Lyme. Former township in Wolstanton ancient parish. Has appeared as Clotone, a manor, in DB, Cnoton (1212), and Cnutton (SPN 73) (SSE 1996 p15). Possible, but unlikely suggestions have been: 'the knot town,' 'the rocky summit town,' 'Cnut's town' - Duignan is unsure (DUIGNAN), Poulton-Smith opts for the latter (SPN p73). Or it means 'Canute's town' i.e; it belonged to King Canute (MR p242). Named after a Norseman called Knut or Canute (POP p149). Or shares the same root as Cannock (NSFCT 1908 p135). In the earlier C13 the tenant held the manor of Knutton of the king for a fee and by the service of performing guard duties at Newcastle Castle (SCSF p116) (VCH vol 8 p13). The church, St Mary, on the corner of Church Lane and High Street, was built in 1872-1874 (BOE p167). Became an ecclesiastical parish in 1875 (LGS p158) (GLAUE p415).

Knutton Heath Former common land, formerly in Keele parish. Part of the heath was a race course for Newcastle-under-Lyme borough prior to 1816; racing had ceased by 1851. Here James Wantling raced (W p300) (OTP p165) (VCH vol 8 p50). Enclosed by an Act of 1816 (VCH vol 8 p49) and is mainly covered by Silverdale village (SHC 1960 p14); Silverdale was known as Knutton Heath until 1854 (Newcastle Times Oct 20 1971).

Knypersley Former hamlet on a bank which formerly overlooked the former New Pool; Knypersley is now a suburb of Biddulph, 21.25m N of Stafford. Former manor and liberty in Biddulph ancient parish (LCAST 1898 p64) (BALH p26 see map). The manor was created in 1189 with the division of the original extensive Biddulph (see) manor. It was held by the de Knypersley family of Knypersley Hall (BALH p21). The name appears in the C13 as Knypresley (SSE 1996 p15). Duignan was unable to make anything of 'knyper.' Ley or lea is pasture-land (DUIGNAN). 'Knyper' is thought to be from Norwegian 'gnipa' meaning 'rocks,' so 'rocks meadow or pasture;' the Norwegians were prevalent in the area in the C10 (BHS p13). Park Lane between Knypersley and Rock End, was formerly Gutter Lane, a name thought to be derived from Guthrum's Lane and of Danish origin (TTTD p162). The church, St John the Evangelist, on the corner of St John's and Tunstall Roads, was built in 1848-1851 (BOE p69). Knypersley became a separate ecclesiastical parish in 1921 (GLAUE p415). Gwenne Price caused a national stir with her ahead-of-its-time, bridal outfit, a white trouser suit, at her wedding in Knypersley church in late March 1967; the vicar said he would never marry

another bride in a similar outfit (ES Jan 3 1967 p15p).

Knypersley End House 1m SE of Knypersley.

Knypersley Hall The original Knypersley Hall at Knypersley, Biddulph, was built in Henry II's reign and was the seat of the Knypersleys, a branch of the Biddulph family. By marriage it passed to the Bowyers. In 1736 it passed by marriage to the Gresleys (TTTD p166). Sir Nigel Gresley, builder of the Apedale Canal 1775-6 (NSFCT 1991 p41), modernised the hall by applying a brick casing to it in 1760. He is said to have been no longer living at it in 1783 (BALH p49), and sold it to James Bateman (d1824) of Salford in 1808 or 1810 (TTTD p166). The Batemans were originally of Tolson Hall, Westmorland (NSFCT 1954 p94) (BGFB p9). His son, John Bateman (1783-1858), lived at Knypersley Hall and his son James (1811-1897) left the hall in 1842 to improve Biddulph Grange (BGFB pp12,13p). The third floor of the house was removed and its size reduced in 1858 (BIOPP p17p). Edward Cooke noted in his diary a curious Etruscan tomb at Knypersley Hall in Sept 1849 (BGFB p15). (BALH pp24, 46, 49, 142-143, 155, 171-172, 175-176). Knypersley Hall and Greenway Bank were connected in the later C19 by a private carriage way allowing members of the Heath family and their guests to travel between their several residences without using the public road through Knypersley (TTTD p167).

Knypersley Hall At Gorsty Hill, 2.25m SW of Marchington. Formerly in Marchington Woodlands township in Hanbury ancient parish (W p563). There was pasture in the N of Abbots Bromley parish near here known as Knypersley in 1483-5 (ABMB p53). Formerly spelt Knipersley (SHOS vol 1 p92) (W p563). The name indicates a 'pasture' preceded by a personal name, possibly a nickname (SPN p8). Shaw thought it may have been one of the lesser seats of the Mynors family. It was still inhabited by a Mynor in the late C18 (SHOS vol 1 p92).

Knypersley Park Former hunting ground of the Bowyers. There was a deer park at Knypersley by the C17, as noted by Sir Simon Degges (1612-1704). The park was disparked in 1795 and restocked with deer in 1859. In 1867 it contained 120 acres (EDP p178) and covered the area of the present Greenway Bank Country Park (BIOPP p19p). The name is preserved in a house 1.25m ESE of Knypersley.

Knypersley Pool A pool and reservoir at the SE end of The Serpentine. They are now collectively known as Knypersley Reservoir. It was originally an eight acre mill pool. In 1805 the son of Hugh Henshall Williamson of Greenway Bank drowned in the pool whilst attempting to swim across it (ONST 1960 p232). The pool was enlarged in 1823 (NSJFS 1974 p124. 1991 p44), or 1825 (ONST 1960 p231), or 1827 (Greenway Bank Country Park. Staffs County Council Leaflet). There was a glacial boulder on the edge of the pool which may have been a parish boundary marker. It disappeared in 1962 having been rolled into the pool by vandals (ONST 1976 p375).

Knypersley Reservoir Collective name for the pools Knypersley Pool and The Serpentine. They were built on the Greenway Bank estate to supply the Trent and Mersey Canal (NSFCT 1938 p62). The water feeds the Caldon Canal and came to be in its present shape after 1823. Both the Serpentine and Knypersley Reservoir comprise 46 acres (English Reservoirs. Bill Howes. 1967 p56).

Knypersley Rocks Outcrop of gritstone rocks S of Knypersley Park. The named rocks comprise: 'The Green Slab' and 'The Pinnacle' (SGM p287). There appears to be a house built into, or close to, one of the outcrops.

Kocholme, Le It is perhaps the island in the Sow to the W of St Thomas Becket Priory. Le Kocholme was given to that priory some time after its foundation (BERK p47).

Kyber Pass Is another name for Lea Road or a passage at the end of Lea Road, Wolverhampton. The name appears on a postcard 1895 (TB June 1978 p3p) (PENOP p62p).

Kynchall Former name for an area around the junction of Lichfield Road and Broad Lane where the late C18 Pipe Grange Farm stands, 1m ESE of Burntwood. The Kynchall family, who lived in the late C13, took their name from this area. Kynchall Lane appears in 1412 and may be the present Broad Lane (VCH vol 14 pp201-202).

Kynnersley's Bank Refers to a stretch of the Abbots Bromley road near its junction with Stafford Road, Blount's Green. The name is from the Kynnersley family of Loxley and Highfields Halls (TRTC p24).

L

Laches, The Minute hamlet on the slopes of a low hill by a tributary of Saredon Brook, 0.5m E of Coven. One house is called Upper Laches Farm, another Lower Laches Farm. An axe-head of Neolithic or Bronze Age was found at The Laches in C17 (ABl p86) (BDH p18). A brass head of a bolt of a catapulta or unlooped palstave was found in a field here (NHS p403) (SHOS vol 2 p294 - just quotes Plot) (HOWM p1) (ASI p86) (SHC 1938 p297) (NSJFS 1964 p17). The name means 'swampy pool' (SPN p23 - spelt Latches).

Ladderedge Lofty ridge rising above the confluence of the Churnet and Endon Brook, 0.25m SE of Longsdon. Formerly in Longsdon township in Leek ancient parish. The ridge forms the southern end of Longsdon Hill, a long hill which may have given Longsdon its name (VCH vol 7 p203). The hamlet of Ladderedge, on former Ladderedge Common, enclosed in 1815 (VCH vol 7 p203), was centred on the junction the Leek road (A53) and the road to Horse Bridge in the C19. By the late C19 this area was considered the centre of Longsdon village, with the area to the S called Ladderedge (SVB p114) (VCH vol 7 p203). On Nov 4 1967 at 4.30am a coach driver at Ladderedge saw for about eight minutes through his windscreen five white lights in a cross or diamond formation about 900 feet high in the sky (FSRP p18).

Ladderedge Common Former area of 310 acres on Longsdon Hill. It was enclosed in 1815 (VCH vol 7 p207).

Ladfordfield N of Seighford airfield, Ellenhall. By the 1990s there was a small industrial estate at Ladfordfield.

Ladford Pool Next to Ladfordfield. Plot says it contains three score acres and is next largest pool in the county to Aqualate Mere (NHS p43). Ladford Pool was a hundred acre swamp. About 1800 it was drained and turned into meadows (SL p129).

Ladies Mile A stretch of road from Wall Heath to Enville or Highgate Common via the Green Forge. This was a favourite ride for the moderately-well-to-do who had a jig or trotting horse on days out from the Black Country. The straight stretch of lane on the route was ideal for them and was known, no doubt, also in a disparaging sense, too, as the Ladies' Mile (BCM July 1968 p11).

Ladies Well Mow Cop. A well which was of the date or dated 1858. It has gone from its position by Woodcockwell School, Church Street (WMC).

Lady Bromley's Oak Still existing in 1834 (1834 OS map) (SPNO p108). At approximately SK 017153 on present OS maps in the centre of Cannock Chase.

Lady Dale Dale nearby to Pickwood Hall, S of Leek. The name implies the dale has been a holy place dedicated to Our Lady the Virgin Mary and there may have been a chapel the Blessed Virgin Mary at Lady Dale. The unlocated 'Cholpesdale,' the site for Dieulacres Abbey before it was moved to its present site, may have been Lady Dale (SMM pp56,57,59,71 see map). Has also appeared as Ladydale. For the well at Ladydale see Lady o' the Dale Well.

Lady Dorothy's Cottage 1m SE of Enville, on the W side of the Chester Road, in Enville ancient parish. Built in 1755 by Lady Dorothy Grey of Enville Hall, a daughter of the 3rd Earl of Stamford, (d1781) as a charity school to prepare 12 girls for domestic service. The school closed shortly after 1925 and became a private residence in c1930 (VCH vol 20 pp93,117 p facing p145).

Lady Edge An edge 1.75m N of Upper Elkstones. Formerly in Fawfieldhead township in Alstonefield ancient parish. Heathland called Lady Edge, which extended NW into Heathylee township, was recorded in the later C14. The last common land on Lady Edge was enclosed in 1839 (VCH vol 7 p29).

Ladygreen House 1.25m W of Cheddleton.

Lady Isabella's Well A stopping place on the perambulation of Brewood in the vicinity of Bishop's Wood and Ivetsey Bank (SCSF p26).

Lady Low 0.25m N of Blore (Ray). Burial mound situated on top of a hill 722 feet high at SK 13894979. It is 20 paces in diameter and three feet high. It was excavated by Carrington in 1849. A cremation with an arrowhead was discovered (TYD pp156-157,163) (VCH vol 1 no 35) (NSJFS 1965 p34), as well as a deposit of calcinated bones (WTCEM p10), and a bronze dagger (NSFCT 1926 p146). It is a listed monument. To the NE of Lady Low at SK 13934985 is another burial mound which is a listed monument. It is 19 paces in diameter and 1.6 feet high. It was excavated by Carrington in 1849. A cremation with a small tanged bronze dagger was discovered (TYD pp150-151,163) (ARCH vol 43 p449) (NSJFS 1965 p34).

Lady Meadow Tamworth. According to tradition Sir Tarquin and Sir Lancelot of the Arthurian legend, fought a tournament in Lady's Meadow (GLS p91). Site where Sir Robert Peel erected his first cotton factory in the area. Has also appeared as Lady's Meadow.

Lady Meadow Former meadow 0.75m ENE of Dudley Castle, formed part of Coneygree Colliery. 'Dudley Castle' was the first steam engine erected in England (reports of two slightly earlier engines erected in Cornwall are inconclusive - SL p207) and Thomas Newcomen's first engine. (SHOS vol 2 pp119-120) (SOSH p296). It was erected in 1712 to drain water out of the coal mines of Lord Dudley and Ward. A near-contemporary source placed it 'at Dudley Castle in Staffordshire' and for many years it was believed to have been situated in the grounds of Dudley Castle, or at one of about six sites in the Black Country. The exact site became a matter of some national controversy (VCH vol 2 pp91,165) (Newcomen Society Transactions vol 13 p12. vol 16 pp155-159). From an engraving of the machine, published in 1719, JS Allen, in 1965, was able to locate the site to Lady Meadow by calculating its distance and angle from the castle (Newcomen Society Transactions vol 37 (1964-5) pp57-84) (BCM Oct 1976 pp40-46. Oct 1977 pp36-37. Jan 1978 pp83-84. July 1980 pp26-28) (The Steam Engine of Thomas Newcomen. LTC Rolt & JS Allen. 1977) (SL pp206-207).

Lady Meadows Lady Meadows Farm is under 1.75m SE of Bradnop. Formerly in Bradnop township in Leek ancient parish. Reputedly, fairies exist in the neighbourhood of Lady Meadow (TOI p172) (FLJ 1941 p236). In the Jacobite Rebellion the Young Pretender's army passed Lady Meadows on Dec 4 1745 (BPCSM p7). Lower Lady Meadows Farm, to the S of Lady Meadows Farm, is of the late C18 (VCH vol 7 p170).

Lady Moor Former hamlet 2m NNE of Sedgley, in Sedgley ancient parish. It was a district of Coseley by 1832 (HC p63) and adjoined the hamlet of Broad Lane (W pp198,200). The church, St Oswald, was built in 1888 of cinder, making it possibly unique as a church structure. It closed in the mid 1970s (BCM April 1982 p50il). Has also appeared as Ladymoor. The old hamlet was demolished from 1938 (BCM April 1982 pp49-52). David Bailey (1834-1917) was born in Lady Moor. He wrote a considerable amount of philosophical and religious poetry; his poem on the 'Cuckoo in Bilston' being an exception. With his wife he opened a school in the Orchard, Bilston, where he was to become famous for his teaching of 'Copper-plate' writing; he was a great friend of Isaac Pitman (HC p92). (BCM April 1982 p50).

Lady Moor Land belonging to the lord of Endon manor in 1399, 1.5m NW of Endon. Formerly mainly in Endon township in Leek ancient parish. By the C17 it was considered common waste, by which time it was being squatted (VCH vol 7 p181).

Ladymoor Farm C19 house 1.5m NW of Endon. Formerly in Endon township in Leek ancient parish. There was a house on the site of Ladymoor Farm by the later C16 (VCH vol 7 p177). The name is from Lady Moor (see).

Ladymoor Gate House or minute hamlet 1.75m ESE of Knypersley. In Biddulph parish. The name is from Lady Moor (see).

Lady of the Lake Boathouse on W side of Rudyard Lake. Built in 1893 for the Davenport family by William Larner Sugden with Pre-Raphaelite influences. 'Lady' is a reference to the statue of a lady erected in a niche in the chimney of the boathouse (The Architect. Dec 29 1893) (RL pp43,62il,ps).

Lady o' the Dale Well A holy well in Lady Dale at the bottom of a hill on which Pickwood stood, probably named in honour of Our Lady from Norman times (NSFCT 1882 p26), or in the Middle Ages (VCH vol 7 p88). The area in which the well stands was known as Lady Wall Dale in the late C16 (VCH vol 7 p88). The well has been called Lady Well (HLS p71), Ladydale Well, Our Lady's Well, Ladymedale Well, and My Ladies' Dale Well (NSFCT 1882 p26). The well was famed for its cure of eye complaints (VBB p20) (SMCC p8), and was given a stone head in the 1850s erected by the owners of Pickwood Hall in memory of their son. Water then flowed through a metal lion's head and the well was surrounded by metal railings, both were removed in WW2 (SMM pp56-58p). Within the memory of some living in the early 1990s there was a May Day procession to the site by children of St Mary's Roman Catholic church (VCH vol 7 p88).

Lady Pool Small pool N of Rushall Hall, Rushall. The pool is of medieval origin and was made possibly to either contain fish or drive a mill. In 1305 Sir Roger de Morteyn gave Sir Thomas le Rous his share of a fish pond called Lady pool (SNAR p58). A furnace existed on the Rushall road, near Ladypool, from very early times; Plot in the later C17 is said to have noted it. It was still standing in 1718 (HOBLL p244) (SNAR p58). The 'mill meadow' near Lady Pool noted by Plot probably commemorates the site of a windmill. A post mill at Rushall was described as 'newly erected' in 1693 and is shown on maps of 1775 and 1778. It was demolished some time before 1834. It seems to have stood on the E side of Lichfield Road; Joseph McKenna in 'Windmills of Birmingham and the Black Country' maintains that it was near the northern junction with Cartbridge Lane (SNAR p60). The same or another windmill stood at SK 028011 at Rushall (see).

Ladysmith House 0.75m SW of Hoar Cross, on the old road from Abbots Bromley to Lichfield. Formerly called The Gullets when the residence of Thomas Bamford (1743-1822) (BUBA pp9,10p). It was re-named Ladysmith after the battle of Ladysmith in the Boar War (SVB p96).

Lady Stone Rock feature at the N end of Ramshaw Rocks at approximately SK 02096285 (1834, 1887, 1900, 1926 OS maps) (SGM p177).

Lady's Walk A medieval track from Stoke-upon-Trent to Hulton Abbey via Northwood. Used by Hulton Abbey monks to get them from the abbey to officiate at Stoke church. Hulton Abbey was dedicated to the Virgin Mary (UDC) (OTP pp156-157) (H p87) (NSFCT 1923 p154. 1989 pp36-37 plan). Has also appeared as Our Lady's Walk.

Lady's Way Route running over Cannock Chase from Teddesley Hall, crossing the Stafford-Cannock road at Shut-the-Gate. It was similar to Marquis's Drive, but has now (1951) disappeared (GCC p24).

Lady's Well A well which was next to Bell's Mill Pits, Etruria Road, Hanley (ROS vol 1 p87).

Lady's Well Tunstall. (OTP p2) (SHST p218). The name is preserved in Ladywell Road. Tunstall had no piped water until 1848 (POP p176).

Lady Well A possible holy well at Bradley, near Stafford. Evidence for a well of this name at Bradley is suggested by the names No. 458 Ladywell Meadow and No. 470 Near Ladywell in the Tithe Apportionment (OSST 1944-1945 p12).

Lady Well Drayton Bassett. Its water was by Drayton Manor (DM p62).

Lady Well A well with curative properties cut into a sandstone outcrop in Ladywell Wood on Orton Hills, Wombourne. It can be identified probably with the 'Wodewell' (VCH vol 20 p200) or 'The Woodwell' recorded in the C13. It was later dedicated to the Virgin Mary when it was said to have medicinal properties; it has also appeared as Our Lady's Well. Hackwood in SR p107 says oblations at the well were received by a hermit who shared them between the churches of Penn and Wombourne. There was a cottage here called Ladywell Cottage (WWW p93 p of the cottage). In the late C19 it was described as a favourite resort for people wishing to take its waters (The Antiquary vol 22 p162) (VCH vol 20 p200). (SCSF p143) (SMM p78) (POAP pp9-10) (PMPD pp75-76).

Lady Well Pool Near Pigeonhouse Farm, Compton, Kinver. It was a public washing place in the early C17 (VCH vol 20 p152).

Lakeside A ward in Perton civil parish by the late C20.

Lamascote Tiny hamlet to E of Stafford (1834 OS map). Has also appeared Lombercote (1273), Lambircote (1439), Lambercotes (1548), Lammascote (1775) (SPNO pp77-78), and Lammascotes. The name preserved in, Lammascote Road, means 'cottage(s) where lambs were reared' (SPNO pp77-

78). Gustav Hamel in a monoplane flew here at Stafford's first flying display Oct 12 1912 (EAS p20) (SAIW pl. 52).

Lamber Low 0.5m NE of Waterhouses. Burial mound at SK 08735085 on a hill. Carrington excavated it in 1849. A stone built cist, a crouched adult skeleton with a flint spearhead were found (TYD pp131-132) (VCH vol 18) (DAJ vol 75 pp75,114,117) (NSJFS 1965 p52) (WOY p1). It is a listed monument.

Lambert's Coppice Wood 0.75m NW of Ingestre Hall, Ingestre.

Lambert's End Small district of West Bromwich 0.75m E of the High Street, near to the Vine Inn, opposite Gads Lane (SOWB p25). There was some settlement at Lambert's End, formerly Cutler's End, by the later C18 (OWB p112) (VCH vol 17 p9). Appears as Lambeth End on 1834 OS map.

Lambskin Dale Dale 1.5m SW of Oakamoor also the same distance E of Cheadle.

Lamb's Warren and Lodge. Rabbit warren laid out by John Lamb, a Lichfield coach-maker, in c1717, on the Hammerwich part of Cannock Chase, W of Hammerwich. The present Lamb's Lodge Farm, 1m W of Hammerwich, was Lamb's second and last lodge. The lodge was one of those attacked in the Rabbit Riots on Cannock Chase (see) in 1753-54 (AFT pp190, 220-236) (LOU p72) (VCH vol 14 p267).

Landers i' th' Wood Lander's Wood Farm is 1m NNE of Sandon. So called probably after being the property of the Landors family in the C17 (SHC 1909 p126), or possibly has the same etymology as Landywood. Has also appeared as Launder's Wood (SHC 1909 p126).

Landywood Suburb of Great Wyrley on a hill above a tributary of Wash brook, 1.25m S of Great Wyrley. 0.75m to the W of Landywood is a hamlet called Upper Landywood. Formerly in Great Wyrley township in Cannock parish, now a ward in Great Wyrley civil parish. Great stones from the top of Barr Beacon are at Landywood (GWY p facing p18). The name has appeared as Laund i' th' Wood (C16), Londewood (1670), Landywood (maps of Plot and Morden) (SPNO p71). It is probably from the Middle English word 'launde' (Modern English is 'lawn') original meaning was a plain sprinkled with trees or bush, an open space between woods, a forest glade (DUIGNAN) or 'the (agricultural) land in the wood' (SPN p148). Whitley Stokes in his Glossarial Index to the Martryrology of Oengus gives the word 'land' Old Cymric 'lann' now 'llan' as area, church (NSFCT 1908 p144), or enclosure (NSFCT 1910 p165). The church, St Andrew, Hilton Lane, dates from c1970 (LDD). Landywood Enterprise Park, in Holly Lane, was opened by Diana, Princess of Wales, in 1987 (South Staffs Council).

Lane, The A narrow winding ribbon of rough road that joined the straggling towns of the Potteries over a distance of eight to 10 miles from Tunstall to Lane End, Longton (SHST p8). The ancient Uttoxeter-Stoke road with its extension to Newcastle-under-Lyme was also simply known as 'The Lane.' It was turnpiked in 1759 (SASR 1987 p105).

Lane Delph Former settlement which developed along the line of the Stoke-Uttoxeter road (the boundary between the ancient vills of Great and Little Fenton) running from Victoria Place to where the Plaza stands (FF pp16,80) (SASR 1987 p101). The first part of the name 'Lane' may be from Richmilde Street (see), the Roman road between Derby and Chesterton (see Lane End). The second part of the name has nothing to do with Dutch pottery but is derived from the Old English word 'delve' meaning to dig; in this case ironstone and coal, which were anciently dug here (POP p107). The area was also called Middle Fenton (HSP pp70,141) (HBST p552). By 1843 it had the character of a respectable small town (HBST p553). It was formerly in Stoke-upon-Trent chapelry in Stoke-upon-Trent ancient parish. The name no longer prevails and Fenpark Industrial Estate covers one part of the area.

Lane End E of Derrington (1834 OS map). The name is preserved in Lane End Farm, now practically merged into Derrington.

Lane End 1m SSW of Longnor (1834 OS map).

Lane End Former township with Longton in Stoke-upon-Trent chapelry and ancient parish and was the name of modern Longton (see) town. A barbed and tangled arrowhead of the Neolithic or Bronze Age was found in Nov 1931 in Goldenhill Road (NSFCT 1932 p192) (NSJFS 1964 p35). Richmilde Street (see), a Roman road between Derby and Chesterton, passed through Lane End. In the Middle Ages this road was known as Mere Passage or Mear Lane. Some have thought the name Mere Passage arose from a trackway over a swamp, connected with a small lake. It is believed Meir to the SE is named after a swamp. Another explanation is that Mere means the 'boundary,' so 'boundary lane.' The road did separate the two hundreds of Pirehill and Totmonslow (HBST pp559-560) (DUIGNAN p83) (SHC 1909 p59 note) (SASR 1987 p104). By the later C17 settlement by the road was known as Meare Lane End. In 1775 the present Uttoxeter Road was known as Meer Lane (maps of Plot and Yates) (HBST p559) (VCH vol 8 p226) (SASR 1987 p96) (FF p16). In time Mear was dropped from the name and the settlement became simply Lane End. Lane End was used to refer to present Longton until at least the late 1830s. Simeon Shaw calls the whole of his chapter on Longton 'Lane End' (HSP pp72-77). 'Lane End' or sometimes 'Longton St John the Baptist' ecclesiastical parish was created from Longton ecclesiastical parish in 1866 (GLAUE p415). But by the late 1830s 'Longton' was in popular usage; 'Lane End' being considered too mean-sounding for a place which was trying to appear respectable (HBST p555) (VCH vol 8 p226). By the 1834 OS map 'Longton' is applied to the built-up area S of Lane End. The name Lane End no longer prevails. Lane End (Longton) had the poorest and most insanitary housing of the Pottery towns and was given the contemptuous name of Neck End by the inhabitants of rival towns, yet paradoxically its people produced the most delicate of ceramic products (SL p225). Authorisation for the Lane End Tramroad to link Lane End with the Trent and Mersey Canal near Whieldon Road, Stoke, was given in 1802 (HCMS No. 5) (VCH vol 2 p306).

Lane End Farm On N side of the Leek-Ashbourne road, 1m SE of Bradnop. Formerly in Bradnop township in Leek ancient parish. Mentioned in 1675. It was an inn called the Red Lion in 1818 (VCH vol 7 p171). Lane End Farm may be identified with Oxhay Farm (see) which was the Red Lion Inn in 1745. Ox Hay Wood lies to the farm's SW on the 1834 OS map.

Lane Ends Area of Brown Edge village. Now called Church Road (BEH pp31,49p,53p).

Lane Ends Small hamlet between Packmoor and Brindley Ford. Formerly in Wolstanton ancient parish. The name is from perhaps where The Lane (see) which linked the Pottery communities ended.

Lane Green Former hamlet, now a suburb of Codsall, 1m ESE of Codsall. Formerly in Tettenhall ancient parish. The green, at the top of Lane Green Road, was mentioned in the early 1640s (VCH vol 20 p12). Some of the green still remained in 1935 (TCOP p146p). The Lane Green estate at Bilbrook was built to accommodate the new Boulton Paul factory workers (HOWU p148).

Lanehead A mostly-C18 house on S side of Holehouse Lane 1.25m NW of Endon. Formerly in Endon township in Leek ancient parish. It was so called in 1648 (VCH vol 7 p177).

Lane Head Small district by Wyrley and Essington canal, 1m NE of Willenhall. Formerly in Willenhall chapelry in Wolverhampton ancient parish, became a part of Short Heath civil parish in 1895 (SNW p25). Lane Head was a little mining community in the C19 (WDY p14). According to David Potts, writing in 1984, the district could be considered a village and is called 'the village' by the some inhabitants (Selective Essays on Willenhall. David Potts. 1984. Copy in Willenhall library).

Lanes End House in one range with Brereton Hall (see), Rugeley.

Lanesfield District 1.25m WSW of Bilston, centred on the old Ettingshall hamlet (LAIW p1), by the Birmingham Canal, Old Cut Old Main Line. In Sedgley ancient parish. A fossil stem, about 30 cms in diameter and 12 cms deep, from the Carboniferous period was found in 1982 as drains were being laid close to Lanesfield School in Newman Ave; these types of fossils are thought to have caused the deaths of many in the Parkfield Colliery (LAIW pages between 29-30). Underhill and others think the name must have previously been simply 'Lane's field;' the Lanes were a prominent family in the area. Lane's Hall which appears on the 1834 OS map may have been a former name of Rookery Hall (AMS p448) (LAIW pp1,2). Lanesfield seems to have been a product of the early C19 expansion of the Black Country (LAIW p2). The Coseley Engineering Co Ltd were or are based in Lanesfield. They were one of the leaders of the world in the supply of steel-framed pre-fabricated buildings in the 1950s. Buildings at the Baghdad Trade Fair were theirs, and at Heathrow Airport (Staffs County Handbook c1958 p47).

Laney Green Small village 1m ENE of Shareshill, to E of junction 11 of M6, Cannock. In Shareshill ancient parish. Has appeared as Loany Green (1704) (SPN p73), Lanes Green (Yates' map), and Lowney Green (OS map 1834) (SPNO pp113-114). If from Loany Green then perhaps monies were collected at this green (SPN p73).

Langley Close Near Stanshope, Alstonefield. In Wetton ancient parish. In the later C17 Plot was told there were quantities of black chalk here (NHS p124).

Langley Farm Near Brewood. An axe-head of Neolithic or Bronze Age was found here in the 1970s. It is kept by Mr K Shropshire of Wood Hall Farm, Codsall Wood (BDH p18 il).

Langley Green Some common land in Armitage parish (OSST 1956-59 p8).

Langley Hall 0.5m NNW of Lower Penn. Formerly in Lower Penn township in Penn ancient parish. Built in the early C18. It appears on Yates' map and the 1834 OS map. Between c1800 and c1875 it was tenanted by the Thurstons, and then by the Beddards to c1930. By 1940 Raymond Harris had moved in

and he was here to c1960. The hall was sold as part of the Lloyd House estate in 1901 (PPTP pp55 il facing, 56). In 1986 the hall was sold separately from the farm (PPTP p56), and by 1988 the house was known as Langley Hall Farm and Langley Farm (PENOP p82p).

Langley Lawn House 1.5m S of Bishop's Wood (1834 OS map). For Langley in a local rhyme see Brewood.

Langot Ancient boundary point of Tutbury (SHOS vol p56).

Langot Valley Valley on either side of the Sow from its source to Blore Pipe at Fairoak. Yonge supported the suggestion that the name was derived from the early British 'llangut' meaning holy stone - giving rise to the legend of a sacred stone on the top of some eminence used by druids - Fairoak Knoll (ROT p11). (BOV p29). Or 'Langot' is an obsolete form of 'Languet' which in turn is derived from Old French 'Languette' diminutive of 'Langue' a tongue - the valley is tongue shaped - the name may have been applied by French glass makers, who were operating in Bishop's Wood in the C16 (NSFCT 1937 p121). On the E side of the valley are many caves. One cave near Greatwood Lodge is supposed to have hidden an escaped murderer in 1948. Another in Pick Field (NW of Wetwood Manor) is large and rectangular and was at sometime fitted with a wooden beam to support the roof, and sheltered cattle. Another cave is behind a yeoman's garden at Croxton, it extends for some distance into the red sandstone. There is another cave near the marl pits on Greatwood Farm which was once inhabited by a hermit called Joe Wilson (MR p18). Another cave, which was inhabited by the Locke family, who were gypsies and who have a headstone in Croxton churchyard, is near Blore Pipe Farm on the left of the road leading to Offley Brook. Buckingham's Cave in Outlands is below New Inn Bank, behind the home of 'Old' Matthews (BOV pp32,33,43-44).

Langton House In SW part of Lichfield cathedral Close. Probably built in the mid C18. Is adjoined on the N by Moat House (VCH vol 14 pp58 see map, 67).

Lapley Ancient parish and former township. The small village of Lapley tops a small rise at a little distance from the former Roman road between Whitchurch, Shrops and Pennocrucium, 7m SSW of Stafford. Lapley has been identified with the Lappeleya mentioned in a charter of 1061 in which Earl Ælfgar grants Lapley to St Remigius (Remy) Abbey of Rheims (SHC 1916 p126-127). Later forms are: Lepelie, a manor held by St Remigius', in DB (under Northants), Lapeleia (1130), Lappeleia (1200), Lappele (1262), Lapleye (1577), Lamplew (SHOS vol 1 p44) (CE p115) (NSFCT 1952 p34) (BS p319 see under Stephen Light Mott) (SPNO p167) (SPN p74) (SSE 1996 p15). The name means probably 'Hlappa's lea' (DUIGNAN), or 'laeppa leah,' 'woodland clearing at the boundary (literally end) of the manor' (SPNO p167) (SPN p74), or 'at the end of the estate or parish' (SSE 1987 p30. 1996 pp15,22) (LSWA p17). The custom of Borough English prevailed at Lapley (NHS pp277,278). Commander Wedgwood thought Lapley ancient parish probably formed originally a part of Church Eaton parish and split away from it soon after 1086 (SHC 1916 p197). Another account states that ecclesiastically Lapley may have belonged to Penkridge at an early date and through the negligence of Penkridge Collegiate Church St Remigius Abbey created it a parish after acquiring Lapley manor in the early 1060s (VCH vol 3 p298). The parish church, All Saints, Cemetery Bank on the W side of the village, is of C12 origin and was the church of Lapley Priory (VCH vol 4 p150). For fairs, markets, and wakes of the parish see Wheaton Aston. There was probably a windmill in Windmill Field at Lapley Hall Farm. It existed in 1291 and was held by Lapley Priory. It was disused by 1358 (VCH vol 4 p149) (WBJ p29) (CE p121). For the parliamentary garrison at Lapley Hall or House and the retaking of the house by royalists see Lapley Hall. Thirteen were involved in an incident of Morris Dancing at Lapley on Aug 5 1655 and were accused of being Papists (LOU p345). By the late C20 Lapley was a ward in Lapley, Stretton and Wheaton Aston civil parish. A sulphur spring, near the southern boundary of the parish, may have a connection with the 'spa' at Wheaton Aston (see). In the later C17 Plot mentions a giant oak at Lapley (NHS p248).

Lapley Court Lapley (NHS p313).

Lapley Hall Lapley. Also called Lapley House (LGS p159) (NSFCT 1911 p227) (LSWA p22). Dates from the late C16 or early C17 although it has been much restored since (VCH vol 4 pp139p facing,144). Squire Peters garrisoned the house in the Civil War for parliament with a force of about 170; it was most unusual for the parliamentarians to garrison houses. However, a servant named Collier, a royalist sympathiser, in Nov 1643 informed the royalists at Chillington Hall of the strength of the Lapley garrison. Royalists under Capt Heavingham or Col Heveningham from Chillington then came over and retook the house on Dec 21 (LGS pp159,160) (HOS 1998 p74) (LSWA p22; says on Dec 1). A contingent of 12 parliamentarians stationed in Lapley church came to the aid of their fellow parliamentarians but to no avail. Subsequently, one of the 12 went to Stafford for reinforcements. Meanwhile, Capt Heavingham asked Col Leveson at Dudley Castle for royalist reinforcements, leaving a certain Lieut Stanley in temporary charge of the house. Both side's reinforcements arrived in Lapley at the same time and a fight ensued in which Leveson's men were able to beat off a parliamentary attack and hold the house for the king (LSWA pp22-23). A captain, thought to have commanded the royalist garrison, who may have died in this skirmish, was buried in the chancel of the church (E&S July 11 1998 p9). (WJO July 1903 xxxiii p) (LGS pp159,160) (NSFCT 1911 p227) (SOP p136) (VCH vol 4 p144). The house was enlarged by Col FH Swinfen in 1875. It was purchased from Col Swinfen with a portion of Lapley Hall and Lapley Wood farms in 1888 by Edward Smith, a Wednesbury tube manufacturer (LSWA p20). The brick garden wall with gothic window and arches was probably built in c1875 (VCH vol 4 p144).

Lapley Hall Farm Lapley. L-shaped timber-framed building with C19 brick additions. It is situated opposite the later C18 Lapley House (VCH vol 4 p144).

Lapley Hayes William Hyven of Lapley Hayes, near Wednesfield, married his third wife at the age of 105, saying it was 'better to marry than burn.' Hyven died in c1810 at Little Bloxwich, aged 115 (W p57). There is a Lapley Close at Horseley Fields close to Neachells.

Lapley House Lapley. It is situated opposite Lapley Hall Farm. Brick, dating from later C18. A boundary wall to the S formerly had the date '1828' worked in dark bricks (VCH vol 4 p145).

Lapley Old Manor House Lapley. Timber framed. Stands N of the church and probably occupies part of the site of Lapley Priory. Traces of a moat remain (VCH vol 4 p144). Said to have been lately restored in 1903. Col Swinfen was in occupation in 1903 (WJO July 1903 xxxv). The Manor House with a portion of Lapley Hall and Lapley Wood farms was bought by Henry Francis Graddon Perry from Col Swinfen in 1888 (LSWA p20).

Lapley Priory Former Benedictine house for monks and a dependency of St Remigius Abbey at Rheims. In 1061 Burchard, son of Earl Alfgar (or Ælfgar), died returning from having accompanied Aldred, Archbishop of York, on a mission to Rome and was buried by the monks of Rheims. In fulfilment of his son's dying promise Alfgar gave the monks land at Lapley and elsewhere in Staffs. The priory was founded sometime between 1061 and 1086. At the suppression of the alien priories in 1415 Lapley was given to the new college at Tong, Shrops (LGS pp37,158-159) (SOSH p105; Alfgar was the son of Leofric and Godiva and he also fathered Earls Edwin and Morcar) (NSFCT 1950 p89; founded in 1063) (VCH vol 3 p340) (HOS 1998 pp56,58). (Staffordshire Domesday Studies. Eyton. p42) (SHC 1916 pp128-129). The priory buildings evidently adjoined the church on the N side and part of the site now occupied by the timber-framed Old Manor House. The church itself contains much C12 work. The priory site and the church were enclosed within a moat (VCH vol 3 p342). Eynon-Williams thinks the base of the tower, the chancel arch, and a portion of the S chancel wall of Lapley church date from the foundation of the priory (NSFCT 1950 p89). The OS map shows earthworks directly to the N of the church. Some remains are in a farmhouse on NE side of church (GNHS pp137,138) (W p463) (CE pp115-121) (Booklet by WD Eynon-Williams) (VCH vol 3 pp340-343) (SGS p116) (LSWA pp17,19).

Lapley Wood Farm House 0.75m SW of Lapley.

Lapwing Hall Shown on 1887 OS map 0.25m N of Meerbrook, approximately at Lea End. Field name derived from an animal name (- the pewit) (APB p48).

Lark Hall House 1m N of Bradnop.

Lark Hall House 2m WNW of Wetley Rocks in Bagnall parish. Large farmhouse in existence by 1851. In the early 1890s the house was demolished and replaced by a large barn (B pp79-80).

Lark Park House to NW of Bottom House, on Morridge (1834 OS map).

Lask Edge Promontory lying between the head of the Trent and Horton Brook, former common and fragmented minute hamlet 1m SE of Biddulph Moor. In Horton ancient parish. Has appeared Laxege (1239) (VCH vol 7 p72), and Lasco Edge in 1807 when a house here was registered for Protestant Dissenters by Hugh Bourne (SHC 1960 p11). The common, which covered 143 acres in 1805, was enclosed in 1815 (VCH vol 7 p72). The area was prospected by Shell for oil and gas, but abandoned in 1984 due to insufficient flow rates (NSFCT 1993-4 New Series vol 19 p32).

Latebrook Area to W of Goldenhill, 1m NW of Tunstall.

Latham Hall House 0.75m SE of Calton. The burial mound 510 metres N of the hall at SK 11344951 is a listed monument.

Lathbury's Hill Hill S of Draycott-in-the-Clay leads up to Needwood Forest.

Latherford Minute hamlet with about two houses on a tributary of Saredon Brook; Upper Latherford Farm and Lower Latherford Farm, 0.75m NW of

Shareshill. In Shareshill ancient parish. Has appeared as Loddereford (1343 to 1511), Lodresford (1358), Lotherford (1442), Latherford (1528-1547) (SPNO p114) (SSE 1996 p15). In Anglo-Saxon loddere, lodre means a beggar. Perhaps, beggar's ford, hill, lake, street, thorn, way, or brook (DUIGNAN) (SPN p104). (SOB p117). Oakden gives 'ford' as the terminal but is uncertain that beggar is the prefix (SSE 1996 p15).

Laughing Cottage Cottage lodge to Bank End Farm, High Lane, Brown Edge. It was built by a member of the Shoobridge family in the later C19. It is so called because of the many laughing faces built into the walls of the cottage (ONST 1979 p398).

Laurels, The Substantial house situated at the corner of Handsworth Wood Road and Wood Lane, Handsworth. It is apparently shown on a map of 1794 at Hunts Green or thereabouts (HPPE p67).

Laurels Farm Brick building at Brineton dated 1678 (VCH vol 4 p64). Palliser mentions a brick house of 1678 at Brineton, which he suspects may be the first brick house in the W of the county (SL p100).

Lawn, The The parkland in Rolleston is now The Lawn (UTR p181). The name is from the word 'lant,' a ploughed strip of field? (UTR p181).

Lawneswood House 1.75m NE of Stourton.

Lawn Farm Bagnall. Has also appeared as Laund Farm (1834 OS map). See Little Lawn Farm and Big Lawn Farm.

Lawn Farm House in Fenton Vivian township surrounded by Botteslow township (HBST p526), SE of Berry Hill. Has also appeared as Lawn (1834 OS map) and The Lawn. The moat near the house may represent the site of Fenton Vivian manor house (HBST p526) (VCH vol 1 p366. vol 8 pp205,207). The moat was excavated in the 1960s (Reports of City of Stoke-on-Trent Museum Arch Soc No. 2 1966) (NSFCT 1982 p19).

Lawn Farm House over 0.75m SE of Endon. Formerly in Endon township in Leek ancient parish. The house is of the C17 (VCH vol 7 p177). There is a priest's hole at The Lawn (STM Dec 1968 p47). In the earlier C17 the house was known as the Laund meaning woodland pasture, possibly a reference to grassland reserved for deer: In this area was the medieval deer park of Hanley Park (VCH vol 7 p182).

Lawn Farm 1m NW of Stramshall.

Lawnhead Minute hamlet on an incline above the head of Lonco Brook 1.5m WNW of Ranton. In Ellenhall parish.

Lawns Farm 0.75m NNW of Branston (NSJFS 1964 p17). Has also appeared as Lawn Farm (UTR p181). In 1942 the tooth of a Steppe horse (similar to wild horse of Mongolia) was found here at SK 216224 (info KL Neal). For other finds nearby see Branston. The name is from the word 'lant,' a ploughed strip of field? (UTR p181).

Lawns Wood Small modern residential hamlet on a ridge above the Stour 1.5m NE of Stourton. Formerly in Kingswinford ancient parish. The site of the house Lawnswood is shown on a map of 1822 as a field; the house was erected in the 1830s (SNSV vol 1 p204). The name appears in the 1851 census.

Lawrence Lane Former hamlet in Rowley Regis parish (BCWJ p86). Lawrence Lane is a prominent street running N to S between Cradley Heath and Old Hill (Birmingham A-Z 1995).

Lawrence Hay Former deer park belonging to the Crown lying beside Stockley Park in Anslow township in Rolleston ancient parish. It was in existence by 1543 and was a park for only a short time. In 1625 it passed into the possession of Sir Edward Moseley. Has also appeared as Lawrence Heyes (ANS pp46,51,77).

Lawton Grange House 1m SE of Wall. At Lawton Park, belonging to one Townley in the later C17, were noted to be quantities of lead ore (NHS p166).

Laythropp's Almshouses Carter Street, Uttoxeter. The original grant of four houses in Carter Street for almshouses was made by William Laythropp, son of Humphrey Laythropp of Crakemarsh, in 1700. The almshouses were rebuilt in 1848 by Thomas Fradgley (AUOPP p27p).

Lazy Hill Hill and road leading out of Aldridge to Upper Stonnall. The name aptly describes the long slow climb up from Stonnall and the Chester Road (SNAR p35).

Lea, River Rises near Lea Head Manor then runs through Madeley (M pp22,30) then on to Wrinehill Hall, where it joins the Checkley Brook. North of Madeley Pool the river flows through a shallow, but clearly defined valley (MHSP p42). Has appeared as The Lea Brook and the water Lee (1621), and the Lea (1656). Dodgson in the Place-Names of Cheshire part 1 p18 has shown that the Lea was the old name for Checkley Brook (SPNO p12).

Lea, The Large farm or compact minute hamlet on a ridge overlooking Lonco Brook 1.25m NNW of High Offley. In Adbaston ancient parish. The house is reputedly haunted by a 'Madam Vernon' (SFL pp127,128). Has also appeared as Gilbert's Lea (W p382).

Lea, The House situated on SW side of Barlaston Green, and former estate, appearing in documents from the mid C13; has also appeared as Barlaston Lea, and can perhaps be identified with Lee Hall, in existence in 1460. In 1849 Francis Wedgwood (1800-1888), grandson of Josiah Wedgwood I of Etruria Hall (see), built Upper House (see) on the eastern part of the estate. The Lea house became the seat of Francis' second son Clement Francis Wedgwood (d1889) (SHC 1909 p82 note) (BAH pp13,33). Clement Francis' second son, Josiah Clement (d1943), MP for Newcastle-under-Lyme, historian and writer for SHC, was born in Barlaston in 1872 (possibly here?), and was created Baron Wedgwood of Barlaston in 1942 (POTP pp225-226).

Lea, The An ancient estate near Graiseley, in the ancient parish and foreign of Wolverhampton (HOWM p44). Has also appeared as the Lea House. There seems to have been a small settlement at the Lea in the Middle Ages (HOWM p6) and the name appears on Saxton's map. The estate and house belonged to the Warings until they moved to Oldbury, near Bishop's Castle, Shrops (SHOS vol 2 p172). Richard Giffard died here in 1606 (HOWM p61). Robert Waring (1614-1658), poet, historian, student of Christ Church, Oxford, and professor at Oxford may have been born at the Lea (NHS p276) (PSS pp472-473) (VFC p139). A house known as the Lea and Lea Hall existed until at least the 1840s and the name survives in Lea Road, built over part of the estate (Mapping the Past Wolverhampton 1577-1986. Mary Mills 1993 p2). Parts of the moat which surrounded an old hall remained to at least 1879 (SSAHST 1982-3 p57).

Lea Brook Former hamlet in Tipton ancient parish (W p709). A Lea Brook, a tributary of the Tame, flows eastwards through Willingsworth to join a Tame head river S of Wednesbury (TMS p127). A Leabrook, in the Wednesbury area, which may be this Lea Brook is mentioned in 1315 (HOWV p108). The name is preserved in Leabrook Road running between Ocker Hill and Wednesbury (Birmingham A-Z).

Leacroft Appears to have been a straggling fragmented hamlet stretching from Rumer Hill, under 1m ESE of Cannock, to slopes above Newlands Brook 1m SE of Cannock. Formerly in Cannock township and old parish. Has appeared as Lecroft (1327), Lee Croft (1327), Leycrofte (1493), Leacroft (1577. 1613. 1834 OS map) (Saxton's map) (SPNO p57). The name is from Anglo-Saxon 'laege-croft,' meaning 'the untilled croft,' but its probable meaning is 'the disused croft' (SPN p74). From his land at Leacroft Dr Birch allowed water from a spring to feed the conduit house in Cannock (W p451). Leacroft Farm at the E end of the hamlet was Hill Farm by 1976 (OS map 1:25,000 1976) and Leacroft Hill by 1989 (Birmingham A-Z 1989). A new development, called Orbital Park, on the N side of Watling Street at Churchbridge was taking the name Leacroft by 1995 (OS Street Atlas of Staffs 1995).

Leacroft Farm Leacroft (CCAP p34p).

Leacroft Hall Stood in the centre of the straggling hamlet of Leacroft, at approximately SJ 996094, and appears to have been demolished; an open cast mine now (1990s) extends to the site. It was the birthplace of Bishop John Hough in 1657. He was the son of John and Margaret Hough, the latter being daughter of John Birch of Leacroft, considered to be the ablest attorney in England in his day. John Hough was bishop of Lichfield between 1699 and 1717, and of Worcester between 1717 and 1743 (HOL p123) (W p643) (CCBO pp173-175) (VB p122). The hall, seat of Dr William Byrrche (Birch) in 1736, appears on OS maps of 1834 and 1889. It had been partially demolished probably by 1851. In the 1950s several buildings associated with it remained. They were a late C17 stable block, a barn dated 1676, an outhouse with a tablet inscribed 'Dr. W.B.' 1737, and another outhouse which may have been a dovecote (VCH vol 5 p56). There is a tradition that the three S windows as well as the S doorway in Cannock parish church came from Leacroft Old Hall; the church S doorway (with the date 1752) was demolished in 1957 (VCH vol 5 p65 note). According to tradition there is a secret tunnel from Leacroft Hall to Cannock church and another tunnel which connected Cannock and Penkridge churches (CCF p60; Wright is very sceptical of the story).

Leacroft Hall House 1m WSW of Cresswell.

Leadendale Dale S of Rough Close, Longton. Has also appeared as Leaden Dale. A house here was the seat of Major Cecil Wedgwood (1863-1916), son of Godfrey Wedgwood of Idlerocks (see) (WCW p337).

Lea Field Rugeley (gravestone in Brereton churchyard).

Leafields House 3.25m ESE of Fradswell.

Leafields Farm House over 0.25m WNW of Abbots Bromley. Dated 1837. Here the Abbots Bromley Horn Dancers performed in the afternoon of Sept 6 1999.

Lea Grange 0.75m SW of Elmhurst, just over 1m NW of Lichfield cathedral. Was the centre of an estate, known as Stychbrook Grange in the C15, which had been given to St John the Baptist's Hospital in Lichfield for the maintenance of a chantry in the C13. There may have been a house here in the C15. The main block of the present house was rebuilt in the early C19 (VCH vol

14 p234).

Lea Hall House over 0.25m NE of Handsworth, on the N side of Wood Lane. The original building, said to be of medieval origin, was of sandstone blocks. In the C16 and C17 it was occupied by the Squire(s) family; a daughter of William Squire married William Harman, and their first child was afterwards John, Bishop of Exeter (1519), later known as Bishop Vesey (John Harman). The hall was rebuilt just prior to 1800 (HPPE p66), and again or in the 1840s, was still standing in 1984 (MNB pp38,40,41,53).

Lea Hall House under 2m SE of Rugeley. Formerly written Lee Hall and situated by Armitage road, in Armitage parish (SHOS vol 1 p210). Once the seat of Hon Robert Curzon. Residence of John Webb an architect and landscape designer in 1804 (SSE 1994 p29). It had become a farmhouse by 1851 (W p555). Occupied by Walter John Landor in c1863 (KD 1863). Gives its name to Lea Hall Colliery (see).

Lea Head Manor Timber-framed house 2m SW of Madeley. Built by local craftsmen in 1671 for William Bucknall and his wife; the Bucknalls are believed to have lived at Lea Head since at least 1565. In c1848 the owner was Rev Thomas Bucknall Lloyd. The house was tenanted in the later C19 and until 1920 when it was acquired by a Sandbach family. The house was extended in 1934 by the then owner Lt Col James Doyle who died in WW2. In 1982 it was the home of John Howle and his wife Miranda (ES June 3 1933 p3p. Sept 9 1982) (DoE II*). (M pp22p,23). The gate piers are late C17 topped by pineapple finials; a curiosity, since pineapples were only introduced to this country in 1660 (DoE). To the W of the hall, still within Staffs, is a moat (CAMS p63), on which stood the manor's predecessor (NSFCT 1945 p95), which was burnt down during the Civil War (JC 39). So called from the River Lea rising nearby.

Lea Heath Tiny hamlet on a small tributary of Bourn Brook 0.75m NW of Newton. Written just Lea on Plot's map. In Stowe parish.

Lea House In Walsall Wood Road, Aldridge. Appears to be a C18 house. It was the residence of some members of the Proffitt family, farmers and maltsters, in the C19. In 1940 the International Furnace Equipment Co was using the house. It was a private residence by 1996 (SNAR p52).

Lea Knowl House 1.5m N of High Offley. Has plaque on front which reads 'I.V.F. 1704. PETER HAND FREE MASON.'

Lea Laughton Fragmented small hamlet on high ground overlooking Horton Brook, 0.5m W of Horton, in Horton ancient parish. Has appeared as Lee (earlier C19), and Lea Lathton (1841) (VCH vol 7 p65).

Leamonsley Large village on a low ridge between Leamonsley and Trunkfield Brooks 0.5m WSW of Lichfield cathedral. Formerly in the county of Lichfield and in the parochial township of St Michael's, Lichfield (W p516). Has also appeared as Lemansley. The name is from probably an Anglo-Celtic compound, with the Celtic 'lemo,' elm, as part of its first element (Medieval Settlement. PH Sawyer. map on p202) (English Place-Name Elements. vol 2. p23) (VCH vol 14 p37). The church, Christ Church, on the N side of Christchurch Lane, was consecrated in 1847 (VCH vol 14 p151). Leamonsley evidently grew up after the opening of a fulling mill on Leamonsley Brook in the early 1790s (VCH vol 14 p28).

Leamonsley Brook Joins the Stowe at Minster Pool, Lichfield. Has also appeared as Pipe Brook (VCH vol 14 p195).

Leamonsley Common Common pasture on Lichfield's western boundary. It stretched S and E from Leamonsley mill pool to Walsall road. An Act authorizing its enclosure was passed in 1815 (VCH vol 14 p111).

Leamore Former hamlet on ground rising above the Wyrley and Essington Canal, now a district of Walsall, 0.75m SSE of Bloxwich. In the foreign of Walsall. Later in Blakenall Heath ecclesiastical parish. 'Leymore' was mentioned in deeds to property in 1420 (BY p27). The name means 'moorland used for pasture' (BY p27) (SNBP p37). There was settlement around Leamore Lane, Broadstone (now Bloxwich Road), and the northern end of Green Lane by 1775. Mining was in progress at Leamore in the 1850s and 1860s (VCH vol 17 p164). Became a ward of Walsall county borough in 1889 (VCH vol 17 p217). Council estates were built in the area in the 1920s and after WW2 (BY p27). The church, St Aidan, Hawbush Road, Forest estate, was built in 1964 (LDD). A house in Kelvin Road to the W of Leamore is allegedly haunted by the ghost of an old man who places his hands around the necks of those whom he dislikes (GOM p23).

Lea Park Situated NW of Wrottesley Hall. It was a park of the Wrottesley family by 1382. It had become effectively disparked by or in the C17 (VCH vol 20 p33). Has also appeared as Le Lee (HOPTT p195).

Leasows, The House 1.5m WSW of Stretton (Penkridge). In Stretton ancient parish. Appears as Stretton Leasows on 1834 OS map.

Leather Hall House in Birmingham Road, Walsall. It was occupied by Samuel Wilkinson, Town Clerk, in 1878. It was so named because it was once owned by a currier (SNWA p66).

Leaton Former manor 0.5m SSE of Bobbington. The Leaton area was inhabited by the later C13 (VCH vol 20 p65). The Dickens family (of which the novelist Charles Dickens is a descendant) held the manor of Leaton in the late Middle Ages (TB June 1994 p17).

Leaton Hall House 0.5m SE of Bobbington. The present hall, succeeding an older hall probably occupied by the lords of Leaton the Dickins family, is of C18 origin but was re-fronted with stucco and enlarged to the rear in the early C19 (VCH vol 20 p70), perhaps in 1817 when Pevsner says the hall was built (BOE p76). The hall was occupied by the Moseley family in the C19 (mems in Bobbington church). It was used by the Air Ministry in the later years of WW2 (VCH vol 20 p70).

Leawoods, The Small hamlet on a ridge overlooking a tributary of Lonco Brook 1.25m SW of High Offley. In High Offley parish. Pitt in c1817 says Leewoods is a manor belonging to Lord Anson in Norbury parish (THS p272). Formerly Leawood Pits (W p391) (1834 OS map) and Leawood Pits appears on graves in Norbury and High Offley churchyards.

'Le cunstablecross' Medieval cross which stood in the early C14 beside the Leek-Congleton road at the W end of Rushton James township, presumably where it was crossed by a road which runs along Long Edge. The cross had gone by 1611 (VCH vol 7 p220).

Lee, La House and manor at Lea Heath, S of Drointon. In 1293 it was the seat of the Lee family (SHC 1909 p189 note).

Lee Brook Runs from Waterfall to Cauldon.

Lee Farm House 0.75m NW of Rushton Spencer church. Formerly in Rushton Spencer township in Leek ancient parish. The present house is of the early C18 (VCH vol 7 p224).

Lee Forge and House. 0.25m N of Biddulph church. Excavation of the large conical earthwork at Lee Forge showed it had been used as a castle mound in the C11 or C12. It was strengthened in the late C12. The dwelling on it was rebuilt in the C13 and probably remained in use until Biddulph Hall was built in the late C16. Iron slag found here suggests there was a forge here in the later medieval period (CAMS p15) (BHS No.1. June 1968 pp6-9). Has also appeared as Lea Forge.

Lee House Mid Georgian house at Waterhouses (BOE p298).

Leek (locally *Leyk* BOJ book 2 p53). Ancient parish in the former Leek and Lowe township. The large market town of Leek on a spur in a valley (NSFCT 1882 p26) (VCH vol 7 p84) is 21.25m NNE of Stafford.

EARLY. Arrow-heads made of Elf-shot have been found at Leek (OL vol 2 pp115,116il). An axe-hammer (which went to the Potteries Museum), and a now-lost arrowhead mentioned by Plot and found by Thomas Gent (NHS p396 tab 33 fig 2), were found in Leek parish (OL vol 2 pp115-116) (NSJFS 1964 p27). Some burial mounds by the former railway line in the Birchall or Compton area were known locally as 'Sheba's Breasts'; the railway line actually cut through one mound (HLS p13) (DPMM p107). For other burial mounds near Leek see Birchall and Cock Low. The line of the **Roman** road from Buxton through Leek, Cheddleton, Blythe Bridge, Hilderstone, and Stafford to Pennocrucium (see) on Watling Street has yet to be established; it did not follow the present Leek-Buxton road, which has its origins as a turnpike road (VCH vol 7 p98). There was perhaps an early Roman castellum or station on the Limes Britannicus (see) of the Notitia in the Leek area. Concangios (or Concangii) of the Notitia has been identified with Leek (VCH vol 1 p186), or the traces of an entrenched camp in fields to the E of Dieulacres Abbey, not far from Leek (NSFCT 1902 pp115-116). However, Concangios has been identified with another place in the north of England (VCH vol 1 p186). In 1776 a Roman coin hoard was found in a hole in the ground 2m S of Leek. Three coins were said to be of Victorinus (269-71) (GM vol 46 pp540,591) (OL vol 1 p326) (VCH vol 7 p85). The hoard has been lost (NSJFS 1964 p27).

600 to 1086. The **name** represents brook or stream from Old Norse 'loekr' (VCH vol 7 p84) (SPN p75) (SHC 1999 p7), or from Norse 'loecko' (NSFCT 1915 p186). (NSJFS 1981 p2) (SSE 1996 p15). Oakden thought it was a stream-name of Scandinavian origin or an unrecorded Old English form which had transferred from an old origin of the stream or river that flows through or by Leek (SSAHST 1967 p34). The brook was perhaps the stream called the Spout Water (see), or its tributary which ran from a spring in St Edward's churchyard down the W side of St Edward Street (formerly Spout Street) (VCH vol 7 p84), or the brook could refer to the healing waters of Lady o' the Dale Well, S of Leek (SMM p63). It was formerly thought by some to be probably of Celtic origin and mean a flag (flat) stone, from either Welsh 'llech' or Irish and Gaelic 'leac' (DUIGNAN) (SPN p75), or Old Irish 'liac' 'liag,' a stone or rocky slope (NSFCT 1908 p135). **Churches**. The parish church, **St Edward the Confessor**, lies on the N side of Church Street. By its

chancel door is a tall cylindrical Saxon preaching cross, erected according to tradition by Bishop Wilfred of Ripon in the C7 (Leek Parish Church of St Edward the Confessor: History and Guide. WF Brooks. post 1972). There is a tradition that the cross sinks lower into the ground every year and there is a local rhyme, which runs

> When the Churchyard Cross shall disappear,
> Leek town will not last another year.

(GM 1780) (SCSF p86) (SMM p28). There are other parts of Saxon preaching crosses in the churchyard. An early Saxon church of wood which stood probably on the church site, was replaced by a late Saxon and late Norman building. That church burnt down in the great fire at Leek in 1297. Its replacement was completed in 1320; the present church is of this date with later additions (Leek Parish Church of St Edward the Confessor: History and Guide. WF Brooks. post 1972) (BOE p168). The church was dedicated to just St Edward in the C16. By the C18 it was believed that the patron saint was Edward the Confessor, but it may have been originally dedicated to Edward the Martyr (d978/9) (SHC 1999 p9). The church, **St Luke**, Fountain Street, was built in 1848 and the chancel lengthened in 1873 (BOE p170) (LDD). The **parish**, formed before 1086, formerly contained the chapelries of Cheddleton, Horton, and Ipstones and the 12 townships of Bradnop, Endon, Heaton, Leek and Lowe, Leekfrith, Longsdon, Onecote, Rudyard, Rushton James, Rushton Spencer, Stanley, and Tittesworth. It was the largest parish in Staffs (SHC 1916 p194) (GLAUE p415) (VCH vol 7 p78). Leek parish feast may have been held on the nearest Sunday to Oct 18 by at least the early C18. It was held on this day by the mid C19, possibly in association with the feast of the Translation of Edward the Confessor (Oct 13), then regarded as the patron saint of the parish church (VCH vol 7 p146). In the mid C19 races occasionally followed on the succeeding Monday and Tuesday in Birchall Dale (W p722).

1086 to 1642. The **manor** of Lec appears in DB. Later forms include: Lech, Leke (SPN p75). At the time of DB the manor included probably Leek town, Tittesworth, the area of the later townships of Bradnop and Onecote, and most of Leekfrith. Bradnop and Onecote became separated from the manor in the C12 (VCH vol 7 pp79-80). Hugh 'd' Avranches,' ancestor of the Earls of Chester, whose pedigree appears under Chartley Castle (see), acquired Leek manor sometime between 1087 and 1093. Leek then became strategically important as one of a chain of manors which linked Chester with the Earl's estates in the east Midlands; Earls Way (see), which connected the Earl's estates, passed through Leek (SSE 1993 p3). Hugh 'of Kevelioc,' Earl of Chester, had a house in Leek, and issued charters from here in the earlier 1170s. He died at Leek in 1180 (PRT p55), or 1181 (The Complete Peerage) (SSE 1993 p3). A charter was issued from Leek by Hugh's son Ranulph 'de Blundeville' Earl of Chester in c1210. Sometime between 1207 and 1215 the same Earl licensed Leek as a borough (SL p80) (MR p206) (SSE 1993 p1) (VCH vol 7 p125). In 1232 he granted Leek manor to his newly-founded Dieulacres Abbey (SSE 1993 p1). (NSJFS 1970 p85). Leek manor remained in the abbey's possession until the Dissolution and the town is a rare example of a Cistercian monastic borough (SL p149). From the end of the C13 Leek manor comprised the townships of Leekfrith, Lowe (later Leek and Lowe), Tittesworth, Heaton, and Rushton Spencer, but lost much of its control over the last two from the C18 (VCH vol 7 pp80,124). The ancient manor house was in Church Street near the house where Thomas Parker, 1st Earl of Macclesfield and Lord High Chancellor, was born (NSFCT 1918 p128). **Conflict between abbey and town**. In 1380 a group was indicted for having beheaded John de Warton of Leek by the command of Abbot William of Dieulacres Abbey for which the abbot was imprisoned, but he was soon pardoned and released. The event of the beheading may have inspired part of the 'Sir Gawain and the Green Knight' poem (VCH vol 3 pp232,233 note). There was a serious riot in Leek in 1516 caused by the abbot of Dieulacres and eight men and was aimed at preventing the arrest of Thomas Hyde, a servant of the steward of Leek, who was accused of complicity in a murder (VCH vol 3 p233). The borough returned to Leek manor after the Dissolution. Leek manor was known as the manors of Leek and Frith from the mid C16 (VCH vol 7 pp80,124). The chronicle of Croxden Abbey records that the whole town and church burnt down in 1297 (LGS p162) (VCH vol 7 p85). **Edward II** visited Leek in 1318 whilst hunting in the Swythamley area (NSFCT 1882 pp26,65) (OL vol 1 p324).

MARKETS. The Earl of Chester was granted a charter on Nov 23 1207 to hold a **market** here on Wednesdays (NSJFS 1971 p50). Miller says 1208 (OL vol 2 p71). The Wednesday market has continued to the present (1991) (OWEN) (THS) (SCSF p95) (LHE p265). There have also been markets on

Fridays and Saturdays since 1850 (VCH vol 7 p105). The cattle market at the corner of Haywood Street and Ashbourne Road between 1874 and 1960 was replaced by the present shopping precinct, Smithfield Centre, officially opened on Oct 31 1962. A **market cross** existed in the C14 (SCSF p91). There is a 20 feet high (KES p127) millstone grit shaft 'Butter Cross' or market cross with a Maltese cross head, probably of early C15 origin (BOE p171), in Market Place (Leek Times Sept 23 1871). Until 1658 it was the custom to publish the banns of marriage at the market cross (OL vol 1 pp118,173,176,325). It has the inscription 'Given by J Jolliffe Esq 1671,' and perhaps replaced an earlier stone. It originally stood at the junction of Sheep Market and Stanley Street at the bottom of the Market Place (PDS&C p25p) until 1806 when a small town hall, which was itself replaced in 1878 (OL vol 1 pp1-6) (SOSH p345), was erected on its site. The market cross was then re-erected at Cornhill, on a site which became the town cemetery in 1857 (VCH vol 7 p106). There it was being ignominiously utilized as a lamp post in the early C20 (LGS p162). It was returned to the Market Place in 1986 (PDS&C p25) (NSFCT 1990 p39). A prediction concerning this cross was once current and is contained in this rhyme

> When this old crosse shall be removed from toune,
> A lying tongue shall rise, and truth be knocked downe.

(SCSF p91). (PS p148) (SOSH p344p of in the cemetery). There is another fluted shaft of a former cross, in Cheadle Road near Leekbrook, set back (DoE) (BOE p171 note). There have been **fairs** at Leek on these days at various times: A fair on the first Wednesday in **Jan** was introduced in 1814, but shortly became the last Wednesday in Dec (VCH vol 7 p106). Wednesday before Candlemas (**Feb 2**) (COOKE) (VCH vol 7 p105), which became Wednesday before Feb 13 after 1752 (Whitaker's Almanac) (SCSF pp98,99). By the mid C18 there was a fair on **Easter Wednesday** (Whitaker's Almanac) (COOKE) (SCSF pp98,99) (VCH vol 7 p105). That for **April 3** was granted in c1700 (OL vol 2 p21). The fair granted to Thomas Jodrell in 1629 for **May 7-9**, was held on May 18 after 1752 (Whitaker's Almanac) (COOKE) (SCSF pp98,99) (OL vol 1 p35) (SOSH p343). At sometime it was granted with a court of pie powder or dusty foot court (FOS pp98-99) and was still continuing in the early 1990s (VCH vol 7 p106). By the mid C18 there was a fair on the Wednesday after **Whitsun** (VCH vol 7 p105). This may be identified with the fair on Whit Wednesday (COOKE) (SCSF p99). In 1207 King John confirmed to Ranulph, Earl of Chester, a seven-day fair three days before the feast of St Edward, perhaps the Second Translation of Edward the Martyr (**June 20**). By 1538 this fair was held on July 18 (VCH vol 7 p105). By the mid C18 there was a fair on **June 22**, moved to the July 3 after 1752 (Whitaker's Almanac) (COOKE) (SCSF pp98,99) (VCH vol 7 p105). **July 17** was a fair day by c1680 and in the mid C18, and moved to July 28 after 1752 (Whitaker's Almanac) (COOKE) (SCSF pp98,99) (VCH vol 7 p105). The fair held around the feast of St Edward was held on, and for seven days after, the feast of St Arnulf (**July 18**) by 1538 (VCH vol 7 p105). In 1207 King John confirmed to Ranulph, Earl of Chester, a seven-day fair three days before the feast of St Edward, perhaps Edward the Confessor (**Oct 10**). By 1538 this fair was held on July 18 (VCH vol 7 p105). By the late 1790s Wednesday after Oct 10 was also a fair day (Whitaker's Almanac) (COOKE) (SCSF pp98,99) (VCH vol 7 p106). This fair has been identified as a remnant of the fair confirmed in 1207 (OL vol 2 p71). In 1622 there was a fair on All Souls' Day (**Nov 2**), which moved to Nov 13 after 1752 (Whitaker's Almanac) (COOKE) (SCSF pp98,99). It later became a pleasure fair and continued until 1960 (VCH vol 7 pp105,106). The fair on the first Wednesday in Jan introduced in 1814 shortly became the last Wednesday in **Dec** (VCH vol 7 p106). The Wednesday before **Christmas** is also said to have been a fair day (Whitaker's Almanac) (SCSF p98). A tradition which occurred during the erection of stalls before fair day was called 'Chalky-back Day' when hoards of children would descend on the fair site and chase madly round, chalking on each other's backs (HLSP p95).

PUNISHMENTS. In 1293 the abbot of Dieulacres as lord of the manor claimed infangetheof and right of **gallows**. Gallows stood probably in Mill Street by the mid C16 (VCH vol 7 p130). A **lock-up** in the market place was pulled down in 1806 and replaced by a town hall containing two cells (VCH vol 7 p130). The old wooden **stocks** were at Overton Bank and were in time replaced by steel stocks fixed opposite the Red Lion Hotel (OL vol 2 p221). Bright records John Harrison of Ipstones Edge and Thomas Shemilt being put in them for fighting with the village (Ipstones?) constables. After they were liberated they went to the Red Lion at Bradnop and renewed the battle (TOI p170). Leek's **brank** was last used in 1824 (OL vol 1 p177. vol 2 pp223-224) (TFTPM pp83-86) (VCH vol 7 p130). Leek's **ducking stool** is said to

have stood by the Churnet off Abbey Green Road near Broad's Bridge in the 1560s (VCH vol 7 p130). A chair claimed to have been a ducking stool is displayed in St Edward's church (SLM Feb 1948 p84) (PDS&C p47p) (DP p68).

CIVIL WAR AND COMMONWEALTH PERIOD. Leek was a parliamentary garrison for some of the Civil War from 1642 (OL vol 1 p191). It was never attacked or besieged by royalists, although royalists threatened to take it. Some Moorland Dragoons returned to Leek after failing to take Stafford in Feb 1643 and shortly received training from qualified parliamentary soldiers sent by Sir John Gell (BFS p13). In 1643 there is believed to have been a skirmish in the vicinity of Leek. Capt Mollanus for parliament was sent to release some Moorland Dragoons captured by Lord Newcastle at Hartington and were sent back to Leek (OL vol 1 p191). Col Rugeley with a parliamentary force fled to Leek from Uttoxeter on hearing of Prince Rupert's advance after Rupert's retaking of Lichfield garrison in April 1643 (BFS pp20-21). By May 1643 there was a parliamentary garrison at Leek (VCH vol 7 p89). It was commanded by Lieut Col Peter Stepkin from perhaps mid April 1643. Stepkin had been a royalist at the Stafford garrison but had changed sides. Rumours of a royalist assault on Leek spurred Stepkin to encourage the parliamentary leader Brereton to counterattack and take Stafford (BFS p21) (LOU p27). In Nov or Dec 1643 royalist forces under Lord Eythin entered Leek. By March 1644, however, a parliamentary committee had been set up in Leek (HOS 1998 p74) (VCH vol 7 p89). One labouring man spoke out against the Protector before a crowd in Leek Feb 11 1657 and was charged (LOU p346). Two cannon balls were found in old Basford Lane in 1820 (OL vol 1 p328). 1660 to 1800. **Appointment of a churchwarden**. By the early C17 each quarter of Leek ancient parish had a churchwarden. By 1725 the churchwardens were appointed by the vicar from lists of three names submitted in writing at Easter by the inhabitants of each quarter. After the creation of new parishes in the early C19 Leek alone retained its single warden and the peculiar method of his appointment (VCH vol 7 pp82-83). In 1970 it was believed that in the whole of the provinces of Canterbury and York there are only two other churches with a single warden (STM Sept 1970 p31). By c1972 it was believed there was no other church with a single warden (Leek Parish Church Guide. c1972). The office of warden of Leek survived the appointment of district wardens following the creation of a team ministry in Leek in 1979 (VCH vol 7 p83). Nominations for the appointment are made at the annual vestry meeting in Holy week and the nominee can be of any religion. If there are more than three nominees, a town election has to take place. According to Leek Parish Church Guide one of these town elections took place some years prior to c1972. The vicar makes his appointment by announcement from the pulpit on Easter Sunday (STM Sept 1970 p31). The earliest known warden is Ralph Mountford who held the office in 1675 (Leek Parish Church Guide. c1972). The **Quakers** acquired a meeting house at Overton Bank in 1693 or 1694. The registers list 240 burials here; the largest Quaker burial-ground in the county. Margaret Lucas is the most noted person buried there (SSAHST 1970 p42) (W p724; Overton's Bank). The **Presbyterian meeting house** in Derby Street was burnt down at Leek Fair on July 28 1715 when a mob of over 100 rioted (OL vol 1 pp214-215) (NSFCT 1917 p69) (VCH vol 7 p142). Subsequently, some of the rioters crossed the county boundary to attend Congleton races and broke into a meeting house there (LOU p96). Leek was electing a **mock mayor** by 1758. The first-known mock mayor held a feast at the Cock Inn in Jan 1759. This may have become the annual Venison Feast held by Leek mock mayors, recorded from 1837 to at least 1889 (VCH vol 7 p146). The **Leek Troop** of the Staffordshire Volunteer Cavalry (later Staffordshire Yeomanry), raised by Capt J Bulkeley in 1794, broke up in 1829 and re-enrolled under the name Leek and Moorland Troop in 1842. This broke up in 1888 (OL vol 2 pp89-95) (FSP p60) (VCH vol 7 p151). The Lincoln Militia passed through Leek on their way to serve in Ireland in Sept 1798 (OL vol 1 p91). **Prophecy**. Lilly made a prophecy in 1680 that the treasure of Anslem Archbishop of Canterbury in King Stephen's reign would be discovered at Leek in 1681 (OL vol 1 pp71-73). **Disasters**. There was an extraordinary flood in Leek Aug 12 1717 and a son of Richard Robton drowned at Abbey Green (OL vol 1 p185). A tub of gunpowder accidentally exploded at a mercer's house on Dec 25 1731 killing the daughter and a maid and blowing the roof off (OL vol 2 p290). **Natural phenomenon: Double Sunset**. From a site in St Edward's churchyard the sun can be seen setting twice, 5.75m away, behind the hill, the Cloud or called Bosley Cloud, at midsummer solstice. This phenomenon is due to the extremely steep western escarpment of the Cloud, around which the sun can re-emerge, after falling behind the hill, to set two minutes later for a second time. The phenomenon, noted by Dr Plot in the later C17, can only be seen in the churchyard from Doctor's Corner (see), and only between June 20 and 22. However, NSFC excursionists positioned in the churchyard on June 21 1877 were disappointed, and in 1884 it was noted that the view from the churchyard was becoming obscured by fir trees on the ridge beyond Packsaddle Hollow. By the mid C20 trees in the churchyard were beginning to obstruct the view from Doctor's Corner; the last sighting from there may have been in 1958, although some say they saw the double sunset in c1962/3. It is a present misconception that the double sunset can still be seen from a raised position 50 yards to the W of Doctor's Corner. This position is too far to the W for the sun to reappear from behind the Cloud. The phenomenon can be seen at certain other places near Leek on three successive days sometime in a fortnight either side of June 21. Dr Plot wondered if someone in the future would measure the distance the sun moves in its daily progress, advancing and receding, around the Cloud to calculate the exact points where the double sunset can be viewed. Several double sunset 'enthusiasts' from the Leek area have, from the 1960s, measured the distance the sun moves in its daily progress, advancing and receding, around the Cloud. The enthusiasts' research has yet to be published. Pickford adds that the position in the churchyard is the traditional and most romantic place to witness the double sunset. Other positions are the Roaches, Leek Moor and Lowe Hill bridge (NHS pp2,3 tab 1 fig 1) (GM May July 1738) (NSFCT 1878 p34) (OL vol 1 pp52, ils,56,57) (PS p148) (Leek Times, week ending July 18 1884) (SC p172) (MC pp28,29) (KES p125) (TTTD p121) (VB p192) (COS p11) (MR p207) (DP p62-63) (GLS p63) (DPEM p138) (ES June 9 1997 p11) (local info). **Persons and visitors. Charles Cotton** and **Izaak Walton** claimed Leek ale to be the best in the country and the French 'Historical Dictionary' by Moreri (1716) commends Leek's excellent beer which the English call 'ale' (IANS p109) (OL vol 1 p319). **Thomas Parker**, 1st Earl of Macclesfield, a relation of the Parkers of Park Hall (see), near Caverswall, was born on July 23 1666/7 in a house in NW corner of the Market Place (OL vol 1 p165), now (1991) known as 2-4 Church Street (VCH vol 7 pp89,91). For Rev **Thomas Loxdale** (d1742) the antiquary and vicar of Leek 1725-1735 see Meretown. For **James Brindley**, the engineer, in Leek see Lowe Hammill, Lowe Hill, and Brindley's Mill. Anna Seward of Lichfield (see) told James Boswell that the father of Dr Johnson of Lichfield (see), **Michael Johnson**, had served his apprenticeship in Leek to one Joseph Needham, a Leek bookseller (SOSH p345) (OL vol 1 p188) (VCH vol 7 p117 note), and that whilst at Leek he courted Elizabeth Blaney (b1694), who reputedly has a memorial in Lichfield cathedral (SHOS vol 1 p251) (HOL p76). For his 'Life of Johnson' Boswell is said to have embellished Seward's information saying the cause of Blaney's death may have been over-love for Michael (Dr Johnson and his Birthplace. A Retrospective and Guide. Johnson Birthplace Committee. 1933 p26). Others say Michael Johnson served his apprenticeship to a London stationer, not at Leek (Johnsonian Gleanings vol 3 pp6-7) (VCH vol 7 p117). **Dr Johnson** visited Leek in 1777 and said of the town that despite it having 'an old church...' it was '....but a poor town' (SOSH p345) (Letters of Samuel Johnson. RW Chapman vol 2 p226) (VCH vol 7 p89). The NSFC library edition of OL p184 notes it was James Boswell and not Dr Johnson who visited Leek in 1777. **John Wesley** visited Leek in 1772 and preached at Leek in 1782 in the club-room of the Blackmoor's Head Inn. He visited again in 1783 and for the last time on April 5 1788 (OL vol 1 pp169,327) (LR p11) (E p57) (VCH vol 7 p144). For the fanatical preacher, **James Nixon** of Goldenhill (see), who wore out the knees of his trousers praying in Leek market place, see Goldenhill. Miss **Harriot Mellon** (subsequently Mrs Coutts and Duchess of St Albans) appeared at the Swan Theatre behind the Swan Hotel before 1792 aged 18 (OL vol 1 p14. vol 2 pp111-112) (VCH vol 7 p149). Another account says Miss Mellon was born in 1777 (HOU). **Richard Badnall** (d1839), author of 'Zelinda: a Persian Tale, in Three Cantos,' was born in Leek in 1797 (PSS pp146-148) (VFC p6).

GRAMMAR SCHOOL. Founded in 1720, with a school building built in 1723 by Thomas Parker, 1st Earl of Macclesfield, a relation of the Parkers of Park Hall (see), Caverswall, on the corner of Clerk Bank and Overton Bank. The school was not, as long thought, endowed by Parker. It closed in 1900 (OL vol 1 pp132-137 il. vol 2 pp65-70 il) (BOE pp28,171) (VCH vol 7 pp89,155-156).

THE 1745 JACOBITE REBELLION. Prince Charles Edward Stuart and his Scottish army with the Dukes of Athol and Perth etc passed through Leek on their way to London to overthrow the Hanoverian monarchy. Lord George Murray, leading a vanguard passed through on Tuesday Dec 3 1745, with the prince and the main force passing through later in the day (W p48) (OL vol 1 p197) (BPCSM p10) (VCH vol 7 p91) (ES Nov 28 1995 p8), or some say the prince passed through on Monday Dec 2 1745. Once in the town the prince proclaimed his father 'King James III of England' from Leek market cross and asked for shelter at St Edward's vicarage. Mary Daintry, the vicar's wife, answered the door. When she saw who it was she is said to have slammed the

door in the prince's face, and collapsed. She died on Dec 15 1745, aged 41, some say out of shock (BPCSM p6). It is thought the prince rested at No. 2 Church Street; a room there was known as the Prince's Room (BPCSM p6). Some say he slept the night at the house of William Mills, a lawyer, which by the 1990s was called Foxlowe (VCH vol 7 p91) (ES Nov 28 1995 p8). Lord George Murray is reputed to have spent the night at Mr Fern's (NSFCT 1925 p58). Some officers were taken to Haregate Hall (BPCSM p6). The army is said to have used the Saxon cross in the churchyard for target practice (JC 10 il). The army left Leek for Derby at 2.00am on the 4th. It passed through the town in retreat on Saturday Dec 7 1745. The prince, now said to be a broken man, is said to have slept again at the house of William Mills (BPCSM p8). The army, now far from orderly, broke into the Friends' meeting house. They forced people to billet and feed them, and stole food, necessities, arms and horses. The next day the Prince's pillow was found to be saturated with tears (BPCSM p8). The rear guard of the army left on the morning of Dec 8 1745. When it had gone a straggler was caught tied to a horse's tail and dragged round the Market Place until he died. He was buried in the pig market. The Duke of Cumberland passed through Leek on Dec 10 1745 in pursuit of the prince (BPCSM pp8,13) (VCH vol 7 p91). There are many relics in the Leek area left by the Prince's army (OL vol 2 pp138-139). Joshua Toft of Haregate had a piece of the original plaid worn by Charles. It came via Miss Ferriar who had it off an old royalist lady of Manchester (NSFCT 1882 p26). A small barrel full of silver coin to pay the Highlanders discovered in Stringer's, the draper's shop, went to the Joliffes of Leek Old Hall (BPCSM p8). A flintlock gun and a piece of tartan said to have been torn from the plaid of Prince Charles were still in the town in 1938 and were shown to members of the NSFC (NSFCT 1938 p120). In the C19 old women held memories that they were among those pretty young girls who caught the prince's eye and shook his hand (LGS p162).

INDUSTRY. Industries principally associated with Leek have included the making of buttons (carried on in Leek by 1485 - OL vol 1 p324), ribbons, handkerchiefs, and shawls (SOSH p346) (IANS p45), mohair working (SCSF p112), clock and watch making (OL vol 2 pp33-43) (VCH vol 7 p116), and in the later C19 the making of cardboard boxes and bobbins for the silk and cloth industry (VCH vol 7 p115). Leek's industry in the C18 and early C19 was **silk-weaving**, which had reached the town by the 1670s (VCH vol 7 p89) or in 1685 (OL vol 1 p325). The tradition that silk working was brought to Leek by Huguenot refugees after 1685 is based on a misreading of the Leek churchwardens' accounts (SOSH p346) (VCH vol 7 p106). In c1800 Thomas Ball introduced a twister's wheel to the silk weaving industry at Leek and carried on in business in a shed or 'shade' behind the parish church. He laid the foundations of the trade in silk sewings and twist which in time brought world-wide renown to Leek. In 1809 he took up **silk-dyeing** in partnership with James Badnall (HOLS 2nd ed pp5-6) (VCH vol 2 pp207,208. vol 7 p109) (VL part 1 p31); Leek became notable for silk-dyeing and still was by at least the late 1960s (VCH vol 2 p208). Huguenots also reputedly introduced dyeing to Leek at the end of C17 (SOSH p346). To praise Leek's silk industry an old rhymer composed this couplet

> For silken fabrics, rich and rare,
> What city can with Leek compare!

(NSFCT 1908 p192). In 1834 the handloom weavers of Leek went on strike for improved rates of pay (VCH vol 7 p92). Murals depicting scenes from the early days of Leek's textile industry were discovered beneath the painted walls of the Quaker meeting house at Overton Bank in 1995. It was planned to restore the murals, believed to have been painted in the 1930s by Walter Crane, a follower of William Morris (ES Feb 9 1995 p12p). In the C20 Leek became an important centre for knitwear (HOS 1998 p105). The remaining silk works in Leek closed in 1994 (HOS 1998 p108). At about this time Leek took to antique selling, specialising in goods 'at the lower end of the market,' and making and reconstituting pine furniture, with many of the former mills providing warehouse space (Heart of the Country. Central TV. Aug 31 1999).

FRENCH PRISONERS IN LEEK. A total of 346 high-ranking French prisoners were garrisoned on parole at Leek between 1803 and 1814 during the Napoleonic wars; the last group arrived in 1812. They included a general captured at San Domingo in the West Indies. As parole prisoners, they were given the freedom of Leek but were allowed to go only a mile from the market place. There was a weekly roll call in the market place. During the course of the war many were exchanged for British prisoners, and 44 escaped. At the end of the war many returned home, but others forged permanent links with Leek by marrying local girls and settling in the area; some say the area they were concentrated in, was known as Petty France (see) (ES Oct 1 1993 p8)

(VCH vol 7 p92). The oldest survivor was Pierre Magnier, a shopkeeper, who died in 1874 (French Connections. Joan Bennett and others. 1995) (ES Oct 24 1995 p8). On March 26 1996 a sandstone memorial to the French prisoners was unveiled in St Edward's churchyard by Baron Gougaud, president of the Foundation Le Souvenir Napoleonien (ES March 27 1996 p4p).

1800 to 1850. The **Blanketeers**, 400 workers from Manchester who wore blankets and not coats, came through the town on March 11 1817 (OL vol 2 p92) and or in Feb 1819 (OL vol 1 p178) marching to London to protest to the Government. They were not allowed to stay in Leek and continued towards Ashbourne. The Leek Troop of Staffordshire Yeomanry caught up with them at Hanging Bridge on the Derbys border where they were dispersed. About 30 were successful in returning to Leek from where they were escorted by special constables to Macclesfield (VCH vol 7 p92). (LOU p381). There was **Chartist unrest** in the town from Aug 13 to Aug 16 1842. A demonstration comprising between 2000 and 4000 men, mainly from Congleton and Macclesfield, took place on the morning of the 15th. On the 16th the remaining men left to protest in Burslem, where in the riots there Josiah Heapy, a 19-year-old Leek shoemaker, was killed (VCH vol 7 p93). **Town improvements.** By an Act of 1825 a body of 34 improvement commissioners was established to light, watch, cleanse and improve Leek town (defined as a circular area with a radius of 1200 yards from the hall in the market place). In 1855 a new body of 24 commissioners with extended powers was set up and the boundary was extended to 1500 yards. Some boundary stones, inscribed 'LIA 1855 LB' (Leek Improvement Act, 1855, Leek Boundary) still remain at this distance. Leek was one of the few towns in the county (if not the only one) which had a circular boundary (IANS p156) (VCH vol 7 p125). The Churnet Valley **railway** opened through the area W of the town in 1849 with a station on the Newcastle road (VCH vol 7 p91). The NSR's Leek to Stoke railway line opened in 1867 (OL vol 1 p331). The railway to Waterhouses closed to passengers in 1935; in 1960 to the Potteries; on Nov 7 1960 to North Rode and Manchester, although railway employees seem to have used this line until June 15 1964 (NSJFS 1964 p79) (CVH p129). **Leek Sunday School Festival.** Annual procession by Leek Sunday school children, with hymns sung in the market place. The procession, originally for children of the Wesleyan Methodist Sunday school and later for children of all dominations, is first recorded in 1828. In that year it took place on the last Sunday in Aug, but was later moved to a Friday in Aug and then to a Saturday in July. It was known as Cap Sunday by the mid C19, from the caps worn originally by the girls, and as Leek Sunday School Festival by 1910 (VCH vol 7 pp146-147) and it has been called Leek Club Day. In the early 1960s it was held on the third Saturday in July (TTTD p132). The festival was still taking place in the early 1990s (VCH vol 7 pp146-147). In the early 1960s the third Sunday in Nov was known as Club Sunday, for on this day all the men's clubs of the town walked in a parade to church (TTTD p132). In 1836 one thousand Leek **teetotallers** dined together (OL vol 1 p329). **Bad weather and illness.** The town experienced a great snowstorm on May 18 1837, a terrific thunderstorm on Aug 28 1838 and a hurricane on Jan 6 1839 (OL vol 1 pp186,187). The town was hit by a diphtheria epidemic in 1857 (OL vol 1 p58). **Wombwell's Circus** visited Leek in 1822 and in 1839. It included Leek in it's last tour in c1930 (VCH vol 7 p149). **Persons and visitors. Abraham K Killminster** (or Killmister or Kilmister - BS p262), poet and playwright, was born in Leek and baptised on Feb 28 1807. As Tom Oakleigh, he is attributed with writing articles on sport and other topics including 'The Oakleigh Shooting Code' (1840); 'Beauties of Derbyshire: Dovedale' (1865); 'The Dalesman,' a five-act play; an article in the Encyclopaedia Britannica on shooting; and collaborated with James Wilson (1795-1856), younger brother of 'Christopher North' in 'The Rod and the Gun.' He also wrote prose and verse for The Mirror and other periodicals between 1830 and 1845, chiefly under the name of Cymbeline. He died at Moorland House, Leek, on Christmas day 1858, and was the subject of some correspondence in N&Q Aug 1924 and May 1925 (OL vol 1 p137. vol 2 pp128-130) (PSS pp154-155) (VFC p79). 'Little' **Jimmy Maddock**, a dwarf of Leek, who stood just two feet tall, caused a sensation in the C19 when, aged 45, he married a girl young enough to be his daughter. Two thousand people attended the wedding (STM April 1969 p31). For **Reuben Jackson** of Leek who set his bull dog on a preacher in 1824 see under Rocester. Sir **Walter Scott** stayed one night in Leek on April 5 1828 (OL vol 1 pp189-190). On Jan 28 1832 **Joseph Mellor**, aged 33, stole bread and cheese from the house of Samuel Kidney of Leek. He was sentenced to death at Staffs Assizes (OL vol 1 p329. vol 2 p235). **William Gould** was assaulted and robbed by three men - Daniel Tipper, aged 22, John Lovatt, aged 21, James Smith aged 23 - on the Leek-Macclesfield road on Dec 22 1832. Smith gave evidence for the Crown and Tipper and Lovatt were sentenced to death (OL vol 2 p236).

1850 to PRESENT. The **arms** of old Leek district showed two coiled serpents around the winged staff, a Caduceus. The Caduceus symbol was changed in the 1950s (SMM p63il). Scott-Giles, writing in 1953, has the arms of Leek urban district as: The seal bears the rod of mercury, symbol of commerce, among bales of goods, with the motto 'Arte favente nil desperandum' (Supported by skill, there is no cause to despair) (CH p340). In **WW2** a huge elm tree in St Edward's churchyard was hit by fire from a German plane and consequently died (Leek Parish Church Guide. c1972). 'The Spirit of Leek,' a Spitfire MK2 R7211 aircraft donated to the RAF by the people of Leek, came into operation on May 15 1941 and was withdrawn on Feb 11 1944 (MD pp75-77). **Britannia Building Society.** The Britannia, the UK's sixth largest building society in 1997 (RL p128), has its origins in the Leek and Moorlands Building Society, which was founded in 1856. By the 1870s that society was expanding nationally (SSE 1993 pp115,117,118). In 1956 it merged with the Westbourne Park Building Society to become the Leek and Westbourne. The name became Leek Westbourne & Eastern Counties after a merger with Eastern Counties Building Society. After more than sixty mergers the society merged with the Oldbury Britannia Building Society in 1974 and became the Britannia in 1975. The society's headquarters moved to Newton House, a new building on the E side of the Cheddleton road at Birchall, in 1970. A further building for the society, Britannia House, was built on the opposite side of the Cheddleton road in 1992 or 3 (ES May 26 1993 p10) (VCH vol 7 p121). **Leek United Building Society,** founded on Jan 1 1863, became Leek United and Midlands Building Society in June 1990 (Building Societies Yearbook 1998-99: Official Handbook of the Building Society Association). The **Leek Embroidery Society** (also known later as the Leek School of Embroidery) was founded by Lady Elizabeth Wardle, wife of Leek silk dyer Thomas Wardle, in 1879 or 1880. As well as designs the society produced finished articles using the naturally dyed silks or other materials from Thomas Wardle's factory, the most famous of which is the copy of the Bayeux Tapestry, recently (1990s) in Reading Museum, but originally exhibited in the Nicholson Institute (see). The society's output rapidly declined after Lady Wardle's death in 1902 (VCH vol 7 p152). Their copy of the Ajunta design was purchased by Leek Museum in 1933 (ES May 31 1933 p6p - article on Leek Embroidery Collection in general). **Some history and cultural societies.** The Leek and District Civic Society was formed in 1978. Leek and District Historical Society, formed in 1984, has published 'Chronicles' since 1988 (VCH vol 7 p152). The Leek and District Field Club was founded in 1956 (info Mrs Beniston). The **earthquake** of 3.21pm July 3 1904 was felt at Leek (NSFCT 1905 p133). **Persons and visitors.** In 1854 George Nadin sold his wife in Leek to an Irish labourer for a quart of ale (STM April 1969 p31). The **Duchess of Teck** is said to have visited Leek in the mid C19 (NSFCT 1882 p26). The Duke and Duchess of Teck visited Leek in 1872 (OL vol 1 p331). **William Morris** (1834-1896), craftsman and designer, was brought to Leek in 1875 by Sir Thomas Wardle (d1909) to experiment on dyes at Wardle's works at Hencroft on the Abbey Green Road, and was a frequent visitor to Leek in the later 1870s. An essay by him titled 'Art and Socialism' (1884) appears in Leek Bijou Freethought Reprints (VCH vol 7 pp96,145 note) (HLSP p49). He reputedly was instrumental in the campaign to save Greystones (see) in Stockwell Street. A Labour Church established at Leek in 1896 was named after him. As the William Morris Labour Church it had a succession of bases in the town, all furnished and decorated in the Arts and Crafts style, and was active politically until at least 1935 (VCH vol 7 p145). **The Nicholsons.** Nicholson Institute (see), Stockwell Street, was founded by Joshua Nicholson in 1884. His younger son, Sir Arthur Nicholson, gave the town the Nicholson War Memorial at the end of Derby Street in the former cattle market; his son Lt BL Nicholson died in action in 1915 in WW1. It is a clock tower and was built of Portland stone in 1924 and dedicated in 1925 (SMCC p2) (VCH vol 7 p97). The clock has been known locally as 'Sir Arthur's Wristwatch' (HLSP pp96-97). Prince George (later **George V**) came to Leek on July 28 1900 to open the Leek Technical Schools and to lay the foundation stone of the William Carr Gymnasium, opened in 1901, which stood next to the Nicholson Institute. He came again as king with Queen Mary on April 23 1913 (R&S p44) (VCH vol 7 p148) (ES Nov 16 1996 p21). **Harold Davies,** Labour MP for the Leek division between 1945 and 1970, was created Baron Davies of Leek, a life peer, in 1970 (VCH vol 7 p132). The world record for beer mat flipping was set by **Roy Clarke,** 36, of Fleetwood, when he flipped 72 on Feb 9 1979 at Leek (GBR 1980 p218).

NEWSPAPERS. Leek's first newspaper, **Leek Times**, was founded on July 30 1870 by Matthew Henry Miller and amalgamated with the Leek Post in 1934 (LR pp28-30) (SHJ spring 1996 p19). Seven issues of a collection of essays and lectures under the general title of **Leek Bijou Freethought Re-**

prints, were published by the Leek architect, Larner Sugden, between 1881 and 1884 (VCH vol 7 p145 note). In 1893 Miller launched the **Leek Comet** a Wednesday weekly paper designed to attract farmers and others attending Leek market. It seems to have discontinued in Feb 1894 (LR pp28-30) (SHJ spring 1996 p19). The **Leek Post, Cheadle Times and Moorland Advertiser** (often simply Leek Post), founded by Leek Conservatives in 1884 (VCH vol 7 p153), amalgamated with the Leek Times to become **Leek Post and Times, Cheadle News and Times and Moorland Advertiser** in 1934 and this is still running (SHJ spring 1996 p19). The **Leek and District Advertiser**, founded on Nov 24 1911, ran until at least Jan 3 1913 (SHJ spring 1996 p19). In 1924 Fred Hill became the publisher and editor of the Leek News an annual (Dec) publication which was still running in 1980 (LR pp28-30). The **Leek Recorder**, founded on Jan 30 1937, ran until at least Nov 6 1937 (SHJ spring 1996 p19).

REFERENCES TO LEEK. Leek has been styled 'Capital of the Moorlands' (1793) (LGS p160) (VCH vol 7 p84), 'Queen of the Moorlands' (OL vol 1 p109) (TSW p21) (LR p8), and 'Metropolis of the Moorlands' (NSFCT 1906 p145). In Arnold Bennett's novels Leek is Axe. 'The Record of the Hills' by AL Gee is about Leek and its surroundings (VFC p53). 'Lay and Lyrics,' by Muriel H Brown, is a collection of poems mainly concerned with Leek and its surroundings (VFC p20). 'Sunbeams and Shadows: A First Book of Poems' (1926) by Nellie Birch of Leek, contains verse about Leek and other local places (VFC p15).

CUSTOMS, SUPERNATURAL AND SUPERSTITION. The folk custom of heaving in Easter week was practised in Leek but had apparently ceased by the later C19 (VCH vol 7 p146). The custom of dragging a plough on **Plough Monday** was still observed in Leek in the later C19 (VCH vol 7 p146). Leek children went begging for **soul cakes** on All Saints' Day until the eve of WW1 (VCH vol 7 p146). Mrs E Edwards and Mrs F Astles claim they saw a ghost or **ghosts** in Leek in the 1930s (ES 16 Sept 1936 p5). In late 1980s or early 1990s Susan Critchlow saw a ghost of a man in a long black cloak with a tall black hat in the the town cemetery (GLS pp65-66). The Co-op on Buxton road, Leek, is haunted by strange sounds and the ghost of an old man with a long grey beard (SMM p46). There is the spectre of an old man seen at a steel scaffolding factory at Leek whose presence is always heralded by the smell of pipe tobacco (SMM p54). **UFO sightings**. Three people saw a very bright white round object, slightly oval, in the open, from Leek on Sept 20 1967 at about 8.30pm; it was possibly a UFO (FSRP p16). Three people saw a very bright single oval-shaped light with a dome on top which changed colours, through binoculars from Spring Gardens, Leek, on Oct 10 1967 at 7.00pm (FSRP p16). **Fairies**, reputedly, once inhabited the now lost Goodfellow Bank (see). Girls in Leek were still (1941) **touching metal** as a talisman whenever they passed a priest. The superstition derives from Bronze Age man's fear of Druids of the Stone Age over whom he had just conquered (FLJ 1941 p237). **Witches**. A witch lived in Getiffe's Yard, Derby Street in the early C17 (GLS p62). She lived next door to an old woman who cooked and sold oatcakes; they often argued. One day the witch materialised as a black cat in the doorway of the old woman's house and cursed the oatcake. This happened many times until the old woman threw a hot oatcake at the cat and it fled. The witch was then seen to have a scold mark on her back (OL vol 2 pp113-114) (FOS pp36,37) (MR p208) (TB May 1993 p5) (GLS pp62-63). There was a Victorian witch of Kiln Lane who practised her art on the machinery of a mill in Mill Street, and who made the bands come off the wheels and loosen the wheels themselves (FLJ 1942 p127). She lived in the 1870s and operated a form of 'protection racket' (DP p69). An old woman, Betty Yates, of Russell's Yard, near the top of Russell Street, was a town character and more of a fortune-teller than a witch. She baked and sold oatcakes in Leek. She stole her fuel from a neighbour, C Wilson, who one day taught her a lesson by sticking gunpowder in one of the sticks, and so Betty blew up her bakestone. Betty immediately ran out of her house crying 'The devil's come down the chimney and taken th' oatcakes' (OL vol 2 p32). **Maids**. There was a rhyme by a poet of the Moorlands alluding to the out-numbering of women to men in Leek which went

> In Leek and Lowe the maids be so many,
> That you can get a wife for a penny.

(OL vol 1 p177) (STM April 1969 p31).
Leek and Lowe Former quarter and township in Leek ancient parish. The quarter comprised Leek town (VCH vol 7 p82). 'Lowe' is always Lowe, not Low. Lowe being a ring of low land or dale lying all round the hill on which Leek town stands. The term 'Lowe' perhaps evolved as a separate watch and ward when the Earls of Chester lived in the district (NSFCT 1905 p159 note) and

was used to describe the tithing without Leek borough at various times during the Middle Ages. After the disappearance of the borough at the Dissolution the whole area came within Leek manor and Leek township, which was known by the later C17, as Leek and Lowe (VCH vol 7 p124). The township then comprised Leek town and some scattered farms surrounding Leek for instance at Birchills, Leek Edge and Westwood (W p719). The civil parish called Leek and Lowe, created in 1866, was renamed Lowe in 1895, and abolished and added to Leek urban district in 1934 (GLAUE pp415,416) (VCH vol 7 p84). For a rhyme about Lowe see Leek.

Leek Branch of the Caldon Canal Authorised in 1797 (IANS p24) completed in 1800 (OL vol 1 p183). Opened in 1802 (IAS p120). Diverges from the Caldon Canal N of Hollinhurst crosses over the Caldon Canal on the Hazelhurst Aqueduct. Ends, according to the OS map, S of Barnfields; the original basin in Leek has been filled in (IANS p24). Its traffic was mainly transporting coal which ended in 1934, and tar which ended in 1939. The canal was abandoned in 1944. The stretch N of the Churnet was bought by Leek urban district council in 1957 and filled in; Barnfields industrial estate was later built on the site (VCH vol 7 p100). (The Trent and Mersey Canal. Peter Lead. 1980. pl 126 shows the N portal of the tunnel on the Leek Canal. pl 127 shows the wharf at Leek c1900).

Leekbrook Small hamlet at the confluence of the Churnet and Cartledge Brook 1.25m NE of Cheddleton. Partly in Leek and Lowe township in Leek ancient parish and partly in Cheddleton ancient parish. Leekbrook has been described as a pretty hamlet (LR p37). Takes its name from a small brook which joins the Churnet S of Leek (SPNO p12). (SMOPP vol 2 p62p of the brook at Leekbrook). The Churnet Valley railway line linking Macclesfield with Uttoxeter, opened in 1849 and closed in 1960, passed through Leekbrook. The line from Stoke to Leek, opened in 1867 and closed to passengers in 1960, joined the Churnet Valley line at Leekbrook (VCH vol 7 pp100,180). The line from Leekbrook to Waterhouses, authorised on March 6 1899, opened on June 15 1905 (VCH vol 2 p324). The line from Leekbrook to Cauldon closed to passengers Sept 30 1935, but was still open to goods in 1983. The line from Leekbrook to Oakamoor closed on Nov 7 1960 but a single track still remained open in 1983 for carrying sand from the British Industrial Sand Works at Moneystone (CVH pp128-129). The area in Leek and Lowe township was developed as an industrial estate from the later 1970s (VCH vol 7 p98). A headless white dog has been seen in the Leekbrook area (NSFCT 1900 p147) (FOS p18) (SCS p6).

Leek Forest It stretched to Swythamley and embodied Lud Church (OL vol 2 pp87,162) (L p5 See Longnor). Has also appeared as Lac Forest.

Leekfrith Former quarter and township in Leek ancient parish covering land N of Leek (W p728) (S&W p297). The quarter consisted of the townships of Heaton, Leekfrith, Rudyard, Rushton James, Rushton Spencer, and Tittesworth (VCH vol 7 p82). The civil parish of Leekfrith, created 1866 (GLAUE p415), encloses part of Abbey Green, Blackshaw Moor, Lud Church, Danebridge, part of Upper Hulme, The Roaches, Hen Cloud, Hazlewood, Gun Hill, Redearth, and Meerbrook, and Newbrook, and Pool End (S&W p297). It once extended to Bridge End on the outskirts of Leek where an upright stone in the wall says 'Leekfrith' (HOLF p1). The manor of Frith, created after the Dissolution and comprising the estate formerly belonging to Dieulacres Abbey, descended with Leek manor after the mid C16 (VCH vol 7 p196). Has also appeared as Leek Frith, and sometimes as Firth. Frith is of doubtful origin, and means a wood (VCH vol 7 p197), or wild land (DA p70). The name is always found on the borders of ancient forests (DUIGNAN p64). It is a common Middle English word meaning woodland with more specific connotations of a royal forest or game preserve (NSJFS 1977 p36). Is from Welsh 'ffridd' forest or park (NSFCT 1908 p139). Frith means a woody vale (HOLF p2). Frith is the 'truce or peace' land - could relate to a Saxon battle in the area, or the Scotch rebels retreat from the area in 1745 (SK p196) (NSFCT 1916 p80).

Leek Moor Common land E of Leek town centre. Formerly covering part of the townships of Leek and Lowe, and Tittesworth (VCH vol 7 p233). There was some settlement on Leek Moor by the 1630s (VCH vol 7 p89) and at Leek Moorside on the E edge of the moor in Tittesworth township by the late C16 (VCH vol 7 p233). Most of the moor was enclosed in 1811 (W p719) (VCH vol 7 p103) and later some remaining common land on the moor became part of the Leek Town Lands (OL vol 1 p262) (NSFCT 1923 p79) (VCH vol 7 p103).

Leek Moorside House 0.75m WSW of Thorncliffe, on the E edge of Leek Moor. Formerly in Tittesworth township in Leek ancient parish. Has appeared as Pool House (1596. Late C17), Leek Moorside (late C17. 1821), The Edge (C18), and Moorside (Yates' map). The present house appears to date from the C17 (VCH vol 7 p233 note).

Leek Park Public park at rear of Ball Haye Hall. It incorporates John Hall's gardens in which was a rustic shelter. John Hall's gardens were much frequented by American soldiers based at Ball Haye Hall in WW2. Much vandalism occurred to the rustic shelter and it was eventually pulled down (ALC p48p).

Leek Town Lands Former common land belonging to the freeholders of Leek and Lowe township. The main part of which was the large medieval open field in the W and S environs of Leek town, called Leek Town Field. The field was extended to include Woodcroft and Westwood Heaths in the later C17. The remaining land is still (1991) administered by a trust, which was set up in 1811; some of Leek Moor was given to the trust in the C19 (VCH vol 7 p103).

Lee Lane Former small settlement represented by the present Lea Lane Farm and or Lea Hall Farm by the head of a tributary of Moreton Brook 0.5m SSW of Admaston, but in Colton parish. It is mentioned in a deed of c1250 as 'del Lee' when the rental was one rosebud at the feast of St James (SHC 1919 pp42-43) and has appeared as Lea Lane. (Plot's map) (OS map 1834) (W p194). It takes its name from an old lane, of which very little now (1919) remains which ran from the Colton-Admaston road near Lea Hall Farm and passed Wilderley Barn and ran perhaps on to Moreton Grange. The present (1919) Lee (or Lea) Lane connecting the Colton-Admaston road with Newton was made in the early C19 to compensate for the loss an old lane running through Blithfield Hall grounds (SHC 1919 pp42-43).

Lees Brook Runs through Alton Towers estate and was dammed to create fish ponds and lakes (Y).

Leese Farm 1.25m SSW of the church at Castle Church. A house may have been on this site by at least the C14. Has also been known as The White House and Lees House. The farmhouse in 1959 appeared to have been rebuilt in the early C19 (VCH vol 5 p93).

Leese Hill Hill 1.5m W of Loxley Green. (HOU p331). In Uttoxeter parish (W p792) and partly in Kingstone parish (SGSAS). Has also appeared as Lees Hill (Plot's map). Here rises Tad Brook. German incendiary bombs fell on Leese Hill in WW2 (TRTC p66).

Leese House Farm House 0.5m S of Cresswell. Plot's map marks Lees approximately here. Preserved in Leese House Farm. Lees with Paynsley, 0.5m to the ESE, may represent the DB estate Lufamesles (see).

Lees Grange Former grange of Croxden Abbey, which may have been situated in the area of Nothill Farm (see) (CDS p18). Granges of Croxden Abbey are recorded by Stuart at Croxden and Crakemarsh (CDS pp7,16). This may be the grange at Croxden, or another way of referring to Grange of the Leys, a grange of Croxden Abbey, thought by some to have been at Crakemarsh (see) (VCH vol 3 p226).

Leeside Minute fragmented hamlet or house 1m SSW of Rushton Spencer village.

Leetech Former settlement? N of Coven (1834 OS map) now merges with Coven.

Le Hyeschute Wednesfield. An old coal working site (VCH vol 2 p72).

Le Leghe Former moated house NW of Aldridge. The earliest record of it is in 1388, and it has appeared as Le Legh. The arms of a branch of the Legh family are marked by Aldridge on Plot's map. In the C18 it was a farmhouse. It was destroyed in the C19 by railway and colliery works (SSAHST 1982-83 p34) (MOA p135). The name, a French form of the Saxon 'leah' (meaning woodland or woodland clearance), need not indicate a Norman origin (MOA p135).

Leigh Ancient parish containing the former townships of Leigh and Field (W p782). (NSFCT 1923 p148). Was identified by Wolferstan, but not by Dugdale and Shaw, as the Lege mentioned in the will of Wulfric Spot (c1002), founder of Burton Abbey (SHC 1916 p35). The manor of Lege, held by Burton Abbey, appears in DB. The parish was formed between 1086 and 1291 probably out of Uttoxeter parish and may at first have formed a joint parish with Checkley, with a church at Leigh; Checkley perhaps becoming a separate parish in the early C13 (SHC 1916 pp194,199). Leigh became a separate civil parish in 1866 (GLAUE p416). It was recommended that Leigh railway station be closed in 1963 (ES March 22 1963). Foot-and-mouth disease broke out in Leigh parish in early 1968 at Withington Farm and Stone House Farm (SN Feb 16 1968 p1. Feb 23 1968 p11).

Leigh House 0.5m W of Enville Hall. Existed by the mid C15 when held by the Leigh family, and was so named by the early C17. A portion of the late medieval timber-framed building still survives (VCH vol 20 pp91,101,103).

Leighlane and Leighlane Bank. Church Leigh.

Leighswood Wood, area, and an industrial estate 0.25m N of Aldridge. In Aldridge ancient parish. A wood called Lees Wood appears in this area in the C19 (OS map 1834) (ALOPPR pp5-10).

Leighton Patch of land in the Pinfold Street area of Uttoxeter 0.25m S of the town centre. Here at Leighton Ironworks Henry Bamford (1819-1896) opened his implement manufacturing firm in 1871. Leighton means market garden (BUBA pp27-28,95,97). The ghost of a woman with dark hair in black who appeared at Bamford's factory in the late 1970s is believed to be the wife of Henry Bamford, Emily Bamford, who died in the 1880s. She used to visit the works and perhaps died at the works (GLS pp103-104).

Leman Syche Lichfield (HOL p5).

Lemon Brook Obsolete name for the head water of Combes Brook. The name occurs on the maps of Yates, Cary (1787) and Stockdale (1794) (NSFCT 1948 p50) (SPNO p12).

Le Mote Wheaton Aston. In Edward III's reign the prior of Lapley had a messuage called 'Le Mote' at Whetenaston (VCH vol 4 p148). The name suggests that the property was surrounded by a moat (SSAHST 1982-3 p44).

Lenches Bridge On the Dudley Road to the E of The Village, Kingswinford.

Leominche Street Roman road. Is mentioned in a deed of C12 and has formerly appeared as Leomirchistrete (SL p40). The Arbour, Mucklestone, lies on it and it may have passed through Market Drayton, Tunstall (Hales), Oakley Park and Madeley (SHC 1945/ 6 p27). DG Harnaman derives the name from the Celtic 'ley maen-gist-hir' meaning 'place (of) the stone cist long' a possible indicator to the presence of a long cairn over a 'kistvean' or cist of which the Devil's Ring and Finger are the two remaining stones (NSFCT 1937 pp117-118).

Leper House A house for the attenders at the Leper Well (see). The original house was mentioned in the PR 1596 as 'ye Lepre House,' and is said to be of C16 origin (TB Feb 1989 p11. Feb 1993 p27p). Hackwood says the Leper House was replaced at a later period by a 'Brimstone Ale-house' so-called because the water was sulphurous (AOW p94). (SMM p77). The original house was presumably on or near the site of the present Leper House Farm over 0.5m N of Codsall church, and NW of the Leper Well (VCH vol 5 p20). Plot implies the house was actually by the well (NHS p101); the present house is not very close to it.

Leper Well Holy well on N side of the road from Gunstone to Codsall Wood, presently at the foot of an old alder tree (TB Feb 1989 p11p) at SJ 871048. Anciently attended by lepers and sufferers from skin diseases, and those with sores and scabs who took the sulphurous waters. Has also appeared as Codsall Well and Codsall Wood Well. (NHS p101) (SHOS vol 2 p290 - just quotes Plot and Dr Wilkes, no mention of it being a leper well) (W p173) (SCSF p141) (AOW p94) (OSST 1944-1945) (SJC p10) (SN June 11 1976 p9) (CPP p23).

Less Brook Runs through Alton Towers estate, and was dammed to create fish ponds and lakes (Y).

Letocetum Most important Roman settlement in the county. Situated at Wall, straddling Watling Street. There was a Roman and later Romano-British settlement at Wall from the C1 AD until the C4, and possibly until the C5 (VCH vol 14 pp284-285). By the C3 the settlement was known by the Romans as Etocetum. The name is a Romanised version of Celtic 'Llwyd Coed' meaning 'the grey wood' (SSAHST 1963 p51) (HOA p2) (MR P353). Or 'Lectocetum' represents the Celtic toponym 'letocaiton,' and means 'grey wood' which reflected the wooded character of the area. From 'letocaiton' evolved the form 'luitcoet' and the place Cair Luitcoit or Caer Lwytgoed (see) (VCH vol 14 p4). (DoE Official Handbook) (JEPS No. 8 p56).

0 to 100. The XIV Legion were stationed on land near the later Letocetum from 48 AD before it advanced to Wroxeter in c58 AD and a large fort was built some time between c43 to 80 AD to accommodate it (SSAHST 1963 p15). The fort was probably on the high ground near the present Wall church (DoE Official Handbook. 1979 p3). Watling Street was built to the S of the fort in the 70s (VCH vol 14 p283). According to archaeological evidence the first fort was succeeded by a succession of forts (DoE Official Handbook. 1979 p3): Gould thinks there were up to four forts used at different times (SSAHST 1963) (NSJFS 1966 p71). A bath house was built on the lower-ground SW of the fort in the late C1 for use by soldiers; it was later re-used by the inhabitants of the civilian settlement (VCH vol 14 p283). It is uncertain whether Letocetum lay in Cornovii or Coritani territory, lying as it does halfway between these tribes' capitals at Wroxeter and Leicester (DoE Official Handbook. 1979 p4). Willmore says it was the chief town of the Cornavian Britons (HOWW p19). Tringham says the Cornovii had a shrine outside the Roman fort in the later C1 (VCH vol 14 p285).

100 to 200. In the C2 the settlement covered about 30 acres W of the later Wall Lane. By the C2 there was a burial area beyond the western end of the settlement (VCH vol 14 p283).

200 to 300. By the later C3 or early C4 the eastern part of the settlement, covering about six acres between Wall Lane and Green Lane and straddling Watling Street, was enclosed with a stone wall surrounded by an earth ram-

part and ditches (VCH vol 14 p285).

300 to 400. By the C4 Letocetum had become a Romano-British town with a hostel and a bath-house, and which provided 'mutatio' and 'mansio' for the traveller on Watling Street (HOS p10). Civilians continued to live inside the settlement and on its outskirts in the late C4 and possibly in the C5 (VCH vol 14 p285). The town possibly became the administrative centre of the district (DoE Official Handbook. 1979 p4). It has been argued that the whole of the Lichfield district (including Whittington, Alrewas, Fisherwick) lay within the territory of Letocetum (SSAHST 1968-69 pp44-43): While it has also been argued that the See of Lichfield may correspond to the late Roman Letocetensium district from the Civitas Cornoviorum to the W and the Civitas Coritanorum to the E (SSAHST 1978-79 p11).

REDISCOVERY AND DOCUMENTATION. Letocetum appears in the C3 'Antonine Itinerary' as Etocetum and in the 'Ravenna Cosmography' of the late C7 as Letocetum. Nennius in the C8 and C9 includes it in his list of 28 British cities (DoE Official Handbook). Salmon tried to show that Wall was Uxacona and that Barr Beacon was the real site of Etocetum (HOWW p19). Camden thought Etocetum was at Uttoxeter (HOU p27) (NSFCT 1908 p110). Plot recorded in 1686 that in a field called the Butts, to the N of the bath-house, he was shown two pavements of Roman origin (NHS p401 fig 4, tab 33 of a Roman pillar). A gold otho was found in 1690 (SSC p129 in the intro). E Arblaster noted in a letter of 1719 Roman coins found at Wall (SSAHST 1963 p21). John Horsley in his 'Britannia Romana' 1732 p420 makes a reference to certain walls which encompass about two acres called Castle Croft (SSAHST 1963 p1). W Stukeley, according to his 'Itinerarium Curiosum' 1776 vol 2 p21, visited Wall in the early C18 and saw parallel walls, 12 feet apart, which were three feet thick and 12 feet high, forming rooms like square cells at Castle Croft but were in the process of being demolished. W Hutton in his 'History of Birmingham' 3rd ed 1793 p218 said the demolition of the 'walls' was continuing. W Pitt noted the whole length of the perimeter wall was visible in 1817 (THS pp128-129). The wall, referred to as 'the castle,' and seen by C18 antiquarians was at Castle Croft (SSAHST 1963) (NSJFS 1966 p71). A Roman military barricade composed of oak trees standing on end was discovered before 1827 (SMC p173). An excavation was made by R Garner in 1859 in the 'Castle Croft' (SA June 18 1859) (JBAA vol 29 p55. vol 46 p227) (LGS p246-247). By 1872 nothing remained above ground (SSAHST 1963 p1), until, in 1873, Col Bagnall revealed extensive foundations in many parts of the field in 'The Butts' and an 11 feet thick wall running W to E for some 150 feet at 'Castle Croft' (BAST 1873 p38) (JBAA vol 29 p53. vol 46 p227). An excavation has tried to locate a subterranean passage supposed to lead from 'The Butts' to 'Castle Croft,' but remained undiscovered. Lomax, in his 'Guide to Lichfield,' says, workmen have found a figure, near the church, of earthenware of a woman, as big as a man, in a strange dress with a helmet-like cap - perhaps, a cult statue of Minerva (DoE Official Handbook). A length of wall was found in 'Castle Croft' in 1887 (DoE Official Handbook). But apparently no excavation was made in 1887 as Masefield, VCH and Webster claim, owing to misinterpreting JBAA vol 46 p227 (NSJFS 1964 p40). The bath-house and a building to the NE, known as the 'villa', were excavated in 1912-14 by the NSFC (NSFCT vol 47 p140. vol 48 p110. vol 49 p132) (LGS p263-266). The 'villa' has been filled in. The bath-house, built of Keuper sandstone, has been left exposed. Its foundations are of Wenlock limestone, possibly quarried from Daw End and or at Linley Farm (VCH vol 2 pp189,192-193. vol 14 pl 55). In 1924 the 'bath-house' site passed to Miss ED Henderson. In 1933 the NT were managing the site and it passed to them in 1934 (NSFCT 1933 p153) (VCH vol 14 p285). In 1922 a small bronze bowl was found embossed with a Chi-Rho symbol, suggesting Christian worship at Letocetum or Lichfield at the end of or after the Roman period (BAST vol 50 pl xiii) (SSAHST 1972 p30. 1992-93 pp1-4 ils, ps). A Roman well was found in 1931. Later, a stone implement, a well-shaped celt, was found 300 yards SE of the junction of Watling Street with Ryknild Street 0.5m E of Wall, close to the Lichfield-Sutton Coldfield railway (NSFCT 1931 pp176-177. 1934 pp59-60). Near Moat Bank at Wall Lane at SK 090066 was discovered a temporary camp near the N side of Watling Street. Part of the S and W ditches and the rounded SW angle were visible (NSJFS 1964 p41). The bath-house was re-excavated by G Webster in 1956 prior to conservation by the Ministry of Works (BAST vol 74 p12). More excavations in 1971 showed the bath-house, courtyard and colonnade had been constructed in the early Antonine period (SSAHST 1973-74 pp13-28 plan). The 'Castle Croft' site was excavated 1961-3 (SSAHST 1963 pp1-7). A fort occupied at various times from the Claudian period was found by SSAS in 1959-60. It measures 185 feet by 400 feet and is situated on the hill in the vicinity of the church. Its SE corner abuts onto the NW corner of the settlement at 'Castle Croft' (BAST vol 69 pp11-23) (SSAHST 1963 pp1-50. 1966

pp1-38. 1969 pp7-29). Excavations took place in the area of Market Lane and NE of Wall church prior to 1979 (SSAHST 1979-80 pp1-14 ils. 1981-82 pp1-67). Various Roman finds were made during excavations at the W end of Wall village, S of Watling Street in 1980 and 1981 (SSAHST 1983-84 pp1-30). Some of the thousands of artifacts found at Wall and at the Shenstone Hall Farm site are in Lichfield City Library Museum, Wolverhampton City Museum and the site museum at Wall, which contains about 60 coins, Iron Age and Roman pottery, querns, brooches, bronze objects, floor tiles, a large column base found in 1912 and a fragment of a milestone with

IMP....

AVR....

inscribed on it (DoE Official Handbook). Slag found at Wall suggests the Romans made iron at Letocetum (SSAHST 1969 p30). The finding of human horned heads carved in stones suggest a pagan temple of the Cornovii formerly on the site. When the Romans re-used them they reversed the stones to spurn the old religion (MR p353).

(SD pp25,51) (SHOS vol 1 General Intro p18. vol 2 p66) (SSC p129 in the intro) (GNHS pp68,69) (W pp517-518) (NSFCT 1912 pp139-143ps, plan. 1914 pp132-147. 1924 pp185-186) (KES pp8,218) (SOSH pp18-19) (LET) (CCC p8) (SLM Dec 1949 p77p of the bath-house before it was open to the public) (The Roman Site at Wall. G Webster. 1958) (SSAHST 1971-72 pp1-8. 1985-86 pp27-34 ps. 1988-89 pp18-20ps. 1990-91 pp1-78. 1991-92 pp1-6) (VB p13) (BOE p292 pl 4) (SL p39p. pl 4) (SGS pp173,174) (WMAG Oct 1979 pp2-3ps) (MR p354p) (AA p259) (BAST vol 74 pp15,23, 28-29).

Letter Box Cavern in the Wren's Nest (BCM Oct 1970 p51).

Lett Low Perhaps a burial mound at SK 091584, or SK 087588, or SK 095588, or SK 076582 near Warslow. Here a bronze dagger was found (NSFCT 1926 p146).

Levedale Tiny village on ground rising above the brook which forms the Bradley Penkridge boundary, 2m WSW of Dunston. In Penkridge ancient parish. Has appeared as Levehale, a manor, in DB (SSE 1996 p15), Levedehale (1198), Levedale (1199-1369), Levedenhal (1242), Leydall (1538), Leddall (1560) (SPNO p89), Lead (Blaeu's map), and Lovedale (THS p258). In the Middle Ages the name was somewhat corrupted and has only reverted to the current form in recent times (SPN p77). Duignan cannot interpret the name. Poulton-Smith thinks 'Leofa's water meadow' (SPNO p90) (SPN p77). A medieval chapel at Levedale does not appear in the returns of 1563 or after. It was discovered in 1552 and 1553 that there was a meadow in Bradley parish belonging to this chapel, called St Laurence meadow (SHC 1915 p150). The site of the chapel may be preserved in the field name 'Chapel Yard' at Levedale mentioned in the PR 1732 (HOP p30). The mission church at Levedale dates from c1920 (LDD).

Levedale Hall Levedale. The capital messuage of Levedale manor. Occupied in 1654. Richard Bartlem is recorded as living in the Old Hall in c1841. The hall, which has appeared as Old Hall and Hall House, was no longer standing by the mid 1950s (VCH vol 5 p115).

Level, The Brierley Hill. Formerly in Kingswinford ancient parish. The name Level was in existence by 1785 (A Plan of the intended Extension of the Dudley Canal in the Birmingham Canal. John Snape. 1785). Presumably Level New Furnaces to N of Merry Hill Shopping Centre is a remnant of this district.

Level Wood Appears on Fowler's map of 1822; it stretched as far W as Delph Locks and as far E as Dudley parish (WFK p17) and covered the present Merry Hill Shopping Centre (BCM spring 1995 p31).

Leveretts Hill Eminence on the W side of Handsworth ancient parish. Now occupied by Handsworth Cemetery (MNB p35). The Leveretts or Leveretts House, a house near the junction of Camp Lane and Park Lane, was built in 1700. It was rebuilt by 1794. In the mid C19 it was the seat of the Pearson family, who later moved to Farcroft. From 1890 to 1906 it was occupied by Samuel Withers JP. Samuel Dawes followed him and lived here until 1925 when he bought and moved to Charlemont Hall (see). The Leveretts was demolished in 1930 (MNB pp41,47,49) (HPPE pp65-66). 70 acres of Leveretts Farm became Handsworth Cemetery in 1910 (MNB p51). The name is preserved in The Leveretts, a residential area, to the NE of the cemetery.

Lewisham Park Public park on S side of Dartmouth Road, 1m N of Smethwick Old Church. Opened in 1905 (VCH vol 17 p93), when it was leased to Smethwick by Viscount Lewisham. It had earlier been a football ground used by employees of Birmingham Railway Carriage & Wagon Works (SMEOP p115p).

Ley, The Ilam. Here is the battle stone cross (NSFCT 1946 p36).

Ley, The NNW of Ingestre Hall, in Ingestre Park (Dower's map).

Leycett (locally *Lease-it*). Former small planned colliery village (MHSP p56) on top of a narrow valley in which lies Walton's Wood, now a small hamlet, 2m NE of Madeley. In Madeley parish. There was coal mining in the Leycett area by the C16 (MHSP p42). Appears in 1733 as Leasit and Leasitt (SHC 1944 p27). The name means 'the ley in the wood' (M p7). For Firmstone's Mineral Railway which ran from Firmstone's coal pits at Leycett to Madeley Heath see Madeley. In 1869 uniform brick terraces were built for local miners (M p58) (SL p252). With the closure of Leycett Colliery, it was difficult to sustain the size of the village and the bulk of it - three streets - was demolished by the Coal Board in 1968-9 (SL p252), with most inhabitants being rehoused in Madeley Heath (Newcastle Times May 22 1968). Permission to rebuild the village in 1975 was refused (ES Jan 10 1974. Feb 13 1974. Nov 28 1974. March 7 1975. March 13 1975. June 13 1975).

Leycett Park Leycett. A medieval deer park enclosed out of forest. Probably came into existence after 1355 and was first mentioned in 1392. Probably founded by the Hospitallers' of Keele and formed a part of Keele manor (MHSP p16); later held by the Earls of Stafford. Walton's Wood was within its bounds (NSJFS 1962 pp73,76. 1963 pp48-52 plan). Ceased being a park in c1400 (MHSP p16).

Ley End Former area of Handsworth ancient parish (HANDR pviii).

Leyfield Park New housing estate, built from 1980s, 1m ESE of Trentham, S of Longton Road.

Leyfields Suburb of Tamworth, 0.5m NW of Tamworth town centre. The area was rural before the mid C20 and formerly lay in Wigginton township in Tamworth ancient parish. The name, which does not appear on the 1890 OS map 6 inch, was used to describe this area by at least 1971 (1971 OS map). It is from Anglo-Saxon 'leage' meaning fallow land (SPN p123). The church, St Francis, Masefield Drive, was built in 1960 (LDD).

Ley Fields House 0.25m NE of Thorncliffe. Formerly in Tittesworth township in Leek ancient parish. Is of C17 origin (VCH vol 7 p233).

Ley Hall Handsworth. Seat of John Spencer (d1825) (mem in St Mary's church, Handsworth).

Leys Minute hamlet 0.5m W of Whiston, Froghall. Has appeared as Lees (Plot's map) (1834 OS map). There appears to have been a colliery at Lees in the early C19 (VCH vol 2 p306).

Leys, The A hill W of Brockmoor, Brierley Hill (TB March 1983 p34 see map). Formerly in Kingswinford ancient parish. Sometimes misspelt as The Lays (1881 OS map). The road the Leys is an old road across Pensnett Chase (SNSV vol 1 p207).

Leys, The The name was used to describe heathland by 1890 W of the centre of Tamworth (OS 1890 OS map 6 inch). The name is from Anglo-Saxon 'leage' meaning fallow land (SPN p123). The Leys was a residential area by at least 1971 (OS map 1971).

Leys Junction Junction of the Stourbridge Canal with its Fens Branch (HCMS No. 2).

Lichfield Cathedral city 15m SE of Stafford. The city has been referred to as the 'Mother of the Midlands' (VB p14), because its cathedral, Lichfield Cathedral (see), was once the mother church of all, or nearly all, the Midland shires (SGS p117). Lichfield occupies a small semi-circular vale in the gently undulating Keuper Sandstone country that lies between Cannock Chase and the valleys of the Tame and Trent. Most of the old city lies below 300 feet (SHC 1950/1 pp139-140).

PREHISTORY. Fragments of **Mesolithic** flints have been found on the high ground occupied by St Michael's churchyard, and they may indicate a flint industry site (SSAHST 1980-81 pp2,70,72) (VCH vol 14 p4). A prehistoric polished flint axe has been found in Gaia Lane. Another axe found in Lichfield was being kept by Lichfield Museum in 1950 (SHC 1950/1 p144). The same or another flint axe found in Lichfield is in Lichfield Museum (NSJFS 1964 p28). The same or another polished flint axe from Lichfield of **Neolithic** origin is now in Lichfield Museum (SSAHST 1980-81 p21). Traces of a Neolithic settlement have been found on the S side of the sandstone terrace occupied by the cathedral (SSAHST 1980-81 pp2,36-37,42-43) (VCH vol 14 p4). A flint arrowhead has been found in Beacon Park (see). A bronze palstave bought at Lichfield went to Shrewsbury Museum (NSFCT vol 61 p143) (NSJFS 1964 p28). The same or another unlooped bronze palstave of early **Middle Bronze Age** (1400-1200 BC) origin is now in Shrewsbury Museum (SSAHST 1980-81 p21). A looped bronze palstave from Lichfield of Middle Bronze Age (1300-1100 BC) origin went to Lichfield Museum (SSAHST 1980-81 p21). St Michael's at Greenhill may have replaced a pagan sanctuary (VCH vol 14 pp4,135).

ROMAN. It is possible Lichfield was in a pre-Roman estate or administrative centre (SSAHST 1968 pp43,49-51) (Signposts to the Past. Margaret Gelling. pp57-59) (VCH vol 14 p4). And later in a 'territorium' of Letocetum

during at least some of the Roman period (SSAHST 1968 pp43,49-51). Icknield Street passes on the SE side of the city: It has been argued that the fact that Icknield Street was built across existing fields suggests settlement in the Lichfield area by the time of its construction (SSAHST vol 22 p97) (VCH vol 14 p4). It is possible that the sub-Roman or Celtic administrative unit of Letocetum moved to Lichfield: The position on Watling Street was exposed and the marshy valley two miles away, remote (SSAHST 1968 pp43,49-51). There have been scattered Romano-British finds in the city (SSAHST 1980-81 pp2,6) (Lichfield Mercury Oct 17 1986 p8 p) (VCH vol 14 p4). The Close may have been an ancient Celtic site, and Bishops Clinton or Langton only deepened an old Celtic Roman fosse when they constructed the defences of the Close (NSFCT 1908 p123). A burial discovered beneath the cathedral in 1751 was possibly of Romano-British origin (GM vol 21 p398) (VCH vol 14 p4). The discovery of a Roman urn, and human remains within a malthouse on the causeway W of the Minster Pool in Aug 1802 is evidence of Roman/British occupation (HOL p511) (NSFCT 1908 p123. 1913 p127). Galacum in the 10th Journey of Antonine a Glamoventa Mediolano (Milan) was identified with Lichfield by Dr Fulk (HOL p301 note). For Roman finds made at Lichfield see GNHS p70. **Massacre of early Christians tradition**. According to tradition in c286 AD St Amphihalus or Amphibalus after the death of his spiritual pupil or teacher, St Alban, left Verulam (St Albans) and fled along Watling Street until he came to the Lichfield area where he held weekly Christian seminars. These were attended by local people and perhaps even wealthy Romans from Letocetum. Emperor Diocletian (284-305) decreed the execution of these Christians. The decree was carried out by a Roman legion, under Maximian, who executed 999 or 1000 Christians. Some say the site of the massacre was at Christianfield, near Stitchbrook, or at Boley, or at Spearhill and that they were left to lie where they fell and were devoured by wolves. Or the Christians were amassed into a funeral pyre and buried at Christianfield, or at St Michael's churchyard, or at Borrowcop Hill, or on the site of the cathedral (NHS pp398-399) (SMC p163) (HOL pp2-3,515) (GNHS pp155,156) (DUIGNAN p91) (SC p125) (History of Names. Mordacque vol 2 p237) (SOSH pp22-23) (VB p14) (FOS pp27-29) (SSAHST 1986-87 pp1-3) (MR pp209,211) (VCH vol 14 pp38,39) (GLS p67) (SMM p153). **Possible origins for the tradition**. By the 1120s Lichfield had become written 'Lichefeld,' a form much removed from the earlier forms. By c1250s the first attempts to explain 'Lichfield' were made. The first element was taken to be 'lich' or 'liches' and the place name to mean 'the field of corpses,' which needed an explanation. The view apparently held at Lichfield in the C13 was that the corpses resulted from a battle. Matthew Paris (d1259) of St Albans abbey linked Lichfield, possibly for the first time, with the fabrications that were accumulating round the British protomartyr St Alban. Geoffrey of Monmouth invented a St Amphilbalus as St Alban's spiritual teacher, whose converts, according to a later C12 'Life' of St Alban, were massacred in Wales. Matthew Paris identified the place of the massacre as Lichfield. His identification was accepted by at least one C14 hagiographer at St Albans, by John Lydgate in 1439, and the Warwick antiquary John Rous (d1491) (VCH vol 14 p38). Rous identifies the massacre story with Lichfield in his work concerning the bishops of Worcester. Shaw believed this work to be Plot's source (SHOS vol 1 p232). Rous's version was perpetuated by Leland. But Leland did not mention the massacre story in his account of his visit to the city in c1541 (VCH vol 14 p38). Succeeding writers perpetuated the story. In 1549 the massacre story appeared on the seal of the newly formed city corporation and found its way onto successive corporation seals, and onto paintings in St Mary's church, and a stone bas-relief on the Guildhall. Archbishop Ussher dismissed Amphibalus and the massacre story as a fabrication in 1639. However many continued to perpetuate the story. A variant of the tradition - given for instance by Raven (MR p209), and Bell (GLS pp66-67) - claims the corpses were the people of or in the army of three Christian kings or chiefs, defeated at Lichfield by Diocletian. Bell says, although the kings' names remain unknown, a rhyme names them as 'Cope,' 'Borrow,' and 'Hill,' and the three spires of Lichfield cathedral represent them (GLS pp66,67). One version of the rhyme is

> Three slain kings named, Borrow, Cope and Hill,
> When the battle was ended, lay quite cold and still.
> Legs, arms and bodies were scattered all about,
> For the battle had been cruel, of that there was no doubt

(FSBC p59). This version of the tradition possibly arose out of a misinterpretation of the design of the C16 and C17 corporation seals (see below under heading 1500 to 1600) (VCH vol 14 pp4,39). (HOS pp13-14). After the Roman occupation Lichfield may have been in Luitcoit (a Celtic territory) (see) or there may have been a Celtic settlement near or at Lichfield called Cair Luitcoit (see) or Caer Lwytgoed (see) (VCH vol 14 p4).

600 to 700. The date of Anglian presence in the Lichfield area may be determined by discovering when Lyccidfelth or Licidfelth - the first Anglian name for Lichfield - was coined. Lyccidfelth or Licidfelth appears in a 'Life' of St Wilfrid written soon after Wilfrid's death in 709, and in Bede's 'Ecclesiastical History of the English People' finished in 731. Tringham thinks these forms were perhaps coined in c600 and certainly in or by the 660s (VCH vol 14 pp37,38). The earliest accounts of the establishment of the bishopric in 669 speak of Lichfield simply as a place. It may be that in the C7 the name Lyccidfelth was used for an extensive area and only later came to be restricted to the cathedral and its environs (VCH vol 14 p4). Raven believes there was a Christian settlement at Lichfield by at least the early 600s (MR p211). Hughes, in 1925, says a settlement at Lichfield may have been built with building material from Letocetum (SOSH p19). (DUIGNAN p92) (SSAHST 1972 p30) (MR p211). Tringham thinks Wulfhere would not have offered, and Wilfrid would not have accepted, a cathedral site in an unnamed spot that was remote and inhabited chiefly by semi-independent Britons, had not there been some Anglian settlement already established there (VCH vol 14 p38). From the time of the establishment of the Mercian See at Lichfield in 669 there has always been some settlement at Lichfield, if only restricted to the cathedral and its environs; a spiral-headed pin of C7 origin was found in dredgings from the Minister and Stowe Pools in 1855 (SSAHST 1980-81 p3 note).

700 to 800. **Former spellings.** Lichfield was written Licitfelda in c710 (SSE 1996 p15); Licetfeld (HOL p1) in the Anglo-Saxon period (HOL p1); Licidfield by Bede; Lecefelle and Licefelle in DB; Lichfeld by Ingulphus and Huntingdon; Licethfeld by Simon Dunelm; Lichesfelde by Bromton; Lichesfeld by Gervas; Lychefeld by Knighton (HOL p1); Leichfeild in an order-letter from Charles I (HOL p19); Litchfeald in a letter from Capt Hunt to Col Bagot 1644 (HOL p27), Lyccidfelth, Liccidfeld, Liccedfeld, and Liccetfeld (SPN p77). All etymologists have disagreed about the **origin of the name.** Theory **one** is that it arises from 'field of the dead bodies,' 'lic' in Anglo-Saxon signifying a body. This theory is supported by the story of the massacre of Christians in Diocletian's reign (284-305). But the theory relies only on a post-Conquest form 'Lichefeld' and therefore can be discredited. The massacre story was discredited in 1655 (VCH vol 14 p38). (History of Names. Mordacque vol 2 p237) (W p486). Theory **two** is that Lichfield means 'field of the marsh, or lake' if from the verb 'leccian' which in Anglo-Saxon signifies to water or to cover land with water (SHOS vol 1 p231) or from the word 'leche' signifying a watery place (Stukeley. Itin. iv. p66). Duignan opts for this theory; Stowe and Minster Pools being anciently one marshy mere, far extending their present bounds. But the theory relies only on a post-Conquest form 'Lichefeld' and is not the earliest form 'Lecefelle' and therefore can be discredited (VCH vol 14 pp38-39). Theory **three**, the one now usually accepted by authorities, is that it is derived from the Roman settlement of Letocetum (see) which in turn is derived from the ancient British city in this area called Cair Luitcoet (see) or Caer Lwytgoed (see) which means 'the place of the grey woods' (HOA p7) or 'city of the grey wood' (DUIGNAN p92). The latter element being from Anglo-Saxon 'feld,' giving the literal meaning as 'field (ie common pasture) in (or beside) the grey wood' (VCH vol 14 p4). Early exponents of this theory appear to be Rev Thomas Barns and CGO Bridgeman (SHC 1916 p321). By the late 1960s CC Taylor thought the 'open land of Letocetum' suggesting Lichfield was in the territory of Letocetum (SSAHST 1968 p49). Gelling's alternative of the early 1980s is that it is 'field or open land near Letocetum' (NSJFS 1981 p3) (MR p209). (GNHS p155*) (GLS p66). **Kings buried at Lichfield.** King Ceolred was buried in the vicinity of the cathedral in 716 (VCH vol 14 p6). Ethelbert, king of the East Angles was buried in the cathedral in 794 (VCH vol 14 p6). It is possible Lichfield was a **literary centre** in the C8 and the C9, when Mercia appears to have been important in the world of culture. But no pre-Norman Conquest text or manuscript, teacher or scholar can be certainly linked to Lichfield (VCH vol 14 p6). The **Lichfield Gospels** is an illustrated C8 gospel book which has belonged to Lichfield cathedral from the C10. It was probably produced in Ireland, Iona, or Northumbria and did not originate in Lichfield. It was possibly produced as a gift for a Mercian church or a Mercian king. It was in Wales by the early C9 (VCH vol 14 p6). The book has also been called St Chad's Gospels, or 'Textus St Cedde' (W p499). The manuscript is in Latin and contains the gospel according to St Matthew, St Mark, and the gospel of St Luke, but only up to chapter iii, verse 9 (RHPS p256) (LGS p173). Marginal notes show that it was acquired by Gelhi the son of Arihtuid from one Cingal, in exchange for Gelhi's best horse, and by him dedicated to God and St Teilo. Another note states that Godwin, the son of

Earwig, publicly cleared himself from the charge of unchastity brought against him by Bishop Leofgar (RHPS p256). Another note states the gospel book was acquired by Llandaff cathedral, and that it has been at Lichfield since c950 (LGS p173). The gospel book was preserved during the Civil War by the Precentor, William Higgins, and then returned to the dean and chapter. Dr Scrivener thought the work was by Chad, himself, if not of some contemporary (MOS p131). In 1994 in the belief that medieval monks from Lichfield stole the gospels from Wales, Rev Patrick Thomas, a Welsh clergyman, requested they be returned to Wales (ES Nov 26 1994 p15). There was a request for the return of the gospel book to Wales from the vicar of Llandeilo in 2000 (BBC 1 Midlands Today April 12 2000). (Wankey's Cat. of Saxon Mss) (Hickes's Thesaurus) (SHOS vol 1 p261) (SHOSA p4 vol 2) (SC pp49-53) (BAST vol xli 1916 pp5-21 6pls) (KES p133) (SOSH pp47p,48) (DRBSC p476) (LPL p) (HOS p45il) (SK pp127,128 il) (AA p257pc).

800 to 1000. A Mercian collection of pedigrees of English kings and lists of popes and English bishops, compiled in c812, may perhaps have originated at Lichfield and may later have been kept here (VCH vol 14 p6). Lichfield came under Danelaw between 886 and 890 when Watling Street was fixed as the boundary between Saxons and Danes (VCH vol 14 p7). The cathedral was presumably despoiled, and the disruption probably led to the communal life of the canons (VCH vol 14 p7). Willmore mistakenly lists Lichfield as one of the burhs of Ethelfleda but neglects Stafford (HOWW p31).

1000 to 1200. In 1039 Bishop Byrhtmaer died at Lichfield (S&W p390). In 1086 Lichfield was also the name of an episcopal manor which covered much of SE Staffs and may have had its origins in the estate given to the See by King Wulfhere and Wilfrid (VCH vol 14 p7). **Settlements comprising Lichfield.** By the end of the C11 it is doubtful whether there was a single settlement called Lichfield (VCH vol 14 p7). At that time Lichfield may have merely comprised three small settlements, collectively known as Lichfield; one in the area of Gaia Lane and Shaw Lane; a second at Greenhill; and the third at Lower Sandford Street (SSAHST 1968 p49. 1984-85 pp11-35). To these can be added three more, one at 'Bech' SE of Stowe; another at the N end of Dam Street near a gate into the Close and a mill on the outflow of Minister Pool; and another at Stowe, extending from the area of St Chad's church and a nearby mill along Stowe Street and Lombard Street (VCH vol 14 p7). The **three city churches** appear to have their origins in three of these settlements: St Michael, on Greenhill (see), over 1m ESE of the cathedral, first recorded in 1190, stands on a religious site of C5 or C6 origin; its parish later included the out-townships of Burntwood, Fisherwick with Tamhorn, Freeford, Hammerwich, Haselour, Statfold, Streethay with Fulfen, and Wall with Pipehill (VCH vol 14 p135): St Chad at Stowe (see), 1m NE of the cathedral; its parish later included the out-township of Curborough and Elmhurst: St Mary in Market Street, under 0.5m SE of the cathedral, is recorded in 1293 but may have its origins in a church of the mid C9; its parish embraced the city without the cathedral Close (VCH vol 14 p135). In the Middle Ages the three city churches had no parish and were treated as chapels of ease by the cathedral. They were served by cathedral clergy as part of the 'parochia' of the cathedral. This system - unique among English cathedral cities - lasted until the parish of St Mary's was created in 1491 (VCH vol 14 p135-140). From the C13 to the C19 ecclesiastical jurisdiction in Lichfield and its neighbourhood was exercised not by the bishop but by the dean and cathedral, or whenever there were vacancies in the deanery, by the chapter. The dean's jurisdiction continued to be exercised over the parishes of St Chad, St Mary, and St Michael until abolished in 1846. The only place in the city over which the dean failed to maintain jurisdiction was St John's Hospital (VCH vol 3 pp93-94. vol 14 pp154-155). Lichfield was laid out as a planned town by Bishop Clinton (d1149) in the 1140s (BOE p189 note) (SL p148) or between 1129-49 (NSJFS 1971 p52). The **planned town** was certainly in existence by 1151 and may have been finished by Bishop Durdent. In 1153 King Stephen granted Bishop Durdent a **mint** at Lichfield. The grant was confirmed in 1154 and in 1189. The mint closed down in 1198. The only surviving coin is one struck during Richard I's reign (VCH vol 14 p10). **Visitors and events. William of Malmesbury** visited Lichfield in c1125, and wrote disparagingly of it (SL p148) (VCH vol 14 p7), then, it was only a small village. Bishop Clinton held a **synod** at Lichfield in 1139 and another in the later 1140s (VCH vol 14 p9). The **Empress Maud** attended the synod held at Lichfield at Whitsun in c1139 (TTH p23). **Henry II** was at Lichfield in 1161 (W p487). William Croc (descended from Richard the Forester and a member of the Croc family, hereditary foresters of Cannock Forest) was hanged in 1167 for the murder of Gilbert, the king's cupbearer in a **brawl** at Lichfield, where the king was holding his court (DUIGNAN p48). In 1173 **Henry II** stayed at Lichfield and while here held meetings of the king's court (SOSH pp113-115). He was in Lichfield in 1175, when he tried the murderers of a royal forester, and in 1181 (VCH vol 14 pp11,85). **Bishop Pucelle** died at Lichfield in 1184 (VCH vol 14 p9). **Bishop Muschamp** (d1208) was the first bishop to be buried at Lichfield after the Norman Conquest (VCH vol 14 p9). **King John** was at Lichfield (R&S p8).

THE BOROUGH. The earliest reference to the town of Lichfield being a borough is between 1155-59 (SHC 1924 p87) (NSJFS 1972 p68) (VCH vol 14 p73). No charter has survived (VCH vol 14 p9). The borough was governed as a separate manor, 'the manor of Lichfield,' probably from its creation, and was held by the bishop until 1548 (VCH vol 14 pp9,67). The old manor courts had taken place in a moot hall, probably at the Moot Hall (see) in Lombard Street, moving to the Guildhall (see Lichfield Guildhall) in 1549 (VCH vol 14 p75). Burgage tenure was in existence before 1176. At no time did borough status lapse (NSJFS 1972 p68). **Charters**. No charter creating Lichfield a borough survives (VCH vol 14 p9). The bishop of Lichfield was granted a charter in **1153** (VCH vol 14 p9) or sometime between 1149-1154 to hold a market at Lichfield on Sundays (NSJFS 1971 p50). Richard I invested Lichfield with the right of purchasing land to the value of ten pounds (W p487). A charter of **1441** exempted the cathedral and Close from shire and town officials but the town continued to be under the authority of the bishop of Lichfield as lord of the manor in many secular affairs (NSJFS 1979 p4). The charter of **1461** confirms the charter of 1441. The charter of **1548** made Lichfield a city and created the corporation. Under the charter of **1553** the city of Lichfield was created a county. Elizabeth I's charter of **1558** confirms and ratifies the charter of 1553 (HOL pp336,337,338). The charter of James I dated **1623** (perhaps the charter of 1622 - VCH vol 14 p76) confirms all previous charters (HOL p344). The charter dated **1624** (perhaps the charter of 1623 - VCH vol 14 p76) confirms all former charters, differing only in a few instances (HOL p346). The charter of **1664** directs that two bailiffs shall be annually elected by the Corporation? on St James' day (HOL p347). Early in 1686 James II procured a surrender of the Corporation's charters. The king granted the Corporation a new charter dated July 9 **1686** reincorporating them by the style and title of Mayor and Alderman. By this charter, they might purchase lands; sue and be sued and have a common seal (HOL 348). James II restored to the Corporation on 17 Oct **1688** their ancient rights, charters, liberties, annulling the charter of 1686, and from this time to the early C19 the Corporation has subsisted as it was left by the charter of Charles II (HOL p348) (W p491) (SOSH p155).

MARKETS AND FAIRS. The bishop of Lichfield was granted a charter in 1153 (VCH vol 14 p9) or sometime between 1149-1154 to hold a **market** at Lichfield on Sundays (NSJFS 1971 p50). By 1293 the market had been moved to Wednesdays (VCH vol 14 p116). A weekly market was granted in 1307 (LAWTT p24). By the early C17 there were markets on Saturdays and Wednesdays (VCH vol 14 p116). The charter of 1622/3 replaced them by ones on Tuesday and Friday (HOL p305) (W p484) (VCH vol 14 pp21,116). The Friday market was the principal market in the 1780s, and the Tuesday market lapsed in the 1840s (VCH vol 14 p116) (OWEN) (THS) (SCSF p94). The Friday market declined in the later C19 (VCH vol 14 p116), so that it could be reported there was no market in 1888 (LHE p265), but a Friday market was still being held in the mid 1980s (VCH vol 14 p116). A **market cross** in the Market Place was erected by Denton, Dean of Lichfield, at a cost of £360 (HOL p300) (SCSF p89) (VCH vol 3 p165). It was compassed with steps and covered with a vault for some to shelter under. This was raised on eight stone arches, surmounted by carved rails or banisters, topped with eight statues of the Apostles, each carrying the emblem of his death. The cross was destroyed by parliamentarians in 1643 and a brick market house built on the site (HOL pp453-454) (VCH vol 14 p18) (LI parts 4 and 5 p100) (LAL p7) in the 1650s. The market house, rebuilt in the early 1730s, was demolished in 1789. A new market hall was completed in 1797 on the site of the former Roundabout House in the Market Place. This was replaced by the Corn Exchange, now with shop fronts, in Conduit Street; a building built as a combined market hall and corn exchange in 1849-50 (VCH vol 14 p117 pl 28). **Fairs**. A fair on the Friday after the **Epiphany** (6 Jan) (Twelfth Day) was granted by the 1622 charter. This fair had lapsed by 1735 but may have been revived in c1790 (VCH vol 14 pp118,119). (SHOS vol 1 p316) (Whitaker's Almanac) (SCSF pp98,99). There was a fair on **Ash Wednesday** by 1409, with an accompanying court of pie powder by 1464. The fair, said to have begun by ancient custom on Shrove Tuesday, was confirmed by the 1622 charter. The fair was known as the Old Fair by the C17. In the later C19 the fair was ordered to be held on Shrove Tuesday only, and that day may have been settled upon in the C20. By the later 1870s the fair had become a pleasure fair. The custom of proclaiming the fair by the town crier in the presence of the mayor and a civic party was still being practised in the mid 1980s (VCH vol 14 pp12,29,118,119). (SHOS vol 1 p316) (COOKE) (W p484) (Whitaker's Almanac) (SCSF

pp98,99,101) (NSJFS 1978 p2). A fair on **May Day** and the day following was granted by the 1622 charter fair (VCH vol 14 p118). (SHOS vol 1 p316) (W p484). The fair was held on May 12 (new style) (COOKE) (Whitaker's Almanac) (SCSF pp98,99). The oldest recorded fair is the **Whitsun** fair, claimed by the bishop in 1293 for the Tuesday, Wednesday and Thursday of Whit week by immemorial right. This fair was extended to 15 days in 1307 (VCH vol 14 pp12,118). White alone mentions a Monday Whit fair (W p484). A fair on the **first Monday in July** was instigated in 1815 but had been discontinued by c1850 (VCH vol 14 p119). A fair on the eve and feast of the **Exaltation of the Cross** (13 and 14 Sept) was granted in 1337 (VCH vol 14 pp12,118). A fair on the **first Monday in October** was instigated in 1852. This fair was still being held in the 1870s (VCH vol 14 p119). A fair on the Friday before the feast of **St Simon and Jude** (Oct 28) and the day following was granted by the 1622 charter fair (VCH vol 14 p118). Shaw places it on the Friday in the week after the feast (SHOS vol 1 p316). (Whitaker's Almanac) (SCSF pp98,99). The fair was known as the goose fair by the later 1740s. In 1752 it was moved to the first Friday in Nov and was in decline in the earlier C19 (VCH vol 14 p119). A fair on the **first Monday in November** was instigated in 1815 but had been discontinued by c1850 (VCH vol 14 p119). A fair on the morrow of **All Saints** and seven days following (2-9 Nov) was granted in 1307 (VCH vol 14 pp12,118) (LAWTT pp24-25). There was a fair on the first Tuesday in Nov for geese and cheese, mentioned by COOKE, and Hackwood (SCSF p99). After the Reformation Lichfield is said to have lost all but one of its fairs. In the C18 there were four fairs but only two were important (VCH vol 14 pp16,21). There was a fair in 1792 (OWEN) and there was one in 1888 (LHE p265).

MEDIEVAL COURTS. The ancient courts of Lichfield were: **St Hilary's Court** held on Mondays near the feasts of St Hilary (Jan 13). It was, by the 1470s, known as a view of the borough or of the free borough (or of the free burgesses) (VCH vol 14 p74). **St George's Court** see Court Baron. The **Court Baron** (or called St George's Court) held on St George's Day (HOL pp351,354). It was, by the 1470s, known as a view of the borough or of the free borough (or of the free burgesses) (VCH vol 14 p74). (FOS p93). The **Court of Array** held on Whit Monday (HOL p351) is a View of Frankpledge or View of Men at Arms (LPL). A law of 1176 (FOS p102) or 1181 (SCSF p34) ordered that a 'view' of arms and armour should be made regularly in every town by those having jurisdiction over it (FOS p102) and to provide armour for the defence of the cathedral walls (VB p26). This law or act was confirmed by the Statute of Westminster 1285 which stipulated that freemen between the ages of 15 and 60 be liable to serve in the national interest (FOS p102). Courts of Array are first recorded in Henry V's reign, when Henry went to France in 1415 he empowered certain commissioners to take in each county a review of all the freemen able to bear arms, to divide them into companies and to keep them in readiness for resisting an enemy. The Statues of Array were repealed in James I's reign (Rymer vol 9 pp254,255) (HOL pp352-354). Ever since James I's reign the review has been nothing more than mere ceremony. The Court of Array has long had associations with the Greenhill Bower festival (see under Greenhill). The festival, which was held at Greenhill, also occurred on Whit Monday. According to Rev Dr Falconer the old Guild Hall became too small for the Court and the growing number of officers and the Court decided to meet on the more spacious Greenhill (SCSF p35). This may explain the Array's association with the Bower. The Court continued to assemble at the Guild Hall and then process to Greenhill, where the Court officials partook of the refreshments at the booths or bowers of the Bower Festival. The Court of Array was noted by Celia Fiennes, and Dr Johnson. According to Pitt's account (1817) the Court assembled at Greenhill. Here the town crier, in the presence of the Sheriff, Town Clerk and Bailiffs, proclaimed the names of all the householders in the 21 wards of the city, and all the persons who owed suit and service to the court of Lichfield manor. After this ceremony the Constables, and men-at-arms leave and march through the streets to a ward and summon the Dozener, or Petty Constable of that ward, to accompany them to the Court. Before they go the armed men fire a volley over every house in the ward, and on this salute the inhabitants invite the constables into their houses for refreshments. The Dozener, carrying his flag or ensign, then accompanies the Constables and armed men back to Greenhill. There in the presence of the Dozener the Town Clerk calls forth from a roll the name of every householder in that Dozener's ward. The Constables and armed men then march back through the streets to another ward and repeat the process going to and forth between Greenhill and the wards until the Dozeners of the 21 wards have all been called. The process took all day (SCSF p35). By probably the C20, the Court's procedure was dramatically reduced in order to make it a 'quaint piece of theatre' for a public audience in the Guildhall. Today (1996) the Court convenes at 11.30 and closes at noon. It has little to do with the Bower of the afternoon, as it once had, except for the Mayor and other Court officials go on to join the Bower procession (FOS p102). (SHOS vol 1 p317*) (SSC p123 in the intro) (W pp492-493) (Long Ago: A Journal of Popular Antiquities. Alex Andrews. ed 1873. vol 1 p220) (S&W vol 1 p6) (BCC vol 1 p166) (Sir Benjamin Stone's Pictures. Records of Natural Life 1906 vol 1 pp39-41) (LGS p178) (SJC p9) (VB p26) (FOS p102). Examples of the English 'Bills' paraded by men at arms have been on show at St Mary's Centre. The **Magdalen Court** (or called Great Portmote Court or Le Dozener's Court) held on the feast of St Mary Magdalen (July 22) (HOL pp351,354) was a view of tithingmen. The tithingmen represented wards in the town and made presentments relating to offences such as assaults, gossiping, and failure to attend the watch (VCH vol 14 p74). The facetiously named **Maudlin's Court**, for administering the oath of office to the dozeners (SHOS vol 1 p318) and for punishing inebriety (HOL p351). The **Court of Pyepowder** (or called Pie Powder, or Court of Dusty Foot) was held by the bailiffs at the May fair and or Old fair and the Ash Wednesday fair (VCH vol 14 p12). It regulated disputes at these fairs. The name is from Pieur Poudreux - see Dr Pettingal's dissertation in Archaeology vol 1 p190 - signifying the dusty feet of suitors; or according to Sir Edward Coke, because justice is done there as speedily as dust can fall from the feet. But Barrington in his observations on the statute says it is from the pied puldreaux (a pedlar, in Old French) and therefore signifying the court of such petty chapmen as resort to fairs. This court was confirmed to the citizens of Lichfield by a charter of Charles II (SHOS vol 1 p318) (PT p115) (HOL pp350, 351). Tutbury, Walsall, Wednesbury also had Pyepowder Courts. **Court of Record** was established by the 1548 charter to meet weekly on Thursdays for the recovery of debts, amounting to 40 shillings or over, but after 1553, of under 40 shillings as well (HOL p354). The court was formally abolished in 1857 (VCH vol 14 p78). There were also the quarter sessions and a court for gaol delivery (HOL p351).

PUNISHMENTS. For the **gallows** see Gallows Wharf. There was a **pillory** in 1305, and it stood on the N side of the market square in 1402-3. In the later C18 it stood at the NW corner of the market house (VCH vol 14 p85). **Stocks** are mentioned in the late 1680s. In the later C18 they formed part of the pillory in the market square. Stocks kept in the Guildhall in 1895 are probably those in the museum opened there in 1986 (VCH vol 14 p85). Hackwood describes the stocks as being in use to a comparatively late period. They were set on wheels and kept in the Town Hall. When required they were wheeled out into the street and placed in front of the Town Hall (SCSF p130). There were also stocks in the Close at the W end of the cathedral near the conduit in 1749. In 1823 the stocks were moved to the S side of the cathedral (VCH vol 14 p85). A **whipping post** stood next to the pillory in the C18 (VCH vol 14 p85). The **scold's bridle** is said to have been in regular use in Lichfield from the C15 (SAL) (SCSF p125). One was bought by the Conduit Lands Trust in 1666-7, and one was still in use in 1781 (VCH vol 14 p85). One went to Greene's Museum in the C18 (SAL) (SCSF p125). A **cucking stool** is mentioned in 1485. Duckings took place in Minster and Stowe Pools (VCH vol 14 p85). If the stool proved ineffectual, it was the custom in Lichfield, to then use the scold's bridle (HOL p383) (SCSF pp125,126). A **branding iron** was available in 1701 (VCH vol 14 p85). There was probably a **gaol** in Lichfield by 1306 and it probably stood in the Market Place. It was attacked in 1459 by men of Henry Percy, Earl of Northumberland. By the C16 the gaol probably stood behind the guildhall. The gaol was closed in 1866 and a magistrates' court built on the site in 1867, but four cells were incorporated into the Guildhall and in 1986 they were opened as part of a small museum (Lichfield Mercury May 23 1986 p11) (VCH vol 14 p84).

1200 to 1400. In medieval times the bounds of Lichfield were beaten on Ascension Day. The custom was revived for the 1300th anniversary of the death of St Chad in 1972 (LTM March April 1972 p26). The **wells** of Lichfield, including St Chad's Well (see), were dressed on Ascension Day (THS i p100) (SAL p133) (HOL pp508-509) (SHOS vol 1 p344) (VCH vol 14 p161). In Lichfield an ancient custom which was long observed at Christmas and New Year was for **roisterers** to call upon the inhabitants with a cup and entreat a contribution either of drink or of 'wassail' money (HOL) (SCSF pp4,49). It was the custom in medieval times for the inhabitants of ancient boroughs such as Lichfield to **'Set the Watch'** on Midsummer Eve. In addition to the standing watch, it was customary for hundreds of citizens, shouldering pikes, partisans, or halberts, or bearing torches of fire to join in an annual Marching Watch, all in military array, which, says Hackwood, made for a weird picturesque night pageant (SCSF p45). For the watch in Lichfield see VCH vol 14 p102. Most of the city was destroyed in a **fire** in 1291 (HOL p302) (W p489), but the Close escaped (VCH vol 14 p11). There were **guilds** attached to the three town churches - St Chad, St Michael and St Mary. **St Chad**. The broth-

ers of St Chad at Stowe existed in c1300, and the guild of St Chad was mentioned in 1365. **St Michael**. In the earlier C16 there was a guild of St Michael (VCH vol 14 p131). **St Mary**. There was a guild of St John the Baptist attached to St Mary's in 1353. There was also a guild of St Mary attached to St Mary's in the mid C14. Both had both male and female membership. These two guilds were amalgamated to form the guild of St Mary and St John the Baptist at Lichfield in 1387 (HOL pp312-335) (VCH vol 14 pp75,131). A master and four wardens were elected at an annual meeting on the feast of the Conception of St Mary (Dec 8). An annual feast occurred for members on the Nativity of St Mary (Sept 8) (VCH vol 14 p131). By the C15 this guild was participating in the government of the town, on behalf of the bishop, and the master was assisted by a group called the Forty-eight (VCH vol 14 p132) (LAWTT p23). The Guild had a guild hall (see Lichfield Guildhall) in Bore Street by 1421 (VCH vol 14 p131). Guild members could trade freely in the city without paying tolls (LAWTT p23). The guild was dissolved in 1548 (NSJFS 1979 pp4-5). The Conduit Lands trust acquired many of the endowments of the guild in 1545 (VCH vol 14 p79). Members included: Richard II, and his queen, Anne (VCH vol 14 p132), the Duke of Clarence (NSJFS 1979 pp4-5), Henry VII in 1487 and his queen, Elizabeth in 1494, and their son Prince Arthur (HOL p304). Also local gentry and the heads of religious houses (VCH vol 14 p132). Priests' Hall (see) was living quarters for the chaplains of the guild (VCH vol 14 p132). **Merchants robbed**. In 1342 some Lichfield merchants and their servants set out for Stafford market with 'spicery and mercery' worth £40. On their way they were set upon by Sir Robert de Rideware and two of his squires who made off with the goods. The merchants escaped back to Lichfield and aroused the Bailiff, he collected men and pursued the robbers. A pitched battle took place, but Rideware helped by his brother, Walter, pursued the Bailiff and got hold of the mercery again. When the merchants tried to seek justice from the King's judges at Stafford the judges unjustly took the side of Rideware. The merchants were kept outside the gates of Stafford and were driven back to Lichfield (SOSH p142) (CCBO pp104-105). There was a **pinfold** in Dam Street near the gate to the Close, but by 1476 it had been removed, probably to Beacon Street. Another pinfold stood at Greenhill in 1498 (VCH vol 14 p75). **Persons and visitors**. **Henry III** was at Lichfield in 1235, 1237 and 1241 and admired 'the new work at Lichfield' - the high wooden roof of the cathedral (VCH vol 3 p149). Others say he was in Lichfield in 1251 (HOL p302) (RVW p9), and for three days in 1257 (R&S p9). (NSFCT p23). **Edward II** as prince of Wales was probably at Lichfield in 1296 and as king in 1309 (VCH vol 14 p14); for one night in 1323 in the Bishop's Palace (VCH vol 3 p153 note); and on March 14-18 1326 (CE p28 note 4) (VCH vol 14 p14). **Bishop Langton** stayed the night at Lichfield on Jan 12 1319 during his visitation of the deanery of Tamworth and Tutbury (SSE 1994 p2). **Richard FitzRalph**, famous theological writer, was a canon at Lichfield cathedral between 1336 and 1346 and spent three years in residence at Lichfield (VCH vol 3 p152). **Edward III** was at Lichfield in 1328. The record of him being in Lichfield in 1331 is probably an error for Lincoln (VCH vol 14 p14 note). He came to Lichfield in April 1348 for a 'Hastilude' in celebration of his victory over the French at Crecy (ARCH vol 31 pp113-16) (VCH vol 14 pp14,161). In June the king held further hastiludes at Windsor and in July he issued orders for building St George's Chapel - the chapel of the Companionship of the Order of the Garter. It is reasonable to suppose that the order had already been envisaged and may have been whilst at Lichfield - he was at Lichfield on St George's day 23 April (LTM March April 1972 p28). (SCSF p133) (SMM p145). At the hastiludes the king is said to have run a tilt against the Duke of Lancaster (SCSF p133). **Richard II** was at Lichfield in 1386 to attend the enthronement of Bishop Scrope, and for Christmas 1397 on which occasion he and his entourage consumed 200 tons of wine and 2,000 oxen (SHOS vol 1 p309) (HOL pp289-290,302) (SMC p163) (W p490) (RVW p9) (SOSH p143) (LTM Dec 1971 pp16-17) (VCH vol 14 p14). Some say he was at Lichfield in 1390 (R&S p13). In May 1398 he concluded a treaty with the Duke of Brittany at Lichfield and attended the enthronement of Bishop Burghill and attended the tournaments laid on in his honour (VCH vol 14 pp14,161). He was at Lichfield as a captive of Bolingbroke (Henry IV) (SSTY p10) on his way to London from Flint Castle in 1399 (HOL p302) (R&S pp13,16) (VCH vol 14 p14). On the last occasion he seems to have stayed in the house of the Archdeacon of Chester outside the Close (VCH vol 3 p153 note).

1400 to 1500. Probably the oldest surviving pieces of dramatic literature in English are the excerpts known as **'The Lichfield Fragments.'** They are contained in a small book of liturgical music, songs and speeches and were written down in c1430. After the Reformation, this book was set aside by those in charge of the services at Lichfield cathedral, since the old liturgies were no longer acceptable, and in c1606 it was bought as part of a 'job lot' by

Shrewsbury School, who still owned it in 1994. The fragments of drama it contains consist of several pages which form the part played by one performer, 'Triplex.' He was the third Shepherd in the play of The Shepherds, and the third Mary in The Resurrection, as well as taking one other part which is harder to identify. The fragments were incorporated into some of the Mystery Plays performed round Lichfield on May 1 and 2 1994. The book, in 1994, still in its medieval binding, was considered virtually priceless (info from the programme for The Lichfield Mysteries Plays. Lichfield May 1994. p22p). **Persons and visitors**. In 1402 **Henry IV** ordered knights, squires, and yeomen from various parts of the country to Lichfield for his campaign against Owen Glyn Dwr (VCH vol 14 p12). He was in Lichfield before and after the battle of Shrewsbury in 1403 and 1404 (SOSH p157) (R&S p14) (RVW p10). He was at Lichfield in 1405 summoning a parliament to be held at Coventry (W p487). In 1414 the King's Bench sat at Lichfield for over three weeks. **Henry V** stayed at Burton Abbey to oversee the proceedings (Henry V. GL Harriss. pp65-66) (VCH vol 14 p12). Others have Henry V spending two months at Lichfield in 1414 (NSFCT 1909 pp156-157) (SOP p92) (R&S p14). **John Grace**, preacher, was in Lichfield. It was in Lichfield that he narrowly escaped death at the hands of the mob in 1425 (HOWW p259). **William de Lichfield**, divine and poet, d1448 (DNB) or d1447, was born in Lichfield; he was the author of 3083 sermons (HWE vol 2 p309). (No entry in VCH vol 14). **Robert Whittin(g)ton** (or Whytynton, Whittinton), the noted grammarian and poet. He was born in Lichfield probably shortly before 1480 and is said to have attended Lichfield Grammar School. He styled himself as 'Protovates Angliae' (fl 1530) (DNB) (HWE vol 2 p309) (NHS p275) (SHOS vol 1 p329) (HOL pp439-440) (SMC p166) (VCH vol 14 p170) (SAL p112) (VFC p142). He may have taught at Lichfield Grammar School sometime between 1513 and 1518 (NSJFS 1979 p4). **Richard, Earl of Warwick**, passed through Lichfield in 1460 to meet the Duke of York at Shrewsbury (VCH vol 14 p12). **Edward IV** was at Lichfield in 1461 (R&S p16) to dine with Bishop Hale. In 1462 he made an agreement at Lichfield with the Earl of Warwick and spent two weeks here in 1473 (VCH vol 14 p14). The **Duke of Clarence** visited Lichfield in 1466 (VCH vol 14 p13). **Lord Stanley** was at Lichfield prior to the battle of Bosworth in 1485 (VCH vol 14 p12). Henry Tudor, Earl of Richmond (**Henry VII**), camped with his army of 5,000 men near Lichfield on Aug 15 prior to the battle, having travelled from Milford Haven by way of Shrewsbury and Stafford (LGS p227). He was received with military honours at Lichfield by Sir William Stanley, younger brother of Lord Stanley (VCH vol 14 p12). On Aug 16 he was, says Harwood, 'joyfully received into the city, which two days before Lord Stanley had evacuated with the appearance of flying before him.' Richmond left Lichfield on the evening of Aug 16, attended only by his private guards (HOL pp302,303). It has been stated that he only arrived at 'The camp near Tamworth' (said to be at Hopwas) on Aug 18 (R&S p18). Richmond's whereabouts in the meantime have been the subject of dispute. The official line was that he lost his way, although it has been surmised, that he stayed with Lord Stanley at Elford (SHOS vol 1 part 1 p50) (HOL pp302,303) (LGS p227) (SOSH p163) (RVW p10).

GRAMMAR SCHOOL. Some have said there was a grammar school in existence at Lichfield by 1440 and it may have been connected to St John's Hospital (NHS p275) (SHOS vol 1 p329) (HOL pp439-440) (SMC p166) (SAL p112). A free grammar school was founded by Bishop William Smith in 1495 as part of his refoundation of St John's Hospital. The school house was opposite St John's Hospital in St John's Street from 1587. New buildings replaced those on the existing site, opened in 1850. The grammar school became part of the mixed comprehensive King Edward VI School after amalgamating with Kings Hill Secondary Modern in 1971 (VCH vol 6 pp159-161). (SHOS vol 1 p322*) (GM vol 64 p413 il of) (SOSH pp175il,179). The old practice of 'barring out' the masters on Shrove Tuesday (or Goodish Tuesday, as it was also sometimes called) prevailed at Lichfield Grammar School (SCSF p10). The custom flourished during the late C17 (FOS p84). Hughes says, a new grammar school was built in Lichfield in 1903 (SOSH p179). Rev Thomas Harwood (1767-1842), author of HOL and publisher of SOS in 1820 and 1844, was headmaster from 1791 to 1813 (SHOS vol 1 p322) (SLM autumn 1953 p26il,28) (SH pp36,123,136 il of facing). **Alumni**: Robert Whittin(g)ton (1480s) (see above); author William Wollaston whose childhood was spent at Great Bloxwich (see); Bishop Smalridge; five judges who sat on the bench at the same time - John Willes (1685-1761), Sir Thomas Parker (?1695-1784), William Noel (1695-1762), Sir John Eardley Wilmot (1709-1792), and Sir Richard Lloyd; Baron of the Exchequer Dr James; Elias Ashmole (1617-1692); Gregory King (1648-1712) (see below); poet Isaac Hawkins Browne the elder (1672-1719); essayist Joseph Addison (1672-1719) (VFC p1); mathematicians John Rowley (see below), and John Colson (1680-

1760); inventor John Wyatt (1700-1766) of Thickbroom Hall (see); physician Robert James (1705-1776); Thomas Newton (1707-1782), bishop of Bristol; lexicographer Dr Samuel Johnson (1709-1784) (see below); Theophilus Lowe, canon of Windsor (d1769), who reputedly equalled Johnson as a scholar (Johnsonian Gleanings. AL Reade. Part III. 1922. p125); actor David Garrick (1717-1779) (see below); Henry Salt (1780-1827), Egyptologist (see below); entomologist and palaeographer John Obadiah Westwood (1805-1893); poet and playwright Thomas LF Livingstone (1829-1891) (VFC p86); poet William Arthur Wood (b1857) (PSS pp307-309) (VFC p145); Tom Langley (b1907), author on pugilist fighters (BCM Jan 1974 p25). (HOL pp496-499) (W p507).

1500 to 1600. In 1548 the bishop surrendered his manorial rights in return for a £50 rent charge (NSJFS 1979 p4). A governmental vacuum would have ensued had not the town been granted a **charter of incorporation** in 1547 (HOL pp312-335; date given is 1549). Lichfield was the first Staffs town to be incorporated (HOL p335) (HOS p56). Henceforth it was to be ruled by two bailiffs to be elected annually, and a council of 24, elected jointly by the bailiffs and citizens; it also acquired a common seal, a steward, a prison, and licence to purchase land to the value of £20 per annum (NSJFS 1979 p5). The charter also dignified the town with the title of 'City' (HOL pp336,337,338). Queen Mary issued a new charter in 1553 which confirmed the 1548 charter, and made Lichfield a county, creating Lichfield County (see). As a county Lichfield had its own sheriff, and was exempt from hundred courts, yet remained geographically situated in the South Division of Offlow hundred (W p482) (NSJFS 1979 p5) (VCH vol 14 p15). The right to use a common **seal** was granted to the corporation by the charter of 1548. The design of 1549 shows three dismembered bodies which were supposed to represent some of the Christians massacred by Diocletian (VCH vol 14 pp85,86il). (NHS p399). The seal was altered slightly in 1622, 1688, and in the C18. The Corporation seal was carved on the pediment of the old Guildhall (SHOS vol 1 p343), fragments of it remain in the Museum Gardens. (HOL p356). The arms of the City of Lichfield appear on the N abutment of the W side of St John Street railway bridge. A heraldic device of chevrons on a checky field was also used as arms by the late C17 (VCH vol 14 p86). The **arms** of Lichfield city, authorized in 1950, are: Checky of nine gold and ermine in each of the gold squares a chevron gules. The supporters are: Dexter, St Chad vestured in alb and amice proper with orphreys vert embroidered in gold, a dalmatic also vert with gold embroidery, and a gold chasuble trimmed with green and embroidered with gold; his gloves white and shoes purple; in the bend of his right arm a gold pastoral staff, and in his right hand a model of Lichfield Cathedral proper; and Sinister, a Guild Master of Lichfield in C15 dress proper, carrying in his left hand a bunch of red roses with stalks and leaves proper. The **motto**, which was Dr Johnson's choice, is: 'Salve Magna Parens' (Hail, Great Parent) (CH pp333il,334) (VCH vol 14 p86il). The **Lichfield Martyrs** refers to three people burnt at the stake in Lichfield Market Place during Mary I's reign. They were Thomas Hayward and John Goreway burnt in Sept 1555, and Joyce Lewis of Mancetter near Atherstone, Warws, daughter of Sir Thomas Curzon of Croxall Hall, burnt at 9.00am on Dec 18 1557 for heresy (VCH vol 3 p46) (LAWTT pp26-27) (LAL p7p of the plaque to the Lichfield Martyrs in Market Place). Another account has Joyce Bowers burnt at the stake in Lichfield after the Reformation (SK p96). In 1563 Lichfield was the **county's largest populated town**, with Wolverhampton next and Stafford next (SL p155). The city was struck by **plague** in 1564, 1593, 1594, 1645, 1646 (HOL pp302,304,306) (SCSF pp134,137). The plague of 1593 took 1000 lives, and the one of 1646 took 821 lives (HOL) (HOWW p227). Alrewas PR records that the steeples of St Mary's and St Michael's blew off in the **storm** of 1593 or 1594 (SHOS vol 1 p138). **Persons and visitors**. **John Leland**, visited Lichfield sometime between 1535-1543, and noted that the pools - Sandford Pool, Minster Pool, and Stowe Pool - divided the city into north and south parts (VCH vol 14 pp1,3). **Edward VI** was in Lichfield on Sept 23 1547 and apparently visited the cathedral (VCH vol 14 p16). **Elizabeth I** arrived at Lichfield from Kenilworth on July 27 1575. She appears to have stayed elsewhere and returned to Lichfield on July 30. Here she stayed until Aug 3, when she left for Chartley Hall (Alrewas PR) (SHOS vol 1 p333) (SMC p164) (HOL p304) (W p488) (R&S pp23-24) (VCH vol 14 p16). Whilst in Lichfield or on another occasion she gave her penknife to a Lichfield family. It was for some years in Greene's Museum and was eventually presented to the BM by Rev Henry White's brother Thomas (SHOSA vol 2 p9). **Sampson Camden**, a native of Lichfield and a house-painter who had moved to London, was the father of William Camden (1551-1623) 'The British Pausanias,' author of Britannia (1586) (Dictionary of Authors. S Austin Allibone. 1859 vol 1) (HOPT vol 1 p5). **Edmund Genings** (or Gennings), a Catholic priest beheaded on Dec 10 1591, was born in Lichfield in 1567 of a Protestant family. He was ordained an RC priest at Rheims in 1590 and returned to Lichfield, but captured in London. He was beatified in 1929 (BSB p223) (VCH vol 14 p155).

SHERIFF'S RIDE. The Sheriff's Ride is the 'perambulation' of Lichfield city or county boundary led by the sheriff on horseback followed by at least one member of every family in the town (MR p215). **Origins**. The ride dates from 1548 when Edward VI gave Lichfield the rights of a city and ordered the bailiffs to make an annual perambulation of the city's bounds. This took place on May 1 and was accompanied by the sheriff of Staffordshire (VCH vol 14 p83). After the creation of the county of Lichfield in 1553 the sheriff of Lichfield headed the ride, and the date was moved to the feast of the Nativity of the Virgin Mary (Sept 8) (SCSF p27) (VCH vol 14 p83). Hackwood implies the ride has its origins before the time of Mary in an ecclesiastical perambulation of Lichfield in Rogation week. He says some believe the date of the ride was moved from Rogation week to the Nativity of the Blessed Virgin some time after the Civil War, probably at the Restoration (SCSF pp27,28). The main **purpose of the ride** was to perpetuate from generation to generation the remembrance of Lichfield's boundary for legal reasons. Gradually it became a social event, with much drinking and gaiety along the way, and collation at the Guildhall at the end. The custom had a practical importance. During the Civil Wars some of the town archives were destroyed, and in 1656 the civic authorities won a boundary dispute with Lord Paget on the evidence of an old man who had 'beaten the bounds' as a youth (MR p215). A Corporation Charter granted or confirmed by Charles II provided that 'the bailiffs and common councilmen shall annually on the Nativity of the Blessed Virgin (Sept 8) perambulate the boundaries of the city and county of Lichfield and the precincts thereof' (SCSF p27). **Description of the ride**. The **length of the circuit** was believed to be 16 miles long and the ride has been described as the 'sixteen jolliest miles in Staffordshire.' But there is no surviving perambulation before the later C18 (VCH vol 14 p1). By 1962 the circuit was thought to be more like 18 miles. In 1978 Jon Raven estimated the length of the ride to be 24 miles (FOS pp116-117). The **route** in 1921 was up Beacon Street, to Cross-in-the-hand Lane, Lyncroft Hill, Lea Grange, Elmhurst, Stychbrook, Curborough, Brownfields, Gosling Lane, Trent Valley Road, Darnford Mill, Freeford, Knowle, Birmingham Road, Aldershawe, Sandyway, Pipe Grange, Maple Hayes, Pipe Green, Abnalls Lane and then back to the Cross-in-hand Lane where the perambulation ended in the presence of the City Mace and Sword Bearers and other uniformed attendants (SCSF p27). **Evolution and documentation**. Dr Johnson's father, Michael Johnson was Sheriff in 1709, and headed the 'ride' the day after his son's birth. 'An Account of the Life of Dr Samuel Johnson, from his birth to his eleventh year, written by himself' relates that when asked by his wife who he would invite to the 'Riding' the following day, Michael Johnson replied, 'All the town now' (Johnson on Johnson. John Wain. 1976 pp1-2) (Young Samuel Johnson. James L Clifford. 1955 1962 ed. pp3,7). According to Hackwood, who seems to have attended the ride in 1921, the ride had taken place without a break since 1553 (SCSF p27). After Lichfield County was reunited with Staffs in 1888 the shrievalty was continued as an office of dignity (VCH vol 14 p83). In 1921 the assembly (which included the Mayor, the Corporation and the city officials) met at the Guildhall, where the sheriff entertained his friends with light refreshments. By 1962, at least one sheriff had used a jeep to complete the ride. The first woman sheriff was Councillor Mary Halfpenny, chosen in 1968 (VCH vol 14 p83). In Sept 1971 Major General JA d'Avigdor-Goldsmid was the first MP to take part in the ride (LTM Oct 1971 p31ps). By 1978 the ride was held on the nearest Saturday to Sept 8 'so that the local pony club can participate' (FOS pp116-117) (MR p215). (SHOS vol 1 p316) (HOL pp356-358,360) (CSL pp26,27,28) (SA Sept 14 1912 p10 col 4) (BCC vol 3 pp63-64) (SOSH p155) (SJC p9) (VB pp26,27) (WMAG Sept 1979 p31) (AA p259). In 1988 the ride took place on Sept 10. The riders (who would have previously applied to take part in the ride) congregated in Market Square by 10.00am. After an assembly at the Guildhall the sheriff then arrived in the Market Square and chose the best 100-150 'turned out' riders to accompany him. At 10.30am the sheriff mounted his horse and 'started' the ride. Lunch and horse racing took place at Freeford Manor, followed by the sheriff's presentation of the Sheriff's Cup and the Stirrup Cup to winners. There was tea at Pipe Hall Farm. At about 6.00pm the ride was greeted in Abnalls Lane by the town Crier and Mace Bearers who then led it in ceremony through the streets to the cathedral Close, arriving at about 6.20pm. Here the ride was met by the dean and chapter. After glasses of sherry the ride was led in ceremony by the Crier and Mace Bearers to the Guildhall, where after further refreshments and congratulations to the sheriff the ride dispersed (info George Kemp - Sheriff in 1988) (Your Horse Magazine. Nov 1988). One of the seven Lichfield Morris dances is called 'Sher-

iff's Ride' (LTM Nov 1971 pp10-11).

1600 to 1648. **Persons and visitors**. The last heretic to burn at the stake in England, **Edward Wightman**, died in the Market Place on April 11 1611 or 1612. Wightman was a puritan and a mercer from Burton who is said to have called himself the Holy Ghost and held heretical and blasphemous opinions. He was about to be burnt in Lichfield Market Place in March 1611 or 12 but recanted. Later he re-asserted his heresies and was burnt on April 11 (Antitrinitarian Biography. Robert Wallace) (Narrative History of King James. Somers Tracts. vol 2) (Magna Britain. vol v. p6) (SHOS vol 1 p17) (HOL pp304-305) (W p535) (VCH vol 3 p59. vol 14 p16) (Loyal and Ancient City. Howard Clayton. pp7-9) (STMSM July 1979 p32p of the plaque to Wightman in Market Place) (ZSB) (LAL p7p of the plaque to Wightman). **James I** passed through Lichfield on several journeys, particularly in 1622 and 1624 (Magna Britannia vol 5 p6) (HOL p304) (W p488). **Michael East**, composer, became Master of the Choristers sometime between 1610-1618, remaining in Lichfield until his death in 1648 (VCH vol 3 p172). **Elias Ashmole**, Windsor Herald to Charles II and founder of the Ashmolean Museum, was born at Priests' Hall (see) in 1617, the son of Simon Ashmole, a saddler. He attended Lichfield Grammar School, and was a chorister in Lichfield cathedral. In 1638 he became a solicitor. In the Civil War he was a royalist and in 1644 the King appointed him commissioner of excise at Lichfield; later he entered Brasenose College, Oxford. In 1660 he was made Windsor Herald, called to the Bar, and in 1669 received the degree of Doctor of Medicine from Oxford. In 1667 Ashmole presented a silver drinking bowl to the bailiffs of the corporation. It has been known as the Ashmole Steeple Cup (PSS pp23-29 il) (Elias Ashmole. CH Josten. 1966 vol 1 p11) (STMSM April 1979 pp10,11). It was made in 1666 and has a cover and three roundels, each depicting a dismembered body; an illusion to the Christians traditionally massacred at Lichfield (VCH vol 14 p87). The cup was on show in St Mary's Centre in the late 1980s (VCH vol 14 p87). Lichfield Corporation promoted Ashmole's candidature for one of the Lichfield seats in the 1685 general election, but he withdrew under royal pressure to make way for Richard Leveson (SHC 1950/ 1 pp215-227) (VCH vol 14 p93). Ashmole observed a ceremonial drinking custom at Lichfield. The first two toasts always were to the reigning monarch and then to 'Weale and Worship' drunk from a massive embossed goblet holding three or four quarts 'The Mayor drinks first, and on his rising, the persons on his right and left also rise. He then hands the cup to the person on his right side, when the one next to him rises the one on the left of the mayor still standing. Then the cup is passed across the table to him, when his left-hand neighbour rises; so that there are always three standing at the same time - one next person who drinks, and one opposite him' (IADC p143). Ashmole died on May 18 1692 and was buried in South Lambeth church. Some money given annually to the poor in the later C18 was known as Ashmole's Charity. It was not established by Ashmole's will, and was interest off a sum, probably accumulated from gifts he had made to Lichfield's poor in his lifetime (VCH vol 14 p190). In the C19 there was a half-length portrait of Ashmole at Blythe Hall, Warws, the family seat of Sir William Dugdale (HOL p446). (NHS pp276-277) (SMC p47) (HOL pp440-442 note) (SHOS vol 1 pp239-330) (SOS ppxlvi, xlvii, xlix) (W pp504-505) (SSW pp55-61) (S p118) (SOSH pp224,225il,226) (Elias Ashmole (1617-1692) 5 vols. CH Josten. 1966) (STMSM Dec 1978 p32p of a print of his bust from a copy in WSL) (SH pp68,69) (VFC p5). Bishop **Edward Wetenhall** (Wettenhall, Whitnall, Whetenhall, Whitnall, Withnoll and Wythnall), was born in Lichfield on Oct 7 1636. In 1679 he became bishop of Cork and Ross, being translated to the bishopric of Kilmore and Ardagh in 1699. He died in London on Nov 12 1713 and was buried in Westminster Abbey (SMC p166) (DNB) (PSS p473) (VFC p141). He appears to be the Edward Wettenhall MD of Cork who came into possession of the High House, Stafford, and Loxdale thought that he might have been born at Tixall (HOT p74).

CIVIL WAR. The cathedral and Close were garrisoned by both sides in the Civil War and besieged three times. The Earl of Chesterfield and Sir Richard Dyott were commanders of the garrison for the king from Feb 1643 (LGS p165) (VCH vol 3 p174), and the **first siege** took place when the parliamentarians besieged the royalist garrison on 2 March 1643. On this day, the parliamentarian leader, Lord Brooke, was shot dead outside a house in Dam Street by John 'Dumb' Dyott stationed on the central tower of the cathedral. The house in Dam Street has become known as Brooke House, and the event is alluded to in Walter Scott's epic poem 'Marmion' (W p488) (BEV p141) (LGS p165) (SOSH pp197-199). Sir John Gell took over as parliamentary leader and with Sir William Brereton's reinforcements the garrison was taken by the parliamentarians on March 5 1643 (VCH vol 3 p174. vol 14 p17). The cathedral was perhaps the first seized by the parliamentarians (SHOS vol 1 p237-243). The **second siege** began immediately after, with the royalists besieging a parliamentary garrison under Col Russell. The royalist Col Henry Hastings made an attempt to retake the garrison on March 21 but failed. Prince Rupert arrived on April 7 and set up his artillery on Prince Rupert's Mound (see) (VCH vol 14 p17). The parliamentary garrison surrendered on April 21 1643 (VCH vol 14 p17), or according to Masefield, was taken on April 20 (LGS p166). The city and garrison then passed to the royalists and was governed by Col Richard Bagot (see Bagot's Bromley). Queen Henrietta Maria passed through Lichfield in July 1643 on her way S from Bridlington. Prince Rupert passed through in March 1644 on his way to relieve Newark and again on his way back (VCH vol 14 p17). Charles I, after fleeing from the battle of Naseby, lodged on Sunday June 15 1645 at the Bishop's Palace (VCH vol 14 p17); leaving for Bewdley (SOB p77) via Wolverhampton (Collectanea Curiosa vol 3. Gutch) (HOL p28). Col Bagot also returned to Lichfield after Naseby and died of wounds in the Close in July 1645 (VCH vol 14 p17). A plague which broke out in July 1645 and continued into 1646 affected the town but not the Close (VCH vol 14 p17). Charles I stayed at Lichfield for two nights in Aug 1645 (VCH vol 14 p17). Or he passed through on Aug 10, and travelled on to Newark (LGS p166) (SOB p77). In Jan 1646 Sir Thomas Tyldesley was appointed governor. On March 9 1646 Sir William Brereton captured the city for the parliamentarians, and immediately after took place the **third siege** of the garrison in the Close (VCH vol 14 p17) (SSGLST pp35-38). Homeshaw says the siege began almost a year prior to the final surrender (SOB p77). The royalist garrison surrendered on July 10 1646 (HOL pp19-26,305-306) (HOS p36) (SOB p77) and the Close was evacuated on July 16 (VCH vol 14 p18). It was the last garrison in Staffs to surrender and one of the last in the country (VCH vol 14 p18). The Lichfield Surrender Articles, dated July 18 1646, are articles for the delivering up of Lichfield Close by the royalists after the third siege. Greene made a transcript of the Articles on March 12 1771 from the original then in the possession of Egerton Bagot of Pipe Hall in Warws; the blank spaces denote the parts which had either been torn off or perished (HOL pp30-34; gives a copy of the Articles) (HS p236 p of the title page). The WSL has an incomplete transcript copy. (WJO Aug 1904 pp210-213) (SOSH pp199-200) (The Siege of Lichfield: A tale illustrative of the great rebellion. 1881 2nd ed. W Gresley).

1648 to 1700. Gilt or silver **maces** to be carried before the bailiffs by the serjeants-at-arms were authorized by the charter of 1622. These were apparently lost during the Commonwealth period. Two were presumably made at the time of the 1664 charter. One of these was lost in 1690 to be replaced by another (VCH vol 14 p86). Queen Victoria is said to have said Lichfield's rare silver-gilt maces were the finest she had seen outside London (STMSM April 1979 pp10,11). By the late 1980s there were two maces of the City of Lichfield on display at St Mary's Centre, Lichfield. Lichfield was one supposed centre for the Yarrington Plot of 1661, and arrests were made in Walsall (Deliver Us From Evil. RL Greaves. p74) (LOU p347). **Religious quarrel**. A disputation between a Quaker and the Muggletonian Thomas Tomkinson took place at a Lichfield inn, apparently in the 1670s (DNB) (VCH vol 14 p157). There were **fires** in Lichfield in late 1681, or early 1682, and in 1697 (VCH vol 14 p21). The Lichfield (Horse) **Races** began in the 1680s on Fradley Heath (see) and moved to Whittington Heath (see) in the 1700s. **Some late C17 notes**. Walter Chetwynd of Ingestre noted in 1689 'the fair ladies of Lichfield' (VCH vol 14 p22). His guest at Ingestre, Dr Plot, thought the city was physically gradually sinking like Newcastle-under-Lyme. In a Lichfield coffee house Plot was shown a raven whose upper mandible was turned downward and crossed the lower, but the under one was straight (NHS pp113,234). **Persons and visitors. Gregory King**, herald, genealogist, engraver and statistician, was born in Stow Street, Lichfield, on Dec 15 1648 (HOL pp446-447,510) (GNHS p165) (DNB). He was teaching in Lichfield in 1669 (VCH vol 14 p181). At the end of 1669 he became the steward, auditor and secretary of the Dowager Lady Jane (Lady Gerard and Baroness Gerard) of Gerrard's Bromley Hall (see) and from then until 1672 he resided at Sandon Old Hall (see), when he returned to London. He became Registrar of the College of Arms in 1683 and conducted several installations of Knights of the Garter. He was the engraver for a new edition of Camden's 'Britannia' and the edition of 'Æsop's Fables' (2 vols. London. 1672-3). In Queen Anne's reign he became Secretary to the Comptrollers of army accounts, and to the Commissioners for stating the public accounts. He died on Aug 29 1712 and was buried in the chancel of St Benet's, Paul's Wharf, London, where there is a monument to him (SHOS vol 1 p330 after L. 16. SHOSA vol 2 p9) (HOL pp446-447) (DNB) (SH p57). **George Fox**, the founder of the Society of Friends or Quakers, visited Lichfield at the beginning of the winter of 1651, shortly after his release from Derby gaol and preaching near Burton upon Trent. In his Journal he describes how he had a vision here of blood flowing through the streets and went about exclaiming, 'Woe unto the bloody city

Lichfield!' (HS p235) (LGS pp178-179) (VCH vol 3 p117) (HOS pp31-32). No one hindered him, and he afterwards concluded that he had been sent by God to 'raise up' the blood of the 999 Christian martyrs who had been massacred by Diocletian (SSE 1987 pp105-106ils) (VCH vol 14 pp38,157). The inscription on a plaque to Fox in the Market Place says, during this visit he stood without shoes in the Market Place and denounced the City of Lichfield (LAL p7p of the plaque). One of the seven Lichfield Morris dances is called 'The Bare-footed Quaker' (LTM Nov 1971 pp10-11). Dame **Joyce Blundell** complained in a petition after the Restoration that she had had her plate, valued at £2,000, seized by Col Richard Bagot to pay the King's troops garrisoned at Lichfield as she travelled through the city (HOS pp34-35). **Thomas Dilke**, playwright, author of the comedy 'The Lover's Luck' (1696) and the tragicomedy 'The City Lady' (1697), was born in Lichfield (VFC p39). The **wife of one Dilk**, a foot-post in Lichfield in the C17, bore five children in a year at two separate births (NHS p277). **James II** stayed at Lichfield on Aug 31 1687 and lodged at Lady Littleton's house in the Close (the Deanery - VCH vol 14 p24) and touched various persons for the King's Evil in the cathedral before going on to Coventry (HOL pp308-309) (Handbook of Lichfield. Hewitt) (SCSF p151) (RVW p13) (R&S pp30-31); a year earlier, after the surrender of the Corporation's charters and the granting of a new charter, he had given the city a civic sword which has been exhibited in the St Mary's Centre in the Market Place (HOL p348) (W p491) (SOSH p155). In June 1690 **William III** passed through Lichfield on his way to Ireland and stayed one night at the Deanery in the Close (HOL p309) (RVW p13) (R&S p32) (VCH vol 14 p24). The writer and traveller **Celia Fiennes** visited Lichfield in summer 1697 and noted the city lay 'low and waterish' (VCH vol 14 p3). She wrongly thought Coventry was still, with Lichfield, the bishop's See (VCH vol 14 p22).

1700 to 1750. Lichfield of the early 1720s was described by poet Isaac Hawkins Browne as 'the Paphos of England' on account of its pretty women (VCH vol 14 p22). In the 1730s or 1740s Dr Wilkes described Lichfield as 'the most genteel place in the county' (VCH vol 14 p22). An infantry regiment was founded at the King's Head Inn (see) in 1705. At a by-election in Lichfield in 1718 a mob supporting the Pretender attacked the Whigs (VCH vol 14 p19), or in April 1717 (LOU pp100,360). For the political disturbances of the Staffordshire County election 1747 at Lichfield Races on Whittington Heath see Introduction. There is a tollhouse on the corner of Beacon Street and Wheel Lane which dates from the early 1730s (LAL p22p) (VCH vol 14 p45). **Persons and visitors. Frances, Countess of Huntingdon**, lived in Lichfield after she was widowed in 1701 until 1705 or later (HOL p469) (VCH vol 14 p22). A man named **John Rowley**, a mathematician, born at Lichfield, is said to have invented the orrery, a clockwork model of the solar system, and to have named it after his patron, the 4th Earl of Orrery (1676-1731). However, Rowley appears to have merely taken up the idea from a Mr George Graham, and made the first instrument for the Earl of Orrery (HOL p448) (GNHS p165) (Johnsonian Gleanings. AL Reade. Part III. 1922. p135). **George Farquhar** (1678-1707), playwright, was billeted at the George Hotel (see) and stayed at the Castle Inn (see), both in Lichfield. Hewitt says Queen Anne visited Lichfield to touch for the King's Evil; on which occasion Johnson, as a boy, was touched by her (Handbook of Lichfield. Hewitt). But others, including Hackwood, say Queen Anne never visited Lichfield (SCSF p151). **Thomas Newton** (d1782), bishop of Bristol from 1761, was born in Bird Street on Jan 1 1707; his brother, Andrew, founded Newton's College (see) (SHOS vol 1 p330) (HOL pp293,448) (GNHS p165 note). Some give 1703 for Thomas Newton's date of birth (W pp499,505) (VFC p98). The plaque on the house says he was born in 1704 (LAL p43p). **Daniel Defoe** visited Lichfield sometime before 1723 and thought it was the best town in the county and noted the city was divided into two by the sheets of water - Sandford, Minister, and Stowe Pools - creating one part called the 'Town' and other called the 'Close' (VCH vol 14 pp3,22). He considered the cathedral 'one of the finest and most beautiful in England' (VCH vol 14 p3). **John Loveday** was a visitor in 1732 (VCH vol 14 p19). **Horace Walpole** visited in 1743 and wrote of it that 'the bog in which the cathedral ....stands stagnates, I believe, midst beds of poppy and makes all its inhabitants as sleepy as its bishops and canons' although he thought the cathedral 'very fine' (VCH vol 14 p3). On Nov 28 1745 the **Duke of Cumberland** reached Lichfield in a bid to stop the Young Pretender in the 1745 Jacobite Rebellion; he took command from Sir John Ligonier (NSFCT 1925 p54). In 1746 the composer **Musgrave Heighington** performed in the city (VCH vol 14 p164).

THE LICHFIELD 'LIONS.' Members of a loose literary circle resident or native of Lichfield covering much of the C18, referred to as the Lichfield 'lions,' may be said to include: Gilbert Walmesley, a native of Lichfield and diocesan registrar from 1707, who lived in the Bishop's Palace from the late

1720s until his death in 1751; Richard Greene who created Greene's Museum (see); prebendary Sneyd Davies, poet and resident in Lichfield from c1751 to 1769; John Alcock (1715-1806), vicar choral and organist at Lichfield cathedral 1749-1760 and author of the novel 'Life of Miss Fanny Brown: a Novel' and church music (BS) (SSAHST 1979-80 pp25-33); Priscilla Pointon, poet, who was born in Lichfield in 1750 and brought up in the city. She became blind at the age of 13 and her 'Poems on Several Occasions' appeared in 1770 (PSS pp387-389) (VFC p107); prebendary Thomas Seward, writer, who took up residence at the Bishop's Palace shortly after Walmesley's death; his daughter Anna who became a celebrated poet; Samuel Johnson and David Garrick, whom Walmesley encouraged in their youth; scientist Dr Erasmus Darwin, resident between 1758 and 1780; and 'literati' Richard Lovell Edgeworth and Thomas Day. The activities in Lichfield of the last six are expanded on in the next four paragraphs.

SAMUEL JOHNSON. **Early Years**. Dr Samuel Johnson, England's greatest C18 literary figure and lexicographer, was born in a house in Breadmarket Street on Sept 7 (or 18 New Style) **1709**. For Johnson's ancestry on his paternal side and maternal (the Fords) side see The Reades of Blackwood Hill with a full account of Dr Johnson's Ancestry Aleyn Lyell Reade (1906). For Johnson's birthplace see Johnson's Birthplace. The PR of St Mary's church, Lichfield, records his baptism **on the** day of his birth (LGS p176) (LAL p7). He was nursed by Joan Marklew in George Lane. When 'not quite three years old' he was reputedly carried **to** Lichfield cathedral on his father's shoulders to hear Dr Henry Sacheverell **preach**. Yet Sacheverell's only recorded visit to Lichfield was in **1710** (VCH vol 3 p63) (Johnsonian Gleanings. AL Reade. Part III. 1922. pp67-71) (**Life** of Johnson. J Boswell. ed. GB Hill and LF Powell vol 1 p39), and **many doubt** the story. Two dame-schools are connected with Johnson. He **attended Dame Oliver's School** (see) in **1714** and afterwards was taught by **Tom Brown**. This may have been in a school kept by Tom Brown, a shoemaker, **or by Thomas Brown**, master at Minor's School (founded in 1670), **which stood** on the corner of Bore Street and St John Street, or as Brown's **private pupil** (VCH vol 14 pp171,173,174). In **1716** Johnson entered Lichfield **Grammar School**. In **1725** he was refused entry to the school after prolonged absence. In autumn 1725 he left for Stourbridge Grammar School. He returned in summer **1726**. Clifford says he may have been in Stourbridge up to the end of Oct 1726. Boswell says he is at Stourbridge for little more than a year. Between 1726-1728 Johnson worked for his father as a bookshop keeper and was a guest in the households of Gilbert Walmesley, Capt Peter Garrick, Theophilus Levett, Stephen Simpson, John Marten, William Butt, and Edmund Hector snr, whose son, Edmund (1708-1794), was Johnson's childhood friend, and whose daughter, Ann, (1711-1788) was Johnson's first love; Edmund jnr later became a surgeon and lived in Birmingham, and his sister Ann later married Rev Walter Carless. In Oct **1728** Johnson left for Pembroke College, Oxford. He left Oxford and returned to Lichfield on Dec 12 **1729**. Boswell says he left Oxford in autumn **1731**. He left to be usher at Market Bosworth, Leics, on July 16 **1732** and returned to Lichfield in Feb **1734**. Boswell relates an incident, for which there is no date, in which Johnson had to forcibly remove a man who had taken his seat at a Lichfield playhouse. Clifford suggests it may have been at a performance of Colley Cibber's farce 'Hob: Or the Country Wake' at the Guildhall in c1734 and the incident concerned a Scots officer and an innkeeper. Between 1734-1735 Johnson went back and forth between Lichfield and Birmingham, attending Mrs Porter his future wife. He worked as a tutor for the Whitbys of Great Haywood (probably those of The Old Manor House, Little Haywood) from May to June 1735. He opened the school at Edial Hall in Dec 1735 or in early **1736**. Edial Academy closed in Feb 1737. Johnson is said to have begun and finished his tragedy 'Irene' at Lichfield (SMC p172), whilst others say he wrote it at Edial Hall (NSFCT 1931 pp84-90). **Visits to Lichfield from London**. Dr G Birkbeck Hill in his edition of 'Boswell's Life of Johnson' records 13 visits Johnson made to Lichfield after moving to London (Dr Johnson and his Birthplace. A Retrospective and Guide. Johnson Birthplace Committee. 1933 p32). Johnson and Garrick left for London on March 2 **1737** and returned, briefly, to Lichfield in summer 1737. Johnson visited Lichfield from autumn **1739** to spring 1740, during which visit he saw his mother for the last time, and meets Molly Aston (DJL). Johnson's mother died in **1759** (DJL). Johnson paid a five week visit to Lichfield from winter **1761** to spring **1762**. Some say he was in Lichfield, or still in Lichfield, in July 1762 (Dr Johnson and his Birthplace. 1933 p32) or in Lichfield for only five days during the winter of 1761-2 (SSE 1988 p17). In summer and autumn **1767** he was in Lichfield for six months (but Boswell says three months) (SSE 1988 p17). During the visit he looked for his nurse's house and had a reunion with his parents maidservant, Catharine Chambers. Johnson visited Lichfield in Aug **1769** and noted how 'in Stowe Street where I left a draw

well I have found a pump.' He also found 'the lading well' in George Lane 'shamefully neglected' (VCH vol 14 p99). He was in Lichfield again in July **1770**. During this visit he probably stayed with Lucy Porter at Redcourt; on successive visits when travelling alone Johnson always stayed with Lucy Porter (DJL p213). He visited Lichfield between June 20 to after Aug 5 **1771** (SSE 1988 p17). According to some Johnson was also in Lichfield between Oct 15 and Dec 7 **1772** (DJL ix) (SSE 1988 p18). Between July 6 and 9 **1774** Johnson visited Lichfield with the Thrales en route to visit Mrs Thrale's birthplace in Wales. The party stayed at The Swan and visited Lucy Porter, Mrs Aston at Stowe Hill, and Greene's Museum (DJL p225). Johnson made a visit to Oxford, Lichfield and Ashbourne between May 29 to some time in Aug **1775** (SSE 1988 p18). Johnson and Boswell arrived in Lichfield on March 23 **1776** (or 22 - DJL p229) and stayed at the Three Crowns (LGS p176). They visited Lucy Porter, Peter Garrick and Johnson's schoolfellow Harry Jackson. During this visit Johnson declared the people of Lichfield 'the most sober, decent people in England, the genteelest in proportion to their wealth, and spoke the purest English.' During this visit Boswell tasted Staffordshire oat ale and oat cakes. On March 25 the date of their departure for London according to Hopkin Johnson alone dined at Mrs Gastrell's house much to Boswell's annoyance (DJL p231). Others say they left for London on March 26 having arrived on March 23. In 1776 and perhaps during this visit Johnson explained in a remark to Boswell why his fellow natives were not industrious (VCH vol 14 p1) see under industry. In **1777** Johnson left London for Oxford, Lichfield and Ashbourne in late July and returned in early Nov (SSE 1988 p18). Boswell visited him at Lichfield in Sept 1777. During a visit about this time Johnson and Boswell called in on Mrs (Moll) Cobb and Miss Adey at The Friary. According to Hopkin, but not Donald Greene, Johnson was in Lichfield in **1778** (DJL ix) (SSE 1988). Johnson was in Lichfield in May and June **1779**. During this visit Johnson went with Mrs Cobb to the Greenhill Bower. Boswell was in Lichfield alone in late Oct 1779 (DJL p232). Johnson visited Lichfield in autumn **1781** and found the 'Great Stile' at NE corner of Levett's field, which he played over as a child. Fondly remembering his time spent here, he succeeded in leaping over it twice. Johnson was the first to bring a copy of Fanny Burney's novel 'Evelina' (1778) to Lichfield (VCH vol 14 p23). Johnson's last visit to Lichfield was in Sept **1784**. He returned two books - 'A Treatise on Astma' by Dr Floyer, and 'The History of the Worthies of England' by Thomas Fuller - to Lichfield cathedral Library on Nov 9 1784 (LTM Dec 1972 p49). He died in London on Dec 13 1784. For the date of Johnson's penance in Uttoxeter market place see Uttoxeter. **After Johnson's death**. After Johnson's death, Johnson's servant, Francis Barber and his family came to live in Stowe Street, Lichfield. Later he moved to a neighbouring hamlet where he kept a school. After his death in 1801, at Stafford Infirmary (probably Staffordshire General Infirmary at Foregate (see)), his wife returned to Lichfield and opened a school (DJL p234); a direct descendent of Francis, Dennis Barber, was working as a bank manager in Market Drayton, Shrops, in 1999 (Sunday Telegraph. Oct 3 1999 p10pc). Lucy Porter died in Lichfield in **1786** (DJL ix). Mrs Piozzi (formerly Mrs Thrale) visited Lichfield in **1787** (DJL ix). In **1798** Shaw notes Johnson was a native of Lichfield (SHOS vol 1 pp323-329). By **1801** Johnson's birthplace was attracting visitors (Tour through Northern Countries of England and Borders of Scotland. R Walker. vol 1 pp104-105) (VCH vol 14 p23). In **1817** Mary Bagot of Blithfield noted that Lichfield was 'unfrequented now except by its regular inhabitants, who form a considerable society, very different from what it was in Johnson's day' (Links with the Past. Mrs Charles Bagot. (SL Bagot). 1901 p165) (VCH vol 14 pp31-32). In **1838**, at the expense of Rev Chancellor Law (W p485) (GNHS p157), a statue of a seated Johnson, to the design of Richard Cockle Lucas, was erected at the W end of the Market Place, Lichfield. The statue is seven feet high on a pedestal 10 feet high all in Yorkshire Magnesian limestone and weighs nine tons (W p485). The three reliefs, one on three of the four sides of the base, show i) the infant Johnson seated on his father's shoulders listening to Sacheverell's preaching in the cathedral, ii) his triumphal progress to school on the shoulders of his school-fellows, and iii) his famous penance in Uttoxeter market-place (LGS p175) (LAL p8p). (DoE II*) (BCGB pp383-385) (KES pp141,142) (SSW p51) (STMSM Nov 1972 p34ps) (BOE p194) (MR p213) (VCH vol 14 pl 25 showing RC Lucas inspecting the statue in 1859). In **1840**, probably in April, Johnson's birthplace was visited by Charles Dickens (Old Curiosity Shop. Biographical Edition of The Works of Charles Dickens in 8 vols. vol 5. 1902. xii). Johnson's birthplace was founded as a museum by Col John Gilbert in **1900** (SSW p52) and opened to the public in May **1901** (STMSM May 1979 p39). In **1908** a bronze statue of James Boswell, by Percy Fitzgerald, was erected at the E end of the Market Place (DoE II*) (LPL p) (LGS pp175-176) (SOSH p245) (CL Oct 3 1957 p662p) (STMSM Nov 1972 p35p) (BOE p194) (LAL p7p)

(MR p213). **Societies and recent customs**. The **Johnson Society of Lichfield** was founded in 1910 (VCH vol 14 p169). It appears to have been associated at an early stage with an annual supper which was occurring at the Three Crowns Inn on his birthday by at least 1910. The venue for it later moved to the Guildhall. It still (2000) continues (LGS p176) (Sunday Telegraph Review Section July 7 1996 p22). It had become a tradition by at least 1934 for a wreath to be laid at the foot of Johnson's statue, annually, on his birthday and for the cathedral choir to recite his last prayer on the steps of his birthplace (ES Sept 18 1934 p1p) (SJC p9). The supper and wreath-laying ceremony had been transferred to the nearest Saturday to Sept 18 by at least 1988 (AA p259) (info Pauline Simkins). Another custom is the raising of a glass of sherry on March 2 to commemorate the departure, for London, of Johnson and Garrick on this day in 1737 (Sunday Telegraph Review Section July 7 1996 p22). The present (2000) **Johnson Society of London**, was formed in 1928, to celebrate and promote the work of Johnson and that of his contemporaries. Unlike the Lichfield society it has regular meetings and lectures, which take place over the winter. Some time after WW2 the society started the custom of annual wreath laying on Johnson's tomb in Poet's Corner in Westminster Abbey at noon on the nearest Saturday to Dec 13 (info Mrs O' Donnell). (Johnsonian Gleanings. AL Reade. Part III. 'The Doctor's Boyhood.' 1922. pp125,193) (KES p175) (Young Samuel Johnson. James L Clifford. 1955 1962 ed. pp3,7,21-22,27,28,48,89,91-92,157,163) (STM Aug 1969 p29) (LTM Nov 1971 p13) (Johnson on Johnson. John Wain. 1976).

PETER AND DAVID GARRICK. Capt Garrick father of Peter (b1710) and David (b1716/7), actor, theatre manager, playwright and friend of Dr Johnson, moved to a house since known as David Garrick's House (see), Beacon Street, shortly after 1716 (LAL p21). Some think David was born at David Garrick's House (STM Aug 1969 p29), but he was in fact born at Hereford. David and his younger brother George were pupils of Dr Johnson at Edial Hall (see). David left for London with Johnson on March 2 1737. He established himself there as an actor principally after appearing as Richard III in 1741. When a Lichfield man went to London he was asked by Peter to deliver a letter to David. On seeing Garrick advertised in a performance he paid to go and see it, but he was so disgusted by 'the mean appearance and mercenary conduct' of the character, which he identified with the actor, that he refused to deliver the letter. David died in 1779 and was buried in Westminster Abbey; Johnson wrote on his tomb; 'His death eclipsed the gaiety of nations, and impoverished the public stock of harmless pleasure' (Life of Garrick. Murphy) (GM vol 71 p389) (SHOS vol 1 p330) (SHOSA vol 2 p9) (SOSH pp241il, 244) (S p118) (Cambridge Biographical Encyclopedia. David Crystal. 1994) (Theatrical Anecdotes. Ned Sherrin. p90) (VFC p52). In 1745 Peter commanded a volunteer company in Lichfield (VCH vol 14 p24). After Peter's death in 1795 a famous trial took between Mrs Docksey (sister of Peter and David Garrick) plaintiff and Stephen Panting of Lichfield, apothecary, defendant, which was held in ejectment before Baron Thomson and a special jury at Stafford lent assizes in 1796. The case was tried in St Mary's church, Stafford, as the town hall was being built. Panting of about 30 years old had been called on to be the man servant to the very aged (80 years old) Peter Garrick, who, in his senility gave all his estate to Panting, which Mrs Docksey rightly thought he never would have done if he was of sound mind instead giving it to his life long friends, Mr Bailye, and Mr Hinckley. The question was was Peter Garrick of sound mind when he made his will in 1795. The verdict proved in favour of the plaintiff (info from Stafford Reference Library).

ANNA SEWARD. Anna (or Anne) Seward, poet, has been described as the centre of a literary circle at Lichfield in the later C18. She was born in Eyam, Derbys, in 1747 when her father, Canon Thomas Seward, was rector of Eyam. Her mother was Elizabeth, daughter of Rev John Hunter, headmaster of Lichfield Grammar School and the teacher of Dr Johnson (DNB). In 1755 Thomas Seward became prebend of Pipa Parva in Lichfield cathedral (SHOS vol 1 p293) (GM vol xlv p192. vol li p624. vol lii p683). From 1749 (DJL viii), or 1754 (BS p396), or 1757 (The Cambridge Biographical Encyclopaedia. David Crystal. 1994) Anna resided in Lichfield: Her father is said to have resided at the Bishop's Palace (see) in the Close from 1754 (VCH vol 14 p22). In June 1764 her sister Sarah died when on the eve of marriage with Mr Porter, Dr Johnson's stepson. Mr Porter then took an interest in Anna, but she did not encourage his advances. After the death of her sister, Anna formed a close family relationship with her adopted sister, Honora Sneyd, who had come to live with the Sewards in 1756. She encouraged the liaison between Honora and Major John Andre (b1751) in the late 1760s. In 1773, however, Honora became the second wife of Richard Lovell Edgeworth, see below. When Andre was hung as a spy by the US military authorities in the American War of Independence in 1780 Seward wrote attacking George Washington in her 'Monody' (1781). After her father's death in 1790 Anna continued

to live in the Bishop's Palace until she died in 1809 (DJL viii) (CL Dec 30 1954 pp2312-2315 ps. Oct 3 1957 fig 4 p662). She was an advocate in having Minister Pool landscaped (LAL p39). At the palace she entertained poet William Hayley in 1782, violinist Wilhelm Cramer in 1796, landscape gardener Humphrey Repton in 1807, and poet Robert Southey in 1808 (VCH vol 14 p23,164); also in her circle were Henry Francis Cary of The Green (see), Thomas Day of Stowe House (see), and Rev George Butt (d1795), poet, novelist, playwright and religious writer, who was born in Lichfield on Dec 26 1741 (PSS pp89-96) (VFC pp22,119); Seward was a visitor to Bernard Granville at Calwich Priory (see), and is said to have had amorous desires for John Saville (d1803), Vicar-Choral of the cathedral. His monument in the cathedral has some verses written by her. She asked in her will to be buried beside him (HOL p89) (LGS p170). Her best known work is the poetical novel 'Louisa' (1784). Her poems were edited by Sir Walter Scott in 1810, with a memoir (The Cambridge Biographical Encyclopaedia. David Crystal. 1994). In her lifetime she was known as the 'Swan of Lichfield' mainly because of her enormous output of turgid (LAL p39) and over-sentimental verse. She is referred to by Boswell in his Life of Johnson as the 'Poetess of Lichfield.' Horace Walpole described her as having 'no imagination, no novelty.' Miss Mitford described her as 'all tinkling and tinsel - a sort of Dr Darwin in petticoats.' Darwin called her the inventress of epic elegy (DNB). But Masefield in LGS (1910) called her 'preposterous' (LGS p169). (SHOS vol 1 pp343,347,348,349) (GNHS p165) (SLM summer 1955 pp12,13,22) (MMH pp70p,71 il of - painting by John Opie) (TOS p83).

ERASMUS DARWIN. Dr Erasmus Darwin MD FRS (1731-1802), physician and botanist, moved to Lichfield in Nov 1756 from Nottingham after a brief time there as a doctor (DJL viii). By 1758 he was occupying a house on the W side of the Close, which has become known as Darwin's House (see). In 1766, while botanising, he accidentally met Rousseau at Wootton Hall (see), with whom he afterwards corresponded. Whilst in Lichfield Darwin associated with the intelligentsia; he met Johnson once or twice, but the two disliked each other. Darwin was close, however, with like-minded Whigs like Matthew Boulton, owner of Soho Manufactory (see), Josiah Wedgwood I born at Churchyard House (see) (for him it is said he designed a windmill at Etruria Works see), James Watt, the Sewards and others; they held monthly meetings, or as Darwin called them 'lunar meetings,' at each other's houses. The **Lichfield Botanical Society** was formed in 1778 by Darwin to promote a translation of the botanical works of Linnaeus. In the late 1770s Darwin created a botanic garden, 1m W of Lichfield near Abnalls in Burntwood, which was maintained after he left Lichfield in 1781 by a fellow member of the society (VCH vol 14 p169). The garden embraced a stone bath house (since known as Darwin's Bath (see)) by a medicinal well there. Another venture was his attempt to try to prevent lightning striking Lichfield Cathedral (see) for which he invented his own lightning conductor. In 1770 Darwin's first wife, Mary Howard, died. By her he had three sons; the youngest son, Robert Waring Darwin (1766-1848) became a physician at Shrewsbury. Robert married Susannah Wedgwood, daughter of Josiah (see above), and their fifth child was Charles Darwin (1809-1882), natural historian; some of Charles' work was carried out whilst staying with his uncle, Josiah Wedgwood II, at Maer (see). In 1781 Erasmus Darwin married the widow of Col Chandos-Pole of Radbourne Hall and moved away from Lichfield, later moving to Derby, and later to Breadsall Priory, N of Derby, where he died of heart disease on April 18 1802. After his death Anna Seward recollected several rather unfavourable anecdotes about him, which many believed were false; Charles Darwin claimed Seward was bitter towards his grandfather for he had not offered to marry her after the death of his first wife (DNB). Desmond King-Hele has written extensively about Erasmus Darwin and many of his works on him, including his 'Erasmus Darwin: A Life of Unequalled Achievement' (1999), are in the WSL.

EDGEWORTH AND DAY. In 1765 Richard Lovell Edgeworth, exponent of railroads and inventor of the odometer (CCHCA p37), visited Lichfield and made several visits to the city in 1769. In 1770 he took a house in Lichfield with Thomas Day (d1789) (DJL viii). The house that Day took in 1770 was Stowe House (see). Often writers make no reference to Edgeworth taking this house with Day. Day had come to Lichfield with his young protege, Sabrina, to consult Dr Erasmus Darwin, and finding he liked the city so much he wanted to stay. After a year of further instruction in Lichfield Day found Sabrina a disappointment and he sent her to school in Sutton Coldfield. He was then introduced to Honora Sneyd, but when she refused to have anything to do with him he took an interest in her sister, Elizabeth. Day went to France to 'improve himself' to be worthy of Elizabeth but when she would have nothing to do with him (Lichfield Miscellany. John Godwin. 1978 p55) Day and Edgeworth went to France in 1771; they returned to Lichfield in 1773

(DJL ix). In 1773 Edgeworth married Honora Sneyd, adopted sister of Anna Seward, see above. In 1780 Edgeworth published in Lichfield 'Practical Education; or Harry and Lucy' a didactic book for children, which he had initially written with his wife for his own children. The book apparently inspired Day to write 'Sandford and Merton.' He eventually left Lichfield and married Miss Esther Milnes of Chesterfield, Derbys (SHOS vol 1 pp345,349 note 3) (HOL p510) (LGS pp175,176) (SOSH p300) (VB p19) (Lichfield Miscellany. John Godwin. 1978 p55) (VCH vol 14 p171) (TB Nov 1992 p10 il).

1750 to 1850. There was a society of **Gentlemen Archers** in the early 1770s. An archery society was in existence in 1824. This was revived in 1846 (VCH vol 14 p162) and probably became known as the Lichfield Society of Archers, who disbanded in 1939 (LTM Sept 1971 p58), and were revived in 1965 (VCH vol 14 p162). Their trophies of a silver horn, belt, quiver and broach (occasionally exhibited at St Mary's Centre, Lichfield) are competed for annually (LTM Sept 1971 p58). Another account says Lichfield has a society of archers, founded in 1851, by Mr Manley of Manley Hall. Richard Greene of Stowe House donated their trophies (CCHCB p12). In 1759 a **canal** was proposed from Minister Pool or Stowe Pool to the Trent at Weston (Derbys), but nothing came of the scheme (VCH vol 14 p47). The **Lichfield Troop** of the Staffordshire Volunteer Cavalry (later Staffordshire Yeomanry) was raised by Major EP Elliot in 1794 (FSP p60) (VCH vol 14 p29). The original **Staffordshire Agricultural Society** (SAS) was founded in 1800. The first meeting was at the Swan Hotel (see), Lichfield. **Persons and visitors. Charles Dibdin**, comedian, singer, and composer of 'Poor Tom Bowling,' appeared at Lichfield Theatre in the 1790s (CCHCA p49). **John Glover** (1767-1849), landscape painter and watercolourist, practised as a drawing master in Lichfield between 1794 and 1805. His most famous pupil whilst at Lichfield was **Henry Salt**, artist, traveller, collector and Egyptologist, who was born in Lichfield on June 14 1780; Salt attended Lichfield Grammar School; he had the bust of Ramases II transported from Thebes to the BM in 1817; he died in Cairo in 1827 (PSS pp133-137 il) (TB Dec 1992 p13) (VCH vol 14 p181) (VFC p117). The famous artist **JMW Turner** (1775-1851) painted a view of the cathedral from the SW. The painting was for sale in Nov 1992 (ES Nov 12 1992 p8p). In 1795 Charles Genevieve Louis Auguste Andre Timothee D'Eon de **Beaumont** (1728-1810), chevalier, emissary, and secretary in Russia and England who caused controversy all his life as it could not be established whether he was male or female, and excelled in fencing, demonstrated his skill in 'the art of attack and defence with a single rapier' in Lichfield; this was one of his last public appearances (DNB) (VCH vol 14 p166). Rev **Rowland Muckleston** (d1897), minor poet, son of Rev John Fletcher Muckleston, DD, was born in The Close on Aug 29 1811 (PSS pp163-165). The 1st **Marquess of Anglesey** passed through Lichfield on his return to Beaudesert Hall after the battle of Waterloo in 1815 (VCH vol 14 p29) and his funeral took place with much pomp in Lichfield cathedral in May 1854 (ILN May 13 1854 p442ils). Miss **Maria Foote**, Prima Donna of Convent Garden, later Countess of Harrington, appeared at Lichfield Theatre in 1817 (CCHCA p48). Mary Evans **'George Evans'** visited the cathedral in 1826, 1840, and 1861; her last visit was in the company of her husband (NSFCT 1918 p122). She also made visits in 1840 and 1859 to visit relations at Eborall's school for girls in the Close (VCH vol 14 p180). **Queen Victoria** was in the Close in 1832 and as queen in late Nov 1843 (ILN Dec 2 1843 p361. Dec 9 1843 p372). **Richard Garnett** (d1906), poet, was born in Beacon Street on Feb 27 1835. When only aged 16 he became assistant in the Printed Book Department of the BM, and rose to be Keeper of Printed Books in 1890 (PSS pp214-219) (VFC p52). **Queen Adelaide**, the widow of William IV, was in the Close in 1839 (R&S p39) (VCH vol 14 p60). The violinist **Nicolo Paganini** (d1840) played in Lichfield in 1833 (VCH vol 14 p164).

INDUSTRY. The city had little important industry before the C19. In the C13, there were goldsmiths, glaziers, a bellfounder, and leather and cloth workers (VCH vol 14 p11). A saddlers' company may have existed since the end of the C13; a vintners' company and a mercers' company since C14 (VCH vol 14 pp12,119-120). For the laws of the mercers' company see Transactions of Royal Historical Society New Series vol VII pp109-125. There was quarrying in the C14 and C15 (VCH vol 14 p12). Lichfield kersey was famous in the early C16 (SSAHST vol 32 pp85-86). The clothworkers' and weavers' company was recorded in 1552, the cappers' in 1575, the tailors' in 1576, and the smiths' in 1601. Capping declined in the later C16 (VCH vol 14 pp16,120-122). In the C18 there was coach-making, clothworking of all kinds, brewing (Lichfield ale had a national reputation), bookselling and printing, and watchmaking (VCH vol 14 pp21,122-127). There were fulling **mills** at Leamonsley by the early 1790s and at Pones Mill (VCH vol 14 p28). But Lichfield has never been thought of as an industrial town: Dr Johnson of

Lichfield (see) remarked in 1776 'We are a city of philosophers: we work with our heads and make the boobies of Birmingham work for us with their hands' (VCH vol 14 p1). From the later C19 Lichfield's most important industry was brewing (VCH vol 14 pp127-128). There was a **windmill** in Gay field in 1343 (VCH vol 14 p115). Land in Castleditch field was described in 1606 as the site of a former windmill (VCH vol 14 p115). There was a windmill on E side of Grange Lane, at SK 109106, over a mile NW of the cathedral, by 1807. It was known as Grange Mill by 1818 (VCH vol 14 p115). In 1905 the tower became part of Windmill House, built by Sir Thomas Blomefield, Bt (VCH vol 14 p115). Some say a Mr Bridgeman, who was involved in restoration work on the cathedral, converted the windmill into a residence (WIS pp11p,20) (WBJ p29 il xxv). For the windmill in Stowe Hill field see under Stowe Hill.

RAILWAYS. Railways put an end to Lichfield's long-distance coaches, even before there was a railway in Lichfield and the last mail coach, the Chester mail, to leave the city, left on April 11 1838 (CCHCB p20) (LAWTT p39) (VCH vol 14 p46). Lichfield was connected to the railway system with the Trent Valley Railway, which ran from Stafford to the Birmingham-London line at Rugby from Dec 1 1847. The station was N of the Burton road SE of Streethay. The SSR line connecting Lichfield to Walsall and Derby opened on April 9 1849 for freight (NSJFS 1962 p99), and on June 1 1849 for passengers (SSR p10). It had a station, the City Station, to the S of the town, (rebuilt in 1884), and another near the Trent Valley Railway station at Streethay. The two at Streethay were replaced by a single station in 1871 (VCH vol 14 p47) (SSR p24). The SSR railway bridge over St John Street was built in the gothic style in 1849. Pedestrian-ways passed through two embattled towers, and there were sweeps on either side. On the W side of the bridge, the N abutment has the arms of the City of Lichfield, the arms of Bishop Hacket and of the See of Lichfield. The S abutment has above the arms of England and below those of Bishops Heyworth and Lonsdale. In this way two of Lichfield's most distinguished bishops are commemorated and also, tactfully, the one who was reigning in 1849. On the E side, the arms, which are above only, are those of local landed families: on the N side are those of Gower and Bagot, and on the S side those of Anson and Wolseley (ILN April 14 1849 il) (NSJFS 1962 p101) (VCH vol 14 p47 pl 29). The bridge was extensively altered when the railway track was widened for the line from Birmingham; the pedestrian-ways were demolished in 1969 (IAS p180 il) (VCH vol 14 p47). The LNWR extended its Sutton Coldfield line to Lichfield in 1884 (VCH vol 2 pp323-324). It was recommended that Lichfield station (High Level) be closed in 1963 (ES March 22 1963).

NEWSPAPERS. The **Lichfield Mercury began as the Staffordshire Mercury**, published from Stafford. In July 1815 it appeared as The Lichfield Mercury and Midland Chronicle and was discontinued in 1833 (VCH vol 14 p170) (SHJ spring 1996 p21). James Broughton wrote his series 'Notices of Staffordshire' for the paper (OPB p9). Copies of the **Lichfield Mercury, Tamworth, Burton and Walsall Gazette, and Staffordshire and Warwickshire General Advertiser** survive from the period Jan 1 1830 to Dec 27 1833 (SHJ spring 1996 p21). The **Lichfield Advertiser and Newspaper for Lichfield, Alrewas, Shenstone etc** ran from Jan 6 1865 to 1866 (VCH vol 14 p170) (SHJ spring 1996 pp19-20). A **Lichfield City and County Record and General Advertiser for the District** was being published in 1869 (SHJ spring 1996 p20). The **Lichfield Chronicle** was being published in 1877 (VCH vol 14 p170). The **Lichfield Mercury and Advertiser for Lichfield, Stafford, Walsall etc** (or simply Lichfield Mercury) was first published on Sept 27 1877 and still runs (VCH vol 14 p170) (SHJ spring 1996 p20). The **Lichfield Herald, City and District News** founded by mid June 1883, became the Lichfield Herald, Hednesford and Cannock Chase News from Dec 4 1868 and then the Lichfield Herald and City Times, Hednesford and Cannock Chase News from Aug 3 1888 to 1897 (VCH vol 14 p170) (SHJ spring 1996 p20). The **Lichfield City Times, Cannock and Hednesford Herald**, founded on Dec 2 1887, ran until at least July 27 1888 (SHJ spring 1996 p20). The **Lichfield Pioneer** appeared between at least Aug 5 1921 and May 26 1922 (SHJ spring 1996 p21). The **Lichfield Times and South Staffordshire Advertiser** founded on Nov 27 1926, ran until at least June 12 1954 (VCH vol 14 p170) (SHJ spring 1996 p21). The **Lichfield, Rugeley & Brownhills Post** was founded in 1983 (Willings Press Guide. 1988). The **Lichfield and Burntwood Midweek Mercury** was appearing in Feb and March 1991 (SHJ autumn 1993 p22).

1850 to 1900. The **South Staffordshire Water Works Company** (SSWWC) was founded by John McClean in 1852 at Lichfield where its first headquarters were situated. SSWWC have had pumping stations at Sandfields (see), Huntington (see), Ashwood (see), Wood Green (see), Hinksford (see) and other places. Early reservoirs of the company were Stowe and Minister Pools,

Lichfield, since when it has built Scout House Reservoir (see), Hanch Reservoir (see), Blithfield Reservoir (see), one on Cawney Hill (see), and others. It has also built a water treatment works at Seedy Mill (see). In 1979-85 the Company, brought together its control room, buildings department, and headquarters onto the present (1999) site at Green Lane, Walsall. In 1992 a new corporate structure was established whereby the water supply company became a wholly-owned subsidiary of South Staffordshire Water Holdings plc (GHC pp8,33,38). A **bell from Burma** was brought to this country in 1854 and used as a fire alarm on the roof of Lichfield Guildhall (see). On Jan 14 1873 a **fire** broke out at a house in the Market Place and killed all the Corfield family (VB pp15-16). The **Lichfield Morris Dance** is a morris dance peculiar to Lichfield. The Lichfield dances are in the Cotswold tradition. The Lichfield dances require eight men (whereas the Cotswold Morris requires six) (LTM Nov 1971 pp10-11). Others say there are ten dancers in the Lichfield morris (NSFCT 1956 p115). There are seven dances, five with names with local associations, these are - 'Castlering' where wakes were held in summer and the dance perhaps first performed; 'The Vandalls of Hammerwich' refers to an incident in Norman times when some of the villeins of Hammerwich set fire to the woods in nearby Cannock Forest; 'The Sheriffs Ride;' 'Milley's Bequest' after Milley's Hospital; 'The Barefooted Quaker' refers to George Fox's visit to Lichfield. Those without local associations are - 'Ring o' Bells' and 'Nuts in May.' The earliest known illustration is by the Lichfield historian Charles Stringer in c1520 (LTM Nov 1971 pp10-11). It is recorded that morris dancers were paid to perform at a parliamentary election in 1761 and dancing at election time remained a custom in the earlier C19. Morris men also danced at Christmas 'masquerades' in the late C18 and early C19 (VCH vol 14 p160). They were at the Greenhill Bower (see under Greenhill) until the 1880s when the group were disbanded owing to the general disorderliness which accompanied them. Lichfield's morris tradition lapsed until some 10 years later it was revived by boys from the Midland Truant School in Beacon Street. Instead of the traditional Cotswold costume of white trousers and shirt and straw hat which the Lichfield Morris men had always worn the boys now appeared in white stockings and black knee breeches, a form of dress peculiar to the Lancashire tradition. By 1907 the dances were again being performed by men. Another peculiar custom they acquired of the Lancastrian morris was the blacking of faces. By 1936 the dances had lapsed again. A morris group was reformed in the 1950s or, as Raven says, in the 1960s. The dances were re-learnt using archive material and by oral information (LTM Nov 1971 pp10-11) (MR p215). (Folklore. 103 (2) 1992 pp131-159). A group called the Lichfield Morris Men was formed in 1979 to perform dances particular to Lichfield. The Three Spires Ladies' Morris was formed in 1981 to perform clog dances. The Ryknild Rappers were formed in 1988 to perform traditional sword dances (VCH vol 14 pp160-161). **Persons and visitors**. **Nathaniel Hawthorne**, the great American novelist, visited Lichfield in 1855 (VCH vol 14 pp29,32). In 1855 George Hodson, Archdeacon of Stafford and Canon of Lichfield cathedral, died. His son, **William SR Hodson** (1821-1858), became famous during the Indian Mutiny (1857). At the head of an irregular body of cavalry known as Hodson's Horse, he took part in the siege of Delhi and after its fall discovered the last Mogul emperor and his two sons (LGS p174) (Macmillan Dictionary of Biography. 1981) (ZSB). **Henry James**, novelist, visited Lichfield in 1872 and thought the city 'stale without being really antique,' but thought the cathedral 'great among churches' (VCH vol 14 p3). The Prince of Wales (**Edward VIII**) visited Lichfield in May 1894 to review the Staffordshire Yeomanry. He was given a tour of the cathedral by the Dean (LOPP p12p).

1900 to PRESENT. **Gardens of Remembrance** are on both sides of the Minster Pool, below the Close. N of the Pool is a garden in memory to those who died in WW1 (LAL p40) and opened in 1920. A stone balustrade originally from Moxhull Hall, Wishaw, Warws, and then removed to Shenstone Court was bought from there by the City of Lichfield for this garden (VCH vol 14 p164). Mee notes a strange coincidence concerning the balustrade. It was noticed when it was being set up that it bore the letter 'V;' the mark used by the mason Vinrace who had built the bridge crossing Minster Pool in 1816 (KES p145). S of Minister Pool is a garden in memory to those who died in WW2 (LAL p40) and it was opened in 1955 (VCH vol 14 p164). **Lichfield Spitfire** was a MK VB serial BL 812 (info St Mary's Centre, Lichfield). The headquarters of the **Mormons'** English church was at Lichfield between 1972 and 1977 (VCH vol 14 p159). By 1980 the most incorrect **telephone** bill was that received by the landlord of the Blue Bell Inn who received a bill for £1,494,000,000 on Aug 18 1975. The Post Office admitted it contained 'an arithmetical error' (GBR 1980 p202). The **Staffordshire University Lichfield Centre**, the UK's only purpose-built integrated further and higher education centre, opened in May 1998. It is designed by Aiden Ridyard (SLM April 1998 p33pc). It is a joint project between Tamworth and Lichfield College and Staffordshire University; the ultra-modern glass design echoes Lichfield cathedral (info Staffs University). There is a Lichfield, Illinois, USA. **Persons and visitors**. **George VI** and his wife Queen Elizabeth stayed several times at the Bishop's Palace during the episcopate of Bishop Edward Woods (local info); in 1946 Dorothy L Sayers's play 'The Just Vengeance,' commissioned by the dean and chapter as part of the Cathedral's 750th anniversary festival (June 13-23 1946), was performed in the cathedral in the presence of Queen Elizabeth (VCH vol 14 p166) (local info). The British Army's tallest soldier was **Benjamin Crow** who was signed on at Lichfield in Nov 1947 when he was seven feet one inch tall (GBR 1980 p185). **Ruth Felicity Chadwick** (b Birmingham 1951) living in Lichfield in 1970 had passed the most GCE exams whilst at school. Between summer 1966 and summer 1969 she passed 17 'O' Levels and 6 'A' Levels, totalling 23 (GBR 1970 p219). In archery the British record highest championship scores for Double Round is 2254 achieved by **Steven Hillard** at Lichfield on Aug 8-9 1987 (GBR 1992 p224). **Elizabeth II** distributed Maundy money in the cathedral in 1988 (VCH vol 14 p60).

LICHFIELD AND LITERATURE. George Farquhar's 'The Beaux' Stratagem' (1707) is set in Lichfield (VCH vol 14 p165). Sir Walter Scott buried 'Marmion,' the hero of his epic poem of that name, at Lichfield (S&W p192). For Thomas Henry Lister (1800-1841/2), novelist, of Lichfield (ZSB) (VFC p85), see Armitage Park (see). 'Harvest in Poland' (1925) by Geoffrey Dennis of Walsall is partly set in Lichfield (VFC p38). The thriller writer, Craig Thomas, born Cardiff in 1942, was living near Lichfield in 1985. His first novel was 'Rat Trap' (1976), others include 'Firefox Down,' and 'The Bear's Tears' (1985). Lichfield Literary Prize, a biennial literary prize worth £5000 for a work of fiction set in the Lichfield area, conceived in 1988, is a unique award for literature as it is the only competition of its kind organised and sponsored by a local authority and competed for on a national basis. Winners have been: Rockabye (1989) by Valerie Kershaw; A Nest of Singing Birds (1991) by John Caine; The Short Caution (1993) by Gary Coyne; The Ladies of the Vale (1995) by Alys Carter, and Lady Gilmore's Cottage (1995) by Sheila White; Ordeal at Lichfield (1997) by Anthony Clarke. All winners' work has been published except for that by John Caine (ES Jan 28 1993 p8) (SLM March 1996 p13) (Sunday Telegraph Review Section July 7 1996 p22) (info Lichfield District Council). 'Lichfield' is a noun amongst funeral directors. A 'Lichfield' is an expensive type of funeral ('In Excess' BBC Radio 4 Dec 27 1994).

Lichfield Canal Is the proposed name for the section of the Wyrley & Essington Extension Canal between Ogley Junction and Huddlesford Junction on the Coventry Canal after it is restored by the Lichfield and Hatherton Canals Restoration Trust, formed in 1988 (Trust leaflet).

Lichfield Castle A castle at Lichfield, fortified by Bishop Clinton (1129-48), is mentioned by a C14 Lichfield chronicler. This may refer to the construction of a wall and gates round the perimeter of the Close. The Close was described as 'castellum' in c1200 and by the C14 the mill in Dam Street was known as Castle Mill (VCH vol 14 p60). (SHOS vol 1 p309 - Info from Godwin p367). This was probably the castle in which Richard II kept his Christmas in 1397 (1398 - MCC) and where he was kept prisoner in 1399 and made an unsuccessful bid for escape (SHOS vol 1 p309). Although, Gould says he stayed in the medieval Bishop's Palace (MCC). The **site of Lichfield Castle** has been in dispute ever since Leland mentioned it in c1541 (NSFCT 1913? pp113-128). Often believed to have been sited near where the section of Lichfield Town Ditch known as 'Castle Ditch' persists (W p490). But Castle Ditch probably received the appellation 'Castle' in consequence of its proximity to an Anglo-Saxon fort on Borrowcop Hill (VCH vol 14 p7). Harwood thought the castle was N of the 'old' Grammar School, since on the N side of Frog Lane leading into Wade Street is a small street called Baker's Lane anciently Baxeter, and in 1523 called Back Cester; cester, caster implying a fort (HOL pp 300,499). Others say the name is derived from Old English 'baecestre,' a baker (VCH vol 14 p41). The name 'Castle Dyke' persists by the Civic Hall in Wade Street (LAL p5). Salter says a castle was built at Lichfield in 1129, and probably stood in the area of Wade Street and Frog Street. It was destroyed under the terms of a treaty of 1148. When Leland visited the town c1540 the name 'Castle Field' was still in use, and he comments on there having been a 'castle of anciente tyme in the south part of the town, but no part of it standeth' (CAMS p22). It was thought that the castle site would be found on the site for the new post office on the NW side of the N end of Frog Lane (now Redcourt Road), but nothing conclusive was found (SSAHST 1968 pp70-71). Another possible site for the castle has often thought to be SE of the W gate to the Close near the ground occupied by Newton's College. There is a small drawing, by Smith, from Elizabeth I's time in the Harl. Mss representing a tower reputed to be on that spot, although Camden affirms he did not see it. Smith's drawing may represent the tower at the SW corner of the Close (HOL p292 note). The Close after 1300 could have been considered a castle argues Gould. Bishop Langton fortified it in c1300, a tower was positioned at each of the four corners and strong gatehouses were added on the W and S sides (MCC) (CAMS p22). (GNHS p157) (W pp483,490). Perhaps, there were two castles of different periods. The Baker's Lane castle probably was the earlier; Richard II being imprisoned in the latter. The mound 'vicus altus' on which the Grammar School built in the 1870s stood is probably part of a prehistoric fort (SSAHST 1968 p71).

Lichfield Cathedral The cathedral and Close may have been an ancient Celtic site (NSFCT 1908 p123). There is a tradition that the legendary massacred Christians slain during Diocletian's reign (284-305) are buried on the cathedral site (VCH vol 14 p39).

SEE OF LICHFIELD. **Establishment of the Mercian See at Lichfield**. In 653 Peada, under-king of the Middle Angles and son of Penda, king of Mercia, became a Christian on his marriage to the daughter of Oswiu, king of Northumbria. He brought back four missionaries from Northumbria, who probably worked among the Mercians as well as the Middle Angles. In 655 Oswiu took control of Mercia, establishing Peada as king of the Southern Mercians. Diuma, one of the four missionaries was made first bishop of the Mercians. In 658 Wulfhere, another son of Penda, gained control of Mercia (VCH vol 14 p5). St Wilfrid was asked by King Wulfhere to perform episcopal duties in Mercia at various times between 666-669 and was given by the king grants of land including Lichfield. Wilfrid decided that Lichfield should become the seat of the hitherto peripatetic bishops of the Mercians (VCH vol 3 p40), others say the See of Mercia was established at Repton. **Reasons why Wilfrid chose Lichfield**. Because at Lichfield there was a church or monastery - perhaps destroyed during the battle at Caer Lwytgoed: A bronze bowl has been found at Wall bearing the Christian Chi-Rho monogram (VCH vol 14 p5). Or because it was close to a Mercian royal centre, perhaps Tamworth, or 'Wulfherecestre' at Bury Bank (VCH vol 14 p5). Or because of its proximity to Icknield Street and Watling Street; Icknield Street was a link with the NE and Wilfred's diocese (VCH vol 14 p5). Or because Lichfield was a good base from which to do missionary work; paganism was prevalent certainly in the Wednesbury, Wednesfield, and Weeford areas (VCH vol 14 p5). **Chad at Lichfield**. The first bishop to reside at Lichfield was Chad (or Ceadda, Cedda, Cedde) who succeeded Wilfrid in 669. Chad's church probably stood on the site of the present cathedral (VCH vol 14 p6). According to tradition Chad, a Benedictine monk, preached at a nearby hamlet called Stowe. Stowe was probably also the site of his retreat, and the place where he died in 672 (VCH vol 14 p6). At Stowe Chad is said to have partaken of the waters of a spring, now called St Chad's Well. Chad was buried near the church of St Mary, presumably the cathedral. In 700 a funerary church was built. It was probably close to the site of the present cathedral and was dedicated to St Peter. Hedda transferred Chad's remains to it (VCH vol 3 pp3-4. vol 14 p6). A **shrine of St Chad** was noted by Bede by the 730s (VCH vol 14 p53). In the C9 a homily was written on the life of St Chad. It may have been written in Lichfield and is in the Mercian dialect of Old English (VCH vol 14 p6). In the Norman cathedral, the shrine of St Chad, probably stood near the high altar (VCH vol 14 pp49,53). Bishop Langton (1296-1321) set up a 'magnificent' shrine for St Chad's relics in the cathedral. By 1335 some of the relics were kept in a portable shrine and his head in a painted box. The shrine was improved in 1378. But sometimes it is said to have been made by Robert Stretton who was bishop in 1378 (SHOS vol 1 p304). By 1445 the head was encased in a gilt reliquary in its own chapel, probably the chamber over St Peter's chapel off the S choir aisle. By 1445 there was another reliquary containing his right arm (VCH vol 14 pp12,53-54). The destruction of the shrine in 1538 brought about the end of pilgrim traffic to Lichfield (VCH vol 3 p168. vol 14 p14). The ornaments were seized by the Crown. The cathedral kept the shrine (VCH vol 14 p54), which was completely destroyed in the Civil War (SHOS vol 1 p253). (HOL p93) (W p494). The **relics or bones of St Chad** were smuggled away by Canon Arthur Dudley, who took them to his sisters, Bridget and Catherine Dudley at Rushall Hall near Walsall (SCHJ No. 9 pp12-15), or Rushall near Walsall (SSE 1987 p129), or to them at Russell's Hall (see) near Dudley. From then on the bones were secreted by various Catholics at Woodsetton Lodge (see), Leveson's Moat (see), Blackladies or Boscobel (see), Swynnerton Hall (see), and at Aston Hall (see), where they were rediscovered in 1837. Some were taken to Flanders in 1669, and by 1671 were in Liege (VCH vol 14 p54). From Aston those that remained in England went to Oscott where their identity was investigated by an official inquiry. The relics were then taken to the Roman Catholic cathedral of St Chad in Birmingham on June 21 1841 and there enshrined above the high altar (SR pp65,66) (RHPS

pp256-259). In 1995 the relics contained the bones of at least one other person; that year the bones were found by radiocarbon dating to be of C7 origin. (HSS pp56-59) (HOS p24) (SCHJ No. 9 pp12-15). St Chad gives his name to a C8 gospel book in Lichfield cathedral (see below); springs at Abnalls, Chadwell, Stowe (Lichfield), and Woodsetton Lodge; to a ditch forming an ancient boundary of Cannock Chase; a house at Bagnall; and a district of NEE Bilston. His image depicted on glass appears in churches at Burton (St Paul), Hoar Cross, Leek (All Saints), Stapenhill, Walsall (St Michael), and Wednesbury (St James). (SHOS vol 1 pp231,262) (HOL pp3-5,129-130) (LC) (SK pp122-128) (LGS pp164,165) (S p112) (SOSH pp38-48) (RHPS pp92-101) (KNS pp53,54,113) (FTWM pp130-134) (VCH vol 3 p2) (BSB pp158-159) (ODS pp82-83). Five years after the establishment of the Mercian See at Lichfield in 669 King Wulfhere died and was probably buried in the vicinity of the cathedral (VCH vol 14 p6). In 679 Mercia was divided into the five Sees of Lichfield, Lindsey, Leicester, Worcester and Dorchester (appendix to Florence of Worcester's chronicle) (VCH vol 3 p3). In 788, under Offa, king of Mercia (757-796), Lichfield was raised to the status of an archbishopric after the diocese was enlarged to incorporate some of the province of Canterbury. It retained this status until 803 (VCH vol 14 p6) (HOS 1998 p28). In 822 Bishop Ethelweald established a cathedral chapter of 20 canons under a provost (HOS 1998 p28). The medieval diocese covered Staffs, Derbys, Ches, and parts of Warws, Shrops, and Lancs. The See has not always been at Lichfield. In 1075 it was moved to Chester. In 1102 it was moved to Coventry. In 1208 it recovered its position as a See, although the style of the diocese was thereafter Coventry and Lichfield. In 1541 the northern part of the diocese was detached to form the new diocese of Chester. In 1661 the style of the diocese was changed to Lichfield and Coventry. In 1836, after the transfer of the archdeaconry of Coventry to the See of Worcester, the diocese was again called simply Lichfield. In 1878 Derbys was removed so that the diocese then only covered Staffs and a part of Shrops. In 1905 part of South Staffs was transferred to the new diocese of Birmingham (VCH vol 14 pp7,10) (HOS 1998 p53). In 1993 Himley deanery was removed to Worcester diocese (info Lichfield Diocesan Office). Lichfield diocese was the first diocese in Britain to advertise on television (on Central (west)) in the week Jan 18 to Jan 25 1993 ('Sunday' BBC Radio 4. Jan 17 1993).

PAST BUILDINGS. According to Gould, Bede relates that Chad built himself a habitation near the church at Lichfield, but does not speak of him building a church; suggesting Lichfield already had a church. Some have suggested Chad's cathedral was near or on the site of the present St Chad's (Bell's 'Lichfield Cathedral' p120) (SSAHST 1972 p31 note) and Chad's 'more retired dwelling place' was on or near the site of St Michael's at Greenhill (VCH vol 14 p135), or that Chad's cathedral was close to the present cathedral and only aligned on an E - W axis with the holy well at Stowe (Lichfield Cathedral Guide 1989). **Saxon cathedral**. The cathedral established by Chad before he died on March 2 672 was presumably the church dedicated to St Mary near which he was buried (VCH vol 14 p49). In 700 Chad's remains were transferred to a funerary church, apparently dedicated to St Peter (consecrated in Dec 700 - VCH vol 3 p140). St Mary's and St Peter's probably stood near each other. The Saxon cathedral may have stood on the site of a side chapel on the N side of the presbytery of the Norman cathedral. The site of the chapel, which corresponds to part of the present N choir aisle, was believed in the C18 to be the burial place of the Mercian kings. The funerary church may have stood on the site of a side chapel on the S side of the Norman presbytery; later St Peter's chapel. It is not known when the churches were incorporated into one cathedral (VCH vol 14 p49). These early churches were built of wood. The **Norman cathedral** begun in 1085, and probably finished by 1148 (VCH vol 14 p49), was built of stone. The overall dimensions of the Norman cathedral are not known. Perhaps, it was similar in size and style to Bishop Clinton's Buildwas Abbey (Lichfield Cathedral Guide 1989). By the time of DB it was known as the Church of St Chad which remained its popular name (VCH vol 3 p143). The present dedication to St Mary and St Chad is found from at least the late 1150s (VCH vol 3 p140). During the restoration of the present cathedral in the 1850s the foundations of the Norman cathedral were uncovered in the choir. There is also Norman stonework in the crossing area and in the wall linking the S choir aisle to St Chad's Head Chapel (Lichfield Cathedral Guide 1989). So a minute part of the Norman cathedral is incorporated into the present cathedral. Evidence that a pagan burial ritual survived in Britain long after it was thought to have died out was discovered in Lichfield cathedral in 1994 when the grave of a priest, believed to be from the late C11 or early C12, was discovered under the vestibule of the Chapter House. The grave, which would have stood outside the Norman cathedral, has a libation hole in a half-moon shape - an aperture through which the living could communicate with the dead (Link supplement in Lichfield Diocese parish magazines. Oct 1994).

PRESENT BUILDING. The rebuilding of the Norman cathedral was begun in the early C13. The rebuilding of the nave dates from 1257-85, with work on the W front beginning shortly afterwards. The two W spires and the central spire were probably finished by 1323. The central spire was possibly the first on the cathedral to be built, and was destroyed in the Civil War (VCH vol 3 p157. vol 14 p51). The Lady Chapel was finished by 1336. The new choir was completed by the later C14. The rebuilding of the cathedral was complete by the beginning of the C15 (VCH vol 14 pp51-52). After 1550 the central tower was restored after being struck by lightning (VCH vol 3 p168). In the Civil War the cathedral was damaged worse than any other and was desecrated by the parliamentarians in 1643 (VCH vol 14 p18). After five days continued parliamentary bombardment during the third siege of Lichfield in the Civil War the central spire collapsed on May 12 1646 damaging the choir and nave. Services in the cathedral had resumed by mid June 1660, and the chapter was reconstructed in Sept 1660 (VCH vol 14 p18). The **first general restoration** of the cathedral took place from 1660 to 1669 (BOE p175) (VCH vol 14 p52). Rededication took place on Christmas Eve 1669 (VCH vol 3 p176). The **second general restoration** took place under the direction of James Wyatt of Blackbrook Farm (see) from 1788 to 1795. It was his first cathedral task and his prime aim was to enlarge the choir (BOE p175) (VCH vol 14 p52). Lichfield was the first cathedral in which Wyatt's plans for restoration were actually carried out, and his aims of uniformity of style and the creation of sweeping, uncluttered 'vistas' (VCH vol 3 p187). The restoration included a stained glass window for the E window after a design by Sir Joshua Reynolds, which was removed in 1803 (VCH vol 3 p188. vol 14 p52). In 1802 the dean and chapter purchased through Sir Brooke Boothby (who had purchased it for £200 - although it was estimated at £10,000) some of the famous **Herckenrode glass**, Flemish glass of c1540, from the dissolved Cistercian abbey of Herckenrode, near Hasselt, near Liege, Belgium. Some of it was then placed in the seven most easterly of the nine windows in the Lady Chapel (W p495) (LGS p172) (HOS p24) (BOE p184). The total glass, numbering 340 pieces (SSC p125 in the intro), has been considered the most beautiful in England (KES p134). Transportation of the glass and fitting it cost £1000 (BCGB p374). That in the Lady Chapel has been much jumbled but presents a splendid glow of colours (LGS p172); for what each window there depicts see LGS p172. Other glass from Herckenrode is in the S choir aisle, the N aisle of the cathedral and at St Mary's church, Shrewsbury (BOE pp184,185) (LCPG pp9-11,28-41,42-44). (HOL pp112-113) (GNHS pp165,166) (The Herckenrode Windows in Lichfield Cathedral. Hugh Bright. 1962). A **third general restoration** occurred between 1842 and 1846 during which period Sydney Smirke restored the S aisle of the nave (VCH vol 14 p53). A **fourth general restoration** began under Sir George Gilbert Scott from 1857 to Oct 1861. In 1861 the cathedral was officially reopened (VCH vol 3 p194). General restoration continued under Scott's son, John Oldrid Scott, until 1901 (BOE p177) (VCH vol 14 p53). The central spire was restored in 1950, the roof and fabric restored between 1956-66, and the Chapter House restored in 1982 (Lichfield Cathedral Guide 1989). The cathedral is built of new red sandstone from quarries near Lichfield, at Borrowcop and at Wheel Lane (Bell's 'Lichfield Cathedral' p35). The present cathedral's **dimensions** are, from the top of the central spire to the floor 252 feet (GNHSS p26: Garner had erroneously given it as 183 feet on p158 of GNHS), from the floor to the top of a western spire 193 feet (Bell's 'Lichfield Cathedral' p39), from the E end to the W end 371 feet (BOE p174). (NSFCT 1913 pp113-122). The three **spires** of the cathedral make the cathedral unique in England; Coventry and Ripon cathedrals anciently had three (Bell's 'Lichfield Cathedral' pp35-36) (SGS p117). Shaw noted on one of the spires at the W end was fixed a conductor to preserve the cathedral and neighbouring houses from lightning, it had been devised by Dr Erasmus Darwin (SHOS vol 1 p26 in the appendix). A brick building to house the **library** was built beside the N transept in the late C15. It was demolished in 1757 and the library was moved to a chamber over the chapter house (VCH vol 14 p56). Amongst the manuscripts of note in it by the late C18, were - a copy of Pope Nicholas IV's Valor Ecclesiasticus, a record of the taxation in 1291 (SHOS vol 1 p261) (HOL p108) (W p499) (LGS p171); a folio illuminated Chaucer; and a beautiful heraldical folio of the Knight's of the Garter (SHOS vol 1 p261) (HOL p108) (W p499) (LGS p171) (KES p133) (DRBSC p476). After 1865 the library was extended into a room over the vestibule (VCH vol 14 p56). During a restoration of the library in 1992 large sections of a tiled floor laid in the late C13 were discovered behind bookcases. The floor has been described as 'one of the finest and most complete medieval examples to have survived' (CL April 30 1992 p75pcs).

The first known statutes for the cathedral date from the time of Bishop Nonant

(1185-1198) and are the earliest to survive for any English cathedral (VCH vol 3 p142. vol 14 p9). Lichfield was one of the last secular cathedrals to secure the right of electing its own dean (English Secular Cathedrals. Edwards. p122) (VCH vol 3 p145 note). Lichfield was nationally known for its cloister in the C13, for the phrase 'Cloister of Lichfield' to arise, according to Thorold Rogers in 'Six Centuries of Work and Wages' 1894 pp105-6. The editor of English Historical Documents vol 3 p882 doubts its authenticity. It was the custom in Lichfield diocese for **Chad pennies** or farthings, payment from parishioners to the mother church for reparation of the cathedral, to be paid to the cathedral on St Chad's day (March 2). But usually such payments in other dioceses were made at Whitsun time. The custom still prevailed in 1996 with the Chad Pennies being placed on the cathedral high altar (SHOS vol 1 p259) (HOL p109) (BCC vol 2 p161) (SR p66). In Medieval times to pay their oblations the ancient parishes of the See processed to the cathedral from their own parish. Collisions sometimes occurred between rival parishes en route to the cathedral, with groups being crushed by large banners. In 1357 the bishop ordered the substitution of a simple cross for the processional banner (SCSF p11). During the **Nebulae** at Whitsuntide light wheaten cakes were scattered from the triforium into the choir (VCH vol 3 p142). By 1306 a **boy bishop**, presumably one of the choristers, was being appointed on Holy Innocents' Day (Dec 28) and the custom still persisted in the earlier C16 (VCH vol 3 p164. vol 14 p160). **Wassailing** was practised by Cathedral choristers at Christmas in 1800, and the custom continued in the later C19 (VCH vol 14 p161). Every three years between 1856 and 1912 **Diocesan Choir Gatherings** were held in the cathedral, bringing together all the parish choirs of the diocese. Lichfield diocese was the first in the country to hold these gatherings (VCH vol 3 p192. vol 14 p165). **Ghosts** have been seen in and about the cathedral (GPCE p33).

Lichfield Cathedral Close The Close may have been an ancient Celtic site (NSFCT 1908 p123). Bishop Clinton enclosed the cathedral surrounds with a defensive ditch (MCC). But Clinton (the NSFCT writers say Langton) may have only deepened an old Celtic Roman fosse (NSFCT 1908 p123). The Close covers 16 acres (VCH vol 14 p57).

FORTIFICATION OF THE CLOSE. The castle fortified by Bishop Clinton (1129-48) mentioned by a C14 Lichfield chronicler may refer to the construction of a wall and gates round the perimeter of the Close. The Close was described as 'castellum' in c1200 and by the C14 the mill in Dam Street was known as Castle Mill (VCH vol 14 p60). The Close ditch probably never contained water (VCH vol 14 p60). In 1299 license was granted for the building of a crenellated stone wall round the Close (VCH vol 3 p150). Bishop Langton is accredited with this work which took place in c1300. Towers stood at intervals in the wall and at each of the four corners. Clockwise there was the NE tower forming the NE corner of the medieval Bishop's Palace; the base still survives and is commonly known as the Bastion of The Bishop's Palace (MCC) (BOE p188) (SK p198) (LPL p) (LAL p26p). The tower in the middle of the E wall formed the SE corner of the Bishop's Palace: A tower stood on the site of Selwyn House: St Mary's House (see) incorporates a turret: The South Gate had two towers: The SW tower recorded in 1312-13 was demolished by 1661: A tower in the W wall was known, in 1315, as the Dean's Tower and had been demolished by 1661: The NW tower had a statue of Bishop Walter, presumably Walter Langton, in the 1390s and was probably demolished in the Civil War (VCH vol 14 p60). There were two **gates** - West Gate (see) and South Gate (see). At a depth of 15 feet a **subterraneous passage** was discovered in 1804 under one of the towers and was supposed to lead from the cathedral and to have been formed in the Civil Wars (W p500). In 1317 and 1322 Edward II ordered the Close to be securely defended on his behalf (MCC), probably in response to the national disturbances of 1321 and 1322. The Close had to be defended again in 1329 when Sir Ralph Bassett and Sir Robert Mauresyn attacked (VCH vol 3 p153). The Close was attacked in 1436 (VCH vol 14 p84). For the Close used as a garrison in the Civil War see under Lichfield.

BUILDINGS IN THE CLOSE. WEST SIDE. **The Vicarage** (see). **Vicars' Hall** (see). **No. 9** the Close was in 1942 occupied by Dean Iremonger and is now (1999) used as the Cathedral Bookshop (info Michael Cockin). NORTH SIDE (from W to E). The house on the site of **No. 12** was damaged during the Civil War. Inhabited by 1666. Remodelled in the early C19 and the third storey added in 1865. Later occupied by the chancellor (VCH vol 14 p64). No. 12 was the first house in the Close to be occupied by the refounded Lichfield Cathedral School (St Chad's) in Jan 1942 and was then known as the School House. Afterwards the school also temporarily occupied the Deanery (see) and then also on a permanent basis the Palace (see) (info Michael Cockin). The School was still using No. 12 in 1989 (VCH vol 14 p64) and in 1999. **Chancellor's House** (see). The **Choristers' House** (see) formerly stood on the sites of No. 13 and No. 14 (later holding Dean Savage Library, but now (1999) flats). **No. 15** the Close was in 1942 occupied by the Custos and is now (1999) privately occupied. A kiosk in the SW corner of the garden of No. 15 was built in 1803 as a water conduit for the Close, and was used from the mid 1980s for the sale of refreshments (info Michael Cockin) (VCH vol 14 p65). **The Deanery** (see). **Bishop's Palace** (see). EAST SIDE (from N to S). **Selwyn House** (see). **St Mary's House** (see). SOUTH SIDE (from E to W). A house on the site of **No. 19** was the residence of Bishop Hacket from c1662 to 1670. After 1670 it reverted to a canonical house. In the later C18 it was occupied by Charles Howard (d1771), a proctor in the consistory court, who built a grotto of shells and fossils in the garden. The house was demolished in 1779. The present house was built in c1800 (VCH vol 14 p65). It is now (1999) used as the Chapter office, office of the Friends of Lichfield Cathedral, and tea rooms (info Michael Cockin). A house on the site of **No. 20**, possibly a banqueting hall, was erected for Bishop Hacket in 1666. Over the fireplace was an oak panel, dated 1669, which bore his arms and those of the diocese. The panel is now in the entrance hall of the Bishop's Palace. From 1692 to 1803 No. 20 was the diocesan registrar's office and muniment room. It housed Greene's Museum from sometime after 1803 to 1806 and was demolished in 1819. No. 20 house was rebuilt in 1833, and was occupied by the cathedral custos in 1990 (VCH vol 14 p66). **New College** (see). **St John's Hospital in the Close** (see). **The Refectory** (see). **Bishop's House** (see). The house on the site of **No. 23** was the courtyard house of Henry Edial, prebendary of Gaia Minor (1480-1520). It was remodelled in c1812. It was occupied by the treasurer (L Hammond, bishop of Stafford) in 1942 (info Michael Cockin). By the late 1980s it occupied by the precentor (VCH vol 14 p66 pls 6,7). At **No. 24** is the house rebuilt by Thomas Milley, the prebendary of Handsacre, in c1461. It was remodelled in c1814. In the late 1980s it was occupied by the treasurer (VCH vol 14 pp66-67 pl 6). By 1999 it was occupied by the archdeacon of Lichfield (info Michael Cockin). HOUSES FRONTING BEACON STREET (from S to N). **Langton House** (see). **Moat House** (see). **Newton's College** (see). **Darwin House** (see). **Dimple House** (see).

GROUNDS. The open space around the cathedral was a **graveyard** for those who lived in the Close. In 1391 the graveyard was considered unconsecrated by an act of violence when an apothecary from Coventry was assaulted on it (MCC). There has been a **conduit**, fed by springs at Maple Hayes, in the Close since the mid C12. It presumably stood NW of the cathedral. There was a conduit there by the C17. It was agreed in 1697 that the conduit, known in the C16 and C17 as Moses' Head (see), should be taken down (VCH vol 14 p95). It, or its successor, was pulled down in Feb 1748 (HOL p292) or in 1786, as it was considered unsightly (VCH vol 14 p96). The reservoir and a stone-encased pump erected in its place proved inadequate and a brick conduit was built in the SW corner of the garden of No. 15 in 1803. Although made redundant in 1876 many residents of the Close preferred the supply from the conduit and it was operational until 1969. It was used as a kiosk by the mid 1980s (VCH vol 3 p189. vol 14 p96). To the S of the cathedral is a **sundial** 14 feet high with four faces. It is placed on a newer column (SLM spring 1957 p29). In 1781 the sundial in the Close was taken down (VCH vol 3 p189). The houses in the Close were decorated with green boughs on **Ascension day**. This custom was revived in the 1920s and was still taking place in the 1980s (VCH vol 14 p161). The **ghost** of a young girl walks by the cathedral (SMM p54).

JURISDICTION OF THE CLOSE. By a royal grant of 1441 and confirmed in 1461 the cathedral close was made juridically exempt from shire and town officials, probably in response to the attack on the Close in 1436 (VCH vol 14 p84). The grant gave the inhabitants of the Close many privileges. The charter of 1461 constituted the dean and canons residentiary sole justices of the peace for the precincts of the Close. The magistrates of the city and counties of Lichfield and Stafford had no jurisdiction here. Neither the sheriff of Staffordshire nor Lichfield could arrest anybody in the Close, unless they had indorsement from a magistrate of the Close first (VCH vol 3 p161. vol 14 p84) (NSJFS 1979 p3). In 1622 James I granted a new charter to the City and, it seems by accident, the traditional clause guaranteeing the independent liberty of the Close was omitted, the Chapter complained and obtained a charter in 1623 not only confirming the privileges granted in 1441 but extending them also. The Close was to be entirely separate from the City and exempt from the jurisdiction of any of the City officials and certain cathedral officers were to be exempt from jury-service. Three days after the issue of the capitular charter the City received a revised version of its own charter in which all passages exempting the Close from civic jurisdiction were restored (VCH vol 3 pp173-174). (SHOS vol 1 p309). The Close was an extra parochial liberty (W p483) and became a separate civil parish in 1858 (GLAUE p416).

The Close remained a liberty until 1836 when it was added to Lichfield under the 1835 Municipal Corporations Act (VCH vol 14 p84). The Close was considered a **place of sanctuary**, the last recorded occasion being in 1532 when a thief sought protection. He was found in one of the Canons' houses and since sanctuary was only granted in the cathedral or graveyard, he was able to be arrested (MCC). There was a **watchman** for the Close by the late C13. The last watchman, Albert Haycock, held the office until his death in 1956, although for some time he was too ill to carry out his duties. He patrolled the Close from 9.30pm to 4.30am, proclaiming the hour and weather (SOSH pp147-148) (Lichfield Mercury June 1 1956 pp6-7) (VCH vol 14 pp84,103).

Lichfield City The town of Lichfield was created a city by Edward VI's charter of 1547 (HOL p356). It was the first town in the county to be made a city. The boundaries of the city of Lichfield are a circuit of about 16 miles (HOL p356).

Lichfield County The city of Lichfield was created a county by Queen Mary I's charter of 1553. The county of Lichfield came into effect from St Thomas' day (Dec 21) 1553. Henceforth, Lichfield was a county in its own right independent of the County of Stafford (SHOS vol 1 p309). The county of Lichfield seems to have been exempt from Offlow hundred court (W p482). Mary possibly did this because the corporation had assisted her in suppressing Northumberland's abortive coup. A sheriff, recorder and coroner - all elected by the citizens - were now added to the city's officers (NSJFS 1979 p5). The first sheriff was Gregory Stonyng (VCH vol 14 p83). Mary's charter stipulated that the sheriff ride the boundaries of the city (or county), a custom which still prevails (8 Sept). The boundaries of the city or county are a circuit of about 16 miles and comprises about 4000 acres, and the out townships about 6000 (W p483 note). Lichfield county was reunited with Staffs by the Local Government Act of 1888; it was one of only four counties of cities not to be made a county borough. The shrievalty survives as an office of dignity (VCH vol 14 p83).

Lichfield Guildhall Bore Street, Lichfield, adjoins Donegal House. From the C13 the Guild of St Mary occupied the site where the Guildhall now stands. The new corporation took over their building at their creation in 1549 (VCH vol 14 p75). The Guildhall served partly as a public assembly room and as a theatre in the C18. William Siddons, later husband of Sarah Kemble, appeared in the 'The Recruiting Officer' in 1770 at the Guildhall (VCH vol 14 p165). In 1773 Sarah Siddons made her first appearance under her married name here (LAL p10). Or and Mrs Siddons made her first appearance here after her husband's death (CL Oct 3 1957 p663). The old Guildhall was taken down in 1846. (VCH vol 14 pl 26 shows the old Guildhall). A large stone carving from the old Guildhall showing the old seal of the Corporation was taken to Beacon Park and has been placed in the Museum Gardens (LAL p20p) (LPL). The present Guildhall was built between 1846-48 by the Conduit Lands Trustees to designs of Joseph Potter the younger (VCH vol 14 p83), and preserves the old condemned cell. The N window is a gift from the dean and chapter. Until 1971 the hall was used as a court for Quarter Sessions and for meetings of the city council until 1973 (LAL p11p). The bell captured in April 1852 as a trophy by the 80th Regiment of the Staffordshire Volunteers when they attacked the Great Dragon Pagoda at Rangoon, Burma, was brought to this country by Lord Wolseley in 1854 and presented to the corporation of Stafford on March 28 1855. It was used as a fire alarm on the roof of Lichfield Guildhall. By the mid 1990s it was at the South Staffs Regt Museum at Whittington Barracks (ES Sept 6 1930 p3) (SLM May 1949 p247).

Lichfield House Bore Street, Lichfield, adjoins Donegal House (VCH vol 14 p43). Timber-framed. The date '1510' is given on the centre gable (LAL p12). Pevsner agrees the house is of early C16 origin (BOE p194). But this date is probably 100 years too early for its construction (LAL 12p). Was the Tudor Cafe by 1974 and still was in 1990.

Lichfield St Chad Ancient parish and township. Sometimes formerly called 'Stow.' Formerly included the township of Curborough and Elmhurst (GLAUE p416). Was a peculiar jurisdiction of the dean of Lichfield cathedral (GLAUE).

Lichfield St Mary Ancient parish containing most of the town or later city of Lichfield (GLAUE p416).

Lichfield St Michael Chapelry in Lichfield St Mary until becoming a separate ecclesiastical parish in 1729. Had separate civil identity early. The parish included the out-townships of Fisherwick, Wall, Pipehill and Streethay, the chapels of Hammerwich, and Haselour, and the hamlets of Burntwood, Edial and Woodhouses (GLAUE p416). Was a peculiar jurisdiction of the dean of Lichfield cathedral (GLAUE).

Lichfield Town Ditch A ditch which marked the limits of medieval Lichfield, presumably dug when the town was established in the mid C12. Probably built by Bishop Clinton (1129-48). A ditch is recorded in 1208 (SHC 1924 pp19,165 pls) (VCH vol 14 p39). On the E side of the town the ditch ran from Stowe Pool to the junction of Lombard and Stowe Street. Then S across the end of Stowe Street, along what later became George Lane, across Tamworth Street, then along the later Gresley Row SW to St John Street. It crossed that street at a point N of St John's Hospital and ran NW to the present Friars Alley. It then turned to Trunkfield brook, following it downstream across Sandford Street and continuing N to join up with the Close ditch, which presumably served as the town ditch on the N and E side. A stretch between Tamworth Street and St John Street became a footpath known as Castle Ditch (see) (VCH vol 14 pp39-40). The ditch almost formed the boundary of the parish of St Mary and is shown on Snape's map (SSAHST 1968 p48).

Lickshead House to the SW of Ramshorn (1834 OS map). Has also appeared Lixhead (W p770). To its SE is a wood Lick's Wood (OS map 1:25,000).

Light Oaks Small residential area 0.75m E of Milton. Two people saw through a bedroom window a bright silver white object or UFO, stationary in the sky at Light Oaks on Aug 2 1967 at 6.00am (FSRP pp5-6).

Light Oaks House 0.5m WSW of Oakamoor (BOE p214). Has also appeared as Lightoakes. It was once the seat of the Bolton family (COPP2 p82p in 1909).

Lightoaks Farm 1.5m NW of Croxden, in Croxden parish. There was a farm at Lightoaks by 1722, when a wood known as Light Oakes Wood existed to the W of the farm (CDS pp19, 89).

Light Oaks Wood Wood to S of Light Oaks, Oakamoor. A character called 'Charcoal Jack' lived in a hut in the wood. He was one of the charcoal-burners employed up to the end of the C19 in Bolton's copper works (VB p174) (MR p180). Has also appeared as Lightoakes Wood.

Light's Yate There is a farm 'Light Gate' marked on a 'Plan of the Parish of Waterfall' 1846 between Waterfall church and the hall (NSJFS 1972 p123).

Lightwood District 0.5m to E of Cheadle. In Cheadle parish.

Lightwood Former hamlet on a high ridge above the Trent and Blithe upper valleys, now a suburb 1.5m SE of Longton. Former township with Blurton in Trentham ancient parish. A handled beaker of the Roman period was found at Lightwood in 1930 on land of Lightwood Concrete Aggregate Ltd (NSFCT 1930 pp141-142 p of facing p142) (NSJFS 1964 p36). In 1960 at No. 698 Lightwood Road a hoard of Roman coins and two silver snake bracelets were unearthed in a garden, wrapped in a coarse weave fabric (BNDA p1). The number of coins varies, some say 2400 (BNDA p1) or 2461 (NSJFS 1963 p19), or 2485 (STM March 1964 p48p of two silver bracelets) (NSJFS 1964 p36). Of which 1,739 were regular Roman coins and 722 irregular pieces and were mainly of the period 253-274 AD (NSJFS 1963 pp19-36 pls), and covering the reigns of Valerian to Probus (NSJFS 1964 p36). (STM June 1969 Supplement p12) (STMSM Jan 1973 p34 p of a small coin of Emperor Valerian from 253-259 AD) (SOK p10). The hoard is currently owned and displayed by the Potteries Museum. William Bailey of Lightwood was one of the first who made lustre pottery (HSP p76). Lightwood was taken into Stoke-on-Trent county borough in 1922 (VCH vol 8 p260).

Lightwood On western edge of Penn Common. The name appears in 1717. Said to be so called from the perambulation of the parish boundary and the lighting of the way by torches. However, Dunphy thinks the name is of either Saxon origin and derive from 'llith' or of Middle English origin and derive from 'lith,' 'lyth' both of which mean slope or hillside (PAIP p84).

Lightwood Common Lightwood, Longton. Waste land formerly in Normacot township in Stone ancient parish. 198 acres of the common were enclosed under an Act of 1793 (SHC 1941 p17).

Lightwood Corner The Penkridge-Broadhurst Green and Cannock-Stafford (A34) crossroads (1834 OS map) (Dower's map).

Lightwood Forest Lightwood, Longton. 650 acres of Lightwood Forest and Blurton banks were enclosed under an Act of 1734 (SHC 1941 p16). White describes it as an enclosed district within the chapelry of Blurton (W p433).

Lightwood Heath May be identified with Threpwode or Threpwoode, a wood in the vicinity of Copshurst Farm long disputed between Normacot and Trentham manors until settled upon Trentham in 1242. Names with Old English 'threap' record long-forgotten boundary disputes (English Place Names. K Cameron) (Discovering Parish Boundaries. Angus Winchester. 1990. p38) (SSE 1994 p77).

Lightwood Hills Longton (NSFCT 1910 p203). May be the hills to the SW of Lightwood and Cocknage.

Lightwoods House In Lightwoods Park at Bearwood, Smethwick. It is said to have been built by Jonathan Grundy of Leics in 1791 (STELE Sept 1 1951) (VCH vol 17 p101) (SMEOP p48p) or by Madame Grundy in 1791; her arms are in Smethwick Old Church (RS p121). Pevsner says the house looks early Georgian, but there is supposed to be a brick inside inscribed '1789' (BOEW p91) (BCM April 1968 p38). Another account says a brick in the wall immediately E of the entrance porch is inscribed 'Jonathan Grundy, June 19 1780' (VCH vol 17 p101). By marriage the house, at times known as The

Lightwoods, passed to the Willett family in 1829. It passed to the family of George Caleb Adkins in 1865 (RS p121) (STELE Sept 1 1951. Dec 29 1951) (VCH vol 17 pp101-102 plan) (SMEOP p48). It was sometime the seat of Francis Galton (WMVB p129). The house and park was bought for the public by AM Chance in 1902 (VCH vol 17 pp101,102). By 1989 the house contained a stained glass studio of world-wide renown (WMVB p129). The name Lightwoods is from the tract of woodland in the area (VCH vol 17 pp101,102). The ancient wood known as Lord's Wood appeared as Great Lightwood in 1709 (STELE Feb 1 1952).

Lightwoods Park Public park 1m S of Smethwick. The park contains a Shakespeare Garden containing flowers, plants and herbs mentioned in his plays (WMVB p129).

Lily Dale A dale by the brook which flows towards Bucknall from Wash Well (FWMBS p4). Lily Dale Farm in Ubberley Road, Ubberley, was for some reason known as Sudden Hall (BUB pp39-40).

Lime House Wisemore, Walsall. Home of Elias Crapper, a local limestone quarry owner of the 1950s. The house was built of limestone rubble and was demolished to make way for a supermarket (WROP p98p).

Lime Pearl Pool In the vicinity of Charlemont Hall; a passage may have lead from the hall to it. Parliamentarians are said to have watered their horses here in the Civil War. Recently (1997) it has dried up (TB Feb 1997 p29).

Lime Pit Bank Former area of Walsall in the present Bank Street area, E of Ablewell Street, under 0.25m E of the parish church. The area was so called by the 1760s. There was metal-working here by 1767 (VCH vol 17 pp153,191). William Siddons, the actor (see under Walsall), performed the play 'Douglas' in an old malthouse in the Lime Pit Bank (SHOS vol 2 p73) (SNWA p9).

Limes, The Sedgley. Here Eliza Tinsley (b1813), business woman and nail factor of Old Hill (see) died on April 18 1882 (BCM July 1982 pp43p-46).

Limes Britannicus Is the Limes Britannicus of the Notitia (Notitia Dignitatum. ed O Seeck. 1876), an earthen wall fronted by a ditch which the Romans constructed from the Don to the Severn, the limits being Doncaster and Gloucester (or Tewkesbury - NSFCT 1902 pp105-106) respectively to mark off the territories of the tribes of the Brigantes, Silures and Ordovices. It was built probably by Ostorius Scapula in 50 AD and acted as a defence barrier for the Fosse Way to the S. It was similar to the Roman structure known as the Limes Germanicus, which ran from the Rhine to the Danube. Limes Britannicus lost its importance with the building of Hadrian's wall. The fosse disappeared under Agricola. Subsequently, it is claimed that it became the mark of the Mercians (Mark-people). The course followed is Doncaster, Sheffield, Buxton, Leek, Stone, NW of Gnosall, Shifnal, Worcester, Tewkesbury and Gloucester. There are sections still visible in the Grey Ditch (since shown to be not Roman) at Bradwell, Derbys; traces of a vallum on Gun Hill; in Abbey Wood, near Dieulacres Abbey; Felt House farm near Cheddleton; and a vallum or raised road near Frankville, Ranton (NSFCT 1902 pp105-106. 1946 pp151-152. 1982 p23) (VCH vol 1 p186). DG Harnaman suggested Lyme in Newcastle-under-Lyme was from the Limes Britannicus (NSFCT 1951 p119). Has also appeared as Limes Britannica (SMM p111), and a stretch in the county appears to have been known as The Mark (OL vol 2 pp15-16). The Limes was serviced by a military road and a supposed chain of forts built by Ostorius Scapula stood at intervals on it; Leek has been identified as the Concagios of the Notitia; Walton (Stone) as the Lavatres; Brough Hall (Ranton) as Veterum or Veteris; Shifnal, Shrops as Braboniacum. However, Prof Haverfield has identified Lavatres, Veteris and Braboniacum with Lavatris, Verteris, and Bravonacis as stations on the second Iter of Antoninus which lay between Isurium (Aldborough, Yorks) and Carlisle, and must have been far removed from Staffs. Prof Haverfield has further shown that the whole theory of the forts of Ostorius Scapula has been founded upon a corrupt text and bad translation of Tacitus (VCH vol 1 p186).

Limestone Hill Hill 0.5m E of Stanton.

Lime Tree House Once fronted the High Street, Bloxwich. The site is now occupied by the car park of a superstore. The house was once the property of Pat Collins 'King of Showmen' (1859-1943) and for many years Bloxwich wakes were held on land behind the house (BY p4) (SNBP p34). Bloxwich wake was still taking place on temporary sites in the early 1970s (VCH vol 17 p250).

Linacre Field name and former settlement. A Ralph de Linacre occurs in Henry II's reign. At or near Linacre may have stood the original Pipe Ridware Manor House; Robert de Pipe, lord of Pipe Ridware, is recorded as residing at or near Linacre in Henry III's reign. The manor house is recorded as Pipehalle (1319), Pypehalle (1420), and Pypehal orcharde (1443); the last form, according to Shaw, can probably can be identified with the later Quintin's Orchard, and therefore places Linacre at Quintin's Orchard (SHOS vol 1 p166*) (THS p71) (GNHS p149).

Linbrook Runs from Byrkley Park to Woodlane joins the Swarbourn and that joins the Trent. Boundary which divides Yoxall and Barton wards of Needwood Forest (VCH vol 2 p352). Has appeared as Limbreuk (1286), Lynbroke (1540), Lynbrooke (1611), and Lintbrooke (1650) (SPNO p12). (SHOS vol 1 p66). The name means 'the noisy brook' (SPNO p12) (SPN p79).

Linbrook A collection of tiny places running N and S of Byrkley from the N - Upper Linbrook Cottages, Middle Linbrook Farm, Lower Linbrook Farm, Linbrook Bridge. In Yoxall parish.

Lincroft Former common land in Tatenhill ancient parish (HOPT vol 1 p135). The land called Lincroft which today (1995) funds a sermon at Barton-un-der-Needwood (see) on Good Friday, initiated by William Key of Sherholt Lodge in 1651, is a field adjacent to the A38 on the area known as 'Fatholme' between Barton Turns and 'Catholme' (UNT pp21-23).

Lincoln Brook Rises at Blymhill Lawn; a tributary of Mottymeadows Brook. Runs E of Blymhill.

Linden Lea The name is preserved in a road name S of Compton Road 1.5m W of Wolverhampton.

Lindens Small district 0.75m N of the earthwork known as King's Standing, Great Barr. (Birmingham A-Z). The area was Perry Barr Common (1834 OS map). There was a farm called Lindens on the present Queslett Road East near the junction with Old Chester Road by 1887 (OS map 1887). The name means lime tree or trees (SNAR p101).

Linedon N of Compton, Enville (Plot's map). The name is taken from Anglo-Saxon 'lind dun' meaning 'lime trees on a hill' (SPN p79). It was the seat of the Grays.

Line House House in Stoney Lane, S of the present Lewisham Street, West Bromwich. In existence by 1699. Demolished in c1820 (VCH vol 17 p23).

Line Houses Former tiny hamlet on top of Harecastle Hill 1m S of Kidsgrove. Settlement built in the 1840s for construction workers on the Harecastle railway tunnel. But one block was in existence by 1839 and may have been built for canal tunnel builders in the 1820s (VCH vol 8 p83) (IAS p173) (IANS p141) (TTTD p196). Has also appeared as Linehouses (IANS p141). Presumably 'line' refers to the railway line.

Linley Tiny district 0.75m NNW of Talke on Ches border.

Linley Over 1m W of Aldridge. In Aldridge ancient parish. There have been limestone quarries at Linley since very early times. Quarries here were possibly worked by the Romans for material used in building Letocetum (SNWA p4); the foundations of the bath-house there are of Wenlock limestone, possibly quarried from Daw End and or at Linley Farm (VCH vol 2 pp189,192-193. vol 14 pl 55) (The Limestone Mines of Walsall. Henry E Green. 1977). At Linley Farm a Roman fibula (clasp or buckle) was found in 1795 and some ancient coins in the cutting of the Daw End Branch of the Rushall Canal (SHOS vol 1 General Intro p35 pl A. fig 13. vol 2 p66) (THS p148) (HOWW pp25,148) (GNHS p70) (CCC p9) (VCH vol 2 p193) (NSJFS 1964 p33). A billion tetradrachma (AD 287-288) was found near the same place in 1957 (MOA p127). Some caverns were here in redundant limestone quarries, which, White noted in the mid C19, were grand and extensive and led to a subterraneous lake visited by tourists in the summer, and were brilliantly illuminated (W p643). The Linley caverns were described in 1856 as 'caverns of immense extent which lead to a large subterranean lake' (ADY p8). In WW2 it is believed the caves were used to store ammunition; the entrances have long since been blocked up (SNAR p36). The name Linley appears in 1432 (SNAR p36). It means 'a place where flax is grown' (SNAR pp36,62). A Linley Lodge stood SE of Barns Road in 1834 (1834 OS map). The name is preserved in Linley Lodge Industrial Estate.

Linley Hall Situated on a hill at Linley Wood, Talke, and was bounded on one side by rocks. A tunnel once existed from the hall to the rocks, but caved in many years ago (Kidsgrove, Talke and Mow Cop. Postcards from the Past. Roger Simmons 1998 p45p). An iron spear with a hammered socket 13 inches in length over all found in a trench near the hall was presented to a NSFC member in the early 1950s. It is perhaps of the medieval period (NSFCT 1953 p106).

Linley Wood At Talke, Kidsgrove. In Talke township in Audley ancient parish (W p428). BB Simms believed there were the terraces here of a pre-Roman agricultural community (NSFCT 1935 p91). Mrs Anne Marsh-Caldwell, poet and novelist, was born at Linley Wood in 1791 and died here in 1874; she was famous in her day as a voluminous novelist (DNB) (PSS p466) (VFC p91). The name is from probably Limeley (Lyme) (HBST p20).

Linthouses, The 1.25m NE of Wednesfield. Formerly in Wednesfield chapelry in Wolverhampton parish. The name, in use by 1750 (WFW p105), is preserved in Linthouse Lane.

Lion Lodges Two lodges now converted into residences at eastern approach to Ingestre Hall, Ingestre. (MR p195).

Lion's Den Cannock Chase. At approximately SK 015186. Here in 1951 a beech tree stood athwart a stream, the water issuing from beneath the well-washed roots (GCC p37). Finlow does not know why it is so called (RRCC p5). Nearby at SK 014184 is an icehouse for Wolseley Hall (IHB p396).

Lion's Den Cavern in Wren's Nest Hill, near Dudley (BCM Oct 1970 p51).

Lion's Den, The A lane to the SE of Hammerwich church (MR p170). The lane was known as Elder Lane from the late Middle Ages to c1881 when it acquired the name Lion's Den (VCH vol 14 p259).

Lion's Den Artificial caves situated on edge of the Common Plot or The Plot, N of Stone, between Mount Road and Old Road. Created by a family named Cartwright quarrying the Keuper sandstone which they sold for cleaning steps (NSFCT 1897 p152 ps. 1910 pp208-209. 1940 p31) (SSBOP p30 p of in 1910). The caves were filled in at some time between 1914 and c1970.

Lions Den A very old cottage on the Birmingham Road, Walsall. The name is from the estate on which the cottage stood (1834 OS map) (SNWA p67).

Lion's Paw Cowall. Bode writes of a Lion's Paw at the turn in the B road from Bemersley to Ladymoor Gate at Cowall (SMCC p6). It is a corruption of Lion Spaw, a spring, which was a resort for sufferers of the King's Evil and appears as Lion Spaw on an old plan of 1771 (ONST 1929 p24). The wood NE of Knypersley Pool has been called Lion's Paw (TTTD p159).

Lion's Rock In Stoney Dale, Oakamoor. Is claimed to have been the hide-out of highwaymen (TFTPM p66).

Lion's Tooth Rock A pointed rock in Pike Pool, which is in the Dove, Dove Dale (PS p107) (ES April 25 1930 p6p. Nov 10 1932 p6. April 5 1934 p8p).

Litley House slightly under 1m SW of Cheadle. Was the first manor to be carved out of the manor of Cheadle. The farmhouse of Litley presumably stands near or on the site of Litley manor house. It took its name from the Lytlehay family who came to it at the end of the C13 (NSFCT 1885 p60. 1913 pp143,145).

Litley Dale Litley (CCT p92).

Litlington Here was anciently (perhaps in the C17?) found the foundation of a wall that enclosed a quadrangular area of 34 yards by 24, which was situated 10 yards from an ancient Roman road called anciently Ashwell Street Newcastle-under-Lyme. The spot was known in old deeds as 'Heaven's Walls' and lies at the bottom of a hill on the summit of which was a tumulus called Limbury or Limbloe Hill, in which was found a Roman coin and the head of Trajan (HSP pp116,117 - Simeon Shaw's source could be Plot?). The only Ashwell (Road) that can be found is in the area of the City General Hospital, Newcastle-under-Lyme. Has also appeared as Lillington.

Little Abovepark House 2m N of Dilhorne. Under 0.25m to the N is the source of the Tean. The source of the Blithe is 0.25m to WNW, at Overmoor.

Little Ankerton House 1.25m NNE of Eccleshall. May formerly have been called Bentham (1834 OS map) (Dower's map).

Little Armshead Farm 1m N of Werrington. Near here a 'Mere Stone,' and a 'stone marked with a cross' are mentioned in an account of the perambulation of Bucknall manor boundary made in 1803 (WJ p19).

Little Aston Village on the slopes of a gentle eminence near the head of Footherley Brook near Ryknild Street, 18m SE of Stafford. Formerly in the Stonnall district of Shenstone ancient parish (W p582). An estate comprising Little Aston and Barr appears in a charter of 957 (SL p61) (SSE 1991 p8) (MOA p127). Another source implies the charter of 957 relates to Aston-by-Stone, not Little Aston (SSE 1996 p10). Little Aston is said to appear in DB from which source it can be deduced that it had split from Barr and become a part of Shenstone (MOA p127). Little Aston was written Little Aston-upon-Colfeld or Colfield or Colefield in the C13 and the C14. The Colefield or Coldfield was an immense heath, partly in Cannock Forest and partly in Sutton Chase (DUIGNAN). The name means East town (DUIGNAN) (SPN p80). Little appears to have been an addition to distinguish it from Aston near Birmingham (THS p163). The church, St Peter, Roman Road, was built in 1874 (LDD). Little Aston became a separate ecclesiastical parish in 1876 (GLAUE p402). Edward VIII, when Prince of Wales, played golf at the course at Little Aston on Dec 5 1932 (GATD p120p).

Little Aston Hall 0.25m W of Little Aston church. The manor of Little Aston was owned by the Aston family (History of the Forest and Chase of Sutton Coldfield. Miss AA or L Bracken. 1860). The first house on the site of the present house was built by Richard Scott of Birmingham in c1660 (SLHT p4). Or the same or another Richard Scott built a house on slightly higher ground than a previous house in 1730 (SVB p111). Pevsner dates the new hall to the late C18, the architect was James Wyatt (d1813) of Blackbrook Farm (see) (BOE p196). 'The Beauties of England and Wales' called this hall a splendid mansion (BOE p196). Shaw made a drawing of it in 1801 (SHOS vol 2 p52 il) (ASE p59 il) (GATD p28 il). (W p583). The hall was rebuilt, encased, or restored between 1857-9 for ES Parker Jervis by the architect,

Edward J Payne, in the Italianate style (GATD p35 il in 1880) (BOE p196 pl 89) (SLHT p4). It was converted into luxury apartments in 1927 (SVB p111). The Morning Room has a beautiful frieze (Birmingham Sunday Mercury 1937) (GATD pp40,41p,42p detail).

GROUNDS. Some beech trees around the lodge in Thornhill Road are said to have been planted by Emma, Lady Hamilton during a supposed visit she made to the hall in 1802 (SLHT p4). Outside the front door of the hall in the 1920s was a flamboyant fountain with an extravagant figure of Pan by Bloye (GATD pp38,39p of c1930). The gatehouse at the corner of Hardwick Road and Roman Road is one of the entrances to Little Aston Hall estate (SLHT p4). There was an ice-house 0.25m S of the hall, close to an area used as the maintenance yard belonging to Little Aston Golf Club. It was situated on a ridge which drops down to the pool. When ESSO took over the hall they used the ice-house as their telephone exchange, but it has since been destroyed (GATD pp49-50). The Orangery still stands but has lost its pediments (GATD p49 p of in 1915).

Little Barr Former manor which emerged by the end of the C12 as a division of Barr manor; Little Barre appears in 1208 (SPN p55) and Great Barr about the same time. In the C14 the manors of Perry and Little Barr were listed together and by 1459 they had become one entity, known as Perry Barr; with the name Little Barr dropping out of use (VCHWA vol 7 pp24,71) (MNB p54). There was possibly a village of Little Barr, probably deserted between 1334-1377 (SSAHST 1970 p34). Has also appeared as Parva Barr.

Little Barr Manor House May have stood on the site of the later Oscott Manor Farm (see).

Little Barr Park Medieval deer park created by John de Pirie in Sutton Chase by 1297 (NSJFS 1968 p50) (MNB p66).

Little Birches On the edge of Cannock Chase, near Rugeley. The remains of a glass kiln of the C16 was found here in 1992. Believed to be the oldest kiln of its kind in England the kiln was taken to the Broadfield House Glass Museum at Kingswinford in 1994 (ES Aug 10 1994 p11). Perhaps Lower Birches is meant.

Little Bishop's Wood Could it be that which is N of main Bishop's Wood, and S of what is called Burnt Wood? BOV p78 says in Little Bishop's Wood there is a very large heap of slag which has lain undisturbed for centuries, also the remains of two dams, one with a wooden sluice pipe in place. The date of the sites was a mystery until a fragment of pottery was found at the largest site, which was identified as of C14 origin by the Potteries Museum. Since then other fragments have been found which all amount to evidence of iron smelting in the area.

Little Blithe Tributary of the Blithe, which it joins 2.25m SE of Blithfield Reservoir.

Little Blore House or minute hamlet 1m SSE of Fairoak.

Little Bloxwich Former hamlet now a suburb of Bloxwich, 0.75m to the NE of Great Bloxwich (Bloxwich). By the later C18 Little Bloxwich lay in the area formed by Little Bloxwich Lane (now Lichfield Road), Stoney Lane, and Selman's Hill (VCH vol 17 p163). The OS map 1834 marks two Little Bloxwichs; one here and one at Fishley Mill. The original settlement may have centred on the stretch of Stoney Lane between Fishley Lane and Selman's Hill where Little Bloxwich Green lay in the later C18. The road between Stafford and Walsall passed through Little Bloxwich until 1766, when it was re-routed through Great Bloxwich (Bloxwich) (VCH vol 17 p163).

Little Bradsholme Field name on the banks of the Trent about Handsacre and Mavesyn Ridware (SHOS vol p181).

Little Bramshall On the S side of Bramshall village (W p771). But is marked to the E of Bramshall on OS map 1834 in the approximate position of The Elms Farm on the S side of Bramshall Road. Has also appeared as Little Bromshall. In DB Little Bramshall formed the moiety of Bramshall manor held by the Crown. It was subsequently severed from Bramshall and added to Uttoxeter ancient parish (SHC 1908 p4).

Little Bridgeford Minute hamlet 0.5m NW of Great Bridgeford. In Seighford parish. Little Bridgeford or Great Bridgeford appears in DB.

Little Brook Runs from Compton joins Mill Brook N of Kinver.

Little Burton Tiny hamlet NW of Burton upon Trent (1834 OS map). The name is preserved in a tiny triangle street at the junction of Horninglow Street and Horninglow Road.

Little Caldmore Tiny street linking Caldmore Road (formerly Caldmore Lane) and Bath Street, Caldmore, Walsall (VCH vol 17 p155).

Little Chell Former vill of Chell township in Wolstanton ancient parish, under 1m ENE of Tunstall, 0.5m NE is Great Chell. Little Chell was still undeveloped by the end of the C19 (VCH vol 8 p83). Although, now merges into Potteries suburbs. The occupants of a house in Scott Road who had heard sounds of an explosion under the floors believed the house to be haunted (ES

Feb 19 1981 p15p).

Little Common Name appears in the 1891 census for an area of Pelsall focused on the houses alongside the High Street end of Pelsall Common as well as those in Green Lane and facing onto Norton Road near the Old House at Home (SNBP p85).

Little Crane Brook Former tributary of Big Crane Brook until Chasewater was enlarged. Now the two brooks join in Chasewater.

Little Curborough Minor former settlement of Curborough, and a township. It lay about Curborough House in the Middle Ages and was later depopulated. A Great Curborough lay about Curborough Hall Farm (VCH vol 14 p229). By 1327 the township of Little Curborough was known as Curborough Somerville (VCH vol 14 p282).

Little Dunstal Farm Dunstal, N of Abbots Bromley. Here the Abbots Bromley Horn Dancers performed in the afternoon of Sept 6 1999.

Little Eaves Forms part of the hamlet of Eaves (see) 0.5m SSE of Hulton Abbey.

Little Fenton At approximately Manor Field Link Road and Lytton Street, Fenton, S of Stoke-on-Trent railway (1834 OS map).

Littlehales Mansion on Buxton Road, Leek. Built by William Spooner Brough, son of Joshua Brough, silk manufacturer, in 1880. The house is probably named after William's mother, the daughter of William Spooner Littlehales of Erdington, Warws (VCH vol 7 pp94,95il).

Little Hardwick Perhaps a farm or small hamlet in existence by 1832 in the area of the present The Downs, a street S of Hardwick Road, to the W of Hardwick. The name, still used in 1920, is preserved in Little Hardwick Road, SE of Barr Common (SNAR pp99,104).

Little Harlaston House SE of Harlaston church. The name appears on the 1884 OS map 6 inch. (OS Street Atlas of Staffs 1995).

Little Hay Hamlet on low ground by Littlehay Brook 1.5m SSE of Shenstone. In Shenstone ancient parish. Over 0.5m N of Warws, but before 1966 the Warws border came up to the S edge of it. Has also appeared as Littlehay (DUIGNAN). The name means little enclosure (or division) (DUIGNAN). A little cottage in the village was haunted by poltergeist activity (GPCE p33).

Littlehay Former manor directly to N of Colton. In Colton ancient parish. Has appeared as Colt (DB) (CWF p5), Luttelhay (C13) (SSE 1996 p15) and Little Hay. The name means 'small enclosure,' although this would not be a reference to the medieval Colton Old Park to the NE of Stockwell Heath as this did not form a part of Littlehay manor (CWF pp153,164). Littlehay manor passed from the Mavesyns to the Blithfields in the period c1287 to 1339 (or 16th Edward II) (SHC 1914 p154 note).

Littlehay Brook Joins Black Brook at Thickbroom which joins the Bourne and runs into Warws. The name appears in 1784 and means 'the small enclosure' (SPNO p12).

Littlehay Manor House Stood on the E side of High Street, Littlehay, Colton. The old manor house, a half-timbered building covered with rough cast, built in the C16 (DoE) was taken down in 1846 (LTM Oct 1971 p35), having become unsafe for habitation, although, the walls were still strong. To mark its site two Tudor chimneys together with the ancient hearth, were spared by Lord Bagot's orders, at the suggestion of Mr HW Holland, then tenant of the manor farm (CWF p161, il of facing p161) (DoE II) (BOE p107). A house of the same name stood in the same area as the former manor house in 1902 (1902 OS map 6 inch).

Little Haywood Village on a bank by the Trent 0.75m SE of Great Haywood. Formerly partly in Colwich ancient parish (W p416) and partly in Stowe ancient parish (SGSAS). Was in Colwich prebend (SSAHST vol 2 1960-61 p44). Little Haywood manor was held under the Gresley family; the well-known family of Grin was seated at Little Haywood between 1200 - 1350, probably later (SHC 1914 p134 note). The earliest reference found by Duignan to Little Haywood was in 1432 (DUIGNAN p77). For etymology see under Great Haywood. Up to the late C18 Little Haywood practically constituted houses known as The Old Manor House (see), The Old Hall (see), The Stone House (see), The Bowyer Arms, The Old House and Mount Pavilion (see), all lay on the slope of Coley Hill and at its base (ie along Coley Lane and the Colwich road) (HAH p41). The Trent and Mersey Canal passes on the S side of the village where along the towpath is a mile stone with 'Preston Brook 55 Miles - Shardlow 37 Miles' (CCF p106). The heaviest or largest pig is thought to have been a British Gloucester Old Spot hog or Midland Plum Pudding hog, which weighed 12cwt 66lbs. In 1774 it stood four feet 8.5 inches high and nine feet eight inches long (GBR 1987 p156) (CL April 9 1992 p63). One GBR account says it was bred by Joseph Lawton of Astbury, Ches, and possibly owned by Joseph Bradley of Little Haywood (GBR 1987 p156. 1993 p145), whilst another says Joseph Lawton of Astbury owned it (GBR 1996 p173). There is an undated painting of this pig titled 'Gloucester Old Spot at

Great Haywood, Staffordshire' painted in the English naive style by an unknown artist (The Times Feb 13 1993 p7pc). Some say the pig is depicted in this painting in front of the Lamb and Flag Inn at Little Haywood (GBR 1986 p158pc). For the highwayman Robert Lander of Haywood see under Great Haywood. For the author, JRR Tolkien (1892-1973), at Little Haywood see Great Haywood.

Little Heath Minute hamlet 1.5m W of Dunston. On the W side of the road between Little Heath and Tofts a field which still (1959) contained pools was known in 1754 as Motes and in c1841 as Moat Bank. It is probably the site of a medieval house. There is a local tradition that stones were carted away from an ancient house which stood N of Dunston Heath near the present Yew Tree Farm (VCH vol 5 p143) (SSAHST 1982-3 p39).

Little Heath Green Hales. Now Little Heathgreen Farm.

Little Hill Former narrow footway leading to Walsall parish church from the top of High Street. It was widened into what is now the street known as Church Hill (VCH vol 17 p149). The name 'Little Hill' arose to distinguish it from the big hill which was Hill Street (SNWA p29).

Little Hill Wednesbury. Here was or is St Boniface's Well.

Little Home In the Penkridge area. Here was common land (VCH vol 5 p127).

Little Ingestre House which was occupied in the late C19 by the Earl of Shrewsbury's agent (COI p42). By 1988 the house was the Balmoral Hotel and restaurant (MR p195). Formerly a small hamlet 0.75m E of Ingestre which may have been the original Ingestre settlement (COI p42).

Little Island The name appears on the 1889 OS map 6 inch, and on 1947 OS map 1:25,000 (sheet 32/99), at SO 974989 in the area of Clarke's Lane ENE of Willenhall, N of Shepwell Green. The area has also been called Island (1841 census) and The Island and is roughly triangular in shape. 'Island' probably arose as the area was bounded by water. The bounds were the Wyrley & Essington Canal from Clarke's Lane to Spring Bank on the N side; a brook from Spring Bank to Stringes Lane on the W side; the Tame from Stringes Lane to the Wyrley & Essington Canal beyond Bentley Cemetery on the S side (TB April 1995 p29). Or more likely the name Little Island arose as the area was once populated by Irish emigrants and thus gained the name of 'Little Ireland,' soon corrupted to Little Island (SNW p17).

Little John's Stride A little to NE of Wetton is Little John's Stride (WTCEM p58). Burial mound? Perhaps, the three burial mounds in a row 0.75m NNE of Wetton. Evidence, perhaps, of Robin Hood's activities in the area? Could also be called Little Low (see).

Little Lawn Farm 0.5m SE of Bagnall. In existence by 1851 when it was occupied by Maria Steele. It may represent a division of Lawn Farm estate (centred on Big Lawn Farm), divided in the early C19 (B pp66-67p).

Little London House which lay at the end of a track running E from Winterdyne Farm over 1m SSE of Harlaston. Formerly in Harlaston township in Clifton Campville ancient parish. It appears on the 1884 OS map 6 inch but not on current OS maps.

Little London Area at the southern end of Sandwell Street, Walsall. It was inhabited by the later C17, and was a spur-making centre by the earlier C18 (VCH vol 17 pp155,156). The lower part of the district was known as the Follet (derived from Folley), a cartway connecting Sandwell Street with West Bromwich Street. The old part, the original Little London, was known earlier as Doveridge Fold, the end of a district called Doveridge (SNWA p69). The name Little London had appeared by 1834 (OS map 1834) and is said to have been given to the district on account of the arrogance of the new residents, who made claim to so many rights that the district was sarcastically called Little London (SNWA p69). The name is preserved in the street Little London between West Bromwich Street and Sandwell Street.

Little London District of Willenhall, under 0.5m N of Willenhall. Formerly in Willenhall chapelry in Wolverhampton ancient parish. The district was so named by the mid C18 (HOWI p186). The name may have arisen from the fact that some of the City of London Companies owned land in this district. There is a farm called Clothiers (see) in the vicinity which may have been owned by the Merchant Tailors' Company, who were often referred to as the Clothiers (HOWI p186) (SNW p18). Close by in Wednesfield chapelry, there was land known as Inlondes Medewe between 1290 and 1376. The medieval term 'lond' means wild and the Old English 'Inlendise' means native or natural (WFW p48). Or the name is from this area having been a stopping place for drovers travelling between London and Wales (TB Sept 1998 p29). A Baptist chapel was built here in 1792. The chapel, demolished in 1994, stood opposite Willenhall's bull ring at the junction of Temple Bar and the Wednesfield and Bloxwich roads (AOW p189) (Little London Baptist Church. Leslie E Burrows. 1997).

Little Longsdon House 0.5m N of Longsdon. Formerly in Longsdon township in Leek ancient parish. Stands on top of a long ridge, which may be the long

hill which gives Longsdon its name (VCH vol 7 p203). The manor of Over Longsdon, in existence by 1278, may have centred on the area of Little Longsdon and Great Longsdon, and the settlement Over Longsdon, recorded in 1278, also may have been in this area (VCH vol 7 pp203, 205).

Little Low Wednesfield. One of the burial mounds thrown up after the battle of Wednesfield (SHOS vol 2 p150). Also noted by Huntbach (AOW p7). (DUIGNAN pp10,97). Has also appeared as Lowe.

Little Low Wetton. Burial mound? (WTCEM p6). There are many unnamed (on maps) burial mounds about Wetton. Although Roberts mentions Little John's Stride (see), as well as this burial mound, this could be another name for it?

Little Madeley Small hamlet 0.75m NE of Madeley. In Madeley parish. In 1817 at Little Madeley Parks Farm was found two urns containing a quantity of Roman copper (or bronze NSJFS 1964 p29) coins. The urns were destroyed. The coins were dated from 235 AD to 340 or said by Pitt to be from Maximinus to Constantine II (THS p447) (GNHS p70) (HBST p17 ils) (SG p19) (VCH vol 1 pp186,191) (M p21). It is possible some of these coins are preserved in Newcastle-under-Lyme Museum (NSJFS 1964 p29). Little Madeley was unrecognised by the Post Office in 1976 (ES Jan 9 1976).

Little Marsh District of Penkridge to the E of the town centre on E side of the canal. The horse fairs seem to have been held in the area of The Marsh to the E of the town by 1754 (VCH vol 5 p129).

Little Moor House under 0.5m SE of Pattingham. It was so called by 1338 and was a settlement by 1439 (VCH vol 20 p173). Appears as Little Moore on Plot's map. 0.25m NE is Great Moor.

Little Moor Partly timber-framed farmhouse of early C17 origin, S of Parkgate Bridge, 0.75m W of Teddesley Hall. By c1841 was known as Park Gate House (VCH vol 5 p184).

Little Onn Hamlet on low ground at the foot of the hill on which High Onn stands, on the E side, 1m ESE of High Onn. Former township in Church Eaton ancient parish. Has appeared as Anne (DB) (identified by Eyton), possibly as Othna (c1130) (SHC 1883 part 2 p52), Parva Onne (1271-1485), Littel Onne (1545) (SPNO p141), and Low Onn. The name Onn means in Celtic, rock or hill (NSFCT 1908 p119) (M p4). In Welsh onn (plural) is ash trees, hence 'little ashes,' although 'little' is probably a Middle English addition (DUIGNAN). Ekwall tentatively suggested that onn may be from the Welsh 'odyn' 'kiln' from older Primitive Welsh 'otn.' Oakden finding Ekwall to be wrong thinks 'river on whose banks ashes grew' (SPNO pp141-142). Rev Canon GTO Bridgeman noted Little Onn was larger than High Onn (SHC 1883 part 2 p52 note). There is a legend that the local witch, Joan Eaton, prevented a church being built here by repeatedly removing the stones to Church Eaton where it was eventually built (OSST 1931 p18). RAF Wheaton Aston airfield at Little Onn, covering the course of a Roman road, was the base for an Advanced Flying Training Unit between 1941 and 1947. In WW2 along with Lichfield it was the most important airfield in Staffs. In May 1944 a staggering 10,837 flying hours (7,964 day and 2,873 night) were flown by aircraft at this airfield; the equivalent of 15 aircraft permanently flying for 30 days. Aneurin Bevin flew to here on Oct 25 1946 for a conference in Stoke-on-Trent. Abandoned in the late 1940s. The site was sold in 1953 and later became a pig farm (info Ron Balding) (WMA pp78,247-258) (Action Stations. David J Smith. 1981. 2nd ed 1990. p203) (SHJ autumn 1989 p64).

Little Onn Hall The manor house of Little Onn manor. The earliest house may have been on the moated site still evident in the gardens. A later house was probably built by Henry Crockett between 1793-1796. The present house was built in c1870-5 by Lt Col CJ Ashton 150 yards due S (VCH vol 4 pp92,95-96). In the grounds are gardens designed by TH Mawson (BOE p104). The summerhouse is by TH Mawson (West Midland Gardens pp170-172). The Dog-bone Pond is a small ornamental pool in the shape of a dog-bone (ACGM pp389-393 fig 476 does not show it where the tennis lawn is depicted). Incorporated into the garden is a small rectangular moat, of perhaps, late medieval origin, about 50 yards NE of the hall (VCH vol 1. vol 4 p92) (SSAHST 1982-3 p38) (CAMS p63). There is a rose garden (ACGM p392p). There is a sundial (ACGM pp389-393 p). Some walling here may be part of the old manor (VCH vol 4 p92). (MR p99p). Also in the grounds a curious glacial boulder with an imprint like a cows hoof on it from Red House Farm (see). (CL April 6 1989 pp162-164 il).

Littlepark House 0.5m N of Okeover.

Little Pipe Hamlet 1m NW of Great Pipe and Pipe Hall (HOL p515). Little Pipe was one of the two post-DB manors of Pipe, the other was Great Pipe (DUIGNAN p119). Has also appeared as Parva Pipa (SPN p95). The name is preserved in Little Pipe Farm.

Little Powder House, The Tipton. A little brick shed associated with mining and pumping operations in the Tibbington area of Tipton. It was strongly built and held the powder explosives used in mining operations. The building may have been erected in the C18. There was a similar one on Wren's Nest Hill. The Powder House ended its days as a stable (BCM July 1977 p28 il by Bert Richards from 1920s).

Little Sandon Appears in DB as *parua Sandone*. Sandon present village represents it (SL p96); however, others have claimed it to have been Burston (BBH p6). It was called 'Little' to distinguish it from the medieval and now depopulated village of Great Sandon 0.5m to the E of present Sandon village (SL p96).

Little Saredon Small village on the southern slopes of Saredon Hill overlooking a tributary of Saredon Brook, 0.5m NNE of Shareshill. Formerly formed a township with Great Saredon, known as Saredon (see), in Shareshill ancient parish. Has appeared as Seredone (DB), or Seresdon (DB) (VCH vol 5 p176), Parva Sardona (c1255) (SSE 1996 p17), Parva Saredoun (1360) (SPNO p113), Littel Sardon (SPN p104), and Little Saredon (Yates' map). Was a separate manor to Great Saredon (DUIGNAN p132). The tenants of the Saredons who had common rights on Cheslyn Hay clashed with John Leveson the owner of the hay when he tried to enclose it in Henry VIII's reign (VCH vol 5 p178). The present windmill may stand on the site of a medieval mill existing in 1332. The present mill was in existence by 1816, towards the end of the century steam power within the mill replaced wind power. It was deserted and derelict during the 1930s. The sails were removed in 1942 the following year it was converted into a cottage (VCH vol 5 p177). In 1976 it was taken over by Mr N Faultless who commenced an extensive renovation. The tower was painted pink (WBJ p30 il xxiv in 1968) (AWM p33) (WIS) (TB May 1993 p21 of it in late 1920s and 1930s).

Little Saredon Manor Little Saredon. The manor house is listed (DoE II). Before the 1940s it was known as Hall Farm and was probably the 'Saraden Hall' mentioned in 1654 (VCH vol 5 p177 note). It is a moated house of stone, brick, and timber, and is of various dates. The central timbered portion is probably of C16 origin. The house was much restored in 1942 (VCH vol 5 p174) (SSAHST 1982-3 p46) (SVB p149).

Little Silkmore Former isolated small hamlet consisting of a collection of cottages to the W of Silkmore Lane, now merged into Stafford suburbs. In 1926 the British Reinforced Concrete Company built a factory next to the hamlet. By the mid 1970s most of the cottages had been demolished to make way for factory extensions (SAC pp11,12 see plan,13).

Little Snape House over 1.75m NNW of Abbots Bromley (1834 OS map) (Dower's map). The house is now called Heatley Bank Farm.

Little Stoke Former hamlet 1m SE of Stone. Formerly formed a township with Burston and Aston-by-Stone in Hilderstone quarter in Stone ancient parish (W p362). Has appeared as Stoca (DB), and Stoke-by-Stone. Keer's Cottage was the local name for the old thatched former Three Crowns Inn here at the junction of the Lichfield and Uttoxeter Roads. The inn was demolished and the present one built nearby. The name was from a Mr Keer who rented it (SSBOP p48p). By the 1960s Little Stoke was a residential area merged with Stone. By April 1998 there was a wooden cross on the E side of the A51 by a gate below the railway line at SJ 919321 to the memory of Keith Wainwright tragically killed here on March 27 1997 aged 17.

Littlestones House on S side of Belmont Road, WSW of Schoolhouse Green, Ipstones. To its ESE is The Stones (OS map 1888 6 inch).

Little Sugnall Tiny hamlet 0.75m NE of Croxton. Former township in the Woodland quarter in Eccleshall ancient parish (W p376). Has also appeared as Sugnall Parva.

Little Tess Cavern Former limestone quarry under Castle Hill, adjoining and on the S side of Dudley Tunnel. It was part of Dark Cavern and they were linked by a new canal tunnel to Dudley Tunnel in 1989; they are now a tourist attraction for boat parties (Dudley Canal Tunnel leaflet).

Little Tixall Appears as a house or minute hamlet 0.25m E of the Trent and Mersey Canal at Great Haywood on OS map 1924 sheet 38 SW. Has now been absorbed by Great Haywood. The name is preserved in Little Tixall Lane.

Little Town In the Level area of Brierley Hill. The name appears in the 1841 census.

Littleton A ward in Huntington civil parish. It appears to be focused on the former Littleton Colliery.

Littleton's Hall Stood behind a row of cottages on the E side of Bromford Lane (VCH vol 17 p23), West Bromwich. Lyttleton Hall Farm a square three-storey brick building of the later C18, believed to be a successor of a house owned by the Littleton family in 1609 (VCH vol 17 pp23-24). It has also been written Lyttleton Hall and was known as Littleton's Hall in 1723. In the early C19 it appears to have been occupied by the Dawes family. The hall was demolished in 1974 (mem in All Saints, West Bromwich) (TB June 1975

p16ps of the hall in 1973 front and back) or 1976 (TB Jan 1988 p17p). (WBOP p108ps).

Littlewood Small district W of the St Mark's church, Great Wyrley. Formerly in Cannock old parish now a ward in Cheslyn Hay civil parish. Has appeared as Luttelwood (1380), and Little Wood (1834 OS map) (SPNO p67).

Littleworth Former hamlet which lay in the area of the Hop and Barley Corn Inn, Mason Street, Coseley (CWBT p70) and it has been described as a village in West Coseley in Sedgley ancient parish (HC p62). The 'Plan of the Mines of Lord Dudley, 1812' shows it to the E of Parkes' Hall. It was a small centre of industry by the beginning of the C19 (HC p62). Littleworth toll house at Woodsetton was built in 1843 and was still standing in 1976 (HC il). It has since been moved to the Black Country Museum (SDOP p95). There is a Littleworth Avenue N of Sedgley Road.

Littleworth Former hamlet and now suburb 0.5m E of Stafford. Formerly in Hopton and Coton out-township of St Mary's parish, Stafford (W p341). The name 'Littleworth,' a derogatory one, appears in 1836 (SPNO p78). The hamlet started to develop after 1880 (VCH vol 6 p193). The mission church, St John the Baptist, in Tithe Barn Road was built in 1902. A new church on a new site on the corner of Weston Road and Westhead Avenue was built in 1928 using materials from the recently demolished Tixall Hall. Littleworth became an ecclesiastical parish in 1928 (VCH vol 6 p249). The area became more populated with the opening of the road and crossing over the Sow known as Riverway in 1914. By 1948 it was one of Stafford's largest suburbs (SKYT p97). An unusual custom which started in 1900 and still continuing in 1951 was the parade of a mock Mayor and Mayoress of Littleworth about Stafford. It seems to have begun in order to raise money for local hospitals and took place annually. The 'Mayor and Mayoress' of Littleworth left and returned to The Gate Inn, Littleworth, where a 'mayoral banquet' awaited them. The banquet was often attended by the Mayor of Stafford and various well-known local citizens (IOM p155).

Littleworth Hamlet, district 0.5m E of St Peter's church, Hednesford. In Cannock old parish. (W). The name is a derogatory one (SPNO p59). Littleworth tramway, opened in 1862, ran eastwards from Littleworth to Heathy Leasows (VCH vol 2 p318). The church, St Michael and All Angels, Littleworth Road, was built in c1990 (local info).

Littleworth 1.75m WSW of Rocester S of Woodhouse Fields, near crossroads (1834 OS map) (Dower's map).

Littleworth Hamlet and extension of Woodseaves, 0.25m to SW. In High Offley ancient parish. There was a windmill at SJ 796250 (WIS p24), which was advertised to be let in 1821 and was a working mill into last quarter of the C19 and said to have existed into the C20 (WBJ p47) (SLM spring 1954 p25).

Little Wyrley Former manor and hamlet on a low prominence by Wash Brook 2m SE of Great Wyrley. In Norton Canes ancient parish. The Wyrley (see) in DB is probably a reference to Little Wyrley, not Great Wyrley. Allowing for inheritance in the female line, the lordship of Little Wyrley manor has changed only once since the Norman Conquest (VB p125). Appears on Plot's map as Little Worley. Early lords of Little Wyrley were the Wyrley family who took their name from the place; this family later acquired land at Hamstead and Perry Barr (GWY p13). But a branch appears to have remained at Little Wyrley: Augustine Wyrley of Wyrley, Staffs and of Netherseal, Leics, was the father of William Wyrley (1565-1618), antiquary and Rouge Croix Pursuivant, and some say he (William Wyrley) was born at Wyrley (Little Wyrley?) (PSS pp1-3) (VFC p147). When young, Wyrley, whose grandfather was William Wyrley of Handsworth, was employed as amanuensis by Erdeswick of Sandon Hall. Whilst working with Erdeswick, he published under his own name a brief heraldic essay entitled 'The trve Vse of Armorie, shewed by Historie, and plainly proued by Example' (1592). Dugdale republished a part of the work in his 'Ancient Usage of Bearing Arms' (1682) and ascribed the work to Erdeswicke. In 1604 Wyrley was appointed Rouge Croix Pursuivant at the College of Arms. Wyrley, who was one of the earliest recorders of the Flitch of Bacon custom associated with Wychnor Manor House (see), also made a survey of Leics churches, which he compiled with William Burton, historian of Leics. Wyrley died on Feb 16 1617-18 and was buried in St Benet's church, near St Paul's Wharf, London (DNB) (SOS p xliv) (SHOS vol 2 p111) (GM vol lxii p417) (SMC p166) (BS p531) (SH p34) (VFC p147). In the C17 Mary Eagle of Little Wyrley reputedly could produce two quarts of milk from her breasts per day, besides what her child sucked. From this amount she could make 2lbs of butter per week during the months surrounding her child's birth. Plot sampled some of her butter (NHS p285) (SD p48). Another case of over-productive breasts is recorded at Rowley Regis (see).

Little Wyrley Hall W side of Little Wyrley hamlet. Has also appeared as Wyrley Grove and Little Wyrley Grove (W p573) (LGS p195) (CCF pp87-91). The core of the house is approximately early C16 (BOE p196). An additional service wing was added in c1660. Further additions were made in 1691. (SHOS vol 2 pp58-59 pl ix) (SLM summer 1954 p7p). Seat of the Fowke family by at least the later C17 (Plot's map) (W p573). Dr Phineas Fowke, who is remembered for walking to Edinburgh returning to the hall after his boots started hurting after 50 miles changing his footware and setting out again, inherited the manor in 1691 (SLM summer 1954 p15) (VB p125) (MR p245). By marriage the hall passed to the Husseys, whose seat it was by at least 1833 (mem in Norton Canes church). In 1851 it was occupied by PF Hussey (W p24). The great-granddaughter of Phineas Hussey, Mrs Wallace, was occupying the hall in 1952. In 1999 the hall was occupied by her son Hamish (SNBP p67) (SNBC p15). Visitors to the hall may have included Dryden in the 1680s (SSAHST 1966 p46). and David Garrick (1717-1779), actor (SNBP p66). In the 1930s Wright noted the coat of arms of the Fowkes was prominently displayed on the external walls of the hall. The windows of the ante room and dinning room have heraldic glass (CL Feb 1952 pp496-499 ps & ps of heraldic glass, Feb 29 1952 pp572-575 fig. 8 of the interior wind vane). There was a rare interior wind vane situated in a cupola in the roof over the entrance hall which told the way the wind was blowing without the inquirer having to leave the house. A spindle operated a golden arrow which revolved on a dial fixed in the floor? of the entrance hall. Wright in the 1930s found it partly dismantled, but the arrow and dial were left (CCF pp88-89). Bird implies it was still there in the early 1970s (VB p125). The library was compiled by Phineas Hussey. It has many first editions including NHS, and four volumes of the letters of Lady Mary Montague (CCF pp87-91). There was an early Renaissance chest with beautiful paintings on the internal lid, of galleons, a rising sun, and a castle-crowned hill. It stood in the hall (SLM summer 1954 p15p). In the grounds is a tithe barn dated 1664 (VB p125), 70 feet by 19 feet (SLM summer 1954 p15) (DoE II). In the barn is or was displayed a great collection of big-game hunting trophies of Frank Wallace, hunter, author and artist (VB p125). The gateway to the hall had a Latin inscription translated 'As to you so to others,' and the date 1687 (GM 1799).

Little Wyrley Manor House Little Wyrley. Former house established in the C12 by the Wyrley family who took their name from the place and afterwards resided at Handsworth (SH p34). Passed to the d' Oyley family who married into the Knighteley family of Little Onn. In 1313 Robert de Knightley was lord of Little Wyrley. John Knightely held the manor in 1339 by the annual render of a rose. The manor passed briefly into the Lee, Peshall, and Blount families (GWY p18).

Littywood Former manor and house at the foot of Butter Hill, on the W side, 1m NE of **Bradley**. In Bradley ancient parish. Has appeared as Lutiude (DB), Lutiwude (1203), Litlewude (1230), Luttlewode (1290), Lytewode (1485), and Littiwood (1616. 1775) (SPNO p135). The name is from probably, the little wood (DUIGNAN) (NSJFS 1981 p3). Or from Saxon 'langan alre,' '(place by) the tall alder tree' (SPN p94). Or of Celtic origin, the first element is composed of two Celtic roots; one is 'loa, lua, lia,' water, Welsh 'lli,' and the other is 'ti, tea, tai,' enclosure or house - hence 'water house' (NSFCT 1910 p160). The ancient timber-framed house, which has also been called Littywood Hall (SAC pp32,33p), is encased in brick in c1800; the core of it may be C14. The manor belonged to the Staffords in the C15 until it passed to Ann, a Stafford heiress. Through her marriage to Willoughby de Broke sometime between 1473 and 1521 Littywood passed to the de Broke family with whom it remained for many centuries. By 1556 the house was tenanted by the Stapletons who were tenants here for many succeeding centuries (NSFCT 1943 p66) (OSST 1956-59 p41). It was occupied by the Cottons in the C18 (mems in Bradley church). The house is situated in the middle of a double circular moat disproportionate to its size (VCH vol 4 pp74,75 dia) (SL p88, pl 16 aerial) (NSFCT 1982 pp9,10,19). The upcast which has been built between the ditches is higher than the platform in the middle (NSFCT 1953 p63). The moat is of unknown origin, but may have surrounded the first 'caput' of the de Stafford family before they moved to Stafford Castle in the C13 (SL p88) (SSAHST 1982-3 p36). The moat, known to have existed by 1175, was excavated in the 1950s (OSST 1956-59 pp40-43). (VCH vol 1 pp358-9 with plan, vol 4 p74 - is 400 feet above sea level) (ESH p59) (BOE p76) (SGS p66) (MR pp46,47, p aerial).

Liverpool to Hull Canal A canal proposed by Richard Whitworth of Batchacre Hall in 1765 to link Liverpool and Hull using the Weaver, Sow and Trent, and passing through Standon, Madeley and Betley. Near Shallowford or Great Bridgeford it was to have joined with the proposed Bristol and Hull Canal, which also was never built (NSFCT 1927 pp32-34) (BVC p170).

Lloyd, The House 0.75m SSE of Hales (W p389). The Lloyd, which formerly appeared as The Loyd, appears to have been in existence by the later C16 and it was occupied by the Ford (or Foord, Fourd) family in the early C17 (SHC

1945/ 6 pp160,191-192).

Lloyd Drumble Deep ravine with a brook running through it 0.25m NE of The Lloyd, Hales. Formerly called Foxholes and Sneyd's Dumble (SHC 1945/ 6 pp83,191).

Lloyd Hill Hill 0.5m W of St Bartholomew's church, Penn. The Stourbridge Road which passes over it was widened in 1972 (POAP p20).

Lloyd House Late C18 house, under 0.75m SW of Penn church. Formerly lay in Lower Penn township in Penn ancient parish. It was joined to the rest of the township by a narrow neck of land through Bearnett. This area was once called Putley after Putte which means a narrow neck of land which joins two large areas (PONP pp24-26,36). Here was a settlement recorded as Lude in the C13 and the C14. It has also appeared as Luyd, Lyde (SHOS vol 2 p221) (THS p186), Luyde (PONP pp24-26), The Lloyd and The Lloyd's (THS p186). The word 'lude' perplexed Prof Skeat and Duignan. Dunphy says Lloyd comes from Anglo-Saxon 'leod' or Middle English 'lude,' which refer to men of the district set apart, or out on a limb, from their countrymen - the Lloyd was situated in a peninsula joined by a narrow strand to the main body of its township (PONP pp24-26). The Marsh family, important local landowners, bought the Lloyd estate in 1771 (VCH vol 20 p206). The late C18 house was built probably by John Marsh. On his death in 1796, his son, Richard Bayley Marsh, inherited the estate. On his death in 1820 the estate passed to his widow who subsequently married Rev Prebendary William Dalton, first vicar of St Paul's church, Wolverhampton, and founder of St Philip's church, Penn Fields. During his period here he held gatherings of local religious men known as the Lloyd Clerical Meetings. With his death and that of his wife the estate passed to Harriet Bradney Marsh. In 1899 she married Col Thomas Bradney Shaw Hellier of The Wodehouse. In 1901 she sold the Lloyd estate at which sale the estate was broken up (VCH vol 20 p206) (PENOP p33p) (PONP pp25 il of c1870, 26,27). Raven erroneously says that by 1988 the house was a St Anthony's Cheshire Home (MR p392); the home, specially built, in fact lies 300 metres to the N of Lloyd House and opened in 1965 (info Angus Dunphy). There is a summerhouse 50 yards NE of the house of early C19 date. It has ogee-headed shape door and windows (DoE II). There is an ice-house at SO 907974 on the E side of a pool by Lloyd House Farm.

Loaf and Cheese Rock An unusual rock feature in Ramshaw Rocks resembling, presumably, a loaf of bread and a cheese (SMCC p2) (SGM pp154 il,155) situated on the Hen Cloud (OL vol 1 pp92,95), or on Upper Hulme bank (NSFCT 1884 p22). Has also been called Cheese Press. (DP p54 ils of megalithic chambered tombs near Rock Hall; one of them could be the Cheese Press).

Locarno Tipton. To E of the railway station.

Lockgate Remote spot on E side of Gun Hill 0.75m WSW of Meerbrook (OL vol 1 p217). There was once a farm here. Here and at Gungate there is supposed to be a fortification where the ancient British took their stand (HOLF p7).

Lockwood Hall Hall 1m SE of Kingsley. Name is possibly from Lock Wood, a wood to the E. Former seat of the Whitehalls (Plot's map).

Lode Mill Dale, Dove Dale. On Staffs side facing Shining Tor. Gunstone's Load Mill is probably a reference to Lode. Near Load Mill he notes two mounds excavated by Carrington in 1849 and 1850, few finds were made in each (TYD pp138, 174) (NSJFS 1965 p32). The name is preserved in Lode Mill and Lode House. Is from Old English 'lad,' meaning a watercourse or a crossing of a watercourse (VCH vol 7 p11). Here the Dove was forded until at least 1658, when Lode was written Lode End. A bridge carrying the Alstonefield-Ashbourne road was built in the C19. Lode was an inhabited place by the 1670s (VCH vol 7 p11).

Lodge, The House at Gospel End Common, on the edge of Baggeridge Wood. Demolished in the 1960s (TB Feb 1998 p16p).

Lodge, The House which was No. 138 Hamstead Road, Handsworth, in 1984. It was built by Melville, the theatrical owner and producer about the mid C19. It was for a long time the home of Walter Schuroff who had it furnished in the most opulent Edwardian manner (HPPE p67).

Lodgedale Tiny dale 1m WNW of Hollington. Appears as Lodge Dale on 1834 OS map.

Lodge Farm 1m WNW of Great Wyrley church. May represent the Lodge of Cheslyn Hay. The farmhouse is of brick, and dates from c1800 (VCH vol 5 p102).

Lodge Farm House 0.5m N of Meerbrook. Residence of the farmer poet Alfred Hine in the late C19. Hine had a book of poems published in 1902 (HOLF p53p).

Lodge Farm A lodge stood at the W end of the present Silvercroft Avenue, Handsworth, by the end of the medieval period. It was possibly a lodge for Hamstead Hall Park. The farm was rebuilt in the later C18 or early C19. In

1862 it was known as Stockwell Lodge, but by 1911 it was known as Uplands. The building had been demolished by 1983 (MNB pp39,41,47,49).

Lodge Farm Former warrener's lodge on West Bromwich Heath, which existed by the 1770s. The house may be identified with the warrener's lodge on the Heath mentioned in the 1650s. The later lodge formed the nucleus of the Lodge estate, which, in the C19, lay to the W of the High Street, West Bromwich. William Izon, ironfounder, lived at Lodge Farm from c1824 until his death in 1867. The District Hospital was built on the lodge site in 1868, and the town hall and other public buildings on another part of the estate in 1874-5 (VCH vol 17 p23).

Lodge Hill Hill 1.5m SW of Cannock. On E side of it is Lodge Farm.

Lodgerail Pool In Teddesley Park, Bednall.

Loggan Rock A rock feature that use to be on the Roaches but had been destroyed by 1891. Has also been called Rocking Stone (OL vol 1 p95).

Loggerheads Large hamlet on high ground near the head of a tributary of the Tern, 1.5m WSW of St John the Baptist's church at Ashley. In Ashley ancient parish. Loggerheads is a provincial word for knapweed (Centaurea migra), and for the bluebottle (C. cyanus), and occurs in many field names (DUIGNAN). Alternatively, the name was, perhaps, from the inn here called the Three Loggerheads (see): In the C19 Ashley was the destination of a day or weekend trip for many from the Potteries, and the inn with its amusing sign may have been erected for their pleasure. This area is marked The Logger Heads on the OS map 1834. A stone water trough was placed in a dip by the Stone-Nantwich road c1842 so horses could be watered before climbing up hills towards Loggerheads or Market Drayton. In the early 1990s it was hit and broken by a car (ES Dec 28 1992 p4p). Cheshire Joint Sanatorium on the S side of the Eccleshall Road in 250 acres of Burnt Wood opened in 1923 and was extended in 1946, 1947 and 1950. It closed in 1969. In 1977 Newcastle borough council purchased the site for housing development (ALW pl 50).

Loggerheads Farm There is a farm at Great Wyrley called Loggerheads Farm in one of whose fields a horse was attacked by the Wyrley Gang (TB May 1993 p18).

Lomey Town Former hamlet on Cradley Heath (TB May 1994 p27. Dec 1995 p30). The name Lorney Town appears in the 1851 census. Sometime after 1901 the street called Lomey Town became the present Lower High Street (OS map Sheet 71.08). Has also appeared as Lomeytown.

Lonco Brook Runs from Knightley to Forton and flows into the Meece. Various objects have been found in it during drainage operations: a skeleton; a silvered bronze spoon; a bronze spearhead; and numerous iron objects (Shropshire N&Q vol 1 p7 Nov 28 1884) (NSJFS 1964 p25). On the edge of Lonco Brook was found a Romano-British bronze spear 5.5 inches long and in fine preservation (Shrewsbury Chronicle Nov 28 1884) (NSFCT 1926 pp142-143). This is probably the same as the spearhead mentioned above. The name is probably of Celtic origin (MR p247). 'Lon' from the root 'loa.' Perhaps 'co' is a corruption of the Welsh 'coch' red (NSFCT 1908 p130). This is the brook Richard Whitworth of Batchacre Hall dammed to create a reservoir or lake for his Liverpool to Hull Canal. Whitworth was taken to court by his neighbours, downstream, for interfering with their head water. Thomas Bowker of Weston Jones Mill on May 22 1780 recovered damages of £232, and Whitworth was ordered to remove his weirs (VB p156).

Londes, The (*The Lons*). Elevated pedestrian footpath which ran parallel to, and at the rear of the houses fronting North Street, Wolverhampton, emerging at the bottom of Camp Street. Together with Deanery Row it dates back to before 1750. Became known as The Lones sometime between 1817 and 1914 (TB July 1995 p24).

Longacres House E of Blithbury 2.5m E of Colton.

Long Acres Medieval field of Willenhall. It covered the area which stretched from Railway Lane to Bilston Road in one direction and Rose Hill to Dilloways Lane in the other (SNW p43).

Long Birch House 1.5m NE of Codsall. In Brewood parish. Has appeared as Longebruch (1425), Longbryche (1540), Longburch (1682) (SPNO p41), and The Long Birch. Has a similar etymology to Birchills (DUIGNAN p15). From Anglo-Saxon 'byrce' 'long new enclosure,' bearing in mind it was in Brewood Forest (DUIGNAN) (SPN p23). Parts of the old house may have dated back to medieval times with others which were certainly parts of the late C16 and mid C17. It was described in c1680 as 'a good house.' It was the dower house of Mary Giffard of Chillington after the death of her husband Thomas in 1718 to her death in 1753 (OHW pl 19) (VCH vol 5 p38 il of in 1838 facing p34). John Hornyold continued to live at Long Birch after becoming vicar apostolic of the Midland District for the Catholic church in 1756. His successor, Bishop Milner, remained here until 1804 when he moved to Wolverhampton (VCH vol 3 p110). Or was the seat of the vicars apostolic until 1819

(OHW pl 19). Long Birch is mentioned in 'The Wanderings of a Pen and Pencil' by FP Palmer and A Crowquill (1846) (WJO Jan 1905 p350p). The house was demolished in 1874 and the present farmhouse was built in 1878. WTC Giffard sold it in 1919 (VCH vol 5 p38). The chapel at Long Birch was used for public worship from at least 1779 and closed in 1844 (VCH vol 5 pp44-45). SE of Chillington Hall opposite Long Birch was a windmill (BDH pp214,215).

Longbridge Former name of Longport (see). An old bridge carrying the packhorse road from Burslem to Newcastle over the marshy Fowlea Brook (NSFCT 1938 p58. 1943 p32). Built or rebuilt in c1544. Was in a poor state of repair in 1624 (VCH vol 8 p109). By the mid C18 it consisted of planks extending for about 100 yards over the marshes about the brook until being turnpiked in the 1760s (AGT p69). Greenslade suggests the reason for the bridge's improvement was the development of the area after the coming of the canal and not that the road was turnpiked (VCH vol 8 p109). Has also appeared as Long Bridge.

Longbridge Brook Runs S of Lichfield in the vicinity of the London road (VCH vol 14 p111).

Longbridge Hayes Former small village in Fowlea valley 1m W of Burslem, on the W side of Longport station. Formerly in Wolstanton ancient parish. The name is from Longbridge (see); the name Hayes suggests an enclosure. By 1965 the village comprised a couple of streets - John and Peel Streets - and was reached by Longbridge Hayes Road off Porthill road (Barrow's Pointer Guide Map of Newcastle-u-Lyme. 1965). By the late 1980s the village had been cleared for industrial development; the row of terrace houses in Peel Street, the last housing in the village, was demolished in 1988 (Newcastle Times Oct 21 1970) (ES May 1 1973. June 9 1982. Aug 1 1998 p2p).

Longchurch Valley Is mentioned in a confirmation charter of 1447 granting Shifford's and Broomhall granges to Combermere abbey. The name may be from depressions in the ground marking out the boundary between Shifford's and Broomhall granges (SHC 1945/ 6 p28).

Long Compton Minute hamlet by a tributary of Butterbank Brook, 1m S of Ranton. In Ranton parish.

Longcroft Longcroft Farm is 0.75m NNE of Yoxall. In Yoxall parish.

Longcroft Hall Presumably was situated at or near Longcroft Farm, which is 0.75m NNE of Yoxall. The estate was granted to Roger de Yoxhale in 1216. In 1576 it was purchased by Simon Arden on the usual conditions that he provide Elizabeth I with one light horse and paid into the Royal Exchequer £1 6s 8d for his land at Yoxall then valued at £10. Mary Arden, William Shakespeare's mother, is said to have lived at Longcroft Hall (YX p7). The hall continued as the seat of the Ardens to at least the early C20 (mems in Yoxall church). The moat surrounding the hall was filled in in 1796 (SHOS vol 1 p102) (SSAHST 1982-3 p58) (BTOP vol 1 p87). In WW2 the hall was requisitioned by the War Office and subsequently became a Home Guard training centre (BTOP vol 1 p87p) (ESNF p51p). It was derelict in July 1954 (NSFCT 1954 p93) and had been demolished by 1983 (BTOP vol 1 p87). Some say the hall was demolished in 1952 (ESNF p51). A curious altar piece comprising ten scenes of sacred history on ten oak panels or compartments was anciently kept at the hall. It went to Mr Greene's Museum at Lichfield in the earlier C18 (SHOS vol 1 p102).

Longdon Ancient parish and village on Shropshire Brook in a narrow valley above the Trent Valley, 12m SE of Stafford.
EARLY. In the later C17 Plot noted a spring on relatively high ground in the churchyard and a 30-yard-deep well in the parsonage on much lower ground. The latter was sometimes in need of water, whereas the spring was not (NHS p86). At the E end of the church was found a square-shaped fortification with the E and S sides still visible. The fort was thought to be of **Roman** origin (NHS p406) (Magna Britianna. Cox. vol 5 p35) (Antiq. vol 2 p272). The remains consist of several short lengths of slopes, but without discernible boundaries (Post 'Ancient Earthworks') (VCH vol 1 p191). Shaw could find no evidence of Roman remains here nor did Pennant mention any (SHOS vol 1 p227). Bernard Smith says there is a fort by the NW wall of Longdon church (S p74).
1000 to PRESENT. Longdon was identified by Dugdale, Shaw, Duignan and CGO Bridgeman with the Langandune mentioned in the will of Wulfric Spot (c1002), founder of Burton Abbey; others have identified it with Longdon-on-Tern, Shrops (SHC 1916 p40) (SSE 1996 p15); Dent and Hill thought Longdon the seat of Wulfric Spot (HS p50). Later forms are: Lanngedun (1158), Langedon (1195) (SPN p80), Langdon (c1540) (LI appendix p171), and Longdon (Bowen's map). The **name** means 'long Hill' (DUIGNAN) (LGS p179) (NSJFS 1981 p3); probably a reference to the lofty ridge between Longdon village and Brereton (OSST 1936 p41). Or 'place at the long hill' (SPN p80) (SSE 1996 p15). From the time of the Saxons until Henry VIII's

reign, the bishops of Lichfield held Longdon manor and its members in free barony, and had here a free court, with Waif, View of Frank Pledge etc, without cognizance of the sheriff (W p565). Longdon is a prebend in Lichfield cathedral (SHOS vol 1 p292) (VCH vol 3 p141) founded by Roger de Clinton in the C12 (SSAHST vol 2 1960-61 p47). The parish was a peculiar jurisdiction of the dean and chapter and certain prebendaries of Lichfield cathedral until peculiar jurisdictions were abolished in 1846 (VCH vol 3 p94). The parish **church**, St James, on an eminence SE of the village, on the N side of the Lichfield-Rugeley road, is of C12 origin (LDD), but has been added to at various periods since (LGS p179) (BOE p197). Behind Longdon Almshouses, in a field N of Longdon Hall at SK 079141, is an **ice-house** constructed in brick (VB p121) (IHB p394). The village is famous for the **proverb**, said to be first recorded by Shaw (LTM Nov 1972 p24), which alludes to its length

> The stoutest beggar that goes by the way
> Can't beg through Longdon on a Midsummer's day.

(SHOS vol 1 p211) (THS p79) (KES p147) (SCSF p166) (FOS p148) (Penguin Dictionary of Proverbs. Allen Lane. 1983. p82). An alternative is to read summer for midsummer. And an old inhabitant at the end of the C19 had another similar saying that 'Long long' has run the beggar to death' (NSFCT 1899 p133). In c1984 Mrs M Piper began the annual Nov **Longdon History Show** in the village hall for local history enthusiasts (info Mrs M Piper). **Persons and visitors.** In the later C17 Plot noted a couple of Longdon who lived to great ages and died within days of each other. **William May** died aged 108 and his wife Joyce died aged 98. They were buried in the same grave on the same day (NHS p327) (SHOS vol 1 p227) (W pp57,565) (NSFCT 1899 p135). **Ann Agon** died at Longdon in Sept 1833 aged 102 and three months (W p565). Sir **William Wolseley**, 3rd baronet, was drowned in a little brook at Longdon during a thunderstorm on July 17 1728. Charles Wedgwood had been visiting him at Wolseley Hall and as a courtesy Sir William accompanied his visitor for some of his return journey. At Longdon on Sir William's return a storm caused the mill dam to burst and the sudden rush of water overturned his carriage and swept it into the swollen stream. According to tradition whilst abroad Sir William had had his fortune told by a Persian or an Egyptian fortune teller who had predicted that he and his four Arabian horses which he had bought previously would die by drowning. Then so as not to tempt fate Sir William sent the horses home separately from himself - only to perish with them years later in the ford near his home (Broughton's Scrapbook p210) (SHC 1914 p146 note) (VB p117) (LTM Nov 1972 p25) (Sir Charles Wolseley: The radical baronet. Anne Bayliss. 1983 p2). In the late C18 **Francis Robinson**, a sculptor, had a studio greenhouse by or in his house on the opposite side of Longdon Green to Lysways Hall (SHOS vol 1 p224); Garner, in mid C19, noted that a portion of the glass from Longdon church adorned a summerhouse in the neighbourhood (GNHS p153).

Longdon Green Tiny village 0.5m SE of Longdon. In Longdon parish.

Longdon Hall Under 0.25m SSE of Longdon church on Church Hill. Erected in 1839-40 (W p568) and formerly known as Longdon House; had become Longdon Hall by 1887 (OS map 1887 6 inch). It was the seat of William Henry Chetwynd and Lady Hannah Marie Chetwynd by 1851; William Henry Chetwynd continued to live here until at least 1872 (W p568) (KD 1872). Occupied by Arthur Chetwynd JP in 1896 (KD 1896 p223). On a path N of the hall stood an underground icehouse in 1971 (VB p121).

Longdon Old Hall 1.5m WSW of Longdon. Belonged to the family of Weedon, who sold it to John Floyer, son of Sir John Floyer Knt, physician to Charles II, who bequeathed it to Richard Burnes of Aldershaw (d c1767), whose son, John Burnes Floyer, succeeded to it (or it was left by John Floyer to John Burnes Floyer - SHOS vol 1 p222). John Burnes Floyer's nephew and heir, Trevor Owen Burnes Floyer, clerk, was the owner in 1819 (SOS p181). By the late C18 the status of the hall had fallen to that of a farmhouse. It is probably the Old Hall occupied by Thomas Cresswell, farmer, by 1872 (KD 1872). Longdon Old Hall was being farmed by Robert Morton in 1896 (KD 1892 p223). Appears as Longdon Hall (Yates' map) (SHOS vol 1 p222) (1834 OS map). The SW corner and S side of a moat at SK 066126 remained in 1958. It had been filled in and built over by 1974 (SSAHST 1982-3 p44).

Long Edge Ridge, rising to 1050 feet high, 1.5m W of Rushton Hall. Formed the western boundary of Rushton James township (TTTD p145) (VCH vol 7 p219).

Longer Moors A 1764 Sutherland map shows the fields between Noose Lane and Waddens Brook Lane as being known as Longer Moors. In the early C20 Fibbersley Colliery stood in this area (SNW p25).

Longfield Cottage Former low-built early C19 stucco house opposite the Noah's Ark Inn, Hartshill Road, Hartshill, Stoke-upon-Trent parish. Has also ap-

peared as Longfields Cottage and Longfields (The Crusade against Crippledom: The Story of Millicent Duchess of Sutherland and the North Staffordshire Cripples Aid Society. Dr Tony Carter 1991 pp27,28p). Longfield Cottage is the birthplace of novelist **Dinah Maria Mullock** (later Mrs Craik) (VCH vol 8 pp177,183). She was born here on April 20 1826 (NSFCT 1925 pp82,84) or June 7 1826 (SK pp120-121). Her father, Thomas Samuel Mullock, an eccentric Irish preacher with a literary bent, died in 1869 and is buried in the churchyard of St Mary's, Castle Church, Stafford. Her novels include 'The Ogilvies' 3 vols (1849), 'Olive' (1851), 'The Head of the Family' (1851), 'Agatha's Husband' (1853), and 'John Halifax, Gentleman' (1857), the last novel is supposedly set in Tewkesbury, Glous, but has names from the Hartshill and Newcastle localities. Longfield is the name Dinah gave to John Halifax's residence but the house was modelled on Detmore House near Cheltenham; of the house in the novel Dinah writes:- 'Longfield! happy Longfield! little nest of love, and joy, and peace - where the children grew up and we grew old - where season after season brought some new change ripening in us and around us. Beloved Longfield! my heart, slow pulsing as befits one near the grave, thrills warm and young as I remember thee!' (The Crusade against Crippledom etc. Tony Carter 1991 p27). In 1864 she married George Lillie Craik. She died at Shortlands on Oct 12 1887 near Bromley, Kent. There is a wall tablet to her memory in Tewkesbury Abbey, Glous (LGS p219) (The Mellards And Their Descendants. Aleyn Lyell Reade. 1915 p77) (NSFCT 1925 pp82-95) (POTP pp161p,162). (SA Oct 15 1887) (BS pp320-321) (HBST p512) (S p122) (DNB) (A Brief Account of the Life and Writings of Dinah Mullock. DG Harnaman) (PSS pp394-404 p) (SHST p597) (SLM summer 1955 pp12,13,22) (SSAHST 1970-1972 vol 12) (Newcastle-under-Lyme Local History Press Cuttings. Book 1. pp76-79p) (VFC p33) (FWNS pp11-14). Dinah's grandmother Jane Mellard had moved to Longfield Cottage in c1816; she moved to the Big House, Bucknall in c1825, but Dinah and her family appear to have lived on at Longfield Cottage until 1831 (PSS p401) (VCH vol 8 pp177,183). Dinah subsequently lived in Lower Street and in Mount Pleasant at what is now No. 7 (NSFCT 1925 pp82,84) (NUL p42). By the mid C19 there appears to have been an estate known as Longfields centred on Longfield Cottage, which between 1842 and 1852 was the home of Herbert Minton, pottery manufacturer (VCH vol 8 p177) (The Crusade against Crippledom etc p26). In 1884 Longfield House, another house nearby to Longfield Cottage, which formed part of the Longfields estate, was occupied by Mrs Samuda (KD 1884). By 1991 it had been demolished and the North Staffordshire Medical Institute built on the site (The Crusade against Crippledom p26). The Cripples' Hospital (or later **Hartshill Orthopaedic Hospital**) moved to Longfield Cottage in 1918, having originated at a convalescent home at Hanchurch, founded in 1911. The hospital was established by the Potteries and Newcastle Cripples' Guild (or Cripples' Aid Society), founded in 1901. The Guild was the inspiration of Millicent, Duchess of Sutherland (d1955) (VCH vol 8 p197) (SVB p91). The hospital was officially opened on July 13 1918 by Sir Robert Jones and on the same occasion Sir Joseph Cook, former PM of Australia, and formerly of Silverdale (see), laid the memorial stone of an operating theatre at the hospital. A new extension to the hospital was officially opened on Nov 13 or 15 1931 by the Prince of Wales. The extension was called the Rosemary Ednam Memorial Extension after Millicent's daughter, Rosemary (later Viscountess Ednam) of Himley Hall (see), who was killed in a plane crash in Kent in 1930. The Cripples' Aid Society continued as managers of the hospital until the hospital was incorporated into the NHS in 1948. On Dec 7 1989, Elizabeth Leveson-Gower, 24th Countess of Sutherland, a grand-daughter of Millicent, opened the new Sutherland ward extension of the hospital (ES Aug 5 1995 p29. Aug 24 1999 p3) (The Crusade against Crippledom etc pp18,25,26,28p,33,35,37). By the late 1990s the Hartshill Orthopaedic Hospital building (containing at its core a much altered Longfield Cottage) had been demolished and a new orthopaedic unit opened in a new surgical block on the City General Hospital site at Hartshill (see): The new Sutherland ward extension has been retained as the Sutherland Library for the storage of patients records. The hospital was believed to be haunted by an old lady who was usually seen by the staff and not by the patients. But in 1991 she was seen by one of the patients (GLS pp49-50).

Longford Hamlet 1.25m SW of Cannock. The name derives from the local name for a portion of Watling Street running between Churchbridge and the Four Crosses (DUIGNAN p96 - recorded in 994 as Lang straet (or Long street)).

Longford House Situated at junction of A5 and A460, Longford, Cannock. Built in c1840 (BOE p93). Duignan refers to it as Longford Hall? Has or had an ice-house situated at SJ 967092 (SSAHST 1980) (IHB p394).

Longford House 200 yards S of of Longford Bridge, in the Penkridge area, perhaps E of Penkridge. Dated 1706 and has alterations of 1872 (VCH vol 5 p108).

Long-Hedge Nook Meir Heath, Longton. House in the Meir Heath area marked on Yates' map.

Long Hurst Hill Bradley-in-the-Moors. Plot says an old cave dweller, Helen Millard, lived in Thors House Cave in Long Hurst Hill in the Peakstones. Helen Millard, a widow, reputedly lived to the age of 115 and she may have lived longer had she not died, probably in the 1670s, in a fire (NHS pp172,321). Peakstones could be taken to be about Peakstone Rock.

Long Knowle Old farm 3m NE of Wolverhampton (DUIGNAN). Formerly in Wednesfield township in Wolverhampton ancient parish. The name formerly applied to land known as Knoll Bruches occurring between 1290 and 1376 and field names known as Long Noles in 1764 (WFW pp48,60). The farm, which stood in the vicinity of Bradburn Road off Long Knowl Lane, was demolished in 1935 (BTW p101). In 1936 some of the old timbers from the house went to the construction of a 'Tudor' house, called Long Knowle, near Compton, built by a Mr Wooddisse (BCM Jan 1978 pp56,57). The elongated pool near the farm may have been the remnant of a moat (WFW p69). The Long Knowle Estate was built in this area after WW2 as an overspill housing estate for Wolverhampton (WHTOP p75p of Long Knowle Estate shopping centre). The area became a separate ecclesiastical parish from Wednesfield in 1964, known as 'Wednesfield St Gregory the Great' (GLAUE p428). The church, St Gregory, on the corner of Blackhalve and Long Knowle Lanes, was built in 1966 (info Helen Baker).

Long Lake Council housing estate in the Longlake Avenue area, Tettenhall. Built in the late 1940s (BTW p69).

Long Lane Head (1834 OS map) (Dower's map). The house Longlane Head is 0.75m SSE of Fulford.

Long Ley Road and small area between Springfield and Heath Town on the S side of the Wolverhampton Road; Long Ley Primary School in Long Ley was formerly St Stephen's Primary School (Wolverhampton Chronicle Nov 19 1999 p24).

Long Low A long burial mound 1.25m SE of Wetton. Situated between SK 12165399 and SK 12105383. It is of Bronze Age origin (HOS 1998 p24) and is two round burial mounds linked by a bank, an arrangement not found elsewhere in England. The NE burial mound is 28 paces in diameter and eight feet high. The SW burial mound is NS 17 paces, EW 20 paces in diameter and five feet high. The bank is 15 feet wide, four feet high and 220 yards long. Carrington and Bateman excavated it in 1848/ 9; Carrington excavated it again in 1851. From Carrington's description the NE burial mound appears to be original, and the bank and SW burial mound later additions (NSJFS 1965 p55). A low drystone wall ran the length of the bank and against this flat slabs were laid and the whole covered with small rubble. At the SW end the wall ran to the centre of the burial mound, where it was terminated by a similar wall built at right angles to it (NSJFS 1965 p56). The larger mound - the NE burial mound - contained 13 crouched skeletons, together with two leaf-shaped arrow-heads (HOS p9), the smaller - the SW burial mound - contained some burnt bones (PDS&C p118p). It is the longest chambered tomb in the Peak District (PDS&C p118p) and a listed monument. (TYD p121,131,144-147,182) (R vol 5 pp26-30) (VCH vol 1 no 26) (OS Megalithic Survey. vol 4. CW Phillips. 1934 pp9-10) (Prehistoric Chamber Tomb of England and Wales. GE Daniel. 1950. p184) (NSJFS 1962 p33) (DAJ vol 75 pp86,114,117) (SC p148) (BOE p308) (MR p373). Fairies are traditionally believed to appear at Long Low on Christmas Eve (FLJ 1942 p127) and behind Castern Hall 1m to the S (FPSB p163) (Witcutt). About 300 yards from Long Low is a burial mound Carrington excavated in 1852. Human bones, pottery fragments, pieces of bronze, an iron awl, and a piece of glass (probably of C17) were found (TYD pp187-188) (DAJ vol 74 p148) (Medieval Archaeology vol 6/ 7 pp49-50) (Gazetteer of Early Anglo-Saxon Burial Mounds. A Meaney. 1964. p222) (NSJFS 1965 p56).

Longly A common W of Eccleshall enclosed 1719 or 1845 (ECC p18).

Long Meadow Half timbered house on Fisherwick road, Whittington (MR p378p), near Lichfield.

Long Mere The larger of the two pools on Milford Common, Cannock Chase. There is a tiny valley called Mere Valley 0.5m to the S.

Longnor Small remote moorland town on a very steep edge between the Dove and the Manifold 28.25m NNE of Stafford, former parochial chapelry and township in Alstonefield ancient parish. With reference to its situation Longnor was described in 1865 as 'quite as beautiful as that of Buxton' (R vol vi p75) (VCH vol 7 p42).

700 to PRESENT. The 'Daily Mail' article of 1971 (probably connected with the no smoking trials - see below) stated that the **battle** between the West Saxons and the kings of Mercian was fought at Longnor in 715 AD (L p2),

although, others state it was fought at Bunbury (Alton Towers) or Bonebury (Wetton). Some have wrongly identified this Longnor with the DB Longnor near Lapley (DUIGNAN) (LGS p179-180). This Longnor appears as Langenoure (1227) (SSE 1996 p15), and Longenovere (C13) (SPN p80). The **name** if it is from Longenovere or Langenoure means 'long ridge' (SSAHST 1967 p33) (L p5 - keen to stress it is 'ridge' not 'alders') (SPN p80). The present **church**, St Bartholomew, S of Church Street, may stand on the site of a church founded in the C12. A church is first mentioned in 1448. The present church dates from the later 1770s (VCH vol 7 pp46,47) (St Bartholomew's, Longnor). Longnor became a separate ecclesiastical parish in 1737 and a separate civil parish in 1866 (GLAUE p416). In 1697 Longnor **wakes** were held in Aug, probably on the feast of St Bartholomew (Aug 24), Longnor church is dedicated to St Bartholomew. By 1772 the wakes began on the first Sunday in Sept and lasted a week. There was still a wakes week in the early 1990s (VCH vol 7 p43). A bull was baited at Longnor wakes in 1831 (SA Sept 24 1831 p4) (OL vol 1 p328) (VCH vol 7 p43). Longnor men were caught **poaching in Leek Forest** during William II's reign and the village was ordered to be burnt down in punishment (W Beresford in Reliquary) (L p5). There were **stocks** in the early C17 and a new pair are said to have been made in 1861 (VCH vol 7 p45). A **lock-up** stood opposite what was the old post office in Carder Green on the road to Glutton. It was a circular beehive-shaped building used in the C18 and C19 and similar to that which survives at Alton. It was demolished in 1886 according to Mr Hyde, late registrar (L p27, p of facing p57) (Bygone Days in the Peak District) (PDS&C p46) (DMV p48p). There was a **pinfold** on the E side of Longnor village in the lane leading to Folds End Farm between at least the late 1820s to 1908 (VCH vol 7 p45). **Markers**. There are possibly five, and certainly four, stones on the edge of the road between Longnor and the Leek-Buxton road. They were set up to guide travellers in snow. A stone used as a gatepost in the locality may have been the fifth stone (PDS&C p77p). There is a legend which found its way into N&Q 1869 that the warrant for a **freemason's lodge** at Longnor was signed by Prince Charles Edward Stuart when in Derbys during the 1745 Jacobite Rebellion (NSFCT 1908 p195). The Longnor freemason's lodge acquired the Moira Apron (considered a most precious possession) in 1814 (L p32 p of opposite p43). A **hoard of medieval silver coins** (English, Scottish, Flemish) were found in Boosley Folly Meadow in 1867. Presumably they had been hidden or lost after the struggle between Edward II and his cousin, Thomas, Earl of Lancaster, in the early C14. Thomas' father, Edmund was overlord of a wide area which included Longnor as part of Alstonefield manor. The discovery was noted by a fellow of the Royal Historical Society (NSFCT 1909 p155) (L p8). The wells of Longnor were formerly dressed. **Well-dressing** was revived in 1950 but not continued. The tradition was revived again in 1983 and has continued ever since on wakes Sunday (VCH vol 7 p43). **On television and in books**. Granada Television's 'World in Action' filmed the people of Longnor in a no smoking trial in 1971. 103 gave up at the beginning of the trial, 29 were left at the end of the year, and only two remained non-smokers a few years later (L p54) (VB p208 - screened Jan 1972?). Longnor was the setting for the ATV series 'The Mallens,' which involved Longnor school children (L p54). Longnor was also the setting for several items in the Innes Book of Records (1980) (L p54). **Persons and visitors**. According to tradition **King John** was at Longnor to sort out thieves taking deer from the forest here (WTCEM pp52,53). **Andrew Bromwich** (c1652-1702), Roman Catholic priest, is believed to have been born at or near Longnor (BEW) (W p744) (OL vol 2 p63) or at Old Oscott (see). Bromwich was tried at Stafford Assizes in 1679 for alleged involvement in the Popish Plot. He was condemned to die, but the sentence was not carried out and he was eventually released (W p744). For **William Billinge** see Fawfieldhead. **John Wesley** visited Longnor on Aug 11 1772 (E p57). **Samuel Fidler** of Longnor walked from his own house to Buxton, upwards of five miles, within three days of his death aged 105 (Westminster Magazine 1780) (OL vol 1 p285) (L p56) (SMOPP vol 2 p106). **Charles Charlesworth** of Longnor, son of Richard Charlesworth, born on March 14 1829 of normal parents, had an extreme aging disorder. At the age of four he had reached the full stage of maturity with whiskers, and at six was old, greyhaired and bearded. He died from senile decay at the age of seven in 1836; at death his voice was reedy, his skin shrivelled and he had the appearance of a man of 70 (GM 1834 p636) (Broughton's Scrapbook p69) (Dublin University Magazine 1868) (OL vol 1 p57) (BCWJ p110).

MARKETS AND FAIRS. The **market** which the lords of Alstonefield manor claimed in 1293 was held at Longnor. In 1595 the Crown granted John Harpur, lord of Alstonefield manor, a Tuesday market at Longnor. There were proposals in the early 1770s to build a market house and there was certainly a market house by 1817 (VCH vol 7 p44). There was a market in 1792 (OWEN)

and a market in 1888 (LHE p265). Sir John Harpur Crewe had the market hall rebuilt in 1873. The table of tolls exhibits a full table of tolls for both buyers and sellers covering a variety of items from livestock to baskets of eggs (L p24) (COS p7p). The market had ceased by 1931 when the market house was converted into a parish hall (VCH vol 7 p44). There is a **market cross** by the road seven metres W of the Harpur Crewe Arms, it is a shaft made out of two pieces of stone possibly of C15 or C16 origin (DoE II) (L p22) (VCH vol 7 p44). The **fair** which the lords of Alstonefield manor claimed in 1293 was held at Longnor. There was a fair in 1478, four by 1549 (VCH vol 7 p44). In the late 1590s there were fairs on St George's Day (April 23), Tuesday in Whitsun week, St James' Day (July 25), and Michaelmas. By 1817 there were eight - Candlemas Day (Feb 2), Easter Tuesday, May 4, May 17, Whit Tuesday, Aug 6, Tuesday before Old Michaelmas (Oct 10), Nov 12 (SCSF pp99, 104) (L 23) (VCH vol 7 pp44-45). The four fairs in 1896 were on Easter Tuesday, May 4, May 17, and Whit Tuesday. These fairs were still held in 1928, but there is no later record of them (VCH vol 7 p45).
SUPERNATURAL AND SUPERSTITION. The **headless horseman** of the Moorlands reputedly has been seen in the Longnor area. He was last seen in 1895 (L pp48,113 pp10-11) (SSGLST p11). This headless horseman is mentioned in the historical romance 'Flash' (1928 p113) by Judge Alfred Ruegg, a native of the locality (L p48) (UHAW p77). The **sounds of a horse** and rider galloping down the High Street, and taking the Heath House Road out of Longnor, have been heard in the middle of the night (L p49). In the 1950s there was a newspaper report of a **haunted lonely cottage** near Longnor, where odd and unexplainable noises occurred according to the two occupants, a Mr Wood and his cousin. The vicar had to carry out an investigation, reported as an exorcism (L p48). Mr Wood and his cousin were eventually driven out of the cottage by the poltergeist activity (GLS pp69-71 - on one sighting in Jan 1960) (EGH pp149-151). **An apparition** was seen by a Longnor man of one of his long-dead female relatives. He could describe every detail of her dress and face although he had never seen a picture of her (L p49). A small **phantom dog** has been seen in Gauledge Lane (L p49). For another phantom dog see Doctor's Trees. Longnor anciently had many **superstitions** peculiar to it. One was to fix a charm to churns to make butter plentiful, and on ploughs to do the work of two. It was unlucky for the church clock to strike three while a funeral was taking place and often the clock was stopped for a funeral service. Another superstition was to never bring a coffin to the church down Back Street, so that however out-of-the-way it may be, funerals always approached St Bartholomew's via the Buxton Road (L pp49,50).
Longnor Tiny hamlet on low land by Longnor Brook 0.75m NW of Lapley. Partly in Bradley and Lapley parishes. Has appeared as Longenalre (DB), Longenare (1236), Lungenalre (1285), Longenhore (1332), and Longnorley (1506) (SPNO p136) (SSE 1996 p15). Longenolre means 'tall alders' (DUIGNAN) (SSAHST 1967 p32) (L pp8,9). Or 'at the tall alder tree' (SPNO p136). By Longnor Hall or over 0.5m to the SSW was possibly a lost village (SSAHST 1970 p35).
Longnor Brook Joins the Whiston Brook at Bickford.
Longnor Hall Longnor, Lapley. Three-storey brick house dated 1726 (BOE p168). Represents the manor-house of the manor of Longnor (VCH vol 4 pp76,82).
Longnor Mill Mill to W of Longnor on the Manifold. In Alstonefield ancient parish.
Longport Former hamlet in the Fowlea valley, now a district 0.75m W of Burslem. Formerly in Burslem chapelry in Stoke-upon-Trent ancient parish. The settlement began in 1773 as a tiny hamlet to serve the new Trent and Mersey Canal, and lay on the W side of the canal. In 1777 it was named Longport, the year the canal opened. It was the model for other nearby canal side settlements - Middleport and Newport. Sometime after the mid C19 Longport merged with the conurbations of Burslem (VCH vol 8 p106) (SL p236). It is said to have taken the first part of its name 'Long' from Longbridge, with 'Port' from the canal wharf (AGT p69). For an incident during the 'Bread Riots' at Etruria which occurred at Longport on March 7 1783 see under Etruria. In 1876 Longport Football Club turned professional and was renamed Burslem Port Vale (TSS p47). Gertie Gitana, music hall artist, was born Gertrude Astbury at 7 Shirley Street, Longport on Dec 28 1887, daughter of Bill Astbury, a porter, and Lavinia Kil Kenny. This house still existed in 1977 (ES April 13 1977; date given for her death is July 11 1964). When a few months old her family moved to 50 Price Street, Burslem (FWNS p23). Her family moved to Frederick Street, Hanley when she was aged three. At an early point in her career she was given the stage name of 'Little Gitana,' Spanish for gipsy. She died in London on Jan 5 1957 (British Music Hall. R Busby) (The Northern Music Hall. GJ Mellor) (Weekly Sentinel Jan 11 1957) (ES April 13 1977) (POP p56) (POTP p102) (PPP p46p) (The Advertiser Feb

17 1994 p13) (TB May 1995 p19p) (TSS pp141,143p) (FWNS p26). Longport is, collectively with Middleport, 'Shawport' in Arnold Bennett's novels. A multicoloured oblong-shaped object in the northeast sky, possibly a UFO, was seen from Longport on Sept 8 1967 at about 8.15pm (FSRP p15).
Longport Hall A stone mansion of early C19 date, to the S of Trubshawe Cross, Longport. In 1843 it was the residence of William Davenport. Was demolished in c1885 (VCH vol 8 p113) (OTP p64). The Burslem Endowed School formerly in the Wedgwood Institute moved to here in 1880, and was attended by Arnold Bennett, novelist; the hall is Shawport Hall in his novels (Arnold Bennett and Stoke-on-Trent. EJD Warrilow. 1966. pp20,29il of c1843, 30).
Longridge Hamlet on a long low ridge overlooking Whiston brook on the road S of Levedale, Dunston. In Penkridge ancient parish. The name has appeared as Langerigge (1199), Longerygg (1307), Longerugge (1315), Langrigge (1399), Longeridge (1588) (SPNO p90) (SSE 1996 p15). It means the long ridge (DUIGNAN) (SPN p92). Prebend of Penkridge Collegiate Church, which had, unusually, two little (probably a reference to minor) canons (SCSF p161) (VCH vol 3 p300).
Longsdon Large village in a narrow steep valley high above Endon Brook 20m N of Stafford. Former manor and township in Leek ancient parish. Aerial photography has revealed a group of four mounds at SJ 969541 over 0.5m SE of the church (NSFCT 1983 p13). Has appeared as Longesdon (1242) (SSE 1996 p15). The name is from Longsdon Hill, the long hill (dun) (VCH vol 7 p202). Gelling thinks 'hill called Long' (NSJFS 1981 p2). The possessive s, as in Longesdon, and its retention are strong evidence of a personal name, suggests this was 'Lang's hill' (DUIGNAN). By the mid C13 Longsdon manor had become split into two halves known as Over Longsdon (centring probably on the present Little and Great Longsdon) and Nether Longsdon (centring probably on present Dunwood) (VCH vol 7 p205). The manor of Longsdon, along with Rushton and half of Ipstones, was held in 1242 by the service of providing a knight for the garrison of Chester Castle for 40 days (VCH vol 7 p205). The present centre of the village at the junction of the Leek road (A53) and the road to Horse Bridge was known as Ladderedge (see) hamlet prior to the late C19 (1834 OS map) (SVB p114) (VCH vol 7 p203). Longsdon was in 'Endon, Longsdon and Stanley' civil parish until becoming a separate civil parish in 1894 (GLAUE p416). The church, St Chad, on the N side of the Leek Road, to the W of School Lane, opened in 1905 (VCH vol 7 p209). Longsdon became a separate ecclesiastical parish in 1906 (LGS p180). The TV presenter, Anthea Turner of Norton-in-the-Moors, married disc jockey, Peter Powell, at Longsdon church in 1990 (ES May 19 1999 p5).
Longsdon Hill Long ridge, rising to 779 feet high, stretching S from Little Longsdon. In the S the ridge is known as Ladderedge (VCH vol 7 p202)
Longsdon Moor Former area of 310 acres on Longsdon Hill. It was enclosed in 1815 (VCH vol 7 p207).
Longshaw Fragmented minute hamlet, area 0.5m SSE of Cotton. Formerly in Alton ancient parish.
Longshaw House 0.5m SSE of Bradnop. Formerly in Bradnop township in Leek ancient parish. The name appears by 1343 (VCH vol 7 p170) and in 1345 as Longshaw (SHC 1910 p438). The present Longshaw Farm is of the C17 (VCH vol 7 p170).
Long-sur-Longe Was probably intended to be Long Furlong. Place on the route of the beating of bounds around Lichfield (SHOS vol 1) (HOL p358). There is a street named Longstaff Croft to NE of the cathedral.
Longton Manor and early settlement in the vicinity of Longton Hall, 0.75m SW of modern Longton. Has appeared as Longeton (1212), and Longetona (1237) (W p302) (SPN p80) (SSE 1996 p15). If from Langeton then 'long town or settlement' (DUIGNAN) (NSJFS 1981 p2), or 'the long farmstead' (SPN p80); was the hamlet about Longton manor house (later Longton Hall, see) considered at some period in the Middle Ages long in comparison with other settlements? From c1830 the name Longton was adopted by Lane End.
Longton (proverbially *Neck End*). Large Potteries town on Anchor Brook 12.75m N of Stafford. Former township with Lane End in Stoke-upon-Trent chapelry and ancient parish.
1500 to 1840. One of the oldest cottages in the town, No. 97 Sutherland Road, was demolished in 1916. It was timber-famed and reputed to have been an RC chapel after the Reformation (NSFCT 1915 p148). Longton was known as Mear Lane End until c1730, and as Lane End (see) (from whence comes Neck End) up to c1830. From c1830 it took the name of Longton after the early settlement of Longton (see) (which Lane End was rapidly merging with) because 'Longton' was considered more polite (HBST p555) (VCH vol 8 226) (SL p228; on the growth of Longton). (FF p16). **Churches**. The church, **St John the Baptist**, King Street, was built as a chapel for dissenters in 1762. It became an Anglican church and was rebuilt in 1795, and partly rebuilt in

1827-1828 (BOE p259). It was demolished in the 1980s and was not rebuilt (local info). Some say Longton became a separate ecclesiastical parish in 1802 (GLAUE p416), whilst others say it became a separate ecclesiastical parish (Longton St James) in 1839, having previously been a chapel in Stoke-upon-Trent ancient parish (LGS p180) (VCH vol 8 p188) (CAST p57). Longton St John ecclesiastical parish was created out of Longton St James in 1866 (CAST p57). The Commissioners' church, **St James the Less**, in Uttoxeter Road, was built in 1832-1834 (BOE pp260-261). The church, **St John**, Rutland Road, attached to the Rectory, was built in 1994 (LDD). Longton had a tradition for **lawlessness** in the early C19 (LOU p293). A bread riot began on April 26 1800, with the stopping of a food cart (LOU pp154-155). Two hundred people were involved. The Newcastle and Pottery Troop of Staffordshire Yeomanry were sent to suppress it. Seven were sent for trial (SA early May 1800). Following the elections of 1837 disruption broke out in Longton on July 24 after news from Hanley told of the success of the Tory candidate (LOU p225). A substantial riot arose in the town against the 'new police' in 1839. The Newcastle and Pottery Troop of Staffordshire Yeomanry commanded by Capt Tomlinson had to be brought in. Later, reinforcements of Uttoxeter and Stafford Troops were brought in. 23 were arrested (SA May 11 1839) (LOU pp236-237). On June 23 1841 Longton was the scene of anti-Tory violence (LOU p226). **Persons and visitors. Rosamond Cook** of Longton died on Sept 23 1774 aged 124 and **Lydia Barber** of Longton died aged 107 (St John's Church Bazaar brochure 1903) (STM Sept 1964 p39). (SSC p122). A woman, aged 20, in a desperate state of poverty in a lodging house in Lane End (Longton) was recognised by a child as the young woman called **Mary Coe Sherriff**, a niece of Rev James Sherriff, Wesleyan minister, late of Lane End, but now (1825) of Congleton, who had lived with her uncle and his wife when they lived in Lane End. On being recognised the woman claimed that she was indeed Mary Coe Sherriff and was accepted as such by the local community, who set about drastically improving her circumstances. The woman related that after the death of her aunt her uncle had raped her and made her pregnant; and that arrangements were then made for her to go home to her father at Kingsbridge in Devon; and that at length her condition was made known to her father, who took her dilemma so much to heart he died; and that she then married a poor pedlar, and when the baby died in infancy he deserted her. At length Rev James Sherriff was brought to Lane End to meet his supposed niece. After a private consultation he disowned her alleging that she was an impostor. The local community then doubted her true identity. Rev Sherriff then proceeded to bring forward his real niece from Devon, and at length the woman was proved to be an impostor and sentenced to three months hard labour (Pottery Gazette Jan 29 1825. Feb 12 1825) (Broughton's Scrapbook pp105-109). **William Cyples** (d1882), poet and novelist, was born in Longton in 1831. He published two volumes of poetry, 'Miscellaneous Poems' (1857) and 'Satan Reformed' (1859), and anonymously, several novels, the last being 'Heart of Gold' (1883) (PSS pp199-206) (VFC p34).

MARKETS AND FAIRS. Longton had a market by at least the second half of the C18 (VCH vol 8 p237). The **first market hall** was built by subscription in 1789 in what is now Times Square. A **second** market hall, known as the Union Market and later as the Old Town Hall, was built in 1814. It became Longton Court House in 1856 and was demolished in 1950 (VCH vol 8 p237). A **third** market hall with town hall was built in Times Square in 1844 and rebuilt 1863 (VCH vol 8 p237). A memorial plaque to Able Seaman John Brown VC of Sandford Hill who died in the raid on St Nazaire on March 28 1942 was erected in the town hall in Nov 1992 (ES Nov 10 1992 p9p). A memorial stone to Trooper Robert Beswick, who died on Christmas day, 1900, while fighting in the Boer War, formerly in the New Primitive Methodist church in Stone Road was erected in the town hall in Sept 1993 (ES Sept 25 1993 p4). By 1829 **fairs** were held on the days following those held at Newcastle. By the mid C19 fairs were held on Feb 14, May 29, July 22, and Nov 1 (W) (VCH vol 8 p238).

INDUSTRY. The industries of Longton have been iron-working, mining, pottery (formerly mainly porcelain, then bone china), brick and tile making, and brewing (VCH vol 8 pp238,245).

1840 to PRESENT. The town became a borough on April 3 1865. The borough was one of the Six Towns which federated in 1910 to form Stoke-on-Trent. Longton adopted the **arms** of the Heathcote family of Longton Hall as its own, but these have never been recognised as official arms for the town by the College of Arms (CH p330) (SHST pp273,280il). **Newspapers.** The United Branches of the Operative Potters was founded in 1843. William Evans (1816-1887), who was instrumental in founding the union, claimed it had a membership of 2,000, most of which were hollow ware pressers. In 1843 the union launched The **Potteries Examiner and Workmen's Advocate**, which

was printed at Longton (see) (POTP p92). The paper shamed the pottery owners into ending the 'allowances' which effectively put up wages, but the physical conditions remained as poor as ever (POP p85). It was printed at Ride's Bank, Longton (H p88). The paper carried on in different directions and under new titles until c1892 (H p88). Copies of the **Longton Times and Echo** survive from the period of 1894 to 1905 (SHJ spring 1995 p9). Copies of the **Longton Weekly Herald** survive from the period of 1898 to 1899 (SHJ spring 1995 p9). Copies of the **Longton Gazette and News** survive from the period Nov to Dec 1937 (SHJ spring 1995 p9). **University extension work** in the form of lecture courses was offered to working adults in Longton from 1892. At first these were organized from Manchester University and subsequently by Oxford University. From 1902 a more intimate form of education was provided by the Extension Lectures Guild whose members worked more systematically at the work outlined in the lecture courses and met each other annually at the University Extension Summer Meetings held alternately in Oxford and Cambridge Universities. Out of this emerged the Longton Tutorial Class of 1908 under the guidance of RH Tawney. This class has been considered the first WEA/ University tutorial class in England. It met at the Sutherland Institute (see), Longton, and under Tawney studied C17 economic history. Enrolled in the class were labourers, clerks and tradesmen as well as some from the lower professions; a portrait of Jack Elkin, miner and member of Tawney's first class, hangs in the library at the Wedgwood Memorial College at The Limes (see), Barlaston (NSJFS 1961 pp101-102) (HOLB p105). Victorian school buildings, known as Tawney House, named after Tawney, in Webberley Lane, were occupied by the WEA in the late 1970s (POP p142). A Russian gun from the **Crimean War** was erected outside Longton Court House in 1867 (VCH vol 8 p180). Longton is Longshaw in the novels of Arnold Bennett, and it is one of his five towns of the Potteries. **Strange phenomena**. The former cinema in Stoke Road is haunted by a former member of staff. In the early 1970s the building was converted into a bingo hall called Tudor Bingo Hall (GOT p145) (GOHK p289) (SMM p52). A pinkish glow in the sky with a red semicircle of light in the middle of this glow, possibly a UFO, was seen from Longton hall Road, at about 11.00pm on Sept 12 1967 (FSRP p15). **Persons and visitors. General Booth**, founder of the Salvation Army (1829-1912), preached as an ordinary minister at the Zion Chapel, Longton in 1855 (TSS p49). The left arm and right hand of **Rupert Simms** (1853-1937), author of BS, severed from him in an accident at Daisy Bank Brickworks as a young man were buried by the wall of Longton church (SHST p446). On June 9 1908 at Longton fete a balloon ascended containing two lady parachutists, Miss **Dolly Shepherd** (1886-1983) and Miss **Louie May**, who intended to descend in a display. But Louie's parachute failed at 11,000 feet and the two descended on Dolly's parachute landing at Church Leigh in what is believed to have been the first mid-air rescue (EAS pp11-12) (GBR 1996 p132. 1998 p334). For Sgt **Albert Edward Egerton** VC see Blythe Bridge. **George V** and Queen Mary visited Longton on April 22 1913 (ES Nov 16 1996 p21). At Longton Whitsuntide fete May 17 1913 **Gustav Hamel** flew in an air display (EAS p21). **Prince Charles** visited Longton on March 3 1998 (ES March 3 1998 p13p).

Longton Brook Trentham.

Longton Hall 0.75m SW of modern Longton. Although not in DB, Eyton thought 'Longton was probably involved in the Domesday manor of Wolstanton,' at this time (SHC 1909 p58). There was a Longton manor by the earlier C13 when it was held of the king on condition of paying a fee and performing guard duties at Newcastle Castle and escorting the king in wartime as far as Wrinehill and back. The manor had many tenants but from at least the earlier C13 until at least 1650 overlordship descended with Newcastle manor (BVC p35) (SCSF p116) (VCH vol 8 p151). There was possibly a manor-house at Longton in the Middle Ages and there was certainly one by the early C17. It was the seat of the Foley family, lords of Longton, in the C17 until 1773, although it was leased out for most of the C18 (VCH vol 8 p229) to the Lane family; Obadiah Lane obtained the lease of Longton manor in 1702 and rebuilt the hall then (BNDA p37). The hall was reconstructed as an imposing Georgian country house in the 1770s (SL p227). John Edensor Heathcote purchased the hall in 1777 (AHJ 1995 p75) and it continued as a Heathcote residence until c1840 and ceased to be owned by the Heathcotes in 1928 (SHST p372). Sir John Heathcote's grandson, the poet and playwright, Thomas LF Livingstone (1829-1891), was born at Longton Hall (PSS p466) (VFC p86). From c1840 it was leased out and had various tenants until JHE Heathcote's death in 1928 (SHST p372). John Henry Clive, nephew of Clive of India, later of Clanway Hall (see), lived with his mother at Longton Hall when a child (POTP p62). The hall was sold by Heathcote's executors in 1933. The new owners, the Wottons, had it demolished in 1939 (VCH vol 8 pp228p facing,231) (POTP p120) or in 1934 (GLS p72) or by 1942; it had been in a decaying condition for many years (NSFCT 1942 p54). (SHST p546p of, p547p of the hall in Jan 1939, p548p front view). The original hamlet of Longton grew up around an early Longton Hall (SL p227). The ghost of a girl in white was seen in 1943 close to the site of Longton Hall in the lane from Longton to Blurton (GLS pp71-72). The ghost of a lady dressed in a cloak and a feathered hat was seen in c1934; she is believed to be the wife of a previous owner of the hall who was murdered on New Year's eve by her husband for having an affair with one of the grooms. This ghost reputedly appears every New Year's Eve (GLS pp72-73). Stables and coach houses were not demolished with the hall in 1939 and were still standing in the 1950s (VCH vol 8 p231). The stables probably occupy the site of the kilns of Longton Hall Works (see). There was a lake in which, reputedly, was found the body of a girl who had worked as a servant at the hall in the C18. According to tradition she became pregnant and committed suicide.

Longton Hall Works Longton Hall. From c1749 a pottery was erected at Longton Hall - the first pottery works in Longton - by William Jenkinson, occupier of the hall by at least 1752 (VCH vol 8 p239). In 1751 Jenkinson went into partnership with William Littler (1724-1784) of Hanley (VCH vol 8 p239) (POTP p140) or of Brownhills, Tunstall (OTP p65) (H p45). Littler had commenced making semi-transparent ware, which he called china in c1750 (OTP p65), and was the originator of the brilliant blue ground colour in ceramics which the later china factories of Longton used to such splendid effect on their Victorian tablewares and figures, known as 'Littler's Blue' (POP p128). During the Jenkinson and Littler period Longton Hall Works made the first porcelain in Staffordshire (S p119) (SL p227). Or rather the first 'soft paste' porcelain works in Staffs and as such the works were one of very few 'soft paste' potteries in England (IANS pp92,149). Some consider 'soft paste' not true porcelain. Bell's Pottery, Newcastle-under-Lyme, also have the claim of being first producers of porcelain (POP p170). With Jenkinson's departure in 1753 Littler took over as manager (VCH vol 8 p239) (POP p128). Financial support was withdrawn in 1760 and the works closed and Littler moved to Scotland (VCH vol 8 p239) (POTP p140). Stables and coach houses were probably built over the site of the kilns of Longton Hall Works. (NSFCT 1956 p87). In excavations Bembrose was unable to find evidence of Littler's porcelain on the site (NSFCT 1942 p55). But in excavations at the site of the hall in 1955 fragments of Longton Hall porcelain were revealed (NSFCT 1956 pp85,87). (Watney's 'Longton Hall Porcelain') (NSFCT 1957 pp19-25).

Longtown Area of Rowley Regis (BCWJ).

Long Walk A walk in the grounds of Loxley Hall. It leads to the grotto, Robin Hood's Chapel (see). A small door from Uttoxeter parish church was erected at the entrance of the walk in c1828 (NSFCT 1922 p128).

Longway House House slightly over 1.5m NW of Lichfield cathedral. In existence probably by the mid C17 and demolished in the C19 (VCH vol 14 pp231,234). Marked on 1834 OS map at approximately SK 098115. The C18 barn, long in ruins and derelict, was converted into a house in c1995.

Longwood Birthplace of Alfred Moss, poet and editor, in 1859. His biography of JK Jerome appeared in 1929 (PSS pp324-330 p) (VFC p95). As Long Wood it is marked on 1834 OS map. The name is preserved in Longwood Bridge over the Rushall Canal.

Lord Hay's Branch of the Wyrley and Essington Extension Canal. Runs from Pelsall Wood to Lords Hay (VCH vol 2 p293). Opened in c1798. Closure sanctioned in 1954 (HCMS No. 2) (BCM winter 1995/ 96 p23). A Bronze Age mace of c1500 BC was discovered near the Lord Hay's Branch in Nov 1953 (SOB p96p facing).

Lords Hay To E of Great Wyrley (Smith's map).

Lordshire House in Werrington 0.5m ENE of the church. The name occurs as Lordshare on 1834 OS map.

Lordsley Fragmented tiny hamlet 1m NW of Ashley. One house is called Lordsley End Farm. It may have formerly appeared as Lords (1834 OS map) and Loran (Dower's map).

Lord's Well Sinai Park. Marked on the present OS map 1:50,000. Is probably the fine chalybeate spring a little below Sinai Park house noted by Shaw in the late C18. Then it was enclosed by a stone wall with steps leading down to the water. On the wall appeared this inscription 'Re-built by William Lord Paget in 1701' (SHOS vol 1 p24).

Lordswood A wood called Lords Wood is marked on the 1834 OS map within the very narrow neck part of the Harborne ancient parish. Lord's Wood has appeared as Great Lightwood (1709) (STELE Feb 1 1952), and Carless Wood, after the Carless family, who resided at The Grove, Harborne, in the C18 (GMH pp3-4,10). There are currently secondary schools by the name of Lordswood in approximately the same area as the wood, long built on.

Lord Ward's Canal Short canal built by 2nd Viscount Dudley and Ward be-

tween 1775 and 1778 purely as access to limestone quarries under Castle Hill. Runs from the Birmingham Canal Old Cut Old Main Line at Tipton Junction to Castle Mill Basin (HCMS No. 2) (info Dudley Canal Trust). See also Pensnett Canal.

Lot's Coppice NE of Newchurch or at SW corner of airfield.

Lount House 1m NE of Anslow. Formerly in Anslow township in Rolleston ancient parish (UTR p181). The name is from common land in existence by 1300. Lount was an inhabited place by 1700 (ANS pp103,116). The name is from the word 'lant,' a ploughed strip of field? (UTR p181).

Lount House 3.25m SE of Hixon.

Lount Farm By Moreton Brook 1m NW of Colton. There is a burnt mound at SK 03792184 (SSAHST 1994-95 p5).

Louse Hill Seighford. Controversial meadow or heath in a C18 tithe dispute (OPB p16).

Love Lane Former short lane in Walsall leading from Whitehall Road to the neighbouring fields and was much frequented by courting couples, now made into a street. Another Love Lane in Walsall (also known as Snake Lane) has become Highgate Avenue (SNWA p70).

Lovers Walks Alias Hobs Hole Lane, Aldridge (ALOPP p30p); a path through Watermills Wood, Apedale (NOPP pl 102 in c1910); a former track now Hinstock (Enstock) Road, Handsworth (HPPE p68); a track from St Peter's church, Harborne, to Weymoor Farm (Whitehouse Farm) via The Hillyfields (OHOPP p11p).

Low, The A burial mound at Elfordlow Farm, Elford.

Low, The House 1.25m S of Longnor. Formerly in Fawfieldhead township in Alstonefield ancient parish. The name was recorded in 1399 and is thought to have been so named on account of the number of burial mounds in the vicinity; 'low' being the common term for burial mound (VCH vol 7 p27). Has also appeared as Thelow (Smith's map) and Low (Bowen's map and others). For the burial mound here see under Boothlow.

Low, The In the C17 Plot and Huntbach noted a large burial mound at The Low; much of it was destroyed (NHS p403) (AOW p9) (NSJFS 1965 p59). Perhaps, it was a prehistoric burial mound or a later one containing those killed in the battle of, or battles of, Wednesfield or Tettenhall in 910 or 91 AD (DUIGNAN p97) (W p205). Smallshire says 'The Low' is a field name near to the early nucleus of Heath Town (WFW p23). 'The Low' may also be identified with Low Hill, near Bushbury.

Low Bent Former area or field at SK 09206228, S of School Clough; the field here is now called The Bent. Formerly in Fawfieldhead township in Alstonefield ancient parish. In the field called The Bent is the burial mound which was excavated by Bateman in 1848 (TYD pp36-37) (NSJFS 1965 p38). It was excavated again in the 1980s by David Wilson and Faith Cleverdon (SSAHST 1985-86 pp8-22).

Lowe Hammill The bottom part of Mill Street, Leek, was once Lowe Hammill or Hamlet. It was once a distinct small hamlet since it was cut off by the precipice known as Lowe Hill, until James Brindley cut Mill Street through it (NSFCT 1905 p159). The bottom of Mill Street may also have been called Lower End in the earlier C19 (VCH vol 7 p142). There is a Hamil Drive off Mill Street. The name is from 'Lowe' as in 'Leek and Lowe' (see).

Lowe Hill Hill 0.5m NW of Leek. In Leek ancient parish. The name is from 'Lowe' as in 'Leek and Lowe' (see). James Brindley built Mill Street through it as a route to Lowe Hammill (NSFCT 1905 p159), and Brindley may have had a farm on it (NSFCT 1882 p26).

Lowe Hill Hill 1.25m SSE of Leek. Was probably an inhabited area by the earlier C14 (VCH vol 7 p85). The name is from 'Lowe' as in 'Leek and Lowe' (see). This may have been the Lowe Hill where James Brindley had a farm (NSFCT 1882 p26). Lowe Hill Bridge is dated 1828 presumably the date when the section of Leek-Ashbourne turnpike road below was made (NSFCT 1948 p53). A tollhouse was built at Lowe Hill on the Leek-Ashbourne turnpike road (built 1762) in 1765. It was replaced by one at Pool Hall (see) near Bradnop in 1828 (VCH vol 7 pp99,171). The name appears on the 1834 OS map as Low Hill. In the Jacobite Rebellion the Young Pretender's army came over Lowe Hill on Dec 4 1745 (BPCSM p7). A phantom coach has been seen in the area (FLJ 1942 p126).

Lowend House 0.75m SSW of Sheen. In Sheen ancient parish. The name may be from a burial mound. There has been settlement at Lowend since at least the later C17; a barn here is inscribed with the date 1666 (VCH vol 7 p241). To the W of Lowend on the W side of the Manifold at SK 097604 is a bargain stone used as a gate post; it is probably not in its original position (PDS&C p73p).

Lower Acre House 2m N of Onecote. Formerly in Onecote township in Leek ancient parish. The present house, dated 1826, acquired its present name, Manor Farm, by 1913 (VCH vol 7 p212).

Lower Bangley House 1m SE of Hints. Perhaps, also is a minute hamlet referring to the neighbouring scattered properties.

Lower Barton Farmhouse 0.5m W of Bradley. Dates from later half of C17 (VCH vol 4 p76).

Lower Biddulph Former manor and liberty covering the Gillow Heath area and the W part of Biddulph town. Has also appeared as Nether Biddulph. The manor was created in 1189 out of the division of the extensive Biddulph (see) manor. It did not have resident lords (NSFCT 1888 p70) (LCAST 1898 p64) (BALH pp21, 26 see map).

Lower Birches House 1m SSW of Rugeley. May have been confused with Little Birches (see).

Lower Bradley A current name, which appears to have arisen as the name for the eastern half of Bradley manor or estate, in Bilston township. The former small canal-side hamlet of Lower Bradley was overshadowed by the industrial expanses of the Bradley Bar, Bradley Hall and Britannia Works (see) (TB May 1985 p1). The Zeppelin L21 dropped five bombs on Bradley on Jan 31 1916 in WW1, one damaged the canal bank and killed Mr and Mrs Frederick or William Fellows who were walking along the canal by a pumping station in Lower Bradley. To their memory local people carved two crosses in the brickwork of the pumping station wall where they were hit. Mr Fellows, aged 23, was killed outright but his wife, Maud, aged 24, lived for a short while and died on Feb 12 1916. The bomb cap has been preserved. A plaque marking the spot of the incident was to be unveiled on July 15 1994 (TB 1983. July 1994 p17p) (BCM summer 1996 pp67-68). Lower Bradley was developed for housing after WW1 (OS map Sheet 67.04).

Lower Clent A manor of Clent as opposed to Church Clent manor, which belonged to the Crown until Charles I's reign. Lower Clent belonged to the de Somery family of Dudley Castle (see) (SHOS vol 2 p247).

Lower Cowley A house at S end of Cowley 1.25m S of Gnosall.

Lower Dippons Wrottesley. W of Tettenhall Wood.

Lower Elkstone Moorland hamlet enclosed by the deep valley of Warslow Brook 1.5m W of Warslow, 0.75m SE of Upper Elkstone; Upper Elkstone is the larger and older of the two Elkstone settlements (VCH vol 7 p57). Formerly in Warslow and Elkstones township in Alstonefield ancient parish (W p742). Appears as Over Elkstone (1272) and Nether Elkstone (1290) (VCH vol 7 p57). It formed a separate manor by the late C13 but was a part of Sir John Harpur's Alstonefield estate by the early C17 (VCH vol 7 p59).

Lower Ellastone S end of the village of Ellastone. At one time it may have existed as a separate tiny hamlet.

Lower Farm Almington. A sword of the late C17 period was found here in c1915 (NSFCT 1931 p189).

Lower Farm To W of Little Bloxwich. A cruck-truss house, built in c1819. Stood near the junction of Stoney Lane and Selman's Hill (SK 005032). Demolished in April 1963 to make way for a housing estate called Lower Farm estate. The actual site of the farmhouse is now occupied by Smith House (SSAHST 1963 pp69-73) (BY p18) (VCH vol 17 p163) (SNBP p4). The church, The Holy Ascension, Sanstone Road, was built in in 1968 and serves the Lower Farm estate (LDD).

Lower Gornal Large Black Country village 20m S of Stafford, former liberty in the Upper Side division in Sedgley ancient parish (W p195). Lower Gornal has appeared as Nether Gournall (1632) (HC p39), Nether Gournal (Plot's map), and New Gournall (Bowen's map). There was a Quaker burial-ground in Lower Gornal, probably in use from 1678. It may have been at SO 921907 or where the Red Cow Inn (see) stood at SO 920909, for some bodies in rows were discovered there (SSAHST 1970 p42). Lower Gornal was renowned for the extraction of sand from local quarries. A chief industry in the area was crushing the sand making Gornal Lily White Sand (BCM Oct 1970 pp20p-21) (WBJ p34) which was used as a scouring powder (MR p162). For the former windmill in Pale Street, Ruiton, which may have ground lily white sand see The Round House. Whilst the men were down the mines it was mainly the women who went about selling the sand from carts drawn by donkeys. The sellers of it had a ditty they sang to sell their ware:

> Get yer sond, get yer sond,
> Ha'penny a bucket, and some in yer 'ond.

(TABC p28). 'Gornal' ecclesiastical parish, formed in 1824, has become known as 'Lower Gornal' (GLAUE p412). The church, St James the Great, at the S end of Church Street near its junction with Temple Street, was built in 1815-1823, and enlarged in 1836 (LDD) (BOE p199). There was a **bull ring** for bull baiting at Lower Gornal (BHOP2 p8). A **mock sun** was witnessed by Col John Lane and Mr Persehouse of Lower Gornal on July 12 1678; the same day others saw it at or near Hopton Heath (NHS pp3,4,5,6,7). **Water**

pump. Children of Lower Gornal sung a song in c1920 about a local woman who diluted her milk with water

> Mrs Morgan's gone to jail
> For milking the cow with the iron rail.

The cow with the iron rail is, of course, a picturesque way of describing the water pump (BCM April 1968 p37). For the Gornal Nailmakers Carol see FOS p92. **Persons and visitors. John Johnson Shaw**, seismologist, was born at 11 Church Street, Lower Gornal on Dec 27 1873 (BCM spring 1995 p51), subsequently lived in West Bromwich (see) and made experiments at Baggeridge Colliery (see). Rev **James Yates Rooker** (d1887), vicar of St James', Lower Gornal, since 1848, was shot at in a grocery store at Five Ways, Lower Gornal, on Aug 8 1879 by Charles Hartland, owing to various grievances held by Hartland against Rooker, one being Rooker had acted as a magistrate in a case brought against Hartland for indecent exposure, another being when the vicar was executor of a will to which Hartland staked some claim. Rooker carried the bullet in his skull until he died (Daily Telegraph 1881) (SR p63) (TB March 1977 p24. Aug 1982 pp1,14ps. April 1988 p5). Rev **JR Windsor-Garnett** was curate in Lower Gornal for two years between 1924-25 and Lower Gornal appears as Nether Maltings in his 'The Village' (1926). He was criticised for portraying Lower Gornal too closely (TB Sept 1986 p14) (VFC p144; date given for publication of 'The Village' is 1931). For **JB Priestley's** comments on Gornal see Gornal.

DERIDING OF THE NATIVES. People from the two Gornals have become known as Gornal Donkeys, a term of abuse implying simplicity (FLJ 1890 p326. 1896 pp366-386). The people of the Gornals have long had a reputation, particularly with those in other Black Country towns, for being dimwitted. Other Black Country townsfolk, no doubt, fed up with accusations of being dimwitted from the rest of the country themselves needed a community to ridicule: This is the traditional home of Aynuk and Ayli (MR p162), see under Black Country. A Gornal man will play a coal shuttle as a musical instrument. A local butcher? had an advertisement showing a pig pulling a trolley loaded with pork with the caption 'Drawing his own conclusion' (John Sparry on BBC Radio 4 April 14 1994 9.45am). A Gornal man could also put a pig on a wall to let it see the village brass band go by. An old picture postcard proves this once happened, although, in fact, it never did. However, this story became Black Country folklore. The postcard, dating from c1900 asks 'who put the pig on the wall to watch the band go by,' with a picture of a pig, possibly super-imposed, resting its trotters on a wall and its head raised stationed next to the man who put him there. It was long claimed this was a Gornal character called Johnny Longstomach, who stood six feet seven inches tall. The origin of the card was lost in time until a correspondent of TB identified the occasion of the band playing, which was also featured on the card, to the visit of Capt Webb of Dawley, Shrops to the village (TB Oct 1974 pp20-21. Aug 1979 pp1,19-20) (BCM Jan 1978 pp17-18p) (BCWJ p110) (MMBCC pp54-61). Another story concerning the village band relates that their drummer was so small and his drum so big he once lost his way trying to follow the band and arrived at Ruiton beating the drum by himself (BCWJ p110).

Lower Gospel End Farm Penn Road, Gospel End. Had a stone inscribed 'HB 1695.' The 'B' may stand for the Bourne family. In 1997 it was the residence of the Pugh family (SDSSOP p22p).

Lower Green NW part of Coven. Has also appeared as Gregory's Green (1834 OS map).

Lower Green Hanley. Small village, which with Upper Green, 0.5m to the NE, formed Hanley up to early C18. The area is now the present Market Square (VCH vol 8 p142) (POP p38). Together they were collectively known as Hanley Green.

Lower Green A green to the S of Tettenhall church half way up a ridge. One centre of Tettenhall village grew around this green; the other centre, probably the younger, Upper Green (see), developed around a green to the W of the church (TCOP p12p) (VCH vol 20 p5). In 1613, when it was known as Old Tettenhall Green, it covered 13 acres. In 1695 it was called Lower Green, but this name was not regularly used until the mid or later C19. It has also been known as Tettenhall Green. By 1980 it covered 3 acres. The stocks of Tettenhall Clericorum manor, made in 1723-4, probably stood on Lower Green (VCH vol 20 p7). The ghost of a police superintendent who had died whilst still in the force was seen by his colleagues on the Upper or Lower Green in c1944 and in Feb 1946 (TB Feb 1988 p17) (GOM pl 8(c)).

Lower Green Farm House 2.25m N of Onecote. Formerly in Onecote township in Leek ancient parish. the present house is dated 1773. There was a house here by 1650, when it was known as the Green or Threewall Green

(VCH vol 7 p212).

Lower Hatton Southern part of the fragmented tiny hamlet of Hatton (see) 1.25m NNE of Standon.

Lower House Farm Stanley village. May stand on the site of the medieval manor house of Stanley manor. The present house is of c1700 (VCH vol 7 pp229,231).

Lower Hurst House 2.5m NNW of Alstonefield, on Archford Moor. Formerly in the detached portion of Fawfieldhead township in Alstonefield township. The house may date to before the C18 and appeared as New Hurst in 1779 (VCH vol 7 p11).

Lower Knightley Fragmented minute hamlet 2m SW of Ellenhall. No Lower Knightley appears on the 1834 OS map. The house Knightley Green seems to be in it.

Lower Lane Former hamlet of Fenton which developed at the junction of the Newcastle-Uttoxeter road and the roads to Bucknall and to Blurton (now Manor Street and Christchurch Street respectively). The hamlet along with Lane Delph was the most populous area of Fenton in 1775. It became known as Church Fenton (see) after the building of Christ Church in 1838-39 (VCH vol 8 p207).

Lower Leigh Tiny hamlet 0.5m W of Church Leigh. 0.25m S of Upper Leigh. Formerly in Leigh township and ancient parish.

Lower Loxley Tiny hamlet 0.25m W of Loxley Hall. Lower Loxley Farm, formerly called Loxley Hall Farm, in c1900 reputedly had a haunted sitting room and milking parlour (Uttoxeter Post and Times Oct 27 1995) (TRTC pp103p,104-105).

Lower Meaford Farm Meaford. Formerly owned by the Earl of Sidmouth. Much of its land was used for the site of Meaford (see) Power Station, built in the 1940s. In c1980 the farmhouse became Lakeside Country Club and later the Lakeside Tavern Inn (Memories of the Downs Banks. Kathleen Day. c1999 p10). This farm appears to have been one of the Meaford Farms (the other being Upper Meaford Farm) (Yates' map), and later Meaford Farm (1834 OS map) and Meafordhall Farm (OS maps 1889 6 inch, 1988 1:25,000), 1.25m SSW of Barlaston.

Lower Moddershall Over 0.25m WSW of Moddershall, by Scotch Brook. Comprises the watermills Mosty Lee Mill and Splashy Mill (SVB p126). Does not appear on current OS maps.

Lower Moors Rowley Regis. Field name (NHS p170).

Lower Nobut Minute hamlet of about two properties 1.5m SE of Church Leigh. In Leigh ancient parish. Nobut was originally from North Butt (W p782).

Lower Oxhay House nearly 1m SW of Rushtonhall. Formerly in Rushton James township in Leek ancient parish. There was a farmhouse here in 1768 (VCH vol 7 p220).

Lower Pendeford Is the northernmost Pendeford, 1.25m SSW of Coven. Preserved in Lower Pendeford Farm.

Lower Penn Village on the crest of the ridge which rises out of the Smestow valley, and former township 1.5m WNW of St Bartholomew's church, in Penn ancient parish. From Upper Penn the village is reached through a cut in the sandstone rock at Spring Hill called The Rock. There was possible Neolithic settlement on Springhill ridge, but there is no evidence to support the speculation (ALP p16). For Iron Age activity in Lower Penn township see Pool Hall. The Roman road from Greensforge to Pennocrucium may have passed through Lower Penn township (ALP p19). Lady Godiva owned the Lower Penn estate or manor of Nether (Lower) Penn before the Norman Conquest (SHOS vol 2 p218) (HOWM p2). Has appeared as Penne (DB), and Penn-Buffar when held by William Buffare (or Buffere), living in 1185; Robert Buffary held Lower Penne in 1316 (SHC 1881 p10. 1911 p413. 1919 p165) (PONP p36). Became a separate civil parish in 1866 (GLAUE p419). The church, St Anne, Springhill Lane, was built in 1888 (LDD); during the foundation ceremony - the foundation stone is dated July 26 1888 (St Anne's day) - a time capsule was concealed in the church structure (Wolverhampton Chronicle Oct 15 1999 p20p).

Lower Reule House 1.25m WSW of Haughton. A branch of the Chetwynd family were living at Reule Hall at Lower Reule by the end of the C17. The house built in 1847 has the date 1847 and the initial 'M' above the doorway. In 1955 it was empty and a new house had been built 100 yards farther E (VCH vol 4 p76). Has also appeared as Nether Reule.

Lower Rowley House 1.5m NE of Hamstall Ridware, S of Rowley Farms.

Lower Snowdon Minute hamlet 1m W of Patshull on the Shrops border.

Lower Stonehouse House 0.25m NNW of Brown Edge.

Lower Stonnall Minute hamlet at the foot of Grove Hill, on the NE side, by a tributary of Footherley Brook, 0.5m ENE of the church at Stonnall. In Shenstone ancient parish. Has appeared as Nether Stonnall (Plot's map) and Stonall Inferior (SHOS vol 2 p54). Lower Stonnall has a tradition of once

having its own chapel. The materials were taken to build Shenstone church; the church contains some carving of the keys of St Peter and Lower Stonnall chapel was dedicated to St Peter (SHOS vol 2 p54).

Lower Tean Village by the Tean in Tean valley 0.75m SE of Upper Tean. Formerly in Tean division of Checkley ancient parish. It remained in Checkley ancient parish after Upper Tean became a parish in 1844 (LGS p231). For wells in Lower Tean see Well in the Wall. The burial mound N of the village at SK 01723874 is 25 paces in diameter and five feet high and a listed monument. It was excavated by Redfern in July 1876. The floor of the burial mound produced evidence of combustion, although no human remains nor funeral pottery were found. A ring in jet, and six worked flints were found. Some Roman pottery fragments were found in the later course of the excavation. Redfern thought the barrow to be Celtic (HOC p191) (HOU 1886 p36) (NSJFS 1965 p35). It or Upper Tean appear in DB as Tene, and as Nether Tean on Plot's map. For a rhyme about Lower Tean see Checkley. But Jon Raven gives a different version which does not mention Upper Tean (FOS p148).

Lowe's Hall Stood at the end of Charlemont Crescent, Charlemont, West Bromwich. It was built in the C18 for Jesson Lowe whose family originated in the Lyndon area. It was demolished in 1948. During the Sacheverell riots Gornet Lowe shot dead two of the mob that attacked the old meeting chapel (WBOPP pl 68).

Low Farm The burial mound at Low Farm at Booth Low at SK 09006283 was excavated by Thomas Bateman in 1848 (TYD p36); considered not 'a barrow' by Gunstone (NSJFS 1965 p38); excavated in the 1980s and confirmed to be a burial mound of late Neolithic or Early Bronze Age (SSAHST 1985-86 pp1-8 ils). (L p51).

Lowfields House 1.25m NE of Stramshall. Near Combridge (HOU p26). There is or was a burial mound here called Lowfields Low or Robin Hood Butts. Robin Hood is supposed to have used it as a shooting target from White Gate at Stubwood near Denstone. Redfern notes the burial mound still existed, although its elevation was only slightly above the surface and it was covered with trees. Fragments of swords are said to have been turned up near it, in the course of draining operations (HOU p26). Gunstone could find no sign of it and thinks it was a natural feature (NSJFS 1965 p50). There is a tradition amongst the local people that a battle was fought at Lowfields, perhaps in Saxon times (HOU p26). (NHS p414).

Low Frith District of Alstonefield ancient parish identified for taxing and rating purposes. In existence by 1611 as a sub-division of High Frith. It covered the township of Fawfieldhead (VCH vol 7 p7).

Low Green In approximately position of Darlaston Green (Offlow hundred) (Dower's map).

Low Hall Low Hill, Bushbury. (TB Sept 1981 p10).

Low Hall Lowe Hill, Leek.

Low Hill Former small hamlet (BUOP p6) now a residential area of Bushbury, 0.75m SSW of Bushbury, in Bushbury ancient parish. There may have been a burial mound on the hill here possibly called The Low (see). There seems to have been a small settlement at 'atte Low' in the Middle Ages (HOWM p6). (SHOS vol 2 p150). The area was developed with a new municipal housing estate built from 1926; by 1939 there were nearly 9,000 houses. Originally all the streets of the new estate were given numbers as names. A Methodist chapel made of iron was opened in Kempthorne Avenue in 1927. With the building of a brick church in 1929 it became the church hall and was demolished in 1966 (WAIW vol 3 p) (BUOP pp35p,36p,124p) (Wolverhampton Chronicle Oct 25 1996 p18p) (E&S May 15 1998 p14) (HOWU pp147,148). The church, The Good Shepherd, on the corner of Second and Dickinson Avenues, was built in 1928. It burnt down in 1946 and was rebuilt on the same site in 1956. This successor building of poor design was demolished in 1998 (info Rev Neil Hogg). Was a ward of Wolverhampton borough by 1982.

Low Hill House Stood at the top of the present Goodyear Avenue, Low Hill, Bushbury (STC p24p). Built in c1760 for Willis Kempson of Bilston and his wife, Bridget, youngest daughter of Walter Gough of Old Fallings. Later, the house had several owners including Henry Lovatt (1831-1913), civil engineer and entrepreneur. The house was demolished in 1926 and Whitgreave School built on the site (BUOP p38p).

Low Plantation 0.75m NNW of Alstonefield. In Low Plantation is a large and irregular mound at SK 12895657 (NSJFS 1965 p31).

Lows, The Burial mound under 1m S of Grindon at SK 08425303. It is 25 paces in diameter and two feet high (NSJFS 1965 p38) and a listed monument.

Loxdale Industrial area marked clearly on OS map 1:25,000, between Moxley and Bradley presumably around Loxdale Street. Prince George visited the Loxdale reclamation scheme on April 24 1933 (BOP p149p). By the late C20 there was an industrial or business park here is called Loxdale Park.

Loxley District on high ground above Dagdale or Picknal Brooks, tributaries of the Dove. The district consists of the hamlets of Loxley Green and Lower Loxley and the houses Loxley Hall and Loxley Bank. Loxley Hall is 10.5m ENE of Stafford. Former constablewick in Uttoxeter ancient parish (W p789). Has appeared as Locheslei (DB), Loksle (C13), Lockesley (C13), Lockesleye (C13) (SPN p81), Nether Loxley (East) and Over Loxley (West) (Plot's map). The name perplexes Duignan, but it possibly represents Loc's or Loxa's lea (DUIGNAN) (SPN p81). Ekwall gives 'Locc's leah' (SSE 1996 p15). The medieval chapel at Loxley is not mentioned in the returns of 1533 or after (SHC 1915 p296). A vessel of Etruscan form is said to have been found in the park of Loxley Hall in the C18. It was reproduced in facsimile by Josiah Wedgwood I in his red ware, 26 copies were made and were known as the Loxley Vase (HOU p329) (SVB p40). On or near Sept 7 1915 a Handley Page bombing aeroplane was compelled, owing to thick fog, to land in a field near Mr Whittaker's farm at Loxley (TRTC p55). The body of Susan Maxwell, aged 11, was found in a wood by the lay-by N of Loxley Hall on Aug 12 1982. She had been abducted from near her home at Cornhill, Northumbria, near Coldstream, Scotland on July 30 1982, by Robert Black, a van driver. He was accused and found guilty of her murder and that of two other children (TRTC pp59,83-89). For Loxley Tunnel see Bromshall Tunnel.

ROBIN HOOD BORN AT LOXLEY. There is a local tradition that Robin Hood was born at this Loxley in 1160 (IAANS p xxxiv). (SOS) (W p792) (GNHSS p8) (WTCEM p58) (SOSH pp116-117) (NSFCT 1935 p92) (AB pp193,194) (TOS p42) (MR p48) (GLS pp99-100) (TRTC pp99-102). Or that Robin Hood often visited this Loxley (HOU pp327-329) (SVB p40). To **support the tradition** there are seven pieces of evidence but none prove he was born at Loxley or even came to this area in his life, if he lived at all. **Firstly** there is the coupling of the names of Robin Hood and Ranulph, 'de Blundeville,' Earl of Chester, in Piers the Plowman, 1362; the earliest known reference to Robin Hood (HS p103). Ranulph was lord of Chartley Castle, 4m to the SW of Loxley. The castle, rebuilt by Randulph 'de Blundeville,' Earl of Chester, passed to the Ferrers family in 1232. **Secondly**, Dent and Hill, found evidence of a family by the name of Odo living in the Uttoxeter area in the early C13. Ranulph 'de Blundeville,' Earl of Chester, was granted by Henry II a wholesale grant of Staffs lordships including all the estates of Radulphus filus Odonis - the Latinized form of Od or Hod (HS p102). **Thirdly**, ballads have claimed Robin Hood had a claim to the Earldom of Huntingdon (in the C18 Dr Stukeley compiled a pedigree to agree with this claim). In Robin Hood's time the Earl of Huntingdon was David St Liz, who married Maud, daughter of Hugh (d1181), Earl of Chester, sister of Ranulph 'de Blundeville,' last Earl of Chester, and sister-in-law of William Ferrers, Earl of Derby, of Tutbury and Chartley Castles (HS p103). **Fourthly**, a horn existed at Loxley Hall, seat of the Kinnersleys, which bore the initials 'R.H.' supposedly referring to Robin Hood (HOU p328 il) (SMM pp141-142). The horn bears three horseshoes (two and one) - the arms of the Ferrers (PS p73) (LGS p180). Redfern says it probably passed from the Ferrers family to the Kinnersleys by the marriage of Johanna, daughter of Thomas de Ferrers, to John de Kynnardesleye, through which marriage it is supposed Loxley also came into the possession of the Kinnersleys (HOU pp327-329) in 1327 (HS p103) - The Kinnersleys claimed the horn had been in their possession since 1327 (S p140). **Fifthly**, there are many Staffs references in a ballad about Robin Hood. The full title of the ballad is 'A new Ballad of bold Robin Hood; showing his birth, breading, valour, and marriage at Titbury Bull-running, calculated for the meridian of Staffordshire but may serve for Derbyshire or Kent' (SHOS vol 1 p55) (HS p105). The date of the ballad is uncertain, but, say Dent and Hill, it is evidently later than Elizabeth I's reign. It is earlier than any allusion to Maid Marian; it asserts 'the father of Robin a forester was,' and contains the first mention of Locksley, said to be in the county of Notts (but as Dent and Hill point out there is no Locksley in Notts). It has many allusions to Staffs, it assumes that Sherwood and Tutbury lie near together; it details a fight near Tutbury; it tells of 'Sir Roger the parson hies from Dubbridge' (Doveridge near Uttoxeter); and of 'the King of the Fidlers' a possible allusion to the King of the Minstrels Court of Tutbury (HOU pp327-329) (HS p105). The ballad was in the Roxburgh Collection in the BM by the late C20 (LTD p116). **Sixthly**, there are separate traditions that Robin Hood was active in the vicinity of the Staffordshire Loxley; in Burton, Needwood Forest, Elford, Swythamley Park, Lud Church, and old Macclesfield Forest. Nor have, according to Dent and Hill, the other places he is said to have frequented - Barnsdale, Sherwood, Plumpton Park, Cumberland, and Ingleton Forest - claimed him as a native (HS p103). **Seventhly**, Robin Hood and Maid Marian are said to be portrayed in the Abbots Bromley Horn Dance (LTD p116). The evidence **against the tradition** is that: the Loxley 3m WNW of Sheffield also claims to be his birthplace, as does Loxley in Warws, and according to Holt, it is not a fact that Robin Hood existed at all or that he was

born in any place called Loxsley or Locksley. It was John Major in 'History of Greater Britain' (1521) that provided Robin with a birthplace - Lockley (RHH). The myth of Lockley as the birthplace was perpetuated by Grafton, Stowe, Camden, and Robinson (HS p101). (Robin Hood. Ritson. pxv).

Loxley Green Fragmented small hamlet approximately 2.5m SW of Uttoxeter. During WW2 a British plane crashed at Loxley Green (TRTC p67).

Loxley Hall To N of Loxley Green, and E of Lower Loxley. Is 10.5m ENE of Stafford. In 1327 it became the seat of the Kynnersley family of Kynnersley Castle, Hereford, after the marriage of John Kynnersley to Joanna de Ferrers, sister and heiress of Thomas de Ferrers, lord of Loxley (TRTC p92). The hall was rebuilt in 1792 (SVB p40). Dr Gomme dates the front to c1795 and another date given for the part-rebuilding is 1797 (TRTC p94). Burke's Seats (1852) refers to the house as being almost rebuilt in 1817, although the room called the hall was kept (BOE p199 note) which may be the entrance hall? (SSC p138). Redfern says the old house was destroyed in c1805 (HOU p328). The room called the hall has panels which date from c1650 and a frieze with the date 1607 (AUOPP p76). The panelling or the frieze shows scenes of; the Saviour; the Virgin and infant; the Flight into Egypt; the Apostles and Evangelists, and the Last Supper. Also on a cornice are the arms of the Stuarts (SSC p138). A heraldic frieze was noted in the big hall. Over the fireplace are more than 100 coats of arms including the royal arms in the centre. According to Redfern the arms painted are those of the principal families in the kingdom in 1608 (NSFCT 1922 p128). (MR p353p of a door in the hall room). Some masonry from the old hall went to build Robin Hood's Chapel (see) situated at the end of the Long Walk (SVB p40). (SHOS vol 2 pl on p27 showing the hall and park) (PS p73p of the hall) (MR p352p). A treasure kept at the hall was a horn reputed to be Robin Hood's. The hall was owned by the Kynnersleys until Clement Kynnersley died childless in 1815. The estate and hall then passed to his nephew Thomas Sneyd (b1774), youngest brother of William Sneyd (b1767) of Ashcombe Park (see). By Royal License Thomas Sneyd took the name of Sneyd-Kynnersley in 1815; his descendants continued to live at the hall. Despite part of or all of the estate being sold in 1916 and or in 1918, the hall remained with the family until it was sold in 1945 (TRTC pp36,94). In WW2 it was partly occupied by the widow Mrs Sneyd-Kynnersley and American servicemen, and then by Italian POWs (TRTC pp66,90p). The Staffs county council purchased the hall in 1945 and in 1954 it became a school for boys with special educational needs. It was still a school in 1988 (SVB p40) (TRTC p94).

GROUNDS. 0.5m SSE of the hall at SK 05853145 is a stone pillar to the memory of Craven Kynnersley, who accidentally shot himself dead on this spot when out hunting on Dec 26 1736, aged 25; his dog having jumped up at him causing his gun to discharge (TRTC pp59,93). (SVB p40). The plaque with an inscription on the pillar had been stolen by the mid 1990s. There is an octagonal dovecote between the main road and the hall (BOE p199) (MR p352). The dovecote is said to date from 1740 (TRTC pp96,97p). See also Robin Hood's Chapel.

Loxley Park Medieval deer park at Loxley enclosed out of forest. In existence by 1505 (NSJFS 1962 p76). Former deer park in 1660 and 1735, and according to Neale in his 'Views of Seats,' in 1821 (EDP p177).

Loynton Former manor (W p465), and minute hamlet on gentle SW sloping ground by the head of a tributary of Lonco Brook 0.5m NW of Norbury. Plot believed the fossilized stumps of firs he found at Loynton in the later C17 were those of the alien Abies Legitima vel mas Bellonii, or Abies of Parkinson, not found in England or Ireland, proving that these types of fir were anciently indigenous to Britain (NHS pp209,216,217). Has appeared as Levintone (DB), Levuntuna (1088), Livintuna (1163), Levynton (1281. 1339), Loyngton (1371), and Loynton (1410-1834) (SPNO p176). The name means Leofa's town or farmstead (DUIGNAN) (SPNO p176) (SSE 1987 p28) (SPN p44) (SSE 1996 p15). Formerly in Weston Jones township in Norbury parish in Cuttlestone hundred; yet Loynton was curiously assessed under Pirehill hundred from the C17 to 1834 when it was returned by order of Quarter Sessions to Cuttlestone hundred (VCH vol 4 p61).

Loynton Hall Red-brick house of three stories at Loynton, 0.75m NW of Norbury. Late C18 to early C19 (BOE p212). Residence of the Higgins family until 1823 when the Loynton Hall estate passed to their relatives, the Burnes of Penn, Staffs. Miss CS Burne, folklorist, born Moreton, Gnosall, in 1850, was of this family. Her nephew SAH Burne was born here on March 30 1879. Described as 'the doyen of Staffordshire history' in the C20, he wrote APB, ESH, OP, OPB, and OPM, contributed to SHC and VCH (vols 4 and 5) and held the office of NSFC President. The hall was his residence in 1956. Some time after his death in 1972 a room in WSL was named after him. The Burnes are no longer at Loynton Hall (mem in Norbury church) (info Douglas Johnson) (VCH vol 4 pp156,159) (SHC 1970 ppviii-ix) (SH pp149-150).

Loynton Moss Former area of wetland to the W of Blakemere Pool, consisting of Big Moss and Little Moss. Plot makes a number of references to Loynton, and the preserved trees found in the moss (NHS p216) (VCH vol 4 pp155-162) (WSS p107). Two ring ditches possibly representing ploughed out burial mounds have been found SE of Loynton Moss (WSS p95). The pool was visited by the NSFC in Aug 1920 (NSFCT 1920 p160). The extensive moss came up for sale in 1969. In 1970 Staffs Wildlife Trust purchased the central core of the moss, comprising about 32 acres about Blakemere Pool; the rest was drained for farmland. The reduced moss, now (1998) managed as a nature reserve by Staffs Wildlife Trust and registered as an SSSI, was visited by the NSFC in July 1998. The name is preserved in Moss Farm 0.5m NNE of Loynton (WSS pp106,107) (NSFCT 1998-99 pp40-41).

Lucepool Single house or minute hamlet 1m ENE of Yoxall.

Lud Brook Former brook which ran near Lud Church. It was a tributary of the Churnet. Has appeared as Lodebroc (C13). The name of its valley has appeared as Luddebroc (1330), and Luddebrok (1346) (SPNO p13). The name is preserved in Lud Church (see), and means 'the loud brook' (SPNO p13).

Ludburn Tributary of the Manifold and house formerly in Fawfieldhead township in Alstonefield ancient parish (W p746), 1.5m SSE of Longnor. There was a house at Ludburn by the early C16 (VCH vol 7 pp27-28). The name may mean 'the loud stream' (SPNO p13). See Lud Well.

Lud Church Large natural chasm or ravine 1m NE of Swythamley hidden in the undergrowth of Back Forest in the Moorlands. It is one of the wonders of the county. **Length**. Plot stated it was approximately 208 yards long. Raven says 100 yards, and Porter says 200 feet, or is 180 metres (253 metres including all surface side passages) (SHJ autumn 1989 p3). **Depth**. At different places it is 30, 40, 50 feet deep (NHS p173). Or, according to Porter, it can be up to 60 feet, or 18 metres deep (SHJ autumn 1989 p3). Or, according to Miller, it can be to 80 to 100 feet deep (OL vol 2 pp162-163p). **Width**. The walls of rock are approximately 20 feet apart at the top (LGS p225). Others say six to ten feet wide (NSFCT 1889 p63) (MR p316). Although its mean width is 3.5 metres it can in places reach 5 metres. The N wall is steeper, more solid and sometimes overhanging. Although the ravine has a total of four entrances, access is normally made via the steps at the southern entrance and from the footpath at the northern entrance. A boulder spanned another entrance at the southern end; by 1989 it had been removed as a safety precaution. At the northern end lies a cave known as Gawain's Scabbard; the entrance is approximately 0.70 metres in diameter (SHJ autumn 1989 pp3-18 ps). Meal Ark Clough is a similar natural chasm to Lud Church in the Dane. AS GREEN CHAPEL. Recently Lud Church has been identified with the Green Chapel of the 'Sir Gawain and the Green Knight' poem written in c1400. In a re-edited version of the poem from the MS Cotton Nero, A. x in the BM by Sir Israel Gollanez (1940) it is concluded that if the 'Green Chapel' is not in a setting in North Wales or Pembrokeshire, then it could be identified with Thor's Cave. In the 1950s Prof RWV Elliott of the University of South Australia, formerly of Keele University, came to the opinion that the 'Green Chapel' bore a marked similarity to Lud Church (STM Dec 1969 pp5,26,27) and the anonymous author of the poem wrote in a dialect peculiar to the NW Midlands (The Times. May 21 1958) (CL Oct 19 1961 p952) (NSJFS 1962 pp86-87. 1977 pp20-49) (SMCC p5) (MR p316) (Daily Telegraph. Weekend Section. Oct 2 1993 pxxxvi) (VCH vol 7 p195) (DP p49) (HOLF p44) (SMM p145). A writer for NSFCT in 1932 did identify Knar, a farm in Cheshire close to the Staffs border near Flash, with its singular and plural forms in the poem (NSFCT 1932 p61). The face of the Green Knight is said to be portrayed on the eastern wall of the cave towering over the steps close to the main entrance at the southern end of Lud Church (SHJ autumn 1989 p8).
AS A HIDING PLACE. The chasm is said to have sheltered Robin Hood (HOLS 1883 p140) (WTCEM p57) (SHJ autumn 1989 p10) (SSGLST p13) (GLS p89) (HOLF p43). He is claimed to have been in Swythamley Park or old Macclesfield Forest (MC p30). Lollards also are said to have hidden in it, giving rise to its occasional name the Lollard Church (LGS pp224p,225). The chasm was a Lollard secret meeting place or hiding place in c1405. The forester of the estate, and himself a Lollard, Henrich Montair, carried food to them and guarded the entrance (NSFCT 1905 p169) (HOLF p42). One day in the early C15 Walter de Lud-Auk, the, or, a Lollard leader, and a Lollard assembly including Walter's beautiful young granddaughter, Alice, were discovered by the authorities and were massacred here, or taken captive. Some say they were given away by Alice's singing; she alone, some say, was killed by the soldiers. Walter de Lud Auk died in prison. Henrich Montair managed to escape to France (NSFCT 1905 p169). An oak tree grew over the grave of Alice at the entrance to the ravine (SHJ autumn 1989 p10) (SSGLST pp13-15).

No part of the chasm is reached by the sun. A Quarnford man is said to have brought snow to Leek market on July 17 from the depths of Lud Church (NHS p173). The antiquarian, Rev Thomas Loxdale of Meretown (see) visited the 'Church' in 1708 (SH p78). Charles Edward Stuart, the Young Pretender, reputedly stopped to rest at Lud Church on his march S during the 1745 Jacobite Rebellion (SMM p145) (DPEM p109); another account says local farmers hid their livestock in the ravine to prevent the same Scots army taking them (SHJ autumn 1989 p10). Sainter, in 1878, noted running water at the bottom of the cave (SHJ autumn 1989 p12).
FISSURE CHASM. At the S entrance was a small slanting fissure chasm. It was explored by a student accompanied by a miner and another man, some years prior to 1860. They left there a newspaper and other items bearing the date of their visit. As they returned a terrible clap like thunder occurred at the small entrance aperture which would have fatally wounded them had they been at that spot at that moment (LMF pp45-76). In c1862 the white figurehead of the ship 'Swythamley,' lost on route to Bombay in Sept 1862, was placed at the entrance to this chasm by Philip Brocklehurst. The figurehead in the form of a woman came to be known as Lady Lud (PDS&C p12p of statue of Lady Lud) (HOLF pp42-43). It resembled many people's idea of Alice, the granddaughter of Walter de Lud-Auk, and was said to be a tribute to her. The figurehead was still there in 1914 (SLM July 1950 p162) (NSJFS 1970 p117) (VCH vol 7 p195) (GLS p90). This fissure chasm appears to have since collapsed (SHJ autumn 1989 p16).
FOLKLORE. Another name for the chasm is Trafford's Leap after one of the Traffords of Swythamley Hall, who, on his horse, leapt over the chasm whilst out hunting, but his hounds all fell to their deaths (STM April 1968 p22) (VB 213) (MR p318) (SSGLST p13) (HOLF p42). The howls of the dead hounds are said to haunt the chasm (UHAW p76), and Trafford's ghost reputedly haunts it. Miss Dakeyne says that there was a subterranean cavern underneath Lud Church which was inhabited by a strange and distinct race of beings (DP p50): These are fairies thinks FLJ 1942 p127. A headless rider spectre or the headless horseman of the Moorlands reputedly has been seen in the vicinity of Lud Church (NSFCT 1882 p40).
ETYMOLOGY. The chasm has also appeared as Lud-Church (NHS p173), Lud Church Cavern, Lud's Church, and may have been called Lud-Auk (NSFCT 1932 p56). The element Lud first appears in the names Luddebroc and Luddebeche (Brook, see) both of which occur in the charter by which land was given for the founding of Dieulacres Abbey, a few miles from Lud Church. Lud either represents a person's name Lud(d)a, or is from Old English 'hlud' 'loud' and occurs in place names like Ludbrook, Ludford, Ludlow and Ludwell all associated with streams (NSJFS 1977 p27). Pickford suggests 'hlud' was applied to the chasm for loud clap noises have been heard emanating from it; Miss Dakeyne reports that men exploring the 'Lady Lud' chasm heard noises like a terrible clap of thunder (DP p50). Others have thought Lud a form of 'lid' from Old English 'hlid' an opening, gap (NSFCT 1932 p56). The chasm may have had some religious significance to ancient Britons and received its name because of an association with the cult of the Chthonian Zeus or Pluto (NSFCT 1922 p171). The name may be derived from Lud or Llud or possibly Nudd, the British name for a Celtic sky or river god. In mythology Lud's wife was Anu, Annu or Dana; her name may be the origin of the nearby river Dane (SHJ autumn 1989 p8) (DP pp46-48p). Or Lud may be from Lugh or Lud, a Celtic chieftain (who took his name from the sun-god Lughasakh). Lugh, known as Lugh the Longhand, is supposed to have kept and tortured his prisoners in the chasm, and on windy nights it is said that the ghostly cries of these prisoners can be heard (UHAW p76). There is a tradition that a Danish Viking known as King Ludd found the cave and gave his name to it (SHJ autumn 1989 p8). It has been suggested that the chasm received its name through Lud being a corruption of Lollard. However Lud Church is said to have been then called Lud-Auk (LGS p225). Auk is perhaps from Old English 'ealh' a temple, or Old English 'healh' a nook, recess, retreat (NSFCT 1932 p56) (DP p47). So the chasm would have given its name to Walter de Lud-Auk (DP p47). Oakden implies that the chasm was given its name in Victorian times from the nearby Lud Brook (see) and its valley (SPNO p13).
(GNHS p65) (OL vol 2 pp162,163 pl, 165) (HS pp105p, 183) (The jottings of some geological, botanical, ornithological and zoological rambles round Macclesfield. J Sainter. 1878. p157) (PS p145) (MC p30) (PS pp145,146p) (Proceedings of the Geologists Association. W Hind. 1891. ppcxxvi-cxxvii) (COEA p of facing p210) (KES p201) (Everymans Dictionary of Non Classical Mythology. E Sykes. 1952. p129) (CL Oct 19 1961 pp954-957) (SMCC p4 il on p5) (VB pp212,213) (Curiosities of the Peak District and Derbyshire. F Rodgers. 1974) (Dane Valley Story. C Rathbone. 1974. pp9-10) (SGS p142) (British Cave Research Association Bulletin No. 16. 1977 p7) (First and Last.

R Smith, M Williams, S Gregory. 1979) (Caves of Derbys. T Ford & D Gill. 1984) (MR pp316,317pc,318) (TB Nov 1994 p19p) (The Circlemakers. Andrew Collins) (The Seventh Sword. Andrew Collins) (DPEM pp135-137).

Luddebeche Brook Rises on the southern slopes of Gun Hill. Joins the Churnet near Foker (NSJFS 1970 pp84 map,85).

Ludwall Appears to have been a well between Longton and Normacot and is named in the Hulton Abbey charter. The name may represent 'the people's well' (SHC 1909 p59 note).

Ludwell Bridge Lud Well. Crosses the Dove (ESH p16).

Luitcoit An estate or administrative centre in the Lichfield area from which Lichfield partly took its name (VCH vol 14 pp4,37). It is possible that the estate pre-dates the Roman period and survived the Roman occupation and was known by the local Celtic-speaking people as Letocaiton and later as Luitcoit (SSAHST 1968 pp43,49-51) (VCH vol 14 p4). There may have been a post-Roman settlement of Luitcoit known as Cair Luitcoit (see), or Caer Lwytgoed (see). In the Welsh poem 'Marwnad Cynddylan' a C7 prince, Morfael of Luitcoet, is mentioned (DUIGNAN p92) (MR p211). The name is believed to have evolved from 'letocaiton' (the Celtic toponym of Letocetum) and means the 'grey wood' (VCH vol 14 p4).

Lum, The Near the Mermaid Inn on Morridge. The Lum is the source of the Hamps (NSFCT 1910 p166). The name represents the Celtic root 'leum,' a spring (NSFCT 1910 p166). There is a circular site near the Lum of sufficient antiquity to bend the parish boundary (NSFCT 1908 p107 note).

Lum Edge Moorland waste 1m NE of Upper Elkstone, mainly in Warslow and Elkstones township, in Alstonefield ancient parish. Enclosed in 1839 (VCH vol 7 p59). The boundary between the townships of Fawfieldhead, and Warslow and Elkstones was marked by stones on Lum Edge in 1837 (VCH vol 7 p27).

Lunn's Almshouses Stowe Street, Lichfield. William Lunn gave houses in Stowe Street for six poor widows in 1654. The old houses were replaced in 1959 with a terrace of six old people's bungalows known as William Lunn's Homes. By 1985 seven more homes had been added (VCH vol 14 pp184-185).

Lunt, The Area 0.75m ENE of Bilston. Formerly in Bilston chapelry in Wolverhampton ancient parish. The name means a lawn or open place in a wood where the game was driven for slaughter (HOBLL pp220-221). Prince George visited the Lunt allotments for the unemployed on April 24 1933 (BOP p149p). A garden shed containing hundreds of pigeons on the Lunt council estate mysteriously disappeared within a few seconds suggesting supernatural activity (GPCE p16).

Lupin Minute hamlet consisting of two farms, or one farm and its out buildings 1.25m ESE of King's Bromley. Lupin Bank is in Orgreave township of Alrewas ancient parish (W p594).

Luth Burn Tributary of the Trent (SPNO p13).

Lutley Tiny hamlet on gentle S-facing slopes above Philley Brook 1m SSE of Bobbington. In Enville ancient parish. Appears in the C12 as Luctelega and Luteleg (SPN p48). The name means 'little lea' (DUIGNAN) (VCH vol 20 p91) (SPN p48). A manor of Lutley had appeared by the later C12 (VCH vol 20 p91). The moated site at SO 816884 (CAMS p63) probably surrounded the medieval manor house of Lutley manor. This had a chapel and some stonework was visible on the moated platform in the early 1970s. Coins and other artifacts, including what was said to be a stone font, were dug up in the area in the early C19 (SHOS vol 2 p276) (SVS pp282-283) (Stour and Smestow Arch Research Group Field Survey Reports vol 1 (1970-3) p3) (VCH vol 20 pp94,104) (SSAHST 1982-3 p41). There was possibly a medieval village N or S of Lutley Farm, probably deserted between 1377 and 1524 (SSAHST 1970 p35). Lutley Farm, which dates back to the late medieval period, may be the Lutley manor house mentioned in the later C16 (VCH vol 20 p104).

Luxmore House on Leek-Buxton road near Leek. Built in 1902 to plans of architects Messrs Sudgen and Son for AH Moore (STC p39p).

Luzlow House 1.75m W of Wetley Rocks. Near Lusse Lees (otherwise Lusselows) an upright stone is mentioned in an account of the perambulation of Bucknall manor boundary made in 1803 (WJ p19). The house at Luzlow used to be an inn (WYV p33).

Lyde Brook Runs SE of Lloyd House. Tributary of Wom Brook which is a tributary of the Smestow. May be identified with the Hlyoe broc which occurs in a charter of 985 (SPNO p13) and has been identified with Lloyd Brook, said to have been one of the boundaries mentioned in Lady Wulfrun's charter of 994 (PENOP p76p). Has also appeared as Lydebroc (1294-1295), and Lodbroke (1424-1425) (SPNO p13).

Lydiate End Former area of Handsworth ancient parish (HANDR pviii).

Lydiates, The House 1.5m W of Kinver. The name is from Lidigate, a gateway in the fence which anciently surrounded the royal Coton estate in Shropshire (KRC p13).

Lyme Brook Rises S or E of Wood Lane runs by Holditch to Hanford and is a tributary of the Trent. Newcastle-under-Lyme is situated on it. Plot noted Lyme Brook in the later C17 (SPNO p13). The name is from Anglo-Saxon 'hlimme,' or 'llimme' meaning a stream, river, torrent (DUIGNAN). Duignan was probably wrong about this in the case of Newcastle-under-Lyme. Morland gives a form Duignan does not; the city of London had in their letter-books 1317 - 'Newcastle Super Are,' suggesting that the brook was alternatively known as 'Are' or 'Ayr,' 'ar' being the Norse word for river (POP p149). Morland is emphatic the Lyme Forest gave its name to the town, and the town gave its name to the brook. The river Lyme is not Saxon but of Celtic origin, related to Welsh 'llif' and Cornish 'lif' meaning 'flood or torrent' (SPN p81). Or is, possibly, from the root 'lleven,' smooth (NSFCT 1908 p129).

Lyme Forest Huge primeval forest stretching from the head of the Trent into Cheshire and covering that now settled by Newcastle-under-Lyme. The name may be from 'elm,' so it is the 'Elm forest.' Named by the Goidels or Gaels in c1100 BC (NSFCT 1946 p149). Or it may be from the C1 Roman boundary wall known as the Limes Britannicus (see); DG Harnaman suggested Lyme in Newcastle-under-Lyme was from the Limes Britannicus (NSFCT 1951 p119). The name may be from the Roman Limes, or limits between the C4 Roman provinces of Britannia Prima on the west and Flavia Caesarensis on the east (TTTD p217). The forest was a boundary of the Palatine of Cheshire (SMM p130). The forest, which has also appeared as Forest of Lyme, lasted until medieval times (SL pp48,67,69) (NUL p158) (SMM p130). It gives its name to the affix in Newcastle-under-Lyme; with Lyme Brook, running through that town, named after the town (POP p149). In medieval times Ashton (Lancs), Betton (Shrops), Chesterton, Laughton (Ches), Madeley, Newbold (modern Astbury, Ches), Norton (Shrops), and Whitmore were affixed 'under-Lyme.' Lyme also appears in Audlem (Old Lyme) (Ches), Burslem, Lyme Handley (Lancs), and Lyme Park (Ches) (NSFCT 1887 p42) (HBST pp20-21). Not only must the forest have covered these places but it stretched across to Beeston Castle, Ches (NSFCT 1941 pp36,37). It possibly reached into Yorks, where it appears in Limb Hill, and into Derbys, where it appears in Morley Lime (SSE 1996 p6).

Lyme House House nearly 1.5m NNW of Longsdon. Formerly in Longsdon township in Leek ancient parish. There was a house here by 1515 and there may have been one here by 1414 (VCH vol 7 p203).

Lymes, The Minute hamlet on hilly ground by Park Brook 0.5m NNW of Butterton (Newcastle-under-Lyme).

Lymford Farm C18 house over 2.25m NW of Rushton Spencer church. Formerly in Rushton Spencer township in Leek ancient parish. The name, in existence by 1333, is from probably a crossing over the Dane to the E. Lymford House, mentioned in 1596, may have stood on this site (VCH vol 7 p224).

Lyncroft 1m NW of Lichfield. Between Elmhurst and Pipe Hill. Lincroft field, a former open field, on the W side of Wheel Lane was mentioned in 1305 (VCH vol 14 p110). Has also appeared as Lincroft. The name means 'flax croft' (DUIGNAN) (SPN p78).

Lyncroft House Lyncroft, Lichfield. On W side of Stafford Road. Was built probably in late C18 (VCH vol 14 p21). The pianist and composer Muzio Clementi (d1832) lived here in c1830 (VCH vol 14 p164).

Lyndon Hamlet, now suburb 0.75m N of the High Street, West Bromwich. The name appears from the earlier C14 and as Lindon on Plot's map and as Lyne at the beginning of the C18. The name is from probably the lime tree or linden. Lyndon was at the centre of West Bromwich ancient parish and was the most populated area of the parish before 1801. A market house for the parish belonging to the lord of the manor existed at Lyndon in 1725 but it seems to have fallen into decay by c1740 (WB p50) (VCH vol 17 p34) (SOWB p23). There seems to have been a lock-up at Lyndon in the C18 (WB p55). The stocks were also kept at Lyndon and they are now in the Oak House grounds (VCH vol 17 pp4,43) (SHWB 13). By the later C18 the main part of the village lay around the junction of the present Hargate Lane and the present Lyndon Street and extended SE to Mayer's Green (VCH vol 17 p4). North of the hospital, probably in Windmill Field, at approximately SP 008925 stood a windmill in the early C19 (WBJ p45). Lyndon ward of West Bromwich borough, created in 1882, was divided into three, Hateley Heath, Friar Park, and Charlemont in 1952 (VCH vol 17 p46).

Lyndon Lyndon Farm, on the head of a brook forming ornamental pools in Enville Hall grounds, stood over 0.75m S of Enville. There was settlement at Lyndon by 1312, and there were five houses here in 1663. The Lyndon estate was held in the C16 and C17 by the Shadwell family, from whom the dramatist and poet Thomas Shadwell (d1692) claimed descent. They sold the estate in 1747 to Lord Stamford who incorporated it into the grounds of Enville Hall. The house was gothicized about this time, perhaps by Sanderson Miller.

It was demolished in c1961 (VCH vol 20 pp93,99,103 pl of Lyndon in the later C18 facing p112).

Lyne Hill Tiny hamlet on low ground by a brook 0.75m SSE of Penkridge. In Penkridge ancient parish. Has been described as a hamlet, as a manor, and as a farm (VCH vol 5 p116). Has appeared as Lynhull (1237), Linhill (1237), Lynehille (1422), Lynylle (1475), Lynell (1551-53) (SPNO p90), Line Hill (Plot's map) (W p468), Linehill Green (1834 OS map) (DUIGNAN) and Lynn Hill. The name is from Anglo-Saxon 'lin hull,' 'the flax hill' (DUIGNAN p95) (SPNO p90). 'Green' was applied later (SPN p82).

Lyng Name for the area about Lyng Lane and Moor Street, West Bromwich. In West Bromwich ancient parish. The name is from a kind of bush which covered this area of West Bromwich Common (SOWB p24). In existence by 1775. By the mid C19 several streets had been laid out in the Lyng area as far S as Sams Lane. Lyng became a ward of West Bromwich borough in 1918. The church, The Good Shepherd with St John, on the corner of Lyttleton Street and Bromford Lane, was built in 1967. The Lyng area was redeveloped by the council in the 1960s (VCH vol 17 pp9,46) (LDD). By 1999 formed a ward with Greets Green in Sandwell metropolitan borough.

Lynn Minute hamlet by a tributary of Footherley Brook over 0.75m NNE of the church at Stonnall. In Shenstone ancient parish (W p583). Appears in the period between C13-C14 as la Lynd (SSE 1996 p15) and has appeared as Lyndon and Lynne (SHOS vol 2 p55). The name is from perhaps, a grove or lime-tree (DUIGNAN) (SPN p106) (SSE 1996 p15). Or is of Celtic origin (HOWW p8). There may have been a Quaker burial-ground at Lynn, but it may have been no more than an individual garden interment (SSAHST 1970 pp42-43).

Lynne Hall At Lynn. Held by the Stanleys, perhaps in Henry VIII's reign. It appears to have passed to the Erpes in the earlier C17. Francis Erpe was a parliamentarian in the Civil War. From the Erpes the hall passed in Charles II's reign to the Persehouses of Walsall. Some small remains of the hall were visible in the late C18 (SHOS vol 2 p55). A Lynn Hall appears on the 1887 OS map six inch at the junction of the Stonnall-Shenstone road and the Hilton road, at SK 075044. A Lynn House on the N side of the Stonnall-Shenstone road, at SK 081044 appears in 1887 and in 1976 (1887 OS map 6 inch. 1976 OS map 1:25,000).

Lyntus Two coppices 1.5m WSW of Fradley are called Big Lyntus, and Little Lyntus.

Lyons, The Over 0.75m W of Enville. The present tall white-brick villa in the Tudor style built in 1847 for Job Bissell, formerly of Tipton, succeeds a farmhouse which was in existence by 1704. The name may be from Lions Meadow, mentioned in 1300 (VCH vol 20 p94).

Lysways Minute hamlet 0.5m SE of Longdon. In Longdon parish. Appears in 1167 as Lisuis (DUIGNAN), and Liswis. Lysways lies in watery meadows and probably has the same root as Leasow place names (DUIGNAN) (SPN p78).

Lysways Hall N side of Lysways Lane, to E of Longdon Green. According to tradition the hall was once a castle built in Henry II's reign with a secret door and underground passage into the forest (LTM Nov 1972 p25). An old hall on this site belonged to the family of Liswis (or Lyswayes) by at least Henry I's reign (SOS pp181-182); the hall has appeared as Liswis Hall. There is a story of a Liswis who murdered his wealthy neighbour over a gambling session in the Middle Ages and was revisited by the skeleton spectre of his victim the following Christmas and died of a heart attack brought on by fright from seeing the ghost (LTM Nov 1972 p25). In Richard II's reign the Liswis' sold the estate to John Legydd (or it passed by the marriage of the Liswis heiress to John Legydd). John's daughter and heir carried the estate by marriage to James Arblaster of Cropston, Leics, after which it was known as Arblaster Hall (SOS pp181-182). In 1769 (THS p87) or in 1772 the Arblasters sold the hall to Francis Cobb who left it to his two nieces, of the name of Tyson, the survivor of which owned the hall in 1819 (SOS pp181-182). It was occupied in 1834 by Col William Berrisford (d1850) (W 1834 p364) (mem in Longdon church). The hall, at some time, was owned by the Austin family. Representatives of the Tyson nieces sold the hall in 1836 to Charles Smith Forster (1784-1850), first MP for Walsall (1832-1837), who made the hall his residence (SOS 1840 p242) (W p568) (SNWA p44). Dinah Mulock spent a fortnight staying here in early summer 1844 when it was the seat of William Parker, who was formerly of Albion House, Shelton (NSFCT 1925 p89). Charles Smith Forster was succeeded by his son Sir Charles Forster (1815-1981), MP JP, who was residing at the hall in 1872. He was created a baronet in 1874 (KD 1872) (SNWA p44). Wright, writing in the 1930s, records that the hall was demolished recently; the Forster succession having failed on the death of Sir Frank Villiers Forster (d1930), 3rd Bart (CCBO pp194-198) (mem in Longdon church). In the hall Wright noted a curious relic which stood at the top of the main staircase. It was an old fashioned eight-stop gallery organ in rosewood case. At the head of another staircase was an antique Sheraton barrel-organ in mahogany case. In the yard outside was a relic of the pre-motor car age - a four wheel omnibus, painted black, picked out in red used for the family to convey them from the railway stations at Armitage and Lichfield (CCBO pp194-198). The present hall, of C18 origin (SGS p125) (CCHCB p of c1890), was divided into two by the early 1970s, by having its centre demolished (SGS p125). The hall was advertised for sale in CL Sept 21 1995. (SHOS vol 1 pp222-224). By the later C19 there was an extensive park attached to Lysways Hall, known as Lysways Park, which stretched to Longdon Green, and followed the Lichfield road to Cheat Hill (OS maps).

Macclesfield Canal Canal which branches off from the Trent and Mersey Canal S of Hardingswood Road, Kidsgrove. Crosses over the Trent and Mersey Canal on the Pool Lock Aqueduct (see) and over the Tunstall-Liverpool road on the Red Bull Aqueduct (see), both are on the Ches Staffs border at Red Bull. Joins the Peak Forest Canal at Marple, Cheshire (IANS p24). Completed by 1831, surveyed by Thomas Telford, the engineer was William Crosley (IAS p172).

Mackillan's Green Near Bell End, Rowley Regis. The name appears in the 1851 census.

Madam's Bridge Former wooden foot bridge over the Trent at SJ 877384, Tittensor, now lost. It has also been called Madame's Bridge (NSFCT 1915 p154). The earliest bridge on, or near, the site was a stone bridge built by Lady Dorothy Wilmot Bridge in 1597. It was blown up in the Civil War on Feb 29 1643 by Capt Stone for the parliamentarians and the stones lay on the Trent bed for nearly half a century. John Bagnall rebuilt the bridge in brick in 1680. It was destroyed again by a maiden, Miss Ann Aston of Parkfields, Barlaston, on Nov 15 1834 at night because she disapproved of two young ladies who were paying attentions to her bachelor brother and used the bridge to come to see him (NSFCT 1940 p34) (STM May 1964 p33). An account of 1915 implies that the present (1915) bridge is a packhorse bridge and the masonry of it is in a somewhat ruinous condition and passengers now (1915) cross by means of a wooden plank and handrail (NSFCT 1915 p154). (BAH p15). The current (1990s) steel and concrete footbridge is its replacement.

Madeley (locally *Meedley* BOJ book 2 p97). Large village situated on the River Lea (MHSP p5), former township and ancient parish 16m NW of Stafford.
EARLY. Two large boulders were noticed by the NSFC in the vicarage grounds, a granite 3 feet by 2 feet 9 inches by 2 feet round, and a trap 4 feet by 2 feet 6 inches by 2 feet 6 inches angular, there were no scratches on either. They were brought here by a Mr Daltry from an adjacent field (NSFCT 1892 p107). Within 200 yards of the village is a mound (NSFCT vol 34 pp47-48), possibly a burial mound now destroyed (NSJFS 1965 p43). For the burial mound 1m S of Madeley see 'Romulus.' At Madeley Manor Farm is a quern (M p21). A half mile stretch of **Romano-British** road was found in Madeley Great Park (see). It was traced by three Cambridge geographers in c1785 and runs from Uriconio by way of Newport, Langot Lane and Maer to Middlewich and the Roman Condate (NSFCT date uncertain). At Madeley was perhaps, the Roman town of Mediolanum (STM May 1963 pp42,43). For a hoard of Roman coins found in Madeley parish see Little Madeley.
700 to 1700. Has appeared as Madanleig (SSE 1996 p15) or Madanlieg (975) (DUIGNAN) (SPN p82) when a charter was made of its bounds (SHC New Series. vol 12 p202 note) (SL p61). The first part of the **name** 'Made' is a mead or meadow, ley is generally a clearance in wooded country (M). Or derived from a river name: Madeley, Shrops is on the Mad Brook (NSFCT 1908 p144). The earlier form 'Madanlieg' suggested to Duignan a proper name (NSFCT 1908 p144). Mills gives 'Mada's woodland glade.' The personal name is a nickname meaning 'foolish' (MHSP p8) (SPN p82) (SSE 1996 p15). The present parish **church**, All Saints, Woore Road on the N side of Vicarage Lane, dates from the C12; there are traditions that a church of Saxon origin existed at Madeley, perhaps on the site of the present church (SVB p117) (All Saints, Madeley: A Short Guide). Madeley was created a parish after 1086 and before 1291 and must have been formed originally out of Wolstanton original parish (SHC 1916 pp192,195). Madeley **wake** was on the nearest Sunday to Nov 6 or on a Sunday if that was Nov 6 in the C19 (W p395). The **manor** of Madelie (Madeley) is recorded in DB and was then

held by the de Staffords of Stafford Castle: Edmund de Stafford, held the manors of Stafford, Bradley, and Madeley of the king by barony on condition he found three armed men with three horses and equipment for war whenever there was war between England and Wales, or Scotland (temp. Edward II) (SMC p122). Ralph de Stafford was granted a charter May 13 1341 to hold a **market** here on Tuesdays. The market may never have taken effect, at all (NSJFS 1971 pp51,57). For Madeley cross see SCSF p87. Madeley has or had a **lock-up** (M p14p of the workhouse and lock-up). A long cross silver penny E.1 1302-7 has been found, presumably in the Madeley area (M p21). Later forms of the name are: Madeley under line (Erdeswick 1593-1603) (SOS p78), Magdalea (Camden) (NHS p44), Great Madeley (Plot's map), and Madeley-under-Lyme (LGS p180).
1700 to PRESENT. Richard Whitworth's Liverpool to Hull **Canal** (see) was to have passed through Madeley but it was never built (BVC p170). Madeley had a station on the Grand Junction **Railway** from its opening in 1837 (MHSP p53). The 2-2-2 Lucifer engine broke the world speed record when it reached 56.75 mph on the GJR at Madeley Bank on Nov 13 1839 (GBR 1974 p146). For the record of the 'Coronation Scot' see under Whitmore. Firmstone's Mineral Railway ran from Leycett to Madeley Heath. It opened in 1838 and closed in c1957. Another tramway operated from the iron works at Madeley Heath to the Nantwich turnpike road from 1854 (NSJFS 1968 p99) (M p7). By 1870 Madeley was linked by rail to Market Drayton (MHSP p55). Madeley station, on the E side of Manor Road to the E of Old Madeley Manor (site), had closed by 1962 (OS map 1962). Near the former railway station, 0.25m S of the church, remains a 33 feet high **octagonal well head** of Caen stone known as the Offley Well Head. It was erected in the mid C19 by Hon Miss Crewe in memory of her aunt Hon Lady Offley (Mrs Cunliffe-Offley) (d1850), a sister of 2nd Lord Crewe (d1837), who was a great benefactor in the area. A fountain issues into basins on three sides (W p395) (BOE p200) (MHSP p71). In WW1 the Zeppelin which had passed over the Potteries on the night of Jan 31 1916 came towards Madeley and dropped a bomb into open country near the village (TB July 1994 p19). There is a **local tradition** that the first man who got drunk at the Offley Arms Inn (see) was made the mayor of Madeley (M p29). For Madeley in a rhyme see Betley. **Persons and visitors**. Willenhall's famous drunken parson, Rev **William Moreton** (1759-1834), was baptised at Madeley on July 7 1759 and he may have attended Madeley Free School (SHC 1970 p171). **John Wesley** (d1790) visited Madeley shortly before his death. It became the custom for the church bell to be tolled each evening after **Samuel Stretch** (d1804) of Shropshire, a pedlar and messenger who resided at Madeley, endowed a bell ringer to ring a bell for a short period each evening so that wayward travellers, like himself, might find their way home. The bell was rung for about five minutes before and after 9.00pm each evening until the 1970s when the custom ceased; there being no volunteer (the original endowment having depreciated to nothing) prepared to carry it on (W p396) (MHSP p81) (info Jane Tellier). The library of the NSFC (founded at Etruria) is named after Rev **TW Daltry**, successively curate (1861-1880), and then vicar (1880-1904) of Madeley, NSFC secretary (1866-1904).

Madeley Brook Runs by Wrinehill Mill (NSFCT 1919 p25).

Madeley Farm House over 1.5m NE of Stramshall. In Checkley ancient parish. May represent the demesne of Madeley Holme (see). Near Madeley Farm some foundations in Cheshire and Madeley fields were thought by Redfern to be of Roman origin (HOU p61) (VCH vol 1 p191) (NSJFS 1964 p21). There was possibly a medieval village at Madeley Farm (SK 055370) or at Madeleypark (SK 065383), possibly deserted in the C18 (SSAHST 1970 p35).

The name has probably the same origins as Madeley near Heighley Castle (SPN p82).

Madeley Great Park Medieval deer park S of Madeley Old Manor emparked by the de Staffords in the C14 (SL p91). For the Roman road in the park see Madeley. The park was in existence by 1293 (NSFCT 1910 p175) or some say by 1272. Referred to as 'Great' in consequence of the de Staffords holding the nearby smaller parks of Leycett and Netherset Hay (NSJFS 1962 p76. 1963 pp39-47 plan). The park comprised about 830 acres and was the largest of the Madeley manor parks (MHSP p16). Has also appeared as Madeley Park, and possibly Madeley Old Park. Stretches of bank and ditch still partly surround the park (SL pp91,92 plan). Plot noted that the timber in the park at Madeley (Old) Manor surpasses that of Bagots Park. And that at Madeley Park pale there was an oven to Madeley Old Manor; it was common to place ovens at some distance from the house (NHS pp223,360). In the C19 the park belonged to the Crewe family (EDP p178).

Madeley Heath Residential area 1m NE of Madeley. In Madeley ancient parish. At cSJ 783454 at Round Hollies was found a flint scraper of Neolithic or Bronze Age (NSFCT vol 67 p125) (NSJFS 1964 p28).

Madeley Holme Former manor, division of Checkley ancient parish and possible lost vill. Madeley Farm (see) or Madeleypark (see) may represent the demesne: There was possibly a medieval village at either place, since depopulated. Has appeared as Madelie (DB), Madeleye (1175) (SPN p82), Madeley Alphon (1316) (SHC 1910 p411), Madeley Ulfac (DUIGNAN), Little Madeley (DB notes. Phillimore edition 1976), Old Holm, and Madeley Old Holm (NSFCT 1940 p25). The name has probably the same origins as Madeley near Heighley Castle (SPN p82). Ulfac, perhaps from Wulfheah (DUIGNAN). The manor was held by Lady Godiva for a while after the Norman Conquest. At the time of DB it was held by Wulfheah of Robert de Stafford. Here there are ancient earthworks which represent the site of a house where Lady Godiva was kept in exile in 1071 during the second insurrection against the Normans. The reason for the lack of Saxon traditions in the area is perhaps due to Norman raids here after 1071 (NSFCT 1940 p25. 1948 p121) (STM March 1967 p31).

Madeley Manor Heighley Castle Way, 1m N of Madeley on the lower slopes of Bryn Wood above Middle Madeley. Is different to Madeley Old Manor (or Old Madeley Manor), which confusingly has also appeared as Madeley Manor. This Madeley Manor was the residence of Mrs Cunliffe-Offley, a sister of the 2nd Lord Crewe, and her husband after it was built in 1820 and before her death in 1850; Offley Well Head in Madeley is to her memory (MHSP p71). Another account of 1834 says the house was lately erected by the Earl of Wilton (descended from the Egertons) and is occupied (1834) by Lady Egerton (W 1834 p645). On 1834 OS map a house here or near here is called Madeley House. Whilst giving drawing lessons to Annabel Crewe, daughter of 2nd Lord Crewe (d1837), William Callow made a watercolour of the house in 1843. The painting was purchased by Newcastle borough council in 1992 by which time the half-timbered section of the house had been demolished (The Advertiser Nov 24 1992 p3) (ES Nov 26 1992 p8. Jan 9 1993 p5). Hon Miss Crewe was residing at Madeley Manor in 1851 (W p21). The acrobat, Charles Blondin (1824-1897), performed in the grounds of Madeley Manor on May 31 1887 (TB June 1993 p36). In the C20 the house has been flats, then offices until becoming a nursing home in c1989 (local info).

Madeley Manor Pool It appears to be the pool to the E of Madeley Manor house. Izaak Walton fished in this pool; hence the name of nearby Walton's Wood (NSFCT 1942 p63).

Madeley Old Hall N of Madeley church on the Woore-Newcastle road. Timber-framed building. It was a farmhouse and not the manor house (SL p98). Has the date 1647 entwined with a mocking inscription

16 Wallk k nave what look est at 47. ISB

carved onto the front of the house. The initials I.S.B. were added during the Civil War by John Bowyer of Stonylow or Sidway (STM May 1967 p26p). This inscription was apparently written because the owner was so annoyed at people staring at the house in reverence because Queen Margaret of Anjou had, reputedly, stayed here on her way to Eccleshall after the battle of Blore Heath (BPS p44 note). Or is a message to fool local parliamentarians into thinking the owners were loyal while in reality they were royalist (PWNS p75). Or simply a reflection of the pride of the new owner (MHSP pp38p,39). (W p395) (LGS p181) (KES p149) (SCSF p168) (STM Oct 1964 p45) (VB p185) (BOE p200 - Old Hall) (SGS p126) (MR p220p).

Madeley Old Manor Ancient house under 1.5m S of Madeley, on the N boundary of Great Madeley Park. Has also appeared as Old Madeley Manor, and formerly Madeley Manor. An early building on the site was the manor house

of the de Staffords, lords of Madeley; Ralph de Stafford, 1st Earl of Stafford (d1372), was granted a license to fortify the house in 1348 (SL p92 note) (CAMS p23p plan) or 1349 (NSJFS 1969 p133). In 1547 Sir Thomas Offley (?1505-1582/3), a native of Stafford and lord mayor of London in 1556-7, came into possession of Madeley manor. The hall then became the seat of the Offley family (M pp2,3). Sir Thomas was a frugal man, of whom it was written:

> Offley three dishes had of daily roast,
> An egg, an apple, and (the third) a toast,

(KES p149) (M p4). Sir Thomas's great grandson, Sir John, was a friend of Izaak Walton who visited the hall in the C17 (NSJFS 1969 p133). In the later C17 Plot noted the hall had a wooden shuffleboard (NHS p383 tab 16 il of the Manor). Sir John's son, John, married the daughter and co-heiress of John Crewe of Crewe. Their son, John, took the name of Crewe in 1708 (M p3). His descendants were created Earls of Crewe. Lord Crewe was created KG in 1908 and Marquess of Crewe in 1911 (M p3). The hall had three portraits of the first Lady Crewe (d1818), two were by Reynolds. In one she appears as a shepherdess and the painting is peculiar in that her eyes are not seen. She looks down at a book giving full effect to her eye-lashes. There is another portrait of her in old age by Sir Thomas Lawrence. A painting by Canaletto, 'The Capitol of Rome,' was hung in the library (SLM April 1948 p92). After the union of the Crewe and Offley families, the estate fell into decay and the house was practically razed to the ground in 1749 (NSFCT 1949 p120) or in 1793 (NSFCT 1976 p13). In 1793 a new manor was built using the stones of the old manor (NSJFS 1969 p133). This appears to be the farmhouse slightly to the N which has appeared as Madeley Manor (Greenwood's map), Madeley Old Manor (Teesdale's map), Madeley Manor Farm (1834 OS map), and Manor Farm (1983 OS map). In the early C20 Masefield noted only a ruined stone gateway and some mounds and trenches remained of the old manor house (LGS p181). The complicated earthworks at Madeley Old Manor in the mid C20, which did not appear to protect or enclose anything, may have been the result of landscape gardening (NSFCT 1953 p 64). In 1967 Madeley Old Manor was owned by the Lord O'niell Settlement Trustees of Crewe (Newcastle Times Dec 13 1967). (GNHS p123) (BN April 7 1932 1 pl) (STM May 1967 p27p) (M p23) (MR p221p). In the later C17 Plot noted that a rare Coccothraustes or Gross-beak bird had been found and killed at about Madeley Old Manor and had been preserved in the collection of Madam Offley (NHS p230). For the burial mound NNE of Madeley Old Manor see 'Romulus.' Had an ice house.

Madeleypark House 1m S of Croxden, owned between the C16 and the C18 by the Madeley family, whose descendants removed to Uttoxeter (HOU p359). May represent the demesne of Madeley Holme (see). There was possibly a medieval village at Madeley Farm (SK 055370), or at Madeleypark (SK 065383); it was possibly deserted in the C18 (SSAHST 1970 p35). The name is from Madeley Ulfac Park.

Madeley Park Farm House over 2m SSE of Madeley. There is a circular earthwork on a knoll S of Madeley Park Farm at SJ 787411, near the centre of which is a rough sandstone block which lies buried with its upper surface showing. The earthwork is 51 yards in diameter and a Roman coin was found near the knoll (NSFCT 1935 pp69,70) (NSJFS 1964 p29). The same or another burial mound, 10 feet high, is by the railway line at SJ 788412 (NSFCT 1983 p11). A rectangular earthwork near the farm is thought, locally, to be a Roman camp - a stretch of Romano-British road runs through Madeley Great Park (see). The sides of the earthwork are roughly 60 feet in length, about 12 large stones were in the ditch on the W side (NSFCT 1935 pp66,67 plan, 68,69).

Madeley Park Wood Wood in the centre of 'old' Madeley Great Park 2m SSE of Madeley; recently became a residential area. A small rectangular earthwork at SJ 782416 with a single bank and ditch was excavated in 1935 and fragments of undated pottery found, now lost (NSFCT vol 70 p66). Excavations in 1961 were inconclusive and it has been destroyed (NSJFS 1964 p29).

Madeley Round Barrow Burial mound at SJ 775428? at Madeley (M p21).

Madeley Ulfac Park Medieval deer park in the vicinity of Madeleypark. In existence by 1316. It belonged to the Bassets (NSJFS 1964 p63). A small part of the park pale or fosse surrounding the old park is evident to the N.

Madge Dale N of The Dale, E of Dilhorne (1834 OS map).

Madge Oak A Madge Oak is marked on 1834 OS map just N of Castle Ring. It was a parochial boundary mark and visited in the Rugeley perambulation (PCC p13). Perhaps, is same as Magic Oak (see).

Madman's Lane Former lane to the W of Norton Canes. Runs from Watling Street at SK 002076 N to SK 004079 (1888 OS map 6 inch) (CCF p222).

Maer Ancient parish, former township and manor. The small village of Maer lies at the head of the Tern valley by Maer Pool, the source of the Tern, 12.25m NW of Stafford (W p363). For a possible **Iron Age** farmstead near Maer see Maer Moss. Various **battles** are said to have taken place at or near Maer in the Anglo-Saxon period. Penda, king of Mercia, reputedly killed Oswald, king of Northumbria, in one in 635 (ES Sept 1936 p4). In a battle in 642 Penda slew Maser or Maserfield at Maerfield (GNHS p74) near Maer. King's Bank in the Maer Hills is the tradition resting place of Oswy, Christian king of Northumbria, slain in a battle in 642 (STM June 1967 p27p). In 705 Kenred, king of Mercia, fought and defeated Osrid, king of Northumbria (SMC p163) (S&W p389) (NSFCT 1888 p35). **Some wrong identifications.** There was formerly some confusion as to whether Maer appeared in DB as Mere or Mera. It was formerly believed that Mere was Meretown in Forton and Mera was Maer (NSFCT 1888 p35) (Domesday Studies. Eyton. p87). But the converse is the fact (SHC 1909 p236) (VCH vol 4 p172). The battle of Bloreheath (1459) was wrongly said to have taken place at Maer by Rev W Snape in his account of 1812 and this was perpetuated by Pitt in his THS (SHC 1945/6 p94). Maer later appears as Mere (1242) (SPN p82). The name is derived from nearby Maer Pool, a mere, a great lake or standing water (DUIGNAN) (LGS p182) (SH p45) (SPN p82) (SSE 1996 p15). The parish **church**, St Peter, on an eminence to the E of Maer Hall, in the village centre, is believed to have been built in 1210 and restored or rebuilt in 1600 (SVB p119) and restored in the later C19 (BOE p201). Maer parish was formed between 1086 and 1291 probably out of Mucclestone original parish (SHC 1916 pp192,195). The **vicarage** is an old house, built in 1580 by Sir John Bowyer, but has been enlarged (LGS p182). On Monday May 10 1756 at 6.00pm a **freak hail storm** occurred at Maer when stones as large as hazel nuts descended (Universal Magazine May 1756) (SMC p78). **Persons and visitors.** In 1286 a court was held at Maer by the **Chief Justice of England** (TTTD pp239-240). It is recorded in Maer PR that in 1639 a **Richard Wilson** of Maer lived to the age of 138. The clerk evidently had his doubts as he entered in brackets (ut ipse dixit) (so he said himself) (MJW p15). The natural historian, **Charles Darwin** (1809-1882), grandson of Dr Erasmus Darwin of Lichfield (see), frequently visited his cousins and uncle, Josiah Wedgwood II, at Maer Hall for social reasons. He was present for the shooting season in Sept on many occasions and was at Maer in Sept 1826, and Sept 1827. He was also at Maer in Oct 1828, July and Aug 1829, Aug and Sept 1830, Aug, Sept and Dec 1831, Nov and possibly in Oct 1836, Sept 1837, July and Nov 1838, Jan and Aug 1839, June 1840, May 1841, May and June 1842, July 1843, April 1844 (STM June 1967 p26) (SLM Feb March 1988 p14) (MJW p20) (Darwin. Adrian Desmond and James Moore. 1991 pp29, 47, 75, 204, 278, 279, 288, 289, 292, 309) (ES Feb 4 1982) (The Correspondence of Charles Darwin. S Smith and F Burkhardt. vol I (1821-36) 1985. vol II (1836) 1986?). Josiah Wedgwood II was instrumental in persuading Darwin's father to allow him to accept the invitation to sail on the Beagle (The Life and Letters of Charles Darwin. pp43-44,59). On Jan 29 1839 Darwin married his cousin, Emma Wedgwood, daughter of Josiah Wedgwood II, in Maer church (she had been baptised in the church on Sept 17 1824) (NSFCT 1987 p41) (SVB p117) (Darwin p19); their signatures appear in an old church register (MJW p21p) (ES May 14 1997 pp1,4p), which by 1998 was kept at the SRO (Spotlight on the Diocese of Lichfield. May June 1998 p4). After the marriage the couple travelled to London on honeymoon from the recently opened Whitmore station on the GJR. From the mid 1820s Darwin took a close interest in the flora and fauna of the area around Maer. From late 1836 to 1842, having returned from the Beagle as a very experienced, internationally-known scientist based in London, he interested himself in natural studies around Maer; the cross-pollination of bees (Darwin pp290,292,509); the identification of rare hybrids of bilberries; the influence of earthworms on the generation of soils alongside William Dabb's cottage and croft (the result of following up conjecture of his uncle, Josiah Wedgwood II, that identifiable debris scattered on the surface of a peaty bog meadow at SJ 780384 to counteract poor drainage 80 years previously had been buried to 12-14 inches depth due to the action of earthworms - an idea known as 'Ye Maer Hypothesis'). He followed up his ideas on the transmutation of species, about which he had been keeping a notebook between 1837 and 1842, by writing in May 1842 a short 35-page preliminary draft of what became known as 'Origin of Species.' Darwin was a visitor to George Tollet's Model Farm near Betley Hall; Tollet's daughter, Georgina, checked the Ms of 'Origin of Species' for spelling, syntax and grammar before publication (1859) (NSFCT 1888 p34. 1939 p76) (STM June 1967 p26) (BOPP). Whilst at Maer Darwin identified a rock-bearing mineral Hornblende which he believed had been carried to the Maer Hills from Aberdeenshire by glacial action (ES Sept 4 1936 p4. Sept 9 1936 p5). Between 1842-44 Darwin was the first to locate the Butterton (see) Dyke, 3m from

Maer. When staying at Maer Darwin may have attended services at the Old Meeting House in Newcastle-under-Lyme (ES May 28 1930 p4). Also he is said to have spent some considerable time at Rowley Regis (BCWJ p134), possibly observing the polygonal basalt columns in the quarries there (this article was written in collaboration with David B Thompson). **Princess Margaret** visited Maer when she attended Stoke Guides Parade on June 16 1973 (TTH p158).

Maerfield There is a house E of Berth Hill called Maerfield Gate S of the Stone-Nantwich road. At SJ 794389 in the corner of a field to the N of Maerfield Gate Farm is a 10-15 feet high burial mound crowned with trees and was probably part of the Camp Hill-Berth Hill-Kings Bank complex, and in 1983 was possibly threatened by road widening (NSFCT 1983 p11). To the S of Maerfield Gate Farm at SJ 794389 is a burial mound which takes the form of three small bowls, nearly at the top of a sloping field near trees and a rocky outcrop (NSFCT 1983 p11). At Maerfield, reputedly, King Penda slew Maser or Maserfield in 642 (GNHS p74).

Maer Hall Represents the manor house of Maer manor. In 1443 Maer manor was granted to Ralph Macclesfield, and his successors held it until his descendant, Ralph Macclesfield, sold it to John Chetwynd of Rudge (d1702) in 1693. He was succeeded at Maer by his second son John (d1767). For Thomas Maxfield (d1616), Roman Catholic martyr, who may have resided at Maer Hall see Chesterton Hall. In 1735 John succeeded to the Ingestre estate on the death of his brother, William, and moved to there letting Maer Hall to Sir Nigel Gresley of Drakelow (COI p225,226il) in. The Chetwynds and their successors, the Talbots, remained owners until 1790 when it was sold to James Bent. He sold it in 1802 (HOE p48) (TTTD pp239-240), or in 1805 (SVB p117) to Josiah Wedgwood II, third son of Josiah Wedgwood I of Churchyard House (see) and Etruria Hall (see). Josiah II was lent the money to purchase the hall by Robert Darwin (father of Charles Darwin), his brother-in-law, and the Wedgwoods moved here in 1807 (Darwin. Adrian Desmond and James Moore. p12). For Charles Darwin at Maer Hall see Maer. The present hall was originally built in the Jacobean style or period (BOE p201) by a member of the Bowyer family (SGS p126). Josiah II made the first alterations and extensions to the hall, which was known as Maer Hall by the mid C19. His wife came from another potting family, the Davenports. The Davenports owned the hall from 1845 (SVB p118) or 1847 until 1892. William Davenport (1805-1869), pottery manufacturer, died at Maer Hall. He is portrayed unsympathetically in 'When I was a Child,' the autobiography of Charles Shaw (1832-1906), as the person who had forced Shaw into the workhouse by sacking his father (POTP p76). William Davenport built extensions to the N which included the morning room, the billiard room and the clock tower (TTTD pp239-240). In 1892 FJ Harrison, Liverpool ship owner, bought the hall and estate from the Davenport trustees and spent vast sums modernising the interior and adding a new entrance at the northern end. In 1898 he installed electricity powered by a steam engine (SGS p126). He was succeeded by his two daughters Miss RHM Harrison OBE (later Master of the North Staffordshire Hunt) and Miss JEL Harrison OBE JP (TTTD pp239-240). During their time the Duke of Rutland, the Earl of Shrewsbury, Lord Combermore, and the Earl of Lichfield and many others were visitors when taking part in the North Staffordshire Hunts here (MJW p23). Miss RHM Harrison died in 1960. On the death of her sister Miss JEL Harrison in 1963 (ES Nov 5 1963) the hall was sold to Dr Michael Tellwright. After much opposition from the Victorian Society Dr Tellwright had the hall reduced in 1972 to its early C19 size. The clock tower went to the US and some of the stones went to building a house at Daisy Lake. The hall was sold to the Fradleys in 1980, the owners in 1998 (local info) (ES July 22 1982). (SLM Feb 1948 pp70,71 about the interior) (MR p222p).
GROUNDS. The square dovecote in the courtyard has 18 holes each side, each hole has its projecting brick as an alighting ledge (SLM summer 1958 pp34-35,37p). There is a stone footbridge linking the hall to the church which passes over the main road through the village. It was built by William Davenport, whose initials appear on it (SVB p118). The gardens were designed by Mawson (BOE p201).

Maer Heath Heath 1.5m NW of Maer. N of Blackbrook. Former common land enclosed in c1812 by the Wedgwoods of Maer Hall (GM 1812) (SL p129). Appears on 1834 OS map. In a wood here is a very large andesite granite boulder (NSFCT 1916 p73).

Maer Hills Hills N of Maer. Comprise Berth, Berry, Burgh, or Byrth Hill, Red Hill, a hillock, Camp Hill, King's Bank, and War Hill (NSFCT 1931 pp91-92), suggest confrontations took place over them; Berth Hill was fortified in the Iron Age. A long trench was located in Feb 1938? to complete the Iron Age citadel on Maer Hills - the site combines a stronghold, camp, cattle-sorting corral and enclosed cultivation areas (NSFCT 1937 p116). Near Berth

Hill is a mound, S of Camphills is another and S of King's Bank is another (NSFCT vol 66 p99). Probably none of these are burial mounds (NSJFS 1965 p44). Since no sign of burials have been found these mounds must be look-out or signalling posts (NSFCT 1938 p114). For other burial mounds on or near Maer Hills see under Baldwin's Gate, Camp Hill, King's Bank, Madeley Park Farm, Maerfield and Sandyford. S of the hills at SJ 78273875 is a sub-rectangular enclosure and other cropmarks (NSJFS 1964 p29). See under Maer for battles which may have taken place over the hills in Saxon times, and for Charles Darwin in the hills. Local inhabitants were fighting to stop developer Willoughbridge Leisure's proposals to build two 18-hole golf courses, 58 houses, and an hotel by the hills in 1993 (ES may 13 1993 p14).

Maer Lane Marked on Smiths map. The name is preserved in Mere Lane Farm on W side of A449 N of Gailey.

Maer Moss Minute hamlet 1m W of Maer, and former wetland. In c1813 an ancient paved road was discovered running across the moss in an NE to SW direction. Ward considered it possibly part of a Roman road between Chesterton and Wroxeter (HBST p589). But the discovery may be connected with a ditched rectangular enclosure on the northern fringes of the floodplain underneath Bury Hill Fort. No firm dating evidence is available for this enclosure but it may represent an Iron Age farmstead (WSS p95).

Maer Pool Small natural lake just W of Maer. It is the last remnant of an extensive Ice Age lake covering the whole Maer valley (TTTD p241). Is the source of the Tern. The pool or mere is probably the origin of the name of the village Maer. (NSFCT 1888 p38). By 1999 the pool was a SSSI (info David B Thompson).

Maerway Lane Former township of Maer ancient parish (W p397). A lane and tiny hamlet 2.25m NW of Maer.

Magic Oak Old tree in Beaudesert Old Park. Had a hollow open trunk 26 feet in circumference (SG p109). (GNHS p409). Perhaps, is same as Madge Oak (see).

Magog Two rock outcrops of Millstone Grit by a series of fishponds above Belmont Hall, near Ipstones (NSFCT 1943 p59).

Mahull Hill on which Heighley Castle stands (NHS p44 & Camden mention it). Mahull Lake is near a village called Magdalea (Madeley) (SMC p119).

Maiden Castle A knoll or bluff, at SJ 927450, in Park Hall Country Park, possibly man-made, as there was mining and sandstone quarrying in the vicinity (Park Hall Country Park. Staffs County Council Leaflet. Pre-1991).

Maiden's Bridge At SO 878904, 0.5m SW of Himley (1834 OS map) (BCM Oct 1988 p32). Takes its name from the brook over which it crosses, which in turn took its name from Saxon '(ge)maere' 'mearc' meaning a boundary and dean; the brook formed the boundary between Himley and Kingswinford ancient parishes (TB Nov 5 1998 p10).

Maiden's Ford The name occurs in Lady Wulfrun's charter of 994. Dr Oliver called it the 'Virgin's Ferry.' It was believed by GP Mander to be where the Birmingham road crossed a stream forming the Darlaston (Offlow hundred)-Bilston boundary (WA vol 2 p92). According to Smallshire Maiden's Ford presumably lay near Bilston sewage works (WFW p30).

Maiden's Well Holy and healing well in Marchington Road (E side) at SK 095328, Uttoxeter. Anciently called Marion's Well, or Marian's Well or Marian's Wall Well (wall having the same meaning as well). Redfern says Marian is a corruption of Mary. Uttoxeter church is dedicated to St Mary, and the well would doubtless have been a baptistry in early times (HOU p264). Redfern thought the well was of Saxon origin (SLM Oct 1951 p20). Maiden's Well lies in the middle of a ley line which stretches from Toot Hill near Croxden to Toot Hill near Croxden (SMM p165 see map). The well was excavated in 1873 and a sandstone column possibly bearing Ogham script was found (LTD p108). The well is believed to be haunted by the ghost of a handsome young lady, and consequently people were much afraid of passing the well at night - a superstition, thinks Redfern, probably arising from a former belief that the well was inhabited by spirits (HOU p264) (SMM p73). (OSST 1944-1945) (SW pp154,156).

Major's Barn West part of Cheadle. In Cheadle parish.

Maker's Lane Formerly originally Mustard Maker's Lane. The lane runs from Hoar Cross Hall to Woodmill (SVB p96).

Malbonck Forest Medieval forest on the top and E of Morridge covering the townships of Fawfieldhead, Heathylee, Hollinsclough, and Quarnford (VCH vol 7 p5), and stretched to the Dove (HOLF pp13-14) and to Swythamley (OL vol 1 p255. vol 2 p87). Milner says the northern part of Cheddleton parish formed the southern extremity of the forest (CVH p150). Has also appeared as Forest of Alstonefield (1227), Forest of Mauban (early C14), Malbank Frith (early C14), Malbane Forest, Malbanc Forest (CVH p150). The name is from the Malbank family, lords of Alstonefield manor until 1176 (VCH vol 7 p5). There were foresters by the later C13. By the early C15 the

Beresfords of Beresford Hall held the office of forester of Malbon Frith. By 1670 there was a tradition that there had been two officers of the Frith, a bowbearer living at Beresford Hall and a keeper living at Boosley Grange in Fawfieldhead (VCH vol 7 p6).

Malbon Frith Remaining fragment of Malbonck Forest. An area of waste, comprising 4,335 acres, in the late C16 (VCH vol 7 p5).

Malkins Meer Field name or pool in central Burslem in the C18, to E of the Market Place, SE of The Jenkins. Appears on a plan of the town in c1750 (SL p213 see plan).

Mamble Square District at the E end of Old Meeting Road, Coseley. Formerly in Sedgley ancient parish. The district, also called Momble Square 1837-1852, was so called by 1851 (CWBT p25) (W p200). By the early C20 the name was being left off maps.

Manifold, River Rises S of The Travellers Rest Inn NE of Flash at SK 033676. Approximately 20m in length. Joins the Dove S of Izaak Walton Hotel. Up stream the river may sink into the ground after dry weather (and during most summers) through a series of holes in the river bed, the first is near Wetton Mill. These holes or fissures are called locally swallow holes or swallets, from the action of the river being swallowed up (AAD pp184-185) (JAT p64) (LGS p185), another local term for them is 'stack' holes (NSFCT 1917 p28). After falling through the holes, which it has mostly done by or at Darfur Crags (SGS p111), or further down stream at Weag's Bridge (NSFCT 1917 p27), the river takes a subterraneous channel under the river bed and re-emerges by Ilam Hall (SHOS vol 1 part 1 p89 - Darwin's poem, or part of it, is given). Plot challenged the local gentry - Rev Port of Ilam Hall and Charles Cotton of Beresford Hall - to test the underground channel by sending corks down a swallow hole and seeing if any re-emerge at Ilam (WTCEM pp71,121,122,123) (NSFCT 1944 pp38-39). This challenge was taken up by a gardener at Ilam Hall and it worked. The test and its result was told to James Boswell and Dr Samuel Johnson of Lichfield (see) on a visit they made to Ilam in the C18. Johnson remained sceptical. The river takes 22 hours to travel underground (PDS&C p8). Sir Thomas Wardle sealed up known swallet holes with concrete to prevent the river flowing underground in c1890 (NSFCT 1917 p30). But the concrete cracked due to a compression of air and a series of ventilation pipes had to be erected along the river bed (PDS&C p8). The Manifold and Hamps have been compared on their underground united courses to the Alpheus and Arethusa famed in Greek mythology (NSFCT 1878 p34). Has appeared as Water of Manifould (1434), Manyfolde (1551), aqua de Manifould (1573. 1618), Manyfold (frequently up to the end of the C19) (Michael Drayton (1563-1631) in Polyolbion) (GNHS p20) (SPNO p13). Manifold was in use by 1899 (NSFCT 1899 p98 note). The river fully justifies its name, i.e. is of many parts, complex, it folds many times (DUIGNAN) (LGS p184) (NSFCT 1946 p159) (SPNO pp13-14) (SPN p83). 'Hyle' is the old name of the Manifold (NSJFS 1961 p137). Manifold may represent 'cam' 'crooked' which occurs in the Cam of Glous and Cambs (NSFCT 1908 pp127-128). Michael Drayton in his 'Polyolbion' described the Manifold as follows

> .... Crankling Manyfold,
> The first that lends Dove force;
> of whose meandered ways
> And labyrinth-like turns (as in the moor she strays)
> She first received her name.

(HLSP p122).

Manifold Valley Valley of the river Manifold. Perhaps, the county's most beautiful valley. Masefield gives a good account of it in LGS p182. The teacher and archaeologist Samuel Carrington reported strange unexplained vapours, and rumblings like explosions emanating from rocks and caves in the valley in a letter to SA, which appeared on Aug 16 1870. A railway line opened on June 27 1904 known as the Waterhouses and Hulme End extension, or Manifold Light Railway, ran from Hulme End to Waterhouses. The first ticket was issued by a Mr Haycock station master at Hulme End (ES March 21 1934 p7p of the first train on the line) (HLSP p116). The Duke of Devonshire cut the first sod at Waterhouses in Oct 1899 (WTCEM p108) (LTD p40). (WOY pp70-71). It was built to transport milk, tourists, and to stimulate a revival of mining at Ecton Hill (SL p249). By 1932 the line was part of the Leek and Manifold section of the LMSR (RM Oct 1932 pp253-259). The line was not a success and the last train ran on Saturday March 10 1934. 'E.R. Calthrop,' and 'J.B. Earle' were the names of the two locomotives which worked the line. Built by Kitson & Co., they were the first 2-6-4 tank engines to run in Britain (SMOPP vol 2 pp88p,89p). Another account has the last train running on Sept 28 1934 (LTD p40). The track between Ecton and Redhurst Halt was turned into a road, but that between Redhurst Halt and Weags Bridge remained a pathway, partly on account of a protest meeting held at Wetton Mill in 1959 (SL p261) (DMV p71). A model of the line made by John Holroyd was to be exhibited at the Manifold Valley Visitor Centre in Hulme End from May 2000 (ES April 21 2000 p11). Much of the valley became NT property in 1936 (NSFCT 1936 p31). In the late 1960s there were proposals to dam a 2.5m stretch of the valley to create a reservoir. It was petitioned against and stopped (SVB pp113-114).

Manley Hall Former house 1m WSW of Weeford, at SK 128035, in Weeford ancient parish, on or near a house called The Grove in 1976 (OS map 1:25,000 1976). The hall was erected by Admiral John Shawe Manley (d1857) in 1833 in the Tudor style. It appears to have been owned by the Manleys to the early C20 (mems in Weeford church) (W p610); the Admiral's brother served in the French Wars as an officer in the Austrian army and later as Adjutant General of the Papal Guard (ASE p28p) (CCHCB p9 p of). It had majestic towers and pinnacles. After some years as a boys' school it was demolished in the 1960s (KD 1936) (CCHCB p9) (SGS p177).

Manley Wood Wood 1.25m SSW of Weeford.

Manor, The White Art-Deco style house, of the 1930s or later, at Gorstybirch near Stallington. By early 2000 the house was a day nursery.

Manor, The Former district about Little London, Willenhall. Appears on 1947 OS map 1:25,000 (sheet 32/99) at SO 960990. Here was Leveson's Moat (see).

Manor Estate Modern housing estate, situated W of Wolverhampton Road, Stafford. Built in the 1950s (VCH vol 6 p196).

Manor Farm Aldridge. House in existence in the C17 and still stood in the C19 (MOA p133).

Manor Farm House 1.5m ENE of Bobbington. Formerly Bobbington Manor Farm. Belonged in the C17 to the Dickins family of Leaton. In 1684 it was bought by the lord of Bobbington manor and descended with the manor until 1821 (VCH vol 20 p68). It seems to appear as New House on 1834 OS map.

Manor Farm House 0.5m ESE of Endon. Formerly in Endon township in Leek ancient parish. Built for Richard and Mary Tomkinson in 1637 (STM Dec 1968 p36p of the stones escutcheon/ inscription built into the front of the house bears the initials R.T / M.T. 1637.) (VCH vol 7 p177).

Manor Farm Leese Hill, near Kingstone. The old beams in the house are said to come from an old galleon. The house was occupied by the Batthew family in the late 1940s (TRTC pp108,115). The house is said to be haunted (TRTC p110). There is said to be a tunnel between Manor Farm and Wanfield Hall, 1m to the S (TRTC p108).

Manor Farm House 1.5m WSW of Flash. The house, mainly of the C19 with a date stone of 1739, was called Quarnford House prior to 1895 and it may stand on the site of Quarnford Farm, in existence by 1597 (VCH vol 7 p49). The manor court met at Quarnford Farm (UHAW pp9,51 il of Manor Farm).

Manor Farm Stood in Penn Road, Penn. Formerly owned by the Childlow family and was sold off for housing land in the 1940s (PENOP p14).

Manor Farm Penn. Formed a part of the Duke of Sutherland estate in 1843. Occupied by the York family between 1890 to 1917 when the Sutherland estate was sold. It was occupied by Reg Massie from 1940 to before 1987 (PPTP pp60-61).

Manor Farm Stafford Street, Walton, Stone, near Walton Bridge over the Trent. May have been the Walton manor house, or on or near its site. In about the early 1980s the farmhouse became a nursing home for the elderly and has been extended on several occasions since. By 1993 it was Manor House Residential Home for the Elderly. By 1999 the memorial to those killed in WW1 which stood near the entrance to the house was in Walton Community Centre. The house is listed DoE II (info JG Beecham) (1993 telephone directory).

Manor Farmhouse Clifton Campville. The house has a big brick square dovecote and a square dilapidated gazebo (BOE p106) (SGS p86).

Manor House, The Modern house built by the Slack family, clock-makers, on the N side of Park Lane, opposite the former Ipstones Manor House in Ipstones Green, Ipstones (TOI p44). The Slack family appear to have been occupants between at least 1884 and 1912 (trade directories). So named by 1900 (1900 OS map 6 inch).

Manor House House which stands opposite Oaken Manor on N side of Oaken Lane, Oaken. It dates from the early C19 (VCH vol 20 p79).

Manor House, The Stands at the northern end of the Bull Ring, Sedgley. The house never was a manor house, merely a gentleman's seat. In 1901 it was the home of Abner Farnworth (OS map Sheet 67.07). It was demolished in 1968-69 (SDOP p48p).

Manor House Upper Green, Tettenhall. Situated on the green between Regis Road and Limes Road. Flats now stand on the site (BTW p79p).

Manor House House which stood at the junction of High Street and Church Street, Wombourne. It was formerly called Old Hall and was the town house

of the Marsh family, important local landowners, in the C18, and probably in the C17. It was demolished in c1968, and had nothing to do with the manor house of Wombourne manor (VCH vol 20 pp206-207).

Manorial Farm On W side of Old Chester Road and N of Bridle Lane, Streetly. Came into existence between 1841 and 1887. In the early C20 it was farmed by Linnaeus Middleton. After his death, and in 1918 the farm was let to his representatives. Mrs Middleton was still running the farm in 1936. The estate was laid out with roads and houses from 1956 (SNAR p99).

Manor of Castre The ancient Saxon manor of Bradley approached the Sow and confines of Stafford borough. Soon after the Norman Conquest it was severed into two parts. The part adjacent to the river was called the Manor of Castre (Castle), afterwards the Manor of Stafford (SIOT p148) (SKYT p35), or the Castle of Stafford (1293) and Castle Manor (1399). The manor was held from early times to at least the mid C20 by the de Stafford family of Stafford Castle at Castle Church, where courts were held. By the C16 they were held partly there and partly in Forebridge, and in the earlier C17 they were held at Forebridge (see) (VCH vol 6 5 pp86,88).

Manor of the Wall A manor containing Wall Grange. Takes its name from 'The Mark' an ancient boundary line (OL vol 2 p15). Mentioned in old Leek deeds. Probably has reference to the wall or vallum or Limes Britannius and the possible Roman station of Concangii (NSFCT 1902 p117).

Mansion House Cheadle. Built in 1869 by Robert Plant, who helped finance the railway line to Cheadle (1901). The house was demolished in 1978 and senior citizens' bungalows in the present Mansion Close built on the site (ACOPP p123p). The ornate stone doorway went to the Les Oakes collection at Hales View Farm (see) (ES Jan 11 1997 p19p).

Mansion House On N side of Lichfield Road, Stone, adjoining the S side of the churchyard of St Michael's church (SIS p70).

Mansty Mansty lies at foot of Shoal Hill (CCBO p92), on the NW side, in Penkridge ancient parish. Lower Mansty is 1m NNW of Hatherton; Mansty Wood lies to its N; Mansty Farm lies to its N, 1.5m N of Hatherton. The name is of Celtic origin (HOWW p8). In a ditch at Mansty Gully the body of Diana Tift, aged ten, was found by Tony Hodgkiss on Jan 12 1966. The next day the police found the body of Margaret Reynolds, aged six, in the same ditch. Margaret, of Clifton Road, Aston, Birmingham, was abducted whilst returning to school after lunchbreak on Sept 8 1965. Diana, of Hollemeadow Avenue, Blakenall Heath, had been abducted near her home in Chapel Street on Dec 30 1965. The cases remain unsolved (Murder on the A34. Harry Hawkes. 1970).

Manwoods Former house 2m NW of Handsworth, formerly in Handsworth ancient parish. It was situated off Park Lane on the Handsworth side. It was originally built as an estate house by Sandwell Priory - probably it was the residence of a priest who acted as the estate bailiff. It was built in the form of a cross and contained a secret hiding place. It was rebuilt in its later form in 1680, by Henry Ford, steward to the Whorwoods of Sandwell Hall. The name Manwoods for the house had appeared by 1794. It has also appeared as Bayers Hall or Bayes Hall, but reverted to its original name. Three generations of Wrights lived here, and in 1836 it was the seat of a Mr Farmer, who assisted Joseph Reeves with his WB (1836). Prior to demolition in 1969 it was erroneously described to a coach party of American tourists as the birthplace of Bishop Asbury of Hamstead (see), and it had become rather dilapidated (MNB pp40,45) (HPPE p85). It appears on the Birmingham A-Z (1989), but no house is marked on OS map 1:25,000 (1993). The name is preserved in Hilltop and Manwood Golf Course.

Manwoods Cottage Forge Lane, Manwoods. Here Francis Asbury preached his first sermon in c1763. The site of it is by the edge of Manwoods Golf Club (250th Anniversary of Bishop Francis Asbury. Aug 1995) (OWB pl No. 24 facing p80) (BCM summer 1995 p45).

Maple Brook Runs S of Chorley. Formerly Chestall Brook (VCH vol 14 p195).

Maple Hayes Estate on gentle SE-facing slope near the head of Leamonsley Brook, 1.25m W of Lichfield cathedral. Formerly in Burntwood out-township of St Michael's parish, Lichfield (W p514). The name means 'the enclosure(s) where maple trees grow' (SPN p25). Takes its name from land called 'Mabbley Hays' which by 1498 was divided into four crofts, one of them in Pipe Park (VCH vol 14 p211). The conduit head to supply water to Lichfield cathedral Close, 0.25m SSE of Maple Hayes House at SK 09230928, is probably of mid C12 origin (DoE II*) (AJ vol 56 part 1 pp73-79). A brick conduit head was built at Maple Hayes in c1780 to replace the existing head, which probably dated from the C13. In 1821 the old head was brought back into the operation to improve the supply. The last conduit in the Close closed in 1969 (VCH vol 14 p96). At SK 102101 is a moated site, said by CAMS p63 to be at Maple Hayes. In a hollow at the head of a stream N of Maple Hayes house Dr Erasmus Darwin created a botanical garden, now lost. The garden was in the vicinity of Darwin's Bath (see), at SK 096099. Harwood says Darwin bought the land in 1777 and started to erect his garden by the bath (HOL pp562-563). Miss Seward wrote a poem in 1779 describing the garden (SHOS vol 1 p347). (SHOSA vol 2 p9) (CCBO pp120-124) (TB Oct 1993 p22).

Maple Hayes House House 1.25m W of Lichfield cathedral. There may have been a house on the site since the beginning of the C18 known as Pipe or Mayle Hayes Farm. The house was rebuilt by 1796 by a Lichfield wine merchant, George Addams. In 1804 the house was sold to John Atkinson who built up a collection of paintings and art works here (VCH vol 14 p211) - Calvert said there was a portrait by Holbein of Edward VI at Maple Hayes (SSC p126 in the intro). In 1839 the house was sold to Sir Thomas Fremantle, Bt, later Baron Cottesloe. In 1851 it was sold to Samuel Pole Shawe of Hints Hall and in 1884 it was sold to Albert Octavius Worthington, a member of brewing family (VCH vol 14 p211) (SGS p69). Sold in 1949 (SVB p47) or 1951 (VCH vol 14 p211), and became a boarding house attached to King Edward VI grammar school, and from 1982 a specialist school (SVB p47) (VCH vol 14 pp211-212 pl 14).

Marcaroni Former area of Etruria. To N of the old racecourse and W of Boothan. Marcaroni bridge, a footbridge over the Trent and Mersey Canal, was the central figure of the locality (H pp109-110).

March End Area to E of central Wednesfield. Formerly in Wednesfield chapelry in Wolverhampton ancient parish. There was an Ice Age granite boulder about four feet by three in a ditch on the S side of the roadway between March End and Perry Hall in 1909 (WJO Nov 1909 p293). Appears as Marshend, a tiny separate hamlet, on 1834 OS map. The name is derived from Marsh; much of the area in the vicinity of Wadden's Brook near Wednesfield was formerly called the Moors or the Marsh (WFW p9). However, some have thought March is probably from Anglo-Saxon 'mearc' meaning boundary (BCTV p78).

Marchington Former manor, township and chapelry in Hanbury ancient parish. Marchington village lies on a gentle promontory above the Dove and one of its tributaries which rises out of Needwood Forest, 14m ENE of Stafford. In Marchington parish was found a bronze palstave of the **Bronze Age** once in William Molyneux's collection (HOU 1886 p45) (NSJFS 1964 p29). Has appeared as Maercham (951), Marchamtune or Maerchamtun (c1002) when mentioned in the will of Wulfric Spot, founder of Burton Abbey, Merchametone (DB), Marchanton-sub-Nedwode (SHC 1916 pp25,90) (SL p61) (SSE 1991 p8. 1996 p15), Mercinton (SHOS vol 1 p89), Merghanstone (HOU p337), and Mercington (SPN p83). The first part of the **name** 'March' is from Middle English meaning boundary, so 'the town on the march;' Marchington is on the border of Staffs and Derbys (DUIGNAN) (SPN p83). Mills interprets the name as Old English 'merece + haeme + tun.' Ekwall says 'tun of the Mercham people.' Or is possibly 'smallage (wild celery) dweller's tun' (SSE 1996 pp15,22) (SMSE p3 note). In 1086 the manor was held of Henry de Ferrers and as such formed the lands appertaining to the Honour of Tutbury. The infamous 'heriot,' a death duty paid by villeins and free tenants to their lord, out of a dead man's possessions, was enforced in Marchington manor (W p561). Marchington became a separate civil parish in 1866 (GLAUE p416). There was a church at Marchington in 1089 (LDD). The present parish **church**, St Peter, on the N side of Church Lane, on the E side of the village, was built in 1742 (BOE p201). Became a separate ecclesiastical parish in 1739 (GLAUE p416) refounded in 1862 (LGS p186). Hanbury **parish feast** was on the Sunday before Midsummer day (W p559). The Marchington Wake cake had the reputation for being nice but not big, which gave rise to the expression

As short as a Marchington Wake Cake

which went into general usage, and implies something is very pleasant but there is not enough of it (SVB p120). **An early occupation.** The place-name 'Potteresleag' found in the Marchington area in the mid C10 suggests pottery making was occurring in the area then (HOS 1998 p95). **Charities.** In the early C19 Henry Chamberlain, a native of Marchington, set up with others the Marchington Charities. The money raised by renting out property in London was given to village poor, and to local children on leaving school, the latter being a practice still carried on in 1988 (SVB p119). The three houses comprising the almshouses, erected in 1860 by Lydia Chawner of Houndhill, were still standing in the village square in 1988 (SVB p120). In the late C18 and early C19 Marchington was known for its **treatment of wife beaters**. Straw could be laid at the door of the persistent offender, or he could be brought before an elected committee of the village. If found guilty he could be paraded through the village astride a wooden pole carried on the shoulders of the villagers. The parade was led by the town crier who recited the villain's

misdeeds. His efforts to keep upright on the pole always caused much amusement (SVB p120). **Aircraft crash.** A Vickers Varsity light aircraft crashed in Staffs near Marchington on Aug 19 1984 whilst travelling from East Midlands airport to an airshow in Liverpool with 14 people on board; 11 people were killed (ES Feb 26 1994 p3). For a **rhyme** which is a play on the place names Marchington and Hound Hill, see Hound Hill.

Marchington Cliff Cliff on N edge of Needwood Forest escarpment and tiny settlement 1m S of Marchington. The battle referred to as taking place near Tutbury Town in the ballad about Robin Hood (see Loxley) is said to have taken place at an old lost inn (called The Robin Hood) on the summit of Marchington Cliff (LTD p116).

Marchington Hall A distinguished late C17 brick house in Marchington (SGS p126). In the 1930s it was occupied by Richard Longdon, a textile manufacturer from Derby, a convert to Catholicism. He converted an outbuilding at the hall into an RC chapel; in c1960 this was replaced by an RC chapel, dedicated to St Thomas a Becket, in Marchington village (AUOPP p91p).

Marchington Park Medieval deer park. In existence by 1346 and was probably short-lived. Belonged to the Earl of Lancaster (NSJFS 1964 p64).

Marchington Ward One of the five wards of Needwood Forest. First mentioned in 1249; was the first Needwood Forest ward to be mentioned. The heirs of the Mynors of Blakenhall were the hereditary foresters of the ward. Marchington ward was bounded on the S side by the Mare Brook and the other sides formed the NW edges of the main body of the forest. The lodge of the ward may have been Eland or Ealand Lodge (HCT p366) (HOPT vol 2 p223) (VCH vol 2 pp349,352).

Marchington Woodlands Fragmented hamlet of Marchington Woodlands lying in undulating country below the northern escarpment of Needwood Forest plateau 1.5m SW of Marchington. Former manor, township and chapelry in Hanbury ancient parish. Marchington Woodlands formerly lay in Needwood Forest (SMSE p4) and has appeared as The Woodlands (HOU p336). For the moated site off Tinker's Lane at SK 10872891 see Moat Spring. The church, St John, on Smithy Hill on the E side of Hodge Lane, was built in 1858-1859 (BOE p202). Became a separate ecclesiastical parish in 1859 (GLAUE p416) refounded in 1860 (LGS p186). Became a separate civil parish in 1866 but this was abolished with parts entering the parishes of Marchington, Newborough, Hanbury, Tatenhill and Anslow (GLAUE p416).

Marchington Woodlands Manor House The original manor house of Marchington Woodlands of probably C15 date stood S of (or some say on the site of - SVB p121) Marchington Woodlands church at Smithy Hill, at SK 109295 (SMSE p6), or on the moated site (a listed monument) with a fishpond and associated closes SSE of the church at SK 10822945. It was the seat of the Thirkells by about the mid C16; they had possibly inherited the manor by marriage into the Mynor family. By the late C16 the manor had passed to the Rugeleys by marriage (maps of Plot and Bowen) (SHOS vol 1 p92) (W p23) (SMSE pp8-12) (SHJ spring 1994 p31). The house, also known as Smallwood Hall, had completely disappeared by the later C18 and was superseded by a now lost house called Smallwood Hall (see), built to the W, near the site of the present Smallwood Manor (see) (SVB p121).

Mareback Former rock feature which jutted out of that part of The Cloud situated in the parish of Rushton Spencer. It was quarried and destroyed (DP p76).

Mare Brook Tributary of the Dove. The name appears in 1804 (SPNO p14).

Mare Brook Runs from Hanbury Park to Far Hoar Cross to the Swarbourn. Boundary which divides Marchington and Tutbury wards of Needwood Forest (VCH vol 2 p352). Has also appeared as Marbrouk (1286), Merebroke (1338), Marebroke (1434), and Marebrook (1798) (SHOS vol 1 p66) (SPNO p14).

Mare Brook Rises S of Streethay, and runs N of Brookhay to join the Tame E of Brookhay (SPNO p14).

Margaret's Lane Former hamlet in Great Barr chapelry in Aldridge ancient parish (W p552). Does not appear on 1834 OS map.

Marlpits Area of Rugeley lying between the railway to Cannock, the line to Brereton Colliery, and the road to Lichfield. The old pinfold was moved from the centre of Rugeley to the Marlpits estate in c1829 and it still stood here in 1878 (VCH vol 5 p152 note).

Marnshaw Head House 1.25m W of Hollinsclough. Formerly in Heathylee township in Alstonefield ancient parish. There was a house here by 1444 (VCH vol 7 p33). Appears as Mount Shaw Head on 1834 OS map. The place name 'shaw' means a copse (VCH vol 7 p33).

Marquis's Drive Five-mile route crossing Cannock Chase. Runs from Beaudesert Hall to the hunting grounds of the Marquises of Anglesey at the N end of Sherbrook Valley (CCBO p65) (GCC pp27,29). Named after the 1st Marquis of Anglesey (VB p114).

Marsh, The Large vanished expanse of water which lay to the E of Newcastle-under-Lyme. Its boundaries were Queen Street up to Brampton House, King Street as far as the Borough Arms, and Marsh Parade, off George Street (NSFCT 1915 p83). Another expanse of water called Colleswaynes Lake lay close by (NM p157) (VCH vol 8 p3). The Nelson Place area was once a common field and by the late C18 it had become a tip and was squatted. The Marsh Lands Trust was set up in 1782 to improve, or some say reclaim, The Marsh and common land (NSFCT 1915 p83). In 1787-88 the Royal Theatre was built by John Pepper between King Street and Brunswick Street. It was demolished after 1960 and the relief medallion of Shakespeare, attributed to John Flaxman, which had hung on its facade, now hangs on the New Victoria Theatre at Stoneyfields (see) (VCH vol 8 p9) (STM May 1964 p43p of medallion on Victoria Theatre, Hartshill) (NUL p158). By 1818 Marsh, Queen, King, Water and Brunswick Streets and Barracks Road (formerly Bagnall Street) were in existence (NM p157) (VCH vol 8 p3). The Independent Building Society of Newcastle-under-Lyme had built a large estate at Marsh Crofts by 1816 (SSE 1993 p108). The Town Walks, a series of public walks in this area were created out of open fields and instituted under the Inclosure Act of 1816. The two walks are Station Walks, formerly Brampton Walks, and Stubbs Walks. The Russian gun from the Crimean War which was presented to Newcastle by Samuel Christy MP in 1857 was erected in Station Walks. It was still standing there in 1960. After 1918 it stood along side a WW1 tank which was removed in 1940 for scrap as part of the WW2 war effort (VCH vol 8 pp4,180 note) (NULOP vol 1 p41p of Stubbs Walks,42p) (SFH p18) (TSS p39p). The Commissioners' church, St George, on the W side of Queen Street, was built in 1828 (VCH vol 8 pp16,20-21). The ecclesiastical parish of Newcastle-under-Lyme St George was created in 1832 (GLAUE p417). St Paul's church in Victoria Road was built in 1905-1908 (BOE p209) and a separate ecclesiastical parish of Newcastle-under-Lyme St Paul was created out of Newcastle-under-Lyme St George in 1905 (GLAUE p417). Nelson Place is perhaps named after a bust of Lord Nelson which was situated in a niche in the pediment of a C18 house which stood at the Barracks Road junction with Nelson Place (NULOP vol 1 p18p).

Marsh, The District of Penkridge to the NE of the town centre by the canal. The horse fairs seem to have been held in the area of The Marsh by 1754 (VCH vol 5 p129).

Marshall's Court Ancient timber-framed building of C15 or C16 origin in Church Street, Tamworth. It became the Old Paregoric Shop and in 1931 was demolished in c1931 (TH April 4 1931. April 30 1932 p & il) (THM vol 5 pp65,74).

Marsh Brook Rises S of Stanton. Joins Ordley Brook.

Marsh Common Common pasture which lay S of Shortbutts Lane on S side of Lichfield. An Act authorizing its enclosure was passed in 1815 (VCH vol 14 p111).

Marshes Hill Ridge some 900 feet high (BEH p10), N of Brown Edge. There is common land at Marsh Hill which may have arisen as manorial waste (OSST 1956-59 p6).

Marsh Green District of Biddulph. 1m N of the shopping centre, 0.25m W of St Lawrence. Formerly in Lower Biddulph liberty in Biddulph ancient parish. The name appears to be from a marsh here (BALH).

Marsh Hall At NE corner of Wolstanton Marsh.

Marsh Lane Hateley Heath, West Bromwich. This was a fen (SOWB p24).

Marsh Meadow A small nature reserve near Adbaston (SVB p11).

Marsh Park Brierley Hill. Park to W of St Michael, described as newly opened in the 1920s (BHOP2 p25p).

Marston Small hamlet on low ground by Marston Brook 1.5m SSE of High Onn. Former township in Church Eaton ancient parish (W p456). Has appeared as Mersetone (DB - under Northants), Merston (c1255), Mershton (1316), Mershton juxta Blumenhulle (1359), Marston (1567), Merston under le Seard (1652) (SHOS vol 1 part 1 p44) (CE p115) (NSFCT 1952 p34) (CE p115) (SPNO p141) (SPN p35). The name means 'the marsh town or tun' (DUIGNAN) (SSE 1996 p15), or 'farmstead near a marsh' (SPN p35). A well at Marston was dressed (SMM p89).

Marston Small fragmented hamlet on high ground near the head of Marston Brook 1m SSE of Yarlet. Former township and chapelry in St Mary's parish, Stafford (W p342). Had separate civil identity early' (GLAUE p417). Appears in DB as Mersetone. Chetwynd thought it was from its flat and marshy situation (SH p45), so 'marsh town or tun' (DUIGNAN) (SSE 1996 p15). The site of its deserted village can be made out from aerial photographs at Marston Farm at SJ 924275 (SPJD p48p). Marston was a prebend of Stafford Collegiate Church (VCH vol 3 p305). There was a church or chapel at Marston in the C16 (LDD). Became a separate ecclesiastical parish with Whitgreave in 1777. The present church, St Leonard, on the W side of the Yarlet road, was built in 1794. Separated from Whitgreave in 1846 but reunited with it in 1850 as 'Marston with Whitgreave' (GLAUE p417) (BOE p202). On Sept 4 1954 a vidya was seen by Mr and Mrs Botham over Marston (The Coming of the Spaceships. Gavin Gibbons. 1956). Foot-and-mouth disease broke out at Marston Hall Farm in early 1968 (SN Jan 26 1968 p13).

Marston Brook Runs from W of Aquamoor joins Wheaton Aston Brook E of Marston.

Marston Brook Runs from Marston (Yarlet). Joins the Sow, at Littleworth.

Marston Field One of the open fields of Stafford. Enclosed in 1807. The neighbouring hamlet Marston had an open field also called Marston Field (NSJFS 1975 p30).

Marston Juxta Tutbury Ancient boundary point of Tutbury (SHOS vol 1 p56). Marston from Marston-on-Dove, Derbys.

Marston Manor Farm Marston, High Onn. Incorporates parts of a timber-framed house of the C16. Represents the manor-house of Marston (High Onn) manor (VCH vol 4 pp92,94).

Marten Hill Hill 902 feet high, WSW of Okeover Hall, Okeover. The bowl burial mound on the top of the hill at SK 14184777 is a listed monument.

Martenslow Farm at Grindon, which probably derives its name from a former habitat of the pine marten (NSFCT 1910 p63).

Martilege Garden In Gaia Lane, Lichfield (HOL p512).

Martin's Low NW of Waterfall. In Grindon parish. Has also appeared as Martins Lowe. Could it be called Morting Low on Smith's map?

Martlin Hill S of Colton. Probably a corruption of marling from the huge marl pit excavated on its south side (CWF pp180, 204).

Mason's Bank Formerly in Coseley division in Sedgley ancient parish, 2m NW of Dudley (W p200). The Mason's Bank mentioned by White could have been in present day Roseville? (W p200).

Mason's End Former hamlet in the Red Hall area of Gornal Wood. The name occurs in the 1851 census.

Mason's Rough A spinney close to the Bishop's Woods (BPS pp86,171).

Maudlin's Well Well approximately W of Milley's Hospital, Lichfield. Shaw says it is down a small lane on the left on the way to Dr Darwin's botanical garden. So called because tradition says someone who had had too much drink had fallen down it (SHOS vol 1 p347). It could be the same as Merlicke's Well at the bottom of Shaw Lane?

Mavesyn Ridware (locally *Mavis-son Rid-ware*). Ancient parish and former manor. The small village of Mavesyn Ridware lies on low ground at a little distance N of the Trent, 10.5m ESE of Stafford. An irregular enclosure of Neolithic origin has been found at Mavesyn Ridware (HOS 1998 p24). The name has appeared as Ridvare (DB), and Ridewale Mauvaisin (1236) (SL p56) (SPN p98) (SSE 1996 p15). There is said to have been 56 spellings and pronouncations of Mavesyn to date (info Peter Clarke). See Hamstall Ridware for origin of Ridware. Mavesyn is from the Mavesyn family, early lords of Mavesyn Ridware manor (SSE 1996 p374) of Mavesyn Ridware Old Hall (see). The parish church, St Nicholas, in Church Lane, was built in c1140. The nave, chancel, S aisle and porch were rebuilt in 1782 (SVB p122) (A Guide to the Parish Church: St Nicholas's Church Mavesyn Ridware). Mavesyn Ridware parish was a peculiar jurisdiction of Alrewas prebend in Lichfield cathedral until peculiar jurisdictions were abolished in 1846 (VCH vol 3 p94) (GLAUE p420). Shaw noted a custom concerning swans perhaps peculiar to Mavesyn Ridware parish: 'It is the rule here,' he says "that if a pair of swans breed on another's royalty, one of the cygnets is claimed by him, as the 'land swan.' And if the swans belong to two different persons, the cygnets are divided between them equally, he who has the odd bird this year giving it up the other the following year; but in some places it is the custom for the pen to take the cygnets, and the cob only two. If not pinioned, they become quite wild, are called 'elks,' and are shot with impunity' (SHOS vol 1 p190) (W p570). George Henry Fourdrinier, paper manufacturer and former resident near Stone (see), died at Mavesyn Ridware on Sept 3 1854 (POTP p99).

Mavesyn Ridware Hall Mavesyn Ridware. Built by Charles Chadwick (d1756), lord of Mavesyn Ridware, in 1718 on the site of Mavesyn Ridware Old Hall (SHOS vol 1 p185) (BOE p204). Charles Chadwick, grandson of Charles Chadwick (d1756), was living at Mavesyn Ridware Hall in 1797 (St Nicholas Church, Mavesyn Ridware guide).

Mavesyn Ridware Old Hall S of Mavesyn Ridware church. The original manor house at Mavesyn Ridware is thought to have been built by Hugo Mavesyn (also styled de Rideware) in the mid C12 (St Nicholas Church, Mavesyn Ridware guide). The original manor house was perhaps rebuilt on at least one occasion in the medieval period. It was the seat of the Mavesyn (or Mauvoisin, Mavesin, Malvoisin) family, lords of Mavesyn Ridware. They may have taken their name from the French malvoisin, 'bad neighbour.' Or from being in

some way associated with a tower or a castle structure erected near a besieged place, which in French is called a malvoisin (SHOS vol 1 p166) (SVB p122). (STMSM Oct 1973 p26) (SPN p98). According to tradition a member of the Mauvoisin or Mavesyn family of Rosny-sur-Seine near Mantes (about 35m WNW of Paris) was awarded the manor for his services to William I in the Norman Conquest. By the earlier C12 the lord was Hugo Mavesyn (also styled de Rideware), believed to have been the grandson of the Norman knight who was awarded the manor. In c1140 he founded in the northern part of the manor, a priory called Blithbury Priory (see), near where it is believed the original manor house stood, perhaps on or near the site of Kileby Hall (see) (SOS p185) (SHOS vol 1 p168) (St Nicholas Church, Mavesyn Ridware guide). Thereafter he established himself in the southern part of his manor, building St Nicholas' church and an early Mavesyn Ridware Old Hall at what became known as Mavesyn Ridware. An effigy in the N wall of St Nicholas' church is said to be of this Hugo. He was succeeded in Henry II's reign by his son Sir William, who lived to King John's reign. He was succeeded by his son Sir Henry (fl 1235), who was succeeded by his son Sir Robert (fl 1256). He was succeeded by his son Sir Henry, the Crusader (fl 1292); the effigy in the N wall of St Nicholas' church adjoining that of Hugo is of Sir Henry, the Crusader. He was succeeded by his son Sir Robert, the Forester (c1272-c1377). He was succeeded by his son Thomas (died c1373) by his second marriage. Thomas was succeeded by his son Sir Robert (born c1360). Sir Robert, a supporter of Henry IV, slew Sir William Handsacre, lord of neighbouring Handsacre manor and a supporter of Henry IV's usurpers, by an oak called Gog (see) near Mavesyn Ridware, before they left to fight each other in the battle of Shrewsbury (1403). Despite being victorious against his neighbour Sir Robert died in the battle. Sir Robert was succeeded by his eldest daughter, Elizabeth, who by her second marriage to Sir John Cawarden, took the manor to the Cawardens. With the death of Thomas Cawarden II in the later C16 the manor was split between his four daughters. In 1594 one daughter, Joyce, married John Chadwick, and he and his descendents eventually acquired the whole manor. John was succeeded by his son, Lewis, who was succeeded by his daughter, Katherine (d1697); the manor remained held by Chadwicks, however, since Katherine married into a different branch of the Chadwick family. Her son, Charles Chadwick (born c1637), succeeded; his son Charles (d1756) succeeded him, and in turn he was succeeded by his son Charles Chadwick Sacheverell (later just Sacheverell) (d1779). He was succeeded by his aunt Dorothy (d1784), who was succeeded by her nephew, Charles Chadwick (grandson of Charles (d1756) by his second wife). He was succeeded by his son Hugo Malvesyn Chadwick (c1793-1854). His grandson, Hugo Malvoisin Chadwick, was born in 1860 (St Nicholas Church, Mavesyn Ridware guide). The old hall was demolished in the early C18 and the present Mavesyn Ridware Hall (see) built on the site.
GROUNDS. A former hall was probably surrounded by a **moat** (SSAHST 1982-3 p44). The 87 feet (CCBO p131 - 85 feet) long **gatehouse** range of Mavesyn Ridware Old Hall remains. It was probably the N side of a quadrangular inner court (SHOS vol 1 pp157,188) (BOE pp203,204). (GNHS p149) (LGS p202) (KES p151) (STM Aug 1970 p29 ps) (VB p110) (SVB p122) (DoE Grade 1). It may have contained a chamber said to have been an oratory (SSC p126 in the introduction). Oliver Cromwell is said to have held a meeting of his council in it the night before the attack on Lichfield (CCBO pp131,132). It was converted into living accommodation in the 1960s or the early 1970s (STMSM Aug 1973 p27 il by W.G. Wright). Is featured in and illustrated in George Griffith's tragedy 'The Two Houses' 1866. Attached to the gatehouse is a **dovecote** or pigeon-cote (LGS p202) of C16 origin (SLM summer 1958 pp34-35,37 p of the interior). A field name, or part of the old quadrangle was called Dovehouse Close (SHOS vol 1 p188).

Maw Green Former hamlet 0.75m S of Walsall. In Walsall ancient parish. Appears on Yates' map and J Cary's map (1805) as Maw Green, and on Smith's map as Mow Green. The area, inhabited by the C18, was centred on the junction of West Bromwich Road, Delves Road, and Highgate Road. Became suburbanised from the 1890s (VCH vol 17 p155). There is a Maw Street at Fullbrook.

May Bank District 0.5m SSW of Wolstanton. In Wolstanton ancient parish. A coin of the Emperor Valerian I was found by an eight year old girl while playing in Stratfold Avenue in 1936. It was found near the old stone wall part of Highfield Farm, which had been pulled down for road improvements. It went to Newcastle-under-Lyme borough police. It was minted in Alexandria in 254 or 255 AD (ES Sept 4 1936 p6). In summer 1941 the Germans made a raid on Newcastle-under-Lyme and Taylor Avenue, May Bank, was hit, killing May Ellen Robertson, aged 22 (ES March 18 1977).

Mayers Green Small district 0.5m NE of the High Street, West Bromwich. In West Bromwich ancient parish. Originally Mare's Green (W p390). The name

is from the family named Mare who lived in West Bromwich from C16 to the mid C18 (SHWB 14) (SOWB p24). There was settlement at Mayer's Green by the 1680s (VCH vol 17 p4).

Mayfield Ancient parish and former township and manor. The large fragmented village of Mayfield covers the W slopes of a long stretch of the upper Dove Valley.
EARLY. Carrington excavated an unlocated burial mound 18 paces in diameter called Mayfield Low in 1849. A stone cist containing an urn had been found some years before. Only a few fragments of pottery were found (TYD p152) (VCH vol 1 no 31) (NSJFS 1965 p44). Hackwood notes a burial mound at Mayfield (SCSF p74). There is a burial mound between Upper Mayfield and Hanging Bridge at SK 15574606 four feet high (NSJFS 1965 p44). A Neolithic or Bronze Age battle axe was found at Upper Mayfield at SK 15114642 in 1854 according to the OS 6 inch map (NSFCT vol 45 p196), but there is no confirmation of this (NSJFS 1964 p29). There are miscellaneous earthworks of pre-Norman Conquest origin in Mayfield parish at or called the Cliffs, and Hollow Lane (SHC 1916 p207). For other burial mounds in the Mayfield area see under Harlow, Rowleys. Plot noted **Roman** coins had been found in Dale Close between Okeover and Mayfield (NHS p404) (AAD p207 note) (NSJFS 1964 p29). Plot also noted that a Roman urn had been found in a bank in Church Townfield in Upper Mayfield prior to 1676 (NHS p404) (AAD p207 note) (VCH vol 1 p186) (NSJFS 1964 p29).
1000 to PRESENT. Has appeared as Madevelde, a manor, in DB, Matherfeld (c1180) (SSE 1996 p15), and Mathfield, which was in use in the C18 (NSFCT 1948 p39) and was still being used by some in 1924 (SCSF p74). (SPN p83). The **name** is from Maethelfield, i.e. the meeting field (DUIGNAN) (LGS p186). The medieval form Matherfield represents 'madder field' (NSFCT 1948 p39). Or 'Open land where madder grows' (NSJFS 1981 p2) (SSE 1996 p15). Or from Anglo-Saxon 'maeth-feld' 'the mown clearing' (SPN p83). The parish **church**, St John the Baptist, on the N side of Church Lane, Church Mayfield, was first built probably in c1125 (Mayfield Parish Church). The **parish**, formed before 1086, may have originally contained the ancient parishes of Rocester, Alton, and Ellastone (SHC 1916 p194). Mayfield **wakes** were held in the third week in August and Wakes Sunday was the first Sunday after June 24 (MOM p6). The large and scattered **village of Mayfield** comprises Upper Mayfield, the northern hamlet, Church Mayfield the southern hamlet, and a hamlet lying to the SW called Middle Mayfield. The area known as Daisy Bank on 1834 OS map at a crossroads linking the Mayfields has grown to be the largest hamlet and is now known as Mayfield. It is 20.5m NE of Stafford. There is a moated site at SK 143453 to the NW of Middle Mayfield (CAMS p64). The **strip lynchets** at SK 156461 are a listed monument. **Stocks** stood by a stone cross between Upper and Middle Mayfield. The same cross or another has been erected on the S side of Mayfield church (Mayfield Parish Church). At Upper Mayfield was a **toll house** on the Ashbourne-Leek turnpike road (NSFCT 1948 p39) (MR pp226p,227). **Rock houses** stood on the right-hand side of Bridge Hill and had their rear walls built into the rock at the back. They were demolished probably before WW1. Evidence can still be seen where the cave-like cellars were hewn into the rock (MR p227) (MOM p23p). **Aircraft crash.** A Wellington 111 BJ 658 crashed at Mayfield on Jan 21 1944 killing the crew of six (MD p33). The present (2000) **Mayfield Heritage Group** formed in c1990 (info Pat Smith). Lowes Cottage, Upper Mayfield, a three-storey stone building of c1750, is reputedly haunted by **poltergeist activity** representing the curse of a milkmaid who reputedly was raped and strangled to death at the cottage in the C19, and a young boy who hung himself from the rafters. In Nov 1993 a Mr and Mrs Smith purchased the cottage but in early 1998 they were granted permission by a county court judge to pursue a civil claim for the return of the rest of their purchase money on the cottage, because they were not told that it was haunted prior to purchase. The vendors meanwhile sued the Smiths for the remainder of purchase money. In Jan 1999 Smiths lost their case (Daily Telegraph March 1998 p3p. Jan 16 1999 p5ps) (ES March 6 1998 p4p. Jan 19 1999 p5p).

Mayfield House 1.25m SSW of Tutbury (OS map 1:25,000).

Mayfield House in Sutton Road, Walsall. Built possibly by a member of the Jesson family in 1796. If so by will it came into the possession of the Windle family who were followed by the Brace family, and subsequently by John George Taylor. In 1921 it was acquired by Walsall Grammar School for use as a Junior Girls School, and is now (1992) a preparatory school for boys (SNWA p63). Formerly known as Discount Hall and Tommy Hall, from the time when employees were expected to accept goods in lieu of a part of their wages (SNWA pp37,103).

Mayfield Cottage On N side of Slack Lane at SK 152457 (1834 OS map). Former name of Stancliffe Farm, when it was the residence of the Irish poet,

Thomas Moore; he lived here from 1813 to 1817 (LGS p187) (STM Aug 1967 p30p). Whilst at Mayfield Cottage he is believed to have written these poems: 'The Woodpecker,' 'Lalla Rooka' (1817) and 'Twopenny Postbag' (1813) (W p784) (KES p5) (VFC p94). His daughter Olivia Byron Moore (1814-1815), who died aged about six months whilst his family were living in Mayfield, is buried in Mayfield churchyard (LGS p187) (KES pp152,153) (STM Aug 1967 p31p) (TFTP pp174-177). Moore visited his daughter's grave, when staying at Alton Towers in 1835 (VFC p95). (AAD p209il on facing page) (GNHS p93) (JAT pp60,61) (PS p124) (UDC book 1 pp8il,9,10,11,12) (S pp140p,141) (SLM Feb 1952 pp11il,12,21) (STM Oct 1963 p53) (VB p175) (BCM April 1977 pp8-10) (ESNF p88p) (MR p227). NSFC visited the cottage in Aug 1966 (NSJFS 1967 p84). It was known as Stancliffe Farm by 1967 (STM Aug 1967 p30p,31).

Mayfield Grange House in Birdsgrove Lane, nearly 1m N of Mayfield. Marked on 1834 OS map, but not on current OS maps.

Mayfield Hall Georgian house at Middle Mayfield. Represents the manor house of Mayfield manor. The present hall dates from the early C18. Inside is a fireplace dated 1608 (MOM p46). Beneath the hall are cellars and passages cut out of the sandstone. There are three main tunnels leading out in the direction of Old Hall Lane and Hollow Lane. They reputedly date from the C12 or C13 and their true extent is unknown. Some have been blocked up and each one is wide enough for four people to stand abreast or for a cart to be pulled through (MOM p54p). In the 1920s the hall was occupied by two families, the Wardles and Barbers. The most distinguished member of the Wardle family was Rear Admiral TE Wardle commander of the cruiser 'Alcantara' which sank a German battleship at the battle of Jutland. In 1993 Mayfield Hall was the property of Mr Butler (MOM pp46,53). The stable range has a tower similar to that of Mapleton church, Derbys (BOE p205) (MR p227p). The pig sty has unusual feeding chutes set into the side (MOM p55p). The gardens are landscaped in the manner of 'Capability' Brown (STM Aug 1967 p30p), and contain unusual steps dating from the Regency period. They are convex and change half way to concave as they ascend. They are reputedly one of only two of these types of steps in the country (STM Aug 1967 p30p) (MOM p54p). There were two giant Wellingtonia Sequoia trees in the gardens, but only one now (1993) survives (MOM p54p).

Mayrick House Stood on site of the library at Hill Top, West Bromwich. Seat of Joseph Hateley, a lawyer. He was known for being the man who refused to take part in the celebrations which followed the suppression of George IV's Divorce Bill of Queen Caroline. These involved the illuminating of one's house with candles. Consequently an effigy of him was hung and burnt in front of the 'Three Crowns' in view of Mayrick House in Nov 1820 (OWB p117). Has also appeared as Meyrick House (VCH vol 17 p7). The grounds were laid out as Hill Top Park in the late C19 or early C20 (VCH vol 17 p7).

Meadleys, The House 1.25m ESE of Patshull. It was an inhabited place by 1327 (VCH vol 20 p162). Has appeared as The Medleys (1905 OS map) (VCH vol 20 p162).

Meadowcroft Park New (1999) housing estate built on the site of the former British Reinforced Concrete works on the N side of Silkmore Lane, Queensville, Stafford.

Meadow Lane Area about Meadow Lane and for a quarter of a mile to the W of Meadow Lane, 1m NNW of Newcastle-under-Lyme.

Meaford (locally *Mef-ford*). Former manor formerly in Kibblestone township and quarter in Stone ancient parish (W p364). By 1872 formed a township with Oulton (KD 1872). The fragmented hamlet of Meaford lies by the Trent and its confluence with a tributary which passes through the Downs, 1.5m NW of Stone. The settlement at the foot of Bury Bank now (1988 OS map 1:25,000) known as Meaford was formerly called Darlaston (Pirehill hundred) (1834 OS map. 1963 OS map 1 inch). The two DB Meaford manors are Mepford (held by St Remigius Abbey, Rheims, and granted to them at the same time as Lapley (Priory), LGS p159) and Metford (held by Helgot of Earl Roger). The ending means 'ford,' the first part is, perhaps, from Anglo-Saxon meadow or from a tiny tributary of the Trent here called Med (DUIGNAN). Or 'ford where the streams meet' (SPN p117). Or 'mea' is from the river-root mi-ad 'ad' 'aud' water and the diminutive prefix 'mi' (NSFCT 1908 p144). Coffin Pound is the nickname for the stretch of Trent and Mersey Canal between the second and third locks here, owing to its shape, whilst Suicide Lock is the nickname for the top lock in the flight of locks. It is said to have gained its name on account of people taking their life here (Canal Town: Stone. John M Bolton. 1981 reprint 1989 p33). 'A' Station of Meaford Power Station opened on former farmland of Upper and Lower Meaford Farms between the Trent and the Trent and Mersey Canal in Nov 1947. It was the first post-war power station in the country to be brought into commercial operation, drawing water from the Trent as a coolant for its con-

densers. A further station, 'B' Station, was built later. Apparently 'A' Station closed in c1976 and 'B' Station in Sept 1990. The five cooling towers of the Station, known locally as the 'Five ugly Sisters,' were demolished by being blown up in Sept 1991 (NSFCT 1947 p164. 1950 p92) (TSS p114) (SPJD p90pc of the towers falling) (SLM Sept 1999 p71) (Memories of the Downs Banks. Kathleen Day. c1999 p18) (info Phil Mellor). Meaford Hall Farm had a horse gin - still quite common in the north of the county where they are known as gin gangs, but are rare in the south and in the midlands (COS p50p).

Meaford Hall House 1.5m NW of Stone. The cellars are very massively constructed and some have thought they show traces of ecclesiastical architecture (NSFCT 1922 p167).

THE JERVIS' AND PARKER-JERVIS'. The second son of James Jervys of Chatcull Old Hall (see) (b c1490) was William of Ollerton, Shrops. William was succeeded by his son John (b c1550), who was succeeded by his son John (b1598). John (b1598) married his second cousin Elizabeth, daughter and sole heir of John Jervis of Chatcull Old Hall. Their eldest son William purchased Darlaston (Pirehill hundred) from James Collier in 1655. He died without issue and his Darlaston and Meaford estates passed to the son of his younger brother John (1631-1680), John Jervis, born at Chatcull Old Hall in 1670. John (b1670) married Mary only daughter and heir of John Swynfen of Swinfen Hall (see), and he is perhaps the builder of an early Meaford Hall, said to have been built by John Jervis in 1686 (SIS p117) (SN May 16 1997 p8). He was High Sheriff of Staffs in 1709. He died in 1746 and was succeeded at Meaford by his fifth son Swynfen Jervis (1700-1771). He married Elizabeth Parker (1698-1784) of Park Hall (see), Caverswall (RHPS pp130,140) (Burke's Peerage 1879, 1967) (Accessions 8144-77/45 in WSL). Swynfen Jervis (d1771) was succeeded by his eldest son William Jervis. He died without issue in 1813 and Meaford passed to his younger brother **Admiral John Jervis**, 1st Viscount and Earl St Vincent (d1823). He was born at Meaford Hall on Jan 20 1734/5 in the upper part of the S part of the hall which has a 'shell-hood' external doorway. In 1782 he was the commander of the 'Foudroyant.' After he captured the French warship 'Pegase' off Brest he was rewarded with a KB. The admiral is remembered for defeating a far superior Spanish fleet off Cape St Vincent on Feb 14 1797. In 1801 he became First Lord of the Admiralty. He retired to Rochetts, Essex, and died there. The admiral has a monument in the crypt of St Paul's cathedral, London; a portrait by F Cotes (1769) in the National Portrait Gallery, and a bust by Sir Francis Chantrey in St Michael's, Stone. In 1897 the Cape St Vincent centenary celebrations included a feast in Meaford village schoolroom; a public procession through High Street, Stone, followed by a service in St Michael's church; a feast at Stone workhouse and a ball at Meaford Hall. In 1932 some artifacts formerly belonging to the admiral were exhibited at Teddesley Hall, Staffs; and in 1935 some were exhibited at St Joseph's Hall, Stone. A strange velvet cap which was worn by the admiral was at the WSL in 1984 (GNHS p116) (PS p54) (S p123) (LGS pp54-55,222) (SOSH pp250-258) (RHPS pp32,103-107,115,116) (ES May 2 1932 p4. Dec 28 1934 p4. Jan 15 1935 p6. Jan 17 1935 p1p. Jan 19 1935 p3p) (KES p198) (STM Oct 1965 pp27,28p of portrait. Sept 1968 pp30-31) (VB p142) (SGS p162) (SLM May 1984 pp15p of velvet cap, 16p of portrait) (SHJ vol 2 pp16-17) (TB April 1994 p18il). In the room below where the admiral was born, formerly the study, was found £200 in notes in a secret draw of a cabinet which had remained there for more than 50 years (RHPS pp103-104). Behind panelling in the study was a secret room. Admiral John Jervis married Martha daughter of Sir Thomas Parker Knt (d1784) of Park Hall (see), near Caverswall, but he died childless in 1823. The Meaford estate then passed through his sister, Mary (d1828), wife of William Henry Ricketts (d1799) to her son who assumed the name of Jervis becoming, **Edward Jervis Jervis** (formerly Ricketts) (1767-1859), 2nd Viscount St Vincent. He married firstly Mary-Cassandra daughter of Lord Saye and Sele and the viscountcy of St Vincent descended with their children. Edward married secondly Mary-Ann, second daughter of Thomas Parker of Park Hall (see), near Caverswall, and the Meaford estate descended to his children by this marriage. Their three children were John Edward Jervis (d1837), Mary-Anne Jervis (1812-1893), and Edward, who succeeded to the estate and the other Parker-Jervis estates of Aston hall, near Sutton Coldfield, and Park Hall, near Caverswall, and assumed the name of Parker-Jervis, becoming **Edward Swynfen Parker-Jervis** (1815-1896). In 1840 **Mary-Anne Jervis** (b1812) married David Ochterlony Dyre Sombre. Sombre, heir to the fortune of the Begum of Sirdhanah in Bengal, was declared mad in 1842 and died in 1851. In 1862 she married secondly George Cecil Weld, who later became the 3rd Lord Forester. In 1872 she and her new husband won the famous five-year long court case with the East India Company over the possession of her late husband's estate, known as the Arms Suit (RHPS p126) (SN June 25 1993 p12). A plaque now (1997) by the front door bears testament to the bitter court battle (SN March 12 1993 pp22-23. May 16 1997 p8). Mary-Anne Lady Forester purchased the Meaford estate in 1873 (SIS pp117,119). Between 1874-7 (BOE p269) she built a N wing, with a clock tower and containing a staircase from Russia, and encased it and the old hall in Corsehill stone from Arran island (NSFCT 1922 p167) (SSBOP p68p in 1905) (SDOPP p58p in 1914). The first hall was then sometimes known as the 'Old Hall.' In 1935 a plaque was erected over the 'shell-hood' doorway to commemorate Jervis' birthplace (ES Jan 22 1935 p8p). On the death of Mary-Anne Lady Forester in 1893 Meaford Hall was left to the son of her brother Edward (d1896) and his descendents (NSFCT 1993-94 pp68-69). Edward's third son William Robert Parker-Jervis (1841-1919), Sheriff of Staffs in 1911, was of Meaford and Park Halls. His eldest daughter Miss Ethel Mary Parker-Jervis OBE (1878-1956), commandant at Sandon Hall Auxiliary Hospital between 1915-18 (Burke's Peerage 1879, 1967) (Accessions 8144-77/45 in WSL), was the last occupant of Meaford Hall before it was taken over by the National Electricity Board (OPB p20); Miss Parker-Jervis was later of Darlaston Hall (see), Stone.

The hall passed out of Parker-Jervis hands in 1943 when the estate was purchased by Victor Roden (ES Dec 27 1985 p8) (SN May 16 1997 p8). The Roden's demolished the N wing erected by Lady Forester (MR p228). There was a plan to site the first University College of North Staffordshire here: Keele Hall was eventually chosen (TSS p94). In 1963 the hall and grounds were bought by Percy Bilton Ltd, builders, who used the hall as offices and the grounds as a heavy plant depot; prior to this the grounds had been used as a market garden and nursery (MR p228). In 1964 the hall was scheduled as a building of historical interest. It was being renovated and converted into flats by 1988 (SSBOP p68). The NSFC acquired a fine sack bottle of end of C17 kept at the hall, which was found in the moat of Painsley Hall c1830s (NSFCT 1945 p82). The hall was in need of repair in 1993 and was purchased by businessman Carl Bailey in c1996. He had restored the hall and converted the stable block into residences by spring 1998 and built three new detached houses close to the hall (SN May 16 1997 p8p) (The Express. June 27 1997 p60p) (local info). (W p364) (LGS pp54,222) (SOSH p251p) (RHPS il. No. 17) (SIS pl 19 facing p119 il of the 'Old Hall').

GROUNDS. The 'Cat Stone,' which existed in the 1940s and 1950s in a corner of the estate, is a memorial to a cat of Admiral St Vincent. The admiral is believed to have written the inscription on the headstone

> 'Tis false that all of pussy's race,
> Regard not persons but the place,
> For here lies one who could she tell,
> Her stories by some magic spell,
> Would from the quitted barn and grove,
> (or Would claim she quitted barn and grove)
> Her sporting haunts to show her love,
> At sound of footsteps absent long,
> Of those she soothed by purring song,
> Flew to their arms with fond embrace,
> For love of them and not for place.'
> St Vincent.

(ES Dec 27 1985 p8). In the 1940s and 1950s there was a pathway running beneath some beautiful larch trees called **Freeman's Walk**. It was named after John Freeman, a slave brought back by Admiral Jervis from Jamaica. Freeman, who appears on the tomb of the admiral in St Michael's, Stone, is said to have planted the larches and created the walk (ES Dec 27 1985 p8). In the 1980s the garden contained a **grotto** by a fountain, both in a poor state of repair, and further to the N a **pets cemetery** comprising eight graves: i). "Diamond.' My Blemheim d. Nov. 23 1900 E.M.P.J.' ii). "Peter' d. May 16 1902 E.SI.V.P.J.' iii). "Trixie.' My Spaniel d. March 1909 C.P.J.' iv). "Robert' d. Sept. 28 1917 aged 16 W.R.P.J.' v). "Wasp' Faithful friend and devoted companion for 15 and a half years of E. SI. V.P.J. d.May 17 1918' vi). "Cymro-Ricky' b. Conway March 27 1920 d. Meaford June 13 1931.' vii). "Tony' b. May 1931 d. Nov. 1931.' viii). "Tiny' d.Oct. 1935.' The **Smoking House** was a little house on a knoll with a sycamore tree at each of its four corners. It stood about 500 yards from the hall by the Meaford Road at the corner of the road down to Meaford Old Hall Farm and the 'watery lanes.' The house was built for men to retire to to smoke tobacco as smoking was forbidden in the hall during the time of Admiral John Jervis and his brother William (SIS pp74-75).

Meaford Old Hall Timber-framed building E of Meaford Hall, and on other side of canal and railway line from Meaford Hall. John Joule of Joules Brewery, Stone, died at the old hall after a lingering illness on May 2 1858 (The

Gazette. Oct 1988 p8) (SSBOP p71p). Joseph Timmis resided here between at least 1872 and 1892. The house was occupied by Joseph Lowe in 1912 (KD 1872. 1892. 1912). Was restored in the 1980s.

Mear Hay Woods Longton (SHST p529).

Mears Coppice Former coppice on steep north bank of the Stour at Dunn's Bank, now a track. The name is probably from Saxon '(ge)maere' 'mearc' meaning a boundary; the coppice by the Stour the former boundary between Staffs and Worcs (TB Nov 5 1998 p10).

Mear Stone In a plan of the boundary of the manor of Handsworth Gallowes Hill is mentioned, also a mear stone, and Sir Robert Holt's Conduit (SHOS vol 2 p108).

Mease, River Rises about Ashby-de-la-Zouch, Leics. Forms the Staffs Derbys border for a short while N of Clifton Lodge, and again N of Haunton. Joins the Trent 0.5m N of Croxall. But before the county boundary changes of 1894 the Mease formed the county boundary all the way from Edingale to where it joins the Trent. Has appeared as Meys (1247), Mese (1577. 1586), Messe (c1600), Meass (1840) (GNHS p23) (SPNO p14), and Maese (UCC). (HOA p10 Mease-Meos) (DUIGNAN). The name is from Anglo-Saxon 'meos,' 'a mossy bog, or marsh' (SPN p83).

Medall Green A green in Compton, Kinver. It was mentioned in 1453 and 1562 (VCH vol 20 p139). Has also appeared as Medenale Green.

Medicine House Stood on the Staffs side of New Road opposite the Blue Bell Inn car park in Wrinehill. Formerly an inn known as the Red Lion. It acquired the name Medicine House after Samuel Johnson, an apothecary, rented it c1880, and sold his patent medicine from here called 'The Staffordshire Cure All.' Johnson previously had a shop in The Summerhouse (see). Sewers in the roadway caused the Medicine House to crack in 1963. The property was sold in 1969 (Newcastle Times Feb 26 1969) (BVC p189) (SVB p186) (BOPP pl 55 photograph of it or The Summerhouse). The house was scheduled for demolition in 1970 owing to road widening. In Aug 1970 there were plans to take it down piece by piece and re-erect it near Holmes Chapel, Ches (ES April 7 1970. Aug 12 1970 p) (BVC p189), and the house was moved for preservation by Alan Garner, writer, to stand alongside his house, Toad Hall, Blackden, Goostrey, Ches, in c1970 (info Ian Bailey). Some years later and by about the mid 1980s the present (2000) house called Old Boundary House was erected on the old house site (info Bill Kimpton).

Mediolanium, Mediolanum and **Mediomanum**. The same or different settlements in Roman Britain which may have been in Staffs. According to Ptolemy in his 'Geography,' c120 AD, Mediolanium is a chief town of the Ordovice tribe (SHC 1916 pp307-308). Mediolanum or Mediolano appears in the 10th Antonine Itinerary, or Route x of the Itinerarium Britannianum, or Iter x (NSFCT 1938 p112). The same or another Mediolanum or Mediolano appears in the 2nd Antonine Itinerary, or Route ii of the Itinerarium Britannianum, or Iter ii. Mediolanum and another place, Mediomanum appear in the 'Cherographia' of the anonymous geographer of Ravenna, whose work is assigned to the C7 (NSFCT 1908 p115. 1937 p125). Some authorities say Mediolanum stands for the central 'llan,' ie: habitation or inclosure; hence churchyard or church. Or Mediolanum is derived from 'med' fertile, 'lan' soil, land (SHC 1916 p313 note). Conjectured sites:

MEDIOLANIUM, or MEDIOLANUM, or MEDIOMANUM has been identified with **Bearstone**, Shrops by a Mr Jones of Market Drayton who sought to identify one of the places with an earthwork at Bearstone (NSFCT 1890 p25): **Chesterton**, Newcastle-under-Lyme, by Garner (GNHS p70; Mediolanum): **Chesterton**, Shrops, 6m SW of Pattingham, formerly in Staffs (SVS p321): **Chesterton Green**, Warws, 6m SE of Warwick on Fosse Way (SVS p321 note): **Clawdd Coch** (near Llanymynech) by the editors of the Monumenta Historica Britannica but was rejected by CGO Bridgeman (SHC 1916 p315): Somewhere in the parish of **Drayton-in-Hales**, Staffs (THS p319): **Knightley**, Staffs (THS p319): **Hales** after the discovery of a Roman villa E of Hales in 1927 (NSFCT 1928 pp109-110): **High Offley** (THS p319) (W p390); W Page rejects this identification (VCH vol 1 pp184,188): **Holditch** after excavations in the late 1950s revealed a very large settlement at Holditch to the S of Chesterton (HOS p12): **Madeley** (STM May 1963 pp42,43): at or near **Market Drayton** by Horsley (Britannia Romana. J Horsley. 1732) (SHC 1916 p315): **Whitchurch**, Shrops; CGO Bridgeman thought this a possibility as did the third edition of the OS map of Roman Britain (1956) which placed one of the settlements at or near Whitchurch. Authorities were still placing one of them here in 1969 (SHC 1916 p312) (NSJFS 1961 p28. 1969 p104). ID Margary in Roman Roads in Britain vol 2 1957 pp249,251,254 noted there were a Mediolanum (which he placed at Chesterton) and a Mediomanum (which he placed at Whitchurch).

MEDIOMANUM has been identified with **Arbour Farm** W of Mucklestone (NSFCT 1908 pp114-115).

MEDIOLANUM of the Iter x (but not of the Iter ii) may be **Chesterton** N of Newcastle-under-Lyme (SA March 16 1912 p5) (SHC 1916 p319): **Festiniog** near an old road called Sarn Hellen, Merionethshire, by Dr Gale (SHOS vol 1 p23): **Gravenhunger** near Woore, by Shaw (SHOS vol 1 p23): **Llanvyllyn**, Montgomeryshire, by Camden (SHOS vol 1 p23).

MEDIOLANUM of the Iter ii and Ptolemy's Mediolanium was identified with **Mathrafal** or Mathraval or Meivod, Montgomeryshire, by Camden but rejected by CGO Bridgeman and others (SHC 1916 pp312,315) (NSFCT 1930 p142).

MEDIOLANUM of the Iter ii and the Iter x has been identified with **Chesterton** N of Newcastle-under-Lyme (SA March 30 1912 p5) (SHC 1916 p312). Dr William Bennet and Rev T Leman were the first to identify it with the Mount Pleasant site in 1789 ('Magna Britannia' vol 2 part 2. 1806-22. p433. D&S Lysons) (AJ vol 30 (1873) p159). Ward attempted to reconcile Ptolemy's 'Geography' and the Antonine Intera ii and x and identify Chesterton with Mediolanum on both routes (HBST pp6,15); Rev Thomas Barns and SAH Burne reiterate the identification (SA Nov 19 1904) (NSFCT 1908 pp103-148. 1912 p142) (SHC 1916 p316).

(HBST p14) (GNHS p68) (NSFCT 1886 pp53-54. 1908 pp103-120. 1911 p142) (Mediomanum; a lost Staffordshire station on Watling Street. Thomas Barns. 1904) (LGS p113) (OTP pp60,63) (WWT pp4,5) (E p8) (S p72) (SA March 16 1912. March 30 1912. April 13 1912. April 27 1912.)

Meece Brook Brook rising in Madeley parish to W of Keele Park (by Racecourse Farm S of Keele?) runs through Whitmore (NSFCT 1916 pp55-59). It drove Chorlton Mill and passes though Stableford. Runs through Cotes Heath, Millmeece, and joins the Sow 0.5m S of Izaak Walton's Cottage, Shallowford. Has also appeared as Mesebrock (1272), Meace and Meese (DUIGNAN) (SPNO p14): Older forms are preserved in former forms of Coldmeece and Millmeece which lie on Meece Brook (SPNO p14). The name is from perhaps Old French Mees meaning meadows (NSFCT 1887 p41). Duignan could find no early forms. Perhaps from the root 'uisage' in Gaelic and Erse and Welsh 'wysg' with the diminutive 'mi' (NSFCT 1908 p130).

Meece House Former early C19 three-storey house at Cold Meece, at SJ 853326. It was occupied by Edward John Wedgwood Wood (d1922) in the earlier C20 (mem in Swynnerton church) (NSF p5) and was used by the MOD in WW2. In c1968 it was bought by Martin Hood. It was identified as a being 'most at risk' in a 1991 Buildings at Risk survey compiled by Staffs county council. The house, listed Grade II, was in a very ruinous state in 1995 and had been demolished by May 1998. In Aug 1998 Martin Hood was facing court action for demolishing the house. But he denies demolition since the building materials remain in a pile on the site (local info) (ES Aug 6 1998 p15p) (SN Aug 6 1998 p19). There was a plaque on the N wall of the house. It commemorated the Daily Mail's London to Manchester Air Race, and that

> Louis Paulhan flew over this house at 4.50 a.m. on Thursday, 28th April, 1910 on his way to Manchester to win the £10,000 prize, which he accomplished.

By 1979, when the house was derelict, the plaque was moss-covered (MMM pp35-38). It was stolen from its place in the wall in about the mid 1980s and has never been seen again (local info) (EAS pp25,29) (VESOP pl 112) (TB May 1994 pp18-19p. Aug 12 1999 pp18-19).

Meerbrook Small village above Meer Brook 24m NNE of Stafford. Former chapelry in Leekfrith township in Leek ancient parish. Meerbrook Coalfield is a coalfield between Axe Edge and the Roaches, four square miles in extent. It was the extreme southern point of the Lancashire and Cheshire coalfields and was one of the highest above sea level in England (HOLF p54). Meerbrook was a grange of Dieulacres Abbey (NSJFS 1970 p85). There was a settlement at Meerbrook in the mid C13 (VCH vol 7 p193). Has appeared as Merebroke (1338) (SSE 1996 p15) and 'le Myres' (1543) which is said to echo 'myre' in the medieval epic poem 'Gawain and the Green Knight' (NSJFS 1977 p36). The name is from the Meer Brook. The church, St Matthew, in the centre of Meerbrook village, was built in 1538. It was enlarged and almost rebuilt in 1873 (St Matthew's Church, Meerbrook. Mary Breeze). Meerbrook became a separate ecclesiastical parish in 1724 (GLAUE p417) refounded in 1859 (LGS p187). Prior to the change in the calendar in 1752 Meerbrook wake may have been held on the Sunday nearest Sept 21, the feast of St Matthew, the patron saint of Meerbrook church. In the mid C19 the wake was celebrated at the end of Sept or the beginning of Oct (VCH vol 7 p195). In the later C17 Plot noted at Meerbrook the local farmers burn the grass when it was green to prevent the fern blowing away if there is a wind, and to extract the oily substance within the fern (NHS p334). Two houses - Waterhouse Farm and Fountain Inn - in the SE part of the village were demolished and

submerged under Tittesworth Reservoir when it was enlarged between in 1959 and 1962. By 1998 Mrs W Hine, associated with Meerbrook Village Hall since 1927, was the longest serving village hall member in the county (Melting Pot. Summer 1998 p15).

Meer Brook Flows from Turner's Pool through Meerbrook and gives its name to Meerbrook. It formerly joined the Churnet at New Grange (SSE 1993 p4), but now runs into Tittesworth Reservoir. The brook was so called by c1220 (VCH vol 7 p193) and it has appeared as Merebroc (1330), Merebroke (1338), Mar Brook, and Markbrook (SVB p123) (SPNO p14). The name means 'boundary brook' (NSJFS 1981 p2) (SSE 1996 p15), or, very appropriately here, the brook by the pool (NSJFS 1977 p36). The boundary referred to would be an ancient line earthwork called The Mark (see) (OL vol 2 p15), or possibly a boundary of an estate based on Rudyard (SSE 1993 p4).

Meer Oak House 1m SW of Wrottesley. In Pattingham ancient parish. The name is from an old oak called Meer Oak or Tynedede Meer Oak (see) which marked the point of junction of the manors of Wrottesley, Perton and Pattingham (HOPTT p154 note) (VCH vol 20 pp10,172). Has also appeared as Mere Oak. There was a windmill about 0.5m W of Meer Oak in the Westbeech (see) area.

Meese, River Rises out of Aqualate Mere (VCH vol 4 p104). Raven suggests it rises S of Aqualate Mere at Outwoods (MR p155). But this is not so (WSS p110). Spends little time in the county. Forms Shrops Staffs border from S of Forton until it leaves Staffs E of Chetwynd Park in Shrops. The name is from Anglo-Saxon 'meos,' 'a mossy bog, or marsh' (SPN p83). Has affectionately been called locally the 'Sleepy Meese' (Yates' map) (WSS p110).

Megacre Tiny hamlet comprising a row of houses 0.5m ESE of Audley. Megacre Lane originally linked Woodlane to the Bignall Hill Road, and was a narrow track until after 1850. Formerly Migacre, probably derived from a field name at one side of the lane (AHJ 1917 p97).

Meg-a-doodles Well A well, that Shaw calls Meg-a Wood's Well, and says was, near the top of Waddam's Hill, Wolverhampton, and which he noted was long neglected (SHOS vol 2 p165). (HOWW). White says there was an arched well at Windham's Hill called Meg-a-Wood's Well, unknown to his contemporaries or fallen into disuse (W p76). (SCSF p140 - calls it Meg-a-doodles Well). Waddam's Hill is probably Wadham's Hill (see).

Meg's Well Whitmore. Is on the Hey Sprink old road to Whitmore (M p28).

Meir Former small hamlet in Caverswall ancient parish (W p752), centred on the crossing of the Leek-Stone and Longton-Uttoxeter roads, 1.75m SE of Longton. Formerly in Normacot township in Hilderstone quarter in Stone ancient parish (W p371). The **Roman** road, Richmilde Street (see), passed through Meir (MRM p3). The lower stone of a rotary quern, probably of the Roman period, has been found on high ground at Meir (NSFCT 1938 p113) (NSJFS 1964 p36). Meir's main road junction was part of a marsh known as the Mere - hence Meir has been referred to as 'the Meir.' The Mere was crossed by a cobbled causeway which formed a section of the Roman road (ES July 16 1996 p8). Meir has also appeared as Meer and Mear. The **church**, Holy Trinity, at the junction of Uttoxeter Road and Box Lane, was built in 1890-1891 (BOE p261). The **expansion of Meir** in every direction from the old centre to create the present large suburb took place in and from the 1920s with many from the Potteries being rehoused in new estates here. Meir was taken into Stoke-on-Trent county borough in 1922 (VCH vol 8 p260) (MRM p39). The ecclesiastical parish of Meir was created out of Caverswall ancient parish and Normacot ecclesiastical parish in 1926 (GLAUE p417). The **municipal airport** for Stoke-on-Trent, opened on May 18 1934 (MRM p7) or in 1935 (SHST p156) (TSS pp121-122). It was sited on the S side of the A50 running from the garden of 912 Uttoxeter Road to the boundary of Blythe Bridge or Catchem's Corner for approximately 1,000 yards - 1,540 yards along Grindley Lane and having three sides of 880 yards (MRM p7). George VI landed at Meir Aerodrome on July 12 1934 to visit Stoke-on-Trent (R&S p46). The aerodrome was used as a turning-point in the King's Cup Air Race in 1937 (ES Dec 5 1994 p8). Amy Johnson may have flown to and from the airfield in WW2 (ES Dec 5 1994 p8). It was used privately after WW2 until closing in 1961 (MRM p8). The runway was taken up in 1979 (MRM p8). The housing estate known as Meir Park had been built on the land by the 1990s (WMA vol 1 p210) (TWWW May 1996 pp18-19) (Airfield Focus. No. 34: Stoke-on-Trent (Meir). Roger Lycett-Smith. 1998). **Transport tunnels**. A tunnel of 847 yards (MRM p3) long was built at Meir for the Stoke Uttoxeter line (1847) of the North Staffs Railway (IAS pp132,142). Meir station opened for passenger traffic in 1892 (MRM p3). It was recommended that the station be closed in 1963 (ES March 22 1963). The Meir tunnel, opened in 1998, is a long underpass taking the new A50 under the Stone-Leek road in the centre of Meir. **Newspaper**. The Stone Gazette and Meir, Eccleshall and Barlaston News, founded on May 14 1937, ran until at least March 18 1938 (SHJ spring

1996 p25). An unusual object resembling a vertical sausage in the sky, possibly a **UFO**, was seen by three people for about three seconds from Sandon Road on Sept 6 1967 at about 9.50pm (FSRP pp14-15). **Natives.** In 1457 a carefully-planned murder took place at Meer on the Friday after Christmas. A band of ruffians arrived in the night at the house of **Henry Whyte** a farmer and set on him and his wife as they lay in their bed. The Coyneys of Weston Coyney were accused and Richard Challoner and John Tomlinson of Chedull (Cheadle) but at the trial they were found not guilty (NSFCT 1913 p149). **David Johnson**, author of 'Sabre General' and 'Promenade in Champagne,' was born in Meir in 1927 (VFC p75).

Meir Green Former small hamlet in Caverswall ancient parish (SGSAS) and in Normacot township in Hilderstone quarter in Stone ancient parish (W p371). Has appeared as Mear Green, and was in the Meir Road area, Normacot (1834 OS map).

Meir Hay Suburb of Longton, 0.75m E of Longton. Former common land?

Meir Heath Former common land in Normacot township in Hilderstone quarter in Stone ancient parish (W p363), but now nearly all built on. The present residential area of Meir Heath on the crest of a high ridge above the upper Trent and Blithe valleys lies 2.5m SSE of Longton, 1.5m S of Meir. From the late C17 to the mid C18 there was an **iron furnace** at Meir Heath (NHS p158) (NSFCT 1953 pp42-45) (MR p229). The name appears in Swynnerton PR in 1756 as Mare Heath (AHJ 1995 p46). A **windmill** stands about 825 feet above sea level at SJ 929402 (STM March 1972 p34p). The mill was used by Yates as a triangulation point for his map (1775), and by the surveyors for the first OS map (SHC 4th series vol 12 1984 vii), and is shown on Yates' map. However, traditionally it has been said that a Richard Ash Broster, who lived to the age of 110 (died sometime between 1950-85?), built the mill, which suggests the present mill was built on an old mill site. Broster and his wife also ran an inn nearby called the 'Dusty Miller.' It is now a butcher's shop and is not to be confused with nearby 'Windmill Inn.' The mill became disused at the turn of the C20. It was sold to SPWWC in 1908 who installed a water tank within the tower for local distribution. It was bought by Joules in 1928. When Karl Wood painted the windmill for a painting in April 1939 it still retained its cap and the remnants of two sails. These were removed by the Home Guard who added a watch tower for the war. This was taken off in the 1960s and the tower now carries an aerial mast for radio communications (WBJ pp30-31 ils. 33 - 35 in 1890, 1900, 1978) (SLM spring 1954 p24) (STMSM Aug 1978 p26p). A man named **Stoddard** who was wounded in the Peterloo Massacre in Manchester on Aug 16 1819 lived in a cottage on Meir Heath. He was a travelling pot seller (PTP pp36-38). The **church**, St Francis of Assisi, on the W side of Sandon Road, S of Church Close, was consecrated in Oct 1940 (info Rev Pawson). The ecclesiastical parish of Meir Heath was created in 1948 (GLAUE p417). The **fine views** from Meir Heath include: to the N Macclesfield Forest and Shining Tor in Ches; to the W and S the Trent Valley; to E the Blithe Valley, Weavers and the Moorlands.

Meir Park The name for the new housing estate built on the old Meir aerodrome. The mission church, St Clare, on Lysander Road, was opened in 1981 (info Rev Pawson) (LDD). The name was also used for a ward of Stoke-on-Trent district by 1991 covering the Meir, Weston Coyney, Normacot Grange, and Lightwood areas.

Mercian A ward of Tamworth borough by at least 1993, covering the area of Coton, Wigginton Park and Lichfield Road Industrial Estate.

Mere Area and former estate in Lutley manor in Enville ancient parish. There was settlement at Mere by the early C14, probably near the present Mere Hall (VCH vol 20 p94).

Mere Name of the manor in which Forton, Mereton, Sutton, Aqualate and Warton are situated. But from 1553 was styled Mere and Forton (VCH vol 4 p106). Appears as La Mare in old documents (NSFCT 1937 p62).

Mere, The L-shaped house which stood to the SE of the present Mere Hall, Enville. It was the seat of the Moseleys in the mid C18 and appears to have also been called Mere Hall at some time. It was demolished or destroyed by fire in the early C19 and has since been covered by a tiny reservoir (VCH vol 20 p105). Part of the mid C18 stable block to the NW of the house was converted into the present Mere Hall sometime in the early C19 (VCH vol 20 p105).

Meredale House Forton. A C18 brick house. Bought by Sir John Boughey in 1816. Used as a dower house during much of the C19 (VCH vol 4 p105). (MR p155p).

Mere Farm House 1.5m N of Enville, on the N side of Mere Lane, in Enville ancient parish. Tall, gabled building of the early C17 with a projecting porch. Late C16 parts of a former house on the site survive at the rear of the present house. The house was known in the earlier C19 as The Mere and as Mere Farm by 1982 (VCH vol 20 p105). (WJO Nov 1905 p295p) (TB Nov 1986

p17p. Dec 1986 p4 il from ILN Dec 26 1857 showing children clementing by the front door).

Mere Hall House 1m SE of Bobbington, in Enville ancient parish. To NW of Mere Farm. The house was created out of the E end of a stable block of mid C18 origin of a nearby vanished house called The Mere (see). Mere Hall was known as Mere House by 1838 and as Mere Hall by 1982 (VCH vol 20 p105).

Mere Hill To W of Throwley Hall, Calton. There is a burial mound on top of it at SK 10535259. It is 20 paces in diameter and a listed monument. Carrington excavated it in 1848. A rock-cut grave, a child's skeleton and two skeletons, a cremation and a heeled bronze dagger (TYD pp113-114) (VCH vol 1 no 3) (BAP vol 1 p158 fig 187) (DAJ vol 75 pp109,110,111. vol 77 p26, B6). Food vessels of the Beaker people, of the Yorkshire type, have been found on it (NSJFS 1962 p33). Has also appeared as Mare Hill.

Merelake Minute hamlet just over the border in Ches 1.75m WSW of Kidsgrove.

Meretown Hamlet by the Meese 0.5m S of Forton. In Forton ancient parish. It was formerly identified with DB Mere, and consequently Meretown has been associated with an Anglo-Saxon battle which is said to have been fought at a place called Mere; however that Mere has subsequently been identified with Maer. Meretown has appeared as Mera (DB), Mere (1198), Meyre (1547), Meeretowne (1551-1553), Meerton (Plot's map), Meer Town (1755) (SPNO p147); it may have also been written Mearton; here the wife of Samuel Ward, who gave birth without any cognizance of being pregnant, lived (NHS p270); and Meer (SGSAS) (W p458). The name is from nearby Aqualate Mere (DUIGNAN). 'Town' is modern and appears from the C17 (SPN p13). Meretown was once a considerable village. It had the 'big house' of the manor of Mere and Forton, situated on 'Bury Hill' in the village (NSFCT 1937 p62). The mermaid of Aqualate Mere reputedly threatens to destroy Meretown if the mere is allowed to go dry (NSFCT 1896 p121). The antiquary, Rev Thomas Loxdale (d1742), son of John or Joseph Loxdale of Meretown, was born in Meretown on October 3 1675. He was curate of Forton (1698-1703), vicar of Seighford (1703-1721 or 1723), curate of Ellenhall (1717 to at least 1720 but not later than 1723), rector of Tixall (1719-1742), and vicar of Leek (1725-1735) (SHJ spring 1991 p7). Another account has him being rector of Tixall from 1735 (SSE 1994 p74). At Seighford he recorded a man aged 124 who became a father again at the age of 100 (SHJ spring 1991 p7). His unpublished history of Leek was begun in 1730; the Ms of about 200 pages has been in the possession of St Edward's church, Leek, since his death; other Mss of his are in the WSL. Loxdale was buried at Seighford on April 21 1742 (SOS pl xiii) (BS p292) (OPB pp16,17) (SL p77) (SH p77) (SHJ spring 1991 pp7,12).

Meretown House Meretown. Occupied in 1851 by Hon Miss Hill (W p22).

Mere Valley Tiny valley ENE of Brocton. Long Mere is a tiny pool 0.5m to the N (GCC p2p).

Merlicke's Well Well at the bottom of Shaw Lane off Beacon Street, Lichfield. It could be the same as Maudlin's Well?

Merridale Former estate and small village by Graiseley Brook now a suburb 1.25m WSW of Wolverhampton. Formerly in the foreign of Wolverhampton in Wolverhampton township, chapelry and ancient parish. Half of a sandstone axe of 1200 BC date was found in the playing field of Wolverhampton Grammar School near the brook at Merridale in 1928 (HOWM p1). There seems to have been a small settlement at Merridale in the Middle Ages (HOWM p6). Appears as Merrydale on Plot's map. The name is from the old meaning of 'merry,' meaning sweet, or pleasant (DUIGNAN). There was a settlement to the S known as Merry Hill. Edward Banks (d1884), architect and poet, was born at Merridale in 1849. A collection of his poems ' Waifs of Rhyme' was published in 1885 (PSS pp264-265) (VFC p8). Emma Dorothy Barcroft 'Auntie Dorothy' of the 1930s BBC radio programme, Children's Hour, is buried at Merridale Cemetery in Jeffcock Road, opened in June 1850 (HOWU pp106-107).

Merridale Manor House Capital messuage of the Merridale estate, Wolverhampton. Merridale estate passed to the Salford family in the C13 on the marriage of William to Agnes, daughter and co-heiress of Henry de Hampton. The Salfords held the estate until the early C17, at which stage ownership becomes confused (HOWM p44) (WMARCH 1994 p116). It seems likely that the estate belonged to the Normansells for a time in the C17 (WMARCH 1994 p116). By the beginning of the C17 there was a house on the estate, sometimes known as Merridale Manor House or Hall, at the junction of Merridale Lane and Road. This was then occupied by William Normansell, mercer. His son, also William, became a magistrate during the Commonwealth, and was one of the nine local voters for the Barebones Parliament, 1653. A house on this site in 1901 was known as Old Merridale Farm (OS map 1901 Wolverhampton (SW) 62.10). In 1930 Merridale Hall, reputedly was demolished, and was replaced by a farm. This house was a ruin by the mid 1960s. By 1998 it had been converted into shops which by then were empty and boarded up. A nearby timber-framed barn belonging to the house converted into a garage and petrol station was demolished in 1961 (HOWM p61) (WOLOP p22p). In the 1970s the Royal Commission on the Historic Monuments of England declared that the old hall had been demolished. However, its remains were discovered during the demolition of a relatively new garage some time prior to 1994 (WMARCH 1994 p116).

Merriden Area in the mid C19 probably near Merridale (later Moatbrook) House which stands at the junction of Strawmoor Lane and Moatbrook Lane, 0.75m W of the church at Codsall (VCH vol 20 p77).

Merril Grove Farm 2.5m W of Longnor. Formerly in Heathylee township in Alstonefield ancient parish. There was a house here by 1439 (VCH vol 7 p33).

Merrill's Hall Former moated homestead (WFW p68), now the name for an industrial area 0.5m ESE of Wednesfield, formerly in Wednesfield chapelry. The name has appeared as Merols Hall, with reference to the moated homestead (VCH vol 1 p368), Merol's Hole Colliery (WFW p68), and Merrils Hole, an industrial area (BCM April 1987 pp52-53). The moated homestead may have been associated with William Boon de Marsh of 1300, owing to the proximity of March (earlier Marsh) End, but have taken its name from the Merrill family, resident in Wednesfield in the C17. The moat, which appears on the 1840 tithe map, lies opposite the eastern end of Hart road, now (1978) within the Hope Gate of the Weldess Tube Works. It was an angle fragment of 130 feet by 50 feet in 1908, but had vanished by the early 1980s (VCH vol 1) (WFW p68) (SSAHST 1982-3 p55). The house of unusual shape nearby may have been dubbed 'Merrill's Hall' by local inhabitants or have some antiquity (WFW p68).

Merrions Wood Wood 0.5m W of the church at Great Barr. Noted for having been laid out by Humphrey Repton for the carriage drive to Great Barr Hall for Sir Joseph Scott, although it was never part of the Great Barr Hall estate. Is now (1997) listed parkland. Blue plaques on timber posts relating the history of the wood have been erected at either end of the carriage drive (Forest of Mercia News. No. 4) (info David Grundy).

Merry Hill Hill and former farm (TB Nov 5 1998 p10), now an area 0.75m ESE of Brierley Hill above Black Hill. Formerly in Kingswinford ancient parish. The hill, 450 feet high, is marked on old maps at the highest point in Ladywood Close, off Coppice Lane, and has a fine view of Rowley Regis church (TB Nov 5 1998 p10). The name appears in the 1851 census and is from Anglo-Saxon '(ge)maere' 'mearc' meaning a boundary; the hill lies close to Kingswinford ancient parish boundary (TB Nov 5 1998 p10). The present Merry Hill Shopping Centre to the NW, erected by Don and Roy Richardson, brothers, was built on the site of the Round Oak Steelworks (formerly Old Level Iron Works), closed in 1982, which in turn was built in the former Level Wood area (map of 1822) (MR pp54p,55p) (BCTV p14) (BHOP p9) (BCM spring 1995 p31). The record for pancake tossing in two minutes was set by Judith Aldridge at the Merry Hill Centre on Feb 27 1990 when she tossed one 281 times (GBR 1991 p181). By 1994 the centre was the largest shopping centre in Europe, with approximately 25,000,000 customers (The Guardian Dec 24 1994 p32).

Merry Hill Small, formerly isolated, district of Smethwick. The soap and red lead works of Messrs Adkins and Nock (later Thomas Adkins & Co) had based themselves here by 1818: This gave rise to the area being known in the C19 as the Soap Hole (STELE Sept 23 1950) (VCH vol 17 p94) (SHCB p7). There is a Merry Hill Court at the S end of Murdock Road off Foundry Lane, 0.25m NE of Smethwick old church.

Merry Hill Former hamlet (PENOP p7), now a suburb of Wolverhampton, 1.25m NNW of Penn. In Penn ancient parish, later in Penn Fields ecclesiastical parish. There were glacial boulders lying about the Merry Hill area (PPTP p37). The name appears as Murrihull in 1340 (HOWM p8). The church, St Joseph of Arimathea, Coalway Road, was rebuilt in 1990 (LDD). Was a ward of Wolverhampton borough by 1982.

Merryton Low Burial mound 1.5m NW of Upper Elkstones at SK 04136099 on a hill by Blakemere 1603 feet high (LGS p3). Formerly in Onecote township in Leek ancient parish. The burial mound is a listed monument. The burial mound could be the one in which was found a brass bolt of a Roman catapulta, as noted by Plot (NHS p403). The burial mound 350 metres SW of Merryton Low at SK 04006067 is a listed monument. To the W of Merryton Low at SK 04866124 was found a stone hammer of Neolithic or Bronze Age origin (NSJFS 1964 p22). Appears in the C13 as Meriloneslowe (VCH vol 7 p211) (SHC 1999 p5 note). The name is from Old English 'hlaw' a burial mound, and 'gemaere lone' by a boundary lane (VCH vol 7 p211). A Stirling 1 N 6075 aircraft crashed at Merryton Low on July 13 1942. The crew of

eight were killed except F/ SGT Regimbal who died some hours later (MD pp20-21). The hill is topped by a trigonometrical station pillar on which is a memorial to former members of the 5th Leek Battalion Home Guard who served in WW2 (HLSP pp72p,73). The pixies of Merryton Low are said to lure travellers away (SJC p5).

Mershac A late timber-framed cottage of the late C16 or C17 construction, beyond Halingdene, Penkridge. Stands next to another timber-framed cottage called Reynard's Cottage (PVH pp23il,24).

Mesty Croft SE district of Wednesbury. In Wednesbury parish. Wysti (see) or Wisti Bridge in a charter of about the later C12 has been identified with Mesty Bridge crossing the Tame, possibly carrying Crankhall Lane (HOWV p103). Believed to be formerly Mansty Croft. If so, Mansty is a Celtic word meaning 'the little path' (WAM p7). A Celtic derivation for Mesty Croft was not endorsed by Duignan (HOWV p5). St Luke's Mesty Croft ecclesiastical district was founded in 1944 (HOWY p313). The church, St Luke, on the corner of Elwell and Oldbury Streets, was built in 1973 (LDD).

Metal House Large farm on N side of Ash Bank road, to the WSW of Ash Hall. There may have been a tunnel from Metal House to the moated site at Simfields (FWMBS pp14-16).

Metchley Abbey House under 0.75m ENE of Harborne church at approximately Abbey Road off Greenfield Road, Harborne, just within the old Staffs border (1834 OS map). Built in c1800. Edward Augustus Freeman (1823-1892) historian and author of 'Old English History for Children' and 'History of the Norman Conquest' was born here (VCHWA vol 7 pp23,50) (PSS pp180-185 il) (GMH p20) (VFC p51). By 1994 the house was used for sheltered housing (OHOPP p25 il from a C19 print).

Metchley Grange In Harborne ancient parish. Was just in Staffs (VCHWA vol 7 pp23,50). Sir Henry Wiggin Bt (1824-1905), Mayor of Birmingham 1864-1865, MP for E Staffs 1880-1885, and Handsworth 1885-1893, High Sheriff of Staffs in 1896, resided here. The trees in the former grounds were still standing on the Metchley Grange housing estate in the early 1980s (GMH p15).

Metchley Lodge Stood in the Bantock Way area of Metchley Lane, Harborne. Occupied by Sir Granville Bantock (1868-1946) between the mid 1920s to 1934. He was Principal of the music school of Birmingham and Midland Institute, and succeeded Elgar as Professor of Music at Birmingham University. As a conductor he popularised the works of Sibelius (HOHE p33).

Mickle Hills 1.5m WSW of Lichfield cathedral on the S side of Walsall Road. There was a farm at Mickle Hills by 1800 (VCH vol 14 p112). Mickle Hill was a place on the route of the beating of bounds around Lichfield (SHOS vol 1).

Mickleholm By the Trent at, or near, Alrewas. From an old Norse word Mikill meaning large (HOA p18). Originally Muckleholm.

Micklewood Heath In Penkridge parish (VCH vol 6 p57). Has also appeared as Micclewood. There is a Micklewood Close, a modern street on an housing estate, S of Wolgaston Way on the S side of Penkridge.

Micklow The name is preserved in Micklow House Farm 1.25m SW of Stone. On the Eccleshall Road here has been seen a greyhound boggart (NSFCT 1900 p142) (FOS p18).

Middle Biddulph Former manor and liberty of Biddulph ancient parish (LCAST 1898 p64) (BALH p26 see map). The manor was created in 1189 with the division of the original extensive Biddulph (see) manor. It comprised the Biddulph church and Greenway Moor areas and was held by the de Biddulphs of Biddulph Old Hall (BALH p21). Has also appeared as Middleton (NSFCT 1898 p70).

Middle Cliffe House nearly 0.75m WSW of Bradnop. Formerly in Bradnop township in Leek ancient parish. There may have been settlement here by the later C13 (VCH vol 7 pp169-170).

Middle Hattons, The The middle farm of The Hattons (see) over 1.5m NE of Codsall, 200 yards S of the farm The Old Hattons. Built by 1775. In 1959 it was known as The Hattons (VCH vol 5 p33), but is referred to as The Middle Hattons on the current OS map 1:25,000.

Middle Hill S of Wedge's Mills, Cannock.

Middle Hills The top part of Morridge, 2.5m NNW of Upper Elkstones. Middle Hills was described as a 'miniature hamlet in the heart of the moorlands' in the early C20 and then contained the Royal Cottage (HLS p4).

Middle Hulme House at the foot of Hen Cloud 0.5m ESE of Meerbrook. Formerly in Leekfrith township in Leek ancient parish. There was a house here by the mid C13 (VCH vol 7 p193). Some say that Dieulacres Abbey had a grange here (HOLF p63), but the abbey had a grange at Nether Hulme to the W. Before the later C18 the road from Leek to Buxton passed through Middle Hulme (VCH vol 7 p195). The present Middle Hulme Farm is said to be the oldest dwelling in Leekfrith on account of the date 1118 appearing over the door. But this is probably a misreading of 1718. The front has been plastered (VCH vol 7 p194) (HOLF p63). Near Middle Hulme at SK 00276047 is a mound with a ditch about 40 paces in diameter and five feet high (NSJFS 1965 p43).

Middlehurst At Turnhurst there is a special school called this (Stoke-on-Trent A-Z)

Middle Ley 0.5m SW of Patshull Hall, Patshull.

Middle Linbrook Farm 0.5m W of Needwood was formerly possibly called Nettlebed (1834 OS map).

Middle Madeley Is the settlement NE of Madeley, between Madeley (or Great Madeley) and Little Madeley. The name does not appear on 1834 OS map.

Middle Mayfield Hamlet 0.5m W of the church at Mayfield. Is written North Mathfield on Bowen's map, and on other C17 and C18 maps written N. Mayfield, possibly N. should stand for Nether, since Middle Mayfield is not the northernmost Mayfield.

Middlemore Over 1m S of Sandwell Hall. Formerly in Smethwick township in Harborne ancient parish. Transferred to West Bromwich in 1966. Middlemore Industrial Estate was developed on the site of the Birmingham Railway Carriage and Wagon Works (built 1864) after it closed in 1963 (VCH vol 17 p93).

Middle Pool Former canal feeder pool on Pensnett Chase. Still survives as part of a recreation area (BHOP2 p106p).

Middleport The settlement in the Fowlea valley near Burslem began in the early C19 as a tiny hamlet to serve the Trent and Mersey Canal, and lay on the E side of the canal. Has become a suburb of Burslem. It was modelled on Longport and was situated N of Newport (see) (SL p236). Is collectively with Longport 'Shawport' in Arnold Bennett's novels. A house in Spencer Street represented the birthplace of Denry Machin for the film 'The Card' (1952) (Arnold Bennett and Stoke-on-Trent. EJD Warrilow. 1966 p118). As a child Bennett lived at No. 175 Newport Lane, which was for sale in March 1993 (ES March 18 1993 property pages).

Middleport Park Middleport. Laid out in 1908 on the site of the garden of St John's rectory house (VCH vol 8 p106).

Middle Ridware Former name for Pipe Ridware; it became Pipe Ridware in the C14. Another name for it about the same time was Parva (or Little) Ridware (DUIGNAN p127) (SL p56). Has also appeared as Media Ridware (Media = Middle).

Middleton Green Small hamlet on S-facing slopes high above Bear's Brook 1.5m ENE of Garshall Green. Formerly in Leigh township and ancient parish.

Midley Pits Tiny mere in marshland 0.5m W of Aspley, Slindon.

Miflins Valley On NW side of Stile Cop, WSW of Brereton.

Mile End Farm on the A53 0.5m SW of Blackshaw Moor.

Mile Flat, The Wall Heath, Kingswinford. In c1833 here was held the last so-called Black Country Blood Sports 'Olympics' (TB Aug 1983 pp1,5. Jan 1984 p29). The road from Wall Heath to Greensforge is called Mile Flat (OS map 1:25,000).

Milehouse Hamlet now merged into the suburbs of Newcastle-under-Lyme, 1m N of the town centre, or 1m WSW of Wolstanton. Part of the Roman road from Rocester to Chesterton was found in a garden in Links Avenue in Aug 1995 (ES Aug 4 1995 p3p). The name, which is preserved in Milehouse Lane, may be from an inn known as The Milehouse, which stood on the Liverpool Road at Cross Heath (ES Nov 5 1960). At a factory known as 'Factory 81' at Milehouse Rolls-Royce produced Britain's first jet engine, the Derwent jet, between Oct 1944 and Dec 1945 (ES Nov 14 1994 p8p).

Mile Oak District around the junction of A453 with the A5 1m WNW of Fazeley. The name refers to the oak which stood at the junction of what are now the A5 and A453; an hotel of this name now occupies the site (SPN p123). The mission church, St Barnabas, Manor Road, was built in c1970 (local info).

Miles Bank Minute district of central Hanley (H p47). There is a street called Miles Bank off Stafford Street. It takes its name from Thomas Miles, who in c1685 was manufacturing brown ware at a works near Foundry Passage and Bostock Square. A bank is another way of referring to a pottery or manufactory. During recent excavations (1910?) a sun-drying kiln was found. He appears to have adopted salt glazed very soon after it appeared on the market (H p47).

Miles Green Tiny hamlet 0.5m NNW of Alsagers Bank. In Audley parish. Formerly Meer Green, Mees Green (C18); had become Miles Green by 1841 (AOPP pl 26) (AHJ 1997 pp96,101). Mees in Early English means 'moss' (AOPP pl 26). However, Mees may be from the Mee family who tenanted a house near Mees Green in the C17 (SHC 1944 p42). According to Parrott it was named after a Thomas Mee who was the major tenant here in the early 1500s (AHJ 1997 pp96,101).

Miles Knoll Hill and area 0.75m SSE of Calton. In 1995 the ghost of a man flagging down traffic was seen on the A523 at Miles Knoll. It is said to have been that of man called Charlesworth, who was killed when his car, a Porsche, cashed at the same spot in 1989 (info from a Traffic Process Officer).

Milestone Edge (by 1983 increasingly *Millstone* CVH p173). In the Cheddleton area (CVH p20). A Bronze Age spindle-whorl, which went to the Potteries Museum, was found at Milestone Edge (NSFCT vol 80 p82. 1953 p107) (CVH p20). The name is from a milestone on the E side of the Leek-Cheddleton road; it marked four miles from Leek (CVH p173).

Mile Tree Place on Leek Moor by the Leek-Buxton turnpike road, where by the early 1770s there was a tollhouse (VCH vol 7 p99). Presumably there was a tree here called the Mile Tree.

Milford Village on the northern edge of Cannock Chase on a bank above the Sow 1m E of Walton-on-the-Hill. In Baswich township and ancient parish (W p439). The mound at cSJ 976208 on S side of Stafford-Rugeley road was recorded by Miss LF Chitty in 1926 (NSFCT vol 41 p141) (NSJFS 1965 p33). Milford is mentioned in documents from 1675, but it is not marked on maps until the C18 (BERK2 p11). The hamlet of Milford grew up round Milford Hall from the late C18 (VCH vol 5 p2). Air Marshal Sir Peter Terry's house at Milford was attacked by the IRA some time in the 1980s or the early 1990s. An arms dump of the IRA's was found on Cannock Chase. At Milford and along the Rugeley road has been seen the phantom cyclist of Weetman's Bridge.

Milford Common Common land 0.25m SE of Milford adjoining the N end of Cannock Chase. The name appears in a deed of 1821 (SPNO p31). Annual fairs were held on the common from the 1880s, and on every bank holiday in spring and summer by 1906, which were mainly attended by excursionists from Stafford who had travelled on the train (HCMBOPP pp63p,64). The original first hole of Cannock Chase Golf Club covered a part of the common (BERK2 p35 plan). On Sept 3 1954 a vidya was seen by Mr and Mrs Reece over Milford Common. It moved at the speed of a jet aircraft and looked like an orange (The Coming of the Spaceships. Gavin Gibbons. 1956).

Milford Hall House on N side of Stafford-Rugeley road, Milford, at SJ 965211. Built on the Mill House estate which was purchased by John Byrd in the early C18. John Byrd died in 1771 and was succeeded by his daughter Lucy. In 1771 she married Rev Richard Levett, vicar of West Wycombe (Bucks). During the last quarter of the C18 the hall seems to have been occupied by Ellen, Lucy's younger sister. The hall may have already been built by 1771 (BERK2 pp13il,14il), or it was built soon after 1771 (VCH vol 5 pp4,6). Pevsner says the hall is in the Georgian style (BOE p205). (MR p359). On Ellen's death in 1806 the whole estate passed to Richard, the son of Rev Richard Levett and Lucy Byrd. The house was enlarged in 1817 and has later additions (VCH vol 5 pp4,6). Seat of the Levetts and Levett-Haszards (SVB p169).

GROUNDS. E of the house there is an ornamental water supplied by the former mill stream. Near its N end, and to the E of the hall by the Stafford-Rugeley road, is a small brick bath house dating from c1803 (VCH vol 5 p4) (BERK2 p16p). This may be the same as a boathouse near the N end of the lake, which is of c1800 (BOE p205). There is a round, colonnaded summer house thought to have been made by Rev Richard Levett who was inspired by the 'temples' in West Wycombe Park (Bucks) (VCH vol 5 p4) (BOE p205) (BERK2 p15p). In the garden are four Ionic capitals probably from the E front of the house and some medieval stone fragments that possibly formed part of the original piers that supported the tower of the Anglo-Norman church of St Mary's, Stafford (OSST 1929 p40) (SKYT p922) (VCH vol 5 p4). In a gateway to the gardens of Milford Hall is stonework from the gateway of St Thomas' Priory (BERK p60) (BERK2 p18p). By a path is the 'Lover's Tryst' seat on which William Byrd Levett and Maud Levett carved the initial of their first name and a love-heart whilst courting in the early 1890s (BERK2 p18ps). The wrought iron entrance gates are from King's Bromley Manor and have the letter 'L' (representing the Lane family former owners of King's Bromley Manor) in the centre of each gate (BERK2 p13).

Milford Lodge On N side of Stafford-Rugeley road, to W of Milford Hall, Milford. Formerly Milford House. Built by John Twigg in the late C18 or the early C19. It passed from the Twiggs to William Swynnerton Byrd Levett in 1897 at which time the house became known as Milford Lodge (BERK2 p11p).

Milk Hill Hill in the Moorlands 2m W of Cauldon, 938 feet high. On it is a burial mound at SK 09034968. It is 13 paces in diameter and five feet high (NSJFS 1965 p52). The burial mound at SK 09284966 is a listed monument.

Milkhill Gate On the old road from Miles Knoll to Waterhouses (NSJFS 1972 p123). Has also appeared as Miskill Gate.

Milking Bank 2m SSW of Coseley, or 0.5m SE of Lower Gornal, or 1.25m W of Dudley.

Milking Bank Incline and tiny district of Heath Hayes 1m SSE of Hednesford. Appears as such in 1821. The name means 'bank where cows were milked' (SPNO p60).

Milking Gate N end of Sutton Park on Warws Staffs border on 1834 OS map. Gould notes that are six burnt mounds in Sutton Park at Milking Gate (MOA p15).

Mill Small hamlet now merged into Leek. Has also appeared as Lowe Hamill. Was cut off from the rest of Leek by Lowe Hill until James Brindley removed Lowe Hill to build Mill Street connecting the town with Mill. The name is from an old mill situated here established soon after the Norman Conquest and was the oldest building in the town at one time. Hamill means hamlet (NSFCT 1905 p159 note).

Mill Brook Tributary of the Dane (SPNO p14).

Mill Brook Runs from Enville Park joins the Stour at Dunsley.

Mill Brook A brook running S of Fazeley.

Milldale Tiny hamlet 0.75m SE of Alstonefield by the Dove, at S end of Mill Dale and N end of Dove Dale. Viators Bridge (see) crosses the Dove here (MR p230p). Formerly in Alstonefield township and parish. The mill from which Milldale took its name existed probably by 1282 (VCH vol 7 p9).

Mill Dale Next named dale, up river on the Dove from Dove Dale. (MR p230p). The W side is in Staffs, the E side in Derbys. Pitt in the early C19 described the dale as 'a long narrow vale or glen of great depth, the sides of which are composed of overhanging precipices of limestone, estimated to be from 100 to 150 yards of perpendicular elevation' (THS p39). Most have thought the 'Happy Valley' mentioned in the novel 'Rasselas' by Dr Johnson of Lichfield (see) was based on a stretch of the Manifold at Ilam. However, Roberts thinks 'Happy Valley' was based on Milldale (WTCEM p63).

Mill Dale Small dale to the E of Balterley. The traditional place for local people to go on Good Friday to eat hot cross buns (AOPP pl 23) (AHJ 1995 p111).

Mill End Minute hamlet under 1m NNW of Audley (NSJFS 1971 p67 see map). In Audley ancient parish.

Mill End Tiny district of NNE Penkridge, between Teddesley Road and the Penk (VCH vol 5 p107). Here was a corn mill, and although the name 'Mill End' does not appear on the 1884 OS map 6 inch, it appears on those of 1902 and 1924.

Milley's Hospital Beacon Street, Lichfield. Founded in 1424 by William Hayworth (or Heywood) bishop of Lichfield and Coventry, and said to have been first built in 1424. So called after Dr Thomas Milley, a Canon Residentiary of the cathedral, who endowed and rebuilt the hospital in 1504. Has also appeared as Dr Milley's Hospital. Consists of a brick building with stone quoins. Contains 15 dwellings and a chapel for the use of poor women (SHOS vol 1 pp234,346-347) (HOL pp512-513) (W pp508-509) (LAL p21p) (LPL p) (BOE p192) (DoE II*) (CL Oct 3 Date? p661). The hospital was referred to as St Katherine's Hospital in 1687 and was often simply known as the Women's Hospital until the C19 (VCH vol 3 pp275-278). The hospital was restored in 1906-7, 1953-4, 1967-8, and 1985-7 (VCH vol 3 p278. vol 14 p184). One of the seven Lichfield Morris dances is called 'Milley's Bequest' (LTM Nov 1971 pp10-11).

Millfields Area in the Black Country about Millfields Road, Bilston. There was a disaster at Millfields Ironworks foundry here when a boiler exploded on April 13 or 15 1862, 28 men died (ILN May 2 1857 p410il) (TB Feb 1977 p7. Dec 1987 pp16-17) (TEBC2 p82) or 27 died (BOP p130). For Millfield furnace see BCM Oct 1990 p62. In Jan 1914 the body of Kent Reeks was found on former waste ground off Millfields Road crossed by a footpath to Wrights Foundry and bordered on the W side by the Birmingham-Wolverhampton railway and on the E side by the former Dudley-Wolverhampton railway. The expensive clothes and possessions on Reeks' person were all that could identify him. Reeks, who had been shot three times, was of Australian birth but an America resident and had crossed the Atlantic on the Canadian Pacific liner, the Empress of Ireland. He had stayed at a Liverpool hotel until Jan 19 1914. It was thought that the killer or killers, who may have travelled with Reeks on the Empress of Ireland and stayed at the same hotel, had transported the body to the waste ground by car and that one of them had been familiar with the area (MMMR pp111-115). But no killer or motive could be found and the case remains unsolved (QMMH pp10-15) (MMBC pp114-128) (MM pp59-64) (TB June 1979 p5. July 1988 p29p. Aug 1988 pp1,5. May 1993 p22). The waste ground has recently been developed for housing and factories (MMMR p115).

Mill Fleam Tributary of the Dane (SPNO p14).

Mill Fleam Flows E of Walsall. Provided the power for a mill known as Peck Mill (IE p76). Leather dressing was carried on by it (SSE 1991 p77).

Mill Green Minute hamlet on Mire Brook consisting of about two houses 0.75m

SSE of Abbots Bromley.

Mill Green Fragmented small hamlet on an E-facing slope overlooking a tributary of Footherley Brook, 1.25m ENE of Aldridge. Formerly in Aldridge township and ancient parish (W p551). The census returns for the C19 show that Mill Green was then quite a thriving community (SNAR p38).

Mill Green Tiny area 0.5m ESE of Cannock about the Lichfield Road. In Cannock ancient parish.

Mill Haft Wood Wood 1m SE of Norbury. Name is from Norbury manor watermill (VCH vol 4 pp155,160). At approximately SJ 801222 was a windmill. It appears on Plot's map, deeds of 1712,1719, Jeffrey's map. It had gone by 1839 when a tithe map records only 'Windmill Field' (WBJ p32) (VCH vol 4 p160).

Mill Hill Hill 0.5m S of Wednesfield parish church. There may have been a burial mound on the summit known as South Low (see) in which some of the dead of the battle of Tettenhall or Wednesfield were buried (WFW p23). On Mill Hill was an early windmill which existed possibly until 1750, at approximately SO 943993 (WBJ pp22,42). Since 1930 the site of the windmill and Southlowfield has been occupied by AE Jenks and Casttell Ltd, manufacturers of metal pressings of all kinds (WFW p130). The same or another mill lay just N of the present Planetary Road (WFW p96).

Mill Hill On High Lane between Little Chell and Stanfield, E of Tunstall.

Millhouse Former hamlet, probably laying E of Patshull Hall, was an inhabited place by 1327. Millhouse was mentioned in 1716 but was subsequently depopulated in the landscaping of Patshull Park which took place in the C18. No settlement of Millhouse is shown on Yates' map (VCH vol 20 p162). A medieval village has been recorded at SJ 809010 to the E of Patshull Hall (SSAHST 1966 p49. 1970 p35).

Mill House Rakeway, at SK 015423. Built by the Mylles family of the old Rakeway House in 1635 (CCT p17). (LGS p109). Stone Jacobean house containing some good panelling and two magnificent oak tables (NSFCT 1921 p138). The house was known as Mill House Farm by 1981 (CCT p17).

Millhurst Name of an estate in 1574. Formerly a detached part of Farewell and Chorley parish. It was added to Streethay parish in 1879. Originated as part of a grant of land called Lindhurst given to Farewell Priory in the later C12. The house on which the estate was centred was N of Curborough House and it had been demolished by the mid 1980s (VCH vol 14 pp278-279).

Millian Brook To E of Seighford.

Million, The The main part of the forest on Enville Common.

Millmeece Hamlet on Meece Brook 0.5m NE of Slindon. Former township in Cotes quarter in Eccleshall ancient parish (W p375). Erdeswick's identification of Millmeece with DB Mess was accepted by Eyton (SHC 1914 p54 note), and has been accepted ever since. Millmeece has also appeared as Mulnemes (1289) (SSE 1996 p15) and Mill Meece. The name means 'mill marsh' (SSE 1996 p15). There was a mill here by 1298 which gave its name to the place (ECC p50). John de Harcourt held Chatcull and over 1000 acres in Podmore, Millmeece, Great and Little Bridgeford and Seighford by the service of bringing four men of Chatcull and Podmore to act as beaters to the bishop's hunt (ECC p13). Mr J Serjeant of Millmeece, whose arms appear on Plot's map, presented Plot with a crystallised stone (selenite) in the shape of the moon, rarely found in the county at the time (NHS p176 tab ii fig i). John Highfield of Millmeece, forger, was captured at his son's house at Johnson's Wood (see) in 1828 (CCSHO pp79-86). In 1914 SPWWC built a pumping station at Millmeece at SJ 830339 to supplement Hatton Pumping Station (see), 2m to the N. Its two steam engines - an Ashton Frost (of Blackburn) installed in 1914, and a Hathorn Davey (of Leeds) installed in 1927 - which pumped water from bore holes ceased commercial work on Dec 22 1979, but are still (1999) operated for tourists at weekends. They have acquired the name 'Gentle Giants' on account of the slow and quiet motion of the flywheels; coal for fuel came by rail to Standon Bridge station. In 1979 the pumping station converted to electricity. In May 1981 Severn Trent Water Authority leased the old engine room to the Millmeece Pumping Station Preservation Trust Ltd who turned it into a museum. By 1999 the museum had acquired a bust of 2nd Duke of Sutherland of Trentham Hall (see) formerly at Wall Grange Water Works by St Caena's Well (see) and the ceremonial spade used to dig the first sod of turf of Deep Hayes Reservoir (see) in 1847 (PWW pp12p of Sutherland bust, 17) (info Millmeece Pumping Station Preservation Trust) (Mill Meece guide) (IAS pp35p,165). From April 1943 there was a RNAS base for training WRNS air mechanics at SJ 838332. It was associated with the Royal Ordnance Factory at Swynnerton (see); it had no airfield and was known as HMS Fledgling (info Ron Balding) (Action Stations. 10. Supplement & Index. Bruce Quarrie 1987). Foot-and-mouth disease broke out at Mill Meece Farm in early 1968 (SN Jan 5 1968 p13).

Millpool Hateley Heath. Name is from a watermill and its pool on the Hobnail

Brook (TB Aug 1995 p6).

Mill Pot Cave Small fissure cave with two entrances opening into small chambers near the road bridge at Wetton Mill, at SK 09665609, partly excavated in 1962. A bucket-shaped urn found during the excavation has been displayed at the Potteries Museum (NSJFS 1971 pp39-47).

Millstone Green Former name for a common contiguous to Hanchurch Heath (THS p385) and the former name for Butterton (Newcastle-under-Lyme) village (gravestone in Whitmore churchyard) (SVB p48). Formerly in Swynnerton and Trentham ancient parishes (W pp425,434). A Birmingham barber called Harper caused a sensation by landing here in a balloon from Birmingham on Jan 4 1785, two years after the world's first balloon flight. The poem 'The Ballooniad' records the event (EAS p7) (TB Oct 1992 p13).

Milton Large village by the upper reaches of the Trent, 17m N of Stafford. Formerly mainly in Norton-in-the-Moors township and parish and partly in Hulton Abbey township in Burslem parish (W p400). Appears in 1227 as Mulneton (SSE 1996 p16). The **name** means 'mill tun' (SSE 1996 p16). The **church**, St Philip and St James, on the W side of Baddeley Green Lane and N of Millrise Road, was built in 1865 (BOE p267). Became a separate ecclesiastical parish in 1848 (ONST 1964 p251) or 1865, and a separate civil parish in 1894 (GLAUE p417). Milton was taken into Stoke-on-Trent county borough in 1922 (VCH vol 8 p260). **Canal.** The Caldon Canal, built through Milford, opened in 1777. The Johnson Brothers, when part of the Wedgwood Group, had three narrow boats specially built to carry ware from Hanley to their packing house at Milton on the Caldon Canal. The boats were called 'The Milton Maid,' 'The Milton Queen,' and 'The Milton Princess.' The Milton Maid turned turtle three times during its working life ('The Trent & Mersey Canal' in the Historic Waterways Scenes series. Peter Lead. 1980. pl 80) (SOTB p28p of the Milton Princess). The **railway** line from Milton to Cheddleton Junction, authorised on July 13 1863, opened to passengers on Nov 1 1867 (CVH p128). **Well-dressing.** There was a well in Milton on the site of the former TSB Bank (ES April 13 1996 p21). The custom of decorating the village well with flowers was observed at Milton on Ascension Day (Holy Thursday). Hackwood gives an instance of the New Well being decorated in 1884 (SCSF p30) (FOS p103). **Natives. Samuel Leigh,** the first Methodist missionary to go to Australia and New Zealand, was born in Milton in c1790. He left for the Antipodes in 1815. The Leigh Memorial Methodist Church, in Milton, was built in 1865 (Milton's Missionary. Pauline Jones) (ES June 20 1994 p9il). The actor, **Alan Lake** (born c1941), who married the filmstar, Diana Dors, is a native of Milton (ES April 29 1981 p3. April 24 1999 p17ps).

Milwich (locally *Mil-ich*). Ancient parish and village in undulating country in the valley of Milwich Brook (SSAHST 1994-95 p3), 6.5m NE of Stafford. A **Neolithic** or **Bronze Age** stone implement has been found in Milwich parish (VCH vol 1 p181) (NSJFS 1964 p30). A burnt mound, cut through by a steam at SJ 97563153 S of Milwich, was discovered in 1990. It is Bronze Age origin (SSAHST 1994-95 pp1-5). The **name** has appeared as Melewich, waste, in DB, Mulewiche, a manor, in DB, and Millewyz (C13) (SPN p84). It means 'mill village.' The mill may have been a salt mill; the village of Salt being only 3.5m away (DUIGNAN) (SPN p84). The parish **church**, All Saints, on a hill away from the main village, on the SW side, may stand on a Celtic pagan site, on account of the dedication to All Saints' which is linked with Celtic pagan New Year fires, and the remote situation of the church (NSFCT 1908 p112). There was a church at Milwich in the C12 (LDD). The font in the present church is of C13 origin and present tower was built probably in the late C15 (LGS p188). The nave is of 1792 (BOE p206). The church is chiefly notable for possessing the earliest dated (1409) **bell** in the county (LGS p188). A small oak model has been made of the bell axle (SLM Sept 1983 p12p). The original axle is thought to have been in use since at least 1409. John Shemilt carved the model. It passed to Shemilt's great grandson Randle Knight of Brookside House. It was for a long time kept at Milwich Hall (local info). Milwich parish formed out of Stone original parish probably after 1147; for about that year Milwich manor was given to Stone Priory. It was certainly founded by 1291 (SHC 1916 p195). In 1256 Milwich **manor** (comprising Milwich, Garshall and Coton) was equally divided between Geoffrey, son of Philip de Nugent, and Robert de Milwich. The castellated house or castle, known as Garshall Castle, of Hervey Bagot or Hervey de Stretton within Philip de Nugent's fee may have stood at the moated site at SJ 965335 between Garshall House and Oulton House. Of this moat, according to SLM, nothing is known (SLM Sept 1983 p11). SAH Burne thought there may have been a Norman castle in the Milwich area, yet to be discovered (ESH p59). (SHC 1909 p156-157 note) (NSFCT 1912 pp183,185) (ESH pp59,60) (CAMS p64). The manor house of the de Milwichs is probably represented by the moat at Milwich Hall. Besides the moats at Garshall and Milwich Hall, there

is another moat at Milwich (SHC 1909 p160 note). This may have been the moat which suggested to SAH Burne that there were two manor houses in Milwich, and that the village lay in two manors (ESH p59). Ranton Priory had land in Milwich and the priory may have had a grange here (VCH vol 3 p253). Robert de Grendon and others were granted a charter dated July 28 1304 to hold a **market** here on Fridays. The market had ceased by 1500 (NSJFS 1971 p51). **Civil War.** According to local legend some parliamentarian stragglers returning to Derby after losing the battle of Hopton Heath in March 1643 broke into Milwich church and attempted to loot the church plate. The churchwardens, however, put up a spirited defence putting soldiers to flight. The only casualty in the 'Battle of Milwich' was a dented chalice which was buried until after the Restoration (BFS p18). The story is doubted by some in the village (local info). Charles I passed through Milwich from Stone to Uttoxeter on March 24 1645 (NSFCT date uncertain, pre-1930 p184). At Milwich in the later C17 Plot noted an 11 year old child called **Franc Philips** who was neither male or female (NHS p268); a mare which unusually gave birth to twins (NHS p266); and an ivy bush at the S end of the vicarage house, which when it had run out of planes to cling to, grew out in branches like an oak or elm (NHS p206). SAH Burne found Milwich had been identified with **Muggleton** (ESH p31) - where, Muggletonians (a sect founded by John Reeve and Lodowick Muggleton (1609-98)) said God made his last revelation to man. Ilam has the same claim (ZSB). The village may be unusual in having had families of the names King, Bishop, and Knight (**names of chessmen**) all living in it at the same time, in the mid C19 (NSFCT 1993 p11).

Milwich Brook Runs through Milwich and joins Gayton Brook S of Coton, near Milwich (SSAHST 1994-95 pp1-5).

Milwich Hall Timber-famed building (DoE II) at Milwich. Built on a moated site which probably represents the manor house of the de Milwichs, who held half the manor of Milwich from 1256 (SHC 1909 pp156-157 note). The core of the present house was probably built by the Aston family of Tixall. Sir John Aston bought part of the Milwich estate in 1493 (NSJFS 1974 p126). The hall had an interesting collection of old deeds, books and firearms (NSFCT 1947 p169). Some items from the C16 to the C18 were found during restoration of the hall in 1969. They were of little interest, except for, perhaps, a glass bottle with the seal of Sandon Hall (NSJFS 1975 pp100-101) (SLM Sept 1983 p11). There is a sundial in the garden dated 1691, which may not have been meant for the hall. The village blacksmith has clamped the post to the base with four angle pieces but the sun and frost have warped them out of place (SLM spring 1957 pp28,29 il).

Mince-pie Hall Combridge, Rocester. Curiously designed house, situated on an eminence, with a turret and observatory, in existence by 1817 (THS p223). Demolished by 1996. Name is unexplainable (SPN p99).

Mincing Lane Blackheath. An old lane. Spelt on old maps Mincen Lane (TB Nov 1979 p25) and Minsin. There is a Mincing Lane at right angles to the Oldbury Road between Whiteheath Gate and Blackheath (Birmingham A-Z).

Minnbank Incline and house 0.5m S of Aston, Mucklestone. Appears as Mill Bank on 1834 OS map and Dower's map.

Minnie Farm 0.75m W of Alsagers Bank. Probably named from Minnie Pit (see).

Minnie Pit A sister pit of Podmore Hall. Halmer End. At SJ 793489. Or otherwise Podmore Hall No. 1 pit in the Bullhurst Seam. Named after Minnie Craig, daughter of a partner in the company of Cooper and Craig (AHJ 1996 p17). It had a disaster on Dec 16 1909 when an inrush of water killed one miner (LWF p117). Another disaster occurred on Jan 17 1915 and killed nine miners (Leigh says Jan 15 - LWF p117). Another disaster occurred in Jan 1918, some say on Jan 12 (SL p252) (TSS pp76,78) (NSFCT 1984 p16) (LWF p117), or on Jan 15 or on Jan 17 (IANS p36 or p38). This disaster was, perhaps, the worst colliery disaster ever of the North Staffordshire Coalfield: 155 (some say 156 - ES Aug 14 1993 p9) men died; 12 died in the explosion, the rest were poisoned by the resulting mixture of carbon monoxide and smoke. One man died in the rescue party. It practically wiped out the male population of Shraleybrook (SL p252). (Weekly Sentinel Feb 8 1980) (ES Dec 1 1980) (A pp126-128). The last body was not recovered until Aug 19 1919 (IANS p36) (LMV pp29-33). The disaster inspired a poem 'Miners' by Wilfred Owen (SL p252) (MR p168 - gives an extract). The mine was owned by 'The Midland Coal, Coke and Iron Company' who also owned the Burley Pit and Podmore Hall pits; it closed on May 1 1930 (IANS p134). 'Yedsticks' was the local name for the winding-gear of the pit (AOPP pl 49). A memorial made of Derbyshire stone to those killed in the disaster of Jan 1918 was erected in early Jan 1981 (ES Jan 8 1981 p1p) (Weekly Sentinel Jan 16 1981) (MR p169p). In 1988 a memorial with seats was erected by sculptors, Holmes and Eglin. There were proposals in Aug 1993 for the memorial to be restored after it had been vandalised in Oct 1992 (ES Oct 23 1992 p3pc. Aug 14 1993 p9p).

Minster Pool Pool lying directly to the SE of Lichfield cathedral and makes the cathedral unique amongst English cathedrals in lying beside a pool (BOE p174). It appears to have grown out of marshy land or water known as The Vivarium in medieval times. Minister Pool was formerly Middle Pool (VCH vol 14 p115) and had become known as Minister Pool by 1781 (John Snape's map of Lichfield). The pool had its own boat in about the C18, kept by the Corporation, to convey the inhabitants of the City to the Close (HOL p295). The view across Minster Pool to the cathedral is most picturesque and much photographed (Lichfield. Bell's Cathedral Series. 1908. p31p). In 1771 it was dredged and reshaped, trees were planted and Minster Pool Walk was created along the S bank (WMLB p86). Anna Seward, the 'Swan of Lichfield (see),' is said to have been an advocate in having the pool landscaped, having been impressed by the new Serpentine in Hyde Park, London (LAL p39). In 1840 a local physician denounced Minster and Stowe Pools as a source of disease and called for them to be filled in (VCH vol 14 p3). In 1855 Minister Pool came under the authority of the SSWWC (WMLB p86), and was a reservoir from 1856 until 1970 (VCH vol 14 pp114,116). In WW1 the pool and Stowe Pool were empty. A German Zeppelin is said to have passed over Lichfield, perhaps intent on a raid and because the pool was empty the Zeppelin lost its direction and Lichfield was spared (GHC p16).

Mires Brook Runs to from Bagots Bromley. Passes on the S side of Abbots Bromley and through Mill Green (ABMB). Tributary of the Blithe. The name means 'bog, swampy ground' (SPNO p14).

Mitchel Ancient estate in Upper Penn. 2.5m SW of Wolverhampton. The name means the 'great hall' (DUIGNAN).

Mitchell's Wood Farm Near High Carr, Red Street. The base of a carved Anglian cross now in Chesterton church was found here in Aug 1958. It had been used as a feeding trough since the end of the C19 (NSFCT 1959 p87).

Mitham House Croxall.

Mitre Cottage House on W side of A515 N of Newchurch and on N side of the B5234. Here was an ancient house, which may have provided refreshment to the monks of Burton Abbey on their way to the cell at Abbots Bromley. There is a small design of a bishop's mitre (hat) inset in the gable end relating to the abbey days (IVNF).

Mitton Minute hamlet 0.75m NW of Whiston, situated by Church Eaton Brook. In Penkridge ancient parish. Has appeared as Mutone (DB), Muton (1194), Motton (1206), Muiton (1221), Mytton (1453) (SPNO p86). The name is from Anglo-Saxon, and represents 'town at the junction of two streams' (DUIGNAN) (SSE 1996 p16).

Mitton Lodge Mitton Lodge Farm is 1m W of Whiston.

Mitton Manor House situated half way between Whiston and Mitton. The house known as Mitton Manor in 1959 was a mid C19 red-brick house with stone dressings (VCH vol 5 p117). It was for sale in 1995 (SLM Christmas 1995 p21p).

Mixon Tiny moorland hamlet high above the Hamps nearly 1.5m NNW of Onecote. Formerly in Onecote township in Leek ancient parish, behind Morridge in the Moorlands (W p729). The name appears in 1197 (VCH vol 7 p211) and as Mixne in 1219 (NSFCT 1908 pp144-145) and Mixen (H p14). It is from Anglo-Saxon and Middle English 'mixen,' 'mixne,' a mixen, dung-heap (DUIGNAN). Or 'the dung-hill' (SSAHST 1967 p34) (SPN p77) (SSE 1996 p16). Perhaps from 'ais' 'as' a mountain with the diminutive prefix 'mi' and the root 'ion' 'ainne' an enclosure (NSFCT 1908 pp144-145). The original settlement seems to have been at Old Mixon Hay (see), 1m to the WNW. The present hamlet of Mixon existed by 1775 and was occupied chiefly by copper miners in the earlier C19 (VCH vol 7 p212). At Mixon was mined lead (NSJFS 1961 p79). Hustings Farm, in the hamlet, used to serve as an inn (SVB p133).

Mixon Hill According to White seems to be the hill, 1394 feet high, to SW of Upper Elkstones, in Alstonefield parish; Upper Elkstones is situated on its eastern slope (W p742).

Moab's Washpot A small pool on the summit of Walton Hill near Clent (CR pp17-18).

'The Moat' House 0.75m NE of Cotton on W side of B5417. Takes its name from the large moated site slightly to its NW. The moat is of unknown origin, but is thought to be of about the C14 (HAF p391).

Moat Bank Farm Alrewas (HOA p33).

Moat Bank House Wall Lane, Wall. Near Moat Bank at SK 090066 was discovered a temporary camp. (Perhaps of Roman origin and linked to the Roman settlement of Letocetum). Part of the S and W ditches and the rounded SW angle were visible (NSJFS 1964 p41). The name is said to be from a rabbit warren which lay near here built by the mid C15 in the medieval form

of an embankment with a protective ditch (VCH vol 14 p292). Lord Henry Paget (later 4th Marquess of Anglesey), first master of the S Staffs Hunt, established in 1865, built the hunt's first stables at Moat Bank House. The kennels were here until 1873 when they moved to Fosseway Court (VCH vol 14 p286).

Moat Brook Runs from Bilbrook to Pendeford to the Smestow. The brook, so called by 1652, probably took its name from the moat surrounding the former Moor Hall; it gives its name to Bilbrook (SPNO p14) (VCH vol 20 pp12,79).

Moatbrook House Formerly Merridale House. Stands at the junction of Strawmoor Lane and Moatbrook Lane, 0.75m W of the church at Codsall (VCH vol 20 p77).

Moat Close Remains of a large rectangular moated site at SK 109187, S of Hamstall Ridware village near the Blithe. Traditional site of the seat of the de Ridwares, lords of Hamstall Ridware (SHOS vol 1 p152) (VCH vol 1) (SSAHST 1982-3 p42).

Moat Farm 1m NNE of Draycott-in-the-Clay. At SK 160304 is a fragmentary moat 240 feet by 210 feet (CAMS p64) (MR p174).

Moat Farm Ocker Hill. Built in c1780. Former home farm to nearby Walker's Hall. It was surrounded by a moat (VCH vol 1) (SSAHST 1982-3 p51) (WBOPP pl 120). Since it was surrounded by a moat the ancient house on this site may have been a manor house. Demolished by 1946 and a new housing estate built on the site (OH pp52-54). On Moat Farm estate a Roman coin a sestertius of Commodus was found in c1953 (NSJFS 1964 p38). (HOTIP pl v) (TB Oct 1996 p11p).

Moat Farm Great Wyrley. Farmhouse dating from c1700; an outhouse carries a keystone inscribed with the name of Thomas Lycett and the date 1758. Here are two sides of a rectangular moat (VCH vol 1. vol 5 p78) (Great Wyrley 1051-1951. J Homeshaw & R Sambrook. 1951) (SSAHST 1982-3 p58). See Moat Hall.

Moat Hall There are two schools called this in Great Wyrley, 0.25m SSE of the church. Possibly formerly called Moat Farm. Two sides of a rectangular moat are said to have been in existence at Moat Farm, Great Wyrley, in the 1950s (VCH vol 5 p78).

Moat Hall House S of Hanbury. Disappeared. Could be same as Moat Hall S of Newborough, or more likely a moat at Woodend, which has not disappeared.

Moat Hall House by Moat Hill, 0.5m S of Newborough. Formerly in Newborough township of Hanbury ancient parish (W p563).

Moat Hall Wednesfield. By Moat House Primary School, off Lichfield Road?

Moat Hill Hill 0.5m S of Newborough. Here is a moat at SK 136246 (CAMS p64).

Moat Hill Area of Walsall about Alumwell, S of Wolverhampton Road (VCH vol 17 p222). The name moat is probably from the moat of Walsall manor-house.

Moat House Timber-framed house at the S end of Acton Trussell village. Stands on the site of the former manor house of Acton Trussell (see) and was the seat of the Trussells until the later C16. In 1575 the lords of the manor conveyed the Moat House to Matthew Moreton of Engleton. In 1593 he sold it to Lewis Dickinson. The oldest part of the present house is the E side (BERK2 p121), and this was constructed in the early C16 (VCH vol 5 pp12,14) or at the end of the C17 when it was owned by the Dickinsons (BERK2 p121). The house stayed with the Dickinsons until 1778 (BERK2 pp122p,123p). It was later owned in trust by the Barlows who sold the estate to the Littletons of Teddesley. Moat House still formed part of the Littleton estate in 1947 (VCH vol 5 pp12,14). In June 1988 the house became a restaurant (PVH pp36,37il) (SLM July Aug 1998 pp48-50pcs). The house was surrounded by a moat (SSAHST 1982-83 p33) (CAMS p63). Brindley used the W side of it for the Staffs and Worcs Canal cutting. (DoE II).

Moat House Large, square moated site 0.5m WSW of Essington, on the N side of Blackhalve Lane on the border with Essington township, at SJ 954030. 'Le Mot' in Essington is mentioned in a grant of 1321. There was a cottage on the site until c1930; VCH vol 1 erroneously states that the moat was filled in in c1890 (WFW p70) (SSAHST 1982-3 p41) (CAMS p64).

Moat House Farmhouse-looking building at Great Wyrley. Seat of the Lycett family. Some windows have been bricked up to avoid window tax (CCAP p18p). The moat to the N may be the site of the manor house of Great Wyrley. The foundation stones were carted away in c1800 (many were used in cottages in Walsall Road near the post office). The area surrounding the moat has the reputation of being the oldest inhabited part of Wyrley and is known locally as Wyrley Town (GWY p facing p21, p22).

Moat House Medieval open hall house on the N side of the Stafford-Newport road (A518) in Haughton. It was built in c1430 and was substantially altered in the C17; there is the inscription 'Thomas Reynolds, 1680' above the doorway. The moat surrounding the house, which may have surrounded the original manor-house (VCH vol 4 pp136,138) (SSAHST 1982-83 p43) (info Alan Appleby), had disappeared by the end of the C20. The house, known as Moathouse Farm prior to 1991, was renamed Moathouse by the Applebys owners and restorers of the house since 1991. The Applebys have felt the presence of the ghost which haunts this house: A lady's maid, she always keeps one room dust free and is known by them as 'Mary from the dairy' (SVB p92) (SMM p53) (info Alan Appleby). It is not the same as Haughton Old Hall (see).

Moat House In SW part of Lichfield cathedral Close. Built in the earlier C18 by Thomas Ame. Is adjoined on the S by Langton House (VCH vol 14 pp58 see map, 67).

Moat House 0.25m WSW of Longdon. To the E of the house at SK 077139 are the remains of a possible moat, which may represent the site of Broughton Hall, if Broughton Hall was moated (SSAHST 1982-3 p44) (CAMS p64).

Moat House 0.75m N of Pelsall church, at SK 024043 (SSAHST 1986-87 pp51-54). In this area there appears on the 1834 OS map a place called The Moat. In the late C18 Shaw noted an estate, place, or field name called the Moat House at Pelsall (SHOS vol 2 p61) which may be identified with this place. The present Moat House or Moat Farm (1981) in the Moat Farm Way and Moats Close area of Pelsall Wood takes its name from a nearby moat, measuring 168 feet by 80 feet (VCH vol 1 p365) (SSAHST 1982-83 p34) (SHOP p2) (MR p253) (SNBP p86p of Moat Farm in 1967). The supposed moated site was excavated prior to housing development in 1982 and no moat was found, nor any evidence for a building earlier than the C17 (SSAHST 1986-87 pp51-54). There is another moat at Pelsall in the vicinity of Pelsall Hall (see).

Moat House C18-looking house with a portico, between Mill Walk and Newport Road, Stafford, approached over a wooden bridge. Near Stafford town watermill; the mill pool may have been mistaken for a moat. Formerly known as Holly House. In the C19 the house was occupied by the mill owner. It appears to have been given the name Moat House in the C20. Between 1903 and 1907 it was a school which became Stafford Girl's High School. Later it became the HQ for the local branch of the NFU. By 1996 it was offices (SSTY p228) (SAC p64). It is haunted by several ghosts, one being a cat, another a figure in white, another a young girl in a head band and shawl (info Bruce Braithwaite).

Moat House House situated on the N bank of the Tame in Lichfield Street, Tamworth. Said to have been built in 1572 by William Comberford (SHOS vol 1 p422) (W p621). Others say it was built by Richard Jekes and passed to the Comberfords in 1591 (LTM Sept 1971 pp18-19). William Comberford entertained Prince Charles here when James I stayed at Tamworth Castle in 1619 (NSFCT 1912 p200). After the Civil War William Comberford had all his estates confiscated and the house passed into the hands of Thomas Fox a former captain of the parliamentary forces. Fox sold the house in 1663 to Sir William Boothby. In the C18 the house passed to the Littletons, and the Wolfertons. In 1752 it was bought by William Abney, Whig barrister of the Inner Temple (SHC 1922 pp280-281). In 1757 he sold it to the 1st Marquis Townshend of Tamworth Castle (see) (or it was purchased by the 2nd Marquis in 1767 - NSFCT 1912 p200) for the use of his steward but the Marquis thought so highly of the house that he moved in himself and lived here until 1811 (LTM Sept 1971 pp18-19il). From 1815 it was the residence of Dr Robert Woody and in 1821 the house passed to him (NSFCT 1912 p200). From 1815 it was a private lunatic asylum until reverting back to a private house in the 1860s. The house was offered to Tamworth Corporation in 1950 (LTM Sept 1971 pp18-19). The hall upstairs was 50 feet by 18 feet but was by Shaw's time divided into two. On the ceilings were the arms of Comberford, Beaumont, Leventhorp, Heronvile, Sutton (alias Dudley) of Dudley Castle (see), and Fitzherbert of Staffordshire. (SHOS vol 1 p422,423 pl 38 shows an engraving of the hall) (W p621) (LGS p230) (BOE pp278-279) (SGS p168) (DoE II) (MR p322) (TDOPP p42p). The moat from which the house takes its name still surrounds the house, and was fed by the Tame (SSAHST 1982-3 p48). There is a C18 gazebo with a pyramid roof in the garden (BOE p278).

Moat House Farm nearly 0.75m NE of Wednesfield, formerly in Wednesfield chapelry. A moated farm here was owned by John Gough in 1661. In the Gough family deeds of 1774 'The old moathouse' is mentioned (THS) (WFW p66). A farm, known as the Moat House in the corner of the present Hyde Road and Moat House Lane East, was inhabited in 1840 but not in 1851 (WFW p66). About 1860 a house was built near the Lichfield Road which assumed the name of Moathouse Farm, despite being at some distance from the original Moat House, which in the C20 became known locally as Hyde's Farm. Hyde's Farm was demolished prior to the construction of the Moathouse Estate, an overspill housing estate for Wolverhampton, in 1953/4. Has also appeared as Moat Leasow (VCH vol 1; confuses old Moat House moat with

the moat of Moat House, Essington) (WFW p66) (SSAHST 1982-3 p55) (WHTOP p72p of Moathouse Estate shopping centre) (BTW p102p).

Moat House Former house on a moated site at SO 963988, Moat Street, in The Manor area of Willenhall. It was the residence of the Leveson family from some time prior to Edward I's reign as leasees of the prebendal manor and holders of a considerable estate in the king's manor of Stowheath. The Willenhall portion of the estate passed to Thomas, younger son of Thomas Leveson, his elder brother Sir Walter inheriting the more important Wolverhampton part. John Leveson, the descendant of Thomas Leveson Jnr died in c1750, leaving his sister, Elizabeth, sole heiress; she proceeded to sell the whole estate (HOWI pp149-150). The Levesons are said to have sold the house in c1763 (SNW pp31,41). In the earlier C17 the house appears to have been a Jesuit boys' school. It was raided in 1635. In or after 1655 John Leveson brought to the school for safekeeping those remaining relics of St Chad given to him by the late Peter Turner SJ who had been entrusted with them by the Hodsheads of Woodsetton Lodge (see). In 1658 parliamentarian soldiers discovered the box with the relics in the house and stole many of them. Not all were taken and before March 2 1661 William Atkins SJ, probably the chaplain, had a new box made for what remained. The relics were last noted here in 1667 and were taken at some later date to Boscobel (see) (SCHJ No. 9 pp12-13). It was assessed for hearth tax in 1666 when it was the largest house in Willenhall. The house was destroyed by 1800; the moat was destroyed by the construction of the Midland Railway in 1876 (HOWI pp150-151) (SSAHST 1982-83 p49). The grounds covered an area extending from the present Leveson Street in the N to Wood Street in the S and from Stafford Street in the W to Cemetery Road in the E. There was a lake in the grounds (SNW p49).

Moat House Bridge Crosses over the Staffs and Worcs Canal 1m NW of Shareshill. To W of the bridge at SJ 930074 is a homestead moat, noted by Shaw in the late C18. Moat House or the moat was the late C18 property of Thomas Philips of Shareshill. The moat was partly damaged when the Staffs and Worcs Canal was constructed (VCH vol 1 p366. vol 5 p173) (SSAHST 1982-3 p47) (CAMS p64).

Moat House Farm Gayton. Or on OS map (SJ 978283) Moat Farm, and has been known as Moat House and may have been the manor house of Gayton (NSFCT 1912 p186). High up on an external side wall of the house is a tablet depicting a monkey and underneath the motto 'Croma Boo' ('I Burn') and the initials 'J.F.C.' or 'J.F.G.' According to tradition the tablet was placed there to commemorate a pet monkey which had rescued a baby or child from the attic during a fire (STM Dec 1965 pp42p,43). But the monkey crest, motto and initials relate to the family of Fitzgerald of Cruim Castle, Ireland, a member of which family was at Gayton as lay-impropriator of the parish church and lived at Moat House (W) (NSFCT 1924 pp102-103. 1933 pp175-176) (STM Dec 1965 pp42p,43). Surrounding the house is an oval moat (CAMS pp10 plan,64). To the W of the house, at SJ 977282, is a three-acre moated site, massively embanked on three sides. This, thought SAH Burne, was a vivarium (fish pond) in the C13 (ESH p27) (NSFCT 1982 p10).

Moat Junction Junction of Wednesbury Oak Canal with its Ocker Hill Branch (BCM autumn 1995 p18).

Moat Meadow Part of a moat was visible at SP 011949, Friar Park, in 1836, but there was no trace of it in 1958. According to tradition the site represented the friary attached to Sandwell Priory (SOWB p23) (SSAHST 1982-3 p51).

Moat Site, The 1m W of Walsall, at SP 001985. Was identified by Frederick Willmore as the location of the medieval manor-house of Walsall (HOWW p239). The location of the hall so far from the centre of Walsall reflects the division of the manor into two parts: Borough and Foreign. The manor house was formerly surrounded by the park belonging to the manor, known as Walsall Park (see). The platform moat was in existence by 1388-9 but the manor buildings probably pre-date this. The Ruffus' were lords of the manor of Walsall to 1247: The Bassetts of Drayton were from 1338 to 1390; Ralph last Lord Bassett was born here (HOWW p239). The house was described as 'The Manor House within the Moat of the Park' in 1380. The Bassetts were succeeded in 1390 by the Beauchamps, earls of Warwick, who probably never lived here. They may have installed their parker at the house. There was a Park Farm (see) a short distance to the S of the moat. The manor house was either a total ruin by 1576 or had disappeared by then. A survey of 1617 implies the manor house had disappeared by then. In 1763 there were two houses in evidence within the moat belonging to a Mr Holmes. In 1859 the public park known as 'Moat Garden' was opened on the site. White mentions the 'Moat Garden' in 1851. The park closed in 1865 and the site was leased out as building land. Soon afterwards the northern side of the moat had to be filled in to make way for houses. The Belle Vue Inn has also occupied part of the site. The rest of the moat site, after being excavated in 1972-74, became the site for the extension of Manor Hospital, built in the late 1970s (W p649) (SSAHST 1974-75 pp19-53. 1976-77 pp29-45. 1982-3 p48) (VCH vol 17 p171) (NSFCT 1982 p19) (HOPL). A Roman brass padlock was found on the site during excavations in 1978 (info Walsall Museum).

Moat Spring Sulphurous spring (HOU p15), at SK 111286, near Buttermilk Hill, Marchington Woodlands. The name is possibly from the listed monument, a quadrilateral enclosure of 3,600 square yards surrounded by a moat off Tinker's Lane at SK 10872891 (CAMS pp10 plan,63). The name of the spring is preserved in Spring Moat Farm at Gorsty Hill, over 0.5m to the WNW.

Mobberley Small hamlet on an undulating bluff above the confluence of the Tean and Cecilly Brook 1.25m S of Cheadle. In Cheadle parish. There is a toll house on the Upper Tean-Cheadle road at SK 006405 (IANS pp19,49p). Mobberley Quarry (sand and gravel) is slightly to the SE.

Mobberley Brook It is joined by Cheadlemill Brook and in its turn Cecilly Brook to the Tean. The name may be from someone with the surname Mobberley, a name from the place, Mobberley in Cheshire (SPNO p15).

Mobb's Bank Formerly in Willenhall chapelry in Wolverhampton ancient parish (W p161). Has been located to the area formerly called Little Island (see), NE of Willenhall, or in the present Rose Hill area (SNW p58), S of Willenhall.

Mocc's Low A long lost burial mound at Moxley. Early forms of Moxley suggest the place was named after a burial mound to one Mocc (DUIGNAN), who, perhaps, was killed in the battle of Wednesbury.

Mockbeggar Hall Former brick, oval-shaped house 1m ENE on or just off, to the W of, Broad Lane, Essington. In Bushbury parish. It was built in the late C18 (RS p122) or between 1730 and 1780 (TB April 1993 p13p) by the Vernons of Hilton Hall for their workmen in the style of an Italian barracks (DUIGNAN) (SPNO p51). Later appears as Colliers' Castle. However, Oakden says Colliers Castle was a reference to coalpits, used sarcastically (SPNO p50). Mockbeggar Hall was demolished in 1936. It received its name from beggars or vagrants who saw the building from a far and mistook it for a gentleman's seat and duly approached it for alms but discovered the occupants were as poor they were, hence it gained the appellation of Mock Beggar Hall (RS p122). LB Jackson implies that the name arose from 'Mockbeggar' one of nearly 200 supernatural beings identified by folklorist Michael Aislabie Denham (TB Feb 1993 p25). (HAS p45) (ESSN pp24p-25).

Mockbeggar's Hall Near Rocester (NSFCT 1927 p168).

Moddershall Village in a pretty dell on a tributary of Scotch Brook 8.5m N of Stafford. Formerly in Kibblestone township and quarter in Stone ancient parish (W p364). Over 0.25m WSW is Lower Moddershall. The manor of Modredeshale appears in DB. The name is from 'Modred's hall' probably being the first Angle to settle there (DUIGNAN) (SOSH p73). Or 'Modred's meadow' (NSFCT 1945 p91). Or 'Modred's nook' (NSJFS 1981 p2), or corner of land (SPN p84), or hollow (SSE 1996 p16). Or 'Modred's settlement in a remote valley' (BNDA p3). Became a township between 1851 and 1872 (KD 1872). With Oulton became a separate ecclesiastical parish in 1879 (KD 1912). The mission church, All Saints, on the W side of the Knenhall road at the N end of the village, was built in 1903 (BOE p206) (LDD). It was taken down and rebuilt on firmer foundations in 1993, owing to mining subsidence (SN May 21 1993 p12p). Foot-and-mouth disease broke out in Moddershall parish at Idlerocks (see) in late 1967. Moddershall has been described as a Little Switzerland, an allusion to the picturesqueness of the village, particularly about the mill pool by the Boar Inn (see), and Idlerocks dell (ES Aug 17 1996 pp20-21). Prospect House or Rose Cottage was haunted, perhaps in the C19, by a lady traveller who had called at the house in a poor condition and died before morning; her ghost only being 'laid' when the roof of the house was taken off (NSFCT 1900 pp142-143). The turn of phrase 'fair to Moddershall,' instead of, presumably, 'fair to middling or moderate' was used as a reply by a Barlaston man living in the 1980s when asked how he was (local info).

Moddershall Grange 1m NE of Moddershall.

Moddershall Oaks Area to the N of Moddershall. A man was thrown from his horse on the road through Moddershall Oaks and died. The next day his body was found on the road and the horse was found grazing in a nearby field. The man's ghost has been seen riding along this road riding a white horse. By the late C19 this locality was known as 'the frightening' (NSFCT 1900 p143).

Moddershall Oaks House on a hill to the N of Moddershall designed and built by Josiah Clement Wedgwood IV, a descendant of Josiah Wedgwood I of Etruria Hall (see), in 1907-8. The house, usually known as the Ark, is a long 'ranch' type wooden bungalow with an open verandah. It was built in South African style; Josiah Clement Wedgwood IV previously having spent time in South Africa (A Personal Life of the Fifth Josiah Wedgwood 1899-1968. John Wedgwood).

Moddershall Old Manor House Moddershall. Is now used as riding stables (SVB p126).

Moddershall Valley Name for valley through which Scotch Brook runs. There were watermills in the valley as early as the C12 (SPJD p78). In the last two centuries there have been at least eight mills situated in the valley. Many started out as cloth fulling mills but were converted to grinding flint for the pottery industry, they are: Boar Mill, Coppice Mill (or Shardlow's Mill) (see), Hayes Mill (or Oulton Mill) (see), Ivy Mill (see), Mosty Lee Mill (see), Ochre Mill (see), Splashy Mill (or Top Mill) (see), Weaver's Mill (see), Wetmore Mill (see) - (IAS p43) (IANS p91) (SPJD pp78-83). In 1979 it was designated a conservation area (SVB p135).

Moden Hill Former small hamlet high on a hillside (AMS p447), S of Cotwall End, N of Ruiton. In Sedgley ancient parish. The name has appeared as Mouidenhill (Sedgley PR 1587) and occurs in Sedgley PR in 1634/5 and 1654/5, and on 1947 OS map 1:25,000 (sheet 32/99) at SO 918927 and has appeared as Modenhill (SNSV vol 2 pp57,72). According to Underhill it stands high on a hillside. The name may be from St Modwen of Burton (AMS p447). Or owing to the very steep incline of the meadow, it has been suggested that it was 'mow-down-hill' (PHS p24).

Modwenstow Shaw says Burton upon Trent was anciently called this (SHOS vol 1 p231). Or more precisely Leland called the Island of Andressey Modwenstow (W p533). The name may refer to Modwen's settlement on the Island of Andressey, or the later medieval settlement situated about the C13 chapel. Modwenstow was referred to as Saint Modwen's Orchard in 1925 (NSSG p12).

Moggs Swampy areas in Lichfield which had been reclaimed from pools about Lichfield cathedral, especially on the W, S and E sides. A part appears to have been known as The Vivarium (see) in medieval times. In medieval times there was a pool W of Bird Street, at some time called Upper Pool. Land about it was known as 'the moggs' in 1498, formerly the word had been a personal name. The southern part of this was in the C17 known as Swan Piece (later Swan Moggs). Swan Moggs was drained under the terms of a lease of 1800. Another stretch of Moggs, known as Stowe Moggs (so called in the late C18 when it existed) was an area of marsh W of Stowe Pool (VCH vol 14 p110). Upper Pool may be identifiable with Clayton's Bishop's Pool (or Bishop's Fish Pool) which by 1730 had slited up completely and was a swamp; it became known as Swan Moggs (CCHCB p76) (LHSB L.6). The Moggs, to the W of Bird and Beacon Streets, is now the Museum Gardens and Beacon Park (LAL p2).

Mole Cop An eminence a little to the S of the old township of Great Fenton. There were some indications that on the top of the hill was an early British burial mound (NSFCT 1926 p136). Appears on Hargreaves Map 1832. It was originally called Culverd's Low and appears as this in an old cartulary of Burton Abbey. It has also appeared as Cop Low (NSFCT 1926 p136). Present site is approximately Brookside Drive.

Molineux Fold Between Molineux House and Molineux Alley.

Molineux House and later Hotel. North Street, Wolverhampton (TB Aug 1989 p17p). Situated across the ring road from the RC church of SS Peter and Paul, and the facade faces the Ring Road. Built before 1720 (TB Nov 1996 p6p) or in c1740-50 by ironmonger Benjamin Molineux (d1772), with later additions (WMAG April 1964 p38. Jan 1965 pp26-27il). Mander says it was built by John Molineux sometime between 1740-50 (HOWM p133). The house was chosen for the S Staffs Industrial and Fine Arts Exhibition which was opened by Earl Granville on May 11 one year (WAIW vol 3). The Molineux family are said to originate from Flanders and to have come to England in the early C14 (TB Aug 1994 p25). The house remained in the Molineux family until the 1860s, when Oliver Edgar McGregor bought the house and converted it into a licensed premises. By 1889 the house had become the headquarters of Wolverhampton Wanderers. In 1901 the hotel was bought by Wolverhampton brewery, W Butler and Co. It was listed Grade II in 1949 and Grade II* in 1977. In 1958 the S wing was demolished. In 1969 the hotel was bought from Bass, Mitchells and Butlers, by Wolverhampton Wanderers FC. In 1979 it closed. It was in a very poor state of disrepair by at least 1995 and was still derelict in Sept 1997 (BOE p319) (SGS p186) (BCM Jan 1982 p40. Oct 1982 pp6-7p of poster of the hotel in its heyday?) (WPOPP vol 1 pp30p of in 1866, 31p of in 1915) (TB March 1995 6p) (Wolverhampton Chronicle Sept 12 1997 p32ps) (WOLOP p93p of in 1950). A 60 feet long long whale, called 'Jonah,' was exhibited on a long, low multi wheeled trailer at the Molineux Hotel in July 1954. It weighed 69 tons. In order to preserve the body 2,200 gallons of formalin solution were pumped through the whale's veins. It was shown in Hanley in the 1960s (TB Feb 1994 p29. March 1994 p9p). The gardens of the house, which have been described as magnificent, swept down to what is now Waterloo Road (HOWM p133). The grounds were acquired by Wolverhampton Wanderers FC in 1901 and became part of the club grounds. The ghost of a young boy dressed in the clothes of the early 1950s and wearing a Wolverhampton Wanderers scarf and carrying one of the rattles popular at the time has been seen in Molineux Alley; he always appears in a slight mist (GOM p16).

Monetvile Appears in DB as Monetvile and has appeared as Montville. Long unidentified. Eyton in Domesday Studies etc; The Staffordshire Survey p72 thought it in Cuttlestone hundred as stated in DB. In 1887 TJ de Mazzingi thought it was at Castlehill, the hill on which Stafford Castle stands, and that it should be read 'Montvile,' 'the mount town' (SHC 1887 part 1 p16). WF Carter, who agreed with Mazzinghi about its situation but disagreed with him over its etymology, thought the name represented 'the vill of the mint' and was the site of Stafford mint (SHC 1908 pp227-230. 1916 p170) (DB. Phillimore. 1976. notes). The site of Monetvile was still unidentified by 1952 (NSFCT 1952 p36). Recently thought to be the village at the foot of Stafford Castle (on SE side) deserted by 1450. The village was found after excavations in the 1980s. Its church may have been the present St Mary's at Castle Church (MR p285) (SAC pp80 plan, 82) (HOS 1998 p32 plan).

Money Lands Formerly in Wigginton township in Tamworth ancient parish. On NW side of Wigginton is a flat of lands so called because, according to tradition, many ancient coins and bones of men have been ploughed up. There is some account of this in Magna Britannia (SHOS vol 1 p432) (W p626). (THM vol 6 p31). Has also appeared as Money Flats, and Low Flat (SVB p180).

Moneymore 1m SSW of Weeford. Has also appeared as Moneymoor (1834 OS map). There is a windmill situated at SK 135020. A windmill existed here in 1775 and 1818. It probably became disused before 1914 (WBJ p31 il vii). (WIS pp13p,23). In 1998 Moneymore Cottages were occupied by ecology demonstrators protesting against the Birmingham Northern Relief Road, due to be built through the site. The cottages stood about 200 yards from the protesters' main camp at Green Wood (see). On Dec 21 1998 after nine months of occupying tunnels underneath the cottages and the cottages themselves, the protesters were evicted so that the road could be built (BBC 1 Midlands Today. Nov 24 1998. Dec 21 1998).

Moneystone Area on the N side of the Churnet Valley 2m N of Oakamoor. In Kingsley ancient parish. Money is a corruption of 'main, moin, muine,' Old Celtic 'meini, menigo,' a stone (NSFCT 1910 p162). Soft pink sandstone was quarried here until 1970 (HAF p17); the last train load of sand from the British Industrial Sand plant at Moneystone left in Aug 1988 (COPP2 p109p).

Monkey Island District of Heath Town, in the vicinity of Old Heath Road. Perhaps from a tool called a monkey used for stamping by ironworkers, who mostly lived in this area (TB Feb 1985 p15).

Monkey Tree Cottage 0.25m NNE of Heighley Castle.

Monkhouse North part of Cheadle. The Abbot of Croxden had a cell on the summit of Cheadle Park (HOC p34). Prince George, Duke of Kent (1902-1942), a younger son of George V, opened the Monkhouse Community Centre in Back Street on July 13 1934. Back Street was renamed Prince George Street, after his visit (ACOPP p24p).

Monk's Coach-house Road Strip of ground outside Cheadle Park (HOC p34) or Abbots Coachway Road (ESH p28). The Abbot of Croxden had a cell on the summit of Cheadle Park (HOC p34).

Monks Clownholm House 0.75m SE of Rocester, in a peninsula protruding into Derbys and on the E of the Dove. Has appeared as Abbots Clownholm (Yates' map), Abbots or Monks Clownholm (1834 OS map), and Monk's Clownholm (1987 OS map 1:25,000). To the N is Abbotsholme School, always in Derbys, the first school in the country to teach human reproduction (GBR). The name seems to be from it probably being once the residence of the dispossessed of Rocester Abbey; in this area was a residence of William Grafton last abbot of Rocester (NSFCT 1932 p113).

Monk's Dock Former canal boat yard near Dudley Road, Tipton. It was owned in the early C19 by a Thomas Monk, boat builder and canal carrier, who was born in Stourport in 1765 and died at Tipton in 1843 (BCM Jan 1978 p6p,8-10,12-14,16). He built the 'Euphrates' a very swift flyboat, locally famous for its record passages to and from Birmingham and Wolverhampton. Captained by John Jevon, it is stated to have been one of the finest packets of its kind ever built. Monk was a past master at boat and barge building and is said to have come to Tipton from the coast of Ireland, where his family were engaged in small craft construction. At the beginning of the C20 some pilot boats were still being called 'Monkey' boats, derived from Monk's boats, he being the pioneer of this type of canal carrier. The name Monk's Dock was in use by 1851 (HOTIP p192) (OH p62). Monk also gave his name to Monk's Wharf and Monk's Basin, if not the same as Monk's Dock (BCM Jan 1978 p6p,8-10,12-14,16).

Monks Green Whittington, Kinver. Mentioned in 1574. The name may be from a connection with Combermere Abbey, Ches, which held land in Whittington in c1200 (VCH vol 20 p137).

Monks Neil Park Public park at Great Chell created on the site of a disused colliery (MR p177). Opened in 1972 (POP p64).

Monks Path Between Trysull and The Bratch.

Monk's Walk Broughton. A walk along a double avenue of limes on the boundary side of some fish pools at Broughton Hall (BPS p52).

Monk's Walk, The Near Lapley Wood Farm, Lapley.

Monk's Wood Small wood 1m E of Cheadle.

Monk's Wood At SJ 980516 under 0.75m SE of Cheddleton (1834 OS map). Seems to have been once the property of Dieulacres Abbey. Nearby, crossing the Churnet is Monk's Ford (CVH pp160,173).

Monmore Field Open field which lay to the E of Wolverhampton prior to enclosure (HOWM p44).

Monmore Green District 1m SE of Wolverhampton on low ground to the E of the Birmingham Canal Old Cut Old Main Line. Formerly in Wolverhampton township, chapelry and ancient parish. Monmore Green was identified by Smallshire as the Wetmere which appears in Lady Wulfrun's charter 994 (WFW p29), and by Mander with Mora, a village mentioned in a C13 survey (HOWM p5). It is the Manna's Lake which appears in 1291 (WFW p29). Monmore Green appears on the maps of Plot, Morden and Bowen, but not on the 1834 OS map. Has sometimes appeared as Monmore. The first part of the name Mon is from Celtic and means a bog, 'more' is rightly 'mere,' hence 'the bog pool' (DUIGNAN) (NSFCT 1908 p135). 'Manna's Lake' has been interpreted as 'man's lake' (WFW p29) and as 'the lake of the men' (BCTV p62) (SPN p144). Here was a sulphur holy well with vitriol. It was unknown or had fallen into disuse by the mid C19 (W p76). (NHS p105) (SHOS vol 2 p165) (AOW p94) (OSST 1944-1945). Monmore was a prebend of Wolverhampton Collegiate Church (W p82) (VCH vol 3 p324). The church, All Saints, Steelhouse Lane, was built in 1877-1879 (BOE p322). Here was a windmill (SLM spring 1954 p25). Lycra jackets for racing greyhounds were first used in Britain at the greyhound race track at Monmore Green in July 1999 (Midlands Today. July 16 1999). In 1815 several thousand people assembled on Monmore Green expecting to see the ghost of John Wilkinson, ironmaster of Bradley (see), Bilston. In more recent times the sound and or vision of horses galloping down Steelhouse Lane has been heard and or seen (GOM p15). In 1829 the 'Greyhound' coach overturned at Monmore Green whilst travelling to Birmingham. One person was killed and four were injured (TEBC2 p33).

Monmore Lane District 0.5m NE of Willenhall. Has also appeared as Mumber Lane (1834 OS map), Monmore Colliery (1834 OS map), and Monmer Lane (DUIGNAN). The name is from land in this district which was originally in the manor of the prebend of Monmore (HOWI p187). Or from Mumber, a word representing 'a great bog;' gypsies inhabiting this area by the early C19 changed the named to Mumper (SNW p49) - the Mumper's Dingle (see) of George Borrow's novel 'Lavengro' (1851). By further corruptions Mumber became Momber and finally Monmer and Monmore (SNW p49).

Mons Hill Hill at N end of Wren's Nest Hill, 1.25m SSW of Coseley. The name which appears on the Plan of the Mines of Lord Dudley 1812 has also appeared as Man's Hill (1851 census). Has the same limestone geology as Wren's Nest Hill, and became a part of the Wren's Nest Hill National Nature Reserve in 1957 (WNNNR p4).

Monster's Wood In Arley Wood, Arley ancient parish. The name records probably the slaying here of some wild animal (perhaps a boar) in medieval times (AOA p19).

Monument Field Field name of field in which is a square memorial or monument marking the site of the hall of the Bagot family at Bagot's Bromley, which they vacated for Blithfield Hall in 1811.

Monument Hill Hill near Tittensor. May also be called Tittensor Hill (see). Under 0.5m WNW of the statue of the 1st Duke of Sutherland at SJ 865390 is a burial mound excavated in 1859. A flint arrowhead and some human bones were found (HOTM p9) (NSJFS 1965 pp48-49). It lies on the lip of a sandstone cliff face at SJ 868388 (NSFCT 1983 p12).

Monway Branch of the Walsall Canal Spurred off the Walsall Canal at SO 9765945 and served The Patent Shaft Steel Works. Completed in 1812 and closed in 1957 (BCM autumn 1995 p22).

Monway Field Large open field, 0.5m W of Wednesbury. A fragment of Roman glass has been found at Monway Field (WAM p8). The field was so named by 1315 (HOWV p108) and was an open field until the end of the C18 (WMLB p100). Has also appeared as Manway Fields (1834 OS map) and Monway Fields. Now not marked on Birmingham A-Z or OS maps. The name means 'bog way' (DUIGNAN). Or 'mon' means separate, so the 'separate way;' but

Hackwood agrees with Duignan that it is probably of Celtic origin and means the 'bog way.' Close by is Hoo Marsh and Broadwaters (WAM p7). There was horse racing on Monway Field in 1778 (HOWV p155). After the Walsall Canal (1786) was constructed through the area Monway Field became industrial (WMLB p100). (VCH vol 2 p162). Tobacco pipe clay could be found here in the late C17 (NHS p121).

Monway Gate In Wednesbury parish. Mentioned in old deeds as a well-known landmark. Hackwood thinks it may have been an ancient watch tower on the Portway - perhaps a rude but massively built gate-house (WAM p53). However, Ede says, the 'Gate' part referred to the road itself (from Dudley and Tipton) leading into Wednesbury by or across Monway Field (HOWV p109).

Moodystreet House 0.5m W of the shopping centre of Biddulph.

Moor Burgess Farm Situated over 0.5m NE of Wilnecote, at SK 230021. In existence in 1888 and in 1971 (1888 OS map 6 inch. 1971 OS map 1:25,000).

Moor Court Neo-Jacobean house 1.25m SSW of Cotton. In 1860 Alfred Sohier Bolton purchased a house and had it extended, he called it Moor Court (SMOPP vol 1 p99p in 1920) (BOE p214). It was an HM Prison by 1975 (OS map 1975. 1:50:000). (COPP2 p24p).

Moorcroft Former small area of Moxley in the mid C19 (W p79). The name, preserved in roads on either side of Moxley Hospital and the canal junction to the ENE of the hospital, is presumably from a croft on the moor (SNDB p70).

Moorcroft Junction Junction of the Walsall Canal with its Bradley Branch (HCMS No. 2). At SO 975951.

Moorehill Field name in Tutbury derived from the Burton family who were resident here (SHOS vol 1 p56).

Moor End The Station Road area of Barton-under-Needwood. The name is from flat moor lands at Barton Turn (UNT p36).

Moor End Farm nearly 1m N of Gnosall. Could be considered a small hamlet in 1680 (VCH vol 4 p111). Has appeared as More Ende (1583. 1677), Moor End (c1680-1833) (SPNO p160). Pools on the W side of the track leading to Moor End, at SJ 830220, probably formed the moat, indicated here by field names (VCH vol 4 p127).

Moorfields Large house in Church Lane, Handsworth (HPPE p23).

Moorfields Caravan park, house, and small industrial estate to the W of Swynnerton. Just prior to WW2 the site was outlined for a residence for the workers at the new Royal Ordnance factory near Swynnerton, but only the foundations of the residence were ever built (info Michael Cockin).

Moorfields Former tiny settlement over 1m S of Wolverhampton. Formerly in Sedgley parish and manor (SHOS vol 2 p221). The name appears in the charter of King Aethelred 985 as 'Scurf's Moor.' In the tithe map of 1840 this district is called the Moors and stretched to Goldthorn Hill (HOWM p10 note). It occurs as Moorfields in the 1841 census. The name is preserved in Moorfield Road, E of the Royal Wolverhampton School.

Moor Green Minute hamlet? 0.5m N of Forsbrook.

Moor Hall House 1m E of Bagnall. The moated site and pond to the W of the hall at SJ 94235093 and SJ 94095095 are a listed monument. The present stone house dates back to the C16 (B pp65-66p). To the S of Moor Hall at SJ 942505 a perforated stone axe-hammer was found in July 1964. It was sent to the Potteries Museum (NSJFS 1965 p121 il) (B p6p). The name is from William Murhull JP of Bagnall Hall (see), or one of his family (MMM p43).

Moorhall House 0.75m SE of Clent.

Moor Hall 0.75m WSW of Codsall church. It stood on a medieval moated site where Strawmoor Lane crosses Moat Brook. It was still occupied in 1690, but had been demolished by 1796. The moat survived in 1849 (VCH vol 20 pp79,82) (SSAHST 1982-3 p39). The name is preserved in Moor Hall Bridge carrying Strawmoor Lane over the railway.

Moorhall One of the four prebends of Gnosall Collegiate Church. Its prebendary lived in Moor Hall, a house, which may have adjoined the churchyard in Gnosall, which appears in 1360 as Morehall and later as Moor Hall (1706. 1748) (SPNO p158). It was still standing in the C18 (VCH vol 4 pp113,115). The name is from 'the hall on marshy ground' (SPNO p158).

Moor Hall Farm 0.5m W of Madeley. In Madeley parish (W p397). Appears on J Phillips & FW Hutchings map (1832). (NSFCT 1932 p125).

Moor Hall 1.25m SE of Penkridge. Moor Hall can perhaps be identified with 'ofer pæne mor' which occurs in a charter of 993 (SPNO p91). The name has appeared as Mora (1227), La More (1261), the More Hall 1578, Moorehall (1598) (SPNO p91). It means 'the barren waste land' (SPNO p91). The prebend of La More held some time in the C12 is probably to be identified with the prebend of Penkridge in Penkridge Collegiate Church. There was a manor of More or La More belonging to the dean and chapter of Penkridge by the end of the C13. Moor Hall is described as a hamlet in 1598. In 1754 a house known as Moor Hall stood on the site of the present Moor Hall Cottages.

(VCH vol 5 pp117,124), which appear to be the only properties in Moor Hall on 1:25,000 OS map.

Moor Head About 0.5m ENE of Uttoxeter on the old Derby road (1834 OS map).

Moor House To the E of Biddulph Old Hall, on the E side of the Overton Road, Biddulph. The Stonier or Stanier family lived in a house on this site by 1560. William Stonier was residing in a house on this site in 1840. By 1843 Francis Stanier, a member of the Newcastle-under-Lyme branch of the family had acquired and rebuilt the house, where his family lived up to the 1870s. It was then leased to the Twyford family. Thomas Twyford, inventor of the one-piece ceramic water closet, lived here. A Cardinal Patent hand basin installed here in 1900 is now at the Gladstone Pottery Museum, Longton. The property was bought by the Leese family, the tenants, in 1920 (BIOPP p16p).

Moorhouse House SE of the medieval town of Leek. The site of it may have been occupied by the C13. By 1503 the house had passed by marriage from the Bailey family to John Jodrell (or Lodrell) of Yeardsley, in Taxall, Ches. It was possibly soon after 1700 when it passed from the Jodrells to the Grosvenors; they still owned the house in the mid C19. The house survived until at least 1940 (VCH vol 7 p85). Appears on Plot's map (1682) as Moorehouse.

Moorhouse Farm 0.75m SE of Uttoxeter. Here, Redfern noted, two burial mounds a few yards from one another, one being 120 yards round and about ten feet high. Redfern thought that if they were not druidical burial mounds, then they were probably ancient hut circles (HOU p25) (HOU 1886 p38). Gunstone only mentions one (NSJFS 1965 p50).

Moorlands, The or the 'Staffordshire Moorlands' or the 'Stone Wall Country' or 'Leek Moorlands' (NSFCT 1908 p196). Is the name given to the NE corner of the county; the southern tip of the Pennine chain; an extension of the Derbys Peak District. Plot designated it as between Three Shires' Head in the N to Draycott or Uttoxeter in the S (CCT p178). It was called 'the Moorlands' in 1329 and was so called by Defoe (A Tour Through The Whole Island of Great Britain. Daniel Defoe. 1724-6. Letter 8) (HOS 1998 p17). **Boundaries.** White said it constituted one-sixth of the county (W p50). The district is approximately 300 square miles in size (SSGLST p10) and bounded by the county border in the N and E and a line from Mow Cop to the northern edge of the Potteries, through Endon to Cheddleton and along the Churnet to the Dove at Rocester (LGS p3). The Roaches, Weaver Hills, Lum Edge, Morridge, Leek - the 'Capital of the Moorlands' (VB p192) - are all included. **Climate and landscape.** Early scientists say that the Leek Moorlands is the coldest part of England from its altitude and distance from the sea (NSFCT 1908 p196). Its landscape is the most different to the rest in the county owing to its geology, which comprise millstone grit and mountain limestone (LGS p2). Except in the valley basins the land is all above 800 feet. It is a landscape considered both beautiful and bleak. **Commentators and visitors.** John Leland noted that the common people of the Moorlands called Sir William Bassett (d1553) of Blore Hall (see) 'the Kinge of the Morelande.' William Camden wrote in 'Britannia' (1586) the area was 'so rugged, foul, and cold that the snows continue long undissolved...' (HOS p7) (VCH vol 7 p78). Later in the C16 Erdeswick wrote of the district round the source of the Churnet as 'one of the barrenest countries I know' (BFS p3). Michael Drayton in 'Polyolbion' (1613) wrote

> But Muse, thou seem'st to leave the Morelands too too long:
> Of whom report may speak (our mighty wastes among)
> She from her chilly seite and from the barren feed,
> For body, horn and hair, as fair a beast doth breed,
> As scarely this great isle can equal.

(OL vol 2 p24) (VCH vol 7 p78). Dr Plot, as well as noting the prevalency of freemasonry in the Moorlands during the later C17 (NHS pp316-318), also noted an unusual tree called Sorbus Pyriformis or Frazinus Sylvestris growing wild on the Moorlands which sometimes people transplanted into their gardens. He says it is more common in France, Italy and Germany and resembles the Ornus or Quicken-Tree. But this tree bears fruit on the sides of the branches. The fruit has the size of a small Jeneting pear. If picked in September it has a strong sour taste and ought to be kept over till October when it tastes as well as a medlar. Many believed the boughs ward off evil spirits. Consequently walking sticks were made of it and boughs were kept about peoples beds (NHS pp208,223) (SCSF p50). It was through the Moorlands Prince Charles Edward Stuart marched to Derby in Dec 1745 in the Jacobite Rebellion (NSFCT 1908 p195). Thomas Bakewell wrote 'The Moorland bard, or Poetical recollections of a weaver in the Moorlands of Staffordshire' 1807 vols 1 and 2. The enclosed fields, were bordered with the stone walls which Pitt, author of THS, so disliked (SL p128). Mrs RS Garnett wrote 'Amor Vincit: a romance of the Staffordshire Moorlands' (1912). Masefield, writing in the early C20, sums up the scenery '-the grey stone farms within the tree-clumps, the heather, the close-bitten thymy turf, the roads that go undaunted sheer up the steepest hill, the lonely churches outlined against the heaven' (LGS p3).

The medieval Malbonck Forest covering much of the Moorlands would have had **primeval** origins. Traces of Iron Age or **Romano-British** field systems N of Ilam suggest early arable farming (SL p37). The tribe inhabiting the Moorlands between the C6 and the C9 were the Pecsaetan, who may have been Celtic rather than Anglian (OL vol 2 p13) (SL p44) (HAF p35). **Agriculture**. DB records many settlements in the Moorlands as 'waste.' Perhaps their inhabitants had resettled in the recently ravaged settlements of the lowlands (SL p58). The first thorough exploitation of the district, agriculturally, was by religious orders, particularly the Cistercians, who had their houses and granges here in the C12 and the C13 (HOS p38) and grazed sheep on the hills. Enclosure mainly took place by statute, rather than by agreement as occurred in the rest of the county (SL p123). The sycamore is a relatively recent introduction and proves to be a valuable quick-growing wind-break (SL p108). Principle **industries** are or have been quarrying limestone at Cauldon, grit at Ipstones, copper mining at Ecton and lead mining at Mixon, and the making of buttons, fine handkerchiefs and small cloths (NSJFS 1961 pp77-84). The dales and moors have been attracting **tourists** since the mid C19. The Peak District National Park which encompasses most of the Moorlands was created in 1950 (NSJFS 1974 p30) (HOS 1998 p17; says 1951). Eighty square miles of the Peak District National Park including the Roaches and Ramshaw Rocks had to be closed to the public from late July 1995 due to fire risk because of the dryness of land (ES Aug 4 1995 p5).

CIVIL WAR AND THE MOORLAND DRAGOONS. Several small troops of horse under the royalist Sir Francis Wortley, pursued by the parliamentarian Sir John Gell, plundered their way through the Moorlands in Nov 1642. Gell captured some of their number and they were tried at Stafford, but the justices there, were lenient and let them go. This apparent injustice incited the Moorlands to raise their own force - the Moorland Dragoons (BFS pp7-8). They were said to be good 'stout fighting men, but the most ungovernable wretches that belonged to the parliament' (OL vol 1 p191). In early Feb 1643 the Dragoons were led to Stafford to demand Sir Francis Wortley and his forces leave the county (LOU pp25-26). They were led by 'a person of low quality' (HOS p35) known as 'The Grand Juryman' who may have been Capt John Watson, or more likely Philip Jackson of the Jackson family of Stanshope Hall (BFS pp10,12). After allowing the sheriff to leave the town, the Dragoons appealed to parliamentary commanders Gell and Brereton in Derbys and Ches for help in attacking it (LOU p27) (HOS p35) (HAF pp118-121). But reinforcements never came and the Dragoons' siege of Stafford had collapsed by the end of Feb 1643 (BFS pp12-13). Boden says they fought for the royalists at Stafford in Feb 1643 (BNDA p27). The Dragoons fought with the parliamentarians at the battle of Hopton Heath, March 19 1643. Some Moorlanders were taken prisoner at (Great or Little) Haywood on March 17 (BFS p18). The Moorland Dragoons are said to have also been at Biddulph Old Hall in the Civil War (BALH p39). They were apparently defeated by a small royalist force near Uttoxeter on Feb 18 1645 (LOU p28). (L p13). Capt John Watson who had been a commander with them was ambushed and killed by royalists near Uttoxeter in Feb 1646 (BFS p23).

SUPERSTITIONS. Moorlanders, geographically isolated, have their own dialect (NSFCT 1882 p27 of Leek and Morridge. 1919 pp44-53), traditions, and are renowned for their frugality (OL vol 2 p134). Superstitions take longer here to die than elsewhere. There has long existed in Moorlands and Peak District folklore the belief that fairies inhabit the many burial mounds, here known as lows or lowes (GLS pp32-33). There are traditions of them existing in Thors Cave, at Bradnop, Cauldon Lowe, Ipstones, Leek and Mixon. Visions of stage coaches, headless horsemen, wandering Jews, phantom black dogs, fairies, and tales of a man-eating family abound (OL vol 1 pp313-314. vol 2 pp299-303). A small spirit or glowing light like a candle flame is known as a Jack o' the Lantern or a Will o' the Wisp in the Moorlands. It is said that when someone in the Moorlands is about to die these spirits or lights are seen to dance nearby (DOG p130) (FOS p16). Witchcraft was practiced in the Moorlands (OL vol 2 pp299-303) (TOI pp165-166). For Moorland sayings see OL vol 2 p252.

WANDERING JEW. The Wandering Jew is a character of medieval legend who is condemned to roam the world externally because he mocked Christ on the day of the Crucifixion by refusing him a cup of water. The earliest recording of him is by Matthew Paris (1200-1259). The Wandering Jew was reported all over Europe in the Middle Ages; many are presumed to have

posed as the figure for monetary gain. The Wandering Jew is said to have visited the Staffs Moorlands on a Sunday afternoon in the 1650s (DPEM p94) or in 1658 (GLS p58) when a poor old man claimed a stranger in a purple shag gown called at his cottage in the Moorlands, said to be near Ipstones (Albion: A Guide to Legendary Britain. Jennifer Westwood. 1985. pp224-225) (GLS p58). The old man had been lame for a long time and the stranger said he could cure him if he take two or three balm leaves steeped in beer for two or three weeks. This he did, and was restored to health. Dr Gilbert Sheldon (a native of Stanton, and later Archbishop of Canterbury) was in the area at the time and told Elias Ashmole the story, who told John Aubrey (1626-1697) of it, who noted it in his 'Miscellenies' (1696). The tale continued to be told throughout the Moorlands; Pickford has had it told to him by four different families in the Axe Edge area, and by a farmer of Wildboarclough, Ches (DPEM p94-95). (DFMAL p112) (OL vol 2 pp268-271) (TOI pp162-163) (FOS pp30,31) (FLJ 1981 p138) (MR p196) (HOLF pp50-51). The Wandering Jew is said to have asked a lame old man for a drink of beer in the Ipstones area in c1850 (HLSP p53).

Moor Pool Estate Garden suburb centred on The Circle and Moor Pool Avenue, 0.75m NNE of Harborne. Under the guidance of John Sutton Nettlefold, Harborne Tenants Ltd began in 1907 to build the estate, vying with Bourneville as a model garden suburb (TB April 1986 p27) (HOHE p32). Takes its name from a pool called the Moor Pool, which the washerwomen of Harborne once frequented. The estate still (1989) centres on this pool (WMVB p78) (OHOPP p20p of Moor Pool c1905).

Moor's Gorse Tiny settlement on the Hednesford-Rugeley road over 2m NW of Beaudesert Hall. Has also appeared as Moors Gorse (1821) and Moores Gorse (1834) (SPNO p108). The SSWWC water pumping station here ceased working in 1955 (PCC p58p) but continued as a museum piece (CCM).

Moorside Minute settlement 0.75m WNW of Hollinsclough. Formerly in Alstonefield ancient parish.

Moorside House on the N side of Eaves Lane on Wetley Moor. Occurs on the 1834 OS map. Another house called Moorside on Wetley Moor lies to the E of Washerwall Lane (Stoke-on-Trent A-Z. 1992).

Moorside Fragmented tiny hamlet 0.5m SW of Onecote, situated on N side of Morridge. Formerly in Leek ancient parish.

Moorside Brook Runs from Moorside, Wetley Moor northwards to the Hole House Brook (a tributary of the Trent).

Moors Well Werrington. (WYV p60 il). Possibly near Moorville Hall?

Moor Top House on Morridge 1m W of Onecote (1834 OS map (Dower's map).

Moor Top Farm House 0.5m W of Hollinsclough on the edge of Hollinsclough Moor. Formerly in Hollinsclough township in Alstonefield ancient parish. The present house was built in the early C19 for John Tunnicliff (VCH vol 7 p38).

Moorville Hall House 1m SE of Werrington.

Moosey Moor Wood Valley Lies to the E of the Hermitage, S of Ipstones (NSFCT 1926 pp116-117).

Moot Hall There was a building called this in Lombard Street, Lichfield in 1708. Here was probably the moot hall where Lichfield manor courts were held until the newly established Lichfield corporation acquired the manor in 1548 and carried on their business in Lichfield Guildhall (see) (VCH vol 14 p75).

Moot House A mid to late C18 house which overlooks the Croft (ALOPP p26p), SW of Aldridge church (BOE p53). Moot House was once the home of the Cooke family (ALOPPR p24p of in c1960). Various members of the Hepburn family lived here from c1900 to the 1950s (SNAR p29). Another account, which says Moot House was built in the Adam style, identifies the house with Portland House (see), and states that Portland House received its name from the Portland stone used to surround the windows. By 1989 Moot House was a nursing home (WMVB p11).

Mopes Ash To E of Birchills, Walsall (SOB p161 see map facing). Appears at the junction of Bloxwich Road and Harden Road in present Leamore on 1834 OS map.

Mopplesford Hills Stood near the site of the present Rose Hill housing estate, Willenhall (SNW p49). The former Morfital Lane (now the N end of Gipsy Lane) may have been derived from these hills (SNW p49).

Moreton Fragmented tiny hamlet in the lower Dove Valley backed by the escarpment of the Needwood Forest plateau, 1m NNW of Draycott-in-the-Clay. Formerly in Draycott-in-the-Clay township in Hanbury ancient parish (W p560). There was a burial mound in the vicinity of Moreton destroyed in 1860. It was of the long variety and no relics were found in it, except for a few pieces of bone and a fragment of corroded iron (HOU p26. 1865 p30). Is not a burial mound (NSJFS 1965 p36). The Mortun mentioned in a charter of 956 was assigned by Birch to a Staffs Moreton; CGO Bridgeman suggests with grave scepticism that it may be Moreton near Marchington, in Hanbury ancient parish (SHC 1916 p95). One of the Staffs Moretons was considered by Shaw the Mortun mentioned in the will of Wulfric Spot (c1002), founder of Burton Abbey; others have thought Morton, a parish in Scarsdale hundred, Derbys (SHC 1916 p36). The manor of Mortune appears in DB. The name means 'marsh settlement' (NSJFS 1981 p2). Or 'Moor tun' (SSE 1996 p16). A lamb called 'Jim Smith' was born to a Suffolk ewe on Moreton Farm in late Oct 1996 (BBC 1 Midlands Today. Oct 29 1996).

Moreton Village lining the foot of a steep W-facing ridge at some distance to the E of Moreton Brook 9m WSW of Stafford. Former quarter in Gnosall ancient parish. In the later C17 there was a raised work of Roman fashion here only a mile to the W of the Limes Britannicus (NSFCT 1902 p119). One of the Staffs Moretons was considered by Shaw the Mortun mentioned in the will of Wulfric Spot (c1002), founder of Burton Abbey; others have thought Morton, a parish in Scarsdale hundred, Derbys (SHC 1916 p36). Has appeared as Mortone (DB), Morton (1242-1652), Moreton (1428-1833) (SPNO p157). The name means 'moor town or tun' (DUIGNAN) (SSE 1996 p16). Or 'marsh settlement' (NSJFS 1981 p3). There was a chapel near Moreton Park in medieval times. It was not recorded at the Reformation and said to be demolished by c1680. The church, St Mary, in an elevated position on the E side of Church Lane, at the S end, was built in 1837 (VCH vol 4 p132). Moreton became a separate ecclesiastical parish in 1845 (LGS p189) (GLAUE p417). Charlotte Sophia Burne (d1923), writer, folklorist and author of SFL, was born on May 2 1850 at the Parsonage, Moreton, the house of her uncle, Rev Tom Burne, the vicar. She was the daughter of Sambrooke Burne (d1861) heir to the Loynton Hall (see) estate (BS p89) (FLJ vol 86 autumn/ winter 1975 p167) (STMSM Sept 1980 p56; born May 2 1855) (MR p234). Another account says she was born at Morton vicarage near Oswestry, Shrops (VFC p21). She later lived in Shrops, but designed a window in Norbury (see) church and resided at Pyebirch Manor (see) in the early 1880s.

Moreton Very fragmented hamlet on high ground above Moreton Brook consisting of about five properties. Moreton House is 2m SE of Hixon. One of the Staffs Moretons was considered by Shaw the Mortun mentioned in the will of Wulfric Spot (c1002), founder of Burton Abbey; others have thought Morton, a parish in Scarsdale hundred, Derbys (SHC 1916 p36). One of the two Mortone manors recorded in DB was held by the bishop of Chester (Lichfield). The name means 'marsh settlement' (NSJFS 1981 p3) (SPN p85). Or 'moor tun' (SSE 1996 p16). In Colwich parish and prebend (SSAHST vol 2 1960-61 p44). There was what was considered a sizeable village in the Middle Ages at either Moreton House or at Upper Moreton at SK 029221 over 0.5m to the SE of Moreton House, possibly deserted 1334-1524 (SSAHST 1970 p35). Walter Chetwynd in 1679 was the first to identify a settlement here from, probably, earthworks (SL p82). There was a branch here of the well-known 'Wymer' family, called Wymers of Morton (SHC 1914 p150 note).

Moreton Brook Runs from Moreton through Colton to the Trent at Rugeley Junction (CWF p219). Appears in 1395 as Mortonbrok and takes its name from Moreton, Hixon (SPNO p15).

Moreton Brook Rises near High Onn, and runs westwards on the S side of Moreton; forms the county boundary, W of Moreton; appears to join Back Brook or Coley Brook which flows into Aqualate Mere.

Moreton House Moreton, 2m SE of Hixon. Occupied in 1851 by William Hanbury (W p22).

Moreton House Set back from the junction of Moreton Parade and Church Lane, overlooking Wolstanton Marsh. Built of brick for Ralph and Anna Moreton in 1743. From the Moretons the house passed to their daughter Mary; on her death it was inherited by Mr Sparrow, who sold it to Rev CC Ellison. By 1940 it was owned by Newcastle corporation and was used as borough education offices (Newcastle Times June 16 1971) (MR p243). It was a childhood home of Sir Oliver Lodge, born at The Views (see), Penkhull; there was a sighting of what was alleged to be Lodge's ghost in 1963 (Weekly Sentinel Aug 2 1963) (Newcastle Times June 16 1971). There were plans to demolish the house in 1971 (Newcastle Times Aug 11 1971) (ES Aug 6 1975 il. Dec 1 1975. July 28 1980). Could be same as Marsh Hall (see).

Moreton Park House 0.5m WNW of Moreton church, in Gnosall ancient parish. Dates largely from the later C19. The lord of Moreton manor lived here in the C19 (VCH vol 4 p121). On a triangular raised plot immediately W of Moreton Park stood a chapel, noted by Gregory King in c1680 as demolished (VCH vol 4 p132). On the road between Wilbrighton and Moreton Park are the remains of a wayside cross (VCH vol 4 p112).

Morfe Area on upland between Philley and Sneyd's Brooks, and former manor N of Enville, in Enville ancient parish; Morfe Hall Farm is 0.5m NNE of Enville; Little Morfe Farm, under 0.25m N of Morfe Hall Farm, was built in

1852 (VCH vol 20 p93). Has appeared as Moerheb (736) (SSE 1996 p16), Morve (DB) (SVS p577). The maps of Saxton to Kip, and Speed all show Morfe Forest to the W in Shrops. The name is probably from Welsh 'morfa' meaning a marsh (DUIGNAN) (NSFCT 1908 p145). Ekwall thinks perhaps a reduction of Old Welsh 'mor - dref' meaning 'big village' (SSE 1996 pp16,22). (SVS p281). The medieval manor house of Morfe manor, in existence by the C14, may have stood on or near the site of Morfe Hall Farm (VCH vol 20 pp93,106). There was possibly a medieval village at either Morfe Hall Farm or Little Morfe, probably deserted between 1334 and 1524 (SSAHST 1970 p35). Yates' map shows a settlement called Morfe near the junction of Morfe Lane and the road from Enville (VCH vol 20 p93). Morftown or Morfe is described as a small village in S&W p362.

Morfeheath Farm House on W side of Highgate Road, 1.5m NE of Enville, in Morfe manor and Enville ancient parish. Built by 1723 on former heath or waste land, enclosed in 1683. The house became the club house for Enville Golf Club in 1968 (VCH vol 20 pp93-94,96).

Moriat Hills At SO 851860 (1834 OS map). Hills on the E side of Hampton Valley, and W side of Smestow Brook. The one at SO 851860 rises to a height of 442 feet above sea level. Others in the range, if a range is meant, may be one of a similar height 0.25m to the N and another of a similar height under 0.25m to the SSW.

Morrey Tiny hamlet on ground rising out of the Trent Valley over 0.75m W of Yoxall. In Yoxall ancient parish. A large tape mill was founded there in 1790s later run by Bend and Co (VCH vol 2 p221). Has appeared as Murrey (Plot's map), Morry, and Morhay.

Morridge (-ridge or -rich SPN p85). Long ridge on an edge of moorland stretching from Winkhill in the S to Morridge Top in the N (NSFCT 1882 p26), rising to a height of 1521 feet (LGS p3) or 1,535 feet (VCH vol 7 p1). The ridge passes through Bradnop and Elkstones districts and gives its name to Morredge-with-Foxt township which formed the E end of Ipstones parish (W p779), Morridge Side (see) and Morridge Top (see) (SGSAS). A **ridgeway**, which may be prehistoric, follows the high curve of Morridge (PRT p24). The largest of three **burial mounds** on Morridge relinquished a brass bolt of a Roman catapulta (NHS p403) (NSJFS 1965 p45), this is probably a Bronze Age palstave found in a barrow on Morridge (NSJFS 1964 p31). The mound may have been Merryton Low. Plot had also heard of an axe head being found on Morridge (NHS p397) (NSJFS 1964 p31). A mound 13 paces in diameter and 1.5 feet high on Morridge was excavated by Carrington in 1850 who found nothing (TYD p165) (NSJFS 1965 p42). The **name** has appeared as Morrugge (1227-1345), Morridge hill (c1233), Morrug (c1256), Morrage (c1278), Morredge (1413, Moryche (C16), Morridge (1570. 1612. 1713) (SHC 1910 p438) (SPNO p23), and Morredge Common (THS p40). Morridge, or Morredge, is a corruption of moor edge (W p779). Or is from from Saxon 'mor hyrcg' and means 'moorland ridge' (SPNO p23) (SPN p85). Probably on the western slopes of Morridge was the **'grave of Thomas'** a point on the boundary of Dieulacres Abbey. Its site cannot be identified (NSJFS 1970 p84). Pitt in the early C19 noted Morredge Common was exploited for its large quantities of peat, cut for fuel (THS p40). On July 22 1882 a **strange phenomenon** in the sky was seen on Morridge by local inhabitants. It looked like an immense factory chimney which moved about with a strong wind that was blowing at the time. After about 15 minutes, the object which appeared to be in the Warslow Hall area, disappeared, to the great relief of those who saw it who believed it was something uncanny, dangerous and boding no good (OL vol 2 p303). A good **view point** is at SK 028596. In the layby by the road is a viewfinder to the memory of Paul Rey (1925-1977), rambler and world traveller. There is another to Rey in Dimmings Dale. To the SW, W and N can be seen Hanley, Jodrell Bank (Ches), and Axe Edge. (HLSP p68p,69).

Morridge Side Fragmented hamlet 1m SE of Bradnop. Formerly in Bradnop township in Leek ancient parish. The settlement began with squatters squatting on the waste land here in the C17 (VCH vol 7 p171). The army of Prince Charles Edward Stuart passed through Morridge Side on Dec 4 1745 in the Jacobite Rebellion (BPCSM p7).

Morridge Top Minute hamlet 3.5m NNW of Upper Elkstones, Elkstones. Formerly in Alstonefield ancient parish. Morridge Top is 1521 feet high (NSFCT 1881 p44) (LGS p3).

Morrilow Heath Heath and fragmented hamlet 1m NE of Garshall Green. In Leigh ancient parish. Children at Hilderstone in the early C19 were told fairies danced in the rings on the Morrilow Heath (NSFCT 1900 p141).

Morris House Morris House Farm is 1m WNW of Endon, 0.5m ENE of Brown Edge. At SJ 914543 is a burial mound in very good condition, 10-15 feet high partly hidden from view, with a tiny brook washing one side between the mound and a cliff (NSFCT 1983 p12).

Morughale Former village in Offlow hundred, unlocated for many years. Probably deserted sometime between 1334 and 1524 (SSAHST 1970 p35). FJ Cope in 1936 placed it on the northern side of the road leading from Trent Valley Station to Lichfield (OSST 1936 p43). Tringham (and possibly others, earlier) located it in the mid 1980s to the same area; that of the former Bexmore Farm, 1m E of Lichfield cathedral, at SK 132100. It has appeared as Morwhale (late C13) (SSE 1997 p84), Morghill, Morghall (1457), Mourghall and Morfall (OSST 1936 p43), and was in existence by the mid C13 and was a more important settlement than nearby Streethay. A charter was dated at Morughale in 1443, but by the late 1480s the hamlet had apparently been deserted. A track in fields which runs from Valley Lane to Streethay was known as Morughale Lane (VCH vol 14 p275). The name means 'nook of land (halh) bestowed as a morning-gift (morgen gifu).' Morning gifts were gifts of land given by the bridegroom to the bride on the morning of their marriage in Anglo-Saxon times (VCH vol 14 p275).

Moseley Former manor and rural tiny hamlet in and above a tiny valley created by a brook which may be called Black Brook or Wybaston Brook, 1.25m SW of Featherstone. In Bushbury ancient parish. Lady Godiva held Moseley before the Norman Conquest (HOWM p2). The manor of Moleslei appears in DB (SHOS vol 2 p183). The name is from perhaps Anglo-Saxon 'mose,' a moss or marsh. But in this case it means 'Moll's pasture' (DUIGNAN) (SPN p144) (SSE 1996 p16). The Devil's Elbow is a stretch of brook at Moseley (BUOP p34p).

Moseley 1.75m E of Wolverhampton. Industrial area in the Willenhall area (BCM April 1987 pp55-57). Formerly in Wednesfield chapelry in Wolverhampton ancient parish. Moseley Hole Farm (in 1978 the old Skin and Hide Factory near the Uplands estate) has been identified with the Kirnesford (see) mentioned in Lady Wulfrun's charter of 994 (WFW p30). Formerly Moseley Hole (1841 census), and Moseley Village (OS map 1:25,000). The name is from Anglo-Saxon mose, a moss or marsh. Hole means a hole, a depression (DUIGNAN) (SPN p144).

Moseley Court Stood about 400 yards NE of Northicote Farm, nearly 0.75m S of Moseley Old Hall. In Bushbury ancient parish. Built by George Thomas Whitgreave (1787-1863) of Moseley Old Hall for himself and his London bride between 1815 and 1820. The house was considerably altered in the C19. From c1870 it was let to various families and was finally sold in 1922. Following the death of the last owner, Mrs AJ Wesson, the house was badly vandalised. It was demolished in the 1960s (BUOP pp7,32p). In the 1820s GT Whitgreave built for himself a Roman Catholic chapel in the grounds on the N side of the house. Two of the Whitgreave children who died young were buried here. The chapel was demolished in the 1920s but its site can be identified by a rectangular piece of lawn (BUOP p31p in 1913).

Moseley Green Junction of the road between Northicote and Slade Green and that between Snapes Green and Moseley. The name appears on the 6 inch OS map 1886.

Moseley Hall Moseley, Featherstone. 0.25m SSW of Moseley Old Hall. In Bushbury ancient parish. Former seat of the Moseley family, later the Hortons, lords of Moseley manor. The house was rebuilt in the early C18 by Thomas Moseley. The present front of the house has some similarities with Old Fallings Hall, which dates from about the same period, and may have been designed by the same architect (BUOP p33p). (On Birmingham A-Z marked Moseley Hall Farm).

Moseley Old Hall Timber-framed house 1m SW of Featherstone. In Bushbury ancient parish. Built in c1600 for Henry Pitt of Bushbury, who had bought the land in 1583 from the Codsall family (BUOP p28p); Pitt's daughter Alice married Thomas Whitgreave of Whitgreave, hence the hall came into the Whitgreave family. The hall, mentioned in 1600 (NT Guide p6), became famous after Charles II took refuge here having escaped from the battle of Worcester (1651). The Whitgreaves moved to Moseley Court in 1820. The hall was encased in brick in 1870; sold by the Whitgreaves in 1925 to the Wiggins of Bloxwich, and given to the NT in 1962 (NT Guide pp6,7) (CL May 16 1991 pp136-139). An unexplainable presence in the corridor near the King's Room chills people and scares animals, also poltergeist activity moves objects of the warden's family and an unexplainable shadow haunts them, which was last seen in 1991 (MGH pp47-49p) (GPCE p61). The spectres of soldiers of the Civil War period are said to appear in the vicinity of the hall (GPCE p61). A tunnel is said to lead from Moseley Old Hall to Bushbury Hall Farm (TB Nov 1981 p27).

CHARLES II AT MOSELEY OLD HALL. Charles II's shelterers at the hall were Alice and her son Thomas (MR p234). Charles left Boscobel for Moseley on the evening of Sunday Sept 7. He was accompanied part of the way by the five Penderell brothers and their brother-in-law Francis Yates; they left him at Pendeford Mill or at Featherstone, to walk the last stretch to Moseley for it was considered unsafe for them to go with him all the way. He arrived early

on the morning of Sept 8 1651 and left for Bentley Hall on the evening of Sept 9; the royalist, Lord Wilmot, was already in hiding here (NT Guide p27). The room in which Charles stayed became known as the King's Room. In it - under the floor boards of a small cupboard (DoE II*) (LGS p100) - is one of the two priests holes of the house. It is maintained Charles hid in it whilst the house was being searched (LGS p100). At Moseley Charles met Father Huddlestone, who dried and warmed the king's feet. Huddlestone preserved a piece of coarse shirt and a handkerchief of the king's, which in 1910 were with the Riddells of Northumberland (LGS p99). Charles II's bed, which had been in the Oak Room at Wightwick Manor from 1913, was returned to Moseley Old Hall in 1962 (CL April 18 1996 p68). There was kept at Tettenhall Towers in 1894 a small oak table from Moseley Old Hall, used by Charles II, when concealed here (HOPTT p277). In the later Stuart period it was customary for the people of the district to make a pilgrimage to one or all of the houses which had sheltered Charles II (SCSF p18). Jon Raven says they made a pilgrimage to all, starting with Bentley and ending with Boscobel (FOS p99). The Monarch's Walk, in existence by 2000, is a circular walk which follows the king's route after the battle of Worcester (Black Country Breaks. Black Country Tourist Board brochure 2000).

(NHS p307) (SD pp41,42) (SHOS vol 2 p184) (GNHS pp82-87) (W pp47,170) (AOW p24 il of, or rather touched up photograph on p facing p64) (OHW pl18) (WJO Nov 1909 pp296-297) (SOSH p217) (HOS pp29,35 map) (SCHJ No. 8 Winter 1966-67 pp1-16) (VB p83) (BOE p206) (SGS p128) (AWM p36) (R&S pp28-29) (Biography of Charles II. Antonia Fraser. 1979 pp116,117, 119-121,175) (AA p258) (Article by RA Chand with many illustrations from unknown magazine in CL box in WSL) (MR p234) (TOS pp114-115) (COS p65p) (National Trust Guide by RA Chand. 1993). See also the bibliography under Boscobel.

GROUNDS. A Knot Garden constructed by the NT in 1963 (NT Guide p16). The last Ice Age reached its maximum southern extent about Wolverhampton and glacial boulders lie in the vicinity of the hall (WJO Nov 1909 p293).

Moses' Head The conduit in Lichfield cathedral Close was known as Moses' Head in the C16 and C17. It was surmounted by a stone cross. A new conduit replaced this conduit in c1697 (VCH vol 14 p95).

Moss Carr House 0.5m SE of Hollinsclough. Formerly in Hollinsclough township in Alstonefield ancient parish. Is probably the Moscure which appears in the earlier C15 (VCH vol 7 p38). Boggarts have been seen near the Moss Carr area (L p49).

Moss Close S of Rushall Hall (VCH vol 2 p196).

Moss Farm Farm 0.5m SW of Fairoak. Near here was found, probably when the moss was drained in 1975, wild horses' teeth of the Pleistocene Age. Also during WW2 a bomb was dropped on the moss, setting fire to the growth and disappearing into the peat. It was still there and unexploded in 1986 (BOV p77). An aircraft refuelling hose dropped from the sky and landed near Moss Farm in Nov 1999 (SN Dec 29 1999 p20p).

Mossfield Tiny hamlet (1834 OS map) 1.25m SW of Bucknall. Now merely a road name at Adderley Green, Longton.

Mossgate Tiny hamlet on high ground in undulating country 1m SSW of Fulford. Formerly in Hilderstone quarter in Stone ancient parish (W p370).

Moss Grove Area of Kingswinford and a stretch of the Wolverhampton-Stourbridge road from the junction of Summerhill and High and Market Streets to the junction of Stallings Lane and Dudley Road. David Piddock, artist, was born at Moss Grove in March 1960 (BCM winter 1999/2000 pp48-52p).

Moss Hall On Moss Hill, over 0.5m SW of Endon. Was called the Moss in 1750 and Moss Hall in 1772. Is currently (1992) called Moss Hill (VCH vol 7 p178).

Moss Hill Hill between Endon Edge and Stockton Brook.

Moss House House 1.25m NNE of Audley. Has also appeared as Mosshouse.

Moss House In Madeley parish (W p396). There is a Moss House Farm is 0.5m WNW of Madeley.

Mossland The property of St Radegund's Chantry, founded in Lichfield Cathedral in 1242, formed a manor which by 1338 included a capital messuage in Pipe called Mossland (VCH vol 14 p212).

Mosslane Lane and minute hamlet on high ground in undulating country 1m S of Fulford.

Mosslee Hall Stone house of 1640 1m WNW of Ipstones. However, the house may have been built in the C16 (NSFCT 1953 p121). Once the mansion of the Hollins family (OL vol 2 p109). Has a fine oak staircase and some beautiful mullioned windows; it has on a water pipe the date 1640 (LGS p154) (MR p196p). (NSFCT 1890 p36) (JSD p246il). Has also appeared as Moss Lee Hall and Mossley Hall. Near the hall is a boulder of Millstone Grit (NSFCT 1916 p74).

Mossley Area of Rugeley, 0.75m SE of St Augustine church. A Mosseley Green

(Grene) appears in 1570 and Mossley Close in 1840 (SPNO p109).

Mossley District in the suburbs of Bloxwich, 0.75m W of central Bloxwich, approximately in the area N of Sneyd lane, E of Creswell Crescent and W of Broad Lane, in the foreign of Walsall. Has appeared as Matteslye (c1300), Mosley (1665), Moseley (1665) (SNBP p41), Mosley Field (1834 OS map). The name means probably 'the mossy glade in the forest,' or 'the mossy bank or slope' (SNBP p41). Much of the suburb is an housing estate dating from the later 1950s (VCH vol 17 p163). The church, St Thomas, Cresswell Crescent, was built in 1959 (LDD).

Moss Pit Former small hamlet 1.5m S of Stafford. Formerly in Castle Church parish and a part of Burton manor (near Stafford) (SAC p22). Has appeared as le Mosse (1548), Mospit (1836) (SPNO p78), and Moss Pits. The name means 'the swampy hollow' (SPNO p78). There was settlement at Moss Pit by c1840. Since 1945 Moss Pit has expanded greatly and has become a suburb of Stafford (VCH vol 5 p84).

Moss Pit Green Former name for the Ford Brook Lane area of Shelfield. The name appears on the tithe map in 1841. By 1883 there is a house Moss Pits and to the N a Mosspits Farm on Ford Brook Lane (SNBC p27).

Moss Pit House On W side of Chain Lane, Moss Pit, Stafford. Built in the mid C19. In the later C19 it was owned by the Morts, owners of the Staffordshire Chronicle and later of the SA. After several other owners the house was demolished in the C20 (SAC p23).

Moss Pool Small pool W of Meretown, Forton, the W bank forms the Shrops border.

Moss Pool Former pool 0.5m SW of Norbury church. In the later C17 Plot noted it foretold a drought or dearth when its water rose (NHS p46) (SD p60). This was Plot's 'old Pewit Pool' and was frequented by black headed gulls or pewits (NHS p231). The gulls deserted this pool on the death of John Skrymsher in 1665 to Offley Moss, 2m away (NSFCT 1927 pp37-38). The 'old Pewit Pool' was identified by SAH Burne with field number 345 (Cow Pasture and Drain) on a Norbury tithe map (StRO D(W) 1718/ 16-18). No pool in this vicinity appears on Yates' map and it has been assumed that the pool was drained between 1686 and 1775 (WSS p109). Another account has the pool in existence in 1775 but reduced to three acres in extent and surrounded by a moss of 23 acres. It had been lost by the 1950s (VCH vol 4 p155).

Moss Side Minute settlement 0.75m WNW of Hollinsclough.

Mosswood Appears to be an area centred on Mosswood Street to the W of Rumer Hill. The church, St Barnabas, Hampton Street, dates from c1960 (LDD).

Mott Close Moat The Heath, Uttoxeter. A moated residence a little distance below the Three Tuns Inn. The Beamhurst road cuts across a portion of the site. The house had been long destroyed even by the mid C19. Nothing but the moat was observable even by c1700. The land on which it stood formerly belonged to the Mynors and was called the Little Park (HOU p236).

Mottley Pits Part of the common plot at Stone. The terms Mudley Pits, Mottley Pits and Motley Pits have been used to refer to the terraces on the common plot. Some have thought the terraces constructed by a Celtic-Anglo agricultural community (NSFCT 1935 p91). Masefield and Cope think they are of Anglo-Saxon origin and may have represented an enclosure and council meeting place or moot, and outside the enclosure, the community's open fields cut into strips or terraces (LGS p222); Cope suggests Mottley is a corruption of moot (SIS pp4,5). But the name has also been used to refer to the high humpbacked mounds with dips in between, also on the common plot, in a small area to the WNW: Mudley Pits was used to refer to these mounds on the 1880 1:25,000 map (NSFCT 1897 see map facing p141): Most think these were thrown up by the Duke of Cumberland to raise his cannons high at his camp made here on Dec 3 1745 to intercept the Young Pretender in the Jacobite Rebellion (SHOS vol 1 part 1 p86 - no mention of the Pits only of the Duke's arrival in Stone with an army) (MOS p25) (RHPS p41) (SSBOP p31p in 1910 - and mentions Saxon field strips) (COS p52p). Some think the terraces or mounds or both were made a century earlier by parliamentarians in the Civil War (W p360) (NSFCT 1940 p32). Raven thinks the terraces could be prehistoric, Roman, Saxon, or Civil War in origin (MR p308). Pits could come from the name of a field 'Sand Pits' to the S, or from the old sandstone workings in the N escarpment of the common plot, which created the caves known as the Lion's Den. (SSC p135 in the intro.) (KES p194). Mottley Pits has also been corrupted to Mudley Pits, and again corrupted to Muddlies. And, confusingly, some use the term 'The Plots' to refer to both Saxon terraces and Civil War or 1745 Jacobite Rebellion mounds. In 1965 a small cannon ball of the 1745 Jacobite Rebellion period as found in a field adjacent to Mottley Pits on the site of the present swimming baths (info Mr & Mrs MC Cockin). In the early C19 or thereabouts a person going from Meaford to

Oulton saw a Will o' the' Wisp (or Jack o' the' Lantern, a fairy) which he followed until he found himself in one of the Motley Pits (NSFCT 1901 p135).

Motty Meadows Field or meadow land 1.5m WNW of Wheaton Aston and Blymhill. It is the most northerly habitat in the British Isles for the Snake's head-fritillary (Fritillaria meleagris, locally falfillary, a chequered lily); here Wheaton Aston villagers came and still (2000) come on the first Sunday in May to pick the fritillary. Motty Meadows was created a National Nature Reserve in 1982 (WAAIW il on back page) (BBC 1 Midlands Today April 26 2000). Has appeared as Mutty Meadows (1682) and (Great) Motty Meadow (1735) (SPNO p130).

Motty Meadows Brook Tributary of the Penk. Runs from Brineton to Wrestlers Farm joins Wheaton Aston Brook at Marston. The brook was named from the field name Motty Meadows (SPNO p15).

Mound, The Waste land at Brownhills in West Midlands close to the border with the new county of Staffs. Scene of a Ku-Klux-Klan gathering on the night of Aug 7 1992. A five feet high wooden cross was burnt. The police and fire brigade were called to the scene (I Aug 11 1992).

Mount, The Ipstones. It was the local poor house before 1834 (JSD p245). It was known as Noggin Hall when occupied by Ralph Hughes, farmer between at least 1884 and 1888. It was known as the Noggin, when occupied by Oakes Ash Jnr between at least 1900 and 1904 (trade directories). The name noggin means a small wooden cup as in a 'noggin of whiskey.' According to tradition an old lady who made the old-fashioned brooms called besoms lived here and was selling besoms with small noggins of unlawfully distilled whisky concealed in them (TOI p45).

Mount, The House in Greatbatch Avenue, Penkhull, in Stoke-upon-Trent parish. Built in 1803/4 by Josiah Spode II (PRA pp43-45p, pp46-48 plan of the Mount Estate pp49-50p of Mount Lodge in 1910) (BOE p264 pl 53). Part of The Mount estate became the site for the new North Staffs Infirmary at Hartshill (see), built in 1866-69. The house, The Mount, became the North Staffordshire Deaf and Blind School in 1897 (VCH vol 8 pp183,197) (PPP p94p) (ES May 29 1980). In the 1870s two ice-houses still existed, one in the shrubbery N of the house and one near the NE corner of the present cemetery (VCH vol 8 p183).

Mount, The House in Mount Road, Tettenhall Wood. Built on the site of an earlier house of the same name for Charles Benjamin Mander in c1865 (VCH vol 20 p9) or c1870 (BOE p311). Enlarged in 1891-1908. Noted for its sumptuous ballroom by Edward Ould (BOE p311) (SGS p188) (MR p327). After the death of Sir Charles Mander Bt (d1951) the house was sold and became an hotel (TCOP p49p) (VCH vol 20 p9). The house stands on a hill, 560 feet high. The hill has a panoramic view which includes the Malverns, Habberley Hill, Kinver Edge, Clent Hills, Barr Beacon, Cannock Chase, Stafford Castle, the Wrekin, the Welsh Hills by Welshpool, and the Clee Hills (STC p45p). A plaque to commemorate CB Mander was erected at The Mount Hotel in 1992 (Commemorative Plaques by the Wolverhampton Civic Society).

Mount, The Brick Victorian villa. Uttoxeter. Seat of Henry Brassington Bamford (1849-1928) to c1909. It was then occupied by his brother Joseph Bamford (1860-1936). By 1978 the house was the Red Cross Home (BUBA pp31,37p,40). It has also been called St Mary's Mount and was a nursing home in 1994 (UOPP pl 59).

Mount Ephraim When Jesson Lowe died in 1758 he is said to have owned a property at Mount Ephraim to the NW of Charlemont Hall (VCH vol 17 p21).

Mount Pavilion House between Little Haywood and Colwich on the N side of Main Street. The old part of the present house was built on the site of an earlier house in c1730 (HCMBOPP p34) by Charles Cope Trubshaw or 1740-2 (HAH p42 il). It was then called Mount Pleasant. In 1791 Trubshaw sold the house to a Mr Brome (HHHC p64). On Brome's death in c1825 Viscount Tamworth, son of the 7th Earl of Ferrers of Chartley Castle (see), bought the house and immediately enlarged it to be a large Gothic mansion and renamed it Mount Pavilion. But both the Viscount and the Earl died before the house was fit to be occupied (HCMBOPP p34p in 1922) (BOE p107). It was then sold to the Benedictine Order of Contemplative Nuns (founded in Paris in 1651) who began to occupy the house in 1834 (SPN p37), or in 1835 (HOSCC p100), or in 1836 (BOE p107 - 1834). The order brought with them the relics of 29 different martyrs. These included one of Venerable Margaret Ward, supposedly unique, the arm of the Venerable Oliver Plunket (now lost). The priory contained the relics of these English saints:- Blessed Richard Thirkeld, Venerable William Harrington, Venerable Thomas Pickering OSB, Venerable Richard Langhorne, and some of Venerable Philip Powel OSB (FS p365 note). Some of the relics have been given to Downside and Erdington Abbeys. The house is now called St Mary's Abbey (HCMBOPP p34). (W p415). It may have been formerly referred to as Mount Priory (S&W p256).

Mount Pleasant Is the section of road from Bilston to Willenhall which is nearest to Bilston town centre. Formerly in Bilston chapelry in Wolverhampton ancient parish. Origin of the name is unknown. Here was Bilston's windmill (BOP p47). It may be the Mount Pleasant which appears in a piece of unpublished writing about body snatching by Sabine Baring-Gould (TB Feb 1995 p17).

Mount Pleasant Former hamlet over 0.5m ESE of Brierley Hill, formerly in Kingswinford ancient parish. A Methodist chapel was built here in 1828 (OS map sheet 71.07). It was described as a hamlet in the mid C19 (W p184). It extends E from the junction of Mill Street, Delph road and Amblecote road to the junction of Thorns Road, Merry Hill, and High Street, Quarry Bank. On the 1881 OS map Mount Pleasant is the name given to an area S of this road in the vicinity of Thorns Farm (SNSV vol 1 p234). The name is preserved in the street Mount Pleasant. California is the former local name for an area near Mount Pleasant (SNSV vol 1 p55).

Mount Pleasant S of Kettlebrook, Amington. N of Dosthill.

Mount Pleasant Mount Pleasant and Lower Castle Street are on the site of the Roman settlement at Chesterton. The site is a flat-topped hill. Perhaps occupied in the Iron Age and later by the Romans. The Roman site at Holditch is 0.75m to the SSE. (MR p242) (OTP p60).

Mount Pleasant House in Ellastone could have been the model for 'Poyser's Cottage' in George Eliot's novel 'Adam Bede' which she set in Ellastone (SVB p73).

Mount Pleasant District over 0.25m SW of Fenton. The area was formerly called Great Fenton. The church, St Paul, Smithpool Road near Whieldon Road, was built in 1885 (info Mrs Bailey) (LDD).

Mount Pleasant House 0.75m NE of Forsbrook.

Mount Pleasant House 1.5m WNW of Grindon.

Mount Pleasant Shelton, Hanley. The name is preserved in Mount Pleasant (Stoke-on-Trent A-Z). Where approximately Bell's Mill (see), a water mill, was situated (OTP p151).

Mount Pleasant District of Kingswinford 1.25m SW of Kingswinford, in Kingswinford ancient parish (SNSV vol 1 p234). The name is preserved in the roads called Mount Pleasant.

Mount Pleasant In Sedgley parish (SGSAS). There is a Mount Pleasant Street off Birmingham New Road, Roseville (Birmingham A-Z).

Mount Pleasant W suburb of Uttoxeter.

Mount Pleasant House 0.25m NW of Whiston, Foxt.

Mount Pleasant House slightly under 1m SE of Cellarhead, at SJ 967466.

Mount Sinai Great Bridgeford. On S banks of the Sow directly W of Creswell chapel ruins.

Mousecroft Small area between Cannon Street and Regent Road, Hanley (POTP p122).

Mousehall Mousehall Farm, 0.75m S of Brierley Hill, between the Thorns and Amblecote Road, may have been built for the ranger of Pensnett Chase (KCPC p13). John Cary, who was Pensnett Chase head ranger, lived here in the early C17 (TB June 1974 p11). The Carys continued to live at Mousehall until the end of the C18. Mousehall Farm still stood in 1950 (KCPC p13), but appears to have been demolished shortly after (SNSV vol 2 p57). The name has appeared as Mousall (1665. 1691), Mousul (1832) (SVS), and Mouse Hole Farm (Fowler's survey 1840) (SNSV p235).

Mouse Hill Area 0.25m WNW of Pelsall. Formerly in Pelsall township. The name, which occurs in the 1841 census, is preserved in the name of a street, S of the Wolverhampton Road. The name may be from an infestation of mice in the area (SNBP p87). Or more likely a corruption of Malthouse Croft; that name appears in this area on the 1843 tithe map (SNBP p87). Pelsall Foundry established at Mousehill by Ernest Wilkes in 1852 closed in 1977 (PTYV pp14,22).

Mouse Low Burial mound said to be near Deepdale. Is 14 paces in diameter and two feet high. Excavated by Carrington in 1848. A crouched male skeleton with a necked beaker, four barbed and tangled arrowheads and a flint dagger were found (TYD pp115-116) (VCH vol 1 no 5) (BAP vol 1 p88 fig p60) (DAJ vol 75 pp76,105,114,118) (NSJFS 1965 p39). A flint arrow-head was found in a bronze drinking-cup (S p45) (SOSH p10).

Mouse Park A field name in the Eccleshall district (ESH p18).

Mousesweet Brook Source is in the Rowley Hills. It runs through the former Pensnett Chase (KCPC p12) and joins the Stour to the SE of Quarry Bank. Scott in the early 1830s called it Watchern Brook (SNSV vol 1 p87). Just S of its confluence with Black Brook it was dammed to form Cradley Pool. Anciently Mootsmeet Brook, a name from an old Saxon boundary name Moot Meet (BCWJ p80); the brook formed the boundary between Rowley Regis (Staffs) and Dudley (Worcs) parishes.

Mow Cop (to rhyme with cow SGS p128). Prominent great rocky hill or crag

1091 feet above sea level (LGS pp3,189) or 1101 feet (NSFCT 1882 p32) made up of Carboniferous Yoredale rocks; the oldest in the area (MR p235). Has appeared as Mowel (c1270) (SSE 1996 p16), Mowa, Mouhul (SPN p85), and Mole Cop (Plot's map). The name is derived from Old English 'muga,' heap (? boundary cairn) and 'copp,' hill (NSFCT 1947 p166). Others say it is derived from 'moel coppa' meaning 'bald hill' (TTTD p172). (MC p20) (SPN p85) (SSE 1996 p16).

Stone from Mow Cop was formerly popular for **millstones**. Stone here was hewn by the Romans for that purpose. Quarrying for millstones flourished in the C13 and C14 (KAIW p2). In the C17 grinding stones were obtained from quarries here by cleaving the rock with a great number of small wedges lest the stone should crack (NSFCT 1979 p17). The curious tall rock pinnacle on the hill called the Old Man of Mow (see) may have been made by this quarrying. On the hill are many **springs** utilized by the inhabitants of Mow Cop village, one is the Parson's Well (see), another is the Squire's Well (see). The other unnamed wells are; a spout well in Church Street; a spring well on footpath around St Luke's church; a well in the top field of Rose Cottage Farm, Close Lane (Ches); a spring in Halls Road (Ches); Well Street or Bakers Lane Well, built into a wall (Ches); wishing wells at Nos. 33 and 53 High Street (Ches); a slab-covered well at No. 28 Congleton Road, and a well in the wall outside No. 126 Congleton Road with inscription on stone plaque 'For the Refreshment of Weary Travellers. God Speed them on their way. J.Y.B. 1861' above a gargoyled cup (WMC p); a freshly-made well at No. 100 Station Road (Ches) (all these wells are mentioned in WMC). Mow Cop was probably the site of a **beacon**. There is a farm on the Biddulph side of the hill called Beacon House farm (NSFCT 1947 p166). The hill, and possibly the folly (see below), was used by Yates as a triangulation point for his map (1775), and by the surveyors for the first OS map (SHC 4th series vol 12 1984 vii). Hugh Bourne of Bemersley Green (see) organised a camp meeting on the hill in imitation of the **revivalist camp meetings** held in America for his followers. The meeting took place on the Cheshire side on Sunday, May 31 1807 and started at 6.00am and continued without a break until 8.30pm (VCH vol 3 p127). This turned out to be the first general meeting for the Primitive Methodists, although the assembly met under the auspices, although not the approval of, the Wesleyan Methodists, of whom Hugh Bourne was a member. The name Primitive Methodist was not adopted by the Society until Feb 1812 (LGS p48) (VCH vol 3 p129). There have been large gatherings of Primitive Methodists on the hill to celebrate anniversaries of the original meeting, for instance, in 1857, 1907, and 1957, and it is believed that a small group of the local Methodist circuit met annually to mark the event, which had by the late 1990s an ecumenical attendance. In 1936 the hill and the folly were given by Joseph Lovatt to the NT, and the deeds were formally handed over to it in 1937 in a ceremony which marked the original meeting's 130th anniversary (info Stephen Hatcher and John Anderson) (ES April 24 1937 p1. May 31 1937 p6. June 3 2000 p5) (STM June 1970 p13p) (TTTD p173) (PWNS p138p). In 1841 the Primitive Methodists erected a chapel in the area of the original meeting, which is on the Ches side (MC p22 pl xxi). A plaque from this chapel, which reads

PRIMITIVE METHODIST CHAPEL. 1841. Hitherto hath the
Lord Helped Us

was re-erected on the outside wall of the later and nearby Primitive Methodist Chapel of 1860, which was enlarged 1882. Above this plaque was placed another which reads

The stone beneath was taken from the first chapel and inserted here
by John Shenton of Silverdale 1903

(MC p39) (TSW p10p). The **Staffordshire Way**, a footpath which runs for 92 or 95 miles across the length of the county from Mow Cop (north) to Kinver Edge (south), was created by Staffs county council. The first stage, that from Mow Cop to Rocester, opened in spring 1977; the second stage, from Rocester to Cannock Chase, opened in 1979; the third stage, from Cannock Chase to Kinver Edge, opened in 1983. The path became a part of the E2 trans-Europe footpath in 1999 (The Staffordshire Way handbooks) (E&S Oct 2 1999 p14). **Views**. Prospects of Mow Cop can be viewed from as far as Oulton Heath, Hanchurch Hills, and even from Yarlet Bank in the S, and from many places on the Cheshire Plain. From Mow Cop Liverpool docks, Beeston Castle, Jodrell Bank, Shutlings Low, the Roaches, and the Clwydian Mountains in Wales can be seen on a clear day.

MOW COP FOLLY. Very prominent circular turret and wall with an arch crowning the summit of Mow Cop hill. It was erected by the Wilbraham family of Rode Hall, Ches, 2m to the W of the summit, as an eye-catcher and summerhouse (DoE II) and is often known as Wilbraham's Folly (TTTD p173) and has been called Mow Cop Castle (SN Oct 28 1999 p9p) and the Castle. According to a tradition the folly was built at the end of the C17, or possibly sometime between 1716 and 1726, but the most likely date is 1754, for the then owner of Rode Hall, Randle Wilbraham (BOEC p285) (ES Oct 20 1980). The folly is 32 feet high and 20 feet in diameter with walls three feet thick. On the S side is a supporting wall with an archway 20 feet high and 12 feet wide (TTTD p173). The folly may also have been used as a beacon, since it was discovered the roof the turret used to have, was concave suitable for holding burning material. There were originally two floors in the turret and it was furnished as befitting a summerhouse belonging to a country house. The windows of the turret were also glazed and the bare ground surrounding the folly was once grass. There were small repairs to the building in 1824 and in 1841. In 1847 the Wilbrahams returned to Ches from Lancs and took steps to restore the building. However, by this time the Sneyd family of Keele Hall who owned the land on the Staffs side on which the folly partly lay, were claiming possession of half the building. The dispute over ownership resulted in a case heard by Justice Patteson at Staffs Assizes on March 19 1850. As a result of this the Wilbrahams and the Sneyds amicably agreed to share the building and keep a key each, with a third key kept at Mow Cop, and allow public assess as before (MC pp10,11,18) (PS p22p) (LGS p189) (KES p154) (NSFCT 1947 p166) (VB p186) (BOE p207) (SL p135) (SGS p128) (ES Oct 20 1980) (SLM Nov/Dec 1983. June/July 1987) (KTM p80il) (MR p235p) (PWNS p138p). By Oct 1999 the NT had fenced off the folly during the week to prevent hooligans and drug-users frequenting it and leaving rubbish in the turret (ES Oct 28 1999 p9).

MOW COP IN LITERATURE. For a poem entitled 'Moule Cop' which appeared in the Pottery Gazette on Nov 9 1822 see Broughton's Scrapbook p89. Noah Heath's much anthologised 'Lines Wrote Upon Mow Cop' appears in his 'Miscellaneous Poems' (1823) (VFC p63). The poem 'Mow Cop' composed by David Oakes begins

> Mow Cop, it is a pleasant place,
> The summer-house stands high,
> Those rugged rocks have braved many blasts,
> And the clouds floating in the sky.

Leese thinks the poem may have been written in the late C19 (KBT vol 2 pp38-40).

Mow Cop Large straggling village, half in Ches and half in Staffs 21.5m NNW of Stafford. Takes its name from the hill, Mow Cop (see) on which it stands. The Staffs Mow Cop was partly in Wolstanton and Biddulph ancient parishes (W p290). In the later C17 Plot was impressed by an automated anvil he found working in a smith's shop a little S of Mow Cop (NHS p390 tab 32 fig 10). There was a windmill at Mow Cop (WMC p). Between 1700 and 1812 the PR of Edgmond, Shrops, contains frequent records of baptism or burial of persons belonging to Mow Cop. There are at least 75 such entries during this period, and 23 different family names are involved. No marriages are recorded of the parties concerned, which indicated to John Dearden, that the people were of nomads or travelling tinkers with their own form of marriage. They perhaps came this way using a prehistoric trackway which runs from the Cloud and follows the ridge along England's main watershed into Shrops (TTTD p175). **Churches**. The Commissions' church, **St Thomas**, Congleton Road, was built in 1841-2; the church in Ches, **St Luke**, dates from 1875 (BOE pp206-207). Staffs Mow Cop became a separate ecclesiastical parish in 1843 (GLAUE p417). **Hillside Chapel**, a Wesleyan Methodist chapel, on Chapel Bank, was built in 1852. It closed in c1986 and was purchased as a private residence by John Anderson in 1991. In 1994 Anderson opened the Chapel Museum, a museum of local history, here, still running in 2000. The chapel is mentioned in both BOE and BOEC and may be unique for having an entry in more than one volume of Pevsner (info John Anderson) (BOE p207; says built in 1865) (BOEC p285; says built in 1862) (ES May 3 1994 p3p). The growth of Mow Cop village may be due the opening of Tower Hill Colliery to the ESE in c1840; hence the building of St Thomas' and the Primitive Methodist chapel (Ches) about this time (info John Anderson). A row of 14 cottages in Mow Cop called Welsh Row commemorates miners brought here from South Wales in c1862 (TTTD p180). It was recommended that Mow Cop and Scholar Green railway station be closed in 1963 (ES March 22 1963). Harper noted in 1907 that there were many wayside bread-baking ovens beside cottages lining the foot of Mow Cop hill. It was the custom amongst cottages to bake in turns or on certain fixed days (MC p22 pl iv shows one). A Slingsby Firefly aircraft crashed in a field near the church on

Oct 20 1998 whilst travelling from Woodford Aerodrome, near Bramshall, Greater Manchester. The French training pilot and his Spanish Air Force student were killed (ES Oct 21 1998 pp1pc,3p).

Moxley Former hamlet now a residential district in a triangle formed by High Street, Great Bridge Road and Bull Lane with Walsall Canal, Darlaston (Offlow hundred). Formerly in Darlaston and Wednesbury parishes and Bilston township and chapelry of Wolverhampton ancient parish. Early forms of Moxley suggest the place was named after a burial mound to one Mocc (DUIGNAN) (SPN p137), or Mocka (SCSF p74). It may be of Celtic 'moc' signifying 'pig.' But Hackwood thinks this extremely doubtful (WAM p7). Became a separate ecclesiastical parish in 1845 (GLAUE p417). (TB Feb 1992 p5). The Commissioners' church, All Saints, at the junction of Moxley Road and Church Street (formerly Holyhead Road), was built in 1850-1851 (HOWY p313) (BOE pp296-297). In 1816 a large number of coins, of the reigns of Elizabeth I, James I and Charles I were found near Moxley. They may have been buried during the Civil War (HOBLL p176). About 1778 finches were first crossed with canaries here to be called Moxley Mules (BCM Oct 1978 p52). (S p141). The Zeppelin L21 aircraft dropped three incendiary bombs on some brick works in Moxley on the night of Jan 31 1916. Two failed to ignite and no damage was done (BCM summer 1996 p68). The spectral figure of a woman in long dark clothes was seen by a man by the canal by the Rocket Pool at Moxley in the late 1940s. It may have been the ghost of Esther Baggott, murdered by her husband in Nov 1867 (TB Dec 1996 p11). On May 10 1999 No. 15 Hughes Road, one half of a modern semi-detached house, unexpectedly collapsed into a forgotten mine shaft, belonging to the former Moxley Colliery (BBC Midlands Today. May 10 1999. May 11 1999. May 24 1999) (Daily Telegraph May 11 1999 p8p).

Moyses Hall Farm in Bilston (W p142).

Muchall Former hamlet (PENOP p7) in Penn ancient parish. Has appeared as Mugehale (1291), Muchehale (1291) (HOWM p8), Muchall (Plot's map), and Mitchell (1834 OS map). There were gravel pits near the Stag's Head and on the Penn Road (PENOP p8). The name is preserved in Muchall Road, on E side of Penn Road, Wolverhampton. The church, St Aidan, Mount Road in Penn Fields ecclesiastical parish, was built in 1962 and serves the present residential suburb covering the former hamlet (LDD).

Muchall Grove Muchall. Built by Charles Clark in c1860 on land formerly part of the Muchall Hall estate. Clark was elected Mayor of Wolverhampton borough in 1860-1. After his death in 1863 his widow, Mary, continued to live here until the early 1870s when the house was bought by Edwin Thomas Wright, iron founder, who died in 1877 (PAIP p21). It was the seat of the Thompson family in 1908. In 1945 it was compulsorily purchased by Wolverhampton borough council for a civil defence establishment for the Civil Defence Corps. In 1962 the house and grounds were taken over by the borough's Welfare Services (Social Services). They demolished the house and built the present fifty-bed home for the elderly; this, opened in 1965, also has the name Muchall Grove (PENOP p29p) (PAIP p21) (PONP pp15-16).

Muchall Hall House which stood at the junction of Mount and Manor Roads, to the E of Upper Penn. It was bought by William Thacker in 1815. With his death in 1854 the estate was sold and broken up. Out of this break up Muchall Grove was created. (PAIP pp20-21). A Robert Thacker is found residing here in the mid C19 (W p191). Has also appeared as Mochall Hall (mem in St Bartholomew's church, Penn). (THS p186) (TB Feb 1988 p3).

Muchall Manor Farm Muchall. The farmhouse, standing in 1901, formed parted of the Lloyd estate (PENOP p26p).

Mucklestone (locally *Muxon* see rhyme under Betley). Ancient parish and former township. The village of Mucklestone lies on a gentle W-facing slope rising out of the Tern backed by undulating country, 15.25m NW of Stafford. For the prehistoric dug-out canoe found at Mucklestone see under Tern. Has appeared as Moclestone, a manor, in DB, and Mukleston (1221) (SPN p85). The **name** was thought to contain an element of 'man' in Mediomanum, on account of the Roman settlement, Mediolanium (see), being in the Mucklestone area (SA April 13 1912 p5). Or the name is derived from 'Mucel's town or tun or farmstead' (SPN p85) (SSE 1996 p160) if of Anglo-Saxon origin, which is likely since it is in DB. But if of Middle English origin then 'great stone' (DUIGNAN). The 'stone' in Mucklestone may represent a lost Neolithic burial chamber in the vicinity (NSFCT 1908 p115) (SL p36), or even a reference to the 'Devil's Ring and Finger'? There was a **church** at Mucclestone in the C11 (LDD). The present parish church, St Mary, at the junction of the Eccleshall Road and Napley road, has a late C13 or earlier C14 tower, but the rest of the church was rebuilt in 1790 (LGS p189) and again in 1883 (BOE p207). Mucklestone **parish**, founded before 1086, originally probably contained the ancient parish of Maer. Later it contained five townships in Staffs and four in Shrops, viz: Bearstone, Dorrington,

Gravenhunger and Woore (a chapelry which became a separate ecclesiastical parish in 1760) (W p398) (SHC 1916 p192) (GLAUE p417). Adam de Muckleston was granted a charter on Aug 3 1309 to hold a **market** here on Tuesdays (SHC 1909 p273 note). The market had ceased by 1500 (NSJFS 1971 p51). **Point-to-point horse races**, organised by the North Staffordshire Hunt, took place near the village from Victorian times until c1980 when the event moved to Sandon Hall (ES April 22 2000 p20p). **Persons and visitors.** From the top of the church tower **Queen Margaret of Anjou** watched the defeat of her forces at the battle of Blore Heath on Sept 23 1459. According to tradition she escaped on a horse, whose shoes were reversed, to mislead her pursuers, by a Mucklestone blacksmith called William Skelhorn. An anvil purporting to be the anvil he used remains in the churchyard. An inscription on a house opposite the church claims the house stands on the site of the smithy. (NSFCT 1884 pp14-16) (SFL p93) (FLJ 1890 p319) (BPS p44) (LGS p189) (STM Oct 1967 p30p. July 1971 pp23,24) (VB p159) (STMSM July 1980 p32) (SLM Oct/ Nov 1988 pp14,15ps) (SVB pp127,128) (COS p28p) (ROT p14) (SSGLST pp25p,26) (MR p236). She is alleged to have gone on to Madeley Old Hall (BPS p44 note) before going on to Eccleshall where she reputedly took refuge in the church (SOSH ppp161-163). Some say she spent the night at Dimsdale Hall (WWT p80). The first legal Catholic emigre priest to settle in Staffs was **Louis Martin de Laistre**, who came to tutor the children of the rector of Mucklestone in c1794 (VCH vol 3 p112). For the **'Mucklestone Idiot'** see Mucklestone Wood Farm. For the 'Mucklestone Folly' see Oakley.

Mucklestone Rectory Mucklestone. Originally built in Tudor times the house was bought from the Cistercian monks in 1539 by John Offley, a wool merchant. The building was practically rebuilt in the C18 (ES Feb 19 1982 p). On the lawn was a weeping larch with a coverage of 100 yards, perhaps the only one of its species in England (BPS p166).

Mucklestone Wood End House 0.5m SE of Mucklestone.

Mucklestone Wood Farm House 1m SE of Mucklestone. In the early C19 the house was occupied by William Smith and his sister who kept their brother, George (b c1781), an alleged lunatic, shut up in the attic half starved and in appalling conditions, so that they could receive £50 a year for keeping him. News of Mr Smith's incarceration came to Rev Henry Delves Broughton JP and Mr Eld JP who set about freeing him. On Jan 28 1826 they came to the house and after being denied access demanded entry. When in the house they searched for Mr Smith and at length found him in the attic, naked, filthy and emaciated. Mr Smith was taken to a Stafford lunatic asylum (St George's?). On the way a pencil drawing was made of him at Eccleshall. An enquiry was made into the case by a commission set up by the Lord Chancellor. After George Smith's death at the Stafford asylum in 1829, his body was returned to the same relations at Mucklestone Wood Farm, at their request. But in 1883, a workman accidentally struck a pick through Smith's coffin in Mucklestone churchyard and it was found to have never contained a body (Remarkable Case of the Mucklestone Idiot. Being a Collection of Newspaper Cuttings, inlaid; a Pen and Ink Portrait of the Idiot: and Trial of Smith-v.-Hodgetts and others for Libel (Birmingham Journal) 1826. Compiled by James Broughton) (BS p410) (BPS pp164-166). By 1981 the house was called White House Farm (1981 OS map 1:25,000).

Muckley Corner Tiny hamlet on Watling Street 1m SE of Hammerwich. Formerly in Hammerwich out-township in St Michael's parish, Lichfield (W p516) and on the boundary with the extra-parochial liberty of Ogley Hay. Has appeared as Muckley (mid C13), and Mucklow (C16-C17), and Muckley Corner (by 1660) (VCH vol 14 p285). Muckley means the great 'leah' (a wood or clearing in woodland) (VCH vol 14 p285). Mucklow may be from 'Mucel's low,' or quite likely 'great low,' from a great low long obliterated for farming, although there is no documentary evidence a burial mound existed (DUIGNAN) (SSE 1996 p16). The inn Muckley Corner House at the junction of the turnpike road and Watling Street was in existence by the 1790s. By the mid C19 and until 1883 petty sessions were held at the inn, where there was a lock-up (VCH vol 14 p285). The lime kilns in existence at Muckley Corner by 1845 are said to have ceased working in the mid 1890s (VCH vol 14 p293).

Mud Dale A dale, N of Coney Dale, now lost to a huge sand and gravel quarry 2m SE of Cheadle (1834 OS map).

Mullet Park Near Pensnett, Kingswinford.

Mumber Lane N of Little London, Willenhall (1834 OS map). It appears to be a past form of Monmer Lane (see).

Mumbles Square House on main Lichfield road SW of Hixon (1834 OS map) (Dower's map).

Mumper's Dingle Place which appears in George Borrow's novel 'Lavengro' (1851). Borrow (1803-1881) is known to have stayed here between June 21

and Aug 1 1825, and its site is said by him to be above five miles from Willenhall. In the novel the fictional Isopel Berners camps at Mumper's Dingle, and here Lavengro fights Jack Bosville ('the Flaming Tinman') and tries to teach Armenian to Isopel Berners (VB p38). In the Dec 1880 issue of the Cornhill Magazine L Stephens enquires about the location of Mumper's Dingle. In 1900 WI Knapp in 'The Life, Writings and Correspondence of George Borrow' (1899) identified it to a spot occupied by the Monmer Lane Ironworks which had totally obliterated it. But Sampson in the Introduction to 'The Romany Rye' 1903 edition says Knapp's conclusion had been too hastily reached, and suggests the more likely site is in the vicinity of Dingle Lane, Dingle Bridge and a field called Dingle Piece (NSFCT 1950 pp16-18,23-24). Masefield says the Dingle was used later in the C19 as a marl pit, and then the Bentley Canal was cut through it (LGS p255) (MR p382). Dingle Lane is off Thorne Road, Little London (Birmingham A-Z). The OS map 1834 does not mark it, leaving its precise position, speculative. Generally, it is thought to be located somewhere between Mumber Lane and Ashmoor Lake, N of Bentley Canal. Although some believe it is a composite of two or three places, one of which lay in the Black Country, at Bilston or Willenhall (TB Oct 1977 p29. March 1979 p27. Aug 1981 pp1,5. Oct 1982 p23. Sept 1988 p16 see map. Feb 1993 p29 - Ambrose Smith was the model for 'Jasper Petulengro.' Nov 1994 p1). Some even believe Mumper's Dingle is about at Pulford, Cheshire where Lavengro crossed to Wales in the novel (ES Jan 17 1930 p4). Or some believe it was at Shrewsbury (TB Nov 1981 p15). (SOSH p317) (NSFCT 1950 pp13-30) (In the Steps of George Borrow. Eileen Bigland. 1951) (BCM July 1972 p71. Oct 1972 p70. Oct 1978 pp54-59. Jan 1980 pp38-41) (AOW p173). Mumper's Dingle is possibly so called after the disease mumps: The children of the gypsies who lived here reputedly had mumps (TB April 1979 p5). See also Monmore Lane.

Murder Bridge In the Dennis Park and Clockfields area, Amblecote (SNSV vol 1 p98).

Murder Bridge Appears to be a former railway bridge at Withymoor Village, in the Plants Hollow area (BCM spring 1999 p75).

Musden Grange House and former extra parochial liberty in the Moorlands on a hillside high above the Manifold, 1.5m NE of Calton. It remained extra-parochial until 1857 (NSFCT 1913 p62), or 1858 when it became a civil parish. The civil parish was abolished in 1886 when it entered Ilam ancient parish (NSFCT 1917 pp41-51) (GLAUE p417). Food vessels of the Beaker people, of the Yorkshire type, have been found at Musden (NSJFS 1962 p33). In a burial mound at Musden was found a bronze dagger (NSFCT 1926 p146). These finds were probably made on Musden Low (see). Musedene, waste, appears in DB. The name may mean 'valley of mice' (NSJFS 1981 p2) (PNPD). The Musden estate, approximately 600 acres including Upper Musden, Doglane, and Musden Low, was given to Croxden Abbey from the later C12. The abbey shortly depopulated the sizeable village, which may have been situated in the Upper Musden area, and turned the estate into a grange. The grange appears to have been leased to the Bassetts by the mid C15. It was granted to Richard Cotton in 1545. In the later C16 Musden passed through several hands until it passed in 1584 to Gilbert Lord Talbot, later earl of Shrewsbury. By the early C18 it was divided into two - Upper Musden and Lower Musden. The grange buildings, which lay at SK 123511 to the W of the present house, did not survive long after the Dissolution. A survey of the site was made in 1985. On account of Musden having been a grange it obtained extra-parochial status (NSJFS 1961 p137) (NSFCT 1913 p62. 1917 p43) (VCH vol 3 p226) (SL p73) (SASR 1995 no 5 pp30-36 plans).

Musden Low Hill high above a bend in the Manifold 0.75m E of Calton. Has at least four burial mounds situated on it. One topping the summit at SK 11845008 is a listed monument. It is 28 paces in diameter and four feet high. Carrington excavated in 1848/ 49 and found a skeleton and cremation (TYD pp118,151) (VCH vol 1 no 7 and 30). The one farthest S at SK 11854991 is 18 paces in diameter and three feet high and a listed monument. Carrington excavated it in 1849/ 50 and found nothing (TYD pp138,139,164). Slightly to its W is one at SK 11785008. It is 21 paces in diameter and five feet high and a listed monument. Carrington excavated this in 1848 and found a cremation, a skeleton and two globular narrow-necked urns, probably of C6 origin (TYD pp119-120) (VCH vol 1 no 9) (Gazetteer of Early Anglo-Saxon Burial Mounds. A Meaney. 1964 p221) (Medieval Archaeology. vol 6/ 7 p45 fig 13b). Slightly to its N is one at SK 11615014. It is 24 paces and three feet and a listed monument. Carrington excavated this in 1849 and found a bronze round heeled dagger and a flint scraper, three decayed skeletons one with a food vessel and two flints and near the surface were two Anglian intrusive burials, one with a pair of annular brooches possibly of C7 origin (TYD pp148-149) (ARCH vol 43 pp460-461) (VCH vol 1 no 9) (DAJ vol 74 p143. vol 75 pp109,110,112. vol 78 pp95-96) (Gazetteer of Early Anglo-Saxon Burial Mounds. A

Meaney. 1964 p221) (Medieval Archaeology. vol 6/ 7 pp44-45) (NSJFS 1965 p53). Pevsner says there are four burial mounds on Marsden Low (BOE p93). Probably, he means, Musden Low.

Mutchill's Gutter Ravine W of Horsepasture Pools, Beaudesert Old Park. Here Mutchell's Oak and Mutchell's Well are situated (1887 OS map 6 inch) (SPNO p109).

My Lady's Farm 1.25m WSW of Swindon.

Myott's Wood Wood 1.5m NE of Milwich. In Milwich parish (W p420).

Myron, The House at Histons Hill, Codsall, where Rex Farran was assassinated on May 3 1948 as he received a parcel bomb from terrorists in Palestine, called the Stern Gang, which was meant for his older brother Capt Roy Farran, an undercover agent for the British Forces in Palestine (MM pp35-42) (MMMR pp67-73) (MCS pp55-60).

Myrtles, The Wolstanton. Seat of A Boulton in 1907 (STC p35p).

Mystylowe The name in the early C17 for a mound on the Staffs Ches boundary on the Cloud. Perhaps a reference to the Bridestones (VCH vol 7 p223).

Mytholm Island created by the rivers Trent, Tame, and Meece 1.5m ESE of Alrewas. (HOA p18). On the other side of the Tame, opposite Mytholm, in the field called Rattlejack, is a strange circle in the land which may have been an ancient pen or pound (HOA pp3,4). At SK 185146 is the site of a round burial mound which is a listed monument.

N

Nabb Brook Runs from Denstone joins Alders Brook at Alders which in turn joins the Dove. The name is from the house called The Nabbs (SPNO p15).

Nabbs, The House 1m W of Denstone.

Nabend House 0.75m ESE of Hollinsclough. Formerly in Longnor township in Alstonefield ancient parish. There was a house here by 1613 (VCH vol 7 p42).

Nab Feet Upper Hulme. On E side of A53.

Nab Hill Hill to W of Leek near Westwood Heath, preserved in Nab Hill Avenue, once a part of the Leek Town Lands (OL vol 1 p262) (NSFCT 1923 p79). A tunnel carrying the Macclesfield-Uttoxeter railway line runs through it. The tunnel entrances were built to resemble a natural cavern in the rock, with no masonry at either side (VCH vol 7 p100).

Nagersfield Area between Buckpool and Brettell Lane where there was a brick works. Nagersfield fireclay mine was reputed to contain 'one of the finest seams of Old Mine fireclay in the world' and be the best equipped and most up-to-date mine in the fireclay industry (TB Jan 1996 p16). The name, which appears as Nagurs field (1774), is from possibly an open field system in Kingswinford manor (SNSV vol 1 p236).

Nag Hill One of the smaller hills in the Clent Hills. Marked on OS map 1:25,000 E of Clent.

Nags Hill Tiny hamlet at the junction of the Rugeley Road and the lane between Creswell Green and Boney Hay, on rising ground above Redmoor Brook on the edge of the former Gentleshaw Common (info Margaret Brookes). Lewis Wright (1889-1985), poet and novelist, lived in a cottage here. His 'The Katty Letters,' (1977) was written in phonetic script in 1937, and purports to be from his cat to his daughter (VFC p146).

Nanny's Rock Rock or cliff face, with five compartments on W side of Kinver Edge, 0.75m SW of Holy Austin Rock. Dr Wilkes supposed it to have been once the retreat of some Christian hermit (SVS p167). Has also appeared as Nannies Rock and Mag-a-Fox Hole. The rock had a cave called Meg-o-Foxhole in c1680. This name probably originated from the cave-dweller of this time one Margaret-of-the fox earth, who died on June 8 1617 (NHS p414) (Kinver PR) (SD p34) (SHOS vol 2 p263) (W p178) (KRH pp16p,17) (VCH vol 20 p122). In the late 1750s it was stated that a few years before a poor man had converted the cave into a dwelling house for himself and his family; it is said that the date 1726 was once legible in one of the rooms (Yates' map) (LHEL vol 2 pp19-20) (Trans Worcs Arch Soc new series vol 6 p144) (VCH vol 20 p122). It was occupied by Sarah Evans in c1820 and Nancy Evans in 1830; a woman recluse was living here in c1890, by which time it was known as Nanny's Rock (VCH vol 20 p122). The name Nanny's Rock, perhaps arose, from a character known as 'Nanny,' a herbalist and potion maker, who operated from one of the caves and was visited by the inhabitants of Kinver, including the novelist, Nancy Price, who recalled visiting her during her childhood (KRH p17) (BCM spring 1997 p16). It has a chimney cut out of the rock, known as the Devil's Chimney (KRH p16). Scott writing in 1832 noted that in a steeper part of the rock is Fox's Harbour, a group of cottages, of the most romantic cast, which form a neighbourhood (SVS p167). (RKE p28). According to tradition it was also the resort of highwaymen at the end of C19 and in the early C20, and that an underground passage led from the caves to another group of rock dwellings about a mile away at Drakelow, Worcs (WJO July 1903 xxxvi) (SVB p107). Below Meg a Fox Hole at cSO 829835 Plot noted a burial mound made of stone (NHS p414), but it is probably not a burial mound (NSJFS 1965 p43).

Nan Tor At Wetton Mill (LGS p185). In the rock is Nan Tor Cave (TD) (KES p3).

Napley Heath Heath and scattered minute hamlet 0.75m NNW of Mucklestone. In Mucklestone parish. 111 acres of Napley Heath were enclosed under an Act of 1807 (SHC 1941 p20).

Napney Field Former open field of West Bromwich by Walsall Road at Hall End (SSAHST 1988-89 p32).

Narrow Dale Short and extremely narrow ravine in the Moorlands 1m NNW of Alstonefield. In Alstonefield township and ancient parish. Narrow Dale is one of the county's most famous, though little visited, dales. The dale is positioned on a north south axis between Narrowdale and Gratton Hills to the W of the Dove. It is so narrow and steep that in winter the sun cannot be seen from the dale bottom. In mid summer it can only be seen from about one 'o clock. Noon here, therefore, could be said to be at 1.00pm and is called the Narrow Dale Noon. Plot noted the local people use the expression 'Narrow Dale Noon,' to proverbially express a thing done late at noon. There is a similar dale at Lanthony, Monmouthshire (NHS p110). It is not in Onecote township or near Onecote as stated by Pitt and Raven (THS p240) (FOS p148). (Pigot & Son map 1830) - spelt Warrow Dale) (W p742) (TPC p163) (AAD p148) (S&W p298) (SCSF p45) (VB pp204,205).

Narrowdale House 1.25m NNW of Alstonefield. Named after the dale to the E of the house. Narrowdale, a settlement and a manor by the later C13 (VCH vol 7 pp11,17), may have been large enough to be considered a hamlet in the

C19. Its decline may have been brought on by the closure of Ecton Mines (AVH p57). The manor is not mentioned after the late C13 and may have been absorbed into Beresford manor (VCH vol 7 p17).

Narrowdale Hill Hill on W side of Narrowdale, Alstonefield. The burial mound on it at SK 12335726 is a listed monument. It is 11 paces in diameter and 3.5 feet high and was excavated by Bateman in 1846. Food vessels, of the Yorkshire type, of the Beaker people were found in it (VAD pp97-98) (BAP vol 1 p158 fig 194. vol 2 pp52,122 fig 477) (DAJ vol 75 pp86,89, 109-110,113. vol 77 p26 B1) (WTCEM p179) (NSJFS 1962 p33. 1965 p31) (MR p11).

Narrows, The A stretch of the Staffs and Worcs Canal at Fordhouses (WPOPP vol 1 p111p).

Nash's Coppice Wood to W of Gospel End (TB Oct 1992 p15 see map).

Nash Elm House to E of Nash End, Upper Arley (Dower's map).

Nash End Minute hamlet on a hill in undulating country at some distance from the Severn, 1m NNE of Upper Arley. Nash End was described in the late C18 as a township of Arley parish (SHOS vol 2 p253).

Natsfield Farm On W side of Stafford Road, Wallington Heath, Bloxwich. The name is from an old field name (SNBP p53).

Navigation Coffee House At Barton Turn, Barton-under-Needwood.

Naychurch House 0.5m NNE of Upper Hulme in Heathylee township in Alstonefield ancient parish. Here is a spring which has the reputation of never freezing and may have been worshipped in pagan times (Some Random thoughts on Ancient History of Leek. ND. Author unknown. From vol 10 of local pamphlets in Horace Barks Ref Lib) (NSFCT 1884 p26). The name is a corruption of the Celtic 'niath' 'nid' strong, fortress-like (NSFCT 1908 p145). A house called Knachurche appears in 1432. The present house called Naychurch retains C17 stonework (VCH vol 7 p33) (UHAW p51 il).

Neachells Former estate and hall - Neachells Hall (see) - 0.75m 1.75m ENE of Wolverhampton, 0.5m S of Wednesfield, in Wednesfield township and chapelry in Wolverhampton foreign and ancient parish (W p156) (HOWM p44). Neachells, which has also appeared as Nechels (1686), Nechells, Neechill and Neachell (Birmingham A-Z), evolved into a hamlet from Neachells Hall and other nearby homesteads (WFW p72); it was described as a village in the later C17 (NHS p415), and appears as an isolated hamlet on 1834 OS map. Place-names Etchells or Nechells, recorded from the C13 near several old-established villages seem to mean 'land added to an estate by reclamation' ('Selected Papers' E Ekwall (Lund Studies in English 33. 1963) pp33-35) (TYS p22) (SL p72). Or is from probably Old French 'echells,' ladders, steps, stairs, meaning, in substance, a two-story house, where the access to the upper floor was by an internal ladder or outer steps; in the C13 a two-storied house was a rarity (DUIGNAN). By the 1980s it had become an wholly industrial district surrounded by Black Country conurbation. A goblin-like figure was seen running across the bridge in Neachells Lane in the 1970s (GPCE p62).

Neachells Branch of the Bentley Canal. Spurred off the Bentley Canal at Merills Hall. Ran to Neachells Hall Colliery. Opened in 1845. Closure sanctioned in 1953 (HCMS No. 2).

Neachells Farm Stood to the S of Neachells Hall on the E side of Neachells Lane. It belonged to Silvester Hayes (bailiff of the Deanery manor of Wolverhampton) who purchased from Thomas Neachells 'The Moat Croft' at Neachells and other lands in that hamlet in 1624 (WFW p79). It later belonged to the Grosvenor family (WHTOP p17p of c1950). It was demolished in the 1970s. Its moat was destroyed by mining at the beginning of the C20 (WFW pp67,74p of c1940) (SSAHST 1982-3 p55) (CAMS p61).

Neachells Hall Former C14 structure of two storeys near the junction of Strawberry Lane and Neachells Lane, at SO 947989 at Neachells. It may be identified with 'the entrenched place of Wulfrin' occurring in a document of 1240 concerning Prestwood (WFW p48). It was owned by the Hopes in the C16, and taxed on six hearths in 1666. The Tomkys seem to have been resident at Neachells Hall in the C17 and C18. A painting was made of the hall (titled 'Wednesfield Old Hall') by Thomas Wood of Great Haywood in 1837. In the 1850s it was used as a beerhouse known as 'The Board' and thereafter fell into disuse and disrepair. Only a part of the gateway remained in the early C20. By 1978 no living person could remember the hall standing. Its rectangular moat survived until the late C19 (HOBLL pp133,134,135) (WFW pp67,74il) (SSAHST 1982-3 p55) (CAMS p61).

Near Clump, The Baldwin's Gate. Bears a very strong superficial resemblance to a long burial mound (NSFCT 1935 p70).

Needwood Ecclesiastical parish and modern minute hamlet 0.75m NNW of Rangemore, near the centre of the former Needwood Forest. A polished flint celt and a bronze palstave with a broken loop are said to have been found in the Needwood area in 1864 (BTIH p9). The hamlet was formerly known as Five Roads End, as it grew at the junction of five straight roads, which were

made at the time of the enclosure of Needwood Forest in c1811. The New Inn, marked on the 1834 OS map, appropriately placed at the convergence of the roads is probably coeval with the building of the roads, and the hamlet developed from this settlement. The ecclesiastical parish of Needwood was created out of parts of Rangemore, Tutbury, Marchington Woodlands, Newborough, Yoxall, Barton-under-Needwood, and Scropton parishes in 1895 (GLAUE p417).

Needwood Forest Said to have been once a large 'natural' forest and to have comprised the entire tract of land on a high plateau between Trent, Dove and Blithe (VCH vol 2 p349) (SL p54) and the later private park of Chartley Park. The forest lay in Rolleston and Hanbury parishes (SGSAS).
EARLY to 1600. On Needwood Forest Lands in Marchington parish was found a polished flint axe of Neolithic or Bronze Age which went to the BM (NSJFS 1964 p29) (see also Forest Banks). A promontory fort existed above Marchington commanding the Dove Valley: According to David Ford the well defined earthworks of it can still (1999) clearly be seen in woodland (LTD p115). For a gold torc found in Hanbury parish in Needwood Forest see under Greaves Wood. An ancient track (HOPT vol 1 p10), or Roman road struck SE through Checkley, Uttoxeter and across Needwood Forest straight for Leicester. It was traceable across the forest at the end of the C18 (NSFCT 1908 p110). The **name** could be a corruption of Neat's Wood - the wood of cattle (HOU p49). In Welsh, nedd, nydd means 'what turns, a dingle, a resting-place' (DUIGNAN) (HOPT vol 1 p137). Mills and Gelling think the 'refuge wood' (NSJFS 1981 p3) (SSE 1996 p16). **After the Norman Conquest** the forest became a hunting preserve of the Ferrers family. Its status then became that of a chase, although it continued to be referred to as a forest: It is only referred to as a chase in one charter, that of April 1248 (VCH vol 2 p349) (SSE 1990 p24). Has appeared as Nedwode (1248) (SSE 1996 p16), and Nedwood Forest (1698) (Illustrated Journeys of Celia Fiennes edited by Chris Morris. 1984. p149). Robert de Ferrers, 6th Earl of Derby, forfeited his lands including Needwood Forest to the Crown in 1266 for his part in the Barons' War (VCH vol 2 p350) (SL p64). In 1267 Henry III granted the forest to his son Edmund, Earl of Lancaster (VCH vol 2 p350). In 1285, Edward I granted his brother Edmund, Earl of Lancaster, the right to appoint Justices of the Forest whenever necessary, after this the forest was administered under forest law (VCH vol 2 pp350-351) (NSJFS 1968 p49). The forest was in the king's hands from 1322 to 1327 as a result of the rebellion of Thomas, Earl of Lancaster, in 1322 (HCT p57) (VCH vol 2 p358). When ownership of the Duchy of Lancaster which included the forest passed to the Crown in 1399 the forest officially ceased being a chase and became a forest (SL p69). The forest remained part of the Crown estates to the Enclosure Act of 1801. Before enclosure it may have been 9,920 acres in **extent** when it anciently enclosed Hanbury, Yoxall, Barton, Tutbury and Marchington (NSFCT 1953 p118) or roughly 9,000 acres (ESNF p8p). At the time of enclosure it covered 9,400 acres with a circumference of 23m (LTD p118), and in 1946 covered 8,000 acres with a circumference of 24m (NSFCT 1946 p149). **Hunting rights**. The granting of hunting rights in Needwood Forest by the abbots of Burton Abbey in the C12, may have initiated the custom of annual horn dancing in Abbots Bromley (VB p107). In 1492 Henry VII granted hunting in the forest (R&S p18). **Royal visitors and travellers**. **Richard II** hunted in the forest. He was often a guest of the Bagot family (AA Book of British Villages, see under Abbots Bromley). **Mary, Queen of Scots**, rode and hawked in the forest when held at Tutbury (VB p91). **James I** hunted in Needwood Forest in 1619, 1621, and 1624 (UTR p99); and **Charles I** did in 1634 and 1634 (HCT pp88,207-8,219) (VCH vol 2 p356). **Robin Hood**. The battle referred to as taking place near Tutbury Town in the ballad about Robin Hood (see Loxley) is said to have taken place in Needwood Forest at Marchington Cliff (see) (LTD p116). According to tradition, as a forester told W Byford-Jones in the 1930s, there is a stone which marks the spot in Needwood Forest where Robin Hood lay hidden in a thicket to escape from the King's men (QML pp156-161). Another tradition tells of a house at Six Lanes End (probably Six Roads End) which was built on the foundations of the one in which Robin Hood was born (QML pp156-161). There is a local tradition that certain houses in Needwood Forest had 'fog bells' and each house rung a particular number of strokes, so that the wanderer might know his locality. The house bell for Yoxall Lodge had the date 1785 (NSFCT 1929 p180). In 1356 **David Kynric** (Kenric) lost his way in Needwood Forest, returning home from the French wars. He emerged out of forest - then stretching across the whole of N Staffs - at Ashley and vowed to rebuild the church there in thanksgiving for his safe delivery (VB p159). **Lady Tansley**, an abbess, whilst journeying from Tutbury to Uttoxeter also became lost in Needwood Forest, but found her way to Uttoxeter after hearing its curfew bell. As a thanksgiving she gave a bell full of money to Uttoxeter (see) to ensure the perpetual ring-

ing of the curfew bell (SCSF p160). **John Leland** in the earlier C16 found Needwood 'mervelusly plenished with dere' (LI vol 5 p22) (HOPT vol 1 p161). In the later C16 **William Camden** (1551-1623), antiquarian and historian, visited the forest (VCH vol 2 pp355-356). **Celia Fiennes** travelled through Needwood Forest on her way to Derby in summer 1698 (Illustrated Journeys of Celia Fiennes edited by Chris Morris. 1984. p149).
ADMINISTRATION. **Wards** were the territories into which the forest was divided by the Ferrers family in order to be administered. Five wards - Barton, Marchington, Tutbury, Uttoxeter, Yoxall - were created sometime between 1086 and 1266 (NSFCT 1929 p180). Each ward had its own hereditary forester (VCH vol 2 pp349,350 see map) (NSJFS 1968 p51 map). The officers for each ward lived in 'lodges' (LGS p191) - Byrkley Lodge (see) in Tutbury ward; Sherholt Lodge (see) in Barton ward; Yoxall Lodge (see) in Yoxall ward; and Ealand Lodge (see) in Marchington ward (ESNF p8). Four woodmote courts were held a year, probably in the chapel at Tutbury Castle, or at Byrkley Lodge. The **woodmote** tried forest offenders until the C17 and comprised a jury of 24 men (SHOS vol 1 p61) (W p571) (UTR p109). From the C17 many of the more serious offences seem to have been dealt with by JPs or at the Assizes (LGS p191) (VCH vol 2 p351). The first **Master Forester** appears by 1306. From 1417 the office was usually combined with that of the steward of Tutbury. There was a holder of this office until disafforestation in the early C19 (VCH vol 2 p358). The **Chief Ranger** and his deputy, with lieutenants and keepers under him had charge of the deer and other game, while an **Axe-Bearer** with his deputy and woodmen, saw to the felling and planting of timber; Robert J Harper of the New Lodge was axe-bearer to Queen Victoria (SHOS vol 1 p61) (W pp560,571) (LGS p191). The prime income from the forest was building timber and major timbers were called 'Houseboote' and smaller timbers 'Hayboote' (LTD p119). According to tradition in the C15 there was a position called **knave of the ward**. The holder of this office went every night to the border of the forest and blew a horn to keep the deer out of men's corn and grass; his fee was a levy of corn from each tenant (HCT pp358-359) (VCH vol 2 p350). Common rights in the forest were claimed by 18 townships each having their own burn identity mark (HOPT vol 1 p161 il). For the administration of the forest see GNHS p145 and VCH vol 2 pp349-358.
GATES AND PARKS. There are said to have been 32 **gates** into the forest (UNT p4). CH Underhill gives 20; there were, starting with Callingwood Gate, on the east, and proceeding clockwise, Tatenhill Gate, Dunstall Gate, Barton Gate, Blakenhall Gate, Wood Lane Gate, Wood Lane Gate, Wood Mill Gate, Hadley End Gate, Mustard Makers' Lane Gate, Ravens' Nest Gate, Dole Foote Gate, Moat Lane Gate, Duffy Lane Gate, Tomlinson's Gate, Buttermilk Hill Gate, Stubby Lane Gate, Draycott Gate, Hanbury Wood End Gate, Blackbrook Gate and Anslow Gate (UTR p114). Twelve deer **parks** were created in the forest (SL p90). White says there were anciently eight parks impaled within the ring of the forest: Agardsley, Stockley, Barton, Heylyns (Highlands), Sherholt, Castle Hay, Hanbury and Rolleston (W p571). Cantor adds these others on the periphery: Rowley, Yoxall and Uttoxeter (NSJFS 1968 p49), and Shirley adds - New Park and Tutbury or Castle Park (EDP).
1600 to PRESENT. The Uttoxeter Ward was enclosed and disafforested between 1636-39 (SL p106). Conscripts raised in SW Staffs to suppress the Scottish rebellion and sent to Uttoxeter, to be escorted to the N, rioted in Needwood Forest in 1639 (VCH vol 2 p352), or July 1 1640 (SHC vol 15 New Series p202) (NSJFS 1966 p15) (BFS p4). They are said to have pulled down the fences of enclosures in the Highwood area in Uttoxeter Ward (BFS p4). Parliament nearly sold the forest in 1654 to raise money to pay its soldiers. 834 signed a petition against the sale (VCH vol 2 pp352-353), which was presented to Oliver Cromwell on Feb 5 1654 (SHOS vol 1 pp62,63). Riots against enclosure occurred on March 25 1654 involving 200 armed commoners (LOU pp68-69,344). Between 1656 and 1658 a Commonwealth commission drew up plans to enclose the forest with 4610 acres going to the Commonwealth and the other 4610 acres going to the 22 townships (including allegedly in Scropton, Derbys) who claimed common rights (SHOS vol 1 pp62,63) (VCH vol 2 pp352-353). There were further riots in 1659 when enclosure of the forest was attempted (VCH vol 2 p352. vol 6 p53). The sale and enclosure was delayed for administrative reasons and by the Restoration of Charles II (VCH vol 2 pp352-353) (NSJFS 1969 pp4-5). There were schemes to sell the forest in 1663 and 1683 (VCH vol 2 p353). In one Charles II nearly sold the forest; a fee was paid for it. To compensate the prospective purchaser, the purchaser was allowed to fell over half the total trees in the forest, this occurred between 1697 and 1701. Proposals for disafforestation and enclosure requested in 1778 by the duchy court were circulated in 1779 but never became law (VCH vol 2 pp353-354). An Enclosure Act was passed

in 1801. The remaining forest was enclosed between 1802 and 1811. The final award was made in 1811 (VCH vol 2 p354) (NSJFS 1969 p5) (SL p119). All common rights were then extinguished. The current straight roads through it are not Roman but made at the time of the enclosures in c1807. **People and Folklore**. Miss Burne wrote in NSFCT 1896 p122 that the local people were still not sufficiently used to enclosures even by 1896 to have learnt to keep gates shut. Local superstitions long prevailed in the forest. About 1893 an old oak in the old deer park at Hanbury in Needwood Forest was struck down by lightning, and people came from all around to get pieces of the stricken wood as a charm to preserve their houses from lightning (FLJ 1896 pp380-381). Forest inhabitants also considered the burning of any green thing unlucky (NSFCT 1896 p122). They also considered the burning of elder boughs bad luck and therefore could not use elder boughs as fuel (FLJ 1896 p380. 1911 p24). It was also believed that holly and ivy must never be burnt and some of it must be kept until the following year to save the house from lightning (BCC vol 3 p245). The Needwood Foresters, an archery society for prominent families living in the Needwood Forest area, was found in 1822 and disbanded in Sept 1827. During this period the society is said to have met four times a year at Blithfield Hall, Byrkley Lodge, Hollybush Hall, and Dunstall Lodge (CCHCB pp10-12). Some curious natural history. In the later C17 Plot noted a vitriolic spring in the forest 1.5m SE of Hanbury near either Needwood House, Lower Castle Hayes Farm, Belmot Farm or Stockley Park (NHS p105) and a buck believed to be living in the forest which had, unusually, four branches of antlers (NHS pp260-261) (SHOS vol 2 p143). Shaw says there were or had been two ancient limes of a vast size in the forest and no others. The limes stood a mile a part from each other (SHOS vol 1 p70). References in literature. Needwood is mentioned in a rare example of early C16 English courtly love lyric verse kept in the manuscript MS Rawlinson C813 in the Bodleian Library, Oxford (Summary Catalogue 12653) (The Review of English Studies. Feb 1990 pp12-44). The forest floor was surprisingly pastoral and good for grazing cattle as Michael Drayton noted in 'Polyolbion':

Of Britain's forests all (from th'less unto the more)
For fineness of her turf surpassing.

(VCH vol 2 p355) (SL p101). Francis Noel Clarke Mundy of Markeaton, Derbys scathingly attacks disaforestion in his poem 'The Fall of Needwood' (1808); his previous poem on the forest 'Needwood Forest' (1776) celebrates its delights (BS p321) (HOPT vol 1 p161). An autumn day in the forest is described in Mary Howitt's poem 'The Chronicle of Wood Leighton; or, A Year in the Country' (1836) (NSFCT 1893 p139) (HOPT vol 1 p162).
Needwood House 1.25m N of Rangemore. In Rolleston parish. Seat of Capt CE Tennant in 1851 (W pp22,575).
Needwood Manor (IVNF photograph). 0.5m ESE of Rangemore. Built in a Scottish baronial castle style. Is now a hotel (MR p260p).
Needwood Parsonage Said to have been near Lichfield. It was a school run by a Rev Humphry Price and was attended by Thomas Smith, when aged 11, from May 1811. He was an heir to a certain property in Ireland (as grandson of William Smith of Carmoyle) and was secretly removed from the school in Sept 1812 and then claimed to be dead. A reward of £200 was put out for news of his whereabouts since his sister Jane, believed him to be still alive in the late 1820s. He was discovered in Jamaica living under the name of Crosby, in c1837. The inheritance had gone to the families of Arthur and O' Brien (Sunday Times Jan 22 1837) (Broughton's Scrapbook pp228-229).
Nellie Dale A dale by the brook which flows towards Bucknall from Wash Well (FWMBS p4).
Nelson Hall Stood S of the church at Cotes Heath. Former hostel built in c1938 for workers, relocated from Woolwich Arsenal, at the new Royal Ordinance Factory near Swynnerton. The hall was never used by them as they preferred to live in the Potteries, and during WW2 the U.S. army used it as a camp. In 1965 the building opened as Stafford Teacher Training College, which closed in 1979 (info St Thomas', Cotes Heath). It was then a hostel for Ugandan refugees. By the mid 1990s the hall had been demolished and the site redeveloped as an housing estate. It is named after Admiral Lord Nelson. (local info).
Netherby Hall Formerly stood in Netherby Road, Gospel End (PAIP pp112,113il), or on the N side of Gospel End Road, near Caswell Road (BCM Dec 1997 p43il), Sedgley. Built in the 1860s by John Millard. Had an impressive gatehouse-looking front with castellated battlements. Sometime home of Major Haden (BCM Dec 1997 p43). Demolished in the 1950s (PAIP pp112,113).
Nether Hall or Low Hall or Lower Hall, Burton upon Trent. This was the Blount

family's town house as opposed to their seat, Blount's Hall, at Blount's Green, Uttoxeter. In time it passed to the Gresley family (SHOS vol 1 p12). Nether Hall at Wetmore, near Burton upon Trent was occupied by a branch of the Blount family of Burton Blount in the later C15 (ANS p45). Richard Almond, steward of Lord Paget, acquired Nether Hall in 1622 (BTIH p49). Nether Hall was pulled down a long time ago (info KL Neal. 1999).

Nether Hulme Medieval settlement 0.5m SSE of Meerbrook at the confluence of the Churnet and Meerbrook, in existence by the mid C13 (VCH vol 7 p193). It may be the oldest Hulme settlement of the three - Nether, Middle and Upper (SHC 1999 p7 note). Had become a grange, known as Nether Hulme Grange and later as New Grange (see), of Dieulacres Abbey by 1291. Has appeared N Holme (Plot's map), North Holm (Bowen's map), and New Grange (1834 OS map).

Netherland Green Minute hamlet 2m W of Marchington. In Uttoxeter parish.

Netherset Hay House 1m SE of Madeley. In Madeley parish. Has also appeared as Netherset Hey. In a field by the house has been found a paved surface (Lancs and Ches Ant Soc. vol 13. 1895. p184) (JBAA series 2 vol 2 p124) (NSJFS 1964 p29). Nearly all the cattle of Netherset Hey Farm died in the Cattle Plague of 1866 (AADB p63).

Netherset Hay Park Medieval deer park which lay to N of Madeley Great Park. The smallest (approximately 430 acres) and the shortest-lived of the parks of the Earls of Stafford at Madeley. In existence by 1401 when described as 'The Littil Park' (NSJFS 1963 pp53-55 plan. 1964 p64) (MHSP p16).

Nether Stowe Small district of Lichfield N of Stowe.

Netherton There was settlement at Netherton, at the foot of Tinacre Hill SW of Wightwick, by 1327 (VCH vol 20 p10). Marked on 1880-6 (2 inch to 1m) and 1905 OS maps. In Tettenhall ancient parish.

Nethertown Hamlet 1.75m E of Hill Ridware. In Hamstall Ridware ancient parish. Shaw called it Walter's Ridware since in DB Walter was the holder of the nether most town of the Ridwares (SHOS vol 1 p151). Has also appeared as Netherton. It was perhaps so called to define it from Hamstall Ridware, the upper town (SHOS vol 1 p151 note).

Nettlebed (1834 OS map). It is now Middle Linbrook Farm? 0.5m W of Needwood.

Newbold Former manor represented by Newbold Manor Farm, over 1m ENE of Barton-under-Needwood. In Tatenhill ancient parish. CGO Bridgeman has identified the Newe Bolde in a charter of 942 with Newbold (SHC 1916 pp84,85) (SSE 1991 p8). The name means 'new house' (HOPT vol 1 p137). Robert de Ferrers (1266) gave the tithes of Newbold to the Abbey of Nostel, Yorks, of which he was a patron. The manor has always been associated with Dunstall and passed in the same descent to the Somervilles, Griffiths and Sir Francis Boynton, who sold it to Sir Francis Brecknock and others (HOPT vol 1 p131). In the fields in or surrounding Newbold, Plot noted in the later C17, cattles' coats turned a different colour (NHS p111). Plot noted salt springs at Newbold grounds, which he says are about midway between Burton and Branston. Here Mr Fownes tried to develop salt making but failed (NHS p98).

Newbolds, The Ancient farm in Wednesfield township, 1.75m NE of Wolverhampton. There is believed to have been a house here since at least the C12. The name, occurring between 1290 and 1376 as Newboldsbruche (c1290), Le Newbolds, and le Newbolt, means 'new house.' In 1595 it was purchased by John Gough and remained a part of the Gough estate with Old Fallings until c1878 (DUIGNAN) (WFW p69). The present (1992) house was built in the C18 and was a working farm until 1933. It is now (1992) divided into flats (WFW p48) (WHTOP p157p). The moat to the E of the farm was quite small (WFW p69) (SSAHST 1982-3 p56). According to the 1834 OS map it stands on the E side of Deyncourt Road near its junction with Fairview Road.

Newborough Village in a narrow valley on Ealand Brook, 13.25m E of Stafford. Former township and chapelry in Hanbury ancient parish (W p561). A Roman Republican coin has been found in Newborough parish, it is now lost (GNHS 1860 p8) (NSJFS 1964 p30). The same or another Roman coin, of base silver, was found in Newborough, which was in the possession of Robert Garner in the C19 (HOU p339). Newborough was originally a hamlet called Agardsley (see) until it was made a new free borough by Robert de Ferrers, 6th Earl of Derby, in 1263 (VCH vol 2 p349). Has appeared as Neuboreg (1280) (SSE 1996 p16) and Neuburgh (1327) (SPN p86). Burgage tenure survived until at least 1609 (NSJFS 1972 p69). The earliest record of a market here is 1150-59? - this could refer to the New Borough at Tutbury (NSJFS 1971 pp52,62). Competition from villages like Abbots Bromley stifled the borough's growth and it never grew beyond the size of a small village. The regular strips of burgage plots - Shaw says there were 101 - survive as gardens (SHOS vol 1 p92) (SCSF p118) (SL pp69,85,149) (MR p239) (ESNF

p24ps c1905). There was a windmill at SK 125252, 0.5m to W of Newborough, marked on maps of 1820 and 1831 (WBJ p32). Newborough became a separate ecclesiastical parish in 1784 (GLAUE p417), refounded in 1862 (LGS p192). The church, All Saints, at the junction of Yoxall Road and Abbots Bromley road in the village centre, was built in 1899-1901 (BOE p208). Sir Arthur Sullivan played the organ in it in 1901 (info Peter Smith). Newborough became a separate civil parish in 1866 (GLAUE p417). A well by the village school gates is dressed on spring Bank Holiday Mondays, a tradition begun in 1978 (STMSM July 1979 pp3,4ps,5) (SW p77) (MR p234) (SVB p129) (SLM April 1996 p21pcs). There have been two earthquake tremors in the last 200 years felt by people in the low-lying parts of the village (SVB p129).

New Borough Name for the planned borough created by the Earls of Derby in c1140 outside Tutbury Castle walls (SHC 4th series vol 4 p75) (VCH vol 2 p349. vol 3 p331 note) (SL p151).

Newborough Brick Hill Minute hamlet above a tributary of the Swarbourn 0.75m SE of Newborough (1887 OS map 6 inch).

Newborough End Minute hamlet 0.75m SSW of Newborough (1887 OS map 6 inch).

Newborough Hall 0.25m NNW of Newborough is Newborough Hall Farm. N of the farm is a rectangular moated site (CAMS p64; ref SK 076471 is wrong). The moated site with millpond, two fishponds and connecting channels at SK 13392592 and SK 13432598 are a listed monument.

Newborough Park Medieval deer park in Needwood Forest. In existence by 1346 and was probably short-lived. Belonged to the Earl of Lancaster (NSJFS 1964 p64).

Newbridge Former estate and hamlet in Wolverhampton township, chapelry and ancient parish. In the foreign (HOWM p44) of Wolverhampton. Newbridge is presently a suburb of Wolverhampton by Smestow Brook, before Tettenhall, 1.25m WNW of Wolverhampton. Appears as Novum pontem in 1327 (DUIGNAN). Is 'new' in the sense it replaced a ford (SPN p145). Erected on a bridge over the Staffs and Worcs Canal at Newbridge in 1988 is a plaque which reads 'When the union with Ireland Act was passed in 1800 the mail coach route from London to Holyhead became very important. Thomas Telford was appointed to improve London-Holyhead road. The earlier road crossed the old bridge which you can see from here. For the new bridge was built in the 1820s. It was replaced by this wider bridge in 1939' (BCM April 1989 pp38-40). The estate belonged to F Holyoake in the mid C19 (W p96). The church, St Jude, on the corner of Tettenhall Road and St Jude's Road, was built in 1867 (LDD).

New Buildings, The (1834 OS map) (Dower's map). Newbuildings Farm is 0.75m SE of Marston, near Stafford.

Newcastle-under-Lyme (locally 'Castle, 'Cassal POP p149, BOJ book 2 p93). Large market town, former manor and ancient corporate borough. The large market town of Newcastle-under-Lyme lies on a slight eminence by Lyme Brook 15.25m NNW of Stafford.

EARLY. For the boulder stone outside the 'old'? library see under Berry Hill, Bucknall. A medium sized Neolithic or Bronze Age axe-hammer was found during excavations in Bridge Street in c1942 (NSJFS 1962 p29. 1964 p30). 1086 to 1200. Newcastle-under-Lyme is not in DB. This fact has led some, like Palliser, to think the town did not exist in 1086, not even as a small village (NUL p2), and that it owes its origins to the castle built in the C12 (HOS p56). But Robin Studd thinks a town at Newcastle did exist in 1086 and that it was omitted by the DB surveyors (SSE 1990 pp11-17). It has long been thought Newcastle derived its **name** from the new fortress built at Newcastle in the C12 by Ranulph 'De Gernon,' Earl of Chester, in lieu of the old castle at Chesterton (expounded by Camden, perpetuated by Erdeswick, Chetwynd and Plot - SSE 1990 p1) (W p302) (SHC 1909 p55) (SPN p86), or of an old castle at Trentham (expounded by SAH Burne in NSFCT 1912 pp144-150 - SSE 1990 p2), or of Stafford Castle (HOS p17) (NSJFS 1966 p44) (NUL). Recently, Robin Studd has argued that 'New' was applied only in the sense of 'recent' or 'novel,' and that the older castles at Chesterton, Trentham and Stafford had little or nothing to do with Newcastle's acquisition of its name (SSE 1990 p3). The affix 'under-Lyme' first appears as 'Novum oppidum sub lima' in 1168, and later as 'Novum castellum subtus Lymam' in 1173 (VCH vol 8 p11) (SSE 1996 p16). This appears to be a reference to the Lyme Forest (see), and 'Lyme' means 'elm tree' (EKWALL 1960 ed) (VCH vol 8 p11). Morland is emphatic Lyme Forest gave its name to Newcastle-under-Lyme, and the town gave its name to Lyme Brook (POP p149). DG Harnaman has suggested Lyme is derived from the Limes Britannicus (NSFCT 1951 p119). Whilst some at Newcastle formerly foolishly thought that 'under Lyme' was derived from the new castle being first seen through or under lime trees (NSFCT 1887 p90). Newcastle was written 'Newcastle Super Are' (or 'Newcastle on the Are') in the city of London's letter-books 1317 suggesting that the brook was alternatively known as 'Are' (or 'Ayr' - 'ar' being the Norse word for river) or 'Lyme' (POP p149) (NSFCT 1991 p60). Studd found Newcastle first recorded in 1140 or 1146 as 'novum castellum de Staffordshira cum omnibus eidem pertinenciis' or 'the new castle of Staffordshire with all its appurtenances' (SSE 1990 p10). Newcastle is recorded in 1166-67, as 'Nouum Oppidum sub Lima' a term that implies non-burghal status, but the roll for 1172-73 called it a 'burgus' and it has been considered a borough ever since (NSJFS 1972 p69). There was a chapel at Newcastle by the late C12. The main old **church** of Newcastle, St Giles, on the N side of Church Street, has some C13 work. Some say Newcastle was an ancient parish (W p300), whilst others say it was formerly a chapelry in Stoke-upon-Trent ancient parish (GLAUE p417) (SGSAS). It had separate civil identity at an early period. The separate ecclesiastical parish, created in 1849, was united with Butterton in 1940 (GLAUE p417). **Beating the bounds** has been practised in Newcastle. In 1887 the bounds were perambulated not in Rogation week but in March (SCSF pp27,28) (FOS pp116,117).

THE BOROUGH. Newcastle acquired burghal status in c1179 and acquired the right to nominate its own mayor at some date between 1235 and 1251 (SSE 1990 p4). In 1323 a series of petty feuds began between the Aldithley (or Audley) family of Heighley Castle (see) (the family had held Newcastle Castle for a time in the C13) and the citizens of Newcastle (POP pp157-158). The body which administered Newcastle certainly by the later C14 was the mayor, the bailiffs and a body of burgesses. After the charter of incorporation in 1590 the governing body was to consist of the mayor, the bailiffs, and 24 'capital' burgesses (VCH vol 8 pp25,26). The Guildhall in the middle of the High Street was built shortly after Nov 1713, replacing an earlier hall, which seems to have stood a little to the N of the present Guildhall (NTS p248) (VCH vol 8 p10). From 1368 (the earliest of which there is any record) up to the Municipal Reform Act of 1835 the mayoral election was held on the Tuesday after Michaelmas day (Sept 29). Then it was changed to the Tuesday after Nov 9. Mayoral-election day was known as **'Clouting-out day'** because boys were 'clouted-out' of their schools by gangs of older boys armed with knotted ropes which they battered at school-doors. Once out the boys would roam the town in the hope that tradespeople and residents would throw apples and nuts into the streets before them to be scrambled for (FLJ vol 25 1914 pp297-298). The election of a **mock mayor** by the ordinary citizens on the same day as the mayoral election was practiced in Newcastle in the C19 and up to the C20. After the election and proclamation of the real mayor at the Guildhall, the ordinary burgesses assembled at the adjacent market cross and proceeded with all the appearance of legal formality to discharge the old mock mayor and appoint a new one. The first recorded mock mayor was Jatty Mayson chosen Oct 1792. This information comes from an inscription on a mould for a china bowl, and there is no evidence that the custom pre-dates this date (VCH vol 8 p54). There is a theory, however, that the custom was begun by the freemen or burgesses at the time of the charter of 1590 in protest against their rights being usurped by the corporation: From 1833 the council ceased to be a self-perpetuating oligarchy when all the burgesses were given the right to elect the mayor and bailiffs, but the custom, accompanied by much horse-play and merriment, continued into the later C19. In 1841 two mock mayors were nominated by two principal hat manufactories. In 1844 RW Buss depicted the Mock Mayor ceremony in a painting (SA Oct 16 1841. Oct 19 1912) (Broughton's Scrapbook p450) (LCAST 1850-51 pp126-131) (Historical Records and Directory of Newcastle-under-Lyme. Jeremiah Ingamells. 1871) (SCSF p163) (H p99) (NSFCT 1929 pp52-53,84 il,84,85-88. 1935 p79) (VCH vol 8 p27) (NUL pp91,92il of RW Buss's painting of 1844,123) (SLM Aug Sept 1987 p29p of RW Buss's painting) (FOS pp120, 121, 122). **Charters**. The exact date of the first charter is unknown for it is lost. It has been thought Newcastle was created a borough in **1173** (Staffs County Handbook c1958) (VCH vol 8 p25) (NUL p5) (NSJFS 1973 pp1-8) (STMSM Feb 1973 p26). Although, some say in **1179**, since that was the year Preston, Lancs, received its charter, which was modelled on Newcastle's (VCH vol 8 p25) (POP pp155-156). (LGS p193 and MR p239 say 1180). A charter of **1216** granted the lord of the manor the right to hang felons on a gibbet and judgment over his bondmen and villeins (SCSF p123). In a charter granted **1235** Newcastle became a free borough (NSFCT 1935 p78) (VCH vol 8 pp25,44) (NSJFS 1962 p108) (NUL p86); the original charter no longer survives (NSJFS 1973 p2). Another of **1251** gave the mayor (here mentioned for the first time) and burgesses the right of fee-farm (VCH vol 8 p25). Preston also had a copy of this charter (NSFCT 1935 p77). One of **1281** granted a fair (VCH vol 8 p47). Another of **1293-6** gives first mention of a Guildhall (NM pp47-49) (VCH vol 8 p44). One of **1336** granted a fair (NUL p14). A charter was granted in **1344**. Preston borrowed this charter (for its wording) and kept it until 1910 (NSFCT 1935 p77) (POP p156). A charter of

confirmation was granted in **1372** (ES 31 July 1935 p4p, 30 April 1937 p8). Another of incorporation confirming the privileges already possessed by Newcastle was granted on May 18 **1590**. It made the borough a 'close corporation,' the council becoming a self-perpetuating oligarchy (VCH vol 8 p26) (NUL pp34p,36). A charter of **1664** insisted royal approval be obtained for certain appointments (VCH vol 8 pp26-27). In **1684** Newcastle surrendered its charters to the Crown and in **1685** a new charter was granted by James II. In Oct **1688** Newcastle recovered its original charters (NUL p59). (VCH vol 8 p27) (W pp303-304) (SK pp199,200). The **arms** of Newcastle-under-Lyme borough as granted in 1951 are: Or, rising for a base barry wavy of four pieces argent and azure charged with three fishes swimming proper, a castle of three towers gules; on a chief azure a lion passant guardant between two fleurs-de-lis all gold. The crest is: on a wreath gold and gules, a demi-lion with a forked tail argent, charged on the shoulder with a Stafford knot gules and supporting a staff proper and there on a banner azure charged with three gold wheatsheaves. The supporters are: two lions guardant sable, each supporting a scythe proper. The motto is: 'Prisca Constantia' (With ancient constancy) (CH p334il). The **seal** is dated 1590 (STMSM Feb 1973 p26p). The civic arms incorporates the arms of Richard, Earl of Cornwall (founder of Hailes Abbey, near Winchcomb, Glous). The link could be that James de Aldithley (or Audley) was in his military service in Germany (ES Jan 22 1930 p6ps. July 3 1930 p6. April 4 1933 p10il) (VCH vol 8 p39il) (STM March 1966 p37) (NOPP pl1).

MARKETS AND FAIRS. Newcastle may be identified with the 'New Market of Trentham' in the Pipe Rolls of the C12; Newcastle was then in Trentham manor (SSE 1990 p17). There was a **market** by 1171-72? (SHC vol 1 p65) (NSJFS 1971 pp51,52). A market is first mentioned specifically in 1203, but may be older (VCH vol 8 p45) (NSJFS 1962 p110). In 1203 Newcastle was amerced for having changed its market day from Sunday to Saturday (THS) (SCSF p95). An armed band of the Duke of Lancaster's men raided the town on a market day in 1320 (POP p157). Newcastle market was raided by Adam Deneys, of Congleton, with 500 unknown men on the Feast of St Gregory in 1325 (POP p158). The medieval **market cross** was restored in 1579. In 1691 it stood in the centre of High Street, opposite the end of Ironmarket, probably on its original site. By 1820 the five circular stone steps forming the base had been removed to the N end of the Guildhall; at some point a lamp standard, a Roman Doric column, was erected on it (W) (SCSF p89) (NTS p203) (VCH vol 8 p11) (NUL p22) (BOE p210). There were **fairs** on: **Jan 13**, a new market (VCH vol 8 p47) (NUL pp14,158). **Shrove Monday** (COOKE) or Shrove Fair (Mar 2) (VCH vol 8 p47) (NUL pp14,158). **Low Sunday**, which was before 1438, held on the Tuesday following the Octave of Easter (granted by the charter of 1336) (VCH vol 8 p47). **April 20** (Easter Fair) (VCH vol 8 p47) (NUL pp14,158). **Easter Monday** (COOKE). **Whit Monday** (COOKE) (June 8) (VCH vol 8 p47) (NUL pp14,158). **Trinity Monday**, which was before 1438, held on Holy Trinity (eve, feast and morrow of) (granted by the charter of 1281) (VCH vol 8 p47). July 13 (Wool Fair) (VCH vol 8 p47) (NUL pp14,158). Monday before **July 15** (COOKE). **Sept 11**, which was before 1753, held on Monday after the feast of St Giles the Abbot (Sept 1) (granted by the charter of 1590) (NTS p63) (VCH vol 8 p47). Cooke gives Monday after Sept 11 (SCSF p99). **Sept 14** (Wakes Fair) (VCH vol 8 p47) (NUL pp14,158). **Nov 2** (Cold Fair) (VCH vol 8 p47) (NUL pp14,158). **Nov 6** (St Leonard's Day) (granted by the charter of 1438) (VCH vol 8 p47) (COOKE) (SCSF p99). In 1840 the town had seven fairs a year as well as six cattle fairs (VCH vol 8 p47) (NUL pp14,158). These cattle fairs may have been on Plough Monday, second Monday in February, May, August, October, and December, White mentions these as well as the others (W p300). By the C17 and possibly earlier the custom of 'walking the fairs' was practised. This later became something of a general procession of the borough council and occurred at the Whit Monday Fair. The custom may have been a vestige of the court of pie powder (VCH vol 8 p47). There was a bull ring in Nelson Place (NUL p158). For the bear ring see Bear Pits.

1200 to 1600. In the early C19 Pitt noted that an erroneous notion had prevailed that the town was hitherto larger in size, and that it once had four churches, but that three of them, as well as a considerable part of the town, were reduced in the wars of the Barons (1258-1265). But the notion could be discounted as these other churches were probably only chantries of St Giles' (THS p364). There was an **anchoress** in the church in 1227, and there may have been a hermit in the town in 1335, but the source (SHC new series viii p154) gives 'Novus Burgus' which may be Newport, Shrops. There was also a hermit in the town in 1465 (Hermits and Anchorites of England. Rotha M Clay pp246-247) (VCH vol 3 p137). It was the custom in medieval times for the inhabitants of ancient boroughs such as Newcastle to **'Set the Watch'** on Midsummer Eve. In addition to the standing watch, it was customary for hundreds of citizens, shouldering pikes, partisans, or halberts, or bearing torches of fire to join in an annual Marching Watch, all in military array, which, says Hackwood, made for a weird picturesque night pageant (SCSF p45). Newcastle had a sheriff's ride (FOS pp116,117). In 1286 four Stafford men were summoned by a man from Newcastle for taking from him in Stafford three skins he was selling there. The Newcastle man pleaded that, as he was a burgess of a free town he had the right to sell in any market in the realm except London. The Stafford men pleaded that their town had received its trading charter before Newcastle, and that by this charter no man was allowed to sell wool by the fleece in Stafford market unless he was a burgess of that town. The Newcastle man lost (SOSH pp154-155). **Persons and visitors.** **King John** visited Newcastle and stayed at the castle during the Ides of March 1206 (ES Jan 19 1934 p13) (R&S p8) (POP p165). **Henry III** passed through en route for Chester and North Wales in 1257 (HOS p48). **Edward II** visited Newcastle on Nov 5 1323 and bestowed one day's food on the 12 Dominican friars at Blackfriars (NSFCT 1882 p26) (R&S p11) (VCH vol 3 p272). **Barnaby Googe,** the poet of the Reformation, appears to have been at Newcastle, and a passage in his 'Itinerary' runs

> Newcastle-under-Line--a
> There I trounced in burnt wine--a;
> None but the wicked there remained,
> Weekly lectures were proclaimed.

(SCSF p166).
PUNISHMENTS. Ranulph 'de Blundeville,' Earl of Chester, lord of Newcastle, obtained a charter in 1216 granting him the right to hang felons on a **gibbet** and to judge his bondmen and villeins (SCSF p123). A **'cage'** or temporary lock-up existed in 1612 (NTS p279) (VCH vol 8 p40) (NUL p122). Newcastle had its own **scold's bridle** made of iron (NHS p389 tab 32 fig 9) (BEW) (SMC pp200-202) (SM pp475,557) (SCSF p125) and **ducking stool** (NHS p389) (SD p66) (SCSF p126). Near the S entrance to the Guildhall stood the town **stocks** (HONUL p145) (VCH vol 8 p10).
GRAMMAR SCHOOL. A free school existed in Newcastle since by least 1565 (VCH vol 6 pp161-162). It became a grammar school in 1602 with the endowment of Richard Clayton (SOSH p179) (W p307), or in 1692 (VCH vol 6 pp161-162), or in 1702 (POP p162). Dissatisfaction with the conversion to a grammar school led Rev Edward Orme, master of the school between 1654-68, to found the Orme School (see below) (NUL p65). The grammar school has also been called the Borough School, the Free School and the Free Borough School (NRS p129). The school had stood S of the tower of St Giles' since probably from its earliest days. The grammar school building was pulled down in 1719-1720. A new building was begun in 1722. About 1820 a new school was built on the corner of Hanover Street and School Street. In 1668 the building was described as 'singularly shabby... and so small that two masters cannot teach in it at once with comfort.' In 1872 the grammar school and the Orme School amalgamated to form Newcastle High School (VCH vol 6 pp161-162) (GSS pp44il-47). **Alumni:** Elijah Fenton (1683-1730), poet (POTP p95); George Cooper (1786-1860), poet and native of Newcastle (PSS pp142-143); David Johnson (b1927), novelist of Meir (see).
ORME SCHOOLS. In 1704 or 1705 Rev Edward Orme, master of Newcastle's Grammar School (1654-1668), founded the Orme School after dissatisfaction with the provision given by it (see above) (SOSH p179) (POP p162) (NUL p65). The school has also appeared as the Charity English School and English School. The school was at first housed in or by the Old Meeting House, and was briefly evacuated between 1715 and 1717 during the rebuilding of the Old Meeting House after it was burnt down by rioters in July 1715. In the early C19 the school moved to the Marsh (by the corner of Hanover Street). In 1851 it moved to new buildings on the site of the old workhouse at Higherland. The school amalgamated with the Grammar School in 1872 to form Newcastle High School (for boys). A middle school (called Orme Middle School) for boys (aged 8-16) was created at the same time and it continued to occupy the Higherland buildings of the old Orme School. It closed down in 1927 in which year it was replaced by a new local authority grammar school at Wolstanton, which was known by 1966 as Wolstanton Grammar School. In 1931 the Orme Boys' Senior School was opened in the buildings of the old Orme Middle School. Orme Girls' School was founded in 1876 (VCH vol 6 pp66-67) (A Short History of the Orme Girls' School. SM Smith. 1961) (History of Orme Boy's School. E Kershaw. 1967) (The Educational Endowments of Newcastle-under-Lyme. T Pape. 1913. pp70-111 p of the school built in 1850 facing p70) (NUL pp65,145p of the school at Higherland, 146,148,150,152p of the old schoolhouse built 1715) (Arnold

Bennett and Stoke-on-Trent. EJD Warrilow. 1966 p24).
NEWCASTLE HIGH SCHOOL. A boy's High School was established in 1872 (VCH vol 6 p161-162) or 1874 with the amalgamation of Newcastle Grammar School and the Orme School. The High School building was built in 1876 and modelled on that of Rugby's. The school magazine is called 'The Firefly.' Attached to the High School was a boy's middle school, and Orme Girls' School, founded in 1876. **Alumni.** The philosopher TH Green was one of its commissioners. Former pupils include: Arnold Bennett, novelist, of Burslem, who attended Orme Middle School from May 1882; George Beardmore (alias Cedric Stokes) (b1908), novelist and children's writer; Sally (Sarah) Ward, Conservative MP for Cannock (1931-35), who attended Orme Girls' School, she was later of Walsall Wood; John Wain, novelist, of Stoke-upon-Trent (NUL p153) (A Short History of the Orme Girls' School. SM Smith. 1961) (Arnold Bennett and Stoke-on-Trent. EJD Warrilow. 1966 p23) (SNBC p46) (VFC p11).
1600 to 1642. **Persons and visitors.** Rev Nightingale states that John Goodwin eminent Puritan divine was born in Newcastle; but this is a mistake. Goodwin was a native of Norfolk (S&W p276). For **Thomas Maxfield** (d1616), Roman Catholic martyr, see Chesterton Hall. **Thomas Harrison,** parliamentarian commander in the Civil War, and most eminent figure in the Fifth Monarchy movement, was born in 1616 in a house on the W side of the High Street on the site of what was the Midland Bank by 1980. A plaque on the wall of the bank commemorates him. He was a signatory of Charles I's death warrant in 1649, and major-general and commander-in-chief of the forces in England in 1650. He was arrested in Merrial Street, Newcastle, in early May 1660 by Col Bowyer, and on Oct 11 1660 he was tried and found guilty by a jury, which did not even bother to retire to consider its verdict. On Oct 13 1660 he was hung, drawn and quartered; Pepys was present at his disembowelling. The house Harrison lived in in Newcastle prior to his execution was visited by the NSFC in Sept 1943 (GNHS p129) (S p114) (LGS pp53,54,193) (SOSH p204) (KES pp157,158) (NSFCT 1943 p74) (SHJ pp14-23) (POP pp169-170) (Weekly Sentinel Dec 5 1980 il. Dec 12 1980) (NUL pp55il,56,58) (SHJ summer 1987 pp14-23). The martyrdom of Venerable **William Southerne** (or Sutheran, Sutherne, Sutheridge, Sudren, Southren) on April 30 1618 was originally thought to have taken place at Newcastle-under-Lyme, but in fact took place at Newcastle-upon-Tyne (SCHJ No. 12 1972 pp1-12). **Henry, Earl of Huntingdon,** visited Newcastle in Aug 1636 and noted it as 'a long town, the street (presumably High Street) very ill paved and houses poor thatched and very few either tiled or slated' (VCH vol 8 p3).
CIVIL WAR AND COMMONWEALTH PERIOD. Royalists made a plundering raid on Newcastle in May 1644 (VCH vol 8 p7). John Bradshaw (b1602) of Congleton, Steward of Newcastle (1641-1659), MP for Stafford and Cheshire in 1654, was President of the High Court of Justice, the court which condemned Charles I to death. He is said to have died at Greenway Hall (see) near Bagnall. There is a plaque to his memory on the wall of the Midland Bank, Newcastle (LGS p193) (ES March 31 1978) (BALH p41) (NUL p55il) (COS p16) (HOS 1998 p76). His ghost and that of Henry Ireton, has been seen in Red Lion Square, London (DOG p129). During the Interregnum banns of marriage were proclaimed at the market cross (HONUL p117) (VCH vol 8 p11).
1660 to 1800. The mayor and others in Newcastle were accused of burning the bill of exclusion in 1683 (LOU p352). **Anglican non-conformity.** The first registration of a dissenter meeting-house in the county was in Newcastle in 1689 (HOS p32). The dissenter meeting house of 1705, just W of St Giles', where Rev Edward Orme founded an English school, was burnt down by anti-dissenters sometime between July 13 and 16 1715 before the Riot Act came into effect at the end of July (NSJFS 1974 p61-79). Another account says George Long's Meeting House for dissenters was burnt in a riot on July 12 1715 (NSFCT 1917 p69). Pointon says the Meeting House was attacked in July 1714 and there was a clear plan for the riot, which had a staged duel as its opening. The duel was staged in the castle which was beyond the borough's jurisdiction. In the succeeding riots there were many oaths to the Old Pretender (LOU pp90,931,359). The Old Meeting House was rebuilt in 1717 and became the Unitarian chapel (NSJFS 1974 p61-79). William Willett who married a sister of Josiah Wedgwood I was minister between 1727 and 1776 (NUL pp63,65p). Elijah Fenton, Joseph Priestley, the chemist, and Josiah Wedgwood I may have attended services here, as may Charles Darwin when staying at Maer. There is a medallion of Josiah Wedgwood I in the chapel. A school room was added in 1925 (ES May 28 1930 p4). (BOE p210). Capt Jonathan Scott, introducer of Congregationalism to North Staffs, took to evangelism in the army with such excessive zeal that his superior officers suggested he resign his commission which he did. In c1776 he began his first

work in the county in the open air at Newcastle which led to the formation of a congregation the following year. He attracted the patronage of Lady Glenorchy, whose benefactions he used to support an academy at Newcastle between 1783 and 1792 (NUL p64). John Wesley is said to have visited Newcastle prior to visiting Leek in 1788 (E p57). Two dragoon regiments were stationed at Newcastle to confront Prince Charles Edward Stuart in the 1745 Jacobite Rebellion but the Young Pretender marched via Leek (NSFCT 1925 p59). The **Newcastle Troop** of the Staffordshire Volunteer Cavalry (later Staffordshire Yeomanry) was raised by Col Earl Gower in 1794 (FSP p60) (info Yeomanry Museum). Newcastle-under-Lyme was chosen as the name of a new peerage as a device to preserve the **peerage** of the Duke of Newcastle-upon-Tyne, which was in danger of dying out. Under a complicated arrangement the title passed into the family of the Earl of Lincoln. Thomas Pelham-Holles (d1768) was created 1st Duke of Newcastle-under-Lyme in 1756. The 2nd Duke (nephew of the 1st) assumed the name Pelham-Clinton in 1768. He died in 1794 (Burke's Peerage 1970). The title became extinct in 1988 when the 10th Duke, Edward Pelham-Clinton, died in Devon (ES March 5 1996 p8). The practice known as **badging the poor** was introduced to Newcastle in 1685 (NUL p40) or 1686, 11 years before it was statute law (VCH vol 8 p32). Those in receipt of poor relief then had to wear a badge (NUL p40p of what the badge would have looked like). In 1717 the form of the badge was altered to the letters 'NP' in red (VCH vol 8 p32). **Persons and visitors. Godfrey Witrings**, a butcher of the town and strong-man who could lift great weights in his teeth, was seen by Dr Plot in the later C17. Plot, incidentally, thought the town, like Lichfield was physically sinking (NHS pp113,293). The **Duke of Monmouth** was given a warm welcome at Newcastle when he passed through to Trentham in Sept 1682 (VCH vol 8 p7) (NSFCT 1974 p64). In 1713 **Thomas Benson**, a native of Newcastle, invented a flint-grinding machine which was supposed to obviate lung disease among pottery workers (VCH vol 8 p8). **Elizabeth Elstob** (d1756), Anglo-Saxon scholar, essayist and linguist, was born at Newcastle in 1683. She later lived in Evesham, Worcs (VFC p45) (no mention in DNB, BS or VCH). **Philip Astley** (d1814), equestrian performer and proprietor of the famous 'Astley's Circus' and considered the founder of the modern circus, was born in Newcastle in 1742. Having received little education he was brought up in his father's trade of cabinet-maker and veneer-cutting. About 1759 he joined the army and served abroad, on his return he became an equestrian showman, later opening equestrian theatres. He was imprisoned in 1783 for not having a licence to perform. In his life he constructed 19 amphitheatres for equestrian exhibition. He died in Paris and was buried in the cemetery of Pere-la-Chaise (DNB) (LGS p193) (VCH vol 8 p7) (VFC p5). **Edward Massey** (b1768), a native of Newcastle, is known as the inventor in 1802 of the patent log for measuring the speed of ships (VCH vol 8 p8). **John Whitridge**, congregational minister at Newcastle in the 1780s, claimed to have established one of the earliest Sunday schools in the county (NUL p64). **Edward Knight** (1774-1826), actor of Stafford (see), appeared as Hob in 'Hob in the Well' at Newcastle-under-Lyme. **Isaac Keeling** (d1869), poet and religious writer, was born in Newcastle on Feb 12 1789, after some time as a designer and engraver at Wedgwood's, Etruria, he became a Wesleyan minister in 1811. In 1871 a volume of his sermons, which included several poems on sacred themes, was published (PSS pp144-145) (VFC p77).
1800 to 1900. Expanses of water known as **The Marsh** (see) and Colleswaynes Lake and common fields nearby on the E side of Newcastle were drained and developed with superior housing in the earlier C19. The **weights and measures office**, a small octagonal stone structure of one story, was erected in High Street to the S of the Guildhall in 1835. It had a low-pitched octagonal roof surmounted by a lamp. Its erection involved the removal of a stone pillar from the site to the centre of Red Lion Square. By 1877 the building itself had been removed to Red Lion Square but in 1926 it was demolished. By 1960 the weights and measures office was at 22 High Street (VCH vol 8 p11) (TWWW June 8 1991 p4p). The Staffordshire Yeomanry were called out to suppress a political riot in 1817 and an election riot in 1823 in the town (LOU). There was an Asiatic **Cholera outbreak** in Newcastle in 1849 which claimed 234 lives in nine weeks (ES Feb 2 1981 p11). As early as 1863 Newcastle inhabitants petitioned the House of Commons in favour of votes for women (VCH vol 8 p7). The sketch made of the town by EH Buckler in 1853 appears in NUL pp75,76. **Persons and visitors. Jane Walker** of Newcastle was charged with publishing and distributing seditious material. She was subsequently discharged. She was the only woman in Staffs so charged in the early C19 (LOU p211). **AW Harrison**, late C19 photographer, a native of Newcastle, is credited with having produced the first X-ray photographs in this country (VCH vol 8 p8). **John Currie** (d1914), artist, was born in Newcastle on May 14 1883. He was a decorator at Minton's in 1903 and won a

scholarship to the RCA. In 1907 he was appointed master of life drawing at Bristol School of Art. At the Slade School of Fine Art he made the acquaintance of Augustus John and Jacob Epstein and other artists. His picture of Penkhull in a post-impressionist style was presented to the Potteries Museum by Arnold Bennett. On Oct 8 1914 at No. 50 Paulton Square, London he shot his model, Dolly Henry, dead then turned the gun on himself (POTP p73) (ES April 3 1999 p10oils). **Vera Brittain** (d1970), writer, was born on Dec 29 1893 in what is now Sidmouth Avenue. Her father, Arthur, was a director of Brittain's paper mills at Cheddleton; her paternal grandfather was a Meigh of Ash Hall. Her family moved to Macclesfield when she was 18 months old (ES July 26 1965. Aug 26 1993. Dec 9 1993 p8p) (SLM Christmas 1995 p39p) (VFC p18) (FWNS pp34-39ps).
INDUSTRY. The residential, rather than industrial, nature of Newcastle is due largely to Newcastle being situated on red surface beds of the Newcastle Series which are barren of coal (NSFCT 1939 pp78-79). The town's industry was anciently wool (SL p86), iron working and nailing. Plot noted flat iron plates (frying-pans) were made here by John Holland (one of only two in the country involved in this trade, the other was at Wansworth, Surrey - POP p159). Greenslade and Stuart say he was actually at Keele (VCH vol 8 p51) (HOS p43). In 1696 a project was approved for the erection of a windmill on Brampton Bank (VCH vol 8 p48). There was a windmill on high ground to E of what is now Seabridge Road recorded by Greenwood (1819/20) and Sherlock (1820), but does not appear after (WBJ p32). In the C17 and the C18 and through into the C19 the town was prominent in clock, felt, hat, silk throwing and pipe making and to some extent tanning. Pipe makers were: Catherall c1637, the Riggs c1649-76 (POP p161), the Braddeleys c1676-17, Jones c1670, William Hand c1780, Ralph Morgan c1780, Pomona, the Bloods, the Tittensors, Ball, Fox and George Larkin (NUL pp87,90). There were mills, too; to the local squire, Ralph Sneyd it was 'that foul smithy Newcastle' (SL pp159-160). The town has quite emphatically never considered itself one of the pottery towns (POP p152), although, in the C18, Dr Pocock wrote to tell his mother that 'Newcastle-on-Lyne' was the capital of the Potteries villages (POP p149). Newcastle had some potteries. Samuel Bell was producing high quality ware from 1724-44 at Bell's Pottery (see). William Steers of London had a pottery in Newcastle. In the C19 and C20 its industries have been the manufacture of uniforms, motor-car harnesses, fluorescent lighting equipment, electric lamps and equipment for the cotton industry. About 1950 Newcastle wires and cable factory supplied all the wiring for the Bristol Brabazon I and was to equip the Bristol Brabazon II (NSFCT 1950 p92). (VCH vol 8 pp50-53).
RAILWAYS. The NSR opened a branch line from Stoke to Newcastle in 1852. It terminated at Knutton Junction where there was a line run by the Silverdale & Newcastle Railway to Silverdale. In 1856 mineral lines were opened beyond Silverdale to Apedale. From 1864 the NSR began to build passenger lines to Madeley and then on to Nantwich and Market Drayton (VCH vol 8 p7). The railway to Market Drayton closed to passengers in 1956, the line then ended at Silverdale (NSJFS 1964 p79). It was recommended that Newcastle station close in 1963 (ES March 22 1963).
NEWPAPERS. The **Newcastle Journal**, founded by mid July 1852, became the **Newcastle and North Staffs Pioneer** from July 5 1856. From Feb 5 1859 it became the **Staffordshire Times and Newcastle Pioneer**. Later it became the Staffordshire Weekly Times, which became the Staffordshire Times from Nov 28 1874 (VCH vol 8 pp53-54) (Newcastle-under-Lyme. An Octocentenary guide to sources of information. 1973) (NUL pp160,165ps) (SHJ spring 1996 pp21-22). The **Newcastle-under-Lyme Free Press** which ran from Sept 2 1882 to 1910, was distributed free every Saturday by its proprietor, AP Bayley (Newcastle-under-Lyme. An Octocentenary guide to sources of information. 1973) (NUL pp160,165ps). The **Newcastle Guardian and Silverdale, Chesterton and Audley Chronicle** (or simply Newcastle Guardian), founded on April 23 1881, ran to 1909, was at first a Liberal paper but later self-styled as an independent paper. It put Newcastle's news in the context of what was happening in the Potteries (VCH vol 8 pp53-54) (Newcastle-under-Lyme. An Octocentenary guide to sources of information. 1973) (NUL pp160,165ps) (SHJ spring 1996 p21). The **Newcastle Times** began as Stoke-on-Trent City Times in Nov 1935. By March 4 1938 it was the Newcastle Times, and became the Newcastle-under-Lyme Times from April 13 1951; this ran until at least 1973 (Newcastle-under-Lyme. An Octocentenary guide to sources of information. 1973) (NUL pp160,165ps) (SHJ spring 1996 p22).
1900 to PRESENT. In July 1930 the House of Lords, after debating the **Stoke-on-Trent Extension Bill**, rejected it: The City of Stoke-on-Trent had proposed to annex Newcastle borough and Wolstanton. The Bill was again defeated in March 1931 by an even more decisive vote against (NSFCT 1931

p194). In **WW2** the Germans bombed Gower Street on June 26 1940 at 1.42am (ES Feb 4 1977). For the bomb which hit the N Staffs Royal Infirmary see Hartshill. For the bombing raid in summer 1941 on Newcastle-under-Lyme see May Bank and Silverdale. Hanslip Fletcher's **view of Newcastle** (1913) appears in NULOP vol 2 p73p. In 1903 a **statue of Queen Victoria** was erected in front of the Royal Theatre in Nelson Place. It was presented by Sir Alfred Seale Haslam and unveiled by Grand Duke Michael of Russia (VCH vol 8 p11) (SHST p88p) (TWWW June 8 1991 p5p). In 1963 it was moved to Station Walks (ES Oct 5 1963. Oct 7 1963. June 24 1981 p9p) (Newcastle Times Oct 9 1963). The **earthquake** of 3.21pm July 3 1904 was felt at Newcastle (NSFCT 1905 p133). Since 1941 a **borough museum** has been in existence. The first rooms were Lancaster Buildings, but since 1956 it has been at the Firs in Brampton Park. The collection contains remains from the Pomona site, remnants of wood from the castle, the borough muniments (NSFCT 1934 pp70-71), and a collection of old prints of Newcastle (NUL p160), an iron bound oak muniment chest of 1560, and part of a past Newcastle market cross shaft. In 1950 was founded the present (2000) **Newcastle Natural History Society** (info Kath Swain). In the 1980s Fine Fare built an orange and green-panelled clad supermarket in Stafford Street. It was dubbed the 'Rubik's Cube' as it bore a similarity to the puzzle of that name and was described as **'Britain's ugliest building.'** After the closure of the supermarket in c1988 the building remained empty until being purchased in 1993. The upper part of the building due to be a cinema complex was re-clad in 1999-2000 (ES July 21 1993 p8p. April 17 1998 p3p. July 7 1999 p11p). By 1980 the **largest flag** (or Union Jack) flown from a public building in Britain was a union flag measuring 40 feet by 20 feet. It was first flown from the Civic Offices at Newcastle Carnival for ten minutes, on April 21 1977 (ES Dec 8 1976. April 21 1977) (GBR 1980 p166). The highest table **skittle score** in 24 hours is 116,047 skittles, set on April 15-16 1990 by 12 players at the Castle Mona, Newcastle (GBR 1995 p290). Two unusual lights in the sky, believed to be a **UFO**, were seen through binoculars from Newcastle on Sept 2 1967 at about 9.30pm for about 10 minutes (FSRP p13). **Persons and visitors**. In 1907 the **Duke of Sutherland** offered Trentham Park and hall to the Potteries at Newcastle's Drill Hall, but nothing came of his offer (PPP p13p). **George V** and Queen Mary visited Newcastle on April 22 1913 (ES Nov 16 1996 p21). Princess Elizabeth (**Elizabeth II**) visited Newcastle on Nov 1 and 2 1949. Elizabeth II came to Newcastle on May 25 1973 and unveiled a plaque in connection with the octocentenary celebrations (R&S p47). **Jackie Trent**, a singer and song writer, was born in Newcastle on Sept 6 1940 as Yvonne Burgess. She later took the name Jackie Tremaine and later became Jackie Trent. Trent and her husband Tony Hatch were known as 'Mr and Mrs Music.' They co-wrote the song 'Where Are You Now,' which reached number 1 in the UK charts in 1965. During the late 1960s Trent and her husband composed several major hits for Petula Clark including 'Don't Sleep in the Subway,' 'My Love' and 'Call Me.' In 1972 they wrote the score for Cameron Mackintosh's first West End production 'The Card' (a musical adaptation of Arnold Bennett's novel). In 1986 Trent and Hatch wrote the theme song for the TV soap opera 'Neighbours' (Newcastle Times May 19 1965) (The Guinness Encyclopaedia of Popular Music. Colin Larkin. 1992) (FWNS pp62-63p). British records in cycling have been set at Newcastle by **Beryl Burton** OBE for women's unpaced standing start when she covered 3km in four minutes 14.9 seconds on July 18 1964; and **Phil Griffiths** for amateur unpaced standing start for one hour on Aug 24 1978 when he travelled 27 miles 979 yards in that time (GBR 1980 p265). **John Golding** when Labour MP for Newcastle made the longest speech in committee in parliament at the committee on small amendments to the British Telecommunication's Bill on Feb 8-9 1983 which lasted 11 hours 15 minutes (GBR 1996 p183). **Eva Morris**, who grew up in Lower Street, Newcastle, was born on Nov 8 1885. By late 1998, aged 113, she was a resident of Autumn House nursing home, Stone, when she was believed to be the second oldest woman in Britain. On her 114th birthday, still at Autumn House, Eva was considered by the GBR Britain's oldest person. By mid Jan 2000 Eva was possibly the oldest person in the world (ES Nov 11 1992. Nov 10 1994 p11p. Nov 10 1995. Nov 10 1997 p4p. Nov 9 1998 p2p. Nov 8 1999 p2. Nov 19 1999 p12. Jan 14 2000 p5pc) (SN Feb 10 2000 p8).

NEWCASTLE IN LITERATURE. Newcastle is Oldchurch in Dinah Mulock's second novel 'Olive' (1850) (NSFCT 1925 p91); Oldcastle in Arnold Bennett's novels; Overcastle in HG Wells' 'In The Days of the Comet' and 'The New Machiavelli' (ES March 5 1996 p5). Newcastle appears in a local rhyme about Betley (see).

Newcastle-under-Lyme Canal Authorised in 1795 to extend the Trent and Mersey Canal to Newcastle-under-Lyme. It was 4m long and went via Stoke-upon-Trent, Boothen, and Trent Vale to terminate just off Brook Lane (IANS

p23) (NSJFS 1973 pp107-114). The Newcastle section ceased operation in 1921 and the canal closed in 1933 or 1935 (Nicholson's Guide to the Waterways No. 5 'Midlands' pp46-47). The last remaining section of the canal in Aqueduct Street was to be covered for car parking in 1963 (ES Dec 17 1963). Road widening S of Newcastle and in Stoke has practically removed all traces. The building of the A500 in the early 1970s destroyed its junction with the Trent & Mersey Canal (SWY p28). Timothy Trow drowned in this canal at Boothen (see) trying to save Jane Ridgeway.

Newcastle-under-Lyme Castle Former castle situated W of Pool Dam, Newcastle-under-Lyme, formerly in a detached portion of Stoke-upon-Trent ancient parish (VCH 8 p15). It seems to have been originally a royal castle and included in the royal manor of Trentham (VCH vol 8 p11). In its early years it could have been referred to as Trentham Castle (see) (SHC 1933 part 2 p6; says it was founded in Wolstanton manor). The first castle was possibly built by Henry I in the early C12; a castle had been built at Newcastle by 1149; that year it was granted to Ranulph 'De Gernon,' Earl of Chester (see Chartley Castle). The site for the castle was chosen because it gave control over the meeting place of routes leading to Chester and the Lyme Brook could be dammed to create a lake to surround the castle (ES Jan 19 1934 p13) (R&S p8) (POP p165) (NSJFS 1962 p108). After Ranulph's death in 1153 the castle appears to have remained with the Crown for many years. In 1215 the castle was granted to Ranulph de Blundeville, Earl of Chester (see Chartley Castle), but on his death in 1232 it was recovered by the Crown. In 1264 Henry III granted it to Simon de Montfort, Earl of Leicester (d1265). In 1267 Henry III granted the castle to his younger son Edmund, created Earl of Lancaster. Edmund's son succeeded to the castle in 1296. His widow held it after his execution in 1322 until her death in 1348. Henry, Earl of Lancaster (created Duke in 1351) succeeded. In 1362 the castle passed to the late Duke of Lancaster's daughter and her husband John of Gaunt, Duke of Lancaster, who held the castle in right of his wife until his death in 1399 (VCH vol 8 pp11,12) (CAMS p24). Gaunt made repairs to it in the 1370s (NUL p28). The Duchy accounts suggest it was maintained until the 1440s after which it was neglected in favour of Tutbury Castle. Minor repairs were made in 1478-9. Leland in c1541 wrote 'Al the castel is doune save one great toure' (LI vol 7 p36) (VCH vol 8 p12). The buildings were altogether decayed by 1610 when leased to the Sneyds (CAMS p24). The Earl of Huntingdon, visiting Newcastle in 1636, said it was decayed. Throughout the C18 the castle grounds, left in a wild state, became something of a fishing and game reserve (VCH vol 8 p15). The Sneyds purchased the site from the Duchy in 1828 and drained the marsh which had been the castle pool (POP p150) (CAMS p24). The castle site was levelled in 1855 when Castle Hill Iron Foundry to the NW of the castle mound was erected (ES June 22 1934 p6p) (NTS p336) (VCH vol 8 p15). The castle enclosure was oval, the long axis pointing roughly NW to SE with the mound at its southern end (VCH vol 8 p13). Workmen digging in the vicinity of the castle site in 1904 revealed two lengths of wall running parallel to each other running N and S, which was thought to be the entrance to the castle with the drawbridge in front of it (NSFCT 1905 p142). The excavations of the 1930s led to uncovering of old masonry, sections of drawbridge, and foundations of a gatehouse in John of Gaunt's Road (ES Jan 19 1934 p13ps. June 22 1934 pp5,6p - parts of the N and S walls. April 14 1938 p5) (NSFCT 1933 p169 plan, 172p. 1934 pp65-70p. 1935 pp71-75) (NUL pp2,4p). By 1935 the castle site had been acquired by the corporation, presumably from the Sneyds (VCH vol 8 p15). The castle site was opened as a public park, Queen Elizabeth Gardens, in 1944, for which some of the castle mound was unfortunately levelled (VCH vol 8 p15). A mound at the NW end of the Gardens is a remnant of the castle. Some of the older houses in the town, for instance the Lamb Inn, have or had red sandstone foundations probably stone pillaged from the castle (NUL pp22,28). An old mansion at entrance of Clayton Lane built of castle stone was knocked down in 1947 (TFTP pp202-224).

By at least the C13 a considerable part of Stoke parish had become a manor of Newcastle-under-Lyme (excluding Newcastle borough which was administratively self-contained and autonomous) which descended with the castle. This was administered at first from the castle, and after it became ruinous from the Courthouse at Penkhull (now the Greyhound Inn). By the earlier C13 it appears that the vills of Knutton with Dimsdale, Hanchurch, Clayton, Hanford, Whitmore, Hanley, Longton, Fenton, Tunstall with Chatterley, Normacot, and Bradwell with Thursfield were held of Newcastle manor by the service of providing men and arms for a certain period to perform garrison duties at the castle (VCH vol 8 pp13,15) (SASR 1987 p97) (NSR p12). (SOS p22 noted by Erdeswick) (SD pp64-65) (SSC pp133 in the intro, 82) (GNHS p128) (W p303) (NSFCT 1887 p90. 1888 pp32-34) (MOS pp28,30) (LGS pp192-193) (SOSH p271) (S p86) (KNS pp127,128) (VCH vol 8 pp11-

15) (NSJFS 1966 p44) (BALH p22) (BOE p208) (NUL pp6,7,8,9p,10 il of what the first castle may have looked like, 12 il of what the castle may have looked like in the C13) (SL pp94,148) (SGS p129) (MR pp240,241p).

Newcastle-under-Lyme Junction Canal Authorised in 1798. Opened in 1799. It joined the Newcastle-under-Lyme Canal with the Gresley Canal. Abandoned in 1851 when the NSR purchased it and laid a line and sidings on short lengths (SWY p29). For its route through Newcastle see IANS p23. (NSJFS 1973 pp107-114) (Nicholson's Guide to the Waterways No. 5 'Midlands' pp46-47) (LHSB 6 p22 see map).

Newcastle-under-Lyme Park Appears to have been N of Newcastle in the vicinity of Chesterton High Carr. A medieval deer park enclosed out of forest. In existence by 1235 (NSJFS 1962 p76).

Newchapel Hilltop village 20.25m NNW of Stafford. Formerly called Thursfield (NSFCT 1924 p34) (SVB p130) or the 'town-stead' of Thursfield township (HBST p130) in Wolstanton ancient parish. There was probably a church here in 1533. In 1610 a new stone chapel was built giving the village its present name. The building on a ridge top on the W side of Station Road was rebuilt in 1767 and again in 1878-80. It is dedicated to St James the Apostle (HBST p130) (BOE p211) (SVB p130). James Brindley (d1772), canal engineer, who lived at nearby Turnhurst Hall, is interred in the churchyard (HBST p130) (BOE p211) (SVB p130) (SSW pp104,105) (STM Nov 1967 p27p) (MC p50) (POTP pp48-49) (SHST p120; how it fell into a state of decay, repaired in 1954). Newchapel became a separate ecclesiastical parish in 1715 (GLAUE p417), refounded in 1846 (LGS p193). The grammar school at Newchapel was founded by Dr Robert Hulme of Sandbach by his will dated 1714 (HBST p130) (NSFCT 1945 p97). It closed in 1877 but interest from the original bequest was still (1988) being distributed annually to students who needed a grant (SVB p130). The village grew from 1850 on account of coal and ironstone mining, an activity which later made the main street suffer subsidence (SVB p130). The first Wesleyan Methodist chapel was built in the main street in 1747. It was here Hugh Bourne, founder of Primitive Methodism, preached one of his last sermons in the Wesleyan Methodist Chapel on Sunday Jan 18 1852. The building became a Sunday school when a new Wesleyan chapel was built in 1876. A new Wesleyan church opened in 1987 (SVB p130). Newchapel became a separate civil parish in 1894 (GLAUE p418). It was recommended that Newchapel and Goldenhill railway station close in 1963 (ES March 22 1963) (MIDD vol 3 pp40,41p). A Natural Sciences Centre with an astrological observatory and exhibition centre was in existence at Newchapel by 1968. Two of its astronomers, Roger Stanway and Anthony Pace, reported on the UFO sightings in North Staffs in the 1960s ('Flying Saucer Report' R Stanway and A Pace. 1968 photograph) (STM June 1969 p33) (ES July 5 1979) (SLM May/June 1992 p20).

Newchurch Tiny hamlet in high ground between the Swarbourn and Lin Brook in the middle of Needwood Forest 1.5m SE of Newborough. Formerly called Christchurch-on-Needwood in Tutbury parish (SGSAS). Or rather Christchurch-on-Needwood was a parish created in 1804 at the time of the disafforestation of Needwood Forest (LGS p192) and what became known as Newchurch was where the parish church, Christ Church, was built in 1809; the church was altered in 1880 (BOE p211). For the nearby airfield see Tatenhill.

Newclosefield House or small hamlet over 0.75m ENE of Dilhorne. Newclose Fields (1834 OS map). Whilst insane John Burndred, a blacksmith at Park Hall Colliery, murdered his wife Sarah Anne, and then himself, at their house at New Close Fields, in Dilhorne parish, on Sept 27 1903. Both were aged 43 (DMF pp39-49).

New College Former collection of houses, hall and chapel surrounding a courtyard on S side of Lichfield cathedral Close. Built after 1414 on land given by Bishop Burghill and improved by Dean Heywood in 1468 (VCH vol 3 p165). The college was a common residence for the cathedral chantry priests. It was a private residence after the dissolution of the chantries in 1548. It was later divided into separate properties which were demolished in the C19. The buildings of Lichfield Theological College were built on the site after 1872. St John's Hospital in the Close, the Refectory (by 1999 called College Hall), and the Bishop's House (No. 21) now occupy the site (info Michael Cockin) (GKMCLC) (VCH vol 14 p66).

New Cottage Former house 1m WSW of Flash, on S side of road between Quarnford and Flash. The datestone from nearby Summerseat went to New Cottage (UHAW p51).

New Cross 0.5m WSW of Wednesfield. New Cross may be the Cross Bruches, mentioned in the C13 (WFW p13). Bruches may derive from 'Braec' meaning 'newly broken (cultivated) land' - Cross Bruches then probably meant 'newly cultivated land at the cross' or possibly 'broken land at the newly erected cross' or similar. The 'cross' must signify a Christian cross as there is

absolutely no evidence of any cross paths, or division of land at this site. Perhaps there was an old cross on Wednesfield village green, or maybe New Cross was the site of the first cross and lay quite close to the village green, which almost certainly was whittled down and down in size throughout the ages (WFW p13). It appears as a house or tiny hamlet on the 1834 OS map. A new Wolverhampton Union workhouse to replace the one on the Bilston Road was built here in 1901 (WHTOP p110p) or 1903 (BOE p321). The original building designed by Arthur Marshall was a hospital by the 1930s (WHTOP p110). What may have been the ghosts of two boys eating fish and chips were seen by two girls near New Cross Hospital in the 1950s (GPCE p57). In 1988 a plaque was erected inside the hospital to commemorate SH Sheldon (1894-1972), Consultant Physician (1920-1958) (Commemorative Plaques by the Wolverhampton Civic Society).

Newfield House 0.5m S of Sheen. In Sheen ancient parish. There has been a house at Newfield since at least 1677 and probably by 1615 (VCH vol 7 p241).

Newfield Tiny hamlet 0.75m N of Tunstall. Formerly in Wolstanton ancient parish. Pitt states that it was formerly part of the extensive Town Fields of Tunstall, in c1613 (THS p393). But Simeon Shaw notes Pitt gives no authority for this information (HSP p20).

Newfield Green In Marchington Woodlands parish (W p563). There is a New Field 0.75m SSE of the Marchington Woodlands church at SK 115287 on the 1834 OS map.

Newfield Hall Stood in the area known as Summerbank, almost opposite to where the upper end of High Street, Tunstall, meets Summerbank Road, on the E side between this corner and Hardy Street (SHST p554). Admiral Smith Child inherited and rebuilt it in 1770 adding a pottery works, Newfield Pottery, to it (VCH vol 8 p101). He died here in 1813 (W p288). John Henry Clive, nephew of Clive of India, later of Clanway Hall (see), lived at Newfield Hall when helping Admiral Smith Child to run Newfield Pottery (POTP p62). Bought by William Adams (1798-1865) master potter in 1858 (POTP p13). Demolished in 1949 (SHST pp552,554p). By 1958 its site was occupied by Beresford Transport Ltd (VCH vol 8 p92) (POTP p60). (OTP p43).

Newfield Old Hall Seat of the Baddeleys. Predecessor to Newfield Hall (VCH vol 8 p91).

Newfields House 1.25m WSW of Wetley Rocks. Appears as Newfield on 1834 OS map.

Newford Valley Between Ford Green and Sneyd Green. Norton Colliery formerly stood in this valley (SOTB p115).

New Forest A short-lived forest created or enlarged by William I or one of the Norman kings. It covered an area of 90 square miles and lay about the upper Trent area. It covered Dimsdale, Tunstall, Abbey Hulton, Trentham, Tittensor, Tixall, Church Leigh, Weston Coyney, and Whitmore (BNDA pp9-10). A 'Nova Foresta' is mentioned near Newcastle several times in the Pipe Rolls (NSFCT 1910 p171). Clive or Cliff Hay seems to have been its only hay. It was disafforested in c1204, except for Clive Hay. Bridgeman says that it may have been called the 'New' Forest because it was reafforested after Newcastle had come back into royal hands in the mid C12 (SHC 1923 pp301-302) (VCH vol 2 pp348-349. vol 5 p26) (NSJFS 1968 p48 fig 1) (SL p69). It has also appeared as Newcastle-under-Lyme Forest.

New Grange Grange established by Dieulacres Abbey by 1291 on the site of a settlement at the confluence of Meer Brook and the Churnet called Nether Hulme (SSE 1993 p4). The house was at some time called Nether Hulme Grange (VCH vol 3 p233) and became known as New Grange. It was bought by Thomas Mountfort from Sir John Bagnall in 1564. A later house had a Jacobean staircase, a studded door, mullioned windows and an inside well. Mr Mountford of New Grange secreted 48 sack bottles of ale with the words 'SACK 1640' in a manure heap at the approach of the Young Pretender's army during the 1745 Jacobite Rebellion (BPCSM pp2,8) (HOLF pp4-5). New Grange was demolished to make way for an enlarged Tittesworth Reservoir in the 1960s (SVB p123) (SHC 1999 p7).

New Guild House 1.5m E of Forton. The name 'Guild' probably has some connection with Guild of Monks (see).

Newhall Seat of the Egertons. Now part of Betley village. Probably same as Betley Old Hall (see). (Plot's map).

New Hall Farm Lichfield Road, Cannock. Brick house dating from at least 1689, the date stone also bears the initials W.H. (CCAP p34p) (CCAP p34p).

New Hall Farm NW side of Onecote village. The present house of the later C19 evidently replaces an earlier house (VCH vol 7 p211).

New Hayes Area of S Bradeley village, near Burslem comprising Hayes Street and Berrisford Street (now Sherratt Street), which were also known as 'Monkey Row' on account of the fact that mortgages were taken out on some of the houses not bought outright. In school days there was keen rivalry between

New Hayes and Bradeley in sports (ONST 1977 p389).

New Hayes Small wood and road 0.5m E of Cannock Wood. Formerly a small hay or estate called le Newe, Neuhey, Neuhaye (1348), New Hays (1834) (SPNO p60), and New Hay (VCH vol 5 p57).

New House House 2m NE of Garshall Green. Has also appeared as St Johns Fields.

Newhouse House 0.5m ESE of Stanley, Bagnall. Formerly New House.

New House Formerly partly in Beech quarter in Stone ancient parish and partly in Swynnerton ancient parish (W pp369,424). There is a New House at Beechcliff (SJ 856387) on the 1834 OS map.

New House, The Ipstones. Formerly called The Grange (TOI p45).

Newhouse House 0.5m ESE of Stanley. Formerly in Stanley township in Leek ancient parish. There was a house here by 1751 (VCH vol 7 p229).

New House Farm On S side of Horton village, in Horton ancient parish. It is of C18 origin (VCH vol 7 p65).

New House Farm On S side of Onecote village, on the Ipstones road. Is dated 1680 (VCH vol 7 p211).

New House Farm 0.75m ENE of Lower Penn. Formerly in Penn ancient parish. Dates from at least the C17 and was the most important farm in the district. The estate was sold in 1909 and broken up with the creation of farms at Hillcroft, Westcroft and Robin's Nest. The old farm then became known as Hillcroft and a new house built slightly to the E became known as New House. Hillcroft (the original New House) was replaced by a bungalow sometime after WW2. New House Farm (the new house) later became known Highfields Farm. In 1949 the land of Highfields Farm was compulsorily purchased and Highfields School and part of the Warstones housing estate built on the site (PONP pp44,46). Highfields Farm was not demolished by 1988 and Highfields Secondary School built on the site as claimed by PENOP p88p. The house, now (1998) not a farm, still stands adjacent to the boundary of Highfields School (info Angus Dunphy).

New Inn Bank Incline at Outlands in Adbaston parish. There is a good view from New Inn Bank which includes the Wrekin and the Caradoc near Church Stretton, Shrops (AADB p32). Below the incline is Buckingham's Cave (see).

New Inn Hall Former mansion and then an inn which stood near Holyhead, Sandwell, and Woodland Roads, Handsworth. The hall was built in 1580. It was bought by Robert Stamford of Perry Hall (d1607) from Thomas Groves of West Bromwich in the late C16 or early C17. Until 1638 it was still the private Stamford residence, but Col Stamford, a royalist officer in the Civil War, converted it into an inn, when it was partly rebuilt. The name 'New Inn' appears on Plot's map. Prior to 1798 the present New Inns Hotel was built and New Inn Hall reverted to a private residence, being then (1798) occupied by Mr Crockett. In c1854 it was the seat of William Potts (HPPE p86). Another account says New Inn Hall was owned by the Wyrleys and Birches, and usually occupied by members of their families until the mid C19. New Inn still stood in 1862 (MNB pp40,47).

New Invention Former hamlet now a suburb 2m NNE of Willenhall at crossroads where the Willenhall-Cannock road crosses that from Wolverhampton to Bloxwich (ESSN pp28-29). Formerly partly in the township and chapelries of Wednesfield and Willenhall in Wolverhampton ancient parish. The name was in use by the later C17. In the baptism of one of his children in 1663 John Poole is described as of 'the New Invention neare the Snead.' At that time New Invention consisted of less than a dozen cottages (HOWI p187). It was a small mining hamlet in the C19 (ESSN pp28-29). In the 1880s there were 31 lock and key makers at New Invention (trade directories) (Black Country Calendar 2000). The hamlet lay in Wednesfield separate parish from 1849 to 1866 when Short Heath Holy Trinity church (established 1855) extended its ecclesiastical parish to New Invention in 1866 (WFW p100). Many have tried to interpret the name. Tildesley thought it may be a corruption of an earlier name (HOWI p187). Some have thought it was an inn (WDY p14), or where a particular new type of machine was used, for on early maps New Invention is prefaced by the definite article THE New Invention (ESSN pp28-29). The name could be from a new kind of pump used in the local mines. Hackwood favoured the theory the invention was a new kind of chimney pot (WDY p15). (AOW p180). It has been suggested that here the new invention of nailing horse's shoes back to front was tried by a highwayman in an attempt to deceive his pursuers. Or simply the word 'invention' was first given to the place in the Middle Ages (then inventre) when the word meant 'to come across or to find' (TB Sept 1998 p29). A Ragged Invention appears on the 1834 OS map W of Codsall. There is a New Invention in Shrops, 2m N of Knighton.

Newlands Minute hamlet 2m NE of Colton. In Colton ancient parish. Appears a surname in 1337 as del newelond (SSE 1997 p82), and has appeared as Newland (W p413).

Newlands, The Hamstead. Originally a row of eight houses built by Isaac Meacham, manager of Hamstall Hall Colliery, in c1902 for his own and his family's residence in his retirement. So called after the land which was called the Newlands (VH p69p).

Newlands Brook Runs at Norton Canes to Wyrley Brook.

Newlands Farm 1.75m S of Uttoxeter. Appears on 1834 OS map as Newlands.

Newlands Green An area in the fork between the High Street and Bearwood Road, 0.25m NE of the Old Church, Smethwick. Said to have been named after William Newland (d1860), a Congregationalist wheelwright who lived here in the early C19 (STELE Sept 15 1951) (VCH vol 17 p89).

Newlands Well Mentioned in a perambulation of Norton Canes, made in 1775, as a gospel place (DUIGNAN p69) (SR p4). There is a Newlands Lane S of Heath Hayes.

New Lodge Georgian mansion (LTD p153) 0.75m SW of Hanbury, now a school? The house belonged to the Duchy of Lancaster by at least 1868 and probably long before. It belonged to the Duchy to at least 1940 (trade directories). Probably on account of it being a possession of the Crown, George III was incarcerated here during periods of his madness (LTD p153), and William IV stayed here. George Edward Anson, keeper of the Privy Purse to Queen Victoria died here in 1849 (mem in Hanbury church) (MR p174); Hon Mrs Anson was in residence in 1851 (W p22). Robert J Harper of the New Lodge was axe-bearer of Needwood Forest to Queen Victoria (W p560). New Lodge was tenanted by Charles Edward Boothby from at least 1868 to at least 1888; Humphry Brook Firman in 1892; Ernest Arliss from at least 1900 to at least 1916; Mrs Arliss in 1924 (trade directories).

New Mills District and former hamlet in the foreign of Walsall (W p649). The name is from mills known as New Mills, built in 1601-03, E of the Wednesbury road between the present Countess Street and Bescot Crescent, at SP 009974 (TMS p72). They were rebuilt in 1788-89 and demolished in the earlier 1920s (VCH vol 17 p185). New Mills railway junction became Pleck Junction (SSR p11). The mills were so named to distinguish them from the Lord's Mill at the Bridge, Walsall, upstream (WROP p114). The name is preserved in New Mills Street, Palfrey.

New Mills House New Mills, Palfrey. Built in 1740 and for many years was occupied by Henry Boys. The house was still standing in 1997 (WROP p114p) of in c1918).

New Oxley Area on the W side of Stafford Road, N of the Goodyear works, Oxley. It appears to have been so called by the 1780s when New Oxley House (see) was built (BUOP pp44,51).

New Oxley House Three-storey house standing near the junction of Stafford Road with Church Road, in the area known as New Oxley. Built in the 1780s for William Warner, founder of a family of distinguished clerics, lawyers and benefactors of Wolverhampton Grammar School. Until 1905 it was the seat of Henry Staveley-Hill for four years when he moved to Oxley Manor. The house, which took its name from the area New Oxley, is now (1993) divided into flats and known as 437 Stafford Road (BUOP p44p).

New Park Medieval deer park in Needwood Forest belonging to the king (EDP p176).

New Park C19 colliery 1.25m ESE of Trentham (OS map 1834). In Trentham ancient parish (W p434). The area is now (1996) a large housing estate.

New Park House Over 1m ESE of Trentham. Former seat of the Tellwright family. There is a large stained glass window on the central staircase depicting an illustrated map of Staffordshire, inscribed 'This window was made for Joseph and Ann Tellwright 1938.' The house became a residential home of the Teachers' Benevolent Fund in 1968 (ES July 2 1997 p8p) and was officially opened on May 7 1969 by Katharine, Duchess of Kent. It was still the home in 1999 (info New Park House).

Newplace Blore (Ray). Seat of the Bassetts of Drayton Bassett in the Middle Ages (NSFCT 1885 p61).

New Pool Tiny hamlet 0.25m W of Knypersley. Formerly in Biddulph ancient parish. The name, in existence by 1482 (BHS June 1972 p29), is from a pool called New Pool and has also appeared as Newpool. The pool was still in existence in 1791 (BALH p15). By 1962 it was covered by Knypersley Sports Club cricket ground and the Congleton Tunstall road, the A527 (TTTD p164). In the later C17 Plot thought the pool was the source of the Trent (NHS p42). In 1791 it was considered the source of both the Trent and Biddulph Brook (BALH p15).

Newport Tiny canalside hamlet which developed in the early C19 to serve the Trent and Mersey Canal situated at the S end of Newport Lane, Middleport. Formerly in Burslem chapelry in Stoke-upon-Trent ancient parish. By the 1970s had been absorbed into Burslem (SL pp216,236). The name is of medieval origin and not modern, as generally thought, and appears in the court leet records (NSFCT 1924 p36).

Newport Branch of the Shropshire Union Canal. Diverges from the Shropshire Union Canal at Norbury Junction, leaves the county at Meretown and joins the Shrewsbury Canal at Wappenshall, Shrops, and was built mainly to carry Coalbrookdale iron (IAS p184). Opened in 1830 (NSJFS 1966 p70) or 1833 (IAS p184) or 1835. Built by Thomas Telford. S of Norbury was a superb flight of 17 locks in 1.5m; derelict by 1975 (SL p244). There is a combined canal and road bridge near Forton. The canal was abandoned in 1944 (IAS p184) (Nicholson's Guide to the Waterways No. 5 'Midlands' p49). Had closed altogether by 1947 (SL p257). Was very much overgrown by 1965 (NSJFS 1966 p70).

Newport House Newport Road, Stafford. Built by George Jones (d1883) in c1881 (SAC pp95-96).

New Road Audley parish (SGSAS). There is a highway called New Road 0.25m NE of Audley leading to Bignall End.

New Springs or New Springe (1733). House nearly 0.75m W of Talke. Formerly in Talke township in Audley ancient parish. It was built in the C17 on land owned by the Eardleys of Eardley Hall known as Talke Hayes (SHC 1944 p71).

Newstead Suburb 0.5m SSW of Blurton. Was a house in the C19. Formerly in Blurton chapelry in Trentham ancient parish.

Newstead House over 1m SSW of Cheddleton.

Newstone Newstone Farm, dated 1773, is 1.75m N of Upper Hulme. Formerly in Heathylee township in Alstonefield ancient parish (SGSAS). A structure known as 'Newstone Chapel,' a stopping place on the Leek Methodist Circuit, was added to the farm in 1816. The chapel which could accommodate about a 100 closed in 1931. The name 'Newstone' is from a 'rocking' stone (DPEM pp47,48,49p of the 'rocking' stone) (VCH vol 7 p36) (UHAW p35). The farm has also appeared as Middle Farm (UHAW p35).

Newstreet Is a road created in the mid C18 between Waterhouses and Bottom House which became part of the Leek-Ashbourne turnpike road (NSFCT 1948 pp46-47). Also is the name of a house over 0.5m NW of Winkhill, on the road.

Newton Minute hamlet on ground rising above the Blithe 0.75m ESE of Cresswell. This Newton has been considered the Niwantune in a charter of 956; others think it Newton Solney, Derbys (SHC 1916 p95). Appears in DB as Niwetone (see), but probably this is a survey of Draycott-in-the-Moors. There is an Upper and Lower Newton.

Newton Former hamlet on a bank above the Tame (MNB p60) now a suburb NW of Hamstead, 2.75m NNW of St Mary's church, Handsworth. Formerly in Perry Barr township in Handsworth ancient parish. The Newton area W of Walsall Road was transferred to West Bromwich county borough in 1928 (MNB p75). The common of Perry manor may have been situated in this area. There was settlement at Newton probably by the end of the C13. The name means 'new farm' (MNB pp64,66). In Newton Road was a station on the GJR which opened on July 4 1837 (IAS p130).
BISHOP ASBURY'S COTTAGE. A cottage, situated on the N side of Newton Road (A4041), facing the junction with Hamstead Road, is believed to date from the mid C17. It is a simple artisan's dwelling, constructed of brick, tile, and timber. When built it was part of a short terrace, but the other cottages were demolished when Newton Road was widened. The parents of Francis Asbury (1745-1816), founder of the Methodist Episcopal Church and first bishop of the American Methodist Church (1785), moved to this house in 1746. Here Francis, born at Hamstead (see), spent his childhood (The Pioneer Bishop: The Life and Times of Francis Asbury. WP Strickland. 1860) (OWB pl 27 showing the cottage adjoining other cottages) (VB p63) (VCH vol 17 p4) (MR p163) (BCM Oct 1984 pp52-60. July 1992 pp33-36) (WBOP p85) (TB May 1994 p25). The cottage was acquired by West Bromwich corporation in 1955 and opened to the public on Nov 27 1959 (TEBC) (VCH vol 17 p72) (Bishop Ashbury's Cottage. Sandwell Borough Council. 1994).

Newton Tiny village on an E-facing slope overlooking the Blithe 7.5m ENE of Stafford. Former manor and township in Blithfield ancient parish (W p412) (SHC 1908 p84). This Newton has been considered the Niwantune in a charter of 956; others think it Newton Solney, Derbys (SHC 1916 p95). The manor of Niwetone appears in DB. A medieval chapel at Newton, certified before 1563, is not mentioned thereafter (SHC 1915 p28). Newton township is loyal to the dedication of the parish church by keeping its wakes in the week in which St Leonard's day (Nov 6) occurs, whilst Blithfield township keeps its wakes early in Sept (SHC 1919 p2). Since the 1950s a Mrs Berta Capewell has voluntarily cleaned and polished the village telephone box. This extraordinarily worthy act was reported in the national media (SVB p37).

Newton House under 1m SSW of Oakamoor. To E of Threapwood.

Newton Hurst Minute and rather fragmented hamlet 1m ENE of Newton. In Blithfield ancient parish (W p412). Newton Hurst appears as 'Le Hurst,' a

wood, in 1257 (SHC 1919 p20). A star-shaped selenite was found in Harley field in the C17 (NHS p177 tab 11 fig 4 - could be an illustration of it).

Newton Junction Junction of the Tame Valley Canal with the Rushall Canal (HCMS No. 2).

Newton's College Former almshouse situated at W end of Lichfield cathedral Close. The almshouse, for the widows, orphans and unmarried daughters of clergy, was founded by Andrew Newton (d1806), the son of a Lichfield brandy and cider merchant, and brother to Thomas Newton, bishop of Bristol. The building, to the design of Joseph Potter the elder, comprises a range of 16 dwellings (VCH vol 14 p67). Bell's 'Lichfield Cathedral' p35 describes it, architecturally, as 'hideous.' It opened in 1803 (HOL p292) (GKCLC). Has also appeared as Newton's Buildings. The almshouse closed in 1988 and the college trustees transferred it to the dean and chapter (VCH vol 14 p67). Masonry from the West Gate (now demolished) is incorporated into part of it (VCH vol 3 p189).

Newtown Fragmented hamlet in the Moorlands 2.25m WSW of Longnor on the edge of common waste, in Fawfieldhead township, in Alstonefield ancient parish. Newtown existed as a hamlet by 1754. Sir George Crewe (of the Harpur-Crewe family), lord of Alstonefield manor, tried to encourage Newtown to grow in the late 1830s; having a mission church, St Paul, built here in 1837. But Newtown remained small (VCH vol 7 pp28,30) (LDD).

Newtown Small housing estate 0.75m W of Brocton. Does not appear on the 1834 OS map. In Baswich parish.

Newtown About Oxford Street, Bilston (1834 OS map). Now obsolete.

Newtown Small hamlet 2.25m SSE of Great Wyrley. Formerly in Bushbury parish, now a ward in Essington civil parish. A Neolithic or Bronze Age macehead was found to the E of Newtown at SJ 996041 which went to Birmingham Museum (BAST vol 71 p135) (Proceedings of the Prehistoric Society vol 25 p139) (NSJFS 1964 p41). Newtown grew up as a result of Lord Hay's extension of the Wyrley & Essington Canal (ESSN p52), which brought the limestone burning plant to Newtown (SOB p124). The name appears on 1834 OS map. A chapel, St Aidan, built in 1897 of corrugated iron was situated at the bottom of Long Lane at the junction with Stafford Road. The chapel was closed in 1969 and a bungalow built on the site (The Beloved Disciple: The Story of St John's Church Essington. Ralph Tomkinson. 1992).

New Town Large housing estate, 0.75m N of Brownhills, 1.25m WSW of Hammerwich. It straggles Watling Street for 1m (from SK 043065 to SK 057065) and spreads N from the street. Does not appear on the 1834 OS map. Was beginning to be settled by miners from the 1860s (VCH vol 14 p261).

New Town Tiny new settlement 1m SW of Hammerwich, on N side of Watling Street (1:25,000 OS map). Formerly in Hammerwich out-township in St Michael's parish, Lichfield.

Newtown Former small hamlet which had grown up near Stapenhill Wharf on the Stourbridge Canal, 0.75m ENE of Stourton, by c1830 (SVS p182) (RKE p19) (VCH vol 20 p124). In Kinver ancient parish. Has also appeared as New Town and the name is preserved in Newtown Bridge.

New Town An area at the N end of Beacon Street, Lichfield. The name prevailed in the 1830s to refer to an area at the junction of Wheel Lane and Beacon Street (VCH vol 14 pp25,27).

Newtown House or minute hamlet 1.75m E of Penkridge. In Penkridge ancient parish.

New Town Former hamlet in Rowley Regis parish (W p194) 1.5m WSW of Rowley Regis. Developed around Bannister's beerhouse (later the Holly Bush Inn) and smithy on the S side of Mousesweet Brook in the early C19. Developed more rapidly in the period 1835 to 1850 to an almost self-contained community (TB Aug 1995 p27). Has also appeared as Newtown. By association, some of the area N of Mousesweet Brook (formerly in Worcs) is currently known as Newtown (Birmingham A-Z).

Newtown Hamlet over 1.5m SW of Rushtonhall. Formerly in Rushton James township in Leek ancient parish. The hamlet grew on former waste land and was so called by 1701. By 1783 there were several cottages, mainly on the S side of a road running between Leek and Congleton via Horton (VCH vol 7 p220).

Newtown Original name for Castletown, Stafford, in the C19 (VCH vol 6 p195) (Stafford Post May 12 1988 p5) (SAC p71). In Stafford ancient parish.

New Town Hamlet or suburb 2m WNW of the High Street, West Bromwich, embracing the Farley Park area. Appears as a hamlet on 1834 OS map. By 1999 was a ward in Sandwell metropolitan borough.

Newtown Row Row of houses in Walsall erected in c1850 by Thomas Bate, builder, a member of Walsall town council. So called because there were few houses in this neighbourhood, and it was said the houses represented 'a new town.' The properties are now Nos. 110 to 114 Stafford Street (SNWA p76).

New Village Residential area to E of Mushroom Green. The place appears in the 1841 census as New Town and Mushroom New Village. Perhaps so called in contrast to the unplanned and haphazard Mushroom Green (OS map Sheet 71.07). The name is preserved in the street called New Village.

New Village Former district of Smethwick. Grew with the opening of the Birmingham Canal New Cut New Main Line in the later 1820s. It lay on the E side of the Birmingham-Dudley road (VCH vol 17 p91). Inhabited by industrial workers (SHCB p8).

New Village An area of small houses, known as New Village by 1871, developed NW of High Street (S of Upper Green), Tettenhall (VCH vol 20 p8).

New Wood Wood and farm 2.75m NE of Kinver church, in Kinver ancient parish. New Wood Farm, which existed by the 1880s, had come to be on the edge of an housing estate dating from before WW2 and the later C20 (VCH vol 20 p124).

New York House 0.25m WNW of Upper Elkstone. Formerly in Warslow and Elkstones township of Alstonefield ancient parish. New York Mine, part of the New York and Royledge Copper and Lead Mines (W p743), closed in 1859 (VCH vol 7 p60).

New Zealand House 1.5m S of Swythamley, E side of Gun Hill.

Nicholson Institute Educational establishment in Stockwell Street, Leek. Founded by Joshua Nicholson (d1885) in 1884. It contains a free library, reading room, and a picture galley (SOSH p346) (ES Oct 17 1934 p4) (VCH vol 7 pp112,153il). In 1885 Lady Elizabeth Wardle, founder of the Leek Embroidery Society, saw the original Bayeux tapestry in Normandy, and had 34 ladies of the Society make a copy of it. The copy, using specially dyed wool to match the eight original colours, was finished in 1886 and was first exhibited in the Institute. Over 1000 visitors came to see it. After touring throughout the country as an exhibit it was bought in 1895 by Octavia Hill's brother Alderman Hill and given to Reading Museum, Reading, Berks, where it was still on show in the 1990s (KES p128) (VB p194) (NI pp42,43). Between 1891 and 1911 William Kineton Parkes, novelist, was librarian at the Institute. His work includes 'Potiphar's Wife' (1908), 'The Altar of Moloch' (1912), and 'Hareware' (1914) (VFC p103). In the 1980s the museum contained: Some embroidery made by the Leek School of Embroidery; a model fairground made by Richard Henry Lomas of Leek made between c1880 and c1940; and the designs for the memorial in Leek to Joshua Nicholson. The institute's visitor's book contains some famous names: Keir Hardie, Mark Twain, GK Chesterton, George Bernard Shaw, Walter Crane, Olave Baden-Powell, George VI and Queen Mary (when Duke and Duchess of York), the Duke of Sutherland, and the Marquess of Ripon (NI p60). An orang-outang's mummified body was found in a barrel in the loft of the institute on March 31 1965. At first it was thought to be the body of a seven to 10 year-old girl. It was sent off to Sheffield University to be examined who declared the body to be that of an orang-outang (NI p64). Joshua Nicholson's younger son Arthur gave Leek the Nicholson War Memorial in 1924 to the memory of his son.

Nield Bank House 0.5m ESE of Flash. Formerly in Hollinsclough township in Alstonefield ancient parish. Appears as Neelde in 1455 (VCH vol 7 p38). The bottle containing the spirit of John or Josiah Gaunt's ghost is said to have been buried on Nield Hill (UHAW p77).

Nine Pins Clump of trees on the top of Hillswood, N of Leek. These had fallen and were replaced in 1953 by a conifer plantation (NSFCT 1978 p37).

Ninety-Nine Steps Limestone rock feature at the southern tip of Wren's Nest Hill. At the top of the steps is fine viewpoint (WNNNR p22).

Niwetone The name appears in DB. It is Newton 1m SSE of Draycott-in-the-Moors. The DB Niwetone entry may really have been a survey of Draycott-in-the-Moors (Draycott-in-the-Moors does not appear in DB); Newton is one of the three hamlets which form Draycott-in-the-Moors ecclesiastical parish (NSFCT 1915 p90).

Noah's Ark House(s) before Dove Bridge, Uttoxeter, just in Staffs. Redfern does not mention it but he says there was a hermitage at Dove Bridge. (HOU p236).

Noah's Ark House to W of Newborough.

Noah's Ark Inn Crabbery Street, Stafford. Originally reputedly built as a residence for the dean of Stafford Collegiate Church (SIOT). However there is no evidence to support this except its nearness to St Mary's (SKYT pp11,12ps). Some say it was owned by the Cradoc family (later known as Craddock) (SKYT p11). Elizabeth I is reputed to have taken wine here en route to Stafford Castle in 1575 (SKYT p11) (SSTY p217). About 1830 it became an inn (SKYT p11). Dr Palmer of Rugeley (see) murdered his mother-in-law, Mary Thornton, to inherit the inn (info Mr Pitt). In 1877 the inn was bought by the corporation who took it down in part and demolished the overhanging porch for a road widening scheme. The original stone was reused in the alterations (FSP p84) (SOPP pl 36p). There a tradition that a tunnel runs from here to Stafford Castle (SKYT p11). The inn closed in 1961 and then became a weights

and measures office for Trading Standards. Later, it was owned by Stafford borough council and associated with the nearby market hall. In 1999 the property became an inn known as The Surgery. (SLM June 1953 p20 il) (ASOP p127).

Nobut Formerly in Leigh township and ancient parish. A UFO resembling the last quarter of the moon lying on its back was seen in the eastern sky from a farm at Nobut at about 5.00am on Sept 2 1967 (FSRP p11). See Upper Nobut, Lower Nobut.

Nobut Hall At Upper Nobut 1m E of Church Leigh.

Noddyfield Valley Valley through which a road runs between Prospect Village to Hayfield Hill road. Has appeared as 'Noady Field' (1682), Noddy Field (OS map 1834) (SPNO p60). The name means 'foolish, silly,' used in a derogative sense (SPNO p60).

Noddy Park Aldridge. Noddy Park Farm was in existence in the C17 and still stood in the C19 (MOA p133). A Noddy Park occurs in 1768 (SNAR p40). It is now a street name N of Aldridge church.

Noel's Almshouses Earl Street, Stafford. Built by Sir Martin Noel in c1640 (SIOT p77 il facing) (LGS p218) (OSST 1934 p21). Or c1660 (BOE p245). Or called 'The College' as the almshouses were built on the site of the court house belonging to Stafford Collegiate College (SKYT p96). The almshouses consist of 12 houses; six men and six women; all had to be over the age of 50. The almshouses were later endowed by John Chetwynd, Philip and Thomas Foley, and Mrs Catherine Abnett (SPP p31p) (SIOT pp77-78).

No Man's Bank 2.5m WNW of Burntwood, on S side of Watling Street.

No Man's Green On the border of Shrops and Enville and Kinver ancient parishes. It is mentioned in 1601 and 1624 (VCH vol 20 p109). Has also appeared as Nomans Green (Royal Kinver p1).

No Man's Piece Bilston. Tradition alleges that this piece of land was left untilled and unrated because it was set aside for the burial of felons gibbeted at the corner of Stow Heath Lane (HOBLL p219).

Noon Sun House 2m NNW of Upper Elkstone. The house, but not the name, occurs on the 1834 OS map. The name perhaps reflects an astrological point in alignment with Merryton Low, 0.75m to the SW. It may therefore be an ancient sacred site (DPMM pp104-105).

Noonsun Common Fragmented tiny hamlet on high sloping ground above a tributary of the Churnet under 0.25m W of Ipstones. Incidentally, like Noon Sun (see above) Noonsun lies on a similar SW-NE alignment with, in this case, standing stones at Sexton Farm.

Noose Lane Lane on the W side of Little London, Willenhall. Appears in the C13 as le Nous. By 1951 the lane divided the urban districts of Willenhall and Wednesfield (HOWI p186) (WFW p48). The name is probably from the medieval name 'Nese' which means a headland or nose and undoubtedly refers to a projection in the boundary of one of the fields (HOWI p186) (SNW p51).

Norbury Ancient parish and former township. The village of Norbury on a slight incline in the middle of low ground formerly surrounded by wetland is 7.5m W of Stafford. Two cropmarks identified as **burial mounds** from air photographs are 0.5m NE of Norbury at SJ 79222417 and SJ 79282418 (NSJFS 1965 p45). For **Bronze Age** bronze implements found in Norbury parish and noted by Shaw see under Warton. The manor of Nortberie appears in DB, where it is recorded as having two priests. From this CH Burne surmises the church was probably a collegiate or portionary church before the Norman Conquest; the townships of Norbury and Weston Jones, which long had been distinct entities for all parochial purposes, representing the portions (NSFCT 1888 pp63,66). Later forms are: Nordbiri (1198), Northbiri (c1255), Northbury (c1291), Northburgh (1316), Norberye (1482), and Norbury alias Nothedbury (1612) (SPNO p174) (SPN p88). The **name** is from 'North Bury' - the 'Bury' was, perhaps, thought CH Burne, the rising ground between the church and the rectory (NSFCT 1888 pp63,66) (DUIGNAN) (SSE 1987 p30) (SPN p88). It may have been considered as 'north' in relation to Stafford Castle (SPNO p174). There may have been a Saxon **church** at Norbury, which may have been founded by St Chad of Lichfield Cathedral (see) (St Peter's Church, Norbury: A History. Rev BT Swinnerton. pre 1975). The present parish church, St Peter, on the E side of the village, is mostly of mid C14 origin (VCH vol 4 p160). The E window was designed by the folklorist, Miss CS Burne (born Moreton, Gnosall, 1850), in 1873 (VCH vol 4 p162) (BOE p212) (MR p244). The parish formed before 1086 and probably originally contained Forton ancient parish (SHC 1916 p192). The **wake** was on the nearest Sunday to St Peter's day in the C19 (W p465). For Norbury **Windmill** see Mill Haft Wood. Norbury was originally on the **Eccleshall-Newport road** until the present road to the N was built by-passing the village (St Peter's Church, Norbury: A History. Rev BT Swinnerton. pre 1975). The poet, **Richard Barnfield** (1574-1627), eldest child of Richard Barnfield and Maria Skrymsher may have been born at Norbury Manor. He was baptised in Norbury church. His adult life was spent at Darlaston Hall, Stone. Some of his work has been mistaken for Shakespeare's (NSFCT 1888 p65) (LGS pp47,194,221) (PSS pp4-11) (RHPS pp155-158) (SLM Nov 1950 p33) (SN May 19 1951 p6) (STM Dec 1967 p38) (SIS pp38,118) (VFC p9). **Norbury Local History Group** formed in 1990 (info Tony Browne). **Customs.** At Norbury many of the schoolboys regularly sported an oak-leaf on Restoration day (May 29). Hackwood implies that this custom had lapsed by 1924 (SCSF p19). The custom of gooding for stacks of wheat on St Thomas' Day (Dec 21) at Norbury was kept up until 1875 (SFL p392) (BCC vol 3 p205) (STMSM July 1980 p33). **Old oak(s).** In the later C17 Plot noted an oak with a girth of six yards growing between the manor and the windmill (NHS p210). On the old village green just below the church, was until the late C19, a remarkable old oak - once no doubt the village trysting-tree, thought CH Burne (NSFCT 1888 pp63,66). A labouring man was attacked by a **boggart** in the Norbury area on Big Bridge (see).

Norbury Junction Junction of Shropshire Union Canal or Birmingham & Liverpool Junction Canal and its Newport Branch 0.5m SE of Norbury (opened in 1833, abandoned 1944) (IAS p184) (SPJD p87pc aerial view).

Norbury Manor Built in the mid C19, to S of Norbury Old Manor. It replaced Norbury Old Manor and re-used its stones (NSFCT 1976 p18). The Old Manor was haunted and some believe the ghosts 'flitted' with the stones. There are stories of a phantom horse in the stables and disturbances in the house (SFL pp50,51) (FOS p20) (STMSM July 1980 p32). (STM Dec 1967 p38p of Norbury Manor - the farmhouse).

Norbury Motte A Norman motte of a lesser lord (SL p65) in the centre of Norbury village.

Norbury Old Manor Ancient seat of the Butlers 0.75m E of Norbury. According to Stebbing Shaw it was built by the elder Ralph le Botiler or Butler, lord of Norbury manor in c1291 to 1307 (GM 1801 vol 81 p231) (CAMS p42 il). The C13 mansion probably consisted of four ranges set round an open court within a wet moat. It was probably never embattled. It was one of the earlier medieval mansions to be built less defensively. Its outer walls were only about a metre thick and iron grilles just protected the outer windows. The Botilers sold it to Thomas Skrymsher in 1521 (CAMS pp7,42). Thomas Skrymsher probably rebuilt the manor house in the C16. Plot noted an echo which rebounded off the mansion which he thought was the best of its kind in the county (NHS p29 tab 19 of the hall) (SD p61). Sir Charles Skrymsher's daughter carried the property to the Boothbys of Tooley Park, Leics. In 1760 it was sold to various owners (NSFCT 1888 pp65,66). In 1775 the Ansons of Shugborough bought the manor and advowson (NSFCT 1888 pp65,66) (CAMS p42). By 1801 it was in a state of decay and was inhabited by farmworkers (GM 1801 vol 81 p231). Demolished in c1820 (LGS pp194-195) or by 1838 (VCH vol 4 p155) (NSFCT 1976 p18) or in 1838 (CAMS p42) (SPJD p46) partly because it had become so haunted (STMSM July 1980 p32). The moat remains (ESH p58) and the foundations were visible when the moat was dry in 1976 (NSFCT 1976 p18) (SPJD pp42pcs,44il). The site of the house was a garden by 1914 (SHC 1945/ 6 p109). A plough in the summer of 1952 turned up some old glass, perhaps from the manor (SLM Oct 1952 p11p of the moat). Remains of the foundations could still be seen on the inner side of the rectangular moated enclosure near Mill Haft Wood in c1955 (VCH vol 4 p155). (STM Sept 1966 p38) (MIDD vol 1 p7p).

Norbury Park 1.25m SE of Norbury. Has also appeared as Norbury Old Park. A medieval deer park enclosed out of forest. In existence by 1342 (NSJFS 1962 p76). Saxton noted it on his map (EDP p179). A short length of vallum was the only survival of it in 1910 (NSFCT 1910 p170).

Norbury Park House 1.25m SE of Norbury.

Nordley Hill Hill and district N of Wednesfield. There may have been a burial mound on the summit in which some of the dead of the battle of Tettenhall or Wednesfield were buried (WFW p23).

Nore Hill Settlement 0.75m NW of Pattingham, nearly 1m SSE of Patshull Hall in Patshull ancient parish. There was settlement here by the mid C13 and the place was known as Nore before the C17. The present farm called Nore Hill is probably of C17 origin (VCH vol 20 pp162, 163).

Normacot Former manor and township in Hilderstone quarter in Stone ancient parish and partly in Stoke-upon-Trent chapelry in Stoke-upon-Trent ancient parish. The former hamlet of Normacot, over 1m SE of Longton, lay on rising ground near the source of Furnace Brook, in the Star-and-Garter Road area. A fragment of the thin tapering butt of a large stone prehistoric axe was found in Mr Rhead's garden in c1935 (NSJFS 1962 p26. 1964 p35). A fragment of polished sandstone celt of the late Neolithic period was found at a quarry in Normacot (NSFCT 1953 p105). Bronze Age. A beaker of the period c1700 BC was discovered at Normacot in 1936 (NSFCT vol 71 p66) (DAJ vol 75 p72) (NSJFS 1964 p35). A cinerary urn of the period c1400 BC was

found in Meir Road in Feb 1927 (NSFCT 1926 p147. vol 70 p85) (Proceedings of the Prehistoric Society. vol 27 p298 no. 195) (NSJFS 1964 p35). A quern of the Iron Age (450 BC) was found at Normacot during quarrying (NSFCT 1938 p114) (STM June 1969 Supplement p12) (BNDA p1). The manor of Normanescote appears in DB. Northman was an Anglo-Saxon personal name, hence, Northman's cot, or the North man's cot (DUIGNAN) (SSE 1996 p16). Or Northman may have been a nickname (SPN p116). Henry de Aldithley (or Audley) of Heighley Castle (see) held Normacot manor by 1227 by the service of performing guard duties at Newcastle Castle (SCSF pp116-117) (VCH vol 8 p13). Hulton Abbey was granted the manor in the early C13 and established Normacot Grange (see) here. The present suburb of Normacot comprising the triangle of land between the Uttoxeter Road, Upper Normacot Road and Meir Road, had been laid out in building plots for the Duke of Sutherland by 1875 and much of it was built up by the late 1870s (VCH vol 8 p227). Normacot became a separate ecclesiastical parish in 1852 and a separate civil parish in 1894 (GLAUE p418). Unlike other Stone townships Normacot township lay in the North Division of Pirehill hundred (KD 1872). The church, The Holy Evangelists, on the S side of Upper Belgrave Road, was built as a chapel of ease to Blurton church in 1847 (VCH vol 8 p235) (BOE p260). Normacot was on the North Staffs Railway Uttoxeter branch line (opened in 1848). A line from Bucknall to Normacot opened in 1875 (VCH vol 2 p309). It was recommended that Normacot station close in 1963 (ES March 22 1963). A tiny one storey property in Uttoxeter Road may have been the smallest house in N Staffs (ES Oct 1 1932 p3p). Reginald J Mitchell, born in Butt Lane (see), spent his childhood in Normacot, living in the school house, which still stands opposite The Holy Evangelists church (MR p219).

Normacot Grange 0.75m SE of Normacot, 2m SE of Longton. Formerly in Hilderstone quarter in Stone ancient parish. The manor of Normacot seems to have been given to Hulton Abbey when the abbey was founded in the early C13. By 1242 there was a grange of the abbey here covering the Meir Heath and Lightwood areas. It was leased out by the mid C15 and was sold to Sir John Giffard of Chillington Hall in 1540. It remained with the Giffards for many generations. The grange farmhouse, with its reputedly medieval cellars, was occupied by the Lane family from the C17 and stood behind the present Grange Middle School, Sandon Road, Meir on the perimeter of the former Meir airfield. It was demolished in 1984 (BNDA p37) (Normacot and its Church. C Beaver. 1972 p5) (SASR 1985 pp58,61,66,68) (SSE 1994 p73).

Normacot Hills A range of low hills which commence at the junction of Meir Road and Star-and-Garter Road, and continue through Lightwood and Shooters Hills (600 feet) to Rough Close. They are composed of the Trias or New Red Sandstone (NSFCT 1910 p83).

Normanswood Farm over 0.5m ESE of Stowe-by-Chartley. Gypsum mining was probably taking place here by the mid C19. There are references to workings intermittently from at least the 1860s. The mine re-opened after a period in 1949 and was abandoned in 1956 (VCH vol 2 p199) (info Hixon Local History Society).

Norris Hill Elevated ground opposite St John's Way, Ashley. Norris Hill Farm, which stood off Church Road, was demolished in the 1960s for the housing development in St John's Way (ALW pls 17 in c1906, 18).

North Buttress Rock feature on NE slopes of The Cloud in Staffs (SGM p266).

Northcote Hall Oscott, Great Barr. Named after Rev James Spencer Northcote d1907 (buried at Oscott. He was author of 'A visit to the Roman Catacombs' 1877). Now part of Oscott College? (POTP p163) (Oscott College, a brief history. JJ Coyne).

North Gate Medieval gateway in the wall surrounding Stafford, on the N side. It was the strongest defended of Stafford's four gates since no marsh land existed in front of it and attacks were most likely to come from the N (SSTY p2). This account is slightly contradicted by inscriptions on metal plates marking the site of the North Gate in Gaol Square, erected in 1982-83. The inscriptions tell that the North Gate guarded the causeway access through marshes on the northern approach. The gate is probably mentioned in 1170 and occurs by name in 1445 (VCH vol 6 p199). By the late C15 the gate was the largest of Stafford's gates (W p325) (LGS p217). There is a tradition that a castle was built by the gate in Henry VIII's reign and that the gate may have been part of it (SKYT p48). By the early C17 the gate was being used as a gaol and had become known as Gaol Gate (W p325) (LGS p217) (VCH vol 6 p199). James I sheltered from the rain under the gate on his visit to Stafford in 1617 (SKYT p3). By 1678 it was in a ruinous state and a house of correction was built on the site. The 'Gaol Gate' gaol had appalling conditions in the late C18 according to John Howard's 'An Account of the Prisons and Houses of Correction in the Oxford Circuit' (SKYT p130). Prisoners were moved to the present Stafford Gaol when it opened in 1794. The old prison was demolished by 1820 (W p325) (LGS p217). Some say the house of correction was built in 1700 and was really a rebuilding of the old gatehouse (SIOT p89) (SKYT p48). Part of the foundations of the North Gate were unearthed in 1959 and further foundations may have been found in the mid 1960s (SN March 14 1959. Feb 26 1965 p9. March 4 1965 p8). Some of the stones from the gate were discovered in Crabbery Street (SN Jan 10 1964 p18p). Has also been called Foregate (SOSH p148). (OSST 1933 pp36-37).

Northicote Former tiny hamlet and old timber-framed farmhouse over 0.5m NE of Bushbury. In Showell manor in Bushbury ancient parish (BUOP p6). (WJO Feb 1906 p41p). Has appeared as Northincote (1255), Northcot, and Northycote (SHOS vol 2 pp182-183). The name means 'Northern cot' (DUIGNAN) (SPN p145). The farm was built in c1600 by the Underhill family, Roman Catholics. The Underhills lived here to 1791. The front of the house was formerly the back (BUOP p30p). Later, Northicote became part of the Whitgreave family estate of Moseley Court (Northycote: 400 Years of a Wolverhampton Farm leaflet by Wolverhampton Council). According to Mark Whittaker Lord Wilmot hid at Northicote Farm after the battle of Worcester (1651) (info Mark Whittaker). But according to Shaw and Broughton he hid in a house of John Huntbach at Brinsford (SHOS vol 1 p79. vol 2 p184) (SMC p170). By the road here in 1983 a driver, reputedly, swerved to avoid the ghost of a cavalier on horseback, and overturned his car (info Bruce Braithwaite). The farm appears on a postcard wrongly attributed to be Moseley Old Hall drawn by J Fullwood in his Etchings at Old Wolverhampton 1880 (SHJ vol 2 p48p). In 1978 Wolverhampton borough council acquired Northicote with 80 acres of surrounding land, and restored the farmhouse; it is now used for educational visits as well as being a venue for displays of country crafts organised by The Friends of Northicote Farm (BUOP p30) (Northycote: 400 Years of a Wolverhampton Farm leaflet by Wolverhampton Council). In 1993 Northicote Secondary School was the first school in the country to be failed by OFSTED inspectors after which the school dramatically improved; the headmaster appointed in 1993, Geoff Hampton, became the first serving head teacher of a state school ever to be knighted when he was knighted in 1998 (BBC Radio 4. World at One. Nov 1 1996) (I Jan 26 1998 p13) (Who's Who 1999).

North Low Wednesfield. This burial mound, South Low and others, reputedly contained some of the dead from one of the battles which took place about the year 907 to 911 at Tettenhall (see) and or at Wednesfield. According to Plot in the later C17, in North Low were buried the defeated Danish Northumbrian noblemen and kings - Eowills, Halfden or Hildein and two of their earls Ohter and Scurfa, also another king, Juvar, and nine other noblemen. North Low had disappeared by the later C17 (NHS p415). In the late C18 Shaw noted North Low was near lands in Croft Lodge (SHOS vol 2 p150). Willmore says North Low was probably in North Low Field (HOWW p30), an open field of Wednesfield, which, according to Smallshire, lay in the Amos Lane and Long Knowle Lane area (WFW p53). (SVS p332) (W p157) (S&W p177) (SC p148) (AOW p7; says Huntbach and Duignan notes them) (NSJFS 1965 p59).

North Quarry Rock feature on NE slopes of The Cloud in Staffs. (SGM p266).

Northwood Former hamlet now a suburb of Hanley, 0.5m E of Hanley. Formerly in Hanley and Shelton townships in Stoke-upon-Trent chapelry and ancient parish (W p232). Northwood was created into a more formerly laid out hamlet by William Ridgway and was known as Northwood by 1832 (VCH vol 8 p143). Northwood became a separate ecclesiastical parish in 1845 (CAST p57) (GLAUE p418). The Commissioners' church, Holy Trinity, Lower Mayer Street, E of Baskerville Road, was built in 1848-1849 (BOE p258). The Duke of Devonshire attended cockfighting at the Cat Inn (see), Northwood. Another Northwood cockfighting inn was the Cock Inn in Providence Square, which was still in existence in 1910 (H p99). Harriet E Fourdrinier, novelist, was a resident of Northwood, identified with this Northwood (note on frontispiece of WSL copy of her novel 'Our New Parish: Its Privileges and Progress' 1852). She was the daughter of Henry Fourdrinier; the Fourdriniers had a paper manufactory at Ivy House Paper Mill (see), Hanley. However, Rosemary Toeman states it is a Northwood in Shrops (VFC p50). The football team, Hanley Swifts, had a football ground at Northwood (H p101).

Northwood Minute hamlet in the C19, now a modern housing estate 1.25m NW of Trentham. In Trentham ancient parish. Now merges with Clayton.

Northwood Tiny hamlet 0.5m NE of Ellastone. Near it is said to have been a circular group of oaks called 'Twenty Oaks;' Rousseau's favourite spot (NSJFS 1966 p58).

Northwood North Wood appears on Yates' map to the E of Meer Oak. In Tettenhall ancient parish, near the Pattingham parish boundary, and was an inhabited area by 1257 (VCH vol 20 p10).

Northwood Brook Runs NE of Ellastone a tributary of the Dove.

Northwood House Formerly Prospect House. Northwood, Hanley. Seat of William Ridgway, pottery manufacturer, in 1829 (VCH vol 8 p143).

Northwood Park Bushbury (Birmingham A-Z). Modern housing estate. Does not appear on the 1834 OS map.

Northwood Park Northwood, Hanley. Public park opened in 1907 as part of the jubilee celebrations of Hanley's incorporation (VCH vol 8 p143).

Northwood Tumulus A Neolithic burial mound by Northwood Farm, Northwood Lane, Trentham, in a field called Cow Pasture at SJ 85954171. Is six or 5.5 feet high and 70 feet in diameter and was reported in very good condition in 1983. Excavated by Molyneux in 1859. Two or three earthen vessels and a cinerary urn and a flint arrow head were found and a large quantity of calcined bones. One cinerary urn is in the Potteries Museum (Annals of the Diocese of Lichfield. 1859. pp20-22) (JGM figs 89, 101) (HOTM p9) (The Ceramic Art of Great Britain. Ll Jewitt. figs 6,51,56) (NSFCT vol 32 pp153-154. 1925 p189. 1931 p191. vol 72 p117. 1983 p10) (HOTC pp1-8) (ES Nov 2 1934 p6p of the cinerary urn) (NSJFS 1965 p49) (STM May 1966 p33) (BNDA p1). The Trentham burial mound Garner mentions is perhaps this or one in Trentham Park (GNHSS p5*). A fragment of an axe-hammer of Neolithic or Bronze Age from Trentham (JGM p112) (NSFCT vol 32 p153) may have been from this burial mound (NSJFS 1964 p35). A mace-head of the Late Neolithic Age or Early Bronze Age was found near Northwood Farm, slightly W of Lyme Brook about 150 yards before it joins the Trent, in the early 1930s (ES Nov 2 1934 p6) (NSFCT 1934 p77) (NSJFS 1964 p35) (STM May 1966 p33).

Norton Bog The area now covered by Chasewater (see) originally formed a part of the extensive Norton Bog (SNBC p11) (1888 OS map 6 inch).

Norton Bridge Small village on a bank above Meece Brook 1m NE of Chebsey. In Chebsey parish. The railway station on the GJR at Norton Bridge opened on July 4 1837. The North Staffs Railway line to Stoke-on-Trent, opened in 1848, branches off the GJR line at Norton Bridge. There was a serious accident to the 'Irish Mail' at Norton Bridge on Dec 8 1899 (Railways In and Around Stafford. Edward Talbot. 1994 p4). The old Norton Bridge station (which also served Eccleshall) was demolished in 1961 (EOP p77p). The mission church, St Luke, Station Road, was in built in 1893 (EOP p76p) (LDD). The architect, Max Hutchinson, proposed a new country town be built at Norton Bridge in the journal 'Building' Sept 15 1989 pp58-61 il.

Norton Canes Ancient parish and large village on a low prominence bounded by Newlands and Gains Brooks 16.25m SSE of Stafford. The Northtune or Nordtune mentioned in a charter of 951 was identified by Birch in his Cartularium Saxonicum with this Norton. But Dugdale identifies it with Norton-in-Scarsdale, Derbys (SHC 1916 p76). The name later appears as Nortone, a manor held by the bishop of Chester (Lichfield) in DB, Norton-super-le-Canok (C13) (SPN pp88-89) (SSE 1996 p16), Norton-under-Cannock (SHOS vol 2 p57) (LGS p195) (DUIGNAN). Erdeswick in the late C16 described it as the third Wyrley and it may have been called Norton (North) in recognition of it being N of Great and Little Wyrley (HOWW p6). 'Canes' is probably synonymous with Gain's as in Gain's Brook and Gain's Lane, which are nearby to the village. The two probably represent the name of a former lord or landowner. (The family name 'Canes' is derived from Cahaianes or Cahagnes, in Normandy) (DUIGNAN). Or 'Canes' is a corruption of Cannock. There was a church at Norton in the C14 (LDD). The present parish church, St James, lies at the end of the roads Church Vale and Church Road on the W side of Norton. With the exception of the tower and outer walls the church of 1832 was destroyed in a fire in Jan 1888, and was rebuilt shortly after (LGS p195) (BOE p212). Beating the bounds was practised in Norton Canes (SCSF p21). The area was anciently part of Cannock Forest. Common land at Norton Canes was enclosed in 1868 (PCC p16). S of Church Road at SK 012076 was a small rectangular moat, destroyed by ploughing in 1983 (SSAHST 1982-3 p38). Norton Canes parish was a peculiar jurisdiction of the dean and chapter of Lichfield cathedral until peculiar jurisdictions were abolished in 1846 (VCH vol 3 p94) (GLAUE p418). Norton was a colliery village from the C19 (SL p118). The present village extends further NE from the original nucleus. The SSR opened a branch railway from Ryder's Hayes to Norton Canes in 1858 (VCH vol 2 p317). A railway was completed from Aldridge through Walsall Wood to Norton Canes in 1882 (VCH vol 17 p278). Civilly Norton Canes partly entered Brownhills urban district when it was formed in 1894, and wholly in 1896 (GLAUE p418). The old Norton charities were: Walker's Dole, Smith's Dole, Green's Dole, Davis' Dole. Roger and Phineas Fowke's Charity, which had 15 penny loaves distributed among the poor, was still operating in the late C19 (CCC p111). William Masfen, aged 29, a farmer of Norton Canes was murdered on July 1 1893 by John Thomas Hewitt, a miner who was poaching. Hewitt was hung (TB Oct 1982 p5).

Norton Common Extensive common in Norton Canes parish which stretched from the A5190 in the N to Watling Street in the S, from Norton Canes in the W to Chasewater, and covering most of the present Chasewater, in the E (SSE 1994 p47). Common land at Norton Canes was enclosed in 1870 (MH 1994 p108).

Norton East District NE of Norton Canes. Built on former Norton Common, anciently part of Cannock Forest. The land now covered by Norton East was enclosed in 1868 (PCC p16). The name appears on the 1888 OS map 6 inch.

Norton Farm Very isolated farm 2m SW of Stone. In 1932 a mace-head of Neolithic or Bronze Age was found and taken to the Potteries Museum (ES Nov 2 1934 p6p) (NSFCT 1932 pp125-126. vol 69 p77) (NSJFS 1964 p19).

Norton Green Hamlet on slopes in the valley of the head of the Trent 0.75m NE of and now merges with Norton-in-the-Moors. Formerly in Norton-in-the-Moors chapelry in Stoke-upon-Trent ancient parish. The firm of T Cope and sons of Norton Green supplied the huge chains which supported the Menai Straits Suspension Bridge in 1826 (ONST 1977 p383) or in 1829 (TFTPM p90). At the beginning of the C20 Norton Green was still an entirely separate village from the adjoining villages of Ball Green and Norton with which it now (1958) merges: In 1955 Leek rural district council started to build houses at Norton Green (ONST 1958 pp216,219).

Norton Green District SE of the church at Norton Canes.

Norton Green Branch of the Caldon Canal. Spurred N off the Caldon Canal near Little Heakley Farm, at SJ 904517. Opened in 1778 (HCMS No. 5).

Norton Green Hall Norton-in-the-Moors. Seat of William de Mere in 1276. Alfred Hales lived in the hall in the 1840s. He committed suicide here on July 6 1842 after the failure of his pit at Limes Kilns, Norton Greens. EW Oldacre occupied the hall shortly after the suicide of Alfred Hales despite the fact that Alfred's son claimed it. Probably EW Oldacre repossessed it as a mortgage on it had not been paid. Oldacres were in possession by 1851 (ONST 1939 pp82-83). Later, Charles Hales, Alfred's son, claimed the property as heir, and Oldacres said that he could resume possession if he would pay off the mortgage. On several occasions however, Hales took the law into his own hands and made attempts to gain possession by force, one of which being on Sept 9 and 10 1861; this or another attempt by Hales at repossession culminated in what has been described as the Norton Green Riot (ONST 1939 pp82-83. 1954 p180).

Norton-in-the-Moors Former township (ONST 1926 p8) and large colliery village on a high escarpment between the head of the Trent and Whitfield Brook Valley 18m N of Stafford. Former chapel in Stoke-upon-Trent ancient parish. EARLY to 1600. A Neolithic or Bronze Age axe-hammer has been found at 57 Leek Road which went to the Potteries Museum (NSJFS 1964 p31). There is a tradition that the **Biddlemoor Men** occupied the Norton ridge area and not the Biddulph Moor (see) area (SMM p106). The Northtune mentioned in the will of Wulfric Spot (c1002), founder of Burton Abbey, may be identified with this Norton (SHC 1916 p27) (SHJ autumn 1996 pp1-5). Later the name appears as Nortone, a manor, in DB, Norton-super-le-Mores, Norton-sub-Keuremunt (see Kenermont Hay) (SPN p77), 'ye town of Norton-in-ye-Moors' (1386), Norton-under-Kermond (1394), Norton i' the Moors (Plot's map), Norton-upon-the-Moors, Norton-le-Moors (1944), Norton-in-the-Moors (1944) (ONST 1944 p110. 1950 p246), and Norton-on-the-Moors (GLAUE p418). The name means 'North town' (DUIGNAN) (SPN p77). There was a **church** at Norton in the C12 (LDD). The present church, St Bartholomew, on a hill top with views to the Moorlands on the corner of Highgate Close and Norton Lane, was rebuilt in brick in 1738, and again partly rebuilt in 1914 (BOE p267). Norton **wakes** were held on the fourth Sunday in August or on the Sunday following August 24 or, if Sunday falls on that day, on that day (ONST 1928 p19). The **village developed** from the Middle Ages by being on a crossroads of the old road from Leek to Burslem and the road from Milton to Biddulph (SVB p131). The village centre was the square standing opposite the old Bell and Dragon Inn (ONST 1926 p9). Norton parish **stocks** stood near the crossroads and was visible from the window of the Old Cock Inn (ONST 1976 pp373-374). Norton **pound**, demolished in the second half of the C19, stood on the upper corner of Pinfold Croft, now (1927) known as Mount Pleasant (ONST 1927 p14). A court case of 1547 describes a quantity of land including two windmills at Norton Le Moors. One was at SJ 895518 (WBJ p32).

1600 to PRESENT. The PR records many **excommunications** by Rev Humphrey Repton (d1695), and by his son Rev John Repton (d1730) (NSFCT 1921 p26). The original **death warrant of Charles I** was kept here when in the hands of Rev Daniel Turner. It passed from the original owner, republican Judge Bradshaw, who appears third on the list of witnesses to the warrant, and who died in poverty at Greenwood Hall, to Ralph Stevenson of Cobridge and it eventually came to Rev Daniel Turner (SMC pp172,181) who had it in 1823. But some say Turner only had a copy of the original (ONST 1939 p78).

Coal mining - there are references to colliers in Norton from 1598 (ONST 1933 p41) - was the reason for the village's continued growth. However, at the beginning of the C20 Norton was still an entirely separate village from the adjoining villages of Ball Green and Norton Green with which it now (1958) merges (ONST 1958 p216). Norton had separate civil identity early. It became a separate ecclesiastical parish in 1779 (GLAUE p418) or in 1807 (W p400), refounded in 1849 (GLAUE p418). Norton was taken into Stoke-on-Trent county borough in 1922 (VCH vol 8 p260). With Bradeley formed a ward of Stoke-on-Trent district by 1991. The open-air camp meeting of the **Primitive Methodists** led by Hugh Bourne at Norton Aug 23-25 1807 was regarded by Bourne as marking the firm establishment of camp meetings in England (VCH vol 3 p128). It was due to this camp meeting that Hugh Bourne and his brother, James, were expelled from the Wesleyan Methodists (ONST 1933 p40. 1952 p166. 1956 p208). A German Howitzer gun captured in **WW1** was given to Norton and stood on a prominent site at Norton Recreation Ground until in c1938 when it was destroyed for scrap metal (ES Sept 14 1996 p21p. Aug 14 1999 p20p). Norton is reputed to have been the **'Gretna Green' of N Staffs** for allowing runaway marriages, ending with the Act of 1754 (SCSF p64) (ONST) (TOS p63). Fulford also had this reputation. The **Old Nortonian Society**, an historical society, was set up at a meeting in 1923 at Ye Old Cock Inn, and has transactions (ONST) from 1925 (POTP p216) (ES April 26 2000 p21). **Natural history**. In the later C17 Plot noted a foxglove that flowered an unusual colour by the wayside near Norton (NHS p203). Garner noted a curious stone under a yew in the village (GNHSS p20). The earthquake of 3.21pm July 3 1904 was felt at Norton-in-the-Moors (NSFCT 1905 p133). **Persons and visitors**. **Charles Bowyer Adderley** (1814-1904) of Hams Hall, Warws, was the son of a Bowyer of Knypersley; the Adderleys were holders of the freehold manor of Norton. He was MP for N Staffs in 1841, and inventor of the expression 'local government.' He entered the House of Lords in 1878 as 1st Lord Norton (ONST 1948 p138) (PPP p63) (NSFCT 1991 p47 notes. 1998-99 pp44-45). The 7th Lord Norton (b1915) died in Oct 1993 (ES Oct 22 1993 p9p). Dr **Thomas Wright**, born in Norton in the C19, was facially disfigured and was dubbed by the local community 'the ugliest man in the world.' He lived in a cottage in the High Street with a built-in date stone bearing the initials 'T.W.' (ONST 1966 p273) (ES April 16 1994 p23p). **Anthea Turner**, presenter of major television shows from the late 1980s, was born at Norton on May 25 1960. Her sister, Wendy, a journalist and television presenter, was born at Norton on June 5 1963 (ES Dec 30 1996 p4) (FWNS pp64-71ps).

Norton Manor House Stood a considerable distance NE of Norton Canes church at SK 015077. Shaw noted that traces of the moat were visible (SHOS vol 2 p57). By 1982 the moat had been levelled (SSAHST 1982-3 p38).

Norton Manor House Norton-in-the-Moors. Built in 1781 by William Lownes, the only known lord of Norton manor to have resided within the boundaries of Norton manor. The house was still standing in 1948 (ONST 1948 p138).

Norton Old Hall Norton Canes. It seems to have stood N of Watling Street, at SK 012076 (SSE 1994 p47). The family of Hanbury who bore arms in the C17 are placed on Plot's map at Norton. A stone, Wright noted, that faced Watling Street had on it the inscription 'Anno Dni 1682. Fr: Hanbury.' The ends of the iron spouting at the eaves had lion's heads at the corners. It suffered from subsidence and had to be demolished in the 1930s. As it was being demolished, sometime in the C18 and C19, coins were found (CCF pp181-184). Has also appeared as Norton Hall.

Norton Springs Branch of the Cannock Extension Canal. Very short canal taking the Cannock Extension Canal into Norton Canes. Closed in 1954 (HCMS No. 2).

Nose, The Rock feature on NE slopes of The Cloud in Staffs (SGM p266).

Nothill Brook Runs from Hollington joins Alders Brook at Combridge and it is not long before this brook joins the Dove.

Nothill Farm 1.5m SSE of Croxden, in Croxden parish. Has been identified with Lees Grange, a grange of Croxden Abbey (CDS p4). A farm at Nothill was in existence by 1722 (CDS p19).

Nottle End The Dunstall Road area of Barton-under-Needwood. The name is a corruption of Nuttall End, from Nuttall House (UNT p36).

Nth Cloud, The At SJ 998635. Twin-faced outcrop of rock lying below the Roaches escarpment and above the minor road, midway between the Five Clouds and Roach End (SGM pp114- 115 il).

Nun Brook Runs by Patshull to the Worfe, which is a tributary of the Severn.

Nun's Walk Two small enclosures adjoining the site of Blithfield Priory still bear the name of the Nuns Walk, and the hollow way from the high road to the nunnery is still called Nuns Lane (SHOS vol 1 p204).

Nun's Well Court Bank Covert, Cannock Wood. An ancient well lined with sandstone and capped with a brick arch erected in the C16 (SSAHST 1965 pp30-31). Thought to have healing properties for eye diseases (MR pp81-82). In the late C18 Shaw noted it seemed to possess no other quality than that of a pleasant softness (SHOS vol 2 p314). Although close to the site of Radmore Abbey, it is thought to have been used by nuns from Farewell Priory (CCBO p32). After the Reformation it was in general use. In the mid C18 it was sold into private hands. The owner built a brick structure round it and charges were made to those wishing to take the waters; this bought about its decline (SHOS vol 2 p314). The well was described as almost choked up in the late 1920s (NSFCT 1930 p143). In the 1930s Wright found the bricks round the well slightly displaced and the roots of a nearby ancient oak had a python-like grip of the surrounding rock (CCF p82). After WW2 the well was covered with corrugated iron sheets and has been buried under four feet of earth (MR pp81-82). (GNHSS p8) (CCC pp22,24,128).

Nurton Hamlet 1.5m SSE of Wrottesley Hall, 1.25m ENE of Pattingham. In Pattingham ancient parish. On West Beach Heath towards Patshull Park is a flat stone about a yard long and of oval form, having a cross moline cut upon it in basso relievo ten inches each way (SHOS vol 2 p206). Nurton existed by 1312 when it was written Noverton (DUIGNAN) (VCH vol 20 p173).

'Noverton' is a shortened expression from 'atten-overton' - upper town, which describes its geographical position (P p160) (SHOS vol 2 p206) (DUIGNAN).

Nurton Brook Runs from N of Nurton to join Black Brook which in turn joins Smestow Brook.

Nurton Hill Hill and minute hamlet 0.5m NW of Nurton. It may have had its origins in the place called The Hill, mentioned in 1392, which was a settlement by 1428. The name Nurton Hill was in use by the mid C18 (VCH vol 20 p173). At SO 835998 is a windmill which was built by 1811. It probably last ground corn in 1880 (WMAG May 1972 p7p). About 1917 it was converted to form part of an extensive house now called the Mill House (SLM spring 1954 p25) (WBJ p32 il xxvi) (WIS pp12p,21) (DoE II). Others say it was restored and added to in 1933 (WMAG May 1972 p7).

Nuttall House Dunstall Road, Barton-under-Needwood. Formerly Yewtree House when it was the seat of the Sanders family; seat of Joseph Sanders in 1691 (UNT pp7,117p). It was rebuilt in the gothic style and changed to Nuttall House (W p605), locally called 'Chimney Pot Hall.' By 1995 the house, a residential home, was known as 'The Towers' (UNT p120).

Oak, The Manor house at Oakfarm, Kingswinford, where Sir Stephen Glynne, Gladstone's brother-in-law, lived. It was reputedly haunted (TB May 1978 p11). Is probably same as Oak Farm Mill (see).

Oak, The West Bromwich (W p686). Former name of the Oak House? The Oake, seat of the Turtons, is marked on Plot's map. The surrounding area may also have been called The Oake or The Oak.

Oakamoor Village lining steep bluffs on both sides of the Churnet 16m NE of Stafford. Formerly partly in Farley township in Alton ancient parish (HAF p82), partly in Cheadle Grange quarter in Cheadle ancient parish and partly in Whiston township in Kingsley ancient parish (Staffs Gazetteer. Staffs Archive Service. 1994). The name has appeared as Okeymoore (1686) (NHS p358) and Oakway Moor (1694) (SHC 1947 p56). So called from being covered with dwarf oaks (THS p36) (PNPD). The church, Holy Trinity, on Church Bank on the W side of the Churnet, was built in 1832 (Holy Trinity Church, Oakamoor: Brief historical notes). Was formed into a separate ecclesiastical parish in 1833 (GLAUE p418), refounded 1864 (LGS p195). This was abolished in 1932 to help create Oakamoor with Cotton ecclesiastical parish (GLAUE p418). The rolling mills of Messrs Patten & Co at Oakamoor were taken over by Messrs Thomas Boulton and Sons of Birmingham. Under Boulton it produced locomotive boiler tubes, brazing materials, brazed copper tubes, the copper rollers used in the printing of calico, sheet brass and copper sheet (HOC p39) (PS p130), as well as the copper core for the experimental submarine cable laid between Dover and Calais in 1849 (NSFCT 1892 pp144-145) and for an attempt at a trans-Atlantic telegraph cable running between St John's, Newfoundland and Valencia, County Kerry, Ireland, in 1857; this failed, but a second attempt in 1858 with Boulton copper core proved successful for a short period, failing in Oct 1858. The Atlantic was permanently crossed with telegraph cable from 1866. Boulton's wire factory later moved to Froghall (HOC p39) (PS p130) (S p142) (KES pp161-162) (VB p172) (TFTPM pp37-45). The Boulton Memorial Chapel is a Free Chapel.

It was built in 1878 off Carr Bank on the E side of the Churnet (BOE p214) and in the main part of the village. Oakamoor station opened on the NSR's Churnet Valley railway line on June 13 1849 (COPP2 p86p of Oakamoor station). The line from Leekbrook to Oakamoor closed on Nov 7 1960 but a single track still remained open in 1983 for carrying sand from the British Industrial Sand Works at Moneystone. The line from Oakamoor to Uttoxeter closed to passengers on Nov 7 1960 and for goods on Jan 4 1965 (CVH pp128-129). It was recommended that Oakamoor station close in 1963 (ES March 22 1963). The civil parish of Oakamoor was created out of Cheadle, Cotton, Farley, and Kingsley parishes in 1896 (GLAUE p418). There were floods in the village in 1927 (COPP2 p85p). In the later C17 Dr Plot noted an inhabited conical house made of turf situated between Cheadle and Oakamoor (NHS p358). For Ann Harvey of Oakamoor, who is said to have lived to the age of 120, see under Ellastone. Many of the poems in the collection entitled 'Between the Churnet and the Dove - Poems of North Staffordshire' written by Samuel J Looker, between 1910 and 1950, allude to the area about Oakamoor (VFC p87).

Oakamoor Lodge Oakamoor. Built in 1761 by George Kendall, the manager of the Oakamoor mill. It was occupied in the early 1800s by the Wragge family. In c1875 it was bought by Thomas Bolton. From c1900 it was occupied by the Bearblocks. It was demolished soon after 1951 (COPP2 p84p).

Oak Cottage Foxt, Ipstones (FX p114).

Oakedge Hall Formerly situated in 'a solitary situation' (THS p313) near Weetman's Bridge on the S side of the Stafford-Rugeley road, E of Beggars Hill, at SK 008204 (OS map 1955). Has also appeared as Oak Edge. It appears that Oakedge passed with other estates of the bishop of Lichfield after the Dissolution to the Pagets and they sold it to the Whitbys of The Old Manor House, Little Haywood (SHC 1914 p133 note). It is not clear whether there was a house at Oakedge before 1750, but: White says William Anson (an ancestor of the Ansons of Shugborough) resided at Oakedge Hall in James

I's reign (W p416). Simms says the poet William Somerville (d1742) was born at Oakedge (BS p420); others say he was born at Wolseley Hall (see). The Whitbys appear to have had descendants who Dr Johnson of Lichfield (see) tutored in 1735. Johnson is said to have written the inscription for the memorial in Colwich church to a John Whitby (d1752/6 aged 34) his former pupil. The same or another John Whitby built a house called Whitby Wood for his bride, Ann ('The Widow of the Wood'), in 1750; the house was said to be newly built in 1768. John Whitby died aged 34 in 1752 and his wife Ann was left a widow, with two small children. Shortly after his death, and still in 1752, Ann courted John Robins, MP for Stafford, and duped Sir William Wolseley, 5th Bt, of nearby Wolseley Hall into marriage. The scandal of how she deceived Wolseley appears in a book titled 'Widow of the Wood' printed for C Corbett opposite St Dunstan's church, Fleet Street, 1755. The author's name does not appear in most editions. The BL has several editions (HOT p72) (OP pp23-24). After the deception was exposed the widow left the district, and died in 1782 (HOSCC p103). (SHOS vol 2 pl at back on p20 shows hall and Colwich church) (W p416) (N&Q 1874-9 vol 2 pp58,136) (HAH pp41,46) (CCBO pp168,169) (The Widow of the Wood. SAH Burne MA. 1964) (WMAG Sept 1965 pp20-22ps). After the departure of the 'Widow of the Wood' the house remained empty until it was bought by Thomas Anson in 1768 who changed the name to Oakedge. The hall, occupied only by a few estate servants in 1817 with the windows of its principle rooms boarded up (THS p313), was demolished in the latter half of the C19 (SNTG p56); the site is now untraceable.

Oakedge Park A deer park near the site of Oakedge Hall belonging to Lord Lichfield (EDP p179) (GCC p7p of as seen from Step Hill).

Oaken Small village on a hill bounded by Moat Brook (VCH vol 20 p79) 1m SW of the church at Codsall. Former township in Codsall ancient parish (W p173). Has appeared as Ache, a manor, in DB, Oce (C13), Oke (C13), Ake (1293) and Oken (C13). WH Stevenson thinks the name is from Anglo-Saxon acum (dative plural of ac), oaks (DUIGNAN). Or 'at the oaks' (SSE 1996 p16). Croxden Abbey held an estate at Oaken by the late C12. They had established a grange at Oaken by 1291. Between 1327 and 1538 it held the whole manor (VCH vol 20 p83). The grange was rebuilt near the road in 1370 (NSFCT 1951 pB34. 1952 pB62) (VCH vol 3 p226). By the early C16 the abbey was leasing the grange (VCH vol 20 p83). At the Stafford Assizes in 1293 the abbot of Croxden complained that the dean of Wolverhampton had disseised him of four acres of wood in Ake. The dean objected that there was no vill in Staffordshire called Ake, and he appealed to a jury. The jury found that the vill was called Oke, and not Ake, and the suit was therefore dismissed (DUIGNAN pp108-109). There was probably a Quaker burial ground at SJ 857027, now part of Oaken Manor (SSAHST 1970 p43) (VCH vol 20 p88). On the N side of the A41 Wolverhampton-Newport road at SJ 855022 is a wind and solar powered telephone box for it was too expensive to bring the power cable to the site. The phone ceased operating by wind and solar power sometime in the mid 1990s (local info).

Oakenclough Brook Rises on the E side of Morridge and runs near Oakenclough Hall to Hardings Booth; it joins the Manifold at Longnor (VCH vol 1 p1). The name means 'the ravine where oaks trees grow;' the stream runs through a deep ravine where oak trees abound (SPNO p15).

Oakenclough Hall House 1.75m SSW of Hollinsclough in Heathylee township in Alstonefield ancient parish. There was a house near the present hall by the early C15. In the C17 it was replaced by a stone house. This was styled Oakenclough Hall in 1747. In the later 1890s it was replaced by the present hall built on an adjacent site (VCH vol 7 p33). (DUIGNAN p42 mentions Oaken Clough).

Oakenfield A road N of Lichfield Cathedral on the boundary route of the Sheriff's ride.

Oaken House Codsall. Arthur Mee saw some elms here with girths of 22 and 24 feet (KES p70).

Oaken Lanes The area E of Oaken hamlet was inhabited by the earlier C17 when it was known as Oaken Lanes (VCH vol 20 p79).

Oaken Lawn Former area of waste W of Strawmoor Farm, 1.25m SW of Codsall. The area was being encroached upon by the later C17 (VCH vol 20 p80).

Oaken Manor House at the top of Oaken Lane, Oaken, Codsall. The present house dates from the earlier C19 but stands on the site of a former house which may date from the C17. There is a stone dated 1677 set into a barn in the grounds (VCH vol 20 p79).

Oaken Park Croxden Abbey had a park in its manor of Oaken, Codsall, by 1329. It was situated at the W end of Oaken Lane in the area of Oaken Park Farm, and was still known as Oaken Park in the C17. Oaken Park Farm, 1.75m WSW of Codsall, existed in the later C18. The present house dates from the early C19 (VCH vol 3 p227. vol 20 pp80,85).

Oake's Well A well at Wednesbury, probably a variant spelling of Oakes Well (see). Or it could be the public one that was close to the entrance gates of 'The Hollies' in c1854 (WP p95).

Oakes Well A well still present in the garden of Oakeswell Hall in 1962 (HOWY p227) and gives its name to Oakeswell Hall. The well was described in March 1969 as soon to disappear (E&S March 6 1969; E&S have a photo of the well).

Oakeswell End Small district of Wednesbury (WAM p53), formerly called Dymmock's End (HOWV p108), and Dimock's Green (WAM p100). S of Walsall Street and N of the railway. Appears as Oakswell End on OS map 1:25,000, but does not appear as a district on Birmingham A-Z. Ann Griffiths, a servant for John Crowther, was beaten to death by William Beard at Oakeswell End on the morning of March 16 1844 (TB Oct 1984 p5).

Oakeswell Hall Stood SE of Wednesbury parish church, on the S side of Walsall Street. In Wednesbury ancient parish. Oakeswell Hall was Wednesbury's second manor house and may have come into being after the death of John de Heronville, lord of Wednesbury manor, in 1315 and the division of the manor between his widow, Juliana, and his son Henry. A house is recorded on the site in 1421. The hall was known as New Hall Place in the C15. In 1591 a court case between William Comberford and Thomas Jennyns disputed the ownership of the house. Thomas stated that the property had been given as a wedding present from his father, William Jennyns, in 1577. The name 'Oakeswell' appeared in the papers of an attorney, William Booth, in 1662 (HOWV p108) (BCM spring 1993 p68). 'Oakes-well' is taken from the ancient water source which still (1993) exists on the site, although now dry (BCM spring 1993 p68). In the C17 the hall was the seat of the Hopkins family (SHOS vol 2 p84 pl xiii); William Hopkins, who fought for Charles I in the Civil War, was captured at Rushall Hall in 1644 (WAM pp53,80) (HOWV p79) (BCM spring 1993 p68). Oakeswell Hall passed from the Hopkins to Richard Parkes, ironmaster and Quaker, sometime between 1689 and 1707, and he was living here from 1708 (HOWV p79) (WP pp95,99). By 1774 the Oakeswell estate was being farmed by the Kendrick family who, in turn, sold it to another farmer, John Hawe (BCM spring 1993 p68). The Hawe family were Quakers (SHOS vol 2 p84). On the death of John Hawe's son, Thomas, in 1825 the hall was purchased by John Beaumont (Aris's Birmingham Gazette March 21 1825). By 1884 the hall had been renamed 'The Rookery' and was the home of Joseph Smith, Clerk to the Local Board, who advocated that it be used at some later date as a museum (WP). The hall was then leased by a succession of doctors, the most notable being Dr Walter Chancellor Garman, who was living here in the late C19. His daughter, Kathleen Esther (1901-1979), was romantically involved with the sculptor, Sir Jacob Epstein (1880-1959) from 1921 and became his second wife in 1955. As part of the Garman-Ryan Collection some of Epstein's work was given to Walsall Museum and Art Gallery in 1973. Some of Dr Garman's grandchildren and other children also achieved notoriety; a daughter, Mary, married the South African poet Roy Campbell and had an affair with the writer Vita Sackville-West, whilst a son, Douglas, was romantically involved with Peggy Guggenheim; Kathleen's daughter by Epstein, Kitty, married the painter Lucian Freud, whilst another granddaughter of Dr Garman married the writer Laurie Lee (The Sunday Telegraph Dec 19 1999 Review p7). The hall was purchased by Wednesbury borough council in 1960 and sold to Staffs county council in 1961 who demolished it in 1962. The site passed to West Midlands county council and lay empty for more than 20 years (DNB 1951-1960) (BCM April 1993 p of on cover, pp8,39-43) (TB March 1980 p14p) (WDOP p118p of in 1897) (TWDOP p106p rear view in 1953). The site of the hall was excavated in 1983 (SSAHST 1985-86 pp64-77. 1990-91 p96).

Oakfarm Area over 0.5m N of Kingswinford.

Oak Farm Mill A former name for the Glynne Arms (see). No, says MR p162p, this was the manor house, where the Glynne family resided; now demolished. If so, is probably the same as The Oak (see).

Oakfields House 0.5m SSW of Blithfield. In Blithfield parish.

Oakham Hamlet in the C19 now a suburb of Dudley 1.25m NNW of Rowley Regis. In Rowley Regis parish. Has always been in Staffs never in Worcs (SHOS vol 2 p240) (SVS p433). Has also appeared as Oakum (W p194). It can be surmised that Oakham was an early settlement on account of its etymology. The name means 'the dwelling in the oaks' (BCWJ p86). Col Barker or Baker, the manager of a colliery at Oakham in the 1920s, was according to tradition a woman, one Lillias Lima Valerie Barber (b1895) who posed as her husband on his death, or reconstructed herself as Col Sir Leslie Victor Gauntlet Bligh Barker DSO, Bart. In this guise she obtained amongst many short term positions the post of groom to a baronet who lived in Hall Street, Dudley. Others say she had no association with the colliery at Oakham. Her identity was exposed on several occasions; she married two women at different times, and went to prison for deception and indecency. She died reputedly in Suffolk in 1960. Her last identity was as a Geoffrey Norton (News of the World) (TB Feb 1994 p5. March 1994 p13. April 1994 p17).

Oakham Hill Hill to NE of Netherton near Darby Hill?

Oak Hill Hill and house? 0.5m NW of Handsworth, marked on OS map 1834. Handsworth Wood School stands on the approximate site of it.

Oak Hill A hill at Penkhull (NSFCT 1891 p54).

Oak Hill Small district between Trent Vale and Boothen 0.75m S of Penkhull, centred on London Road and Trent Valley Road and Oak Hill Hall and Stoke Lodge. The name 'Ochul' occurs in the C13 as one of open fields of Longton (VCH vol 8 p176 note) and has occurred as Oakhill. In Stoke-upon-Trent chapelry in Stoke-upon-Trent ancient parish.

Oak Hill Trysull. Has also appeared as Watt-hill (SHOS vol 2 p207).

Oakhill Hall N of Madeley, S of the Betley road. Appears on the maps of Yates (as Oakehall Hill), Greenwood, and Teesdale.

Oak Hill Hall Newcastle Road, Penkhull. Early C19 house (VCH vol 8 pp176,183).

Oakhill House Upper Tean. Parts of the house were built in 1689. In the early C19 it was occupied by Rev CB Charlewood. It was later the seat of the Philips family (COPP2 p70p), and was for sale in July 1998 (SN July 16 1998 p45p).

Oak House Ancient timber-framed house in Oak Road, Lambert's End, 0.75m W of High Street, West Bromwich (WBOPP pl 14). In West Bromwich ancient parish. Dates from the early C16 (SHWB 7) or mid C16 with brick additions of the 1630s (NSFCT 1959 p102) or the later C16 (WB p156) (VCH vol 17 p9 il facing p16). Seat of the Turton family in the C17. Capt John Turton was a parliamentarian in the Civil War (WAM pp66il,80) (SHWB 16). The last Turton to live here was John Turton (d1768). The house then passed to his natural son William Whyley and remained in the Whyley family until 1837. It then had several occupants (SHWB 7). The house was known as the Oak House by 1725 (VCH vol 17 p25), but seems to have been known as The Oaks in the mid C19 (1834 OS map) (Dower's map). It derived its name from a particularly fine English oak which stood on the green in front of the house which was destroyed by fire in 1846 (BCM Oct 1977 pp42,44) (SHWB 7). John Wesley preached in the courtyard here in 1774 (SHWB 16) (VCH vol 17 p64). It was purchased in 1895 by Reuben Farley, then mayor (LGS p250) and restored and opened as a museum in 1898 (WBOP p62) (SHWB 7). The museum re-opened in 1951 having been refurnished with period furnishings (VCH vol 17 p25 plan). (SHOS vol 2 p134) (SOSH p329) (S p88p) (AWM p38) (HS pp325il,326il) (KES p225) (BOE pp301-302) (SL p176) (MR p364). A rare formal garden of limited dimensions, possibly dating from the C17, was excavated in the vicinity of the house in 1991 (WMARCH 1994 p111).

Oaklands, The House off Church Lane, Handsworth Wood. Built by John Russell, ironmaster, in 1841. It was last occupied as a private residence by Walter Scott, managing director of Ansells Brewery Ltd. He lived here in the 1930s to the 1950s. Later bought by the Swedenborgian Church who turned it into a church? (HPPE p90).

Oaklands, The Large house in Regis Road, Tettenhall. It later became the offices for Tettenhall urban district council, and now (1997) includes the library (TPOP p30p).

Oakley Tiny hamlet 1.5m ESE of Bishop's Wood, in Brewood ancient parish.

Oakley Ancient estate and manor by the Mease, now (1902) a farm (DUIGNAN) - Oakley Farm is 1.5m NNE of Elford. Formerly in Croxall parish, Derbys, but this part of Croxall has always been in Staffs. Oakley was identified by Dugdale, Shaw and Duignan with the Acclea bequeathed in the will of Wulfric Spot (c1002) ultimately to Burton Abbey (SHOS vol 1 p380) (SHC 1916 p27); later appears as Acle, a manor, in DB, and Acley (SHOS vol 1 p387). The name means 'oak pasture' (SSE 1996 p16). There was possibly a medieval village at Oakley Farm, probably deserted between 1334 and 1539 (SSAHST 1970 p35). The Birmingham & Derby railway line which opened on Aug 5 1839 had a station at Oakley (IAS p131).

Oakley Tiny hamlet to S of Oakley Hall and former township in Mucklestone ancient parish (W p399). BB Simms thinks Oakley Park drive follows probably the line of a Roman-British road. Appears in DB as Aclei (NSFCT 1938 p112). The name is from Anglo-Saxon ac = oak, and lea = pasture, so the 'oak pasture' (DUIGNAN). There was possibly a lost village at Oakley Hall, probably deserted sometime between 1334-1524 (SSAHST 1970 p35).

Oakley House to the S of Springfields, Raleigh Lane, West Bromwich. Owned in 1836 by Timothy Kenrick, son of the elder Archibald Kenrick. Demolished in c1960 (VCH vol 17 p10).

Oakley Folly A brick folly, built to look like a church as an eye-catcher for Oakley Hall (see). Situated at SJ 714364, N edge of The Folly wood. The

tower was built by Col D'Avenant, first cousin to Charles Boothby Skrymsher, and sometime of Broomhall Grange. Prior to 1774 he leased much, if not all, of his cousin's unenclosed land at Blore Heath, for, it is said, a training ground for race horses. He built the tower to view the horses from. After his death in 1798 his land and the folly were sold to Sir John Chetwode and then formed a part of Oakley Hall estate (SHC 1945/ 6 pp208-209); Sir Philip Chetwode of Oakley Hall is said to have viewed his horses from it (SLM June July 1987 p15). It was going to be converted into domestic accommodation, but was struck by lightning - DoE II. (MR p237) (F p306) (BOE p207) (JC 40 il).

Oakley Hall Hall by the Tern 1.5m WSW of Mucklestone. Ancient seat of the de Oakley family until the end of the C14 when the Oakley heiress married a Chetwode (SHC 1945/ 6 p174). It was then the seat of the Chetwodes until WW1 when General Sir Philip Chetwode, Bart, sold the estate (NSFCT 1982 p44) (ES Sept 3 1982). John Chetwode, who was created a baronet in 1700, built the present hall in the Queen Anne style in 1710 (SHC 1945/ 6 p211); the building has a datestone with the date 1710 (BOE pp214il-215). Lord Chetwode, 7th baronet, became a Field Marshall. Sometime shortly before 1982 the estate was bought by an American (ES Sept 3 1982). Some workers on the Oakley Hall estate lived at Norton Forge (see). 150 metres N of the N front of the hall is a grotto. It is probably of early to mid C18 origin and was cut out of natural sandstone. It has ashlar facings (DoE II). To the W is a well preserved ice house; the entrance is round-arched with rubblestone voussoirs under coped with stone gable; a short tunnel leads to an egg-shaped cavity, the store is lined with a brick dome - DoE (BOE p215).

Oakley Park Medieval deer park. 2m NE of Market Drayton. In existence by 1322. Belonged to John Hamelyn (NSJFS 1964 p64).

Oakley Park The park of Oakley Park, Mucklestone. Lies to N of the hall. For the prehistoric dug-out canoe found in the river Tern in Oakley Park see under Tern. SW of the hall at cSJ 695365 is a possible burial mound (NSFCT vol 73 p114) (NSJFS 1965 p44).

Oaks, The Former wood and thicket along the boundary of Anslow and Branston townships. In existence by 1300. Part of it was common (ANS p23).

Oaks, The S side of Merridale Road, Wolverhampton. Built in the C18 by Thomas Gibbons of the Wolverhampton 'Old Bank.' Before being bought by John Corser in 1816 it contained paintings of Sir Joshua Reynolds, Gainsborough and others. Bought by Mr and Mrs Charles Corser after their marriage in 1893 (WMAG Aug 1963 p16p). The house was sometime occupied by John Marston, Mayor of Wolverhampton 1888/9 and pioneer of the Sunbeam cycle (WMAG Feb 1964 p47p).

Oakwood House on the E side of Old Meeting Street, Carter's Green, West Bromwich. Built by Thomas Jesson on a site called Oakley's Croft, which he had purchased in 1679. It was for many years the seat of the Jessons, and Rev Thomas Jesson presented it to the borough in 1912. In 1955 the corporation demolished the house, and the grounds were turned into Oakwood Park (VCH vol 17 p26). A new house was then built on the site (WBOPP pl 79) (WBOP p122p) (SHWB 8) (HPPE pp89,90).

Oates' Oak Oak formerly situated at the corner of the old bowling green in front of Tixall Old Hall (see) (NSFCT 1916 p138). Behind this tree in 1678, Stephen Dugdale, a steward of Lord Aston, claimed he concealed himself to overhear his master plotting with Lord Stafford to murder Charles II and install Charles' brother, James, a Catholic, on the throne. Dugdale's evidence, which was most spurious, had Lord Aston imprisoned and Lord Stafford executed. The NSFC visited Tixall and saw the tree in April 1880. The tree has also been called Stafford Oak (NSFCT 1881 p14). Someone maliciously set fire to the hollow trunk and completely destroyed it in 1880 (LGS p236); it stood until 1881 (SLM Feb 1951 p19).

Oat Hill N end of Cannock Chase. 0.75m SSE of Milford. Is some 575 feet high (OSST 1954-56 p17). Twenty two Scots Pine, probably that planted by Thomas Anson to commemorate his brother's World circumnavigation in 'Centurion' 1740-44 (CCM), or that planted in 1780 to add variety to the open heath country - which was within view of Shugborough (WMLB p77) - were still growing on the hill in the 1950s (OSST 1954-56 p18). Is probably the Oak Hill mentioned in STMSM Nov 1972 p41.

Occamsley Pitts Brownhills (NHS p399).

Ocker Hill Former small hamlet called Hocker Hill (early C19 - mid C19) (HOTIP p191), later a village (W p708), and ward of Tipton borough. Now a district in the Black Country conurbation over 1m NE of Tipton, on a slight prominence above low ground. In Tipton ancient parish. The root of the name may be Welsh 'ochr,' 'ochren,' a side, a shelving locality. Ocker, is a somewhat common name, always in relation to a hill or hill-side (DUIGNAN) (NSFCT 1908 p136) (OH p9). Perhaps, from the family of O'Kell or later Ockull, who may have lived in a house on site of Cotterills Farm (TB Jan 1977 p5). From the later C18 Ocker Hill was bounded by many canals - the

Walsall Canal, Birmingham Old Cut Old Main Line, Ocker Hill, Lower Ocker Hill and Toll End Branches - so it justly deserves its description as the 'Venice of the Midlands' (OH p10) (BCM Oct 1974 p8); also Tipton parish has also been described as such. The Boulton and Watt engine (1779) on the Birmingham Canal Old Cut Old Main Line at Smethwick was removed in 1898 to the Birmingham Canal Navigation Company's depot at Ocker Hill in 1898. Here it was seen by Henry Ford, who offered to purchase it and transport it to the United States. But the canal company refused to sell. When the Ocker Hill depot was closed in 1959 the engine was presented to Birmingham Museum of Science and Industry for display. By 1989 it was the oldest working steam engine in the world (OH pp63-65) (SMEOP p6p). Ocker Hill was linked to the railway system from Sept 14 1863 when the SSR constructed a branch line from Wednesbury to Ocker Hill and Princes End to join the London and North Western line for Wolverhampton. The Ocker Hill line was closed for passenger traffic in c1890 and the station had been dismantled by 1946 (SSR p25) (OH p65). The separate ecclesiastical parish of Ocker Hill, created in 1845, was known as Tipton St Mark by 1991 (GLAUE p418). The church, St Mark, in St Mark's Road, was built in 1849 (BOE p304). The site of Ocker Hill power station was established by the Midland Electricity Corporation for Power Distribution and was described at the time as 'the largest electric power installation in England.' The cooling towers were taken down on Aug 18 1985. The Spine Road (opened in 1995), or later known as the Black Country New Road, built by the Black Country Development Corporation, now sweeps through the space between the old and the new sites (TSSOP p72) (TWDOP p21p) (BCM Autumn 1999 p24). By 1998 the Midland Electricity Board had its headquarters in Toll End Road by when it was having installed into its offices the first Design Engineering Geographic Information System in Europe (info Julian Shaw). Rev Hildric Friend, Wesleyan minister of Ocker Hill, published a 352-page work entitled 'Flowers and Flower Lore' in 1883 (BCM July 1975 p45). Hackwood writing in 1924 says that within living memory a caul was sold at Ocker Hill for a 'goodly number' of guineas. A caul being a membrane which was believed to have special properties which prevented one from drowning (SCSF p57).

Ocker Hill Branch of the Birmingham Canal. Spurred off the Birmingham Canal Old Cut Old Main Line at Summer Hill near Moat Road. Built in 1774. A short branch of the Walsall Canal provided a partial link with the Ocker Hill Branch. This small branch is still (1995) detectable near a bowling green and park at Toll End close to the Tame Valley Junction. Ocker Hill Branch Canal would have passed from the Moat Junction along a line between Highfield Road and St Mark's Road. Its whole length closed in 1948 and was built over by 1995 (BCM autumn 1995 p18. summer 1999 p67).

Oddo Hall House to W of Ipstones church. Odda Hall was occupied by James Butteras, farmer, in 1863; Oddo Hall was occupied by John Harrison, farmer, between at least 1876 and 1892. Arthur Johnson was living at Odda Farm in 1900 (trade directories) (MR pp195,196p).

Oddfellows Hall Graisbrook Hall, Shenstone, used to stand behind this house. Built as a reading room - the first in the area - during the Crimean War. The house is now (1993) a hairdressing salon at ground level and a flat above (St John the Baptist, Shenstone. Dick & Audrey Davies. 1993. pp11,12il).

Offandyke Field name near Strongford. The name, which could be interpreted as Offa's valley, perhaps reflects the fact that Mercian kings held Trentham (Annals of the Diocese of Lichfield Past and Present 1859) (SHC 1909 p74 note) (HOTC pp18-19). Has also appeared as Offandyne.

Offa's Wood Rowley Regis. On Haden estate (BCWJ p15).

Offleybrook Tiny hamlet 2.5m N of High Offley. Partly in Adbaston and Eccleshall parishes. Has also appeared as Offley Brook. Offa was a common Anglo-Saxon personal name (DUIGNAN). Offleybrook formerly lay by Greatwood Heath (SSE vol 7 1995 p75). On the road between Walk Mill and Offleybrook on Jan 8 1866 John Poole, a railway labourer from Croxton, was murdered for money by George Bentley, aged 27, with a blow to the head by a stone in a handkerchief. The two had previously been drinking together in the Four Crosses Inn, Offleybrook. Bentley was caught because he took his victim's boots, and was arrested at the Royal Oak Inn, Eccleshall (SA Jan 13 1866) (BPS p155; called Charles Bentley) (ROT pp19-21).

Offley Grove House 1.5m WNW of High Offley, 0.5m S of Adbaston. Formerly Hill Hall (see) and before that Hill House (see). The name was changed from Hill Hall to Offley Grove in c1860 by Valentine Vickers, who purchased the house in 1858 and moved here in 1860. Vicker's widow continued to live here for some time after her husband's death in 1867, after which it was left empty. In WW2 troops were billeted here. Soon after 1956 the house was demolished (NSFCT 1927 p36) (AADB pp60,61). On the Offley Grove estate by the Lonco Brook was found a Romano-British skeleton also a bronze spear head, an iron implement and a bridle-and-bit (STM June 1966 p34).

Offley Hay Fragmented small hamlet on undulating ground above the upper reaches of the Sow, 2m NNE of High Offley. In Eccleshall ancient parish. The common land known as Offley Hay abutted Greatwood Heath to the N and may have been considered a part of that heath (SSE vol 7 1995 p75). There was horse racing at Offley Hay between at least 1705 to 1734 (VCH vol 2 p364). Offley Hay was not enclosed until 1841 (W p376). There is a mission station, at Offley Hay, which also has, or does, serve as a school (LDD). In the later C17 Dr Plot noted a localised typhoon or tornado about 40 yards wide which swept from Offley Hay to Slindon and destroyed many great oaks at Sir John Pershall's house at Sugnall (NHS p27 tab 1, fig 10). In Offley Hay there is a sycamore tree which is said to have grown from the stake that was driven through the body of a giant in an attempt to keep him down (FOS p42) (MR p250).

Offley Marsh Tiny hamlet on marshy ground in undulating country above the upper reaches of the Sow, 2m N of High Offley. In Adbaston ancient parish.

Offley Marsh Common A small nature reserve (SVB p11).

Offley Moss Former stretch of wetland and pools. The famous pewits of NW Staffs came here after leaving Moss Pool in 1665 at John Skrymsher's death. The pewits left for Shebdon Pool in 1668 (NHS p231). The pewits were able to discern between that part of the pool and moss belonging to the Skrymshers not that belonging to another estate since the pool and moss lay over land belonging to two estates. It was probably the western (larger) of the two pools which the pewits occupied; that belonging to the Skrymshers (WSS p109). The two pools are shown on Yates' map as standing on Knightley Common, with the eastern pool lying wholly in Gnosall ancient parish, and the western pool lying partly in Gnosall and High Offley parishes. Knightley Common, including the eastern pool and part of the western pool, was enclosed by an Act of 1806. The common (Woodseaves Common) about the western pool, that lay in High Offley parish, was enclosed in c1822. On the enclosure plan the eastern pool is shown as Roan Pool, on another enclosure plan the west pool is identified with the words 'Land Late the Pewits Pool' (WSS p110). In 1927 the moss was represented by a patch of peaty soil on the northern outskirts of Woodseaves village (NSFCT 1927 p38 see maps). See also Pewit Pool.

Offley Rock Minute hamlet nearly 2.25m N of High Offley. In Eccleshall ancient parish. Here is a deep cutting in the red sandstone through which the road passes on a steep gradient (NSFCT 1910 p199).

Offley Well Head A large monumental well head 0.25m S of the church at Madeley, at SJ 772439. The well head is 33 feet high built of Caen stone erected by Hon Miss Crewe in memory of her aunt Hon Lady Offley in the mid C19 (W p395) (BOE p200). Madeley railway station stood by Offley Well Head.

Offlow Name for the consolidated manors of Cowley and Nethertown in Hamstall Ridware parish (SHOS vol 1 p152).

Offlow A burial mound near Whitehouse Farm at SK 123059 1.75m NW of Weeford, which was 40 feet in diameter. Believed by some to be the burial place of an important person in Roman times owing to its proximity to Watling Street and was later called Offlow (NSFCT 1933 pp154-155). Others have thought King Offa (d796) was buried here (SOSH p58) (CCC p12). According to Matthew of Paris he was buried by the Ouse in Beds, so it could not be to him. Or, perhaps, it is to another Mercian king called Offa, of the pagan period, prior to 654 (In Search of the Dark Ages. Michael Wood. 1987 p102), or to a commander called Offa, or to a member of the Mercian royal family (VCH vol 14 p5). The mound may have become a pagan shrine from which Weeford took its name (VCH vol 14 p5). The mound had been much reduced by 1902, but was still visible (DUIGNAN p110). It was described as almost ploughed away by 1909 (MOS p7), and described as almost ploughed away in 1933 (NSFCT 1933 pp154-155) (SD p24) (SHOS vol 1 pp22-23, vol 2 p30) (SSC p129 in the intro) (HOL p561) (W p609) (VCH barrow list) (NSJFS 1965 p48) (WMMA p144). The mound was important enough to give its name to the hundred of Offlow (GNHS p74) (ESH pp45-50) (VCH vol 14 p5). Has also appeared as Off Low. See also Dugdale's 'Warwickshire' in Knightlow hundred.

Offlow Former administrative division (hundred) of Staffs, covering the SE area of the county. Appears in DB as Offelav. The name is from the burial mound Offlow (see), where the hundred court may have met in late Anglo-Saxon times. Hackwood thought that the hundred court could have been held at Sedgley (WAM p9); however that place was in Seisdon hundred. With the passing of Cannock Forest into royal hands after the Norman Conquest some of Offlow hundred is said to have been transferred to Cuttlestone (GWY p13). Lichfield, although situated in Offlow South Division, was a county for a period between the mid C16 and the later C19, and therefore in no hundred (W p482). Parishes, townships and extra-parochial liberties in the **North Di-**

vision were: Alrewas, Alrewas Hayes (extra-parochial), Anslow, Barton-under-Needwood, Branston, King's Bromley, Burton Extra (Burton), Burton upon Trent, Clifton Campville, Croxall, Curborough and Elmhurst, Draycott-in-the-Clay, Dunstall, Edingale, Fisherwick, Foston and Scropton (the Derbys part of), Fradley, Freeford (extra-parochial), Hamstall Ridware, Hanbury, Harlaston, Haselour (extra-parochial), Marchington, Marchington Woodlands, Mavesyn Ridware, Newborough, Pipe Ridware, Rolleston, Statfold, Streethay, Stretton, Syercote, Tamhorn (extra-parochial), Tatenhill, Thorpe Constantine, Tutbury, Whittington, Wychnor, Yoxall (W pp528-529) (S&W p91). In the **South Division** were: Aldridge, Armitage, Bentley, Burntwood, Canwell (extra-parochial), Chorley, Darlaston, Drayton Bassett, Dudley Castle, Elford, Farewell, Fazeley, Great Barr, Hammerwich, Handsacre (Armitage), Handsworth with Soho, Harborne, Hints, Hopwas, Hopwas Hayes (extra-parochial), Longdon, Norton Canes, Ogley Hay (extra-parochial), Pelsall (formerly in Wolverhampton parish), Pipe Hill (township), Rushall, Shenstone, Smethwick, Swinfen, Statfold (extra-parochial), Tamworth, Tipton, Wall, Walsall, Wednesbury, Wednesfield (formerly in Wolverhampton parish), Weeford, West Bromwich, Wigginton, Willenhall (formerly in Wolverhampton parish) (W pp529, 580-581) (S&W p132).

Ogley Hay Former estate which became a hay, or division of Cannock Forest (DUIGNAN). 2.5m NNW of Aldridge. The northern boundary was formed by a two-mile stretch of Watling Street from Knaves Castle in the W to Wall Butts in the E. A charter was made of its bounds (SL p62), when the estate was given by Lady Wulfrun to the monastery of Wolverhampton in 994 (HOWM p14), when Ogley Hay appears as Ocgintun (SHC 1916 p169). The name means 'Ocga's town' (DUIGNAN). In 1086 according to DB, where it appears as Hocintune, the estate belonged to the canons of Wolverhampton (SHC 1916 p169. 1919 p157) (DB. Phillimore. 1976), and as such it formed a part of Wolverhampton (see) Deanery manor (HOWM p26). Shaw identified DB Hocintune with Essington (ESSN p8). By 1291 the estate had passed to the Crown and was a hay of Cannock Forest (VCH vol 2 p338). Prior to 1837 the estate belonged to Phineas Fowke Hussey and was an extra parochial liberty. It was enclosed in 1835 and 807 acres of it were enclosed under an Act of 1838 (SHC 1941 p18) (APB p6) (BHT) (PCC p16). Others say Ogley Hay was enclosed in 1839 (MH 1994 p108). In 1837 the estate was purchased by Charles Foster Cotterill who over the next ten years set about developing the estate with industry and housing for new collieries, and in doing so had some of the streets of the future town of Brownhills built (MH 1994 p121). A scattered settlement to the E of Brownhills known as Ogley Hay appears to have also grown in the C19. So that, at the beginning of the C20, it could be said Brownhills and Ogley Hay were two coal towns (LGS p195). A separate ecclesiastical parish called Ogley Hay, created in 1852 (GLAUE p418), refounded in 1854 (LGS p195), was later known as 'Ogley Hay with Brownhills.' The extra parochial liberty became a separate civil parish of Ogley Hay in 1858. Civilly it partly entered Brownhills urban district when it was formed in 1894, and wholly in 1896 (GLAUE p418).

Ogley Junction Junction of the Wyrley and Essington Extension Canal with its Anglesey Branch (HCMS No. 2), to the S of Lichfield Road and E of Sadler Road, S of Watling Street, Brownhills.

Og's Barn Near Beresford Hall. Not marked on OS maps. An old stone barn with very thick walls. The name is of Celtic origin (MR p130p).

Oils Heath House under 0.5m W of Warslow, in Warslow township, in Alstonefield ancient parish. There was a cottage here by 1665 (VCH vol 7 p57).

Okeover Parish and tiny estate hamlet at the mouth of a gulley by the Dove 21.5m NE of Stafford. Formerly probably in Ilam ancient parish but perhaps in Blore ancient parish. Okeover was identified by Dugdale and Shaw as the Acofre mentioned in the will of Wulfric Spot (c1002), founder of Burton Abbey (SHC 1916 p35). Has appeared as Acoure (DB) and Oakover (AAD p207). Oke is from Anglo-Saxon 'ac' oak, 'over' is from Anglo-Saxon ofer, ofre, bank, margin, border, hence the oak bank (or border or slope) (DUIGNAN) (SPN p89) (SSE 1996 p16). Oakden and Gelling agree with Duignan (SSAHST 1967 p34) (NSJFS 1981 p3). At the time of DB the manor was held by Burton Abbey. Some time between 1094 and 1113 it was granted to Orm, a tenant of Tutbury Priory. His descendants adopted the name Okeover and the manor remained with them until the death of Haughton Ealdred Okeover in 1955 (SHC 1904 pp3-147) (The Times Jan 25 1955) (English Genealogy. AR Wagner. 1960 p50) (SL pp66-67) (SGS p132); and thus the manor is noted for having been held in the male line of this family for approximately 800 years. At Okeover (SK 158482) was a village in medieval times depopulated by the C16 (SSAHST 1966 p49. 1970 p35) (SL p83). The villagers may have settled in nearby Mapleton, Derbys (SASR 1995 no 5 p43). The church, All Saints, 30 yards from Okeover Hall, was built in the

late C13 or earlier C14 (BOE p216). In the later C17 the church was exempt from all ordinary jurisdiction (as are all Royal chapels) and as such was regulated by the founder and not by the Ordinary (NHS p297). In 1856-1858 the church was restored by Sir Gilbert Scott (BOE p216); the work was carried out by William Evans of Ellastone, a relation of the novelist George Eliot (LTD p50). The Young Pretender's army passed through Okeover on Dec 4 1745 in the Jacobite Rebellion. When in retreat from Derby on Dec 6 1745 the army robbed the hall and the church (BPCSM pp7,8). Okeover had civil identity early and was ecclesiastically independent as donative. Its separate ecclesiastical identity was abolished in 1946 to help create Ilam with Blore Ray and Okeover ecclesiastical parish (GLAUE p418).

Okeover Hall Seat of the Okeovers. The hall Dr Plot visited in the later C17 was Elizabethan or Jacobean. It was surrounded by a moat, which was probably not the moat that still exists in the S of the grounds (NSFCT 1982 p12). Leak Okeover inherited the estate in 1729. His curious first name comes from his mother who was heiress of William Leak of Norfolk (NSFCT 1976 p21). The Highlanders of the 1745 Jacobite Rebellion, retreating from Derby, are reputed to have looted what little there was at the hall. A letter dated Dec 9 1745 from the family chaplain to Leak Okeover complains of Scots stragglers (LGS pp195,196) (NSFCT 1948 p29). In 1745 Leak Okeover formed an ambitious scheme to rebuild the house by adding E and W wings running back from the old house, which became the S front. This was partly carried out. But in 1751 having run into debt he went to Boulogne, where he lived miserably under the pseudonym of Mr Scrimshaw. His major love was Okeover, and he wrote 'I cannot nor ever will be brought to part with Okeover. I will much sooner never see England again than do it.' His debts paid off, he returned in 1753 and carried on building. He had planned to rebuild the S front but died in 1765. A SE corner block was built in his lifetime (NSFCT 1976 p22). In the C19 the then owner demolished a larger part of the property, leaving only the E range and the SE corner and remnants of the W range. A drawing by Buckler shows the result (NSFCT 1976 p22). The next owner found the house too small, and built an Italian style block which became a new W range. (SHC 1904 p of in 1903 facing p3). Finally, the present (1976) owner on taking over in 1955 returned to Leak's original plan of a symmetrical half H, with the old E range restored to match the W range and a new S range (NSFCT 1976 p22). These were completed by 1960 (BOE p215) (SL p132). The hall has or had paintings by Raphael, Titian, Vandervelde, and Rubens (GNHS p98) (LGS p196). Ruben's (SMC p172) or and Raphael's painting of the Holy Family, valued at between 1,000-2,000 guineas in the early C19, is said to have been discovered in an old lumber room, where it is conjectured to have been hidden during the Civil War (AAD pp198-199 il of the hall facing p199) (SSC p137 in the intro). A magnificent china set made in China for Leak Okeover was sold in the 1970s (LTD p50). (CL Jan 23 1964 pp172-176. Jan 30 1964 pp224-228. March 12 1964 pp568-572. March 19 1964 pp645-649) (NSFCT 1893 p140) (STC p13p).

GROUNDS. In the later C17 Plot noted the gardens grew 60 different sorts of apple, 20 sorts of pear, 16 sorts of cherries and 35 sorts of apricots as well as seven sorts of nectarines and peaches (NHS p227). The Bowling Green House was built in the summer of 1746. It did not exist by 1964 (CL March 19 1964 p649). Dawn of Love statue is inside the Temple of Pomona. It represents a young woman with a rose-bud on her bosom. The sculptor is Giuseppe Borgonzoli (BOE p216) (MR p250). The Necessary House or water closet was designed by Sanderson for Leak Okeover and is classical in design (CL March 19 1964 p649) (BOE p216) (SGS p132) (SL p134) (MR p250) (F p321). The Temple of Pomona, goddess of fruit, is to the N of the hall. It was built by Simon File for Leak Okeover in 1747-48 and moved to its present position in 1759 as Leak Okeover could not make up his mind where it should go (CL March 19 1964 p647p) (BOE p216) (SGS p132) (F p321) (MR p250).

Okeover Park Former medieval deer park enclosed out of forest to S of Okeover Hall. In existence by 1225 (NSJFS 1962 p76. 1964 p63). Contains 200 acres (EDP p178). A tree in the park has a hole said to have been made for shooting deer in the days when the park was a deer park (CL March 19 1964 p649). See also Wishing Oak.

Old Abbey, The Cottages on N side of High Street, Abbots Bromley. Called Dandelion by 1939. According to tradition it and a building to its W, Coleridge House, formerly Castle House, was the house of correction for the monks of Burton Abbey, lords of Abbots Bromley; although the two sites may have been part of a grange of the abbey (AB pp11,28).

Oldacre Tiny district of south Brocton. Appears in 1570 as Oldecarre and means 'the marshy land where alders grew' (SPNO p34).

Oldacre Burn Brook running along the S foot of Tar Hill (SMM p173).

Oldacre Hall Oldacre Lane, Brocton, lead to it (HCMBOPP p80). It was standing in the C18 (BERK2 p69).

Old Brook Tributary of the Trent (SPNO p15). Old Brook Valley, otherwise known locally as Abraham's Valley or Vale, is in Cannock Chase, 2.75m WNW of Rugeley. But somewhat oddly some maps give this name to a track going up a spur which drops down near Seven Springs from the high Haywood Warren area (Cannock Chase by Car. Staffs Nature Conservation Trust Ltd. ND, but between 1971 and 1974 p6).

Oldcatgut House on E side of Leek road N of Moorville Hall, in Caverswall parish. Occurs on OS map 6 inch 1890.

Old Chester Road An ancient trackway. Beyond Brownhills it is known as the 'Welsh Way' (HOWW pp17-18). Where it crosses Ryknild Street is a field known as 'Roman's Field' where coins of Domitian, Hadrian and other emperors have turned up (HOWW p24).

'Old Constable Wick Tree' Name for the tree by the stocks in the centre of Caverswall. Its predecessor, planted in 1672 and replaced in 1935, was called 'Town Hall Tree' (SMOPP vol 1 p7p).

Oldcott Farm on N-facing slopes of Golden Hill 1m ESE of Kidsgrove. Former hamlet and township in Wolstanton ancient parish (W p289) (AGT p63) (PPP vol 2 p1p of Oldcott Green). Oldcott was a member of Tunstall manor by c1130 (ONST 1976 p374). Park Farm is formerly the farm of Oldcott Park (TTTD p192). Has also appeared as Oldcote.

Olde House on the Green, The A C17-looking house with a timber-framed upper floor on the W side of Fulford village green.

Old End Former tiny district of Coseley over 0.5m SW of Coseley church, Church Road. The council built houses here after WW1 (HC p75). The name is preserved in Old End Lane.

Old End Hamlet in West Bromwich ancient parish, settled by the later C18 (VCH vol 17 p9). It was in the vicinity of Lyttleton Street, Sams Lane, and Bromford Lane on the southern edge of West Bromwich Common (SHWB 5). Or in the present Richard Street area, slightly to the N of Bromford Lane (VCH vol 17 p9). It apparently received its name, Old End, after the collection of hovels which abounded here (SOWB p25). Has also appeared as Moore's End (OWB p112).

Old End Former small hamlet in Sedgley ancient parish S of Sangwin Road, Roseville. The name was current in the mid C19. Old End Lane still survived in 1904.

Old End Hall Roseville, Coseley. Built by Samuel and Martin Groucutt in the C19. Situated between the end of Castle Street and Groucutt Street. It was demolished to make way for the Clifton Cinema (TB April 1986 p4).

Oldengine Farm To NE of Dilhorne. Named as such by 1800, and seems to have taken its name from several fire engines employed at Dilhorne Colliery in the C18. Little Oldengine Farm, nearby, seems to have been named after Oldengine Farm (CCT p65).

Oldenhal Lone The name Oldenhal lone occurs in the period between 1290 and 1376 in the Wednesfield area. The 'Old hall' may represent 'halh' meaning remote valley or may refer to a lost hall, or Neachells Hall. It could refer to 'the entrenched place of Wulfrin' of the 1240 Prestwood agreement, near Noose Lane or Portobello (WFW p48).

Oldershaw N of Loynton, Norbury. It is possibly the Hildersheaves on the 1834 OS map; Dower's Hildersheayes; and White's Oldershire in High Offley parish (W p391).

Old Fallings Former small hamlet (BUOP p6) now a district 0.75m SSE of Bushbury. In Bushbury ancient parish. Formerly lay on the edge of Cannock Forest. The name is from Anglo-Saxon 'feallan,' meaning 'old falling, felling (of timber), clearing' (DUIGNAN p59) (WFW p6). In the later C17 Plot noted the phallus fungi at Old Fallings and almost anywhere within three or four miles of Wolverhampton and at Bentley (NHS pp200-201,202 tab 14 fig 4, fig 5).

Old Fallings Hall House of an ancient estate at Old Fallings in Wednesfield chapelry in the ancient parish and foreign of Wolverhampton (HOWM p44). An old hall here seems to have been the seat of the Challenors in Elizabethan times (HOWM p44), and a house here appears on Plot's map. The present house, of c1720 (BOE p321) (BUOP p40p), situated on a hill (SHOS vol 2 p187), was built by Walter Gough (whose arms, impaling Harwood, are over the front door). It has also appeared as Old Fallings Manor. Shaw noted in the great parlour, portraits, supposedly by Kneller, of Sir Henry Gough's sisters Anne and Bridget Newbury, of Thomas Harwood of Tern, and others; and in the bedchamber a portrait of the navigator and founder of the Gough Islands, Sir Richard Gough Knt (d1728), when old in a brown coat and neckcloth (SHOS vol 2 pp188,190,191). The custom of placing a hearse on the grave of the deceased head of the family for a year after burial was introduced into the Gough family by Mrs Martha Gough, daughter of Thomas Harwood of Tern, Shrops (SHOS vol 2 p192). The Goughs maintained the hall until 1818 (BUOP p6). With the death of John Gough in 1844 the hall passed to his wife Jane

Elizabeth Paget of Cranmore Hall, Somerset. With the death of Jane in 1848 the estate passed to her brother John Moore Paget (1791-1866). The hall appears to have been let out in the early 1850s, as G Briscoe, was in residence in 1851 (W p22). The Paget family offered the hall for sale in 1916. The hall was finally sold in 1925 and became St Chad's College, a Catholic boys' school. In 1977 this school became a mixed comprehensive school (BUOP pp40p of the chapel, 41p of the dining hall) (MR p71). 400 acres of Fallings Park estate became the site for Fallings Park Garden Suburb or Old Fallings Park (see).

Old Fallings House Stood on the opposite side of Old Fallings Lane to Old Fallings Hall. In the 1920s it was the home of Charles Owen Silvers, manager of Wolverhampton Corporation Transport. In the 1930s it was occupied by Father Woulfe (BUOP p41p of in 1916).

Old Fallings Park Garden suburb built on 400 acres of Old Fallings Hall estate. Formerly in Wednesfield chapelry in Wolverhampton ancient parish. Fallings Park was a ward of Wolverhampton borough by 1982. It was initiated by Sir Richard Paget, the owner of the hall and planned by Thomas Adams who used Hampstead Garden Suburb and Welwyn Garden City as models. The first six houses were started in 1907. There were 75 houses by 1915. But the scheme was never fully completed. The originally tenanted and centrally managed houses were being sold off by the 1920s (WJO Feb 1907 pp41p-47) (MR p71) (WHTOP p154p). The area is now called Fallings Park.

Oldfallow Suburban district 0.75m N of Cannock. In Cannock ancient parish. Has also appeared as Oldefallowe (1257. 1570), Oldfarrow (1834) (SPNO p60). The name means 'old fallow land' in the sense of long or formerly used (SPNO p60).

Old Falls Ancient farm on Cheslyn Common, near Shareshill (DUIGNAN pp15,59). (VCH vol 5 p78). The name appears in 1792 (SPNO p72) in an Enclosure Act of that year. In trying to put into effect the Act a Mr Whitehouse brought a case against a number of squatters on the ex-parochial common land here who were resisting eviction. The case lasted between 1808 and 1815 (GWY pp31-32).

Old Farm Former timber-framed house in Bond End, Burton upon Trent, believed to have belonged to Burton Abbey (W p535).

Old Farm On E side of Sandwell Road, formerly Sandwell Lane, Handsworth. There was settlement at Old Farm by the end of the C13 (MNB pp35,38).

Old Field S of King Street, Fenton, is Oldfield Brick Works (Stoke-on-Trent A-Z).

Oldfields Farm 1m SSW of Grindon. The burial mound 160 metres SE of the farm at SK 08285288 is a listed monument. Appears as Oldfield on the 1834 OS map.

Oldfields Hall Large Victorian mansion on Stone Road, Uttoxeter. The house was built in the late C18 as Oldfields House (AUOPP p48p). It was at some time owned or occupied by the Bladons (TRTC p42). In the C19 it became Martha Bennett's school and then Charles Ford's home before being owned by John Bamfield (possibly Bamford?) (AUOPP p48p). It was the seat of John Bamford (1853-1918) of the Uttoxeter engineering-products firm, after transferring from Dove Bank House by at least 1891. Here he built a cricket pavilion and ground on which the Australian XI and Indian XI have played. Later the residence of his eldest son Henry John Bamford (1891-1947) to at least 1936. By 1978 the house was part of Oldfields Hall Secondary School, successor of the old Grammar school (BUBA pp33,34p,59,70). By 1994 it was a middle school (UOPP pl 57). The name appears to be from a common field known as The Old Field (1834 OS map). Foley says it was named after the family who built it (TRTC p42).

Oldford House over 0.5m SW of Seighford (1834 OS map) (Dower's map).

Old Forge Small area of Swan Village, West Bromwich, off Phoenix Street. Probably applies to the works here.

Old Forge N of Manwoods. Here Francis Asbury, aged 13, was apprenticed to a Methodist blacksmith, Mr Foxall, at the old forge, now part of Forge Mill Farm, just off Forge Lane (250th Anniversary of the Birth of Francis Asbury. Aug 1995).

Old Furnace Tiny settlement at the junction of Stoneydale, Greendale, and Lambskindale, alongside a small nameless stream in an idyllic dell 1m SW of Oakamoor. In Cheadle ancient parish. Iron was made here from the C13. Here iron-making in N Staffs was revolutionised in 1593 when Lawrence Loggin of Ashby and Sir Francis Willoughby of Woolaton Hall built the first water-driven blast furnace in the region. The Old Furnace and the Oakamoor forge were jointly known in accounts as the Okymoor works. The forge closed in 1608 (The Iron Valley or Eight Centuries of Iron Making in the Churnet Valley. Herbert Chester. 1979) (HAF pp287-292).

Old Hag Farm 1m SSE of Swythamley, was probably on the Roman Limes

Britannicus (NSFCT 1902 p116). According to an old legend, related since c1674, it is supposed to be named after the Old Witch of Frith and to have been a wayside inn (HOLF pp23-24) (DPEM p141). The witch could turn herself into a hare and was chased by a farmer called Wood of Frith Bottom (FLJ 1942 p127). Perhaps the same as Hag Cottage (see).

Old Hall Blackwood Hill. Mostly rebuilt by 1932. Seat of the Reades before 1702 when they moved to Fields Farm, Gratton (NSFCT 1932 p30). Also a half timber framed building called Old Hall Farm.

Old Hall Hanley. The cellars of the hall were used by the Old Hall Works, which later occupied the site of the hall (OTP p180). Presumably, Oldhall Street preserves the name.

Old Hall, The Stood close to the entrance of The Old Manor House in Coley Lane, Little Haywood. In the later Elizabethan period it was occupied by a gentleman named Bristowe (later Bristle). It was described as a picturesque ruin in 1830-40 with only a few rooms habitable. The site is now (1924) occupied by a number of small houses (Colwich PR) (HAH pp35-39).

Old Hall, The S of Rugeley parish church (VCH vol 5 p150 see map). It may have had its origins by the C13 when it belonged to the dean and chapter of Lichfield as rectors of Rugeley. From the C16 it belonged to the Chetwynds. In 1780, when the property belonged to Mr Anson, it was described as a very ancient timber-house. Part of the garden wall was still standing in 1957. Apparently it was once called Lower Hall to distinguish it from Bank Top at Hagley (VCH vol 5 pp157 note, 158 note).

Old Hall Farm Stone house which stands to the WSW of Bagnall Hall in Bagnall village. Speake records only occupants since 1851 (B pp76p,77).

Old Hall Farm Middle Mayfield. Jacobean stone house once known as Froggatt's Farm. Built between 1620 and 1630 by Mr Fern, a London merchant. About 1860, Luke Samson, resident at the time took his barometer outside and shot it with his muzzle-loading shotgun after he considered that it had let him down at haymaking time. The gun is still (1993) in the possession of a Mayfield resident (MOM p50ps). (BOE p205) (MR p227p). In the vicinity of the farm is a stone rubbing post, once a legal requirement on farms; few remain today (MOM p51p).

Old Hall Farm Upper Mayfield. Is dated 1680. On one side the windows have been filled in (probably because of the window tax of the 1790s) (MOM p72p).

Oldhall Park Housing estate SW of Moseley Old Hall, Bushbury.

Old Hannah Spring Sandon. Spring at SJ 962302, 0.5m NE of Sandon.

Old Hattons, The The oldest and most northerly of The Hattons (see) over 1.5m NE of Codsall. Was known as The Hattons until at least c1841 (VCH vol 5 p33).

Old Hayes Former enclosure made out of Druid's Heath by the C14. Situated to the S of Kings Hayes (see) (MOA p134).

Oldhay Top House 1m NW of Meerbrook. Probably on the Roman Limes Britannicus (NSFCT 1902 p116). Has also appeared as Old Hay Top.

Old Hednesford (locally *Old Hedgefud* BILP1). Is SE of Hednesford. Is the original small hamlet of Hednesford, situated at Hill Top and a little to the S of Hill Top. Before coal mining it provided local staging services for travellers and facilities for the training of racehorses. Hednesford was described as 'the most noted place for training available to persons in the Midland Counties' by the Sporting Magazine of June 1839 p106 (VCH vol 5 pp49,52). John Wesley preached in Hednesford in 1738. Hednesford was described as a hamlet in the late C18 (SHOS vol 2 p315). Evidence of coal mining in the later C18 has been found at Hednesford Brickworks between Hednesford and Heath Hayes (St John's Heath Hayes 75th Anniversary. JC Oakes. 1978 pp5,7). Ghost Row is the local name for a row of houses a short distance from Cross Keys Inn, Old Hednesford. Reputedly haunted by the ghost of John Cook who was murdered by William Palmer (CCBO p86).

Old Hill Field on which John Wedgwood's obelisk is placed at Bignall End (AOPP pl 36) or an alternative name for Bignall Hill.

Old Hill Former C19 large hamlet on a hill above Mousesweet Brook 1m SW of Rowley Regis, in the Black Country. In Rowley Regis parish. The area's original name was Old Dell (OS map sheet 71.08). The name Old Hill appears on Plot's map. A cross at Old Hill stood by the Trinity Sunday Schools, which were built in 1879 (TB Oct 1993 p20). **The church**, Trinity Church, Halesowen Road, was built in 1876 (ORR pp100-101) (SNSV vol 2 p6). Old Hill was formed into a separate ecclesiastical parish in 1876 (LGS p196) (GLAUE p418) (SNSV vol 2 p6). By the later C20 Old Hill was a district, and with Cradley Hill formed a ward of Sandwell metropolitan borough. **Brick-making.** Old Hill 'claymen' produced many of the bricks with which factories, houses and chimney stacks were built using a type of common red clay (TB March 1979 p26). **Canal burst.** Dudley Canal Line Two burst its banks at Old Hill during the thaw from the severe winter in the period 1879-

1882 (BCWJ p112). The novel **'Ghost in the Water'** by Edward Chitham (1973) is set in and around Old Hill. For **witches** at Old Hill in the early C19 see TB April 1972 p13. **Persons and visitors. Lydia**, wife of Job Green of Cherry Orchard, is said to have been sold in the 1840s in front of the Old Hill courtrooms, now (1996) the Cookey Hotel. This is thought to have been the last known sale of a wife in Staffs (TB Oct 1996 p5). **Eliza Tinsley** (1813-1882), business woman known as the 'Queen of Commerce,' was a nail factor mainly at Old Hill (BCM July 1982 pp43p-46) (TB Dec 17 1998 p21p) or at Cradley Heath. Her chain works produced the longest mine-chain ever made (TB July/ Aug 1973 p25p; born in 1814). **William Eric Hollies**, who has been described as one of the finest bowlers in cricket of his generation, born in c1913 grew up in Old Hill. He played for Warws from 1932 to his retirement in 1957, and for England in the mid 1930s and after WW2; he is perhaps best remembered for bowling out Don Bradman in his last test innings for no runs in 1948 (ORR p124p). A ballad was composed about the drowning of two Gorsty Hill boys - Stanley Barrington, aged 11, and Jesse Lowe, aged 13 - in Dudley Canal Line Two near Waterfall Lane, Old Hill, on July 5 1924 (TB Aug 1976 p7). The actress and comedienne Josie Lawrence was born at Old Hill in 1959 (The Times Magazine Nov 23 1996 p82).

Old Hill The road of this name over the hill of the same name was part of the main road from Bridgnorth to Wolverhampton before a new and less steep way, The Rock, was cut through the sandstone ridge to the N in the early 1820s. There was building along Old Hill by the early C17 (VCH vol 20 pp7,13).

Old Hill Valley Old Hill, Rowley Regis.

Old House Great Barr. The seat of Joseph Scott? (SHOS vol 2 p105, pl xiv facing p101).

Old Lea House 1.5m NW of Norbury. In High Offley parish.

Old Man's Head A mound in Fairoak Valley, supposedly contains some dead from the battle of Blore Heath (1459).

Old Man of Hoy A knoll, at SJ 927448, in Park Hall Country Park, possibly man-made, as there was mining and sandstone quarrying in the vicinity (Park Hall Country Park. Staffs County Council Leaflet. Pre-1991).

Old Man of Mow Pinnacle of Yoredale rock resembling the head and shoulders of an old man (SLM Nov/Dec 1983) situated on the edge of the hill called Mow Cop. It stands 70 feet high (ES Jan 9 1993 p18pc), and has been thought by some to have formed naturally and may have had religious significance to prehistoric man. However, it was probably created by quarrying in c1862, or earlier (TSW p11p) (TTTD p172) (VB p186) (NSFCT 1979 p17) (ES Jan 9 1993 p18), perhaps out of respect for the holy ground on the top surface (MR pp235p,236). However, there is a reference to it and a poem written about it in the earlier C19, when it stood 80 feet high and 20 feet in diameter (Broughton's Scrapbook p90). In 1936 it was given by Joseph Lovatt to the NT (TTTD p173). (W p290) (GNHS p13) (MC p9 pl 2). For a poem about it see OL vol 2 p27.

Old Manor House, The Stood by Coley Lane in Little Haywood. It appears to have been a large house belonging to the Whitby family, who at one time owned half or more of Haywood manor. The house was at one time known as 'The Hall Flats' and afterwards as 'The Old Manor Farm.' Only a part of the building remained after c1720-30. A family named Wells used to reside here. Part of the remains were being used as a blacksmiths shop in 1840. In 1768 Hon Thomas Clifford purchased the Whitby estate but Clifford sold it that year to Thomas Anson, elder brother of Admiral Lord Anson (HOT p72) (HAH pp32,33). The Whitby family bore arms as is shown on Plot's map. But on that map their house is shown at Great Haywood. This is either a positioning error and Little Haywood is meant or they had moved by then (1682). Dr Johnson of Lichfield (see) was tutor to the children of Thomas Whitby of Great Haywood in May and June 1735 and accompanied the Whitbys to Colwich church. One of the children is said to have been John Whitby (d1752/6 aged 34); possibly John's widow was 'The Widow of the Wood' of Oakedge Hall (see). The Latin inscription on his memorial in Colwich church is said to have been written by Johnson (OP p24) (Young Samuel Johnson. James L Clifford. 1955 1962 ed. p152).

Old Manor House Corner of Ebstree and Seisdon Roads, Seisdon. The house is inscribed on the front 'W / HE / 1684' and some of the early part of the house is of this date (VCH vol 20 pp187,190). Represents the manor house of Seisdon manor.

Old Mitre Inn 0.5m E of Essington, at SJ 969034. Dates from the C18. In 1824 the body of a murder victim, Ann Spence, was laid out in the cellar. She had been murdered by Thomas Power. Arbuthnot Bostock exhibited what purported to be the skeletal remains of famous highwaymen William Duce, and Jonathan Wild in the old coach house of the Mitre (ESSN pp32-33p). There is a tradition of a hoard of money, mainly Spanish, secreted in nearby Essington

Wood (see) by a Spanish agent, Emilio Ripoll, before he was captured by counter forces. Ripoll wrote from prison to the Mitre's landlord in 1900, Thomas Cope, asking him to locate the money, but he did not and it may still remain in the wood. The inn may have received its name from a stay made here by a bishop of Lichfield who left his mitre behind, after which the diocese gave permission for it to be used as the inn sign. Ron Butler who took over the inn in 1972 confirmed this story (ESSN pp32-33p) (SNW p49).

Old Mixon Hay House in the moorlands 2m NW of Onecote, at the N end of Onecote Brook Valley. Formerly in Onecote township in Leek ancient parish. Here Hulton Abbey had established a grange by 1237 (VCH vol 7 p211). Is the original settlement of Mixon and was known in 1710 as Mixon Hay (VCH vol 7 p213). It was envisaged that the Consall Plateway be extended to Mixon Hay on the E side of the Churnet, but the line was never completed (CVH p126). 0.5m to SE is New Mixon Hay.

Old Moat Farm Summer Hill, Tipton. Ancient seat of the lords of Tipton. It was noted in a survey of 1690 (HOTIP p24). The name is preserved in the former Moat estate, Moat Colliery and the present Manor Road.

Old Moxley Tiny part of Moxley in the Queen Street and Grocott Road area (Birmingham A-Z 1995).

Oldnall Clent. From Oldenhull, an old hill (TB Jan 1974 p13). There is a Odnall Cottage in Clent parish (W p173).

Old Oscott Former hamlet (MNB p60) on a SW-facing slope rising out of the Tame Valley, now a residential district 1.75m SE of Great Barr. Formerly in Perry Barr township in Handsworth ancient parish. The **name** has appeared as Auscot (Plot's map), Ascott (1775) and Oscott (1884) and is the original Oscott settlement (KPP). It is from perhaps, Osa's cottage (DUIGNAN). Or from the Celtic forest-root 'aos' or 'os' a wood (NSFCT 1908 p141). In the C16 the Stamfords held the Oscott estate. A branch of the Bromwich family were living at Oscott by the 1530s (Maryvale. Beth Penny. 1985 p1). **Andrew Bromwich**, Roman Catholic priest, was born at Oscott House, Oscott, in c1652, son of William Bromwich, a Catholic (Maryvale. Beth Penny. 1985 p1). Some say Andrew was born at or near Longnor (see). In the C17 Bromwich had a Catholic mission at Oscott. He was condemned to death in 1679 in the Popish Plot (see under Tixall Old Hall), but was reprieved and lived at Oscott House to his death on Oct 20 1702 or in 1703. (LGS p236) (FSP p89) (SCHJ No. 2 Spring 1962 pp9-12) (VCH vol 3 p106). There is a chair at Oscott College, New Oscott, traditionally believed to belong to Andrew Bromwich (Maryvale. Beth Penny. 1985 p3p). In 1752 or 1753 a new house was built on the site of Oscott House for the Vicars Apostolic of the Midland District at the Catholic mission at Oscott, but it was never occupied by them and instead was used for a short while as a boarding school. In the later C18 the house was extended. The chapel, existing in the early 1970s, was built in 1778. In 1796 a Catholic college and seminary, known as **St Mary's College**, opened in the house. In 1808 Bishop Milner became the sole proprietor of the college. In 1815 he established the Sodality of the Sacred Heart, and soon afterwards erected here the first altar dedicated to the Sacred Heart in England. In 1816 the college was extended with the erection of a central building (destroyed in a fire in 1860). In 1838 the college moved to New Oscott and the old college was used as a preparatory school. In 1846 John Henry Newman and his colleagues took possession of the house and renamed it Maryvale; Newman's pet name for Maryvale was 'Sancta Maria in Valle.' In 1851 four sisters from the Convent of Our Lady of Mercy, Handsworth, opened Maryvale as an orphanage and branch house to Handsworth. In 1980 the Sisters of Mercy closed the orphanage with the children being moved to Coleshill. The building was then converted into the Diocesan Centre for Catechetics and Evangelisation. It was refurnished in 1983 (KPP pp14-16il,23) (BOEWA p196) (SCHJ No. 20 1981 pp13-14) (Maryvale. Beth Penny. 1985 pp15,22-23). **Housing estates**. Old Oscott was removed to Birmingham, Warws, in 1928. In 1934 First National Housing Trust developed a thousand acres S of Old Oscott with housing (MNB p75). The **church**, St Mark with All Saints, Bandywood Crescent, was consecrated in 1966 (BDD p108). Old Oscott became a separate ecclesiastical parish in 1967 (GLAUE pp415,419).

Old Park Colton. Deer park of approximately 110 acres. 1.5m NE of Colton enclosed by the De Wasteney family in Henry III's reign. About three quarters of the park pale (defensive ditch) survives (CWF pp164-166 il facing p165).

Old Park Medieval hunting ground which belonged to Dudley Castle and was still surviving in the castle grounds in 1913 (VCHW vol 3 p100).

Old Park Park to SE of Patshull Hall, Patshull.

Old Park Former hamlet or district in Sedgley ancient parish (W p200). It may be the same as Old Park W of Dudley which bordered with Sedgley parish. Old Park was developed for housing after WW1 (OS map. Sheet 67.15).

Old Park Area and street N of Wednesbury. The Old Park Works, Darlaston

Road, was one of the earliest examples in industrial history of 'vertical integration' - the participation by one firm in several industrial processes and the making of a varied range of related products (WMLB p105). Old Park Colliery was slightly damaged in the Zeppelin L21 raid on Wednesbury on the night of Jan 31 1916 (BCM summer 1996 pp68-69). A modern engineering-plant occupied the site of the colliery by 1971 (WMLB pp100-101). The name is from an old park belonging to Wednesbury manor house (SNDB p17).

Old Park Hall Seat of the Bassetts of Drayton Bassett at Cheadle in medieval times. The site is moated but no trace of the building is visible (NSFCT 1885 p60).

Oldpark Hill Hill 0.75m NNW of Throwley Hall.

Old Peel House 1m E of Balterley. Originally Old Peel Carr.

Old Perton Recent term to refer to the old settlement of Perton, since an housing estate was built on Perton airfield, which now goes by the name Perton (MR p253).

Old Raven's Hall A farm in the Betley area? Some of it dates from 1632 (BOPP pl 17).

Oldridge Farm House 0.5m SE of Foxt. Here is an outcrop of rock (built into the property?) (Family Walks in the Staffordshire Peak & Potteries. Les Lumsdon. 1990. pp28p,29).

Old Road Former tiny hamlet 0.75m NW of Barlaston new church, in Barlaston ancient parish. Appears on 1834 OS map. The name is from the stretch of road here which once formed part of the old Carlisle road before traffic was transferred to the turnpike road through Tittensor (BAH p16).

Oldry Lane In Brieryhurst liberty in Wolstanton ancient parish (W p289). On 1834 OS map there is a hamlet called Aldery Lane 0.5m ESE of Brieryhurst. This has become Alderhay Lane (Stoke-on-Trent A-Z).

Old Sheldon's Bank Wetton. Possibly the slope leading up to Thor's Cave. A Mr Taylor in the late C19 saw the ghosts? of two light greyhounds, on several occasions in the evening, entering a cave in this bank, later the cave is identified as Thor's Cave (WTCEM pp71,94,144).

Old Springs Tiny fragmented hamlet on a prominence above Coal Brook 1.25m SW of Hales. In Tyrley manor in Drayton-in-Hales parish. A looped palstave of the Bronze Age was found near Old Springs Hall at SJ 70493348 in 1960 (NSJFS 1962 p30. 1964 p39). Both what were believed to be burial mounds at Old Springs Hall at SJ 70013230 and to the N at SJ 70293274 (SHC 1945/ 6 p11) are natural features (NSJFS 1965 p50). Possibly the name 'Old Springs' may be connected with the supposed burial mounds here. Springs means a wood, and refers to the springs or shoots which grow up from stumps or stools, after timber has been felled (SHC 1945/ 6 pp11-12).

Old Springs Hall Hall of early C19 origin 1.25m SW of Hales (BOE p138). Occupied in 1851 by Edgerton Harding (W p22).

Old Stallings Farm Stallings Lane, Kingswinford. Dismantled in 1973/74 (TB March 1974 p25).

Old Star Cluster of properties 0.75m S of Cotton on the old main road from the Moorlands to Oakamoor. Garner noted two burial mounds at Old Star (GNHSS p5). Formerly Blazeing Star (Plot's map) (HAF p396) (COPP2 p95p of the Star Inn). Some have thought the name 'Star' is from the shape of roads which join here, or from a beacon on Weaver Hills (NSFCT 1879 p27). The name 'Blazing Star' is from an inn of this name here, which in turn took its name from a nearby C16 furnace. Later a turnpike road (present B5417) was constructed to the N and the Blazing Star Inn was then removed to the new road and is now called The Star Inn (HAF p396).

Old Street Old highway which was identified by Duignan as the old Lichfield to Wolverhampton road running E of New Invention, across Pool Hayes towards Broad Lane South to Noose Lane, to perhaps Watery Lane and on to Neachells village (WFW p31).

Old Timbers Half timbered house on Fisherwick road, Whittington (MR p378).

Old Town Hall Cruck and brick cottage on the corner of College Road and Slack Lane, Handsworth. Former residence and office of the overseers of Handsworth parish. Said to have been built in c1460 (HANDR pviii, p1p). It has also been called Cruck House (HHHW p54p in 1936).

Old Warley By 1999 was a ward in Sandwell metropolitan borough. Presumably embraces the Warley area.

Old West Bromwich 1m NE of West Bromwich. The old settlement of West Bromwich as opposed to the new settlement 1m to SW.

Old Wood Hamlet 1m ESE of Colton. In Colton parish (W p414).

Oldwood House at Toot Hill, Croxden. Also a house 1m NW of Stramshall.

Olive Green Tiny hamlet at the mouth of a small valley formed by a tributary of the Blithe 0.75m SE of Hamstall Ridware. Partly in Hamstall Ridware and Yoxall parishes. Has appeared as Gallows Green and Olive Green (1887 OS map 6 inch). (SHOS vol 1 p152).

Oliver Hill Flash. At 1684 feet high is the highest point of Staffordshire (BEV p20) (VB p210) (VCH vol 7 p1).

Oliver's Green Area to W of Denstone. A story based on oral tradition is that a baggage train in the Civil War was ambushed at Denstone and the casualties were buried at Oliver's Green. There may be some truth in the story as Oliver's Green lies in close proximity to the old packhorse road from Uttoxeter to Alton (HAF p124).

Oliver's Mounds Two grassy mounds at Denstone which are believed to be the remains of hollows formed for an old packhorse route or saltway; one of the mounds is a diversion around wet or muddy ground (ESNF p103p). (S pp97,98p of) (KES p78).

Olton Former hamlet in the centre of Patshull parish. Has appeared as Oldington (C13-C17), Olton (1374. C17-C19), and Oulton (Plot's map). It was in existence by the mid C13. The settlement of Olton disappeared in the C18 with the landscaping of Patshull Park. A farmhouse called Olton survived until the early C19 (VCH vol 20 p162). Oulton Garden is 0.75m SSW of Patshull Hall.

Oncote Former hamlet on low ground by Gamesley Brook 1m W of Great Bridgeford in Horsley division in Eccleshall ancient parish (W p379).

Onecote (*On-cut* PNPD). Small moorland village in the upper Hamps valley 21.5m NE of Stafford. Former township and chapelry in Leek ancient parish, but in 1604 said to be in Grindon parish (SHC 1915 p199). The **name** appears in 1199 as Anecote (SSE 1996 p16). It means 'one cottage' (DUIGNAN). Oakden agrees (SSAHST 1967 p34). Or 'remote' (VCH vol 7 p211) or 'lone cottage,' perhaps the home of a shunned eccentric, or place avoided for superstitious reasons (SPN p90). It is said that a soldier named Burnett with the army of the retreating Young Pretender during the 1745 Jacobite Rebellion on seeing that Onecote only had 'One Cote' decided to settle here, as there was plenty of room for him! (BPCSM p8). The **original settlement** may have been to the N of the present village centre, at the confluence of the Hamps and Onecote Brook, where, at Onecote Grange, Croxden Abbey had a grange apparently by 1223. There was settlement at the present village centre at the junction of the road from Bradnop with the Ipstones-Butterton road by the earlier C17 (VCH vol 7 p211). At Onecote is a rectangular moated site with house on site (ESH p58). The **church**, St Luke, On the S side of Douse Lane in the NW end of the village, was built in 1753-1755 (BOE p216). Became a separate ecclesiastical parish in 1783 (GLAUE p419) and was ecclesiastically united with Bradnop in 1862 (LGS pp196-197). Became a separate civil parish in 1866 (GLAUE p419). The **headless horseman** of the Moorlands reputedly was seen at a crossroads near Onecote in 1935 (SSGLST pp10-11) (GLS p43) (HLSP p123).

Onecote Brook Rises N of Old Mixon Hay. Joins the Hamps N of Onecote village (VCH vol 7 p211).

Onecote Grange House 0.25m NW of Onecote, at the confluence of the Hamps and Onecote Brook. Formerly in Onecote township in Leek ancient parish. Built on or near the site of a grange of Croxden Abbey, here apparently by 1223. The present house is dated 1884 and stands on the site of an earlier house, which was probably of the later C17; a datestone of 1654 on an outbuilding possibly comes from a still earlier house (VCH vol 7 pp211,213).

Onecote Lane End House 1m WNW of Onecote. Formerly in Onecote township in Leek ancient parish. The house here probably existed by 1641 and certainly by 1690 (VCH vol 7 p211). The case of Gridley in chapter xv of Charles Dickens' 'Bleak House' (1852-3) is based on the Chancery lawsuit brought by Joseph Cook of Onecote Lane End Farm in 1844 in an attempt to obtain £300 bequeathed to him by his father. It became very protracted, and four years later far from resolved, William Challinor of Pickwood Hall (see), a Leek solicitor involved with it, sent Dickens a pamphlet urging Chancery reform, based on the case (NSF pp115-116) (VCH vol 7 p212) (VFC p25) (SHC 1999 pp177-199).

Onecote Lane Head House 1m WNW of Onecote. Formerly in Onecote township in Leek ancient parish. The house here was so called by 1670 (VCH vol 7 p211).

Onecote Old Hall House 0.25m NE of Onecote. Formerly in Grindon parish.

One Hundred and Forty Four Steps A cavern in Castle Hill, Dudley. Originally known as the Dark Cavern (BCM Oct 1970 p51).

Onneley Small village in undulating country to the N of the source of the Lea 1.5m SW of Madeley. Former township in Madeley ancient parish. Onneley is said by Paffard to appear in DB as Anelege (SSE 1996 p16), and has appeared as Anneley (C16) and Onniley. In Welsh 'onn' (plural) is ash-trees. Perhaps, 'the lea of the ash trees' (DUIGNAN). Or 'ash-tree river' (SPN p90). Oakden thinks Duignan is incorrect (SSAHST 1967 p33). From Celtic 'onn' meaning rock or hill (NSFCT 1908 p136) (M p4). Mills gives 'Onna's or Anna's or isolated wood clearing' (SSE 1996 p16). There was a pilgrimage

chapel of the Virgin at Onneley by the later C14 (HOK p13). It is mentioned in the Valor Ecclesiasticus 1535 as Onnley St Mary, but not in the 1563 return (SHC 1915 p184). It is shown on Saxton's map. No shrine is mentioned, it may have been a journey of penance from Madeley church (M pp5,6). It is believed to have stood by the lane running N from Onneley to Betley (OSST 1949-50 p13). A modern chapel, on the N side of the Woore-Madeley road, was the parish hall by the 1990s. **'Boring village'?** In April 1996 some young people of the village hung a notice beneath the village sign on the roadside warning 'Beware! You are now entering the most boring village in England.' The story was taken up by ES and then by the national press and Onneley was 'officially' dubbed England's most boring village (ES May 1 1996. May 10 1996. Aug 4 1998 p9). However, at 5.30am on Sept 17 1998 animal rights activities released into the wild about 2,500 mink farmed at Kelbain Farm, Onneley. Most were recaptured or destroyed shortly after being released, but a few reached distances of 15 miles or more four days after being released (ES Sept 17 1998 p1. Sept 21 1998 pp1,3).

Orchard Brook House in Shareshill. Has a timber-framed annex of c1600 (VCH vol 5 p173). Is perhaps the Orchard Farm on the OS map 1:25,000 on the N side of the village. The name may be from the brook which runs to the N.

Orchard Common Former common land (UHAW p11) 1.25m N of Flash. Most northerly named feature in Staffs. There is an Orchard Farm over 1m NNW of Flash.

Orchard Hills Large private development of E Walsall built by McCleans in three phases starting in 1958. Streets here have an agricultural theme (SNWA p78) - which suggests the area of Fallowfield Road and neighbouring streets in Daisy Bank.

Orchards, The House 0.75m SSW of Okeover.

Orchbrook House Shareshill. One of the few old buildings surviving in Shareshill. Has some features which date from the C17 (SVB p149).

Ordish's Farm On S side of Park Street (Pinfold Lane) 1m W of Burton upon Trent, at SK 231225. The house, on the site of Bond End Grange, is said to have been built by Henry Watson, a tanner, in 1649 (BTIH p52 il of in the mid C19). Ordish's Farm was still standing in 1947 (1947 OS map 1:25,000 (sheet 43/22)).

Ordley Brook Rises above Mayfield near Stanton joins Northwood Brook at Ousley and this joins Tit Brook which flows into the Dove. The name means 'a corner or spit of land in the stream' (SPNO p15).

Orgreave Small hamlet on low ground in the Trent Valley near the confluence of the Trent and Bourne Brook 1.5m WNW of Alrewas. Anciently lay in Alrewas Hay (DUIGNAN), later a township in Alrewas ancient parish (W p593) and was in Alrewas prebend (SSAHST vol 2 1960-61 p43). E of Lupin Bank was found a Neolithic or Bronze Age stone axe in 1955 (BAST vol 73 p118) (NSJFS 1964 p14). The name appears in 1195 as Ordgraue (SSE 1996 p16). It means 'Ord's grove (or wood)' (DUIGNAN) (SPN p11). Mills and Gelling think probably 'pointed grove' (NSJFS 1981 p3) (SSE 1996 p16). Or means 'the edge of the wood' (LTM Dec 1971 p63). Orgreave became a separate civil parish in 1866 (GLAUE p419). During a robbery at Mr Bakewell's house at Orgreave on May 31 1895 Mr Bakewell and his son were shot dead by Thomas Bond of Hixon. Mrs Bakewell, also in the house, would have been shot only the bullet ricocheted off the herring bone of her corset. She was able to identify Bond, and he was arrested in Nottingham by a policeman who noticed him whilst shaving at home and ran out into the street and caught him. He was found guilty and hung (HOA p188) (CCSHO pp53-67). John Hall of Orgreave had a cow which delivered a calf with two heads on 11 May 1644. It lived for one day then died (SHOS vol 1 p139 - mentioned in PR and by Plot).

Orgreave Hall Orgreave, Alrewas. Probably built in 1668, and was considerably enlarged during the next 60 years or so (BOE p54); it appears to have been built by William Turton and remained in the Turtons until at least his death in 1683 (Plot's map) (SHOS vol 1 pp128,133). John Gisborne, poet (1770-1851) lived here for a while (NSFCT 1947 p100). Samuel Winter (d1847) lived at Orgreave Hall (mem in Croxall church). It was last privately owned by Col Harrison. It is now (1992) a residential home for the elderly (MIDD vol 4 p38p).

Oriel Cottage Stafford Road, Ford Houses, Bushbury. Built in the early 1860s in the Neo-Tudor style. It has been completely restored (BUOP p49p).

Orslow Tiny hamlet on upland near the head of Orslow Brook 2m N of Blymhill. Former township in Church Eaton ancient parish. Has appeared as Horslage (1195), Horselawe (1203), Orselowe (1242), and Orsloe (c1680) (SPNO p142) (SSE 1996 p16). Horsa was an Anglo-Saxon personal name, and in Anglo-Saxon 'hors' is a horse. Perhaps, 'Horsa's low' (burial-mound), or 'the horse low' (DUIGNAN) (SPNO p142) (SSE 1996 p16). In c1208 there was recorded a windmill at approximately SJ 818156 (WBJ p15). Midway between

Bromstead Heath and Orslow a 'Mill Hills' is recorded on 1817/ 1833 OS maps at SJ 800159, suggesting here was a windmill (WBJ p16).

Orslow Brook Runs from Orslow then to Moreton, joins Moreton Brook.

Orslow Manor Orslow. A square farm-house of red brick and appears to date from the late C18 or the C19. Represents the manor-house of the manor of Orslow (VCH vol 4 pp92,97).

Orton Tiny village nestles beneath the Penn Hill, on the S side and beneath Orton Hills, on the W side, over 1.25m NNW of Wombourne, 2.25m WSW of Penn. Former township in Wombourne ancient parish (PONP p26). The last Ice Age reached its maximum southern extent about Wolverhampton and glacial boulders lie about Orton (WJO Nov 1909 p293). Has appeared as Overtone, a manor, in DB (SVS p577), Overton (C13. Plot's map. SHOS vol 2 p215), Orton (C13), Overdon (1327) (VCH vol 20 p134), and Oreton (DUIGNAN). The name means probably, 'the upper town or farmstead' (DUIGNAN) (SPN p145). The centre of the village was at the crossroads formed by the road from Lower Penn to Wombourne and the road from Trysull to Upper Penn and Wolverhampton (VCH vol 20 p200). A manor house at Orton was held by tenants of the Greys at least between the 1580s and the 1620s (VCH vol 20 p204). There was probably a pound NE of Orton before the early C19 (VCH vol 20 p216). A finger post pointing the way to Trysull Workhouse was still standing in Orton Lane in the 1960s (TB July 1998 p13p).

Orton Grange House on W side of Orton Lane, S of Orton. Property of the Marsh family, important local landowners, by 1700. Has a cross wing dated 1685, and a three-storeyed C18 block on the site of the main range (VCH vol 20 pp200,207). The core of the original building is thought to have been built in the early C12 (S Staffs Walks: A Three Mile Walk Around Orton. S Staffs Council 1993).

Orton Hall House on W side of Orton Lane, Orton. Now called Orton Hall Farm. Built in 1754 (VCH vol 20 p200).

Orton Hills Hills S of Orton, Wombourne, comprising Edge Hill (PPTP p58), Orton Hill and others. Lady Well (see) is situated on one hill. Views of the Sedgley, Sedgley Beacon, Cambrian Mountains, Clents, Malverns, Abberleys, Woodburys, Clees, Wrekin and Welsh borders can be obtained from them (POAP p3) (S Staffs Walks: A Three Mile Walk Around Orton. S Staffs Council 1993). Comprise Lower Keuper Sandstone (S&WC p114).

Orton House House on N side of Showell Lane, Orton. Dates from the C18 (VCH vol 20 p200).

Oscott Manor Farm Stood at the junction of Birdbrook Road and Lingfield Avenue, near Oscott Community Hall, Old Oscott. May represent the site of Little Barr Manor House (MNB pp54,62). A building was standing here by 1840. In 1884 it was known as Manor House (KPP p13p).

Osier Bed Between Bilston and Willenhall was a small mining hamlet where William Hanbury Sparrow had blast furnaces (BCM Oct 1990 p61). There is an Osier Place at Horsley Fields.

Osierbed Wood Butterton (Newcastle).

Ossams Hill Near Ossoms Hill, Grindon.

Ossoms Cave Cave situated about 27 metres above the Manifold in Ossoms Hill. Flint implements believed to be of Palaeolithic Age have been found in it during excavations between 1954 and 1956 (NSJFS 1964 pp24,56) (HOS p9) (SASR 1987 pp25-59, 86-93 ps ils). Finds of Roman origin include fragments of animal bone and pottery (PASN vols 11, 12) (British Caving. 1962 2nd ed. CHD Cullingford. p320) (NSJFS 1964 p24). Has also appeared as Ossums Cave (HOS p9),

Ossoms Eyrie Cave Is a rock shelter in an almost inaccessible position in Ossums Cliff (NSJFS 1964 p24). In Ossums Hill? It has displayed traces of prehistoric occupation (HOS p9). Finds of Roman origin included a small fibula, a tanged knife, a decorated bone pin, fragments of bronze and glass, and Derbys ware pottery (PASN vols 8, 14) (British Caving. 1962 2nd ed. CHD Cullingford. p320) (NSJFS 1964 p24).

Ossoms Hill Hill 0.75m NE of Grindon, over looks the Manifold. The name is perhaps linked with the cult of Esus, which in Anglo-Saxon is Oslac, Osbeorn and in English Osborne (NSFCT 1908 p109). An American Skytrain (or 'Dakota') made an emergency landing in a field at Ossoms Hill in WW2; one crewman went to Ossoms Hill Farm to telephone and some walked to Wetton Mill; eventually a group walked into Grindon (MD p62).

Otherton Former manor (W p466) and minute hamlet comprising one house (Otherton Farm) 1.25m SSE of Penkridge, on marshy upland above and at some distance from the Penk. Has appeared as Orretone or Oretone (DB) (there is no other Orretone in DB), Ooerton (1167), Otherton (1167), Oterton (1262), Oddarton (1572) (SPNO p91). Duignan thinks it could be upper town, but is unsure. Oakden gives 'other (second) tun' (SSE 1996 p16). There was possibly a medieval village in the vicinity of Otherton Farm, or 0.25m to the W of Otherton Farm (SSAHST 1970 p35), since depopulated.

Otherton Brook Rises S of Penkridge (PVH p12).

Oulsclough House 0.75m NE of Oakamoor.

Oulton Village on S-facing slopes beneath the high ground of Oulton Heath and above Scotch Brook 6.5m N of Stafford. Formerly in Kibblestone quarter in Stone ancient parish. The rare find of a **Roman** metalworking die has been found at Oulton. The artifact is recognizable as a small decorative boss applied to Roman helmets and segmented form of armour cuirass (Antiquaries Journal. 70 (2) 1990 pp456-459 il tabs). A large hoard of **Saxon** treasure was discovered on the site of Oulton Abbey by a gardener of Mr Shelley in 1795. But the hoard was lost as soon as it was found due to being distributed amongst the local inhabitants (SOK pp11,39,40) (SG p19). The **name** has appeared as Oldeton (1251) (SSE 1996 p16), and Oldington (C13). WH Stevenson says the 'ing' and 'e' show that it was 'Ealdantun.' The Anglo-Saxon form, if the place was of Anglo-Saxon origin, would be 'Ealdantun' (dative). Perhaps, from the personal name Ealda, so 'Ealda's town' (DUIGNAN). Or from Anglo-Saxon 'old tun' meaning an old settlement or enclosure (SVB p134) (SSE 1996 p16). Or the first element is a personal name of Scandinavian origin 'Ouldulf's farmstead' (SPN p90). In the **Civil War** the parliamentary force comprising 500 which took Stafford in mid May 1643 came through Oulton prior to their attack. With their approach a royalist force, apparently encamped on Oulton Heath, fled in the night (BFS p22) (HAF p122): The Gamuls of Oulton Old Hall may have been royalists (SOK pp23-25). **Trade.** For Oulton Mill see Hayes Mill. Blakeman's Gravel Quarry created the cliff face at the rear of the village hall at the beginning of the C20 (SDOPP p68p). Seems to have been formerly in Kibblestone township. But by 1872 formed a township with Meaford (KD 1872). Ecclesiastically became a part of the new parish of Christ Church, Stone, in 1837 (The Church of St John the Evangelist. Fred Leigh). The **church**, St John the Evangelist, on the W side of Church Lane, was consecrated in July 1878 (The Church of St John the Evangelist. Fred Leigh). With Moddershall Oulton became a separate ecclesiastical parish in 1879 (KD 1912) (LGS p197) (GLAUE p419). **The Flash** is a colloquialism for the newer road from Stone to Oulton. It is the name for the dip in the road (NSFCT 1908 p143. 1930 pp38-39). The village was a noted cockfighting centre (NSFCT 1915 p156). A **sampler** made at Oulton went to the County Museum at Shugborough (SOK p57). **Supernatural.** Oulton Vicarage is said to be haunted by a miser who died in some tragic way (burnt to death). His ghost returns to the study each month to count his money (NSFCT 1900 p143) (FOS p21). Two extra-terrestrials were seen late at night by Mrs Wood and her children in a field near her home in Oulton in approximately Sept 1971. The entities were at least six feet tall, dressed in 'diving suits' and moving like 'astronauts on the moon.' One of the entities strode around and kept squatting as if looking for something; the other was mostly stationary. They were luminous in the darkness, and one glowed more than brightly than the other (Northern UFO News 66 p6) (MMSE pp199,288). **Leslie Bishop**, poet and journalist, was born in Oulton in 1908; John Galsworthy, novelist, admired his collection of essays, published in 1929. After spending many years working as a journalist in Canada Bishop returned to England in 1982, and lives in Stone. His 'Until Tomorrow, The Collected Poems of Leslie Bishop' was published in 1999 (ES April 17 1999 p3p). He is probably the Les Gurney Bishop, author of the novel 'Paper Kingdom' (1936) (VFC p15).

Oulton Tiny hamlet in undulating country surrounded by former wetland above Wood Brook 0.75m SSW of Norbury. Formerly in Norbury township and ancient parish. For Bronze Age bronze implements found near Oulton noted by GM see under Warton. Has appeared as Oldington(e) (1286), Upper and Lower Oldington (1305), Oldyngton (1364), Oulton (1413), Over Wolton alias Over Olton, Nether Wolton alias Nether Olton (1572), Upper Norbury (W) and Lower Norbury (E) (Plot's map), Upper and Lower Oulton (1834 OS map) (SPNO p174) (SSE 1996 p16). The name means 'old tun or farmstead' (SPNO p174) (SSE 1996 p16). Mrs Estwick of one of the Oultons, is believed to have lived to the age of 120. She died in c1678 before Dr Plot could meet her (NHS p321).

Oulton Oulton Farm is nearly 1m WNW of Rushton Spencer church. Formerly in Rushton Spencer township in Leek ancient parish. The name appears in 1651 to describe a close. But there may have been settlement here in medieval times for the name derives probably from 'ald tun' meaning old farmstead (VCH vol 7 p223). From 1723 rent from the fields, Great and Little Oulton, helped endow the Ash almshouses in Leek (W p725) (VCH vol 7 p166).

Oulton Abbey Oulton, Stone. Formerly Oulton House. Built by Thomas Dent, solicitor, in c1720 (SDOPP p66p in 1906, p67) or by William Dent who bought a farm on the site in 1756 and rebuilt it (SOK pp35,73il). The house was given a new front by the Stone brewer John Joule in 1822. In 1835 it was bought by the Duke of Sutherland, who lived here for three years whilst alterations were being made to Trentham Hall. In 1838 it became a private lunatic asylum run by Mrs Sarah Bakewell, and was then known as Oulton Retreat (A History of Psychiatry in North Staffordshire. Dr Edward D Myers. 1997). In 1853 it was sold to a group of Benedictine nuns. During their occupancy the house became known as St Mary's Abbey, the dedication being to St Mary. An alternative name since has been Oulton Abbey (SOK p74) (SDOPP pp66,67). By the late 1960s the nuns had a children's nursery at Oulton Abbey; later they were running a home for the elderly and the nursery at the abbey. In their library is St Alban Roe's missal, 1605 (SOK p66).

Oulton Cross Tiny district 0.5m SW of Oulton. Formerly in Kibblestone quarter in Stone ancient parish. Marked on OS map 1:50,000, but not on 1:25,000. There was a plague cross and a large sandstone trough for the washing of coins to prevent infection for cattle dealers from Stone's neighbouring villages at Oulton Cross (MOSP pp23-24).

Oulton Grange 0.25m WNW of Oulton, Stone. Built by 1889 (1889 OS map 6 inch) (SVB p134). Residence of William Adams (1868-1952) master potter, before he moved to Oulton Cross (ES March 19 1994 p15). It had a lavatory suite with printed decoration painted over the glaze made by Johnson Brothers, 1895, installed in the billiard room. DP Shelley donated it to the Gladstone Pottery museum.

Oulton Heath District and former common land 0.25m NW of Oulton, Stone. The area may have been occupied by Kibblestone Park in medieval times (SOK p15). The heath was enclosed in 1770 (SOK p75). 578 acres of Oulton Heath were enclosed under an Act of 1779 (SHC 1941 p17). Stone Golf Club had a course on the heath between by at least 1896 to 1916 (SOK p75).

Oulton House House 0.5m SW of Garshall Green, 0.75m NNW of Milwich. In Milwich ancient parish.

Oulton House NNW of Oulton Abbey, Oulton, Stone. Built in c1841 and purchased by JW Bishop in 1891. It stands about 300 feet above sea level and has fine views of the Wrekin and the Church Stretton Hills (STC p36p). Another account has the house built in the later C19 by a master potter, wanting to retreat from the smoky Potteries (SVB p134).

Oulton Old Hall NNW of Oulton Abbey, Oulton, Stone. Built in 1613 from local sandstone (SVB p134), perhaps with stone from the demolished Kibblestone Manor House (SOK p18). It has two storeys. Seat of the Gamuls to 1670 and the Shorts (Plot's map) to 1699 when bought by the Beech family. The Beeches were Roman Catholics and there was probably a Roman Catholic chapel of theirs at the hall in the C18. The present third storey was added sometime between 1774 and 1782. The Old Hall seems to have been owned by the Shelley family from 1782 and was a school from this time until 1858 when it was bought by Thomas Andrew Potter (1824-1880), first editor of ES, as a private residence. In 1896 Francis Elliot Kitchener (d1916) became the owner, headmaster of Newcastle High School and brother of Lord Kitchener of Khartoum. Subsequent owners have included two Pottery families; the Senhouse family who were connected with Mintons, and the Woods of Burslem (POTP p172) (SOK pp19,28il,65,72) (ES April 15 1998 p13p).

Oulton Rocks NE of Oulton, Stone. House built in the later C19 by a master potter, wanting to retreat from the smoky Potteries (SVB p134). Residence of Capt Victor Goss (b1865), son of William Henry Goss, pottery manufacturer, from the late C19 to his death from a fall from a horse in March 1913; the horse is believed to have trodden on a wasps nest which it knocked from a hedge (William Henry Goss. Lynda and Nicholas Pine. 1987 pp112,113p). Has also appeared as Oultonrocks.

Ounsdale Area above Wom Brook 0.75m W of Wombourne. In Wombourne parish. There was a house at or near Ounsdale in the hollow on the Sedgley-Bridgnorth road by the mid C17 (VCH vol 20 p199). Ounsdale was described as a small village in the mid C19 (W p210). From the 1950s it was an industrial area (VCH vol 20 p199).

Ousal Brook and Dale. Lies to the N of, and runs into Dimmings Dale, S of Oakamoor. (NSFCT 1922 p34).

Ousley Brook Runs near Stanton in the Moorlands. Is a tributary of Rangemoor Brook which in turn is a tributary of the Dove. The name is from perhaps wase 'a muddy place, a marsh' and leah (SPNO p15).

Ousley Cross Minute hamlet in a small valley at the confluence of Rangemoor and Ordley Brook 1m S of Stanton (ESNF p111p). The name is from a wayside cross shrine of which only the base remains. It was erected by the monks of Calwich on the road between Calwich and Ilam or else it marked the site of some now forgotten skirmish, which tradition says was fought between Lord Ouseley and Lord Audley, which, Nicholls says, took place in the Wars of the Roses (NSSG p18). The nearby names of Audley Bank and Harlow (N of Calwich) support the latter tradition (LGS p135) (KES p186) (NSFCT 1918 p117) (STM July 1965 p41) (APB p41). Ousley Cross has several references

coupled with the Langford family, who may have been related to the Longfords who had links with Calwich Abbey. Perhaps the cross was brought from Calwich Abbey by a Longford or Langford. The farmhouse here has the date 1424 cut into the stone lintel of the front door and is probably an import, too. Eleanor Langford committed suicide at her house at Ousley Cross in Sept 1642 (NSJFS 1972 p127).

Ousley Wood To W of Ousley Cross, Stanton.

Outlands Tiny hamlet on a high bluff above a narrow stretch of the upper Sow valley, 2m S of Fairoak. In Adbaston parish. Has also appeared Outwoods (W p382). William Wakeley, born Shifnal in 1590 came to live in Outlands and here he died in 1714 aged 125. A memorial to him hangs over the door in Adbaston church, and a stone was by his grave near the ancient preaching cross in the churchyard. This was moved when the churchyard was being cleared and levelled in 1947; it now (1975) stands by the S side of the church tower (AADB p58). Adbaston PR reveals another old man of Outlands, Richard Amies, who was buried on Nov 19 1781 aged 101 (AADB p58). Here is Buckingham's Cave (see). For other caves near Outlands see EOP p51p and MR pp18,19,20p,21.

Outlanes Fragmented minute hamlet on ground rising out of the Trent 0.5m W of Oulton (W p371). Formerly in Kibblestone quarter in Stone ancient parish. Also a footpath from Meaford Old Hall across the meadows to Oulton (NSFCT 1917 p143).

Outwoods Former tiny hamlet in the C19 on the W side of an expansive stretch of the Trent valley on slopes leading up to the Needwood Forest plateau, 1.5m W of Burton. Formerly in Burton ancient parish. Became a separate civil parish in 1866 (GLAUE p419). Former common land which has appeared as Outewoode (1499), Outwoode, and reputedly Abbot's Outwood. The ownership of the common, which may have originally included Rough Hay and Henhurst Wood and extended into Anslow township in Rolleston ancient parish, was disputed in 1598 when Sir William Paget brought an action in the Exchequer Court against the tenants of Rolleston who claimed common rights here. Paget claimed it was called Horninglow Outlands and lay in Burton manor and therefore belonged to him. Outwoods was enclosed in 1771 (ANS pp23,59-61,104). Outwoods is now a large suburb of Burton upon Trent.

Outwoods Hamlet nestles underneath a steep escarpment by Back Brook 0.75m NW of Moreton. Formerly in Moreton quarter in Gnosall ancient parish (VCH vol 4 p111). Has appeared as the Outhwoods (1674), and Outwoods Common (1797). The name means 'wood on the outskirts' (SPNO p161).

Over Bradnop Name used to refer to Upper Bradnop (maps of Plot and Yates). But the 1834 OS map uses the name 'Over Bradnop' to refer to present Bradnop (alias Nether or Lower Bradnop).

Over End Former area or liberty in Handsworth ancient parish (HANDR pviii).

Overend Name in the C15 for the area about the S of the High Street, Kinver about the church. This area was known as Kinver Hill in the C17. In the C17 Kinver Hill was a township of Kinver parish. In this area may have been an early settlement by the church (VCH vol 20 pp121,149).

Overend Hamlet in West Bromwich ancient parish at SE end of the High Street (OWB p112). It was formerly a strip of waste land near to where the Central Police Station now stands. The land was enclosed in c1690 (SOWB p25). There was settlement here by the 1780s (VCH vol 17 p4).

Over Furnace One of William Paget's forges on Cannock Chase, another was Over Forge. They were leased to the Chetwynds in 1614 (VCH vol 2 p111).

Overhang Rock feature on the Roaches, Upper Hulme (VB p209).

Over House Finchpath Hill (Hill Top), West Bromwich. It came into the Jesson family in the mid C15 and remained with them until at least the end of the C18 (VCH vol 17 p26).

Overhouse House Burslem. Has the Overhouse Manufactory attached? By the early C17 the Overhouse estate belonged to the Burslem family. In the C17 the estate fragmented and later in the century the Colcloughs were living at the Overhouse, just N of the market place (SHJ winter 1987 p26). The house was rebuilt as a small double-fronted structure of brick in the late C18 or the early C19 on 'the site of the old timber-built manor house' (Life of Wedgwood. Eliza Meteyard. vol 1 p181 note 1 fig 49). It was occupied by the Twigg family in the mid C19 and was still a private residence in 1924. It was offices in 1960 (VCH vol 8 p120).

Overhouses Farm 0.5m SE of Heaton. Formerly in Heaton township in Leek ancient parish. Dated 1853 and stands W of a house of the same name in existence by 1656 (VCH vol 7 p187).

Overley Minute hamlet of about two properties 0.5m NW of Alrewas. Formerly in Orgreave township in Alrewas ancient parish.

Over Low Burial mound 0.75m WNW of Stanton at SK 11464624, 38 paces in diameter and six feet high. Carrington excavated it in 1848 finding two crouched skeletons (TYD p127) (VCH vol 1. no 12) (NSJFS 1965 p47). It is a listed monument. The name means perhaps, the upper burial mound.

Overmoor Tiny hamlet 1.5m E of Werrington. The Blithe rises to SSW of it.

Over Sale Bagot's Bromley. Formerly a hamlet and an estate in Marchington Woodlands township in Hanbury parish (W p561). Has also appeared as Oversale, The Sale, and Lower Sale House.

Overton Former manor and liberty in Biddulph ancient parish, stretching north of Biddulph to the Cheshire border (LCAST 1898 p64) (BALH p26). The manor was created in 1189 with the division of the original extensive Biddulph (see) manor and was held by the de Overtons to 1365 when it passed to the de Biddulphs of Biddulph Old Hall (BALH p25). Has also appeared as Over Biddulph (W p386) and Upper Biddulph (NSFCT 1888 p70). The name is preserved in Higher Overton and Overton Hall 1.5m NNE of the church at Biddulph.

Overton Minute hamlet on the slopes of a promontory on E side of Broadgatehall Brook 1.5m SW of Croxden. In Checkley parish. Near Overton was found a damaged circular lead case of uncertain date (HOU p63). It has been destroyed (NSJFS 1964 p19).

Overton Hall Overton, Biddulph. At SJ 897606. May have been tenanted by two brothers in the early part of the C19 who terrorised the local area (DPEM p32). In the cellar is a bricked up archway and there is a legend that a tunnel ran from here to Biddulph Old Hall (DPEM p32).

Overton Manor Overton, Biddulph. House reduced to the status of a farmhouse by 1917, but dating from Elizabethan times (NSFCT 1917 p144).

Overton Manor House In the Overton area of Hammerwich, at SK 064076. Formerly Overton Manor farm. Brick and dates from the mid C18, but it has an earlier cellar (VCH vol 14 pp259,264).

Overwoods House on Hockley-Wood End road, at SP 234999. Formerly in Wilnecote township in Tamworth ancient parish. In existence in 1884 (1884 OS map 6 inch).

Owen Park Richard Street, Darlaston, Offlow hundred. Has appeared as the Owen Memorial Garden and Owen Recreation Ground and was originally laid out to the memory of Alfred Ernest Owen, co-founder of the firm Rubery Owen (1893), and a local councillor (Staffs County Handbook c1958) (SNDB p76).

Owen's Bank Tiny district 0.75m SSW of Tutbury.

Owletts Hall Owlett Hall Farm is 1.25m NE of Stonnall. In 1955 a Neolithic or Bronze Age axe was found at Owlett Hall which went to Birmingham Museum (BAST vol 73 p117) (Proceedings of the Prehistoric Society vol 25 p141) (NSJFS 1964 p33). The hall is of the late C17 or early C18 origin. Has also appeared as Birchley Farm, Owl's Hall, and Owlet Hall (1887 OS map 6 inch). It was the childhood home of librarian and writer of Staffs ghost stories, Rosalind Prince. Here her mother saw the ghost of an old woman in a long dress in the hall and persistently heard sounds like a hand trying to feel its way along the wall of the landing. In the early 1950s here was tested the Lucas Freelight system, a wind powered electricity supply (MGH pp62-64).

Oxbarn To E of Merry Hill S of Bradmore. In Penn ancient parish. Ox Barn Farm fronted the lands now occupied by Warstones schools. It was sold with the Burne estate in 1878. Ox Barn estate was developed with housing between 1920 and 1955 (PONP pp40,43).

Oxbury A small area of Lichfield N of Borrowcop Hill by the town ditch (HOL p513) (VCH vol 14 p7). The Old English 'burh' element may refer to an Anglo-Saxon fortification on Borrowcop Hill (VCH vol 14 p7).

Oxenholm Pole Name of field on the banks of the Trent about Handsacre and Mavesyn Ridware (SHOS vol 1 p179).

Oxensitch House over 0.5m N of Flash. Formerly in Quarnford township in Alstonefield ancient parish. There was a tollgate here between 1829 and 1839 (VCH vol 7 p51).

Oxford Housing estate 0.75m SE of Newchapel (Stoke-on-Trent A-Z) built on the site of the old hamlet of Wedgwood. Formerly in Wolstanton ancient parish. Oxford, as a place, is mentioned in 1853 (ONST 1934 p48). There was at this time or later a colliery called Oxford (ONST 1975 p365).

Oxhay There was settlement at Oxhay, Biddulph, by 1500. Formerly in Middle Biddulph liberty in Biddulph ancient parish (BALH). The name is preserved in Ox-Hey Crescent and Drive on the E side of the Congleton Road.

Oxhay Farm nearly 0.5m W of Meerbrook. Has date stones of 1754 and 1765. The farm has a large storage area, possibly for fodder, possibly for the nearby former packhorse way (VCH vol 7 p193).

Ox Hay Burton upon Trent. Between Burton Abbey and Horseholme island. Has also appeared as The Hay.

Oxhay Farm Bradnop. Was called the Red Lion Inn in 1745 when the Young Pretender's army passed through in the Jacobite Rebellion. Here two of the Jacobites quarrelled and one slew the other. A Jacobite was buried behind the farm and ever since a black dog ghost or boggart has been sighted here (FLJ 1942 p126) (DPEM p110). Oxhay Farm may be identified with Lane End Farm which was the Red Lion Inn in 1818. Ox Hay Wood lies to the farm's SW on the 1834 OS map.

Oxhill Area 1m W of Handsworth. There was settlement here by the end of the C13. Oxhill House was built by 1794 and was still standing in 1862 (MNB pp38,41,45,47). It was situated not far from where the RC St Augustine's church now (1984) stands and was approached from the lodge in Rookery Road. The house stood empty for a while and was eventually demolished in c1900 or even before (HPPE p91).

Oxleasows House 1m NNW of Chebsey.

Ox Leasowes Bridge Crosses the Birmingham Canal at Swan Village, Coseley.

Oxley Former manor and hamlet on ground rising up from the Penk at some distance from the Penk, now a suburb of Wolverhampton 1m WSW of Bushbury. Formerly in Bushbury ancient parish. Appears in DB as Oxelie. The name means 'ox lea' (DUIGNAN) (SPN p144). Created a separate ecclesiastical parish in 1953 (GLAUE p419). The church, The Epiphany, Lyme Road, was built in 1960 (LDD). Oxley was a ward of Wolverhampton borough by 1982. Goodyear Tyre and Rubber Company opened their present factory on the E side of the Stafford Road in 1927 (BUOP pp8,96). Ashley Milner (b1881) of Oxley was a very productive short story writer for periodicals and newspapers (VFC p94).

Oxley Farm Former estate at Oxley. Passed into the Leveson family in 1534. Remaining with the Levesons in the C17: William Fowler, probably a member of the Fowler family of Pendeford, made a map of the estate in 1649 (SSAHST 1979-80 pp15-24il).

Oxley House Oxley. Large neo-classical villa built probably in the 1820s for John Henry Sparrow of the local iron-making family (BUOP p45p). In 1851 it was the seat of Alexander Hordern (W p22). At some time it was the seat of John Shaw, a Wolverhampton industrialist, founder of Tettenhall College. By 1860 it was the seat of Richard Shelton, a timber merchant. The house then sank slowly into dereliction. In 1983, after a devastating fire, it was rebuilt and converted into flats (BUOP p45).

Oxley Manor Stood on what is now Oxley Park golf course, Bushbury. At Oxley Manor a bed of boulder clay yielded five species of shells. Rev W Lister, a vicar of Bushbury, thought the shells may have been brought to Oxley from the Arctic by glacial action in the Ice Age (WJO Nov 1909 p295). The last house to occupy the site of the medieval manor-house was built in 1854 for the Wolverhampton banker, Alexander Hordern. With his death in 1870 the estate passed to his late wife's brother, Henry Hill, another banker. His son Alexander Staveley-Hill MP and JP took an active part in parliamentary affairs and local government (BUOP p42p). It was he who erected the memorial stone at Wulfruna's Well (TB July 1988 p6p). In 1880 with his second wife, he donated the combined Anglican chapel and schoolroom in Bushbury Lane (known as the 'Concrete Chapel'). With his death in 1905 the estate passed to his son, Henry, an MP and JP. He served in WW1 as Lieut Col of the Staffordshire Yeomanry. In 1920 the family left Bushbury and the house was demolished in 1929 (BUOP p42). The house was at some time the seat of Rt Hon William Huskisson (BS p242).

Oxley Moor S part of Oxley suburb, Bushbury.

Oxneford Appears to have been an ancient estate in the foreign of Wolverhampton, centred on the house that became Chapel Ash Farm (HOWM p44), presumably at Chapel Ash. There seems to have been a small settlement at Oxneford in the Middle Ages (HOWM p6). The name, occurring in the C14 (DUIGNAN p113), has also appeared as Oxeneforde.

Oxonbury Field near Greenhill, Lichfield (NSFCT 1922 p69).

P

Packington Hamlet on a slight incline above Brook Leasow 3.5m ESE of Lichfield, 1.25m NW of Hopwas. Former township with Swinfen in Weeford ancient parish. Became a separate civil parish with Swinfen in 1866 (GLAUE p425). Has appeared as Pagintone, a manor held by the bishop of Chester (Lichfield) in DB, Padintone (SHOS vol 1 p233), Pakenstone and Pakinton (SPN p124). The name means 'Paga's town' (DUIGNAN), or 'farmstead of Paga's people' (SPN p124), or 'tun of Pac(c)a's people' (SSE 1996 p16). A medieval village is recorded at SK 164063 to the NW of Packington hall. It was deserted probably between 1379 and 1524 (SSAHST 1966 p49. 1970 p35) (IHB p395). Yet according to Palliser's map Packington is placed 0.5m WSW of Hopwas (SL p84 see map). Near Packington Mr Walter Ashmore of Tamworth first observed the fuss ball fungi - Fungus Pulverulentus, Cute Membranacca, Substantia Intus Spongiosa, Pediculo brevi Crassiori, in Oras fere ducto - has a texture resembling a sponge. Ashmore went on to observe the same at Alrewas Hayes (NHS p200 tab 14 fig 3).

Packington Hall Packington Hall Farm is 1.25m NW of Hopwas. In Weeford parish. The hall standing in 1907 was in the Gothic revival style, a la Strawberry Hill. It was built in c1810 and replaced a former house about which very little is known, only that it may have stood in the park not far from that hall. The later hall appears to have been the property of the Levetts; it was occupied by Rev Thomas Levett in 1834; Robert Thomas Kennedy Levett is recorded as residing at the hall in 1868, 1876, 1892 and 1904; it was the seat of George Arthur Monro Levett in 1924. The hall appears to have also been tenanted for periods; William Kendall was in occupation in 1851; Walter Fisher was living at the hall by 1884 to at least 1888 (W 1834). In c1910 it was owned by Rev T Levett but occupied by Brigadier-General Hugh James Archdale CB (b1854). It was unoccupied in 1932 and in 1940 (trade directories) (SHBP p193). By 1978 the hall was being used as a factory (SGS p177). In the later C17 Plot noted extraordinary cherries grown here, planted in the quincunx order (NHS p227). Ice-House Plantation to ENE of Packington Hall Farm at SK 164064 suggests the hall had an ice-house (IHB p395).

Packington Moor House 1.25m NNE of Weeford. It perhaps preserves the name of common land of Packington township.

Packmoor Large modern hamlet on a high narrow escarpment above a head brook of the Fowlea 0.25m E of Newchapel. Formerly in Wolstanton ancient parish. John Harold Rhodes (1891-1917), miner, was born in Mellor Street. On Oct 9 1917 in WW1 he stormed an enemy pill box and captured nine prisoners single handed for which he received the VC and Croix de Guerre. He was wounded in action on Nov 27 1917 and subsequently died. A memorial plaque was erected to his memory at the Chatterley Whitfield Coal Mining Museum at Whitfield Colliery (see) on April 20 1984 (ES Feb 7 1983) (POTP p177). The wooden folly resembling a summerhouse in the garden of Elm House, Mellor Street, was made by the owner of the house, Philip Hardaker, an artist, in 1991.

Pack Saddle Hollow Just N of Rudyard Manor marked on Yates' map. 2m from Leek on Macclesfield Road (ESH p17). Here some highway robberies occurred in 1835 (OL vol 1 p329).

Padbury There was evidently a settlement in the Padbury Lane area (0.75m N of Burntwood) by 1298. Padbury Way was mentioned in the early C16 (VCH vol 14 p199).

Paddock Area of Walsall to ENE of St Matthew's church and S of Holtshill Lane. Occurs as a separate common field in the C16 (VCH vol 17 pp148 see map, p of c1974 facing 161,180). Became a ward of Walsall county borough in 1889 (VCH vol 17 p217).

Paddock, The Former tiny area of Coseley, S of Coseley church (CWBT p44p). The Paddock is mentioned in 1832 (HC p63). The name is still preserved in a street of this name.

Paddock Farm 0.75m S of Ipstones. An old tree in front of the farm house was curiously growing out of a circular stone base in the 1990s.

Paddock House Farm House dated 1828, 2m NW of Alstonefield on W side of Archford Moor. There may have been a house on this site by 1775 (VCH vol 7 p11).

Padwells Place on the route of the beating of bounds around Lichfield (SHOS vol 1). Is somewhere in the vicinity of Pipehill.

Padwick Padwick Farm is 1m SSE of Leek on A523. Has been described as waste between Ipstones and Cheddleton (SHC 1910 p439). There has been a house at Padwick since Norman times. When it was first built it was the only place between Leek and Ipstones (TOI p41). Has appeared as Parnwic (c1240-50) (SHC 1910 p439) and Paddock (Pigot and Son map 1830). Seat of the Turner family from Norman times to c1830 (TOI p41); and possibly can be identified with The Paddock, seat of the Turner family (NSFCT 1870 p37) (OL vol 1 p212); there is a Paddock Farm S of Ipstones.

Pagets Bromley Abbots Bromley became Pagets Bromley when Sir William Paget was granted the manor in 1544 (VCH vol 3 p297 note) or in 1546. It was written Pagets Bromley in 1584 (SSE 1996 p20). In time (c1730) Abbots Bromley became prevalent again. However, Yates' map marks both Abbots and Pagets Bromley, which is placed to the W of Abbots Bromley, at approximately Yeatsall.

Painleyhill Farm and hill 1.5m SSE of Church Leigh. Formerly in Leigh township and ancient parish. The hill may be the ridge which runs S from Painleyhill Farm and stands on the E side of the Blithe. The medieval chapel at Field, certified in 1548, but not mentioned in 1563 or after (SHC 1915 p150), is thought to have been at Painleyhill. It is thought to have stood on a site which was, by the mid C20, occupied by a house; a large key found at Painleyhill was kept formerly at Leigh Rectory (OSST 1949-50 p14).

Painter's Rock Rock feature at SK 061429, Oakamoor.

Pale Flatts Farm 0.75m N of Stramshall.

Palfrey Former hamlet centred on Milton Street near the confluence of Fullbrook and the Tame, now a suburb 1m SW of Walsall. In Walsall ancient parish. Palfrey Green occurs in 1386 (VCH vol 17 p157). The name is from Middle English (from Old French) and means a riding horse, generally a lady's. But Duignan and Poulton-Smith prefer, from a fine as in 'the king's palfrey' (DUIGNAN) (SPN p135). It may be from Old English 'pall' 'still or firm' of the ground perhaps, or even of the character of a person (BCTV p72). The church, St Mary and All Saints, in Sun Street, was built in 1893 (VCH vol 17 p237). The ecclesiastical parish of Walsall Palfrey was created from Caldmore ecclesiastical parish in 1902 (GLAUE p427). Palfrey became a ward of Walsall county borough in 1931 (VCH vol 17 p217).

Palfrey Green Lay at the southern end of what is now Lord Street, Palfrey, Walsall. Palfrey Green occurs in 1386. There was evidently iron-working near Palfrey Green in the later Middle Ages (VCH vol 17 pp157,192). Duignan remembered seeing a fragment of the green. By 1902 'Green' had been dropped. Poulton-Smith thinks it was at the green that the monies were collected which gave the place its name Palfrey (SPN p135).

Palfrey Park S of Dale Street, Palfrey. Opened in 1886. Extended in c1935 (VCH vol 17 p157).

Palin's Farm Near Knighton Hall, Knighton, Adbaston. Brick and half-timbered farmhouse probably of C17 origin. It has been considered the oldest farmhouse in Adbaston parish. The owner in 1841 was Sarah Palin, since when it has been known as Palin's Farm (AADB p32). It may once have been the original manor house. It was for sale in April 1998 (SLM April 1998 p9pc).

Palmer's Almshouses Stafford. Prior to 1638 Rev Robert Palmer rector of St Mary's, Stafford, left a cottage or cottages situated in St Martin's Lane (Martin Street) then inhabited by elderly poor to be continually used as a home for the poor. After c1800 the almshouses moved to the top of Broad Street at Broad Eye (OSST 1934 pp22-23). (VCH vol 6 pp265-266).

Palmer's Cross Suburb of Tettenhall 2m SE of Codsall. In Tettenhall ancient parish. It was in Pendeford prebend of Tettenhall Collegiate Church (SHOS vol 2 p198). Shaw noted it was represented by a single large farmhouse of no great age. The word 'Palmer' suggests a pilgrim (SHOS vol 2 p202). The name referred to a farm in Codsall Road opposite the end of Windermere Road which existed by the mid C18 (VCH vol 20 p12).

Panniers Pool Weir or winding in the Dane at Three Shire Heads (SMCC p3). The name is first recorded in 1533, when possibly there was no bridge and packhorses with their panniers had to ford the small rock pool (PRT p78). At Three Shire Heads (see) Staffs, Ches, Derbys met.

Paper Mill End Former hamlet 0.5m N of Perry Bridge. Formerly in Perry Barr township in Handsworth ancient parish. The name, from a paper mill at Grindleford on Holbrook in the C19, is preserved in the road called Paper Mill End (W p702) (MNB p70).

Paper Mill Farm S of Winkhill, Onecote.

Paradise A weir and stretch of wooded valley through which the Manifold runs at Ilam (TD p) (MOS p20p) (KES p114) (SGS p110). Its scenery so impressed Dr Johnson of Lichfield (see) he used it in his novel 'Rasselas' (VB p202). 'Paradise Walk' is just below Ilam Hall, a cross called the 'Battle Stone' is in it (SMOPP vol 2 p115p) (HLSP p171). A little wooden footbridge over the Manifold here was hit by a tree in a gale in 1962 (DMV p85p).

Paradise District on the old Stafford road in Coven parish, but formerly in Brewood ancient parish. In the early C19 Pitt described Paradise as a small village or hamlet (THS p255). It was in the area of the Manor House at SJ 923060, 0.5m E of Cross Green under 0.5m SSE of Slade Heath (grave of Thomas Bickford in Shareshill churchyard, but not appear on current OS maps) (The Observer Magazine March 30 1997 p25).

Paradise House 0.5m SSE of Alton, in Nabb Lane. In existence by 1841 (1834 OS map) (HAF p197).

Paradise A small area and name of cottage to W of Hollington.

Paradise Wood A copse. Remaining part of the lost Bishop's Wood. SE of the village of Bishop's Wood (SVB p34).

Parchfield House and field name NE of Rugeley railway station. Mentioned from the C14, if not before (CWF p81).

Parchment Hall Alias Spring Hill House, Jesson Road, Walsall, when it was occupied by the Jesson family, the head of the family was a lawyer who used much parchment in his profession (SNWA p78).

Parchments House and Gardens. On N side of Stowe Pool, Lichfield. Here Michael Johnson had a small parchment manufactory, near by is Johnson's Willow commemorating his son Samuel (HOL p510) (SSAHST 1970 p51).

Pardoe's Cottage Former C18-style 'artisan's' cottage in Pardoe's Lane (now Victoria Road), Darlaston (Offlow hundred) (BCM July 1985 p52). Pardoe is an Old English word 'parlur' meaning a small piece of enclosed ground, possibly a croft (BCM July 1985 p33).

Park Ward of Hanley from 1895 (VCH vol 8 p158).

Park Ward of Tipton borough embracing the Victoria Park area.

Park Ward of Wolverhampton borough by 1982, covering Compton, and part of Finchfield.

Park Brook The brook which runs into The Black Brook at Thickbroom? (SHOS vol 2 p47). The brook that does join the Black Brook at Thickbroom is called Littlehay Brook.

Park Brook Former name for the upper reach of the Trent as it flowed through Knypersley Park (NSFCT 1991 p47 note).

Park Brook Runs from Keele to join the Trent (HOTC p1).

Park Dale To W of West Park, Wolverhampton. Formerly in Wolverhampton chapelry and ancient parish.

Park End Minute hamlet near a head brook of the Weaver 1.75m ENE of Balterley, 1m NW of Audley. Former township in Audley ancient parish (W p428) (NSJFS 1971 p66). Here was possibly a medieval village, probably deserted between 1334 and 1524 (SSAHST 1970 p35).

Parkes' Hall Stood where Parkes' Hall Reservoir lies, S of Tipton Road, Woodsetton. In Sedgley ancient parish. The hall demolished in the early C19 was built in the C18 but incorporated some medieval work (HC p78). It was once the seat of the Persehouse family, and hence has often been referred to

as Persehouse Hall (SR p121) (TB April 1983 p15). The Persehouses have resided in the Woodsetton area since at least 1439 (HC p78). The hall was still standing in 1835 (SDSSOP p34il of in 1835) (SDOP p42) (BCM spring 1999 p42il) (SNSV vol 2 p97). By 1901 there was a small hamlet known as Parkes' Hall in the vicinity of the site of the hall (OS map Sheet 67.07). The name may be from the Parkes family of Willingsworth Hall who acquired Sedgley (see) manor in 1600.

Parkes' Hall Pool Reservoir Tiny reservoir on the N side of Parkes' Hall Road, Upper Gornal. Conceived in 1835 and built shortly after. At one point was the only remaining works left of the Dudley Water Works Company. Owned in 1999 by Dudley MBC (BCM spring 1999 pp64-65). The Tipton Slasher's first fight was fought near Park's Hall Pool. It was fought between 'Skim Skinny' of Gornal and lasted two days. The 'Slasher' won the stake which was a donkey and a bag of sand (AMS p455).

Park Farm 0.5m NW of Fradswell.

Park Farm Ancient site for a house at Oldcott, Tunstall, 0.5m SW of Newchapel (VCH vol 8 p82 map at SJ 858538). Does not appear on current OS maps. Known as Black Park in the early C16. The house that existed in 1960 was probably built in 1840 by Smith Child. The porch, which incorporated brick ornament similar to that at St John's Goldenhill, carried a date tablet with Smith Child's initials (VCH vol 8 p92). The name probably preserves Audley Park, for Newchapel lay in the Audley manor of Thursfield. Morden's map shows a park here (NSFCT 1910 p173).

Park Farm Stood on the N side of Rocky Lane, near Lymedene Road, facing the path that leads into Perry Hall Park, Hamstead. In existence by 1794 (MNB p62).

Park Farm 0.75m ENE of Sandwell. The 'Park' is a survival of Hamstall Hall Park which had been disparked by 1798 (VCH vol 2 p24).

Park Farm Stood a short distance to the S of The Moat Site (see), Walsall. Also known as Craddock's Farm, Charles Craddock having lived here for over 50 years (SNWA p78). The name is from the medieval Walsall Park (see).

Parkfields Former hamlet at a little distance from the Trent in Barlaston ancient parish (W p411), now the W part of Barlaston village. Parkfields Farm is 1m WSW of Barlaston old church. Near Parkfields was found a Neolithic or Bronze Age stone implement (NSFCT vol 41 p147) (NSJFS 1964 p15) or celt (NSSG p6). (VCH vol 1 p181; mentioned under Trentham and in Masefield's collection) (NSFCT vol 43 p194 in the Potteries Museum, formerly in Masefield's collection). The hamlet developed in the C17 or C18, and a road to the N running between Barlaston and Tittensor via Madam's Bridge appears to have been re-routed S through Parkfields and Heyfields (its present route) about this time (BAH p15). Sarah, wife of Josiah Wedgwood I, resided at Parkfields Cottage from 1805 until her death in 1815 (HOE p48) (BAH p30). Miss Ann Aston was of Parkfields, Barlaston (Nov 1834). She disapproved of two young ladies paying attention to her bachelor brother, and had the bridge - Madam's Bridge - they were crossing to see him, destroyed (STM May 1964 p33). John Carey pottery manufacturer between c1803-1843 died at Parkfields. He had the Rectory House in Longton built which was attacked in the Chartist riots (1842) (POTP p57).

Parkfield Suburb 1.75m SSE of Wolverhampton. In Sedgley ancient parish. Near the Birmingham New Road at Parkfield at cSO 921963 was found a flanged axe in Oct 1969 (SSAHST 1971 pp47il,48). The area, so called by 1851, was made up with small mines and unplanned miners cottages prior to the mid C20 when it was developed with housing (1851 census) (WOLOP p19p). There has been a Parkfield Ironworks (W p95), and Parkfield Furnace (BCM Oct 1990 p62). Parkfield took its name from Parkfield House on Dudley Road (Wolverhampton Chronicle Nov 12 1999 p15). The name for the house may originally have come from Sedgley Park (see), an old deer park.

Parkfields House to E of Hales Hall, over 1m ENE of Cheadle. Ten metres W of the house is a mid C19 gazebo (DoE II).

Parkfields Tiny hamlet over 0.25m ENE of High Offley.

Park Fields House 1.25m WNW of Uttoxeter.

Parkgate House 1m WSW of Newborough. In Abbots Bromley parish.

Parkgate Minute hamlet on hilly ground near the head of several small streams, 0.5m S of Wootton.

Park Hall Very ancient and long lost timber-framed hall 0.5m NNW of Brookhouses, Cheadle. In the Middle Ages it was a seat of the Bassetts, a branch of the Bassetts of Sapcote, and anciently of Drayton Bassett. John Bassett of Park Hall inherited Blore manor by his wife Joan Brailsford and his son Sir John Bassett (1345-1411) was of Blore Hall (see) (NSFCT 1906 p165. 1913 p145. 1982 pp14,19) (Swinscoe, Blore, and the Bassett. David & Martine Swinscoe. 1998). In the C17 Park Hall was owned by the Banks family, lords of Cheadle, and occupied by a family called Bamford until c1686 (CCT pp25-26,32). In c1881 Plant noted the moat and portions of the foundation remained (HOC p11). For the stained glass from here see NSFCT 1922 pp78,84-90 ps. To the S is Parkhall Farm.

Park Hall House 0.5m NNE of Church Leigh. There was a house on the site in medieval times; the present house is moated and access is over a bridge. A fireplace and panelling in the present hall confirm that it was built in the 1690s (AUOPP p75p). Has been the seat of the Leighs, Astons, Whitehalls of Sharpcliffe, Ashenhursts (by at least the earlier C18), and Browns (NSFCT 1922 pp149-150) (mems in Church Leigh church). For a rhyme about Park Hall see Checkley.

Park Hall In High Offley parish (W p391). Park Hall Farm is 0.75m ENE of High Offley.

Park Hall House over 1m ENE of Longton. In Weston Coyney manor in Caverswall ancient parish (W p752) (HOC p242). Seat of the Parkers from at least the later C17 to at least the mid C19. George Parker (d1663) purchased Parkhall from the Coyneys of Weston, and rebuilt the hall here. His younger son Thomas Parker married Anne, daughter of Robert Venables of Antrobus, Ches. Their younger son **Rt Hon Sir Thomas Parker**, said to have been born at Leek (see) on July 23 1666/7 and baptised there on Aug 8 1667. He was created Baron Parker of Macclesfield in 1716 and created 1st Earl of Macclesfield in 1721. He was Lord Chancellor of Great Britain (1718-1724/5), and was impeached in 1725 for corruption, found guilty and fined £30,000. His reputation was then very low, and a saying about Staffordshire concerning him then prevailed throughout the country:- 'Staffordshire had produced the three greatest rouges ever known in England - Jack Sheppard, Jonathan Wild (of Wolverhampton) and Tom Parker' (OL vol 1 p166). He died of strangury in Soho Square, London on April 28 1723 (DNB) (HS p284) (SSC pp101-104) (LGS p161) (TFTP p124) (VCH vol 7 pp89,91). George (d1663) was succeeded by his son William Parker (d1663), who was succeeded by his son George Parker (d1716). He was the father of Elizabeth (b1698), who married Swynfen Jervis (1700-1771) of Meaford Hall (see). George (d1716) was succeeded by his son William Parker, who died in 1723 without issue. He was succeeded at Park Hall by his brother **Sir Thomas Parker Knt** (d1784), Lord Chief Baron of Exchequer. By Sir Thomas' second wife, Martha, he had a daughter Martha, who married John Jervis, 1st Earl St Vincent, of Meaford Hall (see). Sir Thomas (d1784) was succeeded by his son Thomas (d1797), sheriff of Staffs in 1786. He was succeeded by his son Robert Parker (d1808), sheriff of Staffs in 1802, who was succeeded by his brother Thomas Hawe Parker (d1856), sheriff of Staffs in 1836 (OPB p23) (HBST pp560,561 see pedigree) (mem in Caverswall church). The old hall was gutted by fire and rebuilt as a large brick mansion in c1793 (HBST p560). (PPP vol 1 p133p of c1912) (STP pp174p of the ruined hall, 238). In the later C17 Plot was shown an oat mill here whose main wheel drove other wheels used for further stages in grinding (NHS p337). Plot also noted a very copious spring which could drive a mill situated less than a bow's shoot from it's rising and made an excessive noise in its exit (NHS p90) (SMC p142). Perhaps this was the oat mill. The park to the NNE of the house was officially opened as Park Hall Country Park on 10 April 1981 (ES April 9 p12p).

Park Hall Shenstone Woodhouse, Shenstone (SHOS vol 2 p46). Former seat of the Hill family (SVB p151).

Park Hall Former name for a Georgian house which stood in Park Street near Townend Bank, Walsall. Built in 1775 and still stood in 1930. The name is from the medieval Walsall Park (see) (SNWA p81).

Park Hall House over 1.5m SE of Walsall, on N side of Park Hall Road. Built in 1863 and from c1897 was the home of WJ Pearman Smith (d1939), mayor of Walsall 1899-1902. Demolished in the 1950s and a primary school, Park Hall School, opened on the site in 1970 (VCH vol 17 pp154,155) (SNWA p81). Has also appeared as Old Park Hall. There was an ice-house belonging to the hall at SP 033970, thought to have been destroyed (IHB p144).

Park Hall Country Park NW of Weston Coyney. Public country park of 333 acres officially opened in April 1981. Formed out of part of Weston Coyney Old Park (see) and as such went on to form part of the estate of the Coyney family and then the Parker family of Park Hall. The exploitation of the area for sandstone and coal which began in the C19 came to an end in 1970. The derelict land started to be reclaimed for the country park from 1973 (Park Hall Country Park. Staffs County Council Leaflet. Pre-1991) (PCCSC p243) (MIDD vol 1 pp28,29p).

Park Hall Hills Hills to the W of Weston Coyney (NSFCT 1910 p83). By 1993 it was the custom for three crosses to be erected on the hills at Easter. On Easter Sunday in 1993 a service was held by the crosses at sunrise (ES April 8 1993 p14p. April 21 2000 p1pc). In 1967 from the hills people claim they saw on Oct 12 at 7.30pm for ten minutes a bright object shaped like a bowler hat with a large brim over Caverswall Common, and on Oct 22 between 4.50am and 6.00am a bright star-like object which appeared like an eight to ten inch

dinner plate (FSRP p17).

Park Hall Old Park Medieval hunting ground at Cheadle. Belonged to the Bassets of Park Hall. Was three miles in circumference, according to a contributor to GM 1794 (NSFCT 1910 p175).

Park Hayes House 0.5m WSW of Gratton. Appears as Park Hays on 1834 OS map.

Park Head Lower and Higher Parkhead are 0.75m E of Ipstones. In Morridge and Foxt liberty in Ipstones ancient parish (W p780). William Beresford of Park Head died in 1704, aged 116 (OL vol 2 p220).

Park Hill Hill 0.25m S of Goldthorn Park. At SO 9188957 was found a Roman coin - a denarius of Caracella - in 1951 (NSJFS 1964 p20). Probably the same as Sedgley Park Hill, a hill 600 feet high (HOWM p6).

Park Hill House in Park Hill Drive on W side of Hamstead Hill, Handsworth (MNB pp41,49). Built in the late C18 or early C19, possibly by a Mr Vaughan, the owner in 1801. He appears to have been followed by Edward Lewis, mentioned in W (1834) as the occupant of the house on Hamstead Hill, which must be Park Hill. Between 1891 and 1899 the house was owned by Mr Walton. Later it was owned by Charles Palmer, and later occupied by Palmer's sister-in-law, Mrs Pountney. It was later used by the Ministry of Works as offices for the Ministry of National Insurance. The house was re-faced in 1953 (HPPE pp92,93). The original drive was from Hamstead Hall Road.

Park House House over 0.5m N of Consall. John William Sneyd (b1822) of Basford Hall was also of Park House, Consall (County Biographies: Staffordshire. Frederick B Ludlow. 1901).

Park House House on SE slopes of Gun Hill, by Franklins, 0.75m SW of Meerbrook (OL vol 1 p217). It was on the NE boundary of an old park which once belonged to Dieulacres Abbey. The ancient earthwork line called 'The Mark' runs through the middle of the park (OL vol 2 p201).

Park House Partly late C18 house (BOE p168) at Lapley. Col GS Tudor altered the house in c1867. He was a keen supporter of the Rifle Volunteer movement and near the house built Fort St George (see). The house is known locally as 'The Castle' (VCH vol 4 p145). (LCWA p79) (SPNO p170).

Park House House at the N end of Bishop's Wood, 0.75m SW of Fairoak. Preserves the name of Blore Park (NSFCT 1933 p93). The spirit of a mother transmuted into the form of her little daughter appeared to a preacher at a gateway leading into Bishop's Wood just below the Park House at the same time as her mother's death (the writer's mother). The preacher was returning home to the 'Lees' from taking Sunday School at Fairoak (BOV pp50-51).

Park House Grove Lane, Handsworth. At first, this large white house, was known as The Grove until it was bought by Handsworth urban district council and used in association with Handsworth Park from 1887. The house was demolished in 1968 (HHHW p100p).

Park House Large Victorian villa at Stafford. Seat of Henry Brassington Bamford of Uttoxeter (1849-1928) from c1909 (BUB pp30p,31).

Park House Willoughbridge. Preserves the name of Willoughbridge Old Park (NSFCT 1910 p175).

Park House Farm 0.75m SW of Meerbrook. Formerly in Leekfrith township in Leek ancient parish. The site of the house was occupied by the earlier C16 (VCH vol 7 p194).

Park Lane In Audley parish (W p430). Road running NW from Audley (1834 OS map); the hamlet of Park End lies on it.

Park Lane Fragmented hamlet 1.25m ENE of Chillington. In Brewood parish.

Park Lane Estate Housing estate built N of Park Lane, Knypersley, Biddulph, between 1945 and 1957 (BALH p235).

Park Nook House over 0.5m WSW of Ranton. In Ranton parish (W p402).

Park Pool 0.5m SW of Weston Hall, Weston-under-Lizard. Has also appeared as New Park Pool.

Parkside Modern residential estate 1.75m NNW of Stafford.

Parksite Modern housing estate 0.75m W of Silverdale. Has also appeared as Park Site Estate.

Park Springs Park Springs Farm is over 1.25m ESE of Hales. Occurs as Goatman's Hill in the late C17 (SHC 1945/ 6 p190). The house of 1933 is modern (NSFCT 1933 p93).

Park Springs Wood Wood 1m ESE of Hales, to W of Burntwood. Once part of the forest of Blore (NSFCT 1933 p93). Here was found a paved area of uncertain date at a depth six feet at cSJ 730330 (HOMD p69) (NSJFS 1964 p39. 1969 p105). It could be of Roman origin (STM April 1966 p30).

Parkstile House 2m NE of Bagot's Bromley.

Park Village Suburb 1m W of Wednesfield. Is about 0.5m from Heath Town, adjoining Fallings Park in the Wood Street area (WPOPP vol 1 p99p). Formerly in Wednesfield chapelry in Wolverhampton ancient parish. The name had appeared by 1891 (OS map 1891).

Park Village Is the present Roebuck Street, on E side of Roebuck Lane near the

M5, West Bromwich. It was laid out in the 1850s (VCH vol 17 p10).

Parnell House House 1m NNW of Meerbrook. So called because the farmer who built it admired the Irish politician, Charles Stewart Parnell (HOLF p25).

Parrott's Dumble Wooded valley 1.25m NE of Audley in Audley ancient parish. Leased by the Staffs Nature Conservation Trust from the Coal Board (NSFCT 1989 p42) (MIDD vol 1 pp44,45p). Said to be named after Richard Parrott, who wrote a survey of Audley parish and Talke hamlet in 1733 (AHJ 1996 p50), or a member of his family (SHC 1944 pcviii).

Parr's Warren Warren 2m SE of Brocton, Cannock Chase.

Parsonage House Church Leigh. In the later C17 Plot noted a tremendous pear tree growing in the moat of Parsonage House, which cast a shade on 244 square yards (NHS p225) (NSFCT 1923 p150. 1982 p12).

Parson and Clerk Inn, The Public house at the junction of Sutton Oak Road and Chester Road North, Streetly, at SP 083964. It was known as the Royal Oak until the mid C18 (GATD pp102,104). The name is said to have been changed after a dispute between the rector of Handsworth, Rev T Lane, who had some interest in the house, and the landlord Walter Gough who succeeded to the Perry Hall estates in 1773. The dispute culminated in a law suit. Mr Lane not only kept Gough out of possession of the house but withheld his licences. Gough in return arranged for at least two of his servants to attend Handsworth parish church every day to form a congregation to compel Mr Lane to read the services daily, which he was compelled to do, if sufficient attended. Eventually Gough won the law suit and in 1788 rebuilt the house. To commemorate his victory he had a caricature placed on one of the gable ends of the property (THM vol 4 p55), or on a barn door (TBS p23). It resembled a parson bending his head in an attitude of prayer and his clerk standing behind him with an uplifted axe. These figures remained on the wall until c1860 (THM vol 4 p55). A variation of this story is that a rector of Handsworth had been annoyed by a tenant farmer's failure to pay his rent. Accompanied by his clerk, the parson then attempted to remove the tenant from the house. That caused much indignation, and a local wag drew the caricature of the parson and his clerk on the end of the inn wall, thus giving the inn its name. The farmer's friends took further revenge by sending one or two people daily to Handsworth parish church to make the parson read the daily services (The Handsworth Herald. 1904) (TBS pp23-24). The inn had reverted to being the Royal Oak by 1834 and it was still called this in 1903 (OS maps) but appears as the Parson and Clerk on the OS map 1881-8 revised 1906 2 inch to 1m and on the 1912 OS map. (IOM pp99,102p) (MNB p64).

Parson's Brake Farm and wood 2.5m NW of Rangemore.

Parsons Green This was an area close to the Old Town Hall, Handsworth, and consisted of an acre of ground extending towards Laurel Road (HPPE p37).

Parson's Park Slightly N of Tatenhill (HOPT vol 1 p134).

Parson's Well, The Well near the Primitive Methodist Chapel, and post office, Mow Cop. It bears the inscription 'Keep thyself pure. The Parson's Well. 1857.' At sometime it belonged to the Sidebotham family (PS p24) (TSW p83) (WMC p) (MC p25 pl vi). The Parson's Well is mentioned in the poem 'Mow Cop' composed by David Oakes (KBT vol 2 pp38-40).

Pasford Minute hamlet by Pasford or Nun Brook 1m W of Pattingham. In Pattingham ancient parish. Here was Pattingham manorial mill, in existence by 1314; it was known as Basford or Pasford Mill by 1717 (VCH vol 20 p173).

Pasford Brook Rises N of Patshull. Has been dammed to form ornamental pools in the grounds of Patshull Park in the C18 (VCH vol 20 pp161, 172). After briefly forming the county boundary W of Pattingham it appears to become Nun Brook, a tributary of the Worfe, a tributary of the Severn.

Pasturefields Small hamlet by the Trent 2.5m NW of Colwich, 1.5m NW of Great Haywood. Formerly in Colwich ancient parish. By 1999 the saltmarsh at SJ 994247 was a SSSI nature reserve in the care of the Staffs Wildlife Trust.

'Patch, The' Name for an old area about Lower Walsall Street to Horseley Fields and centred on Hill Street South, nearly 1m ESE of Wolverhampton (TB Jan 1997 p29. April 1997 p11. May 1997 p4. June 1997 p29).

Patshull Ancient parish and tiny estate village on a low promontory between two head streams which merge to form Nun Brook, 15.5m SW of Stafford. The parish formerly lay in the southern division of Seisdon hundred but was transferred to the northern division in 1845 (VCH vol 20 p161). For the **'lost city'** between Wrottesley and Patshull see Wrottesley Old Park. The **name** has appeared as Pecleshella (DB), Patleshull (1200), Patteshull (W p189), Petesey (c1540) (LI appendix p170), Pateshull or Patshall (Bowen's map). It means 'Paecgel's hill' or 'Pyttel's hill' (DUIGNAN) (SPN p91), or 'Paettel's hill' (NSJFS 1981 p3) (VCH vol 20 p162) (SSE 1996 p16). There was a **church** at Patshull by 1200. The present parish church, St Mary, in Patshull Park SW of Patshull Hall, was consecrated in 1743; its predecessor stood

half a mile away, probably further S at or near the former hamlet of Olton (VCH vol 20 p170). The church closed in 1992 after the congregation dwindled to just seven. It has occasionally opened since for special occasions (E&S July 11 1998 p13). In the C18 the parish **wake** was held in Sept (VCH vol 20 p163). A **medieval village** is recorded at SJ 809010 to the E of Patshull Hall on the county border; it was possibly deserted in the C17 (SSAHST 1966 p49. 1970 p35), approximately in this area was the former hamlet of Millhouse (see) (VCH vol 20 p162). **Manorial tenure service**. In Edward II's reign, Robert Maunsell granted to Sir Ralph de Pickeford, after his decease, all the vill of Patshull, (except the dower of his wife, and foreign service due to his lord), on condition he pay a pair of gloves at Easter at Patshull church (SCSF p119). There is possibly a **moated site** at SJ 819012 over 1m ENE of Patshull Hall (SHOS vol 2 p286) (SSAHST 1982-3 p45). There was a pinfold at Burnhill Green (see) in the C19. A Patshull **Volunteer company** was raised in 1860 by the 5th Earl of Dartmouth. It was still running in 1891 (VCH vol 20 p163).

Patshull Hall Patshull. The present house, the successor of Patshull Old Hall (see), forms a quadrangle. The original house on the S side and the wings on the E and W sides (which were at first free-standing) were built for Sir John Astley (d1772) in the mid or late 1730s to designs by James Gibbs (d1754); Francis Smith of Warwick (d1738) supervised the work (SGS p133). William Baker created the quadrangle c1750. He is responsible for linking the E and W wings to the original house and for building a N range with a central entrance. Further work in the C19 added rooms onto all sides (BOE p218) (VCH vol 20 pp165-166 plan). In 1765 Sir John sold Patshull to Sir George Pigot, Bt, a nabob and owner of the famous Pigot diamond (VB p72) (VCH vol 20 p165); it has been said that he was able to buy the estate on the proceeds of the sale of the diamond (MR p252). The manor then descended with the Pigot baronetcy until Sir Robert Pigot sold Patshull to William Legge, 4th Earl of Dartmouth of Sandwell Hall (see), in 1848. Lord Dartmouth came to live here in 1853, but died later that year (VCH vol 20 p165). There were great festivities at Patshull Hall for the majority of Viscount Lewisham in May 1872 (ILN May 18 1872 p472il). In 1900 George V and Queen Mary (then Duke and Duchess of York) stayed here for four days. Queen Mary stayed here again in 1939 (SA July 21 1900. July 28 1900. March 14 1936) (STC p12p) (SLM autumn 1954 p12) (VCH vol 20 p163) (TPOP p119p). Patshull remained with the Legges until after the death of the 7th Earl of Dartmouth in 1958. He was succeeded by a cousin (or brother), and most of the estate passed in lieu of death duties to the Crown, still the owner in 1980 (VCH vol 20 p165). (LGS p197) (VB p71). The 7th Earl's widow lived in one wing of the hall until her death in 1966; the 7th Earl's fourth daughter Lady Barbara (b1916) lived with her husband Capt Adam W Kwiatkowski at Hack Cottage in Patshull Hall grounds between at least 1967 and the late 1990s (Burke's Peerage 1967) (local info). The hall became an orthopaedic rehabilitation hospital in WW2 and Wolverhampton area health authority were still running it as such in 1980 (VCH vol 20 p165) and in 1988 (MR p252p). There were plans in 1999 to convert the hall into flats.

INTERIOR. In the hall was a painting of the combat fought at Paris Aug 29 1438 on horseback, in the presence of the royal family, between John de Astley and Peter de Masse in which the later was defeated. In the same piece is painted another combat, fought at Smithfield on foot on Jan 30 1441 between Sir John Astley and Sir Philip Boyle, in which the former obtained victory (GNHSS p31). In Dugdale's History of Warws there is an engraving of it (SHOS vol 2 p285). Lord Dartmouth gave the original to Arley Castle but kept a copy on wood at the hall (SLM autumn 1954 p12). The hall also contained paintings of the Washington family - portraits of 1) Sir George Villiers 2) his daughter the Lady Anne Washington 3) her eldest son Henry, as a child 4) her daughter Elizabeth, as a child 5) another daughter Susannah Washington who married Reginald Grahme 6) Col William Legge. Also Hoppner's and Romney's portraits of Lady Feversham formerly Lady Charlotte Legge, Huysman's Col William Legge, Vivien's Lord Dartmouth (1st Baron) and Gainsborough's 2nd Earl of Dartmouth and other portraits by Reynolds. The hall also contained a fine collection of seals, the Legge family often holding the office of Lord Privy Seal (NSFCT 1931 p34) (ES Feb 19 1932 p6) (SLM autumn 1954 p12. winter 1954 pp10,11 ils). On the new wing of the hall was a six-quartered stone coat of arms. In the second quartering are the arms of Washington. The Washington arms have been quartered by those of Legge ever since Col William Legge married Elizabeth Washington of Kensington (daughter of Sir William Washington) in 1642. Elizabeth Washington and William Legge were the parents of Admiral George Legge, 1st Baron Dartmouth (NSFCT 1931 p31). The house has also appeared as Patshull House (VCH vol 20 pp161-172 il of from the S front in the late C18 and p of from the N front - both face p176). The ghost of a lady in white is said to haunt the hall. She has been seen by a patient who was convalescing at the hall. She could be the late Lady Dartmouth (TB April 1993 p13). A pool in the grounds is said to be haunted by a gypsy girl or the spirit of a gypsy girl which inhabits a large fish (GOM p23 p of the pool 3 (c)).

GROUNDS. Oil bombs were dropped on Patshull Park in WW2 (PPTP p26). There are two **boathouses**, one 400 yards S of the church of the mid C19 with a Kings Post roof (DoE II), and the other 25 yards N of the Temple of the late C19 (DoE II). The **Doric Temple**, perhaps by James Gibbs, stands on the W side of the Great Pool, 0.75m S of the hall. It was incorporated into the Temple Hotel in 1980 (VCH vol 20 p167) and is now a licenced bar (DoE II*). Lord Dartmouth brought a C18 stone **fountain head**, three feet wide and originally five feet high, from Upper Pepperhill, Boningale parish Shrops c1880. It was broken when a branch from a tree fell on it in 1978, but it was still standing on the lawn below the W wing in 1980 (WORF p90) (DoE II) (VCH vol 20 p167 note). A fountain from Patshull Park is presently (1997) in the garden of Upper or Lower Pepperhill in Boningale parish, Shrops (TPOP p116p). There is another **fountain** of cast iron with figures and dolphins (DoE II). The **Great Pool** was begun in 1768. It was extended into its present Y-shape later in the C18 (VCH vol 20 p167). Shaw at the end of C18, noted the lake of near 100 acres which he said was newly finished (SHOS vol 1 part 1 pp90, painting of the hall facing 284,285). NE of the hall in the southern corner of the walled garden was a cylindrical **ice-house** partially sunk into the ground and having a thatched roof. It was used into the C20, but was demolished prior to 1980 (IHB p395). By 1988 grounds to the S of the hall had become a **golf course**. That year Colin Young, using a buggy for transport, completed 1260 holes (6412 yards) between July 2-9. This achievement broke the world record for the most holes in golf in a week (GBR 1995 p259).

Patshull Old Hall The manor house of Patshull manor and predecessor to Patshull Hall. It is said to have stood on low ground near water (SHOS vol 1 p70. vol 2 p283). This was possibly S of Patshull Hall by Pasford Brook near the medieval hamlet of Olton (see) (VCH vol 20 p162), or possibly to the E of Patshull Hall at the medieval hamlet of Millhouse (see). The old hall was moated (VCH vol 20 p165). The manor was inherited by Thomas Astley in 1451; his wife was Joan Gresley, Henry VI's nurse. The manor then descended in the Astley family for over three centuries. During the Civil War Walter Astley (d1654), a papist, garrisoned the old hall for the king (VCH vol 20 p164) but it was captured by Capt Stone for the parliamentarians in Feb 1644 (GNHS p77) (LGS p197), or in 1645 and Walter was taken prisoner (SHOS vol 1 p70) (VCH vol 3 p105. vol 20 p164). Plot noted that Sir Richard Astley (d1688) had invented a device like a pillory for measuring game-cocks here (NHS p387 tab 32 figs 6,7) (SD p43) (SHOS vol 2 p285). In 1698 the hall was considered 'old and low.' Patshull Hall (see) or known as Patshull House was rebuilt for Sir John Astley (d1772) on a new site in the mid or later 1730s (VCH vol 20 p165).

GROUNDS. Two ornamental gamecocks in ornate gateposts beside the churchyard are said to commemorate an occasion when an Astley lost the estate and won it back all in one day on cockfighting wagers (VB p71). In the later C17 Plot noted tunnels between the barn and the stables for oats to be put down to feed the horses (NHS pp388-389). An engraving of the hall was left out of NHS because trees hid its facade (NHS p359) (SH p60). Plot noted a fountain, which threw up a great column of water bigger than that at Trentham. It was within a large rotunda which was fenced with a high brick wall with iron gates for the entrance. Also in another garden a 'bird cage' in which was a wind-cock which directed a cistern. Also an ornamental canal, at the S end of which was a grotto, in the process of being built when Plot was at the hall (NHS pp338,339) (SD pp42,43).

Patshull Park A game park for the lords of Patshull manor existed by the C14. By the earlier C17 the park occupied the NE corner of the Patshull parish, as it did in 1775. It was walled by Sir John Astley in the mid C18. Lord Pigot landscaped much of the park in the later C18 (VCH vol 20 p168). The Legges are said to have had a deer park at Patshull in the C19 (EDP p180).

Pattingham (*Pattinjam* DUIGNAN). Ancient parish and former township. The village of Pattingham lies in undulating country by the heads of several tributaries of Nun Brook, 16.25m SSW of Stafford.

EARLY. A Middle Bronze Age four-foot long gold torc was found N of the church in a field called Fantley Hill in 1700 (SD p43) (SHOS vol 1 General Intro p33. vol 2 p279) (SVS p322 note) (GNHS p70) (LGS p25) (KES p165) (CCC p9) (P pp9-10) (THS p188) (ARCHJ vol 11 p54) (NSJFS 1964 p31). In 1780 a D-shaped gold ingot, two inches long was found in Pattingham parish. It was worth £152 but the ploughman who discovered it sold it in Birmingham for only 1L.18 shillings. 'Golden' is a local field name (SHOS vol 2 p279) (SVS p322 note) (THS p188) (NSJFS 1964 p31).

1000 to PRESENT. The parish **church**, St Chad, by the junction of Patshull

Road and High Street, stands on or near the site of a Saxon church. The present church contains some Norman work (The Church of St Chad, Pattingham). The present spire on the tower was added in 1865 (Friends of Ancient Staffs Churches showing views from WSL collection. JS Roper. 1970). The parish, formed before 1086, formerly included the township of Rudge, Shrops. Pattingham township formerly lay in the southern division of Seisdon hundred but was transferred to the northern division in 1845 (SHC 1916 p193) (VCH vol 20 p161) (GLAUE p419). There was mention of a **wake** day in 1610-11. In the mid C18 the wake was held early in March, presumably in connection with the feast of St Chad, the patron of the Pattingham church (March 2) (VCH vol 20 p175). The **name** has appeared as Patingha, a manor, in DB, Pattingeham (C12), and Patingeham (C12) (SPN p91). The origin of Pattingham confused Duignan. Stevenson says from the personal name 'Peatta' as in Peattingtun, found in an Anglo-Saxon charter, said to be Patton, Shrops (DUIGNAN). The 'ham (homestead) of Peatta's people' (VCH vol 20 p173) (SSE 1996 p16) (SPN p91). The custom of inheritance by **Borough English** was practiced in Pattingham (VCH vol 20 p178). Pattingham parish was a **probate jurisdiction** of the lord of the manor until abolished in 1846 (VCH vol 3 p94 note). The lord of the manor Ralph, Lord Basset of Drayton, was granted a charter on Aug 6 1316 to hold a **market** here on Tuesdays. The market had ceased by 1500 (NSJFS 1971 p51). In 1316 the lord of the manor was granted a **fair** on the vigil, feast, and morrow of the translation of St Edward the Confessor (Dec 12-14) (VCH vol 20 p179). There was a fair in 1792 (OWEN). By 1845 there was an annual Meeting on last Tuesday in April (for cattle, horses, sheep, pigs) (SCSF p99) (VCH vol 20 p179). The cattle fair was still being held in the 1890s (VCH vol 20 p179). There was a **bull ring** in front of the Pigot Arms, formerly the King's Arms (WMAG Feb 1968 p26). The centre of Pattingham village was known as the Bull Ring (TPOP p99p). The **gallows** of the manor stood in the Woodhouses area (VCH vol 20 p180). There was mention of a **pillory** in 1384 (VCH vol 20 p180). By the late C18 the **stocks** and mounting block were situated by the corner of the churchyard facing the post office and are depicted in Richard Paddey's aquatint in SHOS vol 2 pl facing p279. (P p164). The ancient custom of tolling a **curfew bell** at Pattingham at 8.00pm was still being kept up in 1829 (Wolverhampton Chronicle Nov 4 1829) (Broughton's Scrapbook p312). On Holy Innocent's day (Dec 28), a muffled peal was rung at Pattingham (BCC vol 3 p281). There was a **pound** on the N side of Newgate near the junction with Westbeech Road. It was demolished in c1961 (WJO July 1908 p148p) (VCH vol 20 p180). For Pattingham **windmills** see under Nurton Hill and Westbeech. The great **fire** of Pattingham occurred on Sept 10 1698 and burnt down the church and part of the village. It broke out in the workshop of William Taylor, locksmith (WMAG Feb 1968 p26). **Sculpture from Houses of Parliament.** On the S wall of Pattingham church near the porch is a carved stone in the form of an angel holding a shield with a cross. The inscription is 'From the Houses of Parliament. Presented by G le Mander MP 1934' (P p56).

Pattingham Hall At Hall End, Pattingham. Stone and brick building, partly dating from the C17. In 1935 a timber-framed wing, incorporating old materials, was added to the existing building. The hall which may have stood on the site of Pattingham manor house, was demolished in c1968 (VCH vol 20 p176).

Paul's Coppice Former hamlet on W side of Walsall Wood Common. Formerly in a detached portion of the foreign of Walsall ancient parish. There was settlement here by 1763 and the area was so named by 1805 (VCH vol 17 p278). The name appears on 1834 OS map and has appeared as St Paul's Coppice (MH 1994 p115). In the street called Paul's Coppice on E side of Lindon Road (formerly New Street) there is a house inscribed 'By the Sweat of a Miner's Brow 1895' (VCH vol 17 p278 note).

Pavier's Row Row of cottages made for miners slightly SE of St Anne's church, Chasetown. Built by John Pavier of Hammerwich Place Farm, Hammerwich in the 1850s. The row was renamed Pavior's Road in 1962 (VCH vol 14 pp261,269).

Paxton House Former residence of Smethwick's first mayor, Alderman Jabez Lones, in South Road, Smethwick (SMEOP p49p). The house was standing in 1928.

Paynsley Former estate at Cresswell on the W side of the Blithe, 2.75m NW of Church Leigh. In Draycott-in-the-Moors ancient parish. Has been identified since 1915 with DB Lufamesles (NSFCT 1915 pp90-91) (SHC 1916 p167) (DB. Phillimore. 1976). Has also appeared as Painsley.

Paynsley Hall House at Paynsley, 2.75m NW of Church Leigh, in Draycott-in-the-Moors ancient parish. Here are numerous earthworks and entrenchments in the surrounding fields which may have been the disused moat of some old castle (NSFCT 1888 p58). (ESH p58). Seat of the Draycotts from the Norman Conquest to the beginning of the C18 when the estate (or Draycott-in-the-Moors manor) passed by female descent to the Lords Stourton; Lady Stourton (d1841) was lady of the manor in the 1830s. By 1851 Sir Edward Vavasour Bart was lord of Draycott (Plot's map) (GNHS p91) (W 1834) (W pp773,774). The Draycotts were recusants and Dr Anthony Draycott was chancellor of Lichfield diocese in Queen Mary's reign and is said to have been extremely cruel towards Protestants. A daughter of the Draycotts married Anthony Babington (see Chartley Hall) (LGS p126). In the Civil War the Draycotts garrisoned the hall for the king and it was ordered to be demolished on March 2 1643 but the order was not carried out (NSFCT 1888 p61. 1913 p197) (LGS p126), and the hall was then made a parliamentary garrison (GNHS pp77,91) (HOS 1998 p72). In the C19 Paynsley Hall was occupied by farmers and this was still the case in the early C20, retaining nothing of the old building except an enormous stone chimney (trade directories) (LGS p125). Richard Morfe, who worked for the Draycott and Fowler families at Paynsley Hall and St Thomas' Priory had the ability to predetermine or prognosticate the changes of the moon, the times of eclipses, and at what time Easter and Whitsuntide fall, or even any other movable feast, but also on what day any future movable feast will fall in years to come (NHS p303) (SD p107). Has also appeared as Painsley Hall.

Paynsley Park Medieval hunting ground surrounding Painsley Hall and by the banks of the Blithe (EDP p177). The park may have suffered in the Civil War because Paynsley Hall was captured by the parliamentarians. Is the 'Wastegate Farm' the site of the west gate in the park fence? (NSFCT 1910 p176). The park was disparked before the time of Sir Simon Degge (EDP p177). Has also appeared as Painsley Old Park.

Peacock Hay Minute hamlet on a hill between the upper reaches of Fowlea Brook and a tributary 0.25m W of Tunstall. Formerly in Chatterley liberty of Wolstanton ancient parish (W p297).

Pea Hill Hill. Sandon Bank, 1m NW of Salt.

Peakhouse Former homestead which stood at the top of Sargent's (or Sergeant's) Hill, Walsall. So called from being situated on the 'peak' of Sargent's Hill. It gave the name 'del Peak' (of the Peak) to a yeoman family (SNWA p14).

Peakstone Rock Rock feature 0.5m NW of Bradley-in-the-Moors, at SK 051422. Is an unweathered crop of Keuper stone. The Himlack Stone near Nottingham is a parallel example (S pp31p,32). Peakstones, an area or house, appears as Peykestonys in 1541 (HAF p84), and, according to Oakden, gives its name to Peake Rivulet, now Croxden Brook (see). In the later C17 Plot noted a rock house called Thurse House in Long Hurst Hill near Peakstones (NHS p172). Raven calls it Rock Farm (MR p47p). Perhaps, the house to the N is called Rock Farm. There is a house called Peakstone Farm on Alton Common to the N of Peakstone Rock on the 1834 OS map. The old Peakstones Inn was originally near the Peakstone but was moved to the N side of the new Alton-Cheadle road when it was built (HAF p358) (OS Staffs Street Atlas. 1995).

Pea Low Burial mound 0.75m N of Alstonefield at SK 13085645. It is 38 paces in diameter and 10 feet high and was excavated by Bateman in 1845 and Carrington in 1848. It is a listed monument. A fragment of an ornamented drinking cup was found. Near the surface was a hoard of some 50 Roman coins, the latest was of the early C4. Also an undatable globular urn with several holes drilled in the side containing a cremation. Villagers have found an Anglian inhumation with an iron spearhead, a lancehead, and a knife, and an iron arrowhead, and another spearhead were recovered later (VAD pp76-77) (TYD pp121-122,125-126) (VCH vol 1 p208) (BAP vol 2 p52,122 fig 483) (The Arts in Early England. GB Brown. 1915 vol 4 p772) (Gazetteer of Early Anglo-Saxon Burial Mounds. A Meaney. 1964 p222) (Medieval Archaeology vol 6/ 7 p43) (NSJFS 1965 pp30-31).

Pearl Brook Tributary of the Sow. The name of the lower part of Sandyford Brook (VCH vol 6 p185). Runs on the E side of Stafford. Has appeared as Pirlewallsiche (c1300) (SPNO p15). The name is derived from Old English 'pyrle' and Mercian dialect of Old English 'wælla,' 'the bubbling spring' (SPNO p15).

Pearl Hill One of the Rowley Hills range (SVS p436).

Pearl Well Lyndon, West Bromwich. In the mid C19 it was noted to be a remarkably fine spring of pure water belonging to the parishioners and was lately repaired by Mr Wilkes and others (W p682).

Pearse Hay Farm 0.5m S of Bishop's Wood. The name is said to be from a former hay in Brewood Forest (BDH p72). The farmhouse is a building of the early C17 with additions of c1835 (VCH vol 5 p38) and has appeared as Priests Hay, Peirce Hay (1723) (BDH 1992 pp81, 142) and Pearce Hay Farm. The name means 'the enclosure of Piers or Pearce' (BDH 1992 p351), or according to tradition it was named from the piecing of ricks of hay by parliamentary forces with lances when searching for Charles II after the battle of Worcester in 1651 (SVB p35) (info Mark Whittaker). For Pearse Hay in a

local rhyme see Brewood.

Pear Tree Estate Large residential suburb on the SW fringe of Rugeley, S of the Hednesford Road. It was built in the mid 1950s to house miners at Lea Hall Colliery. The church, The Good Shepherd, Hislop Road, was built in the early 1960s (info Rev MJ Newman).

Pear Tree Farm On S side of Greyhound Lane, Lower Penn. Built by Ellen Persehouse, daughter of Thomas Bradney of Penn Hall and wife of William Persehouse. Has an inscribed stone over the doorway reading 'E.P. 1821.' In the C19 the house was sold to the Lloyd estate, which in turn was sold and broken up in 1901. The name is said to be from the Tettenhall Pear. In the 1990s there were three Tettenhall Pear trees growing here (PPTP pp57,84).

Pear Tree Farm Penn Common. The Parker family ran a milk round from here between 1910 and 1963. The named is said to be from the Tettenhall Pear. Two Tettenhall Pear trees were growing here in the later C20, but by 1996 one had been blown down (PPTP pp31,84).

Pear Tree Lake Farm Over 0.25m WNW of Balterley and E of Pear Tree Farm.

Peaseland Rocks Rock feature on Staffs side of Wolfscote Dale. At SK 140569.

Peasley Bank Hill 2.25m NE of Great Bridgeford.

Peatswood Hall House 1.5m W of Hales. In Drayton-in-Hales parish. The name is from a wood here called Peats Wood, which occurs in 1669, which was formerly called Skelhorne Spring, or Payt's Hill, and John Preston's Hill. It seems to have taken this name from the Peat (or Peyt, or Payt) family in the late C16 or C17 (SHC 1945/ 6 pp86-87,131,136). Another interpretation is that it is from 'Peot's wood' (SPN p57). The first mention of a house at Peatswood is in 1695, when the Bannister family are said to be of Peatswood. It was the seat of Thomas Dicken, a lord of Tyrley manor, in the later C18 and he considerably added to the house, between 1787 and 1800. He was declared bankrupt and sold Peatswood to a branch of the Twemlows of Twemlow, Ches in 1808, who continued to live here until at least 1914, with Col Francis Randle Twemlow (b1852) being the author of the article on the manor of Tyrley which was presented to the WSL in 1927 and which appears in SHC 1945/ 6. The house was altered and improved in 1881-4 and in 1903-4 (SHC 1945/ 6 pp189, 205,251-252). The brick stables with a domed cupola were built in c1900 (BOE p138) (MR p168). The clockhouse is listed II (DoE). Some of the grounds was landscaped by Gilpin in c1825 (SHC 1945/ 6 p250).

Peck's House House 1m NW of Rushton Spencer church. Formerly in Rushton Spencer township in Leek ancient parish. The house here was so called in 1662 (VCH vol 7 p224).

Pedestal, The Rock feature on The Roaches (VB p209).

Peggs, The Peggs Farm is 0.5m SW of High Offley.

Peggy's Lantern Bridge A stone railway bridge over a brook about 200 yards on the Macclesfield side of Rushton Spencer and has a sturdy wooden footbridge beneath. Perhaps named after a silk weaver who passed over the bridge to work with a lantern (SVB pp145,147).

Pellwall Neo-classical house under 0.5m S of Tyrley overlooking the Tern. Formerly in Drayton-in-Hales ancient parish. Built on former Tyrley Heath purchased by Purney Sillitoe, solicitor, in 1820 (SHC 1945/ 6 p257-258). The house, which has also appeared as Pell Wall, was built to designs by Sir John Soane, Sillitoe's friend, between 1822-1828 (BOE pp219-220) (OVH p32). It was Soane's last country house (SGS p102) (OVH p32). Its offices are underground (SHC 1945/ 6 p258). Sillitoe is said to have named the house Pellwall, after a field on his new estate. It is thought to mean 'The spring or well (wall) in the hollow (Pell)' (SHC 1945/ 6 p258). When he died in 1855 the house passed through his niece to the Griffin family who made certain alterations to it between 1861 to 1880. From 1891 to 1901 the property was let. It was then sold to James Munro Walker of the whiskey family for whom the swimming pool and bachelor wing had been added. It seems to have been acquired by the Brothers of Christian Instruction in 1928 and used as a boys' boarding school until 1962. The property was purchased by a Mr Rolf in 1965. Mr Rolf was unable to acquire planning permission to turn the house into an entertainment and exhibition centre or have it demolished. He then left it empty (OVH pp31-37 ps). In 1986 the interior was gutted by a fire which some allege was started deliberately by Mr Rolf. It was discovered to be on fire at 8.00pm, but out by midnight, but ablaze again three hours later. The North Shrops district council responded by putting a compulsory purchase order on the property in 1988 and handed over responsibility for renovation to Pell Wall Hall Preservation Trust ('Silent Houses' The Way We Were. Central TV. July 19 1993. 10.40pm) (ES May 25 1994 p25p). At the end of the N drive is a small triangular lodge designed by Soane in a vague Egypto-classical style (F p314). It is surmounted by a hexagonal lantern with weather vane. It is described by Thorold in 1978 as recently restored, added to, and converted into a house (SGS p102p of the lodge). (CL Sept 17 1992 p118p).

Pelsall Large village on a low plateau between Ford Brook and a tributary 14m SE of Stafford. Former out-township and chapelry of Wolverhampton ancient parish. There was a burnt mound probably of the **Middle Bronze Age** by Ford Brook 0.5m ENE of Pelsall parish church at SK 02800319. It was discovered in 1911 but could not be found in 1985 (MOA p15) (SASR 1987 p17). According to an old tradition **Lady Wulfrun** made her way to Pelsall after escaping from the sacking of Tamworth in 943; here she rested her horses and was treated kindly by the local inhabitants (SHOP p14). A charter was made of Pelsall's bounds (SL p62), when Lady Wulfrun gave the estate to the monastery of Wolverhampton in 994 (HOWM p14). The **name** has appeared as Peoleshale (994) (WMVB pp124-5), Peleshale, (DB. c1215-1224) (SHOP p2), Peleshala (SPN p91), Peolsford, Pyshalle (SHOP p2), and Pelshall (W p155). It means Peol's hall (DUIGNAN), or Peol's nook (NSJFS 1981 p3), or 'Peol's corner of land' (SPN p91). 'All' may be from 'halh' which may mean 'land between two streams,' which in Pelsall's case may refer to the area which falls between the Ford Brook and Clock Mill Brook (SHOP p2) (WMVB pp124-5). In William I's reign Pelsall **manor** was held by the canons of Wolverhampton (having held it since Wulfrun's grant in 994). It continued to be held by Wolverhampton Collegiate Church until the Dissolution and as such lay in the Wolverhampton (see) Deanery manor (HOWM p26). In William I's reign Robert de Corbeuil is described as the tenant - his descendants assumed the surname 'de Pelsall' and this name appears to have survived until the C18 when the heiress of the family, the granddaughter of the last Sir Thomas Pelsall was married to the Earl of Breadalbane (SHOP p2). There was a **church** at Pelsall by 1311. It was probably a small chapel built close to Pelsall Hall in what is now Paradise Lane (PTYV p3). The present Commissioners' church, St Michael and All Angels, at the junction of Church Road and Hall Lane, was built in 1843-1844 (BOE p220). A fair or wake in Pelsall came at the end of Aug. For many years it was held in Stanley's Fields at the rear of the High Street. At other times it was held at the rear of the White Lion or Bush Inns (SNBP pp71,73). **Growth from tiny village**. The original village may have centred on the mill at Pelsall, mentioned in c1215-1224, which may have been situated on Clock Mill Brook in the Old Town Lane area (SHOP p2); the main centre of Pelsall by the later C18 was still this area, now known as Old Town (PTYV p11). The expansion of Pelsall from a tiny village into an industrial boom town dates from the opening of Pelsall Ironworks on the Wood Common by the Wyrley & Essington Canal in c1832. The ironworks were at first owned by Mr Fryer, a Wolverhampton banker, and gained a reputation for making bar and sheet iron of the best quality. It closed in 1892. The remaining chimney stacks on the site were demolished in the 1920s (SHOP pp4-5) (ADY p24) (WMVB pp124-125). Pelsall became a separate ecclesiastical parish in 1766, and a separate civil parish in 1866. It became a part of Aldridge and Brownhills urban district in 1966 (GLAUE p419) (PTYV pp6,8,22). **Cookery Corner** is the colloquial name for the corner of Old Town Lane and High Street, Pelsall, from there having been a building where cookery was taught. It is also known as a Silver's Corner (SNBP p70). There was a fingerpost with four arms at the junction of the Norton and Wolverhampton Roads. Successive signs were still known as the **fingerpost** which became a fare-stage on local bus routes (SNBP p73); on a very foggy night a coach and horses vanished completely into the pond by the fingerpost and were never seen again (SHOP p14). Pelsall **railway** station on the Lichfield-Walsall line opened on April 9 1849 (SSR p10). There was an epidemic of **scarlet fever** in Pelsall township in 1886 (PTYV p18). **Newspaper**. The Cannock Chase News, founded in May 1889, became the Cannock Chase Courier and Pelsall News from June 25 1889, later in the year its title changed and Pelsall was dropped (SHJ spring 1996 p17). In **WW2** in 1940 German bombs were dropped on the Pelsall North Common and demolished a house in Highbridges (PTYV p21). **Princess Anne** officially opened the flats in Old Vicarage Close in Sept 1986 (SNBP p91). On the front of an old house at Pelsall, sunk in the brickwork, was the lettering:-

VT. TIBI SIC. APIS. An'o Dom'i
TH. 1687.

A thrifty Staffs man has rhymed it:

One that would own his own roof-tree
Must emulate the busy bee.

(SCSF p168).

Pelsall Common Former wasteland belonging to the church (SHOP p11), on either side of Norton and Walsall Roads to the NE and SE of Pelsall church. Has also occurred as Pelsall Heath (1834 OS map) (SNBP p79). In 1884 the

principal landowners of Pelsall tried to enclose some of the unenclosed common, but the scheme was abandoned (SHOP p11).

Pelsall Hall The present hall is situated in Paradise Lane, Pelsall. A moat in fields called Park Fields opposite the present hall perhaps represents the site of an earlier hall. The sides of the moat had become mutilated by old coal pits by the late C18 (SHOS vol 2 p61) (SSAHST 1982-83 p34). There is another moat near Moat House (see) near the junction of Norton and Wolverhampton Roads to the NE. There appears to have been a hall by 1311 and in 1634. In 1785 Phineas Hussey of Wyrley sold the hall to the Charles family of King's Bromley; the present hall was their seat until 1917 or 1918 when it was sold to Walsall Health Authority for use as a tuberculosis sanatorium. The patients were transferred to Goscote Hospital in 1930 and the hall then became a nurses' training centre. By 1981 it was used by ambulance personnel. That year there were plans to build an ambulance training centre in the grounds. In 1988 the hall opened as a private residential home for the elderly (SHOP p20) (PTYV pp11,20,21,23) (SNBP pp75-76ps,77).

Pelsall House Pelsall. The house was sold in 1930 when the estate of the Barnett family was sold (PTYV p21).

Pelsall Junction Junction of the Wyrley and Essington Extension Canal with the Cannock Extension Canal (HCMS No. 2).

Pelsall Wood District of Pelsall 0.75m N of Pelsall. A common (W p155). May have formerly been called Wood Common. Pelsall Ironworks opened at Wood Common in c1832.

Pendeford Former estate in Tettenhall ancient parish. The present fragmented hamlet of Pendeford by the Penk and on a hill overlooking the Penk is 3.5m NW of Wolverhampton, 2.25m SSW of Coven. A **Roman** road from Pennocrucium on Watling Street can be traced SE of the site of Pendeford Hall (VCH vol 20 p3). The first element of the **name** is thought to be composed of the roots 'pen' a height and 'ti' 'tai' house (NSFCT 1910 p162), or it is from the personal name Penda (VCH vol 20 p12) (SSE 1996 p16), perhaps from Penda, king of Mercia (625-655) (SPN p144). The second element is from ford, presumably from a crossing of the Penk (VCH vol 20 p12) (SSE 1996 p16) (SPN p144): hence Penda's ford. However, Upper Pendeford Farm where the original settlement may have been, is not on the Penk, but on high land S of Pendeford Hall. The ford is probably on the old road to Penkridge from the S: hence - 'hill-house near the road' (NSFCT 1910 p162). The **manor** of Pendeford appears in DB (SSE 1996 p16), and is one of the few places in England the orthography of which has remained unchanged since DB (HOPTT p91). Pendeford manor, although forming a part of Tettenhall ancient parish, lay within the bounds of Cannock Forest. Between 1278 to 1536 it belonged to St Thomas' Priory, Stafford, and had passed to the Fowlers by the end of the C16. It remained with branches of the Fowler family, with those who became the Fowler-Butlers in the C19 holding the manor at the end of the C19 (HOPTT pp93,96-98) (VCH vol 20 pp23,30). There was possibly a **deserted village** in the vicinity of Lower Pendeford Farm or 0.75m to the SSW where a caravan park is, possibly deserted in the C17 (SSAHST 1970 p35). Pendeford was one of the prebends of Tettenhall Collegiate Church (HOPTT p67) and was in Tettenhall Regis manor (W p205) (VCH vol 3 pp319,320). Near Pendeford Bridge at SJ 887034 was a **windmill** on a small hill. Its earliest reference occurs in 1819 and it does not appear on the OS map of 1883 (WBJ pp47-48) (VCH vol 20 p34). Another mill may have also existed at Upper Pendeford Farm (WBJ pp47-48). A **strange pool** at Pendeford, perhaps near Pendeford Hall, which became troubled prior to rain, with bubbles rising in it and a yellow scum forming on the surface, which the rain washes away, was noted by Dr Plot in the later C17. Plot thought the bubbling was created by fish or eels having sensed a change in the atmosphere (NHS p45) (SHOS vol 2 p202). **Wolverhampton Municipal Airport**. Boulton Paul Aircraft Ltd set up on a site 2.5m NNW of Wolverhampton in 1936. They occupied a new factory next to the forthcoming Wolverhampton Airport, which opened to the W of it on June 25 1938 (EAS p16) (VCH vol 2 p171. vol 20 p12) or on June 27 1938 (Wolverhampton Chronicle March 19 1999 p17) and was at first operated by The Midland Aero Club until requisitioned by the RAF at the beginning of WW2 (TCOP pp83-98). During WW2 a mock factory was erected to fool enemy bombers. It has since disappeared (BDH p188). The airport hosted the King's Cup Air Race in 1950 which included Group Capt Peter Townsend in his Hurricane. The action shots for the film 'The Man in the Sky' starring Jack Hawkins were filmed here in 1950 (WF p51) or 1956 (TCOP p95). The airport also featured in the former TV soap opera, Crossroads, during the 1960s (TCOP p95). In its history there have been about five air crashes. The worst was on April 9 1970 when a De Havilland Dove flew in to pick up the Dowty Boulton Paul directors. The plane crashed in Redhouse Drive killing the two pilots and the occupant of the house; this accident led to the closure of the airport on Dec 31 1970 (WMA vol 1 pp119-

128) (BCM April 1971 p69) (VCH vol 20 p14) (Wolverhampton Chronicle March 19 1999 p17). The airport was converted into an industrial estate in the 1970s (EAS p16), and an housing estate. An area of the housing estate is known as 'Dovecotes' after a dovecote, the sole remains of Barnhurst Hall (TCOP p97). The **church**, St Paul, Whitburn Close behind Safeway supermarket, opened in 1981 serves the new housing estate (Collegiate Church, Tettenhall. 1989) (LDD). **PC Henry William Browne** was murdered on the tow path of the Staffs and Worcs Canal at Pendeford Bridge on Aug 7 1887. His killer was never found (TB July 1977 pp33-34. July 1978 pp33-34. Aug 1978 p3).

Pendeford Hall Stood on the W side of Pendeford Hall Lane, 2.25m N of Tettenhall. In Tettenhall ancient parish. Seat of the Fowlers (later the Fowler-Butlers) for 400 years until 1935 (VCH vol 20 p23 il of c1835 from the south facing p33) (TCOP p98p). The old hall was rebuilt in 1670; this date was over the principal door. Over the chimney piece in the dinning-room was cut the arms of the Fowlers. Shaw also noted an excellent cartulary relating to the manor and the priory of St Thomas at Stafford (SHOS vol 2 p202). In 1851 the hall was occupied by Richard Evans (W p22). After being requisitioned during WW2 it was partly demolished in 1953 and what remained was demolished in 1968 (VB p73) (VCH vol 20 p24). The site is currently (1990) occupied by a mobile home park (TCOP p98). In the early C19 William Pitt noted an echo which seemed to reverberate off the front of the house (SHOS vol 2 p203).

Pendeford Mill 2.25m SW of Coven, at SJ 889035, on the confluence of the Penk and Moat Brook. Has been variously called New Mill, Barnhurst Mill, and Pendeford Mill (VCH vol 20 p33). Here on Sept 8 1651 Charles II in flight after the battle of Worcester between Boscobel and Moseley Old Hall dismounted from his horse and continued to Moseley on foot; three of the five Penderell brothers who had accompanied him to here then returned to Boscobel (VCH vol 20 p5) (Moseley Old Hall. National Trust Guide. RA Chand. 1993). The mill house was converted into two cottages in 1912. The mill itself was demolished in 1961 (VCH vol 20 p33). Rev Henry Higginson, the 'Roving Ranter,' was born at Pendeford Mills in 1805 (BS p224) or 1806 (TB Dec 1980 p23). He was educated at Brewood Grammar School. Became a Primitive Methodist minister in 1833, superannuated in 1866. Simms considered him one of the most original characters of his day. He died at Aston, Worcs in 1871 (BS p224), and is buried in the cemetery attached to Round Oak Chapel (TB Dec 1980 p23).

Pendrell Hall House 1m NW of Codsall. Built in c1870 by Edward Viles of Bilston, editor of the Gentlewoman's Journal. The Gaskells moved here from the Birches in 1910 (TCOP p136p of in 1912). Has appeared as Pendryl Hall (VCH vol 20 p79) and Pendry Hall (1905 OS map). In 1926 the estate was bought by Frank Gaskell, the son of a Lancashire industrialist. He remodelled the house. In 1955 his family sold it to Staffordshire county council, which opened the hall as a residential adult education college in 1961 (VCH vol 20 p79) (SVB p58), still running in 1997 (Wolverhampton Chronicle May 23 1997 p32). There was a sulphur spring by the Newport road N of Wood Hall Farm. Its medicinal properties were noted by Plot in c1680 (NHS p101). The spring continued to attract visitors until the later C19. In the mid C19 water from the spring ran to the courtyard of an inn on the site of the present Pendrell Hall lodge (Wanderings of a Pen and Pencil. FP Palmer and A Crowquill. 1846. pp36-37) (Transactions of South Midland Institute of Mining, Civil and Mechanical Engineers vol 3 (1871-3) pp16-17) (ABW pp51-52) (VCH vol 5 p20 note. vol 20 p79).

Pendrell Oak Codsall. An old oak, long disappeared (CPP p24p of in 1900).

Penfield At or near Acton in Swynnerton ancient parish (W p425). Pen Fields, S of Keele, occurs on Dower's map. Penfields Wood is 1.5m NNW of Acton.

Penhole Area W of Kinver (1834 OS map). In Kinver parish (SGSAS). There were some houses here by 1841 (VCH vol 20 p121).

Penk, River Rises in the area between Yew Tree Lane and Wrottesley Road, N of Tettenhall, formerly occupied by a meadow called Penkridge Well; the southern end of the meadow is marked by the modern street named Penk Rise (VCH vol 20 p1). Its first appearance above ground is out of a drain at SO 876996. It runs past Dippons Farm, through Perton new housing estate, on the N side of Wergs Hall and on to Pendeford, where there is a spring from where one of its tributaries comes called Penkridge Wells? or it may be the actual source of the Penk? (SHOS vol 2 p198). From Pendeford it runs on the W side of Coven, Somerford, Penkridge and Acton Trussell and joins the Sow at St Thomas Priory to the E of Stafford. Length is 15.5m. Has appeared as 'on lang Penchrich' (996), Pencrigh (c1175), Pencriz (c1250. 1286), Pencke (1568. 1606), Penke becke (1577), and Penk (Saxton's map) (SHC vol 5 part 1 pp166, 177. 1916 p319) (SPNO p16) and Pink (1698) (Illustrated Journeys of Celia Fiennes edited by Chris Morris. 1984. p147). In the later C17 Plot

noted that it was slower than the Trent and the Sow (NHS p43). Bird was told that it was thought the fourth best trout stream in England in 1896 (VB pp78-79). It is said the entire Penk was dredged in 1857-8 by the Moncktons of Stretton Hall who owned much land along its banks (VB p78). Gives its name to Pendeford and Penkridge. Duignan and others think it takes its name from Penkridge (DUIGNAN) (NSFCT 1908 p131) (SPNO p16) (SPN p93).

Penkholm Name of field on the banks of the Trent about Handsacre and Mavesyn Ridware (SHOS vol p183).

Penkhull Large hill-top village above the confluence of the Lyme and the Trent 0.75m WSW of Stoke-upon-Trent, now a suburb merging into the Potteries. Former township with Boothen in Stoke-upon-Trent chapelry in Stoke-upon-Trent ancient parish (W p224).
EARLY. A polished stone axe implement of the **Neolithic** period was found by Mr G Heath the headmaster of Penkhull County Middle School (NSFCT 1953 p105). A leaf-shaped arrowhead of Neolithic period was found in a garden in Chamberlain Avenue, length is 1.25 inches and one inch wide (PRA pp15,17p). A Neolithic or Bronze Age stone axe was found at Penkhull many years before 1962 which went to the Potteries Museum (NSJFS 1962 p26. 1964 p35) (PRA pp15,17p). A Neolithic flint arrowhead was discovered in 1979 by Kenneth Shotton of Leawood Road, Trent Vale, and went to the Potteries Museum (PRA pp15,17p). A small pygmy incense cup of the **Middle Bronze Age** two inches high, 3.25 inches wide at its widest with circular impressed decoration was found in 1910 or 1911 during the building of Penkhull Garden Village which went to the Potteries Museum (Staffs Weekly Sentinel Oct 31 1925) (NSFCT vol 60 p188. 1931 p191) (JBAA series 2 vol 37 p254) (NSJFS 1964 p35) (STM June 1969 Supplement p12) (History of Stoke-on-Trent. R Nicholls p40) (VCH vol 8 p174) (SHST p439p) (PRA pp15,17p). Penkhull may have originated as an ancient **British settlement**. It has been suggested that the name is a compound of the British 'pencet' ('end of the wood') and the Old English 'hyll' so 'hill at wood's end' (VCH vol 8 p174) (NSJFS 1981 p2) (SPN p88) (SSE 1996 p16). Ward says it may be equivalent to pink, a name in the past given to primrose, there is a Primrose Hill (see) in the vicinity of Penkhull. Or is of British origin 'pen' (the head), and 'cyl or kyl' (a kiln or oven) (HBST p508). The prefix may represent the Anglo-Saxon personal name 'Pinca' (DUIGNAN). In pagan times the inhabitants of Penkhull were known as 'Penkhull Piles' but had to go though an initiation ceremony to obtain the title which consisted of being drawn through a pool which existed in the grounds of Stoke church until it was filled in (CAST p7).
1000 to PRESENT. The manor of Pinchetel appears in DB. From 1086 until the development of Stoke-upon-Trent town in the C19 Penkhull was the **centre of the population** in this area (VCH vol 8 p174). During and after the Commonwealth period Newcastle-under-Lyme manor courts were held at Penkhull since Newcastle Castle was in ruins (NSFCT 1943 p18). In Mill Street was a windmill. The earliest reference to a miller is in 1818, although Penkhull probably had a windmill long before this date due to its high position (WBJ p33). One may have existed from the C14 (PRA pp81-82). By 1891 it had been dismantled when the spindle was said to be in a stable at the end of Penkhull Terrace (WBJ p33) (SK p95). The windmill was pulled down in late 1830s (VCH vol 8 p202). There was a **lock-up** in Penkhull in 1829 which served Penkhull and Stoke (VCH vol 8 p195). Became a separate ecclesiastical parish in 1845 (GLAUE p419). The **church**, St Thomas the Apostle, in Rothwell Street, was built in 1842 (VCH vol 8 p192). For Sir Oliver Lodge see The Views. The famous artists, **Ellis Roberts** and the brothers Rhead, all lived at Penkhull in their younger days (NSSG p47).

Penkhull Garden Village Residential garden suburb 0.5m S of Penkhull, which developed from 1910 along Trent Valley Road. The first house opened in The Croft area in March 1910. The project, which failed to reach its envisaged size, collapsed soon after WW1 with only 95 houses built (VCH vol 8 p174) (PPP vol 1 p91. vol 2 p97) (Local Historian 27 (1) Feb 1997 pp30-47).

Penkhull Green Open space in centre of Penkhull village, in the centre of which the church stands (History of Penkhull. VG Aston p41) (VCH vol 8 p174).

Penkhull Hall Penkhull. Deaconess BI Smee owner of The Views (see) believed that Penkhull Hall had stood on the site of The Views (PRA p77).

Penkridge Ancient parish and former township. The small town of Penkridge lies by the Penk at its confluence with Whiston Brook, 4.75m S of Stafford. EARLY. Penkridge may have been the site for an **ancient British settlement**, the name of which was something like 'Pencric,' which the Romans stole and Latinised to 'Pennocrucium' and applied to their settlement on Watling Street at Stretton. Penkridge may be associated with the worship of the Celtic 'fearsome deity' - the Dark One, for the god Pennocrucion is the same as the Gaelic god of the Irish harvest, Cenn Croich or Crom Dubh, the Dark One (The Life and Death of a Druid Prince. Anne Ross and Don Robins. 1989) (SMM p175). Camden wrongly believed Penkridge was the site of the Roman 'Pennocrucium' (W p466) (NSFCT 1908 p116). A brass head of the bolt of a catapula of **Roman** origin was found at Penkridge in the mid C18 (W p466).

600 to 1086. The **name** has appeared as Pencric (958), Pencric (1000), Pancriz (DB), Pencriche (1156), Peichriz (1158), Pencris (1203), Penkriche (1271), Penkeriche (1360), Penckereche (1428), Penkrigge (c1430), Penckrige (1578), Penkarich (1674), Panckeridge (1698), and vulgarly as Pankrage (1724-47) (Illustrated Journeys of Celia Fiennes edited by Chris Morris. 1984. p148) (SPNO p87) (SPN p92). The early form 'Pencric,' is probably of Celtic origin. Duignan separates the word into two - 'pen' and 'cric.' In Welsh 'pen' means 'the head, extremity, or upper part (of anything),' in Gaelic 'crioch, criche' (Irish 'crioc, criocans') means a boundary, end, limit, frontier, giving 'the head or end of the border or frontier' (SHC 1916 p321) (SPN p92): The Penk was an ancient boundary of Cannock Forest. Or if derived from Irish 'Cenn Crudich' then 'chief of the mound' or in Modern Welsh 'Pen Crug' formerly written 'Pen Cruc' and earlier possibly as 'Pennos Cruci' and 'Pennocruc.' Rev Thomas Barnes thinks the 'chief of the mound' is a reference to the Celtic Zeus (NSFCT 1908 p118). In the absence of a hill (at Penkridge), Anne Ross and Don Robins take, 'head of the mound' or 'chief mound' to be a burial mound (The Life and Death of a Druid Prince. Anne Ross and Don Robins. 1989) (SMM p175). The Romans probably Latinised 'Pencric' or its earlier forms to produce Pennocrucium, the name of their station situated in Pencric district (DUIGNAN) (LGS p198). The Brythonic form 'Penn' occurred in Pennocrucium (NSFCT 1922 p170). Some have thought the name from the Anglo-Saxon name Pinca or from 'benn' a mountain and 'uig' an enclosure (NSFCT 1908 p145). There is no authority for regarding Penkridge as being the 'ridge on the Penk' (NSFCT 1908 p145). **Mercian royal residence.** The description of Penkridge in the test of the charter of 958, as 'the famous place which is called Pencric,' shows that it was then a place of importance, and an occasional residence of the Mercian kings (LGS p198) (VCH vol 3 p298) (SSE 1987 p23). King Edgar (d975) is said to have made Penkridge his headquarters during a campaign to deal with a combined Danish-Irish force entering the country by way of Cheshire; and since at that time, the seat of government was with the king, Penkridge for a brief period held the distinction of being the capital of England (St Michael and All Angels, Penkridge: Royal Collegiate Parish Church. R Cheadle). There is an ancient thoroughfare leading from Penkridge to the W (Newport, Shrewsbury, Chester), known as 'King Street' (DUIGNAN p117). There was a medieval tradition that Penkridge Collegiate Church was founded by King Edgar (957-75) out of a church here said to have been founded by King Eadred (946-55) (VCH vol 3 p298). Perhaps this church had its origins in a chantry chapel said by tradition to have been established at the burial place of Saxon dead who died in a skirmish at Bull Bridge (see) as they went after Danes retreating from the battle of Tettenhall (see) in c910 (St Michael and All Angels, Penkridge: Royal Collegiate Parish Church. R Cheadle p2).

1086 to 1500. The manor belonged to Edward the Confessor, and as a royal manor was inherited by William I (HOS p17). The parish **church**, St Michael and All Angels, near the junction of Pinfold Lane and Church Road, was formerly the church of the Penkridge Collegiate Church. There was a church, Our Lady, probably on this site by 920. The present church has some early C13 work (St Michael and All Angels, Penkridge: Royal Collegiate Parish Church. R Cheadle) (BOE p220). Became a separate ecclesiastical parish in 1551 which included the chapels of Coppenhall, Dunston, Shareshill, and Stretton (GLAUE p419). **Beating the bounds** was practiced over three days in Rogation Week in Penkridge parish until 1820 (SCSF pp25-26) (HOP pp29-30). The earliest reference to Penkridge being a **borough** is in c1290 and the last is in 1471 after which borough status lapsed (NSJFS 1972 p69). The **lock-up** was in Bellbrook not far from the Court House, now a library (HOP p84) (PVH p22il) (SOP p128 opposite p of) (SVB p136). The **stocks** were in Bellbrook not far from the Court House, now a library (HOP p84) (PVH p22il) (VCH vol 5 p106) (WMAG March 1976 p16p) (SOP p128 opposite p of) (SVB p136). According to Hackwood, the stocks were outside the Police Station (SCSF p130). A **cottage** at Penkridge, said in 1976 to be about 500 years old, contains a priest hole (WMAG March 1976 p16p). **Sundials.** In Main Street is a sundial in which figures are cut. It rested on an elaborate octagonal stone which in turn was supported by a square sandstone shaft bearing no relation to the other work. It probably came from the church. There was another sundial in a garden behind houses in Earl Street. It was probably a rnillstone worn thin and was smashed up into pieces and taken away in the late 1950s (SLM spring 1957 p29). **Persons and visitors.** In 1212 **Henry of London**, Archbishop of Dublin, came to reside in the Penkridge Deanery and remained at Penkridge until 1228 (WMAG March 1976 p18).

Richard le Pencriche, a pupil at the college in the C14, became notable in English literature. He decreed that students should construe their Latin and Greek into England instead of Norman French (PVH p17).
MARKETS AND FAIRS. Andrew le Blund (or Blounts) was granted a charter on May 23 1244 to hold a **market** here on Thursdays. The right was confirmed in 1364. The market had lapsed by 1584 and was revived when Sir Fulke Greville was granted a market here in 1617. This was evidently held on Tuesday; it had been discontinued by 1680 but had been resumed by 1747. Market day was still Tuesday in 1817 (SCSF p95) (VCH vol 5 p129) (NSJFS 1971 pp51,62). Stock and general markets were held on Mondays by at least 1868 to at least the 1950s (VCH vol 5 p129). The market in 1988 was held on Wednesdays (MR p254). A **fair** in the vill of Penkridge was granted with the manor by Hugh Hose or Hussey to the Archbishop of Dublin in 1215 (VCH vol 5 p129). There was a fair on April 30 by 1817. It was reputed to be the best in England for saddle and draught horses (THS p256) (OWEN) (SOP p172) (HOP p67-71), and was still being held in 1912 but not by 1924 (VCH vol 5 p129). A fair was granted to the lord of the manor in 1617. It was, by 1680, held on **May Day** and seems to have lapsed by 1817 (VCH vol 5 p129). Another fair was granted in 1617. It was by 1680 held on **Midsummer Day** and seems to have lapsed by 1817 (VCH vol 5 p129). By 1834 Penkridge had a fair, held on **Sept 2** (which added to the two existing fairs). It was still being held in 1912 but not by 1924 (VCH vol 5 p129). A fair on **Sept 28 and 29** and three days following was granted to Hugh le Blund in 1278 (VCH vol 5 p129). The grant was confirmed to Hugh le Blund or Blount or Flavus, lord of Penkridge, and his heirs in 1312 (VCH vol 5 p129) or 1316 (SCSF p103). Various dates from Sept 21 to Oct 2 have been given for the holding of this fair in the period from the C13 to the mid C18 (SCSF pp97,103) (VCH vol 5 p129). Lord Broke sold the manor in 1519 but reserved to himself the profits of the fair (NSJFS 1974 p26). Others say the fair descended with the manor until at least 1617 (VCH vol 5 p129). By 1522 horses were being dealt in at the fair and were the sole merchandise in 1598. In the late C16 Penkridge was described as 'a small village famous for a horse fair' (Britannia. Camden. p530) (VCH vol 5 p129). Penkridge horse fair became nationally famous gaining coverage in the London Gazette of Sept 1674, Daniel Defoe's 'Tour through Great Britain' of 1734, in which he describes it as the 'greatest horse-fair in the world' where 'an incredible number of gentlemen attended with their grooms to buy gallopers, or racehorses,' and 'Schofield's Middlewich Journal' of Aug 1756 which tells that the fair was not considered as highly as it once was (SCSF p103) (MR p254). In 1756 the first Monday and Tuesday in Sept were fixed upon for the fair. But by 1817 the fair seems to have lapsed (VCH vol 5 p129). There was a fair on **Oct 10** by 1817. It was reputed to be the best in England for saddle and draught horses (THS p256) (OWEN) (SOP p172) (HOP p67-71), and was still being held in 1912 but not by 1924 (VCH vol 5 p129). A fair was granted to the lord of the manor in 1617. It was, by 1680, held on **Oct 28** and seems to have lapsed by 1817 (VCH vol 5 p129).

1500 to PRESENT. Penkridge's several **trades** were brick making, stone quarrying (from C13 to 1940) and at Springslade Pool (MR p254) iron working from the C16 (SCSF p112) (VCH vol 5 p106). There was a **windmill** which appears on maps between 1775 and 1820 shortly before Cuttlestone Bridge to E of the Water Eaton road (WBJ p33). In the **Civil War** Royalist troops quartered here were worsted in a small skirmish in May 1645 (HOP p18 note) (VCH vol 5 p106). At Penkridge many of the schoolboys regularly sported an oak-leaf on May 29 to celebrate the Restoration of Charles II; Hackwood implies that they were still participating in the custom in 1924 (SCSF p19). The earliest recorded **horse racing** in the county was at Penkridge in 1680, held after the Midsummer Fair (HOS p64). Horse racing continued until 1734 and was revived in the C19 (MR p254). There was a three-quarter mile race course to the E of Preston Hill where September races were held in c1825 and were still being held in 1834 (VCH vol 5 p106). In 1737 there was a large fire at Penkridge (ADD p30). Penkridge church tower was used by Yates as a **triangulation point** for his map (1775), and by the surveyors for the first OS map (SHC 4th series vol 12 1984 vii). For the **Penkridge Troop** raised in 1803 see Teddesley Hall. **Railways.** Sherlock says, Penkridge Viaduct, which spans the Levedale Road and the Penk at SJ 920144, is the most notable work of the GJR in Staffs. It was built by Thomas Brassey (1805-1870) and completed for the opening of the line in 1837. Each of the seven arches has a span of 30 feet and is 37 feet high (SA Sept 26 1885 p6) (VCH vol 5 p105) (IAS p185). Penkridge had its own airfield which operated in **WW2** (WMA vol 1 p213). In 1931 **demolition of the old High Street** and Bucknals Bury (road leading to Stafford), which together resembled the characterful narrow high streets of Cheadle and Stone, was proposed by the county council for widening the Wolverhampton-Stafford road; a bypass was

considered unfeasible as the land about Penkridge was too marshy. Despite protests by the town work went ahead and by 1937 the road was significantly widened with 38 buildings having been destroyed (SOP pp165 see map, 188p of the old thoroughfare) (The Good Old Grit: A History of the People of Penkridge 1270-1939. Robert Maddocks. 1994 pp208-210). **Strange sights**. A flock of Scandinavian birds rarely seen in Britain landed at Penkridge in January 1975 (SN Jan 24 1975 p9). Pickford and his wife saw the ghost of a little girl dashing in and out of headstones in the churchyard. One of the graves was of a five-year old named Sarah Elizabeth (SMM p174). **Persons and visitors**. **Elizabeth I** passed through Penkridge in 1575 (Penkridge PR) (VCH vol 5 p106). There is a tradition she stayed at the White Hart Inn (see). There is another tradition that Mary, Queen of Scots, was refreshed at the White Hart on two occasions during her captivity in Staffs. For **William Southall**, a Catholic priest hunter of Penkridge in the later C17, see Tixall Old Hall. **John Wesley** visited Penkridge on Oct 9 1745 (HOP p83) (PVH p14). **Cecil James Croydon Tildesley** (d1963), poet, was born at Penkridge on Aug 2 1877, the younger son of James Carpenter Tildesley (d1907), poet and author of HOP. CJC Tildesley was still residing in Penkridge in the late 1920s. His reputation rests on the poem 'Cannock Chase' about Cannock Chase (see), which appeared in Chamber's Journal in 1918 (PSS pp233,369) (VFC p130).
NEWSPAPERS. The **Penkridge Courier and West Staffordshire Counsellor**, an edition of Cannock Chase Courier and West Staffordshire Counsellor, was appearing between at least Nov 9 1961 and April 9 1964 (SHJ spring 1996 p22). The **Penkridge Advertiser**, an edition of the Cannock Advertiser, was appearing between at least Feb 27 1969 and June 27 1974 (SHJ spring 1996 p22).

Penkridge Bank Incline 1m W of Slitting Mill on the Rugeley-Penkridge road, N of Birches Valley (1989 OS map 1:25,000).

Penkridge Collegiate Church The college may have originated in the C10, see under Penkridge. In 1086 there is evidence of a religious community at Penkridge, suggesting a collegiate church. The Crown gave the church of Penkridge to Bishop Clinton of Lichfield in 1136. By the early 1180s Penkridge had been recovered by the Crown and restored to the status of a Royal Free chapel. In 1215 King John bestowed the advowson of the deanery on the Archbishop of Dublin, so each archbishop until 1548 was automatically Dean of Penkridge (VCH vol 3 pp298,299) (VB p79) (SL p95) when it reverted to the Crown (LGS p198). John also bestowed on the Archbishop the manor and fair of Penkridge which had been granted by Hugh Hose or Hussey (VCH vol 3 pp298,299). The college has appeared as St Michael's College. These prebends are mentioned as belonging to the college during its duration: Pillatonhall (1272), Cannock (to C14), Bold (1342), Coppenhall (1365), Shareshill (1365), Dunston (1365), Penkridge (1365), Congreve (1365), Longbridge (1365), the King's Chantry (1365), the Chantry of the Blessed Virgin Mary (1365), the Chantry of the Sacrist (1349), Brennydhalle (1396) (VCH vol 3 p300). Some of these were the seven prebends which the college possessed at its dissolution in 1548. In Aug 1548 the site of the college house and all the deanery possessions in the tenure of Edward Littleton, were granted to John Dudley, Earl of Warwick; his lands were forfeited to the Crown in 1553. In 1581 the Crown granted the college to Edmund Downynge and Peter Aysheton who sold it in 1583 to John Morley and Thomas Crompton. They conveyed the estate to Sir Edward Littleton in 1585 and it remained with the Littletons until sold in the C20. Despite the dissolution the peculiar jurisdiction of the former college over the parish of Penkridge survived until peculiar jurisdictions were abolished in 1846. It is said that Edward Littleton, as tenant, thwarted John Dudley's attempts to sell the estate and in revenge Dudley had all the collegiate buildings destroyed save the church. Some stone from collegiate buildings is said to have been used in the lower parts of housing in Market Street. For possible sites of college property see Deanery Hall (VCH vol 3 pp93,298-303,301. vol 5 p111) (St Michael and All Angels, Penkridge: Royal Collegiate Parish Church. R Cheadle). (SA Aug 22 1885 p3).

Penkridge Heath Lay to the E of Longridge within Penkridge manor and the deanery manor. The common on it was enclosed in 1827 (VCH vol 5 p127).

Penn Ancient parish covering several ridges and hills to the E of the Smestow 18m SSE of Stafford. Present name for the settlement formerly known as Upper Penn.
EARLY. The last Ice Age reached its maximum southern extent about Wolverhampton and glacial boulders lie about Penn (WJO Nov 1909 p293). Penstones Lane to the W of Lower Penn was formerly Pennstones because of the glacial debris (PAIP p61).
1000 to PRESENT. Algar held the Upper Penn estate before the Norman Conquest, whilst Lady Godiva owned the Lower Penn estate. On the S side

of the church, on the corner of Church Hill and Vicarage Road at Upper Penn, is the base and stump of an **ancient cross** said to have been erected by Lady Godiva as a preaching cross in c1050. Itinerant priests of St James' Priory, Dudley, provided occasional services at it until the church was built in c1200. The cross was found under another cross in 1912 (Church Guide photograph) (MR p257) (SMM p177). The present church, of late C12 and early C13 origin, was dedicated to St John the Baptist; the present dedication of the church to St Bartholomew dates to at least 1801 (St Bartholomew's Church, Penn: A Guide. Rachel Hampton. 1997). The **parish**, formed between 1086 and probably 1200 and certainly by 1291, may have formed originally a part of Wombourne or Sedgley or Tettenhall parishes (SHC 1916 p197). Later it just comprised the townships of Upper and Lower Penn. Both anciently lay within the limits of Kinver Forest and both appear in DB, both as Penne. Some say the **name** is from Anglo-Saxon 'penn,' a pen, fold (DUIGNAN) (AMS p448) (SPN p145): The pen may have been a cattle pen which some early settler made in Kinver Forest (LGS p200). Whilst others say Penn is from Welsh 'pen' from the root 'beann' 'benn' mountain, a reference to the high ground in this district (SHOS vol 2 p218) (NSFCT 1908 p136) (EKWALL 1966) (SPN p145). Dunphy gives 'head of the hill,' the original settlement being at Upper Penn, on higher ground (PAIP p45). Mills gives '(place at) the hill' (SSE 1996 p16). Money was left by Raphael and Anne Sedgwick in 1747 for the building of five **almshouses** in Penn. But Sedgwick's successor Thomas Bradney failed to honour their bequest which was to have commenced in 1751. It took an order in chancery in 1760 to compel Bradney to build the almshouses. They were erected in Pennwood Lane and are still (1998) used as almshouses (PENOP p8) (info Angus Dunphy). For Penn **windmills** see Penn Fields and Goldthorn Hill. Dr Wilkes in the later C18 described Upper Penn as a small town (SHOS vol 2 p218). **Food riots** occurred at Penn on April 29 1800 and were directed at farmers. 150 were involved (LOU pp152,375). **Residential growth**. By the mid C19 Penn Road and Penn village were becoming residences for wealthy industrialists and professionals from Wolverhampton (PENOP p8). The Penns became separate civil parishes in 1866 (GLAUE p419). The middle class Penn Court, Penn House and Woodlands estates were all laid out as building land in the mid 1930s (PENOP pp9,70). Penn generally now refers to the area formerly known as Upper Penn. Penn was a ward of Wolverhampton borough by 1982. For the cottage whose second storey was a **railway carriage** see Bradmore. For the **toll house** in Penn Road see 'Investigating Penn' by Wolverhampton WEA. 1975. BCM April 1975 p58p. Some **motor cycles** built by WH Boulton of Penn in the 1920s were called Penn Nibs (PVBC p63p). **Strange sights**. A dark brown cat about four feet long, perhaps a puma, was sighted in the Compton, Aldersley, Lower Penn, Wombourne area in July 1980 and exploring a partly built house in March 1981 (Shropshire Star March 17 1981) (Birmingham Evening Mail March 20 1981) (MMSE pp94-95,99,288). In Penn Road the ghost of a tall woman appeared beside a mother walking in fields with her daughter. The ghost was only noticed by the daughter. The next day at about the same time the mother was taken ill and died (SR p107) (TB April 1988 p5). **Natives and visitors**. According to Dunphy no arch of coal was erected across Penn Road for Queen Victoria's visit to Wolverhampton in Nov 1866 as claimed by PENOP p51p, instead it was erected on the Wednesfield Road (info Angus Dunphy). **Elizabeth Gough**, a nanny from Penn engaged to work at the Kent household in 1859 at Road Hill House, Road, Somerset, was suspected of murdering her charge, baby Francis Saville, but the real murderer was Constance Kent, the baby's step sister (TB April 1982 p5) (SMML pp96-99). **Vera Isabel Arlett**, poet was born in Penn in 1896 and lived here until c1906. In 1927 she published a selection of her lyrical poems, some of which seem to have been inspired by her childhood (PSS pp416-421 p) (VFC p4).

Pennard House Walsall Wood Road, near Druids Heath. Built by 1834 (1834 OS map) (SNAR p50). If an old place name, is from the root 'beann,' 'benn' Welsh 'pen' a mountain, and 'ard' high (NSFCT 1908 p145).

Penn Brook Rises at Goldthorn Park runs to Wodehouse.

Penn Common Common land 0.5m SE of Penn. Formerly stretched as far N as St Bartholomew's church, Penn (PENOP p7), and as far S as Gospel End in Sedgley ancient parish. The growing of malt and barley on the common is remembered in the name of the Barley Mow Inn in Pennwood Lane (PENOP p94p). In the mid C19 bare-fist pugilist fights and annual races took place on the common (AMS p471) (PENOP p9). The plan to build the Midland, Birmingham, Wolverhampton and Milford Junction Railway's main line across Penn Common in 1883 failed (PPTP p28). The brewery tower at the bottom of Penn Common was built by John Millard of Netherby Hall, Sedgley, in the later C19 (PAIP pp112,114il) (PPTP p30). Penn Artisans Golf Club opened a course on the common in 1897 and closed in 1993. The club produced several professionals including Charlie Stowe who represented Britain in the 1937 and 1945 Walker Cups, and Archie Compston, who was born at No. 11 Turf Cottages, above the duck pond on Penn Common on Jan 14 1893. He came second in the British Open in 1925, third in 1928 and sixth in 1930. He was runner-up in the French Championship in 1929; winner of the News of the World Tournament (PGA) in both 1925 and 1927 as well as the Gleneagles Tournament in 1925 (PONP pp113-114) (Wolverhampton Chronicle Jan 7 2000 p14). By the early C20 the common was popular as a place of recreation (PENOP p9). It has been also a stopping-place for gypsies (PENOP p77p). There were numerous disputes in the C19 and C20 about the use and ownership of the common. One such case in 1912 gave rise to an enquiry in the High Court (PENOP p74p). One night in WW2 incendiary bombs were dropped on the common (PPTP p26).

Penn Court Former estate in Upper Penn (info Angus Dunphy). The house called Penn Court was occupied by William Hanbury Sparrow in 1844 who was succeeded by his son William Mander Sparrow who was succeeded by his daughter Mrs Emma Fowke until c1899. At the beginning of WW1 it was used as a temporary barracks and demolished after WW1 for housing land (PMPD p48). Developed with housing in the 1930s (PENOP p9).

Penn Craig House at Lower Penn. Built in 1895 (PAIP p52).

Penn Fields Residential suburb 1m NNE of Penn. Shaw records a **burial mound** near the turnpike on the Worcester road, a little N of Grazeley Brook (SHOS vol 2 p165). This is a possible reference to Dead Lad's Grave? Gunstone was unable to locate the mound in the 1960s (NSJFS 1965 p59). To the W of the Stourbridge road at SO 902969 was a **windmill** advertised to be let in 1813 with a dwelling and bakery and advertised again in 1837 (SA Sept 23 1837) (WBJ p47). With the building of the **church**, St Philip (1859), Church Road, the Penn Fields area became a ecclesiastical separate parish, known as Upper Penn. This was renamed Penn Fields in 1966. Modern churches in this parish include one at Muchall and another at Merry Hill (PENOP p9) (GLAUE p419). **Residential development**. By the late C19 the focus of Penn Fields had moved from Coalway Road and St Philip's to the Lea Road area where numerous streets had been laid out. Because of difficulties with operating trams on the route to Stubbs' Road, Penn Fields, a **motor bus service** was inaugurated in 1905 making Wolverhampton the first municipal tramways undertaking in Britain to operate a bus service. This operated until the construction of the tram route in 1909. Birches Barn and the Beckminster estates remained open land until after WW1 when they were selected for the site of Wolverhampton's first municipal housing under the 'houses for heroes' scheme (PENOP pp9,70). **Natives. Marjorie Crosbie** (1892-1971), poetess, was born at Worcester Lodge, Penn Fields; she later lived at Codsall (PSS pp434-439 p) (VFC p33). For Able Seaman **Douglas Morris Harris** (d1917) of Pennfields see Wolverhampton. **Judith Glover**, historical novelist, travel and exploration writer, journalist, and author of Tiger Lilies (1991) was born in Penn Fields in 1943. She was educated at Wolverhampton Girls' High School.

Penn Hall W of the church in Vicarage Road, Penn. A former hall stood on the site of the present hall (POAP p43). The present house was built originally as a hospital by Raphael Sedgwick (d1747) and his wife Anne (d1728) in the C17 (BOE pp323-324) (SGS p188) (PENOP p25p). Dunphy says it was built by Thomas Bradney (d1782), possibly Raphael Sedgwick's brother-in-law (POAP p48) or son of William Bradney (probably Anne Sedgwick's cousin) (PAIP p104), in accordance with the wishes of the Sedgwicks. The architect was William Baker (POAP p48, il on front cover). Others say Thomas Bradney, who was High Sheriff of Staffs in 1752, only encased the house after the Sedgwicks built it (BOE pp323-324) (SGS p188) (PENOP p25p). In 1782 the estate passed to Thomas Bradney's daughters, Ellen and Esther, by his third wife. It was Ellen (d1829) and her husband William Persehouse who made Penn Hall their home. Their son, William Bradney Persehouse, inherited the house. After his death in 1843 it was occupied by John W Sparrow, the industrialist, who was living here in 1851. When the next tenant, William Underhill, died in 1899, the Persehouses sold the estate (POAP p48). In 1899 (STC p16p) or 1902 it was bought by Lt Col Thomas Francis Waterhouse of Sedgley (b1865). He employed HT Hare to remodel and improve the hall. In 1923 Waterhouse was found guilty of fraud and sold the house. It was bought in 1924 by Francis JJ Gibbons who resided here to after WW2. In 1947 it was purchased by Wolverhampton's Watch Committee. They opened it in 1948 as a Residential and Training Hostel for the Borough Police. In 1974 the Police Authority moved out and the hall became Penn Hall Special School, officially opened by Joan Lester MP, in June 1975. The Education Authority planned and built a completely new school in the grounds between 1975 and 1981 (POAP p62). By 1990 the hall was the residential part of the school (PENOP p25). Has an Art Nouveau style sundial above one of the entrances (BOE p323) (MR p257). (TB Dec 1997 p10il from SHOS). In the grounds

are an early C18 pedimented summerhouse and an early C19 octagonal Gothick summerhouse, which was in ruins in the early 1970s (BOE p324).

Penn Hill Former name for the 300 feet high hill on the N side of Seisdon village. This may be the 'hill of the Saxons' from which the name Seisdon is derived. About 1300 it was known as Penn Hill, a name derived from the Celtic 'penn' meaning a hill. By the late C16 it was called Round Hill or Whitney Hill (VCH vol 20 p185). The Penn Hill on the 1834 OS map is the incline between Upper and Lower Penn and that which Springhill Lane runs along (ALP p12).

Penn House Former estate in Upper Penn (info Angus Dunphy). Developed with housing in the 1930s (PENOP p9).

Penn Manor Formerly stood in the present Manor Close, on S side of Penn Road, N of Manor Road, Upper Penn. Was built probably after 1840 by a wealthy industrialist or professional from Wolverhampton. By the late 1880s it was occupied by Mrs Thompson. She was followed by Edward Whitehouse Lewis. After 1910 the house was occupied by Frederick William Paddey. The house was pulled down in the 1950s (PONP pp4,8,10).

Penn Moor Farm Georgian farmhouse situated on an elevated ridge and fronting Vicarage Road, Upper Penn. Throughout the C19 it was inhabited by the Jenks family. Sold with the Lloyd estate in 1901. The name is from Haddocks Moor, the name of a field forming part of its land (PPTP p1 il facing).

Pennocrucium Former Roman settlement 1m SE of Stretton (Penkridge). Pennocrucium is mentioned in the Itinerary of Antoninus of the C3. (SD p50) (Itinerarium Curiosum. W Stukeley. 1776. vol 2 p23) (SHOS vol 1 p30) (VCH vol 1 p192). The **name** is probably a Latinised version of 'Pencric' the name for the ancient British settlement at Penkridge (DUIGNAN) (LGS p198) (NSFCT 1922 p170) (The Life and Death of a Druid Prince. Anne Ross and Don Robins. 1989) (SMM p175). Until recently its site remained unlocated with only conjectures from various writers as to its location. It was thought to be at the Roman villa (see below) near **Engleton** after the villa was discovered in 1937 (OSST 1936 pp30-38); at or near the Spread Eagle Inn, **Gailey**, by Mr Codrington and CGO Bridgeman (Roman Roads in Britain. Codrington. p79) (SHC 1916 p321); at Penkridge by Camden, Garner and Langford (GNHS pp68,134) (S&W p379) (NSFCT 1908 p116); at or near **Stretton** by Plot, Stukeley, Horsley and Masefield (NHS p401) (Britannia Romana. J Horsley. 1732. p419) (W p466) (SH p59) (LGS p223) (VCH vol 1 pp187,192); at **Teddesley Park** by Calvert, after a Roman short dagger was found there in 1780 (SSC p121 in the intro). A brass head the bolt of a catapulta was found there in mid C18 (SSC p117) (W p466). The true site, astriding **Watling Street**, 1m SE of Stretton, was first identified from an air photograph taken in 1946 (NSJFS 1964 p17). BAS excavated the site in 1948 after which Dr JK St. Joseph concluded it was Pennocrucium (NSFCT 1948 p109) (BAST vol 74 pp1,6,10). Pennocrucium appears to have been a collection of Roman forts and settlements from various periods to the N and S of Watling Street situated around the junction of many Roman roads; to Whitchurch (NW) (OSST 1936 pp30-38), Wroxeter (W), Wall (E), Metchley (SE) (WFW p32), Greensforge (S) (Roman Roads in Britain. ID Margary. 1957. vol 2. pp27-28), and Buxton (NE) (VCH vol 7 p98). They are: **A fort**. At Stretton Mill at SJ 897111, 1000 feet N of Watling Street consisting of 3.5 acres, about 470 feet by 450 feet, and with a single ditch on one side, double ditches on three sides; was occupied sometime between 50 - 200 AD (OSST 1945-47 pp23-27) (VCH vol 4 pp163,164) (BAST vol 69 p50) (NSJFS 1964 p37) (HOS p12) (BOE p271) (BDH pp30,31). A second fort has been discovered on the same site; both forts are possibly of the C1 period (LSWA p7). **A fort**. On the same site as former, occupied sometime between 50 - 200 AD, but at another time to former, noted by Pevsner (BOE p271). **A fort**. Of rectangular form between Water Eaton and Kinvaston at SJ 909114, consisting of 26.5 acres; with dimensions NS 780 feet and EW 1475 feet. The fort is enough to house half a legion. It was built sometime between 60-80 AD (HOS p12). A recent air photograph shows evidence for two periods in this fort (BAST vol 69 p52. vol 73 p100) (NSJFS 1964 p32). The fort was excavated in 1947 (BDH pp30,31). **A villa**. At Engleton at SJ 894104, 500 yards S of Watling Street with a small bath wing. It was discovered and excavated in 1937 (WAS 2nd Field Study Trip pp1-6) (SHC 1938 pp267-293 ps ils) (NSJFS 1964 p17) (HOS p12) (BOE p79), at which time it was thought, wrongly, to be the true site of Pennocrucium (OSST 1936 pp30-38). Is said to have been inhabited probably between the late C2 and C4 AD (VCH vol 5 p21). A Roman pillar said to come from it has been utilised as the shaft of a sundial in the grounds of Engleton Hall Farm (BDH pp24,25il, 26il,27,28). A coin of Eadred (946-995) was found here (BDH p27). A cross-bow type brooch has been found at the Engleton villa (BDH p27 il). **Civil settlement**. Or fortified village with a posting station where travellers could change horses astriding Watling Street at SJ 905107; occupied throughout most of the Roman period or Pevsner says between the C2 to C4; measuring 700 feet by 450 feet and surrounded by three ditches. Excavated in 1948 (NSFCT 1948 p109) (HOS p12) (BOE p79). **Brooch finds**. A dolphin brooch has been found at Pennocrucium, a fibula brooch was found at the Bell Inn on the A5, a C1 AD brooch was found at Bradshaw's farm, and fibula brooches, dating from C1 to C2 AD, have been found near Blackladies (BDH pp28,32).

Pennover House at the corner of the Avenue and Vicarage Road, Penn. Seat of Theodore Addenbrooke (b1867) (PMPD pp55-56).

Pennycrofts The name is preserved in Pennycrofts Court, 0.5m E of Stafford. Pasture owned by the widow Crossapeny in 1535. By 1670 the area was known as Pennycrofts (SPN p111).

Pennycroft Well Holy well E of The Wharf on E side of disused railway, Uttoxeter, on left hand side of road to Doveridge. Is sulphurous (HOU p15) (LTD p108). Good for weak eyes (OSST 1944-1945) (SJC p10). Was decorated in early May by Marsh Mallow flowers. So called because a penny was given to the afflicted who came to it for its healings virtues (HOU pp263-264). When Redfern visited the well in 1881 it was completely hidden under a bog (SLM Oct 1951 p20). (R 1860-1861) (BCC vol 2 p110) (MWN Sept 23 1893).

Penny Hill The top end of Wales Lane, Barton-under-Needwood, was known as Penny Hill (UNT p121).

Pennymore Hay At Deepmore S of Calf Heath. Marked on 1834 OS map.

Pennyquart Well Pennyquart Farm, Croxton. A well in the Woodland division in Eccleshall ancient parish. So called as the farmer sold water from it for one penny a quart in c1800 during a drought (BOV p48) and it was the only well in the area not dry (BPS p150) or the water was so pure it could be sold for this (SFL p70). (STMSM July 1880 p32) (SW p107).

Pensnett Former district parish (W p184) 1m ESE of Kingswinford. In Kingswinford ancient parish. The area now known as Pensnett appears as Commonside on the 1834 OS map. The name is from Pensnett Chase. Became a separate ecclesiastical parish in 1844 (W p184) (GLAUE p419). The church, St Mark, N of High Street on Vicarage Lane, was built in 1846-1849 (BOE p222). It contains a sword which once belonged to William Ewart Gladstone (BCM summer 2000 pp9,26).

Pensnett Canal Spurs off the Dudley Canal at Parkhead at S end of the Dudley Tunnel. Built in 1839-1840 by Lord Dudley's Trust to serve the Round Oak and other iron works belonging to his lordship, and terminated at the Wallows. Disused in the 1940s except for a short section to the Hart's Hill Iron Company which lasted until 1950 (BCM summer 1995 pp25-27). Has also appeared as Lord Ward's Canal (VCH vol 2 p297 see map) (SWY p10).

Pensnett Chase Lay over high undulating country between Kingswinford and Dudley. Private medieval forest which descended with Dudley manor and consequently was mainly owned by the de Somery family and their successors, the Suttons (alias Dudley) of Dudley Castle (see). The chase started perhaps as part of Kinver Forest and was granted to the de Somerys by the Crown. It stretched from just S of Himley in the N to the Stour in the S and from Kingswinford in the W to Dudley manor in the E (NSJFS 1968 pp42,50 fig 1). Pensnett has appeared as Pensnet (1244), Peninak (1247), Pennak (1271), Penynak (1292), and Pensned (1327) (SPN p94). 'Pen' may be from Welsh 'pen' head, end (Pensnett occupies high land). 'Snett' may be from Anglo-Saxon 'snead,' detached - the chase having been detached from Kinver Forest (DUIGNAN). 'The wood on the hill' (KCPC p8), or 'the wood on Pen Hill' (WMVB p126). 'Hill, or enclosure, of the woodland area' (SPN p94). First mention is made of the chase in 1291, although it may have been referred to in 1275 (VCHW vol 3 p100) or in 1254 when Roger de Somery was reported to be claiming a free chase 'in the hay of Sedgley and the wood of Penn.' The chase seems to have been accepted by the Crown by at least 1273 (SSE 1990 p25). At the end of C15 the chase is sometimes known as the Chase of Dudley (SSE 1990 p46). In the mid C16 men of Wordsley, Himley and Kingswinford in a concerted action against enclosure broke 50 perches of hedge erected around Merry Hill Coppice on Pensnett Chase (KCPC pp26,28) (NSJFS 1974 p48). Notionally, the hays of Ashwood and Chasepool of Kinver Forest were considered an extension of the chase with Kinver Forest's demise in the C17: the ownership of the two hays having passed to the Dudleys (VCH vol 2 p348). Two of the Gunpowder Plotters, Lyttleton and Winter, after fleeing Holbeche House (see), remained at large on Pensnett Chase and other places in the vicinity until being caught at Hagley Hall or House, Worcs, on Jan 9 1606. At the beginning of the C17 Dud Dudley of Dudley Castle (see), managed a forge on the chase for his father and is said to have discovered or practised smelting iron with coal instead of charcoal here and or at Cradley Forge (see) (VCHW vol 3 p100). In the mid C18 commoners violently protested against enclosure. The part of Pensnett Chase in Dudley parish called Pensnett Wood was enclosed with other commons in 1783

(VCHW vol 3 p100). The last official mention of the chase appears in 'The Pensnett Chase Enclosure Act' of 1784 (KCPC pp9,11).

Pensnett Line Mineral railway lines. The original line was the Shut End Railway of 3.25m. It opened on June 2 1829 and linked the Earl of Dudley's coal pits at Shut End with the Staffs and Worcs canal at Ashwood Basin. It passed N of Kingswinford village, and through Wall Heath. An extension line to Round Oak was built in 1859. The lines closed in 1937. The first locomotive to run on the original line was the Agenoria, made by Messrs Foster, Rastrick & Co at Amblecote. The locomotive worked the line until 1860. In 1885 WO Foster presented 'Agenoria' to the Science Museum, where it remained until WW2, when it went to the National Railway Museum at York. It was still an exhibit at York in 1990 (Birmingham Gazette June 1829) (VCH vol 2 pp306,310) (TB March 1975 p28. Nov 1982 p23) (A History of the Pensnett Railway. WKV Gale 1975) (BHOP pp7,8) (BCM Jan 1979 pp35p-42). Some earthworks of the railway line could still be seen in 1999 (BCM winter 1999/ 2000 pp24-26).

Penwie, The The name occurs in Lady Wulfrun's charter (994) and means probably Pen-way; the way to Penn (HOWM p2). It reputedly connected Penn and Moseley (near Featherstone) manors of Lady Godiva, via the boundary of Bushbury manor. Park Lane towards Scotlands formed a part of it (WFW p31).

Pepper Alley Former area of Walsall Wood. The name only occurs in the 1841 and 1851 census returns. It is uncertain where exactly the area lay but may have been in the Hall Lane area (SNBC p41).

Pepper Slade Slade 2m SE of Brocton, Cannock Chase.

Pepper Street Street 0.75m NNW of Keele. Here is a toll house at SJ 803457 (IANS p19).

Percy Ratcliffe's Cottage Back Lane, Hixon. Tiny cottage which measured only 16 feet by 12 feet. It was demolished in 1986 and replaced by a house called 'Chartley Corner' (info Hixon Local History Society).

Peril Hole A cavern at the bottom of an airshaft created for quarrying purposes in Wren's Nest Hill. Is some 200 feet below the surface. Was named Peril Hole by the Cave Rescue Team following a close shave there. Since 1960 this shaft has been filled in due to the death of a 13 year old Wolverhampton boy who fell down it (BCM Oct 1970 p50p).

Perry Former manor and township in Handsworth ancient parish and hamlet, now a suburb 1m ENE of Handsworth. Some writers claim the **Romans** had a camp at Perry village. Some Roman pottery was found behind the Boar's Head Inn, Perry Barr, and Icknield Street is nearby (THM vol 4 p55). The **name** Perry, a manor, has appeared as Pirio (DB), Pivio, Pirie, Piri and Pyrie. It is from Middle English 'pirige,' a pear tree (DUIGNAN). Krausse thinks 'Perry' is derived from 'ber' or 'pyr' which are Welsh forms of the Gaelic 'bar' 'barr' and 'bre.' Hence Perry and Barr are merely duplications of the same root (NSFCT 1908 p136). Barr is from the manor of Little Barr (see) (VCHWA vol 7 p24). Morland thinks Barr from the product, bar-iron, as in Shelton Bar (POP p38). **Creation of Perry Barr manor**. In the C12 and C13 there emerged another manor, close by, known as Little or Parva Barr (see). In the C14 the Perry and Little Barr manors were listed together and by 1459 they were regarded as an entity, Perry Barr. In 1541 the owner of the manor, Thomas Smith, sold the eastern half to William Stamford of Perry Hall and so divided the manor until it was united in the mid C19. As Catholic recusants the Stamfords forfeited their property in 1644, and it was bought in or before 1659 by Henry Gough. The western half eventually went to the Wyrleys, and later to their heirs, the Birches. The two divisions became known as Perry Warren (Wyrley) and Kingstanding Warren (Gough/ Birch). The two families who held the respective halves were invariably involved in squabbles with one another. In 1780 a dispute between them occurred concerning the boundary between the two divisions (VCHWA vol 7 p24) (MNB pp54,67). **Extension of the name Perry Barr by association**. Perry Barr has been used to describe the whole area N of the Tame. It was the name of the municipal ward and a parliamentary division which did not extend S of the river. Although, after the naming of the railway station S of the Tame 'Perry Barr' in c1837, the area to the S of the Tame also became known as Perry Barr, by association (VCHWA vol 7 p24) (MNB p44). Perry Barr became a separate ecclesiastical parish in 1862. The separate urban district of Perry Barr was created in 1894 out of that excluded from Handsworth urban district. In 1928 some of the urban district was transferred to West Bromwich county borough (Staffs), some to Sutton Coldfield metropolitan borough (Warws) and the rest entered Birmingham county borough, (Warws) as Perry Barr civil parish. This was abolished in 1930 (GLAUE p419). There was a **hamlet of Perry**, perhaps settled in Anglian times, N of the footbridge (later Perry Bridge) over the Tame, by Stuart times and certainly by 1775. It is now (1983) lost (MNB pp60,66,67). From the C18 to the present day 'Perry' has referred to that part of Perry Barr just N of Perry Bridge and near Perry Hall and Perry Mill (VCHWA vol 7 p24). The foundation stone of the **church**, St John the Evangelist, on the S side of Church Road, was laid in 1831 (BOEWA p195), but the church was not consecrated until 1862 (BDD). At SP 073917 a **windmill** is shown on the preliminary OS map of 1814 and on 1831 edition (WBJ p33). A quantity of **forged coins** believed to be those of coiner William Booth were unearthed in 1956 in the garden of the parents of Derek Cherrington at Perry Barr (FSBC p29). The **highest score in football** between English clubs was when Aston Villa beat Accrington 12-2 at Perry Barr on March 12 1892 (GBR 1995 p252).

Perry Barr Common Common land in the NE part of Handsworth ancient parish. Formerly known as Little Barr Common it formed a part of Sutton Chase (MNB p55). It covered the present Kingstanding, and Lindens areas (1834 OS map). The mound, King's Standing, stood on it (TBS p10). 1300 acres of the common were enclosed in 1814 under an Act of 1811 (SHC 1941 p18) (A History of Greater Birmingham - down to 1830. Victor Skipp. 1980 p89).

Perry Beeches Residential suburb 1.25m SE of Great Barr. Former agricultural land belonging to the Perry Hall estate. In the 1920s there was some housing development at the top end of the estate. In 1928 the Perry Beeches area entered Birmingham and the estate was sold. In 1934 the land was acquired by Birmingham city council. The First National Housing Trust began building much of the present housing shortly afterwards (WMVB p127) (MNB p75). Brick Kiln Lane became the present Beeches Road sometime between 1917 and 1937. Has also appeared as Perry Beaches (GLAUE p419). Became a separate ecclesiastical parish in 1957 (GLAUE p419). The church, St Matthew, on the corner of Aldridge and Birdbrook Roads, was consecrated in 1964 (BOEWA p196) (BDD).

Perry Bridge Crosses over the Tame 2.75m SE of Great Barr. Known locally as Zig Zag Bridge (VCHWA vol 7 p51) because of the line of its parapets. There was a footbridge here by 1612. The present bridge was built in 1690 (HPPE p93), 1709 or 1711 by Sir Henry Gough of Perry Hall; in 1932 a concrete bridge w18/6/00as built beside it (VCHWA vol 7 p51) (MNB p37). The old bridge still stood in 1984 (HPPE p93).

Perry Crofts Modern residential district 0.75m NNE of Tamworth. Formerly Perry Croft. It lay in Warws but was in Tamworth ancient parish. Perry Croft manor was held of the king by the service of finding coal and litter for the king's chamber when he should come to Tamworth (VCHWA vol 4 p249). There was a moat possibly at SK 212050 (SSAHST 1982-3 p48). In 1890 Perry Crofts was heathland or common land E of the Ashby Road (1890 OS map 6 inch). The modern residential district, centred on Perry Crofts Crescent by 1971, is built in the area where only Perry Crofts Farm stood in 1902 (OS maps 1902, 1971). By 1995 the name was used to describe the area formerly called Gillway (Birmingham A-Z 1995).

Perry Hall Former moated mansion on the N side of the Tame at the W end of the present Perry Avenue, 1m NNE of Handsworth, said to have replaced Perry Manor House (see). The house was gabled and of three stories enclosing a courtyard with massive projecting chimneys on its E side. It bore the date 1576 and is said to have been built by Sir William Stamford, lord of Perry Barr in the later C16, to succeed Perry Manor House (MNB p54). In 1610 Edward Stamford of Perry Hall is described as joint lord of Great Barr manor (MOA p54). The Stamford (or Stanford) family sold the Perry Hall estate to Richard Best, a bookseller of Gray's Inn Gate, in 1659 (HPPE p94) (Maryvale. Beth Penny. 1985. p1). From 1669 Perry Hall was occupied by the Gough family after it was bought by Sir Henry Gough Knt of Old Fallings from either Richard or William Best (THM vol 4 p55). After the purchase of Edgbaston manor by the Goughs (Lords Calthorpe from 1796) in the early C18 Perry Hall was often the residence of a younger son (MNB p54). In the late C18 Shaw noted it had many portraits of the Gough family (SHOS vol 2 p190). Additions in the Tudor style were made to the hall in the 1848 by the eccentric local architect SS Teulon (MNB p62). In 1851 the hall was partly owned or occupied by FHWG Calthorpe and Hon F Gough (W p22). In 1871 it was occupied by Hon Susan Calthorpe (HPPE p94). In 1875 the owner, Hon GC Calthorpe, sold or leased the estate to Hamstead Colliery Co Ltd who promptly opened Hamstead Colliery on the estate (VH p1). The Gough-Calthorpes sold the Perry Hall estate to Birmingham corporation in 1928 (MNB pp54,62). Shortly afterwards the hall was demolished and the corporation turned the moat into a boating pool (VCHWA vol 7 p71) (MNB p62), and the grounds into playing fields (BOOP p32p). In the later C17 Plot noted a mysterious circle in a field in the grounds near the Tame. It was, or grew to be, 50 yards in diameter, and in growing in size ran into the river. It was locally believed that the circle had been made by witches (NHS pp9,10,17).

Perry Hall Former ancient house in Wednesfield chapelry in Wolverhampton

ancient parish over 1.25m ENE of Wednesfield. The Pyrye, Pirige, Perye and Perry family who are mentioned frequently at Wednesfield from the C13 to the C20 had extensive holdings from the C17 to the C19 much in the part of Wednesfield associated with the hall (DUIGNAN) (WFW p70) (SNW p54). A house, Perry Hall, is marked on the 1834 OS map and the name occurs in the 1841 census. The elongated pool along side the road near Perry Hall Farm, on the W side of Broad Lane North near the Wyrley & Essington Canal, appears to be a moat associated with the ancient house, but, according to Smallshire, this is uncertain (WFW p70). The name has for some years referred to a residential district in the approximate area. A church serving this district, St Augustine and St Chad, on the corner of Lichfield Road and Stubby Lane, was built in c1957 (info Margaret Stevens). In 1909 an Ice Age granite boulder lay in a ditch on the S side of the road between March End and Perry Hall (WJO Nov 1909 p293).

Perry Hill Former estate in the Brennand Road (Brandhall Road) area, Warley. The estate was laid out with housing from 1949 (ORR p49).

Perry Manor House Apparently of Tudor date with four gables it stood in Rocky Lane, Perry. It was replaced as the residence of the lord of the manor by Perry Hall (see) and thereafter served as a bailiff's house. By 1983 the site was occupied by a line of shops (MNB pp54,62).

Perry Park Large municipal park S of the Tame 1m N of Handsworth. Birmingham Alexander Sports Stadium is in it.

Perry Park Former estate belonging to the Perry family, prominent in the Old Hill area since the C17 (TB Dec 1997 p25). For Perrypark House, Blackheath, see the map in TB Feb 1985 p10. The name is preserved in Perry Park Road 1m S of Rowley Regis (Birmingham A-Z).

Perry Pont House Stood in the area of the present Nash Square on the W side of Aldridge Road and the E side of the Tame, Perry. In the C19, after the discovery of sandstone rubble in the grounds, it was considered that there had been a large Roman camp here. The house was built in the later C18 or early C19 (MNB pp38,41). In 1838 it was occupied by William Harry Osborn, a Birmingham wine and spirit merchant (HPPE p93). William Osborn erected grottoes and statues throughout the grounds. In 1838 the garden is referred to as having been arranged with great taste and care to make 'one of the most perfect little paradises which any man could desire' (HPPE p93).

Perry's Croft 'Perry's Croft Bull Bait' was a ballad, probably of the earlier C19, describing a bull bait in the period c1790s to c1840s. The first verse goes:

> From Gornal, un from Sedgeley,
> Likewise from Tip'un tu,
> The sportsmen crowded to ther town
> They'd nothin' else ter du.

(UBCB p117).

Perrys Lake Appears to have been a hamlet in the City Road-Popular Rise area, in Rowley Regis parish. Formerly Perry's Folly (OS map 1834) (BCWJ p86). The name, which appears in 1851 census, is from the Perry family of Perry Park (see), prominent in Old Hill area from the C17 (TB Dec 1997 p25).

Perry Warren The name for that half of Perry manor which was granted to George Birch, joint lord with John Gough of Perry Barr manor by 1779 (KPP p8).

Perry Wood Large medieval wood which lay in the area between Newton and Perry Beeches, laying on high ground reaching 480 feet at its highest. The wood had been greatly reduced by Tudor times, and was reduced by the late C19 to remnants in the present Perry Wood Road area on the E side of Walsall Road (MNB pp55,61,66).

Pershall Hamlet lining the foot of some rolling countryside by the Sow 1m NW of Eccleshall. Former township in Horsley division of Eccleshall ancient parish. A flint arrowhead of the Neolithic of Bronze Age was found at Pershall in 1938 (NSJFS 1964 p21). The Blest family held land in Pershall from 1298 to the present day (1964). In 1530 Roger Blest of Pershall held two tenements. The main one of these was undoubtedly the freehold, which Roger held by the nominal service of one sixteenth part of a knight. This descended in the family to John Blest who held it in 1622. He had to provide the bishop with two pairs of gloves with two pence yearly and send two beaters to the bishop's hunt for three days, three times a year. The rent had thus remained the same for over 300 years (ECC pp42-43). Pershall was thought by Chetwynd to have been a prebend in Lichfield cathedral (SHC 1914 p51).

Pershall Pool Pool E of Cop Mere, to W of Pershall.

Perton Former manor and hamlet lining the edge of a S-facing escarpment overlooking Black Brook 2m WSW of Tettenhall. In Tettenhall ancient parish.

Later in Tettenhall Wood ecclesiastical parish. A **Bronze Age** palstave found at Perton in 1834 went to the BM (HCCW p141) (HOPTT p7) (NSJFS 1964 p45) (VCH vol 20 p3). Perton has been identified with the Pertune mentioned in a charter of the period between 1062 and 1066 in which it is granted to St Peter's, Westminster (SHC 1916 p130). Later, the **name** has appeared as Pertone, a manor held by St Peter's, Westminster, in DB, Pertona (1167) (SSE 1996 p16), Pirton (W p207), and Purton (OS 1834 map) (DUIGNAN). It is from probably Perigtun, the town of the pear tree; the district is still (1894) famous for a peculiar kind of pear only found in Tettenhall parish (HOPTT p103) (DUIGNAN), or 'pear tree tun or farmstead' (VCH vol 20 pp10,30) (SPN p145). **Prebend.** Perton-with-Trecott was one of the prebends of Tettenhall Collegiate Church (HOPTT p67) and was in Tettenhall Clericorum manor (W p205). It is not styled in VCH as Perton-with-Trecott (VCH vol 3 pp319,320). **Manorial tenure service.** John de Perton held the manor of Perton in c1332 from the king by grand serjeantry to wit, by the service of one man, armed with a chain of armour composed of small rings of iron woven together, and leather protective undergarments, a steel cup and a lance in the king's army, when he was in a war with Wales (Madox's 'Baronia' 1741 p243) (SMC p122) (SCSF p117). The centre of the **old hamlet** lay round a green where the present Jenny Walkers Lane was joined by a road running NW from Tinacre Hill and passing in front of the moated Perton Hall (VCH vol 20 p10). Sir **John Wollaston** (1595-1658), lord mayor of London in 1643-4, was the son of Edward Wollaston of Perton (VCH vol 20 p5). From c1986 the **'Tough Guy' competition** has been held once a year at South Perton Farm, presently known as Tettenhall Horse Sanctuary. The competition is an eight-mile obstacle course testing endurance and strength of both sexes. Prior to the event in 2000, on Jan 30, Christians protested against a particular challenge in the competition in which contests can carry a crucifix, claiming it trivialises the Christian story (The Sunday Telegraph. Dec 26 1999 p3p) (BBC 1 Midlands Today Feb 1 2000).

PERTON MODERN VILLAGE. There was an **airfield** in WW1, possibly the oldest military aerodrome in Staffs, on the N side of Pattingham Road at SO 860995. It was operation in 1916/17 (info Ron Balding). The WW2 airfield 0.75m NE of the old village of Perton opened in 1941. It probably closed in late 1945 and was abandoned by the RAF in July 1947 (VCH vol 20 p11) (WMA vol 1 pp215-230). Some have erroneously claimed that a Dutch force was based at the airfield in WW2 (TCOP) (TPOP pp87-90ps) (Wolverhampton Chronicle June 5 1998 p15ps). However, the force appears to have been at Wrottesley Hall not Perton airfield (Wolverhampton Chronicle June 26 1998 p10). The **building of the modern village** of Perton on Perton airfield was in progress by 1976, after long-running indecision and controversy over the airfield's future use. When plans to turn it into a civil and military air base in 1946 failed, councillors looked to building an housing estate on it, but squatters, who were here to the mid 1950s, came and occupied the site. A proposal in 1956 to build a psychiatric hospital on the site was opposed by local residents. Sir Charles Mander's proposal for an housing estate in 1963 resulted in the public inquiries of 1964 and 1969; such was the vehemence of local opposition. In Oct 1970 the High Court dismissed Staffs county council's application for an housing estate. But in 1974 the proposal of developers, Galliford, to build a new village with its own facilities was accepted. Residents began moving in May 1976. Development continued throughout the 1980s. In 1982 a six ton granite boulder was erected in the village centre to commemorate the past presence of the air force. Perton civil parish was created in 1986. In 1988 the inhabitants decided to stay in South Staffs district in Staffs instead of being incorporated into Wolverhampton borough in West Midlands (VCH vol 20 p11) (Wolverhampton Chronicle Oct 11 1996 p20ps). By 1988 Perton referred to the new village and the original settlement had become known as Old Perton (MR pp253,380); by the late 1990s some new Perton inhabitants preferred to call new Perton Perton Village (Wolverhampton Chronicle Nov 26 1999 p20). The **church** at new Perton, Anders Square, was built in 1983 (LDD). Cosford and not Perton may be mentioned in the book **'The Face'** (John Petty. 1972. Gentry Books. pp120 onwards) (info Angus Dunphy). Gareth Morris of Perton set a record by completing 1873 **step-ups** in an hour on Jan 30 1993 using a 15 inch high exercise board (GBR 1995 p210).

Perton Court Jenny Walkers Lane, Old Perton. The fragment of a moat here at SO 860986 (CAMS p64) was part of a moat which once surrounded Perton Hall (SSAHST 1982-3 p58).

Perton Farmhouse Jenny Walkers Lane, Old Perton. Has a listed dovecote (DoE II).

Perton Grove Former villa in Perton Road, Wightwick. Built in c1855 for Henry Underhill, a Wolverhampton solicitor. Demolished in c1964 (VCH vol 20 p10).

Perton Hall Medieval house on a moated site occupied by the Pertons, lords of Perton, near Perton Court, at Old Perton. It was probably enlarged in or soon after 1364 by Sir John Perton. The manor had passed to Sir Humphrey Stafford of Southwick, in North Bradley (Wilts) by 1398. It passed to Sir William Compton in 1519 who sold it to the Levesons of Wolverhampton in 1523. The manor was inherited by Vice-Admiral Sir Richard Leveson (d1605) in 1602. It has been suggested that the Vice-Admiral may have installed his mistress and cousin Mary Fitton (1578-1641), here. She was a former maid of honour to Elizabeth I, and may be the 'dark lady' of Shakespeare's sonnets. The manor of Perton was sold to the Wrottesleys of Wrottesley Hall in 1664. For a period in the C18 the hall served as a dower house for the Wrottesleys. It was still habitable in the early C19, but most of it had been demolished by 1820 (VCH vol 20 pp5,25) (TPOP p81 il of). Shaw noted the solid stone horse-block, near the kitchen door was hewn out of a cistern from Wrottesley (SHOSA vol 2 p19).

Perton Park There was a park at Perton by 1423; it may have been created by Sir John Perton, living in the mid 1360s. It lay W of Perton and extended almost to Tettenhall parish boundary. It had been disparked by 1654. In Perton Park was a sandstone quarry of Lower Keuper sandstone (VCH vol 2 p190. vol 20 p33).

Perton Ridge Ridge along which Old Perton is situated; the Tettenhall Wood-Pattingham road runs along it and there are fine views from it (Wolverhampton Chronicle Nov 26 1999 p20).

Pessall Farm 1m E of Croxall. Removed to Staffs with Croxall in late C19.

Peter's Hill Hill and district overlooking the Stour nearly 1.25m SSW of Brierley Hill, in Amblecote parish. The name is said to be from Peter Hill who had a house and land here in 1805 (VCH vol 20 p51) (SNSV vol 1 p259). Peter's Hill Primary School, just S of Hillfields Road, built in the 1970s, had 12 sets of twins in May 1994: The British record was set by Farmor Comprehensive at Fareford, Glous, which had 14 sets of twins in 1987 (SNSV vol 1 p259) (Daily Express May 26 1994 p27p).

Pethills Farm at the N end of Morridge, NE of Morridge Top, over 1m NNE of Royal Cottage. Formerly in Heathylee township in Alstonefield ancient parish.

Pethills Pethills Farm is 2m SSE of Onecote. Formerly in Onecote township in Leek ancient parish. There was land called Pethills in 1251 and there was a house at Pethills by 1539. The present house is dated 1799 (VCH vol 7 p212). Pethill is marked on Smith's map.

Pethills Ford Under 0.5m WNW of Waterfall Cross. The ancient Earls Way (see) from Chester to Derby forded the Hamps here (NSFCT 1948 p47).

Pethillshead Farm 1.5m S of Onecote. Formerly in Onecote township in Leek ancient parish.

Petrifactions, The At Cotwalton Dumble, Moddershall. Supposed petrifaction in Hilderstone Brook where erosion of a softer sandstone strata has allowed the formation of a waterfall (SSBOP p60p in c1910) (ES July 21 1937 p8ps).

Pettyfields 1.25m SW of Ipstones (1834 OS map); it may now be Glenwood House.

Petty France Former tiny district of Leek N or NW of St Edward's church reputedly settled by French prisoners of the Napoleonic Wars (1803-14) (ALC). It was so called by 1816 (VCH vol 7 p92) and called Petite France by 1906 (HLS p72). (SL p152 shows map with it marked) (LR p36). Others think the name refers to a section of St Edward's churchyard where the French prisoners were buried (ES Oct 1 1993 p8p. Oct 24 1995 p8) (French Connections. Joan Bennett, Colin Parrack, Ray Poole and Cathryn Walton. 1995) and the name was given to this area owing its proximity to that part of the churchyard (VCH vol 7 p92). Petty France was cleared of its terrace cottages in the 1960s (VCH vol 7 p98 pl 37).

Pewit Hall House 0.75m S of Onecote. Formerly in Onecote township in Leek ancient parish. The present house is probably of the early C19 (VCH vol 7 p211).

Pewit Hall In approximately position of Rough Close Farm, Rough Close (1834 OS map).

Pewit Pool (*Pewet Pool*). Refers to several pools (now all vanished) that the black-headed gulls, Black Caps, or sea crows (Larus ridibundus) frequented on the Skrymsher estates in Staffs after returning from migration to breed. They had a reputation for displaying superstitious tendencies by always choosing a pool on the Skrymsher estates when coming to Staffs and leaving a pool to go to a new one on the death of the head of the Skrymsher family. Plot in the later C17 noted they frequented Moss Pool (see) (or Old Pewit Pool) but deserted this after the death of James Skrymsher to a pool at Offley Moss (see) and returned to Moss Pool after three years. Here they continued until the death of John Skrymsher (1665) which occurred at egg laying time, but despite this, they still left their nests. They went again to Offley Moss and the following year to Aqualate (another Skrymsher seat) and continued there for two years and then (1668) went to another pool - Shebdon Pool (see) - of the next heir Sir Charles Skrymsher Knt (NHS pp231-232). Plot says the catching of them with nets was a great spectator sport and one with four legs was caught at Norbury and there was a certain old pewit, who may have been their leader, who attacked the catchers suggesting they had some government amongst them (NHS pp232-233 tab 19, p234) (Man and the Natural World. K Thomas p62). Shaw noted they had scarcely bred on a Skrymsher estate since 1794 (SHOS vol 1 part 1 p96). (W p391) (NSFCT 1927 pp37-38). One of the pools (or all of them) had strange properties which deterred birds from flying over it (SJC p6). Richard Whitworth noted pewits over and nesting on his pools at Batchacre Hall between at least 1773 and 1806 (OSST 1931 pp31-37). Plot believed the fossilized stumps of firs he found in the old Pewit Pool were those of the alien Abies Legitima vel mas Bellonii, or Abies of Parkinson, not found in England or Ireland, proving that these types of fir were anciently indigenous to Britain (NHS pp209,216,217).

Pheasant Hall Over 1m W of Alsagers Bank. For the murder which took place near the hall in 1844 see The Hays.

Pheasants Clough House NW of Upper Hulme. Seat of the Doxeys in the C17 who probably gave their name to Doxey Pool (OL vol 2 p145). Pheasants Clough Farm was the birthplace in 1831 of the sculptor, Richard Hassal (d1868) (VCH vol 7 p196) (HOLF p20).

Pheasey Modern residential district on high undulating land above the Tame basin over 1m E of Great Barr, NE of Queslett, built on Pheasey Farm estate on the ancient common of Barr Lea (MOA p139). Formerly in Aldridge ancient parish. The name is from perhaps a Simon Veysie (or Vesey) who bought a property and land in Great Barr in 1557. A document of 1610 describes the land as Veysies Farm (MOA p139) (ADY p19) (SNAR p69). Pheasey Farm was enlarged when Great Barr Common was enclosed in 1799. Pheasey remained part of Great Barr manor until the Scott estates were sold in 1918. In autumn 1935 the First National Housing Trust, a subsidiary of Henry Boot and Sons of Sheffield, which had already built a number of housing estates on farmland N of Birmingham, purchased Pheasey Farm, then consisting of about 340 acres, as a site for housing estates. The first sod was cut by Sir Kingsley Wood on July 13 1937. By the start of WW2 1,724 houses had been built. British and American troops were billeted in 400 of the houses in WW2. In 1946, the trust began building again and the estate was virtually complete by 1981 when about 3,800 houses had been built (ADY p19). The housing estate was originally called Pheasey Farm Estate, and its streets are named after British artists (SNAR p75). The church, St Chad, Collingwood Drive, was built in 1964 (LDD).

Philley Brook Runs N of Enville to the Smestow. Part of Philley Brook W of Mere Mill divided the manors of Morfe and Lutley (VCH vol 20 p91) (SPNO p16). For the name see Filley Brook, Stone.

Philleybrook There was an inhabited area called Philleybrook at SO 811884 1.25m NW of Enville in the early C14. A house here was known as Philleybrook Hall in the late C17 and earlier C18 (VCH vol 20 p94).

Phoenix Park Public park E of Goldthorn Hill, 1.25m SSE of Wolverhampton.

Piccory Tor Dovedale. Rock feature(s) (GNHS p12). Could be same as Pickering Tor.

Pickards House 0.5m N of Upper Arley on a moated site. Former small estate and manor held of Arley manor in the Middle Ages, later descending with Hextons manor in the C13 (SHOS vol 2 p258) (VCHW vol 3 p7). Also known in the C15 as The Wodehouse or The More (VCHW vol 3 p7), and has also appeared as Picards. The name is from a native of Picardy, France (DUIGNAN).

Pickfords Bank Short stretch of road from Job's Pool to the road which runs down the W side of the St Anne's Vale, Brown Edge. It was so named because a family named Pickford built a cottage near the top of this short connecting road and in order to get drinking water sank a well in front of the cottage. The well was filled in in c1939 (ONST 1979 p399).

Picknal Brook Runs from Loxley to Uttoxeter to the Dove. Has also appeared as Picknalls Brook (UTP p4p).

Pickwood Hall House over 0.5m SE of Leek, in Leek and Lowe township, Leek ancient parish. Situated at foot of Lowe Hill. Is part C17 and C18 but mostly late C19 origin. Existed by 1705. Samuel Toft, a button merchant, had property here in the early C18 (VCH vol 7 p89). It has been mainly the seat of the Challinor family since at least the mid C18 (NSF). It was the seat of William Challinor (1821-1896), poet, critic and solicitor who had a case at Onecote Lane End (see) which was used by Charles Dickens in 'Bleak House' (PSS pp176-179) (VFC p25). Col William Francis Challinor was the last Challinor to live here and he left in 1928 (info Mr C Parrack). From a field close to Pickwood can be seen the double sunset over The Cloud (NSFCT

1882 p26) (see under Leek). (JSD p192p).

Picmoor Wood Wood in Weston-under-Lizard ancient parish, 1.5m WNW of Weston-under-Lizard. Has appeared as Pikemore (1380), Pike More (1834 OS map), and Pikemeres (1840) (SPNO p181).

Piddock Farm House and estate between the Birmingham Canal and Cranford Street, Smethwick. Formerly owned by the Piddock family probably from the late C16, perhaps earlier. Soho Foundry (see) was built on part of the estate in 1796. The farm was also known as Cranford Farm by this time. It was demolished in c1852 (VCH vol 17 p102-103).

Piggot's Bottom A dell SE of Beaudesert Hall.

Pigsty Park This name applied to a part of Ryecroft Street, Walsall, formerly Ryecroft Park, and was given to this part because it was 'less respectable' than the other section of the Park (SNWA p82).

Pikelow Burial mound on a hill 0.25m ESE of Waterfall. Carrington excavated the possible burial mound in 1849 (TYD p157). It is now destroyed (NSJFS 1965 p52). Has also appeared as Pike Low.

Pike Pool Still water enclave in the Dove in Beresford Dale. So called after the grey monolithic pointed rock jutting out of the 'pool,' resembling a pike, which is called the Lion's Tooth Rock (PS pp106,107). Charles Cotton and Izaak Walton liked to fish here in the C17 (Dovedale Guide. Keith Mantell. 1985. p24). Mr Edwards wrote a poem on Pike Pool (AAD pp147-148). (GNHS p19 il) (CCR) (JAT p56) (HS pl p277) (TPC p162) (TD p) (DMV p30p).

Pilgrim's Way or Portway. Highway for pilgrims to St Chad's shrine in Lichfield cathedral. It ran from Burton Abbey, through Harlaston, Elford Lowe, and Fisherwick (THM vol 1 p69) (TH Dec 27 1941).

Pilgrim's Well Well behind Hanbury church. Is so called after the pilgrims who came to St Werburgh's shrine and is still called this (MR p171).

Pillar Box Oak An oak with a shapely and beautifully bevelled letter-hole placed about three feet from the ground in Court Bank Covert, Cannock Wood. Wright says he playfully posted a letter through the hole - it was so inviting (CCF p84).

Pillaton Small hamlet on the gentle incline between the Penk and Cannock Chase highlands, 1.5m SE of Penkridge. Former manor and quarter in Penkridge township and ancient parish (W p468). The now extinct place Bedintun(a), Beddintone (DB), or Beddington adjoined Pillaton and was situated at SJ 942130 by the hall (SSAHST 1966 p49. 1970 pp34,35). Land at Bedintun was granted in 993 by King Ethelred to Wulfric Spot (VCH vol 5 p118); there is a C11 copy of the charter granting the land in the WSL (SL p62). The same land was granted by Wulfric Spot to Burton Abbey by 1004. This land is probably the same as the 'Bedintona' and 'Pilatehala' mentioned between 1100 and 1113. In 1114 or 1115 'Bendintona' was waste while 'Pilatehala' was inhabited; nothing further is heard of 'Bedintona' after 1135 at the latest (SHC 1916 p31) (NSFCT 1955 p79) (VCH vol 5 p118) (SSE 1996 p16) (SPN p94). In 1185 the Pope confirmed Burton Abbey in its possession of Pillaton. The overlordship still belonged to Burton Abbey in 1535, passing to the king at the Dissolution; he granted the manor in 1546 to Sir William Paget, whose family remained overlords until at least 1769. The manor was held of the overlords by the de Broks (early C13); the de Elmedons; the de Wrottesleys (early C14); the de Wynnesburys (C15). Alice de Wynnesbury (d1529), heiress, married Richard Littleton taking the manor to the Littletons. Her son Sir Edward (d1558) succeeded. He was succeeded by his son Sir Edward (d1574), who was succeeded by his son Edward (d1610), who was succeeded by his son Edward (d1629). He was succeeded by his son Edward, who was created baronet in 1627. He and his successors lived at Pillaton Hall (see) (VCH vol 5 pp118-119) (DUIGNAN). It is thought that the settlement at Bedintuna was deserted when the inhabitants moved to Pillaton (SPN p94) (DUIGNAN). The curved ditch W of Pillaton Hall considered by VCH vol 1 to be a moat of a former Pillaton Hall is probably a hollow-way of the deserted village (SSAHST 1982-3 p46). There was a short-term landing field for the RAF at Pillaton in WW2 (SHJ autumn 1989 p64). **Name meanings**. 'Bedintun' is from Beda's town or farmstead (DUIGNAN) (SPN p94). Pillaton has appeared as Pillenhaul (c1540) (LI appendix p169). Oakden and Gelling think 'pilatan' represented 'pilled oats' with 'hale' as 'corner,' so 'nook or corner where pilled oats grow.' It probably arose as a field-name, which by confusion of the second elements 'hale' and 'hall' attached itself to Pillaton Hall (SSAHST 1967 p32) (NSJFS 1981 p3). Other interpretations are: 'Pilla's farmstead' or 'Pilla's corner of land' (SPN p94), or from Anglo-Saxon 'pil' (Latin - pilum) meaning 'pile' as the hamlet rested on wooden piles (SLM spring 1957 p25), or a Celtic derivation and from Celtic words meaning 'swamp' or 'swampy' and the root 'aite' meaning 'house,' with the word 'hale' being a later addition (NSFCT 1908 p146). According to tradition it derives its name from the biblical Pilate (DUIGNAN), but this can be discredited.

Stevenson says you cannot get the genitive 'en' from 'Pilate' (NSFCT 1908 p146).

Pillaton Green Tiny hamlet to the N of Pillaton Hall (VCH vol 5 p108).

Pillaton Hall House at Pillaton 1.5m SE of Penkridge. The present hall is built on the moated site of an earlier hall which may have been the seat of some of the lords of Pillaton and the bailiffs of Teddesley Hay (SSAHST 1982-3 p45) from the late C12 (see above). The whole Forester family at Pillaton Hall died in the Black Death (COEA p221). The hall was rebuilt in brick by the Littletons in the late C15 (BOE p222) or in the early C16 (VCH vol 5 pp119-120). The chapel was largely rebuilt in c1480 (LGS p199) (NSFCT 1927 pp88-92) or in 1488 (BOE p222). The hall was quadrangular around a square courtyard with the gatehouse forming the N range (BOE p222) (OHW pl 15) (NSFCT 1982 p14). Edward Littleton (d1629) was succeeded by his son Sir Edward Littleton (b1599), who was created a baronet in 1627 and became the 1st baronet. He was succeeded by his son Sir Edward Littleton (d c1709), 2nd Bt, MP for Staffs 1663-78. His son, Edward, died in 1704 before his father and Sir Edward was succeeded by his grandson Sir Edward Littleton, 3rd Bt, Sheriff of Staffs in 1712-13. On his death in 1741-2 he was succeeded by Sir Edward Littleton (d1812), 4th Bt, the son of his brother Fisher Littleton. Sir Edward (d1812) had Teddesley Hall built after 1742 and by 1754, for his own occupation, preferring not to live at Pillaton Hall. For his descendants (who later took the title of Lord Hatherton) see Teddesley Hall. A rearguard action in the Civil War was fought at or near Pillaton Hall after the battle of Naseby in 1646, a number of cannon balls have been unearthed near Pillaton giving support to this view (PVH p6). The hall was still intact by 1754 when occupied by Lady Littleton (VCH vol 5 p120). Others say much of the hall was pulled down in 1741 or in 1749 (NSFCT 1924 p197), or between 1741 and 1749 (WJO April 1905 p105). A visitor in 1786 reported that only a farmer lived here and that the chapel was ruinous and that demolition was imminent. At this period the great hall, probably in the S range, still contained some old stained glass (possibly now in the chapel) some showing subjects from the Old and New Testaments and some in circular panes showing the signs of the Zodiac and others in circular panes showing emblematical devices not easily understood - one represents a man crowned with his legs in stocks. In a kitchen window, thought formerly to have been in the chapel, was a representation of St Modwen, flanked by smaller kneeling figures (GM Dec 1789 pp1087-89 pl iii) (GNHSS p21) (HOP p65) (HSS p50) (NSFCT 1925 p191) (VCH vol 5 p120). The E, S, and W ranges of the quadrangle were pulled down in 1799, leaving eight tall chimneys standing. John Buckle made extensive drawings of the remains in 1841. Between 1884 and 1888 Lord Hatherton restored the gatehouse range and largely rebuilt the chapel. By 1910 to at least 1959 a caretaker resided in the gatehouse range (LGS p199) (VCH vol 5 p120). The gatehouse range was restored in 1976 for a residence of the eldest daughter of the 5th Lord Hatherton (SGS p136p) (CL Sept 2 1993 pp54-55 pl 5 painting by JC Buckler of the gatehouse in early C19). (SHOS vol 2 pl) (W p468) (HOP pp16,62-66) (LGS p199) (NSFCT 1927 pp88-92 p facing p89 is of armorial glass at Pillaton Hall) (CCBO pp53,55) (AWM p41) (SOP p102) (SLM spring 1957 p27). An old oak door and some armorial bearings carved in oak from Crabbery Hall, Stafford have been removed to Pillaton Hall. Tildesley says an old woman told him, who lived in the house at Pillaton, that she had seen in the lumber attic a beautiful image of the Virgin Mary in an old trunk (HOP p63). Masefield says there is a stoup outside the door of the chapel and in the chapel a squint and a piscina (LGS p199). A stone quern is placed in the archway of the gatehouse (LGS p199) (CCBO p56). The chapel of Pillaton Hall was a prebend of Penkridge Collegiate Church in 1272 (VCH vol 3 p300).

DISCOVERIES MADE AT THE HALL. Treasure reputed to have been secreted here by Robert Devereux, Earl of Essex, in 1599 was searched for in 1741 by Sir Edward Littleton who virtually pulled the hall down brick by brick to find it. At length he discovered a **hoard of coins** behind an oak casement in a chimney breast. Possibly one of the chimneys that remain and stand isolated. In 1886 the words 'JESUS MARCY' stood over the great chimney. The letters were formed of flowers and scroll work (HOP p65), possibly this was the chimney where the treasure was found. Yet Wright in 1930s says the room where the treasure was found still existed and was used to exhibit various interesting relics including the curious oak carvings which were described in GM Dec 1789, and others which were found in an old cottage in Penkridge (CCBO p56)). The coins were found in 25 leather purses and consisted of English guineas, French pistoles, Spanish moidores and other foreign coins. Its value estimated at £15,749 (in 1886 £60,000) was used to build Teddesley Hall (HOP p63) (NSFCT 1924 p197) (NSFCT 1955 p79) (SLM spring 1957 p27). Some coins were preserved by the Littletons and some went to the BM (CCBO p53). A **chalice and paten**, dated 1525 (VCH

vol 5 p134) (BERK p59; said to have originally belonged to St Thomas' Priory), and a wooden effigy of C13 origin have also been found at Pillaton Hall. Perhaps at the same time and in the same place as the coins. But others say at a different demolition (SVB p135). Some say they were found in the walls of Pillaton in George II's reign (VCH vol 5 p134), or found at Pillaton in 1794 (BERK p59). Round the bottom of the chalice are the words 'Sancti Maris ora pro nobis,' and round the rim 'Pater de calis Deus miserere noblis' with the letters IHS in larger characters in the centre. At one time the chalice stood on the mantelpiece in the study of Teddesley Hall. The first Lord Hatherton had it placed in a cabinet with the paten. On the cabinet door was a silver plate with an inscription written specially by Cardinal Wiseman (CCBO p53). The original chalice and paten went to the V&A, replicas were in Pillaton Hall chapel in 1956 (VCH vol 5 p134) and or are used at St Mary's, Stafford (ES April 22 1932 p9p) (31st Annual Report of the Pilgrim Trust 1961 and Hibberts Dissolution pp229-232) (SOP p108) (HOP pp63-64). The 19 inch high **wooden effigy** of some dignitary was thought at first to be of C15 origin, like the hall, until it was sent to the Society of Antiquaries for examination. They suspected it of being 200 years older. The figure is in a sitting position with hands on knees. Opinions still differ as to its identity. Some think it is of a saint or of King Herod or of a Roman ruler or, considering where it was found, of Pilate (SC p36) (NSFCT 1924 p197) (SG p1) (CCBO pp54,55 p of facing p55). If it is a piece of English wooden sculpture of the C13 then it is extremely rare (BOE p222). After the discovery of the figure it remained for many years at Teddesley Hall. By the mid 1950s it was mounted on the S wall of Pillaton Hall chapel (VCH vol 5 p134).

Pillaton Park Former deer park at Pillaton (EDP p179).

Pilstones Area S of Swynnerton. The name is preserved in Pilstones Wood 1m SSE of Swynnerton.

Pinchley Barn Or Pinchley (1834 OS map) 0.75m NW of Okeover.

Pinfold A ward in Cheslyn Hay civil parish.

Pinfold House In Aldridge ancient parish, probably in Great Barr township. In existence by the C17, and could be earlier (MOA p139). There is a Pinfold Lane running N from Great Barr Old Hall.

Pink Pool Off Prouds Lane, Bilston. Was created out of old mine floodings (BOP p67).

Pinnox Tiny area 1m NNW of Burslem. Perhaps, from Pinnox Pottery.

Pipa Major Nothing has been written of this prebend in Lichfield cathedral, except for a mention in the Lincoln Cathedral Statutes and in VCH vol 14 p135 where it is said it takes its name from Pipe in Burntwood parish. No mention of it is made in Willis Browne's Diocese of Lichfield, Fasti Ecclesias Anglicanae, SHOS vol 1, HOLJ, HOL, VCH vol 3 and SSAHST vol 2 1960-61. Its existence appears to explain why there is a prebend called Pipa Minor.

Pipa Minor Prebend in Lichfield cathedral. See Prees, Shrops.

Pipa Parva Prebend in Lichfield cathedral founded by Bishop Roger de Meiland in c1280 (VCH vol 3 p144). (SHOS vol 1 p291). Its main revenue was derived from Pipe and Wall, although it also had association with Farewell (SSAHST vol 2 1960-61 p47). Rev Thomas Harwood identified the prebend with Little Pipe (HOL p515), one of the two post-DB manors of Pipe (DUIGNAN p119). Thomas Seward, father of the poetess, Anna Seward, held this prebend in 1755 (SSAHST vol 2 1960-61 p47).

Pipe Former manor, estate and settlement which centred on the manor house (later Pipe Hall), covered Edial and Woodhouses, and was first mentioned as a place in c1140 (VCH vol 14 pp198,205). From the mid or later C12 water was piped to Lichfield cathedral Close from Maple Hayes in Pipe manor (VCH vol 14 p95). There was a manor of Pipe by 1235 which was also known as the manor of Great Pipe (or Magna Pipa, giving its name to the prebend of Pipa Major) as distinct from Little Pipe (Parva Pipa), a detached part of St Chad's parish, Lichfield (VCH vol 14 p205). Gives its name to the de Pipe family, who in turn gave their name to Pipe Ridware and Pipe Hay (SHOS vol 1 p83). The name may have derived from the conduit S of Pipe Hall which supplied water to Lichfield cathedral Close (DUIGNAN), or the watercourse (Leamonsley or Pipe Brook) which rises near the conduit (VCH vol 14 p198). (HOL p515) (SPN p95) (DUIGNAN p119).

Pipe Brook Tributary of the Trent. Rises W of Lichfield. Has appeared as Pipebrouk (1286) (SPNO p16) (SPN p95). Duignan suggested the name was from an artificial water-pipe. However, the name means probably 'the channel of a small stream' (SPNO p16).

Pipe Grange N of Pipehill. The site has been occupied since the Middle Ages. The prior of St John's Hospital, Lichfield, held the estate in 1298. He held it by the service of stocking the larder of the bishop of Lichfield as lord of Longdon manor. The present house dates mainly from the C18 and the early C19. Canon Hugh Bailye, chancellor of Lichfield cathedral was the tenant in the 1820s (VCH vol 14 pp286,289-290). Gen Robert Newton Philips (d1895) was of Pipe Grange (mem in Christ Church, Leamonsley). There was a dovecote near the house in 1398 (VCH vol 14 p290).

Pipe Green 0.75m W of Lichfield cathedral, it may have been a part of Pipe Moor (VCH vol 2 p220. vol 14 p111).

Pipe Hall Bilston. Sir Richard Pipe, who became Lord Mayor of London in 1578, built a 'splendid mansion' near the site of the later Pipe Hall (built in the C18?). His ancestors (the Pypes), who may have originated from Pipe Ridware, appear to have been at Bilston by the C14. His son acquired Bradley manor (near Bilston) in James I's reign (HOBL pp143,146,148,159) (HOBLL p48) (BOP p8). Their original hall was probably in the vicinity of Hall Street. Pipe Hall eventually became the Pipe Hall Academy, a private school, and is now a public house (BOP p65).

Pipe Hall House 1.5m W of Lichfield cathedral. Formerly in Burntwood outtownship of St Michael's parish, Lichfield (W p514). Represents the manor house of the manor of Pipe. There was a manor house at Pipe by the mid C12, which probably contained a chapel by the second half of the C14. Pipe Hall is mentioned in 1436. The Pipe family, lords of the manor, probably resided here until the manor passed to the Staffords in the C15. The manor passed to the Heveninghams in the mid C16 and to the Welds of Lulworth Castle, Dorset, in 1775. As Roman Catholics the Heveninghams and the Welds allowed the hall to become a RC centre. In the C18 the Bates family, Catholics, tenanted the hall. When the manor passed to the Wolferstans of Statfold in 1800 the RC centre closed down. The Shawe family had the hall and manor by 1884 when they were sold to AO Worthington. The hall was rebuilt in c1770 and there were some extensions and some internal remodelling to it in the early C19 (SSE 1987 pp131,132p) (VCH vol 14 pp206-207,222-223).

Pipe Hay Former medieval enclosure in Needwood Forest. It appears to have been formerly known as Ris Hay, but became Pipe Hay after it passed into a branch of the de Pipe family of Pipe (see) (SHOS vol 1 p83). The name is preserved in Pipehay Farm on the E side of Pipe Hay Lane, Draycott-in-the-Clay.

Pipe Hayes In Pipe manor and township near Lichfield (DUIGNAN p120). Maple Hayes House may have been known as Pipe or Maple Hayes Farm in the early C18 (VCH vol 14 p211).

Pipehill Small hamlet on a marshy ground by a low hill to the N of Watling Street 1.75m SW of Lichfield cathedral. Former out-township of St Michael's parish, Lichfield (W p517). In the late C18 (probably during the construction of the Wyrley and Essington Canal) on Pipe Place Farm estate at Pipehill a **palisade of oak trunks** was traced for some 500 yards below ground with a 'V' shaped ditch running parallel, apparently respecting the contours of the ground (SSAHST 1980-81 pp2-3) (WSS p116) and therefore not quite in a straight line. It was brought to Stebbing Shaw's attention by William Pitt, author of AOS. It was thought at the time to have been a Roman vallum or military barricade which extended northwards from Wall and to have stood 12 feet high above ground and flanked with bastions (SHOS General Intro pp19-20 vol 1 p356). Harwood in SOS thought it was of British construction (SOS p302); in HOL he thought it was of Roman construction (HOL p565) (SSAHST 1980-81 pp2-3). It is ascribed to the Romano-British period by VCH vol 1 p191, and undated by NSJFS 1964 p41. Recently it was thought to have been built as a boundary or a form of aqueduct in the Roman period (WSS p117). A copper coin of Hadrian (120 AD) was found at the site (Ms Min Soc Ants London vol 26 (1794) p317) (BAST 1873 p41) (VCH vol 1 p191). The **hamlet** of Pipehill, situated on Pipe Marsh, has appeared as Pipe (C12), Pype (C12) (SSE 1996 p17), Hardwick (C14), Pipe Hardwick (C14-C17), and Pipe Hill (VCH vol 14 p286). Pipe could be from the Celtic forestroot 'feabh' a forest, this would easily be corrupted into Pipe (NSFCT 1908 p140). Or from Anglo-Saxon 'Pipe' inferring a channel (often filled with water) (SPN p95). Hardwick means a livestock farm (VCH vol 14 p286). There was a house for the preparation of **tobacco** in Pipehill in the early 1700s (VCH vol 14 pp292-293). The separate **civil parish** of Pipehill, created in 1866, was abolished in 1894, and removed to the civil parishes of Lichfield St Michael and Wall (GLAUE pp419-420). In the later C17 here Dr Plot found a glowing sort of earth and made up with silver coloured Laminac which came off on the hands, also the same could be found at Brereton Hill (NHS p118).

Pipehill Farm SW of Pipehill. The site has been occupied since the mid C14 and the present house is partly medieval (VCH vol 14 p286). The estate which centred on Pipehill Farm was given to Canon Thomas Milley, archdeacon of Coventry, who in 1504 included it in his re-endowment of Dr Milley's Hospital. By the mid C17 part of the rent from the farm was 15 horseloads of coal delivered on Midsummer Day or 7 shillings 6d in lieu. The coal remained part of the rent until the late C18. The hospital sold the farm in 1920 (VCH

vol 14 p290).

Pipe Hill House SW of Pipehill. Dates from the mid C18 but replaces a house in existence by the later C17 (VCH vol 14 pp286,290). Has also appeared as Pipe Hill Manor (OS map 1:25,000).

Pipe Marsh Area of waste which lay about the crossing of the Lichfield-Walsall road with the Burntwood to Lichfield and Wall road. Pipehill hamlet was built on it (VCH vol 14 p286).

Pipe Moor Barren land S of Lichfield on the boundary with Pipehill township, was recorded as common pasture in 1298. Probably Pipe Moor became the later Pipe Green (VCH vol 14 pp110-111).

Pipe Park Medieval deer park. In existence by 1498. Formerly owned by the lord of Pipe. Situated SE of Pipe Hall (VCH vol 14 p214).

Pipe Place Farm 1.25m E of Hammerwich. The house is of c1700 (BOE p292). Is dated 1764 (VCH vol 14 p290). The estate of Samuel Bradurne, where an ancient military barricade (see under Pipehill) was found, was centred on Pipe Place Farm (SHOS vol 1 part 1 p19) (WSS p116).

Pipe Place Farm S of High Bridge, under 0.5m NNE of Handsacre.

Pipe Ridware Small hamlet at the confluence of Bentley Brook with the Trent 1m E of Hill Ridware. Former chapelry in Alrewas ancient parish. Has appeared as Riduuare, a manor held by the bishop of Chester (Lichfield) in DB, Pipe Ridwale (C13); Pipe did not appear until 1236-42 (SL p56) (SPN p99), Parva Ridware, Little Ridware, Media Ridware, Middle Ridware (DUIGNAN p127), and Pipe Ridware (C14). The name is from the de Pipe family of Pipe near Lichfield (DUIGNAN), who were lords of the manor by at least 1285 (SPN p99). In 1259 Pipe Ridware was said to be included in Alrewas prebend (SSAHST vol 2 1960-61 p43). Pipe Ridware parish was a peculiar jurisdiction of Alrewas prebend in Lichfield cathedral until peculiar jurisdictions were abolished in 1846 (VCH vol 3 p94) (GLAUE p420). The old church, St James, on the S side of Pipe Lane and S of the Hamstall Ridware road, of Norman origin, was rebuilt in 1842 (LGS p203) (SGS p140). The church became disused and was turned into a theatre in 1985, known as Ridware Theatre (SLM April 2000 p56p). Pipe Ridware became a separate ecclesiastical parish in 1726. The separate civil identity which it had early was abolished when the civil parish entered Mavesyn Ridware civil parish in 1934 (GLAUE p420).

Pipe Ridware Manor House The original manor may have stood at or near Linacre (see) (SHOS vol 1 p166*) (GNHS p149), to the NW of Pipe Ridware. The manor house moved to Pipe Ridware by the Trent when John Whitehall purchased Pipe Ridware manor in c1677. The house at Pipe Ridware was still standing at the end of the C18 (NSFCT 1933 pp64-65). Shaw says it was lately occupied by Rev John Arden of Longcroft and was previously not stuccoed (SHOS vol 1 pp161 pl, 166). The house has since been pulled down leaving its walled garden which has become the garden of Hall Farm. In the wall still remain one or two of the alcoves in which John Whitehall used to place his skeps (for beekeeping). His pigeon house (is this the dovecote?) also remain but was in 1933 in a forlorn condition (NSFCT 1933 pp64-65). Two sides of the moat which surrounded the house, fed by streams from the Trent, existed in 1908, no traces were visible in 1983 (VCH vol 1) (SSAHST 1982-3 p45).

Pipes Meadow House or cottage at Bilston. Name comes from the Pipe family, lords of Bilston manor (BOP p71).

Pire Hill Hill 462 feet high 1.75m SSW of Stone. Formerly in Fulford chapelry in Hilderstone quarter in Stone ancient parish (W p363). Between Yarlet and the foot of Pire Hill was found a socketed spearhead (NHS p404 tab 33 fig 8) (SMC p174) (NSJFS 1964 p44). As a hundred of Staffs it appears in DB as Pireholle, Pirehel, Pereolle, Pereholle, Pereoll. Pire is from pyre or fire, from there having been a beacon on the hill (SPP p33). Or 'the hill of the pear tree' (DUIGNAN) (MOS p7) (SPN p118), although the probable root is the same as Barr Beacon or Perry Bar (see) (NSFCT 1908 p136). Gelling thinks, possibly, 'look-out hill' (WMMA p144) (NSJFS 1981 p2). Pirehill Hall or House, at the foot of the hill, was occupied from 1941 by the National Fire Service as a Fire Force Headquarters for Shropshire and much of Staffordshire (SIS p141) (MR p26) (ADD p137p). Under the 1947 Fire Service Act which became law in 1948 the Staffordshire Fire Brigade Service was founded out of an amalgamation of existing town and district fire brigades. Its headquarters have been at Pirehill Hall. In 1986 the service became the Staffordshire Fire and Rescue Service (ADD pp144,175). Prince Charles visited the Staffs Fire and Rescue Service station at the house on March 3 1998 (SLM April 1998 p15). In March 1999 a statue representing firefighters past and present was erected in front of the house (SN April 1 1999 p21p).

Pirehill Former administrative division (hundred) of Staffs, covering the NW area of the county. The name is from Pire Hill SSW of Stone (GNHS p74) (ESH pp45-50), where the hundred court appear to have met in late Anglo-

Saxon times. Parishes, townships and extra-parochial liberties in the **North Division** were: Adbaston, Ashley, Audley, Balterley, Betley, Biddulph, Bucknall and Bagnall, Burslem, Butterton (Newcastle), Chesterton, Chorlton, Drayton-in-Hales (Shrops), Eccleshall, Fenton, Hanford, Hanley, High Offley, Keele, Longton, Madeley, Maer, Normacot (township), Norton-in-the-Moors, Standon, Stoke-upon-Trent, Swynnerton, Trentham, Tunstall, Tyrley (township), Whitmore, Wolstanton (W pp212-213) (S&W p224) (GLAUE p427). White lists Newcastle-under-Lyme parish and borough in the northern division, but Langford places the borough in the southern division. In the **South Division** were: Abbots Bromley, Barlaston, Blithfield, Chartley Holme (extra-parochial), Chebsey, Colton, Colwich, Creswell (extra-parochial), Ellenhall, Fradswell, Gayton, Hopton and Coton, Ingestre, Marston, Milwich, Ranton, Ranton Abbey (extra-parochial), Salt and Enson, Sandon, Seighford, Stone (except Normacot township), Stowe, Tillington (extra-parochial), Tixall, Weston-on-Trent, Worston (extra-parochial), Yarlet (extra-parochial), Stafford (the town) (W pp212-213) (S&W p252).

Pitchings Farm near the Hamps, Waterfall. Has also appeared as Pitchen (W p787).

Pit Graves Hill A copse, a remnant of the lost Bishop's Wood, SE of Bishop's Wood village (SVB p34).

Pitmoor Pool Sheriffhales (SHOS vol 1 part 1 p99).

Pitts Hill Former hamlet beside a head stream of the Fowlea Brook 0.75m NNE of Tunstall (SHST p484). Formerly in Wolstanton ancient parish. Occurs as the home of a branch of the Bourne family in 1678 (VCH vol 8 p83). Has also appeared as Pits Hill (1834 OS map), and Pittshill. See Elizabeth Belwood in BS p52. It was recommended that Pitts Hill railway station close in 1963 (ES March 22 1963).

Pitts Top Hill W of the main road at Townend, Sheen. In Sheen ancient parish. Was so called by the 1730s. The hill was quarried probably in the C18 and certainly in the C19 (VCH vol 7 p245).

Plantation House House under 1.25m SSE of Cheadle. Built in 1855 for the family of Thomas Mackenzie by Charles Lynam of Colwich, over the doorway is the Mackenzie crest 'Luceo non uro' meaning 'Enlightenment before law.' When the Mackenzies left the house was used as a vicarage to St Chad's church, Freehay, until 1927. It is now (1994) a private residence (SMOPP vol 1 p49p) (ACOPP p60p) (COPP2 p80p).

Plant's Green Former hamlet S of Newtown in Rowley Regis parish. The name, which appears in the 1851 census, seems to be preserved in Plant Street, Cradley Heath (BCWJ p74) (BCM autumn 1989 p45) (TB Aug 1995 p27).

Plants Hollow The name is preserved in Pants Hollow street in Withymoor Village. It is named after a well-known local family and lies on the former boundary of Brierley Hill and Quarry Bank urban districts (SNSV vol 1 p261). There were mines and clay banks still in operation in the 1920s at Plants Hollow (BHOP2 p32p).

Plardiwick House 0.75m WSW of Gnosall. Formerly in Cowley quarter in Gnosall ancient parish (W p460) (VCH vol 4 p111). Has appeared as Plerdewick (1199), Pardewyk (1378), Plardswicke (1585), Plordewicke (1607), and Plardewick (1834 OS map) (SPNO p157) (SSE 1996 p17). The ending is from Old English 'wic' meaning a dairy farm (SSE 1987 p28).

Plardiwick Hall The manor-house of the reputed manor of Plardiwick. It existed until c1680. Plardiwick Manor Farm may be the site of it (VCH vol 4 p122).

Plashes Farm 0.5m E of Acton Trussell. Built c1650 using ship's timbers. It was formerly known as Puddle Hole Farm, but was known as Plashes Farm by at least the early 1970s (BERK2 p102p) (1972 OS map 1:25,000).

Platt Bridge An area? 1m W of Eccleshall. Marked on OS map 1:25,000.

Platts, The Area 0.5m NNW of Amblecote. It was an inhabited area by the later C12 or early C13 when a family by the name of Platte lived here (VCH vol 20 p49). Here was a glasshouse. The name is preserved in Platts Road, Crescent and Drive at W end of Brettell Lane.

Platts, The House and estate on W side of the Stourbridge-Wolverhampton road opposite Dennis Hall, in Amblecote parish. In the early C18 it was the seat of the Joshua Henzey, who ran a glasshouse to the N of it. About 1760 a new house was built. It was demolished in 1967 and houses built on the site (VCH vol 20 p51). John Pidcock of the Dial glassworks inherited the estate, from whom it was acquired by glass manufacturer Thomas Webb. He is recorded as living here in 1851 but is said to have moved shortly after to Dennis Hall (SVS p108) (W p167) (SNSV vol 2 p30).

Pleck Former hamlet near Walsall Brook now a district 1.25m WSW of Walsall. In the foreign of Walsall. Has appeared as The Pleck (VCH vol 17 p157), Fleck on Smith's map, and as Walsall Pleck on 1834 OS map. The name is from Anglo-Saxon 'plaecca' meaning 'piece' or 'parcel' of land (SNWA p82) (HOPL) (VCH vol 17 p157). Or from a Welsh family who had settled at Pleck in the early C18 (Walsall Red Book. 1875). Malcolm McDevitt thinks the theory of Walsall Red Book fanciful and totally incorrect (HOPL). Pleck was entirely in Walsall Park in medieval times (HOPL), and appears as a small area of waste in 1576 and 1617. The Pleck was an inhabited area by C17 (VCH vol 17 p157). The former tiny hamlet centred on Horseshoes Lane (Wellington Street) and Narrow Lane (HOPL), by the early 1970s the main shopping of the district was in Wednesbury Road and its adjoining streets, developed from the late C19 (VCH vol 17 p159). For Pleck's industry see Walsall. The ecclesiastical parish of Pleck and Bescot, created in 1860, was called 'Walsall St John' by 1991 (GLAUE p420). Became a ward of Walsall county borough in 1889 (VCH vol 17 p217). The church, St John the Evangelist, in Pleck Road, was completed in 1858 (VCH vol 17 p237) (BOE p297), and rebuilt in Scarborough Road in 1976 (LDD). The Zeppelin L19 which made a raid over Walsall on the night of Jan 31 1916 dropped a bomb in Pleck Road. It fell on a stable killing a horse, four pigs and about 100 fowl (BCM autumn 1996 p57).

Pleck, The House 0.75m NNE of Whitmore.

Pleck Junction Railway junction S of Walsall, formerly known as New Mills Junction (SSR p11).

Pleck Park Park 1m NE of Wednesbury. Former parkland for Bescot Hall (SSAHST vol 33 1991-92 p49). The old hamlet of Bescot was at the N end of the park.

Plot's Giant Oak Large oak at Lapley noted by Dr Robert Plot, author of NHS, in the later C17 (NHS p248) (VCH vol 4 p144).

Plough Farm By the Staffs and Worcs Canal, Gailey. The earthworks at SJ 922109 to the NNE of the farm have been identified with the medieval settlement of Rodbaston (see).

Plumpton House 0.25m SW of Wootton Lodge (1834 OS map). The name is preserved in Plumpton Banks Plantation.

Podmore Remote and obscure (OSST 1949-50 p15) minute hamlet on a promontory between Chatcull and Bromley Brooks 1.25m NNE of Charnes. Former township in Broughton chapelry in the Woodland quarter in Eccleshall ancient parish (W p376). Has appeared as Podemore (DB), and Podemor (SPN p44). The name means 'Podda's moor' (DUIGNAN), or 'Pod's moor' (SPN p44). Gelling thinks 'frog marsh' (NSJFS 1981 p2) or moor (SSE 1996 p17). John de Harcourt held Chatcull and over 1000 acres in Podmore, Mill Meece, Great and Little Bridgeford and Seighford by the service of bringing four men from Chatcull and Podmore to act as beaters to the bishop of Lichfield's hunt (ECC p13). These lands probably comprised the manor of Gerrard's Bromley, and its tenure custom was that the lord had to find four men three times a year to accompany the bishop when he hunted in Eccleshall Park (HOG p194). In 1921 SAH Burne identified a ruined cottage here which occupied the site of a Pre-Reformation chantry chapel. The site has the field name 'Chapel Yard' on an estate map of 1684. The cottage lies E to W and has some old moulded and decorated masonry (NSFCT 1922 p161) (OSST 1949-50 p15). The Gaywoods, minor gentry, were of Podmore and Bishop's Offley (ECC p41).

Podmore Audley ancient parish. By the early C16 there was a manor of Podmore which was formed out of Audley manor. The manor was united with that of Apedale after 1602 (SHC 1944 pxix). Is represented by Podmore Hall (see).

Podmore Bridge Bridge at Consallforge at SK 002487. Built in 1952. Named after the Podmore family who had a flint grinding mill here. It replaced a bridge called London Bridge - so called because it was erected by a London Company, who mined ore in the valley (MR p111).

Podmore Green Was common land at Podmore, Gerrard's Bromley, of which there was one acre remaining in the 1950s (1889 OS map 6 inch) (OSST 1956-59 p13).

Podmore Hall Formerly stood close to the Scot Hay road near Alsagers Bank (IANS p136) at approximately SJ 802482. It was registered and licensed as a Methodist meeting house in 1693 (NSJFS 1971 p66). It was occupied in the early C18 by the Eardleys of Miles Green (SHC 1944 p25). Has appeared as Podmode Hall (Yates' map).

Podmore Pool Pool 1m N of Charnes.

Pointhorne House 0.75m ESE of Croxden, in Croxden parish. Fields at Pointhorne show clearly the ridges of former open fields (CDS p18). The name appears as Poynthorn in 1694 and there was a farm at Pointhorne by 1722. The farm known as Upper Pointhorne had gone by 1913. The site was marked in 1978 by a hollow over the former well (CDS pp19,22,65).

Pone's Brook On boundary of Lichfield City (HOL p357). It could be the brook which runs through Stowe and feeds Stowe Pool.

Pool, The Pool S of Pool Hall, 1.5m NNE of Trysull.

Pool Dole In the present Fenpark Road and Pool Street area of ENE Fenton (1834 OS map). In Stoke-upon-Trent chapelry in Stoke-upon-Trent ancient parish.

Poolend Small hamlet over 0.75m E of Rudyard. Formerly in Leekfrith township in Leek ancient parish. Here was a great pool; the ancient dam of which was still evident in c1900 (NSFCT 1885 p54) (OL vol 2 p203). Has also appeared as Pool End.

Pool Farm On the N side of Turner's Pool. Formerly in Leekfrith township in Leek ancient parish. Built for William Armett in 1669 (VCH vol 7 p194).

Pool Farm Former farm at SP 025880 in the present Victoria Park area of Smethwick. There may have been a moated site here (SSAHST 1982-3 p51).

Pool Field Medieval field boundary of Newcastle-under-Lyme (NUL p107). One of the four fields comprising the pasturage belonging to the burgesses of Newcastle (W p304) allotted to them under the Enclosure Act passed 1816.

Poolfold Small hamlet 1.25m NNE of Biddulph shopping area. In Biddulph ancient parish.

Pool Green Tiny district of SW Aldridge, 0.5m from the centre. In Aldridge ancient parish. The original Saxon settlement of Aldridge may have been at Pool Green where a number of roads meet and where there was large pool (MOA p129): Aldridge takes its name from alder trees, and the alders like wet situations (SNAR p42). The pool was largely destroyed when the railway was built in 1872 and has subsequently been completely destroyed by further building (MOA p129). The church, St Mary, Tynings Lane, was built in 1936 (LDD).

Pool Green House and minute hamlet 0.25m N of Tatenhill, on a promontory in between some small dales.

Pool Hall House which stood in Beacon Street outside Lichfield cathedral Close on the site of Westgate House. Pool Hall was annexed to Wolvey prebend in the later 1270s and was known as Pool Hall by 1438. Was probably destroyed in the Civil War and rebuilt by 1670. It was rebuilt again in the later C18, possibly by the lessee, Peter Garrick (VCH vol 14 p68). (HOL p511).

Pool Hall Formerly in Bradnop township in Leek ancient parish. There was a cottage called Pool Hall on the Ashbourne road by 1663. It was rebuilt in the Gothick style in the earlier C19 (VCH vol 7 p171) and may be the present Pool Hall Farm, 0.5m NW of Bradnop. The tollhouse to the SE of the farm was built in 1828 to replace the one at Lowe Hill (see) to the N (built in 1765) (VCH vol 7 pp99,171). The last toll was taken in 1858 (NSFCT 1948 pp33p facing, 53. 1956 p111; implying that there was only one tollhouse) and the house was demolished in the 1970s (VCH vol 7 p170). A phantom coach has been seen along the Ashbourne road here (FLJ 1942 p126). The coach is pulled by two horses and is said to visit various parts of the Moorlands. Some have seen it, but not heard the tramp of the horses' hooves, whilst others have heard both, but not seen it (OL vol 2 p302) (ES Sept 16 1936 p5).

Pool Hall House 1m NW of Lower Penn. Formerly in Lower Penn township in Penn ancient parish. The small square enclosure at SO 86209740, E of the house, is possible Iron Age activity, and was revealed by aerial photography in 1964 (NSJFS 1964 p28) (ALP p16).

Pool Hall Bridge Crosses the Dove to E of Bridge End, Sheen. There was a bridge here probably by 1506, and certainly by the early C17 when it was called Pool Hall Bridge. Pool Hall (later Moat Hall) stands not far away in Derbys and was until the mid C17 the manor house of Sheen (VCH vol 7 pp242,244).

Pool Hayes Residential suburb and a large comprehensive school 1.25m NNE of Willenhall. The Pool Hayes housing estate was built in 1965 (SNW p55), some or part of this estate is known as Summer Hayes village (Selective Essays on Willenhall. David Potts. 1984. Copy in Willenhall Library). The name is from a farm at Ashmore Lake, known as Pool Hays in the 1840s. The farm takes its name from an enclosure near a pool; the pool may have been that which stood near Pool Hayes School, which was filled in some years ago to make way for housing development (SNW p55).

Pool Head A house at Pool Head, Eccleshall, was registered for Protestant Dissenters by George Pool of Stafford in 1817 (SHC 1960 p42). There is a house called Pool House 0.5m N of Eccleshall (1834 OS map).

Pool House House and former estate 0.75m N of Audley in Eardley End township in Audley ancient parish. An old house called this or the present house belonged to the Eardleys in 1733, and formerly by the early C17 it belonged to the Eardleys of Eardley Hall (SHC 1944 p51).

Pool House Farm Over 1m NNE of Great Barr. Is of C17 (WMARCH 1995 p114) or earlier (MOA p139). Has also appeared as Pool Farm.

Pool Lock Aqueduct Kidsgrove. Built in 1829 to take the Macclesfield Canal across the Trent and Mersey Canal (NSJFS 1965 p92 pl VIb) (IAS p172).

Pool Meadows Industrial area in the Willenhall area (BCM April 1987 pp52-53).

Popehouse Lane Place which occurs in a deed of the C16 relating to Upper Arley (VCHW vol 3 p5).

Popinjay Farm House at SK 075323, near Blount's Green, Uttoxeter (Yates' map). Has also appeared as Poppingey and Popinjay Fields. The house may have been an inn. In the Middle Ages a popinjay was a target in the shape of a parrot used by archers. On May 21 1983 two cars collided at Popinjay Hollow killing one of the drivers (TRTC p52).

Poplar House A Georgian house in King Street, Darlaston (Offlow hundred). Mrs Henry Wood (nee Ellen Price) stayed here with relatives Samuel and Pheobe Mills and wrote part of her novel 'East Lynne' (1861) in the summer house in the large garden. The house later became a private girls school and subsequently a shop known as Stanburys. It was demolished in Sept 1977 (WDY p25 p of in c1880) (TWDOP p145p) (SNDB p66p) (photograph in the Walsall Local Studies Centre). The site is now occupied by Darlaston Neighbourhood Office in the modern shopping centre. A plaque is erected on the site to commemorate the house (BCM April 1985 p14. Oct 1989 pp55-56) (MR p122). The Columbarium a dovecote (Darlaston Town Trail. Malcolm Timmins), may have belonged to Popular House.

Poplars An old opencast mining area S of Cannock near Kings Wood. Restarting mining on the site was prevented by a residents' protest. Instead, a £40 million historical theme park was proposed (VB p123).

Poplars Farm 0.25m N of Anslow. The farm was created by Joseph Davis (1734-1811) in the later C18 (ANS p107).

Poplars Farm On E side of Fishley Lane in Walsall ancient parish. The farm at SK 006038 was formerly moated (VCH vol 1 p368. vol 17 p163) (SSAHST 1982-83 p49).

Porter's Farm House 1.5m NW of Horton, situated on former Horton Hay, in Horton ancient parish. May have been created when Horton Hay was divided into farms in the later C17. It existed by 1805 (VCH vol 7 p72).

Porter's Hill Hill 2.25m ENE of Colton.

Portfields House by Blithfield Reservoir, 1m SW of Abbots Bromley.

Portgate Field One of the open fields of Stafford. Enclosed in 1807 (NSJFS 1975 p30).

Porthill Former hamlet on a hill by the Fowlea Brook, now a district 0.75m NNE of Wolstanton. In Wolstanton ancient parish. A Neolithic or Bronze Age small axe with incomplete perforation in the Potteries Museum said to come from Porthill is probably from Church Lawton, Ches (NSFCT vol 66 p193) (JBAA series 2 vol 37 p254) (NSJFS 1964 p30). The church, St Andrew, at the junction of Watlands View, High Street, and Porthill, was built in 1886 (BOE p313). Porthill became a separate ecclesiastical parish in 1913 (GLAUE p420). In June 1946 Ivy Griffiths was killed whilst walking across waste ground to her home in Arnold Grove. There seemed to be no motive and the case is still (1990) unsolved. Up to at least 1963 a detective returned to the scene of the crime on the anniversary of the murder to see if the murderer had also returned (STM July 1963 p39). In 1953 a Meteor flown by RAF pilot Percival Boulton disintegrated in mid air crashing in flames on Porthill Park cricket ground just missing Wolstanton school; part of a wing came down outside May Bank school. Boulton was killed (info Ron Balding) (ES Nov 28 1994). The BBC Radio One disc-jockey, Bruno Brookes (b1960), from Stoke-on-Trent lived at Rhodes Court, Porthill, while broadcasting on Radio Stoke before moving to London in 1984 (ES Jan 27 1993 p12p). Porthill is 'Hillport' in Arnold Bennett's novels. A bright yellowy white object or UFO long and oval in shape lying horizontally in the sky in the northeast was seen from Porthill on Aug 23 1967 (FSRP p6).

Porthill House Stood on the S side of Porthill road, Porthill, at the top of the hill, and apart from Shelton Hall and Westlands Hall it was the nearest thing to a mansion in this area. It was once occupied by William Clowes, whose daughter Anne married Hugh Henshall Williamson of Greenway Bank House. In c1840 Edward Wood bought it. The house is shown on maps between at least c1885 to 1945. It is Hillport House in Arnold Bennett's 'Anna of the Five Towns' (OS maps 6 inch) (WWT p66) (Arnold Bennett and Stoke-on-Trent. EJD Warrilow. 1966 p122).

Portland House Aldridge. It was the seat of Frank James, who became MP for Walsall in 1892. The house later became known as Aldridge Court (ALOPPR p32p), and has perhaps erroneously been identified with Moot House (see), Aldridge.

Portland House Stood S of Newcastle Street, Burslem. Home of the Riley family in the early C19 (HBST p267). Was being used as a technical school in 1960 (VCH vol 8 p112).

Portobello District on low ground near the stream which joins Sneyd Brook near County Bridge 1m N of Bilston. Formerly in Willenhall chapelry in Wolverhampton ancient parish. The name occurs in the 1841 census in Willenhall parish. White, in the mid C19, described it as a large and improving village (W p161). The church, St Alban, built in the C19 stood on the site of St Alban's Court, on the S side of Willenhall Road near Wesley Court at the N end of New Street. The site was sold in c1955 and the church demolished (info Rev David Hartland). There was a windmill in Portobello at SO 951986. It was possibly used for drainage in the C19. Has not been traced on any map. The mill is said to have been demolished in c1918 (WIS p25). Here occurred a railway accident on Oct 19 1899 when a goods train from Wednesfield Heath collided with a passenger train from Wolverhampton High Level Station on the LNWR line at the junction near Neachells Bridge (WDY p10p).

Portstreet The Portstreet mentioned in Lady Wulfrun's charter (994) as at Kirclesford (Moseley Hole) must be as traced by Duignan a northern section of the road from Portway Road, Wednesbury, via Dangerfield Lane and Catherine's Cross (Darlaston) via Darlaston Lane to Portway Road (Bunker's Hill, Bilston). The highway branched at Moseley Hole (i) via Dean's Road, Church Street (Heath Town), Bushbury Road, Newbolds, Old Falling Lane, and Bushbury Hill to Northycote (ii) via Neachells Lane, Amos Lane, Long Knowle Lane, Pear Tree Lane, Underhill to Northycote. Beyond Northycote the single road proceeded to Stafford via Standeford. It has been thought that the highway formed part of the Anglo-Saxon Stafford-Warwick road (HOWM p2) (WFW p30). Whilst Hackwood thought that Portway Road, Wednesbury, was either of Anglo-Saxon or Roman origin, and may have been a part of the 'salt-way' from Droitwich, through Oldbury and Wednesbury to join the Chester Road beyond Bloxwich (WAM p8).

Port Vale Former wharf on the Trent and Mersey Canal (AGT p69), in the Burslem area, in Burslem chapelry in Stoke-upon-Trent ancient parish. The name is perhaps from 'port' as in wharf and 'vale' from Ravensdale or Fowlea Vales. **Port Vale Football Club.** Longport Football Club had its first headquarters at Port Vale House in Scott Lidgett Road (formerly Alexandra Road), Longport, in 1876. The club became professional in 1885 and was renamed Burslem Port Vale after the house. Its first ground was in meadows near the house. In 1881 it moved to the area now covered by Westport Lake and in 1884 to Moorland Road. In 1886 the club moved to Cobridge. In 1911 it moved to a ground off Bryan Street, Hanley, and stayed there until moving to their present (2000) ground in Hamil Road (0.5m NE of Burslem) in 1950; known as Vale Park by at least 1963 (VCH vol 8 pp141,171) (TSS pp47,123; says the club have had six grounds between 1919 and 1968). By 1969 the greatest number of appearances in Association Football for Ireland was 56 by Billy Bingham (a player for Sutherland, Luton, Everton, and Port Vale) of which 34 were for the International Championship, between 1951 and 1963-4 (GBR 1969 p311). The club is still (2000) known locally as The Valiant.

Portway On the eastern edge of Arley village. A part of the Roman road from Worcester to Wroxeter (W p168).

Portway Ancient way from Cromford, Derbys through Ashbourne, Hanging Bridge, down Port Lane to Ellastone (and then perhaps, to Uttoxeter) (NSFCT 1976 p44).

Portway Part of Harlaston is known as the Portway (THM vol 1 p69 (TH Dec 27 1941)).

Portway Part of the highway through Hopwas has been described as 'Port Way' (THM vol 1 p69 (TH Dec 27 1941)).

Portway Pilgrim's Way (see) has been described as Portway (THM vol 1 p69 (TH Dec 27 1941)).

Port Way The road between Tutbury and Burton upon Trent, which was a Roman road (HOU p342). The name is not necessarily from it having been of Roman origin. The word 'port' in Old English meant simply 'town;' in Anglo-Saxon times 'portway' was a way leading to a town (DUIGNAN) (NSFCT 1976 p44). The Portway Cross, a boundary cross, appears to have stood at the junction of the Tutbury Road with Longhedge and Anslow Lanes, SW of Rolleston. It was similar to Horninglow Cross (UTR p167) (IVNF p of the present day site on the main Burton-Tutbury road).

Portway Hamlet on SE side of Turner's Hill, 0.75m NNE of Rowley Regis. In Rowley Regis parish. When on one of his visits to Himley Hall the Prince of Wales (Edward VIII) visited a slum in the Portway area (BCM April 1971 pp56-57).

Portway An ancient way from Newport to Stafford and Coventry (NSJFS 1969 p11).

Portway Name for a stretch of Roman road in 1618 from Forton to Newport and to Tong and Chesterton (probably Shrops) and on to Worcester (NSFCT 1937 p63).

Portway Name for the Roman road at Uttoxeter (NSFCT 1908 p110).

Portway Hall Stood on the S side of Newbury Lane close to the 'Four Ways' and boundary with Oldbury near Turner's Hill, Rowley Regis (TB Feb 1988 p5). Built of brick, later stuccoed, and was dated 1674 (SL p177); some say it was built in 1671 (ORR p79p). Built by Daniel 'Ironside' Johnson, a disciple of Oliver Cromwell. It was he who is supposed to have brought Cromwell's

skull to the hall which was stolen from here by Theodore Russell and sold to John Wilkinson in 1787, who presented it to a leading antiquary who kept it in his private museum until handing it over to Cromwell's old college - Sidney Sussex, Cambridge, where it now lies in an unmarked grave. The hall was occupied by the Woodhouse family - the most famous of whom was James Woodhouse (1735-1820), the 'Cobbler Poet' of Rowley Regis (see). In the early 1800s the hall was sold by the Johnsons to the Williams family. The hall may be identified with Portway House, occupied in 1851, by John and SH Blackwell. Later in the C19 it was the residence of the Ramrod Colliery manager, Joseph Baker. The Pardoe family occupied the hall from 1900 to 1952. The hall, which had sunk some 20 feet due to mining subsidence since it was built, was for sale in 1974 (W p22) (TB July 1974 pp18-19p, p of Cromwell's skull. Aug 1974 pp18-19p of the hall in c1919, 29 - on Cromwell's skull. Sept 1974 p26p. Nov 1979 p5p of. May 1995 p13p. July 1995 p27. Sept 23 1999 p25p) (ORR p79p). It was derelict by 1975 (SL p177) and demolished shortly after 1979 (ORR p79) (TB May 1995 p13).

Postern House Postern House Farm is 0.75m N of Tatenhill.

Pothooks Brook Tributary of the Penk. Forms the E boundary of Coppenhall civil parish (VCH vol 5 p138). Potte means 'the deep holes in a river-bend' whilst 'hoc' means 'a spit of land in a river-bend' (SPNO p16).

Pottal Valley A valley in SE corner of Teddesley Park, 2m SSE of Bednall.

Pottal Pool 2.25m SSE of Bednall, 0.75m N of Huntington. Pottal Pool and Slade occur in 1814 and the name means the 'valley with a deep pit or hole' (SPNO p121). Pottal Pool was a reservoir for Staffs and Worcs Canal (CCBO pp116,117). Pottal Pool Lido was opened on Aug 3 1933. The place is mentioned in Cecil J Tildesley's poem titled 'Cannock Chase'

'....They drop their slender shadows cool
About the banks of Pottal Pool,'

(TB April 1996 p11).

Potteries, The Collective name for the pottery manufacturing districts in North Staffordshire in recognition that the area had a staple trade. The area focuses on the Six Towns - Burslem, Fenton, Hanley, Longton, Stoke-upon-Trent, and Tunstall. In these towns - federated to form Stoke-on-Trent in 1910 - pottery manufacturing predominated. The term 'The Potteries' was applied to the district for the first time in the latter half of the C18 (Staffordshire pottery and its History. Josiah C Wedgwood p2) (SHC 1934 p6) and was in use by the early C19 (POTP p239) and seems to have been imposed from above. The area has also appeared as The Pottery (POTP p239). By the early 1990s Staffs pottery from the Potteries still held world-wide prestige. The area was then producing 75-80 per cent of the UK's pottery (HOS 1998 p107), and the industry was, and still (2000) is, the leading employer in the district. However as the 1990s progessed there was strong foreign competition, especially from the Far East, recessions, bankruptcies and further mergers. Where once it could be said the industry employed more than all the other industries of the district combined this was no longer the case by the end of the 1990s with many service and telecommunications industries having moved into the area. Despite the diminishing potteries Potteries people of all occupations still have the habit of turning up their crockery at restaurants to see who made it, and there is a Potteries saying that Potteries people have slip in their veins not blood! (BBC Radio 4 July 15 1994 9.30pm).

The development of the Potteries is based on the presence of quick-burning coal in the N Staffs Coalfield in conjunction with locally-found clay (HOS 1998 p15). Holes made in clay roadways in the Potteries by local inhabitants digging to steal clay may have given rise to the general term 'pot hole,' a hole worn in the road surface (local info). A Roman kiln has been found at Trent Vale (see); the Romans may also have had a kiln at Burslem; the monks of Hulton Abbey may have initiated potting at Burslem. Medieval kilns have been found at Sneyd Green (see). As a consequence of Burslem's early involvement in pottery-making it has been referred to as the 'Mother of the Potteries.' The earliest evidence of pottery-making in the other towns is recorded: in 1348 at Tunstall; in c1540 at Hanley; in the 1680s at Stoke; in c1710 at Fenton; and in the mid C18 at Longton (VCH vol 8 p99,163,202,217,238). According to tradition glazing ware with salt was discovered by accident in c1680 to the W of the Potteries at Stanley Farm (see), or was introduced to the region by the Elers brothers of Dimsdale Hall (see) in c1700. In 1720 potters went up to London to petition for the prohibition of the import of china-ware (SSAHST 1967 p52). The first porcelain works in Staffs was built at Longton Hall in the mid C18 (VCH vol 8 p238). Pottery-making was carried on in domestic workshops until at least the later C18 when Josiah Wedgwood started to industrialise the process at his specially-built Etruria Works (see). Perhaps as a consequence of domestic workshops individual factories in the Potteries have always been known as either, a pot-bank, a bank, a works, a pottery, a potworks, or a manufactory, but rarely, if ever, a factory.

BOTTLE OVENS. From at least the C19 to the mid C20 the Potteries was dominated by bottle-shaped brick kilns, known as bottle ovens. That no other large industrial buildings prevailed is remarked upon by JB Priestley in his 'English Journey' (1934): 'The pottery manufactories - known locally as 'potbanks' - have nothing big about them, no six-storey factories or towering chimneys.' Longton had the most; there it was said it was a fine day if you could see the other side of the street, such was the density of smoke from kilns (there is a Potteries expression 'to see the smoke' ie: to be born or 'to see the light'). As well as firing pottery many kilns were used for calcinating flint. It is believed there was about 4,000 bottle ovens in the Potteries in the C19; in c1900 there were 2,600; in 1936 there were 2,500 (there were then about 300 potteries in the City of Stoke-upon-Trent - SHC 1934 p7)' (Notes on 'The Card' by IL Baker) (WMLB p65) (The Times Aug 18 1999 p8) (ES Aug 18 1999 p8). Firing fuelled by coal gradually died with the introduction of gas and electricity and the traditional bottle oven became obsolete. Most were demolished, and the familiar skyline crowded with bottle ovens and smoke, was lost. A further blow to bottle ovens came in the 1950s with Clean Air Acts; the last firing of a bottle oven for commercial purposes was in 1978. In 1964 there were only 200 bottle ovens in the Potteries; by 1999 there were only 47. In August 1999 the Potteries Heritage Society received lottery funding to repair and stabilise 12 of 21 bottle ovens in danger of collapse (WMLB p65) (ES Dec 12 1994 p8. Aug 18 1999 p8) (The Times Aug 18 1999 p8). (NSFCT 1939 pp22-28).

In 1862 26 manufacturers signed a 'Memorial of Employers in the Potteries' and sent it to Sir George Grey, Home Secretary, complaining that young children were still working in the pot-banks injurious to their education (POP p105). The independent Royal Pottery, or Stanley Troop, raised by Capt Josiah Spode in 1798 (FSP p62) was a part of the Staffordshire Yeomanry from 1803 (info Yeomanry Museum). The Potteries Provision riot of 1800 may be a reference to the food riot of that year at Longton (see). There were fears of riots by the colliers of the Potteries in May 1831 and requests were made to Manchester to send a troop of cavalry (LOU p206). The potters' ancient hiring-time was Martinmas, whereas the agricultural hiring-time in the rest of N Staffs was at Christmas (NSFCT 1896 p126) (OTP p18). Factory girls in the Potteries were still touching metal as a talisman whenever they passed a priest in 1941. The superstition derives from Bronze Age man's fear of Druids of the Stone Age over whom he had just conquered (FLJ 1941 p237). For the Potteries in literature see 'The Frobishers: a story of the Staffs Potteries' (1901), and 'The Rival Potter' by R Randall (1990), and Burslem and Hanley.

CHARTISM IN THE POTTERIES. Social unrest arising out of the failure of the 'People's Charter' of the Chartist movement had its roots in the Potteries. The movement had came to prominence in Britain in 1838. The petition for the 'People's Charter,' including universal suffrage, vote by ballot, annual parliaments, equal electoral districts, the abolition of all property qualification for members, and payment for their services, with over three million signatures was rejected on May 2 1842. When a coal owner, 2nd Earl Granville of Stone Park (see), gave notice to his men of a pay reduction a meeting of all colliers in Hanley agreed to call out the pits in N Staffs from Monday July 11. A central committee of Operative Colliers was set up and throughout the next fortnight hundreds of colliers roamed the streets forcing turn-outs in the pits, stopping the colliery engines by raking out the boilers and pulling out their plugs. The disturbances became known as the Plug Plot riots or Operative riots. Nearly the whole Potteries were forced to close for lack of fuel, but potters showed no antagonism towards colliers and their aims. As time progressed colliers' demands surpassed the mere restoration of the cuts and they began to demand a basic regular wage. Renewed turn-outs occurred at two pits from August 6 and a crowd of 200 colliers attacked Burslem Town Hall. During the course of the strike N Staffs colliers extended their actions into adjacent districts and the Black Country. Something like a general strike in the country for the Charter began on Aug 12. At the height of the unrest 15 English and Welsh and eight Scottish counties were affected. FC Mather went so far as to call it a general strike. At the same time as the Potteries were influencing other parts of the country, the workers of the area fell under the influence of those from outside, particularly Thomas Cooper who arrived in Hanley on Saturday August 13. At Winchester, a trades conference called for a general strike for the Charter and urged other towns to do the same. Within the Potteries crowds gained confidence through attacks on Hanley police station, pottery court of requests offices in Stoke, Thomas Allen's house in Fenton, the house of TP Rhodes (a stipendiary magistrate in Penkhull), Stoke workhouse, Longton police courts, the house of Rev Benjamin Vale, rector of

Longton, the houses of pottery manufacturers Charles Meigh, and Charles James Mason (but not that of the Ridgeway's who were liberals), Forrester, Granville's agent, Albion House (William Parker, magistrate), Hanley Parsonage (Rev Atkins), the home of the chief bailiff. On Aug 16 several marches rendezvoused at Burslem when the George Inn was attacked. The Riot Act was read, when turn-outs from Leek arrived, the magistrate, Capt Powys, gave the order to fire and one man died and others were seriously wounded and the crowd dispersed, pursued by soldiers. Subsequently, there was a massive crack down by the authorities who flooded the Potteries with soldiers. Ultimately a Special Commission of Assize was set up at Stafford which sat between Oct 1-15 and dealt with 276 accused (including the elderly blacksmith agitator Joseph Capper of Tunstall (see)?), who were often tried in batches. Nobody was sentenced to death but 116 were imprisoned and 56 transported. The Chartist movement had disappeared by 1850 (A Short History of the English People. JR Green. 1898 p840) (LOU pp243-249) (The Crisis of 1842: Chartism, the colliers' strike and the outbreak in the Potteries in The Charter Experience. J Epstein & D Thompson pp194-200. Robert Fyson).

Potter's Cross Former tiny hamlet overlooking a bend in the Stour 0.75m NNW of Kinver. In Kinver parish. Now merges into Kinver. By the late C20 was a ward in Kinver civil parish. There was a cottage here by the early 1620s and the area had many houses by 1841 (VCH vol 20 p121). A lesser noble was caught poaching deer in Kinver Forest in medieval times and was punished by being flayed; his skin left exposed upon the site of Potter's Cross (BCWJ p106).

Pottery Coalfield A coalfield covering most of the Potteries and beyond. 'The first recorded discovery of organic remains in the coal-measures of the Pottery Coalfield dates as far back as 1835, when Sir Philip Egerton read a paper before the Geological Society of London, 'On the Discovery of Ichthyolites in the SW portion of the N Staffs Coalfield" (J Ward in W Gibson and other 'op, cit.' p285) (NSFCT 1944 p55 note).

Pouchers Pool Former pool which seems to have been approximately at over 1.5m NE of Enville near a warrener's lodge, which was in existence probably by 1623 (VCH vol 20 p93). The name is preserved in Pouchers Pool Road.

Pouk Hill Small rounded hill by Sneyd Brook 0.25m ENE of Bentley, 1.75m NW of Walsall. Formerly in Bentley township in Wolverhampton ancient parish. Formerly the hill resembled a huge mole hill some 300 or 400 yards in circumference and comprised of dolerite (or basalt, a type of black marble like Rowley Rag). In 1565 a pasture here was known as Poukeloftons (SNWA p84). In the later C17 Plot noted a large witch elm growing on the hill, that had embraced and lifted up from the ground with its root a great stone of at least 200 weight (NHS p212). Quarrying which had taken place from the later C17 had by the early C20 practically obliterated the hill (NHS p174) (WJO Aug 1908 p211p) (VCH vol 2 pp203,204. vol 17 p160) (WDY p13). In the initial stages of quarrying fine hexagonal basaltic columns were created, similar, but on a smaller scale to those seen at Giants Causeway and the Isle of Staffa. By 1862 the sides of the quarry (which were perpendicular) were formed of pentagonal columns which in some places rose to 20 feet high. The columns bent over to a common centre so creating a gigantic hall (Walsall Observer 1862) (SNWA p84). The hill has given up many delights for geologists. Dr Cooper of Bilston had a huge fossil fish (Megalichthys Hibberti) from it and put it in the BM (SOB p201) (SNWA p84). There may have been a moat at SO 991988, S of Pouk Hill, which would have been destroyed when the M6 was built (SSAHST 1982-3 p49). The name, which appears on the 1889 OS map 6 inch, has also appeared as Powke Hill. 'Hob' and 'pouke' have the same meaning. 'Hob' is a Middle English word for a sprite, an elf, a hobgoblin (DUIGNAN pp80,121).

Pound Green 1m SSW of Arley, on W side of the Severn. In Upper Arley parish.

Poverty Knob Hill, probably in the Birchills area of Walsall (HOPL).

Poverty Wicket Ride or gate through or at the edge of Swynnerton Old Park, suggestive of medieval superstitions and of the woodman (NSFCT 1917 p152).

Powke Hillock In the vicinity of The Eagle Colliery, Rowley Regis (TB Nov 1986 p5). Quagmire Hall at Powke Hillock was the local name for the seat of the Suttons (TB June 1972 p17. Nov 1997 p13).

Powke Lane Former settlement or hamlet by Dudley Canal Line Two 0.5m SW of Rowley Regis. In Rowley Regis parish (W p194) (1834 OS map). Is said to be derived from Puck's Lane, a relic of belief in woodland spirits (BCWJ p100). The name is preserved in Powke Lane (Birmingham A-Z).

Presford Brook Runs to Coton Clanford where it joins Doxey Brook which in turn joins the Sow. Or Prestford Brook runs by Prestford Meadows, tithe land historically paid to the vicar of Seighford which caused a dispute in the C18 (OPB pp14-17). The name of the brook may be from prost 'a priest' compounded with ford (SPNO p16).

Preston Former manor and liberty (W pp466,468) near Whiston, Penkridge, on low ground by Whiston Brook, in Penkridge ancient parish. Is mentioned in c1215. Described as a hamlet in 1598. Comprises the houses Preston Hill and Preston Vale. The name means 'the farmstead or the manor of the priests' (SPNO p92).

Preston Hill Mid C18 house at Preston 1m ENE of Whiston. In Penkridge ancient parish. Penkridge had a three-quarter mile race course to the E of Preston Hill in the 1820s and 1830s (VCH vol 5 p106).

Preston Vale House at Preston 0.5m ENE of Whiston. In Penkridge parish. A late C17 farmhouse (VCH vol 5 p120); the tall chimney at the end of the buildings is a former steam-mill (PVH p59). There was a chapel at Preston Vale sited in a field on the left of the lane approaching Preston Vale. By 1732 it was described as 'a little house inhabited by the widow Wooley.' It was also a 'Gospel Place' (PVH p59). The name is from Anglo-Saxon 'preost tun,' 'the priests' farmstead' (SPN p95).

Prestwood Farm 1m N of Wednesfield (SVS p120 note). Formerly in Wednesfield chapelry in Wolverhampton ancient parish. It lay within the bounds of Cannock Forest. The name occurs in 1240 and the wood, Prestwode, later dominated much of the Wednesfield area (WFW pp6,45). Edward II granted it to the dean and chapter of Wolverhampton, but the monks of Wolverhampton monastery had held it long before (DUIGNAN). The name is from it having been held by Wolverhampton Collegiate Church (DUIGNAN). In Elizabethan times the Prestwood estate was in the foreign of Wolverhampton and belonged to the Levesons (HOWM p44). To the E of the farm is a moated site which seems to have been occupied until 1612 when as the residence of John Hope it was burnt down. Another house was built and this house is shown on an estate map of 1661 as lying on the site of the present farmhouse. The estate map of 1661 was made by William Fowler, probably a Fowler of the Fowler family of Pendeford. In 1661 Prestwood Farm was the residence of George Perry (SSAHST 1979-80 pp15-22) (WFW p64). The moat, 250 feet by 190 feet in 1908 (VCH vol 1 p368), remained until 1972 when a change of ownership and occupier caused its extinction (WFW p64) (SSAHST 1982-83 p41).

Prestwood Tiny hamlet on N-facing slope of a hill above the confluence of Hole Brook and a tributary 1.25m SW of Ellastone. Former township in Ellastone ancient parish. Ecclesiastically severed in 1860 to help create Denstone ecclesiastical parish. Became a separate civil parish in 1866 (GLAUE p420).

Prestwood Small settlement on the side of a ridge between the Smestow and the Stour overlooking the Stour under 1m NNE of Stourton. Formerly in Kingswinford ancient parish (SGSAS) removed to Kinver ancient parish in 1934 (VCH vol 20 p118). It lay within the bounds of Kinver Forest (DUIGNAN). At Prestwood (probably at Prestwood House) Shaw was shown a small glass annulet adorned with red and white streaks which may have been a Roman ornament (SHOS vol 2 p236). The name means 'the wood of the priests' (SPN p95), and is from it having been held by the bishops of Worcester in the C8, C9 and C10 (DUIGNAN). For the wharfhouse serving some ironworks by the canal see under Gothersley.

Prestwood Hay Former hay or division or deer enclosure of Kinver Forest in the Prestwood area; it existed in the Middle Ages (NSJFS 1968 p40 fig 3). Is not listed as such by VCH vol 2 p344. Perhaps, was mistakenly thought to have been a hay, for the Prestwode family held a house and land at Prestwood by the service of keeping Ashwood Hay from the later C13 to c1500 (VCH vol 2 p346 note).

Prestwood House Set on the N bank of the Stour at Prestwood, Stourton. A house stood here by Richard III's reign when it was occupied by John de Somery (KEOP p56). In the late C16 a new house was built by Sir John Littleton. He forfeited the estate, having adhered to Robert Dudley, Earl of Essex, in his abortive rebellion in 1600 (BOE p223) (NSFCT 1976 p14). 'Red' Humphrey Littleton hid at Prestwood, his old home, after being found to have hidden the Gunpowder Plot conspirators Robert Winter and Stephen Littleton at his home Hagley House or Hall. Here he was found by justices from both Staffs and Worcs and taken to Worcester for trial (HOWM pp64,65). The house had passed to the Foleys by 1672. It remained with them to the mid C18 when it passed by marriage to the Hodgetts, and by marriage it passed from them to another branch of the Foley family. Their heirs assumed the name Hodgetts-Foley until Paul Henry Hodgetts-Foley changed his back to Foley. He was a keen cricketer and prime mover in seeing Worcs CCC become a first class county club. He sold the Foley estates, including Prestwood, in 1913 (NHS tab 9 il of the house) (SHOS vol 2 p234 pl xxxv) (SVS pp120-123) (NSFCT 1976 p14) (VCH vol 20 p130) (SNSV vol 2 p80) (TB June 1998 p6p). The house has also been the seat of the Sebrights and

Hodgsons (perhaps Hodgetts is meant?) (KEOP p56). The house may have contained a small piece of black velvet in a paper, inscribed

> This is a piece of King Charles the First's coate
> that hae was beheaded in, given to Dr Holinton.

Also in the house was a letter sent from Charles II at Brussels to the Foleys or Herbert Price, dated Oct 16 1658 (SHOS vol 2 p236). The Elizabethan house was demolished in 1766 (NSFCT 1976 p14). The house standing in the early C19 was remodelled in the Gothic style (BOE p223); it was stuccoed in 1821 (RKE p17). It was bought in the mid 1920s for a hospital for chest diseases but during the alterations a fire broke out and the building had to be demolished. A new hospital building was then built on the site of the former house; the few stone edgings to the flower beds are all that remain of the Gothic house (NSFCT 1976 p15) (TB Feb 1984 p23p). By 1996 the hospital building was being used as a nursing home (KEOP p56p). There was a chapel surmounting a gothic gateway in front of the old house dedicated to St Peter. This was taken down in 1821 (RKE p17). Garner says the gateway was the gateway to an older house and was still standing in his day (GNHS p181). The grounds were landscaped by Humphry Repton in 1790 (BOE p223).

Price's Cave Cave slightly to the N of the Devil's Staircase at SK 001493 above the Churnet and Caldon Canal, 1.25m ENE of Consall. Called Price's Cave after a Mr Jack Price, butler at Belmont Hall, who lived in it for 11 years after retiring. Some say Belmont Hall kept him supplied with food (SMCC p11 il), others say he stole food from the hall (NSFCT 1906 p167).

Priestfield Former hamlet on low ground by the Birmingham Canal Old Cut Old Main Line formerly partly in Wolverhampton and Bilston townships in Wolverhampton ancient parish, 2m SE of Wolverhampton (1885 OS map 6 inch). For Priestfield Furnace see BCM Oct 1990 p61. The name is from a field where prisoners from the north, on their way to transportation or the gallows, were rested over night and visited by the local priest (TB Jan 1987 p5). But an entirely different explanation is given by others. That it belonged to the priest (HOBLL p236) or more precisely partly to the church at Penkridge, partly to the church at Stretton and partly to the chantry at Bilston (S&W p334) (DUIGNAN). Or that it was the Priests' land of Wolverhampton mentioned in the charter of Burton Abbey 1004 (WAM p21).

Priests' Hall Opposite the W door of St Mary's church and next door to the Three Crowns Inn, Breadmarket Street, Lichfield. It was the living quarters for the chaplains of St Mary's guild in medieval times (VCH vol 14 p132) (CCHCA p34). The house is thought to be of C16 origin and has many C18 and C19 alterations. It was the birthplace of Elias Ashmole (see Lichfield) on May 23 1617. There has been a very long Latin title for the house and it has also appeared as Le Priesthale; in the 1960s it was known as No. 5 Breadmarket Street (HOL p478) (PSS p24) (Elias Ashmole. CH Josten. 1966 vol 1 p11. vol 2 p309) (LAL p10p of plaque on wall).

Primrose Hill The name is preserved in a street to E of Hanford church (NSFCT 1891 p54).

Princefield Penkridge. There is a Princefield Avenue SE of Penkridge town centre.

Prince Rupert's Mound High ground N of the Close, Lichfield. Named after Prince Rupert who raised his artillery on it from April 7 1643 during the second siege of Lichfield in the Civil War. The ground was still known as Prince Rupert's Mound in 1990 (1882 OS map 6 inch) (VCH vol 14 p17).

Prince's Corner Name for the junction of High Street and Harborne Park Road, Harborne. Said to have been so called after the visit of the Prince of Wales, later Edward VIII, to nearby Bishop's Croft in 1923 (HOHE p33).

Princes End Former hamlet, now a district over 1m NNE of Tipton Green, Tipton. Formerly partly in Tipton and Sedgley ancient parishes, the boundary followed the High Street. White wondered whether the prebend of Prees in Lichfield cathedral could be Prince's End, suggesting Prince's End is a corruption of Prees End, and supported by the fact that the prebendary belonged to the tithes of the adjoining parish of Tipton (W p200) (PHS p24). The name appears on the Plan of the Mines of Lord Dudley 1812, and erroneously as Printer's End on J Phillips & WF Hutchings map (1832). Clay was obtained from the Sedgley parish part of Princes End in the C18 (HC p53). TE Lones of Princes End was the author of 'A History of Mining in the Black Country' (1898) (BCM July 1975 p45). Princes End was linked to the railway system from Sept 14 1863 (SSR p25) (WAM p112). Six boys drowned when they fell through ice on a pool at Princes End in c1890s (TB March 1986 p27). For the discovery of the body of Mrs Eliza Jane Worton in Wednesbury Oak Loop Canal see Murder Bridge. Tom Barratt VC, Pte of the 7th Batt S Staffs Regt, died July 27 1917 aged 22. He had was known as the 'Princes End VC' and had a memorial in Darkhouse Baptist Chapel which went to Whittington Barracks (TB Jan 1981 pp1p,29). It was the custom in Princes End (as perhaps at other places) for shrines comprising flowers and a cross to those who had died in WW1 to be placed on the walls of houses in the 1920s (TB March 1977 p11). By 1999 Princes End was a ward in Sandwell metropolitan borough.

Princes Park Tiny public park by Christ Church, Burntwood. Is said to date from the 1840s. Measures only 29 feet by 15 feet and was considered in 1998 the smallest public park in Britain and was due to be entered in the GBR (ITV. Central News. March 24 1998 10.30pm).

Pringle Gate and Lane. N of Hammerwich (1834 OS map).

Priory, The Small farm under 0.25m E of Shredicote Hall Farm, in Bradley ancient parish. Has appeared as Priory (Dower's map). Represents the small estate of the prior and canons of St Thomas' Priory, Stafford, held by them from the C13 to their suppression. The old half-timbered house was replaced by a brick one, probably in c1838 (VCH vol 4 pp76,85). William Aston was from Priory (mem in Penkridge church).

Priory, The Former rectory built on part of Stone Priory (see) site shortly after 1758. Has also appeared as the Parsonage House (1844). By 1972 the house was called The Priory (SIS p30). In the mid C20 the house ceased being a wholly private residence when Robert S Heywood, auctioneer and estate agent, opened offices on the ground floor. Some remains of Stone Priory exist in the cellar (local info).

Priory Farm 2.75m ENE of Colton.

Prioryfield Former area N of Roseville, Coseley. The name has appeared as Prioryfield (1834. 1887) and Priorfield (1938) (OS maps). The present Birmingham New Road cuts across the former Priorfield Colliery, situated to the N of Upper Ettingshall, which was in operation between at least 1834 and 1938 (OS maps). Priorfield Foundry was situated S of Biddings Lane at Deepfields. Priorfield Furnace belonged to HB Whitehouse. Its bricks were used to build houses in the Lanesfield area (BOP p128 c1912).

Priory Housing Estate Coseley. Built in c1930. Stretches from near The Priory at Dudley to the foot of the Wren's Nest (MR p135).

Prison Barr Field Shelton. Rev Thomas Barns writes it Brison Barr Field. Behind Wedgwood's Etruria Works; here the game Prison Bars was played (SHST p673) (NSFCT 1910 p167).

Prospect Hill House which stood roughly where Wretham Road joins Soho Hill, Handsworth. It was home and factory of Francis Eginton, who left Boulton & Watt in 1784 and here he brought the art of painting on glass to perfection. The house was visited by Lord Nelson, with Sir William and Lady Hamilton in 1802, when Eginton selected six of the prettiest girls in Handsworth to strew flowers in the path of the Lord Nelson (HPPE p95).

Prospect House Top of Snow Hill, Shelton. Seat of pottery manufacturer, John Clementson. Demolished in 1898 (SHST p644p).

Prospect Village Small modern village 1m WSW of Cannock Wood. The housing estate, which entirely makes up the village, was built in c1926 (VCH vol 5 p51). A house in this area, or this area, was known as Fiddlers Corner in 1888 (1888 OS map 6 inch).

Providence Former ward of Hanley. Created in 1895 (VCH vol 8 p158).

Providence Square Formerly in Stoke-upon-Trent chapelry in Stoke-upon-Trent (SGSAS). There is a Providence Square off Town Road at Far Green, Hanley.

Pryors Hall Former moated house, documented from 1704 (info Peter Lesley), at Walton, Stone. By the 1930s, Priory Farm by then the only moated farm in

the district (NSFCT 1935 p90), was occupied by the Brandon family, farmers. The house was demolished in c1962 and the present (1998) shopping arcade in Eccleshall road by Tilling Drive then erected on the site (SIS pp48,50 note) (info Jim Brandon).

Pudding Green Junction Albion, West Bromwich. Where the Wednesbury Branch Canal of the Birmingham Canal diverges from the Birmingham Canal New Cut New Main Line (SWY p11). But before 1829 it diverged from the Birmingham Canal Old Main Line at Spon Lane Junction (Galton Valley. A Walkers Guide. Sandwell Metropolitan Borough Council. 1993).

Pudding Hill S of Spring Hill, Cannock Chase (PCC p77), at SJ 975205. A granite boulder, weighing 3 tons, found in a gravel pit in WW2 was placed on the top of Pudding Hill in 1949. It was moved to the top of Spring Hill on Nov 14 1954 (PCC p89).

Puddle Hill To NE of Hixon. Had been built on by 1981.

Pullins Hall To S of Tividale. Marked on John Ogilby's 'Britannia' (1675) as Pullins Hall or Pullons Hall (STELE Feb 11 1955; W Ellery Jephcott was unable to locate it). This could be a reference to Brindleford Hall?

Punch Bowl, The 0.75m SE of Milford. A hollow, shaped like a punch bowl. (TSW p55p) (HCMBOPP p46p).

Puppy Green Approximately by Coneygee Engine House, at Park Lane Dudley Port. Possibly the Birmingham Canal New Line obliterated it (Plan of the Mines of Lord Dudley. 1812). Appears in the 1851 census as Duppy Green.

Pur Brook Tributary of the Blithe. Runs at Bagot's Park to Hamstall Ridware. Has appeared as on pire broc, of pirebrok (951), in pire broces heafde, æfter pire broc (996), Pirebroc (c1205), Pirbroke (1548), and per brooke (1559) (SPNO p16). Ekwall thought the name perhaps represented 'a pear-tree.' He also suggested a word cognate to Norwegian 'pira' 'to trickle' (SPNO p16). The root is 'bior' 'feor' (NSFCT 1908 p128).

Pur Brook Tributary of the Sow.

Purleyhill House 1m NNE of Hamstall Ridware. In Hamstall Ridware parish.

Puthull's Described as 'by the water of Hanse.' Land owned and enclosed by Croxden Abbey (VCH vol 3 p226 note). Has also appeared as Puttelles.

Puzzle Garden A maze of houses at the back of Middle Madeley (M p27).

Pyat's Barn House under 1m WSW of Rushtonhall. Formerly in Rushton James township in Leek ancient parish. Is perhaps named after the Pyatt or Pyott family recorded in the late C16 (VCH vol 7 pp219-220).

Pyebirch Manor House 1m SE of Eccleshall. May take its name from the nearby field 'Pipebriche,' which is mentioned in the C13 (ECC p13). Residence of folklorist Sophia Charlotte Burne (d1923), born Moreton (see), Gnosall, author of SFL, after 1876 but by 1884 to at least 1892 but not by 1900 (trade directories; appears in KD 1884 as Birch Manor) (VE pp146).

Pye Clough Pye Clough and Pye Clough Head are 3m W of Longnor (1834 OS map) (DUIGNAN p42).

Pye Green Modern residential district on a high point of Cannock Chase 2.5m NNE of Cannock. In Cannock parish. The name has changed little over centuries. Perhaps from Anglo-Saxon 'pie' meaning 'gnats' used her in the sense 'the green where gnats abound' (SPN p30). Here is a Post Office tower built in 1970, 258 feet high, on land 775 feet above sea level (WMAG Aug 1979 p21); it is the most conspicuous object of Cannock Chase (BOE p94) (SL p253) (STMSM Aug 1979 p25p) (MR p269pc).

Pyegreen Valley Green Heath. Valley S of the Pye Green wireless mast. Appears to have been formerly Huntington Valley (1834 OS map).

Pyford Brook Runs by Alrewas Hayes joins the Trent at Alrewas.

Q

Quarnford Former moorland township (W p744) and chapelry (GLAUE p420) in Alstonefield ancient parish. Became a separate ecclesiastical parish in 1752, and a separate civil parish in 1866 (GLAUE p420). It is the highest parish in England (DVOPP p2); the present centre of the population for the civic parish is Flash (VB p210). An outlying boulder of Eskdale granite is at Quarnford at the northern end of Goldsitch Moss (NSFCT 1916 p73). The **megalithic chambered tomb** Langford notes between Flash and Quarnford is not the one referred to by Loxdale in SHOS. It must certainly be in part of artificial construction, and is a very remarkable curiosity. Each stone would weigh many tons (S&W p384). Others also note a megalithic chambered tomb stone between Flash and Quarnford (GNHS pp66il,416) (WTCEM p10) (SC p147). A small perforated **mace-head** with faceted ornamentation on one face has been found in Quarnford parish which went to the Hunterian Museum, Glasgow (The Antiquary vol 37 p99) (Proc Soc Ants of Scotland vol 43 p383) (NSJFS 1964 p32). The township was covered by Malbonck Forest in medieval times (VCH Vol 7 p5). The **name** has appeared as Querneford (1227) (SPN p96) (SSE 1996 p17), Warneford (1564) (SSE 1996 p69) and Wharnford (maps of Jan Jansson (1646), Morden and Bowen). 'Quarn' is thought to derive from Old English 'cweorn,' a quern or millstone (VCH vol 7 p49). Most have thought 'ford by the mill' (DUIGNAN) (SL p71) (NSFCT 1932 p57) (SPN p96) (SSE 1996 p17). Oakden agrees with Duignan (SSAHST 1967 p34). The ford was probably over the Dane near Manor Farm (formerly Quarnford House) and the name may refer to a stopping place on a route for the carriage of millstones (VCH vol 7 p49). **Coal** was mined out of the Goldsitch Moss coalfield in Quarnford parish by at least the late C14 to the mid C20 (SSE 1996 pp66-95). There was a manor of Quarnford by at least 1321 to 1597 (VCH vol 7 p51) (SSE 1996 p69). The former place called Quarnford is now represented by Manor Farm, 1.5m WSW of Flash. There was possibly a **medieval village** of Quarnford there, deserted towards the end of the Middle Ages (SSAHST 1970 p35). Later, Quarnford has been described as a little village (NSFCT 1895 p154), and a house (DUIGNAN), but the main centre of the population in the township is now Flash; Quarnford Post Office there, is the highest in England (VB p210); Quarnford parish hall at Flash was built by international volunteers in 1959 (Staffs Village Halls Directory. Susan Miles. 1994). **Sir George Crewe**, lord of the manor of Alstonefield, on his first visit to his estates in the Quarnford area in 1818 or 1819 likened the area to 'the very end of the civilised world' (SSE 1996 p66). It was a Wharnford (Quarnford) man who was supposed to have brought **snow to Leek market** on July 17 from Lud Church (NHS p173). A farmer near Quarnford when plagued by the **witch**, Jennie Roberts, in the mid C19 protected himself with witch elm and remained unharmed. Roberts then turned her black art on the farmer's livestock with such dire consequences that the farmer and his wife had to move out of the area (DP p68).

Quarnford Park A medieval deer park enclosed out of forest. Created in c1200 by Peter the clerk, a member of the Earl of Chester's household. It was still in existence in 1227 but was then disparked. It was to the SW of Flash in the Gradbach area (NSJFS 1962 pp74,77) (VCH vol 7 pp51-52).

Quarry, The In Audley township in Audley ancient parish. Occurs in Richard Parrott's Survey (1733) as Quarre and Quarrel (SHC 1944 pp15,23) (AHJ 1997 p96).

Quarry, The Hartshill, Stoke-upon-Trent. Home of Charles Lynam of Colwich, architect, who married Lucy Emma, the daughter of Robert Garner, author of GNHS. Garner lived here with his daughter's family from 1885 to his death in 1890 (NSFCT 1949 p27) (POTP p101).

Quarry Bank Small village on a sharp bluff that rises from the Stour and Mousesweet, giving the settlement a stepped or terraced appearance (WMLB pp118,124), 1.25m ENE of Brierley Hill, but now merges into the Black Country conurbation. The area lies on the most westerly coal basin of the Black Country (WMLB pp118,124). It was formerly in Kingswinford ancient parish (W p184) and then in Brierley Hill ecclesiastical parish. Became a separate ecclesiastical parish in 1844 (GLAUE p420). The Commissioners' **church**, Christ Church, High Street, was built in 1845-1847 (BOE p80) (BHOP p107). Quarry Bank urban district, a separate civil parish, was created in 1894 (GLAUE p420). For the so-called 'Quarry Bank Food Riots' of WW1 see TB Sept 2 1999 p4. **Persons and visitors**. **Joseph 'Big Joe' Chivers** murdered David 'Titus' Taylor at the Wagon and Horses Inn, Quarry Bank on March 10 1856, owing to longstanding hatred between the two men. Chivers was arrested on the day (June 10) he had expected to witness the execution of William Palmer of Rugeley (see) (TB Sept 1981 p17. June 1982 p5). **Caroline Pearson**, of near Turners Lane, was murdered. Her body was found in a cornfield near the present (1973) Birch Tree Inn, Quarry Bank (TB Dec 1973 p7). There was an outbreak of small pox at Quarry Bank in 1894 (BCM Oct 1970 pp45-46). **Joseph Jones** murdered his son-in-law, Edmund Clarke, in Dec 1906 at his cottage in Victoria Street, Quarry Bank, where they both resided. Jones was hung in 1907 (TB July 1976 p26p). **Henry 'Blind Harry' Griffith** (d1930) of Quarry Bank was the Quarry Bank town crier, despite being a short man and blind (TB July/ Aug 1973 p11p) (MMBCC pp62p-55). Prof **John R Woodhouse**, the FIAT -serena professor of Italian studies at Oxford, was born at Quarry Bank in 1937 (BCM Sept 1998 pp8-12p).

Quarry Bank Tiny hamlet on the W side of a hill N of Keele 1.5m S of Alsagers Bank.

Quarry Heath Minute hamlet on ground gently rising from the Penk to the Cannock Chase highlands, and old quarrying area, 1.25m ESE of Penkridge. In Penkridge parish. Occurs as common land in 1598, but the area was inhabited by at least 1635, the heath being enclosed in 1827 (VCH vol 5 p106) (SPNO p92). Stone from this quarry was used for the C19 restoration of Lichfield cathedral (KD 1892 p267) (VCH vol 5 p106) (NSJFS 1967 p47). (SPN p96).

Quarry Hill Small hamlet and hill by Kettle Brook 2m S of Amington, on road to Polesworth. Formerly in Amington and Stoneydelph township, in Tamworth ancient parish, Warws. The area, which has also appeared as Quarry Bank, was not built up until just after 1900 (TDOPP p68p).

Quarry Hills Low hills by the stream which was anciently forded at Darnford, E of Borrowcop Hill, Lichfield. In 1235 Henry III granted to the dean and chapter a licence to dig stone to repair Lichfield cathedral out of the Forest of Hopwas and the site became known as Quarry Hills (VCH vol 14 ?).

Quarry House Stood at the junction of the old, Walsall Road and Wood Lane (now Walsall Road), Hamstead. May be the 'Short House' on a map of 1775 and in existence by 1794 as Quarry Farm (MNB pp62,67). Residence of Thomas Barber Wright, the Birmingham manufacturer, who first suggested the Hospital Sunday movement in 'The Midland Counties Herald,' and founded the movement in 1859. In his memory a hospital at Hammerwich (see) was erected (TBS p26).

Quarry Lodge A stucco mansion whose battlements, castellations and turrets were like a cross between Strawberry Hill and Windsor Castle (IE p125). Stood at the junction of Tamworth Road and Quarryhills Lane, S of Lichfield. Presumably built on the site of Freeford Cottage, seat of Thomas Rowley, physician, in 1834. Known as Lower Borrowcop Villa in the later 1840s and as Freeford Villa in the 1850s. Renamed Quarry Lodge by 1861 (VCH vol 14 p25). Residence of Major Henry Elwell (b1816), son of John Elwell of Heath House, Wombourne, in the final years of his life to his death on Dec 30 1872 at the Shire Hall (see) (IE pp120-125).

Queelane Queelane Farm is 3.5m W of Marchington.

Queen Low Is probably the same as Queen Low on the Weaver Hills mentioned by Plot in the later C17 (NHS p404). The mound is now (1984) lost (SPNO p24). (SCSF p74). It may be identifiable with Queen's Knoll (see).

Queen's Bower Area covered with a few oak trees and shrubs 0.5m SSE of Cotton. On the tithe map schedule No. 518 it is called Holly Wood (HAF p393).

Queen's Cross At junction of Holehouse Lane and Gratton Lane (Stoke-on-Trent A-Z).

Queen's Garden Tutbury Castle. The daughter of the king of Castile and Leon Constantia became the second wife of John of Gaunt and they in turn became king and queen of Castile. She brought a continental atmosphere to Tutbury Castle, and introduced the custom of bull-running. She made a garden outside the castle, one of the mounds overlooking the priory being taken for the purpose. Until then gardens had almost exclusively been restricted to monasteries (UTR p64).

Queen's Gardens Station Walks, Newcastle-under-Lyme. A statue of Queen Victoria was moved from Nelson Place to here in 1963 (ES Oct 7 1963) (ES June 24 1981 p9p).

Queens Gardens Holyhead Road, Wednesbury. Has a plaque to record the fact that Telford built the Holyhead Road in c1826 (BCM Jan 1969 p6p).

Queen's Low Burial mound over 1m NW of Tixall, near Lower Hanyards Farm at SJ 964239. There is a burial mound called King's Low at SJ 955237, 0.5m to the W. 42 paces in diameter and 1.5 feet high. Their origin is unknown although two urns were found near them in the beginning of the C18 (W p426). (SOS p70) (SC p148) (KES p207). Another near Lower Hanyards Farm has been destroyed (NSJFS 1965 p49).

Queen's Oak Bagot's Bromley (STMSM April 1973 p24).

Queen's Oak Appears on the OS maps 1884, 6 inch and 1925, sheet 31 SE as 'on the site of an ancient Queen's Oak,' at approximately SK 014306, over 1.25m NNE of Chartley Castle in Chartley Park. It is said to have been named after Mary, Queen of Scots, who was confined at Chartley Old Hall in the later C16. In early Aug 1586 she was removed from Chartley to Tixall Old Hall so her apartments could be searched to implicate her in the Babington Plot. In order to lure her away from the hall so neither she nor her servants would suspect anything, Sir Amyas Paulet, her guard, is said to have invited her to hunt in Chartley Park, where, at the oak later called Queen's Oak, a force to escort her to Tixall made a surprise appearance (info Tim Moss of Hixon Local History Society).

Queen's Park Public park 0.75m NW of Harborne. Opened in 1897 (HOHE p31).

Queen's Park Public park at Longton given by the Duke of Sutherland in honour of Queen Victoria's Jubilee. Opened in 1888 (POP p145).

Queen's Purse Wood Wood to E of Fauld, Hanbury. Formerly in Tutbury ancient parish (late C19 OS map 6 inch).

Queensville Suburb of Stafford on low ground by the Penk, 1.25m SE of the town. Formerly a hamlet called Spittal Brook in Castle Church parish. The name Queensville was adopted in 1838 to commemorate Queen Victoria's coronation (VCH vol 6 p194).

Queen's Well Dunstall, Tatenhill. White noted the salt marsh, which enriched by saline springs, was celebrated for its beneficial effects on sickly horses (W p607).

Queen Tree Tree over 0.5m S of Gorsty Hill, Marchington Woodlands. Appears on OS map 1925 sheet 32. Slightly to the SW of it is King Tree.

Queslett Former tiny hamlet beneath the high ground of the former Barr Lea Common, now a residential suburb 1.25m SE of Great Barr. Formerly in Great Barr township and chapelry in Aldridge ancient parish (W p552) and partly in Perry Barr township in Handsworth ancient parish (SGSAS). The original hamlet, in existence as Queestley by 1775 (MNB p67), centred on Aldridge, Beacon and Queslett Roads. Has also appeared as Queeselet (DUIGNAN). The name is from Middle English 'queest, queast, quease, queece' wood pigeon, and Anglo-Saxon 'slaed' slade. So the slade of the wood pigeon (DUIGNAN).

Quintin's Orchard House by a moated site 0.5m NE of Hill Ridware. Quintin's Orchard was identified by Shaw with the site of the original Pipe Ridware Manor House (see) and consequently may formerly have been called Linacre. Said to have been built in 1319. After being known as Pipehall and Pipehall Orchard in the C15 the place later acquired the name Quintin's Orchard from farmers or occupiers called Quinten or Quinton living here in 1606 and afterwards (SHOS vol 1 p166*). In the early C19 Pitt noted there were still remains of its ancient moat and adjoining orchards (THS p71) (GNHS p149) (SSAHST 1982-3 p45).

Quixhill Hamlet on the N bank of Churnet Valley facing Denstone, 0.25m N of Denstone. In Rocester ancient parish. Has appeared as Quikeshull (1227. 1272) (SPN p96) (SSE 1996 p17), Quixhull (1496) (OSST 1935 p41), and Quickshill: The ten references to Quixhill from 1590 to 1720 have eight different spellings (NSJFS 1972 p124). The name means 'Cwic's hill' (DUIGNAN) (SPN p96). Ekwall says Cwic is a short form of names such as Cwichelm (SSE 1996 p22). Or from Anglo-Saxon 'cwic,' meaning 'living' but the suffix 'hill' is peculiar for a hamlet in a valley bottom (NSJFS 1972 p124). In 1496 John Madeley, a local farmer, sued his neighbour, John Fitzherbert of Norbury (Derbys), for theft of corn and hay, an action arising out of the fact that both men claimed the freehold of Quixhill. The case was heard in the Star Chamber. There is no record of the judgment given (OSST 1935 pp41-43). Quixhill Lodge, a free-standing arch between two lodges, at the S end of Quixhill Lane, is a former lodge to Alton Towers (ESNF p108p).

Quonians Lane Quaint tiny lane off Dam Street, Lichfield. The name Quoniames is recorded in 1283 in Quoniames well and is possibly derived from the Latin word 'quoniam' meaning 'since, seeing that' (VCH vol 14 p42). Here was Dame Oliver's school which was attended by Samuel Johnson of Lichfield (see). Since 1879 R Bridgeman and Sons Ltd, architectural and ecclesiastical craftsmen in wood and stone, have had a premises in Quonians Lane (LAL p49p) (LPL p7p) (STMSM July 1980 p17p).

R

Racecourse Farm House 1.5m N of Whitmore.

Rad Brook Tributary of the Churnet. Runs S of Heaton to Ryecroft Gate. Feds Rudyard Lake. Was so called by the early C14 (VCH vol 7 p223). The name is from probably 'the brook with peat-stained water' (SPNO p16).

Raddle Farm 1m NE of Edingale, Staffs (Yates' map).

Raddlepits Earthwork of pre-Norman Conquest origin 0.5m NNE of Wootton-under-Weaver (SHC 1916 p207).

Radford Former hamlet by the Penk 1.5m SE of Stafford. Formerly in Baswich township and ancient parish (W p439). The name appears in 1836 and means 'ford suitable for riding over' (SPNO p31) (SOB p117); Ratford or Radford Bridge was a medieval meeting point for those wishing to travel SE through Cannock Forest (see). The name is preserved in Radford Bank and Radford Rise on the E side of the Penk between Queensville and Weeping Cross. On Aug 4 1795 there was a riot by a mob who had congregated at Radford Bridge to detain a quantity of corn which they thought was to leave the county on the Staffs and Worcs Canal. The Staffordshire Volunteer Cavalry (later Staffordshire Yeomanry) were sent to quell it (SA Aug 8 1795) (FSP p61; says the 8th, the date of the SA report). There was a railroad between Stafford and Radford wharf on the canal operating from as early as Nov 1 1805 (SIOT p51) (VCH vol 2 p306).

Radford Field name in N area of Stone town (SIS pp25 see map,29). Also known as The Radfords (local info). The name is preserved in Radford Street.

Radhurst Grange Main Street opposite Wales Lane junction, Barton-under-Needwood. Built in c1760. In the mid C19 it was occupied by a surgeon (UNT pp120-121).

Radleys, The Former farm on N side of the Daw End Branch of the Rushall Canal, S of the present street called The Radleys, at Daw End. The farm appears on the 1887 OS map but not on Yates' map (1775). The name also appears on the 1825 Rushall estate map as fields called Big Radlies, Little Radlies etc (SNAR p63). It means 'red clearing' and may relate to the colour of the local soil, especially as clay has been dug not far from there for many years (SNAR p63). Iron ore impregnated with a milky liquid set in a bed of limestone found in Radleys Limestone Works was noted by Plot (NHS p188 Tab 12 Fig 1). Here was a limestone works; 'Old Limekilns' appears to the W of the farm on the 1887 OS map. The name is preserved in several street names and Radleys School.

Radmore Moorish bog, originally in Cannock Forest, 0.5m SW of Cannock Wood. In Cannock ancient parish. Has appeared as Rademor (1154), Redamore (1157), Redemor (c1250), Raddemor (1313) Rodmores (1602), The Redmore (1682) (SSE 1996 p17) (SPNO p61), and Red Moor. Ekwall gives 'red moor' (SSE 1996 p17). See Duignan's explanation for Radley Moor.

Radmore Abbey Radmore, Cannock Wood. Believed to be at approximately SK 042118 (MR p81 plan). Formerly a hermitage (VCH vol 3 p136). King Stephen endowed it in the late 1130s (HOS 1998 p56). Empress Matilda in defiance of Stephen persuaded the hermits to adopt the Cistercian order in c1145 (HOS p26) and St Mary's hermitage became St Mary's Abbey (VCH vol 3 p225). It was the first Cistercian house in the county. Soon the monks found Cannock Forest royal foresters a great nuisance and they left for Stoneleigh in Warws in 1155, which Henry II had given them in exchange for Radmore in 1154. Henry II turned the priory into Radmore Hunting Lodge (see). (SHOS vol 2 pp313-314; Plot placed the priory in Offlow Hundred, but Yates' map places it in Cuttlestone hundred) (W p450) (GNHSS p8) (SOSH p110) (CCC p22) (CCBO pp31-32) (SSAHST 1965 pp30-31).

Radmore Hunting Lodge Radmore, Cannock Wood. Henry II turned Radmore Priory, believed to be at approximately SK 042118, into a hunting lodge in c1154 (HOS p26); he is said to have used it in July 1155 (MR p82). From 1161 the canons of Llanthony were installed as custodians (SSAHST 1965 pp30-31). The second hunting lodge, which King John had built 200 yards SE of the priory is clearly defined by a rectangular moat earthwork at SK 043117 (SSAHST 1982-3 p38). Within a part of the earthwork are the sandstone foundations of the lodge (MR p80). By 1230 the estate seems to have passed out of royal hands (VCH vol 5 p57). (CCF pp82-83,84) (CCC p22; on the moat) (SOSH p113 note).

Radmoor Lane Partly in Gnosall and Forton parishes (SGSAS). Radmore Lane Farm is 2m W of Gnosall. Has appeared as Redamora (1157), Radmore (1227), and Radmoore Lane (1481). The name means 'the red peat-stained marshland' (SPNO p175).

Radmore Wood Tiny hamlet on the slopes of a hill between Dunstal and Ash Brooks, nearly 1m NE of Abbots Bromley. In Abbots Bromley parish.

Radnor Lane S of Oulton, Norbury. Has also appeared as Rednor Lane (Plot's map). Radnor Lane Farm is 1.5m SSE of Norbury.

Radway Hall To W of Gothersley.

Radway Hill Hill on W side of Smestow Brook at SO 857869, 0.75m NW of Prestwood.

Radway House House in Aldridge ancient parish mentioned in the will of Alice Scott (1588), although Alice who inherited the house did not live here. It should not be confused with Radway Manor, which is a timber-framed house erected in 1934 on a different though nearby site, using old materials (MOA p139).

Radwood Radwood Hall Farm and Radwood are 2m S of Madeley. In Maer ancient parish. There was possibly a medieval village in the vicinity of Radwood Hall Farm (SSAHST 1970 p35).

Ragged Invention At approximately Wheatstone Lodge Farm 0.75m W of Codsall (1834 OS map).

Raikes Moorland area over 1m S of Sheen. In Sheen ancient parish. There was a farm at Raikes by 1651, when the area was known as Bartine Edge (VCH vol 7 p242), later the area was known as Rakes. James Wall of Rakes perished in the snow on his way to market at Leek or Longnor with a sow fastened to his hand, the incident is recorded in a register of 1689 (APB p41). The present Raikes Farm dates from c1800 (VCH vol 7 p242).

Rails Farm 1.75m WNW of Horton, on the W side of Horton Hay, in Horton ancient parish. It is said to take its name from the fence which once surrounded the hay. The house may have been inhabited by Thomas Challinor (d1577) and may have been the seat of successive Challinors until William Challinor (d1721) (VCH vol 7 p67).

Railswood Copse Former wood on E side of Norton Road, Pelsall. The Rails Coppice in the 1843 tithe belonged to the Charles family of Pelsall Hall. Some of the wood was lost when Copse Crescent was built in 1963 (SNBP p70).

Rainbow Hill Beaudesert Old Park. S of Moor's Gorse (PCC p77).

Rainbow Valley Valley running N to S, S of Rugeley Road (A460) N of Rawnsley Hills (Geographia Cannock & Hednesford Street Plan).

Rainroach Rock Oakamoor, at SK 064429. To the E of it at SK 06064290 what was believed to be a man-made mound appears to be a natural rock outcrop (NSJFS 1965 p32). Nevertheless it is a listed monument.

Rake End Former hamlet (THS p77). Now a district of N Hill Ridware. In Mavesyn Ridware ancient parish. The name has appeared as Le Rake (1334), Rakeynd (1523) (SHOS vol 1 p200). It is from Middle English 'rake' 'raike' a way, path (DUIGNAN). The field name Chapel Croft here may represent the site of a chapel for the lords of Mavesyn Ridware when they resided at Kileby Hall (see) before moving to Mavesyn Ridware Old Hall before the mid C12 (SHOS vol 1 p200). There was a pinfold at Rake End (SHOS vol 1 p200). It was noted Rake End was contiguous with Hill Ridware by the early C19, so much so that it was then often considered to be a part of it (THS p77). For the murder of William Charlesworth of Rake End in 1857 see Abbots Bromley.

Rakegate Centred on Elmdon Road and Sheldon Road, Dunstall, 2.25m NNW of Wolverhampton. Also has appeared as Rake Gate. Rakegate was developed with housing from the late 1940s. Oxley Library in Probert Road stands on the site of the old Rakegate Farm (BUOP pp46-47ps,146p of Rakegate Farm).

Rakes, The Area of N of Alstonefield village. It was an inhabited area by the later C17 (VCH vol 7 p9).

Rakes Dale Dale 0.5m W of Alton.

Rakes Hill Road 1m WNW of Burntwood. There was a waste called Rakehill in 1597, and Rakehill Lane was mentioned in 1670. There was a settlement in the Rake Hill area in 1775. The road now called Rake Hill was known as Stephen's Hill in the early C19 (VCH vol 14 p199).

Rakeway Tiny hamlet on high ground which rises above Cecilly Brook 1m SE of Cheadle. And Rakeway Castle Farm to the N. In Cheadle ancient parish. From Rakeway Head is a particularly good view of the Cheadle basin (NSFCT 1921 p138).

Rakeway Grange A house on this site known as Rakeway House at Rakeway at SK 017422 was the seat of the Mylles family; who were mining ironstone in the Lightwood district of Cheadle in the 1590s. They built Mill House, Rakeway in 1635 and moved there. Old Rakeway House had a remarkable small rectangular staircase of oak in the Elizabethan style (CCT p17).

Ramrod Hall Stood W of Whiteheath Gate, Rowley Regis. Was so named from the manufacture of gun ramrods during the American Civil War (O pp226-227) (BCWJ p66) (TB Sept 1978 p29. Sept 1986 p27).

Ramshaw Minute hamlet comprising scattered cottages at the N end of Ramshaw Rocks 1.25m NE of Upper Hulme. Formerly in Alstonefield ancient parish. The name means 'clearing within a wood where rams roamed' (PNPD) (DPMM p92).

Ramshaw Rocks Outcrop of rocks 1m NE of Upper Hulme, and are considered not part of The Roaches. At the peak of the outcrop, at about 1500 feet or more, the rocks become more massive and continuous, and the resemblance of a toad can be discerned in one of the larger masses (TTTD pp103p, 104p) (see also Winking Man and Lady Stone).

Ramshaw (*Ramser* SVB p136). Hamlet on a high slope leading up to the Weaver Hills nearly 1.5m SE of Cotton. Former township in Ellastone ancient parish. A cup-marked stone at Ramsor Farm, Ramshorn, was found by an earth-moving machine in 1993 at SK 08444543. The slab of stone averages about 20 cm in thickness. It is a piece of early art from Neolithic to Early Bronze Age in date (SSAHST 1994-95 pp16-20). Ramshorn has appeared as Rumesoura (1197), Romesovere, Romesor (SPN p96) (SSE 1996 p17), and Ramsor (W p775). Ramshorn first appears in 1723 (NSJFS 1972 p124). Corruption to Ramshorn was occurring in the 1920s (NSFCT 1925 p197). Oakden suggests it was OS maps which perpetuated the modern spelling (SSAHST 1967 pp35-36). The name means 'the ram's bank' or possibly 'Hraefn's, Hraemn's, Hrem's bank' (DUIGNAN). 'The hillside where rams are kept' (SPN pp96-97) (SSE 1996 p17). Gelling thinks 'wild garlic promontory' (NSJFS 1981 p2) (SSE 1996 p17). Thomas Burton of Ramsor was buried on Feb 5 1654, aged 111 (NSJFS 1972 p127-128). Ramshorn is said to be one of the first Primitive Methodist strongholds in the county (SVB p137). Ramshorn became a separate civil parish in 1866 (GLAUE p420).

Ramshorn Common Common land 0.5m NW of Ramshorn. Is the Anglo-Saxon burial at Ramshorn mentioned in HOS p13 Eid Low, or the burial mounds at Threelows, or at SK 099449?

Range Corner The centre of WW1 Rugeley Military Camp on Cannock Chase. There are four ways at Range Corner (CCF p229). The camp stretched between White House, Marquis Drive and Penkridge Bank (Discover Cannock Chase. Follow The Great War: Motor and Foot Trail. Staffs County Council). Whether now Rifle Range Corner which is at SJ 998168?

Ranger Former common on the N side of Dimmings Dale 1.25m WNW of Alton (THS p36). The area appears as Range Moor on 1834 OS map. The name is preserved in The Ranger, a youth hostel, at SK 053436.

Rangemoor House 1.5m E of Werrington.

Rangemore Small village on upland in the centre of Needwood Forest plateau between Lin Brook and streams rising in Knightley Park (Rangemore) (see) 16m E of Stafford. Formerly known as Tatenhill Gate, a former entry into Needwood Forest (1834 OS map), Ravenwolmesmore, Ravenesmore, and Raven's moor (HOPT vol 1 p137). Formerly partly in Tatenhill and Hanbury ancient parishes. Rangemore ecclesiastical parish was created in 1884 from part of the Staffs part of Scropton ancient parish (Derbys) and from the parishes of Tatenhill, Tutbury, Anslow, and Dunstall (GLAUE p420). The church, All Saints, on the S side of Tatenhill Lane, was built in 1867 (HOPT vol 1 p32).

Rangemore House Georgian house 0.5m SW of Rangemore. Later became Rangemore Hall (IVNF photograph), when, perhaps, it was sweepingly enlarged in 1879. It was enlarged again in 1900 (BOE p224) (STC p12p). Residence of Michael Arthur Bass (1837-1909), later first Lord Burton. Edward VII was a visitor here (SVB p139) in Feb 1902 (BTOP vol 1 pp41,83p of the Billiard Room) and in Nov 1907. On at least one of his visits to the hall the king, an ardent bridge player, was partnered by Lady Burton's sister, Miss Jane Thornewill, considered to be 'the best woman bridge player in England' (ESNF pp23p, 91p of the library). By 1988 the hall was Needwood School (MR p260). In 1997 a wing of the hall, then Grade II listed, was bought by three brothers named Manjinder, Parmjit and Kuldip Gill. In April 2000 they were charged of conspiracy to defraud an insurance company. It was alleged they falsely claimed that five ornate fireplaces from the hall had been stolen when in fact it was believed they had sold them to a New York antiques dealer (Daily Telegraph April 5 2000 p11). In the grounds is a brick-lined ice-house approached by a long tunnel still remains (BOE p224), and a cedar tree planted by Edward VIII during his visit to the hall in Feb 1902 (ABTOP p128p).

Rangemore Wood Wood 0.75m SSW of Stanton.

Ranton (*Ronton*). Ancient parish and village by Clanford Brook 3.5m WNW of Stafford. Ranton manor lies in Pirehill hundred, on the border of Cuttlestone hundred (DUIGNAN). Ranton has appeared as Rantone, a manor, in DB, Ramton (c1540) (LI appendix p169), Rontun, and Ronton (C19-C20) (SPN p97). The name is from probably Anglo-Saxon 'rand' an edge, or border, so 'border town' (DUIGNAN). Or 'farmstead on the slope' (SPN p97). Mills suggests 'ram tun' (SSE 1996 p17). There was a hermitage at Ranton in the later C12 (NSFCT vol 50 pp95,97) (VCH vol 3 p136). The parish church, All Saints, on the W side of the main road in Ranton village, is of C13 origin with a chancel of 1753 (BOE p224). A past vicar is said to have caused controversy by feeding children dog biscuits (SVB p139). There is a tradition that during the outbreak of cholera at Stafford a small market was held here and all coins were passed through water in a shallow stone basin, now lost (NSFCT 1915 pp166,171). Murder and strange sights. Richard Tomlinson, aged 22, murdered his girlfriend, Mary Evans, aged 20, on Dec 16 1833. The murder took place on a road approaching Ranton as the couple, both of Ranton, were returning from staying with relations at Knightley. Tomlinson took a stone to Mary's head and suffocated her to death after she would not retract a taunt. Tomlinson was found guilty of murder and hung in March 1834 (MM pp86,88p of the execution notice) (STMSM Sept 1974 p14) (MMM pp51-54) (SMML pp52-55). At Vicarage Farm Mrs Jessie Roestenberg and her two young sons saw a round UFO hovering over their cottage at Ranton on Oct 21 1954. Inside were two men. The craft was tipped forward as if to enable the men to see Mrs Roestenberg better. They had high foreheads, white skin and long hair, and wore blue clothes and transparent helmets (The Coming of the Space Ships. Gavin Gibbons. 1956. pp64-75) (MMSE p130). In the later C17 Plot noted an extraordinary rennet (local dialect runnet) at Ranton (NHS p388).

Ranton Green Fragmented hamlet 1m SW of Ranton. Is Banton Green on Smith's map.

Ranton Hall Former manor house 0.5m W of Ranton. Seat of the Noel and Harcourt families. Has or had a fire oak staircase said to be about 200 years old in 1908 (NSFCT 1908 p176). An unusual sundial was noted at the hall by Plot in the later C17. It represented an open book; the leaves acting as dials (NHS pp332-333) (SD p88). Immediately to the E of the house is a moated site (CAMS p64).

Ranton House 0.5m SSE of Ranton.

Ranton Priory Former Augustinian house (SOSH p109) by Clanford Brook 1m W of Ranton.
EARLY. The priory was founded prior to 1166 (NSFCT 1908 p175). It was founded by Robert and Celestia Fitz Noel of Ellenhall for Augustinian canons from Haughmond Abbey, the 'mother house' after 1138 and by 1166 (BOE p224) (MR p260). It was dependent on Haughmond Abbey (NSFCT 1947 p168). It was at first known as 'St Mary of the Assarts,' then generally as 'St Mary of the Clearings' or 'of the Riddings' (NSFCT 1908 p175) (LGS pp37,200) (SL p70) as it was built on cleared forest land, and it has been known as Ranton Abbey. It was surrounded by a rectangular moat, there are traces of it on the N side (ESH p58). The cartulary of Ranton Priory appears

in SHC vol 4 1883 pp264-295. The principal surviving part is the abbey church tower of C15 origin. A portion of the nave S wall also survives (BOE p224). Perhaps, the upper part of the tower was used as a pigeon-house when the priory was a monastic institution (NSFCT 1908 p175). A C14 tower removed from Ranton Abbey is said to have been built on to the gamekeeper's cottage at Seighford Hall (F p306). There is a tradition the bells were transferred to Gnosall (NSFCT 1915 pp92-112,167-169). A bell was found beneath the archway of Ranton Priory House (EF pp73, 75). (SOS p136; noted by Harwood) DoE II* (SD p88) (In Gough's Collection in the Bodleian dated 1731 there is a sketch of the church) (SSC p135) (GNHS p117) (GNHSS p17) (STM Aug 1965 pp30-31) (SFH p40) (The Priory and Manor of Ranton. JW Bradley) (VED p138) (KES p10) (SGS pp136,137) (SVB p140).
AFTER THE DISSOLUTION. After the priory was suppressed in 1536 it was acquired by Sir Simon Harcourt (a descendant of the founder) (HOS p28. 1998 p58) who lived in the priory refectory (SL p95) (VCH vol 3 pp251-255) (Daily Telegraph. July 25 1992 Weekend Section p15). Harcourt's descendant Robert Harcourt mortgaged all his Staffordshire properties several times over before setting off to found a small English colony in Brazil in 1609 (a venture which floundered for lack of funds). The house, which has also appeared as Ranton Priory House and Ranton Abbey House, then passed to the Copes (Daily Telegraph. July 25 1992 Weekend Section p15). In the later C17 it was the residence of Anne Cope (NHS p112; on the red soil to be found in a particular spot near the abbey). Sir Jonathan Cope commissioned William Baker to remodel the house in stages (Daily Telegraph. July 25 1992 Weekend Section p15). The house assumed its present form in the 1820s or the 1830s when it was remodelled by the 1st Earl of Lichfield as a hunting lodge (SNTG pp46pl,74; painting at Shugborough Hall by Sir Francis Grant titled 'A shooting Party at Ranton Abbey' (1840) shows the house in the background) (SL p95, pl 17 shows an illustration of the same house in 1812). It was the residence of ED Moore in 1851 (W p22). It was accidentally burnt down in 1942 when a squadron of Dutch airmen were billeted here (ASOP p90 c1928). They are supposed to haunt the property (EF p48). Or one room is reputedly haunted and that room remained, strangely, undamaged by the fire of 1942 (info Bruce Braithwaite). Ranton Priory House was in ruins by 1974 (BOE p224) and totally covered in ivy by 1988 (MR p260p) (MIDD vol 1 pp34p,35). In 1992 it was purchased by the 5th Earl of Lichfield who planned to build a house for his son near the Priory House and reduce the old house to one storey (Daily Telegraph. July 25 1992 Weekend Section p15) (ES April 5 1993 p4). The house was extra-parochial (until 1857) as it was formerly monastic property (NSFCT 1913 p62) (APB p6). The separate civil parish of Ranton Abbey, created in 1858, was abolished and entered into Ellenhall ancient parish in 1885 (GLAUE p420). Appears as Banton Abbey on Smith's map.

Ratcliffe's Stable Cave A small cave lower down in the rock than Thor's Cave. In Manifold Valley, Wetton. Named after a farmer who hid himself and his horse here to escape the Scots in 1745 (LGS pp184-185) he was called Ratcliffe. Has also appeared as Radcliffe's Stable Cave. After the farmer's pursuers left the area he remained in the cave and took up cobbling; it was remarkable how many caves were workplaces for cobblers. According to legend Ratcliffe was really Charles II or Charles Edward Stuart the Pretender in disguise, as it is known he lagged behind his troops for fear of treachery and as much as being recaptured (WTCEM pp7,71,144,145) (KES p3) (SJC p1).

Rattlejack On the other side of the Tame, opposite Mytholm, in the field called Rattlejack is a strange circle in the land which may have been an ancient pen or pound (HOA pp3,4).

Raven Hill Brereton (VCH vol 2 p160). In Rugeley parish. Has also appeared as Ravenhill.

Ravenhill House Raven Hill, Brereton. The oldest part of the house is on the S side and dates from the late C18. There are numerous additions mostly of the mid C19. In WW1 the house was a military hospital (AR p114). During WW2 it was the property of Rugeley urban district and in 1948 was taken over by British Electronic Products Ltd (since 1950 the Lancashire Dynamo Electronic Products Ltd) who erected factory buildings in the grounds (VCH vol 5 p158). The house is supposed to be haunted (STMSM March 1973 p27) (GOT p144) by the ghosts of an elderly lady, galloping horses, coaches and a voice shouting out, 'Halt ! Who goes there?' (GPCE p39). Perhaps, the ghost of Rev George Talbot builder of the house who died in a hunting accident in 1812.

Raven Rock Rushton Spencer. A lost rock feature. It jutted out of that part of The Cloud situated in Rushton Spencer parish. It was quarried and destroyed (DP p76).

Raven Rock Rock outcrop on The Roaches. Rockhall cottage is built into it

(SGM p19).

Raven Rock or Riven Rock. Is the most prominent and lofty rock in the Wickenstone Rocks (BGFB p31).

Ravenscliffe Hamlet 1m S of Kidsgrove. Former township (W p291) (S&W p251) in Wolstanton ancient parish (AGT p63). Has also appeared as Ramscliffe, a manor and a member of Tunstall manor by c1130 (ONST 1976 p374), Ranscliff (1834 OS map) and Rainscliff. 'Raven' occurs as a prefix in several places in N Staffs and probably preserves the Old Norse personal name 'Hrafn,' although it was not only used by Norsemen (NSFCT 1916 p82).

Raven's Clough House over 1.25m NW of Rushton Spencer church. Formerly in Rushton Spencer township in Leek ancient parish. The house was so called by 1596 (VCH vol 7 pp223-224). Has also appeared as Raven Clough. The name is from probably 'the clough frequented by ravens' (SPNO p17).

Ravensclough Brook Rises on the E side of the Cloud. Flows eastwards to join the Dane E of Raven's Clough. Takes its name from the house, Raven's Clough (SPNO p17).

Ravensdale Valley Through which the Fowlea runs (OTP p8). Raven Heath had an ironworks at Ravensdale (IANS p43).

Ravenshall Houses on the road between Wrinehill and Betley, 0.75m SSW of Betley. In the C19 it was a small hamlet. In Betley parish. The name is from the valley of the raven (BOPP pl 16) (BVC p34).

Ravenshurst Former small hamlet in Harborne parish. Appears on OS map 1834 1m N of Harborne. The name is preserved in Ravenshurst Road. Cardinal Newman was present at the death of Father Ambrose St John in an upper room of Ravenshurst Farm on May 22 1875 (HOHE p28).

Ravensitch Brierley Hill. Appears as a small hamlet on 1947 OS map 1:25,000 (sheet 32/98), at SO 914854, 1m ENE of Amblecote. Here were ironstone deposits (VCH vol 2 pp120, 226).

Ravens Lane Former country lane and hamlet in Audley township and parish (SGSAS) (AHJ 1997 p98). The name is preserved in the road Raven's Lane at Bignall End.

Raven's Nest To E of Merryton Low (1882 OS map 6 inch).

Ravensnest Gate Hoar Cross. Raven's Nest (1834 OS map) a wood is to the W of Hoar Cross hamlet by Mare Brook.

Raven's Tor Giant buttress on the Staffs bank of Dove Dale between Hall Dale and Mill Dale, but closer to Hall Dale (Dove Dale Guide. Keith Mantell). (TPC p165) (TD p) (MR p128).

Rawnpike Oak Very old oak which was situated a few feet outside the fences of Beaudesert Park at the foot of Castle Ring (DUIGNAN) by side of a path which leads from Cannock Wood to the Wood Pit. 26 feet in circumference. Had twisted branches in shapes of serpents and lions (SG p109; Roan Pike) (GNHS p409; Roan Pike). By the 1930s had a girth of 28 to 30 feet (TB Feb 1995 p3). There are traditions that the Duke of Wellington and the Marquess of Anglesey on their horses sheltered under it as they were making their way across Cannock Chase (TB March 1995 29p). Believed to be about 800 years old when struck by lightning and destroyed by fire in 1932. It had stood 80 feet high and its branches had a measurement from tip to tip 120 feet (NSFCT 1916 p85 see map facing) (CCBO pp23il of facing, 24,25,26 note) (CCF pp96,203). The tree was hollow and about 23 boys could fit inside it. It gave its name to Rawnsley, 2m away (TB Feb 1995 p3). Probably same as Roan Oak. 'Rawnpike,' 'Ranpike' and 'Rampick' as it is occasionally pronounced and spelt, is a dialectic word for a stag-headed or dead-headed tree. The tree was hollow and stag-headed by 1902 (DUIGNAN). Or perhaps 'the conical hill frequented by the raven' (SPNO p60).

Rawnsley Mining hamlet in a marshy valley surrounded by the Cannock Chase highlands 1.5m ENE of Hednesford, in Cannock parish. The name is from Rawnpike Oak (see). Or perhaps means 'woodland glade of the raven' (SPNO p60). Rawnsley was considerably increased in size when a colliery company built a hundred terrace houses here in 1914 (VCH vol 5 p51). For the church see Littleworth (Hednesford). For the Staffordshire Millennium Embroideries made by Sylvia Everitt of Rawnsley see Introduction.

Rawnsley Hills Beaudesert Old Park. Over 0.5m N of Rawnsley.

Ray Hall House 1.5m WSW of Great Barr, near to the Tame. Formerly in Great Barr township in Aldridge ancient parish. The hall has also appeared as Rea Hall (SHOS vol 2 p106, the 2nd p106). Isaac Taylor regards 'Rhe' as one of the five primary river roots and connects it with the Gaelic 'rea,' rapid and the Welsh 'rhe,' swift (NSFCT 1908 p131). Duignan doubts whether it is of Celtic origin. It is simply Anglo-Saxon 'ea', a stream, with 'r' added to it. In Anglo-Saxon charters 'on thaere ea', on the river, is common (DUIGNAN). Formerly the residence of a branch of the Stamford family, who were residing at Perry Hall in 1610 (MOA p139). A building known as Ray Hall was standing on the approximately site of Ray Hall in 1995, on land surrounded on all sides by the junction of the M6 with the M5. (Birmingham A-Z 1995). The area was transferred to West Bromwich county borough in 1931 (GLAUE p402).

Reacliffe House Farmhouse 0.75m NNW of Rudyard. In existence by 1675 (VCH vol 7 p67). Seat of John Haworth before he built and moved to Cliffe Park Hall in c1811 (RL pp5,13-14). Has also appeared Rea Cliffe Farm.

Readyleech Green House 0.75m N of Flash. There was a house here by 1770 (UHAW).

Reaps Moor Former moor and very fragmented small hamlet on a hill above Blake Brook in the Moorlands 2m SSW of Longnor. Formerly in Fawfieldhead township in Alstonefield ancient parish (W p743). The moor was recorded as Reaps Moor in 1595 and the settlement appears as Repemoor Top on Yates' map (1775) (VCH vol 7 p29). A mission chapel, St John, built in 1842, occupies the upper floor of a house at SK 084621 (BOE p225) (VCH vol 7 p30) (LDD). Here was a cheese factory opened in the 1870s, closed in 1950 or 1958, which made Derby cheeses (PDS&C p103p) (VCH vol 7 p29). Isaac Ball was born at Fieldshead (possibly Fieldhead, a house, 0.5m E of the Longnor road) in Reapsmoor in 1812. He emigrated to America and worked as a bricklayer in Illinois and married a descendant of a Mayflower Pilgrim (John Howland) in 1838. He went to Missouri then Oregon with 64 others, and acquired some 640 acres there. He became active in making Oregon a progressive state; Ballston is named after him (L p31). George Smith (d1895), social reformer, born at Clay Hills in 1831, worked here for some years when married as a brickmaker until 1855. He later lived at Coalville, Leics (SOSH p346) (VCH vol 7 p29).

Reckoning House Appears on Yates' map (1775) near Wood House Farm on the edge of Hawksmoor Park. Mentioned in a deed of 1694 as The Counting House, and seems to have become known as the Reckoning House shortly after. The Barkers lived in the Reckoning House and accounted for all the coal sold from the mines (CCT p19) (SHC 1947 p56, 57 note).

Rectory Farm Church Lane, S of Checkley village, S of the Tean. Has a beautiful panelled room known as the Monk's Room for monks visiting from Croxden Abbey before Checkley had a priest. The path they are said to have taken is still in use going past High Ridges Farm (or marked Highridges on OS maps) through Hollington to Croxden (CJF p81). Has a mid C19 dovecote (DoE II).

Reddal Hill A hamlet from 1600 (BCWJ p101) on the W side of Old Hill. Has also appeared as Readhall Hill (BCWJ p74), Redhall, Rednall, Redall Hill and Reddall Hill (1834 OS map). The name is preserved in Reddal Hill Road. In 1844 a separate ecclesiastical parish was created for the S Rowley Regis parish region, covering Cradley Heath, Old Hill, Spinners End and other hamlets. It was given the name of Reddal Hill (W p193) (S&W p353) (GLAUE p420). Spinners End is apparently an alternative name for the Reddal Hill area (TB Dec 1997 p27).

Reddal Hill House Reddal Hill. A farm here was recorded in 1734. Formerly Macefields Farm, built 1759, rebuilt 1819 (TB Oct 1974 p25p. Nov 1974 p7ps, il of in 1840).

Redbank Sometime name of Dresden, Longton (GLAUE p410). Its choir sang with those of Hanford, Blurton, Trentham and Swynnerton at Queen Victoria's Silver Jubilee Celebrations (TTH p72). Also a Red Gate; both are marked on 1834 OS map. Has also appeared as Red Bank.

Red Brook Tributary of the Swarbourn (Staffs Farming 1700-1840. Staffs County Council Local History). However, if it runs through Brereton it runs to the Trent; there is a Redbrook Lane in Brereton. Has also appeared as Redebroke (1262. 1603) (SPNO p17). The first element is from probably 'hreod' 'a reed' (SPNO p17).

Redbrook Estate An housing estate at Raven Hill, Rugeley. Built by the National Coal Board in 1953 (VCH vol 5 p149).

Red Bull Minute hamlet on upland 1m NW of Hales.

Red Bull Hamlet 1m NNW of Kidsgrove on the Ches border in a gap near the head of a tributary of the Wheelock which runs in Cheshire. There is a trough spring well close to Red Bull (WMC).

Red Bull Aqueduct Carries the Macclesfield Canal over the Tunstall-Liverpool road (A50) on the Ches border. Built in 1828 (IAS p172). (WMC).

Red Court House on S side of Tamworth Street, Lichfield. Built in 1766 by Lucy Porter, the step-daughter of Dr Johnson of Lichfield (see) (LGS p176) (VCH vol 14 pp19il of in 1819,21). Dr Johnson stayed here if unaccompanied on visits to Lichfield. Demolished in 1929 or 1930 (Reades of Blackwood Hill. AL Reade. private print 1906. pp242-243) (VCH vol 14 p21) (DJL p225).

Red Cross Reddish gritstone cross in Biddulph parish. The cross is of C15, or earlier, origin (DoE II), and is in the form of a pillar. It has the sign of the cross near the top, front and back. Lower down and both sides is the sign of an anchor. In 1943 it was presented to Knypersley church by Mr and Mrs

Arthur Goodwin of Red Cross Farm (TTTD p165). By 1968 it was standing in the churchyard at Knypersley, but it is believed to have formerly stood at the cross roads (itself formerly known as Red Cross) of Newpool and Tunstall Roads, High Street and Park Lane Knypersley (BHS June 1968 p15). However, it is marked on J Cary's map (1805) SW of Gillow Heath, Biddulph. (W p387) (NSFCT 1890 p26) (BALH p26; map marks an Anglo-Saxon cross N of Knypersley Hall, shown in the centre fold of book the area 'Red Cross' just N of Brindley Ford).

Redearth Area 1.5m SW of Meerbrook. Formerly in Leekfrith township in Leek ancient parish. The name is from the earth being red (NSFCT 1885 p54). There were two houses at Redearth by the later C16; only one survives. It was rebuilt in the C17 and may have been used as a weaving workshop (VCH vol 7 p194).

Redgate Presumably near Red Hall Farm to ESE of Craddocks Moss. The name is from a gate to Heighley Park, a medieval deer park (BVC p35).

Redgreet Minute hamlet to the W of Sugnall.

Red Hall House 1.5m SW of Clent, to SE of Broome. Land at Redewall was granted to Black Ladies Priory in 1373. The name has also appeared as Redewell. It is from red wielle 'a red spring' (Broome: A Worcestershire Village. Geoffrey Parkes. 1978 p13). Perhaps the same as Red House, which was for a time the residence of Noah Hingley (d1877) anchor, chain and cable maker at Primrose Hill (see) (TB Feb 1981 p4).

Red Hall House and former estate 0.5m SW of Alsagers Bank, at SJ 786478 (IANS p134). Formerly in Halmer End township in Audley ancient parish. The estate belonged for many generations to the Egertons of Betley Hall until c1715 when it was sold to Mr Tollett, later of Betley Hall (SHC 1944 p26).

Red Hall Former hamlet between Gornal Wood and Lower Gornal. The name appears in the 1851 census.

Red Heath Redheath Plantation is 0.75m WSW of Silverdale.

Red Hill Hill N of Berth Hill in the Maer Hills. John Dearden thought Red Hill the meeting point of the watersheds separating the Trent, Weaver, and Severn (TTTD p238).

Red Hill Tiny area of SW Eccleshall, on the Stafford Road. According to a local tradition there is supposed to have been a battle here; much red blood was spilt (local info).

Red Hill S of Upper Longdon, by Shropshire Brook.

Red Hill Stone (SSBOP p9). Field name in NE area of Stone town (SIS p25 see map).

Red House Stood on the corner of the present Redhouse Lane and Paddock Lane, Aldridge. The house appears on the 1834 OS map. The Redhouse Farm, which appears in 1887, stood at some distance away along Redhouse Lane. It seems to have disappeared by 1958 (SNAR p43). Gives its name to Redhouse Industrial Estate.

Red House Newton Road, nearly 1m SSW of Great Barr. A former Red House was the seat of William Brasebrygge in 1541 (MOA p139). The present house is of c1841 (HPPE p98), and was built by Robert Wellbeloved (or Wildblood - HPPE p98) Scott, a liberal and Stourbridge industrialist, who won the general election for Walsall borough in 1841 or 2 (SOB p162) (TBS p27). Amongst the later occupiers and owners were Thomas Bagnall (1851) (W p22), and Robert Bagnall, of the Golds' Hill Iron Works, and John Marshall, ironmaster, famous for his connections with the Wednesbury Patent Shaft and Axle Tree Company (TBS p27). Goods worth £1,000 were taken from the house in a serious robbery which occurred here. Sir Henry Meysey Thompson was one of the last private residents of the house and was living here when he contested the Handsworth Division in 1892 (TBS p28) (VH pp38,41p). In 1902 it was taken over by Birmingham Hospitals Saturday Fund as a convalescent home for children. West Bromwich corporation later took the property for use as a sanatorium but the Medical Officer of Health ruled it was not suitable for the purpose. In WW2 the house was occupied by the military, and by 1951 was being converted into flats (TBS pp27,28). In 1929 the grounds were opened as a public park (TBS p26). The obelisk said to commemorate the death of Princess Charlotte, daughter and heir of George IV, who died in childbirth on Nov 6 1817, lies in a meadow below the house. It was still standing in 1984, although then badly cracked. It is of Egyptian character and 30 feet high (SLM Nov 1950 p15p) (SOWB p25) (VH pp38,41p) (HPPE p98). According to a local legend the obelisk was erected to the memory of a famous black horse, once owned by a Bagnall (HPPE p98).

Red House, The The Village, Kingswinford. Formerly belonged to the Earl of Dudley. By 1999 the house was a nursing home. It has round rods and corner plates because it is tilted and there is evidence of subsidence (BCM autumn 1999 p58).

Redhouse, The Brick mid C18 house W of Trysull church. Has Venetian windows (BOE p287) (SGS p172) (MR p339).

Red House Farm Farm 0.75m E of High Onn. It once had on its land a curious glacial boulder with the impression of a cow and calf hoof on it. The legend accompanying it concerns the witch of Church Eaton, Joan Eaton. There was once a cow at the farm, known as the Dun Cow, which had a reputation for never milking dry. Joan Eaton is said to have challenged the local community that she could milk Dun Cow dry. But it ran from her to Worcester where it died and was buried near the cathedral (NHS p197), or it ran to Delamere Forest where it was shot (OSST 1931 p20). Joan then put a spell on the farm, saying that if the stone was ever removed all the farm's cattle would died. When the farm was owned by Little Onn Hall, the owner of the hall, Col Ashton ordered the stone to be removed to the grounds of the hall, where it remains today. However, this done, that season the occupier of Red House Farm lost all his cattle (OSST 1931 p20) (VB pp150-151). It was probably the stone Plot noted in the later C17 lying in the middle of the street at Little Onn. Plot thought the imprint on it was the fossil mark of the orchites or lapides testiculares (NHS p197).

Redhouse Farm Redhouse Road, Tettenhall. Had been demolished by 1997 (TPOP p56p).

Red House Park A public park, nearly 1m SSW of Great Barr. In 1929 the grounds of Red House were opened as a public park (TBS p26) (WMVB p68).

Redhurst Cave Cave in Redhurst Gorge. Has also been called Old Hannah's Cave or Hole, or Old Anna's Cave after a woman (SJC p1; a witch) called Hannah or Anna, who lived here, and or is believed to haunt it (NSFCT 1899 p99); or someone hid in it; or from a woman called Anne Wyndham author of 'Ye King's Concealment at Trent' who alleged a monarch hid in it; or she lived in it, as a hermit, herself. It is also haunted by a hobthrust (who may be the same as Anna?) (WTCEM pp7,27,71,88,94) (KES p3) (TD). It was first excavated by Sir Thomas Wardle 1898. Some human bones were discovered here (SJC p1), a skull went to the Potteries Museum. (NSFCT 1899 pp105-113. vol 44 p227) (NSJFS 1964 p44). Some unexplainable explosion noises were heard issuing from the cave in 1855, 1868, 1896 (NSFCT 1899 pp98-105) (Leek Post Aug 13 1896) (National Speleological Society Bulletin 44 pp11-14, reproduced in 'Pursuit' vol 15 No. 4 pp157-160) (MMSE pp216,288). (LGS p185).

Redhurst Gorge Veers off the Manifold Valley near Darfur Bridge Cave, runs round the foot of Wetton Hill (LGS p185). (SMOPP vol 2). The name is from probably Red Deer Hurst corrupted to Redderhurst (NSFCT 1899 pp97-116, p of facing p97). Redhurst Gorge is reputedly haunted by the Hob i' th' Hurst or Hobhurst ghost (NSFCT 1899 pp113-116). The headless horseman of the Moorlands has been seen as far as Redhurst (WTCEM p93).

Red Lion Hotel or Inn. Situated on E side of Market Place, Leek, and is reputedly the oldest inhabited building in Leek. Said to have been built by Thomas Jolliffe in 1607 (VCH vol 7 p88), or in 1627 (OL vol 1 pp176-177. vol 2). Thomas Jolliffe was a wool merchant (VCH vol 7 p88), and the Joliffes were parliamentarians in the Civil War (BFS p9). Leek manor court leet was held here every Oct in the earlier C19, and a Leek county court was held here every month in the mid C19 (NSFCT 1990 p39) (VCH vol 7 pp124,130). It has been variously called Hall House (VCH vol 7 p88), Leek Old Hall (NSFCT 1990 p39), Joliffe House and Leek Hall (BPCSM p8). The house was known as the Red Lion by 1751 (VCH vol 7 p88), and was re-fronted, apparently in 1791 (VCH vol 7 p88), in the Georgian style. On Oct 11 1836 Manuel Matthews Egidia da Silveria, of Rio Janeiro, Brazil, shot himself in its lavatory after alighting from a coach (OL vol 1 p177). The inn sign was painted by Isaac Findler, artist, of Cheddleton (see). An ornamental plaster ceiling, with a representation of the triumph of death, from the inn is now (1991) preserved at Leek School of Art (VCH vol 7 p88). Some panelling from the inn was taken by Matthew Millar to Swainsley; other pieces were taken to Leek Technical School in the 1890s (OL vol 2 pp102 ils,104,105). The last man to be hanged in Leek (1631) is said to have been held prisoner here. The inn is reputedly haunted (Real Ale in and around the Potteries. CAMRA. p41).

Red Lion Square Open space at the junction of several thoroughfares in central Newcastle-under-Lyme; at the junction of Church, High and Merrial Streets and Lad Lane. The name is from an inn (local info).

Red Lion Square Junction of Audley and Apedale Roads, and Castle, Church and Victoria Streets, Chesterton, N of Newcastle-under-Lyme (Borough of Newcastle-under-Lyme Street Atlas. post 1974).

Redmoor Brook Tributary of the Trent (SPNO p17).

Redshaw House 1.5m ESE of Rushton Spencer village.

Red Street Hamlet on the eastern extremity of Bignall Hill high above a tributary of Fowlea Brook 1m N of Chesterton. Formerly in Talk o' th' Hill township, Audley ancient parish and partly in Chatterley liberty, Wolstanton an-

cient parish (W pp289,430). The name must be taken together with Rode Heath or Rudheath (Cheshire). Is sometimes read Ridge Street. From the Celtic forest-root 'rithead,' 'roed,' 'rud,' 'rus.' It was a road through the forest (NSFCT 1910 p163). There is a local tradition it is 'red' after a battle here in ancient times (The Times Nov 22 1967). A stone preaching cross of c800 of millstone grit, 36 inches by 26 inches, was found at Mitchell's Wood Farm, Red Street, in 1958. It went to Holy Trinity church, Chesterton (NSFCT 1959 p87). What is commonly called the 'Redstreet Monument' is an obelisk memorial on the top of Bignall Hill to John Wedgwood (1760-1839) (DoE II) (KTM p11p) (BOE p64) (Silverdale and Chesterton in Old Photographs. Dave Adams. 1988. pl 53). There is a mission church, St Chad, at Red Street (LDD).

Red Street Park Talke. In c1980 a couple claimed to have witnessed a UFO in the form of a massive orange and blue light whilst sitting in their car at Red Street Park (SMM p95).

Redway Approximate site of the present Oxensitch, N of Flash (1834 OS map).

Redwood House on a hill above Rudyard village on top of the southern end of Whorrocks Bank. It was called Bank House by 1613. The house was rebuilt in the Gothick style, probably for James Challinor, who lived here in 1851. The house was renamed Redwood in the 1920s (VCH vol 7 p67).

Reedswood Park Public park 1.25m NW of Walsall. Former derelict mining ground (VCH vol 17 p160). Formerly known as Reed's Wood. The Countess of Mountrath's map (1763) shows several plots of land in this area belonging to Widow Reed including an area of coppice (SNWA p89); the same or another map of 1763 implied it is only open to the public every seven years. In 1775 Richard Reed paid £5 annual rent to agents of Lord Mounthrath for his cattle to graze the land. Opened as a park in 1877 (SOB p201) or in 1885 (VCH vol 17 p160).

Reeve End Cottage N end of Yoxall village at SK 14101918 (SSAHST 1985-86 pp48-52). Dates from pre-1350 and is the only known aisle hall remaining in Staffs (SVB p186).

Refectory, The Former chapel of Lichfield Theological College, built in 1885, on S side of Lichfield cathedral Close. Converted into an educational and social centre, known as the Refectory in 1980, and known as College Hall in 1999. The buildings of Lichfield Theological College, closed in 1972, stand on a site once occupied by New College (see) (info Michael Cockin) (VCH vol 14 p66).

Regent's Wood Wood 1.5m NW of Beaudesert Old Park, Beaudesert Old Park. To W of Stile Cop. It was planted by the 'Waterloo' Marquis of Anglesey to commemorate the visit of Prince Regent and Duke of Clarence to Beaudesert in 1815 (PCC p73).

Reule Upper Reule (see) is 1m W of Haughton and Lower Reule (see) is over 1m WSW of Haughton. Formerly partly in Bradley and Gnosall ancient parishes; transferred to Haughton parish in 1934 (SPNO p136). Has appeared as Rohale (1168), Ruhale (1199), Rewelle (1272), Rewle (1286-1439. 1686), Rewol (1340), Rule (1363-1372) (DUIGNAN p129) (COI) (SPNO p136) (SPN pp97,112). The name means 'the rough spring' or 'the rough knoll' or 'the rough ditch' or 'the rough hedge' (DUIGNAN). Or 'the rough corner of land' (SPNO p136) (SPN p97). Or 'the rough spring' (SPN p113). The Reule manor held by the de Muttons prior to c1284 then passed to the Chetwynds; they had a manor house at Upper Reule (COI pp42,53) (VCH vol 4 p82). At Reule Plot noted a calf just cast with five legs (NHS p262).

Reule Brook Presumably rises near Reule, Haughton, and contributes to the Trent (NHS p42).

Revedge 1m SSW of Bradnop in the Moorlands. Formerly in Bradnop township in Leek ancient parish. There was settlement here by the later C13 (VCH vol 7 pp169-170). The present Revedge Farm is dated 1691 (VCH vol 7 p170).

Revidge Former waste land in the Moorlands 1m NW of Warslow. Formerly in Warslow and Elkstones township in Alstonefield ancient parish. The name means 'edge frequented by foxes' (PNPD). Enclosed in 1839 (VCH vol 7 p59).

Rewardine Ruiton, Upper Gornal. A stone windmill called Rewardine Field Mill was at SO 919921. It was situated at the junction of Windmill Street and Hill Street. It was built in 1702 by Peter Persehouse. (This was probably on the Windmill Bank Thomas Cox mentions at Gornal (SD p40)). Persehouse sold it to Thomas Maullin (a nailmaker from Coseley, whose descendants also owned Maullin's Mill at Coseley) in the second half of the C19 a stone quarry was working round the mill, and following heavy rain on Jan 31 1872 it began to collapse and crashed into the ground (WBJ p34) (SNSV vol 2 p81). But according to BCOPP vol 1 pl 79 a Edward Jones demolished a mill which stood on the corner of Windmill Street and Hill Street due to its general state of disrepair, perhaps, at some time later than 1872, and a drawing was made of it in 1907. Gornal Lily White Sand was probably ground by the mill at some time (WBJ p34). (SLM Spring 1954 p25). The name Rewardine cannot be found on the 1834 OS map or Birmingham A-Z (1995), and it seems to be a form of the name Ruiton. The terminal 'wardine' is a form of 'worth' so often found in Shrops and signifies 'a property' or 'a farm.' Ru or Reu may have been a proper name of the original owner (SR p106).

Rewlach House 2m S of Longnor. Formerly in Fawfieldhead township in Alstonefield ancient parish. Is recorded in the early 1420s (VCH vol 7 p27). The name means possibly 'rough, boggy area' (PNPD).

Reynard's Cottage Late C16 timber framed house beyond Halingdene at Penkridge. Stands next to another timber framed cottage called Mershac (PVH p24).

Reynolds Hall Stood near the present Arboretum Road, Walsall (VCH vol 17 p151), access to it was from the lower end of Rushall Street (SHOS vol 2 pp74-75). The Reynolds family had an estate in Walsall in the C15. By 1575 it included the house known as Reynold's Hall. By marriage the estate passed to the Walkers in the early C16, and to the Persehouses in 1546; it was their seat until 1771 (VCH vol 17 p177) (BCM July 1977 pp20-22). John Persehouse (d1636), succeeded to the Reynolds Hall estate in 1605; his Persehouse family history begins in the 1580s (SH pp19,20). It was seat of John Persehouse in 1651 (HOWV p119). The mob brought John Wesley here to see Mr Persehouse JP in Oct 1743 (SOB pp142-143). Appears on Yates' map (1775) and has appeared as Renards Hall. The last Persehouse left the hall and estate to his godson John Walhouse. With the death of John Walhouse in 1835 the remaining estate passed to his nephew, Edward John Littleton, who was created Baron Hatherton in 1835. The hall had been demolished by 1800 in order for the limestone underneath to be quarried. In the C19 the Hathertons were responsible for much of the residential development of NE central Walsall. The home farm, S of the former hall was occasionally known as Reynold's Hall in the C19 (VCH vol 2 p197 note. vol 17 pp151,177,191).

Reynolds Hay Farm House over 1m SE of Endon. Formerly in Endon township in Leek ancient parish. The house is of the C17 (VCH vol 7 p177). The hay part of the name may refer to an enclosure associated with the medieval deer park of Hanley Park formerly in this area (VCH vol 7 p182).

Reynolds Orchard Controversial piece of land lost in a gambling match at SJ 768335, 0.25m SE of Broughton church (1889 OS map). It was lost in the C17 or C18 by a Yonge to a Broughton on condition the other could have it for three harvests only. Lady Broughton determined to keep the land, seeded it with acorns. Some oaks were cut down after WW2, but some still remain so even now the Yonges cannot claim the land (BOV p15). Lumsdon and Rushton say a Lord Gerrard lost his estate in gambling to a Meynell, but make no mention of the orchard (PWNS p49). Has also appeared as Reginald's Orchard? The moated site in the orchard at SJ 76813339 is a listed monument.

Ribden Minute hamlet on the southern slopes of the Weaver Hills 1.5m S of Cauldon. In Farley township of Alton ancient parish. A polished flint axe of the Neolithic or Bronze Age was found in the moat in 1880 (HOU p44) (NSJFS 1964 p22) (HAF p28). A perforated stone axe hammer (celt or macehead) was found 'on the heath' at Ribden Farm in 1892. It was at the Potteries Museum in 1996 (HAF p29). There is a moated site at SK 076471 at 1005 feet, which was perhaps never water-filled (GNHSS p5) (NSFCT 1982 pp9,10) (CAMS p64). The lead and copper ores in the limestone under Ribden have been mined since at least the C17 (NHS pp166,404; the low on Ribden) and possibly since Roman times (HAF p292). An engine house tower (connected with the mines?) which stood here, and was in a ruinous state for a while, was pulled down and its materials used in the building of a lime kiln at Ruelow. The engine was moved about quite a bit (PSM pl 76). Takes its name from Ribden Low or hill.

Ribden Low Hill forming part of the Weaver Hills (SPNO p23), and burial mound at SK 07624777, 1m S of Cauldon, 0.5m N of Ribden. The hill is 1190 feet high. The mound is 28 paces in diameter and seven feet high. Carrington excavated it in 1849. Three barbed and tangled arrowheads and a crouched skeleton were found (TYD pp127-128) (VCH vol 1 no 13) (DAJ vol 75 pp114,118) (NSJFS 1965 p35) (HAF pp390-391). It is a listed monument. The name appears in 1328 as Wrebedun (SPNO p23) (SPN p97). It means 'Wrybba's hill' (SPNO p23) (SPN p97). Said to be named after a local tribal chieftain of the Saxons (SPN p97).

Richmilde Street Roman way between Littlechester (or Derventio) (near Derby) and Chesterton (near Newcastle-under-Lyme). It went via Rocester, Woottons, Hollington, Upper Tean, Draycott-in-the-Moors, Blythe Bridge, Meir, Lane End (Longton), Lane Delph, Stoke-upon-Trent and Wolstanton. From Chesterton it carried on to Middlewich, Ches. It has appeared as Via Devana, Richmilde (1257), Richnilde, Rycknield, Rikeneld, Mear Lane (the part in the Longton area) (DUIGNAN p83) (VCH vol 2 p275) (MRM p3) (HOS 1998 p26). Cobbled pavement found at Stoke-upon-Trent and at Wolstanton

may be remains of it (NSFCT 1908 p106).

Richmoorhill Hill and house on road between Cellarhead and Kingsley, at SJ 968470. Appears as Rich Moor on 1834 OS map.

Rickerscote Hamlet near the Penk 2m SSE of Stafford. Former township in Castle Church ancient parish (W p343). Has appeared as Ricardescote, a manor, in DB, Rycardescote (1217-37), Rycardscote (1557), Rikerscote (1560) (SPNO p76), Ricarscote (1686) (NHS p120), and Rickerscote (Yates' map 1775). The name is from the Anglo-Saxon personal name 'Ricard' - so 'Ricard's cottage' (DUIGNAN) (SPN p112) (SSE 1996 p17). Or the name arose after the Norman Conquest as 'Richard' was a typical Norman personal name (SHC 1908 p229 note). A copper alloy seal-matrix was found at Rickerscote in c1995. It has been identified as a matrix for an alnager's seal for Warwickshire and probably dates to the early C15. Its inscription, in Lombardic lettering, may be translated as 'Seal of tax on cloth in the county of Warwick' (WMARCH 1995 p95). In the later C17 Plot found Brick-earth at Rickerscote (NHS p120). A spa found on the estate here was claimed to have similar properties to the waters of Bath, Cheltenham, Harrogate, and Leamington. In 1817 its waters were recommended for the afflictions of the liver and digestive organs, for jaundice, and for scrofula, and for various forms of chronic debility (SA April 1817) (THS) (SIOT p80) (SCSF p145) (VCH vol 5 p84) (SPN p112): Because of those coming to take the water here Rickerscote became a considerable hamlet in the earlier C19 (VCH vol 6 p196). Since 1945 Rickerscote has expanded greatly and become a suburb of Stafford (VCH vol 5 p84). The church, St Peter, on the S side of Rickerscote Road, was consecrated in 1957 (VCH vol 6 p249). Rickerscote was created a separate ecclesiastical parish in 1962 (GLAUE p420). There was a serious railway accident at Rickerscote at 11.15pm on March 8 1996 when a Royal Mail train collided with a derailed south-bound freight train carrying chemicals. One man died and 19 were injured (ES March 9 1996 pp1,4).

Rickerscote Hall At the end of a lane to the E of School Lane, Rickerscote. Some of the hall, in 1959, which was timber-framed, dated from the C16 (VCH vol 5 p89). The hall, mostly of c1690, may have been built on the site of Rickerscote Old Hall and may include parts of the old hall (SAC pp20-21p).

Rickerscote House Unimpressive red brick house of the early C19 on N side of Rickerscote Road, Rickerscote (SAC p18,19).

Rickerscote Old Hall There was a hall at Rickerscote by the C14 when it was occupied by Reynold-de-Waite. Roger Hinton, whose will is dated 1685, may have lived in Rickerscote Old Hall or Rickerscote Hall (SAC p20).

Rickthorn Area 1m SSW of Bobbington which was inhabited by the later C13 (VCH vol 20 p65).

Ridding Possibly a former open field to the W of Anslow village (ANS p23) and a small hamlet SW of Anslow. The name, which has also appeared as Riddings, had appeared by the mid C13 (ANS p23). Riddings Farm is 0.5m SW of Anslow.

Ridding Field Former small open field of Wednesbury which lay to its SE end. The field is marked on the 1799 map of Wednesbury. The name is preserved in Ridding Lane (SSAHST 1990-91 p98).

Ridding Lane Near to Hateley Heath, West Bromwich. The name is derived from 'La Ruddinge,' a field mentioned in ancient documents (SOWB p24). A le Rudynnge, in the Wednesbury area, which may have been an early form of Ridding, is mentioned in 1315 (HOWV p108).

Riddings Dunstall, in Barton-under-Needwood parish (NHS p197). Whether Duignan refers to this when he mentions Ridding. Ridding, he says, is equivalent to Birchills, meaning a clearing in the wilderness (DUIGNAN p15).

Riddings Lies S of Denstone College, Denstone. Originally Ridings.

Riders Ease Common The name occurs in the 1841 census in Pelsall township. See Ryder's Hayes.

Rideware Brook Tributary of the Trent. Has appeared as aqua de Rideware (1255). Takes its name from the Ridware villages (SPNO p17).

Ridgacre Area S of Hateley Heath in West Bromwich ancient parish. It was apparently an inhabited area in the earlier C14. Church Lane was originally called Ridgacre Lane. The area was densely wooded until the earlier C19 when it became an industrial district. By the mid 1970s the area was covered by housing estates (VCH vol 17 p7 note).

Ridgacre Branch of the Wednesbury Old Canal. Runs from the Wednesbury Old Canal at Swan Junction, terminated at Ridgacre Lane (now Church Lane). Opened 1826 (VCH vol 2 p297 see map. vol 17 p14). Halford Branch was a branch off it. The upper reaches of it were remaining in 1995 (BCM autumn 1995 p20). Seems to take its name from the area called Ridgacre.

Ridge End Ridge End Farm is 1.25m NW of Sheen. In Sheen ancient parish. There was a farm at Ridge End by 1648. It was rebuilt in 1744 (VCH vol 7 p242).

Ridge Hill In Madeley ancient parish (W p396). A Ridge Hill appears on 1834 OS map 1m ENE of Madeley to S of Madeley Heath.

Ridge Hill Hill 1.5m WSW of Kingswinford church. Has appeared as 'Ridge Hill or Ash Wood' (1834 OS map). It appears to give its name to Ridge Hill Hospital at Buckpool. Has also appeared as Rudge Hill (BCM Oct 1988 pp32-33). Ridgehill Wood is a wood on the summit; the E edge of the wood forms the West Midlands boundary.

Ridge House, The Estate and old timber-framed manor house on Cobridge Road, Etruria. Probably owned by the Homersleys in the early C17. In 1745 the house was occupied by Ralph Leigh (VCH vol 8 p152), who reputedly on hearing that the Young Pretender Prince Charles Edward Stuart had reached Leek hid his fortune (worth 60 guineas) under an oak tree. The oak was still standing in 1829 in fields which became the ground on which the Potteries races were held and on which now (1952) stands the old Racecourse Colliery tip of the Shelton Company (HOE p15). In 1767 the house was occupied by a Mrs Ashenhurst. In 1767 she and her son sold the Ridgeway House estate to Josiah Wedgwood I and Etruria Hall was built on part of it. As a memorial to the estate two stones or earthenware pillars with the letters R.H. cut deeply into them were placed on the site and were there as late as 1876 (HOE pp13, 15,16, 57,187, 188,380; pp305,307 on Ridge House Farm) (VCH vol 8 p152).

'Ridgeway' Lower Penn. Built in the 1930s with original materials by Major Hutchinson Smith (POAP p14).

Ridgeway Minute hamlet 1.5m N of Norton-in-the-Moors. Formerly in Norton chapelry in Stoke-on-Trent ancient parish. Where the Ridgway family, potters, are reputedly from (OTP p174).

Ridgeway Hall Ridgeway, Norton-in-the-Moors. Built in 1669 and rebuilt in 1859 (ONST 1932 p39). Or built in 1687 (NSFCT 1957 p66). Has also appeared as Ridgeway Farm.

Ridings Brook Rises near Hednesford Park. Flows on the E side of Cannock to Wyrley Brook at Bridgtown.

Ridware Hall To W of Hill Ridware.

Rileyhill Minute hamlet on low ground in the Trent Valley by Bourne Brook 1m SSW of King's Bromley. There is an irregular D-shape enclosure around a circle: a pit alignment nearby, at SK 125155 (MOT pp31,55) (NSJFS 1964 p27).

Rine Brook Runs into the Swarbourn from the Newchurch and Woodlane Road.

Ring, The Circular row of 14 (HHHC p77) or 16 cottages between Great Haywood and Little Haywood, at SK 002220. The cottages were an example of some of the earliest experiments in rehousing (STM March 1966 p24). Designed by Samuel Wyatt of Blackbrook Farm (see) for the Ansons to rehouse the displaced inhabitants of Shugborough Village. Each cottage had a garden and there was a communal wash-house, bake-oven and school room in the centre of the circle. The Ring was demolished in 1965 (SHC 1970 p88) (SNTG p41). By 1996 the Ring had been replaced by modern houses (HHHC pp77,78ps).

Ringstone Farm On Wetley Moor 0.75m NNW of Werrington. It may have been named from the 'large stone with a round hole in it' mentioned in an account of the perambulation of Bucknall manor boundary made in 1803 (WJ p19).

Rising Brook Tributary of the Trent; appears to flow in the Rugeley area of Cannock Chase. Has appeared as Rysond brooke (1538), and Rysombrooke (1585) (SPNO pp17,19). The first element is perhaps from 'hrisen' 'growing with brushwood' (SPNO pp17,109).

Rising Brook Tributary of the Penk. Rises at Hyde Lea and runs in the S Stafford area and gives its name to Risingbrook hamlet. Has appeared as Rysembrooke (1590), Risonbrook (c1680), Rising Brook (1788) (SPNO p78). The name means 'the brook growing with brushwood' (SPNO p78).

Risingbrook Small hamlet by Rising Brook 1.25m S of Stafford. In Castle Church parish. Formerly written 'Risom Brook.' Since 1945 Risingbrook has expanded greatly and become a Stafford suburb (VCH vol 5 pp84,92). The nucleus is at the junction Rowley Bank, Burton Manor Road, and Rising Brook. The name is from the brook, Rising Brook (SAC p38). A round hazy mass of glowing orangy-red light, slightly larger than a sixpence at a maximum height of about 300 to 400 feet was seen from Risingbrook on Aug 25 1967 at approximately 11.00pm (FSRP p7).

Rising Valley A valley running through Cannock Chase created by Rising Brook (SL p105).

Riverdale House on N side of Main Street in Colwich village. Occupied by Sir Graham and Lady Balfour some time between 1900 and 1938 (HHHC p43).

Riverside Doveleys A pleasant mansion on Staffs side of the Dove 1m SSW of Ellastone. In Rocester parish. Formerly the residence of Col Riddlesden, then Benjamin Heywood (AAD p294). Has also appeared as Dove Leys (1834

OS map. 1851), Doveleys, and Riverside Doveleys (1981 OS map). The original small farm here was occupied by Thomas Percival Heywood in 1851. He appears to have rebuilt the farm as his country house in 1856, the year he succeeded to the knighthood. His son, Sir Arthur Percival Heywood of Duffield Bank, near Derby, was a well-known narrow-gauge railway-engineer and made his first experiments here. Sir Arthur Percival Heywood gave the land for Denstone College. The house was occupied by Sir Graham Heywood Bart DSO by 1924 to at least 1940. In 1946 Doveleys became an educational establishment (W p19) (trade directories) (The Story of The Woodard Schools. KE Kirk. 1937. p124) (ESNF p107p).

Riverway Bridge Built in 1914 over the Sow at Stafford (ROT p42). Is it the bridge from Forebridge district to Littleworth.

Rivoli Originally two cottages called Peewit Castle in Suckling Green Lane, Codsall. It is now (1990) painted white and stands at right angles to the road (TCOP p110p).

Roach End 2.5m NNW of Upper Hulme. At the NW end of The Roaches.

Roaches, The Large ragged outcrop of rocks and former waste in Leekfrith township in Leek parish, in the Moorlands, 1.5m NNW of Upper Hulme. The highest point is 1657 feet (S p13) (LGS p3) or 1658 feet (OS map 43/06) (VCH vol 7 p191). The Roaches are geologically the Goldsitch Coalfield and its surrounding grit escarpments covering an area of nine square miles (NSFCT 1920 pp76-87; geology of The Roaches). They form the ridge part of the E boundary of the Cheshire Triassic Plain (NSFCT 1868 p13). (LGS p163). From the Upper Tier on a clear day the panorama includes Bosley Cloud, Jodrell Bank, Cannock Chase, the Welsh mountains and reputedly, Pen-trwyn on The Great Orme (SGM p30).

A number of megalithic chambered tombs have been found on the Roaches. The round cairn near the peak of the Roaches at SK 00106388 is a listed monument. One large boulder has steps cut into it (PS p150p). The asymmetrical-shaped Neolithic or Bronze Age axe-hammer found 0.25m N of Roaches Hill on the W side of the road in 1925 went to Reading Museum (NSJFS 1962 pp30-31) another or the same is in the Potteries Museum (NSJFS 1964 p25). A faceted stone axe-shaped amulet, and a spindle whorl have been found near the Roaches (Scientific Rambles in the Macclesfield District. J Sainter. 1878 p43). A plaster cast of the amulet is preserved in the BM (NSJFS 1964 p28). Amulets or lucky charms made from stone carved from these rocks were sold as neck charms; evidence that the area was, once, thought to be sacred (DP p51p). Raven believes the Roaches are 'the rocheres' in the medieval epic poem 'Gawain and the Green Knight' (MR p316). The Roaches were so named by 1358 (VCH vol 7 p191). The name is from the French 'roche,' meaning a rock or cliff (VCH vol 7 p191). Or from Old Norman French 'les roches' (NSFCT 1882 p26) (COS p10). The correct spelling should be Roches, Roaches is a misspelling (S p138). Some say the Roaches were christened Les Roches - the Rocks - by French prisoners from the Napoleonic wars (VB p209) (JC 5).

At the sight of Hen Cloud and the Roaches Dr Plot in c1680 said 'my admiration was still heighten'd to see such vast rocks and such really stupendous prospects, which I had never seen before, or could have believed to be, anywhere but in picture' (NHS pp170-171) (VCH vol 7 p78). In 1708 Thomas Loxdale, the antiquarian and vicar of Leek, visited the Roaches and found them 'one of the most romantick prospects in Nature, far beyond Dr Plott's description' (VCH vol 7 p78). William Pitt, the agronomist, visited the Roaches in 1794 and considered them and Sharp Cliffe Rocks as 'stupendous piles ...... a sublime lecture on humility to the human mind' (AOS p199) (VCH vol 7 p79). In the late 1880s Miller noted that The Roaches rock features called the Rocking Stone or Loggan Rock, the Sun Dial and the Tip Cat had been destroyed (OL vol 1 p95). In the late C19 the Roaches were described by a Mr Brough, leader of a NSFC expedition to the area, as 'Lonely, weird and romantic.' It was noted at this time that there existed two rock features resembling the Duke of Wellington and Lord Brougham (NSFCT 1895 pp153,154). In the 1920s it was noted that there were no better examples of wind sculptured rocks than those on The Roaches; that they were the most impressive outcrops in the country, and that the great castellated masses, the undercut pinnacles, the protuberant blocks, looked like wondrous examples of cyclopean architecture (NSFCT 1922 p50). The Roaches appear in Pamela Hurst's romantic novel 'Angel of the Moorlands' (1995) (ES May 30 1995 p19). Some consider Five Clouds (see), Hen Cloud (see) and The Nth Cloud (see) as part of The Roaches, but technically they are not.

Three thousand acres of the Roaches were enclosed under an Act of 1805 (SHC 1941 p17) in 1811, at which time The Roaches were added to the Swythamley estate (VCH vol 7 p195). In 1860 a footpath was made along the ridge of The Roaches (SSGLST p21). The Duke and Duchess of Teck (Princess Mary Adelaide of Cambridge, granddaughter of George III, mother of

Mary of Teck future wife of George V) visited the Roaches when guests of the Brocklehursts, owners of the Swythamley estate, on Aug 23 1872. The Royal Standard was erected on the rocks of the third summit (in the Lower Tier area - SGM p24) where a special seat, called the Queen's Chair, was cut in the rock for the Duchess (HOLF pp18-20ps) (HLSP p154) (Cambridge Biographical Encyclopaedia. David Crystal. 1994). Having encouraged tourism in the C19 (VCH vol 7 p195) the Swythamley estate forbade climbing and trespassing on the Roaches from the 1930s (SSGLST pp19,21). For Brocklehursts' private zoo and its wallabies see Roaches House. There were five aeroplane crashes on the Roaches in WW2. A German Junkers JU88-A5 crashed on the Roaches on May 8 1941 all four crew were killed (MD pp70-72). A Wellington Bomber 'Z for Zebra' crashed into the Roaches in Nov 1942 (ES July 14 1981 p9): This perhaps relates to the crash at Hen Cloud (see). On Jan 3 1945 a Lancaster 1 flew headlong into the back of the the Roaches only a few feet below the summit, all seven crew died (MD pp16-17). In 1977 the Swythamley estate was broken up and in 1980 The Roaches were purchased from the Swythamley estate by the Peak Park joint planning board (SSGLST p19) (SGM p31) (VCH vol 7 p195).

THE TIERS. The Roaches comprise a S escarpment, which comprise two tiers. One is called the **Lower Tier** which is situated behind Rockhall (see) and comprise these named crags: 'Bengal Buttress' 'Raven Rock' 'Valkyrie.' To the E behind this tier is the **Upper Tier**, which comprise these named crags:- 'Calcutta Buttress' 'Blushing Buttress' 'The Great Slab' 'Central Massif' 'Maud's Garden' 'Jeffcoat's Buttress' 'Rotunda Buttress' 'Bachelor's Buttress' 'Kelly's Shelf' 'Beckermet Slab.' The escarpment to the N of this tier, which comprise a long edge, is called the **Skyline**, it comprises these named crags: 'Condor Buttress' 'Tower Buttress' (one of the Skyline's steeper bastions) 'The Trio' 'Cave Buttress' 'Skyline buttress' (the Skyline's largest face) 'The Pinnacle' 'Alpha Buttress' 'Far Skyline Buttress' 'Very Far Skyline Buttress' 'Hard Very Far Skyline Buttress' 'Window Buttress or The Cube or Back End Boulders' (SGM).

Roaches House House 0.25m N of Upper Hulme. Near the house was found a Celtic interment in 1883. The bones and fragments of two pots went to the Nicholson Institute, Leek (HOLF p15). The house was formerly called Argyle Cottage (1887 OS map 6 inch) (VCH vol 7 p194), Argyle House (HOLF p15), The Roches House (1900 and 1926 OS maps 6 inch) (HOLF p15), Roche House (ES Oct 12 1936 p5), The Roaches House (OS The White Peak Outdoor Leisure Map 1980). It was built in 1876 (VCH vol 7 p194) by John Hall, a wealthy manufacturer (TTTD pp106-107). Some say it was built by a Scottish couple (HOLF p15). It was here Lt Col Courtney Brocklehurst (member of the Brocklehurst family of Swythamley Hall; there is a memorial to him on Hangingstone Rock) kept a private zoo in the 1930s which appears to have covered Hen Cloud. A kangaroo escaped on Oct 8 1936 and roamed the Roaches and neighbouring areas until captured at Scholar Green on Oct 11 1936. By or shortly after the outbreak of WW2 the zoo appears to have contained wallabies evacuated from Whipsnade Zoo. Brocklehurst left to take part in the war - he was in Burma by 1942 - and the animals were released into the wild. Once wild on the Roaches they started breeding. At its height the wild wallaby colony numbered about 60. By the mid 1960s it was believed to have died out, killed by the cold weather of 1962-3. But sightings of wallabies were common in the 1970s. By May 1997 they were thought to have died out, although some claim to have seen them since (ES Oct 12 1936 p5. July 16 1965. May 8 1996 p3ps. May 21 1997 p13p. May 31 1997 p9p. Dec 20 1997 p9. March 14 1998 p11) (SGM p22) (Daily Telegraph May 12 1997 p4) (DP p39) (HOLF p16) (COS p10). Yaks (HLSP p154) and llamas (SMM p136p) are also said to have survived for a while on the Roaches. Bird says Sir Philip Brocklehurst introduced wallabies into Swythamley deer park, but the wallabies escaped from it in 1938 (VB p213) (GLS p91).

Roberts Green Former hamlet near Upper Gornal. The name, which appears in the 1861 census, is preserved in the street called Roberts Green to the W of Jew's Lane. The old farmhouse called Robert's Green at Lower Gornal was still standing in 1963 (SDOP p21p).

Robin Hill Hill and tiny hamlet 0.75m SW of Biddulph Moor. Here is a reddish-coloured gritstone outcrop of rocks known to local children in the early 1960s as the 'Ticking Rock' (TTTD p158). A sampler in memory of Sarah Brookes of Robin Hill (died Oct 21 1891 aged 59, buried Biddulph Moor), was displayed in an exhibition in the Potteries Museum, Hanley, autumn 1994.

Robin Hood Farm On the Audley Road on W side towards Bignall Hill from Chesterton, at SJ 824502.

Robin Hood's Butt Former burial mound which was situated in a field called Thelow Flat SW of Wigginton at cSK 208062. (SHOS vol 1 p432) (HTCT p60 map) (THM vol 6 p31). It was one of the Robin Hood Shooting Butts, the other is Elford Low (see). Garner thought it was of Celtic origin and

reported that it had been levelled (GNHSS p9). Destroyed in the late C18 (NSJFS 1965 p58).

Robin Hood's Chapel Grotto at the end of the Long Walk, 0.5m SSE of Loxley Hall, Loxley. It is made out of remaining ornamental stone from the old Loxley Hall, which was destroyed in c1805 (HOU p328). The arms of the Sneyd-Kinnersleys are incorporated into the facade. So named with regard to the tradition which relates Robin Hood was born at Loxley Hall. (NSFCT 1922 p128). There is a tradition that Robin Hood became engaged to Maid Marion in the surrounding woodland (TRTC pp59,95p,96).

Robin Hood Shooting Butts Collective name for Elford Low and another burial mound about a mile away, facing it, called Robin Hood's Butt (see), Elford. They were so called from the belief that Robin Hood practiced here and was able to shoot an arrow from one to the other (W p603). But, apparently, an estate map of 1845 shows them close together on the left hand side of the road near Wigginton Lodge and Lycett's engraving factory. They could not be found in the early 1970s (LTM Nov 1971 p12) (THM vol 6 p75).

Robin's Nest Farm Lower Penn. The name is no doubt connected with the spring that bubbles up constantly at the side of the road (SVB p115).

Rocester (*Roaster* VB p164, MR p264). Ancient parish and village at the foot of a promontory between the rivers Dove and Churnet slightly N of their confluence 15.5m NE of Stafford.

EARLY. A necked beaker of the **Neolithic** or **Bronze Age** was found during road construction in 1939 (DAJ vol 75 p77) (NSJFS 1964 p32). A bronze flat axe, possibly of the **Early Bronze Age**, was found at the mill to the E of the church in 1792 (SHOS vol 1 General Intro p34 note) (NSJFS 1964 p32). Richmilde Street (see), the **Roman** road between Derby and Chesterton, passed through Rocester. On it at Rocester was the Roman station, of possibly, Veratinum (NSJFS 1976 p94). From 1792 many Roman items have been discovered at several points within and near Rocester including three coins of Domitian (HOU 1865 pp356-357. 1886 p66) (NSFCT vol 46 p113. 1913 p109. 1914 pp97-98,103-108. 1931 pp179-182. 1932 pp113-115. 1959 p85) (PS p126). The foundations of Roman baths, it has been supposed, have been discovered at Rocester (GNHS p70). Masefield placed the Roman settlement near Barrowhill (see), 0.75m to the N of Rocester (LGS p203). Yet a site was found centred on the present church (itself on the site of the former abbey), and excavated in 1961 (NSJFS 1962 pp37- 52) and in c1987 (SHJ vol 4 pp26-39; excavation report) (SLM April/ May 1987 p51. Oct/ Nov 1987 p69p) (SVB p141) (MR p264p of excavations). The Queen's Arms Inn may stand on part of the Roman settlement (ES April 6 1994 p4). There are believed to have been several successive Roman settlements on the site centred on the church, some say up to four (MR p264). The earliest pottery finds from it date from c70 AD suggesting that the first fort was built in the period of Agricola (HOS p12). The military garrison was later withdrawn and the fort abandoned c120-150 AD. A civil settlement occupied the site after 200 AD (NSJFS 1964 p33) (SASR 1986 pp20-51 ps ils). More fortifications were built in c280 AD (HOS p12). Here at some time during the Roman period was the chief 'mansio' between Chesterton and Derby (NSFCT 1908 p108. 1913 p110). (S p74) (KES pp167,168) (STM March 1968 p26). In 1985 a copper alloy plate broach of Roman origin depicting a horse and rider, and various pieces of Roman pottery were found during excavations at New Cemetery, Church Lane (SSAHST 1984-85 p1 il). The same or another copper alloy mount in the form of the lion's head of Roman origin was found in 1986 during excavations at the New Cemetery, Church Lane (SK 111395). A similar mount, found in 1913 at Dove School, Rocester, was in the Potteries Museum in 1988 (SSAHST 1988-89 p11 ils).

1000 to PRESENT. The **name** has appeared as Rowcestre, a manor, in DB, Rouecestre, Roveecestre, and Rocestre (SPN p99), and Rossetter (HOC p253). It means 'Hrof's castle.' 'Hrof' an Anglo-Saxon personal name, modern 'Ralph' and 'cester' indicative of the Roman station here (DUIGNAN) (SPN p99). Mills suggests 'rough Roman fort' (SSE 1996 p17). The parish, formed after 1086 and probably about the time Rocester Abbey was founded, was originally a part of Mayfield parish (SHC 1916 p198). Rocester itself once contained the chapelries of Bradley-in-the-Moors, and Waterfall (GLAUE p420). The parish **church**, St Michael, W of West View and N of Mill Street, rebuilt in 1873, was formerly a part of the abbey church of Rocester Abbey (see) (LGS p203). Rocester parish **wake** was on the Sunday after Oct 11 in the C19 (W p786). Rocester Abbey was granted a charter on July 4 1283 to hold a **market** here on Thursdays, and with that market, probably, having lapsed, a Friday market was granted in 1440 (NSJFS 1971 pp51,53) (SVB p141). The butter cross is in the churchyard. The late C18 Arkwright's Cotton Factory (see), with later additions, may have made Rocester seem like **'a small town'** to Masefield in c1910 (LGS p203), although later in the C20 Rocester was described as a village. During the 1960s the place lost alot of its character when many of the houses in the village centre were demolished to make way for shops and flats (SGS p140) (SVB p141). For JCB see under Rocester Green. The **railway** line (Churnet line) from Uttoxeter to Macclesfield via Leek opened on July 13 1849 passed through Rocester (NSJFS 1962 p99) (CVH p128). In 1852 the NSR built a branch line from Rocester to Ashbourne (VCH vol 2 p309). The Ashbourne passenger service ended in 1954, with regular passenger trains on the Churnet line ending in 1960 (ESNF p98p of Rocester station). It was recommended that Rocester station close in 1963 (ES March 22 1963). A 70 feet wide **crop circle** was found in a field between Rocester and Uttoxeter. It had been made by Aug 17 1996 (ES Aug 17 1996 p11p). **Natives and visitors.** In the later C17 Dr Plot noted a **James Plimmer** of Rocester who was able to refrain from spitting whilst smoking a pipe (NHS p302). **Rueben Jackson** was a bull dog fighter and mean character from Leek who set his dog on a preacher in 1824 called George Bull saying 'My dog has pinned many a bull and he shall pin another tonight.' However, the dog turned on his master and this action led Jackson to believe there was something in religion after all. He became a preacher at Rocester and here died in peace (TOI pp172-173).

Rocester Abbey Rocester. An Augustinian house (SOSH p109) (LGS p37) dedicated to St Mary (SVB p141). (KES p10). Founded by Richard Bacon, nephew of the Earl of Chester, in 1140 (GNHS p93), or about 1146 (LGS p203) (BOE p225) (MR p265), or between 1141 and 1146 (VCH vol 3 p247). Few English houses of Austin Canons ranked as abbeys. Some have found it surprising to find Rocester, a small house, titled an abbey. The abbey was suppressed in 1538. The 'house or site' of the monastery, leased in March 1539 for 21 years to Edward Draycott, one of Cromwell's servants, was sold the following July to Richard Trentham. In c1570 Thomas Trentham of Rocester Abbey was sheriff of Staffs (SHOS vol 1 xxxvi). Part of the abbey church was retained as the parish church (SOS pp491-492) (VCH vol 3 pp247-251). The exact site of the abbey was still uncertain in the 1930s. See the Frameyard (NSFCT 1932 p113). The site was found to be immediately to the SE of Rocester church. Traces of the buildings remain in the shape of mounds (LGS p203). Fragments of stained glass from the priory are preserved in the S window of the church (GNHSS p11). (HOC pp192,193,194) (STM March 1968 pp26,27). Has also appeared as Rocester Priory.

Rocester Green Former tiny hamlet to W of Rocester on W side of the Churnet (1834 OS map) (W p786). Rocester railway station was here. **Bamford's Factory.** Joseph Cyril Bamford (JCB) brought his company for the manufacture of traction and digging excavators from Crakemarsh Hall to Rocester Green in 1950 (SVB p141). The famous logo of the company, which first appeared in 1953 on the JCB Loadover, was based around the side swath bar of the 1951 JCB Hay-Mower, the shape of which meant the letters were all of different heights (TRTC p15). By 1970 the first phase of the present JCB works at Rocester Green had been developed. A second stage was complete by 1972. Prince Charles visited the factory in Nov 1977 (BUBA pp119,120,121p). The surrounding ground has been landscaped with pools and sculptures made out of JCB excavators (COS p38p of the metal birds sculpture, p39p of the Fossar sculpture by Walently Pytel). A 24 feet long and 17 feet wide bronze sculpture called Opus by Mark Delf was placed in the grounds of JCB in May 1992 (SN May 15 1992 p5p). (VCH vol 2 p145).

Roche Grange Hamlet on the W side of the Roaches 2m NW of Upper Hulme. Formerly in Leekfrith township in Leek ancient parish. There was a grange of Dieulacres Abbey here by 1246 (SVB p123) (VCH vol 7 p194). By 1600 it was the seat of the Hulmes (OL vol 2 pp158-159) (HOLF p5). Appears as Roach Grange on Plot's map.

Rock, The Sandstone cutting between Upper Penn and Lower Penn (SVB p115).

Rock, The Sandstone ridge separating the two settlements of Tettenhall. In making improvements to the London to Holyhead road (A41) Thomas Telford cut through The Rock, using gunpowder, between 1820-23. The Rock now refers to the stretch of road running through the cut (Tettenhall Village Trail. History Dept, Regis School, Tettenhall).

Rockcliffe Near Huntley and Cheadle. According to Hackwood, situated on the side of a hillock here is a well said to contain many remarkable properties and famed for the cure of many disorders. It seems to have been formerly resorted to more by the superstitious than the ailing. The superstitious professed to obtain prognostications of future events by the appearance of bubbles on the surface when stones or pebbles were dropped into it. There was once an engraving with an inscription on the wall of the well, but in c1800, the stones were utilised as building material elsewhere (SCSF p144).

Rock Cottage Endon Edge, Endon. Built as a cottage orne in 1846 for Abner Wedgwood. He died here in 1869. It was enlarged after being bought in 1890 by James Slater, Art Director at the Doulton Pottery works at Burslem. Became a private nursing home in 1983 (VCH vol 7 p179).

Rock Cottages Three cottages built into a rock face on the road from Standon church to Standon old post office. The cellars of the Rectory House are cut entirely out of rock (HOPS p15).

Rock End Small hamlet below and behind the Wicken Stones rocks 1m E of Knypersley. The hamlet starts at the top of Park Lane, known locally as Gutter Lane (Guthram's Lane?) (CIOPP pp21p,23p).

Rockery Hall Rockery Road, Lanesfield. Appears in 1834 as Lane's Hall and Ettingshall Hall in 1844. Purchased in 1898 by James Charles Bates. By the 1990s the property was the base for the 44 Club, a society established after WW2 for those formerly active in civil defence in the war (SDSSOP p42p).

Rocket Oak At SK 195219 on OS map 1:25,000. ESE of Rangemore. A wood or single oak?

Rocket Pools Lower Bradley, Bilston (TB Sept 1978 p5. May 1984 p1).

Rockets Dingle 0.75m NE of Dunstall, Tatenhill. Dingle which breaks the line of rising banks of Needwood Forest plateau (HOPT vol 1 p134).

Rock Farm 1.25m W of Winkhill. The Rock (1834 OS map).

Rockhall Cave under 1m NE of Upper Hulme, in Raven Rock below the Lower Tier on the Roaches, at its S end, at SK 006622. The cave is fronted with ashlar. The natural chamber or caves - one was known as the 'Rock Cave' (SSGLST p19) - was occupied by Solomon Bowyer and his descendants from the C16 until the C19. The property was known as Rockhall in 1770 (VCH vol 7 p194) and has also appeared as Rock Hall Cottage. The freebooter or moss-trooper 'Bowyer of the Rocks' and his daughter Bess (c1785-1860), a besom maker, were the most famous characters who lived here. Bowyer was a terror to the neighbourhood, and Bess was a noted harbourer of smugglers and deserters. Bess's children were John Robinson Bowyer (b1815), Hannah Bowyer (b1825), and Eliza Bowyer (1831-1836). Hannah probably was nicknamed Doxey and after giving birth to a son in c1845 she disappeared. Some say she was abducted by an Irish vagrant others that she left of her own accord; reputedly, her voice still haunts the locality (SVB p124) (SGM pp19-20) (HOLF pp16p-17) (DPEM pp50,51,53p). Another account says the cottage was taken over for a few years in 1810 by a family named Bradley; possibly at this point the cave was fronted with ashlar and made into a cottage. The ashlar front is of early C19 origin: The cottage was from this time possibly used as a shooting box (DoE II). At the death of a tenant, who was a female descendent of the Bowyers, it was enlarged and restored by PL Brocklehurst (killed in a railway accident at Stoke) (NSFCT 1868 p23 note. 1884 p21) for his gamekeeper (MR p348) in 1850 (SSGLST p19) or in 1861 (DPEM p50) (ES Jan 7 1993 p17p) and a toll of a penny or twopence had to be paid to its occupant before walking up to the Roaches (HOLF p17). Rockhall was visited by the Duke and Duchess of Teck (see the Roaches) when guests of the Brocklehursts on Aug 23 1872 (SSGLST p22). The Duchess planted a Scotch fir at the entrance (OL vol 2 pp208,209p) (HOLF pp18-20ps). After lying derelict for many years the cottage was bought by the self-styled Lord of the Roaches, Doug Moller, and his wife Anne in 1978. In Dec 1989 the Mollers agreed to leave after the building was condemned as being unfit for habitation. In association with the British Mountaineering Council the Mollers converted it into a climbers hut with accommodation for 12 people. This was officially opened to the memory of the famous climber Don Williams (d1985) on Jan 23 1993 (ES Jan 3 1987 p. Jan 7 1993 p17pc. Jan 14 1994 p18p) (SSGLST pp20p,21). Rockhall was listed in 1987 (MR pp346,347pc). A legend connected to Rockhall is that a flat stone to the right of the cottage was used by pre-historic man as a place of sacrifice (MR p348). There is a poem about Rockhall in Lays and Legends of the Moorlands (HOLF p17). (NSFCT 1942 p62) (PS p150p) (VB p209). Surrounding the cottage on the W side is a walled enclosure creating a 'garden' area. By 1999 this 'garden' had, as well as a particularly huge boulder erratic, a ha-ha, and a sundial, and in the SW corner of the enclosure was a small stone roofed building.

Rockhouse Red-brick house with a Tuscan porch which stands back from New Road, Penkridge, in a large garden. Built in the late C18, probably by a member of the Croydon family (VCH vol 5 p108).

Rockmount House in Dark Lane, E of the Old Grammar School House, Kinver. Built in or shortly before 1624. It was known as the Stone House by 1672 and as Rockmount by the 1860s. Nancy Price (alias Mrs Maude) (d1970), stage and film actress and novelist, was born here in 1880 (VCH vol 20 pp121,126) and lived here until the age of 15 (RKE pp19,32,35-37) (KRC pp26,27) (BCM spring 1997 p15) (VFC p108). In her autobiography 'Into an Hour Glass' she tells of the ghost of a former vicar of Kinver, Rev John Newley, that haunts the house (KEOP p62p of the house).

Rocks Hill Former 'fine' house near to the present Church Hall, which stood in Mill Street, Brierley Hill. In 1822 it was occupied by James Pagett and owned by Benjamin Brettell (WFK pp12,15).

Rock Tavern An inn which stood approximately by Stourton Hall, and situated by, or enveloped, some caves which were used for storage space (and the building backed onto a rock?). For a long time its exact location was not known (KRH pp25,29 see map), although it has now been determined (TB Feb 1990 p12p of the possible location, which is now just a bare rock). It was the inspiration for the inn in Baring-Gould's novel (KRH p25). It was described by the criminal, John Poulter, hung in 1755, as the 'greatest rendezvous in England for thieves,' when Edward and Margaret Lyne were the licensees, as it stood near the boundaries of three counties facilitating easy escape out of any county's jurisdiction (OP pp4-5).

Rock Well A well on W side of Cheadle Road, Alton (DoE II).

Rodbaston Fragmented small hamlet near marshy ground at some distance to the E of the Penk 1.5m S of Penkridge, mainly comprising what is now Rodbaston Farm Institute. In Penkridge ancient parish. The name has appeared as Redbaldestone (DB), a manor of Richard the Forester, whose seat may have been Rodbaston Castle (see), Rembaldeston (1195-96), Redbaldeston (1198), Rodbaston (1221), Rodebaston (1300) (SPNO). It means 'Redbald's town or tun' (PVH p46) (SPN p93) (SSE 1996 p17), or 'Rodbeald's town' (DUIGNAN). The possible medieval village, since deserted, at Rodbaston in the later C11, may have been at approximately SJ 922109, to the S of Rodbaston Hall where earthworks have been mistaken for a moated site (SSAHST 1970 p35. 1982-3 p59). John of Gaunt granted to John Eggington a lease capsulated within this rhyme

> I John o' Gaunt do give and do grant
> To thee John Eggington right heir of Rodbaston,
> So long as the water flows under Bull Bridge.

(S&W p567) (HOP p13) (SCSF p167).

Rodbaston Castle 0.5m N of Rodbaston, on the site of the moat, at SJ 921124 (SSAHST 1982-3 p46). Wilkes thinks here was a fortified homestead of Richard the Forester (or Richard Chenven - VCH vol 2 p339), holder of Rodbaston in DB (SOP p38), and residence of his descendants (the de Crocs, the de Brocs, and the de Loges - DUIGNAN), hereditary chief foresters of Cannock Forest. One is recorded having a castle in this area, in 1154. In 1199 it is mentioned as a manor house, and as a castle again in 1215 (VCH vol 5 p121). Has also appeared as Rodbaston Manor House and The Roundabout. John de Saundersted, a later lord of Rodbaston, c1322-1353, is said to have built a crenellated house during his lordship (SOS p178) (NSJFS 1966 p44) (CAMS p25). This may have been on this site or on the site of Rodbaston Old Hall (see) 500 yards to the SE.

Rodbaston Hall 1.5m S of Rodbaston, about 500 yards S of Rodbaston Old Hall. A house existed here by 1841, but the hall may date from some years later (VCH vol 5 p122). It was occupied in 1851 by C Holland (W p22) and later in the C19 by the Wards (mems in Gailey church). The Staffs College of Agriculture has its origins in an agricultural training depot opened by the War Agricultural Committee in 1919 at Dunston, S of Stafford, at their former tractor depot. Later that year Staffs county council bought Rodbaston Hall, and the neighbouring houses of Hall Farm, and the Grange, and the depot moved there. In 1921 it became known as Rodbaston Farm Institute, which became the Staffs College of Agriculture in 1967. In 1994 it became independent of the county council and was renamed Rodbaston College (1972 OS map 1:25,000 called Staffordshire Farm Institute) (PVH pp46,48il) (HOS 1998 p94).

Rodbaston Old Hall Formerly lay on or near the site of Rodbaston Stables at SJ 925120 (VCH vol 5 p121). John de Saundersted, a lord of Rodbaston (c1322-1353), is said by some - SOS p178; NSJFS 1966 p44; CAMS p25, but not by VCH vol 5 p121 - to have built a crenellated house during his lordship. This may have been on this site or on the site of Rodbaston Castle (see) 500 yards to the NW. The Eginton family were tenants in Rodbaston from the 1380s until c1768 and probably they inhabited the manor house which was possibly at first at Rodbaston Castle and later here; they are said to have been here by 1690. The house, which had a private chapel, had disappeared by 1959 (VCH vol 5 p121). Has also appeared as Rodbaston Manor House. (NHS p449; is possibly referring to it) (SD p59).

Roddige Minute hamlet on low ground at some distance from the Tame 0.75m E of Fradley, 1m S of Alrewas. Near Roddige was found a stone axe of the Neolithic or Bronze Age (NSJFS 1964 p14).

Rodney Hall Now Moorfields, Cotes Heath. A hostel built in c1938 for workers, relocated from Woolwich Arsenal, at the new Royal Ordnance Factory at Swynnerton. The hall was never completed and was therefore never used by them; instead they resided to live in the Potteries. Named after Admiral Rodney.

Rodney's Rest A wall which was at Gornal (whether Upper Gornal or Lower Gornal?). Reputedly this wall was frequented by loungers of the community

who liked to lean over it and gawk at ladies going passed. They were frequently moved on by the police, and tar was even spread over the top surface to prevent them leaning on the wall. Nothing seemed to work until someone wrote 'Rodney's Rest' in white paint over the wall. In time it was demolished to make way for a shopping precinct. In the West Bromwich Building Society office in Abbey Road, Gornal Wood, is a ceramic mural depicting the words 'Rodney's Rest' (BCM Jan 1978 pp17-18).

Roebuck House at the N end of Roebuck Lane, West Bromwich ancient parish. Existed in 1684 and was demolished in c1855 (WB p157) (VCH vol 17 p10). Probably gave its name to Roebuck Lane.

Roggin Row Former name for an area or row of cottages which stood in the later C19 on the W side of Audley Road at SJ 822503 (OS maps 1:2500) (SVB p55).

Rolfe Street Area of Smethwick N of the old village centre and name for the Smethwick east railway station, as opposed to the station at West Smethwick. Rolfe Street is said to have been a hamlet in the 1830s (BCM Dec 1998 p32). On 1834 OS map the area, unnamed, appears built up and not connected to Smethwick. Rolfe Street railway station moved to its present position in Stoney Lane in 1979. The old station is haunted by the ghost of Thomas Chandler, captain of Smethwick Fire Brigade, who committed suicide by taking gas in July 1923. A plaque to Chandler's memory, erected in the old station, has been re-erected in the new station. The plaque has mysterious properties initiating unexplainable phenomena (TB May 1993 p31p). For the Theatre Royal, Rolfe Street, see Smethwick. The little-known Rolfe motor cycle, made between 1911 and 1914, took its name from the street, but was originally made in nearby Bridge Street (PVBC p36).

Rolleston Ancient parish and former township. The large village of Rolleston on Alder Brook on the S side of the Dove Valley is 20m ENE of Stafford. There was an Anglo-Saxon **church** at Rolleston (UTR p217). The present parish church, St Mary the Virgin, on the S side of Church Road near its junction with Burnside, dates from c1100 (UTR p217). In 1910 Sir Oswald Moseley requested all the seats in St Mary's aisle in the church for his family. The parishioners resented this and removed the hassocks and placed bent pins on the baronet's pew, but the Consistory Court awarded the Moseleys 38 seats (VB p102). There is a tradition of a secret passage leading from the church to the Spread Eagle Inn (local info). The parish **wake** was on the first Sunday after new Christmas day in the C19 (W p575). **Name**. The Rothulfeston which appears in a charter of 942 has been identified with Rolleston (DUIGNAN) (SSE 1991 pp7,8,17. 1996 p11) (BTIH pp13-14). Rolleston has been identified with the Rolfestun mentioned in the will of Wulfric Spot (c1002), founder of Burton Abbey; and if so it was acquired by the monks of Burton abbey from King Æthelred in 1008 (SHC 1916 p25); in which year a charter was made of its bounds in which it appears as Rolvestun (SHC 1916 p121) (SL p62). Later forms are: Rolvestune, a manor, in DB, Rodulfeston (SPN p26), and Rolleston-on-Dove. The name means 'Hrothwulf's town, tun' (DUIGNAN) (UTR p165) (LGS p204) (SSE 1996 p17), or 'Hroald's farmstead' (SPN p26). The free **grammar school** founded in 1520 by Robert Sherbourne, bishop of Chichester, is the oldest such foundation in the country. The school room by the church, dated 1640, housed it (SVB p142). The original endowment letter, written in black letter, is kept in a wooden box in the school room (SMC p172). The **almshouses**, a row of six cottages beside Alder Brook, were built in 1712 as part of a charitable bequest to the village by William Rolleston (SVB p142), there is a hand pump in front of them (UTR p206). Rolleston **railway** station opened in 1894 and closed to passengers on Jan 1 1949 (ABTOP p131). **Loss and gain**. A small part of the parish (without population) was considered to be in Derbys in and before the C19. In 1903 it was transferred to Marston-on-Dove parish, Derbys (GLAUE p420). For many years the wheel cross of C10 origin in the churchyard was part of the floor of Tatenhill church porch. It was moved to Rolleston by Sir Oswald Mosley, and was placed in its present position in 1897 (info KL Neal).

Rolleston Hall Rolleston. An early hall was of Tudor origin and the seat of the Rolleston family, lords of Rolleston (SVB p142). In c1615 Sir Edward Mosley (d1638), son of Sir Nicholas Mosley (Lord Mayor of London d1612) bought the hall from the Rollestons (LGS p204). In the Hearth Tax returns of 1665 the hall is described as demolished; it may then only have been partly demolished or reduced in status, for it was then occupied by a farmer named Bond (UTR p201). Rolleston Hall appears to have passed to the Ancoats branch of the Mosley family in the later C17 or earlier C18 (UTR pp196-197). Sir Oswald Mosley of the Ancoats branch, and described as of Rolleston, was created a baronet in 1720. On his death in 1751 he was succeeded by Sir Oswald Mosley, 2nd Bt. He died unmarried and was succeeded by his brother Sir Rev John Mosley, 3rd Bt. He died unmarried and the estates passed to his cousin Sir John Parker Mosley, who was created a baronet in 1781. His son Oswald

Mosley (d1789) is said to have had Rolleston settled upon him and he had the hall modernised and altered by Thomas Gardner of Uttoxeter; thereafter Rolleston was the chief Mosley seat. Sir John Mosley died in 1798 and was succeeded by his grandson, Sir Oswald (1785-1871), 2nd Bt (new creation), founder in 1842 of BTNHAS (see under Burton upon Trent), and author of HCT and NHT. His successor was his son Sir Tonman (1813-1890), 3rd Bt, who in turn was succeeded by his son Sir Oswald (1848-1915), 4th Bt. The well-known profile of the 4th Bt and his love for all things English resulted in him being used as the model for the Punch cartoon of 'John Bull.' He was a friend of Edward VII, who he met at agricultural shows. The 4th Bt allowed Rev Tyrwhitt, Canon of Windsor, who the King favoured, to succeed to the Rolleston living. But during his time as Rolleston vicar Tyrwhitt sort to diminish the Mosley's influence in practices to do with the church. The 4th Bt threatened to dismiss him. Resulting court cases lasted years but were finally won by Tyrwhitt. The 4th Bt was succeeded by his son Sir Oswald (1873-1928), 5th Bt. He had been banished from the hall by his father for debauched behaviour, subsequently taking up residence in Tutbury and becoming known as the 'Tutbury Tup.' He was succeeded by his son Sir Oswald Ernald Mosley (1896-1980), 6th Bt. He was MP for Smethwick 1926-1931 and formed the New Party in 1931; his first wife, Cynthia (d1933), was a MP for Stoke-on-Trent. His second wife, Diana, was residing at Wootton Lodge (see) in 1939 (Burke's Peerage 1967) (DNB 1971-1980) (LTD pp205-206,207). The hall was damaged by fire in 1871 and rebuilt in 1872-3 (UTR pp201-202) (BOE p227; in 1871) (MR p266; in 1870). It was sold in the late 1920s after the succession of the 6th Bt and then demolished in 1928 (LGS 4th ed. (1930) p204) (UTR pp201-202) (SGS p141) (SVB pp142-143) (ABTOP p124) (ESNF p35p) (LTD p203). Bits of the facade were incorporated into houses built on Rolleston Road, two miles from the village centre (SVB pp142-143). (W p575). Parts of Horninglow Cross were possibly removed to a rockery at Rolleston Hall by Sir Oswald Mosley (UTR p167).

Rolleston-on-Dove Is either a different way of referring to Rolleston, or, as marked on OS map 1:25,000, is a recent extension to the village situated about 0.75m to the E. Nothing existed here in 1834 (1834 OS map).

Rolleston Park Former medieval deer park enclosed out of forest, 1.5m WSW of Rolleston, 0.5m E of Tutbury Castle, in Tutbury parish. The park was created by Robert de Ferrers, 1st Earl of Derby, d1139 (UTR p36), and was certainly in existence by 1285 (VCH vol 2 p350) (NSJFS 1962 p76). Contained in compass 1.25m. It was sold by the Crown in 1628 (ANS p92) or 1629 (EDP p175) and purchased by Sir Thomas Leigh and others in trust for Sir William Powell. From this time on the park was farmed by a manager or lessee. The park was the possession of the Moseley family in 1806 (ANS pp92,134). A farmhouse known as Rolleston Park was in existence by the late C18 (SHOS vol 1 p61). This or a later building was sold in 1919 with the break up and sale of the Rolleston Hall estate (ANS p147).

Roman Well A well, believed to be of Roman origin, on N side of Aqualate Mere, to the E is Anc's Hill (see) (VCH vol 4 p105). It seems to have been bored out of the solid rock, its interior is 19 inches in diameter (NSFCT 1928 p134). (SLM spring 1956 pp27,28).

Romblelowes House 1.5m NE of Wolverhampton (SHOS vol 2 p170) appears on 1834 OS map but is now lost. Fallings Park Industrial Estate occupies the site.

Rome Hall On Knightley Common where the Lesser Thrumwort is found (SHOS vol 1 part 1 p99). Presumably this is Knightley near Ellenhall.

Romer In Sandon parish (W p404). Romer Farm is 0.25m N of Burston. The name is from probably - 'ro,' strong and 'mir,' a hill (NSFCT 1908 p146; it is, after all, on a hillside above the Trent).

'Romulus' Burial mound NNE of Madeley Old Manor at SJ 77504287 is a mound 38 paces in diameter and 10 or 12 feet high. Had six mature sycamore trees rooted into the top in 1983 and has been partly excavated by Keele Summer School (NSFCT vol 34 p41. 1983 pp10-11) (NSJFS 1965 p43).

Rookery, The Hamlet in the shadow of Mow Cop hill 1.25m NE of Kidsgrove. In Wolstanton ancient parish. There is a mission church, St Saviour, at The Rookery (LDD). Has a number of wells. There is one in the field behind No. 20 High Street, dated 1850; another in front of No. 3 High Street, dated 1750; and in front of No. 7 High Street (all these wells are mentioned in WMC).

Rookery, The Small hamlet near Graisley, Wolverhampton (W p95). Probably area around Rookery Lane off Penn Road and Goldthorn Hill. Rookery Lane is otherwise known as Cut-throat Lane, since a murder was committed there.

Rookery, The Pensnett. In the late C19 the Rookery was occupied by George Glaze, a partner in an iron foundry at Corbyn's Hall. Later occupied by David Bryce JP, a coke and breeze merchant, who was succeeded here by his daugh-

ter and her husband (SNSV vol 1 p286).

Rookery, The C18 house 0.25m S of Yoxall (BOE p331) (MR p399).

Rookery Farm Rookery Lane, Aldridge. House in existence in the C17 and still stood in the C19 (MOA p133) (SNAR pp43p,44).

Rookery Green Former area of Handsworth (HPPE p37), near to Rookery House?

Rookery House Stood at the junction of Holyhead Road and Rookery Road, Handsworth. Built by 1794 but not standing by 1862 (MNB pp41,45,47).

Rook Hall The name is preserved in Rook Hall Farm 0.5m SE of Butterton (Newcastle-under-Lyme).

Roost Hill House and hill 1m SSW of Bradnop. Egg Well is on the N side.

Rose Bank Farm Probably stood in the area of Rose Bank Street, SW of Ball Haye. Formerly in Tittesworth township in Leek ancient parish. The farm was in existence by the earlier C18 (VCH vol 7 p233).

Rosebank House Two-storey brick house in Rose Bank Street, on the E side of Leek. Built in 1837 to the designs of an acclaimed local architect, William Sugden. It was at sometime occupied by a Leek silk manufacturer, and in 1961 was converted to offices. In c1985 it became a private house. In early 1999 the last occupant left and in Nov 1999 the house, by then a listed building, was moved in one piece on hydraulic jacks along greased tracks to a new site 30 metres away so that a new Co-op supermarket could be erected on the original site of the house (Daily Mail Nov 17 1999 p43) (ES Nov 18 1999 p3pcs).

Roseford Place on the old road between Wolverhampton and Penkridge. Perhaps between Somerford and Penkridge (SHC 1934 p19). There is a Roseford Farm over 1.25m N of Acton Trussell on the E side of the Penk (1834 OS map).

Rosehill House on N side of Town End, 0.25m WSW of Cheadle. In 1814 John Blagg bought a converted farm cottage in Cheadle, then called Primrose Hill. He extended it and renamed it Rose Hill. The Blaggs appear to have been succeeded by the Masefield family, who resided here until 1946 (COPP2 p122p). It was the residence of John Richard Beech Masefield (1850-1932), father of Charles JB Masefield (1882-1917), author of LGS, and uncle of John Masefield (1878-1967), Poet Laureate (NSFCT 1931 pp144-148p) (STM July 1971 p25).

Rose Hill An industrial area of S Willenhall (BCM April 1987 pp55-57). The name is from the firm of Rose & Hill which owned collieries in this district about the mid C19. Hincks frequently refers to them in his account book (HOWI p188). The area was formerly called Mobb's Bank (SNW p58).

Rose Hill Name which was applied to the slope to the E of Wednesbury church until the end of the C19, according to Hackwood (WAM p8). The name is from probably a corruption of Rhos Hill, 'rhos' signifying 'moorland' and is a cognate word with 'rush' (WAM p8).

Rose Hill House Stood near the old Toll Gate, at the junction of Soho Road and Villa Road, Handsworth. It was the residence of William Creighton, a scientist employed at the Soho Manufactory. To pursue his astronomy he had a small observatory erected on the roof. The house was demolished to make way for the church at the top of Villa Road (HPPE p101).

Rosemary Hill The name appears on the N side of Keele Road, W of Newcastle-under-Lyme (maps of Greenwood and Teesdale) and as a farm on S side of Keele Road on 1834 OS map. Rosemary Hill Colliery, Silverdale, was formerly owned by the tile manufacturer, John Nash Peake (1837-1905), who was sharply criticised by George Smith author of 'The Cry of the Children from the Brickyards of England' (1871) (POTP p169).

Roseville Suburb on ground rising to the watershed at Sedgley 0.75m SW of Coseley. Formerly in Sedgley ancient parish. The name may be from Roseville House, which stood by 1861 on the S side of Avenue Road at the junction with Bayer Street. By 1901 there was a hamlet called Roseville centred on Jevon, Ebeneezer and Ward Streets (1861 census) (OS map 1901 sheet 67.07. 1904 sheet 67.08). Roseville now (1995) covers the area which was the former hamlet of West Coseley (Birmingham A-Z 1995). There was a windmill 100 yards N of the Providence Baptist Chapel at SO 936936. It is shown on maps of the early and mid C19 but not by 1885 (WBJ p19).

Ross Area of W Blackheath about Ross road, Rowley Regis. Appears as a separate hamlet on 1947 OS map 1:25,000 (sheet 32/98) at SO 967868. (BCWJ p73).

Rough Close Residential district in hilly country at the tail end of the Potteries, 2.75m SSE of Longton. Formerly partly in Kibblestone quarter in Stone ancient parish and partly in Barlaston ancient parish (W pp364,411). There was a farm here by the late C17 and a tiny hamlet by the 1720s (BAH p31). Appears as a hamlet on 1834 OS map. John Daniels, a farm labourer, shot his brother, William, dead in a fit of passion at Dale House Farm, Leaden Dale Road, on Feb 27 1886. Daniels was found guilty of manslaughter and sentenced to 20 years imprisonment (DMF pp50-61). The land to the N of Common Lane has always been in Blurton township in Trentham ancient parish, and the old mission church, St Matthew, on the corner of Lightwood Road and Common Lane, built in the 1890s, was in Blurton parish. The old church was abandoned because of mining subsidence in the 1950s and rebuilt slightly to the E in 1961 (info Rev Pawson) (LDD).

Roughcote Fragmented minute hamlet on a promontory above a bend in the Upper Blithe 1.25m NNW of Caverswall. In Caverswall ancient parish. Here was a residence of the Cheddleton Wolfes (NSFCT 1923 p34). There is a possible burial mound here (WJ p28). At Roughcote Farm at SJ 944444 is a 15 feet high burial mound. Described as in perfect condition in 1983. Keele University is alleged to possess an aerial photograph of the site. It is said to have historical associations with the Cromwellian period (NSFCT 1983 p12).

Rough Hay Former woodland and waste on the edge of Needwood Forest belonging to Burton Abbey (ANS pp12-13), later a minute hamlet 1m N of Tatenhill now made large by modern housing lining the roads to Burton. Formerly partly in Anslow township in Rolleston ancient parish and partly in Branston township in Burton ancient parish; the latter was removed to Anslow parish in 1984 (ANS p9). Has appeared as Rohay (1305), Rugh Hey (1518) and Rowhey (1707) (ANS p102). It is likely that some of the abbey tenants in Wetmore held certain rights of common at Rough Hay (ANS pp12-13).

Rough Hay NW area of Darlaston (Offlow hundred). Former barren heath which may have been alluded to in a document of c1255 (Darlaston Community History Project. 1984. p2. Copy in Willenhall library). In the C18 and C19 Rough Hay was extensively mined for coal and was left 'waste land of clay, pit mounds and waterlogged holes' until the late 1920s when the council began to develop a housing estate here (SNDB p84). Rough Hay Ironworks were in operation in the mid C19 (W p598). Rough Hay House is of the late C19 (SNDB p84p). There is a mission church, St Christopher, at Rough Hay (LDD).

Rough Hill NE of Springfield, Rowley Regis (OS map 1:25,000).

Rough Hills Area N of Ettingshall and Parkfield in undulating country by the Birmingham Canal Old Cut Old Main Line, over 1.5m SE of Wolverhampton, preserved in Rough Hills Road, Ettingshall. Formerly in Bilston chapelry in Wolverhampton ancient parish. 'The Thorn where the three boundaries meet' mentioned in Lady Wulfrun's charter of 994 has been identified with Rough Hills (WFW p29). In the C19 Samuel Fereday had mines at Rough Hills (BCM Oct 1990 p62). Rough Hills colliery, in existence in the mid C19, lay near Goldthorn Hill village in Wolverhampton township (W p95). Rough Hills became a separate ecclesiastical parish in 1938, when the church, St Martin, Dixon Street, was built. The parish name had become 'Wolverhampton St Martin' by 1991 (GLAUE p420) (LDD).

Rough Park House 0.75m ENE of Hamstall Ridware. In Hamstall Ridware parish. Rev Gisborne found the very rare Lily of the Valley plant or Convallaria Majalis in Rough Park (SHOS vol 1 part 1 p102. vol 1 p66).

Rough Stockings 0.5m NNE of Streethay. The name is recorded in 1632. The name indicates an area cleared by trees (VCH vol 14 p275). A small farmhouse, which was derelict in 1986, was built here probably in the mid C18 (VCH vol 14 p275).

Roughstone Hole 1.75m N of Ipstones. On E side and near the head of Combes Valley (TOI p11). Has also appeared as Rough-Stone-Hole House.

Rough Wood Wood in existence in the later C19 (OS map 6 inch). Situated in a bend in the Wyrley and Essington Canal SW of Bloxwich. Formerly in Bentley township in Wolverhampton ancient parish. Is probably a remnant part of Bentley Hay. By the later C20 the area was a Country Park.

Roundabout, The A circular entrenchment on Whitmore Common known locally as 'The Roundabout.' Is about 25 yards in diameter (NSFCT 1934 p81). Excavated in 1935 (NSFCT 1935 pp64-65).

Roundabout, The Former ancient free-standing building which stood at High Green, Wolverhampton, until being demolished in 1885? (HOWM p79).

Roundabout House Built on an island site in the C17 near SE side of Cannock churchyard. Close by stood or stands Cromwell House (CCF pp123-124).

Roundabouts, The Area said to apply to the houses around the junction of the Old Church Road and Harborne Park Road, Harborne. The name occurs in 1834 (STELE June 26 1953).

Roundabout Tumulus, The 0.25m NE of Norbury. On the top, at SJ 78852384, is a Bronze Age burial mound with a 'dimple' in the top, which is perhaps the work of a C19 archaeologist (SPJD pp8p,9) (WSS p95). It is 25 paces in diameter and four feet high (NSJFS 1965 p44) a listed monument. Roundabout is a common field name (NSFCT 1910 p164).

Round Barrow Near Madeley Farm, Madeley. Whether at SJ 775428 ?

Round Hill Earthwork 400 feet high by 370 feet near Great Barr (OSST 1949-50 p18) is of pre-Norman Conquest origin (SHC 1916 p207). It is the Round Hill near Loaches Bank on the W side of the Chester Road (VCH vol 1 p372)

(History of Birmingham. W Hutton. 1835. p476). According to Hutton it was surrounded by a ditch, but there was no trace of this in 1860 when the mound was described as 210 feet in diameter and 10 feet high (History of the Forest and Chase of Sutton Coldfield. AA Bracken. 1860. p3). The size of the mound suggests that it is a natural feature, possibly a glacial drift deposit, rather than a burial mound, but the ditch, if one ever existed, would suggest that it was not of natural origin (SSAHST 1990-91 p90).

Round Hill A hill. 0.5m SSE of Hoar Cross.

Round Hill, The Small round hill topped with an earthwork 0.5m ENE of Kingsley.

Round Hill House 1m S of Flash, in Quarnford parish (1834 OS map) (Dower's map) (UHAW p51 il).

Round Hill Hill 1m SE of Stourton. Round Hill Farm existed by 1851 (VCH vol 20 p125).

Round Hollies Madeley. A hill? Near top of here was found a fine round large flint scraper in the late C19 which went to the Potteries Museum (NSFCT 1932 p125).

Round House Former railway engine shed at Whieldon's Grove, Fenton. Has been described as the 'monster engine stable.' It was said when first built in 1848 to be the largest 'stable' in the country (SA April 22 1848) (W) (POP p100). It was still standing in the 1950s and was circular in form and had a diameter of 200 feet within the walls. Within the building was another circle 87 feet in diameter, divided into 24 archways, corresponding with compartments for that number of engines (VCH vol 8 p209).

Round House Stood in the area of the present Queen's Road, near the entrance to Victoria Park, Tipton. It was the seat of a branch of the Parkes family of Willingsworth Hall. The Round House is referred to in 1714 as 'ye round house' and in many deeds and conveyances (HOTIP pp93, 187).

Roundilow Burial mound 0.75m WNW of Meaford, on N side of A51 at SJ 873358. Possibly the same as Round Low (see). Was gradually being ploughed away by 1983 (NSFCT 1983 p11).

Round Knoll Burial mound near Ribden, at SK 070472 (HAF p392). Carrington excavated in 1849. It has been damaged by a limekiln (TYD p157) (NSJFS 1965 p35).

Round Knowl Hansley Cross, near Alton. A field, the highest point of which was considered by VJ Burton in 1957 a possible burial mound of Bronze Age origin. Gunstone in 1961 thought it no more than a natural rocky mound. Lately (1996) it has been recorded as a possible Bronze Age bowl barrow by the Staffs Sites and Monuments Record. It has never been excavated (HAF p30).

Round Low Possible burial mound. Possibly the same as Roundilow (see). Approximately 0.5m W of Bury Bank, Stone (SIS p2 see map). Damaged by the tenant clearing ground for ploughing. Evidence of burning was discovered (Mss Hist of Tittensor. f. 270b in WSL) (NSFCT vol 41 p142) (NSJFS 1965 p48). The mound consisted of various kinds of stones collected from the neighbourhood and promiscuously thrown together (The Shrops & N Wales Natural History & Antiquarian Society 1835-37) (NSFCT 1926 p142).

Round Low Burial mound at SK 08475284, 1m S of Grindon. It was excavated by Carrington in 1848 and is 24 paces in diameter and three feet high. Several pottery fragments were found but no burial (TYD pp114-115) (NSJFS 1965 p38). Is a listed monument.

Round Oak Area 0.5m NNE of Brierley Hill. Formerly in Kingswinford ancient parish. A glasshouse was here (VCH vol 2 p226). There were two Methodist chapels erected near to the Round Oak (SVS p142). Round Oak Steelworks, built by William 11th Baron of Dudley, was demolished in the early 1980s and the site used for the Merry Hill Shopping Centre. It was known locally as the Earls' Works and one of the flagships of his mineral empire before becoming part of British Steel (MR p54). George Lovatt, the 'Fat Man' of Brierley Hill, but later resident at Round Oak, was born at Saltney, near Chester, on Oct 26 1869 and came to work for Thomas Sitch, chainmakers of Cradley Heath, in 1889 (BCM April 1985 pp30-35 p). Later he appears to have been a hay and straw dealer in the Brierley Hill area; eventually he had to take orders for this business from a seat in the upstairs window over the shop, since he could hardly move because of his enormous size (TB Oct 1993 p5). He died at his brother's house in Dudley Road (formerly the Unicorn Inn) on March 12 1933. His weight at death has been put at 42 stones (BCM April 1985 pp30-35) or 60 stones (TB Oct 1993 p5). At his funeral attended by hundreds of local people, on March 16 1933, he was described by the rector of Brierley Hill, Rev JH Herbert, as 'an unprecedented spectacle.' His coffin was seven feet four inches long and three feet six inches wide and two feet two inches deep. He was buried in the churchyard at St Michael's, Brierley Hill (TB July/ Aug 1972 p5. June 1980 p1p. Jan 1981 p26p of his funeral. Oct 1993 p5. Aug 26 1999 p18. Sept 16 1999 pp18-19) (BCM April 1985 pp30-

35) (John Sparry on BBC Radio 4 April 14 1994 9.45am) (MMBCC pp46p-53p of his coffin template).

Round Rock Remarkable bold mass of red sandstone in the woods to the E of Biddulph Grange (BGFB p30).

Rounds, The The name The Rounds appears in 1655 and was probably near what is now Rounds Road, Coseley (HC p48). Rounds Hill and Colliery appear in this area on a map of 1904 (OS map 1904 sheet 67.08).

Round Well The name is preserved in Roundwell Street, Tunstall (OTP p2). Tunstall had no piped water until 1848 (POP p176) (SHST p218).

Rousend Marked on maps of Plot and Bowen in the approximate position of the tithe barn NNW of Goosemoor Green, at SK 062124.

Rousseau's Cave An arched grotto originally at Wootton Hall. It was still at Wootton in 1924 (NSFCT 1924 p201). In it the French philosopher Rousseau is reputed to have written 'Confessions' when he was staying at Wootton Hall between 1766-7. At Wootton it was situated beneath a terrace (LGS p133) (AT p32). It has been removed to Consall New Hall (KES p243) (SLM Feb 1951 p13p).

Rouster Farm 0.75m E of Swythamley. The Irish word 'rausen' means fine or magnificent and 'ster', Norse 'saefer,' a chalet, or Summer farm (NSFCT 1916 p82).

Roway Near Brades Village, preserved in Roway Lane (W p686). In West Bromwich ancient parish. Is an ancient name for the Tame in the Greets Green area (TB May 1995 p27).

Roway Branch of the Birmingham Canal New Cut New Main Line. Spurred off the Island Line N of Roway Lane and ran to Union Furnaces. Or called Union Branch (VCH vol 17 p13). Opened in c1810. Closure sanctioned in 1954 (HCMS No. 2).

Rowden Lanes Former hamlet where the old road to Essington crossed the present Cannock Road, 1.5m W of Essington, in Bushbury ancient parish (BUOP p6). Has also appeared as Rowdon (1306), Roudoun (1314), Rowdons (1549) (SPNO p51), Rouden Lanes (Plot's map) (Yates' map), Rowdon Lanes (1834 OS map). The name means 'the rough hill' (SPNO p51).

Rowe, The Hamlet on the E side of Meece Valley S of Stableford Bridge, Chapel Chorlton. In Swynnerton ancient parish. All the houses are on the E side of A51. Has also appeared as The Row.

Row Hill Hill 1.25m NE of Draycott-in-the-Clay. A tiny seam of gypsum outcrop has been found here (VCH vol 2 pp197,198).

Rowley Former estate 1m SSW of Stafford. At Rowley Bank at SJ 918216 was found a perforated pebble of the Neolithic or Bronze Age which went to Manchester Museum (NSJFS 1964 p34). Rowley formed a separate vill by at least 1452. Has appeared as Rowelowe (1300), Rowleye (1335), Roweley (1401) (SPNO p76), Rowlowe (C16) (VCH vol 5 pp84,90).

Rowley Former estate and fragmented tiny hamlet on fairly level ground at some distance from the Blithe. It comprises the farms - Rowley Farms and Lower Rowley - 1.5m NE of Hamstall Ridware. In Hamstall Ridware ancient parish. Has appeared as Rouueleia (DB), Roweleye (1291) (SSE 1996 p17) and mentioned by Plot in the later C17 (NHS p205). Gives name to Rowley Park (see). For the name Oakden gives 'rough woodland clearing' (SSE 1996 p17).

Rowley A ward by 1999 of Sandwell metropolitan borough. Presumably embraces the Rowley Regis area.

Rowley Gate House 1m N of Longsdon. Formerly in Longsdon township in Leek ancient parish. The house probably stands on or near land called 'Throwleyate' in 1515. The present later C17 house has a porch with a doorhead bearing the name Anne Hulme and date 1686, now illegible (VCH vol 7 p203).

Rowley Hall Hall at the S end of Rowley Avenue 1m SSW of Stafford. In Castle Church parish. There was a hall at Rowley by the late C15. The Rowley estate was owned by the Stanfords or Standfords or Staunfords from then to the early C17. Later the Berringtons owned it and a Berrington was living at the hall in 1679 or 1680 (VCH vol 5 p90). The present hall was built by William Keen c1812 (Stafford Past: An Illustrated History. Roy Lewis. 1997 p70p of in 1868) or in c1817 (BOE p250). George Keen was the occupant in 1851 (W p22) (VCH vol 5 p90). In the 1860s and 1870s it was occupied by the Hand family. Between 1882 and 1892 Capt Hon George Augustus Anson lived at the hall. He was followed by Benjamin Armitage JP (SAC p106p,107). The Home Office reformatory for girls, formerly the County Industrial Home in Sandon Road, moved to Rowley Hall in c1930. Rowley Hall was being used as a Home Office remand home for girls in 1957 (VCH vol 5 p90. vol 6 pp195,205). It has been an old peoples home (MR p294) and now (1996) a private hospital. The villas of Rowley Park (see) at Stafford were built in the part of the grounds W of Wolverhampton road after it was sold off before 1868 (VCH vol 5 p84. vol 6 p195).

Rowley Hall Formerly situated close to St Giles church, Rowley Regis (TB Oct 1995 p27il of c1883); there is a road called Rowley Hall Avenue off Church Road off Hawes Lane (BCWJ p66). There was a hall probably on this site in Saxon times (HORV p7). The hall mentioned in the Hearth Tax of the C17 may have been partly of C16 origin (BCWJ p66) or the hall that was rebuilt during the C17 (HORV p9). It is perhaps the hall of Christopher White who sheltered the Gunpowder Plot conspirators, Stephen Littleton and Robert Winter, as they fled from Holbeche House (see) across the Rowley Hills to Hagley (BCWJ p66) (HOWM p63; Mander makes no identification with Rowley Hall). Others say Christopher White was of Bullfield Farm (see) and sheltered the Gunpowder Plotters there. It has been occupied by the Groves, then by marriage, Francis Eld (HORV p9), and was occupied by John Beet from 1825 to 1844. Mary Beet was living at the hall in 1851 (TB Oct 1995 p27il). It was plagued by an outbreak of horse mutilation similar to that occurring in the Great Wyrley area, between 1888-1892 (TB Oct 1974 p19). During the early C19 the old hall was pulled down and a smaller building erected. Brick and stone fragments of the old hall remained until the 1950s (HORV p9). The hall stood close to a basalt quarry (ORR p6p). Rowley Hall was demolished in 1970 (TB Aug 12 1999 p25p. Aug 26 1999 p13).

Rowley Hill House 1m ENE of Stretton (Penkridge). Nearby at SJ 90251180 to E of Rowley Hill is a burial mound 32 paces in diameter and 1.5 feet high. (GM vol 67 part 1. 1797. p111) (NSJFS 1965 p48). Mr Dickenson, who considered it to be a military station, discovered it in 1746 (S&W p382) or in 1796, or it was excavated by a Mr Dickson in 1796 (LSWA p7). Celtic remains are said to have been found during its destruction in the C19 (ABW p9). Some Roman finds were discovered; part of the Roman Station of Pennocrucium (see) (VCH vol 4 pp163,164). The name has appeared as Rowleyfeld (1284-1358), Rowley Field (1606-1608), Rowley Hill Field (1606-1608), and Roley Hill (W p469) (SPNO p179). It means 'the rough glade' (SPNO p179).

Rowley Hills Range of hills about Rowley Regis. The hills were formed by a titanic volcanic eruption more than 130 million years ago (TB April/ May 1973 p16). The range comprise eight hills - Turners, Cawney, Tansley, Coxes Rough, Timmins, Derbys, Oakham and Kate's (TB Jan 1983 p13). The first glacier intrusion into the Midlands in the Ice Age left boulders of volcanic ash and felsite from the Arenig Mountains in North Wales on the top of the Rowley Hills (WJO Nov 1909 p295). The range has also been called the Dorsal Ridge (TB Feb 1998 p11).

Rowley Park Former medieval deer park enclosed out of Needwood Forest. Is mentioned in c1223 (VCH vol 2 p350) and appears in 1253 as Parcus de Rugehel, Rughel and Rughl (BCWJ p21). In existence by 1297 (NSJFS 1962 p76). It belonged to the king and was later granted to Sir Thomas Leigh (EDP p176). The name is from the vill, Rowley, and is preserved in Rowley Farms, 1m NE of Hamstall Ridware.

Rowley Park Suburban district of Stafford at Rowley. 1m SW of Stafford. The suburb is a garden suburb development 'of suburban residences of a superior class' built by Staffordshire Land, Building, and Investment Co Ltd on part of the park of Rowley Hall W of the Wolverhampton road, which the company had bought before 1868. The earliest development, the terrace villas in Lawn Road of c1870 are formal in size and style. Those in Crescent Road are informal (VCH vol 5 p84. vol 6 p195). (MR p294). Pevsner calls the 'High Victorian' terraces in Lawn Road 'atrocious without a doubt, remarkable without a doubt' (BOE p250). The name Rowley Park has been used for some years to embrace an area wider than the original development. Paul Butters (b1908), novelist and playwright, lived most of his life in Rowley Park. His work includes a play 'Search No More' (produced in 1950), a novel 'Price of Admission' (1965) and SSTY (VFC p23).

Rowley Regis (locally like to row, to quarrel). Former manor and chapelry, later a parish comprising an odd amalgam of Black Country mining and nailing hamlets, hills and districts in hilly country.
EARLY. Roman coins found in the area suggest the Romans may have had a station here. In April 1794 a boy, pulling down a stone wall, found an earthen pot of a globular form containing about 1200 silver Roman coins of the C1 AD (SHOS vol 1 General Intro p35. vol 2 p240) (THS p203) (GNHS p69) (W p193) (O p222) (VCH vol 1 p186) (NSJFS 1964 p33). For other Roman finds in the area see Cakemore, Worcs, and Hawes Hill.
1000 to 1700. A possible Saxon well existed to the late C18 where the Municipal Buildings stand (BCWJ p16). The **name** has appeared as Roulea (1169), Roelea (1173), Ruelega (1174), Ruleye (1272) (SPN p99). It means 'the rough lea' (DUIGNAN). Hackwood thinks it is rough lea as opposed to smooth wick (Smethwick) (RS p20). It appears that Rowley manor, held by the de Somerys of Dudley Castle, was divided into two on the death of John de Somery (d1322). That which remained with the barony of Dudley (held by the de Suttons)

came to be known as Rowley Somery. That which was granted to Halesowen Abbey came to be known as Rowley Regis (SHOS vol 2 p239) (BCWJ p31). Regis as an appellation starts to appear from 1330 (Staffs County Handbook c1958 p119). There is no clear reason why it was suffixed Regis. Most have thought that because the manor does not appear in DB it must have been in the king's demesne and consequently received the appellation Regis. Although there is no evidence of it being in the king's demesne later than DB it may have lain in a royal forest, such as Kinver (DUIGNAN) (The English village community' F Seebohm. 1913 ed) (BCWJ pp20-21). There is no truth in the tradition that it received the appellation in recognition of Charles II (called 'Old Rowley') naming his horse Rowley (MR p267) (SPN p99). Rowley Regis **manor**, with a manor house at Brickhouse Farm, included the village of Rowley, Whiteheath, Blackheath and up to Coombs Wood and Hayseech Common (BCWJ pp37,42). The **church**, St Giles and St Michael, stands on a hill 21.25m SSE of Stafford. There has been a church on this site since Saxon times. A church was built sometime between 1199 and 1216. In 1840 this church was taken down and a new church built with a tower added in 1858. The church was deemed unsafe owing to mining subsidence in 1900 and rebuilt, except for the tower, in 1904. On June 18 1913 this church burnt down. The present church was built in 1922-1923 (BCWJ pp21-27). The **chapelry** was in Clent ancient parish (a detached portion of Staffs in Worcs before 1844) in Worcester diocese by at least 1284 (BCWJ p22). Rowley remained in that diocese after becoming a separate ecclesiastical parish in 1848, but was removed to Birmingham diocese in 1905 (VCH vol 3 pp92,96) (GLAUE p420). Rowley Regis held its **wake** on St Giles' day (Sept 1) (SCSF p106). There was an old saying concerning Rowley Regis wakes, before the clocks were subject to summer time:

It's dark at eight at Rowley wake

Rowley wakes were often the scene for brutal bull baiting (BCWJ pp106-107). A **windmill** between Rowley church and Brickhouse Barn could have been used for grinding corn (BCM Jan 1979 p17). For other Rowley Regis windmills see under Hawes Hill Mill, Primrose Hill, Rowley Mill. In or some time prior to the later C17 a **lamb** belonging to Thomas Grove of Rowley Regis was found at the butchers to have another lamb in its belly (NHS p261) (BCWJ p108). In the later C17 Plot noted some **double-eared wheat** had been sown at Rowley Regis and in neighbouring parts of Worcs. It was also called 'Poland' from where it was thought to have originated and grew four or five feet high. Plot could find no descriptions of it elsewhere (NHS pp204-206 tab 14 fig 6). **Persons and visitors. Elizabeth I** is supposed to have passed through Rowley Regis on her way from Halesowen to Dudley in 1557 (BCWJ p134), although the date may have been 1575. In the C16 **Leah Aynsworth** of Rowley is said to have been able to produce an over-abundance of breast milk during the months surrounding a birth (BCWJ pp107-108). Another case of over-productive breasts is recorded at Little Wyrley (see). The Gunpowder Plot conspirators, Stephen Littleton and Robert Winter were fugitives in the Rowley Regis area, and were sheltered by **Christopher White**, who is believed to have been of Rowley Hall (see), or Bullfield Farm (see). After sheltering with White they were led by Thomas Smart and John Holyhead to a barn in Hagley, Worcs. For nine days they hid in a barley mow in the barn where they were fed by a man named Peck or Perkes, before being sheltered by 'Red' Humphrey Littleton at Hagley House or Hall where they were caught on Jan 9 1606 (HOWM pp63,64).

1700 to PRESENT. Rowley was created a **municipal borough** in 1934 (BCWJ p103). Separate civil identity was lost in 1966 when the civil parish was taken into the new county boroughs of Dudley, West Bromwich, and Warley, and the metropolitan borough of Halesowen (GLAUE p420). The **arms** of Rowley Regis borough, granted in 1933, are: Gules, on a pale ermine between two gold lions' faces, a human leg azure cut off at the thigh, and on a chief azure a gold lion passant. The crest is: On a wreath argent and gules a gold castle with three towers, and issuing from the battlements a demi-lion vert with a forked tail, charged on the shoulder with a gold fleur-de-lis and holding between the paws a gold anchor. The supporters are: Dexter, a Smith standing in front of an anvil; and Sinister, a miner holding in his left hand a pick resting on the shoulder, and with a safety-lamp hanging round his neck; all proper. The motto is: 'Loyal and Industrious' (CH p335il). Rowley Regis Central School was by the late 1940s Rowley Regis **Grammar School** (BCWJ p118). The principal **industries** of Rowley Regis have been in coal mining, nail and chain-making, and the quarrying of **Rowley Rag**. 'Rowley Ragstone' and 'Rowley Rag' are local common names for what is basically a blue, hard basalt, Olivine Dolerite, an igneous rock (TB Jan 1983 p13). It is devoid of grit and not at all calcareous (S&W p353). It was mined from, and mainly in,

the C19 and was used for street paving, channelling and for a road-metal (WMLB p113) (MR p267). It occurs in a restricted area between Dudley and Rowley Regis; Palliser says, evidence of its quarrying occurs everywhere around Turner's Hill, creating an almost lunar landscape (SL p192). The Hailstone was made out of it. Wilson Jones believes the first of the four churches at Rowley Regis was built out of it (BCWJ p21). A black basalt similar to Rowley Rag has been found at Pouk Hill, near Bentley, Walsall (SVS pp435 note,441). (SHOS vol 1 part 1 p91. vol 2 p240*) (GM Dec 1812) (GNHS p235) (W p192) (O pp15,224) (LGS p204) (KES p169) (QBSS pp109-113) (VCH vol 2 p203,204) (DOB p273) (SGS p141) (BCM Oct 1979 pp55-56; article from GM Dec 1812 with engraving) (WDY p13). **References to Rowley Regis.** The novel 'Ghost in the Water' by Edward Chitham (1973) is set in and around Rowley Regis. A carol, 'Rowley Regis' was composed by Joseph Parkes, a nailer of Blackheath in the 1860s. An earlier song, concerning Rowley, called 'The Poor Nailmaker' seems to have died out by 1840 (BCWJ p111). This rhyme, possibly from an old ballad, features Rowley Regis

Rowley Rowley - Thunder Noise
Take the girls and leave the boys

(BCWJ p8). **Supernatural**. For the story of a curious infected needle (compass or magnet) see Freebodies. Wilson-Jones noted a beautiful little road or lane on Hawes Hill (see) which he and others claim they had walked along but were unable to relocate on subsequent visits (BCWJ p106). The cure of placing a potato in a pocket and allowing it to remain until it became as hard as a stone to cure rheumatism is said to have originated in Rowley Regis (BCWJ p109). Jane Hingley of Rowley Regis claimed three tiny entities with wings flew into her living room and sat and talked with her before taking off in an UFO. The case became known as the Mince Pie Martian Case (ABDUCTION pp73,74) (MMSE p292). **Natives and visitors. James Woodhouse**, the poet, known as 'the Poetical Shoemaker' or 'the Cobbler Poet,' was born in Rowley Regis in April 18 1735, the son of Joseph Woodhouse; the Woodhouse family are said to have occupied Portway Hall (see). Joseph Woodhouse, who died in 1776, is buried in Rowley Regis parish church churchyard, and the inscription on his grave is by his son, James, the poet (DNB) (BCM Jan 1979 pp44il-48). Woodhouse left school at the age of eight and became a shoemaker. Having married early he added to his means by elementary teaching. At some time Woodhouse, who was six feet six inches tall, was a carrier of goods between Rowley and London. In 1759 he addressed an elegy to William Shenstone of nearby Leasowes in Shrops (detached). Shenstone became much interested in him and sent the elegy to his friends in London, and had it printed in Dodsley's edition of his own poems. A collection was made for Woodhouse and he was able in 1764 to publish a volume entitled 'Poems on Sunday Occasions.' Woodhouse was now celebrated. He was invited to Mrs Thrale's house in London in 1764 to meet Dr Johnson of Lichfield (see). On this occasion or at some other time Johnson told him to 'Give days and nights, Sir, to the study of Addison.' In 1770 Johnson spoke disparagingly of Woodhouse, saying 'He may make an excellent shoemaker, but can never make a good poet. A schoolboy's exercise may be a pretty thing for a schoolboy, but it is no treat for a man.' Soon after 1766 Woodhouse was appointed by Edward Monagu to be his land bailiff on either his Yorkshire and Northumberland estates. He held this post until c1778 when he returned to Rowley. His 'Norbury Park and other poems' appeared in 1803 (DNB). In later life Woodhouse lived in London and was killed in 1820 after being knocked down by a pole of a carriage whilst crossing Orchard and Oxford Street. He is buried in the churchyard of St George's chapel, near Marble Arch, London (BCSG vol 4 pp45,131-132). (Blackwood's Magazine. Nov 1829) (The Life and Works of James Woodhouse. Rev RI Woodhouse. 1896) (O pp239-244) (PSS pp81-85) (TB Aug 1994 p13p) (VFC p145). The highwayman, **'Rowley Jack,'** operated in the Rowley Regis area in the mid C18. He may have formed a brief partnership with the famous highwayman, Dick Turpin, who is said to have stayed at nearby Whiteheath Gate. 'Rowley Jack' and his accomplice, Rebecca Fox, went missing in 1754; their skeletons are said to be those found at Brindleford Hall (see) (TB Sept 1976 p17. March 1978 pp18-19). Admiral Jervis (d1823), born at Meaford Hall (see), came to Rowley Regis to observe the making of nails and chains, both required for his ships (BCWJ p134). Rev **George Barrs** (1771-1840) of Haden Old Hall (see), curate of Rowley Regis and ardent campaigner against bull baiting, caused the funeral bell in the church to be tolled each minute throughout the day, with a muffled peal following at 10 o' clock at night, on the death of Princess Charlotte of Wales in Nov 1817 (BCM Oct 1968 pp55-57) (TB Nov 1978 pp20-21. May 1993 p15). **Charles Darwin** is said to have spent some considerable time at Rowley Regis (BCWJ p134). On Sept 20 1802

Alice Robinson died after a red hot nail rod was thrust into her side whilst at work in a nail shop; although perceived as an industrial accident the coroner returned a verdict of murder (PR) (BCWJ p113). For the murder of **Matilda Stringer**, a maidservant of Rowley Regis, in the 'The Hailstone Murder' case see under Hailstone. **Kaigy Nate**, an old man of Rowley Regis, was sentenced to 19 years imprisonment for the attempted murder of his wife (BCWJ p91). For **Lord Henderson** of Rowley (the title being taken from Rowley Regis) see under Kingswinford.

Rowleys Burial mound 1.5m WSW of Church Mayfield, to ENE of Calwichbank Farm at SK 13814417. Is 44 paces in diameter and eight feet high (NHS p404) (VCH barrow list) (NSJFS 1965 p44).

Rowley Somery Former manor, which was one half of the division of Rowley manor, the other being Rowley Regis. It was originally held by the de Somerys of Dudley Castle (see) (SHOS vol 2 p239). Rowley Somery manor included from below the church on the Dudley side including the demesne, the warrens of Old Hill, Cradley Heath, Tividale and Oakham (BCWJ p42).

Rowley Village Former main settlement of Rowley Regis parish 21.25m SSE of Stafford. It centred along a stretch of road running S from Rowley church; the road is still called Rowley Village. According to Chitham Rowley Village was an attractive and unusual with a unique feeling until the 1950s (HORV p7). With the growth of Blackheath, to the S, as a commercial and residential district from the mid C19 Rowley Village declined. By the late 1950s the old village had been demolished (ORR pp8,73p).

Rowley Water A brook. Gnosall is said to be situated on it (SCSF p161).

Rowlow Burial mound on the former Calwich Common, to NNE of Calwich Abbey, at SK 13814417. It was noted by Plot who considered it of Roman origin. Is a listed monument. Its name suggests that it was the burial place of some petty king (NHS p404) (AAD p207) (SCSF p74). Although Plot noted a burial mound here, it is possible that he wrongly called it Rowlow, and that the mound of that name is on or at Rue Hill 4m to the NW (SPNO p24).

Row Moor In Norton chapelry in Stoke ancient parish. Is said to have been situated beneath the dirt mounds at Ford Green (ONST 1938 p76).

Rownall Small hamlet on high ground on the edge of Wetley Moor 0.75m WNW of Wetley Rocks. Has been identified with DB Rugehala (DB. Phillimore. 1976). But Gen Wrottesley and Col Wedgwood thought it DB Bughale (SHC 1916 p167. 1919 pp157,158). And has appeared as Roughenhale (C13), and Rowenhale (C13) (SPN p34). The name means 'the rough meadow' (DUIGNAN), or the 'rough nook' (NSJFS 1981 p2), or 'rough hollow' (SSE 1996 p17). Formed one of the four divisions of Cheddleton manor (CVH p21) and parish (W p763). N of Rownall Hall was possibly a medieval village (SSAHST 1970 p35). Henry, who may have been the steward of the de Verdun family in the Middle Ages, styled himself as 'the King of Rownall' and seems to have frequently quarrelled with the Sherrards of Cheddleton (CVH p19). Milner says Rownall had a witch in the early C19 who was nearly as well known as Molly Leigh of Hamel Grange (see). She was a herbalist and dealer. Her cottage was burnt down in c1820 by a band of neighbours led by landlord Capt Powys (CVH p162).

Rownall Hall S of Rownall, Wetley Rocks. Seat of the Arblasters of Longdon, near Lichfield, after they became lords of Cheddleton manor in c1620 (CVH p72). It was the seat of Smith Child MP for N Staffs from 1851 (W p763). By the late C19 Edward John Ridgway, formerly of Hanley, is described as of Rownall Hall (mem in Wetley Rocks church).

Rowney Gate The corner site at Loggerheads, between the road to Newcastle and the road to Mucclestone, is known as Rowney Gate. By 1933 the old name of Rounhay had been superseded by Brand or more commonly Burnt Wood (NSFCT 1933 p93). There is a Rowney Farm to W of Loggerheads.

Rowney Wood Large wood W of Loggerheads. Is now called Burnt Wood (see) and was more extensive than Burnt Wood. Here the Earl of Salisbury's forces camped on the night of 22-23 Sept 1459, the night before the battle of Blore Heath (NSJFS 1980 p11). The name is preserved in Rowney Farm 2m WSW of Ashley.

Royal Cottage Former name for Tollgate House on Ashbourne Road, WSW of Middle Mayfield. It reputedly gained the name Royal Cottage after the Princess Royal commented on it as she passed by on her way to Calwich Abbey (MOM p48p).

Royal Cottage Inn 2m NE of Upper Hulme situated on E side of A53 (former turnpike road) at 1410 feet high, at Middle Hills. It is uncertain whether the inn ever existed before the turnpike road was made in the 1760s. The inn is known to have existed by 1805 and was called Royal Cottage by 1833 on account of the belief that a royal person had once slept here (VCH vol 7 p33). Some believe it was Charles I (R vol v p134) (OL vol 1 p50. vol 2 pp290,291il) (PS p149) (SMCC p2), or Charles II (WTCEM p7; and that he stayed at the Royal Oak, Wetton), or Prince Charles Edward Stuart (Bonnie

Prince Charlie) slept here one night in 1745 and the settle on which he lay is still (1938) preserved here (NSFCT 1938 p121) (VB p207) (SMM p123) (UHAW pp18,51 il) (PNPD), or just some of the Young Pretender's army stayed here in the 1745 Jacobite Rebellion (DPEM p109), or either Charles I or Prince Charles Edward Stuart (HLS p4). The ghost of an elderly lady was offered a lift by a motorist on the road near Royal Cottage. The ghost accepted the lift but on approaching the car, she disappeared leaving only her foot prints in the snow (SMM p48). Close by is the source of the Churnet (OL vol 2 p290).

Royledge House 0.75m WNW of Upper Elkstone. Royledge copper mine closed in 1862 (VCH vol 7 p60).

Ruck of Stones Farm which stood in Lewisham Road, formerly Ruck of Stones Lane, Smethwick. Seems to have taken its name from a heap of stones which marked the parish boundary (STELE June 9 1951) (VCH vol 17 p103). The farm belonged to the Hunt family to 1734, and seems to have belonged to them by the later C16. It seems to have been demolished in the later 1880s. The Surrey Works of Evered & Co Ltd were built on the site by 1900 (VCH vol 17 p103).

Rudge, The Former out-township and outlying manor of Standon ancient parish (HOPS p4) (COI p219) (NSFCT 1913 p60), on undulating land near the head of Bromley Brook 3m W of Standon. Rudge has appeared as Rigge (DB), Rugge, and Ridge (COI p219) (DUIGNAN). Ridge means a ridge of elevated land, sometimes slight elevations (DUIGNAN p126). There was possibly a village in the vicinity of Rudge Manor (see), now lost (SSAHST 1970 p35). Jesuits are recorded as being active in the Rudge during the C17, and afterwards as Gerrards Bromley (ALW pl 24).

Rudge Manor Represents the manor house of Rudge manor, formerly in Standon ancient parish, 3m W of Standon. In the C12 the manor was held by the de Muttons passing by marriage with Ingestre to the Chetwynds. In 1541 Sir William Chetwynd settled the part now centred on the house known as Rudge Manor on Anthony, his second son. This descended with Ingestre and eventually passed to the Talbots. In the C19 it was purchased by Hon Mrs Meynell-Ingram. The Chetwynds, descendants of Anthony, occupied the house in the C16 and the C17. At some time prior to 1892 it was reduced in size and status to a farm house (COI pp119-223 il of in 1885).

Rudgeway, The The old Chester road between Castle Bromwich and Stonnall was anciently, and was still, known as the Rudgeway in 1902 (DUIGNAN). It marked the boundary of Staffs and Warws and ran through part of Sutton Chase known as 'Coldfield' (NSJFS 1968 p50) (VCHW vol 4 pp235-236). Has also appeared as Rugeway (NSJFS 1968 p50).

Rudlow The manor of Rudlowe is supposed to have been sited near Tatenhill Lane or Tatenhill Common. About 0.5m W of Callingwood Hall. Has also appeared as Rudlowe. The manor belonged to the Knightleyes in the C13 and C14 (HOPT vol 1 p113); they partook in the strange manorial tenure custom of Birdshall and Tutbury (NHS pp414,441-442). The wood called Knightley Park preserves the name (HOPT vol 1 p113).

Rudyard Ancient parish, former manor and township. The hamlet of Rudyard on the SW slopes of Gun Hill in Leek ancient parish (W p729) (GLAUE p421) is 2m NW of Leek. The separate civil parish of Rudyard, created in 1866, was abolished in 1934 and amalgamated with Horton civil parish (GLAUE p421). The estate called Rudegeard mentioned in the will of Wulfric Spot (c1002), founder of Burton Abbey, was identified by Dugdale, Shaw, and Duignan as Rudyard (SHC 1916 p35) (VCH vol 3 p201) (SSE 1993 p4). Later the name appears as Rugehala (DB), and Rudierd (SPN p100). Some have formerly thought the first element is from 'ruddy' with reference to the redness of the soil: Or from the growth of rods of young trees here: Or from a road through the lost forest of this area, from the Celtic root 'rithead,' Old Irish 'road' (NSFCT 1885 p54) (SSAHST 1967 p34): Or from Rudda, an Anglo-Saxon personal name (DUIGNAN) (SPN p100) - the personal name 'Rudda' may appear in nearby Rudheath, Ches (SSE 1996 p3); Or from 'rue,' (Ruta graveolens) a non-native herb from the Mediterranean area (SSAHST 1967 p34) (MR p268), whose medieval forms are 'ruda' and 'rude' (SSE 1996 p3): Or from 'rue' (Thalictrum flavum), an unrelated British meadow plant (SSE 1996 p3): Or from rudd, a popular sporting fish (EKWALL) (MR p268) (SSE 1996 p3). Generally, the terminal is considered to be a 'yard' or 'garden.' Ekwall thought it may represent 'pond' and that Rudyard is 'pond where rudds are kept' since 'Rudyard is on Rudyard Lake (but the lake is a C19 reservoir) (SSE 1996 p3). He also thought it might be 'yard or garden where rue was grown' (SSE 1996 p3). Rudyard may be of Old British origin 'yr Rhyd-yeard' 'the ford of the height' (S&W p319). Some say there was a **hamlet** centred on Rudyard Hall (see) (HHHL p100). But by the late C18 there was a hamlet on the road between Leek and Macclesfield centred on Rudyard Manor. This was gradually deserted in the C19 and replaced by the present

Rudyard village at the S end of Rudyard Lake, see below (Yates' map) (VCH vol 7 p216). In early 2000 there were sightings in the Macclesfield Road area of a possible **'big' cat** wild in the countryside (ES March 24 2000 p3. April 20 2000 p23).

Rudyard C19 village by Rudyard Lake, formerly called Harper's Gate, 22.5m N of Stafford. Formerly in Horton ancient parish. For Rudyard township and the old settlement of Rudyard to the NE see above. **Creation of modern Rudyard.** After the construction of Rudyard Reservoir (or Lake) in c1800 and the arrival of the railway in 1850 Harper's Gate expanded as a popular resort with Rudyard Lake attracting people to the area. The reservoir keeper's house was opened as Rudyard Lake Hotel by 1851. The hotel was renamed Hotel Rudyard in c1886 (VCH vol 7 p68), by which time Harper's Gate was being referred to as Rudyard (RL). The NSR built the Churnet Valley **railway** line connecting Macclesfield with Leek and shortly afterwards opened a station at Rudyard on Aug 18 1850. Rudyard Lake station closed to passengers on Nov 7 1960 (RL pp23,116). A steam 10.25 inch gauge railway following some of the old track bed along Rudyard Lake N from Rudyard station was set up in 1978 and has sporadically run ever since (RL pp117,127p). **Well-dressing.** A well, known to have existed by the late C18, on the western bank of the dam end, near to the present tourist information centre was first dressed in 1871. Well-dressing here was later promoted to encourage tourists to Rudyard by Rudyard Lake Hotel (VCH vol 7 p69) (RL p26). The custom had ended by the beginning of the C20. The well was cleaned and renovated in c1984 (RL p26). At the junction of Lake Road and Horton Bank in the centre of Rudyard is a 10 feet high, four feet wide rock sometimes known as **'The Jubilee Stone'** quarried from the top of Hole House Bank. It was erected in 1897 to celebrate Queen Victoria's Diamond Jubilee and shows Victoria in bass relief. It also records her death and the births, coronations and deaths of all subsequent monarchs, and those who fell in the Boer War, WW1 and WW2 (ALC p61p) (SVB p144). The WW1 memorial curiously records that that war ended on Aug 31 1921 (not Armistice Day Nov 11 1918), for a technical state of war still existed between America and Germany until Aug 21 1921 when the US Government signed in Berlin, a separate treaty of peace with Germany, after President Harding had signed a joint resolution of Congress declaring the end of WW1 on July 2 1921 (MMM p95) (HLSP pp110-111). The stone was broken during its transportation from the quarry up Horton Bank and a small join is still visible near the top of the monument (RL p44). There were services in the **church**, St Gabriel, on Whorrocks Bank, built in 1903-1905 on poor foundations, to 1928. The church was demolished in c1946; some of the stone went into the extension of the Memorial Institute and some into Wit's End, on Horton Bank (RL pp48-49,88p). **'Rudyard Rock,'** a candy stick, was only available from the shops and cafes of Rudyard and was on sale to tourists by at least the 1920s. By the early 1950s the village had 'lost its gentility and tranquillity and began to look tatty' (RL pp23,103p,115,116). (TWWW March 1997 p4). **Gwen Massey** of The Willows, Rudyard, aged 34, murdered her lover's wife, Mary Elizabeth Walton, with blows of a hammer to the head on Feb 8 1963. She took the body in a red Morris mini-traveller to High Street, Mow Cop, and left it in the car there where it was discovered the next day (MCS pp84-95). Pickford and his family saw a **UFO** above Rudyard in the form of a golden ball. The object was sighted by others in the district (SMM p93).

Rudyard Hall House nearly 1.5m NE of modern Rudyard village. Formerly in Rudyard township in Leek ancient parish. Lies high on the slopes of Gun (NSFCT 1908 p141). Represents the capital messuage of Rudyard manor, a manor held by the Rudyerds or Rudyards, a family who took their name from the place, by at least the C13 (VCH vol 7 p217). Notable of this family were: Richard Rudyard, a crusader in Henry II's reign (HOLF p11): Ranulphus de Rudyard, who according to tradition, killed Richard III at the battle of Bosworth Field (1485) (NSJFS 1962 p86) (HOLF p11): Edward Rudyerd, a minister of Uttoxeter, who published 'The Thunderbolt of God's Wrath against the hard-hearted and stiff-necked Sinners' (1615): Sir Benjamin Rudyerd, noted wit, poet and statesman of Charles I's reign, nicknamed the 'Silver Trumpet of the Long Parliament.' He was the friend of Lord Pembroke, Pym, and Hampden, and upon whom Ben Jonson wrote several epigrams: and John Rudyerd, the architect of the second Eddystone lighthouse in 1706 (R 1861) (HOU p228) (NSFCT 1885 p54) (BS p383) (HOLF pp11-12). In 1723 the manor was sold by the last two surviving Rudyard heiresses to Thomas Parker, Earl of Macclesfield. The manor remained with the Earls of Macclesfield until 1919 (NSFCT 1905 p157) (VCH vol 7 p217). The present house was built mainly in the earlier C17 (MR p267) (RL p11p of west front in 1919). In 1854 during the residence of Robert Needham Methodist services were transferred to Rudyard Hall and remained here until 1892 (RL p300).

Rudyard House House over 0.5m NE of modern Rudyard village. Formerly in Rudyard township in Leek ancient parish. Built in the C18. Formerly called Green Tree Farm and Greentree Farm (NSFCT 1885 p54) (1979 OS map 1:25,000) and stands in the area of the old hamlet of Rudyard (VCH vol 7 p216).

Rudyard Lake Reservoir lying to the E and N of modern Rudyard village. Originally 1.75m long and more than 0.125m wide (OL vol 303). Constructed by the damming of Dunsmore Brook in 1793 (LGS p205) (SHST p128p) (SVB p144) or Dingle Brook in 1799 (VCH vol 7 p65), or rather authorised in 1797 (BOE p227) (SL p244) (MR p267) (NSFCT 1991 p44) and completed by 1800 (RL p13). It was built as a feeder for the Macclesfield, Trent and Mersey, and Caldon Canals (LGS p205) (BOE p227). And is itself fed by Dingle Brook and Rad Brook (VCH vol 7 p68). Some say it was built in 1831 (VB p214) (SGS p141). The lake was commonly known as Rudyard Reservoir to about the mid C19 (RL p14). Its area has been given as 170 acres (LHSB No. 6 p26) or 164 acres (RL p5). Pitt says it can feed a 100 miles of canal. It was described in 1813 as 'little inferior to some of the Cumberland lakes' (Staffs. J Nightingale. p1169. Beauties of England and Wales. xiii) (VCH vol 7 p68). The lake was widened and deepened in 1907 to two miles long and 0.25m wide (SHST p128p). It was emptied in the drought of Sept 1933 (SHST p128p). A coffin-shaped wharf at the start of the canal feeder at Rudyard Lake is known as Giant's Coffin (HLSP p109p). In WW2 American servicemen had a camp E of Cliffe Park Hall from where they tested amphibious landing craft. Wires were set across the lake designed to prevent enemy invasion. A Sterling Bomber crashed at Cliffe Park Hall (see) in 1944 (RL pp98,114). The Mersey Weaver River Authority's plans in c1971 to raise the height of the lake by about 40 feet were never carried out (ES March 25 1981 p12p). The Rudyard Lake Users' Forum, founded in 1989, founded Rudyard Lake Ltd who took over the management of the lake in 1995 (ES May 22 1995 p9). Rudyard Lake Ltd seems to have been refounded as Rudyard Lake Trust in Sept 1996 (RL p119). **The Lake as a tourist attraction.** The NSR acquired the lake when the company purchased the Trent and Mersey Canal in 1847 (ES June 29 1996 p21). With the completion of the Churnet Valley railway line along the eastern bank of the lake between 1848 and 1850 the lake became a popular resort for excursionists and Potteries people (RL pp23,24). The station at the N end of the lake, opened in 1905, was at first called Rudyard Lake. About 1925 its name changed to Cliffe Park, when Rudyard station at the S end of the lake, opened in 1850, took that name. Both stations closed to passengers in 1960 (VCH vol 7 pp217,220). There were regattas held on the lake on April 21 1851, June 9 1851 (RL p24) and April 21 1856 (OL vol 1 pp303-305,329). Fanny Bostock of Cliffe Park Hall, at the N end of the lake on the W side, brought injunctions against the railway company for promoting the regattas of the early 1850s. Her argument that the company was not entitled to use the reservoir for any other purpose than its original one was supported by the Queen's Bench in 1855 (VCH vol 7 p68). The lake was so frozen in Feb 1895 as to allow a fire engine to cross from one side to the other to attend a fire, and the Leek Volunteers to march the full length of the lake and back (RL p44). At the turn of the C20 a steamboat called the Countess of Ellesmere operated on the lake. It or another steam craft caught fire and sank and its remains lie at the bottom of the lake (ES May 26 1993 p8). In 1913, 20,000 people visited the lake in a single day (ES June 29 1996 p21). The lake has often been described as a silver lake. **Visitors and victims of the Lake.** George Allen, George Davenport and Samuel Harrison drowned in the lake in 1838 (OL vol 1 pp303-305,329). **The Kiplings.** The lake is said to give its name to the novelist, Rudyard Kipling (born on Dec 30 1865) given to him by his parents who first met here on a picnic in the summer (RL p25) or spring of 1863 (BEV p21) (VB p214) (STMSM Sept 1980 p15) (PS p138) (PWIS p57) (HLSP p107). Rudyard's father John Lockwood Kipling had come to Burslem (see) to be a ceramic designer after studying in London (POTP vol 1 p136). Some say it was at Rudyard Lake that John Lockwood Kipling proposed to Rudyard's mother, Alice Macdonald, of the Macdonald family of Wolverhampton (see 1848-1870), having previously met her (TTTD p137) (POTP vol 1 p136) (TFTPM pp124-125), or they just came on a visit here as a married couple, in 1864 (SVB p144), whilst others say it was here Rudyard was conceived. Rudyard's parents were married on March 18 1865 (BEV p21) (RL p25). **Charles Blondin** (1824-1897), acrobat, tried to cross the lake on a rope suspended 100 feet above the water on Sept 26 1864, and visited the lake again in June 1878 (RL pp25,26). W May drowned in the lake in 1869 and Hyde and Stretch drowned in it in 1870 (OL vol 1 p331). **Capt Webb** swam in the lake on June 25 1877. Thousands came in trains to watch him (TSW p20) (RL p26). On July 14 1907 **James Bennett** and **John Bode** both private soldiers in the 1st Volunteer Batt of the N Staffs Regt, and of Leek, drowned in the lake when their boat capsized as they were returning from the Hanging Gate Inn, Rushton;

it was Bennett's 26th birthday. A third occupant of the boat James Hill, aged 23, was saved (SMOPP vol 2 p41p of the funeral).

Rudyard Manor House over 0.75m NE of modern Rudyard village. Formerly in Rudyard township in Leek ancient parish. Built in the C18. Formerly called Green Farm and stands in the area of the old hamlet of Rudyard (VCH vol 7 p216).

Rudyard Villa S of Rudyard Villa. Built in the mid 1860s (VCH vol 7 p68).

Rudyard Villa Near Horton Lodge, N of Rudyard village. Built in 1860 by Matthew Gaunt, magistrate and landowner, to designs by William Sugden. At first called Rudyard Vale and was changed to Rudyard Villa by 1871, presumably to distinguish it from another Rudyard Vale, built in the mid 1860s to the S (VCH vol 7 p67). By 1865 Keepers Cottage or Spite Hall (see) had been built a few yards in front of it (RL p27).

Rue Barn Rue Barn Farm is 1.5m NE of High Offley. There is a Rue Hill 1m SSE of High Offley. The field 'Ruyl Field' in Horsley township occurs in 1298 (ECC p14). Rue Barn occurs on the 1834 OS map.

Ruebury A round hill detached from the rest of the Clent Hills. On the hill is the site of an ancient encampment (SVS p295). Has also appeared as Rubury.

Rue Hayes Farm 1.25m NW of Onecote. Formerly in Onecote township in Leek ancient parish. The present house is partly of the C17 (VCH vol 7 p211).

Rue Hill Hill 1m SSE of Cauldon. There was a turnpike gate here (IANS p18). Has appeared as Rowlow (1686), Rowlow (Yates' map), and Rue Hill (1838 OS map) (NHS p404) (SPNO p24). Close to the Weaver Hills and may be said to be part of the Weaver Hills range.

Rue Hill Eminence to the N of Blakemere Pool, Norbury.

Ruelow Ruelow Wood is 1.25m S of Ipstones and runs along the Churnet (TOI p11). Has also appeared as Rhuelow.

Rufin's Well Holy well within the boundaries of Tamworth Castle on the E side. The well was recorded in 1276 when a man was fined for obstructing the pathway to it (VB p29). Rev Henry Norris remarked that 'it affords a copious supply of water to a bath house erected over it' (KNS pp82,83). Named after Rufin one of the two sons of King Wulfhere of Mercia. Perhaps, Wulfhere dedicated it to his son in remorse after he slew him for converting to Christianity (VB p29). Has also appeared, incorrectly, as St Rufin's Well; for Rufin was never a saint. (NSFCT 1902 p161) (Ut Supra p32) (SCM April 1988 p10p).

Rufford House 1.75m NNE of High Offley.

Rugeley (locally *Ridgeley* DUIGNAN). Ancient parish and town by the Trent in the Trent Valley 8.5m ESE of Stafford.

1000 to 1750. The **name** has appeared as Rugelie, a manor, in DB, Ruggele (C12), Rogeley (C12) (SPN p100), Riggele (1311), Ryggeley (1389), Riddesley (1577) (SPNO p105), Rydgeley (later C16) (SHC 1938 p146), Ridgly (1698) (Illustrated Journeys of Celia Fiennes edited by Chris Morris. 1984. p148). Other forms before the C19 include Rudgelie, Ridgeley, Riddsley and Rugeley (LGS p205). It means 'Ridge lea,' the ridge being what Cannock Chase is situated on; the greater part of the former manor of Rugeley covered Cannock Chase (DUIGNAN) (SPN p100) (SSE 1996 p17). Dr Wilkes thought the 'ridge' was the hill a little above the town standing about a 0.25m S of the Trent (Etching Hill?) (SHOS vol 2 p321). It takes its name from Rugeley Hay (Staffs County Handbook c1958 p120). Others have interpreted the name as 'red pastures' (VB p117) (MR p268). Rugeley parish was a **peculiar jurisdiction** of the dean and chapter of Lichfield cathedral until peculiar jurisdictions were abolished in 1846 (VCH vol 3 p94) (GLAUE p421). The old parish **church**, St Augustine, stands on the N side of Station Road and dates from the late C12. In 1823 a new church was built on the opposite side of the road. The tower and chancel of the old church remain (VCH vol 5 p163) (BOE p227) (SGS p141). The ancient stone **pinfold**, situated apparently on the N side of Sheep Fair, was partly converted in c1774 to a **lock-up**. The pinfold was moved in c1829 to a site on the Marlpits estate where it still stood in 1878 (VCH vol 5 p152). In 1346 the **Black death** came to Rugeley (LTM Nov 1971 p9). In the **Civil War** a parliamentary garrison seems to have been set up at Rugeley in 1645 (VCH vol 5 p152). Rugeley's inhabitants were fined by the parliamentary committee at Stafford for their support of the royalists in the Civil War (LTM Nov 1971 p9). In the **1745 Jacobite Rebellion** the Duke of Cumberland's army spent one night in Rugeley on Dec 1 (LTM Nov 1971 p9). **Pestilence, fire and flood.** There was a fire in the town on May 20 1646 (SHOS vol 2 p322) and or on May 20 1649 (LTM Nov 1971 p9) (ADD pp23-24). The plague came to Rugeley in 1665 (LTM Nov 1971 p9). There was a fire in the town on Feb 1708 (SHOS vol 2 p322) (ADD p24) when 29 people lost their homes (LTM Nov 1971 p9). The town was also hit by a 'great rain' on Sept 15 1708 (VCH vol 5 p152). In or shortly after 1760 a **maypole** was set up between Sandy Lane

and Horse Fair for George III's coronation and it was still standing in the mid C19 (VCH vol 5 p152 il of in 1856 facing). **Persons and visitors. William Creswell**, a C17 apprentice to Antony Bannister of Rugeley, who could whistle so artificially like a flageolet that nobody could distinguish him from one at a distance if he was out of sight (NHS p284). Mrs **Mary Knowles** (d1807), eldest daughter of Moses and Mary Morris of Rugeley, was born at Rugeley on May 5 1733. She was a Quaker, painter and poet and so outwitted Dr Johnson of Lichfield (see) in conversation that Boswell, his biographer, refused to record her triumphs in his biography (DNB) (GM June 1791. Oct 1791) (PSS pp385-386) (CCBO p68) (VCH vol 5 p152) (VFC p80).

MARKETS AND FAIRS. The bishop of Lichfield was granted a charter on June 2 1259 to hold a **market** here on Thursdays (NSJFS 1971 p51). The charter of 1259 was confirmed some time between 1387 and 1390. The Thursday market was still being held in 1747 and 1851. By 1868 general markets were held each Saturday as well as Thursday, with a cattle market every alternate Tuesday (VCH vol 5 p160). At the County Museum at Shugborough is a market toll board with list of tolls for the district of Rugeley, dated 5 July 1879. **Fairs**. A cattle fair on **April 14** had been introduced by 1834 but had lapsed by 1912 (VCH vol 5 pp160,161). The charter of 1259 included a grant of a fair to be held annually on the Vigil, Feast, and Morrow of St Augustine of Canterbury, **May 25-27**. By 1747 saddle horses were being dealt in at this fair (VCH vol 5 p160). There is a tradition that the legendary highwayman, Dick Turpin, stole his mare, Black Bess, from Rugeley horse fair (AB p50) (ABAB p50). With the introduction of the Gregorian calendar the May fair seems to have moved to early June. Whitaker's Almanac gives June 1 (SCSF p98) and Cooke gives June 6 (SCSF p99). Others say it was a large fair and ran from 1 to 6 June (VCH vol 5 p160). In the C19 the old May fair was for colts and horses of a superior quality and attained importance through Rugeley's position on the trunk railway from Holyhead, which brought fine consignments of Irish horses, for which the British Army and foreign armies were often the purchasers (SCSF p104) (Staffs County Handbook c1958 p120). It was still being held in 1932 but had lapsed by 1940 (VCH vol 5 p161). By 1747 there was a fair held on **Oct 10**. With the introduction of the Gregorian calendar this seems to have moved to Oct 21 (SCSF pp98,99) but had lapsed by 1912 (VCH vol 5 pp160,161). A cattle fair on the second Tuesday in **Dec** had been introduced by 1834 but had lapsed by 1912 (VCH vol 5 pp160,161).

INDUSTRY. Rugeley's main industries from the Middle Ages have been tanning, iron production and some glass making. Rugeley also participated from the early C18 in the clothing trade and made hats and felts (SCSF p112). Its chief manufacture by 1817 was hatmaking (VCH vol 5 p161). There was probably a **windmill** at approximately SK 039180. A messuage within the manor of Hagley was recorded as 'Le Wyndmayle' in 1600 indicating an old mill site (VCH vol 5 p160) (WBJ p34).

GRAMMAR SCHOOL. The school probably existed by 1567 with lessons being held in the church (VCH vol 6 pp162-164). Walter Wolseley, on June 6 1610, was seized in fee of certain lands in Staffs, for the maintenance of a schoolmaster to teach scholars at Rugeley (LHSB 14 pp51il,52,53). A school building was built in 1707 at the junction of Wolseley Road and Colton Road; the first stone was laid by Richard Hollinhurst, mason, on Sept 9 1707. The school and the master's house were rebuilt in c1820. In the mid C19 Rev Thomas Bonney father of Cambridge geologist Prof TG Bonney (1833-1923), was master here (VCH vol 5 p152). Another account says Charles Bonney was the brother of HT Bonney, headmaster. When he was 21 Charles Bonney went to Sydney, Australia. He became the first man to 'overland' sheep moving 10,000 of them vast distances across unexplored areas. He pioneered many new routes for overlanding cattle (AR p62p). The school became a maintained secondary school in 1931 and merged with Fair Oak comprehensive school in 1968 (VCH vol 6 pp162-164). The school building had disappeared by the 1950s but the master's house was still surviving then (VCH vol 5 p153). **Alumni**: John Landor of Colton (see); TG Bonney (1833-1923) the geologist (STMSM March 1974 p28; said to be buried in Rugeley churchyard); William Palmer, poisoner (1824-1856) (MMM p24); Jack Martin, footballer for England in WW2 and for Aston Villa; Trevor Saunders, footballer for Walsall FC (TB Dec 1994 p20).

1750 to PRESENT. Rugeley was described in 1747 as 'a handsome clean well-built town of exceeding pleasant and healthful situation' (W). By 1834 Rugeley was considered 'the largest and handsomest market town in the Cuttlestone hundred' (W) (VCH vol 5 p149). A square brick **Town Hall** was built in the centre of the Market Place in c1790. It had an open arcade of three bays to the ground floor and a cupola on the roof. The town hall was extended in c1850. The inquest on William Palmer, the famous poisoner, was held here in 1856. A new town hall was opened in 1879 on the corner of the Market Place and Anson Street on the site of the Shoulder of Mutton Inn (VCH vol 5 p153). Rugeley was linked by **railway** to London and Liverpool in 1847 and to Walsall via Cannock in 1859 with a line known as the Cannock Mineral Line (VCH vol 5 p151) (NSJFS 1964 p86). Trains collided at Rugeley Trent Valley station on Nov 12 1905 (AR p92p). The station closed in 1965 and a new station opened on the line at Rugeley on May 30 1997 (Staffs County News. July 1997). In 1859 a **company of volunteers** representing Rugeley was enrolled (VCH vol 5 p152). The Rugeley **urban district** was formed in 1894 (VCH vol 5 p152). For **WW1** Rugeley Military Camp see Range Corner. Rugeley **power station**, 1m SE of Rugeley, built on the site of Boothurst house, for the Central Electricity Generating Board, opened in 1963 (SL p253), drawing water from the Trent as a coolant for its condensers (SLM Sept 1999 p71). By 1967 the tallest cooling tower in Britain was one of its dry cooling towers at 350 feet tall (GBR 1967 p139). The two power stations there in 1988 were known as Rugeley 'A' and Rugeley 'B' (MR p268). Rugeley 'A' was being demolished in 1997 (E&S Aug 16 1997 p33). For curious Rugeley **street names** see VB p118. A fat cigar-shaped silver **UFO** with portholes surrounded by a golden halo was seen over Rugeley in summer 1980 (ES Sept 21 1998 p8). **References to Rugeley**. The town is Trentford in Richard Bagot's novel 'Casting of Nets' (1901), and is Riddsley in Stanley Wayman's 'The Great House' (CCF pp187,188) (CCBO p69). **Persons and visitors. Edward Bamford**, known as the 'Staffordshire Giant,' was born at Rugeley, and was living in c1782. He is said to have stood seven feet six inches tall. He was a remarkably stout and strong man, with a cheerful and good temper. His trade was a hatter. Such was the enormous size of his hand that he could take up a foot-rule endways with his finger and thumb. After having travelled the country some time as an exhibition, he retired to a public house in London. In 1834, long after his death, there was a life-size model of him in the shop of John Porter, hatter, of Burton upon Trent (SA Nov 15 1834) (BUBA pp125-126). According to the inscription below a drawing published on May 4 1771 (in the WSL portrait collection in 1999), a Mr Bamfield was the Staffordshire Giant. The drawing shows Mr Bamfield standing beside 'the Norfolk dwarf,' a Mr Coan. According to the inscription, Mr Bamfield, who lived the latter part of his life in Sheare Lane near Temple Bar, London, was seven feet four inches tall, whilst Mr Coan was said to be not exceeding three feet high; and the two men both died aged 36; so presumably Mr Bamfield was dead by 1771 (WSL portrait collection). **Thomas Holcroft** (1745-1809), writer and playwright, author of the play 'The Road to Ruin,' lived some of his childhood at Rugeley (SHJ spring 1990 pp6-13). **Walter Savage Landor** (1775-1864) poet and author of 'Imaginary Conversations' born at Warwick was related to the Landors of Rugeley (DNB) (BS). His relation, **Walter Noble Landor** (1864-1955), historian who contributed 'Stafford Incumbents and Parochial Records (1530-1680)' to SHC 1915, and wrote an unpublished history of Rugeley up to the C18, gave his name to Rugeley's present (2000) local history society, the Landor Society, formed in 1954 (info Mrs MK Neal) (SH p149). **Thomas Sidney** or Sydney (d1889) of Stafford (see) who became Lord Mayor of London in 1854 was an apprentice to a grocer in Rugeley from 1817 (MMM p79). For the 'Rugeley Murder' case, the murder of **Christina Collins** on the Trent & Mersey Canal in 1839, see Hoo Mill. **William Palmer**, the famous poisoner, was the second son of Joseph Palmer, a prosperous timber merchant of Rugeley (TPP p7). He was born in 1824 at Church Croft House (see), Rugeley. After a medical training which included an apprenticeship to Edward Tylecote, a surgeon of Great Haywood and a short spell as a walking pupil in Stafford Infirmary, during which time it is alleged he tried to poison a man called Abley in a local inn (TPP pp9,11). Palmer finished his medical training in London in 1845 (TPP p11) and returned to Rugeley in 1846 to practice as a doctor. At the Beggar's Oak (see) and in Abbot's Bromley Palmer is said to have courted his future wife, Anne Brookes Thornton (b1827), who he married in Abbot's Bromley (see) church in 1847. She was the illegitimate daughter of William Brookes, a retired colonel who had settled in Stafford, and Mary Thornton, the colonel's housekeeper. With the capital acquired by his marriage Palmer began to breed race-horses and by 1850 he had abandoned his practice run from his house in Market Street, Rugeley, to concentrate on his racing interests. He is considered to have poisoned with strychnine or antimony a succession of relatives and acquaintances; his first victim was Mary Thornton, so, it is said, he could inherit Col Brookes' property in Bath Street, Stafford, and Mary's inn, the Noah's Ark Inn (see). Later victims, also poisoned for financial gain, were his wife, Anne in Sept 1854; his brother, Walter, in Aug 1855, and finally his friend, a solicitor, John Parsons Cook of Lutterworth, Leics, in Nov 1855, the poison taking its affect at the Shrewsbury Arms Inn (see), Rugeley (Cook's ghost haunts Ghost Row see) (VCH vol 5 p152) (SHCST 1971-73 pp22-24) (MMMR pp7-14) (SOPP pl 37) (TPP p21). As well as Abley, Palmer may also have poisoned four of his children by his wife, Anne, who died in in-

fancy; the family nurse, Ann Bradshaw, believed that he had poisoned them; his illegitimate child by Jane Mumford; Mr Bladon of Ashby-de-la Zouche, Leics (1850); Joseph Bentley, his uncle; Mr Bly of Norfolk, who Palmer was indebted to; his illegitimate son by Eliza Tharme (Dec 1855) (TPP pp12-21); and a navvy at Cross Keys Inn (see), Old Hednesford. The total number he poisoned is not known but is thought to be at least 13 and probably 16, making Palmer the most prolific murderer in England to at least 1974 (GBR 1974 p196). National hysteria surrounded the last case which indicted him of being a serial poisoner. He was found guilty and hanged outside Stafford Gaol on June 14 1856. It is said, that as he approached the gallows platform Palmer enquired whether the platform was safe: It is also said, the townsfolk, led by Alderman Sidney, petitioned the prime minister, Lord Palmerston, to have Rugeley's name changed; the doctor having brought shame on the town. Palmerston agreed, but only on condition they named Rugeley after him! A ballad entitled 'A New Song on the Recent Murder with which William Palmer now stands charged' was sold during Palmer's trial (ILN May 24 1856 pp560ils, 561, 562, 563, 564il) (WA Marson's scrap book in WSL; vol 1 pp21,23) (UDC book 2 pp64-77) (LGS p206) (The Life and Career of Dr William Palmer of Rugeley, together with a full account of the murder of John P Cook and a short account of his trial in May 1856. George Fletcher. 1925) (Palmer, the Rugeley Poisoner. Dudley Barker. 1935) (CCF pp150-152) (KES pp171-172) (QMMH pp1-9) (SLM summer 1956 p13 il, 14 il,28) (STM Sept 1968. May 1969 pp30,31) (STM March 1974 p43) (VB pp119-120) (UBCB pp243-244; ballad on Palmer) (FSP p92) (MMM pp24-27) (One Hundred Years of Medical Murder. John Camp. 1982) (SOPP pl 52) (TB May 1972 pp8,17. July 1993 p18. Sept 1993 p5. Oct 1993 pp18-19 ils) (MR p270) (MCGM pp119-122) (TOS pp45-50) (MMMR p14) (SAC pp97-102) (MCS pp20-28) (SMML pp39-42) (John Godwin on 'Open Country' BBC Radio 4 Aug 14 1999) (SN Feb 10 2000 p18). Palmer's house in Rugeley became the town post office and then a shop with a shop front put in on the ground floor. The house was still standing in 1988 (AR p39p in 1900). The story has been made into a novel 'They Hanged My Saintly Billy' by R Greaves published sometime between 1945-60, and a television drama made by Granada in early March 1998 and screened in Nov 1998. His ghost has also made an appearance (TB July 1979 p15). **John Porter** (1838-1922), a racehorse trainer at Rugeley, wrote the novel 'Kingsclere' (1896) (VB p120) (VFC p107). **George VI** visited Rugeley in July 1934 (R&S p46).

NEWSPAPERS. The **Rugeley Advertiser**, founded on Sept 20 1882, ran until at least Aug 14 1897 (SHJ spring 1996 p22). The **Rugeley Mercury**, founded by Sept 30 1882, is still running (SHJ spring 1996 p23). The **Rugeley Pioneer** appeared between at least Aug 5 1921 and May 26 1922 (SHJ spring 1996 p23). The **Rugeley Times and South Staffordshire Advertiser** appeared between at least Nov 20 1926 and 1985 (SHJ spring 1996 p23): Willings Press Guide (1988) implies that the Rugeley Times then amalgamated with the **Rugeley Newsletter**, an edition of the Staffordshire Newsletter. The **Lichfield, Rugeley & Brownhills Post** was founded in 1983 (Willings Press Guide. 1988).

Rugeley Hay Former estate which became a hay or division of Cannock Forest (MR p268). The hay was in existence by the reign of Henry II and certainly by the 1230s (VCH vol 2 p338. vol 5 pp58-59, 155). It seems to have comprised most of present Cannock Chase, Gentleshaw and Radmore Hunting Lodge (Staffs County Handbook c1958 p120). It may give its name to the town, Rugeley. The hay was abolished with the grant of Rugeley to the bishop of Lichfield (SSAHST 1963 p27), and the creation of Cannock Chase, in 1290 (VCH vol 2 p338). After the creation of the chase the keepership of the hay or bailiwick of Rugeley followed the same descent as the manor of Hagley, which was held in sergeanty by the keepers until 1588 (VCH vol 5 p159).

Rugeley Oak Approximately at SK 009165 (1834 OS map). Slightly N of Fair Oak Lodge. (SPNO p109; was in Beaudesert Old Park).

Rugeley Turn Road junction 0.75m NW of Abbots Bromley at the junction of the Abbots Bromley-Uttoxeter road with the Admaston road. Here the Abbots Bromley Horn Dancers have performed on Horn Dance day. Abbots Bromley airfield at SK 075255 was known as Stone airfield in Nov 1940. It was later known as Abbots Bromley. No trace of it remained by the later C20 (WMA vol 1 p147) (SHJ autumn 1989 p64) (The Airfields of Britain. vol 1 A-Bur. Kenneth P Bannerman. 1994 p20).

Ruiton Tiny district of W Upper Gornal. In Sedgley ancient parish. Ruiton occupied a lofty eminence which had formerly a beacon. Cox in the early C18 noted that the mountains of North and South Wales may be seen from Ruiton with a telescope (SD) (AMS p447). White says it is this Ruiton that is a joint prebend with Prees of Lichfield cathedral (W p200). Shaw says it was a Ruiton in Warws. Ruiton has appeared as Rewardine (1702), and Rewarden (1795) (AMS p446). It is thought to have been derived from Rui, which is akin to the

Welsh rhiw, a hillside, and ton, Anglo-Saxon, town or place (AMS p446). The 'wardine' part in an earlier form may be from Anglo-Saxon weorthyn meaning 'farm' or 'estate' (AMS p446). There is a windmill on the E side of Vale Street about 0.75m S of Sedgley, built in the 1830s. The mill reputedly ceased work in 1872 and proceeded slowly to decay. Demolition was threatened in the 1950s but this was prevented after 700 people signed a petition in its support. This resulted in a Building Preservation Order being placed on it (WBJ p35 il viii). The mill served for a time as scout headquarters (WIS p22) (WJO Aug 1906 p212p) (SLM spring 1954 p25) (SDOP p18p of in the 1950s). It was probably this mill whose future was in the balance in 1978? (BCM July 1978 p3). In 1979 the Black Country Society took over the lease (WBJ p35). The mill was restored by 1984 (WBJ pl viii) (MR p162). Raven says according to tradition there were two mills in Ruiton, but one was taken down because there was not enough wind for both of them (MR p162p) and the 1834 OS map only shows two. For other Ruiton windmills see under Rewardine, the Round House, and Sandyfields (Sedgley).

Ruiton Farm Old stone farmhouse built of local stone of C16 or C17 origin (SDOP p18p).

Ruiton House Vale Street, Upper Gornal. Built in about the later C18. Had been split into four properties by 1997, one of which is No. 80a Vale Street (TB Jan 1997 p3).

Rumbow Cottages Tiny hamlet in a valley of a stream that flows between the Clent Hills and Romsley Hill (SNSV vol 2 p104) over 0.5m ESE of Clent. F and KM Somers interpret Rumbow as meaning a low bridge over a river (SNSV vol 2 p104).

Rumer Hill Hill, estate and residential district in undulating hilly ground overlooking Ridings Brook 0.75m SE of Cannock. In Cannock ancient parish. Has also appeared as Rugemor (1245-50), Rouwemer (1355), Romehill (1570), Rowemore (1610), Rumere Hill Farm (1730) (SPNO p61), Romer Hill (Yates' map), Reaumore Hill (W p449), Romer Hill, and Rumour Hill (1834 OS map). The name means 'the rough marshland' (SPNO p61). Here was a chalybeate spring, once much frequented by the late C18 (SHOS vol 2 p317) (THS p262) (W p449). The water which fed the conduit at Cannock came from here (CCBO p99). Lord Hatherton was taken to court by the Marquess of Anglesey over his coal mining on the Rumer Hill estate, an estate held by Hatherton of the marquess by copyhold. The marquess, the plaintiff, believed Hatherton, the defender, had no right to mine the coal here without his permission; Hatherton on the other hand believed he did. The case held on March 9 1842 at Worcester was one of the most celebrated of the C19 for it was a dispute between two noblemen with counsels containing the most famous advocates of the day. For Hatherton were Sir T White, Sergeant Ludlow, and WJ Alexander. For the marquess were Sir William Webb Follett (the Solicitor General), RV Richards, Whately, Whitmore, and Justice Talfourd; his account of the action in verse is believed to be the only one known to have survived of the trials he recorded in verse. Two lines run:

I was a Collier in my youth, and still
I work the Colliery at Rumore Hill;

The case proved in favour of the marquess. Hatherton later failed with his appeal (SHC 1947 pp3-46). Romer Hall at Cannock (NSFCT 1908 p146) may be a misspelling of Romer Hill.

Rumford Hill Hill on W side of Smestow Brook 2m ENE of Enville.

Ruscote Appears in DB. Eyton thought it somewhere near Blymhill. Commander Wedgwood at first thought it might be connected with Rosecroft Lane in Haughton, but he later agreed with Rev E Bridgeman that it was Brockhurst (see) (SHC 1916 p170).

Rushall Old parish and former village by Ford Brook now a suburban district of Walsall 15.25m SSE of Stafford. Rushall was a chapelry of Walsall ancient parish until at least 1446. For a hoard of **Roman** coins found at Rushall see under Linley Lodge Industrial Estate. The manor of Rischale appears in DB (SOSH p90). The **name** means 'the rushy pasture,' and unlikely to be a hall made of rushes (DUIGNAN). 'Dwelling on a low marshy site' (HOWW p249). Or 'rush nook' (NSJFS 1981 p3), ie 'the isolated farm by the rushes' (MR p272). Or 'the corner of land overgrown with rushes' (SPN p134). There was a **church** at Rushall possibly in early Norman times and certainly by 1220. The early church may have been attached to Rushall Hall (ROR p88). The present church, St Michael the Archangel, in Leigh Road, was built in 1856 (LDD). The church, Christ the King, Lichfield Road, was built in c1885 (LDD). The **Rushall Psalter** is a large folio volume in leather-covered boards, originally chained in Rushall church. It is made up of 197 leaves of vellum, 370 x 246 mm; pasted in at one end is a leaf from a large notated and illumi-

nated antiphonal of late C15 English manufacture. The volume is said to have received new covers in the C17. One part seems to have been a service book written for John Harper (probably of Rushall Hall) in the C15. Many pages are illuminated. It contains the Sarum Kalender, Horae BVM, Litany, Vigils of the Dead, a liturgical psalter with litanies, prayers etc. When Shaw saw the volume in the late C18 it belonged to Rev William Leigh (SSAHST 1981-82 pp59-91). The **Mollesley Dole** paid out one penny to every man, woman and child in Rushall as well as in Walsall (SL p179 note). There was a **village of Rushall** at the intersection of Walsall-Lichfield road and Bloxwich-Daw End lane 0.75m to the N of the original Rushall containing the hall and church at least by 1775. There were limestones quarries to the E (limestone was used in Walsall's tanning industry - VB p59). A windmill in this area at SK 028011 was described as 'new erected' in 1698. It stood in 'Windmill Field,' opposite 'The Villa' (HOWW p239), and was dismantled in the early C18 (WBJ p34). Another windmill, a post mill, stood near Lady Pool (see) to the S in c1775. Rushall village grew dramatically after WW2 from a small village to a large suburb, and in the C20 housing has been built along the Walsall-Lichfield road towards old Rushall (ADY p20) (SNAR pp54,55). Rushall **railway** station on the Lichfield-Walsall line opened on April 9 1849 (SSR p10). Rushall station was in use until 1909 (SNAR p65p) and the line has been long closed. A clock and drinking fountain were set up in the village square near the Coffee House to mark Queen Victoria's Diamond Jubilee in 1897 (ADY p21p). **Murder**. On Sept 21 1941 Violet Richards, aged 24, and Kitty Lyon, aged 18, both from Paddock, Walsall, were shot to death by Pte Douglas Peach, who robbed them of their handbags, as they were walking through the cattle bridge carrying the railway N of Rushall Hall. Peach was hung at Winson Green Prison, Birmingham, on Nov 26 1941 (MMMR pp79-82).

Rushall Canal The Daw End Branch of it joins the Wyrley and Essington Canal at Catshill. Spurs off the Tame Valley Canal at Rushall Junction; joins its Daw End Branch at Longwood Junction. Constructed in 1840-43 (VCH vol 2 p296) or built in 1847 (SWY p16).

Rushall Hall House 0.75m to the S of the northern district of Rushall. The Rushall Hall site has been occupied continuously since Anglo-Saxon times. Saxon coins are said to have been found in the mound by the hall (MOA p15). The first hall, of which there is no record was built in the C12 and parts of this sandstone building can be detected in the present gateway (ADY p21). The first halls were probably fortified and could be described as castles; one or some were moated; a moat lies N of the present hall (SSAHST 1982-3 p50). There was probably a hall belonging to the Rushall family who held the manor from c1160s to the 1230s. The manor then passed to the Boweles family. Work on a hall here may have been going on in 1292. William de Boweles had a house here in 1323, for a notorious trouble-maker, John de Wetales, attacked it. A new hall was built in c1400 by Geffrey Ive (CAMS p56) or by the Grubbere family (ADY p21). By the mid C15 the hall came by marriage into the Harpur family who added the gatehouse, on the western side of the enclosure, still remaining (SD p22) (SSC p129 in the intro) (GNHS p172) (HOWW pp257-258) (BOE p295) (SGS p141) (WOPP pl. p134) (SSAHST 1981-82 p79) (MR p271p). The Harpur arms appear above the arch in the gatehouse (CAMS p57). The Leigh family obtained the manor by marriage in 1540 and they had a third storey added (to the gatehouse?) by the end of the C16 (CAMS p56). (WJO Nov 1907 pp293-296ps). In the Civil War Rushall Hall was a parliamentary garrison. In spring 1643 it was besieged and captured by the royalists. It was retaken by the parliamentarians on May 22 1644 under the Command of Lord Denbigh (HOWV p85) (HOS p36) (AOW pp66-69) (WPP pp82,83p of gateway). Capt Tuthill became the commander of the new parliamentary garrison. Col Leveson of Dudley Castle then used a man named Pitt of Heath Town, or Wednesbury, or Wednesfield, or Wolverhampton, to bribe Tuthill to surrender the garrison by offering him a sum of £2,000. But Pitt was discovered, and hanged at Smithfield, London, on Oct 12 1644 (WFW pp90-92) or on Dec 12 1644 (W p578) (WAM p81) (LGS p207) (HOWM pp88-89) (MOA p50). Some say Pitt or Pytt was called Francis, a yeoman farmer. Smallshire says it was Francis's second son, Thomas (b1619) (WFW pp90-92). The hall seems to have been dismantled in 1646 (LGS p207). Two canon balls, relics of the war, were long preserved in the hall (SHOS vol 2 pp65-66 pl. x of the hall) (WJO Nov 1907 pp295-296) (LGS p207). The siege of 1643 was re-enacted in Oct 1970 (info Walsall Local History Centre). Edward Leigh, author of 'A diatribe of Mony or Coyn' (1671), lived at Rushall Hall and was MP for Stafford in 1640. In 1811 the hall passed from the Leighs to the Mellishes by marriage. Soon after the Mellishes' arrival, George Canning, Prime Minister in 1827, a near relation of the family, slept in the tower of Rushall Hall whilst on a visit (WJO Nov 1907 p294) (SSAHST 1981-82 p80). Subsequently, the hall passed to the Buchanans (ADY p21p). By 1845 a farmer was occupying the hall. He took down the upper part of the gatehouse and part of the curtain wall. The curtain wall enclosed a court 90 metres by 56 metres and is some 6.3 metres high in places (CAMS p57). The current Rushall Hall built in the C19, into the NW corner of the court, may have been the hall the antiquarian WH Duignan lived in between 1857 and 1889. At SP 02539992 NW of the hall is a burial mound NS 14 paces and EW 16 paces in diameter and seven feet high. Desultory excavations in c1955 produced clay pipes, black glazed pottery and fragments of human bone (ROR p6) (NSJFS 1965 p50). By the late 1970s the ruins of the gatehouse were becoming unstable and dangerous, and was repaired from 1980 (SSAHST 1981-82 pp79,92-99 ils, ps).

Rushall Junction At Ray Hall S of Walsall. Junction of the Rushall Canal with the Tame Valley Canal.

Rushall Park There was a medieval park in the area to the N and E of Rushall Hall. Leland, writing in c1540, noted a park at Rushall (ROR p31). Plot describes the furnace near Lady Pool as standing 'in the park.' The Park Pits (1887 OS map) were limes pits to the E of Rushall Hall (SNAR pp58, 61 see map).

Rushford Slang 0.5m NE of Wombourne. In Wombourne parish.

Rushley Settlement to the N of Musden in Ilam parish. At SK 11985147 is a burial mound, 12 paces in diameter and 2.5 feet high. It was excavated by Carrington in 1850. Few bone fragments were found (TYD p162) (NSJFS 1965 p54). It is a listed monument. The name appears on Smith's map.

Rushy Marsh Coppice in Pattingham ancient parish, 1.25m SSE of Pattingham. It probably preserves the name Marsh. There was a settlement called Marsh in Pattingham parish by the 1590s (VCH vol 20 p173).

Rushton Medieval manor, former chapelry and settlement at Rushton Marsh (VCH vol 7 p219) in and above the upper Dunsmore Brook valley. The chapelry contained the townships of Heaton, Rushton James, and Rushton Spencer. It became a separate ecclesiastical parish in 1726, refounded in 1865 (LGS p207) (GLAUE p421), and is now called Rushton Spencer (see) (GLAUE p421). The manor which appears in DB as Risetone belonged to the Crown and may have centred on Rushtonhall (Rushton James). It had passed from the Earls of Chester to the de Verduns of Alton Castle (see) by 1153. In the C13 the manor divided with a part, known at first as Hugbridge, going to the Dispencers. This became Rushton Spencer. The remaining part, which became Rushton James, was retained by the de Verduns who granted it to the de Aldithleys (or Audleys) of Heighley Castle (see), sometime in the mid C13. James de Aldithley (or Audley) (d1272) was an early holder of this manor and he probably gave his name to it (SSE 1993 p7) (VCH vol 7 p219). Others attribute the Fitz James family with giving their name to the manor (NSFCT 1932 p52) (HOLS p134).

Rushton Bank Tiny hamlet under 0.5m W of the village of Rushton Spencer. Formerly in Rushton Spencer township in Leek ancient parish.

Rushton Grange 0.5m S of St John's, Burslem. Former township in Burslem chapelry in Stoke-upon-Trent ancient parish (W p269). The old vill and hamlet Risctone appears in DB. The name means 'the rushy town (enclosure)' (DUIGNAN) (VCH vol 8 p107). It was given to the Cistercian abbey, Hulton Abbey, at its founding in the early C13. It was a grange of the abbey by 1235 (HBST pp280,287 pl) (VCH vol 3 p236. vol 8 pp107,113) (SASR 1985 pp58, 61). After the Dissolution the grange was sold to James Leveson in 1539. In 1540 it was resold to Richard Biddulph of Biddulph Old Hall. The grange remained with the Biddulphs, Roman Catholics, until the C19 (SASR 1985 p67). The area was once marshy and here the Biddulphs went wild-fowling. After the Civil War they leased the grange to the Bagnalls, also Roman Catholics. An infection, perhaps, brought from Italy by the governess to the Biddulph family caused a plaque at Burslem in 1647 and the dead were buried in pits near Rushton Grange (SOSH pp203-204) (NSFCT 1921 p27); although the governess is said to have been buried with the Biddulph household in Kate's Hole (see) behind Biddulph Old Hall. The plague also spread to Stone (SCSF p137). A protestant mob sacked the grange in 1688 (HBST p287 il in 1800). The grange farmhouse, part of which was used as a Roman Catholic mass-centre during the C18 and the C19, was still functioning as a farm as late as the 1920s, but had disappeared by 1958 (SASR 1985 p67). By 1820 a new church had been built to replace the chapel at the grange which had by then become 'a mere thatched shed.' The new church was demolished in 1936 (POP p36) and St Peter's, Waterloo Road, was built on the site in 1937. Rushton Grange is the Manor Farm in Arnold Bennett's 'Clayhanger' (VCH vol 8 p116 note 44).

Rushton Grange Old Park Enclosed by Ranulph, Earl of Chester. It enveloped Sneyd Wood. The park was not kept up after 1232 (NSFCT 1910 p173).

Rushtonhall Small hamlet 4m NW of Leek, on the old Earlsway (see) (SL p80), and the main settlement of Rushton James township. The DB manor of Rushton, and the later manor of Rushton James, probably centred on Rushtonhall; the medieval manor house probably stood on the site of Rushton Hall Farm (see) on the W side of the hamlet. Has also appeared as Rushton James (Dower's map) and Rushton Hall.

Rushton Hall Farm May stand on the site of Rushton James manor house. The manor was acquired by the Rode or Road (Plot's map) family at the end of the C15. It remained with that family until being sold to George Lee in 1752. In 1773 the estate was inherited by Richard Ayton. By the early C19 it had passed to the Antrobus family. The present house is of the C17 with C19 alterations (VCH vol 7 pp221, 219).

Rushton James Former manor and hamlet 0.5m SW of the chapel at Rushton Spencer, now called Rushtonhall. Former township in Rushton chapelry (GLAUE p421) in Leek ancient parish. The manor evolved as a division of Rushton (see) manor. There was possibly a village at Rushton James in medieval times (SSAHST 1970 p35). 'James' is after possibly the Fitz James family (NSFCT 1932 p52) (HOLS p134) or after James de Aldithley (or Audley) of Heighley Castle (see), an early holder of the manor (SSE 1993 p7) (VCH vol 7 p219).

Rushton Marsh Small village by Dunsmore Brook 0.25m ENE of Rushton Spencer chapel on the turnpike road (W p730). Formerly in Rushton Spencer township in Leek ancient parish. The name appears in the mid C17 and may then have applied to a hamlet (VCH vol 7 p223). The hamlet perhaps evolved on the township common waste land; most of it lay in the Rushton Marsh area (VCH vol 7 p225). The hamlet is named Rushton Marsh on the 1834 OS map, but the village is now called Rushton Spencer (1980 OS map 1:25,000).

Rushtons Barn NE of Milwich (1834 OS map) (Dower's map).

Rushton Spencer Small village by Dunsmore Brook 24.5m N of Stafford. Former manor in the Forest of Leek created out of the division of Rushton manor in the early C13. Rushton Spencer manor, at first known as Hugbridge, was held by the le Despenser family of the Earl of Chester from the early C13 for a chief rent of 1 lb of pepper (SSE 1993 p5) (VCH vol 7 pp223,225). The appellation Spencer was added in the C14 to define the manor from the neighbouring manor of Rushton James. Some say it was Hugh le Despenser, Earl of Winchester, who gave his name to the manor (SVB p145); he was attainted of high treason and all his lands were forfeited to the Crown in 1330 (NSFCT 1932 p52). (NSJFS 1962 p86 note). Rushton means 'the rushy town (enclosure)' (DUIGNAN) (SPN p101) (DP p10; there was or is a rush bearing ceremony at the Forest Chapel in Macclesfield Forest). Oakden agrees with Duignan (SSAHST 1967 p34). There was a **church** at Rushton Spencer by 1368 and that church may be identifiable with the present church, St Lawrence, which lies on a hill 0.5m WSW of Rushton Marsh in isolation. It retains medieval timber framings and was rebuilt in stone in the C17 (VCH vol 7 pp227-228). In the later C19 Rushton Spencer **wake** was held on the Sunday nearest Old St Lawrence Day. It was probably held on or near the feast of St Lawrence (10 Aug), the patron saint of the church, before the calendar change in 1752 (VCH vol 7 p225). Later Rushton Spencer was the name for a township in Rushton chapelry in Leek ancient parish (W p729). The chapelry became a separate ecclesiastical parish, which is now called Rushton Spencer (GLAUE p421). The name Rushton Spencer now also applies to the hamlet formerly called Rushton Marsh. At SJ 931630, 0.5m NW of Rushton Spencer was an **ice factory**, which drew its water from a spring and mechanically frozen (IHB p395). Rushton Spencer station on the NSR's Churnet Valley **railway** line, opened with the line in 1849. It closed to passengers in 1960 (VCH vol 7 p225). In the later C19 and early C20 Rushton Spencer practised the customs of begging for soul cakes on All Soul's Day (VCH vol 7 p225), the dressing of St Helen's Well (see), and maypole dancing (DP p14). **Persons and visitors**. In the later C17 Plot was told of a man here who lived to the age of 105 (NHS p324). **Thomas Meaykin**, born in c1760, son of Thomas and Mary Meaykin, took work as a groom in Stone, Staffs, in c1780. His employer was an apothecary, whose daughter, had designs on him (MMMR p49), or both loved each other (KES p173). In July 1781 Meaykin died, reputedly of natural causes, and was buried in St Michael's churchyard, Stone, on July 16. Meaykin's ghost and a pony he had been fond of in life, who is said to have scraped on his gravestone, alerted the local community to the suspicious circumstances of his death. In summer 1782 his grave was opened and Meaykin was found to be buried face down, a sign that he had been buried alive. On July 17 1782 his parents reinterred him in St Lawrence churchyard, Rushton Spencer, with his feet facing W in order to lay his ghost. It was thought he had been poisoned by the apothecary who had disapproved of his daughter's advances to him. The inscription on Meaykin's present gravestone at Rushton Spencer implies he was murdered (GNHSS p13) (FLJ 1941 p236) (SLM Spring 1955 pp18,19) (VB p214) (STMSM Dec 1974 p23) (MMM pp72-75) (SVB p145) (DP p18) (GLS pp86-87) (SSGLST pp7-9p of Meaykin's grave) (MMMR pp48-50p of Meaykin's grave) (SMML pp35-

38). **Joseph Godson** broke into the parochial chapel at Rushton Spencer on Dec 14 1832 and stole a bible, prayer book and other church property. He was sentenced to death, aged 27 (OL vol 2 p235).

Rusty Brook Common name for a tributary of the Tame. Perhaps ran in the Portobello, Moseley Hole area of Bilston (TB Oct 7 1999 p27. Oct 14 1999 p21)

Ryders Green Former hamlet at some distance from Greet Brook 1m W of the High Street, West Bromwich. Near Swan Village S of Harvills Hawthorn. The name is from presumably the Rider or Ryder family of Dunkirk Hall (SCSF p158) (SHWB 14) (VCH vol 17 p8).

Ryders Green Junction Junction of the Wednesbury Branch of the Birmingham Canal with the Walsall Canal.

Ryder's Hayes Ryder's Hayes Farm is 1m NE of Pelsall. The 'hunter's track' mentioned in a charter of Pelsall's bounds of 994 may relate to Ryder's Hayes (SNBP p93). The field name 'Rydders Heys' occurs in a perambulation of Pelsall boundaries in 1643 and is confirmed in the 1843 tithe. In the 1841 and 1881 census returns the enumerator translates the local pronunciation as 'Rider's Ease' (SNBP p93). The modern form could be a corruption of the Anglo-Saxon landmark 'Ordesheah' which appears in the charter of Pelsall's bounds of 994. Alternatively it could have been enclosed land belonging to the De Ridder family (SNBP p93). Ryder's Hayes station on the SSR opened in April 1856 (SSR p17). The SSR opened a branch railway from Ryder's Hayes to Norton Canes in 1858 (VCH vol 2 p317). Since the 1960s housing has been built on the E side of the Norton Road at Ryder's Hayes; the streets of the estate are named after saints and the estate is colloquially known as 'The Saints' (SHOP p20) (PTYV p22) (SNBP p94).

Ryebrook Tributary of the Hamps. Runs at Grindon. The name is from probably 'the brook by which rye grows' (SPNO p17).

Ryecroft Penn parish (SGSAS). There is a Ryecroft Avenue at Goldthorn Hill.

Ryecroft District overlooking Ford Brook over 1.5m SE Bloxwich, 1m N of Walsall. Formerly in Rushall ancient parish. The urban part was taken into Walsall borough in 1876, a further part was added in 1890 (VCH vol 17 pp150 see map, 161). Is probably the Roycroft Plot noted in Rushall parish (NHS p262). By 1834 it was noted for its sand quarries (VCH vol 17 p161) (SNWA p91). At Ryecroft a signalman Mr Brookes was killed by a train taking a short cut home on Oct 10 1922 from Ryecroft Junction signal box to Butts. His body lay on the track between 10.00pm and 3.00am and was mutilated by five trains passing over him (BCM Jan 1985 p17). For its industry see Walsall.

Ryecroft Street of brick terraces in Newcastle-under-Lyme. The street dates from pre-1845 (NULOP vol 2 p53p of in 1955). The name is preserved in the name of the N part of the ring road.

Ryecroft Gate Small hamlet at the confluence of Rad and Dunsmore Brooks 0.5m S of Rushton Spencer village. Formerly in Rushton James township in Leek ancient parish. There was settlement here by the C17 (VCH vol 7 p219).

Rye Hill House 1.5m S of Church Eaton. In Church Eaton parish. It was the residence of Charles Ashton in 1851 (W pp22,456). Ryehill Bridge is SE of Little Onn.

Rye Hills Minute hamlet over 0.75m NE of Alsagers Bank.

Rye Low Burial mound at SK 10526128, 0.25m ENE of Brund. It is 40 paces in diameter and a listed monument. Excavated by Bateman in 1849. Traces of burning were found. Sheldon in 1894 found nothing (TYD p62) (Proceedings of the Society of Antiquaries of London series 2 vol 15 p425) (NSJFS 1965 p46).

Ryland Aqueduct Carries the Birmingham Canal New Cut New Main Line (Island Line) over the road called Dudley Port. An access point to the canal here is known locally as the Devil's Hole (see) (BTRA p15). The aqueduct, built in 1836, was replaced by a modern aqueduct in 1967 when the old one was demolished (TSSOP p54p). The Devil's Hole is the local name for an access point to the canal in the Ryland Aqueduct (BTRA p15).

S

Saddlesall Island in the Trent, created by a new cut, 0.25m NW of King's Bromley.

Saint Amon's Heath John Sutton thinks it can be identified probably with Blackheath, near Stafford, SE of Beacon Hill. Here some of the royalist forces camped prior to the battle of Hopton Heath. Harwood and others have mistakenly identified St Amon's Heath with Hopton Heath itself and claim the battle took place here (SOS pp54-55) (GNHS p77) (W p341); at least one modern historian, LA Verity, in an unpublished biography of Sir John Gell deposited at Hopton Hall, near Wirkswick, Derbys, accepts this location (SHJ winter 1987 pp1,7).

Saint Anne's Vale Picturesque valley that runs from S to N through one part of Brown Edge village. It seems to have been first called this in an entry in the church registers made by the Rev RG Young in 1871. It is likely that it took its name from the dedication of Brown Edge church in 1844. In 1960 most of the older residents were still referring to this vale as the 'Hollow.' It is thought that the dedication name - St Anne - was taken from the wife of Lord Norton whose name was Anne and from the eldest daughter, born in 1843, who also bore that name (ONST 1960 p231. 1979 p399) (SGSAS) (BEH pp7,52p,55p). The name still prevails, appearing on a signpost in Brown Edge in 1998.

Saint Anne's Well Holy well opposite the main entrance to the house, Sinai Park (OSST 1944-1945). Burton upon Trent (SJC p10). If not Lord's Well (SW of Sinai Park), then, perhaps, an unnamed well to the NNW (1:25,000 OS map).

Saint Anne's Well Anne's Well Wood, Ranton. It had a great reputation as being good for the eyes and from at least 1890 to at least 1928 people came from as far away as Stone to fetch its water (NSFCT 1928 p166).

Saint Ann's Well In Combes Valley. Near Cheddleton flint mill? (NSFCT 1877 p5).

Saint Ann's Well In the Quarnford area and may take its name from Dana or Anu, the earth mother goddess of the Celts (UHAW p75).

Saint Anthony's Flat One of the four common lands comprising the pasturage belonging to the burgesses of Newcastle allotted to them under the Enclosure Act passed in 1816 (W p304). Nine acres of which were still common land in the 1950s (OSST 1956-59 p9).

Saint Augustine Iron Spring Situated in the grounds of Batchacre Hall, just 'out of the South West Park gate by the Crossing Dam over the Brook.' The spring is of strong chalybeate water (OSST 1931 p31). Has also appeared as St Anns Well in the Lake.

Saint Augustine's Priory Former medieval friary at Stafford Green, Forebridge, Stafford. Has also appeared as St Austin's Friary (SIOT p88). There is no mention in VCH vol 3 pp273-274 that it was ever dedicated to St Augustine. Founded by Ralph, Lord Stafford, in 1343 (VCH vol 5 p92) or 1344 who gave land to the Augustinian Canons of St Thomas' Priory; it was the last religious house founded in the county before the Reformation (HOS p25). Its church was described as 'the grandest in Stafford.' Edmund, 6th Baron Stafford (d1403) was buried here (SSTY p139). The tomb of Ralph, Lord Stafford, the founder, was brought here from Stone Priory in 1537 when Stone Priory was suppressed. Leland says in St Augustine's Priory hung a pedigree of the Staffords (SIOT p88). St Augustine's was suppressed on Aug 9 1538. The friary site extended SW from the Green in Forebridge and street names on that side of Wolverhampton Road preserve the memory of the friars. The RC church of St Austin is so named because it stands on part of the site (VCH vol 3 pp273-274). Cherry says the site of the priory was at the back or S side of the Green Brewery, where, in 1890, some ancient walling could be found. And in the brewery garden some ancient masonry was found (SIOT p88). Some stone from the friary church went to Bradley church, SW of Stafford (CHMS p21) (ACOB p8). (SOS pp153,154) (GNHS pp109-110) (W p326) (LGS p217) (VCH vol 5 p92) (SAC pp40-47).

Saint Bertram's Ash Very old ash tree situated by St Bertram's Well (see) near Ilam. It was considered sacred and much venerated by the common people (AAD p187 note). It was believed that it was dangerous to break a bough from it (NHS p207) (Man and the Natural World. K Thomas p75). It had a narrower shaped leaf than Plot had seen on an ash before (NHS p409). Named after the Saxon hermit and Mercian prince, Bertram, whose shrine is in Ilam church, and whose name can be variously spelt, see under Stafford (SMC p171) (W p778) (APB p30) (TPC p172) (SC p142) (LGS p153) (SW pp99, 208,209) (MR p193).

Saint Bertram's Bridge Footbridge over the Manifold S of Ilam Hall and church (APB p30) (SW p209). It used to carry the old road to Blore. It was restored in 1839 (MR p193p). Stand on the bridge and you look up the 'Happy Valley' (Paradise Walk) of Dr Johnson's 'Rasselas' (NSFCT 1936 p28). The name Bertram can be variously spelt, see under Stafford.

Saint Bertram's Chapel Former medieval chapel at Stafford, built in the late Anglo-Saxon period (BOE p240), in c1000 (MR p289), perhaps, on the site of St Bertram's Hermitage, by his cross, and to contain his shrine. There is some evidence that it was the parish church until St Mary's church, built to the E of it by 1086, replaced it. It was built in contact with the W end of the nave of St Mary's and abutted on the SW corner of St Mary's (SIOT p90). The documentary evidence of the chapel dates from 1227 to 1820 (NSFCT 1954 p83). St Bertram's is termed a separate church and never classed among the dependent chapels. There is no record of an incumbent, advowson or any endowments, so presumably it was served by a priest of Stafford Collegiate Church, and in 1524, a dean is in fact appointed to the deanery of SS Mary and Bartholomew in Stafford Collegiate Church. In the C15 there was a guild of St Bertram (or Bertelin) which continued until the Dissolution (OSST 1953-54 pp3-13). Stafford Grammar School was first housed in St Bertram's Chapel (SIOT p90). Part of the chapel was fitted up as a council chamber in 1605 and used for nearly 200 years for council meetings. It was taken down in 1800 (TNE p256) (SL p51), or 1801 (SSTY p133), or 1802 (HOS p66). In 1954 the site was excavated and the foundations of three buildings of different periods were found (NSFCT 1954 p83. 1966 pp7-8) (BOE p240). The earliest was a wooden post structure, the next a church of stone of C11 date with alterations of C13, and the last the church altered in the late C16 or in 1605. Other finds included Bertram's Cross, coins of Ethelred II, Edward I, Henry VIII and a series of C16 and C17 Nuremburg castings counters and paving tiles of 1300 to 1600 (OSST 1953-54 pp18-60 plan and ps) (NSFCT 1954 p83). Some of the stone remains are left on display (DoE II) (SL p144). The end wall of the chancel is missing. For its dimensions see MR p289.

Saint Bertram's Cross A cross at which the Saxon hermit and Mercian prince, Bertram preached; his name can be variously spelt, see under Stafford. The cross reputedly existed at Stafford in the Anglo-Saxon period. It was probably situated near St Bertram's Hermitage and Chapel (HOS p66). A seven feet long wooden cross, which may have been it, was discovered when the chapel was excavated in 1954. It had been intentionally buried and disintegrated soon after exposure (OSST 1953-54 pp14-18 plan and ps) (NSFCT 1954 pp82-83). A replica of the cross is currently displayed in the middle of the exposed chapel foundations (SL p144) (MR p289).

Saint Bertram's Hermitage Stafford. According to tradition the Saxon hermit and Mercian prince, Bertram, his name can be variously spelt (see under Stafford), had a hermitage on the island of Betheney (see) or Bethnei in c705 (HOS p65) (SSTY p132) (MR p289). St Bertram's Chapel (see) was prob-

ably built on the site (SSTY p133). Evidence of a former wooden chapel was discovered beneath the stone foundations of St Bertram's Chapel, when it was excavated in 1954 (SL p144).

Saint Bertram's Shrine Tomb of the Saxon saint and Mercian prince, Bertram in Ilam church. Stafford also had a shrine to St Bertram.

Saint Bertram's Shrine Stafford is recorded as having the tomb of the Saxon hermit and Mercian prince, Bertram, in the C12. It was probably in St Bertram's chapel, which was at the W end of St Mary's church) (HOS p66). Since the C14, Ilam has also had a shrine to St Bertram. (Bertram can be variously spelt. See under Stafford).

Saint Bertram's Well Small holy spring 0.5m NE of Ilam at SK 137514, on W slopes of Bunster Hill under St Bertram's Ash (see). Has also appeared as Holy Ash Well (Holiwallesiche) (WTCEM p40). Named after the Saxon hermit and Mercian prince, Bertram, whose shrine is in Ilam church, and whose name can be variously spelt, see under Stafford. The shrine and well were places of pilgrimage in the Middle Ages (NHS p207) (SMC p171) (W p778) (AAD p187 note) (APB p30) (TPC p172) (SC p142) (LGS p153) (OSST 1944-1945) (SLM Oct 1951 p20) (SJC p10) (SW pp99, 208p,209) (MR p193) (SMM pp65p,66,67p). Roberts thought it was near Wetton (WTCEM p41). Near the well has been found a bronze flat axe of the early Bronze Age which went to the Ashmolean Museum (NHS p403) (NSJFS 1964 p26). The well is at the end of a 16.25m long ley line starting at Foolow in the High Peak, Derbys, and passes through Arbor Low (The Ley Hunter's Companion. Paul Devereaux and Ian Thomson. 1979) (SMM p67). By the well was found the head of a Roman securis (NHS pp403-404 Tab 33 Fig 6) (SD pp70,103,104). On the lawn of Ilam Hall, between the church and St Bertram's Bridge, is another well, which, perhaps, shares the same name (S p137) (SW p209).

Saint Boniface's Well Former public well in Wednesbury on Little Hill (SCSF p141) (HOWY p227).

Saint Caena's Well Wall Grange, Longsdon; perhaps the well at SJ 972539 on the E side of Hollinhay Wood. It has also appeared as St Ann's (1849), Senus (1849), Sinner's (1849), Caena's, Cere's, and Coena's Well (1870s), and may have been known as St Agnes Well (VCH vol 7 p203). In 1846 it was determined by a local engineer, Liddle Elliot, that the spring was of excellent quality and sufficiency to supply the Potteries. It lay on an estate belonging to the 2nd Duke of Sutherland of Trentham Hall (see), who allowed the newly-formed SPWWC to build Wall Grange water works (built 1848-9) to the W at Horse Bridge. The works pumped the water to a reservoir at Ladderedge which in turn was piped to the Potteries. The Duke became the first patron of the company; a bust of him by Matthew Noble was unveiled at Wall Grange Water Works on July 29 1863. In 1935 it was presented to Newcastle-under-Lyme Corporation; by the 1990s it was on display at Millmeece Pumping Station museum (PWW pp8p,11,12) (SHST p220) (SJC p10) (AGT p124) (Cheddleton Remembered. Vera Priestman. 1978 p23). The name may be from St Agnes or St Ann (VCH vol 7 p203), or from the Norman St Cene (or the Holy Supper) in France (NSFCT 1882 p26).

Saint Catherine's Well Big Wood, Sugnall Park. The structure round it is of the early C19 (DoE II). It is probably the same as Holy Well. Holy Well is surrounded by stonework surmounted by a cross in woods between Copmere and Sugnall. Local tradition asserts it was blessed by one of the Popes (NSFCT 1884 p32. 1910 p198) (NSSG p18).

Saint Chads District of NE Bilston, near The Lunt.

Saint Chad's House Bagnall. There is an inscription on the house, which is in Welsh and translates as 'What Owen has he holds' - Samuel Owen Wrexham (B pp43,44).

Saint Chad's Well Chadwell, Blymhill. A holy well named after Saint Chad and gives name to the village it is in (W p460) (SJC p10). Probably the same as the Elder Well and the Brineton mentioned by Plot (OSST 1944-1945).

Saint Chad's Well Well, reputedly containing pure water (LAL p36) situated in the garden of Well Cottage, Stowe, Lichfield. By the well Chad or Cedd in the late C7 built his hermitage and performed his baptisms. There is a stone at the bottom of the well, on which Chad is reputed to have stood when performing baptisms (LI Parts 4 & 5. p99) (MR p214p). The well gained in popularity after Chad's death and gained a reputation as a healing well attracting large numbers of pilgrims to it during the Middle Ages (SW p35). In the earlier C18 the water was thought to be good for sore eyes (VCH vol 14 p147). But the water was said to have caused ague if drunk (SW p110). The ancient custom of dressing it with boughs and reading the gospel by it on Ascension Day was still practised in 1800 (THS i p100) (SAL p133) (HOL pp508-509) (SHOS vol 1 p344) (VCH vol 14 p161). The well was covered with an octagonal stone shelter, which had the inscription 'CE EP DCLXIX,' in the 1830s at the instigation of James Rawson, a local physician (MOS p facing p124) (HS pp21p,22) (SOSH p46p) (VCH vol 14 p147). After the water had dried up in the early 1920s, the well was lined with brick and a pump was fitted to the spring which fed it. The pump was inaugurated with a service in 1923. An annual RC pilgrimage to the well commenced in 1922 and ended in the 1930s, and an Anglican pilgrimage to it took place in 1926 (Lichfield Mercury June 30 1922 p5 p) (History of St Chad's Church. P Laithwaite. 1938. p28) (VCH vol 14 p147). The octagonal stone shelter was demolished in 1949 (STMSM July 1973 p26), and by 1952 the present open four post structure supporting a pyramid tiled roof had been constructed (SLM Oct 1951 p20. Jan 1952 p24p). DoE II* (HOL pp300,504) (SSC p126 in the intro) (W p503) (GNHS p26) (SCSF p142) (KES p139) (LGS p177) (ES June 23 1930 p1p) (KNS p83) (ESS pp45,46,150,162) (VB p24) (SGS p118) (LOPP p34p). There is a chalybeate **spring** 40 yards NW of the well (SW p209) or 100 yards NW of the well (STMSM July 1973 p26). Chad is believed to have also performed his baptisms here (SW p209). It was promoted by the Conduit Lands Trust and Sir John Floyer, one of its trustees. Work was carried out at the spring to make it accessible in the mid 1690s. There was mention in 1717 of people resorting to Stowe 'to drink the waters' (VCH vol 14 p107). The spring was enclosed with a brick building in 1725. After Floyer's death in 1734 it fell into disrepute, in which state it remained many years, but recovered its reputation by the 1780s (SHOS vol 1 p345) (HOL pp508-509) (ESS pp45,46,150,162) (VCH vol 14 p107). In 1818 and 1824 its water was analysed and declared similar to that of Tunbridge Wells (VCH vol 14 p107). The spring was dressed with green boughs and flowers on Ascension Day from, and perhaps before, the Reformation at a service attended by the clergy of St Chad's (SCSF p29) (STMSM July 1973 p26) (Garland for the Year. Timbs). The brick structure survived until 1968 when it was demolished and built over (CCHCA p41) (VCH vol 14 p107). The spring, or St Chad's Well, is the head of Stychbrook (SJC p10).

Saint Crudley's Well Well situated just off Lichfield Street, Bilston, near to the entrance to Proud's Lane (HOBLL pp173-174) (SCSF p141). It was Bilston's water supply and a healing well. Probably formerly known as St Chad's Well (SMM p77). The well is said to have borne a Latin inscription, which translated read:

> Who does not here his alms bestow,
> At him the demon laughs below.

(HOBLL p174). Has also appeared as Crudeley Well and Cruddley Well.

Saint Edith's Well Holy and healing well 0.5m ENE of High Onn and 1m SW of Church Eaton, at SK 835165. It had a reputation for curing the king's evil and eye problems (SW p208). Its water did not reveal any minerals in experiments Plot undertook on it (NHS pp99,106; it is probably one of the three wells he mentions near Shuston House (Shushions Manor?)). Stood on land once belonging to High Onn Manor. Believed to have been anciently blessed by the bishop of Chester. It had a wooden rustic pyramidal covering with a thatched roof, which was rebuilt in the early 1950s, which has since dilapidated. A man rebuilding the covering in the 1950s says his tools were turned shiny and glistening after being, accidentally, left in its water (The Countryman. autumn 1992. pp127-129il). The well is dedicated to perhaps St Edith, the daughter of King Edgar and Wulfrida, of Kemsing, Kent (The Countryman), or of Wilton (The Year 1000. Robert Lacey & Danny Danziger. 1999 p170). However, some local inhabitants believe that the well is dedicated to the St Edith of Polesworth and Tamworth (local info). (SC pp141,142) (SCSF p143) (OSST 1944-1945) (NSFCT 1946 p146) (SLM Oct 1951 p20) (SJC p10) (S p130) (VCH vol 4 p91) (Stafford Post July 21 1988 p1) (SN July 29 1988 p5) (MR p99p) (SMM p73).

Saint Eloy's Hospital Medieval hospital which stood in the area known as the Spittles, at the junction of Newcastle Lane and London Road, to the W of Penkhull (CAST p11). It appears in records spasmodically between 1409 and 1590 (NUL pp26,27), but may have been in existence as early as the C13 and may have been an almshouse (CAST p11). Has appeared as the hospital of St John, St Louis, St John the Baptist and St Louis, St John the Baptist and St Eloy, or by 1485, St Leo (VCH vol 3 p289), and St Loye (VCH vol 8 p188). It seems even by 1409 to have stopped sheltering the poor (NUL pp26,27). The land of the hospital may later have formed the estate known as Spittles (CAST p11).

Saint Erasmus's Chapel Pre-Reformation chapel built by William Chetwynd III (SHC 1909 p150 note) or Walter Chetwynd in the early C16 (OSST 1949-50 p13). It was built close to St Erasmus's Well on Ingestre waste, probably at the edge of the park opposite Shirleywich and built to cater for an increasing number of pilgrims visiting the well, some of whose recipients would hang their crutches on the side of the chapel (COI pp133-134) (OSST 1949-50 p13) (SLM Oct 1951 p20).

Saint Erasmus's Well Sulphurous olegagenous holy well with healing powers, in the grounds of Ingestre Hall (SJC p10). The structure containing it was built in the time of Henry VII by William Chetwynd (SH p46) and it was closely associated with a nearby chapel dedicated to St Erasmus (SLM Oct 1951 p20) (SW p91), dissolved at the Reformation. The well had become neglected by the later C17 (NHS pp99,100). Dr Wilkes rebuked Plot's account, and thought it did not exist (SH p46). Dr Murray found both iodine and bromine in the Ingestre Well (GNHSS p4). (OSST 1944-1945).

Saint Francis de Sales Chapel Roman Catholic chapel at Woodlane, Yoxall. It was built in 1795 by Charles Talbot, Earl of Shrewsbury of Hoar Cross Old Hall. It represents one of the earliest Catholic centres in Staffs and was built to resemble an out-building to the Presbytery to which it is attached in order to hide the fact that it was a Catholic place of worship. The building was restyled to look like an ecclesiastical building after the Catholic Emancipation Act of 1829. A priest, endowed by the earl, resided at the Presbytery until 1966. By 1978 the church was being served from Barton-under-Needwood (BOE p327) (BUBA pp2-3).

Saint George's One of three wards of Walsall municipal borough (W p639) (VCH vol 17 p217).

Saint George's Hospital S of Corporation Street, Stafford. Formerly Staffordshire General Lunatic Asylum. Designed by Jospeh Potter. Opened on Oct 18 1818 by the Duke of Sussex, sixth son of George III. It was then one of only four asylums in the 52 counties of England and Wales. An early notable patient may have been George Smith of Mucklestone Wood Farm, the 'Mucklestone Idiot.' In 1837 Monsieur le Dr Fairet, chief physician of the Salpetriere Hospital, Paris, visited Stafford Mental Hospital. The hospital was enlarged in 1849-50 and renamed St George's in the late 1940s (VCH vol 6 p235) (SKYT pp71,74). It had been closed for a time by 1999 when it was proposed to use the building for a national food and catering centre.

Saint Giles Green Area around where four roads meet at Blithbury. The name is obsolete after the C16. The priory at Blithbury was dedicated to St Giles (CWF p11 note).

Saint Helen's Well Spring S of of the vicarage house at Rushton Marsh, Rushton Spencer. Has variously been called St Helen's Well and St Daniel's Well (VCH vol 7 p225). A former vicar of Rushton, Rev William Mellard, maintained it was St Daniel's Well, not St Helen's (DP p14). Plot mentions two springs here which supplied an overshot mill, situated not far from their rise. It has long been renowned for going dry after a period of eight or 10 years, and always about the beginning of May, when springs should be at their highest, and not returning until the following Martinmas. The spring always goes dry before some calamity, war, or drought. It has been so reliable that villagers have come to depend on it to foretell evil. It foretold the English Civil War, the beheading of Charles I, the great corn dearth of 1659 (STM April 1968 p31) or of 1670 (SW p89), the disturbances of 1679 (NHS pp49-50), the death of Edward VII, and WW1 (DP p14) and WW2 (SMM pp73-74). Plot believed that the well seized up at eight or 10 year intervals, anyway (SH p59). The timing of its seizure, at the beginning of May, connects with the Celtic feast of Beltaine (May 1) (DP p14). It was a Mr Peter Goostry, an intelligent man, whose influence in the area was considerable, who helped materially to bring the superstitions connected with the well into contempt (S&W p299). The well was dressed, up to the 1920s (SMOPP vol 2 p24p of in 1907) (DP p16p) (SMM p74) or to 1933 (VCH vol 7 p225). Thereafter the well became neglected and overgrown but had been tidied up by 1995, by which year dressing of the well had resumed (DPEM p113p). (SD pp107,108) (W p730) (SCSF p144).

Saint James' Hospital 1m N of Tamworth. Founded by Philip Marmion of Tamworth Castle (see) in 1274 or 1275 (VCH vol 3 pp294-296) (SVB p180) or in 1285 (LGS p230) and served by priests of the Premonstratensian Order (LGS p230). The hospital, which has also appeared as Hospital of St James, was built after 1266 (VCH vol 3 pp294-296). Gould thinks the hospital building is represented by the remaining chapel-looking building called Spittal House (see) or The Spittal. He thinks it is of Norman origin and was rebuilt shortly before 1274 and that it functioned as a hospital for a very short time, if at all, and served for the rest of the medieval period as a chantry. Hospitals dedicated to St James, were often set up after a pilgrimage to St James, Compostella (SSAHST 1968 pp23-31).

Saint John's Hill Hill at Shenstone on which is situated the modern house called 'Viewpoint' (BOE p235).

Saint John's Hospital House at Alton designed by AWN Pugin. It is one composition with the C19 Alton Castle (see); the two are linked by a bridge over a moat-ravine (MR p13). The hospital was begun seven years before the castle in 1840 (W p766), but was built more slowly, being completed in 1846 (SGS p51); some of it was finished in 1843 (BOE p60). Pugin was prouder of this and of Cheadle church than of any of his other buildings (BOE p60). It is three sides of a quadrangle, open to the castle. On the left side is a chapel whilst the right side has the guildhall (a village hall). The centre range is the entrance (BOE p60) (SGS p51). Sister Mary Joseph Healy (d1857 aged 31) and another sister (d1868 aged 41) are buried in the cloister (HAF p275). (W p766) (JAT p13 il of) (CL Nov 24 1960 pp1226-9) (MR p13p). **Chapel**. Formerly used as part of St John's School (HAF p274). Pevsner says the monumental brasses to 16th Earl of Shrewsbury (d1852) and the 17th Earl of Shrewsbury (d1856) are in this chapel (BOE p60), whilst Thorold says they are in the castle chapel (SGS p52). (W p767) (JAT pp15,16) (CL Nov 24 1960 pp1227p,1229). **St John's School**, a school for local Catholic children, was housed at the hospital shortly after it's completion. It was supported by the Earl of Shrewsbury. The girls were taught in the chapel, whilst the boys were taught in the guildhall. From c1855 it was staffed by nuns from the convent of Sister of Mercy at Carlow, Ireland. They were succeeded in 1868 by the Sisters of Mercy of St Anne's Convent, Birmingham. During their time at St John's Hospital the sisters opened a boarding school for girls. During WW2 girl boarders from St Anne's Convent, Birmingham, were evacuated to the hospital and other evacuees from Manchester were taught in the guildhall. In 1949, St John's which had been an all-age school, became a Primary. It closed in 1994 (HAF pp274-280p). The ghost of an Irish nun on a small bridge in the vicinity of the primary school has been seen by many, including a female former pupil at the primary school returning to visit the school (MS&S p65). The **St Aloysius' School for Little Boys**, later St John's Prep School, a prep school for Catholic boys, was founded by the Sisters of Mercy in 1898. The school moved from St John's Hospital to Alton Castle in 1920 (HAF pp281-286).

Saint John's Hospital Former medieval hospital in St John's Street, Lichfield. Has also appeared as the Hospital of St John the Baptist (LAL p15p). In existence by 1208. Bishop Roger de Clinton may have been the founder (VCH vol 3 p279. vol 14 p10). Some say he founded it in 1135 (LAL pp15-16) or in c1140 (VCH vol 3 p279) (BOE p191). Some say Roger, bishop of Lichfield, was the original founder, and he may have been Roger Weseham, or Roger Molend, both of the C13 (HOL pp537-556). Freeford prebend originally included the hospital (VCH vol 14 p153). St John's was formerly a hospital but by the C15 had become an almshouse (VCH vol 14 pp153,184). In 1495 Bishop William Smith gave St John's a new body of statutes, a school with a master (Lichfield Grammar School, see), and accommodation for 13 almspeople and a chapel (tablet over the entrance erected in 1720) (W p509). Freeford prebendary was then granted the right to appoint one of the 13 almsmen (SSAHST vol 2 1960-61 p46). In the late C15 or early C16, and probably after Bishop Smith's re-foundation, the hospital was extended with new accommodation with eight chimneybreasts abutting onto St John's Street (BOE p191). There was a foolish tradition that the chimneys were not incorporated into the hospital properly because chimneys had not been invented by the time of the hospital's construction (LGS pp177-178). Some restoration of the hospital occurred in 1929, 1966-7, 1970-71 (VCH vol 3 pp279-289). The hospital had a **chapel** by the mid C13 (VCH vol 14 p153). In the S wall of the present chapel are possibly traces of the former chapel (BOE p191). The glass in the E window, erected in 1984, is by John Piper and depicts Christ (Lichfield Mercury June 29 1984 p45 p). (SHOS vol 1 p322 pl.xxxi) (GNHS p157) (The Hospital of St John Baptist without the Barrs of the City of Lichfield: some notes on its history. Harry Baylis. 1960) (St John's Hospital, Lichfield. 1984. Howard Clayton) (COS p48p). A St John's Priory, built by Clinton, said to have been an Augustinian house (SOSH pp109,167p), may be identifiable with this hospital. In 1981 the trustees of St John's Hospital opened a new almshouse in Lichfield cathedral Close known as St John's within the Close (see), and from 1989 the old almshouse in St John's Street was called St John's without the Bars to distinguish it from the new almshouse (VCH vol 14 p184).

Saint John's Hospital Medieval hospital situated at the junction of Lichfield Road and White Lion Street, Forebridge, Stafford Green. Founded in 1208, for the sick and aged (SSTY pp139-140). Or first mentioned in 1208. Founded probably by one of the Stafford family (VCH vol 3 pp290-293). A pictorial record of its chapel is preserved on a C14 seal (SKYT p60il). The court house of the Manor of Castre (see) appears to have been built on or near the site reusing some materials from the hospital. The court house was also used by Castle Church parish church wardens for meetings. By the early C19 the house was converted into the White Lion Inn. Two ancient buttresses built into the inn are said to have formed part of the chapel (SKYT pp60,61p) (VCH vol 3 pp290-293. vol 5 pp88,91) (SAC pp130,131il of the inn). Or the hospital was situated near St Augustine's Priory, where the Grapes Inn now stands on the S side of Lichfield Road, near to the Green (SIOT p88) (LGS

p217) (VCH vol 3 pp290-293). According to Leland the hospital lay hard by the Sow (L vol 5 p21). In 1929 a large number of skulls and bones were dug up at the inn, leading some to believe that the inn stood on the hospital burial ground (SKYT p60). Forebridge lock-up is said to have been built with some stone from St John's Hospital (SKYT 58). (SOSH p173).

Saint John's Square On the S side of Fountain Place on the W side of Burslem town centre. Nos. 15 and 15a were 'John Bain's Shop' in Arnold Bennett's novel 'The Old Wives Tale' (DoE II).

Saint John's Well Healing well at Shenstone (SCSF p143) (SMM p80).

Saint John's within the Close Almshouse on S side of the Lichfield cathedral Close built in 1981 by the trustees of St John's Hospital, St John's Street, Lichfield, on the site of the Theological College which closed in 1972 (VCH vol 14 p184) (GKCLC). In the C15 this was part of a site on which was the New College (see). Has also appeared as St John's within the Close (VCH vol 14 p58 see map).

Saint Kenelm's Furrow Patch of grass greener than ordinary running up to the Knoll Hill 0.5m NNE of Clent, in Staffs (NHS pp411-413) (CR p71). Or an old hedge bank running up Knoll Hill which was in existence in 1876 (STELE Feb 24 1955). Traditionally believed to be the site where Kenelm was murdered in the C9. Knoll Hill may be Clent Hill.

Saint Kenelm's Pass Extremely narrow gorge. The road from Clent to St Kenelm's Chapel runs through it and this is Clatterbatch Road? Marked on OS map 1:25,000.

Saint Lawrence's Well At Grazeley Brook, Wolverhampton. Was situated in an enclosure a little eastward of the Worcester Road (SHOS vol 2 p165). White says it was either unknown or had fallen into disuse by 1851 (W p76). (SCSF p140).

Saint Leonard's Hill Piece of land in Bilston. Given by Thomas Perry in 1494 to the church (St Leonard's chapel). In 1623 it was the subject of a lawsuit since the sole surviving trustee had claimed it as his own (HOBLL p236).

Saint Leonard's Hospital Medieval hospital for lepers and persons with skin disease at Queensville, Stafford (LGS p217) (FSP pp97,98-100). It was the belief in the C16 that Ralph, Earl of Stafford (d1372), had founded the hospital (VCH vol 3 p294). The hospital, sometimes called Spittle Chapel (OSST 1929 p18), was in existence by 1386-7 when it was in the patronage the Stafford family (VCH vol 3 p294). It was possibly a refounding of the Holy Sepulchre Hospital (see) at Radford. The site of the hospital has never been precisely identified but is probably to the E of Lichfield Road between St Leonard's Avenue and the railway (VCH vol 3 pp293-294) or as some have said near to what is now Queensville Avenue (SSTY p140), and was partly incorporated into the old tavern called Holly Bush, which existed in the C18 (SIOT p88). Dudley Wilks writing in c1939 says a silver chalice was dug up some years ago on the site of the burial ground of the hospital (FSP pp97,98-100) (SOSH p173). (SAC pp149-150). The hospital appears to have given its name to the hamlet of Spittal Brook, which became Queensville in the C19.

Saint Leonard's Well Formerly situated below Anslow church (in the centre of Anslow village?), at the road junction (IVNF). About 1946, Underhill noted, the trees planted to give shade to it were still standing and a pump in a railed enclosure. He says the well stood to the W of Mount Pleasant Farm by the old chantry dedicated to St Leonard (UTR pp214,237).

Saint Mary Bridge Crosses the Tame at Tamworth; whereas Bole Bridge crosses the Anker. Leland in c1540 noted it had 12 arches and led to Coventry. He presumed it to be built by Lord Basset of Drayton since on it was a (five-sided?) stone cross bearing the Basset arms (LI part 5. p105). The cross had been reduced to a stump by the late C18. It was later placed in Tamworth Castle (see) and has acquired the name Marmion's Stone (LGS p228). The bridge was damaged beyond repair in the great flood of Feb 1795 and had to be blown up, and rebuilt in 1796 (SHOS vol 1 pp141,420) (SHC 1934 p91). A time capsule casket was placed in one of the parapets on Nov 7 1839 and taken out 100 years later (THM vol 1 pp38-39p). Has also appeared as Lady Bridge. (SK p199) (Topographer vol 1 p532, and vol 3 p117) (GM vol 62 pp981,1184)

Saint Mary's Bridge Bridge over the Dove leading from Ilam to Thorpe. An earlier bridge probably replaced the present bridge, which is dated 1790. It probably led to Musden Grange (a grange of Croxden Abbey). Every Cistercian house was dedicated to the Blessed Virgin Mary (NSFCT 1917 p46).

Saint Mary's College Is Oscott College at Old Oscott (1794-1838) and at New Oscott, Warws (1838).

Saint Mary's Hospital Cannock. In existence by 1220. It probably ceased to exist sometime after 1230 (VCH vol 3 p274).

Saint Mary's Hospital It may have stood about 0.25m SE of St Peter's church, Wolverhampton. Founded in 1392-5 by Clement Leveson, chaplain, and William Waterfall. Perhaps suppressed at the Dissolution and the property perhaps passed to the Levesons (VCH vol 3 pp296-297). It may have stood by Pipers Croft (HOWM pp34,35).

Saint Mary's House At SE corner of Lichfield cathedral Close; overlooks Stowe Pool. The house incorporates one of the turrets positioned at each of the four corners of the wall that surrounded the Close in the Middle Ages. Incorporates an early C14 house, perhaps built by Bishop Langton. In 1626 the house, formerly occupied by the prebendary of Freeford, was known as 'the old palace.' This name is difficult to explain as St Mary's House stood outside the grounds of the medieval palace (VCH vol 14 p65 pl 11). Remodelled inside in 1710 and again in 1804-5 (VCH vol 14 p65). In May 1804, about 15 feet under the tower, was discovered a subterranean passage running E from the cathedral (HOL p295) (Fuller's Church History. Book iv. p174). From 1851 to 1965 it was the vicarage for St Mary's, Lichfield, when it became the Diocesan Office (GKCLC). Has also appeared as St Mary's Vicarage. (BOE p189).

Saint Mary's Vicarage House in Bath Street, Bilston. Birthplace of Sir Henry Newbolt. Demolished in 1968 to make way for a sports centre (BOP p66p).

Saint Mary's Well or Mariwell. Formerly situated opposite the W end of St Mary's church in Breadmarket Street, Lichfield. Existed in the late Middle Ages (HOL p478 note) (VCH vol 14 p99).

Saint Michael's Well There are or were several springs in the churchyard of St Michael's church, Lichfield (and even under the church?) (NHS p86).

Saint Modwen's Well A well dedicated to Modwen, situated on the island of Andressy, Burton upon Trent, at SK 254228. Modwen is reputed to have drank from the well (SJC pp4,10). It had a reputation for curing the King's Evil, but proved to contain no minerals in Plot's experiments in the later C17 (NHS p106). The well is dressed on the anniversary of St Modwen's death (STMSM Sept 1973 p26) (FOS p103). It was probably situated on the flat meadow opposite the Church Yard, as this spot is still known as Annesley or Andressey (HOBTW p11) (OSST 1944-1945). (SD p14) (SHOS vol 1 pl.) (SC p140) (SCSF p142) (KNS p83) (SLM Oct 1951 p20).

Saint Modwen's Well Holy well dedicated to Modwen, 0.5m E of the church at Canwell, at SK 149006. Had a reputation for curing the King's Evil, but proved to contain no minerals in Plot's experiments in the later C17 (NHS p106) and used for debility (OSST 1944-1945) (SJC p10). (SD p14) (SHOS vol 2 p22 - the 2nd p22) (KNS p83) (SCSF p142). Has also appeared as Modswell's Well (SMC p170).

Saint Paul's By 1999 was a ward in Sandwell metropolitan borough. The ward takes its name from, and covers the area about, St Paul's church, Owen Street, Tipton.

Saint Peter's A ward of Wolverhampton borough by 1982, covering central Wolverhampton.

Saint Peter's Bridge Crosses the Trent at Burton. Built in 1985 and connects Bond End with Stapenhill (ABTOP pp11p,141).

Saint Stephen's Hill Tiny hamlet on a hill above the Blithe Valley (at this point now dammed to form Blithfield Reservoir) 1.25m SE of Blithfield. In Blithfield ancient parish. Near St Stephen's Farm was found a perforated stone hammer or mace head, oval in shape of Neolithic or Bronze Age origin found at The Rookery about 200-300 yards from the house (NSFCT 1934 p59) (Proceedings of the Prehistoric Society. vol 25 p139) (NSJFS 1964 p16). The Steven's Hill which formerly had a chapel on it (LTM Oct 1971 p35) is probably a reference to this place. The 1955 OS map shows the site of a chapel, St Stephen's Chapel, at SK 061230 ENE of the hamlet St Stephen's Hill, now on the edge of Blithfield Reservoir or submerged under it.

Saint Thomas Former small hamlet which grew up on the site of St Thomas Becket Priory. Formerly in Hopton and Coton out-township of St Mary's parish, Stafford (W p341).

Saint Thomas Becket Priory (locally *Senthomas* LGS p80). Former medieval priory 1.25m NNW of Walton-on-the-Hill, 2m E of Stafford.
ABBEY. Founded in c1175 (some say 1174, 1179 or 1180) by Richard Peche, bishop of Lichfield (1161-82) (SOSH p109), for Augustinian Canons in memory of his friend Thomas Becket, murdered at Canterbury in 1170. (It was one of the earliest foundations under Becket's name - BOE p247). Others say there was another founder, with Peche, one Gerarp, a wealthy burgess of Stafford (LGS p80), or that he was Gerard fitz Brian (VCH vol 3 p264), or that he was Gerard Stafford (SKYT p81), or that he was Brian, father of Gerard Stafford (BERK p45). Peche and Brian, in effect, founded the priory when they brought six Black Canons of the Augustinian Order from Darley Dale to start the building of the priory. The buildings were, however, started by Brian's son, Gerard Stafford, in 1174. According to records the first buildings were demolished and Bishop Peche rebuilt the priory in 1180, dedicating it to St Thomas the Martyr. The Canons were replaced by monks in 1191 (BERK pp45,47). Bishop Northburgh visited the

priory in 1347 (BERK p54) and or in 1356 (VCH vol 3 p264). Henry IV visited the priory after the battle of Shrewsbury in 1403. Bishop Blythe visited in 1524. Bishop Lee secured the site after the dissolution in 1538 (HOS p28) (BERK pp43-57 ils dias ps). The priory has also been called St Thomas the Martyr Priory, and Stafford Priory (VCH vol 3 pp260-267), and has been commonly called Senthomas, Sentimus and Stewmas. The cartulary of St Thomas Priory appears in SHC vol 8 1887 pp125-201. (SHC 1914 pp127-128 note).

AFTER THE DISSOLUTION. After the death of Bishop Lee in 1543 his nephew, Brian Fowler, acquired St Thomas' (BERK p57). Fowler, a Catholic, established an important Roman Catholic centre here which lasted to 1715 (NSFCT 1945 p88) or 1717 (BERK p58). The Catholic ex-bishop of Peterborough was given sanctuary here in c1564. On the death of Brian Fowler in 1587 the priory passed to his son, Walter (d1621). One of Walter's sons, William, became a Dominican priest and served as chaplain at St Thomas', and, on his death was buried here. Another son Brian (d1658) had a son Walter (d1683), who in turn had a son Walter, who married Constantia, the daughter of Walter, first Lord Aston of Tixall (BERK p59). A house was built on some of the priory site in the late C17 and incorporates masonry of the priory (BOE p247). This has become known as St Thomas' Hall (FSP p96) (SKYT p83), St Thomas' Farm, Senthomas (LGS p80) and Priory Farm (OSST 1963-5 p6) (VCH vol 3 p266). For the Fowler family's involvement in the Popish Plot see Tixall Old Hall. A gatehouse for the hall was built. This was taken down in c1717 (BERK p60). Celia Fiennes noted the priory (SKYT p83), as did Chetwynd and Loxdale (SH pp44,81). On the death of Walter son of Walter in 1695 the priory passed to his brother William. On his death in 1717 the priory passed out of the hands of the Fowlers to William's niece Kath Casey and her husband John Betham Fowler. Their daughter Catherine came into possession in 1719 (BERK p59). Roxburgh says soon after the priory had been dismantled as a residence, part of the ancient mansion was utilised by a company of cotton spinners (SKYT p84). The cotton spinners stayed only a few years in the early 1700s (BERK p59). From 1703 to 1716 it was the residence of the Catholic bishop for the Midlands, Dr George Witham (SKYT p83). In 1726 Catherine married Thomas Belasyse, (Viscount Fauconberg). In disgust at having to surrender part of the estate to Rebecca Grove, niece of William Fowler, Fauconberg sold the priory to the notorious Sara, Dowager Duchess of Marlborough in the 1730s (NSFCT 1945 p88) (BERK p59), perhaps in 1739 when the priory passed into Protestants hands (HOS p30). On Sara's death in 1744 the priory passed to her grandson Hon John Spencer, who was created Earl Spencer in 1765 (BERK p59). In 1765 the priory passed to the ancestors of Earl Talbot (SKYT p83). The Talbots left it to the Shrewsburys and it was still part of the Shrewsbury estate in 1948 (SKYT p83).

REMAINS. Some of the windows may have gone to Weston-on-Trent church; the Fowler family were lay impropriators of Weston (NSFCT 1879 p40 two plans facing, 1885 p24). Some stone pillars which formed the entrance to the Chapter House were used in the building of Brocton Hall in c1717 (BERK p60), and some gothic arches also went there (BOE p81) (MR pp58,296p) (F p313). Stonework from the gateway is said to be in a gateway to the gardens of Milford Hall (BERK p60). The chalice and paten are believed to have gone to Pillaton Hall where they were rediscovered in the C18 (BERK p59). Six marble panels representing the life of Christ which were formerly part of the altar at Tixall Priory (St Thomas' at Baswich?) (SAIW pl 38) were at Stafford Castle in the C19. Charles Lynam of Colwich once visited the site by boat and traced a part of wall which was formerly the N transept of the church (NSFCT 1945 p88). In 1877 Lynam plotted what he considered to have been a plan of the priory (SKYT p83). In 1902 workmen digging a pit on the site of the priory to bury two dead cows uncovered two sandstone coffins containing skeletons; one skeleton had a full and perfect set of teeth. One skeleton was buried faced down (Staffordshire Chronicle. Jan 18 1902) (SKYT p84). Other remains were discovered when a cesspit was dug in the priory's burial ground (ROT pp51-54). The old pavement of the church was discovered in about the 1930s during an excavation (FSP pp94,95-97,98-100). The OSS excavated the site in the 1930s and threw doubt on Lynam's measurements without actually disproving them (SKYT p83). Priory Farm is certainly on the exact site of the medieval entrance to the precinct. By the 1960s the most considerable remains on site were those of the conventual church and the western and southern ranges of the cloister court. Part of the conventual church was to be seen in a stretch of walling some 39 feet long on the N side of the garden of Priory Farm. The W end of the church may be in line with the W end of Priory Farm (OSST 1963-5 p6) (VCH vol 3 p266). (W p326) (GNHS pp109,130) (GNHSS p15) (S p91) (KES pp29,153) (HOS p25) (SSTY pp140p,141) (SGS p157) (ASOP p94 St Thomas' Mill Farm near Baswich in 1910). St Thomas' was considered extra-parochial in 1851 (W). There is a tradition of a passage leading away from the priory cellar in an unspecified direction (SKYT p84). The original seal is in the BM. For an illustration of the seal see S p of opposite p90. The priory is supposed to be haunted by the ghost of a damsel who was murdered by soldiers in the precincts. She returns to haunt at various times of the year such as Halloween and Candlemas (SKYT p84) (FSP p10) (ROT p54).

Saint Thomas Spring Baswich. A weak brine salt spring (NHS p97), presumably near St Thomas Becket Priory.

Saint Thomas Trees Hill 0.25m SE of Dilhorne church. Here is a burial mound at SJ 973432. It has been excavated by Stoke-on-Trent Museum Archaeological Society (NSFCT 1983 p13). It is a listed monument. In the early 1920s some Roman coins were found on top of the hill (NSFCT 1987 p25). Has also appeared as Saint Thomas's Trees.

Sale, The Tiny hamlet on low ground S of Pyford Brook 0.5m NW of Fradley. In Alrewas ancient parish. (SHOS vol 1 p46). The causeway enclosure NE of The Sale at SK 154144 is a listed monument.

Sale Brook Runs in the Saverley Green, Fulford, Moddershall area.

Salisbury Hill Hill 0.75m SW of Tyrley Castle Farm, Tyrley, Staffs, formerly in Drayton-in-Hales ancient parish. The old deer park of the Pantulfs (1086-1232) included Salisbury Hill and Tyrley Heath. Named after Richard Neville Earl of Salisbury the Yorkist commander who encamped here after the battle of Blore Heath (STC p9) (NSFCT 1913 pp207,208). But W Beamont, said wrongly, that Salisbury camped here prior to the battle (SHC 1945/ 6 p94).

Sally Harding's Valley Near Bednall, Cannock Chase.

Sally Moor N of Ramshorn. Marked on Pigot and Son map (1830).

Salt Village by the Trent lining the foot of the northern edge of Salt Heath upland 3m NE of Stafford. Former out-township with Enson of St Mary's parish, Stafford. Has appeared as Halen (1004) (DUIGNAN), Selte, a manor, in DB, Salte, and Saute (SPN p102). Halen is Old Welsh for salt (DUIGNAN) (SPN p102). It takes its name from the nearby salt springs (LGS p207) (SH p45) (SGS p142) (SVB p147) (SSE 1996 p17). But salt has never been at Salt village (WMARCH 1993 p72). Was a prebend of Stafford Collegiate Church (VCH vol 3 p305). The church, St James the Great, at the junction of Trentfield Lane and Salt Road in the W end of the village, was built in 1840-1842 (BOE p229). Salt became a separate ecclesiastical parish in 1843 (GLAUE p421) or 1844 (LGS p207). It became a separate civil parish in 1866 (GLAUE p421). Foot-and-mouth disease broke out at Salt Hill Farm in early 1968 (SN Jan 26 1968 p13).

Saltbox Former farm on S side of Queslett Road (formerly Queslett Lane) and N of King's Road (MNB p71). An illegal prize fight took place between Tom Lane and Patrick Perry at Saltbox. The fight, undisturbed by police, probably took place in Feb 1879 (Birmingham Gazette Feb 1879) (TBS p32). The farm was demolished by 1940 when Sundridge School, Sundridge Drive, was built on the site (MNB p73).

Salt Brook Rises in Needwood Forest runs through Draycott-in-the-Clay to the Dove.

Salt Brook Tributary of the Trent. Runs at Salt. (SPNO p17).

Salterholme Field name in or near Alrewas. In this field, according to Alrewas PR, Robert Nevill and his son were killed by lightning whilst they sheltered under an oak (W p592).

Salter's Ford Farm To E of Newtown, 1.5m SW of Rushtonhall. Formerly in Rushton James township in Leek ancient parish. The house may stand on a packhorse way (VCH vol 7 p220).

Saltersford Lane E of Alton may be presumed part of a long-distance saltway, perhaps from Nantwich to Derby by way of Newcastle and Cheadle (SL p111).

Salters Hall 3m SW of Dudley (DUIGNAN) (ESH p16), just over 1m SE of Kingswinford church, in Kingswinford ancient parish. It appears on the 1834 OS map to the W of Dingle Road on the S side Bromley Lane.

Salters Lane There is a Salter's Road in Walsall area.

Salter's Street Wigginton. Name of field near Money Lands or Flats (SHOS vol 1 p432).

Salter's Way Medieval pack horse road from the brine pits at Weston-on-Trent to Bagnall by way of Washerwall and Wetley Moor (NSFCT 1957 p68).

Salter's Well At Salter's Well Farm, Wetley. 0.5m S of Bagnall. The part of the Roman way which runs through Bagnall is known as Salter's Wells (STM July 1970 pp26,27p).

Salter's Well Holy well near Newcastle-under-Lyme, which has also appeared as Salterswell. No doubt so called for it was frequented by salt carriers in medieval times travelling between Cheshire and the S (SMM p78). Had a reputation for curing the King's Evil, but would not prove to contain any minerals in experiments Plot carried out in the later C17 (NHS p106). (SCSF p143) (OSST 1944-1945) (SLM Oct 1951 p20) (SJC p10).

Salt Heath Heath 0.5m S of Salt, above Sandon Bank. The battle of Hopton Heath partly took place on this former wasteland (SHJ winter 1987 p1).

Salt Library, William Library housing William Salt's collection, manuscripts and historical works mainly relating to Staffs. The library is situated on the N side of Eastgate Street, Stafford. It is named after William Salt, third son of John Stevenson Salt, banker of London, who lived at a house later occupied by Baswich House (see), Weeping Cross. William Salt was born in London in 1808; however, SAH Burne in a newspaper article, stated erroneously that he was born at Weeping Cross (info Randle Knight). Salt spent his life collecting historical documents and paying for the transcribing of large sections of the Public Records and BM holdings relating to the county. The collection cost him between £35,000 and £40,000 to compile and was easily the most comprehensive of its kind (SKYT p75). Salt died in 1863 and it had been his intention to sell the collection. In 1868 his wife, Helen Salt resolved to sell it: Sotheby's even went so far as to make a catalogue (SKYT p74). Protracted negotiations with Mrs Salt stopped the collection from being sold immediately and she was persuaded to try and keep it together for the county. In 1868 a trust was formed to find funding to purchase the work and for a permanent library for it. For two years between 1868 and 1872, whilst funds were being found, the work was housed at Shugborough Hall (SKYT p75). In 1870 Mrs Salt was informed that the trust was unable to find the necessary funds and she should let the collection go to the BM. With the loss of the collection imminent John Sneyd of Ashcombe Park was galvanized into convening a meeting comprising the trust members and notable persons of the county in Dec 1870 to save the collection for the county. At the meeting a new committee was formed and an appeal sent out. In March 1871, with only half the money needed raised, Mrs Salt had begun to grow impatient; the Bodleian was willing to take it. Then Thomas Salt MP, nephew of William Salt, presented the Old Bank House in Market Square, Stafford, which he possessed, to the county for a library, as well as a substantial donation. Mrs Salt finally agreed to sell the collection to the county for £6,000; £4,000 less than her original asking price (SKYT p76). The library opened at Old Bank House in 1872 and moved to its present location in Eastgate Street in 1918 or 1919. The library building was extended when a house, adjoining, was obtained in 1934 (SKYT p76). (MOS pp259-265) (LGS p218) (OSST 1934 pp33-38) (OPB pp7-10,24-26) (VCH vol 6 p258) (SLM autumn 1958 pp32-33. Feb March 1986) (DRBSC p477) (SKYT pp74-78) (SH p137) (HOS 1998 p134p). In 1879 the **William Salt Archaeological Society**, named after William Salt, was founded by Major-General George Wrottesley (d1909) of Wrottesley Hall (see) to publish documents, local and national, relating to Staffs history, mainly in the series known as SHC. In 1936 the name was changed to the Staffordshire Record Society. The society was still continuing under that name in 1999 (Staffordshire Record Society membership form). There had been the suggestion of a Staffordshire Topographical Society earlier in the C19 which had come to nothing (SA Dec 24 1841) (OPB p10). The original Salt collection, which also contained some non-literary artifacts relating to Staffs, has been greatly added to since it was purchased. Some of the non-literary artifacts include: **Catapula head** found at Bushbury, mentioned in NHS and SHOS. **Wax impressions** of 20 conventual and other ancient seals illustrative of Staffordshire. Model of a **stone coffin** lid found at Burton upon Trent in the foundations of the abbey church. Some Staffordshire **clogg almanacs**. A stained glass noted for having Mary Queen of Scots insignia scratched onto it often known as the **'Mary Pane'** and originally from Hall Hill House (see), Abbots Bromley. An **order from Charles I** to Prince Rupert dated 18 Sept 1642 ordering him to send troops from Stafford to Nantwich (FSP p22). A **portrait of David Garrick**. A **tally (wooden)** of Edward Sneyd, Sherriff of Staffordshire, 1825. The **death mask of William Palmer**, the Rugeley poisoner. The **scrap book of William Albert Marson** (d1918?) containing valuable information about Stafford covers the period c1865 to 1915; Marson kept a grocers shop in the High House (Staffordshire Books, Prints, Drawings - catalogue for intended sale in 1868) (info Dominic Farr) (VCH vol 6 p266).

Saltmoor On N side of Goose Brook, Oxley. Retains the name 'Saeffan Moor' which appears in the charter of King Athelred dated 985. The name occurs as part of the boundaries of Tettenhall Regis in 1300 in the form of 'Saffemoor' (HOWM p9 note). To Shaw 'Saltmore' was land at the foot of the incline to Tettenhall. It had been boggy, which, thought Shaw, would have been helpful in the defence of Tettenhall in the battle of c910. By the early C19 'Saltmore' had been drained (SHOS vol 2 p194).

Saltwell At the E end of Flash village at junction of road with the A53. There is said to have been a cock pit beside the road between the present Old Vicarage and Saltwell (NSFCT 1952 p101) (UHAW p20). Has also appeared as Salt's Well (UHAW pp20,49).

Sampson's Cave Small cottage of three rooms built into a rock knoll, and is only ten feet across between Enville and Kinver. It lies just off a public footpath, on the Enville Hall estate at SO 828852. It was constructed by Sampson Allen, who was alive in 1768; in 1770 it was occupied by Thomas Brook. It was still inhabited in 1861 and in the C20 (VCH vol 20 p93). It was abandoned in the 1930s (TB May 1994 p15p of interior. Oct 1994 p15p of exterior), or occupied from time to time in the 1950s, and was boarded up in the 1960s (TB April 1988 p3. Sept 1989 p29). According to tradition it was the home of the Enville Giant (WJO July 1903 xxxv) (FOS p42). Like other caves in the area it was occupied by local labourers, but unlike most of the others it had a rapid turnover of tenants. Close by, at SO 829854, is an icehouse for Enville Hall (KRH pp23,24 plan,27) (IHB p442). Barbara Jones seems to have mistaken the icehouse or cave for Shenstone's Chapel (a folly in the grounds of Enville Hall (see)). She noted a long passage led from the cave to a round chamber with a domed roof, which she thought was possibly an icehouse (F&G p388). Has also appeared as Samson's Cave.

Sams Lane S of High Street, West Bromwich. Takes its name from Samuel Partridge who lived here in 1780 (SOWB p24).

Sandbank Street in central Bloxwich. The name first appears on the electoral register in 1874 (SNBP pp49-50p).

Sandbeds Little mining community near Lane Head (WDY p14), Willenhall. The name is from rich red sand beds (SNW p62). Became a part of Short Heath civil parish in 1895 (SNW p25). Appears on 1889 OS map 6 inch and 1947 OS map 1:25,000 (sheet 32/99). The name is preserved in Sandbeds Road.

Sandborough Minute hamlet on the other side of the Blithe Valley from Hamstall Ridware, 0.5m ESE of Hamstall Ridware. In Hamstall Ridware parish. A house at Sandborow was registered for Protestant Dissenters in 1758 (SHC 1960 p121).

Sandfields Small residential area on ground rising above Trunkfield Brook just under 1m SSW of Lichfield cathedral. Here was built the first pumping station of the SSWWC. The works was officially opened by Lord Ward on Oct 26 1858. A plaque at the works commemorates the opening - the last name on the plaque, that of the Company Secretary, was chiselled off, allegedly after financial malpractice (GHC pp10p of plaque,11p).

Sandford Gate Situated in Lower Sandford Street, Lichfield, which was the old road to Walsall. It was erected by Bishop Roger de Clinton (1129-1148). Has also appeared as Sandford Bar. The bar remained until the end of the C18 (LAL p18).

Sandford Brook Joins the Mill Brook running into the Dove.

Sandford Brook Runs at Lichfield. Is sometimes known as Trunkfield Brook (CCHCB p76).

Sandford Gate or Standford Street Gate. One of the five gates in Lichfield Town Ditch. Recorded in c1200. The gate was probably of wood (VCH vol 14 p40).

Sandford Hill District of Longton and just under 0.5m N of Longton, on the slopes of a ridge above Cockster Brook. Formerly in Stoke-upon-Trent chapelry and ancient parish.

Sandford Pool Former pool which lay to the W of Minster Pool, Lichfield. Separated from Minster Pool by a causeway. It later became known as Upper Pool and Over Pool. Drained and landscaped by the 1780s. The site is now Beacon Park (VCH vol 14 pp1,3,115).

Sandhills Tiny 0.75m ESE of Brownhills. In Shenstone ancient parish.

Sandhills Branch of the Stourbridge Extension Canal. Spurred off the Stourbridge Extension Canal in the Tunstall Road area of Bromley. Ran to Ketley Colliery (HCMS No. 2).

Sandhills Branch of the Wyrley and Essington Canal. Short canal running from the Wyrley and Essington Canal at Catshill to The Sandhills (HCMS No. 2).

Sandon Ancient parish and former manor. The village of Sandon on the N side of the Trent Valley overlooking the Trent is 3.75m NE of Stafford.
EARLY. The **Roman** Buxton-Pennocrucium road may have passed through Sandon. Sandon has been identified with the Roman Sandonium (NSFCT 1908 pp112,113 see Milwich). In the lane leading up to the church is an artificial semicircular cutting in the rock, by the road side. It would have contained a shrine to the patron deity, positioned at the entrance to all Roman stations (NSFCT 1908 p113). Perhaps Plot notes it when he writes 'as you pass through the hollow way at Little Sandon; and in another cut in the rock.....' (NHS p171). But no Roman remains have been found to prove there was a Roman station at Sandon (NSFCT 1908 p113).
1000 to PRESENT. The present village of Sandon is DB Little Sandon (see) (parua Sandone) (although some have claimed DB Little Sandon is Burston) and consists mainly of Sandon Hall estate buildings of 1905 designed by Sir

E Guy Dawber (BOE p231). The other Sandon in DB, Sandone, is Great Sandon, a village at SJ 953295 (see) situated by the church and Old Hall, deserted some time between 1539 and 1666 (SSAHST 1966 p49. 1970 p36) (DB notes) (SPJD p47pc). However, others believe the old village was deserted no earlier than 1717 (Jesus be our Spede: The Parish Church of All Saints', Sandon. 1986 p7). The **name** is from Anglo-Saxon 'sand dun' sand hill (DUIGNAN) (NSJFS 1981 p2) (SPN p102). Sandon parish formed out of Stone original parish after 1086 and probably before 1170 (SHC 1916 p195). The parish **church**, All Saints, at the top of School Lane in the area of the old village, has some fragments of C11 work (Jesus be our Spede: The Parish Church of All Saints', Sandon. 1986). Cooke gives Nov 14 as Sandon's **fair** day (SCSF p99). There was a fair in 1792 (OWEN), but no fair in 1888 (LHE p265). In the **Civil War** parliamentarians may have mutilated the tomb of Sampson Erdeswicke of Sandon Old Hall (see) on their way to the battle of Hopton Heath (1643). The PR records the burials of soldiers killed in this battle as does Weston-on-Trent PR (LGS pp208-9). For a **windmill** at Sandon see under The Shruggs. Sandon was on the main **London-Holyhead-Carlisle route** from the Middle Ages to the end of the stage-coach age. There was a verse scratched onto a window at the 'old' Dog and Doublet in the village suggesting travellers preferred to stay at Sandon rather than at Stone (VB p134). The **railway** line of the NSR opened through Sandon in 1849 (VCH vol 2 p309). That year was built the railway station at the request of the Earl of Harrowby of Sandon Hall so that he could be picked up by the express through-train to London, whenever necessary (SVB p148). It is in a T-plan shape, the stem incorporates a porte-cochere for the Earl (IAS p187) (MIDD vol 3 p30p). Edward Thomas, the village schoolmaster in 1849, often referred to the trains in his diary and recorded special excursions from the Potteries to Sandon Park (NSFCT 1980 p47). Sandon station closed in 1955 and became a private residence after 1985 (SSBOP p57p). **Freemasonry.** The Earl of Harrowby Lodge No. 2625 100 F.M.U. banner made of silk of c1890 was rediscovered in c1975; it had lain on the floor of the balcony of Sandon Hall for many years. It is thought to be the only one in the Stafford district (STMSM Oct 1975 pc on front cover) (SLM Feb 1950 p96p of lime kiln at Sandon). For the Lancaster bomber which crashed in a field between Burston and Sandon see Burston. The **Staffordshire Wildlife Trust** was formed in 1969. In 1999 the Trust was a part of the national organisation known as The Wildlife Trusts. It then cared for 30 wildlife reserves within the county and had its headquarters at Coutts House, Sandon (Trust leaflets). A great number of the rare and curious **Haw-gros-beak bird** (Coccothraustes) (as noted by Plot at Madeley Old Manor) migrated into S Staffs towards the end of the C18. A strong easterly wind was observed to prevail before their arrival. Three were killed in Sandon plantations near Sandon Hall in 1795. Two specimens were given to Shaw by Rev Bonney in 1797 (SHOS vol 1 part 1 p94).

Sandon Bank Tiny hamlet 0.75m WNW of Salt.

Sandon Castle Sandon. Mr Scrivener thought Sandon Old Hall was castellated, or some even earlier fortified structure existed at Sandon owned by the Staffords in the C14 (NSFCT 1910 p212).

Sandon Hall Sandon Old Hall (see) was replaced by a new hall built in 1770 by Archibald Hamilton (1740-1819), 9th Duke of Hamilton, grandson of the 4th Duke (SGS p144) (SPJD p52). HE Chetwynd-Stapylton says this hall was built on the site of the original old hall (COI p193). However, John Darling says this hall was located further down the valley (SPJD p52). It was designed by Joseph Pickford (SGS p144) (SPJD p52).
THE RYDERS. In 1776 (COI p193) or 1777 (SGS p144) (SPJD p52) Archibald Hamilton sold the Sandon estate to Nathaniel Ryder (1735-1803). He was created Lord Harrowby of Harrowby, Lincs, in 1776. His third son, **Henry Ryder** (1777-1836), became bishop of Lichfield and Coventry. Nathaniel was succeeded by his eldest son **Dudley Ryder** (1762-1847), who was created Earl of Harrowby and Viscount Sandon in 1809. He married Susan daughter of the 1st Marquess of Stafford (Granville 1721-1803) of Trentham Hall (see). Dudley was Governor of the Charter House, Trustee of the BM, High Steward of Tiverton, DCL, FSA. He died on Dec 26 1847 (W p404) (SSW pp165-168), shortly after the death at Sandon Hall of his granddaughter, Charlotte-Mary, second daughter of Granville-Dudley Ryder, second son of Dudley, who died on Dec 13 1847 after being burnt at the hall owing to her muslin dress accidentally taking fire (W p404). Dudley was succeeded by his son Dudley Ryder (1798-1882), 2nd Earl. The hall burnt down on June 6 1848 (W p403) and a new hall was begun in 1848 and completed in 1852 (NSFCT 1910 p212) (SPJD p52). In the intervening years the Ryder family and the Earl lived at Sandon Lodge (W p404). Dudley (d1882) was succeeded by his son Dudley Francis Stuart Ryder (1831-1900), 3rd Earl, who died without issue. He was succeeded by his brother Henry Dudley Ryder (b1836), 4th Earl, who was earl for only six months until he died later in 1900. He was

succeeded by his son John Herbert Dudley Ryder (1864-1956), 5th Earl, who was succeeded by his son **Dudley Ryder** (1892-1987), 6th Earl, author of 'Geography of Everyday Things' and contributor to 'England at Worship.' By the time of his death in 1987 he had been the longest serving Deputy Lieutenant of Staffs. He was succeeded by his son Dudley Danvers Granville Coutts Ryder (b1922), 7th and present (1995) Earl; Dudley Danvers' eldest son in 1967 was Dudley Adrian Conroy Ryder (b1951) (Burke's Peerage 1967) (SN May 15 1987 p3) (Who's Who 1995). There is a tradition the poet Lord Byron stayed at Sandon Hall to visit Lady Susan Ryder (BCM April 1977 pp8-10); perhaps she was Lady Susan (d1827), eldest daughter of Dudley, 1st Earl of Harrowby (Burke's Peerage 1967). One of the participants in the Cato-Street Conspiracy, an attempt to assassinate the Government in 1820, was a carpenter at the Sandon Hall (info Michael Bossom).

THE PRESENT HALL. The present hall was built 0.75m SE of the present Sandon village, 0.5m S of Sandon Old Hall. It was built to designs of William Burn and is in the Jacobean style (STC p8p) (SPJD p52). In the hall is a Polish 'States' tapestry and Polish Vestibule satin wood furniture, and in the library a Chippendale table (CL June 13 1991 pp178pc, 180,181). The hall was Sandon Hall Auxiliary Hospital between 1915-18; the hospital comman-dant was Miss Ethel Mary Parker-Jervis OBE (1878-1956), of Meaford Hall (see) and later of Darlaston Hall (see) (Burke's Peerage 1967). HRH Prince Henry visited the hall on Sept 30 1927 (RHPS p283). The hall was still occu-pied by the Ryder family in 1998 (ES Oct 2 1992 p3. Oct 8 1992 p16) (E&S Oct 3 1992) (LGS p209) (SGS p142p) (Daily Telegraph. Weekend Section. Nov 12 1994 p40p). If the aloe in the gardens flowers this portends a death of the Lord Harrowby (FLJ 1896 p385). See also Sandon Park.

Sandon Old Hall An ancient timbered edifice which was defended by strong walls and a deep moat 0.5m ENE of present Sandon village.

THE ERDESWICKES AND GERARDS. The Erdeswickes, originally of Erdeswicke Hall in Minshull Vernon, Ches, inherited Sandon by the marriage of Thomas Erdeswicke to Margaret Stafford, daughter and heir of Sir James Stafford, in 1338/9; Sandon then became the Erdeswicke seat. Thomas' great great grandson, Hugh, was succeeded by Hugh, who was succeeded by his brother Sampson. He was succeeded by his son Hugh (c1520-1596), who was succeeded by his son **Sampson Erdeswicke** (c1539-1603), the antiquary. Both Hugh and his son remained Catholic in Elizabeth I's reign, and Sampson has been described as one of 'the most obstinate and dangerous recusants' in Staffordshire.' Dugdale ascribed the brief heraldic essay entitled 'The trve Vse of Armorie, shewed by Historie, and plainly proued by Example' (1592) by William Wyrley (whose family originated from Little Wyrley (see)), Erdeswicke's amanuensis, to Erdeswicke. In c1593 Erdeswicke began work on SOS. This work, originally titled 'A View of Staffordshire,' is considered the first attempt at a comprehensive history of Staffs. It was not, however, published until 1717. The first version was compiled from various transcript copies including one by Dugdale. It was reissued in 1723. The title was changed to 'A Survey of Staffordshire.' In 1775 George Tollet of Betley Old Hall described the first editions as 'famously incorrect. I know no book more erro-neous and defective.' A new edition was published by Thomas Harwood of Lichfield in 1820 and a second improved edition in 1844. In 1601 Sampson designed his own tomb which still remains in the chancel of Sandon church. In niches above the recumbent effigy of himself kneel his first wife Elizabeth Dixwell, and his second wife Mary, widow of Everard Digby of Stoke Dry, Rutland; she brought him several step-children, of whom the eldest, Everard, was executed in 1606 for complicity in the Gunpowder Plot; he with the other conspirators, went to hide in Holbeche House (see), in Staffs. The hands of the effigy of Sampson are missing, they reputedly were cut off by parlia-mentarian soldiers on the way to the battle of Hopton Heath (1643). On the N wall of the church Sampson had painted a heraldic tree showing coats of arms of the Erdeswicke pedigree from 1086. Sampson was succeeded by his son, Richard Erdeswicke (b1594) (DNB) (SH pp24,25,34) (SPJD pp49p,50p; says Sampson's wives were Elizabeth Dikeswell and Maria Neale). Richard sold Sandon manor to his half-brother, George Digby (d1675), whose daugh-ter and heiress, Jane, brought it to the Gerards of Gerrard's Bromley Hall, by her marriage to Charles, Lord Gerard. The herald Gregory King of Lichfield (see) stayed at Sandon Old Hall with George Digby (d1675), between the end of 1669 and 1672 whilst serving as steward, auditor and secretary to his daugh-ter the Dowager Lady Jane, Lady Gerard, Baroness Gerard, whilst she re-sided at Gerrard's Bromley Hall (see) (DNB). In 1680s the old hall was the seat of Jane, Lady Gerard, Baroness Gerard. The son of Charles and Jane, Digby Gerard (b1662), 5th Baron Gerard of Gerrard's Bromley, was suc-ceeded by his daughter, Elizabeth. In 1698 she became the second wife of James Hamilton (1658-1712), 4th Duke of Hamilton. Her quarrel with her first cousin Charlotte, wife of Lord Mohun, over their respective shares in the

division of the Gawsworth estate, Ches, led to a celebrated duel in Hyde Park, London, on Nov 12 1712 between their husbands; both Lord Mohun and the Duke of Hamilton were killed (Jesus be our Spede: The Parish Church of All Saints', Sandon. 1986 p7).

The old hall was probably deserted after a new hall - the first Sandon Hall (see) - was built in 1770 by Archibald Hamilton (1740-1819) grandson of the Duke of Hamilton killed in the duel of 1712 (NHS Tab 4) (THS part 2 p221) (SGS p144) (The Complete Peerage) (Jesus be our Spede: The Parish Church of All Saints', Sandon. 1986 p7) (SPJD p52). In 1854 a small portion of the inner wall was the only remnant of the old building (NSFCT 1910 p212. 1912 p182). Darling says the old hall was demolished during the latter half of the C19 (SPJD p51). The moat remains (ESH p58) (CAMS p64) (SPJD pp47,50,51pcs).

Sandon Park Park of Sandon Hall and former deer park noted by Sir Simon Degge (EDP p179). The present park was designed by William Emes. Many of the follies were erected by Sir Dudley Ryder, 1st Earl of Harrowby (SPJD p53). A replica statue of the **Artemis of Versailles** was presented to the 5th Earl of Harrowby in 1908 by his aunt and erected in the grounds. It was destroyed in a storm in 1976. A new replica of the statue made in bronze by sculptors Miranda Wakeman and Hannah Northam was erected in the grounds in 1999 (ES Sept 3 1999 p11pc) (SLM Oct 1999 p19pc). **Black Hill** is a natural tree-covered oblong-shaped knoll to the N of Sandon church. **Erdeswicke's Pool** is in Sandon Hall estate. The **Giant's Seat** is a peculiar seat cut out of the rock near the Perceval Shrine. According to tradition it was carved by a giant (HOSCC p120) (IAANS p xxix or xix). **Harrowby's Folly** see Trentham Tower. **Helen's Tomb** is a folly cum reservoir, on the southern tip of Black Hill (1881 OS map) (SPJD p53p). A **hunting lodge** is said to have stood on the site of the present hall. It is implied it was built by the first Hamilton to come to Sandon; therefore this would be James Hamilton, 4th Duke of Hamilton, and building would have occurred sometime between 1698 and 1712 (Jesus be our Spede: The Parish Church of All Saints', Sandon. 1986 p7). There was an **ice house** at SJ 956292. Dates from c1780 (DoE II). (SEDG Feb 1988 pp6,7) (IHB p395) (SPJD pp53,54pc). **Lichfield Lodge** is at SJ 966280. **Miss Ann Ryder's Steps** is a series of rock-cut steps on the E side of Black Hill in a panoramic walk around the hill; the walk passes Helen's Tomb (1881 OS map) (SPJD p53). The **Perceval Shrine** or Seat at SJ 958292 is an alcove in the Gothic style in a hillside and commemorates the Prime Minister Spencer Perceval assassinated in the House of Commons in 1812. It was erected by the 1st Earl of Harrowby who was a friend. There is a bust of Perceval in a niche at Wellington School (GNHS p112) (W p403) (KES p174) (LGS p209) (IAANS p xxix or xix) (F & G p390) (BOE p231) (VB p134) (SGS p144) (F p315) (DoE II) (SEDG Feb 1988 pp6,7) (SPJD p52p). The **Pitt Column** or Pitt's Column, 0.5m SE of Sandon Hall, commemorates the Prime Minister William Pitt the younger who greatly furthered the career of 1st Earl of Harrowby who erected it in 1806. In 1798 he was one of Pitt's seconds in his duel with Tierney. It is a 75 feet high column in the Doric order with an urn on the top and modelled on Trajan's Column. There is an inscription on the southern pedestal (SSC p135 in the intro. p30) and on one of the sides is this inscription 'Mourned as a citizen for the father of his country and a friend for a friend' (SEDG Feb 1988 pp6,7 p of). (DoE II*) (GNHS p112) (W p403) (SOS p48) (PS p56) (LGS p209) (KES p174) (VB p134) (BOE p231) (SGS p142) (SSBOP p52) (IAANS pxxix or xix) (F p315) (SPJD pp53,54pc). For a William Pitt Club see Wolverhampton. **Pulpit Rock** a presumed natural rock feature slightly N of Helen's Tomb (1881 OS map). **Sandon Home Farm** under 0.5m ESE of the hall was designed by Samuel Wyatt (d1807) of Blackbrook Farm (see). Pevsner describes it as 'an excep-tionally fine example of a Georgian model farm' (BOE p231). **Shepherd's Hut** on Shepherd's Hill over 0.25m due S of Trentham Tower. Appears on the 1887 6 inch and 1925 sheet 31 SW OS maps. **Summerhouse** is a struc-ture by Pulpit Rock (1881 OS map). **Temple of the Winds**. Appears on an OS map of 1881 to the SE of Sandon church. **Trentham Tower** (OS map 1925 sheet 31 SW) or Trentham Hall Tower Top. An eye-catcher or shooting box 0.5m NE of the hall, at SJ 961292. Italianate in style (BOE p231). Was the top of the tower from Trentham Hall and was erected here as Trentham Hall was being demolished in 1905-1912 (KES pp174,211) (LLST p208p of on Trentham Hall). It has been called Lord Harrowby's Folly (F&G p390) (FZ p112) (F p316). Lord Harrowby is said to have paid £100 (F&G p268) or £175 (SEDG Feb 1988 pp6,7) (SPJD pp54,55pc) for it. It cost £107 for haul-age and re-erection (SEDG Feb 1988 pp6,7) and was presumably transported here by canal (SPJD pp54,55pc). (DoE II*) (S p148) (North Staffs Land-scape p97) (SSBOP p52). **Wigan's Knoll** is to the E of Sandon Home Farm and N of Pitt's Column. Appears on the 1887 6 inch and 1925 sheet 31 SW OS maps. Along the **'Winter Walk'** may be seen specimens of mature beech, oak, sycamore and sweet chestnut (SST). Point-to-point horse races, organised by the North Staffordshire Hunt, have taken place at Sandon Hall since c1980 before which the event took place at Mucklestone.

Sandon Wood Wood 1m E of Sandon.

Sandown To E of Perton.

Sandpits Name for a field of 20 acres, enclosed in 1801, in W area of Stone town between the Trent and the old Chester and Carlisle road (SIS p25 see map). Has now been developed.

Sandwell Former ancient estate 21m SSE of Stafford on the NW-facing valley slope of a tributary of the Tame (SSAHST 1989-90 p1). In West Bromwich ancient parish. There is evidence of **Mesolithic** (represented by flints found during excavations in 1982) and **Middle Bronze Age** activity in Sandwell Valley (see) and near the site of Sandwell Priory (SSAHST 1989-90 pp8-25). It has been suggested that Sandwell Priory was established in one corner of a pre-existing double-ditched rectangular enclosure (SSAHST 1986-87 pp14-38); **Iron Age** and **Roman** objects found during excavations in 1982 could be associated with a settlement inside this: A Roman road which ran SE from Pennocrucium to Metchley possibly passed the site of Sandwell Priory (SSAHST 1989-90 p24). A Roman coin has been found at Sandwell Park Farm (see). An **Anglo-Saxon** settlement at Sandwell was presumably at the site of Sandwell Priory (see) and is said to have been first settled by a hermit in c980 (OWB p24). The **name** is from the Holy Well (see) here, from Latin 'sanctus fons' (SHOS vol 2 p128) (MR p365). Or from sand spring or well (DUIGNAN). A manor of Sandwell existed from medieval times with Sandwell Priory exercising a separate manorial jurisdiction over its estate, and the Whorwoods and their successors the Legges regarded their Sandwell estate as a manor (VCH vol 17 pp43-44). In the C19 an **industrial and residential area** S of Three Mile Oak and N of the Birmingham Canal, developed, which sometime in the C20 took the name of Sandwell. Sandwell became a ward of West Bromwich borough, when created in 1882 (VCH vol 17 p45). In 1974 Sandwell was chosen as a name for the new West Midlands metropolitan borough comprising West Bromwich, Smethwick, Oldbury and Rowley Regis (SL p176).

Sandwell Green Former area of Handsworth near the boundary with Sandwell Park, near Island Road (HPPE p37).

Sandwell Hall After the suppression of Sandwell Priory in 1525 the ruined priory and its estate passed to Wolsey's Oxford college. In 1530 Wolsey's property passed to the Crown, which granted it to Dame Lucy Clifford. In 1557 it passed to John Cutte, the grandson of Dame Lucy by her first husband, Sir John Cutte (d1528). In the mid C16 and until c1567 a succession of minor gentry and yeoman farmers seem to have occupied the 'priory house.' In 1569 John Cutte sold the estate to Robert Whorwood (or Wharwood), a London mercer and a younger son of John Whorwood of Compton, Kinver, who lived here until his death in 1590. Sandwell then descended in this branch of the Whorwoods (VCH vol 17 p18). Erdeswick noted a Thomas Whorwood living here (SOS p415). The Whorwoods were royalist in the Civil War (SHWB 16). In 1701 Thomas Brome Whorwood sold the estate and hall to William Legge, who had Sandwell Hall built.
THE LEGGES. William Legge (d1670), Groom of the Bedchamber, married Elizabeth, daughter and coheir of Sir William Washington of Packington, Leics. He was succeeded by his son George Legge (1647-1691), who was created Baron Dartmouth of Dartmouth in Devon in 1682, and became 1st Lord Dartmouth. He was succeeded by his son William Legge (1672-1750), 2nd Lord Dartmouth. He was created Earl of Dartmouth and Viscount Lewisham in 1711. His eldest daughter Lady Barbara married Sir Walter Wagstaffe Bagot (1702-1768), 5th Bt, descendent of the Bagots of Bagots Hall (see). The 1st Earl was succeeded by his grandson George Legge (1731-1801), 2nd Earl of Dartmouth and 3rd Lord Dartmouth, son of George Legge (d1732). The 2nd Earl was succeeded by his son George Legge (1755-1810), 3rd Earl and 4th Lord, who was succeeded by his son William Legge (b1784), 4th Earl and 5th Lord. The 4th Earl developed and owned several collieries in the West Bromwich area including The Cronehills (see), The Terrace (see), Heath Colliery (see), and Pitt Street Colliery (see). On his death at Patshull Hall in 1853 he was succeeded by his second son William Walter Legge, 5th Earl and 6th Lord. He was born at Sandwell Hall in 1823 and served as MP for South Staffs (1849-1853). He was succeeded by his son William Heneage Legge (1851-1936), 6th Earl and 7th Lord. As well as being the first president of the Staffs County Cricket Club, formed in Stafford in 1871, the 6th Earl became president of the Staffordshire Parish Register Society on its foundation in Jan 1901. His son and his successor William Legge (b1881), 7th Earl and 8th Lord, succeeded his father as president until his death in 1958; the society, still (2000) runs and is one of the few in existence still regularly printing PRs. The 7th Earl's only son was killed in action in the

battle of El Alamein (1942) and the 7th Earl was succeeded by his brother (or cousin) Humphry Legge (1888-1962), 8th Earl and 9th Lord. He was succeeded by his son Gerald Humphry Legge (b1924), 9th Earl of Dartmouth and 10th Lord Dartmouth, who was Earl of Dartmouth in 1967 (Burke's Peerage 1967) (VCH vol 17 p18) (SA Jan 19 1901). William (born c1949), inherited the earldom of Dartmouth in 1998 (The Sunday Telegraph Sept 19 1999 p38).
THE HALL. Baron Dartmouth had William Smith of Tettenhall build Sandwell Hall between 1703-c1712 (VCH vol 17 il facing p16 from the SE c1810) (BOE p303-304) (SGS p178) (OWB pl No. 6 as it was in 1710). (SHOS vol 2 pp130-132 catalogue of the pictures in all the rooms). It was reconstructed in 1805 (SLM Feb 1959 pp18,19) (OWB pl No. 6). The Legges left Sandwell Hall for Patshull Hall in 1853 because of increased industrialisation in the area (VB p71) (VCH vol 17 p20) (TEBC2 p68). It was then let for a time to GF Muntz, the metal manufacturer and political reformer. After his short stay it stood empty until 1857 when the 5th Earl allowed it to be used by an Anglican educational institution. It was a lunatic asylum from 1897 to 1906, then a school for mental defectives, and in the 1920 a boys' borstal (VCH vol 17 p20). It was demolished in 1927 (SLM Feb 1959 pp18,19), or 1928 (VCH vol 17 p20) (WBOP p102ps of Sandwell Park Farm) (WBOPP pl 33, pl 32; Sandwell Park Lodge c1900) (SL p176) or 1929 (LGS p250). (W p685) (DOB p275) (HPPE pp102-106) (BCM April 1990 pp13-16; Sandwell Park Farm). GROUNDS. All that remains of the hall is Arch Lodge, a park entrance gateway, 0.75m SW of the site of the hall, situated in the middle of M5 Junction 1 (VCH vol 17 p10). Two ice-houses stood in the grounds, the one to the E at SP 022912 on S bank of Ice-house Lake, about 150 yards from the hall, was restored in 1982. The other was at SP 020913, at about 400 yards from the hall, and was destroyed when the M5 was constructed (IHB p444) (SSAHST 1985-86 pp78-82 ils plan).

Sandwell Park Park for Sandwell Hall which was filled with deer by 1735 (EDP p180). The 1834 OS map shows it as the land mainly to the S of the hall.

Sandwell Park Farm Over 0.25m WNW of Sandwell Hall. A Roman coin, a sestertius of Gordian III, which was found here went to Birmingham Museum (NSJFS 1964 p42).

Sandwell Priory There was a hermitage at Sandwell associated with Holy Well (see) before Sandwell Priory was built (VCH vol 3 p136) (OWB p24); there is a tradition that the spring was visited and sanctified by St Augustine (OWB) (SSAHST 1989-90 p2). Sandwell Priory, a Benedictine monastery dedicated to St Mary Magdalen (VCH vol 3 pp216-219 note), was founded in c1180 or in c1190 by Guy de Offini (or Offney, Opheni, Offeni, LGS pp37,250, OWB pp36-39, SHWB 9), or by Guy's son, William, a principal tenant of Gervase Paynel, lord of Dudley (VCH vol 3 pp216-219 note). The priory was possibly built on the site of a Romano-British settlement, see under Sandwell. The priory had a tiny community in residence, sometimes, by the later C14, only one monk (VCH vol 3 pp216-219 note). Bishop Langton stayed at the priory on Jan 9 1319 (SSE 1994 p2). The priory was suppressed by Wolsey in 1525 and secured to benefit his new college at Oxford, the present Christ Church. By which time the priory church had fallen into decay (VCH vol 3 pp216-219 note. vol 17 p18) (SL pp95,176) (HOS 1998 p58). (SHOS vol 2 p128) (GNHS p173) (S p90 p facing shows the priory seal, now in BM) (BCM Feb 1968 pp60-64. April 1975 p53 il of the seal. April 1992 pp49-52; archaeological survey) (Sandwell Priory. D Dilworth. 1975) (SHJ vol 4 pp52-61 pls, dias, maps). Some of the priory foundations seem to have been incorporated into Sandwell Hall and Shaw noted that some foundation was traceable in the back part and offices of the hall (SHOS vol 2 p130), whilst a few fragments of the priory came to light on demolition of Sandwell Hall in 1929 (LGS p250). The Holy Well and a stone coffin also existed in the C18 (SLM Feb 1959 pp18,19). Masonry, including window moulding, may have been used in the building of Toll End Hall (see) (alias Wharwood's Hall).

Sandwell Valley Valley 1m NNW of the site of Sandwell Hall, Sandwell. For the geography of Sandwell Valley see SSAHST 1986-87 pp14-38. There is a burnt mound probably of the Middle Bronze Age in Sandwell Park at SK 02309163. It was discovered in 1983 (SASR 1987 p18). Another burnt mound probably of the Middle Bronze Age on Dartmouth Golf Course at SP 01589256 was discovered in 1983 (SASR 1987 p18). Heat-shattered pebbles of a possible former Middle Bronze Age burnt mound over an area about 4.5 metres long and about three metres wide were found at Hillhouse Farm at SP 01869255 (SASR 1987 p18).

Sandyfields Estate and tiny hamlet is to W of Cotwall End, Sedgley. Sandyfields Farm is an old building; it was still standing in 1997 (SDSSOP p25p). In 1786 Father Perry added an RC chapel to his house at Sandyfields. Its name of St George's became synonymous with the tiny hamlet in which it stood. The hamlet still exists, amongst modern housing along Sandyfields Road (SDOP p64). A post mill at Sandyfields was sketched by R Noyes in 1817; it appears in 'Industrial Archaeology - Molinology' A Dunphy. Ellowes Hall Scholey Teachers' Centre. At a later date there was a mill at SO 912933 which may have replaced the post mill. But neither appear on the 1834 OS map (WBJ p35).

Sandyford Name for a house or burial mound at SJ 785404, 0.5m NW of Baldwin's Gate. The burial mound here was described as in good condition in 1983 and 20 feet high (NSFCT 1983 p11).

Sandyford Former name for a district of NNE Stafford, about Sandon Road by Sandyford Brook, when it was entirely rural. Here public executions were carried out to 1793 before being moved to outside the new Stafford Gaol. The gibbet stood near Sandyford Bridge (HOS p67) which crossed Sandyford Brook at the E end of Victoria Terrace (OS map of Stafford 1900). The last to be hung here were three convicted of the murder of Mr Ward, attorney, at Yarlet (SIOT p80) (SKYT p133) (SSTY pp118-119).

Sandyford Hamlet on the S slopes of Golden Hill 0.5m N of Tunstall. (W p288). Rev Thomas Wilde died here in 1861 (BS).

Sandyford Farm and fragmented minute hamlet 0.5m NE of Swynnerton. Marked in John Ogilby's 'Britannia' (1675).

Sandyford Brook Tributary of the Dove (SPNO p17).

Sandyford Brook Ran by Sandon Road, Stafford (OS map of Stafford 1900). Tributary of the Sow. Has appeared as le Sondyford (1432) (SPNO p17) (SSE 1997 p82). The name means 'the sandy ford' (SSE 1997 p82).

Sandy Lane Part of Brown Edge village adjacent to the old Newcastle-Leek turnpike road. It would probably take its name from the amount of sand brought down by storms from the higher ground on each side (BEH pp31,89p). Appears on 1834 OS map and Dower's map.

Sandy Lane In Drayton-in-Hales parish (W p389). There is a small lane called Sandy Lane 1.75m SW of Mucklestone at Red Bull.

Sandy Slade 1m NNE of Hednesford. In the sand quarry off Hednesford Road was found the upper and lower millstone grit rotary quern of Roman origin (NSJFS 1964 p17).

Sandy Town Kinver. Langford noted between the Warren House and Sandy Town a small plain covered with sand, where there were the remains of a camp (S&W p362).

Sandyway Minute hamlet 1.25m WSW Lichfield cathedral. Grew up on the road from Lichfield to Walsall and was already inhabited in the late C16 (VCH vol 14 p21).

Sankey's Corner Area around the junction of the Cannock Road and the Rugeley Road, Chase Terrace, formerly heathland in Cannock Chase (CCF p223). Since at least the 1960s it has become the administrative and commercial centre of Burntwood urban parish. Possibly named after one of the Sankey family who lived at Bridge Cross Farm (dated 1864), situated slightly to SE of the crossroads (VCH vol 14 p201).

Saredon Former township in Shareshill parish containing Great Saredon and Little Saredon. Saredon became a separate civil parish in 1866 (GLAUE p421). The name Saredon is used to refer to the settlement 1m N of Little Saredon on the 6 inch OS map 1884.

Saredon Brook Runs N of Great Saredon. Tributary of the Penk, which it joins N of Coven. Has appeared as Searesbroc (996), Searesbrocesforde (996), Sarebroke (1290), the Sarebrok water (1338), and Sarebrook (NSFCT 1908 p129) (SPNO p18) (SSE 1996 p22). The Saredons are on or near it (SSE 1996 p22) and give their name to it (SPN p105), or rather the hill (don) (which gives its name to the Saredon villages) gives its name to the brook (SPNO p18).

Saredon Hill Hill 1m NNE of Shareshill. Is 500 feet high (VCH vol 5 p173). According to local tradition Shareshill (see) church was originally built on this hill.

Saredon Low In the later C17 Plot noted a Roman burial mound in a field E of Great Saredon (NHS p403). In the late C18 Shaw noted that the mound had been nearly levelled by the plough, but the spot was still marked (SHOS vol 2 p310).

Satan's Stone In 'Stone Field' just below Rushton Spencer chapel is a stone with pagan associations, known as Satan's Stone. According to legend it stood on the hill where the church stands and was thrown down by the monks of Dieulacres Abbey in contempt of the old religion. They then built the chapel on the top. Another story is the Devil moved the chapel foundation stones down the hill and the determined chapel builders moved all the stones back up, but one stone was left and this is it. Marks on the stone are said to indicate where the Devil sat on it and the grooves are his apron strings as they burned into the stone. At the entrance to the chapel are two ancient rounded stones of a similar type (DP pp10-11) (SMM p11). Has also appeared as Devil's Stone.

Satnall Hills Small range of hills 0.5m SE of Milford at N end of Cannock

Chase. The hills are named as such by Plot (1686) and on the 1836 OS map (SPNO p31). Perhaps, once topped with Scots pines, reputedly, planted by Thomas Anson to commemorate his brother's World circumnavigation in 'Centurion' 1740-44 (CCM), or planted in 1780 to add variety to the open heath country, which was within view of Shugborough Hall (WMLB p77). The Satnall Hills remained in Cannock Chase and unenclosed despite the diversion of the Stafford-London road from the N side of them to the S side of them in the early C19. This was mainly due to the protestations of John Twigg of Barnfields who threatened Thomas Anson of Shugborough Hall, who was the instigator of the diversion, that his men would tear down Anson's fences for as long as necessary to keep the hills in the chase (BERK2 p47). Satnall Hill is 475 feet high (OSST 1954-56 p17).

Saul's Crack Crack in a rock face on The Roaches (VB p209). Situated in the Upper Tier (SGM p62).

Savage Hays Probable original name of a point called 'Savagees' on a broad slope of Gun Hill below Park House where some traces of a battle between the Britons and the Romans c22 BC were found. Miller thinks one could paraphrase this as 'the fields of fierce struggle' (OL vol 1 p217).

Saverley Green Common land and tiny village on the W side of the Blithe Valley 1m WSW of Cresswell. In Hilderstone quarter in Stone ancient parish. Formerly known as Saley Green which is derived from the nearby Sale Brook (NSFCT 1917 pp144-145). There was 1.5 acre of common land remaining at Saverley Green by the 1950s (OSST 1956-59 p13). Saverley Green was famous for its cock fighting. The police made a raid in c1850 but the participants escaped to a neighbouring house and evaded capture. It retains its village green (NSFCT 1917 pp144-145). Saverley Green is home of one of the mystics Pat and Terry Shotton, a UFO investigator. Patricia was convinced of the importance of a remote pond some miles across fields to the W of Saverley Green (GS p175). In the Old Orchard is the well they call the well of sacred blood (EF pp162-163p). In 1998 the House of Lords was to pass judgment on a disputed strip of land, 87 feet by six feet, lying between two properties at Saverley Green. The land has been claimed by both Mr Insley of Saverley Cottage and Mr Wibberley of Yew Tree House since 1987 (The Guardian Oct 5 1998) (ES Oct 6 1998 p2). By 1998 it had become a tradition for a spectacular bonfire on a theme to be built for Nov 5 celebrations in the grounds of the Greyhound Inn at Saverley Green (ES Nov 5 1998 p1pc).

Saverley House Saverley Green. Residence of Mr and Mrs HJ Colclough (ES June 4 1931 p8p of the rock garden).

Saville's Botanic Gardens, John On N side of Stowe Pool, Lichfield. Between the Parchments House and Stowe Pool. Belonged to John Saville, a Vicar Choral, the beloved of Anna Seward. Developed after 1773 (SHOS vol 1 pp345-346) (SSAHST 1970 pp52-53 see map).

Saxonfields In the Bambury Street area, Longdon. N of Sandford Hill.

Saxonfields Street on S side of Wergs Road, Tettenhall (Wolverhampton Chronicle March 18 1999 p3)

Saxons Lowe Conical-shaped hill 1m S of Tittensor about 40 feet high, thought to be a burial mound itself or to have one on top of it; fragments of urns of the Bronze Age have been found in the burial mound (VCH vol 1 pp376-377 dia, 181) (SIS p1). But Gunstone found no confirmation of this and no burial mound on the hill (NSJFS 1965 p48). Pickford thinks the hill is far older than the Saxon period (SMM p18p). There is a tradition that King Wulfhere is buried here (SK p193) but others say he is buried in a mound at nearby Bury Bank hillfort. (GNHSS p5) (STM May 1964 p32) (BNDA p1) (MR p399). Saxon Lowe lies on a ley line between Stone church and Grounds Lowe (SMM p23 see map). The hill has been commonly called Hangman's Hill (NSFCT 1887 p57. 1915 p115).

Scaldersitch C19 house 1m S of Sheen. In Sheen ancient parish. A date stone inscribed IOM 1661 on the present house suggests that it has earlier origins (VCH vol 7 p242).

Scalpcliff Hill Between Winshill and Stapenhill, at SK 258225. Is 300 feet high. There was a village here in pre-Roman times (HOBTU p2). Scalpcliff, which has also appeared as Scalpcliffe, has been identified with the Mount Calvus, or in English 'Calvecliff,' mentioned in 'Vita Sanctae Monennae' (a life of St Modwen) written by Conchubranus, an Irish monk, probably between 1000 and 1050 (BTIH p11) (HOBTU p7).

Scamnell House over 0.75m N of Chebsey. Appears as approximately The Samnill on 1834 OS map and as Scammill on Dower's map.

School Clough House 1m SSW of Longnor, in Fawfieldhead township, Alstonefield ancient parish. Appears as Scoldeclogh in 1331 (VCH vol 7 p27 note). It was hit by a German bomb in 1941 (L p53). The name incorporates a word of Scandinavian origin (VCH vol 7 p27).

School Farm C19 house in Birch Lane near the junction with Mill Lane,

Shelfield. St Peter's Chantry in Lichfield cathedral had property in Shelfield, including a house and land which was granted to Queen Mary's Grammar School, Walsall, in 1554. It became known as School Farm and continued in their ownership until 1944 (SNBC p22p).

Schoolhouse Green Southern (now central) part of Ipstones where the Onecote Froghall road intercepts with Church Lane.

Schoolhouse Lane Cross Cross in the hand at the end of Aldershaw or St John's Lane, anciently Schoolhouse Lane, Lichfield (HOL p537). Perhaps not the Cross in the Hand in the N of the city, where perambulations started and finished.

Scolding Green Former hamlet on Cradley Heath by the Mouse Sweet Brook (TB June 1982 p15. May 1994 p27). The name appears as Scholding Green or Skelding Green in the 1851 census. Scolding Green Road, existing in 1901, became an extension of Dudley Wood Road before becoming the present St Anne's Street (OS map sheet 71.08) (SNSV vol 2 p104).

Scotch Brook Rises at Hartwell and after about two miles joins the Trent at Stone (SIT). It has been described as 'rapid' (W) and in its three mile length it powered nine watermills in the Moddershall Valley (SVB p135). Has appeared as Scotia Brook (SPNO p18), River Moddershall (SIT) and was formerly known as Cottars' Brook, from cottar a lower type of villein, sometimes called a bordar. Cottars' became corrupted to Scottars' (SIS pp20-21 note) (SK p167 facing p166 are photographs of icicles beside the brook Jan-March 1895). For the origin of the name see Shushions.

Scotch Hill Hill 1.5m WSW of Rangemore. In Needwood Forest. Formerly Scotshills, and Skoteswallehull (HOPT vol 1 p137).

Scot Hay Tiny village in undulating country under 1m SSW of Alsagers Bank. Formerly partly in the ancient parishes of Keele, Madeley and Audley. There are excellent views of the Cheshire Plain from Scot Hay (TTTD p223). Has also appeared as Scott Hey (1851) (W p396) and Scott Hay (BOJ book 2). Birthplace of Wilf A Bloor (d1993) in 1916, who wrote the 'Jabez' stories (BOJ) written in Potteries dialect which appeared in ES, except for a few years in the 1970s, from 1968 to 1993. He wrote under the pseudonym, A Scott, possibly a play on his birthplace (ES July 2 1993 p8p).

Scotia District 0.5m N of Burslem. Scotia Bank was in Burslem chapelry in Stoke-upon-Trent parish.

Scotia Brook Rises S of Tunstall joins Fowlea Brook in the Longport area.

Scotia Valley Between Longport and Tunstall (VB p191). Around the area of Scotia Brook.

Scotlands, The House in Bushbury. Formerly partly in Bushbury parish and partly in Wednesfield chapelry in Wolverhampton ancient parish. The name, in use by 1750 (WFW p105), is not from Anglo-Saxon or Middle English 'scot' tribute, payment, nor from a Scots person, but from Anglo-Saxon sceatlandes, corner lands. The house is situated at the corner of a triangular piece of land bounded on all sides by roads (DUIGNAN) (SPN p145).

Scotland Yard Former cottages in a courtyard approached by an alley at the N end of Lichfield Street, adjacent to Stafford Street, Stone. The name is from Scotch Brook which runs close by (SIS p21 note) (MOSP p4). The cottages were demolished in c1937 (info Mrs JG Beecham). It is now (1999) mostly the site of a car park; the Scotch Brook running in a culvert beneath the car park (info Michael Cockin).

Scott Arms Inn Public house in the junction of Newton Road and Walsall Road, formerly in Great Barr township in Aldridge ancient parish. There appears to have been a Scott Arms by 1710, for when the Hoos were lords of Wednesbury from 1710 to 1791, much Wednesbury magisterial business was carried on here (TBS p12). But Hackwood says it was when the Scotts were lords of Wednesbury, from 1777, that the inn was used for manorial business (WAM p94). The first (or second?) inn was built by Sir Josiah Scott in c1800, when it combined an inn, a brewery and a butcher's shop (MNB p64). The beer made, used water from a well at the inn (IOM pp67-68 p facing) and was legendary. In Victorian times cattle auctions were held here (SPN pp55-56). Great Barr Association for the Prosecution of Felons, founded in 1824, held annual dinners here (TBS pp16,24-25). In the mid C19 Scott Arms was described as a hamlet (W p552). A Roman Catholic community held services in a barn at the Scott Arms before the community had their own chapel, Holy Name, Great Barr (TBS p25). Near the inn was the house where Dr Gorman lived (VH pp37p c1900, 38, 40p c1897). The inn, known as Scott Arms Hotel in 1921, was demolished and replaced by a palatial roadhouse in 1966 (BCP pp20ps,77ps) (MNB p64; says 1930s). In the C20 a Roman phalera was found by the Scott Arms (MOA p16).

Scott House Stood off Walsall Road in Hamstead, in Perry Barr township. Residence of John Charles Addyes Scott (d1888). He was no relation, however, of the Scotts of Great Barr Hall (WAM p94).

Scounslow Green Small hamlet in undulating country rising to the Needwood

Forest plateau 2.25m WSW of Marchington. Formerly partly in Uttoxeter and Hanbury parishes. The Cundesley mentioned in a charter of 951 may be identified with Scounslow (SHC 1916 p90), becoming, from Cundesley, Scounsley then Scounslow Green (SMSE p3). White spells it Scoundslow Green (W p792) and Redfern spells it Scownslow; named from a burial mound (HOU p26). There is a moated site at Scounslow Green (SMSE p6).

Scout House Reservoir Former circular reservoir 0.75m E of Hednesford. Built by SSWWC in 1878 (MR p180) or by 1880 (VCH vol 5 p52). The name is from Scout House (1834 OS map). In 1887 a burst main pipe caused a chain reaction, and 43 million tonnes of water cascaded through the Hednesford Hills (CCAP p104p) (Cannock Chase: The Second Selection. June Pickerill. 1997. p8p). It was abandoned in 1916 due to settlement fractures (MR p180). Other accounts say the reservoir closed in 1930 and stock car racing was taking place within it by 1954. The raceway closed in 1956 but was re-opened in 1962; known as, Hednesford Raceway, it was still open in 1997 (CCAP p104p) (MR pp180-181) (Cannock Chase: The Second Selection. June Pickerill. 1997. p8p). Another account describes the reservoir as disused in the 1950s (VCH vol 5 p52) and derelict in the early 1970s (Cannock Chase by Car. Staffs Nature Conservation Trust Ltd. ND, but between 1971 and 1974 p6). Has also appeared as Rawnsley Reservoir.

Scrip Low Burial mound 0.25m W of Stanton at SK 12264609. 22 paces in diameter and two feet high. Carrington excavated it in 1850 and found a cremation (TYD p163) (NSJFS 1965 p47). Has also appeared as Script Low.

Seabridge Old hamlet on a ridge overlooking Park Brook 1.75m SSW of Newcastle-under-Lyme. Former township mostly in Stoke-upon-Trent, but partly in Trentham and Swynnerton ancient parishes (Staffs General & Commercial Directory 1818) (W p236). Has appeared as Sheperugge (C13) (SSE 1996 p17), and Shea Bridge on the maps of Plot and Smith. The name means sheep bridge (DUIGNAN) (SPN p88), or sheep ridge (NSFCT 1944 p98) (SSE 1996 p17). The 'bridge' would be a bridge over Park Brook. A mill at Seabridge is mentioned in 1386 as devastated. It may have been a windmill (NSFCT 1944 p98). William Boulton (1825-1900), pioneer in ceramic engineering, was born in Seabridge. Between 1860 and 1897 he took out 23 patents including a rope-drive jigger (1868), a mechanical lathe (1874), lathes thrower's wheels, an encaustic tile apparatus, a dish-washing machine and a machine for making electric insulators. He is buried in Burslem cemetery. His eldest son became engaged to Arnold Bennett's sister Tertia Bennett, but was drowned at Barmouth while on holiday with his fiancee (Pottery Gazette Oct 1 1896. Dec 1 1900) (ES Oct 1 1952) (VCH vol 2 pp146-148) (IANS p102) (POTP pp42-43). Seabridge now merges into the suburbs of Newcastle.

Seabridge Hall Seabridge. (NSFCT 1890 p11; in occupation). Seabridge House is described as a respectable old mansion occupied by John Wedgwood in 1843; it had formerly belonged to Lady Pilkington (HBST p525).

Sealpey House Burton upon Trent. Formerly in Derbys.

Sedgley Ancient parish and former manor. The town of Sedgley on a ridge 500 feet above sea level on England's main watershed (TTTD) is 18.5m S of Stafford. Mander puts the High Street area at 756.7 feet high, which is higher than Sedgley Beacon, at 700 feet high (HOWM p6).
EARLY. In the Pitt Rivers and Oxford University Museum, Oxford, there is a cast of a Wenlock Limestone fossil of a Euucladia Johnsoni from Sedgley. JT Fereday of Sedgley had a fossil tree trunk in his garden (SVS p461 note). Druidical sacrifices are believed to have taken place in Sedgley in ancient times according to Burritt. Robert Hobbes mentions a druids' altar was here. Druids at Sedgley are alluded to in Disraeli's 'Sybil' book 3, chapter 4 (BCM autumn 1993 p56).
700 to 1600. The **name** means Secga's lea, the pasture belonging to Secga (DUIGNAN) (SPN p103). Secga is an Anglo-Saxon personal name meaning 'one who tells anything, an informant' (SR p3) (TB Jan 1981 p23). Another theory is that Sedgley is derived from Sigge's lea; Sigge being the real name of the Teutonic conqueror who, in overrunning North West Europe assumed the name of Woden for the sake of prestige; he was the founder of Sigtuna otherwise, Sigge's town, in Sweden (AOW pp13-14). Twamley in his History of Dudley Castle says Sedgley is from 'sedge' and 'ley' - a sedgy field. Duignan disagreed with this, pointing out that Sedgley is situated on a lofty ridge. However, Underhill opts for Mr Twamley's theory noting that owing to a sub surface of clay in parts of the district, water is held as by a sponge, hence the ground would be sedgy. To support this theory a Sedgley tenant paid for the privilege of seeking cranes, and also made something from the sale of rushes to cover floors of the mansions of the manor (AMS p1) (WMVB p130). Sedgley was identified by Birch in his Cartularium Saxonicum with the Soeges lea mentioned in a charter of 866 (SHC 1916 p78). Later forms are: Segleslei, **manor**, in DB, Secgesleage, Seggeslegh (SPN p103). The custom for the lord to take cash rather than service from his villeins was occurring at Sedgley

from as early as before 1300 (HOS p39). The custom of Sedgley manor was, if a copyholder made a lease, without a licence of the lord, for one year, and died within the term, it should be made void against the heir. This was adjudged by the court to be a good custom in the case of 'Turner and Hodges' (Litt. Rep. p233) (SHOS vol 2 p221*) (SMC p122) (SR pp36,38,39,40). The custom of Borough English prevailed in Sedgley manor (HC p28). Sedgley parish was a probate jurisdiction of the lord of the manor until abolished 1846 (SR pp42-43) (VCH vol 3 p94 note). In 1600 the manor was bought by Thomas Parkes, of the Parkes family of Willingsworth Hall (SOS pl viii) (WW p23) (SR p30) (HC p36) (VCH vol 2 pp112,113,239). Manorial court business was carried on at Court House Inn (see). Hackwood thinks that Offlow hundred court could have been held at Sedgley (WAM p9). But Sedgley was in Seisdon hundred. The **parish**, formed before 1086, formerly contained Coseley (GLAUE p421) and probably the ancient parishes of Kingswinford and Tipton, and may have contained the ancient parish of Penn (SHC 1916 p193). There is a tradition that at night fairies moved the parish **church** to its present position from a former site near the abbey, where Ellowes Hall stands (SR p108). There was a church at Sedgley in the C11. The present parish church, All Saints, Vicar Street, was built in 1826-1829 (BOE p232). Sedgley **wakes** were celebrated in early Nov, following All Saints day. Wakes of a similar nature, although on different weeks, were also held annually at both Upper and Lower Gornal. These ceased to be held in c1930 (PHS p11). Sedgley **curfew bell** tolled to c1810 (PHS p10).

INDUSTRY. Ironstone and surface-coal mining is recorded at Sedgley in 1273 (HOS p42), and Sedgley grew owing to mining in the C19 (SL pp173,184). Although Sedgley was a big nail-making centre - Plot noted the parish had 2000 nailers in the later C17 (SL p109) - it had a rather distinctive industry compared to other Black Country towns, owing to the rich deposits of fireclay, that of making fireclay goods (Staffs County Handbook c1958 p123). Sedgley nailers also made ploughs, cart and fire irons, horse shoes, bolts, hinges and buckles. Steel pens were made at Sedgley as early as 1806 by J Fellows, several years before the celebrated Joseph Gillott was making them by machine in Birmingham (AMS p158) (STELE Feb 25 1955. March 4 1955) (TTTD p297). For Sedgley windmills see under Rewardine, The Round House, Ruiton, and Sandyfields.

1600 to PRESENT. The Dudley **plague** of 1616 spread to Sedgley (SCSF pp134-135). An **anti-dissenter riot** occurred at Sedgley in 1789, about three or more were involved (LOU pp168,379). **Food riot.** In the Sedgley region armed crowds paid menacing 'visits' in the search for food on April 29 1800 (LOU pp152,375). The **cholera epidemic** of 1832 reached Sedgley parish on Aug 10 and claimed 290 lives in the parish (SCSF p139) (TB May 1978 pp20-21. Feb 1998 p17). **Chartism.** 'Sedgley is a little Tory-ridden village in which the petty authorities have insolently and illegally threatened to arrest the first Chartist who entered,' said a Chartist, after an incident concerning Samuel Cook at a Chartist rally in support of the Sedgley Nailers Strike at the Bull Ring, Sedgley, in which he and his supporters were charged with holding an illegal meeting (TB Oct 1979 p5). John Mason, a shoemaker and Chartist orator was arrested at Sedgley (BCM Jan 1986 p40). **Local government.** Sedgley town was in the Upper Side division of Sedgley ancient parish (W p195). From 1894 it was in Sedgley urban district until 1966 when it was removed to Dudley county borough (GLAUE p421). For **Sedgley charities** see SR pp61-63. For **body-snatching** a man was whipped at the cart's tail from Sedgley to Bilston in 1826 (SCSF p129). Three houses in Sedgley were hit by **lightning** in the dreadful thunder storm on Monday April 23 1797; a fireball came down the chimney of the house of Stephen Cox, a nailer, at the time he and his wife were sitting and their child was sleeping on a chair by the fire. The mother providentially snatched up the child and saved its life, but the pillow on which it lay probably scorched as many of the bricks from the top of the chimney had fallen upon and about it. The electric charge passed through two houses adjoining and melted the leads of the windows, and appeared to travel sideways attracted by a nail in a back door and cut out a portion of it (SHOS vol 2 p222) (THS p192) (W p198) (SR pp108,109) (TB April 1988 p5). Hackwood notes that a few years prior to his writing (1898) it was the custom for the clergy and choristers of Sedgley church to ascend the tower on **Ascension morning**, where they sang a number of appropriate hymns, including 'Hail the day that sees Him rise' the celebration attracted considerable attention from parishioners (SR p108). The custom seems to have been still practised in the 1970s (TTTD p296) (WMAG March 1976 p17). A black **phantom dog** of an immense size has been reported at Sedgley (FSLBWM p44). **Natives and visitors.** It has been stated that no one can claim to be born a native of Sedgley unless they were born within the sound of the parish church bells (PHS p10). Mrs **Martha Southall** of Sedgley, born on April 20 1819, lived through six reigns from George III to George V (E&S

May 21 1910) (BCM Oct 1973 pp13-14). **Abel Hill** (d1820), collier and murderer, whose victims were drowned in the canal at Capponfield (see), is said to have lived in Abigail Lane (unlocated), Sedgley (TB Dec 3 1998 p5). Rev **Charles Girdlestone**, vicar of Sedgley (1826-1837), was a biblical commentator, hymn writer, classicist and pamphleteer (IE p116). He wrote 'Farewell Sermons' (1837) on his departure from Sedgley (BCM July 1992 pp42-43il-45). For the murder of **Eliza Silleto**, aged 6, in 1864 see Daisy Bank. **David Bailey** (1834-1917), poet and phonetist associated with Sir Isaac Pitman, was born in Broad Lanes, Sedgley on Oct 25 1834 (BS p39) (PSS pp211-213) (KES p176) (ZSB) (VFC p7). **Elizabeth II** visited Sedgley in her Jubilee tour in 1977 (SDOP p125p).

SEDGLEY IN LITERATURE. Sedgley appears in Ellen Thorneycroft Fowler's novel 'The Farringdons' (1900/1) as Sedgehill (BCM July 1978 pp44-46) (PPTP p34) (Wolverhampton Chronicle Sept 19 1997 p12); and as Sedgebury in Francis Brett Young's novels (BCM April 1980 pp10-15); his 'Dr Bradley Remembers' is set in Sedgley (SDOP p118). Sedgley is Rushley in Rev JR Windsor-Garnett's 'The Village' (1926) (TB Sept 1986 p14). EA Underhill's poem 'Around the Beacon' which appears in a collection of his poems called 'Patchwork' (1932) is about the Sedgley area (VFC p135). For Joseph Darby, and John Cornfield, poets, see Hurst Hill. For Sedgley as a verb see BCM April 1971 p27.

RHYMES.

> Walsall town for brandy legs,
> Bilston town for bulls,
> Hampton town for fancy girls,
> And Sedgley town for trulls.

(SCSF p165) (SJC pp2,3). Jon Raven gives a different version:-

> Walsall for brandy legs,
> Baggeridge for nuts,
> Bilston for dust and dirt,
> And Sedgley for sluts.

(FOS p149). The allusion to the devil in another rhyme is said to refer to the harsh, foul language of the nailers of Sedgley:-

> The Devil ran through Sedgley,
> Booted and spurred,
> With a scythe at his back
> As long as a swerd (sword).

(SR p107) (SCSF p167) (SJC pp2,3) (FOS p35). For a long rhyme on the inns of Sedgley see BCM July 1968 p45.

Sedgley Beacon 0.5m NE of Sedgley at SO 92299439. Sedgley Beacon seems to be a reference to a ridge called the Sedgley Ridge (see) or Beacon Hill (see) which forms part of the Severn-Trent watershed (SL p172), or England's main watershed and has an altitude of nearly 700 feet (HOWM p6) above mean sea level. The beacon is the highest cultivated land in England (WJO Aug 1906 p211). Underhill says the beacon is not the highest cultivated land in England, only the highest inhabited tableland in England (AMS p2). Commands views of the Wrekin, Malverns, the Clee Hills, and Welsh Mountains (PHS p17). Sedgley Beacon is supposed by some antiquaries to have been the site of Druidical sacrifice. The Romans may have used Beacon Hill as an observation post (SR pp1,2) and it has been used as a beacon site to warn of the Danish invasion and invasions since (AWM p45). An underground reservoir was built on Sedgley Beacon in 1970. It was operational by 1972 (SDOP p124p). In Aug 1925 three unidentified disc-like objects could be seen flying over Sedgley Beacon (TB March 1981 p16).

BEACON TOWER. Sedgley Beacon seems to be also a reference to the tower on Beacon Hill, commonly called Beacon Tower. The present tower was built for Lord Wrottesley as an astrological observatory in 1846 (WJO Aug 1906 p211p) (KES p205) (BOE p232; it must be closer to Sedgley than Pevsner's 1.5m) (BCOPP vol 1 pl 53. vol 2 p48), although there was a tower on the site previously, according to Shaw (TTTD pp295-296) (TB Sept 1982 p22p). Sedgley Sundries 1786-1870 attributes the tower to a Mr Petit. It is a stone structure 50 feet high by seven feet diameter; the top being reached by a winding staircase (PHS p17). The tower was said to be unsafe in 1978 (WMAG Nov 1978 p27p).

Sedgley Hall Former timber-framed building 0.25m W of Sedgley town centre, at SO 912938. Seat of the Gevons or Jevons and appears as 'the Hall' in 1614 (AMS p) (BCM spring 1999 p42il). Richard Gevons bought Sedgley Hall in

1573 (BCM autumn 1989 p46). Appears to have been the seat of John Elwell (1785-1859), ironmaster, in the earlier C19 (IE p116; if so this house has also been known as the Manor House and Sedgley House). William Shade died in 1827 at Sedgley Hall (mem in All Saints, Sedgley). It was the home of Stephen Wilkes in 1924 (SDOP p15) (SNSV vol 2 p80). Demolished in 1966 to make way for a modern housing estate called Sedgley Hall, although the land remained undeveloped to at least the mid 1990s (SDOP p15p).

Sedgley Hay Roger de Somery of Dudley Castle (see) was reported to be claiming a free chase (Pensnett Chase) 'in the hay of Sedgley and the wood of Penn' in 1254 (SSE 1990 p25) or in 1255. Sometimes the hay is considered a hay of Kinver Forest. Greenslade and Kettle could find no other reference to Sedgley Hay, nor, they say, was Sedgley in Kinver Forest, and the term probably implies an inclosure. Sedgley Hay may be identifiable with Baggeridge Hay or Wood which occurs from the earlier C13 (VCH vol 2 p344 note).

Sedgley Park An old deer park of the Ward family. Erdeswick describes it as 'a large goodly park' (EDP p180). Sedgley Park (see) and Parkfields preserve the name (RS p13).

Sedgley Park House 1.5m S of Wolverhampton. 1.5m N of Sedgley. The name is possibly from Sedgley Park (see), an old deer park. The early C18 house was the seat of the Dudley family (BOE p232) (SGS pp144-145) (SDSSOP p33p). In 1763 the house consisted of three unconnected buildings which were joined over the next 80 years. The central house, known as 'High House,' was given the name the 'Lantern,' because its long windows lit by candle-light gave it that appearance as viewed from Penn Common. The lodge to the hall gives its name to the present Lodge Farm (PPTP p33). The house was an hotel known as Park Hall by 1962 (TTTD p295), and approached by a road from Goldthorn Park, Wolverhampton.

SEDGLEY PARK SCHOOL. From 1763 Sedgley Park housed the famous Roman Catholic college and seminary founded by William Errington at Betley in 1762 (HOS p30) (VCH vol 6 pp156-157). The school was perhaps the first Roman Catholic college established after the Reformation. In 1774 William Ward inherited the hall but allowed the school to continue. The school moved to Cotton Hall (see) in 1873 (VCH vol 6 pp156-157). (SHOS vol 2 p221 pl.xxix) (History of Sedgley Park. Canon FC Husenbeth. 1856) (SR p65) (WJO May 1904 pp125il-133) (Sedgley Park and Cotton College. Canon Willibrord Buscot. 1940) (A History of Sedgley Park and Cotton College. Frank Roberts. 1985) (MR p276) (WPOPP vol 2 p73p). Alumni: John Milner (1752-1826) divine and historian, vicar apostolic of the Midland District 1803-1826; John Philip Kemble (1757-1823), celebrated tragedian; John Kirk (1760-1851) divine and historian; John Chetwode Eustace (?1762-1815) classical antiquary; Rev George Oliver (1781-1861) historian; Rev Frederick Charles Husenbeth (1796-1872), writer, Grand Vicar to Bishop Walsh of the Midland District and author of 'The History of Sedgley Park School, Staffordshire' (1856); Robert Garner, author and doctor of Foley House (see); Lt Gen Sir Alfred Keogh (1857-1936) director general of the Army Medical Service 1905-1910; Cardinal Bernard William Griffin (1899-1956), archbishop of Westminster 1944-1956 (VCH vol 5 pp157-158) (HOWM p135) (SNSV vol 2 p15).

Sedgley Priory Priory Lane, Sedgley town. Is believed by some to have been the sister building of St James' Priory, Dudley, and there is a tradition of a tunnel running between the two. The building was being used for housing accommodation in 1941 (AMS p445). Others say there was never a priory at Sedgley; that the name and that of the nearby Ladies Walk reflect the fact that St James' Priory once owned this land (OS map Sheet 67.07) (SDOP p57p).

Sedgmoor Park Between Deepfield and Lanesfield (Centro Dudley Map).

Seedy Mill Seedymill Farm is 1.25m SE of Longdon, S of Hanch Hall. Seedy Mill on Bilson Brook S of Seedymill Farm was recorded in the mid C13 as 'Synethimilne' (VCH vol 14 p236). A township liable to pay tithes to the vicars of the parishes of St Mary, St Michael and St Chad, Lichfield (HOL p456). SSWWC built a water treatment works at Seedy Mill in 1939-1943 (GHC p20pc aerial view). Greg Peters, aged 11, achieved two holes in one on one day at Seedy Mill Golf Course in Jan 1999 (BBC 1 Midlands Today. Jan 21 1999).

Seggersley House 0.25m NE of Ellenhall (1834 OS map).

Seighford Ancient parish and village in pastoral country on Gamesley Brook 2.25m NW of Stafford. A small relict moss exists to the E of Seighford village. It was created in the Late Devensian period (WSS pp102,104p). There may have been a **church** at Seighford in Saxon times (LGS p209); there was a church here in the C11 (LDD). The present parish church, St Chad, on the E side of the Cooksland road in the village centre, has some work of c1100 (LGS p209). The parish was formed out of Stafford ancient parish after 1086

and probably before 1150 (SHC 1916 pp192, 196). It was reformed as Seighford with Derrington and Cresswell ecclesiastical parish in 1930 (GLAUE p421). The parish **wake** was on the last Sunday in June in the C19 (W p406). Seighford had a hobby-horse which was used in some ceremony to raise money for repairs to the church (SMC p169) (SCSF p6) (NSFCT 1947 p167) (FOS p79). Seighford has appeared as Cesteforde, a manor held of the bishop of Chester (Lichfield) in DB, Cesford (1291) (Eyton p79), Cesterford, and Seteford (SPN p104). The **name** Cesteforde implies an unlocated Roman community (SL p45) (MR p277). Mills gives '(Roman) fort ford' (SSE 1996 p17). If of Anglo-Saxon origin then Seohtre is Anglo-Saxon for a brook, hence the ford of the brook or ditch (DUIGNAN) (ROT p32). The 'ford' is where the Gamesley Brook is crossed by the lane off the village green, opposite the school (MR p277). **Manorial tenure service**. John de Harcourt held Chatcull and over 1000 acres in Podmore, Mill Meece, Great and Little Bridgeford and Seighford by service of bringing four men of Chatcull and Podmore to act as beaters to the bishop's hunt (ECC p13). A report in the Staffs Chronicle tells of a freak **hailstorm** here on July 3 1719. Hailstones of 11 inches circumference and others measured nine, 10 and 11 inches in a later storm in the afternoon (ROT p32). For Rev **Thomas Loxdale**, the antiquary, vicar of Seighford from 1703 until 1721 or 1723 see Meretown. Rev William Jordan, first tutor of Dr Johnson of Lichfield (see), was vicar here between 1731 and 1739 (OSST 1935 p46). AIRFIELD. Seighford airfield (WMA pp234-238) opened in Oct 1942. No. 30 Operational Training Unit flew Vickers Wellington III bombers from Seighford to Feb 1945; here was the base for the 'D-Day' gliders - Horsas and Hotspurs (SHJ autumn 1989 pp63, 64). The airfield was used by the RAF to 1946, and by civilian aircraft from 1956. Boulton Paul used the airfield to test fly jet aircraft. In 1959, when Canberras were used, the runway was lengthened to 2,000 yards. It closed in 1966 (Wolverhampton Chronicle Feb 25 2000 p14) (ROT p34). In Feb 1945 a crash crew at the airfield saw on the ceiling of their billet the faces of a crew of a Wellington bomber which had crashed. In 1969 someone saw lights on in the old control tower, long after the lights had been removed (info Bruce Braithwaite). A memorial plaque to airmen who died flying from Seighford was erected in Seighford church in 1993 (ES April 13 1993 p8). In July 1996 a glider crashed at the airfield, the pilot, Stephen Taylor of Little Haywood, was killed. There was a mid-air collision between gliders over the airfield on May 2 1998. The pilots of both gliders, Ian Stuart Andrews and George Leonard Askew, were killed (ES May 4 1998 p9). A large illuminated crab-like object shinning like gold with 'a dome like half an orange about 25 feet wide and with a halo above it' was seen 80 feet in the sky from Seighford Vicarage by Rev Cedric Wright on June 25 1954 (The Coming of the Spaceships. Gavin Gibbons. 1956).

Seighford Hall Timber-framed house 0.5m NW of Seighford. In 1559 Elizabeth I gave the hall to Richard Eld or Elde, paymaster to her forces in Ulster (VB p139). Said by others to have been built in 1587 (info Bruce Braithwaite). Elizabeth I's coat of arms is over the fireplace in the current lounge. She is said to have stayed at the hall (STM Aug 1965 p37p) (VB p139) (IOI p36). Col Peter Stepkin, a royalist in the Civil War, was shot dead here in 1648 in an action against the parliamentary garrison at Stafford. He had defected to the parliamentary side after the battle of Hopton Heath, but later returned to the royalists (BFS pp23-24) (ROT p48). The antiquary, Rev Thomas Loxdale (d1742), married Elizabeth, daughter of Francis and Elizabeth Eld of Seighford Hall, in 1720 (SHJ spring 1991 p10). John Eld of Seighford Hall founded the Staffordshire General Infirmary at Foregate (see) in 1772 (SHJ spring 1991 p21-22). The Elds were still residing at the hall in the mid C19. By 1876 it was tenanted by Frederick Lyon JP; by 1880 by William Williams; by 1884 by Joseph William Williams JP. Francis Frederick Eld JP was in residence between at least 1888 and 1896. Between at least 1900 and 1940 the hall was occupied by William Warrington Dobson JP. Ownership of the hall and lordship of Seighford belonged to the Elds to at least 1928, thereafter, to at least 1940 it was held by trustees of their estate (mems in Seighford church) (trade directories) (STC p14p) (OSST 1935 pl facing p45, p46). Additions were made to the hall in the late C19 (BOE p233). The Staffs Constabulary used the hall as a motor training school after WW2 (NSFCT 1947 p167). In the 1970s it was a restaurant and a night club (info Bruce Braithwaite), and then an hotel, then a home for the elderly (MR pp278pc,279). A **ghost** called the 'gentle governess,' a former deceased governess, is said to have checked on new governesses, shortly after their appointment (HIE p176) (IOI p36) (VB p139). The ghost of the same or another governess is said to have appeared at the hall to avenge the wife of a past owner, who allegedly murdered her after discovering she had had an affair with her husband, and deposited the body in a pool in the grounds. Another, or the same, was the figure of a lady carrying a basket who was seen disappearing into a wall of the hall by campers in the grounds (info Bruce Braithwaite). To the SW of the hall is a brick C18 **gamekeeper's**

cottage. A C14 tower removed from Ranton Abbey has been built on to it, giving the effect of a converted Norman church (F p306). Has been referred to as a barn (DoE II). (BOE p233) (MR p277) (SGS pp144p,145).

Seisdon (locally *Seize-don* Stan Hill). Small village on a small hill by Smestow Brook 1m NW of Trysull. Formerly in Trysull chapelry in Wombourne ancient parish; in Trysull parish after 1888. The last Ice Age reached its maximum southern extent about Wolverhampton. Glacial boulders lie all about in the tract of ground extending from Wolverhampton to Trescott, Trysull, and Seisdon. Large walls at Seisdon are built of boulders of granite, syenite, felsite and quartzite. Boulders also form the foundations of walls and are used as corner stones, horse blocks, gates posts, and boundary marks (WJO Nov 1909 p293). Has appeared as Seisdone, a manor, in DB, and Seyxden (1236) (SSE 1996 p17). 'Seis' and 'Sais' is Welsh for Saxon, so 'Saxon's hill' (DUIGNAN), or 'Saxon hill' (NSJFS 1981 p3) (SPN p146), or 'Saxons' hill' (SSE 1996 p17). But WH Stevenson thinks this unlikely. For, although, the Welsh may have called a hillfort here, taken from the Saxons, after them, the English, were unlikely to adopt the Welsh name, when they came to reoccupy (DUIGNAN). The reference to 'Saxon' may not refer to the presence of English amongst Welsh but to the presence of some Saxons in a predominantly Anglian community (WMMA pp143-144). According to Krausse the name would mean the 'hill-fort' (NSFCT 1908 p147). The hill referred to is probably that formerly called Penn Hill (see). A stone house in the village was the original court house for the Trysull area (SVB p166). Trysull and Seisdon became a separate civil parish in 1866 (GLAUE p426). The arms of Seisdon urban district, granted in 1952, are: Argent fretty gules with gold roundels at every point of intersection, a bordure vert charged with twelve Stafford Knots or. The crest is: On a wreath argent and gules rising from flames proper a silver demi-unicorn with gold horn, hoofs, mame, and turfs, supporting a Roman sword, points downwards, proper, its pommel and hilt gold. The motto is - 'Honeste progrediemur conando' (Let us progress by honour endeavour) (CH pp340il,341).

Seisdon Former administrative division (hundred) of Staffs, covering the SW part of the county (GNHS p74) (ESH pp45-50). Appears in DB as Saisdon(e), and Seiesdon. The name is probably from a small hill which over looks Seisdon village. This hill was presumably the meeting-place for the hundred court in late Anglo-Saxon times (WMMA pp143-144). It was formerly believed that the name was from Seisdon village (DUIGNAN). Parishes, townships and extra-parochial liberties in the **North Division** were: Bushbury (part of), Himley, Kingswinford, Patshull (after 1845), Penn, Rowley Regis, Sedgley, Tettenhall (Regis and Clericorum), Wolverhampton (W p61) (S&W p331) (VCH vol 20 p161), and the townships of Oaken, and Codsall (after 1845) (VCH vol 20 p76). In the **South Division** were: Amblecote, Bobbington (the Staffs part of), Bovenhill (but in Tettenhall parish), Broom, Clent, Enville, Kinver, Patshull (before 1845), Pattingham, Pendeford (but in Tettenhall parish) Trysull, Upper Arley, Wombourne, Woodford Grange (extra-parochial), Wrottesley (but in Tettenhall parish) (W p61) (S&W p331) (VCH vol 20 p161), and the township of Codsall (before 1845) (VCH vol 20 p76).

Seisdon Hall Substantial red-brick house in Seisdon village. It has heavy stone dressings and shaped gables. Reputed to be Elizabethan with a half-timbered core. In 1992 it was occupied by the Foster family (MIDD vol 3 pp38p,39).

Seisdon House House with five bays in Seisdon village. It is a low red brick Georgian house with a columned porch (MIDD vol 3 p39).

Selman's Hill Hill and road on N side of Lichfield Road, Little Bloxwich. Lower Farm (see) stood at the corner of Selman's Hill and Stoney Lane. The first official record of the name is in 1889, and it is believed to be from Thomas Selman, a blacksmith appearing as a resident of Little Bloxwich in the census returns between 1851 and 1871 (SNBP p50).

Selwyn House House at E end of Lichfield cathedral Close. Built by Canon James Falconer in 1780 in the ditch which formed part of the ancient fortifications of the Close. In 1908 it became a hostel for students of Lichfield Theological College and was named Selwyn Hostel in memory of a previous resident, Harriet (d1907), widow of Bishop Selwyn. In 1922 the students moved into the Bishop's Palace and Bishop Kempthorne moved to Selwyn House. In 1931 the bishop moved back to the palace and the students back to Selwyn House. The college closed in 1972 and the house was divided into flats (VCH vol 14 p65) (GKCLC). There is tradition of one of the Aston sisters building Selwyn House to ruin the view of the cathedral for her sister living across Stowe Pool at Stowe House. The tradition is she was unmarried and not wanted by her sisters and was shuttled about by them between Stowe House and Stowe Hill Mansion, year after year, until, out of spite or hate, she built Selwyn House. Dorothea, Lady Charnwood, in 'An Autograph Collection' (1930) could find no foundation or authority for the story, nor could F Marston in SSAHST. Besides, Selwyn House does not lie directly on the axis

line between Stowe House and the cathedral (SSAHST 1970 pp49-53). Has also appeared as 'Hate House' and 'Spite House'. (BOE p188).

Serpentine, The Pool and part of a reservoir on the former Greenway Bank estate. On NW side of Knypersley Pool. The Serpentine and Knypersley Pool are now collectively known as Knypersley Reservoir. Created by Hugh Henshall Williamson after he purchased the Greenway Bank estate in 1778 and before 1883 as a feeder for the Caldon Canal and as a lake to ornament the grounds of Knypersley Hall (SL pp244-245) (Greenway Bank Country Park. Staffs County Council Leaflet) (NSFCT 1991 pp41,46).

Serpentine Drive Carriage drive made specially for the Earl of Shrewsbury between Cheadle and Alton Towers, through Dimmings Dale (NSFCT 1944 p103).

Serpent Stone, The Serpent-shaped stone with an eye marked in it in the appropriate place. It lies near the Bawd Stone and the Roaches. It is said to be on an astrological alignment with the Bawd Stone (see) (DPEM p56p).

Seven Arches Viaduct Carries the railway over the Penk at Penkridge. Completed by Thomas Brassey in 1835. It became a prototype of the many viaducts he went on to build for the French Railways (PVH pp7p,20).

Seven Ashes Marked on Saxton's map, near Hilderstone, and copied on the maps of Kip, Speed, Blaeu, Blome until Plot's map when it ceases to appear. An illustration of seven ash trees are always shown and the feature has been written on maps Ye 7 Ashes. They were probably a feature on a prominence overlooking the Trent Valley and were marked to help travellers find their way who were on the highway in the Trent Valley. The ashes were, probably, gone by the later C17, and Plot's map was the first to totally discard Saxton's map as a model (NSFCT 1919 p60).

Seven Chimneys Cottage at Seven Chimneys on the W side of Warslow village was a police station by 1871, and it still (1994) retains part of the original cell with its wooden bed (VCH vol 7 p58).

Seven Dwellings At The Delph near Amblecote (TB Jan 1982 p5). The name is preserved in a street name (Birmingham A-Z 1995), crosses over the Stourbridge Canal.

Seven Houses Suburb 0.5m S of central Wolverhampton which arose in the C19 (W p96). Formerly in Wolverhampton township and ancient parish. There is no evidence of this name persisting.

Seven Oaks Beaudesert Old Park, at approximately SK 038142. The name appears on 1834 OS map and 1887 OS map 6 inch.

Seven Sisters Huge limestone cavern on the SW side of Wren's Nest Hill, near Dudley. It was created by mining in the 'pillar' and 'stall' method and was known in the C19 as the Light Cavern. It receives its present name from the seven pillars of limestone which supported the mouth of the cavern; by 1990 there were only five pillars left. David Cox made a now famous engraving of the cavern in 1829 (BCM April 1970 p60 il on p61. Oct 1970 p51) (VB p45; spelt Severn, probably erroneously) (WNNNR p23).

Seven Springs Seven springs at the N end of Cannock Chase, S of Weetman's Bridge, at SK 005206. A tall lady in black of beautiful complexion haunts the vicinity of the springs (SN Dec 24 1949 p7). This Seven Springs is a tourist spot and was the camp for a large group of hippies in 1985 (SN Aug 6 1998 p6). On April 27 1986, Gavin Hall, aged five, fell down a nine-inch wide hole to a depth of 23 feet at Seven Springs. Seven hours after falling down the hole Gavin was rescued by the Staffordshire Fire and Rescue Service, who dug a separate shaft to reach him (ADD pp177,178p). (SSC p121 in the intro; whether a reference to this seven springs?)

Seven Springs Middle of Cannock Chase. At SK 006182. Here are, presumably, seven springs.

Seven Springs S end of Cannock Chase, near Marquis Drive. At SK 032147. Here are, presumably, another seven springs. It was from these springs that miners at the Cannock Wood Pit drew water for their own supplies (CCBO p of facing title page, pp65,66).

Sevenways Cave Cave at SK 098549 on E side of Manifold 0.75m ENE of Grindon in the Manifold Valley. It has traces of pre-historic occupation (HOS p9) in that a disarticulated skeleton accompanied by two leaf-shaped arrowheads of the Neolithic period have been found in it (NSJFS 1964 p24) and several finds of what may be of Roman date (PASN vols 8,9,10) (British Caving. 1962 2nd ed. CHD Cullingford. p275) (NSJFS 1964 p24).

Severn, River A three mile stretch of this long river formerly ran through the county before Arley parish was transferred to Worcs.

Sexton Farm Ipstones Edge, 1m ENE of Sharpcliffe Rocks. The 'Sun Stone' standing stones, forming a rough quadrilateral, lie on land owned by Sexton Farm. They were discovered some time before 1980 by Harold Bode, who thinks the stones may be of ancient origin and are on an alignment with the setting sun behind Sharpcliffe Rocks at the summer solstice, and with other nearby stones at the equinox sunrise and sunset. The stones may be the origin of the name Ipstones (ES 1980) (DPEM pp72-74p). It is perhaps an astrological marker in alignment with Noonsun Common to the SW.

Shackamore At the confluence of the Trent and the Sow, close to Shugborough (SL p42). The name is of pagan origin.

Shadwell Spring A spring, which never freezes, which serves Clayers Pool, Enville Hall. Even a vessel of frozen water will be thawed out if placed in it (NHS p91).

Shaffalong House 0.5m WSW of Cheddleton. In Cheddleton parish. Shaffalong is the name for a coalfield in this area. Ceased being worked in c1912 (IANS p35). Its extent is shown on a map in IANS p32. Has also appeared as Shafferlong. Here the Cheddleton Wolfes had a house (NSFCT 1923 p34). Joseph Preston, aged 48, of Shaffalong but formerly of Macclesfield, Ches, was executed for incestuous rape of his youngest daughter, Mary, aged 11, in April 1828 (CCSHO pp47-51).

Shakes Castle Early meeting place of Darlaston Green (Offlow hundred) Methodists before their removal to a new nearby chapel on the corner of Perry Street and Castle Street, built in 1844. The name 'Shakes' may be from the the fact that Methodists were often mocked and 'shakers' suggests the energetic hymn singing and hellfire preaching often practiced by them (SNDB p28).

Shaky Bridge Footbridge over the Sow to W of Cresswell Chapel ruins (VB p138) (ROT p32). Has also appeared as Shaky Bridges.

Shallowford Hamlet in pastoral country by the Sow 1m ENE of Chebsey. In Chebsey township and ancient parish (W p388). Appears in the C13 as Schaldeford (SSE 1996 p17). Chetwynd says from a ford in the Sow (SH p45). The shallow ford (DUIGNAN) (SSE 1996 p17). Here is Halfhead (see), Izaak Walton's cottage. See also Shawford. Some have thought Izaak Walton was born at Shallowford (SHC 1914 p62 note), but he is thought by most to have been born in Eastgate Street, Stafford. There is a private family Quaker burial-ground at SJ 872292, represented by a clump of trees about 0.5m from Norton station on N side of the Shallowford-Chebsey road (SSAHST 1970 pp43-44 p). The last burial was in 1859 when a man from the Potteries was buried, making a total of 10 burials (info Bruce Braithwaite). There have been sightings of Quaker ghosts in the vicinity, one sighting was by a couple in 1969, and there has been at least one further sighting (ROT p30) (SN April 15 1994 p5) (further info from Bruce Braithwaite). In the early C19 a skeleton was found in a field at Shallowford at a depth of four feet; it was thought to have been that of someone murdered (Broughton's Scrapbook p171; article is dated Sept 22 1814).

Shallowford Brook Blymhill (SHOS vol 1 part 1 p109).

Shallowford Brook Shallowford. (An Izaak Walton Guide).

Shallowford House House on the W side of the Norton Bridge road, Shallowford. By the late C20 it was the diocese of Lichfield's Retreat House (Chebsey Website 2000).

Sham Chapel Farm overlooking Cotton Dell. Perhaps, the site of a vanished pre-Reformation chapel in the old parish of Kingsley. The building lies E to W and has some old masonry (NSFCT 1922 p160). Sham Church Farm is the site of a chapel (NSSG p15). Could be now Side Farm at SK 058465.

Shamrock Yard Bilston. Named by the large numbers of Irish workers who came to live in Bilston in the C19 (BOP p68).

Shareshill Large village on a hill in a valley formed by a tributary of Saredon Brook, 9m S of Stafford. Former chapelry in Penkridge ancient parish. The last **Ice Age** reached its maximum southern extent about Wolverhampton and glacial boulders lie about Shareshill (WJO Nov 1909 p293). In 1966 a bronze unlooped palstave of the early **Middle Bronze Age** was found during ploughing of a field in the vicinity of the church (SSAHST 1971 pp47il,48-49). Shaw mistakenly identified Shareshill with DB Stagrigesholle, otherwise identified with Stramshall (SHOS vol 1 pxii appendix to General History); the manor Servesed (Shareshill) appears in DB. Later forms are: Sarneshull (1213), Saresweshull (1225), Sarsculf (1227), Shareweshulf (1252), Schareshulle (1271-1657), Sarueshulf (1298), Shareshall (Morden's map), Shareshill (Yates' map) (SPNO p116) (SPN p104) (SSE 1996 p17). The **name** originates from Old English 'scraef-scylf,' 'a hill by a narrow valley' (SVB p148), or from Anglo-Saxon 'scylf hyll,' 'the shelved terrain' (SPN p104). Gelling says it is partly unexplained (NSJFS 1981 p3). Mills gives hill or shelf (SSE 1996 p17). Or it represents 'Moor heath, or moor hill, or heath lead, or hill stead' (DUIGNAN). The parish lay in Cannock Forest between at least 1167 and 1301 (VCH vol 5 p178). There are encampments on the N and S sides of the village. The N side earthwork seems to be at SJ 946067, to the NE of the village and partly obliterated by the school playground (VCH vol 5 p173) (BAST vol 77 1959 pp45-58) (SSAHST 1982-3 p46) (NSFCT 1982 p19). Excavations have shown this to be the site of a C12 mansion abandoned by c1400. It was claimed in the early C20 to be of

Roman origin (VCH vol 1 pp346,348) (SSAHST 1982-3 pp46-47) (CAMS p44). White noted a square form thought to be of Roman construction (W p479); relics found out of it and the earthwork on the S side of the village were kept in the church in the C19 (SMC p172). The S side earthwork is similar to that on the N side of village. By the mid 1950s it had disappeared (VCH vol 1 p192. vol 5 p173). The same or another moated site was said by Shaw to lie SW of the village and was considered by him to perhaps represent the seat of the ancient family called Shareshill (SSAHST 1982-3 p47). The **church,** St Mary the Virgin and St Luke, in St Mary's Close, was rebuilt in 1743, but has some C14 work in the lower parts (A Sketch of the History of Shareshill Church. Shareshill WI). According to local tradition the church was originally built on Saredon Hill but 'as fast as the workmen put it up by day, the pixies took it down by night and re-built it in Shareshill' (Spotlight. Nov/ Dec 1999 p3). Former **prebend** of Penkridge Collegiate Church (VCH vol 3 p300). The peculiar jurisdiction of Penkridge Collegiate Church over Shareshill survived until peculiar jurisdictions were abolished in 1846 (VCH vol 3 p93 note). Shareshill became a separate parish in 1551. Formerly formed a township in Shareshill parish (GLAUE p421). Shareshill had an annual parade and a **feast day**. At the head of the procession was a man carrying a mop with a bunch of flowers decorating the top. Halts were made at all the public houses (CCF p144). The village grew to its present size mainly from the mid C20. **William Henry Havergal** (1793-1870), the composer of sacred music and writer on the subject, was vicar of Shareshill from 1860 to his death, although he was absent for much of his incumbency owing to blindness and infirmity. His daughter, **Frances Ridley Havergal** (1836-79), a hymn writer, is remembered for her hymn 'Take my Life, and let it be Consecrated, Lord to Thee' (BS p215) (LGS p211) (KES p178) (VCH vol 5 p174) (CCBO pp178-179) (CCF pp144-146) (VB p83) (TB Dec 1990 p7p).

Sharpcliffe Hall House and estate 1.25m NNW of Ipstones. In Ipstones ancient parish. At Sharpcliffe is a small burial mound, which may be the place of a child's burial (NSFCT 1911 p207). On the Sharpcliff estate has been found a stone implement and either a palstave or spearhead of Neolithic or Bronze Age origin (NSFCT vol 1 p164) (VCH p181) (NSJFS 1964 p26). Also on the estate a cist and pottery were found in a burial mound and destroyed by workmen for gravel before 1911 (NSFCT vol 46 pp135,207. vol 50 pp164-165,187) (NSJFS 1965 p42). Sharpcliffe is said to have been an ancient British encampment (TOI pp39-41). A residence here, recorded in 1280, was anciently the seat of the Sharpcliffes, passing to the Whitehalgh or Whitehough family of Park Hall, when a James Whitehalgh married into the Sharpcliffe family in the C15 (LGS p154). James' great grandson and successor, Robert, changed his name to Whitehall. Robert's daughter-in-law, Elizabeth (nee Hollins), was living at Sharpecliffe in 1647. The present hall appears to have been built by her son, John Whitehall (d1684), in c1630 (TOI p40) or 1673 (NSFCT 1890 p37. 1915 p165) or in 1679 (STC p15p). (BOE p157). An inscription over the porch reads 'This house builded by John Whitehall of Park-hall, Esquire, sonne to James grandchilde to Robertm great grand-childe to James Whitehall; which John by Frances heire to William Aston of Park-hall, Esquire had Elizabeth and Ann and James by Frances Gresley.' Sharpcliffe then passed to John's son by his second wife Frances Gresley, James. James was succeeded by his two daughters Frances (who married Fisher Littleton d1740) and Ann (who married Thomas Parker, Lord Chief-baron Court Exchequer d1784). The two families (Littletons and Parkers) appear to have held Sharpcliffe to the early C19 (TOI pp39-41). It was occupied by Ralph Debank Sneyd in 1851 (W). In 1860 DH Sneyd of Ashcombe to some extent remodelled the hall (TOI p39-41). In 1874 he sold it to Hugh Sleigh JP (TOI p40). It was occupied by farmers Thomas Bailey in 1876, and James Citchlow in 1884 (KD 1876. 1884). It was occupied by Arthur S Boucher JP between at least 1907 and 1916. In c1907 the hall was being enlarged and restored (STC p15) (KD 1916). Residence of RM Argles by 1940 (NSFCT 1939 p80). Owned for a time by the YHA. The hall is mentioned in a poem by Ralph de Tunstall Sneyd about Combes Valley (see). In a shrubbery on the estate in 1955 was found a cast-iron fireback, bearing the arms of the Hollins of Mosslee Hall, the initials of Phillip and Elizabeth Hollins and 1671; the date of their wedding. It was believed to come from an old house that used to stand in a field known as Greener's Croft (NSFCT 1955 pp39-40il).

Sharpcliffe Rocks Rocks which lie on the crest of a ridge in the grounds of Sharpcliffe Hall, over 0.25m ESE of the hall (SGM p202). Pitt in the early C19 noted the rocks comprised coarse plum-pudding stone (breccia arenacea), creating a surface which 'seem like sand and small pebbles cemented together' (THS p40). The geology of the rock is Triassic Conglomerate (SGM p202).

Sharpley Heath Heath and fragmented minute hamlet 1m NNW of Garshall Green. In Hilderstone quarter in Stone ancient parish.

Shatterford An eminence (SHOS vol 2 p254) and small hamlet in very undulating country at some distance from the Severn, 1.5m ENE of Arley. In Upper Arley parish. Has appeared vulgarly as Shatterfoot (SHOS vol 2 p254). According to Joseph Chillingworth, minister of Arley, the name is derived from schytenford, or the passage of the archers, scythians or Saxons (SHOS vol 2 p254) (DUIGNAN). Or from Anglo-Saxon 'scytere' meaning 'shooter,' used to refer to river rapids or a fast-flowing stream, or used to refer to an archery training ground, or possible competition site (SPN p105). The gospel oak on the green at Shatterford had burnt down not so many years prior to 1914 (AOA p92). There was coal mining at Shatterford sometime prior to 1850 (AOA p90). Shatterford is not in Staffs according to Yates' map.

Shatterford Wood A wood in the E of Arley parish, and formerly in Kinver Forest (VCHW vol 3 p5).

Shaver's End Situated at the southern tip of the former detached portion of Walsall ancient parish, on the W side of Lichfield Road. There was a house here by 1775 and Shavers End appears on 1834 OS map. It stood on the site of Shelfield Farm (VCH vol 17 p277). Has also appeared as Shaw's End (SNBC p29). The farm, over 1m NNE of Rushall church, appears on the Birmingham A-Z 1989 edition but not on the 1995 edition where it is replaced by Deepwood Close.

Shaw There are a number of houses prefixed Shaw E of Fradswell Heath; Shaw Farm, Shaw Lodge, Shaw Lane, Shaw Cottage, also a Withyshaw S of Fradswell Heath.

Shaw Barn 1.5m SW of King's Bromley. Appears 1834 OS map.

Shaw Bottom House 1.75m N of Upper Hulme.

Shawe Hall or Shaw House. 0.5m SSW of Kingsley. There seems to have been an old Shawe Hall occupied by the Ladkins in the Civil War and later in the C17 by the Stubbs family. Shawe Hall was rebuilt in 1821 in red brick (CCT pp54,57). It was at some time also occupied by the Beech family (ACOPP p63p). It was in a derelict state and covered with ivy in 1966 (STM Dec 1966 p33p) and was demolished in 1987 (SMOPP vol 1 p69p in 1919).

Shawfield Fragmented small hamlet about the head of Blake Brook in the Moorlands 2.5m SW of Longnor. In Fawfieldhead township in Alstonefield ancient parish. Shawfield Wood on the former waste was planted by Sir George Crewe (or Harpur-Crewe), lord of Alstonefield manor, in 1834 (VCH vol 7 p29).

Shawford and Shawford Brook. Mentioned in Izaak Walton's 'Angler's Song.' Some think it is an allusion to Shallowford. But there is a Shawford in Walton's other county Hampshire (LGS p210).

Shaw Hall Shawhall Farm stands at the junction of Shaw Hall Lane with the road to Coven Lawn, N of Coven Heath, in Bushbury ancient parish. The name Shaw Hall occurs in the 1841 census.

Shaw House Greengate Street, between the High House and the Swan Hotel, Stafford (VCH vol 6 p190). Or has been called Shaw's House (OSST 1933 p44), and the Charles House, after Charles I once slept here. Stands between the ancient High House and the Swan Hotel proper. By at least 1948 the Swan was using its first, second and third storey rooms. 'Shaw House' has been shown to be older than the High House. It was stuccoed some time after John Robert Ferneyhough's sitograph of 1781, which shows its half timbering. In 1947, the stucco was removed and the original 'quite straightforward' framing underneath revealed. The structure was re-stuccoed and the surface painted exactly as it had appeared in Ferneyhough's sitograph (SKYT pp8,9il,24p).

Shaw House House 1.5m N of Upper Hulme. Formerly in Leekfrith township in Leek ancient parish. A scattered settlement of coal miners grew up in the C19 around Shaw House (VCH vol 7 p194). (BS between pp523-531; Shawhouse - Could be this Shaw House, or in Shawfield to W of Longnor. Is it in Staffs?).

Shaw Lane (*Shay*). Lane running through Forton. Part of the Roman road which ran from the Cheshire salt district. So called in 1640. Shay is a corruption of salt (NSFCT 1937 p63).

Shaw Lodge Farm 1.5m NW of Gratwich.

Shawmoor Former farm 1m NNE of Hulme End on the W side of the Manifold. Formerly in Fawfieldhead township, in Alstonefield ancient parish. The name may have derived from Schal Moor, common waste mentioned in 1392 (VCH vol 7 p29).

Shawms, The Substantial house in the Voysey style, off Radford Bank, Radford Rise, Stafford. Built in 1905 by T Sandy (BOE p248). Occupied by HJ Bostock between at least the years 1935 and 1946 (SHC 1934. 1944 List of Members), it was for sale in 2000 (DoE II) (SLM April 2000 p10pc). The name is possibly from a place where shawn players traditionally played (SPNO p31).

Shaws, The In King's Bromley parish (SGSAS). Is shown on the 1834 OS and Dower's maps 2m SW of King's Bromley at Shaw Lane Farm.

Shawside House 1.5m NNW of Upper Hulme.

Shawtop House under 1.5m NNW of Upper Hulme.

Shaw Wall Small hamlet 0.5m ENE of Foxt. Has also appeared as Shaw Walls.

Sheath House, The (1834 OS map) (Dower's map). Sheath House Farm is over 0.75m NNW of Hopton.

Shebdon Small hamlet in a bend in Lonco Brook at some distance from the brook, 1.25m S of Adbaston. In High Offley ancient parish and was in (High) Offley prebend (SSAHST vol 2 1960-61 p47). Appears in 1267 as Schebbedon (SSE 1996 p17). The name may mean 'Sceoba's hill' (SSE 1996 p17).

Shebdon Heath N of Shebdon on N side of Shrops Union Canal (1834 OS map).

Shebdon Pool Pool formerly situated N of Shebdon by Shebdon Bridge (S of Shrops Union Canal). It had completely disappeared by 1922 although it was only drained and enclosed in the mid C19 (NSFCT 1922 p124 map showing the outline of the pool c1800). Appears regularly on maps from the later C17 (ESH p31) and has appeared as Shebdon Moss Pool and Shebben Moss Pool (WSS p108). Plot noted that it was the favourite breeding spot of the Black Headed Gull or Pewit; they always returned here to breed, failing to do so meant something ominous was about to occur (NHS p233) (Man and the Natural World. K Thomas p62). They were here between 1668 and 1770 before leaving for the meres of Flashbrooke Common (NSFCT 1927 p38). In the later C17 Plot believed the fossilized stumps of firs he found in Shebdon Pool were those of the alien Abies Legitima vel mas Bellonii, or Abies of Parkinson, not found in England or Ireland, proving that these types of fir were anciently indigenous to Britain (NHS pp209,216,217). The pool was described as drained and enclosed in 1817 (THS p23).

Sheen Ancient parish, manor, and high moorland village between the Dove and the Manifold 16.75m NE of Stafford. There is possibly a **burial mound** W of Sheen village (VCH vol 7 p241). For other burial mounds in Sheen parish see Brund Low, Rye Low, and Townend. Sheen was identified by Wolferstan as the Sceon mentioned in the will of Wulfric Spot (c1002), founder of Burton Abbey (SHC 1916 p40); has also appeared as Sceon (DB) (SSE 1996 p17), Shone (1272), and Shene (1272) (SHC 1904 p116). The **name** is from possibly Anglo-Saxon 'scine, scene, sceone' meaning 'beautiful' or 'a delusive appearance' a reference to one of the nearby rivers (VCH vol 7 p241), or the Manifold's disappearance under ground; the Manifold forms the W boundary of the parish (DUIGNAN). Or the name means 'the shining one' (SVB p150). Mills and Oakden think it is from an unrecorded Old English word 'sceon' meaning 'shed' or 'shelter' (SSAHST 1967 p34) (VCH vol 7 p241) (SSE 1996 p17). There was a settlement at Sheen village by 1175. The **parish**, which has been described as 'one immense hill,' was a chapel of Ilam ancient parish, itself a possession of Burton Abbey; Sheen was granted to Burton upon Trent collegiate church in 1541. Sheen chapelry split away from Ilam probably shortly after Burton college possessions were sold off in 1546 (SHC 1915 pxxxi) (VCH vol 7 p240,246). With the curacy becoming a perpetual curacy in 1743 Sheen became a separate ecclesiastical parish. It had separate civil identity early (GLAUE p422) (VCH vol 7 p247). The present parish **church**, St Luke, on the E side of the main road in the village, stands on the site of a chapel which was at Sheen by 1185. It was rebuilt in the C16, and again in 1828-1832, and again in 1852 (VCH vol 7 p248). Before 1752 the **wakes** were held on the Sunday before Oct 18, the feast of the patronal saint of the parish, St Luke. After 1752 they were held on Oct 29 (VCH vol 7 p243). There was a fair at Sheen in 1771 (VCH vol 7 p245). The oldest surviving houses in the village mostly date from the C17 (VCH vol 7 p241). In the 1850s AJB Hope, heir to the Beresford estate, tried to make the village into an **'Athens of the Moorlands'** by giving it new facilities to attract residents 'of means and religion.' To some extent his plans were fulfilled, for a new church, parsonage, and school were built, and the C15 village cross, 50 metres W of the school, was restored. But his plan to enlarge the village with new high-quality villas was not realised (DoE II) (LGS p211) (VCH vol 7 p241). The **Parsonage**, designed by William Butterfield in 1852, was the last building visited by Sir Nikolaus Pevsner during his final tour in 1970 to complete his Buildings of England series (BOE p234) (The Guardian. Oct 10 1970 p8) (VCH vol 7 pp247-248) (The Times. Weekend Section. Nov 20 1999 pp1-2). In 1996 the village **post office** opened for one day a week in the living room of the cottage of Pat Sutton, the postmistress; hitherto it had been in the Staffordshire Knot Inn in Sheen (ES Nov 20 1999 p17pc). The Sheen Farmers **Tug-of-War team** were world champions in 1975, 1977 and 1980 (SVB pp150-151) (GBR 1988) (Real Ale in & around the Potteries. CAMRA. p63) (PWNS p157). Of the 20 **lime trees** planted in Sheen village in 1761 19 survive. The body of **Thomas Bassett**, a native of Sheen and immigrant in the USA, was transported back to the village for burial at the expense of his fellow immigrant and friend, Adolphus Frederick Bleathman. It was then considered an extraordinary act of friendship; Bassett had fallen to his death from scaffolding in Memphis, Tennessee, in 1867 (HLSP p80).

Sheen Hill Hill 0.75m N of Sheen, 1247 feet high (VCH vol 7 p240). From the top on a clear day can be seen nine church spires and towers and the Wrekin (SVB p150). The view from it was praised by Langford in S&W p319.

Sheen Moor Common waste land in the N part of Sheen parish. Piecemeal enclosure of the common was taking place in the later C17 (VCH vol 7 p244).

Sheep Fair Rugeley, an area preserving the site of the sheep market (SPN p100). A street of this name runs from Church Street to Elmore Lane.

Sheephouse House 2.25m S of Leek. Formerly in Leek and Lowe township in Leek ancient parish. Held by Dieulacres Abbey until the abbey was dissolved in 1538, in which year it was known as Sheephouse (VCH vol 7 p88).

Sheepwalks, The Area of high ground 0.75m SW of Enville Hall, and the higher reaches of Enville Park (SGS p98) (MR p146). It has been identified with the pre-Norman Conquest settlement of Cippemore (see). The area was occupied in the earlier C14. There was a warrener's lodge on the southern edge of the Sheepwalks at approximately SO 812852, probably by 1623 (VCH vol 20 pp92 see map, 93). The warrener's lodge, on or near the site of a building known as Sheepwalks House in c1880 (VCH vol 20 p101 see map), has been identified with the Shepherd's Lodge of Enville Hall (see) (TB Sept 1989 p29 il by Ron Davis); the warrener's lodge, known as Enville Lodge by 1623, was gothicized in the C18, perhaps by Sanderson Miller; the ruins of a C17 building stood there in 1982 (VCH vol 20 pp99,111). The Sheepwalks area was known as 'the hills' in the C17 and was beginning to be referred to as Sheepwalks in c1800; Shaw calls it Sheep Walk (SHOS vol 2 p271) (SVS pp279-280) (VCH vol 20 p93). By 1880 Enville Hall grounds had been extended to include the Sheepwalks (VCH vol 20 p101 see map).

Sheepwash Tiny hamlet 1.5m N of Caverswall situated on the upper Blithe. In Caverswall ancient parish.

Sheepwash Area 1.75m W of the High Street, West Bromwich, in West Bromwich ancient parish (VCH vol 17 p8). Sheepwash Mill, in Sheepwash Lane, was a mill on the Tame (SHWB 14).

Sheldon Farm Grindon Moor. Farm 1m WNW of Grindon. Near here, on Feb 13 1947, the Halifax RT 922 aircraft trying to dispatch food to snow-bound Grindon crashed killing the crew of eight (MMM p22).

Shelfield (*Shelfill* DUIGNAN). Large village on raised land between Ford Brook and a tributary 1m SE of Pelsall. Formerly in a detached part of the foreign of Walsall ancient parish. Scelfeld is described in DB as wasteland. The name means 'shelving hill' (DUIGNAN). Or 'shelf hill' (NSJFS 1981 p3). Or 'the enclosure on a shelf of land' (SPN p134). Shelfield was originally part of the manor of Walsall and became a separate manor in the C16. It was an inhabited area by the earlier C13 and was called a hamlet in 1276. The original village centre was the Mill Road, Field Lane, Birch Lane junction (VCH vol 17 p277) (ADY p25p). There was a pound at the junction of Four Crosses Road and Lichfield Road in the later C19 (VCH vol 17 p281). Wakes in the detached part of the foreign of Walsall ancient parish were held, sometimes at Shelfield and sometimes at Walsall Wood (see). By the C18 Shelfield had spread NE to a district known as 'Irondish' near the junction of New Street and Walsall Road. Shelfield remained largely wooded until at least early C17, but by the mid C19 only a few isolated coppices remained (ADY p25). There was a windmill at Shelfield between 1744 and 1786, but its location is unknown. By 1816 there was a windmill on the N side of Mill Lane (VCH vol 17 p280), at SP 028025. It was shown on OS map 1831. Its equipment was for sale in 1843, perhaps indicating its demise, although millers are recorded at Shelfield in 1868 and 1872 (WBJ pp35,36). It was rebuilt as a steam corn-mill by the early 1880s and worked as such as a corn-mill until the mid 1930s (VCH vol 17 p280). Shelfield became a part of the new ecclesiastical parish of Walsall Wood in 1845 (GLAUE p427) and of Brownhills urban district in 1894 (ADY p25p). The church, St Mark, at the S end of Green Lane, was built in 1965 (info Mrs Male) (LDD). In the late C17 Dr Plot noted a goose at Shelfield with three legs (NHS p234).

Shelfield Lodge Farm on S side of Mill Road, Shelfield, at SK 031023. Was an early C18 brick building retaining part of its predecessor, a late-medieval hall house. It was demolished in 1961 to make way for an housing estate (SSAHST 1968 pp63-69 p ils) (VCH vol 17 p277) (ADY p25) (SNBC p26p).

Shelmore Great Bank Canal embankment on the W side of Shrops Union Canal 1m SSE of Norbury. The name Shelmore may be from 'scelf' from Old English 'shelf,' and 'mor' from Old English 'marsh,' or 'barren upland.' The name may therefore mean wide, nearly level, marsh (Place-names in the Landscape. 1984. M Gelling. p186) (WSS p110). Lord Anson who owned Norbury Park at the time of the building of the Shrops Union Canal insisted it avoid his estate and Telford had to take the canal to the W on low ground. In 1829 he started to build a high 1.5m long embankment to support the canal (SWY p33) (PWIS pp28,30). Slip after slip occurred in the early 1830s.

Two major collapses occurred, one in Aug 1832 and another in May 1834 (WSS p110). At length Telford's deputy, William Cubitt, ordered large quantities of hard core (broken stone) to be tipped into the treacherous clay with the intention of stabilising it (TTTD pp264-265). The embankment did not consolidate until six months after Telford's death in Sept 1834 and only then traffic had to go slow on the stretch (SWY p33) (PWIS pp28,30). The canal opened in 1835.

Shelmore Park Woodland area in Norbury parish (VCH vol 4 p155), possibly synonymous with Shelmore Wood.

Shelmore Wood Wood 1m SE of Norbury. Shelmore House is to the S. Also a Shelmore Valley Farm. The name Shelmore here appears on the 1834 OS map (SPNO p175).

Shelton Former hamlet which centred upon the brow of the hill adjacent to the modern church, overlooking Fowlea Valley (HBST p412), now a suburb of Hanley, 0.75m SW of Hanley. Former township in Stoke-upon-Trent chapelry and ancient parish. According to Commander Wedgwood, Eyton wrongly identified this Shelton with the Scelftone in DB; whilst according to Commander Wedgwood the correct identification of Scelftone is with Shelton-under-Harley (see) (SHC 1916 p168). The **name** means 'town on the shelve or slope' (DUIGNAN). Or 'shelf settlement' (NSJFS 1981 p2). The centre of old Shelton hamlet was probably in the vicinity of Shelton Old Hall. By the second half of the C18 there was settlement in Shelton township in the Snow Hill and Broad Street area and the Marsh Street area, the latter is and has been long considered the W side of Hanley town. In 1813 an Act of parliament formed Shelton and Hanley into a market town. There was continual conurbation from Hanley to the S end of present Snow Hill by at least the 1830s (1834 OS map) (H p18) (VCH vol 8 p144). Shelton was ward of Stoke-on-Trent district by 1991. The Commissioners' **church**, St Mark, on the S side of Broad Street, was built in 1831-1834 (VCH vol 8 p155) (BOE p258). Became a separate ecclesiastical parish in 1843 (CAST p57) (GLAUE p422). A **pinfold** stood to the E of Cleveland Passage in c1880 and may be identifiable with the pinfold owned by the corporation in 1907 (H p10) (VCH vol 8 p162). Between Shelton and Hanley **tobacco pipe clay** could be found (NHS p121). Some C18 pottery has been excavated in College Road (ES April 4 1992 p1p). **Shelton Iron Works**, roughly to the W of Cobridge Road and N of Etruria Hall (VCH vol 8 p169; gives the original exact site), was erected by 2nd Earl Granville of Stone Park (see) in 1841. A Shelton Iron Works commemorative jug dated Jan 4 1841 was rediscovered in the 1930s? in an old second-hand shop in Birmingham and went on show in the works headquarters, which was Etruria Hall (HOE p179). An incident occurred at Shelton Bar Ironworks in April 1855 when a 20 feet diameter flywheel at the mill crushed a man to death. HG Wells is believed to have based his short story 'The Cone' on an incident at Shelton Bar Ironworks. The incident occurred in May 1871 when John Sherratt, a single man of 32 and a blast furnace stone-breaker, threw himself into the furnace. He was thought to be of unsound mind (SHST p630) (ES March 5 1996 p5). Arnold Bennett's review of 'The Cone' for 'Woman' journal instigated his lifelong friendship with Wells (info Peter Cheeseman). In WW2 the Germans attempted to bomb the works on June 30 1940; a man, his wife, and their 19 year-old son were killed when their house was hit in Shelton (ES June 11 1977). Shelton Bar Steelworks became part of British Steel after nationalisation in 1967. A campaign in the 1970s to save the works from closure lasted eight years, during which time Shelton Bar became something of a cause celebre. The drama documentary entitled 'Fight for Shelton Bar!' created by the Victoria Theatre Company (later based at Stoneyfields (see)) was staged at the old Victoria Theatre, Hartshill, in Jan 1974 (BBC Radio 4. Start the Week. Dec 6 1993) (info Peter Cheeseman). A 'tin man' statue sculpted by Colin Melbourne was made to celebrate it entitled 'The Fight for Shelton Bar' (POP pl 24). The final blast furnace closed in 1978. British Steel was privatised in 1989 and the works closed in 2000 (ES Dec 12 1994 p8. April 28 2000 pp2-3). The suffix 'Bar' comes from the product, bar-iron, to distinguish it from a sheet-rolling mill (POP p38). Although, it may not necessarily be from bar-iron. There may have been a field name called Prison Barr in Shelton. The game, known as Prison Barr, may have originated here, or the field may have been named after the game which was played here. The present (1999) **Staffordshire University** has its origins in the Central School of Science and Technology which opened on College Road (junction with Station Road) in April 1914. This later became the North Staffordshire Technical College and then, in the 1960s, the College of Technology. The North Staffordshire College of Technology, Staffordshire College of Technology, and Stoke-on-Trent College of Art merged in 1970 to form North Staffordshire Polytechnic, under the control of Staffs county council. In 1978 the polytechnic and Madeley College of Education merged. In 1988 the name of the Polytechnic changed to Staffordshire Polytechnic. In 1989 the polytechnic was granted corporate status as a higher education corporation, free from local authority control. In 1992 it became Staffordshire University. The university still occupies some of the original college buildings at its now large College Road campus in Stoke-upon-Trent. It obtained the campus at Beaconside, Stafford, after amalgamation with Staffordshire College of Technology in 1970. It has had a campus in Leek Road, Stoke-upon-Trent, since the early 1970s. In the 1990s the university moved its School of Health and part of its Business School to buildings in Blackheath Lane, Stafford. Staffordshire University Lichfield Centre opened in Lichfield (see) in May 1998. **Alumni**: Susie Cooper, ceramic designer who trained at Stoke-on-Trent College of Art; Mike O' Brien MP; John Mayock and Joanne Jennings, Olympic athletes; Jim Davies, guitarist (info Judith Robinson, Staffordshire University) (AGT pp136,137 il of the old Central School of Science and Technology). **1981 riots**. The riot in Stoke Road on Saturday July 12 1981 in which about 150 were involved was thought to have been a copy-cat incident of national rioting (ES July 13 1981 p1ps). 75 acres of the former Shelton Bar Steelworks were reclaimed for the National Garden Festival site opened by Elizabeth II on May 8 1986 (JC 30). After the festival had finished in 1987 the site, which became known as Festival Park, was converted to a leisure complex and trading estate. Shelton is **Cauldon** in Arnold Bennett's novels. **UFO sightings**. Two bright orange eliptical lights side by side hanging motionless in the western sky was seen from Howard Place on Aug 24 1967 at approximately 10.40pm. Another UFO high in the sky travelling at an incredible speed was seen from Shelton on Aug 29 1967 at 6.16am (FSRP p7). **Persons**. **Edward Lane**, a Shelton schoolmaster, patented an improved steam-engine in 1809 which would raise water and grind corn (Chronicle of Industrial Patents of Invention No. 3,256) (VCH vol 2 p167). In Newland Street in 1921 **James Bowman** grew a twelve feet, five and a half high inch sunflower and won a wager with a man in Kent who said that a sunflower could not be grown higher in the Potteries than one in Kent. The event made national news (Sunday Illustrated. Oct 9 1921) (ES June 25 1996 p8p).

Shelton Hall It stood between Cemetery Road and Caledonian Road, Shelton. Built by Charles and Ephraim Chatterley in 1782 (OTP pp145,176) (HBST p386) (VCH vol 8 p150). Demolished in 1958 (POTP p60) or 1959 (VCH vol 8 pp150,153). However, Warrilow says, Ephraim Chatterley built it in 1872 and it was pulled down in March 1959 (SHST pp357,471 il of in c1825, 571,572p). Here the young Sir Oliver Lodge and his parents lived (OTP p147). Also known as Chatterley Hall (or House?).

Shelton Heath Heath 1.5m SE of Shelton-under-Harley (Smith's map). Is not marked on current OS maps where the names Hatton Common, Hatton Rough, Old Waste Plantation, New Waste Plantation appear.

Shelton New Hall Stood by Newhall Street, Hope Street, Sampson Street and top portion of Century Street, Shelton. The hall was demolished in 1920 (VCH vol 8 p167), or soon after WW2 (SHST p569). Formerly called Shelton Hall, and later called New Hall, Shelton (although, this area is now considered Hanley). The name New Hall was used by at least 1801, presumably to avoid confusion with the Old Hall in Hanley and the other two halls in Shelton (VCH vol 8 p166 note). Others say 'New' is after the New Hall Company who bought the hall for a pottery (POP p51).

Shelton Old Hall Old house which overlooked Wellesley Street, Shelton. Birthplace of the poet Elijah Fenton on March 25 1683 (BS p165). His poem 'An Ode to the Sun for the New Year' is perhaps the most celebrated (POTP p95). He died at the home of his patroness, Lady Trumbull, on July 16 1730 in Easthampstead, Berks, and was buried in the churchyard there. Elijah Fenton's travelling writing case was given to the NSFC through the WSL by Major CJ Jacobs (NSFCT 1953 p107). (Lives of the Poets. Dr Johnson) (SMC pp187-188) (Life of Elijah Fenton. Robert Fenton) (PSS pp41-46 il) (CAST p46) (POP pp38-39) (OTP p68) (STM June 1966 p29il) (VFC p48). The Fentons left in 1695 and moved to the Steps, Newcastle-under-Lyme. Jacobean oak panelling went to Betley in Queen Anne's reign (BVC p121). Shelton Old Hall remained Fenton property and was owned by Sir Thomas Fletcher Fenton Boughey of Aqualate Hall in the mid C19 (HSP p48) (GNHS p131) (VCH vol 8 pp150,153). The hall was destroyed by fire on May 22 1853. The fire was attended by Etruria and Hanley Fire Brigades who are said to have fought each other for water to put it out, such was the rivalry between the two brigades (HOE pp322,323) (HBST il facing pp409, 412) (POTP p95) (ADD p40). The carved oak mantelpiece was salvaged and went to Ernest JD Warrilow's home (SHST pp540 il - 542 il, 543).

Shelton-under-Harley House 2.75m NW of Swynnerton, just N of Stableford. Former township in Swynnerton ancient parish. Shelton was identified by Commander Wedgwood with the Scelfitone in DB (SHC 1916 p168). Later appears as Shelton-under-Airley (W p424). It may be this Shelton (rather than Shelton near Hanley) where William Murrell held a quantity of land (15

to 40 acres) in Edward II's reign by the sergeanty of keeping the King's Clive Hay in the former New Forest (see) (SCSF p116). John Dimmock, pottery manufacturer, was born here in c1819. His works in Hanley escaped the rage of the Chartists because he was considered a friend of the working class (POTP p79).

Shenstone Ancient parish and large village on a low hill by the confluence of Crane and Footherley Brooks 17m SE of Stafford.
EARLY. A glacial boulder was used in the foundations of the church (STMSM Nov 1972 p41). At Shenstone and at Drayton Bassett were found a hand axe from the **Upper Palaeolithic** (pre-Ice Age) period; the earliest evidences of man in the county. It was found 0.5m NNW of Shenstone Hall cSK 111054, and was in a private collection for many years prior to 1972 (SSAHST 1972-73 p5 fig 1) (NSJFS vol 12. 1972. pp1-20) (SL p35) (MR p280). A polished stone axe was found at SK 111065 by Mr Foden of Shenstone Hall in autumn 1965 (SSAHST 1965 p40). A **Neolithic** or **Bronze Age** stone axe was found in Whatley Field in 1930 (NSFCT vol 69 p60) (NSJFS 1964 p34). A hoard of bronze weapons was discovered at Gainsborough Hill Farm (see) in 1924 (LGS p25). A Roman farmstead has been found at Shenstone (HOS p12) - probably either one to the N of the village at SK 111054 see Shenstone Hall Farm, or one at SK 108061. (The Roman Site at Shenstone, Staffs. HR Hodgkinson & PB Chatwin. 1944).
900 to PRESENT. There was a **church** at Shenstone possibly in Saxon times (SSAHST 1973 pp43-49) and certainly by 1129 (SSAHST 1970 p25). The old parish church, St John the Baptist, at St John's Hill, may have contained materials from a chapel at Lower Stonnall. The old Shenstone church contained some carving of the keys of St Peter and Lower Stonnall chapel was dedicated to St Peter (SHOS vol 2 p54). The old church was pulled down and the present church built slightly to the S in 1853-4 (ILN Dec 3 1853 p476il) (St John the Baptist, Shenstone. Dick & Audrey Davies. 1993). Some parts of the old church remain (BOE p235). The parish formed between 1086 and 1291 probably out of either Lichfield or Walsall parishes (SHC 1916 pp194, 198). **Beating the bounds** was practised in Shenstone parish (SCSF pp21,22) (BCC vol 1 p135). The **name** has appeared as Scenstan (C11), Seneste, a manor, in DB, Shenestan, Schenestane (SHOS vol 2 p31) (SPN p105), and Sheinston (c1540) (LI part 5 p99). Senestan or scenestan mean shining or beautiful stone; originating, from perhaps, its proximity to the Roman city of Letocetum - wondrous to the Saxons - or a particular Roman carved stone considered beautiful (DUIGNAN) (SPN p105), or the red sandstone on which the village is built (SVB p151). The custom of decorating the village wells with boughs and flowers was observed at Shenstone on Ascension Day (Holy Thursday) (RHS) (SCSF p29). **Newspaper**. The Lichfield Advertiser and Newspaper for Lichfield, Alrewas, Shenstone etc ran from Jan 6 1865 to 1866 (VCH vol 14 p170) (SHJ spring 1996 pp19-20). The Shenstone **savings bank**, started in 1818, was the first in the area, the chief depositors coming from the Black Country. The reading room in Oddfellows Hall (see) built during the Crimean war was also the first in the area (SVB p151). **Reliant** car manufacturers of Two Gates (see) had a works at Shenstone. Norton Motor Cycles are based at Shenstone. In New Road are two houses with the names **'Defiance' and 'Victory'** etched on the walls. The houses are the result of a gentleman's victory at the High Court overturning his neighbours objections to build them (SVB p152). **Husbandry**. In the later C17 Plot was told by Mr Frith of Thornes that the people of Shenstone used Erica Vulgaris, or heath or ling instead of hops to preserve their beer, and that they sometimes make malt of oats which mixed with that of barley is called dredg-malt (NHS p379). **Bishop Langton** stayed at Shenstone on Jan 11 1319 (SSE 1994 p2). **Henry Lea** (or Lee) of Shenstone died in 1660 aged 107 (SHOS vol 2 p40) (W p583).

Shenstone Court 0.5m S of Shenstone church. Former manor house for a separate manor which was given by Henry D' Oyley to the Abbey of Oseny in Oxfordshire. In Henry VIII's reign it passed through Richard Cox DD Dean of St Mary's, Oxford to Thomas Stanley of Little Aston; then to the Corkes; then to the Swanhursts, or Dolphins; there was a monument to Richard Dolphin in Shenstone church defaced in 1593, because it prayed for his soul (ASE pp8, 132p of Shenstone Court, 134il of Shenstone Moss). The estate subsequently passed to the Bagnalls. It was owned by Thomas Bagnall, ironmaster, in 1851 (W p582). Between at least 1899 and 1907 it was the residence of Sir Richard Cooper, MP for Walsall and inventor of Cooper's sheep dip (STC p22p) (ASE p8) (SVB p151). Demolished before WW2 (BOE p235) (SGS p146) and a smaller house built on the site by 1993 (St John the Baptist, Shenstone. Dick & Audrey Davies. 1993. p10). Dr Wilkes in his Collections called the house the Manor of The Moss (SHOS engraving pl vii vol 2 p47), and it has been called The Moss (THS p162) (1834 OS map) (SVB p151), Moss House, and Shenstone Moss Park (1851) (W p582). By

1899 it was known as the Court (ASE p8). There was a feature in the vicinity of the house known as the Moss Lake. Had a stone balustrade originally from Moxhull Hall, Warws. By at least 1937, it was bought by the City of Lichfield for the Garden of Remembrance on the N side of Minister Pool, Lichfield, where it is now situated (KES p145). The Lodge, according to Pevsner, must be of c1840 and has a canted bay between two porches or verandas of two Ionic columns (BOE p235).

Shenstone Hall House 0.5m NE of Shenstone, by the A38 and by the Black Brook. The former house on this site, Shenstone Old Hall, was built by the Rugeleys and the house passed to the Brandreths who were living here by c1650. Michael Brandreth sold the hall in the early C18 to Samuel Hill, who let the hall out. John Egginton of Rodbaston was a tenant (ASE p7) (SHOS vol 2 pp41-43,44. pl.vi). By 1851 the hall was owned by Hon F Gough of Perry Barr (W p582). By 1899 it belonged to Mr Foster of Canwell Hall (ASE pp7, 110il). By 1993 the hall was a nursing home for the elderly (St John the Baptist, Shenstone. Dick & Audrey Davies. 1993. p11). (BOE p235) (SGS pp146,147p of porch) (MR p280p).

Shenstone Hall Farm A Neolithic or Bronze Age polished flint axe was found at Shenstone Park Farm (NSJFS 1964 p34). A Roman site was found on the land of Shenstone Hall Farm at over 0.5m N of Shenstone at SK 110054, 0.5m SE of junction of Watling Street and Ryknield Street, 1,500 metres SE of Letocetum. First excavated and probably discovered in c1929. Then excavated between 1930-36. Believed at first to be a fort and more recently a small farmstead surrounded by cattle ditches. Occupied from the early C2 to C4 AD and linked to the township of Letocetum. Air-photographs showing crop-marks show evidence of farming and other Romano-British farms (BAST vol 63 p1) (Roman site at Wall. G Webster. 1958 p13) (NSJFS 1964 p34) (SSAHST 1971 pp1-8 ps plans) (Roman site at Wall. DoE Official Handbook. 1979). A piece of Samian ware probably of Antonine date was found and a coin struck c37 AD of Agrippa (NSFCT 1932 pp108-110. 1933 pp153-154). There is a rectangular cropmark at SK 11350528 (NSJFS 1964 p34). And a pit alignment at SK 116057 (MOT p31) (NSJFS 1964 p34).

Shenstone House Shenstone. Is said to have been inherited by Thomas Neville from his uncle, Nigel. Thomas Neville, who was in residence by 1851, greatly improved the house. By 1899 it had been inherited by Nigel Neville (W p23) (ASE p8).

Shenstone Lodge The house built by John Strickson in the early C18 with the materials from the house called Shenstone Park (see), if not the same as the Shenstone Lodge, see below.

Shenstone Lodge House 0.75m S of Shenstone near or on the site of a house now called Oakwood (1976 OS map 1:25,000). The families connected with this house were the Wards (1640), Colliers, Parkhursts, Pagets and Parkers (ASE p8). Robert Parkhurst (d1764), third son of of Dormer Parkhurst of Epsom, Surrey and of Catersby, Northants, was a page to the Princess of Wales, wife of George II, and later fought at the battle of Minden (SHOS vol 2 p46). The house was purchased by Admiral Sir William Parker in 1812; he resided here when in England and was still the owner in 1851, when it was occupied by EL Maw (W pp22,582) (KES p179). It may be identifiable with the house formerly called Wood End Park Hall, which was called the Lodge by 1899 (ASE p8). The house called Shenstone Lodge was the residence of Thomas Addison Negus in 1899 (ASE p122p). In 1993 Shenstone Lodge was owned by Sandwell Education Authority (St John the Baptist, Shenstone. Dick & Audrey Davies. 1993. p11)

Shenstone Moss Former area 0.25m S of Shenstone church. Here the house called The Moss (later Shenstone Court) stood (THS p162).

Shenstone Park An ancient deer park. First enclosed in 1236 by Sir Ralph de Grendon. It was three miles in circumference and lay E of the A5127, embracing the present house called Shenstone Park (SSAHST 1988-89 pp46-48 il). The park was noted by Leland and Erdeswick. Disparked in Charles II's reign (SOS 1st ed p421) (EDP p180) (SSAHST 1982-3 p47).

Shenstone Park House 0.75m SE of Shenstone, situated on a bank by Black Brook. The original house was built by a Grendon in Henry III's reign. It then passed to the Nevils, who forfeited it in 1471; then to the Lakes and Wards, and then to the Heads; from Mr Head the estate was purchased in c1700 by John Strickson. He had rebuilt the hall (the Shenstone New Hall?) by the time he sold the estate in 1723; the materials from the old hall were taken for the building of Shenstone Lodge (SHOS vol 2 pp43-46 il of Strickson's house). Strickson appears to have been followed by the Hills of Huntstone (of whom Lord Berwick was one), and Hoskins until the estate was sold in 1797 to Edward Grove of Stretton and Lichfield (d1845). His heir sold it in 1851 to John Shawe Manley, who had pulled down most of the hall by 1899. It was called New Hall from at least 1817 to at least 1899 (THS p162) (W p582) (ASE p8).

Shenstone Park Moat At SK 119035 to the SW of the house called Shenstone Park. Here may have been a hunting lodge first established in the late C11 by the D'Oyley family. Henry III licensed a park here in 1236. Some excavations produced little of interest (SSAHST 1982-3 p47) (CAMS p44). The moated site is a listed monument.

Shenstone Woodend Hamlet between Footherley and Littlehay Brooks 1.25m S of Shenstone. In Shenstone ancient parish. Woodend as an addition usually implies a settlement found in a clearance, made by men from the place whose name it succeeds, in this case Shenstone, out of Cannock Forest (SL p71). It has been said that Shenstone Woodend was the northernmost end of the Forest of Arden (SVB p111). Susanna Southwell, mother-in-law of Joseph Jobbern of Shenstone Woodend, married aged 112. Just before she died she was able to talk rationally about several transactions to which she was an eye witness about a 100 years previously (SHOS vol 2 p40) (W p583). The redundant 'tin tabernacle' church on the W side of Birmingham Road still stood in 1999.

Shepherd's Abbey Rocks Rock feature on Staffs side of Dove Dale opposite Dove Holes. So called because the rock formation resembles an abbey (Dovedale Guide. Keith Mantell. 1985 p15pc) (EF pp73,75). Has also appeared as The Church Rock and Captain's Rock (DMV p28p).

Shepherd's Cottage Acton Hill, at SJ 946193. Said to have been occupied by the shepherd, Richard Burton (BERK2 p133p). He and his wife, Mary, lost five children between the ages of two and 17 in 11 days in March 1835. A son died in 1838 and two more in 1840. Others say Burton occupied Acton Hill Farm to the N at SJ 946196. The ghosts of the Burton children are said to haunt Acton Hill Farm (SKYT p89) (VB p81) (MR p6).

Shepherd's Cottage Drayton Bassett (DM p19). Presumably at Drayton Manor.

Shepherd's Cross 1.2 metre high, very worn wayside cross 150 metres S of junction with Biddulph Park road and is said to have been erected in the C14 (DoE II). It is situated in the old manor of Overton and may be of Saxon origin (BALH p26 map), in Biddulph Park (DPEM p29). Or was carved into a cross out of a stone which has been on this site since ancient times and preserves the site of a possible Druids Grove (SMM p38p). The Shepherd's Cross is at the N end of a ley line stretching from the Old Man of Mow and running through Beacon House and Biddulph Old Hall (SMM p122 see map). On the opposite side of the road is a fountain (STM Oct 1965 p31ps) (SMM p121p).

Shepherd's Farm Lynn, Stonnall (1:25,000 OS map).

Shepherds Fold Small lane N of High Street, at its W end, Blackheath, Rowley Regis. The name is from a shepherd's fold by the former common land here (BCWJ p73).

Shepherd's Row Row of terrace houses in Kingsley on the road leading to Hazles Cross. They were also known as Parliament Row and were built in the mid 1800s by Miss Shepherd (COPP2 p90p).

Shepherds Stand At Alton (HAF p193).

'Sheppertons, The' Dower house near High Bent House. Perhaps, fictional. Appears in Cedric Stokes's 'The Staffordshire Assassins' p15.

Shepwell Green Former hamlet (before the mid C20) now a residential and industrial district of Willenhall by a tributary of Sneyd Brook, 0.5m E of Willenhall. Formerly in Willenhall chapelry in Wolverhampton ancient parish. The area appears to have been common land and the name Shepwell may indicate that the commoners once enjoyed grazing rights here (SNW p63). Plot says there is a stinking sulphur well between Willenhall and Bentley (NHS p104).

Sher Brook Rises on Cannock Chase joins the Trent and the Sow at Shugborough. Has appeared as Sherbrok (1290) (SPNO p18). The name is perhaps not a corruption of Shirebrook. It may be derived from the bilation of the root 'caor' (NSFCT 1908 p129). Is from 'scir' 'bright, shining' (SPNO pp18,109).

Sherbrook Valley Valley created by the Sher Brook 1.5m SE of Brocton. A burial mound, 159 feet in diameter and nine feet high, in Sherbrook Valley by an ancient trackway between Colwich and Milford was excavated by Mr Molyneux in 1862. He discovered ash, burned bones and three damaged ancient British pottery beakers in it (OSST 1949-50 p20). Another mound on the Milford side of the trackway was opened by Mr Cherry in the C19. It was of irregular shape and measured about 75 feet by 66 feet. He discovered in it three separate and distinct layers of human bones all showing fire action. They were surrounded by coarse fragments of ancient British pottery (OSST 1949-50 p20).

Shereland Brook Tributary of the Tame (SPNO p18).

Sherholt Lodge House 1.75m SW of Rangemore. In Tatenhill ancient parish. The lodge was the residence of, or held by, the keepers of Barton Ward of Needwood Forest, William Key (d1651), and from 1670, George Vernon of Sudbury Hall, Derbys (SHOS vol 1 p67) (UTR p106) (GNHS p145) (W pp571,605) (HOPT vol 1 p152) (SVB p30) (ESNF p8). Beside the lodge is a moated site (CAMS p64). The name 'holt' means a copse (HOPT vol 1 p137).

Sherholt Park Medieval deer park enclosed out of forest which lay in the area of Sherholt Lodge (see). In existence by 1374 (VCH vol 2 p350) (NSJFS 1962 p76. 1964 p63). Contained in compass 10 furlongs (EDP p176). Has appeared as Shireholt Park and Sherrold Park. The name is preserved in Sherholt Lodge.

Sheriffhales Ancient parish and village on the S slopes of a ridge N of Watling Street 12.25m SW of Stafford or 17m E of Shrewsbury. It has been suggested that the Halen mentioned in the will of Wulfric Spot (c1002), founder of Burton Abbey, is Sheriffhales (SHC 1916 p34). Appears in DB as Hales, and has also appeared as Sheriff Hales. The parish formed before 1086 (SHC 1916 p193). The parish church, St Mary, in the SW corner of the village, is of C13 origin (LDD). The western part of the parish including the manor house of the Trussells lay in Shrops, while the eastern half lay in Staffs. As late as 1666 for the Hearth Tax Leveson Fowler's house was surveyed within the Cuttlestone hundred, but with a note attached saying 'it is in Shropshire by decree in chancery.' The matter was settled by the Local Government Act 1894 which consigned the whole parish to Shrops (VCH vol 4 p61) (SL p29). John Wesley appears to have been quite often at Sheriffhales, for instance in 1782, 1784 and 1786 (SA Jan 31 1885 p6. Feb 14 1885 p6) (SKYT p125).

Sherra Cop Lane Track almost dividing Admaston, Blithfield and Colton parishes. It possibly arose from 'the Path of the Sheriff' as a sheriff of Staffs was asked to settle a dispute in 1250 over the pulling down of a hedge along this track. A Blithfield deed mentions this lane as 'Semitam Vice Comitis' meaning 'the path of the Sherrif' (CWF pp40-41). The name is preserved in Sherracrop Plantation.

Shifford's Bridge Area and bridge 1.5m WNW of Hales and 2.5m SW of Mucklestone. Former horse-bridge carrying the Market Drayton-Newcastle-under-Lyme road, mentioned in a deed dated 1476. The present (1914) bridge dates from c1768. Appears as Shepherd's bridge in 1633 and 1649 (SHC 1945/ 6 pp9,176). The name is from sheep ford (SHC 1945/6 p28).

Shifford's Grange House 2.25m SW of Mucklestone. There was a grange here between the C12 and the Reformation belonging to Combermere Abbey. After 1545 the property, described as a manor in 1606, passed to the Needhams, later Viscounts of Kilmorey, who continued to hold it through the C17 until the mid C19 with Francis Jack Needham selling the estate to Peter Broughton of Tunstall in c1850 (SHC 1945/6 pp12,120-121,175-176, 206-207, 259).

'Shift End' Alias Wolverhampton Street, Bilston. Apparently, so called from local nomenclature 'shifted' meaning removed, with reference to the extension or removing out of the end of the town when the area was first developed with housing (HOBLL p220).

Shingle House Elizabethan house at or near Gospel Oak, in Wednesbury Oak Road. Former seat of the Nightingale family (living in the early C17). The house appears to have stood to at least 1800 (HOTIP pp93, 188).

Shining Ford Crossing over Oakenclough Brook and hamlet 1.75m S of Hollinsclough; the brook forms the boundary between Fawfieldhead and Heathylee townships. A hamlet existed at Shining Ford in the earlier 1630s (VCH vol 7 p27).

Shippy House 1.25m NW of Haughton. Formerly known as the Isle of Shippy (VCH vol 4 p76) and appears as this on 1834 OS map (SPNO p166).

Shire Brook Rises in the Lozells area and joins the Tame at Witton. Formed the Warws Staffs border (MNB p35).

Shire Hall Market Place, Stafford. A shire hall stood on the S side of Stafford market place (now approximately Market Square) by the 1280s (HOS pp65,66) (VCH vol 6 p201). As well as being used for the county court it was probably also used as the town hall, or guild hall, and as a market hall (HOS pp65,66,68). In the later C16 the assizes were often held for periods outside Stafford, at Wolverhampton, partly on account of the inadequacy of the old shire hall; a new shire hall in the middle of Stafford market place was built in 1586 (NHS pp371-372 tab 31 shows it) (HOS pp65,66) (VCH vol 6 p201). That building was replaced by the present hall. Completed in 1799 it was designed by the little-known John Harvey and stands E of the former hall, on the E side of Market Square (BOE p246) (VCH vol 6 p202). The stone for it was quarried at Tixall (HOT p68). Renovation of it was complete by July 1993 (ES July 2 1993 p5). On March 13 1854 Sir Thomas Noon Talfourd, judge, poet, and friend of Charles Lamb, died of apoplexy while actually upon the judgment seat in the county court in the Shire Hall, where there is a bust to his memory. He had been staying with Edward John Littleton at Teddesley Hall (LGS p218) (CCF p147) (KES p184) (VFC p127). On Dec 30 1872 Major Henry Elwell (b1816) of Quarry Lodge (see), Lichfield, died unexpectantly whilst attending the Quarter Sessions (SA) (IE pp121-122). In 1855 Alice Grey, the famous fraudster, was tried at Stafford by Grand Jury at the assize court (OP pp5-8). Edward VII was entertained by the mayor at the Shire Hall on Nov 23

1907 (SSTY p16). The last assizes were held at here in 1971 and replaced by the Crown Court in 1972. In 1991 the Crown Court moved to new premises at the present Stafford Combined Court Centre in Victoria Square (SN Oct 22 1971 p19. Jan 21 1972 p10) (VCH vol 6 p201). A procession of Crown Court judges escorted by police officers, 'armed' with wooden halberds, through the streets of Stafford to the Shire Hall has long taken place. The custom has its origins in medieval times when the High Court Judge on his circuit around the country would be met at the county boundary by the sheriff and his armed escort of 'javelin men' to protect the judge. At the town boundary the party would be met by the mayor and continue to the Shire Hall. From 1890 policemen have replaced the 'javelin men.' In the early 1990s the custom was said to be taking place twice a year. In 2000, when it was occurring three times a year in Jan, May and Oct to the Combined Court, there were plans to reduce the number of annual processions or abandon the tradition on account of the Mounted Police Branch being disbanded (A History of Staffordshire Police. Commemorative Issue 1992) (info FN Morris and JG Beecham).

Shireland Hall Two halls of this name standing side by side, stood on E side of Shireland Road, between Florence and Edith Roads, 0.75m ESE of Smethwick chapel. Land in this area was known as Shireland by the mid C16. **Old Hall**. The hall of the mid C18 may have been the one occupied by a family called Jennen in the later C17. Plot's map links the Jennens to a house at 'Shire lanes.' The house had become known as Shireland Hall by 1765. Its subsequent history is uncertain, but it may have survived as Shireland Hall Farm, a house 30 yards SW of the new Shireland Hall (VCH vol 17 pp103-104). **New Hall**. A house which also went by the name of Shireland Hall was built at the end of the C18 close to the site of the former hall. It served at certain times as two residences. In 1852 TH Morgan, a Baptist minister, ran a school here for the sons of clergy of all denominations. The school was attended by George Newnes (1851-1910), publisher and founder of Tit-Bits, The Strand Magazine, and Country Life, in c1865. The hall was later a girls' school, and unoccupied in the 1880s. It was demolished in c1887 (STELE July 29 1950. Nov 7 1952 il of c1850) (VCH vol 17 pp88,103-104). (SHOS vol 2 pp125-126).

Shire Lanes Marked on the maps of Plot and Bowen in the area of Shireland Hall, Smethwick, and could be a former spelling of Shireland.

Shire Oak Former ancient oak which stood at approximately SK 053038 on S side of Lichfield-Walsall road, a short distance from the summit of Shire Oak Hill (BLHT). Believed to be 2000 years old when the stump was removed in the 1890s (CCC p64) (HOWW p15). Described as an old Druid's oak in WPP p111. It marked the boundaries of Shenstone and Walsall ancient parishes. The tree is mentioned as early as 1533 (WOPP pl p122) (BLHT). It appears on Saxton's map as 'The Shire Okes' (BLHT). In the Civil War Prince Rupert may have used the oak as a rendezvous and possibly camped his army here in early 1644 (BLHT). There is a tradition Dean Swift sheltered under it in a storm on a journey to or from Ireland. Under the tree Swift was joined by a tramp and his woman-friend. Their conversation revealed they had only just made love together. This so scandalised Swift he married them immediately. The woman asked for a marriage certificate, where upon Swift wrote the following

> Beneath this oak in stormy weather
> I joined this whore and rogue together:
> And none but He who made the thunder
> Can put this whore and rogue asunder.

(IADC p220). The wood in which it was stood was a refuge for highwaymen and described as 'a den of thieves' (SHOS vol 2 p53) (SVB p157); a Mr Jones of Tipton, a carrier, was attacked near the tree in 1756 (Broughton's Scrapbook appendix p3). Its remains were removed in the mid 1890s (SHC 1910 p35) (Walsall Observer May 9 1896) (VCH vol 17 p277). (GNHS p409) (SG p109) (SMC p173). A portion of the oak was presented to Shire Oak Grammar School, Walsall Wood, in March 1966 and was in the school library in 1969 (photograph of the oak portion in Walsall Local History Centre) (SNBC p46p). The name is from 'scyre,' to divide (SHOS vol 2 p53).

Shire Oak The S district of Brownhills on ground rising to Shire Oak Hill. In Shenstone ancient parish. Civilly became separated from Shenstone when joined Brownhills urban district when it formed in 1894 (GLAUE p422). The name is from the ancient oak called the Shire Oak (see).

Shire Oak Hill Hill which rises 540 feet above sea level. The Shire Oak (see) stood a short distance from the summit and gave its name to the hill (BLHT).

Shire Stone Stopping place on the perambulation of Brewood in the vicinity of Bishop's Wood and Ivetsey Bank (SCSF p26).

Shirkley Hall Farm 1.5m NW of Horton, situated on former Horton Hay, in Horton ancient parish. May have been created when Horton Hay was divided into farms in the later C17 (VCH vol 7 p72). Is marked on Yates' map.

Shirle Hill Incline and house by Handsworth Park, Handsworth, about 500 yards from St Mary's church. The house was occupied by the Pepper family in 1900 (HPPE p55).

Shirley Farm, Hollow and Common 0.75m ESE of Foxt. In Kingsley ancient parish. The first Cotton Plane (see) plateway went through Shirley Hollow.

Shirley Brook Rises on Black Heath. Runs SE of Foxt. Joins the Churnet at Froghall. Appears on 1837 OS map as Shirley Hollow (SPNO p18).

Shirleywich Tiny hamlet by the Trent under 1m NE of Ingestre. In Weston-on-Trent ancient parish. Formerly called Brine Pits (NHS pp66,93), owing to the salt workings here. A Shirley of Chartley Castle (see) - probably Sir Robert Shirley (1650-1717) - manufactured salt here in the C17 and re-named Brine Pits Shirleywich, in honour of his family (SL p109) (WMARCH 1993 p72) (SPJD p73). Hackwood says salt was discovered here in c1670 (SCSF p145). In c1705 a new, stronger brine stream was tapped and a new works built (SIOT p7). Production increased with the construction of the Trent and Mersey Canal between 1766 and 1777; in 1810 a tiny spur called the Shirleywich Canal Arm was built to serve the works. By 1998 only a small portion of this arm remained and it was unconnected to the main canal (SPJD p74) (info Hixon Local History Society). In the C19 there was a decline in the production of salt at Shirleywich. From 1827 there was competition from Earl Talbot's Weston Salt Works 0.5m to the N, and later from new works at Stafford (SPJD pp73-76pcs). The Shirleywich works were closed by 1901. Some believed that the salt in the air was the reason why the local people lived to great ages (MR p280).

Shirrall Minute hamlet on lane leading to Shirrall Hall on rising ground above Gallows Brooks 1.5m W of Drayton Bassett. In Drayton Bassett parish. Has also appeared as Shirral.

Shirrall Hall House 1.5m W of Drayton Bassett.

Shirrall Park Medieval park at Shirrall. The 'Park of Sheralf' is mentioned in the late C15. 'Sherrolde Park' occupied about 443 acres adjoining the Canwell estate. It was disparked by 1756 (SHOS vol 2 p9). It lay bounded on the N side by the A453 and on the NE side by Drayton Lane and embraced Shirrall Hall, the later Shirral Farm, marked on Yates' map (SSAHST 1988-89 pp45-46).

Shirts Mill Basin Underground basin in Tipton Canal before Castle Mill Basin is reached. Like that basin, it was probably a former limestone quarry (Dudley Canal Tunnel leaflet).

Shoal Hill 656 feet high hill (Cannock Chase by Car. Staffs Nature Conservation Trust Ltd. ND, but between 1971 and 1974 p16) 2m NW of Cannock. Has also appeared as Le Sholle (1286. 1300) and Shore Hill (1834 OS map) (SPNO p124). The name means 'the sloping or slanting hill' (DUIGNAN), or 'the hill with a twisted shape' (SPNO p68) or 'the hill with a curled appearance' (SPN p30). The boundary of Gailey Hay probably began at Shoal Hill (VCH vol 5 p182). Wright describes the view from the top of it in CCBO pp91-93.

Shoal Hill Common Unenclosed common land in the triangle W of Cannock parish boundary, S of Huntington parish boundary and E of the Cannock-Penkridge road (PCC p17) (MH 1994 p108).

Shobnall Large hamlet by Shobnall Brook beneath the escarpment forming the edge of the Needwood Forest plateau 1.5m WNW of Burton upon Trent. In Burton Extra township in Burton upon Trent ancient parish (W p540). A Roman urn was found at Shobnall (HOBT p23) (NSJFS 1964 p18) (STMSM Sept 1973 p26) (BTIH p10). A much eroded Roman coin of the period 275-280 AD was found in a garden in Shobnall Street in 1984 (info KL Neal). Has appeared as Sobehal (1114), Sobenhal (C12. C13), Scobenhal (C13), Schobinhale (1295), Shopnall, Shobenhale (C13), Shopunhale (1320), Shobenall (1531) (SHOS vol 1 pp23-24) (BTIH p22). The name means 'hall of Sceoba' (DUIGNAN) (SPN p27). By 1325 it was a grange of Burton Abbey (VCH vol 3 p204). In the early 1540s overlordship of Shobnall manor passed to Sir William Paget of Beaudesert (SHOS vol 1 p24). The church, St Aidan, on Shobnall Road, was built in 1884 (BOE p87). The separate ecclesiastical parish of Shobnall, created in 1916, had become known as 'Burton upon Trent St Aidan' by 1991 (GLAUE p422). In 1887 the range of maltings at Shobnall, at SK 234229, belonging to Bass was said to be the largest in the world belonging to any one firm (IAS p155). Lord Burton's Daimler crashed into a dingle of the Forest Road at Shobnall on Dec 7 1907. The only occupant was the chauffeur who escaped serious injury (BTOP vol 1 p59p).

Shobnall Brook Runs from Shobnall through Burton to the Trent.

Shobnall Grange SW of St Aidan, Shobnall. The house has a C17 part with old brickwork and mullioned and transomed windows (BOE p87). It perhaps stands on the site of the grange at Shobnall belonging to Burton Abbey, or the house may have formed a part of the grange buildings. It was the seat

of one of the ancient Rugeley family in the earlier C17 (SHOS vol 1 p24). The house was for sale in 2000 (DoE II) (SLM April 2000 p12pc).

Shooting Butts Cannock Chase. Shooting Butts Farm is 1.5m WSW of Rugeley. Name is from some old shooting butts here. The now closed Shooting Butts School was one of the pre-WW2 National Camps Corporation schools (TB Jan 1997 p7. Feb 1997 p7).

Shooters Hills In the Meir Heath-Lightwood area. Are 600 feet high (NSFCT 1910 p83). Shootershill House appears between Lightwood and Sandon Roads at SJ 927406 on 1890 OS map 6 inch, formerly in Hilderstone quarter in Stone ancient parish.

Short Heath Heath and area of Bloxwich. Appears on 1834 OS map, between High Street and Elmore Green Road and Elmore Row. Traditional working place of the locksmiths of Bloxwich (SOB p144).

Short Heath Area N of the Wyrley and Essington Canal 1.75m NE of Willenhall. In Willenhall chapelry of Wolverhampton ancient parish. Short Heath was a small mining hamlet in the C19 (WDY p15). In 1984 Short Heath, broadly speaking, was the area between New Invention and Willenhall town centre (Selective Essays on Willenhall. David Potts. 1984. Copy in Willenhall library). The area became a separate ecclesiastical parish known as 'Willenhall Holy Trinity' in 1846 (GLAUE p429). The Commissioners' church, Holy Trinity, on the corner of Coltham Street and Church Road, was built in 1854-1855 (HOWI p20) (BOE p295). Short Heath became a separate civil parish in 1894 (GLAUE p429) or 1895 (SNW p25). A mysterious sandstone column was found in the vicarage garden of the nearby Holy Trinity church, close to the boundary of the churchyard. Perhaps, a crude burial stone (TB July 1985 p1p). A clever young man was turned into a mumbling fool for the rest of his life after cruelly throwing a cat into the canal at the top end of Clark's Lane.

Shortwood Minute hamlet consisting of about two properties under 2m NNE of Charnes. In Standon parish. At SJ 79543555, 0.5m SSE of Shortwood Farm, is a mound 34 paces in diameter and eight feet high, thought not to have been a burial mound, and which was, in 1935, covered with trees (NSFCT vol 57 p151. 1935 pp65-66) (NSJFS 1965 p46). By 1983 it had had a bite taken out of it on the S side, leaving it kidney-shaped and is listed as a burial mound (NSFCT 1983 p11).

Shotwood Hill 0.5m W of Rolleston. Has also been called Shooter's Hill, Shotter's Hill and Shot-at-Hill. It received its name during the Civil War after an attack from the hill (SHOS vol 1 p34) (LTD p195). Underhill is sure the name is from 'shotts' a name for a block of lants or ploughed strips (UTR pp120,181).

Showells, The Old house and manor 1.25m NNE of Wolverhampton (BUOP p6). In the foreign and parish of Wolverhampton (HOWM p44), or in Bushbury parish (SGSAS). Between Wolverhampton and Seawall was a spring called Spaw Spring (see) noted for curing eye diseases (NHS p106). There used to be a strong spring running through Showells Moat (filled in in 1935) (HOWM p9 note) (SSAHST 1982-3 p52). The Showells has been identified with the 'Seofan wyllan' in the charter of Ethelred of 985 (HOWM p9 note); later appears as Seawall (Plot's map) (DUIGNAN), Sewell (HOWM p9 note), Show Hill (1834 OS map), and Showell (BUOP p6). If from 'Seofan wyllan' then means 'the seven wells:' A tradition of seven springs is common (Ekwall's Concise Oxford Dictionary of English Place-names. p391) (HOWM p9 note). Or sewels 'hanging devices' put on the periphery of parks or forests in medieval times - The Showells lay within the bounds but on the border of Cannock Forest - to frighten deer and keep them within the bounds of the forest (DUIGNAN). The unnamed estate owned by Lady Godiva before the Norman Conquest may have been Seawall (The Showells) (HOWM p2). There seems to have been a small settlement at Showells in the Middle Ages (HOWM p6). In c1340 the estate passed from the de Seawallfields to the Everdons. In Henry VIII's reign it appears to have passed from them to the Levesons who sold it in 1700 to the Huntbachs of Featherstone (SHOS vol 2 p187); however the Huntbachs appear to have been occupying the house from an earlier period. Margery, the second daughter of John Huntbach, married Dugdale, the herald, on March 17 1623 and Dugdale spent the first year of his married life here. Dugdale spent the night of April 10 1663 at Seawall, whilst making his heraldic visitation as Norray King of Arms, when the house belonged to his nephew John Huntbach, the antiquary (HOWM pp96-97). In the early C18 the hall and the estate passed from the Huntbachs to Sir Samuel Hellier's father by marriage. Shaw noted at the end of the C18 that the old hall, surrounded by a moat, had been dilapidated for many years and a new farmhouse had been erected on or near its site (SHOS vol 2 p187) (HOWM p134). In 1851 Showell House was the seat of W Mannix (W p23). In the earlier C20 a large housing estate was built on the Showells estate. Showell is preserved in one of its streets, Showell Circus.

Showell Circus Circular row of shops and public house - the Bushbury Arms - built for the Low Hill housing estate, Bushbury (BUOP p137p), built by 1929

(HOWU p147). The name is derived from The Showells.

Shraley Former estate to the W of Audley in Knowl End township in Audley ancient parish. It belonged for many years prior to c1716 to the Bougheys and thereafter the remainder of it belonged to the Vernons (SHC 1944 p37).

Shraleybrook (locally *Shraley Bruk* BOJ Book 3 p82). Thriving colliery village in the C19, but shrank to its present tiny size after most of its inhabitants, who were miners, were killed in the Minnie Pit disaster (SL p252). Formerly in Knowl End township in Audley ancient parish. Here is a toll house at SJ 780503 (IANS p19). Has also appeared as Shaleybrook (W p428), and Shraley Brook (SL p252).

Shredicote Minute hamlet near Church Eaton Brook consisting of about three properties 1m SW of Bradley. Former township (THS p279) in Bradley ancient parish. Has appeared as Shradicote (1221), Schradyncot (1336), and Shredicot (1561-1775) (SPNO p137) (SSE 1996 p17). The name means 'cottage on a piece of land cut off.' The property was probably a detached, isolated, or outlying portion of a manor or estate (DUIGNAN) (SPN p112) (SSE 1996 p17). At Shredicote Plot noted a calf just cast with five legs (NHS p262).

Shredicote Farm 0.25m S of Shredicote Hall Farm. Could date from the later C17 and have been the seat of the Brown or Browne family in the C17 (VCH vol 4 pp76,83). The old farmhouse, which may have been surrounded by a moat, was destroyed and rebuilt in the 1960s (SSAHST 1982-3 p36).

Shredicote Hall Farm 2m NW of Whiston. A former hall here may have been the seat of the Brown or Browne family in the C17. Largely rebuilt in the early C19. By 1847 was owned by Ann Parkes. Subsequently was the property of the Morris-Eytons. Sold to Lord Newport in 1948 and sold to a tenant farmer soon after. The earthwork S of the farm may have been a house platform; the ditch there may have surrounded an orchard, not a moat, but the depression SW of the farm may have been a moat (VCH vol 4 pp76,83) (SSAHST 1982-3 p36).

Shrewsbury Arms Inn or hotel in Market Street, Rugeley. Parts may date from c1700 (VCH vol 5 p153). Formerly The Crown to at least 1810 (IOM p78) (VCH vol 5 p153) (SPN p100). Then renamed the Talbot Arms. Remodelled in the early C19 (VCH vol 5 p153). It became famous after its associations with Dr William Palmer of Rugeley (see), who obtained national notoriety for being a serial poisoner and was hung in 1856. He is said to have poisoned John Parsons Cook (VB p118) or Joseph Cook (CCF p196), his last, or fourteenth, victim (SPN p100) at Shrewsbury races in 1855, where Cook's horse won. Cook then came to stay at the inn and here Palmer's poison took its effect. Raven says Palmer brought a bookmaker (unnamed) back to the inn having administered poison to him at Shrewsbury races, and here he died (MR p270). (ILN May 24 1856 pp560il,561,562,563,564il). Owing to the ignominy of being associated with Palmer the inn was renamed the Shrewsbury Arms, probably after the Talbot family, Earls of Shrewsbury. The inn was kept for eight years by Noah Corbett, a Shropshire man, who would show people round the room where Cook died (CCF p196). The inn was still standing in the 1950s (VCH vol 5 p153) and is said to be haunted by the ghost of Dr Palmer or John Parsons Cook (GPCE p38). By 1992 the inn was Shrew Kafe Bar (TPP p3).

Shropshire Brook Rises N of Beaudesert Hall. Flows through Longdon to Handsacre where it joins the Trent. The name has nothing to do with Shropshire, but could be from a tenant of that name (SPNO p18).

Shropshire Covert Covert on N side of Shropshire Brook, Beaudesert Old Park.

Shropshire Row Former street name at Bradley, Bilston. The street appears to have been built originally for workers at John Wilkinson's ironworks in Bradley, in the later C18, and named after the inhabitants, workers who Wilkinson had brought from his Broseley ironworks in Shrops. It was still Shropshire Row in 1839 (Map of Bilston Township - R Timmis 1839), but by 1885 had been renamed Salop Street (OS map) (The Black Country Iron Industry. WKV Gale. 1966 p34).

Shropshire Union Canal Runs from Autherley Junction to Ellesmere Port, Ches. Leaves the county N of Tyrley Castle. 39.5 miles long (IAS p197) or 66m, of which 23m lie in Staffs (SWY p30). The Shropshire Union Canal was formerly four entirely separate canals which, through various amalgamations, eventually became the Shropshire Union Canal in 1845, and later affectionately called the 'Shroppy' (VB p151) or 'Shroppie' (PWIS p28). The four constituent canals, in order of construction, were: the Chester Canal from Chester to Nantwich opened in 1779; the Wirral Line of the Ellesmere Canal from Ellesmere Port to Chester opened in 1795; the Middlewich Branch of the Chester & Ellesmere Canal Company (an amalgamation of the aforementioned) opened between Barbridge Junction and Middlewich in 1833, and the Birmingham & Liverpool Junction Canal from Nantwich to Autherley Junction opened in 1835 (Shropshire Union Canal Cruising Guide 1985). The last section, built by Thomas Telford, was built between 1826-32 (VCH vol 4

pp111,112,155,163-4) or 1826-35 (WMLB p53), and opened in 1834 (W), or on March 2 1835 (VCH vol 2 p295 note) (TTTD pp264-265). In 1847 it was proposed to convert the canal into a railway, which was to run from Wolverhampton to Calveley on the Chester and Crewe railway. But the idea was abandoned (SHC 1945/6 p268). The 'Shropshire Union Canal' in Arnold Bennett's novels is, in fact, the Trent and Mersey Canal. For the story of the man monkey boggart who haunts a bridge over the canal see Big Bridge.

Shrubbery, The Former area of Willenhall, S of the town centre in the New Road area and land to the S of it. In the early C19 it was considered an area of outstanding beauty (SNW p50).

Shrubbery Hall Hall which may have stood at Bloomfield. It may originally have been the residence of Robert de Blome (HOTIP p187).

Shruggs, The Tiny district above Jolpool Brook 1m NW of Sandon. At SJ 945306 was a windmill shown on the maps of Plot and Jeffrey (WBJ p34). Shugg Lane formed part of an old way from Stone, through Aston, Burston, Hilderstone, Milwich to Uttoxeter (NSFCT 1938 p120).

Shude Hill Old cattle market site in Leek (SMOPP vol 2).

Shuffalong Minute hamlet overlooks a valley created by a tributary of Endon Brook, 0.5m WSW of Cheddleton. Or a name for a coalfield (VCH vol 2 p70).

Shugborough (locally in late C19 *Shukborough* DUIGNAN). Ancient estate 3.75m ESE of Stafford at the confluence of the Trent and the Sow. In Colwich ancient parish. The area S of the confluence formerly lay in Haywood manor and was a bailiwick of the manor by the C15 (SHC 1970 p89). The manor belonged to St Chad before the Norman conquest and afterwards to the bishops of Lichfield (BERK2 p38). They built Shugborough Manor House (see) here. At the dissolution Shugborough passed to the Pagets. They sold it, along with Haywood, Coley, and Oakedge, to the Whitbys who sold Shugborough to William Anson of Dunston in 1625 (SHC 1914 p133 note). Shugborough Manor House was superseded by Shugborough Hall (see). From medieval times a village, Shugborough Village (see), grew about the manor house. The village was swept away by the Ansons of Shugborough Hall to create Shugborough Park (see). Has appeared as Shukburgh (C14) (SSE 1996 p17), Shokkeburgh (SPN p106), Shut-borowe (1493), Shubbrow (1495), Shutborowe (1496) (HAHS pp46,48), Shuckesbyry, Shuckesborough (c1540) (LI appendix p169), and Shutborow (C16) (BERK2 pp40-41). According to legend the area is believed to have been at first a hermitage, occupied, according to Leland, by a hermit called Shuckborough (NHS pp447-448), who gave it to the bishops of Lichfield. According to Chetwynd Shugborough is a corruption of Sow-borough, from the nearby river Sow (HOT p58) (SHC 1914 p129). Others have thought the name is of Saxon origin, from 'Sug,' Saxon for Sow, and 'broc,' Saxon for brook (HAHS p48). Others say it is from a burial mound of portentous significance, 'bewitched barrow' or 'demon low' (DUIGNAN) (SPN p106) (SSE 1996 p17); it is of pagan origin (SL p42). Or it might be from the root 'coid,' but rather the root 'sceach' 'sgeach' thicket, forest (NSFCT 1908 p147).

Shugborough Hall Two-storey brick house, built at Shugborough to the S of Shugborough Manor House (see) in c1693 or 1694 (BERK2 p42), or 1695 (SNTG p19) (ROT p58) by William Anson (1656-1720). The hall has subsequently been the seat of the Ansons.

THE ANSONS. William (d1720) was succeeded by his eldest son, Thomas (1695-1773). William's younger son, **George Anson** (1697-1762), was the famous admiral who made a voyage around the world in HMS Centurion between 1740 and 1744. Thomas, who died unmarried, was succeeded by his nephew, George, by his sister, wife of Sambrooke Adams. George assumed the name and arms of Anson in 1773. He was succeeded by his son Thomas (1767-1818) who was created Viscount Anson and Baron Soberton in 1806. He was succeeded by his son, Thomas (b1795), who was created Earl of Lichfield in 1831. Thomas, 2nd Earl, succeeded his father on his death in 1854. He was succeeded by his son Thomas, 3rd Earl, in 1892, who was succeeded by his son Thomas, 4th Earl, in 1918. The 4th Earl was succeeded on his death in 1960 by his grandson, Thomas (b1939), 5th Earl, better known as Patrick, a professional photographer and cousin of Elizabeth II (W p416) (SNTG pp7,9,93).

THE HALL. The original house remains in the centre of the present house (SL p132). The wings of the present house are of c1748, heightened after 1768. In 1794 Samuel Wyatt, the architect, was employed to add the portico, with eight Ionic columns to the front of the house (W p417). Between 1803-6 he designed and had built the convex-shaped saloon extension to the rear of the house (BOE p237), reputedly in preparation for a visit by the Prince Regent (SNTG p38ps). (SHOS vol 2 pls on pp18,19 at back) (GNHS pp114,115) (CCF pp112-115). Thomas Pennant, author of PT, made the hall his centre for most of his Staffs excursions and he was here a few hours before the death of Thomas Anson (CCF pp113-114). Queen Victoria, as Princess Victoria, visited Shugborough Hall in Oct 1832 (S&W p260) (SIOT p74). Sir Edwin Landseer (1802-1873), painter, was at Shugborough in 1863 and possibly in the 1820s. Lady Harriet who married the 2nd Earl of Lichfield in 1855 brought the painting of her mother, Louisa, Duchess of Abercorn and herself as a baby to Shugborough. In 1863 he sketched Viscount Thomas Francis Anson, son of the 2nd Earl. Also whilst at Shugborough he made drawings of dogs and horses (SNTG p49pc,70). Capt Lt Col Hon Sir George Augustus Anson (d1947) was born at the hall in 1857. He prosecuted and condemned George Edalji in the Wyrley Gang case; his wife Lady Blanche and their only daughter were killed by a bomb falling on their London house in April 1941 (SHJ vol 2 pp36-40). JRR Tolkien (1892-1973), author, walked through the estate in 1914 and later referred to the hall as 'the house of 100 chimneys' in one of his books (ES Aug 9 1997 p21). Tolkien stayed for a while during some of WW1 at Great Haywood (see). The hall was open to the public for the first time in summer 1957 (SLM summer 1957 p15). On the death of the 4th Earl in 1960 Shugborough was offered to the Treasury in lieu of death duties. The Treasury passed it to the NT, which leased it to Staffs county council, who in collaboration with NT still (2000) maintain Shugborough; the Anson family still have rights to reside in a private part of the house (NSJFS 1967 p82) (SNTG p54) (HCMBOPP p47p) (HOS 1998 p48). Elizabeth II visited Shugborough on May 25 1973 (R&S p47). On the jambs of the door to the Anson Room may be seen the pencilled heights of successive generations of Anson children (SNTG p76). Following Anson family tradition there were celebrations at Shugborough Hall in 1999 for the 21st birthday of Thomas William Robert Anson, Viscount Anson (b1978), during which the tenants presented a painting to the Viscount and a cannon was fired (SLM Oct 1999 p19). The **Bird Room**, an upstairs saloon, is so called because it was used by the 3rd Earl of Lichfield, a keen naturalist and ornithologist, to display his large collection of stuffed birds. Is now the drawing-room of Lord Lichfield's private quarters (SNTG p68p). In the passage by the **Verandah Room** hangs a fragment of HMS Centurion. It is the lion figurehead from the ship. It passed through many hands, including those of George VI who had it Windsor Castle, before being presented to 3rd Earl of Lichfield (SSW pp32,33) (ES May 2 1932 p4) (SNTG p72). The **Ante Room** contains an arched recess for a large-scale model of the Centurion, made for Lord Anson in 1747. The model was sold in 1842 and is now in the National Maritime Museum at Greenwich (SNTG p8p,31,56). A chandelier at the hall takes two people two days to clean (Central TV Feb 9 1993 'Heart of the Country' 7.30pm). **Ghosts**. The hall is allegedly haunted by a former lady of the manor named Harriet, who was often seen by one member of staff. The building is also said to have several cold spots, the unexplained fragrance of old-fashioned perfumes, aromatic tobacco, cheese and fish (GPCE p43). A certain bedroom is believed to be haunted; a decorator from Penkridge experienced unexplainable knocking sounds in 1990 (info Bruce Braithwaite). GROUNDS. The stables are to the left of the front entrance of the hall and date from the mid C18. The clock and bell are of 1767, which may also be the date of the whole block. The architect could be Charles Cope Trubshaw of Great Haywood. The Staffordshire County Museum (see below) opened in the stables in 1966. Under the trees in front of the stables are a dogs' graveyard instituted in 1910 with little memorials stones to Anson pets (SNTG p85). In the midden yard were being grown in 1989 the blue sweet peas 'Admiral Anson' (Lathyrus nervosus). They are descendants of seeds reputedly brought back to Shugborough from Juan Fernandez by Lord Anson's cook (SNTG p85). For further afield in the grounds see Shugborough Park. COUNTY MUSEUM. The County Museum opened in the stables in 1966 and is run by Staffs county council (SNTG p85) (HOS 1998 pp48-49,135). It contains many artifacts from Staffs including - a fingerpost from the Wilkin (see), and reputedly, a shoe from a farm in the Abbots Bromley area, which brought ill-luck on the farm when removed (local info).

Shugborough Manor House Former moated manor house or palace built by a bishop of Lichfield at Shugborough in Haywood manor. It existed by the reign of Edward I (HOL pp124-125) (NSFCT 1881 p15) or by 1313 and was built here for Shugborough lies between the bishop's palaces at Eccleshall and Lichfield (BERK2 p38). The house lay just S of the confluence and to the N of the present hall. Shugborough Village (see) grew about it. The stone to build the original manor house may have come from Heywood Park, where hewn walls remained in the C19 (HAHS p8). At the Dissolution Haywood manor was bought by the Pagets. They preferred to reside at Beaudesert. In 1624 or 1625 the Pagets sold Shugborough to Thomas Whitby, who sold it in the same year to Thomas (SNTG p19) or William (BERK2 p42) Anson of Dunston, a lawyer. Anson and his son William (1628-1688) lived in the manor house. But William (1656-1720) the son of the second William built the core

of the present Shugborough Hall (see) in 1694 (BERK2 p42).

Shugborough Park Park created by the Ansons of Shugborough Hall in the C18 to beautify the estate about the hall. In WW2 the USA had a military hospital in Shugborough grounds. Some ghostly presence at the site of the hospital or another past military base in the grounds is so terrifying to dog-guards that they are not taken there (info Bruce Braithwaite). The 'Vale of Shugborough' is a way of referring to the Park of Shugborough (W p417). The **Arboretum** was established in the C19 and contains Wellingtonias and a recent unique collection of different varieties of oaks (SNTG p79). **Arch of Hadrian** see Triumphal Arch. The **Blue Bridge** or called Chinese Bridge, was erected in 1813 by Charles Heywood, it leads across the Sow to the Arboretum (CGE p42 pl 73a) (F&G p389) (BOE p238, pl 51) (SNTG pp21,79) (F p311). Has for many years been painted red. **Boathouse** see Chinese House. **Bowling Green** see Orangery. The **Cascade and classical colonnade** stood about 440 yards S of the hall on the N side of the now lost mill pool at approximately SJ 988221. The classical colonnade was possibly an adaptation of the Temple of Saturn in the Roman Forum. Both were erected in c1750 and probably disappeared between c1780 and 1800, possibly at the time of the Great Flood in 1795 (SHC 1970 facing p110) (SNTG pp22,79) (F p310; called a ruined colonnade). The **Cat Monument** or Cat's Monument on a small island in the Sow, access is by the Blue Bridge. Plinth topped with a large urn, the whole is 20 feet high. Around the base are four rams' heads - perhaps representing the herd of Corsican goats Thomas Anson (1695-1773) introduced at Shugborough (F p311). On the urn a cat sits with a curled tail - perhaps represents Admiral Anson's favourite cat which toured the world with him (VB p117), or was one of a breed of Persian cats, pets of his brother, Thomas (BOE p238), the last one of which died at Shugborough soon after 1768 (F p311), Sir Joseph Banks saw him in 1768 (F&G p389) (SNTG pp82pc,83). The urn is said to contain the ashes of the cat (CCF p114). The plinth bears a Coade stone tablet with a heraldic device in bas-relief. Artificial stone was only used after 1767 (F p311), but the tablet is a later addition, probably of the 1770s (SNTG p83). (DoE II) (CGE p42,86 pl 74) (SGS p148) (STMSM June 1980 pp20-22p). **Chinese Bridge** see Blue Bridge. **Chinese House** is by the Blue Bridge. Built in 1747; Thomas Wright may have had something to do with its building. It was one of the first pieces of Chinoiserie in Britain (CL Aug 1 1996 p43). It was copied from a design by Sir Percy Brett, Anson's First Lieutenant on the 'Centurion' and inspired by architecture seen in Canton (SNTG p80) (F p310). Its purpose was partly to house the collection of Chinese porcelain, painted mirrors and other artifacts brought from China by the admiral. They were removed to the hall in 1885 (SNTG p21). The exterior was painted pale blue and white with fret patterns. The interior had a richly lacquered colour scheme of red, green, blue and gold. The house was noted by Thomas Pennant (PT) and greatly admired by Anna Seward who wrote a long poem about Shugborough in c1760

> Here mayst thou oft regale in Leric Bower,
> Secure of Mandarins' despotic power....
> Safe from their servile yoke their arts command
> And Grecian domes erect in Freedom's Land.

(SNTG pp20,21). (GNHS p114) (W p417). Described by Siren in c1950 as in need of repair (CGE p42 pl 73b). It was once surrounded by the water of 'The Lake' (see), with a boathouse attached and was reached by a pair of bridges of Chinese design (SHC 1970 facing p110) (CL Aug 1 1996 p43) (DoE II) (F&G pp112,389) (SGS p148). The Sow was re-routed after the floods of 1795 since when the Chinese House has stood by the Sow (old cut) (SNTG p80). Lanthorn of Demosthenes (see) has also been called **Choragic Monument, Dark Lanthorn, Demosthenes Lanthorn** and **Diogenes Lanthorn**. The Grecian **Doric Temple** has been attributed to James 'Athenian' Stuart, but there is no documentary evidence. It was built in 1760s and was conceived as the entrance to the kitchen garden, which at the time occupied the space between it and the Shepherd's Monument. The old kitchen garden wall, which adjoined it, was demolished in 1805 leaving it in its present isolated position. The Temple is now nothing more than an alcove. It has a six-column portico, and a pediment. It is the earliest monument of the Greek Revival in Europe after Stuart's one at Hagley Hall, Worcs, built in 1758. They are both based on the Temple of Hephaistos, known commonly as the Theseion, and dedicated to Athena. It crowns the hill overlooking the Agora in Athens (DoE I) (SGS pp148,151p) (SNTG p83) (BOE p238) (CGE p86) (F&G p389) (F p311). The Temple may have been called the Temple of Diana (see). The **Druid figure** is situated on a crag in the remaining part of the Ruins. It is made of Coade stone and was found to be leaning in the 1960s and was restored in 1969 (SNTG pp79,81p). **Gates of Jerusalem** see railway tunnel. **Greenhouse** see Orangery. The circular **ice-house** at SJ 984218, was possibly built by Wyatt. It is half dug into the Bunter pebble beds and rises half above the ground, is situated at the edge of the parkland high on the side of the Sow Valley (IHB p395). In the reserve collection at the County Museum is an iron hook found on the floor of the corridor of the ice-house in Sept 1991. **'The Lake'** was a vague L-shaped pool which stood to the N of the hall, and may have been the remains of the medieval moat which surrounded the manor house. The Chinese House stood on an island at the N end of it. After 1795 the original course of the Sow was diverted to follow one arm of it, whilst the other arm was filled in (SHC 1970 facing p110). **Lanthorn of Demosthenes** was built in 1764-71 by 'Athenian' Stuart and lies 0.5m WSW of Shugborough Hall. The Lanthorn is a replica of the Choragic Monument of Lysicrates in Athens (built in the late C4 BC, or 334 BC). Stuart discovered an inscription on the Athens monument saying that it was erected by Lysicrates of Kikyana as a memorial to the victory of the tribe of Akamantis in a dramatic contest. Consequently Shugborough's has sometimes borne the name Lysicrates Monument. In the early 1750s the Athens monument was embedded in the walls of a Capuchin convent between the SE angle of the Acropolis and the Temple of Jupiter, and in the C18 it was invariably known by British travellers as the Lanthorn of Demosthenes. Shugborough's replica, therefore, has usually had this name. The original was supposed to have been built by the orator as a place of study and retirement, and hence Shugborough's is sometimes known as the 'Dark Lanthorn.' Other names for Shugborough's have been Dark Lantern, Lantern of Diogenes (or Diogenes Lanthorn), Demosthenes Lanthorn and Choragic Monument. Shugborough's differs from the original in that it lacks a square podium, or base, and a sculptural frieze representing the myth of Dionysus and the Tyrrhenian pirates. The latter, however, was probably reproduced by means of a painted frieze. Alton Towers also has a replica of the same monument. The trophy above Shugborough's consisted of a metal tripod and a Wedgwood bowl. They disappeared and were replaced by fibreglass replicas in 1965. The Lanthorn was restored in c1975 (DoE I) (GNHS p114) (CGE p86) (BOE p58) (SL p134) (SGS pp148,151p) (SNTG pp25-26 il of the original,74 painting by M Griffith, 89pc,90) (F p312) (1977 OS map 1:25,000). A pair of **lion columns** at the E end of the terraces are from a Hindu temple in South India, thought to date from c800 AD (SNTG p79) (ES Aug 9 1997 p21pc). **Lysicrates Monument** see Lanthorn of Demosthenes. An **oak tree** of great antiquity at Shugborough in the C19 was noted by Garner, who claimed the circumference was 21 feet at smallest part of trunk (GNHS p409). Its circumference in 1842 was 19 feet (SG p109). There was an **obelisk** on Brocton Hill (see). **Orangery** or Greenhouse. First built in 1750 but reconstructed by 'Athenian' Stuart in 1764. Was situated at right angles to the Sow in front of the hall facing over a bowling green, and screened the S side of the garden. As well as housing exotic plants the Orangery was intended to display Anson's collection of antique sculpture as well as two 'modern statues' of Hymen and Narcissus. This sculpture was sold off in 1842. The Orangery was demolished in c1855 when Nesfield's terrace was laid out (SNTG pp22,83). A small timber **pagoda** built in 1752 as an afterthought to the Chinese House (F p311), stood on the Sherbrook as it flowed out of the now lost lower mill pool towards its confluence with the Sow. It was built c1752 and appears in the views of Nicholas Dall and Moses Griffith. It disappeared between c1780 and 1800 (SHC 1970 facing p110), and may have been swept away in floods in the later C18 (SNTG p21), possibly in the floods of 1795. The **railway bridge** at SJ 997211, carrying the Trent Valley Railway over the approach road to Shugborough from Lichfield has battlements or stone walls above the level of the railway line of a sufficient height to prevent the danger of horses being alarmed. The seahorses and lions represent the supporters of the Lichfield arms. The shield-of-arms of the first Earl of Lichfield (Lichfield impaling Phillips) and the Lichfield crest are represented (NSJFS 1962 p100) (IAS p160) (HCMBOPP p52p in 1924). The **railway tunnel** between SJ 981216 and 988215 for the Trent Valley Railway which runs through the park is 777 yards long (IAS p160) (HCMBOPP p51p). Has ornamental entrances. The W portal near the Stafford approach road is more elaborate and carries the date 1847 (NSJFS 1962 p103 pl viii). It is Norman in style and was known by engine drivers as the 'Gates of Jerusalem' (IAS pp140il,160) (BERK2 p41p). The E portal seems intended to resemble the entrance to an ancient Egyptian temple. (ILN Dec 4 1847 il). The **Ruins** by the Sow is from the first phase of the park's landscaping in the 1740s and 1750s and are in part the work of Thomas Wright. Reputedly consists of stones from the bishops' ancient manor house and various chinoiserie structures recalling Admiral Anson's visit to Canton in 1743. Originally the Ruins was far more extensive, stretching westwards and including a Gothic pigeon house and comprised a complex with the now lost classical colonnade (see) and Orangery (see) (SGS pp148,151p) (SNTG pp20pc shows Nicholas Dall's

painting of the The Ruins in 1775, 56,75,79). (SD p89) (SOS p186) (CCF p115) (F&G p389) (BOE p238) (F p310). The **Shepherd's Monument** is situated to the N of the house and faces the Cat Monument, only trees obstruct the view between the two. The monument has been attributed to Thomas Wright, since it closely resembles one of his 'Six Original Designs for Arbours' (1755) (CL Sept 2 1971 p548). It resembles a sort of Boeotian temple. The flanking rustic Doric columns and entablature may have been added by Stuart, but the monument itself, with a carved stone rustic surround, predates the work, being in existence in 1756 when it was described by Anna Seward in her long poem on Shugborough (SNTG p31p). The present complete monument or the earlier part of it was probably completed in c1750. When first built the monument backed onto the outside of the old kitchen garden wall and was not freestanding as it is now. Pennant described it (SNTG p83). The centrepiece, a Scheemakers bas-relief of Poussin's 'Et In Arcadia Ego' (1640-42), still in place in the early 1970s (BOE p238), had gone by 1986 (F p309), and was in place again by 1989 (SNTG p31). The exact significance of the mysterious inscription 'D O.U.O.S.V.A.V.V. M' is not known. The separate terminals D.M. possibly stand for 'Dis manibus (sacrum) - 'sacred to the dead' - which would suggest that the monument is commemorative (SNTG p31). The builder of the monument, Thomas Anson, actually refused to reveal to his contemporaries the meaning of the inscription. Some believe the monument is a memorial to Admiral George Anson's wife, Elizabeth, although it was built 10 years before she died, others believe it is a romantic memorial to a lost love of Thomas Anson. The figure of the goddess Isis is said to adorn the monument. There is a belief, expounded by Andrew Baker and others, that there is profound occult significance in it; that it records a 'great and genuine secret tradition transmitted by men like (Isaac) Newton and (Andrew) Ramsay and bequeathed to us (in the monument) by Thomas Anson:' According to the book 'The Holy Blood and the Holy Grail' it can be linked to the Holy Grail. Anson is said to have often hung over the monument in a meditative and emotional sort of way (HOT) (SN Sept 1 1989 p9p. Sept 8 1989 p9). (DoE II*) (SSC p14) (GNHS pp114,115) (W p417) (CCF p114) (CGE pp42,86 pl 75) (F&G p389) (SGS p148) (SN Oct 28 1999 p23). The **Stafford Lodge** is the lodge by the start of the drive to the hall at Milford, it was designed by Samuel Wyatt (HCMBOPP p48p). The **Temple of Diana** (ASOP p25p of in 1863): has this disappeared or is it the same as the Doric Temple (see)? **Tower of the Four Winds** or Temple of the Winds (DoE II*) (F p312). An octagonal two-storeyed tower, with two Corinthian porches, and a coffered dome in the upper room (SGS pp148, 151p), said to have been built on the site of the pound of Shugborough Village (see) (SHC 1970 facing p110) (BOE p236) (SNTG p40), to the N of the present Park Farm at the S end of the now lost lower mill pool. When built it faced the Cascade and classical colonnade and the Pagoda (SNTG pp24il, 88): Gilpin thought it should have been built on a hill (F pp312-313). It is a copy of the Horologion of Andronikos Cyrrhestes in Athens. An illustration of the original in situ was made by James Stuart, Nicholas Revett, and Le Roy, French archaeologist, between 1748 and 1755. Their drawings of it appear in GM in 1757 and in Antiquities of Athens (vol 1. 1762) (STMSM Oct 1973 p22). The Tower here was built in c1765 by Charles Cope Trubshaw of Great Haywood; the date 1765 and the name John Fowler, a plumber (STMSM Oct 1973 p22), or James and Thomas Warreley, plumbers (SNTG p85), are inscribed on the roof leadwork. The tower differs from that of the original in that there are windows on both storeys; the porticoes are set diametrically opposite each other and what in Athens, a segmental wing, here covers an axial staircase and runs to cornice height. The tower may have had windows only in the upper storey, and reliefs depicting the Winds on the outside of the upper storey as shown in Moses Griffith drawing of the tower, reproduced in Pennant's 'Journey from Chester to London' (1782). However, ground-floor windows are depicted in Moses Griffith's watercolours in the Verandah Passage in the hall and in one of Dall's paintings (SNTG p85). Dr Johnson of Lichfield (see), who had no liking for Admiral Anson nor the family on account of their Whig tendencies, once visited Shugborough and on seeing the Tower of the Winds gave vent to an epigram:

> 'Gratum animum laudo, qui debuit omnia ventis
> Quam bene ventorum surgere templa jubet'

> I praise the grateful wit which thus bestows
> A temple for the Winds by which he rose.

(Life of Johnson. Boswell. ed 1860 p624) (Shugborough. Staffs. 1966 p32). The lower wing may have been added in c1805 by Samuel Wyatt, when altering the tower into a dairy for Lady Anson. The 1st Earl of Lichfield used the upper floor for gambling - the tower being at a discreet distance from the house. Other versions of the tower are at West Wycombe (by Revett 1759), Badger Hall, Shrops (by James Wyatt), Radcliffe Observatory, Oxford (by James Wyatt), the banqueting house at Mount Stewart, County Down (by Stuart), and at St Pancras church, Marylebone (STMSM Oct 1973 p22) (BOE p237). It was restored or reconstructed in 1969 (E&S Aug 5 1969 p24p). Stuart's decoration in the first-floor room was restored in 1987-9 (SNTG p86). (CGE p86) (F&G p389) (TSW p53) (SL p134) (SNTG pp85,86p, 87p). The **Triumphal Arch** or Arch of Hadrian or Hadrian's Arch. 0.5m SSW of the hall, at SJ 987214. It may have been one of the first of the park ornaments to have been built by 'Athenian' Stuart. It is a copy of the Arch of Adrian in Athens (GNHS p114) (VB p117) or some say the Arch of Hadrian in Athens (CGE p86) (BOE p236) (SNTG p90pc) (F pp311,312). Built of Tixall sandstone (VCH vol 2 p190) in the Roman style (SL p134), work on it began after Nov 1761 (SNTG p90). Whilst it was being built Admiral Anson died (1762) and it was turned into a monument to him and his wife; their busts, carved by Peter Scheemakers, were placed in the upper stages (HCMBOPP p50p). The monument was probably completed in 1766 (SNTG p90). The nature of the embellishments to be placed on it were apparently decided by Stuart, Matthew Boulton, Josiah Wedgwood I, his partner Thomas Bentley, and Dr Erasmus Darwin meeting at Shugborough on Christmas eve 1770 (CCF pp112-113). (DoE I) (SSC p14) (W p417) (SSW p32) (FZ p112) (F&G p390) (SGS p148). The famous 1000 year old **yew tree**, behind the Shepherd's Monument on the banks of the Sow, reputedly the largest in England, has a circumference of 525 feet or 50 yards and is claimed to be unique in England (CCF p115) (SLM Oct 1947 p35. Feb 1951 p19). Said to be 45 yards high and 160 yards in circumference in 1973 (SST), and a circumference of 183 yards in 1997 (ES Aug 9 1997 p21). At charity garden parties between WW1 and WW2, an admission charge was made and special tickets issued for visiting the tree (SNTG p83). The yew may occupy the site of the ancient burial mound, 'bewitched barrow' or 'demon low,' which forms part of the name Shugborough (SN Oct 28 1999 p23). For Shugborough Park follies, generally, see STMSM Feb 1973 pp24-25. In late 1996 or early 1997 a stone carved with the figure of a man and an ox pulling a plough was found by a garden in the grounds. The carving appears to be oriental in style and is perhaps from one of the garden ornaments (ES Jan 11 1997 p5p).

Shugborough Village A village, with medieval origins, was at SJ 990217, S of Shugborough Park Farm, near the Sow. By the early C16 Shugborough village was a much larger place than Colwich as the muster rolls of Henry VIII prove, having double the population (SHC 1914 p131 note). At one time there seems to have been a village street lined with cottages running from the Essex Bridge to Shugborough Hall. The lanes S and W to Cannock Chase projecting from the hall also had cottages beside them. The village was deliberately cleared to beautify the surroundings of Shugborough Hall between 1737-1773 (SSAHST 1966 p49. 1970 p36) (SNTG p19). To the S of the hall was a mill, and there was another mill, the Upper Mill, in the village. The village also had its own pound (said to have stood on the site of the Tower of the Four Winds) and pastures called 'Magmoor' and 'Lamoor.' Thomas Anson began demolishing cottages in 1737 as the leases fell in. Nicholas Dall's painting of the grounds in the late 1760s shows some cottages still standing incongruously amongst the follies of the park. The last small remaining group of cottages clustered round the Tower of the Four Winds was demolished from 1795. The villagers were removed firstly to another part of the grounds; then in the early C19 Thomas Lord Anson moved them again to new terraced cottages in Trent Lane, Great Haywood and The Ring (see) (SL p156) (SHC 4th series, vol 6. 1970 pp86-110) (BOE p237 note) (SNTG p40) (BERK2 p44).

Shur Hall Stood at the southern end of Spout Lane, S of Caldmore Green, Walsall. Existed by the early C19. By 1974 it was used as commercial premises (VCH vol 17 p155). Has also appeared as Shut Hall (SNWA pp30,96).

Shushions Minute hamlet and former manor by the confluence of Marston and Wheaton Aston Brooks 1.5m SE of High Onn. Former township in Church Eaton ancient parish. Has appeared as Sceotestan, a manor, in DB, Schuston (c1255-1566), Shiston (1283), Scuston (1293), Chuston alias Schuston (1310), Shuston (1686), and Shushions (1834) (NHS) (SPNO p142) (SPN p107). The name means 'Sc(e)ot's stone;' Sc(e)to being an Anglo-Saxon personal name, probably given to people or their descendants who were good shots at archery (DUIGNAN) (SPN p107) (SSE 1996 p17). Or may be derived from the root 'coed' (NSFCT 1908 p146). The DB village may have been in the area of Shushions Manor (SSAHST 1982-3 p38). A watermill at SJ 843144 existed in c1300 (VCH vol 4 p98) (WBJ p17). In a water course in c1780 near or at Shushions was found a skeleton in a full suit of armour of the Civil

War period. It was similar to that found at Hall Farm, Bushbury, in c1770 (SHOS vol 2 p182). Near Shuston House Plot noted three wells (perhaps one being St Edith's Well - see) which had the reputation for curing the king's evil, but he could not prove they contained any minerals (NHS p106) (SCSF p143).

Shushions Manor Shushions. Represents the manor house of Shushions manor. The present house dates from the early C19. To E of the house a deep curved moat and other earthworks suggest a fortified site (VCH vol 1. vol 4 pp92,98), or the remains of the DB village (SSAHST 1982-3 p38).

Shustoke Ancient moated homestead and farm by a tributary of Full Brook 0.75m WNW of Great Barr. Has appeared as Scotescote, Shitestok, and Sustock (SPN p56). The name means 'Scot's fenced-in place or town' - for Scot see Shushions (DUIGNAN), or 'Sceot's cell (or monastery)' (SPN p56). May be derived from the root 'coed' (NSFCT 1908 p146). There is a possible moated site at Shustoke Farm at SP 036962 (SSAHST 1982-3 p50). For Shustoke's appearance in a poem by Sir Joseph Scott see Great Barr.

Shute Hill Hill on which Chorley lies, and a house nearby known as Shutehill (OS maps 1887, 1902).

Shut Heath Tiny hamlet on N side of Brazenhill 0.75m NNW of Haughton. In Haughton ancient parish.

Shut Hill S of Acton Trussell church (1834 OS map), Teddesley Hay extra-parochial. Appears in 1814 and 1834. The name means 'hill with a steep slope' (SPNO p121). The name is preserved in Shutthill Bridge carrying the Teddesley Road over the Trent and Mersey Canal.

Shutlanehead Tiny hamlet on a ridge above the head of Meece Brook 0.75m W of Butterton (Newcastle-under-Lyme). Formerly in Swynnerton ancient parish. At the crossroads was found a sandstone Stone Age (Palaeolithic-Neolithic) axe-hammer in Sept 1953 (NSFCT 1953 p105) (NSJFS 1962 p26. 1964 p44) (STM May 1966 p33).

Shutt Cross House In Walsall Wood Road, Aldridge. Originally a C17 farmhouse with many additions and improvements made in the C18 (SNAR pp50,52). It was once the home of Joseph Shutt, a curate at Aldridge church (DoE II) (ALOPPR p23p).

Shutt End Former liberty in Kingswinford ancient parish (BHOP p5), and an area of Pensnett bound by two inns 'The Four Furnaces' just below High Oak, 'The Talbot' at Lenches Bridge, and Corbyns Hall and Shutt End House (TB June 1990 p5). The name appears in the 1851 census and has appeared as Shutend (WFK p33). For Shutt End Railway see Pensnett Line. The puddlers at Bradley, Foster & Co at Shutt End went on strike in 1852; some were prosecuted, fined and imprisoned (TEBC2 p66). There is no longer an area of Shutt End (WFK p11).

Shutt End Hall Stood on W side of Tansey Green Road, Shutt End, at approximately SO 904897 (WFK p10 see map). Seat of the Bendys (also owners of the Holbeche House) in the C17 (BCM March 1908 p22); it was occupied by the Bendys for many generations prior to 1851 was still occupied by them in 1851 (W p182). Another account say Shutt End Furnaces had replaced the Shutt End Hall by 1840 (WFK pp11,31).

Shutt End House Stood on S side of Dudley Road by the junction of Corbyn's Hall Lane (WFK p10 see map), Shutt End. Built in 1760 (BHOP2 p105p). John Hodgetts (d1741) was of Shuttend House (mem in Kingswinford church) (SHOS vol 2 p232). Residence of Capt John Belcher in c1780. He died of a fever at a friend's house in Stourport in 1783 (TB June 1974 p11). George William Gibbons died in 1846 at Shutend House, aged 15 (mem in Kingswinford church). The house became known as The Plantation. It was bought in 1915 by Dr HW Plant. Demolished in the 1960s for house building plots (BHOP2 p105).

Shutt Green Tiny hamlet on a low hill between Belvide Reservoir and the Shrops Union Canal 1m NW of Brewood. In Brewood parish. Has also appeared as Le Shutegrene (1320), Shetgrene (1338), Shutgrenelane (1461), Shutt green (1723), Shut Green (1834 OS map) (SPNO p42). The name is from the sibilation of the root 'coid' 'coed' forest (NSFCT 1908 p146).

Shut-the-gate Bednall. At SJ 966165.

Shutthill Bridge Crosses the Staffs & Worcs Canal, 0.25m S of the church at Acton Trussell.

Shuttington Bridge Amington. In Warws prior to 1910.

Siche Hall Leek. In 1870 the hall was the venue for a lecture given by Mr Sleigh to members of the NSFC (NSFCT 1870 p37).

Sideway (*Sid-a-way*). House and small industrial district near the Trent 1.25m S of Stoke-upon-Trent. In Stoke-upon-Trent chapelry and ancient parish. The name may have referred to a side way route from Stoke-upon-Trent to Longton by-passing Fenton (ES Aug 1 1998 p6). Or 'a settlement by the side of a long hill' (BNDA p3). The Trent and Mersey Canal has burst its banks at Sideway. Some of the area is now (1998) known as Trentham Lakes, a business and leisure park in the vicinity of Britannia football stadium.

Sideway Hall Sideway?, Stoke-upon-Trent. (SHST p129).

Sidon Hill Area S of Hemlock Way, W of Hill Street, SW of Hill Top, Hednesford (OS Street Atlas Staffs 1995).

Sidway Minute hamlet 2.5m NE of Mucklestone. In Maer parish. Here Dora Twyford OBE 1880-1924, social reformer, daughter of TW Twyford died (POTP p212).

Sidway Hall House 0.25m WNW of Mucklestone. Anciently the seat of the Bowyer family from the late C14 (MJW p13).

Silkmore Former hamlet on low ground by the Penk, now merged into the Stafford suburbs. Silkmore Lane and Crescent are 1.25m SSE of Stafford. In Castle Church parish. Has appeared as Selchemore (DB) (W p343) (it is the only Selchmore in DB, and Duignan believes it to be unique), Selkemore (1224), Selkemer (1255), Silk Moor (Yates' map) (SPNO p77), and Ikemor (SPN p112). The name may be from 'silken' in the sense of soft, smooth, after all, it lay in soft fertile meadows. But 'silk' cannot really be used in conjunction with 'moor.' Duignan thinks it is more likely to be 'Seolca's moor' in agreement with WH Stevenson (DUIGNAN). Palliser gives 'fen with a drain' (SL p71). Gelling gives 'drain marsh' (NSJFS 1981 p3). Or 'marshland with slow drainage' (SPN p112) (SSE 1996 p17).

Silkmore Hall Silkmore, Stafford. Built in the late C18 by Thomas Mottershaw on or near the site Silkmore Old Hall (W p343) (S&DOP p58p in c1905). Has a symmetrical front. Additions were made to it in 1820 (SOPP pl 66p) or c1820 (S&DOP p58) or c1825. It had been divided into flats by 1957 (VCH vol 5 p94), and was demolished in 1962. Hall Close, a small estate of council bungalows and old peoples' flats was built on the site in 1967 (VCH vol 6 p196) (SOPP pl 66p) (S&DOP p58) (SAC pp16p,17) (Stafford Past: An Illustrated History. Roy Lewis. 1997 p77).

Silkmore Old Hall Stood on or near the site of Silkmore Hall. There appears to have been a hall at Silkmore by the C12 which was occupied by the de Doxeys, who held Silkmore manor until 1572. The manor then passed to Matthew and William Craddock. In 1578 the manor passed to Sir Anthony Colclough. By 1629 the Colcloughs had sold the manor to Thomas Backhouse. It then passed through several hands. By 1788 the manor was held by Sir George Chetwynd of Brocton Hall who appears to have occupied the hall whilst alterations were made to Brocton Hall (SAC pp15,16).

Sillimor's Hall Name of a croft, also known as Sylymore, at Dimock's Green alias Oakeswell End, Wednesbury (WAM pp79, 101).

Silverdale (locally Silverdeele BOJ book 2 p26, a native is a Daleian Pit Boy to Prime Minister. G Bebbington. c1986 p1). Large former coal mining village in a valley created by a tributary of Lyme Brook 1.75m WNW of Newcastle-under-Lyme. Formerly partly in Keele and Wolstanton parishes and situated on the former Knutton Heath; Silverdale was known as Knutton Heath before 1854 (Newcastle Times Oct 20 1971). The **name** Silverdale does not appear on Yates' map, but does appear on maps from at least 1830 and on Greenwood's map. It appears to be a fairly recent creation (The Future of the Staffordshire Village. The Council for the Protection of Rural England Staffs Branch 1977). Some believe that it came from the silver birches that lined the valley here; others that it is from the wealth made from local mining (Newcastle Times Oct 20 1971). Silverdale was known locally as Silvan Dale (Newcastle Times April 18 1960); 'silver' may be then a corruption of sylvan, a poetical or literary word for woodland and romantically rural. Another possibility is that Knutton Heath village adopted the name Silverdale which was applied only to the dale and hamlet (and the nearby Silverdale Iron Works) farther to the W than the village (the name is shown in that area on the 1834 OS map). In 1853 Silverdale became a separate ecclesiastical parish, refounded as 'Silverdale and Knutton Heath' in 1855. The **church**, St Luke, on the N side of Church Street, was built in 1853 (BOE p239). The Silverdale **Iron Works** vase is shown in IANS p65 pl34. The first **railway** in Silverdale was a private mineral line constructed by Ralph Sneyd from his ironworks to a wharf at Pool Dam, Newcastle, in 1849-50; the railway was also used by passengers from 1859. The passenger service between Silverdale and Stoke was withdrawn in March 1964 (S&COP pl 19). The line from Silverdale to Market Drayton, opened in 1870, closed in 1956 (TWWW Feb 1990 p12). It was recommended that Silverdale station close in 1963 (ES March 22 1963). Silverdale became a separate civil parish in 1894 (GLAUE p422). **WW2.** A German unexploded anti-aircraft shell dropped by German bombers on a raid on Newcastle-under-Lyme in summer 1941 killed Eunice Stubbs, aged 20, at Silverdale (ES March 18 1977). **Newspaper.** The Newcastle Guardian and Silverdale, Chesterton and Audley Chronicle, founded on April 23 1881, ran to 1909 (SHJ spring 1996 p21). **References to Silverdale.** Silverdale is Silverton in Arnold Bennett's novels (Arnold Bennett and Stoke-on-Trent. 1966. EJD Warrilow. p131). The film, 'The Proud Valley' starring Paul

Robeson, about a Welsh mining village made in 1939 was partly shot in a cottage, one of a row of stone cottages in Church Street, known as 'The Gothics,' erected between 1851 and 1853, which were demolished in 1960 (Newcastle Times May 18 1960) (S&COP pl 28). 'Goldmoor' is the name for a soap opera based on life in and after coal mining in Silverdale, which started on BBC Radio Stoke and later on other BBC stations in the Midlands. For a poem about Silverdale by Harold L Whittaker see ES March 17 1981 p6. **Natives. Joseph Cook**, Liberal PM of Australia between 1913 and 1914, was born at Silverdale on Dec 7 1860. He was born at Vale Pleasant and lived at Brookside, another street nearby, from the age of three months. By 1871 his family had moved to what is now 86 Newcastle Street. At the age of nine he worked in local coal mines. He married in Chesterton and emigrated to Australia in 1885. There he did not realise his original ambition of becoming a Methodist preacher and instead turned to politics. In 1909 he became Defence Minister. As well as serving as prime minister he is remembered as the 'father' of the Australian Navy. In 1918 he laid the memorial stone for an operating theatre at the Cripples Aid Society's hospital for children at Hartshill (see). Later in his life he served as Australian Commissioner in London before retiring to Australia where he died in 1947 (SLM Feb/ March 1987 p27p) (Pit Boy to Prime Minister. G Bebbington. c1986 p2) (ES Aug 24 1999 p3p). For **Lord Cadman** of Silverdale see Silverdale House. **Fanny Deakin** (nee Davenport) (d1968), political activist known as 'Red Fanny,' was born at Spout House Farm at the end of Abbey Street, Silverdale, on Dec 2 1883. She joined the Social Democrats and when they broke up she joined the ILP in 1919. Four years later she joined the Communist Party. Twice between the World Wars she visited Russia on the sponsorship of Silverdale people. She married a miner in 1901 and lead strikes and hunger marchers. The maternity hospital in Newcastle-under-Lyme for which she campaigned, opened in 1947, bears her name (NUL pp116,120) (FWNS pp27-33p). At Silverdale lived twin sisters **Agnes** and **Ethel** (maiden name unknown). They claimed to have telepathic powers between them, and to have seen in their Silverdale home the ghost of their Uncle Jim who was killed in WW1 (GLS pp81-82). **Michael Howells** (b1963) of Silverdale was the 1994 world clay pigeon champion (ES Aug 2 1994 p3p).

Silverdale House Victorian stone villa at Silverdale. Former home of the Cadman family; James Cope Cadman was general manager of The Butterley Co Ltd, coal and ironworks at Silverdale. His son, John (1877-1941), professor of Mining and Petroleum at Birmingham University pioneered the exploration of the Persian oil fields in the Middle East and became Chairman of the Anglo-Iranian Oil Company. He became 1st Baron Cadman of Silverdale in 1937. He was succeeded by his son John Basil Cope Cadman (d1966), 2nd Baron. The house was converted into the Park Site Workingmen's Club after WW2 (ES April 6 1966) (S&COP pl 25).

Silver End Former small hamlet on a hill in a bend in the Stourbridge Canal, now a district of Brierley Hill, over 0.5m WSW of Brierley Hill, centred on Brettell Lane and Bull Street. So named by 1901 (OS map Sheet 71.06). The area is known as Lower Delph on Fowler's map of 1822; but the present Silver Street then existed, on the N side of Bull Street (WFK p16p see map).

Silverhill House between Barton Gate and Barton-under-Needwood on N side of the road. Built in the C18 and was renovated by the architect, Giles Scott, in 1820 (UNT pp37,118p,121). Occupied in 1851 by CW Lyon (W p23) and by Miss Lyons in 1896. Later, the house was occupied by Col and Lady Ritchie (UNT pp39,121).

Silver Jubilee Park Bounded by Birmingham New Road, Mason and Oak Street, at Roseville, Coseley. The area formerly formed part of the site of 'Holeridding' mentioned in an old lease (HC p23).

Simfields Area by a tributary of the Trent by several spurs of land 1m WSW of Werrington. At Simfields is a rectangular moated site, which possibly marks the house of the de Verduns before the de Verduns were able to settle at Alton Castle (see) (NSFCT 1926 p136). Johnstone thinks the moat could have surrounded a house belonging in the C13 and the C14 to either a member of the de Werynton family, or the de Buckenhale family, or the de la Halle family, or that it had been formerly held by a Sir Leon de Layn (WJ pp11-12). (CAMS p64). It has been a cattle-pound or paddock. The present house stands well clear of the moat (NSFCT 1953 p64). To natives of the district the moat is known as Hall Court (WJ p11). There are references to three excavations of the moat, in 1905, 1935 and 1956 (WJ p11) (NSFCT 1982 p19). There is believed to be a tunnel from the moat to the Metal House (see).

Sinai Park Former medieval deer park enclosed by Burton Abbey out of Needwood Forest (ANS p17), 1.75m WNW of Burton upon Trent. Formerly in Branston township in Burton upon Trent ancient parish. The **park**, in existence by 1410 (NSJFS 1962 pp73,76) (AFT p194 note; spelt oddly Sainai), remained until at least the mid C18 and passed with Burton manor at the

Dissolution to the Pagets (SHOS vol 1 pxxiv) (EDP p177). A park keeper is recorded in 1707 (ANS pp58,102). It may be identifiable with Shapenhale Park (alias Shobnall Park) (SHOS vol 1 p24). But later appears as Seyne Park (1534), Sennye Park (1550), Seney Park (1707), and St Seyney Park (SHOS vol 1 p24) (NSSG p12) (ANS pp42,102). **Name.** According to Burton in his Description of Leicestershire the estate was so called by the abbot of Burton Abbey because it reminded him of 'a vast, rough hillie ground, like the wilderness of Sinai of Arabia' (HWE vol 2 p301). In old documents it is written 'Seyne.' This is said to be a corruption of an Old French word, meaning 'a holiday and its associated privileges' (GLS p81). The present E-shaped timber-framed house, which appears to have been attached to the park, certainly had some association with Burton Abbey. It may have been a summer retreat or pleasure house or sanatorium of the abbots, or the Great Lodge of their grange at nearby Shobnall. The moat surrounding it has been dated to 1334 (SSAHST 1988-89 p26) (BOE p77). The two wings, formerly detached, have been dated to the C15, and the central portion to the C17 or C18 (IHOBT p21). According to local tradition Sinai was used by Henry VIII as a hunting lodge, and it was considered as a prison for Mary, Queen of Scots. In the C18, the structure was fashionably medievalised and given Georgian additions (Daily Telegraph. Weekend Section July 29 1995 p9). The house was stuccoed by 1798 (SHOS vol 1 p24) (BTOP vol 1 p38p). In the later C18, when known as Seany Park, the house was the residence of William Wyatt, steward to the Pagets, commissioner in the case of the inclosure of Gailey Common in 1773, and a member of the Wyatt family of Thickbroom Hall (see) or Blackbrook Farm (see) (Staffordshire Farming. 1700-1840. Staffs. County Council. Local History Source Book. p13) (info KL Neal). (KES p43). In WW2 the RAF were billeted here. After WW2 it was used to house homeless families, then it was used by the local farm (Daily Telegraph. Weekend Section July 29 1995 p9). The house was badly neglected after 1945 and fell into extreme decay (IHOBT p21); Pevsner wrote of it being derelict in the early 1970s. It appears to have remained derelict under various owners; some of whom used it as a pigsty (southern wing) (SGS p66) (MR p48) ('Silent Houses - The Way We Were' Central TV. 19 July 1993 10.40pm) (info KL Neal). It was bought in c1993 by Kate Newton, who is restoring it (GLS pp79-81), starting with the N wing (IHOBT p21). An old wooden door belonging to the property has been located to the house of Mr Evans at Alrewas (info KL Neal). (DoE II*) (BTOP vol 1 p38p). There is a spring to the SE of the house called Lord's Well (see), which according to legend, has a tunnel leading off it to Burton Abbey (BTOP vol 1 p38); the BTNHAS have searched for this tunnel but as yet have found nothing (info KL Neal).

Singing Cavern Former limestone quarry under Castle Hill, adjoining and on the S side of Dudley Tunnel (BCM Oct 1970 p51). In 1984 a new canal tunnel was made from Dudley Tunnel to it. It was the first new canal tunnel in Britain for 130 years. In 1989 a former rock tunnel was re-opened to the adjacent Dark Cavern. The caverns are now a tourist attraction for boat parties from the Black Country Museum at Tipton (Dudley Canal Tunnel leaflet) (MR p135).

Singing Kate's Hole Spot where the dead of the Burslem plague of 1647 were buried at Rushton Grange, Burslem. So called after Kate, the Italian governess of the Biddulph family, who is said to have brought the plague over from Italy (HBST p217) (TB July 1998 p19).

Singing Nellies Lane Hanchurch Hills. Leads up to the edge of Swynnerton Old Park (NSJFS 1971 p121).

Sittles House on W side of the Tame 1.25m NW of Elford. For a Romano-British farmstead complex 0.25m NE of Sittles see under Alrewas.

Six Ashes Tiny village in undulating country on Brantley Brook on Staffs Shrops border 2m NW of Enville. Formerly in Bobbington chapelry in Claverley ancient parish, Shrops. At Six Ashes was a gate in the fence or boundary which surrounded the ancient royal Coton estate in Shrops (KRC p13). There was a settlement at Six Ashes by 1775. The name is from six ash trees which marked the county boundary; these were still standing in 1793 (VCH vol 20 pp64,67).

Six Roads End Minute hamlet in Needwood Forest at the junction of six roads over 0.5m SSW of Draycott-in-the-Clay. The six straight roads radiating from here were almost certainly created at the time of the parliamentary enclosure (SL p69). The hamlet has also been called Six Lanes End (ESNF p26p). There is a tradition that a house at Six Lanes End was built on the foundations of the one in which Robin Hood was born (QML pp156-161) (SMM p142).

Six Ways Central area of Bilston (BCM Jan 1985 p40).

Six Ways Former commercial district of Smethwick. The district grew in the C19 and was inhabited by industrial workers (SHCB p8). On 1834 OS map six roads are shown meeting at approximately the meeting of Windmill Lane,

Grove Lane, Soho Way, and Cranford Street. No trace of the district remained by 1989 (SMEOP p14p).

Skeath House Sandon Bank. House 1m WSW of Salt.

Skelhorne Spring Former enclosure or woodland known as Skelhorne's Spring was situated in the present Peatswood area of old Tyrley parish in the C16 (SHC 1945/ 6 p86).

Skidmore's Row Hamlet in Sedgley ancient parish (W p200). There is a Skidmore Road, off Harding Street, Coseley.

Slack Hillock Former hamlet in Rowley Regis parish, close to the Shrops border. The name appears in the 1851 census and has appeared as Sleck Hillock (BCWJ p73). Is now the Station Road area of Old Hill. Slack Hillock Farm became the Sportsman & Railway Hotel (TB Nov 1995 pp20-21p. Dec 1995 p30), which later became the Wharf Public House (OS map Sheet 71.08).

Slade, The House, area or tiny hamlet on Colliery Road under 1m WSW of Brereton in a valley on the E side of Cannock Chase. It may be identifiable with Baudy Slade or Bawdy Slade N of Beaudesert, W of Upper Longdon (maps of Plot, Morden, Bowen and Yates). To the E of The Slade is an area known as The Glen.

Slade Heath Heath by the Staffs and Worcs Canal and fragmented hamlet 0.5m ESE of Coven. In Brewood ancient parish. 55 acres of Coven Heath and Slade Heath were enclosed under an Act of 1850 (SHC 1941 p19).

Slade Hill Farm 1.5m NW of Wolverhampton on Tettenhall Road. In Wolverhampton township, chapelry and ancient parish (W p96).

Slade Hollow Hollow and minute hamlet under 0.25m NW of Stanton. In Ellastone ancient parish.

Slade House NE of Calton (W p778). Thomas Tomkinson (1631-1710), poet, was born at Sladehouse, the son of a farmer. He was a member of the Muggletonian religious sect. His work includes the 26-stanze poem 'Joyful News from Heaven, for the Jews are Called' (PSS p472) (VFC p131).

Slade Mans Hole 1.5m of Draycott-in-the-Moors. Perhaps, half way between Tean and Draycott. Here during a battle, soldiers were slain, and legend has it that if something was thrown up into the nearby rocks a soldier would appear (SVB p68) (SMM p54).

Slain Hollow Reputedly, here King Ina (Ine) of the West Saxons fought against Ceolred, King of Mercia in 716. The battle is known as the battle of Benebury and the site for it has never been truly identified, due to uncertainty whether Benebury was really Bunbury (see) or Bonebury (see). Roberts, Plot, and Abbot Jourval all thought it took place near Alstonefield at possibly above Thor's Cave (WTCEM p35). The Daily Mail 1971 thought it took place at Longnor in 715 (L p2). The ornamental lakes and Canton Pagoda of Alton Towers are presently situated in this hollow, which has also appeared as Slade Valley (BATR). (MR p14).

Slaney's House Timber and plaster house, reputedly the oldest in Cheadle, situated in the High Street facing Church Street formerly called Paradise Street. Occupied for many years by a Mr Slaney, saddler and harness maker (HOC p51il).

Slang Drumble Near Park Hall, Church Leigh.

Slang Oak Ancient oak which stood 1.25m from Elford (NSJFS 1962 p148). It is said to have been in existence for over 1000 years and to have stood in Elford Park (see) (HS p159p), or on Elford Low (see) (NSJFS 1962 p148). It was dead but still standing when Mee saw it (KES p90). Seems to have been in existence when visited by NSFC in June 1961 (NSJFS 1962 p148).

Slang Park Existed in the first quarter of the C19 in the region of John, Vine and Mollart Streets, Hanley (H p107). The name is perhaps from a field.

Slate House Farm House beneath Sheen Hill 0.5m N of Sheen. In Sheen ancient parish. Is mentioned in 1611 (VCH vol 7 p241).

Slater's Hall Bromley, Kingswinford. Scott wrote in the late C18 it had become a farmhouse by his time and it contained several rows of arches and modern embellishments which had 'effaced the marks of antiquity' (SVS p134).

Slimersdale In Maer parish. Probably former name for Slymansdale. White suggests it was the name for a hall which became called Camp Hill Hall (W p397). This is probably the Camp Hall marked on the current 1:25,000 OS map. Slymansdale, also marked on the current 1:25,000 OS map, is a house to the ESE of Camp Hall.

Slindon Tiny village in the Meece Brook valley in a gap leading to Brockton 7m NW of Stafford. Former manor (SCSB p1) and township in Cotes quarter in Eccleshall ancient parish (W p375). For a crystallised formed stone found near Slindon see Mill Meece. Has appeared as Slindone (DB), Slindon (1242) (SPN p107), and Slyndon (1679) (SHC 1914 p41). The name is derived from the Old English (or Old Swedish - SPN p107) 'slind' meaning 'a slope' or 'the side of a hill' the hill, the remnant of a river terrace, rises modestly towards Aspley on the western side of the village (SCSB p1). 'Sloping hill' (NSJFS 1981 p2) (SSE 1987 p32. 1996 p17). Duignan could make nothing of the prefix, but agreed the terminal represented 'hill.' The stone well head erected by John Charles Salt dated 1884 on the grass verge by the A519 originally stood opposite Villa Farm on the corner of the road to Aspley (DoE II) (EOP p63) (SCSB p7, pl 18 shows it in its original position). The church, St Chad, on the E side of the main road, was built in 1894 (BOE p239). Thorold described it as 'a little church of rare beauty' (SGS p148). Graham Balfour visited the village school in 1908 (SCSB p36).

Slip Low Burial mound near Wetton (WTCEM p6). Possibly the same as Scrip Low. Excavated by Bateman in 1846 and by Carrington in 1851. Two skeletons, one crouched, were found (VAD p97) (TYD p181) (NSJFS 1965 p56).

Slitting Mill Village and former hamlet on the E side of Lady Hill overlooking rising Brook in Cannock Chase 1.25m SW of Rugeley. In Rugeley ancient parish. There was a burnt mound probably of the Middle Bronze Age 0.5m S of Slitting Mill at SK 02941689. It was noted in 1913 and 1930 but has not been located since (SASR 1987 p16). Slitting Mill was formerly called Stonehouse or Stone House (VCH vol 5 p149), from the large stone house situated at the entrance to the village. The present name derives from an iron slitting mill which was situated here - one of the earliest in the Midlands - started by Thomas Chetwynd in 1623 (VCH vol 2 p111) (Iron and Steel Industry. Schubert p306) (SVB p152). Appears as Slitting Mill on Yates' map (SPNO p107). The mission church, St John the Baptist, in Church Close, was built by 1892 and is unusual in that it is attached to a private house (built in 1970 on the site of the old school house) (St John the Baptist Church, Slitting Mill near Rugeley. Sheila M Simpson. 1993).

Sloth, The Rock feature on top of the Great Slab in the Upper Tier of The Roaches and one of the most difficult rocks of any there to climb, involving the technique of roof-climbing (VB p209) (SGM p57).

Slough, The Area of Pelsall just N of the former Pelsall township. It is alluded to in the charter of Pelsall's bounds in 994 (PTYV p4). (SNBC p20).

Slowe Moor The name occurs from the early C17 in the Wellington Street (formerly Slough Lane) area of Smethwick. The name may have been in use in c1275 when Agnes de Slouf occurs among the tenants of Smethwick manor. It was stated in 1884 that the name derived from the sloes that had abounded in the area within living memory, the earlier existence of Fenfield in the area suggests 'slough' as an alternative derivation (VCH vol 17 p94).

'Slowgreaves' Little hill between Little Stoke and the crossroads at Hilderstone. The name may be derived from 'Soldiers Graves' from a battle which had taken place in the area (PHH p9).

Slymansdale House 1m NNW of Maer.

Smallbridge Formerly probably the footbridge that carried the road from Tunstall and Wolstanton over Scotia Brook near Burslem Mill (VCH vol 8 p109). A bank between Brownhills and Trubshaw Cross was known as Smallbridge Bank in the C17 (VCH vol 8 p108). Name, which has also appeared as Small Bridge, was the name for a wharf on the Trent and Mersey Canal in existence by 1802 (VCH vol 8 p110) (AGT p69). Some time was owned by George Appleby and Co (HBST p154).

Small Brook Tributary of the Smestow. Has appeared as Smalbroke (1416) (SPNO p18).

Smalley's Moor A piece of moor which seems to have been exchanged with a piece of land called Brickholt on Nov 5 1576 by the custom of livery of seisin. The symbols by which these lands were represented in the ceremony of livery of seisin were a bough of an oak and a piece of turf from the respective properties, which were then hung from a hedge and an oak on these properties (SCSF p121).

Smallrice Fragmented small hamlet in undulating country at the head of Stocking Brook 2m S of Hilderstone. In Sandon ancient parish. Appears in the C13 as Smallris (SSE 1996 p17). The name is from 'small rise,' which is, in contrast to Hardewick or Hardiwick - the high homestead (DUIGNAN) (NSFCT 1910 p163) (SPN p118) (SSE 1996 p17). Smallrice was described in 1591 as a manor (SHC part 2 1934 p18). Smallrice Farm had a horse gin, still quite common in the north of the county, where they are known as gin gangs, but are rare in the south and in the midlands (COS p50p).

Smalls Farm Occurs on the 1834 OS map 0.5m WNW of Red House, Great Barr, slightly to the E of Newton Junction on the Tame Valley Canal. The M6 now passes in this area.

Small Silver Green Minute hamlet on the NW side of Hound Hill under 0.25m S of Marchington. In Hanbury parish.

Smallthorne Small hamlet in the mid C19 (ONST 1967 p280) on a NW-facing slope overlooking the Trent, now a suburb of Burslem 1m ENE of Burslem, in Burslem chapelry in Stoke-upon-Trent ancient parish. A stone mace-head of **Neolithic** or **Bronze Age** has been found here and is listed in Masefield's collection (NSFCT 1908 p194) (NSJFS 1964 p35). The name has appeared as 'Smallthorneheede' (1569) and Smallthorne (1666) as the name of land in

Sneyd township. The **C19 settlement** of Smallthorne developed just in Norton township (VCH vol 8 p107). From 1779 Smallthorne was in Norton-in-the-Moors ecclesiastical parish until becoming a separate ecclesiastical parish in 1859 (LGS p212) (GLAUE p422). Became a separate civil parish in 1894 (GLAUE p422). Smallthorne became a part of the City of Stoke-on-Trent in 1922 (ONST 1964 p251). There was a church at Smallthorne by 1850; St Saviour's stands on the S side of Ford Green Road, and N of Saturn Road (LDD). A German gun captured in **WW1** stood outside the old council offices at Smallthorne in the 1920s and 1930s (ES Sept 14 1996 p21p). Smallthorne is 'Moorthorne' in Arnold Bennett's novels. A **UFO** was seen over Birches Head, Hanley, and Bentilee by Mrs Kathleen Paszek of Whatmore Street on Aug 30 1967 (FSRP pp29,32). Two people saw a bright round light about the size of a two inch ball held at arm's length from Nettlebank, Smallthorne, on Aug 30 1967 (FSRP p9). **Natives and visitors. Hamlet Emberton** (d1890), street musician, popularly known as 'Klondyke,' was born at Smallthorne in c1818 (SHST p672p) (POTP p90). **Arthur Berry** (b1925), author, playwright, artist was born at Smallthorne. He is the author of 'A Three and Sevenpence Halfpenny Man' (1984) and 'The Little Gold Mine' (1991). After time in London and Manchester Berry came to live on a farm at Biddulph (ES Jan 12 1981) (VFC p14).

Smallwood Former estate and area 2m WSW of Marchington. Formerly in Marchington Woodlands township in Hanbury ancient parish. First or earliest documentary mention of Smallwood is in a rental of 1382 where there is mentioned a Elizabeth de Smalwode (SMSE p4). The name may be derived from an island of woodland detached from the much larger Needwood to the S and designated 'small' (meaning 'narrow' rather than 'little') (SMSE p4).

Smallwood Hall Georgian-style house at SK 109295 which superseded Marchington Woodlands Manor House (see), to the E. The hall was occupied by the Webbs of Tutbury Cotton Mill in the C19; Thomas Webb was occupying the hall in 1851, when the house was called Smallwood Manor. There is said to be an illustration of it by F Redfern in 1864 (W p23) (HOU p336) (SMSE pp13 il,14-15) (SHJ spring 1994 p31). The house was superseded by Smallwood Manor (see), built nearby in 1884.

Smallwood Manor House at Smallwood, Marchington Woodlands. Built in 1884 by the Hodgson family (SHJ spring 1994 p31) or in 1886, and had electricity from the start (BOE p202 note). The style of the house is said to deliberately reflect that of holiday villas in Eastbourne, for that is where Mrs Hodgson spent her holidays (SVB p121). Leased by Denstone College in 1937 to house its preparatory school (VCH vol 6 p158). (SMSE) (AUOPP p77p).

Smart's Buildings Minute hamlet in the centre of Cannock Chase, over 2m SW of Rugeley. There is a burnt mound probably of the Middle Bronze Age on the E bank of the Rising Brook NE of Smart's Building at SK 02541591. There is another of the same period to its NW at SK 02481612 (SASR 1987 p16).

Smedley Sytch House 0.5m NE of Shawfield, in Fawfieldhead township in Alstonefield ancient parish. Appears as Snethlesych in 1406. There was a road from it to Boosley Grange until the earlier C19 (VCH vol 7 p27 note).

Smestow Hamlet on Smestow Brook at its confluence with Wom Brook 0.5m NNW of Swindon. In Wombourne ancient parish. The hamlet, also known as Smestall, existed as a nailers' settlement by 1816 (VCH vol 20 p200). Smestow was the home to farmer Tommy Tucker who, when accused of selling diluted milk, claimed it was because his cows had been outside over a very rainy winter (MMBCC p104). The bore-hole near Smestow Bridge was built by Germans in 1912 to allow underground water to be extracted and so lower the level of water in the Earl of Dudley's mines at Baggeridge and Himley is 2842 feet (866 metres) deep and claimed to be the deepest well in Britain. It has a steel cover (TB Jan 1991 p6p) (GBR 1996 p79). The same or another well, 1,650 feet deep, in the Smestow Valley (see) made by Germans between June 25 1912 and July 31 1912 created a rivulet called 'Hun River' (BCM summer 1994 pp24-25). For the origin of the name see Smestow Brook.

Smestow Brook Brook rising E of Wolverhampton and flowing for 13 miles to the Stour near Stourton. It has been described as a river (SHOS vol 2 p165) (SVS p373 note) and is full of twists and curves, and running in a dilatory fashion (ALP p13). It has appeared as Tresel (985) (SPN p130), Trisel (pre 1066) (BCM summer 1994 p22) (SSE 1996 p23), Smethestall (1300), Smestow (1576) (VCH vol 20 p185), Smestall (Saxton's map), Smeltall (c1600), and The Smestal (1844) (ALP p12) (SPNO pp18,22) (SPN p107). It also appeared as Trysull Brook in the late C18 (VCH vol 20 p185). Tresel is of Celtic origin and means meandering (VCH vol 20 p185); Welsh 'tres' is toil, labour (BCM summer 1994 vol 27 No. 3 p22) (ALP p13). The name Smestow, an Old English one meaning a still pool (VCH vol 20 p185), was probably the name, according to TR Bennett, of a small pool in a stretch of the river near Smestow hamlet (ALP p12) (SPNO p18). According to others Smestow is of Middle English origin and does not signify a pool, but means 'the stalls or places of the Smiths or Smithies' (DUIGNAN). It has been thought that the name Smethestall was at first applied to one arm of the river or to one of its tributaries, and later transferred to the main arm (ALP p12). Another theory is that the two elements (both Saxon in origin) in the present word Smestow - 'staell' either meaning stagnant or a place for catching fish, and 'smethe,' smooth - were applied individually to one or the other of the two rivers which unite to make up the present Smestow (SPN p107). One of its sources is the Cullwell Well at Springfield, E of Wolverhampton. Shaw and Jones say it rises at Showell Farm, Bushbury (SHOS vol 2 p198) (HOPTT p2), whilst Drayton implies in Polyolbion (1613) that Wulfruna's Well is the source (HOWM p4). Some say it rises on Dunstall Racecourse (Midland Rivers. John Roberts and John Drewett p81), whilst others say it rises in Fowler Park, Heath Town (TB April 1998 p9). From Dunstall it passes in a south-westerly direction through Compton, Wightwick, Old Perton, and Trescott, where it is joined by the Black Brook. At Smestow hamlet it is joined by Wom Brook. It joins the Stour near Stourton, which in turn joins the Severn at Stourport (HOPTT p2). (GNHS p23). The river has inspired the poem by Eustace Lees 'The Staffordshire Stream which Indicated a New Era' (1929). The old forms of Smestow give name to Trescott and Trysull.

Smestow Gate To the NW of Smestow (TB Sept 1986 p30).

Smestow Valley The valley of the Smestow (SL p101) (BCM summer 1994 vol 27 No. 3 p22). The 'Hun River' in Smestow Valley is the local name for a rivulet created by the 1650 feet well dug by Germans between June 25 1912 and July 31 1912. The well was created by a syndicate prospecting for coal, and in WW1 provided water to the Birmingham Metal and Munitions Company (BCM summer 1994 pp24-25). The well may be the same as the well at Smestow (see), which, at 2842 feet deep, is claimed to be the deepest well in Britain.

Smethwick (*Smeth-ick*, locally *Smerrick* The Black Country. Edward Chitham. 1972 p173). Large town on the South Staffs plateau (VCH vol 17 p87), and most easterly of the Black Country, 23m SSE of Stafford, 23.5m NE of Worcester, 21.25m NW of Warwick, or 3m WNW of Birmingham. Former township in Harborne ancient parish (SHCB p3).

EARLY. Situated in the field (site of the old reservoir between Old Church and Thimble Mill Pool) is an Ice Age boulder. Tradition says that every time the bells of the Old Chapel ring it turns round once. Another popular tradition connected with it is that two horses bought it here at night, but could not move it afterwards (RS p7). There were two glacial boulders in the area of the footpath from Old Church to the Thimble Mill (SMEOP p127p). Four boulder stones embedded in the footpaths at the junction of Astbury Avenue and Davison Road were to be moved to Victoria Park in 1952 (STELE Feb 22 1952). There was another boulder near the Summit Bridge at the corner of Holly Lane and Oldbury Road in 1952 (HAS p2) (RS p7) (STELE Feb 29 1952).

900 to 1750. The manor of Smedeuuich (Smethwick) is recorded as being held by the bishop of Chester (Lichfield) in DB. Later forms are: Synewkh (1291), Smethwik (1576), Smithwyke (1618), Smethewicke (1664), Smithwich (John Cary's map 1787) (STELE Sept 29 1951. Dec 22 1951) (SHCB p3). Smethwick is said to have also appeared as Smedewich, Smeythwik, Smethewyke (SPN p107). The **name** arose because it was the wic or village on smooth heathland. That is, it was smooth by comparison (RS p12) (DUIGNAN) (SOSH p330). Kenward and others think it was because of the numerous smithies here. Falmouth in 1653 was known as Smithwick (RS p12) (SPN p107). Smethwick **manor** formed part of manor of Longdon. Overlordship was formerly held by the bishop of Lichfield, then after 1546 by the Pagets (VCH vol 17 p98). The manors of Smethwick and Harborne were granted to Halesowen Abbey sometime before 1229. After the Dissolution they passed to Sir John Dudley, later Earl of Warwick and Duke of Northumberland, and were forfeited on his attainder in 1553, and were granted in 1554 to his relative Edward, Lord Dudley. His son Edward sold them in 1604 to Sir Charles Cornwallis, whose grandson, also Charles, sold them to Thomas Foley in 1661. In 1709 Thomas' son, Philip, of Prestwood House, sold them to George Birch of Harborne and Henry Hinckley of The Beakes. In 1710 Birch and Hinckley divided them up with Smethwick going to Hinckley. Smethwick manor stayed with the Hinckleys (or branches of the family) until 1766 when it was sold to John Baddeley of Birmingham. It then became divided. In the earlier C19 Smethwick manor was united in the Reynolds family who are recorded holding it until the 1830s (VCH vol 17 p98) (SHCB pp3,4). **Civil War**. In 1643 the final stages of the battle which resulted in the royalists under Prince Rupert capturing Birmingham, took place along the old road to Handsworth; part of which was Shireland Lane

(present Waterloo Road) (RS p40) (VCH vol 17 p89). There was a **pound** at the junction of Bearwood Road and Birmingham-Halesowen road in 1877 and another in Oldbury Road. A smithy was built on the site of the latter in c1878 (VCH vol 17 p119).

1750 to 1850. Smethwick comprised a collection of small hamlets to the mid C18. There was no church or manor house for the village to grow around in medieval times (SHCB p3). Before the C19 the main centre of population seems to have been at Bearwood Hill (see) (VCH vol 17 p88). Smethwick increased in size after Boulton founded the Soho Works in 1764 and after the building of the Birmingham Canal Old Cut Old Main Line cut through to the N between 1768 and 1772 and Telford's Birmingham Canal New Cut New Main Line cut 1824. Smethwick increased rapidly in the 1830s and over the period 1840 to 1900; a new centre of Smethwick emerged to the N of Bearwood Hill in the 1830s (VCH vol 17 pp88,91). **Churches**. The oldest church in Smethwick is **Parkes' Chapel** or Smethwick Old Chapel or Old Chapel, at the junction of Uplands and Church Road. It was built in 1732 (VCH vol 17 pp123,124). **Holy Trinity** church for the northern part of Smethwick was consecrated in 1838 (VCH vol 17 p125). A **wake** at Smethwick, held in mid October, existed by 1826; Harborne, Smethwick's mother parish, held its wake in September (VCH vol 17 p134). The Cape Fair of the 1860s was presumably held at Cape Hill (see). Bull baiting at Smethwick was prohibited by an order in council as early as 1773. However, it continued. In 1798 a baiting was started on Snow Hill at the Salutation Inn, but the Loyal Association of Birmingham Volunteers, came out and put a stop to it. Bull baiting was finally abolished with the Act of 1835 (RS pp115,116-118). Smethwick became a separate ecclesiastical parish (known as North Harborne) in 1842 (VCH vol 17 p88) (GLAUE p422). Harborne ancient parish was 'hour-glass' in shape; the township of Smethwick represented the northern 'side,' whilst Harborne formed the south 'side.' By at least the beginning of the C18 it was usual to appoint one or more officers for each 'side' of the parish. Eventually, in alternate years each 'side' was able to appoint a constable for the whole parish (SHCB p9). For Harborne and Smethwick **charities** see RS pp63-66 and VCH vol 17 pp141-142. **Daniel Hall**, aged about 29, believed to be of West Bromwich, with Edward Green and John Stokes, broke into the house of Samuel Bull of Smethwick on Dec 21 1789 stealing five silver table spoons and a pair of silver tea tongs, two silver watches and a great coat: Hall was executed at Stafford on March 26 1791 (Crime broadsheets in the WSL).

INDUSTRY. The **windmill** with three pairs of stones in Windmill Lane at SP 029882 was built by William Croxall in 1803. It lost its cap and sails in a gale in 1880s? The wooden machinery and mainshaft were removed in 1890. It then became a store for the Windmill Brewery. After serving as a Civil Defence Observation post in WW2 it was considered unsafe and dismantled in 1949 (WBJ p36) (VCH vol 17 p109) (SMEOP p28p) (WIS p25). There was another windmill in Smethwick at Cape Hill (see). As well as iron working practiced at the **Soho Foundry** (see) and other places, Smethwick's other industries have been the production of tubes, soft drinks, beer, soap, and pens; working in brass; the building of gun barrels, marine engines, weighing machines, specialised glass and glass painting (LGS p21) (SHCB p7) (VCH vol 17 pp109-118). **Chance's Glass Works** on the W side of the S end of Spon Lane was operated by Chance Brothers and Co from the late 1820s. In 1851 it was thought to be the largest crown and sheet glass works in England (W p704) (VCH vol 2 p229. vol 17 pp115-116). Its lighthouse works, opened in 1851, was the country's only works dedicated to lighthouse machinery (LGS p21) (SHCB p7). The works also produced all the glass for Joseph Paxton's 'Crystal Palace' in Hyde Park for the Great Exhibition (1851). The works were visited by George VI and Queen Elizabeth in WW2 (TB Aug 1995 p3p). The company was acquired by Pilkington Bros Ltd in 1955 (VCH vol 2 p229). There is a statue of James Chance (b1814) in West Smethwick Park (see). (History of Chance Bros & Co. JF Chance. 1919). The iron work for the same 'Crystal Palace' was made at the **London Works** (see) Smethwick (SHCB p7). Hydraulic presses and jacks were made by Tangye Ltd at their **Cornwall Works**, built on the site of Smethwick Hall (Rabone Hall), from 1864 to 1969 (VCH vol 17 p112). **Heath Street Works** in Cranford Street made screws when occupied by the firm of JS Nettlefold and Joseph Chamberlain (1836-1914), Mayor of Birmingham (1873-5) and statesman (VCH vol 17 pp88,113). During the later C19 the making of nuts, bolts, and screws became Smethwick's most important industry (VCH vol 17 p112). Fine art pottery was made by **Ruskin Pottery** (named in 1904 after art critic John Ruskin, and formerly Birmingham Tile and Pottery Works) in Oldbury Road, West Smethwick from 1898 to 1935 (VCH vol 17 p118) (Ruskin Pottery: The Pottery of Edward Richard Taylor and William Howson Taylor, 1898-1935. Paul Atterbury and John Henson. 1993) (BCM winter 1999/2000 pp9-15ps). (CL Aug 12 1993 p82). The **Carfield** motor cycle was made at Windmill Lane, Smethwick between c1919 and c1927 (PVBC p15).

1850 to PRESENT. **Local government.** In 1888 some Smethwick residents sought to have the town incorporated with Birmingham. The matter was only decided against by the Local Board by the casting vote of the Chairman (SHCB p10). Smethwick became a separate civil parish (an urban district) in 1894 (VCH vol 17 p88) (GLAUE p422). On June 12 1899 the town obtained its Charter of Incorporation and became a municipal borough, with Jabez Lones, who was the prime mover of the scheme, becoming the first mayor (SHCB p10). On April 1 1907 Smethwick became a county borough. Smethwick county borough **arms** were granted in 1907, and according to Scott-Giles were, in 1953: Or, a caduccus and a club laid saltire proper, on a chief azure a beacon fired between two symbols of the plant Mars, all gold. The crest is: On a wreath gold and azure, a demi-lion gules charged on the shoulder with a gold Stafford Knot and holding in the paws an arrow point downwards proper. The motto is: 'Labore et ingenio' (By industry and ingenuity) (CH p329il). In 1927 571 acres of Oldbury urban district were transferred to Smethwick. When Smethwick comprised 2496 acres it was said to be the most densely populated county borough in England: outside London it was exceeded only by Salford in 1951 (Staffs County Guide c1958 p125) (VCH vol 17 p88). Proposals to amalgamate Smethwick with Oldbury in 1920, and with West Bromwich in 1945 came to nothing. On April 1 1966 Smethwick county borough was dissolved and the borough of Warley constituted and Smethwick transferred to Worcs (SL p170) (SHCB pp10-11). By 1999 the name Smethwick was used for a ward in Sandwell metropolitan borough. **Social change.** In the 1950s many immigrants settled in Smethwick. They were mainly Sikhs from the Punjab. Their temple, the Guru Nanak Gurdwara, in the old Congregational chapel in High Street, which they had purchased in 1961, was considered to be the largest Sikh temple in Western Europe in 1962 (The Times July 31 1962) (VCH vol 17 p134). In the evening of July 10 1981 rioting occurred in Smethwick, similar to the riot at Handsworth (see); a large crowd protested in Victoria Park; 17 shops were damaged in the Windmill Shopping Centre with four arrested there; overall 17 were arrested in Smethwick (Birmingham Mail July 11 1981) (Birmingham Post July 11 1981). A **cholera epidemic** affected Smethwick in 1853 (SHCB p9). The station at Smethwick on the Birmingham, Wolverhampton and Stour Valley **Railway** opened in 1852. The Stourbridge Extension Railway, opened in 1867, linked Smethwick with Stourbridge (Galton Valley. A Walkers Guide. Sandwell Metropolitan Borough Council. 1993). No. 115 High Street is an old **toll house** (BCM July 1987 pp38-40). Smethwick **Theatre Royal**, Rolfe Street, built in 1896 by Charles Barnard boasted the largest auditorium in the country (BCM winter 1998/9 pp36-38 il). It had a fire disaster on Sept 2 1929, which claimed the lives of 11 or 12 people who are buried in a mass grave in Uplands Cemetery (STELE Nov 6 1953) (TB Oct 1979 p15; that the fire occurred on Sept 3) (BCM winter 1998/9 p38). Or the fire occurred on Sept 2 1939 (SMEOP p148p). **Floods.** Smethwick flooded on July 11 1927 (SMEOP p150). In the early 1950s John Cross saw the **ghost** of the late Mrs Peters, a confectioner, in the door of her old shop in Ballot Street (MS&S p28). **Natives and visitors.** A resident of Smethwick, **Samuel Johnson**, a labourer aged about 40, a native of Harlaston, Staffs, hung one of his children, stabbed his other child, and took his own life by hanging in the back yard of his house. The two children were Benjamin, aged 9, and Thomas, aged 5 (Bell's Messenger June 18 1837) (Broughton's Scrapbook p135). **Edward Caswall** (1814-1878) divine and poet, was a founder of the Roman Catholic mission at Smethwick (VCH vol 17 p88). **Henry Pettitt** (d1893), writer and playwright of 'light theatre pieces,' was born in Smethwick in 1848. His work includes the play 'Golden Fruit' (1873) and the pantomime 'Harlequin King Frolic' which had the longest recorded run at the Grecian Theatre in 1880/1 (VFC pp105-106). **Sydney Francis Barnes** (d1967), who has been described as the finest bowler ever to play for England in cricket, was born in Smethwick on April 19 1873. He was made an honorary member of Stafford CC when he went to live in Stafford after WW2 (SSTY p186) (STM June 1965 p43p) (NOPP pl 62) (TB Feb 1994 p35p. Aug 1997 p10). **Sydney Fowler** (d1965), writer (pseudonym of Sydney Fowler Wright), was born in Smethwick in 1874. His crime novels include 'The Bell Street Murders' (1931) and 'Who Killed Reynard?' (1947); 'The Throne of Saturn' (1952) is a collection of short stories (PSS pp367-368) (VFC p50). In 1874 **Alphonse Bertillon** (1853-1914) inventor of the forerunner to fingerprinting was teaching French at the Collegiate School in South Road (VCH vol 17 p88). In the C20 Smethwick has had a number of colourful MPs and contestants: In the 1918 election the suffragette Christabel Pankhurst contested the seat, which was won by the Labour candidate (HOS 1998 p84). Sir **Oswald Mosley** (1896-1980), of Rolleston Hall (see), was MP (Labour) from 1926 to 1931. He was leader of his own newly formed party, the New Party, during the last months he repre-

sented the borough (VCH vol 17 p123). **Patrick Chrestien Gordon-Walker** (1907-1980) held the seat for Labour from 1945 to 1964. In the early 1960s he led his party's opposition to the Conservative government's Commonwealth Immigrants Bill, and on account of this it seems they made immigration the issue for the seat in the 1964 general election. The slogan "If you want a nigger for your neighbour, vote Labour" was allegedly coined for the campaign for this seat and their candidate Peter Griffiths went on to win it. Despite losing his Gordon-Walker was made Foreign Secretary in the Labour administration and was made a life peer in 1970 (HOS 1998 p84) (Oxford Dictionary of Political Biography. Dennis Kavanagh. 1998) (Daily Telegraph June 2 2000 p31). In the 1966 general election the seat was taken back by Labour's **Andrew Faulds** (1923-2000), an actor. He held it (redrawn and renamed Warley East in 1974) until 1997. As a politician he was outspoken and an individual (Daily Telegraph June 2 2000 p31p). **Gladys (Sally) Lunn**, athlete, was winner of the 800 metres in the World's Games for Women's Championships 1930. She was also winner in about 30 other events in various championships (TB April 1983 p7p). **William A Savage** of Smethwick was awarded the VC for bravery during the raid on St Nazaire on March 27-28 1942. A plaque at the Council House, Smethwick, commemorating him was unveiled on April 18 1953 (TB March 1989 p4p. April 1989 p20p). **Ken Wharton** of Hume Street, Smethwick, was well-known in the motor racing world. In 1951 he won the Hill Climb Championship and he was also successful in long-distance sports car races. He was killed in New Zealand in 1957 (SMEOP p145p). The actress **Julie Walters** was born in Smethwick in 1950 and attended a school at Holly Lodge (see). The comedian, **Frank Skinner** (real name Chris Collins), is from Smethwick. He took up comedy aged 30, making his debut in 1987. In 1991 he won the Perrier Award at the Edinburgh Festival Fringe. He has had a chat show on BBC Radio One and has appeared in the TV sitcom 'Blue Heaven' written by himself and in the Channel Four show 'Pack of Three (1991/ 1992) and in the BBC show 'Woodcock' (1994) (Radio Times Guide to TV Comedy. Mark Lewisohm. 1998).

NEWSPAPERS. The **Smethwick Telephone**. A Weekly Newspaper for Smethwick, West Bromwich etc (or simply Smethwick Telephone) (STELE), founded on Feb 9 1884, became the Smethwick Telephone and Warley Courier from March 1 1963 and the Warley Courier and Smethwick Telephone from April 1 1966, and the Warley News Telephone in October 1966 (VCH vol 17 p135) (SHJ spring 1996 p23). The Oldbury paper Weekly News brought out the **Smethwick Weekly News** from 1890 to 1895 and from 1906. The **Smethwick Globe** appeared briefly in 1895, and the **Smethwick Advertiser and Three Shires Indicator** briefly in 1909 (VCH vol 17 p135) (SHJ spring 1996 p23).

Smethwick Castle Cottage with castellated towers, perhaps of the late C19, which stood in Queen Street, Smethwick. It is shown on an old postcard with the caption 'Smethwick Castle' (TB Nov 1996 p29p). The building was still standing in 1931.

Smethwick Common Mentioned in 1631. Lay probably in the N or NE part of Smethwick township (VCH vol 17 p107).

Smethwick Great Reservoir Created in 1769 and drained in 1835 (HCMS No. 2) (1834 OS map) by the damming of Thimblemill Brook to feed the Birmingham Canal Old Cut Old Main Line. It lay in the Rosefield and Cheshire Roads area to the NE of Parkes' Chapel.

Smethwick Grove Large mansion on E side of Grove Lane, Smethwick. Has been described as a Georgian house (VCH vol 17 p105 il of c1830 facing p128) and has been called the Grove (STELE Feb 20 1953. March 6 1953). James Keir, chemist and industrialist, may have been living here in the mid 1780s. JL Moilliet, a Swiss merchant, may have been living here in the first years of the C19 (STELE March 20 1953. Dec 3 1954); he was settled in Birmingham by 1801 and purchased the house in 1813. In 1801 he married Amelia Keir, daughter of James Keir. Maria Edgeworth, novelist and friend of Amelia Moilliet, visited Smethwick Grove in 1819 and 1821. The Moilliets moved to Hamstead Hall in 1826. The house was demolished in the 1860s by which time the area surrounding it had become industrialised (VCH vol 17 pp104-105). (SHCB p4).

Smethwick Hall The Smethwick Hall of the mid C18 N of Birmingham Canal Old and New Main Lines on W side of Rabone Lane may have been the Smethwick Hall which existed in 1660 (VCH vol 17 p105), perhaps on or near the site of a moat for a former hall (SSAHST 1982-83 p50). The mid C18 Smethwick Hall was occupied by the Rabone family from c1780 to 1850. The family had sold the hall by 1859, by which time it was known as Rabone Hall. Sometime shortly after 1862 Tangyes Ltd built their Cornwall Works on the site (SR p97) (VCH vol 17 p105) (SHCB pp4,8). (STELE Oct 13 1951) (VCH vol 2 p160) (SMEOP p46p). In the later C17 Plot noted a yew tree here with bright yellow leaves not caused through disease. The yellow foliage brought forth berries whereas the green did not. Plot could not account for its yellow colour (NHS p207).

Smethwick House Stood at the W end of Stoney Lane, 0.5m from Old Church, Smethwick, formerly on the western flank of a little valley. Said to have been built in 1746 by Thomas Hanson (perhaps misspelt as Ansell in RS p121 and is confused there with Smethwick Hall - at one time known as Rabone Hall). Smethwick House was called Smethwick House by the 1830s, but in the later C19 became known as Smethwick Hall. The last mention of a Hanson at the house occurs in 1834 (W). By 1840 the house belonged to Thomas Darby. It was occupied by a John Samuel Dawes in 1855 and apparently remained in the possession of the Dawes family to later in the C19. They appear to have let it to various tenants including a school which occupied the building between 1875 and 1885. It was later purchased by the Tangyes. It housed Belgian refugees between c1914 and 1916 and was the residence of Benjamin Shakespeare, clerk to the Smethwick Justices, between 1916 and 1925. The house was bought by Smethwick corporation in 1928 and was demolished in 1937. Smethwick Hall Boys and Girls High Schools were built on the site in 1939 (STELE Oct 27 1951. Oct 13 1951. Oct 20. 1951. Nov 3 1951. Oct 3 1952 il of c1850) (VCH vol 17 pp89,105-106) (SHCB p4) (SMEOP p47p). Smethwick corporation opened the grounds as the public park, Smethwick Hall Park, in 1930. A pool, a feature of the former grounds, remains (VCH vol 17 p106).

Smethwick Junction Canal junction to the W of Soho Foundry. Here the Birmingham Canal Old Main Line diverges from the Birmingham Canal New Main Line (Galton Valley. A Walkers Guide. Sandwell Metropolitan Borough Council. 1993).

Smethwick Old Hall Mid C18 building near SP 012883 (a site near Smethwick House). Plot is said to have noted a predecessor to Smethwick Old Hall, which may have stood on a moated site E of Smethwick Old Hall (SSAHST 1982-3 p50).

Smethwick Summit High heathland of about 1000 yards long about 491 feet high connecting the heaths of Smethwick and Bromwich. Brindley built the Birmingham Canal Old Cut Old Main Line over it in 1772 following the 491 contour line. A series of six locks on either side were built to raise it over the Summit. However, the locks caused bottlenecks and in 1789 Smeaton built a cut nearby, 18 feet lower, making some of Brindley's locks redundant. Smeaton's canal is now the Birmingham Canal New Cut Old Main Line. This in turn was superseded by a 20 foot still lower cut, built by Telford in 1829, now the Birmingham Canal New Main Line. It ran to the S of Smeaton's cut and achieved for Telford a constant level from Birmingham to Tipton without locks. The Brindley Canal over the Summit has now gone; three of his locks on the Smethwick side still exist (Galton Valley. A Walkers Guide. Sandwell Metropolitan Borough Council. 1993).

Smith Hills Small range of hills 0.5m N of Barton-under-Needwood. Preserves the name or profession of a former owner or occupier of land here (HOPT vol 1 p138).

Smith's Pool Pool in a public park S of the railway line, Mount Pleasant, Fenton. Bert Mycock, a 16 year old colliery surface worker drowned in it on June 10 1939 (ES June 12 1939 p7). Probably same as Smithpools (SHST p487).

Smithy Moor Smithy Moor Farm is 0.5m SE of Stanton. Mentioned in 1683 (NSJFS 1972 p124). A raised circular area over a bloomery slag heap becomes visible on the farm after any dry period. The slag suggests here was a furnace from the C17 or later (NSJFS 1975 p101).

Snails End Former name for the N end of Yoxall village (1834 OS map).

Snails Green Former hamlet comprising a straggle of houses (MOA p137) in Aldridge ancient parish. The hamlet was situated in the area of Junction 7 on M6, S of Great Barr church. It is marked on a map of Morden. Bishop Francis Asbury went to school at Snails Green (250th Anniversary of Birth of Francis Asbury. Aug 1995).

Snake's Hill A hill near Hints.

Snape Hall Built by 1794 W of Wellhead Lane N of Witton Road, Handsworth. It was standing in 1862 but not in 1911 (MNB pp41,45,47,49).

Snapehall Snapehall Farm is 1m WNW of Whitmore.

Snape Marsh Shelton, Hanley (SHST p25).Gives its name to Marsh Street, Hanley.

Snapes Green Former small hamlet on Greenfield Lane W of the railway in Bushbury ancient parish. The name occurs on maps by at least 1886 to at least 1952.

Snelles End Hamlet in Yoxall parish (SHOS vol 1 p98).

Snelsdale Okeover. 1m NW of Mayfield.

Sneyd Former township crowning a ridge overlooking the upper Trent in Burslem, also called Hamil, which was by the C18 the most populated part of the township (VCH vol 8 p106). Sneyd was member of Tunstall manor

by c1130 (ONST 1976 p374). Appears in 1256 as Sned (SSE 1996 p17). Snede means a piece, fragment, something cut off. The property was probably a detached, isolated, or outlying portion of a manor or estate (DUIGNAN) (NSSG p10). Or Saxon 'forest clearing' (VCH vol 8 p107). The Sneyd family originated from Sneyd (SNEDE). Sneyd became a separate ecclesiastical parish in 1844 (GLAUE p423). The church, Holy Trinity, at the N end of Nile Street, built in 1851-1852, became unsafe and was demolished in 1959. It was transferred to St Werburgh's church, Hamil Road, which was reconsecrated Holy Trinity in 1958 (VCH vol 8 p124).

Sneyd, The Former hamlet in the low Sneyd Brook valley by the Wyrley and Essington Canal 2.5m NNE of Willenhall. Formerly in Willenhall chapelry in Wolverhampton ancient parish; that part of Sneyd centred on Sneyd Farm has remained in Staffs and is now a ward in Essington civil parish. Appears as the Snead in 1663 (HOWI p187). The name is from Anglo-Saxon 'snaed' which can mean, depending on context, 'piece of land,' 'clearing,' or 'piece of woodland' (SPN pp134-135). Common land at Sneyd was enclosed in 1815 (MH 1994 p108). There was a mineral line from Essington Wood Colliery to the Wyrley & Essington Canal at Sneyd (VCH vol 2 p323).

Sneyd Brook Rises in the Sneyd area, Willenhall. Runs southwards forming the NW the boundary of old Walsall borough. It joins one of the head rivers of the Tame in Bentley Mill Way and proceeds as the Tame (or in the C18 as Bescot Brook). The lower part of the brook was known as Bentley Brook in the C14 and as both Bentley Brook and Park Brook in the C18 (VCH vol 17 p143).

Sneyd Green (locally *Snayd Grayn* SSE 1997 p88). Suburb of Hanley and nearly 1m NNE of Hanley. Pottery was made here in the early C13 and again between c1650 to 1730 or later. Two medieval kilns were discovered to the NW of the junction of Sneyd Street and Crossway Road by children of Sneyd Green County Primary School in 1954. One was described as 'the most perfect example of a medieval pottery kiln known in England' (NSFCT 1954 pp83-86. 1956 p85) (VCH vol 8 pp131-132) (SASR 1984 pp41-47 plans ils). Sneyd Green was a hamlet before the C20, appearing as Snead Green in the C17 (mem in St Margaret's, Wolstanton) and probably arose as common land belonging to Sneyd hamlet in medieval times (SNEDE). A bull ring at Sneyd Green was described in 1925 as being fixed in front of the inn at Sneyd Green (NSFCT 1925 p190). The ecclesiastical parish of Sneyd Green was created in 1955 from Cobridge ecclesiastical parish (GLAUE p423). The church, St Andrew, S of Sneyd Street to the W of Hanley Road, was built in or by 1962 (LDD). It is Toft End in the novels of Arnold Bennett (Arnold Bennett and Stoke-on-Trent. 1966. EJD Warrilow. p151). Bennett mentions that he went for a walk up to Sneyd Green on Sunday Dec 22 1907 in his Journal. Noah Heath, poet, was born at Sneyd Green in c1780. He was a potter by trade and worked as a modeller and mould maker for Joseph Mayer. His poems 'Miscellaneous Poems' vol 1 1823 and vol 2 1829 are very rare (BS p219) (ROS vol 2 pp101-123) (OTP pp140-141) (PSS pp131-132) (BALH p177) (VFC pp63-64). Mrs Isabelle Thompson who had taken the part of Mrs Pearce in the original 1914 production of 'Pygmalion' settled with her husband AW Thompson, manager of the old Theatre Royal, in Sneyd Green; she died here on Jan 15 1981 (ES Jan 16 1981 p24p).

Sneyd Hill Park Public park on N side of Leek New Road, Sneyd Green.

Sneyd House Formerly situated at the top of Moorland Road, Burslem. Said to be the birthplace in 1816 of Robert Heath, later MP for Stoke-on-Trent (OTP pp91,107il).

Sneyd Junction Junction of the Wyrley and Essington Canal with its Birchills Branch (HCMS No. 2).

Sneyd Reservoir Reservoir at The Sneyd, Willenhall, at SJ 981023.

Sneyd's Brook Runs by Lutley N of Enville. Part of it formed the boundary between Enville and Morfe manors (VCH vol 20 p91).

Sniddles Head Isolated farm on the E side of Gradbach Hill, 0.75m SE of Gradbach. Appears on the 1834 OS map. Sniddles Cottage is illustrated in UHAW p51.

Snipe Cottage over 1.5m NE of Heaton. Formerly in Heaton township in Leek ancient parish. Part of the present cottage is possibly of the C17. It was called Snipe Hall in 1756 (VCH vol 7 p187).

Snout's Gap Walsall Road, Cannock. Here was sited the first Cannock parish workhouse (VCH vol 5 p52).

Snowdon Settlement in the NW of Patshull ancient parish. Snowdon was mentioned as a member of Patshull manor in 1279. The names Upper Snowdon and Lower Snowdon were in use by 1861. Upper Snowdon, a house which had disappeared by 1982 1m WNW of Patshull Hall, was the former Snowdon; Lower Snowdon is a group of cottages 1m W of Patshull Hall (VCH vol 20 p162).

Snowdon Pool Former fish pool 1m WNW of Patshull Hall, partly in Staffs and partly in Shrops. It was perhaps constructed in the mid C13 by Sir Ralph of

Pitchford. The pool was drained in the 1850s and planted with trees (VCH vol 20 pp162,169).

Snow Hill Hill and street name in Shelton, Hanley.

Snow Hill Hill, 513 feet high, and formerly higher (HOWM p6), and street name in Wolverhampton under 0.5m S of St Peter's church. May be identified with 'the snows' mentioned in the charter of Ethelred of 985 (HOWM p10 note). White noted a medicinal spring near Snow Hill that had either fallen into disuse or was unknown by 1851 (W p76). Houses were first constructed on Snow Hill in the C18 (WP&P p19).

Sodom Small hamlet adjoining Can Lane 1m ENE of Sedgley (W p200) (HC p54). In Sedgley ancient parish. It is not marked on 1834 OS map and the name no longer prevails. Hell Lane terminated at Sodom, at its S end. The old folk of Coseley had a saying that 'Sodom begins where Hell ends' (TB Nov 1976 p24). The name alludes to the evilness of the place and perhaps paganism (BCM Oct 1993 p56).

Sodom Former name for the E end of Wombourne village. In use in 1867 (VCH vol 20 p201).

Sodom Hall Stands at Upper Ettingshall. Built in c1800 (HC p62).

Softlow Softlow Wood is 1m WNW of Stanton.

Soho, The Area of Bond End by the Trent about the present Technical College, Burton upon Trent (BTOP vol 1 p16p). Here were hat factories and the Soho Wharf which was developed to deal with the increased trade which resulted from the improvement of the navigation on the Trent after 1712. Sailing barges of up to 40 tons capacity used its facilities. With the development of the Trent and Mersey canal, from 1770 onwards, river trade declined and eventually the wharf fell into disuse and disrepair (IHOBT pp38il,45).

Soho Mainly an industrial district on an upland plain stretching from the top of Soho Hill westwards - Hockley Brook passes through the district - 0.5m S of Soho Foundry, under 0.5m E of Windmill Lane, Smethwick (VCH vol 2 p165). Former township with Handsworth in Handsworth ancient parish. The name appears to have at first been applied to an inn, formerly a hut or cottage of a warrener on the summit of common land. By association the name, Soho, was then applied to the surrounding common (Soho Heath alias Crabtree Flat) and hill (Soho Hill), forming part of Handsworth Heath, a vaguely defined common ranging across three parishes (SHOS vol 2 p117) (SHCB p6) (MNB p40). 'Soho' is an old hunting term. It could have derived from an inn sign depicting a hunting scene with the huntsman represented with the word 'soho' issuing from his mouth (RS p16) (SHCB p6). In Aug 1854 a tubular bridge between Soho and Handsworth designed by John Robinson Maclean collapsed and fell into the road during the construction of the Birmingham, Wolverhampton and Dudley Railway line (SSR p14). The nearest station to Soho was on this line in the Benson Road area to the S of Soho (1834 OS map). The Handsworth, Soho and Perry Barr Junction Railway opened in 1889 (VCH vol 2 p310). The church, St Michael and All Angels, St Michael's Road off Soho Hill, was built in 1855 (Old and New Birmingham. Robert K Dent. 1879. p619) (BOEWA p181). William Murdock (1754-1839), engineer and pioneer of coal gas for lighting, lived at No. 13 Foundry Row, one of a row of small cottages built for Boulton's workers workers in Soho (SHCB p6), during or after his association with the Soho Foundry. By 1999 Soho formed a ward with Victoria in Sandwell metropolitan borough.

Soho Foundry 1.5m SW of St Mary's church, Handsworth, approximately 1m W of Soho Park, by the Birmingham Canal New Main Line. Towards the end of the C18 it became evident that Matthew Boulton's Soho Manufactory (see) could not cope with existing business and Boulton and his partner James Watt of Heathfield Hall (see), decided to build the Soho Foundry. Built on part of the Piddocks Farm estate (VCH vol 17 p102), it opened in 1795 or 1796 and provided castings for the Soho Manufactory. It was the first factory to be built solely for engineering products and has been described as 'the first factory in the engineering industry in the world' (HOS p45). It was largely under the control of the sons of the founders of the Soho Manufactory, Matthew Robinson Boulton and James Watt, junior (SHCB p6). Produced complete steam engines; the first engine completed is said to have been ordered by John Wilkinson of Bradley (see), Bilston. From 1798 William Murdock, inventor of gas lighting, of No. 13 Foundry Row in Soho (see) and of Sycamore Hill (see) (from 1816), was manager of the foundry. The foundry was gas lit before 1800 (SHCB p6) or in 1803 (The Cambridge Biographical Encyclopaedia. 1994. see under Murdock) and was one of the first industrial complexes to be so lit. Or the Soho Manufactory was lit by gas in 1802 to celebrate the Peace of Amiens (MNB p44): The remains of the gasometer thought to have been used by William Murdock in his early experiments with gas lighting could still be seen at the Foundry in 1921 (SMEOP p19p). William Buckle is said to have invented the first lead screw for a lathe of any considerable size at Soho Foundry in c1825 (STELE Feb 19 1954). The foundry

produced the 4-cylinder engine which powered the screw of Brunel's 'Great Eastern,' launched in 1858 (VCH vol 17 p110). A mint was added in 1860 (SHCB p6). In 1895 the foundry was acquired by WT Avery, weighing machine manufacturer. The foundry ceased casting operation in 1956 (VCH vol 17 p113) (Galton Valley. A Walkers Guide. Sandwell Metropolitan Borough Council. 1993). (Soho Foundry 2nd ed. 1948. WKV Gale) (VCH vol 17 p110).

Soho Hill Eminence 450 feet high 0.5m S of St Mary's church, Handsworth ancient parish. The hill was a place of execution and was known as Gibbet Hill up the end of the C18, by when the name Soho Hill was being used (SHOS vol 2 p117) (KD map of Birmingham) (MNB p44). By 1840 Soho Hill, formerly a part of Soho Heath, was lined with mansions (MNB p50).

Soho House Soho Avenue, Handsworth. Built for Matthew Boulton, founder of the Soho Manufactory (see), on the former Handsworth Heath by William Wyatt II (b1734) of Blackbrook Farm (see) in c1766. Boulton referred to the house as 'l' hotel de l' amitie sur Handsworth Heath.' It was extended and remodelled by Wyatt's brothers, James and Samuel, between 1796 and c1805. The dining room vaulted plaster ceiling and its columns are a reduced version of James Wyatt's design for Canwell Hall. The house had a central heating system installed in c1810. Matthew Boulton lived here between 1766 and 1809. The house remained Boulton property to after WW2, but Boulton's descendants mainly lived at Great Tew, Oxon, after 1815. The house was at some later date a lady's college; the vicarage for St Michael's church; and a private hotel, Soho Hall Hotel. It was unoccupied in 1851. In the C20 it was acquired by Birmingham city council for use as a police hostel, and a new block was built in the garden in the 1960s (W p696) (CL Feb 27 1997 pp40-43pcs) (HANDR p50p) (The Wyatts: An Architectural Dynasty. John Martin Robinson. 1979 p19) (HHHW p24ps). The end sections of the wings were removed in the early C20 and some say the house was demolished in 1927 (BOEWA p184) (VCHWA vol 7 pp50-51). The house was restored and opened to the public in Oct 1995 (Soho House. A Short Guide. Birmingham City Council). The museum was broken into and some artifacts taken in the early morning of July 2 1999 (BBC Midlands Today. July 2 1999). The house is believed to be haunted (HANDR p50). In the garden is a replica of Boulton's 'Hermitage,' a small thatched hut, first built in c1775 (Soho House. A Short Guide. Birmingham City Council).

Soho Manufactory Built by Matthew Boulton on Moneybank Hill, Handsworth Heath, in 1762 (SHOS vol 2 p117) (SHCB p6) to designs by Benjamin Wyatt I (d1772) and his sons of Blackbrook Farm (see), when the original architect T Lightoler proved unsatisfactory (The Wyatts: An Architectural Dynasty. John Martin Robinson. 1979 p19). The manufactory stood in the South Road area of Soho, on the Hockley Brook which it crossed by Factory Road. The manufactory was extended in 1765 (SHCB p6), with a front range, consisting of five spacious brick-built squares with a facade 19 bays wide, resembling an inflated stable block. The extensions were designed by Benjamin Wyatt I's eldest son, William Wyatt II (b1734). It was then the biggest factory in Europe if not the world and contained areas for the workers to live. When completed the manufactory was the first Wyatt building to be seen by a large public. Wyatt relations, John Wyatt II (1700-1766) of Thickbroom Hall (see), 'the inventor,' worked for a while for Boulton at the manufactory; his eldest son, Charles (1750-1819) and his second son, John III (b1752), were also Boulton employees (The Wyatts: An Architectural Dynasty. John Martin Robinson. 1979 pp4,5). With the completion of the manufactory Soho became the centre of industry in Britain for a period as celebrated in the following epigram -

> Soho ! - where GENIUS and the ARTS preside,
> EUROPA's wonder and BRITTANIA's pride;
> Thy matchless works have raised Old England's fame;
> THINE ! ever blended with a BOULTON's name.

Matthew Boulton told Dr Johnson of Lichfield (see) and James Boswell on a tour of the manufactory in 1776 that 'I sell here, Sir, what all the world desires to have - Power'! Soho also, to an extent, replaced Lichfield as the social and intellectual centre of the North Midlands; it became a meeting place of the Lunar Society (The Midlands. Past-into-Present series. Clive Gilbert. 1978 p44) (The Wyatts: An Architectural Dynasty. John Martin Robinson. 1979 p19) (Channel 4. Time Team. Jan 18 1997) (CL Feb 27 1997 p40). Towards the end of the C18 it became evident that the manufactory could not cope with existing business and Boulton and his partner, James Watt (d1819), an engineer originally from Scotland, later of Heathfield Hall (see), decided to build the Soho Foundry (see) (SHCB p6). (W p696). For the Boulton and Watt engine which pumped water up locks at Smethwick see Birmingham Canal Old Cut Old Main Line. For the inn which workers frequented and where rivals engine builders supposedly sent spies to gather information on the latest innovations at Soho Manufactory and Foundry see Waggon and Horses Inn. Boulton had a mint in brick buildings near the manufactory in the South Road area. (W p696). In Dec 1800 a group of constables and detectives entrapped five robbers who broke into the counting room of the mint. One, William Fould, alias the Little Devil, got away with 100 guineas. He was apprehended and imprisoned in Stafford Gaol (SHOSA vol 2 p16). The manufactory was **lit by gas** in 1802 to celebrate the Peace of Amiens (MNB p44). The manufactory finished operations in 1848 with the death of the young James Watt and was completely demolished in 1862-3 (VCHWA vol 7 p259) (BOEWA pp183-184) (SOSH pp296 il from SHOS, 297 il of 'Old Bess' the first engine employed in the factory) (SL p170) (HPPE pp107-109). The manufactory and mint sites were later built over. Parts of the foundations of both were rediscovered in excavations made by the Channel Four Time Team at Easter 1996 (Channel 4. Time Team. Jan 18 1997).

Soho Park Formerly lay S of Soho Hill on the old border with Warws. Soho Pool (see) and Shell Pool formed parts of this park; Shell Pool lay near to South Road. It was still in existence in the 1890s and was later filled in and the site built on with houses (HHHW pp9p,16p) (Kelly's Directory Map of Birmingham).

Soho Pool Pool in S part of Soho Park constructed in 1759 and used for power purposes for Ruston and Eaves and later for working machinery at Boulton & Watts Soho Factory. With the coming of steam power the pool was turned into a pleasure resort of 23 acres. By 1837 it was known as Knibbs Pool after a Mr Knibbs who had a cottage near the pool and who organised the pool facilities (HPPE p64) (HHHW p22p in 1868). The old county boundary went through it. Marked on Charles Henry Blood's map of Birmingham and its environs 1857. The pool was situated in the valley between what is now Soho and Park Roads, now (1984) the site of coal wharves, railway sidings, and offices (HPPE p64).

Soldiers' Hill Former burial mound, which seems to have been on or near Wombourne Common, 0.5m N of three other burial mounds on Wombourne Common. They were all noted by Dr Wilkes (d1760) and have been noted by others since. Soldiers' Hill seems to have also been called Battlestead Hill, and Battlefield Hill. Some have speculated that the mounds were thrown up to bury the dead after a battle in Roman or Anglo-Saxon times; some have thought the battle of Tettenhall and or Wednesfield took place here (SHOS vol 2 p211) (SVS p329) (GNHS p73) (TOS p80) (TB April 1982 p18).

Soles Hill Hill 1.5m N of Calton overlooks the Hamps. 1164 feet high.

Soles Hollow To E of Soles Hill.

Solomon's Hollow Hollow under 1m WNW of Thorncliffe. Formerly in Tittesworth township in Leek ancient parish. The hollow is deep but the stream is small (NSFCT 1908 p147). The hollow was formerly called Edge End Hollow (VCH vol 7 p235), and possibly took its present name from Solomon Ash who held land here in the C19 (HOLF p39). Another suggestion is: there is a Salomon's-born near Erfurt, Thuringia (Germany?), which is derived, by Krausse, from 'siol' a river root followed by the diminutive 'min' (NSFCT 1908 p147). It was here, according to an old tradition handed down by the Rudyerd (Rudyard) family, that Liulf of Aldredeslega (either Audley near Newcastle or Alderley near Leek) discovered his wife being adulterous with his kinsman Gamel of Tittesworth in the early C12. In his rage he killed Gamel, without giving him a chance to defend himself (ALC p74p). These names do appear in the Staffs Pipe Roll 1129-30 and Gustavus Sneyd thinks there may be some truth in the old tradition (OL pp178,179il-181).

Somerford Tiny hamlet by the Penk 1m E of Brewood. Former liberty of Brewood town in Brewood ancient parish and was included in Brewood prebend (SSAHST vol 2 1960-61 p43). Has appeared as Sumerford (1204) (SSE 1996 p17), and Somerford (c1275. 1346. 1603. 1723) (SPNO p39). In Celtic signifies the meeting of two brooks or rivers cymmere, summer or somer (SHOS vol 2 p306). If from Anglo-Saxon, then 'summer ford,' presumably because the Penk could only be forded here in summer (DUIGNAN) (SPN p23) (SSE 1996 p23). William de Somerford held Somerford manor in 1313 or 1314 by the service of finding a man with a horse worth half a mark and with a sack of hemp, to follow the lord for 40 days when there was war in Wales; by attendance at the lord's three-weekly courts; by presentation of a tithing man at the twice-yearly great courts of Brewood; and by the rent of four shillings a year (VCH vol 5 p34). At approximately SJ 899089 was a mill, which was recorded on the 1817 OS map (WBJ p15).

Somerford Area W of Willenhall, near Portobello. The name, which has also appeared as Summerford, is preserved in the road Summerford Place or Somerford Place. It is certainly a reference to a ford in the stream here, but

probably not a ford only used in summer. The original form may be Stoniford. This may have been corrupted to Stomfords by the error of a clerk; a 'Stomfords Lone' appears in 1371. In turn this form may have been corrupted to Somerford (WA vol 2 p91 note) (HOWI pp186-187). Or the name may be from Somerford (see), Brewood (SNW p64).

Somerford Bridge Formerly Stone Bridge. Carries the road from Brewood to Four Ashes over the Penk. Is recorded in 1605 (VCH vol 5 p19).

Somerford Grange Somerford, Brewood. Tall house in the neo-Gothick style, similar to Speedwell Castle. Said to have built as an eyecatcher for Somerford Hall by George Barbor some time after 1761 (VCH vol 5 pp24-25) (BOE p239) (NSJFS 1976 fig 8 facing p43. p45). Has the appearance of a folly (SGS p67) (F p307). In the late C18 Shaw writes of Somerford Hall Grange and the large drawing room on the left side being the old part erected by Mr Barber (SHOS vol 2 p306 pls).

Somerford Hall House S of Somerford 1m ESE of Brewood. The Somerford family lived at the old hall(s) from the C13 to 1705. Seat of Sir Walter Wrottesley of Wrottesley by 1707 to his death in 1712. The estate was bought by Robert Barbor of the Inner Temple in 1734. He built the present hall in the second quarter of the C18. The estate passed, probably in 1779, to the Hon Edward Monckton (VCH vol 5 p35), a younger son of Viscount Galway in Ireland (W p447). Edward altered much of the building in the late C18 (VCH vol 5 p35 il of in 1820 facing). The hall was the seat of the Moncktons until 1845 when they moved to Stretton Hall (VB p78) (SGS p67). After the death of George Monckton in 1858 the hall was held by tenants until at least 1928, but it was unoccupied in 1932 and 1940. It was converted into flats in c1945 (VCH vol 5 p35). (BOE p239). The dovecote built in Robert Barbor's time is incorporated into a range adjoining the house on the W (VCH vol 5 p35) (info Phil Williams).

Songles, The Residence of James Leggeye, a French glassmaker, and Judeth Tyzake who he married according to Eccleshall PR. On Fairoak Grange (farm) are some fields called 'the Songes,' near Hookgate (Songles meaning the fields where ears of corn are gleaned according to New Oxford Dictionary) (NSFCT 1930 p146. 1933 pp92,97).

Sotshole Former coalmining district just W of Great Bloxwich (SOB pp59,124), close to Bloxwich centre (W p649) and at end of Station Street (SNBP p54). In Walsall ancient parish. The name, which appears on the 1834 OS map and has appeared as Sots Hole, no longer prevails.

Sot's Hole Small area of West Bromwich (OWB p43). Said to be so called after a Richard Reeves, whose nickname was 'Old Sot,' who kept an inn situated in the hollow of Dagger Lane which was called 'The Bear and Ragged Staff' during the period 1719-69 (SHWB 13) (SOWB p24). Has also been called Sinkh or Sink Hole (OWB p43), and Sinkhole has also been called Bird End (see). The Sot's Hole area seems to have become known as Church Vale (see) (VCH vol 17 p4).

Sot's Hole Shown on a map of 1774 as a tiny settlement in High Street, Amblecote, between what became Vicarage Road and the former gas works. There is no reference to Sot's Hole in LO Davies' 1853 Survey of Amblecote (SNSV vol 1 p305. vol 2 p22).

South Gate Defensive stone gateway in SE section of the wall surrounding Lichfield cathedral Close. It lead out on to Dam Street. Built after c1300, or perhaps after Edward II ordered the Close to be securely defended on his behalf in 1317 and 1322 (MCC). It was far greater in size and strength than the West Gate, the other main gateway to the Close. The south gateway had two towers. It was built by Bishop Langton and taken down in the time of Dean Addenbroke in the mid C18 (HOL p295) (Fuller's Church History. Book iv. p174) (W p500) (VCH vol 3 p189. vol 14 p60). The base of one has recently been revealed in the garden of St Mary's House after excavation. Bishop Hacket's stables, which became the Diocesan Registry and Muniment Rooms and now a Visitors Study Centre covers the site of the other tower (GKCLC).

South Gate Medieval gateway in the wall surrounding Stafford, on the S side. It stood between Mill Bank and Back Walls South slightly to the N of Green Bridge and the Sow, at the junction of Greengate and Bridge Streets, Backwalls South, and Mill Bank (SIOT p89). It commanded the crossing over the Sow and was not as strongly fortified as the North Gate, since, before it, lay marshy land (SSTY p2). South Gate was known as such by the late C14 and known as the Green Gate by 1612. Both names were still in use in 1674 (VCH vol 6 p199). The road through the gate led out onto the Green or Stafford Green. The gate was taken down in 1777 (SKYT p49) (VCH vol 6 p199) or 1780 (W p325) (SIOT p89). Richard Whitworth of Batchacre claimed that the demolition was carried out on his initiative 'to make a noble opening at the entrance of the town.' Between 1804-1807 he converted adjacent premises to the SE into Castle Whitworth (see) (VCH vol 6 p199). (LGS p213) (SOSH p148) (OSST 1933 p46) (SOPP pl 26) (ROT p40).

South Low Wednesfield. This burial mound, North Low and others, reputedly contained some of the dead from one of the battles which took place about the year 907 to 911 at Tettenhall (see) and or at Wednesfield. According to Plot South Low still existed in the later C17 (NHS p415). Shaw says South Low lay near Mr Hope's Windmill (SHOS vol 2 p150); probably the mill on Mill Hill (see). Willmore says South Low probably lay in South Low Field (HOWW p30), an open field of Wednesfield, was the same as that called Windmill Field (WFW p51). (SVS p332) (W p157) (S&W p177) (SC p148) (AOW p7; says Huntbach and Duignan notes them) (NSJFS 1965 p59).

Southlow Tiny hamlet on high undulating ground near the head of a tributary of Endon Brook 0.75m SSW of Wetley Rocks, in Cheddleton ancient parish. The ring burial mound of this name is opposite to the entrance to Wetley Manor at SJ 955484 by Little Southlow Farm. TE Moore and JD Johnstone excavated it in 1936 but found neither charcoal nor flint (CVH p18). It was described as in good condition in 1983 (NSFCT 1936 p73. 1983 p12) (WJ p28).

Southlow Manor Southlow. House originally built to be a public house to serve two pits which were to be developed on the Cheadle Road opposite Consall Lane end in the late C19. Neither the pits nor the inn came to fruition (CVH p188).

South Street Old track which ran over Cannock Chase from Cannock to Rugeley (NSFCT 1908). Is marked on current maps SW of Wolseley Park (PCC pp61,64). Has also appeared as Sow Street (OS map 1:25,000). The Roman road leading down to a ford in the Trent at or towards Colwich is called South Street (SHC 1914 p136 note).

Southwell A Southwell house and farm S of Stafford Street, Eccleshall (1889 OS map 6 inch). The name is also a modern road called Southwell Estate to the S.

Sovereign Lane Lane in Ashley. The name commemorates a visit to the area by James I (VB p160).

Sow, River Tributary of the Trent. Rises on rough land to N of Fairoak Grange (BOV p98), over 0.75m W of Broughton. The river is approximately 17m in length. An Iron Age spindle whorl of millstone grit was found in a meadow by the upper reaches of the river (NSFCT 1959 p86). Has appeared as Sowa (1118), Stouue (c1130), Sowe (c1174-1699), Sovve (1401), Sow (c1540. Saxton's map) (SPNO pp18-19), and Sore (1698) (Illustrated Journeys of Celia Fiennes edited by Chris Morris. 1984. p147). The name is of Celtic origin (CCC p8) (SDW p9). The Cent(ury?) (enary?) Dictionary assumes 'sough' to be of Norse origin (DUIGNAN). It is from a Celtic root 'sab' 'sa' or 'sua' water (NSFCT 1908 pp130-131. 1916 pp55-59). Or derived from the Gaulish word 'seu' meaning 'to flow, liquid' (ROT p3) (SPN p108). Ekwall has claimed that Sow is the British river name, derived from British Souo (RN ppp375-376). K Jackson in Language and History in Early Britain (1953), disputes this. Oakden is unsure (SPNO p19). The Sow drove the fulling mills between Outlands and Cop Mere. It provided the water for the moat around Eccleshall Castle. Chebsey is situated on the Sow. Meece Brook flows into it S of Shallowford. It drove Worston Mill. Stafford is situated on it. The Penk flows into it N of Baswich. It flowed through Shugborough Park. After the floods of 1795 a new cut was made at Shugborough by Thomas Anson. It is 0.5m long and runs to the N of the old course. After the construction of the new course the old course then became an ornamental feature in the grounds of Shugborough. On the island created by the two cuts stands the Cat Monument (SNTG p80) (ROT pp58-59). Just below Essex Bridge the Sow flows into the Trent. In the later C17 Plot noted the Trent was more rapid than the Sow, but it was more rapid than the Penk (NHS p43). (GNHS p17) (ROT).

Sowe A manor containing some of the Fowler lands. Formerly used to comprise part of what was occasionally called the manor of Baswich (VCH vol 5 p5).

Spade Green 0.5m W of Pipe Hall, 1m S of Farewell. Partly in Farewell parish and in an out-township of St Michael's parish, Lichfield. The area around Spade Green was known as Childerend Pipe in the late C13 and Childerhay End in the later C16 (VCH vol 14 p198). Spade Green was mentioned in 1538 and was an inhabited area by 1690 (VCH vol 14 p202). Thirteen poplar trees were planted at Spade Green to commemorate the battle of Waterloo (1815); the last was cut down in 1930 (Lichfield Mercury Feb 7 1930 p5) (VCH vol 14 p202).

Span Approximate position is Gallows Green, Alton (Plot's map). Lost.

Spanton's Bank A bluff by Parkfields, Barlaston.

Sparrowlee On a stretch of Manifold Valley. In Waterfall parish (W p787). There was a station on the Manifold Valley Light Railway at Sparrowlee (HLS p44).

Sparrow Park Former cattle market area at Leek in front of the Talbot Inn (formerly the Spread Eagle). In 1874 the cattle market moved away from Sparrow Park to Smithfield Cattle Market, a site bounded by Ashbourne Road and Haywood and Leonard Streets (this area became the bus station after 1960). Sparrow Park is now occupied by the Nicholson War Memorial (HLSP pp91-92).

Sparrow's End Brewood. It may take its name from Sparrow's Cottage mentioned in 1829 (BDH p224). Sparrows End Lane is on the SE side of Brewood leading to Tinkers Lane.

Sparrows Forge Lane Former lane in the Wednesbury-Darlaston area. The name is from probably a forge called Sparrows. There is a Swallows, or should not it be Sparrows, Close off Wood Green Road. An old lady of Old Park Road saw on a New Year's eve the ghost of a man in this lane. He was wearing light-coloured breeches, dark coat with tails and top hat with a curled brim of the 1830s period (TB Dec 1983 p23. Jan 1984 p11).

Spath Tiny hamlet on low ground near the Tean backed by rising ground 0.5m SE of Stramshall, in Uttoxeter ancient parish. Mary Blood of Spath is said to have been the last person baptized at Crakemarsh church. She died a few years prior to 1865, aged 106 (HOU p244).

Spaw Spring Springfield, Wolverhampton. Has also appeared as Spa Well. In the later C17 Plot wrote of a spring in a narrow lane about midway between Wolverhampton and Sea Wall (Showell) called the Spaw, which anciently had a reputation for curing eye diseases (NHS p106) (AOW p94), perhaps this is similar or the same as a spring called Culwell (see). Shaw wrote Spa Well (or otherwise Seawall) was nothing to do with Cull Well (SHOS vol 2 p165). The boundaries of Wolverhampton, Bushbury, and Wednesbury meet at Spa Well (HOWM p2).

Spear Hill By Boley, Lichfield, on route of the perambulation of the City boundary (HOL p357). In the 1570s it was claimed that Boley and Spear Hill alluded to the bows and spears used in the massacre of Christians at Lichfield in the reign of Diocletian. According to Gelling Spear Hill is probably derived from the felling of wood for spear-shafts or from a surname (VCH vol 14 p38 note).

Spectacles, The Ponds S of Aqualate Mere. The 'black-lakes near Aqualat' frequented by avocets according to Plot (NHS p231) may have been the Spectacles (WSS p111).

Speedwell Castle Brick town house in Market Place, Brewood, facing the end of Stafford Street. The house was built in c1750 in the neo-Gothick style which has been described as Carpenters' Gothic. Has the appearance of a folly and was built by local apothecary, William Rock, d1753, on a whim out of proceeds of betting on 'Speedwell,' the Duke of Boulton's horse - the horse is featured in John Cherry's 'Portraiture of horses' (1740). The house has been known as Lantern House (E&S: On The Map p3 June 20 1997) and was known as Castle Flats by 1959 (VCH vol 5 p23 p facing p24). (DoE I) (LGS p91) (VB pp39p,78) (BOE p78 pl 44) (SL p134) (NSJFS 1976 fig 4. fig 5 of a detail of Chinese Chippendale staircase. pp43-44) (SGS p66,p) (SVB p42) (F p307pc) (BDH pp182-184p) (COS p69p).

Spellow Meeting place for the people of Alrewas in Saxon times within the water triangle - could be between the Tame, Trent and Mease? The name still exists in field names along Croxall Road - Wet Spellow, Dry Spellow, Wiggespellow (HOA pp13,14).

Sphinx Rock Rock feature which has the appearance of a sphinx, on Ramshaw Rocks (ES July 5 1968 p14p). Situated behind Lady Rock Farm.

Spicers Stock Wednesbury. In 1728 the lane now called Ladbury's Lane (unlocated) was described as leading from High Bullen to 'Spicers Stock' or Spicers Stock Street (WAM p53).

Spicers Stone 1m NE of Cheddleton (Dower's map) (OS map 1:25,000).

Spill Meadow Inhabited area of Upper Gornal in 1901 (OS map sheet 67.07). The name is preserved in the street Spills Meadows on the N side of Kent Street.

Spion Kop Wood near Hoar Cross planted during the Boer War and named after the place in South Africa where a battle was fought in that war (SVB p96).

Spinners End Former hamlet on Cradley Heath. The name has also appeared as Spinner's End (BCWJ p101) and appears in the 1851 census. Flemish spinners are said to have settled here after the St Bartholomew troubles on the Continent (BCWJ p101). Sometime after 1901 the street of this name was renamed Upper High Street (OS map sheet 71.08). Spinners End gave its name to a railway depot at the end of a very short branch line, slightly N of Cradley Heath (VCH vol 2 pp310 see map,325). Spinners End is apparently an alternative name for the Reddal Hill area of Cradley Heath (TB Dec 1997 p27).

Spirit Hole Area of Cradley Park, Cradley. Reputedly so called after a courting couple were frightened here by a bloodstained ghost in about the C18 (TB March 1996 p5).

Spital A ward of Tamworth borough by at least 1993, covering the area of north Tamworth, N of the railway and W of the Anker.

Spite Hall Large cottage near Horton Lodge, N of Rudyard, on W side of Rudyard

Lake. Built in c1865 a few yards away from Rudyard Villa and said to have been built to ruin the prospect of Rudyard Lake for the owner of Rudyard Villa. Formerly, the cottage had a barn-like appearance and was decorated with ugly gargoyles pulling out their tongues in the direction of Rudyard Villa. Some are now (1988) lost (SVB p144) whilst some are now (1997) in the rockery in the garden (RL p27). It is unknown who erected the cottage, formerly called Keepers Cottage. According to some as the land adjacent to the villa did not form part of the same estate the villa owner was just unable to stop the cottage's construction. Another story tells of two warring brothers who quarrelled over a beautiful old tree in the grounds of the villa which obstructed the view of the lake. When the brother who owned the villa cut the tree down his brother built the cottage to ruin the view. It became a tea room from 1873 and also served as a guest house from the 1890s (RL pp27,29,38il, p).

Spittal Brook Runs in the Checkhill area, Kinver, and joins Smestow Brook at Gothersley. The name may be from the Hospitallers who were granted land in Kinver parish in 1189 (VCH vol 20 p137).

Spittal Brook Brook and former name for Queensville, Stafford. The Spittal Brook area was renamed Queensville in 1838 to commemorate Queen Victoria's coronation. The brook formed the southern boundary of Forebridge and crossed under the Lichfield road at this point (VCH vol 6 p194). The name, which formerly appeared as Spital Brook (SAC p149), is probably from St Leonard's Hospital, which was situated in this area in medieval times.

Spittal House Ancient two-cell chapel 1m N of Tamworth, in Wigginton Road. Said to be the Hospital of St James or a chapel attached to the hospital, or after being the hospital became a chapel. Dent and Hill say it is probably the Sanatorium built in 1345 during a plaque which killed a third of Tamworth's population. It may have been used afterwards as a hospital by the Guild of St George or another semi-religious brotherhood (HS p177p of before restoration). Gould says it is of Norman origin, rebuilt anew before 1274, and functioned as the hospital (not a part of it) for a very short time, if at all, then used as a chantry until the Reformation. In 1534 it was called a free chapel. By 1550 the chantry was closed and the property sold. It served as a barn in the C18 and then a cottage before falling into ruins. The Guild of St Albans bought the chapel, also known as Spital Chapel and The Spital, intending to set up a College of St James here. In 1906 it was bought by Dr Joy. A restoration appeal ensued. HC Mitchell claimed to have restored it in 1909 but it was not until 1914 that the W wall was encased and a fire-place removed and it was reopened for worship (SSAHST 1968 pp23-31 plan) as the mission church, St Peter (LDD). (SHOS vol 1 p430) (NSFCT 1906 p147. 1922 p168) (Archaeological Journal 1908 vol 65) (LGS p230) (OSST 1949-50 p13). Excavations in July 1968 failed to find any traces of earlier structures, but an illicit medieval burial was found (SSAHST 1968 p23). (TH Sept 5 1914) (THM vol 4 p4, 72ps, 103 sketches, 104,105,107) (BOE p277).

Spittleford Brook Tributary of the Meese Brook. Has appeared as Spittleford Brook (1731) (SPNO p19).

Spittle Brook Tributary of the Smestow. Has appeared as Spittel broc (1300), Spitelbrook (1342), and Spittell brooke (1609). The name is from a hospital or religious house (SPNO p19). It is perhaps identifiable with Spittal Brook in the Checkhill area.

Spittles Former estate and the name for an area of Newcastle-under-Lyme about the junction of Newcastle Lane and Newcastle Road to at least 1849, W of Penkhull (VCH vol 8 p188) (CAST p11). Has also appeared as The Spittal (W p223). The name is from a medieval hospital in this area called St Eloy's Hospital (see); its land may have comprised the estate called the Spittles in existence by 1653 to at least 1834 (VCH vol 8 p188) (CAST p11).

Spittles Brook, The Penkhull (NSFCT 1910 p165).

Spode Factory Church Street, formerly High Street, Stoke-upon-Trent. Formerly known as Turner's Works when run by John Turner. From 1762 the young Josiah Spode I was a manager here. In 1770 he bought the works and became the sole owner in 1777. Josiah Spode II became potter to the Prince of Wales in 1806. Josiah Spode III succeeded in 1827 but died in 1829. In 1833 Spode's executors sold the firm to his partner William Taylor Copeland. Since 1932 his firm, which has worked here ever since, has been styled WT Copeland and Sons Ltd. The ware they make is often known as Spode ware. The original ranges facing Church Street were demolished in 1938. Copeland's have another site facing City Road, often referred to as Copeland Pottery or Works (IANS p147). (HSP pp215-221) (SLM April 1951 p19p - Early Spode china) (VCH vol 8 p203) (NSJFS 1965 p89) (Spode. A History of the family, factory and wares 1733-1833. L White (The Story of Spode. G Bernard Hughes) (POP pp75-76) (AGT pp56,151il) (AA p258). In the principal corridor at Buckingham Palace are some of the Chinese Porcelain pagodas supported on enamelled pedestals made by WT Copeland in bone china and

fitted with ormolu pedestals as well as other Staffordshire ware (SLM June 1953 p12p). Prince Charles visited Spode factory on March 3 1998 (ES March 3 1998 p13). A ghost reputedly haunts the works (ES March 8 1967) (GOT p141).

Spode House Present name for a hall 0.75m W of Armitage, formerly called Armitage Park (see). In 1859 Josiah Spode IV, son of Mary and Josiah Spode III, renamed Armitage Park Hawkesyard. He converted to Catholicism and left it to the Dominican Order after his death (1893). The Dominicans built a house Hawkesyard Priory (see) on a site above the hall between 1896-1914. On completion of the priory Hawkesyard was occupied by a series of schools (VCH vol 3 p115). In 1924 the Dominican school for boys was moved to Laxton Hall, Northants, and was succeeded by a succession of preparatory schools conducted by Catholic laymen independent of the priory; a Mr Stafford-Northcote moving the last such school to Bishton Hall after WW2 (LTM Dec 1972 p36). The house then became a youth centre and was renamed Spode House. In 1954 it became a conference centre. When the Dominicans left Hawkesyard Priory in 1967 the Priory also became a part of the conference centre. The whole Spode House centre was closed in 1987 (VCH vol 3 p115) (LTM Dec 1972 pp33,36) (SVB p19) (HOS 1998 p60).

Spon Area named Spon in the S of West Bromwich ancient parish existed by 1344 when William atte Sponne held land in West Bromwich (VCH vol 17 p9). Spon Brook occurs in 1585, Spon Heath in 1633, Spon Coppice in 1695 and Spon Lane in 1694. The name is from possibly a holy well called Spon Well, thought to have stood where the celebrated Spon Lane pump stood 1840-1890. Spon is from 'Spona' a splinter of the supposed cross of Jesus Christ brought back from the Holy Land in the Crusades and set over the well (OWB p34) (SOWB p24). Or from the Spon family (SOWB p24).

SPON LANE. Runs from West Bromwich ancient parish in the N to Harborne ancient parish in the S (W pp681,704). By the later C18 the area of **Spon Lane in West Bromwich parish** was one of the most populous parts of that parish. There was much settlement along Spon Lane itself, particularly the eastern side, and eastwards along the Birmingham road. The Salters family, bayonet and light spring makers, built their first works in the Birmingham road area in the 1770s. In the early 1790s Archibald Kenrick built a foundry E of Spon Lane Bridge. By 1798 there was a brassworks between Kenrick's foundry and Spon Lane. In the 1790s John Houghton, clerk to the Birmingham Canal Company, was building Houghton Street and a canal wharf on the Birmingham Canal. William Bullock opened a foundry W of Spon Lane in 1805. Samuel Kenrick opened the Summit Foundry to the E of Archibald Kenrick's works in 1830. To the E of Spon Lane Kenrick's Village (see) had been built by 1837, and an area of it was known locally as Monkey Green (see) (VCH vol 17 pp9,10). Spon Lane became a ward of West Bromwich borough, when created in 1882 (VCH vol 17 p46). The Rusty Lane of JB Priestley's 'English Journey,' (1933) a book describing a journey he made through England in the autumn 1933, is Grice Street on the W side of Spon Lane (VCH vol 17 p10). Of Rusty Lane Priestley says 'I have never seen such a picture of grimy desolation as that street offered me....The whole neighbourhood is mean and squalid, but this particular street seemed the worst of all.' On the W side of the S end of **Spon Lane in Harborne parish** Chance Brothers and Co's operated their huge glass works (see under Smethwick) from the late 1820s. The Birmingham, Wolverhampton & Stour Valley Railway, opened in 1852, had a station in Spon Lane in the Harborne parish. It closed in 1964 (VCH vol 17 pp14,91-92). (O p19).

Spond, The Farm over 0.5m SSW of Alton. In Alton ancient parish. Has appeared as Sponne (1271), Sponberne (1372), and Spon (1642). The first mention of a farm here is in 1573 (HAF pp202-205).

Spon Drumble Glen through which Fradswell Brook runs S of Coton Hayes.

Spon Lane Branch of Titford Canal. Spurs off Titford Canal at Engine Street, Tat Bank. Runs to Rood End (HCMS No. 2).

Spon Lane Junction Canal junction to the W of Spon Lane under the M5. It was originally the junction of the Wednesbury Branch of the Birmingham Canal with Brindley's Birmingham Canal Old Main Line. After Telford had built the New Main Line in 1829 and had amalgamated the last couple of miles of the Wednesbury Branch into it it became a New Main Line Old Main Line junction; the other being to the W at Bromford Junction (Galton Valley. A Walkers Guide. Sandwell Metropolitan Borough Council. 1993).

Spot, The Part of Clayhanger Common, near Brownhills, was known as The Spot. The name is preserved in Spot Lane (SNBC p20).

Spot, The By Spot Farm 1m NNW of Hilderstone. In Kibblestone township and quarter in Stone ancient parish (W p364). By 1872 it was situated in Moddershall township (KD 1872).

Spot Acre Tiny hamlet on a high ridge overlooking Sale Brook dell and in the far distance the Trent Valley, 1.75m NNW of Hilderstone, in Kibblestone quarter in Stone ancient parish (W p371). There was said to be a hospice in the Spot area (SIS p13) built in the C7 and connected with Stone Priory (NSFCT 1910 p161) or a hospice built in about the C13 by the Knights of St John at Keele (STM Nov 1965 p39) or connected with Burton Abbey and its founder Wulfric Spot (IHOBT p5). In old deeds it is 'le spot grange.' The name may be from Wulfric Spot founder of Burton Abbey (SIS p13) and or he may have taken his own name from the land here called Spot (SOK p11). Or Spot is a corruption of the Latin 'hospitum' through the Celtic 'yspytty' (NSFCT 1910 p161). Or, thinks G Harnaman, a corruption of 'Spittals' or Spittles.' He thinks Acre was from Acre in Palestine the headquarters of the Knights of St John of Keele (STM Nov 1965 p39).

Spot Grange House 0.75m NNW of Hilderstone. In Kibblestone township and quarter in Stone ancient parish. By 1872 was in Moddershall township (KD 1872). In the later C17 Plot noted at Spot Grange a spring which ran if there was to be a drought or dearth, having not run for three or four years previously (NHS p49). Francis Beardmore of Spot Grange was the author of a treatise on the management of horses etc (1832) (BS p50). Foot-and-mouth disease broke out at Spot Grange Farm in early 1968 (SN Jan 26 1968 p13).

Spot Lane Lane from Hilderstone school, Hilderstone to the Spot, now called Hilderstone Road. A boggart has been seen by the bridge over the brook close to Hilderstone in Spot Lane (NSFCT 1900 pp144,146) (FOS p18) (SCS p6) (PHH p18).

Spout, The A well or spring (SVB p49) at Butterton (Newcastle-under-Lyme).

Spout, The Spring at Spout House, Cotwall End (AMS p445).

Spout Hall St Edward Street, Leek (SMOPP vol 2). The old hall was the seat of Francis Needham in the C16 (OL vol 1 p281). The present house was designed by Norman Shaw in 1871 (BOE p172 note) and built for Hugh Sleigh (d1901) in 1873 (VCH vol 7 p96).

Spout House House 0.5m NNW of Consall.

Spouthouse The name of this farm is preserved in Spouthouse Lane, running between Walsall Road and Hamstead Road, Hamstead. Formerly in Perry Barr township. The name is from a spout to which spring water was piped for convenience (MNB pp62,66). Spout is marked on the maps of Morden and Plot.

Spout House, The Taylors Lane, Smethwick. It was at one time known as the Spread Eagle Inn. Demolished in 1937 (SMEOP p47p).

Spout Water Brook running through Leek. Runs down what is now Brook Street (formerly Spout Lane) and the N side of Broad Street. The brook may have given its name to Leek (VCH vol 7 p84).

Spragg House Spragg House Lane, Norton-in-the-Moors. Has an iron grille of c1840 the occupants erected to protect themselves at night from Chartist rioters. It seals off the upstairs from the ground floor and is placed across the banisters (STM June 1966 p21p).

Spratslade Former hamlet in Blurton chapelry in Trentham ancient parish (W p433). The name is preserved in Spratslade Drive in Dresden. Evidently the hamlet was important enough for a police station to be situated here, for it is mentioned in a letter from Mr Steward to Mr Loch, land agent of Trentham Hall, dated 16 Aug 1842, the time of the Chartist riots (info Rose Wheat).

Spread Eagle Former name of Gailey hamlet, in Water Eaton liberty in Penkridge ancient parish (W p468). The site of the Roman settlement known as Pennocrucium has thought to be at or near the old Spread Eagle Inn (Roman Roads in Britain. Codrington. p79) (SHC 1916 p321), but its true site has since been discovered further W, astriding Watling Street. Gailey was an alternative name for the hamlet by 1834 (VCH vol 5 p104). The railway station here on old LNWR line or GJR was called Spread Eagle when it first opened in 1837; it was renamed Gailey in Aug 1881. It closed in 1951 (SA June 17 1837) (CWF p11 note) (NSJFS 1967 pp46,55) (Railways In and Around Stafford. Edward Talbot. 1994 p4). An hotel called the Spreadeagle stood at the crossing of the A449 with Watling Street until it was rebuilt away from the junction during the conversion of the A449 to a dual carriageway in the 1930s (Gailey Crossroads in the 1920s. Alex Chatwin. c1995) (SHJ spring 1995 p17).

Spreading Tree Hill On other side of A38 from Canwell.

Spring Bank District of Willenhall, 0.5m NE of Willenhall. Formerly in Willenhall chapelry in Wolverhampton ancient parish. The area became a separate ecclesiastical parish known as 'Willenhall St Ann' in 1860 (GLAUE p429). The church, St Anne, Ann Street, was built in 1856-1858 (BOE p312).

Spring Coppice Former wood N of the Stour, at the S end of Coppice Road, Hayseech. The name is preserved in Spring Crescent (SNSV vol 2 p20).

Spring Croft There is a County primary school called this at Blythe Bridge (Stoke-on-Trent A-Z).

Springfield District of Rowley Regis covering the lower half of the W side of Turner's Hill, 1m NW of Rowley Regis. In Rowley Regis parish. Here, up to

the C18, there existed a holy well. The water was reputed to be good for eyes (BCWJ p115). Here is Bullfield Farm (see). Presumably near Bullfield Bridge.

Springfield N of Sedgley are streets called Springfield Grove, Garden, Avenue situated on W slopes of Beacon Hill.

Springfield District of Wolverhampton on upland near the source of the Smestow, 0.75m ENE of Wolverhampton, formerly in Wolverhampton chapelry and ancient parish. Springfield Estate, built in the late 1870s, centred on Culwell Street. It was planned by Wolverhampton council to rehouse people from the centre of Wolverhampton under the Artisans' Dwelling Scheme of the 1870s. Of the 290 planned houses only 75 were built by 1880 (WHTOP p128p). The church, St Barnabas, was built in 1892-1893 (BOE p321) on the N side of Wednesfield Road after Springfield Road. It became the New Testament Church of God in the 1960s (info Rev French). The church, St Stephen, Hilton Street, was built in 1907-1909 (BOE p321).

Springfield Cottage Stood in Walsall Road, Darlaston (Offlow hundred), immediately adjacent to Well Street. The supermarket (in 1993) nearby, was formerly called Springfield House and there is also a Springfield Tavern in the area. The name is from a spring near the tavern (SNDB p95).

Springfield Farm Stood on the N side of Springfield Lane, Ford Houses, Bushbury (BUOP p26p).

Springfield House Springfield House or Hall is situated on N side of Oaken Drive, 0.25m NE of Oaken, Codsall, by the Staffs Way (TSW p67). Witches' Cottage in Oaken Drive, between Oaken and Codsall, is the local name for the lower lodge to the house. It was built in c1850 (TCOP p148p).

Springfields Tiny hamlet by Meece Brook, also known as Springfield, 1m N of Chapel Chorlton. Here is an old stone mill unusual in design rebuilt by the Duke of Sutherland. Long undiscovered, only listed in 1987 (MR p87p). The name Springfield Hall, Chapel Chorlton, can be found on a gravestone in Whitmore churchyard.

Springfields Old mansion situated at the N end and on the W side of Roebuck Lane, West Bromwich. Seat of Archibald Kenrick, ironmaster, by 1795. After his death in 1835 his son Archibald lived here. It was probably rebuilt about this time. In the 1850s it was the seat of W Bullock, ironmaster. By at least c1860 to c1906 it belonged to the Salters family. In 1970 it was the social club of G Salter & Co Ltd (Kenricks in Hardware. RA Church. 1969. p28) (VCH vol 17 p10) (HPPE p109).

Springfields District of Newcastle nearly 0.75m SW of Penkhull. Formerly in Stoke-upon-Trent chapelry and ancient parish. In the vicinity of Spring Fields and Trent Vale was a Roman fort (POP p90). There was settlement at Springfields or Spring Field in existence by 1775 (VCH vol 8 p176). The first police surgery held in a supermarket in the country was held by PC Neil Russell at Tesco supermarket, Newcastle Road, on Oct 2 1998 between 9.00am and 11.00am (ES Oct 1 1998 p3p) (BBC Radio 4. You and Yours. Oct 2 1998). Springfields Hotel and the area about it is reputedly haunted (Real Ale in & around the Potteries. CAMRA p72) by a monk (TFTP pp206-207). The ghost of a cowled figure which haunts Clayton Lane and Springfields has been seen by every member of a particular family (SFH pp19,21).

Springfields Estate Housing estate on the outskirts of Rugeley, between the town and Etching Hill (VB p118).

Springfields Hall Springfield, Stramshall. Seat of W Phillips in 1851 (W pp23,792).

Springfields House Georgian brick house on the W side of the Newcastle Road, Springfields, Newcastle-under-Lyme. The house was an inn known as the Springfields Hotel by at least the early 1990s. In 1998 there were plans to demolish the inn and build a larger inn on the site (ES March 14 1998 p13p). Has a secret passage in which was found an old sword - something to do with Newcastle Castle (TFTP p205). For the ghost which reputedly haunts the house see under Springfields.

Spring Field Spring At foot of Etruria 'Woods,' which were just beyond the foot of Basford Bank. At the foot of the woods there was a sharp bend then right to Wolstanton (HOE p324).

Spring Head Spring which has a basin in Biddulph Grange gardens in 'China' 15 metres SW of the 'Great Wall of China' (DoE II survey made in 1984).

Spring Head Spring which has a basin on W side of Overton Road 10 metres N of the the gates to Biddulph Grange. Is of early to mid C19 and neo-Norman in style (DoE II).

Spring Head Spring which has a basin and cover at Thorncliffe, is of the late C18 (DoE II)

Spring Head Wolverhampton Road, Sedgley. Spring which has been described as a source of the Tame which came from under Sedgley Hill (PHS p18); is perhaps AE Underhill's Spring Well (AMS p445).

Spring Hill Hill at Brocton Field, slightly N of Womere, on W side of the Chase, 2m SE of Brocton, on Cannock Chase. The hill here (SJ 980181) is unnamed on OS maps and its name is uncertain; it may be called Spring Hill or Chase Hill. It is 637 feet high. It was originally topped by a water tower for the WW1 Brocton Army Camp. Still in the ground are the concrete post holes for it. A glacial boulder on a cairn of stones is situated on the site of the water tower. The boulder had two plates bolted onto it. The smaller of the plates probably bore an inscription telling the history of the boulder. Another, of disc shape on the top side, was probably a viewpoint finder. The boulder was found in Brocton quarry and had been carried from SW Scotland in the Ice Age (STMSM Nov 1972 p41) (SVB p44) (TSW p54). According to the Friends of Cannock Chase the same or another granite boulder, weighing three tons, was found in a gravel pit in WW2. In 1949 it was placed on the top of Pudding Hill until it was moved to Spring Hill or Chase Hill on Nov 14 1954 (SN Sept 10 1949 p7. Sept 17 1949 p5. Nov 20 1954 p8p. Aug 22 1959 p14p) (PCC p89il). Another account says the boulder was set up here to commemorate Lord Lichfield's gift of 1,784 acres of chase to the public in 1956 (WMAG Feb 1968 p15p). There was no boulder on the top of the Spring Hill at the N end of the Chase in 1996, so it is presumed this hill is meant by the Friends of Cannock Chase, although the boulder may have stood on that hill from 1954 until being moved to this hill in 1956. Some remains of concrete sleepers for the railway which carried stores to the WW1 Brocton Army Camp can still be found in the vicinity (info Bruce Braithwaite). Slightly to the S is a triangulation pillar.

Spring Hill Hill at N end of Cannock Chase, N of Pudding Hill, over 1.75m NNE of Brocton or 0.5m SE of Milford, at SJ 976207. Is 675 feet high and topped with a 'saucer' burial mound known as The Bury (see). It was on the top of this hill that the Friends of Cannock Chase placed a granite boulder on Nov 14 1954, removed from the top of Pudding Hill (PCC p89il). But no boulder can now (1996) be found here. See entry above.

Springhill Fragmented tiny hamlet on Ryknild Street 1.25m S of Hammerwich. Formerly in St Michael's parish, Lichfield.

Springhill Modern hamlet on either side of B4210, 1m NE of Essington.

Spring Hill Outliner hill of the larger Penn Hill, and a suburb of Wolverhampton, over 0.5m WNW of Upper Penn. Formerly in Penn ancient parish. The Spring Hill area was developed with housing in the mid 1930s (PENOP p91p). In Warstones Crescent in 1969 remained a pillar box with the cypher of the uncrowned Edward VIII (WMAG Feb 1969 p21p).

Spring Hill Walsall. There was a windmill at Spring Hill, built, according to the maps of Yates, between 1775 and 1799. It existed in 1816 but probably disappeared soon after (VCH vol 17 p186). It stood at SP 023977, 0.75m SE of Walsall (WBJ p42). Closer to the town centre on either side of Birmingham Road stood two houses, Spring Hill House (on W side), and Springhill (on E side) (VCH vol 17 pp148 see map, 154).

Springhill House Springhill Lane? Lower Penn. At some time occupied by Edward Bagnall Thorneycroft (PAIP p52).

Spring Hill House House in Jesson Road, Walsall. Existed by 1813 as Springfield, the home of Richard Jesson, an attorney (VCH vol 17 p154). It was occupied by the Jesson family and once known as Parchment Hall (SNWA p78), and possibly also once known as Cheat Hall (SNWA p29). Now stands in the part of Jesson Road now occupied by St Mary's RC school (VCH vol 17 p154).

Springpool Wood Wood 1m SE of Keele.

Spring Slade Dell, Pool, and Lodge on W side of Cannock Chase 1.5m ESE of Bednall, in the former Teddesley Hay extra parochial estate. Appears in 1300 as Springewall (SPNO p121). Liz Hodgkiss who came to Cannock Chase in the 1880s and took up the local occupation of picking the young growth of birch trees for broom-making became known as the 'Besom of Spring Slade.' She was reputed to be the last of the besoms of Cannock Chase (PCC pp80-82).

Springslade Pool 0.5m SE of Bednall. Here iron was worked from at least 1585 (MR p254).

Spring Vale House 0.75m S of Tittensor. Formerly in Beech quarter in Stone ancient parish (W p369). In 1808 it was bought by Thomas Bakewell of Cheadle (see) from the Jervis family for his asylum (Broughton's Scrapbook pp270il,271) (SIS p101) (History of Psychiatry. 4 (1) March 1993. pp107-127) (A History of Psychiatry in North Staffordshire. Dr Edward D Myers. 1997) (ES May 31 1997 p19). It was sold to the Duke of Sutherland in 1840 (RHPS il. No. 12, pp287-288).

Spring Vale At Spring Bank is a street called Springvale, Willenhall.

Spring Vale District 2.25m SE of Wolverhampton. Formerly partly in Bilston township in Wolverhampton ancient parish and partly in Ettingshall liberty in Sedgley ancient parish. The name is from a spring here called Wulfruna's Well or Spring Vale Well (HOBLL p175) (AOW p92). Lady Wulfruna's spring at Coseley noted by a C16 writer (WMVB p49) is possibly a reference to this

well. The name Spring Vale, which appears in the 1851 census under Ettingshall, was used for a ward of Coseley urban district created in 1912 (HC p71). That part of Spring Vale formerly in Bilston township formed Spring Vale ward in Wolverhampton borough by 1982. Spring Vale Furnaces were purchased by Alfred Hickman in 1866 and operated as an ironworks until 1884 when he converted to steelmaking. By 1895 it was the largest integrated works in Staffs. In 1920 it was sold to Stewart & Lloyd. Became a part of British Steel on nationalisation, who closed it in 1979 despite fierce local opposition (BOP p126).

Springwall Brook Tributary of the Penk. Has appeared as Springewallbrouk (1286) (SPNO p19).

Spring Well Spring renowned for its sweetness and purity, in the vicinity of Washerwall Lane, Washerwall (FWMBS p4).

Springwood Tiny hamlet on a ridge looking down on the upper Lyme Brook valley 0.5m NW of Chesterton. In Wolstanton ancient parish. In Springwood Road at SJ 821499 remains a 40 feet high brick furnace called Partridge Nest or Throstles' Nest (NSJFS 1964 p116) Furnace (preserved in Partridge Nest Farm on Audley Road?) for the production of iron. Said to be the earliest blast or oldest coke-fired furnace in N Staffs, dated at c1760 or 1768 (NSJFS 1964 p116. 1965 p91), and by it a pair of workers cottages, which look mid C19 in origin (BOE p211). (IAS pp183-184) (IANS pp26, 42, 43, 44, 62p figs 28, 29) (MR pp242, 243p).

Sprink House 0.75m WNW of Sheen. In Sheen ancient parish. There was a house here by 1755 (VCH vol 7 p241).

Sprink Brook Runs S of Morrilow Heath.

Sprinks Farm House over 1.25m WNW of Horton, situated on former Horton Hay, in Horton ancient parish. In existence by 1665 and may have been created when Horton Hay was divided into farms in the later C17 (VCH vol 7 p72).

Squire's Well, The Well by the roadside near to the Old Man of Mow, Mow Cop, at the other end of the summit, opposite The Town Inn (MC p25 pl viii), with this inscription

To do good forget not,
The Squire's Well. 1862

(PS p24). WMC p says it is in High Street and dated 1808.

Squitch House House 1.5m ENE of Bagot's Bromley, in Abbots Bromley parish, at SK 089265. Squitch appears as Le Queche in 1404 (SHC 1914 p175 note). The name means 'land infested with couch grass.' A farm which formerly stood here was taken into Bagots Park between 1744 and 1762 (ABMB p53).

Squitch Oak Ancient and former oak with a circumference near the ground of 43 feet and a height of 61 feet (NSFCT 1901 p74). In 1832 it had 1012 feet of timber, 12 feet more than the Swilcar Oak (MOS p51). It seems to have been situated near Squitch House, in Bagot's Park (LGS p192). Has also appeared as Squitch Bank Oak (AB p200). (GNHS il) (SC p171) (SG p109) (KES p16) (CCBO p26) (SLM Oct 1947 p35 with drawing by JG Strutt from 1824) (STMSM April 1973 p24).

Stableford Tiny hamlet by Meece Brook in a narrow valley over 0.5m NNE of Chapel Chorlton. Formerly partly in Chapel Chorlton chapelry in Eccleshall ancient parish and in Swynnerton ancient parish (W pp377,424). The hamlet is mentioned by Chetwynd (1679). In the 1980s a protester against Cruise missiles wrote over the railway bridge here - 'Cruise out - Fly back!' - for the view of train passengers travelling S. This was noted as a clever play on the common expression.

Stadmorslow Minute hamlet consisting of two houses called Upper (or Stephens Farm), and Lower Stadmorslow. The latter is 1.5m SSE of Mow Cop. Former township in Wolstanton ancient parish (W p291) (AGT p63). A member of Tunstall manor by c1130 (ONST 1976 p374). Has appeared as Stadmerslow, Stodmorelowe (NSFCT 1926 p44) and Stodmerslow (ONST 1976 p374).

Stadon Hole A tiny mere? at SK 020693 (1947 OS map sheet 43/06) on the Derbys Staffs border over 1.25m NNW of Flash.

Stafford Ancient parish and the county town, lying approximately in the centre of the county.
EARLY. Stafford probably owes its origin to its situation at a crossing of the Sow. The loop in the river at this point and the streams and marshy ground to the E formerly made the area virtually an island. As such the area was easy to defend and made an attractive dwelling place. The surrounding land is a plain bounded by rising ground at a very short distance (VCH vol 6 p185). For **Neolithic** activity in Stafford see King's Pool. During excavations in May 1929 on the site of the Grapes Hotel a number of skulls and other skeletal remains of the Beaker period were found. From this it has been surmised that

Stafford was on a track taken by the Beaker folk from the E coast to North Wales (NSFCT 1929 pp174-175). Most of the line of the **Roman** road from Buxton through Leek, Cheddleton, Blythe Bridge, Hilderstone, and Stafford to Pennocrucium (see) on Watling Street, has yet to be established (VCH vol 7 p98), but a 15-mile stretch of it running from Pennocrucium to Blythe Bridge, passing through the centre of Stafford, was discovered in June 1991 (SN June 21 1991 p3. Aug 20 1993 p9) (ES June 22 1991 p4). In 1961 a Romano-British jar was found in Market Square (SPJD p23pc). In 1976 evidence of Roman settlement was discovered on a site in Clarke Street (The Archaeology of Stafford to 1600 AD. Alison J Walker. Bradford University MA dissertation. 1976) (VCH vol 6 p186); Roman pottery (SN June 21 1991 p3) and two coins, dated 330-335 AD, were found (SPJD p23). Excavations at St Mary's Grove by St Mary's church in the 1980s uncovered three structures which were Roman or earlier. The structures were interpreted as granaries, suggesting Stafford was a Roman storage centre (SPJD p23pc). Roman pottery has been found during excavations on the site of Yates' Wine Lodge in Gaolgate Street in 1998 (ES July 31 1998 p71), and at Castle Church (see).

600 to 800. Early forms of Stafford such as 'Staeth' 'Stae' 'Staeths,' meaning jetty, shore, waterside, or bank, occur on coins minted at Stafford in the Anglo-Saxon period (kept at museums at Stockholm and Copenhagen). Stafford was, perhaps, Staethford before being recorded in DB as Stadford and Statford - so, 'the shore where the ford is, where a landing could be made' (DUIGNAN) (MOS p6) (LGS p212) (SH p74) (NSJFS 1981 p3); the ford is either one formerly at Green Bridge or at Broadeye, both over the Sow (info Michael Greenslade). In the later C17 Plot thought the **name** derived from 'a shallow place in the river (Sow) here about that could easily be passed with the help of a staff only.' For Sir Simon Degge, a contemporary of Plot, it was 'a childish conceit to talk of a staff and a ford; what help could a staff do in passing a ford? But the true etymology is Stadeford, that is the strand, shore or bank of a ford, and we find it in Doomesday Booke writ Stadford' (SH p74). From time immemorial Stafford has been associated with **St Bertram** (or spelt variously Bartelinus, Bartellen, Beccelin, Bernard, Bernerd, Bertelmus, Bertelin, Berthelm, Bertelline, Bertillinus, Bereterum, Bertolin, and Bettelin). According to tradition St Bertram was born near Stafford in c680, of royal Mercian blood. Rejecting the dissolute life of the court, and having religious leanings, he travelled to Ireland and lived in the household of an Irish king. He fell in love with the king's daughter, an Irish princess. They both returned to England, where they led a nomadic life in forests. As the princess was about to give birth to their child, Bertram left her in the forest to fetch a midwife. When he returned she was being devoured by wolves, whereupon, in remorse, Bertram became a hermit. He may have stayed for a while on the Wirral (churches at Thurstaston and Runcorn were dedicated to St Bertoline) before finally making his way home. On his way home at a place called Bertelmesley (identified as Barthomley, Ches) he was challenged by the Devil to change a stone into bread, but he did the opposite and turned the bread into a stone. At Barthomley can still be seen Bertram's stone. He was given some land, an island at Stafford known as Betheney (see), by his father and in c705 he built a hermitage on it. Some years later a new king came to the throne. He wanted Bertram evicted from Betheney and sent a gigantic knight to challenge him. But with angelic help Bertram fought off the knight. Such was his fame as a result, that the island became over populated. This made Bertram leave for a deserted and mountainous place, believed to be at Throwley or Ilam, where there is an ash, bridge, cave and well named after him. On Sept 9, in a year unknown, he died. His burial place is supposed to be an ancient rebuilt tomb in Ilam church, the subsequent site of many miracles. His feast day is Aug 10 (ODS p42) (Barthomley - The story of an estate village. Robert Speake. 1995 pp24-27). In Stafford, what may have been his preaching cross was discovered in 1954 on the site of the church of St Bertram or Bertelin behind St Mary's. A replica of this is displayed on the site (VCH vol 6 p243) (MR p289). The earliest reference to a saint, believed to be St Bertoline, was written by Felix, a monk of Crowland, Lincs, between 730 and 740, but his life does not fit later accounts relating to the Stafford St Bertram and he is believed to have been a different saint, although some accounts confuse the two. The earliest account of St Bertoline, in association with Barthomley, is in a book printed by Wynkyn de Worde, in 1516, the Nova Legenda Angliae (Barthomley - The story of an estate village. Robert Speake. 1995 p25). Bertelin appears at the beginning of a record of affairs in Stafford compiled between 1604 and 1624 by the town's mayor Thomas Worswicke. Some aspects of St Bertram's life are similar to those of St Berthelme of Fecamp (SH p10). In 1888 Bishop Browne identified St Bertram of Ilam with St Bertelin of Stafford (An Account of the Three Ancient Cross Shafts etc. Bishop Browne. 1888). (HSS pp1-24) (LGS p212) (VCH vol 3 p136) (HOS pp65-66) (SSTY p1) (St Bertelin of Stafford and the Conversion of the heathen Mercian Folk.

Lionel Lambert) (St Bertelin of Stafford. Michael Fisher. 1977) (MR p289).

800 to 1066. Excavations on a site in Salter Street in Dec 1994 revealed artifacts of c800, showing Stafford had been occupied 100 years earlier than previously thought (SN Jan 20 1995 p11). Saxon pottery has been found during excavations on the site of Yates' Wine Lodge in Gaolgate Street in 1998 (ES July 31 1998 p71). According to the Anglo-Saxon Chronicle having good defensive possibilities Stafford was fortified by Ethelfleda or Æthelflæd, daughter of King Alfred, in 913; one of a chain of fortified 'burhs' she built in the Midlands against the Danes (AASE p134) (KNS p110 p facing shows Lady Ethelfleda founding the burh at Stafford at the millennium anniversary 1913). Willmore mistakenly lists Lichfield as one of the **burhs** of Ethelfleda but neglects Stafford (HOWW p31). The early fortifications developed into Stafford Town Walls (see) with four gates - East Gate (see), North Gate (see), South Gate (see), West Gate (see). Stafford has appeared as Stæth (958-75), Stæ (979-1016), Stæths (C11), Stæfford (mid C11), Stadford (DB), and Statford (DB) (SPN p108). Stafford possessed a **mint** which issued coins at intervals from the time of Athelstan (924-939 or 925-941) until that of Stephen (W p321) (GNHSS p15) (SIOT pp140-146 ils facing) (MOS p6) (LGS p212) (OSST 1944-45 pp13-18 lists the coins minted here in Saxon times minus those in the BM collection) (SSTY p3) or that of Henry II (VCH vol 6 p186). At Stockholm is a coin of Edgar (958-75) bearing on the reverse 'Stæth;' and there are also three coins of Ethelred (979-1016), two bearing 'Stæth' and one 'Stæ.' At Copenhagen there is an Ethelred marked Stæth, and a Canute (1016-35) marked Stæths (DUIGNAN p141). In 1800 between two and three hundred pieces of ancient silver coins in excellent condition were discovered in a small jug in Mr Kingstone's tanyard in Stafford. They had been coined during the reigns of Ethelred, Canute, and Hardicanute (SIOT p56). **Churches.** There was a church at Stafford by the C10. This probably stood on the site of the Saxon church, St Bertelin, on the W side of Greengate Street. Slightly to the E of it was built its successor, the present parish church **St Mary**, which dates from the early C13. These churches were minster churches and on them Stafford Collegiate Church (see) centred (VCH vol 6 pp238-239). A parish of Stafford formed before 1086 and probably originally included Seighford ancient parish and may have included Bradley ancient parish (SHC 1916 pp192,196). The later parish centred on St Mary's was a peculiar jurisdiction of Stafford Collegiate Church until the college was dissolved (VCH vol 3 pp93,94). The church, **St Chad**, on the E side of Greengate Street, slightly to the S, was built by at least the C12 to serve a small parish covering the E side of Greengate Street in the town centre; it was possibly built by the bishop of Lichfield to serve his tenants on his estate in Stafford. St Chad's was mostly rebuilt in the C19 and C20. St Chad's parish was a peculiar jurisdiction of the dean and chapter and certain prebendaries of Lichfield cathedral until peculiar jurisdictions were abolished in 1846 (VCH vol 3 pp93,94). The parish was united with St Mary in 1973 (VCH vol 6 p245). St Chad's had a great bell that called the parishioners together in all things pertaining to Stafford town, and a ring of bells in its central tower (COEA p226). **Wakes**, known as Green Wakes, were held in August on the Green (see) at the S end of the town. Other wakes have been held at Foregate (see). Hobby horse dancing, as at Abbots Bromley, was practised in the town from medieval times until the Civil War. By Tudor times it was a means of raising funds for the church and was practised at New Year (SMC p169) (SCSF p6) (VCH vol 6 p256) (HOS p69) (FOS p79).

1066 to 1200. William I ravaged Stafford and other parts of Mercia on his way to suppress a rebellion in the N in 1069. When a second insurrection, led by Edric the Wild, followed in less than a year, he defeated the rebels in a battle at Stafford in 1070 (SSTY p5) or in 1069 (VCH vol 6 p187) (BALH pp20,21). Others just say on his march S from the campaign in Yorkshire William I built a castle at Broad Eye in 1070 which had a short life (LGS p212) (HOS p65). In DB Stafford is recorded as 'walled' (see Stafford Town Walls) and containing 179 houses, but about 51 were unoccupied (LGS p212), a collegiate college and a mint (SSTY p7; 164 houses in total with 52 unoccupied). The king's sheriff lived at Stafford; his castle was here; his judges sat here (SOSH p148). Stafford town grew up mainly along a street on a north south axis within the town walls (HOS p65). Foregate (see), the first suburb of the town without the town walls, is mentioned in 1170, another, Forebridge (see) is mentioned in the C13 (VCH vol 6 p191) (HOS p65). The 'Stanford' besieged in 1153 by the future Henry II was formerly identified with Stafford but has since been shown to be Stamford, Lincs (VCH vol 6 p187). Henry II is reputed to have come to Stafford to meet 'a remarkably handsome girl.' The story comes from a biographer of Thomas a Becket (SIOT p71) (Stafford Survey. TH Higson. 1949 p16) (SSTY p10). The county court at Stafford is recorded in 1176 (VCH vol 6 p200). There was a **watermill** on the Sow in the town as early as 1164, at SJ 921229. The final mill was a three-storey brick building with a tablet inscribed 'G.B. 1834.' It was demolished in 1957 and the two undershot waterwheels with their pit-wheels retained for display in Mill Bank (VCH vol 6 p facing p193) (IAS p188) (ROT pp37,38p). The Town Mill was known for generations as Brookfield's Mill (SKYT pp17 il of from 1845, 18).

THE BOROUGH. In DB Stafford is described as a borough, and once as a city (NSJFS 1972 p69) (SIOT p110; Stafford is said to have been styled a city in 1219). In 1206 King John granted Stafford a Charter of Liberties making it a free borough and confirmed its ancient privileges (W pp327-328) (LGS p213) (SOSH pp151,152,153p of the Charter) (Staffs County Handbook c1958 p129; there have been at least 14 royal charters to present, since) (HOS p66) (SSTY p7) (NSJFS 1972 p69). The charter may have have been recognising the custom of Borough English in which land passed to the youngest son, brother, daughter or sister. The custom appears to have been in use in Stafford in 1390 and certainly by the C16. It was still observed in the 1830s, although it was stated in 1851 to have been abandoned, a share in a house in Eastgate Street was described that year as held by the custom of Borough English (VCH vol 6 p222). (SD p68) (SHOS vol 1 p130) (SMC p173) (W p326) (CE p73) (S&W vol 1 p6) (SCSF p120). By 1206 there appears to have been a borough court (VCH vol 6 p223) (HOS p66). Borough courts were held in a guildhall in the C15; in part of the Shire Hall and in part of St Bertram's or Bertelin's chapel from the C16 to the mid C19. A guildhall was built on W side of Market Square in 1854 and rebuilt in 1935. A borough hall was built in Eastgate Street between 1875-77 (NHS pp371-372 tab 31 shows it) (SKYT p2il) (VCH vol 6 p227) (HOS pp65,66). In 1977 Stafford borough council offices were built on the site of the Royal Brine Baths in Greengate Street (built in 1892 and demolished after a lake of brine was found under Stafford Common) (SN Feb 16 1996 p20ps). By the 1290s the town was governed by two bailiffs, chosen annually (HOS p66). In 1593 Thomas Fitzherbert was elected a burgess for Stafford, and the Commons, after a great debate, voted that a person outlawed might be elected. John Wilkes cited this case to a friend in 1767 to prove he was eligible to become an MP (SIOT p52). In May 1613 Tom Warwick went to London to try and secure a new charter for the town and had an interesting letter from his wife longing for him to return (OP pp11-12). The town did receive a charter on April 8 1613 which initiated the role of mayor; Matthew Cradock was its first. For a list of mayors from 1614 to 1885 see HOSCC pp31-32. In 1687 James II had a Catholic appointed alderman and later the same year had him elected mayor. **Charters.** The first charter, one issued by King John on May 1 **1206**, made Stafford a free borough, corporation and confirmed its ancient privileges. The charter granted the burgesses freedom from toll throughout the kings lands, save at London (VCH vol 6 p215 - a privilege made use of in 1286 at Newcastle). The charter was confirmed by a charter granted April 11 **1228** (SIOT p57) (VCH vol 6 p222). The charter granted June 1 **1260** (SIOT p57) or 1261 (SKYT p113) was a confirmatory charter and granted Stafford its first fair. The charter granted on July 4 **1314** (SIOT p57) and or 1315 was a confirmation of the 1206 charter with new privileges (VCH vol 6 p222). Charters were granted on Feb 10 **1327** (SIOT p57), in **1341** (VCH vol 6 p222), and **1375**. The one of 1327 or 1375 exempted the burgesses from jury service, murage, and granted them the right to elect a coroner and have a prison in the borough (SIOT p57). Further charters were granted on June 24 **1378** (SIOT p57), and or 1379, and in **1390** (VCH vol 6 p222), January 9 **1400**, March 10 **1413** (SIOT p57), and or 1415 (VCH vol 6 p222), March 30 **1434** (SIOT p57), **1440** (VCH vol 6 p222), Feb 4 **1477** (SIOT p57), and or 1478 (VCH vol 6 p222), Jan 27 **1511**, May 10 **1526**, and Aug 24 **1545** (SIOT p57) and **1548** (VCH vol 6 p222). The charter of Dec 18 **1550** formally incorporated the borough, granted the burgesses the liberty to appoint a justice of the peace for the borough, and a grammar school (SIOT pp59-60). A charted was granted in **1554** (VCH vol 6 p222). The charters granted on Nov 15 **1560** and March 27 **1604** (SIOT p57) or 1605 (VCH vol 6 p222) were confirmation charters. The charter of April 8 **1613** stipulates that the borough be incorporated by the name of the Mayor and Burgesses of the Borough of Stafford, with perpetual succession and to comprise of a mayor, a recorder, 10 aldermen (two of which were to be justices of the peace within the borough) and 10 chief burgesses (SIOT pp61-62) (LGS p213). Some say this charter was issued in 1614. The Corporation's privileges were confirmed in **1664**-5 (VCH vol 6 pp222-227). In **1685** the charters were surrendered and a new one issued (SIOT pp63-64). In Oct **1688** the old charter was restored (VCH vol 6 pp222-227). Another confirmation charter was granted on March 27 **1767** (SIOT p57). The charter of Sept 6 **1827** was, at length, obtained after a petition by Stafford's freemen in protest at the oligarchical nature of the Corporation council (SIOT pp62-63). Stafford borough **arms** was first noted at the Heraldic Visitation of 1614 and shows:

Gules, a square castle with four domed towers in perspective argent, a gold pennon on each tower, in chief two Stafford knots and in base a lion of England all or (VCH vol 6 p229il) (SIOT p149 il No. 1, 150) (CH p336 il). The arms of the new Stafford borough, created in 1974, also feature the Stafford Knot (ES Aug 14 1993 p33). Stafford Borough **seal** was first noted at the Heraldic Visitation of Staffs made by Glover in 1583 and shows a castle triple-towered, on the dexter and sinister sides four lions passant guardant, and in base a fifth lion (SIOT p149). The seal at the Heraldic Visitation of 1614 is the same as that of 1583 only with the legend of 'Sigillvm Commvne Ville de Stafford' (SIOT p149 il No. 2).

MARKETS AND FAIRS. Stafford anciently had its **market** by prescription. There was a market-place in Stafford in the later C12 (VCH vol 6 p213). Mention of a market is not until 1230. Or in c1175 (SHC vol 8 part 1 p131) (NSJFS 1971 p52). The market day was on Saturday (THS) (SCSF pp93,94). There was a market in 1792 (OWEN), and a market in 1888 (LHE p265). A **market cross** stood in the middle of the market place (now approximately Market Square) by the early C15. It was removed when the new Shire Hall was being built in 1587, but there was still a market cross in the mid C17 (HOS p68) (VCH vol 6 p213). There were **fairs** on: **St Matthew the Apostle** held between Feb 23-25 (SKYT p113), or Sept 20-27 (SCSF p100) (VCH vol 6 p214) was the first of Stafford's many fairs and was founded by the 1261 charter and known nationally in the late C17 as the 'Hop Fair' (SKYT p113). Its dates were changed to Sept 16-18 in 1781 (COOKE) (SSTY p199) (VCH vol 6 p214). It had lapsed by 1851 (VCH vol 6 p214). (SOSH pp151,152,153) (HOS p68). A fair on **Shrove Tuesday** (Whitaker's Almanac) (COOKE), or Tues before Shrove Tuesday (W p332) and three days following was granted in 1614 (VCH vol 6 p214). **April 3** (Whitaker's Almanac), or first Tues in April, or at the beginning of April and was still being held in 1851 (W p332) (VCH vol 6 p215). **Finding (or Invention) of the Holy Cross** May 3 - Founded by charter March 30 1412, became May 14 after 1752 (Whitaker's Almanac) (COOKE) and was for cattle and horses (W p332) (SKYT pp55,113) (SSTY p199), held in conjunction with a pleasure fair from the 1820s (VCH vol 6 pp214,256). By 1315 there was a fair on the feast of **St Peter and St Paul** (June 29) (Whitaker's Almanac) (COOKE) for wool (W p332). The date of this fair was changed to June 24 in 1683 (SCSF p100) (SIOT p26). The June fair later reverted to June 29, but after the change in the calendar in 1752 it moved to July 10, but was moved to the Saturday before June 29 in 1781 (VCH vol 6 p214). (COOKE) (SSTY p199). **Oct 2** a statute fair (Whitaker's Almanac) for colts (W p332) (SKYT p55). **Dec 4** (granted by the charter of 1685) (SCSF p100), for cattle and swine (COOKE) (W p332) (SIOT p26) (VCH vol 6 p214). **Dec 14** (Whitaker's Almanac). There was a fair in 1792 (OWEN), and a fair in 1888 (LHE p265). The custom of Walking the Fair was instituted at Stafford by the charter of 1412 (SKYT p114) (VCH vol 6 p214). PUNISHMENTS. For the **gallows** see Forebridge and Sandyford. For the lock-up see Forebridge. Stafford had two **stocks**, one pair were placed in the old Butter Cross, and the other pair was on the Green opposite the Ivy House, Forebridge (SIOT p79) (SCSF p130). At one time there were stocks in St Mary's churchyard (SKYT p95). Stafford's **cucking stool** which was repaired in 1620 and again in 1623 was usually kept in a 'penthouse' at the 'Gaole syde' (SCSF p126). There was a **pillory** in the Market Place by 1575 (VCH vol 6 p228) (SCSF p127). A **whipping post** or place was in operation in the C17 and C18 (VCH vol 6 p228) (SIOT p79). The **scold's bridle** was used in Stafford up to 1838. The same bridle was in the Wragge Museum in 1890 (VCH vol 6 p228) (SIOT p79). In 1250 the dean and chapter of Stafford Collegiate Church had a renewal of their right to hold their own courts and to have their own gallows for men and pit for drowning women, in St Mary's churchyard. It is said that these stood in the NE corner nearest Averill's old shop (VCH vol 6 p205) (SKYT p96).

1200 to 1500. During the Barons' Wars Stafford was apparently royalist at first; but seems to have changed sides and was captured by royalist forces in 1263 (VCH vol 3 p242. vol 6 p187). The Black Death had reached Stafford by the summer of 1349 (SSTY p7). Towards the end of the C14 a slackness of the town watch resulted in Stafford being raided by 'evil-doers from Wales and Cheshire' (HOS p66). Edward III granted to Simon de Ruggelei and his heirs the vineyard or orchard near Stafford (or fish pond without East Gate - SCSF p119) by holding the king's stirrup whenever the king came to Stafford and was mounting his palfrey (SMC p122). King's Pool (see) by East Gate was held by a curious tenure (SD p68) (SHOS vol 1 p130) (SMC p173) (CE p73) (S&W vol 1 p6). There were two **religious guilds** in Stafford in the Middle Ages (NSJFS 1979 p15). A **miracle** consisting of the restoration of the sight of a blind man is said to have been performed in 1386 in the church of St Bertram or Bertelline at Stafford (HOSCC p11); and in c1386 the same or another wonderful miracle occurred at the altar of St Bertram in Stafford according to Cassgrave (S&W p277). Henry, Lord Scrope left money to an anchorite at Stafford in 1415 (VCH vol 3 p137). **Persons and visitors. Henry III** visited the town on March 5 1223 (SIOT p71) (SSTY p10). Bolingbroke (Henry IV) led the captive **Richard II** through on his way to London from Flint Castle in 1399 (SIOT p71) (SSTY p10). **John Stafford**, a Franciscan Friar, was born in Stafford. He was a philosopher and divine, but chiefly an historian, writing a Latin history of England's affairs (c fl 1380) (HWE vol 2 p309) (NHS p275) (SMC p166). **Henry IV** passed through Stafford to the battle of Shrewsbury in July 1403 (SIOT p71) (R&S p14) (VCH vol 6 p187). In Aug 1485 Henry Tudor, Earl of Richmond (**Henry VII**), is said to have met Sir William Stanley at Stafford Castle (SSTY p10) (VCH vol 6 p187) before the battle of Bosworth Field, having travelled from Milford Haven. (Lord Stanley changed his allegiance from Richard III to the Earl during the battle). Others say that they met on Cannock Chase (STMSM Nov 1972 p41), or at Lord Stanley's seat, Elford Old Manor House (R&S p18) (HOL pp302,303).

INDUSTRY. In the C10 Stafford was a place of pottery manufacture (WMMA p153). Stafford industries between the C12-C14 were wool, cloth, iron, and gold. Between the C14-C17 some of the former and capping; woollen caps gave way to beaver hats, felt-making and hats (SIOT p78). There was a windmill at Foregate (see) in the later C16, and one at Broad Eye (see) by the end of the C18. Between the C18-C20 Stafford produced much of the former items, and took to brewing, and through its tanning industry, embraced the making of boots and shoes mainly for the home market (chiefly ladies' ware), wooden soles, and gloves. By 1796 there were five shoe makers in Stafford with that of William Horton of The Hough (see), much the biggest (SAC p142). The building at the back of Chetwynd House (the Post Office) in Mill Street lately (1934) taken down for alterations of the General Post Office has been identified as Horton's Shoe Factory, the first factory for the manufacture of boots and shoes in Stafford. During the alterations quite a number of the Horton copper penny and half penny tokens were found under the floors (OSST 1934 p19). The town's involvement with the production of boots and shoes gives rise to this verse:-

For boots, and shoes, and slippers rare,
What shire with Stafford may compare.

(S&W vol 2 pl xxvii). In the early part of Sheridan's connection with the borough someone wrote:- 'Stafford is famous for the manufacture of Cloth, which enriches the pocket, and for excellent ale, which revives the spirits of the Inhabitants' (SIOT p78). Ribbon-weaving was a short-lived occupation at the end of the C18 (SIOT pp78-79). Later the town took to making railway locomotives (at Castletown) and wagons, when William Gordon Bagnall started Castle Engine Works at Castletown in 1875. The company made the locomotive 'Isobel,' 'Isabel,' or 'Isabella' for Cliff Hill Granite Co of Markfield, Leics in 1897. In 1953 it was returned to Stafford and put on display in Victoria Park (VB pp132-133) (STMSM March 1976 pc on front cover) (SAC pp73-75). From 1993 it has appeared on the sign of the Railway Inn at Castletown (ES Aug 19 1993 p4p). One family carried on the business of stocking weaving in the C19 (SIOT p79). Salt was worked at Stafford Common between 1877-1963 (MR p287). In the C20 Stafford produced electrical parts, concrete products, tools and chemicals (VCH vol 6 pp215-222). By the mid C20 English Electric Co Ltd (later GEC) were based at Stafford in one of the largest electrical engineering factories in the country (NSFCT 1950 p92).

1500 to 1642. In 1542 Stafford was made an open-air secular sanctuary, and the borough authorities assigned certain places of sanctuary, including buildings in Tipping Street on the S side of St Chad's churchyard (VCH vol 6 p228) (ESS p36). In 1593 a man died in the town well (HOS p68). The spire of St Mary's - thought to be one of the highest in England, says Plot - fell in a storm in 1593 and was repaired in 1594 (NHS p369), or according to Masefield fell on March 21 1594 (LGS p215). (Alrewas PR) (SHOS vol 1 p138) (SKYT p92). Outbreaks of plague in Stafford in 1604 and 1610 were serious enough to cancel the Sessions (SCSF p134) (SSTY p8). Hackwood implies plagues occurred at, or threatened, Stafford in 1621, and 1630 (SCSF p135). A plague broke out in Stafford in 1637 according to Ashley PR (SCSF p136) (NSFCT 1975 p35). A plague broke out in Stafford in 1642; relief was called for from the hamlet of Greatgate (SCSF p136). **Persons and visitors. Sir Thomas Offley** (?1505-1582), a native of Stafford who came into possession of Madeley manor and resided at Madeley Old Manor (see), was lord mayor of London in 1556-7 (VCH vol 6 p186). Although **John Leland** mentions Stafford in his Itinerary in c1540 he never visited the town. **Elizabeth I**, coming from Chartley, passed through Stafford on Aug 6 (S&W p278), or

Aug 8 1575 to dine at Stafford Castle; the furthest north she had ever been (SIOT p71) (SSTY pp10,11). There is a tradition she stayed at the Noah's Ark Inn (DoE). Her visit resulted in the Statute of Capping, and the restoration of the county assizes which had been temporarily removed to Wolverhampton and Lichfield, and she received a silver cup from the town (SMC p164) (W pp325-326) (S p144) (LGS p213) (SOSH pp181,347) (FSP p34) (SSTY pp10-11) (HOS p68) (ROT p36). The PR of St Mary's records the visit (SIOT p72). **Sir Hugh Homersley** (?1565-1635), a native of Stafford, was lord mayor of London in 1627-8 (VCH vol 6 p186). **Father Sutton**, Catholic recusant, of Burton upon Trent (see), was executed at Forebridge (see) in 1588 after being caught saying Mass in Stafford. **Izaak Walton**, author, was born in Eastgate Street, Stafford, on Aug 9 1593 (SOSH p204). His father, an alehouse keeper named Gervase Walton, died in 1597; he is thought to have been the son of George Walton of Yoxall. Izaak's widowed mother later married another local innkeeper (ROT p28) (SN Millennium Special Jan 2000 p3). Walton served as an apprentice to a London clothier and draper. By 1618 he had his own shop in Fleet Street and was a Freeman of the Ironmongers Company. In 1626 he married Rachel Floud (d1640) at Canterbury. In 1646 he remarried, secondly, Anne (d1662), half-sister of Bishop Ken and then returned to Stafford. In the Civil War his sympathies lay with the royalists. In 1651 he smuggled Charles II's diamond 'Lesser George' from its hiding place at Blore Pipe House (see) to Col Blague imprisoned in the Tower of London; he subsequently escaped and took it to Charles II on the continent. In Staffs Izaak Walton was friendly with Sir John Offley, who he visited at his seat Madeley Old Manor (see); a wood, Walton's Wood (see), in the vicinity is named after him. In the company of another Staffs friend, Charles Cotton, poet and author, of Beresford Hall (see), he enjoyed his passion for angling and country pursuits; fishing in the Dove (see), in Dove Dale (see) and Beresford Dale (see). In his best known work, a treatise on fishing and country life, 'The Compleat Angler, or the Contemplative Man's Recreation etc' (1653), dedicated to Sir John Offley of Madeley, Walton is Viator and Cotton Piscator Junior. There were five editions of 'The Compleat Angler' published in Walton's lifetime. In c1654 Walton purchased Halfhead Farm (see) at Shallowford near Stafford, as an occasional residence. After the restoration of Charles II Walton embarked on a new career as steward to the bishop of Winchester, living at the bishop's residences at Winchester, Chelsea, and Farnham Castle. He kept the post of steward until he died on Dec 15 1683 during a great frost. He was buried in Winchester cathedral (LGS pp60-61,80) (ROT pp28-29). His biographies include: Donne (1640), Sir Henry Wotton (1651), Richard Hooker (1665), George Herbert (1670), and Robert Sanderson (1678) (LGS pp60-61). A cottage in Eastgate Street which survived into the C19 was, according to tradition, thought to have been Walton's birthplace. By 1880, when it was photographed, it had been converted into stables and a coach house. The cottage was demolished shortly after 1880 (Broughton's Scrapbook p266 il of) (SAIW pl 66) (SN Aug 14 1964 p6). In 1953 a plaque was erected by OSS on the site believed to have been Walton's birthplace in Eastgate Street. It was re-erected on the wall of the present police station built on the site, and was still there in 2000. In 1878 a bust of Walton was placed in St Mary's church, Stafford (LGS p215). Every year flowers are placed on it and a special service held in the church to commemorate his birthday (Aug 9) (Stafford Past: An Illustrated History. Roy Lewis. 1997 p51p). (NHS p245) (SMC p166) (SM pp423,442) (AAD p140) (SSW pp1-9) (ILN March 9 1844 p157il of Walton's house at Stafford) (S pp114-116) (DAJ vols 4,39,44,46,47) (SOSH pp204-210) (PSS pp15-22 il) (KES pp184-186) (SLM Feb 1950 p96p) (GMS pp48-70) (NSFCT 1958 pp14-25) (VB p132) (SGS p154) (SEDG Oct 1987 p10) (TOS pp64-67). **William Shakespeare** may have visited the town; his company did on seven occasions between 1610 and 1628 (SSTY pp46-47). **James I** visited Stafford in Aug 28 1617 and described it as 'a little London' (SIOT pp72-73) (SKYT p3). He was very taken with the immensity of the town mace and ordered that it should never be allowed to rest in a horizontal position, and his command is carried out today (SSTY pp11-12) a unique privilege it shares with the City of London (FSP p53). **John Speed** in the early C17 considered Lichfield 'more large and of far greater fame' than Stafford as well as 'much her ancient' (Theatre of Empire of Great Britaine. J Speed. 1611 p69). **Sir Martin Noel** (1614-1665), founder of Noel's Almshouses (see), was born in Stafford (VCH vol 6 p186). **Charles I** was in Stafford in 1641 (SIOT p73).

GRAMMAR SCHOOL. The burgesses petitioned Edward VI for an adequately endowed school and in 1550 he established 'the Free Grammar School of Edward VI' (LGS p213) (HOS p66) (VCH vol 6 p164-167). The charter establishing a grammar school was granted in 1551 (SKYT p67). The school may have had its origins in a school attached to the collegiate church of St Mary started in medieval times (SSTY p225). The earliest known document in which the school is mentioned is dated 1473 (SKYT p66). Leland writing between 1535 and 1543 noted a 'schole for grammar in Stafford' (SKYT p66). He was told that Thomas Counter (or Countre) (died in c1500) and 'Sir Randol' a Stafford chantry priest founded the grammar school. In 1548 the chantry commissioners decided that Counter's foundation was a free grammar school, but he may just have endowed an existing school attached to St Mary's (VCH vol 6 pp164-167). The first building the school is known to have occupied is believed to have been in the SW corner of St Mary's churchyard. About the time the school received its foundation or refoundation charter the school was transferred to St Bertelin's chapel. Here the school stayed until the chapel was demolished in 1800 or 1801. It was then temporarily moved to the chapel of Noel's almshouses in Mill Street. Later in 1801 it was moved to new premises in Gaol Square. In 1813 the building was taken down and re-erected at the Gaol Square entrance to North Walls (VCH vol 6 pp164-167) - Roxburgh gives a photograph of it. In June 1859 (SSTY p227), or in 1860 (VCH vol 6 p166), after a Public Enquiry at the Guildhall, the debauched headmaster of King Edward's Grammar School, George Norman, was ordered to retire (SSTY p227). A new school, designed by Henry Ward of Stafford, was built in Newport Road in 1862 (SKYT p67,68p,69-71). The school was absorbed into a co-educational comprehensive school called King Edward VI High School in 1976 and opened in West Way in buildings formerly occupied by Stafford Girls' High School (VCH vol 6 pp164-167). (W p335) (SOSH p178) (History of King Edward VI Grammar School. J Sydney Horne. 1930) (SAC pp57-62). **Alumni**: George W Gough (1869-1948), novelist (see below); Most Rev Alfred Walter Averill primate of New Zealand (1925-1940) died Christchurch July 6 1957 aged 91 (SN July 13 1957 p8p); Leslie Gardiner, navy historian and writer, who attended the school in the C20. GIRL'S HIGH SCHOOL. Had its origins in Moat House School opened in 1903 at Moat House (see), Stafford. In 1907 that school became Stafford Girl's High School. Girl's High School amalgamated with the boy's Grammar School, becoming King Edward VI High School in 1976 (SSTY p228-229). **Alumni**: Carol Ann Duffy, poet, born in Glasgow on Dec 23 1955, who moved with her family to Stafford when a child; previously she attended St Joseph's Convent, Stafford (Contemporary Poets. Fifth edition. Tracey Chevalier. 1991) (SN Sept 16 1994 p10). STAFFORD GRAMMAR SCHOOL (second creation). Another school called Stafford Grammar School, founded in 1982 with the aim of resurrecting a co-educational grammar school for Stafford, was in existence in 1996 (SLM Sept 1996 p62).

CIVIL WAR. Charles I and Prince Rupert were in Stafford on Sept 17-19 1642 (VCH vol 6 p187), both quartered at the High House (see), and Prince Rupert picked off St Mary's steeple weathercock with his pistol (BFS p7). An order preserved in the WSL from Charles I to Prince Rupert dated 18 Sept 1642 still exists. It requires Rupert to give orders for eight troops of horse and five troops of dragoons to march towards Nantwich from Stafford (FSP p22). From this time Stafford was a royalist garrison. (SIOT pp65-67) (FSP pp19-24) (NSJFS 1966 pp16-17). In early Feb 1643 the Moorland Dragoons were led to Stafford to demand Sir Francis Wortley and his forces leave the county; Wortley had plundered the Moorland region in Nov 1642 (LOU pp25-26,340). After allowing the sheriff to leave the town, the Dragoons appealed to parliamentary commanders Sir John Gell and Sir William Brereton in Derbys and Ches for help in attacking it (LOU p27) (HOS p35). But reinforcements never came and the Dragoons' siege of Stafford had collapsed by the end of Feb 1643 (BFS pp12-13). After taking the royalist garrison in Lichfield cathedral Close on March 5 1643 the parliamentarians made a second attempt to take Stafford. But royalists were forewarned of Brereton's rendezvous with Gell on Hopton Heath near Stafford and a royalist force under the Earl of Northampton and Col Hastings rode out to confront them on March 19 1643 (BFS pp14-15). A battle then took place known as the battle of Hopton Heath (see) in which the royalists were victorious. At the height of the battle Hastings was called back to Stafford to settle a dispute between the governor, Col Cumberford, and his second-in-command, Lieut-Col Peter Stepkin. This dispute flared up again and Prince Rupert, in Stafford in mid April 1643, replaced Cumberford with Col John Lane. Stepkin left Stafford and changed sides. Stepkin advised Brereton to attack the town in mid May 1643. A parliamentary force of above 500 men then proceeded to Stafford. Before dawn on about May 16 Stepkin and Capt Bowyer with some 50 or 60 foot soldiers by stealth crossed over the town walls and were easily able to open one of the gates letting in the rest of their force after the guard had fled. The parliamentarians then took Stafford with only the loss of one of their side and about three royalists. Royalist gentlemen taken prisoner included Capt Bagot, Capt Ralph Sneyd, and Sampson Cumberford (a relative of William Cumberford?). Some say Stafford was taken on the night of May 4 1643 (LOU p27). Another account says Stafford was taken after daybreak on Dec 3 1644 by Henry Stone and Sir William Brereton (SHJ summer 1987 p35). One account states Col Lane was slain, but this is untrue since he later served as governor of Rushall Hall (BFS pp21,22,23) (SPJD p26). Stafford then became the seat of the parliamentary county committee (VCH vol 6 p187). Stafford Castle remained a royalist garrison for a little longer. Isabel, the elderly Lady Stafford who had garrisoned it for the king in the absence of her grand-daughter's husband, William Howard, Viscount Stafford, refused to hand it over. A minor skirmish was fought in the vicinity of the castle in May 1643, followed by a siege until July, when the garrison withdraw (ROT pp48-49). A Vernon Yonge was executed in front of it (FSP pp55-57). On Dec 22 1643 the parliamentarians ordered the demolition of the castle (LGS p214) (SIOT pp12-13, 67) (VCH vol 5 p85) (HOS p20) (NSFCT 1983 p40). Stafford remained in parliamentary hands until the Civil War ended in 1646 (BFS p23). On Dec 3 1644 Col Lewis Chadwick of Mavesyn Ridware the parliamentarian governor of the town was arrested under suspicion of having neutral sympathies and replaced by Capt Henry Stone (SHJ summer 1987 p27) (HOS 1998 p74).

1643 to 1800. For the custom arising out of the terms of Hale's Charity, founded in 1643, see Turk's Head. A **plague** which also raged elsewhere in the country broke out in Stafford in 1646 (SCSF p137) (OSST 1934 pp28-29). The regicide John Bradshaw was elected MP for Stafford in 1654 (SSTY p14). In 1654 in compliance with the Cromwellian law the mayor of the borough, Thomas Backhouse, performed the ceremony of marriage of the Rector of Stafford, Rev Robert Palmer, after the usual proclamation made in the market on three successive Saturdays (SCSF p65). **Presbyterians** of Stafford were among the first to make an application for registration after the Test Act of 1672. That year a house in Stafford was licensed as a meeting house. After the Toleration Act of 1689 a purpose-built Presbyterian meeting house opened in Balk Passage (VCH vol 6 p255) (Trinity Church, Stafford: A Short History. Hilma Wilkinson. 1991). Roxburgh says the original building dated back to 1674, making it the oldest congregations of the Presbyterian church of England (SKYT p42). In the Sectarian riots of 1715 rioters were unduly incited by the rector of St Mary's, Rev Joseph Walthorne, MA, a member of the High Church, who was so intolerant to Dissenters he even forbade Christian burial to their infant children (SKYT p44). The meeting house was attacked on July 7 1715 and rioting continued off and on for another fortnight. Some of the furniture from the church was burnt in the Market Square. 47 rioters were brought before a Sheriff's court, but only 10 were found guilty. The other rioters who sought to have them released were thwarted by a troop of Dragoons and two troops of cavalry from Shrewsbury (SIOT p12) (SKYT pp43,44-45) (LOU p86). The restored meeting house became famous in 1720 by being made one of the two garrison churches in the country for the Scottish troops incorporated into the British army. A painting of the Royal Arms given to the church as a symbol of constitutional loyalty survives and has been hung at the top of the staircase of the present brick Holy Trinity church (for three of Stafford's non-conformist congregations, Methodist, Presbyterian and Congregational), Mount Street, which was built in 1988 on the site of the old Presbyterian meeting house; that building having by then become empty and having fallen into disrepair (Trinity Church, Stafford etc). A 'gang' caused a disturbance in Stafford in 1716 with the Tory constable going about the town with a gang and fiddlers playing a pro-**Jacobite** tune (LOU pp99,360). Such was Tory resentment against Lord Gower for joining the Whigs and turning against the Stuart cause there was a contest for the **1747 election** for the County seats, and there was agitation during voting for the boroughs seats. During the vote for Stafford borough - in which William Chetwynd (a Whig) and John Robbins were returned members - a riot occurred and Chetwynd House, the town house of William Chetwynd, was broken into and damaged by the crowd (LOU p103). As a consequence it appears that 18 were convicted at the Stafford Assizes (SIOT p53; Cherry gives the date Aug 1748, and a reference to an article in Morning Advertiser dated Aug 28 1748, but the general election was in Aug 1747). Hanoverian troops in Stafford incited a Jacobite riot on June 10 1749 (LOU p104). In Sept 1754 there was a riot between troops and townsmen with Jacobite sympathies (LOU p109). From 1785 to 1808 the Holyhead post route lay through Stafford (VCH vol 6 p196). A traveller in 1787 thought Stafford 'a dull idle place' (VCH vol 6 p201). Stafford declared itself against the slave trade at a county meeting held on Feb 5 1788 (SIOT p51). The Staffordshire Volunteer Cavalry (later Staffordshire Yeomanry), which later had their headquarters at Yeomanry House (see), formed in Stafford in 1794. The Stafford Troop, raised by Lt Col Hon E Monckton in 1794, was a part of the Cavalry (FSP p60) (info Yeomanry House). An earthquake was felt in the town on the Wednesday before Nov 21 1795 (SA Nov 21 1795). The famous trial between Mrs Docksey and Mr Panting of Lichfield (see) took place at St Mary's church in 1796. **Persons and visitors**. Armstrong, the C17 poet wrote of Stafford -

'_____such, through the bounds of pastoral Stafford, Runs
the brawling Trent,'

(SIOT p78). Charles II's illegitimate son, James, **Duke of Monmouth**, was
appointed Lord High Sheriff of the town by the Corporation in 1677 (SSTY
p14) (VCH vol 6 p224). He was arrested at Stafford by John Ramsey, the
king's sergeant in arms, after dinner at a mercer's house on Wednesday Sept
20 1682 (LCAST 1894 p95) (OSST 1930 pp26-27. 1932 pp21-29) (Biography of Charles II. Antonia Fraser. 1979 p424). The Tory mayor, Sampson
Birch, had collaborated in the duke's arrest (VCH vol 6 p224). Cherry says
the proclamation for the Duke of Monmouth's arrest and the arrest of three
others, including Sir Thomas Armstrong, MP for Stafford, was issued on June
28 1683 (SIOT p5). In 1687 the Catholic **Bishop Leyburn** visited Stafford
(VCH vol 3 p107). **William III** passed through Stafford in 1690 on his way
to Ireland (VCH vol 6 p187). In 1690 there was a large fire at Stafford (ADD
p30). In 1698 the writer and traveller **Celia Fiennes** visited Stafford and described it as 'an old built town timber and plaister pretty much in long peaked
roofes of tileing.' She noted it was the custom in Stafford to be given food
and drink in every house (SIOT pp91-92) (VCH vol 6 p186) (Illustrated Journeys of Celia Fiennes. Edited by Christopher Morris. 1984. p148). **Daniel
Defoe** had visited Stafford by 1724. He had expected it to be larger, although,
he noted it had lately increased in size and some had prospered by recently
taking to the clothing trade (VCH vol 6 p186) (A Tour Through The Whole
Island of Great Britain. Daniel Defoe. (Penguin. 1979). pp400-401). **John
Wesley** stayed a night in Stafford on March 16 1738 and on Feb 20 1746. He
was in Stafford to preach for the first time on Aug 29 1783 and preside at the
opening of the original Wesleyan Chapel, in Cherry Street (SSTY pp146-
147). Wesley was in the town to preach again in March 1784 and March 29
1785. On the last of these occasions he declared in his diary 'This was the
more strange, because there are few towns in England less infected with religion than Stafford.' Wesley's last visit to Stafford was on March 31 1788
(SLM Sept 1950) (SKYT p125). (SIOT pp139). In Dec 1745 the **Duke of
Cumberland** stayed at Chetwynd House when in pursuit of the Young Pretender in the 1745 Jacobite Rebellion (SIOT p44). **Richard William Vaughan**,
a Stafford linen draper, was in 1758, the first man to forge Bank of England
notes (SIOT p43). He is said to have forged twelve £20 bank notes to impress
his fiancee. He was hanged at Tyburn in 1758 (FSP pp91-92). **William Withering** (d1799) practiced at the Staffordshire General Infirmary at Foregate
(see). The comedian **Edward Knight** (d1826), commonly known as 'Little
Knight' was born in Brighton in 1774. He appeared as Hob in 'Hob in the
Well' at Newcastle-under-Lyme, and was engaged by Nunns, the manager of
the Stafford Theatre. He worked at the Stafford Theatre from 1799 to 1802.
He married a Miss Clews, the daughter of a local wine merchant. Knight's
son, the portrait painter, John Prescott Knight (d1881), was born in Stafford
in 1803 (DNB) (VCH vol 6 p186) (VFC p80). From 1780 to 1806 one of
Stafford's MPs was playwright **Richard Brinsley Sheridan**. Sheridan kept
the Stafford seat in the general elections of 1796, 1801, and 1802 (HOSCC
pp23-26) (SIOT p84). Whilst electioneering Sheridan is said to have occupied two rooms on the first floor of No. 6 Eastgate Street, and from one of the
first floor windows Sheridan is said to have made his maiden speech to the
Stafford voters in 1780. The house later belonged to the author of SIOT, JL
Cherry (SIOT p87), and later was rented as an office by Paul Butters, author
of SSTY, and had been demolished by 1979 (SSTY pp84,85p,86). Sheridan
is said to have occupied Chetwynd House (see) (FSP pp13-19) or was merely
entertained there as a guest of shoe manufacturer, William Horton (SSTY
p202) and his ghost is said to haunt that house (FSP pp13-19). Stafford was
more attracted by Sheridan's 'five guineas' bribes for a vote than his elo-
quence. At the 1806 general election he stood for the Westminster seat but
was defeated (SIOT p84). Having lost his fortune he stood again for Stafford
borough in Sept 1812 but did not get in (LGS p214). He put this failure down
to the refusal of Mr Whitbread to advance him £2,000 out of the sum due to
him by the committee of the Drury Lane Theatre for his share of the property
(SIOT p84). He is remembered by Stafford for his toast which ran:

May the trade of Stafford be trod under foot by all the world,

(LGS p214) (HOS p69) (SL p115) (SSTY p202), although his constituents,
foolishly, convinced themselves they were being insulted (LGS p214). Financially ruined, Sheridan was forced to sell a handsome cup presented to
him by his Stafford electors. He died in poverty on July 7 1816 (SIOT p85).
(SLM Oct 1951 pp12-13,24). **William Wordsworth** came to Stafford in 1789
to visit his old schoolmaster Joseph Shaw then headmaster of King Edward

VI's School (SSTY p227). The **Prince of Wales** attended Stafford Races at
Coton Field in 1790 and gave a purse of £50 (R&S p38). **George Baker**
(?1773-1847) musician was organist of St Mary's from 1790 to 1800; he was
repeatedly reprimanded by the Corporation for neglecting his duties and was
prohibited from playing his own favourite composition 'The Storm' (VCH
vol 6 p187). In 1792 the 5th **Viscount Torrington** thought Stafford 'very
mean, though the county town' with inns that were 'merely ale-houses and fit
for the market folks only' (VCH vol 6 p201). The actress, **Harriot Mellon**
(b1777), who first appeared on the stage at Uttoxeter (see), came to live in
Stafford in 1792 for a few years. Here, aged 14, she made her debut in 'The
Jealous Wife' and in Oct 1794 was spotted by Sheridan in 'The Wonder.'
Sheridan promptly forgot her, but she went to London anyway and appeared
as Lydia Languish in 'The Rivals' (SSTY pp51-53). A Staffordshire newspaper of about the end of the C18 reported the extraordinary marriage in Stafford of **William Chapman** and Matha Stafford both of Stafford, whose combined ages computed to 160 years (SCSF p62).
1800 to 1900. On Sept 14 and 15 1800 riots took place in Stafford owing to
the scarcity and excessive price of flour. The 17th Light Dragoons were sent
out on both days to suppress the mob and the Riot Act was read (FSP p63)
(SIOT p10). The bank of Messrs Omar Hall and Co of Stafford was robbed
of nearly £2,000 in March 1808 (SA March 18 1808) (SIOT p8). On June 11
1823 a total of between four and 600 were involved in an attempt to rescue
prisoners from the custody of constables (SA Nov 15 1823) (LOU p234).
The Staffordshire Yeomanry were sent out to suppress the Stafford Radical
riots in 1819 (FSP p63) (SIOT p10), and the Stafford Election riots in 1826
(FSP p63) (SIOT p10). The failure of Wellington over the Reform Bill led to
demonstrations in the county, and an effigy of the Duke was burnt in Stafford
market place in the evening of the day the bill failed (SA Oct 19 1832 p4)
(LOU p218). After the Chartist riots had subsided special commissions were
held at Liverpool and Stafford in 1842. What became known as the Stafford
Commission transported 54 men and imprisoned 154 (mainly these from the
Potteries?); the Liverpool Commission transported 11 men and imprisoned
115 (The Age of The Chartist 1832-1854. JL and B Hammond. p272). A
Russian gun, captured at Sevastopol, was placed in Stafford Market Square
in 1856. This was subsequently removed to Eastgate open market, and finally sent to Chester in c1876 (OSST 1932 p47). In 1858 when the **shoe
manufacturers**, Bostocks, introduced machinery the workers went on strike
for five months (SIS (paperback ed. 1980) p39). Bostock's 'Lotus' Company
HQ and main factory in the centre of the town, founded in 1834, was destroyed by fire in 1902. The Sandon Road factory dates from 1903 (NSJFS
1965 p74). **Libraries and museums**. The William Salt Library (see) opened
at Old Bank House in 1872 and moved to its present location in Eastgate
Street in 1919; it contains the valuable scrap book of William Albert Marson
of the High House (see) documenting the C19 history of Stafford. The Wragge
Museum (see) opened in 1879. The **County Refuge** (later the County Industrial Home) was opened in Sandon Road in 1878. It was built by subscription
to provide work for friendless women and had three main departments, for
cooking, sewing, and laundry. It was thought to be the first of its kind in the
country. By 1928 it had become a Home Office reformatory for girls, which
in c1930 moved to Rowley Hall (SA Sept 21 1878) (VCH vol 6 p205). Staffordshire County Cricket Club formed at Stafford at a meeting held on Nov
24 1871. Lord Dartmouth (see Sandwell Hall), who presided over the meeting, was elected president. The club played at various grounds in the county
(VCH vol 2 p369). A great **fire** hit the town on Oct 1 1887 (SN Oct 2 1987
p9. Oct 9 1987 p9). Figures representing peoples of tea-growing countries,
such as India, China, Burma, and Ceylon adorned a tea warehouse in Market
Street. They were originally painted (SN Jan 18 1958 p3p). **Persons and
visitors**. **Thomas Sidney** or Sydney (d1889), lord mayor of London 1853-4,
was born in Stafford in 1805 (VCH vol 6 p186). All eight children of his
second marriage had Stafford as one of their first names (MMM p79). He
was Sheriff of London and Middlesex in 1844, MP for Stafford between
1847-52, and 1860-65, and Lord Mayor of London in 1853-4 (SHJ spring
1989 pp31-32) (VCH vol 6 p186). A charity given by Sidney constituted by
a deed of Nov 21 1857 is commonly known as 'Sidney's Sovereign;' £1
having been given annually to 60 poor widows and widowers. In the 1930s
each recipient was nominated in turn by the Mayor, the Rector, and the Vicar
of Christ Church at Epiphany Tide, whenever a vacancy occurred (The Charities of Stafford. Lionel Lambert. c1931-1955? p25) (VCH vol 6 p270). In
1889 his widow erected a drinking fountain to his memory in Gaol Square or
Sidney Square (now lost). The fountain was surmounted by a shaft bearing
lamps and a figure of Samson (VCH vol 6 p193). Sidney's shield (displaying
13 oak trees surmounted by a hedgehog, and the motto '_____ eo agere')
was affixed to the fountain. The lamp was replaced by a clock by 1916. On

May 8 1928 a motor van backed into the fountain and smashed it to pieces (FSP pp75,76) (SOPP pl 21p) (SMML pp66-69). In 1818 **NW Cundy** (b1778), husband of Frances Stafford Cooke, sister of Richard Stafford Cooke, claimant to the title of Baron of Stafford (see above), stood unsuccessfully in the election for Stafford borough. Mr Cundy was ridiculed in the press being called disparagingly 'Mr Chip' on account of being labelled a carpenter, although by profession he was a civil engineer (OP pp19-20). In 1819 the future **Lord Campbell** then barrister on the Oxford Circuit described Stafford as 'the dullest and vilest town in England' (VCH vol 6 p201; also other references to how awful Stafford was considered). **Junius Brutus Booth** (father of the assassin of President Lincoln) played at Stafford in Oct 1819; the Wilkes family were of Aldersley (see). **Edward Henry Hengler** (d1865), the true founder of Hengler's Circus, was born in Stafford on Aug 15 1819; he and his father, Henry Michael Hengler, were famous tight-rope walkers and circus performers of their day (SHJ spring 1989 pp7-21). **Henry Erskine Johnston** played at Stafford in April 1821. **Clara Fisher** played at Stafford in May 1821 (SSTY pp46-83; gives thorough history of theatre in Stafford). The **Duke of Wellington** received the Freedom of Stafford in Nov 1821 (CCBO p75). **George Borrow** (1803-1881), author, stayed at Stafford in Aug 1825, and may have been employed at the Swan Hotel (see) in Stafford. In 1826 **Monsieur Ferrus**, physician to Napoleon, visited Stafford Mental Hospital (SKYT p74). **Maria Foote** played at Stafford in Aug 1827. **Queen Victoria**, as Princess Victoria, passed through Stafford in Oct 1832 on her way from Shugborough Hall to Lord Liverpool's seat in Shrops (Broughton's Scrapbook appendix p2) (SIOT p74). In 1859 Queen Victoria lunched at Stafford station (SIOT p74) (SSTY p16), and again took refreshment at the station in 1865 (SIOT p74). **Signor Paganini**, violinist, played at Stafford in May 1834 (SSTY pp46-83). **Thomas Brassey**, engineer, was working on the GJR at Stafford when his son Thomas, 1st Earl Brassey (d1918), politician and colonial governor, was born here in 1836 (VCH vol 6 p186) (SOP p172). **Edward Ilsley** (d1926) was born in Appleyard Court, S of Tipping Street in 1838. From 1888 he was the RC bishop of Birmingham, and from 1911 to 1921 the RC archbishop of Birmingham (VCH vol 3 p115 note. vol 6 p186) (info Michael Greenslade). **Queen Adelaide**, wife of William IV, arrived by the GJR at Stafford in July 1840 and left for Alton Towers (R&S p39) (SIOT p74). In April 1852 **Charles Dickens** stayed a night at the Swan Hotel in Stafford. He liked to call the hotel 'The Dodo.' He called Stafford 'as dull and dead a town as anyone could desire not to see' (SL p155) (SHC 1999 pp201-216). He called the Lyceum Theatre in Martin Street 'a mouldy little theatre' (SSTY p87). (HOSCC pp85-88) (KES p181). In 1873 **Prince and Princess Christian** were welcomed in Stafford before going on to Ingestre (SIOT p74).

RAILWAYS. A railroad opened in 1805 connecting Stafford with Radford wharf on the Staffs and Worcs Canal (VCH vol 2 p306). In Oct 1880 at the junction of the Lichfield and Wolverhampton roads workmen found a quantity of timber sleepers which may have formed part of the tramway (SIOT p51). From July 4 1837 Stafford was connected to Liverpool and London via Birmingham by the GJR (NSJFS 1962 p99) (MR p295). The Trent Valley line was officially opened on July 26 1847 but delays meant Stafford was not connected with London (via Tamworth) until Dec 1 1847 (NSJFS 1962 p99) (SL p246). The Stafford-Wellington, Shrops line opened on June 1 1849 connecting the town with Shrewsbury on the Shropshire Union Railway (S&UR p5). The line between Stafford and Newport closed in 1964 (VCH vol 2 p333. vol 6 p198). The Stafford-Uttoxeter line was opened on Dec 23 1867 and closed to passengers in late 1939 and closed in 1957 (NSJFS 1964 pp78,79) (VCH vol 6 p198). In March 1957 the Stephenson Locomotive Society (Midland Area) ran a special 'last train' over the Stafford-Uttoxeter line (info Hixon Local History Society). The stationmaster of Stafford was able to wear a silk hat; a privilege accorded to stationmasters at only six other stations in England (FSP p32). Charles H Lea (d1888), of Stafford, invented automatic gates for railway level crossings in 1868. A year later he patented his invention (Alphabet Index of Patentees 1869 No 121) and at the London International Exhibition of 1874 his 'automatic apparatus for opening and closing gates at railway level crossings in connection with signals' was on view (OSST 1932 p45) (VCH vol 2 p164). In 1877 the Stafford Railway Building Society, joined the Building Society Association, although the society was formed some years earlier, by a member of the Dean family, local accountants, to enable railway workers in Stafford to acquire mortgages. By 1999 the society had a branch in Old Bank House in Market Square, Stafford, the former William Salt Library premises (local info). There was a serious accident on March 12 1906 when the midnight express from Euston to Liverpool and Manchester derailed and collided with Newport Road bridge (Railways In and Around Stafford. Edward Talbot. 1994 pp4, 44-45). An

accident occurred at the station in Aug 1990 which killed the train driver of a train which drove into the back of a stationary train (ES March 9 1996 p4). There was a serious accident at Rickerscote (see) on March 8 1996. Tony Davies of Stafford set the time record for visiting the northernmost (Thurso), southernmost (Penzance), westernmost (Arisaig), and easternmost (Lowestoft) stations in Great Britain in 37 hours 34 minutes on April 14-15 1993 (GBR 1995 p124).

NEWSPAPERS. For the many county newspapers published in Stafford see Introduction. The weekly **Stafford Mercury**, the first Stafford-focused paper, ran for 17 issues from Jan 1863 (VCH vol 6 pp258-259) (SHJ spring 1996 p24). The weekly **Stafford Chronicle** established in 1877 became the Staffordshire Chronicle in 1884, the paper was bought by Powysland in 1955 and merged with Staffordshire Advertiser (SN Millennium Special Jan 2000 p8); a paper called the **Stafford Chronicle** was being published in 1997 (Willings Press Guide. 1997). The **Stafford Newsletter**, founded in 1906, became the Stafford and Mid Staffordshire Newsletter from Jan 22 1955, but reverted to the title, Stafford Newsletter, from Jan 14 1966 and still runs (VCH vol 6 pp258-259) (SHJ spring 1996 p24). The **Stafford Observer** was founded in 1908 but had ceased by 1916 (SN Millennium Special Jan 2000 p8). **Bell's Weekly Reporter** ran from 1910 to 1916; it incorporated the **Stafford Free Press** from 1912. The free **Stafford News Shopper** ran for 34 issues from 1970 (VCH vol 6 pp258-259). The free **Stafford and District Trader** was founded in 1981 (Willings Press Guide. 1988). The **Stafford & Stone Chronicle**, founded in 1981, was still running in 1997 (Willings Press Guide. 1988. 1997). The free weekly **Stafford & Stone Trader**, founded in 1981, was still running in 1997 (Willings Press Guide. 1988. 1997). The weekly **Stafford Post** was launched in 1984. The **Stafford and Stone Shopper** had ceased publication by 1988 (Willings Press Guide. 1988. 1997).

1900 to PRESENT. **HQ of national organisations**. To 1996 Stafford was the centre for the country's only crime prevention centre before moving to Yorkshire (info Carol Galpin): Stafford was also the headquarters for these national charities: one to help mothers overcome the abduction of their children: the Portia Trust (founded 1971), which helps people who commit offences due to extreme emotional distress (ES July 8 1994 pp4,18): and the National Association of Widows, founded by June Hemer of Stafford (Handbook for Widows. June Hemer and Ann Stanyer. 1978). **Historical Societies**. Old Stafford Society (OSS) was founded in 1924 and published transactions (OSST) from 1928 to 1960, when the society changed its name to the Stafford Historical and Civic Society; its transactions (SHCST) continue to date. The Stafford & Mid Staffs Archaeology Society, founded in Feb 1971, still (2000) meet in Stafford (info Kath Wood). In 2000 these two and about 18 other heritage groups were members of the umbrella Stafford Borough Heritage Group (formed in 1994) (info Alan Appleby). In c1929 a small **hoard** of 15 coins comprising 12 English coins (mainly half pennies, counterfeit, and of the 1770s), and three Anglo-Irish coins (all halfpennies, counterfeit and of 1766), was found resting on a beam of the Old Bakehouse situated on the E corner of Mill Street and Church Lane, when the building was being demolished. The coins went to the OSS and were on permanent loan to Stafford Museum and Art Gallery in 1972 (The Dunchurch and Stafford Finds of Eighteenth-Century Halfpence and Counterfeits. PH Robinson. Reprinted from The British Numismatic Journal. vol LXI 1972 p152). There was an outbreak of **Legionnaires disease** in Stafford in April 1985 at Kingsmead Hospital and at Stafford District General Hospital at Coton Hill (see). By June 7 1985 39 had died of the disease (SN May 3 1985 p1. May 10 1985 p1. June 7 1985 p16). **Earthquakes** have been felt at Stafford at 3.21pm July 3 1904 (NSFCT 1905 p133); on Jan 14 1916 (SSTY p18); on Oct 5 1993, measuring 2.3 on the Richer scale, about 2.5 miles beneath the town (Daily Telegraph Oct 6 1993 p3). On Feb 8 1946 the railway station and streets about the Green were badly hit by **floods** and buildings damaged when both Sow and Penk banks burst and left the town isolated. The town had been and was to be flooded many times (SSTY pp19,20ps,21) (ROT pp44-45) (SN Feb 9 1996 p9ps) (SAC pp120-121p). The first shop in Stafford to have an **escalator** was Allied Carpets who opened in July 1978. **Supernatural**. The apparition of a man floats through the front door of a cottage, built in c1882, in Garden Street. It is believed to be William Elton who lived in the cottage in the 1880s (MGH p58). A house in Newport Street is reputed to be haunted (GLS pp84-85) and an undisclosed nursing home in the town has had paranormal activity (MGH pp59-61). A house in North Walls is said to have been haunted (SN Nov 20 1981 p28). In about Aug 1954 the first of several **UFO sightings** at Stafford was made from Stone Road. On Aug 31 1954 a bright yellowish ball in the sky was seen from Weston Road by Wilfrid Daniels. It later disappeared behind Stafford Castle. The same object was seen in the evening from Stone (see). On about Sept 8 1954 Mrs Rita Rogers saw a clearly-defined vuna from her garden in Stafford. It was cigar-shaped and dark against the bright sky (The Coming of the Spaceships. Gavin Gibbons. 1956). Sometime between Aug 6 and 9 1967 after hearing strange sounds outside two people of Grey Friars saw from their bedroom window an object in the sky which appeared to be the size of a rugby ball, which may have been a UFO (FSRP p6). A bright orange flare-like light, possibly a UFO, was observed by six witnesses from two different localities at Stafford (one being Lawns Road) on Sept 23 1967 (FSRP p16). A parachute-like object, with a bright orange light beneath was seen from Brunswick Terrace on Oct 6 1967; a bright orange object that split into two was seen from Young Avenue on Nov 11 1967 at 8.32pm (FSRP facing p17 p19). A number of people at Stafford saw in the sky what one of them describe as a white parachute-like object with a bright orange light beneath, on Oct 6 1967 at 9.42pm (FSRP p16). In early 1977 four Stafford policemen claim they saw a UFO (ES Feb 8 1977) (SMM p98). **Persons and visitors.** Sir **Bernard Spilsby** (1877-1947), pathologist, lived in Stafford in the early C20 (info Alan Walker). **Arthur Conan Doyle**, creator of Sherlock Holmes, was in Stafford in Dec 1906 to unravel the case against George Edalji in the Wyrley Gang case at Great Wyrley (see). **Gustav Hamel** gave a flying demonstration at Lammascotes on Oct 12 1912 (EAS p20). **George Constantinesco**, a Romanian by birth later a British subject, whilst working at WH Dorman (former shoe manufacturers later engineering parts), invented the machine gun synchronising gear for aircraft used in WW1 (info Ron Balding) (The Times March 27 1919) (Dorman Centenary 1870-1970 p9). General **Charles de Gaulle** visited Stafford in Oct 1941 (Around Stafford. Roy Lewis. 1999 p128p). **Sydney Francis Barnes** (1873-1967), famous cricketer born in Smethwick (see), was made an honorary member of Stafford CC when he went to live in Stafford after WW2 (SSTY p186). **David Horne** of Stafford, strongman, was winner of the World All-Round Weightlifting title in 1992 and produced his own booklet titled 'David Horne's Iron Grip Course' (TB Oct 1993 p15p). A member of the Searchers pop music group, **John McNally**, appeared before Stafford County Magistrates in Dec 1967 charged with speeding (SN Dec 15 1967 p15). The actor, **Neil Morrissey** (born c1963), who has appeared in TV sitcoms 'Stuck on You,' 'Roger Roger,' 'Men Behaving Badly' is from Stafford (ES July 1996 p1p. April 26 1999 p13p) (Radio Times Guide to TV Comedy. Mark Lewisohm. 1998). **Prince Charles** visited Stafford in 1978 (SSTY p16) and in early June 1981 (ES June 3 1981 p1p) and on March 3 1998 (SLM April 1998 p15). **Tim Healey shook** hands with 10,291 people in 10 hours 10 minutes in Stafford on Feb 24 1962, breaking a world record (GBR 1962 p220). **Christopher Wood** of Buxton, Derbys, aged 53, notorious serial robber of high street building societies in the Midlands and the North of England between late 1995 and 1999 wearing a flat cap, and consequently known as the 'Flat cap' robber, was sentenced to 14 years imprisonment at Stafford Crown Court on May 24 1999. In Staffs he robbed Birmingham Midshires, Rugeley on Sept 17 1996 and on May 29 1997; Staffordshire Building Society, Uttoxeter on Nov 26 1996; and from the Leek United Building Society, Uttoxeter on July 30 1997 he took nothing. The long hunt for Wood was led by Staffs Police. Their life-size cardboard cut-out photograph of him to help the public detect him is believed to be the first in the country; the cut-out is to go to Staffs Police Museum at Baswich House, Weeping Cross (Daily Telegraph May 25 1999 p4ps) (SN May 27 1999 p9) (ES May 28 1999 p2).

STAFFORD AND LITERATURE. TE Jackson author of the novel 'The Voice in the Wilderness' (1914) lived in Stafford (VFC p73). George W Gough (1869-1948), author of the novel 'The Yeoman Adventurer' (1916), was born in Stafford (VFC p55). Joseph Price, an authority on bee-keeping, was born at Halesowen in 1872, but died at Stafford in 1947. His 'Price on Beekeeping' was published in 1949. Jim Hunter, writer, was born in Stafford in 1939. His novels include 'The Sun in the Morning' (1961), 'The Flame' (1966), and 'Walking in the Painted Sunshine' (1970) (VFC p71). Trevor S Jennings, author of books on bell ringing, for instance, 'A Short History of Surrey bells and ringing customs' (1974), lived in Stafford. Audrey Smith, whose illustrations appear in 'Giuseppe; translated' (by Ray Ockenden. 1963), 'Candy in the Alps' (by Maud D Reed. 1964), 'The Wrong Track' (by Timothy Morgan. 1966), lived in Stafford. Valerie Greeley, author of 'Farm Animals' (1981), 'Pets' (1981) and 'Zoo Animals' (1981), lived in Stafford. Frederick Clitheroe, poet, author, librarian at Keele University and author of 'Meerook' (1980), 'Ellipsis' (1981), 'Harecastle Mint' (1982), lived at Stafford. A prospective novel 'Rogue Element' scheduled to be written by best selling author Terence Strong in 1995 was to be set in Stafford (SN Aug 25 1995 p9). For Stafford as a verb see BCM April 1971 p27. 'Stafford' is a variety of Day Lily, but it may have been named after someone with the Stafford surname.

Stafford Branch of the Staffordshire and Worcestershire Canal. Built in 1816. Diverged from the Staffs & Worcs Canal at 0.25m NW of Baswich church, at SJ 944227 and followed a widened and deepened Sow to the centre of Stafford. Used until the 1920s (IAS p120) (Nicholson's Guide to the Waterways No. 5 'Midlands' p48) (VCH vol 6 p198). A lock connected the two canals, the brick work of which was still visible in 1971, but not by 1986 (SWY p40).

Stafford Brook Rises by Wolseley Park House, Cannock Chase, joins the Trent at Wolseley Hall. A tributary is called Little Stafford Brook. There is a burnt mound probably of the Middle Bronze Age 0.75m NW of Slitting Mill near Stafford Brook Farm at SK 01921517. It is about 16 metres in diameter and about 1.5 metres high and was discovered in 1988 (SASR 1987 p16).

Stafford Castle There were several successive royal castles in the Broad Eye and Stafford town area. It is possible that on the rare occasions when 'Stafford Castle' is mentioned in the early C14 Bridgnorth is intended as the Staffs sheriff was also sheriff of Shrops up to 1344 (VCH vol 6 p200). Some writers have argued that all the Stafford castles, even the Norman ones, were situated at Castle Church (The Early Norman Castles of the British Isles. ES Armitage. 1912. pp213-214) (Stafford Hist and Civic Soc Trans 1971-73 p3). **Edward the Elder's fort.** There was a tradition in Elizabethan times that the mound known as Castle Hill and standing SE of Broadeye Bridge was the site of a tower built in 913 by Edward the Elder, brother of Ethelfleda (Britannia. Camden. 1695 pp531, 538). But this tradition is improbable (VCH vol 6 p200). **Ethelfleda's fort.** There is a tradition Ethelfleda built a fort in the Broad Eye area in 913 (LGS p212) or 918 (GNHS p103). Norman fort. A fort or castle was built by William I, when, either returning from the Yorkshire campaign, or after, going to Yorkshire, crushing a rebellion at Stafford in 1069 (HOS p17) or 1070 (SSTY p5) (VCH vol 6 p200) on the way. The site belonged to the manor of Chebsey (VCH vol 6 p200). It was perhaps only of wood and lasted about 10 years (LGS p212) (SL pp58,59). It had been destroyed by 1086 and is described in DB as recently destroyed (VCH vol 6 p200). (SOS p140) (NHS p416) (W p321) (SHCST 1971-73 pp9-11) (ROT p36). **Norman castle.** The fort, mentioned above, may have been rebuilt as a castle by William Rufus (LGS p213), or by Henry I, when he was faced with a rebellion (HOS p17). Orderic Vitalis declared that Henry I entrusted 'custodiam Stephordi castri' to William Pantulf in 1102 (VCH vol 6 p200). It has been disputed whether this does refer to a castle at Stafford, and if so, whether the castle was in Stafford town or at Castle Church; Palliser and Salter and others have argued that it was built at Castle Church. If it was in Stafford town, it is thought to have been replaced within 50 years by a new castle at Newcastle-under-Lyme, and subsequently used merely as a gaol (SHC vol 8, part 2, 1887 p7) (NSJFS 1966 pp44-45). **Tudor castle.** There is a tradition that there was a castle built by the North Gate in Henry VIII's reign which contained part of the gate (SKYT p48).

SITES. It is not known whether these castles or forts were all on the same site, or exactly where the sites were. Three sites have been identified. They are 1) at Castle Hill, Broad Eye (presently occupied by the windmill) (DoE II) (SKYT p3) (SSTY p217) (VCH vol 6 p200) (info Bruce Braithwaite). Sir Simon Degge says in his Ms notes on NHS that there was a castle within the town near the Broad Eye, and in his time a bank, called the 'Castle Bank,' which Cherry supposes was the later Castle Hill (SIOT p90). Or 2) not far away at Bull or Bully Hill, off Gaol Square (presently occupied by Sainsbury Supermarket), for it can be assumed Boley, Bullie and Bully are merely modifications of Bailey (SKYT pp48-49) (VCH vol 6 p200). Or 3) in the Mount Street or Mount Row area. Both the finding of large blocks in an old wall during street-widening work in c1932 and the name 'Mount' suggest that in this area was an old fort or possibly the Saxon mint (FSP pp78,79). The site of the castle is still called 'The Mount' (MOS p8). Traces or memories of its site survived until c1600 (VCH vol 6 p200) (CAMS p25). Cherry says Rev W Beresford is of the opinion that there are the remains of a castle in the garden of the house of the Misses Wogan, opposite the rectory (SIOT p90).

Stafford Castle Former baronial castle at Castle Church, in the Manor of Castre (see) or manor of Stafford (SIOT p148). The castle was the caput of the Stafford barony, one of the great baronies held direct from the king as lord paramount, by a tenant-in-chief or tenant in capite (SCSF p117).

DESCENT OF THE STAFFORDS AND THEIR DESCENDENTS. **Robert de Stafford** (or Robert Teoni), younger son of Roger de Teoni, of the French family Teoni (or Toeni, Tonei), who were standard bears to the Dukes of Normandy, accompanied William of Normandy on the Conquest of 1066. After William I had put down the insurrection at Stafford in 1070 he granted land near Stafford and the hill on which Stafford Castle stands and a manor (later to become known as the manor of Castle Church) to Robert. Robert, or a descendant, built the first Stafford castle at Castle Church some time after 1071 (HOS pp17,20). No castle at Castle Church is recorded in DB (1086) (VCH vol 5 p84), but certain evidence from DB suggests to Dr Philip Morgan that a castle may have been in existence there then (SHJ summer 1987 p47). Others say the first castle at Castle Church was probably Henry I's castle built and entrusted to William Pantulf in 1102 (SHCST 1971-73 p2) (CAMS p25). Robert, who was the most important Staffs landowner in 1086 after the king (HOS 1998 p32), died in 1088 and was buried in Evesham Abbey. He was succeeded by his son **Nicholas** de Stafford (d c1138), who was buried at Stone Priory (see). He was succeeded by his son **Robert** (still living in 1220-1), who was succeeded by his sister Millicent (who died before 1224/ 5 and is buried with her husband at Stone Priory). She married **Hervey Bagot**, who assumed the name of Stafford and died before 1193. Their son **Hervey** (died before 1237), succeeded. He was succeeded by his son **Hervey**, who died before 1241 without issue. He was succeeded by his brother **Robert**, who died before 1261. He was succeeded by his son **Nicholas**, who died at the siege of Deresloyn or Droslan Castle, Wales, in 1287 and was buried at Stone Priory. He was succeeded by his son **Edmund**, who married Margaret, the daughter of Ralph Lord Bassett. Edmund was created a baron in 1299 and became 1st Lord Stafford, and died before 1308, and was buried in the Friars Minor of Stafford. Edmund (SMC p122), or Edward (SCSF p117), Lord Stafford, held the manor of Stafford, and the manors of Bradley, and Madeley of the king by barony on condition he find three armed men with three horses and equipment for war whenever there was war between England and Wales, or Scotland (temp Edward II) (SMC p122). Edmund was succeeded by his son **Ralph**, 2nd Lord Stafford. His younger brother Sir Richard (d1381), was of Pipe Ridware and Clifton Campville (see). Ralph obtained a weekly market for Madeley in 1341, rebuilt Stafford Castle (see) (allegedly resided at Hyde manor house at Hyde Lea Mottes during the rebuilding), founded Saint Augustine's Priory (see), Stafford Green, fortified Madeley Old Manor (see), and may have been a benefactor to the nearby St John's Hospital (see), Stafford Green. He was created 1st Earl of Stafford in 1351. He married Margaret, daughter of Baron Audley, Earl of Gloucester, and died in 1372. He was succeeded by his second son **Hugh**, 2nd Earl of Stafford, who married Phillipa, daughter of the Earl of Warwick. He died in Rhodes in 1385 on his way home after making a pilgrimage to Palestine. He was succeeded by his second son, **Thomas**, 3rd Earl of Stafford, who died in 1392. He was succeeded by his younger brother, **William**, 4th Earl of Stafford, who died in 1395. He was succeeded by his younger brother, **Edmund**, 5th Earl of Stafford. He married Anne Plantagenet, granddaughter of Edward III. On his death at the battle of Shrewsbury in 1403, he was succeeded by his son, **Humphrey**, 6th Earl of Stafford. He married Lady Anne Nevill, sister of the Earl of Salisbury, aunt of Edward IV, and was created the Duke of Buckingham in 1444, and died at the battle of Northampton in 1460. He was succeeded by his grandson, **Henry**, 2nd Duke of Buckingham and 7th Earl of Stafford, a ward of Edward IV, and brought up by the king's sister. He married Catherine Rivers, sister of Elizabeth, the Queen of Edward IV, and was beheaded in Salisbury market place in 1483, for conspiracy to usurp Richard III and place the Earl of Richmond on the throne. The titles were then forfeited. However, Henry VII restored the titles to Henry's son, **Edward**, who became 3rd Duke of Buckingham and 8th Earl of Stafford. He married Lady Eleanor Percy, daughter of Henry, Earl of Northumberland, and built Thornbury Castle, Glous. He made an enemy of Cardinal Wolsey with the prank of pouring water into the Cardinal's shoes. In revenge Wolsey laid false charges against Edward that he was planning to assassinate the King. He was consequently charged with treason and beheaded at Tower Hill on May 15 1521. The dukedom, other titles, and estates were then forfeited. In 1532 the King gave Edward's son, **Henry**, Stafford Castle and the manor of Stafford the title of Lord Stafford. In 1547 he was restored to the barony as 1st Lord Stafford and died in 1563. He was succeeded by his son, **Edward**, 2nd Lord Stafford, who died in 1565. he was succeeded by his son **Edward** (d1603), 3rd Lord Stafford. He was succeeded by his second son **Edward** (d1625/6), 4th Lord Stafford. He was succeeded by his grandson, **Henry**, 5th Lord Stafford. He died without issue in 1637, aged 16. He was succeeded by **Roger** Stafford, son of Richard Stafford (or Floyde), second son of Henry 1st Lord Stafford (d1563). Roger Stafford, 6th Lord Stafford, surrendered the barony in 1639 and died in 1640 (his sister married a joiner, and their son was a cobbler in Newport, Shrops). From Roger Stafford the barony was bestowed upon Sir **William Howard**, husband of Mary, sister and heiress of Henry, 5th Lord Stafford. He was created 1st Viscount Stafford in 1640. In the Civil War Viscount Stafford was a royalist. In 1680 he was beheaded for his alleged involvement in the Popish Plot (see under Tixall Old Hall). After the execution the Stafford lands were restored to his widow, and a new earldom of Stafford was created for her son, **Henry** (b c1648), who became 1st Earl of Stafford in 1688 (and would have been the 2nd Baron and Viscount but for the attainder). He died without issue in 1719 and

the title then passed to his nephew, **William** (Stafford-Howard) (d1733/4), 2nd Earl of Stafford (3rd Baron and Viscount but for the attainder). He was succeeded by his son **William Matthias** (Stafford-Howard) (1718/9-1750/1), 3rd Earl of Stafford (4th Baron and Viscount but for the attainder), who died without issue. He was succeeded by his uncle **John Paul** (Stafford-Howard) (b1700), grandson of 1st Viscount Stafford (d1680) and brother of the 2nd Earl. He was the 4th Earl of Stafford (5th Baron and Viscount but for the attainder), and died without issue in 1762. The earldom then became extinct, as did the right to the (attainted) Viscountcy of Stafford, but the barony of Stafford devolved to the niece of John Paul (or daughter of William, 2nd Earl of Stafford), Lady **Anastasia** Stafford-Howard (1722-1807), a nun (who would have been the Baroness Stafford (6th Baron) but for the attainder). With her death the title devolved to Sir **William Jerningham**, who was the son of Sir George Jerningham and his wife Mary (daughter of Francis Plowden and his wife Mary, sister of John Paul, 4th Earl of Stafford). Sir William Jerningham died in 1809, having made some attempts to reclaim the title of Baron Stafford; he would have been 7th Baron but for the attainder. He was succeeded by his son Sir **George** William Jerningham, who made further attempts to reclaim the title, even having Stafford Castle rebuilt. In 1824 there appeared a rival claimant, Richard Stafford Cooke, a cabinet maker of Chelmsford, Essex, who in his pursuit of the title stayed briefly at the Dolphin Inn (see), Stafford, in Dec 1822. He appointed his younger brother, James Stamp Sutton Cooke, a man of some legal training, to act as his press agent. But James rather too bombastically and antagonistically promoted his brother and the two received much ridicule in pamphlets and newspapers (many of which are kept in the WSL). Sir George was successful in his claim and became 8th Baron Stafford and 2nd Viscount Stafford when the reversal of the attainder was obtained on June 17 1824. Despite losing the claim Richard maintained his right, and in 1830 was charged with sending letters bearing the forged frank of the Baron of Stafford. He was considered an amiable lunatic and discharged. Nevertheless he kept an action of ejectment on foot against the new and official Lord Stafford until 1833 when it lapsed for want of funds (OP pp20-22). In 1851 Sir George, who took the name of Stafford before that of Jerningham becoming Stafford-Jerningham in 1826, died. He was succeeded by his son from his first marriage, Sir **Henry Valentine Stafford-Jerningham** (b1802), 9th Baron Stafford and 3rd Viscount Stafford. He died without issue in 1884 and was succeeded by his nephew, Sir **Augustus Frederick** Fitzherbert (Stafford-Jerningham) (b1830), 10th Baron Stafford and 4th Viscount Stafford. He died unmarried in 1892 and was succeeded by his younger brother Sir **Fitzherbert Edward** (Stafford Jerningham) (b1833), 11th Baron Stafford and 5th Viscount Stafford. He died in 1913 and the title passed to his nephew (his sister's son) **Francis Edward Fitzherbert-Stafford** of Swynnerton Hall, who became the 12th Baron Stafford. He died in 1932 and was succeeded by his brother **Edward Stafford** Fitzherbert, 13th Baron Stafford (1864-1941). He died without issue and was succeeded by his nephew **Basil Francis Nicolas** Fitzherbert, 14th Baron Stafford (1926-1986). The present baron, 15th Baron Stafford, is his son **Francis Melfort William** Fitzherbert (b1954) (The Complete Peerage) (HOS p20) (SAC pp153-156) (Who's Who 1993).

STAFFORD KNOT. The Stafford Knot was the badge of the Stafford family. **Origins**. The tradition that the Stafford Knot was devised so that three people could be hung at the same time can be dismissed (NSFCT 1918 p31) (FSP p46) (ES Aug 14 1993 p33). A knot resembling the Stafford knot appears on the cross shaft in Stoke-upon-Trent churchyard, which can be dated to 750 to 850 AD (ES Aug 14 1993 p33). The Stafford family seem to have adopted it from Joan, Lady of the Wake, daughter of Hugh de Stafford, 2nd Earl of Stafford (d1385) (MOS p15 handwritten note in WSL copy) (NSFCT 1918 p33) and a direct descendent of Hereward the Wake. An early appearance is on a seal of Joan, currently in the BM, which clearly shows a cordon of Stafford knots. It was then known as the 'Knot of Hope.' On her death in 1443 her possessions passed to her nephew Humphrey, 6th Earl of Stafford, who adopted the knot as his badge and used it as personal cognisance. **The knot as a Stafford family emblem**. The Earls of Stafford (or Dukes of Buckingham) gave it to their retainers and servants as a livery and means of recognition. The Staffords used the badge to decorate their buildings, furniture, and hangings; it appears on a chasuble worn by Edmund, 5th Earl of Stafford at his wedding in 1398, which was displayed at the V&A, London in 1997. It also appears at Thornbury Castle, Glous, the residence of Edward, Duke of Buckingham, who appeared on the Field of the Cloth of Gold in 1520 at the head of the king's retinue (SC pp10-21). A most elaborate example can be seen in the chapel of St Edmund in Westminster Abbey, upon a curious marble mural slab in memory of John Paul Howard (d1762), Earl of Stafford (NSFCT 1918 p33). **The knot as a county emblem**. The knot had been incorporated into the arms of the borough of Stafford by 1583 (VCH vol 6 p229), and has been adopted as the emblem of the county and has become known as the Staffordshire Knot. The county took it from the coat of arms of Stafford borough: It appears on Green Bridge, Stafford (VB p130). It has been an emblem of the North and South Staffordshire Regiments, Staffordshire Yeomanry, Staffordshire Police Force, Staffordshire Agricultural Society, in most coats of arms of Staffordshire boroughs and urban districts and the Staffordshire Guides (ES Aug 14 1993 p33) (BCM Jan 1977 pp6-10ps). The knot is carved on Cheswardine church tower (Shrops, formerly Staffs) (NSFCT 1974 p125). It is embroidered on the back of a chair in the State Sitting room at Shugborough, and on the shirts of Rushall Rovers football team of 1878 (WOPP pl p136), and appears on many horse brasses. EC & J Keay Ltd of James Bridge, Darlaston (Offlow hundred), engineering works, used the knot in their name plates (TB Nov 1993 p29). A giant steel Stafford knot was made at Hingleys, Netherton, Worcs (see), for the Great Exhibition at Crystal Palace in 1851. The steel bar was five inches in diameter and the knot was described in newspapers of the time as 'the eighth wonder of the world.' It was cut up for scrap and transferred to Round Oak steelworks in 1970 (TB Nov 1986 p1p. July 1993 p1p).

THE CASTLE. A castle at Castle Church is mentioned in the 1140s (CAMS p25). Recent evidence suggests a stone rectangular tower keep was built on the mound sometime in the C12, probably by Robert de Stafford (d1188). The castle is unusual in having two baileys. In the reign of Henry II the free chapel of St Nicholas was described as being 'within the castle of Stafford.' This is thought to have been at the castle of Castle Church (SIOT p148). During the Barons' Wars, in 1263, forces under William la Zouche, Justicier of Chester, and David, brother of Llewelyn, Prince of Wales captured the castle (SIS p22). There was probably a chapel in the castle by 1147 and the chapel dedicated to St Nicholas is recorded in 1292 and was in use until the mid C16 (VCH vol 5 pp85,97). In 1347 Ralph, later 1st Earl of Stafford, constructed on the now disused Norman motte (SL p87) a substantial rectangular stone tower house with octagonal corner towers and a fifth tower in the middle of the W side and walls seven feet thick at the base. The design was very unusual, probably being based on a continental model, and the Norman keep had to be partly excavated to provide a larger foundation (VCH vol 5 p84) (HOS p20) (NSFCT 1983 pp39-40). In 1348 Edward III granted a license for it to be embattled (VCH vol 5 p84). The castle reverted to the Crown on the execution of Edward Stafford, Duke of Buckingham, last High Constable of England (The Guinness Book of Lasts. Christopher Slee. 1994. p142), in 1521. In 1531 it was restored to Henry, Lord Stafford, and his wife Ursula (VCH vol 5 p85). In 1575 Elizabeth I was entertained to dinner at the castle. In 1603 it was described as the 'rotten castle of Stafford' and in 1634 as 'somewhat ruined.' For the castle in the Civil War period see Stafford. (SOS p140) (SH p31; on Erdeswick considering the age of the castle) (NHS p416) (GNHS p103) (W p324) (MOS p28) (OSST 1932 pp31-35. 1951-52 pp10-14) (TNE p256) (SHJ vol 2 pp11-15. vol 5 pp42-48) (SHCST 1971-73 pp1-9. 1991-92 pp14-20) (SGS p154) (ROT p35p) (AA p258) (SAC pp82-86).

JERNINGHAM'S CASTLE. The castle foundations or tower bases survived the Civil War. In the C18 the NE corner tower of the tower house, which had remained standing higher than the rest after slighting, was converted into a folly. The same or a different stretch of remains, described as a 'fragment of walling,' was also standing when Sir William Jerningham succeeded in c1788 (VCH vol 5 p85 il of c1800 facing p86). Sir William intended to strengthen this but decided to clear the site and expose the plan. A full excavation was made. Sir William's son, Sir George Jerningham, and his brother, Edward Jerningham, rebuilt the castle in the Edward III style in Tixall stone from c1812. The scheme was never completed and only the western towers and a suite of rooms at the western end were built. Edward Jerningham was living at the castle by Oct 1817 when the antiquary, William Hamper visited in here (VCH vol 2 p190. vol 5 p86 frontispiece). (SSC p135 in the intro. p11 etching by F Calvert c1830) (W p24) (HS pp45p, facing 164,170p) (LGS pp218-219) (SOSH p87il) (SOPP pl 54 in 1904) (SSTY pp6p,34p of in c1920, & p of interior of the Main Hall) (SL p135) (F p307) (F & G p391) (FZ p111) (SN April 5 1996 p18) (SAC pp87-89). Many cannon balls of the Civil War period were found when the castle was being rebuilt by Jerningham (SLM summer 1956 pp18,19). The castle was used as a triangulation point by surveyors for the first OS map, and the site had been used by Yates for his map (SHC 4th series vol 12 1984 vii). In the interior glass cases displayed at the castle in the C19 were six marble panels representing the life of Christ which were formerly part of the altar at Tixall Priory (St Thomas' at Baswich?) (SAIW pl 38 shows interior of the Great Hall). The castle ceased to be the Jerningham seat later in the C19 (the barony passed to the Fitzherberts in 1913). It was used as an observation post in WW2. Gales dislodged castel-

lated battlements of the S tower on March 16 1947 (SKYT pp15p,16ps showing towers). The turrets and upper rooms were then sealed off (SSTY p17). The castle was declared unsafe in 1950 up to which time it had been occupied by a caretaker. In an abandoned state it became vandalised (STMSM Nov 1979 pp30,31ps). In 1961 a boy was killed by the collapse of the mullions of the main E window (MR p286). It was given to the Stafford borough council in 1960 (SLM Aug/Sept 1988 p25). They demolished the towers and curtain walls in 1950 (SAIW p37p), or 1961 (info Bruce Braithwaite), or 1963 because they were considered unsafe (DoE II) (STM July 1963 p49p just prior to demolition of the towers. July 1970 p30ps) (CAMS pp25,26p,27 plan,28). By 1974 only the shell of the ground floor remained (BOE pp249-250). Whilst staying with the caretaker's family in 1936 a visitor heard sounds of a horse on several occasions, which could not be explained (info Bruce Braithwaite). In July 1968 there was a ghost sit-in at the castle but nothing was seen (Stafford Advertiser July 4 1968 p5). The sound of a blacksmith working at an anvil has been heard in the vicinity of the castle, and archaeologists have found evidence for a blacksmith's stable and smithy by the castle (info Bruce Braithwaite). In a wood that surrounds the castle have been found some cannon balls, a plain silver cross, a lobster Cromwellian helmet, still to be seen at Haughton, the lower portion of a large font, and silver coins of Edward VI (FSP pp55-57). Excavations below the castle took place from 1979. Some pottery finds were made (STMSM Nov 1979 pp30,31ps) (MR p286p shows the excavations-287). There a tradition that a tunnel runs from the Noah's Ark Inn to Stafford Castle (SKYT p11). (NSJFS 1966 pp44-45).

Stafford Collegiate Church A Royal Free chapel at Stafford. It was in existence before 1086, since the existence of canons in Stafford in DB suggests there was already a college here. It is recorded in 1546 and 1548 that King John founded the collegiate church. The first mention of it is in his reign and he may have promoted the dedication to St Mary. In 1258 Roger de Molend, bishop of Lichfield, disregarding St Mary's status as a Royal Free chapel attempted to subjugate it, under Bozo de Clare, the dean, by arms. Both sides refused to plead at the assizes. The bishop eventually obtained entry but he was unable to bring any disciplinary powers over the clergy (SIOT p98) (LGS p215) (SKYT pp94-95) (SSTY p136). In 1280 Archbishop Pecham came to Stafford and was physically prohibited from entering the St Mary's by the sheriff (VCH vol 3 pp304,305). The privilege of sanctuary in St Mary's was infringed in 1300 by the violent capture and imprisonment of Adam Coly and William de Offleigh. The men had committed certain felonies and were imprisoned in Stafford Gaol; from this they broke out and took sanctuary in St Mary's, but were captured and re-imprisoned. The dean and chapter of St Mary's complained to the king, and the justices of the gaol delivery were commanded to return the men to the Dean and Chapter (SCSF p158) (SKYT p95). In Oct 1929 the controversy over St Mary's status as a Royal Free Chapel arose again, when the Rector of St Mary's Rev Lionel Lambert tried to have it's status reaffirmed in the Chancery Division but the action proved in favour of the bishop of Lichfield (LGS p215) (SKYT p96) (SSTY pp136,138). The college has also appeared as St Mary's College and St Mary's Collegiate Church. The collegiate buildings stood on the S side of the churchyard and eventually came into the hands of Stafford corporation. Known as the College House it was normally held by the master of the grammar school from at least 1615 until the 1720s. A workhouse was established in some of the outbuildings after it was mostly demolished 1736-38 (VCH vol 3 pp206,303-309). The main gateway to the college estate was **St Mary's Gate**. This was an ordinary building with an archway under wooden gates which were closed at night, with a room or lodging for the gate-keeper. It was situated on the E end of the passage leading across to St Mary's Grove and the present (1933) passage to the backs of the High House (OSST 1933 p50) or across the passage bearing the name of St Mary's at the gable of the former Brookfield's shop (SKYT p96), on the site of the present McDonald's restaurant. The college estate was of considerable size. Starting from St Mary's Gate, it followed through the houses along the main street, then ran W to Victoria Park, S along Kitling Brook and the Tenterbanks, and then turned E to run under 'the lower part of the Swanne' back to St Mary's Gate (SKYT p96). The site of the Vicars' College, with its garden, was, in 1948, covered with the Conservative Club and cottages adjoining it in St Mary's Lane, St Mary's Schools and schoolyard (SKYT p96). Noel's Almshouses (see) was built on the Court House of the canons. The dean resided at the Deanery (see), and what became Noah's Ark Inn (see) was reputedly a residence for him. Notable incidents relating to the college occurred in 1258, 1280, 1300, and 1929.

Stafford Common Common land of 125 acres (OSST 1934 p28) approximately 1.25m N of Stafford town, administered by the Stafford Common Lands Trustees (info Michael Cockin). Is the remainder of a larger common, enclosed in

1800 (OSST 1934 p28), and some of it is the remainder of Foregate Field, enclosed in 1807. The railway station at Stafford Common on the Stafford & Uttoxeter Railway line, the old 'Clog and Knocker' was opened on July 1 1874 (VB p133) (Railways In and Around Stafford. Edward Talbot. 1994 p4).

Stafford Gaol Foregate, Stafford. The county prison or gaol at Stafford is first mentioned in 1185 (VCH vol 6 p203). The Staffordshire sheriff was also sheriff of Shropshire (until 1344) and prisoners were sent to prison in Shrops, usually at Bridgnorth Castle, in the mid C13 (VCH vol 6 pp200,204-205). In 1390 County prisoners were kept in the borough gates in Stafford. A new County prison was built at the end of or 'near' Crabbery Lane and 'towards' Broadeye in c1391 (VCH vol 6 p203). In 1414 three prisoners escaped from Stafford gaol and claimed sanctuary in St Chad's church, Stafford. The church was besieged, and on attempting to escape one of the men was killed (SHC vol xv p27) (COEA pp225-226). In the early C17 the lower part of the North Gate in Stafford was used as the county gaol. A new gaol by the town wall, E of the North Gate, probably came into use in 1621 (VCH vol 6 p204). By the end of the C17 a new county house of correction was built on the site of the North Gate in Stafford. The gate was ruinous in 1678 (VCH vol 6 p204). Stafford Prison was built in Gaol Road in 1793 to designs by William Blackburn, replacing the old gaol in North Gate (BOE p247). At the time of its opening it was one of the largest in the country (SKYT p130). The prison was extended in c1819, 1832-3, 1852-4 and 1864-6 (VCH vol 6 p204) (SKYT p132). Four round towers (or keeper's lodges) were built by 1856 in the angles of the surrounding wall (VCH vol 6 p204); some had to be taken down when they became unsafe probably due to brine pumping underneath Stafford for salt (SKYT p132) (ASOP p55) (SSTY pp119,121). On Sunday night, a few days before Aug 15 1795, there was a break-out attempt (SA Aug 15 1795) (SIOT p53). For a curious suicide at the gaol in 1800 see Greenfield. Early **hangings** at the gaol appear to have taken place in public. The last execution for forgery took place at Stafford in 1828 (TB March 1975 p15). William Beard was executed at Stafford Gaol on Aug 17 1844 after being found guilty at the last assizes of the murder of Elizabeth Griffiths, domestic servant of Mr Crowther (ILN Aug 24 1844 p115) (TB June 1993 p19; Beard's victim was Ann Griffiths). In June 1856 an estimated 35,000 came to see the execution of William Palmer, the serial poisoner of Rugeley (see) (SSTY p122). The last person to be hung in public at the gaol was William Collier in 1866. The last execution at the gaol was on March 14 1914 (SKYT p133).

Stafford Green Alias The Green, in Forebridge, Stafford. In the later C17 Plot noted a maid lived at Stafford Green to the age of 122. Her diet was chiefly scraped cheese, sugar and brown bread (NHS p321).

Stafford Park Medieval deer park enclosed out of forest, held by the Earls of Stafford. In existence by 1284. Lay to the W of Stafford (NSJFS 1962 pp73,76).

Stafford Port Wharf on the Staffs & Worcs Canal, centred on the Trumpet Inn, Radford Bank, Stafford. Buildings on the opposite side of the road from the Trumpet were known as the 'The Port of Stafford' until their demolition in the 1960s (BERK pp15-16,17) (SAC p117p). The wharf has also appeared as Radford Port and The Port of Stafford. (VCH vol 2 p288. vol 6 p198).

Staffordshire and Worcestershire Canal Opened in 1772 to link the Severn at Stourport with the Trent and Mersey Canal at Great Haywood. The canal, a contour canal (SVB p182), was formerly known as the Wolverhampton Canal and is 46m long. Dr Johnson of Lichfield (see), who called it the Stafford Canal, wrote how he 'crossed the Stafford Canal, one of the great efforts of human labour and contrivance which passed away on either side to lose itself in distant regions, uniting waters that nature had divided, and dividing land which nature had united.' The canal never came under railway control as did so many canals (VB p82). The stretch through Wombourne and beyond is reckoned to be one of the most beautiful lengths of canal in England (SVB p182).

Staffordshire Moor Enclosed common land to W of Lud Lane, Tamworth, S of the railway, formerly in Wigginton township in Tamworth ancient parish (1890 OS map 6 inch). Since Tamworth lay in two counties it had two pieces of common land, Warwickshire Moor and Staffordshire Moor. By the C13 the town house owners of Tamworth had the right of pasture on one or other of the commons depending on their residence being in Warws or Staffs. The moors were greatly enclosed in the C18 (WMLB p90). According to Shakespeare's 'Richard III' Henry VII's forces camped here prior to the battle of Bosworth, in 1485 (HS p158). Some 62 acres of the common remained in the 1950s (OSST 1956-59 p14).

Staffordshire Pool Former pool on Shire Brook near Witton. It stretched into Warws and was approximately 4.5 acres in extent. It may have been made in

Georgian times or perhaps in Stuart times. The pool was in filled when Shire Brook was culverted in the later C19 (MNB p35).

Stafford Town Walls DB suggests Stafford was a walled town by 1086. The suggestion comes in the phase 'within town walls' under the heading 'In the Borough of Stafford;' as such Stafford was the only one of seven walled towns in England, and the only walled town in the county (SIOT p89) (SOSH p148) (VCH vol 4 p37) (SPJD p26). However, B Wilson could find no reference in DB to Stafford being a walled town (OSST 1948-49 p8). The walls were re-built or strengthened in 1224. Early town walls were built mainly of timber. By 1600 the walls were mainly of stone, but stretched on the NW and NE sides consisted of wooden palisades (VCH vol 6 p199) (SSTY p3). The walls ran along (clockwise) North Walls, South Walls, Mill Bank, Tenterbanks and Chell Road. In the Civil War in 1643 and 1644 they were strengthened (VCH vol 6 p199) (SIOT p89). They were in ruins by 1680 (W p325) (HOS p65) (SSTY p17). (OSST 1938 pp38-42) (SAIW pl 34p) (FSP pp78,79). Streets named North Walls, formerly Back Walls North (NE side of the town), South Walls, formerly Back Walls South (S side), Mill Bank (S side), Tenter Banks (W side) preserve the line of the walls (SOPP pl 35). Uncovered or **remaining** sections of walling are at the **S end of North Walls**. This is a fairly long stretch topped by modern brickwork (SSTY p2p) (SOPP pl 27p; it adjoined a chocolate shop at the Lammascote end of North Walls in the 1920s?). Remains of the North Wall were offered to the County Museum in 1974 (SN Feb 22 1974 p7). At the **end of Eastgate Street** is a small piece containing a groove of a portcullis. It was originally part of the East Gate at the junction of North Walls and Lammascote Road and removed in c1938 to relieve a traffic bottleneck (ES Jan 20 1938 p7p). June 6 1938 p4p shows excavations of a section of the old wall (SKYT p48p) (HOS p65) (SSTY pp17-18) (SOPP pl 27) (SN Feb 15 1974 p5) (BOE p245) (MR p288) (SPJD p27p). At the **end of Lichfield Road** is a small piece adjacent to the re-erected Lock-up next to the White Lion Inn, (MR p293) - it must have been re-erected here. From the **South Gate to the Coach and Horses Inn**, is a portion, 50 yards long, uncovered and covered up again in 1928 when old buildings (a mercer's shop) on corner of Mill Bank were taken down because of road-widening (NSFCT 1928 p148) (SSTY p3) (SOPP pl 26) (SPJD p27p). None of the four gates in the town walls survive. They were the East Gate (see), North Gate (see), South Gate (see), West Gate (see).

Stag Caves Caves to W of Kinver church and N of Anchor Hotel are at the rear of and part of the Stag Inn at the bottom of Mill Lane close to the Stourbridge Road. The inn was demolished in 1975. The largest cave is over 30 feet in depth (KRH p28).

Stake Bank 0.75m NW of Ipstones (1834 OS map). Stakebank Wood (OS Street Atlas: Staffs 1995) lies by Collyhole Brook.

Stake Gutter NE of Upper Hulme at SK 024633 on the Roman road to Buxton there is a rectangular camp discovered in 1938 (NSFCT 1938 p114). The camp either did not exist by 1964 or never existed (NSJFS 1964 p25).

Stallbrook Hall House 1.25m WNW of Castle Church, in Seighford parish. Said to date from the C14 and was moated. In the C16 it was the seat of the Bowyer family of Knypersley. Sold in Charles II's reign. In disrepair in the later C20 it was restored in the late 1990s (DoE II) (SVB p66) (The Way for the Millennium. 2000. p5).

Stallings 0.5m NNE of Kingswinford. In Kingswinford ancient parish. Stallings was a hamlet in the mid C19 (W p184). The name, which persists in Stallings Lane which runs E from Wall Heath, was probably named after Stawlings Farm, mentioned between 1822 and 1851. In 1840 it was occupied by William Cox and owned by the late Earl of Dudley (SNSV vol 1 p307). That farm is probably identifiable with Stallings Farm (1834 OS map) on the N side of Stallings Lane.

Stallington Hamlet on the E-facing slope of the Blythe valley made large by its hospital, formerly Stallington Hall (see) 0.75m NNE of Fulford. Former township in Stone quarter in Stone ancient parish (W p364). Former manor belonging to Stone Priory (W). Appears in 1251 as Stalenton (SSE 1996 p17). The name means 'tun of the Staelingas' or 'stony hill tun' (SSE 1996 p17).

Stallington Hall Stallington. By 1834 to at least 1851 it was the residence of Richard Clarke Hill (d1852) (mem in Fulford church) (W 1834) (W p23) whose daughter married Sir Smith Child. The Hill Childs lived here for many years. It was a hospital for the mentally handicapped between 1930 and c1998 (ES Sept 3 1930 p4. Sept 17 1930 p6p. April 3 1998 p5p) (JSD p97p).

Stallington Heath Heath over 0.5m SW of Fulford.

Stamp's Bridge Crosses the Manifold at Swainsley. Takes its name from the old mine stamps yard which was situated in the field below the bridge on the Ecton Hill side of the river (DMV p65).

Standeford Small hamlet on Saredon Brook over 0.5m N of Coven. In Brewood ancient parish. An axe-head of Neolithic or Bronze Age was found at Standeford

Mill House in 1987 (BDH p19il). Has also appeared as Staunford (1245-50), Stawntiford (1506), Stantiford (1644) (SPNO p39), Standerford and Stanford. The name means 'the stony ford' (SPN p23). This may be a reference to a Roman road (between Pennocrucium and Metchley) which forded the brook here (WFW p32). The Anglo-Saxon Portstreet (the Warwick-Stafford road) is thought to have passed through Standeford.

Standeford Green Minute hamlet to W of Standeford.

Stand Hill The hill is a ridge between Wordsley and Kingswinford. (SVS p134). The suburb on it is known as Standhill or Standhills.

Standhills House House on Standhills estate 0.5m S of Kingswinford church. Residence of successive coal and ironmasters. Appears on a map of 1822. Occupied by George Firmstone, ironmaster, in 1834, and by Thomas Oakes, ironmaster, in 1851, and at the end of the C19 by William Peers. In the mid C19 the Standhills estate was owned by HE and J Bradley, a Dudley family (SNSV vol 1 p309). Some say it was demolished by 1881 as it does not appear on the 1881 OS map (SNSV vol 1 p199), or demolished sometime after 1900 owing to mining subsidence. Now built over with housing estates (TB Oct 1996 p19). There seems to have been a summer house in the grounds; a modern inn called The Summerhouse stands on or near the site (TB Oct 1996 p19p).

Standon (vulgarly *Stawe*, *Staun* SHC 1914 p7, Michael Cockin; there is a Staun Wood, 0.5m WNW of the church). Ancient parish and former township (HOPS p4). The village of Standon at the foot of a long ridge by Meece Brook whilst some of the old settlement is on the crest of the ridge overlooking Chatcull Brook 8.25m NW of Stafford. The **name** has appeared as Standune (C10) (SPN p114), Stantone (DB), Standon (1190) (SSE 1996 p17), and Standon Rock (later C20); 'Rock' was applied to Standon by the Post Office sometime after WW2 to help telephone operators distinguish Standon from Sandon (see), the word is from the sandstone rock cutting and cottages in the village (info Michael Cockin) (telephone directory 1999). The name means 'stone town,' probably because the original settlement was built of stone (DUIGNAN). Mills and Gelling think 'stone hill' (NSJFS 1981 p2) (SSE 1996 p17). Or 'stoney hill' (SSE 1987 p32) (SPN p114). There was a church at Standon in 1086. The present parish church, All Saints, at the crossroads of Mill Lane and Church Lane, has some Norman work (BOE p250-251). There is a tradition that the church was built of stones brought by angels at night from a hill above the village (HOPS p145). Standon ancient parish, once said to be completely bounded by water (NSFCT 1913 p50), was formed before 1086 (SHC 1916 p192). The **parish feast** was on the nearest Sunday to All Saints day in the C19 (W p407). Richard Whitworth of Batchacre Hall had proposals in 1765 to build the Liverpool to Hall **Canal** through Standon but it was never built (BVC p170). There was a station at Standon Bridge on the former Grand Junction **Railway** until Feb 4 1952 (Railways In and Around Stafford. Edward Talbot. 1994 p4). It was recommended that Standon station close in 1963 (ES March 22 1963). For a **rhyme** about rivalry between Cotes Heath and Standon see Cotes Heath. **Persons and visitors.** Rev **William Jorden**, rector of Standon 1729-1733, was the tutor of Dr Johnson of Lichfield (see) tutor at Pembroke College, Oxford. Johnson abhorred his lectures and is reputed to have said of him on being fined for non-attendance 'Sir, you have sconced me two pence for non-attendance at a lecture not worth a penny' (Life of Johnson LLD. James Boswell edited by W Croker LLD vol 1 p48 note) (HOPS p168). Standon Farm Approved School, built in 1885 for the homeless, became an approved school in 1938 for boys aged 13 to 16. **William Peter Fieldhouse**, aged 21, assistant gardening master at the school was shot dead by a group of 10 boys in an attempted break out from the school on Feb 15 1947. The boys were apprehended on the railway line between Madeley and Crewe later that day. Since no boy would admit to the killing all were charged with the murder; four boys were found guilty. The school closed later that year (MCS pp50-54) (A History of Staffordshire Police. Commemorative Issue 1992). **Jacquie Lewis**, who died in 1975 of cancer, lived at Standon old Post Office; her 'Let me tell you how I live with cancer' was published posthumously in 1977 (info Michael Cockin) (copy in WSL).

Standon Hall Hall 0.75m WNW of Standon. Built in 1910 to designs by J Francis Doyle of Liverpool (BOE p251) for Sir Thomas Anderdon Salt (1863-1940), 2nd Bt of Standon and Weeping Cross, Stafford, who became bankrupt and never lived at the hall (SKYT p80) (EOP p68p) (see under Baswich House). However, some say he merely experienced financial difficulties shortly after moving into the property, and did live here for a time (info Michael Cockin). The hall was bought by Staffs county council in 1928 (EOP p68) and officially opened as an orthopaedic hospital in 1932 (SVB p154). The hospital closed in the late 1970s. The hall is now (1998) a nursing home.

Standon Old Hall Hall 1m WNW of Standon. Timber-framed, half is C16 and half is C17. The hall was formerly Standon manor house (HOPS p61) (EOP

p67). There has been a house on the site since the Norman conquest; the sandstone cellars being older than the present house (EOP p67p). Some have thought there was a chapel in the cellar, but there is little evidence of there ever being one (NSFCT 1922 p159). It may have been the seat of the Vyse family in the C17 (mems in Standon church) (Plot's map). The peculiar custom of hanging a dead calf on a wall so that cows might look at it to prevent them aborting their young prematurely prevailed at Standon Old Hall. Also the custom of the household assembling round lighted bundles of straw in wheat fields after dark on Jan 6 to scare off witches, who were believed to give mildew to the young wheat and kill lambs, was practiced at the hall in the mid C19 (Old Customs and Tales of My Neighbours. 1898. Fletcher Moss. pp52,53,200 pl of the hall). Thomas Woolf (d1892) was of Standon (Old) Hall (mem in Standon church). There is a mound about 0.5m W of Standon Old Hall, situated on high ground. From N to S it is 50 feet and from E to W 60 feet. The width of the ditch averages about 20 feet (NSFCT 1922 pp152-153).

Stanfield Hamlet in the C19 on ground rising above a tributary of Fowlea Brook, now a suburb of Burslem, 0.75m N of Burslem. Formerly in Burslem chapelry in Stoke-upon-Trent ancient parish. Two good specimens of fossil trees were found in their actual positions of growth in a small clay pit at Stanfield. They were due to be removed because of quarrying in the 1960s (NSJFS 1964 pp104,106-107). Stanfield has also appeared as Stanfields. The Tellwrights had a house here known as Stanfields from the mid C16. By the early C19 the house was situated on the hillside below High Lane (VCH vol 8 p121) (NSSG p10). The church, St Werburgh, built in 1895, stood in Hamil Road and was replaced by the church, St Werburgh, at the junction of Haywood Road and High Lane, built in 1953 (VCH vol 8 pp124-125). Susie Cooper (1903-1995), ceramic designer, was born at Stanfield. Her parents later moved to Milton. She was employed at AE Gray & Co, Hanley, from 1922, and founded her own pottery firm in 1929. The company was at Crown Works (see), Burslem, by 1942. Susie Cooper Ltd was absorbed into Wedgwood Group in 1966. She was awarded an OBE in 1979, and an honorary degree by Keele University in 1993. She spent some of her retirement at Dilhorne (see) (FWNS pp49-55ps). Lance-sergeant John (Jack) Daniel Baskeyfield VC, born on Nov 18 1922 in Burslem, was of Carson Road, Stanfield. He became a butcher, later serving in the Staffordshire Regiment and was posthumously awarded the Victoria Cross for heroically manning an anti-tank gun at Oosterbeck in the battle of Arnhem in WW2 on Sept 20 1944. Between 1933 and 1936 he was a chorister at Christ Church, Cobridge, in which church there is a collection of photographs of him to his memory. In spring 1969 a film entitled 'Baskeyfield V.C.' was shown at the Manchester Film Theatre. On Sept 20 1969 a plaque to his memory was unveiled in the Market Square Gardens, Burslem. In 1996 a bronze statue of Baskeyfield was unveiled at Festival Heights (see) (STM Oct 1969 p25p) (ES April 29 1977) (TSS p118p) (MMM pp93-94) (SMML pp63-65).

Stanley Small village on the NW slopes of a hill overlooking Endon Brook valley, and former manor and township in Leek ancient parish, 15m N of Stafford. Has appeared as Stanlega (1130), (SSE 1996 p17). The name means 'the stony cleared open-land' (SSAHST 1967 p34) (VCH vol 7 p229), 'a stoney hill or clearing' (E p10) (SSE 1996 p17), 'stoney ground' (SVB p154). Or possibly a corruption of the Old English phrase 'stone legh' meaning stone-laden ground. Or some, locally, think from the Stanley family, Earls of Derby (PWNS p114). Or that that family and others of the name Stanley take their surname from Stanley (SVB p154). The medieval manor house may have stood where Lower House Farm (see) now stands. Glazing pottery by means of salt was accidentally discovered at Stanley in 1680 (SVB p155). A class which formed at Stanley in March 1810 resulting from the activities of Hugh Bourne of Bemersley Green (see) is regarded as the first Primitive Methodist class, although, the society did not adopt the name Primitive Methodist until 1812 (LGS p48) (ES March 11 1980). The village grew up in the C19 in connection with flint mills and further expansion has taken place in the C20 (VCH vol 7 p229). By the mid C19 Stanley formed a township in Leek ancient parish with Endon and Longdon townships (W p370); this became a civil parish, excluding Longsdon, from 1894. Ecclesiastically, Stanley was in Endon chapelry (VCH vol 7 pp229,232). There is a mission church, St Agnes, at Stanley (LDD).

Stanley Farm Near Bagnall (said to have been a short mile from the small pottery of Mr Palmer at Bagnall, 5m E of Burslem). According to a tradition it was at Stanley Farm the process of salt glazing was discovered when here in c1680 Joseph Yates' servant was boiling in an earthen vessel, a strong lixivium of common salt to be used some way in curing pork. But during her temporary absence the liquid over-boiled running over the sides of the vessel, quickly causing them to become red hot; the muriate acid decomposed the surface, and when cold, the sides were partially glazed. Mr Palmer then took up the process and it was introduced into the local pottery industry (HSP pp108-109) (H p130). But salt glazing was already a long-established practice by the later C17 (The Pottery Trade and North Staffordshire. 1660-1760. Lorna Weatherill. 1971 p29). The Elers brothers of Dimsdale Hall (see) are alleged to have introduced a method of salt glazing into England (HSP p111).

Stanley Field Farm 1.75m NNW of Norton-in-the-Moors, between Ridgeway and Bemersley. Formerly in Norton chapelry in Stoke ancient parish. Here John Wesley preached more than once (ONST 1933 p42).

Stanley Head House over 0.25m ESE of Stanley. Formerly in Stanley township in Leek ancient parish. There was a house here by 1743 (VCH vol 7 p229).

Stanley Moor Hamlet on rising ground on the S side of Endon Brook valley 0.75m N of Bagnall, 0.25m WSW of Stanley. Formerly in Bucknall and Bagnall chapelry in Stoke-upon-Trent ancient parish.

Stanley Moss Low-lying ground to the W of Stanley. Formerly in Stanley township in Leek ancient parish (VCH vol 7 p230).

Stanley Pool Small reservoir 0.5m NNE of Bagnall. Formerly partly in Stanley township in Leek ancient parish and partly in Bagnall township in Stoke ancient parish. Built out of a former mill pool at a height of nearly 600 feet above sea level on a narrow plateau below the 1,000 feet hills of Baddeley Edge and Bagnall as a feeder for the Caldon Canal (SVB p155) (VCH vol 7 p230) or the Trent and Mersey Canal (NSFCT 1938 p62) (B p123) in 1783 (B p123) or 1786 (VCH vol 7 pp229, 230 note) and finished by 1787. The former eight acre reservoir was enlarged to 33 acres in 1840-41 (NSFCT 1991 pp41,46) (VCH vol 7 p230). It is now (1990) 80 acres (B p123). Reputedly it gave its name to Sir Stanley Baldwin (1867-1947), prime minister, after his parents Louisa Macdonald (see Wolverhampton and Swindon) and Alfred Baldwin made a visit to it. Baldwin's cousin, Rudyard Kipling, was named by his parents after their day-out by Rudyard Lake (NSFCT 1938 p62) (TTTD p137).

Stanshope Small hamlet on high ground in the Moorlands at the head of Hall Dale 1m SSW of Alstonefield. In Alstonefield ancient parish. In Ramscroft Field at SK 13205426 E of Stanshope is a burial mound 36 paces in diameter and four feet high in which was found a rock-cut graves with skeletal remains of Beaker pottery and a bronze dagger (TYD pp158,160) (VCH vol 1 no 25) (BAP vol 1 p88 fig 56, fig 71) (DAJ vol 75 pp106,112) (NSFCT 1926 p146) (NSJFS 1965 p30). It is a listed monument. The burial mound in Stanshope Pasture at SK 13505421 ESE of Stanshope is 20 paces in diameter and seven feet high and a listed monument. It was excavated by Bateman in 1846 and Carrington in 1849, and burial remains of Beaker people were discovered (VAD p86) (TYD pp142,143) (VCH vol 1 no 25) (NSJFS 1962 p33. 1965 p30). Another 0.75m ESE of Stanshope at SK 1385569, 17 paces in diameter and seven feet high, has been excavated (NSJFS 1965 p30). A burial mound at Stanshope Pasture excavated by Bateman in 1846 revealed a skeleton and pieces of Samian pottery (VAD pp86,87) (NSJFS 1965 p30) (VCH vol 7 p9). For the burial mounds S of Stanshope see under Damgate. Appears in DB as Stanespe. 'Hop' is Anglo-Saxon for 'valley' - the stoney valley (DUIGNAN), or enclosure (SSE 1996 p17), or '(place at) stony valley' (SPN p114). Gelling thinks 'Stan's valley' (NSJFS 1981 p2). The estate of Stanshope, which existed prior to the Norman Conquest, had become a part of Alstonefield manor by 1307 (VCH vol 7 p1). It was a hamlet by the beginning of the C13 (VCH vol 7 p9). There was a pinfold at Stanshope in 1713 (VCH vol 7 p20). Here, in the later C17 Plot was told there were small quantities of yellow and red ochre and marble (NHS pp124,174).

Stanshope Hall C17 stone house (BOE p55) at Stanshope, 1m S of Alstonefield. An estate at Stanshope was held by the Jackson family from the C16 (VCH vol 7 p17). Some say the estate was purchased by John Jackson some time during the 1560s (AVH p56p). Capt Philip Jackson (d1675) was a parliamentary commander in the Civil War and may have led the Moorland Dragoons in the attack on Stafford in 1643 (BFS pp12 il,24). He was succeeded by his son William (d1679), who was succeeded by his brother Capt Henry Jackson, a parliamentarian in the Civil War, who Charles Cotton considered 'an admirable fly angler' (VCH vol 7 pp17-18), or who is said to have taught Cotton the art of fly-fishing (NSFCT 1936 p30). He sold the estate to John Jackson, a London merchant, in 1699, but continued to live here until 1702. By 1704 John Jackson had been succeeded by his niece Mary, wife of of Sir Raphe Assheton. By her will of 1720 Dame Mary left the estate to Strelley Pegge, great-grandson of Philip Jackson's sister Ann (VCH vol 7 pp17-18). He sold it to William Manley in 1767 and the house was re-styled about this time. There is a date 1789 on the west gable. The hall fell into disrepair after Manley was declared bankrupt in 1799. It was restored by Ralph Beardmore,

the owner, in the 1850s (AVH pp56-57) (VCH vol 7 p18 pls 29,30).

Stansley Wood Wood in a stretch of land surrounded on three sides by Blithfield Reservoir, 0.75m E of Newton. In Blithfield ancient parish.

Stansmore Hall Stone three-gabled hall 1m WNW of Dilhorne (BOE p116), in Dilhorne parish, 1m NE of Caverswall. Positioned near the Limes Britannicus, hence the name (NSFCT 1902 p117). Built at the same time as Caverswall Castle in c1620. It was the residence of the potting family of Wolfe from the early C17 (NSFCT 1923 p34). It was likened by the leader of an NSFC outing to 'Wuthering Heights' (NSFCT 1940 p29).

Stanton Village on high ground in the Moorlands overlooking Marsh Brook 19m NE of Stafford. Former township in Ellastone ancient parish (AAD p246). For the two gold torcs found near Stanton see under Thorswood House. Appears in DB as Stantone. The name means 'tun or farmstead or tun on stony ground' (SPN p47). The mission church, St Mary, on the S side of Marsh Lane on the SW fringe of the village, was built in 1846-1847 (BOE p251) (LDD). Became a separate ecclesiastical parish in 1849, but its separate status was not sustained and it returned to Ellastone ancient parish. Became a separate civil parish in 1866 (GLAUE p423). There is a rhyme relating to Stanton which goes;

Stanton-on-the-Stones,
Where the Devil broke his bones

(SCSF p167) (SJC pp2,3) (STM July 1965 p40) (FOS p35). For folklore about here still prevailing in 1925 see NSFCT 1925 p197. Archbishop Gilbert Sheldon (1598-1677) was born in a cottage in the centre of the village. In 1664, whilst bishop of Lichfield, John Hacket, made a pilgrimage to Sheldon's birthplace and wrote eulogistic verses in iambic form on a plaque over the chimney piece. Plot recorded the verses in the 1680s and gives them in NHS p273. It has been noted that Plot's version may be inaccurate for another version in AG Matthews' 'Congregational Churches of Staffordshire' is different and seems less clumsy (NSFCT 1925 p197 note). (SHOS vol 1 p276) (AAD p210) (SMC p173) (GNHS p99) (STM July 1965 p41). By 1925 the original script had worn out and the verses had been rewritten in white paint on either the original wooden board over the old print, or on a new board (NSFCT 1925 p197 note). The board with the verse was riddled with woodworm in the early 1990s (local info). The site of the birthplace is still (1996) occupied by a cottage. It is recorded in Ellastone PR on July 17 1625 that John Slater of Stanton was 'killed by thunder.' Was he really killed by thunder, should the recorder have written lightning? (NSJFS 1972 p127).

Stanton Moor Covered a large area N of Stanton and appears to have adjoined Calton Moor by the Swinscoe road (Smith's map). In the early C19 Pitt described Stanton Moor as a considerable waste on a limestone surface (THS p37).

Stapenhill Stapenhill, in Kinver ancient parish, is mentioned as an area of pasture in 1293. It was the name of a farm by the 1630s. The present Stapenhill Farm, 2.5m NW of Kinver church, appears to date from c1840 (VCH vol 20 pp123-124). The name was later applied to a small wharf on the Stourbridge Canal, where the small hamlet of Newtown (see) had grown up by c1830 (SVS p182). By the 1830s sandworking was in progress in the Stapenhill area (VCH vol 20 p124).

Stapenhill Ancient parish and former village on a low bluff by a wide stretch of the Trent beneath rolling country 0.5m SE of Burton upon Trent, on E side of the Trent, but now a suburb of Burton. Formerly in Repton and Gresley hundred, Derbys, but partly in Burton parish and partly its own parish (which included the hamlet of Cauldwell and the township of Stanton-and-Newhall) (W pp530,542). There was possibly a **pre-Roman village** at Stapenhill (HOBTU p2). In 1881 a **Saxon cemetery** was discovered by men working in a brickyard in an area between Rosliston Road and Stanton Road; 31 skeletons and five cinerary urns were found (LGS p220) and traces of some 36 burials, of which 34 were inhumations and two cremations. Also among the finds were a small copper coin of Constantine the Great dated to c327 AD, and a barbarous imitation of a coin struck in honour of Antonia, the mother of Claudius, of unknown date (NSJFS 1964 p18) (BTIH pp11-12ps,13ps). (HOS p13) (STMSM Sept 1973 p26). In 1953 a short length of ditch of the Saxon cemetery excavated in 1881 was shown to be also of Roman origin (BTNHAST vol 1 1889 p156) (DAJ vol 75 p1) (NSJFS 1964 p18) (BTIH p10). The Stapenh' mentioned in a charter of 942 has been identified with Stapenhill (SHC 1916 pp86,87) (SSE 1991 p8) (BTIH pp13-14). Has appeared as Stapenhille (DB) (SSE 1996 p18), and Stapenhyll (SPN p27). The **name** means 'at the steep hill' (SSE 1996 p18), or 'Steep hill' (SPN pp27,72). The parish **church**, St Peter, in Stapenhill Road near St Peter's Street, was built in 1880-1881 (BOE p88), replacing an earlier church at Stapenhill; there was a medieval, and possibly a Saxon, church at Stapenhill. Stapenhill was removed to Staffs in 1894-1895 (SL p29). The railway bridge over the Trent at SK 246210 was protected in WW2 by four two-man rectangular pillboxes designed to look like buttresses (WMARCH 1993 pp35-36). **Natives.** In Feb 1595/6, a 13 year old boy called **Thomas Darling** fell ill. He was living with his uncle and aunt at Burton, and he claimed that he had been bewitched by a woman named Alse Gooderige from Stapenhill. He was believed to be possessed of the devil and subsequently underwent exorcisms. In June 1597 the Stationers' Company in London published a pamphlet, nearly 50 pages long, about the case; Alse's mother Elizabeth Wright was also believed to be witch. Alse died in Derby gaol (SSE 1997 pp1-17) (SMC pp81-87). **Mrs Abney** of Stapenhill had a natural history collection which was housed by BTNHAS in a museum in High Street, Burton upon Trent (SH p151). The brewing family of **SH Evershed**, early aeroplane builders, were natives of Stapenhill (EAS p15).

Stapenhill Farm House 1m ENE of Stourton (RKE p19). The name means 'the hill of the stapol.' Stapol is Anglo-Saxon for a pole or pillar marking the boundary of a manor or estate. Stapenhill adjoins the borders of Staffs and Worcs (DUIGNAN). Gelling thinks the name means 'steep hill' (NSJFS 1981 p3).

Stapenhill House Stapenhill. The house was demolished in 1933 (ABTOP p137p) and the site given by WH Goodger in 1935 for the creation of Stapenhill Pleasure Gardens (BTOP vol 1 p3). The sundial in the Pleasure Gardens is said to stand on the site of the house (ABTOP p137).

Stapenhill Spring Cottage Formerly in Derbys (Yates' map).

Stapylton House Old Church Road, Harborne. Built in 1840 by Rev James Towry Law for his curate Rev Stapylton Bree. Demolished in 1966 and Stapylton Court built on the site (OHOPP p27p).

Staresmore Near Rowley Village, Rowley Regis. Here there was a seat of a family named Staresmore (SHOS vol 2 p239).

Start's Green Over 2.5m NE of Upper Arley, on the SW boundary of Kinver. Consists of just Start's Green Farm. Is beyond the current county border, but was within Staffs before 1894 or 1895. It has been suggested that Cynefares Stane, a boundary stone mentioned in 964, was at Start's Green (BAST vol 53 pp108-109) (VCH vol 20 p119 note).

Startley Head Hill 2.5m S of Rugeley. To Shaw in the late C18 Startley Head was a charming place on Cannock Chase (SHOS vol 1 p214). Has also appeared as Startley Piece (1840) and Startley Hill (SPNO p109). The name means 'woodland pasture on a projecting piece of land' (SPNO p109).

Star Wood Wood covering lower reaches of Cotton Dell, 0.75m SW of Cotton, 0.5m NE of Oakamoor. Otherwise better known as Cotton Dell (NSFCT 1892 p144). By Jan 2000 the wood was considered to have been continuous woodland since the early C17 and is a Site of Biological Importance (Staffs Wildlife Jan 2000).

Statfold Tiny ancient parish and former manor. The minute hamlet of Statfold, on ground gently rising above the Anker and at some distance from the Anker by one of its tributaries, is 22.25m SE of Stafford. There may have been a Saxon **church** at Statfold (Mr Wolferstan's notes. 1974). The later church is a prebend, often written Stotfold, in the chapter of Lichfield cathedral, founded by Bishop Roger de Clinton (SHOS vol 1 p293) (HOL p567) (VCH vol 3 p141) (SSAHST vol 2 1960-61 p49). The church lies on the N side of Statfold Hall and is a small chapel. It may have been first built in the C12, or in later C13; much of the older fabric is of C14 origin. It fell into disuse in the C19; Harwood noted that divine service at the church had been discontinued by the mid C19 (HOL p567). The chapel was restored in 1906 and is now (1990s) maintained privately (Mr Wolferstan's notes. 1974). The parish, formed between 1086 and 1291, originally formed a part of Tamworth parish (SHC 1916 p198). Later the parish was ecclesiastically sometimes claimed to be in Lichfield St Michael parish (VCH vol 14 p135), or Lichfield St Mary parish (GLAUE p423), but by the C18 it was included in Clifton Campville with Chilcote ancient parish (GLAUE p423). In 1967 the parish was absorbed into Clifton Campville ancient parish ('Brief Notes' compiled by Mr Wolferstan of Statfold Hall. 1974). Statfold's separate civil identity was lost in 1934 when it entered Thorpe Constantine ancient parish (GLAUE p423). **The manor** is not mentioned in DB; although Shaw supposed it to have then been a member of the bishop of Lichfield's barony of Longdon. The manor was held by at least Henry II's reign to the C14 by the Salveins (later Selveyns and Salveyns); followed by the Ardens; Stanleys; Hercys (early C16). It was then divided and by the later C16 had wholly fallen to the Wolverstons or Wolferstans, who had Statfold Hall (see) built (SOS) (SHOS vol 1 pp410-412). Has appeared as Stotfold (1291), Stottesfold (1293), and Stotfolt (1327) (SPN p115). The **name** is from Anglo-Saxon 'stod-fald' meaning the stud enclosure or horse field (SHOS vol 1 p410) (DUIGNAN) (SPN p115) (SSE 1996 p18), or the shore of a river, but this does not answer the geographical situation of

Statfold (SHOS vol 1 p410). A **medieval village** was at SK 238073, it was probably deserted after the plague of 1348 or between 1334-1524 (SSAHST 1966 p49. 1970 p36) (SL p83) (Mr Wolferstan's notes. 1974). **Natural history**. In the later C17 Dr Plot noted an exceptionally sized hog at Statfold. Mr Wolferstan sent him one of its teeth which had another tooth growing out of it, which appears in his book (NHS p255 tab 22 fig 9). Mr Wolferstan also showed Plot a loon bird killed at Comberford, which had some curious variations from the norm (NHS p229 tab 22 fig 1). Plot was told about a toad which lived in the top of the chapel spire at Statfold until, on being revealed to the air, it died (NHS pp247-249).

Statfold Hall In Statfold hamlet. The Wolferstans are said to have had a seat here by 1465 (SPN p115). In 1550 the Wolferstans obtained Statfold manor by marriage with the heiress of the Stanleys (W p604). The core of the present house is Elizabethan. The thin polygonal tower had, according to a newspaper account of 1899, a datestone 1571 over its doorway, but this no longer survives. However, the brickwork is said to suggest a late C17 date. The tower was probably built as an observatory by Francis Wolferstan (SHOS vol 1 p415). In the late C18 Shaw noted that 38 churches or chapels in five counties could be seen from the top of it. (W p604). A lintel with 'F.W. 1681,' found when the N wing was demolished in 1939 (BOE p252 - says 1937), has been placed at the base of the tower. Major alterations occurred to the house in the late C18. In the early C19 the N and S wings were added ('Brief Notes' compiled by Mr Wolferstan of Statfold Hall). Stanley Pipe Wolferstan was in residence between at least 1844 and 1851. Francis Stanley Pipe Wolferstan was living at the hall in 1868 (SOS p453) (W p604) (KD 1868). The house is still (1998) occupied by the Wolferstans. A large dovecote existed in the garden in the late C18 bearing the inscription 'ANNO D'NI 1571.' Shaw gives an illustration of it (SHOS vol 1 p410). Plot noted the gate piers in front of the house in c1675 on which Francis Wolferstan had placed a pair of globes, painted with maps of the world (so that he might see how night and day passed over them) but in Jan 1677 they were both struck by lightning, one one day, the other the following, both struck in the same place (NHS p9, tab 1, fig 5) (SHOS vol 1 p414).

Steel House Under 0.5m ESE of Horton, in Horton ancient parish. So called by 1561, but its site was probably occupied by the late C13, when the toponym Style was used by a tenant of Horton manor (VCH vol 7 p65).

Steen Wood In Blithfield ancient parish. Steenwood Cottages is 1.25m SE of Blithfield.

Steeple House Over 0.5m N of Ilam (1834 OS map). Has also appeared as Stapleshouse.

Steep Low Hill in the Moorlands 0.5m NW of Alstonefield topped by an Anglo-Saxon burial mound at SK 12345612 (HOS p13). No trace of a barrow was found during field work (NSJFS 1965 p30). Near Steep Low is a burial mound excavated by Carrington in 1848 no finds of any significance were made (TYD p126) (NSJFS 1965 p31). Raven says the burial mound at Steep Low was opened in 1845, and some smelted iron-iron ore, a drinking cup, animal bones and three Roman coins, one undeciphered, one of the Emperor Constantine (307-337 AD), and one of the Emperor Tetricus (768-773 AD), were found in it (MR p11). (VCH vol 7 p9). Some believe nearby Alstonefield may take its name from 'One-Stone Field,' a reference to Steep Low, for in winter the summit of the hill represents a sharp dome of almost bare rock (AVH P2).

Stencill's Farm House 1m ENE of Walsall.

Stepmother Stone Monolith situated on the Staffs Ches boundary on the Cloud, Ches. Noted in the early C17 (VCH vol 7 p223).

Stepping Stones, The The name could apply to two famous places in the county where stepping stones are situated. One set cross the Dove N of Thorpe Cloud. The stones here were not in existence in the early Victorian period, but were in existence by 1875 (DMV pp5p,7ps). Another set cross the Sher Brook on Cannock Chase at SJ 987200 (SLM Spring 1958 p27p) (TSW p57).

Steps, The House in Ironmarket, Newcastle-under-Lyme, next door to Arlington House (see). Built by John Fenton in 1700-2 (VCH vol 8 p9) and was subsequently the residence of the Fenton family (formerly of Shelton Old Hall). The present (1963) house was built by Thomas Fletcher soon after 1784. The house became the National Provincial Bank in the early C20 (VCH vol 8 p9) (BVC p121). A house called Steps House or The Steps was still standing in 1966 (ES Oct 17 1966 p).

Step Walk Short-cut footpath leading off from the carriage drive from Quixhill Lodge at Alton Towers. It leads up through the woods in a zig zag fashion (JAT p36). It is reputedly haunted (EGH p86). Has also appeared as The Steps.

Stevens Park Public park of 21 acres 1m SE of Brierley Hill, between Thorns Road and Park Lane, on part of the former Thorns Colliery. The land for it was given by local industrialist Ernest Stevens in 1919. The park opened in 1921 (OS map Sheet 71.07) (SNSV vol 1 p251).

Steward Aqueduct Aqueduct to the W of Spon Lane, Smethwick. Constructed in 1828 by Telford to take the Birmingham Canal Old Main Line over his New Main Line. The M5 passes over it (Galton Valley. A Walkers Guide. Sandwell Metropolitan Borough Council. 1993). The aqueduct has also been called Stewart Aqueduct (SWY p10).

Stewponey Area of Stourton; that part on the E side of the Stour, and the name for a lock on the Staffs and Worcs Canal (SGS p158). In Kinver ancient parish. The name is unique (DUIGNAN), and is, perhaps, the most perplexing in the county. Most writers think it is from the old tavern called Stewponey (VCH vol 20 p124), although, the name could pre-date the inn. The most popular belief, and the one propagated by the current inn, and by Baring-Gould's novel 'Gladys (or Bladys) of the Stewponey' (1897), is that it was named after the town called Estepona in the S of Spain where a soldier (a local man), was quartered in the wars of Queen Anne or Peninsula Wars. The native returned with a Spanish bride and became landlord of the tavern re-naming it the 'Estepone Tavern' in honour of his wife. Estepone being difficult for the English to pronounce it soon became Stewponey (SCK p1) (VCH vol 20 p124) (MR p298) (SPN p72). Stewponey is actually mentioned in a letter 34 years before the Peninsular War (BCM July 1968 pp53-54il. Oct 1968 p71). Or perhaps the inn or area is named after 'stew pones,' fish pools of religious property in the Middle Ages (SVS p173) (SCK p1) (VCH vol 20 p124). Perhaps, from Epona, the horse fertility goddess known as the lady of the foals, who protects horses, donkeys and all equine creatures. The Romans would have images of her along their roads as good luck symbols and there was a Roman road under 1m to the E. The inn may have taken its name from the Latin for bridge, and 'Stour Ponte' was corrupted to Stewponey (N&Q 3rd series vol 6 p298) (SCFK pp42-43) (RKE p22) (SCK p1) (VCH vol 20 p124). The Stour is marked on old maps as 'Stewri' (SCK p1). Another theory is that it derives its name from Stewpony ale, a well known drink which was sold here (N&Q 6th series vol 2 pp308-309. vol 3 pp97-98,130. vol 4 pp155,457. vol 7 p131) (VCH vol 20 p124). (SHOS vol 2 p267) (SVS p172) (KRC pp28-29). The ghost that haunts the area around the Stewponey Hotel is said to be that of William Howe (GLS p61). Stewponey is 'Far Forest' in Francis Brett Young's novels (BCM autumn 1989 p58).

Stewponey Inn Old tavern situated at the junction of the Wolverhampton-Kidderminster and Stourbridge-Bridgnorth roads. Has also appeared as Stewponey Tavern and Stewponey Hotel. The present inn certainly dates from the early C18 (VCH vol 20 p124). But the first tavern on the site is believed to have been built in the Middle Ages to accommodate a royal entourage when a sovereign was staying at Stourton Castle, and to have been a posting station and haunt of fleeing royalists and highwaymen, who took refuge in its secret rooms and smugglers who hid goods in its vaults (SCK pp1,2). It was described in 1744 as 'the house of Benjamin Hallen, being the sign of the Green Man and called the Stewponey.' Thereafter it was known simply as the Stewponey until c1840 when it was known as the Stewponey and Foley Arms. It was then a posting house (VCH vol 20 p124 il of in 1828 facing p129) (KEOP p8ps). Rev Sabine Baring Gould's novel 'Bladys of the Stewponey' (1897) features a legendary daughter of one landlord. The film of the novel was shot in the area in 1919 (SCK pp1,2). As part of the Prestwood estate the inn was for sale in 1913. In the later 1990s the inn was threatened with demolition on account of road widening (TB June 1998 p6p). For how the inn received its name see Stewponey.

Stickley Here is Ellows Hall School, and Stickley Lane, NW of Lower Gornal.

Stile Cop Hill 2m S of Rugeley on Cannock Chase. 679 feet high. In Rugeley ancient parish. There are exceptional wide views from the top, particularly to the N, E, and S. Tobacco pipe clay was excavated here (NHS p121), by a Dr Stiles between the early to the mid C17. When Stiles left he planted 58 beech saplings from his native Bucks on the summit. They were felled in 1946 (Cannock Chase by Car. Staffs Nature Conservation Trust Ltd. ND, but between 1971 and 1974 p7) (PCC p71). In the summer of 1698 Celia Fiennes said she went to Stiles Coppice. From the top she said she could see into seven counties: Warws, Leics, Glous (she must have meant Worcs), Derbys, Staffs, Shrops, Ches (Illustrated Journeys of Celia Fiennes. Ed by Christopher Morris. 1984. p148) (CCBO p69). The name is from Dr Stile. Cop may be 'the top of the hill' (CWF p41), but it may be an abbreviation of coppice. In CCF pp221-222 Stile's Coppice is Stile Cop.

Stile House House 0.75m N of Bradnop. Formerly in Bradnop township in Leek ancient parish. Is of the C18 with an extension dated 1859 (VCH vol 7 p171). Has also appeared as Steel House (1834 OS map). There is an early C17 cross shaft, three metres high on a 10 cm high base, 0.5m ENE of Stile

House. It has a dowelled head, the cross is missing (DoE II). It was, perhaps, a meeting place for the parishioners of Bradnop quarter in Leek parish (OL vol 1 p190) (HLS p117) or where the parishioners of Onecote could meet the vicars of Leek (MOS p268). Or was a cross for travellers on the Morridge road, an ancient pre-Roman track (NSFCT 1948 p119). Or possibly a plague cross, or because it is so remotely positioned moved here from elsewhere (DoE II). Sir Thomas Wardle had it re-erected after it had fallen over (MOS p268). It had fallen over in 1930 or 1940 and was restored by Lt Col WF Challinor (NSFCT 1948 p119. 1956 p111). (TOI p173; very vague mention and not named) (VBB p18il) (PDS&C p56p) (DPEM pp111,112p).

Stinking Lake Former lake which lay by the Watling Street between Ivetsey Bank and White Pump Farm (Yates' map). In a hedge between here and Ivetsey Bank was growing the rare Wood reed or Arundo Epigeios in the late C18 (SHOS vol 1 part 1 p99). Here is or was a sulphur well (NHS p104) (BDH pp276,277). The name is preserved in Lake Plantation (SPNO p170).

Stockings, The House 1m W of Codsall. In Codsall ancient parish.

Stockings Brook Runs to Small Rice round back of Sandon Park to Weston-on-Trent to the Trent. Stockings means the grubbing up or clearing in the wilderness or wood (DUIGNAN p15) (SPNO p19).

Stock Lane Lane which links Marchington with Marchington Woodlands (SVB p121). Formerly in Marchington Woodlands township in Hanbury ancient parish (W p563).

Stockley Park Former medieval deer park formerly in Tutbury ancient parish, removed to Anslow parish in 1984 (ANS p9). Appears as Stoc lega in 1008 (SHC 1916 p123). The park at Stockley was created by Robert de Ferrers, 1st Earl of Derby, d1139 (UTR p36) and in existence by c1170 (VCH vol 2 p350) and certainly by 1297 (NSJFS 1962 p76), having been emparked out of Needwood Forest by Robert Ferrers in the C12 (UTR p100). Contained in compass 21.5 furlongs. It was sold by the Crown between 1628 and 1630 (ANS p92) or in 1631 (EDP p175) to John Tunstall, Matthew Lister, and Robert Smethwicke. From this time the park was farmed by a manager or lessee. It was leased by the Buxton family from c1660 and there was a house at Stockley Park by 1679 (ANS pp77,92). Ownership of the farm in Stockley Park changed in 1712 to Sir William Oldes. It was then occupied by Joseph Stevenson. Rev Thomas Gisborne of Yoxall Lodge inherited the estate from his father in 1771 and sold it to the Crown in 1806 (ANS p126). Some say Gisborne sold it to the Crown (as part of the Duchy of Lancaster) in 1802. Stockley again left the hands of the Duchy in 1901 when it passed to Sir Oswald Mosley. The estate was sold in 1920 with the break up and sale of the Rolleston Hall estate (UTR p100) (ANS p147).

Stockley Park House nearly 2.5m N of Tatenhill.

Stockton Former small hamlet now submerged into Walton-on-the-Hill, 0.75m SE of Baswich church. In Baswich or Berkswich parish. Has appeared as Stokton (1284), and Stokton juxta Cannok (1306) (SPNO p30) (SPN p18) (BERK pp63,64). It formerly belonged to St Thomas' Priory (VCH vol 5 p5) (SSE 1996 p23).

Stockton Brook Small village in a valley created by a tributary of the Trent (possibly called Stockton Brook) and on a hill on the N side of the brook 1.25m NNW of Milton. Formerly in Norton-in-the-Moors chapelry in Stoke-upon-Trent ancient parish. Thomas Cope beer seller of Stockton Brook was hit and killed by a stone thrown by some riotous people at his beer house in Oct or Nov 1835. Seven men were accused of his murder and attempts were made to apprehend them (Broughton's Scrapbook p436). The railway station at Stockton Brook opened in 1896 and closed in 1956 (VCH vol 7 p180).

Stockton Common To E of Stockton, Baswich (BERK p63). (Before the Houses Came: The Story of a farming family in the Rural Parish of Berkswich. Marjorie Knight. 1992. p7).

Stockwell There was settlement at Stockwell, Handsworth, on the S side of the present Friary Road, by the end of the C13. The name is preserved in Stockwell Road, S of Friary Road (MNB p38,44).

Stock Well Stopping point in the perambulation of Tutbury. The well was, perhaps, situated near Tutbury church and was the watering place for cattle (SHOS vol 1 p57).

Stockwell End Hamlet on ground above Tettenhall overlooking Smestow Brook now merged into Tettenhall, 0.25m NW of Tettenhall church. In Tettenhall ancient parish. The last Ice Age reached its maximum southern extent about Wolverhampton and glacial boulders lie about Stockwell End (WJO Nov 1909 p293). The area was so named by the 1640s (VCH vol 20 p7).

Stockwell Heath Hamlet 1m NE of Colton. In Colton parish. There is 0.253 acres of common land here abutting the road in the village. It has a pond in the middle (OSST 1956-59 p8).

Stoke Grange House formerly on the E side of Lichfield Road, Stone (1834 OS map). Seat of Josiah Wedgwood V (1899-1968), son of Josiah Clement IV, a descendant of Josiah Wedgwood I of Etruria Hall (see), from about the 1930s to at least 1948 (SHC 1944. 1947 List of Members) (A Personal Life of the Fifth Josiah Wedgwood 1899-1968. John Wedgwood). The name may be preserved in Grange Road.

Stoke Hall Lay S of Stoke-upon-Trent church beyond the road to Fenton. Former rectory or parsonage. It had a moat encircling it and a bridge across the moat. Built in the Elizabethan style, it, or a former house on the same site, was in existence by the mid C15 as the residence of James Moseley, the rector's proctor. According to his own relation John Lightfoot, the distinguished Hebrew scholar, later of Uttoxeter (see), was born at the Rectory House at Stoke on March 29 1602 (HBST p482). The hall was occupied by a curate at the beginning of the C17, and by 1666 John Mainwaring lived here as rector. By 1794 to 1801 George Steedman, who was churchwarden at Stoke, lived here. In 1818 it was rented out to a tenant farmer, but was again occupied by a curate in 1828. It was repaired in 1829, and occupied by the rector in 1834 and a curate in 1851. Rt Rev Sir Lovelace Tomlinson Stamer (1829-1908), who succeeded as rector of Stoke in 1858, lived here until 1864, when Cliffville (see) was acquired as the rectory; Sir Stamer later lived at Halingdene (see), Penkridge. The hall was demolished in 1891 (CAST p34) (POTP p199). By the 1950s P.M.T. offices and garage were occupying the site. The approach gates were on the line of the main road opposite the Red Lion (VCH vol 8 p186) (CAST pp33-34) (NSFCT 1982 pp11,17). Garner noted here was found the carved head of a friar, probably a dripstone termination from the old church (GNHSS pp19,20). Some fossils from Stoke Hall Quarry went to Buxton Museum.

Stoke-on-Trent Collective name for the six pottery towns of Burslem, Fenton, Hanley, Longton, Stoke-upon-Trent, and Tunstall, which federated in 1910. For information about this area prior to 1910 see individual towns and The Potteries.

FEDERATION OF STOKE-ON-TRENT. **Leading to Federation**. The six towns were envisaged in a union as early as 1817 (VCH vol 8 p253) (HOS p58). An article which appeared in SA on Feb 4 1871 argued against federation of the pottery towns (TTTD p188). The idea of a 'County of the Potteries' gained much support with the creation of county councils in 1888, but Hanley's acceptance of county borough status for itself killed the plan (VCH vol 8 pp253-254). Between 1900 and 1903 meetings were held to discuss federation with a view to making a representation to the Local Government Board. But towns gradually withdraw when proposals were unacceptable to them (POTP p240). From 1905 polls were taken in most of the towns. The main contentious issue was the fear of a flat rate. By 1908 with all the towns generally in favour of federation (except for Fenton), federation in the near future seemed likely (VCH vol 8 pp254-257). Arnold Bennett forecast the towns federated before they actually were in his novel, 'The Old Wives' Tale' (Oct 1908). **Federation**. The Potteries Federation Bill became law on Dec 21 1908 (POTP p242). On March 31 1910 the county borough of Hanley, the boroughs of Burslem, Longton and Stoke-upon-Trent, and the urban districts of Fenton and Tunstall were federated (POP p74; on why the federation was called Stoke-on-Trent). It was a federation unique in English local government (VCH vol 8 p252) (HOS p58). The federation had the status of a county borough. The first meeting of the council was at North Stafford Hotel, Stoke-upon-Trent. Major Cecil Wedgwood, a member of the Wedgwood family of Etruria Hall (see) and a keen supporter for federation, became the first mayor of the new county borough (VCH vol 8 p257). **After Federation**. After federation it was found all six towns had some streets with the same name as one of the other five towns. To prevent confusion for the services within the new single authority these streets were renamed. In 1922 Abbey Hulton, Bentilee, Blurton, Bucknall, Chell, Hanford, Lightwood, Meir, Milton, Norton-in-the-Moors, Smallthorne, and Trentham were added to the borough; Strongford was added in 1929 (VCH vol 8 p260). On June 5 (ES April 4 1933 p10) (R&S p44) or July 25 1925 George V raised the status of the federation to a city when visiting to lay the foundation stone of the extensions to the North Staffordshire Royal Infirmary at Hartshill (see) (LGS p221; Jowitt, Masefield's reviser, misleadingly implies it is Stoke-upon-Trent which was created a city) (HOS p58). The letters patent to confirm and create the title of Lord Mayor became effective in July 1928 and Thomas Clarke Wild, then mayor, became first lord mayor of the City of Stoke-on-Trent (POTP p249). Proposals, in 1930, 1946, and 1948, to include Newcastle-under-Lyme and Kidsgrove in the borough all failed (VCH vol 8 p259). In 1974, with local government reorganisation, power was transferred back to the county council in Stafford, but the six towns remained united in one authority, Stoke-on-Trent district council (POTP p249). On April 1 1997 Stoke-on-Trent became a unitary authority separate from the county council (Daily Telegraph July 5 1994 p4). The **arms** of Stoke-on-Trent city and county borough granted in 1912 are:

Silver, a cross gules fretted with gold; in the first quarter a representation the Portland Vase; in the second, a kneeling camel proper charged on the body with a silver shield bearing a red cross; in the third, an eagle displayed sable; and in the fourth, a scythe proper; on a chief gules a boar's head torn off between two Stafford Knots all gold. The crest is - On a wreath argent and gules, a potter of ancient Egypt seated and working at his wheel, silver. The motto is - 'Vis unita fortior' (Strength is the stronger for unity) (CH pp329il,330). (SHST p280il). For what the arms represent see STM Dec 1965 p50 and VCH vol 8 p263.

There was a Zeppelin raid on Stafford Coal and Iron Company's blast furnace on the night of Jan 31 1916. The half dozen bombs dropped landed on spoil banks (TB July 1994 p19). By 1978 the largest bottle in the world was considered to be a sherry bottle made in May 1958 in Stoke-on-Trent, which was five feet tall and had a capacity of 20.5 Imperial gal. It was named an 'Adelaide' (GBR 1978 p79). By 1980 the highest price paid for a piece of pottery was £15,015 for a Staffordshire C18 salt-glazed pew group, which sold at Christie's on Dec 15 1975, and the highest paid for a pot lid was £2,000 by Richard Cashmore for a C19 Staffordshire Porcelain example, which sold at Phillips, London, on Oct 18 1978 (GBR 1980 p168). The teapot commissioned by Stoke-on-Trent city, exhibited at the 1988 Glasgow Garden Festival, has been considered the largest in the world. Made by ANMAC of Nottingham, it was 12 feet high with a diameter of 16.5 feet, and depicted scenes representing Stoke industries (GBR 1990 p141). 'The Greatest Show on Earth' was filmed in the Potteries. Potteries Motor Traction (PMT) were the first company in Britain to introduce the Global Positioning System (GPS) for its buses in Feb 1993 (Sunday Telegraph March 7 1993 p5). For the Potteries Museum and Art Gallery see Hanley. **Natives and visitors**. The nephew of Arnold Bennett, **George Beardmore** (alias Cedric Stokes), was born in 1908 in Stoke-on-Trent. Some of his work includes 'The Staffordshire Assassins,' 'Madame Merlin' (1946), 'A Tale of Two Thieves' (1947), 'A Lion Among the Ladies' (1949), and 'A Thousand Witnesses' (1953) (VFC p11). **George V** and Queen Mary visited Stoke-on-Trent on April 23 1913 (SOSH p276) (R&S p44). **JB Priestley**, author, touring England for his 'English Journey' (1934), was in the Potteries in March 1934 (ES March 26 1934 p6). **George VI** visited Stoke-on-Trent on May 22 1924, July 12 1934, and Feb 14 1941 (R&S p46). **John Toft**, writer, was born in the Potteries in 1933; much of his later work, including 'The Dew' (1981), is set in the Midlands (VFC p131). **Bob Taylor** MBE, cricketer, was born in Stoke-on-Trent in 1941. Princess Elizabeth (**Elizabeth II**) visited Stoke-on-Trent on Nov 1 and 2 1949 (R&S p47). A bone china vase, which has become known as the Queen's Vase, showing the highest skills in the North Staffs ceramic industry, was presented to Elizabeth II by the British Pottery Manufacturers' Federation in 1954. It was one of the most complicated pieces of bone china ever to be created and symbolised the Commonwealth (TSS p111p). On Nov 2 1955 Elizabeth II and the Duke of Edinburgh toured the Potteries. Elizabeth II was again in Stoke-on-Trent on May 25 1973 and to open the National Garden Festival at on former land of Shelton Bar Steelworks at Shelton (see) on May 8 1986 (R&S p47). By 1993 the longest interval between test tube twins was 18 months, between the births of **Amy and Elizabeth Wright**, the daughters of Mrs Mary Wright, aged 38. Elizabeth was born at Stoke-on-Trent on April 22 1987 from an egg which had been in frozen storage for 29 months (GBR 1993 p59). **Prince Charles** visited Stoke-on-Trent on March 3 1998 (ES March 3 1998 p13p).

Stoke Park Deer park noted by Sir Simon Degge (EDP p179). It possibly can be identified with Stone Park which could be said to be by Little Stoke, Stone?

Stoke-upon-Trent Ancient parish and Potteries town at the confluence of the Trent and Fowlhay Brook (CAST p7), 14.25m NNW of Stafford. The town lay in Penkhull-with-Boothen township (W p224).

EARLY. Richmilde Street (see), the Roman road between Derby and Chesterton, passed through Stoke-upon-Trent. Parts of an ancient roadway were excavated near the Red Lion Inn in 1887 and a pavement of boulder stones excavated by Charles Lynam of Colwich in 1903 by the former site of the Colin Minton Campbell statue in the middle of Campbell Place (NSFCT vol 38 p158. vol 39 p140) (NSJFS 1964 p36) (CAST pp8-9).

800 to 1086. There was a **church** at Stoke-upon-Trent possibly by the early C9, for when the Norman church was pulled down in c1830, a stone corbel head was found embedded in the walls bearing the date in Roman numerals, apparently DCCCI (801) (CAST p8). Two fragments of a **stone cross** (which, in all probability, replaced an even earlier one of wood), dating from not later than the mid C9 (CAST p9) or from c1000 (VCH vol 8 p191) of millstone grit was discovered by the sexton in 1876 when digging a grave. In 1935 the cross was erected on a mount in the SW corner of the churchyard to commemorate George V's Silver Jubilee (VCH vol 8 p191) (CAST pp9-10). There

is a tradition an abbey once stood in the Church Fields, to the front of what would later be Stoke Hall (see) (SHST p524). There was certainly a church at Stoke by 1086. The old parish church, St Peter Ad Vincula, to the E of Glebe Street, was built in 1150, or in the early C13. A new church was built on or near the site in 1826-1829. Some stones from the old church were rediscovered in the overflow course of the millpond at the old Boothen Mill, and in 1887, were erected to the S of the new church to create some arches (VCH vol 8 pp188,189) (BOE p262) (AGT p142il of the arches) (CAST p8). The ancient parish was very extensive, containing the parishes of Bagnall, Bucknall, Burslem, Longton, Newcastle-under-Lyme, Norton-in-the-Moors, and Whitmore (GLAUE pp423-424). Stoke **wakes** were held on the first Sunday dedicated to St Peter ad Vincula (Aug 1) and from the mid C19 a week's holiday after the wake was instituted for the whole parish (W p226) (VCH vol 8 p205). August 1 corresponds with the Lugnassed, fair of Ireland, associated with Lug the Sun hero, and represents an ancient Celtic festival associated with the Sun god, Lug or Lleu (NSFCT 1908 p107).

1086 to 1874. Stoke does not have a separate entry in DB but appears under Caverswall (NSFCT 1952 pp34-35) as Stoche. It appears in the C13 as Stoke (SPN p115). Stoke is a very common English place-**name**, it means a 'place fortified by a stockade or fence.' Hughes says Stoke would have been a defensive place for Anglo-Saxons. Here they could ward off Britons who had taken to the Moorlands (DUIGNAN) (SOSH p270). Or, perhaps, from stock, stoke, as in Norway, where a staff of a cross was planted by Olaf - a zealous missionary who would stick his cross-staffs in the ground for the inhabitants to gather round and hear him preach (SK p193). From Anglo-Saxon 'stoc' which could mean 'holy site' 'monastery' or 'cell,' or alternatively just 'place' (SPN p115). What was properly called Stoke until c1780 consisted of only five houses including Stoke Hall and was situated to the E of the church; the main population lived in Penkhull village. There was a pinfold in Stoke which also served Penkhull erected in 1839 or 1840 (VCH vol 8 pp173,201) (SL p217). The town developed to the W of the church (W p224) and was encouraged by the opening of the Trent and Mersey Canal in 1777; it passes through Stoke and several wharfs were built here (VCH vol 8 p173). There was significant development after WT Copeland's purchase of the Spode Works in 1833, which he soon expanded (AGT p156). The first **town hall** was built in 1794 and demolished in c1938. The present town hall, in Glebe Street, by Henry Ward, has been considered the most impressive of the municipal buildings of the six towns. It was begun in 1834 and still not quite finished in 1850 (VCH vol 8 p180) (AGT pp140il,141). In Aquinas Street formerly Thomas Street there is a **Quaker burial-ground**. It has burials from the 1820s to 1951 (SSAHST 1970 pp44-45). The Staffordshire Yeomanry were sent out to suppress the Stoke Election **riots** in 1837 (info Yeomanry Museum). **Horse-racing** occurred from 1850 to 1860 in wakes week on a site now occupied by Michelin tyre factory. There is still a Racecourse Road off London Road (VCH vol 8 p205 note). A **Russian gun** from the Crimean War was presented to Stoke-upon-Trent by WT Copeland in 1857. In 1858 it was set up opposite the Wheatsheaf Inn. It was moved to a site in Hill Street by the old Town Hall in c1874 (VCH vol 8 p180) (PRA p78). **'West End'** is a local term for the W area of the town bordering with Penkhull (GLS p85). **Persons and visitors.** To **Charles Dickens** in 1852 Stoke was 'a picturesque heap of houses, kilns, smoke, wharfs, canals and river lying (as was most appropriate) in a basin' (VCH vol 8 p174). **Joseph Edwards** (d1931), Principal and Professor of Mathematics and Physics at Queen's College, London, was born at Stoke on March 16 1854 (NSSG p47). At the 'Poor House' Stoke **Hannah Bourne**, a deformed dwarf of 25 inches high, gave birth to a baby daughter measuring 21.5 inches high (SHST p634).

RAILWAYS. Stoke was connected by rail to Stafford from April 17 1848 (the only one of the five towns on a main line - the others were served by the Potteries Loop Line); to Uttoxeter from Aug 7 1848; to Crewe and Congleton from Oct 9 1848 (NSJFS 1962 p99) (CVH p128); to Leek from 1867 (OL vol 1 p331). The line from Leekbrook to Stoke closed to passengers on May 7 1956, but was still open to goods in 1983 (CVH pp128-129). A station in Winton Square (see) opened in 1848. For an enormous railway engine shed by the station see the Round House. In the later C20 so many vehicles became stuck on the Stoke Road under the bridge which carries the railway that the bridge was claimed in 1997 to be the fourth most damaged one in Britain. Ten vehicles were stuck in 1996 (ES Feb 15 1997 p9).

STOKE CITY FOOTBALL CLUB. Stoke City Football Club was founded in 1863, and it is the second oldest in the country (VCH vol 8 p205) (TSS p47) (Introduction to Arnold Bennett's The Old Wives' Tale. John Wain). 'Stoke End' referred to the N end of Stoke City's former football ground, the Victoria Ground (ES 15 Nov 1994 p9). Britain's worst sports disaster to 1968 was when 33 were killed after a section of the barriers collapsed at the

Bolton Wanderers' ground at Burnden Park, Bolton, Lancs, during the Cup tie match against Stoke City on March 9 1946. The game was played to a finish (GBR 1968 p258). Another account says 28 were killed in the disaster (TSS p94). The most protracted FA Cup tie in the competition proper was that between Stoke City and Bury culminating with Stoke winning 3-2 in a match on Jan 24 1955, after five meetings and after nine hours 22 minutes of play (GBR 1969 p313. 1974 p270). In 1997 Stoke, known locally as the Potters, moved to the Britannia Stadium at Sideway, 0.75m to the SSE.

1874 to PRESENT. Stoke-upon-Trent was made a **borough** on Jan 1 1874 (SOSH p276) (POP p74). For the seal of the borough see SHST p281il. The town was one of the six towns which federated in 1910 to form Stoke-on-Trent. The building for the new county borough council of Stoke-on-Trent, King's Hall, was built at Stoke behind the present town hall in 1910-11 (VCH vol 8 p182). **Strange sights.** The skeleton of an elephant was discovered whilst constructing Michelin's tyre factory, Campbell Road, in 1927: It had possibly been a circus elephant (SHST p634). A house in Sheppard Street is believed to be haunted (GLS pp85-86). Two people saw a UFO in the shape of a bright orange glow like an egg or a boat on its side in the sky from Michelin's factory on Aug 31 1967 (FSRP p10). **Persons and visitors. Herbert Stansfield**, a freemason, has a curious grave in Stoke-upon-Trent churchyard known by the local boys as the Devil's Grave because of the figures of death which are on it (CAST p45). Dr **Edward Kenealy** (1819-1880), barrister and founder of Staffordshire News and Trade Advertiser, was MP for Stoke-upon-Trent from Feb 18 1874 to 1880, being elected as an independent. When he first took his seat in the House of Commons no member could be found to present him, which brought about the ending the ceremony of being 'introduced' (POTP p134) (William Henry Goss. Lynda and Nicholas Pine. 1987 p64p cartoon). A statue to **Colin Minton Campbell** (1827-1885), pottery manufacturer and MP, was unveiled in the centre of Campbell Place by the Duchess of Sutherland on Jan 1 1887. The sculptor was T Brock ARA. It is of bronze, eight feet high, and erected on a pedestal of grey Cornish granite nine feet high. Amongst the distinguished persons at the unveiling ceremony was the Marquis of Lorne. In 1954 the statue was moved to its present site near the Minton Works in London Road (SSW pp132,133) (PPP p76p of in Campbell Place) (POTP p56). The composer **Havergal Brian** (d1972), born Dresden (see) in 1876, was married in St Peter's church in 1899. In the early C20 Brian lived for a short while at 50 James Street (POTP p47p). **George V** and Queen Mary visited Stoke on April 22 1913 (ES Nov 16 1996 p21). Rev **Douglas Henry**, rector of Stoke-upon-Trent from 1924 (bishop of Chester between 1938 and 1955), at six feet four and half inches high was believed to be the tallest Anglian bishop or clergyman in England. He was the chief mover for a new church at Stoke (CAST pp27-31). **Eliza Gregory** (nee Jones), born in Stoke in c1897, died at Trentham in 2000 aged 103 (ES April 26 2000 p5p).

STOKE-UPON-TRENT AND LITERATURE. Stoke, one of Arnold Bennett's five towns of the Potteries, is Knype in his novels (Notes on The Card by IL Baker). Paul Breeze, author of 'While my guitar gently weeps' (1979), and 'Back Street runner' (1980), was born in Stoke and later lived in Hanley. John Wain (d1994), novelist, poet and critic, was born in Stoke-upon-Trent in 1925. He attended Newcastle High School. Some of his work includes 'Hurry on Down' (1953), 'A Travelling Woman,' and 'The Living World of Shakespeare.' The novel, 'The Contenders,' has a local theme (VFC pp136-137) (TWWW Feb 27 1999 p2p). For a rhyme from Stoke see FSBC p55.

Stokeville Garden suburb 0.25m SE of Penkhull. It comprises streets W of the S end of London Road in Boothen and contains 24 Italianate-style villas (SSE 1993 p110). Built by the Stokeville Building Society from c1850 (VCH vol 8 p183), or in 1840s (BOE p265) (SL pp223,224 plan) (SSE 1993 p110). The architect is said to have been the young Charles Lynam of Colwich (POTP p143). This middle-class development was known as The Villas from at least 1880 (VCH vol 8 p183). The development also contained a communal tennis court and park. The area was declared a conservation area in the 1970s. In 1998 some National Lottery money was awarded for the restoration of some of the houses. According to a local tradition a former occupant of one of the houses died choking on a garlic bulb which he had taken to bed with him to ward off vampires (ES April 2 1998 p21p).

Stone Ancient parish, former manor, township, quarter and market town 6m NNW of Stafford, situated on a terrace on the E bank of the Trent (SIT), at its confluence with Scotch Brook.

EARLY. A **fossil** of sand with perfect ripples marks in rock of the Triassic Age was found at Stone (ES Nov 25 1930 p4p). For a collection of antiquities and **mammalia** found about Stone by W Wells Bladen see NSFCT 1896 p106. Stone **celts** have been found near Stone (NSFCT 1908 p194). In Stone parish a large stone **axe-hammer** was found before 1886 which went to the BM (ASI p202) (VCH vol 1 p181) and a small **axe** with unfinished perforations found before 1892 which went to the BM (ASI p202) (VCH vol 1 p181 il) (NSJFS 1964 p36). One is possibly illustrated in SIS p2. On the E side of Stone was a **burial mound** opened up in the C18 and a cinerary urn containing a cremation found (SHOS vol 1 General Intro p35) (R vol 6 p64) (JGM p93 fig 94) (The Ceramic Art of Great Britain. Ll Jewitt. vol 1 p8 fig 14) (Proceedings of the Prehistoric Society vol 27 p298 no 196) (NSJFS 1965 p47). A cremation in a collared urn of the **Bronze Age** was found in a gravel pit in Stoke Lane (SHOS General Intro p35) (R vol 6 p64) (Proceedings of the Prehistoric Society vol 27 p298 No. 196) (NSJFS 1964 p36). Stone parish church has been found to lie at the S end of a ley line stretching from Groundslow and running through Saxon's Lowe and Bury Bank (SMM p23 see map). Stone was a possible site for the unlocated **Roman** settlement of Rutunium (see) according to Shaw (SHOS vol 1 p23); whilst Walton (see), near Stone, has been identified with the Lavatres of the Notitia on the Limes Britannicus. For Roman finds in the area see GNHS p70. A Roman road ran from Stone through Hanford to Chesterton (TTH p15). During the building of a housing estate in c1942 a Roman coin of Trajan was found (NSFCT 1942 p54) (NSJFS 1964 p36).

600 to 1086. In the High Street was found an iron spearhead possibly of Saxon origin which went to the Potteries Museum (NSFCT vol 30 p108) (VCH vol 1 p179) (NSJFS 1964 p36) (SIS p2 il may be of it). **Legend of Wulfad**. King Wulfhere of Mercia (d675), lived at the fortified palace at Wulfherecester at Bury Bank (see), about two miles from Stone. Like his father Penda, Wulfhere was a pagan, but was converted to Christianity on his marriage to Ermenilda, a daughter of the royal and Christian house of Kent. However, he later reverted to paganism and refused to allow his sons Wulfad (or Wolfad, Wolf-fed, Wulfflad) and Rufin to be brought up as Christians, but his daughter Werburgh of Trentham (see) was brought up as a Christian. The two princes were converted to Christianity by Chad of Lichfield Cathedral (see), when one day they were out hunting they followed a white hart which led them to Chad, who was living as a hermit. Chad preached to them and baptised them. One of Wulfhere's noblemen, Werebode (or Werbode, Werebod), who was also a pagan sought to marry Werburgh, but she refused having vowed to devote her life to piety. She was supported in this decision by Wulfad and Rufin. In revenge Werebode informed Wulfhere that his sons had defied him and had become Christian. Wulfhere then swore that he would kill his sons. The princes managed to flee but the king rode after them and killed Rufin at Burston (see) and Wulfad at Stone. Their mother had their bodies buried together on the spot where Wulfad had fallen, and in accordance with Saxon custom a large cairn of stones was placed over the grave. Later Werebode was taken ill and died miserably. Wulfhere himself was overcome with remorse and eventually visited Chad to receive absolution and in c670 allowed Ermenilda to build a small priory on the site of her sons' grave (NHS p408) (HOTC p14) (NSFCT 1881 pp24-25) (KNS pp52-55) (SIS pp8,15) (A Short Guide to St Michael's Church, Stone. PA Leason. c1990s) (MR pp306-307). (SOS p33) (SMM pp20-24). Another account relates that Wulfad was murdered at Stone in 650 (HOE pp288,297p) or in about the 660s. Byrne and others suggest that Rufin was also murdered at Stone (TFTP p74). Another tradition has both princes being slain by their father in Eccleshall church (W p373) (BPS p93). Some say Christians built the cairn of stones, as it was a Saxon custom for them to do so (Magna Britannia et Hibernia Antiqua et Nova, vol 5 in the Savoy, 1730) (SIS pp7, 10 note). The tradition may have arisen from Bede's 'Ecclesiastical History of the English Nation' or Bede's 'Anglo-Saxon Chronicle,' Book 4, ch 16 p253 (RHPS p37) where it is stated two royal princes, brothers to Attwald, king of the Isle of Wight, fled a battle occurring on the island and took refuge on the mainland at a place called At the Stone, thought to be Stoneham, between Winchester and Southampton (RHPS p37), or Stonestat in the S of England (HOS p14) (VCH vol 3 p240). The princes were betrayed and ordered to be killed by the victor of the battle. Before their execution, however, they were allowed to receive Christian instruction given by a certain priest. This story was perhaps linked to Stone by monks of Stone Priory to provide a story for the founding of the priory believing that Stone was At the Stone (History of Lichfield Diocese. Beresford). There was a strong belief in medieval times that the legend was really true. A tablet which hung in Stone Priory at the dissolution told of the legend, and mention is made of the tomb of the blessed martyr St Wulfade in the Stone Chartulary Folios 41, 42, and 43 (SHC 1885) (RHPS p36) (SIS p10 note). A version of the legend, taken from a Peterborough book written in c970 in the BM, appears in Dugdale's 'Monasticon Anglicanum' vol 6 part 1 pp230-232 (SIS p10 note). The story has been perpetuated by Henry Bradshaw in 'Life of Saynt Werburga of Chester' (1513), Erdeswick (SOS pp33, 36 note by Harwood) (SH p31), Speed (Historie of Great Britaine. 1632. p305), Chetwynd (SH p46), Plot (NHS pp406-408) and others (SD pp71,72) (SHOS vol 1 p232

note) (SMC p170) (HOL p4) (The Holy Lyfe and History of Saynt Werburge. Ed Edward Hawkins. Chetham Society xv (1848)) (CSL pp106-114) (The Archdeaconry of Stoke-on-Trent. Hutchinson) (LC p89) (SK pp193,198) (PS p53) (HSS pp39-43) (MOS pp106-110) (LGS p222) (Publications of the Modern Language Association of America. vol xxxii (1917). pp323-337) (SOSH pp34-35,36-37) (KNS pp52-66) (SJC p4) (HOTC p13) (KRC p15) (BSB p733) (STM May 1966 p32) (SIS p7) (Anglo-Saxon England vol vii (1978) p11) (BNDA p5) (Saints and Relics in Anglo-Saxon England. David Rollason. 1989) (TTH p15). Despite some of the above having shown some skepticism it was not until the 1960s that the legend was firmly denounced on the grounds that it was based on a misunderstanding of Bede's 'Ecclesiastical History of the English Nation' (HOS p14) (VCH vol 3 p240). This view was, however, challenged in a lecture given on Feb 19 1993 by Dr Philip Morgan to the Stafford and Mid Staffs Archaeology Society. Although Greenslade and Stuart do not believe the legend of Wulfad they believe Wulfhere did convert to Christianity and founded a priory at Stone in the C7 (HOS p14) (VCH vol 3 p240), apparently Wulfhere had converted to Christianity by 659, when he is said to have appointed Triumphere, bishop of the Mercians (RHPS p23). Some kind of hermitage, religious house, small community of nuns, or church continued here until Stone Priory (see) was founded in the C12. Stone **parish** was formed before 1086, probably then containing the ancient parishes of Draycott-in-the-Moors, Milwich, Sandon, and Swynnerton (SHC 1916 pp192,195). **Churches**. Stone Priory church, **St Mary and St Wulfad**, beside the present Lichfield Road, just on the N side, and at its junction with Church Street, served as the parish church from the dissolution of the priory. An aisle was built onto it in 1572. The old church collapsed on Dec 30 1749 and was replaced by the present church, St Michael, on a site slightly to the NE, in 1753-1758 (SIS pp18 see map, 19,61) (BOE p267). The church, **Christ Church**, Radford Street, was built to serve northern Stone and Darlaston (Pirehill hundred), Meaford, Tittensor, Oulton and Moddershall, in 1838-1840 (SIS pp91-92). It was added to or rebuilt in 1885 and again in 1899 (BOE p268). Stone **wake** or parish feast was held on the feast of St Michael and All Angels (Michaelmas day Sept 29), to whom Stone church is dedicated. Bull and bear baiting took place at Stone wakes as did cock-fighting. The last bull baiting took place in c1830 (RHPS pp65,66-67) (SEDG Feb 1988 p9il). By 1851 wakes were being held on the Sunday after Michaelmas day (W p359). Stone wakes were held in a field on the site of the present Stonefield Park before it opened in 1928 (RHPS p250) (MOSP p25). 1086 to 1700. Stone does not appear in DB, yet was in existence then. Cope thinks it was included in the manor of Walton; the priest mentioned under Walton was probably at the church in Stone (SIS p13). Appears in 1187 as Stanes (SSE 1996 p18). The **name** is from Anglo-Saxon 'stan or stanas' 'the stone or stones' and means 'at the stone(s).' Since one document gives Stanes, this would suggest the name was originally plural. The majority of English places with this name stand on, or near, a river (SSE 1996 p18) (SPN p116). The tradition is the stones are a reference to the stones Queen Ermenilda set up over her son, Wulfad, and some say, also over her other son Rufin (murdered at Burston) in c670 (W p359) (RHPS p31) (SK p198). Duignan is unaware of the legend and cannot say what 'stone' or 'stones' gave the town its name. In medieval times Stone manor was held by Stone Priory (see). It was later held by the Colliers of Darlaston Hall (see) near Stone and passed from them to the Cromptons, of Stone Park (see); the manor then descended with that estate and its owners until at least the late C19. Bird says in the **Barons' Wars** (1258-65) royalist forces attacked Stone to retaliate against Simon de Montfort, custodian of Kenilworth Castle, Warws; Kenilworth Priory being attached to Stone Priory (VB p141). Is this the same event Cope refers to when he says in 1263 forces under William la Zouche, Justiciar of Chester, and David, brother of Llewelyn, Prince of Wales burnt Stone after returning from capturing Stafford and Chartley Castle and destroyed Stone Priory muniments? (SIS p22) (VCH vol 3 p242). Palliser says a fire destroyed the town in 1264 (SL p153). The earliest reference to Stone being a **borough** is 1364. Burgage tenure still existed in 1536 (NSJFS 1972 p69). The town **pound** stood in the car park area in Stafford Street (SIT). The **stocks** were at Walton Bridge near the Lamb Inn, which was at the end of Elm Terrace. The last stocks were made by a wheelwright, Isaac Dutton, who ironically was the first person to be placed in them. Also the town had a pillory which was in the Market Place. The last man in them was in 1848 (RHPS p65) (SIS p76). These **bell ringing customs** were discontinued shortly after the abolition of Church Rates, in 1868; the curfew bell, rung each night from Lady day to Michaelmas at 8.00pm, and for six months an hour earlier; the rising bell, rung on week days at 6.00am, on Sundays at 7.00am, after which the day of the month was tolled; the parson's bell, rung on Sundays at 1.00pm for ten minutes, perhaps for when the parson distributed loaves of bread to the poor

(RHPS p66). **Great North West Road**. Stone lay on the main route from London to Chester, the former port for Ireland; for Carlisle and Scotland and for North Wales (SIT). In medieval times the road (which had the name King's Highway) followed some of present Lichfield Road, Abbey, Crown and Newcastle Streets. The giving of hospitality to travellers was financially burdensome to Stone Priory by the 1340s (SIS pp17-19). In 1573 Stone is the only town in Staffs mentioned in a list of postmasters (SIS p38). In the C17 the town, a principal changing station for coaches, was the first over-night stop from Chester, or the third overnight stop from London, conse-quently there were a large amount of public houses, and many with large stable accommodation (RHPS p244) (SIT). What is said to be the first coach-ing advertisement mentions Stone: The journey from London to Stone is advertised in the Mercurius Politicus of April 9 1657 as taking three days and costing 30 shillings (RHPS pp241-242). In Britannia (1675) John Ogilby says the old Chester road which ran through Stone is 'one of the six prime post ways, and readiest for Ireland, and one of the most frequented roads of the kingdom.' In 1729 the road through the town was turnpiked (SIT). In 1834 no fewer than 38 stage coaches passed through Stone, daily (W p358) (SIS (paperback ed. 1980) p28). There was a verse scratched onto a window at the 'old' Dog and Doublet in Sandon that suggested stage-coach travellers preferred to stay at Sandon than at Stone (VB p134). As a consequence of its position Stone had had many noteworthy persons passing through it and commenting on it. **William the Conqueror** came through from Chester to Stafford during the revolt of the north of England in 1069: **Henry III** came through (NSFCT 1896 p106), and **Henry VIII** travelled through going be-tween Lichfield to Stoke (RHPS p296). **John Taylor** known as the 'Water Poet' who travelled on foot from London to Edinburgh, passed in 1620. Af-ter receiving much hospitality, he had a rough passage between Lichfield and Newcastle:

> At night I came to a stony town called Stone,
> Where I knew none, nor was I known of none:
> I therefore through the streets held on my pace,
> Some two miles further to some resting-place.

In 1638 **Richard Braithwaite**, author of 'Drunken Barnaby's Four Journeys to the North of England,' also visited Stone. He was suspected of being a Jesuit, and was searched, but his bundle of papers turned out to be playing-cards (NSFCT 1911 p249) (SIS p40). **Daniel Defoe** calls Stone a consider-able town in his tour of Britain (1723). Defoe's Moll Flanders passes through Stone in his novel titled after her; although, to make her appear vague, he has her say Stone was in Cheshire. In 1792 the 5th **Viscount Torrington** travelled through Stone (SIS p68).
MARKETS AND FAIRS. Stone Priory, lords of Stone manor, was granted a charter on July 13 1251 to hold a **market** on Tuesdays (NSJFS 1971 p51). The market allowed the town to expand outside the priory gates (VCH vol 3 p243) (SL p147) (SIS (paperback ed. 1980) p20). The market was revived under the licence granted to Robert Collier, lord of Stone manor, in 1549 (SIS p34). Stone was described as 'a great parish and market town' in 1604 (SIS p40). There was a market in 1792 (OWEN). In 1817 the market was held on Tuesdays (THS) (SCSF p95). In the early C20 there was a labour hiring market or fair, known as 'Gorby's Market' in the market square in May (MOSP p14). The cattle market in Mill Street closed in c1994 and Safeway supermarket was built on the site in 1999. A **market cross** stood at the bottom of Church Street in c1670. Sleigh in HOLS says banns were proclaimed from Stone market cross in the C17. By 1929 the cross site had been built on (RHPS pp161,241). A **fair** was granted to the prior of Stone Priory with the charter of 1251 for the vigil, feast, and morrow of St Wulfad the Martyr (SIS p17). Cooke gives Tuesday after Mid Lent, Shrove Tuesday, Whit Tuesday, May 29, Aug 5 (for cattle) (SCSF p99). A pie powder or dusty foot court associated with the fair was held at the Crown Inn in 1810 (SIS p85). Two cheese fairs were introduced in 1840 on the third Tuesdays in Oct and May (SIS p99). There was a fair in 1792 (OWEN), but no fair in 1888 (LHE p265).
GRAMMAR SCHOOL. A grammar school was founded by Rev Thomas Alleyn (d1558) when he left his estates in trust to Trinity College, Cam-bridge, with directions to found three free grammar schools - at Uttoxeter, Stone, and Stevenage, Herts. The school was at first housed in a single room of Stone Priory (SIS pp35,37) (VCH vol 6 pp167-168). Thomas Chaloner, finding no master at the school in Feb 1649, effectively restarted it. By June 1650 he had left Stone (SIS pp43-44). The old school room was replaced by a new stone or brick building in c1758. It was still standing in the parish churchyard by c1800 and was described as a 'heap of ruins' in the early

1840s (SIS pp80 il,92) (VCH vol 6 pp167-168). In the early C19 no master seems to have taught at the school, and there was effectively no school. In 1844 Trinity College had a new school house built in Station Road. The house was called Cambridge House. The school moved to new premises and its present site at Oulton Cross in 1889. It converted to a co-educational gram-mar school in 1936. In 1969 the school merged with Granville Secondary Modern School, Stone, to form the comprehensive Alleyne's School (VCH vol 6 pp167-168) (SIS p80 il). Cambridge House was derelict by at least the 1980s to 1999 when restoration began on the building.
CIVIL WAR AND COMMONWEALTH PERIOD. No side appears to have made Stone a garrison in the Civil War, but both sides passed through the town. Sir William Brereton from Cheshire with a parliamentary force passed through en route for the battle of Hopton Heath in March 1643. After the battle Brereton quartered his troops here before leaving for Nantwich on March 23 (BFS pp14,18). After the parliamentarians took Stafford in May 1643 and made it the seat of their parliamentary committee for the county the Stone district came under parliament's control and had to make weekly money pay-ments to them; quarter their troops; have their goods requisitioned; and give salt for gunpowder (SIS pp42,43). Charles I spent two nights at Stone Park in 1645 (SIS p42). A plague which occurred at Rushton Grange and Burslem in 1647 then spread to Stone (SCSF p137). Thomas Chaloner MA a royalist and former master of Shrewsbury School taught at Stone Grammar School be-tween Feb 1649 and no later than June 1650 during his alienation from Shrews-bury School; his wife died whilst he was at Stone and is buried in St Michael's churchyard. In the second Civil War Prince Charles (Charles II) quartered his army at Stone on Aug 19 1651 en route for Worcester (SIS pp43-44).
1700 to 1800. Damage was done to Stone's dissenter meeting house on July 8 1715 (SIS p49) (LOU pp88,359). For the Duke of Cumberland and his army quartered at Stone during the 1745 Jacobite Rebellion see Cumberland House, and Mottley Pits. The **Trent and Mersey Canal**, which passes through the town, completed in 1777, had its headquarters in Stone (SIS (paperback ed. 1980) p20). It was noted within 10 years of the canal's completion that the town felt like a 'little seaport' (SL p236). The canal mile post at The Top Lock, Star Inn, Stone, dated 1819, reads 'Shardlow 49 miles: Preston Brook 43 miles' (DoE II) (IANS pp24,44 fig 7) (SEDG May 1988 p4p). The **Town Hall** built in early C19, stood on the N side of High Street. After serving as the Assembly Rooms and Town Hall it doubled in the C20 as a cinema (SIT). In about the 1980s the building was demolished and shops built on the site. Mr C Foden of Lightwood came into the possession of the old town **fire en-gines** one dated 1787 and the other is dated 1800 (ES Jan 2 1931 p5 ps). **Natives and visitors.** Sir **Sampson Wright**, writer, was from Stone. He be-came an assistant to Sir John Fielding. He appears to have died in the later C18. He does not appear in DNB or BS (SHOS vol 1 p67 note; suggests he became as famous a writer as Fielding). Rev **Stebbing Shaw**, author of SHOS, the son of Rev Stebbing Shaw, son of John Stebbing Shaw of Stone was born in Stone in 1762 (RHPS p39) (BS p397). Others say he was born in or near Stone (SA Feb 16 1799) (GM 1803(1) pp9,10) (SHC 1970 p224 p facing) (SH pp98-113), whilst others say he was born in Fulford (STM Nov 1965 p39) in Stone ancient parish. For the case of **Thomas Meaykin** see under Rushton Spencer. The parents of the watercolourist, **Peter de Wint**, a young doctor Henry de Wint, an American of Dutch descent, and his wife, Caroline Watson of Scotland, came to Stone in 1781 and had ten children. Peter, their fourth son, was born in a house adjoining the Crown Inn on Jan 21 1784 (LGS pp64-65) (SIS p77). Pearson says the house stood behind, what was in 1981, Boots the Chemist (MOSP p14). As a young man he had drawing lessons from a Mr Rogers of Stafford (LGS p65). Peter left Stone to be apprenticed to John Raphael Smith in London on April 1 1802 (SIS p77). In c1806 he returned to Stone for a brief stay, returning to London in autumn 1806 (RHPS p159). In 1807 he exhibited for the first time at the Royal Academy, his pictures includ-ing one of Tittensor Common and two views of Trentham Hall; daughters of the Duke of Sutherland were at one time his pupils (SEDG Nov 1987 pp9-10). In 1810 he married Harriet Hilton of Lincoln, the sister of his life-long friend William Hilton, RA (LGS p65) (RHPS p159). He lived in Lincoln from 1814 (SEDG Nov 1987 pp9-10). Apart from a visit to France in 1828 and to North Wales in 1829 he painted only the English landscape, especially land-scapes in the vicinity of Lincoln (The Penguin Dictionary of Art & Artists. Peter and Linda Murray. 1978). He also lived in London, and died there in 1849 (LGS p65). In c1984 there was discovered a memoir written by de Wint's wife in which she clearly states that her husband was born in Hanley, but there is no other documentary proof to substantiate the claim. There are no records to show he was baptised at St Peter's, Stoke, or St Michael's, Stone, where registers show his younger brothers and sisters were baptised. His painting titled 'A View Near Stone' was purchased by Stone town council in 1984

(SEDG Nov 1987 pp9-10). (SSW pp84-90) (S p121) (Great Artists. Gilbert R Redgrave) (STM May 1968 pp24,37) (Drawings and Watercolours. Peter De Wint. David Scrase. 1979). **George Cooper** (d1834), pugilist gypsy, was born in a caravan by Redhill Lane, on Red Hill in c1791. Cooper, known as the 'Bargeman' because of his work on canal boats at Stone, was rated one of the most complete boxers of his time. He was beaten in a famous boxing match with Dan Donnelly at 'Belcher's Hollow,' Curragh of Kildare, Kildare, Ireland on Dec 13 1815 (Dan Donnelly, His Life and Legends. Patrick Myler). He is said to have been the model for the Flaming Tinman in George Borrow's 'Romany Rye' (SN May 15 1992 p9).

1800 to 1850. The independent **Stone and Eccleshall Troop**, raised by George Steedman of Cold Meece in 1798, disbanded in 1814, appear to have been a part of the Staffordshire Yeomanry between c1814 and c1816 (FSP p62) (SIS p73) (info Yeomanry Museum). Owing to its proximity to the Potteries the town was warned to take precautions against the proposed **Chartist insurrection** and it is said barricades were actually erected at Stone for Whit Monday 1839: It was unusual that the authorities of the Potteries did not take any measures (LOU pp229-230). Stone was warned to take precautions during the Chartist riots by a notice dated Aug 18 1842 (SIS p99). The first meeting of the **North Staffordshire Agricultural Society** was held at The Crown (see), Stone in 1844 (The History of Staffordshire Agricultural Society. Brenda Greysmith. c1978). **Floods.** Stone flooded after a terrific thunderstorm on June 25 1830 (SA July 3 1830) (Broughton's Scrapbook p235). **Natives and visitors. The Fourdriniers.** A French Protestant family of paper-makers called Fourdrinier emigrated to England in the C18. They erected a paper-making factory in Herts (POTP p99). Two sons of the family - Henry Fourdrinier (1766-1854), and Sealy (d1847) - worked for many years on paper-making machinery, the first patent being taken out in 1801 (SIS p100). Henry established a paper-making mill, N of Stone - now known as Coppice Mill (see) - in the C18 (SSBOP p61). By 1807 Henry and Sealy had perfected their machine for making continuous paper, of any size. In c1814 two machines were erected in Russia at the behest of the emperor of Russia but they were never paid for. To compensate the Fourdriniers £7000 was paid to them in 1840 by the British parliament. Many people thought this inadequate and The Times organised a subscription which purchased annuities for Henry Fourdrinier (SIS p100). In 1827 George Henry Fourdrinier (Henry's son?) established a factory at Ivy House Paper Mill (see), Hanley (VCH vol 8 p170). There the firm made the tissue paper used by potters in printing copper-plate engravings. Henry Fourdrinier patented a machine for producing paper from pulp in a few minutes in wide sheets and capable of endless extension. In 1846 George Henry Fourdrinier (Henry's son?) patented an improved printing press, using steam, hot air or water, a paper-cutting machine, potters' steam presses and slip softeners (POTP p99). By 1840 Henry Fourdrinier lived at Burston Hall (see), near Stone. In 1841 his wife died and was buried in St Michael's churchyard, Stone. Fourdrinier died at Mavesyn Ridware on Sept 3 1854 (RHPS pp159-160). Mr L' Estrange in the novel 'Our New Parish' by Harriet E Fourdrinier is modelled on her father Henry Fourdrinier (ILN) (SA Oct 21 1824) (Note in front of WSL copy of the novel) (BS p176) (GM vol 49 pp102,103) (Sentinel Summer No. 1907) (H p55) (SEDG Sept 1988 pp6,7) (Links of the Past. TG Adie) (VCH vol 2 pp148-149. vol 8 p170). For the case of **Daniel Collier**, seen to move in Stone after being executed in Stafford in 1820, see under Hanley. Elizabeth Prout, born at Shrewsbury in 1820, came to Stone with her parents in the 1830s. Whilst in the town she came under the influence of the Catholic missionary, Father Dominic Barberi of nearby Aston Hall (see), who converted her to Catholicism. In 1851 she founded the 'Sisters of The Cross and Passion' in Manchester. She died of consumption on Jan 11 1864 and was interred at St Anne's, Sutton, near St Helens, Lancs. In June 1973 her remains were brought to a shrine in the new church of St Anne and Blessed Dominic at Stone (SCHJ No. 19 (1980) pp28-36). **Richard Smith**, inventor of Hovis bread, was born at the Old Mill, Mill Street, and baptised in St Michael's church in Feb 1836. Smith left Stone as a young man. His process for bread with the brown wheat germ flour was sold to Samuel Fitton & Sons of Macclesfield, who patented it in 1887 as Smith's Patent Germ Bread. This name was replaced by that of 'Hovis' on the suggestion of an Oxford schoolmaster, Herbert Grimes, who adapted the Latin tag 'hominis vis' - 'the strength of man.' The firm eventually became the Hovis Company; Smith remained on the board of the company until his death in 1900 (SEDG Nov 1987 p13p) (WTMS p147).
INDUSTRY AND RAILWAYS. Stone's industries have been shoe manufacturing (to rival Stafford), tanning, brewing, fustian working, and brass working between 1794 and the 1830s (SIT). Bent's Brewery, to the NW of the town centre, closed in 1958, and the site had become the Mount Industrial Estate by 1980. Joule's Brewery, in the centre of the town, won the right to

use 'Stone Ale' as its copyright and the red cross as trademark (provided it was always on a green background) after a lawsuit taken to the House of Lords in 1888. The brewery, later taken over by Bass Charrington, closed in 1972 (SIT) or 1974 (SIS 1980 pp28,43,48). The three-storey brick Town Mill by Scotch Brook is dated 1792. By the mid 1970s it was derelict (SIT). But it was still standing in 1999 by the modern Christchurch Way. A windmill was built in 1803 on low-lying land adjacent to the canal 0.25m S of the church at SJ 905335. F Calvert sketched it behind a large barn in 1830 (SSC) (RHPS pl 1 shows view of Stone) (WBJ pp37-38). It was demolished in 1847. In a ceremony Viscount St Vincent cut the first turf for a Stoke and Stafford railway line which was to run through Stone, in a field adjoining the Gosdells, now Stone Golf Course on Feb 11 1847: Stone was connected with Stoke and Stafford from April 17 1848 and with Colwich from May 1 1849 (NSJFS 1962 p99) (SIS p95. and (paperback ed. 1980) p37).
NEWSPAPERS. The **Stone and Eccleshall Advertiser and Staffordshire, Shropshire and Cheshire Chronicle**, founded by March 2 1889, became the Stone, Longton Fenton & Eccleshall Advertiser and Uttoxeter and Cheadle Gazette from May 16 1896, and the Stone and Eccleshall Advertiser from Aug 29 1903; this paper ran until at least Dec 26 1914 (SHJ spring 1996 p25); a Stone and Eccleshall Advertiser of Sept 5 1957 is referred to in SIS. The **Stone Weekly News** ran between at least Oct 4 1901 and June 30 1911 (SHJ spring 1996 p26). The **Stone Gazette and Meir, Eccleshall and Barlaston News**, founded on May 14 1937 ran until at least March 18 1938 (SHJ spring 1996 p25). The **Stone Guardian**, founded in 1948 or 1949, became the Stone and Eccleshall News from Oct 4 1958, and the Stone Guardian and Stafford Newsletter from Jan 14 1966. In 1969 or 1971 it appears to have amalgamated with **Stone Newsletter**, a Stone edition of the Stafford Newsletter; this was still running in 1997 (Willings Press Guide. 1988) (SHJ spring 1996 pp25,26). The free weekly **Stafford & Stone Trader** was founded in 1981. But the Stafford and Stone Shopper had ceased publication by 1988 (Willings Press Guide.1988). The **Stone Gazette**, founded by John Butterworth, was in existence at least over the period between Nov 1987 and Oct 1988 (SN April 20 2000 p8).
1900 to PRESENT. The Russian burial anthem, the 'Contakion' was sung for the first time in England at the funeral of Mrs Elizabeth Brisco-Owen, mother of Rev AE Brisco-Owen in St Michael's church, on July 17 1899 (RHPS p232). The earthquake of 3.21pm July 3 1904 was felt at Stone (NSFCT 1905 p133). For Stone **airfield** see Rugeley Turn. The device of Stone **urban district** is of heraldic character: A black shield charged with a gold chevron between in chief a wheatsheaf and a tun, both gold, and in a base a shoemaker's knife and an awl crossed saltirewise proper, their handles gold; and on the chevron a Staffordshire Knot proper between two black lozenges. Above the shield is a gold naval crown and issuing therefrom a silver demi-pegasus, its wings spread, holding between the hoofs a black lozenge. The motto is 'Sit Saxum Firmum' (May the Stone be Firm) (CH p340). From April 1 1974 Stone formed a part of a new enlarged borough of Stafford. The first time the Freedom of a borough was presented at a ceremony outside the city or main town of the borough was at Stone on March 31 1979 when HMS Collingwood, a descendant of the first HMS Collingwood of the early C19 and a successor of HMS St Vincent, was presented with the Freedom of the Borough of Stafford at a ceremony in St Michael's church. Also the ceremony was believed to be the first at which a council meeting occurred during a church service. HMS St Vincent was named after the sea battle, Cape of St Vincent, in which Admiral John Jervis of Meaford Hall (see) was victorious. By 1979 HMS Collingwood was the Royal Navy's floating Weapon Engineering School at Fareham, Hants (Order of Service book in WSL) (STMSM July 1979 pp57,58,59ps) (info George Beecham). A **film** called 'Kent the fighting man' was made in and around Stone in 1916 (MOSP p22). **Stone Historical and Civic Society**, an amenity and historical society, formed in 1995 (info Philip Leason). **Foot-and-mouth disease** broke out in late 1967 and early 1968 in Stone parish at these farms - Berry Bank Farm, Aston Hall, Aston Lodge Farm, and Mount Pleasant Farm (SN Dec 22 1967 p15. Dec 29 1967 p13. Jan 5 1968 p15). **Cuisine, superstition and phenomena.** The special dish to celebrate mid-Lent 'Mothering Sunday' in Stone parish was a roast veal and custard, eaten at mid-day. This occurred on the fourth Sunday in Lent (FOS p86). Stone was a famous Staffs centre of gooseberry growing in the C19. It held the record for the premier prize from 1860 to 1901, until it was taken by an Harborne grower in 1901 (STELE May 11 1956). The tradition of all wedding parties approaching St Michael's church by the Priory Gate, and all funerals by the West Gate (at the bottom of Church Street) still prevailed in 1929 (RHPS p66). A UFO was seen over or near Stone (UFO Study p31). In the evening of Aug 31 1954 three boys saw from Stone a what resembled a Mexican hat in the sky. One boy, Keith Billinge, cycled to Meaford to get a

closer look at it. The same object had been seen from Stafford (see) earlier in the day (The Coming of the Spaceships. Gavin Gibbons. 1956). **Natives and visitors. Cardinal Newman** was present at the opening of St Dominic's Convent in 1854, and was a visitor to Stone on subsequent occasions. The **Prince Imperial of France** assisted at a High Mass at St Dominic's during Christmas 1881; he was later killed in the Zulu War (RHPS p309). **Edward VII** came through Stone in 1880, and again when king in a motor car in 1907 going to Alton Towers. On Oct 18 1913 **Gustav Hamel** flew in an air display at Stone (EAS p21) (TB March 1994 p18p) (ES Oct 18 1997 p21p). **Edward VIII** passed through Stone in 1924, and Prince Henry in 1927 (RHPS p296). **Mark Hughes**, author of SOSH, appears to have been headmaster of Christ Church School, Stone, by 1925. By 1930 he had moved to Malvern (SOSH title page) (ES Jan 1930 p6. Jan 24 1930 p6p). **Pauline Miller**, whose family lived in High Street, was the second wife of the artist Sir James Gunn from c1930. He painted many portraits of her; his portrait of her was one of the successes of the RA 1930 Summer Exhibition; his 'Pauline waiting' painted in 1939 'reflects perfectly the aura of the age' (CL March 30 1995 pp66-67) (local info); his 'Pauline in the Yellow Dress' was at Preston Art Gallery, Preston, Lancs, in 1999. **Joe Louis**, the heavyweight champion of the world, visited American forces based at Stone in WW2 (MOSP p27). **Andrew N Wilson** (b1950), author of The Healing Heart (1980), Wise Virgin (1982), Hilaire Belloc (1984), Tolstoy (1988), Eminent Victorians (1989), Jesus (1992), The Faber Book of Church and Clergy (1992) spent some of his childhood at Stone. The Wilson family lived at Stonefield Cottage, Newcastle Road, between at least 1957 and 1958, during which time Wilson attended the junior part of St Dominic's Convent School, Station Street (info Sister Mary Henry. St Dominic's Convent). **Prince Charles** visited Stone on March 3 1998 (SLM April 1998 p15).

Stone Cross Former small square at the end of Pinfold Lane, Penkridge, which was lost when the A449 road was widened in the 1930s. The name is from an ancient cross which stood here at least until 1740 and afterwards said to be re-erected in the churchyard (PVH p18p of the cross in the church yard) (SCSF p87). It was where the perambulation of Penkridge in Rogation Week went to on the first day after starting at the church (PR 1732) (HOP p29). The cross in the churchyard is partly C14 and C19 (DoE II).

Stone Cross Minute hamlet on ground gradually rising from the Tame and a tributary 1m NNE of the High Street in West Bromwich. The nucleus seems to have been an inn called Stone Cross Inn. Now, wholly merged in Wednesbury-West Bromwich suburbs. Was under 0.25m E of West Bromwich manor house at Hall Green, near Charlemont. The name is from a wayside cross outside Stone Cross Inn, in existence until 1894 (SHWB 8 p, 13) (BCP pp17,18-19ps of the inn); the base survived as part of a signpost until c1897 (VCH vol 17 p6). Some say the cross was a preaching cross (SOWB p23) or a shrine. In 1794 a minister wrote that he had seen a stone pillar at Stone Cross, and that it was higher and vaster than the kind that sun dials were placed on. There were also two others at one time and there were stone steps (SMM p30). Goods were left at the cross for local people in times of plague, or the markets of Walsall and Wednesbury were held here in times of plague (RHS) (SCSF pp87,88) (WAM p53) (BCM April 1969 p53) (BCOPP vol 1 p42 pl of the 'Cross Inn' c1908; the inn sign shows picture of a cross) (BCOPP pl 71 shows the original red sandstone cross where the lamp post was). The church, The Ascension, in Walsall Road, was built in 1938 (VCH vol 17 p60). Stone Cross was the last place in West Bromwich to hold may pole celebrations. The maypole stood in a field near to Stone Cross Inn. The last observance of the custom was in 1915 (BCM April 1969 p54). The Stone Cross area was bombed in WW2 (TB Jan 1996 p3. Feb 1996 p3).

Stone Cross Conduit Conduit, in existence by 1482, situated at the junction of Lombard Street and Tamworth Street, Lichfield. Named after a stone cross which had stood here in the later C13. A dial was set on the conduit in 1675. The conduit was rebuilt in 1750 and was still standing in 1795, but not by 1806 (VCH vol 14 pp96,97).

Stonefield Former very large 'open' field stretching across N Stone from the Trent to Oulton Road, Stone. Formerly in Kibblestone township and quarter in Stone ancient parish (W p359). In Meaford and Oulton township by 1872 (KD 1872). The field, also known as Stone town Field, was mostly built on after it was enclosed in 1798 (NSFCT 1940 p32) or 1801 (SIS (paperback ed. 1980) p28). However, the Common Plot in NW area of the town (SIS p25 see map) is a remaining part of it. The view from the Common Plot takes in the Wrekin, the Bredons, and in favourable conditions, the Montgomeryshire Hills (NSFCT 1910 p208). On the Common Plot are straight terraces, the remains of Saxon field strips, and mounds created by encampments of the Civil War or the 1745 Jacobite Rebellion, both are called the Mottley Pits (see). Also there were fish ponds near Old Road believed to

be of medieval origin (NSFCT 1897 map facing p141 and ils facing p150). Coins (especially those of the reign of James I), cannon balls and artifacts of the period have been unearthed here since.

Stonefield Park Tiny public park at the N end of Stone, enclosed by Field Terrace, Albert St, and Old Road, opened in 1928. Before the opening of the park Stone wakes were held here on land known as 'The Wakes Field' (MOSP p25). (SSBOP p27).

Stone Heath Fragmented small hamlet 1.5m E of Hilderstone. Partly in Hilderstone township and quarter in Stone ancient parish and partly in Leigh parish. The name is from perhaps former common land of Stone.

Stone House On or near the site of the present College Cottages 1.25m SSW of Bobbington (1834 OS map).

Stone House On the road to Denstone College, at Denstone. Dated 1712 (BOE pp28,116).

Stone House, The Off Coley Lane, Little Haywood. Probably built in the early Tudor times and at one time in the possession of the Whitby family of The Old Manor House. The Stone House (Farm) was still standing in 1924 and was owned by John Charles Moore by 1930 (HAH p39) (HAHS p54).

Stone House 0.5m NE of Horton in Horton ancient parish, on top of Grindlestone Edge. Existed by probably 1559 (VCH vol 7 p65).

Stone House Stone house at Slitting Mill on the N side of Rugeley-Broadhurst Green road. The oldest part of the house is a roughly square stone block at its SE corner dating from the late C16 or C17. Seat of a branch of the Weston family of Hagley Hall by 1757. Between 1807 and c1842 it was owned by Thomas Pickering or his trustees. Residence of Sarah Hopkins of 'The Forge' (later Fair Oak House) between 1808 and 1844. The Gardners were living here by 1854 to at least 1928. Shortly before the WW2 it was converted into a country club and in the war taken over by the Air Ministry. It was still MOD property in 1957 (VCH vol 5 p158). The house was still standing in 1998; a stone sign at the entrance to the drive declares that the property was built in 1584.

Stone House Farm Old house in Brown Edge in Norton chapelry in Stoke-on-Trent ancient parish (ONST 1932 p39).

Stonehouses Tiny hamlet on the W side of the Blithe Valley 0.5m SSE of Forsbrook.

Stone Lowe Anglo-Saxon burial mound on a promontory to the W of Stonelowe Hall (SVB p114). Appears like an hexagonal pile of boulders and consists of a natural outcrop of sandstone, surmounted by three flights of rough stone steps conjoined. The tradition is that they point respectively to Endon (whence came the Bulkeleys), to Cheddleton (where the Sherrards lived), and to Stonelowe Hall (NSFCT 1926 p137). The name means 'grave among the stones' (SVB p114).

Stonelowe Hall 0.25m W of the church at Longsdon. Formerly in Longsdon township in Leek ancient parish. There was probably a house on this site by the C13. The present house is mainly of the C17 (VCH vol 7 p203), or of the Elizabethan period (SVB p114). The Stonelow estate was held by the Stanlowes, who were living here by at least the early C13, and then by the Sherrards or Sherratts by 1434. From the Sherratts it passed by marriage in the C16 to the Bulkeleys or Buckleys; they held it until the C19 (VCH vol 7 p207). Others say the hall was at sometime occupied by the Britles, and the Breretons (NSFCT 1870 p37. 1926 p137) (OL vol 1 pp251-254). The supposed arms of Sir Robert Bulclough and of the Bulkeley family can still be seen faintly on a pillar at the entrance to the house (NSFCT 1916 p142). The hall was restored in 1866 by Editha Pigot; her name appears on the dated pediment over the main door (VCH vol 7 p207). The hall is sometimes spelt Stanlowe Hall. It derives its name from Stone Lowe (see).

Stone Old Hall Formerly in Station Road, Stone. Seat of the Barbour family. Stone rural district council offices later occupied the building (SIS pp48; called Old Hall, 50 note). Stone Old Hall can probably be identified with the Old Hall in Stone which was the birthplace of John Richard Beech Masefield in 1850, father of Charles JB Masefield (1882-1917), author of LGS, and uncle of John Masefield (1878-1967), Poet Laureate (STM July 1971 p25).

Stone Park Medieval hunting ground 0.5m ENE of Stone (Plot's map) (NSFCT 1910 p176). Stone Park, or Stone Old Park, was once in the possession of Stone Priory. After the Reformation it was owned by the Crompton family, who had their seat here. In the Civil War Thomas Crompton favoured the Puritans but refused to raise a force for the parliamentarians without the King's authority. In fact, in May 22 and 23 1645 Charles I was an uninvited guest here prior to the battle of Naseby (SIS p42). During the Commonwealth the house became a place for non-conformist preaching (SIS p44). Thomas Compton died in 1673 and in 1683 or 1684 his son, William, purchased Stone manor from James Collier, thereafter the manor seems to have descended with Stone Park. On the death of William's granddaughter, Elizabeth Crompton, in 1747 the house and manor passed to her sole executrix and adopted heir, Miss Mary Browne of Broseley, Shrops (SIS p46). Later, the house and park were owned by Lord Gower (Leveson-Gower of Trentham Hall); he was keeping deer in the park here in c1735 (EDP p179). In 1771 Lady Katherine Leveson-Gower made over some of the rent from the Stone Park estate to charity (KD 1912). The younger son of Granville Leveson-Gower (1721-1803) of Trentham Hall, Granville Leveson-Gower (1773-1846), minister plenipotentiary to the Court of St Petersburg in 1807, was created Viscount Granville of Stone Park in 1815 and Earl Granville and Baron Leveson of Stone, Staffs in 1833. He was succeeded as lord of Stone manor by his son Granville George Leveson-Gower (1815-1891), 2nd Earl Granville, colliery owner in the Potteries and principal owner of Shelton Iron Works at Shelton; his decision in July 1842 to reduce miners' wages, precipitated a miners' strike, which partly lead to the Chartist riots in the Potteries (see) in Aug 1842 (W p360) (SIS p83) (POTP p140). The trustees of the late Earl held Stone Park and Stone manor in 1892 (KD 1892). The 2nd Earl was succeeded by his son Granville George Leveson-Gower (1872-1939), 3rd Earl Granville (styled Lord Leveson until 1891). He died without issue and was succeeded by his brother William Spencer (1880-1953), 4th Earl Granville, who was succeeded by his son Granville James Leveson-Gower (b1918), 5th Earl Granville, Viscount Granville of Stone Park and Baron Leveson of Stone, still living in 1993 (The Complete Peerage) (Burke's Peerage) (Who's Who 1993). The old house is now replaced by Stone Park Farm (SIS (booklet 1980 ed.) p17).

Stonepit Hill Hill W of Sheen Hill. In Sheen ancient parish. Was so called by the 1730s. The hill was quarried probably in the C18 and certainly in the C19 (VCH vol 7 p245).

Stone Priory Former Augustine Priory (LGS p37) at Stone and has been called Saint Augustine's Priory. A church of some sort existed at Stone by c670 (SMC p173). From this date there was a nunnery or hermitage here founded by Queen Ermenilda (or King Wulfhere, after his conversion to Christianity), to commemorate, according to tradition, her son, Wulfad, murdered for converting to Christianity by her husband, Wulfhere, on the site in c660s (SIS pp8,15). The priory was one of only four monastic foundations in Staffs prior to 1066 (HOS p14). DoE says the priory was founded in 1135. Some say it was founded by Enisan de Walton (SAS p11). In the early C12 Geoffrey de Clinton, Henry I's chamberlain and treasurer, bought the church and granted it to his Augustine priory at Kenilworth, Warws, founded in 1122. After Geoffrey de Clinton's death the overlord Robert de Stafford II patronised the church. During his time it's status was raised to a priory. The charter dated between 1138 and 1147, granting to the canons at the church more land, may be its foundation charter (SIS p15) (VCH vol 3 pp240-247). In July 1251 the prior was granted a charter to hold a weekly market for Stone. The priory remained dependent on Kenilworth until 1260 (SIS p20). The priors possessed rights of free warren in the C13 (NSFCT 1910 p175). The seal is a pointed oval, 2.5 inches by 1.5 inches and shows the Virgin, crowned and seated, with her Child on her left knee, and holding a flower in her right hand with the legend: 'Sigillum ecclesie sancte Marie et sancti W...... (M)artiris de Stanis' used on documents in the C13 (SIS p31).

AFTER THE DISSOLUTION. The priory was suppressed in 1536 (SIS p27) or in spring 1537 (VCH vol 3 p246). It was one of the first Staffs houses to be suppressed (SIS p27). Lord Stafford then had all his ancestors monuments removed from the priory church to St Augustine's Priory (see) at Forebridge, Stafford (SIS p29). The priory, which straddled the current Lichfield Road, and its land, were sold to George Harper, Sir William Pykering and George Robinson, mercer of London. The priory church, dedicated to the Blessed Virgin Mary and St Wulfad, was to remain as the parish church until the 1740s. In a short time the property was re-sold to William Crompton of Stone Park and James Collier of Darlaston (Pirehill hundred) and parcels of land went to others of the merchant and tradesmen class. In the mid C16 William Crompton is accused of striping the priory buildings (SIS (booklet 1980 ed.) p15). In Edward Arblaster's note-book (1719) the remains are described as 'ample' (NSFCT 1922-23 pp63-64) (SIS p30). A Parsonage House was built on part of Stone Priory site in 1753-8, now called The Priory (SIS p30). About 1770 Lichfield Road was built through the site to High Street and some subterranean passages and walls were discovered (RHPS pp31,32). By 1789 the remains were much reduced (SIS p30). In 1828 a tiled pavement was found and below it a grave near the Parsonage House (SIS p30). A remaining arched doorway of the Norman period was drawn by Peter Orlando Hutchinson in Oct 1833 (NSFCT 1910 frontispiece) and was sketched in June 1841 by JC Buckler (GNHS il facing p89 - original is in the WSL). Garner wrote in 1844 that several rudely formed coffins had been found, but gives no details (GNHS p116). The principal remains surviving are two bays of the vaulted undercroft

or crypt with ribs springing from moulded corbels. This was in a section between the priory church and the chapter house. It now forms the roof of the cellars of the house called The Priory (see) JH Beckett drew it in 1911 (RHPS il No.10, il No. 26) (SIS p28 il) (SPJD pp34-35ps) (DoE II). Two stone figures, one of an Austin canon and one of a lady, in the W porch of the present church were in the priory church (KES p195) (SIS pl 6). In 1962 a length of old wall was revealed beneath the corner of Lichfield Street and Church Street (SIS p30). (SSC p135 in the intro) (SOS p36) (W p359) (NSFCT 1881 pp25-27) (LGS p221) (SOSH p106) (BOE p267) (SIS pp15-32) (SIS (booklet. 1980)) pp9-14).

Stones, The House S of Belmont Road, SW of Schoolhouse Green, Ipstones. To its WNW on S side of Belmont Road is Littlestones (OS map 1888 6 inch).

Stonesteads Burial mound N of Waterhouses at SK 08415054. It is 16 paces in diameter and two feet high. It was excavated by Carrington in 1849. A crouched male skeleton was found (TYD p131) (VCH vol 1 no 17) (DPTB p10). It is a listed monument.

Stone Villa House which stood WNW of Lark Hall in Bagnall parish. Built in 1787 on land known as Gold's meadow. It was demolished in 1970. The name may have been from Thomas Stone who lived here in the late C18 (B pp78-79).

Stoney Bridge Bridge 1m NNE of Wheaton Aston, 2.25m W of Whiston.

Stoney Cliffe House 0.5m SE of Upper Hulme. Lay in a detached portion of Bradnop township in Leek ancient parish. Was transferred to Heathylee civil parish in 1934 (VCH vol 7 p31). There was a house here by 1586 (VCH vol 7 p33).

Stoney Croft Became the present Market Square, Tunstall (SHST p268).

Stoney Dale Dale SW of Oakamoor.

Stoneyfields 'A handsome mansion' on the N side of Etruria Road, Basford. Built in 1780 (Newcastle Times Dec 20 1972). In 1801 the house was owned by Mrs Hatrell and was then for sale; it was perhaps purchased by William Bent; he was the owner in the earlier C19. By 1832 Nigel William Heathcote lived here. Thomas Firmstone, ironmaster, became the occupier in 1836; he left sometime after 1853. During some of his occupancy the house belonged to JS Caldwell. By 1857 to at least c1889 it was owned by the Peakes. By 1892 Percy Frederick Meakin was living here. For a short while the house was leased to John Goddard. Stoneyfields was purchased from Fanny Meakin by Eric Ernest Young in 1923; Young's widow lived here until her death in 1965. The estate was then divided with the house being purchased by Morgan Insurance Brokers who had their offices here to the early 1990s (Pigot's Directory 1832) (HBST p513) (Newcastle Times Dec 20 1972 p of Stoneyfields House) (ES Feb 13 1974) (info from New Victoria Theatre). By c1997 the house had been converted by the Tom Cobleigh Pub group into an inn called the Polite Vicar.

GROUNDS. Some of the gravestones of Mr Young's dogs (info Peter Cheeseman). The **New Victoria Theatre** on land to the E of the house has its origins in the Studio Theatre Company, founded by Stephen Joseph (d1967) in London in 1955 to explore the creative potential of theatre-in-the-round. In 1962 the company converted a cinema at Hartshill, built in 1914, to a theatre-in-the-round for its permanent home, and called it the Victoria Theatre; hitherto the company had been a touring one using a portable theatre-in-the-round. Shortly after the conversion Joseph left the district to lecture at Manchester University. In 1966 administration of the theatre passed from the company to the new Stoke-on-Trent and North Staffordshire Theatre Trust Ltd. In 1984 the former paddock and tennis court of Stoneyfields (which was sold in 1965 to the Staffs county council and passed to Newcastle borough council), was leased by Newcastle borough council to the trust for the site of a new theatre. The New Victoria Theatre, a purpose-built theatre-in-the-round, was built on the site between 1984 and 1986; the first performance was on Aug 12 1986. Peter Cheeseman CBE, Theatre Director at the old and new Victoria Theatres from 1962, is noted for the eleven documentaries he compiled and directed with the Victoria Theatre Company. Many of those documentaries, for instance 'Fight for Shelton Bar!' and 'Nice Girls,' depicting protests against the closure of, respectively, steelworks at Shelton (see), and Hem Heath Colliery (see), were challenging and pioneering. 'Come On Stan: The Remarkable True Life Story of Stanley Matthews' of Hanley (see) was written by Rony Robinson and opened at the theatre in 1994. Cheeseman retired in 1998 and was then said to be the longest-serving theatre director of an English provincial theatre in modern times. By the late 1970s the national reputation of the Victoria Theatre was high. By 1998 it had fostered the careers of many famous actors in film and theatre, including: Robert Powell (1964), Fiona Walker (1964-6), Ben Kingsley (1965), Roy Barraclough (1965-6), Anton Vogel (1965), Anne Raitt (1966-9), Shane Connaughton (1967),

Bob Hoskins (1968), Carol Drinkwater (1970), Bill Thomas (1973-5), Kevin Whately (1976-7), Gerda Stevenson (1978), Shelly Willetts (1988-9), and Matthew Cottle (1992); the directors and writers Alan Ayckbourn (1962) and Mike Leigh (1966); RSC director, Ron Daniels (1965), and designer, Alison Chitty (1974). The work of local writers Paul Gater, John Wain and Arthur Berry of Smallthorne (see) has been staged at the old and new Victoria Theatres (info Peter Cheeseman) (Stars from the Vic. 1998) (VFC pp14,53) (I Feb 25 1998 p13) (ES Feb 28 2000 p3). For the origin of the relief medallion of Shakespeare on the external wall of the theatre see The Marsh.

Stoneyford House over 1.5m SW of Hales. There was a house in the SW corner of Bayley's Spring called Stonyford as early as 1635 (SHC 1945/ 6 p184).

Stoneyford Minute hamlet by Stonyford Brook 1m NNE of Yoxall. Has also appeared as Stonyford.

Stoney Low Tiny isolated settlement on a hill above a tributary of the Lea 1.25m ESE of Madeley (W p396). It can only be approached by a long track from the Keele-Whitmore road. At Stoney Low Farm is a boundary stone or and burial mound (M p30). A Robert Beach of Stoneylow is mentioned in 1643-4 (MHSP p46). (NSJFS 1974 p51).

Stonnall Village on upland above Grove Hill near the source of a tributary of Footherley Brook 15.25m SE of Stafford. In Shenstone ancient parish. Has appeared as Stonehala (1140) (SHOS vol 2 p53), Stanahala (1143), Stanhala (1167), Stonhal (C13) (SPN p118) (SSE 1996 p18), Stonall (Plot's map) and Upper Stonnall, which centred on the junction of the Chester Road and the Vigo-Lower Stonnall road (1887 OS map 6 inch). The name is from the Stony hill on which it stands, or from stone hall (DUIGNAN). Gelling thinks 'stone nook' (NSJFS 1981 p3), or 'the stony corner of land' (SPN p118). Mills gives 'stone halh (hollow)' (SSE 1996 p18). The church, St Peter, was built in 1822 on an isolated hilltop position to the S of Stonnall, at Thornes, on a piece of land considered unsuitable for farming and only suitable for a church (BOE p269) (SVB p157; built in 1826). Stonnall became a separate ecclesiastical parish in 1823, refounded in 1845 (GLAUE p424). There is a notice listing tolls from the Stonnall toll gate in four fragments at the County Museum, Shugborough.

Stony Brook Tributary of the Rising Brook, a tributary of the Trent (SPNO p19). There was a burnt mound probably of the Middle Bronze Age 1m SW of Slitting Mill at SK 02081655, has appeared as Le Stonybrooke (1584) (SPNO p109). In 1930 it was said to be 33 feet in diameter. It was in an area that has been planted by the Forestry Commission since the 1920s and it is possible that it has been destroyed (SASR 1987 p16).

Stonydelph Stonydelph Farm, on high ground above a tributary of Kettle Brook, is over 2m ESE of Tamworth. The former township of Amington and Stonedelph was in Hemlingford hundred, Warws, in Tamworth ancient parish (THM vol 6 p31). The name first appears as an assart in Wilnecote (VCHWA vol 4 p247) (THM vol 6 p31) and has also appeared as or Stoneydelph and Stonedelph. The name is from Anglo-Saxon 'stan-delph' 'stone quarry' or 'stone-diggings' (SPN pp122-123). Stonydelph was created an ecclesiastical parish in 1864 but reunited with Tamworth parish in the 1870s. Became a separate civil parish in 1866. Parts of the civil parish began to be taken into Tamworth borough from 1932 and the whole civil parish was taken into the borough and into Staffs in 1965 (GLAUE pp402,425,436). Stonydelph was a ward of Tamworth borough by at least 1993. The church, St Martin in the Delph, St Martin's Centre, Ellerbeck, was built in 1990 (LDD).

Stonyford Stonyford Covert, House, Lane are over 1.75m NNW of Mavesyn Ridware, in Mavesyn Ridware ancient parish.

Stonyford Brook Tributary of the Swarbourn, which it joins at Wood Lane N of Yoxall. Runs SE of Woodlane (SPNO p19).

Stony Lea Former small hamlet under 0.5m NE of Cannock, on Old Hednesford Road (1889 OS map 6 inch). In Cannock parish (SGSAS).

Stonylow Stonylow Farm is 0.5m SW of Waterfall. Appears as Stony Lane on the 1834 OS map.

Stonyrock Minute hamlet at the N end of Milk Hill in the Moorlands 1m ENE of Cauldon, which has also appeared as Stoneyrock (NSJFS 1962 p31). In the garden of Stoney Rock Cottage an axe-head or adze was found in 1954 (NSFCT 1959 p86) (NSJFS 1962 p31. 1964 p41). Was on the Leek-Ashbourne turnpike road and here is a toll house (NSFCT 1948 p33p facing).

Stonywell Small hamlet in the narrow Ben Brook valley 0.5m NNW of Farewell. In Longdon ancient parish. Appears in the C13 as Stoniwelle (SSE 1996 p18) and has also appeared as Stoneywell. The name is from a large stone in Stonywell Well (see). According to local traditions if the stone is removed from the well some injury will befall the cattle of the hamlet (SHOS vol 1 p222) (DUIGNAN) or the spring will dry up (SPN p79). John Stanywell or Stonywell, was born at Stoneywell. He entered Pershore Abbey, Worcs, a

Benedictine monastery, as a youth. He later became a doctor of divinity and became abbot of Pershore Abbey. He built a new chapel attached to the S aisle of St James' church, Longdon, for his burial (SHOS vol 1 p222) (SMC p166) (W p565) (NSFCT 1899 pp134-135) (LGS p179).

Stonywell Well According to Shaw Stonywell was a roadside near-circular well from which Stonywell takes its name. So called from there being a large stone at the bottom and in the middle of it. There was a local tradition that if the stone was removed something ominous would befall the inhabitants' cattle (SHOS vol 1 p222) (NSFCT 1899 p134) (CCC p22). In 1999 this well was believed to be under the kitchen of New Stonywell Farm (info from a local farmer).

Stormy Hill Hill S of Moorville Hall, nearly 2m N of Caverswall. It appears to have been the western terminal on the Consall Plateway, a mineral railroad which ran from here to the Caldon Canal (VCH vol 2 p306).

Story Brook Tributary of Ash Brook rises in Bagot's Forest. The Staffordshire Way follows it for a mile.

Stour, River Rises 0.25m N of St Kenelm's chapel on the NE side of the Clent Hills, Worcs. Halesowen is situated on it. Forms the Staffs county boundary for 10m from S of Haden Hill to E of Bellsmill. Then enters the county fully. Leaves the county S of Whittington. Kidderminster is on it. Flows into the Severn at Stourport. Has appeared as Stur (736), Sture (866), Stoure (1300), Store (1344), and Stowre (c1540) (SPNO p19). The Stour was made navigable to Stourbridge by 1667 (HCMS No. 2). (SHOS vol 1 p89) (SVS pp366-371) (BCWJ pp79-80). The name is from perhaps 'ys dwr,' the water (DUIGNAN) (NSFCT 1908 p132) (BCWJ p79) but Duignan thinks this is unlikely as 'dwr' is a modern colloquial form of Old Welsh 'dwfr,' which could only appear in English as 'dover' or 'duver.' Or is from the Gaelic root 'sturr' rough or uneven (NSFCT 1908 p132). The root is thought to be something like 'steu,' literally 'firm,' although in this context would be 'strong or powerful' (SPNO p19) (SPN p119) (SSE 1996 p23). (SVS p364).

Stourbridge Canal Built in 1776 (MR p53). It was open by 1779 (BCM summer 1994 p47). The main arm runs from Brockmoor to join the Staffs and Worcs Canal at Stewponey. There are two further arms, one which runs from Wordsley Junction to Delph Junction at the bottom of Nine Locks (HCMS No. 2). Another arm runs from Amblecote to Stourbridge.

Stourbridge Extension Canal Former canal which spurred off the Fens Branch of the Stourbridge Canal at Brockmoor Junction (HCMS No. 2), or of the Stourbridge Canal at Ley Junction near Buckpool (BCM summer 1995 pp23-25), continued beyond Commonside to Oak Farm Basin (HCMS No. 2). Built in 1839-1840 (BCM summer 1995 pp23-25). Closure sanctioned in 1935 (HCMS No. 2).

Stourmoor Former considerable waste on limestone (Nightingale's Staffordshire) (S&W p310) to the E of Cheadle.

Stourton Fragmented village at the confluence of the Smestow and the Stour and on high ground to the W, 24.5m SSW of Stafford. Former township in Kinver ancient parish. The Stur mentioned in a charter of 855 AD was identified by Birch in his Cartularium Saxonicum with Stourbridge. But CGO Bridgeman suggests Stourton, or else Sture, Worcs (SHC 1916 p76). Appears in 1227 as Sturton (SSE 1996 p18). The name means 'tun or town or farmstead on the Stour' (DUIGNAN) (SPN pp72,119) (SSE 1996 p18). (SVS p172). The old settlement is on the W side of the Stour, W of the castle. Stourton also applies to new housing on E side of the Stour, an area formerly known as Stewponey. Stourton possibly gave the title to a nobleman (SVS pp175-179). Stourton formed a township with The Hyde from 1830 to the mid C19 (VCH vol 20 p149). By the late C20 it was a ward in Kinver civil parish. There is a mission church, St Peter, at Stourton (LDD).

Stourton Castle Former royal hunting lodge for Kinver Forest, later the seat of the lord of Kinver manor and latterly a country house. It stands on the W side of the Stour on an outcrop overlooking the the Stour, E of the old settlement of Stourton.

1066 to 1500. References to royal visits to Kinver, hunting lodges at Kinver, and the king's chamber at Kinver throughout the later C11 and most of the C12 may all relate to a hunting lodge on or near the site of Stourton Castle. A royal hunting lodge was built at Stourton between 1195-6. It was at first referred to as at Kinver, but was referred to as at Stourton in 1207 (VCH vol 2 p347. vol 20 p123). The lodge was fortified by a ditch or moat subsequently lost by successive development (SSAHST 1982-3 p43) (CAMS pp5,29). King John stayed here to hunt on Aug 18 and on Aug 19 1207 (NSFCT 1909 p183) and in 1215 (VCH vol 2 p347) (BCM Oct 1971 p51). By 1222, when the lodge was known as the castle of Kinver, it was the seat of the keeper of Kinver Forest and the lord of Kinver manor (VCH vol 20 p131). It was fortified during Henry III's reign (CAMS p29), or in the 1370s (VCH vol 2 p347). The present buildings occupy the site of the keep; the bailey or outer court lay to the NW (VCH vol 20 p132). Edward I stayed at Stourton in 1277 (VCH vol 20 p126), probably at the castle. Sir Thomas Murdak was murdered at the castle at Easter 1316. A few days after the murder Murdak's widow, Gillian, married Sir John de Vaux, of Stourton Castle and keeper of Kinver Forest; they were subsequently accused of the murder. He was sent to the Tower of London and subsequently acquitted and she was sentenced to be burnt (SCFK pp19-22) (VCH vol 2 p344 note. vol 20 p131) (BCM Oct 1971 pp55-58) (CAMS p29). In 1360 the prior of Dudley was held at Stourton for an offence against forest laws. The Hamptons were living at Stourton Castle by 1391 when John Hampton was licensed to build an oratory at the castle (VCH vol 20 p131). The castle was rebuilt by John de Hampton probably between 1430 and 1461, of which some remains. The present rendered W tower is of about this period (CAMS pp29p,30). In 1461 Hampton was deprived of his estates by Edward IV, but restored to them in 1470; he died 1472. Edward IV gave Stourton to his brother George, Duke of Clarence, and it was briefly alienated to Tewkesbury Abbey, but recovered by Henry VII (CAMS p29). 1500 to PRESENT. About 1500 the castle was occupied by Sir Richard Pole and his wife, Margaret Plantagenet (later Countess of Salisbury), daughter of the Duke of Clarence and niece of Edward IV and Richard III. According to an early tradition their son, **Reginald Pole** (d1558), was born here in 1500 or 1501 (VCH vol 20 pp126,131). After receiving several high posts in the Church of England Reginald Pole fell out of favour with Henry VIII in opposing the king on divorce, and left for Italy. In 1536 in exile he was made a cardinal. In revenge for Pole's opposition to the king his mother was kept in the Tower of London for two years and finally she was found guilty of treason and beheaded in 1541; she was beatified in 1886. In 1554 in Mary I's reign Pole was made papal legate in England, and as archbishop of Canterbury between 1555 and 1558 was principally responsible for returning England to Catholicism (SD pp46,47) (SVS pp175-176) (GNHS p181) (SOSH p180) (KES pp121,122) (BSB p467) (SGS p158) (STMSM Aug 1980 pp12,13) (RKE pp13-16) (Cambridge Biographical Encyclopaedia. David Crystal. 1994) (TB Sept 30 1999 pp18-19). The ranges around the former court are of brick and were built in the mid to late C16 (CAMS p30). Sir Thomas Whorwood had moved from Compton Hall to the castle by 1602. Until the late C17 it was often the seat of the Whorwood family, who were neutral in the **Civil War**. Probably during their time the gables were built. On March 30 1644 the castle was taken by Col John 'Tinker' Fox for the parliamentarians but it was surrendered back after they were routed on Stourbridge Heath (VCH vol 20 p131) (SOB p75). An old bullet-ridden door from the Civil War is still preserved at the castle (NSFCT 1909 p183) (KRC pp22-24) (TB Oct 1985 p15p of and of the castle. Jan 1992 p21p). Rt Rev **William Talbot** (d1730), was born at Stourton Castle in c1659, son of William Talbot 'of Whittington,' a relation of the Talbots of Alton Towers (see). He was successively bishop of Oxford, Salisbury and Durham in 1699, 1715 and 1722. In the debate in the House of Lords following the trial (1710) of Henry Sacheverell he was one of the four bishops who spoke for his condemnation (SVS pp177-178) (SMC p166) (DNB) (KRC p23; born at Stourton Castle in 1650). For his successors see under Alton Towers. Noise from a local forge made the house unsuitable for the gentry in the C18, when the Hollins family, farmers, lived here (CAMS p29). In the C19 the house was the seat of a succession of industrialists (CAMS p30). In 1832 foundations of a pair of round towers of an outer bailey to the NW were discovered - perhaps - of the 1220s - during the implementation of Sir Robert Smirke's alterations and additions, when the porch tower of the hall (to E of W tower) was demolished. The neo-Jacobean projecting W wings are Smirke's (CAMS p30). In the C20 and until 1974 it was the seat of the Grazebrooks (VCH vol 20 p132); of whom **Francis Grazebrook** (1884-1974), writer, and author of the novel 'Nicanor of Athens' (1946), was one (VFC p56). (NHS pp151,448) (SHOS vol 2 pp265-267 pl xxxvi - a NE view and a W view) (SVS p174) (GNHS p181) (W p179) (MOS p37) (NSJFS 1966 p45) (BOE p252) (STMSM Aug 1980 pp12,13) (RKE pp13-16) (KEOP p60ps) (DoE II). In 1838 a gothic lodge of red brick was built at the entrance to the drive from the Bridgnorth road (VCH vol 20 p132).

Stourton Court House in Stourton on the Stourbridge-Bridgnorth road. Built in 1850. Destroyed by fire in 1877. Rebuilt by Capt Foster in 1883 (VCH vol 20 p123) (RKE p24).

Stourton Farm N of the old settlement of Stourton.

Stourton Hall 0.25m W of the old settlement of Stourton. Stands on or near the site where there was a house by the 1730s. It was built in c1850 by William Bennitt who was living here in 1851. The house was later extended (VCH vol 20 p123). It was also the home of Mrs Downing, poetess, in the 1920s (RKE p24). The hall may have been known as Stourton House, which was part of the Prestwood estate for sale in 1913 (TB June 1998 p6p). Noted for its famous glasshouses to grow tomatoes which supplied Covent Garden markets

(RKE p24).

Stourton Hill Is about 360 feet above sea level (RKE p24). Is probably the hill on E side of Enville Common at SO 851860, but this is 443 feet high.

Stourton Junction Junction of the Stourbridge Canal with the Staffs and Worcs Canal at Stewponey.

Stourton Park Seems to have been the only park allowed in Kinver Forest. It belonged to John Hampton, keeper of the forest. Was 300 acres (NSJFS 1968 p48).

Stowe Former hamlet, now suburb of Lichfield, 0.5m NE of Lichfield cathedral. Stowe has been identified as the 'more retired dwelling place' and place of death of Chad, early missionary and bishop of the Mercians (d672), in Bede's Ecclesiastical History of the English People. A holy well, St Chad's Well (see), now in St Chad's churchyard, is traditionally associated with Chad. Consequently, Stowe has been considered sacred (Anglia Sacra. H Wharton. vol 1 p459) (LI vol 2 p99) (SHC 1924 p15) (VCH vol 3 p140. vol 14 p134). The church, St Chad, on the N side of St Chad's Road, is recorded in c1190. It was later the parish church of St Chad's parish, see Lichfield St Chad. It has been suggested that the church stands on the site of Chad's cathedral (hitherto identified as close to the present cathedral) and Chad's more retired dwelling place was on or near the site of the church of St Michael at Greenhill. In the late C12 the church contained a statue of St Chad (VCH vol 14 pp134,135). In 1242 Stowe appears as Stowe (SSE 1996 p18). The name means a holy place or a church (VCH vol 14 p134) (SSE 1996 p18). A C13 canon of the cathedral considered Stowe 'that sacred spot.' A C13 topographer, who claimed there were two minsters at Lichfield, implied Stowe was the eastern one (SHC 1924 p51) (VCH vol 14 p134). In 1321 the cathedral chapter and Lichfield Franciscans processed to St Chad's to pray there for the sick Bishop Langton (VCH vol 14 p134). There was an anchorite named John Mede at Stowe in 1504. 'The Ancker's House' in the churchyard occurs in 1571. The anchorite's house was built against the NW corner of the church (History of St Chad's Church. P Laithwaite. 1938. pp15-16,28) (VCH vol 3 p137. vol 14 p144). In the C18 St Chad's stood on an island in the eye of Stowe Pool and there was a chalybeate spring to the NW of St Chad's Well developed by Sir John Floyer (Young Samuel Johnson. James L Clifford. 1955 1962 ed. see map p28).

Stowe Ancient parish and village on the W side of Cage Hill near Amerton Brook 5.75m ENE of Stafford. Stowe is not in DB. Appears in the C13 as Stowe (SSE 1996 p18) and has appeared as Stowe-by-Chartley. The name is from old Anglo-Saxon 'stoe' or 'stow,' a place or habitation (NSFCT 1886 p39). Or 'stow,' 'an enclosed place' (DUIGNAN). 'Stowe' is an Old English word meaning 'hermitage' or 'holy place' (WMLB p93). Or just 'place' or 'inhabited place' (SPN p119). The parish church, St John the Baptist, near the corner of Drointon Lane and Station Road in the village centre, was built in the C12 (LDD). The parish, formed before 1086, was curiously entangled with that of Colwich and originally probably contained the ancient parish of Weston-on-Trent (NSFCT 1913 p60) (SHC 1916 p192). The old custom of ringing the curfew bell was kept up at Stowe to within a few years of 1886 (NSFCT 1886 p39). Hand stocks stood in the open space at the junction of the roads. The post was six or seven feet high with iron fastenings near the top on each side. The stocks are believed to have been moved in c1870 by some navvies working on the construction of the Stafford & Uttoxeter Railway for a lark (NSFCT 1886 p39). Alabaster was worked here; the only other place in the county where it can be found is about Tutbury (MR p309). In the County Museum, Shugborough is a stone ware beer bottle from Uttoxeter collected from the Cock Inn. For the aircraft crash near the village in 1994 see Chartley Moss.

Stowe Gate One of the five gates in Lichfield Town Ditch. Erected by Bishop Roger de Clinton (1129-1148). Is recorded in the later C13 (VCH vol 14 p40) and has appeared as Stowe Bar. It was situated at the junction of Lombard and Stowe Streets, George Lane, and Stowe Road. The bar remained until the end of C18 (LAL p37). The gate was probably of wood (VCH vol 14 p40).

Stowe Hill Stowe, Lichfield. Small hill to ENE of St Chad's church, at NE end of Stowe Pool (SHOS vol 1 p345). In St Chad's parish, Lichfield. By 1574 there was a windmill in Stowe Hill field, evidently on the E side of the later Brownsfield Road; it had been pulled down by 1649 (VCH vol 14 p115).

Stowe Hill Mansion Georgian house at the E end of Stowe Pool, on Stowe Hill, Lichfield. Is to the NNE of Stowe House (SSAHST 1970 p50 see map). Built in the 1750s, and by 1756, by Miss Elizabeth Aston, who also built Stowe House and another house at Stowe, about which very little is known. Anna Seward in 'Lichfield: an elegy,' written in 1781, mentions only two houses:

> We mark the villa, rising near the lake,
> And fairer she, that 'midst the verdant brake,

From sultry gleams, and wintry tempest
shrill,
Stands softly curtained on the eastern hill.

(VCH vol 14 p71). (LAL p36) (DoE II*) (BOE p195). Miss Elizabeth Aston was probably in residence in 1777, whilst her widowed sister, Mrs Jane Gastrel, lived at Stowe House. On Elizabeth's death in 1785 the house passed to Magdelen Walmisley, widow of Gilbert Walmisley, but she died in 1786 and the house passed to Jane Gastrel who let it to Lady Carhampton. It was empty in 1788 and sold in 1792. Later occupants were Phoebe Simpson until 1816; Frances Dorothy Furnivall between c1821 and c1854; Arthur Hinckley between c1859 and c1889; FH Lloyd to 1916; and from 1978, Mr and Mrs PL Rule (VCH vol 14 p133 pl 13). The house has also been called Hill House and Upper Stowe House (LGS p176). There was an icehouse in grounds, now built over (IHB p395). In the late 1980s there was a grotto, built partly from medieval stonework, and a sunken fernery (VCH vol 14 p72).

Stowe House Georgian house E end of Stowe Pool, on Stowe Hill. Is to the SSW of Stowe Hill Mansion (SSAHST 1970 p50 see map). The house was built in the earlier 1750s and by 1756 by Miss Elizabeth Aston (VCH vol 14 p71 pl 12), or in the early C18 (BOE p195). (SHOS vol 1 p345) (W p503) (LAL p36p) (DoE II*). The house was at first occupied by Thomas Hinton, perpetual curate of St Chad's (d1757). Thomas Day, author of 'Sandford and Merton,' took up residence in 1770. Bird and Howard Clayton say, at some time Richard Lovell Edgeworth lived here. Here Thomas Day attempted, unsuccessfully, to educate a foundling girl on Rousseausque lines in the hope of turning her into a perfect wife for himself (LGS p176) (SLM Feb 1951 pp14,15,16) (VCH vol 14 pp71,171) (VB p19) (CCHCA pp33,37). Day and Edgeworth are said to have been living in a house in the Close in 1771 (LGS p175). Mrs Jane Gastrel, widow, was living at Stowe House in 1777 whilst her spinster sister Miss Elizabeth Aston lived at Stowe Hill House (SSAHST 1970 p51). Later occupants included Fairfax Moresby in c1800; Richard Gresley in c1817; William Gresley in c1830; and Charles Holland MD to 1876. Stowe House was known as St Chad's House from c1860 until the late 1870s (VCH vol 14 p71). Later occupants included WF Gordon to c1902; and GR Benson, Baron Charnwood, and his wife Dorothea Benson, Lady Charnwood, an autograph collector (SSAHST 1970 p49) from c1903 to 1933; their daughter Theodora Benson spent her childhood here (CL Nov 14 1957 pp1028-1029p of; the article is by Theodora Benson). Their son John Benson occupied Stowe House until c1937. Stowe House was occupied in 1940-44 by Belmont School from Hassocks, Sussex. From 1951 it has been a nurses home and management training centre (VCH vol 14 p72). There seems to be no truth in the story that Selwyn House was deliberately built, across Stowe Pool, to spoil this house's view of the cathedral (SSAHST 1970 pp49-53). The house has also been called Lower Stowe House (LGS p176).

Stowe Pool The larger of the two pools in Lichfield about the cathedral. It is NE of the cathedral. The W end of the old extensive pool gradually became marshland, which was known in the C18 as Stowe Moggs. In 1840 a local physician denounced Minster and Stowe Pools as a source of disease and called for them to be filled in (VCH vol 14 p3). The pool was let to or bought by the SSWWC in 1855 (WMLB pp86,93 plan showing its former extent), and was a reservoir from 1856 until 1970 (VCH vol 14 pp114,116).

Stow Heath Small district on ground rising above Willenhall brook 1.5m SE of Wolverhampton. Formerly partly in the townships and chapelries of Bilston and Wolverhampton in Wolverhampton ancient parish. The name probably originated from the manor of Stowheath (see) and has appeared as Stowe Heath. In Gibbet Lane is a tollhouse reputedly once kept by William Perry, the 'Tipton Slasher.' It partly still survives (BOP p92p).

Stowheath Very extensive manor created probably in the early C13 by uniting the local royal manors of Bilston, Willenhall and Wolverhampton (WA vol 2 no 2 p103). It has been known as the 'manor of Wolverhampton.' It stretched as far W as the Halfway House on Tettenhall road, and covered the whole of Bilston and a considerable part of Willenhall (W p159) (HOWM p27) taking in Horseley Fields, Rough Hills, and Monmore Green. The overlord was the king and the position of tenant-in-chief or bailiff of the lordship of Wolverhampton seems to have been held by the lords of Dudley in the C12 to 1204 (HOWM p27). The position eventually came into the family of Lovel and was held by them until forfeited on attainder by Francis, Lord Lovel, in 1485. He appears in Shakespeare's Richard III and was one of the most romantic figures of his time. The position passed to Thomas Taillour in 1489. Sir John Gifford, Gentleman Usher of the Chamber, obtained the office of joint bailiff in 1512. Later, the Leveson family purchased the manor. By the 1830s the manor was jointly owned by the Levesons and the Giffards of Chillington; both exploiting the rich coalfield lying under the manor in the C19 (HOWM

p27) (MH 1984 p63). The 'lord of the Heath' occurring in medieval times has been thought to be a title taken by the lord of this manor, although it may have been the title assumed by the lord of Wednesfield Heath (WFW 72). The moated **manor house** which stood on the site of the Chillington Tool Manufactory or Chillington Iron Works (later Tool Co Ltd), 1m ESE of Wolverhampton, at SO 928982, was probably first established in the early C13 by Robert Burnell, bishop of Bath and Wells, Chancellor to Edward I, as a stopping place on the way to his house at Acton Burnell, Shrops (SSAHST 1982 p56) (BCM April 1987 pp52-53) (CAMS p62). Francis, the last Lovel who was lord of Stowheath, reputedly resided here in the later C15. Its status as a manor house then lapsed owing to its bleak situation and the future lords of Stowheath had houses elsewhere (HOWM p41). The moat remained until 1788, with a furnace close by, and was destroyed in the early C20 (SSAHST 1982-3 p56) (BCM April 1987 pp52-53) (CAMS p62).

Stow Lawn Former area now a suburb, 0.75m N of Bilston. The name appears on Greenwood's map and on J Phillips & WF Hutchings map (1832), but it is not on the 1834, or 6 inch 1885 OS maps.

Stowman's Hill 0.5m SW of Neachells, at cSO 941983. Here was a burial mound possibly containing some of the defeated of the battle of Wednesfield or Tettenhall (NHS pp45,415) (SHOS vol 1 General Intro p37. vol 2 p150) (AOW p9) (NSJFS 1965 p59) (WFW p23). According to Pitt it was removed to mend the roads and nothing remarkable was discovered in it (HOWW p30). According to Mander the burial mound was set up here because this was the meeting place of the townships of Wolverhampton, Bilston, Willenhall and Wednesfield (WA vol 2 pp90,91). Stowman Hill is mentioned in 1733. Mander in the 1930s noted that a field name in Bilston preserves the name of Stowman's Hill (WA vol 2 pp90,91). There is a Stowman's Close near Lanesfield and Stowlawn and Stow Heath SW of Neachells.

Straits, The A stretch of the Dove in Dove Dale. Formerly known as Tissington Straits (HS pl p273) (DMV p13p).

Straits, The Steep narrow road between Sedgley and Himley in Sedgley parish, also a district which is the lower part of Cotwall End village. The name has appeared as Streights and The Streights (1834 OS map). A short road between The Straits road and Cotwall End Road is called Straits Green. The name is from the French word 'Estorit' meaning 'a narrow passage' as in 'the Straits of Gibraltar' (DUIGNAN) (TB Sept 1976 p14) (SPN p104). Underwood suggests that the name may be from an old saying in Gornal 'in great straits,' which alludes to trouble or poverty, and therefore the name may have been given originally to a district not a road (AMS p448). The old mission church, St Andrew, at The Straits, was known as the Crooked Church on account of it becoming awry. It was rebuilt in 1923 (BCOPP vol 1 pl 62 shows it in 1906) (BCM Jan 1977 p22) (LDD).

Straits Hall Straits Green, The Straits, Gornal. Built by Alexander Gordon in the first half of the C19. Occupied in 1898 by Mr Wones (SR p111).

Straits House The Straits, Gornal. Was an inn by 1976 (TB Sept 1976 p15ps).

Stramshall Village on a hill overlooking the Tean and Dove Valleys 12.5m NE of Stafford. Former constablewick with Creighton in Uttoxeter ancient parish (W p789). Redfern claims that a burial mound was destroyed when Stramshall church was built (HOU 1886 p38) (NSJFS 1965 p50). NE of the church is a burial mound 120 feet by 90 feet. It is possibly of Saxon origin (NHS p414) (SD p109) (MR p310). An air photograph taken in 1976 shows crop marks NE of Stramshall at SK 08053600 believed to represent the site of a Roman camp. The site was investigated in 1985 (SASR 1986 pp13-19 p plans). Redfern recorded a find of Roman pottery in the Stramshall area at cSK 080358 (JBAA vol 29) (HOU 1886 p59). Gunstone thinks this may be of medieval or later date (NSJFS 1964 p40). Fragments of what may be Romano-British pottery have been found in a field near the village (MR p310). Has appeared as Stagrigesholle, a manor, in DB, Strangricheshall (1221), Strangricheshull (1227), Strongeshulf (1269), Strangeshide (Erdeswick c1600), Stranshull (Erdeswick c1600) (SOS p380) (SPN p119) (SSE 1996 p18), and Strogsihull (SHC 1908). Shaw erroneously identified Stagrigesholle with Shareshill (see). The name means 'Stranglic's hill' (DUIGNAN) or 'Stronglic's hill' (NSJFS 1981 p2), or 'Stongric's hill' (SPN p119-120). Mills says Strangric means strong-ruler (SSE 1996 p18). There is documentary evidence of remains of open fields in Stramshall as late as 1735 (CDS p18). There was a Quaker burial-ground at SK 076358, the SW angle of the field in which the church stands in an area known as 'Quakers' Bit' (HOU 1886 p246). When the road to the A50 was widened it was cut into it. Some say it was on the N side of this road, and some on the S (SSAHST 1970 p45). The church, St Michael and All Angels, on the corner of St Michael's Road and Hollington Lane, was built in 1850-1852 (HOU p431) (BOE p270). Became a separate ecclesiastical parish in 1853 (GLAUE p424) or 1854 (LGS p223). For a rhyme about Stramshall see Checkley.

Stramshall Hall Thomas Trobeshaw said to be living at Stramshall Hall in the later C15 moved to Shugborough Village (HAHS p47).

Strangleford Birch House near a tributary of the Penk 1.5m W of Brewood. In Brewood ancient parish. Has appeared as Strongelford (1315) and Strangleford (1327) (SPNO p39). 'Strangle' (weed) is a provincial or dialectic word for the 'Orobanche' and 'Cuscuta' or choke-fitch, chokeweed. 'Ford' is ford. 'Birch' is a later addition, it means 'a breaking up of wild land, a new enclosure' (DUIGNAN) and did not appear until the C18 (SPN p23).

Stratford Former manor and depopulated place by the mid C17. It was situated on Watling Street 'where it thwarts the river towards Fazeley.' Occurs as a manor held with Lea Marston (Warws?) by the family of La Launde in the C13 and C14 (VCHWA vol 4 p250).

Strawberry Hill Hill on E side of Old Brook 2.5m WNW of Rugeley on Cannock Chase.

Straw Hall Brick farmhouse on the Penn Road near the Royal Wolverhampton School. It was called this by the mid C19 (W p95). One story tells of how the owner of this house was robbed and murdered by highwaymen just as he was approaching home. His body was thrown into a sandpit opposite the house. Early maps show a number of sand and gravel pits in the area of Straw Hall. There is a local tradition that one pit in front of Goldthorn Terrace, which has never been built on, is a plague burial place (PENOP p49p).

Strawmoor Farm 1m SW of Codsall, in Codsall, at the junction of Oaken and Strawmoor Lanes. The farm appears to date from the early C19 (VCH vol 20 p80).

Streethay Hamlet on a low prominence above Mare Brook 1.5m ENE of Lichfield cathedral. Formerly a township in St Michael's parish, Lichfield (VCH vol 14 p273). Appears as Stretheye in 1262 (SSE 1996 p18). The name means 'the hay, or enclosure, on the Street (Ryknild Street)' (DUIGNAN) (VCH vol 14 p275) (SSE 1996 p18). There was settlement at Streethay by the mid C13. There was a green by the later C16, and at the green a pinfold (VCH vol 14 pp275,282). There is a well head probably of C17 origin 25 yards SW of the Manor Place, Ryknild Street (DoE II). Became a separate civil parish in 1866 (GLAUE p424). Louis Paulhan and Claude Grahame-White, participants in the Daily Mail challenge to fly from London to Manchester landed their planes at Trent Valley station on April 29 1910 (VCH vol 14 p240).

Streethay Hall Streethay (SHOS vol 1 pl xxxiii). Is probably a reference to the present Streethay Manor House, at SK 143108. A manor house of Streethay manor was probably in existence on this site by the mid C13 and occupied by the Streethays, lords of the manor. They sold the manor to the Pyotts in the late C16. The medieval house, which was surrounded by a double moat, was rebuilt probably from c1620 by Richard Pyott (d1667). In the mid C18 the hall passed to the Wilmots. The Hollands, who had been tenants from the mid C18, became the owners in 1796. They held the hall until 1887, and it was held in trust until 1920. Most of the C17 house, except the back range of an enclosed courtyard, was demolished by 1792. In the later C20 the house was remodelled (VCH vol 14 p277 pl 51 shows the hall in the 1790s). The double moat of the old hall formed a feature of the later hall (VCH vol 14 p277). In the late 1980s a stone bath house with a corbelled roof, probably of the C17, stood W of the house (VCH vol 14 p277). There was a dovecote in the grounds in the early C18 (VCH vol 14 p277).

Street House Stood at the corner of Halford's Lane and the Birmingham Road (A41) in West Bromwich ancient parish, close to the border with Handsworth. It occurs from 1661. In 1818 it was the seat of Joseph Halford. Between c1833 and c1846 Henry Halford, an iron merchant, resided here. It was rebuilt about this time. By the 1850s the new house was called the Hawthorns (see) (VCH vol 17 p10).

Streetly Very large residential district on the former upland Coldfield or Great Barr Common 3m NE of Great Barr. Formerly in Aldridge ancient parish.
EARLY. A flint arrowhead was found in a garden in at the N end of Thornhill Road, at the junction of Foley Road East (The Royal Town of Sutton Coldfield: a commemorative history. DV Jones. 1973). A Roman coin has been found in Foley Road near Besom House (SSAHST 1990-91 p89). A sandstone block carved into a head, and subsequently squared off, was found in a garden in Thornhill Park in 1972 and went to the BM. It has been dated to the first or second centuries AD (SSAHST 1990-91 p89).
1500 to PRESENT. 'Streetly Hill' is mentioned in a perambulation of Aston Coldfield manor in 1537 and occurs on the 1834 OS map. The name possibly arose on account of the hills close proximity to Ryknield Street (Chester Road) (ADY p15) (SNAR pp85,96). Streetly Wood, Little Streetly Wood and part of the Warder's belt at Sutton were almost completely destroyed in a fire on Aug 3 1868 (TBS p29). On July 1 1879 the Midland Railway Co opened a station on open land on the NW edge of Sutton Park. It is said that the first

train to arrive at the station (at the junction of Foley Road East and Thornhill Road) carried passengers who were attending a race meeting at nearby Four Oaks Race Course (ADY p15) (SNAR p85). The name Jervis-town was favoured by the directors of the Midland Railway for their new station because it bordered on the Little Aston Hall estate owned by ES Parker Jervis, but the station and the later residential district took the name Streetly from the nearby hill (ADY p15) (SNAR pp85,96). That there was no village or settlement at Streetly before 1879 is illustrated by a report of 1881 in a local paper which recalled that the few residents in the district between Barr Beacon and Little Aston had, in the past, been the last people in the Midland counties to be made to pay 3d. delivery money for every letter addressed to them, even if it was a demand to pay taxes (TBS p24). The first houses of Streetly were villas built along Streetly Lane, Thornhill Road, and in the Foley Road area. After WW1 large estates were developed across Chester Road into the Blackwood Road area, and by the 1960s housing was being built in the Hundred Acre Wood (ADY p15p). The church, All Saints, situated on the N side of Foley Road East by Foley Church Close, was built in 1908 and enlarged in 1950 (SLHT p11) (SNAR p93; built in 1918). Streetly was created a separate ecclesiastical parish out of the ecclesiastical parishes of Great Barr and Little Aston in 1918 (GLAUE p424). An article in The Sutton Coldfield Observer on Jan 27 1989 tells of a coven of witches at Streetly (FSLBWM p29).

Streetway House On S side of Watling Street 1.25m ENE of Shenstone.

Stretton Large village on the E-facing slope of the Trent Valley near the Trent's confluence with the Dove 21.25m E of Stafford. Former township in Burton upon Trent ancient parish (W p541).
EARLY. Broken antlers of red deer, the upper part of two skulls of Bos longifrons and the broken bone of Bos primigenius was found in 1942 in gravel pits at SK 261258 (info KL Neal). An extended inhumation burial has been found in Stretton parish (NSJFS 1964 p37). A portion of a bronze necklet about 12 centimetres in length was found in another gravel pit at Stretton at SK 266265 in Feb 1944 and was said, by the BM, to be probably of Balkan manufacture dating from the Late Bronze Age or Early Iron Age (BTIH p9). Stretton has been identified with the Roman settlement of Ad Trivonam (see).
900 to PRESENT. In c1860 during the construction of the railway on the S side of the village several urns containing cremations have been found, believed to be of Anglo-Saxon origin (VCH vol 1 p206) (NSJFS 1964 p37) (BTIH p11). At Mr Gretton's house at the Beach numerous urns containing ashes and bones were found in gravel pits of Anglo-Saxon origin (HOBT p21) (VCH vol 1 p206) (NSJFS 1964 p37). There is a miscellaneous earthwork of pre-Norman Conquest origin in Stretton parish at or called the Vicarage (SHC 1916 p207). A charter of 942 grants a block of estates, one of which is 'Stretton,' to a thegn (DUIGNAN) (SSE 1991 pp7,8. 1996 p18), or the charter is dated 941 (SL p56). Stretton was identified by Dugdale, Shaw and Duignan with the Straettun mentioned in the will of Wulfric Spot (c1002), founder of Burton Abbey (SHC 1916 p31). Stretton later appears as Stratone, a manor held by Burton Abbey, in DB (SHOS vol 1 p25). Takes its name from Icknield Street on which it is situated (LGS p223). It was a **grange** of Burton Abbey by 1325 (VCH vol 3 p204). In the early 1540s overlordship of Stretton manor passed with other Burton Abbey estates to Sir William Paget of Beaudesert (SHOS vol 1 p8). Ecclesiastically severed 1825 to help create Burton upon Trent Holy Trinity ecclesiastical parish, refounded 1842. Became a separate ecclesiastical parish in 1844. This was refounded as 'Stretton cum Wetmore' in 1873 (GLAUE p424) (LGS p223). Dudley Fowkes says Stretton did not become a separate ecclesiastical parish until 1873 (SHJ autumn 1991 p2). The **church**, St Mary, on the corner of Hillfield Lane and Church Road, was built in 1895-1897 (BOE p270), replacing a chapel of ease (LTD p213). Stretton and Clay Mills **railway** station opened in 1901 and closed to passengers on Jan 1 1949 (ABTOP p131p); the railway and the close proximity of Burton upon Trent were principal factors for the growth of Stretton in the C20 (LTD p213). **John de Stafford** (d1280), Abbot of Burton Abbey (1260-1280) and builder of Monk's Bridge was born at Stretton in c1200 (SHOS vol 1 p6).

Stretton Small village on the gentle E-facing slope of the Penk Valley 8m SSW of Stafford, 0.5m N of Watling Street. Former township and chapelry in Penkridge ancient parish (W p469). An axe-head of Neolithic or Bronze Age was found at Stretton (NHS) (BDH p18). A Celtic burial mound to the N of Stretton was excavated in the C18 (LSWA p6). A Bronze Age looped palstave was found at Stretton in 1717. It was exhibited at the Society of Antiquaries, London in 1726 (Magna Britannia. T Cox. vol 5 p51) (ARCH vol 5 p113) (SHOS vol 1 General Intro p31). Shaw gives the impression that two implements were found, but this results from his confusion of the sources (NSJFS 1964 p37). Until 1948 many thought Stretton was built on the Roman settlement of Pennocrucium (see). A Roman artifact found in the vicinity of Stretton is a brass head of the bolt of a catapulta (NHS tab 33 fig 5) (SD p51). Has appeared as Estretone, a manor, in DB, Strettona (1158-1165), Stretton (1166), Stretton juxta Brewode (1285), Stretton juxta Horsebrok (1300), and Stretton juxta Lappeley (1330) (SPNO p178); Shaw described this Stretton as Stretton on Dunsmore (SHOS vol 1 p203). The name means 'the farmstead on the Roman road (Watling Street)' (SPNO p178) (SPN p120). The church, St John, near Stretton Hall, has a C12 tower, the rest is mainly of c1753 and 1860 (VCH vol 4 pp168,169). Became a separate ecclesiastical parish in 1722, and a separate civil parish in 1866 (GLAUE p425). By the late C20 was a ward in Lapley, Stretton and Wheaton Aston civil parish. The wake was fixed in 1761 as the Sunday after Sept 8 (VCH vol 4 p164) (LSWA p12). The nucleus of Stretton is between the church and the Lapley road (LSWA p6). Stretton was a prebend of Penkridge Collegiate Church (VCH vol 3 p300). Stretton's market, held every Tuesday, had been obsolete for many years by the C20 (LSWA p12). In the C19 there were three fairs at Stretton, April 30, Sept 2, Oct 10, for horses and cattle. One, held under a grant of Edward II, is thought to have been one of the earliest in the country for saddle and draught-horses (LSWA p12). Stretton Bridge over the Penk is presumably on the site of a stone bridge that crossed the Penk at Stretton by end of the C16. That bridge may correspond with the 'Eton' Bridge mentioned in the late C13 and the early C14 (VCH vol 4 p163). For Stretton in a local rhyme see Brewood.

Stretton Hall House NE side of Stretton (Penkridge). Rebuilt soon after 1700 (VCH vol 4 p166) (BOE p271) by John Congreve of Congreve - the Congreves had acquired Stretton in the C14. It is said the playwright, William Congreve (1670-1729), stayed at Stretton Hall with his paternal grandfather, Richard Congreve, in 1689 (VFC p30). In the mid C18 it was sold to the Conollys; of whom Thomas Conolly was one. In 1758 he married Lady Louisa Lennox (daughter of the 2nd Duke of Richmond, great-granddaughter of Charles II). She and her sisters are the subject of the book 'Aristocrats' by Stella Tillyard, upon which the 1999 TV series 'Aristocrats' is based. The Conollys, who had seats in London, Dublin, and Castletown, County Kildare, sold Stretton to the Moncktons of Somerford Hall in 1845 (VB p78) (SGS p164) (Sunday Telegraph Magazine, July 11 1999 pp36-39). It was the seat of Lieut-Gen Henry Monckton in 1851 (W p23). It was much improved in c1835 (W p469). Extensive alterations occurred in c1860 (VCH vol 4 p166p facing c1800). (LSWA p13p). For the mantelpiece see SLM Dec 1951 p14p. There was a copy of Reynold's portrait of Lady Cork at Stretton Hall in 1951 (SLM Dec 1951 p14). In the grounds there is an ornamental bridge of the mid C19 adjacent to the hall (DoE II). Congreve's Oak according to tradition is named after William (d1729), the playwright, who may have sat under it to write his comedy 'The Old Bachelor' (1693). Congreve is said to revised the play whilst staying with his friend Robert Port at Ilam Hall (VFC p30). (SLM Dec 1951 p14). There is an ice-house with a small circular opening of C18 origin 300 metres NW of the hall (DoE II).

Stretton Mill 0.75m SE of Stretton (Penkridge). An axe-head of Neolithic or Bronze Age was found at Stretton Mill Bridge. It is kept by David Horovitz (BDH p19). For the Roman forts near Stretton Mill see Pennocrucium. Has been the site of a watermill since the mid C18 (VCH vol 4 p167).

Stretton Wharf Wharf on W side of Shropshire Union Canal 1m SW of Stretton (Penkridge). The wharf is mentioned by 1851 and was still in use in 1928 (VCH vol 4 p163). Here is Telford's aqueduct of iron, built and dated 1832, carrying the canal over Watling Street (BOE p271) (IAS p197).

Stretwyle Name in 1286 for the place where Watling Street crosses the Penk, SE of Stretton (Penkridge) (SHC 1916 p319).

Strine Brooke Tributary of Moreton Brook, a tributary of Blymhill Brook. The name is from Middle English 'strind' meaning 'a stream' (SPNO p20).

Strines House 1.25m E of Upper Hulme in Heathylee township in Alstonefield ancient parish. There was a house here by 1415 (VCH vol 7 p33). The name may be of Scandinavian origin (UHAW p75).

Stringers Corner Under 0.75m NNE of Hednesford.

Stringes Former area of Willenhall. The name is of ancient but unknown origin (HOWI p188). Stringes Lane and Close lie on the W side of Clarke's Lane in N Willenhall. The name Stringes is from Stringes Meadow, formerly situated in this area, but the origin of the name is unknown (SNW p68).

Strongford Minute hamlet on low marshy ground near the Trent over 0.5m N of Tittensor. In Trentham ancient parish. Strongford has appeared as Stranford (Annals of the Diocese of Lichfield Past and Present 1859). Strongford Bridge or Tittensor Bridge was an ancient bridge carrying the London Carlisle road over the Trent (SHC 1934 p82). The bridge was carried away by a flood in 1655 (SIS p52) or 1665 (SHC 1934 p23) and was replaced only by a six foot wide horse bridge. It was not reconstructed properly until 1709 when converted into a cart bridge (VCH vol 2 p279). It fell down in 1790, was rebuilt

and fell down in 1792 and was rebuilt in 1793. The bridge was damaged in 'harty rains' in 1796 (SHC 1934 pp89,90) (SIS p69).

Stubbers Green Small hamlet on mossy ground near a tributary of Ford Brook and the Daw End Branch of the Wyrley and Essington Canal 1.5m NE of Rushall. In Aldridge ancient parish. Has also appeared as Stubbocks Green (1610) (DUIGNAN p15) (MOA) (SNAR pp35,46), and Stubber's Green (1889), when Stubber's Green Colliery was working. The name implies a clearing in the wilderness or wood (DUIGNAN). Stubbers Green was considered quite a large settlement in the C19 and earlier C20, with inhabitants employed in brick making and in mining, but had become a small hamlet by the late C20 (SNAR pp46,47p).

Stubbs Field Medieval field boundary of Newcastle-under-Lyme (NUL p107). One of the four fields comprising the pasturage belonging to the burgesses of Newcastle allotted to them under the Enclosure Act 1816 (W p304).

Stubby Lane Hamlet S of Marchington on Draycott Road. Formerly in Draycott-in-the-Clay township in Hanbury ancient parish (W p559). Appears on Plot's map, and Shaw frequently mentions it. The name is preserved in a lane to the WNW of Draycott-in-the-Clay at SK 148288. It lies beneath the northern escarpment of the Needwood Forest plateau.

Stubby Lane Formerly in Wednesfield chapelry in Wolverhampton parish (SGSAS). There is a Stubby Lane over 1m ENE of Wednesfield (Birmingham A-Z).

Stubby Lea Tiny hamlet on W side of the Tame 2m ENE of Whittington. Here was the medieval settlement of Tymmor (VCH vol 14 p239). Has appeared as Stubby Lee and Stubby Leas.

Stubwood Hamlet on the E-facing slope of the lower Churnet Valley 0.5m S of Denstone. In Rocester parish. At White Gate, Robin Hood is reputed to have stood and fired his arrows at a burial mound at Low fields (HOU p26).

Stumps, The Bagnall. Name given to the remains of an old Roman road from Bagnall to Abbey Hulton. The part of the Roman way which runs through Bagnall is known as Salter's Wells (STM July 1970 pp26,27p).

Stunsteads Cluster of houses SW of Bradnop village by the Leek Ashbourne road. Has appeared as Tunstedes (earlier C14) (VCH vol 7 p170), and Stunsteads (1834 OS map).

Sturbridge Small hamlet on rising ground to the N of the mossy Sow Valley 1m SSE of Slindon. In Eccleshall ancient parish. The community is made larger by the complexes of Raleigh Hall and Drake Hall. Appears as Stourbridge on 1889 OS map 6 inch.

Sturgeon's Hill Hill on S side of Lichfield. The junction of Cherry Orchard, Rotten Row, and Boley Lane is called Sturgeon's Hill. (VCH vol 14 p163).

Stych At the crossroads at Blakeley, Wombourne (1834 OS map).

Stychbrook House and former settlement 1.5m N of Lichfield. Formerly in Curborough and Elmhurst out-township of St Chad's parish, Lichfield (W p514). Has appeared as Tichebroc (DB), Stychbrook and Stitchbrook. The ending is brook. This may be a reference to Circuit Brook (VCH vol 14 p229), or to the small rivulet which rises at St Chad's Well, Stowe, Lichfield (SJC p10). The beginning is unexplainable (NSJFS 1981 p2) (VCH vol 14 p229). Is 'Ticc's brook' (SPN p79). There was a settlement here by the mid C13. The settlement lay in the vicinity of the present farmhouse and was probably deserted some time after the C15. The present farmhouse at Stychbrook was built in the later 1730s and was ruinous or had been pulled down by 1990 (VCH vol 14 p235). In the later C17 Plot noted a small stream which began at Stychbrook, so strong with aluminous sulphate, a residue had collected at the spring head (NHS p106).

Stychfields Hall Opened as a factory of the English Electric Co in 1962 at The Hough, Stafford. Ceased in May 1994 as the canteen for the GEC Alsthom factory (SN Aug 26 1994 p25). The name is from the land here (SAC p147).

Sudden Dale In the vicinity of Abbey Green and Dieulacres Abbey. At the top of the dale is a burial mound (OL vol 2 pp16,18). Or called Chopesdale?

Sugar Loaf, The A bluff of limestone by the Dove in Dove Dale (DMV p16p).

Sugarloaf Hill in the Maer Hills (NSFCT 1891 p41). Has also appeared as Sugar Loaf Hill (1834 OS map) (Dower's map).

Sugarloaf A reef limestone knoll 1m NW of Wetton, NNE of Dale Farm, 0.5m NW of Wetton Hill (OS map 1:25,000) (DMV p68p). It is probably identifiable with a limestone rock of the same name mid way between Wetton Mill and Butterton (PS p99).

Sugarloaf Farm 2.5m SE of Stourton.

Sugar Rock Rock feature on the Roaches (MC p30). But Harper could be referring to the rock feature on the Cloud.

Sugar Rock Former rock feature cut by quarrymen, which jutted out of that part of the Cloud situated in the parish of Rushton Spencer. It was quarried and destroyed (DP p76).

Sugar Well Spring below Ellowes Hall, just in Lower Gornal (SDSSOP p122p).

Sugar Well Mow Cop. Situated below the folly on Mow Cop. It was 74 feet deep. Now partly filled in (WMC).

Sugar Well Spring issuing from the side of the canal cutting near Roebuck Lane, Smethwick. So called from the white deposit left by the water. It was said to be good for eye complaints (STELE May 7 1949) (VCH vol 17 p93).

Sugar Well Tunstall. (OTP p2). So called because the water was always sweet and clear. Tunstall had no piped water until 1848 (POP p176). (SHST p218).

Sugnall Hamlet on upland overlooking a dell formed by a small tributary of the Sow, 1.25m SE of Croxton. Former township in the Woodland quarter in Eccleshall ancient parish (W p376). Has appeared as Sotehelle, a manor held by the bishop of Chester (Lichfield), in DB, Sugenhulle (1222) (SSE 1996 p18), Sogenhul (SPN p44), Great Sugnall, and Sugnall Magna. Sucga's hill, this Anglo-Saxon personal name means a bird (DUIGNAN) (SPN p44). But 'nall' may represent Old English 'halh' 'nook, corner of land' and 'sucga' was not only a personal name but also a type of bird (SSE 1987 p32). Mills suggests 'sparrows' hill' (SSE 1996 p18). Gelling gives 'sparrow's hill' (NSJFS 1981 p2). Sugnall was on a turnpike road from the later C18. In 1807 a driverless coach pulled up in Eccleshall. The driver had fallen off, asleep, at Sugnall. The horses had proceeded to Eccleshall, instinctively. The driver was later found dead by the roadside at Sugnall (GM 1807) (PWNS p30). In Feb 1999 John Myatt, aged 53, of Corner House, Sugnall, an artist, was found guilty of forging paintings by famous artists such as Alberto Giacometti, Ben Nicholson and Graham Sutherland between 1986 and 1996 for a dealer called John Drewe of Reigate, Surrey, and sentenced to one year imprisonment (Daily Telegraph Feb 16 1999 p5) (ES Feb 16 1999 p13p). In the later C17 Plot noted an ash and an elm near Great Sugnall which intertwined from about one foot above the ground (NHS p213).

Sugnall Hall Croxton. According to OS map 1:25,000 is N of the Eccleshall road, off a lane to Little Sugnall. Richard Hodges was in residence at Sugnall Hall in 1851 (W p23). It was owned by the Lowe family in the mid C20; Susan and Edwin Lowe of Sugnall Hall, had improvements made to Eccleshall church to commemorate their second daughter, Mary, who died of meningitis in the 1920s aged 20 (Holy Trinity Church: A Brief History. Rev Stephen Cooke).

Sugnall Old Hall The hall stood S of the Eccleshall road, Croxton (1834 OS map); Sugnall Home Farm may now occupy the site. Built by Sir Thomas (COI p39) or Sir John (ROT p21) Peshall to replace Horsley Old Hall (see) (ROT p21) in 1611 (COI p39) after it had burnt down. Sir John or Sir Thomas was created a baron in 1611 and became the Sheriff of Staffs in 1616 (SAS p14). The hall passed by marriage from the Peshalls to Lord Glenorchy in 1730. The Turtons afterwards built a large square house here, which had disappeared by the late C19 (COI p39). The Turton hall appears to be identifiable with Great Sugnall Hall; Lt John Turton (d1803) was born at Great Sugnall Hall (mem in Eccleshall church). See also Walk Mill.

Sugnall Park Park of Sugnall Old Hall.

Suicide Lane Lane which runs from Wallows Lane, along the side of the allotments and the 'blackboards' to Wood Green. It is usually known as the road 'along the black boards,' although some know it as the "Running Lane." It includes a railway crossing where lives have been lost, accidentally or wilfully (SNWA p100).

Sukerhall One of the four prebends of Gnosall Collegiate Church. Its prebendary lived in Sukars Hall, a house adjoining the churchyard in Gnosall, which appears as Seukesworth (1359), Sukerhall (1395), Sewkarsworth Hall (1451), Sukars Hall (1645), and was probably no longer standing by 1677. A later house on, or close to, the site became known as 'The Manor' by 1851 and later as the 'Manor House' (SPNO p158) (VCH vol 4 pp113,115-116). It was being used as an egg packing station by 1962 (TTTD p260). The original form means 'the enclosure of Sukar or Shuker' (SPNO p158).

Suker's Lodge Former lodge for Beaudesert Hall (BPW p24), 2m NE of Hednesford, N of the Rugeley Road. The name Suker has appeared as Seukesworth (1369) (SSE 1996 p18) and Sugars Lodge (OS map 1834) SPNO p110. It means 'Sukar's or Shuker's enclosure' (SSE 1996 p18). A Richard Suker appears in PR for 1580 (SPNO p110). Suker's Lodge had been demolished by 1992 (BPW p24).

Summerbank N of Tunstall. Newfield Hall was situated in this area (SHST p552).

Summerfield Nos. 7 and 8 Summerfield Road, S of West Park, Wolverhampton, were built in 1839 by George Benjamin Thorneycroft, born in Tipton (see), at the back of his mansion Chapel House in Tettenhall Road for the use of his daughters when they married. In 1857 his daughter, Ellen Thorneycroft, married Henry Hartley Fowler, 1st Viscount Wolverhampton (1830-1911), son of a Wesleyan minister, Mayor of Wolverhampton, MP from 1880, Cabinet Minister, and knight from 1895. No. 7 Summerfield Road was the birth-

place on April 9 1860 of their daughter, the novelist, Ellen Thorneycroft. In c1867 the Fowlers moved to Woodthorne (see) (BCM July 1978 pp44-46. Spring 2000 p46) (Wolverhampton Chronicle April 30 1999 p31).

Summerford House at Willenhall. Birthplace of James Carpenter Tildesley (d1907), author of HOP, on June 14 1840 (PSS p233) (VFC p130).

Summerford Place Suburb of Willenhall (OS map 1:25,000 1988). See Somerford.

Summerhill House and area (DPMM p104) 0.25m S of Gambles Green. Formerly in Hollinsclough township in Alstonefield ancient parish. The present house here is dated 1757 and was built for John Gaunt, a button merchant, known locally as 'the king of the Flash,' a reference to Flash village, the centre of the area's button trade (VCH vol 7 pp38,39). Another account says Josiah Gaunt built the house, and his ghost reputedly was said to race around the yard at midnight. When the vicar failed to dislodge the ghost, someone else was sent for, who captured it's spirit in a bottle which he then buried on Nield Hill (UHAW p77). Fleeting glimpses of a little girl with hair down her back and wearing a long frock who fell down a well in the corner of a field on the farm has been seen on a number of occasions at the bottom of the well (UHAW p77). The name perhaps reflects an astrological point in alignment with the Ballstone (see), nearly 2m to the SW. Summerhill may therefore be an ancient sacred site (DPMM p104).

Summerhill Hill over which the Lichfield-Walsall road passes 1m SSE of Hammerwich.

Summerhill A hill to the W of Kingswinford. In Kingswinford ancient parish. Shaw referred it as 'a pleasant eminence' (SHOS vol 2 p233). Scott refers to it as an area containing several elegant residences (SVS p124) (SNSV vol 1 p319).

Summerhill Three-storey high Georgian mansion on the corner of Swindon Road and Summerhill, Kingswinford. In the earlier C19 it was occupied by Mrs Diana Briscoe (Baugh's map of Shrops 1808) (Fowler's map 1822). In the 1890s it was occupied by Edward Webb, the Wordsley seed merchant. After WW2 it was the home of Sir Sidney Barratt, chairman of Albright and Wilson, chemical manufacturers, Oldbury. The house was converted into Summerhill House Hotel by 1988 (BHOP2 p94) (SNSV vol 1 p319).

Summer Hill District 1m NE of Tipton. In Tipton ancient parish. The area was so named by 1834 (W 1834). Sir Alfred Hickman, the 'Iron King of the Midlands,' was born in a small house adjacent to the former Moat estate offices (HOTIP p7).

Summer Hill Area and farm 1m N of Upper Hulme. The name perhaps reflects an astrological point in alignment with the Bawd Stone (see), to the SW. It may therefore be an ancient sacred site (DPMM p104).

Summer Hill Summerhill Farm is 1m SE of Warslow, on E side of the Manifold.

Summerhill Court Former Victorian brick villa on the corner of Cot Lane and Lodge Lane, Kingswinford. Demolished in the early 1990s (BHOP2 p93p).

Summerhouse, The Georgian brick 'lodge' on E side of the main road (New Road) to Betley, at Wrinehill. It is on a slight hill, opposite the former Wrinehill post office (BVC p189), and slightly above the former Medicine House. The core of the building was built in 1580 (STM June 1968 p15p of it in a derelict state) (BOPP pl 55 photograph of it or the Medicine House) and is timber-framed. (BTC pp34,35p) (DoE II*). Some say it was built in 1700 (BVC p189), or c1710 (BOE p329), others that the original building was encased in brick at this time. It was an occasional pied-a-terre of the Egertons (of the family of the Earl of Wilton - BVC p189) of Wrinehill Hall (SGS p126). The house is said to have been built with a flat roof so the Earl of Wilton could follow the progress of the hunt through the countryside (ES Nov 28 1996 property pages p4p). There is an inscription on a pane of glass which reads; 'Thomas Egerton/ WB Egerton, July 13 1727.' Since when it has had several uses. It has been a barracks, and a workshop. In 1869 the apothecary Samuel Johnson rented it from the Earl of Wilton and opened it as a shop to sell his cures. About 1880 Johnson rented another building, nearby, known as the Medicine House (see). A granddaughter of this Samuel Johnson was living at the house in 1980 (BVC p189). The house, restored in 1975-6, was for sale in Nov 1996 (ES Aug 4 1982. Nov 28 1996 property pages p4p) and was unoccupied and awaiting further restoration in 2000.

Summerseat Former house 1m WSW of Flash, on N side of road between Quarnford and Flash. Had a datestone with the date 1769. The house was occupied in the mid C19 and after it was demolished the datestone went to New Cottage, situated nearby (UHAW p51il).

Summerstreet Lane Long stretch of broad lane visible S of Spot leading to Cotwalton anciently part of the Roman vallum of Limes Britannicus (NSFCT 1902 p118. 1933 p181).

Summit Bridge Smethwick Summit. Carries Roebuck Lane over the Birmingham Canal Old Main Line. Built of brick 1789 or 1790 by John Smeaton. (Galton Valley. A Walkers Guide. Sandwell Metropolitan Borough Council. 1993). Palliser is wrong in attributing it to Brindley (SL p242).

Summit Lock Etruria. Lock where the Caldon Canal joins the Trent and Mersey Canal (IANS p24).

Summit Rocks Rock feature on NE slopes of The Cloud in Staffs (SGM p266).

Summit Tunnel On the Birmingham Canal Old Cut or New Cuts at Smethwick. Is 103 yards long (OS map for canal navigations 1977).

Sunday Bridge Spans the Tame at Newton, Hamstead. Appears on 1834 OS map 2 inch to 1m.

Sun Dial Rock feature that used to be on the Roaches. It was still standing by 1891 (OL vol 1 p95).

Sun Dial House Great Barr. Stood in Queslett Road, now demolished (WBOP p112p).

Surey Place S of Abbey Green. Formerly in Leekfrith township in Leek ancient parish. The name is recorded in the earlier C16 (VCH vol 7 p198). Has also been described as a little village at the entrance to Dieulacres Abbey (HOLF p6).

'Surey Pavement' Causeway raised by the monks of Dieulacres Abbey, so that in times of flood they could still walk up to Leek (OL vol 1 p150) (NSFCT 1978 p37). There was a tradition it was called 'The Surey' because it was the sure way to relief for beggars (OL vol 2 pp184-185). At the Quarter Sessions in 1724 the inhabitants of 'the village of Surrey in the Parish of Leek' were judged responsible for the road from the end of 'Surrey Pavement to Gun Gate' (PRT p56).

Surfeit Hill Hill and former settlement over 0.25m S of Cradley Heath, at SO 953857. The name, which appears in the 1851 census, is preserved in Surfeit Hill Road.

Sutherland Institute Technical school and library at the S end of The Strand, Longton. Built on land given by Cromartie, 4th Duke of Sutherland (POTP p204). The foundation stone was laid by Edward Prince of Wales (Edward VII) on Feb 7 1897 (SOSH pp290,291p) (HOLB p105il of the Prince of Wales laying the foundation stone from ILN). Officially opened on Oct 27 1899 (AGT p169il). (BOE p261). For the first WEA tutorial class in England which was held at the Sutherland Institute in 1908 see under Longton.

Sutton Tiny village on the S-facing steep escarpment of a low ridge overlooking Aqualate Mere under 1m NE of Forton. In Forton ancient parish. Has appeared as Sutton (1202), Suthon (1332), Southetonne (c1540) (SPNO p147) (SSE 1996 p18). Is Anglo-Saxon for south town (SOSH p76) (SPNO p147) (SSE 1996 p18). In the woods of Sutton in the Middle Ages may have lived a hermit whose habitation was given to the Benedictine Abbey of Shrewsbury in the C12. That estate may be represented in the name of the modern house Guild of Monks (VCH vol 3 p136. vol 4 p107). In a cottage here was said to be a figure-head from a man-of-war ship which floated on the artificial lakes of Whitworth's Batchacre Hall (NSFCT 1927 p35).

Sutton Chase The area later covered by this medieval chase probably formed the southeastern part of Cannock Forest until granted to the Earl of Warwick as a free chase in 1125. At this time, its bounds seem to have extended from Salford Bridge by Perry Barr and Barr Beacon to the source of the Bourne (or Black) Brook and along it to the junction with the Tame at Drayton Bassett and so back to Salford Bridge, Warws. About 12 square miles of it lay in Staffs (SSE 1990 p24). The chase also stretched over the later Great Barr Common and Little Barr Common (later Perry Barr Common), to the Holbrook in Perry Barr (MNB p55). Drayton Bassett Park, Little Barr Park and Weeford Park were created in it (NSJFS 1968 p50). In 1528 Bishop Vesey granted the chase to the burgesses of Sutton Coldfield. However they did not exercise their hunting rights over the Perry Barr Common until 1730 (MNB p66).

Sutton House House at top end of Water Lane in Endon village. It is of the C16 and was built possibly by Richard Sutton (d1547). It was enlarged in the C17 and C18 (VCH vol 7 p177). Has been incorrectly identified with the tanyard where Tam, the drummer boy with the Pretenders army in the 1745 Jacobite Rebellion, was tanned (STM Dec 1968 p37p) (E pp93,94-95).

Sutton Oak Corner 2m E of Great Barr. At Kingstanding (Birmingham A-Z).

Swag, The Stubbers Green, Aldridge. Created as a result of flooded mineral workings (SNAR p46).

Swags, The Kingswinford. Former partially filled-in marl holes. Now part of George V Park (TB Sept 1978 p24p).

Swainsley Minute hamlet in the Moorlands 0.75m SE of Warslow, situated in a loop in the Manifold. Has also appeared as Swanslee (W p785). The first part is from Sweyn, first Danish king who conquered the Saxons in 1010 (STM Nov 1966 p30). Or 'clearing for pigs' (PNPD). A railway tunnel at Swainsley was 154 yards long (IAS p136).

Swainsley Hall Swainsley. The original house was built in 1864, but extended in the 1890s and in c1910. It was occupied in the late C19 by Sir Thomas Wardle, a friend of several Pre-Raphaelites; William Morris and Sir Edward Burne-Jones were guests here (PDS&C p8) (DMV pp65p,66ps,67). Some panelling from Leek Old Hall (see) was brought to Swainsley by Matthew Millar, at the demolition of Leek Old Hall (OL vol 2 pp102ils,104,105). The NSFC visited in 1930 and saw a life-size wooden bear at the hall (ES June 23 1930 p5p). (NSFCT 1908 p64p of facing). The dovecote in the grounds was built in c1920 to house 200 birds. It is copied from a design in Brittany, France. By 1958 it was used as a fishing lodge (SLM summer 1958 pp34-35,37p - roof was thatched).

Swainsmoor House 2.5m NW of Upper Elkstone, in Heathylee township in Alstonefield ancient parish. There was pasture to the N called Swains Moor by the early C14. There was a house on the site of Little Swainsmoor Farm, under 0.25m to the SE of Swainsmoor, by the early C16 (VCH vol 7 p33). Has also appeared as Swansmoor.

Swallow Moor Name of field derived from an animal name (APB p48). Probably same as Swallow Moss (see).

Swallow Moss Wild waste land 1.5m NW of Warslow, in Warslow and Elkstones township in Alstonefield ancient parish. Enclosed in 1839 (VCH vol 7 p59).

Swan Bank Small area of Bilston (BOP p33). Here was situated the Overas Cross (SCSF p92).

Swan Bank Earthwork 0.25m SW of Cookshill (WJ p28). Richards is probably referring to this when he writes of a mound perfectly round, with its sides having a 45 degree slope and a true truncated top which is not due to weathering. It is sited in a dip between two ridges. It was probably not a windmill base and there is no approach road. Richards considers it has Roman characteristics and is not prehistoric (NSFCT 1983 p13).

Swan Bank Penn parish church is situated on Swan Bank (Birmingham A-Z). In Penn ancient parish (SGSAS). The name is from the Swain (or Swenes) family, who were living in Penn in Tudor times (PPTP p46).

Swan Hotel Old coaching inn W side of Greengate Street, Stafford, next to the High House. The inn is said to have been erected on the ruins of the old college buildings of St Mary's in the mid C18. In the cellars are traces of windows below street level. A priest's hole was discovered in an upper room in 1946. Charles I is said to have slept a night in the High House. The room he slept in is now incorporated into the Swan (SSTY pp210-211). The hotel is recorded in Lord Torrington's diaries, covering the period 1781-94. Lord Torrington found great fault with the 'farming' people who frequented the hotel, especially for their habit of always, as he says, whining and complaining (SKYT p25). In early 1794 a committee of Deputy Lieutenants and Staffs magistrates met to launch an appeal for monies and equipment for the founding of the Staffordshire Volunteer Cavalry (later Staffordshire Yeomanry) (info Yeomanry Museum). The Swan Hotel has been identified as the inn in 'Romany Rye' and 'Lavengro' at which George Borrow (1803-1881) was employed for a few weeks as an ostler from Aug 3 1825 (LGS p217) (OSST 1934 p16). WI Knapp in 'The Life, Writings and Correspondence of George Borrow' (1899) makes no attempt to identify it. In the definitive edition of 'Romany Rye' published by Murray 1900 there is a picture of the Swan. Sampson in the preface to Methuen's 1903 edition, takes it for granted that it is the Swan. Jenkins, a later biographer, concludes in 1912, it is not (NSFCT 1950 p25). Charles Dickens stayed a night here in 1852. He was very scathing of it and called it 'The Dodo' in 'A Plated Article' from Reprinted Pieces (OSST 1934 p16) (SN June 28 1974 p20) (SSTY pp210-212). (SKYT pp22il, 23p,24p,25). The head waiter of this inn was forewarned of his imminent death by the tolling of a certain bell (SA Oct 4 1890) (FLJ 1909 p220).

Swan Junction NE of Swan Village. Junction of the Wednesbury Old Canal (or Balls Hill Branch) with the Ridgacre Branch of the Wednesbury Old Canal (BCM autumn 1995 p20).

Swan Passage A path which took its name is from an old inn called The Swan (demolished in c1845) (SHST p643) at Hanley. It was known as Swan Walk in 1808 and was doubtless a foot road across the Swan Meadow which continued across the churchyard and along side the playground to Union Street and High Street. Swan Passage was a street in 1987 on the site now covered by the Potteries Centre (Stoke-on-Trent A-Z). In 1820 three men convicted of an assault on a woman in the Lamb Inn were hanged and their bodies brought back to Hanley and buried under the road way in Swan Passage, where they would undergo the further supposed indignity of being walked over. The bodies have since been re-buried, having been disturbed during excavations (H pp94,111). On the corner of Swan Passage the illustrious and industrious Michael Huntbach, draper, had a shop. His attempts to purchase another property formed the basis of Arnold Bennett's story 'The Feud' in 'Tales of the Five Towns' (POTP p129). (Stoke-on-Trent A-Z).

Swan Pool Stubbers Green, Aldridge. Was marshy ground on the 1920 OS map (SNBC p30). Became a pool as a result of flooded mineral workings (SNAR p46). Swans have nested here since the 1980s (SNBC p30).

Swan Pool In Sandwell Park, 0.5m N of the site of Sandwell Priory. Former mill pool of Sandwell Mill. The pool is known locally as Warstone (pronounced Wosson) Pool but often appears on maps as Swan Pool (TMS p39) (HHHW p10p in 1899).

Swansmoor House 1.25m SE of Hixon, to its SE is another house, Lower Swansmoor Farm. In Colwich ancient parish. A bronze implement ploughed up at Swansmoor went to Ingestre and is now lost (Trent Valley Magazine Feb 2 1869 p7) (NSJFS 1964 p20). Has also appeared as Swans Moor, Swanmoor (W p418), and Swainsmore (HV p3). The name may be from a mire at SK 0165252, which may have been created in the Devensian period (WSS p104).

Swan's Neck, The A near complete loop in the Trent 0.75m E of Ingestre.

Swan Village Former hamlet NE of Mons Hill, in Sedgley ancient parish. The area was formerly Coseley Moor. There was a hamlet called Swan Village, which centred on the junction of Sedgley Road with David Street (now Vicarage Road West) by 1861 (1861 census).

Swan Village Area around the junction of Swan Lane, Phoenix Street, and the Tipton road, 1m NW of High Street, West Bromwich. In West Bromwich ancient parish. The old portway came through Swan Village along the site of the gas works (OWB p12). Swan Village takes its name from the Swan Inn (see) (SHWB 8) (SOWB p24). Mining and iron-working became established in the neighbourhood in the early C19 (VCH vol 17 p8). The Birmingham & Staffordshire Gas Light Company built its works here in 1825. It is said to have been the largest gas works in the country and 'consequently in the world' - by a guide book dated 1838 (W p682) (WAM p111) (VCH vol 17 p8) (Portrait of the Black Country. Harold Parsons. 1986 p105) (WBOPP pl 77). A gasholder at Swan Village, which had been built in the early 1930s, was demolished by being blown up on Sept 5 1999 (TB Sept 23 1999 p10p). The Birmingham, Wolverhampton & Dudley Railway, linking Birmingham with Wolverhampton, opened in 1854, had a station at Swan Village. The branch line linking Swan Village with the SSR at Great Bridge, opened in 1866, closed in 1964 (VCH vol 17 pp8,14).

Swarbourn, River Tributary of the Trent. Runs through Needwood Forest (SHOS vol 1 p66). The low-lying parts of Newborough get flooded when the Swarbourn bursts its banks (SVB p129). Has appeared as Swerborn (1192-1247), Suereburn (C13), Swereburne (1252), Swerbourn (1337), and Swarborne (1414) (SPNO p20) (SPN p121). If from Swereburn then the meaning is 'sluggish stream' from Anglo-Saxon 'swar burna' (SPNO p20) (SPN p121).

Sweethills Farm 1m SE of Dilhorne. Perhaps from the hills here.

Sweeting's Field Opposite the Victoria Football Ground, Stoke-upon-Trent. Stoke City football ground from 1875 (TSS p47) until 1997.

Swilcar Lawn Swilcar Lawn Farm is 4.25m ENE of Bagot's Bromley.

Swilcar Oak Ancient oak which stood 1000 feet WNW of Swilcar Lawn Farm at cSK 128283 in Marchington Ward of Needwood Forest (OS map 1925 sheet 32). Believed to be upwards of 700 years old when uprooted in a storm in 1941 (SLM Feb 1951 p19) or destroyed by lightning in 1944 (LTD pp114p,123); it was next largest oak in the county to the Beggar's Oak (NSFCT 1915 p160). Celebrated in FNC Mundy's poem 'Needwood Forest' and in Dr Erasmus Darwin's poem in SHOS (SHOS vol 1 p70) (CCBO p26). (W p572). Described in Marshall's 'Rural Economy of the Midland Counties' (vol ii 1798) as 'the father of the Forest' (NSFCT 1927 p167) (LTD p122), and has also been called Swilcar Lawn Oak. In 1802 it was measured and valued at approximately £31 (SLM Feb 1951 p19 il of in 1807). In 1832 it contained 1000 cubic feet of timber, 12 feet less than the Squitch Oak (MOS p51). White in the mid C19 recorded a girth of 21 feet at a height of five feet, the lower stem being 10 feet high; the whole height 65 feet and the extent of the arms 45 feet and it was bound together in many places by leaden clasps (W p572). In Victorian times the oak was a favourite spot for picnickers. By the late C19 the trunk appears to have been affected by fungal infection (LTD p123). In 1901 it had a girth of 22 feet at six feet high (NSFCT 1875 p7 il of in 1900 facing p74). JE Nowers in 1905 recorded a girth of 25 feet five feet from the ground and a height of 60 feet (UTR pp106-107) (ESNF p39p in 1905). (SSC p127 in the intro, p125) (GNHS p408il) (NSFCT 1875 p7 il of in 1900 facing p74) (HOU p359) (SC pp171,172) (SG p109) (CCC p66) (SMC p172). A Bronze Age looped palstave has been found near it (JBAA vol 14 p266) (HOU 1886 p45) (NSJFS 1964 p29).

Swinchurch Brook Rises at Western Meres. Passes SW of Chapel Chorlton. Joins Meece Brook N of Bowers Bent (SPNO p20).

Swindon (commonly *Swin* W p211). Village by Smestow Brook in low undu-lating country 20.75m SSW of Stafford. In Wombourne ancient parish (W p211). Four burial mounds have been noted N of Swindon on Wombourne Common (see). Has appeared as Swineduna (1167), Swinnerton (C18) (VCH vol 2 p118), and Sevindon (J Cary's map 1801). Some believe the first part of the **name** is from Sweyn, first Danish king who conquered the Saxons in 1010 (STM Nov 1966 p30), whilst others think it represents swine, hence 'the swine's hill' (VCH vol 20 p200); Swindon was in Kinver Forest and the pasturage of swine in a forest was an important privilege. Or Sigewine's hill, this Anglo-Saxon personal name means a 'wise friend' and would become shortened to Siwine, Swine (DUIGNAN). Mills gives 'swine hill' (SSE 1996 p18). Swindon was a **manor** by the time it was first mentioned in 1166; by then there may have been a settlement here. It was an inhabited area in the early C14 (VCH vol 20 pp200,207). There were **stocks** in Swindon in 1732 (VCH vol 20 p216). The **church**, St John the Evangelist, on the E side of Church Road, was built as a chapel of ease to Wombourne. It was consecrated in 1854 (VCH vol 20 p221). Swindon became a separate ecclesiastical parish in 1867 (LGS p223), and a separate civil parish in 1896 (VCH vol 20 p217) (GLAUE p425). A **wake** was held at Swindon in late October or November 1808 (VCH vol 20 p201). **Ironworks**. At Swindon in the 1620s Dud Dudley of Dudley Castle (see) smelted iron ore by burning coal rather than by charcoal, and was the first in the country to do so (MR p311); Raven may be mistaken, for others say Dud Dudley claimed that it was near his house, Greens Lodge, coal was first used in glass-making (VCH vol 20 p215), and others say the first use of coal for smelting iron was at Cradley Forge (WMLB p122). Bowen's map says 'Here is a noted Blade Mill.' There is a tradition that parliamentarian soldiers in the Civil War came to the Swindon Forge to have their swords sharpened after the battle of Dudley (TB May 1975 p30). **Steelworks** at Swindon were owned by Richard Thomas and Baldwin - Stanley Baldwin of Bewdley, Worcs (d1947) (said to have been named after Stanley Pool (see)), PM in 1923-24, 1924-29, 1935-37, was a frequent visitor to Swindon and a governor of Swindon School (notice board at South Staffs Council offices). The Baldwins gave the area of Cookley (see) near Brockmoor its name when they removed their works from Cookley, Worcs, to there. **Rick-burning**. John Swatkins, aged 22, and Thomas Lloyd, aged 53, Thomas Timmins, aged 19, and Thomas Wilcox were charged with setting fire to a stack of barley of Richard Powell Williams at Swindon (TB June 1978 p38. June 1986 pp10-11) (VCH vol 6 p120) on Jan 14 1831 in protest at increased mechanisation of agricultural implements. Timmins was acquitted and Wilcox was exonerated (TB June 1978 p38). The other two were executed at Stafford. This was the only case in the county where there was a prosecution and conviction for rick-burning (Wolverhampton Chronicle Jan 19 1831) (International Review of Social History xix (i) pp86-99) (TB June 1986 pp10-11). **William Hawkeswood** of Pedmore, Worcs, was hanged for the murder of his employer, Mr Parker, at Swindon in 1808 (TB June 1984 p29).

Swineshead House on a steep S-facing slope above Swinchurch 4.5m NNW of Eccleshall, 0.5m SSW of Chapel Chorlton. In Eccleshall ancient parish. Has appeared as Suesneshed (DB), Suineshefet (C12), Suinesheued (C12) (SPN p44), Swynesheverd (1327) (SSE 1997 p91), Swynchurch, Swines Head and Swyneshead. The name may mean 'swines's head' (NSJFS 1981 p2), or 'pig hill' (SPN p44). Perhaps it is a reference to the pagan worship of animal heads which were once a prominent part of Saxon sacrificial feasts (SSE 1997 p91). See also Swindon. Here was possibly a village in medieval times, since depopulated (SSAHST 1970 p36). Swineshead gives rise to the Staffs surname Swingewood and various forms (SSE 1996 p23. 1997 p91).

Swineholes Wood Heather moorland and upland woodland 1m SW of Winkhill. By 1999 the wood was a SSSI nature reserve in the care of the Staffs Wildlife Trust (Staffs Wildlife Trust leaflet).

Swinfen Hamlet above a tributary of Fisherwick Brook 1.25m NNW of Weeford. Former township with Packington in Weeford ancient parish. Became a separate civil parish with Packington in 1866 (GLAUE p425). Appears as Swyneffen in 1232 (SSE 1996 p18). The name means 'the swine's fen' (DUIGNAN) (SPN p78). Ekwall gives 'swine fen' (SSE 1996 p18). An early form of the name of Henry I's reign (RHS) is said by Shaw to relate to Sinfin near Derby (SHOS vol 2 p29). Here was possibly a medieval village, probably deserted in the C18 (SSAHST 1970 p36).

Swinfen Hall House 1.25m NNW of Weeford. Built in 1755, designed by Benjamin Wyatt (1709-1772) of Blackbrook Farm (see), and said to have first brought him into repute (SHOS vol 2 pl v, p30) (W p610) (BOE p271) (CCHCB p108 ps of the hall front and rear 1900) (The Wyatts: An Architectural Dynasty. John Martin Robinson. 1979 p18pc of Swinfen Hall) (SPN p138). The Swinfen estate passed on the death of Charles Broun in 1883 to his son Col Michael Alexander Swinfen-Broun. On his death in 1948 the estate was sold and purchased by the Crown. By 1974 it was in part one of Her Majesty's prisons (CCHCB p133) (BOE p271) and is now (1988) a youth custody centre (MR p363). The hall has Art Nouveau bathrooms which are listed (DoE II*). There was an ice-house in the grounds, which has not been located and is almost certainly destroyed (IHB p394).

THE SWINFENS. Swinfen was held by the Swinfens (or Swynfens) from an early period and in this family it remained for several centuries. William Swynfene (d1549) was succeeded by Thomas Swynefen (dead by 1560). He was succeeded by Richard Swynfen (dead by 1595), who was succeeded by John Swynfen (d1632), who was succeeded by Richard Swynfen (d1659). His successor **John Swynfen** (1612-1694), was of some note. He was MP for Tamworth during the Commonwealth and Restoration periods, and was one of the MPs excluded from parliament by 'Pride's Purge' (1648). In Samuel Pepys' diary for Nov 10 1662 Pepys notes 'the great Mr Swinfen.' John helped draw up a bill which was brought into the House of Commons in 1679, for disabling the Duke of York, as a Papist, from succeeding to the Crown. He died in 1694 and was buried at Weeford (DNB) (RHPS p128) (SGS p177) (CCHCB p109). The elder son of John (d1694), John Swynfen (d1671), was the father of Mary Swynfen (b1670); she married John Jervis of Darlaston and Meaford Hall (see) and her grandson was Admiral John Jervis (d1823). However, Swinfen Hall appears to have passed to the second son of John (d1694), Francis Swynfen. His eldest son, Richard Swynfen MP, died without issue and the Swynfen estate passed to his brother Samuel Swynfen (c1686-1736), physician who resided at Swinfen Hall and later at Birmingham. He sold Swinfen to a Samuel Swynfen, who claimed to be in some way related to the Swynfens. He had the hall rebuilt in 1755 and left Swinfen to his nephew Samuel Grundy who assumed the name of Swinfen. He left Swinfen to his nephew John Grundy who assumed the name and arms of Swinfen. By his first wife he had sons, Samuel and John. By his second wife, sister of Sir Francis Ford, he had several sons and daughters (SHOS vol 2 pp29,30). The John Swinfen of Swinfen (d1828), who has a memorial in Weeford church, may be identifiable with John Grundy (later Swinfen). **Swinfen v. Swinfen**. John (d1828) was succeeded by Samuel Swinfen. He died in 1854 leaving the estate to his widowed daughter-in-law, Patience (nee Williams) (d1876), a former parlour maid, who his son, Henry, had met in a London boarding house; Patience had nursed old Swinfen through the last years of his life at Swinfen Hall. However, old Swinfen's will was contested by the new heir-at-law, Capt Frederick Hay Swinfen, the son of the eldest of Samuel Swinfen's half-brothers. At the ensuing trial at Stafford assizes on March 13 1856 Mrs Henry Swinfen was advised by her counsel, including Sir Frederick Thesiger, to agree to a settlement whereby she would gain an annuity but lose the estate. When her counsel settled without her consent she refused to accept the verdict. On Sept 29 1856 Capt Frederick Swinfen came to repossess the hall but retreated after Mrs Swinfen fired a pistol at him from a hall window. Despite Capt Swinfen turning many of the estate tenants against her, the people of Lichfield are said to have supported Mrs Swinfen. A ballad dedicated to the Lady of The Manor of Swinfen appeared in 1857; the last verse runs

> Success to the Lady of Swinfen's old Hall
> Ha! Ha! Bad'un
> Long, long may she live, may her Enemies fall
> Sad'un, Bad'un and Mad'un

In Nov 1857 Charles Rann Kennedy (1808-1867), lawyer, offered his services to Mrs Henry Swinfen to reverse the first verdict. By the time of the retrial at Stafford on July 23 1858 it had attracted national interest. After the verdict went in favour of Mrs Swinfen, Kennedy then proceeded to bring an action for damages against Sir Frederick Thesiger, now Lord Chelmsford and Lord Chancellor, on her behalf. But this case, which came before a jury of the Court of Exchequer on July 4 1859, brought a verdict in favour of Sir Frederick Thesiger. The national fervour in support of Mrs Swinfen then waned and Kennedy lost his reputation and became almost destitute. In the summer of 1860 Kennedy managed to persuade Mrs Swinfen to a scheme whereby she would devise the Swinfen estate in his favour, so that on her death it would go to him. On the back of this scheme he would find it easier to borrow money. But in Dec 1861 Mrs Swinfen married the widower, Charles Wilsone Broun of Linnburn, Scotland. In his fury Kennedy then brought a case against Mrs Swinfen (now Mrs Swinfen-Broun) at Warwick assizes suing her for £20,000, the costs he had incurred at previous trials on her behalf. He won his case and was awarded the full amount of £20,000. The last case in the series resulting from the original Swinfen versus Swinfen case was that brought by Charles Broun against Kennedy at the court of

Common Pleas. It proved in favour of Charles Broun and made legal history in that it established the principle that a barrister cannot sue for his fees (ILN July 9 1859) (CCHCB pp108-133) (GMH p27).

Swinfen Lake Lake 0.5m NE of Swinfen Hall, 1.5m NNW of Weeford.

Swinfen Wood Is described in a poem by Frederick Price entitled 'A Summer Evening in Swinfen Wood' (S&W pp164-165 poem in full).

Swingbridge Park Housing estate? N of Clayhanger, near Brownhills, by the Wyrley & Essington Canal built in 1998. The name is from nearby Swingbridge Farm, which dates from the late C18 (SNBC p20).

Swingle Hill In Stoke-upon-Trent chapelry and parish. Swingle Hill Road is 0.75m WSW of Longton.

Swinscoe Small village on the SW slopes of a high hill above Ellishill Brook in the Moorlands 0.75m SSW of Blore. In Blore Ray parish. At Commonend Farm, 0.5m NW of Swinscoe, was found a Neolithic or Bronze Age axe-hammer (NSFCT vol 61 p146. vol 62 p153. vol 64 p179) (NSJFS 1964 p16). For the burial mound over 0.5m NE of Swinscoe see Top Low; for the one 0.25m SE of Swinscoe see Cliff Top. There are two more 0.75m SE of Swinscoe. One at SK 14194777 (20 paces in diameter and 2.5 feet high) was excavated by Carrington in 1852, well baked pottery and Samian ware were found (TYD p186) and another at SK 14174780 (seven paces in diameters and 1.5 feet high) which may not be a burial mound (NSJFS 1965 p45). Swinscoe appears in 1248 as Swyneskow (SPN p121) (SSE 1996 p18). Some believe the first part is from Sweyn, first Danish king who conquered the Saxons in 1010 (STM Nov 1966 p30), whilst others think it represents swine. The terminal 'coe' is very rare in Staffs, but common in Yorks and Lancs. It is of Danish origin, meaning a wood. So probably 'the swine's wood' (DUIGNAN) (SPN p121). Oakden agrees with Duignan (SSAHST 1967 p34). Swinscoe Green (1834 OS map) to the S of the A52 is the present village centre. Town End (1834 OS map) to the W of Sinscoe Green is preserved by Townend Farm on Bullgap Lane; Bull Gap (1834 OS map) being a tiny settlement slightly to the S. Three marauding Jacobites were shot down at Swinscoe by the Smith family during the 1745 Jacobite Rebellion. They were buried in the 'Flatts' behind the lime Kilns tenanted by Mr Thomas Stannah. People were afraid to go there for fear of ghosts (WTCEM p144). There is a black dog ghost which haunts the Jacobite graves (FLJ 1942 p126. 1958 p185) (DPEM p109). Diana Dors stayed in a C16 cottage in the village in 1962 whilst appearing in a show in Ashbourne and claims to have seen the ghost of a Jacobite (GLS pp87-88) (SBB p190) (ES April 29 1981 p3; Alan Lake of Milton married Diana Dors).

Switzerland North Staffordshire as a whole is sometimes described as a miniature Switzerland (APB p39). In 1896 a Rudyard hotelier promoted the Rudyard village area as 'the Switzerland of England' (KD 1896 p53) (VCH vol 7 p69). Grand Duke Michael of Russia, when residing at Keele Hall (see), described Keele as the 'Switzerland of England.' On the Newcastle road, Loggerheads there was an 'AA' or 'RAC' sign which advertised Price's Guest House as 'The Switzerland of England' (ALW). The 'Illustrated Guide to Kinver' (Birmingham and Midland Tramways. 1904) referred to Kinver as 'the Switzerland of the Midlands' (VCH vol 20 p118) (RKE p29) (PWIS p8). The Churnet Valley about Alton has been described as Little Switzerland (TSW p36). As has Moddershall, an allusion to the picturequeness of the village, particularly about the mill pool by the Boar Inn, and Idlerocks dell (ES Aug 17 1996 pp20-21).

Swynnerton Ancient parish, township, and village at the S end of a ridge in the hills between the Trent and Meece valleys 7.5m NNW of Stafford.

EARLY. The butt end of a stone axe hammer was found at Swynnerton during excavations in summer of 1941. Also a coin or token of lead rather like a long-cross penny (NSFCT 1942 p56) (NSJFS 1964 p38). For the burial mound 0.25m SW of the village see King Clump. Two other burial mounds mentioned by NSFCT in the Swynnerton area were not found by Gunstone (NSJFS 1965 p48). Richards gives two references for two burial mounds in the Swynnerton area at SJ 844344 and SJ 841425. This would place the first on the perimeter of Swynnerton Training Area and the latter at Butterton (NSFCT 1983 p12).

600 to PRESENT. Swynnerton is noted as formerly a royal seat (Bowen's map) (ESH p31). This appears to be merely a reference to King Wulfhere of Bury Bank hillfort or one of his descendants, and that the people of the hillfort migrated to Swynnerton to found the village (SAS p8). The village was first built on lower ground to the S of the present village near the residence of a Saxon prince and removed to the higher ground by Swynnerton Hall in 1812 (SAS p8). The Sulueston mentioned in a charter of 942 has been identified with Swynnerton, or else Snelston, Derbys (SHC 1916 pp86,87). Has appeared as Sulvertone, a manor, in DB, Suinnerton (1242), Swynafterton (1272), Swynforton (1272) (SPN p121), Swilveston, Silveston (SHC 1886 p3), and

Swinerton (c1540. 1682) (LI appendix p172) (Plot's map). The early forms of the **name** suggested to Duignan 'silvertown;' the later forms were extraordinarily different and hard to account for. Some believe the first part is from Sweyn, first Danish king who conquered the Saxons in 1010 (STM Nov 1966 p30). 'Farmstead of the swineherd' (SPN p121). The parish **church**, St Mary, N of Swynnerton Hall in the village centre, was built in the C12 (LDD). Swynnerton parish formed sometime between 1086 and 1291: Commander Wedgwood thought the southern part of the parish formed originally out of Stone original parish and the northern part out of Stoke original parish (SHC 1916 p195). The parish was very extensive up to 1845, it included Yarnfield, Keele and Butterton (Newcastle). Roger de Swynnerton was granted a charter on Oct 19 1306 to hold a **market** here on Wednesdays. The market had ceased by 1500 (NSJFS 1971 p51). (Bowen's map) (THS) (SCSF p95). The charter of 1306 also granted an annual **fair** to be held on Aug 15 (SVB p162). A silver groat struck by Wolsey at York (the issue which led to his impeachment) was found at Swynnerton and went to the Potteries Museum (NSFCT 1940 p26). **Clearance of the old village.** The old village, to the S of Swynnerton Hall, was moved in the C18 to provide a clear view from the hall (SVB p162), and redeveloped on the high ground to the N of the hall. From the terrace at Swynnerton Hall can be seen Wolverhampton, Stafford Castle, the Wrekin, and the borders of Cheshire (W). Swynnerton church tower was used by Yates as a triangulation point for his map, and by the surveyors for the first OS map (SHC 4th series vol 12 1984 vii). At Swynnerton in the later C17 Plot found a blue sort of **marl** with red veins (NHS p119) and a hard slate-like marl (NHS p120) (SL p129). For Swynnerton water tower and how Swynnerton received a **water supply** in the late C19 see Hatton Pumping Station. **Royal Ordnance Factory.** The Royal Ordnance evacuated Woolwich Arsenal, London, and built a factory to the S of Swynnerton village at the beginning of WW2. The site was chosen for it was rural, well wooded, close to a main railway line and frequently veiled in the thick fog which settles in the Meece Valley. The factory invariably manufactured its own fog when there was none to camouflage it from enemy aircraft. The factory, which is said to have gained Swynnerton the derisive name of 'Swinerton' from William Joyce, Lord Haw Haw, in his propaganda broadcasts from Germany in WW2, was toured by George VI on Feb 26 1942. At its peak there were 23,000 workers at the factory. For them were built houses and flats at Walton (see), Stone, and halls of residence known as Frobisher Hall (see), Howard Hall (see), Duncan Hall (see), Beatty Hall (see), Raleigh Hall (see), and Drake Hall (see); that proposed for Moorfields (see) was started but never finished. The factory closed in c1959 and has subsequently been partly a landfill dump and industrial estate (R&S p46) (ES March 1 1977) (info Mr & Mrs JG Beecham and others). **Foot-and-mouth disease** broke out in late 1967 and early 1968 in Swynnerton parish at these farms - Swynnerton Heath Farm and Lodge Burn Farm (SN Dec 22 1967 p15. Feb 23 1968 p11). There is a tradition that the chestnut tree opposite the Fitzherbert Arms Inn is the model for the chestnut in 'The Village Blacksmith' by American poet, **Henry Wadsworth Longfellow** (1807-1882). The poem (1839) runs

> Under the spreading chestnut tree
> The village smithy stands;
> The smith, a mighty man is he,
> With large and sinewy hands;
> And the muscles of his brawny arms
> Are strong as iron bands.

(NSFCT 1918 p112) (IOI p14). Dr Charles Swann, reader of American Studies at Keele University, says despite Longfellow having been a guest at Swynnerton Hall his smithy and chestnut were in Cambridge, Massachusetts (ES March 28 1992 p20p). Similar traditions surround a smithy and chestnut at Dunchurch near Rugby, Warws (ES Aug 20 1938 p3p).

Swynnerton Grange House 0.75m SE of Swynnerton.
Swynnerton Hall In Swynnerton village. Built in 1725-29 probably by Thomas Smith of Warwick for Thomas Fitzherbert, and replaced Swynnerton Manor House as the Fitzherbert's seat. Major alterations were carried out in c1810; some of these had been pulled down by 1978 (BOE p272) (SGS p165). The relics of St Chad are believed to have been brought to Swynnerton Hall from Boscobel (see) (or Blackladies) by the Fitzherbert family, owners of Boscobel to 1812. It is certain that the relics were taken to Aston Hall (see), Stone, when the Fitzherbert family ceased to reside at Swynnerton Hall, possibly at the end of the C18 (RHPS pp258-259) (SCHJ No. 9 p14) (VB p24). In 1913 the Fitzherberts inherited the title of Baron Stafford (see Stafford Castle at Castle Church). Swynnerton Hall is said to be one of only two houses in the county which has remained consistently Catholic since the Reformation to

the present (local info). There is a fine prospect of the hall from Red Hill, Eccleshall. In the grounds was built an ice-house in c1812 S of the hall at SJ 853354 (IHB p395). (MR p312p). A tree, known as the Serpent Tree, because of its serpent-like shape, was growing in Swynnerton Park in 1950 (SLM July 1950 p168p).
Swynnerton Heath Swynnerton Heath Farm is 1m NNW of Swynnerton.
Swynnerton Manor House The former hall, to the present Swynnerton Hall, stood at the centre of the old Swynnerton village, S of Swynnerton Hall (SVB p162). Said to be begun by 'Alan' the first of the Swynnertons and first lord of Swynnerton (1086). Formerly also known as Swynnerton Castle (SAS p8); a license to crenellate the manor house was granted in the Middle Ages (CAMS p7). By the mid C16 the manor appears to have passed to the Fitzherberts; Thomas of Swynnerton was sheriff of Staffs in c1543 (SHOS vol 1 pxxxvi) (Plot's map). The house appears to have been a royalist garrison in the Civil War and was destroyed on March 1 1643 (GNHS p71) (NSFCT 1940 p34). It was in parliamentary hands in 1644 (HOS 1998 p72), and was rebuilt in 1667 (SAS p8). Thomas Fitzherbert built a new house, the present Swynnerton Hall (see), on higher ground in 1725. By 1900 the moat of the manor house had been expanded into a lake with the site (still containing the foundations) then forming an island in the middle of it (SAS p8).
Swynnerton Old Park Former medieval deer park enclosed out of forest, extending northwards for 1.5m from 2m NNW of Swynnerton. Said to date back to Saxon times (NSFCT 1946 p161). Certainly in existence by 1324 (NSJFS 1962 p76). A striking feature of the park is the way in which it is intersected by many miles of 'rides' most of which, and their entrance gates, having local names (NSFCT 1917 p152). It was reduced in size in the Napoleonic wars, WW1 and WW2. 'Old' may have been applied after the creation of the new park when Swynnerton village was cleared (NSFCT 1946 p161).
Swynnerton Park S of Swynnerton Hall. Former site of the old village of Swynnerton.
Swythamley Very fragmented hamlet in a ravine formed by a tributary of the Dane, surrounded by hills. The centre of the hamlet is represented by Swythamley Hall and its estate buildings which are 26.25m NNE of Stafford. Formerly in Heaton township in Leek ancient parish (W p728). The name is from perhaps a form of 'swithen' a moor which has been cleared by burning (cf. Old Norse 'svitha,' to burn) (NSFCT 1932 p56) (NSJFS 1977 p30) (VCH vol 7 p187) (SHC 1999 p7), and the Old Norse word 'holmr,' or its English equivalent, meaning raised ground in marsh land (VCH vol 7 p187). The Swythamley area was a great hunting ground of the Norman earls Palatine of Chester. Hugh 'of Kevelioc,' Earl of Chester, is said to have died in the manor of Leek at the hunting-lodge at Swythamley in 1180-81 (HOLS) (NSJFS 1962 p85 note) (NSJFS 1977 p30). In the autumn of 1318 Edward II and Earl of Lancaster, reputedly, exchanged a kiss of peace in the presence of two cardinals, nine English bishops and other lords here (NSFCT 1870 p33). There was a chapel of ease erected at Swythamley in 1833, but it was mainly used as a school (W p744). In 1905 a church was built on the Swythamley Hall estate by the main road, SW of the hall. It closed in 1977 (VCH vol 7 p190); it had bells which were uniquely pulled by water-power (SMOPP vol 2). A Liverpool ship owner called one of his vessels 'The Swythamley.' The sailors nicknamed it the 'Sweet Emily.' It was wrecked on the Blenheim Reef near the Cape of Good Hope (DP p39). Its figure head was placed in a chasm in Lud's Church; it resembled many people's idea of Alice the granddaughter of Walter de Lud Auk, mercilessly slaughter there in the C15, and was said to be a tribute to her (GLS p90).
Swythamley Hall The site of the hall, or approximate site at Swythamley, has been traditionally considered the site of the Green Knight's white castle in the medieval epic poem 'Sir Gawain and the Green Knight' (VCH vol 3 p233 note) (NSJFS 1977 pp20-49) (MR p229) (SMM p131); later the hunting lodge of the Earls of Chester (NSJFS 1977 p35); later still, possibly by 1246 and certainly by 1291, a grange of Dieulacres Abbey, where lived the lay brothers (SVB p123) (NSFCT 1932 p56) (VCH vol 7 pp187,188). The first hall was the grange building (NSJFS 1977 p30). In 1534 it was the residence of John Whitney, brother to the abbot of Dieulacres Abbey (HOLF p2). After the Dissolution the Swythamley estate was granted to William Trafford of Wilmslow. The estate remained with the Traffords until it passed to the Brocklehursts in 1832: Sir Philip Brocklehurst, a surveyor and map maker on Sir Ernest Shackleton's 1907 Antarctic expedition, appears to have been a relation of these Brocklehursts. In 1975 on the death of Philip Brocklehurst the estate passed to his sister's nephew, John van Haeften, who broke up and sold the estate in 1977 (OL vol 2 pp81,83p) (ES April 1 1976. Oct 25 1977. June 17 1989 p15) (VCH vol 7 p189). The hall, and its parkland, was then bought by the World Government for the Age of Enlightenment, followers of the guru Maharishi Mahesh Yogi, and the hall became the Maharishi Interna-

tional College. In 1987 the estate was bought by businessman, Richard Naylor (ES June 17 1989 p15p), who modernised the hall and sub-divided it into high class country residences (DVOPP p11) (VCH vol 7 p189 pl 28 view of the W front). Throughout its history the hall is said to have been occupied at various times by the Mill, Nedham, Rede, Stonier, Strangman, Toft, and Trafford families and Constance, the mother of the ill-fated Prince Arthur (NSFCT 1870 p37. 1905 p168). On Dec 26 1813 (STC p19p) (BOE p273) (HOLF pp2,3il, p facing p26) a fire burnt down the C17 part of the hall leaving that which had recently been added by Edward Nicholls (VCH vol 7 p189). In the mid C19 Philip Lancaster Brocklehurst (d1904) is said to have enlarged (VCH vol 7 p189) or rebuilt the house, although the centre block may be a remnant of the old hall (MR pp314,315pc). The ghost of a mistress of a member of the Trafford family walks in the 'haunted' bedroom, searching, it is said, for the baby she lost during childbirth (SMM p45p). (W p728). GROUNDS. Some relics of the 1745 Jacobite Rebellion found on Gun Moor (see) and some Roman gold objects found on the Swythamley estate (at Bartomley Farm see) were still preserved at the hall in 1931 (OL vol 2 p86) (NSFCT 1931 pp182-184il,185) (Roman Cheshire. W Thompson Watkin. 1886). For wallabies that escaped from Brocklehursts' private zoo see Roaches House.

Swythamley Park Deer park at Swythamley enclosed out of forest which probably existed in medieval times; although no record of a park appears in the surveys of Saxton and Speed. But in 1537, the abbot of Dieulacres Abbey leased to Robert and Elizabeth Hulme seven pastures, including the 'parklaunde' in the vicinity of Swythamley Grange (EDP p178) (NSJFS 1962 p77). Robin Hood is said to have been in Swythamley Park or old Macclesfield Forest (MC p30) and to have sheltered in nearby Lud Church (HOLF p43) (WTCEM p57) (GLS p89).

Swythamley Park Small park belonging to Swythamley Hall situated to the W of the hall. The burial mound at SJ 96776483 is a listed monument. In the park at SJ 969648, 350 metres WNW of the hall, is a cylindrical cross shaft with square head, similar in type to those at Cleulow (Ches) and Chebsey. The shaft is perhaps of C8-C9 origin or of C12 origin. The square head is of mid C19 origin. The cross was removed in c1874 from Wincle Grange, Ches (DoE II) (OL vol 1 p16 il) (NSFCT 1920 p160) (VCH vol 7 p189). For the balloon which descended in 1826 near Swythamley Park see Gun Hill.

Sycamore There was settlement at Sycamore, in the Sycamore Road area of Handsworth, on the S side of the present Holyhead Road, by the end of the C13 (MNB pp38,45).

Sycamore Hill It stood W of Queens Head Road, Handsworth (presumably near Sycamore Road). Built in 1816 for and by William Murdock (1754-1839), engineer and inventor of coal-gas lighting, who worked at Soho Foun-

dry (see). The house, said to have been the first house ever to be lit by gas, was demolished in 1927 (VCHWA vol 7 p51) (DNB) (MNB p41). Has also appeared as Sycamore Hill House (HHHW p32p) and Sycamore House.

Sycamore Park In the 1880s was the residence of George Parish, a well-to-do brick manufacturer (TBS p26). Could be in the Old Walsall Road, Hamstead.

Sycamores Hill Hill on Cannock Chase 0.75m S of Brocton. Has also appeared as Sycamore Hills (1821) (SPNO p34); nearby was perhaps a house called The Sycamores (1834 OS map).

Syerscote Fragmented minute hamlet on a low promontory by the head of a tributary of the Anker 1m WNW of Statfold. Former township in Tamworth ancient parish. There is a burnt mound probably of the Middle Bronze Age NE of Syerscote Manor next to a stream at SK 227083. It was excavated in 1976 (SASR 1987 p17). Has appeared as Fricescote, a manor, in DB, Siricescotan (1100) (SSE 1996 p18), and Sierscote (1817) (THS p143). The name means 'the cottages of Siric,' this Anglo-Saxon personal name means 'victorious' (DUIGNAN). Ekwall gives 'Sigeric's (or Siric's) cottages' (SPN p124) (SSE 1996 p18). At SK 223076, by Syerscote Manor, was a small medieval village. In the 1330s there were at least 10 houses. It was deserted between 1334-1524. Aerial views show the pattern of the village and the ridges and furrows of strip farming (SSAHST 1966 p49. 1970 p36) (SL pl 12, pp77,83-86). Syerscote estate was anciently a prebend of Tamworth Collegiate Church (W p626) (VCH vol 3 p310). Syerscote became a separate civil parish in 1866. This was abolished in 1934 when Syerscote entered Thorpe Constantine ancient parish (GLAUE p425). Syerscote features in a derisory rhyme about Tamworth (see).

Syerscote Manor House 1m WNW of Statfold. Syerscote Manor is all that remains of a small medieval village (SHOS vol 1 p110). By 1817 the farm and estate of Syerscote belonged to Joseph Grundy (THS p143). Residence in the later 1840s of Mary Elizabeth Smith, the plaintiff in the trial against Washington Sewallis Shirley, 9th Earl Ferrers of Chartley Castle (see) for breach of promise of marriage. From Syerscote she wrote 'A Statement of Facts respecting the Cause of Smith v. the Earl Ferrers etc' (1846), and 'Moscha Lamberti or, A Deed Done Has An End. A Romance' (1849) (copies in WSL). She was possibly resident at Syerscote in connection with her aunt - possibly Fanny Smith - who had a ladies boarding school in Tamworth.

Sytch Brook Runs N of Burslem (Enoch Wood's Plan of Burslem. 1750).

Sytch Farm Oldest house in Bradnop village in 1992. It incorporates a cruck truss that was part of a medieval hall (VCH vol 7 p170). In 1973 two medieval or packhorse horseshoes were found at Sytch Farm (NSJFS 1974 pp139-140).

Sytch Valley Between Brownhills Toll House and Burslem (SHST pp23,487,523p of Sytch Watermill c1948).

T

Tackeroo Cannock Chase. Former name for a part of Brindley Heath near Bean Farm (PCC p77) (SLM Oct 1996 p13), NE of Hednesford. 'Tackeroo' Pit was an alias for No. 5 Mine of the West Cannock Colliery (VB p122). Tackeroo Railway was a line built in WW1 to transport men and goods from the main railway system at West Cannock Colliery at Tackeroo to Brocton Camp. It passed by Brindley Village, sometimes also known as Tackeroo, over the site of the later military cemeteries, passed the E side of Ansons Bank, and ran N to Milford Common. The 'Tackeroo Express' was a train which ran on it (BERK2 p81) (Discover Cannock Chase: Follow the Great War Motor and Foot Trail. Staffs County Council).

Tacker's Well Former public well in Wednesbury at the bottom of Church Street (HOWY p227).

Tad Brook Tributary of the Blithe, which it now joins in Blithfield Reservoir. Rises on Leese Hill N of Kingstone and flows through Kingstone (SVB p106). Has appeared as Tappebroc (C13), Tadbrooke (1349), Tabbrook (1402), and Tade Broke (1543) (SPNO p20). There is in the Martyrology of Oengus a word 'tade' which means 'steath' or 'concealment' (NSFCT 1908 p129). Or means 'stream where toads are found' (SPNO p20) (SPN p20).

Tadgedale Dale 0.75m SE of Mucklestone. Tag Dale (1834 OS map).

Tadpole Hole Coombes Wood, Haden Hill area. In Rowley Regis parish. One of the springs of Hawes Hill, or Springfield or Cradley Springs, which in spring became covered with reeds and live tadpoles (BCWJ pp69,71). Has also appeared as Tadpool Hole.

Tagg Moor Moor which formerly covered the area now covered by Dairy House Farm, 1m SSW of Hales, called 'Derihouse' in 1644 (SHC 1945/ 6 p187).

Talke Large former mining village on a hill overlooking Parrot's Dumble and Bath Pool valley 1m SW of Kidsgrove. Former township in Audley ancient parish (W p428). A Bronze Age axe hammer head was found at Talke (STM June 1969 Supplement p12p). Has appeared as Talc (DB), and commonly as Talk on the Hill (1834 OS map) and Talk o' th' Hill. The **name** is derived from the Irish 'tulach' a hill, or the Welsh 'twlch' 'a height, hill, a knoll, high place' (DUIGNAN) (NSFCT 1908 p136) (SGS p165) (MR p318) (SPN p122). James de Aldithley (or Audley) of Heighley Castle (see), was granted a charter on Nov 16 1252 to hold a **market** here on Tuesdays. The market had probably lapsed by 1299 (NSJFS 1971 pp51,53). According to a plaque on the market cross in the High Street the cross was erected in 1253 and restored in 1887, and still stands on what was probably the market place (LGS p226) (SL p154) (AGT pp56-57il) (KAIW p2) (JC pl 36) (KTM p30p) (DoE II). There was a **fair** at Talke of three days' duration at the feast of St Martin. There was a **church** at Talke in the C16 (LDD). The church, St Martin, on the corner of Audley Road and Crown Bank, was built in 1794 (BOE p273). Talke became a separate ecclesiastical parish in 1741, refounded in 1859. Became a separate civil parish in 1932 (GLAUE p425). Talke lay on the **London-Carlisle road**, turnpiked in 1714. The Plume of Feathers at Talke was considered 'a great wagonners' inn' in 1733 (KAIW p2). On Aug 4 1781 two tons or 39cwt of gunpowder and other things exploded while being conveyed through the village in a wagon (LGS p226) (CCHCA p20) (ADD p30). The man attending the wagon, Joseph Fallows, a coachman relieving the driver (who was taking refreshment in an inn), and all the horses were killed. The inhabitants of adjacent cottages were injured. A brief was issued by order of George III commanding collections to be made throughout England and Wales for the relief of the sufferers (KD 1872). The fob watch of Joseph Fallows was reduced to a solid mass and eventually went to H Williamson of Greenway Bank (AGT pp56-57) (A p61). Some torn and twisted metal from

the wagon went to Sir Ashton Lever's Museum (GM Sept 1781 pp421-422). Leese thinks the exact site of the explosion was on Coalpit Hill (KBT vol 2 pp21-22). Masefield and others say the event took place in 1782 (LGS p226) (St Martin's Church parish Magazine July 1980). The **Talke Ash**, a very large ash tree, was said by Richard Parrott in 1733, to have fallen down in a wind in c1683. Parrott claimed that it was the highest in the country and that it could be seen from Delamere Forest and most of the hills in Cheshire (SHC 1944 p62). In early July 1781 a **fire** destroyed nine houses and five barns in the S end of Talke (GM Sept 1781 p422) (KBT vol 2 pp19-20).

Talke Pits Hamlet now suburb 0.5m SSE of Talke, 1m SW of Kidsgrove.

Tallash House 2.25m NNW of Horton, situated on former Horton Hay, in Horton ancient parish. May have been created when Horton Hay was divided into farms in the later C17. It existed by 1805 (VCH vol 7 p72).

Tame, River Has three principle head rivers, which in turn have many head streams all converging at Bescot. Has appeared as Tame (c1025. 1228. 1300. 1509. c1540. 1592. 1695), Tama (1232. 1285), Tome (1379), Thame (1282. 1292. 1350. 1509) (SPNO p20). The name is of pre-English origin, and the meaning is uncertain (SPNO p20). It has been thought to be from Anglo-Saxon 'tam' meaning tame. Prof Skeat thinks it is older in origin, probably irrecoverable (DUIGNAN). The root is 'tam' which means 'spreading,' 'still.' Although Krausse drives it from 'taom' 'tain' 'tann' the same root as Tean (NSFCT 1908 p131). Or 'dark river' and said to be related to Welsh 'taff,' Irish 'temen,' and even Sanskrit 'tamas' (HPPE p114) (SPN p122). Before coalmining basket making was an industry for those living close to the banks of the head rivers (OWB p103). There was a scheme to make the Tame navigable from the Trent to Tamworth in 1759, but it was proved to be too expensive (HTCT p6). By 1854 the Tame had become contaminated with Black Country pollutants and this was written:-

> The Tame was foul as it could be with
> sewage black as dye
> It ran with garbage in the wet and
> stank when it was dry.
> No fishes lay beneath its bank,
> there were no fish to lie.

(WMVB p75).

FIRST HEAD RIVER. The first head river rises on Stow Heath. Dilworth calls it Willenhall brook (The Tame Mills of Staffordshire. D Dilworth. 1976. p112). At Portobello it is joined by a head stream from Marshend. Runs through Willenhall. Then is joined by two more head streams from S of Essington and New Invention. It flowed under the original County Bridge. It is joined by Bilston Brook at Darlaston Green (Offlow hundred). Flowed under the original James Bridge. It is joined by Sneyd Brook in Bentley Mill Lane. From here to Bescot it was known as Bescot Brook in the C18 (VCH vol 17 p143). At Bescot it becomes the main Tame and receives the second and third head rivers. Water from the Tame was an element used in Walsall's tanning industry (VB p59). Length 4.5m.

SECOND HEAD RIVER. The second head river, possibly formerly Greets Brook (TB May 1995 p16), rises near Whiteheath flows NE to Oldbury, where it is joined by a head stream from Tipperty Green. Further downstream is joined by a head stream which arose from several springs in the Roebuck Lane and Spon Lane areas. Then passes under the Birmingham Canal S of New Town. At SE of Horseley Heath is joined by a head stream which rises out of several springs about Tividale. After flowing under the original Greet or Great Bridge flows through Mesty Croft. Finally joins the main Tame at Bescot Junction. Length 6m.

THIRD HEAD RIVER. The third head river, or called Ford Brook on OS maps, rises on Brownhills Common and is joined at Shelfield by a head stream which rises from several streams from Walsall Wood. Another head stream from Huddocks Moor joins slightly further downstream; another head stream joins in Walsall, having risen on the slopes of Barr Beacon. Finally joins the main Tame S of New Mill. Length 6m.

THE UNITED RIVER. The united river proceeds to Holford Mill where it passes out of the old county into Warws. Dilworth, in TMS, notes, up to this point it, and its river heads, have driven as many as 47 water mills. N of Coleshill the river turns N, and re-enters the county 0.5m SW of Dosthill. Before Wilnecote and Glascote's removal to Staffs, it formed the county border from this point and re-entered the county fully below Tamworth Castle. About at Tamworth the Tame is considered generally shallow and slow in its course, whilst the Anker is deep, narrow and winds considerably (HTCT pp5-6,8). Flows on W side of Tamworth and E side of Tamhorn; giving them their names. Passes Comberford, and Elford. The old salter's way crossed it W of Croxall. It enters the Trent 1.5m E of Alrewas. Length from Bescot to the Trent is 26m. (SHOS vol 1 p89) (GNHS p18) (TMS).

Tame Bridge Former old bridge at SP 016955 on Sandy Lane, 1m S of Walsall. It probably existed by the later C15 and was a main crossing point over the Tame. Although the bridge lay outside Walsall borough, for many centuries its upkeep was the responsibility of Walsall corporation. It was rebuilt in c1783 and disappeared in the late 1960s (VCH vol 17 p13) (The Delves. Henry E Green. 1983). At Tame Bridge the three ancient parishes of Wednesbury, Walsall, and West Bromwich met (SCSF p24). At Tame Bridge was an old tannery (IE p43). The name, Tame Bridge or Tamebridge, was also applied to a hamlet situated just to the E of the M6 where it starts to diverge from the M5. There is an industrial estate of this name in the area (Birmingham A-Z). Near the Bulls Head Inn at Tambridge, Mathew Adams, aged 74, was murdered on Dec 1 1841. Thomas Boswell, aged 22, (who later confessed to committing the murder), George Giles, and James and Joseph Wilkes were accused (Crime broadsheets in the WSL).

Tame Meadow On Aug 9 1777 there was a meeting of the basket makers of Warws and of Staffs at Tame Meadow. A song was written for, and sung, at the meeting. The Tame Meadow is described as a large plantation of osiers. There were nine or more verses, one verse went:

> To the humble old trade, though few better there be;
> To Tame Meadow, that fair, happy Staffordshire vale,
> We'll drain the brown jug of its nappy, good ale.

(OWB pp103-104).

Tame Valley Canal Diverges from the Walsall Canal at Ocker Hill runs through Hamstead. Joins the Birmingham & Fazeley Canal at Salford Junction N of Birmingham (SWY p16) (VCH vol 17 p14). Initiated under an Act of 1839. Opened in 1844 (SWY p16) (TEBC2 p54). On Sept 9 or 29 1881 Sgt George Bates, aged 34, drowned trying to rescue Kate Grainger, aged 11, who had fallen into a wharf on the S side of the canal at Hall Green. Both died; Bates is buried in Wood Green Cemetery (TB Aug 12 1999 p27. Sept 30 1999 p17).

Tame Valley Junction Ocker Hill. Junction of the Walsall Canal with the Tame Valley Canal.

Tamhorn Minute hamlet on the E-facing gentle slope of Tame Valley 1.25m NNE of Hopwas. The name has appeared as Tamahore (DB), Thamenhorne, Tamenhorn (C12), or Tamehorn (SHOS vol 1 p379) (CE p95). In the C16 it became confused with Tymmor, and such spellings as Tympehorn and Tymhorne related to Tymmor (VCH vol 14 p239). The name is from its situation near the Tame. Tamenhorn is Anglo-Saxon for 'the horn of Tame' (DUIGNAN). Or 'horn-shaped land by the Tame' (NSJFS 1981 p3) (VCH vol 14 p239). Ekwall gives 'the bend of the Tame' (SPN p124) (SSE 1996 p18). Tamhorn formed a township with Horton in St Michael's parish, Lichfield, by the late C13. Tamhorn, an extra-parochial liberty since the 1830s, was transferred to Whittington ecclesiastical parish in 1967 (VCH vol 14 p252) (GLAUE p425). A village was at SK 180070 by Tamhorn House Bridge, on W side of canal. It was deserted some time between 1334-1524, leaving only the manor house by the late C17 (SSAHST 1966 p49. 1970 p36) (SL pp46,84,103) (VCH vol 14 p239). By the later C20 there were only about two properties at Tamhorn.

Tamhorn Park Park to S of Tamhorn.

Tamhorn Park Farm Tamhorn, 1.5m ESE of Whittington. Formerly the manor house of Tamhorn. The Tamhorn family, lords of Tamhorn, had a house in

Tamhorn in 1500. It was occupied by the bailiff, Walter Astley, by the end of the C16 and was the seat of his descendants until the later C18 when the house passed by marriage to the Dyotts. In 1815 General William Dyott briefly came here to live. The present house dates from the early C18. Remains of a dovecote were visible in c1990 (VCH vol 14 p247).

Tamworth (locally *Tamworth* see rhyme at bottom of entry). Large market town and former borough, township and ancient parish 21.75m SE of Stafford, situated at the confluence of the Anker and Tame.

PREHISTORY. An axe-hammer, of c1800-1400 BC, was found in Thackery Drive, 0.75m NW of the town centre, in 1962 (NSJFS 1964 p38) (SSAHST 1973-74 pp3-4 ils). A Bronze Age spear-head found in the Anker at Tamworth appears in a catalogue of Tamworth Castle Museum of 1906 (SSAHST 1973-74 pp1,3 ps).

600 to 800. The **name** has appeared as Tomtun (late C7), Tomeworthig (mid C8) (In Search of the Dark Ages. Michael Wood. 1987 p86), Tamouuorthig (781) (SSE 1996 p18), Tamouuordi, Tomewordig, Tameworthig, Tamuuorde (SPN p122), Tameneordige, Tameumdina (W p617), Tameworthe (c1540) (LI part 5 p105); and has been identified with the Tamwurthin mentioned in the will of Wulfric Spot (c1002), founder of Burton Abbey (SHC 1916 p27). It means 'the farm estate on the Tame' (DUIGNAN). Or 'the enclosure by the Tame' (NSJFS 1981 p3) (SPN p122). The Mercians built a 'worthig,' a defensive ditch with stakes in the inner face of a bank perhaps with an enclosing palisade, at Tamworth in the mid C8 (In Search of the Dark Ages. Michael Wood. 1987 p86). The earliest reference to Tamworth is probably contained in a Memorandum written at Peterborough which records a transaction of 675-692 AD (WMMA pp146-153). Tamworth may have been a **royal seat of Mercian kings** from as early as the late C7. King Offa (757-796) had his palace at Tamworth, possibly built in 757 (WMLB p86) and certainly by 781 (SSAHST 1972-73 p41), when Offa issued several charters from Tamworth. Tamworth is mentioned as a town in 799 and 50 years later another charter refers to it as 'the famous town that is called by many, Tamworth' (SSAHST 1970 p17). It was probably no more than an enclosure around the palace complex (SSAHST 1968 p37). In 816 Ceonulf granted a charter from Tamworth (NHS pp410-411); there were three charters issued from Tamworth before 900 (SHOS vol 1 p415 - the 2nd p415) (W p618). The charters show that from then on the Mercian kings regularly kept Easter and Christmas at Tamworth. From the C9 there was a permanent treasury here for the receipt of royal dues. Perhaps the royal archives were kept here (SSAHST 1972-73 pp42-44 p). The situation of the palace buildings has not been located; they may have been situated N of the church; there was a search for the palace in 1960 (WMLB p86). Excavations to the NE of Bolebridge Street in 1968 revealed evidence of substantial buildings, which may have been the palace; the site lies close to the C8 watermill (see below). It is possible, but unlikely, that the defensive enclosure of 50 acres of Ethelfleda's 'burh' of the later Saxon period, revealed by excavations in 1967, was built on the former palace enclosure of the early Mercian kings (AASE pp102,121,134,135,146 note - 164) (WMLB p86) (SSAHST 1972-73 p41). In 1971 a two-storey **water mill** of c760 was discovered in Bolebridge Street. It would have stood at the SE corner of the Saxon defences by the Anker (pp48,49) ('In Search of the Dark Ages' Michael Wood. 1987 p86p,87). It was probably powered by a horizontal overshot wheel, and is one of two Saxon watermills discovered in the country (SSAHST 1971 pp9-16 ps plans) (AASE pp54,68,70,85,88,89 plan of, 90 plan of section from side 93,97,254,276,442 pl xii). There was a **mint** at Tamworth from the reign of Offa to Henry I (HS p77ils of coins) (LGS p227), or from the reign of Athelstan to 1154, or from Canute in 1017, and renewed by William II (W p617). Some say the mint lasted from the reign of Athelstan to Henry I (THM vol 4 p57) or to King Stephen (SSAHST 1969 pp32-53). Twenty eight coins are in the Castle Museum (WMLB p89). But the best examples are at Stockholm, sent no doubt as part of the Danegeld (SOSH pp113,351). (SSC p93) (KNS p70) (TH May 18 1940) (THM vol 1 pp48-49) (SLM autumn 1957 p18). A hoard of nearly 300 silver coins from the reigns of William I and II (with 33 from Tamworth mint) were unearthed during the erection of the Marmion Street schools in 1877 (THM vol 1 p48 (TH May 18 1940)). Saxon finds were revealed during excavations by the Peel Arms Inn in King Street in summer 1994 (SSAHST 1992-93 pp5-20 ils plans). For other Saxon finds in Tamworth see AASE p334, SSAHST 1967 pp17-19.

800 to 1066. When Tamworth was taken and controlled by the Danes in 874 it was the only town in the county (SL p50). Mercia was then abolished and Tamworth lay on the frontier of Wessex and Danelaw. Millward and Robinson imply this frontier formed the Staffs Warws boundary (WMLB p92). The Danes' defeat at Tettenhall (see) in c910 enabled the West Saxons and Mercians to consolidate on the frontiers of their regained territory. With the death of

Mercian ealdorman Aethelred, his widow Ethelfleda or Aethelflaed (King Alfred's daughter, and Edward the Elder's sister) was given charge of Mercia in 912. In the early summer of 913 Ethelfleda built a defensive ditch and bank enclosing a 'burh' at Tamworth. In 1960 and again in 1967 small sections in the N of this enclosure were excavated; in the earlier excavation a rare cut halfpenny of Edward the Martyr (975-978) was found; the later excavation took place S of Albert Road and showed that the ditch and bank enclosed an area of 50 acres, and that the bank had been re-enforced in the later C10, perhaps to make repairs after the storming of Tamworth (see below). The coin was of great interest to numismatists (NHS p406) (SOSH p64) (KNS pp108,109,116,117) (Numismatic Chronicle 1960 p7) (Sylloge of coins of the British Isles. AJH Gunstone. 17. 1971) (WMLB p87) (SSAHST 1967 pp17-29. 1968 pp32-42. 1972 pp32-37, 38-42. 1974-75 pp54-57) (STMSM June 1979 p20) (AASE pp102, 121, 134, 135,146 note - 164). **Ethelfleda's 'burh'** seems to have had a hand in the shaping of the later county boundary which ran through the centre of Tamworth town. Her 'burh' was to form the nucleus of a Saxon settlement in the town. An already existing Danish community remained to the N. When the Staffs Warws county boundary was made it followed the borders of the two communities street by street; hence it zig-zagged through the centre of the town, running down Holloway, Ladybridge St, Church St and Gungate (WMLB p92) (SSAHST 1971 pp18,25). Gould finds little evidence for the theory that the placing of the boundary was a deliberate act by the king of Wessex to prevent Mercian nationalism (SSAHST 1971 p42). The town and borough remained divided until the two halves were brought together into Staffs in 1890 (SL p29). Ethelfleda died at Tamworth in 918, or June 12 920 (WAM p20). The present statue to her in the Castle Grounds was carved by EG Branwell RBA (THM vol 6 p51p). **Tamworth sacked.** A great council held at Tamworth in 924 appointed Ethelfleda's nephew, Athelstan, the first king of all the English. Athelstan died in 939 and subsequently the Danes marched S from York and sacked Tamworth and the Five Burhs. They are said to sacked the town in 939 under Anlaf (Olaf) Guthfrithsson (SSAHST 1969 p34). Simeon of Durham puts it in 939 (SSAHST 1967 p25 note). Gould and Wood think the date of the sacking is more likely to be 940 (SSAHST 1967 p25 note) (In Search of the Dark Ages. Michael Wood. 1987. pp130,133,153) (WMMA p149). Broughton says in 941 (SMC p163). According to the Anglo-Saxon Chronicle and other sources the Danes under Olaf Sihtricsson sacked Tamworth in 943 (HS p71) (VB p30) (SGS p165) (CAMS p31) (MR p320). Lady Wulfrun, who founded Wolverhampton (see), is reputed to have escaped from the town during the sacking, resting for a while at Pelsall (see). The late king's brother and successor, Eadmund, recovered the lost Mercian territory in 940 (SSAHST 1969 p34). **St Edith** or St Editha is a shadowy historical figure with Tamworth associations about whom there are several different legends. **Edith's Identity. Firstly**, she has been identified (by Goscelin in c1080) with the sister of the West Saxon king, Edgar (959-975) (SSAHST 1985-6 pp35-37). **Secondly**, she has been identified (by John of Tynemouth in 'Sanctilogium Angliae' and 'Historia Aurea') with the sister of the West Saxon king, Æthelwulf (839-858). This king reputedly founded Polesworth Abbey, Warws, three miles E of Tamworth, after St Modwen had cured his son of an obscure illness and placed Edith under her for training. Edith later became abbess of Polesworth (W p617) (SSAHST 1985-6 pp35-37). **Thirdly**, she has been identified (by Roger of Wendover, perpetuated by Matthew Paris and others) with the sister of King Athelstan (924-939), who married Sihtric Caoch, the Hiberno-Norse king of Northumbria, at Tamworth in 925 (LGS p226), or 926 (SSAHST 1969 p33. 1985-6 p36) (VCH vol 3 pp309-315), or 927. Roger of Wendover represents her as being cast off by her pagan husband who died soon afterwards. Edith, he claims, preserved her chastity and retired to Polesworth, ending her life in good works. **Conclusion.** Gould, writing in the 1980s, agrees with the second identification and dismisses the first on the grounds that Edith probably lived earlier than the mid C10 and Edgar is not known to have had a sister called Edith. He rejects the third identification because the Anglo-Saxon Chronicle omits the name of Sihtric's bride, nor does it state what became of her in widowhood; and whereas Athelstan did have a sister called Edith, she lived mainly on the continent following her marriage to Emperor Otto (SSAHST 1985-6 pp35-37). **Edith's resting place and ghost.** Edith was buried probably at Polesworth Abbey, but had been moved to Tamworth, possibly by c1155, probably by a member of the Marmion family of Tamworth Castle (see) (SSAHST 1985-6 pp37-38). In 1640 William Dugdale discovered a 'very old' parchment belonging to the Ferrers family of Tamworth Castle. The document alleged that a Sir Robert Marmyon had been granted Tamworth Castle by William I and that the same Sir Robert had expelled the Abbess Osith and all her nuns from their abbey at Polesworth; that the same Sir Robert was visited one night at Tamworth Castle by St Edith's ghost threat-

ening to punish him if Polesworth Abbey was not returned to the nuns; that the ghost struck him with her crozier and told him his wounds would not heal unless he restored the nuns to their convent. William Dugdale mentioned the legend in his Monasticon Anglicanum and it has since appeared in other histories. It has been established since, however, that St Edith's ghost visited Robert Marmion (d1143/4) in 1139 to avenge him for the confiscation of her abbey by one of his ancestors: It was during Robert's life that nuns at Polesworth were restored to Polesworth church and other property; and Marmions after Robert became devoted to the cause of St Edith (SHOS vol 1 pp118,423) (SOSH p112) (HS pp71-72) (TNE pp259,260-261) (SOSH p112) (The Complete Peerage) (SLM Feb 1959 p30) (STMSM May 1973 p25. Sept 1980 p20) (SSAHST 1985-6 p37). The ghost of a lady in black habit, known as the Black Lady, who repeatedly haunts Tamworth Castle (see) is said to be St Edith. Someone claimed they photographed her in c1950. She is said to appear in the 'Haunted Room' (STMSM Jan 1979 p21) (THM vol 4 p51) (VB pp30-31) (HB p122) (GBG pp223,224) (GOT p145) (GLS pp92-93). St Edith's feast day was July 15, moved to July 26 after 1752. The parish churches of Polesworth (Warws), Pulverbach (Shrops), and Tamworth are dedicated to her (SSAHST 1985-6 pp37-38), as is St Edith's Well (see) near High Onn. In 1873 three stained glasses by Ford Madox Brown depicting themes on St Edith's life were placed in the chancel clerestory windows in St Edith's, Tamworth (SLM Feb 1959 pp25-26,30) (BOE p276). She is also depicted on glass at St Paul's, Burton and there was a portrait of her at Aston Hall, near Stone, which went to the RC church in Fountain Street, Leek (BSB p222) (St Editha and Tamworth Church. FR Willington). The parish church, St Editha, on the N side of Church Street, may stand on or near the site of a Saxon church in existence by 943. This church was rebuilt reputedly in 963 and extended in 1080. Fragments of C12 work remain in the present church (NSJFS 1966 pp8-9) (The Collegiate and Parish Church of St Editha. George G Pace). **1066 to 1500.** Tamworth does not appear in **DB** but its burgesses are mentioned as living and working as other villagers in the neighbouring manors of Coleshill, Drayton Bassett and Wigginton. Apparently space was left for a Tamworth entry in DB. It would have been inserted after the entry for Stafford at the beginning of the Staffordshire section (SSAHST 1968 p39) (DB. Phillimore. 1976. Notes). The reason for Tamworth's omission from Staffs DB was perhaps because the Staffs half of the borough, had the church, and was always considered only a parish of the county; DB deals with manors not parishes (NSFCT 1952 p35). The **parish**, formed before 1086, may have originally included Statfold ancient parish (SHC 1916 p194). It also included the chapelries of Wigginton and Wilnecote, the townships of Fazeley, Syerscote, Amington and Stoneydelph, Bolehall and Glascote, the liberty of Tamworth Castle, and the hamlet Hopwas Hayes (GLAUE p425). The parish also lay in two counties yet both parts were in the archdeaconry of Stafford (VCH vol 3 p92). The Staffs and Warws sides of the town were held by the Crown in the Norman period. Staffs Tamworth was administered on the king's behalf through the royal manor of Wigginton (SSAHST 1971 p20). The Warws half of the borough was removed to Staffs in 1888 (VCHWA vol 4 p246) or in 1890 (SOSH p355). The bounds of Tamworth ancient parish were beat on June 1 1697 (THM vol 1 p1 (Sept 18 1937) vol 1 pp25,27 (Oct 9 1937)). Millward and Robinson, wrongly, say 1899 (WMLB p90). **Fire.** The church and the town burnt down in 1345 (HS p176) (SOSH p352) and there was another fire in 1460 (SSAHST 1971 p39). There was one **religious guild** in Tamworth in the Middle Ages (NSJFS 1979 p15). There was a case of **heresy** at Tamworth in 1454 (VCH vol 3 p43). A curious relic of medieval times, an alabaster plaque or table, was discovered by H Charles Mitchell in an old mansion near Tamworth. The table shows the head of St John lying on a charger with, below, the mutilated figure of Jesus shown emerging from the Tomb. Jesus is flanked by the full-length figures of St Peter and St William of York (NSFCT 1927 p150). **Royal visitors.** Henry I was in Tamworth sometime between 1109 and 1116 to grant Lapley church to the Abbey of St Remigius, Rheims. He was in the town before 1115 (NSFCT 1902 p163). He probably came to the town again in 1129 and 1133. In 1157 royal prisoners were sent from Oxford to Tamworth. Whilst at Tamworth in 1158 **Henry II**, with Thomas Becket as his chancellor, confirmed a grant to Merevale Abbey, Warws, during the lordship Robert Marmion (died c1181) of Tamworth Castle (see) (SOSH pp113-115) (R&S p6) (SSAHST 1971 pp20-21) (TGT p12). **Henry III** probably visited the town in 1257 (HS pp75,76) (TGT p12). **Edward II** was at Tamworth Castle in 1325 (R&S p11) (TGT p12). He was at Tamworth on March 13 and 12 1326 before going on to Lichfield (CE p28 note 4). Henry Tudor (**Henry VII**) came through the Tamworth area in 1485 to the battle of Bosworth.

THE BOROUGH. Tamworth is a borough by prescription; that is its recognised rights are so ancient that their foundation is lost in the distant past

(THM vol 1 p3). In the later Middle Ages Tamworth apparently fell 'into so great decay, that it had lost the name of a borough town almost' (SHOS vol 1 p420) although burgage tenure certainly survived (HATC pp28,36-37). Tamworth was nationally known for its villeins in the C13 for the phrase 'Villeins of Tamworth' to arise, according to J Tait in 'Medieval English Borough' pp83-84; Tamworth's villein-burgesses were evidently a curiosity (English Historical Documents vol 3 p884). In the early C17 Tamworth had two town halls to serve the two local governments of the two halves of the town in separate counties. The Staffs one stood in Lichfield Street and the Warws one stood on the site of the Peel Arms Hotel at the junction of Market Street and Ladybridge Street (SSAHST 1971 p26). The Corporation originally met at the Warws town hall? moving to the current town hall in the Market Place in 1701, built at the expense of Thomas Guy (BOE p278 pl 43) (SGS p167p) (MR p320p). Being divided into two counties, Tamworth, had two pieces of common land, Warwickshire Moor (see) and Staffordshire Moor (see). By the C13 the town house owners had the right of pasture on one or other of the commons depending on their house being in Warws or Staffs (WMLB p90). **Charters**. Tamworth received a charter of incorporation in **1560** (WMLB p92) (NSJFS 1972 p69). A second charter was granted in **1588** which constituted the Corporation guardians and governors of the Grammar School. The 1560 charter united the two 'sides' of the town under one corporate body, although the county boundaries remained as before. The new corporate body later became self elective and was styled 'The Bailiffs and Commonality of the Town of Tamworth in the counties of Stafford and Warwick.' A small contention arose after the 1588 charter was granted in that the lord of the manor continued to claim his exclusive right to grind the people's corn at the Castle Mill; a claim which the townsmen contested by boycotting the mill (THM vol 1 p3). The charter of 1588 was renewed in **1663** and surrendered in **1688** (THM vol 1 p3). The **seal** of Tamworth borough in 1953 bore a fleur-de-lis, probably from the royal arms of Queen Elizabeth I, by whom the town was incorporated (CH p336).

MARKETS. Tamworth held a weekly **market** on Saturday by prescription, from the time of the Mercian kings (SCSF p95). Tamworth probably never received a market charter. A market is first recorded in 1249 (SSAHST 1968 p39. 1971 pp21-22) (NSJFS 1971 pp51,52). Until Elizabeth I's reign Tamworth possessed two markets, for the two halves of the town, before moving to one, on the Warws site. The Staffs one, originally serving the Danish quarter, was held at the junction of Butcher Street (later Church Street), Cross Street (later Colehill) and Gumpigate (later Gungate). The Warws one, originally serving the Saxon borough, was held on the present market place and gives its name to Market Street (SSAHST 1971 p33) (WMLB p92). There was a market in 1792 (OWEN), and a market in 1888 (LHE p265). From Richard I's reign there was a **market cross**, long vanished, at the Staffs market site (SCSF p89). In 1516 the butchers were forbidden to sharpen their knives on the cross (Around Tamworth in Old Photographs. Richard Sulima. 1994 p47).
Fairs. Monday before **St Paul's Day** (Jan 25) established after 1792 (SHOS vol 1 pp420,421) (COOKE) (SSAHST 1971 p37). **St George's Day** (April 23 old style) (May 4 new style) (and three days after) (granted by the charter of 1337) (SHOS vol 1 pp420,421) (OWEN) (COOKE) (SSAHST 1971 p37). **St Swithin's and St Edith's Day** (July 15 old style) (July 26 new style) was Tamworth's original fair (SHOS vol 1 pp420,421) (Whitaker's Almanac) (OWEN) (COOKE) (SSAHST 1971 p37). First Monday in **Sept** established after 1792 (SHOS vol 1 pp420,421) (COOKE) (SSAHST 1971 p37). Some say there is a fair on Oct 6 which is called **St Faith's day** fair (BCC vol 3 p93) (SA Oct 11 1913 p8 col 1). Feast of **St Edward the Confessor** (Oct 13 old style) (Oct 24 new style) (and three days after) (granted by the charter of 1337) (SHOS vol 1 pp420,421) (OWEN) (COOKE) (SSAHST 1971 p37). (SCSF pp98,99,104). There was a fair in 1792 (OWEN), and a fair in 1888 (LHE p265). SLM winter 1954 p19 says Tamworth's 'Cherry Fair' is not what it was. For some Tamworth **street names** see SA May 23 1885 p6.
PUNISHMENTS. There were stocks in the market place, and a pillory in the market place until the end of the C18. Tamworth also had a ducking stool (THM vol 1 p11).
1500 to 1800. A plague broke out in Tamworth in 1560 and continued until at least 1563 and, perhaps, longer. Others broke out in 1596, 1606, and 1636 (SCSF pp134,135). For the Civil War in Tamworth see Tamworth Castle. In 1664 there was a large fire at Tamworth (ADD p30). **Appointment of vicar case**. It was the practice for the lay deans to appoint the minister - a claim they eventually substantiated in the law courts. Yet the Corporate body, as Governors of the Grammar School, claimed the appointment of the curate - or 'the two curate places.' In practice, the minister and the curates were one and the same person: ie, the vicar. When the living became vacant the lay dean appointed a new minister, followed by the Corporation appointing the

same man to the 'Two curate places.' Occasionally the town got their man first. This arrangement worked well so long as both parties agreed. In 1694 there was a case where the two parties disagreed concerning the lay dean's appointment of Rev Samuel Collins (THM vol 1 p7). Another case was when the lay dean refused to accept Rev Simon Collins and presented Rev William Sawley in 1759. The case was settled at Stafford assizes in 1761 in favour of the lay dean. The Corporation continued to appeal to 1764. The Repingtons as lay deans continued to exercise their right until 1898 when the gift was transferred to the bishop of Lichfield (THM vol 1 p19). A **Quaker meeting house**, which had a graveyard attached, was erected behind No. 101 Lichfield Street in 1753 (SSAHST 1970 pp45-46). A number took part in the food riot in Tamworth on July 1 1740, an assault was made on a miller's house (LOU pp270,363). There was a hunger riot in Tamworth in 1766 (MH autumn 1976 p262). The independent **Tamworth Troop** raised in 1798 (FSP p62), was a part of the Staffordshire Yeomanry from 1813 (info Yeomanry Museum). **Persons and visitors**. For **John Leland's** visit to Tamworth in 1541 see Tamworth Castle. There is a tradition **Elizabeth I** visited Tamworth (STMSM Sept 1980 p21). **James I** and Prince Charles were at Tamworth Castle on Jan 18 1619 (SHOS vol 1 pp421,430). James I was probably at the castle again in 1621 (R&S p25), and Aug 1624 (SHOS vol 1 p47). (AA p259). **Thomas Fletcher** of Tamworth died in 1590 aged 102 (W pp615-616). **Thomas Guy**, a native of Tamworth, built almshouses in Gungate in 1678 to accommodate six poor women. In 1693 he enlarged it to accommodate 14 men and women and added a library (LGS p231). The almshouses were rebuilt in 1913 (BOE p278), or 1914 (LGS p231). During **Dr Plot's** visit to the town in the later C17 he was shown a great collection of skulls in the Charnel House. The clerk showed him a way of telling the difference between male and female skulls, but Plot was not very convinced of his method (NHS p330). Plot noted a strange custom frequently practiced about Tamworth to remedy a disease affecting cattle called the Foule, the symptoms of which were excessive fatness in the legs and feet. The site where the cow or heifer lay is identified and the turf cut out and hung on a tree facing N, which, if the cow or heifer blows on it (or the wind blows on it?) cures the cow or heifer in three or four days time (NHS p388). **John Meggs**, died in 1769, aged 101 (W p615).
GRAMMAR SCHOOL. Leland noted a grammar school in the mid C16. It was endowed in the 1530s by John Bailie or Bailey (VCH vol 6 p168il of in 1820s facing p145). Queen Elizabeth I refounded the school in 1588 (W p622), when she made the Corporation governors of the school. From then on it took the name of Queen Elizabeth's Grammar School. The grammarian Samuel Shaw MD was headmaster between 1708-1730. The school stood in Lower Gungate between 1678 and 1867. New premises were built in 1867/8 on the Ashby Road near Upper Gungate (TDOPP p31p). New buildings opened there in 1937. In 1960 the grammar school was merged with Tamworth Girls' High School to form a mixed grammar school (VCH vol 6 pp168-171). The school was known as Queen Elizabeth Mercian High School by 1994 (TDOPP p31p). The school magazine was called 'The Fleur-de-Lys' vol 2 No. 1 is Dec 1922 (THM June 22 1940) (THM vol 1 pp50-51p). **Alumni**: Rev William Whiston, translator of Josphus (b1667 at Norton Vicarage near Twycross), entered 1684; Thomas Guy pupil c1665 (LTM April/ March 1972 p45).
1800 to 1900. By the later C19 Tamworth was described as a 'well-to-do town.... but we cannot call it an interesting place' (SA May 23 1885 p6). **Tamworth Manifesto** was a manifesto issued by Robert Peel in 1834 which laid out rethinking on the Tory party's principles after the Tories defeat in the general election of 1832. It was so called because Peel read it from the balcony of Tamworth Town Hall (HOS p61) (DM p40). The manifesto was also important for in it Peel re-named his party 'Conservative' instead of 'Tory' (TB March 1993 p3). Peel's second Tamworth Manifesto was published after his fall from power in 1847 and was again addressed to the electors of Tamworth (THM vol 1 p104). A **statue** of Sir Robert Peel (d1850) was erected in Market Street at the W end of the Town Hall in 1852 (SLM autumn 1957 p15) or 1853 (BOE p278) (SGS p167p). It was erected by public subscription at an estimated cost of £1,100. The bronze figure by Matthew Noble, was due to be eight feet high, have its right hand uplifted as if addressing the House of Commons, be set on a granite pedestal and surrounded by an iron railing (W pp579,619). The statue was restored in 1986 (SLM April 1953 p9p. autumn 1957 p15. Oct Nov 1986 p12). (DoE II) (KES p204) (VB p32). **Tamworth Civic Society**, formed in c1973, and out of it in 1979 formed the national **Peel Society**, to not only commemorate the work of Sir Robert Peel PM but also the whole Peel family. In 2000 the society were seeking premises for a museum (info Marion Hine and Janet Lees). By the mid C19 the payment of **church rates** had become resented by non-conformists. The refusal to pay the church rate by a prominent Tamworth non-conformist, Mr Haskew, resulted in legal proceedings being taken against him by the churchwardens in

c1861. No rate was levied in Tamworth during 1862, but on July 2 1863 the vestry was again summoned to levy a church rate. By this time the Nonconformist minister, T Burgess, had promoted the anti-church rate cause far and wide and Tamworth became nationally known for its anti-church rate feelings. The Court of Arches judged in favour of Haskew. Church rates in Tamworth were abandoned on Dec 27 1867 (THM vol 1 p112 (Aug 17 1946)). For two days in late Sept 1809 Tamworth played host to a large-scale **music festival** organised to raise funds for alterations to the parish church of St Editha and the enlargement of the organ. It was an isolated event for Tamworth, unprecedented and without sequel. Around 130 of the leading musicians of the day were involved in four concerts of choral and orchestral music (SSE 1993 pp81-106 ils). **Persons and visitors. Robert Bage** (d1802), novelist, retired to Tamworth (THM vol 1 p21). The itinerant philosopher and lecturer on antiquities and chemistry, **John Warltyre**, died in great poverty at Tamworth, and was buried on Aug 23 1810 (OL vol 2 p217) (SMML pp83-85). **W Farr**, a Tamworth carrier, is said to have lived to at least the age of 144 and bequeathed 10,000 L to charitable uses (Broughton's Scrapbook p444). **George Borrow** when aged nine stayed in Tamworth with his father's regiment from April 8 and May 3 1812, during which time he first met the tinker, Bosville, the Flaming Tinman of 'Lavengro.' On July 26 1825 he went to a horse fair with the gypsies of Mumper's Dingle, probably this was at Tamworth (NSFCT 1950 pp13,15,22-23). **Gage Earle Freeman** (d1903), poet and writer on Falconry, was born in Tamworth in June 1820 (PSS pp170-172) (VFC p51). **Mary Kirton Roby** (d1867), poet, was born in Tamworth in 1828; her father and uncle compiled T (PSS p469) (VFC p114). **Queen Adelaide**, wife of William IV, visited Tamworth in Nov 1839, and stayed at Drayton Manor (R&S p39). **Charles Dickens** passed through Tamworth in 1840, probably in April, and was joined in the town by his younger brother Alfred who was sent to Birmingham to retrieve Dickens's gold watch from a pawnbrokers (Old Curiosity Shop. Biographical Edition of The Works of Charles Dickens in 8 vols. vol 5. 1902. xii). **Queen Victoria** and Prince Albert visited Tamworth on Nov 28 1843 accompanied by the Duke of Wellington, and again on Dec 1 1843 on their return (ILN Dec 2 1843 p361. Dec 9 1843 p372) (THM vol 1 p1). **Edward Farmer** (born Derby 1809), poet, author of 'Little Jim,' and a detective for a railway company, was long a resident in Tamworth and died here on July 10 1876. He is buried in the new cemetery at Derby (FLJ Dec 4 1918 p329) (PSS pp160-162) (TB Sept 1975 pp18-19ps. March 1993 p1p. April 1993 p3p) (VB p32) (STMSM Sept 1980 p21) (VFC p46).

INDUSTRY AND RAILWAYS. Tanning was the town's principle industry for a very long time until about the C19. Tamworth also made superfine narrow woollen cloths, and linen, and practiced the printing of calicos (SCSF p112). For the production of Reliant Robin cars see Two Gates. The Birmingham and Derby **railway** line which opened on Aug 5 1839 had a station at Tamworth (IAS pp130,132). The first sod of the Trent Valley line of the London and North Western Railway was cut at Tamworth by Sir Robert Peel on Nov 13 1845 and the line opened on June 26 1847. The line linked Tamworth with London and Stafford (IAS pp131,133) (WMLB p90). For the locomotive called 'Tamworth' which ran on the Birmingham and Derby railway line see Barton Turn.

NEWSPAPERS. The **Tamworth Advertiser and Trent Valley News** appeared between at least Jan 16 1869 and Sept 27 1913 (SHJ spring 1996 p26). The **Tamworth Herald and General Advertiser** (or simply Tamworth Herald), founded by 1871, still runs (SHJ spring 1996 p26). The **Tamworth Miners' Examiner and Working Men's Journal**, founded on Sept 13 1873, became the Tamworth Examiner and Working Men's Journal from Dec 27 1873; this paper ran until at least Jan 15 1876 (SHJ spring 1996 p27). The **Tamworth Mercury**, founded Feb 22 1878 ran until at least May 31 1957 (SHJ spring 1996 p27). The **Tamworth Chronicle and Midland Counties Advertiser**, founded on April 19 1884, ran until at least Aug 16 1884 (SHJ spring 1996 p26). The **Tamworth Times**, founded on Dec 3 1892, ran until at least Dec 27 1895 (SHJ spring 1996 p27). The **Tamworth Times** (new version), founded on June 9 1905, ran until at least Feb 17 1912 (SHJ spring 1996 p27). The **Tamworth News and Four Shires Advertiser**, founded on Sept 21 1934, ran until at least Jan 3 1936 (SHJ spring 1996 p27). Some Burton upon Trent (see) and Lichfield (see) newspapers have Tamworth in their title.

TAMWORTH PIG. The breed of pig known as the 'Tamworth' or 'Tamworth Sandies' (LTM March/ April 1972 p9), or 'Sandy backs,' is a sandy red colour and is the nearest of British breeds to the European wild hog. The breed resembles the Old English Forest pig and has forequarters more fully developed than the rear and a distinctive long snout. Its peculiarly-shaped pricked ears were evidently so formed so that when in its lair in the forest it would be notified of the slightest movement. Its short body, well-sprung ribs, strong

loin, thick shield and long tusks make it both a powerful and a dangerous enemy. The 'Tamworth' is thought to have originated in Spain, arriving in England in c1797 and immediately adapting to the forested areas of the Midlands. 'Tamworth' breeders, with those of the 'Large White' and 'Middle White,' founded the National Pig Breeders' Association in 1884 (VCH vol 6 p129 facing pl x2) (MR p281p). Another account says the Tamworth Pig is thought to be a variant of the Berkshire breed, produced by crossing with imported stock, perhaps from India, in the early C19. Sir Francis Lawley of Middleton, Warws, near Tamworth, and Sir Robert Peel of Drayton Manor, have been credited with its introduction (HOS 1998 p94). The breed was improved in c1860 and had been changed again by c1912 (THM vol 4 p26). In the early 1960s 'Tamworths' were the most common breed on British farms but had dwindled to only 150 sows in Britain by 1997 (The Times. March 29 1997 p8p). Tamworth people were still referring to Tamworth natives as 'Sandy Backs' or 'Sandies,' a colloquialism for Tamworth Pig, by the end of the C20 (local info).

1900 to PRESENT. **Floods**. The Anker and Tame both overflowed on Dec 31 1900 and flooded Tamworth (THM vol 4 p121). The Anker broke its banks in May 1932 and again flooded Tamworth (THM vol 4 p123). In 1965 Tamworth was designated an **Expanding Town** to absorb the population overspill from Birmingham (MR p319). In the initial years there was much antagonism between the natives and the newcomers, who the natives called '021s,' being the Birmingham telephone code. The Rev John Withers was compelled to preach a sermon of peace and reconciliation from the pulpit on Aug 18 1967 (Anderson Country. BBC Radio 4. March 8 1994). Tamworth **Snow Dome**, at Leisure Island, Riverdrive owned by First Leisure Corporation, is Europe's first real snow indoor ski centre. It opened in April 1994 (The Birmingham Post & Mail Year Book and Who's Who 1998). On Sept 13 1994 a rare **albino frog** called 'Tom Tom' was found at Tamworth and taken to Drayton Manor Park. For the escaped **'Tamworth Nine'** cattle see Hopwas Hay. There is a city called Tamworth in New South Wales, Australia (City on the Peel. Roger Millis. 1980). **Supernatural**. The Mason family of Tamworth claimed their modern council house was haunted by a strange phantom cat in autumn 1976 and January 1977 (EGH pp207-208). **Persons and visitors**. In 1908 **Mrs Hutton** of Dosthill erected a drinking fountain to the memory of her late husband. Known as the Hutton Fountain it was erected at the junction of the Ashby and Comberford Roads on a piece of land known as The Hand. There were three drinking troughs, one for people, one for dogs, and one for horses. The inscription read 'I was thirsty and ye gave me to drink.' It was temporarily removed in the 1960s but has now (1994) been replaced (TDOPP p30p). **George VI**, when Prince George, opened the war memorial extensions of Tamworth Hospital on May 29 1924 (R&S p46). On June 6 1980 **Elizabeth II** visited Tamworth and opened the Ankerside Shopping Centre (TGT p12). In 1988 **Princess Anne**, the Princess Royal, visited Tamworth (TGT p12). **Marjory E Mitchell**, young authoress and poet whose first novel was 'Yet in My Flesh,' is a native of Tamworth (THM vol 5 pp48,49p). **Gregory Cordell** of Tamworth, aged 27, and Carla Germaine of Sutton Coldfield, Warws, aged 23, married without ever having any contact with each other prior to the wedding on Jan 25 1999. The wedding, the prize in a competition held by the BRMB radio station in Birmingham, is believed to be Britain's first in which the couple never met or saw each prior to the ceremony. By July 1999 the couple had separated (Daily Telegraph Jan 26 1999 p3ps) (Daily Mail July 17 1999 pp26-27).

BALLADS AND RHYMES. The **Tanner of Tamworth** ballad is the name of a famous long ballad purporting to record a meeting at Bassets Pole (R&S p16) between Edward IV, hunting in Drayton Basset Park, and a Tamworth tanner returning from Birmingham market (HS pp148-156). After some bargaining they exchanged horses, the king giving his valuable hunter for the tanner's mare 'Brocke,' a sorry beast worth four shillings. But the poor tanner soon found that he could not ride the fiery spirited animal, and forfeited a sum to get his own mare back. When the king revealed his true self the tanner expected to be hung for his impertinence but instead the king gave him the manor of Plumpton Park with 300 marks a year (WAM pp52-53). The ballad is well documented from 1596 onward, and achieves some authenticity by being included in Bishop Percy's 'Reliques.' A shorter version (only 23 verses long) is the most popular version (TOS pp106-108). (LGS p227) (FTWM pp112-115). In the ballad known as the **'Tamworth Minstrel's Complaint'** a Tamworth man who travelled round singing and playing a harp whilst his wife visited markets selling drapery claims to have been robbed of a large sum of money (SSAHST 1971 p34). These rhymes contain the name of Tamworth:-

Sutton for mutton,
Tanworth for beef,
Wasall for bandy legs,
And Brum for a thief.

Tamworth and Uttoxeter -
Both sold the Church Bible to buy a town bear.

There's Bitterscote and Bonehill,
And Dunstall upon Dunn,
Hopwas and Coton,
And miry Wigginton;
Little Amington and Great Amington,
With the Woodhouses by,
Glascote and Wilnecote,
And merry Faseley;
Comberford and Syercote,
and Bole Hall Street -
And Tamworth is the head town,
Where all the cuckolds meet.

(HTCT) (SCSF p165) (SJC pp2,3) (FOS pp149,150-151).

Tamworth Castle Lies in the SW angle of the Anglo-Saxon burh of Tamworth and is protected by the Anker to the S and covered the ford or bridge at the confluence of the Anker and the Tame. The castle stood in Warws prior to 1890.

THE MARMIONS, FREVILLES, AND FERRERS. The Saxon castle became the property of William I at the Norman Conquest. According to a legend in a 'very old' parchment belonging to the Ferrers family of Tamworth Castle, discovered by William Dugdale in 1640, a Sir Robert Marmyon had been granted the castle by William I. However, it has been shown William I gave the castle to Robert le Despencer (or Dispensator) (who has been identified with a Robert the Bursar who held land in Warws in 1086). Although Robert le Despencer held the castle, he does not appear to have held the town of Tamworth, and although the castle lay within the borough defences, the castle and its liberty were kept distinct (HS pp71-72) (The Complete Peerage) (SSAHST 1971-72 p19. 1985-6 p37) (SHJ summer 1987 p47) (TGT p1) (HOS 1998 p41). **Robert Marmion** (died c1106) of Fontenay-le-Marmion, Calvados Dept, Normandy, was the father of **Roger Marmion** (died c1130). By Roger's marriage to Robert le Despencer' niece (SSAHST 1971-72 pp18-20. 1987-88 p2), the castle passed to the Marmions, passing to them by c1100 (HS p72). Roger (died c1130) was succeeded by his son **Robert Marmion**. He was one of the staunchest supporters of King Stephen against the claims of the Empress Matilda to the throne. In 1141 Matilda gave the town and castle to one of her adherents, Sir William de Beauchamp. In 1143/4 Robert was killed in warfare with the Earl of Chester. He was succeeded by his son **Robert Marmion** (died c1181), who was restored to the castle in c1148 by King Stephen, for services rendered by his father to the king. He was succeeded by his son **Robert Marmion**. He is said to have resisted a royal order for the castle's destruction for he had sided with the barons against King John; it is said the Sheriff of Staffs and Shrops, who was sent to carry out the order, was besieged himself in the castle by the people of Tamworth on behalf of Robert, and was starved into submission. Robert had died by 1218 and was succeeded by his son by his first wife **Robert Marmion** (d1241-43); to him the castle was restored in 1220. He was succeeded by his son **Philip Marmion**, who was engaged in building at Tamworth Castle in the 1260s, and founded St James' Hospital (see) to the N of Tamworth; he had died before 1291 (HS p74) (LGS p227) (CAMS p31) (TGT p1) (SSAHST 1987-88 pp2,43). (SSAHST 1987-88 p43). The castle then passed, briefly, to Philip's eldest daughter, Joan (who died childless), and then to Philip's second daughter, Mazera and her husband Ralph de Cromwell. Philip's daughter, Joan, by his second wife became tenant of Scrivelsby manor, Lincs, which had been held for some time by the Marmions of the king in chief by grand serjeanty of being armed on the day of the king's coronation for the defence of the king's estate. This service to be performed at each coronation became known as acting as the King's Champion. At the coronation of Edward III, in or after 1327, Joan's second husband Henry Hillary claimed the right to perform the service, but it was dispensed with on that occasion, possibly because of the rival claims of Alexander de Freville (see below). The right of King's Champion then descended to Joan's son, Thomas, by her first marriage, then to his daughter Margaret, who took it to her husband Sir John Dymoke. In 1377 Sir John Dymoke after a prolonged contest before the Court of Claims established the right of his wife Margaret against a claim by Sir Baldwin de Freville

(see below). From that date, although again disputed by the Freville claimant in 1399, the right of the Dymokes was maintained and performed by them at subsequent coronations, the last being at the coronation of George IV in 1821 (The Complete Peerage). Another account says the Dymokes last performed the act at the coronation of William IV (The Guinness Book of Lasts. Christopher Slee. 1994. p166). The Dymokes were still holding Scrivelsby manor in 1977 (SGS p165). The daughter of Mazera and Ralph, Joan, married **Alexander de Freville** (d1328) and the Frevilles held the castle by 1327/8 (The Complete Peerage) (HS p75) (SSAHST 1987-88 pp2,3) (VB p31) (CAMS p31). Their son **Baldwin de Freville** (d1343), was succeeded by his son Baldwin de Freville (d1375), who was succeeded by his son Baldwin de Freville (d1387), who was succeeded by his son Baldwin de Freville (d1400). He was succeeded by his son Baldwin de Freville (d1418), who was succeeded by his sister Elizabeth Freville (HTCT p362). By her marriage in 1423 to **Thomas Ferrers**, the castle passed to the Ferrers of Groby, Leics. They were descended from the Ferrers of Tutbury Castle (see) (who by marriage into the family of the Earls of Chester inherited Chartley Castle). Thomas Ferrers died in 1459 and was succeeded by his son Sir **Thomas Ferrers** (d1498), who was succeeded by his grandson Sir **John Ferrers** (d1515), son of Sir John Ferrers. Sir John (d1515) was succeeded by his son Sir **Humphrey Ferrers** (d1553), who was succeeded by his son **John Ferrers**. He was succeeded by his son Sir **Humphrey Ferrers** (d1607), who was succeeded by his son Sir **John Ferrers**. He was succeeded by his son Sir **Humphrey Ferrers** (d1633), who was succeeded by his son **John Ferrers** (d1680), who was succeeded by his granddaughter **Anne Ferrers**, daughter of Sir Humphrey Ferrers (d1678). By her marriage in 1688 to Hon Robert Shirley (d1699), a relation of the Shirleys of Chartley Castle (see) she united the representatives of the senior line of the Ferrers of Chartley with the junior line of the Ferrers of Groby, and Tamworth Castle. Their descendents succeeded to the barony of Ferrers, created in 1299. Their daughter and heir **Elizabeth** was suo jure Baroness Ferrers from the death of her grandfather Sir Robert Shirley of Chartley Castle (see) (d1717) to her death in 1741. In 1715 she married James Compton, 5th Earl of Northampton (d1754). Their daughter **Charlotte** (d1770), was suo jure Baroness Ferrers, from 1749 to 1770. In 1751 Charlotte married George Townshend of Rainham, Viscount Tamworth (and afterwards (1787) Marquess Townshend). Their son **George Townshend** (d1811), Lord Ferrers, succeeded. He was created Earl of Leicester in 1784 and succeeded as Marquess Townshend in 1807. On his death in 1811 he was succeeded by his son **George Townshend**, Marquess Townshend. He died without issue in 1855 and the barony of Ferrers then fell into abeyance between his sisters and their issue (The Complete Peerage) (WMLB p89) (SSAHST 1987-88 p3).

THE CASTLE. The motte, nearly 100 feet high and 50 feet wide on the summit (SSAHST 1977-78 see plan on p16), is of Norman construction. However, it is erroneously accredited to Ethelfleda by LGS p228p, SK p199, and SGS p165. The herring-bone masonry appearing in the lower portions of the curtain wall is of 1070-1100 (BOE p277) and is one of the finest examples of herring bone walling in the country (WMLB pp89,91) (TNE p261). The circular, though irregular, shell-keep and tower is c1125-1160 in origin (BOE p277) (CAMS p32) (MR p320). At the base of the tower is Marmion's Stone a weathered stone named after one of the Marmion family. It was once the base of the cross which stood on St Mary's Bridge, Tamworth (KES p203) (LGS p228). The curtain wall, which links the keep to a gatehouse over a dry moat, is 50 metres long, 25 feet high, 10 feet thick and topped by the approach walkway to the keep and manor house. The gatehouse was situated to the NE and built between the 1250s and the 1270s. The gatehouse was demolished probably between 1715 and 1730 and certainly by 1741. The Bull Inn (later Town Hall Vaults Inn) was built on the site about this time and the lower portions of the gatehouse were incorporated into the inn. The inn was demolished in c1970. The foundations of the gatehouse were discovered between 1972-4, and have been left exposed (SSAHST 1977-78 pp15-28. 1987-88 pp5,7,43,47) (CAMS p33). The Ferrers continued to use the keep as an occasional residence and were carrying out repairs to it in 1541 (TGT p12). The castle was a royal garrison in the **Civil War**, from 1642. It was taken by parliament after a two day siege on June 25 1643 (LGS p227) (SOB p75); the keep suffering no damage (CAMS p31). A Capt Waldyve Willington was placed in command of the castle (Tamworth Castle Guide. 1993 p1). From the late C17 the Shirleys, Cromptons, and Townshends all had seats elsewhere, and rarely lived at the castle. The tightly packed apartments of the manor house within the keep are of various periods from about the C14, but essentially Jacobean. In 1786 the S side of the keep was faced in ashlar, and other additions in the Gothic style, made. The Great Hall built in Henry VIII's reign (WMLB p89), was rented to Robert Peel (father of the PM) in 1790 for some months for him to use as a forge while he was building his first cotton mill at Tamworth. Others say he rented it between 1790 to 1792 (HOS P22) (VB p32). It is the Banqueting Hall or State Drawing Room which has the frieze of heraldic shields in 52 panels (Staffs County Handbook. c1958. p139p) (BOE pp277-278) (STMSM May 1973 p25) (VB p31), or 55 panels (KES p201), in it is an inscription recording that Sir John Ferrers was descended from David, king of Scotland (LGS p228), and the sword used by Lord Thomas Ferrers at Bosworth, which is inscribed 'He who loses me loses honour' (VB pp31-32). There is a minstrels' window in the State Drawing Room at Tamworth Castle (STMSM Sept 1980 p20). The Oak Room also has an heraldic frieze (BOE p278). From 1814 to 1831 the castle was owned by John Robins, a London auctioneer, until returning to the Townshend family (THM vol 1 p78) (SSAHST 1987-88 p3) (Tamworth Castle Guide. 1993). In 1897 they sold it to Tamworth Corporation for £3000 (TGT) and turned it into a museum holding the town's collection (SGS p165). The grounds have been turned into a pleasure park and gardens (HOS P22). (SHOS vol 1 pp416-419,420) (GNHS p169) (SMC ils opposite p149 two engravings from 1780 and 1789) (SM p407) (SSC p94 with an etching by P Cormouls c1830) (W pp619-620) (HS pp33 il, il facing p39, 40il,41,70p247 il of 1780) (NSFCT 1902 pp159-161. 1910 p216; the pike and halberds used by the old watchmen are kept in the Castle Museum) (S p66p) (SOSH pp66,67p 352, 353p of the Great Hall) (KES pp202,203) (KNS pp68,p,69, p of the Great Hall facing 80,81,82) (SLM Nov 1950 pp22-23il) (STMSM May 1973 p25 interior) (SHJ vol 5 pp45-48). **Supernatural**. The ghost of a lady in black habit, is said to be that of St Edith of Polesworth and Tamworth (see). There is another ghost of a white lady, who walks the battlements. She, reputedly, mourns the death of her lover Sir Tarquin of the Arthurian legend, defeated in a tournament against Sir Lancelot, which took place in Lady's Meadow below the castle (GLS p91). (RPG pp5-10; includes the 1949 investigators report) (AA p259). A reputedly haunted staircase is called the 'Haunted Staircase' (HB p123p) (STMSM May 1973 p25). **Visitors. Henry II** was entertained at the castle in 1158 (VCH vol 1 p224) (NSJFS 1966 p45). **John Leland** visited in 1541. **James I** stayed at the castle three times - Jan 18 1619, 1621, Aug 1624 (R&S p25) (SHOS vol 1 pp47,421,430) (TGT p12). On the second occasion with his son, Prince Charles (who stayed at the Moat House). Another account says it was on James I's first visit to Tamworth that he was accompanied by his son (SHOS vol 1 pp421,430). Sir **Walter Scott** visited the castle in 1828 (TGT p12) and left his signature, scratched onto a piece of glass. This has been removed from its window for safety and is kept somewhere at the castle (VB p31). After his visit Scott wrote his poem 'Marmion;' the hero of which, 'the good Lord Marmion' lives at Tamworth Castle (AA p259) (TGT p12). Tamworth is mentioned in several instances, including

> And there, with herald pomp and state,
> They hailed him Lord of Fontenaye,
> Of Lutterward and Scrivelsbaye,
> Of Tamworth tower and town;
> And he, their courtesy to requite,
> Gave them a chain of twelve marks weight
> All as he lighted down.

In the same poem, Scott makes King James of Scotland suggest that:

> ....if within Tantallon strong
> The good Lord Marmion tarries long
> Perchance our meeting next may fall,
> At Tamworth, in his castle hall.

(VB p31). (TGT p12). (SOSH p112) (STMSM May 1973 p25).

Tamworth Collegiate Church The collegiate church at Tamworth is said to have been founded out of a nunnery or convent at Tamworth, thought by various writers (including Leland and Tanner) since the C16 to have been founded by St Edith in her widowhood (LGS pp226-227) (VCH vol 3 pp309-315) (SSAHST 1985-6 p36), or by Lady Wulfrun (or Wulfruna), of Wolverhampton, the mother of Wulfric Spot, whose will reputedly mentions a religious community at Tamworth in Anglo-Saxon times; it has been suggested Wulfrun was buried in the nunnery (SHC 1916 pp10,15,40) (HOWM p4). There is no conclusive evidence that there ever was a nunnery or convent at Tamworth, nor that one was founded by Edith (W p617) (SSAHST 1985-6 p36). Some say King Edgar founded Tamworth Collegiate Church in c963, when he refounded the church after being devastated by the Danes (HATC p46), whilst others say William I founded it, and others that the Marmions founded it in the C12 and C13 (LI vol 2 p104) (VCH vol 3 p309 note). It was

not a royal free chapel until the C14 (SL p52). The college consisted of six prebendaries. The customs of the college were to publicly declare the Assize of Bread in the church on Relic Sunday, when the High Bailiffs and Serjeants at Mace attended in 'great procession,' to hold mystery plays on Corpus Christi day, and to, perhaps, hold a service from the battlements of the church tower on May morning similar to the one still held on Magdalen Tower, Oxford (HS p174). Bishop Langton visited the college on Jan 13 1319, and stayed the night at Tamworth (SSE 1994 p2). A transcript of a supplementary set of statutes for the college promulgated by Dean John Bate in Sept 1442 survive. The originals are lost. In it the dean cites earlier Tamworth statutes. No medieval statutes survive from the other Staffs collegiate churches (SSAHST 1968 pp55-62). The college was dissolved in 1548 (VCH vol 3 pp309-325). See also the Deanery, Tamworth.

Tamworth Gate Gate to Fisherwick Park. It stood on the site of the present Copes Lodge, 0.75m ESE of Fisherwick Hall Farm (VCH vol 14 p245).

Tamworth Gate One of the five gates in Lichfield Town Ditch. Erected by Bishop Roger de Clinton (1129-1148). Is recorded in c1200 (VCH vol 14 p40). It was situated at the junction of Tamworth Street and George Lane. The gate, also known as Tamworth Bar, had a bar which remained until the end of the C18 (LAL p52). The gate was probably of wood (VCH vol 14 p40).

Tanhouse The farm of this name which stood in Hamstead Road, Hamstead, may have been in existence as Taners in 1775 and as Tanhouse in 1794. Gives its name to Tanhouse School (MNB pp62,67,68) and the Tanhouse housing estate; the church, St Bernard, there at the junction of Broome Avenue and Greenfield Road, opened in 1961 (VCH vol 17 p60).

Tan House Meadow An island in the Tern, immediately S of Market Drayton churchyard, adjudged to be in Staffs in 1885 after a long dispute as to which county (Shrops or Staffs) it lay in. So called after its proximity to the Drayton tanyard. A bridge carrying the Newport road crosses over it (SHC 1945/ 6 p4).

Tansey Green Former hamlet now a suburb 1m E of Kingswinford church. Formerly in Kingswinford ancient parish. The name appears in the 1851 census. Here is Tansey Green House.

Tansley Hill An outlier hill of Barrow Hill on the W side, Kingswinford ancient parish.

Tantany Became a ward of West Bromwich borough in 1918 (VCH vol 17 p46). Tantany Lane is W of All Saints Way and N of The Expressway.

Tappeley A carucate of land in Bagot's Bromley manor. Mentioned in 1198 and 1432. Obsolete by 1908 (SHC 1908 p15 note).

Tar Hill Hill 0.25m SSE of Brocton. On NW edge of Cannock Chase. The name may be a corruption of tor 'rocky hill' (SPNO p34). Or may be derived from the days when burning tar was used to appease the Beltaine god; at the foot of the hill is a spring known as Oldacre Burn (SMM p174).

Tatenhill Ancient parish and former township. The village of Tatenhill nestles in a narrow dale (HOPT vol 1 p134) in the steep escarpment leading up to the Needwood Forest plateau 17.75m E of Stafford.
EARLY. The enclosure 350 yards N of Tivey's House at SK 202207, 0.75m SSW of Tatenhill is a listed monument. Tatenhill has been identified with the Roman settlement of Ad Trivonam (see). A Roman ornament and possible road remains were discovered to the E of Tatenhill church in 1819 (BTIH p10). Some Roman pottery has been found at Tatenhill (GNHS p70). A hoard of Roman coins has been found at Tatenhill. The hoard consisted of 30 coins dating from BC 29 to AD 96 (VCH vol 1 p185).
900 to PRESENT. Has appeared as Tatenhyll in a charter of 942 which grants it as one of a block of estates to a thegn (SSE 1991 pp7,8. 1996 p18), and as Tattenhul (1251) (SPN p125). The **name** is from an Anglo-Saxon female called Tate, so 'Tate's hill.' Tat means 'joyous, cheerful' (DUIGNAN). Or means 'the hill of the spies' (HOPT vol 1 p137). Perhaps has associations with the Saxon deity Toutates, or thought, Sir Oswald Moseley, Tuisto or Tiw (NSFCT 1908 p111). Gelling thinks 'Tata's hill' (NSJFS 1981 p3) (SPN p125). The parish **church**, St Michael and All Angels, on the E side of Main Street in the village centre, was built by 1296 (HOPT vol 1 p17), but was mainly rebuilt in the C15 (LDD). Commander Wedgwood could not decide whether it was an original **parish** from which Burton upon Trent broke away or that Burton was the original parish from which Tatenhill broke away (SHC 1916 p197). The ancient parish formerly included the chapelries of Barton-under-Needwood, and Wychnor, and the township of Dunstall (GLAUE p425) and the manors of Barton, Wychnor, Dunstall, Newbold, Birdshall and Tatenhill, and the Rectory Manor of Tatenhill, all of which, except for Wychnor, were subordinate to the manor of Barton (HOPT vol 1 pp5,13). **Manorial tenure service**. Sir Philippe Somerville held of the Earl of Lancaster this manor and that of Draycott-in-the-Clay on condition he went to Tutbury Castle on St

Peters Day (Aug 1 or Lammas) to hunt geese for which he was provided with a horse, saddle, and one hound. From St Peters Day to Holy Rood Day (Sept 14) he went (with the earl's steward?) hunting for all the geese he could find on the earl's land with the assistance of all the foresters and small tenants. On his return he had to dine with the steward and then return the horse and hound and saddle and depart kissing the porter (SD p62) (SMC p123) (Baronage vol 2 p108) (GNHS p148) (HOA pp31,32). On the E side of Postern Road, 40 metres N of the Old Rectory, is a **dovecote** (DoE II). Tatenhill **Airfield**, 3m WNW of Tatenhill at Crossplain, was built by the RAF in 1941 and was operational between 1942-45. The B5234 road was closed from the New Inn until being re-opened in the 1950s (WMA vol 2 p242) (ESNF p25p). **Natural history**. In the later C17 Plot noted a sulphur well on the main road near the pound, which in summer time lays down a sediment of many colours, and gives off a stinking smell (NHS p104) (SD p47) (SJC p10). This could be a completely different well to the one that has now a stone covering. Plot also noted an echo near the church, which he called the Nymph Echo (NHS p28) (SD p47) (SHOS vol 1 p109) (HOPT vol 1 p9) (SCA p131). Cox noted a storm of large hail stones here (SD p47). For a **rhyme** about Tatenhill see Barton-under-Needwood. **Natives and visitors**. **Bishop Langton** stayed the night of Jan 16 1319 at Tatenhill (SSE 1994 p4). This verse in Latin appears on the monument of **Thomas Leeson** (d1539), parson of Packington, Leics, at Packington, Leics:

> Tatenhill my birthplace,
> Ashby was my nurse,
> Packington my sepulchre,
> So on from better to worse.

(SOS) (HOPT vol 1 p108).

Tatenhill Common Hamlet above the brook that runs through Tatenhill, in Needwood Forest, 0.25m W of Tatenhill. There was common land of Tatenhill ancient parish here (HOPT vol 1 p135). Here, the grass, Plot noted in the later C17, turned cattles' coats a different colour, perhaps, owing to the salt wells hereabouts (NHS p111). At SK 192224 on S side of Tatenhill Lane was a windmill, recorded in documents between 1842-1861, but not marked on any of the early maps (WBJ p38).

Taylors Green Over 0.5m NW of Longsdon. Formerly in Longsdon township in Leek ancient parish. The name occurs in 1482 (VCH vol 7 p203). Hugh Bourne registered a house at Taylors Green for Protestant Dissenters in 1815 (SHC 1960 p36) (VCH vol 7 p 209). Appears as Tailors Green on 1834 OS map.

Taylor's Low Burial mound near Wetton. Excavated by Bateman in 1845, but was previously disturbed. A crouched female skeleton was found in a stone cist and in a large rock-cut grave two more skeletons (VAD p66) (Barrow digging by a Barrow-Knight. Rev S Isaacson. 1845. Frontispiece) (NSJFS 1965 pp56-57).

Tean Former division in Checkley ancient parish. See Lower Tean and Upper Tean.

Tean, River Rises N of Little Abovepark. Passes by Parkhall. At Mobberley the river is joined by Cecilly Brook. Some say Cecilly Brook is one of two head waters of the Tean and both are called Tean Brook. The Tean starts with their confluence (NSFCT 1948 p123) (VB p174). Has appeared as Tene (1389. 1686), Teine (1577), Tayne (Saxton's map), Tayne (c1600), Taine (1613), and Teane (Speed's map) (SPNO p21). The name is from the Welsh 'tain,' 'taen,' 'tan,' Irish 'tain' meaning a spread or expanse (of water) (DUIGNAN). From the Goidelic 'tain', water (NSFCT 1908 p127). The word appears to relate to Welsh 'taen' 'a sprinkling' and may mean in this sense simply 'the river or stream' (SPNO p21) (SPN p126). Some have said the name is from the taken or ta'en (ie: defeat) received by the losers in a battle reputedly fought (between Danes and Saxons) at Deadman's Green (see) which lies by the Tean (HOC p188). Gives name to Teanford, Upper and Lower Tean. Joins the Dove at Dove Bridge. Length 11.5m or 15m (Survey Gazetteer of the British Isles John Bartholomew 9th ed post 1951). In the Tean Brook in the later C17 Plot found a red sort of magnetic graphite which he thought was an iron ore called Haematities (NHS p164).

Tean Hall Upper Tean. Timber-framed house of 1613 (BOE p280). In the early C18 a brick house was added on to the E end (IAS p60) (SGS pp168,169p) (MR p324p). In 1747 Messrs John and Nathaniel Philips set up a tape mill in it; one of the earliest in the country. The hall later became the Manager's House of the mill.

Teanford Hamlet on a steep bank above the Tean 0.5m NNW of Upper Tean. Partly in Checkley and Cheadle parishes. Has also appeared as Tenford.

Tean Leys House 1.5m NW of Church Leigh. The house Far Teanleys is 0.25m

to the SW.

Teddesley Hall Built near the site of Tedgley Lodge (see) at SJ 951156, just under 1.5m SSW of Bednall. Tedgley Lodge may have been the lodge for Teddesley Hay and that estate had come to the Littletons of Pillaton by 1610. Soon after 1742 and by 1754 Sir Edward Littleton (d1812), 4th baronet, built Teddesley Hall, for his own occupation, preferring not to live at Pillaton Hall. The hall was designed by Charles Cope Trubshaw. There were plans to extend the hall in 1814 (VCH vol 5 p of facing p179, pp183,184) (BERK2 pp107p,109). According to tradition Sir Edward Littleton used the treasure found at Pillaton Hall between 1742 and 1749 to finance the original building (HOP p63) (SHC 1927 pp34-36) (VCH vol 5 p183). (SHOS vol 2 pl) (SOP p100p of the hall) (W p481) (IHB p396; the hall was built in 1820). The Teddesley (or called Penkridge or Cannock) Troop of Staffordshire Yeomanry was raised by Mr Littleton in 1803 (FSP p63) (info Yeomanry Museum). When Sir Edward Littleton died childless in 1812 the baronetcy expired. The estate then passed to his grand nephew Edward John Walhouse (b1791) of Hatherton Hall (see), who took the name of Littleton and took up residence at Teddesley Hall with his wife Hyacinthe Wellesley, daughter of the Marquis of Wellesley, the eldest brother of the Duke of Wellington (CCBO p74). He was created a baron in 1835, becoming the 1st Baron Hatherton (Burke's Peerage 1879). During his occupancy many notable guests stayed here. The Duke of Wellington was a frequent visitor. He stayed when receiving the Freedom of Stafford in Nov 1821. He visited the house again, with Sir Robert Peel and Croker, Secretary to the Admiralty ('Coningsby' in Disraeli's novel) on Dec 8 1825. William Huskisson stayed the night prior to his fatal accident at the opening of the Liverpool and Manchester Railway. Lady Wilmot, described by Byron as the lady 'who walks in beauty like the night', was a visitor (CCBO pp75,76). Thomas Babington Macaulay (1800-1859), essayist and historian, was a visitor (CCF pp53-57). Anna Jameson, noted art critic before John Ruskin, was another visitor, as was Mary Russell Mitford of our 'Our Village'; she had won £200,000 in a lottery aged 10 choosing the number 2224 which computed to her age. Dr Buckland, the geologist Dean of Westminster, John Peter Labouchere, father of the editor of 'Truth,' Lord Redesdale, Speaker of the House of Commons, were all visitors as was Charles Greville, the famous diarist, in Sept 1843 (CCF pp147-149). At one time the chalice found at Pillaton Hall stood on the mantelpiece in the study of Teddesley Hall. The 1st Baron Hatherton had it placed in a cabinet with the paten. On the cabinet door was a silver plate with an inscription written specially by Cardinal Wiseman (CCBO p53). After the death of the 3rd Baron Hatherton in 1930 the Littletons left the hall for Hatherton Hall (see) (SOP p186) (PVH p6) (BERK2 p112). The chalice and paten were on public show at the hall in May 1932 (ES April 22 1932 p9p). During WW2 the hall was requisitioned for troops and POWs, it then stood empty until it was demolished 1954. The service and stable block was retained (VCH vol 5 p184) (PVH p32). A Snetzler organ from the hall went to the church of St Andrew-by-the-Wardrobe in the city of London (SGS p134) (MR p255). By early Jan 2000 there were plans to build a 79-bedroom hotel and conference centre on or near the site of the hall (SN Jan 13 2000 p21).

Teddesley Hay Former estate which became a hay, or division of Cannock Forest (DUIGNAN), 2m ENE of Penkridge. The hay was in existence probably by Henry I's reign and is mentioned by name in 1235 (VCH vol 2 p338. vol 5 pp75-76,119,183) and or in 1236 as haya de Teddesl, and as the kings haye of Teddesleye in 1461 (SPNO p120) (SSE 1996 p18). Other forms between 1236 and 1275 are: Teddesly, Tudeslegh, Teddesleg, Teddesleg Hay, Tedeslegh and Tidesleye (SPN p126). The name means 'Theodric's or Tedric's lea' (DUIGNAN). Or 'Tydi's leah (woodland glade)' (SPN p126) (SSE 1996 p18) (SPNO p120). In 1300 the hay boundary on the W side was the Penk. The N boundary was formed by the 'Springewell' Brook as far as 'Springewall.' The S boundary is along the Huntington boundary. The E boundary follows the road that is now the A34 (BERK2 p103). Lordship of the manor of Huntington, or just a property owner in Huntington, anciently entailed the condition that the lord, or property owner, look after Teddesley Hay in Cannock Forest for the king. (M.S. Mus. Brit. temp. Hen. 7) (SMC p122). The bailiff of the hay had his seat at Pillaton Hall (SSAHST 1982-3 p45). Leland, in c1535, mentioned the hay. It ceased being a hay in 1550 when the Crown granted it to John Dudley, Earl of Warwick. It subsequently passed into and descended with the Littleton family (VCH vol 5 p183), who started extensive enclosing of the hay from the second half of the C16 (BERK2 pp103,105). The hay was enclosed in 1814 or and in 1827 the area to the W of Blake Street was enclosed (PCC p16) (MH 1994 p111). Although Teddesley was part of the parish of Penkridge for the purpose of tithes in 1252 the only other record shows it was extra-parochial liberty to Bednall and Acton Trussell in 1817 (W p468) (BERK2 p103). It became a separate civil parish in 1858

(GLAUE p425).

Teddesley Head Bednall. The maps of Plot and Bowen mark this hill to the E of Teddesley Park. Could be former Warren Hill (see).

Teddesley House Lichfield Street, Walsall. The Council House was built on the site in 1902-5 (VCH vol 17 p151).

Teddesley Park Former deer park in Teddesley Hay (EDP p179), later the park of Teddesley Hall. Formerly stretched up to the A34. A Roman short dagger was found in King Dick's Encampment (see) in the park in 1780. Lord Hatherton told NSFC excursionists that many of the oaks of the park were planted in King John's reign (NSFCT 1926 p151). A park in Teddesley Hay is mentioned in 1589 (VCH vol 5 p183). There is a C18 conical ice-house at SK 948158 for the hall beneath an earthen mound five yards N of the stable block (DoE II), 25 yards from the site of the hall. Built in 1820 (IHB p396). Home Farm to the NE of the hall was built in 1767. In 1820 an over-shot water mill with a wheel of 29 feet in diameter, which drove a stationary threshing machine, was built within the farm complex. This particular type of mill was thought to be the first of its kind in the Midlands; but the Ansons at Shugborough claimed they had the first at their White Barn Farm. In 1838 Lord Hatherton replaced the wooden wheel with an iron one 38 feet diameter by two feet eight inches wide, with 13 arms with a brace between each; the whole wheel was below ground level (IAS p200). It was claimed this wheel was the largest in the country. It ran until 1942 before it was replaced (BERK2 p105). Foot-and-mouth disease broke out in Dec 1967 at Teddesley Home Farm (SN Dec 29 1967 p13). In the 1840s Lord Hatherton claimed his rickyard was the largest in the country (BERK2 p106). An airfield at SJ 960150 was operational in Teddesley Park 1942-45 (WMA vol 2 p244) (SHJ autumn 1989 p64).

Tedgley Lodge Moated medieval house which may have been the lodge of Teddesley Hay. It stood about 200 yards NW of Teddesley Hall. By 1650 the house on this site was known as Tedgley Lodge and was occupied by Fisher Littleton a kinsman of Sir Edward Littleton of Pillaton Hall. The moat was mentioned in 1754 but had been obliterated by the 1950s (VCH vol 5 p183) (SSAHST 1982-3 p48) (BERK2 p107).

Tene Brook Flows in the Warstones area westwards towards the Smestow (PONP p45). The name, which does appear on any OS maps, is debatable. In the 1647 Manorial Survey of Penn there are references to 'Tynn Meadow' which abuts this brook in Upper Penn. TR Bennett in IP proposed that this brook was formerly known as the Tynn or Tene (IP) (ALP p3).

Tennal Hall Half-timbered building of the C14 (HOHE p34) or of the Elizabethan period (OHOPP p24p of c1910) nearly 1m NW of Harborne. Elizabeth I is reputed to have stayed here in 1575 (HOHE p34) (OHOPP p24), and the wife of Charles I is reputed to have stayed here (HOPP pl 38). In the 1750s it was the home of farmer Job Freeth, said to be Harborne's biggest man at 40 stone (OHOPP p24). The hall was demolished in 1937 (HOHE p34). The name is preserved in Tennal Approved Boys School. In the later C17 by the wayside near the hall Plot found a red sort of earth, which discoloured hands and strongly adheres if put to the tongue (NHS p124). David Cox, artist, painted a picture of a lane near the hall (HOHH p2).

Ten Row and Seven Row A row of ten terrace cottages behind a row of seven terrace cottages, although one has been added to make eight, Penkhull New Road, Penkhull. They were built by Josiah Spode after 1812 (PRA pp80p,81p). (VCH vol 8 p184).

Tenter Banks Street running from Broadeye on W side of Stafford. The name, which has also appeared as Tenterbanks, is from the process of stretching cloth carried on here as part of the cloth and cap industry of Stafford (SIOT p78), or from the tinting or dyeing of cloth for the same industry; the phrase 'Tainter Bank Walk' is mentioned in an old deed (1688) (OSST 1930 p28. 1933 p38).

Tenterhill Minute hamlet in a narrow tiny dale near the upper Dove 1m WNW of Hollinsclough. The name is used for the hill between the Dove and Golling Gate in 1775. The name suggests that cloth working may have been carried on here (VCH vol 7 p38).

Tern, River Tributary of the Severn, which it joins at Attingham, Shrops. Rises out of Maer Pool, Maer. Has appeared as Tirn (1228), Terne (1232-1686), Tirne (1316. 1360), Teryn (1439), and Tyren (1477) (SPNO p21) (SPN p126). The name is from perhaps the Welsh 'ter' clear, pure, the 'n' is excrescent (DUIGNAN). Or is perhaps a corruption of the root 'dor' the Welsh 'dwr' (NSFCT 1908 p126). Is from a word related to Welsh 'tren' meaning 'strong' or 'forcible' (SPNO p21) (SPN p126) (SSE 1996 p18). The first three miles has been straightened and deepened to be used as a drain (MR p224). A ten foot long canoe was found in the Tern in Oakley Park at SJ 703375 in 1922 which went to Birmingham Museum (LGS p190) (NSFCT vol 45 p157. 1926 p141. 1943 p73) (Staffs Weekly Sentinel Oct 23 1926) (Shrops Arch Soc

Trans series 4 vol 11 p131) (BAST vol 77 p1) (NSJFS 1964 p30). It is probably prehistoric; Raven says of Iron Age origin (MR p236). Others say the canoe, a dug-out one, was found during the summer of 1926 (OSST 1956-59 p39). By the late 1990s archaeologists believed the canoe to be in fact a water trough (info Debbie Ford, Potteries Museum). W of Willoughbridge Wells the Tern forms the county boundary and continues to until it leaves the county W of Salisbury Hill (now in Shrops), except for a 0.5m stretch where Staffs protrudes into Shrops to include Knighton. (GNHS p23). The first part of the name is preserved in Terley or Tyrley Castle (DUIGNAN).

Terrace, The House to the E of Oaken hamlet. Built in the early C19 for Henry Wood, a Wolverhampton distiller. In 1983 the house was owned by the National Coal Board (VCH vol 20 p79).

Terrace, The Mansion off Dandy's Walk on the N side at the N end of Birmingham Road (formerly King Street), Walsall. Built by John Forster by 1834. White called this area Wood End (W p428. 1834 ed). The house was sold to the trustees of the Blue Coat school in 1931 (VCH vol 17 pp154,227 il facing p176).

Tettenhall Ancient parish and large village on the slope of an abrupt hill, rising above Smestow Valley (HOPTT p1), 15m SSW of Stafford. Has been, for about the past 200 years, a prosperous suburb of Wolverhampton, 1.75m to the SE of Wolverhampton. Tettenhall ancient parish was partly in the south and north divisions of Seisdon hundred until 1845 when the whole parish was transferred to the northern division (GLAUE p425) (VCH vol 20 p1).

EARLY. In the later C17 Plot noted springs which rise within three yards of each other on the hill above the church and wells 20 yards below, near the church, all of which were 20 to 30 yards deep (NHS p86). The last Ice Age reached its maximum southern extent about Wolverhampton and glacial boulders lie about Tettenhall (WJO Nov 1909 p293). North of Wergs Road in the open field called Low field Shaw noted a burial mound (SHOS vol 2 p194) (VCH vol 20 p3); Gunstone could not locate it (NSJFS 1965 p49).

BATTLE OF TETTENHALL. According to the Anglo-Saxon Chronicle, and Asser, a battle took place at Tettenhall in 910 on the eighth of the Ides of August in which the Danes failed in their attempt to invade Saxon England and were defeated under Edward the Elder (SMC p163) (S&W p389). According to Lappenberg this battle had the important consequence of freeing England from Danish attacks (HOWW p30), and it started the process by which the Danes were pushed eastwards (VCH vol 20 p5). Some claim, including Aethelweard, a C10 western earl, who said in his 'Chronicles' the battle took place on Aug 5 910, that it occurred at Wednesfield (DUIGNAN p169) (WFW p5) (MR p325). Various dates and locations have been given for the battle: According to Rogeri de Hoveden 'Analium Parte Priori' it occurred in 907; according to Simeon Dunelmensis, John Brompton and Florentius Wigorn it occurred in 911 (NHS p415); Leland in one volume says that it took place in 907, and in another in 933 (SMC p163). Plot says there were two battles in 910; the first at Tettenhall the second at Wednesfield (NHS p415). Willmore says a battle took place at Tettenhall in 910 and another battle took place at Wednesfield in 911 (HOWW p29). Jones thought one battle took place, and it started at Wednesfield and ended with the Danes retreating and taking up a position at Tettenhall, three miles away (HOPTT p9). Mander and Tildesley in HOWM are alleged to have suggested that the battle may have taken place at Wolverhampton before it became a settlement (A little bit of Heath Town. Stephen J Beardsmore. 1989. p6). Greenslade and Stuart said it could have happened at either Tettenhall or Wednesfield (HOS p16). Smallshire thought the battle took place to and fro between Tettenhall and Wednesfield, but perhaps the main battle took place on the heath between Stowheath and Old Fallings (WFW p23). Others have thought it took place in the Wombourne Common area. Another alleged site is the Danes Court (see) area. According to tradition prior to the battle the Danes left their stronghold in Stafford and made a raid following the Roman road through Brewood, Chesterton Walls and Bridgnorth, but were brought to battle at Danes Court (St Michael and All Angels, Penkridge: Royal Collegiate Parish Church. R Cheadle. p3; returning to Stafford after the battle a skirmish occurred between Saxons and retreating Danes at Bull Bridge near Penkridge). In the main battle three Northumbrian (or Danish) kings were killed (MR p325). The Anglo-Saxon Chronicle lists these as slain: King Ecwilf (a Dane), King Healfden (a Dane), Earl Ohter, Earl Scurfa, Othulf, Benesing, Anlaf the Black, Thurferth, Osferth, Guthferth, and Agmund (HOPTT p9). The burial of the dead of these battles, if two, have been mixed up, and it cannot be decided which burial mounds belong to which. Broughton says the dead were buried in two mounds at Wednesfield. He noted the one in Southlow Field remained whilst the one in Northlow Field had been flattened (SMC p163). White says the dead were buried under a mound in Lowhill Field (W p205). Masefield says some burial mounds in the fields below Tettenhall Wood are probably where some of the slain were buried (LGS pp26,232). Jones says a burial mound at Wightwick probably contains many of those killed in the battle (HOPTT p10). Soldiers' Hill burial mound at Wombourne is alleged to contain dead from this battle. Smallshire says the dead were buried in mounds at Southlow Field (Mill Hill, Nechells Lane), Northlow Field (Nordley Hill), Stowmans Hill (near Moseley Hole), Rumblelows (now Thromblelowe), Ablow (Wolverhampton), Low Hill, and Horseley Fields also Horselow Field in Wednesfield, and 'The Low' a field name near to the early nucleus of Heath Town (WFW p23). (SHOS vol 2 pp150,194) (SSC p136 in the intro) (GNHS p73) (VCH vol 1 p219. vol 20 p3) (WJO Sept 1904 p240; it occurred at Tettenhall in 911) (KNS p107) (KES p205) (TOS p80) (AOW p8) (Anglo-Saxon England. FM Stenton. 1971) (SH p1).

900 to 1750. According to ancient local tradition a **church** at Tettenhall was founded to celebrate the Saxon victory over the Danes at the battle of Tettenhall in 910. No evidence of a Saxon church survives except for an ancient yew tree in the churchyard (Collegiate Church, Tettenhall. 1989). The church of the former Tettenhall Collegiate Church, which became the parish church, had late C12 parts. That church, St Michael and All Angels, was gutted by fire on the night of Feb 2 1950 and rebuilt in 1955 (VCH vol 20 p41). The **wake** was on the first Sunday and Monday after old Michaelmas day (W pp74,205). With the passing of the Town Act of 1777 bull baiting moved out of central Wolverhampton to occur at Tettenhall wakes and other places (HOWM p164). The wake continued to be held in the 1860s (VCH vol 20 p14). The DB **manor** of Totehala (Tettenhall), then held by the king, appears to be the later Tettenhall Regis manor, whilst the DB manor of Totenhale (Tettenhall) appears to be the later Tettenhall Clericorum manor (VCH vol 4 pp38,45. vol 20 pp18,15). The prefix in the **name** is from the personal name Tota, Teota, Teotta, so: Tota's hall (LGS p238), or Teota's valley (English Place Names. Ekwall) (VCH vol 20 p7), or Teota's nook (NSJFS 1981 p3), or Teota's corner of land (SPN p144). The prefix could be from the Anglo-Saxon verb 'totian' or Middle English 'toten,' to project, stick out, so the 'look-out place by the meadow-land' with particular reference to being a reconnaissance place for Tettenhall battle in 910 or a common observation post in time of war. Prof Skeat thought the 'hall or dwelling on a look-out hill' if the terminal 'heall,' hall, is to be considered (HOPTT p8) (DUIGNAN). Camden says it was called Theotenhall ie; the house of the Pagans or of the Danes (SHOS vol 2 p194) (S&W p354). Dr Oliver thought it the 'hall of the sun;' Tetan being another name for that luminary. However, Hackwood says, Oliver ignores the possibility of a terminal in the form of 'heale,' a meadow land, or of heath, so the 'enclosed land on a river-side' (SR p5). Tettenhall parish was a peculiar jurisdiction of Tettenhall Collegiate Church until peculiar jurisdictions were abolished in 1846 (VCH vol 3 p93). The **medieval village** was extensive, being centred on two greens (Upper and Lower Greens) bisected by a sandstone ridge (Tettenhall Village Trail. History Dept, Regis School, Tettenhall). Lower Green nearer the Smestow is probably the older settlement of the two (VCH vol 20 p7). (Staffs County Handbook. c1958. p140). For **windmills** in Tettenhall parish see Aldersley, Pendeford, Tettenhall Wood, and Wightwick.

1750 to PRESENT. By the later C18 Tettenhall's rural charm was attracting excursionists from industrial Wolverhampton, and that town's wealthy as a place of residence; the wealthy of Wolverhampton appear to have been sending their children to Tettenhall to be nursed in the 1750s and 1760s. In 1816 Thomas Telford improved the steep, crooked and narrow road between the two greens for the London to Holyhead mail coach route. In 1798 an **Association of Volunteer Cavalry** was formed at Tettenhall under the title of 'Loyal Volunteer Cavalry' but disbanded in the early C19 (HOPTT p286). On May 22 1860 the first **Rifle Volunteer Company** was formed at Tettenhall, and was named the 30th Staffordshire Rifle Volunteer Corps (HOPTT p286). **WW2**. Tettenhall suffered from four air raids in 1941; two civilians were killed and 208 houses damaged (PPTP p26). In 1946 36 prefabricated bungalows were built in Henwood Road (VCH vol 20 p38). Most of those surviving in the early 1990s were encased in brick by 1996. Apparently the occupants refused the authority's request for their demolition: Some of the houses have been left in their original state (TPOP p79p). The Wolverhampton & Kingswinford **Railway**, opened in 1925, passed through Tettenhall; it closed to passengers in 1932 (NSJFS 1964 p79) and to goods in 1964 (VCH vol 20 p14). For the clock tower at Upper Green see Upper Green. The **arms** of Tettenhall urban district (VCH vol 20; formed 1894, abolished 1966), granted in 1938, are: Vert, a chevron engrailed between three uprooted oak-trees all gold, and on the chevron three roundels barry wavy argent and azure. The crest is - On a wreath gold and vert, a silver windmill on a green in front of it two battle-axes crossed saltire wise gules. The motto is: 'Respice, aspice, prospice' (Look to the past, the present, and the future). Scott-Giles notes

that the axes refer to the battle of Tettenhall in 910 (CH pp339,340il). A **Swiss chalet** from the 1902 exhibition at West Park, Wolverhampton, was removed after the closure of the exhibition to opposite the Dog and Gun Inn, Tettenhall. Here it was utilised as a shelter for passengers at the old tram terminus. It was demolished in the early 1970s (WMAG Nov 1969 p11p) (TCOP p23p) (Wolverhampton Chronicle Oct 18 1996 p22p). **Supernatural**. Beacon/ WABC Radio Station, situated in a former orphanage in Tettenhall, is said to be haunted. The vision of a little girl sitting by a fireside has been in the area which used to be the chapel of the orphanage (GPCE p61). A very large old house in Wrottesley Road is said to be haunted by the smoky outline of the head and shoulders of an elderly lady who would peer from one of the windows (GPCE p62). **Natives and residents**. In 1791 **William Pitt** (1749-1823), native of Tettenhall and author of THS and AOS, noted Tettenhall contained 'many pleasant houses and genteel families' (PSS p468) (VCH vol 20 p3) (VFC p106). For novelist **Ellen Thorneycroft Fowler** see Woodthorne. For **R Lewis Wright** (d1985), poet and novelist, born Tettenhall in 1889 see Nags Hill, Burntwood. Joyce Coombes (pseudonym of **Joyce Hales**), novelist, was born in Tettenhall in 1906. Her work includes 'George and Mary Sumner, Their Life and Times' (1965), 'Judgement on Hatcham' (1969), and 'One Hundred Years on the Hill' (1970) (VFC p30). **Rachel Heyhoe-Flint**, champion and leading exponent of women's cricket, was living in Tettenhall in 1991 (BCTV p64).

TETTENHALL PEAR. The Tettenhall Pear, or called Tettenhall Dick, is a wild cooking pear peculiar to Tettenhall and its adjacent parishes. The variety had originated by the C15. It is a small fruit, of between 30 to 45 millimetres in breadth, but grows on a large tree, some being 50 or 60 feet in height. It is golden yellow with russet dots; occasionally there is a patch of green. According to Dunphy the fruit is plentiful but lacking in taste, however, Shaw in the late C18, thought it well flavoured. According to him it baked and boiled well, but did not keep long; there were many hundreds of the trees growing in Tettenhall parish in the late C18, but rarely elsewhere. This particular pear tree may be the pear tree used as the device in the Perton family arms; the Pertons held Perton, 2.5m WSW of Tettenhall, from Henry III's reign to Henry V's. The fruit was noted in the Gardeners' Chronicle in 1841 and it is listed in 1862 as one of the fruits in the Royal Horticultural Society's garden at Chiswick (SHOS vol 2 p199) (AOS p89) (GNHS p178) (Proceedings of the Royal Horticultural Society 1862) (POAP p67) (PPTP p84). According to Bryan Fowler, in the later C20, there were upwards of 70 Tettenhall Pear trees within a 10 mile radius of Tettenhall. Some are at Pear Tree Farm (Penn Common), Straits Green, Lower Gornal, and at Lower Penn (at Pear Tree Farm and Orchard Farm) (POAP p67, il on p68) (PPTP p84) and at Saxonfields (Wolverhampton Chronicle March 18 1999 p3). In 1996 there was another in the orchard in the grounds of Wightwick Hall (CL Aug 15 1996 p46). In 1999 a horticultural company called Bees and Trees based at Leintwardine, Heres, were trying to re-establish the variety. It was then planned that 2000 Tettenhall Pear trees be planted in the Black Country (BBC Midlands Today. Oct 6 1999).

TETTENHALL AND LITERATURE. Dickens in 'Old Curiosity Shop' gives a melodramatic description of the journey Little Nell and her grandfather make through the Tettenhall area on their way to Tong, Shrops (WMAG Oct 1963 p35. April 1964 p42). Tettenhall is Tetleigh in the novel 'Fuel of Fire' (1902) by Ellen Thorneycroft Fowler of Woodthorne (see); the novel is set in Tettenhall (VCH vol 20 p5). For the poem 'Tettenhall' by Marjorie Crosbie of Penn Fields (see) see PSS p437. In 1789 Rev William Fernyhough wrote a poem titled 'On the Beautiful Village of Tettenhall, near Wolverhampton.' It ends:

> 'Tettenhall, thy still engaging scenes conspire,
> To wake the sages, and the poet's fire.
> From noisy town, with worldly cares replete,
> To ease the mind, lo ! this the choice retreat.
> Here Hampton's sons in vacant hours repair,
> Taste rural joys, and breathe a purer air.'

(HOPTT p5) (VCH vol 20 p3).

Tettenhall Clericorum Manor forming W side of Tettenhall parish formerly belonging to the dean of Tettenhall Collegiate Church and one which included Bilbrook, Aldersley, Barnhurst and the prebends of Perton-with-Trescott and Wrottesley (W p205) (HOPTT p10). The name Tettenhall Clericorum came into use only in the early C16 (VCH vol 20 p18).

Tettenhall Collegiate Church The collegiate church of Tettenhall was reputedly founded by King Edgar (957-975) (HOPTT p66) (VCH vol 20 pp18,39); some in 1546 and 1548 ascribed the foundation to Edward III. Priests are recorded at Tettenhall in DB (VCH vol 3 pp315,316. vol 20 p39). A dean is first mentioned in c1176 (VCH vol 3 p316). The college was a royal free chapel by 1295 (SL p52). It consisted of five prebends by the mid 1250s; Pendeford, Tettenhall, Perton, Wrottesley, and Codsall. Tettenhall prebend was later known as Tettenhall and Compton; and as Compton in 1373 and in 1401: Bovenhill (or Bovenhull) became the styling of the prebend thereafter (HOPTT p67) (VCH vol 3 p318. vol 20 p19). Dissolved in 1548 (SL p95). Some living in c1800 remembered that some of the collegiate buildings stood to the E of the church (SHOS vol 2 p195) (VCH vol 3 pp315-321). For the seal of the college see SHOS vol 2 pp195,196. (W p205).

Tettenhall Hill It may be the Church Hill of the C18, the hill on which Tettenhall church stands. Mentioned in the late C14 (VCH vol 20 p7).

Tettenhall Regis Manor forming the E side of Tettenhall parish formerly belonging to the king and one which consisted of two detached parts. One extended N from Old Hill and the ridge above Tettenhall church to the later Woodthorne Road South, Keepers Lane at Wergs, the Penk as far E as Dam Mill, the Cronkhall area, and the later Pendeford Avenue. The other extended SW from Lower Green to include Compton, the Finchfield area on the high ground to the S and Wightwick (VCH vol 20 p15). The prebends of Bovenhill and Pendeford were included in this manor: There never was a manor house for this manor (W p205) (HOPTT pp10,13). A building described as the manor house in 1760 was an inn used for meetings of the court (VCH vol 20 p17). The manor has also appeared as King's Tettenhall (VCH vol 20 p15). The name Tettenhall Regis was used for a ward of Wolverhampton borough by 1982, covering the Tettenhall area.

Tettenhall Towers Mansion on E side of Wood Road, Tettenhall, built in the C18 and before 1763 by Thomas Pearson on the site of 'The Holly Bush' Inn (WMAG Aug 1963 p17il) (VCH vol 20 p8). Birthplace of Judge John Pearson in 1771. The house was tenanted by the Corbett family to 1841, and then, for a short time, by W Fleeming Fryer. Col Thomas Thorneycroft (b1822), son of GB Thorneycroft of Tipton (see), occupied the house from 1851 and purchased it in 1854 (BTW pp74-75ps). Col Thorneycroft, who died in 1902 (HOPTT pp269,270 p facing) (TPOP p34p) or on Feb 6 1903 (TB Jan 1986 p14p), was probably the builder of the two polygonal towers which were added in 1866 (BOE p326): A poet, eccentric and great inventor of gadgets, Col Thorneycroft, made a sock and shoe warmer attached to the heating system (TPOP p35p of); installed a telegraphic communication between rooms and signalling equipment in the tower (HOWU p141); built a private theatre in the hall by 1880 (BTW pp74-75ps); and flew over the Towers in a balloon on Sept 11 1882 (WJO March 1903 xi) and wrote a poem about the experience (PSS p472) (VFC p129). His niece, Ellen Thorneycroft Fowler, refers to the Towers in her novel 'Place and Power' as Tetleigh Towers, the country seat of Sir Conrad Clayton (BCM Spring 2000 p47). In 1894 there was kept at the hall a small oak table from Moseley Old Hall, used by Charles II, when concealed there, panelling from Tewkesbury Abbey, and St Peter's Wolverhampton, old suits of armour from Alton Towers, and firedogs used by Elizabeth I (HOPTT p277). The main hall fireplace is reputedly haunted. The ghost may be a maid who had fallen from the upper gallery during the period of Thorneycroft occupation (WMAG Nov 1975 p13). The same or another ghost is that of a lady in grey dressed in the period of the late 1870s (BBC 1 Midlands Today Sept 8 1998). At least four other ghosts are said to haunt the house and grounds, including that of Col Thomas Thorneycroft (E&S Aug 31 1998 p10) (BBC 1 Midlands Today Sept 8 1998). The house is now (1977) part of **Tettenhall College**. A Free Church boys' boarding school, opened as Tettenhall Proprietary School in Aug 1863. The name was changed to Tettenhall College in 1869. The school first occupied the Hall (see), Tettenhall. A school building in the gothic style was built close by in College Road in 1865 (BOE p326) or 1867 (VCH vol 6 pp171-172) to designs by George Bidlake. The Hall then became the headmaster's house. The school purchased Tettenhall Towers in 1943-4. By 1963 the Towers housed seven forms, music rooms, a library and a gym (VCH vol 6 pp171-172). (SGS p187) (BCM spring 1995 p41il). **Alumni**: CE Shaw MP for Stafford; Sir Dr Arthur Harden (1865-1940), scientist who discovered the essential part played by phosphorylation and dephosphorylation in the breakdown of sugar by yeast and in fermentation by other micro-organisms, and who shared the Nobel Peace prize in 1929 (info Angus Dunphy) (National Biography 1901-1970); J Lloyd Morgan MP for Carmarthen; Dr RF Horton MA, late Fellow of New College, Oxford (HOPTT p285); Thomas Pitfield (1903?-) composer, artist taught at the school (BBC Radio 4. Sept 9 1993. 11pm); Prof Peter Radford (b1939), athlete (info Angus Dunphy); David Sumberg (b1941), Conservative MP for Bury South since 1983 (Who's Who 1997). In the grounds Col Thorneycroft built squash courts, a swimming bath and Turkish baths (HOWU p141).

Tettenhall Wightwick Name used for a ward of Wolverhampton borough by 1982, covering the Tettenhall Wood and Wightwick area.

Tettenhall Wood District and former village on the top of a abrupt hill, rising above the Smestow Valley, 1m SW of Tettenhall. In Tettenhall ancient parish. The area, originally known as Kingsley Wood and known as Tettenhall Wood by 1613, was formerly the northern part of a large common stretching from Lower Green, Tettenhall, to Kinver Chase (WJO July 1905 p183) (VCH vol 20 pp8,29). This in turn was a remnant of the ancient Kinver Forest (NSJFS 1968 p47). Petitioning for the enclosure of the common occurred in c1805. By then there was extensive encroachment on the common (there was settlement in The Holloway (see) by 1586) (VCH vol 20 pp3,8). (HOPTT p268). The common was enclosed in 1809 and the present centre of Tettenhall Wood village, at the junction of Mount, Wood, School and Church roads, then developed (VCH vol 20 p8). On the E side of Mill Lane, at SO 873991 0.25m of Tettenhall Wood church, is a windmill. It was first shown on Greenwood's map, and was described as 'Windmill House' on OS map 1886. The tower was probably shortened on its conversion into a residence. The octagonal pyramidal roof was originally of slate but is now of tile (WBJ p38 il xix) (WIS pp13p,22) (VCH vol 20 p34). The church, Christ Church, in Church Road was built in 1865-1866 (BOE p324). Tettenhall Wood became a separate ecclesiastical parish in 1868 (GLAUE p425). AG Matthews (1881-1962), the ecclesiastical historian, was Congregational minister at Tettenhall Wood from 1907 to 1922 (VCH vol 20 p5). Roger Ormerod (born Wolverhampton 1920), author of over 20 crime, mystery and suspense novels between 1972 and 1993, lives in Tettenhall Wood (VFC p100).

Tettenhall Wood House Castellated Gothic villa on N side of Wood Road, near the end of the present Grange Road, Tettenhall Wood. Built by Thomas Rickman in 1835 for Theodosia Hinckes (d1874), traveller and collector and founder of St Mary's church, Wolverhampton. After her death in 1874 the house passed to HT Davenport, Conservative MP for North Staffs (1880-1885) and Leek (1886-1892) who changed his name to Hinckes in 1890. The house was occupied by Samuel Bayliss, a Wolverhampton industrialist, from at least 1900 to 1912. It was occupied by the Hickman family from at least 1915 to 1969. Sometime shortly after 1969 the house was demolished and houses and a school built on the site and former estate of the house. The lodge on Wood Road was still remaining in 1990 (TCOP p48p) (VCH vol 20 p22) (BTW p78).

Thatch Moor Former minute hamlet 1.25m NE of Yoxall, 0.5m S of Yoxall Lodge on Lin Brook. Appears on 1834 OS map and has appeared as Thatchmore. The name is preserved in Thatchmoor Lane (Staffs OS Street Atlas. 1995).

Thatchmoor House 1.5m S of Fradley. In Whittington parish.

Thickbroom Minute hamlet on a bank above Black Brook of about three properties 1.5m ESE of Shenstone. Formerly in Weeford township and ancient parish. Appears in the C13 as Thykebrom (SSE 1996 p18) and has appeared as Thickbroome. So called from the quality of broom formerly growing upon it (SHOS vol 2 p25) (DUIGNAN) (SPN p79). Here was possibly a medieval village, deserted in the C17, and now lost (SSAHST 1970 p36).

Thickbroom Hall Thickbroom. Appears in the Weeford PR 1562. It was then owned and occupied by the Wyatts. John Wyatt I (1675-1742) was described as of Thickbroom. Many of his eight sons became notable, mainly in the fields of invention, building, architecture, and land agency; they themselves headed dynasties with descendents successful in those fields; between 1746 and 1946 the Wyatts produced no fewer than 28 architects, five sculptors and carvers, five painters, a President of the RA, and a President of the Royal Institute of British Architects. John Wyatt I's eldest son, John Wyatt II (1700-1766), 'the inventor,' attended Lichfield Grammar School. He invented mechanical spinning, the level weighing-machine, ball bearings, and a button-making machine. For some of his career he worked for Matthew Boulton at Soho Manufactory. His eldest son, Charles (1750-1819), also worked for Boulton at Soho and was later an architect in London. John II's second son, John III (b1752), also worked for Boulton. His eldest son John Francis (Frank) patented a new type of brick in 1814. John III's second son, Walter Henry (Harry) Wyatt, was an inventor. John I's second son, William, was agent to Lord Uxbridge. John I's third son, Samuel, was a stay-maker in London. John I's fifth son, Benjamin (1709-1772), lived at Blackbrook Farm (see); his descendents were perhaps the most illustrious of all the Wyatt branches. The seventh son, Job, founded a screw factory at Tatenhill. The eighth son was Edward. His grandson was Benjamin Wyatt, the builder, of Sutton Coldfield (1755-1813) (The Wyatts: An Architectural Dynasty. John Martin Robinson. 1979) (A Biographical Dictionary of British Architects 1600-1840. 3rd ed Howard Colvin. 1995).

Thicknall Former minute hamlet, appears to be represented by Thicknall Farm, 1.5m W of Clent, on the border of Broome and Clent parishes in Staffs until

1844, now in Worcs. Has appeared as Thychenaile (1304), Thikenolre (1327), Thicknall (1592. Yates' map), and Thickhall (C & J Greenwood's survey map of Worcs 1822) (SNSV vol 2 p76). Here was Lower Clent Common (alias Clent Heath) (SNSV vol 2 p76).

Thick Withins House 1.25m WSW of Hollinsclough, in Heathylee township in Alstonefield ancient parish. There was a house here by 1406 (VCH vol 7 p33).

Thieves Ditch Ditch behind North Walls, Stafford (SOPP pl 35). A pasture called Thevesdych is recorded in 1399 and 1404 (VCH vol 5 p94) (SPNO p78). (SAIW pl 33p). According to OS map of Stafford 1900 Thieves Ditch runs along the back of the residences in Back Walls North.

Thistleberry Small hamlet over 0.5m WSW of Newcastle-under-Lyme. Now submerged into the suburbs of Newcastle. Between Keele and Newcastle-under-Lyme Dr Plot found Brick-earth (NHS p120).

Thistleberry House House at the junction of Keele Road and Thistleberry Avenue, Newcastle-under-Lyme. Built sometime between 1785 and 1847 by Samuel Mayer. The house stood until c1955 (NSFCT 1979 p35). It was the birthplace of Joseph Mayer (1803-1886) (son of Samuel Mayer), the antiquarian collector, many of his collections went to Liverpool (VCH vol 8 p8). A tower known as **Thistleberry Castle** was erected in the grounds for Mr Mayer's pleasure. An old photograph in c1900 shows an overgrown tower surrounded by a moat approached by a bridge. The tower was pulled down in c1919 and its bricks used to fill in the moat. In 1942 a bomb fell on the site so no traces of the buildings or moat remain (NOPP pl 9 of it c1905) (NSFCT 1979 p35) (NULOP vol 1 p46p).

Thistley Field name in SE area of Stone town between the Trent and the Lichfield road.

Thistley Hough District of W Penkhull now just a road. In 1938 a girl's high school was built here (SHST p386). In 1939 a by-pass was built through here to avoid Newcastle (ES 19 Jan 1939 p7).

Thornberry Hall 1.5m NE of Cheadle. S of Lockwood Hall and near Hales Hall. Seat of William Thornbury (d1689) in 1667 (HAF p128). Was for sale in 1832 (CCT p79). Has also appeared as Thornbury Hall.

Thorncliffe Tiny village in a deep ravine formed by Tittesworth Brook 2m N of Bradnop. Is 1505 feet high (LGS p3). Formerly in a detached portion of Bradnop township in Tittesworth township of Leek ancient parish (W p730). Nearly 0.5m ESE of Thorncliffe at SK 02265837 on the slopes of Morridge is a burial mound 8.5 paces in diameter and two feet high (MOS p267) (NSJFS 1965 p49). Has appeared as Thorntileg (C13) and Thorncliffe (end of the C16) (VCH vol 7 p233). Thorntileg is of Old English origin and means a clearing amid thorn trees. The 'Cliffe' part may be a reference to the deep ravine (VCH vol 7 p233). Or 'Thoni's slope' (PNPD). Thorncliffe was an inhabited area by the 1230s (VCH vol 7 p233). A Master DK 912 force-landed at Thorncliffe on July 1 1943. The pilot, who was alone, survived (MD p55). A P47D Thunderbolt crashed at Easing Lane, Thorncliffe, in WW2. The American pilot was killed (MD p66).

Thorncliff Low Burial mound 0.5m N of Caltonmoor House at SK 11344951, 28 paces in diameter and six feet high. Excavated by Carrington in 1848 and by the Leek and District Field Club in 1959. A rock-cut grave, a male skeleton with a bronze round heeled dagger were found. The later excavation produced nothing (TYD pp118-119) (VCH vol 1 no 8) (DAJ vol 75 p112) (NSJFS 1965 p53).

Thornes Tiny hamlet on high ground overlooking the Chester Road 0.25m S of Stonnall. Former manor in Shenstone parish. At or near Thornes grew a thick wood on a hill which fell down one night in c1718, perhaps blown down by a strong wind, or the trees were up-rooted by an earthquake, since the roots of the thickest and firmest had been strangely torn up and laid on the ground (SHOS vol 2 p54). For Stonnall church at Thornes see Stonnall. The name is of Anglo-Saxon origin and denotes thorny, uncultivated land (SHOS vol 2 p53).

Thornes Hall Thornes, Stonnall. Erected by Thomas de Thornes; it was a mansion of some note in Edward IV's reign. This house was either added to or rebuilt by Robert Jolliffe. In about the later C17 another house was built by the Friths (or Fryths). That house had been reduced in size by the later C18 and was then tenanted (SHOS vol 2 p54).

Thorneyedge House 1m SE of Bagnall. The house has also appeared as Thorney Edge. Thought to have been a property owned by Robert Garner, author of GNHS, from the 1850s (NSFCT 1949 pp24-25).

Thorneyfields In Castle Church parish (SGSAS). Thornyfields Farm is 0.75m S of Castle Church.

Thorney Hills House 3m ENE of Bagot's Bromley, 1.25m S of Marchington Woodlands church.

Thorney Lane Former ancient hamlet near a tiny tributary of Pur Brook 1m

NW of Newborough in Hanbury parish (W p562). Lay to SW of Agardsley Park. Has also appeared as Thorney Lanes, the present name of the lane there (OS Street Atlas Staffs 1995).

Thorneyleigh Minute hamlet at the foot of Gun Hill on the NE side, 1.5m NNW of Meerbrook comprising Thorneyleigh Hall Farm and Thorneyleigh Green Farm. Formerly in Leekfrith township in Leek ancient parish. Appears as Thorneylee on J Cary's map (1805). 'Thorn' represents the shrub hawthorn which grows in abundance here (NSJFS 1977 p36).

Thorneyleigh Hall Thorneyleigh, Meerbrook. Once the seat of the Armetts or Armitts. Has often appeared as Thorneylee Hall (OL vol 1 p212. vol 2 pp86,87). The present C17 house, Thorneyleigh Hall Farm, has inscriptions above the doorways reading 'WA.IC. 1691' 'A.GC.IC. 1670' (HOLF pp24-25) (VCH vol 7 p194).

Thornhill The house Lower Thornhill is 1.25m NW of Madeley. In Madeley parish. Higher Thornhill is 1m NW of Madeley.

Thornhill Former woodland and house a little way from the junction of Thornhill Road with the Chester Road, Streetly. The housing area known as Thornhill Park was developed from 1955 (SNAR pp104-105).

Thornhill House House 0.5m SW of Handsworth church, S of Holyhead Road, at its junction with Thornhill Road. The house had been built by 1794 and was still standing by 1862 (MNB pp41,45,47). Other accounts say Thornhill House was built in 1826 for Matthew Boulton's daughter, and that the house was situated on the Grove Lane side of Thornhill Road. It was for many years the residence of Miss Boulton, who bought the nearby Coalbank Tavern in order to pull it down to stop the rowdiness associated with the inn. But the price she had to pay was so high that the area was called Golds Hill, and this name is preserved in the name of a nearby street. Thornhill House was demolished in 1900 (HPPE pp115-116) (HHHW p47ps).

Thorns Hamlet N of Lye on Staffs side of the Stour (W p184) 1m SE of Brierley Hill. Formerly in Kingswinford ancient parish. The name, which appears in the 1851 census, is preserved in The Thorns School and Thorns Primary School.

Thorntree Hall Thorntree Hall Farm is 0.5m SW of Newborough.

Thorn Tree House Thorn Tree Farm is 2m SSW of Uttoxeter. To the N of the house at SK 086303 are some traces of two rectangular moated sites (CAMS p64) (NSFCT 1982 p10). It differs from Blithewood in not being concentric. The two island moats lie side by side (ESH p59).

Thorpe Constantine Ancient parish and minute village on a low promontory beside a tributary of the Mease 23m SE of Stafford. The manor appears in DB as Torc (SHBP p229), or Torp (DB John Morris. Phillimore. 1976). The **name** is of Scandinavian, Danish origin (SHOS vol 1 p405). It means 'village farm' (SPN p126). Ekwall gives 'outlying or secondary farm' (SSE 1996 p18). The Anglo-Saxons may have borrowed the word off the Danes. If from Torc (alleged DB spelling), then 'a pretty village' (SHBP p229). The Constantines were a Norman family, and Earls of Breteville, Pacey, Constantine, and places in Normandy and were lords of Thorpe in the C13 (DUIGNAN). Galfrid de Costetin held a fee in 1212 (SSE 1996 p23) (SDW p12). In 1255 Geffry Costentine held the manor of the king, as the honour of Lancaster. Afterwards it was held by Gilbert, Earl of Lincoln. In 1328 John Hotham, bishop of Ely, held it from whom it passed to the Scroops of Marsham. In 1514 it was held by Thomas Fitzwilliam. It was held in 1516 by his son William who lived at Aldworth, Warws. From the Fitzwilliams it passed by marriage to the Foljambes who sold it in 1574 to John Aylmer afterwards bishop of London, whose son Samuel sold it in 1598 to Robert Burdett of Bramcote, Warws. In 1631 or 1632 Sir Thomas Burdett Bart of Foremark, Derbys, sold it to William Ives of Leicester whose only daughter, Jane, married Richard Inge of Leicester; he built Thorpe Hall (see). Their son, William, who at length succeeded his father, was one of the judges of Leics appointed by parliament in 1654. A long succession of Inges have held the shrievalty of Staffs, and of their family was William Inge, the distinguished scholar and antiquary (SOS pp454-455) (SHBP pp227-229). There was a **church** at Thorpe Constantine in the C13 (LDD). The present parish church, St Constantine, SE of Thorpe Hall, has a medieval-looking tower (BOE p281). Most of the church was rebuilt in 1801 (LDD) and again, or in 1883 (BOE p281). A deserted **medieval village** is recorded here at SK 260089, slightly to the N of the church (SSAHST 1966 p49. 1970 p36). The village was not mentioned by Erdeswick (SOS p454). There are **good views** from the village to the E and W (SGS p168). **Natural history.** An unexplained block of ice, two metres square, fell from the sky to land at Thorpe Constantine in March 1975 (MMSE p288) (The World Atlas of Mysteries. Francis Hitching). In the later C17 Mr Inge of Thorpe Constantine sent Dr Plot a bone out of the caul of a female swine, which was of an exceptional size and appears in NHS tab 22, figs 10,13,16. Also Inge told him of a cow who revealed the skeleton of a calf it never bore when slaughtered, and a mare with a bony substance growing out of its ear (NHS pp255,262,266) (SHOS vol 1 p407).

Thorpe Hall In Thorpe Constantine village. Built by Richard Inge in 1651 (SOS p455) (SGS p168) and subsequently occupied by the Inge family, lords of Thorpe Constantine, until at least the early C20; it was Inge family tradition to call its heirs William (SHOS vol 1 p407). The hall, the centre of which is of c1651, also had three shaped gables, lost in the C18. The N wing is of c1800, the S of c1812 (SHBP p230) (BOE p281). In 1844 it was the property of William Phillips Inge (SOS p454,455). In 1851 the hall was the seat of Capts W and C Inge (W p23). A billiard room was built in 1870 (SHBP p230). In 1881 William Frederick Inge JP succeeded his uncle. After his death in 1903 his widow Mrs Mary (Caroline) Inge (b1865), lady of the manor, continued to live at the hall until at least c1910 (SHBP p227p of the hall facing). Inside the hall is oak panelling from Drakelowe Hall, Derbys (demolished 1934) (MR P328).

Thor's Cave Most spectacular and perhaps the largest cave in the county situated in Thor's Cliff (or Thor's Cave Tor, or formerly Thorshouse Tor) on the E side of the Manifold, 0.75m WSW of Wetton. The cave is situated 250 feet above the river bed and 100 feet below the top of the rock (WTCEM pp17,37,38). The total height of the rock is 919 feet high (OL vol 1 p156). EARLY. Being close to water and high up and therefore easy to defend the cave made an attractive dwelling place for peoples of the Palaeolithic, Neolithic, Bronze and Iron Ages and Roman period; finds from these periods have been made in it. It was occupied by Iron Age refugees until Hadrianic-Antonine times (NSJFS 1962 p33) (info Michael Greenslade). Carrington and E Brown made excavations in it between 1864 and Oct 1865, finding two perforated bones (JAT pp64,65,66il,76). A bronze armilla and fibula was found and went to Derby County Museum (WTCEM p18). Many finds are now in Sheffield Museum (SGS pp180-181). (Trans Midland Scientific Ass 1864/ 5) (R vol 6 p201) (VCH vol 1 p198) (S p46) (HOS p9) (NSJFS 1964 pp43,44). A whetstone of uncertain date was found in c1942 at the entrance by a school boy (NSFCT 1942 p55). Gunstone was unable to locate two **burial mounds** excavated by Bateman and Carrington in the C19 near Thor's Cave. One, a small circular barrow in Wettondale was excavated by Bateman in 1846 and revealed a heap of river cobbles and animal bones and pieces of flint. The other mound, a 'long barrow' of oval form on less elevated ground nearer to Wetton village than the former one revealed no cist or receptacle for a body, but did reveal some animal bones (VAD pp85-86). An interment or mound of nine paces in diameter of considerable importance was opened by Carrington in 1850 near Thor's Cave. It revealed a stone vessel and a bronze bucket with an iron handle of uncertain date (TYD pp172-173) (VCH vol 1 no 38) (LGS pp24,25) (SOSH p10) (DAJ vol 74 p145) (Medieval Archaeology vol 6/ 7 p52) (Gazetteer of Early Anglo-Saxon Burial Mounds. A Meaney. 1964. p223) (NSJFS 1965 p57). **Druids**. Roberts noted the cave had a megalithic chambered tomb called 'The Altar' (WTCEM pp17,37,38). Broughton noted druids performed rites in the cave (SMC p173).
500 to PRESENT. The cave has also appeared as Tor's Cave, Thur's House, Thursehole, Darwin Thor's Cavern, Hobthurst, and Hobhurse Cave or Hobhurst Cave (NHS p172) (WTCEM p126). The name is a corruption of Tor (NSFCT 1883 p22). Or from the god Thoth (HYB pp435-9). Or Thor who was worshipped by the Moorlanders at Grindon (NSFCT 1908 p109). Or is from Thurse or fairy, hence Thursehole; Thurse came from the same root as the Greek theos, a god (FLJ 1941 p236). The wind screeching in the cave gives rise to the tradition of the 'Fiddling Hobthurse' whose fiddling was thought to be more than a harmless sprite (FLJ 1941 p236. 1942 p127). In the later C17 Plot noted in the roof shapes created by the rock formation, one represented a man with a curled beard, looking out of a hole (NHS p172) (SD p110). A poor man, Titterton Mycock or Tissington Mycock, in an inebriated state, fell off the top of the rock above the cave in 1825 and was dashed to pieces on rocks below. His ghost, reputedly, haunts the cave (W p788) (AAD pp159-160). In 1874 a woman was thrown into a pit in the cave by a man and died. Henry T Brown of Canada heard her screams as she fell and went to her assistance. The man then pushed Brown into the pit. Both his legs broke in the fall and he died stranded there about a week later. His body and that of the woman's were later discovered by a Mr Hawkins, who found a notebook kept by Brown recording his time in the pit (LTD p43). In the 1930s Ralph de Tunstall Sneyd of Fair View (see) used the cave for religious ceremonies, choosing it for the Gorsedd ceremony at midsummer (HLSP p119). The Manifold Valley Light Railway had a refreshment room and shelter on a platform below the cave until 1917 (SMOPP vol 2 p87p c1929). (IAANS p xviii) (PS p94p of interior) (LGS pp24,25,184) (S p70p) (KES pp3,227) (CCOP p84) (SCA pp68,179) (HOS p9) (DAJ vol 4) (S&W p329) (TD p) (BOE pp307-308) (PDS&C p8p) (MR p373ps) (SLM April 2000 p56pc).

Thor's Fissure Cave Cave at SK 098549, close to Thor's Cave. Excavated by GH Wilson in 1933-34. Some Palaeolithic finds, fragments of Beaker and other Bronze Age pottery, animal bones including those of a dolphin, pottery of Iron Age and Roman periods and human remains in shallow graves were found (Cave Hunting Holidays in Peakland. GH Wilson. p13) (Caves and Caving vol 1 p61) (Trans Cave Research Group vol 1 No. 4,47) (British Caving. CHD Cullingford. 1962. p274) (NSJFS 1964 p43) (HOS p9).

Thors House Hollow or cave in the Peakstone Rock in Long Hurst Hill, Bradley-in-the-Moors. Traces of habitation dating from the Roman period have been found here (NHS p172) (HAF p34). It was latterly inhabited by a family and previously by the centenarian, Helen Millard (NHS p172). Has also appeared as Thurse House (HAF p34).

Thorswood House House under 1m NW of Stanton. Probably the same as Thorswood House Farm. At SK 121467, 0.5m to the SE was found in 1853 a gold torc of the Middle Bronze Age (1350-1000 BC). Rev H Bainbridge found it and it went to the BM (GNHSS p5; was discovered in 1854) (ARCHJ vol 11 p54) (NSFCT 1928 p147 p facing) (NSJFS 1964 p35) (STM July 1965 p41) (HOS p9). A simple gold strip bracelet was found in Sept 1953 100 yards S of Thorswood House. Perhaps of the late Bronze Age and made of Irish gold and weighs under an ounce. After being found it was declared treasure trove at Uttoxeter and purchased by Stoke-on-Trent City who still possess it (NSFCT 1953 p106) (NSJFS 1964 p35) (STM March 1964 p48; muddles the two finds) (HOS p9). Over 0.25m WSW of Thorswood House at SK 11114678 is a possible burial mound nine paces in diameter and three feet high (NSJFS 1965 p47). Over 0.25m W of Thorswood House are three possible burial mounds at SK 11184709 (11 paces dia, 3.5 feet high) at SK 11124723 (nine paces dia, three feet high) and at SK 11214725 (12 paces dia, two feet high) (NSJFS 1965 p47). These three were all listed monuments by 1994. There are four others about Thorswood, none of which Gunstone could locate. Carrington excavated them all between 1848 and 1850. One, 14 paces in diameter and two feet high, in 1848 revealed nothing (TYD p124). Another, 28 paces in diameter and described as high, constructed round a natural rock outcrop revealed found nothing (TYD pp124-125). A third revealed nothing (TYD p165). The fourth, 13 paces in diameter and about five feet high, which had been previously disturbed, revealed burnt bones (TYD p165) (NSJFS 1965 p47). The name commemorates the Norse god Thor (NSFCT 1916 p82).

Threapwood Small hamlet on a hill overlooking Dimmingsdale to the N, 1.5m SW of Oakamoor. In Cheadle parish. Appears as Reap Wood Head on 1834 OS map. Usually, names with Old English 'threap' record that the area was once the focus of a boundary dispute (English Place Names. K Cameron) (Discovering Parish Boundaries. Angus Winchester. 1990. p38). There is a mission church at Threapwood (LDD).

Threapwood Woodland which appears to have formerly belonged to Trentham Priory and has been identified with the present Lightwood, an extension of Cocknage stretching down toward the present Dresden (BNDA p9), and a wood in Longsdon parish which was added to Trentham Priory's estate at Wall Grange in 1275. The name means disputed wood, presumably a reference to a conflict over ownership or pasture rights (VCH vol 7 p208).

Three Crosses, The Local name for a stopping place on the Penkridge perambulation between Pillaton Hall and Penkridge. On the S side of the road at the Three Lanes' Ends (HOP pp29-30).

Three Crowns Inn Former inn which stood in Breadmarket Street, Lichfield. Elias Ashmole of Lichfield (see) was born in the Priests' Hall (see) which stood next door (SPN p78). At the Three Crowns Dr Johnson of Lichfield (see) stayed on some of his visits to Lichfield and according to Boswell 'lorded it with no less than three crowns over his head' (CCHCA pp27-28). Boswell and Johnson stayed in 1776; Johnson's chair and the knocker with which he called for drinks could still be seen in 1951 (IOM p81). An annual supper was still being held here in Johnson's honour on his birthday (Sept 18) in 1910; the dishes served are always of the substantial character which pleased him (LGS p176). (SLM May 1949 p243) (CL Oct 3 1957 p663) (LAL p10ps of plaque). The Amicable Society of Lichfield had its headquarters here (IOM p80). With the closure of the inn in or by the 1970s Johnson's chair was removed to his birthplace museum (CCHCA pp27-28). Perhaps named after the three crowns of the three wise men; St Mary's church is opposite the inn. Or the name is from the three slain British chieftains buried under Borrowcop Hill (IOM p81) (SPN p78).

Three Farms Former township in the Woodland quarter in Eccleshall ancient parish which included the farms - Ankerton, Baden Hall, Brockton Hall (SCSB p1) and Hill Farm (W p376). It may be a medieval creation (NSFCT 1913 p51). Three Farms has also been called Badnall (NSSG p5).

Three Hammers Farm S of Coven, S of Cross Green.

Three Lane Ends Three Lane Ends Farm is 3.25m ENE of Bagot's Bromley.

Threelows Fragmented minute hamlet on high ground under the southern flank of the Weaver Hills 0.5m E of St Winfrid's College, Cotton. Has also appeared as Three Lows. The Wrekin, Shrops, can be seen on a clear day from Threelows to the SW (HAF p392). Thomas Bateman opened five burial mounds near Threelows during the period 1849-50. The first, at SK 07524634, is 19 paces in diameter and five feet high. Burnt human bones were found (TYD p164). It was damaged by 1965 (NSJFS 1965 p37) (HAF pp27,28). Is a listed monument. The second, at SK 07674629, is 18 paces in diameter and two feet high. A cremation with rough flints was found (TYD p164) (NSJFS 1965 p37) (HAF pp27,28). Is a listed monument. The third, unlocated, revealed four skeletons, one crouched, a food vessel, part of a bronze bracelet and other artifacts. The fourth, unlocated, revealed a cremation and flint implements. The fifth, unlocated, revealed nothing (HAF p28). Here was a turnpike gate (IANS p18). Speake thinks the three lows (burial mounds) referred to in the name are:- Round Knoll (see), one at SK 077463 or SK 07674629 (listed the 'second' above), and one at SK 07524634 (listed the 'first' above) (HAF p392-393).

Three Lows Wetton (NSJFS 1962 p33). Perhaps the three burial mounds 0.75m NNE of Wetton. Gunstone lists those under Brownslow (see). He is unable to locate the Three Lows. Bateman and Carrington excavated one in 1845 and 1850, respectively. A crouched skeleton and three other skeletons, a barbed and tangled arrowhead, fragments of three beakers, a cinerary urn, remains of a food vessel, part of a bronze bracelet and a considerable remains of a funeral pyre were found (VAD pp69-70) (TYD pp167-168) (DAJ vol 75 pp86,91,114,119. vol 77 p26, B8) (NSJFS 1965 p58). The food vessels, of the Yorkshire type, were of the Beaker people (NSJFS 1962 p33). Carrington excavated another in 1849 and found a stone built cist with a cremation, flint implements, a bone pin, a small cinerary urn and an old person's skeleton (TYD p161) (DAJ vol 75 p119) (NSJFS 1965 p58). He excavated another mound, which was possibly not a burial mound, in 1851 and found nothing in it (TYD p178) (NSJFS 1965 p58).

Three Mile Oak Ancient tree 0.5m SSW of Sandwell Hall, near Sandwell Park boundary. The name was later applied to a hamlet in Handsworth ancient parish (W p698). The ancient tree known as the Three Mile Oak formerly stood on the N side of the Birmingham Road (A41) (VCH vol 17 p10), and was a stopping place for coaches on the turnpike road. It is shown on the turnpike map of 1771 (BCM July 1985 p36). By the 1830 it had gone but the name was preserved by the nearby inn (on the corner of Roebuck Street and the Birmingham Road - HPPE p116) and toll-gate (mentioned by 1756) (WB p159) (OS map 1834) (SLM Oct 1947 p35) (VCH vol 17 pp10,11). On June 20 1836 Mark Robinson was thrown from the Alexander Omnibus at Three Mile Oak. The name 'Three Mile Oak' puzzles Hall (HPPE p116). Perhaps so called for the oak was three miles from Birmingham.

Three Parish Wood Wood 1m E of Canwell.

Three Penny Bit House Lodge to Barlaston Hall on corner of Queen Mary's Drive and Longton Road, Barlaston. So called because it is shaped like a coin (SSBOP p82p in 1907). Built in c1856 (info John Mould). The drive is so called as it was officially opened by Queen Mary, wife of George V (local info).

Three Shire Heads Place at Pannier's Pool at SK 009686, to the NW of Flash, at the confluence of Ffirestoen Brook and the Dane. Here in 1533 Ches, Staffs and Derbys are said to have met. But maps of the C17 and C18 show the three counties meeting at Staffordshire's most northerly point, 1m or 2m N of Flash (where the Three Shire Stones (see) have been marked). (SMCC p3). This was owing to uncertainty over common land belonging to Hartington parish, Derbys. When this land was enclosed in 1804 the counties meeting point was re-established to be at Pannier's Pool or Three Shire Heads (VCH vol 7 p49). Coin forgers are alleged to have made their base in the locality because they found the proximity to the counties' meeting convenient as they could easily evade the authorities of every county. Walter Smith wrote a poem dated 1923:

> Of Three Shires Head strange tales are told
> Of coiner, thieves, and bandits bold,
> Who long defied the country reeve
> By hiding in some neighbouring greave;
> Or, crossing o'er the border stream,
> Which here with rapid waters teem,
> His jurisdiction might deft
> And their nefarious burdens ply.

(DP pp6il,7). In the 1870s Three Shire Heads was the scene of a bare fist contest long after the abolition of pugilism. The fight was between the 'Burslem Bruiser' and the 'Preston Pet.' A Leek magistrate tried to stop the fight but the participants just crossed into Cheshire and continued fighting. The Leek magistrate also crossed over and, apparently, became an enthusiastic spectator (SLM April 1996 pp16-17). Has sometimes appeared as Three Shires Head (NSJFS 1965 p115)

Three Shire Mere At Three Shire Stones (Saxton's map).

Three Shire Stones By the early C17 there were three standing stones on top of Cheeks Hill which were said to mark the boundaries of the three counties of Ches, Derbys and Staffs (VCH vol 7 p49). Three stones are shown on Stent's edition of William Smith's map (1602). They are shown, one in each county, on Speed's map. They were recorded in 1621 (DP p6). On Blaeu's map they are shown on Axe Edge. Called the Three Meer Stones, where there was a farm by 1750 (UHAW), they are shown at the Travellers Rest Inn at Flash Gate on Yates' map and also then on the 1834 OS map. They are said to have still been in existence in the early C19 (VCH vol 7 p49). One pillar-like stone was standing near Flash Bar, on a mound (a possible burial mound), in the later C20 (W p717) (PRT p78) (DP p6) (DPMM p105p). It is unknown whether the stones were situated all in one county to mark a place where the authorities of each county could meet on equal terms or one stood in each county. The county boundary in this area was much disputed in the C16 and C17 (SSE 1996 p71). In 1804 the meeting place for the counties was re-established to be at Panniers Pool or Three Shire Heads (see).

Three Shires Oak Oak which stood near the Bear Inn, over 0.5m S of Smethwick. It was supposed to have stood at the junction of Three Shires Oak Road, Thatchers Hill (now Abbey Road), Love Lane (now Wigorn Road), and Thimble Mill Lane (now Thimble Road) and to have marked the meeting point of Staffs, Worcs (a detached portion in the detached portion of Shrops), Shrops (a detached portion). A popular misconception is that it marked the meeting point of Warws, Staffs, and Shrops. Some say it was cut down in c1895 when believed to be only about 80 years old (STELE Jan 5 1952. Oct 17 1952 il c1850). Others say it was cut down by Smethwick corporation in 1908 (O p22) (SLM Oct 1947 p35).

Three Trees Common Former common land near Brindley Village on Cannock Chase. The common was described in 1957 as rapidly disappearing (PCC p79).

Thromelowe 1.5m N of Wolverhampton, in the Fallings Park area, formerly in Wednesfield chapelry in Wolverhampton ancient parish. Burial mound thrown up over the dead killed in the battle of Tettenhall (or Wednesfield) in c910. It has appeared as Tromelows (c1290), Rumblelows (commonly called in the later C17), Rumballows (as a house on the 1834 OS map), and Tromelowe (1902) (AOW pp7,10). The name is from possibly Anglo-Saxon 'truma' a legion, troop, army, host. So 'the burial mound of the army or host' (DUIGNAN). Thromelowe farm, which stood in Park Lane near the present Guy Motors, formed a part of the Gough estate and may have been moated (WFW p23). (SHOS vol 2 p150) (SVS p332).

Throne Former small hamlet 0.5m NE of Rowley Regis. Appears on 1947 OS map 1:25,000 (sheet 32/98), at SO 976880. The name is preserved in Throne Road, Throne Close, and Throne Crescent.

Throstle's Nests A place S of Bradnop: A field name at Okeover, derived from an animal name (APB p48): A place NWW of Sheen.

Throwley Fragmented minute hamlet, mainly comprising Throwley Hall, 1.25m NNE of Calton, situated in a tongue of land between the Hamps and the Manifold in the Moorlands. Former township in Ilam ancient parish (SASR 1995 no 5 p1). For burial mounds near Throwley see Arbor Hill. In a narrow valley by the Manifold between Castern and Throwley is a burial mound excavated by Carrington in 1848. It was composed of sand and river cobbles; a crouched and a burnt skeleton were found in it (TYD pp120-121, 189-190) (NSJFS 1965 p42). At least one of the burial mounds about Throwley is an Anglo-Saxon burial site (HOS p13). In 1856 a glass bead with yellow decoration was found near Throwley which may be of Anglian origin and went to Sheffield Museum (NSJFS 1964 p42) (WOY p2). The first mention of Throwley is in 1208 (SL p71), and it has appeared as Truele (SPN p127), Truleg (C13) (SSE 1996 p18), Througley (c1540) (LI appendix p172). The prefix is from Anglo-Saxon 'thruh,' or Middle English 'throwe,' a sarcophagus, tomb. So the 'ley or pasture of, or by, the tomb, burial mound or stone-coffin' (DUIGNAN) (SSE 1996 p18) (SPN p127). Or means 'clearing with a conduit' (SL p71) (MR p328). In medieval times there was possibly a village of Throwley by Throwley Old Hall, possibly where there are earthworks to the E and NE of the Old Hall (SASR 1995 no 5 pp20,26). Or at 0.5m to the SSW at Throwley Cottage. It was probably deserted between 1377-1524 (SSAHST 1970 p36). The medieval field system at Throwley was still evident in 1991 (SN Jan 25 1991 p55). Local folklore says that Oliver Cromwell and some of his troops were stationed at Throwley or lodged at Throwley Old

Hall, and that royalists were stationed at Tissington, Derbys (NSFCT 1878 p12). But Cromwell has been confused with Thomas Cromwell of Throwley Old Hall of Henry VIII's reign (SBB p190). In the later C17 Charles Cotton showed Dr Plot an earwig of a milk colour at Throwley; earwigs are normally a chestnut colour (NHS p237). A phantom coach has been seen above the Manifold ravine between Ilam to Throwley (FLJ 1942 p126).

Throwley Barracks A seven bay range, built in the C17. It was one of the service buildings of Throwley Old Hall and stands 90 metres W of the Old Hall (SASR 1995 no 5 p27). The building has also been called 'The Barracks.'

Throwley Hall House which stands next to the ruins of Throwley Old Hall. It is likely to have been built sometime between 1838 and 1878 (SASR 1995 no 5 p26). Although it has been said, probably erroneously, to have been built by the Meverells of Throwley Old Hall in the C18 (SN Jan 25 1991 p55).

Throwley Moor Moor about Soles Hill, 0.75m W of Throwley Hall. Over 0.5m WSW of Throwley Hall is Throwleymoor House. There is a burial mound to the W of it at SK 09845218, 12 paces in diameter and three feet high. Carrington excavated it in 1849/ 50. A cremation in an urn, a bronze awl and a perforated axe-hammer were found (TYD pp154,162) (VCH vol 1 no 34) (ARCH vol 75 pp96-97) (NSJFS 1965 p55). Another, behind Throwley Moor House, 13 paces in diameter was excavated by Carrington in 1849. A large plain globular urn with two holes perforated through one side was found (TYD pp157-158) (VCH vol 1 no 32) (NSJFS 1965 p55).

Throwley New Park Lay to the E and SE of Throwley Old Hall. A new deer park at Throwley of some 60 acres was enclosed in 1508. It belonged to the lords of Throwley. It was still in existence in the later C17. A park at Throwley is described as long disparked in 1867 (EDP p178). Some of the pale earthworks of this park were still remaining in the later C20 (SASR 1995 no 5 p21).

Throwley Old Hall The Meverells, later lords of Throwley manor, built a hall on or near the site of the Old Hall in the C13 (CL Feb 14 1991 p75) after acquiring land here in 1208 (SASR 1995 no 5 p21). Arthur Meverell was the last prior of Tutbury Priory (LTD p40). In 1603 Sampson Meverell built the Old Hall (LGS p184 p facing); Pevsner thinks it was probably built in the early C16 (BOE p281). It was occupied by the Meverells until Robert Meverell died in 1626. The estate then passed to his sole daughter, Elizabeth, and through her husband Thomas Cromwell, 4th Baron Cromwell, later Viscount Lecale and Earl of Ardglass in Ireland (of the family of Oliver Cromwell), the estate passed to the Cromwells (W p777) (MR p328,330p,373) (SASR 1995 no 5 p21). A shield from the old hall was traced by Mr Pape to Throwley Hall and duly photographed. It is the coat of Cromwell impaling Meverell (NSFCT 1922 p78). Throwley Old Hall was destroyed in the Civil War (WTCEM pp53,85) with Thomas Cromwell and his son serving the royal cause (SASR 1995 no 5 p26). For the tradition of Oliver Cromwell at Throwley Old Hall see Throwley. In 1704 Throwley was part of the marriage settlement for Lady Elizabeth Southwell heiress of Vere Essex, Earl of Ardglass. It remained with the Southwells until 1790 when it passed to Sir Samuel Crompton and in 1851 an S Crompton was the owner. By the early C18 the Old Hall was tenanted. The interior is said to have been gutted by fire in the mid C19. It then appears to have been left to decay to its present ruinous state (W p777) (SASR 1995 no 5 pp25-27). (DoE II* scheduled AM) (TD ps) (S p11) (PS pp90,92p) (SGS p111) (ES Jan 26 1991) (CL Feb 14 1991 p75) (DMV pp77,78p) (WOY2 p19; that in c1660 Wingfield Cromwell sold the hall to Theophilus Biddulph of Cheapside, London). The pool and terraces of the C17 gardens to the SE and S of the Old Hall still remain and were surveyed in 1987 (SASR 1995 no 5 pp26-30).

Throwley Old Park Medieval deer park enclosed out of forest which lay to the W of Throwley Old Hall in the area of Oldpark Hill. In existence by 1306 (NSJFS 1962 p76). It belonged to the lords of Throwley. It was still in existence in the later C16. A park at Throwley is described as long disparked in 1867 (EDP p178) (SASR 1995 no 5 p25).

Thundering Well A well from which the local inhabitants claim they can hear noises on the Sharpcliffe estate, Ipstones (NSFCT 1906 p170), in Combes Valley (NSFCT 1915 p164). An NSFC expedition visited the well, but did not hear any noises. Some members thought the noises were created by old mine workings in the vicinity in which occasional falls took place (NSFCT 1906 p170). Near it Mr Boucher of Sharpcliffe Hall found a bronze spearhead, four feet down. On another part of estate he found a stone axe (NSFCT 1915 p164).

Thursfield Former name of Newchapel (see) (NSFCT 1924 p34). Former township of Wolstanton ancient parish. Has appeared as Turvoldesfeld, a manor, in DB, Turnedesfeld (W p302), Thurfredesfeld (C13). The name means 'Thorold's open land' (SSE 1996 p18). Or Thurfredesfeld is similar to the

female name Thorfritha (DUIGNAN). Or Tur is from Thor, the god of thunder (HBST p130) (NSFCT 1908 p118) (SVB p130). Was a member of Tunstall manor by c1130 (ONST 1976 p374). In 1236 Henry de Aldithley (or Audley) of Heighley Castle (see), held the vill of Thursfield by the service of performing guard duties at Newcastle Castle (SCSF pp116-117) (VCH vol 8 p13).

Thursfield Lodge NE of Newchapel.

Tibbets Garden Area of Cradley Heath in 1901. Is now covered by the street called Northgate (OS map Sheet 71.08).

Tibbington Former name of Tipton (see), and a ward of Tipton borough (Staffs County Guide. c1958. p141). It is the name used for a district 1m NNE of Tipton Green or 1m NW of St Martin's church. This district lay within Tipton ancient parish and Tipton parish church originally stood here. The mission church, St Joseph, Newhall Street, was active between 1913 and 1921 (TSSOP p11p). The Tibbington housing estate earned itself the nickname 'Abyssinia' possibly because its construction coincided with Italy's invasion of Abyssinia in 1935 (TSSOP p20).

Tibbington Hall The hall which existed by this name in the C19 lay at the end of Newhall Street, Tibbington, Tipton. In 1825 it was occupied by Richard Smith and was subsequently tenanted by Daniel Turner. The owners at that time were Samuel Walker & Co of the Gospel Oak Iron Works. The hall had been demolished by 1915 (HOTIP pp186-187 pl ii). There appears to have been a hall in this area in medieval times, known as the 'Hall of Tibinton.' From documents it can be deduced that Dud Dudley of Dudley Castle (see) was the owner and perhaps occupier of the same or a later hall in the area; he is recorded as living at Tipton in 1631 and 1663. Another possible occupier of that hall about this time was the mother of Dud Dudley, Elizabeth Tomlinson. That hall appears to have been called at some time 'Colonel's Hall' after Dud Dudley (alias Col Dud Dudley). In the mid C18 the same or a later hall in this area may have been known as Tipton Hall (HOTIP pp26,186-187 pl ii).

Tickhill House 1.25m NNE of Caverswall.

Tickle Belly Entry Passageway at Burslem. Its course has been in dispute for some time. It is thought by Jim Morgan to run alongside Burslem Park between Moorland Road and Hamil Road (ES Sept 5 1995 p8p).

Tillington Former hamlet on a bank above the marshy low Sow Valley, now a suburb of Stafford, 1m NNW of Stafford town. Former extra-parochial estate attached to St Mary's parish, Stafford (W p343). It received its name according to Chetwynd because it was a place of note for husbandry and tillage (SHC 1914 p105). 'Tilla's town' (DUIGNAN). Or 'the farmstead of the people of Tylla (or Tylli)' (SPN p111). Has appeared as Tillintone, a manor, in DB, Tillinton, and Titlingeston (SPN p111). There was a sizeable medieval village at SJ 910250, which was deserted between 1334 and 1524 (SSAHST 1970 p36). Walter Chetwynd in 1679 was the first to identify a former settlement here from, probably, earthworks (SHC 1914 p105) (SL p82). The note in SOS (Harwood) about a circular entrenchment here is an error - it is to be seen at Billington, Bradley parish (SHC 1914 p105 note). According to Chetwynd the tithes of Tillington formed a prebend in Stafford Collegiate Church (SHC 1914 p108). The separate civil parish of Tillington, created in 1858, was abolished in 1917 when it entered into Stafford municipal borough and civil parish, and Creswell ancient parish (GLAUE p426). There is a church in Rowley Street (LDD). The Staffordshire Ambulance Service formed after 1948 as an amalgamation of local ambulance services. By the later C20 its headquarters were at No. 70 Stone Road; the service had the best record in the country for reaching patients in the quickest time in 1998 (Today Programme. BBC Radio 4 Sept 24 1998).

Tillington Hall Tillington, Stafford (SOPP pl 25). Could be same as Tillington House, which appears on 1834 OS map and was occupied in 1851 by William Thomas Locker (W p23). The hall was occupied by Mrs Carder between at least 1935 and 1946 (SHC 1934. 1944 List of Members). In the 1960s it became an hotel (local info).

Timbertrees Tiny district at Cradley NW of Corngreaves Hall, Rowley Regis. The name is from Timber Tree Piece a field over seven acres situated S of Barrs Road and running between Old Hill Cricket Club ground to the E and the Timbertree Colliery land to the W. Timbertrees Road was laid out in c1922 (SNSV vol 2 p76).

Timmins Hill Hill in the Rowley Hills range (SVS p437). Has also appeared as Blower's Hill.

Tinacre Hill Sir Alfred Hickman's Wightwick Hall stands on top of it; a road of this name runs to the E of the hall (Birmingham A-Z). At the foot of the hill was a settlement called Netherton (VCH vol 20 p10).

Tinings, The Former waste land SW of Pool Green, Aldridge. It was partly enclosed in 1605 when William Wiggin received permission to erect a cottage here (MOA p135).

Tinker's Borough The name seems to apply to a house 0.75m SE of Salt. In St Mary's parish, Stafford. Raven says it takes its name from some cave dwellings once inhabited by tinkers that lie to the W (MR pp195,273p,274). Others say the caves were the cottages of workers on a nearby sandstone quarry (ASOP p28). (SAIW pl 69p) (SL p100). Others imply Tinker's Borough is all the wooded heathland S of Salt. In Tinkerborough there is an engine house with a classical facade dated 1823 in Brick Kiln Lane at SJ 960267. The coal-fired engine drove a water pump and supplied water to the whole of Ingestre estate (DoE II) (MR pp195,273p,368). The engine house seems to have formerly served as the office for the old Tinkerborough Quarry before being adapted to an engine house. There seems to have still been a beam engine in the building in 1935, which was then in a good state of preservation (OSST 1935 p51).

Tinker's Castle Another name for Abbot's Castle Hill (see) (LGS p238). Tinker's Castle is also the name for a colour-washed house on the county boundary near Abbot's Castle Hill under 1m WSW of Seisdon, 1.75m W of Trysull at end of Tinker's Castle Road (The Staffs Way. Cannock Chase to Kinver Edge. p15). It probably dates from the late C18 and it has a cellar carved into the sandstone rock (VCH vol 20 p187). According to local tradition the house may have received its name from a tinker having once inhabited the cellar (POAP p79). This house may also be called the 'House that Jack built.' If so, it stands at the corner of Toads' Nest Lane: In Toads' Nest Lane was a cottage in which, according to tradition, Charles II took refuge after escaping the battle of Worcester (1651). The cottage was described in 1908 as recently standing but in ruins (WJO July 1908 p184p). To the SE is Tinker's Castle Farm.

Tinkersclough Vale (SHST p521) and former area of Hanley parish reached by way of Clough Street, Etruria. Formerly in Stoke-upon-Trent chapelry and ancient parish. Toft pottery was probably situated at Tinkersclough (NSFCT 1953 pp108-109). The area has been described as a rough one (H p108). Bridge Street is in it (HOE p147). (SHST p140p of Tinkerclough Slag Mound in 1957).

Tinkers Green Former triangular open space S of Watling Street at Wilnecote (1834 OS map) (TDOPP p70p). The name is preserved in Tinkers Green Road.

Tinney Green N of Little Madeley on J Cary's map (1801).

Tinsell Brook Tributary of the Dove. The name probably arose as a fairly recent pet-name (SPNO p21).

Tip Cat Rock feature that use to be on the Roaches but had been destroyed by 1891 (OL vol 1 p95). (DP p54 ils of megalithic chambered tombs on the Roaches and one of them could be 'Tip Cat').

Tipperty Green Former hamlet N of Rowley Regis, NE of Old Hill, and W of Portway. In Rowley Regis parish. The name has appeared as Isabel Green, Iberty (Plot's map), Ibberty Green, Tippity Green and Tipperty Green. Isabel Green may be from Isabela de Botetourt's house, the remains of which existed for some time after its demise (BCWJ p67). Or is said to have been called Tippity Green because of the sloping or tipping nature of the green near the Bull's Head Inn (TB Sept 1997 p19). The name Tipperty Green prevails on 1:25,000 OS map referring to an area between Rowley Regis church and Hailstone Quarry. The hamlet grew partly in consequence of the manorial mill here (BCWJ p86). For the post mill here see Rowley Mill. There was a quarry here extracting Rowley Rag (VCH vol 2 pp203,204)

Tipsyford Brook Runs at Saltwells, where it formed the former Staffs and Worcs border (OS map Sheet 71.07).

Tipton (*Tip'un* UBCB p117). Former ancient parish and Black country town on ground gently rising out of a head brook of the Tame 18.5m S of Stafford. EARLY to 1850. The **Roman** forts at Pennocrucium and Metchley were connected by a road which passed through Tipton and Oldbury according to E Chitham in his 'The Black Country' (WFW p32). A Roman coin, an as of Claudius, was found at SO 97629215 in 1961 (NSJFS 1964 p38). The **name** is from perhaps the Anglo-Saxon female personal name Tiba, Tibbe. Or from St Tibbe or Tybba herself, patroness of hunting and hawking (d696); after all Tipton was anciently hunting country (DUIGNAN). Or 'Tibba's farmstead' (SPN p127). Means the 'tun of the family of Tibbe' (SOSH p332) (WAM p9). Or if the original name was Tipstone, then this related to a stave or spear shaped stone - a megalith of prehistoric origin - which may have stood about Tipton (MR p331). The manor of Tibintone (Tipton) is recorded as being held by the bishop of Chester (Lichfield) in DB. Later forms are: Tibintone (1151), Tybinton (1224. 1293), Typinton (1293), Tybington (1312), Typton (1332. 1723), Tibinton (1435), Tybenton (1526), Tebbingeton (1562), and Tibberton (1723), Tippington (1798) (HOTIP p10) (BCM April 1968 p14). The parish formed between 1086 and 1291 probably originally formed a part of Sedgley parish (SHC 1916 pp193,197). Tipton parish was a peculiar juris-

diction of Prees prebend in Lichfield cathedral until peculiar jurisdictions were abolished in 1846 (VCH vol 3 p93 note, 94) (GLAUE p426). **Churches.** The original parish church, St Martin, stood on the site of the present, **St John the Evangelist**, at the N end of Upper Church Lane, Tibbington (LGS p234). It was abandoned in 1797 having become too small, and a new church was built in 1795-1797 on the E side of Lower Church Lane at Horseley Heath. This was dedicated to **St Martin**, and because of its shape became known locally as the 'pepper box.' By 1992 it was redundant (LDD). The old St Martin was rebuilt incorporating the medieval tower (possibly of C13 origin, and drawn by TP Wood in the C19 - TP Wood's Staffordshire. 1990) and rededicated St John the Evangelist in 1854 (TSSOP pp18il,98). St John's had a reputation as a runaways' church (BCM Jan 1978 p22). Tipton **wakes** were originally held on St Martin's day (Nov 11) but changed to July 4 this being the date on which the relics of St Martin were moved to Tours (473 AD) (BCM April 1968 pp60-61) and because the winter date was considered unsuitable for outdoor celebrations (SCSF p106). Tipton wake was as well known as those of Enville up to the early 1800s (BC p149). Tipton wakes survived as a fun fair until 1959 (BCM April 1968 pp60-61). **Beating the bounds** was practiced in Tipton parish (BCC vol 1 p135). Tipton **parish register** had the claim of being the oldest in the country, as it was formerly believed to have been started in 1513. The first entry is dated Dec 20 (the general order for keeping registers was not issued until 1538 - Encyclopaedia Britannica. 11th ed. see under 'Register') (LGS pp233-234). Parkes believed it dated from 1513 (HOTIP pp1-5). However, GP Mander, exploded the claim in Staffs PR Society 1923 ppiii,iv. The entries ascribed to 1513-19 are really of 1573-9, the figure 7 having been ambiguously written and misread (NSFCT 1921 p24) (SL p206 note). Some, including Raven writing in the late 1980s, still perpetuate the claim (GBR 1960 p115) (MR p332). The Dudley **plague** of 1616 spread to Tipton (SCSF pp134-135). **Methodism.** The first Methodist chapel in the county was built at Tipton in 1755 (HOS p32). In the 1860s Tipton had 13 Methodist chapels to four Anglican churches (SL p193). Tipton, a mere village until mid C19, has several centres. The original settlement was Tibbington (see) at about Tibbington Road and Tibbington Terrace. Tipton Green (see) is the shopping centre, and it has its own churches. **Civil unrest.** There was food rioting in Tipton in 1800 (HOWV p122) (OH p69). At Tipton in Sept 1811 five people and possibly another 200 people, were involved in a riot and expulsion of one William Trisham and a subsequent assault on a constable (LOU p233). The **cholera epidemic** of 1832 reached Tipton parish on June 15 and claimed 404 lives in the parish, with one family of 14 losing 12 members. Tipton parish is said to have been where the epidemic started in the Black Country (TEBC2 p37) (TB Feb 1998 p17). Tipton was linked to the **railway** system from Sept 14 1863 (SSR p25). Tipton is said to be the first town in England to introduce **street lamps** (OH p11). **Natives. George Benjamin Thorneycroft** (d1851), first mayor of Wolverhampton (1848), was born in Tipton in 1791 (TB Oct 1977 p4 il) (VB p53); his son an inventor and eccentric owned Tettenhall Towers (see); his youngest daughter, Ellen, was the mother of the novelist Ellen Thorneycroft Fowler of Woodthorne (see) who was born at Summerfield, Wolverhampton. **William Perry**, champion prize fighter, was born in Park Lane, Tipton in the last quarter of 1819, or in early 1820 (TEBC) (The Tipton Slasher: His Life and Times. Tom Langley). He obtained the nickname 'Tipton Slasher' at the age of 17 by thrashing a Birmingham rival (E&S June 14 1997). He was bare-knuckle champion of England from 1850 to 1857 and the first Staffs man to hold the title. (W p708) (BCSG pp52-53, 110) (The Tipton Slasher. 1969. Tom Langley) (WP p64). Lord Dudley was a patron. On the proceeds of his winnings Perry opened an inn called 'The Champion of England' in Spon Lane, West Bromwich. After failing with the inn Perry returned to work on the canals (E&S June 14 1997). He died poor in the workhouse in 1878 (ZSB), or on Dec 24 1880 reputedly at the old Toll House at Gibbet Gate (Gibbet Lane) near Bilston which ran from Stowheath to Millfields and followed part of Ward Street. He is buried in St John's churchyard, Kate's Hill, Dudley (TB Sept 1974 p17. April 1977 p1. April 1979 p7p of his watch-chain. March 1979 p7. Oct 1979 p18. Dec 1980 p13. Oct 1986 p6. Nov 1986 p27il of the Toll House. Aug 1989 p20. July 1993 p1p) (MMBCC pp105-158) (E&S June 14 1997). In the late 1970s a portrait of Perry was found and bought for £700 and was hung in the boardroom of the Tipton and Coseley Building Society, Tipton (Birmingham Evening Mail Nov 22 1979) (BCM July 1981 pp38-40. April 1984 p54). A bronze statue of Perry designed by Bill Haynes was unveiled in the tiny park, Coronation Gardens or William Perry Gardens, Owen Street, Tipton, on May 3 1993 (E&S Nov 30 1992. April 5 1994 p5) (BCM spring 1993 p73p). A plaque in these gardens says his remains lie here. John Broom was a pugilist prize fighter who lived at the same time as the Tipton Slasher (W p708). **Hugh Lewis**, pawnbroker, character and foxhunter, born at Tipton in

1819, lived at Woodfield House, Hill, Sutton Coldfield, in later life. In the grounds of that house he embarked on a red brick tower to be used for fire work displays. The tower, 80 feet high, was never completed and became known as 'Lewis's Folly.' Lewis was buried at Little Aston (BCM April 1971 pp41-42). Sir **Alfred Hickman**, industrialist, known as the 'Iron King,' was born in Tipton in 1830. He became an MP for W Wolverhampton and is known for his writings on railway rates (BS p223) (BCM July 1975 p44).

INDUSTRY. Tipton expanded owing to coal mining, canals, railways, tinplating and iron. At Lady Meadow (see) in 1712 was erected the first working Newcomen steam-engine to pump water out of mines. Robert George Hobbes (1821-1899), who wrote a series of articles in the weekly 'The Leisure Hour' in 1872 about a tour of the Black Country he had made in 1871, noted Tipton presented 'to the eye flame capped towers, heaps of furnace dross, a soil black, loose and muddy, and pools of dirty stagnant water' (BCM autumn 1993 p56). Joseph Hall who lived at Tipton was the first to refine iron using a process known as 'pig boiling' (The Iron Question. Joseph Hall. 1858) (HOTIP p7). In 1825 a Joseph Hall of Tipton invented the sand bottom puddling furnaces (OH p69). The **Aaron Manby**, the world's first iron steamship, was made by Mr Manby and Capt Napier (afterwards Sir Charles Napier) at the Horseley Iron Company at Great Bridge (HOTIP p7) (BCM Spring 2000 p71; built 1820) in 1821 (MR p332), or 1822 (VCH vol 2 p167) (HOS p45). The name is preserved in Aaron Manby Court at Tipton (Birmingham A-Z). (Newcomen Society vol 29 pp77-91) (TFWH p46) (BCM July 1972 pp11-14 il of, 15-17). **The Star**, the first railway engine to be made with a solid plate frame, the first with its reversing motion controlled directly by a reversing lever, the first incorporating arc or link motion with fixed centres, and the first with a boiler free to expand on its frame, was made by a Tyneside engineer at Tipton. It won a competition for a locomotive engine promoted by the Liverpool and Manchester railway in 1833 (Story of Railway Pioneers. S Snell. 1921. pp21,24) (VCH vol 2 p162). **The Monarch** was built at the Tipton works of Horseley Coal and Iron Co (VCH vol 2 p163). The chain anchor for the **Great Eastern** was made by the firm of Messrs HP Parkes of Tipton in 1866. The anchor, the patented invention of Mr Joseph Beterley of Liverpool, weighed 8 tons. The length of the shank was 20 feet 6 inches. The length of wood stock was 19 feet 6 inches. The tread of arms was 7 feet 4 inches (BCM Oct 1978 pp47-50). The iron used was made by Barrows & Sons, Bloomfield, and it was 'proved' at the Tipton Proving House of the Staffs Chain and Anchor Testing Company (BCM autumn 1996 p19). When completed it was described by the Wolverhampton Chronicle as 'the largest anchor in the world' (Wolverhampton Chronicle Jan 2 1867). **The Thunderbolt** car was made in Tipton and in 1938 it set the world speed record of 357 mph, the driver was Capt George Eyston (BCM July 1977 p59. July 1993 pp50-54ps) (TB Jan 1981 p11. March 1981 p9p) (ZSB). **Bean cars**. The long-established Tipton engineering firm, Harper Sons and Bean, took over the Perry Motor Co of Tyseley, producers of the Perry light car. Harper Sons and Bean produced their first Bean model in 1920. A Bean car made the first double crossing of Australia in 1924. After a takeover in 1927 the cars were known as Hadfield Bean. Bean Industries, a part of British Leyland, were still in Hurst Lane, Tipton in 1976 (PVBC pp11-13) (BCFF p203). Beans Engineering appear to have taken over the Reliant car company at Two Gates (see) and consequently were producers of the Reliant Robin. In Nov 1994 Bean Engineering went into receivership (The Times. Nov 19 1994 p6).

CANALS. Through Tipton have run: the Birmingham Canal; Old Cut Old Main Line; New Cut Old Main Line and New Cut New Main Line as well as the Tipton Green Branch Canal. At Tipton was also Monk's Dock (see). Thus for its canals Tipton has been described as the 'Venice of the Black Country' or the 'Venice of the Midlands' (SC p170) (BCSG vol 5 p64) (BCM April 1968 pp57-59) (VB pp41,49) (MR p332). Ocker Hill has also been called the 'Venice of the Midlands' (BCM Oct 1974 p8). The Mission, a bargee's mission house by the canal at Factory Bridge, has a foundation stone with inscription

> To the Glory of God
> And for the Good of the Souls
> of those who pass on the canal
> This Stone is laid
> November 26 1892

(BCM Jan 1975 pp26p-29) (TWDOP p22p). On Sept 9 1899 a 100 yard stretch of canal at Tipton burst its banks, two miles of canal was drained (VB pp49-50).

NEWSPAPERS. The **Tipton and Great Bridge Times**, was published in 1889 (SHJ spring 1996 p28). **The Leader**, founded by Sept 5 1908, became

The South Staffordshire & North Worcestershire Leader, from Nov 11 1908; this paper continued until at least Dec 8 1911 (SHJ spring 1996 p27). The **Tipton Herald** was founded by the proprietor of the Dudley Herald in 1897 (TEBC2 p142). The **Tipton Herald and Tipton Leader**, founded by Jan 25 1919, became the Tipton Herald from May 28 1955 and continued as such until at least 1974 (SHJ spring 1996 p28). The **Tipton and Coseley Times and South Staffordshire Advertiser**, founded on Dec 1 1928, ran until at least Dec 27 1930 (SHJ spring 1996 p28). Some Wednesbury (see) papers had Tipton in their title.

1850 to PRESENT. On Oct 1 1938 Tipton **urban district** was created a municipal borough and received a charter of incorporation. The **arms** of Tipton borough, granted in 1938, are: Gules, a castle between in chief three wheels and in base a Stafford Knot all gold. The crest is: On a wreath gold and gules, a rock proper and issuing there from three spearheads, also proper, with gold hafts. The supporters are: Two gold lions, each holding in the mouth a scrap gules and hanging therefrom a shield sable charged with a gold thunderbolt. The motto is: 'Salus populi suprema lex' (The welfare of the people is the highest law) (CH pp336,337il). The arms of the borough could be seen on a pub sign on the corner of Baker Street and Birmingham and Wolverhampton New Road (BCM July 1977 p58p. April 1989 p60). Tipton ceased to exist as a separate local authority in 1966, when it was absorbed into the county borough of West Bromwich, which itself, was absorbed into the metropolitan borough of Sandwell in 1974 (BCM July 1977 p59. April 1989 p60). In **WW1** Tipton was bombed by two Zeppelin aircraft - L21, L19 late on Jan 31 and in the early hours of Feb 1 1916. The L21 dropped a bomb on Waterloo Street killing one person, and another bomb on Union Street killing 14 and injuring 27. It dropped three incendiary bombs on Bloomfield Road and Barnfield Road. The L19 dropped 11 high explosive bombs in the western part of the town between the L&NW Railway station and Bloomfield, where the Bush Inn at No. 127 Park Lane West was hit. For many years some bomb damage was visible on its facade. Tipton Green Junior School now stands on the site of the house first hit (BCM Jan 1976 p40. autumn 1989 pp57-58. summer 1996 p66. autumn 1996 pp56-57) (TB Sept 1995 p30ps. Nov 1995 p3. May 1996 p15p of the bomb) (TSSOP p53p). Tipton Central Schools opened in Oct 1927 on reclaimed mining land. The school later became Tipton **Grammar School** and by 1995 had become the Alexandra High School (TSSOP p122p) (BCM autumn 1995 p18). **Tipton & Coseley Building Society** has its origins in a society established in June 1901 at 30 Owen Street, Tipton. By 1939 the Tipton & District Permanent Benefit Building Society was located at No. 60 High Street, Tipton. In March 1939 in consequence of opening a branch office at Coseley the name of the society was changed to the Tipton & Coseley Permanent Building Society. In March 1972 the name was changed to the Tipton & Coseley Building Society. The society is still (1999) active and has headquarters at No. 70 Owen Street, Tipton (info Edward C Bridgewood, Tipton & Coseley Building Society) (Building Societies Yearbook 1998-99: Official Handbook of the Building Society Association). Tipton has an annual **pram derby** (TB June 1979 p29p). **Neptune Health Park** being built in 1998 at the junction of Neptune Street with Sedgley Road West is said to be the UK's first health park development. The name Neptune is probably from the Neptune Works of Joseph Wright & Co manufacturers of chains and anchors at Tipton (TSSOP p92). **Gambling wins**. Eight Tipton workmates smashed the world record for a pools win when they shared more than £1.5 million from Littlewoods in Aug 1990 (WF p54). By Oct 1999 a family from Tipton had had three separate jackpot wins in the British National Lottery, winning a total of £3.25 million, and defying odds of 350 million to one (The Sunday Telegraph Magazine. Oct 31 1999 p22). **References in literature and elsewhere**. In Ellen Thorneycroft Fowler's novel 'The Farringdons' (1900) Tipton is Slipton (BCM July 1978 pp44-46). Tipton is Tilton in Francis Brett Young's novels (BCM April 1980 pp10-15). There are five Tiptons in the USA, which probably take their name from this Tipton. There is a New Tipton in West Virginia and a Tipton in Wyoming (TB Dec 1975 p30. Jan 1976 p5). **Persons and visitors. George Baker** of Tipton (1881-1955), was a ballad writer who composed ballads on the Hamstead Colliery disaster (1908) and the Dudley Port disaster (1922) (TB March 1974 pp16p-17). The Tipton Harriers are a nationally known athletics club possibly in part due to **Jack Holden**, born at Tipton on March 13 1907, long distance runner, who won the AAA Championship (1950), the Commonwealth Games and European Games marathons. The Jack Holden Garden between Walton Street and Queen's Road was officially opened on July 23 1952 by Alderman AE Bolton, mayor of Tipton. The Duke of Edinburgh met Holden at the opening of the Tipton Sports Union, Gospel Oak Road, on June 4 1971. There is a plaque to his memory on the wall of Tipton Sports and Social Club headquarters in Sedgley Road East (MR p333) (BCM Jan 1987 pp54-57. April 1991 p63) (BCTV p66) (TSSOP pp78p of Holden meeting Duke of Edinburgh, 96p of Holden's Gardens in 1962) (SNSV vol 2 p49). **Princess Marie Louise** of Schleswig-Holstein visited Tipton on Aug 3 1909 and opened the Staffordshire Training Home for Nurses in Lower Church Lane, Tipton. It was demolished a few years prior to 1977 (BCM April 1977 p61) (WBOPP pls 117,118) (TSSOP pp12p,13p). The Prince of Wales (**Edward VIII**) officially opened the Birmingham New Road, which passes on the W side of Tipton, on Nov 2 1927 (TSSOP p12p). Sir **John Chalstrey** born March 17 1931 in Tipton grew up in Wrens Avenue, Tipton. He attended Dudley Grammar School, became a pioneering surgeon at St Bartholomew's Hospital, London, and was Lord Mayor of London 1995-6 (TB April 1996 p7ps) (BCM spring 1997 pp37-42ps). The heaviest woman ever recorded by 1995 was Mrs **Muriel Hopkins** (b1931) of Tipton, who weighed 43 stone 11lb (height 5 feet 11 inch) in 1978. Shortly before her death on April 22 1979 she reportedly weighed 52 stone but this was proved to be an over estimate, and her actual weight was found to be 47 stone 7lb. Her coffin measured 6 feet 3 inches in length and 4 feet 5 inch in width and 3 feet 9 inch deep (GBR 1995 p56). For Tipton characters **Tim the Tatter**, and 'Dennifer' the Tramp see MMBCC p78 and TB Nov 1974 p22.

Tipton Green Area about West Street and Dudley Road and ward of Tipton borough. Formerly in Tipton ancient parish. Tipton Green is the shopping area of Tipton, although the original Tipton (Tibbington) is 0.75m to the NNE. The battle of Tipton Green in the Civil War was an engagement on June 12 1644 in which parliamentarian troops under Lord Denbigh intercepted and routed royalist troops going to defend Dudley Castle. Lord Wentworth, Lord Cleveland, Lord Wilmote, Col Sands and 4,000 horse and many foot soldiers, and other incendiaries were taken prisoner and 100 slain and many wounded (HOWM p87) (BCM April 1987 pp24-27) (OWB pp72-73) (MR p332) (HOS 1998 p74). The battle lasted three hours (TB June 1977 p5. May 1995 p16). At SO 958925 1m NNE of Dudley Castle was a windmill, first shown by Plot's map, then the maps of Jeffrey, and Bowen (WBJ p21). The church, St Paul, on the N side of Owen Street, was built in 1837-1838 (BOE p282). Another church, St Matthew, on the W side of Dudley Road, was built in 1876 (BOE p282). The ecclesiastical parish of Tipton St Paul, created in 1842, is sometimes called Tipton Green (GLAUE p426). By 1999 Tipton Green was a ward in Sandwell metropolitan borough.

Tipton Green Branch of the Birmingham Canal Old Cut Old Main Line (HCMS No. 2). Spurred off the Old Main Line at Tipton Green Junction near Owen Street, Tipton. Passed under Union Street, had a junction with the Island Line at Watery Lane, passed under Alexander Road, and Lower Church Lane and had a junction with the Toll End Branch of the Walsall Canal in the Jubilee Park area. Ran to Horseley Furnaces. Opened in 1805. Closure was sanctioned in 1966 (HCMS No. 2). The canal, which has also been called Green Branch (BCM autumn 1995 p18), is now (1997) totally lost. At Horseley it joined the Toll End Branch of the Walsall Canal. The completion of the Tipton Green Branch and the Toll End Branch in 1809 gave the first link between the Walsall Canal and the Old Main Line.

Tipton Green Junction Junction of the Birmingham Canal Old Cut Old Main Line with its Tipton Green Branch (HCMS No. 2).

Tipton Junction Junction of the Birmingham Canal Old Cut Old Main Line with Lord Wards Canal (HCMS No. 2). To E of Dudley Road.

Tipton Tunnel Forms a part of Lord Ward's Canal (see) and runs to Castle Mill Basin where the Dudley Tunnel, and the Wrens Nest Tunnel start. It is 196 yards long (HCMS No. 2). Completed in 1778 by the 2nd Viscount Dudley and Ward to carry limestone from workings in Castle Hill and Wren's Nest (VB p45). The tunnel has appeared as Lord Ward's Tunnel (VB p45), and is now often considered to be a part of the Dudley Tunnel; the Tipton portal may be haunted; the sound of children's voices were heard there on the water in 1978 (GOD pp17-19).

Tit Bridge Bridge on main road to Mayfield over Tit Brook or formerly Northwood Brook. The bridge was formerly called Tipp Bridge. Isabel Worthington was drowned at Tit Bridge on Sept 30 1671 according to Ellastone PR (NSJFS 1972 p124).

Tit Brook Runs to Mill Brook to the Dove.

Tithebarn Tiny district of Alton, 0.25m SE of Alton. In Alton ancient parish. Takes its name from the parish tithe barn, which probably stood near the present Tithe Barn House (HAF pp201,202).

Tittensor Village on a promontory overlooking a bend in the Trent and a pretty dell formed by a brook which joins the Trent here, 8.5m NNW of Stafford. Former township in Beech quarter in Stone ancient parish. (W p362). The spring that fed Tittensor mill never froze according to the maps of Plot and Bowen, even in the severest frosts (NHS p91) (ESH p31). A diorite axe-hammer Neolithic or Bronze Age has been found at Tittensor and went to the

Potteries Museum (NSJFS 1964 p38). Has appeared as Titesoure, a manor, in DB, and Titneshovere (1236) (SSE 1996 p18), Titesovere (1272), Tentenhall (1617), Tentenshale (1617), Tytenshall (1617), and Titensore (1617) (SHC part 2 1934 p50) (SPN p127). The ending of the name is Anglo-Saxon 'ofer' 'ofre,' a border, margin. So 'Tidwine's border' i.e. the boundary of his manor or land; the exact name is uncertain (DUIGNAN). Its etymology is difficult to solve (ESH p36). Mills gives 'Titta's ridge' (SSE 1996 p18). Gelling thinks 'Titten's ridge' (NSJFS 1981 p2). Or 'Titten's (place) on a slope' (SPN p127). Garner was shown by Mr Molineux a medieval bronze key found at Tittensor (GNHSS p9). The Nuns' Walk is a local name for a track from near Bury Bank Farm to Tittensor church. There is said to have been a nunnery in a house by the farm (SMM p17). There is a tradition of a tunnel from the nunnery to the church. Pickford found a ley line on this course (SMM p17). There was a manor of Tittensor in 1617 (SHC part 2 1934 p50). The London-Carlisle road took a course through Barlaston until c1600 when it was transferred to the higher route through Tittensor (VCH vol 2 p278). The first section of a turnpike road in Staffs ran from Tittensor to Talke. On Oct 8 1799 there was a serious accident at Tittensor when the 'Balloon' coach from Birmingham to Liverpool overturned into a swollen Trent, three passengers drowned (SA Oct 12 1799) (SIS p69). For a landmark stone (unlocated) with the date 1822 at or near Tittensor see Trentham Park. There is a tradition of a tunnel from the nunnery, that was near Bury Bank Farm, to Tittensor church. Pickford found a ley line on this course (SMM p17). In 1840 an organised band of poachers from Longton and Shelton entered the Duke of Sutherland's estate at Tittensor and a riot ensued in which a dog was stabbed (SA March 21 1840) (LOU p191). The annual wake was on the first Sunday in Aug in the C19 (W p362). The present church, St Luke, on the W side of Stone Road, was built in 1880-1881 (BOE p282). Tittensor became a separate ecclesiastical parish in 1882 (GLAUE p426). Willi (sic) Moore broke the men's cycling record in the Tittensor area when he rode 10 miles in 20 minutes 36 seconds on July 29 1972 (GBR 1974 p264). A cigar-shaped object about 40 feet long and 10 feet across tapering at both ends which had a 'pill box' type of dome on top, was seen over Tittensor by a Tittensor farmer, Arthur Johnson, in Dec 1977 (MMSE pp288,62) (FSR vol 24 No 3 p29). For a rhyme from Tittensor see FSBC p55.

Tittensor Chase Neo-Tudor villa 0.75m S of Tittensor, built in 1856 on high ground overlooking the upper Trent Valley on Tittensor Chase estate, which was owned in the C19 by the Duke of Sutherland of Trentham Hall (see). It was known as Tittensor House in 1889, by when it was occupied by the Marquess of Stafford. Between at least 1901 and 1937 it was known as Titensor Chase, although the house appears as Chase House on an old photograph of c1909 (TTOPP p85p). By at least 1896 to at least 1904 it was occupied by Lord Henry George Grovenor (trade directories). The quaint thatched lodge to the house in Spring Vale on the N side of the A34 is now called Wren's Nest Cottage (TTOPP p84p).

Tittensor Common Former common land marked on 1882 OS map in the area of the present Tittensor Chase, 0.75m S of Tittensor. Saxon's Lowe was situated on it. There is a painting by Peter de Wint titled 'Titerson Common' (The Gazette. 1988). The common has also appeared as Tittensor Heath.

Tittensor Hill Hill, 0.5m NNW of Tittensor, on which a large bronze statue of the 1st Duke of Sutherland (1758-1833) of Trentham Hall (see) stands, raised on a high stone plinth. The statue designer was CH Winks and the sculptor Sir Francis Chantry (BOE p285). Erected in 1834 (AGT p20) (CL May 9 1996 p68), or 1836 (BOE p285). In 1999 the monument, then in a state of decline, was scheduled for restoration by the then major shareholder in Trentham Gardens, St Modwen Properties plc (ES April 10 1999 p13p). Has excellent views of Trentham Hall and Lake.

Tittensor Manor 'Tudor' Victorian villa on the E side of A34, Tittensor, said to be built on the site of an older house. Tittensor Manor was reputedly built by a Duke of Sutherland. Supposedly has two tunnels leading under the road to the church with entrances bricked up (MR p334p). In the later C20 it was the property of Staffs county council who used it as a home for the elderly. By 2000 they were using it as office space and a storage depot (info Malcolm Walls).

Tittensor Old Manor House Formerly situated behind Tittensor church, to the SW. The first hall on the site was built by Sir Peter Gerrard in 1405 and razed to the ground on Sept 24 1459. About one third was rebuilt in the late C16 by Sir Peter Gerrard, but was dismantled in 1834. Its fireplace and some of its panelling went to Tittensor Vicarage (illustration of in Staffs Views in WSL) (NSFCT 1940 pp34-35) and to the church (TTOPP p80p). Others say it was probably of early C17 origin. The Lords Gerrard resided here before moving to Gerrard's Bromley Hall. It was later the seat of the Orme family of Hanch Hall (one of whom was a founder of the Orme School, Newcastle-under-

Lyme) (NSFCT 1915 p154) until c1890. The building became ruinous in c1904 (RHPS pp305-306) (LGS p234) (SLM Feb 1959 pp10-11 p of ruins). The remains of the house were visible in 1909, 1915, and 1949 (SHC 1909 p85 note) (NSFCT 1915 p154. 1949 p122). The hall, which has also been called Tittensor Old Hall, was totally demolished in c1963 to make way for a new housing estate (TTOPP p80) (MR p334). In the barn of Tittensor Farm was a roof beam supposedly from Tittensor Old Manor House or from the old church. One beam bore the inscription '1667 Anno Caroli Secundi C.19' (NSFCT 1940 p34) (SLM Feb 1959 p11). Tittensor Old Manor House is said to have had a **chapel** attached to it at its E end. Charles, Baron Gerrard, is stated either to have restored this chapel or to have built an entirely new one on its site in c1667, which survived until 1810. The same year the graveyard was turned into the hall meadow and the gravestones removed and the ground levelled (NSFCT 1940 p34).

Titterton Name of a tollgate, built in the 1840s, on the Warslow-Hartington turnpike road, 0.25m E of Hulme End, by the road to Alstonefield. In Sheen ancient parish (VCH vol 7 p242).

Tittesworth Former township on W-facing slopes of the upper Churnet valley (now dammed for Tittesworth reservoir) in Leek ancient parish (W p730). The house, Upper Tittesworth (see), is 20m NNE of Stafford, the house, Lower Tittesworth, now called Troutsdale Farm (see), is 0.5m to its NW. Has appeared as Teteworth (C13) (SSE 1996 p18), and Tittisworth (W p730). (maps of Bowen and Dower). The name is from the Anglo-Saxon female personal name Tette, Tete, Tetta. So 'Tette's farm or estate' (DUIGNAN), or 'Taetel' (SSAHST 1967 p34), or 'Teot's estate' (SPN p77) or enclosure (SSE 1996 p18). There was possibly a medieval village at Tittesworth, since depopulated (SSAHST 1970 p36). Tittesworth was ecclesiastically severed in 1845 to help create Leek St Luke ecclesiastical parish. It became a separate civil parish in 1866 (GLAUE p426).

Tittesworth Brook Flows through Thorncliffe and joins the Churnet N of Haregate (VCH vol 7 p232).

Tittesworth Farm Tittesworth. Here was found a prehistoric camp (KES p125). Could be now submerged under Tittesworth Reservoir.

Tittesworth Reservoir Lies S of Meerbrook. Built in 1858 by the damming of the Churnet and Meer Brook and at first called New Pool. The boundary between Tittesworth and Leekfrith civil parishes (formerly townships) passes through its centre, as it formerly followed the Churnet. The reservoir, which has also appeared as Tittesworth Lake (NSFCT 1905 p162), was enlarged between 1959 and 1962 (SSE 1993 p11) (SMOPP vol 2 p28). The dam was constructed in 1958 and the water level raised (NSJFS 1967 p85). The raised level destroyed the SE part of Meerbrook village, New Grange (see), Fountain Inn (see), Waterhouse Farm, two farms at New Grange, a garage and several cottages (SVB p123) (HOLF p38). The enlarged reservoir was inaugurated by Princess Margaret in 1962 (VCH vol 7 p235). The reservoir comprised 189 acres in 1967 (English Reservoirs. Bill Howes. 1967 p56). In 1994 an island was created in it for a habitat of the plover at a cost of £10,000 (ES 9 Sept 1994 p11). In a field on the W side of it, Mr W Hall found a mace-head of Neolithic or Bronze Age origin (NSFCT 1945 p82) (NSJFS 1962 p29. 1964 p28) (VCH vol 7 p193).

Tividale (*Tivvy-dale*). Former hamlet now mainly an industrial area by a tributary of the Tame 1.75m SE of Tipton. Formerly in partly Rowley Regis, Tipton (W pp194,707), and Harborne parishes (SGSAS). The original hamlet was about the old Dudley-Oldbury road (1834 OS map). That part of Tividale in Rowley Regis parish appears to have been developed on Sheldon estates (BCWJ p86). **Churches**. The church, **St Michael the Archangel**, on the S side of Tividale Road, was built in 1877-1878. It contained a window depicting the Virgin Mary, beneath which was the legend 'Queen of the Black Country' (TSSOP p26p). This church was demolished in 1984 and the adjoining church hall served as a temporary church until a new one was built in 1996 (info David Mawson). Tividale became a separate ecclesiastical parish in 1879 (GLAUE p426). The mission church, **St Augustine**, a 'tin tabernacle' of 1883, was still standing S of the junction of Dudley Road West and Tipton in 1999 pending demolition. The church, **Holy Cross**, on a hill on Ashleigh Road, was built in 1966 (info David Mawson) (LDD). A large piece of **coal** weighing over five to six tons from Mr Round's colliery at Tividale was exhibited at the World's Exhibition in London in 1851 (W p708). **Tram crash**. On Feb 20 1908 a tram belonging to the Birmingham and Midland Tramway Company travelling from Dudley to Oldbury became derailed and overturned opposite the end of Gypsy Lane (lost) between the Boat Inn at Tividale and the Blue Ball Inn at Brades Village. All the passengers were slightly injured, the conductor James McCabe lost his life. He had been literally crushed by the tram but did not die instantly (BCM Jan 1988 pp50-54). By 1999 Tipton was a **ward** in Sandwell metropolitan borough. For Tividale as a **verb** see

BCM April 1971 p27. **Natives and visitors**. A mile from Tividale on the road to Oldbury (at the present junction of Tipton Road, Dudley Road East and Dudley Road West) there was a white fingerpost which was daubed with the blood of **Elizabeth Dyson**, murdered on June 26 1902; the day Edward VII was due to be crowned (he was crowned in Aug). A cross was drawn with her blood and the name Kate Bryan, who, it was implied, was the one who had been murdered. Elizabeth Dyson was a divorcee from Bradford and a public house pianist known as 'Madame George.' She had moved to West Bromwich with her lover William Lane. Lane murdered her after a break-up in their relationship, and made no attempt to flee. He was hung at Stafford (TB Aug 1984 p5). **Susan Price**, children's writer, was born in Tividale in 1955. She won the 1971 Daily Mail Literary Competition when a pupil of Tividale Comprehensive School. Subsequently she has written 'The Devil's Piper' (c1972/3), 'Twopence a Tub' (1974/5), 'Ghost Song' (1992), and 'Heads and Tales' (1993) (BCM July 1975 pp61-62; she was born in 1956) (VFC p109).

Tividale Hall Is an area S of Tividale, 1.5m N of Rowley Regis. Named after the hall once here, Brindleford Hall (see), or called Tividale Hall.

Tivity Green Rowley Regis. Could it now be Cock Green. Is it the same as Tippity Green?

Tixall Ancient parish and small village on rising ground at the mouth of a small wide dale above the Trent 3m E of Stafford. Aerial photography has shown cropmarks near Tixall believed to represent an enclosure: Its plan, a 'dented' square, indicates it is not Iron Age in date but possibly of the earlier **Bronze Age** (SPJD pp13p,15). For both enteries in DB Tixall appears as Ticheshale. One **manor** was held from Earl Roger de Montgomery by Henry de Ferrers and the other far larger manor was held from Robert de Stafford by Hugh. On Robert de Belesme's forfeiture in Henry I's reign this division of Tixall may have ceased, the whole becoming part of the Stafford barony (SHC 1909 p195). For the later history of the manor see Tixall Old Hall. Tixall was written Tixhaul in c1540 (LI appendix p169). The **name** is from the Anglo-Saxon personal name Ticce, pronounced tich. So 'Ticce's hall.' This was probably a short form of 'ticcen,' a kid (DUIGNAN). Gelling thinks 'kid's nook' (NSJFS 1981 p3) (SPN p128) (SSE 1996 p18). Could be from a Dane called Tyche, Tyche's hall (HAH p58 note). There may have been a wooden Saxon **church** at Tixall. There was certainly a chapel by c1199. In 1772 an earlier small stone church was rebuilt (A History of Tixall. volume 1: Tixall's Churches. Anne Andrews. 1995 pp4,6,43). This may have stood on the site of the present church, St John the Baptist, on the S side of the Ingestre road, SSW of Tixall Old Hall gatehouse. The present church was built in 1849 (BOE p282). As a separate **parish** Tixall is not listed in the Papal Return of 1291 but it probably had separate ecclesiastical identity by then, perhaps even by 1248. But it remained a peculiar jurisdiction of Stafford Collegiate Church until the college was dissolved in the C16 and was then a royal free chapel of St Mary's until 1846 (SHC 1909 p195. 1916 p199) (VCH vol 3 p93) (GLAUE p426). For the Tixall Tithe Cause, Parish and Manor, see OPM pp11-19. In the later C17 Plot found a **spring** near the church which served the village with water and was found to ascend up the village, and along the Trent a red sort of marl with blue veins (NHS pp87,119). The **stone** quarried at Tixall had a high reputation for the beauty of its grain and colour in the early C19, having been used by then for Tixall Hall, the Shire Hall in Stafford, for the new (1817) bridge at Radford and for buildings at Worcester and Birmingham. It was soft, and easily worked when first taken out of the quarry, but after being left exposed to the air became hard and durable (HOT p68) (HOSCC p97). The remains of an **ancient bridge** were discovered between Great Haywood and Tixall in 1938 (SN July 2 1938 p5). The **Bottle Lodge**, or pepper-pot lodge (SGS p171), a tollhouse-looking octagonal stone building, is on the S side of the Great Haywood road facing Tixall Farm at SJ 98452313. It has an ogee roof and resembles the turrets on Tixall Old Hall gatehouse. This led Pevsner and others to wonder if it was built at the same time, in c1575 (BOE p283) (MR p335). It may have been part of Shugborough estate (SN July 26 1996 p8p) or used as a toll house. Others think it was built in c1800 as a lodge for Tixall Hall, as it stands at the junction of the old drive to the hall with the main road (HCMBOPP p55p). It was inhabited until 1927. The last inhabitant before its recent restoration was Mrs Ann Statham (ASOP p92). Its fireplace is a later addition and the chimney was originally a finial (DoE II). (STMSM June 1980 pp17p,18). There were plans to move the building away from Tixall in 1985 (SN May 17 1985 p7p). The building, still on its former site at Tixall, was restored between 1996 and 1998 (SN July 26 1996 p8p. June 25 1998 p23p) (SLM July Aug 1998 pp20-21 pcs) (ES Sept 5 1998 p10p). At a crossroads in the centre of the village is an 18 feet high hexagonal **obelisk** brought from S Wales in 1803. Has been used as a mile post. Has inscribed on it '1776. Stafford 3.5 miles'. DoE (listed II) says the date is 1770; 6 must have worn to a 0? Some say the obelisk was erected when a new front was put to Tixall Hall in 1776. Dr Tylecote believes it marks the site of an ancient preaching cross (NSFCT 1881 p14). Harwood may have confused it with the Tixall Heath assassination cross (SOS p70). Mee calls it a cross (KES p207). (GNHS p111) (BOE p283) (SGS p171) (STMSM June 1980 pp17p,18) (ASOP p26) (Tixall Conservation Area Booklet). At the end of a lime avenue to the E of the obelisk is a **rotunda** moved from Ingestre Park (see) in 1960. **Ingestre and Tixall Local History Group** formed in 1997 (info Dr Anne Andrews). **'Povey's Seedling'** a variety of apple may have had its origins in the Tixall area (ZSB). **Foot-and-mouth disease** broke out at Collier's Farm, Tixall, in late 1967 (SN Dec 8 1967 p10). People have reported **strange experiences** whilst walking through Tixall late at night; for instance, being transported back in time (GLS p97). **Persons and visitors** (and a camel). For **Mary, Queen of Scots,** and **James I** at Tixall see Tixall Old Hall. For Rev **Thomas Loxdale,** the antiquary and rector of Tixall from 1719, or from 1735, see Meretown. For Bishop **Edward Wetenhall** who may have been born at Tixall see Lichfield. **Ann Moore,** the fasting woman of Tutbury (see), was a servant to Mrs Savage, a widow, in Tixall village. She started to work for Mrs Savage in c1777, aged 16 (HOT p76). **Francis William Webb** (d1906), civil engineer mainly for railway locomotives, second son of William Webb, rector of Tixall (1831-1883), was born at Tixall Rectory on May 21 1836. He was the inventor of the steel-headed rail, and the curvilinear slotting machine; he patented more than 75 inventions between 1864 and 1903 (DNB) (A History of Tixall. volume 1: Tixall's Churches. Anne Andrews. 1995 pp59-68). **Thomas Hartshorne.** By the side of the Stafford road on Tixall Heath are two stone seats with this inscription on them

These seats in the place of others...First set up here by him for the Comfort of Travellers .... Are erected in the memory of Thomas Hartshorne Esq

A **camel** brought to this country in a travelling menagerie in the C17 died due to the negligence of his keeper and was buried where he died in Tixall Field (NHS p267).

Tixall Hall Replaced Tixall Old Hall, after it had burnt down in the C18 (SGS p170) or in c1780 (S&W p274). James, 5th Lord Aston, started to build this hall in 1750, but died in 1751 before it was completed. The estate passed to his daughter, Barbara, who married Hon Henry Thomas Clifford (NSFCT 1881 p13. 1945 p89) (Complete Peerage). Their son Sir Thomas Hugh Clifford (1762-1829) completed the house. Several dates are given for it completion; 1780 (THS p297) (BS pp110) (HOSCC p97) (NSFCT 1976 p24) (MR p336) (SN Jan 14 1994 p20) (SPJD p58ps) (HCMBOPP p54p), or 1782 (ASOP p93), or 1787 (NSFCT 1881 p13). Some say it was built on a new site beside the old hall's gatehouse (MR p336) (ASOP p93). The hall was built of stone hewn locally (HOSCC p97), and had a handsome Doric portico, flanked by a lion and lioness (SOS p68; Harwood on the hall) (W p426) (SOSH p223p). Sir Thomas Hugh Clifford let the hall in 1808 to Granville Leveson-Gower (1773-1846) formerly of Trentham Hall (see) (afterwards 1st Earl Granville) and his wife Lady Harriet Elizabeth Cavendish, second daughter of William 5th Duke of Devonshire. Their youngest daughter **Georgiana Fullerton,** poet, novelist and philanthropist, was born at Tixall Hall on Sept 23 1812. A great part of her early life was spent in Paris. In 1833 she married AG Fullerton. Her first novel was 'Ellen Middleton' (1844), followed by 'Grantley Manor' (1847), 'Lady Bird' (1852), and 'Too Strange not to be True' (1852). She died on Jan 19 1885 in Bournemouth (DNB) (PSS pp390-393) (ZSB) (VFC p52). Sir **Thomas Hugh Clifford** was created a baronet in 1814 or 1815 at the especial desire of Louis XVIII King of France. From 1821 he assumed the surname and arms of Constable (Burke's Peerage) (SMC p173; referred to as Sir Thomas HC Constable) (Complete Peerage) in collaboration with his younger brother the poet and antiquarian, Arthur Clifford (1778-1830), author of 'Tixall Poetry; with Notes and Illustrations by Arthur Clifford, Esq' (1813) (BS p109) (PSS pp123-128) (VFC p27). Sir Thomas Hugh Clifford (Constable) died in 1829 and was succeeded by his son Sir Thomas Aston Clifford Constable, who was living at Tixall Hall in 1834 (W 1834 p688). He died in 1870 and was succeeded by his son Sir Frederick-Augustus-Talbot Clifford-Constable (Burke's Peerage). The Chetwynd-Talbots of Ingestre bought Tixall Hall in 1840 (BOE p144) (NSFCT 1945 p89). Another account says by 1844 the hall was in ruins and in 1855 the estate was sold to the Chetwynd-Talbots (NSFCT 1976 p24). By 1851 it appears to have been let; James Tyrer, was the occupier by at least 1851 to at least the early 1860s (W p23) (SAC p72). Tixall Hall became the headquarters of the Staffordshire Yeomanry in WW1 (NSFCT 1945 p89) (HCMBOPP p56p) and was pulled down in 1926 (SGS p170) (MR P335) (SPJD p59) others say the hall was demolished in 1927 (KES p208) (STM

Aug 1964 p34) (NSFCT 1976 p24) (VB p136) (SL p258) (HCMBOPP p54) or in 1962 (NSJFS 1967 p82). Some of the stone from the hall went to build St John's church, Weston Road, Littleworth (see), Stafford (VCH vol 6 p249) (HCMBOPP p54).

ART AT THE HALL IN THE C19. In the 1830s it was said Tixall Hall reputedly once contained Holbein's portrait of Thomas Cromwell (1485?-1540), statesman and Earl of Essex (SSC p126 in the intro) (SOS p68). Broughton says at Tixall Hall was a tapestry depicting the marriage of Prince Arthur. Walpole had mentioned it (SMC p173). In the possession of Sir TA Constable Bt at Tixall Park in the mid C19 were two of the largest paintings by the artist Edward Bird, a native of Wolverhampton (see). One represented the embarkation of Louis XVIII at Dover in 1814, and the other represented his debarkation at Calais (W p92).

GROUNDS. Tixall Park (see) to the N of the hall, and a stretch of the Staffs and Worcs Canal to the S, known as Tixall Wide, were landscaped in the C18 for the purpose of beautifying the hall surroundings. The Cliffords, who were Catholics, built a chapel at the hall in 1828. (Masefield says, the chapel had been used by the later C17 Lord Aston, a Catholic - LGS p236). The Talbots were not Catholic and had the chapel moved to Great Haywood in 1845 (BOE p144), or in 1855 (NSFCT 1945 p89), where it still stands (HCMBOPP p17p). There is an ice-house at SJ 993236, 1m ENE of the hall (IHB p396). The stables laid out in a crescent in the early C19, still remain, and have been converted to residences.

Tixall Heath Former common land lying in the area of Tixall Heath Farm 1m WNW of Tixall, in Tixall parish. Two urns of Bronze Age origin have been found on the heath; they were destroyed (Britannia. Camden. R Gough ed 1789. vol 2 p390) (NSJFS 1964 p39). The same or other urns excavated from burial mounds on Tixall Heath were noted by Loxdale as being in Lord Aston's possession at Tixall Old Hall in the early C18 (SHJ spring 1991 p13). In 1492 or 1494 (SHC 1909 p150 note) (COI) Sir Humphrey Stanley of Pipe, Lichfield, had Sir William Chetwynd of Ingestre Hall (see) murdered on Tixall Heath. The reason is said to be because of Stanley's jealousy of Chetwynd. Stanley had been instrumental in putting Henry VII on the throne, but when king, Henry VII showed preference for Chetwynd by making him gentleman usher. Stanley tricked Chetwynd onto the heath, asking him in a letter, purporting to be from a Randolph Brereton, to meet at Stafford the next morning. The letter was sent on the Friday night before the Feast of the Nativity of St John the Baptist. Stanley and 20 others intercepted Chetwynd as he went to his appointment and murdered him (PT) (HOL pp98-99) (SMC p173) (SOS p70) (GNHS p111) (S&W p273) (COI pp118-122) (LGS p234) (ROT pp56-57). The spot where the murder took place is near the Halfway House, where the lane from Ingestre joins the road from Tixall, at SJ 951234. An ancient cross of hard moor stone about three feet high, said to have been brought from a ruined mansion in Wales was placed on the site just E of King's Low in c1803. By 1887 it had been broken down (SOS p70 note) (COI p120) (1905 OS Map) (SCSF p87). The cross is now in Tixall church.

Tixall Old Hall Built at Tixall, N of the church, in 1555 by Sir Edward Aston (NSFCT 1881 p13) or in c1575 (the Astons moved to Tixall leaving their former seat, Haywood Hall (see), in c1500 - HHHC p68). Tixall Old Hall probably succeeded an earlier hall of medieval origin; Tixall was held by the De Wasteney family from the mid C12 to 1468, then the Littletons, until by marriage, it passed to the Astons (SPJD p56), with the marriage of Joan Littleton to Sir John Aston of Haywood Hall (see) in 1507. For the descent of the Astons see Haywood Hall (A History of Tixall. Anne Andrews. 1995. p8). Tixall Old Hall was the Aston seat to the mid or later C18 when the Cliffords, their successors, moved to build Tixall Hall (see), begun in 1750 by James, 5th Lord Aston. During her captivity at Chartley (Old) Hall, **Mary, Queen of Scots** (1542-1587) was kept prisoner at Tixall Old Hall for two weeks between Aug 8 and 28 1586 (NSFCT 1886 p35) (LGS p235) (SIOT p11) (SGS p170) (SPJD p58) or 17 days (VB p136), so her apartments at Chartley (Old) Hall (see) could be searched to implicate her in the Babington Plot. On leaving the hall, she disappointed the poor, who accosted her for alms, saying she had nothing to give (NSFCT 1881 p13). (W p45) (LGS p235) (STM Aug 1964) (Mary Queen of Scots: the Captive Years. J Keith Cheetham 1982) (TOS p53) (ROT p55). For Sampson Erdeswick of Sandon Old Hall (see) on the old hall see SOS pp68-70 or SH pp29,79. Sir Walter Aston (d1639), 1st Lord Aston, Ambassador to Spain (1620-1625), entertained James I at Tixall Old Hall in late Aug 1617. James I was en route between Stafford and Hoar Cross (LGS p235) (CWF p131) (SIOT p73) (R&S p25) (HOS p37). Aston was a friend of Michael Drayton; Drayton visited the hall and Tixall appears in his 'Polyolbion'

Trent, by Tixall graced, the Astons' ancient seat,

Which oft the Muse hath found her safe and sweet retreat.

(LGS p235) (SL p104). Some poetry by Gertrude Aston, fourth daughter of Sir Walter Aston, and wife of Henry Thimelby, appears in 'Tixall Poetry; with Notes and Illustrations by Arthur Clifford, Esq' (1813) (PSS pp471-472) (VFC p128). Walter Aston (d1678), 2nd Lord Aston, who remained Catholic, was a royalist in the **Civil War** (HOS p37). After losing the battle of Hopton Heath some of the parliamentary force ransacked the hall en route for Lichfield. Lord Aston was absent at the time and his wife and young daughter were advised by the parliamentary commander to lock themselves in a closet for safety (BFS p18). In 1644 parliamentary troops occupied the hall (NSFCT 1945 p89). Walter Aston (d1678) was patron of Izaak Walton, and a copy of Walton's 'Lives,' dated June 14 1670, given to Aston, was kept at the hall for many years (LGS p235). Charles Cotton's poem 'Duke of Espernon' published in 1669-70 was in the hall library; a letter, believed to be by Cotton, was included in the folio (LPCC p34). **Tixall Old Hall and the Popish Plot.** In Aug 1678 Titus Oates, a former Baptist minister who had been converted to Catholicism after being sheltered in Jesuit houses on the continent but who later nursed a grievance against Catholics when expelled for misconduct, brought to public attention a supposed plot contrived by Catholics to overthrow Charles II and install his brother, James, a Catholic, on the throne. All over the country troops were sent to keep watch on houses where Catholics were meeting in secret. Catholic meetings at Tixall Old Hall were arranged by Walter Aston (d1720), 3rd Lord Aston, and attended by his friend, a fellow Catholic, William Howard, Viscount Stafford, and others in the 1670s. Whilst troops were near the hall Aston's steward, Stephen Dugdale, a 38 year old Catholic, fled into their company after being discovered to have embezzled a large sum of his lordship's money. He was arrested as a suspect and imprisoned in Stafford Gaol in the North Gate. He was persuaded by William Southall of Penkridge to turn informer and implicate Aston and Stafford in a plot to murder Charles II. Dugdale swore that he had been promised by Viscount Stafford 1000 crowns and enrolment in the calendar of saints to secure the murder of the king. Elizabeth Elde, a servant of Lord Aston, then reputedly supplied further information to Dugdale in prison, which further incriminated Lord Aston: That there had been a secret meeting between Aston and a priest called Fitter, the RC chaplain to the Fowler family at St Thomas' Hall, a house built on the site of the former St Thomas' Priory (see). In the meeting, which took place at a place called Brancot (see), Aston reputedly confided to Fitter that he regretted letting Dugdale leave with such dangerous knowledge in his possession. The contents of the meeting were then related by Fitter to his master's daughter, Miss Fowler, who then supposedly told Elizabeth Elde, who went straight to Dugdale. Dugdale's information was used as further evidence in Oates' Popish Plot, and Aston and Stafford and the others were tried for treason. The former was impeached and committed to the Tower of London for six years, whilst the latter was beheaded on Dec 29 1680; two Catholic priests named Ireland, and Gavan of Wolverhampton (see) were beheaded; another priest, Andrew Bromwich of Old Oscott (see), said to have been beheaded, was in fact reprieved; another priest named William Atkins of Wolverhampton (see), was condemned to death, but died in Stafford Gaol; and a number of other Catholics suffered prison terms. According to Stephen Dugdale it was whilst he was concealed behind an oak tree at Tixall - since known as Oates' Oak (see) - he overheard the treasonable conversation between Aston and Stafford (SMC pp67-70) (GNHS p409) (A Short History of the English People. JR Green 1898 p650) (LGS pp235-236) (SG p109) (SOSH pp221,222-224) (KES p209) (STM Aug 1964 p34) (VCH vol 3 p106) (FSP pp88-91,96) (STMSM June 1976 p28) (ROT p56). **Dr Plot's visit.** In the early 1680s Plot noted scarcely two windows in the hall were alike. He reported a frog rain on the bowling green in front of the hall. The frogs as spawn may have been swept off the moors in clouds (NHS pp24,359 tab 29). The stalagmite Plot noted in Lord Aston's possession was used as an illustration in NHS p182 tab II fig II. Reputedly there was a **secret tunnel** from Tixall Old Hall to Haywood Hall (see), Great Haywood. The hall was destroyed by **fire** in the C18 (SHOS vol 2 p17; at back a plate showing remains of a beautiful Gothic window and fireplace and coat of arms). As well as stone from the Georgian hall, demolished in 1926/7, going into the building of St John's church, Weston Road, Littleworth (see), some from this hall was found then and it went into that church (LGS p265). (CL Oct 24 1957 pp876ps,877).
GROUNDS. The massive stone gatehouse was built by Sir Walter Aston in 1530 (NSFCT 1881 p13) or in c1575 (BOE p283) (SL pp97 pl18). It is in the classical style. Erdeswicke in 1598 said it was 'one of the fairest pieces of work made in late times.' Bannister-Fletcher on Renaissance Architecture considered it one of the purist examples of early renaissance architecture in

England (HAH pp78-79). Pevsner thought it perhaps the most ambitious gatehouse in England (BOE p283). In 1721 the gatehouse walls were beginning to show signs of crumbling, and Richard Trubshaw, who called it the 'great Archway,' undertook a restoration. In 1808 Trubshaw's great-grandson made a sketch of what he called 'the great Arch of Gateway' (HAHS p51). The chimneys that used to be on it were removed before 1896. Two Tudor fireplaces remain. In 1968 it was bought by the Landmark Trust. Their work to restore it started in 1976 (SGS p171) (STMSM June 1976 p28. June 1980 pp17ps,18) (NSFCT 1976 p24) (SLM Christmas 1995 p30pcs). It still (1998) survives incongruously isolated in a field. (GNHS pp110,111) (W p426) (HOSCC p98il) (NSFCT 1924 p87il) (VCH vol 2 p190; built of local Tixall sandstone) (STM Sept 1970 p23p) (ASOP p93) (AWM p28) (ANE) (ROT pp54p-56) (SN Jan 14 1994 p20p).

Tixall Park Medieval deer park enclosed out of forest (EDP p179). In existence by 1497 (NSJFS 1962 p76). The park, of 600 acres, appears to have been situated N of Tixall Old Hall (HOT p69); Hanyards may be derived from 'Haguna's gate,' which may have been an entrance to it (DUIGNAN p74). In the C18 the park may have been landscaped by Lancelot 'Capability' Brown (SL p133). Tixall Park Pool lies 0.5m NW of Tixall Old Hall gatehouse.

Tixall Wide Deliberate widening of the Trent and Mersey Canal at Tixall in order to beautify the view southwards from Tixall Hall; to provide the illusion of a lake (HOT p71) (SL p245) (SWY p39p) (SPJD p58). Or known as The Broad Water (1977 OS map 1:25,000).

Toad Hole Dell at Branston, close by Paget School 1.25m ESE of Tatenhill, leading down to the Trent. A loop in the river possibly a landing place for access to Shobnall (IVNF).

Tobacco Box Hill Name for the area immediately S of the junction of Brettell Lane with the Stourbridge Wolverhampton road in the late C18, in Amblecote parish. The name was still in use by 1871 and survived into the C20 as Box Hill and Bacca Box (VCH vol 20 p51).

Todd's End In Staffs but close to the Dudley enclave of Worcs. At NNE end of Dudley Castle Hill. There was a tiny hamlet of Todd's End by 1901 (OS map Sheet 67.12). The name is now lost.

Toft House 1.5m WNW of Dunston. Built in c1700 and in its original form was a T-shaped house. Was known in the early C19 as Old Toft (VCH vol 5 p143). To the SE is Toft Farm, a C18 house, formerly New Toft House (VCH vol 5 pp142-143), and has also appeared as The Toft.

Toft House 1.25m SW of Trentham. In Trentham parish (W p434). At SJ 852397 was a burial mound which has been ploughed out but was four feet high (NSFCT 1983 p12). Has also appeared as The Toft.

Toftgreen Farm House 2.25m NW of Rushton Spencer church. Formerly in Rushton Spencer township in Leek ancient parish. Has also appeared as Toss Green (OS map 1834). There were houses in the Toftgreen area by the later C18 (VCH vol 7 p224).

Tofthall Farm House under 0.5m E of Heaton. Formerly in Heaton township in Leek ancient parish. The present house retains some C17 features. In 1741 it was the seat of William Armett or Armitt, sheriff of Staffs in 1764; he improved the house and laid out a walled garden (NSFCT 1870 p37) (VCH vol 7 p187); another branch of the Armitts lived at Thorneyleigh (OL vol 2 p86) (HOLF p24). In 1775 the house was known as Toft Hall. It was remodelled and extended in the mid C19 (VCH vol 7 p187).

Tolldish Extremely tiny hamlet in mossy ground above a tributary of the Trent, if not a single house, 1.25m SSE of Hixon.

Toll End Former hamlet near the head stream of the Tame now a residential district 1.5m ENE of Tipton. Formerly in Tipton ancient parish. Toll End was a hamlet in the C19 and a ward of Tipton borough. It is now submerged into the Black Country. There was a Joh'e atte Tella in 1327 and 1332 and a John Tolle in 1460 and a Richard Tole in 1597. The name has appeared as Tullerds End (1754) (HOTIP pp15,181) (TMS p129). There was a pound on the Toll End Road (BCM Oct 1972 pp29-30. April 1975 p44) (TWDOP p50p). The name is not necessarily from a tollhouse here, but could be from a person with a surname like O' the' Hulle' or Atte Holle, perhaps they lived at a clay hole or sand pit and the name of the place they named became corrupted to Tole (which it is on Plot's map) or Toll (BCM Oct 1972 pp29-30, April 1975 p44).

Toll End Branch of the Walsall Canal. Spurred off the Walsall Canal at Toll End Junction. Passed N of Alexandra Road, Horseley Heath. It terminated at Horseley, where it had a junction with the Tipton Green Branch of the Birmingham Canal Old Cut Old Main Line: The completion of these two branches in 1809 gave the first link between the Walsall Canal and the Birmingham Canal Old Cut Old Main Line. Closure was sanctioned for the two branches in 1966 (HCMS No. 2). Some say the Toll End Branch continues to join the Birmingham Canal New Cut New Main Line (or Island Line) N of Victoria

Park, Tipton (BCM autumn 1995 pp18-19) (Canals of The West Midlands. Charles Hadfield. vol 5 of The Canals of The British Isles. see map p67). It is now abandoned and in places filled in. Has also appeared as the Toll End Communication Canal (TSSOP p55).

Toll End Hall Toll End. Said to have stood near Cotterill's farmhouse on the S side (OH p59); this hall is different to the other Toll End Hall (HOTIP p185). Seat of Gerard Wharwood in the C16. The Wharwood (or Whorwood) family were the owners of Sandwell Hall and were strong royalists in the Civil War and probably their house at Toll End was partly destroyed in the war, for the family appear to have left Tipton at about this time. The house, also called Wharwood's Hall, may have been partly restored for it is said James Bagnall lived here. According to tradition the western wall was still standing in 1800 showing a large gothic window similar in design to a large window of a church; it may possibly have been brought here from the ruined Sandwell Priory (HOTIP p185) (OH p59).

Toll End Hall Toll End. May have faced the Horseley Road overlooking the Toll End pound (OH p58); this hall is different to the other Toll End Hall. This hall was built in c1760 and has been known as Toll End Castle. It was the seat of the Bagnalls, ironmasters. Later on it was owned by James Solly, industrialist of Great Bridge, and still later it was the property of Richard Mason. It had been demolished by 1915 (HOTIP p188 pl III) (TWDOP p51p).

Toll End Junction Junction of the Walsall Canal with its Toll End Branch (HCMS No. 2) at Moors Mill Lane, S of Tame Valley Junction.

Tom Knocker's Wood Formerly situated around the junction of Quinton Road West and West Boulevard, on the western edge of Harborne parish. It was mostly felled in the mid 1930s to make way for new estate building. Said to be so called after an agricultural labourer who hung himself from a tree in the wood (OHOPP p17p): His ghost is said to haunt the area (HOPP pl 46).

Tomlinson's Corner House 3.5m ENE of Bagot's Bromley.

Tompkin Small hamlet on high ground above the valley containing Stanley Pool 1m ENE of Bagnall. Formerly in Bucknall and Bagnall chapelry in Stoke-upon-Trent ancient parish. Has also appeared as Tomkin. The name is said to be a corruption of 'Tom or Tam's skin.' From Tom, a local boy, captured and skinned alive by roundheads in Civil War at Tomkin Farm (STM July 1970 p27). Or from Tam, a 15 year old drummer boy in the Young Pretender's army in the 1745 Jacobite Rebellion, who Squire Murhall had skinned in revenge for the way Highlanders had been billeted on him or treated him. Tam's skin was intended to make a drum. On being proved unworkable at a tannery in Endon (see) it was buried at this place now called Tompkin. Although some say the skin was made and hung for a time in Endon church until it was thought unlucky, for there had been cattle deaths and crop failures in the district. Motorists have claimed to have seen Tom's ghost on the Leek Road (STMSM April 1978 p20p of an old gravestone with the old spelling Tomkin) (BPCSM p8) (SVB p25) (GLS p98).

Toot Hill Minute hamlet in undulating country near the head of a tributary of the Tean 1.25m SSW of Croxden. The burial mound near Oldwood Farm at SK 05763796 is 12 paces in diameter and six feet high. It was excavated by Redfern in 1863; nothing was found. Excavated again in c1933 and some flints and a half penny dated 1806 were found. Formerly the mound was much larger and probably round and dome-shaped. By the 1930s it was flat-topped. It is a listed monument. Toot Hill lies at the N end of a ley line stretching to Toot Hill near Woodgate running through Maiden's Well (SMM p165 see map). (HOU p352. 1886 p36) (NSFCT 1933 pp163-165. 1908 p108) (NSJFS 1965 p36). The name is from the burial mound, here, which Redfern learnt was in a field called 'Tootle Field' which convinced him the mound was called Toot Hill and dedicated to the Celtic god Toth or Teut (HOU pp17-19,352). Writing about Tettenhall Duignan says 'tote-hill and 'toot-hill' could be construed in Middle English as 'mount of observation' (DUIGNAN p151). Or is derived from Tota's hill (LGS p238).

Toot Hill Hill at Woodgate, over 1m SE of Uttoxeter, with fine views over the Dove Valley (LTD p113). The burial mound at SK 10143184 was excavated by Redfern in 1860. It is 25 paces in diameter and 5.5 feet high. Two cremations were found and Celtic and Roman pottery and a Roman storage jar (JBAA vol 29 pp264-265) (HOU pp22,23,24il,25il,26) (HOU 1886 pp33-35) (VCH barrow list) (NSFCT 1908 pp110,111) (NSJFS 1965 p50). The mound is a listed monument. Toot Hill lies at the S end of a ley line stretching to Toot Hill near Croxden running through Maiden's Well (SMM p165 see map). The name is from the mound which was dedicated to the Celtic god Toth or Teut (HOU pp17-19,20,352). Or is from Tota's hill (LGS p238).

Toot Hill Hill 0.25m W of Alton. In Alton parish. (NSFCT 1908 p108). Toothill Woods are NT property. The name is from Tota's hill (LGS p238).

Toothill Rock On Toot Hill, Alton, at SK 068425. (BATR).

Top Farm On Sheen Moor nearly 1.5m NNW of Sheen. In Sheen ancient par-

ish. There was a house here by 1716 (VCH vol 7 p242).

Top Field Low Burial mound. Said to be near Deepdale. Excavated by Carrington in 1848. A few fragments of bone and pottery were found (TYD p115) (NSJFS 1965 p38).

Top Low Burial mound 0.5m WSW of Blore (Ray). Found to contain 14 skeletons of Beaker people in a crouched or contracted position resembling the pre-natal attitude and suggesting that these people believed in a rebirth after death. Is 309 metres above sea level at SK 12964914. It is N to S 19 paces wide and E to W 13 paces wide and three feet high. It was excavated by Carrington in 1849 who found 14 interments, and re-excavated by Pape in 1929 who found a stone axe fragment which went to the Potteries Museum. It is a listed monument (TYD pp133-138 plan) (VCH vol 1 no 20) (BAP vol 1 p88 fig 59) (NSFCT 1926 p146. vol 64 pp89-97) (DAJ vol 75 pp107,114,119) (NSJFS 1962 p33. 1965 pp33-34) (HOS p9).

Top Moor Farm 1m ENE of Kingstone. Has also appeared as Top Moor (1834 OS map).

Top of Ecton 0.5m SSE of Ecton. For the burial mound to the SW see Ecton Hill.

Top o' the Cross In Quarnford parish. There was a house here by 1770 (UHAW).

Top o' th' Edge E end of Longnor. Formerly in Alstonefield ancient parish. Ghostly apparitions have been reported in this area (L p49).

Top o' th' Hill Area in the vicinity of the school, Gallowstree Lane, Upper Mayfield (MOM p26p). However, the 1834 OS map shows a Top of the Hill in the area of Ashfield Farm, to the W of Middle Mayfield and to the S of Dydon.

Totmonslow Tiny hamlet in a hollow in undulating country above the Blithe under 1m ESE of Draycott-in-the-Moors. In Draycott-in-the-Moors ancient parish. The name is from a burial mound on Oak Hill to some Anglo-Saxon chief (W p774), probably called Tatmann or Totman 'the bright and happy fellow' (DUIGNAN) (MOS p7) (E p9), or Tatmonn (WMMA p144). Or the mound may have associations with the Celtic deity, Toutates, identified with the war-god, who was a sort of Celtic Zeus. Zeus is associated with oak trees and the mound is on Oak Hill (NSFCT 1908 p108). Or 'deadman's low' (SPP p33). Or 'Tatmann's enclosure' (SPN p33). (SD p110) (BNDA p1). A shepherd, Joseph Lees (NHS), Rees or Reeves (W), of Totmonslow, living sometime prior to the late C17, lived to the age of 127 on account, so he claimed, of never smoking, never consulting a doctor and never taking medicine, never drinking between meals and by alleviating his thirst by rolling pebbles in his mouth (NHS pp325-326) (W pp57,774). Broughton, writing earlier in the C19 than White, says he lived to the age of 120 and was examined by Dr Morton (SMC p173).

Totmonslow Former administrative division (hundred) of Staffs, covering the NE area of the county (GNHS p74) (ESH pp45-50). Has appeared as Tatemaneslav (DB), Tateslav (DB) and later as Tatemanneslawa (SPN p33). The name is from a burial mound at Totmonslow, where the hundred court appear to have met in late Anglo-Saxon times. Parishes, townships and extra-parochial liberties in the **North Division** were: Alstonefield, Blore (with part of Calton), Bradnop, Butterton (formerly in Mayfield parish), Cauldon, Cheddleton, Consall, Elkstone, Endon, Fawfieldhead, Grindon, Heathylee, Heaton, Hollinsclough, Horton, Ilam, Ipstones (with part of Foxt), part of Kingsley, Leek, Leekfrith, Longnor, Longsdon, Okeover, Onecote, Quarnford, Rushton James, Rushton Spencer, Sheen, Tittesworth, Warslow, Waterfall (with part of Calton) (W p718) (S&W p284) (GLAUE p415). Dilhorne is placed in the North Division by Langford (S&W p284). In the **South Division** were: Alton, Bradley-in-the-Moor, Bramshall, Caverswall, Cheadle, Checkley (with part of Foxt), Cotton, Croxden (with part of Calton), Denstone, Dilhorne, Draycott-in-the-Moors, Ellastone, Farley, Forsbrook, Gratwich, part of Kingsley, Kingstone, Leigh, Mayfield (with part of Calton), Musden Grange, Rocester, Rudyard, Uttoxeter, Wetton (W p718) (S&W p300) (GLAUE p415). Sheen and Warslow are placed in the south division by Langford (S&W p300).

Totnall Hall E of Cherry Orchard, Old Hill. Seat of colliery owner John Henry Higgs. Ironically mining was also the hall's downfall; it was a victim of subsidence (TB April 1983 p5 see map).

Tower Hill Former tiny hamlet on rising ground above the Tame, now a suburb, over 2m S of Great Barr. Formerly in Handsworth ancient parish. The name, marked on Plot's map, may be from a folly erected on the long slope here running up to the former Perry Wood. The folly may have been erected by the Wyrleys of Hamstead Hall as an eye catcher for the hall (MNB p55). There was a hamlet at Tower Hill by 1775 (MNB p67). The area was developed with housing between 1917 and 1937.

Towland House 0.5m NW of Longsdon church. Only marked on maps of the C19.

Town Croft Hilderstone. Perhaps refers to the old village settlement (NSFCT 1910 p165).

Townend Area 0.25m SSE of Fulford.

Town End Former area of Handsworth ancient parish (HANDR pviii).

Townend Minute hamlet on a promontory overlooking the Manifold 0.5m SSW of Sheen. At SK 10926040 S of Townend is a burial mound which was excavated by Carrington in 1851. It had previously been disturbed. A cremation was found. EW 20 paces, NS 25 paces in diameter and two feet high (TYD p179) (NSJFS 1965 p46). It is a listed monument. To the W is Lowend.

Town End District of Wednesbury (WAM p53). The name is not found in medieval documents (HOWV p108). John Wesley complained in his diary in Nov 1745 that his horse stuck fast in a quagmire near 'Wednesbury Town End' on the Wednesbury-Bilston road from which he had to be rescued by his friends by the light of several small candles (HOWV p146).

Townend Bank District of NW Walsall. Has its centre on Blue Lane (so named by 1768) over 0.5m NW of Walsall parish church (VCH vol 17 p160). This area is now considered to be Birchills (OS map 1:25,000 1993) (Birmingham A-Z 1995). Here fork roads to Wolverhampton, Bloxwich and Stafford. The name occurs in 1557, but it may be the 'head of the town' mentioned in 1309 (VCH vol 17 p147). Here was a Methodist chapel (W p643). A pinfold stood at the corner of Stafford Street and Wisemore Lane (now Wisemore) (SNWA p82). By the mid C19 there were Irish immigrants in the Blue Lane area (VCH vol 17 p145); Potato Square was a court in this area derogatively named in consequence of Irish immigrants at Townend Bank (SNWA pp84,103). Had become a very bad slum area by 1876, when redeveloped (VCH vol 17 pp160-161,221). The name is preserved in tiny streets called Townend and Townend Bank.

Town Field Wolstanton. Perhaps refers to the old village settlement (NSFCT 1910 p165).

Townfields Pleasant cluster of cottages beyond Lower Sandford Street, at the western edge of Lichfield (LAL p18).

Town Fields 600 acres anciently belonging to the burgesses of Newcastle-under-Lyme which they gave up at the time of the enclosure Act of 1816 (W p304).

Townfields Rownall, Wetley Rocks. Here are still the signs of the old strip farming system (CVH pl 29).

Town Hall Became a ward of West Bromwich borough, when created in 1882 (VCH vol 17 p45).

'Town Hall' Tree Name for the predecessor to 'Old Constable Wick Tree,' the tree by the stocks in the centre of Caverswall village. It was planted in 1672 and replaced in 1935 (SMOPP vol 1 p7p).

Town Head District of Alton, to the E of the church.

Town Head 0.25m NE of Foxt. Minute hamlet and now an extension of Foxt. Perhaps, the settlement started here as a grange to Croxden Abbey (SVB p78). It has also been called Foxt Town (SVB).

Town Hill SE of Yoxall church. Here, at SK 143188, is a damaged moat. It probably surrounded a property of the clerk Roger de Yoxall, who obtained land here in the C13 (SSAHST 1982-3 p58) (CAMS p64). Is the original site for the Yoxall manor house, now lost, but the gatehouse still exists incorporated or connected into a house (IVNF photograph of gatehouse).

Townhills To N of Stockton, Baswich, but on S side of the Sow (BERK pp13 see map,63).

Town Pool Weston Park, Weston-under-Lizard.

Townsend District of and 0.5m E of Bucknall. Does not mean the end of the village rather the boundary field. It is quite a common field name (NSFCT 1913 p46).

Town's End Eccleshall. Here the royalists attacked in the Civil War (ROT p23).

Town's End Kinver. Area about the junction of High Street and Stone Lane (VCH vol 20 p121).

Townsend Penkhull. Perhaps refers to the old village settlement (NSFCT 1910 p165).

Town's End Walsall. A hamlet in the foreign of Walsall? (SHOS vol 2 p73). Perhaps was at Townend Bank (see).

Townsend House High Street, Sedgley (BTBC p61p of c1905). Seat of Charles Kemp Homer, grandfather of Frederick Augustus Homer in 1851 (SDOP p43p). Frederick Homer, remembered for his fight against the evils of drink and founder of the local temperance movement, was born here. The 'Band of Hope' in Sedgley was known as 'Homer's Army' (OS map Sheet 67.07). Later the house became the residence of Henry Bickerton Whitehouse, owner of Priorfield Ironworks, Deepfields (SDOP p43).

Townwell Fold Street off Darlington Street, Wolverhampton, behind the Cock Inn. In this street were the town's wells - Pudding Well, Horse Well, Washing Well and Meat Well (W p76) (WJO April 1905 p88). 'Fold' is a remnant of the town's involvement in the wool trade. It was in Townwell Fold on Easter Tuesday 1838, Hinde, making for Darlington Street, experienced the old custom of heaving when he was unexpectedly carried aloft by a group of women who would not put him down until he had paid the 'forfeit' (GW) (SCSF p13). Joseph Whittaker (b1871), lived in Townwell Fold between c1875 and c1915, then a slum area; his novel 'Tales of Tumble Fold' (1903) details the hard lives of Wolverhampton's poor in the 1870s and 1880s (PSS pp357-360) (SOSH p308) (WOLOP p50p of in 1913).

Toye's Well Well at Great Haywood. The pump to this well was remaining in 1997 near to Rock Cottages in Great Haywood (HHHC p10).

Toys, The Over 1m WNW of Enville, in Enville ancient parish. In existence by 1496 (VCH vol 20 p94) and has also been called Toy's Farm.

Toy's Green Former small hamlet in the area of present Corngreaves Trading Estate 0.5m SSE of Cradley Heath. The name appears in the 1851 census and on 1947 OS map 1:25,000 (sheet 32/98) at SO 943854. The name Toy frequently appears in the Halesowen PR in the early C18 (SNSV vol 1 p334).

Travellers Rest Inn Inn 0.5m NE of Flash, at the junction of the Buxton and Longnor roads at Flash Bar (TTTD p97) or called Flash Gate. Situated at 1534 feet and is considered the third highest inn in England after Tan Hill Inn, Yorks (1727 feet) and Cat and Fiddle Inn, Ches (1690 feet) (NSFCT 1947 p168). The inn was in existence by the later 1820s and was so called by 1834 (VCH vol 7 p51). Some say it was once called the Dun Cow (Real Ale in and around The Potteries. CAMRA. 4th Ed. p30). The inn was reputedly frequented by pedlars and coiners who allegedly occupied the area in the C18 (BEV p20). In Feb 1834 some female button makers of the locality used the inn as a meeting place for the setting up of a trade union. The promoters of the trade union were brought to trial at Stafford in July 1834, and the case was heard by Sir John Williams, the judge who had sentenced the Tolpuddle Martyrs to transportation. However in this case the women were released without punishment, owing to their plea of guilt, and because of their good character (SA Aug 2 1834 p2) (VCH vol 7 p53). It was to this inn that the Flash Loyal Union Society or 'Teapot Club' paraded (DP p58). Two young men died after their car crashed into the inn in Feb 1994 (ES Feb 21 1994 p1).

Trench Brook A trench cut for the scheme for making the Stour navigable from Stourbridge to the Severn under an Act of 1662. It ran from Bells Mill (formerly Willetts Mill) to Prestwood. It seems never to have been operational and was superseded by the Stourbridge Canal, completed in 1779. In the C18 it was known as the Navigation Cut and later as Trench Brook. In 1983 the cut, though dry, was visible for most of its course (VCH vol 20 p127).

Trent, River Third largest river in England (HOT p21) and chief river of the Midlands and is one of the few rivers in the world to flow from S to N. The total length of the river is 170 miles; 40 miles of it are tidal and 90 miles are navigable (TTTD p155). In Staffs it flows for 11 miles from the source to its confluence with the Lyme at Hanford; 22m to the Sow at Shugborough; 30m to the Blithe at Nethertown; 34m to the Swarbourn at Wychnor; 36m to the Tame; 36.25m to the Meese; 36.5m to the Derbys border; 43m to its leaving the county, and 43.5m to where the Dove joins it in Derbys. The upper reach through Knypersley Park was called Park Brook on account of it flowing through the former deer park (NSFCT 1991 p47 note). The downward gradient of the river flattens out after Stone to pass through the central, low-lying region of the county (HOS p8). Hence the Upper Trent flows quite rapidly. The bed drops 10 feet a mile between Stoke and Shugborough after which the river becomes more sluggish (WMLB p16). Its constant flooding in this valley and plain creates excellent fertile land for cattle, providing the butter once sold at Uttoxeter market and the leather for the boots and shoes made at Stafford and Stone. Its regular flooding at Alrewas helped to make the osier beds which provided the village with willow to make baskets (VB p37). At a point between Alrewas and Wychnor Bridges the Trent becomes the Trent and Mersey Canal for a short distance (NSJFS 1975 p100).

Ptolemy's river Trisanton was identified with the Trent until Henry Bradley identified it with River Arun, Sussex, in 1883. Tacitus' Annals, xii, c.31 (115-117 AD) mentions another British Trisantona which identifies with the Trent (DUIGNAN) (NSFCT 1946 p159). The Trent is mentioned twice by Bede, the first time in c655 as Treanta, as the boundary assigned by Oswin, king of the Northumbrians, to the kingdom of the South Mercians (lib vol iii cap 24), and the second time as the scene of a battle between Ecgfrith, king of Northumbrians, and Æthelred of Mercia in 679 (lib vol iv cap 21) (SHC 1916 p133). Later the Trent has appeared as Trentan (956), Trent (1267-1559), Trente (1268-1595); it was called Trent and Treant by Leland in c1540 (SPNO p21). **Name.** It possibly shares the same root as the Derwent. Derwent is probably from dwr-gwyn, 'the clear water' (NSFCT 1908 p127). Trisantona is a genuine British word having the force of 'trespasser,' ie; a river prone to overflow its banks (NSFCT 1946 p159) (SPNO p21) (SSE 1987 p32) (SPN p26). Is of Celtic origin (SDW p9). Duignan agrees, but says if treated as a Latin word 'Trisantonam' can only be translated 'Three Santoni,' or 'Thrice Santonian,' the Santoni being a Gaulish tribe from what is now the Charente-Inferieure Department in France (DUIGNAN). Sir Reginald Hardy thinks the name is probably from Anglo-Saxon 'Treonta.' Others have said it is so called from the thirty rivers that fall into it. Whilst others have derived the name from thirty several sorts of fish bred in it (HOPT vol 1 p135), or the thirty abbeys which lie by it (HOT p21). Rev Thomas Butt even thought it took its name from the village of Trentham (Annals of the Diocese of Lichfield Past and Present 1859).

SOURCE. The Trent rises in N Staffs and flows S for some 34 miles before turning in a northwesterly direction to the Humber. There was some confusion over the location of its source in the C17. Plot says it rises out of New Poole (NHS p42), possibly the now lost pool to the W of Knypersley; on his map it is shown rising at Mow Cop and flowing through Brindley Ford and Ford Green to Carmountside; this brook is in fact Whitfield Brook (see) (ONST 1971 p310). It has been said to rise from three springs or heads; two at the foot of Mow Cop and another out of New Pool near Knypersley (SHOS vol 1 part 1 p89) (HOT p21). The true source is under 0.25m S of Biddulph Moor, in fields at SJ 905579, on land 930 feet high (TTTD p155) (HLSP p180). There is an old belief that the waters of the spring at the true source had medicinal qualities (SMOPP vol 2 p17p). There were plans to restore the stone trough, dated 1935, into which the spring flows at the source in 1994 (ES 24 Nov 1994 p5p).

In 1100 the Trent suddenly became dry at Nottingham and no where else on its course from the morning till three in the afternoon (NHS p69). The Trent dried up at Alrewas on Dec 21 1581 (HOPT vol 1 p144); the driest year on record according to 'Nature' Dec 1930 (NSFCT 1930 p160). In the later C17 Plot noted the Trent was more rapid than the Sow (NHS p43). At Rugeley he noted a strange sort of swan on the river whose legs were never black but of a blushy red colour like those of a tame goose (NHS pp228-229). The Trent flooded Burton in 1771, 1792, 1795, 1798, and 1829 (W p535). In the early C19 Broughton noted it is peculiar for being once up over its bank it flows over the fields for four or five days (SMC p119). In Feb 1929 the Trent froze at Burton (ABTOP p133p) (BTIH p161). In the 1950s the Trent was regarded as a dead river (ES Oct 6 1998 p1). In 1970 a national survey listed the Upper Trent as the most polluted river in England (VB p191). For fishing in it see SK pp31-39. Shakespeare in 'Henry V' act one mentions the Trent

'And here the smug and silver Trent shall run....'

(HOPT vol 1 p5) (SLM autumn 1955 pp5,9) (ZSB). Izaak Walton says 'The Trent washing the skirts and purlieus of the Forest of Nedwood, runs down to Burton.' Milton wrote

'Trent, who like some earthborn giant spreads
His thirty arms along the indented meads.'

(HOT p21) (HOPT vol 1 p135). The Trent has been described as the 'Sulky Trent' (HOS p7). (The River Trent. JH Ingram) (Portrait of the River Trent. Peter Lord. 1972) (SOS p3) (GNHS pp16,17,18) (NSFCT 1907 pp93-100) (STM Oct 1963 p49) (SMCC p6).

Trent and Mersey Canal Surveyed by James Brindley in 1758 and envisaged to link the Mersey and the Humber using the Trent downstream from Burton (HOS 1998 p113). The route is from Wilden Ferry on the Trent, Derbys (at Shardlow), to the Bridgewater Canal at Preston Brook near Runcorn, Ches. The canal is 93 miles long (NSFCT 1991 p57); 49 miles are in Staffs (IAS p117). It was authorised in May 1766 (IAS p117). Josiah Wedgwood I cut the first sod at Brownhills, Tunstall on July 17 (LHSB No. 6 p15) or July 26 1766 (HSP p33). The main line, formerly called the Grand Trunk (HSP p33) (HOS 1998 p113), was substantially completed by May 1777 (IANS p20) (NSFCT 1991 p57). The stretch between Wilden Ferry and Burton was open by 1770 (SWY p50) and between Burton and the lock at Trent Lane, Great Haywood, by June 24 1770 (HCMBOPP p10p), and between there and Stone by Nov 1771 (IAS p117), and between Stone and Etruria by 1772 (NSFCT 1991 p41). A barge was able to pass on part of it on Jan 1 1773 (HSP p33). The common dimensions of the canal are 29 feet in breadth at the top and 16 at the bottom, and four feet deep. In 1788 it contained 75 locks - 35 locks to Harecastle Tunnel and another 40 to the Trent - (HSP p33), 189 cart bridges and 11 footbridges (LHSB No. 6 p15). The canal is at its highest at Etruria, at 408 feet (HSP p33) or at Harecastle Tunnel, and drops 316 feet from there to Wilden Ferry (NSFCT 1991 p57). Josiah Wedgwood I had the canal in front of Etruria Hall widened in order to beautify the view from the hall and to

provide the illusion of a lake. Tixall Wide (see) is another instance of the canal being widened to beautify a country park (SL p245). At a point between Alrewas and Wychnor Bridges the Trent is used as the canal for a short distance (NSJFS 1975 p100). The NSR bought the canal in 1856 (HOE pp59,60). The canal is the 'Shropshire Union Canal' in the novels of Arnold Bennett. (SHC 1934 pp104-111).

Trent Bridge Bridge over the Trent at Burton, built in 1863 to 1864 to replace Burton Bridge (see). This bridge, far shorter and wider than Burton Bridge, was built slightly further down stream from the old bridge. The first stone for it was laid on Feb 23 1863 by John Richardson, High Bailiff of Burton. The bridge was opened in 1864 and was widened between 1924 and 1926 (ABTOP pp10,11p).

Trent Bridge Yoxall (W p612). It is now called Yoxall Bridge? Close by is Trentbridge Farm.

Trentham Industrial area in the Black Country in the Willenhall area (BCM April 1987 pp52-53). In 1851 the Duke of Sutherland (of Trentham Hall) was lord of the manor of Stow Heath (W p138), which covered this area.

Trentham Ancient parish and former township. The village of Trentham at the confluence of the Trent and Park Brook is 11.75m NNW of Stafford. It is now submerged into the suburbs of the S Potteries; what is now considered Trentham includes the once tiny hamlet of Ash Green (see), yet the old settlement was by Trentham Hall.

EARLY to 700. The Trentham burial mound mentioned by Garner is probably the same as the burial mound at Northwood (see). A late **Bronze Age** rough piece of ware half an inch thick has been found in the Trentham area (NSFCT 1931 p192). An implement of Neolithic or Bronze Age was found in Albert Road in 1907 (NSFCT 1907 p97) (NSJFS 1964 p35). A socketed bronze celt of late Bronze Age was found by a boy, Reginald Owen, in a Trentham gravel pit in July 1938 and went to the Potteries Museum (NSFCT 1938 p112 pl viii) (NSJFS 1964 p38). A burial mound in Trentham Park was destroyed about 1820 during road building and an urn found (HOTM p10) (NSJFS 1965 p49). A Neolithic or Bronze Age stone implement has been found near Trentham Hall (HOTM p10) (NSJFS 1964 p37). Rev Dr Fulk of Cambridge identified Trentham with the **Roman** station of Brementonacis on the 10th Journey of Antonine (NHS p402) (TTH p15). A Roman road ran from Stone through Hanford to Chesterton. In the C19 some of it was still visible along the top part of Trentham Ley (TTH p15). A perfectly carved outline of a Roman spear has been found on the underside of the praying stone of the Saxon cross in Trentham churchyard (TTH p15). Trentham has been identified with **Tricengeham**, an early spelling of the place where St Werburgh reputedly founded a priory and died, but it has since been identified with Threckingham, Lincs (SHC 1916 p134) (VCH vol 3 p255). Tricengeham has since appeared as Triccingham, Triccengaham, Trykingham, Tickingham and Trickingham (SHOS vol 1 p71) (W p431) and possibly Trytengham (SHC 1890 p295 note). In any event owing to this identification **St Werburgh** has been closely associated with Trentham for a long time. She was the daughter of Wulfhere, king of Mercia (657-674), and was born in c650 reputedly at nearby Stone (RHPS pp19,29) (presumably at Wulfhere's palace on Bury Bank). After the death of her father she became a nun at Ely, to which convent her mother, Ermenilda (or St Ermingild, Erminhilda, Ermenhilda), eventually followed her. The religious houses she either reformed or founded were Weedon (Northants), Tricengeham Priory, and Hanbury Priory (see). Werburgh died at Tricengeham Priory on Feb 3 699 and was buried at Tricengeham. However, it had been her wish to be buried at Hanbury and shortly after burial Hanbury people came and removed her body to their village by stealth. In 708 her body was laid in a shrine at Hanbury, in the presence of Coelred, king of Mercia, his council and many bishops. According to Malmesbury (c1090-c1143) she was buried at Chester. However, according to Higden (c1280-1364), a Benedictine monk of St Werburgh's monastery in Chester, Werburgh's relics were taken to Chester in 875, and placed in the church of SS Peter and Paul to preserve them from violation from the Danes who had advanced as far as Repton, Derbys, not far from Hanbury. According to Goscelin who wrote her life in 1095, at one of these convents a flock of wild geese devoured produce from the convent kitchen garden. Werburgh called the flock to her and preached to them. Despite the flock promising to mend their ways the geese attacked the garden the next day. Their reason for doing so was that the convent cook had continued to use geese in pies. Werburgh agreed this was not fair and called the cook and the pie in question before her. Her prayers for the geese in the pie revived the geese. She then ordered that no goose be eaten in the convent, so long as the geese did not raid the garden. Goscelin may have borrowed this story from the Life of the Flemish saint Amelburga. Geese are nevertheless associated with St Werburgh; they are represented in a picture of St Werburgh in Chester cathedral, and in the middle of a misercord in the choir of Chester cathedral. A former cross in the churchyard on or near the site of the present cross is said to have marked Werburgh's resting place at Trentham. The 'Holy Life and History of Saynt Werburge' was written by Henry Bradshaw (d1513), a monk of St Werburgh's monastery at Chester. St Werburgh is depicted on glass in St Michael's, Stone (SHOS vol 1 p71) (SMC p171) (GNHS p129) (ROS vol 2 pp140-155) (HSS pp43,44) (SOSH pp50,52) (TNE p263) (RHPS pp19-20,29-30,90-91) (KNS pp42,66,67) (KES p104) (FTWM pp130-134) (ESS pp15,16) (HOTC pp13-16) (Penguin Dictionary of Saints. Donald Attwater. 1965. p340) (VB p97) (TTH p16) (BSB p723) (ODS pp401,434).

700 to PRESENT. The Mercian kings held Trentham and it was the only manor of the old royal domain in Pirehill hundred still held by the Crown at the time of DB, in which survey it appears as Trenham; the name appears as Trentham in 1156 (SPN p129). The **name** according to Gelling may mean 'village by the Trent' (NSJFS 1981 p2). Or 'the small village on the river' (BNDA p3). Or 'The home or hamlet on the Trent' (DUIGNAN) (SPN p129). 'Ham' was an early name given to estates of some importance and Trentham was a royal estate (SSE 1987 p32). Or as 'ham' names are so scarce in Staffs 'ham' may be from Old English 'hamm' meaning 'land hemmed in by water or marsh or higher ground, land in a river bend, river-meadow' (SSE 1996 p23). Rev Thomas Butt (1806-41) thought if from Trikingham then 'the dwelling at three meadows' and the village gives its name to the river Trent (Annals of the Diocese of Lichfield Past and Present 1859. Rev JE Edwards (1841-86) thought 'the home of the sons of Tringa or Triga' (TTH p13). According to Eyton 'the mention of a resident Provost, or Reeve, in 1086 (DB), proves Trentham's importance for he was the King's officer, governing the estate independently of the Sheriff'. In 1192 Trentham was absorbed in the rest of the county; and farmed by the Sheriff (SHC 1909 pp74-75 note). Trentham parish was formed before 1086 (SHC 1916 p192). The present parish **church**, St Mary and All Saints, has some remains of the late C12 church of Trentham Priory, a priory which is said to have its origins in a nunnery of c680 (St Mary and All Saints, Trentham) (TTH pp14,17) (BOE p285). There is an old **legend** which relates Trentham church was carried from Hanchurch by white oxen, white swans or white mice, accounts differ as to which, but it was something white. Or that Trentham people helped by fairies spirited away the Hanchurch church for their own village. Probably the meaning of these stories is that at one time Hanchurch had a chapel of ease or cell attached to Trentham (Priory?) and when it closed the sacred vessels were carried by white robed clergy and choristers to Trentham (SOS p27) (Notitia Monastica. Bishop Tanner. p489) (HOTC pp17,18) (NSFCT 1900 p141) (OSST 1931 p22). The cushion and cloth in the pulpit in Trentham church are said to been been once the saddle cloth of the Emperor of Morocco (W p432). **Civil War.** The holes in a panel of the royal arms in Trentham church are said to have been made by bullets fired by parliament troops (KES p211). Trentham PR shows that a type of **plague** occurred at Trentham between April 1728 to March 1729 killing 40 people (TTH p47). Trentham had a **windmill** built at a time when corn prices were high. When prices resumed normal levels the mill was dismantled in c1819. William Hazledine, engineer from Shrewsbury drew up plans for it dated 1801. It was proposed that it should be erected near The Toft (WBJ pp38-39), presumably The Toft in Trentham parish. **Trentham Thursday** was a day out on Wakes Thursday for people of the Potteries to Trentham Gardens (see), specially opened for them for the occasion (TSS p45). Trentham station on the Pottery **railway** line just before the Hem Heath railway bridge carrying Longton Road was built in 1848 and replaced by an Italianate-villa like building designed by Sir Charles Barry in 1851 (TTOPP pp62p,63). It was recommended that the station close in 1963 (ES March 22 1963). Trentham Park station off Stone Road on a tiny branch railway line to the Pottery line opened in 1911 and closed in 1957 (VCH vol 2 pp308,325) (TTH p133; says opened in 1910). Trentham was taken into Stoke-on-Trent county borough in 1922 (VCH vol 8 p260). The **novel** 'A Lion Among the Ladies' (1949) by George Beardmore (alias Cedric Stokes) is set in Trentham (VFC p11). **Natural history.** During Dr Plot's visit to Trentham in the later C17 he noted the jaw of a young elephant which had been discovered somewhere in the grounds of Trentham Hall. It may have been a performer in a menagerie (NHS p267), or a baby mammoth from the Ice Age. **Persons and visitors.** At the end of the C13 **John Peckham**, archbishop of Canterbury, visited Trentham. He stayed long enough to write several letters to the king which are still recorded (TTH p28). The **Duke of Monmouth** came to Trentham in Sept 1682 (NSFCT 1974 p64). **Daniel Defoe** calls Trentham a small market town in his tour of Britain (1723). For Rev **Thomas Moss**, whose poem 'The Beggar's Petition' became very popular, see under Brierley Hill. A painting of Trentham by **Peter de Wint**, titled 'Trentham,' was exhibited at the Royal Academy in 1807 (SIS p78). Trentham

gives its name to a house called Trentham in Baltimore, USA, after Rev **Thomas Cradock**, believed to be the schoolmaster of Trentham (he founded St Thomas', Baltimore 1741); and Trentham, Upper Hutt Valley, New Zealand founded 1839 by **Richard Barton** the Duke of Sutherland's estate superintendent; also a Trentham 40 miles from Melbourne, Australia (TTH pp147,155). The composer, **Havergal Brian**, born in Dresden (see), lived for a short while at 9 Leyfield Road in the early C20 (POTP p47). On June 29 1940 **General de Gaulle** is said to have reviewed the Foreign Legion's Light Mountain Division encamped in Trentham Park (TTOPP p23). It has been said that **Winston Churchill**, and **Queen Elizabeth** wife of George VI stayed overnight in (royal) trains at Trentham Park sidings (TTH p133). For **JF Kennedy** at Trentham see Dairy House under Trentham Hall (Estate Buildings). The Leveson-Gowers were hosts at Trentham Hall (see) to many famous people.

Trentham Castle Some have thought there was a castle at Trentham in the Middle Ages on the strength of a castle called Trentham Castle being mentioned in the Pipe Rolls for Michaelmas 1168 which show the sheriff withholding one shilling for payment for one knight at Trentham Castle; he also charged 3/ 5 of a penny daily per men at arms as part of the cost of guarding Trentham Castle. Also there was a field called 'Castlefield' alongside the Trent, which appears on an estate map of 1714 (HOTC p25) (SHC 1909 pp74-75 note) (NSFCT 1912 pp144-150). Or the same or another called 'Mountfield' (CAMS p34). Although called Trentham Castle the castle referred to could have been at Newcastle, since Newcastle appears to have been under Trentham's jurisdiction (some say Newcastle Castle perhaps lay originally in Wolstanton manor). Newcastle was not granted a charter until 1173 (TTH p25). Again, it could have been the 'old' castle to Newcastle's 'new' castle, although Camden and others thought this was at Chesterton (S p86). No remains of the Trentham Castle have been found (ESH p52).

Trentham Forest An undefined forest in the Trentham area, existing in the C7. Here Chad, early missionary and Mercian bishop, is said to have had a hut whilst converting King Wulfhere's sons, Rufin and Wulfade, to Christianity (NSFCT 1881 p15).

Trentham Gardens Trentham Hall. In the later C17 there was a fountain S of the hall with a basin 10 yards in diameter, in which Plot found several dead frogs and their bones (NHS pp90-91,338). Later gardens, in whole or part, have been attributed to Sir Joseph **Paxton** (HOTC p39), WA **Nesfield** (BOE p284), **Barry**, who designed the formal terrace linking the lake with the remodelled house (CL May 9 1996 p70), and George **Fleming**, head gardener, appointed in 1841, who created an arboretum and experimented with planting shrubs in colour groupings (CL May 9 1996 p70). The formal terrace is divided into two, an upper flower garden which formed a platform for the house and a larger, lower terrace in which two sunken parterres with fountains flank a broad central walk which leads to the lake's edge (CL May 9 1996 p70).

PARTIAL OPENING of the gardens to the public occurred in wakes week from 1835 (TTH p95). 'Trentham Thursday' seems to have started in c1840 (TTH p95). This was the day in wakes week (first Thursday in Aug) eventually settled upon by the Sutherlands for the annual opening of the gardens. As many as 30,000 visited at its height. The custom of 'Trentham Thursday' continued until c1910 and had faded out by the 1970s (POP p143) (TTH p95) (TSS p45) (ES Aug 5 1995 p29p). In 1857 the standard guide to Trentham Gardens was published (TTH p95). The gardens are featured in 'The Gardens of England' by E Adveno Brooke, 1857, and at least 30 articles on the gardens were published in the horticultural press of the C19 (CL May 9 1996 p70). From the 1870s many Potteries people favoured Ashley (see) as a rural resort over Trentham.

FULL OPENING of the park and gardens occurred after the house's demolition, and the gardens were maintained as a public park. '**The Versailles of the Midlands**' was the slogan on posters advertising Trentham in the late 1920s (CL May 9 1996 p70). By the 1960s, there were 250,000 annual visitors (CL May 9 1996 p70). Trentham Hall estate including the gardens were sold to John Broome for £4 million in June 1981 (ES June 18 1981 p1p).

GARDEN ORNAMENTS. In 1976 the '**Banker's Clearing House**' statue was erected on a plinth (on which once was placed an urn) in the Italian Garden in front of the Grecian Temple (TTOPP p14p). The statue commemorates the clearing banks' stay at Trentham Hall in WW2. It is a curled figure of fibreglass in a 50 pence-shape drum made of fibreglass and bears the crest of 12 banks involved in wartime clearing (ES May 22 1995 p8p). Restored and returned to Trentham in 1996 (SLM March 1996 p13). Before the **bridge** in the gardens existed to take one from the road to the courtyard the only means of crossing the Trent at this point was by a ferry boat operated by a rope (HOTC p49). Heathcote Tatham designed an **Egyptian-style green-**

house for the gardens but it was never built (F p316). The **Grecian Temple** was one of a number Grecian temples which originally contained marvellous examples of antique sculpture (TTOPP p14p). The **iron bridge** over the Trent opposite the orangery was built in 1794 and is believed to be the second iron bridge ever built (TTH p97). Is the **Italian Garden** (TTOPP pp17p,18p) the same as parterre? The **Lady of the Sea statue** stood in the centre Rose Garden (DoE II). On the W side of the parterre is a large three-bay **Loggia** (BOE p285). An **Orangery**, a low C19-looking building (and not that by Charles Heathcote Tatham by the hall?) (BOE p284) (TTOPP p29p), stood to the ESE of the hall by the Trent. In 1931 the **ballroom** was built onto it. The ballroom was extended in 1938 and 1964. In its heyday it is said to have been one of the finest in the country, and attracted performers such as Joe Loss and Sydney Thompson (TTOPP pp30p,31p) (TTH pp123,147). Between the hall and the lake is the **parterre** by WA Nesfield (BOE p284). At the head of the lake facing the hall is the **Perseus and Medusa statue**. It is a replica of a statue sculpted by Benevenuto Cellini in 1550 in Florence. The 2nd Duke of Sutherland commissioned the replica after being granted permission by his friend the Grand Duke of Tuscany. It was erected in 1840 and was later removed for renovation and spent some time at Sutton, Surrey, and was returned in 1966 (DoE II*), meanwhile a sundial was erected on the plinth (TTOPP pp21p,22p of the sundial). There was a **rose walk** in the gardens (TTOPP p20p).

Trentham Hall Stood to the W of the main road at Trentham.
THE LEVESONS, LEVESON-GOWERS, SUTHERLAND-LEVESON-GOWERS. The Levesons of Wolverhampton bought Trentham Priory (see) estates in 1540. The **first hall** existed from 1540 to 1630. It was built on the site of, or into the buildings of Trentham Priory by the Levesons. Mary, Lady Leveson, occupied it as a dower house until her death, after being widowed in 1560. Sir William Cecil, later Lord Burghley, and later still Lord Treasurer, may have stayed here on his return from Scotland in 1560. After the death of Sir Walter Leveson in 1602 the hall seems to have been briefly occupied by his second wife, Susan. In 1605, after the death of Sir Walter's son (by his first wife), Sir **Richard Leveson**, the estate passed to Sir **John Leveson** of another branch of the Leveson family. He had to deal with Sir Richard's great debts and having to pay a large levy imposed by the Crown, which alleged Sir Richard had illegally taken treasure from his ship the Great Carrack, the St Valentine in 1602. To this end in late 1607 Crown Commissioners came to the hall attempting to seize it but were turned away by servants. After Sir John's death in 1615 the estate passed to his son, Sir **Richard Leveson**. He at length became free of financial troubles and inherited estates in Kent and Essex. In 1629 he married Katherine Dudley and started to built the **second hall** in 1630; it was finished by early 1639 (VCH vol 2 p193) (BOE p283) (SHJ autumn 1996 pp6-14). The main entrance of this hall was on the W side (NSFCT 1976 p20). It had curious bannisters leading up to the hall containing Roman capital letters, which read

CAROLO BRITANIAE REGE RICARDVS LEVESON
EQVES BALNEI AE DESHASCE HIC FIERI VOLVIT

and relate that the house was built in the time of Charles I (NHS p360 tab 23,24). Stone was hewn from a quarry at Beech for building it in the 1630s (IANS p99; mistakenly says 1680s?) and limestone was used (VCH vol 2 p193). The house was a parliament garrison in 1644 and at some point in the Civil War it was damaged (NSFCT 1976 p20) (HOS 1998 p72). In 1668 Sir Richard Leveson died without issue and was succeeded by his grand-nephew. He took the name of Leveson and added it to his own, that of Gower, and became Sir **William Leveson-Gower** (d1691). He was already 4th baronet of Sittenham, Yorks (CL March 5 1898 p274) (HOS p23). The third and fourth halls were the seats of the Leveson-Gowers; the richest family in the country in the C19. Sir William (d1691) was succeeded by his son Sir **John Leveson-Gower** (1674-1709), 1st Baron Gower. He was succeeded by his son **John Leveson-Gower** (1694-1754), who was created 1st Earl Gower and Viscount Trentham of Trentham in 1746 for services rendered to George II in the 1745 Jacobite Rebellion; he was chief protagonist in the Elibank Plot of 1747 (see Introduction). Sir John or his son John was the builder of the **third hall**, built in c1707 (CL Jan 25 1968 p178) (SHJ autumn 1996 p12) or in the 1730s (HOS p23) or in 1740 (IANS p96) to designs by Francis Smith after 'the model of the Queen's Palace in St James's Park' ie; Buckingham Palace ('The Beauties of England and Wales') (W p432). The hall had nine bays (BOE p284), and a brick kiln had to be erected on the site at its building such was the demand for bricks (IANS p96). John (d1754) was succeeded by his third son **Granville Leveson-Gower** (1721-1803), who was created Marquess of the county of Stafford in 1786. He was responsible for effectively creating a **fourth hall**, an enlargement of the third hall to 15 bays, undertaken by Capa-

bility Brown and Henry Holland between 1768-78 (BOE p284) (AGT p21). (SHOS vol 2 p26 pl showing SE view of hall) (NSJFS 1981 p64 il of Trentham Hall in 1781). A younger son of Granville (d1803) was **Granville Leveson-Gower** (1773-1846). He resided at Tixall Hall (see) from 1808, was created Viscount Granville of Stone Park (see) in 1815 and Baron Leveson of Stone, Staffs, in 1833 and Earl Granville. Granville (d1803) was succeeded by his son **George Granville Leveson-Gower** (1758-1833), 2nd Marquess of Stafford from 1803 (styled Viscount Trentham until 1786, and Earl Gower 1786-1803). He added an orangery in c1808 to designs by Charles Heathcote Tatham (later incorporated into the Grand Entrance, see below) (BOE p284) (SHST pp610,611p,612p,613-617). In 1785 George Granville married Elizabeth, suo jure Countess of Sutherland, and was created 1st Duke of Sutherland in 1833. After his death on July 19 1833 a statue of him to his memory was erected on Tittensor Hill (see). He was succeeded by his son **George Granville Leveson-Gower** (later Sutherland-Leveson-Gower) (1786-1861), 2nd Duke of Sutherland and 3rd Marquess of Stafford (in 1833 only). He was responsible for the additions to the C18 house, creating in effect a **fifth hall**. These additions were carried out between 1833 and 1842 to designs by Sir Charles Barry, architect of the Houses of Parliament (SHST p614). (GNHS p129). The main addition was a tower in the Italianate style and a range to the E which imitated the existing C18 house (BOE p285). On the W side of the house Barry had erected an impressive semicircular one-storey Grand Entrance with a porte-cochere in the centre, and with wings on either side (one of which is Tatham's orangery). The Grand Entrance was not demolished along with the hall, but was unstable and near collapsing by Feb 2000 (BOE p284) (ES Feb 2 2000 p5). George Granville married Harriet Elizabeth Georgiana (1806-1868), third daughter of George Howard, 6th Earl of Carlisle. By the duchess' influence, Stafford House, the London residence of the Sutherlands, became an important centre of society. As mistress of the robes to Queen Victoria Harriet was the principle consoler to the queen immediately after the death of Prince Albert in 1860. She entertained Garibaldi at Trentham Hall in April 1864. Her letters were published by her son Lord Ronald Gower (DNB) (TTH p87). George Granville died at Trentham Hall in 1861; as first patron of the new SPWWC a bust of him was unveiled at Wall Grange Water Works by St Caena's Well (see) in 1863. He was succeeded by his eldest son **George Granville William Sutherland-Leveson-Gower** (b1828), 3rd Duke of Sutherland (Viscount Trentham until 1833 and 4th Marquess of Stafford 1833-1861). The great wealth in estates amassed by the family by this time made him the United Kingdom's greatest-ever private landowner; he owned 1.4 million acres in 1883 (GBR 1995 p163). On Dec 28 1857 an important agricultural draining match took place on the Duke of Sutherland's estate at Trentham, 0.5m from Trentham station (ILN Jan 8 1858 p36il). In the 1860s the 3rd Duke developed an area of S Longton with housing calling it Florence (see) after his eldest daughter. George Granville was succeeded on his death in 1892 by his son **Cromartie Sutherland-Leveson-Gower**, 4th Duke of Sutherland (5th Marquess of Stafford 1861-1892). In 1884 he married the charismatic Millicent Fanny St Clair-Erskine (1867-1955), daughter of 4th Earl of Rosslyn, later an author, who was known during her years at Trentham as 'Meddlesome Millie,' having acquired a reputation as a social reformer in local politics; she founded a holiday home for poor Potteries children in 1898 at Hanchurch (see) and helped found the Potteries and Newcastle Cripples' Guild (or North Staffs Cripples' Aid Society, or Cripples' Aid Society, or Potteries' Cripples' Guild) in 1901, which had a convalescent home at first at Hanchurch and later at Longfield Cottage (see); Arnold Bennett caricatured her in several of his novels as 'Interfering Iris, the Countess of Chell'; Trentham Hall is 'Sneyd Hall' in Bennett's novels (POTP p204) (FWNS pp15-21p). In 1905 the Sutherland-Leveson-Gowers left the hall owing to the smell from the Trent made noxious by pollution from the Potteries (LGS p236); Thorold says, they left in 1907 (SGS p171). It has been said that they then offered the hall to the Potteries to celebrate Potteries' Federation and that it was also offered to be used as a teachers' training college (local info). Between 1910-12 the hall was demolished (BOE p283). The West Gates went to Lilleshall, Shrops (TTOPP p1). The top of Barry's Italianate tower went to Sandon Hall (see) in c1911. Rosemary, daughter of the 4th Duke of Sutherland and Millicent, married William Humble Eric Ward, 3rd Earl of Dudley, of Himley Hall (see). She died in a plane crash on July 21 1930 and there is a stone to her memory in the Memory Garden at Himley Hall, and the extension to Hartshill Orthopaedic Hospital at Longfield Cottage (see) is named after her. In 1913 Cromartie erected a memorial stone on the site of the hall, which had an inscription relating incidents connected with the hall (STMSM March 1973 p36p). On the death of Cromartie later in 1913 the titles passed to his elder son **George Granville Sutherland** (1888-1963), 5th Duke of Sutherland and 6th Marquess of Stafford. He was succeeded by Sir **John Sutherland Egerton** (b1915), 6th Duke of Sutherland and 7th Marquess of Stafford, great great grandson of Francis, younger brother of the 2nd Duke of Sutherland (The Complete Peerage) (Burke's Peerage).

OTHER AND LATER HISTORY. John Dryden (1631-1700), poet and dramatist, was a visitor to the hall in the 1680s (SSAHST 1966 p46). In the later C17 Plot noted a huge tapestry at the hall made by nuns, which may have been made at Trentham Priory. It consisted of square panels, some great, others little, yet presenting uniformity, the one half plain, the other chequered. Plot counted 3317 squares. He describes it as a linen suit of hangings (NHS p389). Benjamin Disraeli visited the hall in the C19, and 'Brentham' in his novel 'Lothair' (1870) is modelled on it (HOTC p50) (VB p182) (MR p338) (TTH p87) (VFC p39). Celebrations for the coming of age of the Marquis of Stafford at Trentham Hall were illustrated in ILN Aug 3 1872 p117il. The Shah of Persia visited the hall on June 26 1873 after visiting Liverpool (ILN July 12 1873 p41ils) (SHST p614). Edward VIII visited the hall in June 1880; on the 18th he was present at the laying of the foundation stone for St Luke's, Tittensor (RHPS p305). After the departure of the Sutherland-Leveson-Gowers from the hall in c1905 the family portraits painted by Romney went to Stafford House and Dunrobin Castle (TTOPP p11). In WW2 the grounds of the former Trentham Hall and the ballroom (see Trentham Gardens) were used as a transit camp for the French Foreign Legion and as the London clearing banks headquarters (Trentham at War. Graham Bebbington. 1995) (SLM Jan Feb 1996 p12). In June 1981 the trustees of the will of the 4th Duke of Sutherland sold the estate to John Broome (ES June 18 1981 p1p). Broome's plans to create a conference centre, an hotel, and houses on the estate came to nothing when planning permission was refused and subsidence discovered under the lake. The estate was then sold to the National Coal Board in 1986, who were trying to sell it in 1996 (TTH p163) (CL May 9 1996 p70) (ES Aug 13 1996 p11). In summer 1999 St Modwen Properties Ltd had plans to rebuild the hall for a luxury hotel and demolish the ballroom and adjoining function room in the gardens for the site of a 'speciality brands shopping village' (SN July 29 1999 p17). The Grand Entrance, which had not been demolished along with the hall, was unstable and near collapsing by Feb 2000 (ES Feb 2 2000 p5). There was a painting of the hall by Wootton which was once in the hall (SSC p134 in the intro). There is a painting of Trentham Hall by Peter de Wint (The Gazette. 1988). John Constable's oil sketch of the hall was on display in the Potteries Museum in Feb 1997, as was 'Trentham from the Lake' by James Holland (1799-1870). A portrait of the hall on an earthenware flask of the mid C19 made at Dale Hall Pottery was shown at the museum in May 2000. Other views of the hall include: 'Trentham Hall' 1912 by EJB Evans (ES March 24 1994 p8p): 'Trentham Hall' 1918 by John Malkin, and paintings by Charles William Brown (1881-1961): A painting which has been in CL (BOE pl 77): Etching of the hall, artist unknown (NUL p111): The hall before demolition (S p148p): From the West Gates in c1910 (TTOPP pp1p,2p): From the S (TTOPP pp4p,5p): From the E end (TTOPP p6p): The hall being demolished (TTOPP p11p): The hall in ruins in May 1912 (TTOPP pp12,13ps). (CL Jan 25. Feb 1. Feb 8 1968).

ESTATE BUILDINGS ADJOINING OR CLOSE TO THE HALL. The **Riding School** is generally a reference to the courtyard complex surrounding a large cobbled stableyard on the NE side of the hall. The 'Riding School' was built between 1840 and c1850 and consists of a stable range and a sculpture gallery on the top floor, and a clock tower. The complex, which still survives, is in a style less faithfully Italianate than the additions to the hall of 1833-42 (BOE p285) (AGT p21 il). **Pullo's plaque**, a memorial to a dog of a servant at the hall, is in the courtyard about six yards from the end of the wall nearest the steps which lead to the site of the former hall. The inscription on the plaque reads

Here Pullo is laid
On purpose 'tis said
To wait on fat Dick if he's able
When to cellar he's been
And filled up to ye brim
He'd wait on him to ye coach stable

Fat 'Dick' is presumed to be Richard Beasley, coachman (d1722 aged 63), whose dog was in the habit of waiting for him at this spot each time Beasley when down the cellar (HOTC pp49,50). Part of the **Poultry House**, a mid C19? Italianate complex of buildings to house game?, is now (1987) part of the church car park (TTOPP p37p). The **Smithy** in Park Drive still remains but is in a neglected state. It has a horse-shoe-shaped entrance (TTOPP p40p). The **'Bothie'** was a mid C19? 'Tudor' cottage situated between the old main gates and the ballroom (see below). It was built to house young estate gar-

deners, and was designed by Mr Roberts, the Sutherland's architect and surveyor (TTOPP p32p of c1909). The **Dairy House**, a quaint 'Tudor' villa with adjoining octagonal cooling room, stood roughly NW of the hall by Park Brook. It was used as a dairy and as a residence for the dairy maids and was designed by Sir Charles Barry in the mid C19. It was extended in the later C19 and used for a time as the headquarters for the Potteries and Newcastle Cripples' Guild. After 1919 it was used as a private residence by the Sutherland's agent and sometimes by Sutherland family members when briefly staying at Trentham. The house was used by Sir Hugh Frazer MP when he was conducting his first campaign for the Stafford and Stone constituency. He was joined for one week in his campaign in July 1945 by John F Kennedy (TTOPP pp35p,36p) (TTH pp93,95,135). See also Trentham Gardens, Trentham Mausoleum, Trentham Park and Tittensor Hill.

Trentham Hills Hills in Trentham Park to the W of Trentham Gardens. George Leveson-Gower (1888-1963), 5th Duke of Sutherland, celebrated his majority with a bonfire in Trentham Hills in 1909 (TTH p122). Up to about the 1970s there was a clump of seven trees known as the Seven Sisters on one of the hills (info the Shaw family). By the late 1980s a Christian service was held at dawn on Easter Sunday on a hill overlooking the M6; by the mid 1990s this service was preceded on Good Friday by the erection of a cross on the same hill, the cross being brought by a procession from Trentham parish church.

Trentham Ley To the SE of Trentham and formed part of Trentham Hall estate. In 1891 the present Trentham Golf Club on the Ley by Barlaston Old Road was founded according to tradition by Millicent, Duchess of Sutherland, as a ladies only club; she is said to have played golf on the Ley prior to this. By May 1894 there was a men's club. In 1991 the club came first in the County Championship; first in the English Club Championship; third in the European Club Championship (info Geoff Marks) (Trentham Golf Club: Centenary 1894-1994).

Trentham Mausoleum Mausoleum at SJ 868410, on E side of the A34. Built by the Leveson-Gowers of Trentham Hall to designs by Charles Heathcote Tatham 1807-8 (BOE p286, pl 63) or 1808-10 (TTH pp76-77). It is influenced by Egyptian architecture and is on a plan of a Greek cross. It was built with large blocks of stone and is in general appearance very cyclopean. The interior has an apartment for performing funeral services and 20 catacombs on each side faced with Derbys marble (W p432). Funeral services continued in it to the end of the C19 (TTH pp76-77). One bell from Trentham church, cast in 1707, which was at Wolstanton church 1767-8 came back to Trentham and went into the mausoleum (HOTC pp38,50). A description of the mausoleum written in 1808 describes it as 'situated on the road-side: the Ancients usually built their tombs near the highways, which reminded them of their ancestors....' (SGS pp171p,172). In 1907 the bodies of the five or six members of the Leveson-Gower family deposited here in catacombs were removed and laid to rest in special lead coffins which were buried in the ground within the compound; descriptive tablets were placed above each of the graves (AGT pp22,23il). The mausoleum, derelict for much of the later C20, was hit by an arson attack in 1993 (ES Oct 16 1993 p3). In 1994 the Duchess of Sutherland gave it to Stoke-on-Trent council, only to discover later it belonged to Lichfield diocese. In 1998 the diocese was still negotiating with Stoke-on-Trent city council about the transfer of ownership to the council (Lichfield Diocese 'Link' May 1998 No 209). The city council had plans in 1998 to re-use the mausoleum by renting out the space in it to the general public as a repository for family urns to raise funds for its restoration and upkeep (The Times May 2 1998 p3pc) (ES Jan 12 1999 p9p. May 26 2000 p19; plans for restoration in summer 2000). (DoE I) (F p316) (MR p338).

Trentham Park Former deer park to W and S of Trentham Hall stretching to Black Lake and incorporating The King's Wood (see). Enclosed by Lord Gower in c1735; the Gowers also had Stone Park (see) at Stone at the same period (EDP p179). A granite **marker stone** with the date '1822' situated on the Trentham estate had gone by Aug 1991 (ES Aug 10 1991 p15p). Some of the park was partly landscaped by Lancelot 'Capability' Brown probably between 1768-78 (SL p133) (AGT p21). The **Lake** stretches southwards from Trentham Hall. Brown proposed it in 1759, to replace the 'canals' of the C17 formal garden. It was built in 1763 (CL May 9 1996 p70) and altered when the hall was being added to 1768-78. The Trent formerly flowed through it. In 1853 the Trent was diverted to run along side the lake (BOE p284) (AGT p21) (NSJFS 1974 p113). Shaw noted the lake was about 80 acres (SHOS vol 1 part 1 p90). (SL p133). It is 'Sneyd Lake' in Arnold Bennett's novels. From the mid C19 gravel was worked in Trentham Park (NSJFS 1974 p115); and **Gravel Pit Lodge**, a 'gothic' stone and wood cottage designed by Sir Charles Barry, stands on the W side of the park at SJ 85194073. Dated 1859, it was under threat of being demolished by the M6 being widened in 1992 (ES April

4 1992 p5p). The **first ice-house** at SJ 865412, under 0.25m NW of the hall, is cut into rock with a brick-lined chamber (IHB p396). There seems to have been a **second ice-house**, probably of C18 and or C19 origin, S of the road to Hanchurch Pools. The structure had a semi-circular roof of brick, six feet high, and was three 10 inches wide. The passage was blocked off after nine feet. It was discovered whilst the M6 was being built and was at first mistaken for the secret passage from Trentham church to Hanchurch Manor prevalent in local tradition (TTH p143). An Art Deco-style **swimming pool** was opened at SE corner of the Lake in 1935 (ES Feb 18 1935 p5p of the model of the pool. July 4 1935 p9p advert for proposals). (TWWW Feb 1990 p20p). The pool measured 130 feet by 60 feet and was fed by the natural spring from Spring Valley. It closed in 1976 and was demolished in 1986 (TTOPP p28p). Trentham estate was purchased in 1981 by John Broome and then by the Coal Board who sold it in 1996 (TTH p163) (CL May 9 1996 p70). The name 'Trentham Park' was used for a ward of Stoke-on-Trent district by 1991 covering the Trentham, Hanford, Sideway and Northwood areas. The poem 'Trentham Park' (1789) is by Rev William Ferneyhough born in Great Fenton (see).

Trentham Priory According to tradition in c680 a nunnery was founded at Trentham by King Ethelred. His niece, the future St Werburgh of Trentham (see), daughter of King Wulfhere, was the first prioress. Werburgh died here in c700 (LGS p237), when aged 50 (FWNS pp7-10) and her body was taken to Hanbury Priory (see) for burial. Some claim Werburgh founded Trentham Priory (SVB p165) (FWNS p9). The first priory was destroyed by the Danes in the C9 (TTH p17). Possibly there was a small cell of the priory at Hanchurch until the Danish invasion (HOTC p17). However, there may never have been a Saxon priory at Trentham as early as the late C7. Trentham has been erroneously identified with 'Tricengeham' where there was a priory founded by Werburgh, and Tricengeham has been identified with Threckingham, Lincs (VCH vol 3 p255). If an early Saxon priory existed at Trentham it may have been rebuilt by Ethelfleda in c907 (TTH p17); this then continued until after the Norman Conquest, when it was refounded (LGS p237). Excavations in 1858 revealed the foundation stones, walls about six feet thick. The top was Norman, the lower was of Saxon origin, although, probably, not old enough to be of c680 (TTH pp17-19). The priory is thought, by others, to have originated in c1100 as a foundation of Hugh 'd' Avranches,' Earl of Chester, but even this tradition has been proved to be unlikely (VCH vol 3 p255). It was refounded for Augustinian canons by Ranulph 'De Gernon,' Earl of Chester, possibly on his death bed in 1153/4 (SOSH pp106,109) (HOS p27) (VCH vol 3 p255). Trentham Priory possessed Wall Grange (DUIGNAN p158) and 'the hermitage of the well of Dunstall' and land then cultivated by Walter the Hermit, mentioned as being a possession of Trentham Priory in 1162. This was at first thought to have been at Holly Wall, Goldenhill, Tunstall. But after some land was discovered to have been called Tunstall at Trentham it was thought to have been close to the priory (VCH vol 3 p136 note. vol 8 p93). In the C13 the priory possessed rights of free warren and may have enclosed for the purpose of preserving (NSFCT 1910 p175). The priory was surrendered in 1536. The property was a royal possession until sold to Charles Brandon, Duke of Suffolk, in 1538. It was sold to Sir Thomas Pope in 1539 and to James Leveson of Wolverhampton in 1540 (VCH vol 3 p259) (SVB p165). Malkin says Brandon came into the property in 1539 and sold it two days later to Pope (AGT p21). (W p431) (PS p52) (S p148) (STM Oct 1969 p31) (BNDA pp8,9) (SLM July 1984 p11). The priory buildings were to the S of the present church. Trentham Hall occupied the site of the priory building. The cloister area between the church and the hall was never built on (NSFCT 1976 p20). The lower E side of the churchyard wall is considered coeval with the nunnery (HOTC p17). A tapestry hung in Trentham Hall in the C17 made by nuns, perhaps of Trentham Priory (NHS p389). The ruins of the Priory Farm were finally demolished in 1947 (SFH p21 il on facing page shows an archway). The cartulary of the priory appears in SHC 1890 pp295-336.

Trenthaye Former old farmhouse 1.25m S of Hanley, on the E side of the present Leek Road approximately facing Cauldon Road. It was built in c1530, and was for centuries the home of the Amys or Amies family, who occur in records in the C14 (NSFCT 1923 p155) (H p109) (SHST p248p, 252p of the farm). The farm, also known as Trent Hay, was occupied in 1668 by a John Leigh, who was dead by 1712. In 1718 his daughters and coheirs sold the farm to John Fenton in whose family it then remained, though held by a tenant (VCH vol 8 p153). The tenant or a labourer at the farm in 1757 was a carrier between the Potteries and Congleton (taking perhaps pots to Ches and returning with corn). During the corn dearth of 1757 he is said to have led a mob through the Potteries in Nov to Congleton and there raided the market (PTP pp25-29). The farm was bought in the late 1870s by Hanley borough as the site of the new sewage works and the house converted into two workmen's dwellings

(VCH vol 8 pp153-154).

Trent House Crown Street, Stone. Name for the Stone workhouse, built in 1792-3, after it ceased to be a workhouse (RHPS p296). It later became a hospital, since when it has been known as Trent Hospital (BOE p269). In the 1980s the ghost of a neat figure in a dark dress and thought to be Sister Simpson, a former nurse, was seen in a corridor (info Bruce Braithwaite).

Trentside Pool Stoke-upon-Trent. Anciently Manor Fields Pool, or fishermen today (1992) call it Seven Arches Pool (NSFCT 1992-3 New Series vol 18 p26. 1993-4 New Series vol 19 p32).

Trent Vale Former hamlet near the confluence of Lyme Brook and the Trent now a suburb under 1m SSW of Penkhull. Formerly in Stoke-upon-Trent chapelry and parish.

EARLY. A **Neolithic** flint arrowhead was discovered in 1979 by Kenneth Shotton of Leawood Road, Trent Vale and went to the Potteries Museum (PRA pp15,17p). The **Romans** had a settlement here into the C2 AD (NSFCT 1933 pp155-158). A Roman fort may have been here on high ground guarding the crossing of the Trent at Hanford and may have been abandoned at the time of Boudicca's revolt (HOS p12). Pottery found here dates from the third quarter of C1 (HOS p12). Has been described as Romano-British. Between 1925-35 Roman coins of Augustus, Claudius, Nero, a few fragments of old pottery and a Roman brooch were found at Trent Vale during marl digging (ES Nov 21 1930 p6) (NSFCT 1930 pp140-141. 1931 pp178-179. 1932 pp111-112. 1933 pp155-158. 1934 pp61-63il. 1935 pp63-64) (NSJFS 1964 p35). A Samian bowl was found in late 1950s (NSFCT 1959 p84 p facing p85). A cinerary urn was found in it in about 130 fragments (STM June 1969 Supplement p12) (HOS new edition p85il). A Roman up-draught kiln was discovered at Trent Vale Brick Works in March 1956 still loaded with eight rough cast globular cooking pots and lids. The kiln is believed to date from c65-75 AD or the early Neronian period (NSFCT 1956 pp88-91plan,92,114) (VCH vol 8 p176) (NSJFS 1964 p35. 1968 pp19-38ps, dias) (IANS p89). During the 1956 excavations a globular 'face' pot was found in 128 fragments (NSFCT 1956 p90). Five copper studs nielloed in silver were found in 1957; the BM could find no British parallel (NSFCT 1959 p84 p facing). Excavations were made to the E of the kiln at SJ 868433 (NSJFS 1965 p121).

1800 to PRESENT. Trent Vale developed as a residential district along the Newcastle road from the early C19 (VCH vol 8 p176). The **church**, St John the Evangelist, Newcastle Road, was built in 1843-1844 (VCH vol 8 p193). A chapel at Trent Vale was registered for Wesleyan Methodists in 1842 (SHC 1960 p95). Became a separate ecclesiastical parish in 1844 (CAST p57) (GLAUE p426). The RC grammar school, **St Joseph's College**, on S side of London Road, opened for boys in Nov 1932 by Christ Brothers at the 'fine old house' known as, High Grove, opposite to Flash Lane. The school later moved to the present larger premises nearby. The school became partly co-educational in c1987 (SHST pp386-387) (ES Jan 2 1999 p3) (info Mrs Broki). Tom Byrne (c1907-1998), author of TFTP and TFTPM, was a master at the school from c1940 to at least 1977 (dust jacket notes in TFTP). Trent Vale is **'Sneyd Vale'** in Arnold Bennett's novels. A bright oblong-shaped object or **UFO** was seen from Leawood Road, Trent Vale in March 1967 (FSRP p5). On Jan 18 1881 a **Kittiwake gull** was shot down at Trent Vale, having been blown so far inland by the force of a storm (NSFCT 1881 p70).

Trent Valley The valley of the Trent in Staffs is loosely land near the Trent between Burton upon Trent and Stoke-upon-Trent. After WW2 power stations at Meaford (see) and Rugeley (see) in the valley were built by the Trent so that they could use its water as a coolant for their giant condensers. In consequence of the power stations the valley has been known locally as 'Megawatt Alley' (SLM Sept 1999 p71). A ley-line is said to follow the valley in the Shugborough area and UFOs are said to have followed this line (SN Oct 28 1999 p23).

Trentville Tiny hamlet near Austin's Cote 1m E of Lichfield cathedral.

Trescott Small hamlet by Smestow Brook 1.75m NNE of Trysull. Partly in Penn and Tettenhall ancient parishes. Was a ward with Kingswood in Perton civil parish by the late C20. The last Ice Age reached its maximum southern extent about Wolverhampton. Glacial boulders lie all about in the tract of ground extending from Wolverhampton to Trescott, Trysull, and Seisdon (WJO Nov 1909 p293). Has appeared as Treselcotum in a charter of 985 (SL p62), when it was granted to Lady Wulfrun by Ethelred (or Aethelred) 'The Unready' (king 979-1016) (HOWM p3) (SL p54) (SSE 1991 p8). It was identified by Mr Bridgeman with DB Cote (SHC 1916 p171). Later appears as Trescot (Yates' map), and Trecott. Has same root as Trysull, with the English translation 'cote' (NSFCT 1908 p147). Is from Tresel or Trisel, the Anglo-Saxon for Smestow Brook, itself derived from Welsh tres 'toil, labour' (VCH vol 20 p11) (BCM summer 1994 p22) (SSE 1996 p23). Perton-with-Trescott was a prebend of Tettenhall Collegiate Church (W p205).

Trescott Grange House 0.25m SSE of Trescott. William Buffary, lord of Lower Penn, granted Trescott to Combe Abbey, Warws, in c1190-1199 (PPTP pp9-13). It passed from Combe Abbey to the Wollaston family sometime during Richard II's reign (HOPTT pp134,135) or to William Wollaston in 1557 (SHC 1908 p102). It had passed to the Bagots of Bagot's Bromley by 1616; sometime residence of Sir Hervey Bagot (d1660) (SHC 1908 p97) (PAIP p49il) (ALP p10). It first appears in Penn PR as 'the Grange' in 1591. The present brick house is said to have been erected in 1682 by John Muchall, since 'Grange new house' is recorded in Penn PR in 1682. However, the present house, may be a little earlier (IP p30) (ALP pp21-23). There is a dovecote in the grounds (PONP pp72-73).

Triangle Area bounded by three roads 1m WNW of Hammerwich, 0.75m ESE of Chasetown. The area was settled by miners from the 1860s and had further development in the C20 (VCH vol 14 p261).

Triangle House 0.75m ENE of Thorncliffe (1834 OS map).

Trickley Coppice Wood 5m SW of Tamworth, S of Carroway Head, on Staffs Warws border. Has also appeared as Crickley Coppice (DUIGNAN p116). Duignan says 'Crick' perhaps, represents Gaelic 'crioch, criche' or Irish 'crioc, crioch' meaning a boundary, end, limit, frontier (DUIGNAN p116).

Trinity A ward of Tamworth borough by at least 1993, covering the area of E of the Tame and W of the railway comprising Two Gates and Dosthill.

Trinity Fields The most NNW suburban district of Stafford, 1.75m from Stafford.

Troughstone Hill, 1,017 feet high, and farm 1m N of Biddulph Moor. There are excellent long views from the top of Troughstone to the Welsh Hills and Liverpool (SVB p33) (CIOPP p25p). It is believed that the stone blocks used to support the rails of the very early railways were quarried out of Troughstone Hill (TTTD p158).

Trouse Lane An ancient lane between High Bullen and Darlaston Road, Wednesbury. Hackwood thinks the lane may have been called by the Celts 'the Tros', meaning the road running high and dry 'above' the level of the marshy land which stretched for some miles to the W of it (WAM pp7-8).

Troutsdale Farm House 1.25m SSE of Meerbrook. Formerly in Tittesworth township in Leek ancient parish. Prior to 1859 the house was called Lower Tittesworth and stands in the area of the medieval settlement of Lower Tittesworth, recorded in 1292 (VCH vol 7 p233). The house, Upper Tittesworth, stands in the area of the medieval settlement of Upper Tittesworth and is 0.5m to the SE. The present Troutsdale Farm dates from the later C20 (VCH vol 7 p233).

Trubshaw Fragmented tiny hamlet in undulating country at the foot of Mow Cop hill on the S side, 1.25m S of Mow Cop. Formerly in Wolstanton ancient parish. There is a well in front of Trubshaw Farm (WMC).

Trubshawe Cross Tiny district 0.75m W of Burslem, in Longport. Name is from an ancient cross at the divergence of the roads to Burslem and Tunstall. The plinth on which it was situated, dated 1750, was rediscovered in 1949. By 1977 the plinth, positioned on a roundabout where the roads diverge, was supporting a new 12 feet high cross of Kerridge stone to a design from a cross in Ruthwell (SLM May 1949 p247p) (VCH vol 8 p113) (OTP p64) (SHST pp655p,656). Near by was Longport Hall.

Trumpers Hays Ancient enclosure in the Harpfield Road area of Springfields, Newcastle-under-Lyme (VCH vol 8 p201).

Trunkfield Brook Joins the Stowe at Minster Pool, Lichfield. Is sometimes known as Sandford Brook (CCHCB p76).

Trussway Ancient trackway which can be traced from Cleulow Cross, Ches, over Gun Hill to Fould, through Leek to Leekbrook, Cheddleton, and as far as Basford Green, its course being marked by a series of crosses. It may have been used by the Earls of Chester when visiting their estates round Leek (NSFCT 1959 p96). AE and EM Dodd identify it at Gungate (PRT p56). This appears to be identifiable with a packhorse way believed to have passed over Gun Hill. Monks of Dieulacres Abbey may have used it for transporting wool to Ches. A cobbled way, by Fold Farm (Fould?), by a deep hollow known locally as Old Roman Way, has been excavated (HOLF p5). A packhorse way for Dieulacres Abbey monks over Gun Hill has also been known as The Hollow Way. It is said to have continued to Bearda Hill, the grange at Swythamley Hall, Danebridge and across the border into Ches to Wincle Grange (a grange of Combermere Abbey), Bennettshill, Cleulow Cross, Sutton and then to Macclesfield (DP p22).

Trysull (*Treezle* DUIGNAN, *Tree-sull* LGS p237). Village on a low knoll above a bend in the Smestow 19m SSW of Stafford. Former chapelry in Wombourne ancient parish. The last Ice Age reached its maximum southern extent about Wolverhampton. Glacial boulders lie all about in the tract of ground extending from Wolverhampton to Trescott, Trysull, and Seisdon (WJO Nov 1909 p293). Has appeared as Treslei (DB), Tresel (985-1300), Trisel (SPN p130),

Tressul (1307) (ALP p13), and Treosle. The **name** is unique in England (DUIGNAN). It is from the Anglo-Saxon form of Smestow Brook, Tresel (SPN p130). Probably from Welsh 'trestl,' a trestle, and appears in Middle English as 'trestel.' Early household tables commonly consisted of boards laid on movable 'trestles' (DUIGNAN). The prefix is probably the Irish 'treb' a homestead, the Cymric 'trev,' Modern Welsh 'tre;' the terminal may be traced to the river root 'sil' 'siol' water, the word then means 'the homestead on the water' now the Smestow Brook (NSFCT 1908 p147). Gelling thinks it is a pre-English river-name (NSJFS 1981 p3). There was a **church** at Trysull by the later C12. The church, All Saints, in the centre of the village, has some work of the early C14 and may have some work of the later C12 (BOE p286) (VCH vol 20 pp193,194). There was a **deanery** of Trysull by 1224. The area it covered mainly comprised the hundred of Seisdon. It was united with Lapley in the late C13, but became a separate deanery again in the mid C19 (VCH vol 20 p188). In 1888 Trysull became a separate ecclesiastical parish. With Seisdon it became a separate civil parish in 1866 (VCH vol 20 p215) (GLAUE p426). Trysull **parish feast** was on the nearest Sunday to Nov 5 in the C19 (W 1834 p290) (W p209) (VCH vol 20 p188). Thomas de Tresell was granted a charter on May 6 1251 to hold a **market** here on Tuesdays. It was recorded in 1254-5. Nothing more is heard of it after 1293 (NSJFS 1971 p51) (VCH vol 20 p192). Thomas de Tresell was granted a charter on May 6 1251 to hold a **fair** on the eve, feast, and morrow of Holy Trinity. It was recorded in 1254-5. Nothing more is heard of it after 1293 (VCH vol 20 p192). There were probably **gibbets** N of Trysull, where the name Gibbet Bank occurs and to the NW of Seisdon, where the name Gibbet Plantation occurs (VCH vol 20 p188). A brick **pound** stood on the E side of School Road N of Hunters Green by the early 1880s. It was restored in c1970. The building which stood nearby in c1979 used as a summer house may have been the pinder's house (VCH vol 20 p193). The Smestow Brook drove a **watermill**, here. It was built of brick in 1854 and belonged to Lord Wrottesley. It worked until 1940 (BOE p287) (VCH vol 20 p192) (MR p339). On the E side of the bridge at Trysull over Smestow Brook is a **notice** which reads

> Motor Car Act 1903
> Heavy Motor Car Order 1904
> Notice
> This Bridge is insufficient to carry a
> heavy motor car the registered axle weight
> of any axle of which exceeds 4 Tons
> By order of Staffordshire
> County Council
> Walter H Cheadle
> County Surveyor
> March 1905

(DoE II). For Trysull **canal** lock keeper's cottage see under The Bratch. Seisdon Union **workhouse** was built on the Penn road 0.75m ENE of Trysull in 1859 or 1860 and closed in the 1936. It was destroyed in a fire and partially demolished in c1965 (VCH vol 20 p193) (TB July 1998 p13p). **Natural history**. A mock sun was witnessed by William Barnesley of Trysull in c1654 (NHS pp3,4,5,6,7). In the later C17 Plot noted a white sort of pebble containing a mealy substance at Trysull, which he had mentioned in his 'Oxford' pp26,30 (NHS pp124-125). Dr Johnson's mother's cousin, **Elizabeth Harriotts**, lived at Trysull Manor House (see).

Trysull Common Former common land which stretched along the western and southern boundary of Trysull parish (VCH vol 20 p191).

Trysull Manor House W end of Trysull village. Timber-framed. Dated 1633 (SGS p172) (MR p339) (SPN p130) or dated 1653 and has been restored (SVB p166). It may have been the manor house of Trysull manor. It was the seat of the Barnesley family by the C17. Elizabeth (nee Barnesley), wife of Robert Harriotts (or Harriots), came to occupy the house from 1690. She was Dr Johnson's mother's cousin, or some say aunt and Johnson stayed here at least once (The Reades of Blackwood Hill with a Full Account of Dr Johnson's Ancestry. Aleyn Lyell Reade. 1906. pp141-145) (SGS p172) (MR p339) (VCH vol 20 p189) (SPN p130). In 1711 Johnson is said to have been brought here to be seen by the young Roman Catholic occultist physician Dr Thomas Attwood of Powick (Worcs) to be remedied for deafness and blindness on his left side. Johnson probably visited Elizabeth Harriotts during his time at Stourbridge in 1725-26 (Young Samuel Johnson. James L Clifford. 1955 1962 ed. p9) (VCH vol 20 p189). Mrs Harriots died in Feb 1728 and left Johnson £40, which partly funded his time at Oxford (Johnson on Johnson. John Wain. 1976. p14) (VCH vol 20 p189). The Manor House has this inscription on the porch

Stranger, should this catch your eye
Do a favour, passing by
Bless this house.....

(SGS p172) (MR p339). By 1860 the house was known as the Manor House (VCH vol 20 p189).

Tucklesholme Meadow or island by or in the Trent. Tucklesholme Farm is on E side of railway to Burton, N of Walton-on-Trent, by the Trent, E of Newbold Manor House. The remains of a barrow cemetery 350 yards SW of Tucklesholme Farm is a listed monument. Has also appeared as Tuklesholme and Tok-les-Holme. The name may have some reference to the family of Tok, who lived at Anslow before 1300 (HOPT vol 1 p139). Or represent Thorkil's holme (HOBTU p9).

Tudor House Timber-framed house in High Street, Cheadle. Built in 1558 and by 1999 was said to be the oldest house in Cheadle. The stucco was removed from the facade in 1907 (NSFCT 1991 p53) (COPP2 p120p).

Tunnel Farm House 0.5m SSE of Wetley Rocks. The Consall plateway passed it. From a tunnel here, at SJ 967485, through which it passed (NSFCT 1945 p87) (IAS p161).

Tunstall (locally *Tunster* BOJ book 2 p53, POP p177). Former scattered hamlet until the C19 on a ridge overlooking the upper Fowlea Valley and the valley of a tributary which joins the Fowlea at Westport 18.25m NNW of Stafford. Tunstall is now the most northerly of the six pottery towns of the Potteries. Former township in Wolstanton ancient parish.
EARLY. An Ice Age granite boulder of about 6.5 tons was unearthed near the Chatterley Whitfield railway, the boulder has marks, of probably, a ploughshare cut into it (SHST p485). It may have gone to Tunstall Park.
1000 to 1800. Has appeared as Tunstal (1212) (SSE 1996 p18), Tunestale, Tunestal, and Tonstal (SPN p130). Scarratt thinks the **name** Tunstall is literally from the town (or Anglo-Saxon 'tun') with stalls, i.e; a market (OTP p59). Or has been thought to be a compound of tun (town) and stall as in an elevated seat (NSFCT 1888 p86). Or 'place at the farmstead' (SPN p130) (SSE 1996 p18). According to Vertigan or Verstegan Tunstall's etymology should be Tuns-deal the word 'deal' signifying 'part' hence forming a part of Wolstanton ancient parish (WWT p83) (NSFCT 1888 p86). Tunstall does not appear in DB but was considered then a member of Thursfield according to Erdeswick and Eyton, but considered a member of Chell according to Ward (SHC 1909 p36). By 1212 a **manor** of Tunstall was held by Henry de Aldithley (or Audley) of Heighley Castle (see) of Newcastle manor on condition he pay a fee and perform guard duties at Newcastle Castle. In the later C16 most of the manor passed from the Audleys to Sir William Sneyd of Bradwell. From the late C18 the whole manor was held by the Sneyds until at least 1940. Tunstall Old Manor House appears to have been superseded by Tunstall Manor House (see), which survived until the late C19 (VCH vol 8 p230). The manor was a large administrative area and stretched beyond Wolstanton parish to take in much N of Cobridge including Burslem in Stoke ancient parish, and land as far as Mow Cop (NSFCT 1943 p18) (SASR 1987 p97). A **lock-up** was part of the Town Hall of 1816 and at one end of it (HOS p58). Tunstall's oak double **stocks** were situated by it (SHST p489), but were removed in 1858 (OTP p74). They were last used in 1852 (SHST p489), and ended up in front of the new town hall built in 1883 (MR p340). By 1899 the stocks were to be found in a corner of the police yard. They had formerly been at the lower High Street end of the Market Place (SHST p646). Another account says the old Town Hall and lock-up were pulled down in 1892. Hughes, writing by 1924, says the stocks have gone (SOSH p287). A tailor named Bailey was often in them and allowed to carry on his trade whilst being punished (WWT p102). The 'King of Tunstall' was a title honoured to one of the special constable for the township of Tunstall in 1823 - either George Tollet or F Twemlow (HSP p140). Tunstall had a **market** by 1525 (VCH vol 8 p98). The six **open fields** of Tunstall were enclosed by agreement among nine owners in 1614 (HOS P40) (WMLB p51) (SL p107). For Tunstall **windmill** see under Clay Hills. **John Wesley** was at Tunstall on March 29 1790 (NSFCT 1888 p87). When in Tunstall he preached in a house in America Street (OTP p10).
1800 to PRESENT. The **Primitive Methodists** first met at Tunstall, in March 1808, in Joseph Smith's kitchen (POP p180). Scarratt was told they first met at the Globe Pottery, (Brownhills?) (OTP p15). Their chapel at the corner of Claver and Oldcourt Streets was one of the earliest Primitive Methodist chapels in the country, and was demolished by 1976 (VCH vol 3 p128) (POP p180) (ABS No. 5 p10). The **Town Hall**, or known locally as the Stone House (locally Ston Hus) was erected in 1816 (HOS p58) (OTP p74). A new town hall built in 1883 in Tower Square was designed by AR Wood (BOE p265)

(MR p340). **Churches**. There may have been a church at Tunstall before the C19; a former open field called Church Field, lay to the W of the town, and human bones have been found at various times in that area (HBST p88) (VCH vol 8 p93). The Commissioners' church, **Christ Church**, on the corner of High Street and Furlong Road, was built in 1830-1831 (VCH vol 8 p93) (BOE p265). Tunstall became a separate ecclesiastical parish in 1837 (LGS p238). **St Mary the Virgin**, Hammond Street (SW Tunstall, name now changed), was built in 1858-9 (VCH vol 8 p94) (BOE p266). The mission church, **St Chad**, was founded by Louisa Wain (d1907) in King William Street (the area has been called Chatterley Crossings) in 1906 (VCH vol 8 p94) (POTP p216). The red brick mission church, **St Aidan**, in Summerbank Road, was built in 1906 and closed in 1973. Subsequently it has had several uses and was still standing in 2000 (ES Jan 14 2000 p71pc). The **wakes** were on the first Sunday after the feast of St Margaret (20 July). In a bid to bring the wakes of the pottery towns into unison with Stoke's in Aug, it was banned in 1879, but resumed the following year after protests (VCH vol 8 p104) (HOS p63). (W p288). Tunstall **railway** station at the S end of the Harecastle railway tunnel was opened in 1864 and renamed Chatterley Station in 1873. In 1873 a station opened in the centre of Tunstall on the Potteries Loop Line (VCH vol 8 p85). It was recommended that Tunstall station close in 1963 (ES March 22 1963). The old Town Hall and lock-up were pulled down in 1892 and a yellow-tiled **clock tower** erected on its site in 1893 to the honour of Sir Smith Child, Bart of Stallington Hall, MP for Tunstall (d1896). The tower has a bronze portrait bust of Sir Smith Child by JS Cartlich (WWT p102) (VCH vol 8 p85) (POTP p61) (BOE p265). It was cleaned and restored in Feb 1993 (ES Feb 18 1993 p13p). There is another clock tower in Tunstall Park (see). For Tunstall Union **workhouse** see Westcliffe. The separate civil parish or **urban district** (POP p74) of Tunstall, created in 1894, was abolished and entered into Stoke-upon-Trent ancient parish in 1922 (GLAUE p426). The town was one of the Six Towns which federated in 1910 to form Stoke-on-Trent. The **arms** Tunstall adopted were never recognised by the College of Arms. The arms are: Chevron between in chief a soup-tureen and in base a vase; on the chevron a Stafford Knot and two scythes, and a canton two furnaces (CH p330). (SHST p280il). Tunstall was one of Arnold Bennett's five towns of the Potteries. It appears as **'Turnhill'** in his novels. The **first purpose-built cinema** in North Staffordshire was built in Station Road (now The Boulevard), Tunstall, by the orphan George Barber (1860-1946) (POP p179). It opened in 1909 and was called Barber's Palace (POTP p29). A building in Art Deco style called Barber's Palace at Tunstall closed in Nov 1998 prior to demolition (ES Nov 24 1998 p3p). (POP pp177-179) (STMSM Oct 1980 pp22,23) (SMOPP vol 2 p10p) (TSS p80). In **WW1** a Zeppelin dropped a bomb over Tunstall in the early hours of Nov 28 1916 which landed in the backyard of No. 6 Sun Street, and destroyed the sculleries and outhouses of Nos. 2, 4, 6 and 8, but shards hit other houses, as well as a nearby RC church. One person was injured (TB July 1994 p19). **Persons and visitors**. **Joseph Capper**, blacksmith and political reformer, born near Nantwich, Ches, in c1778. He later settled in Tunstall and operated a smithy in or by Tunstall market-place. He converted to Primitive Methodism at the camp meeting held at Mow Cop in 1807. He was an early member of Tunstall Building Society, founded in 1816, and resided in a dwelling erected by the society in Piccadilly Street. During the first election in the Potteries (1832) he took up the cause of George Miles Mason, the radical candidate. He vehemently supported the 'People's Charter' of 1838. On June 24 1842 he was at a meeting with other Chartists at Tunstall and preached for the Charter, allegedly urging the crowd to take up arms to fight for their political rights. In mid Aug 1842 he is said to have taken an active part at a meeting held on the Crown Bank on the occasion of Thomas Copper's visit to the Potteries. The meeting was followed by rioting. Capper was held partly responsible although at the time he claimed he was at home. He was arrested on Aug 21 1842 and tried in Oct and was sentenced to two years' imprisonment for sedition. In 1843 he was again put on trial for conspiracy. After serving his sentence he is said to have returned to Tunstall a broken man and died there in c1848. He is buried in Tunstall churchyard (PTP pp53-62) (TFTP pp108-111). Rev **George Castriot De Renzie** (1851-1928), was descended from George Castriot Skanderbeg, prince of Epirus, an Albanian hero of the C15. De Renzie was appointed vicar of St Mary's, Tunstall, in 1898 and is buried in Tunstall cemetery (POTP p78). Another descendant of this family was living at Clayton (see) in 1992. **Clarice Cliff** (d1972), pottery designer and noted for her art deco styles, was born in Meir Street, Tunstall on Jan 20 1899. She attended the High Street Elementary and Summerbank Schools in Tunstall until 1912. Her famous designs were created whilst she was working at Newport Pottery (see) (Clarice Cliff. P Wentwent & K Johnson) (ES May 24 1976) (POTP p62) (FWNS pp41-45). The protagonist in Peter Whelan's play 'The Bright

and Bold Design' is loosely modelled on her (ES Feb 1 2000 p12). **George V** and Queen Mary visited the Alfred Meakin pottery at Tunstall on April 23 1913 (ES Nov 16 1996 p21). **Muriel Pemberton**, painter and fashion designer, who founded Britain's first fashion course at St Martin's School of Art, London, in the 1930s was born in Tunstall in the period 1913-23 (ES June 5 1993 p13pc). Miss **Elsie James**, a native of Tunstall, was still living at Gorsefield Residential Home, Tunstall, aged 103 in 1998 (ES Sept 23 1998 p10p). For **Robbie Williams**, pop musician, see Greenbank.
INDUSTRY. Tunstall's industry from the Middle Ages has been coal and ironstone mining (HOS p42). In the C17 and C18 Tunstall was producing bricks and tiles; the 'Staffordshire Blue' engineering bricks are from Tunstall (MR p341). It then turned to pottery (OTP p41).

Tunstall Tiny hamlet on a shelf of land above Lonco Brook 1m NW of High Offley. Former township in Adbaston ancient parish. Appears in DB as Tunestal. The name is from Anglo-Saxon 'Tuna's Nook' (MR p247). Or 'place at the farmstead' (SPN p131). Was included in Adbaston prebend (SSAHST vol 2 1960-61 p42). A medieval chapel at Tunstall, certified in 1548, is not mentioned thereafter (SHC 1915 p5). Foot-and-mouth disease broke out at the Laurels Farm, Tunstall, in Dec 1967 (SN Dec 22 1967 p15).

Tunstall Hall Tunstall, High Offley.

Tunstall Manor House Formerly stood in Cross Street, Tunstall. Built in the C13, and later encased in brick, was finally pulled down in 1887 (SOSH p285p) or 1888 (VCH vol 8 p88). It probably incorporated part of the original Tunsall manor court house. By the time of its demolition it had been altered many times. Scarratt remembered it existing in c1840 (OTP pp58-59,61 il). It has also appeared as Tunstall Court Leet. Greenslade makes no link between the court house in Cross Street with a house called the Manor House in the centre of Tunstall. The latter was occupied by Thomas Child, yeoman, in the mid C18 (VCH vol 8 pp87,88)

Tunstall Old Manor House The lord of Tunstall manor had a house at Holly Wall to the N of Tunstall by the late C14 (VCH vol 8 p87).

Tunstall Park Park, which has also appeared as Victoria Park, to the E of Tunstall. Begun in 1897 but not officially opened until 1908 (VCH vol 8 p81). The gates are inscribed 'In memory of Thomas Peake, by his children AD 1904' Peake was a noted Tunstall tile manufacturer (d1881) (ES June 19 1995 p19). In the park is a clock tower erected in 1907 to the memory of William Adams (d1905) and his predecessor William Adams (d1805) (SOSH p287) (BOE p265). There is a fountain in the park to the memory of George Cumberlidge (1825-1904), local government officer (POTP p73). Some stones which formed part of the Bridestones (see) found their way to Tunstall Park, where some still (1998) remain (DPTB pp19,20-21ps)

Tunstead House 0.75m NW of Longnor. Formerly in Longnor township in Alstonefield ancient parish. There was a house here by 1415 (VCH vol 7 p42).

Tuppenhurst Minute hamlet by a tributary of the Trent in the Trent Valley floor, 0.5m ESE of Handsacre. In King's Bromley ancient parish. Has also appeared as Tubney (Morden's map), and Tappenhurst (W p556).

Tuppers Pool S of Fairoak, Cannock Chase (Bowen's map).

Turls Hill Hill 613 feet high 0.5m E of Sedgley. The appearance of a John de Terhull in medieval times may indicate that there was settlement on Turls Hill then. Has appeared as Turles Hill (1575. 1582. 1603/4) (HC pp10,38) (SNSV vol 2 p76), and reputedly 'Turleys Hill' (1580. 1608) (SR p4). The name is said to be from the family name Turley (AMS p441).

Turls Hill House The approach to the house was by Turls Hill Road, 1m WSW of Coseley. An early large house on this site was built by a branch of the Persehouse family of Parkes' Hall in the C16; some parts of this building were incorporated into the house which was built on the site in the gothic style in the early C19 (AMS p) (HC p78). The house has been the seat of the Turley family, then the Whitehouse family (industrialists and ironfounders), during whose time the house was called Wallbrook House. In 1901 it was the seat of Benjamin Whitehouse an influential iron-master with works at Deepfields and Coseley (OS map Sheet 67.07). In WW1 it was occupied by Belgium refugees, hence its later name Belgium House. The ghost of a veiled lady in a long black frock carrying a lantern reputedly haunts the perimeter wall. She is thought to be a Turley and is searching for her husband who shot himself in business in the C18. She was seen in the 1920s (TB June 1984 p16. Aug 1984 p1. June 1985 pp10-11) (GOM p19) (GPCE p16). The house, still standing in 1976 (HC il of in 1976), had been demolished by 1994 (TB Oct 1994 p6).

Turn Croft Former important house in Kingswinford ancient parish. The manorial courts for Kingswinford manor were at some time held here (BHOP p6).

Turnditch Farm near Gallows Green, 0.5m SW of Alton. Turnditch Farm is

mentioned in 1789 (HAF p203).

Turn Edge Above Three Shire Heads, 1m to WNW of Flash. The edge presumably is the very steep side of the hill, here, rising to 1424 feet high. (UHAW p51 il). The name means the edge where the thorn bushes grew (NSFCT 1932 p58).

Turners Hill Hill on which Ellowes Hall stands, 0.5m NW of Lower Gornal.

Turner's Hill Hill in the Rowley Regis range over 0.75m N of Rowley Regis. In Rowley Regis parish. At 876 feet above sea level it is the highest peak of the Rowley Regis range and in the S of the county (SHOS vol 2 p240) (GNHS p183). Greatly quarried for Rowley Rag, creating, as Palliser noted in the 1970s, an almost lunar landscape (SL p192). George Smith, a hangman in the C19, who lived at Hangman's Hall (see), was born at Turner's Hill in 1805 (MMBCC pp8p-34). The Downing family were formerly of Turner's Hill and resided at a house known, probably in the C19, as Cloudland House (TB Feb 1998 p11). Has also appeared as Tanner's Hill (S&W p353). Aynocks Quarry is the local name for The Central Quarry on top of Bury Hill Park, Turners Hill (TB Jan 1983 p13).

Turner's Pool Pool over 0.5m SE of Swythamley. Reputedly made by one of the Earls of Chester (NSFCT 1884 p23), probably by the damming of Meer Brook (VCH vol 7 p193). Loxdale says it was made by the monks of Dieulacres Abbey for the purpose of a stew (HOLF p22). Has appeared as Thornhurst Pool (1535) (VCH vol 7 p193), Thurnehurst-pole (1541), and Thornehurst-pole (1543) (NSFCT 1932 pp58-59). The farmhouse, close by, was once Swythamley School, closed in c1870 (HOLF p23). The name represents 'thornwood pool' or 'pool by the thorn bushes' (NSFCT 1932 pp58-59).

Turnhurst Small hamlet above a tributary of Fowlea Brook on a hill facing Goldenhill, 0.75m S of Newchapel. Formerly in Wolstanton ancient parish. Appears as Turnhurste in 1539 (SASR 1995 no 6 p6). For the workhouse at Turnhurst some time known as the Bastille and Turnhurst Institution see under Westcliffe.

Turnhurst Hall It lay across the N end of the present Silverstone Crescent at Turnhurst, Newchapel (SHST pp119, 575p). The hall may have stood on or near the site of a previous hall, which may have been the seat of the Rowley family by the mid C16. The Rowleys were here until the end of the C17 but the house was occupied towards the end of their time by the Bellot family (SASR 1995 no 6 p3). According to Smiles the hall is said to have been the last house in England in which a family fool was maintained (Lives of the Engineers. Samuel Smiles. 1861. pp468-469) (SASR 1995 no 6 pp3,5). The present hall, built of brick in c1700, seems to have passed by the marriage of Rowley heiresses to the Alsager and Bowyer families. It was occupied by John Bowyer and Frances Egerton when it was conveyed to Mary Alsager in 1752; she owned it throughout the period it was tenanted by James Brindley, canal engineer. He may have resided at the hall from as early as 1760. But he is believed to have lived here from 1765 to his death on Sept 27 1772 (SASR 1995 no 6 pp5,9-10,11,13). George Frederick **Handel** (1685-1759) is reputed to have composed the 'Harmonious Blacksmith' whilst on a visit to the hall. He is supposed to have been inspired by the clanking of a smith in the neighbourhood (GNHSS p19) (NSFCT 1938 p64) (HOE pp65,66,127) (WWT p90 p of facing) (SHST p576p of Brindley's experimental locks). After Brindley's death the hall was occupied by the Cole family, who seem to have lived at it to at least the mid C19 and who may have occupied a part of it during Brindley's tenancy. After Mary Alsager's death in 1795 the hall was held by her trustees until 1846 (SASR 1995 no 6 pp11-12). It was demolished in 1929 due to mining subsidence (LGS p193) (SASR 1995 no 6 p25). The staircase was sold to an American for £500, but on the night of the sale youths broke into the hall and did considerable damage to the woodwork (HOE pp65,66). Mr Lovatt refers to the hall as Thursfield Hall in NSFCT 1933 p176. Turnhurst Hall Farm was built on the site of the hall. By 1995 this too had been demolished to make way for an housing estate (SASR 1995 no 6 p25).
GROUNDS. In the garden of Ford Green Hall is a finial from the hall gateway, built in c1700 (SASR 1995 no 6 p25). In Turnhurst Hall grounds on the E side of the hall was a long channel pond thought to have been built by James Brindley to act as a model canal to test locks for the Bridgewater Canal or the Trent and Mersey Canal or the Droitwich Canal (The Staffs Times July 17 1880) (WWT p23) (TFTP pp152-153) (SASR 1995 no 6 p17). The pond was filled in after the house was demolished (SS Sept 10 1929). The site was excavated in 1993. Warrilow, in HOE p65, says the lock gates used in the experiments went to the BM, but in SHST he just says they are in a London Museum; they have never been located. It cannot be proved that Brindley ever built a model canal in the grounds or tested locks here (SASR 1995 no 6 pp22,27,28). He, reputedly built model locks whilst staying at Union Hall (see) in S Staffs. There was a little summer house with a small

tower in the SE corner of the front garden, which is said to have been Brindley's office; it had a clock in it by which many checked their watches. This had been demolished by 1933 (NSFCT 1933 p176. 1938 p64). The reputed clock face from it went to the Brindley Mill Trust Museum, Leek (SASR 1995 no 6 p25). The ruined outbuildings of the hall were remaining in 1967 (STM Nov 1967 p27p).

Tutbury Ancient parish and small town on and about a steep knoll above the Dove 18.75m ENE of Stafford.

EARLY to PRESENT. Tutbury may have been the capital of some past Celtic kingdom, see Tutbury Castle (LTD p169). The bank and ditch which protected the town centre on the S may have formed the defences of a pre-Norman Conquest burh, unrecorded by the Anglo-Saxon Chronicle (SL p146). By the time of Toteberie's appearance in DB the manor and castle had been to granted by the king to Henry de Ferrers. Tutbury manor then descended with Tutbury Castle (see). Other forms of the name are: Toteberia, Totesbery, Totesberie, Stutesberia, Stuteberia and Tuttebury (SHOS vol 1 p37) (SPN p131), and Tedbery (1698) (Illustrated Journeys of Celia Fiennes edited by Chris Morris. 1984. p149). The **name** means 'the look-out, or watch, town' (DUIGNAN). WH Stevenson and Sir Reginald Hardy think it is from the personal name Tutt, so 'Tutt's burgh' (HOPT vol 1 p137). Or 'Tota's burh' (LGS p238). Or 'Tutta's (or Stut's) fortified place' (SPN p132). Or said to take its name from the British deity, Teutates (HOPT vol 1 p137), or the Saxon god, Tuisto, who gave the name to Tuesday (NSFCT 1908 p111) (AOW p13). Redfern, on similar lines, thinks it could be from an altar here to the Gaulish god, Tutas (HOU p340). Mills gives 'Tata's fort' (SSE 1996 p18). Tutbury was one of only three towns of the county where some sort of urban life existed by 1086 (SL pp77,146). Tutbury **parish** formed after 1086 and probably by the later C11 and certainly by 1291 out of Rolleston or Hanbury parishes (SHC 1916 p197). The parish **church**, St Mary the Virgin, on an elevated position above Church Street to the E of Tutbury Castle overlooking Tutbury town, originally formed part of Tutbury Priory, founded in 1080 or in the late 1080s (UTR p32) (BOE p288). In 1972 a female skeleton in an alabaster coffin of medieval origin was found in the N aisle (info KL Neal). **Beating the bounds** was practiced in Tutbury parish (SHOS vol 1 pp56,57). There may have been a **hermitage** by the bridge over the Dove at Tutbury in the Middle Ages (SHOS vol 1 p57) (VCH vol 3 p137 note). Robert Ferrers of Tutbury Castle (see), possibly the 2nd Earl of Derby, created a **new borough** outside Tutbury Castle walls in c1140 as a planned extension to Tutbury. It was called New Borough, but was not the present Newborough (SL p151). There were granted 182 burgages (SCSF p118), and burgesses enjoyed freedom from all toll, tonnage, package, poundage, and other exactions with all their possessions (W p586). At some date burghal status disappeared. Many inhabitants were still styling themselves 'burgesses' in 1611. By 1798 Shaw described Tutbury as 'an antient borough and market town, now only worthy of the name of a pleasant village' (SHOS vol 1 pp56-57) (NSJFS 1972 p69). (SHC 4th series vol 4 p75) (VCH vol 2 p349) (SL p151). Edmund, Earl of Lancaster, claimed from Henry III the right of erecting a **gallows** at Tutbury (SCSF p123). It was still the **custom** in the C18 (an ancient custom) for the vicar to receive a guinea fine for everyone buried in the church and two shillings eight pence for the burial fees (SHOS vol 1 p58). A **railway** line between Burton upon Trent and Stoke-on-Trent via Tutbury opened on Sept 11 1848 (VCH vol 2 p309) (LTD p198). The branch service to Burton in 1881 was known as the 'Tutbury Jenny' the first locomotive being named after the famous Swedish singer, Jenny Lind. The fate of the locomotive was debated in the House of Commons in 1960. But on June 11 1960 at 8.12pm it ran on the line for the last time (VB p96) (ABTOP p101p) (LTD p199). Tutbury station which appears to have been to the N of the town at Hatton in Derbys (1834 OS map) closed in Nov 1966 and was demolished but re-opened on April 3 1989 (ESNF p32p; says reopened in 1990) (LTD p198). After the Burton branch line closed some of the line became a countryside footpath known as Tutbury Jenny (LTD p199). For Tutbury **charities** see UTR pp133-134. **Persons and visitors.** King **John** was at Tutbury in 1201 and 1204 (UTR p38) (R&S p8). **Henry III** was at Tutbury on Nov 23 1251 and in 1257 (UTR p39). **Henry IV** was at Tutbury in Aug 1404 proceeding to Lichfield. He returned to Tutbury on Sept 1 1404 where he received two commissioners from Robert III of Scotland and took an oath to observe a truce with him (R&S p14) (CAMS p35). The tradition that **Robin Hood** was at Tutbury fair is based on an extract from 'Robin Hood's Garland' a ballad describing the marriage of Robin Hood with Clorinda, Queen of the Tutbury Feast, a shepherdess (IOI p13); Robin having been charmed by her dexterous manner of killing a buck in the forest (HS p104). The full title of the original ballad is 'A new Ballad of bold Robin Hood; showing his birth, breading, valour, and marriage at Titbury Bull-running, calculated for the meridian of Stafford-

shire but may serve for Derbyshire or Kent' (SHOS vol 1 p55) (S&W pp120-122) (HS p105). The date of the ballad is uncertain, but, say Dent and Hill, it is evidently later than Elizabeth I's reign. It is earlier than any allusion to Maid Marian (who may have been modelled on Clorinda - SOSH p116). It has many allusions to Staffs, it assumes that Sherwood and Tutbury lie near together; it details a fight near Tutbury; tells of 'Sir Roger the parson hies from Dubbridge' (Doveridge near Uttoxeter); and of 'the King of the Fidlers' a possible allusion to the King of the Minstrels Court of Tutbury (HOU pp327-329) (HS p105). (UTR p73) (MOS p49) (LGS p244) (QML pp156-161). Supporting this tradition are others that Robin was born at Loxley near Uttoxeter; that he was active at Elford, and Burton, and was in Needwood Forest, Swythamley Park, and old Macclesfield Forest. **Piers Venables** from Aston, near Sudbury, Derbys had a gang of local men who, engaged in criminal activities, terrorised the Tutbury area. Tutbury tenants were among those who complained about them in a petition to parliament in 1439 (RHH pp147,150,151). **James I** visited Tutbury from Aug 16 to 20 1619, Aug 19 1621, and Aug 16 to 19 1624 (UTR p99) (R&S p25) (STMSM May 1973 p25. Sept 1978 p24). White says he only once visited Tutbury Castle (W p587). The Duchy of Lancaster had a stud at Tutbury which produced racehorses in Charles I's reign (HOS p64), perhaps that at Castle Hayes Park. Tutbury PR records that **Robert Berkins** of Tutbury died aged 104 a few years earlier than 1797 (SHOS vol 1 p58). **Ann Moore**, nee Pegg, was born on Oct 31 1761 at Rosliston, Derbys, the daughter of a labourer named Pegg. She married James Moore in 1788 but he soon deserted her. She then came to Tutbury with a large family and very poor. By 1808 Ann Moore was claiming that she had eaten nothing since 1806 (SSGLST pp41-44) or from 1807 (UTR p125) or from July 17 1807 (VB p98). In c1777 to at least c1782 Ann was in service to Mrs Savage, a widow, in Tixall village (her aunt (her mother's sister) had been a nursery maid at Tixall-house) (HOT p76; that Ann's father was Thomas Pegg, and Ann married John Moor). The claim of her abstinence from food was brought to public attention in the Medical Journal 1808 by doctors Robert Taylor and John Allen. A committee set up in Sept 1808 believed her (SSGLST pp41-44). A committee who watched her for 16 days in 1811 claimed she had been telling the truth (UTR p125). But Dr Alexander Henderson and a friend, Mr Lawrence, did not believe her in Aug 1812 and another commission was set up consisting of Dr Garlic, Sir Oswald Moseley, and Rev Leigh Richmond, Rector of Turvey, Beds, who surveyed her over a nine day period from April 21 1813 (SSGLST pp41-44) or from April 23 1813 (UTR p125). When they detected she had been lying she was made to sign a confession that she was a fraud, and she and her children were driven out of Tutbury. They turned up in Macclesfield and Knutsford courts on various charges (SSGLST pp41-44). Anne Moore died at Macclesfield in her seventy-sixth year (Broughton's Scrapbook p97). The house in which she lived in Ludgate Street, Tutbury, had been demolished by 1946, by which time the site formed part of the Tutbury Glass Works (UTR p125) (ABTOP p121p). White devotes a whole page to her which is unusual for him (W pp588-589). In the early 1990s there was an illustration of Anne Moore in the Dog and Partridge Inn, Tutbury. (Staffordshire Gazette May 11 1813) (THS p52) (SSC p110) (SM pp361 il,262) (SMT p13) (S&W vol 1 p8) (LGS p244) (BCWJ p108) (SLM Dec 1958 pp12,13) (Weekly Sentinel May 3 1963) (STMSM Dec 1973 pp26-27. Sept 1978 p24. May 1980 p53 il of (original in WSL)) (TB July 1994 p7 il of (original in WSL)). For the 'Tutbury Tup' alias Sir **Oswald Mosley** (1873-1928), 5th Bt, see Rolleston Hall. **Roger Woolley** of Tutbury was a leading authority on fishing flies. His 'The Fly-Fisher's Flies' appeared in 1938 (LTD p168). **Elizabeth II** and the Duke of Edinburgh, journeying from Sudbury, planted two trees at Tutbury on March 28 1957, before leaving for Burton (R&S p47).

MARKETS AND FAIRS. Tutbury's was the only Staffs market recorded in DB and it may never have received a market charter (NSJFS 1971 pp51,52). The market day was altered from Tuesday to Saturday in 1624 (SCSF p96). There was a market in 1792 (OWEN), but no market in 1888 (LHE p265). **Fairs.** Feb 14 (Whitaker's Almanac) (COOKE). **Aug 15** (at which was performed the Court of Minstrels (see Tutbury Castle) and Bull Running (see below)) (COOKE). On the **second Monday in Oct** there was a Statutes fair at the Wheel Inn, a semblance of which continued until the 1950s (LTD p191). **Dec 1** (Whitaker's Almanac) (COOKE). There was a fair in 1792 (OWEN), but no fair in 1888 (LHE p265). In medieval times a great livestock and horse fair was held in a field called the Big Close on the edge of Tutbury (LTD p191). (SCSF pp98,99). Tutbury had a court of Pyepowder (or called pie powder, or court of dusty foot) held by the bailiffs at fairs (UTR p66). For the origins of the word Pyepowder see under Lichfield. There is a local tradition that Robin Hood attended Tutbury Fair. (UTR p73) (MOS p49) (LGS p244) (QML pp156-161).

BULL RUNNING. Tutbury was renowned in the Middle Ages for a custom whereby a bull was chased, caught, slayed and feasted upon in Tutbury. **Origins**. The custom was introduced from Spain after the marriage of John of Gaunt, Earl of Lancaster, to Constance, daughter of Pedro the Cruel of Castile in 1374 (SCSF p41) (FOS p110) and Gaunt being made King of Castile and Leon. The event was in existence by c1377 (FOS p110). It was performed in the afternoon and evening of the morrow of the Assumption (Aug 16). The minstrels of the Honour of Tutbury (see Court of Minstrels under Tutbury Castle), an unrelated Tutbury institution, played an important part in the procedure - the reason for their involvement is unknown, save for when their court was instituted it seems to have been fixed to coincide with the Bull Running. Bull Running began, in fact, after the dinner which concluded the court held on the morning of the same day. According to the minstrels' charter of 1381, only the minstrels were entitled to engage in the sport, the spectators being positively restrained under severe penalties from approaching the bull nearer than 40 yards (SCSF p42) or 40 feet (FOS p112). After the minstrels' dinner the minstrels gathered at a barn, previously at Tutbury Priory gate (FOS p112), where they received a soaped and pepper-nostrilled bull without horns, ears and tail. The bull was ceremonially released by the prior of Tutbury: This office passed to the Duke of Devonshire after the Reformation (FOS p112). The minstrels then had to catch the bull before nightfall and stop it escaping across the Dove to Derbys. If the bull escaped it became the property of the Duke of Devonshire (FOS p112); before the Reformation the prior kept it? If successful, the minstrels could keep it. They brought it to the High Street and baited it with dogs. Then it could be sold or divided among themselves. Plot implies with his description of the custom, in c1680 - his information was supplied by Dugdale (SH p56) - that its rules were strictly kept. Thereafter, the sport became something of a 'free-for-all' with the occasional death. Rev Pegge's account of the custom to the Society of Antiquaries in 1765 appears in SHOS. In 1777 (LOU p181) or in the mid to the late 1770s a quarrel broke out during the bull running between Burton men, headed by John Ludlow, and Tutbury men. One of the latter, William Bennett, died of a fractured skull causing considerable local dissatisfaction with the custom. A petition was drawn up and presented to the Duke of Devonshire and the custom was abolished by the Crown (UTR pp70-73) (HOS p63) in 1778. The rites of the custom are or were on the wall of the Dog and Partridge Inn in Tutbury. There was a custom not unlike Tutbury's at Stamford, Lincs, and in a small respect at Kidlington, Oxon, where on Monday after Whitsun week the maids of the town having their thumbs tied behind them have to run after and catch a lamb with their teeth and she who holds the lamb becomes the Lady of the Lamb (SHOS vol 1 pp52-55). (NHS pp436-440) (GNHS p142) (W pp586-587) (FLJ 1904 p199) (MOS pp54,55) (LGS pp243-244) (SOSH pp138,140) (SCSF pp40-43) (PS p83) (SLM autumn 1958 p28) (FOS pp110-114) (STMSM Sept 1978 p24) (Country Walks around Britain. Holly Ward. p15) (MR p344) (TOS p16).

INDUSTRY. The alabaster of the Tutbury area was worked from the mid C12. Its use in the priory church W doorway in c1160-70 is the earliest known example in England (HOS p42). Tutbury Gypsum is an irregular seam of gypsum outcrop in thickness 8-10 feet ranging on the bluff above the Dove traced from about 1m SW of Tutbury to S end of Draycott-in-the-Clay (VCH vol 2 pp197,198). Woolcombing, and later silk spinning, were Tutbury's traditional industries, giving way in the late C18 to cotton (SCSF p112). There was cotton production at Tutbury Mill (see) by the Mill Fleam of the Dove to the N of Tutbury from the C18. Tutbury was a glass-making centre between 1720 and the present (VB pp95,97) (LTD pp192-193).

TUTBURY HOARD. After Edward II defeated his powerful cousin, Thomas, Earl of Lancaster, at the battle of Burton Bridge (see) in 1322 Thomas returned to his seat Tutbury Castle (see) and gathered his valuables together, including a treasure chest containing money to pay the Scots levies, and fled to Pontefract Castle. In crossing the Dove the treasure chest was lost. It was commonly thought Thomas hid his treasure in the river, but this is unlikely because retrieving it would have been difficult. It is more likely that at a ford in the Dove just below the present bridge the waggon horses probably became unstable in the current and the waggon with the chest overturned (LGS p240) (VB p90). On June 1 1831 Mr Webb's workmen whilst trying to remove gravel from the river on the S side of the bridge to accelerate the flow to a mill found the first silver coins from the chest (Staffordshire Mercury July 2 1831) (Broughton's Scrapbook pp432-433) (MR p344). Duchy of Lancaster officials found 1,500 in the first search. Part of those first found were claimed by the Duchy and are now in the BM (LGS p240). Another part of the collection went on show, or are in the possession of, the Potteries Museum (SOSH p133) (ES June 12 1931 p6). A notice, dated 1831, was placed in the church warning against further searching. But despite this and soldiers

patrolling the river banks - the Staffordshire Yeomanry were sent to suppress a riot created by the excitement and looting of the hoard - many came to hunt for coins. In one day two men on the Derbys bank picked up 5,000 coins (VB p90) (info Yeomanry Museum). In 1838 a large number of coins were found after further diggings (MR p345); Raven could be in error and mean 1883, for Masefield only says in 1883 (LGS p240). In 1832 Sir Oswald Moseley of Rolleston Hall (see) felt compelled to publish his historical researches on Tutbury - HCT - such was the great public interest in the hoard (SH p130). There are 70 coins (excluding the one stuck fast to the stone) of which nine were struck after the accession of Edward II in 1307. 32 were minted at London, 15 at Canterbury, five at Durham, four of Bury St Edmunds, two of York and one of each of these towns - Bristol, Berwick, Chester, Exeter, Kingston-upon-Hull and Lincoln. One was struck at Waterford, Ireland, two of Alexander III (1249-85) of Scotland, and three 'deniers' the continental equivalent of the English penny - including one of Count Robert of Bethune in Flanders (1305-22) and two of Count Gaucher of Chatillon (NSFCT 1937 p115). The total number of coins have been estimated at 20,000 (GBR 1974 p203) or over 100,000 (LGS p240) or some put it at about 200,000 (NSFCT 1937 p115). By 1974 it was the largest hoard of coins ever found in the United Kingdom (GBR 1974 p203) (ZSB). (W pp589-590) (HOU p341) (PS p82) (S p84) (FSP pp65-67) (UTR pp51-54) (DAJ vol 50) (SLM autumn 1958 p27) ('Some Thoughts on Ancient History of Leek' author and date unknown from vol 10 of Local Pamphlets in Horace Barks Ref lib. il of a cluster of coins , then 8 ils of 8 coins) (STMSM Jan 1973 p34 p of silver penny found in 1832 of Edward I's reign. Dec 1973 pp26-27) (TOS pp11-13).

Tutbury Castle The lofty site of the present ruined castle at Tutbury forming the original settlement of Tutbury may have first been fortified in the Iron Age. The castle site was excavated in 1974 and revealed concentric earthworks earlier than the Saxon-Norman period, as well as Iron Age pottery (STMSM Jan 1973 p24. Sept 1974 p38ps. April 1976 p4. May 1980 pp8,9) (LTD p169). (LGS p238) (UTR pp14,15,16 plan facing). Others think the first defences and motte were made shortly after the Norman Conquest (SL p64) (CAMS p35). William Humberston who produced a topographical survey of the Duchy of Lancaster's estates in 1558 and 1559 could find nothing in writing to show whether the castle was built before the Conquest or not (SH p14).

1066 to 1150. After the Norman Conquest William the Conqueror gave Tutbury manor and castle to his nephew Hugh 'd' Avranches,' Earl of Chester. In or soon after 1071 the king gave it to Henry de Ferrers (or Ferrieres) of Normandy. He was a DB commissioner in 1086 when he held some 210 lordships or manors, most in Derbys, but the caput of his **'Honour of Tutbury'** was at Tutbury Castle, near which he founded Tutbury Priory (see). Among his Staffs possessions were Burtone (see) and Uttoxeter (see) (LGS p238) (HOS 1998 p39). The 'Honour of Tutbury' was the group of manors, of which Tutbury manor was one, with peculiar rights and privileges which descended with descendents and then the holders of Tutbury Castle. The Tutbury Coucher is the common name for the Coucher of 1415, because it contains a survey of the administrative system of the 'Honour of Tutbury.' The original is lost, although numerous copies survive in the BM (VCH vol 2 p351 note). The lord of Tutbury had the privilege of taking an **amercement**, or fine, for every bastard born within the lordship. The cognisance of the bishop of the diocese and ecclesiastical courts could be avoided if an oath was made that the bastard was conceived within the lordship, and a payment of ten shillings made to the lord (SCSF p121). The **Agard Horn** is a symbol by which Tutbury manor was held in cornage tenure. The Agard family of Foston (MOS pp58-59), in 1569, claimed the office of escheator and coroner for Tutbury and the bailiwick Leyke (East and West Leake, Notts) (SMC p124), or to be Hereditary Steward of Leyke and Tutbury (SCSF p116) by possessing a white hunter's horn. The horn was 14.75 inches long, seven inches round the mouth, and 2.25 inches at the narrow end (MOS pp58-59). It was decorated in the middle and at each end with silver gilt, to which was affixed a girdle of fine black silk, adorned with certain buckles of silver. The arms in the centre of the horn, were thought by Broughton, to be most likely those of John of Gaunt, Duke of Lancaster, or those of, Edmund Crouchback, 1st Earl of Lancaster (2nd son of Henry III), who received the 'Honour of Tutbury' by forfeiture of Robert de Ferrers, 6th Earl of Derby, in 1266 (SMC p124). The marriage of Nicholas Agard of Tutbury to Elizabeth, daughter and co-heir of Roger Ferrers in 1569 suggests that the horn had previously been in the Ferrers family (SMC p124); the Ferrers may have retained Tutbury and Leyke manors after losing the 'Honour of Tutbury' in 1266, or they were granted the manors at a later date. From the Agards the horn passed to the Stanhopes of Elvaston (Blount. ed 1815), who sold it, in 1753, to Samuel Foxlowe of Staveley, Derbys. It then passed to Mr Greaves-Bagshawe of Ford Hall, Chapel en le Frith (MOS pp58-59) (ESNF p30p). (SHOS vol 1 p44 notes) (DAJ vol 8 il) (Chester

Arch Soc Trans 1905 pp85-128, 129-166 il of the Delamere Horn opposite title page. But nothing on the Agard Horn).

DESCENT OF THE EARLY FERRERS'. **Henry de Ferrers** was succeeded by his third son, **Robert de Ferrers**, a commander at the battle of the Standard (1138) and for his services was created 1st Earl of Derby. He is said to have created the hunting grounds of Barton Park (see), Castle Hayes Park (see), Highlands Park (see), Rolleston Park (see) and Stockley Park (see). He died in 1139 and was succeeded by his son **Robert de Ferrers**, 2nd Earl of Derby, or Earl of Ferrers. He founded Darley Abbey near Derby, and Merevale Abbey, Warws, and may have founded a new borough outside the walls of Tutbury Castle. He was buried at Meredale Abbey, dying before 1160. He was succeeded by his son **William de Ferrers**, 3rd Earl of Derby and Earl of Ferrers. He was an adherent of the younger Henry in his rebellion in 1173 and sacked and burnt Nottingham in 1174. He made a submission to the king at Northampton in 1174 and surrendered Tutbury Castle. He died on a Crusade at the siege of Acre in Palestine in 1190. He was succeeded by his son **William de Ferrers** (d1247), 4th Earl of Derby or Earl of Ferrers. He married Agnes, sister and coheir of Ranulph (d1232), Earl of Chester, and inherited his wife's lands including Chartley Castle and manor. The 4th Earl was succeeded by his son **William de Ferrers** (d1254), 5th Earl of Derby. He married Margaret de Quincy, heiress of Groby, Leics. Their eldest son **Robert de Ferrers** (c1239-c1279), 6th Earl of Derby, was his father's successor at Chartley; for his descendents see Chartley Castle. Their younger son William Ferrers (d1287) inherited Groby. He was succeeded there by his son William Ferrers (d1325), who was summonded to parliament in 1299 and created Lord Ferrers of Groby. The second son of his great great grandson William Ferrers (d1445), was Thomas Ferrers (d1459) who married Elizabeth Freville, heiress of Tamworth Castle. Their descendents held Tamworth Castle until Anne Ferrers, heiress of Tamworth Castle, reunited her junior branch of the Ferrers family of Groby and Tamworth Castle with the representative of the senior branch of the Ferrers family of Tutbury Castle and Chartley Castle by her marriage in 1688 to Hon Robert Shirley, a relation of the Shirleys of Chartley Castle (The Complete Peerage).

1150 to 1560. In the rebellion of 1173/4 Tutbury Castle was seized, taken and destroyed (LGS p239) (CAMS p35). In the Barons' Wars in 1263 (CAMS p35) or in 1264 (LGS p239) Prince Edward attacked the castle in reprisal for the Ferrers' opposition to Henry III. In 1266 Tutbury Castle and the 'Honour of Tutbury' passed to the Crown when Robert de Ferrers, 6th Earl of Derby, forfeited his lands for his part in the Civil War (VCH vol 2 p350) (SL p64). In 1267 Henry III granted the castle and 'Honour' to his second son, Edmund Crouchback, 1st Earl of Lancaster (VCH vol 2 p350). Edmund's son Thomas, Earl of Lancaster, became a powerful opponent of his cousin Edward II and in 1322 the two fought a skirmish on Burton Bridge (see). Thomas lost, and in his escape from Tutbury Castle to Pontefract Castle, Yorks, he lost a chest of money in the Dove, which was rediscovered in 1831 and subsequently known as the Tutbury (see) Hoard. Thomas forfeited the castle in 1327 and it passed to his brother, Henry, and was left dismantled for 40 years. In 1361 it came to Edward III's fourth son, John of Gaunt, who rebuilt the castle, not essentially as a military fortress, but as 'a comfortable castellated residence.' In 1371 John married secondly Constance, Princess of Castile (LGS p240) (SOSH p138). She brought some continental innovations to the castle, introducing a vineyard, a garden and bull-running. When Henry Bolingbroke, son of John of Gaunt, Duke of Lancaster, succeeded to the throne as Henry IV in 1399 the castle and the 'Honour' passed to the Crown and has since descended with the duchy estates in the possession of the Crown to Elizabeth II. Henry IV made visits to his castle in 1404 and 1405 (SL pp64,69,151,154) (The Honour of Tutbury in the 14th and 15th centuries. Dr Birrell. Unpublished thesis). **Fabric of the castle.** The **shell keep**, originally of wood, which stood on the motte, and the **chapel** in the bailey were, subsequently, rebuilt in stone (CAMS pp35,38il of the chapel foundations). The chapel was called the chapel of St Michael on the Hill in Saxon times, but rededicated to St Peter by the Normans (GLS p102). Some of the Ferrers family are buried under it. (UTR p25). Edmund, Earl of Lancaster, or his son, Thomas, built a suite of apartments at the S end of the bailey, which included a **hall** and a **great chamber**; they stood to the end of the C16. The **NE gateway** tower, or N gateway (LGS p242), or called John of Gaunt's Gateway, although he probably had no hand in its building, was built between 1313-1314 (SOSH p140p) (VB 91). John of Gaunt's gateway is illustrated in George Griffith's tragedy 'The Two Houses' (1866). The great rectangular buttresses of the N gateway are Stuart additions (LGS p242). (W p587) (UTR pp18-19). Work on a new piece of **curtain wall** was begun in 1413. Work started on the southern end in 1420. In Henry VI's reign much of the present curtain wall around the bailey was built. The **S tower** was begun in 1442 and finished in

the 1450s (UTR p22). The **dungeons** (UTR p23). The **N tower** or called Margaret's Tower (Tutbury Castle Guide. 1994), or commonly called the high tower or even John of Gaunt's tower (SGS p172) was in construction between 1457-60. (UTR pp20-21). It originally housed a succession of fine chambers and it is thought that it was intended for Queen Margaret of Anjou during the Wars of the Roses (LTD p191). The **shell keep** was totally ruinous by the end of the C15. Major repairs were carried out on the castle from 1561. A sketch of the castle in c1560 shows it looking magnificent (CAMS p35). **Lawlessness.** The bailiffs of Edmund, 1st Earl of Lancaster, at Tutbury Castle captured a robber named William Knout, who turned King's Evidence and charged Richard Astell of Rolleston with being one of his companions. Richard was arrested but gave the bailiffs ten shillings to connive at his escape. Knout then charged Ralph de Aunsedeley (Anslow) with robbery, and he also paid to obtain his freedom. Another, John Walcepot, was also charged, but he was acquitted by the steward of the manor court. The sequel to this series of accusations came when Ralph Young of Rolleston accused Knout of stealing a cow which was still in his possession, and the issue was to be tried by ordeal of battle. They fought at Tutbury and Ralph Young was the victor, thus proving beyond possibility of doubt that Knout was guilty. He was hung (UTR p43). The Stafford Assize Roll of 1293 records the case of William de Tissyngton (or Tyssington), a priest, who murdered William de Lenton, the Janitor of Tutebur (Tutbury) with an axe to the head in Tutbury borough. Tissyngton fled to the church and took sanctuary and thereafter had ecclesiastical privileges and the right of being tried by an ecclesiastical court. His defence was that a robber imprisoned in Tutbury Castle had escaped and he and his victim had both gone after the thief, in the confusion they had mistaken each other for the thief and struck each other (UTR pp41-43) (ESS p25).

COURT OF MINSTRELS. The Court of Minstrels was an annual court to keep order over the musicians of the Honour of Tutbury. The organisation and assemblage of which is thought to have been unique in England (MR p344). **Origins.** The castle became a centre of musical activity in the mid C14, especially after the marriage of John of Gaunt to Constance, daughter of Pedro the Cruel of Castile in 1374 (SCSF p41) (FOS p110); musicians came from all parts of the Honour of Tutbury to take part in festivities arranged for visitors and they inevitably fell out. A court was needed to keep them in order and give them respect. By 1377 (FOS p110) John of Gaunt had established a **Tutbury Court of King's Minstrels.** John of Gaunt granted a charter to the King of the Minstrels dated Aug 22 1381. The original charter was written in Norman French and entitled Carta le Roy de Minstralx. Plot gives a translation. The original charter was confirmed in 1443 (SCSF p41). The charter gave the 'King' and his officers under him power to apprehend and arrest any minstrels who refused to carry out service to the Honour, and who broke the laws of the charter, once a year on the day of the Assumption of the Virgin Mary. In due course it was found that the 'King' could exceed the bounds of justice and it was deemed expedient to institute a **Court of Minstrels.** The Court was fixed for the morrow after the Assumption (Aug 16) and in time the Minstrels also changed their day of service to this date (FOS p111). On this day the minstrels, Steward and the Bailiff of the Lordship congregated outside the Mansion House of the Bailiff and then walked in procession to Tutbury parish church in the following order:-

Music.

Minstrels, two and two.

Steward - King of the Minstrels - Bailiff.

Steward and Officers of the late King of the Minstrels, with white wands in their hands.

Inhabitants of the Borough and Honour of Tutbury.

(SCSF p41). At the church divine service was performed by the vicar of Tutbury, who received one penny from each minstrel as a fee. The assembly then processed to Tutbury Castle hall, where, the Court was officially opened and the various plaints and pleas entered. The Musicians Court Roll was called and two juries were appointed; a jury of 12 for Staffs and another of 12 for the other counties of the Honour (Derbys, Leics, Notts, and Warws). The Steward of the lordship then gave an address. He reminded the minstrels of their importance, and ended by asking them to proceed with the appointment of officers for the following year. The two juries then left the Court to make their decisions. While they were gone the rest of the company took part in a banquet. The 'King' was chosen out of the four stewards of the proceeding year. He had to be from the other county that the 'King' was from that year. In choosing the stewards two had to be from Staffs and two from Derbys (three of them were chosen by the jurors and the fourth by 'him that keeps the

Court'). Upon the juries' return the new officers were appointed. The old 'King' then handed the new 'King' his white wand and then drank his health in wine, and the retiring stewards did the same. The new officers were then able to levy the fines inflicted by the juries of the day. Some of the fines went to the 'Kings Majesty' and the other to the stewards (FOS p112). A **dinner** was attended by the company once this part of the proceedings had been completed. The minstrels' participation in **Bull Running** (see under Tutbury), another unrelated Tutbury institution of Aug 16, began after their dinner when they departed and gathered at a barn, previously at Tutbury Priory gate, where they received the bull. The reason for the two institutions being associated is unknown. According to the minstrels' charter of 1381, only the minstrels were entitled to engage in the sport. It was also the custom for minstrels to serve a seven year **apprenticeship** before playing for gain (MR pp343,344). The **demise** of the Court of Minstrels seems to have begun in the C18. In Tatenhill church is a small memorial to Henry Coxon, a clerk, died 1739, who is described on the memorial as 'The last of the Tutbury Minstrels' (UTR pp67-70) (IVNF). In 1772 a Petition from the Court was sent to the Cavendish family, then the ducal owners of the manor. It requested the return of rents from a piece of land known as Piper's Meadow which funded the minstrel's dinners; the withholding of which would spell the end of the Court of Minstrels (SCSF pp42-43). Despite the abolition of Bull Running in 1778 the Minstrel's Court continued in attenuated form, annually, in the Steward's House at Tutbury Castle for some time after (SCSF pp43) (FOS p113). A procession through Tutbury streets to Tutbury parish church, resembling the old procession headed by minstrels, was briefly revived on the morning of the Feast of Assumption (Aug 15) in the 1940s by the vicar and Rev N Edwards (LTD p181). (NHS pp435-440) (SHOS vol 1 p56) (W p586) (SC pp110-117) (LGS pp243,244) (CBD vol 2 p225 il) (DAJ vol 32) (SLM autumn 1958 p28) (STMSM Dec 1973 pp26-27).

1560 to PRESENT. **Mary, Queen of Scots' imprisonment**. After Mary, Queen of Scots (1542-1587), had fled Scotland in 1568 she was kept prisoner first at Bolton and then in the medieval hall and great chamber at Tutbury Castle from Feb to June 1569 (VB p91). Masefield says she was at the castle for the first time from Feb 4 to April 1569 when she was removed to Wingfield Manor, Sheffield, but was back at Tutbury between Sept and Nov 1569. She was at Coventry between Nov 1569 and Jan 1570 and then at Tutbury until May 1570, and then taken to Chatsworth and later Wingfield Manor (LGS p241). Underhill says she left Tutbury in 1572 for Wingfield Manor where she stayed for nearly 12 years under the care of the Earl of Shrewsbury and from where she made short visits back to Tutbury in 1578, and 1581 (UTR pp21-22,92-98). She was in Coventry for a period until arriving at Tutbury on Jan 14 1585 (VB p91) (LTD p186). Underhill says, later in 1585 she spent a short time back at Wingfield and then returned to Tutbury (UTR pp21-22,92-98). A freestanding timber and plaster lodge, which stood to the S of the N tower and known as the Queen's Lodgings (VB p91), was her accommodation during her last incarceration. She bitterly complained about the lodgings for being too near a privy. Her gaoler at Tutbury was the Chancellor of the Duchy of Lancaster, Sir Ralph Sadler (LGS p241) (VB p91). Coal was brought to her from the mines on Cannock Chase (CCBO p45), and she is said to have hawked on Hanbury Hill (see). Sadler was replaced by Sir Amyas Paulet in April 1585. Paulet tightened security surrounding Mary. This included the opening of her letters and the prevention of her almsgiving to the local poor (VB p91). Mary was at Tutbury at the time of the Duke of Norfolk's intrigues, and listened to his proposals of marriage as the only means of obtaining her liberty, but declared herself adverse to further matrimonial connections. FNC Mundy in 'Needwood Forest' refers to this (SHOS vol 1 part 1 p51. vol 1 pp28,47; the appendix contains much on the confinement of Mary at Tutbury from documents and letters in the possession of Thomas Clifford of Tixall). It has been said certain treasonable letters were conveyed to Mary in beer barrels whilst she was at Tutbury (SOSH p357). At Paulet's instigation Mary was removed to Chartley Old Hall on Dec 4 1585 (LGS p241) (LTD p188). Possibly because Chartley was more secure for being surrounded by a moat and her attendants could be lodged within the compounds and would not be able to secrete letters into her (NSFCT 1886 pp35-36). (GNHS p142) (W p587) (PS pp84p,85) (TOS pp51-52) (SLM winter 1959 pp22,23) (STMSM Dec 1973 pp26-27). **James I** stayed at the castle whilst hunting in Needwood Forest in the early C17, for the dates of his stays see under Tutbury. The medieval hall and great chamber to the S of the motte were replaced by the King's Lodging built in 1631-5. Its S wall was the castle's outer wall and this remains with its inserted classical windows. **Charles I** and Queen Henrietta were at Tutbury in 1634. He stayed again in 1636 (UTR p100). In the **Civil War** the castle was a royalist garrison in 1642. In Feb 1643 Henry Hastings, Lord Loughborough, held it against a short siege

(LGS p242). Charles I and Prince Rupert on their way from Lichfield to Ashbourne were at the castle on Aug 12 1645 (UTR p100) (GLS p101). The castle surrendered to parliament after a three week siege in 1645 (CAMS p37) or on April 20 1646 (LGS p242) (NSFCT 1976 p17). The royalist commander was Sir Andrew Kniveton and he surrendered to Sir William Brereton (LGS p242). In 1647 parliament ordered the castle to be demolished. The order was not implemented, and after the Restoration, repair work was done in 1662 (NSFCT 1976 p17). Salter says demolition of its walls began in 1647 (CAMS p37). Redfern says it was demolished in June 1648 (HOU p87). **After the Civil War**. Some of the castle's accommodation was patched up in 1662 and leased to the Duke of Ormonde (CAMS p37). In the later C17 Plot met with a person who remembered the removing of the old wooden drawbridge (NHS pp39,383435 tab 36). It was so built that no piece of wood used was more than a yard long, and the more weight on it the stronger it was (W pp586-587). In 1681 Ormonde passed the lease to Col Edward Vernon of Sudbury Hall, Derbys and the lease remained with the Vernons until 1864 (NSFCT 1976 p17) (CAMS p37). The Vernons built a house in 1750 on the site of the King's Lodging, later used as a farmhouse. There is an 123 feet deep **well** within the castle precincts. It is circular for the first 12 feet - circumference is 19 feet - then square. It was still in use in 1912 for Vernon's farmhouse (UTR pp17-18) (NSFCT 1912 pp189-191) (LTD p191). There is believed to be a **tunnel** from the well to Tutbury Priory. In an exploration in 1955 nothing was found (LTD p191). Fourth Lord Vernon built a mock mini shell keep on the top of the motte after 1760 or in c1775 or in 1777 as an eye-catcher to be viewed from Sudbury Hall. This is known as **'Julius's Tower'** (SHOS vol 1 p47) (LGS p242) (SL p135) (F&G p391) (F p318). The name may be from an earlier tower. William Humberston in his survey of the Duchy of Lancaster's estates of 1558 and 1559 notes there was an ancient tower on the outer wall of the castle called 'Julius Tower' which the local inhabitants believed had been erected by Julius Caesar (SH pp13,14). In 1832 there was a proposal to use the castle as a prison and the duchy carried out some repairs (NSFCT 1976 p17). **Visitors** to the castle had to pay from as early as 1847 because of the wear and tear from tourists (CAMS p37). In 1913 extensive preservation was carried out and its use as a farm ceased in 1952. Elizabeth II, as Duke of Lancaster, visited the castle on March 28 1957 (NSFCT 1976 p17). There is **Danewort**, Dane's bane, Dane's blood, or Sambucus Ebulus, a rare species of dwarf elder in the castle grounds, only found elsewhere in the county at Wootton near Eccleshall (NSFCT 1885 pp69-70). **Supernatural**. Ghosts which haunt the castle are: A monk-like figure in a brown robe seen in the area known as the Vinecroft; a lady in white, often wrongly ascribed to being Mary, Queen of Scots, she is thought to be a Lady M___ and inhabits the watch tower; a grey lady; a Norman knight who may be a member of the Ferrers family;' a paranormal force which scares animals from going into the banqueting room (GLS pp100-103). (SSC pp108,109 with etching by Shaw, Calvert and Samuel and Nathanial Buck) (SMC p163) (GNHS pp140,141,142) (GNHSS p22) (PS pp80, 82p of the moat,85,86p of the tilting ground) (S p of the N tower, pp84,85) (KES pp213,214) (UTR pp24,103-105) (SLM Nov 1950 pp22-23il) (Guide to Tutbury Castle. Sir Robert Somerville. 1964) (NSJFS 1966 pp39 plan, 45) (BOE pp287-288) (VB pp190-92) (SL pp64,65,66,87) (SGS p172) (SHJ vol 5 pp45-48) (AA p259).

Tutbury Elm A witch elm in the road leading from Tutbury to Needwood Forest at Dun's Cross. In the late C18 Shaw noted the bole of the elm was remarkably straight, thick and lofty, having eight noble branches (SHOS vol 1 p58). It was not the same as the gospel tree at Dun's Cross. Is probably the same as the 'Great Elm' marked on 1834 OS map at SK 211281, just over 0.5m S of Tutbury.

Tutbury Priory Benedictine priory dedicated to the Virgin Mary. It was founded by Henry de Ferrers (fl 1086) of Tutbury Castle (see), or it was co-founded with his wife, Bertha (The Complete Peerage) (LGS pp242-243). On the authority of a couplet in the Tutbury Cartulary the foundation of the priory is generally accepted to be in 1080 (HOS p26) (VCH vol 3 p331) (MRH p79). This is partly confirmed for in DB mention is made of monks holding the Derbys manors of Doveridge and Marston-upon-Dove (VCH vol 3 p331). But some say it was founded in 1089 (Church Guide. BJ Welsh), or in 1121, when it came under the Benedictine order (UTR p82). The priory was colonised by and dependent on the Abbey of St Pierre sur Dives, Normandy. The priory buildings were destroyed after a dispute in 1260 (VCH vol 3 p333). Bishop Langton visited the priory on Jan 17 1319 (SSE 1994 p4). The priory was not suppressed with other alien houses in 1415 although the link with St Pierre had waned by the C15 (VCH vol 3 pp331,337). The priory church was in memory of the recently dead William the Conqueror and of his wife Matilda of Flanders and it was a thanks offering to God for Henry Ferrer's wife Bertha and their children and his father and mother (Church Guide. BJ Welsh).

The monastic building lay to the N and on the N side of the church (VCH vol 3 p337). From the start the church did double as both priory and parish church. Soon after the priory surrendered, on Sept 14 1538, the priory estate passed to the Crown; the monks pensioned off; and the last prior transformed into the first vicar of the parish. The Crown leased the estate to Sir William Bassett. In 1552 the Crown granted it to Sir William Cavendish who built a house on the site using priory stone for it (SHOS vol 1 pp52,59) (SOS p534) (VCH vol 3 p339). The monastic buildings and monastic part of the church were pulled down to leave a church for the parish. That which was demolished included two bays at the E end of the church, the nave N aisle (its arcading was then walled up), the transepts, the central tower, a monk's choir and side chapels, and to the N of the nave the monk's quarters with their cloister and attendant buildings. The roof and clerestory of the nave was removed and over the triforium, which was then glazed, a plain domestic ceiling was constructed with a flat roof. This left about one third of the original structure (Church Guide. BJ Welsh). The site of Chapter House may be in a certain area of the present churchyard where in 1972 an alabaster sarcophagus was found (LTD p179). The much photographed decorated W door in the church still survives and dates from after 1150. It has seven orders; the outer-most represents the earliest use of alabaster in England (BOE p288). BJ Welsh's Church Guide implies it is the inner-most, closest to the door. Bird says it is the second in from the door (VB p92). (GNHS pp543,544) (W pp587-588) (LGS p242p) (UTR pp30-31) ('English Medieval Sculpture' A Gardner p290) (VCH vol 2 p201) (STMSM Jan 1973 p24. Dec 1973 pp26-27). The S doorway was re-stored to being a door in 1913 after being a window for a long time. The lintel is made from a tympanum taken from elsewhere in the priory or may pre-date the priory coming from the old Saxon church (STMSM Sept 1978 p24) and shows a boar hunt (Church Guide. BJ Welsh). (TNE pp258,259) (NTL ppxxi,xliv,xlvii,lxxviii) (UTR p31) (PS p81) (BOE p288) (CHMS p55). (GNHS p143il) (SOSH p106) (KES p213) (SL p75) (BTOP vol 1 p80). The original priory seal is in the BM (S pp90 p facing and p of obverse side,91). The priory narrowly escaped being demolished by a bomb (in WW2?) which landed in the churchyard (STMSM Sept 1978 p24). There is a tradition of a tunnel running between the priory and Tutbury Castle. A wayside chapel set up and maintained by the priory was erected for travellers on a lane to Needwood Forest. The approximate site of it is represented by Chapel House Farm (see).

Tutbury Ward One of the five wards of Needwood Forest. The heirs of the Annesley family were the hereditary foresters of the ward. Tutbury Ward was bounded on the W side by the Mare Brook and on the S by Aylewardsley Way, the other sides formed the NE edges of the forest. Byrkley Lodge was the lodge of the ward (HCT p366) (HOPT vol 2 p223) (VCH vol 2 pp349,352).

Tutbury Woodhouses A manor based on Woodhouses (see) near Tutbury. It was held by the service of making and repairing the wooden vessels used within Tutbury Castle; a custom which persisted for many hundreds of years. In 1201 the manors of Drakelowe and Tutbury Woodhouses were confirmed to William de Ferrers by King John and he in turn passed both manors to William de Gresley (UTR pp38-39).

Tuters Hill Hill 0.5m WNW of Pattingham. In Pattingham ancient parish. Here may be the site of a hillfort (VCH vol 20 p172). The name means 'a look-out place' (Signposts to the Past. M Gelling p147) (VCH vol 20 p173). Tuters Hill was an area of waste in the C14. Enclosure of the common was occurring by the mid C17. By the later C18 there were several houses here (VCH vol 20 p173).

Tween Town Field name at Church Leigh, perhaps, refers to the site of the old village settlement (NSFCT 1910 p165).

Twelve Apostles Group of rocks 0.5m NNW of the Stepping Stones, Dovedale, on Staffs side. The group resembles the twelve Apostles; St Peter foremost (Dovedale Guide. Keith Mantell. 1984. p6pc). (NSFCT 1885 p67) (PS p120) (TPC p170) (MR p127).

'Twelve Apostles' Clump of twelve trees on high ground overlooking Foxlowe near Ball Haye Green, Leek. Miller writes of four remaining (OL vol 1 p282).

Twenty Oaks Circular cluster of oaks near Northwood, said to have been frequented by Rousseau when staying nearby at Wootton Hall (NSJFS 1966 p58). Some say here he wrote some of his 'Letters on Botany' (LGS p133). Mee claims it was here Rousseau wrote the unjust and bitter letters to David Hume accusing him of conspiracy (KES p243). They are referred to in Gisborne's poem 'Vales of Wever' (AAD p248) (Jean-Jacque Rousseau in Staffordshire. 1766-1767. JH Broome 1966. p20). (GNHS p5) (TFTP p183).

Twenty Trees Tiny district of Neachells around Neachells Lane (TB Aug 1987 p17).

Twerlow House N of Sandon. In Sandon parish. Has also appeared as Twirlow (1834 OS map) (Dower's map).

Twichills House 3m W of Barton-under-Needwood.

Twin Ash Tree on Cannock Chase 'which stands near a very large old oak' and was a parochial boundary mark (PCC p13).

Twin Oaks Farm On Staffs and Worcs Canal 1m W of Lower Penn.

Twist, The House 0.5m SW of Butterton (Moorlands). Has also appeared as Twist.

Two Gates S of Colley Gate, Cradley, Rowley Regis.

Two Gates Former hamlet on a bank above the Tame at junction of Watling Street with road to Tamworth, now a district of Tamworth, 2m SW of Amington. Formerly in Castle Liberty, Warws, but in Tamworth parish (W p627). **Colin Grazier**, born and brought up in Two Gates, Able Seaman of HMS Petard, helped retrieve vital information from a German U-boat which his ship had just sunk on Oct 30 1942, aged 22. This information enabled experts to crack the Enigma code and chart the movements of German troops and U-boats so helping the Allies to win WW2. Grazier and an officer lost their lives shortly after the information was discovered, as they remained on the submarine, which was targeted and sank. Grazier, the officer, and a third man responsible for taking the information to the Allies, received George Crosses. In late 1999 a plaque commemorating Grazier was to be erected by the site of his former family home at Two Gates, whilst funds were also being raised for the erection of a statue of him in Tamworth town centre (info Jim Welland and Phil Shanahan) (TH Aug 13 1999 p4p) (Navy News Sept 17 1999). **Reliant Engineering Co**, three-wheel car manufacturers (later makers of the Reliant Robin), had works on Watling Street at Two Gates from 1935. The firm, founded by Tom Lawrence Williams, a former employee of Raleigh Cycle Co, produced cars from 1935 to 1939, and from 1946 to the present, also had works by the 1970s at Kettlebrook and Shenstone (opened in 1963). By 1992 only Two Gates works remained (BCFF pp159-160). At some point Reliant appear to have been taken over by Beans Engineering of Tipton (see). The church in Tamworth Road is dedicated to St Peter (LDD).

Two Oaks Bank At approximately SK 042105, Chase Terrace (1834 OS map) Name is now lost.

Tybenton West Bromwich (SHOS vol 2 p128). Is it Tipton?

Tymmore Fisherwick and Tymmor together formed a township in St Michael's parish, Lichfield, by the late C13 (VCH vol 14 p239). Has appeared as Timmor (DB), Tymmor, and Tynnor. In the C16 the name became confused with Tamhorn, with such spellings as Tympehorn and Tymhorne. There were only two houses at Tymmor in 1635. By the later C18 the name was used only for a notional manor (SHOS vol p375), and the sole surviving farm was, according to Greenslade, Stubby Leas (VCH vol 14 p239). Palliser places the lost medieval settlement S of Tamhorn (SL p84 see map). Some place it 0.75m N of Tamhorn, at SK 178082 (SSAHST 1970 p36). Greenslade places it at Stubby Leas Farm at SK 188096 (VCH vol 14 p239). Some say it may have been deserted between 1327-1524 (SSAHST 1970 p36), others that it was in decay by 1584. John Smith of Timore, near Whittington left all his goods, valued at £81.13.10, to his wife, because, in the words of his will 'My wife hath been the best spoke in my cart' (Staffordshire Farming. 1700-1840. Staffs County Council. 1973. p6).

Tymmor Manor House The Tymmor family, lords of Tymmor from the C12 to the C14, probably had a house at Tymmor. At the end of the C18 the site of the house was stated to be a moated site 'on the right side of the road between Whittington and Elford, opposite to Fisherwick Park.' The site could not be identified in 1990 (VCH vol 14 pp245-246).

Tyndede Meer Oak Name in the C13 of an oak which marked the point of junction of the manors of Wrottesley, Perton, and Pattingham. The tree was described as long lost in 1894. The name still (1894) exists in Meer Oak Lane and Meer Oak Cottages (HOPTT p154 note).

Tyrant's Dale Near Buckingham's Cave. Local tradition has always connected this place name with the Duke of Buckingham. After the Restoration the Duke acquired the name 'Tyrant Duke' (BPS p29 note). Because Buckingham's Cave is at Outlands, Tyrant's Dale must be here also.

Tyrley Former manor centred on Tyrley Castle on a small escarpment overlooking the Tern. The farm on the site of Tyrley Castle is 16.5m NW of Stafford, 0.25m SE of Market Drayton. Former township in Staffs, although in Drayton-in-Hales ancient parish in Shrops. An ecclesiastical parish of Hales, comprising the township, appears to have formed in 1856 (LGS p142) and the township became a separate civil parish from Drayton-in-Hales in 1866. In 1965 the area comprising Tyrley Castle Farm and land W of the Shrops Union Canal was removed to Sutton upon Tern civil parish in Shrops (GLAUE p427). The **name** has appeared as Tirelire (DB) (SSE 1996 p18), Tirley, Turley, Tireley, Tyrlighe, Thyrlegh, Tirle, and Trileg (SHC 1945/ 46 p1). Rev JR Lee thought it might be derived from a Saxon word meaning 'a tower' (HOMD) (SHC 1945/ 6 p1). But most have thought 'pasture on the Ter or Tern'

(DUIGNAN p154) (SHC 1945/ 6 p1) (SPN p126). Tyrley was annexed by its lord to Staffs from Shrops between 1099 and 1135. It was annexed because the Tern was obviously the better boundary for the two counties; and William Pantolf, the lord, had parted with Market Drayton, the nearest Shrops manor to Tyrley; but still retained Almington, the nearest Staffs manor; and to throw the two latter into the same fief was naturally convenient (SHC 1909 p269 note). When in Shrops it was in Hodnet hundred (SHC 1945/ 6 p25). There was a **curious custom of the manor** which exonerated bastard children, known as Lotherwits or Lyerwits, which had been passed down from a Saxon leger or logher. If applied to its full extent the parents of a bastard could receive total exoneration from manorial and ecclesiastical fines if they swore the child was conceived under the umbrage of a certain oak in Knoll Wood, three miles S of Tyrley Castle, but within the manor. The custom was still practiced by the lords of the manor - Lord Gerard of Bromley, Sir Charles Skrymsher Knt, and Richard Church - in the later C17. If 10 shillings were paid to the lords they kept the information from the bishop and all ecclesiastical courts and prevented the father from being discovered. If £1 19 shillings 11 pence were paid to the lords they take no further cognisance of it either, and (for no payment?) if it can be sworn that the bastard was conceived under the oak then both lord and bishop take no cognisance of it (NHS p279). (SMC p123) (FLJ 1896 p381) (RS p17). Tyrley was a probate jurisdiction of the lord of the manor until abolished 1846 (VCH vol 3 p94 note). There was an **oratory** in Tyrley manor by 1361. It is thought to have been a private chapel erected by the le Botelers lords of Tyrley manor and situated in Tyrley Castle or manor house. Eyton and Lee thought it at Hales (HOMD p159) and it was found to be ESE of Hales, in the former Tyrley Park, after excavations in 'Chapel Field' in 1926 (SHC 1945/ 6 pp54-55). At SJ 715342 was possibly a **medieval village** (SSAHST 1970 p36), since depopulated.

Tyrley Castle Former medieval castle at Tyrley. Built by the Pantulfs, a powerful Shrops family. In the C13 it came to the Botelers (LGS pp244-245). The castle, probably built soon after the Norman Conquest, never had any very great strength or military importance (SHC 1945/ 6 pp33-34). It was enlarged and improved in last quarter of the C13 when Welsh raids became

troublesome and probably fell into disuse in the C14 (SHC 1945-6 pp33-36) (NSJFS 1966 p45). A farm was built on the site and its remains were incorporated into it (SLM Nov 1950 pp22-23p of the remains). When Tyrley manor was sold in 1532 no mention was made of a castle (NSFCT 1913 pp208-209). It was occupied by the Collye family in Elizabeth I's reign, and by the Waltons in the later C17 (SHC 1945/ 6 pp178,179). Erdeswick omitted it from SOS (SH p46), but it was noted by Chetwynd and Plot in the later C17 (NHS p448) (SHC 1909 pp268-269). (KES pp101,102). For some time it was wrongly thought that Lord Audley had owned the castle in subsequent years (SHC 1945/ 6 p94). Near the castle farm in 1824 grew a chestnut with a circumference of 24 feet (SG p109) (GNHS pp410,411). It was probably the same as the Spanish chestnut, noted by FR Twemlow in 1914, as having formed a part of an orchard which was part of the old castle garden; the chestnut itself fell down in c1864 (SHC 1945/6 p49).

Tyrley Heath Former heath lying in the SW part of Tyrley quarter of Drayton-in-Hales parish, Staffs, and partly in Hinstock parish, Shrops. The heath had been part of the demesne of the lord of Tyrley, and his tenants had no rights of common here. Enclosed in 1775 (SHC 1945/ 6 pp5,19,150 note).

Tyrley Park Medieval deer park enclosed out of forest. In existence by 1247 (NSJFS 1962 p76). The park was not officially known as Tyrley Park, but as 'The New Park' (SHC 1945/ 6 pp18 note, 83) and Tyrley New Park. It was situated to the W of Blore Park or 'great' Bishop's Wood (NSFCT 1933 p93), on the SE side of Hales. The name park is preserved in the wood called Park Spring (SHC 1945/ 6 p18).

Tyrley Wharf Wharf on Shrops Union Canal 1m SE of Tyrley Castle Farm, Tyrley. Here also are a series of five locks known as Tyrley Locks and a row of Tudor style cottages, built, not by the Shropshire Union Railways and Canal Company, but by the owner of Peatswood Hall. The cottages had been restored by 1985. By the side of the cottages is a memorial to the men of the Peatswood estate who died in WW1. Apparently a bunch of poppies appears by the memorial mysteriously every Armistice Day (Shropshire Union Canal Cruising Guide 1985 p24) (MR p168p).

Tywall Green Near Hardwick, Pattingham. The lord of Pattingham manor had a grove here by 1405 (VCH vol 20 p178).

U

Ubberley Former hamlet on a ridge by a small tributary of the Trent 1.25m NNW of Bucknall. Formerly in Bucknall and Bagnall chapelry in Stoke-upon-Trent ancient parish. Ubberley is now part of the large Bentilee residential suburb (NSJFS 1975 p59-76) (TSS p127).

Ubberley Hall Old stone mansion on the E side of Ubberley Road in Bucknall township. An old house on or near the site is thought to have been the seat of the de Verdun family before they were able to settle at Alton Castle (see); they moved to Alton in Henry II's reign. The hall demolished in the 1950s was probably built in the mid C16 (HBST p527) (SHC 1909 p33 note) (BUB pp2il,3,5). Ubberley Hall or Ubberley Hall Farm was the seat of the Allens, later the Forresters (FWMBS back cover p); in 1843 that of Rev W Clarke (HBST p527), and some time that of the Sherratts (WYV p8). The hall, said

to have some old oak including a good staircase in the 1920s (NSFCT 1926 p136), was demolished sometime between 1953 and 1956. In 1953 it was being used as a mission for the new Ubberley housing estate. There may have been priest holes at the hall; there is a tradition of a tunnel leading from the hall to Hulton Abbey (BUB pp2,3) (info in St Mary's, Bucknall, where there is a photograph of the hall).

Underbank House 0.25m N of Thorncliffe. Formerly in a detached portion of Bradnop township in Tittesworth township in Leek ancient parish. The present house dates from the late C18 but an outbuilding of probably C17 origin suggests that a former house may have occupied the site of the present (VCH vol 7 p233).

Underhill Small hamlet lying at the foot of Bushbury Hill on the E side, 1.25m

SSW of Featherstone. In Bushbury ancient parish. The name is from the fact that it lies at the foot of Bushbury Hill (DUIGNAN) (SPN p145). It has given its name to a large and well-known South Staffordshire family. The Underhills held the estate from the C14 or before until c1617, when Sir Hercules Underhill sold it (DUIGNAN p157).

Under the Hill Tiny area and house 0.5m S of Upper Elkstone. Formerly in Alstonefield ancient parish.

Under the Hill Tiny area 0.25m NNW of Longnor.

Under the Low House 0.25m SSW of Waterfall Low, at Back o' th' Brook, in Waterfall parish. This was one of the 12 farms sold in 1660 to help pay off the debts of Charles Cotton, poet of Beresford Hall (see) (WOY2 pp27p,104).

Under Wetton House 0.5m NE of Wetton.

Underwood Old hamlet to the W of Gillow Heath; only Underwood Hall Farm seems to survive (W p387). In Biddulph parish.

Union Cross S of Greets Green, 1.25m W of West Bromwich High Street, at junction of Union Road with Oldbury Road (1834 OS map).

Union Hall To S of Bannut Tree Road, Compton, Kinver. Built in c1790 by William Hodgetts, brother of John Hodgetts of Prestwood. William Hodgetts was killed in a riding accident on Kinver Edge in 1798. It was the seat of the Brindley family for much of the C19 and was known as Brindley Hall by the end of the C19 (VCH vol 20 p123). (SVS p172). It has been stated, wrongly, that this was the residence of the canal engineer, James Brindley (TSW p73). Some say James Brindley stayed here with relations whilst surveying for the Staffs and Worcs Canal and reputedly built a model lock on a local brook (S&WC p107). He, reputedly, built model locks whilst staying at Turnhurst Hall (see) in N Staffs.

Unite Well Spring at Abnalls, Lichfield. Here Sir John Floyer built a bath house as part of his general promotion of cold bathing in c1700. The bath house had two baths and was collectively known as St Chad's Bath (VCH vol 14 p107). Floyer noted his baths at Unite Well were far colder than the spring at Stowe (HOL p562) and had the reputation for being the coldest in England, yet they never froze (STMSM May 1978 p20). A special keeper looked after the bath house and a charge of not more than two pence was levied for any resident of Lichfield city or Close. Poor persons were accepted free (Young Samuel Johnson. James L Clifford. 1955 1962 ed. p28). (History of Cold Bathing. Sir John Floyer. 1709. pp16-26). In 1780 a surviving bath was let to Erasmus Darwin who incorporated it into his botanic garden and in the C19 the bath was known as Darwin's Bath (see). It has also been called Unett's Well (VCH vol 14 pp107,202).

Untillee Former minute hamlet E of Tunstall (1834 OS map). Huntilee Road probably preserves the name.

Uplands, The Stood in Redmoor Gardens off Muchall Road, Penn. Built in the late 1850s on land owned by Mr Underhill and Samuel Loveridge, the latter perhaps being the occupier. He was followed by Randle Shaw Walker, a local auctioneer. He was followed by Mrs Griffin in the late 1880s. She was followed by the Thompsons, boilermakers at Ettingshall, in the 1890s. Major Steven John Thompson, son of the first Thompson at The Uplands left in 1919. He was followed by the Crawford family. According to local tradition the house was built with money made at card gambling and consequently has been known as the 'House of Cards.' To support this belief there were said to be two sandstone carvings, one on each side of the front door, each representing the face of a playing card, one for a king, the other for a queen (PONP pp17,18il,19).

Uplands House in Hales Lane, 0.25m WNW of the Old Chapel, Smethwick. Built in 1847 by Samuel Thompson, a member of a family of maltsters from West Bromwich. It was presented to Smethwick corporation by his son Samuel Nock Thompson in the 1930s. It was used as offices by the Public Health Department until it was demolished in 1958. Thompson Gardens, a 15-storey block of flats, was erected on the site in 1961 (SMEOP p50p). Gives its name to the Uplands ward of Smethwick (TB July 1995 p21), the road The Uplands and a junior and infant school. The Uplands area was formerly known as Bosoms End (STELE June 26 1953)

Uplands, The To the S of High Onn.

Upmeads House in the Modernist style in Newport Road, Stafford. Built in 1908 to designs by Edgar Wood. Pevsner claims it is one of the most interesting houses of 1908 in the country. The name refers to a view across lawns and fields (BOE p250) (SAC p94p). It is the earliest flat-roofed house in England (SOPP pl 56p). The house was for sale in 1984 when it was listed Grade II (SLM July 1984 p7).

Upper Acre House 2m N of Onecote. Formerly in Onecote township in Leek ancient parish. There was a house here by 1775 (VCH vol 7 p212).

Upper Arley Ancient parish and village on either side of a dell by the Severn nearly 30m SSW of Stafford and 17m NNW of Worcester. Has appeared as

Earnlege (963) (SHC 1916 pp99-100) (SSE 1991 p8), Earnleia (C10), Ernlege (C11), Erlei, Ernelea (C12), Arleg, Erdele, Arnlee (or Arnley) de Port (C13), Aerley (C15), Over Areley (C16. 1801) (SHOS vol 2 p253), Over Arley (Yates' map), Arley (Yates' map 1799), Upper Arley (VCHW vol 3 1913 p5). In the **name** the first syllable Ar is British and signifies high. Ley is probably Anglo-Saxon signifying ground untilled (SHOS vol 2 p253), so 'the high untilled ground.' Prof Skeat thinks Eagle's lea. Duignan thinks from the personal name Earn (DUIGNAN). The appellation 'Upper' may have been added to define Arley from Areley Kings, 5.5m SSE in Worcs, which at sometime was known as Lower Arley. **Manor**. A charter was made of Arley's bounds in 994 (SL p62), when the estate was granted by Lady Wulfrun to Wolverhampton Collegiate Church (HOWM pp11,14). The estate, which appears in DB, passed out of the possession of the college of Wolverhampton to the de Ports sometime between 1135 and 1167 (VCHW vol 3 p5). In 1172 it was forfeited and remained with the Crown until 1194. It belonged to the de Burghs from certainly 1227 to sometime between 1260 and c1301 when it was sold to Robert Burnel, lord of Acton Burnel, Shrops, Bishop of Bath and Wells and later Chancellor of England, who held it for ten years. From Burnel it was conveyed to Edward I who granted it to his Chamberlain, Leotard de Henyn; he sold it to the Mortimers. It remained in the Mortimer family until 1449 when it passed to William Burley whose daughter took it to the Lytteltons. The manor passed from the Lytteltons on the death in 1779 of 2nd Lord Lyttelton to his sister Lucy who married Arthur Annesley Viscount Valentia (afterwards created 1st Earl of Mountnorris d1816). He was succeeded by his son George, 2nd Earl of Mountnorris, a great traveller in Egypt and shell collector. On his death in 1844 Arley Castle and manor passed to his sister Lady Hester Annabella, wife of Major General Norman Macleod. Their eldest son, Arthur, assumed the name of Annesley. In 1852 the Annesleys sold their Arley property to R Woodward, and his son was lord of the manor in 1914 (SOS (1844) p388) (AOA pp21,33,82,85). The parish **church**, St Peter, Apostle and Martyr, on a hill to the NW of Upper Arley village and overlooking the village, is perhaps of Saxon origin, but the present church was built in c1100. It was restored in 1885 and 1886 (AOA pp110-116). The ancient **parish**, formed between 1086 and 1291, probably formed originally a part of Kinver parish (SHC 1916 p197). It had a large stretch of land on the W side of the Severn, stretching S to Dowles, 0.75m NNW of Bewdley, Worcs (Yates' map 1799; shows the stretch on the W side of the Severn to be in Worcs). The parish, under the peculiar jurisdiction of the dean and chapter of Lichfield cathedral until peculiar jurisdictions were abolished in 1846 (VCH vol 3 p93 note) (GLAUE), was removed to Worcs in 1895 and put into the Worcs hundred of Halfshire (VCHW vol 3 p5), and transferred from Lichfield to Worcester diocese in 1905 (VCH vol 3 p96) (SL p29). Arley **wake** was on the Monday nearest June 29 (feast of SS Peter and Paul) and was held to c1824 (AOA p95). The lords of Arley claimed and exercised the privileges of a **fair** and **market** (AOA p38). They also claimed and exercised the privileges of **gallows**. A gallows is believed to have stood on the highest part of the ridge between Nash End and Baynhams called 'Gloser' or 'Gallows-Tree Hill' (AOA p38). **Stocks** in Arley village stood at the head of the village street by the gate leading to the church. They had been removed by 1914 (AOA p38). There was a **ferry crossing** the Severn at Upper Arley by 1323-7 (The River Severn: A Pictorial History. Josephine Jeremiah. 1998). Leland, writing in c1541, called Areley 'a good uplandish town' (SHOS vol 2 p253). In the later C17 Dr Plot noted the area was good for growing apples and making cider, the commonest apple was the **'Janet Moyle'** which grew so well it was exported aboard (NHS p226) (NSFCT 1948 p65). **Natives and visitors**. The father of **Thomas Churchyard** (d1604), poet, born at Shrewsbury in 1520, may have had a farm at Arley (AOA pp51-58). By the later C17 **Margaret Mousole** of Arley had been convicted of killing her bastard child and hung by the neck at Stafford, but she came to life again (NHS p291) (SD p35). A Black Country industrialist, **Roger Turner**, owner of a 1,600 acre estate at Upper Arley since 1959, died in April 1999 leaving £15 million to charity (BCM Autumn 1999 p31).

Upper Barton Farmhouse 0.5m W of Bradley. Has a keystone inscribed 'PWE' and another dated 1719. The symmetrical garden front is of the late C18 and has a pedimented doorway (VCH vol 4 p76).

Upper Berkhamsytch Minute hamlet above the head of Black Brook in the Moorlands, 0.5m E of Bottom House, 0.25m NE of Lower Berkhamsytch. The ancient Earls Way (see) from Chester to Derby passed through here (NSFCT 1948 p47). The Young Pretender's army passed by Upper Berkhamsytch on Dec 4 1745 in the Jacobite Rebellion. A pistol and dirk left by them have been found at Upper Berkhamsytch Farm (BPCSM pp7,9il at Upper Berkhamsytch Farm). Rev Bright thought Upper Berkhamsytch Farm was the probable site of Bottom House Inn (see) (TOI pp166-167).

Upper Bradnop Obsolete name for a settlement in the area of Hare House at the N end of Bradnop Valley. Appears as Upper Bradnop in the 1260s and as Over Bradnop on the maps of Plot and Yates. By 1343 Hulton Abbey had a grange at Upper Bradnop; it's site remains unlocated (VCH vol 7 pp170-171).

Upper Bradley Appears to have been the name for the western half of Bradley manor or estate, in Bilston township. The name occurs on 1834 OS map in the Bradley Lane Cross Street area. The area appears to have been developed with housing for workers at the iron works of John Wilkinson, lord of Bradley, in the later C18. The workers appear to have been segregated according to their place of origin or occupation, for streets such as Clerks Row, Workmens Row, Caledonia Street (for Scots), Shramrock Yard (for Irish), and Shropshire Row (see), are said to have existed, but none, apart from Shropshire Row (and French Row running off it to the S), can be found on the on the Map of Bilston Township - R Timmis 1839. The Upper Bradley area was cleared in c1960 for new housing (The Bradley Ironworks of John Wilkinson. GR Morton and WA Smith. reprint from Journal of the Iron and Steel Institute. vol 234. July 1966 p663) (John Wilkinson. Ron Davies. 1987. Copy in Walsall Local History Centre. p19) (BOP).

Upper Castle Hayes Farm 0.75m E of Hanbury. The house, which has also appeared as Upper Hayes Farm (GLS p45), was totally obliterated by the Fauld explosion on Monday 27 Nov 1944 (The Guardian. Weekend Section. March 11 1989 pp2-3). The other farm affected by the explosion was Hanbury Fields Farm (GLS p45). Lower Castle Hayes Farm is 1m SSE of the Fauld Crater.

Upper Cotton Minute hamlet at the head of Cotton Dell in the Moorlands 1m NNW of Cotton.

Upper Crowley Is the N part of Cowley, on E side of Shropshire Union Canal, 0.75m S of Gnosall.

Upper Dales House 0.75m WNW of Longsdon. Formerly in Longsdon township in Leek ancient parish. Has also appeared as The Dales (1980 OS map 1:25,000). The old house, or cottage, which may have taken its name from the Dale family, who were living in the area in the C18, was rebuilt in the mid 1980s in the C17 style (VCH vol 7 p203).

Upper Elkstone Larger and older (VCH vol 7 p57) of the two Elkstone settlements, 2m WNW of Warslow, 0.75m NW of Lower Elkstone. The settlement lies on the E-facing slopes of a high hill in the Moorlands overlooking Warslow Brook. Formerly in Warslow and Elkstones township in Alstonefield ancient parish (W p742). The hill, 1394 feet high, with three burial mounds on it 0.5m SW of Upper Elkstone is thought to be the 'dun' or hill in an early form of Elkstone (VCH vol 7 p57). The two mounds at SK 05165855 are 85 metres N of the one at SK 05135842. All three are listed monuments and of Bronze Age origin (VCH vol 7 p57). One was excavated by Carrington in 1850. 16 paces in diameter and three feet high. A crouched skeleton, burnt bones and a bronze awl were found (TYD p171). Another 20 paces in diameter and one foot high excavated by Carrington in 1850. One crouched and one decayed skeleton and a boar's tusk were found (TYD pp171-172) (DAJ vol 75 pp108-109. vol 77 p26, C2). These two may be burial mounds which Gunstone located at SK 05165857 (20 paces in diameter and four feet high) and at SK 05165854 (23 paces in diameter and two feet high) (NSJFS 1965 p51). Upper Elkstone has appeared as Elkesdon (c1215. 1227), and Elkesdun (C13) (SSE 1996 p13) (SPN p46), and Elkstone (early C14) (VCH vol 7 p57). The 'don' in Elkesdon, is presumably 'dun' a hill. Perhaps, 'Elc's hill,' but Duignan is unsure about the prefix (DUIGNAN). Elk is Ealac (OAKDEN) (SSAHST 1967 p34). Or 'Ea(n)lac's hill' (SSE 1996 p13) (SPN p46). The hill in question has been identified as the hill SW of Upper Elkstone (VCH vol 7 p57). The Upper Elkstone area formed a manor by the mid C13 until at least the C19. It was mainly in the possession of Trentham Priory in the Middle Ages (VCH vol 7 p59). Copper ore had been discovered at Upper Elkstone by c1680 (NHS p165) and was being worked by 1750 (VCH vol 7 p60). The church, St John the Baptist, in the centre of the village, dates from the late 1780s, replacing an earlier church, mentioned in 1682 (VCH vol 7 pp61,63). Elkstone had its own wake by 1903, when it was held on the second Sunday in July. In 1947 the date was changed to the Sunday nearest the feast of St John the Baptist (June 24), the patron saint of the church. After the closure of the Cock Inn in Upper Elkstone in 1976 the wake ceased (VCH vol 7 p58).

Upper Ellastone The northern-most settlement of Ellastone on a slight promontory between Sandford and Tit Brooks. Here is Ellastone church.

Upper Ettingshall Former small hamlet in Sedgley ancient parish, just over 1m ENE of Sedgley, centred on the Upper Ettingshall Road area. It was still a separate hamlet in 1901. Now (1989) the area is known as Hurst Hill (OS map Sheet 67.03) (Birmingham A-Z). Thomas Salt, born at Coseley in 1867, began broadcasting under the name 'Joe Gutteridge' at the age of 67. Apart

from several talks about the early history of Upper Ettingshall and its church he took a leading part in two local plays by Coseley writer, Harold Small - 'The Nailers' and 'The New Road.' He died in 1948 (HC p93) (TEBC2 p91).

Upper Gornal Large Black Country village on a ridge forming a part of England's main watershed 19.75m S of Stafford, former liberty in the Upper Side division of Sedgley ancient parish (W p195). Upper Gornal has appeared as Upper Gournall (1632) (HC p39), Over Gournal (Plot's map), and Old Gournall (Bowen's map). The church, St Peter, Kent Street, was built in 1840-1841 (BOE p289). Became a separate ecclesiastical parish in 1844 (GLAUE p412). For the wakes see Sedgley. Upper Gornal lock up was a stone building and was demolished in the 1970s (SDOP p86p). Upper Gornal was as involved with the sand extraction and crushing industry as Lower Gornal (see) (BCM Oct 1970 pp20-21 p of the primitive method of sand crushing at Upper Gornal). In the later C17 Mr Persehouse of Upper Gornal showed Plot a parcel of what was believed to be silver ore in a rock in digging a well in his garden and was shaped like a scallop shell (NHS p186). For the ridiculing of Gornal people as simpletons see Lower Gornal. EA Underhill (1869-1944), poet, was born in Upper Gornal. His collection of poems 'Patchwork' (1932) contains the poem 'Around the Beacon (Sedgley)' (VFC p135). For the comments of JB Priestley on Gornal see Gornal. Elizabeth II passed through Upper Gornal on her Jubilee tour in 1977 (SDOP p125p).

Upper Green Small village, which with Lower Green, 0.5m to the SW, formed Hanley up to the early C18. Situated at the junction of Keelings Lane and the present Town Road (H p43) (VCH vol 8 p142). Comprises the area around Hulton Street, Merrick Street and Town Road (POP p38). Together they were collectively known as Hanley Green, and have also been known as Far Green.

Upper Green and **Lower Green** Medieval common land by Newcastle-under-Lyme town. Upper Green, which may have been a medieval market site, appears to have been land in the area of the present junction of Lower Street, Knutton Lane and Ryecroft (VCH vol 8 pp3,46) (POP p165).

Upper Green Green to the W of Tettenhall church on top of a ridge. One centre of Tettenhall village grew around this green; the other centre, probably the older, Lower Green (see), developed around a green to the S of the church (VCH vol 20 p5) (MR p327p) (TCOP p18p). Upper Green, which may be a surviving part of the Kingsley Wood, was known as Marsh Green in the early C18. The name Upper Green had come into use by 1780 (VCH vol 20 pp7,8). On the old green in 1837 at the E end of the present Clifton Road was the pinfold for Tettenhall Regis manor (VCH vol 20 p36). In 1861 there was a proposal to enclose most of the common land of Upper Green and sell it off, but a campaign by villagers defeated the proposal and so preserved the green for posterity (Tettenhall Village Trail. History Dept, Regis School, Tettenhall). A clock tower on the green was presented to Tettenhall urban district council by Mr and Mrs Edward Swindley on June 22 1912 in honour of George V's Coronation (Wolverhampton Chronicle Oct 18 1996 p22p). Underneath the clock there is a WW2 air raid shelter which was completed before the outbreak of war (Tettenhall Village Trail. History Dept, Regis School, Tettenhall. p). The ghost of a police superintendent who had died whilst still in the force was seen by his colleagues on the Upper or Lower Green in c1944 and in Feb 1946 (TB Feb 1988 p17) (GOM pl 8(c)).

Upper Green House nearly 2.5m N of Onecote. Formerly in Onecote township in Leek ancient parish. The house is dated 1830 (VCH vol 7 p212).

Upper Hatton Northern part of the fragmented tiny hamlet of Hatton 1.75m NNE of Standon.

Upper Hoar Cross Fragmented tiny hamlet on the W side of the Swarbourn Valley over 0.5m W of Hoar Cross. The name Upper Hoar Cross is used in IVNF. The principle house is Hoar Cross Hall. Plot noted two springs one situated by a Pur Brook to the W of Hoar Cross Hall and another by the hall, both aluminous (NHS pp105-106).

Upper House 0.75m S of Barlaston old church. Built by Francis Wedgwood, grandson of Josiah Wedgwood I, on the Lea estate in 1849 (BAH p33) (WCW p) (SN April 21 1995 p13). In 1854 Lajos Kossuth, the Hungarian national leader was entertained here (BAH p33). Originally called Barlaston New Hall (W p411) (1889 OS map 6 inch), but by at least 1901 had become known as Upper House. The Wedgwoods were succeeded by the Johnsons, potters, in c1906. The house was Staffs county council's Barton Land Home for the Blind from 1954 to at least 1966 (BAH p35). Some time after 1963 the house became known as Barton Land. It was renamed Upper House when it became an hotel in c1994.

GROUNDS. In 1850 at SJ 896379, on the top of a 500 feet hill (SMM p19), by an ancient track between the Downs and Barlaston (SOK p10), in a rock-cut grave were found fragments of the burial of an Anglian warrior of the C7 which included a 33 inch long iron sword, a small iron knife and numerous pieces of a bronze hanging-bowl and two hooked disc escutcheons cast in bronze with Celtic designs in chempleve enamel. The pottery showed a relationship with the pottery discovered at Middleton-by-Youlgreave. The finds are in BM. This grave is only two miles from the hillfort on Bury Bank. (JGM p258) (ARCH vol 46 p44) (VCH vol 1 p209) (Antiquity. vol 6. p168) (Celtic Ornament. ET Leeds. 1933 p147) (Anglo-Saxon Art. TD Kendrick. 1938. p54) (NSFCT 1905 p140. 1906 p148 plans, 150) (SOSH pp49,51plan) (PASN series 2 vol 22 p67) (NSJFS 1964 p15) (STM April 1963 p29p of iron sword. May 1964 p32) (HOS p13) (SMM pp19-20). The Welfare Committee of the Staffs county council agreed to preserve the site in c1955 (NSFCT 1905 p146. 1954 p88). (NSSG p6). At SJ 896380 was believed to be an icehouse used as an ammunition dump in WW2, located in a spinney adjacent to the house (IHB p392).

Upper Hulme Small village in a ravine formed by Back Brook which joins the Churnet S of the village (NSFCT 1884 p21), 24.5m NNE of Stafford. Formerly partly in Leekfrith township in Leek ancient parish and in Fawfieldhead township in Alstonefield ancient parish (W pp728,746), divided by Back Brook. In the later C17 Plot noted a **spring** which fed the millpool here and never froze (NHS p91). At Upper Hulme was found two urns, one of collared urn type and bone and flint fragments of **Bronze Age**. One urn is in the Nicholson Institute, Leek. Gunstone implies they came from a burial mound (NSFCT 1884 p21) (JBAA series 2 vol 2 p84) (NSJFS 1964 p25. 1965 p39). The **hamlet** of Upper Hulme on the Leekfrith side of Back Brook existed by the mid C13 (VCH vol 7 pp32,194). Has appeared as O:holme (Over Hulme) (Plot's map), and Old Holm (Bowen's map). Described as a village 'without a church' by one lamenting historian (NSFCT 1884 p22). Here from 1869 to 1969 was Tatton's factory, **yarn dyers**, famous for their black eyes. The factory was largely destroyed by fire in April 1891 (MR p346) (HOLF p62p). The fatal boiler explosion at Upper Hulme in 1874 (OL vol 1 p331) may have something to do with this factory. Before the later C18 the **Leek-Buxton road** passed through Upper Hulme (VCH vol 7 p195). **Aircraft crash.** A Spitfire 11A crashed at Upper Hulme on Nov 17 1940. The pilot, who was alone, died. The engine was to remain in waterlogged ground until excavated by Derby Historical Aviation Society in 1975 (MD p39). For a **haunted house** said to have been at or near Upper Hulme see Gradbach Old Hall. **Natives.** Upper Hulme is said to have been the birthplace of **Richard Caldwell**, an eminent physician, died in 1515 (W p728) (NSFCT 1884 p22) (HOLF p52), or died in 1584 (VCH vol 7 p196). A modern street light where the roads to the village and the Roaches fork is known as Harold's Lamp and is in memory of **Harold Shufflebotham**, a former councillor on Heathylee parish council and local farmer who died in the later C20 (plaque by lamp and local info in 1999).

Upper Hurst House 2.5m NNW of Alstonefield, on Archford Moor. Formerly in the detached portion of Fawfieldhead township in Alstonefield township. Existed by 1839 but has been rebuilt since (VCH vol 7 p11).

Upper Leigh Hamlet on a hill overlooking the Blithe 0.75m NW of Church Leigh. Formerly in Leigh township and ancient parish.

Upper Ley Trentham. There are signs of terracing made by the pre-Roman occupants of the area alongside the Stone Road (TTH p13).

Upper Longdon Large hamlet covering an undulating ridge overlooking Shropshire Brook in country rising to the Cannock Chase highlands 1.25m E of Longdon. Formerly Over End (Plot's map), Overton (Bowen's map) and Longdon Upper End (1834 OS map). There is a windmill, now Cosy Cottage (WBJ p30) or Windmill Farm (STMSM Aug 1978 p26p, June 1980 p40p) or Windmill Cottage (OS map 1:25,000), to the W of the village. First notice of it being advertised (for rent) was in 1806. The mill had probably ceased work by the beginning of the C20, and by 1902 it had been converted into a simple cottage. It became derelict and was converted into a luxury home with a circular brick bungalow round the mill base in 1973. A coarse grit runner stone of four feet seven inches forms a garden table (WBJ p30 il xxii in 1962 & il xxiii in 1978). (WIS pp11p,20) (DoE II). From the windmill top in 1952 Bird could see a tremendous view which included Charnwood Forest, Leics, and Kinder Scout, Derbys (VB p120). The village is renowned for Reg Hollinshead's racing establishment (VB p121).

Upper Meaford Farm 1.25m SSW of Barlaston. Formerly owned by the Earl of Sidmouth and was sold to the Electricity Board in the mid 1940s and Meaford (see) Power Station built partly on the land. The farmhouse was occupied by John Ainsworth in 1940. By the late 1940s it appears to have been demolished and the site was lost under power station spoil (KD 1940) (Memories of the Downs Banks. Kathleen Day. c1999 p18). Has also appeared as Meaford Farms (along with Lower Meaford Farm) (Yates' map), Little Meaford (1834 OS map) (Dower's map) and Meaford Upper Farm (1889 OS map 6 inch).

Upper Moorside House 0.5m SSW of Onecote. Formerly in Onecote township

in Leek ancient parish. The present house is probably of the early C19 (VCH vol 7 p211).

Upper Musden House 0.5m SSW of Musden Grange. In the Upper Musden area may have been the village of Musden, depopulated when Croxden Abbey turned Musden into a grange (SASR 1995 no 5 p31). The old road to Upper Musden from Musden Grange is mostly still used, about halfway along it is a place called 'Abbot's Gate' (NSFCT 1917 pp46,51).

Upper Nobut Minute hamlet on a promontory overlooking a tributary of the Tean 1m E of Church Leigh, 0.75m NW of Lower Nobut. In Leigh parish. The name is from perhaps Irish 'noeb' holy. The holy grove or sacred wood (NSFCT 1908 p145).

Upper Pendeford Upper Pendeford Farm is 2.25m SSW of Coven.

Upper Penn Former township in Penn ancient parish. Became a separate ecclesiastical parish in 1859, and a separate civil parish in 1866. Upper Penn ecclesiastical parish was renamed Penn Fields in 1966 (GLAUE p419). In 1933 Upper Penn became administratively part of Wolverhampton borough (PENOP p9). The manor appears in DB. The settlement of Upper Penn is generally now known as just Penn (see).

Upper Reule Farmhouse 1m W of Haughton. The medieval manor-house of Reule may have stood near this house. Close by, parts of a large moat still existed in 1958. By 1847 the ground within this moat was known as 'Old House Orchard.' The house formerly appeared as Reule Lodge (VCH vol 4 p85). There are stories of stones being carted away from this site in the late C19. The manor-house was the seat of the Chetwynds from the end of the C13 onwards. Sir Walter Chetwynd lived at Reule from 1595 to 1612 when he moved to Ingestre. The manor-house was probably abandoned or demolished after this, in the C17. A branch of the Chetwynds were living at Lower Reule by 1680 (VCH vol 4 p76).

Upper Tean Small town by the Tean 11.75m NE of Stafford. Formerly in Tean division in Checkley ancient parish. Richmilde Street (see), a Roman road between Derby and Chesterton, passed through Upper Tean. A possible Roman urn was found at Upper Tean in 1728. It was at a place on the W side of the river, S of the tape mill and formed a part of a garden. However, the urn has been considered to be of Celtic (GNHS p70) (HOC p192) or Bronze Age origin (SHOS vol 1 General Intro p35). (NSJFS 1964 p19). Upper Tean or Lower Tean appears in DB as Tene. Nicholas de Beck was granted a charter on Nov 30 1355 to hold a market at one of the 'Teans' on Tuesdays. The market had ceased by 1500 (NSJFS 1971 p51). There was no market in 1792 (OWEN), nor in 1888 (LHE p265). For fairs Cooke gives April 10, and Nov 12 (for pedlary) (SCSF p99). There was a fair in 1792 (OWEN), but no fair in 1888 (LHE p265). For wells in Upper Tean see Well in the Wall. Tean Hall housed one of the oldest and most extensive tape manufactures in the country, which commenced in 1747, belonging to Messrs John and Nathaniel Philips and Co (W p761). (HOC pp43-44). Three and four storey factory ranges to the W were added at various periods in the C19, known as the New Tean Hall Mills. From 1959 the entire complex was called Tean Hall Mills Ltd (MR pp324p,325). The church, Christ Church, on the corner of Hollington and Vicarage Roads, was built in 1843 (BOE p279). Became a separate ecclesiastical parish in 1844 (LGS p231) (GLAUE p425). The railway from the Potteries to Cheadle reached Tean in 1892 (VCH vol 2 p319). The Upper and Lower Tean by-pass (the new A50), envisaged as early as 1938, was not completed and opened until April 3 1985 (COPP2 p71). The Cheadle and Tean Times first appeared in 1896. The Tean and Checkley History Society was formed in 1985 (info Mrs Johnson). For a rhyme about Upper Tean see Checkley. The ghost of a man carrying a lamp, perhaps a miner, has been seen by several people in or near Upper Tean (MS&S pp65-66).

Upper Tittesworth House 1.75m SE of Meerbrook. Formerly in Tittesworth township in Leek ancient parish. The house stands in the area of the medieval settlement of Upper Tittesworth, recorded in the 1250s (VCH vol 7 p233). The house, Lower Tittesworth, now Troutsdale Farm (see), stands in the area of the medieval settlement of Lower Tittesworth and is 0.5m to the NW. The present farmhouse dates from c1700 and was so called by the mid C19 (VCH vol 7 p233).

Upper Whittimere Minute hamlet on a slight promontory at the S end of Abbot's Castle Hill 2m NE of Bobbington, 0.5m E of Whittimere. NE of Halfpenny Green. A vineyard was started by Martin and Elaine Vickers at Upper Whittimere Farm in 1983 (PONP pp144-146). A medium dry white table wine from the vineyard known as 'Staffordshire Silver' was being sold in 1998. It is the county's only vineyard (TSW p71).

Utter Hill Main Street, Barton-under-Needwood, from Church Lane to Efflinch Lane was once known as Utter Hill (UNT pp36,88p).

Uttoxeter (*U-toxeter*, *Ukseter* by middle class, *Utchiter* by working class, *Ug* by Smallwood Manor pupils VB p163). Ancient parish and market town on a gentle eminence on the W bank of the Dove (THS p205), 12.5m ENE of Stafford.

EARLY. In Dove Valley S of Uttoxeter was found a stone axe of **Neolithic** or **Bronze Age** thought to have been in Masefield's collection and now in the Potteries Museum (HOU 1886 p44) (NSJFS 1964 p39). A small looped palstave of the Bronze Age was found in Uttoxeter district and was in Redfern's collection (HOU 1886 p46) (NSJFS 1962 p29. 1964 p39). Near Uttoxeter was found a bronze spearhead (NSFCT 1908 p194). In Uttoxeter district a small wedge-shaped amulet with a hole for suspension has been found of uncertain date (HOU 1886 p44) (NSJFS 1964 p39). Uttoxeter is believed to have been a British settlement (S&W p321). Druids may have been active in the Uttoxeter area in ancient times for a meadow bore the name of Beale or Bean, evidence, perhaps, of the druidical worship of Baal (HOU p21). **Roman**. There is believed to have been a Roman settlement on the site of Uttoxeter (S&W p321) on the strength of the town's name (LTD p106) and an assumed Roman road from Leicester to Chesterton passing to the S (HOU pp27-28). If there was a settlement at Uttoxeter it was possibly a 'mansio' or 'mutatio' (NSFCT 1908 p110), or an outpost of the garrison at Rocester (LTD p106). Uttoxeter has been identified with Letocetum (later discovered to be at Wall) (NSFCT 1908 p110), Uxacona (LGS p245), and Uriconium (NSFCT 1911 p142). In High Wood a Roman vessel was found in 1788, which perhaps went to Greene's Museum (see), Lichfield (GM) (HOU pp32,33il). In the Market Place area was found in 1856 a well about 10 yards deep said to be of Roman origin (HOU pp31-32). In Carter Street a number of drain tiles said to be of Roman origin were found (HOU p32). In 1927 coins, pottery and an inscribed stone, perhaps of Roman origin, were unearthed in the NE of Uttoxeter (LTD p106). In fields to the S of the town a large quadrangular earthwork has identified as a possible Roman defensive position. The N entrenchment is the best preserved and lies in a field called Sandfort. The S and W sides were also discernible. Pottery has been found on the site and nearby an amphora was located. Bradley Street (N of Market Place) may contain the site of a Romano-British pottery (MR p349). (JBAA vol 29 p263) (VCH vol 1 p193) (SOSH p346) (DUIGNAN p158; Uttoxeter never was a Roman town) (NSJFS 1964 p39; Redfern's Roman artifacts were probably of medieval or later date; nothing of Roman origin has been found since Redfern wrote).

600 to 1000. Uttoxeter is said to have been called Uttok-cestre by the Saxons (S&W p321), and has appeared as Wotocheshede (DB), Uttokishedere, Wittokeshather, Utittokesather, and Huttokesather (SPN p132), Uttockeshedere (C12), Uttoxatre (C14), Uttoxeshather (C14), Utcester (C14), Uttokcester (C14), Utcester (C16), Uttokcester (by Leland) and Uttoxater (Plot's map) (HOU pp4-7) (DUIGNAN). Some have thought the **name** derived from DB Wotocheshede derived from 'wudu' wood and 'seade' shade (HBST) (HOU p5). Or 'Wot's homestead on the heath' (Official Uttoxeter Town Guide. 1993. p13). Or 'Hwittuc's heath' (DUIGNAN). Mills suggests 'Wuttuc's heath(er)' (SSE 1996 p18). Or 'Wittuc's house on the heath' (SPN p132). Or 'Wittuc's homestead in the heather' (MR p349). The termination may be from Latin 'castrum,' a camp (HOU pp4-7), but others say not. 'Cester' only appears from the C14 and is probably a fancy of antiquarian scribes (DUIGNAN) (MR p349). The prefix is, perhaps, from Anglo-Saxon 'mattock' an implement used to disforest, or from Anglo-Saxon 'stocca,' meaning the trunk or stem of a tree. The prefix has also been supposed to mean an outtake from Needwood Forest or an out-take of a camp (perhaps one the Romans had recently departed from) (HOU pp4-7). According to tradition and a find believed to be of Saxon origin there was a **church** at Uttoxeter by the C8 or later. There was certainly a church at Uttoxeter by 1251 (HOU pp151,152) (HOU (1881) p199). It stood probably on or near the site of the present parish church, St Mary the Virgin, Church Street. The present church has a tower of c1325-1350, said to have been built by Henry Yevele, 'the greatest English architect,' son of a Uttoxeter freeholder; his work includes the nave of Westminster Abbey and Canterbury Cathedral (VB pp26-27). In 1828 the nave was rebuilt (BOE p290). The parish, formed before 1086, may have originally contained the ancient parishes of Leigh, Kingstone and Gratwich, and Checkley (SHC 1916 p194). There are **miscellaneous earthworks** of pre-Norman Conquest origin in Uttoxeter parish at Hill House (see) Stramshall, and Cottage Holding (SHC 1916 p207).

1000 to 1500. Uttoxeter was a **manor** owned by the Earls of Mercia. After the Norman Conquest it became a royal manor. The manor was given to Henry de Ferrers of Tutbury Castle (see) after 1086. His son, Robert Ferrers, 1st Earl of Derby, made the town a borough with a market in c1140 (SL p151). Robert de Ferrers, 6th Earl of Derby, had the manor confiscated from him in 1266. It was given to Henry III's son, Edmund Crouchback, and eventually to John of Gaunt, Duke of Lancaster. In 1399 the manor passed with the

Duchy of Lancaster to the Crown. Charles I sold the manor in 1626 to four speculators (Official Uttoxeter Town Guide. 1993. p16), probably, Lord William Craven and his friends who presented it to the townspeople of Uttoxeter (Staffs County Handbook. c1958. p142). The court leet building was in the Market Place close to the Old Talbot Inn (Official Uttoxeter Town Guide. 1993. p13). On Aug 15 1252 Uttoxeter was granted a charter by William de Ferrers, 5th Earl of Derby, making it a **free borough** with 127 burgages. A confirmation of this charter was granted in 1308 (S&W p322) (LGS p245) (SCSF p118) (NSJFS 1972 p69) (Official Uttoxeter Town Guide. 1993. p13). A confirmation may also have been granted in 1292 (HOU p273) (Staffs County Handbook. c1958. p142). The period of the end of burghal status has not been discovered (NSJFS 1972 p69). **Springs**. A conduit above the town spring stood in Uttoxeter Market Place until 1852. In 1854 it was replaced by the present combined conduit head and weighing machine (Official Uttoxeter Town Guide. 1993. p31) (AUOPP p15p). There was a chalybeate or iron-containing spring of Messrs Copes in Pinfold Lane in 1865 (HOU p15). See also Maiden's Well and Pennycroft Well. **Punishments**. Edmund, Earl of Lancaster, claimed from Henry III the right of erecting a **gallows** at Uttoxeter (SCSF p123). Uttoxeter gibbet was situated in the Highwood area, and was last used in c1660 (LTD pp112-113). According to Uttoxeter PR the **stocks** were repaired in 1672 (SCSF p126). According to Uttoxeter PR a **cucking stool** was repaired in 1672 (SCSF p126). The **curfew bell**, rung apparently from at least the later C11 was still being rung in 1865. According to tradition Lady Tansley, an abbess, whilst journeying from Tutbury to Uttoxeter became lost in Needwood Forest, but found her way to Uttoxeter after hearing its curfew bell. In remembrance of this she gave a bell full of money to Uttoxeter to ensure the perpetual ringing of the curfew bell. For centuries after the curfew was regularly rung, preceded always by three tangs of the bell in honour of the abbess, both night and morning, until a newly appointed sexton forgot the preliminary tangs which, according to tradition prompted the abbess's ghost to appear and ascend the bell-rope. The legend is recorded in Mary Howitt's 'The Chronicle of Wood Leighton' (1835) (HOU p185) (SCSF p160) (FOS p21) (LTD p111). Other traditions concerning the abbess are: that she was fleeing from Hanbury Priory after it was sacked by the Danes; that she was accompanied by another nun; that she fell mysteriously ill and died three days after arriving in Uttoxeter; and that she was buried in Uttoxeter church (LTD p111). The recumbent alabaster effigy of a lady in St Mary's church is reputed to be that of the abbess (NSFCT 1940 p38). However, Michael Moss and Mr Jeavons say the effigy is of Elizabeth, daughter of Henry Hussey of Kings Bromley; she died in 1523. By 1999 it was situated on the S side of the W tower. It was moved from another position when the church was rebuilt in 1826-28 and in order to make it fit under the staircase to the gallery the feet were sawn off; they were restored in 1889 when the effigy was placed in its present position (info in the church). A considerable part of the revenues of **Uttoxeter Rectory** was made over to the Chapel of the Garter in St George's, Windsor, when the Order of the Garter was founded in 1348 (SOSH p347) (SCSF p133). For Uttoxeter **charities** see HOU pp315-326 and 'Uttoxeter Charities' PM Turner 1987.

MARKETS AND FAIRS. The Earl of Derby was granted a charter on Dec 14 1251 to hold a **market** at Uttoxeter on Wednesdays (S&W p322) (NSJFS 1971 p51). The Wednesday market was confirmed in the charter of 1308 (THS) (SCSF pp94-95). There was a market in 1792 (OWEN), and a market in 1888 (LHE p265). The cattle market on Wednesdays and Saturdays at the Smithfield Livestock Market behind the Town Hall was described in 1993 as 'one of the largest livestock markets outside London.' A damson market was held in Balance Street until the C20 (Official Uttoxeter Town Guide. 1993. pp24,32,33). The 1308 charter granted the right to hold **fair** on the eve, day and morrow of St Mary Magdalene (July 21 and 22) (S&W p322) (Official Uttoxeter Town Guide. 1993. p13). Whitaker's Almanac gives these fair days - May 6, Sept 19, Nov 11 and 27. Cooke gives May 6, July 5, Sept 1, and Nov 27 (SCSF pp98,99). There was a fair in 1792 (OWEN), and a fair in 1888 (LHE p265). A horsefair was held in Balance Street until the C20 (Official Uttoxeter Town Guide. 1993. pp24,32). In mid Sept a special fair was held to accommodate the damson harvest (LTD p105). A bull ring stood a few yards SE of the conduit or weighing machine in 1865 (HOU p268). For a rhyme about bear baiting at Uttoxeter, probably at fairs, see Tamworth.

1500 to 1640. Uttoxeter was considered a large, wealthy and notable town in the C17; one of the largest in the county (SSE 1987 pp113-128). **Persons and visitors**. John Leland in his Itinerary (c1540) noted 'The inhabitants (of Uttoxeter) are graziers because there are marvellous pasture grounds beside the Dove' (ESNF p77). **Elizabeth I** visited the town on her tour of the county in 1575 (SOSH p347). On Aug 21 1596 a fire destroyed the W side of the town (SOSH p347); Wilkes noted it (SH p92). **John Archbold** of Uttoxeter parish died in 1629 aged 103, but his burial does not appear in Uttoxeter PR (HOU p191). **The Lightfoots.** Rev Thomas Lightfoot (c1577-1653), vicar of Uttoxeter, by his wife Elizabeth Bagnall (d1636), had five sons, three of whom became notable. Thomas, the eldest who became a tradesman in the town, and did not achieve celebrity. Dr John (1602-1675), the second son, said to have been born at the Rectory House, Stoke, or Stoke Hall (see), became a distinguished Hebrew scholar and died at Ely, Cambs. Dr Peter, the third son, became a surgeon in Uttoxeter and made a valuable map of the town in 1658. As well as being the author of a tract called 'A Battle with a Wasp's Nest' he intended to write a life of his famous brother, John, but was prevented from doing so by death. A model of Uttoxeter based on his map was made in Derby. It was rediscovered in Uttoxeter town hall attic in 1992, and put on display in the heritage centre in Carter Street in 1993. Samuel, the fifth son, was a member of Christ's College, Cambridge. After graduating he entered into holy orders but died young (HBST p482) (GNHS p132) (GNHSS p10) (HOU pp173-175, 257,258,260) (BS pp282-283) (H p143) (S p118) (STM Jan 1964 p27) (ES Feb 2 1993 p4p).

GRAMMAR SCHOOL. The grammar school was founded in 1558 under the will of Thomas Alleyne, who was a school teacher here in his lifetime, as he was at Stone. The original school stood in what came to be known as School Lane, later Bridge Street. It was rebuilt in 1735-1736 and extended and altered in 1765 (AUOPP p42p). A new school house was opened in Back Lane or Dove Bank in 1858 or 1859. It was built in the Elizabethan style by HI Stevens of Derby and a London architect named Robinson. In 1921 it became a maintained secondary school. It merged with the girls' high school in 1964 and became a comprehensive school in 1974 (VCH vol 6 pp172-174). Nothing of the old school was left by 1921 (NSFCT 1921 pp37-38). (W p791) (HOU pp303-306) (GSS pp63il-66). A carved sundial with signs of the Zodiac on a gable end of the old school went into the large schoolroom of the new school building when erected in 1858 (UTP p35 il of the free school) (SLM summer 1958 p13p). **Alumni:** Samuel Bentley (1722-1803) (see below); Samuel Bamford (1845-1932) and Henry Brassington Bamford (1849-1928), members of the Bamford family of Bamfords Ltd, agricultural implement manufacturers (BUBA p27, 31).

CIVIL WAR AND COMMONWEALTH PERIOD. Three hundred men of the county were ordered to assemble at Uttoxeter on July 1 and 2 1640 to help suppress the rebellion in Scotland. A mood of anger prevailed as the men gathered and some ran riot digging up fences in Uttoxeter High Wood. The offenders were put under armed guard and the force was marched off to Scotland three days later (HOU pp67-72) (BFS p4) (LOU p340). The town did not declare itself for either the king or parliament in the Civil War. For a brief period the king's ordnance was housed in the town (Official Uttoxeter Town Guide. 1993. p16). Charles I passed through Uttoxeter on Sept 15 1642 en route for Shrewsbury and stayed at Mr Wood's house on Dove Bank (demolished by 1985) (BFS p6); Prince Rupert burnt houses in the town of those who refused to join the royal army (HOS 1998 p73). Redfern has Charles I in the town again in 1643 (HOU pp73,77). The parliamentarian Sir John Gell and his army were in Uttoxeter for three days after the battle of Hopton Heath, March 19 1643, en route for Derby (BFS p18). Col Rugeley with a parliamentary force fled Uttoxeter to Leek on hearing of Prince Rupert's advance on the town after his retaking of Lichfield garrison in April 1643. Uttoxeter seems to have found it expedient to have colluded with the royalists on their arrival as it had with the parliamentarians (BFS pp20-21). John Scott, was killed in the streets of Uttoxeter in 1644, but his burial is unrecorded in Uttoxeter PR. According to tradition his assailant was hung at the pillory in Uttoxeter (HOU p191). Charles I passed through Uttoxeter on May 24 1645 from Stone with Prince Rupert and a large army; he captured the town and stayed at Uttoxeter Hall and was entertained at The Crown Inn with Lord Stanhope and his son (W p790) (HOU pp78-79) (SOSH pp347-348) (HOS pp35,36). The Moorland Dragoons were apparently defeated by a small royalist force near Uttoxeter on Feb 18 1645 (LOU p28). Capt John Watson who had been a commander with the Moorland Dragoons was leading a party against Tutbury Castle when he was ambushed and killed by royalists near Uttoxeter in Feb 1646 (BFS p23). In 1646 a plague hit the town (W p790), but according to Redfern Uttoxeter escaped this plague (SCSF p137). In Oct 1647 46 travelling Egyptians with a pass from parliament came to the town (S&W p324). The Duke of Hamilton and his royalist Scottish force fleeing after the battle of Preston arrived at Uttoxeter on Aug 24 1648. He was ill and unable to march (LGS pp30,245). On Aug 25 he surrendered to the parliamentary commander, General Lambert, concluding the Civil War (S p149) (SOSH p348).

1660 to 1800. The **Quakers** acquired land for a meeting-house and graveyard, in Carter Street, in 1700 (SSAHST 1970 p46). The Duke of Cumberland

stayed two nights at Uttoxeter in his pursuit of the Young Pretender in the **1745 Jacobite Rebellion**, and is believed to have stayed at Uttoxeter Manor House (see) with an ancestor of Sir Alan Gardner (HOU (1865) p93). **Lawlessness**. In 1716 tension between Hanoverian troops and the locals in Uttoxeter caused a riot, 30 were involved (LOU pp100,359). At Uttoxeter in 1762 a group was charged with contemptuously refusing to obey the constable when they refused to accompany him to the local lock-up (LOU p182). There was an anti-Dissenter riot in Uttoxeter on Dec 13 1792 involving about 12. An attack on the meeting house was made (LOU pp170,374). **Fire and lightning**. In 1672 a fire destroyed the lower part of the town (W p790) (HOU 1865 pp237-238) (Staffs County Guide c1958 p142) (MR p350). But neither Richard Blome, who visited the town, and wrote about it in 'Britannia' (1673), Plot, or Celia Fiennes mention the fire (SSE 1987 p127). According to Plot a thunderbolt struck the town in 1678 and pierced the roof of Thomas Kinnerley's new stable, passed through two floors and through a saddle which hung on the wall and at last struck the pavement (NHS p19). Uttoxeter was renowned for its **inhabitants living to great ages**. Sir Simon Degge noted that the town was a healthy place to live and its inhabitants lived to great ages (S&W pp321-322). Inhabitants were considered young at the age of 60. Two women died here in 1702, one was aged 103, the other was 126 (W p788). (PS p68) (STMSM Oct 1980 p18). **Residents and visitors**. **Samuel Bentley** (1722-1803) has been described as 'the Uttoxeter Poet.' One of his poems starts 'Uttoxeter, sweet are thy views!' (JAT p68) (HOU p3,211-217 ils of Bentley's house and signature) (PSS pp76-80) (VFC p13). **Edward Knight**, comedian, born in Birmingham and brought up as an artist but chose acting as a profession instead. He appeared in Uttoxeter in 'Arno Silvester Daggerwood' and 'Signo.' It was from an incident in Uttoxeter that he got his break. A Mr Philips of Uttoxeter recommended him to the manager of a York theatre who in correspondence gave him an awful rebuff to which Knight replied with equal curtness which impressed the York manager and he was given the job. Knight died in 1826 (HOU pp270-272). In 1784 **Dr Johnson** of Lichfield (see) told Henry White that he had gone to Uttoxeter a few years earlier and stood bareheaded in the rain on the spot where his father's stall had stood to atone for refusing to accompany his father as a boy to sell books in the town market place. Clifford says that the occasion of Johnson's insubordination occurred much later. His account says that Johnson was in his early twenties after leaving Oxford. His father, being ill, asked him to go to Uttoxeter market in his place, but Johnson thought keeping a stall in the open market was beneath the dignity of an Oxford man. Johnson left Oxford on Dec 12 1729 and his father died in early Dec 1731 (Young Samuel Johnson. James L Clifford. 1955 1962 ed. p130). Some believe the penance was made in Walsall Market Place as recorded in an early edition of Boswell's 'Life of Johnson' but in later editions Uttoxeter was substituted (WPP p87). It is now generally thought that the penance was made in Uttoxeter Market Place, by the stocks, now occupied by the present conduit (Official Uttoxeter Town Guide. 1993. p31) (S p117p) (KES pp216,217) (BOE p290) (SGS p173) (SL pp131,132) (MR pp350p,351) (COS p42p): It was a custom to remember the penance by laying a wreath on the Weighing Machine on Johnson's birthday (ES Sept 18 1931 p1ps). Or at Bear Hill, for Redfern had interviewed a man named Joseph Twigg who recollected as a child a man doing penance at the pillory, which was at Bear Hill, where there was a pig market. On the bas-relief on the Weighing Machine a pig obtrudes itself into the picture (HOU pp112-121). The precise date of his penance is uncertain. An inscription on the Weighing Machine says 1759 which is generally considered too early. The date is more likely to be 1775 or 1777 (ES Sept 10 1931 p8p. Sept 12 1931 p3). Some say when he was 70 in 1779 (SGS p173), or in c1780 (MR p351) (TRTC p11). Redfern and Greene think he made it whilst staying with Miss Seward in Lichfield in 1784 (HOU pp104-106) (SSE 1988 p15). In 1857 Nathaniel Hawthorne, the great American novelist, tried to visit the spot and was thoroughly disappointed at the natives' ignorance of the event. He later complained about it in writing. The subject was taken up in The Era (HOU p290) (VFC p62). With no history of Uttoxeter to explain it Francis Redfern was compelled to publish HOU in 1865. There is a poem by Walter Thornbury about the penance in 'Once a Week' (1861). Capt Astle made a sketch of Johnson and himself which was in the possession of Mr Norris, stationer. The inn at which Michael Johnson stayed, Redfern thinks, was the Red Lion, and not the Nag's Head (HOU pp107-112,115-119il). (ROS vol I pp15,16) (UTP p21 il) (PS p72) (LGS pp245-246) (SOSH pp348-349) (COS p42). **John Wesley** was an intimate friend of Rev Mr Davenport, curate of Uttoxeter church, and their correspondence appears in the 'Armenian Magazine.' Wesley may have preached in Uttoxeter Market Place and on another occasion stayed at the White Hart and Old Star Inn in the Market Place (HOU p200). Miss **Harriet Mellon** (b1777) (subsequently Mrs Coutts and Duchess of St Albans) made her first debut on stage at Uttoxeter. At the time she stayed at a house in Church Street (HOU pp269-270). Shortly afterwards she appeared on the stage at Leek (see) and Stafford (see). **Mary Howitt** (nee Botham) (1799-1888), the poet lived her childhood in Uttoxeter. Some say she was born in the town (HOU pp196,222-228) (JAT pp68,69il), others that she was born outside the county but moved from Hanley (H p142) to Balance Street with her parents when in infancy (NSFCT 1896 p147). Another account says she came to Uttoxeter in 1798 when a little girl (LTD p111). The house of the Bothams in Balance Street is now called Howitt Place (AUOPP p23p). Mary seems to have left Uttoxeter after marrying William Howitt in 1821 (PS p70) (WTCEM pp25,26,159,160,161) (KES p215) (SOSH p350) (SLM summer 1955 pp12,13,22) (Staffs County Handbook c1958 p92) (STMSM Oct 1980 p18) (SHJ spring 1992 pp19-22) (Mary Howitt: Another Lost Victorian Writer. Joy Dunicliff. 1992) (VFC p69). Howitt's elder sister, Mrs Anna Harrison (1797-1881), was a poet and diarist (PSS p465) (VFC p60).

1800 to PRESENT. The independent **Uttoxeter Troop**, raised by Claude Bagot in 1803 (FSP p63), continued until c1815. It reformed in 1819 and from then on was part of the Staffordshire Yeomanry (info Yeomanry Museum). Uttoxeter was linked to the **canal** system in 1811 by the Uttoxeter branch of the Cauldon Canal (VB p164). The **Town Hall** in High Street was built in 1854 to the design of Thomas Fradgley. The building housed an assembly room, magistrates court, police station and library (Official Uttoxeter Town Guide. 1993. p33). Uttoxeter **urban district** was founded in 1896 (GLAUE p427) or 1898. Scott-Giles gives the **arms** of Uttoxeter urban district as: The Device on the seal consists of an escutcheon with the word 'Floreat' above a Stafford Knot, and the 1896, and a fleur-de-lis in base. In 1974 Uttoxeter became a part of East Staffordshire borough (CH p341) (Official Uttoxeter Town Guide. 1993. p12). In 1940 Uttoxeter became a reception area for **evacuees** from Ramsgate (ESNF p52). AWN Pugin described his **St Mary's church**, Balance Street, he built in 1839, as 'the first Catholic structure erected in this country in accordance with the rules of ancient ecclesiastical architecture since the days of the pretended Reformation' (Orthodox Journal July 20 1839 p33) (VCH vol 3 p113) (A Vision of Splendour: Gothic Revival in Staffordshire 1840-1890. Michael Fisher. 1995. p73). There has been **horse racing** in the Uttoxeter area sporadically since 1720. Originally race meetings were held at Netherwood (see) (TRTC p19). There was horse racing at Uttoxeter on the Town Meadow in 1839, and later at Lambert's Farm off Byrd's Lane. The present racecourse on the Town Meadows at Wood Lane with custom-built stands opened on May 3 1907 and was owned and run by Uttoxeter urban district council. Racing resumed there in 1921 after WW1. The course was requisitioned in WW2. In April 1952 racing resumed. On June 15 1967 champion jockey Josh Gifford equalled Fred Winter's record of 121 winners (set in the 1952-53 season) in a season at Uttoxeter. In 1988 Stan Clarke, businessman, became a major shareholder. With investment made by Clarke a new grandstand was built and officially opened by Prince Edward in Oct 1994. By then the course had become the venue for the Midlands Grand National event held in March each year; it has been also voted Regional Racecourse of the Year (Official Uttoxeter Town Guide. 1993. p17) (UOPP pl 53) (TRTC p19) (AUOPP p21p of Prince Edward at Uttoxeter races) (info Lynda Fletcher). Uttoxeter had a **Hospital Saturday** when, annually, local inhabitants donated flowers to be sold for hospital funds. A stall was set up outside the Town Hall and volunteers with baskets and collecting boxes sold flowers on the streets (AUOPP p12p in 1910). There is a **Uttoxeter in Canada** (LTD p106). **Persons and visitors.** The spire of Anglican St Mary's church was struck by lightning in 1814 and had to be replaced. During its rebuilding two girls - **Mary Allport and Sarah Adams** - who worked at the Red Lion Inn, ascended the spire and kissed the two workmen - Henry Smith of Uttoxeter Heath and Henry Adams. A great crowd gathered round the church to see the spectacle. Henry Smith later married Mary Allport and they settled at Wetley Rocks (HOU pp160-161) (STMSM May 1980 p41). In 1964 **B Austin** of Uttoxeter is said to have grown the largest tomato ever, weighing 3 lb. In 1965 **P Hayes** of Uttoxeter is said to have grown the largest cabbage ever, weighing 69 lb 8 oz; other claims earlier, cannot be substantiated (GBR 1970 p51). The medium, **Doreen Shadbolt**, was told in a vision, in c1980, by a 2000 year-old Egyptian law giver, called Jethro, to move to Uttoxeter from Middlesex, which she was able to do in just six weeks (SN Aug 29 1980. May 8 1987 p9).

RAILWAYS. The NSR opened the Uttoxeter Branch line to Stoke on Aug 7 1848 (S&UR p5); a line was opened to Burton upon Trent from Sept 11 1848; with Macclesfield via Leek from July 13 1849 using some of the Uttoxeter Branch of the Cauldon Canal bed (NSJFS 1962 p99) (CVH p128) (HCMS No. 5). The Stafford & Uttoxeter Railway linking Uttoxeter with Stafford opened

on Dec 23 1867 and closed to passengers in late 1939 and closed in 1957, with the last 'special' train running on the line on March 23 1957 (NSJFS 1964 pp78,79) (S&UR p32) (Railways In and Around Stafford. Edward Talbot. 1994 p4) (TRTC pp173-174). The line to Ashbourne closed in 1954 (NSJFS 1964 p78). Uttoxeter had three railway stations. Two on the Churnet Valley railway (1849) at Dove Bank, and Town Meadow, and the present one, built in 1881, by Highwood Road (SLM summer 1957 pp23-25) (VB p164) (ESNF p72p of the station of 1881). The original Bridge Street station was closed down in c1881 (S&UR p30). George Wakefield (1828-1888), poet of Uttoxeter, was porter at Uttoxeter station and later stationmaster at Blythe Bridge (PSS pp173-175) (VFC p137). In 1908 there was an accident at Uttoxeter station when a runaway train from Bramshall crashed into a stationary train on the Churnet Valley line. Several were hurt (UOPP pl 52).

NEWSPAPERS. Uttoxeter's first paper was **Uttoxeter New Era and General Advertiser** (or simply The Era), founded by Mr Kelly in 1855 (HOU p290). It ran until at least July 27 1910 and then sometime after merged with the Uttoxeter Advertiser (info Clare Prad). To at least 1994 it was known by local inhabitants as 'The Stunner' (UOPP intro). The **Uttoxeter Weekly Times** appeared in early 1875 (SHJ spring 1996 p29). The **Uttoxeter Journal and North Staffordshire Advertiser**, founded on June 21 1876, ran until at least May 30 1877 (SHJ spring 1996 p28). The weekly **Uttoxeter Advertiser**, founded in 1882, became the Uttoxeter Advertiser and Ashbourne Times from July 1 1896 and still (1997) continues (SHJ spring 1996 p28). The Cheadle & Tean Times brought out the weekly **Uttoxeter Echo** in 1955 and it still (1997) continues (SHJ spring 1996 p28). The **Uttoxeter News** appeared between at least 1973 and 1979 (SHJ spring 1996 p29). The Staffordshire Newsletter brought out the weekly **Uttoxeter Newsletter** in 1984 and it was still running in 1997. The Leek Post and Times brought out the weekly **Uttoxeter Post and Times** in March 1992 and it still (1997) continues.

INDUSTRY. The industries of Uttoxeter have been, from the C13, ironworking (SCSF p112), cattle and hence markets for leather (SSE 1987 p119), beef, cheese (Plot noted was sold in London) and butter (gave impetus to the pottery trade of Burslem); in the C18 lapidary and jewellery; from 1868 the manufacture of agricultural implements by Henry Bamford (1819-1896), ironmonger in Uttoxeter from c1844. The firm moved to the Leighton Ironworks at Leighton (see) in 1871 (BUBA pp95,97) (Official Uttoxeter Town Guide. 1993. p17). In 1945 Henry Bamford's great-grandson, Joseph Cyril Bamford (b1916), left Bamford & Sons Ltd and set up his own firm manufacturing excavators, known as Joseph Cyril Bamford Excavators (JCB). The firm's first premises were a lock-up garage at No. 28 Derby Road which it was obliged to leave for Crakemarsh Hall in c1947 as the elderly landlady objected to Sunday working being carried on there (BUBA pp113p,114). Elkes Biscuits supplied the cake for the wedding of Elizabeth II and Prince Philip (LTD p109). There was a watermill opposite Uttoxeter railway station, off Brookside Road, known as Wooliscrofts' Mill and Vernon's Mill (TRTC p134). There was another watermill on the Tean called Titley's Mill (see). For Uttoxeter windmill see The Heath. For Uttoxeter trade tokens see HOU pp290-293 ils and 'Uttoxeter Tokens' John Higgins.

CUSTOMS AND SUPERSTITIONS. **May day customs.** There was a maypole at Uttoxeter in the C16 where the Wesleyan Chapel stood in the C19 (HOU p263). At Uttoxeter garlands and flowers were carried around the town by groups of children on May Day. The garlands consisted of two hoops, one passing through the other, which gave the appearance of four half-circles (HOU p262). Sometimes the children carried a little pole or stick with a bunch of flowers attached to the top of the pole (CSL pp25,26) (BCC vol 2 p216). **Guising.** Guisers still (1993) perform in the town at Christmas and New Year. Morris men dance in the town on Boxing Day (Official Uttoxeter Town Guide. 1993. pp24,32). Girls in Uttoxeter were still **touching metal** as a talisman whenever they passed a priest in 1941. The superstition derives from Bronze Age man's fear of Druids of the Stone Age over whom he had just conquered (FLJ 1941 p237). A 70 feet wide **crop circle** was found in a field between Uttoxeter and Rocester. It had been made by Aug 17 1996 (ES Aug 17 1996 p11p).

UTTOXETER IN LITERATURE. Mary Howitt (see above) calls Uttoxeter Wood Leighton in her novel 'The Chronicle of Wood Leighton' (1835); the town is probably the Deckerton in 'Deckerton and its Last Generation' by her husband (Staffs County Handbook c1958 p92) (SHJ spring 1992 pp20-21). 'Treddleston' is Uttoxeter in George Eliot's 'Adam Bede' (1859) (VB p168). Mabel Leigh Hunt's novel 'Beggar's Daughter' (1963) is set in Uttoxeter.

Uttoxeter Branch of the Caldon Canal. Former canal which ran from Froghall to The Wharf at Uttoxeter. Authorised in 1797 (IANS p24). Work began in 1807. Said to have been completed from Froghall to Oakamoor by Aug 1808, to Alton by May 1809 and to Uttoxeter by Sept 1811 (NSJFS 1963 pp59-67)

(LTD p77). Closed in 1847 (Nicholson's Guide to the Waterways No. 5 'Midlands' p49). Length 13m. John Farrey noted the standard of workmanship was very high on the locks of the Uttoxeter Branch Canal (The Trent and Mersey Canal in the Historic Waterways Scenes Series. Peter Lead. 1980. pls 101, 128). The NSR Churnet Valley railway (for the Uttoxeter-Macclesfield line) made use of the canal bed (IANS p24). (Uttoxeter Canal and nearby Waterways. John Dunnicliff. 1987) (HAF pp227-232).

Uttoxeter Manor House High Street, Uttoxeter. Has also appeared as Uttoxeter Hall, Uttoxeter Old Hall, Uttoxeter House, and the Manor House. In spring 1645 Charles I with Prince Rupert stayed here (SOSH p347). Birthplace of Admiral Lord Alan Gardner (d1809 or d1810 at Bath) on April 12 1742. Gardner left Uttoxeter to be a sailor in 1755 (W p790) (UTP p22p) (HOU pp217-222) (HOU (1881) p271) (JAT p68) (SOSH p350) (KES p215) (STM Oct 1965 p29). The Duke of Cumberland may have stayed here in the tapestried room when at Uttoxeter in his pursuit of the Young Pretender in the 1745 Jacobite Rebellion (HOU (1865) p93) (NSFCT 1940 p38); another account says the Duke stayed at the White Hart Inn (see). There is a priest's hole in the attic. There was an old tapestry in one of the bedrooms showing Elijah being carried up to heaven in a chariot with Elisha watching from the ground (NSFCT 1934 p78). The house was in a state of decay when the novelist, Mary Howitt, noted it in the C19. She described it as a large, irregular brick mansion, standing by the roadside outside the town (SHJ spring 1992 pp23-24). In 1865 and some years previously it was occupied by Dr Taylor (HOU (1865) p93 il facing). In 1881 it was occupied by Misses Marion and Dorothy Hawthorn, who ran a school for young ladies at the house in the late C19 (HOU (1881) p271) (AUOPP p39p). In the early C20 it was the residence of the novelist, Judge Alfred Ruegg KC, JP until he moved to Highfields Hall (see) near Uttoxeter (ESNF p74). The site next to the manor house became a cinema in c1934. It has been a convent and a gentleman's seat (NSFCT 1934 p78). The Manor House is now (1993) Brooke Vernon Advertising (Official Uttoxeter Town Guide. 1993. p33).

Uttoxeter Park Medieval deer park. In existence by 1303. Belonged to the Earls (later Dukes) of Lancaster. Was mentioned in c1603 (NSJFS 1964 pp63,64).

Uttoxeter Ward One of the five wards of Needwood Forest. First mentioned in 1262. It was separate from the main body of the forest. The heirs of the Mynors family of Uttoxeter were the hereditary foresters of the ward (HCT p366) (HOPT vol 2 p223). In 1637 the enclosure and disafforestation of the ward was greeted by riots (VCH vol 2 pp349,352. vol 6 p53) (SL p106).

Uxbridge Ward and suburb S of Shobnall, Burton upon Trent. Christ Church, Uxbridge Street, with adjoining National School were opened in 1844 for this district (HOS 1998 p96).

V

Vale Head Former house on the corner of Mount Road and Wightwick Bank, Tettenhall Wood. In the 1930s the Bruford family lived here. Vale Head was later demolished and replaced by a block of flats called Wightwick Court (TCOP p75p).

Valentine's Brook Flows at Upper Cliff and Lower Cliff on Cannock Chase. May flow into Rising Brook, a tributary of the Trent (GCC pp29,53).

Vale of Frith Tittesworth Reservoir lies in it (SMCC p2), stretches up to Swythamley and Turner's Pool. Gun Hill and the Roaches form the sides (HOLF p24).

Vale of Rudyard Rudyard Lake lies in it.

Vale of Tinkersclough and Etruria (SHST p521).

Vale of Trent Appears to be a reference to the lower Trent Valley in the Lichfield area (VB p13). May also have been referred to as Lichfield Plain (LPL) and Vale of Lichfield. The expression 'The Ladies of the Vale' refers to the three spires of Lichfield cathedral. FNC Mundy in his poem 'Needwood Forest,' 1776, refers to the spires as the 'triumphant ladies of the vale.' Honora Sneyd is said to have called them 'the ladies of the valley' in 1779 (VCH vol 14 p3 note). (Bell's Lichfield Cathedral. AB Clifton. 1908. p30) (LGS p167) (AA p257) (LAL p23). It perhaps came about from someone seeing the cathedral at a distance nestling in the Vale of Trent: Only its three spires, or 'ladies,' are visible at a distance.

Vale Pleasant Shelton, Hanley. Samuel Hollins had a pottery factory here beside Caldon Canal (POTP p124). Marked on 1834 OS map in approximate position of E side of Etruria Vale Road.

Valley Park 156 acres of public open space between Castlecroft and Aldersley along the Staffs and Worcs Canal, and the Smestow and Graiseley Brooks. More than 10,000 people visit the park every year. In 1996 the park was put forward to English Heritage for official designation (E&S Oct 8 1996 p16).

Vandykes, The Spring Lane, Lower Penn. Built in c1911 by the Hills, who were related to Van der Collins, the actress (PAIP p52).

Vauxhall Former hamlet 0.75m NW of Wolverhampton, in Wolverhampton township and ancient parish. The name occurs in the 1841 census and White described it in 1851 as a large modern village (W p96). The name is preserved in a few road names to W of West Park on the N side of Tettenhall Road.

Venison Oak An old oak in Bagot's Park (SLM Oct 1947 p35. Feb 1951 p19) (STMSM April 1973 p24).

Veres House at Footherley. It passed to the Simpsons of Lichfield. In 1899 it was the property of Mr Cooper of Shenstone Court (ASE p8).

Vermin Valley Small valley 1.75m W of Kinver. Appears on 1949 OS map 1:25,000 (sheet 32/88), at SO 815832.

Vernon's Branch of the Wyrley and Essington Canal. Built in c1796, closed in 1954. Seems to have spurred off the Wyrley and Essington Canal near Sneyd Colliery and ran to near Hilton Park. It was the highest the level (536 feet) on the Birmingham canal system (HCMS No. 2).

Viator's Bridge Twin-arch packhorse bridge over the Dove at Milldale, N end of Dovedale. Or called Wheelbarrow Bridge (TPC p164). So called from Viator, the main character in Izaak Walton's 'The Complete Angler; or the Contemplative Man's Recreation' (1653). Viator, reputedly Walton himself, and Piscator Junior (Charles Cotton) ride down from the Derbys side and cross the river here. With reference to its narrowness Viator says to Piscator Junior 'Do you use to travel with wheel-barrows in this country? This bridge certainly was made for nothing else. Why a mouse can hardly go over it; 'tis not two fingers broad' (LGS p124) (VCH vol 7 p10). Scheduled by HM Office of Works as an ancient monument (NSFCT 1936 p30). Bird, writing in 1974, implies the present bridge is a successor to the one of Walton's day (VB p204). Others say the present bridge is probably of the early C16 and replaced a bridge which carried the road to Alstonefield, mentioned in the late 1420s (VCH vol 7 pp9-10). (TD p) (KES pp4,5) (MR p230p) (BZ p108).

Vicarage, The Vicars' Close, NW corner of Lichfield cathedral Close. The residences of the vicars' choral. Built in the C14 and the C15, near their common hall, called the Vicars' Hall (see). They comprise low-built houses in two quadrangles (HOL p291) (VCH vol 14 p58 see map). The houses have inward-looking aspects, with backs to the Close. Some houses in the southern courtyard were changed to face the Close when the new Vicars' Hall was built in Nov 1757 (HOL p291). One quadrangle is called Nether Vicarage (BOE p188 note). The upper courtyard is now called the Vicars' Close (VCH vol 14 p58).

Vicarage Farm Timber-framed house with a priest's room (LGS p200 note) at Ranton. The origins of the house are unknown (NSFCT 1915 pp170-171).

Vicarage Moor On the SW of Walsall. Here were springs which supplied central Walsall with water from the C17 (VCH vol 17 p222).

Vicarage Well Well in Dimble Lane, Alton (HAF p359).

Vicars Choral Area of land on W side of Forge Lane, Little Aston (GATD p88).

Vicars' Close Present name of the upper courtyard of The Vicarage, Lichfield cathedral Close (VCH vol 14 p58 pl 8).

Vicars' Hall Originally probably the residence, and then the common hall, of the vicars' choral. The hall stood in the NW corner of Lichfield cathedral Close in a complex including The Vicarage (see) now known as the Vicars' Close. Bishop Langton granted the vicars' choral the hall or land in 1315 (VCH vol 14 p62) (GKCLC) or 1317 (HOL p291) (VCH vol 3 p156). Here they lived in collegiate style. A hall appears to have been built for them in c1374 (HOL p291). In 1458 the hall was rebuilt by canon residentiary, Thomas Chesterfield (d1452) (SHOS vol 1 p308) (HOL p291). The Duke of Cumberland's soldiers were quartered here in Dec 1745 in pursuit of the Young Pretender in the Jacobite Rebellion (LTM Jan Feb 1973 p10p). The hall was taken down in 1756 and rebuilt in Nov 1757 (HOL p291). In the late C18 it was a spacious and handsome room, usually lent for the purpose of assemblies and other amusements (SHOS vol 1 p308). The hall's main entrance is now incorporated into No. 4 Vicars' Close (S courtyard, by the West Gate): No. 4 used to be the Vicars' Muniment Room (BOE p188 note).

Vicar's Hill Hill and farm 2m NW of Rangemore.

Victoria Ward situated between Horninglow and Shobnall in the Outwoods to Little Burton area, Burton upon Trent.

Victoria Name for an area covering the Windmill Lane to Victoria Park area of Smethwick. By 1999 formed a ward with Soho in Sandwell metropolitan borough.

Victoria Hall Concert hall in Lichfield Street, Hanley. The original part was built at two different times, the front portion was at first an hotel called the Queen's Hotel opened in 1867. Bought by Hanley town council and the Victoria Hall was added to its rear in 1887 (SOSH pp277p,278,280). Officially opened on Oct 4 1888. Elgar's 'King Olaf' received its first performance here in 1896 and Sir Thomas Beecham conducted the first performance of his 'Sea Drift' here in 1908 (VCH vol 8 p172) (POP p54). Frederick Delius, composer, conducted at the hall in 1907 (POP p54). George Bernard Shaw lectured to local Fabians in the Victoria Hall in 1911 (SHST p430) (TSS p64). Some of those that have appeared here are Joachim, Busoni, Madame Patti, McCormack, Delius, Gigli, Tauber, Robeson, and Gracie Fields (VCH vol 8 p172) (AGT pp116,117il) (ES Nov 7 1998 p19). The longest symphony ever written, The Symphony No. 2 (the Gothic), composed from 1919 to 1922 by William Havergal Brian (d1972), born in Dresden (see) in 1876, was played by over 800 performers (four brass bands) here on May 21 1978. The conductor was Trevor Stokes (GBR 1994 p169). The hall, said to have the best acoustics in Britain (local info), was extended, renovated and refurnished between c1995 and 1998 (ES Sept 29 1998 p16pc).

Victoria Institute Tunstall. Built in 1889 (SOSH p287). It housed a museum of Adams ware and other early Staffs potters (LGS p238).

Victoria Park Public park between Dudley Port and Tipton Green.

Victoria Park Public park 0.5m NE of Smethwick old church. Laid out in 1887-8 (VCH vol 17 p89).

Victoria Park Public park between Station Road and the Sow, Stafford. Completed in 1910 (SAC pp69p,70).

Victory Farm 0.75m SE of Kings Bromley.

'Vicus Altus' Mound mentioned by Harwood (HOL p500 note 17) on which Lichfield Grammar School building in the 1870s stood. It was probably part of a prehistoric fort (SSAHST 1968 p71).

Viewpoint St John's Hill, Shenstone. Built in c1939-40. Pevsner says it is decidedly modern for its date, at least, in English architectural terms (BOE p235).

Views, The Penkhull New Road, Penkhull. Built in c1780. Birthplace of Sir Oliver Lodge, wireless telegraphy pioneer, on June 12 1851. In 1863 the Lodge family moved to Moreton House (see), Wolstanton. In 1875 they moved to Watlands Hall (see) (AGT pp28-29 il) (POTP p142). In the 1870s the Lodge family also lived in Old Hall Street, Hanley (OTP p157). He was an exhibitor at the bazaar for the opening of the North Staffs Infirmary, aged 16, with 'exhibitions of electric illuminations which were wholly new to the district.' After a spell in London Lodge studied at the Athenaeum, Stoke-upon-Trent, and at the Wedgwood Institute (see). He was awarded the degree of Doctor of Science in 1877. At the British Association meeting in Oxford on Aug 14 1894 he was the first man to transmit a message by radio telegraphy. He was also the inventor of the method of electrical spark ignition for the internal combustion engine. He was knighted in 1902 and died at Normaton House, near Salisbury, Wilts, in 1940 (Vanity Fair Feb 2 1904 colour il) (ES Sept 24 1931 p6p. Nov 26 1931 p6) (SLM June 1951. spring 1958 p8) (SHST p169) (PRA pp78-80,87) (STM Oct 1964 p49p. Dec 1968 p37) (POTP p142) (photograph in the Warrillow Collection, Keele University showing Lodge receiving the Freedom of the City of Stoke-on-Trent). By 1965 The Views was the home of Deaconess Bl Smee. She believed that the house occupies the site of a Saxon fortress where Lady Godiva was born (Newcastle Times Aug 25 1965); and later Penkhull Hall (PRA p77). She was instrumental in having The Views saved from demolition in 1967 on account of its connections with Oliver Lodge (ES Jan 27 1965 p of The Views. Sept 9 1967) (POTP p142). The house is reputedly haunted (Newcastle Times Aug 25 1965). Glacial boulders of the Ice Age lie in the grounds and may have been used in ancient religious worship (ES May 21 1968 p5p).

Vigo Former hamlet in a marshy valley formed by a tributary of Ford Brook, 1.5m WSW of Stonnall, formerly in Walsall Wood township, Walsall ancient parish. There are two burnt mounds probably of the Middle Bronze Age about 30 metres apart at SK 02081655 on the S side of a stream, separated by marshy ground (SASR 1987 pp16-17). By 1805 the settlement on the S side of Holly Bank Common was known as Vigo (VCH vol 17 p278). Raven says Vigo takes its name from the Vigo Brickworks (BCTV p76). Betty Fox suggests the name may be from the battle of Vigo (1702) (SNAR p50) (SNBC p48).

Village, The Area about Kingswinford church, 0.5m E of the junction of the A491 with the A4101. Here, facing the church, still (1990) stands the Court House. The house was the meeting place for the manorial courts of Kingswinford manor in the time of Lord Dudley and Ward, until abolished in 1850 (BHOP p6) (BHOP2 p89p).

Vinecroft Tutbury (GLS p100). Is within Tutbury Castle precincts?

Vinegar Well Well at the corner of Well Lane and Marsh Green Road, Mow Cop. It is said the local people used to wash their coins in the water during the Great Plague of 1665 (WMC).

Vinegar Well Well on S side of Manor Road, Hall End, Wednesbury. It was originally called Vineyard Well since it adjoined the vineyard of Wednesbury Manor House. It was always a free well (WAM p6).

Vine Tree Croft Near Tutbury Priory. From a vineyard established by Queen Constantia, second wife of John of Gaunt (UTR p64).

Virgins End Area to S of Mayer's Green, West Bromwich ancient parish. Was in existence by 1768 when the Virgin Inn is said to have been built here (VCH vol 17 p4). Said to take its name from the three virgin daughters of John Ward who once kept an ale-house near the top of Bull Street (SOWB p25).

Virgin's Row Former small hamlet near the Birmingham Old Main Line at Lanesfield. Appears on 1947 OS map 1:25,000 (sheet 32/99), at SO 933955.

Vivarium, The Former name for the marsh and sheets of water dividing Lichfield cathedral and Lichfield town. The Vivarium was remodelled to be Minster Pool and Swan Moggs (now Beacon Park).

Vivarium Bridge Links Bird Street with Beacon Street, Lichfield. Bridge over the former Vivarium, and only link between the Lichfield cathedral and the city. The first known crossing here was built by Bishop Langton in c1312, although it evidently replaced an earlier one (VCH vol 14 p11). The causeway of c1312 was a seven feet wide seven arch causeway suitable for pack-horses. Langton probably made the other, shorter, causeway linking the South Gate of the Close with Dam Street, as well (LI part v p101). CC Taylor says the causeway was built in c1296, before which, travellers to the cathedral had to go via Stowe Street, St Chad's church and Gaia Lane (SSAHST 1968 p45). The causeway was widened to 12 feet c1765-1775 and replaced by the present bridge in 1816-17, financed by a special commission (HOL p11) (LAL p39 p of the plaque on present bridge).

Waddam's Pool Former tiny hamlet in the SE part of central Dudley. The name, which appears in the 1841 census, is preserved in the street called Waddam's Pool.

Wadden's Brook Runs SE of Wednesfield. Much of the area in the vicinity of Wadden's Brook was formerly called the Moors or the Marsh from which March End is derived, and an earlier hamlet called Moor End (now untraceable). Has also appeared as Waddamsbrook (WFW p9).

Wade Lane House Rake End. It was considered an ancient stone building at the end of the C18 (SHOS vol 1 p200).

Wadham's Hill Former hill which Whitmore Hill and Molineux Alley led to at SO 913988, Wolverhampton. Appears in the Middle Ages as Wadham's Hill and Othams Hill (WAIW vol 3 p). It may also have appeared as Waddam's Hill, and as Windham's Hill, where there was a well called Meg-a Wood's Well or Meg-a-doodles Well (see). The hill was destroyed when a further section of the inner ring road was built (WAIW vol 3).

Waggersley 0.25m S of Tittensor. Marked 1834 OS map but not on the current OS map 1:25,000.

Waggersley Hall House 0.75m S of Tittensor. May have become known as Tittensor Chase (see) by 1888. Between at least 1860 and 1872 it was owned by the Duke of Sutherland (KD 1860. 1872). Occupied by George Loch in 1868 (KD 1868).

Waggs Brook Forms the county boundary with Shrops from its rising near Mosslane, Bishop's Wood. Flows N of Ellerton Grange, Adbaston on to Ellerton and joins the Meese S of Sambrook, Shrops.

Wain Lee Tiny hamlet below Mow Cop hill on the SE side, 1m SSE of Mow Cop.

Wakelam's Fold A yard or court enclosure at Lower Gornal (SDOP p90p).

Wales End The Wales Lane area of Barton-under-Needwood. The name, also appearing as Whales End, is from Wales End Farm, the seat in 1509 of Johannes Holand de Walessend (UNT pp36,118p), a half timbered hall house of the mid C15 (NSFCT 1959 p90).

Walford Former estate in Penn Fields, adjoining the Birches Barn estate on the W side. Walford Green and Walford Avenue preserve the name (PAIP p44).

Walford Minute hamlet on a steep promontory overlooking Chatcull Brook 0.75m S of Standon. Former township (HOPS p4) in Standon ancient parish. Salt says there are about two or three wells at Walford (HOPS p131). Between at least 1872 and 1916 a Mrs Madan is recorded as living at Walford (trade directories). A phantom cat reputedly haunted the house occupied by the Madan family. Some relations of theirs saw it whilst at dinner in c1893 including their cousin Rev FJ Salt of Winterbourne Manor, Newbury, Berks, who wrote about it in a letter. At least five witnesses say they saw the cat, described as a tabby, and some saw it repeatedly. One included Viscountess Hanworth. The Madans sold their house to a farmer in 1925. The owner in 1939 said he had never seen the cat (AHH Case No. 99 pp353-355) (MMSE p288).

Walk, The Hill in the Weaver Hills at SK 097473 (1834 OS map). Is incorrectly marked at SK 095464 on 1985 OS map 1:25,000; this is in fact the position of another hill called Beacon Stoop (see).

Walker Hall The drive to the hall was from the Ocker Hill road, Tipton. The hall stood near to Moat Farm, its home farm. This hall was of Georgian style, although it is probable a much older hall preceded it. It was occupied by three bachelor brothers, John, Edmund, and George Walker in 1825, who also owned the adjacent works. Many distinguished dignitaries stayed at the hall including Marshall Soult of France, when minister for war in c1830. Many of the dignitaries left orders with the local works for cannon. The hall, called Gospel Oak Hall in 1851 (census), was in a dilapidated condition in 1883 (HOTIP pp187-188). It was demolished in c1900 (TB Oct 1996 p11), and certainly by 1946 when it was covered with an housing estate (OH p55). It has also appeared as Ocker Hill Hall (HOTIP pp187-188). Clayton's Folly (see), West Bromwich, is said to have been an exact replica of Walker Hall on a smaller scale (HOTIP p188).

Walker's Green To SE of Boney Hay, W of Chorley Green, S of Cold Well (Phillips and WF Hutchings map 1832).

Walker's Hill Ocker Hill (WBOPP pl 120).

Walker's Springs Springs 0.5m WSW of Blithfield, at SK 035237.

Walking Stick Oak Former peculiar slim columnar oak in Bagot's Park (LGS p192) towards Dunstal, just N of the concrete estate road. Has also appeared as Bagot's Walking Stick. The oak, 60 feet (NSFCT 1909 p197) or 70 or 80 feet (LGS p192) high, was also peculiar in not having a branch until its top, so having the appearance of a walking stick. It was believed to be 250-300 years old in the 1930s (CCBO p26). There is a tradition which relates the first Bagot was given as much land as he could walk round in a day by William the Conqueror. At the end of the day, being exhausted, he set his stick in the ground and it grew into this oak. The story could relate to Beggar's Oak (ES Dec 29 1932 p4). It was the last surviving of the ancient oaks of Bagot's Park (AR p27), and it is interesting to note that although many of the finest timbers in Bagot's Park were sold in 1933 to alleviate death duties, Lord Bagot specifically excluded Walking Stick Oak from the sale (LTD p128). Raven, in 1988, describes it as white and dead (MR pp4p,5). It blew down in a wind in Feb 1988 (AR p27p c1950s) (LTD p124) which completely uplifted the roots (local info). (NSFCT 1900 il of facing p74. 1915 p161) (KES p16) (SLM Oct 1947 p35p. Feb 1951 p19) (STMSM April 1973 p24).

Walk Mill By Wyrley Brook 1.5m S of Cannock. The Walkmill Bridge crosses over Wyrley Brook. The name is from a mill where walking (or fulling) cloth took place (DUIGNAN).

Walk Mill Hamlet in a dell by the Sow 2.25m NNE of High Offley. In Eccleshall ancient parish. The name is from a mill where walking (or fulling) cloth took place (PWIS p33) (ECC p50). Braithwaite in ROT p18 says the mill was mentioned in DB. A mill existed here by 1298. For the present mill at SJ 791297 see IAS p164. There was in the early C20 a brick building here with Ionic capitals of stone forming the lintel of a doorway. It looked of C17 origin and is perhaps from Sugnall Old Hall (NSFCT 1910 p199). 'J.D.' appears on a barn at Walkmill House (MR p248). For the murder of John Poole in 1866 on the road between Walk Mill and Offleybrook see Offleybrook.

Walk Mill Pool Little pool between Cop Mere and Bishop's Offley Pool, Walk Mill.

Wall, The Estate in Audley township. It belonged to the Boughey family for many generations up to 1733 (SHC 1944 p5).

Wall Small village by a tributary of Crane Brook by Watling Street 15.25m SE of Stafford. Former township of St Michael's parish, Lichfield (VCH vol 14 pp283,285). A flint axe was found on a house drive in Wall. It probably came in a load of gravel from Cannock Chase (NSJFS 1964 p40). A bronze palstave of the Bronze Age was found in Wall parish in 1725-6 (Magna Britannia. T Cox. vol 5 p51) (ARCH vol 5 p113) (SHOS vol 1 General Intro p31) (NSJFS 1964 p40). There was Roman and later Romano-British settlement at Wall from the C1 AD until the C4, and possibly until the C5. By the C3 the settlement was known by the Romans as Etocetum, and later as Letocetum (see). Has appeared as Walla (1167) (SSE 1996 p18), and La Wal (SPN p133).

According to John Horsley in 'Britannia Romana' 1732 p420 Wall is derived from certain walls which encompassed about two acres of ground called Castle Croft - the last remains above ground of Letocetum (SSAHST 1963 p1). (Roman site at Wall. DoE Official Guide. 1979). (DUIGNAN). The earliest medieval settlement may have been on the higher ground around Wall House (VCH vol 14 pp283,285). A pre-Reformation chapel may have stood on 'the ground leading to Chesterfield, and in the parish of Shenstone' (SHOS vol 1 p356). The church, St John the Baptist, on the W side of Green Lane, was built in 1843 (VCH vol 14 p293). Became a separate ecclesiastical parish in 1843, refounded in 1845. Became a separate civil parish in 1866 (GLAUE p427). There is a hand pump adjacent to a barn, 25 metres N of Wall House (DoE II).

Wallacre House 0.75m ESE of Butterton (Moorlands).

Wallash Tiny district on rising ground above the Dove 0.25m NE of Church Mayfield. At the County Museum at Shugborough is reconstructed the interior of the Woodward Smithy from No. 22 Wallash, Mayfield. It was a working smithy until 1964, and was removed after 1974 (info from Christopher Copp) (MOM p57p of the smithy at Wallash).

Wall Bridge Bridge carrying the Newcastle-Leek road over the Churnet. The first known bridge here was built by the monks of Dieulacres Abbey in c1244. The wooden horse bridge which was here at the beginning of the C18 was replaced by a stone bridge in c1712, which was widened in 1929 (VCH vol 7 p99). Probably gives its name to Wall Bridge Farm and Wallbridge Park.

Wall Bridge Farm Stood on E side the Newcastle road, 1.5m SW of Leek, in Leek and Lowe township, Leek ancient parish. Existed by 1775. Demolished in 1974 and is now (1991) covered by Barnfields Industrial Estate (VCH vol 7 pp89,98). The name is probably from the bridge, Wall Bridge (see), to its SW.

Wallbridge Park Modern suburb of Leek, 1m SW of Leek. The private Wallbridge Park housing estate was begun in the 1963 and extended in the early 1970s (VCH vol 7 pp97-98). (SK p196). See also Hostage Lane.

Wallbrook Small suburb at the foot of England's main watershed on the E side, 0.25m S of Coseley. In Sedgley ancient parish. There is a mission church, St Cuthbert, at Wallbrook (LDD).

Wall Brook Runs E of Milwich. Joins Gayton Brook.

Wall Butts Tiny hamlet on Watling Street 1m W of Wall. The name appears on the 1888 OS map 6 inch, and may be from a field called Butts belonging to Wall township.

Wall End Formerly to the SW of Great Bloxwich. Had a chapel dedicated to All Saints (SOB pp2,57,133, 161 see map facing).

Wallface Hill Top, West Bromwich. Here was the lodging for a monk of Sandwell Priory when performing services at West Bromwich church (OWB p36).

Wall Grange Tiny hamlet on a small promontory in a bend of the Churnet 1.25m ENE of Longsdon. Formerly in Longsdon township in Leek ancient parish. At Wall Bridge Farm at SJ 980555 is a burial mound from which came a Middle Bronze Age cinerary urn (NSFCT 1983 p13). Has appeared as Wal (C13), Wal juxta Lek (1293) (SSE 1996 p18), and Wall Grange (possibly by 1439. 1510) (VCH vol 7 p205). 'Wall' is from probably the Old English word for well or spring, with reference to St Caena's Well (VCH vol 7 p203). Some say 'Wall' is from an ancient line earthwork called The Mark alias Limes Britannicus (OL vol 2 p15). At Wall Grange Farm was possibly a medieval village (SSAHST 1970 p36), since depopulated. Trentham Priory owned an estate at Wall by the early C13 and had a grange here. After the Dissolution and until 1911 the estate was held by the Leveson, later Leveson-Gower, family of Trentham Hall (DUIGNAN p158) (VCH vol 3 p256. vol 7 pp203,205-206). It was leased to the Egertons of Wrinehill at various times from the late C15 to the mid C17, and to the Debanks from the late C17 to the mid C18; they built the present Wall Grange Farm, which is of c1715 (NSFCT 1870 p37) (VCH vol 7 p206). There was a railway station at Wall Grange on the Caldon Canal (SMOPP vol 2). In response to the need for sufficient pure water in the Potteries the **Staffordshire Potteries Water Works Company** (SPWWC) was formed in 1847. In 1849 the Company started pumping water from the Wall Grange Water Works from springs by Saint Caena's Well (see) to the Potteries. The Company built Hatton Pumping Station (see) in 1891, and works at Meir in 1868; Stockton Brook in 1884; Millmeece (see) in 1914; and Cresswell in 1928-32 (PWW). By 1849 SPWWC had built Wall Grange Water Works at Horse Bridge to supply water to the Potteries; water was extracted from springs which fed Saint Caena's Well (see) (W p230) (NSFCT 1876 p12). The works closed in the 1980s (VCH vol 7 205).

Wall Hall The old hall, in Castle Croft, Wall (Lichfield), was owned by the Jackson family of Chesterfield, near Shenstone, by the late C16. A new hall was built to the N in the present centre of Wall at the junction of Market Lane and Green Lane and the Jacksons were living in it by 1666. The new hall was extensively rebuilt in the mid C18. It was the seat of the Jacksons until the mid C19. Richard Croft Chawner, fostered since childhood by Edward and Mary Jackson, lived at Wall Hall until the 1850s (BCM vol 10 No. 4 p26. vol 11 No. 1 p30. vol 11 No. 2 p44. vol 13 No. 4 p41). In 1900 the hall was called White House (VCH vol 14 pp285,290-291 pl 54 shows the hall in 1961).

Wall Heath Village, centred on the High Street area, on ground rising above Dawley Brook 1m NW of Kingswinford and merges into Kingswinford. In Kingswinford ancient parish. By end of the C13 there was a hamlet on the edge of Kinver Forest known as Kings-Wall-huh (SVB p168). The name is from probably the Roman earthworks at Greensforge also known as the Walls. (DUIGNAN) (SPN p146). The Heath forge allegedly mentioned in 'Metallum Martis' (1665) by Dud Dudley of Dudley Castle (see) may be a reference to Wallheath, but more probably Heath Forge (see), Wombourne (SNSV vol 1 p123). The common of 1400 acres of Wall Heath and Ashwood Hay were enclosed under an Act of 1776 (SHC 1941 p16). The church of the Ascension at Wall Heath was built in c1893 (BHOP p96). In a tiny field near the Navigation Inn parallel to the famed Mile Flat was an airfield used from 1916 to 1917 by the Royal Flying Corps (WMA p258b). In 1807 William Griffiths, a gamekeeper was murdered at or near Wall Heath. His murderer may have been a poacher named Bossack (TB Aug 1977 p29). General Booth (d1912), founder and general of the Salvation Army, passed through the village in a car on Aug 16 1909 (BCM Spring 2000 p63). Jack Bolhuis of Wall Heath and formerly of Holland built a model windmill in his garden (E&S July 26 1969 p3p).

Wall Heath House Wall Heath. Demolished in the 1960s and a shopping precinct built on its site (SVB p168).

Wallhill Half-timbered house 0.75m N of Rushton Spencer. Formerly in Rushton Spencer township in Leek ancient parish. For centuries the seat of the Yardleys, lords of the manor of Rushton Spencer. The present house bears the date 1621. An earlier house on the site is thought to date from c1400 (NSFCT 1951 p112) (VCH vol 7 pp223,225). Has also appeared as Wall Hill. The name is from 'warhill.' The hill may have been a 'look-out hill' (NSFCT 1932 p53).

Wall House E side of Green Lane, Wall. Is probably on the site of the medieval manor house, and manorial rights have descended with the house (VCH vol 14 p285). A rainwater head on the S side is dated 1761. This may be the date of the building of the house; Sheldon Porter was lord of the manor in 1761 and he may have been the builder (VCH vol 14 p287-288).

Wallington Heath Former hamlet on ground rising out of Sneyd Brook, now a suburb 0.75m N of Bloxwich (W p649). Formerly in the Foreign township in Walsall ancient parish. (W p649). The name is said to have appeared in the C13, and an early form of it is Wale(n)ton (SNBP p58). If it is of Anglo-Saxon origin, then possibly is from 'wealh' meaning a stranger or Celt (SNBP p58). There was a settlement at Wallington Heath by the latter C18 (VCH vol 17 p161).

Wallington House Wallington Heath, Bloxwich. Formerly the King's Arms, a coaching inn in the C18. Is reputedly haunted by the ghost of a young girl who stayed at the King's Arms in the 1720s and was murdered in her room, perhaps, by an ostler, who made off with her roll of French silk (SOB p154) (BY p19) (GLS pp22-23). By 1814 the house had become a private residence known as Wallington House owned by JA Russell; the Russells entertained the Gladstones (Capt Gladstone and WE Gladstone) at Wallington House for the bye-election of Feb 1841 (SOB pp154-155il,162,208 p facing) (SNBP p53). Sold in 1904. Became the convent of St Paul of Chartres which closed in 1964. Demolished in 1964 to make way for an housing estate. The wall surrounding the house is still (1997) in situ (TB March 1997 p13p of house in 1910). Or was demolished in 1968 (SNBP p53). For many years outside the house, and opposite it, were two granite Ice Age boulders (SOB p2).

Wall Lane According to OS map 1:25,000 is a tiny district 0.75m W of Wall, on Watling Street: Moat Bank House is here. But no such district is recognised by VCH vol 14. There is a lane called Wall Lane on the E side of Wall which runs N from Wall Manor Farm at SK 102065 to Pipehill.

Wall Manor Farm On Watling Street, at SK 102065. T-shaped brick house built in 1669 and replaces an earlier house (SVB p167) (VCH vol 14 p285), which has also appeared as Manor Farm.

Wallmires 0.75m SE of Werrington (1834 OS map).

Wallnock Near Axe Edge on the Limes Britannicus, hence Wall (NSFCT 1902 p116).

Wallows, The Small district in undulating fen land 0.75m N of Brierley Hill. Here was a glasshouse. The name, which has also appeared as Wallows, is preserved in The Wallows Industrial Estate. The Wallows was on the Pensnett Line railway (TB March 1975 p28). The name may be from Wallows Well.

Wallows Well Spring at The Straits, Lower Gornal. Its water was used for drinking purposes. Presumably it lay in the Wallows Wood area; the spring may have given its name to the Wallows area. The name is from 'waller' or wallow meaning the hole in the wall (AMS p445). Or from to 'wallow' in (PHS p18).

Wallows Wood At Straits Green (TB Feb 1979 p29). Lower Gornal.

Walls, The House and square enclosed area 0.5m ESE of Enville Hall. It was built as a retreat for Harry Grey, Earl of Stamford (d1739), on part of the former Enville Common. The first house here was built of wood for the earl believed lime was unwholesome. When this building was struck by lightning in 1728 he built another with several rooms and a cellar and enclosed it with a high brick wall forming a square with sides of 400 yards. By 1982 the house had gone but most of the wall remained (SHOS vol 2 pp269-270) (VCH vol 20 p93).

Walls Roman earthwork about Wall Heath (SVB p169). Gives its name to Wall Heath (DUIGNAN p159). 'Walls' probably refers to the Roman fort at Greensforge.

Wall Well Rowley Regis. On Haden estate (BCWJ p15).

Walnut Cottage Betley. (BTC p27il).

Walsall (locally *Wasall* see rhyme under Tamworth). Ancient parish and large town on a large knoll by Walsall Brook 16.25m SSE of Stafford. Lies by the Tame.

EARLY. There is an Ice Age boulder in Walsall Arboretum (SOB p2). Willmore thought the hill on which Walsall parish church is situated may have been enclosed with a ditch or wall and used as a defensive position (HOWW p10). Some **Roman** coins have been found in Walsall: In 1949 a follis of Maximinian near the parish church and an as of Agrippa (63-12 BC) at 51 Emery Street; in 1953 or 1955 a sestertius of Commodus (186-9 AD) at 14 Bernard Road (Arch Newsletter vol 2 p51) (SOB p8) (NSJFS 1964 p41). A Roman brass padlock was found at The Moat Site (see) in 1978.

1000 to 1642. Walsall is not in DB, and it was almost certainly a C12 new town (SL p91 note). But Willmore thought Walsall was in existence at the time of DB, and that it may have been taken in by Bescot, or could have been 'terra regis' or a royal borough and therefore it was not necessary for a record to be made of it, or it was left out in error (HOWW pp44-45). Some have recently thought it did exist as a quasi-urban centre before the Norman Conquest and was included in DB under Willenhall (SSE 1990 p14). Most of the ancient parish lay within Cannock Forest in medieval times (VCH vol 17 p145). Walsall has appeared as Waleshale (1163), and Waleshal (1201) (SPN p134). The prefix in the **name** may be interpreted as 'weal' a wall or well. If a wall then this may have some reference to a Roman fortification (HOWW p34). Or the personal name Wales, Wealh, or Wahl. Or wahl, a foreigner (ie: a Celt) (HOWW p36) (DUIGNAN) (SOSH p28) (SOB p11). The terminal may represent Old English 'heall' or 'heale,' house, hall, palace (HOBLL p2) (S&W p332). Or the Gothic 'alh' indicating some ancient pagan temple here (HOWW p34). Or 'halh,' a shallow valley or nook (NSJFS 1981 p3) (SPN p134). (VCH vol 17 p144) (BCM July 1990 p45). Willmore, Duignan and others have supported Dugdale's suggestion that Walsall is the Walesho mentioned in the will of Wulfric Spot (c1002), founder of Burton Abbey - an estate he bequeathed to his brother Morcar (HOWW p41) (SOSH p322) (VCH vol 17 p144). But CGO Bridgeman and others have suggested Wales, a township in the parish of Laughton-le-Morthen, Yorks (SHC 1916 p28). The manor house was at the Moat Site (see). The parish **church**, St Matthew, on Church Hill, has an uncertain foundation, but it was in existence by 1200 (VCH vol 17 p226). It has a tradition of being moved to its present commanding site from an objectionable position by fairies (SR p108), or from the Chuckery area by witches in the shape of white pigs (N&Q 4th series vol 12 p245) (VCH vol 17 p153 note). It was formerly dedicated to All Saints and has some late C13 work (VCH vol 17 pp230-231), and an unusual vaulted passage leading under the chancel, similar to that of St Peter Mancroft, Norwich (SHOS vol 2 p78) (W p641) (Staffs County Handbook. c1958) (SGS p174). The parish was formed before 1086 and may have originally contained the ancient parishes of Aldridge, Shenstone and Wednesbury (SHC 1916 p194). The **wake** was combined with St Matthew's day (Sept 21) fair (SCSF p106) from 1627 (VCH vol 17 p249). Or commenced on the Sunday before the fair (W p640). In time the wake was fixed for the Monday following the patronal festival, and the next day, Tuesday was a legal fair day. Horse racing, at a course situated between the railway station and the Wednesbury road, was practiced on the following Thursday and Friday; the grandstand at the course disappeared in c1879 (SCSF p106). The wake was discontinued in 1895; it had originally started in 1612 (VCH vol 17 p249) (TEBC). The Easter Monday custom of 'clipping the church' was practised at Walsall in the early C19. The custom involved school children in the forenoon dancing or walking round the church. The symbolism of this activity was thought to represent the

watch of soldiers set round the tomb of Christ by the Roman authorities. The custom was always bought to an end in Walsall with the children being rewarded with Hot Cross buns (SCSF p14) (FOS p91). The custom of **beating the bounds** of the parish was practiced in Walsall (SCSF p24). Parishioners anciently processed to Lichfield cathedral, the mother church, to pay their oblations in 'St Chad Farthings' or other money (SCSF p11). There were two **religious guilds** in Walsall in the Middle Ages which amalgamated in 1520 (NSJFS 1979 p15). By the C15 the hall of St John's guild in High Street was used as the town hall (VCH vol 17 p218). There was a **conduit house** over the water supply from Vicarage Moor (see) in High Street, built in c1677. The conduit house was inscribed in gold letters and adorned with the arms of Walsall (VCH vol 17 p222). In the later C17 Plot noted a well in the grounds of John Carberlege's house, which was aluminous, hence acidic (NHS p106). A **pound** at Walsall occurs in 1361-62. A **pound** stood on the E side of Stafford Street, Townend, in the later C18 and the earlier C19. In 1861 a new pound was built in Freer Street by the pig market (VCH vol 17 p219).

Mumming case. A case brought by the mayor, Roger Dyngley, and inhabitants of Walsall against some men of Wednesbury was heard in the Star Chamber in 1498. Two men, John Cradley of Wednesbury and Thomas Morres of Dudley, were accused of beating the mayor of Walsall and another Walsall man, Thomas Rice, in Walsall. They were captured and imprisoned. The leading men of Wednesbury and Wolverhampton gathered 200 Wednesbury men and threatened riot at the forthcoming Trinity fair at Willenhall in order to obtain their release. The mayor of Walsall petitioned the High Court to restrain the Wednesbury rioters. The defence of the leading men of Wednesbury and Wolverhampton was that they had a right to be at the fair since a mumming play was to be performed there - the moneys collected going to the church - and the mummers had always traditionally comprised the inhabitants of Walsall, Wolverhampton, and Wednesbury. It is not known in whose favour the case terminated (SCSF pp37-40). The mayor and burgesses protested against **ship money** in 1636 (SOB p71) (HOS p34). Walsall had the plague of 1636 (SCSF p135). **Persons and visitors.** Bishop Langton stayed at Walsall on Jan 10 1319 (SSE 1994 p2). There is a belief **Elizabeth I** came to Walsall in June and July 1586 (WPP p80) and slept in a house in Ablewell Street, where the Red Lion stands, but, Shaw could find no authority for this (SHOS vol 2 p74). Col **John 'Tinker' Fox**, well-known parliamentary leader, was born in Walsall in 1610, the son of a tinker of the same name. He became a blacksmith. In the Civil War he took the royalist strongholds of Edgbaston Hall, Hawkesley House, Clent, Aston Hall, and Stourton Castle. He was at the siege of Dudley Castle and the battle of Tipton Green. Parliament awarded him with two thirds of Edgbaston manor and two thirds of Robert Middlemore's lands in King's Norton. Some have speculated that he was Charles I's executioner (WPP p81) (TB Oct 1985 p15).

THE BOROUGH. Various dates are given for the town's first charter granted by the lord of the manor, Sir William Rufus or William le Rous which created Walsall a borough and granted the burgesses quittance from every service, custom, and secular demand except tallage; **1100** (WPP pp74,75); 1159 (Staffs County Handbook. c1958); c1197 (HOWW p159) (SOSH p324) (NSJFS 1972 p69); c1235 (VCH vol 17 p212); in Edward III's reign (SSAHST 1975-76 pp65-71) (SGS p176). The charter of **1309** discharged the burgesses from tallage and pannage. The charter of **1627** appointed a mayor and 24 capital burgesses. This charter was surrendered in 1683 and restored in 1688. It remained in force until 1835 (VCH vol 17 pp212-216) (Staffs County Handbook. c1958) (HOS p56) (WPP p77). Walsall cartulary documents are in BM (WH Robinson's 'Transactions of Ancient Documents in the Walsall Cartulary' 1914) (W p638) (SSAHST 1982-83 pp1-7) (WPP pp75-77). Walsall's roll of **mayors**, dating back to 1377, is the most complete of any borough in the county (Staffs County Handbook. c1958). Willmore thinks the office of mayor pre-dates 1377 (HOWW p164). **Clement's Accompt** is the name for the custom of drawing up of the borough's accounts, which took place on St Clement's eve, and the presentation of the accounts by the mayor on St Clement's day (Nov 23): Burgesses who had not paid their dues by then were heavily fined. The business concluded with a peculiar custom. Apples and nuts were thrown, to be scrambled for, from the windows of the Guildhall. It was also a custom to admit the Grammar School boys into the Guildhall to scramble for apples thrown from the magistrates' bench. The custom was discontinued in 1860. The wardens of the Guild showed their accounts three weeks later on St Katherine's day (HOWW pp428-429) (BCC vol 3 p176) (FLJ 1914 p296) (VCH vol 17 p250). The **arms** of Walsall county borough, granted to Walsall corporation in the C15, are: Royal Arms of England (France and England quarterly) flanked by two lions seated with their backs to the shield and with their tails intertwined, and ensigned by an open crown of fleur-de-lis. Grassy mount inside the crown and seated there on a bear supporting a ragged staff (CH p331il). Walsall owes its arms of the 'Bear and Ragged Staff' to the Earls of Warwick, lords of the manor (SOSH p325) (BCM Feb 1968 pp41-42il). **Bayard's Colts.** Walsall has a set of 17 clubs, halberds and pikes which may be the survivors of the thousand 'Colts of Bayard' mentioned in a document dated 1524-5. In the document the mayor threatened that if the lord of the manor of Walsall attempted to prosecute him and his burgesses for alleged misdemeanours, they would ring Bayard's bell and summon Bayard and his thousand colts to deal with him: 'these coltes being great clubs which have been of long time set and hanged up on high in the Guildhall and be at certain times borne about the town in great reverence, which thing to be suffered is a great abomination.' There may never have been a thousand colts as such: merely, that number was picked out of the air by the mayor to illustrate the strength of the corporation. Bayard may have been alluded to, since he was then, as a French king who had taken part in the wars between Francis I of France and Charles V of Spain, and who was killed in 1524, famous for chivalric virtue. The name colts may be from the fact that two of the present club heads represent horses or colts. There may then have been no more than the present number of colts, which were, probably, at various stages copied from the originals. The colts now comprise 12 clubs with carved heads (mostly of C17; one has the date 1712), two halberds (of C17 and C18), two pole-axes (of C16), and a bill (of C15 or C16). The clubs may have originated as mummers' staves and never formed part of an armoury. They are on average five or six feet long, the carved heads being six or eight inches in size. The carvings portray two demon-like faces, a lamb's head, a placid horse and an angry horse. There are three heads, possibly representing a king, a nobleman and a priest, whose countenances are calm and it could perhaps be said that they are almost smiling. Two other characters show gnashing teeth and fearsomely angry faces. It has been suggested therefore that the clubs can be divided into 'good' and bad' characters - the essentials of medieval morality plays. A bell and a box are also associated with the clubs - these were possibly used for collecting money during plays. Since medieval times until the early C19 the clubs, halberds etc have been used for the maintenance of order and ritually accompanied the mayor to markets, fairs and other ceremonial processions. When not in use they were hung up in the guildhall: Shaw, White, Willmore and Hackwood noted them there. The painting, 'Walking the Fair' showing the colts, painted by Alfred Mudge in 1859, is owned by Wolverhampton Art Gallery but is usually on loan to Walsall Museum. In 1969 two of the colts fell from their hanging place while the court at the Guildhall, High Street, was in session, and were found to be infested with furniture beetle. They were then all transferred to Walsall Museum, Lichfield Street, and restored. After at least a 100 years the colts were carried again in a 'Walking the Fair' re-enactment in 1996, which had been instigated by Councillor Cyril Leaker; Tony Sawbridge's painting of this event hangs in Walsall Museum. By the late 1980s 15 colts were displayed at the new Magistrates Courts in Stafford Street, whilst two (the king and the 'angry' horse) were displayed at Walsall Museum (info Walsall Museum and Carl Franklin) (SHOS vol 2 p73) (W p640) (HOWW pp90-91,183) (CCC p81) (FLJ 1970 pp266-267 ps) (VCH vol 17 p220) (WPP p76).

BOROUGH AND FOREIGN. With borough status established for Walsall, apparently in the C13, the rest of Walsall ancient parish or manor became known as the foreign (or Walsall Foreign) (VCH vol 17 p209). The relationship between Walsall's borough and foreign seem to have been more colourful than those of Dudley and Wolverhampton. The borough consisted of Walsall town and consisted of about 100 acres, whilst the foreign, which consisted of 7,782 acres (HOWW pp5-6), contained the town's out-lying hamlets of Bescot, Blakenhall Heath, Bloxwich, Bloxwich Lane, Broadstone, Caldmore, Coalpool, Dead Man's Heath, Fishley, Goscote, Harden, Short Heath, Wallington Heath and Woodend (SOB pp107,113). In the charter of William Rufus to the burgesses of Walsall the term 'forin woods' occurs (SOB p106). A lease in 1485 contains the words 'of the Manor of the Forren of Walshall' (SOB p106). By the earlier C17 parish government was divided into borough and foreign townships, each with its own rates, vestry meeting and relief for the poor (SHOS vol 2 p73*) (SOB p107) (VCH vol 17 p210). The **boundary** of the foreign was uncertain. For many years the word 'Borough' referred to the Hill of Walsall but no clear boundary had ever existed defining the two. Park Street was in the borough but Townend Bank lay in the foreign (SOB p107). This was in itself a matter of contention. The foreign won a case for fixing the boundaries in 1814 (SOB p116) (VCH vol 17 p209). The **inhabitants** of the borough were mainly tradesmen and metal workers, whilst the foreigners were farmers, cattle producers, tanners, miners, weavers, tailors, bitmakers and locksmiths (SOB p107). Over the **Civil War** period the foreign was royalist and Presbyterian the borough staunchly parliamentarian and puritan (SOB p10). One dispute between the two after the

Civil War was a complaint made to the Crown in a petition by the mainly royalist foreign that the borough was sympathetic to nonconformity in the town. This may have been the reason why the proposed mayor was taken ill on election day 1680 and no mayor was then appointed. In this state the charter of 1627 became null and void and Walsall lost its ancient rights. A writ was issued by the Crown against those carrying on government in the town, and they had to beg for the king's pardon, and ask for a new charter or a confirmation of the old one. This, the last charter, was obtained in 1682 and is printed in a pamphlet by Smart (SOB p111) (SHOSA vol 2 p15). The **rents** were collected differently between the foreign and borough. The lord of the manor's stewards collected individually from those in the foreign, but collectively from those in the borough. This, too, was a contentious matter: As was the use of **public charities**. It was often queried whether the charities were fairly distributed over the borough and foreign: The foreign contending that their inhabitants did not receive due proportion of the charities. Commissions were set up in 1614, 1682, 1726, 1804, 1823 and 1855 to solve the distribution of charities (SOB p111). The **poor rate**, by tradition, was collected by each authority from its own inhabitants for its own poor. But it was considered unjust by the borough that borough men who inhabited the borough, but were also tenants in the foreign, could be rated twice, once by foreign overseers and once by borough overseers. But foreign men, who inhabited the foreign and were property holders in the borough, were only rated by foreign overseers. Also contentious was the inconsistency between levies; the foreign having fewer poor charged less. In 1752 the borough tried to implement a single collection and rate and dispense with the foreign overseers. Samuel Wilks, one of the two foreign overseers, protested and was sent to prison. The borough used Walsall's charter of incorporation (1627) to prove its case. It stated that Walsall should be 'one body corporate and politic in deed, fact, and name.' The case for the foreign was taken up by the wealthy and powerful of Bloxwich. Their case rested on past practice and they were incensed by the imprisonment of the respectable Mr Wilks. After a court case the foreign won in 1754 (SOB p116) (VCH vol 17 p211). The long-running poor rate dispute ended with the establishment of the Walsall Union of Parishes in 1835; Walsall Borough and Walsall Foreign becoming two of the eight townships (W p636) (SOB p116). In 1866 the two townships were created civil parishes. In 1894 these were abolished to help create Walsall county borough (GLAUE p427). Foreign Ward, created in 1835 with the creation of the new municipal borough of Walsall, ceased to exist with the establishment of Bloxwich as a ward of the new county borough and any form of the foreign's political independence ceased to exist (SOB pp106,107).

MARKETS AND FAIRS. William Ruffus (or Le Rous), lord of the manor, acquired a **market** for Walsall sometime between 1219-20 to be held on Mondays (SCSF p102) (NSJFS 1971 p50) (VCH vol 17 p187) (SL p174). Mention of market tolls is made as early as 1283 (SCSF p94). The market was confirmed in 1399 (VCH vol 17 p187) and by a charter of 1402 (THS) (SCSF p94) (SOSH p325). In 1417 the market was changed to Tuesday (VCH vol 17 p187). There was an additional market on Saturdays by 1845 (VCH vol 17 p187). (OWEN) (LHE p265) (SCSF p93). There was **market cross** by 1386. By the C16 it stood at the top of High Street and shortly before 1589 was replaced by a market house (known as the High Cross or High Cross House) built on the same site. This also served as a judgment hall, charity school (SCSF p90), and gaol (VCH vol 17 pp187,219) at various times. It was rebuilt in half timber in 1692 by the corporation. By 1734 it was reported to be in disrepair (SCSF p90) and was demolished in 1800 (SHOS vol 2 p74) (WBF p111) (VCH vol 17 p187) or 1802 (HOWW pp193-4) (SCSF p90). Pearce, writing in 1813, says it was still standing and there were plans to demolish it. While Glew, writing in 1856, says it was demolished in 1809 (SCSF pp89-90). In 1809 the corporation replaced it with a smaller house a few yards uphill, adjoining the steps leading to St Matthew's church. It was demolished in 1852 (VCH vol 17 p187). **Fairs.** A charter of 1417-18 granted a weekly market and two annual fairs (SOSH p325) (SCSF p102). **St Matthias' Day** (Feb 24) (granted by the charter of 1627) (OWEN) (COOKE) (SCSF pp98,99). This fair was popularly known as the Orange Fair (VCH vol 17 p188). **St John before the Latin Gate** (May 6), granted in 1417 (VCH vol 17 p187). **Whit Tuesday** held by prescription, not charter (OWEN) (COOKE). **Nativity of St John the Baptist** (June 24) (and eve of) granted in 1399. It was replaced by another fair in 1417 (VCH vol 17 p187). **St Matthew the Apostle** (Sept 21) (eve and day of), granted by the charter of 1219-20 (SCSF p102) (VCH vol 17 p187). This fair was originally combined with the wake (SCSF p106). In time the wake was fixed for the Monday following the patronal festival, and the next day, Tuesday was a legal fair day (SCSF p106). Hence White giving the fair as the Tuesday after St Matthew's day (W 640). It was replaced by another fair in 1417 (VCH vol 17 p187). Tuesday before the feast of **St Michael** (Sept 29) (granted by the charter of 1627) (OWEN) (COOKE) (SCSF p102). This fair was popularly known as the Onion Fair (VCH vol 17 p188). Shaw says, some say erroneously Oct 10 (SHOS vol 2 p74). (This may be a confirmation of the fair of St Matthew the Apostle). **St Simon and St Jude's** day (Oct 28), granted 1417 (VCH vol 17 p187). Walsall had a court of pyepowder (or called pie powder, or court of dusty foot) held by the bailiffs at fairs (W p638) (VCH vol 17 p188). For the origins of the word Pyepowder see under Lichfield. Walsall had an annual 'walking the fair' procession at which were borne Bayard's Colts (see below) (HOWM p43); the mayor was walking the fair by the 1640s. In 1647 it was decreed that the 24 capital burgesses should walk with him, wearing their gowns; they were accompanied by escorts carrying the Bayard's Colts from the C17 to probably the early C19 after which the practice of carrying the colts died out. The custom of walking the fair was abolished in the early 1870s (VCH vol 17 p188). There is a painting 'Walking the Fair' by A Mudge in c1840, depicting a scene on The Bridge, Walsall (BCM April 1990 p25).

INDUSTRY. There was mining of iron and coal at Walsall by the end of the C13 (VCH vol 17 p189) (SL p78), and limestone was quarried close to the town centre into the C20. Leland in his Itinerary notes all three being mined in c1540 (SL p94). There has been cloth-making, tanning and leather-working in Walsall parish since the mid C15 - in view of which Walsall had called itself 'the leather capital of Britain' (The Guardian. Society Section. Sept 23 1998 p6) - ; brick-making and lock-making since the C17; file-making and tinning since the late C17; brush-making from the latter half of the C18; tube-making from the early C19; organ-building from the latter half of the C19 (VCH vol 17 pp192-208). In 1600 all the town's metal workers were still helping with the harvest and agreeing to avoid their trade at that time (SL p156). Generally Walsall has manufactured bits, bridles, spurs, stirrups and whip-thongs for riding. It has worked pewter, copper and brass, especially making buckles for the Birmingham leather industry. When that trade slumped in the early C19, the town took to saddle making. Its production of metal components for harnesses led to making harnesses and whips from the mid C19 (VB p59) (MR p357). In the early C19 it made gun barrels, like Wednesbury, and, when that trade slumped after the Napoleonic Wars, it made tubes for gas and water (HOS p45). White, in 1834, said the grey limestone E of Walsall was surpassed by none in the kingdom for its extraordinary adhesive qualities and its strength and durability, hence it was then in great demand (HOWW p241). In the early C20 Walsall manufactured motor cars (the Crescent between 1911 and 1915 - PVBC p20), motor car fittings, electrical components, steel and iron tubes (LGS p247) (VCH vol 17 p208). Different industries were often confined to separate districts of the town: leather dressing along the Mill Fleam in the E, bridlebitmaking and saddlers' toolmaking to the N in Bloxwich, chain and gearmaking around Butts, Ryecroft and east Birchills, saddlery and saddlers' ironmongery around Caldmore and Windmill districts to the S, and heavier, large scale industries in west Birchills, Pleck and Hatherton (SSE 1991 p77). The expression 'He waddles like a Walsall duck' refers to the fact Walsall men are suppose to be bandy-legged, owing to the way the men held the saddler's wooden vice between their knees, with feet touching at work (FLJ 1896 pp366-386). The manorial **watermill**, Town Mill, stood on Walsall Water to the N of what is now the Bridge (VCH vol 17 p185), at SP 013988 (TMS p72). It has been variously known as Walsall Mill, Ford Mill, Port Mill, Old Mill, and Malt Mill. It was part of Walsall manor by 1247 and was demolished or converted to other uses by 1763 (VCH vol 17 p185), others say it was demolished in 1813. Hughes, writing in 1925, noted the corporation still paid the lord of the manor two shillings a year in acknowledgement of his legal right still to grind their corn (SOSH p325). For New Mills see New Mills. There was a **windmill** in West Bromwich Road near the White Lion Inn in the C19. A painting by Billy Meikle, a local historian, photographer and artist, shows it to have been a four storey stone-built tower with single tail pole projecting from the rear of the cap frame. When recorded in c1870 the cap had gone and only the remnants of the four common sails were left. It was demolished in c1885 (WBJ p41) (Walsall Chronicle No. 4 1982 'Billy Meikle's View of Walsall'). Plot's map shows two windmills in the area between Goscote, Shelfield, and Pelsall (VCH vol 17 p186). For other windmills in Walsall ancient parish see Blakenall Heath, Bloxwich, Goscote, Highgate, Shelfield, Spring Hill, Blackham's Mill, Persehouse's Mill, and Morteyn's Mill. These references - SLM spring 1954 p25 and WIS pp13ps,23 - refer to Walsall windmills, but it is uncertain as to which.

MOSELEY'S DOLE. A defunct charity for the giving out of pennies or penny loaves to every person living in the ancient parishes of Walsall and Rushall. Provided for at some time out of the estate of Thomas Moseley (or Mollesley). The charity was administered on the eve of Epiphany or Twelfth Eve (Jan 5) (SCSF p7), or on Epiphany or Twelfth Day (Jan 6) (HYB pp54,55). Accounts

vary as to when and how Moseley's estate became appropriated to charity use. The **traditional account** says whilst riding through the town on the eve of Epiphany Thomas Moseley, a native of Walsall, heard a child crying for bread. Moseley resolved to settle his manor of Bascot or Bascote in Long Itchington, Warws, upon the town to provide a penny loaf for every person within the liberties of Walsall on Epiphany Eve forever (SCSF p7) (VCH vol 17 p266). **Plot's account** dispels the tradition (SH p59) and puts forward that Thomas Moseley, of Moxhull, by deed of feoffment, dated St Nicholas day 1452, granted his manor of Bascote to the church of Walsall and Halesowen Abbey for an annual obit for his soul and that of his wife, Margaret. And that the rental from his estate at Bascote did not fully come into the corporation until after the Reformation when it was sold to one Shaw and Headcock and they sold it to the mayor and communality of Walsall (NHS pp314-315). No mention is made in the deed of any dole to be given. The first record of Moseley's estate being bestowed on the poor is in 1539 when the bellman summoned people to go to the church to pray for the souls of Thomas and Margaret Moseley when the dole was given. It is uncertain whether the church gave any bread dole out of Moseley's estate before this date (SCSF p8). After the Reformation obits were abolished. The Bascote manor remained Crown property until 1586, the town, however, renting the land and continuing the dole. Elizabeth I then gave the manor to Sir Jacob Crofts, the Controller of her household, who sold it to two men, named Shaw and Headcock respectively, who in turn sold it to the Walsall corporation, in whose hands the property still was in 1924 (SCSF p8). Sir William **Dugdale's account**, from his History of Warws, says nothing about the dole while giving an account of the Moseley gift to Walsall. Dugdale says Moseley gave his manor of Bascote in trust in 1452 to William Lyle and Thomas Magot, for the use of the town of Walsall. Lyle outlived Magot. When Lyle himself died, his son John claimed it as his own land, denying the trust. A suit was commenced by the town against him in 1515. The suit adjudged to Richard Hurst and John Ford, for the use of Walsall, who soon after made a new feoffment. The manor then continued in the hands of trustees to at least the later C17 (History of Warwickshire. William Dugdale. p347). From this account, says Hackwood, it has been thought that Hurst and Ford were the first beginners of the dole, and that they gave it the name of Moseley's Dole (SCSF p8). **Shaw's account** (SHOS vol 2 pp67,73) (SHOS vol 2 p15). Dr **Wilkes' account** says in 1726 a commission inquired into the charity. It was established that the lands then belonged to the corporation and the dole was only customary, continued at the corporation's discretion. There had been one attempt to end the dole but the populace so vehemently petitioned for its continuation that the corporation reinstated it (Universal Magazine. Jan 1788). **Later accounts** say in the years leading up to the discontinuation of the dole a penny was paid to each inhabitant of Walsall and Rushall by a man who went round with a bag of pennies, and having ascertained the number of persons in each house, left as many pence. The distribution day was regarded by the children as a day of rejoicing (SCSF p8). The dole continued until 1823 (HOWW pp197,259-261) (VCH vol 17 p267), or 1825 (BCC vol 2 pp68-74), or 1832 (HYB pp54,55), when Charity Commissioners raised objection to the method of distribution. With the endowment the corporation built 11 almshouses for widows in Bath Street in 1825 (HOWW pp197,259-261). There was one house for Rushall, and five each for the borough and the foreign. Each occupant received 2s per week, paid out of the general borough funds (SCSF p8). The Bath Street almshouses were demolished in 1952 and replaced in 1955 by seven bungalows in Heather Close, Bloxwich and four in Sandbank, Bloxwich. The bungalow occupants were still receiving a weekly allowance out of the Mollesley Dole fund in 1972 (VCH vol 17 p267). (SD pp10,11,22,23 - at Rushall) (SMC pp173,174) (SSC p51) (Old English Customs. Edwards. 1842 p55) (W p645) (WPP p76) (FOS p80). For other Walsall charities see VCH vol 17 pp267-275.

PUNISHMENTS. **Stocks** stood by the Market Cross (High Cross) in the C17. There were stocks on show in Walsall Arboretum between at least 1924 and 1974 (SCSF pp127,129-130) (VCH vol 17 p219). The **whipping post** stood by the Market Cross (SCSF p127). (VCH vol 17 p219). The lord of the manor claimed the right to gallows in 1293. A pasture called Gallows Leasow probably in the Bloxwich area may preserve the site of the **gallows** (VCH vol 17 p210). The lord of the manor claimed the right to **pillory** in 1293 (VCH vol 17 p210). A pillory stood by the Market Cross (SCSF p127). (VCH vol 17 p219). The lord of the manor claimed the right to **tumbrel** in 1293 (VCH vol 17 p210). Walsall's **scold's bridle** went to Greene's Museum at Lichfield (HOWW) (SCSF p125). (VCH vol 17 p219). Walsall's **cucking stool** was retrieved from the town brook in 1661 or 1662 (SCSF p126). For the **lock up** see Ablewell. (VCH vol 17 p219).

GRAMMAR SCHOOL. Was founded in 1554 (W pp644-645). It stood in St

Matthew's churchyard until 1813 (HOWW pp215-216). In the churchyard it occupied an old timber building known as the Burgess Hall (see) (SNWA p30). In 1813 (HOWW pp215-216) or in 1815 (VCH vol 6 pp174-176) the school moved to Park Street where it was situated until 1847 when it moved to the grandstand on the race course. In 1850 it moved to a new brick building in Lichfield Street, designed in the Tudor style by Edward Adams, a former pupil (VCH vol 6 pp174-176) (SGS p176). The name of the school changed from 'The Free Grammar School of St Mary at Walsall' to 'Queen Mary's Grammar School' in 1909. The school moved to Mayfield estate on the Sutton Road, Walsall in 1964 (VCH vol 6 p176, il of c1854 facing p145. vol 17 p255) (WROP pp45il,46il,49p). The school maintains an annual Founder's Day tradition of laying a wreath on Mary I's tomb in Westminster Abbey. Another tradition connected with the school was the ringing of St Matthew's church bell each day at seven in the morning and again at noon to call boys to meals. The custom continued until the early C20, long after the grammar school had left the churchyard site (SNWA p30). The school magazine is 'The Marian' (BCM April 1991 pp15-20). **Alumni**: Possibly Lord John Somers (1650-1716), Solicitor-General, Attorney General, Lord Keeper, and Lord High Chancellor and patron of Locke and Newton (SHOS vol 2 p74; some say he was educated privately at Sheriff Hales) (W p643) (SNWA p98); Phineas Fowke of Little Wyrley Hall, physician, theologian, classical scholar; John Hough, bishop of Lichfield (and Coventry); Thomas Newton (1810-1889), writer for the Walsall Observer and South Staffordshire Chronicle; John Edward Gray (1800-1875), Keeper of the BM's Zoological Collections (BCM autumn 1993 p57); Sir Henry Newbolt (1862-1938), poet (VB p56); James A Aldis (1842-1936), poet, taught at the school between 1879 and 1897 (VFC p2) and sometime headmaster of the school (SNWA p5); George Woden (alias George Wilson Slaney) (1884-1979), novelist of Wednesbury (see); Harold Parry (1896-1917), poet of Bloxwich (see); Herbert Bennett (d1918), poet (VFC pp12-13); Maurice Wiggin (b1912), editor and novelist of Bloxwich (see); Lord Harmar-Nicholls (b1912), Conservative politician and MEP (BCM Dec 1997 pp10-12); Douglas Orgill (b1922), novelist, journalist and military historian and native of Walsall (VFC p100).

BLUE COAT SCHOOL. Walsall Blue Coat School, Bridge Street, is of uncertain origin. It existed in Walsall by the earlier C18 and may date back to the mid C17 (VCH vol 17 pp254,256). Formerly the school was held in a room over the High Cross, which stood at the top of High Street (HOWW pp223-224). After its demolition in 1800 the school moved to Digbeth (VCH vol 17 p256). Money raised for a plate to present to Queen Caroline (wife of George IV), which she could not receive for she died in 1821, paid for the two statues executed by a local sculptor situated in niches either side of the entrance. They represent a boy and a girl in the school uniform (W p645) (HOWW p224). The effigies were removed by Henry Taylor, one of the managers of the school, and were used as ornaments in his garden at The Hawthorns (see) (there since lost) (SNWA p19). The school amalgamated with the National School in 1820 (HOWW pp223-224) or formally in 1826. In 1859 the schools were transferred to St Paul's Close, which was demolished in 1933 and became the bus station. The senior school, which became secondary modern after 1944, moved to its present site between Birmingham Road and Springhill Road in 1965 (VCH vol 17 pp256-257) (WROP p53il of c1828).

CIVIL WAR AND COMMONWEALTH PERIOD. The town was not garrisoned for either side during the war (VCH vol 17 p146). Queen Henrietta Maria stayed at George Hawe's House (White Hart Inn) in Caldmore in 1642 (LGS p248) (OWB p71) (VCH vol 17 p146). Another tradition says she stayed at the old Red Lion Inn in Ablewell Street on site of Ablewell Street Wesleyan chapel (OWB p71). Others say she was in the town in July 1643 en route to take reinforcements to the king (SOSH p325) (SOB p75) (HOS p34) (VCH vol 17 p146). In 1644 the parliamentarian army under the Earl of Denbigh were quartered in Walsall during the siege of Rushall Hall (VCH vol 17 p146). Such had been the support for Republicanism in the borough at Charles II's Restoration 14 out of 24 members of the corporation refused to take the Oath of Allegiance and thereby lost their positions (SOB p110).

1660 to 1800. In 1665 Walsall took precautions against receiving the **plague** from London (SCSF pp138-139). In 1684 a quarrel between Cavaliers of the foreign and puritans of the borough over the borough's conduct during and after the Civil War-Commonwealth period was resolved with the signing of a **concordat** between the two. The Town Clerk had to recite it at a borough council meeting to quell bitterness between Labour and Independent members on one occasion before WW2 (SOB p111). **Riots**. The Presbyterian meeting house owned by John Godley in Bank (later Fox's and Cox's) Court on N side of High Street was attacked on July 8 1715 (VCH vol 17 p248) (LOU pp87,359). The Walsall riots on 'Oak Apple day,' May 29 1750, were in protest against the reign of George II. Three hundred people are said to have

gathered round the effigy of the monarch and mocked and attacked it (HOWW pp367-369) (Walsall Records. 1914) (TB Aug 1988 p6. Sept 1988 p5) (LOU pp105-107,366). There was another riot at Hill Top (see) in 1751. There were food riots in Walsall in 1800 (HOWV p122). The **Walsall Troop** of the Staffordshire Volunteer Cavalry (later Staffordshire Yeomanry) was raised by Capt W Tennant in 1794 (FSP p60). **Persons and visitors. George Holden**, a butcher at Walsall in the C17, suffered badly from periodical asthma. A postmortem after his death revealed no phlegm on his lungs nor any natural cause for the asthma, but many stones in his gall bladder which may have upset the nerves to his lungs or to some part of his breathing apparatus (NHS pp301-302). At Walsall Dr Plot also noted a tallow from the suet of a bull from Rugeley which shone like a beacon for 10 days continuously and drew great crowds to see it (NHS p265). **John Reynolds** (1667-1727), writer of tracts and hymns, was assistant minister at the Presbyterian meeting-house from 1721 until his death (VCH vol 17 p145). **Josiah Owen** (1711-1755), author of sermons and anti-Jacobite tracts, was minister of the Presbyterian meeting-house in the 1730s (VCH vol 17 p145). **John Wesley** (or Charles Wesley) was pelted at the market house on May 21 1742 and thrown to the ground on three occasions (LOU p113). John Wesley had a rough reception on his first visit to the town on Oct 20 1743 (WPP p86). He visited Walsall on March 26 1764 despite the advice of an itinerant preacher, James Jones. He went to a newly formed branch of the Wesleyan Society at the Castle Inn, Dudley Street (SOB p144). Of this, his second visit, he noted 'There was no opposer, no, nor a trifler to be seen. How is Walsall changed! How has God either tamed the wild beasts or chained them up!' (LGS p247). The actor, **William or Colin Siddons** (d1808) was born in Russell Street, Walsall in 1744; his father kept the inn 'The London Apprentice.' Siddons Snr died by accident, in sparring or wrestling with a man called Denston (SHOS vol 2 p75) (W p644) (TEBC) (TEBC2 p14). In 1766 Siddons Jnr gave a performance of 'Douglas' at a malt-house in Lime Pit Bank (SHOS vol 2 pp75 and app. 15) (VCH vol 17 p250) (SNWA p9). In 1773 he married Sarah Kemble, the famous tragic actress (The private life of Mrs Siddons. Naomi Royde-Smith. 1933) (Sarah Siddons: Portrait of an Actress. Roger Manvell. 1970) (TEBC) (The Cambridge Biographical Encyclopedia. David Crystal. 1994); their son, Henry (d1815), born in Wolverhampton on Oct 4 1774, became an actor and playwright of some note (PSS p470) (VFC p122). **James Gee** (d1827), who supplied Stebbing Shaw with an account of Walsall for SHOS, was born in 1746 (BCM Oct 1992 pp76-79). Some believe **Dr Johnson** of Lichfield (see) made his penance in Walsall Market Place as recorded in an early edition of Boswell's 'Life of Johnson' and not at Uttoxeter as in later editions (WPP p87); he is said to have frequented The Old Still Hotel (see) in Digbeth, Walsall. **Thomas Haskey**, a celebrated ventriloquist, was born in Walsall in c1770. In the summer of 1796 he appeared at Sadler's Wells, London. His stage name was 'Askins' (SHOS vol 2 p75) (W p644). For Rev **John Darwell**, hymn composer, who died in Walsall in 1789, see under Haughton. **Thomas Jackson**, writer and soldier in the Staffs Militia, was born in Walsall in 1786. He was taken prisoner in the Napoleonic wars in Holland in winter 1813-14 and lost his leg. On his return to England he was discharged. His autobiography (c1845) is a document of social life in Walsall and the cholera epidemic of 1832 (BCM July 1978 pp54-59) (Old Walsall and district in years gone by. Walsall Observer. March 1999. p31).

1800 to 1850. The new **municipal borough** of Walsall, created in 1835, was divided into three wards, Bridge, St George's, and Foreign (VCH vol 17 p217). The church, **St Peter**, in Stafford Street was consecrated in 1844 (VCH vol 17 p236). The church, **St Paul**, Darwell Street, was built in 1893 (LDD). **Political unrest**. The failure of the Duke of Wellington to support the Reform Act in 1832 led to numerous demonstrations against him. At Walsall on May 23 an effigy of him was paraded through the streets of Walsall and several people fired at it; one person was hurt in the face (SA May 19 1832 p4) (HOWW p409) (LOU p218). A bye-election for Walsall occurred in Feb 1841. It excited much national interest as it was made the occasion of an all out battle between the Tories and the Liberals over the issue of the abolition of the Corn Laws. Such were the frenzied emotions of the parties, the Yeomanry and a troop of the Scots Greys were in readiness to maintain order. Capt Gladstone, a Tory, was returned with a majority of 20 votes, but only held the seat for a week as parliament was dissolved for a general election. CS Forster, the Liberal candidate, said he would like to see 'all the horses in the world harnessed by Walsall saddlers; all the soles of all the boots pierced by Bloxwich awls; all the boxes fastened by Walsall locks; all the world's dust swept by Walsall brushes' (SOB pp161-162). The **cholera epidemic** of 1832 reached Walsall parish on Aug 13 and claimed 85 lives in the parish (TB Feb 1998 p17). **Manor Hospital** in Moat Street and Pleck Road was built as the workhouse in 1838-42 (BOE p297). It is said to be haunted by the ghosts of a

grumpy old matron, a very pretty nurse, an ambulance and general polter-geist activity (GOM p27) (GPCE p49). **Coach accident**. In 1834 the 'Albion' stage coach was involved in an accident in Park Street, Walsall, while con-veying a party of convicts to Portland. The Deputy Governor of Chester Gaol was killed and two convicts escaped (HOWW) (TEBC2 p40). Walsall was connected to London and Liverpool via Bescot by **railway** from Nov 1 1847 (SSR p10); with Derby from from April 9 1849 and with Dudley via Bescot from May 1 1850 (NSJFS 1962 p99). In Dec 1854 a goods train ran into the back of another at Walsall and a third goods train coming in the opposite direction ran into the wreckage. The driver of the third goods train was killed (SSR p22). **Persons and visitors**. **AM Roe**, poetess, born deaf and in great poverty in Walsall, was the author in her teens of 'Poems on Several Occa-sions' published by subscription in two volumes in 1807 (PSS p469) (VFC p114). **George Holden**, Snr, prize fighter, was born in Adams Row, off Digbeth, in 1821 (BCM July 1972 pp45-51). For Rev **George Fisk**, poet and vicar of Walsall in the mid C19, see Darlaston (Offlow hundred). Walsall's mayor, **John Hyatt Harvey**, accidentally drowned on the July 8 1845 whilst bathing in a worked-out limestone quarry pit which had been filled with wa-ter then situated in Lichfield Street. This pool has been incorporated into Walsall Arboretum (TEBC2 p55) (Portrait of the Black Country. Harold Par-sons. 1986. p98). An explosion at St Matthew's just after the departure of the congregation on Sunday morning Oct 10 1847 blew out the W window and killed the beadle, **James Lunn**, aged 43, who accidentally ignited gas escap-ing from under a pew (W p642) (SHC 1970 p26 il facing).
NEWSPAPERS. The weekly **Walsall Courier and South Staffordshire Ga-zette** ran for a short time from 1855. The weekly **Walsall Guardian and District Advertiser**, founded on April 12 1856, ran to 1869 (VCH vol 17 pp252-253) (SHJ spring 1996 p30). The Liberal weekly **Walsall Free Press and General Advertiser**, founded in 1856, became the Walsall Free Press and South Staffordshire Advertiser from Jan 7 1882 (SHJ spring 1996 p29); in 1903 when it was incorporated into the Walsall Observer (VCH vol 17 pp252-253). The **Walsall Advertiser and Newspaper**, founded in 1857, be-came the Walsall Advertiser in 1892, and this became the Walsall Pioneer and District News in 1916. In 1922 this was incorporated into the Walsall Observer. The weekly **Walsall Herald**, founded on Jan 5 1861, became the Walsall Herald and District Intelligencer from April 13 1861, then as Walsall Herald and Willenhall and Bloxwich Advertiser from June 29 1861 to at least June 25 1862 (VCH vol 17 pp252-253) (SHJ spring 1996 p30). The Liberal weekly **Walsall News and General District Advertiser**, founded on Sept 23 1865, ran to 1872 (SHJ spring 1996 p30). A **Walsall Standard** was founded in the 1850s or the 1860s (VCH vol 17 pp252,253). The weekly **Walsall Observer and General District Advertiser**, founded by late Oct 1868, be-came the Walsall Observer and South Staffordshire Chronicle from Jan 4 1873 (VCH vol 17 pp252,253) (SHJ spring 1996 p30); this was still running in 1988 (Willings Press Guide. 1988; stating, wrongly, it was formerly the Walsall Times & S Staffs Advertiser). Thomas Newton (1810-1889), wrote for this paper under the nom de plume 'Autobiographies Verbosperimpateaubiquitos.' It was for the Observer he wrote the 'Annals of Walsall' (BCM July 1986 pp6-10. Oct 1986 pp39-44. Jan 1987 pp35-40. April 1987 pp44-46. July 1987 pp14-19. April 1991 pp15-20). The **Walsall Spec-tator**, founded on Nov 7 1874, ran until at least Oct 30 1875 (SHJ spring 1996 p31). **Walsall Illustrated Journal and Effective Advertiser**, founded on Oct 1895, ran until at least Dec 1915 (SHJ spring 1996 p30). The **Walsall Recorder**, founded on April 6 1906, ran until at least April 19 1907 (SHJ spring 1996 p31). The **Walsall Pioneer and District News**, founded on Jan 1 1916, became the Walsall Pioneer and South Staffordshire News from April 24 1920; this continued until at least March 31 1922 (SHJ spring 1996 p31). The **Chase Pioneer and South Staffordshire News** (Walsall edition), founded by Jan 29 1921, became the Chase Pioneer from April 29 1921, and this ran until at least March 31 1922 (SHJ spring 1996 p29). The **Walsall Times and South Staffordshire Advertiser**, founded on Jan 17 1925, ran until June 12 1954 when it was taken over by the Observer (VCH vol 17 pp252-253) (SHJ spring 1996 p31). The free papers, the **Walsall Advertiser** (founded 1979), and the **Walsall Chronicle** (founded 1986), were still running in 1988 (Willings Press Guide. 1988). For Walsall magazines see VCH vol 17 p252. **1850 to 1900**. In 1888 Walsall was granted **county borough** status and the three wards of the municipal borough were replaced by eight, Bridge, Birchills, Bloxwich, Caldmore, Hatherton, Leamore, Paddock, and Pleck (VCH vol 17 p217). Hayden Sanders, elected to the borough council, is said to be the first socialist to hold elected public office in Britain (On the Trail of the Walsall Anarchists. Barrie Roberts. 1992). **Walsall Anarchists**. The Walsall branch of the Social Democratic Federation started a club in the 1880s called the 'Walsall Socialist Club.' The club house was in Goodall Street from 1889.

Some of their members achieved national notoriety for being found in pos-session of bomb-making materials when the house was raided by Special Branch officers on Jan 7 1892. Their leader, Joseph Deakin, who had been arrested in London on Jan 6, admitted in a statement to manufacturing bombs which he thought were going to be used to bring down the Czar in Russia. Frederick Charles, Victor Cails, Jean Battolla and Deakin served prison sen-tences. John Westley and William Ditchfield were acquitted. The trial and conviction at Stafford Assizes in spring 1892 was the most important terror-ist trial in Britain of the period. The accused became known as the 'Walsall Anarchists.' Some believed the men had been framed by police spies. Walsall council presented Chief Constable Taylor with £50 and legend says the Czar presented him with a diamond tiepin (Walsall Observer March 26 1892. Jan 9 1982) (TB May 1986 p5) (On the Trail of the Walsall Anarchists. Barrie Roberts. 1992) (BCM autumn 1994 pp45-47). At an exhibition at Walsall Library held to celebrate the centenary of the bomb plot in 1992 were a cast-ing pot (six pots were discovered under the floorboards at a factory in Algernon Street), a bomb, the book of depositions, the witness box used at the first trial in Walsall Magistrates Court and a journal called the 'Walsall Anarchist.' In 1893 Walsall was only the second town in the country to have **overhead wire electrification**, and it was the first town in the country to have wire running down on one side of the road (TEBC) (TEBC2 p136). **Town clocks**. Walsall's first town clock was presented by Major FB Overton in the mid 1850s and placed in the centre of The Bridge (Bridge Street). In 1886 it was moved nearer Park Street to make way for Sister Dora's statue. It was moved again in 1957. Walsall's oldest clock, however, is the Walsall Arboretum clock started by the mayor in Sept 1887 (is the date correct?). It cost £50 and was illumi-nated by gas (BCM April 1986 p8). **Walsall Football Club** was founded in 1896, having been the Walsall Town-Swifts, founded in April 1888 with the amalgamation of the Walsall Swifts (formed in 1877) and Walsall Town (formed in 1879). The club moved to Fellows Park in 1896 (VCH vol 17 p253) (TEBC) (Portrait of the Black Country. Harold Parsons. 1986. p99). In 1990 the club, known locally as the Saddlers, moved to Bescot Stadium in Bescot Crescent. **Persons and visitors**. Dr **Henry Joseph Hamblin** (c1810-1864), surgeon in Walsall by 1835, and from 1843 the Falkland Island's first Colonial Surgeon. He died at sea on June 23 returning from the Islands (HOWW; says he was made Governor of the Falklands) (BCM) (Black Coun-try Essays and Reviews. Charles JL Elwell 1998. pp95-98). **William 'Billy' Meikle** (1858-1943), local historian, artist and photographer lived at 26 Lichfield Street (plaque on house) (BCM April 1990 p61) (BCP p21p of Meikle). **Jerome Klapka Jerome**, novelist, was born in Belsize House (see) in 1859. After his father had suffered financial losses in a coal mine disaster at Norton Canes in 1860, the family moved to London where JK Jerome appears to have been brought up. He left school aged 14 to become a railway clerk at Euston Station, London. His popular novel 'Three Men in a Boat' (1889) was written at Flat 104 Chelsea Garden Flats, London, where there is a plaque to his memory. He was joint editor of The Idler (1892) and founded his own weekly, 'To-day.' JK Jerome was given the Freedom of the borough of Walsall in 1927, the year he died. In Staffs his memory is preserved in Jerome Road, Pleck and in the Three Men in a Boat Inn (see) (KES p219) (CCF p49-52) (BCSG vol 4 p42) (VB p59) (BCM Jan 1976 p46. July 1981 p43. April 1986 p42. July 1989 pp43-45. July 1990 p69) (WMAG Dec 1979 p17p) (The Cambridge Biographical Encyclopaedia. David Crystal. 1994). **General Booth** (1829-1912), founder of the Salvation Army, lived at No. 5 Hatherton Street for a time. In 1990 there was a plaque to his memory on Kennings Garage, built on the site of No. 5 Hatherton Street (BCM April 1990 p61). Sir **Henry Newbolt** (1862-1938), poet, author and naval histo-rian, of Bilston (see), lived in Doveridge Place between 1866 and 1869 (plaque on house), and in Birmingham Road from 1869 to 1873 (VCH vol 17 p145) (BCM April 1990 p61). **Pat Collins**, funfair proprietor, born 1859 at Broughton Heath, Chester, settled in Walsall in 1882. He was a councillor for Birchills, MP for Walsall in 1922-24, mayor of Walsall in 1938-9, and died on Dec 8 1943 and is buried in Bloxwich (BCM July 1986 pp25-30) (TEBC). **Dorothy Wyndlow Pattison**, who became known as Sister Dora, was born in Yorks in 1832 and was the sister of Mark Pattison. She is noted for her work at Walsall Cottage Hospital, Bridge Street, between 1865 to 1878. In 1875 she took charge of the isolation hospital in Hospital Street, Walsall. She attended the wounded of the Pelsall Colliery disaster in 1872 and the wounded of the blast furnace explosion at Jones & Son in Green Lane on Oct 15 1875; Kenyon Jones, one of the two brothers who owned the works, became her admirer (VCH vol 17 pp145,222-223) (TOS pp117,121). He resided for a while in c1900 at No. 71 Fairfield Mount, Walsall (SNWA p41). Pattison died on Christ-mas eve 1878 and was buried in Queen Street cemetery (BCM April 1971 pp23-25. July 1977 pp44-49. Jan 1979 p60p. April 1990 p61 p of plaque on gate posts of Queen Street Cemetery. March 1998 pp43-47. June 1998 pp39-45) (TB Oct 1978 p1. Dec 1978 p17il. Feb 1992 p15p of her grave) (SMML pp109-114). The cemetery closed in 1969 and the land was opened as a public garden known as Sister Dora Garden in the early 1970s, with Sister Dora's grave being preserved. The successor of the Cottage Hospital, Walsall General Hospital, is known locally as the Sister Dora Hospital (VCH vol 17 p223). When a **statue** to her on the bridge in Bridge Street, was erected in 1886 it was the first statue of a woman, not of royal birth, to be erected in Britain. It was designed by FJ Williamson and was seven feet 10 inches high and made of bronze and Sicilian marble and was destroyed by pollution (ILN Oct 16 1886 p405il) (LGS p248). A replacement in Peterhead granite was unveiled in 1957 (SGS p176) (WOPP pl 61) (WPP p101il) (MR pp355pc,356p,357). (Sister Dora. Margaret Lonsdale. 1880) (S p124) (KES p14) (SOSH p327p) (RSL pp54-56) (SLM May 1950 pp138p-139. Spring 1954 p9) (In as Much as .... Millicent Price. 1954) (Dora Pattison: the nurse from the Black Country. Wyndham Charles. 1966) (Sister Dora; The Life of Dorothy Pattison. Jo Manton. 1971) (STMSM Jan 1979 p50 p of her uniform) (WOPP pl p59) (Sister Dora: her life and work. Florence Burleigh). **George Cotterell** (d1898), poet and editor, was born in Walsall on Sept 8 1839 (PSS pp224-228) (VFC p31). The father of John Major, Conservative politician and PM (1990-1997), **Abraham Thomas Ball** (alias Tom Major-Ball) (d1962), circus artist, baseball player and gnome designer, was born in Walsall in 1879, leaving with his parents for America in c1884 but returning to Walsall by 1896 (John Major: The Autobiography. 1999 pp1-3) (Daily Mail Oct 2 1999 pp28-29). **Maria May Harris**, born in Walsall in 1897, was brought before magistrates at Tipton in late Aug 1922 accused of obtaining goods and money from people in Blackheath and Old Hill by falsely pretending to be a wealthy cattle baroness from Californian, USA (TB Annual 1999 pp87-88).

1900 to PRESENT. In WW1 the Zeppelin L21 aircraft which made a raid on Walsall on Jan 31 1916 dropped a bomb which damaged the Wednesbury Road Congregation Church on the corner of Wednesbury Road and Glebe Street. Thomas Merrylees, 28, was killed by flying debris. An incendiary bomb landed in the grounds of the General Hospital. Another bomb damaged houses in Mountrath Street while another blew a hole in the wall of the Elijah Jeffries Saddlery Works. The last bomb from the L21 landed right in the town centre, by the public toilets, outside the Science and Art Institute in Bradford Place. The Mayoress, Mrs Mary Julia Slater, was killed on the No. 16 tram by the bomb which hit Bradford Place. She died later on Feb 20 1916. Also killed in Bradford Place were Frank Thomas Linney 36, and Charles Cope 34. There is a plaque on No. 17 Newport Street (Bradford Street elevation) which records the Zeppelin raid. Another Zeppelin, the L19, which also made a raid over Walsall on the night of Jan 31 1916 dropped bombs on Dora Street, and Pleck Road in Pleck (see) and at Birchills (see) (BCM April 1990 p61. summer 1996 p69. autumn 1996 p57) (TB July 1994 p19) (WROP p64p of Wednesbury Road Congregational Church after raid). For **Walsall Airport** see Aldridge Lodge. The **Garman-Ryan Collection** is a collection of fine art collected by Kathleen Esther Garman (1901-1979), daughter of Walter Chancellor Garman of Oakeswell Hall (see), and Sally Ryan (d1968), sculptress and the daughter of a wealthy American. The collection was made from about the mid 1930s. In 1973 Kathleen Garman gave it to Walsall, since when it has been housed in Walsall Museum and Art Gallery. From Feb 16 2000 the collection was housed in the New Art Gallery, on Walsall's town wharf. The collection includes paintings by Durer, Goya, Rembrandt, Picasso, Monet, Van Gogh, Degas, and some of the work of the sculptor Sir Jacob Epstein. The new gallery was officially opened by Elizabeth II on May 5 2000 (DNB) (The Sunday Telegraph Dec 19 1999 Review p7) (BCM summer 2000 pp25-26p). A **museum of leathercraft** opened in the library in Lichfield Street in 1967-8. It was enlarged with the entire collection of the Museum of Leathercraft in London in 1971 (VCH vol 17 p252). In 1996 **Beechdale housing estate** to the N of Walsall transferred from council control to England's only tenant-controlled housing association, the Beechdale Community Housing Association. The transfer was voted for by a majority of tenants in March 1995. However, since then a former Labour councillor has been hoping to prove that the council under-priced the estate and that council information was secretly leaked to favour the transfer in an attempt to try and return the estate to council control (The Guardian. Society Section. Sept 23 1998 pp6-7). **Easter custom.** A re-enactment of stages in Christ's way to Calvary had become an annual custom along Park Street, Walsall, on Good Friday by 1997 (Spotlight on the Diocese of Lichfield. May June 1998 p1). The greatest concentration of people in Britain in 1999 with the **surname Cooper** is in Walsall (Daily Mail July 17 1999 p35). **Ghosts.** The Town Hall is said to be haunted by a grey form that moves across the stage and middle of the hall, which may be the wife of a former curator (GPCE p48). For the ghost of

Kelvin Road, see under Leamore. **Persons and visitors.** Air Vice Marshall **Norman Sidney Webster** (d1982) who won the Schneider Trophy Race in Venice in 1927 was born at No. 41 Borneo Street in 1902. Webster's average speed was 273.01 mph, and Webster also set the fastest lap at 284.1 mph, a new world record (BCM Oct 1984 pp60-62). **George Loake,** of Walsall, murdered his wife Elizabeth at a cottage of a friend in Warwick Street where she was staying on Sunday Aug 6 1911. Loake, who had lost his job after 50 years service with the LNWR as an engine driver for running his train into a set of stop-breaks and may have had a disturbed state of mind when he committed his crime, was hung at Stafford in Dec 1911 (TB May 1985 p5). The world shorthand record was broken on Nov 9 1920 by **Arnold Bradley** who achieved 309 wpm without error using the Sloan-Duployan system, with 1,545 words in five minutes in a test at Walsall (GBR 1998 p24). The Prince of Wales (**Edward VIII**) visited Walsall on June 13 1923 to open the Ring Road, which in 1931 was renamed Broadway; Princes Avenue commemorates his visit (SNWA pp84,89). In 1939 Miss **Mollie Orgill** was the first female in the country to chair a junior chamber of commerce, when she chaired the one at Walsall; in c1969 she became president of the senior chamber of commerce (Old Walsall and district in years gone by. Walsall Observer. March 1999. p19p). **Sue Harmer-Nicholls**, actress who plays Audrey Roberts in the TV soap opera Coronation Street, daughter of Lord Harmer-Nicholls of Darlaston (see) (Offlow hundred), was born in Slaney Road, Walsall. **Neville Holder** alias Noddy Holder, vocals and guitarist with the 'Glam' Rock pop music group, Slade (formed 1966), was born in Walsall on June 15 1950; Don Powell (born Bilston Sept 10 1950), drummer, and Jimmy Lea (born Wolverhampton June 14 1952, presently (2000) resides in Brewood), bass guitarist, also play for the group. In late 1971 Slade reached number one in the hit parade with 'Coz I luv you'; the group have had hits with 'My Oh My' (1983) and their everlasting festive song 'Merry Xmas Everybody' (1977) (The Encyclopedia of Popular Music. Colin Larkin. 1998). By 1962 the British record for squatting on a barrel on top of a pole was held by **Victor Reeves**, aged 23, of Walsall. He squatted on a barrel 28 inches in diameter on a 40-foot pole for 31 days seven hours, ending on Aug 19 1952 (GBR 1962 p220). **Elizabeth II** visited Walsall on May 24 1962 (WHTOP p36p) (WROP p89p). The world record for brick carrying was set by **Reg Morris** of Walsall (or of Brownhills see) when he carried a 9 lb brick in a nominated ungloved hand in an uncradled downward pincher grip over 61.75m on July 16 1985 (GBR 1991 p176). At Walsall in 1986 he set the world record for fastest sausage meat eater when he ate 2.72 kg (6 lb) in three minutes 10 seconds (GBR 1999 p60). At Walsall on Oct 31 1985 he broke the world record for fastest kipper eater when he ate 27 weighing 16 lb 15 oz (self-filleted) in 35 minutes 24 seconds (GBR 1987 p310). At Walsall in 1988 he beat his previous record by filleting and eating 27 kippers in 16 minutes 52.66 seconds (GBR 1999 p60). The woman's record for brick-carrying was set by **Wendy Morris** of Walsall when she carried a 9 lb 12 oz brick over a distance of 22.5m on April 28 1986 (GBR 1991 p176). Walsall has the highest number of pigeon fanciers in Britain ('Woman's Hour' BBC Radio 4 Oct 12 1993). **Tom Holmes** of Walsall is the United Kingdom champion grabatologist (tie) collector with a collection started in 1928 (GBR 1998 p70). In 1995 he had 8,421 different ties, and 10,624 in 1998. The term 'grabatologist' was coined specially for him in 1993 by the Guild of British Tie Makers. The collection includes ties sent to him annually by British Prime Ministers (GBR 1996 p218. 1998 p70).

WALSALL AND LITERATURE. For **Jerome K Jerome** see Belsize House. A 40-page booklet entitled 'Reasons for withdrawing all connection with the Walsall Cottage Hospital in its Present Form' (1857) by Rev Alexander Gordon (1808-1889), vicar of Bridge Street Chapel, may have been used by **George Eliot** for her novel 'Middlemarch' (1871), in which one of its central themes is intrigue over the chaplaincy of a new hospital in a Midland town (BS p192) (BCM Jan 1976 pp45-46. July 1977 p47). For the novelist, **CF Keary** (d1917), who may have lived in or near Walsall, see Burton upon Trent. **Geoffrey Dennis**, author of the historical novel, 'Mary Lee' (1922), and a mystery novel, 'Harvest in Poland' (1925), was born and brought up in Walsall (VFC p38). Some of the incidents in 'Nightlights: or Shadows from a Doctor's Reading Lamp' (1895) by **Arthur B Frost**, a doctor who practiced in Walsall, may relate to Walsall (VFC p51). 'Love is not so Light' (1898) and 'The Honest Trespass' (1911) are by **Constance Cotterell**, who was a resident of Walsall (VFC p31). **Noreen Dilcock** (wrote under the pseudonyms Norrey Ford, Jill Christian and Christian Walford) (1907-1985), came to Walsall from Yorks in 1945. She is the author of the novel 'The Little Masters' (1970) set in the Black Country, and many other novels (BCM Jan 1970 pp18p,19) (VFC p39); her contemporary, the novelist, Stella Nowell, a resident of Walsall, dedicated her novel 'The Waterfall' (1972) to Dilcock (VFC p99). Walshaw in the novel 'Sowing of Clover' (1913) is Walsall; this novel has been attributed to **George Wouil** of Walsall (VFC p146) and to **George Woden** of Wednesbury (see). Wallchester in **Alfred R Williams'** novel 'Wallchester in The Minutes' (1927) is Walsall (VFC p143). Wallgrove in **Dorothy Baker**'s novel 'The Street' (1951), may be based on Walsall (VFC p7). The novelist, **John Petty** (1919-1973), was born in Walsall, and lived most of his life in Kent Street, Walsall. His novels include 'Five Fags a Day' (1956), possibly immortalises Hatherton Furnaces (see), 'A Flame in my Heart' (1958), 'The Last Refuge' (1966), and 'The Face' (1972). He died at Dawley, Shrops, in Dec 1973 (BCM April 1974 pp61-62. April 1990 p61; there is a plaque to him on his former residence 40 Kent Street) (TB Aug 1984 p30) (VFC p106). **Marjorie Green**, author of the plays 'Heads You Win' and 'The Peaceful Days' (both appeared in 1972), and romantic novels, has resided in Walsall (VFC p56). The historical novelist and author of 'Cavalier Courtship' (1974), **Marina Oliver**, was born in Walsall. She is a graduate of the University of Keele at Keele Hall (see). **Catherine Fellows**, author of the romantic novel 'Leonora' (1972) is a resident of Walsall (VFC p47). **Craig Thomas** (b1942), novelist, taught in Walsall between 1973 and 1977; his work includes 'The Rat Trap' (1976), and the bestseller 'Firebox' (1977) (VFC p128). **Aileen Quigley**, novelist and short story writer, and contributor to BBC national radio programmes, lives in Walsall (VFC p110). **Catherine Fox**, whose first novel 'Angels and Men' was a big success, moved to Walsall when her husband, Rev Peter Wilcox, became vicar of St Paul's, Walsall in 1998 (Spotlight on the Diocese of Lichfield. May June 1998 p8). For rhymes about Walsall see Sedgley and Tamworth. The skin of a Walsall pig is praised in this rhyme

> A Wedgbury cock or a Darlaston duck
> May be a tender morsel
> But none can compare from out of the ruck
> With the skin of a pig from Walsall

(BCM Oct 1968 p67). For the rhyme about Sally Du Da a fishmonger from Walsall see BCM July 1970 p9.

Walsall Arboretum Opened on part of the Hatherton estate 0.75m NE of Walsall in 1874. Prior to this the area had been quarried for limestone. The NE stretch was in Rushall ancient parish until taken in to Walsall borough in 1890 (VCH vol 17 pp152,191 il facing p160). The Walsall Illuminations, by the late 1990s a display of 25,000 light bulbs lighting the lakes, trees and gardens of the arboretum annually in Sept and Oct, began in 1951 as part of the celebrations for the Festival of Britain (Black Country Breaks. Black Country Tourism brochure 2000).

Walsall Brook The united brooks, Ford Brook and The Holbrook, proceed under Walsall as Walsall Brook and joins Bescot Brook close to its confluence with the Tame (VCH vol 17 p143).

Walsall Canal Short sections of the canal were built at three different periods. Starts at Pudding Green Junction on the Birmingham Canal New Cut New Main Line, and follows Brindley's Wednesbury Branch of the Birmingham Canal for just over 0.5m to Ryders Green Junction. The next 2m to Broadwaters Engine were built by John Smeaton by 1786 (authorised by an Act of 1783). The remaining 13m to Walsall were completed in 1799 (VCH vol 2 pp291,292) (SWY p16). Terminated at a wharf in Marsh Lane to the SW of Townend Bank, Walsall (VCH vol 17 pp160,168). In 1841 the Walsall end was joined by the Walsall Junction Canal (or Walsall Branch of the Wyrley and Essington Canal) which links it with Birchills Branch of the Wyrley and Essington Canal at Birchills (SWY p16) (HCMS No. 2).

Walsall Junction Junction of the Walsall Canal with the Walsall Junction Canal (HCMS No. 2) at Bridgeman Street, Walsall.

Walsall Junction Canal Joins the Birchills Branch of the Wyrley and Essington Canal with the Walsall Canal. Opened in 1841 (HCMS No. 2). Is seven furlongs long and has eight locks. Runs from the Wyrley and Essington Canal at Birchills to the Walsall Canal near Manor Hospital. Built in 1839-1840 (VCH vol 2 p296). Has also appeared as the Walsall Branch of the Wyrley and Essington Canal (VCH vol 2 p296).

Walsall Park Medieval hunting ground 1m to W of Walsall. It belonged to Walsall manor and Walsall manor house (see The Moat Site) stood in the middle of it. Emparked by the end of the C12. Partly enclosed in 1385-6. Leland in the earlier C16 noted it 'scant half a mile from the tow ne yn the way to Wolverhampton' (LI part 9 p23) (SSAHST 1974 pp21 note,23) (VCH vol 17 p184) (SNWA p81). A gate to it stood at the junction of Pleck Road and Wolverhampton Road. From there the park's limits ran westward to the brook near Bentley Mill Lane then S to James Bridge where its natural border was at Darlaston Road. Pleck Road formed the easternmost boundary, so in shape the park was an almost rectangle of some 260 acres. In 1557 the park

and manor passed out of royal hands when Queen Mary sold them to Richard Wilbraham a Master of the Queen's Jewel House. The park was disparked soon after passing to Wilbraham but held together as a single plot until at least 1576. The park and manor changed hands many times until they passed to the Bradfords. By the early C17 the park was split into units to accommodate 20 tenants and became known as 'Parklands.' Park Farm (see), Park Hall (see) near Town End Bank, and Park Street are remainders of the park (HOPL).

Walsall Water Tributary of the Tame. The name Erdeswick and Willmore give to Clock Mill Brook (see) and Ford Brook (see) (SOS pp399-412) (HOWW p6) (VCH vol 17 p143 note).

Walsall Wood Growing village on gentle ground rising on the E side of a tributary of Ford Brook, now a suburb over 1.5m E of Stonnall. Formerly a detached portion of Walsall Foreign township in Walsall ancient parish (W p648). The area was anciently in Cannock Forest and the 'wood of Walsall' had occurred by 1200. Squatting on the extensive commons of this detached portion of Walsall parish was in progress by the later C16. The village of Walsall Wood had become the main settlement by the early C19; hitherto Shelfield had been. The industry of the area in the earlier C19 was nailing and chainmaking (VCH vol 17 pp277,278). Walsall Wood was not included in the new borough of Walsall created in 1835 (VCH vol 17 p143). The church, St John, High Street by St John's Close, was built in 1837 (BOE p297) with rebuildings in 1886 and 1895 (LDD). Walsall Wood became a separate ecclesiastical parish in 1845 (VCH vol 17 p275). Wakes in the detached portion of the foreign of Walsall ancient parish were held, sometimes at Walsall Wood and sometimes at Shelfield, on the last Monday in October or the first in November between at least 1894 and 1913 (VCH vol 17 pp278-279). The opening of Walsall Wood Colliery greatly helped Walsall Wood expand as a settlement (MH 1994 p115). A railway was completed from Aldridge through Walsall Wood to Norton Canes in 1882. A station opened in High Street in 1884. It closed for passengers in 1930 and for freight in 1962 (VCH vol 17 p278). Walsall Wood became a civil parish within Brownhills urban district when created in 1894 (VCH vol 17 p275). Brownhills urban district was abolished in 1966 when Aldridge Brownhills urban district was created (GLAUE p405). Sally (Sarah) Ward, Conservative MP for Cannock (1931-35), daughter of John Ainsworth Meaford of Stone and former pupil of Orme Girls School, Newcastle-under-Lyme, was living at Grange Farm, Walsall Wood by 1947 (Who's Who 1947) (SNBC p46). In pigeon racing the pigeon 'Champion Breakaway' owned by R Green of Walsall Wood had the best world career record by 1992, having won 59 first prizes between 1972 and May 1979 (GBR 1992 p285).

Walsall Wood Common Former very extensive common. Situated E of Paul's Coppice and S of the Chester Road, Walsall Wood. It once formed a single continuous waste with Clayhanger Common. The part S of Lichfield Road was known as Holly Bank Common by 1805. Any remaining common was enclosed under an Act of 1865 (VCH vol 17 p280). Common land at Walsall Wood was enclosed in 1876 (MH 1994 p108).

Walstead Hall The C16 Walstead Hall may have been preceded by two halls. These halls may have stood on the site of the C16 hall, on the N side of Delves Common, or near it; one may have stood on the site of Westwood Hayes Farm. The hall appears to have been the seat of the Walsteads, lords of Great Barr manor to the early C17. In the early C17 the manor was purchased from them by the Scott family. During the tenancy of William Clift, between c1850 and 1893, the hall was known as Westwood Hays and was then considered a glebe land farm belonging to Dudley church. During the tenancy of James Bodley in c1902 the hall was known as Bodley's Farm. The area in which the hall stood was acquired by Walsall corporation for new housing land and the hall was demolished in 1932 (WAM p112p) (The Delves. Henry E Green. 1983 pp5-6,9) (TB Oct 1983 p4). The name is from the Walstead family (DUIGNAN p49). At one period the ancient boundary between Wednesbury and Walsall ancient parishes was marked by a ditch in front of the hall (The Delves. Henry E Green. 1983 p5).

Walton Fragmented small hamlet at the foot of Walton Hill on the SW side, 0.25m SE of Clent. In Clent parish. The name means 'serf's farm' (TB Jan 1974 p12).

Walton Fragmented small hamlet on a bank on the S side of the Sow 2m ESE of Eccleshall. Former township in Horsley division in Eccleshall ancient parish (W p379). Appears in DB as Waletone. The name means 'the walled town' (DUIGNAN). Or is of Romano-British origin and means the settlement of the Welsh (ECC p8).

Walton Former small village by the Trent, and township in Beech quarter in Stone ancient parish, 0.5m SE of Stone. A Roman castellum or station may have been at Walton at the junction of the Stafford and Eccleshall roads. It could have been the Lavatres of the Notitia on the Limes Britannicus (see) of the Notitia (NSFCT 1902 p117) and its remains may explain Walton's name. However, Lavatres has been identified with another place in the north of England (VCH vol 1 p186). Has appeared as Waletune (942) (DUIGNAN), Waletone (DB), Waleton juxta Stanes (1285) (SSE 1996 p19), and Walton-by-Stone (c1875) (Charities of Staffordshire further report p331). The name means 'the walled town' (DUIGNAN). Or 'the village of the Britons' (SL p45), or 'farmstead of the Welshmen' (SSE 1987 p32) (SPN p118). For Walton as a place name see ESH pp32-35). Walton was described as a pretty little village in 1929 (RHPS p199). The building of the Royal Ordnance Factory at Swynnerton resulted in the creation a Ministry of Supply housing estate at Walton: 220 houses, 220 flats and 40 staff-houses were built in little over a year (SIS 1980 p46), effectively making it a suburb of Stone and later a dormitory for Stafford and the Potteries. Local children believed the dead were really buried under the community's war memorial (STMSM May 1974 p43p. June 1974 p7).

Walton Bridge Crosses over the Trent at Stone. By the bridge was the original ford across to Stone. The site was bridged by 1317 (SIS p25 see map). Repaired in c1660 (SHC 1934 p23) (SIS p52). With the opening of a new wider bridge on the N side of the bridge on June 28 1984, the old bridge became a footbridge (SSBOP p42p of in 1908). Has also appeared as Trent Bridge.

Walton Bury House in the old part of Walton-on-the-Hill (SVB p169). Built in 1880. The first occupants were Capt Hon HT Allsopp and his wife Hon Mrs EM Allsopp (nee Okeover of Okeover). In both World Wars the Bury was used as a First Aid Centre. It was occupied by the Allsopp's spinster daughter Cynthia until her death in 1974 (BERK pp90p,91).

Walton Grange House on a pastoral plain by a small brook 0.75m ENE of Moreton. Formerly in Moreton quarter in Gnosall ancient parish. Has appeared as Waltone (DB - 1410), Walton (1189), Walton Grange (1422-1833) (SPNO p157) (SPN p135). The name means 'the walled town' (DUIGNAN). Or from Saxon 'wald tun,' 'farmstead in the woodland' (SPN p153). Oakden suggests 'wood or wold tun' (SSE 1996 p19). Was a grange of Buildwas Abbey, Shrops (SPN p135). Is the manor-house of Walton manor. A carved bracket inside the house at Walton Grange is dated 1605 and initialled 'G.O.' It was probably built in 1605 by George Onslowe. In the late C19 it was encased in brick (VCH vol 4 pp122-123). The house was adjacent to the head of Fanlizard Lane which betrayed some high site in the neighbourhood (NSFCT 1922 p170). In the later C17 Plot noted two ashes from different roots growing together, which started growing eight feet apart and joined about four feet from the ground at a spot between Gnosall and Walton Grange (NHS p213).

Walton Grange Stood SW of Walton Bridge, Walton, Stone; a lodge to it stood by Walton Bridge (SSBOP p42).

Walton Hall Hall 1.5m ESE of Eccleshall (W p379). Built in 1848 in the Italian style for Henry Killick (d1874), later occupied by Col Francis Chambers (d1891). In 1948 became a school and is now a special school administered by Staffs county council (mems in Eccleshall church) (EOP p79p of in c1920) (MR pp94-95). Has also appeared as Walton Villa (W p23).

Walton Heath Former common land above the Trent Valley with a few scattered houses 1m SW of Stone. In 1827 the North Staffs Hunt hunted a stag named 'Nimrod' which had been turned out at Walton Heath (The North Staffordshire Hounds 1825-1902. CJ Blagg. 1902. p11). Some of the heath remained on the 1887 OS map by Clement House (now Walton Heath Farm), S of Micklow House. There were ten acres of common land remaining by the 1950s (OSST 1956-59 p13).

Walton Hill Hill (977 feet) 1m ENE of Clent in the Clent Hills range. For the battle of Walton Hill between the Romans and the Britons see Clent Heath. The owners of certain land in Clent still had the rights of common on Walton Hill in 1913 (VCHW vol 3 p50). It is Ulfdown in the novels of Francis Young (History Around Us. Halesowen. John Billingham).

Walton House Clent. Occupied in 1851 by Misses M and A Durant (W p23).

Walton Hurst House 0.75m SW of Walton, Eccleshall. (NSFCT 1902 p119).

Walton Manor House Walton-on-the-Hill. Possibly occupied by the Hardings from the C17. Occupied by Col JA Fairhurst until Helen, Lady Salt, came to live here from Baswich House after her husband's death in 1904. She renamed the house 'Walton-on-the-Hill.' This name was eventually applied to the village. Lady Salt left the village in 1920. The next occupant of 'Walton-on-the-Hill' was Miss Brace (BERK pp21,68p, 69,83p).

Walton-on-the-Hill Village on a hill overlooking the Sow 2.5m SE of Stafford. Formerly in Baswich township and ancient parish (W p439). Walton is said to have been a township (Lewis Topographical Dictionary of England 1840). Has appeared as Waletone (DB), Waletona (c1166), Walton (1285), Walton super Canoke (1326), Walter under Cannock (1587) (SPNO p31). Walton means 'the walled town' (DUIGNAN) or 'farmstead of the Welshmen' (SSE

1987 p28). Walton-on-the-Hill was the name Lady Salt gave to Walton Manor House after she moved there in 1905 (but Oakden found the name in 1812 - SPNO p32). The name was eventually applied to the village after Lady Salt erected signposts on the by-pass, at the bottom of Walton Bank, and at the entrance to School Lane, to direct people to her new home (BERK pp21, 68p, 69, 83p). The village grew owing to it being considered a healthier place for the wealthy of Stafford to live in the C18; the old part of the village, known as 'The Village,' being high up (BERK p72). The area known as the Pinfold may have been the Village Green. In 1801 it was decided that stocks should be erected on the green (BERK p72). Between 1817 and 1820 the Lichfield road was diverted to the N (now the present A513) to lower ground (SVB p169). The church, St Thomas, in School Lane, was built in 1842 as a chapel of ease to Baswich (VCH vol 5 p9). On May 9 1845 lightning destroyed the spire of Walton church (ILN May 24 1845) (BERK pp74-75il).

Walton Pool The main part of the small hamlet of Walton, Clent.

Walton's Wood Wood 1m NE of Madeley, now lines the E side of the M6. Is named after Izaak Walton of Stafford (see) who frequently visited the Offleys at Madeley Manor and fished at Madeley Pool (NSFCT 1942 p63. 1954 p92). (SLM winter 1957 p15). Walton's Wood Pool (M p21) may be the pool to the SW of the Wood on the W side of the M6.

Wandon On Cannock Chase 1.25m NW of Beaudesert Hall. In Rugeley parish. Wandon Lodge was a lodge for Beaudesert Hall and former keeper's cottage on the Marquis of Anglesey's estate. It was later a private resident and for sale in March 1996 (CCBO p67) (SLM March 1996 p6pc) (BPW p24). The YHA had built a hostel at Wandon by 1951 (GCC p29).

Wandon Corner Wandon.

Wanfield Hall (locally *One-field*) Hall 0.75m WSW of Kingstone. In Kingstone ancient parish. The hall belonged to Sir Walter Chetwynd; his son Alexander Chetwynd lived here in 1660. Subsequently, the hall was purchased by Rowland Manlove. In 1725 Rebbecca Manlove married Dr Wilkes, the antiquary. It was at some later date the property of the Lawrence family and was purchased in 1851 by JB Jessop and at some date it was a boarding school (W p23) (TRTC p110). It was occupied by William Bathew who gave the lectern to Kingstone church in 1911 (mem in Kingstone church). Since 1960 (MIDD vol 2 p18p) or at least 1985 it has been the residence of the Rt Hon Charles Henry Chetwynd-Talbot (b1952), 22nd Earl of Shrewsbury, related to the Talbots of Alton Towers (see) (Sunday Mercury. Jan 8 1995 pp62p-63) (TRTC pp91,111). There is said to be a tunnel between Wanfield Hall and Manor Farm at Leese Hill, 1m to the N (TRTC p108).

Warder's Tower Built in 1828 for Knypersley Park, Knypersley, an old deer park (NSFCT 1954 p94), probably by John Bateman for his father's house, Knypersley Hall. It is a prospect tower with a wing attached (CIOPP pp19p,20p in 1930). Perhaps influenced by Clytha Castle, Gwent (DoE*). (HBST p182il) (BALH p173) (SMCC p6) (BGFB p31) (SOTOPP pl 137) (ES 'Plus' June 10 1989 p22).

Wardlow Hill and quarry works 1.25m SSE of Cauldon. There is a burial mound Gunstone calls 'Ward Low' at SK 08544727 (probably destroyed by the quarry) excavated by Carrington in 1848 and by Stoke-on-Trent Museum Archaeology Society in the 1950s. The crouched skeleton of a child was found. (TYD p124) (VCH vol 1 p375) (NSFCT vol 89 pp86-88) (NSJFS 1965 p38). At 08804708 is another, 1.5m SSE of Cauldon, 27 paces in diameter and three feet high, which Gunstone says is near Ward Low Quarry, excavated by Stoke-on-Trent Museum Archaeology Society in 1955 (NSFCT vol 89 p86) (NSJFS 1965 p59). The OS map 1:25,000 marks another at SK 08604695. Another or one of the previous is Wardlow Pasture Barrow. It was excavated in 1955. Another or one of the previous was 56 feet in diameter and three feet high and has been destroyed. Eleven fragments of a pottery incense cup, flints and burnt bone were found, all thought to be of the Middle Bronze Age c1400 BC. Further excavations in 1959 revealed the crouched skeleton of a child lying on its right side (NSFCT 1959 p87). (STM June 1969 supplement p12p) (HAF p390). Another or one of the previous is Wardlow Quarry Barrow this was probably excavated by Thomas Bateman in 1851 and again in 1952/ 53. The name means 'the look-out hill or low' (SPNO p24) (PNPD).

Ware Well A well in Walsall, mentioned in the C17. It was apparently situated near the junction of Lower Rushall Street and Ablewell Street. Gives its name to Warewell Street (VCH vol 17 p221).

Warhall End In the Hill Top district of West Bromwich (SOWB p25).

Warm Entry Passage at bottom of Oxford Street, Bilston. The boiler of a Japanning works made the wall on one side warm. It was an attractive place for courting couples (BCM April 1968 p29p. Oct 1983 pp22-23). Reputedly here a drunken Irishman murdered his adulterous wife after finding her with her lover (TB May 1980 p1).

Warming Castle Former building at SJ 909451, S of Glover's Farm, 0.5km

NNW of Edge Fields Farm (formerly Hedge Fields Farm) between Hall Hill and Pool Dole farms, Fenton. It appears on Hargreaves' Map of the Potteries and Newcastle (1832), and the 1834 OS map and has appeared as Warmers Castle. The NSFC visited the site in 1926 and found no indication that the field ever contained a large building (NSFCT 1926 p136). The site was excavated between 1970 and 1971 and revealed a cobbled floor of about 15 metres by 5 metres and finds from the period c1700 to c1840. It was concluded that a modestly constructed cottage had stood on the site. The origin of the name is unknown (SASR 1984 pp49-61).

Warren Farm Bandy Woods, Kingstanding. Called Warren House in 1840. The house, known as Kingstanding Lodge by 1884 (KPP p12p), had been demolished by 1935 when Kingsland School was built on the site (MNB pp62,73).

Warren Farm Stood at the end of Charlton Road, Perry Barr. Originally built by 1840 as a warrener's lodge, known as the Lodge or Warren House, by the Gough family to guard their rights of common here (MNB pp62,66,67). The name is preserved in Warren Farm Road.

Warren Hill Hill on Cannock Chase, 3.5m N of Cannock. Formerly in Teddesley Hay and could have been called Teddesley Head (see) as marked on the maps of Plot and Bowen. The name appears to have been derived from a warrener's house which was situated on the hill (SPNO p121).

Warren Hill Marked in John Ogilby's 'Britannia' to W of Swynnerton. Could be the hill on which is the water tower.

Warrens Handsworth. Land leased by John Wyrley in 1757 to Matthew Bolton which he purchased and built the Soho works on in 1762 (SHOS vol 2 p117).

Warren's Hall Warren's Hall Farm is 1m NNW of Rowley Regis. But there is a Warren's Hall Road 0.75m to the WSW at Dixon's Green (BCWJ p72).

Warrenshall Park Springfield, Rowley Regis.

Warren's Hill In the approximate position of Warren's Hall (1834 OS map but not on current OS maps).

Warrilow Brook Runs to Bradley-in-the-Moors joins Nabb Brook at Jeffrey Meadow S of Alton. The name means 'near where felons were hanged' (SPNO p22).

Warslow Moorland village on high ground above the Manifold Valley, 25m NE of Stafford. Former chapelry, and with Elkstones a township in Alstonefield ancient parish (W p744).

EARLY. Near Warslow is a burial mound excavated by Carrington in 1849. Two male skeletons a yard apart with flint implements were found (TYD pp161-162) (NSJFS 1965 p51). For other burial mounds in Warslow parish see Blakelow, Brownlow, and Lidlow; the last remains unlocated and may be identified with either of those unnamed E of Warslow at SK 091583 and SK 094587. Pickford says there was a Cock Low (or Cocklow) at Warslow as well as at Leek: the road near the Warslow Cock Low being haunted by the ghost of young boy (SMM p16). But his facts about it are confused with the mound of the same name formerly at Leek.

900 to PRESENT. Warslow has appeared as Wereslei (DB), Werselow (1300) (SSE 1996 p19), Wereselow (1327) (SPN p135), and Warnslow (THS p243) (W p744). The **name** means 'Waer's burial mound' (DUIGNAN). Or Ekwall thinks 'hill with a watch-tower' from Old English 'weardsetlhlaw' (DEPN 4th ed 1960) (SPN p135) (SSE 1996 p19), others say 'weard' represents guard, and 'setl' habitation; Warslow is situated on a hill from which there are views down the Manifold Valley as far as Thor's Cave (VCH vol 7 p57). Oakden dismisses Duignan and is uncertain about Ekwall's derivation (SSAHST 1967 p32). There was a chapel at Warslow by the C13. The **church**, St Lawrence, in the centre of the village, replaced a church of early C17 origin. That church or an earlier church at Warslow was dedicated to St Katherine in 1533 (VCH vol 7 p62). Became a separate ecclesiastical parish in 1785 and a joint ecclesiastical parish with Elkstones in 1902 (GLAUE p427). In the earlier C19 Warslow **wake** took place on the second Sunday in August, near the feast of St Lawrence (Aug 10), the patron saint of the church (W 1834 p719) (VCH vol 7 p58). There are some cast iron **stocks** situated where the lane to Ivy House Farm leaves the main road, close to the school (PDS&C p43) (L p27) (VCH vol 7 p61). In the late 1870s a **pinfold** stood on the NW side of the village near the former workhouse on the road to Fawfieldhead; it had been removed by the late 1890s (VCH vol 7 p61). **Enclosure of land**. In an unusual move the lord of the manor in c1548 agreed to enclose some of the waste on his manor, at the request of, and for his tenants, for arable land (SL p104) (MR p360). **Village expansion**. The village expanded in the C18 owing to the Duke of Devonshire's copper mines at Ecton, and after their decline in the 1820s, by the lead, copper and lime mines at Warslow which survived until 1874 (VCH vol 7 p57, 60). Became a separate civil parish with Elkstones in 1866 (GLAUE p427). The **first telecottage** in Britain opened in Warslow in 1989 (SLM Oct 1996 p17). It was housed in Manifold Primary School

(VCH vol 7 p57). The custom of oratories which originated in Saxon times from Christmas festivities and took the form of house parties and harvest homes was kept up at Warslow in 1900 (WTCEM pp29,30). **Supernatural**. The Hartington Choral Society travelling through Warslow claim they saw the headless horseman of the Moorlands here (Leek Post and Times Aug 1980) (Hartington News and Views Aug 1980) (L p50) (GLS p43). He is said to be the ghost of a knight whose horse brought his headless body home after a skirmish with the Scots (The Good Ghost Guide. John Brooks. 1994) (ES Sept 16 1994 p10). There is still a legend at Warslow that the ghost of a young boy can be seen on the road by Cock Low (SMM p16).

Warslow Brook Tributary of the Manifold. Runs by Merryton Low. The name is from Warslow village (SPNO p22).

Warslow Hall Georgian-style house 0.5m NE of Warslow. Formerly called Brownhill (see) (OL vol 1 p199). Brownhill was rebuilt and renamed Warslow Hall by Sir George Crewe (of the Harpur-Crewe family of Calke Abbey, Derbys, lords of Alstonefield manor) in 1830. It was principally rebuilt for the agent of his Alstonefield estate, Richard Manclark (d1850), but also as a summer residence for himself and his family. After Manclark's death it was used as a shooting lodge (CL June 1 1989 pp168-171 il) (VCH vol 7 pp57,59 pl 35). In 1991 the estate passed with the death of Henry Harpur-Crewe to his sister Airmyne Harpur-Crewe. With her death in 1999 the estate passed to her fourth cousin Andrew Johnson, a Canadian (ES May 8 1999 p10). The grounds were landscaped in the early 1830s. There was a grotto by 1835. Two pools feed a series of small cascades in the steep-sided valley S of the hall (VCH vol 7 p59). For the strange phenomenon in the sky in 1882, perhaps over Warslow Hall, see Morridge.

Warstone Small hamlet 1m ENE of Hilton. In Shareshill ancient parish. At Warstone is a boundary stone between the parishes of Essington and Hilton (DUIGNAN p161). Oakden (SPNO) does not make the identification between Warstone and the Harstan mentioned in a charter of 994, as do Duignan and others (DUIGNAN) (SSE 1996 p19); later Warstone appears as Horeston (1300), Wereston (1428), Horestones (Yates' map) (SPNO p114). The name is from Anglo-Saxon har-stan 'the boundary stone' (SPN p136).

War Stone Great triangular stone, which lay in a hedge at the corner of a field near Seisdon Common, 2m NW of Swindon; in 1988 the stone lay adjacent to the layby at Blackhill still marking a field corner (PMPD pp79,80 il). A Bertram Attehorstone was taxed at Bobbington in 1327 (WAS p3 of first field study). The name is from possibly Anglo-Saxon har-stan meaning boundary stone (SVS p328) (SPN p136). It was mentioned in deeds of 1676. Mr Hamps thought the stone marked the site of the Roman station of Bremenium (SVS p328 note). Prior to 1895 it marked the county boundary (VCH vol 20 p64) and it stood at the meeting point of the parishes of Bobbington, Trysull and Swindon. Many of the local lose granite boulders (remains of the 'great northern drift' in the Ice Age) form village boundaries (GNHSS pp31,32). Wolverhampton Archaeological Society saw it on June 26 1926. (SHOS vol 2 p210) (GNHS p67) (W p209) (S&W p365).

Warstones Farm Formerly stood opposite Warstones Inn. Formerly in Penn ancient parish. Built for Percy Albert Collins by Charles Hill, his father-in-law. Percy married Florence Hill of the Vandykes in Spring Lane, Lower Penn. He left Warstones in 1932 to farm New House Farm (PONP pp47il,48). Wolverhampton council built a huge housing estate at Warstones in the 1930s (PENOP p9), and the name is now used to describe this district.

Warstones Green A park at War Stones, Penn.

Wartell Field Former ancient open field covering land between the Village (Kingswinford) and Moss Grove. Mentioned in the 1775 enclosure survey. The name is preserved in Wartell Bank, Kingswinford, which links Water Street and Dawley Brook Road (SNSV vol 1 p356).

Warton Minute hamlet on the SE side of a low hill at some distance from Lonco Brook 1.25m WSW of Norbury. In Forton ancient parish. Shaw noted the discovery of a number of Bronze Age bronze implements, which appear to have been looped and unlooped palstaves and fragments of rapiers or swords 2m SE of Batchacre Park c1800 (SHOS vol 2 Additions p2). Probably the same as the arms found near Oulton in c1800 mentioned in GM 1801 part 1 pp127. 1812 part 2 p606 (NSJFS 1964 p31). Has appeared as Wavertune (1272), and Warton (1322) (SSE 1996 p19), and Wharton. The name could be derived from 'war town,' where the Romans had a battle with the British (NHS p395). Or it is from Old English 'waefer' - which WH Stevenson did not know the meaning of. It could mean the aspen poplar ('Populus tremula'), from its waving or wavering habit (DUIGNAN). Or 'farmstead near swampy ground, or at a wavering tree' (SPNO p147). The common fields of Norbury and Forton parishes about Warton were intermingled, so that the parish boundary formed an intricate and complicated pattern, which was quite unusual (NSFCT 1913 p62 see plan facing p45). The situation was resolved by the

Staffs Review Order of 1934 which transferred detached portions to the parish in which they lay (VCH vol 4 p155). In the later C17 Plot noted, near Warton, the rare Abies Legitima vel mas Bellonii or Abies of Parkinson fir, whose cones always stand upright. The fir is common in Russia, Poland, Denmark, Germany, Greece, and Scotland, but thought by Plot not to exist in England or Ireland (NHS p209). Plot noted the firs at Warton grew about 40 yards high, and one, 47.5 yards, was six yards round; seven yards higher than the wych elm at Field (NHS p212).

Warton Grange House at Warton, 3m NE of Newport. In the later C17 Plot noted a fallen old pear tree at Warton Grange in the orchard of Edward Low from which had grown six or seven young pear trees, each one another foot in diameter and most of them reaching 40 feet high (NHS p225).

Warwell On Broom Hill S of Wharwell Farm, Landywood. A well believed to have been constructed by parliamentarian troops of Wyrley when encamped on Broom Hill in the Civil War; hence the name War Well (GWY p24).

Warwickshire Moor Enclosed common land to E of Tamworth on the E side of the Coventry Canal. Formerly in Bolehall and Glascote township, Warws. Since Tamworth lay in two counties it had two pieces of common land, Warwickshire Moor and Staffordshire Moor. By the C13 the town house owners had the right of pasture on one or other of the commons depending on their residence being in Warws or Staffs. The common was mentioned by name in 1585 (OSST 1956-59 p14). The moors were greatly enclosed in the C18 (WMLB p90). Some 56 acres of the common remained in the 1950s (OSST 1956-59 p14).

Wash Brook Tributary of the Churnet. Has appeared as Washeye Brook (1676) (SPNO p22). The name is ether from Old English wæsce 'a place for washing' or from Old English wæsse 'a swamp or marsh' (SPNO p22).

Wash Brook Rises on Huddocks Moor runs on W side of Little Wyrley. Runs at Churchbridge, and at some point joins Sardon Brook, a tributary of the Penk.

Washerwall Former small village high up on the S edge of Wetley Moor 1.75m E of Bucknall, in Bucknall and Bagnall chapelry in Stoke-upon-Trent ancient parish. The name appears to be from Wash Well situated at SJ 934478 on an old saltway over Wetley Moor. Nearby in Washerwall Lane is a worn broken cross shaft possibly of late medieval origin (NSFCT 1924 pp187,188) (CVH p155) (WJ p16). It may have been erected by Hulton Abbey monks (WYV p32). It has perhaps served as a butter cross (WYV p32), a boundary mark (WJ p16; the cross is recorded in 1803), or as a mark for the nearby Wash Well (NSFCT 1924 pp187,188). At a short distance from it in a field near the lane leading to the common there is a low squared stone marked with the letters B.B. probably a stone of Bucknall boundary, this being where Bucknall and Cheddleton parishes meet (NSFCT 1914 p170). A quarry here was noted for building stone and another for sand (WJ p16). Washerwall now merges with Werrington, which is to its S. Mary Jane Bonnell (Bonell, Bonnel) of No. 8 Washerwall Lane was murdered by her jealous lover Thomas Clewes, a collier, by a blow to the head with an axe at her house on Sept 17 1888. She died three days later (DMF pp33-38). A UFO in the form of a red pulsating light in the southeastern sky was seen through binoculars from Hewitt Crescent, Washerwall, on Sept 5 1967 at 10.28pm (FSRP p14).

Washgate Bridge Packhorse bridge over the upper reaches of the Dove at Tenterhill, 1m NW of Hollinsclough at SK 053674, or at SK 061670 (COS p8p). (PDS&C p67p shows the packhorse road leading away from the bridge on the Derbys side).

Wash Well Spring at SJ 934478 on the ancient saltway over Wetley Moor (CVH p155), Washerwall Lane, Werrington. The brook rising out of it flows to Bucknall (FWMBS p4). There was a plan in c1800 for it to supply the towns of Hanley and Shelton (HBST p529). Opposite to the well and behind a little shop dated 1834 is the cross (see under Washerwall) (WJ p16). The well has also appeared as Washer-wall-well (SHST p217).

Waste Farm An old farm in Ellastone parish. There is a local belief that the name resulted from parliamentarians laying waste to this area in July 1643. However the name appears in Ellastone PR several times from as early as 1646, and because this is so soon after the incident, the local belief for a derivation of its name can be discredited. By 1972 the farm was derelict (NSJFS 1972 p124). It is probably the Waste Farm over 1m W of Ellastone in Wootton township.

Waste Gate The name Waste Gate appears on a gravestone in Draycott-in-the-Moors churchyard. There is a Wastegate Farm near Painsley Hall see Painsley Old Park.

Watch Box Huge cube of rock high above Lion's Head Rock and close to Picking Tor, Dove Dale, which, in Victorian times, had a reputation for being capable of being rocked (PS p121) (DDI p15) (TPC p168) (PDS&C p10) (MR p127) (DMV pp19p,25p). Has also appeared as Watch Tower.

Water Eaton Tiny hamlet N of Watling Street by the Penk 1m ESE of Stretton

(Penkridge). In Penkridge ancient parish. Eton (Water Eaton) has been described as a vill or township (SHC vol 5 part 1 pp166, 177. 1916 p319). A large Roman fort, part of the Roman township of Pennocrucium, is NE of Water Eaton. Has appeared as Eatun (994) (SSE 1996 p13), Etone, a manor in DB, Eton (1242), Watereton (1360-1420), Watereyton (1506), Water Eyton (1527) (SPNO p92). The name means 'farmstead by the river' (SSE 1987 p28. 1996 p21). There are slight traces of a moat W of farm buildings, at SJ 905113, which may represent the site of the manor house (VCH vol 5 p123) (SSAHST 1982-3 p46) (CAMS p64).

Waterfall Small village on a hill overlooking a tributary of the Hamps in hilly country in a huge bend in the Manifold, 20.5m NE of Stafford. Originally a chapelry in Rocester ancient parish. A Roman crucible was found at Earls Cement works in 1961 (WOY p2). Commander Wedgwood thought Waterfall was in existence by the time of DB and that it had been mistakenly left out of the survey; the manor was acquired by Burton Abbey between 1115 and 1125 (SHC 1916 p168). Appears in 1201 as Waterfal (SSE 1996 p19). The name is not from a waterfall, but from the action of the Hamps falling into a subterranean course about between Winkhill to Waterhouses (maps of Saxton and Bowen) (THS p239) (DUIGNAN) (WOY). Oakden agrees with Duignan (SSAHST 1967 p34). (SVB p171) (SPN p136) (SSE 1996 p19). The church, St James and St Bartholomew, on the W side of Broadway Lane opposite Newhall Farm, is believed to date back to 1100. It was partly rebuilt in 1792 and restored in 1887 (BOE p298) (WOY p63). Became a separate parish with curates early (GLAUE p427). The churchyard is unique in the county, belonging since James I's reign to a lay rector (SVB p171). Stocks are in front of Stocks House (DoE II) (SVB p171) (WOY pl 1, p16) (MR p360p). In the garden of Stocks Green Cottage is the village well, fronted with three rough stone steps (WOY p87). The pinfold was filled with litter until 1971 and then cleared out and supplied with a gate. C18 coins were found beside it in 1948, probably dropped by farmers claiming their cattle (WOY p16). For a rhyme about Waterfall see Cauldon. Waterfall entered Waterhouses civil parish in 1934 (GLAUE p427). Thomas Mycock antiquary and collector lived at Waterfall in the C19. In his collection were many ancient coins, the travelling trunk of Richard III, the escretoire of Elizabeth I and coins of Queen Anne (OL vol 2 p174).

Waterfall Common To the W of Waterfall.

Waterfall Cottage Endon Edge, Endon. Occupied by 1841 (VCH vol 7 p178).

Waterfall Cross Minute hamlet on a hill high above the Hamps in the Moorlands 1m W of Waterfall. The Earls Way (see) from Chester to Derby passed through here, until turnpiked and diverted via Winkhill (NSFCT 1948 p47). A Mr J Clark of Waterhouses believes that the cross of Waterfall Cross is now used as a footbridge at Back-of-the-Brook. The cross may have been a medieval direction post (NSFCT 1920 p162). The Young Pretender's army passed through Waterfall Cross on Dec 4 1745 in the Jacobite Rebellion (BPCSM p7).

Waterfall Lane Hamlet and road extending off Beauty Bank (which runs off Halesowen Road) to Holly Road, Blackheath (BCWJ p73). In Rowley Regis parish.

Waterfall Low Burial mound on a hill 0.5m NE of Waterfall. The mound, at SK 08615230, is 28 paces in diameter and seven feet high and is a listed monument. Carrington excavated it in 1848. It only revealed a robbed rock-cut grave (TYD p114) (NSJFS 1965 p52) (WOY p1).

Waterfall New Hall Stands in Waterfall village on the E side of Broadway Lane, facing Waterfall church. Built by 1666 (WOY2 pp82p,89).

Waterfall Old Hall Stands in Waterfall village on the W side of Broadway Lane, SE of Waterfall church. Owned by Edward Oakden in 1694 (WOY2 pp82p,90).

Waterfalls House Residence in c1900 of William 'Butcher' Mills, a coalmaster, in Waterfall Lane, Rowley Regis. Mills' ghost with a quill in his hand is said to have been seen from a window of a room believed to have been his bedroom (TB May 1981 p11). The house was demolished in 1984 (TB Sept 1984 p22p).

Waterglade Central Willenhall. (W p161). The name is preserved in Waterglade Lane very close to Dimminsdale.

Waterhays Village Large new housing estate, to W of Crackley, NW of Chesterton (A-Z Stoke-on-Trent 1992) covering the area of the former Glasshouse Colliery and Glasshouse farm. The name is from a farm called Waterhays, which stood in the area of the present Longdon Close and Aston Road, between at least the later C19 and 1962. It was possibly demolished to make way for the housing estate which was built in c1989 (OS maps 1:2500).

Waterhead Brook Tributary of the Penk. The name means 'the source of a small stream' (SPNO p22).

Waterhouse Farm 0.75m SSE of Longnor. Formerly in Heathylee township in

Alstonefield ancient parish. There was a house here by 1571 (VCH vol 7 p33).

Waterhouse Farm To the SE of Meerbrook. Formerly in Leekfrith township in Leek ancient parish. A house here existed by the earlier C16. Sometime between 1959 and 1962 it was submerged under Tittesworth Reservoir (VCH vol 7 p193).

Waterhouse Farm 0.75m NW of Onecote, by Onecote Brook. Formerly in Onecote township in Leek ancient parish. The present house, dated 1639, replaced a house recorded in 1609 (VCH vol 7 p211).

Waterhouses Village lining bends in the Hamps 0.75m S of Waterfall. Formerly partly in Waterfall and Cauldon ancient parishes (W p787). Remains of a mammoth were found in a limestone quarry at Waterhouses in 1864 (NSFCT 1931 p193). A macehead of the Later Middle Stone Age has been found at Waterhouses (HAF p25). Hall of Waterhouses excavated a burial mound in the Waterhouses area. A female skeleton was found (TYD p245) (NSJFS 1965 p52). A damaged socketed axe of the late Bronze Age has been found in Waterhouses parish (VCH vol 1 p181) (NSJFS 1964 p42). For burial mounds near Waterhouses see Stonesteads. At Waterhouses the Hamps disappears under ground. Perhaps Waterhouses is named after the curious 'housing' of the water of the river (OL vol 2 p287). Following the Leek-Ashbourne road the Young Pretender's army passed through Waterhouses on the afternoon of Dec 3 1745 in the Jacobite Rebellion (NSFCT 1925 p58), or in the early hours of Dec 4 1745 (BPCSM p7). The road was later turnpiked and at the bridge which crosses the Hamps formerly called Gilbert Bridge was a toll-house known as Waterfall Gate. It demolished in 1926 (NSFCT 1948 pp45-46). The railway from Leekbrook to Waterhouses, authorised on March 6 1899, opened on June 15 1905 (VCH vol 2 p324) and closed to passengers in 1935 although it continued to transport limestone (NSJFS 1964 p79). The civil parish of Waterhouses was created from the parishes of Calton, Cauldon, Waterfall and part of Ilam in 1934 (GLAUE p428). An Oxford R6271 aircraft crashed at Waterhouses on May 21 1943. All three of the crew died (MD p45). A freak whirlwind swept through Waterhouses on May 20 1997. It tore part of the roof off the school swimming pool before travelling up to Winkhill where it caused further damage (ES May 20 1997 p1pc) (ITV. Central News. May 20 1997 10.30pm).

Waterings Farm 1m W of Blore Ray. Appears on the 1834 OS map as Waterings.

Water Linch Name of field in which was found the Dosthill Spa, a chalybeate spring, near Wilnecote. It was inferior to none in England, noted Shaw in the late C18 (SHOS vol 1 p433).

Waterloo SE corner of Hanley (1834 OS map).

Waterloo SE end of Longton (1834 OS map).

Waterloo Clump Hill, which has also appeared as Waterloo Mount, 1m E of Burton upon Trent, formerly in Derbys at SK 266227. 400 feet high. Named after the battle of Waterloo (1814) (CBHBT p16). In the early C20 a water tower was built on the summit (BTOP vol 1 p7).

Waterloo Farm House 0.75m W of Stramshall. And Waterloo Cottage to the E of Comberford.

Waterloo Road Road connecting Burslem and Cobridge. It is Trafalgar Road in the novels of Arnold Bennett (Arnold Bennett and Stoke-on-Trent. 1966. EJD Warrilow. p151), and he lived at No. 198 Waterloo Road after living at Newport Road. No. 205 Waterloo Road was from 1960 until recently the Bennett museum (POP p37).

Watermills Farm Farm 0.5m SE of Alsagers Bank.

Waterside A ward of S Burton upon Trent. The Trent forms its western boundary.

Water Wending It appears to have been the stretch of the Sow before its confluence with the Penk 1.5m ESE of Stafford (1834 OS map), or the confluence point of the Sow and Penk (ROT p51). (BERK p47).

Watery Lane Junction Junction of the Island Line with the Tipton Green Branch Canal (HCMS No. 2).

Watford Gap Tiny hamlet on ground rising up to the hill on which stands the BBC's Sutton Coldfield television transmitter, on Warws border 2m S of Shenstone. In Shenstone ancient parish. The name means 'Wada's ford' (DUIGNAN). Or 'the hunting ford by the gap' (SPN p106).

Watlands Hall Watlands View, Wolstanton. Built in c1815 by a member of the Rogers family. In 1843 was the seat of Spencer Rogers (HBST il facing p159). Seat of Lewis Adams (b1805) pottery manufacturer from 1842 to his death here in 1850 (POTP p11). Sir Oliver Lodge lived here in his childhood. Demolished in Sept 1951 (HOE pp229-230) (SHST pp445, 608il, 609p of in 1940 in a state of demolition) (POTP p142). Has also appeared as The Watlands.

Watling Street Major Roman road from SE to NW England. 30 miles of it run through the county from Fazeley Bridge, S of Tamworth in the E to Weston-under-Lizard in the W. The Staffs section was built in the 70s AD (VCH vol 14 p283). The Staffs section of the road was clearly visible and used up to the C18 except for a curious break in the line where it intersects Icknield or Ryknild Street. Elias Ashmole noted this break in a letter to Sir William Dugdale in 1657 (VCH vol 2 p275). A stone marked the supposed site of the intersection of Ryknild Street and Watling Street in 1888 (1888 OS map 6 inch). In 1928 the exact cross roads was rediscovered (NSFCT 1928 pp147-148) (BAST vol 60 p53) (NSJFS 1964 p34). (SSAHST 1966 pp39-41). Watling Street was known as 'Street Way' in Camden's day (HOWW p24). On the length from Wall to Weston-under-Lizard (20 miles) the raised causeway was so clearly visible in 1727 that Dr William Stukeley forbade any of his companions from riding upon it 'to save it as much as possible from being worn out' (VCH vol 2 p275). (SHC 1916 pp301-324). The name means 'the way of the sons of Waetla' (DUIGNAN). It takes its name from an early form of St Albans, Herts, a city on Watling Street. To the Anglo-Saxons St Albans was known as Waetlinceaster, which in turn came from the local tribe Waeclings (SPN p136). Or from a pure Welsh word equivalent to 'the work of the legion' (HOWW p8). For Watling Street in a local rhyme see Brewood.

Wattville Small district 1.5m SW of Handsworth. Has also appeared as Woodville.

Wawell Lane 0.5m W of Ranton Abbey.

Wayside Distinctive group of 26 houses, built for employees at the Branston Pickle factory, at Branston, when Crosse and Blackwell were there in the 1920s (ABTOP p123p).

Waywarden's Well Originally situated in Station Road, Mow Cop. In 1905 it was taken down and removed and rebuilt near Mow Cop station. An inscription on the old well was omitted in the new erection (MC p25). It has also appeared as Warden's Well (WMC).

Weag's Barn House 0.75m ESE of Grindon, 0.25m SW of Weag's Bridge. The grassland, scrub and woodland at SK 100542 was by 1999 a SSSI nature reserve in the care of the Staffs Wildlife Trust (Staffs Wildlife Trust leaflet).

Weag's Bridge Crosses the Manifold, under 1m ESE of Grindon. (MR p166). Roberts hints it crosses the Dove and spells it Weeg's Bridge, where, he says, just in Derbys a skeleton was found some years ago. The teeth were in a perfect condition and were carried around for weeks in the pocket of a resident. Some say it was the skeleton of an ancient Briton, whilst others the victim of an evil crime, and others a victim of the 1745 Jacobite Rebellion (WTCEM p93).

Weaver Hills Range of hills on the southern edge of the Moorlands, reputedly, the southernmost point of the Pennines or Pennine Chain (NSFCT 1868 p13). The hills are the same age as the Mendip hills and are far older than any of the European or Asiatic mountains or of the Andes, and comprise mountain limestone (NSFCT 1894 p154). Plot in the C17 noted the range comprised Ribden Low (see), Wredon Hill (see) (2m NW of Wootton) and Caldon Low (see). On these hills he noted Queen Low, Gallows Knoll and Castlow Cross (SPNO p23). Other hills in the range are:- Beacon Stoop (at SK 095464; 1217 feet high and said by Masefield to be the highest hill in the range (LGS p3); incorrectly called The Walk on 1985 OS map 1:25,000), Three Knowls (at SK 101464), Queen's Knowl (at SK 104467), The Walk (at SK 097473) (1834 OS map) (NSFCT 1879 p27). Quarrying from at least 1960 has obliterated much of the range.

EARLY. The axe head found on the Weaver Hills is now lost (NHS p397 tab 33 fig 33) (NSJFS 1964 p45). All the burial mounds on the hills are listed monuments. The first four listed below were excavated before 1845. One was excavated in 1795 and revealed several large urns containing cremations, also a bronze fragment, the point of a knife or spear were found (The Vales of Weaver. J Gisborn. 1797. 40n) (NSJFS 1965 p59). One is to the E of The Walk at SK 09754635, 26 paces in diameter and five high (NHS p404) (VCH barrow list) (NSJFS 1965 p59); one on the eastern-most hill, at SK 10184611, is 22 paces in diameter and five feet high; one, at SK 10134616, is 22 paces in diameter five feet high; one, at SK 10074614, is 25 paces in diameter and six feet high. To the E of Weaver Farm, at SK 10524665, is another about 14 paces in diameter and five feet high (NSJFS 1965 p59). Another is at SK 09754642, another at SK 09414653, another at SK 09114641, and another at SK 09454639.

Has appeared as Wever Hills (1682. 1795), Wever (1686) (NHS) (SPNO p23), and Weever Hills (LGS p3). It seems the name refers not to the hills but to a small stream which rises here. Weaver, as a river name, has been defined as 'winding stream' (SPN p137). Mr Edwards in his 'Tour of the Dove' alludes to the Wever

> Lo, the round Wever Hills that bound the sight.
> Hang like a bed of clouds in sombre blue.

They appear in a lengthy poem by Gisborne (NSFCT 1879 p28). And are the model for the Binton Hills in George Eliot's 'Adam Bede' (NSFCT 1918 p122) and presumably appear in the work 'Weaver Hills and other poems' by AE Dodd (1967). A field at the base of the Weaver is known as Target Field since it was used for target practice by the army in WW1 and by the Home Guard in WW2 (SVB p184).

Weaver Lodge Uttoxeter. Seat of Robert Bamford (1860-1936). By 1978 the house was an inn (BUBA pp36,37p).

Weavers Hill Hill 2m SSE of Norbury.

Weaver's Mill N of St Michael's church, Stone. On the lower reaches of Scotch Brook. By c1975 it was a large corn mill, and not associated with the flint-grinding mills of the Moddershall Valley (SIT). However another source suggests that it may have been a flint mill (IAS p43). By the late C20 it was used as a restaurant displaying the former mill machinery. Adjoins Mill Farm formerly owned by AJ Weaver (info Michael Cockin).

Weaverslake Small hamlet on ground gently rising out of the Swarbourn Valley 0.25m WNW of Yoxall and now merges into Yoxall. In Yoxall parish.

Webb Stone Largest of three glacial boulders in a rough line in and near Bradley village, SW of Stafford. In 1999 one lay outside the Red Lion, another by the old Post Office, and the largest, the Webb Stone, by a bungalow on a track leading to White House Farm (VCH vol 4 p76) (ACOB p5). They may be route markers before roads existed (ACOB p5). However, according to tradition they were stolen by the Devil from the church to build up hell, but as he ran with them they became heavier and he tripped and fell, and they rolled away down to their present position (ACOB p5). The Webb Stone, also known as the Wanderer, has a number of traditions connected to it: That it was on an old track which branched off from the old 'King Street' (NSFCT 1908 p119). That a farmer at White House Farm once moved it and all his cattle died, so he replaced it in its present position by the bungalow (VB p151). That spinsters and or maidens should bow before it as they pass on pain of never marrying, and it is said to turn completely round at one minute to midnight (VCH vol 4 p76) (VB p151). That village maidens would take gifts of little cakes to the stone on the night of Oct 31 and in the early morning of Nov 1 they would know the name of their future husbands (ACOB p5pc). The name of the stone has puzzled some (NSFCT 1927 p157). But it seems to have been from the Webb family, local farmers; it once marked the boundary of their land (SN July 13 1957 p5p).

Wedding Fields Former name for the avenue of trees running between the pitches of the Harborne Cricket Club, now called Old Church Avenue, Harborne. It was called Wedding Fields as here the brides used to walk from the village to the church. The avenue was noted by Burritt (HOHE p24).

Wedge's Mills Hamlet by Wash Brook 1m SW of Cannock. In Cannock parish. Dates from the foundation of William Gilpin's edge-tool works in 1790. The site of the mill itself lay between the canal bridge and Watling Street (VCH vol 5 p49). Has also appeared as Wedges Mill (1834 OS map) (SPNO p61). The name is from possibly the Wedge family (VCH vol 5 p61).

Wedgwood Area 0.5m NW of Barlaston containing the present pottery factory of Josiah Wedgwood & Sons Ltd, who moved from Etruria Works (see) to a new factory here in 1940. The area also includes the housing estate known as Wedgwood Garden Village or Barlaston Park (see). Both the factory and the housing estate were built on the former Broughton Adderley estate of Barlaston Hall. The area obtained its name by association with the factory. A new station, called Wedgwood Halt, was specially opened on the nearby railway for Wedgwood factory and the housing estate in 1940, and it opened to the public in 1965? (A Regional History of the Railways of Great Britain. vol 7. The West Midlands. Rex Christiansen. 1973. p277).
WEDGWOOD FACTORY. The factory was designed by Keith Murray and CS White, ceramic designers for the company. For the foundation stone laying ceremony on Sept 10 1938 eight Black Basalt vases specially designed by Victor Skellern, Wedgwoods art director, together with an inscribed china plate, were deposited under the foundations of the entrance to the office building. Each vase was autographed by the layer and each contained a pottery cameo bearing the name of a member of the Wedgwood family (HOE pp361-364p-368). Production at the new factory began in 1940 (BAH p36) (SL p256) (The Story of Wedgwood. Alison Kelly. 1975 p64). In 1954 the Wedgwood Society was formed (Wedgwood: The New Illustrated Dictionary. Robin Reilly 1995). Elizabeth II and the Duke of Edinburgh made a visit to the factory on Nov 2 1955 (R&S p47). Josiah Wedgwood & Sons Ltd started acquiring other pottery companies in 1966 and became a public limited company in 1967. Wedgwood Group was taken over by Waterford Glass Group Plc in 1986 and the two companies were renamed Waterford Wedgwood in 1989 (DDBP pp79-87). The Wedgwood Visitor Centre has been opened for many years at the Wedgwood Factory.

WEDGWOOD AND ITS SUBSIDIARY COMPANIES IN 1999. Wedgwood Group have taken over these North Staffs pottery companies; **William Adams & Sons Ltd** of Greengates Pottery (see) in 1966; **Susie Cooper Ltd** and **RH & SL Plant Ltd** in 1966; **Coalport** of Foley Pottery (see) in 1967; **Johnson Brothers Ltd** of Hanley in 1968; **J&G Meakin Ltd** (which had merged with WR Midwinter in 1968, which in turn had taken over AJ Wilkinson Ltd (for whom the famous designer Clarice Cliff had worked) and Newport Pottery Company Ltd in 1964) in 1970; **Mason's Ironstone China Ltd** (formerly Patent Ironstone China) in 1973; **Crown Staffordshire Porcelain Company Ltd** of Minerva Works (see) in 1973; **Enoch Wedgwood (Tunstall) Ltd** in 1980 (DDBP p79-87) (info Trustees of Wedgwood Museum).

Wedgwood Former tiny hamlet in undulating country above a tributary of the Trent under 1m SE of Newchapel, and township in Wolstanton ancient parish (W p291). Ward thought the name may be from Woden's Wood considering that nearby Thursfield may have its name from the old Norse god Thor (HBST p131). Was a member of Tunstall manor by c1130 (ONST 1976 p374). The name is lost; an housing estate called Oxford now occupies the site. (AGT p63). Reputedly, the Wedgwood family, potters, are from here (W p291) (SSW p65) (OTP p174), and took their name from the place (HBST p428).

Wedgwood Institute Educational institute with art and technology school and library in memory of Josiah Wedgwood I at Burslem, built on the site of the Brickhouse Works (see). Designed by R Edgar and JL Kipling (BOE pp254-255). Decision to acquire the land made in 1859. WE Gladstone MP, Chancellor of the Exchequer, laid the foundation stone in Oct 1863, under which was placed a china casket containing a record on vellum of the building to be erected. Completed in 1869 and officially opened by Earl de Grey and Ripon (ILN May 1 1869 p445il). Burslem was the second place in the country to take advantage of the Free Libraries Act ensuring the institute an annual income of £200 (AGT p79). The facade contains reliefs of the Months of the Year represented by signs of the Zodiac modelled by Rowland J Morris (VCH vol 8 pp113,141) (AGT p79), or according to Gunnis, by H Blanchard (BOE p255). (SSW pp79,80) (SOSH p282) (HOE p300) (STM Oct 1963 p48) (STMSM Sept 1980 p15p) (POP pp22-23). There were plans in 1998 for the institute to be restored with money from the National Lottery (ES Sept 30 1998 p9p). Has also been referred to as the Wedgwood Memorial Institute.
Alumni: Arnold Bennett attended the Burslem Endowed School in the Institute between 1877 and 1880; thereafter the school moved to Longport Hall (Arnold Bennett's Bursley Trail leaflet. 1999) and won a book prize for physics at an evening class here (SHST p371p); it is Bursley Endowed School in his novels 'The Old Wives' Tale' and 'The Card' (Arnold Bennett's Bursley Trail leaflet. 1999); Reginald Mitchell who gained a Maths prize here (EAS p36).

Wedgwood's Tree Huge tree trunk incorporated into the building of the Etruria Works, Etruria. Its upturned base end rose into an upper room and was used as a solid unmovable workbench proving a good surface for making moulds on. Many were misled into thinking Wedgwood had had the tree preserved as it stood on the site previous to the building of the works. But this was not true. It had been incorporated into the structure. Many thought the initials JW carved onto the bench were Josiah Wedgwood's, but they were really those of one Jesse Wilbraham who had carved his initials onto the bench about 140 years after Wedgwood's death (HOE pp318,319ps,321).

Wednesbury (properly *Wensbury*, locally *Wedgbury*, *Wedgebury* MR p360, WDOP p19). Large Black Country town on the South Staffs plateau between two major headstreams of the Tame, which unite at Bescot (HOWV p101) (The Delves. Henry E Green. 1983. p4) 18.25m SSE of Stafford.
EARLY. Hackwood thought 'Rhos' might have been its Celtic name as the ancient British probably made a fort on Church Hill (WAM p8). There may have been a **Roman** settlement at Wednesbury; the Romans usually utilised Celtic forts (WAM p8). Hackwood thought a Roman road ran NE from Droitwich and passed through Oldbury and Wednesbury (WAM p8) (RW pp7,13), whilst Ede thought that a Roman road never passed through the town and suggested the road identified by Hackwood may have been a pre-Roman trackway (HOWV p4). In Wednesbury parish in c1817 was found a hoard of Roman coins containing coins of Nero, Vespasian and Trajan (GM vol 87 (1817) part 2 p551) (WB p88) (WAM p8) (SOB p8) (HOWV p4).
500 to 900. It has been supposed for at least a century that Wednesbury was the site for a **battle in 592** in which the West Saxon King Ceawlin was defeated by the British. Wednesbury's association with this battle is on account of its identification with 'Woddesheorge' and 'Wodensheorge' of the Anglo-Saxon Chronicle, and subsequent versions of the Chronicle or histories compiled by Ethelweard in the C10 (which gives Wodenesbyrg), and Henry of Huntingdon (died c1154) (which gives Wednesburie). The placing of the bat-

tle of Woddesbeorge (or its variant forms) at Wednesbury dates back to at least Hackwood in 1884 (WP p5). It was favoured by Duignan (DUIGNAN pv-ix) in c1900, and was perpetuated by CGO Bridgeman (SHC 1916 pp132,145), Hackwood again (OCHW pp8-15,20-28), and Major PT Godsal in his 'Conquests of Ceawlin.' Some have identified Wodenbeorg with Wimbleton (WP p5). Others, including Camden (1551-1623) and Sir RAC Hoare, identified it with Woodborough, Wilts (DUIGNAN pviii) (HOWM p3); and it has been identified with a place N of Alton Priors, Wilts, which is 1.5m N of Woodborough (SHC 1919 p189). More precisely Dorothy Whitelock identified it with 'Woden barrow' alias 'Adam's Grave' 2m N of Woodborough (0.5m N of Alton Priors) (English Historical Documents. vol 1 c500-1042. Dorothy Whitelock. 1955 p147) (HOWV p6). Kemble, Dr Guest, Gough, Elton (in his Origins of History), and others thought it took place at Wanborough, Wilts (DUIGNAN pviii) (HOWM p3). A **battle in 713** (S&W p389) in 715 (LGS p249) (SHC 1916 p132) in which the West Saxon King Ine or Ina (688-726), fought Ceolred, king of Mercia has been thought to have taken place at Wednesbury. But others thought this battle took place at Wanborough, Wilts (DUIGNAN pix). The site for it was identified by Dorothy Whitelock with 'Woden barrow' alias 'Adam's Grave' 2m N of Woodborough, Wilts (English Historical Documents. vol 1 c500-1042. Dorothy Whitelock. 1955 p147) (HOWV pp7-8). Assuming that these battles did take place at Wednesbury, Hackwood says, according to local traditions, the precise site for one of them was at Wigmore, whilst another was at King's Hill (WAM pp17-18). Assuming that the battle of 592 had been fought at Wednesbury Hackwood and Godsal concluded that the town was founded by Ceawlin (OCHW pp8-15,20-28). However, Ede thought that it may have been founded by the Mercian King Penda (632-654), but nevertheless, Wednesbury probably originated as a military camp and only subsequently became a civil settlement (HOWV pp8-9). There may have been a pagan Anglo-Saxon temple dedicated to the god, Woden, at Wednesbury; it possibly stood on the site now occupied by the parish church (University of Birmingham Historical Journal 1962 vol 8 pp10-11) (Signposts to the Past. Margaret Gelling. 1978. p161) (SSAHST 1990-91 p96). The **church**, St Bartholomew, on Church Hill is of C12 origin, but may occupy a pagan religious site (Wednesbury Parish Church of St Bartholomew. Cyril Willetts. 1988). Hackwood believed that there was a church at Wednesbury in Saxon times - in 1765 the roof of the N aisle fell down, a beam, still (1962) to be seen in the vestry, was noticed to have on it the figures DCCXI - it was then eagerly claimed as a timber from a Saxon church founded in AD 711. The present church, although heavily restored and largely rebuilt in the C19, dates from the late C15 or early C16 (HOWY pp54,301) (BOE p298). Wednesbury appears to have been an independent church before 1248, but after this date is often described as a chapel of the Abbey of Walsall Church, or conflictingly, an independent church. In 1535, for the first time never challenged again, it is described as a parish church (SHC 1916 p198) (HOWV p59). Wednesbury **wake** lasted a week from St Bartholomew's day (4 Sept or 24 Aug old style) (SCSF p106) (WP p15) (BCM Jan 1969 p20; is in Black Country dialect). Or was on the nearest Sunday to St Bartholomew's day (W p671). The wake was formally abolished in 1874 (WAM p116). The custom of **beating the bounds** of the parish was practiced in Wednesbury until c1830 (SCSF p24) (WAM p108) (WP p60). It began and ended at the Elephant and Castle, High Bullen, where it was followed by a dinner (HOWV p149). Parishioners anciently processed to Lichfield cathedral, the mother church, to pay their oblations in 'St Chad Farthings' or other money (SCSF p11). Portway Road on the W side of the town has been identified as a stretch of the Anglo-Saxon way Portstreet (see). **900 to 1086.** It has been asserted for many centuries that Ethelfreda (d918), daughter of Alfred the Great, built a large **burh**, or graff or fighting platform, against the Danes, on Church Hill. However, Ethelfreda's association with a possible burh here is only supported by Wednesbury's identification with Weardbyrig in C11 versions of the Anglo-Saxon Chronicle, and this identification may be erroneous (HOWV p12). In the Chronicle it was noted that Ethelfreda built a burh at Weardbyrig in 915. In the Chronicle of Florence of Worcester (d1118) Weardbyrig appears as Weadbyrig and the founding of the burh there given as 916. In the history of Henry of Huntingdon Weardbyrig is Wordebirh and the date for the burh given as 916. Camden identified Weardbyrig or Weadbyrig with Wednesbury. His identification was perpetuated by Plot (1686), Shaw (1801), Nightingale (1813), Pitt (1817), Harwood (1820), Garner (1844), Bagnall (1854), and Hackwood (1920). Various dates have been given for its construction - 914 (Roger of Hoveden) (SHOS vol 2 p83) (WAM p20) and 916 (GNHS p172) (W p671) (CCC p12). It has been commonly called Wednesbury Castle (SSC p130 in the intro). Some believe Ethelfreda merely repaired the fort and it was originally built by Dudo (HOWW p31). Sharon Turner in his 'Anglo Saxons' says it was built to co-

erce the Welsh (WAM p20). Ede believed a fort, possibly of Iron Age origin, did exist on Church Hill, and it was perhaps utilised by King Penda (HOWV pp13,14). Shaw was able to see some remains of the defences in the late C18 (SHOS vol 2 pp83,86). Scott in 1826 claimed there were no signs of it (SVS p332). Calvert in 1830 claimed he saw no trace of it, only the foundations (SSC p130 in the intro). Willmore (HOWW p31) and Hackwood claimed they saw traces of the earthwork in 1887 and 1902, respectively. The graaf at the W end of the churchyard is accepted by many as part of Ethelfleda's fortifications (WAM p8). The Weardbyrig in the Anglo-Saxon Chronicle, wherever its location, was a mint in Athelstan's reign (924-939) (HOWV p12). The W slopes of Church Hill became Ethelfleda Memorial Gardens in 1953. A **brown stone vessel** about eight inches high with a slightly raised design of a man's head with a beard on the surface was found on a building site in about the early 1970s by Mr Alan Golcher (BCM July 1974 p8p). **1086 to 1660.** The royal manor of Wadnesberie (Wednesbury) appears in DB erroneously under Seisdon hundred; Wednesbury also appears in Seisdon in some early C17 county maps (HOWV pp14,15). Later Wednesbury appears as Wodnesburi (1171-72), Wodnesberi (1183. 1398), Wodnesbyri (1271), Weddesbyrie (1538), Weddesbury (1552) (WAM p11) (HOWV p41). The **name** means 'Woden's mount or hill,' Woden being some chief (DUIGNAN). But others think it is from Woden, the Anglo-Saxon god of battle (SHOS vol 2 p83) (W p671) (WAM p8). 'Woden's fortified place' (SPN p137). Cannock Forest and forest law extended as far as Wednesbury in 1166 (WAM p31) (SHC 1923 pp294-295) (HOWV pp23,103). In 1186 three-fourths of Wednesbury **manor** was not subject to tallage. The feudal custom of 'merchetum' or 'the maiden's fee' was enforced in Wednesbury manor as proved by records of a court held in 1310 (RS p17) (SCSF p61). In 1398 the men of Wednesbury were declared free of tolls upon their goods and property on account of Wednesbury having anciently been a Crown demesne; the mandate was reissued in 1399 and again at various times in the C15. By the end of the C15 the men were also acquitted of 'the expenses of Knights coming to Parliament.' In 1404 William de Bermyngham prosecuted certain Wednesbury tenants for refusal to pay tolls on their goods sold at his market and fairs in Birmingham (WAM pp29,38) (HOWV p41). According to Hackwood the manorial court was kept up every year until recently (1902). It was always terminated with a substantial banquet or leet dinner, provided at the expense of the ladies of the manor. By at least the mid C19 all those invited to participate for the first time were expected to pay a fine, the proceeds of which paid for a second dinner about Christmas time. This second dinner was known as 'Shoeing the Colts' (WAM p98). The main streets, focusing on Market Place and High Bullen, follow the lines of medieval lanes (WMLB p99). **Wells.** There was a well at the bottom of Hollies Drive and another known as the Talbot Tavern Well (near the present (1962) Brunswick Terrace) (HOWY p227). As well as the Market Well, a public well near the Shambles (HOWY p227), there was also St Boniface's Well (see), Tacker's Well (see), and Oakes Well (see). Wednesbury **pinfold** a square stone-built enclosure existed at the corner of Pound Road until it was demolished in 1899 (WAM p88p). For a case brought by the inhabitants of Walsall against some men of Wednesbury heard in the Star Chamber in 1498 see **Mumming Case** under Walsall. There is a tradition that **John Paget**, father of William Paget, first Baron Paget of Beaudesert (see) (1505-1564), was born in Wednesbury (WAM pp70-74) (HOWV p127) (HOS 1998 p47).

MARKETS AND FAIRS. John Hoo, lord of Wednesbury, obtained a **market** charter for Wednesbury in 1709; the market had hitherto been prescriptive (HOWBA pp148-154) (WAM p89) (HOWV p147) (BCM Jan 1972 pp26-28). Another market was established sometime during the C18 or the C19 for Saturday night (SCSF p95). The **market cross** or butter cross, a brick building, was in Market Place opposite the Golden Cross Inn from 1709 to 1824. The upper storey stood on pillars and served as a town hall. A butter market was held in the lower storey. The 'Cross' was demolished in 1824 and its bricks used to repair the churchyard walls (HOWBA p154) (OWB il No.15 facing p48) (SCSF p90) (WAM pp101il, 102). The site was occupied by a triple headed gas lamp in c1900 (WDOP p19p). The Charter of 1709 also granted two annual **fairs** on April 25 (May 6 new style) and on July 23 (Aug 3 new style) (W p671) (Whitaker's Almanac) (OWEN) (COOKE) (SCSF p98) (HOWV pp147-148). There was a fair in 1792 (OWEN), and a fair in 1888 (LHE p265). The old custom of Walking the Fair was practised at Wednesbury (HOWBA p153) (WAM p108) (HOWV p149) (BCM Jan 1972 p26). A Court of Pyepowder (or called Pie Powder, or Court of Dusty Foot) was held by the bailiffs at Wednesbury fairs (SOSH p322) (BCM Jan 1972 p26). For the origins of the word Pyepowder see under Lichfield.

PUNISHMENTS. Hangman's Lane, the later Holden Road, preserves the site of the manorial **gallows** elm tree (SCSF p123). Near the market cross were the **stocks** (HOWBA p154) (WAM pp101il, 102). After the market cross was demolished in 1829 the stocks were removed to the foot of High Bullen (SCSF p130), or near the Shambles and later they were fixed to the pinfold at High Bullen where a Public Weighing Machine was to be erected. Their last location was on private land in Hitchen's Croft near the corner of Union Street and Upper High Street (WAM p104). Also near the market cross was a **whipping post** until disappearing in c1829 (HOWBA p154) (WAM pp101il, 102) (SCSF p130). According to tradition there was a rotting and rusty remnant of a **cucking stool** in a cattle pond near the old manor house of Wednesday (SCSF p126).

INDUSTRY. From the C14, Hackwood says, there may have been about three windmills in Wednesbury. The site for one was known to be in Windmill Lane, Church Hill (see), a second in Reservoir Terrace (unlocated, but perhaps on Church Hill) and a third at King's Hill (see) (WAM p54). Wednesbury lies on a rich seam of the Thick Coal and coal-mining has been its main industry. Coal-pits are first documented in 1315. In the later C17 Plot noted Cannel and Peacock coal being mined at Wednesbury (NHS p125). Opencast mining survived until the late C17 (SL p177). The dependence of the Birmingham metal workers on Wednesbury Coal was well understood in the C18, receiving acknowledgement in verse:

> Beneath old Wedgbry's Banks it lies
> which thousands of the slaves with glaring eyes
> Around him wait or do reside
> In Subterranean Caverns deep and wide
> Where by their Chiefs command they sap like Moles
> Supplying every Smithy Hearth with Coals

(OW pp25-27) (HOWV p117). A Black Country term for coal is 'Wednesbury Dirt' (BCSG vol 4 pp68-69). There was pottery making at Wednesbury between the C15 and the C17 (SSAHST 1990-91 pp96,112-114). Another industry was iron-working; there was nailing probably by at least 1500 and certainly by 1600 (HOWV pp134-135). A German, Frederick de Blewstone, experimented at Wednesbury with a method of using coal in the blast furnace to smelt ore in c1675. He constructed a furnace so built that only the flame of the coal fire could reach the ironstone. Although he took out a patent, he was quite unsuccessful (NHS p128). The solution was not discovered until the early C18 by Abraham Darby at Coalbrookdale, Shrops (HOWV p129). By 1785 there were four forges at Wednesbury. In addition to Wednesbury Forge at Wood Green there were Adam's Forge at Camp Hill Lane, Sparrow's Forge at Fallings Heath, and the iron mill at Wednesbury Bridge (HOWV pp130-131). In the C18 Wednesbury's most important industry was manufacturing gun barrels and gun locks which steadily declined after the French Wars in the earlier C19 but continued in a small way until at least 1935. The 'Lilliputian Gun' on show in the Great Exhibition of 1851 was made by Thomas Griffiths in a Wednesbury workshop. It was 4.5 inches long and had a lock weighing five grains and could fire a tiny pellet through a piece of half inch timber (HOWV pp141-142, 143) (MR p361). Thomas Walker, ironmaster, took out a patent for 'Manufacture of Sheet Iron' No. 13,028 on March 26 1850 (WAM p130). Other industries in the C19 was the manufacture of exquisitely beautiful trinkets in enamel ware, such as snuff-boxes, patch-boxes, tea-caddies, salt-cellars, brooches, breast pins, links, studs, hussifs, and a variety of other small wares. Hackwood, writing in 1924, describes the trade in trinkets, as long obsolete. Many of these enamels have been mistaken for 'Battersea Enamels' (SCSF p112). Later the town produced gaslights and piping (SL p185). Tube Town is Wednesbury's nickname in lieu of its close associations with the metal tube industry (VCH vol 2 p273), an early notable manufacturer of tubes was James Russell later of the Crown Tube Works (see), another innovator in tube making was Cornelius Whitehouse of Wednesbury Forge (see). The 'Wednesbury skelp' and 'Wednesbury twist' are technical terms used in metal-tube manufacturing. 'Skelps' are strips of iron from which barrels are made, and 'Wednesbury twist' was used to describe another process by which a narrow strip of iron was wound round a madril in a spiral direction, the edges being welded together to form a barrel (WW p35) (HOWV p141). The Patent Shaft and Axletree Company was established in 1834 or 1838 by the Rev James Hardy, a Baptist minister in the town. Operating from the vast works at Brunswick, Monway and Old Park in 1959 it became known as the Patent Shaft Steelworks and in 1971 was described as one of the biggest engineering companies in the Black Country. The closure of the works in 1980 was a major blow to Wednesbury (WMLB p102) (WDOP p8). For Wednesbury trade tokens see HOWV pp136-137. For miners' customs and superstitions see below.

CIVIL WAR. Wednesbury parish church was allegedly desecrated in the Civil

War by parliamentarians (HOWV pp86,87). The parliamentarian commander, the Earl of Denbigh, was in Wednesbury on June 2 1644 when he dispatched a letter to the Committee of Safety of Both Kingdoms in London (HOWV p86). Charles II accompanied by Jane Lane possibly passed through Wednesbury to Bristol in his escape after the battle of Worcester (1651) (HOWV p87). The bells of Wednesbury church were rung in the C18 and the C19 on May 29 to celebrate Restoration Day 1660 (SCSF p20).

1660 to 1860. **Social unrest.** The colliers of Wednesbury and neighbourhood invaded Birmingham and rioted on July 16-17 1791. It was a 'patriotic' demonstration against the Radicals, who, as sympathisers with the French Revolutionaries were thought to be anti-English; Joseph Priestley's house was sacked and his scientific instruments and apparatus destroyed (OW pp29-30) (HOWV pp121-122). The Assizes records for the county refer to a disturbance in Wednesbury on July 24 1791. Upwards of 40 were involved and threats were made to destroy a certain meeting house (LOU pp169,373). In 1801 riots occurred in the town on account of the high price of provisions (WAM p104). In 1826 colliers rioted in the town against the reduction of wages and the Riot Act was read (WAM p104). In Nov and Dec 1831 the colliers of Wednesbury rioted on account of short work and low wages. Many Wednesbury men were involved in the riots at West Bromwich in Aug 1842 (WAM p104). **Cholera epidemics** came to Wednesbury parish on Aug 9 1832 and claimed 95 lives in the parish (TB Feb 1998 p17). Another occurred at Wednesbury in Oct 1848 (WP) (WAM p114) (SOSH p322). The **Wednesbury Loyal Volunteer Association** was formed on April 30 1796 (HOWV p122). The **Quakers** had a meeting house in Lower High Street from 1680 with an attached burial ground. The same building or another was the British School from 1810. It was rebuilt in 1862. The Wednesbury Quaker Meeting was in the Warws movement, not the Staffs (SSAHST 1970 pp46-47). '**Quaker's Gutter**' was an artificial watercourse from Hobs Hole Colliery, Wednesbury, to the canal at Willingsworth. The name is thought to be from Samuel Lloyd (1795-1862), a quaker, builder of the watercourse. The gutter was filled with rubbish by 1877 (HOWV pp152,265). **New churches.** The church, St James, St James Street, was built in 1845 (LDD). The church, St John, Lower High Street, built in 1845-1846 (BOE p299), was redundant in the early 1990s. Roads. For the story of how a curmudgeonly Wednesbury ironmaster took his revenge on a **turnpike** keeper who made him buy another ticket just after midnight for another day's toll see BCSG vol 5 pp80-82. The two **railway** stations of Wednesbury were within yards of each other. The SSR from Dudley to Alrewas opened on May 1 1850 (WAM p112). On Sept 19 1853 a passenger train went into the back of a goods train waiting at Wednesbury station (SSR pp21-22). When the Birmingham, Wolverhampton, and Dudley Railway (later GWR) from Birmingham to Wolverhampton via Wednesbury opened on Nov 14 1854 large crowds gathered to watch the first train 'Wildfire' (WMVB p161). Branch lines to Darlaston (Offlow hundred) and Princes End via Ocker Hill were opened on Sept 14 1863 (WAM p112) (SSR p25). **Boiler explosion.** On Dec 9 1824 a large steam boiler at a gun factory in Wednesbury burst and killed the owner, Richard Adams, and four of his workmen (W p673). **Strange sights and sounds.** Rev Miller and two others witnessed a meteor at the W door of Wednesbury church at 12 or one at night on Nov 22 1672. It was so bright it lit their way home. After half an hour there was a great storm (NHS p28) (SHOS vol 2 p84). Rev Miller also noted an echo at Wednesbury. The church bells were said to resound off two windmills on Church Hill, only when the windmills' windows were open towards the church (NHS p28) (SHOS vol 2 p84). **Natives and visitors. John Wesley** preached regularly at Wednesbury between 1743-90, and is said to have visited the town at least 33 times, including six at which he did not appear to preach: 1743 (Jan, April, Oct), 1745 (May, Nov), 1746, 1747, 1748, 1749, 1751, 1752, 1755, 1756, 1757, 1760, 1761, 1764, 1767, 1768, 1770, 1773, 1779, 1780, 1781, 1783 (March, Aug, Sept), 1784, 1785, 1786, 1787, 1788, and March 22 1790 (HOWY p211) (VCH vol 17 pp64,65). On Sunday Jan 5 1743 he made his first visit to the town (VCH vol 3 p64) preaching at the old Town Hall (the market butter cross) at 7.00pm (OWB il No. 15 facing p48) (SCSF p90) and staying in the neighbourhood five days. On Jan 9 he preached there again, at 5.00am, and later, at 8.00am, at 'The Hollow,' forming the first Methodist society in South Staffs at John Sheldon's house 'Crabb's Mill' (see), Holloway Bank. There was a scuffle when he returned to preach at 'The Hollow' on April 19. In May rioting against dissenters broke out and continued intermittently until March 1744. On Oct 20 1743 John Wesley made his third visit to Wednesbury. He preached in the open air at High Bullen (see). In the same afternoon, whilst he was writing at Francis Ward's cottage, a mob arrived. It later dispersed but returned at 5.00pm demanding Wesley be brought to them. He went out and spoke to them and agreed to go with them to a see a magistrate. With a crowd of 200 to 300 he was taken to Bentley Hall, where it was found Justice Lane was not available. The mob then proceeded to Walsall in search of Justice Persehouse of Reynolds Hall: There they found he had retired for the night. On its return it met a Walsall mob, and a conflict between the two groups ensued, the Walsall mob eventually succeeded in capturing Wesley. He was at length rescued by four members of the Wednesbury Society, who had accompanied him from Wednesbury - William Sitch, Edward Slater, John Griffiths and Joan Parks - and a leader of the crowd, **George Clifton** (1704-1789), a local prize fighter, who is believed to have converted to Methodism on the way to Bentley Hall: He became known as 'Honest Munchin.' These followers ultimately succeeded in escorting Wesley back to Francis Ward's house. The following Tuesday 'Honest Munchin' presented himself to a member of the Society and became a Methodist. The incident is supposed to have impressed several local inhabitants, including John Rosley, vicar of Darlaston (Offlow hundred), who now promised to join any measures to punish the rioters (LOU pp117-118) (WDOP p88p of the painting of Wesley with the mob by Marshall Claxton RA). (SHOS vol 2 p86) (W p675) (OWB p90) (WP pp35-40) (HOWV pp204-214) (BCM Jan 1974 pp7-11. Jan 1993 pp51-55) (The Bitter Sacred Cup (Wednesbury Riots 1743-44). J Leonard Waddy. 1976) (TB July 1983 p14) (MR p361) (WOPP pl p107). A couplet which the working men sang at the time of Wesley's early visits goes

Mr Wesley's come to town,
To try and pull the churches down

(BCSG vol 5 p65). Rev **Charles Wesley** paid his first visit to the town in Sept 1742, preaching in 'The Hollow' (Holloway Bank) near Wednesbury Bridge. He was also in Wednesbury on Feb 2 1744 (BCM spring 1993 pp60-63). After his departure the Methodists were attacked and windows were smashed (SOB pp141-143). From Wednesbury PR are found these two entries - on Oct 10 1752 **'Jemima Wednesfield'** (a child left at Taylor's) was baptised, and on April 15 1827 a man of unknown name was found drowned and was buried (BCM July 1981 pp58-59). Rev **Richard Thursfield**, born on Oct 19 1827, author of several religious works, was of Wednesbury. He is the author of 'Rest in Jesus' (1866), 'Helps for School Boys in True Religion' (1879), and 'Bethany or Thought in Verse' (BS p457) (FLJ Dec 4 1918 p329). **John Goddard**, poet and playwright, was born in Wednesbury in c1845; he was the author of 'Jack and the Beanstalk' (1869), 'Old King Cole' and several other pantomime pieces (PSS p464) (VFC pp54-55). **Wyatt Earp** (1848-1929), gunfighter at the OK Corral (1881), may have been born at Alrewas; the Earp family later moved to Wednesbury (E&S Oct 28 1998 p18). **FW Hackwood**, author of many works about the Black Country, was born in Wednesbury on April 18 1851 and later lived at Comberford Lodge (see), in Wednesbury (BCM spring 1993 pp16-21).

NEWSPAPERS. The **Wednesbury Observer and District Advertiser** appeared between at least Sept 19 1857 and Aug 21 1858 (SHJ spring 1996 p33). The **Wednesbury and West Bromwich Advertiser, Tipton and Darlaston Gazette**, founded by late Oct 1869, became the South Staffordshire Advertiser from Nov 30 1872, then as Midland Advertiser from Dec 14 1872, then as Midland Advertiser and Wednesbury Herald from June 10 1916, then as Midland Advertiser, Wednesbury Borough News and Darlaston Chronicle from June 14 1924, then as the Wednesbury Borough News, Midland Advertiser and Herald from Aug 5 1966 and as such continued until at least 1974 (SHJ spring 1996 p32). The **Wednesbury, West Bromwich, Tipton and Darlaston Times**, founded on July 6 1872, ran until at least Sept 14 1872 (SHJ spring 1996 p33). The **Wednesbury Times**, founded on July 6 1872, ran until at least Sept 14 1872 (SHJ spring 1996 p33). The **South Staffordshire Examiner**, founded on May 2 1874, ran until at least Nov 21 1874 (SHJ spring 1996 p32). The **Wednesbury, West Bromwich and Darlaston Examiner and Tipton and Great Bridge Times**, founded on Sept 19 1874, became the Midland Examiner and Times from Jan 10 1877 and as such continued until at least Oct 6 1877 (SHJ spring 1996 p33). The **Borough of Wednesbury Herald**, founded on May 20 1876, became the Wednesbury Herald and South Staffordshire Recorder from June 29 1878 and this ran until at least June 3 1916 (SHJ spring 1996 p31). Two issues of the **Wednesbury Watchman** appeared in Nov 1885 (SHJ spring 1996 p33). The **Wednesbury Free Press**, founded on Aug 9 1884, ran until at least Oct 8 1887 (SHJ spring 1996 p33). The **Wednesbury Leader**, founded on July 16 1898, ceased in 1908 (TEBC) (SHJ spring 1996 p33). The **Wednesbury Borough News and Darlaston Chronicle**, founded by Jan 25 1919, ran until at least Oct 27 1923 (SHJ spring 1996 p32). The **Wednesbury and Darlaston Times and South Staffordshire Advertiser**, founded on Feb 15 1947, ran until at least April 23 1966 (SHJ spring 1996 p32).

1860 to PRESENT. Wednesbury was created a **borough** under the Reform Act of 1867 which allowed it to send a member to parliament (HOS p62). The new Town Hall was opened in 1874 (WAM p116). Wednesbury became a municipal borough when it received a Charter of **Incorporation** in 1886. The municipal borough was abolished 1966 and Wednesbury entered the county boroughs of Walsall, and West Bromwich (WAM pp106,119) (GLAUE p428). The citizens of Wednesbury held a **mock mayor** ceremony when the town received its municipal charter in 1886 (SCSF p164) (FOS p123). The **Town Hall**, in Holyhead Road, was built in 1872 (BOE p299). The **arms** of Wednesbury borough, granted in 1904, are: Sable, at between two silver lions passant each with a gold crown, and on the fess the symbol for Mars between two lozenges all sable. The crest is: On a wreath argent and sable, in front of the rising sun a tower with flames issuing from the battlements proper, the tower charged with the symbol for Mars, also sable. The motto is: 'Arte, Marte, Vigore' (CH pp337,338il). Several Wednesbury men were involved in the **Puddlers' strike** of 1883 and were tried at Stafford (WAM p104). In WW1 the Zeppelin L21 aircraft made a bombing raid on Wednesbury on the night of Jan 31 1916. In King Street, near the Crown Tube 14 people were killed including: Joseph Horton Smith 37, and his children Nelly aged 13, Thomas aged 11, Ina aged 7; also Edward Shilton aged 33, Betsy Shilton aged 39, Mary Ann Lee aged 57, Richard Higgs aged 36, Miss Rebecca Sutton aged 51, Matilda Mary Birt aged 10, and Susan Howells aged 50. The houses hit were demolished in 1958. Other bombs which were dropped by the Zeppelin fell at the back of the Crown and Cushion Inn in High Bullen, and along Brunswick Park Road. Damage was done to Hickman & Pullen's Brewery, railway waggons and buildings in Mesty Croft Goods Yard, where one person was killed. Slight damage was also done to Old Park Colliery. Another Zeppelin, the L19, also made a raid over Wednesbury that night and dropped a bomb on the Axle Department of the Monway Works (TB Jan 1996 p29) (BCM summer 1996 pp68-69. autumn 1996 p56). Next to the Town Hall in Holyhead Road is **Wednesbury Art Gallery**, built in 1890-1 (BOE p299); it was the headquarters of the Wednesbury Society of Arts in the late 1950s (Staffs County Handbook c1958 p145); the gallery has 200-300 paintings (WP p99). For its sculptured busts see BCM July 1981 pp41-42. Wednesbury has two **town clocks** both are to celebrate the coronation of George V. The main clock in the Market Square is the coronation memorial clock built in 1911. The clock had no heavy weights and was driven by an electrical master clock in the entrance hall of the municipal offices 150 yards away. This master clock was in turn synchronised by a signal from Greenwich Observatory sent at 9.00am once a day via the post office telegraph wires. The second clock was presented by William Hunt in 1912 and stood in Brunswick Park (BCM April 1986 p12). **Cricket record**. A Cricket Test Record World Cup team score of 348 for 9 was achieved by Bermuda v. Malaysia in the ICC Trophy Matches at Wednesbury on June 16 1982 (GBR 1983 p261). **Ghosts**. Walker's Bingo Hall in Walsall Street is said to be haunted by several ghosts and poltergeist activity. The building was built as a cinema in 1938 on the site of an old large family house (MS&S pp116-118). **Persons and visitors**. John **'Babbacombe' Lee** 'the man they couldn't hang,' sentenced to death in 1885 aged 19 at Exeter appeared at Wednesbury Theatre after release from prison in 1907 (TB June 1981 p9). **Amy Lyons**, daughter of a former vicar of Wednesbury, published BCS in 1901 (BCSG vol 5 p66). **Ruby and Wilfrid Westwood** of New Zealand visited relatives in Wednesbury in summer 1907; they were child giants and were described as the tallest (and heaviest) children of their ages, in the world at that time. Ruby, aged 13, weighed 17 stone and 4lbs, whilst Wilfrid aged 11, weighed 20 stone 6lbs (TB Annual 1999 pp41,42ps). **Emillie Hammond**, composer of the 'The Women's Institute Song,' was born in Wednesbury, but lived most of her life in Wolverhampton (VFC p59). The Prince of Wales (**Edward VIII**) visited Wednesbury on June 13 1923 (SCSF facing title page). **Elizabeth II** visited Wednesbury borough on May 24 1962 (WDOP p126). **Frank Hartland** of Wednesbury, born April 1 1882, was still living in 1984, aged 103 (TB June 1984 p17p). Rev **David Kirk Beedon** vicar of St Bartholomew's was one of the first vicars in the country to introduce 30-minute 'quickie' services for new worshippers. The new services began at St Bartholomew's on Sept 29 1996 (Daily Telegraph Sept 11 1996 p5).

WEDNESBURY AND LITERATURE. Robert George Hobbes (1821-1899), a correspondent for the weekly 'The Leisure Hour' in the 1870s, mused whether Wednesbury was Wodgate in Benjamin Disraeli's novel 'Sybil' (1846) (BCM autumn 1993 p57), but the novel, set in 1837, is said to have been based on a commission's report on Willenhall (see). Others have identified Wodgate with Wednesfield (see), and Wemsbury in the novel with Wednesbury (AOW p167). 'Original Poems' by Thomas F Bissell (1843-1910), a local poet, appeared in 1871 (WP p83) (PSS pp284-286) (VFC p15). Wednesbury is Wednesford in the novels of Francis Brett Young (1884-1954), and Wednesbury is the setting for his 'My Brother Jonathan' (BCM April 1980 pp10-15) (Portrait of The Black Country. Harold Parsons. 1986 p129) (BCTV p38). George Woden, alias George Wilson Slaney (d1979), the novelist, was born in Wednesbury in 1884. He was a pupil at St Mary's Grammar School, Walsall, and was the author of 'Sowing of Clover' (1913), 'Paul Moorhouse' (1919), 'The Great Cornelius' (1926), 'Our Peter' (1934), and 'Ruffy and Sons' (1945) (TB Nov 1980 p12p) (TEBC) (TEBC2 p120) (BCM April 1991 pp15-20) (VFC pp144,146; the novel 'Sowing of Clover' (1913) has been attributed to George Wouil of Walsall (see)). Henry Treece (1911-1966), novelist, children's writer and poet, was born in Wednesbury (VFC p133). The novels 'Abel's Daughter,' 'A Promise Given' and 'A Bitter Seed' by Meg Hutchinson, a native of Wednesbury, are set in and around the town (TB Nov 12 1998 p11). For Wednesbury as a verb see BCM April 1971 p27.

CUSTOMS AND SUPERSTITIONS. It was a Wednesbury custom to add roasted apples to the Wassail at **New Year**. The white pulp of the apples was known as 'Lambs-wool' (SCSF p4). Wednesbury miners would not work on **old Christmas Day** (Jan 6) (WP p57). The special dish to celebrate **mid-Lent** 'Mothering Sunday' in Wednesbury parish was a loin of veal and custard, eaten at mid-day. The custard pudding was baked in layers with various fruits and other ingredients. This occurred on the fourth Sunday in Lent in the C19 (SCSF p12) (FOS p86). **Wednesbury miners and iron-workers** practised a transference cure until the early C20. It was believed that croup in a child would transmit to a pigeon if it were held to the child's throat until it's death (MR p362). Wednesbury miners would not work in the mines until a dead colleague had been buried if he had died in a mining accident. Nor would they work on Good Friday or old Christmas Day (WP p57). The custom of rolling eggs down a grassy slope at **Easter** was practiced in the first quarter of the C19 in the undulating open space called the Mounts (SCSF p14) (FOS pp91-92). Hackwood remembers the old Easter custom of heaving prevailed in the narrowest part of the High Street near to Rollastons Fold in c1875 (SCSF p13). By 1974 a wooden cross was erected in Wednesbury market place at Easter (E&S April 6 1974; E&S have a photograph). The custom of lighting a 'boon-fire' or bonfire on **Midsummer** night, according to Hackwood, was not unknown in Wednesbury. It was supposed to be a relic of a heathen ritual performed around ancient Baal fires (SCSF p45). The strange sound of migrating birds at night were interpreted by Wednesbury colliers in the C17 as a pack of hounds in the air, and were given the name **Gabriel's Hounds**; colliers refused to go to work the next day if they heard Gabriel's Hounds in the night. In the N of the county they are known as the Seven Whisperers (or Whistlers) (NHS p22) (WP p57) (OW p29) (BCM April 1972 p35) (FOS pp153,154) (SCSF p146). At Bilston the miners called the sound, the Seven Whistlers (GT Lawley in the Bilston Mercury) (FLJ 1896 pp366-386); the sounds were taken as a portentous sign and warned miners to stay away from the pits. At Wednesbury superstition accompanied the **St Clement's day** (Nov 23) game of biting the apple, practised widely in the Black Country. A young girl would pare an apple, taking care to remove the whole paring in one-unbroken piece. Then, standing away from the others, she would throw the paring behind her over her left shoulder. Whatever capital letter the apple paring assumed on the floor foretold the first letter of the name of her future husband (SCSF pp46-47) (FOS p131). For the **Christmas dinner** known as Shoeing the Colts see above.

BALLADS. There is a famous C19 broadside ballad called 'The Wedgebury Cocking' relating the story of a barbaric cock-fighting match. It seems to have been written in the C18 or early C19 to ridicule cock fighting. The ballad, which runs to 13 verses (some versions give 12 verses), could have been so well known by the mid C19 as to give Wednesbury some national notoriety. The ballad appears in a broadsheet in the 1820s published by TR Wood of Birmingham; in Pierce Egan's 'Book of Sports' 1832 and 1844; in the appendix to 'Alps and Sanctuaries of Piedmont and the Canton Ticino' (1881) by Samuel Butler (1835-1902); in Broughton's Scrapbook p466 in the WSL is a version of the ballad (with amendments); in 'The English Ballad: A Short Critical Survey' by Robert Graves (1927); in 'The Faber Book of Ballads' edited by Matthew Hodgart in which it is called the most famous of English provincial ballads; in BC pp146-149; and in UBCB pp110-113. The 'Spittle's,' a public house kept by the Spittle family, mentioned in the ballad has been identified as the Old Blue Ball Inn (see) at Hall End. This is the full ballad as given by Phil Drabble in BC

> At Wedgebury there was a cocking,
> A match between Newton and Scrogging;
> The colliers and nailors left work,
> And all to Spittle's went jogging

To see this noble sport.
Many noted men there restored,
And though they'd but little money,
Yet that they freely sported.

There was Jeffr'y and Cobbur from Hampton,
And Dusty, from Bilston, was there,
Frumity, he came from Darlaston,
And he was as rude as bear;
And there was old Will from Walsall
And Smacker from West Bromwich came;
Blind Dobbin, he came from Rowley,
And staggering he went home.

Ruff Moey came limping along,
As though he'd some cripple been mocking
To join the blackguard throng
That met at Wedgebury cocking;
He borrow'd a trifle of Doll,
To back old Taverner's grey,
He laid fourpence ha'penny to fourpence,
Lost, and went broken away

But soon he returned to the pit,
For he borrowed a trifle more money,
And ventur'd another bet
Along with blubber-mouth Coney;
When Coney demanded the money,
As was usual upon such occasions,
He cried, "B---- you, if you don't hold your rattle
I'll pay thee as Paul paid the Ephesians."

Scrogging's breeches were made of nankeen,
And worn very thin in the groin;
In stooping to handle his cock,
His linen hung out behind.
Besides, his shirt-tail was wet,
Which 'casioned a great deal of laughter;
He turned himself round in a pet,
And cried, "B---- you, what's the matter?"

The morning's sport being over,
Old Spittle a dinner proclaim'd,
That each man should dine for a groat,
If he grumbled, he ought to be damn'd;
For there was plenty of beef,
But Spittle swore by his troth,
That devil a man should dine,
Till he'd eaten his noggin of broth.

The beef it was old and tough,
Of a bull that was baited to death;
Bunny Hide got a lump in this throat,
That had like to have stopp'd his breath;
The company fell in confusion,
To see poor Bunny Hide choke;
They took him into the kitchen,
And held his head over the smoke.

They held him so close to the fire
That he frizzled, just like a beef steak,
Then threw him down on the floor,
And had like to have broken his neck;
One gave him a kick on the stomach,
Another a thump on the brow;
His wife cried, "Throw him in the stable,
And he'll be better, just now."

Then soon they returned to the pit,
And the fighting went on again;
Six battles were won on each side,
The next was to decide the main;
For these were two famous cocks

As ever that country bred,
Scrogging's a duck-wing black
And Newton's a s----- wing red.

The conflict was hard on each side,
Till brassy wing'd blacky was chok'd,
The colliers were nationly vex'd
And the nailors were all provok'd;
Peter Stephens he swore a great oath,
That Scrogging had play'd his cock foul
Scrogging gave him a kick on the a-----
And cried, "Yea, God damn thy soul."

The company rose in disorder,
A bloody fight ensu'd;
Kick, b---- and bite, was the word,
Till the Walsall men subdu'd;
Ruff Moey bit off a man's nose,
It's a wonder no one was slain,
They trampled both cocks to death,
And so made a draw of the main.

The cockpit was near the church,
An ornament to the town,
On one side an old coal-pit,
The other was well goss'd round;
Peter Hadley peep'd through the goss,
In order to see them fight;
Spittle jobb'd his eye out with a fork,
And cried, "B----- thee, it served thee right".

Some people may think this strange,
Who Wedgebury never knew,
But those who have ever been there,
Won't have the least doubt but it's true;
For they are all savage by nature,
And guilty of deeds the most shocking,
Jack Baker whack'd his own father,
And so ended Wedgebury cocking.

(WP p82) (BC pp146-149) (BCM July 1975 pp14-16. Jan 1976 pp28-30. Jan 1982 pp14-20) (MR p362). Jon Raven found two additional verses of 'The Wedgebury Cocking' in Bilston Library which he gives on p113 of UBCB. The ballad 'Wednesbury Concert,' a lampoon on 'The Wedgebury Cocking,' is given in UBCB pp248-249. Another ballad alluding to cockfighting at Wednesbury wake goes

In Wednesbury town, a town whose name
Is coupled with its cocking fame,
Was yearly held by custom's right
A wake where colliers met to fight,
Where bulls were baited, torn, abused
And dogs were killed, which much amused
Those sturdy knights of coal and hammer
Who scoff at peace and joy at clamour

(BCSG vol 5 p64) (HOWV pp153-154). 'The Wooing of Wednesbury, a political ballad by a rejected suitor' dated Oct 30 1868 appeared in the form of a brochure signed 'Q.C.' at the 1868 general election. It was thought to have been written by Dr Kenealy, who was a candidate, but was in fact the work of an Owen Street shopkeeper (BCM July 1975 p44). For a rhyme about Wednesbury see Walsall.

Wednesbury Branch of the Birmingham Canal. Built by Brindley in 1769 (WMLB p101). The southern section of it, which diverged from the Birmingham Canal Old Cut Old Main Line at Spon Lane Junction (now under the M5), ran, in a winding fashion, to the W of the main road at Hill Top, Golds Green. The southernmost half mile section was incorporated into Telford's Birmingham Canal New Cut New Main Line in 1829 (after which the canal started at Pudding Green Junction). The next half mile section, to Ryder's Green Junction, now forms the southernmost section of the Walsall Canal. Has also appeared as Wednesbury Old Canal (OS map for canal navigations 1977) (HCMS No. 2), Wednesbury Loop (Canals of The West Midlands. Charles Hadfield. vol 5 of The Canals of The British Isles. see map p67), and

Balls Hill Branch (VCH vol 17 pp13-14) (BCM autumn 1995 p18). Its **branches** were: i). a two mile spur from Ryder's Green Junction to Broadwaters Engine built by John Smeaton by 1786 (authorised by an Act of 1783) which later was incorporated into the Walsall Canal. ii). the Dartmouth Branch. iii). the Ridgacre Branch. (VCH vol 2 p291) (WMLB p106) (Galton Valley. A Walkers Guide. Sandwell Metropolitan Borough Council. 1993). Much of the Balls Hill Branch or northern section was abandoned in stages between 1954 and 1960 and filled in (VCH vol 17 p13).

Wednesbury Bridge Bridge Street, Holloway Bank. Crosses the Tame 0.75m S of Wednesbury. The bridge by Telford of 1821, which has since been widened, replaced an older and narrower one (WAM p36). There may have been a bridge here in medieval times (HOWV p108). There was a water-driven iron mill at Wednesbury Bridge in the C18 and possibly by the end of the C17; it may have been the mill William Comberford is known to have contemplated building in 1606 (OCHW) (HOWV p131). In 1761 the mill at Wednesbury Bridge was owned by John Wood, son of William Wood of Wolverhampton, well-known for being the contractor for a new Irish coinage called 'Wood's halfpence.' John Wood obtained a patent in 1761 for a new method of making malleable iron from pig iron (WW pp112-117). For his colliery John Wood employed John Wesley's well-known Wednesbury disciple, Francis Ward as underground manager; however, Wood was an opponent of the Methodists (HOWV p132). By the bridge in the C18 was the house of Francis Ward, from which the mob fetched Wesley in 1743 (OWB il No.18 facing p18). Also not far away was Honest Munchin's Cottage (see).

Wednesbury Forge Former industrial hamlet at Wood Green, 1.25m NE of Wednesbury. Grew out of an iron works established at the end of the C16 at the junction of the headstreams of the Tame. First documented 1597 (HOWV pp124-126) (WMLB p100). In the late C18 the forge made gun barrels. The forge was taken over from the Willett family by Edward Elwell in 1817 who turned it into an edge-tool factory (WMLB p105). Edge-tool maker Cornelius Whitehouse (d1883) was a very innovative employee of Edward Elwell. He may have invented the modern bicycle here by 1818 (IE p73) and invented or perfected the method of making metal tubes longer here, in 1825; the patent for which (No. 5109) was bought by James Russell of the Crown Tube Works (see). In 1843 with Henry Russell he took out a patent (No. 9723) for welded iron tubes. In 1849 he set up his own works the Globe Tube Works in competition to James Russell (WAM pp129-130) (VCH vol 2 pp272,273) (BCM Jan 1988 pp6p-15) (IE p73) (MR p361). The factory had one of the tallest and best proportioned chimney's in the country until the 1880s when subsidence caused the top to tilt and it had to be removed (IE p72). In 1971 the site of the forge was occupied by Bescot Drop Forgings (WMLB p105).

Wednesbury Hall Situated about 0.25m NE of Wednesbury church on N side of St Mary's Road. In 1164 the Crown exchanged Wednesbury manor for that of Stonesfield, which adjoins Woodstock, Oxon. The barons d' Oyley (later Earls of Warwick) were the overlords of the tenant at Stonesfield, one Ralph Boterel, and they remained his overlord after he became lord of Wednesbury. Boterel was still lord in 1181 but by 1182 the manor had passed to William Heronville with William's marriage to the Boterel heiress. The manor remained with the Heronvilles until 1406 when Henry Heronville died and was succeeded by his daughters Joan, Alice and Margaret. By 1420 Joan was married to William de Leventhorp, son of her guardian, who saw to it that her other sisters did not inherit the manor by entering them into a convent. By Joan's second husband, Sir Henry Beaumont, the manor passed to her grandson, Sir Henry Beaumont II (1446-1471). By right of marriage Joan's third husband, a Noel (or Nowell) of Ellenhall, held the manor up to at least 1460. Sir Henry Beaumont II's son, John (d1502) would have inherited the manor only his mother out-lived him. Her second husband, George Stanley of West Bromwich, held the manor by right of his wife. He was eventually succeeded by John's second daughter and her husband, a Comberford of Comberford, near Tamworth. The manor remained with the Comberfords up to the Civil War. It was purchased by John Shilton (or Shelton) of West Bromwich Manor House sometime between 1657 and 1663. It remained with the Shiltons until c1709 when it passed to the Hoos of Bradley, Bilston. The manor remained with them until Thomas Hoo died childless in 1791. It then passed to the descendants of his sister, who were holding the manor at the end of the C19 (HOWV pp22-23,48,70,82,88,93-94). A medieval building appears to have been re-built in the Tudor period (WAM p53). The Shiltons (or Sheltons) lords of Wednesbury (1647-1701), lived here (WAM pp80,87-88). Richard Shilton sold the hall to William Ward in 1700; it having possibly already passed out of the ownership of the holders of the manor (HOWV p128). After 1777 the lord of the manor resided at Great Barr (WAM p94). By the early C19 the hall, an old brick mansion, was considered nothing more than a farmhouse (THS p153). By the mid C19 it was owned by Sir Horace St Paul (W p671). Has also appeared as Wednesbury Manor House.

Wednesbury Hill Hill on which Wednesbury parish church is situated. Is 537 feet high (HOWV p102). Presently called Church Hill.

Wednesbury Manor House A manor house at Wednesbury is known to have stood in the Manor Road area to the N of Wednesbury parish church, with open fields around it (SSAHST 1990-91 p96).

Wednesbury Oak District over 1m WSW of Wednesbury. In Sedgley parish. 'Oak' implies not only a stopping place on the perambulation of Wednesbury parish but of some sacred tree where the ancient folk-mote met in Saxon times to discuss village affairs (WAM p9).

Wednesbury Oak Loop Canal Former winding section of Brindley's Birmingham Canal Old Cut Old Main Line which became a mere branch after Whitworth, Smeaton and Telford completed the New Cut from c1800 (VCH vol 2 p292). The canal S of Bradley Lane is now (1997) closed and has mainly been filled in. Sanction for closure was given at various times between 1955 and 1961 (HCMS No. 2). (Canals of the West Midlands. Charles Hadfield. vol 5 of Canals of The British Isles. see map pp66-67) (SWY p9) (BCM autumn 1995 p17).

Wednesbury Old Park Medieval hunting ground. In existence by 1166 and still in existence in 1340 and merged into Cannock Forest (WAM p27). Ede says the park is first mentioned as late as 1484; it had disappeared by the end of the C17 (HOWV p109). Has also appeared as Old Park.

Wednesbury Wood Described in DB as two miles long and one mile in breadth or woodland 2 leagues long and 1 wide. It probably commenced, thinks Hackwood, at Wednesbury Old Park and stretched towards Cannock (WAM p24).

Wednesfield (properly *Wensfield*, locally *Wedg(e)field* UBCB p116, SL p42, MR p362, SHOS vol 2 p150). Black Country town on a plain that gradually descends to Portobello and Moseley Hole at the Wolverhampton to Willenhall road (WFW p9), close to Wadden's Brook, 14.25m S of Stafford. Former township and chapelry with Wednesfield Heath in Wolverhampton ancient parish.

EARLY. A disproportionate quantity of rock of basalt, and basalt or glacial boulders, lay about and in Wednesfield (WJO Jan 1908 p5. Feb 1908 pp34-35. March 1908 pp62-63. April 1908 p101. May 1908 p120). A fragment of a damaged and corroded unlooped palstave of the Bronze Age was found in a garden in Mercer Grove at cSJ 95090148 and went to Birmingham Museum (NSJFS 1964 p42) (SSAHST 1971 p50). The **Roman** forts at Pennocrucium and Metchley were connected by a road which passed through Wednesfield (WFW p32). The Roman road may be identified with the 'Beorgyth's Stone Street' in Lady Wulfrun's charter of 994 (WFW p22).

500 to 1750. There was possibly a pagan shrine to Woden, the Anglo-Saxon god of battle or war (W p156), set up in the vicinity of Wednesfield, perhaps in a grove in or near Wednesfield. According to tradition the shrine was represented by a stone, known as the Woden Stone. It was a sacred altar on which human sacrifices were offered to Woden. Later the stone was removed to the interior of the temple of Woden at Wednesbury (AOW p13) (WMVB p162). **Battle of Wednesfield**. The Anglo-Saxon Chronicle records that Edward of Wessex defeated the Danes at Tettenhall (see) in 910 (DUIGNAN p169). According to Lappenberg this battle had the important consequence of freeing England from Danish attacks (HOWW p30). Florence of Worcester (d1118) and others - Plot, Cox, Garner, Palliser - say this battle took place at Wednesfield (SD p27) (GNHS p73) (HOWW p30) (SL p50). Others give other dates for the battle of Tettenhall. The battle could have taken place at Wednesfield in 910, or in 911 or at some other date. It could have started at Wednesfield and progressed to Tettenhall. Or there could have been two battles in the same year or in different years, one at Wednesfield, and one at Tettenhall (HOWW p29). Wednesfield is first mentioned in the C10 by Aethelweard, western earl, in his 'Chronicles' transcribed by Savile in the C16 and in modern times by Campbell (WFW pp5-6). A charter was made of Wednesfield's bounds (SL p62), when the estate was given by Lady Wulfrun to the monastery of Wolverhampton in 994 (HOWM p14), and the canons of Wolverhampton were holding the manor of Wodnesfelde (as Wednesfield appears in DB) in 1086. Nearly the whole of Wednesfield anciently lay in the Wolverhampton (see) Deanery manor (HOWM p26). Later the town appears as Wodnesfeld. It was not until the 1251 Close Rolls that the 'o' is converted into an 'e' (WFW pp5-6); it has also appeared as Weddysfelde (1530s), and Weddisfeld (1539) (WFW p51). The **name** means 'Woden's field or open land' (DUIGNAN) (NSJFS 1981 p3) (SPN p138). Smallshire says 'feld' clearly relates to open land, being a natural field, not woodland cleared by the axe. It has been suggested that it may have meant 'Woden's plain' which would indicate reference to the entire heathland, including Wednesfield Heath to Stowheath, but according to Smallshire, the geological evidence suggests

that it referred to only Wednesfield village and New Cross area (WFW pp5,6).

Churches. For the tradition of a Saxon church between Bilston and Wednesfield being moved by fairies see Church Hole. An Act of Parliament was passed on Dec 1 1741 for founding and building a chapel at Wednesfield (WFW p98). There appears to have been a church at Wednesfield in 1745 (LDD). The present church, **St Thomas**, on the corner of Church and High Streets, was built in 1751. It burnt down in 1902 and was rebuilt in 1903 (BOE p300). The chapelry became a separate ecclesiastical parish in 1755 (GLAUE p428). The ancient **wake** was held at Midsummer (WFW pp12,128). There was possibly a bull baiting area in ancient times, as the junction at the Dog and Partridge Inn was called the 'Bull Ring' in the C19 (WFW p12). There was cock fighting at the wake in the C19 as the C19 street ballad below shows.

1750 to PRESENT. **Slow growth of the town**. Some have said Wednesfield is one of the oldest, if not the oldest, of the Black Country townships. The present town of C18 Wednesfield remained a small hamlet until the C18 (Staffs County Handbook. c1958. p146). The late enclosure of Wednesfield lands combined with its geology appear to have held back the development of the town in the C19 (WFW p54). There were no deaths in Wednesfield in the 1832 cholera outbreak; one case was reported on Aug 7 (TB Feb 1998 p17). By 1840 Wednesfield still mainly comprised just two streets - High Street and Rookery Street (WFW p125). In 1866 the township became a separate civil parish (GLAUE p428), possibly on account of the growth of Heath Town in the W part of the township? Accounts show that Wednesfield remained small for some time to come: JC Tildesley in the 'The Gazette' of June 29 1868 noted 'Wednesfield is the beau-deal of an old Black Country town. It presents a quaint mixture of town and country, garden and workshop, toil and ease, which distinguished other nearby towns more than half a century ago.... Toil and enterprise have lifted the others to rivalry with Wolverhampton and even Bilston, but Wednesfield has pursued a tortoise pace of progress. Heath Town of rapid growth, like a mushroom town since the coming of the Grand Junction Railway - has bypassed its parent. Wednesfield having neither railway or coalmine of its own' (WFW p112). In 1902 Dr Arthur Hands, Medical Officer of Wednesfield urban district, noted the slow progress of Wednesfield (WFW p112). Wednesfield urban district was abolished in 1966 when Wednesfield entered the county boroughs of Walsall, and Wolverhampton, and the parish of Essington (GLAUE p428). The **arms** of Wednesfield urban district were: The device consists of fighting men in Saxon armour, one wielding a battle-axe and the other with a sword and round shield. It is supposed to represent the battle of 'Woden's Field' 910 - Edward the Elder's defeat of the Danes (CH p341). In **Cycle Speedway** the record for the most British Senior Team Championships (instituted 1950) is six by Wednesfield Aces (1974, 1976-8, 1981, and 1983) (GBR 1985 p265). **Ghosts**. A vision of a man with a bear's head was seen at the site of the old churchyard near Wood Street in the 1970s. A tall, dark ghostly figure that floated several feet off the ground was seen in Wood Street in the 1970s (GPCE p60). Wednesfield is **Wodgate** or Wogate in Benjamin Disraeli's novel 'Sybil' (1846) (AOW p167) (WP p81). **Persons and visitors. John Morrison**, poet, was born in Wednesfield in 1773. He was educated at Wolverhampton Grammar School and seems to have been something of an infant prodigy as his verse translation of the 'Aeneid' (Books II and IV) is recorded as being published in 1787 (VFC p95). **W Iven** of Wednesfield died in 1778 at the alleged age of 115, having retained all his mental faculties and having married four times, lastly aged 105 (Broughton's Scrapbook p425). A house in Church Street backing to the canal which was demolished in the 1960s may have been occupied by **John Wood**, a friend of Dr Wilkes, an antiquary of the C18 (WFW p72). **Enoch Peers**, born in Hall Street, Wednesfield in 1877, was the first All-England Crown Green Bowls Champion, when first held at Fleetwood, Lancs (TB Sept 1983 p1p). **Theresa (Tessa) Sanderson** (b March 14 1956), athlete, was educated at Wards Bridge Comprehensive School, Wednesfield. Sanderson is the only British athlete to compete at five Olympic games from her tenth place in 1976 to fourth in 1992. She was the Olympic javelin champion in 1984 and awarded the MBE in 1985 (My Life in Athletics. Tessa Sanderson 1986) (The Guinness International Who's Who of Sport. Peter Matthews, Ian Buchanan, Bill Mallon. 1993). **Elizabeth II** visited Wednesfield on May 24 1962 (WHTOP p36p).

INDUSTRY. Wednesfield's industries, mainly concentrated in the S of the town, have been lock and key making, but its main industry was the production of vermin traps from the end of the C17 (LGS p249) (Staffs County Handbook. c1958. p146) (WFW pp118-119). One of the old trap works has been re-erected at the Black Country Museum (MR p363). Perry Hall and Castle Bridge Collieries were unsuccessful in the later C19 owing to the local geology and were soon abandoned. But the shafts sunk by Bowmans Harbour Colliery (closed by the early 1990s - BTW p108p) and Barnfield Colliery between New Cross and Dean's Road in the early C20 were very successful (WFW p115). Steelpark, on Steelpark Way, off New Wednesfield Way, off Neachells Lane, built on a former 50-acre seamless tube works which shut down in 1995, was the most efficient and modern steel distribution centre in Europe when officially opened on Oct 29 1999. The site was developed by Corus, the company formed by the merger of British Steel and Koninklijke-Hoogovens (BBC Midlands Today Oct 29 1999) (E&S Oct 29 1999 p1. Oct 30 1999 p18). For Wednesfield windmill see Mill Hill (WBJ p42). BALLAD.

> At Wedgefield at one village wake,
> The Cockers all did meet,
> At Billy Lane's the cockfighters,
> To have a sporting treat.
>
> For Charley Marson's spangled cock,
> Was matched to fight a red,
> That came from Wil'n'all o'er the fields,
> And belonged to 'Cheeky Ned'.
>
> Two finer birds in any cock-pit,
> There never yet was seen.
> Though the Wednesfield man declared,
> Their cock was sure to win.
>
> The Cocks fought well and feather fled
> All round about the pit,
> While blood from both of 'em did flow,
> Yet ne'er un would submit.
>
> At last the spangled Wednesfield bird,
> Began to show defeat,
> When Billy Lane he up and swore,
> The bird shouldn't be beat.
>
> For he would fight the biggest mon
> That came from Wil'n'all town,
> When on the word old 'Cheeky Ned'
> Got up and knocked him down.
>
> To fight they went like bull-dogs,
> As it is very well known,
> Till 'Cheeky Ned' seized Billy's Thumb,
> And bit it to the bone.
>
> At this the Wednesfield men begun,
> Their comrade's part to take,
> And never was a fiercer fight
> Fought at a village wake.
>
> They beat the men from Wil'n'all town
> Back to their town again,
> And long they will remember,
> This Wednesfield wake and main.

(WMAG July 1968 p37) (FOS pp172-173) (MR p362). For a children's rhyme from Wednesfield see FSBC p53.

Wednesfield Green According to Smallshire Wednesfield Green stretched from some point between the Dog and Partridge Inn, High Street to New Cross and was anciently not merely hallowed Christian ground but the site of a pagan shrine (WFW p13).

Wednesfield House A house of this name, shown on a 1932 for sale plan, may have been the residence of the Lane family in the mid C17. It had a central position in Wednesfield village opposite the church. According to Smallshire, the Wednesfield House demolished in the 1930s to make way for the Regal Cinema, was probably not the original (WFW p72).

Wednesfield Junction Junction of the Bentley Canal with the Wyrley and Essington Canal.

Wednesfield Townend The name, occurring in 1627, refers to March End or that part of Wednesfield near March End (WFW p79).

Weeford Ancient parish, small village in a valley below the elevation of Watling Street by a small tributary of Black Brook, and former township 18m SE of

Stafford. The name has appeared as Weforde (DB), Weford, Weoford (SPN p138), and Wiford, Wifford (c1540) (LI part 5 p103). 'Wee' may represent Anglo-Saxon 'waed,' shallow, a shallow ford. Or it is from Anglo-Saxon 'weg' (g=y) a way or road (DUIGNAN). Or from Old English 'wig,' or 'weoh' meaning 'an idol' which is usually translated as 'heathen temple' (SSE 1996 p23). Erdeswick thought 'ford' was from the London-Chester way which passed here over a ford of the Black Brook (SOS p154 - probably 1717 ed) (SHOS vol 2 p23) (SPN p138). If the meaning of Weeford is 'ford by a heathen temple' then here may have been a sacred pagan site (HOS p14). The shrine could have been associated with the burial mound Offlow (VCH vol 14 p5). There was a church at Weeford in the C14. The present parish church, St Mary the Virgin, in Dog Lane in the village centre, was rebuilt in 1802 (BOE p300) (LDD). The prebend of Weeford in Lichfield cathedral was founded by Roger de Clinton (SHOS vol 1 p294) (SSAHST vol 2 1960-61 pp50-51) (VCH vol 3 p141). Edmund de Stafford (1344-1419) of Clifton Campville (see), bishop of Exeter, was prebendary of Weeford in 1377. The parish was a peculiar jurisdiction of the dean and chapter of Lichfield cathedral until peculiar jurisdictions were abolished in 1846 (VCH vol 3 p94) (GLAUE p428). A Purefoy was slain here by Sir Henry Willoughby (of Middleton S of Drayton Bassett) in the cause of Edward IV; and Sir Henry, in the same place, fought and was wounded by Lord L'Isle (LI part 5 pp103,105) (SHOS vol 2 p23) (W p610) (PT p126). Other accounts say there was a fight at Canwell between these two according to a document dated 1417 or 1477. It had arisen out of an alleged breach of Drayton Bassett Park (TH July 27 1912) (THM vol 4 p35). Robert Weston born in c1515, a descendant of the Westons of Weston Hall (see), Weston-under-Lizard, lived at Weeford. He was Lord Chancellor of Ireland from 1566 to his death in 1573 (HOL p362 note) (DNB). For Weeford windmill see Moneymore. For the Wyatts of Weeford see Thickbroom Hall and Blackbrook Farm.

Weeford Hall A deed of 1586 refers to 'the capital messuage called Weeford Hall and the Mote there.' The location of Weeford Hall is not known. It may have stood on or near the site of Hill Hall (see), near Swinfen Hall (SSAHST 1982-3 p60). Weeford Hall was the seat of John Brandreth, whose son, Richard, resided at Shenstone Hall , and whose other son may have been Henry who helped disperse the Rump Parliament (SHOS vol 2 pp24,42). A Weeford Hall is shown near Weeford church on Greenwood's map.

Weeford Park Medieval deer park 1.5m S of Weeford. Created in Sutton Chase. In 1288-89 William de Beauchamp, Earl of Warwick, allowed Ralph de Limesay to make a park in Ash Hay in Weeford (SHOS vol 1 p23). The park appears to have covered the land now covered by the woodland called Weeford Park (SSAHST 1988-89 pp49-50). (NSJFS 1968 p50).

Weeping Cross Former hamlet on rising ground above the confluence of the Sow and the Penk on the edge of Cannock Chase, now a residential district 0.75m WNW of Walton-on-the-Hill. In Baswich township and ancient parish. The cross from which this place takes its name is believed to have been set up to mark the parish boundary; it was a stopping place of the Rogation Day procession (SCSF p87). In the course of time, according to tradition, the church authorities made it a public penance place for offenders against canonical law (SCSF p87). Oakden says it was used for this purpose according to tradition in Edward VI's reign (SPNO p32). These 'weeping' crosses for penitents making their supplications had hollows in the base to support the knees of penitents (NSFCT 1937 p48) and were abolished at the Reformation (DUIGNAN): 'To return by Weeping Cross' or 'to come home by Weeping Cross' denoted repentance of an undertaking (SSC p120 introduction pages) (SCSF p87) (SPN p113). The name appears in 1668 and on Yates' map (SPNO p32). Garner says it was also a place of execution (GNHS p104). Pickford thinks the name 'weeping' is derived from the weeping of the relatives of those executed here (SMM p28). Weeping Cross was developing as a residential district in the 1830s (VCH vol 6 p196). A large housing estate known as Weeping Cross Estate (centred on Porlock Avenue) was built in 1959. In 1959 it was described as one of the largest such estates in Staffs (SLM Feb 1959 p27).

Weeping Cross Farm Fine old Georgian house at Weeping Cross. Owned by the Grindleys in the earlier C19. Sold to the Stubbs family in 1890. Occupied by the Mailee family between 1913 and 1925. Tenanted by the uncle of Marjorie Knight (nee Malpass) from 1925 to 1956 (Before Houses Came: The story of a farming family in the Rural Parish of Berkswich. Marjorie Knight. 1992 pp4-5). It has curious outbuildings known as 'The Grotto' and a summerhouse decorated with shells (Before Houses Came etc).

Weeping Cross House Walton-on-the-Hill. Built by a member of the Twigg family in c1850 on the old foundations of the Mansion House. Perhaps was on a site opposite Baswich House. Later the home of JP Ward. Demolished in the 1950s (BERK pp20,24p,25).

Weetman's Bridge Narrow cobbled bridge which crosses the Trent at the end of Meadow Lane, 0.5m S of Little Haywood, and leads onto the Rugeley Road. There was a wooden trestle bridge at this crossing by c1830 (PCC p60 il of, drawn from a photograph taken in 1870) (HCMBOPP pp28p of old bridge,29p of new bridge) (HHHC p58ps). The present bridge was erected in 1887-8 (plaque on bridge). The present or past bridge was called Little Haywood Bridge (HAHS p54) and locally Wheatman's Bridge (SMM p53) or Wheetman's Bridge, since the largest subscriber who helped pay for its erection was a man called Wheetman Pearson (HAHS p54). However, the plaque erected on the present bridge says it was erected by Joseph Weetman with money raised by subscription. (CCF p106). **Supernatural**. The ghost of a weeping woman (SVB p84) (SMM p53) or a woman in grey who raises her hand to travellers as if hitch hiking on the road has been seen at the S end of the bridge (RRCC p8) (info Bruce Braithwaite). In the vicinity of Weetman's Bridge has been seen a phantom cyclist who appears and disappears before the witnesses eyes. It was seen by Wilf and Violet Daniels in June 1949, who saw it first at Milford (GLS pp75-76). Or seen by a family of four in July 1949 (EGH p120). It is supposed to be the ghost of a water engineer who fell to his death in a shaft at a pumping station in a walled garden opposite Weetman's Bridge. The dead engineer had always cycled to work along this road (GOM p17) (EGH p120) (The Good Ghost Guide. John Brooks. 1994) (GLS pp75-76). Or the engineer fell to his death cycling to work on the Stafford-Rugeley road, and sightings of him have been made on average every four or five years (info Bruce Braithwaite).

Well, The The well from which Well Street, Hanley, took its name. The well may be remembered as that from which an old man drew water and sold it round the town for one half penny per bucketful (H p108).

Wellhead There was settlement at Wellhead, Handsworth, at the junction of Wellhead Lane and Aldridge Road, by the end of the C13 (MNB pp40,45).

Wellings, The House 1m NNE of Ashley in Ashley parish (1834 OS map).

Wellings Cave Cave with three rooms worked out of solid rock at The Wellings. The cave has a long subterranean passage which was explored for nearly 200 yards in the C19 and is supposed to extend to Maer Pool (W pp383-384). The entrance was blocked up by 1935 when thought to be only 20 yards deep. Hounds of the North Staffs Hunt often became lost in this cave (NSFCT 1935 p86). (STM Feb 1964 p31).

Wellington To E of Bradnop (W p730). The name is preserved in the isolated Wellington Farm on Morridge.

Wellington Hanley. Formerly in Stoke-upon-Trent chapelry and parish. Became a new ecclesiastical parish in 1845 (CAST p57) (VCH vol 8 p143). Was called 'Hanley St Luke' by 1991 (GLAUE p428). Also was a ward of Hanley from 1895 (VCH vol 8 p158). Presumably the area contains Wellington Street. (FF p31).

Wellington Belt Long coppice stretching from W to E, S of Acton Trussell church to Gypsy Green. Appears on 1834 OS map. Said to be so named after the Duke of Wellington's visit to Teddesley Hall (SPNO p122).

Wellington House House in the Wellington Road area of Handsworth. The house was built in the later C18 or early C19 (MNB p41). It gives its name to Wellington Road.

Wellington Place Road forming part of the highway between Willenhall and Wednesfield (SNW p74) and a NW area of Willenhall in Little London. The name is from the Duke of Wellington and appears to have been given to this stretch of road at about the time of his death in 1852 (SNW p74).

Well in the Wall Spring rising from under a rock between Upper and Lower Tean on W side of the Tean. In the later C17 it was situated on a part of Mr Thomas Wood's estate (NHS p90). Cox says it is at Nether Tean (SD p109). Redfern says there is a spring called 'Willey Wall Well' at Major Ashby's garden at Over (Upper) Tean - in which garden a Roman vessel was found in 1728 (HOU p347). Foley says it is never known to go dry. He notes a well in Mill Lane, Lower Tean (CJF pp96p,112). Plot and others noted that the Well in the Wall flowed all the year round except in July and August, and that small bones of young sparrows and very young chickens and pigeons could be found in it (NHS p90) (England's Gazetteer. 1778). But Langford, in 1880, says nobody had ever seen any of these bones (S&W p313). (SSC pp87,88) (SMC p142) (SCSF p143). So called in consequence of it rising under a rock (S&W p313).

Well Leason Spring in a field called 'Well Leason,' Croxton, which supplied drinking water for many houses in Croxton. Situated in the lane behind Croxton church (BOV p48).

Welsh House House over 0.5m W of Harborne. Has also appeared as Welch's House. Named after the owner Welch (VCHWA vol 7 p23).

Welshmans Hill Hill 524 feet high 2.5m ESE of Great Barr. Just in Staffs on border of Sutton Park, Warws. The hill apparently received its name for be-

ing on the route taken by Welsh drovers going to London; being common land the hill was a regular campsite for them (MNB p55).

Welsh Row Row of houses mainly inhabited by coal miners in the Towerhill Road area of Biddulph. Built after 1805 and before 1851. Formerly called Williamson's Row. Demolished in 1974 (BALH pp69,143).

Wemberton Brook Brook N of Blore, Hales over which the battle of Blore Heath was fought 1459 according to a contemporary chronicler, Jean de Waurin (NSJFS 1980 p13). Others say it is Hemphill Brook or Hempmill Brook.

Wentlow, The Burial mound on the very top of Gorsty Hill, Gorsty Hill Road at SJ 1019408, N of Upper Tean (NSFCT 1983 p12).

Werburg's Wood Small wood 0.75m SSW of Keele (M p28).

Wereton Area of, and 0.25m SW of, Audley.

Wergs (*Words*). Former hamlet on rising ground above the upper Penk 1.25m ESE of Wrottesley, now a suburb of Tettenhall. Former manor in Tettenhall ancient parish. In the late C18 Shaw noted a burial mound between Tettenhall (see). Wergs was an inhabited area by 1304 (VCH vol 20 p12). It has appeared in 1362 (HOPTT p52), 1441 (WMAG April 1964 p19), as Wirges (1551) (VCH vol 20 p13), and The Werg (Yates' map). The Anglo-Saxon 'Wearg,' means i) a wolf, or ii) a criminal, or iii) an outlaw (HOPTT p52). Or is 'The withy hedges' (DUIGNAN). From Saxon 'witheges,' willows (VCH vol 20 p12) (BCTV p64) (SPN p144). At Wergs the old road from Tettenhall forked to Shrewsbury and to Newport and there was still a cross, Bell Cross, at the junction of Keepers Lane, Woodthorne and Wergs Roads in 1613 (VCH vol 20 pp12,13).

Wergs New Hall Large Italianate house with a tower, N of Wergs, 1.75m S of Codsall, in Tettenhall Regis manor. Built in c1860 by William Fleeming Fryer (d1891) on or near the site of Wergs Old Hall. After 1872 it was the property of TJ Perry, a Bilston ironmaster, and it remained in the Perry family until 1908 or 1909 when it was acquired by Col TE Hickman, a younger son of Sir Alfred Hickman. It became the regional office of the McAlpine construction company in 1964 (VCH vol 20 p18) (TCOP p33p) and it still was in 1988 (MR p103p). (BOE p106) (WPOPP vol 2 p52p of c1914) (BTW p72p).

Wergs Old Hall N of Wergs, 1.75m S of Codsall, in Tettenhall Regis manor. Predecessor to Wergs New Hall (VCH vol 20 p17).

Werrington Large village on high undulating ground on the edge of Wetley Moor above tributaries of the Trent, 15m N of Stafford. Former tiny hamlet in Weston Coyney and Hulme manor (W p752) and a ward of Caverswall parish (WJ p7). Boys from the Approved School (Werrington House) whilst digging in the garden in 1936 discovered small pieces of flint. Two were identified as scrappers (WJ p28). These are probably the same as the **Bronze Age** and early Iron Age flints, knives and scrapers NSFCT 1938 p114 mentions. Has appeared as Werynton (1272) and Wherrington (WJ pp9, 12). Is of Anglo-Saxon origin and means the home of the Werrings who were the followers or kinsmen of a chief called Werra or Wherra (WJ p9). On the N side of Werrington Road is a **windmill** said to date from 1730. Werrington Home Guard used it as their HQ in WW2. In 1952 the MEB took over the site (SMOPP vol 1 p78p in 1906). (WJ pp7,8) (SLM spring 1954 p24p) (STMSM Aug 1978 p26p) (STP p142) (WBJ pp43,44 dia intersection showing main shaft with grooves and mortices il xxxi in 1905 and xxxii in 1962) (MR p363p). The **church**, St Philip, on the corner of Salters Lane and Bank Road was built in 1906-1907 (info Rev John Humphreys). The **growth of Werrington** dates from c1925 when the Ash Hall estate was broken up and sold (WJ p8). Werrington became a separate ecclesiastical parish in 1964 (GLAUE p428). **UFO sightings**. An object like an inverted cup with bright light underneath was seen in the sky from St Philip's church at 10.00pm on Oct 26 1967 (FSRP p18). A glowing orange red cigar-shaped object, stationary and low in the sky, was seen from a Werrington bedroom window at about 10.35pm Oct 31 1967 (FSRP p18). A bright round light which alternated in colour from bright to red to bright green was seen from Stone House Crescent on Nov 9 1967 at 7.15pm. On the same night at 8.35pm three people at Werrington saw an oval object with a small dome on top. It had a red flickering below the centre and a smaller white light to the side (FSRP p19). A couple driving claim they were abducted by aliens and taken by them unconsciously from Werrington to outside Ipstones (SMM p93).

Westacre House on W side of Finchfield Hill, 2m NNW of Penn. It was for sale in 1963 (VCH vol 20 p10). By the mid 1990s the house was an inn.

Westbeech Tiny hamlet by a tiny brook under Nurton Hill 0.75m NNE of Pattingham, in Pattingham ancient parish. Grew on former common land, known as Westbeech Common. There were people living at Westbeech by 1682. There was a windmill at Westbeech in c1680 which was still in operation in the early C19 (Plot's map) (R Baugh's map of Shrops 1808) (WBJ p33) (VCH vol 20 pp175,179). The lost city in Wrottesley Old Park (see) is thought to have extended S to the heath here (NHS p394). Shaw noted a flat oval stone about a yard long with a cross moline cut into it in basso relievo ten inches each way near Patshull Park on Westbeech Heath (SHOS vol 2 p206). Has also appeared as Westbach and West Beach.

Westbridge House Stone. The house was the head office of the Trent and Mersey Canal Company (IANS pp24,150). It stood near the present Westbridge Park entrance gates, Stafford Street, at Bottom Lock (SPJD p85). The house was the council chamber for Stone until the 1920s and then a chocolate factory (MOSP pp19-20). The office shelves were made of slate to reduce the risk of fire damage (SIS pp69,70 note). Demolished by 1981 (MOSP p19). By at least the early 1980s the grounds, known as Westbridge Park, were used for fun fairs. By the late 1990s a leisure centre had been built in a part of the park near the canal; an old red brick building to the S was being used by the district scouts; and a canoeing club were occupying a wooden hut by the Trent.

West Bromwich Large town and parish in the Black Country 21m SSE of Stafford, but up to 1802 West Bromwich was a hamlet centred on the parish church 1.5m to the N, at Churchfield.

EARLY to 1800. There was until c1952 a glacial boulder in Overend Street (STELE Feb 29 1952). The **parish** was formed in c600AD or 643 (OWB p19), and was, according to some, originally a part of Harborne parish, but was a separate parish by the C12 (GLAUE p405). Commander Wedgwood and others think West Bromwich parish, formed by 1291, was probably formed out of Handsworth parish (SHC 1916 p198) (VCH vol 17 p50). The **name** 'Bromwich' is from the quantities of broom which grew here in great abundance (SHOS vol 2 p127). 'Broom-wic' the village of the broom (DUIGNAN p27) (OWB p18) (SPN p139). 'West' was applied to differentiate it from Castle and Little Bromwich in Warws (OWB p33). The earliest surviving document in which 'West' appears is dated 1293 (OWB p33). It was becoming known as West Bromwich by the early C14 (VCH vol 17 p2). The 'Britannia Depicto' (1753) has West Bromwich as West Bromeham or West Birmingham (DOB p336). From the C16 to the C19 West Bromwich is often written in the vernacular - 'Bramege' and 'Brammidge' (OWB p33). The parish **church**, All Saints, by Newton Road and All Saint's Way, was built by the C12 or earlier (NSFCT 1950 p102). It was dedicated to St Clement in and before the C19, and was rebuilt in 1871-1872 (VCH vol 17 pp50,53,54). By the 1830s the **wake** usually began on the first Monday in Nov and by the 1850s often lasted a week (VCH vol 17 p70). Another wake was held at Cutler's End (see). The **manor** appears in DB under Northamptonshire (OWB p26) (NSFCT 1952 p34). West Bromwich Manor House (see) lay nearly 1m NNW of All Saints. Hackwood found two examples of a fancy tenure in West Bromwich. Both are from West Bromwich lease indentures, one, dated October 16, 1649, which mentions as rent a payment and the provision of 'one rose flower,' and another, dated June 7 1658, concerning a property in West Bromwich parish known as Bridge End Croft, mentions the rent as 'one rose flower to be given at or upon the feast day of St John the Baptist' (SCSF p119). In or by 1293 the lord of the manor claimed the right of **gallows** and infangetheof (VCH vol 17 p43) (SOSH p328; said to be claimed by Walter de Everens - perhaps Devereux is meant?). About 1830 **stocks** and **whipping post** which had stood at the corner of Hollyhedge Road and Heath Lane opposite All Saints church were then moved to in front of the Ring of Bells at the junction of All Saints Street and Church Vale. They were apparently taken away when the police force was established in 1840. In 1970 the stocks were preserved in the grounds of the Oak House (VCH vol 17 p43). The custom of **well decorating** was observed at West Bromwich (FOS p103). The West Bromwich **riots against Protestant dissenters** occurred from 12 to 20 July 1715. In the rioter's evidence to the coroner 140 are said to have been killed and wounded. Some newspaper reports say only 14 died, others that three died (LOU pp88-89). Cornet Lowe of Charlemont shot one of the rioters. The evidence of Mr Bayley of West Bromwich at the Bar of the House of Commons is believed to have resulted in the passing at one sitting of the 'Riot Act' of 1715 (OWB pp86-89) (WBOPP pl 68, 78). In Nov 1743 an anti-Methodist crowd took off the roof of a shop next to the meeting house. No action was brought against the rioters (LOU p117). A severe **earthquake** was recorded in West Bromwich on Jan 4 1676 (SHWB 16). A rare pamphlet in existence, dated 1676, is entitled 'A True Relation of the Terrible Earthquake at West Brummidge in Staffordshire, the places Adjacent' (SOWB p16). **Persons and visitors**. For the author **Simon Ryder** (or Rider) (b1558) see Dunkirk Hall. **Charles II** disguised as William Jackson escaped through West Bromwich in 1651 (OWB p facing p16). **Walter Parsons**, of West Bromwich, a giant, was born in the Hall End area of West Bromwich in c1580. His height has been put at variously seven feet four inches; seven feet six inches; eight feet; and nine feet. From his wrist to the end of his middle finger he measured 11 inches. The palm of his hand was six inches wide. He was at first a black-

smith or served with another, for which employment a hole had to be dug for him so that he could stand at the anvil. A generous and gentle man, at length he became a porter to James I and then to Charles I, being succeeded in that office by William Evans, a native of Monmouthshire. Whilst in the employment of the king he occasionally used his immense size, in a playful sense, to the detriment of others. He once lifted a man onto a hook high in a street who had challenged him to fight. He would also in spirit take two of the tallest yeomen of the guard under his arms and carry them about the Guard's Chamber. Parsons died in the 1620s. Plot, in the later C17, noted what was reputed to be his measure or hand print upon a piece of wainscot at Bentley Hall (see). According to Plot, a picture reputed to be of him hung in the Guard's Chamber, and another hung at the Popeshead Tavern in Popeshead Alley, London (Common-Place Book of John Collett (b1633) in the BM) (HWE vol 2 p312) (NHS pp294,308 tab 27) (SHOS vol 1 General History pl. vol 2 pp95,96. vol 2 p134) (HYB) (SCC pp64,65) (N&Q 1849-55 vol 2 pp135,314) (W pp143,685-686) (Book of Giants and Dwarfs. Edward J Woods. 1868) (ROS vol 1 pp68-70) (Book of Giants. FW Hackwood. 1916) (KES p225) (BCWJ p108) (ES Feb 14 1958) (BCM Oct 1981 pp48-49). In the C17 a collier called **Dashfield** at Wednesbury fell down a disused mine shaft. The earth about the shaft then caved in, burying him alive. To the astonishment of the local community he was able to tunnel himself out, by transferring the soil above him to beneath him, for about nine yards in an hour. His neighbours were so suspicious of his extraordinary tunnelling powers they named him 'Witch' Dashfield (NHS p306). **Moses Bennett** of West Bromwich refused to take off his hat until the parson took off his 'devil's garb' (a surplice) for which he was excommunicated (ZSB). **Francis Asbury** (1745-1816), founder of the Methodist Episcopal Church and first bishop of the American Methodist Church (1785), when aged 17 was a Methodist class leader for a group which met in a small building facing what was then called West Bromwich Heath and is now Paradise Street (VCH vol 17 p4) (BCM summer 1995 p45). **David Parkes** (1763-1833), artist, taught in the West Bromwich area between 1789-90 (TEBC p39).

1800 to 1860. **Development of modern West Bromwich**. In 1802 (WMLB p2) or 1804 (VCH vol 17 p3) West Bromwich Common or Heath was enclosed. In a very short time the share holders had erected buildings along the Holyhead turnpike road, which cut across the heath. This became the High Street of West Bromwich (WMLB p52). About 1830 the post office was moved from Hill Top to the High Street. By 1868 the High Street was a busy thoroughfare. The High Street area may be considered to have received official recognition as the new centre for West Bromwich with the opening of the town hall in 1875 on part of the Lodge estate (VCH vol 17 p5). Such was the rapid growth of West Bromwich it was likened to an American city and dubbed the 'Chicago of England' (BBC 1 Midlands Today Feb 1 2000). **Some new churches**. Christ Church, to serve the High Street area of modern West Bromwich, was built in the 1820s (VCH vol 17 p55). It was consecrated in 1829 and was destroyed by fire on Oct 23 1979 (BOE p301) (WBOP p76) (WBOPP pl 5). St Philip, Beeches Road, was built in 1899 (LDD). By 1840 there was a street **market** in the High Street, prior to this markets were held at Lyndon (see). From 1840 until at least 1970 markets were held in a market-place between High Street and Paradise Street. There was a market hall on the site of the present public library between 1874 and 1899 (VCH vol 17 p34). The **cholera outbreak** of 1832 affected West Bromwich. From July 15 to Oct 15 1832 there were 297 cases in the parish, resulting in 62 deaths (SOWB p19) (TB Feb 1998 p17). In 1842 the Riot Act was read at West Bromwich due to the **frequent strikes and disturbances** brought on by the strikes of the colliers (SOWB p19). There was a strike by West Bromwich miners for better wages in 1845 (TEBC2 p55). **West Bromwich Building Society**, founded on April 23 1849, is still (1998) active (Building Societies Yearbook 1998-99: Official Handbook of the Building Society Association). The **first steam coach** - the Hancock Steam Coach - passed through West Bromwich on Sept 17 1832 (TEBC2 p38). The Birmingham, Wolverhampton & Dudley **Railway**, opened in 1854, linking Wolverhampton with Birmingham, had two stations in West Bromwich; one off Paradise Street to serve the new centre, and another at Swan Village (see) (VCH vol 17 p14). The line closed sometime between 1976 and 1989 and had become a path called West Bromwich Parkway by 1995 (Birmingham A-Z. 1989. 1995 editions). Newton Road station on the GJR was called West Bromwich for a few months when first opened in 1863 (VCH vol 17 p14). An **earthquake** was distinctly felt at West Bromwich in April 1805 (Broughton's Scrapbook p81). In c1830 a **pound** stood at the corner of Hollyhedge Road and Heath Lane opposite All Saints church and was then moved to in front of the Ring of Bells Inn at the junction of All Saints Street and Church Vale at Lyndon where it was still standing in 1970 (VCH vol 17 p43) (BCP p16p of in c1898).

Perhaps as a further consequence of the new-isolated position in which All Saints church at old West Bromwich found itself **body-snatchers** were attracted to its churchyard (SCSF p83). **Heaving**. At West Bromwich Heath tollgate on Easter Tuesday in c1850 a group of women hijacked a coach and made the male passengers alight and 'heaved' them until they had paid a forfeit (SCSF p13). In 1857 **Wombwell's Circus** visited West Bromwich and a tiger battered down the dividing wall of its cage shared with a lion which it fought and killed. This was seen by many people and caused much excitement in the town (SOWB p20). **Persons and visitors**. **Robert Spear Hudson** (d1884), inventor of Hudson's Dry Soap Powder, founded his business in High Street, West Bromwich, in 1837. Eventually the works were sold to Leverhulme Bros, Port Sunlight, Ches (TEBC2 p45). **David Christie Murray**, the novelist, was born in a house in High Street, West Bromwich, in 1847. He began his career on the Wednesbury Advertiser and became a leader writer for the paper. When working for the Birmingham Morning News he covered the Pelsall Hall Colliery disaster. For the same or another paper he covered the Black Lake pit fire at West Bromwich. 'A Novelist's Notebook' appeared in 1887. 'Joseph's Coat' (1892) is set in West Bromwich and Birmingham. His best known novel, 'Capful o' Nails (1896), and The Church of Humanity' (1902) are set in the Black Country. Autobiographical works include 'A Life's Atonement' (1879), 'The Making of a Novelist: An Experiment in Autobiography' (1894), and 'Recollections' (1908) (BCSG vol 4 pp41,42) (BCM July 1973 pp61-63. Oct 1977 p47. Jan 1978 pp50-54. Oct 1988 pp26-29. Jan 1991 pp62-67) (VB pp62-63) (ZSB) (VFC p97). He described West Bromwich about the time of his birth as 'a rather doleful hybrid of a place - neither town or country.' He died at his home in Hampstead, London on Aug 1 1907 (Recollections. DC Murray. 1908 p9) (VCH vol 17 p3) (WBOP p155p). **Frederick William Willmore** (d1902), son of Rev Benjamin Willmore, was born at Trinity Vicarage, West Bromwich, in 1848. He was the author of HOWW and ROR, a long poem 'The Chieftain's Grave' in Alfred Moss' anthology of Walsall poetry, and a history of Staffordshire freemasonry which appeared in 1905 (SHC 1928 pp248,249-250) (PSS p473) (BCM Jan 1978 pp79-80) (SH p135) (VFC p143).

INDUSTRY. The iron-workers of West Bromwich produced buckles, rings, bridle bits, and nails in the C16 and C17. West Bromwich was noted for its iron-smelting and nail-making in the C18 and the early part of the C19, but some of the other former industries moved to Walsall over this period. Arthur Young passing along the main road from West Bromwich to Birmingham in 1776, found it 'for five or six miles.....one continued village of nailers' (The Midlands. Past-into-Present series. Clive Gilbert. 1978 p39). Metal toys, and locks and steel bayonets for pistols and guns were made in West Bromwich from the end of the C18. From 1829 boiler-making and engine-making were established in West Bromwich. Also in the C19 West Bromwich was known for the manufacture of soap, bricks, corrugated-iron sheets, metal tubes, steel bars, axles and axle-trees, screws and castings of all kinds. The spring trade expanded greatly in the later C19. In the C20 West Bromwich produced motor cycles (the Sharratt motor cycle produced by John Sharratt between 1911 and 1930 at Carters Green - PVBC pp36-37), motor cars and parts for motor cars, lubricants, and office equipment (Staffs County Handbook c1958 p59) (VCH vol 17 pp34-38,41,42,43). Jensen Motors Ltd, formed in 1935, produced the Jensen car from works at Carters Green between 1935 and 1953. In 1955 the company moved to Kelvin Way, West Bromwich, and production continued to 1976. Production resumed in 1983 (BCFF p204). Mining occurred only from the early C19 (HOS p46). For West Bromwich windmills see Crabb's Mill, The Cronehills, Hall Green, Lyndon, Rider's Mill.

NEWSPAPERS. The Wednesbury Advertiser, founded in 1859, appeared as the **Wednesbury and West Bromwich Advertiser** between 1868 and 1872 (VCH vol 17 pp72-73). **West Bromwich Reporter and General Advertiser for the District** probably existed from 1863 and was a weekly in 1869. No more is known about it (VCH vol 17 pp72-73) (SHJ spring 1996 p35). The **West Bromwich Times**, founded in 1867, had ceased production by 1872 (VCH vol 17 pp72-73) (SHJ spring 1996 p35). **West Bromwich Weekly News**, probably founded in 1871, became the West Bromwich, Smethwick and Oldbury Weekly News (subsequently the Oldbury Weekly News) in or after 1904 (VCH vol 17 pp72-73) (SHJ spring 1996 p35). The weekly **Midland Free Press**, founded in 1875, became the Free Press from Oct 16 1875; in 1933 it was merged with the Midland Chronicle for West Bromwich and Oldbury (VCH vol 17 pp72-73) (SHJ spring 1996 p34). The weekly **West Bromwich Echo** appeared briefly in 1879 (VCH vol 17 pp72-73) (SHJ spring 1996 p35). The **West Bromwich and Oldbury Chronicle**, founded by mid Nov 1896, became the Chronicle for West Bromwich, Oldbury and District from May 12 1905, then the Midland Chronicle for West Bromwich, Oldbury, Smethwick and District from Oct 25 1912, then the West Bromwich, Oldbury

and Smethwick Midland Chronicle and Free Press from July 7 1933, then the West Bromwich and Warley Midland Chronicle Free Press from Feb 4 1966, then the West Bromwich Midland Chronicle and Free Press from July 29 1966 to the present (VCH vol 17 pp72-73) (SHJ spring 1996 p34). The Wednesbury Times became the **West Bromwich News and Wednesbury Times** in April 1966 and ran as such until at least Nov 1972 (VCH vol 17 pp72-73) (SHJ spring 1996 p35). Some Wednesbury (see) papers had West Bromwich in their title.

1860 to PRESENT. The **town hall** in High Street was designed by Alexander & Henman in 1874-5 (ILN Aug 21 1875 p172il) (BOE p301). West Bromwich was incorporated as a **county borough** in 1882. To celebrate the occasion Rev James Silvester (or Sylvester) (b1858), a native of West Bromwich, wrote the poet 'West Bromwich Town' (PSS pp310-313). The arms of West Bromwich county borough were granted in 1882. The **arms** are: Azure, a stag's face and antlers argent between three gold millrinds, within a silver border charged alternatively with four molets and fleurs-de-lis all azure. The crest is: On a wreath argent and azure, in front of four features azure a silver stag lodged, resting its forefoot on a millrind sable (CH p331il). In **WW2** Richard Street South was bombed on Nov 19 1940; 32 people were killed (TB Feb 1996 p3). West Bromwich has two **town clocks**, one at Carters Green (see) and one in Dartmouth Square. The oldest is the one at Carters Green. The Dartmouth Square clock was presented by the Mayor John Archibald Kenrick in 1912 (BCM April 1986 pp7,10). In 1875 John Blackham, a Congregationalist deacon at West Bromwich, invented the **Pleasant Sunday Afternoon**, a regular Sunday afternoon meeting in a chapel or public hall for an assorted programme of song, prayer, reading, and addresses. PSA Societies were founded throughout the nation in the late C19 (VCH vol 3 pp133-134). The inhabitants of West Bromwich are traditionally known as **'throstles.'** The name is said to derive from the 'numberless donkeys who browsed upon the open common lands and whose discordant bray was thus satirically alluded to under the name of the sweet-voiced thrush' (HOWB p115) (VCH vol 17 p2). **West Bromwich Albion Football Club** (formerly known locally as the Throstles, now (2000) known as the Baggies) is believed to have been founded by Rev William Marlborough Carter (d1941), later Archbishop of Cape Town, when curate of Christ Church. He encouraged a boys bible class to play football. At first they called themselves West Bromwich Strollers (SHWB 15). Another account says the club was founded in 1879 by a group of men from Salter's spring works. Several of the early players lived in the Albion area. The club took its present name in c1880 (VCH vol 17 p74). The club won the 1888 FA Cup, beating Preston North End 2-1; the 1892 FA Cup, beating Aston Villa 3-0 (TEBC); and beating Birmingham in the 1931 FA Cup (BCP p23). The highest score by one side in a Football League (Division 1) match by 1974 was 12 goals when West Bromwich Albion beat Darwen 12-0 at West Bromwich on March 4 1892 (GBR 1974 p269). The fastest goals scored in a football match by 1995 were those by William 'Ginger' Richardson of West Bromwich Albion when he scored four goals in five minutes from 'kick-off' against West Ham United at Upton Park on Nov 7 1931 (GBR 1995 p253). The club moved to its present ground, the Hawthorns (see), in 1900 (VCH vol 17 p74). The club supporters were voted the worst dressed in the country in 2000 (BBC 1 Midlands Today. April 25 2000). The highest score in **basketball** in a Senior National League Match by 1991 was 167 by West Bromwich Kestrels v Milton Keynes (69) on Feb 13 1983 (GBR 1991 p241). **North Bromwich** in Francis Brett Young's novels is Birmingham? An **apparition** of a woman nicknamed Mildred has been seen by some of the staff of a ladies fashion shop called Van Allen (GOM p27). **Natives and visitors**. The American, Colour Sergeant **Gilbert Bates**, veteran of the American Civil War, passed through West Bromwich in Nov 1872 carrying out a wager to walk the length of England (SOWB p22). **The Willetts**. Mary Willett, published HOWBW in 1882. She was the daughter of John Nock Bagnall. She was married to the infamous Rev Frederick Willett, vicar of All Saints, West Bromwich (1865-1881), he was charged with immorality by a female penitent of which he was acquitted (SH p134). Mr JW Proctor, a member of the Handsworth Historical Society, related the story of Rev Willett of All Saints, West Bromwich, who died in 1939, aged 101. As a boy he had shaken hands with an uncle, who had fought at Trafalgar, and then about 100, and who, also as a young boy had shaken hands with his uncle aged 101. This latter uncle as a child, had witnessed a progress of King Charles II through the City (of London?), so that three generations of one family covered the period from Charles II to George VI (HPPE p8). **Samuel Lees** died suddenly in 1890 at the age of 42 whilst in office as mayor. There is a bust of him in the Central Library, West Bromwich (BCM July 1982 pp27-28p). The seismologist, **John Johnson Shaw** (d1948), CBE, was born in Lower Gornal (see) in 1873, lived at 'Sunnyside' on the Birmingham Road, West Bromwich (BCM summer 1995 pp59,60p) and made experiments at Baggeridge Colliery (see). A seismograph which he built can be seen in the Science Museum, London. A short road leading to an industrial estate in West Bromwich is named Shaw Street (TB Feb 1993 p27). **Edwin Radford**, journalist and novelist, was born in West Bromwich in 1891. His work, which belongs to the thriller genre, includes 'The Heel of Achilles and Death on the Broads.' The detective novels featuring Inspector Manson, amongst them 'Inspector Manson's Success' (1944), 'Who Killed Dick Whittington?' (1947), 'Death at the Chateau Noir' (1960), and 'Murder Magnified' (1965), were written in collaboration with his wife, Mona Augusta Radford (VFC p111). The unsolved deaths or murders of **Mr Hassal** and his housekeeper, **Mrs Hall**, at Mr Hassal's house, No. 31 Herbert Street, in June 1894 posed many unanswerable questions and the case was sensationalised in the Illustrated Police Budget of June 1894 (MMMR pp14-16). A miner named **Corbett** of Walsall Street, West Bromwich, killed his wife by cutting her throat (TB Feb 1978 pp18-19). **Madeleine Carroll**, film actress (1906-1987), was born in West Bromwich. She starred in 'The Thirty Nine Steps' (1935), and 'The Prisoner of Zenda' (1937) (BCTV p82) (HOS 1998 ed p22 il). It is said that 'It's a long way to Tipperary' was the song that **Jack Yorke** of West Bromwich came up with after being challenged to write, produce and perform a song on the same day on New Year's Day 1912. Yorke was sometime manager of the Eight Locks Inn, Greets Green (West Bromwich Yesterdays. RD Woodall) (SOWB p22). Others have attributed Jack Judge of Oldbury (see) with writing the song. **Keir Hardy** visited West Bromwich on April 13 1913 during a strike here to speak to workers. About 300 took part in the procession through the town (SOWB p22). Prince of Wales (later Edward VIII), visited West Bromwich in June 1923 (WBOP p60). The first time the BBC broadcast a description of a murderer on the radio was to describe the murderer of **Charles William Fox** who was killed on Aug 27 1933 at Fox's house in Moor Street. The broadcast brought a response from the Cheshire police; the vehicle of Stanley Eric Hobday, the murderer, had been abandoned at High Legh near Lymm, Ches, and Hobday was seen by a landworker at Townsend Farm near Carlisle. He was arrested at Radcliffe, Cumberland (MCGM pp162-164) (TB Feb 1986 p5) (MCS pp42-44). **Dorothy Mills**, aged 32, of Bernard Street was murdered on Jan 21 1961. Her body was found by a shed at Wesley Tennis Club in Bratt Street, where she had been to play tennis. The motive for the killing was at first thought to be robbery; her handbag was found in a nearby street minus four pounds. But a postmortem, revealed that Dorothy, a reserved, single person with no known boyfriend, was 13 weeks pregnant. The case remains unsolved (MM pp65-74) (MMBC p172) (MMMR pp101-104). For **Ian Hill** of West Bromwich from the rock music band 'Judas Priest' see Hill Top, West Bromwich. The Black Country Ale Tairsters of West Bromwich - **Peter Hill**, **Joseph Hill**, **Rob Jones** - visited and consumed a drink in 4200 different pubs throughout Britain in aid of local hospital funds between Nov 2 1984 and May 6 1992 (GBR 1993 p93). **Tarsem King** (b1937), Leader of Sandwell metropolitan borough, was created a peer on July 28 1999 as Lord King of West Bromwich; he was the first Sikh to enter the House of Lords (BBC 1 Midlands Today. July 28 1999).

West Bromwich Common Former barren heath of some 387 acres, urbanised by 1850. The common is marked on the maps of Plot, Bowen and Smith and has also appeared as West Bromwich Heath. An old track which ran across the ivy-leaf shaped common like a stem was part of the route from London to Shrewsbury by the beginning of the C16. In the Civil War parliamentarians are said to have thrown up an encampment on the heath near what is now Oak Lane during the siege of Dudley Castle in June 1644 (WB p9) (VCH vol 17 p9), in consequence of which a C19 inn in Wood Lane, Lambert's End, is called the Oliver Cromwell Inn (TB March 1998 pp18-19p). The road was turnpiked in 1727 and was used by the Holyhead mail coaches from 1808 (VCH vol 17 p11); there was a horse block in front of the Farley clock tower, from 1760 (OWB p101). Troop reinforcements camped on the common in Dec 1745, ready to advance to meet the 1745 Jacobite Rebellion. John Wesley was at Westbromwich Heath in 1768 and 1770 (SA Jan 24 1885 p6). The common was enclosed in 1802 or 1804, after which in a very short time the shareholders built along the road (now High Street) and it became the centre of West Bromwich. (W p681) (VCH vol 17 p3). One solitary house for a warrener, the Lodge, was demolished in 1868 and the District Hospital built on the site (VCH vol 17 p9) (SHWB 5).

West Bromwich Manor House Hall Green Road, Hall Green, West Bromwich. Has also appeared as Manor House, Old Manor House, Bromwich Hall (1605), Bromwich Hall, West Bromwich Hall (C18) (OWB p19) (SSAHST 1975-76 p1), and perhaps Old Hall (OS map 1:50,000). Overlordship of West Bromwich manor descended with the Dudley Barony until the death without issue of John, Lord Somery, in 1322. The barony was then divided between his sis-

ters. The ownership then descended with Weoley Castle, Worcs, until at least 1560. The Offini family, founders of Sandwell Priory, held West Bromwich manor in the later C12 to the mid C13 when it was divided between female heirs. A part went by marriage to the Devereux family and eventually passed to the Vernons of Haddon, Derbys. It eventually passed to the Skeffingtons of Fisherwick and is not heard of again after the end of the C16. The other part went by marriage to Richard de Marnham (VCH vol 17 pp14-15). It may have been his sons who squabbled in the early C14 with one son taking his brother's life (OWB pp40-41). The Marnhams held their share of the manor until c1420 and it eventually descended to the Freeman family and then to the Frebodys and then to the Stanleys who held it (or what could be said to be now the whole manor of West Bromwich) from the earlier C16 to 1626. The manor was then purchased by Sir Richard Shilton (or Shelton) (d1647), solicitor-general to Charles I (VCH vol 17 pp15-16) (SGS p178). Between 1706 and 1710 John Shilton mortgaged or sold all his lands. The manor was sold by Order of Chancery to Sir Samuel Clarke in 1720. The Clarkes, who became the Clarke-Jervoises, held it until 1820 or 1823, when it passed to James Smith, and on his death in 1829, to his trustees. There was a manor house at West Bromwich by the early 1220s. The date of the Great Hall, the earliest part of the present hall, is approximately 1290-1310. The filled-in moat was re-excavated as part of the restoration. Significantly no material earlier than the C16 was found. From about the 1830s it was turned into tenements and kept in a poor state. In 1949 and 1950, by which time it had been encased and reduced to the status of a farmhouse, the hall was purchased by West Bromwich corporation for demolition, but on being found to be of historical and architectural importance was saved. The bill for restoration was estimated to be £9,000 in 1956. Restoration began in c1957 and was completed by 1961 (WMAG Dec 1963 pp34-35ps) (VCH vol 17 pp16-17 plan p facing p17) (BOE p303) (SSAHST 1975-76 pp1-63 ils, ps. 1978-79 pp29-38. 1982-3 p51. 1991-92 pp21-41) (SGS p177) (SL p88 pls 14,15 before and after renovation) (NSFCT 1982 p19) (WBOPP pl 73) (WBOP p152p) (SHWB 6) (E&S Oct 2 1999 p19ps). In 1961 the house opened as a restaurant run by Ansells brewery, tenants of the corporation (VCH vol 17 p18) (SGS p178). Said to be haunted (HIE p179) (FSLBWM p37). (SHOS vol 2 p128) (NSFCT 1959 p102) (MR p365p).

West Brook Tributary of Onecote Brook, a tributary of the Hamps. Rises near the house, Westbrook, 2m NW of Onecote, formerly in Onecote township in Leek ancient parish. The present house is of the C19, but there was a house here by 1710 (VCH vol 7 p211). The brook takes its name from being the more westerly arm of the Hamps (SPNO p22).

Westbury Park Modern housing estate, suburb of Clayton, 2m S of Newcastle-under-Lyme.

West Chadsmoor Modern housing estate 1.25m N of Cannock. Is 0.5m NW of Chadsmoor. The church, St Aidan, in Pye Green Road, was in use between 1947 and 1956 (VCH vol 5 p67). Another church, St Aidan, Albert Street, Broomehill, was built in 1956 (LDD).

Westcliffe Small district 1m SSE of Newchapel. The present Westcliffe Hospital on the E side of Turnhurst Road, stands adjoining the site of the Wolstanton and Burslem Union workhouse or called the Tunstall Union House (1834 OS map). The workhouse was built by 1841. Between WW1 and WW2 it became known as the Turnhurst Institution. In the 1940s it became the Westcliffe residential home and served as a home for the poor until 1975. It was demolished in 1993 (W p286) (SASR 1995 no 6 p18) (ES Dec 27 1997 p17). It was abhorred by Arnold Bennett who called it the Bastille in his novels (TSS p46) (ES Dec 27 1997 p17). The 'cinema king,' George Barber, was sent into it aged seven (POTP p28). The Claybourne Centre, opened by Methodist Homes next to Westcliffe Hospital in 1997. It is the third purpose-built home in Britain for dementia sufferers. Prince Charles visited the home on March 2 1998 (ES June 17 1999 p17p) (info Annmarie Walton).

West Coseley Former hamlet centred on the junction of Mason and Oak Streets, Portland Place and Chad Road, in an area now known as Roseville, Coseley. The name first appears in the 1861 census. The ecclesiastical parish of West Coseley was created in 1884 and renamed 'Coseley St Chad' in 1956 (GLAUE p409). Joseph Nicholds, composer, born near Birmingham in or c1784, was landlord of the Hop and Barleycorn Inn (see) at West Coseley.

Westcroft Farm and modern housing lining the Featherstone Road 1m S of Featherstone. Formerly in Bushbury ancient parish, now a ward in Essington civil parish. Merges with Underhill. Westcroft Farm, a timber-framed structure, was formerly known as Werlescroft. It was one of three farms in the possession of the Underhill family, along with Northicote and Underhill farms (BUOP p31p). Westcroft Farm was surrounded by a moat (VCH vol 1) (SSAHST 1982-3 p42).

Western Downs Modern housing estate and suburb of Stafford, built after 1977,

0.5m S of Castle Church.

Western Meres Farm 0.5m SSE of Maer.

Westfields Armitage parish (W p556). The house, West Fields, is over 0.5m S of Armitage.

West Fields House 1m SW of Keele (1834 OS map) (Dower's map).

West Gate Defensive stone gateway on W side of Lichfield cathedral Close built after c1300, perhaps after Edward II ordered the Close to be securely defended on his behalf in 1317 and 1322 (MCC) and completed by 1358 (VCH vol 14 p60). It was through this gate that parish processions, each preceded by a cross, brought offerings to the cathedral at Whitsuntide. There was much rivalry between parishes and in order to prevent scuffles it was decided that all crosses must be left at the gate (MCC). Thomas, the beggar, trampled to death near it in 1293, suggests there was an earlier gate on the site (MCC). It was taken down in April 1800 to widen the road to the Close and for the building of Newton's College (HOL p292 il of facing p293) (GNHS p158) (W p500) (VCH vol 14 p60). Some of its stones went to building Newton's College (VCH vol 3 p189). The base of splayed angle buttress is listed by DoE II*.

West Gate Medieval gateway in the wall surrounding Stafford, on the W side, at Broad Eye. Leland noted a gate at Broad Eye. John Speed stated that there was a fourth gate on the W side of Stafford, and his plan of 1610 shows one at Broadeye Bridge (VCH vol 6 p200). Celia Fiennes, who noted that there had been a gate here, saw the ruins in 1698 (VCH vol 6 p200) (Illustrated Journeys of Celia Fiennes. Edited by Christopher Morris. 1984. p148). Some say it was merely an entrance in the town walls (to the drawbridge?), which, had no defensive properties (SKYT p49) (SSTY p2). It secured the main road to the W prior to the building of the Newport Road in c1700 (ROT p36). There was some doubt in the early C19 as to where this gate had stood (THS p289).

West Heath Now in Cheshire near Doddlespool Hall, originally in Staffs. In Barthomley parish, Cheshire.

West Hill Tiny district and hill on high ground above the heads of Ridding and Rising Brooks 1.75m NNE of Cannock. In Cannock old parish.

Westland Gate Near Sugnall. It formerly lay by Greatwood Heath (SSE vol 7 1995 p75).

Westlands Large private housing estate 1.25m S of Newcastle-under-Lyme. A Roman coin of Claudius has been found in Sutherland Drive (NSFCT vol 1 p49). The housing estate was built after 1920 on Hill Farm estate in Clayton Griffith manor, (a detached portion of Trentham ancient parish in Stoke-upon-Trent ancient parish until 1896) (VCH vol 8 p76) (PCCSC p152p aerial photograph in 1945). Named after Westlands Farm which was situated in the present Sneyd Avenue area (OS map 1882). 'The Westlands' became a separate ecclesiastical parish in 1966 (GLAUE p428). The church, St Andrew, Pilkington Avenue, was consecrated in 1962 (info WGH Gardiner), and has been called The Church in the Westlands.

Weston A ward of Stoke-on-Trent district by 1991 covering the Sandford Hill, Weston Coyney, Normacot, and Meir Hay areas.

Weston Coyney Former manor (W p752) and hamlet on ground rising out of the Blithe backed by the Parkhall Hills, now a suburb of Longton, 1.5m E of Longton. In Caverswall ancient parish. There is said to be a large granite boulder of the Ice Age in the side of the Bucknall road at Weston Coyney (WJ p16). There is a possible burial mound here (WJ p28). Probably the one thought to have been at cSJ 937439 which was probably destroyed by modern housing estate and may not have been a burial mound (NSJFS 1965 p35). Appears in DB as Westone. First appears with an addition, sub Keveremont (see Kenermont Hay), in 1242 (SPN pp31-32). The name means 'west town' (DUIGNAN), or 'western farmstead' (SPN p31). Coyneys (rightly Coignet) were lords of the manor in the Middle Ages (DUIGNAN). Johannes Koyne was lord in 1242 (SSE 1996 p23) (SPN p32). The moated site at Weston Coyney was missed off a list prepared by NSFC for preservation under the Ancient Monuments Act 1911. An housing estate was built over it and a road called The Moat built along side it (Geographia Street Atlas and Index, Stoke-on-Trent, p43) (NSFCT 1982 p16). The church, St Andrew, St Andrew's Church Centre, 375 Weston Road, was built in 1984 (LDD). For the custom of erecting crosses at Easter at Weston Coyney see Parkhall Hills. During the 1984-85 miners' strike the wives of miners at Hem Heath and Florence collieries marched from Weston Coyney to Longton in support of their striking husbands (SSE 1987 p232). An object which dropped vertically in the sky and stopped abruptly when about 100 feet from the ground, where it remained stationary for 10 seconds, then accelerated towards the north, and then disappeared in half a minute was seen from West Coyney at about 7.15pm on Oct 27 1967 (FSRP p18). A round light, bright red in colour, with indistinct edges that shone constantly was seen for about five minutes by two people at Weston Coyney on Nov 10 1967 (FSRP p19).

Weston Coyney Hall Weston Coyney. Seat of the Coyneys in the later C17 (Plot's map). In the early C19 it appears to have been still the seat of the Coyneys, Catholics. Miss Coyney, the heiress, married Walter Hill, on condition he take the name of Coyney and agree that his daughters be brought up as Catholics; his sons could be brought up as Protestants (HOC p243). He was succeeded by his son Col Coyney, probably the C Coyney who was in residence in 1851 (W p24), and the Col Coyney who was the occupant in 1881 (HOC p243). There was armorial glass at the hall at beginning of the C19 but it had vanished by 1922 (NSFCT 1922 p79). The hall was bought by F Pattison in c1910. It was sold in c1938 and demolished in c1944. It is now (mid 1990s) the site for an housing estate (local info).

Weston Coyney Old Park Medieval deer park enclosed out of forest at Weston Coyney. In existence by 1449 (NSJFS 1962 p76). Park Hall, Upper Park Head and Lower Park Head indicate three sides of the old park. The straight length of the Stoke and Caverswall parish boundary probably indicates the remaining W end. In 1449 Robert Coyney sued a carpenter from Baddeley 'for breaking into his park of Weston Coyney' (NSFCT 1910 p175). Bolton Gate may represent one of its gates. The park was owned by the Coyney family and then by the Park family of Park Hall and became absorbed into the rest of their estate between the C17 and the C19. The area became Park Hall Country Park (see) in 1980.

Weston Hall Former manor house of Weston manor, Weston-in-the-Hedge, Standon. In existence by 1327 when occupied by Sir John Chetwynd III (d1354). With the marriage of his granddaughter, Joan, Weston passed to the Peshalls. By marriage it passed from them to the Grosvenors in the C15; they sold it to the Roos family who were owners by 1578. The old hall had disappeared by the late C19 (COI pp30,32,37,39). Here was possibly a village in medieval times, possibly deserted between 1327-1524 (SSAHST 1970 p36).

Weston Hall Very large stone house built in c1630 (SL p97) or the early C17 (SGS pp178,179p) or the late C17 (LGS p251) (NSFCT pp23-24), on Weston Bank 0.5m W of Weston-on-Trent. (BOE p305). Has also appeared as Weston Old Hall. Probably built by William and Lady Dorothy (nee Devereux) Stafford, although local tradition has sometimes attributed it to William Stafford of Chebsey, who married a daughter of Lord Stafford (COI pp162il -163) (NSFCT 1912 pp209-210). Others have said it was built as a dower house for the Talbots, Earls of Shrewsbury (info Bruce Braithwaite). Lady Dorothy (nee Devereux) lived here in the later C17. She was the youngest daughter of Robert Devereux of Chartley Castle (see), 2nd Earl of Essex (NSFCT 1912 pp209-210). She was the mother of Sir Robert Shirley (d1656), Bt, of Chartley Castle (see). Her second husband was William Stafford of Blatherwyke (SHC 1909 p166). It was occupied by a tenant farmer in the later C19 and was sold to settle a gambling debt. William Stubbs was occupying the hall in 1851 (W p23); the Stubbs family of Weston Hall have graves in Salt churchyard. Sometime shortly before 1892 it was purchased by the Earl of Shrewsbury and became a part of the Ingestre estate. About 1910 Masefield noted it was derelict and empty. In c1912 it became the county lunatic asylum of Stafford (COI p163) (AR p30p of c1912). During WW2 the hall was requisitioned and occupied by land army girls; some of whom, reputedly, feeling the hall was haunted, preferred to camp in the grounds (AR p30). The ghost of a lady in green has been seen entering the front door, and the ghost of a nurse has also been seen (SN Oct 29 1993 p8) (info Bruce Braithwaite). The ghost of a woman in white has been seen near the hall (TRTC forward), and a lady in grey is said to haunt the hall (TRTC p177). By at least the late 1990s the hall had been restored and turned into a restaurant.

Weston Hall Weston Hall and earlier halls on the same site at Weston-under-Lizard have been the seat of the lords of Weston-under-Lizard from medieval times (WPG 1974 p32). Hamo de Weston was lord of Weston in 1175. The manor remained with the de Westons until the death of John de Weston, who had died by 1349. The manor was then divided between his daughters. A share of the manor had passed to Sir Adam de Peshale by 1386.

THE MYTTONS AND THE BRIDGEMANS. Adam's youngest daughter married into the Mytton family and the manor passed to the Myttons. John Mytton, lord of Weston, died in 1500 and was succeeded by his son, John (d1533). He was succeeded by his daughter Joyce, wife of John Harpesfield. Their son Edward, assumed the name of Mytton. He was succeeded by his son John (d1615), who was succeeded by his son Edward (d1638). He was succeeded by his daughter Elizabeth, by his second marriage. In 1651 she married Sir Thomas Wilbraham of Woodhey, Ches. In 1686 Elizabeth and Sir Thomas settled their Staffs estates on their third daughter Mary, who in 1681 had married Richard Newport, 2nd Earl of Bradford (Bradford in Shrops) (1644-1723). Their son Henry Newport (1683-1734), 3rd Earl, succeeded. He was succeeded by his brother Thomas Newport, 4th Earl. He died unmarried in 1762, and the manor passed through his sister, Anne and her husband,

Sir **Orlando Bridgeman**, 4th Bt, to their second son Sir Henry Bridgeman (1725-1800), 5th Bt and 1st Baron Bradford (Bradford, Shrops). He was succeeded by his second son **Orlando Bridgeman** (1762-1825), 2nd Baron Bradford, 1st Earl of Bradford (second creation), who was succeeded by his eldest son **George Augustus Frederick Henry Bridgeman** (1789-1865), 2nd Earl of Bradford. Successive Earls were all succeeded by their eldest son: The 2nd Earl was succeeded by **Orlando George Charles Bridgeman** (1819-1898), 3rd Earl. He was followed by **George Cecil Orlando Bridgeman** (1845-1915), 4th Earl, who was followed by Sir **Orlando Bridgeman** (b1873), 5th Earl. On his death in 1957 his son **Gerald Michael Orlando Bridgeman** (b1911), 6th Earl, succeeded (WPG 1987 p18) (VCH vol 4 pp171-172). In 1981 the 6th Earl died and was succeeded by his eldest son, **Richard Thomas Orlando Bridgeman**, 7th Earl. The 7th Earl was unable to pay the massive death duties on his father's death and in 1986 he gave Weston Hall and grounds to the Weston Park Foundation to ensure the preservation of the hall (Daily Telegraph Aug 24 1999 p7). Since then the Foundation and the estate's operating company Weston Park Enterprises have hired out the hall and grounds for public and private events on many occasions: For six hours on May 16 1998 the hall was the venue for a meeting between world leaders, Bill Clinton (USA), Boris Yeltsin (Russia), Tony Blair (Britain), Jacques Chirac (France), Helmut Kohl (Germany), Ryutaro Hashimoto (Japan), Romano Prodi (Italy), Jean Chretien (Canada) for the G8 Summit: Talks took place in the Orangery (E&S May 14 1998 p7) (SLM July Aug 1998 p13). In Aug 20-21 1999 the grounds hosted its first pop music festival, called the V99 festival, with an audience of 50,000 people, many of whom camped the night. The unruly behaviour of some upset the 7th Earl, who lives at Woodlands, a farmhouse on the estate. The Earl expressed his concerns on television without permission from the Foundation's chief executive to do so. The chief executive of the Foundation then berated the Earl and so in protest the Earl instantly resigned his positions as chairman of the operating company and as a trustee of the Foundation, and so severed his links with the hall (Daily Telegraph Aug 24 1999 p7) (Daily Mail Weekend magazine Sept 11 1999 pp10-13).

THE HALL. The hall which preceded the present hall had a four-gabled S front (VCH vol 4 p170). The present house, which has sometimes appeared as Weston House (mem in Blymhill church), was built in 1671 by Sir Thomas and Lady Elizabeth Wilbraham; the latter is credited with the design. For some reason Sir Thomas did not want it engraved for an illustration in Plot's history (NHS p359). (SHOS vol 2 pl of the hall). It incorporates one very thick stone wall and a carved shield (which may date from the mid C16) from the previous hall (VCH vol 4 p170). Originally, the main doorway to the present house was on the S side. The E side was made the entrance in 1825 (BOE p305), or after 1865 when important alterations to the house were made by Orlando, 3rd Earl, after his succession (VCH vol 4 p170). The stucco was stripped from the older parts of the house, revealing the original red brick of 1671, shortly before WW2 (VCH vol 4 p170). Weston Park has been open to the public since May 9 1964 (WMAG April 1964 pp26-27). In the **Library** in late Nov 1858 Lady Lucy, aged 32, daughter of the 2nd Earl, died of burns when the fire set her dress alight. Her sister, Charlotte, aged 31, died trying to rescue her (mem in Blymhill church) (WPG. 1974. p10). Here is kept Lady Wilbraham's copy of an early (1663) translation of Palladio's 'First Book of Architecture' with her own notes and costings clearly visible in the margins. Made into a firescreen is the Bag of the Great Seal of England. Sir Orlando Bridgeman (1608-1674), great great grandfather of Sir Henry Bridgeman (d1800), was Lord Keeper of the Great Seal 1667-1674 (Burke's Peerage) (SLM April 1959 pp12p,13) (WPG pp10,11p). In the **West Marble Hall** is a letter from Charles II Sir Orlando requesting its return (WPG 1987 p10p). On the S wall Bassano's painting 'The Way to Golgotha' (WPG. 1974. p15pc). In a case a selection of 1,100 letters written by Disraeli to Selina, 3rd Countess of Bradford, between 1873 to 1881 (SLM summer 1957 pp10,11,12) (WPG 1987 p10). They were formerly in a despatch case in the library (NSFCT 1955 p81; 110 letters are mentioned). Disraeli gave the countess a yellow parrot, which one day in 1903 laid an egg, an unusual feat for a cock bird. After laying eggs for the next 23 days it died. The bird was stuffed and is exhibited outside the small salon. In the **Second Salon** are some of Gould's books on birds published between 1832 and 1861. They are said to be second only in importance in their field to Audubon's 'Birds of America' (WPG p19). The **Tapestry Room** contains some priceless tapestries from the Paris Gobelin factory, originally made to fit in a first floor bedroom (VCH vol 4 p170) (WPG p5pc) (MR p371). The same room contains dishes made in the Yung Cheng period (1723-35), a drawing of Anne Boleyn by Holbein, containing a memorandum in Holbein's handwriting which reads 'Anne Boleyn, beheaded in London 19 May 1536' (only mentioned in WPG. 1974) and the C18 cut

glass chandelier found in pieces in the Temple of Diana (WPG. 1974. p6). The **Breakfast Room** contains Holbein's portrait of Sir George Carew, Capt of the Mary Rose and the Triple portrait of Charles I by Carlo Maratta. There are portraits in the hall by Constable, Hoppner, Gainsborough, Kneller, Lely, Reynolds, Romney and Van Dyck. (SLM July 1953 pp14-15,18,19,20ps) (The Connoisseur Year Book 1955). One room contains a set or an individual cock-fighting chair (WPG p23p). For the grounds see Weston Park.

Weston Hawes Cuttlestone hundred. Possibly the site for a village in medieval times (SSAHST 1970 p36). According to PV Bate and DM Palliser it could be at SJ 795243, at Weston Wood 0.75m SSW of Woodseaves. However, Weston-under-Lizard was written Weston Hewes in the early C14 (SHC 1914 p182 note).

Weston Heath Hamlet on the N side of a hill 1.5m NE of Sheriffhales. In Sheriff Hales parish. Name appears in 1666 (SPNO p182).

Weston-in-the-Hedge Tiny hamlet on the steep slopes of the Swinchurch Brook valley 1.5m NW of Standon. Former township (HOPS p4) in Standon ancient parish. Has appeared as Westone (DB), Weston-juxta-Standon and Weston-in-Standon (SHC 1914 p12). At Weston Hall (see) may have been a village in medieval times. The name means 'west town.' No reference to Weston-in-the-Hedge is made (DUIGNAN).

Weston Jones Hamlet on rising ground by a tributary of Lonco Brook near Lonco Brook 1.5m WNW of Norbury. The name is perhaps significant as marking a halting place in the Anglian advance westward. There is a tradition of St Martin here. There may have been a Celtic or Welsh church dedicated to St Martin for there is faint tradition here of observing a wake at Martinmas (ESH p45). According to Eyton and Wrottesley a manor at Weston Jones is the anonymous entry recorded in DB as the two hides held of Robert de Stafford by Urfer listed between entries relating to Ridware and Haughton; others have identified the anonymous entry with Hyde manor at Hyde Lea (OSST 1951-52 p16). Has appeared as Weston Johannis or Johannes (1236), Westone Jhones (1245. 1327), and Weston (1242) (DUIGNAN) (LGS p194) (SPNO p176) (SPN pp140-141) (SSE 1996 p19). The name means 'west town;' Weston Jones lies in the most westerly portion of Norbury parish (SPNO p176). Jones was probably a local landowner or lord of the manor. A John de Weston held the manor in 1316 (DUIGNAN) (SPNO p176) (SPN pp140-141). Said to have taken an appellation to distinguish it from Weston-under-Lizard (SHC 1914 p182 note). For Weston Jones earthwork see 'Gregory.' Weston Jones was an extra-parochial liberty (ESH p45). By 1851 it was a township in Norbury ancient parish (W p465). The separate civil parish of Weston Jones, created in 1866, was abolished in 1934 when it entered into the civil parishes of Adbaston, Norbury, and High Offley (GLAUE p428).

Weston Jones Mill 0.5m W of Weston Jones.

Weston-on-Trent Ancient parish and village in the Trent Valley backed by the uplands of Hopton Heath, 4m NE of Stafford. Weston-on-Trent was identified by Duignan, but not by Dugdale, Shaw and others, with the Westune mentioned in Wulfric Spot's will (c1002) (SHC 1916 p38); has also appeared as Westone (DB) and Weston-under-Trent (GLAUE p428). The name means 'west town' (DUIGNAN). 'West' may be from it being on the western boundary of the Chartley estate (SVB p172). The parish was formed out of Stowe parish, probably in the latter C13 (SHC 1916 pp192,196). There was a church at Weston by 1220 (LDD). The parish church, St Andrew, on the N side of Stafford Lane, has some work of c1210 (LGS p250) (BOE p304). Has an exceptionally large village green (VB p136) of three acres which have remained common land (OSST 1956-59 p12). A royalist account of the Hopton Heath battle, published in the year the battle took place 1643, states the parliamentarians had drawn up their forces 'upon a heath, called Hopton Heath, neere a towne called Weston' (SHJ winter 1987 p1). Weston PR records names of those buried here who were killed in the battle (LGS p251). Earl Talbot of Ingestre opened a salt works in Salt Works Lane, Weston in 1821 which shortly overtook in production the salt works at Shirleywich. The works closed in c1900. A small arm from the Trent & Mersey Canal served the works, which closed in c1900 (SPJD p75) (info Hixon Local History Society). Weston Local History Group formed in 1998 (info R Green). On Sept 3 1954 James Penton Leighton saw a UFO from his car on Weston Bank. It was cigar-shaped (The Coming of the Spaceships. Gavin Gibbons. 1956). The ghost of a man named Preston Moore was seen in a lane in Weston-on-Trent in c1860 very shortly after he had died (NSFCT 1900 p142). Theo Douglas, ghost writer and author of 'Behind a Mask' (1898), 'Cousin Hugh' (1910 2nd ed), and 'The Death-mask, and other ghost stories' (1920), lived at Weston. In the early C19 the curate wrote a poem about his departure from the village complaining of the poor condition of the vicarage, it starts:

My Straw-crowned cot, farewell to thee,

Thou shelter of my poverty:
Thou boast of Weston and the shame,
Where I have slept to winds exposed,

(VCH vol 3 p69) (NSFCT New Series vol 18. 1993. p11).

Weston-on-Trent Manor House Weston-on-Trent. Has been split into cottages (AR p31p).

Weston Park Deer park at Weston-under-Lizard, belonging to the lords of the manor. Was stocked with deer in 1570 and in the Civil War (SOS p xxi) (SHC new series vol 2 pp130-133) (VCH vol 4 p173).

Weston Park The grounds of Weston Hall, Weston-under-Lizard. Covers an area of nearly 1000 acres surrounded by an eight mile wall (WPG 1987). An axe-head of Neolithic or Bronze Age was found at in the park and is kept in the Countryside Museum at Weston Hall, Weston-under-Lizard (BDH pp17,18). The park was landscaped by Lancelot 'Capability' Brown in the 1760s (VCH vol 4 p170) (SL p133). The Earl of Bradford introduced deer into the park sometime in the C19 (EDP p180). For the WW2 airfield in the park see Weston-under-Lizard. Weston Park has been open to the public since May 9 1964 (WMAG April 1964 pp26-27). **Flag Tower** see Prospect Tower. The **Little Temple** is a stone shelter overlooking Temple Pool and dates from 1938 (VCH vol 4 p170) (WPG p30). Close to the hall is the **Mausoleum** built in 1870 by the Earl and Countess of Bradford in memory of her son Hon Gerald Bridgeman (VCH vol 4 p176). (SHC 1899 new series vol ii p335). It is in a Beaux-Arts Grecian style and has a portico of two pairs of Tuscan columns (BOE p306). At SJ 816098 1m SE of the hall is a **Moat** which may relate to an abandoned medieval settlement (SSAHST 1982-3 pp51-52). In the middle of the lawn on the lowest terrace is the largest **oriental plane tree** (Platanus orientalis) in the country (The Trees of Great Britain and Ireland. Elwes and Henry. vol 6. 1913 il). The tree must be one of the earliest in Britain; oriental planes were introduced to Britain in the early C16 (SST il on front cover). It has a circumference of 23 feet and is some 70 feet high and its branches span a circumference of more than 130 yards (NSJFS 1969 p133) (WPG p27). At SJ 807106 is a 10 metre long tunnel of C19 origin called **Pausilisp Tunnel** (DoE II). **Pendrill's Cave** is in Shrewsbury Walk at SJ 804107 and is so called after a hermit who occupied it in the C18, it is of late C18 or early C19 origin (DoE II) (WPG p28) (VCH vol 4 p170) (SHC 1899 new series ii p335). The **Prospect Tower** or Shooting Tower or Flag Tower (F&G p391p), is a square folly-tower on Tong Knoll over the border in Shrops, SSW of the hall, at SJ 803092. It is built of red sandstone quarried at Weston, possibly designed by Thomas Rickman, who worked at Weston in 1830-1. It is battlemented and flanked by a slender octagonal stair turret. In it is a plaque dated 1631, which probably refers to a fireplace. From it can be seen both Weston and Tong in Shrops (BOE p306) (F p308). Others say it dates from 1883 (SHC 1899 new series vol ii p332) (VCH vol 4 p170). (SHC 1899 new series vol ii p332). **Roman Bridge** is designed by James Paine. The stone used to build it was quarried in the park (VCH vol 4 p170). (DoE I) (Plans etc of Nobleman's and Gentleman's House. London 1783. vol 2 pp22-23 pls, 68-71) (BOE p306) (SGS p180) (F p308) (MR p371). **Raven Oak Stew** slightly to the NE of the Waterloo Obelisk (1884 OS map 6 inch). A **rustic cottage**, possibly converted from an earlier brickmaker's dwelling, lies at the E end of Temple Pool and dates from the late C18 or early C19 (VCH vol 4 p170). At SJ 814104. Listed in 1953 (DoE II). Seems to have been called by others the Swiss Cottage (1884 OS map 6 inch) (WPG pp30-31,32p) (BOE p306) (F p308). A stone **shelter** overlooking Temple Pool dates from 1938 (VCH vol 4 p170). **Shooting Tower** see Prospect Tower. Shrewsbury Walk is one of the approach drives to the park (VCH vol 4 p170). A **sundial** at SJ 808105 is of early C19 origin (DoE II) (1884 OS map 6 inch). **Swiss Cottage** see rustic cottage. The **Temple of Diana** incorporates an oval orangery, an octagonal music room, and a circular 'tea room.' Designed by James Paine. The stone used to build it was quarried in the park (DoE I) (CL Feb 13 1948 p329) (VCH vol 4 p170 p of on opposite page of the circular 'tea room') (BOE p306) (SGS p178) (MR p371p) (F p308) (WPG pp30,31p). A C18 cut glass chandelier in pieces was found in the Temple in the mid C20 and re-assembled in the Tapestry Room in the hall. Has been designated a conservation area (SL p261). The **Temple Pool** dates from 1795 and was part of the later improvements to the grounds. The Swiss Cottage lies to the E end of the pool (SCH 1899 new series vol ii p334 note) (VCH vol 4 p170). **Waterloo Obelisk** is an obelisk at SJ 81100975. It is 10 metres high and was erected in the late C18 (DoE II) or was erected in 1815 to celebrate Wellington's victory at Waterloo (VB p151). (BOE p306) (F p308).

Weston Spring Longton.

Weston Sprink Shrink Field 1.25m E of Longton (SHST p529). This is probably the same as Weston Spring. Or just Weston Sprink (NSFCT 1900 p91 on its geology).

Weston-under-Lizard Ancient parish, manor, and estate village on an elevated stretch of Watling Street under Lizard Hill on the ENE side, 10.75m SW of Stafford. Has appeared as Guestona (1081) (SSE 1996 p19), Westone, a manor, in DB, Westona (1167) (SPNO p180), Weston juxta Brewode (1236), Weston-under-Brewood (1254), Weston Houwe (1285), Weston Harald (1316), Weston Hewes (1327) (said to be after Hugh de Weston d1305 - SHC 1914 p182 note, SSE 1996 p23), Weston subtus Lusyerd (1349), Weston subtus Luseyord (1349), Weston juxta Blumehulle (1359), Weston Hues (1379-1381), Haraldeswestone (1410), Weston Hughwes (1534), Weston Huys (1547), and Weston subtus Lyzyard (1672) (SHC 1916 p196) (VCH vol 4 p65 note) (CE p123) (SPNO p180) (SPN p140). The **name** means 'the west farmstead;' the parish is in the western portion of Cuttlestone Hundred (SPNO p180). Lizard (appearing as Lusgeard in an Anglo-Saxon charter - SHC 1916 p131) is from Lizard Hill, a hill to the SW in Shropshire (VCH vol 4 p169) (SPNO p180). Lizard is from Middle English 'luce-geard,' a fish-yard (DUIGNAN). Or from 'lazar,' a leper. There was once a leper colony on the hill (VB p151). Bridgeman and Commander Wedgwood thought Weston ancient parish, formed between 1086 and 1291, formed originally a part of Brewood original parish (SHC 1916 p196). The parish **church**, St Andrew, adjoining Weston Hall on the NW side, has a C14 tower but the rest was rebuilt by Lady Wilbraham of Weston Hall in 1700-1701, and restored in 1876 (VCH vol 4 p174). The lords of Weston-under-Lizard **manor** have mainly occupied Weston Hall (see), and the earlier manor house(s) on the same site. Early lords of the manor, the de Westons, took their name from this Weston (WPG 1987 p19). An **abandoned settlement**, probably of medieval origin, lay near the moated site at SJ 816098 1m SE of Weston Hall (SSAHST 1982-3 pp51-52). At SJ 807107 lying to the S of the village and Watling Street was a **windmill**. 'Windmill Field' appears on a plan of 1658. It is shown on the maps of Plot and Bowen, but not on Yates' map (VCH vol 4 p173) (WBJ p45). There was another windmill in similar position in the mid C18 (VCH vol 4 p173). The **Weston Troop** of the Staffordshire Yeomanry was raised by Lord Bradford in 1800 (FSP p63). There was an **airfield** from June 1941 at SJ 810085 adjacent to Weston Park. From early 1944 it had a duel roll as a satellite for RNAS Hinstock who called it HMS Godwit II. Closed summer 1945 (info Ron Balding) (Action Stations. David J Smith. 1981. 2nd ed 1990. p203) (SHJ autumn 1989 p64). The novel **'Miss Fallowfields Fortune'** (1908) by Ellen Thorneycroft Fowler (d1929) (see Woodthorne) is set principally in Weston-under-Lizard (BCM Spring 2000 p49). For Weston in a local **rhyme** see Brewood. The greatest distance covered by a **model steam locomotive** in 24 hours is 167.7m (269.9km) by the 18.4cm 7.25 gauge 'Peggy,' on Weston Park Railway in Weston Park in 10 shifts between June 17 and 18 1994 (GBR 1996 p125).

Weston Wood House 2.75m WSW of Ellenhall. 0.75m SSW of Woodseaves (Plot's map). According to PV Bate and DM Palliser the possible medieval village (now lost) of Weston Hawes could have been here (SSAHST 1970 p36). (W p465).

Weston Yonge Area about Madeley. From a person of this name who inhabited Madeley Manor to 1834 when the manor was sold (M p30).

West Park Public park 0.5m WNW of Wolverhampton, laid out over Broadmeadow Field (see). West Park was designed by Richard Hartland Vertegans (WP p19) (TB Sept 1996 p7ps) (Black Country Calendar 2000). Opened on Whit Monday (June 6) 1881 (WAIW vol 3 ps) (WP&P pp33-34ps). It is widely regarded as one of England's finest Victorian municipal parks (The History of West Park. Wolverhampton Council). (BCM spring 1993 pp23-26). In the park is a bridge of 1880; a bandstand; a clock tower, presented in 1883 by Councillor John Ross, originally known as the 'four faced liar' for telling the incorrect time; a pavilion to the S, of 1890; a lakeside pavilion of 1891 and a conservatory of 1896. The three boulders in the park in 1909 were i). a large felsite boulder 11 feet high, erected vertically like a monolith, with an inscription stating that it is a block of felsite carried in the Ice Age from Arenig Mountains, Merionethshire and that it was found in a clay bed in Oak Street, in 1881 (SMM p25p), others say it is of andesite and from the Lake District, ii). a huge grey granite block from Criffell Mountains, Kirkcudbrightshire, found in Wolverhampton Cemetery in 1880, iii). a syenite boulder situated near West Park lake, is probably from Red Pike, Cumberland (WJO Nov 1909 p293). The Wolverhampton Art and Industrial Exhibition was held in the park in 1902 (WJO April 1902 ?), to celebrate the coronation of Edward VII (TB April 1985 p29) (Wolverhampton Chronicle Sept 4 1998 p13ps). A Swiss chalet, a relic of the exhibition, was removed to Tettenhall (see) (WMAG Nov 1969 p11p. Aug 1978 pp20-21ps). The statue of Charles Pelham Villiers MP sculpted by William Theed in 1878 was moved to the park in 1931 (MR p391). The park was listed by English Heritage in

1986.

Westport Small district developed as a port on the Trent and Mersey Canal, 0.75m WNW of Burslem.

Westport Lake 0.75m WNW of Burslem. Originated as a result of mining subsidence in c1880; its existence was confirmed by the embankment of the former Pinnox Branch Railway (NSJFS 1974 p129). In 1881 Port Vale Football Club moved their ground to the area now covered by Westport Lake and in 1884 they left for Moorland Road (VCH vol 8 p141). The lake was used for a time as a reservoir by Shelton Steelworks (NSJFS 1974 p129). Frederick Cooke aged nine fell through the ice covering it on Dec 27 1950. The first to rescue him, Ronald Hickton, fell through the ice himself and both were rescued by Thomas Byrne, who cycled across the ice to them. Hickton was awarded a certificate for bravery by the Hero Fund Trust. It hangs in the Smallthorne home of his descendants (ES May 12 1994 p10ps). The reclamation of Westport Lake had commenced by 1970, and Westport Lake Water Park was opened by Edward Heath PM in 1971 (SOTB p114), subsequent phases in the reclamation programme were completed by 1979 (PCCSC p243). However, bacteria in the lake prevents leisure activities taking place on, or in, it (POP pp172-173).

West Side Westside Mill is 1m ENE of Warslow on the E side of the Manifold. In Alstonefield township and ancient parish. Lies on the W side of Archford Moor and is a former encroachment on the moor. There was a mill here by 1584 (VCH vol 7 p11).

West Smethwick Residential district on rising ground above a head brook of the Tame over 1m WNW of Smethwick. The area had become known as West Smethwick by 1857. It developed in the C19 as a distinct community focused on the Chance glass works in Spon Lane, with shops around the southern end of the lane (VCH vol 17 p91). The church, St Paul, in St Paul's Road, was consecrated in 1858 (VCH vol 17 p125). The ecclesiastical parish of West Smethwick (St Paul) was created from North Harborne ecclesiastical parish in 1860 (GLAUE p423). In 1969 a council estate containing 586 three-storey terraced houses was built at West Smethwick N of Oldbury Road, S of the canal and to the E of Spon Lane. By 1982 the modern houses were considered locally very undesirable and the area was dubbed 'The Concrete Jungle.' The estate was demolished in or by the mid 1990s and new housing built on the site (info Smethwick Library) (E&S March 22 1982).

West Smethwick Park Opened in 1895 on land given by James Timmins Chance (later Sir James Chance, Bt) (b1814) of Chance glass works, eldest of the six sons of William Chance (1788-1856) (STELE Sept 2 1955) (VCH vol 17 p92) (SMEOP p113p). There is a bronze statue to him by Hamo Thornycroft near the park gates (KES p179) (BCM Jan 1986 pp51-54p).

Westwood Former estate, now a suburb of Leek to E of Westwood Hall. Formerly in Leek and Lowe township in Leek parish (W p721). The Westwood estate was granted to Dieulacres Abbey possibly in the earlier C13. They had established a grange here by 1291 (NSFCT 1885 p53) (NSJFS 1970 p85) and possibly by 1246 (VCH vol 3 p233. vol 7 pp85,101). The name means 'wood west of Leek' (NSFCT 1885 p53). The present Westwood Hall (see) is the chief residence of the estate. The private Westwood housing estate was begun in the 1950s (VCH vol 7 p97).

Westwood Hall Chief residence of the Westwood estate 1m WSW of Leek. After the Dissolution the estate passed through several hands until passing to the Trenthams of Rocester in 1604, who held it for most of the C17 (VCH vol 7 p101). Appears as Wilwood on Plot's map. By the early C18 it belonged to William Jolliffe of Caverswall Castle. On his death in 1709 it passed to his daughter, Lucy (d1742), wife of William Vane (Viscount Vane from 1720) (VCH vol 7 p101). The ghost of Lady Vane is said to haunt the hall (NSFCT 1885 p53). White says a Lady Vane was in residence in the mid C19 (W p721). In 1759 Lucy's son, William Vane, sold Westwood to Mary, Countess of Stamford. Her descendants, the Greys, held Westwood until they sold it to John Davenport, potter of Longport, in 1813 (OL vol 1 p312) (VCH vol 7 p102). He lived here until his death on Dec 12 1848 (POTP p76); during the period 1818 to 1834 he remodelled the house in neo-Elizabethan style. The hall, known as Westwood Hall by 1834, was rebuilt or extended in 1851 by his son, John (1799-1862), a poet (PSS p149) (VFC p36). John's son, George sold the hall in 1868 to John Robinson (OL vol 1 p312 il) (VCH vol 7 p102 pls 24 a view of the hall from the SE c1835, 25 a view of the hall from the S after 1851). It had passed from Robinson's widow to HJ Johnson by 1912. In 1920 he sold it to Staffs county council who turned it into a girls school. In 1965 this school merged with St Edward's Secondary School, which had a new building built for it in 1965 close to the hall. The amalgamated school then became the mixed comprehensive Westwood County High School (VCH vol 7 pp102,162). (JSD p62p). In the grounds is a summer house (BOE p173) (MR p209). The entrance lodge, dated 1852, is of sandstone. It comprises an

arch over the driveway with a room above, and perhaps on account of the 'giant' arch it has been called Arch Lodge (BOE p173) (ES April 11 2000 p8).

Westwood Manor House 1m NNW of Wetley Rocks. The old house known was Westwood Hall (CVH p16), and Westwood House when the seat of Capt Thomas Powys in 1851 (W p24); a Col Thomas Powys of Westwood Manor is said to have served under the Duke of Wellington (SVB p174). The old house was a square greystone structure. It was pulled down and the present neo-Elizabethan house built in 1870 by William Meakin, potter, who altered the name to Westwood Manor, being lord of the manor and in the manor of Cheddleton; Meakin was still the owner in 1907 (STC p26p). Later, the house came into the possession of Enoch Haughton, who eventually gave it the Stoke-on-Trent Education Authority to be used as a special school for children (SVB p174).

Wet Hay Wood 0.5m S of Bishop's Wood. The name is said to be from a former hay in Brewood Forest (BDH p72) (SVB p34).

Wetley Abbey House 0.75m S of Wetley Rocks. Called 'recently built' in 1836 and may have been built for George Miles Mason (1789-1859) by 1824 (CVH p157). Is cruciform in shape (BOE p306). The Mason family, pottery manufacturers, moved into the house in 1824 (CVH p157). One of the sons of the family, the painter, George Heming Mason (1818-1872), born at Fenton Park, lived here between 1858 and 1864 before moving to Westbourne House, Shaftesbury Road, Hammerwich; subsequently he occasionally resided at Wetley Abbey. He was buried at Brompton cemetery (SSW pp106-116) (S p121) (KES p98) (STM Oct 1971 p24p. Nov 1965 front cover pc) (CVH pp157-158) (DNB) (SGS p180; called George Mason Mills) (George Heming Mason. Rosalind Billingham. 1982) (MR p151) (TFTP p120 il of the abbey) (FF pp57,58) (POTP p147). The window mouldings in the exterior walls are said to be from Hulton Abbey (SASR 1985 p77). Is now (1988) a private nursing home (SVB p174).

Wetley Moor High barren former common land and fragmented settlement between the Trent and the Churnet 2.25m WSW of Wetley Rocks. Formerly in Bucknall and Bagnall chapelry in Stoke-upon-Trent ancient parish. The moor is first mentioned in 1226 as Wythemor and in 1529 covered some 1000 acres (NSFCT 1957 p68) and has also been called the Waste (FWMBS p44). **Common rights**. The moor was far more extensive than later and stretched nearly to Wetley Rocks. It lay in Weston Coyney, Caverswall and Cheddleton manors. Each of which had its own rights to the moor. This, and the lack of defined boundaries caused much feuding between the lords and commoners and lords and commoners of the different manors. One case concerned the enclosure of the Cheddleton section by its lord in 1540 and the subsequent riots by commoners (WJ p18) (CVH p161). The **cotton grass** on Wetley Moor was thought to have grown from seeds of cotton plants brought back by two soldiers from 'Werynton' fighting in the American War of Independence. It is however, no more than cotton grass (Eriophorum Vaginatum) (STP pp160, 161p). **Squatting on the moor** may have been taking place in and by the C19 when the inhabitants were described as mainly 'coal-getters' with a lawless reputation and harbourers of criminals (NSFCT 1900 p143); after WW1 the area was inhabited by squatters in makeshift cottages (ES Aug 9 1996 p8). The remains of **bell pits** made by striking miners during the General Strike in 1926 can still be seen on Wetley Moor, at SJ 930484? (IANS pp31,37). Most of the pits are probably a maximum of six feet in depth; a pony was trapped in one (ES June 19 1995 p9. Aug 9 1996 p8). **Superstition**. Maidens in the Wetley Moors area may have long followed a tradition current by the earlier C19 that one could imagine the appearance of their future husband if they stand on the spars of a gate or stile and look at Wetley Moor in the evening after the first appearance of the new moon immediately after New Year's day and recite the lines

> All hail to thee moon
> all hail to thee
> I beg the moon
> to reveal to me
> This night who my
> husband shall be

This information was given by the daughter of a Mr Brown of Eaves, Bucknall, in a log book of the 1830s (ES Jan 15 2000 p17). **Views**. From the Moor's highest point (900 feet) in the E can be seen the Churnet Valley and the Weaver Hills beyond; to the NE, the Morridge, Merryton Low, Hen Cloud, and the Roaches; to the N, Shutlings Low and Macclesfield Forest; to the NW, Biddulph Moor; to the W, the Potteries; to the SW, the Wrekin and the Welsh Mountains; and to the S, Cannock Chase (WJ p17).

Wetley Rocks Long straggling village, partly built beneath a length of mill-stone grit rock crags (of similar formation to though in a less highland situation than the Roaches), rising to a height of 100 feet (LGS p252) (HLS p17), 16.75m NNE of Stafford. Formerly in Cheddleton township and ancient parish (W p764). The **name** Wetley appears to mean 'wet pasture or meadows' (SVB p174). Rocks refers to the crags behind the village (LGS p252). The alleged boundary stone at SJ 963478, 0.25m S of Wetley Abbey, on the boundary between Cheddleton and Consall quarters is possibly the base of a **medieval wayside cross**, not a boundary marker (CVH p155). According to tradition when the Young Pretender in the **1745 Jacobite Rebellion** retreated northwards some of his soldiers while resting on land on top of the rocks, carved his initials on a stone, which now lies in the grounds of a private garden (SVB p174). The village only began to grow at the end of the C18, developing around the stone quarries here (Cheddleton & District Official Guide p31). The **church**, St John the Baptist, on the N side of Mill Lane, was built in 1834 (Cheddleton & District Official Guide p31). Wetley Rock became a separate ecclesiastical parish in 1862 (GLAUE p428). For **beating the bounds** of Cheddleton township through Wetley Rocks see Cheddleton. **Easter custom**. A regular custom of Wetley Rocks is the Palm Sunday procession. To commemorate Holy Week three wooden crosses are carried through the streets to a spot high up and erected on the gritstone edge called Wetley Rocks (JC 14). The custom was being practised by at least 1981 (ES April 17 1981 p12p) and crosses were still being erected on the ridge in 2000. Wetley Rocks had a **fair** in 1888 (LHE p265). The name over the **village well** is Thomas Dawson (CVH p51). **Footpath through house**. In 1998 the Bakers of Rock Cottage on a rock outcrop above the village had to build a 40 feet long 10 feet high tunnel to accommodate the public footpath which ran alongside the cottage when they extended it over the footpath. The footpath then became what is believed to be the only countryside footpath in Britain running under a house (Daily Telegraph Nov 10 1998 p7pc). **Mary Allport** who climbed the spire of Uttoxeter church with a friend in 1814 to kiss two workmen settled at Wetley Rocks after she had married the one called Henry Smith (HOU pp160-161).

Wetmoor Wetmoor Farm is 0.5m NNE of Gayton, in Gayton parish. Has also appeared as Wetmore (W p420).

Wetmore Former manor and hamlet on low ground by an arm of the Trent, now a district of Burton upon Trent, 0.75m N of Burton upon Trent. Formerly in Burton ancient parish. The Withmere mentioned in a charter of 1012 has been identified as Wetmore: The mention of the thieves' hanging place in the boundary description in the charter led Shaw to identify Withmere with the Gallows Flat and Gallows Lane at Wetmore in the late C18 (SHOS vol 1 p20) (SHC 1916 pp124-125) (DUIGNAN) (SL p62). Has appeared as Witmere, a manor held by Burton Abbey, in DB, Wihtmere, Wismera, Withmere, Wichtmere (SPN p27), and Wightmere (SHOS vol 1 p8). The name means 'withy mere' (DUIGNAN). Ekwall gives 'mere by a bend (on the Trent)' (SPN p27) (SSE 1996 p19). In the early 1540s overlordship of Wetmore manor passed with other Burton Abbey estates to Sir William Paget of Beaudesert (SHOS vol 1 p8). The separate ecclesiastical parish of Stretton was refounded as 'Stretton cum Wetmore' in 1873 (GLAUE p424).

Wetmore Hall The name is preserved in Wetmoor Hall Farm, 1.5m NNE of Burton upon Trent. Formerly called Wightmere Farm (SHOS vol 1 p21) and has also appeared as Wetmore Farm. Is situated on the site of Wetmore manor house. The old house formerly belonging to the abbots of Burton Abbey was taken down some years prior to the late C18 and a smaller farm house built. Over the parlour chimney remained, curiously embossed on stone, the name of Thomas Feylde (d1493), an abbot (SHOS vol 1 p21).

Wetton Village on a high limestone plateau rising steeply from the Manifold but backed by moorland hills 23.25m NE of Stafford (SSE 1996 p23). Originally a chapelry in Mayfield ancient parish.
EARLY. In Wetton parish was found a pottery spindle whorl in 1857 and a stone spindle whorl in 1885, one or both went to Sheffield Museum and are of uncertain date (NSJFS 1964 p44). Bateman excavated a burial mound between Wetton and Ilam in 1845. A crouched male skeleton with a dog at his feet was found (VAD pp79-80) (NSJFS 1965 p41). He excavated another, described as a long barrow, near Wetton, in 1846. Only the jawbone of an ox was found (VAD p86) (NSJFS 1965 p57). The village may have its origins in a **Romano-British** settlement 0.75m to the SW known as Borough Hole (see). 1000 to PRESENT. Has been considered the Waddune mentioned in the will of Wulfric Spot (c1002), founder of Burton Abbey, by Wolferstan and CGO Bridgeman; others, including Shaw, have identified Waddune with Long Whadden, Leics (SHC 1916 p40). Wetton appears in 1252 as Wettindun (SSE 1996 p19). The **name** may mean 'wet hill' (SSE 1996 p19). Or may be derived from any of these: wet town, wet stone, Wodin's town, Wrade's town,

Wuotan's town, Odin's town (Odin the Saxon deity) (WTCEM pp18,32,34,44,45). Had separate parish status before 1535 (GLAUE p428). The **church**, St Margaret, in the village centre, has a tower of an early date (BOE p307), or of the C16 (LGS p252). The main body of the church was rebuilt in 1820 (BOE p307). Wetton **wake** was on the first Sunday in Sept in the C19 (W p788). Wetton **stocks** were placed by Messrs Henry Bowden and William Adams. One of the stones which supported the stocks in the wall surrounding the tree was still evident in 1900. The only person ever placed in them was George 'Harvey' Heywood, uncle to Solomon Havey, the 'David' of William Howitt's story of John o' Clamps ghost in Wetton (WTCEM p158). **Customs**. The custom of oratories, which originated in Saxon times from Christmas festivities and took the form of house parties and harvest homes, had lapsed at Wetton by 1900 (WTCEM pp29,30). The custom of 'Seeing' at Wetton in 1900 was thought to have been probably a remnant of Wives' Feast Day, in which wives would arrange an evening to meet together and visit any poor woman of the parish recovering from an illness or in trouble (WTCEM pp96,97). The Ring, a large boulder in the village centre, was noted as the old man's 'seat of custom' (WTCEM pp95,158). **Visitors and residents**. There is a belief that **Charles II** stayed at the Royal Oak at Wetton (WTCEM p7). **Samuel Carrington** (d1870), a school master at Wetton, excavated Thor's Cave in 1864-5, and opened many burial mounds in the Staffs Moorlands with the archaeologist, Thomas Bateman. His note book contains drawings of 150 species of wild flowers. His grave carved with shells and fossils in Wetton churchyard, was erected by friends and the Geological Society of which he was a member (WTCEM pp14,15,23) (PS p94) (LGS pp184,252) (SOSH p9) (KES p227) (NSFCT 1946 p123) (VB p201).

Wetton Hill Hill 1174 feet high, 0.5m NNE of Wetton. On the summit at SK 10495626 is a burial mound which was excavated by Bateman in 1845 and Carrington in 1849. A male skeleton and two crouched skeletons were found (VAD pp83-84) (TYD pp139-140) (VCH vol 1 no 21) (BAP vol 1 p159 fig 225) (DAJ vol 75 pp109,110,120. vol 77 p26 C5) (NSJFS 1965 pp57-58). It is a listed monument. To the NE, 650 metres NW of Under Wetton at SK 11295659 are burial mounds. See also Redhurst Gorge.

Wetton Low Burial mound on a hill 1056 feet high 0.5m SSE of Wetton, at SK 11215474. It is 20 paces in diameter and six feet high and damaged (NSJFS 1965 p57). It is a listed monument. Gunstone records another close by at SK 11075470, from NS 16 paces in diameter and four feet high. It may be a quarry spoil-heap (NSJFS 1965 p57).

Wetton Mill House by the Manifold nearly 1m NE of Wetton. A cave shelter here at SK 096563, excavated in 1974, revealed flints of the Mesolithic period (SASR 1986 p4) (LTD p42): In Buxton Museum are flints found in a rock shelter at Wetton Mill.

Wetwood Small hamlet above the upper Sow Valley, 0.5m ENE of Fairoak. In the Woodlands division in Eccleshall ancient parish (W p380). The Wetwood which appears as Wetwode in 1291 (SSE 1996 p19) is probably the Wetwood in Leekfrith. This Wetwood has appeared as Wetwood Cross (BPS p143). The name means 'wet wood' (NSJFS 1981 p2). Greatwood Heath formerly lay by Wetwood (SSE vol 7 1995 p75).

Wetwood Small hamlet 0.5m NW of Meerbrook comprising the houses Higher Wetwood and to its E Lower Wetwood. Formerly in Leekfrith township in Leek ancient parish (W p732). Possibly by 1246 and certainly by 1291 Dieulacres Abbey had a grange at Wetwood (then Wetwode - SSE 1996 p19). The grange building may have stood on the site of Lower Wetwood (VCH vol 7 p194).

Wetwood Manor Mid C17 house, Wetwood, Fairoak. The seat of the Nevill family between the C17 and the C18. It was restored and added to in 1920. Beneath the crazy paving behind the house is a 90 feet well (BOV p46il of). The house was occupied by WL Pakenham in 1935 (SHC 1934 List of Members). It was advertised for sale in CL May 26 1994 and again in summer 1999 (Style Magazine (Sentinel Publications) Summer 1999; it has been said that the house was built in 1642).

Weymoor House or area or field name S of Harborne. It appears in 1587, when the occupant of a house here appeared at Stafford Assizes (OHOPP p13). The name is preserved in Weymoor Road.

Wharf, The Residential area of NE Uttoxeter. The name is from a wharf where the Uttoxeter Branch of the Caldon Canal terminated. The inn called The Limes was the Wharfmaster's house (Official Uttoxeter Town Guide. 1993. p36).

Wheatlow Brooks Tiny hamlet in a small gorge at the confluence of several small streams N of Garshall Green. Has also appeared as Whitelow Brooks (W p420). It was still known as Whitelow by Milwich's older generation in the early 1990s (info Randle Knight).

Wheatlow Brook Runs from Sharpley Heath to join Gayton Brook at Milwich.

Wheaton Aston Village on a pastoral plain N of Watling Street and S of Wheaton Aston Brook, 7m SW of Stafford. Former township in Lapley ancient parish. Does not appear in DB (LSWA p30). Has appeared as Estona (1167), Wetenaston (1248), Aston (1272), Whetenaston (1347-1571), and Whetynaston (1477) (SPNO p169) (SSE 1996 p10). **Name.** Aston means east town. Probably it was a wheat-growing locality in the C14 and a second name was needed to distinguish it from other Astons (DUIGNAN) (MR p374) (SPN p140). The prefix implying 'where the wheat grows' had appeared by 1248 (SSE 1996 p10), or by 1338 (VCH vol 4 p148). The abbot of Lapley Priory, as lord of Lapley, was granted a charter on April 12 1292 to hold a **market** on Tuesdays at Wheaton Aston. The market had ceased by 1500 (NSJFS 1971 p51) or by 1817 (VCH vol 4 p144). The priory was granted a charter on April 12 1292 to hold an annual **fair** on the vigil and feast of St Peter ad Vincula (July 31, Aug 1) and the vigil and feast of All Saints (Nov 1) at Wheaton Aston. The fairs were being held on April 20 and Nov 1 by 1834 and had lapsed by 1872 (VCH vol 4 p144). At the SE end of Wheaton Aston is a flat-topped mound, which with two adjacent earthworks, probably represents the ancient dwelling known as **'Le Mote'** in the C14 (VCH vol 4 p148). The **church**, St Mary, on the N side of Frog Lane, replaced a chapel in 1857 built of local sandstone in the C14 style (VCH vol 4 p153). The **wake** was on Trinity Sunday (W p463), but by at least 1912 was changed to the first Sunday in May. It was then known as the Fritillary Wake, on account of inhabitants and those of neighbouring villages meeting at Motty Meadows (see) near Marston to gather Snake's head-fritillary (VCH vol 4 p144) (LSWA p32il) (SVB p109). The **ridge and furrow** of the old farming system can still be traced in several fields surrounding the village (VCH vol 4 p144 p facing). There was a **postmill** which stood 150 yards S of the church, at SJ 851125. It was an old mill but the first record of it was in 1854. The mill existed in 1912 but is said to have been burnt soon after (SLM spring 1954 p25) (VCH vol 4 p149) (WBJ p45 il I) (WAAIW p19p) (WIS p24). There was a school described as a free **grammar school** at Wheaton Aston in 1703; thereafter the school is never referred to as a grammar school (SHJ autumn 1989 p29). Up to the C18 Wheaton Aston was regarded as something of a **spa**. There is evidence of a mineral spring in one of the village gardens (SVB p109). A sulphur spring, near the southern boundary of the parish, has been described as a 'healing well' (LCWA p2) (VCH vol 4 p144). On April 9 1777 a terrible **fire** destroyed most of the village. It spread quickly owing to every house being thatched (VCH vol 4 p143) (LSWA p30). The **lock up**, a small brick outhouse NE of the church, was last used in c1910 (VCH vol 4 p143). For **RAF Wheaton Aston** see Little Onn. For Wheaton Aston in a local **rhyme** see Brewood. A **poachers' union** was formed in Wheaton Aston in the late 1960s (WAAIW p22p, il of the 1969-70 membership card). By the late C20 Wheaton Aston was a ward in Lapley, Stretton and Wheaton Aston civil parish.

Wheaton Aston Brook Runs N of Wheaton Aston to join the Longnor Brook at Longnor.

Wheaton Aston New Hall 150 yards N of the old hall, Bishop's Wood. Built by George T Hartley, author of LCWA, in the late C19 (VCH vol 4 p146) (STC p44p). Became a boarding house for Brewood grammar school in 1950 (VCH vol 6 p151).

Wheaton Aston Old Hall 1.5m SW of Bishop's Wood, on N side of Watling Street. The entrance hall contains stained glass bearing the arms of the Thorneycroft and Hartley families. George T Hartley author of LCWA lived here until he built Wheaton Aston New Hall. In WW2 it was a hostel for workers from Wolverhampton. In 1955 it was a boarding house for Brewood grammar school (VCH vol 4 p146). (MR p374p).

Wheatstone Park Villa at the W end of Wood Road, 0.75m WNW of Codsall church. It dates from the 1850s (VCH vol 20 p77). To the SW is Wheatstone Lodge Farm. In this area on the 1834 OS map appears the name Ragged Invention.

Wheeler's Fold Street off Princess Street, Wolverhampton. Remnant of the town's involvement in the wool trade, appears on a map of the town of 1750 (SOSH p308) (WMAG Jan 1965 p27il). The painter Edward Bird was born in Wheeler's Fold in 1772, see Wolverhampton.

Wheel Lane Lane situated N of Lichfield cathedral. From a quarry here stone was hewn to build the cathedral (Bell's 'Lichfield Cathedral' p35).

Whetstone Field Former common field of Aldridge. The name, which appears in 1611, is preserved in Whetstone Lane, which runs S from Aldridge (SNAR p53).

Whetstone Green Wetstone Green is 0.5m W of Bushbury, W of Low Hill (1834 OS map). In Bushbury ancient parish. Survives in Whetstone Road and Grove (Birmingham A-Z).

Whetstone Hole Near Gib Tor and the entrance to Ann Roach 1.5m SSW of

Flash (UHAW p51). Appears on the 1834 OS map as Wetstone Hole.

Whieldon's Grove House situated S of City Road, Fenton, in an area formerly known as Fenton Grove? Built by Thomas Whieldon (b1719) potter in the mid C18 and occupied by him until his death in 1795. Its two-storied front of five bays faced W and had a central doorway. The railway was built by it in 1847 and it was used as a temporary station until the opening of Stoke station in 1848. By the 1950s it was being used as the motive power depot in the Stoke-on-Trent district (VCH vol 8 pp209-210,214, il of c1845 facing p228). For Whieldon's pottery works at Fenton see Potteries in Appendix.

Whistle Oak Old oak NNW of Jockey Hills, Beaudesert Park. It existed in 1834, marked on OS map 1834. (SPNO p110).

Whiston Small village on a hillside overlooking a tributary of the Churnet 1m S of Foxt. Former township in Kingsley ancient parish (W p781) in North Totmonslow hundred division (THS p233). This Whiston is said to have appeared as Witestun in 1002 (SSE 1996 p19). Eyton tentatively identified this Whiston with the Witestone in DB, but it has been shown to be Whiston, Penkridge (SHC 1916 p167). The name means 'Wite's town' (DUIGNAN), or 'Witi's tun' (SSE 1996 p19). Here was a smelting works for ores of lead, zinc and copper (HOC p37), some of the ores being transported by packhorse from the Ecton copper mines (PRT pp70,71). (SVB p175). Foxt and Whiston became a joint ecclesiastical parish in 1898 (LGS p138). The church, St Mildred V Abbess, on the N side of the Froghall-Cauldon road on the W side of the village, was built in 1910 (BOE p308) (LDD).

Whiston Hamlet and liberty in Penkridge ancient parish (W p469), 5m SSW of Stafford. Was identified by General Wrottesley and Duignan with the Witestun mentioned in the will of Wulfric Spot (c1002) (SHC 1916 p31); later appears as Witestone, a manor held by Burton Abbey, in DB, Witastona (1116-33), Wistona (c1176-84), Wyston (1240), Whiston (1333-1479) (SPNO p103). The name means 'Wite's town' (DUIGNAN). Whiston Cross was a gospel place on the Penkridge perambulation mentioned in the PR 1732 (HOP p30).

Whiston Barn SE of Whiston, Kingsley.

Whistonbrook To W of Whiston, Kingsley.

Whiston Brook Runs by Shushions Manor to Longnor.

Whiston Bridge Crosses the Churnet, under 1m W of Whiston, Kingsley.

Whiston Common NE of Whiston, Kingsley.

Whiston Eaves Small hamlet overlooking the Churnet Valley 0.75m SSE of Whiston, Foxt. Formerly in Kingsley parish. Probably here was the burial mound mentioned in TYD p154. (NSJFS 1965 p35). Has appeared as Eaves (Plot's map). On the road to Oakamoor there is a cottage built against a rock outcrop (MR p375p,376).

Whiston Eaves Farm Stone and brick house at Whiston Evaves. Built in the C18 and later (DoE II). Derelict from the mid 1980s. There were plans to demolish the house and rebuild a part of it at Whiston in Dec 1996 because of the encroaching Moneystone Quarry (ES Dec 28 1996 p25pcs).

Whiston Eaves Hall Whiston Eaves. Raven was told it had been demolished and the stone reused to build houses for British Industrial Sand senior management, one is at Hollington (MR p375). Could be same as Whiston Eaves House, a Georgian country house, which had fallen into disrepair before being demolished (SVB p177). The house was haunted (SVB p177).

Whiston Farm On July 5 1866 the body of Thomas Smith Jnr of Whiston Farm, son of the lord of Whiston Eaves manor, Thomas Smith, was found in Black Planting Wood on his father's farm. He had been shot dead by a poacher William Collier, aged 35, early in the morning of July 5. Collier was condemned only on circumstantial evidence and a great many believed he was innocent, so when during the execution on Aug 7 1866 outside Stafford Gaol the noose untied itself they were further convinced. But he was still rehung. He was the last man to be hanged outside the prison (BCM Oct 1968 pp29-30) (SLM April 1983 p26) (RPM pp14-17) (MCS pp31-32) (TB Feb 1978 pp18-19. Aug 1993 p18) (SMML pp5-8). References in QMMH pp22-27 and SLM April 1983 p26 to a murderer called William Collier may relate to a William Collier of Hanley (see).

Whiston Hall To NW of Whiston, Penkridge. Name appears in 1652 (SPNO p104). Is square in plan and of three distinct periods - of the late C16, the late C17, and the C19. As the manor house of Whiston manor it was the property of the Giffards of Chillington, lords of the manor until c1877, but inhabited by tenants (VCH vol 5 p124).

Whiston Hall Whiston, Foxt. Dark stone house, now the club house of a golf course (SVB p175) (MR p374).

White Barn Farm Shugborough. Its farmbuildings contained the first stationary threshing machine in the county; it was worked by water power (SNTG p42p); but the Walhouses at Teddesley Hall claimed they had the first at their Home Farm in Teddesley Park (see) (BERK2 p105).

White Chimney House on Cowall Moor, 1.5m SSE of Biddulph Moor (Yates'

map). The name is preserved in a house called White Chimneys. A mail guard on the Great Eastern Irish Railway called Hulme was a native of White Chimnies. Perhaps a reference to this White Chimney or White Chimneys near Ipstones? He caught the criminal Smith O' Brien and received the reward of £500 and retired to Leek (OL vol 1 p318).

White Chimneys House on Ipstones Edge 0.5m NE of Ipstones.

Whitecross Minute hamlet on low ground by a tributary of Butterbank Brook 1m N of Haughton. On a slight mound at the crossing of four roads near the boundary of Haughton parish, there stood a venerable oak which was dying in 1915. An oak may have been planted on the site of a wayside cross. The cross may have been erected by the White Cross knights, or by the White Friars, or was a white-washed preaching cross used also as a signpost at crossroads, white-washed to be seen at night. The puritans obtained an order in 1643 for the destruction of all crosses (NSFCT 1915 p171).

White Cross Farm On W side of Orton Lane, Orton between Orton Hall and Orton Grange. Built in 1730. Has been called Fox Hall (VCH vol 20 p200), seat of William Chinnery in 1851 (W p20).

Whitecross Pool Whitecross Pits are 0.5m NNE of Bagot's Bromley. Has also appeared as Whitecross Pits.

White Farm Isolated house on the edge of Bishop's Wood, 1m SSW of Fairoak. In the Woodland quarter in Eccleshall ancient parish. Spelt Whitefarm by White who describes it as an isolated hamlet (W p380).

Whitefields Near High Bent, Biddulph Moor. Farmhouse where John Brough, murderer, lived (CCSHO p12) (MCS pp32-35).

White Hall Greet's Green, West Bromwich. Stood in White Hall Road on the site occupied by Farley Park (SHWB 13).

White Hall On the W side of Stourbridge Road, Himley.

White Hall House which overlooked a wharf at Hardingswood, Kidsgrove. The hall, also known as Brick Hall, was built probably by John Gilbert, the younger, in c1765. Gilbert had moved to Clough Hall by 1800 (KAIW p6).

White Hall Near Whitehall Road, Summerhill, Kingswinford. It is shown on Fowler's map 1822 when it belonged to Mrs Diana Briscoe who also owned Summerhill mansion. In 1840 it was still owned by Diana Briscoe but occupied by Samuel Hassall. It was occupied in the 1880s by Frederick William Cook. In the C20 the house was occupied by JW Higgs-Walter JP and J Rushton (SNSV vol 1 p367).

White Hall House on N side of Dr Milley's Hospital, Beacon Street, Lichfield. A house of the vicars' choral in 1497-8. Rebuilt in the earlier part of the C18 as the Coach and Horses Inn. But was again a private house in 1806 when occupied by wine merchant, John Fern; in 1848 another wine merchant, Henry Hewitt, occupied this house. Either Fern or Hewitt built the present house (VCH vol 14 p68). Shaw says White Hale was the house of the archdeacon of Chester and the houses in Beacon Street were mostly burnt down in the Civil War (SHOS vol 1 p319). Harwood says it was anciently called Le White Hale and situated on N side of Shaw Lane (HOL p512). Shaw Lane is off Beacon Street. May have become the White Hart Inn (see in the Appendix).

Whitehall Hamlet S of Caldmore in the foreign and parish of Walsall (W p649). Seems to have been an inhabited area by 1770. A house called White Hall, which probably gave the area its name, still stood in 1843 at what is now the junction of Dale Street and Alexandra Road (VCH vol 17 p157) (SNWA p109). The name is preserved in a street name at Palfrey.

Whitehall Branch of the Walsall Canal. Spurred off the Walsall Canal at Ryders Green Locks and ran to Whitehall Road (HCMS No. 2).

White Hart Inn Substantial Jacobean brick house (BOE p294) (MR p358p) at Caldmore Green, Walsall: Masefield says it is in Vicarage Lane (LGS p248). The house is said to have formed part of an estate belonging to the Hawes in the C17 (BAST 1871 p11). If so, it was probably built by George Hawe (d1679) (VCH vol 17 p178). The house has been known as Hawe Hall (SNWA p54). The Hawes were royalist in the Civil War (WAM p80). Many believe it was here Queen Henrietta Maria stayed when in Walsall in 1642 or July 1643 (OWB p71) (KES p220) (WPP p82); she was in Lichfield in July 1643 (VCH vol 14 p17). The house passed from the Hawes by marriage to the Parkers of Park Hall, Caverswall, in 1764 (VCH vol 17 p178). It became an inn in 1801 (BCP p27p), or was an inn by 1818 (VCH vol 17 p178). The white hart was a Lancastrian badge in the Wars of the Roses; Staffs was mainly Lancastrian, hence the quantity of inns with this sign (LGS pp28-29). By 1997 the building had been restored and opened as a heritage centre and flats after being badly damaged by fire (GPCE p49). In the later C17 Plot noted 'a remarkable pear-tree at the house of the heirs of Thomas Hawe, which (like the Glastonbury Thorn) through frost and snow, puts forth blossom at Christmas' (SNWA p55).

SUPERNATURAL. A human child's arm and a C17 sword were discovered here in 1870. The arm is known as the **Hand of Glory** or Arm of Glory. It is

perhaps the arm of a dwarf child chimney sweep (TB May 1976 p24p), or a hanged villain pickled, dried and used as a candle holder (TB Dec 1981 p1) or in witchcraft (MR p358), or a medical specimen for students of anatomy (MR p358) (GLS p105). It went to Walsall Museum, Lichfield Street, in 1965 (TB Dec 1981 p1. Dec 17 1998 p25p) and, in 1994, was in the Central Library, Lichfield Street (SMM pp45-46); it was on display in the museum in 1999. (HIE p171) (HB p122) (EGH pp170-171) (Believe It Or Not. Cyril T Oxby) (FOS pp18,19) (GOHK pp289-290) (GOM p21) (WOPP pl p71) (GPCE pp49-50). The house is reputedly haunted by the **ghost of a young girl** who killed herself in the late C18 (TB Dec 1981 p1) (SMM p46), or the C19 (FSLBWM p37), and in 1955 the print of a small hand was found in the locked attic, which could only be entered with a key (GLS p105) (SMM p46). The house is also haunted by the **ghost of an elderly maid** who committed suicide here in the early 1900s (GBG p44). A ghostly apparition has appeared at the bedside of the licensee (SMM p46).

Whiteheath Gate Large suburb 1m SSW of Oldbury built on a former heath in Salop, then Worcs; some say it was just in Staffs (TB Oct Nov 1972 p17) and in Rowley Regis parish (W p194). On Yates' map the heath marks the boundary of Staffs with Worcs or Salop. The word Gate is from a toll gate (TB Feb 1985 p17). The place has also appeared as White Heath Gate. In Oct 1978 a tape recorder played back the sounds of an old mining disaster that had occurred at the Black Bat mine, closed in 1883 after several men and boys had been killed in a roof fall. The tape recorder belonged to the McCarthy family who, it turned out, lived more or less on the mine site (Sunday People Oct 8 1978) (Fortean Times No. 28 p15) (TB Sept 1978 p1) (MMSE p292). The ghost of a grey lady has been seen by the residents of a tower block in Whiteheath (TB Feb 1979 p7). The highwayman, Dick Turpin, may have stayed at a Whiteheath tavern under the assumed name John Palmer. He was for a brief period in partnership with 'Rowley Jack' of Rowley Regis (see) (TB March 1978 pp18-19). For the murder of Samuel Whitehouse in 1822 on the Oldbury-Halesowen turnpike road see under Bearwood. Jack Judge, born in Oldbury (see), writer of the popular song 'It's a long way to Tipperary' (1912) and who had a fishmongers shop near the 'Junction,' Low Town, died at 30 Harold Road, Whiteheath Gate, in 1938 (TB Oct 1987 pp12-13. Nov 1987 p13p. Jan 1988 p16) (ORR p129p) (BCM June 1998 pp73-74).

White Hill Hill and residential district 0.75m ENE of Kidsgrove. Formerly in Wolstanton ancient parish. A bright metallic disc with a bright red dome or UFO was seen from Whitehill on Aug 4 1967 at approximately 11.00pm. A bright red light or UFO high in the sky travelling from the northeast in a circular path was seen from Whitehill on Aug 7 1967 at approximately 10.15pm (FSRP p6).

White Hill Farm 1.25m NW of Kinver church. Land to the W of this farm was known as Windmill Hill in the earlier C19 and may be the site of a windmill (VCH vol 20 p145). The White Hill area of Kinver was still fairly undeveloped by 1917 (KEOP p44p of in 1917).

Whitehough Old house, the seat of the Whitehalgh family, over 0.5m N of Ipstones. Formerly known as Whitehalgh. The present house may stand on the site of an older house, a William de Whythalk appears in 1293; a William de Whitehalgh appears in c1380 (TOI p37 p facing p36). The present house was built in c1570 (TOI p37) and bears several dates, the earliest being 1620 (LGS p154) (BOE p157). In c1650 it was held by Quakers (TOI pp36p,37). Reputedly has a secret room (NSFCT 1906 p169) (SMCC p9 il). In the grounds is an early C18 gazebo (DoE II*) and an early C18 sundial, with a chamfered square shaft two feet high (DoE II). (NSFCT 1890 p36). For the black dog which haunts near Whitehough see Inde Font Well.

Whitehouse There was settlement at Whitehouse, on the S side of Moody Street, Biddulph, by 1500 (BALH or possibly BHS?). Formerly in Knypersley liberty in Biddulph ancient parish.

White House House 3.75m NNE of Cannock. On Cannock Chase. South Street passes by it. Originally called New House it was built by c1877 for an old couple from Rugeley by a Hednesford man named Samson Blewitt. The couple had saved the necessary money by collecting wood and picking and selling bilberries and blackberries. The old man is said to have died returning from one of his many drinking jaunts with companions in Rugeley. The next occupiers were named Byford and they called the house Byford's Lodge. After their departure the house was an isolation hospital for victims of the flu epidemic at the end of WW1. It was then taken over by the Hill family who were living here in 1957 (PCC p65). In WW2 is it said to have been used by American servicemen. The house burnt down in c1990. A new brick house, built adjacent to the site of the old house in c1994, is now (1998) an hotel called the White House Hotel. The foundations of the old house still (1998) remain in the hotel car park. There is a picture of the old house inside the hotel (info from White House Hotel).

White House Brick farmhouse and eyecatcher for Chillington Hall (1m away to the NNE). Stands just outside Chillington Park proper. The N facade is classical with Tuscan columns and appears as a folly from the hall, from where it could probably be seen, but is a sham and hides a farmhouse. Thought to have been the work of either James Paine (c1770) or Sir John Soane (c1786) (VCH vol 5 p24). Pevsner says it was built in the c1770s (BOE p103). But later writers have thought it built earlier in 1724 by Francis Smith (F p308). Has also appeared as Whitehouse Farm. (DoE II*) (SGS p66) (F&G p135) (MR p51) (BDH p188) (FZ p111).

White House Situated on the W corner of Brierley Hill Road and Mill Street, Audnam. Residence of Owen Gibbons, tile manufacturer of Brockmoor, and Dr William Tweddell (b1897), a local doctor and golf champion. Demolished in the 1930s for the widening of Brierley Hill Road (SNSV vol 2 p48).

White House Farm Bradley, near Stafford. The Webb Stone (see), a glacial boulder, was on its land. The farmer moved it which put a curse on his cattle, so he replaced it by a bungalow at the drive to the farm (VB p151).

White House Farm Great Wyrley. The house was built on land which formed part of a farm in Stuart times; the owners still pay an annual portion of the pension awarded to the Penderell family by Charles II (GWY p facing p39).

Whitehurst Minute hamlet 1m N of Dilhorne. In Dilhorne parish.

White Lea Farm Nearly 1.5m NW of Onecote. Formerly in Onecote township in Leek ancient parish. There was a house on this site by the late 1530s. The present house is dated 1786 (VCH vol 7 pp211,213).

White Low In the vicinity of Saxon's Low (NSFCT 1926 p142). There is a Whitemoor Farm at Yarnfield and Whitehouse Farm at Norton Bridge.

White Middle Hills Small farm, probably slightly S of the Royal Cottage Inn. Here is the source of the Churnet (HOLF p14). For a haunted house said to have been at or near here see Gradbach Old Hall.

Whitemoor Small hamlet 1.25m NNW of Biddulph parish church. Formerly in Lower Biddulph liberty in Biddulph ancient parish. There was settlement at Whitemoor by 1500 (BALH). The Whitemoor area was occupied by parliament forces in the Civil War during the siege of Biddulph Old Hall (Congleton and District: A Portrait in Old Picture Postcards. Mary & Colin McLean. 1988 p76).

Whitemoor, The House 1.5m SW of Bishop's Wood. In Brewood ancient parish. Has also appeared as Whitemere (1327), Wytemor (1327), Long Whitemore (1390) (SPNO p43) and Whitemore.

Whitemoor Hayes House 1.75m NNW of Elford.

White Pits Pools Weston Park, Weston-under-Lizard.

White's Bridge Bridge carrying the Macclesfield-Leek road over the Churnet, and former small hamlet 0.5m NW of Leek. In Leekfrith township in ancient Leek parish (W p728). Now merged into Leek. Has appeared as Conyngre Bridge (1430), White's Bridge (1630) (VCH vol 7 p99) and Whites Bridge.

White's Hill NE of Cannock (1834 OS map) (PCC p77). The name means the shinning hill (SPNO p61).

White's Hill Hill traversed by Watling Street 2.75m SE of Tamworth, formerly in Warws.

Whitesich Brook Tributary of the Penk. The name means, presumably, 'the light-coloured stream' (SPNO p22).

White Sike The name occurs in Lady Wulfrun's charter of 994. Duignan identified White Sike with 'Cold Lanes' near Bunkers Hill, Bilston (WFW p30). 'Cold Lanes' may be identified with the hamlet known as Cold Lane (see).

White Sitch Large pool 1m W of Blymhill, in Weston-under-Lizard ancient parish (SPNO p182). Has appeared as Whitseche (C13), Whitesiche (1356), and the White Sitch (1834 OS map) (SPNO p182). Samuel Dickenson LLB rector of Blymhill refers to many rare, and not so rare, plants existing in the vicinity of it. For instance, the very rare Agaricus Deliciosus in fir plantations near the pool. On the dam at White Sitch Pool is the rare Agaricus Cantharellus, linn, and Merulius Cantharellus (SHOS vol 1 part 1 p97). Very curious and rare is the Conferva Pegragrophila - globe c. or moor balls, which, despite reports of it, could not be found after two years searching (SHOS vol 1 part 1 p102).

White Well At SO 805874 to SE of Four Ashes.

Whitfield Tiny hamlet in Whitfield Valley 1m NNW of Norton-in-the-Moors. In Norton-in-the-Moors parish.

Whitfield Brook Rises at Mow Cop and flows through Brindley Ford and Ford Green to Carmountside where it joins the Trent. It is commonly called Banky Brook. Plot's map incorrectly shows this brook to be the head of the Trent (ONST 1971 p310. 1978 p386).

Whitfield Colliery Whitfield. The Chatterley Iron Company, owned by the Chatterley family, acquired the leasehold of the colliery in 1872 (IAS p192) and subsequently it became known as the Chatterley Whitfield Colliery. The colliery had a disaster on Feb 7 1881, 25 miners died (IANS p38). Leigh says

21 died (LMV p112), or 24 died (ONST 1941 p93) (LWF pp1-5,119). In 1937 the colliery became the first in the country to extract more than a million tons of coal a year and was one of the first collieries to have electric lighting and electrically-driven coal cutters (BBC 1 Midlands Today. Jan 13 1999) (Heritage Today. Magazine of English Heritage. June 1999 p38). In 1977 it closed and the site opened as the **Chatterley Whitfield Coal Mining Museum**, Britain's first ever mining museum, and in this respect a unique enterprise (ES Aug 25 1978. Feb 23 1994 p1. Sept 7 1994 p16p. Feb 11 1998 p3). The museum closed in 1993 (NSFCT 1993-4 New Series vol 19 p32). The museum had a Hesketh Steam winding engine (AA p255pc) and a memorial plaque to John Rhodes VC, of Packmoor (see). The colliery still with many late C19 and early C20 over-ground buildings and winding gear was listed for preservation by English Heritage in Jan 1999 (BBC 1 Midland Today. Jan 13 1999).

Whitgreave Small village on a hill overlooking a tributary of the Sow to the S, 1.25m NE of Great Bridgeford. Former township in St Mary's parish, Stafford. Has appeared as Witegraue (1193) (SSE 1996 p119), Witegrave, Whytegrave, Witegreve (SPN p112), and Whitgrove (W p343). The name means 'white thicket or grove' (DUIGNAN) (NSJFS 1981 p2) (SSE 1996 p19) (SPN p112) (ROT p28). Chetwynd says the name signifies 'a grave of withs, or willows' (SHC 1914 p101) (SH p45). The name of Whitgreave prebend in Stafford Collegiate Church, embraced many separate prebends. The Whitgreave prebends in 1535 were given as: Swetrnam, Blurton, Hervy, Walsall, Sandall, Orberton, Denston, Potrell and Croft (VCH vol 3 p307). The Whitgreave family of Burton Manor and Moseley Old Hall take their name from this place (SHOS vol 2 p184). Whitgreave became a separate ecclesiastical parish with Marston in 1777, disunited from Marston in 1844, refounded with Marston in 1850 (GLAUE p428) (LGS p253; says became a separate parish in 1838). The church, St John, in the village centre, was built in 1844 (LDD). Whitgreave became a separate civil parish in 1866 (GLAUE p428). A superstition by which maids could know the identity of their future husband was practised at Whitgreave. A maid here was told to take a 'lock of an ash' which is an ash leaf without the final leaflet, to her house and hang it above the door and notice the name of the man who first came in; his name would be the same as the one she would marry (SFL p180) (FOS p57) (STMSM July 1980 p33).

Whitle Sheen ancient parish. The Whitle area, a detached portion of Alstonefield manor in the Middle Ages, was settled by the early C15. The C19 house, Under Whitle, 1.5m NNW of Sheen, stands on the site of a house in existence by 1711. The C19 house, Upper Whitle, 0.5m to the NW, may stand on the site of a former house also in existence by 1711 (VCH vol 7 p1 note, 241).

Whitleyeaves Tiny hamlet on a bank above Lonco Brook 2m E of High Offley, NNW of Whitley Heath.

Whitley Ford House 1m N of Forton. Formerly in Weston Jones township in Norbury ancient parish. Whitley Manor is over the border in Shrops. Appears on Yates' map (SPNO p177). In 1927 there was a conflict of opinion between Staffs and Shrops officials as to the exact course of the county boundary at Whitley Ford Bridge. Entries in the Weston Jones constables accounts for 1788 show that at that date the bridge was wholly in Staffs (NSFCT 1927 p40).

Whitley Heath Heath and fragmented minute hamlet on Lonco Brook S of Whitleyeaves. In Eccleshall ancient parish. Whitley was a common until enclosed in 1719 or 1845 (ECC p18).

Whitmore Small village on the upper reaches of Meece Brook; not the Sow as Mee says (KES p228), 13.25m NNW of Stafford. Former detached chapelry in Stoke-upon-Trent ancient parish, but had separate civil status early (GLAUE p428) (LGS p253; a chapel of Trentham ancient parish). Has appeared as Witemore (DB), Wytemore-under-Lyme (1242) (DUIGNAN) (LGS p253), and Whytemore (C13) (SPN p141). The **name** means 'white moor' (SK p92) (NSJFS 1981 p2) (SPN p141) (SSE 1996 p19), or Stevenson thinks 'Wita's moor' (DUIGNAN). There was a **church** at Whitmore before the Norman Conquest (LDD). The present church, St Mary and All Saints, S of Whitmore Hall on the N side of the Shrewsbury-Newcastle road, has some Norman work, but was mostly rebuilt in 1676. It has a timber-framed bell-turret, and one gable timber-framed (LGS p253) (BOE p308). Commander Wedgwood thought Whitmore had become separated from the rest of Stoke-upon-Trent ancient parish when Swynnerton was formed; Swynnerton's present northern territories once forming a part of Stoke and therefore linking Whitmore with the rest of Stoke parish (SHC 1916 p195). Whitmore chapelry became a separate ecclesiastical parish in 1725, refounded in 1849 (GLAUE p428) (APB p5; became a separate parish in 1807). The **pudding bell** was rung at Whitmore to remind housewives when to take Sunday lunch out of the oven (TTTD p230). The village is situated on England's main watershed

(TTTD p230), and there was a **windmill** at Whitmore which was bought second hand from Newcastle by Edward Mainwaring for £12. However, the cost of moving it seems to have been more - £21. 6s 1d (SLM spring 1954 p24). Whitmore was on the original **Shrewsbury-Newcastle road**. But when in 1846 the present section of road (A53) was made to the E and S of Whitmore Hall, cutting out Acton village, the Mainwarings are said to have asked for it to be built low enough so as to be unseen from the hall (SVB pp177,178). There was a station at Whitmore (at Baldwin's Gate to the W) on the former Grand Junction **Railway** line, opened on July 4 1837, which closed on Feb 4 1952 (Railways In and Around Stafford. Edward Talbot. 1994 p4); at first it was the only railway station in the Potteries area and consequently was of much importance (AHJ No. 2 1996 p52). Another account says the first train passed through in 1839, and large crowds from the Potteries flocked to see it (NSFCT 1921 p72). Whitmore Summit of 380 feet is said to be the highest point on the railway between London and the Lake District, but at Tring a summit of 420 feet is passed when traversing a gap through the Chiltern Hills (TTTD p234). There was an accident at Whitmore station in early Feb 1841 when two trains collided on account of mist and poor visibility; one man was killed (SA Feb 13 1841). In June 1937 the LMS 'Coronation Scot' on its first run broke a speed record at Whitmore approaching Crewe when it reached 112.5 mph (ES June 29 1937 p1p) (TTTD p234) (SGS p126). A violent **hurricane** or tornado struck Whitmore on Sept 23 1811 (Broughton's Scrapbook p455). **Vicar and a vicar's son. John Ball**, who would not sign the Thirty-Nine Articles and was known in scorn as 'the Presbyterian's Champion,' was minister of Whitmore from 1610 to his death on Oct 20 1639. He lived with the Mainwarings at Whitmore Hall (SMC p174) (S&W p251) (TTTD p229). **Samuel J Stone** was born at Whitmore Rectory on April 25 1839, son of Rev William Stone MA. He spent some of his childhood at Colwich and became a scholar, poet and parson and wrote many hymns, the best-known being 'The Church's One Foundation' which he wrote whilst curate at Windsor (BS p437) (PSS pp229-232) (KES p228) (VB p185) (TTTD p230) (VFC p126).

Whitmore Common Snapehall, to the E of Madeley Park Wood (SL p92 see map). Perhaps synonymous with Whitmore Heath. NSFCT records a burial mound here which was excavated but revealed nothing (NSFCT vol 70 pp64-65). Gunstone thinks this was probably not a burial mound (NSJFS 1965 p58). There is a mound 1.5m NNW of Whitmore, to the SW of Racecourse Farm. A gravel pit on Whitmore Common obliterated a recorded rectangular 'camp' in c1938, near which were found a 'bowl' and 'disc' type burial mound from which came two calcinated flints, one a knife and a piece of human calvarium. The later displayed medieval characteristics and probably had no relation to these earthworks (NSFCT 1938 p114).

Whitmore Hall Whitmore Reans, Wolverhampton. A house of this name was situated on the S side of Lowe Street, W of Manby Street in 1901 (OS map Wolverhampton (NW) 1901 62.06).

Whitmore Hall Brick house encasing a timber framed house at Whitmore. Whitmore manor was held by the Whitmores from sometime after DB until 1195 then by the de Verdon family until 1385 when it passed by marriage to the de Boghays (or Bougheys). Whitmore passed from the Boghays to John Ireland in 1544. But he soon died and it was settled on Edward Mainwaring (d1586) in 1546. Sir Edward Mainwaring (d1647) fortified the hall against royalist troops in the Civil War. He was secretary to Lord Strafford and a portrait of Lord Strafford and Sir Edward by Van Dyck was still being kept at the hall in the C18. Edward Mainwaring (d1703) had the present S front of the house built in 1676; it merely fronts the old hall. The hall ceased to pass by direct male line in the Mainwaring family (all the heirs from Edward Mainwaring (d1586) being called Edward) when Edward Mainwaring died without issue in 1825. It then passed to his cousin Rear Admiral Rowland Mainwaring (1783-1862). He was succeeded by his son and heir Charles Henry Mainwaring, d1889 without issue, who was succeeded by his younger brother Frederick Rowland Mainwaring, d1891 without issue, who was succeeded by his sister Ellen Jane who married Wentworth Cavenagh in 1865. Their descendants, the Cavenagh-Mainwarings from 1892, now reside at the hall (SHC 1909 p195 note. 1933 part 2 pp3-182) (SGS p181) (SVB p178) (TTTD p228-229) (BOE p309) (ES June 30 1983; the Mainwarings became Cavenagh-Mainwarings in 1920). Thomas Twyford, the sanitaryware pioneer, was a tenant for 30 years until his death in 1921. Whilst in residence Twyford installed one of his baths, believed to be unique. The bath weighing half a ton was removed in Sept 1996 and put on show at Twyford's factory in Alsager, Ches (ES Sept 13 1996 p3). James Gordon Cavenagh-Mainwaring the son and heir of Ellen Jane, born in 1865, came to live at the hall in Dec 1928 (SHC 1933 part 2 p125). The proposed marriage of Edward Cavenagh-Mainwaring (b1962) to Jane Burgess of Lordsley was the subject of a BBC television documentary. But in May 1994, after a year of filming, the couple

could still not set a date for the wedding giving the documentary makers some anxiety (Daily Express May 10 1994 p5pcs). The stables are of c1620-30 origin (DoE II*) (NSFCT 1919 pp88-89. 1931 pp194-195) (SLM autumn 1958 p13p of interior) (STM July 1965 p31p of interior). A new dovecote was built in 1684 (SHC 1933 part 2 p76). The very rare bird in the UK the Hoopoe (Epupa, Epops, Linn) a migrant from Egypt was seen and shot dead in the grounds of Whitmore Hall by a gamekeeper of the Mainwarings (SA Oct 20 1832) (Broughton's Scrapbook p455).

Whitmore Heath Modern and 'desirable' residential district of NE Whitmore. Probably, formerly known as Whitmore Common, and was common land. Formerly in Whitmore chapelry in Stoke-upon-Trent ancient parish. In Whitmore Heath Lane at SJ 797404 is a five feet high burial mound described as in good condition in 1983 (NSFCT 1983 p11). There is another burial mound, 10-15 feet high, in Greenways House garden at SJ 798405. It is a long irregular mound orientated E to W. In 1983 one end had eleven trees on it and one side had been sliced to make way for a drive (NSFCT new series vol 9 1983 p11). The heath was enclosed in 1841 (SHC 1933 part 2 p144).

Whitmore Reans Suburb of Wolverhampton, 1m NW of St Peter's church. Formerly in Wolverhampton chapelry and ancient parish. The area, part of barren land known as Hungry Leas in the C16, was by the late C18 cultivated and appears to have been then known as Whitmore-ends (SHOS vol 2 p165). Whitmore Reans may be from 'white-moor-reans' a swampy area prone to white fogs or mists and drained by reans, gutters running parallel with the furrows of ploughed land (WOLOP p11). The church, St Andrew, St Andrew's Close, Hunter Street, was built in 1865 (LDD; rebuilt in 1967). The area was developed for housing from about then until at least the 1880s. The name New Hampton was given to the development but did not catch on with Whitmore Reans remaining the area's name; New Hampton only survives in Newhampton Road. One of the first terraces to be built was Waterloo Terrace; the development was completed by 1901 (Mapping the Past Wolverhampton 1577-1986. Mary Mills 1993 pp20,28) (WOLOP pp10p,11p) (HOWU p114).

Whitmore Reans Hall Whitmore Reans. Built in c1850 by Councillor Samuel Griffith, who went bankrupt in 1857 for £160,000 and it is said he built a high wall around the hall to keep out his creditors (WF p46).

Whittamoors, The House and coppice 1.5m SW of Dunston.

Whittimere House 1.5m NE of Bobbington. 0.5m W of Upper Whittimere. Formerly in Shrops. Transferred to Bobbington parish, Staffs, in 1895 (VCH vol 20 p64). A Roman road running from Ashwood to Bridgnorth passed through the Whittimere area (VCH vol 20 p64). A vill of Whittimere existed by the later C13 (VCH vol 20 p65).

Whittimere Hill Near to the War Stone, Seisdon, in Bobbington parish. Here are two small camps of ancient origin (SHOS vol 2 p278) (SVS p328 note) (VCH vol 20 p64).

Whittington Small hamlet on a low hill by a tributary of Brockton Brook 1m E of Charnes. In the Woodland quarter in Eccleshall ancient parish (W p380). Whittington was formerly a small village, later only a solitary farm in Charnes manor, which belonged to a family of that name, but passed by marriage to John Broughton, a younger son of Richard, in Henry VIII's reign, whose great grandson sold it to John Jervis of Chatcull (COI p224 note). Has appeared as Whittenton (1679) (SHC 1914 p29).

Whittington Former manor (W p179) and township (VCH vol 20 p149) in Kinver ancient parish. The small hamlet of Whittington by the Stour is 1.5m SSW of Stourton. The name means perhaps 'Wita's town' (DUIGNAN). Whittington was an inhabited area by the 1180s and became a sub-manor of Kinver in c1200, with a manor house which became Whittington Hall (see) (VCH vol 20 p125). Earthworks S of the hall at SO 858826 represent possibly a medieval deserted settlement (SSAHST 1982-3 p44). Whittington church, in existence in medieval times, is not mentioned in the 1563 or subsequent returns (SHC 1915 p107).

Whittington Ancient parish and village on low ground by the Coventry Canal and at some distance from Fisherwick Brook 16m SE of Stafford, 2m ESE of Lichfield. The Hwituntun mentioned in a charter of 925 was identified by Birch in his Cartularium Saxonicum with this Whittington. But CGO Bridgeman identifies it with Whittington, Worcs (SHC 1916 p76). However, others have stuck with Birch's identification (SSE 1991 pp7,8. 1996 p19). Whittington may have formed a part of Longdon in 1086 but does not appear in DB. In c1255 land at Witinton, identified with Whittington, formed part of the manor of Longdon which was held by the bishop of Chester (Lichfield) (SHOS vol 1 p376) (SPN p141). The name means 'the tun or farmstead of Hwita's people' (SPN p141) (SSE 1991 p19). There was a church at Whittington in the C13 (LDD). The present parish church, St Giles, on the S side of Church Street, has a tower of medieval origin. The rest of the church was rebuilt or added to in 1761 and 1881 (BOE p309). Wakes were on the first Sunday after Sept 11 in the C19 (W p611). The prebend of Whittington in Lichfield cathedral was founded by Roger de Clinton in the C12 as Berkswich. The prebend did not possess any tithes or land at Whittington, but the dean and chapter did acquire the greater tithes as part of their general fund. In consequence of this the prebendary has often been termed as of Berkswich and Whittington, or of Whittington and Berkswich (SHOS vol 1 p294) (SSAHST vol 2 1960-61 p51) (VCH vol 3 p141). The parish was a peculiar jurisdiction of the dean and chapter of Lichfield cathedral until peculiar jurisdictions were abolished in 1846 (GLAUE p428).

Whittington Barracks 1m SSW of Whittington, near Lichfield. The headquarters and museum of the **Staffordshire Regiment** (The Prince of Wales') are currently (1999) at Whittington Barracks. The Regiment has evolved from the amalgamation of four old regiments of foot. The earliest regiment to be raised was in 1705 by Col Luke Lillington at the King's Head Inn, Lichfield. Regiments took the title of their Colonel until 1751 when Lillington's old regiment became the 38th Foot. The second regiment was the 2nd/11th, later 64th Foot, formed in 1756. The two regiments were given the subsidiary titles of (1st and 2nd Staffordshire) in 1782 but had little regular contact with the county. The third regiment, the 80th Foot (Staffordshire Volunteers), was raised in 1793 by William Henry Paget of Beaudesert Hall, later 1st Marquis of Anglesey, mainly from the Stafford Militia, then commanded by his father. The fourth regiment originated as the 98th Regiment, raised at Chichester in 1824, which had no county links at that time. In 1872 the 38th & 80th and 64th & 98th were linked under the Cardwell Army Reforms and in 1881 this process was completed as the former became the South Staffordshire Regiment and the latter the Prince of Wales' (North Staffordshire Regiment). The Prince of Wales' title had been conferred on the 98th in Malta in 1876. The South took crown and Stafford Knot as its badge and the North the Prince of Wales' plumes and Stafford Knot. The two regiments, which raised 35 battalions in WW1 and 21 in WW2, were amalgamated in 1959 to form The Staffordshire Regiment (The Prince of Wales') (info Major E Green) (LAL p42p of the plaque about the 38th Regiment) (VCH vol 14 p24) (Histories of the regiments in WSL). The War Department built new barracks on Whittington Heath in 1877 (CCHCB p161) and are said to have purchased the heath from the Marquis of Anglesey in 1881 (SVB p179). The barracks was built initially to be the Depots of the South and North Staffordshire Regiments, which were to be formed in 1881 under the Cardwell Army Reforms. It was extended to take the Militia Battalions of the South Staffords in 1894 and after further extensions in the early 1900s two Infantry Battalions were stationed there as well (LGS p253). The American 10th Replacement Depot occupied the Barracks from 1942-46 and it was re-occupied by the South and North Staffords in 1948. Subsequently, it also housed the Army Catering Corps Depot (1950s) and then as the Army reduced its size it became the Training Depot for a number of Regiments, firstly the Mercian Brigade and, in 1967, the Prince of Wales' Division - both were regional groupings of which the Staffordshire Regiment was a part. In 1992 the Army changed its system of training recruits and the barracks was taken over by the Army Training Regiment Lichfield in 1992. There it carries out first-phase military training for recruits going to The Prince of Wales' Division, The Parachute Regiment and The Army Medical Services. The most imposing building in the Barracks is the Grade II listed 'Keep' which was a feature of all Cardwell Barracks. A plaque on the wall to the left of the Keep reads 'In memory of JACK THE SOUTH STAFFORD GUARD DOG. DIED MARCH 20 1895' (info Major E Green). (SVB p179) (MR p378) (AWM p29).

THE MUSEUM. The current museum for the Staffordshire Regiment was built at Whittington Barracks in 1969. It tells the story of the old county regiments - the North and South Staffords - and their successors in the Staffordshire Regiment. In 1999 the museum re-opened after a major re-fit and some of its current exhibits include: a **bell from Burma** brought by the 80th Regt of Foot later used as a fire alarm on the roof of Lichfield Guildhall (see). **Colours of** i). the Loyal Pottery Infantry raised in 1798 (disbanded in 1802), subsequently carried by the Lane End Volunteer Infantry raised in 1803: ii). the 64th Regt in use from c1808/9 to 1819. The **Diorama of the battle of Ulundi**, the decisive battle in the Zulu War 1879. **Key of the lower gate of the Citadel at Cairo**, opened on its surrender 1882. **EOKA flag** taken in Nicosia by the 1st South Staffs Regt. Regimental **flag of the Uganda Rifles** captured by 1st Staffordshire Regiment during the mutiny in Jan 1964 before independence. Piece of **earthen ware from Castle Hill in Korea** dug up by the 1st North Staffs Regt when building a defence line in 1953. **List of Regimental recipients of the Victoria Cross**. Small **canon taken from the Mutineers at Lucknow** and presented to Lord Clyde. **Piece of wood taken from**

the hulk of the **'Briton'** which was wrecked on the Andaman Islands in 1844 when conveying a detachment of the 80th Regt from Sydney to India. **38th Foot Shako Plate** dug up in the Crimea and presented to the 1st South Staffs Regt by the 38th Russian Regt in 1916. Ruler said to be made from a tree on which mutineers were hanged during the Indian Mutiny. Formerly the Museum exhibited: A **bust of the Marquis of Anglesey**; he raised the 80th Regt of Foot in 1793. **Colours of** those carried during the Sikh War (a fragment of). Photograph of the **memorial to those who fell at Intombi Drift** in 1879, erected on Jan 1 1911 at Intombi Drift. The **collars of regimental mascots** - 'Baron' (1915), 'Stafford' (d1943), and 'Tyke' (probably WW1). The original **pike heads and descriptive plate of the 80th Regt** (1814) taken from Lichfield cathedral. **Painting of the Staffs Militia at Windsor Castle** in 1804. The original oil painting is at Arbury Hall, Nuneaton, Warws. Exhibited outside the Museum: An **Iraqi M.T.L.B. tank** (Gun Tower APC) captured by the 1st Staffordshire Regiment in the Gulf War in 1991.

Whittington Common 1.5m SSE of Stourton. In Gibbet Wood (see), a part of the common, Benjamin Robins was murdered by William Howe in 1812. Howe was later hung at the murder scene. Since then the ghost of either Howe or Robins or both has been sighted on the common.

Whittington Hall On S side of Whittington Hall Lane, nearly 1m ESE of Kinver church. There was probably a manor house on this site in medieval times, and it was occupied by the lords of Whittington, the Whittingtons to 1351-2, the Lowes from 1351-2, and from 1475 the Greys; the Greys of Enville held it from the early C16. Thomas Grey was described as of Whittington in 1538, but he later moved to Enville Hall. In the later C17 the hall was let to the Talbot family. Their son Thomas (d1730), bishop successively of Oxford, Salisbury, and Durham, was probably born here in 1658 or 1659. The lord of Enville, John Grey (d1709), lived at the hall between 1684 and 1692; his successors, who were Earls of Stamford, lived at Enville Hall (VCH vol 20 pp135-136). The present hall is a brick house of the early C18 (VCH Vol 20 p136), and has also appeared as Whittington Hall Farm and Whittington Manor Farm. Palliser says it was built in 1788 by Lord Stamford of Enville Hall after he vacated the old manor house, now Whittington Inn (SL p96). Earthworks S of the hall at SO 858826 represent possibly the moat of a former hall or a medieval deserted settlement (SSAHST 1982-3 p44). The circular dovecote or pigeon house in the grounds is of medieval origin with C18 additions (DoE II) (VCH vol 20 p136).

Whittington Hall (1) Whittington, near Lichfield. Seat in the later C16 of a junior branch of the Everard family of Leics (SHOS vol 1 p376).

Whittington Hall (2) In the middle of Whittington village, near Lichfield. Built in brick by Zachary Babington. Shaw noted on one of the pillars in front leading into the court is sculptured 'Z.B. 1673.' Was the property of the Hawes family in the late C18 (SHOS vol 1 pp376il - house on the left? 377). Babbington Close, a collection of detached modern houses of the C20, now (March 2000) occupies the site?

Whittington Hall (3) Whittington, near Lichfield. Seat of the Fullwoods in the 1680s. Shaw was unable to identify the house in the late C18 but it may have been one of the houses opposite Whittington Hall (2) (SHOS vol 1 p377).

Whittington Hall (4) Whittington, near Lichfield. Seat of the Harveys in the 1680s. Shaw was unable to identify the house in the late C18 but it may have been one of the houses opposite Whittington Hall (2) (SHOS vol 1 p377).

Whittington Hall (5) In the middle of Whittington village, near Lichfield. Described in the late C18 as an old house with large stone bay windows in the front and a round arched door. In several of the windows were painted the initials H.R.D. It was the property of the Astleys of Tamhorn whose heiress carried it to Richard Dyott. In the late C18 it was occupied by his mother Mrs Dyott, widow of Richard Dyott of Freeford (SHOS vol 1 pp376il - house on the right? 377). The same house appears to have been the seat of John Baggaley between at least 1851 and 1872 (W p24). It was occupied by Lord Berkley Paget in 1880; by George Alex Baird in 1884. The hall was vacant in 1888 (trade directories). It appears to have been largely rebuilt between 1889 and 1891 for Samuel Lipscomb Seckham (creator of Park Town at Oxford) by Holding of Northampton. Some of the original hall appears to have been kept; a C17 stone porch from the old hall is incorporated into the garden side (BOE p309) (SGS p183) (STC p17p). Seckham continued to live at the hall, now The Old Hall (perhaps the old part of the hall), until his death in 1901; in 1910 Masefield described the Old Hall as 'a fine Tudor mansion of red brick, with looped-holed walls and wainscoted rooms' (LGS p253) (mems in Leamonsley and Whittington churches) (trade directories). The house was the seat of Col Bassett Thorne Seckham DSO JP until his death in 1925 (mem in Whittington church) (trade directories) (STC p17p) (The Mercury Supplement July 21 1899). Edward VII stayed at the hall when attending racing on Whittington Heath (SVB p179). Later occupants have included Harold de

Vahl Rubin (1928); Capt Thomas Henry Lawley (1932); Edmund Richards Corn (1940) (trade directories). The hall was still standing in the early 1970s (BOE p309), with some listed stained glass from the old hall with the motto 'WHERE 'ERE/ WE ROAM/ AN ENGLISH MOTHER/ IN AN ENGLISH HOME' (DoE II*). GROUNDS. A garden gateway of C17 origin and two gatepiers dated 1673, probably from the old hall (BOE p309).

Whittington Heath Former common land (SVB p179) SW of Whittington, near Lichfield. Formerly owned by the Marquis of Anglesey and stretched to Freeford (DUIGNAN). Lichfield races were moved to Whittington Heath from Fradley Heath (see) in 1702. By the early 1740s races were held in Sept and lasted two days. They were extended to three days in 1744, by which time Lichfield races were one of the leading meetings in the Midlands (VCH vol 14 pp22,161). For the political disturbances of the Staffordshire county election 1747 at Lichfield races see Introduction. The Tories organised their own rival races a week prior to the normal races between and including 1748 and 1752 (HOS p64). In Aug 1748 George II seems to have rewarded the Whigs by consenting to the inauguration of a Royal Plate of 100 guineas for the winner of the 'Whig' race (VB p15). In the WSL is a handbill advertising the races for the year 1752 stating the race will occur on the consecutive days of 1st, 2nd, and 14th September, for this was the year the Gregorian calendar was introduced to Britain (VB p14). In 1753 the rival Whig and Tory races were amalgamated. In 1769 the famous horse Eclipse won the King's Plate. In the 1830s a course at Broadmeadow Field (see) at Wolverhampton took over from Lichfield as the county's premier meeting (VB p15). The War Department built new barracks on the heath in 1877 (CCHCB p161) and bought the heath in 1881. Racing continued until 1890 (SVB p179) or 1895 (VB p15) (One Hundred Years of Racing at Dunstall Park 1887-1987. Richard Onslow p4; 1895 was the year Dunstall Park became the only course in Staffs to offer flat racing). The grandstand at SK 148071 became a 'Soldiers Home' or recreational club and was used as such until 1955. In 1958 the old grandstand became the club house for a golf course (WMAG Nov 1979 p17p) (SVB p179). In 1999 it was the club house for Whittington Heath Golf Club (info Major E Green). In Aug 1944 a peculiar rain-shower of frogs occurred on the A51 opposite Whittington Barracks. After the shower the road was found to be covered with frogs who promptly jumped into the gutter (MMSE p288).

Whittington Hurst Fragmented minute hamlet on gentle rising ground on the W side of the Tame 1.25m NNE of Whittington, near Lichfield. In Whittington parish. Seems to have also been The Hurst (SGSAS). In Nov 1838 Charles Hand, farmer of Whittington Hurst, was burgled and threatened with his life (Staffordshire Mercury Dec 1 1838) (Broughton's Scrapbook p261).

Whittington Inn Whittington, Stourton, in Kinver ancient parish. Built by Sir William de Whittenton in 1310; his grandson was Lord Mayor of London, Dick Whittington, and it reputedly was his residence, and his ghost is said to haunt the inn (GOM pl 2(b)) (Pub Guide). Lady Jane Grey (1537-1554), a relation of the Greys of Enville Hall (see) and queen of England for nine days in July 1553, reputedly spent some of her childhood here and her ghost reputedly walks the first floor corridor (Pub Guide) (IOM p77 p of inn facing p77) (KEOP p42p of the inn). The inn is also haunted by the ghost of a monk (HPG pp173-174). Charles II stayed a night here after his flight from the battle of Worcester (1651) before going to White Ladies. In 1711 or 1712 Queen Anne reputedly stayed here. It was her custom to have her iron seal fixed to premises which gave her hospitality. The 'Anne R 1711' iron seal on the front door is one of only two remaining in the country (R&S p33) (IOM p77) (KRC p25) (Pub Guide). The inn is probably Elizabethan, not of 1310, as some have claimed, and was the former manor house of an Earl of Stamford of Enville Hall (see), before he built Whittington Hall (or now Farm) in 1788 (SL p96). Others say the present inn was not the manor house (VCH vol 20 p125 note). From a private residence it was turned into an inn in 1788 (SL p96) (VCH vol 20 p125) (KEOP p43ps of the interior).

Whittington Old House Formerly Bathpool Cottages. Horse Bridge Lane, Whittington, Kinver (VCH vol 20 p125).

Whit-well Appears to have been a well between Longton and Normacot and is named in the Hulton Abbey charter. The name may represent 'the white well' (SHC 1909 p59 note).

Whitwell Spring Spring on the W side of Sedgley Beacon, in fields behind Cotwall End House (SDOP p16p). Has also appeared as Whit Well (SDOP p16). It was used for consumptives and also for bathing sore eyes (AMS p445). Gives rise to a brook which is a tributary of the Smestow (AMS p2) (PHS p18).

Whorrocks Bank Escarpment on the W side of Rudyard village. A house in the later Rudyard village was described in 1607 as at Whorrocks (VCH vol 7 p67). The bank derives the first part of its name from a word meaning hoar

(or grey) oak trees, used as a toponym in the later C13 (VCH vol 7 p67). The bank is now (1997) known as Horton Bank (RL p27). The name is preserved in Whorrocks Bank Road.

Wibbilde Moor Barren area near Knowle on S side of Lichfield. Recorded in c1200 and surviving in 1440. Has appeared as Wibbelle Moor (VCH vol 14 p111).

Wickenlow SE of Flash on E side of A53. Wicken is a dialectic word of unknown origin for the mountain ash (DUIGNAN).

Wicken Stones Long thin gritstone ridge of intermittent character lying on England's main watershed (TTTD pp158,161p) below Rock End at the top of Park Lane, Biddulph Moor (BALH see map p13) (BGFB p31) (SVB p33). Some of its crags, 'Garden Buttress' and to E of Wickenstones Farm 'Erf Rocks' (named after the Erf Plastics factory - SGM p290), have been named by rock climbers in recent times. One of the stones is nearly circular and resembles a double plinth or base of an immense column which appears like a druidical monument (HBST p182). Has also appeared as Wicking Rocks (NSFCT 1888 p68), and Wicking Stones (HBST p182). There are excellent views from this ridge (NSFCT 1906 p156). The Wicken Stones are said to have given James Bateman the inspiration for the grandiose rock work at Biddulph Grange (CIOPP p22p). It may have been a local tradition to expose new-born infants under the Wicking, or Wickenstones as Cedric Stokes implies in 'The Staffordshire Assassins' p52.

Wicken Walls Farm in Quarnford parish, to W of Flash, below Turn Edge. 'Walls' is from it having formerly stood on the Limes Britannicus (NSFCT 1902 p116). Or means 'wells where the mountain ash grows' (NSFCT 1932 p58).

Wiggin's Farm Tipton. Occupied by George Brain and owned by Edward Wright in c1815. It was demolished in c1820 and the materials utilised for rebuilding a portion of Hawkin's Farm near Owen Street crossing, Tipton (HOTIP p192).

Wigginstall There is a Higher and a Lower Wigginstall by a small tributary of the Manifold nearly 1.5m WSW of Sheen. Formerly in Fawfieldhead township in Alstonefield ancient parish (W p743). Land called Wigginstall was recorded in 1396. There was a house at Higher Wigginstall by the early C16 (VCH vol 7 p28). For etymology see Wichens.

Wigginton Small village on a hill overlooking Tamworth 21m SE of Stafford. Former township and chapelry in Tamworth ancient parish (W p626). A Saxon highway ran through Wigginton, thought to have been a salt track. There are still signs of the old track and a road called Salters Lane on the Tamworth side (SVB p180). Has appeared as Wigetone, a manor, in DB, Wicgintun, Wyggenton, Wichintona, and Wikenton (SPN p141). The **name** means 'Hwita's town' (SVB p178), or 'Hwita's farmstead' (SPN p141), or Stevenson thinks it may be 'Whitestone' (DUIGNAN). Mills gives 'tun of Wicga's people' (SSE 1996 p19). Former **prebend** of Tamworth Collegiate Church, which was sometimes called Wigginton and Comberford (VCH vol 3 p310). There was a **church** at Wigginton in 1770 (LDD). The church, St Leonard, on the W side of Main Road, N of Comberford Lane, was built in 1777 and added to in 1830 and 1861-1862 (BOE p310). Became a separate ecclesiastical parish in 1778, refounded in 1856 (GLAUE pp428-429). Wigginton **wake** was on the Sunday after Nov 5 (old style) in the C19 (W p626). Hanging Hill to N of Wigginton, at SK 205076 (1889 OS map 6 inch), may represent the site of the manorial **gallows**. There was a **windmill** at Wigginton Farm 1m SW of the church first shown on Greenwood's map. In 1827 it was for sale in conjunction with a property called Tamworth Mill. The windmill had gone by 1883 (Birmingham Gazette Feb 25 1828) (Simmons' notes) (WBJ p46). Became a civil parish in 1866 (GLAUE pp428-429). The SE portion of the ancient parish was in Tamworth municipal borough by 1971, by which time the same area had been developed as a NW suburb of Tamworth (OS map 1:25,000). Wigginton features in a derisory **rhyme** about Tamworth (see). **Murder case**. Judith Roberts of Tamworth, aged 14, went missing from her home on June 7 1972, and her body was found in a field at Wigginton. At length Andrew Evans of Longton, discharged from army training at Whittington Barracks on medical grounds, confessed to the murder although a great deal of doubt as to whether he had committed the crime remained. Despite the poor state of his mind - one given to delusions - and his evident inadequate personality Evans was found guilty of murder and sentenced to be detained for life. In 1997 his conviction was quashed and he was released; he had, until then, been the longest serving prisoner for a miscarriage of justice in Britain (MCS pp111-120) (ES June 9 2000 p5). In the C17 **Mary Vaughton** of Wigginton was famed locally for her ability to survive on exceptionally small amounts of food and drink. She had this ability from birth. Plot noted her diet consisted of bread and butter morsels the size of a half crown coin, or if meat a pigeon's leg, and her liquid intake was nothing more than a spoonful of water or milk a day (NHS pp287-288) (SHOS vol 1 p432) (SVB p181). **Gene Kemp,**

children's writer, was born in Wigginton in 1926 (VFC pp77-78).

Wigginton Lodge Early C19 house 1.25m SW of Wigginton (BOE p310). Formerly in Wigginton township in Tamworth ancient parish. The house is of brick, with a stucco front representing ashlar. Seat of John Clarke MD (d1818) (mem in St Edith's, Tamworth). From 1845 to at least 1851 it was the seat of Sir Charles Mansfield Clarke MD, created a baronet in 1831 (W p626). In 1860 it was occupied by Capt Leigh (KD 1860); by 1872 it was the seat of Richard Moon (KD 1872). The house, called Wigginton Park in 1880, was occupied by Charles Henry Cope JP between at least 1880 and 1896 (KD 1880. 1896). It appears to have also been called Wigginton Hall between at least 1890 and 1932 (maps of 1890, 1902, 1932). There is a grave to Peter Bayley Sehmer (d1911) son of Ernst and Nellie Sehmer of Wigginton Lodge in Wigginton churchyard. In 1940 Wigginton Lodge was the residence of Egbert Alexander de Hamel MC (KD 1940). The house, painted white, was still standing in 1998 with a modern low-lying brick extension for Tamworth Rugby Union Football Club.

Wigginton Manor House A manor house is known to have existed at Wigginton but its site has not been located (SVB p180).

Wigginton Park Public park lying to the S of Wigginton Lodge, surrounded by the modern suburbs of Tamworth. Formerly in Wigginton township in Tamworth ancient parish.

Wightwick Former estate (W p206) and village on either side of a dell formed by a tiny tributary of the Smestow overlooking the Smestow, now a suburb 1.75m SW of Tettenhall. In Tettenhall ancient parish. A burial mound at Wightwick probably contains many of those killed in the battle of Tettenhall (HOPTT p10). The mound near Wightwick Mill at cSO 875986 was excavated in 1955 and shown to be of recent date and not a burial mound (HOPTT) (NSJFS 1965 p49). Has appeared as Wisteuuic (DB) and Whightwick (1834 OS map). The name is from perhaps, but unlikely, 'west village.' Stevenson thinks 'Wihta's or Wiht's village' (DUIGNAN) (SPN p142). It may be also from Old English and mean a village (wic) at a bend (wiht) in the brook (VCH vol 20 p34). There is a windmill on the W side of the present Windmill Lane. It has graffiti on an outside brick which proclaims 'This Windmill was built by John Chamberlain 1720.' It ceased work in the 1880s and was converted into a house, probably by 1905. It was still standing in 1980 (WIS pp13,22) (VCH vol 20 p34). Another windmill stood on the E side of Windmill Lane in the later C18 and the early C19 (Yates' map) (Map of Salop. R Baugh. 1808) (VCH vol 20 p34). Job confuses the two mills (WBJ p46 il xviii of one of the mills). A plaque to commemorate Sir John Morris, an industrialist and only mayor of Wolverhampton to be knighted, was erected at Elmslie Bank, Wightwick in 1994 (Commemorative Plaques by the Wolverhampton Civic Society).

Wightwick Hall Stands on top of Tinacre Hill to W of Wightwick Bank. Built by Sir Alfred Hickman (d1910), a S Staffs coal and iron master and Conservative MP for Wolverhampton West 1885-6 and 1892-1906, in the mid 1890s. The hall became a special school in 1956 and still was in the early 1980s (VCH vol 20 p11) (STC p27p).

Wightwick Manor Wightwick Bank, Tettenhall. Huge neo-Tudor mansion in the Cheshire tradition (SL p141) built by Edward Ould for Theodore Mander (1853-1900), paint manufacturer immediately SW of Wightwick Old Manor, and to the E of Wightwick Hall on Tinacre Hill. Built in two halves, the first in 1887-88, the second in 1893 (SGS p183). In 1894 the house was chosen to host a bazaar, opened by the Countess of Dartmouth, in aid of the Orphan Home (Wolverhampton Chronicle May 30 1997 p24). George V and Queen Mary (when Duke and Duchess of York) visited Wightwick Manor on July 23 or 24 1900 (Wolverhampton Chronicle May 30 1997 p24) (TCOP p76p). Mander's widow, Flora, lived to 1905. She was succeeded by her son, Sir Geoffrey (1882-1962). The Oak Room contained Charles II's bed from 1913 to 1962 when it was returned to Moseley Old Hall (CL April 18 1996 p68). Sir Geoffrey and his wife Lady Mander (Rosalie Glynn Grylls) (1905-1988), experts on the Pre-Raphaelites accumulated much art from that period. Inspired by WG Constable, Slade Professor of Fine Art at Cambridge, and director of the Courtauld Institute of Art, they decided to have Wightwick preserved as a period piece in 1935 (BOE p310). In 1937 Wightwick was visited by William Morris's daughter, May. On Dec 19 1937 the Manders gave Wightwick Manor to the NT (SGS p185) (CL April 18 1996 p68). (CL 1963) (A Very Private Heritage. Patricia Pegg. 1997). Wightwick contains much Pre-Raphaelite fine art both made for it and brought to it since 1937; Burne-Jones, Benson, Henry Treffry Dunn, Arthur Hughes, CE Kempe, Millais, Minton, De Morgan, Morris, Rossetti, LA Shuffrey, Marie Spartali Stillman, Swinburne, and Woolner are all represented. Between 1989 and 1991, the entire family wing was restored (The Independent Dec 7 1991 p50p) CL April 18 1996 pp66-71pcs).

GROUNDS. The garden, created from c1887, is by Alfred Parsons, RA Partridge, and W Partridge (CL Aug 15 1996 pp46-49pcs); the terrace and garden seats are by TH Mawson. **Grigg House** is a little summerhouse with a heather-thatched, conical roof and approached by the Yew and Holly Walk. It appears on Mawson's designs between 1900 and 1910 but may have been made recently (CL Aug 15 1996 p46). **Ice Age boulders**, collected locally, were laid out along the Long Walk bordering the orchard in Sir Geoffrey's time (CL Aug 15 1996 p48 see map). The **Long Walk** to the W of the house is by Alfred Parsons (CL Aug 15 1996 p48). At the end of the **Lower Lawn** is a lime tree planted by George V and a purple beech planted by Queen Mary when Duke and Duchess of York (CL Aug 15 1996 p48) when visiting the house in July 1900 (Wolverhampton Chronicle May 30 1997 p24) (VB p70). The bridge which crosses Wightwick Bank lane is a copy of the **Mathematical Bridge** at Queen's College, Cambridge. The one built in the 1950s replacing an earlier bridge, which was lower and simpler in design, was itself replaced in c1991 (CL Aug 15 1996 p49pc). The **Nuttery** is a woodland area to the E of the house. The **Orchard**, E of the hall, may contain an ancient pear tree, a Tettenhall Dick (CL Aug 15 1996 p46). The **Poets' Gardens**, which face S below the high terrace wall was the idea of Sir Geoffrey and Lady Mander. Each garden, separated by clipped yew buttresses, has plants derived from the homes of writers - Shelly, Dickens, Tennyson and Morris (CL Aug 15 1996 p48). The **South Terrace** runs along the S side of the house. At the W end are pieces of masonry from the Houses of Parliament (SGS p184p). Pevsner says the fragments from the Houses of Parliament were obtained after bombing raids in WW2 (BOE p311). Bird wrote of stonework from Big Ben, brought to Wightwick by Sir Geoffrey Mander, on a terrace (VB p69). John Sale, writing in 1996, says that the crowns off Big Ben's clock tower flank the Yew Walk (CL Aug 15 1996 p46). **Yew and Holly Walk**. Runs to NW of the house. Was perhaps part of Parson's plan. Composed of alternating Golden Queen hollies and Irish yews and leads to the Grigg House (CL Aug 15 1996 p46). (AWM p53) (ACGM p14 fig 5) (TB April 1986 p14p).

Wightwick Old Manor Situated immediately NE of Wightwick Manor (see). This was the seat of the Wightwicks, lords of Wightwick manor from at least the C13 to 1815, and they took their name from their manor here. They became prosperous during the C15; Rev Richard Wightwick was co-founder of Pembroke College, Oxford, in 1624. Francis Wightwick was the last Wightwick to occupy the estate, when it was leased to relations in 1659. In 1815 it was sold to the Hinckes family from whom it was bought by Theodore Mander in 1887. He started building the nearby Wightwick Manor that year. There is said to have been a manor house here from 960. A portion of a former brick house of the late C16 or early C17 remains (1980). That house probably had a central range and two cross wings. Only the western portion, containing one wing and part of the centre was surviving in 1980. Behind there is a range of the same period which may have contained stables. Both buildings were much restored by Ould in the late C19. Wightwick Old Manor has also appeared as Manor House (c1885 OS map 6 inch), and Wightwick Hall (WMARCH 1993 pp10-17 plans il of c1760) (local info) (HOPTT p44 il of facing, 45-46) (BOE p311) (VCH vol 20 p18). On the Wightwick estate Plot found a red sort of magnetic graphite which he thought was an iron ore called Haematities (NHS p164).

Wigmore Small residential district on rising ground near a bend in the Tame by the start of M5, approximately 3m NE of West Bromwich. In West Bromwich ancient parish. At Wigmore, according to local tradition, was fought one of the battles said to have been fought at Wednesbury in 592 or 715 (WAM pp17-18); or in 591 when Ceawlin was succeeded by his nephew Cedric (HPPE p128). Or that a battle was fought here between the Saxons and the Britons in 560 (SOWB p23), or in c560 (SHWB 13). In Anglo-Saxon 'Wig' signifies a battle, perhaps with reference to the battles that may have taken place here (SOWB p23). There was also a natural spring here which was thought to be medicinal and very beneficial to health (SOWB p23). At Wigmore a Mr Henry Bunn utilised the carburetted hydrogen gas he discovered in his garden, at a depth of 15 feet, to light several rooms of his house (W pp682,686).

Wilbrighton Minute hamlet at the foot of Windmill Bank on the S and E sides, 0.75m N of Moreton. Formerly in Moreton quarter in Gnosall ancient parish (W p461) (VCH vol 4 p111). Has appeared as Wilbrestone, a manor, in DB, Wilbritone (1166), Wilbricton (1208-1236), Wylbrighton (1227), Wolbrichton (1285), Willbrighton (Speed's map) (SPNO p157) (SPN p55). The name means 'Wilbriht's town' (DUIGNAN), or 'Wilbeorht's farmstead' (SSE 1987 p28. 1996 p19) (SPN p55). Or perhaps from the term Villiam Britonum, as it is thought the Romans were here (NHS p395). At SJ 795187 there was possibly a medieval village, probably deserted in the C17 (SSAHST 1970 p36). On the road between Wilbrighton and Moreton Park are the remains of a wayside cross (VCH vol 4 p112). There was a windmill on Windmill Bank at SJ 792186 300 yards W of Wilbrighton Hall. The mill appears to have been constructed between 1775-1787. In 1958 a few stones were said to mark the spot (WBJ p46) (VCH vol 4 p128).

Wilbrighton Hall Wilbrighton, Moreton. The manor-house of Wilbrighton manor. Has a wide view to the N (VCH vol 4 p125). It was described by Erdeswick as 'a proper Gentleman's House of Brick' (SOS p178). The S, W, and part of the N walls are of Tudor brickwork with stone quoins (VCH vol 4 p125). This is probably Raven's Wilboughton Hall which he assigns to the neo-Jacobean period (MIDD vol 3 p60p).

Wildblood's Holm Place on the Tame near Alrewas. Here Mary Wilcox was drowned according to the Alrewas PR Nov 19 1692 (SHOS vol 1 p140).

Wildcoal Rock Near Goldsitch in Quarnford parish (UHAW p51).

Wilderhope On Tinker's Castle Road W of Seisdon.

Wilderley Woods In Colton parish lying near Blithfield parish boundary. The wood of Wilderdelaye is mentioned in a deed of Edward I's reign (SHC 1919 p43 note). In the C13 Wilderley Woods was described as one 'in which all the freemen of the circumjacent vills intercommon throughout the year' (NSFCT 1913 p49).

Wilderly 'Hall' 1m WSW of Admaston. Wilderleyhull is mentioned in a grant dated 1348/ 9 (SHC 1919 p43 note) (CWF p178). There is a Wilderley Barn only accessible by a long track from Lea Hall Farm.

Wilderness Hill N of Patshull Hall on Shrops Staffs border.

Wildgoose Farm Over 0.5m WNW of Bradnop. Formerly in Bradnop township in Leek ancient parish. There may have been settlement here by the later C13 (VCH vol 7 pp169-170). Perhaps derived from a field name which in turn is derived from an animal name (APB p48).

Wildhay House over 0.5m SW of Stanton. The name appears in 1742 as Will Hay (NSJFS 1972 p124). From the nature of the terrain 'Wild Hay' would seem to be the correct form of this farm name (NSJFS 1972 p124).

Wildhay Brook Tributary of the Dove. Joins Rangemoor Brook at Wildhay (SPNO p22).

Wildmoor Over 2m WNW of Trysull in approximate position of Wolmore (1834 OS map). In Trysull ancient parish (SGSAS).

Wild Moors Norbury. A Royal waste which stretched from Knightley well into Shropshire. But this moorland has long been enclosed and cultivated (W p464).

Wildmore Hollies Cannock Wood. Lost. Marked on the maps of Morden and Plot approximately at Prospect Village. Could be Wimblebury.

Wildstone Rock House 0.75m SW of Flash. Possibly also a rock feature. There is a field called 'the Cock Pit' beside the Ridge Road near Wildstone Rock (UHAW p20).

Wildwood 1m W of Walton-on-the-Hill. SE suburb of Stafford near Baswich.

Wilkes Green There was settlement at Wilkes Green, Handsworth, at the junction of Rookery Road and Antrobus Road, by the end of the C13. By the C16 there was a small hamlet here (MNB pp40,45) (HPPE p37); and by 1834 when it appears as Wilk's Green (1834 OS map). The name is preserved in Wilkes Green or and Infant School over 0.5m W of Handsworth.

Wilkin Area at the junction of Watling Street and the Chester Road at Brownhills West (Staffs County Handbook c1958 p20 see map). The road known as The Wilkin, N of the present Wilkin Road, dates back to the time of the early collieries in this area; it then appears as a track. It is said to be from a personal name, but the origin is unknown, and first appears in c1850. Wilkin Colliery appears on early OS maps. A Wilkin Inn appears in the 1871 census (SNBC pp14,16). At the County Museum, Shugborough, is a wooden finger post which stood at the junction of the A5 with A452. Its three fingers read - i) 'Birmingham 13m, Oxford 40m' ii) 'Tamworth 11m, Atherstone 17m, ____5m' iii) 'To Chester, Newport 21, Salop 35.5.' Wright noted a finger post at The Wilkin, bearing the date 1770, and recently (1930s) restored. Wright believed it the oldest in the county (CCBO p52).

Wilkins Pleck House 0.75m NNE of Whitmore.

Willenhall (locally *Wylnal*, *Wil'n'all* SNW p36, UBCB p116). Black Country town on Willenhall Brook with gently rising ground to the N 15.75m SSE of Stafford. Former township and chapelry in Wolverhampton ancient parish (W p159).

EARLY. A polished flint axe-head was found in Stafford Street in c1920 (HOWM p1). An unlooped palstave was found in Stafford Street before WW2 whilst a gas-main was being laid (NSJFS 1962 p30. 1964 p44).

700 to 1650. Willenhall has been identified by Duignan as the Willanhalch where two charters were tested by Aethelbald, king of Mercia (716-757), in c732, c738 or c747 (Cart. Sax. 149,150) (DUIGNAN). But Commander Wedgwood prefers the Willenhall near Coventry (SHC 1916 p145). The **name** means 'the meadowland of Willa' (DUIGNAN) (AOW p1). Gelling thinks 'Willa's nook' (NSJFS 1981 p3), or 'Willa's corner of land' (SPN p142).

Perhaps from Anglo-Saxon 'velle,' a fountain, spring or well or purling water (SHOS vol 2 p147). Could be from the Anglo-Saxon word 'vin' for victory, a fight, or a victory (S&W p332). Could be the 'hall of the victory' in consequence of the Saxons winning the battle of Wednesfield in 911 (HOWW p30) (HOBLL p2), but Hackwood says this derivation has been generally discarded, the 'hall of the victory,' having been identified with the lost city of Wrottesley (AOW p4). Although Willenhall is mentioned in Lady Wulfrun's charter of 994, in which she makes a grant of land to the monastery of Wolverhampton, Mander thinks Willenhall was not part of Lady Wulfrun's gift to the monastery (HOWM pp14-15). However, a part of Willenhall (Winenhale) appears as Wolverhampton church property in DB (HOWM p15), whilst a part of Willenhall (Winehala) appears as land held by the king in DB. By the mid C13 the DB Wolverhampton church property lay in Wolverhampton (see) Deanery manor, whilst the DB king property had been merged into the royal Stowheath (see) manor; there was also some of Willenhall in the Wolverhampton (see) Prebendal manor (WA vol 2 no 2 p103) (HOWM pp26,27). The prebend of Willenhall in Wolverhampton Collegiate Church, first mentioned in 1291 (VCH vol 3 p324), was abolished in 1846 (W p82). For the only moated site in Willenhall see Leveson's Moat. Later forms of Willenhall are: Willenhalch, and Willenhale (SPN p142). There was a **church**, St Giles, at Willenhall by 1298. That church appears to have been the one on or near the site of the present church, on the S side of Walsall Street by Church Walk. Except for the tower the old church was taken down in 1748 and rebuilt in 1750. This church was demolished and the present one built in 1866 (HOWI pp17-18) (SNW p60) (BOE p312). Willenhall held its wake on St Giles' day (Sept 1) (SCSF p106). Bull baiting occurred at Willenhall (AOW pp186,188). For Willenhall bull ring see Little London. Willenhall had a fair but not a market in medieval times (NSJFS 1971 p58). There was a case brought by the mayor and inhabitants of Walsall against some Wednesbury men heard in the Star Chamber in 1498 which cited this fair. Two men were accused of beating the mayor of Walsall and another Walsall man in Walsall. They were captured and imprisoned. The leading men of Wednesbury and Wolverhampton gathered 200 Wednesbury men and threatened riot at the forthcoming Trinity fair at Willenhall in order to obtain their release. The defence of the leading men of Wednesbury and Wolverhampton was that they had a right to be at the fair since a mumming play was to be performed there and the mummers had always traditionally comprised the inhabitants of Walsall, Wolverhampton, and Wednesbury (SCSF pp37-40) (HOWM pp42-43). For **Stocks** see AOW p153. GT Lawley states that the **scold's bridle** which formerly belonged to Willenhall was preserved in the possession of John Harper JP of Brueton House, Bilston (SCSF p125). For Willenhall **charities** see AOW pp129-134.

INDUSTRY. Willenhall's smiths were given the order to make all the state locks required by Elizabeth I's government departments. The town could boast by the mid C20 it made 90 per cent of the country's locks, latches and keys (WMAG Sept 1968 pp19,20). Employees in this industry were invariably bent over their work and consequently developed humped backs and hence Willenhall became known locally as Humpshire and Upshire, possibly a corruption of Humpshire. (BCM Oct 1973 pp24-25. Oct 1986 pp35-36) (MR pp380-381) (TB Jan 1996 p15. Sept 1997 p21). Since the C18 it has also produced currycombs, guns, bolts, files, traps, hooks, door furniture, screws, hasps, staples, brass and iron castings and manufactured die-sinking, pressings, drop forging, steel rolling, Bakelite and plastic products and components for refrigerators, typewriters, cycle and motor cars (Staffs County Handbook c1958 pp59,149,151). James Carpenter (1775-1844), was the first manufacturer of locks in Willenhall to use machinery in lock-making from his works, the Somerford Works in New Road. With inventor, John Young of Wolverhampton, from 1830 Carpenter produced a lock in which the action of the latch bolt was perpendicular instead of horizontal. The patent subsequently became the sole property of Carpenter, with the exception of that part which applied to mortice locks; this was retained by Young (AOW pp162-163,165) (Webster's Report of Patent Cases vol 1 p530) (VCH vol 2 p252). By 1974 JE Reynolds of Willenhall had produced the largest padlock in the world, ERA No. 1212 Close shackle 6 lever lock, which weighed 100 lb 45 kg 30. It was used for locking dock gates and boats (GBR 1974 p157p). There was a windmill in Morfittal Lane (approximately Tyler Road, SE of the centre) at SO 968982. It is shown on maps of Greenwood, Yates and the OS (1831/4). It was disused by 1880 (SA Jan 19 1861) (WBJ p46).

1650 to PRESENT. In 1659 a **fire** destroyed most of the important buildings of the town, apart from the church (ADD p22). Willenhall blossomed as a spa in the C18. The **spa** on the N of Willenhall Brook had a cover with this inscription

Fon Oculis Morbisque
Cutaneis diu celebris AD 1726

and was known as Dr Richard Wilkes's Well, 200 yards above it were springs, one of which was dedicated to St Sunday (SHOS vol 2 p148) (GNHS pp249,250; gives 1728 instead of 1726) (AOW pp90,91) (OSST 1944-45). It or another was dedicated to St Dominic (AOW p188). It or another was the Brimstone Well (SHOSA vol 2 p17). The spa well or another situated between the church and the manor house had been a holy well in the Middle Ages (AOW p179). (W p160) (HOSW) (SLM Oct 1951 p20) (SMM p77). Ochre cakes were made out of the yellow colouring in the white clay found in and about the Willenhall spa. Shaw said it appeared like deep yellow veins in the clay, and was also used to dye leather yellow (SHOS vol 2 p148) (W p160). The Asiatic **Cholera outbreaks** of 1832 and 1849 claimed 310 lives in Willenhall (TB March 1994 p20). The outbreak of 1832 reached Willenhall parish on Aug 7 and claimed a total of eight lives (TB Feb 1998 p17). The **church**, St Stephen, on the corner of Wolverhampton and Field Streets, built in 1853-1854 (BOE p312), was demolished in 1978. It was rebuilt in 1979 slightly to the W on the back of an existing church hall (info Rev David Hartland). The separate ecclesiastical parishes of Willenhall St Stephen and Willenhall Holy Trinity were created in 1846 (GLAUE p429). Willenhall became a separate civil parish in 1866 (GLAUE p429). Willenhall **urban district** was created in 1891 (Staffs County Handbook. c1958. p149) or 1894 (GLAUE p429). The **arms** of Willenhall urban district, granted in 1935, are: Parted chevronwise azure and gules, in chief two gold padlocks, and in base a female figure representing Justice, seated and facing to the Sinister, clothed in white, holding in the right hand a sword proper with gold pommed and hilt, point downwards, and in the left a gold balance; and turned toward the centre of shield. The crest is: On a wreath or and azure, a demi-tiger gules holding between the paws a gold Stafford Knot, and in front of the tiger two gold keys crossed saltirewise. The motto is: 'Salus populi suprema lex' (The welfare of the people is the highest law) (CH p341 il). The urban district was abolished in 1966 and transferred to the county boroughs of Wolverhampton, and Walsall, and the parish of Essington (GLAUE p429). **Newspapers**. Copies of the Willenhall Reporter survive in the BL from the period Nov 1885 to July 29 1887 (SHJ spring 1996 p36). The South Staffordshire Times, published at Bilston, became the Bilston and Willenhall Times from Sept 20 1924 and that paper ran until at least April 1 1966 (SHJ spring 1996 p12). Willenhall was connected to London and Liverpool by the Grand Junction **Railway** from July 4 1837 (NSJFS 1962 p99). In 1845 a **boiler explosion** occurred at the Willenhall works of George Thorneycroft in which he and 16 people were injured (TEBC2 p55) or at a Willenhall colliery where 16 people were killed (Wolverhampton Chronicle Dec 17 1845) (WMAG p16). **Willenhall in literature**. It is said that Benjamin Disraeli used the Children's Employment Commission (1843) evidence on Willenhall to produce his picture of the conditions of children working in the lockmaking workshops of 'Wodgate,' the fictional town, in his novel 'Sybil' (1845) (TEBC2 p55). Others have thought Wodgate based on Wednesbury. Willenhall is Wilnon in the novel 'Old Convict Days' published by T Fisher Unwin (AOW p172). For Willenhall as a verb see BCM April 1971 p27. **Natives and visitors**. The poetry of **Stephen Chatterton** (1753-1795), a native of Willenhall, has local themes (PSS pp102-103) (VFC p26). Rev **William Moreton** (b1759), who became curate in Willenhall in 1789 and vicar in 1795, seems to have had the worst reputation of any Staffs clergyman that ever lived. He would deliver his sermons inebriated and then go off to cock fights. His nickname was 'Old Mowton' and he is remembered in this rhyme

A tumbledown church
A tottering steeple
A drunken parson
And a wicked people

In 1791 he was even fined 'for sporting with a gun and two setting dogs upon the manor of H Vernon of Hilton Park.' Moreton was declared bankrupt in 1812 and died in July 1834 and was buried in St Giles' churchyard, Willenhall. At his funeral his curate, Rev George Fisher, contrived not to mention him in the sermon. His pedigree was unknown, and some have thought he was a 'nephew' of George III (SCSF p166) (STELE April 22 1955) (BCSBG) (FSBC p32il) (WMAG Sept 1968 p25) (VB pp51-52) (FOS p149) (Wolverhampton AdNews. April 11 1996 p7), but he was a native of Madeley, Staffs. When he first came to Willenhall Moreton lodged with Jane Pinson, the wife of a farmer living at Portobello, and later on with Mrs Mary Riley at the Swan Inn. After his appointment to the curacy he rented a cottage in Dimminsdale where he

spent the rest of his life (SHC 1970 pp171-185 p). (WAM pp122-123) (AOW pp98,100-104) (HOWI pp45-51) (VCH vol 3 p69) (WDY p2) (TOS p16) (MR p380). **George Lister**, strongman of Willenhall, was born on Aug 16 1832. His nickname was 'Big Hitter.' He died on April 28 1905 and was interred in Bentley cemetery (TB May 1982 p1p. June 1982 p5). Two policemen were murdered whilst on duty in Willenhall in 1864 and 1865; the murderers in each case were never identified: PC **William Lyons** was beaten to death whilst attending a brawl outside the Hope and Anchor Inn on May 7 1864, whilst PC **Enoch Augustus Hooper** was stabbed to death on Dec 8 1865 at the entrance to Love Alley, near Bilston Street, in pursuit of some involved in disturbances at the Royal George Inn, Walsall Street (MMMR pp3-7). On a wall in a corner of the alley beside the Railway Tavern is said to have appeared a glowing red handprint thought to be associated with Hooper who placed his blood-stained hand on this wall after being murdered. The handprint was seen in the earlier C20, and is said to have later appeared on the new wall which replaced the original one (TB Feb 1998 p10. March 1998 p3). **Christopher Edwards**, a locksmith of Church Street, murdered his wife, Rosannah, with a poker on April 30 1872. Edwards was hung on Aug 13 1872 (TB Dec 1980 p5. Aug 1993 p19) (MMBC pp80-96) (The Common Hangman. James Bland. 1984 pp152-158) (MM pp75-83). Willenhall town clock, Market Place, is in memory of **Joseph Tonks** MRCSE LAH, the 'Peoples Doctor' (TB April 1992 p17p). He died in 1891 aged 36 from injuries received in a balloon ascent in 1888/ 9. The clock was designed by Messrs Boddis of Birmingham and was presented by the Friendly Societies of Willenhall 1892. Its overall height is 26 feet (BCM April 1986 pp13-14). **Ike Howell** (1896-1978), born in Willenhall, won the Medaille Militaire in France in WW1 (MMBCC pp35-37). **Martin Ashton** and **Graham Stokes** kept a see-saw in constant motion for 100 hours at Willenhall from June 1-5 1971 (GBR 1971 p308). On March 17 1987 **Reg Morris** extinguished 20,035 torches of flame in his mouth in one hour 48 minutes 14 seconds at Cinders Night Club, Willenhall (GBR 1988 p20).

SUPERNATURAL. Wellington Villa, which stood on the corner of Walsall Road and the Bilston Road, was reputedly haunted by a **very tall man in dark dress** and top hat carrying a black silver-topped stick, and the sound of horses emanating from stables at the rear of the house; it was said to have been one of the most haunted houses in Willenhall (GPCE p60). Strong **poltergeist activity** in a house in Albion Road made national news (GOM p19). In Gipsy Lane unexplained noises such as **Rock 'n' Roll music**, loud motorcycles revving up and teenagers' voices have been heard late at night in the vicinity of the British Road Service haulage company, where stood a night club in the 1950s (GPCE p60). A **big black cat** with bright red eyes seen in Willenhall in April 1975 could have a puma (MMSE p292). Owen Road, to the S of Willenhall, is haunted by the ghost of a **young girl** dressed in a white flowing dress, which crosses the road sometimes stopping to smile at an individual before vanishing before their eyes (GOM p16).

Willenhall Branch of the Walsall Canal. Spurred off the Walsall Canal at The Lunt at SO 965967 and thereafter ran northwards towards Willenhall. Completed in 1803, closed in 1953 (BCM autumn 1995 p22) (HCMS No. 2).

Willenhall Brook Dilworth calls one of the head waters of the Tame which runs through Willenhall Willenhall Brook (The Tame Mills of Staffordshire. D Dilworth. 1976. p112). Has appeared as Wilnalbroc (HODW p18).

Willenhall Old Hall A C17 building which formerly stood on site of Willenhall Branch Library and Fire Station. Built by Dr Richard Wilkes's father, Richard Wilkes. Dr Richard Wilkes, author of HOSW, was born in the hall in 1690. On Dr Wilkes' death in 1760 his widow left Willenhall for London and the hall appears to have been sold after her death in 1798. The mansion then passed through several hands and was demolished in 1934 to make way for the council offices now occupied by the library and fire station (WMAG Sept 1968 p28il) (WDY p3p) (SNW p76). Formerly known as Wilkes Mansion (WMAG Sept 1968 p28il).

Will Gate Willgate Farm is 0.25m ENE of modern Rudyard village and stands in the area of the old Rudyard hamlet in Rudyard township in Leek ancient parish. Has origins dating back to at least 1669 or is on the site of a house dating back to that period (RL pp5,10p) (VCH vol 7 p216). The name speaks of forest enclosure (NSFCT 1885 p54).

William Hardings House Corner of Bellbrook and Mill Street, Penkridge. Rough-cast brick house dated 1673 (VCH vol 5 p107) (PVH pp20,21p). Is now (1998) a restaurant.

Williford By the Tame, N of Whittington Hurst in Whittington parish (W p611).

Willingsworth About 1m W of Wednesbury is the former hamlet by Lea Brook (TMS p127) or source of Lea Brook (BCM Oct 1983 p42). Formerly in Brierley liberty in Sedgley ancient parish. Willingsworth is mentioned in 1555 (HC p36). (NHS p121) (VCH vol 17 p33). The name means 'The Worth, or estate founded by the clan of Willan' (DUIGNAN) (AMS p442) (WAM p9), or the 'farm of Wealh's descendants' (DUIGNAN) (AMS p442), or 'settler's or foreigners farm' (AMS p442), and is preserved in Willingsworth High School S of Moxley and Willingsworth Close at Lanesfield.

Willingsworth Hall Former substantial brick and grey sandstone house at Willingsworth built by Thomas Parkes (d1602) (BCM Oct 1983 p43), and is mentioned in a document of 1598 (WMLB p105); it has been thought that it was built about then (HC pp78-79) (SDSSOP p34 il of). The hall was the seat of the Parkes in the C17, lords of Sedgley manor from 1600 (HC p36). Thomas was succeeded by his son Richard (d1618), who was succeeded by his son Thomas (d1660), an ardent parliamentarian in the Civil War (WAM p80), and the hall was for a time taken by royalists (HOWV p85). Thomas was succeeded by his daughter Anne, who as heiress, took the hall to the Wards by her marriage in 1672 to William Ward, younger son of Lord Ward (BCM Oct 1983 p43. spring 1999 p43il); Lord Dudley's father was born here, his mother being a Parkes (WAM p80). William Ward was succeeded in 1720 by John Ward (b1704) who became the 6th Baron Ward in 1740 and became Viscount Dudley and Ward of Dudley in 1763 (AMS p108). By the late C18 the hall was only a farmhouse (SHOS vol 2 p87 note) and by the end of that century it was already threatened by encroaching industrialisation (WMLB p105). Some parts of the hall were still standing in 1865 when a tunnel was discovered from it leading in the direction of Wednesbury church (HC pp78-79) (BCM Oct 1983 p43).

Willmerhill Gate Formerly in Knowl End township in Audley ancient parish. Seems to have been between Heighley Castle and Cooksgate (SHC 1944 pp34-35).

Willoughbridge Fragmented tiny hamlet straggles upland on the S side of the Tern, 2m NE of Mucklestone. Partly in Ashley, Maer and Mucklestone parishes. At SJ 743393, N of Willoughbridge Lodge is a moated site (CAMS p64). Has also appeared as Willowbridge (NSSG p4).

Willoughbridge Lodge Hunting lodge 1.25m NE of Mucklestone. Built by the Gerards in the C16 or the early C17 as a hunting lodge. From the Gerards the lodge passed to the Meynells. The N front has a central porch tower with staircase turret, the stone cap oddly decorated with a scale pattern (GNHS p547) (STM Jan 1964 p27) (BOE p207) (SGS p185) (ES Jan 6 1981 p6il. Sept 16 1982 il) (DoE II*).

Willoughbridge Park Medieval deer park enclosed out of forest. In existence by 1363. At first thought to be not the same as Ashley Park (NSFCT 1910 p175). Later thought to be the same as Ashley Park, its former name (NSJFS 1962 p76. 1964 p62). Has also appeared as Willoughbridge Old Park. At the time of the Civil War it belonged to the Earl of Shrewsbury but was without deer (EDP p179).

Willoughbridge Wells House 2m NE of Mucklestone. Partly in Ashley and Mucklestone parishes. Warm sulphur springs were discovered here in the 1620s (DoE II) or in c1650 by Jane Lady Gerard, Baroness Gerard of Gerrard's Bromley Hall; the name 'Wells' is from these springs (OSST 1944-45). There is a tradition that James I, whilst at Ashley in 1617, bathed in a spring here for his rheumatism (ALW pl 69). Here Lady Gerard built a bath house and lodgings for the sick trying to create a large fashionable spa resort (SL p110). In the later C17 Plot computed 60 springs rising within 10 yards of this place, several of which, he noted, had been enclosed with squared stone to keep them pure (NHS pp61,63,64,102-103). In 1676 Mr Samuel Gilbert published the 40 paged 'Healing spring at Willow Bridge in Staffordshire.' It tells of those cured by the water. The skin of Mary Wood of Rugeley, aged 19, who had leprosy, was turned beautiful and soft. Margaret Russell of Offley was cured of aches in her bones. Lawrence Key of Stoke, a collier, was cured of maggots in his head as well as his legs. Dorothy Moreton of Stafford was cured in one month of sore legs. Capt John Broughton of Whittington witnessed a man's swollen leg reduced to its normal proportions (SMC pp63,64,65,66). Willoughbridge never became a large spa and declined into oblivion in the C18. The surviving bath house near a pool, now roofless but which formerly had a roof, was probably built in the 1620s; the dates 1690, 1701 and 1864 inscribed onto this bath house probably refer to repairs or rebuildings. On the E side it has carvings of two males heads (DoE II). The house is now (1989) occupied by the Wright family (ALW pl 69 of the house in c1920). (SSC p132 in the intro) (GNHS p26) (SCSF pp143,144) (BPS pp111,112) (LGS p76) (NSFCT 1926 p116) (SLM April 1948 p100) (BOV pp39,40) (VB p161) (BOE p207) (SGS pp185,187p) (F pp306,307) (MR p382p, 384).

Willow Dale At Wetley Abbey, appears on 1834 OS map.

Willowmore Hill Hill 1.25m NE of Bradley, 475 feet high (VCH vol 5 p82,83).

Willshaw 0.75m W of Hollinsclough. Has also appeared as Wilshaw (W p747), and Wiltshaw (1834 OS map). Formerly in Hollinsclough township in Alstonefield parish. Here there appears Willshaw Hill and a house, Willshaw Bottom.

Willslock Small hamlet in undulating country rising to the Needwood Forest plateau 1.25m ESE of Loxley. In Uttoxeter parish. Has appeared as Wills Lock (Smith's map). On Feb 25 1955 Donald Lainton, an insurance agent, was found dying in his car on a farm track off the Abbot's Bromley-Uttoxeter road at Willslock. Lainton had been stabbed ten times in the chest, neck and face and later died. Frederick Cross, who had been seen leaving the Coach and Horses Inn, Great Haywood, with him shortly before the incident, was found guilty of his murder and executed (TRTC p36) (MCS pp80-83).

Wilnecote Village on a ridge on the W side of Kettle Brook 2m SE of Tamworth, now an industrial suburb of Tamworth. Former township and chapelry in Tamworth ancient parish but lay in Hemlingford hundred, Warws. Has appeared as Wilmundecote (DB) (SSE 1996 p19), Wilmecote (1224), Wilmondecote (C13), Wylmyncote (1356) (DUIGNAN Warwickshire 1912). The name means 'Wilmund's cottage' (SSE 1996 p19). Former prebend of Tamworth Collegiate Church (VCH vol 3 p310). Wilnecote became a separate ecclesiastical parish in 1770 (GLAUE p425). There was a church at Wilnecote in the C18 (LDD). The present church, Holy Trinity, at the junction of Ninefoot Lane and Glascote Lane, N of Watling Street, was built in 1821 (BOE p312). Beating the bounds was revived by Wilnecote parish council on July 17 1946 (TH July 13 1946 p3). The township Wilnecote formed with Castle Liberty became a separate civil parish in 1866. Parts of that were taken into Tamworth borough in 1932 and the whole civil parish was taken into the borough and into Staffs in 1965 (GLAUE p425). Wilnecote was a ward of Tamworth borough by at least 1993. Reliant Robin and Scimitar motor cars are made at Beans Engineering, in a factory on the A5. They also had a plant in Tipton (SGS p185) (MR p384). Wilnecote features in a derisory rhyme about Tamworth (see).

Wilnecote Hall Wilnecote. Is S of the A5, 0.25 SE of the church. Probably of early C18 origin (BOE p312) (MR p384). Occupied in 1851 by Major TB Bamford (W p24).

Wimblebury (locally *Wimbleb'ry* BILP2 p30). Modern hamlet on the NW slopes of a hill overlooking the head of Riddings Brook valley 1m ESE of Hednesford. In Cannock ancient parish. The name is from Wimblebury Farm, 0.25m to the NE. Wimblebury, which appears on the 1834 OS map (SPNO p62); Wimblebury is from Anglo-Saxon 'Winebald's fortified place' (SPN p30). The original Wimblebury developed as a mining village presumably in the 1850s and the 1860s. By 1871 it had 700 people (LHSB 50 p6). The church, St Paul, dates from 1889-1890 (VCH vol 5 p67). The old village was once called the 'Holy City' because of the number of churches and chapels here (CCAP p31p of in 1949). By the late 1950s mining subsidence had made the brick terraces of the old village, which dated largely from 1890 to 1910 (VCH vol 5 p51), uninhabitable and the village was evacuated (Sunday Mercury Oct 3 1958), but has since been rebuilt (LHSB 50 p88).

Wimundsway Road from Anslow to 'The Acorn' through Rough Hays. Robert de Ferrers disafforested a considerable portion of the township of Anslow as far as this Wimundsway road (UTR p239).

Wincote Fragmented tiny hamlet in undulating country near the head of Gamesley Brook 1.25m SSW of Eccleshall, near Wootton. Wincote Grange, 1.5m SW of Eccleshall, was the residence of 2nd Lord Nelson of Stafford in the later C20 (local info).

Wind-horn Field Open field which lay to the E of Wolverhampton prior to enclosure. The other Wolverhampton open fields were Broadmeadow, Horseley, Windmill and Ablow (SHOS vol 2 p165) and Monmore (HOWM p44). Has also appeared as Wyndfield and Windfield Field (HOWM p44).

Windledale Hollow 0.75m W of Alstonefield.

Windmill Residential district 0.25m S of Walsall, in the foreign of Walsall (SHOS vol 2 p73) (HOWP p155) (SSE 1991 p77). Grew up on the old road to West Bromwich and is present Sandwell Street (VCH vol 17 p155). At Windmill resided Capt Henry Stone, a parliamentarian in the Civil War. He inherited the property from his uncle on condition he reside in it. By the late C18 it was an inn known as the Wheatsheaf, but still identified by his and his wife's initials in a large brick on the front 'H. S. S. 1662.' (SHOS vol 2 p74) (GNHS p78) (W pp46,643,647) (Civil Strife in the Midlands 1642-1651. RE Sherwood. 1975). For the industry of Windmill see Walsall.

Windmill Bank Near Croxton. In a field here is a deep hole or cavern (NSFCT 1928 p134). For the windmill here see under Croxton.

Windmill Bank Tiny hamlet 0.25m NE of Gentleshaw. Here was a windmill recorded on maps of 1883 and 1902 (WBJ p24 il ix). There is another windmill at Gentleshaw (see).

Windmill Bank Former area of Rowley Regis near Netherton (BCWJ p38).

Windmill Bank At Wilbrighton, Moreton.

Windmill Bank At Lower Gornal (VCH vol 2 p192).

Windmill End Former hamlet on a hill near the head of Mousesweet Brook, N of Darby End. Seems to have formerly been partly in Dudley parish, Worcs and partly in Rowley Regis parish, Staffs. Could be the site of the manorial mill at Darby End, and the hamlet would have grown in consequence of this (BCWJ pp38,86). A windmill had stood on the site of the former railway station here (NEE p6). The name appears on the Plan of the Mines of Lord Dudley 1812. A small house here had a small inserted stone over the door which bore the inscription:

Beware of false spies,
And black-legged ones.

The meaning of the words is unknown, but is thought to recall the Gunpowder Plot conspirators who were brought to bay and captured in this locality (SCSF p168). Joe Darby champion all-round spring jumper (1861-1937) was born in Windmill End. He set records for jumping at Dudley (see), and Wolverhampton (see) (WMAG May 1972 p7p) (TB June/ July 1972 p5. Sept 1975 pp10-11) (MMBCC pp38p-45). There was a fire disaster at No. 5 Pit, Windmill End (which has also been described as Russell's Hall Colliery), on April 17 1910; Thomas Robinson of Baptist End, aged 34, and John Davies of Netherton, died (TB Sept 9 1999 p18).

Windmill End Junction At S end of the Netherton Tunnel. Junction of the Netherton Tunnel Branch of the Birmingham Canal and Dudley Canal Line Two.

Windmill Field Open field lying to the N of Wolverhampton prior to enclosure. Or formerly called Quabbe field (HOWM p44). The other open fields of Wolverhampton were Broadmeadow, Horsely, Wind-horn, and Ablow (SHOS vol 2 p165): Mander adds a sixth, Monmore (HOWM p44).

Windmill Hill Hanley (SHST p217).

Windswell Pool Tiny pool between Forton and Sutton. Has also appeared as Wynsewall (1242), Windswall pool (1618) (SPNO p149), and Winswell. The name is from Wine's well. The name 'Wineshul' is used to describe the hill on which Forton Monument stands is recorded in 1242 (NSFCT 1937 p63).

Windy Arbour Street name to ENE of Cheadle church, off Oakamoor road.

Windy Arbour House 0.75m NE of Madeley.

Windycott House nearly 1.5m ESE of Werrington.

Windy Fields House or tiny hamlet 2m WSW of Church Leigh. In Leigh parish. Appears on 1834 OS map.

Windygates House 0.75m NW of Upper Hulme. Formerly in Leekfrith township in Leek ancient parish and called Bourke Grange (HOLF p21p). There was house probably on the site of the present house by the later C16 (VCH vol 7 p194), and Windygates is said to have been the seat of the Broughs from the early C16 to 1833 (NSFCT 1942 p62). The present house has been called Windy Gates and Windygates Hall. It is dated 1634 and has Yorkshire characteristics. It is built of warm red stone with blocked upper windows to reduce the amount of window tax (HOLF pp21-22) (BOE p205) (VCH vol 7 p194).

Windy Hall Kingstone (Yates' map). Could it now be Wanfield Hall?

Windyharbour House over 1m SE of Alton. In Alton parish. Has also appeared as Wind Harbour.

Windy Harbour 1m WSW of Cauldon. Carrington excavated a mound at Windy Harbour in 1849. It had been, or was to be, damaged by a limekiln (NSJFS 1965 p36). Porter calls her C18 way-mark stone on Ipstones Edge Windy Harbour Cross (PDS&C p77p). Has also appeared as Windy Arbour. This is either a reference to the cross at Windywaycross (see), or Hoften's Cross (see).

Windy Harbour Former estate in Talke township of Audley ancient parish, 0.5m S of Talke (SHC 1944 p59). The name is preserved in Arbour Street.

Windywaycross House 1.25m WNW of Foxt, 0.25m N of Cabbage Hall. At the SE end of Ipstones Edge, at SK 058490, is a rough stone shaft cross about 10 feet high, probably a medieval direction post, sometimes called 'The Long Stoup' (NSFCT 1920 p162), or was a guidestone for packhorse trains (PRT pp69p,71). This might be the way-mark stone on Ipstones Edge (see) mentioned by Porter (PDS&C p77p).

Wineshill Hill on which St Mark's church, Winshill, is situated. Has also been called High Winshill, Wheadley Knob and Gorby's Knob (CBHBT p17).

Wingfoot Park Public park 0.75m WSW of Bushbury.

Winghouse There is a Winghouse Inn and Lane by the Stone Road at Tittensor. Winghouse may be identified with the Windhouse near Tittensor in Beech quarter in Stone ancient parish (W p369).

Winkhill Small moorland village at the confluence of Black Brook and the Hamps 1.5m WNW of Waterhouses. In Waterfall ancient parish. For the burial

mound here see Blackbrook Farm. Appears as Winkle Hill on Plot's map. John Wesley preached at Winkhill (SVB p171). Wilfred Holdcroft, aged about 17, was found hanging in a cow-shed at Long Dytch Farm, Winkhill (ES March 15 1939 p1). A freak whirlwind having swept through Waterhouses on May 20 1997 made for Winkhill. Here it threw a caravan 50 feet up into the air (ES May 20 1997 p1pc) (ITV. Central News. May 20 1997 10.30pm).

Winking Man Rock feature ten-feet high in Ramshaw Rocks to the E of the Roaches, at approximately SK 01996240. Formerly in Heathylee township in Alstonefield ancient parish. It resembles a man's face from the side, particularly if viewed from the Leek-Buxton road (A53). A hole naturally worn in the rock is the man's eye. The eye winks, presumably, in certain lights, or the eye appears to wink as you pass along on the nearby. Alternatively some may have considered the rock represents a woman's face and therefore it has been called Lady Rock? and it lies by another rock feature called the Loaf and Cheese (see) (SMCC pp2,3). The Winking Man may be identifiable with the Winking Witch, a rock feature in Quarnford or Heathylee parishes, thought by some to represent the Celtic god Thor (UHAW p77). (VB p209) (PDS&C p12p) (COS p10p) (JC 4 il). The name may be of Scandinavian origin (UHAW p75). The Winking Man is said to have lost an eye because he saw a virgin walk past from Leek and he blinked so much through the shock of it that it blinded him (DPMM p99p). To climbers the feature is known as the Winking Eye (SGM p153).

Winnington Minute hamlet at the foot of undulating country N of Mucklestone by the confluence of two tributaries of the Tern, 0.75m N of Mucklestone. Former township in Mucklestone ancient parish. The manor of Wennitone appears in DB. The name means 'Wenni's town' (DUIGNAN). Ekwall gives 'tun of Wynna's people' (SSE 1996 p19). From 1183 the Cistercians from Combermere Abbey had a farm in the Mucklestone area (SVB p128); Grange Farm at Winnington may take its name their grange?; by aerial photography, a moated site at Winnington was located in 1937/38 (NSFCT vol 72 1937-8 p117. 1982 p15).

Winnington Glen A pretty dingle some half a mile from Mucklestone church (BPS p157).

Winnothdale Settlement straggling the side of the head of a dale, 2.25m WNW of Croxden (PS p63p, p65p). Partly in Croxden, Cheadle and Checkley parishes. Appears as Winworth Dale on 1834 OS map. The name is from Winnoth Dale, and is from a contraction of wind-worth dale (NSFCT 1917 p150). Winnoth Dale Methodist chapel, known locally as 'The Chapel in the Valley,' opened in 1899, closed in 1969, and was still standing in 1999 (COPP2 p81p).

Winshill Village on a hill overlooking Dale Brook and the Trent Valley 1m ENE of Burton upon Trent. Former township in Burton upon Trent ancient parish but in Repton and Gresley hundred, Derbys (W p530). There was possibly a pre-Roman village at Winshill (HOBTU p2). The Wineshylle mentioned in the will of Wulfric Spot (c1002), founder of Burton Abbey, is probably Winshall (SHC 1916 p31) (SSE 1996 p19) (CBHBT pp15,16); later appears as Wineshalle (DB), and Wineshulla (SPN p27). The **name** means 'Wine's hill' (NSJFS 1981 p2) (BTOP vol 1 p6) (SPN p27) (SSE 1996 p19). Winshill remained a **manor** of Burton Abbey after it came into the abbey's possession in the early C11; it had its own mills, manor house, and gallows (CBHBT pp15,16), which appear to have been at Hanging Hill at the Winshill end of Trent Bridge, near the bottom of Ashby Road (IHOBT pp16,21). By 1325 it was a grange of Burton Abbey (VCH vol 3 p204). Winshill was ecclesiastically severed in 1825 to help create Burton upon Trent Holy Trinity ecclesiastical parish, refounded in 1842. The separate ecclesiastical parish of Winshill was created in 1867 (GLAUE p429). The **church**, St Mark, Church Hill Street, was built in 1869 (BOE p88). The ancient township, which was formerly larger, with the northern boundary being formed by the sky-line from Bladon Hill across to Brizlincote Valley, became a separate civil parish in 1866 (CBHBT 14-16) (GLAUE p429). **Transferred to Staffs**. In 1878 that S of Dale Brook was taken into the newly-created municipal borough of Burton, but the whole township remained in Derbys. In 1894 the 'rural' part of the township was transferred to Newton Solney, Derbys, whilst the 'village' part was transferred to Staffs. These changes are said to have taken place after much debate but mainly because the rate was one penny less in Staffs; the prevailing rate in Derbys was 5.5d, whilst the rate in Staffs was only 4.5d (CBHBT pp15,16) (SL p29). Up to the early 1850s Winshill village was confined to the Church Hill area, an area still called 'Old Winshill.' By the 1861 census there was a new village of Winshill starting from North, West and East Streets (CBHBT pp15,16). Due to poor water pressure a spring still served the village into the C20 ending when a **water tower** was erected on Waterloo Clump in 1904 (BTOP vol 1 p7p of the old spring). Burton **Grammar School** moved to Winshill in 1957 and became the comprehensive, co-educational Abbot Beyne School in 1975 (VCH vol 6 pp154-156).

Winshill Heath Winshill. By 1608 there was coal mining on Winshill Heath (BTIH p49). There is a Common Farm on the N side of Bretby Lane in Derbys just beyond the present county boundary.

Winses Ground A piece of land of Gregory Woodwarde of West Bromwich conveyed by the custom of livery of seisin to John Parkhouse of Hurst Hill. The symbols by which the land was represented in the ceremony of livery of seisin were a bough of an oak which grew by the Tame and a piece of turf (SCSF p121).

Winter Croft S of Dods Leigh, S of Uttoxeter, Stone Road, W of the Blythe. Marked on Pigot & Son map (1830).

Winterside Former house at Moor Side, 0.75m WNW of Hollinsclough. There was a house here called Winterside in 1400 and a house still here in 1924 (1924 OS map 6 inch) (VCH vol 7 p38).

Winter's Walk In Sandon Park at foot of Pitt's Column.

Winton Square A town square 0.25m N of Stoke-upon-Trent built on the former Winton Woods. The square built from 1847 was created with the building of Stoke railway station and North Stafford Hotel which faces it. Pevsner describes it as 'the finest piece of Victorian axial planning in the county.' The station designed by HA Hunt of London opened on Oct 9 1848. On the first floor of which, occupying the same width as the booking-hall, is the board room with a window said to be modelled on one at Charlton House, Wilts, and claimed in 1848, to be 'in size and magnificence unrivalled perhaps in modern times in this or any other country.' The hotel opened in 1849 and was at first called the Railway Hotel. It is referred to as the Five Towns Hotel in the novels of Arnold Bennett (SHST p135) (IAS pp192-193) (BOE p262) (AGT p138il). The nearby former North Stafford Hotel Lake was a reservoir for water for steam locomotives at the station. It was filled in in 1959 and a post office and car park built on the site (SHST p128p,646p). A statue of Josiah Wedgwood I, born at Churchyard House (see), Burslem, by Edward Davis stands in the middle of the square (BOE p262). It was unveiled by 2nd Earl of Harrowby on Feb 24 1863. It is eight feet high and made of bronze. The facial likeness was derived from Sir Joshua Reynold's portrait. A model of the Barberini or Portland Vase is in one of his hands (ILN March 7 1863 p249il) (OTP p193) (HOE pp115 il of the unveiling ceremony, 131) (SOSH pp268p,269) (POP pp99,100).

Winton Villa Corner of Stoke Road and Station Road, Stoke-upon-Trent. Home of Robert Garner author of GNHS from sometime in the 1850s to 1885 (OTP p149 il of in 1860 (1906 ed)). Formerly part of the National Coal Board's N Staffs Area Marketing Office by 1949 (NSFCT 1949 pp24,45).

Wisbar House Checkley. On a wall at the back is a plaque depicting a lady in Georgian period costume with long black hair. Its significance is a mystery (CJF p7p).

Wisemore Street and area 0.5m NNW of Walsall. Occurs as a field name between 1409 and 1689; the field lay between Park Street, Ford Brook, Walsall Brook, and probably by the present Stafford Street. The Wisemore area was densely built up by the 1830s. Most of Wisemore was cleared of slums in the 1930s and obliterated by the technical college, built in stages from 1949 to 1969 (VCH vol 17 pp160, 161,180) (SNWA p111).

Wisemore House Wisemore, Walsall. Listed in 1997 so that the building could be saved from being included in a site for clearance for a proposed supermarket (WROP p123p).

Wishing Pool In Baggeridge Wood (BCM July 1968 p38) (TB Oct 1994 p15p). It was a local custom for people to stand on a particular stone at the water's edge with their backs to the water and throw a penny over their shoulder into the water and make a wish (SDOP p119p).

Wishing Well In Knightley Park, near Callingwood Hall (SJC p10).

Wissage Tiny hamlet by 1881 (VCH vol 14 p27). Now submerged into the SE suburbs of Lichfield.

Wissage Hill To E of the Stowe Pool, Lichfield.

Withington Hamlet on a low ridge between Dagdale Brook and the Blithe 0.5m SE of Church Leigh. Formerly in Leigh township and ancient parish. Is perhaps the parent hamlet of the parish and therefore is even older than Church Leigh (NSFCT 1923 p148). Foot-and-mouth disease broke out at Withington Farm in early 1968 (SN Feb 16 1968 p1).

Withington Green Tiny hamlet 0.5m NE of Withington.

Withnall Moddershall. A 1100 acres of Withnall Heath were enclosed under an Act of 1808 (SHC 1941 p18). Portions of the Forest of Withnall remained as common land in Moddershall until recent times (SOK p14).

Withymoor Former waste to the NE of Amblecote manor house, in the area of Lakeside Court and Kirkstone Way, in Amblecote chapelry (formerly part of Old Swinford parish, Worcs). Has also appeared as Whithymoor (SGSAS), Whittymore (c1760) (SNSV vol 1 p374), and Whitmoor (1834 OS map). The name suggests that at one time the area was moorland which was sufficiently

wet to allow a profusion of willow trees - locally known as withy - to grow (SNSV vol 1 p374). There were houses and a glasshouse here in the later C17 (VCH vol 20 p51). Gives its name to the present Withymoor Village to the E.

Withymoor Village (locally *Wittimer* BCM spring 1999 p75). Modern housing estate 0.5m S of Brierley Hill built on former open cast mining land which was being worked in the Withymoor area in the 1960s (BHOP p9) (BCM spring 1999 p73). A windmill marked on a map dated 1775 is situated in this area (TB May 1977 p9). Probably takes its name from the waste known as Withymoor to the W (BCM spring 1999 p75).

Withysitch Hamlet in the mid C19 in Milwich ancient parish (W p420). Now amounts to no more than a farm, 0.5m NE of Milwich.

Withystakes In 1946 was the name of a cluster of houses between Werrington and Cellarhead, 0.75m ENE of Werrington. Had its centre at the junction of the Armshead-Cellarhead road with the Werrington-Rownall road. These crossroads were so dangerous that in 1935 the main road was diverted to the S. The river Blithe rises here (WJ p23).

Witnells End Small hamlet over 2m ENE of Upper Arley. Has appeared as Whitnells (C16) (VCHW vol 3 p5), Whitnells End (late C18), a township of Arley parish (SHOS vol 2 p253) and Witnals End (1834 OS map).

Wobaston Former farm and manor in Bushbury ancient parish (BUOP p6); Wobaston Cottages are 1m WNW of Bushbury. The prebend of Wobaston in Wolverhampton Collegiate Church, first mentioned in 1291 (VCH vol 3 p324), was abolished in 1846 (W p82). Has also appeared as Wybaston. The hamlet of Ford Houses grew by a ford across Wybaston Brook (SHOS vol 2 p184). The name means 'Wilbald's town or farmstead,' Wibald being a short form of Wigbeald, meaning bold in battle (DUIGNAN) (SPN p144).

Wobaston Manor Wobaston. According to BUOP it is not known when and who built the house, but it was built probably in the late C18 or early C19. The manor was farmed by the Forster family for many generations. It was sold to John Corser in 1787 and repurchased by a niece of the Forsters, Catherine Davenhill, in 1838. It was leased to the Sidney family in the mid C19 and was the home of the Petit family at the beginning of the C20. Frank Watson farmed here in c1925. In 1930 the fields about the house were used for the annual Sunday School Treat (BUOP p27p).

Wodehouse, The House and estate which nestles against the N end of a small ridge in a dell created by Wom Brook, 1m ENE of Wombourne. In Wombourne ancient parish. About 1180 William le Coq (or the cook) was granted a clearing in the forest and later built his 'house in the wood.' The house was inhabited by his descendants, the Woodhouse (de la Wodehouse or atte Wodehouse) family, who lived here to the beginning of the C18 (LGS p260) (VCH vol 20 p204) (SVB p182). By 1708 the Wodehouse estate had passed to Samuel Hellier. His son and heir, Samuel (d1751) resided here and he was succeeded by his son, Samuel. On his death in 1784 the property passed to his friend Rev Thomas Shaw, minister of St John's, Wolverhampton. He later changed his name to Shaw-Hellier. On his death in 1812 the estate passed to his grandson. It then passed with the Shaw-Hellier family but was let to tenants. A tenant in the later C19 was the Wednesbury Liberal MP the Hon Philip Stanhope, who entertained William Ewart Gladstone, PM, here in Nov 1888. From here Gladstone made a brief visit to Himley Hall and to the Drill Hall at Wolverhampton. In 1981 the estate passed from the Shaw-Helliers to John Phillips, a first cousin twice removed of Dorothy Shaw-Hellier, who died in 1981 (SGS p189) (VCH vol 20 pp204-205) (SVB p182) (POAP pp69-71) (Wolverhampton Chronicle May 28 1999 p22ps). The present house incorporates parts of the late medieval timber-framed house. By the mid C17 gabled wings had been added to each end of the S side. GF Bodley restored the house in the 1870s, shortly after which the house was given the archaic spelling 'Wodehouse,' having been previously called 'Woodhouses' or 'Woodhouse.' CR Ashbee and his Guild of Handicraft added a chapel against the E end of the S front c1896-8. He also rebuilt the chimneys, replaced two gables by a parapet bearing the motto 'Domum Dulce Domum' 'Home, Sweet Home' and remodelled the other gables. In 1912 a service wing was added on the E side (BOE p327) (SGS p189) (VCH vol 20 pp205-206) (MR p393). In c1910 the house contained a curious carved figure of the Elizabethan period inscribed with the following lines

> 'Be frugal, ye wives, like in silence, and love,
> Nor abroad ever gossip and roam;
> This learn from the keys, the lips, and the dove,
> And tortoise, still dwelling at home.'

(SHBP p203). The Wodehouse appears in Ellen Thorneycroft Fowler's novel 'The Farringdons' (1901) as The Moat House (PPTP p34).

GROUNDS. A **dovecote** still stood in the grounds in 1784 (VCH vol 20 p206). The **Druid's Temple**, built by 1773 and perhaps inspired by a visit to Stonehenge by Sir Samuel Hellier and Thomas Shaw in 1768, no longer exists (VCH vol 20 p206 il facing p193). The **Grotto**, built by 1767, no longer exists (VCH vol 20 p206 il facing p193). **Handel's Temple**, built to the memory of the composer in 1768 to designs by Gandon, no longer exists (VCH vol 20 p206 il facing p193). The **Harvest Gate** is an iron gate with small farm tool implements attached, mostly scythes and shears (WMAG Aug 1966 p19ps) (WWW p33p). The **Hermitage**, built by 1767, had several rooms one of which contained a life-size model of a hermit called Father Francis; it was noted by Shaw, but no longer exists (SHOS vol 2 p215) (VCH vol 20 p206 ils facing p193). The **Music Room**, built by 1767, was equipped with an organ; it was noted by Shaw, but no longer exists (SHOS vol 2 p215) (VCH vol 20 p206 il facing p193). The **octagon**, built in 1754, no longer exists (VCH vol 20 p206). The **Root House**, built by 1767, no longer exists (VCH vol 20 p206). (AWM p54 of Wodehouse Farm).

Woden Suburb of Wednesfield, 0.5m NW of the church.

Woise Lane 0.5m S of Ranton Abbey.

Wolf Dale Dale and C18 house 0.75m SSE of Rushton Spencer (NSFCT 1885 p54. 1905 p160) (VCH vol 7 p219). Has also appeared as Wulvedale (1322-3) (SHC 1911 p437), Oldall Grange (HOLS 1862 p171), and Wolfdale. Formerly in Rushton James township of Leek ancient parish (W p733). The house may stand on a site occupied in medieval times (VCH vol 7 p219).

Wolf Edge Edge on NW slope of Oliver Hill under 0.5m NW of Flash. (VB p211). Rises to 1575 feet (1947 OS map 1:25,000 (sheet 43/06)). Name of cottage where the counterfeiters of Flash, making 'Flash Money,' were reputedly based (SVB p77). Has also appeared as Wolfe Edge.

'Wolf Pit, The' Occurs in the perambulation of Stoke parish boundary in 1689 and was apparently near Trent Vale. 'Wolvedale bruche' is a boundary mentioned in a charter of Trentham Priory (NSFCT 1910 p176).

Wolf Low Farm C18 house 1.25m WSW of Rushton Spencer. Formerly in Rushton James township in Leek ancient parish (VCH vol 7 p219).

Wolfscote Dale Dale, 1.25m long, created by the Dove. It lies S of Beresford Dale. The name is from Wolfscote Hill and Grange to the E in Derbys, and means 'Wulfstan's cottage' (PNPD). Has austere beauty in contrast to the sylvan beauty of Beresford Dale (VB p205).

Wolgarston House 1m E of Penkridge. Old manor in Penkridge ancient parish (W p466). Has appeared as Turgarestone (DB), Wulgarestone (C12) (SSE 1996 p19), Wolgareston (1215), Wulgastone (1304), Woolgarstone Farm (1834 OS map) (SPNO p93). The name means 'Wulfgar's tun or town' (DUIGNAN) (SPN p93) (SSE 1996 p19). There are faint traces of three arms of a moat 0.5m to the SSE at SJ 936135 (SSAHST 1982-3 p45) (CAMS p64). There is a well at the Upper House at Wolgarston which was a stopping place in the Penkridge perambulation, where the gospel was read (HOP p29).

Wollery Green Former small hamlet situated roughly where the Oxley Arms stood in Bushbury Lane, in Bushbury ancient parish (BUOP p6).

Wolmore House 2m WNW of Trysull. In Trysull ancient parish. On a ridge NE of Abbots Castle Hill. May have been formerly written Wildmoor (see). 0.25m to the E is Moat Rough, a coppice, where there was a moat by c1300. The rectangular moated site was levelled by the farm by 1958 (VCH vol 1 p368. vol 20 p187) (SSAHST 1982-3 p48) (POAP p79).

Wolseley Small hamlet by the Trent and the Great North Road at the foot of a stretch of escarpment rising to the Cannock Chase highlands on the N side, 1m SE of Colwich. In Colwich ancient parish. Wolseley **manor** is noted for having been held by the same family for approximately 1000 years. The Wolseley estate was granted by King Edgar in 975 to an ancestor of the Wolseley family, who according to legend had rid Staffs of wolves (Daily Telegraph Dec 14 1995 p8) (BBC Radio 4. Start the Week. Jan 22 1997). Or others say the manor gave its name to the Wolseley family (SL p66). Has appeared as Ulselei (DB), Wasselega (1167) (SHC 1934 part 2 p55), Worseley (c1540) (LI appendix p171), and Woolsely (1698) (Illustrated Journeys of Celia Fiennes edited by Chris Morris. 1984. p146). The **name** represents 'Wulfric's woodland glade' (SPN p101), or 'Wulfsige's leah' (SSE 1996 p19); Wulfsige meaning 'victorious wolf' (DUIGNAN). At SK 021203 200 yards along the Rugeley road from the Wolseley Arms, on the right, there is a narrow road which leads past Mill House and an alleged **hermit's cave** carved out of the red sandstone rock face (Cannock Chase by Car. Staffs Nature Conservation Trust Ltd. ND, but between 1971 and 1974 p6). **Chapel**. The Trinity chantry at Wolseley, certified in 1546-48, was founded by Geoffrey Wolseley, clerk (d c1341). It may have stood in a field known as Chapel Field between Wolseley Hall and the main road, but probably stood near one end of Wolseley Bridge (SHC 1915 p75. 1934 part 2 p76). Wolseley was in Colwich **prebend** (SSAHST vol 2 1960-61 p44). There were violent **anti-enclosure disturbances** at Wolseley between 1466 to 1481 (SHC 1934 pp78-94. 1941

p6). There was a skirmish in the **Civil War** by Wolseley Bridge when a parliamentary force was routed by royalist troops under Major Scudamore before the battle of Hopton Heath in 1643. A cottage near the scene, formerly part of Roebuck Farm, was given the name 'Cromwell House' when it became a cafe in the 1930s, by 1993 it was known as 'Oliver Restaurant' (HCMBOPP p43p) (HHHC p42). Wolseley was well known for the posting house and inn on the **Great North West Road** in the coaching period (SHC 1914 p146). Mr Pope of Rugeley made a **gazebo** to enclose the electricity and gas meters on his land at Wolseley Bridge and topped it with a thatched dovecote. In 1993 Stafford borough council requested the building be removed for Mr Pope had built it without planning permission (ES Oct 20 1993 p4p). It was still there in Dec 1998.

Wolseley Bridge Important crossing over the Trent carrying the London-Holyhead road, 0.75m SE of Colwich. Grants of pontage for its repair were issued in 1380, 1387 and 1430. It is mentioned in Leland's unpublished notes as 'Worsley or Worseley Bridge' (ABMEE p3) and appeared in many entries as Ousley Bridge, a name used also by John Ogilby (SHC 1934 p24). The Trinity chapel at Wolseley may have stood at one end of the medieval bridge (SHC 1934 part 2 p76); Mr Parker thought it was at the Bishton end (OSST 1949-50 p14). It was rebuilt in 1725 by Richard Trubshawe (HAH pp65,66 il of the old bridge c1700) (SSE 1987 p48il by Stebbing Shaw). The bridge of 1725 was so severely damaged in the extremely harsh winter of 1794/95 it could not be repaired and had to be blown up (SHOS vol 1 p141. vol 2 pls show a ruined Wolseley Bridge). The collapse of a later bridge drowned several men in 1799 (HAH p65). The present bridge of c1800 is by Sir John Rennie (BOE p107). The bridge is haunted by the figure of a man who walks across it at dusk. On the Rugeley-Stafford road W of Wolseley Bridge travels a ghostly ambulance attending a past accident. Also in the same area has been seen the ghost of a quaker (info Bruce Braithwaite).

Wolseley Hall Former house, seat of the Wolseley family, which stood by the Trent to E of Wolseley Bridge.

THE WOLSELEYS. The Wolseleys of Wolseley can prove by authentic evidence an unbroken descent from Saxons times and show the inheritance of the same lands in the male line from some time prior to the Norman Conquest (Burke's Peerage) (AR p37). **Ralph** Wolseley, a Baron of the Exchequer, had licence to crenellate Wolseley Hall in 1469 or 1470 (SHC 1914 p142 note); the document granting crenellation was still being preserved at the hall in the 1930s (CCBO pp165-168). The Wolseleys were strong Yorkists in the War of the Roses; this was unusual in a county where Lancastrians flourished (SHC 1934 part 2 p77). Ralph Wolseley of Shugborough was succeeded by his eldest son John living in 1614, who was succeeded by his second son Sir Robert, 1st baronet (created in 1628). He died in 1646 and was succeeded by his eldest son Sir **Charles** (1630-1714), 2nd baronet, who took a seat in Cromwell's House of Lords and stood high in the favour of the Protector. He was succeeded by his third son Sir **William** (b1660), 3rd baronet, who accidentally drowned in a little brook at Longdon (see) in July 1728. The estate and title then passed to his brother Sir **Henry** (b1663), 4th baronet. On his death in c1730 he was succeeded by his nephew, Sir **William** (c1692-1779), 5th Bt (Burke's Peerage). In the 1745 Jacobite Rebellion he was about to join the cause of the Young Pretender; but while entertaining some of the Government troops was saved just in time by receiving news of the Pretender's retreat from Derby (Colwich. Prebendary Harland) (SHC 1914 p146 note). In 1752 Ann Whitby of Oakedge Hall (see) duped Sir William into marriage, whilst she continued to have liaisons with the local MP. Sir William was succeeded by his son Sir **William** (1740-1817), 6th Bt. He was succeeded by his eldest son Sir **Charles** (1769-1846), 7th baronet (Burke's Peerage). Sir Charles Wolseley was considered a radical baronet and converted to Catholicism in 1837; he had been convicted of holding an illegal meeting and sedition in Stockport, Ches, in 1819. At the meeting he implied he assisted the assailants at the taking of the Bastille (1789) in the French Revolution. He was an advocate of reform in laws which prohibited Catholics from holding offices (Broughton's Scrapbook pp209-212) (DNB) (Sir Charles Wolseley: The radical baronet. Anne Bayliss. 1983). Sir Charles was succeeded by his son, Sir **Charles** (1813-1854), 8th Bt, who was succeeded by his second son, Sir **Charles Michael** (1846-1931), 9th Bt. He was living at the hall in 1907 (STC p18p), and was succeeded by his eldest son Sir **Edric Charles Joseph** (1886-1954), 10th Bt, who was succeeded by his grandson Sir **Charles Garnet Mark Richard** (b1942) (his father Stephen being killed in action in 1944 in WW2). Sir Charles, 11th Bt, the last Wolseley to own the estate, was experiencing financial difficulties in 1992 after opening Wolseley Garden Park, a public garden centre, on the estate in 1990. He was declared bankrupt in 1996 and was living on state benefit in 1998 (ES Aug 5 1992 p10. Aug 4 1998 p9) (Daily Telegraph. Aug 4 1998 p9p).

ASSOCIATED WITH WOLSELEY HALL. **Dryden** was a visitor to the hall in the 1680s (SSAHST 1966 p46). The eldest son of Sir Charles, 2nd Bt, **Robert Wolseley** (1649-1697) is remembered for his poetical warfare with Mr Wharton, brother of the future Marquis of Wharton, which ended in a duel which ended in the death of Mr Wharton. Later Robert Wolseley acted as envoy of King William III in Brussels (PSS pp36-38) (VFC p144). The eldest daughter of the same Sir Charles, Elizabeth, married Robert Somerville of Edstone, Warws, and was the mother of **William Somerville** (d1742), author of 'The Chase' (1735). He was born at Wolseley Hall on Sept 2 1675 (SMC p166) (GNHS p136) (LGS pp59-60) (CCBO p167) (ZSB) (VFC p124); according to Simms he was born at Oakedge (see Oakedge Hall) (BS p420). A niece of Ann Fiennes, wife of the same Sir Charles, was the writer and traveller **Celia Fiennes** (1662-1741). During her stay at the hall for six weeks in summer 1698 (and or 1697) Fiennes made several small journeys across Staffs; to Lichfield (see), across Cannock Chase (see) to Penkridge (see); through Needwood Forest (see) to Derby, via Colton (see) and Tutbury (see). She noted the hall both partly old and newer built, and much admired the hall's Grindling Gibbons staircase (CCBO pp165-168) (Illustrated Journeys of Celia Fiennes edited by Chris Morris. 1984. pp112,146-148). Sir Richard, a younger brother of Sir William, 5th baronet, was created a Baronet of Ireland in 1744-45 and from him descend the Wolseleys of Mount Wolseley, County Carlow, Ireland. His third son was William (d1800). The fifth son of this William (d1800) was Garnet Joseph (d1840). Garnet's eldest son was **Garnet Joseph Wolseley** (1833-1913) the Field Marshal. He was created Baron Wolseley of Cairo and of Wolseley, Staffs, in 1882 and Viscount Wolseley of Staffs in 1885; on his death in 1913 the barony became extinct (Burke's Peerage). In the 1930s Wright noted at Wolseley Hall a large silver rose bowl, whose plinth had pictures of the campaigns of the Field Marshal (CCBO pp160,165-168) (SLM July 1980 p20).

One of the past halls was built in the C17 (SL p258). In the later C17 Plot noted the fine oak panelling in the drawing room, which was then new (NHS p383). This hall seems to have been abandoned and rebuilt in the C18 (HCMBOPP p44p in 1910), or the C19 (SGS p88). The hall burnt down in the 1950s (HCMBOPP p44p) (AR p37p) and the Wolseleys moved to Wolseley Park House. The hall was then left derelict until being demolished in 1966 (SL p268) or 1967 (IHB p396) (ES Nov 21 1995 p9 il and p of before demolition) (Daily Telegraph Dec 14 1995 p8). In the 1930s Wright noted the hall contained two framed documents, one dating from the C12, and a picture of the battle of the Boyne and boots and spurs worn at the battle by Rt Hon General William Wolseley, commander of the Inniskillen Horse, who rode beside William III (CCBO pp160,165-168) (SLM July 1980 p20). (GNHS p136) (SLM June 1948 pp116-117) (WMAG Sept 1965 pp20-22ps) (STMSM July 1980 p20p of the hall).

GROUNDS. In the late C17 there was a walk named after Celia Fiennes' mother (Illustrated Journeys of Celia Fiennes edited by Chris Morris. 1984. p112). There is an **icehouse** for the hall, 1.25m to the SW, at SK 014184, probably of C19 origin. It was renovated in 1988 (IHB p396). After the house was abandoned in the 1950s the gardens became overgrown until being laid out and opened as **Wolseley Garden Park** in 1990 (HCMBOPP p44). A tablet in the new Garden Park has the lines from a poem, by Dorothy Frances Gurney, titled 'God's Garden' (TB July 1991 p25p). The garden has a **maze** ('Mazes' Shire Album Guides. Adrian Fisher and Diana Kingham. p23) called the Britannia Maze. With Sir Charles Wolseley's financial downfall in 1992 Wolseley Garden Park closed and became overgrown.

Wolseley Park Late medieval deer park 2m WNW of Rugeley held by the Wolseleys of Wolseley Hall (see). Licence to enclose was granted to Ralph Wolseley, one of the Barons of the Exchequer in Edward IV's reign (EDP pp179,191), in September 1468, not 1469 (CCF p44), but Palliser says 1469 (SL p90). The park - never a part of Cannock Chase (PCC p12) - still existed in 1867 with its right of deer-leap from Cannock Chase. The deer-leap with its privileges still in practise in 1867 was thought by some to be unique in Britain (EDP pp179,191il); deer leaps were still being kept in repair up to the 1930s (NSFCT 1933 pp76-77) (ESH p29) (FLJ 1896 p382) (HOP p83). In 1838 in the park was a remarkable knot in an ancient oak which resembled the head and face of a bull dog wearing a wreath and a ruff (Staffs Views in WSL vol xii 68). The park may have been also known as Wolseley Wood (NSFCT 1933 pp76-77).

Wolseley Park House House 1.75m W of Rugeley. Became the Wolseley seat in 1967 after Wolseley Hall was demolished (ES Nov 1995 p9) (Daily Telegraph Dec 14 1995 p8p).

Wolseley Plain (VB p117). Seems to be to W of Wolseley Park, to Abraham's Valley.

Wolseley Wood Thousand acre 'hay' or enclosure at Wolseley enclosed by Tho-

mas and Ralph Wolseley in the C15 and disputed at court. Thomas Wolseley claimed that he had only enclosed 300 acres and the parcel of land had always been in the demesne of Wolseley manor. One parcel of land was called Glass House Hay. The wood may be the same as Wolseley Park (NSFCT 1933 pp76-77).

Wolstanton Large village on a ridge overlooking the Fowlea Valley, and former township and ancient parish 15.75m NNW of Stafford, now merges into the Newcastle suburbs.

EARLY. A Neolithic or Bronze Age stone implement has been found at Wolstanton (NSFCT vol 42 p97) (NSJFS 1964 p30). Richmilde Street (see), the **Roman** road between Derby and Chesterton, passed through Wolstanton. The line of it has been discovered at Wolstanton Marsh (see) and in a garden to the rear of Links Avenue by Wolstanton Golf Course at SJ 84694792 (WMARCH 1995 p74).

700 to PRESENT. Wolstanton manor was held by the Crown at the time of DB; Newcastle Castle and borough were probably founded in this manor (SHC 1933 part 2 p6). Others say they may have been founded in Trentham. The **name** has appeared as Wlstanetone (DB), and Wulstaneston (C12) (SPN p142). It means Wulfstan's tun or town (DUIGNAN) (SSE 1996 p19), or 'Wulstan's farmstead' (SPN p142). Wulfstan is said to be from Wolstan or St Wolstan, prior of Worcester Abbey, bishop of Worcester from 1062, and founder of Wolstanton church (WWT p9) (HBST pp114-117). The tradition that Wolstanton took its name from Wolstan is supported by the tradition that some of St Wolstan's ancestors were born at Dimsdale near Wolstanton (NSFCT 1886 p53). There was a **church** at Wolstanton probably in the Saxon period. The present parish church, St Margaret, at the junction of Church Lane and Chetwynd Street, may stand on the site of the church at Wolstanton which was in existence by 1086 and certainly by 1200 (HBST pp110,117). The church was rebuilt in 1859-1860, but the N steeple has some C14 work (BOE p313). The original **parish**, formed before 1086, was very extensive and probably contained the ancient parishes of Biddulph, Audley, and Madeley (SHC 1916 p192), as well as the chapelry of Keele, and the Tunstall, Chesterton, Kidsgrove, Goldenhill, Silverdale, Chell, Newchapel and Mow Cop area (GLAUE p429). The parish was reduced in size in 1851 (APB p5). The **pound** was halfway down Wall Lane (otherwise Knutton Road). It was on the site of the **stocks** (WWT p34). There was **glass making** in the area in the late C17 and C18 at the Glasshouse (see) at Red Street. **WW1.** A Zeppelin was heard passing over Wolstanton on the night of Jan 31 1916. A bomb from another Zeppelin raid in the area on the night of Nov 27 1916 landed in Bradwell Lane, Wolstanton (TB July 1994 p19). **Natives and visitors. Samuel Davies** and Mrs **Ann Turner** were married in Wolstanton church on Dec 31 1811 after three days courtship. Together their ages amounted to 140 years. The bridal party were preceded to the church by a band of musicians in token of the high esteem in which they held the bride (Wolverhampton Chronicle Jan 1 1812) (SCSF p61). **John Leech**, well-known draughtsman and caricaturist of 'Punch,' was married in Wolstanton church in May 1842, his wife being Anne, daughter of Charles Eaton, of Knutton (ES March 7 1932 p4). Dr **Henry Faulds** (1843-1930), a leading finger print expert and police surgeon spent his retirement in Wolstanton and is buried here. **Sid Rowe** (b1918), an Indian novelist, taught at Wolstanton Grammar School (see Orme School under Newcastle-under-Lyme); his 'It's a Wog Life,' by Golly,' appeared in 1966 (VFC p115).

Wolstanton Marsh Green open space to SW of Wolstanton church. A cobble surface was found at cSJ 854477 at Wolstanton Marsh during drainage, which was thought to be part of Richmilde Street (see), the Roman road between Derby and Chesterton (NSFCT 1908 p106) (NSJFS 1964 p31). Here the North Staffs Hunt Pack was at one time kept (OTP pp147-148). Some or all of Wolstanton Marsh, which has also appeared as The Marsh, was enclosed under an Act of 1898 (SHC 1941 p19).

Wolverhampton (BBC announcers and non-natives stress first syllable, locally 'Ompton as in the ballad 'Foxy Southall' UBCB p102, The Book of Wolverhampton. Frank Mason. 1979 p9). Large town, former township and ancient parish 15.25m SSW of Stafford, situated on a hill, 529 feet high (HOWM p6), at some distance from a brook. Wolverhampton and the Wolverhampton Collegiate Church estates, despite falling in Seisdon or Offlow hundred, seem to have formed their own hundred, which was independent of the hundred courts, but not of the sheriff (HOWM p5 note).

EARLY. The last **Ice Age** reached its maximum southern extent at Wolverhampton, between about 26,000 and 15,000 BC (NSJFS 1972 pp8,9 see map) (SL p35). Glacial boulders lie all about in the tract of ground extending from Wolverhampton to Trescott, Trysull, and Seisdon. This area has been described as an 'open-air petrological museum on a grand scale, but devoid of arrangement' (WJO Nov 1909 p293). Some large boulders have been put on show in

East Park (see) and West Park (see). A fragment of an adze of **Neolithic** or **Bronze Age** was found at Wolverhampton Grammar School, Compton Road, in 1895 (Proceedings of the Prehistoric Society vol 25 p139) (NSJFS 1964 p44). It has been suggested that the hill on which St Peter's and the town art gallery stand was the site for a hillfort (WMARCH 1995 p121). Prehistoric implements have been found at Merridale (see) and at Finchfield (see). A gold or bronze (VCH vol 1 p198) ring set with an engraved cornelian of **Roman** origin has been found in Wolverhampton parish (NSJFS 1964 p44). A pottery vessel with a girth of two feet found in April 1783 near St Peter's church and said to be of Roman origin, sold at auction in 1895, proved to be of medieval date (SHOS vol 1 General Intro p35) (WA vol 1 No. 1 pp8,53. vol 2 No. 3 p83 il) (NSJFS 1964 p44). (GNHS p70).

600 to 985. **Cross**. Close to the S door of St Peter's church is a circular red sandstone, tapering shaft, 14 feet high or 3.5 metres high with a lower diameter of 76 centimetres tapering to 56 centimetres at the top. It is perhaps of Roman origin, taken from the Roman City of Wroxeter, Shrops, about 25m WNW of Wolverhampton. It would have been erected to commemorate a special event or to mark a preaching place before the community could afford to build a church (St Peter's Trail. Wolverhampton Council and Wolverhampton Civic Society) (BCM autumn 1995 p48). However, Sue Whitehouse, believes that the cross was almost certainly erected whilst a church was already in existence; the church may have been too small for large congregations and the cross was erected as a focus for outdoor services for large congregations (BCM autumn 1995 p48). The date of its erection at Wolverhampton is uncertain. The carving covering the whole surface of the shaft was thought in the 1940s and 1950s to be of mid C9 origin and was inspired by the decoration of the Charlemagne (742-814) period (ARCHJ vol CXVII 1960) (BOE p315). Or it has been thought to have been commissioned by Lady Wulfrun in the late C10 (BCM autumn 1995 p49); or is the work of c1190 (LGS p257). The decoration is in zones. There is rope moulding near the base, and beneath five half-lozenges, one of which contained foliage and the other four the emblems of the evangelists. The rest of the carving consists chiefly of grotesque beasts and birds (LGS p257). The shaft which survives today was almost certainly surmounted by a cross head of some kind which may have been located at the top of a further section of shaft mounted onto the cap stone (BCM autumn 1995 p49). The earliest pictorial representation of the cross accompanies Isaac Taylor's map of Wolverhampton (1751). Shaw, at the beginning of the C19, estimated that the cross was about 20 feet high (SHOS vol 2 p161 pl xxiv). In 1877 a cast was made of the cross which was on display in the V&A, London, in 1995. The cross was in some state of deterioration in 1913 (Proceedings of the Society of Antiquaries. 1913) (BCM autumn 1995 p49). It was washed down and the cap stone was repaired in 1952. In 1995-6 the cross was cleaned and fragile sections were repaired (BCM autumn 1995 pp48-50). (W p81) (The Builder. 1872 il) (SOSH p307) (S p151p) (Romanesque Architecture in England. AW Clapham. 1930 pl 57) (WA vol 1 No 12 p361) (SLM Aug 1948 p153ps). The 'Hampton' attacked by the Danes before Tamworth in 943, has been identified as Northampton, not Wolverhampton (VCH vol 1) (HOWM p3 note). Wolverhampton has appeared as Heantune (985), Hamtune, Hantone (994), Heantun (1006), Wolvrenehamptonia (1074) (SPN p143), Wlurenehamton (appears in the grant of the collegiate church to Sampson c1078 and is considered by Mander the first record of the full name - HOWM p12), Hantone, Handone (DB), Wrehanton, Wrehantune (Worcs DB), Wulfrunehanton (1169), Wulfrunhamtun (C12), Wolverenehampton (C12), Wolvernhampton (C12), Heantune (1317) (SPN p143), U(V)luorhampton (c1540) (LI appendix p170). The suffix of the **name** is of Anglo-Saxon origin and represents 'High town or farm' in recognition of Wolverhampton standing on high table-land (DUIGNAN) (SOSH p68). Harnaman disputes that the suffix is of Anglo-Saxon origin, and argues that it is from Celtic 'hearn' meaning 'iron,' a suggestion supported by the Romano-Celtic bloomeries (NSFCT 1937 p125). Or the suffix signifies 'free' (S&W p366). It is generally accepted that prefix 'Wolver' is from Wulfruna (see above), an Anglo-Saxon noblewoman, who, according to tradition, founded Wolverhampton (DUIGNAN) (SOSH p68). Wulfrun, a female personal name, means 'wolf council' (SPN p143).

985 to 1000. **Lady Wulfrun in Wolverhampton**. In 985 or 986 (WF p7) a grant of land at Wolverhampton, and at Trescott, was made to Lady Wulfrun by Ethelred (or Aethelred) 'The Unready' (king 979-1016) (HOWM p3) (SL p54) (SSE 1991 p8). The grant of 985 comprises a charter of Wolverhampton's bounds (SL p62) and is the earliest surviving reference to Wolverhampton (HOWM p3). The charter was thought to refer to Southampton until it was proved to relate to Wolverhampton by CGO Bridgeman in SHC 1916 pp101-104 (HOWM p14 note). In 994 Lady Wulfrun made a grant of land to the monastery of St Mary (later St Peter's) in Wolverhampton (WF p7) (SL

pp52,54). The grant comprised the Staffs estates of Arley, Ashwood, Bilston, Hatherton, Hilton (by Ogley), Hilton and Featherstone, Kinvaston, Ogley, Pelsall, and Wednesfield (HOWM p14). **Identity of Lady Wulfrun**. According to Erdeswick Lady Wulfrun (or Wulfruna) lived in the reign of King Edgar (973-975) (SOS p261); Dugdale thought Lady Wulfrun may have been the sister of King Edgar (d976) (LGS p257) (WF p7) (WFW p27), and she may have been advanced in age when she made her grant (HOWM p3). She may have been the Wulfrun captured in the storming of Tamworth in 943 (DUIGNAN) (SHC 1916 pp9-10) (VCH vol 3 p321 note), for she is the only Wulfrun mentioned in the Anglo Saxon Chronicle (HOWM p3). Plot, who thought she lived in the reign of King Ethelred (979-1013), considered her to be the widow of Althelm or Aldhelm, Duke of Northampton (NHS pp416-417) (WFW p27). This Wulfrun was the mother of both Wulfric Spot, founder of Burton Abbey (SHC 1916 pp9-10) (VCH vol 3 p321 note), and of Aelfhelm (or Aldhelm?), ealdorman of Northumbria: Aelfhelm wedded another Wulfrun (HOWM p3) (HOWU p5). However, according to Masefield and Hughes, it was Aelfhelm's wife who was the Wolverhampton Wulfrun and according to Hughes she was the same Wulfrun taken prisoner by the Danes when they sacked Tamworth in 943 (LGS p257) (SOSH pp68,307). **The death of Lady Wulfrun**. Wulfrun, who had received and made grants of land in the late C10, was elderly in 996 (WFW p27); where she is buried is not known. If she had been buried at Wolverhampton some tradition of the fact would have remained. An alternative burial place is Tamworth, where there was a convent mentioned in Wulfric's will, which she may have founded (SHC 1916 pp10,15,40) (HOWM p4). **After the death of Lady Wulfrun** her beneficence lived on in Wolverhampton legend. She had given her name to the college of St Peter, by 1080 known as 'the church of Wolvrenehamptonia;' from this name Wolverhampton is derived (VCH vol 3 p321). Her name also persists in fields and meadows lying to the N of the town at Dunstall, where she may have lived, and being attached to Wulfruna's Well (see) at Dunstall, and Wulfruna's Well (see) at Spring Vale (HOWM p4). A place known as 'the entrenched place of Wulfrin' occurs in a document of 1240 concerning Prestwood. It is thought to be near Noose Lane or Portobello (WFW p48). The rediscovery of her charter in 1560 in the rubble of a wall, lapped in a sheet of lead, revived the traditions surrounding her (WA p194) (HOWM pp4,58). Holinshed (1577) was the first to use the charter as evidence to support the theory (known in the C13 but long forgotten, apparently) that she gave her name to the town (HOWM p58). It is probably through Holinshed that Michael Drayton half remembered her as St Wilfrun. In Drayton's map of Staffs river sources in his Polyolbion (1613) he depicts Wolverhampton and St Wilfrun's Well with a water jar sitting by it (HOWM p4). In the early C18, a tablet, dated 1719, was erected close to the S door of St Peter's church, Wolverhampton stating that in 996 in Ethelred's reign, Wulfruna or Ulfruna, widow of Athelme, Duke of Northampton, founded St Peter's church (SHOS vol 2 p160); the date 996, was later revised to 999 (SLM Feb 1959 p30). By 1880 there was this rhyme about Wolverhampton:

> A thriving town, for arts Vulcanian famed
> And from its foundness, good Wulfruna, named.

(S&W p366). A statue of Lady Wulfrun by Sir Charles Wheeler of Codsall (see) was erected in front of St Peter's church, at the W end, in 1974. It is eight feet six inches high and was the gift of the E&S, and was erected to commemorate the centenary of the E&S (WMAG Dec 1974 p45p) (St Peter's Trail. Wolverhampton Council and Wolverhampton Civic Society).

1000 to 1500. **Alice of Wolverhampton tradition**. King Canute (c995-1035) fathered Harold I (or Harold Harefoot) (c1016-1040) by a concubine called Ælgifu, or Algive, or Alice, or Elgina. There is a tradition that she was a native of Wolverhampton. An annotation by either Hurdman, Loxdale, or Huntbach on p242 of Dr Wilkes's copy of Erdeswick of c1720 in the WSL (No. XXI) allude to affirmations of her existence by Speed (who calls her Algive, Ulfranc's daughter), and Weever in Funeral Monuments (ed 1631) (who calls her Alice, a shoemaker's daughter), both affirm this; Weever's source was Stow's Annals. Other accounts have suggested that Alice's baby was a changeling (HOWM pp3,4). Another account by Ranulf Higden (d1364) (ed 1495 Book vi chapter 20) has Canute fathering Suanus (Sweyn) by Elgina of Hampton (HOWM p4) (WFW p27). A recent account says Harold I was the son of Canute and Ælgifu of Northampton (The Cambridge Biographical Encyclopaedia. 1994. see under Harold I). In the C11, confusingly, both Northampton and Wolverhampton were written 'Hampton' in the various Early English forms (HOWM p3 note). The church of Wolverhampton Collegiate Church (see), which is Wolverhampton's parish **church**, crowns the hill in the centre of the town. In Lady Wulfrun's time the church was dedicated to St

Mary. It was still St Mary's in 1086, but by the mid C12 the change to St Peter had occurred (VCH vol 3 p321). Some work of the late C13 survives. The church was restored in 1852-1865 (BOE p314). The custom at Wolverhampton on Christmas Eve to commence a peal upon the bells, noted by Dr Oliver in the C19, dated from the late C12 (HCCW) (SCSF p48) (TB June 1980 p19). The parish, formed before 1086, may have originally contained Bushbury ancient parish (SHC 1916 pp193,197). The custom of beating the bounds of the parish was practised in Wolverhampton parish on Monday and Tuesday in Rogation Week and prevailed until 1765 (W p68). But is recorded in 1824 (AOW p24). (SHOS vol 2 p165) (SCSF pp21,22) (PA) (BCC vol 1 p135). Parishioners anciently processed to Lichfield cathedral, the mother church, to pay their oblations in 'St Chad Farthings' or other money (SCSF p11). There were four **religious guilds** in Wolverhampton in the Middle Ages (NSJFS 1979 p15). For the medieval **hospital** in Wolverhampton see Saint Mary's Hospital. Payments for ringing the **curfew bell** at Wolverhampton were made until at least 1748 (SCSF p161). **Persons and visitors. Hubert Walter** (c1140-1205) visited Wolverhampton whilst Archbishop of Canterbury (appointed 1193) to sort out the affairs of the collegiate church (HOPTT p18). Hubert Walton, Archbishop of Canterbury, possibly the same as above, is supposed to have been born at Wolverhampton in c1200 (SMC p166). **Stephen Jenyns** (or Jennings) (d1524), founder of Wolverhampton Grammar School, and lord mayor of London (1508), was born in Wolverhampton in c1448 (SOSH p179). **Viscount Lovel**, Lord Holland Deincourt, Burnell and Grey, KG, Chamberlain of the Household and Chief Butler of England, and lord of the manor of Stowheath fought at Bosworth Field and with the Yorkists at Stoke (June 16 1487) and was last seen trying to swim the Trent on horseback. Lovel forfeited the manor and manor house of Stowheath with his other property. The skeleton discovered at Minister Lovel in 1708 is reputed to have been his (HOWM p41).

MARKETS AND FAIRS. Mention of a **market** at Wolverhampton is first made in 1179 (WF p7). In 1180 the inhabitants of the town were ordered to pay a fine to Henry II for holding a market without a licence. In 1204 King John took exception to the existence of a market without a royal charter. Henry II granted a charter for a market to lord of the manor, Giles de Erdington, the dean of Wolverhampton on Feb 4 1258 (HOWM p47) (NSJFS 1971 p51) (WF p7) (SL p146) or 1238 (WMLB p44). The market was held on Wednesdays (WF p8) (THS) (SCSF p94). There was a market in 1792 (OWEN), but apparently none in 1888 (LHE p265). The earliest **market cross** in Wolverhampton would date from 1258 (SCSF p90). A market cross building built at the charge of the town replaced this earlier cross in 1532 (HOWM p46) or in 1552. This building was demolished under the provisions of the town's first Improvement Act, 1777 (SHOS vol 2 p161) (SCSF p90 (HOLK). The key to the building was kept in remembrance of it. G Price in HOLK gives an engraving of it (SCSF p90). A charter for a **fair** was granted on Feb 4 1258 (HOWM p47) (NSJFS 1971 p51) (WF p7) (SL p146) or 1238 (WMLB p44). The annual fair was held on the vigil of the feast of St Peter and St Paul for eight days (SCSF p90) (WF p8). The fair sometimes lasted for 14 days (SCSF p101). Hackwood says the most important of the ancient fairs of Staffs was undoubtedly the Wolverhampton Wool Fair, held on days surrounding July 10. The fair became very important after 1354 when it was made a Staple Fair, after which it had to follow strict Government regulations. Its status as a Staple Fair probably lapsed during the Civil War (SCSF p100). Owen and Cooke give July 10 as Wolverhampton's only fair day (SCSF pp98,99). There was a fair in 1792 (OWEN), but apparently no fair in 1888 (LHE p265). At Wolverhampton fair in 1764 a fight developed following bets on a game of ninepins. In the ensuing affray, sticks, stones and cudgels were used and one man was apparently kicked to death (LOU p180). The annual custom of **'walking the fair'** was a procession through the streets of Wolverhampton on July 9 (the eve of the Wool Fair) by men in antique armour, preceded by musicians playing the fair-tune, followed by the steward of the deanery manor, the peace-officers and many of Wolverhampton's principal inhabitants. The ceremony may have originated out of the necessity of an armed force to keep order at the fair, when Wolverhampton was a great wool emporium. The armed men, numbering 20 or 24, were furnished by the burgesses, who, annually appointed a bailiff of the staff, whose job it was to preside over and receive the tolls of the fair. The ceremony was first omitted in c1784 (SHOS vol 2 p165) and abolished in the late 1870s having attracted too much rowdiness (SCSF p101) (WF p22).

WOLVERHAMPTON MANORS. Wolverhampton comprised three manors; two belonged to the church (the Deanery manor and the Prebendal manor) and one to the king (what became the royal Stowheath (see) manor) (HOWM p25) (NSJFS 1972 p69). On July 11 1263 the dean of Wolverhampton created a borough out of his manor and granted to his burgesses the liberties of

Stafford. The grant covered only the dean's manor and not Stowheath manor. Burgage tenure survived until at least 1657 (NSJFS 1972 p69). A Court Leet and Copyhold Court, known as the Deanery Court of Wolverhampton, were granted in Edward III's reign (WF p8). The **Prebendal manor** comprised the prebends of Featherstone, Hilton, Wobaston, Willenhall, Hatherton, and Monmore, which were ultimately farmed together, by the Leveson family and their successors. Some of these prebends had property in other prebends and there were many portions of prebendal property in the centre of Wolverhampton and the centre of Willenhall. The Prebendal manor was sold by the Levesons to Francis, Earl of Bradford, in 1702 (HOWM p26). Kinvaston, another prebend of the Prebendal manor, ultimately passed into the hands of the owners of Oxley (HOWM p27). The **Deanery manor** included the northern part of the town of Wolverhampton, nearly the whole of Wednesfield, part of Codsall, a small part of Willenhall, Ogley Hay, Lutley (Halesowen), and Pelsall. The deanery manor eventually passed into the hands of the Dukes of Cleveland and when the lease expired and the last Duke died in 1891 the manor reverted to the Church Commissioners (HOWM p26). For **Stowheath manor** see Stowheath.

PUNISHMENTS. For the **gallows** see Gallows Lane. Wolverhampton's stocks were removed from the churchyard to the market place in 1552, and remained near the market cross until 1670, when they were returned to their old position (SCSF p129). Wolverhampton's brank or **scold's bridle** was long kept in the Old Town House on the High Green, along with the pillory and the stocks and other punishment instruments. The scold was paraded on the steps of the Old Town Hall (SCSF pp125,127). The **pillory** was kept in the church down to the C19 and when used fixed in the market place (HCCW) (SCSF p127).

WOLVERHAMPTON WOOL STAPLERS. Some time before the establishment of the 'staple' at Wolverhampton, if a 'staple' was established at Wolverhampton, raw wool from the Welsh Marches was probably being brought to the town and possibly being dealt in by staplers (loosely meaning merchants) and subsequently spun into yarn and woven into cloth here. It has been claimed that in 1354 parliament fixed Wolverhampton along with Westminster, Bristol, Hull, and Canterbury, as a place where the 'staple of wool' could be carried on after its removal from Flanders (HS p241) (SCSF p100). This meant Wolverhampton had been selected as a depot and assessment place for wool, where wool was subjected to toll before export, or the king's taxes (WA vol 1 p169). According to Dent and Hill there were no wool merchants in Wolverhampton in 1340, but the introduction of the 'staple' in 1354 brought many to the town. There was a period of a few years when it was returned to Calais (HS p241). Hackwood implies that the 'staple' at Wolverhampton lapsed during the Civil War (SCSF p100). Others say Wolverhampton was never a 'staple' town for it is not mentioned in the Ordinance of the Staple itself (1354) nor in the Staple Rolls of c1354 to 1460, preserved in the Public Record Office (WA vol 1 p169). Another account says at the beginning of the C15 many of the leading families of the town were trading in wool and some of the more important citizens were members of the Staple of Calais (HOWM p35). In the late C18 Shaw noted the Leveson arms in the upper window of Mrs Normansell's house. James Leveson was a merchant of the staple (SHOS vol 2 p163). Dent and Hill give a list of Bailiffs of the Staple of Wolverhampton between 1483-1499, which was printed in 1868 by G.T.L. (GT Lawley?) (HS p241 note). The wool merchants most probably had a wadehall, or cloth hall, or **guildhall** - Wolverhampton's first public building - where they could attend to their corporate business. This was perhaps the building which stood on the N side of old Lichfield Street and on the site of the present (1951) fountain and gardens. Most of the building was destroyed in the C18, but a chimney breast of the Tudor period survived until July 1859 when it was revealed during the demolition of an adjoining building (HOWM pp36,46). The chimney bore a plaster armorial insignia of commerce. The emblem consisted of the Royal Arms with a garter surmounted by a crown of the period 1509-1603. On the left were the arms of the Drapers Co and on the right the ones of the City of London. It was removed and preserved by Mr Turner. It disappeared after Mr Turner left the county (Wolverhampton Chronicle July 20 1859. July 27 1859) (WA vol 1 No. 1 frontispiece pp15,16). **Folds.** John Roper says, the name 'Fold' has been indiscriminately used in Wolverhampton, and it is difficult to know which: if any, of the existing so-called folds ever had anything to do with the town's wool and cloth trades (WAIW vol 3). Many courts were renamed folds and first appear on a map drawn by George Wallis in 1827 (WOLOP p50). See Blossoms Fold, Farmer's Fold, Molineux Fold, Townwell Fold, Wheeler's Fold.

GRAMMAR SCHOOL. Wolverhampton Grammar School was founded by 1512 by Sir Stephen Jenyns (or Jennings) (d1524), lord mayor of London (1508) (SHOS vol 2 p162) (W p90) (SOSH p179) (History of Wolverhampton School. GP Mander) (VCH vol 6 p177) (WF p9) (WPOPP vol 1 pp50p,51p). Jenyns apparently built the school on the site of his family home in St John's Lane, later St John's Street (VCH vol 6 p177). On Jenyns' death in 1523 the school's affairs were entrusted permanently to the London Company of Merchant Taylors (NSJFS 1979 p8). In 1531 the Company took over management of the school. In 1590-1 they paid for the building of a new school house on the site of the old, which had been burnt down. Isaac Backhouse was master between 1658 and 1685, when he resigned. In 1681 he was accused by Titus Oates, a former school fellow, of involvement in the Popish Plot (VCH vol 6 pp177-179). The school in John Street rebuilt by William Smith of Tettenhall in 1713 (VCH vol 6 pp177-179), or by Francis Smith of Warwick in 1714, was pulled down in 1964/5 (HOWM p137) (WMAG Sept 1965 p17p. Dec 1975 pp20-21. May 1978 pp22-23). But the school had moved to new buildings, built in the Gothic style by Giles and Gough of London, at its present location at Merridale in 1875 (VCH vol 6 pp177-179). **Alumni**: John Abernethy, surgeon; Sir William Congreve Bart, engineer; Rev Thomas Moss (c1740-1808) of Brierley Hill (see); Judge John Pearson, Advocate General in India (1771-1841); John Pearson (1772-1841), poet (PSS p467) (VFC p105); John Morrison (b1773), poet of Wednesfield; Lieut-Col Thorneycroft, poet and war-ship inventor (b1822); Alexander Hordern barrister of the Temple; Richard Tooth late fellow of Trinity College; Vernon Lee Walker of Bromley House, Penn, murdered in the New Herbrides in 1887; J Beete Jukes (1811-1869) geologist; Alfred Hayes (1857-1936), poet, born at Chapel Ash (see); Lewis Allen (b1905), Hollywood film maker; John S Roper (1924-1980) local historian and author of HC; Philip Oakes (b1928) TV scriptwriter (VFC pp99-100); Keith Aldritt (b1930s) novelist; Dr Chris Upton, author of HOWU (The News (Wolverhampton) Dec 3 1998 p20). (W p91) (HOPTT pp269,274) (WJO July 1905 p183) (BCM Jan 1981 pp39-42) (SNSV vol 2 pp102-103).

1500 to 1642. To the puritans Wolverhampton was known as **'little Rome'** for the abundance of Roman Catholics living here, although other places were also called this (NSJFS 1966 p13). During the years of Catholic suppression the shortage of Protestants of suitable rank in Wolverhampton had the curious effect that there were no resident magistrates in the town (HOWM p62). The Staffordshire **Assizes** seem to have been held in Wolverhampton from c1547 to 1593 (SHOS vol 1 pp161-162) (HOWM p47). The Elizabethan parish of Wolverhampton was divided into two districts, **town and foreign**. The town comprised the concentrated settlement on the hill, whilst the foreign comprised the surrounding country estates of The Lea, Graiseley, Oxneford, Merridale, Newbridge, Dunstall, Seawall (The Showells), Old Fallings, Neachells, Prestwood, Ashmore, and Bentley (HOWM p44). The relationship between Wolverhampton's town and foreign seems to have been less colourful than that of Walsall's. In 1590 a **fire**, which lasted five days, broke out in Barn Street (Salop Street) and destroyed 104 houses and 30 barns and a large quantity of grain and left nearly 700 homeless (W p76) (WF p9) (SL p155). The first record of the species the **Bay-leaved Willow** (Salix Pentandra) for Britain was found by Thomas Johnson at Wolverhampton in 1639 (NSFCT 1946 p82). **Persons and visitors**. Wolverhampton was not visited by Leland in his itinerary in the 1540s (HOWM p58). During Mary I's reign **a cardinal** of the Roman Catholic church visited Wolverhampton and stayed with Francis Whitgreave at Moseley Court (Old Hall?); he was the last cardinal to visit Wolverhampton until Cardinal Wiseman in 1855 (HOWM p56). In 1606 **Thomas Smart** and **John Holyhead** were charged with sheltering the Gunpowder Plot conspirators and tried in Wolverhampton by a judge brought specially from Ludlow, and executed in High Green (HOWM p64) (WF p9). **William Perry**, the 'Boy of Bilston,' was baptised at Wolverhampton on Oct 11 1607 (HOWM p60). **Thomas Parr**, 'Old Parr,' of Winnington, Shrops, was conveyed in easy stages to London to be presented to Charles I at the age of 152 in 1635. He passed through Wolverhampton in mid Sept 1635 and stopped at Joan Planckney's Inn (WA vol 1 No. 3 pp83,84,85). **Elisha Coles** (d1680), linguist and poet was born in Wolverhampton in c1640. He compiled an 'English Dictionary' (1676). The DNB describes the verse in his 'Metrical Paraphrase on the History of Our Lord' (1671) as ridiculous doggerel (PSS p463) (VFC p29).

CIVIL WAR AND COMMONWEALTH PERIOD. **Early years**. The town was regarded as having royalist sympathies in the Civil War. There were two garrisons in the town. Prince Rupert passed through Wolverhampton on Oct 11 1642. Charles I arrived in Wolverhampton accompanied by his sons Charles and James on Oct 15 1642 en route from Bridgnorth to Alston Hall and stayed three nights (HOWM p78). He is said to have stayed on Oct 17 1642 at an Elizabethan house, which became the coaching inn the 'Star and Garter,' or stood on the site of that inn. The inn was rebuilt in 1836 and it stood in Victoria Street (plaque on present building). The king is said to have left the town on Oct 18 (HOWM p80). The royalists held the parish church for five

days in the course of which the chest was rifled and tombs were destroyed (HOWM p79) (HOWV p86). In 1643 Prince Rupert visited the town. A parliamentary force led by Sir William Brereton captured the town on March 20 1643 (W p65; White gives the date 1642) without resistance (HOWM p84). But by August it seems to have been a royalist stronghold with Charles I here on Aug 17 1643 (W p65). **Later years**. In May 1645 Wolverhampton was Prince Rupert's headquarters. On May 16 Charles I stayed at Bushbury (W p65). On May 17 1645 Capt Stone of the parliamentary army fell upon the rear of the king's army at Wolverhampton (HOWW p330) (HOWM p90). On June 16 1645 Charles I was back in the town and gave a bag of gold to Mr Gough and offered him a knighthood but he refused it (W p65) (WF pp11,12). Another account has Henry Gough giving Charles I a purse containing £1,200 and being offered a knighthood in return, which he refused; Charles II later gave knighthoods to two of his grandchildren (SOSH p203). Charles I slept, according to the Itur Carolinum, at Mrs Barnford's, a widow, who seems to have had a house on the W side of Cock Street, and left the town for Bewdley on June 17 (HOWM p90). Parliament rallied their forces of some 1,800 foot and 1,200 horse to meet at Wolverhampton on Feb 18 1646. From here the force was employed to break the siege of Lichfield and other places (HOWM p90). The 'whole town' rose and rioted against excise collectors in July 1646 (LOU p340). During the **Commonwealth period** marriage banns were read in the market place (SCSF p63-65). The 'High Riots' of papist gentry occurred in Wolverhampton in 1654 (HOWM p94) (LOU p343). There seems to have been an instance of two holding the living of Wolverhampton between 1655 and 1661. In 1655 Cromwell appointed to the living Rev John Reynolds, a Presbyterian and a liberal. He seems to have allowed the existing minister Ambrose Sparry to carry on working alongside him as a coadjutor. Both sign the register for different entries of marriage and baptism. GT Lawley has suggested that the royalist portion of the congregation preferred the services of the old minister, while those with parliamentarian sympathies preferred Reynolds' services. Reynolds was ejected for Nonconformity in 1661 (SCSF p65). The bells of Wolverhampton church were rung in the C17, C18 and C19 on May 29 to celebrate Restoration Day 1660 (SCSF p19) (FOS p99). Fifteen to seventeen ex-Cromwellian soldiers were accused of associating on market days in Wolverhampton in 1663 after undercover investigations by Sir Brian Broughton (LOU p348).

1660 to 1700. There was an attack upon a load of corn being sent to a baker in the town causing a **riot** in 1692 (LOU p72). On Sept 10 1696 a **fire** broke out in Barn Street and destroyed 60 houses in five hours (WA vol 1 No. 12 p366) (HOWM p107) (WF p14). (WMAG Aug 1969 p25). By the later C17 the four **springs** which came together behind the Cock Inn were given different names appropriate to their uses - Pudding Well, Horse Well, Washing Well and Meat Well (NHS p38) (SHOS vol 2 p163). In the later C17 Plot noted the **phallus fungi** could be found at Bentley and almost anywhere within three or four miles of Wolverhampton and at Old Fallings (NHS pp200-201,202 tab 14 fig 4, fig 5). **Persons and visitors**. Two Roman Catholic priests, residents of Wolverhampton, **Gavan** (or Gawan) (born London 1640) and **William Atkins** (or Atkyns) (born Cambs 1601) were implicated in the Popish Plot (see under Tixall Old Hall) and arrested in 1679. Gavan was executed on Tyburn Hill in 1679, whilst the death sentence imposed on Atkins was never carried out and he died in Stafford Gaol in 1681 (BS pp30,183-184) (LGS p257) (FSP p89) (VCH vol 3 p106). **Thomas Wall** of Wolverhampton was so strong in the teeth he could easily bend a large nail or tenterhook and set it straight again. Plot examined the man's teeth to see if they were all molars, but found they were not. Only his incisors were of an unusual thickness (NHS p293). **Jonathan Wild** or Wilde or Wildy 'The Prince of Robbers' and informer is said to have been born in Walsall Street, Wolverhampton, in 1682 (LGS p64) (MMH pp58,59) (TOS pp35-37), or in 1683 (TB Nov 1985 p14) or c1684 (WA vol 2 no 1 p2; notes there are references in Wolverhampton PR to the birth of a John son of John 'Whily' (1680) and of a Johnathan son of John Wiley, Joyner (1683)). Masefield says Wild's father was a wig maker (LGS p64). Another account says his father was also a seller of herbs in the fruit market (WMAG June 1964 pp16-17). Shaw says Jonathan Wild was born at Boninghale, Shrops (SHOS vol 2 p163). According to Masefield Wild became a buckle-maker in Wolverhampton, and married, but after the birth of his son he deserted his wife and went to London and there began his disreputable career (LGS p64). Mander thought he had traced the son and daughter of Jonathan Wild - Abraham born on June 23 1703 and buried on Oct 8 1713, and Elizabeth buried on March 4 1715-6 (WA vol 2 no1 pp1,2) - presumably both were born in Wolverhampton. In London he was imprisoned for debt, where he remained for about four years. There he became acquainted with Mary Milliner, a lady of doubtful character, with whom he lived, on obtaining his release. While in prison he realised that the condition of the underworld of London provided great opportunities for commercial exploitation. Subsequently he organised the majority of thieves in London and more or less compelled them to bring their booty to him, and if they failed to do so he denounced them to the authorities. It is said he was responsible for bringing to trial 35 highwaymen, 22 housebreakers and ten returned convicts, the majority of whom were hung. Eventually Wild was arrested for receiving some stolen lace. He was tried on May 15 1725, hung at Tyburn on May 24, and buried in St Pancras churchyard beside his third wife, Elizabeth (TB Nov 1985 p14). His skeletal remains may have been exhibited by Arbuthnot Bostock in the old coach house of the Old Mitre Inn (see), Essington. At the time Masefield was writing (1910) his skeleton was on show in the Royal College of Surgeons museum (LGS p64). William Harrison Ainsworth wrote 'Jack Sheppard' (1839) based on his life (BS p6). There were two portraits prints purporting to be of him in Wolverhampton Art Gallery in the earlier C20 (WA vol 2 no 1 pp1,2). By 1999 the gallery had two portrait engravings (cuttings from books) purporting to be of Wild (info Marguerite Nugent). (S p114) (KES pp239,240) (Jonathan Wild: Prince of Robbers. Frederick J Lyons. 1936) (QMMH pp100-105 il) (SLM July 1953 pp22,23) (BCM April 1968 pp33-35) (Thief-Taker General: The Rise and Fall of Jonathan Wild. Gerald Howson. 1970) (TB July/ Aug 1973 pp8-9) (WF p45) (TOS pp35-37 il) (The Thieves' Opera. Lucy Moore. 1997). A highwayman, **William Duce**, was born in Wolverhampton in 1698. He was a part of the 'Croaker Gang' and was executed on Tyburn Tree, on July 23 1723 (TB March 1992 p10). In 1687 the Catholic **Bishop Leyburn** visited Wolverhampton (VCH vol 3 p107). For **William Wood** (1671-1730) of the famous 'Wood's Halfpence' case see under The Deanery. For Rev **Thomas Moss**, whose poem 'The Beggar's Petition' became very popular, see under Brierley Hill.

1700 to 1800. The **Quakers** had a meeting-house in what is now Broad Street from 1704. The site of the Quaker burial ground survives at the junction of Broad Street and Westbury Street. A plaque in a wall commemorates the land being given to Wolverhampton corporation in 1905 (SSAHST 1970 pp47-48). The chapel in John's Lane (later John Street?) was attacked by the mob in early July 1715 and although much damaged it survived (HOWM p130) (LOU p85). **John Street Chapel case**. The first nonconformist meeting-house in Wolverhampton was erected in John Street in 1701-2 for a Presbyterian congregation and conveyed to a body of trustees. During the C18 the congregation and trustees drifted away from Trinitarianism towards Unitarianism. In 1781 the Unitarian majority managed to bar the new Trinitarian minister, elected by a Trinitarian minority, and installed a Unitarian minister. In 1816 a succeeding Unitarian minister, John Steward, converted to Trinitarianism. Due to support from one Trinitarian trustee, Benjamin Mander, Steward remained minister against the wishes of the Unitarians. Mander opened proceedings in Chancery in 1817 to prove the Unitarians had no right to the chapel since it was founded for Presbyterians; moreover, Unitarianism was not legalised until 1813. The Lord Chancellor ordered them to vacate the chapel until the further order of the court. The case created a vigorous national pamphlet war between Trinitarians and Unitarians. The implications were that the Unitarians risked losing a number of other chapels besides John Street. In 1835 the Chancery judged against the Unitarians and their appeals were dismissed. The Unitarians by this time were practising elsewhere in the town and the Trinitarians at John Street, had themselves become split. In 1863 any antagonism which remained was ended by the building becoming the Church of England chapel of ease to St Peter's. In 1890 it became part of the works of Mander Bros (VCH vol 3 pp130-131). (Facts connected with the Old Meeting House etc. 1818) (An Appeal to the Public in Answer to the Remarks of the Rev James Robertson by the Dissenting Ministers who originally signed the case. 1819) (Infringement of Religious Liberty exposed etc. James Robertson. 1819) (Old Meeting House, Wolverhampton. Thomas Eyre Lee) (Detail of the Circumstances relative to the Old Meeting House in John Street, Wolverhampton etc. Charles Mander) (WJO Dec 1902. Jan 1903) (HOWM pp110-113) (WMAG Aug 1963 p42p) (The Wolverhampton Chapel Case. Stella M Blazier. MA Thesis 1985). In 1758-1776 the **church**, St John, in St John's Square was built to serve the western margin of the town (BOE p315) (St John's Church, Wolverhampton: Brief History and Guide). In 1777 an Act of parliament listed 125 residents of Wolverhampton as commissioners responsible for the **government of the town** (WF p15). The Town Act of 1777 made bull baiting illegal and the activity in Wolverhampton had to move outside the town boundaries to Tettenhall where it was a popular feature of the Michaelmas wakes (LOU p239). **Canals**. A proposal for a canal between the Trent and the Severn was published by Dr Thomas Congreve of Wolverhampton in 1717 (VCH vol 2 p285) (SL p234). The Staffs and Worcs Canal was completed between the Severn and Compton in 1770 (VCH vol 2 p288). Until the rest of the canal was completed in 1772 Compton was the terminus

for Wolverhampton goods (WF p44). In 1772 the Birmingham Canal (Birmingham Canal Old Cut Old Main Line) from Birmingham to the Staffs and Worcs Canal at Aldersley Junction was completed (VCH vol 2 p290). **Roads**. The main highway from London to Holyhead ran through Wolverhampton from 1752 before which it had gone through Brownhills (WAM p35). **Food riots** at Wolverhampton occurred in 1766 (MH autumn 1976 p262) and in late 1800 when a ladened barge was stopped near the town, and the barge was stopped from getting to Birmingham (LOU p157). Thomas Turton built the **fine mansion** known as No. 19 Bilston Street before he died in 1733. The house was demolished in 1954 (HOWM p117); a fine house of the Queen Anne period in Bilston Street was demolished in 1953 (WAIW vol 3 p). Dudley Wilks says the **'Reformed Order of Old Women'** originated in Wolverhampton (FSP p79). **Persons and visitors**. **William Vernon**, minor poet and contributor to GM, was born in Wolverhampton, reputedly in 1756; before moving to London he was a buckle-maker (PSS pp109-112) (VFC p136). **John Wesley** first visited Wolverhampton on March 8 1760, again in 1761 and preached at the Angel in High Green. His next visit was on March 23 1768, the next on March 22 1770 when he preached to a large gathering in the High Green from the doorway of one Denman, the printer of No. 44 Queen's Square. During this occasion he was reputedly hit on the head by a stone flung by the locksmith named Moseley, a notorious drunkard, pugilist and gambler, who converted and became a preacher and lived to the age of 90. Wolverhampton was formed into a separate Methodist circuit in 1786. John Wesley was in the town on March 28 1787 and for the last time on March 23 1790 (HOWM p132). **Button Gwinnett**, born in Down Hatherley, Glous, in 1732, traded in Wolverhampton, where he found his wife, who he married in St Peter's church, Wolverhampton, in 1757. He left for America in 1765 and opened a shop in Savannah, Georgia. As one of the three delegates of Georgia to Congress he was one of the 56 signatories of the United States' Declaration of Independence in 1776. He died in 1777. As a signatory of the Declaration Gwinnett's signature subsequently became much sort after. By 1937 there were only 36 Gwinnett autographs known to exist, and 27 of these were already owned by collectors with complete sets of Declaration autographs. One of his signatures appears on his record of marriage in St Peter's PR (KES p235) (SLM March 1952 p21p) (WF p45) (VB p56) (BCM summer 1995 p48). An autographed letter of Gwinnett made $51,000 in 1927, breaking the world record for the most-valuable autograph. It sold in 1979 for $100,000, setting a new world record (GBR 1965 p137. 1981 pp95-96). In 1985 a plaque commemorating Gwinnett was placed on St Peter's House, Exchange Street (Commemorative Plaques by the Wolverhampton Civic Society). **Edward Bird** RA, the celebrated painter, painter to Princess Charlotte, and Royal Academician was born in Wolverhampton, in Wheeler's Fold, on April 12 1772, his father was a carpenter. He died in Bristol on Nov 2 1819. Some of his work was at Tixall Hall in the mid C19 (GNHS p177) (W p92) (BS p60). On Jan 8 1776 the celebrated tragedian, **John Philip Kemble** (1757-1823), made his debut on the Wolverhampton stage in the character of Theodosius (WF p15) in Lee's 'Theodosius' (HOWM p135). Mander says his sister Mrs Sarah Siddons (1755-1831) made her first public bow at Wolverhampton market cross (HOWM p46). In 1987 Embassy Hotels erected a plaque to his memory at Park Hall Hotel, Goldthorn Hill (Commemorative Plaques by the Wolverhampton Civic Society). **Nathaniel Withy** (fl 1778), a minor poet, was born probably in Wolverhampton (PSS pp97-99) (VFC p144). In 1790 **Princess Carbristka** of Poland with the prince, her son, visited Bradley (see), Bilston, to see John Wilkinson's works, staying at the Swan in Wolverhampton (Wolverhampton Chronicle July 7 1790) (John Wilkinson. Ron Davies. 1987. Copy in Walsall Local History Centre. p18). There was a charge of sedition against **Joseph Josbury**, a Wolverhampton chapman, who is said to have denounced to a crowd the king and the monarchy in Easter 1794 (LOU p161).

NEWSPAPERS AND JOURNALS. For the many county newspapers published in Wolverhampton see Introduction. For the **Wolverhampton Chronicle** see Introduction. An **Eagle and Staffordshire Courier** ran from Oct 28 1848 to Feb 24 1849 (SHJ spring 1996 p36). The **Wolverhampton Herald**, founded on Feb 5 1851, became the Wolverhampton and Staffordshire Herald from Oct 29 1851 until Sept 29 1869 when it was incorporated with the Wolverhampton Journal (Wolverhampton & Its Press 1848-1948) (SHJ spring 1996 p39). A later title of this name (WJO), a journal, ran from Jan 1902 to Dec 1909. The **Wolverhampton Municipal Guardian** ran from Jan 3 to March 27 1852 (Wolverhampton & Its Press 1848-1948) (SHJ spring 1996 p39). The **Wolverhampton Journal and Mining District Advertiser**, founded on Sept 3 1853, became the Wolverhampton Journal, Willenhall and Bilston News from Nov 13 1858, then the Wolverhampton Journal from June 1 1861 until it ceased on Oct 12 1872 (Wolverhampton & Its Press 1848-

1948) (SHJ spring 1996 p39). The **Wolverhampton Spirit of the Times**, founded on July 9 1859, became the Wolverhampton Advertiser and Spirit of the Times from Jan 2 1869 and as such ran until at least July 10 1869 (Wolverhampton & Its Press 1848-1948) (SHJ spring 1996 p39). It continued as the Wolverhampton Advertiser from Jan to July 10 1869. The **Midland Mercury: Wolverhampton, South Staffordshire, Shropshire and Worcestershire Journal** ran for a week in early June 1866 (Wolverhampton & Its Press 1848-1948) (SHJ spring 1996 p37). The **Wolverhampton Monthly Messenger** ran between Nov 1872 and May 1873. The **Midland Counties Saturday Evening Express**, founded in Birmingham in 1861, moved to Wolverhampton in 1863 and became the Midland Counties Express in Dec 1866. In 1930 it incorporated the Wolverhampton Chronicle and became the Midland Counties Express and Wolverhampton Chronicle from Jan 3 1931. But the paper closed in May 1947 when it was itself incorporated into the revived Wolverhampton Chronicle to become the **Wolverhampton Chronicle and Midland Counties Express** from May 2 1947 and as such ran until at least Feb 22 1980 (Wolverhampton & Its Press 1848-1948) (SHJ spring 1996 p37). The **Midland Counties Evening Express**, founded by Nov 2 1874, became the Evening Express from Jan 17 1876, then the Evening Express and Star from July 6 1884, then the **Express and Star** from July 24 1889, and this still runs (SHJ spring 1996 p35). The **Wolverhampton Times** ran from Nov 28 1874 to Sept 27 1879. The Wolverhampton Daily News ran from Dec 7 1874 to Feb 6 1875 (Wolverhampton & Its Press 1848-1948) (SHJ spring 1996 p38). The **Wolverhampton Weekly News** ran from Dec 12 1874 to Feb 6 1875. The **Daily Midland Echo** ran from Dec 11 1877 to Jan 2 1879. It continued as the Midland Echo from mid Jan 1879 until at least June 30 1883 (SHJ spring 1996 p36). The **Midland Examiner and Wolverhampton Times**, ran from Oct 13 1877 to Sept 28 1878, and continued as the Midland Examiner and Times which ran from Oct 18 1878 to Sept 27 1879 (Wolverhampton & Its Press 1848-1948). The **Evening Star**, founded on June 28 1880, ran until June 27 1884 when it amalgamated with the Evening Express to become the Evening Express and Star (Wolverhampton & Its Press 1848-1948) (SHJ spring 1996 p36). The **Wolverhampton Guardian** ran from July 3 to Dec 24 1880 and continued as the Midland Counties Guardian from Jan 1 1881 to June 28 1884 when it was incorporated with the Midland Counties Express (Wolverhampton & Its Press 1848-1948) (SHJ spring 1996 p38). The **Staffordshire Herald** was published in Wolverhampton from June 7 to Dec 13 1882 (Wolverhampton & Its Press 1848-1948) (SHJ spring 1996 p38). The **Midland Evening News**, founded on April 3 1884, became the Midland Evening News and Birmingham Evening News from Jan 31 1902, and as such continued until at least July 3 1915 (SHJ spring 1996 p38). The **Midland Weekly News**, founded on April 5 1884, ran to 1915 (Wolverhampton & Its Press 1848-1948) (SHJ spring 1996 p37). The **Midland Wednesday News**, founded on April 22 1884, ran to Dec 16 1908 (Wolverhampton & Its Press 1848-1948) (SHJ spring 1996 p37). The **Wolverhampton Times** ran from July 1930 to July 1931 (Wolverhampton & Its Press 1848-1948). The **Wolverhampton AdNews**, founded in 1973, is a free weekly. The **Wolverhampton Chronicle Trader**, founded in 1980, was a free paper which was still running in 1988 (Willings Press Guide. 1988).
1800 to 1848. Smart's Trade Directory for 1827 noted Wolverhampton was the largest and most populous town in the county of Stafford (Mapping the Past Wolverhampton 1577-1986. Mary Mills 1993 p10). **Some new churches**. The church, St George, in Bilston Road, a Commissioners' church, was built in 1828-1830 (BOE p315). In 1978 it closed and fell into disrepair. It opened as the present (1999) Sainsbury supermarket in 1987 (Nostalgic Wolverhampton. 1999). The church St Mary, in Stafford Street was built by Miss Hinckes of Tettenhall Wood House (see). It was built by 1842 (The Book of Wolverhampton. Frank Mason. 1979 p25) and closed in 1948 (HOWM p178). In 1821 **gas lighting** was installed in the streets. To celebrate the event a 40 feet light column was erected in the market place on High Green (WF p19). **Social unrest**. On market day May 30 1810 a Wolverhampton mob threw butchers' meat from the stalls. On May 31 the Bilston, Teddesley, and Weston Troops of the Staffordshire Yeomanry arrived to suppress the riot (SA June 7 1810) (FSP p64) (BEV p49) (LOU p196). A Wolverhampton alehouse keeper in 1810 attempted to incite troops to mutiny, but the attempt failed (History of the English Alehouse. P Clarke p325) (LOU p214). The Wolverhampton miners' riots were against economic depression and against the Corn Law Bill. Some 300 or 400 miners and ironworkers marched on Wolverhampton on Nov 13 1815. Mr Fereday, whom they had followed from Bilston, addressed them from the window of the Swan Hotel, and at the Angel Inn (Dudley Street) and was able to pacify them, though the danger of riot still remained. Two Staffordshire Yeomanry troops arrived on Nov 14 and were called out to Coseley in the afternoon where a great number of miners had gathered (FSP

p64) (HOWM p151). In 1819 five members of the Tin Plate Workers Society (later the Craft Sector of TASS (Technical Administrative Supervisory Staff, now (1999) part of MSF, Manufacturing Science Finance) were apprehended by the Bow Street Runners in Horsefair (the site is now occupied by Wolverhampton Civic Centre off St Peter's Square), and subsequently transported to Tasmania for the crime of belonging to a union (plaque in Civic Centre) (WAIW vol 3 p of c1880). There was a disturbance caused by colliers demonstrating in the town on April 17 1822 which necessitated the call out of the Scots Greys from Birmingham (Wolverhampton Chronicle April 24 1822 editorial). Riots occurred at the South Staffs County bye election at Wolverhampton in May 1835 during which the Riot Act had to be read twice. Four people were wounded when the troops fired into a crowd (LOU pp223-224). The Asiatic **Cholera outbreaks** of 1832 and 1849 claimed 913 lives in Wolverhampton (TB March 1994 p20). The outbreak of 1832 reached Wolverhampton on Aug 8 and claimed a total of 193 lives (SCSF p139) (MR p387) (TB May 1978 pp20-21. Feb 1998 p17). The **Blood Money case** is an incident which occurred at Wolverhampton which attracted local condemnation and which brought about the repeal of the parliamentary Rewards Act (passed 1693 and 1694), popularly known as the Blood Money Act. Two soldiers, John Hall, aged 22, and Patrick Morrison, aged 25, of a detachment of the 95th Foot, quartered in Wolverhampton were alleged to have robbed an unemployed bricklayer's labourer John Read on the night of July 22-23 1817 in a drunken brawl in the churchyard. Read claimed they had taken 13d (6 pence). His complaints came to the attention of George (HOWM p156) or John (TB Sept 1985 p14) Roberts 'keeper of the house of correction.' Roberts and two witnesses, knowing, it is claimed, that it was a good case and they would benefit by the Blood Money Act for a conviction of felony, had the soldiers arrested and charged with highway robbery. The case went to the Stafford Assizes on July 28 and the two soldiers were found guilty and sentenced to death on Aug 16: Roberts and his two witnesses received £20, £40 and £10 for their testimony. The case was reported in the Wolverhampton Chronicle on Aug 6 and stirred public opinion to intervene. Charles Mander, varnish manufacturer, and George Tompson, his solicitor, and others arrived in London on Aug 12 to petition the king and the Home Secretary, Lord Sidmouth. On Aug 13 they found Sidmouth had just sent a respite to Stafford by special messenger and was generally sympathetic; he even wrote out a copy of the original respite for Mander in case the original was mislaid. Hall and Morrison were pardoned in Sept 1817. The case and others which had preceded it had the Blood Money Act repealed on June 13 1818 (HOWM pp156-158). (Wolverhampton Chronicle Nov 26 1817) (Romance of the Forum. series 1, vol II, p18) (Con. Churches. WH Jones). The youngest recorded death from **alcoholic poisoning** is said to have been that of a four year old, Joseph Sweet, in Wolverhampton in 1827 reported in the Stafford Assizes case R. v. Martin (GBR 1979 p21). Wolverhampton had a **William Pitt Club** set up in 1813 which ceased in c1830 with the death of the secretary, Mr Tindell (WA vol 2 No.1 or 2 pp10-25). In 1825 **horse racing** was first established at Broadmeadow Field (see), and in the 1830s Wolverhampton took over from Lichfield's course on Whittington Heath as the county's premier meeting (VB p15). A severe **pugilist contest**, which was still indecisive after 50 rounds, took place near Wolverhampton on Sept 22 1814 (HOWM p164). **Persons and visitors** (and a lion). The vicar apostolic of the Midland District for the Catholic church was in residence at Giffard House (see) Wolverhampton from 1804 to 1841. The notorious mailcoach robber **Huffey White** escaped the grasp of a team of Bow Street runners in Wolverhampton on Jan 25 1813 (TB June 1984 p1). **Joseph Barney**, a native of Wolverhampton, painted the altar piece in St John's church representing the descent of Christ from the Cross, and was painter in fruit and flowers to George IV (W pp83,85,92). **William Cobbett** (1763-1835) journalist, reformer, and author of Rural Rides (journals covering the period 1821-1832), lectured at the Assembly Room and at the Peacock Inn, Wolverhampton, in late April and early May 1830 (Wolverhampton Chronicle April 28 1830) (BCM winter 1998/9 pp52-55). For **Henry Hartley Fowler**, 1st Viscount Wolverhampton, see Summerfield and Woodthorne. **'Wallace,'** a lion in Wombwell's menagerie, died at Wolverhampton in 1838. His carcass was sent by stage coach to the curator of Saffron Walden museum, Essex. It was still on display there in 1993 (TB Aug 1985 p15p. April 1993 p19p).
1848 to 1870. Wolverhampton was **incorporated** as a borough on March 15 1848. After which the town was governed by a mayor, 12 aldermen and 36 councillors (S&W p370). The corporation mace, over three feet long, was presented by its first mayor, GB Thorneycroft, but it originally belonged to the now extinct borough of St Mawes, Cornwall (Staffs County Handbook. c1958 pp154,157) (WMLB p44) (WF p20). Wolverhampton was the largest borough in the county before the Pottery towns were federated in 1910 (LGS

p256). In 1850 there was a **Wolverhampton tin-plate workers strike**. The ballad 'Song of a Strike' sung to the tune of 'King of Cannibal Island' was a result of this strike. The first verse goes:

> There is a strike in Hampton town,
> caused by two men of great renown,
> who hope to do the tin men down,
> And so reduce their wages.

(UBCB pp83-84). There was a **boiler explosion** at the smoothing iron manufactory of Ben Mason of Walsall Street at 3.40pm on April 24 1857. About four people were injured and two died - Tom Holdridge aged 61 and Isabella Hall aged 12, who was walking past the factory (TB Nov 1982 p14). The Wolverhampton Battalion 3rd Staffs Regt founded in 1859, disbanded in 1908 (WJO Aug 1908 pp212-215. Sept 1908 pp237-240). Yeomanry. From 1893 Himley and Wolverhampton formed 'D' Squadron in the Staffordshire Yeomanry (info Yeomanry Museum). (WJ Aug 1908 p212). The **Wolverhampton Troop** of the Staffordshire Yeomanry, said to have been raised in 1798 (FSP p62), may be a reference to the Bilston Troop. **Wolverhampton Popery Riots**. On Feb 22 1867 a man named Murphy lectured in the town against Popery, a riot was anticipated and the Staffordshire Yeomanry under Capt Perry were called out (FSP pp69-70). This was the last public order duty performed by the Staffordshire Yeomanry (info Yeomanry Museum). The **Deakin Charity** comprising a bread dole was administered and distributed by the churchwardens at St John's every Sunday after morning prayer (WAIW vol 1 p). The 1849 Asiatic **Cholera outbreak**, resulted in the founding of what became The Royal Wolverhampton School (see below), an asylum for the orphans (MR p387). In 1867 Wolverhampton became one of the earliest towns to arrange for its sewage to be irrigated over the land in the form of a sewage farm, which was situated at Barnhurst (TTTD p294). The area about Worcester, Brickkiln and Salop Streets in the SW corner of the town was considered a **'rough district'** with its brothels and 'low pubs' in the C19 (Wolverhampton Chronicle. Feb 18 2000 p18). For the **Blue Coat School** see WJO Jan 1904 p15p of in 1878. In 1854 a Government sponsored **School of Art** was built in Wolverhampton, the first such school in the country (University of Wolverhampton Website. 1998). A row between two water companies, one owned by Wolverhampton and the other private, was settled in favour of the private by parliament. The corporation had to pay £6,500 in legal fees and the town was made almost bankrupt in c1855. The matter was settled by the citizens paying an extra voluntary rate (WF p62). **Early cycling fatality**. On Oct 9 1869 the 'Vale of Evesham News' reported five friends were returning from practising at the Vauxhall Gardens, Cannock Road, when riding their velocipedes along Pipers Row, one William Jones, a carpenter, swerved to miss a pedestrian and ran into a wagon killing himself (WF p34). About 1870 the first person was summoned for riding a bicycle on a public street in the town, yet the chief magistrate ruled that people had as much right to ride a cycle as a horse 'If they were foolish enough to do so' (WF p22). In 1870 an early bicycle and cycle racing was demonstrated in the grounds of Molyneux House (WF p21). **Lightning** on Jan 3 1841 struck the wooden cross on the tower of St Peter's church (TEBC2 p50). A **fire** destroyed Snow Hill, Griffin's Street and Garrick Street in 1857 (WF p21). **References to Wolverhampton**. In March 1848 The Lyceum in Stafford played the farce 'Did You Ever Send Your Wife To Wolverhampton?' (SSTY p87). The lifeboat called 'Wolverhampton' raised by public subscription in Wolverhampton was launched on Aug 27 1866 on Bushbury Pool. It was stationed at The Mumbles, near Swansea. It was lost in a storm in 1883 (BUOP p87p). **Persons and visitors**. In 1832, when Princess Victoria, (**Queen Victoria**), passed through Wolverhampton whilst in progress round the country with her mother, the Duchess of Kent and took refreshment at the Red Lion Inn (WJO Jan 1904 p14). The Queen and Prince Albert passed through the High Level railway station in 1852 (WJO July 1904 p182). On the death of Prince Albert in 1861 the widows of Wolverhampton wrote to the Queen expressing their sympathy. The Queen was deeply moved and promised that if she ever made a public appearance again it would be in Wolverhampton (WF p21). In 1866 Queen Victoria kept her promise and visited the town on Nov 30 (WMAG Nov 1966 p9p). For her arrival the people of Wolverhampton erected an arch of coal, known as the Triumphal Arch of Coal, at the railway station (BCM April 1976 p34 il). At High Green (see) she unveiled a statue of Prince Albert (WJO July 1904 pp181-188) (WMAG Aug 1969 p21). After the unveiling ceremony she unexpectedly knighted the mayor of Wolverhampton, John Morris (WF p21); to whom there is a commemorative plaque at Elmslie Bank, Wightwick (see). **Harry Paulton** (d1917), comedian, was born in Wolverhampton in 1842. Known for his dry and droll wit he was very popular with

Victorian audiences. He was interred at Morden cemetery, London (TB July 1990 p6p). **OG Rejlander** (1813-1875), 'father of Art Photography,' lived and practised between 1845 and 1862 at a premises near the present junction of Darlington Street and Ring Road St Marks (plaque on offices near site). **Charles Dickens**, novelist, appeared at the Exchange Theatre in 1851 (WF p50). About 1855 **Alice Grey**, the famous fraudster, was committed for trial at Wolverhampton. Outside the court a crowd of 4,000 is said to have gathered. She was tried at Stafford in 1855 (OP pp5-8). **John Fullwood** RBA artist, was born in Wolverhampton in 1855 and died in London in 1931 (POAP pp41-42). Rev **George Browne MacDonald** and his four daughters lived at No. 32 Waterloo Road between 1862 and 1863. The daughters went on to have either famous husbands or children: Georgiana (1840-1920) married the painter Sir Edward Burne-Jones: Louise married Alfred Baldwin MP and was the mother of Stanley Baldwin: Agnes married the painter Sir Edward John Poynter: Alice married John Lockwood Kipling and was the mother of Rudyard Kipling (The Macdonald Sisters. AW Baldwin. 1960) (WMAG Oct 1963 pp30-31. Nov 1963 pp26-27. Dec 1963 pp26-27) (POTP p136). In trying to study atmospheric phenomena on Sept 5 1862 **Henry Coxwell and James Glaisher** (d1902 or 1903) climbed to 37,000 feet - a claim strongly disputed by modern experts - in a hydrogen balloon which took off from Wolverhampton Gas Works in Stafford Road. They set the world's highest altitude record and landed at Ludlow (WMA vol 1 p6) (EAS pp8,11) (TB Oct 1992 p13) (Sunday Telegraph Oct 30 1994 p42) (Wolverhampton Chronicle Oct 25 1996 p18p) (BUOP p86p) (info Ron Balding). The height of 25,400 feet is given by GBR 1974 p216; although some writers accept 30,000 feet. There is a poem to celebrate the balloon flight in TOS p106. The ballad about a balloon at Wolverhampton in FSBC p60 may relate to this event. In 1997 a plaque to commemorate the feat was erected at the Science Park in Stafford Road (Commemorative Plaques by the Wolverhampton Civic Society). On July 17 1862 Coxwell and Glaisher made a balloon ascent from Wolverhampton, landing at Langham, Rutland; another ascent from Wolverhampton that year? took them to Solihull (info Ron Balding). **Charles Robinson** of Wolverhampton, aged 18, was hung at Stafford on Jan 9 1866 for the murder of his lover in 1865; he had cut her throat with a razor (TB Jan 1978 p24. Aug 1993 p18).

ROYAL WOLVERHAMPTON SCHOOL. The 1849 cholera outbreak resulted in John Lees, a Wolverhampton lock and key manufacturer, founding in 1849 or 1850 an asylum for the orphans (VCH vol 6 pp179-181) (MR p387). (WMAG Dec 1974 p24). The pupils wore a dress modelled on that of Christ's Hospital in London. Lees bought a site for the school in Penn Road, Goldthorn Hill, in 1852. The new building was known as the Wolverhampton Orphan Asylum and was opened in 1854. The name was changed to the Royal Orphanage of Wolverhampton in 1900 by agreement with Queen Victoria (VCH vol 6 pp179-181). Royal Princess Henry of Battenberg visited the school on July 3 1903 (WJO Aug 1903 xxxvii-xiv). In 1914 the name changed to the Royal Wolverhampton School (VCH vol 6 pp179-181) (PENOP p118p). The Duke of York visited the school on July 20 1922 to distribute prizes (WPOPP vol 1 p80p of in 1908. vol 2 88p). The playing fields of the school were bombed by the Germans in WW2 (PPTP p26). Elizabeth, Queen Mother, the school's patron, visited the school in 1969 (Nostalgic Wolverhampton. 1999).

INDUSTRY. Wolverhampton was a major wool producing town in the C14 and C15; street-names ending with 'Fold' testify to this (SL p86) and in the names of inns (SOSH p308). Lying to the N of Wolverhampton church at SO 916996, Stafford Street, two **windmills** existed in 1775, one of these, a brick tower mill was still in position in 1813. It stood on the opposite side of Stafford Street to Summerhill Lane. An old photograph shows a four storey tower with a boat-shaped cap exposed luffing wheel and four derelict sails. It was demolished in 1893 (WJO Feb 1904 p43p) (WAIW vol 1 il) (WBJ pp46-47). A third mill lay to NE and is shown on maps from Plot to the OS (1832). It could have been the windmill that was struck by a thunderbolt of lightning on July 1 1810 reported in the Warwick Advertiser of July 7 1810 (WBJ pp46-47). In the centre of the town was the Wolverhampton Mill at SO 916984 and shown on Plot's map (WBJ p47). Wolverhampton's main industry in the C18 was lock making (SL p180). Since when it has manufactured buckles, steel, jewellery, toys, tinplating, paper, art metal ware, cast iron hollow ware, safes, boilers, galvanised tanks, bearings, edge tools, machine tools, stampings, pumps, paint, chemicals, tyres, aluminium ware, tyres (see Oxley) and castings for the motor trade, rayon, batteries (Ever Ready had a factory in Park Lane after taking over Efandem by 1925) and much else (Staffs County Handbook. c1958 p159) (Wolverhampton Chronicle April 9 1999 p20).

CYCLES, MOTOR CARS AND CYCLES. The first Wolverhampton cycles were probably built in c1858 by **T Jackson** (WF p34). **Hart** Cycle Company claim to have manufactured cycles since 1863 (WF p63). The **Forder** Company, carriage builders (1860-1910), produced and manufactured the final design to the Hanson Cab, which became the most popular design. They occupied premises in Cleveland Road, now (1984) used by Dixons (BCM Jan 1984 p84). In 1985 a plaque to commemorate C Forder Ltd was erected in Cleveland Road (Commemorative Plaques by the Wolverhampton Civic Society). The **Turner** Motor Manufacturing Company of Great Brick Kiln Street (later with works in Lever Street), were early manufacturers of velocipedes and horseless carriages, producing cars from 1908 to 1928 (PVBC pp58-59). The original **Star** Company was founded by Mr Sharratt and Edward Lisle (1852-1921), designer and builder of bicycles, motor bikes and cars, commercial vehicles and aeroplanes. Star built bicycles from 1869; cars from a factory in Frederick Street from 1897; motor bicycles (an off-shoot of Star Engineering at a works in Pountney Street - BCM Jan 1981 pp37-38) from 1902; aeroplanes from 1910. The first Staring car, a product of a subsidiary company, Star Cycle Co in Stewart Street, appeared in 1905. By 1910 the Star company was the sixth largest car-producer in Great Britain. Star were taken over by Guys in 1928 (PVBC pp39-45) (Wolverhampton Chronicle July 11 1997 p24. April 16 1999 p5). By 1993 in Frederick Street a blue plaque had been erected to commemorate the company, and later bronze sculptures commemorating 'Star' cars were exhibited in the street. When Guys took over the company they moved the business from Frederick Street to a new factory in Showell Road, just off Park Lane (Wolverhampton Chronicle April 9 1999 p20). **Daniel Rudge** (1841-1880), an inn keeper in Wolverhampton, was a builder of high-class cycles from 1870. Later, the firm became Rudge Whitworth and made cycles at Coventry. In 1902 Dan's son, having left his father's company and set up with a fellow employee C Wedge, produced the first **Rudge Wedge** motor cycle from works in Mander Street, Wolverhampton. The company did not last long (VCH vol 2 p151) (PVBC p34). In 1990 a plaque to commemorate Dan Rudge was erected on the Telecom Buildings, Church Street (Commemorative Plaques by the Wolverhampton Civic Society). The **Sunbeam** Company was founded by John Marston, a tinplate and japan-ware manufacturer. The first Sunbeam bicycle was built in 1887; the first car in 1899; the first motor cycle in 1912. In 1911 a Sunbeam was the first British car to top 70 mph and in 1923 the firm won both the French and Spanish Grand Prix. In a Sunbeam V12 Henry Seagrave became the first man to drive a car at over 200 mph on March 29 1927; the car is now at the Motor Museum at Beaulieu, Hamps. Sunbeam ceased car production in 1934 and were taken over by Guy Motors after WW2. The original factory was in Upper Villiers Street. A new factory was built on the other side of the street in 1907, christened the 'Moorfield Works.' However, the bicycle side of the business in Paul Street used the name 'Sunbeamland' in its promotional literature (PVBC pp47-56) (HOWU p117) (BCM Autumn 1999 p17). In 1994 plaques to commemorate Sunbeam were erected in Paul Street (for the Sunbeamland Factory) and Upper Villiers Street (for the Moorfield Works), and another was erected to commemorate the Sunbeam Studios in Sunbeam Street in 1996 (Commemorative Plaques by the Wolverhampton Civic Society). At St John's Retail Park are bronze sculptures featuring Sunbeam World Land Speed Record Cars. **AJS** Motors was founded by the son of a Wednesfield engineering blacksmith and took the initials of one of them, Albert Jack Stevens (PVBC p5). The first Stevens motor cycle was made in 1897 when the brothers fitted an American Mitchell engine to a Wearwell Cycle possibly creating the first motor cycle in England. The company operated in Pelham Street and then from c1909 in Retreat Street (backing onto Penn Road), where AJS also produced delivery vehicles specifically for side-cars. AJS carried on in business at Retreat Street until 1930. In the later C20 the site became Safeway supermarket, and a stone sculpture of an AJS motor cycle by Stephen Field called 'Lone Rider' was erected on the site. In 1998 a plaque to commemorate AJS Motors was erected in Retreat Street (PVBC pp5-10) (Wolverhampton Chronicle July 11 1997 p24. April 16 1999 p5p of former factory) (Commemorative Plaques by the Wolverhampton Civic Society). The **Villiers** Cycle Company was founded by Sir Charles Marston in 1898, son of John Marston, founder of the Sunbeam Company. Villiers quickly specialised in magnetos and carburettors (PVBC pp59-60) (Wolverhampton Chronicle April 16 1999 p5). **Wearwell** were producers of bicycles in Colliery Road by the later C19. They produced motor cycles from 1901 to 1939. The company traded under various names over the years including, Wearwell Motor Carriage Co, Wearwell Cycle Co, with works in Horsley Field, and Wolfruna Engineering Co, the factory then being in Great Brick Kiln Street (PVBC pp60-62). **Juckes** motor cycles, produced by Efficient Engineering and Motor Co owned by TC Juckes, were first made in 1902 from their East End Works, Bilston Road. Production ceased in 1925 (PVBC pp30-31). The **Olympic** motor cycle was made by Frank Parkyn for a short while from 1903 at works in Granville Street. Production was re-

sumed after WW1 but ceased in 1923 (PVBC p31). The **Diamond** cycle was made by DH & S (later DF & M) Engineering from Sedgley Street in the early 1900s. After WW1 production was re-commenced in Vane Street. The company moved to St James Square after 1928, and ceased production in c1931 (PVBC p22). The **Omega** motor bicycle, designed by S Dorsett and BS Roberts, appeared in 1909. It was designed to appeal to the pedal cyclist who just wanted a little extra power. The works are thought to have been in St James Square, Wolverhampton. The Wolverhampton Omega had no connection with the Omega made in Coventry by WJ Green (PVBC p33). **Briton** Motor Company was formed in Wolverhampton in 1909, with Edward Lisle Jnr, in charge. The Briton was conceived as a good quality car selling at a comparatively low price. At first, production was at the Star Co works in Frederick Street, moving to a new factory in Lower Walsall Street in 1913. The company was taken over by Charles Aaron Weight of Sebco. Car production ceased in 1929 when the company became Tractor Spares (PVBC p14). In 1998 a plaque to commemorate Briton Motors was erected in Lower Walsall Street (Commemorative Plaques by the Wolverhampton Civic Society). The **Sedan** commercial van was produced from premises in Lichfield Street in 1909 (PVBC p38). The **Orbit** motor cycle, founded by Mr Dorsett, occupied the old Diamond factory in Sedgley Street. Production ceased in 1924 (PVBC p34). **Clyno** moved from Thrapston, Leics to Pelham Street in 1913 making motor cycles. The company ceased making cars in 1923, and ceased production in 1929 (PVBC pp16-19). In 1997 a plaque to commemorate Clyno was erected in Pelham Street (Commemorative Plaques by the Wolverhampton Civic Society). **Guy** Motors was set up by Sydney Guy (1884-1972) who left Sunbeam in 1914. Guy Motors was taken over by Jaguar in 1961, and ceased operation in 1974 (BCM July 1974 pp36-39ps); the Guy factory was closed in 1982. Their factory in Park Lane, Fallings Park, was demolished in 1984 (PVBC pp23-26) (Wolverhampton Chronicle April 9 1999 p20). In 1997 a plaque to commemorate Guy Motors was erected in Park Lane, Fallings Park (Commemorative Plaques by the Wolverhampton Civic Society). The Hill brothers were founders of **HB** motor cycles produced from premises in Walsall Street between 1919 and 1923 (PVBC p29). Howard R Davies, founder of **HRD** motor cycles, began making his own motor cars in 1924 having worked for AJS Motors. He was bought out in 1928 (PVBC p27). (VCH vol 2 p151) (Story of Japan, Tinplate Working, Bicycle and galvanizing Trades in Wolverhampton and District. WH Jones. 1900 pp152-153) (BCM April 1971 pp5-9. Oct 1971 pp12-13. July 1978 pp18-19. Oct 1978 pp35-41. Jan 1979 pp6-10,50-52. April 1979 pp38-42. July 1979 pp10-14. Oct 1979 pp26-31. April 1980 pp40-45. Oct 1992 p26. winter 1996/7 pp31p,32) (The Book of Wolverhampton. Frank Mason. 1979 pp120,130p of Star motor bike,131p of Star car and Sunbeam car and Sunbeam bicycle) (WF pp36,45) (HOWU pp117-119) (TB July 1980 p5p of a Sunbeam. Aug 1980 p11. Nov 1993).

RAILWAYS. The GJR, opened in 1837, had a station at Wednesfield Heath, 1.25m to the ENE of Wolverhampton. The first station in Wolverhampton was a temporary one - on or near the site of the later Low Level station - for the use of the Shrewsbury & Birmingham Railway whose line connecting Wolverhampton to Shrewsbury opened on Nov 12 1849 (NSJFS 1962 p99) Great rivalry soon developed between the London North Western Railway (LNWR) and the Shrewsbury & Birmingham Railway over the new Birmingham, Wolverhampton & Stour Valley Railway or Stour Valley Railway which would link Wolverhampton to Birmingham New Street. The LNWR had a controlling interest in the construction of the line but the Shrewsbury & Birmingham were to have running rights over it. Anxious that the Shrewsbury & Birmingham would form an alliance with GWR and give GWR a service between Birmingham and Wolverhampton LNWR slowed construction on the line. In what has been described as the **'first battle of Wolverhampton'** a violent confrontation occurred between the two rival companies when the Shrewsbury & Birmingham tried, in June 1850, to circumvent the blockage by the use of the canal at Wolverhampton. The confrontation was only quelled by police and troops (BCM spring 1994 p24). For the new Stour Valley Line was built Wolverhampton's first permanent station in 1852 (or 1854 - Angus Dunphy). Situated at the end of Queen Street, it was at first known as 'Queen Street Station,' becoming 'High Level' station in 1885 (WP&P p5) (WAIW vol 2 p of in early 1900s). The Stour Valley Railway officially opened in Nov 1851. Shortly after its opening, on the morning of Nov 29 1851, in what has been described as one of the most spectacular events of English railway history and the **second battle of Wolverhampton**, a Shrewsbury & Birmingham train tried to push away a LNWR engine called 'Swift' at the High Level station. It had been deliberately placed with its breaks tightly screwed down by the LNWR to obstruct passage of the Shrewsbury & Birmingham train. A large crowd gathered, including the mayor clutching a copy of the Riot Act, which he never read (IAS pp134-135). Disreputable methods like this were continued by LNWR until May 1854 when the Court of Chancery declared in favour of the Shrewsbury & Birmingham Railway, and then, apparently worn out by the struggle, Shrewsbury & Birmingham sold out to the GWR (BCM spring 1994 p24). The Oxford, Worcester & Wolverhampton Railway, linking Wolverhampton to Dudley, opened in 1852-54 (VCH vol 2 p310). The temporary station at the low level was replaced by a permanent structure in 1853 (WP&P p43p) (WOLOP p119p), or 1856 (info Angus Dunphy). The Birmingham, Wolverhampton & Dudley Railway (later part of GWR) built a line, opened in 1854, which ran from the Low Level station to Birmingham via Bilston, Wednesbury and West Bromwich. There was a collision at the High Level station on or near July 8 1863. Travellers from Wolverhampton took LNWR lines via Willenhall, James Bridge and Pleck to reach Walsall before the more direct Wolverhampton & Walsall Railway, through Wednesfield, opened in 1872 (VCH vol 2 pp310,316); it closed to passengers in 1931 (NSJFS 1964 p79). The low level line still had broad gauge lines in 1869, 23 years after the Gauge Commission had reported against it (TTTD pp277, 291-293). Wolverhampton was connected to Brettell Lane with the Wolverhampton & Kingswinford Railway, opened in 1925, closed in 1932 (VCH vol 2 p325). In the 1960s the High Level station was served by trains of British Rail's London Midland, whilst the Low Level station was served by their Western Region (Staffs County Handbook. c1958 p157) (Wolverhampton Chronicle Nov 1 1996 p20). The High Level station was modernised in 1964 (WOLOP pp118-119p of the old High Level station). All that remains of the old High Level station, a Tuscan facade, is at the corner of Railway Street and Horseley Fields (IAS p138). The Low Level station closed in 1969; the last train passing through on July 27. In 1970 it became a parcels depot. This closed in 1972 (WOLOP p119). In 1985 there were plans to turn it into a transport museum. In 1996 there were plans to turn it into a leisure complex (Wolverhampton Chronicle Nov 1 1996 p20ps).

1870 to 1910. In 1888 Wolverhampton became a **county borough** (HOS p58) (WF p22) or on April 1 1889 (Staffs County Handbook. c1958 p157). The arms of Wolverhampton county borough, granted in 1898, are: Gules, a gold cross formally between a pillar, a woolpack, an open book, all argent, and a gold padlock. The crest is: On a wreath gold and gules, in front of a beacon sable with flames proper, two gold crossed keys, wards upwards. The motto is: 'Out of Darkness cometh light' (CH p332il) (Wolverhampton The News Sept 2 1999 p43pc). Wolverhampton corporation arms appear on the Broad Street Bridge which went to the Black Country Museum. The bridge was designed by Eastlake Thomas, borough engineer of Wolverhampton, and built in 1879. It is an 'oblique' or 'skew' bridge, the angle quoted on the drawings being just over 61 degrees (BCM April 1978 front cover). There was a **cholera outbreak** in 1872 (MR p387). The **Staffordshire Building Society** had its origins in the South Staffordshire Permanent Building Society, which opened an office at No. 5 Princess Street, Wolverhampton, on Feb 17 1902. The person believed to have suggested the formation of the society was Francis H Hinde, of the printing firm Alfred Hinde Ltd; Francis Hinde was the first vice-chairman of the society. The word 'Permanent' was dropped in 1951. In 1959 the society merged with West Midlands Permanent Building Society and the Sedgley Building Society. In 1969 it was suggested that the name of the society should be changed to 'Mercian' but the suggestion was not taken up. In 1975 the society merged with the Stafford and County Permanent Building Society, and 'South' in the title of the society was dropped. (The First £100 Million: A History of the Staffordshire Building Society. 1977. ppv note, 44). The **Grand Theatre**, Lichfield Street, was built in 1893-1894 (BOE p318). The theatre closed in 1979, reopened in 1983 and was restored in the late 1990s (Nostalgic Wolverhampton. 1999) (St Peter's Trail. Wolverhampton Council and Wolverhampton Civic Society). **Wolverhampton Art Gallery** in Lichfield Street, by St Peter's Close, was opened in 1884 by Lord Wrottesley using a gold key made by the Chubb Company (St Peter's Trail. Wolverhampton Council and Wolverhampton Civic Society), or it was opened in 1889 (WF p22); in 1998 it won best museum of Fine Art in the Museum of the Year awards. **Wolverhampton Art and Industrial Exhibition** was held in West Park (see) in 1902, to celebrate the coronation of Edward VII (TB April 1985 p29). **Cultural societies**. The Naturalist and Archaeological Department of Wolverhampton Free Library was inaugurated on May 6 1876. A new society with the title Wolverhampton Naturalist and Archaeological Society was formed by Arthur Webb in 1895 with Lt Col Thorneycroft as president. This became the Wolverhampton Archaeological Society in 1911. The society lapsed in WW1, reformed in 1920, and was renamed the South Staffordshire Archaeological Society on April 6 1938. This society still (1998) continues and publishes SSAHST (SSAHST 1976-77 pp91-92). A separate society, the South Staffordshire Naturalist's Society, founded in 1894, is Wol-

verhampton-based (info JAW Downing). The Wolverhampton Literary and Scientific Society, known locally as 'The Lit,' formed in 1880 and still (2000) continues (info HR Rhodes). **Wolverhampton Wanderers Football Club**. The club was founded as Goldthorn Football Club out of pupils at Blakenhall St Luke's. The first general meeting of the club was on Nov 10 1876 and the first competitive match took place on Jan 13 1877. Between 1877 and 1879 the club played on the Windmill 'field' off Goldthorn Hill. In summer 1879 it amalgamated with Blakenhall Wanderers Cricket Club becoming Wolverhampton Wanderers and moved to John Harper's field, situated in Lower Villiers Street, opposite Stoud's Nipon works. The club moved to Dudley Road in 1881 and in 1889 it moved to its present ground, the grounds of Molineux House (The Wolves. Tony Matthews with Les Smith 1989 p7) (The Story of Wolverhampton Wanderers. Tony Matthews with Les Smith 1994 p7) (PONP pp115-118). The club was one of the 12 original members of the Football League (TTTD p293) and won the English Cup (FA Cup) in 1908 beating Newcastle United by 3 goals to 1 (WPOPP vol 1 p32). By 1969 the greatest total of full international caps in Association Football was 105 by William (Billy) Ambrose Wright (b1924) of Wolverhampton Wanderers who had 38 international championship appearances (1946-1959) and 67 foreign international and world cup matches (1946-1959). He was captain in 85 matches. Wright also had four caps for 'Victory' internationals in 1946 (GBR 1965 p276. 1969 p311). The club reached the final of the 1939 FA Cup, but lost to Portsmouth 4-1 (WOLOP p88p). The Club, known locally as the Wolves, won the war league in 1942 after playing two legs against Sutherland 6-3. Wanderers became the first team to have been champions of all four English league divisions in 1988 when they were top of the fourth division (Wolverhampton the 1930s and 1940s. Elizabeth Rees. 1988. pl 52) (WF p61). **Persons and visitors**. In 1877 **James Beattie** founded Beattie's department store, when he opened in a little shop in Victoria Street. It was at first known as the Victoria Drapery Supply Stores (TEBC2 p108). The famous opera singer **Maggie Teyte** was born in Dunstall House (see) in Wolverhampton in 1888. The world record for billiard table jumping was set by **Joseph Darby**, born at Windmill End (see) in 1861, at Wolverhampton on Feb 5 1892, when he cleared a full-sized 12 feet billiard table lengthwise, taking off from a four inch high solid wooden block (TB June/ July 1972 p5) (GBR 1980 p218) (MMBCC pp38p-45). **Dora Powell**, author, who lived in Wolverhampton, was the Dorabella of Edward Elgar's 'Variations on an original theme (Enigma)' 1899 (Edward Elgar; memories of a variation. Dora Powell. 1937. 1979). As a child in 1902 **Charlie Chaplin**, film actor and director, appeared at the Grand Theatre in a Sherlock Holmes play (The Book of Wolverhampton. Frank Mason. 1979 p121). **Henry Irving** played at the same theatre in 'The Bells' in 1903. For another visit to Wolverhampton by Irving in 1905 see Star and Garter Inn (WF p49). **John Hanson**, and the famous actress **Marlene Dietrich** have also played at the Grand Theatre. On Nov 23 1918 the Prime Minister, **David Lloyd George**, received the freedom of the borough at the theatre. In his speech he made his famous quote 'What is our task? To Make Britain a fit country for heroes to live in' (The Times Nov 25 1918) (WF p51). The oldest 'father' of the House of Commons by 1995 was the Rt Hon **Charles Pelham Villiers** (Wolverhampton South) when he died on Jan 16 1898 aged 96 years 13 days (GBR 1995 p186). The **Chinese Ambassador** visited Wolverhampton in 1900 (Wolverhampton Chronicle Feb 12 1999 p20p). **John Masefield** OM (1878-1967), Poet Laureate, stayed at No. 141 Tettenhall Road in 1902, whilst commissioned to organise an exhibition at Wolverhampton Art Gallery (plaque erected on house by Wolverhampton Civic Society in 1985). **Jane Doley**, a middle-aged woman who lived separately from her husband in a Stafford Street lodging house, was murdered on Dec 22 1902 and her body found in the Victoria Canal Basin. Her murderer was never discovered. It has been suggested she was a prostitute (TB Jan 1986 p5). **Harry Lauder** appeared at the Hippodrome Theatre on Oct 29 1906 (WF p49).

1910 to 1950. Star Aeroplane Company, an offshoot of Star Engineering Company in Steward Street, started making **aeroplanes** from 1910 (EAS p16). The Wolverhampton Aviation Meeting occurred in June 1910 at Dunstall Park (WPOPP vol 1 pp118p,119). In **WW1** 1916 Zeppelins appeared over the town (WF p25). In 1935 Wolverhampton was the only British town to participate in the Brussels International Exhibition (WF p26). Wolverhampton's **municipal airport** opened at Pendeford (see) in 1938. The **University of Wolverhampton** has its origins in the Wolverhampton and Staffordshire Technical College which opened in 1933 on and near the site of the former Deanery (see) in central Wolverhampton. In 1948 the college took over the National Foundry College. In 1952 it became the Wolverhampton and Staffordshire College of Technology. In 1956 or 1957 the college was given an electric digital computer from the Atomic Energy Research Establishment (AERE) at Harwell. It was built there in 1949-50 and was known as the WITCH, standing for the Wolverhampton Instrument for Teaching Computing at Harwell. In 1973 the computer was transferred to the Museum of Science and Industry, Birmingham, in full operational condition. By 1978 it was considered the oldest operative computer in Britain and probably in the world. It had 827 'Dekatron' cathode tubes (Staffs County Handbook. c1958 p157) (GBR 1973 p95. 1977 p156p. 1978 p153) (University of Wolverhampton Web Page. 1998). By 1969 the college had become Wolverhampton Polytechnic. That year it merged with the local College of Art. In 1987 the polytechnic merged with the Dudley College of Education, the Wolverhampton Teachers' College of Day Students and Wolverhampton Technical Teachers' College; in 1989 it merged with the West Midlands College of Higher Education. In 1992 the polytechnic became the University of Wolverhampton. In 1996 Wolverhampton Science Park (see), opened, partly funded by the university (University of Wolverhampton Web Page. 1998). The longest Rugby 'try' ever executed was that over 166.5 miles from Wolverhampton Polytechnic to Cardiff Arms Park, Wales, by 15 players from Wolverhampton Polytechnic RFC in 23 hours 29 minutes on March 9-10 1973 (GBR 1974 p277). **Alumni**: Trevor Beattie (early 1980s), creative director in advertising and marketing; Wilf O' Reilly (1995), Olympic speed skater; Vernett Bennett, pop singer with 'Eternal'; Densign White, Olympic judo bronze medalist (info University of Wolverhampton). **Traffic records**. The first experimental traffic lights in Great Britain were set up for a one-day trial at Five Ways (HOWU p137) or in Princes Square on Nov 5 1927 (WF p25) (WOLOP p121p) (BCP p112p) or Feb 11 1928 (GBR 1995 p120). They were permanently installed there in Oct 1928 (plaque on building on corner of Princes Square and Princess Street) (WF p25). The first permanent traffic lights in Britain were set up in Leeds in March 1928 (GBR 1995 p120). During the 1930s Wolverhampton had the biggest trolleybus system in the country (The Black Country. Edward Chitham. 1972 p167). A **captured Messerschmitt** was displayed outside the Molyneux House on Oct 21 1940 (WF p51). An **earthquake** was felt in the Wolverhampton at 4.58am on Aug 15 1926 (WAIW vol 3), and or in 1927 (WF p25). **Persons and visitors**. A memorial bust of Able Seaman **Douglas Morris Harris** RNVR VC of Penn Fields still (1999) stands in St Peter's Garden's, Wolverhampton. It is sculpted by RJ Emerson. The inscription on the plaque on the plinth reads: 'The heroic wireless operator who continued to record messages in the log of the shell-torn Drifter 'Floadi' until killed by enemy gunfire. Adriatic Sea May 15 1917.' He died aged 19 (BCM June 1998 pp36-37p. March 1998 p8p). Miss **Margaret Gibson**, eccentric, who sang in the streets of Wolverhampton at the top of her voice during the 1920s, was known as 'Singing Margaret' (MMBCC pp74p-75); her ghost haunts the market area in Salop Street (Wolverhampton Chronicle May 22 1998 p12). The Duke of York (**George VI**) visited Wolverhampton in 1922 and the Prince of Wales (**Edward VIII**) visited the town in 1923 (WF p25). On Jan 17 (MMBC pp158-171) or on Jan 18 (TB July 1991 p5) 1925 PC **Albert Willitts**, aged 25, was shot dead at Bilston Road by Edward Patrick (Jock) Heggerty, aged 17, William Crossley, aged 19, and George James Dixon, aged 14. All had escaped from a remand home at Leyton Green, Harpenden, Herts. Willitts is buried in Merridale cemetery (MM pp43-48) (MMBC pp158-171) (TB July 1991 p5). **George Arthur Rowley**, footballer, born Wolverhampton in 1926, had scored the most goals in League matches by 1974, scoring 434 for West Bromwich Albion, Fulham, Leicester City and Shrewsbury Town between 1946 and 1965. He had also scored 32 goals in the FA Cup and 1 for England 'B' (GBR 1974 p269). The **Queen of Spain** visited the church of SS Mary and John, Snow Hill, in 1927 (WF p25). In 1928 Sergeant-Major **John Stratford** a veteran of the Indian Mutiny was saluted by the 14th/ 20th Hussars outside his house in Newhampton Road. Sergeant-Major Stratford died on Jan 16 1932 aged 102 (Wolverhampton the 1930s and 1940s. Elizabeth Rees. 1988. pls 6,7). By 1980 the oldest mother in Great Britain reliably recorded was Mrs **Winifred Wilson** (nee Stanley) of Eccles, Lancs, born Wolverhampton on Nov 11 1881 or 1882, died in 1974, who gave birth to her tenth child, a daughter, Shirley, on Nov 14 1936 aged 54 or 55 and 3 days (GBR 1980 p16). **Rachel Heyhoe Flint**, cricketer and broadcaster, was born in Wolverhampton in 1939, and attended Wolverhampton Girls' High School (BCM April 1991 pp10-14). The **Duke of Edinburgh** visited Wolverhampton in Dec 1948 as part of the borough centenary celebrations (Wolverhampton the 1930s and 1940s. Elizabeth Rees. 1988. pl 57). **Winston Churchill** attended a mass election rally at Molineux Stadium in 1949 (Wolverhampton Chronicle. March 17 2000 p14p. March 31 2000 p14).

IMMIGRATION IN WOLVERHAMPTON. Immigrants have settled in Wolverhampton for centuries. In the Middle Ages some Dutch, Welsh, French, and Germans settled in Wolverhampton; Irish immigrants began to appear at the end of the C18; there were immigrants from Shrops in the mid C19; after WW2 European displaced persons settled in Wolverhampton; Jamaicans and Afro-Caribbeans settled in the Waterloo Road area in the early 1950s; Sikhs and Ugandans settled in the town in the 1960s; Chileans in 1976 (HOWU pp126-134). In July 1967 Tarsem Singh Sandhu returned to work with Wolverhampton Transport, after a three-week illness, with a beard and turban. Beards and non-regulation headwear were forbidden by Wolverhampton Transport Department and Mr Sandhu was barred from work. For support he turned to the IWA, the Indian Worker's Association (formed by Mohan Singh Basra in Wolverhampton in 1956). In Feb 1968 a march against the turban ban of some 6,000 Sikhs from across the country took place from the gurdwara on the Cannock Road to Wolverhampton Town Hall, but the ban was not lifted. In his 'Rivers of Blood Speech' in Birmingham on April 20 1968 Enoch Powell, Conservative MP for Wolverhampton SW constituency at the time, mentioned the ban. Subsequently, there were further protests in Wolverhampton both in support of and against Powell; Wolverhampton became of national interest for race relations thereafter and written about in the national press in the 1960s. In April 1969, after the intervention of a government junior minister, and the take-over of the Transport Department by the regional Passenger Transport Executive, the turban ban was lifted. The Shromani Akali Dal, a national body created after this dispute, safeguards Sikh interests (The Observer July 1968) (BBC documentary 'Strangers in a Town') (HOWU pp132-134).

1950 to PRESENT. In 1965 Wolverhampton became one of the four large county boroughs of the Black Country area (SL p265). Wolverhampton's **first high-rise flats** were in Dale Street, built after 1955. The flats still (1996) stand (WOLOP p20p). A site adjacent to the new ring road in the School Street area was a slum area known as Brickiln Croft. It was cleared away in April 1957. New development in the area was to contain both offices and shops and an **open-air market**, as well as an underground carpark, which would also serve as an air-raid shelter in the event of a Third World War. Herbert (Lord) Morrison noted that the development was the first integrated new market in the country, when he officially opened it on June 22 1960 (HOWU p155). The name Brickiln in this area appears on Isaac Taylor's map of Wolverhampton (1750). The **Mander Centre**, described by Palliser in 1975 as 'one of the best post-war shopping centres,' opened on March 6 1968, was hit by fire on Christmas eve 1970 (SL pl 44) (HOWU p158). The late C20 building called **Wolverhampton Civic Centre** is derisively known locally as 'the Kremlin.' In the evening of July 10 1981 **rioting** occurred in Wolverhampton, similar to the riot at Handsworth (see); 30 shops were damaged in the Mander Centre, in Tettenhall Road, and in Dunstall; 23 were arrested (Birmingham Post July 11 1981). **Crime busting and ecological measures**. The installation of CCTV in Wolverhampton town centre in 1988, at that time unique in a town centre, helped rid the streets of gang warfare (HOWU p166). In July 1999 it was announced that Wolverhampton police were to pilot the first Dealership Watch in the country to prevent car crime and fraud (E&S July 26 1999 p5). As the culmination of a 'Let's get leadless' campaign organised by the E&S 1,115 cars were converted to lead-free petrol on a single site in Wolverhampton on April 30 1989 (GBR 1990 p113). **Carpark roof fall**. Part of the roof of the National Car Park carpark in Pipers Row collapsed in March 1997 owing to age. Nobody was using it at the time and nobody was injured (Central News July 24 1998). The greatest concentration of people in Britain in 1999 with the **surname Turner** is in Wolverhampton (Daily Mail July 17 1999 p35). **Persons and visitors** (and a dog). On June 14 1958 **Brian Stanford Hewson** beat the 880 yard running record at Wolverhampton with one minute 47.8 seconds (GBR 1966 p251). On May 28 1960 **Peter Frank Radford** broke the United Kingdom men's running record at Wolverhampton, running 100 yards in 9.4 seconds, 220 yards (turn) in 20.5 seconds, and 200 metres in 20.5 seconds (broken in 1972) (GBR 1970 p235. 1974 p330). On June 18 1960 Peter Frank Radford beat the 100 metres running record at Wolverhampton with 10.3 seconds (GBR 1966 p251). **Elizabeth II** visited the town on May 24 1962 (WF p52) (WHTOP p36) and on her Jubilee tour of the West Midlands in 1977 (WMAG Sept 1977 front cover). **The Beatles** played a concert at the Gaumont, Wolverhampton, in 1963 (Wolverhampton Chronicle. Jan 28 2000 p18). The British record for cycling (professional unpaced standing start) for 20 km was set in 27 minutes 24.4 seconds by **Phil Bayton** at Wolverhampton on June 10 1975 (GBR 1980 p265). By 1983 the oldest member of the House of Commons was **Robert Edwards** MP (Labour) for Wolverhampton South East (b Jan 16 1905) (GBR 1983 p212). On Feb 11 1984 **Edward Hodson** of Wolverhampton landed a 3,956,748 to 1 horse racing bet for a 55p stake. But the bookmaker had a £3000 payout limit (GBR 1993 p253). The United Kingdom record for the male Hammer field event was set by **Martin Girvan** (b1960) who achieved a distance of 254 feet five inches at Wolverhampton on May 12 1984 (GBR 1995 p227). **Josef Stawinoga**, a Pole born in 1921 or 1922, has lived as a vagrant in Wolverhampton since the late 1960s. Since the late 1970s the authorities have allowed him to live in a tent on the central reservation of the ring road near St John's church. He was still living there in early 2000. He is affectionately known as 'Fred' by Wolverhamptonians and revered as a 'Holy Man' by the local Asian community (Telegraph Magazine Feb 22 1997 pp50-52 pcs) (Wolverhampton Chronicle June 26 1998 p10). The record for the largest surviving dog litter was set by **'Trudi'** an Irish Setter owned by Alan Jenkins of Wolverhampton, when she gave birth to 17 puppies in Feb 1977 (GBR 1978 p32).

WOLVERHAMPTON AND LITERATURE. Little Nell and her grandfather in Dickens' 'Old Curiosity Shop' are believed to have passed through the town (BBC Radio 4 'Old Curiosity Shop' Dec 31 1996). Wolverhampton appears as Silverhampton in Ellen Thorneycroft Fowler's novel 'The Farringdons' (1900/1) (BCM July 1978 pp44-46) (PPTP p34) (Wolverhampton Chronicle Sept 19 1997 p12), and as Wolverbury in Francis Brett Young's novels (BCM April 1980 pp10-15). George Griffith (b Bewdley), working between the 1830s and 1880s, lived in Wolverhampton. He was the author of 'The Two Houses, A Staffordshire Tragedy (founded on facts)' (1866), and 'Charles the Second: an Historical Drama in Five Acts' (1867). Rev Henry Bull, poet, hymn writer and sketch writer, was born on June 11 1859. He wrote many Black Country sketches in dialect, such as 'That's Him to a T' (1890). He also contributed dialect poems to Wolverhampton newspapers (PSS p463) (VFC p21). Herman H Chiltern, author of the novels 'The Mind of the Mark' (1924) and 'The Main Chance,' lived in Wolverhampton (VFC p26). Lawrence Meynell (pseudonyms Robert Elton and Geoffrey Ludlow) (1899-1989), novelist, was born in Wolverhampton. Most of his work belongs to the mystery genre (VFC p93). For Marjorie Vernon, novelist born in Wolverhampton, see Warley Woods. Margery Lawrence (d1969), poet, short story writer and novelist, was born at Wolverhampton. Her novels include 'Red Heels,' and 'Nights of the Round Table.' Her collections of short stories include 'Snapdragon' and 'Bohemian Glass' (which was banned) (PSS pp455-456) (VFC p83). Winifred Mantle (c1911-1983) writer of children's novels and romances attended Wolverhampton Girl's High School and lived in Wolverhampton. She has appeared under the pseudonyms Francis Long, Jane Langford and Anne Fellows (VFC p90). Wolverhampton is thought to be the backdrop for some of the scenes in the novels of Roger Ormerod of Tettenhall Wood (see), and is the setting for three of the novels of Keith Aldritt (b1930s), 'The Good Pit Man' (1976), 'The Lover Next Door' (1977), 'Elgar on the Journey to Hanley' (1979). The late C20 novelist, actress and comedian, Meera Syal, was born in Wolverhampton and attended Queen Mary's High School, Walsall; her first novel 'Anita and Me' is semi-autobiographical; her 'Life isn't all ha ha hee hee' appeared in Oct 1999. See also under Chapel Ash and Penn Fields. For Emillie Hammond, composer of the 'The Women's Institute Song,' see Wednesbury. For rhymes about Wolverhampton see Sedgley and Tettenhall.

CUSTOMS AND TRADITIONS. It was the custom on Christmas Eve at Wolverhampton to place mistletoe on the altar of Wolverhampton Collegiate Church to be blessed by the priests, after which it was distributed by them among the congregation (BCC vol 3 p224) (SCSF p49). Lawley records the Easter Monday custom of 'clipping the church' practised in the early C19 and up to the early C19, at both St Peter and St John churches. At Walsall the same custom involved school children in the forenoon dancing or walking round the church. The symbolism of this activity was thought to represent the watch of soldiers set round the tomb of Christ by the Roman authorities. The custom was always brought to an end by loud 'Huzzahs' from the children (SCSF p14) (FOS p91). The special dish to celebrate mid-Lent 'Mothering Sunday' in Wolverhampton parish in the C19 was a roast veal and custard, eaten at mid-day. This occurred on the fourth Sunday in Lent and the same food was still being eaten in the town in the 1930s (FOS p86). In the 1930s there was a tradition among choirboys of St Peter's church that the lion statue at the foot of the pulpit yawns if the preacher goes on over half an hour (KES p233).

SUPERNATURAL. It was said of **Wolverhampton** in 1998 that it was the fifth most haunted place in England (Wolverhampton Chronicle Sept 11 1998 p5); a black phantom dog of an immense size is said to haunt the town (FSLBWM p44). The **town centre** is said to be haunted by past battalions of the South Staffs Regiment marching (Wolverhampton Chronicle May 22 1998 p12), and a gentleman in a bowler hat who asks passers-by the time. This ghost is reputedly that of Kent Reeks, whose body was found prior to 1914 in a ditch on Millfields Road, Bilston. He was last seen alive in Liverpool and no one knows how his body came to lie in Millfields Road (Wolverhampton

Chronicle May 22 1998 p12). The market area in **Salop Street** has a number of ghosts, including 'Singing Margaret' (see Margaret Gibson above). Along **Steelhouse Lane** there have been sightings of horses that inexplicably appear galloping before suddenly disappearing into thin air (GPCE p61). The Central Library, on the corner of **Garrick Street** and Bilston Street, is said to have a ghost that the staff sense whenever they alter things: Books have inexplicably fallen off shelves (GPCE pp62-63). The Green Room in Wulfruna Hall in the Civic Hall, in **Mitre Fold**, which was built on the site of the old Wolverhampton morgue, is said to be haunted. A ghostly figure has also been seen on stage at both the Wulfruna and the Main Civic Halls (GPCE p62). The BBC Radio Studios, **Queen Street**, are said to be haunted (GPCE p62). The Grand Theatre, **Lichfield Street**, is said to be haunted by the ghost of Mr Purdey (or Purdy), a former manager (GPCE p63) (GLS pp110-111); and by a lady in grey (GPCE p63); and by a mysterious waft of lavender perfume of unexplained origin, which may be from the wife of possibly a mayor who had a fatal accident in the theatre when she fell from the stage into the orchestra pit (GLS pp110-111). Peppers wine bar, in a former bank in Lichfield Street, is reputedly haunted by a former resident and his wife (Wolverhampton Chronicle May 22 1998 p12). Spirits from the former graveyard by St George's church, **Bilston Road**, now Sainsbury supermarket, are said to be responsible for the technical problems in Sainsbury supermarket (Wolverhampton Chronicle May 22 1998 p12). The Mander Centre in **Dudley Street** is haunted by the ghost of a little boy called Pipkin who has been frequently seen behind the gates after the centre has closed at night (Wolverhampton Chronicle May 22 1998 p12). The Tap House public house, formerly the Exchange Vaults, in **Exchange Street**, has several ghosts (Wolverhampton Chronicle May 22 1998 p12. Sept 11 1998 p5).

Wolverhampton Collegiate Church There is a tradition King Wulfhere founded the abbey of St Mary in Wolverhampton in 659, although there is no proof (HOWU p3). The probable founding of the collegiate church at Wolverhampton was in 966 (WF p7), or in 994 (VCH vol 3 p321 note), or, according to Dugdale and others, in 996 (W p82) (SHC 1916 pp43,114): The charter by which Lady Wulfrun endowed a minister at Wolverhampton, discovered in 1520, puts the foundation or refoundation date at 994; but the charter may be a forgery (VCH vol 3 p321 note) (SL p52). The first charter of the college is one of Edward the Confessor and probably dates between 1053-57. In it he pledges his troth to his priests at Hampton and wills that their monastery be free, as their possessions (HOWM p12). William I granted the church to Sampson, his chaplain, and made him bishop of Worcester in 1067 (WF p7). (WJO March 1905 pp79-80). The Church of Worcester lost the church of Wolverhampton with the succession of Henry II in 1154 (HOWM p22). On May 31 1205 King John granted a charter to the church which effectively suppressed the deanery and made the church a monastery granting to it the royal manors of Stowheath and Tettenhall but in 1207 the king took back his manors and cancelled the grant (HOWM p27). In 1261 Henry III confirmed the church of Wolverhampton as an exempt jurisdiction (HOWM p29). The college shared the dean of St George's, Windsor, from 1457 (VCH vol 3 pp321-331). The deanery was annexed to Windsor in 1465 (WF p8), and united with Windsor in Feb 1480 in the interest of securing more income for the then dean of Windsor, a favourite of Edward IV (HOWM p41). The college was dissolved in 1547 (VCH vol 3 pp321-331) or in 1550 (NSJFS 1979 p9). At the Reformation there was a 'hermitage chapel' in the collegiate church (SHC 1915 p322) (VCH vol 3 p137). After being dissolved the college was granted to John, Duke of Northumberland. It was restored by Mary I in 1553. This restoration was confirmed by a royal charter in 1564. The college was again dissolved in c1645 and restored in 1660 (VCH vol 3 pp321-331). The deanery remained annexed to Windsor until 1846 when it was abolished (W p82) (AOW pp22-26) (SOSH p307). Wolverhampton parish was a peculiar jurisdiction of the college until peculiar jurisdictions were abolished in 1846 (VCH vol 3 p93). The college was dissolved in 1848 (VCH vol 3 pp321-331). It has also appeared as St Peter's Collegiate Church. For the seals of the college see WA vol 1 No. 7 pp197-203. An old house in old Lichfield Street belonged to a religious house connected with the collegiate church (OHW pl 2).

Wolvern Meadows Meadows below Wulfrun's Well, Dunstall, Wolverhampton (SHOS vol 2 p175).

Wombourne Ancient parish, former manor, and township. The now very large village of Wombourne in Wom Brook valley is 19.25m SSW of Stafford and has merged with the out-lying former hamlets of Blakeley, Ounsdale and The Bratch, on account of C20 housing and industrial expansion.

EARLY. **Post-Mesolithic** flint artifacts have been found at Smallbrook Farm, NE of of Wombourne village, and at Greensforge (see). A stone axe has found at Greenhill Nurseries (see) (VCH vol 20 p197). An **Early Bronze Age** flint arrowhead was found by two-year-old Cherry Griffiths at the Blakeley end of Giggetty Lane Lane in 1951 (WMAG Feb 1972 p31p) (VCH vol 20 p197). **Roman** armoury has been found at Wombourne (GNHS p70). Dr Wilkes noted three burial mounds on Wombourne Common (see) and another known as Soldier's Hill (see) (SHOS vol 1 General Intro p38) (VCH vol 20 p197). 900 to PRESENT. Wombourne can be spelt Wombourn or Wombourne (SPN p146). Wombourne with an 'e' is becoming the accepted form (VCH vol 20 p197 note). The **name** Wombourne is generally thought to be from the Wom Brook (see). However, Dr Wilkes thought it from 'Won' and 'Bourne' from a victory over the Danes at Wombourne (SHOS vol 2 p211). (SVS p329). There was a **church** at Wombourne by 1086. The present parish church, St Benedict Biscop (believed to be a unique dedication in England - BOE p326), on the N side of Church Road, has a C14 tower (VCH vol 20 p220). The **wake** is said to have been originally held in connection with the feast of St Benedict Biscop (Jan 12), to whom the parish church is dedicated. By 1834 the wake was celebrated on the last Sunday in October (W p210) (VCH vol 20 p201). Wombourne parish included Trysull for ecclesiastical purposes until 1888, but in civil matters the two were separate (VCH vol 20 p215). The **manor** of Wamburne appears in DB. The site of the manor house has never been located (VCH vol 20 p204). **Stocks** stood outside the entrance to the churchyard and were still there in 1837 (VCH vol 20 p216). A **pound** was built in the garden of the poorhouse in Rookery Road, Wombourne in 1827 (VCH vol 20 p216). For the **rick-burning case** in Wombourne parish in 1831 see under Swindon. **Trees.** In the later C17 Plot noted by the brook at Wombourne a yew which grew on top of an ash tree (NHS p213). An ancient elm stood opposite the lychgate of St Benedict's church; by 1840 the top had been blown down (GNHSS p31). The tree known as Ye Old Tree was a village landmark, and seems to have been standing in the early C20 (WMAG Feb 1972 p30p). In **WW2** German bombs fell on Wombourne in July 1941 (PPTP p26). By early Feb 2000 a 22 metre-high **telecommunications mast** for the company One2One had been erected on a prominence in Wombourne. By the order of South Staffs district council the mast was disguised with plastic trunk and foliage as a Scotch pine tree; still it was an affront to some and a petition was got up by the North Wombourn Tree Mast Protest Group to have it removed (BBC Midlands Today Feb 9 2000) (Daily Telegraph Feb 14 2000 p9). **Persons and visitors.** **John Sugar,** who was executed for refusing to take the Oath of Supremacy and beatified in Nov 1987, was born in Wombourne in the C16. He was an Anglican vicar of Cannock, but converted to Catholicism and was ordained a Catholic priest. He returned to Staffs in Oct 1601 (SCHJ No. 23 1988 pp1-8). In the later C17 **William Ketley** and **William Cox** lived to the age of 106 (NHS p324) (SHOS vol 2 p215). **Billy Bunn,** a rhymer from the Black Country, was a regular attender at Wombourne fairs. He gives his name to Billy Buns Lane on N side of Wombourne (TB July 1990 p16. Nov 1997 p11). The longest continuous sausage on record by 1995 was one of 21.12km made at the premises of **Keith Boxley** at Wombourne in 15 hours 33 minutes on June 18-19 1988 (GBR 1995 p214). INDUSTRY AND RAILWAYS. Ironmaking was in progress in the parish by the late C16 and continued until 1976. One of the occupations in the village by the early C17 was nailing, another by the late C18 was sand quarrying. A variety of modern industries established themselves in Wombourne in the 1930s and particularly after WW2 (VCH vol 20 pp213-215). A windmill may have stood on Windmill Bank near the centre of the village; Windmill Bank was so named by 1816, but no mill existed then (VCH vol 20 p213). Another windmill stood at SO 877933 between the present School Road and Withymere Lane in 1840 (VCH vol 20 p213) (Greenwood's map) (OS map 1831/34) (WBJ p47). Another windmill stood at Blakeley (see), and at Cockshoot Hill (see). The Wolverhampton & Kingswinford **Railway,** opened in 1925, had a station N of Bratch Road in Wombourne; the station became a visitor centre and latterly a tea room. The line closed to passengers in 1932 and to goods in 1964, and is now (1999) a public footpath known as the Kingswinford Railway Walk (NSJFS 1964 p79) (VCH vol 20 p201) (info Michael Cockin).

Wombourne Common Former common land which has also appeared as Wombourne Heath. Dr Wilkes (d1760) noted three burial mounds on Wombourne Common and another known as Soldier's Hill (see) (SHOS vol 1 General Intro p38) (VCH vol 20 p197). Erdeswick (SVS p329) or Wilkes thought that the battle of Tettenhall had been fought in this area and that the slain from the battle were buried in them (VCH vol 20 p197). In the later C17 Plot thought the mounds were thrown over some eminent commanders and were in some way still evident (SVS p329). Langford thought the mounds may have had an association with the settlement at Abbot's Castle Hill and may contain high-ranking Romans slain in attempts to dislodge the ancient Britons from the settlement (S&W p365). Gunstone could find no mounds in the 1960s (NSJFS 1965 p59).

Wom Brook Rises on Penn Common and joins Smestow Brook at Smestow. Runs through Wodehouse and Wombourne. The stretch running through Wodehouse was anciently known as Lude or Lyde Brook, and that through Wombourne was formerly known as Bate Brook. Gives its name to Wombourne. It was mentioned as Wombourne Brook in 1322 (SPNO p22) (VCH vol 20 p197). Between Wombourne and Smestow the brook has powered at least four mills, viz: Wodehouse Mill, Mill Lane Mill (Wombourne), Wombourne Common Road Mill, and Heath Mill (TB April 1998 p5). The name means 'winding stream' or 'crooked stream' (NSJFS 1981 p3) (VCH vol 20 p197) (SPN p146) (SSE 1996 p19). Or 'wom' is perhaps Anglo-Saxon and Middle English 'wambe, wombe,' belly, womb, here used in the sense of 'hollow.' The terminal is from Anglo-Saxon 'burne,' a brook. So the 'brook in the hollow' (DUIGNAN). 'Hwoman' or 'huwannm' in Saxon means 'a corner or nook' (SR p5).

Womere Swampy pool N of Anson's Bank 1.25m SE of Brocton. This upland bog is a rare feature in Central England and it was originally thought to be bottomless (CCM). The pool was dry in May 1996, but the ground was not completely dry.

Wood, The Is Wood Farm 1m NNW Adbaston. At Wood Farm was found glass fragments suggesting here was a furnace (NSFCT 1933 p104).

Wood, The To the E of Grubber's Ash (Dower's map).

Woodbank Oakamoor. Built in 1833. It was occupied in 1834 by Joseph Ingleby, 'master' at the brassworks at Oakamoor. It was later purchased by the Bolton family (COPP2 p83il).

Wood Bank Tiny hamlet by the Staffs and Worcs Canal and the Penk 1.25m NE of Penkridge. In Penkridge parish.

Woodbank House Stood almost at the bottom of the wide access road westwards from the first bend of Sandyfields Road, Cotwall End (SDSSOP pp32-33ps). It was much extended by the industrialists, Ben Whitehouse, and a member of the Thompson family, and others. Demolished in the late 1950s (BCM Dec 1997 p43il).

Wood Brook Crosses under the Shropshire Union Canal at Norbury Junction, runs into Aqualate Mere.

Wood Brook In the Penkridge area. Here was common land (VCH vol 5 p127).

Woodcock Heath Heath and fragmented tiny hamlet overlooking Kingstone and Tad Brook 0.5m NW of Kingstone.

Woodcock Hurst House 0.75m NNE of Endon. Formerly in Endon township in Leek ancient parish. There was a house here by the later C17 (VCH vol 7 p177). The name is from a field name which in turn is derived from an animal name (APB p48).

Woodcock Well Well at the top of Church Street, Mow Cop, now filled in (WMC).

Wood Croft Small suburb of Leek, 0.5m SW of the St Edward's, on W side of the Newcastle road. There may have been settlement here by the early C13 (VCH vol 7 p85). Former grange of Dieulacres Abbey (VCH vol 3 p233). The late C19 house on the W side of the Newcastle road called Woodcroft had been demolished by the later 1930s when a private housing estate was built over it and its grounds (VCH vol 7 pp95 il of Woodcroft house, 97).

Woodcroft Grange Late C19 house in Leek, probably by the Newcastle road. By the later 1930s a private housing estate had been built over its grounds (VCH vol 7 p97). So called probably after the medieval grange of Dieulacres Abbey in the Wood Croft area.

Woodcross Residential district on ground rising to England's main watershed at Sedgley over 0.75m ENE of Sedgley. In Sedgley ancient parish. There was a small mining settlement here by 1600. Woodcross appears in 1614 as Woodcrosse (HC p24).

Woodcross Farm Stood on the N side of Woodcross Lane, Woodcross. Some of the farm, also at some time known as Head's Farm, may date back to the C17. It was still standing in 1958 (SDSSOP p29p).

Woodcross House Woodcross. Seat of Edward Jones the proprietor of the London & Victoria gun barrel works in Birmingham in 1901 (OS map Sheet 67.03).

Wood Eaton Tiny hamlet by a tributary of Church Eaton Brook 0.5m WNW of Church Eaton. Former township in Church Eaton ancient parish. Has appeared Wudeton (1199), Wodeyton (1284), and Wodde Eyton (1553), (SPNO pp140,142). The name means 'wood near a farmstead' (SPN p146).

Wood Eaton Castle The old house, known in the mid C19 and in 1891 (1891 OS map 6 inch) as Wood Eaton Manor, was demolished in 1937. Wood Eaton Castle may represent the site of Wood Eaton manor house (VCH vol 4 pp92,94). The house known as Home Farm, 1m NW of Church Eaton, stood on or near the site in 1972 (1972 OS map 1:25,000).

Wood Eaton Hall Brick hall 0.75m NW of Church Eaton. Designed by William Baker, in 1754-5 (BOE p104) (MR p99).

Woodeaves House 0.75m ENE of Barlaston old church. It can be traced in documents from the 1480s (BAH p14). Has also appeared as Woodseaves (W p411).

Woodedge Tiny hamlet on a steep slope leading up to the Needwood Forest plateau 1m WNW of Draycott-in-the-Clay. Formerly in Hanbury ancient parish.

Wood End The Main Street at Barton Gate end area of Barton-under-Needwood (UNT p36).

Woodend Hamlet 1m SSE of Hanbury. In Hanbury parish. The present name of the easternmost of the two Hanbury Woodends marked on the 1834 OS map. The W one is still called Hanbury Woodend. At Woodend at SK 176266 is a moated site (CAMS p64).

Woodend 1.75m W of Fradley. In Kings Bromley ancient parish. Includes Woodend Common Barn, Woodend Lock, Wood End Farm.

Wood End Hamlet overlooking a tributary of a head brook of the Tame in the foreign of Walsall, 2m E of Walsall. It was an inhabited area by 1317 and there was limestone quarrying here by the later Middle Ages (VCH vol 17 pp153,154). Wood End Farm on the Sutton Road (W p649) (DUIGNAN p67) formed the centre of an estate which from 1554 to 1894 was an endowment of Walsall grammar school. The present (1974) house dates from 1836. It replaces an earlier house, and this in turn replaces an earlier house of the C15 which apparently stood within a moat about 100 yards W of Sutton Road (VCH vol 1. vol 17 p179) (SSAHST 1982-3 p50).

Wood End Former hamlet now a suburb 0.75m N of Wednesfield. Formerly in Wednesfield township and chapelry in Wolverhampton ancient parish. Wood End, which may be the Woodrugginge occurring between 1290 to 1376, takes its name from the extensive wood of that period called Prestwood. The name occurs in its present form in Wednesfield PR in 1607 and there was a hamlet here by the mid C17 (WFW pp48,72,81,95). Children here played hide and seek in an unusual way in the early C20. The child 'on it' hides his face and counts in the customary way while others in the group hide, he then has to find and catch them in the usual way, but to help him the children hiding from time to time call out a special rhyme

Ile, ile, oller
me dog cor foller

(BCM Oct 1968 pp36-37).

Wood Farm House 0.75m NNW of Adbaston. Formerly in Croxton township in Eccleshall ancient parish. In this area lay the medieval deer park called Bishop's Park (AADB p2). The farm was occupied by the Sharrod family from c1820. The last of the Sharrods was Mrs Edith Ball. When her husband died in 1953 she moved into a caravan and continued to live near the grounds (AADB pp59-60). In the later C19 the Sharrods made a wonderful garden and grotto called 'The Dingle' adjacent to the stackyard at Wood Farm. It was situated in and around a gravel pit and contained a beautiful summer house decorated lavishly with sea shells. It was situated on a little island in the large pool, approached by a decorated footbridge. The garden also contained a tree house in a large tree and a room in a cave approached by an underground tunnel at the entrance to which there was a door comprised of a huge block of sandstone which was mounted in such a way that it swung open quite easily. There was another huge stone contrived as a gate across a path and mounted on a single pivot in the centre. This was so accurately balanced that it could be opened by the pressure of one finger. The Dingle had fallen into a state of decay by 1975 (AADB pp59-60). The rustic wooden tree house near Eccleshall by lanes leading to Shropshire noted by AE Dodd in SLM winter 1956 p22p may be a reference to the tree house here.

Wood Farm Nearly 0.5m Cotwall End. Is situated on the site of the ancient house of Moysi le Forrester, who was living in the C13. His rent was worth 'two pounds of two pounds of cumin;' this remained the rent to at least 1742; Wood Farm was once part of Himley Park (SDSSOP p23p).

Wood Farm House over 0.75m N of Onneley. A large granite glacier boulder, eight feet by seven feet 10 inches by three feet six inches and perhaps originally from Galloway, was said to be buried in a field on this farm (NSFCT 1926 p118).

Woodford House 1.5m WNW of Marchington. From which the family of Woodford took its name (SHOS vol 1 p86 note 3). In 1453 Woodford belonged to Ralph Woodford. In the C16 or C17 Walter Jeffreys held Woodford Farm (HOU p336).

Woodford Grange Former tithe free estate centred on Woodford Grange, a house, 0.5m SE of Trysull. The estate belonged to St James' Priory, Dudley, from the end of the C12 until the priory was dissolved in 1540. The priory had established a grange here by the later C13. After 1540 the estate passed

on through several secular owners until it passed by marriage to the Wrottesleys in 1576; they held it until 1929. In the mid C17 the house may have been a Wrottesley family dower house. The estate remained tithe free and sparsely populated and because of this was considered an extra parochial place. It remained so until it was created a civil parish in 1858. This was abolished in 1900 when it entered Trysull and Seisdon civil parish (W p211) (GLAUE p430) (VCH vol 20 p225). At SO 856936 there was possibly a medieval village at some time depopulated (SSAHST 1970 p36).

Woodford Hall Woodford, near Marchington. Seat of the Jeffreys who were sympathisers with the Young Pretender, a member of the family fled to the USA. The family member took with him a signet ring cut with the family crest. The ring passed down the generations to the present day (SLM March 1952 p21).

Wood Gate Hamlet to W of, and now merges into Draycott-in-the-Clay. Formerly in Hanbury parish.

Woodgate Hamlet 1m SE of Uttoxeter. In Uttoxeter parish.

Wood Green Former small village by the Tame now suburb of Wednesbury, 1m NE of Wednesbury. In Wednesbury ancient parish. A Roman coin of Carausius was found at Wood Green in c1835 when the railway was being cut (WAM p8) (NSJFS 1964 p42). A Richard atte Grene is mentioned in 1315 (HOWV pp108-109). The name is said to be from this area having been a green in Cannock Forest (WAM p32). The GJR opened in the Wood Green area on July 4 1837 (WAM p112). There was a station at Bescot Bridge (see) from 1881 to 1941 known as Wood Green (VCH vol 17 p168). The church, St Paul, Wood Road, was built in 1874 (HOWY p313). The ecclesiastical parish of Wednesbury St Paul or Wood Green was created in 1875 (GLAUE p428). For a remarkable bell ringing achievement at the church see IE pp99-100. By 1898 SSWWC had a pumping station at Wood Green (GHC p14p). The village hall has murals by Edward Payne and Robert Baker (1909-1992) born at Ladymoor, Bilston (BCM Jan 1993 pp41-45 ps). For a children's rhyme from Wood Green see FSBC p53.

Wood Green House House, probably at some time, occupied by members of the Elwell family at Wood Green. Became a part of Wednesbury Boys' High School. It was demolished in 1960 (IE p99) (WDOP p30). Has also appeared as Wood Green Lodge.

Wood Hall Wood Hall Farm is 1m WNW of Codsall. An estate centred on this property can be traced back to the C13 (SVB p58) or early C14 (VCH vol 20 p82). The old hall which stood in a moat at SJ 849044 had been demolished by 1835 by which time a brick house had been built to the N (SSAHST 1982-83 p39) (VCH vol 20 pp79,82) (CAMS p64). The hall was so named by the early C17 and the name is possibly from the Wood family who were living here in the C16 (VCH vol 20 p82). It was bought from the Ward family, owners since at least 1896, by the Gaskell family in the later 1920s (VCH vol 20 p82) (TCOP p113p).

Wood Hayes Former hamlet by a tributary of the Penk, now a suburb 1.25m NNW of Wednesfield. Formerly in Wednesfield township and chapelry in Wolverhampton ancient parish. The name was in use by 1750 (WFW p105).

Woodhead House 3m W of Wetley Rocks, formerly in Burslem township in Stoke-upon-Trent ancient parish. The old Woodhead farm here was part of Hulton Abbey property at its dissolution. The house, which existed in the 1950s, was built in 1865 on the site of an earlier house (VCH vol 8 pp250-251) (B p84). Has also appeared as Wood Head (OS map 1834) (Dower's map).

Woodhead Hall Built by WS Allen in 1873 almost upon the site of Woodhead Old Hall, near Cheadle (HOC pp154-155 il, 156), which William Allen was occupying in 1851 (W p24). The new hall was designed by William Sugden of Leek. Since 1937 it was used by the MOD, and was a wireless communications centre in WW2. By 1994 the property was owned by the Crown; it was for sale in 1995 (ACOPP p61p) (SLM Christmas 1995 p21p) (DoE II).

Woodhead Hill Rock In the vicinity of Knowlend and Royal Cottage, opposite Gib Torr, 1.5m S of Flash (NSFCT 1920 p142).

Woodhead Old Hall Predecessor to Woodhead Hall, near Cheadle. Built by a Mr Lea in 1719. Demolished by Mr WS Allen in c1873 (HOC pp154-155 il, 156). (NSFCT 1906 p166).

Woodhead Plateway Railroad built to carry coal from Shower Pits (closed in the 1890s) at Woodhead Colliery to East Wall to join the Uttoxeter Canal (NSJFS 1965 p112). In the opposite direction went lime for transfer to the Cheadle road at Woodhead Wharf (IAS pp122,157). The plateway was completed by 1827, work having started on it by 1812 (CCT pp55 il, 59).

Wood Hills Site for the first infirmary in the Stoke-upon-Trent district opened in Etruria Vale in 1819 transferred to Hartshill in 1869 (VCH vol 8 p150) (SHST p450).

Woodhouse Former estate in Bignall End township in Audley ancient parish

(SHC 1944 p42). It may be identified with Woodhouse Farm at Wood Lane, Audley, which had been a part of Apedale manor from the C12 (AHJ 1997 p47).

Woodhouse Former moated house, in existence by 1326 and then owned by the Greenway family, 0.25m SE of Biddulph parish church (BALH p25). The area, now a suburb, merges with Biddulph. The house gave its name to Woodhouse Farm and Woodhouse Lane, known as Greneway (Greenway) in c1300 (BHS June 1972 p28).

Wood House Wood House (1834 OS map) and Wood House Farm (1985 OS map) is 1.75m NE of Cheadle and 1.5m SSE of Kingsley, near Gibridding Wood. Cecil Wedgwood (1863-1916), son of Godfrey Wedgwood, a descendant of Josiah Wedgwood I of Etruria Hall (see), lived 'at the Woodhouse near Cheadle,' and had there in the dining room George Stubbs' painting of Josiah Wedgwood I and his family (1780) (A Personal Life of the Fifth Josiah Wedgwood 1899-1968. John Wedgwood).

Wood House House 1m S of Moddershall. On S side of Stone to Fulford lane. Is possibly the Woodhouses on Plot's map. In Kibblestone quarter in Stone ancient parish (W p371).

Wood House Former small hamlet 0.5m SW of Amington (1834 OS map). The name, which appears as Woodhouses in a derisory rhyme containing the name of Tamworth (see), is preserved in Woodhouses Comprehensive School and Sports Centre to the N of Woodland Road.

Woodhouse Hamlet 0.75m NE of Wombourne, in Wombourne ancient parish. It existed by the late C13, evidently as a result of assarting (VCH vol 20 p199). The hamlet is presently represented by a collection of properties called Wodehouse (see) (VCH vol 20 p205).

Woodhouse, The House which lay N of Longton and E of what is now the junction of Anchor Road and Wood Street. The name occurs in 1649. It was leased to the Boultons from 1729 and later owned by them. In the C19 it was owned by the Heathcotes (VCH vol 8 pp232-233).

Woodhouse Council housing estate in Woodhouse Road and Woodhouse Road North area, Tettenhall. Built in the late 1940s and early 1950s (BTW p69).

Woodhouse Farm Farm-house with medieval features 0.75m NW of Haughton. Appears to lie outside and slightly to the W of a moated site (SSAHST 1982-3 p43). May have descended with Haughton manor (VCH vol 4 pp136,138,139). Has appeared as Wodehous (1327), Wood House (Yates' map), and The Wood House (OS map 1836) (SPNO p166).

Woodhouse Field Fragmented minute hamlet in undulating country by Nabb Brook 1.5m SW of Denstone.

Woodhouse Green Area on a promontory overlooking the head of Endon Brook 0.75m to WSW of Endon village. In Endon township in Leek ancient parish. There was a house here by 1607. Clay Lake Farm is in this area (VCH vol 7 p177).

Woodhouse Green Hamlet on N-facing slope of a hill overlooking the Dane to the N, 1m WNW of Rushton Spencer. Formerly in Rushton Spencer township in Leek ancient parish. The Wodehouse, where there were tenements in 1413, may be a reference to Woodhouse Green (VCH vol 7 p223). Here is a C18 burial ground and a farm formerly used as a Baptist meeting house (NSFCT 1943 p64).

Woodhouses Hamlet 0.5m E of Burntwood. Formerly in Burntwood out-township of St Michael's parish, Lichfield (W p515). Appears as Wodehousleye in 1374 (VCH vol 14 p202).

Woodhouses House under 0.5m SSE of Blore (Ray) (Plot's map). Former small tithe free township in Mayfield parish (AAD p210) (W p784). The separate civil parish of Woodhouses, created in 1866, was abolished in 1916 when it entered Okeover civil parish (GLAUE p430).

Woodhouses House under 0.5m NW of Pattingham, on Tuters Hill. In Pattingham ancient parish. The name presumably means 'a clearing in woodland' (VCH vol 20 p173). It was an inhabited place by 1311 (VCH vol 20 p173) (Plot's map).

Woodhouses Hamlet on a hill overlooking the Swarbourn 0.75m E of Yoxall. In Yoxall parish.

Woodhouses Former manor near Tutbury. In existence by 1201 (SHOS vol 1 p58) (UTR). Has also appeared as Tutbury Woodhouses. Woodhouse farm still exists W of Tutbury.

Woodland Hall House 2m WNW of Marchington.

Woodland Hall 0.5m SE of Ashcombe Park, Cheddleton. Can possibly be identified with The Woodlands (see), SSE of Cheddleton.

Woodlands House which stood on N side of Woodlands Street, Smethwick. It existed by 1814. From c1912 to the early 1950s the house was Smethwick Working Men's Club. It was then demolished (VCH vol 17 p106).

Woodlands Former extensive township of scattered houses one to three miles SE of Uttoxeter, in Uttoxeter ancient parish (W p792).

Woodlands House over 0.5m W of Weston-under-Lizard, in Weston-under-Lizard ancient parish. Has appeared Wodelands (1380), the Wadlandes (1666), and Wadland (1840) (SPNO p182). The name means 'lands where woad was got' (SPNO p182).

Woodlands, The House situated in the grounds of Burton Girl's High School, Burton upon Trent. Residence of the headmistress of the school Miss Winifred Mulley, aged 52, who was murdered on July 30 1951 by an army deserter, John Fenton of Derby, aged 20, who had broken into the house looking for shelter and food. His sentence to hang was commuted to life imprisonment (MCS pp61-69).

Woodlands, The House 1.25m SSE of Cheddleton. Occupied by Rev Henry Sneyd in 1851 (W p24). Can possibly be identified with Woodland Hall (see), SE of Ashcombe Park.

Woodlands, The Former estate in Upper Penn (info Angus Dunphy). On the N side of Penn Road, N of Penn church. Developed with housing in the 1930s (PENOP p9).

Woodlands Hall Residential home in Bignall End Road, Bignall End (ES Jan 12 1996 p9). Probably formerly Woodlands Farm, 0.5m N of Diglake (Stoke-on-Trent A-Z).

Wood Lane Hamlet in upland undulating country near the source of Lyme Brook 1m SE of Audley. In Audley parish. Takes its name from the woodland anciently in this area or Woodhouse, an ancient estate here (AHJ 1997 p47). The lane is the former route, now called Apedale Road, which linked Audley to the Woodhouse Farm, by way of Peggy's Bank. In 1733 Parrott reported only eight dwellings here excluding the farm. Peggy's Bank is from Peggy (Margaret Berks) (1761-1842) who took over the tenancy of Miles Green Farm, at the foot of 'her' bank, when her husband died (AHJ 1997 p97).

Wood Lane Road at Lambert's End, West Bromwich. Named after the wood which was on the Cutler's End side and reached as far as Greets Green (SOWB p24).

Woodlane Hamlet on a hill above the confluence of Stoneyford Brook and the Swarbourn 1.25m N of Yoxall. In Yoxall parish. Has also appeared as Wood Lane (BUB p23). Henry Bamford (1819-1896) founder of the Uttoxeter agricultural implement business, came from Woodlane; he moved to Uttoxeter in 1845 (Official Uttoxeter Town Guide. 1993. p17) (BUBA p23p).

Wood Mill Hamlet in the foreign and parish of Walsall, 2m to the E of Walsall. The name is preserved in Wood End Farm on the Sutton Road (W p649).

Woodmill Tiny hamlet on the Swarbourn 1.25m NNW of Yoxall. In Yoxall parish (Plot's map).

Woodroffe's Timber framed house on a T-plan 1.5m WSW of Marchington (BOE p202). Formerly called Bank Top (SVB p121), Bank Top Farm (NSFCT 1915 p160), and Bank House, until its owner Miss Dorothy Longdon (or Methuen - SLM May June 1998 pp53-55pc) discovered the builder's name through research into its history in the 1940s; since then the house has appeared as Woodroffe's and Woodroff's. The clues were names scratched onto windows of the children of Robert Woodroffe, they were Hannah, Elizabeth, Anne and Joseph, who made a deed mentioning the children Robert and Mary in 1673. Another scratch mark says 'I Love Joseph.' However, Miss Longdon found references to Bank House since 1650 (SLM winter 1953 pp23,24ps). The house was built in 1622 by Joseph Woodroffe, a yeoman, whose initials are on a window. The house has remained largely unchanged since. Most of the glass is old and could have been made in nearby Bagots Wood (SVB p121) (IVNF p of) (MR p226) (AUOPP p80p). In the rear section on the ground floor there is a door four feet six inches high (SLM winter 1953 pp23,24ps). In 1759 the house and an estate of 100 acres was sold to a clergyman, Thomas Goodwin of Loughton, Bucks, but the Woodroffes stayed on as tenants until 1800; there are a few of the Woodroffe family buried in Abbots Bromley churchyard. The house was bought by Thomas Gerrard in 1809. It was for sale at £395,000 in May 1997 and appears to have been purchased by Christopher and Lesley Smith who were living at the house by May 1998 (CL May 15 1997 pc property pages) (SLM May June 1998 pp53-55pc). The house was for sale in Sept 1999 (SLM Sept 1999 p14).

Woodroffe's Cliff House 1.75m SW of Marchington.

Woods, The Residential district 1m ENE of Wednesbury. The area, known as Friar Park Wood in 1887, was known as The Woods by 1980 (1887 OS map 6 inch. 1980 OS map 1:25,000).

Woods Bank Lapsed name for a stretch of road from Catherine's Cross to Moxley (SNDB p98) and district S of the centre of Darlaston (Offlow hundred) at SO 976962. The name is from the Wood family. Russian Colliery, disused by c1920, was situated at Woods Bank (SNDB pp98,100).

Woodseat House 1m WSW of Rocester. In Rocester parish. Built in the late C18. Occupied in 1851 by Thomas Wardle (W p24). Colin Minton Campbell (b1827), pottery manufacturer and MP, died here on Feb 8 1885 (SK pp178-

179) (POTP p56). Beaman and Roaf say the house was demolished in the 1930s (IHB p396). It was in ruins in the early 1970s (BOE p226). There is an ice-house to E of the house near a pond is shown on OS maps of 1901 and 1924 (IHB p396).

Woodseaves S of Upper Arley, on W side of the Severn (Plot's map). Shaw described Woodseaves as one of the five townships of Arley parish (SHOS vol 2 p253). The name could be preserved in the Woodhouse Farm and Wood Farm on Dower's map.

Woodseaves Village on a high knoll overlooking and at some distance from Lonco Brook 1m ESE of High Offley. Former township (THS p319) in High Offley parish and was in (High) Offley prebend (SSAHST vol 2 1960-61 p47). A medium polished prehistoric axe of grey-white banded flint was found in May 1939 at Home Farm and is now in WSL (NSJFS 1962 p29. 1964 p25). For Woodseaves Windmill see Littleworth. For the story of the man monkey boggart who haunts a bridge near Woodseaves see Big Bridge.

Woodseaves Common Woodseaves in High Offley parish. Enclosed in c1822. A pool frequented by pewits who had left Moss Pool (see) for Offley moss may have been situated on part of this common (WSS p110).

Woodsetton Former hamlet at the foot of the N end of Mons Hill and liberty now a suburb 0.75m ESE of Sedgley, in the Lower Side division of Sedgley ancient parish (W p195) (HC p71). In the Open Works at Woodsetton were found fine erect fossil trees (AMS p11). Most have thought the Joh' o atte Wodesende who appears in 1327 was of Woodsetton, but Roper thinks he was probably of Wood's End (HC p14). Woodsetton is mentioned in 1537 (HC p19). The name is from wood and Anglo-Saxon 'soetan' people; 'people who settled in the wood' (SR p4) (AMS p442) (SNSV vol 2 p83). The relics of St Chad were secreted at a house which may have stood on the site of Woodsetton Lodge (see) in the early C17. Woodsetton had become a small centre of industry by the beginning of the C19 (HC p62). There is a well in the Dingle of Rough Lane, Woodsetton (PHS p18).

Woodsetton Lodge The house was standing by 1898 when it was the residence of Mr Waterhouse, solicitor (SR p66) (HC p50). Woodsetton Lodge may stand on the site of the brothers Henry and William Hodshead's house at Woodsetton. It was the Hodsheads who accepted the relics of St Chad from Bridget and Catherine Dudley of Russell's Hall, near Dudley (or Rushall Hall near Walsall); they were entrusted to them in fear of the Penal Laws. The brothers divided the relics; William's share has vanished, but Henry kept his, giving his share to his wife at his death in Sept 1615, she in turn gave them to Peter Turner SJ. But according to tradition Henry was waited upon by Turner on his death bed and in Turner's presence Henry called repeatedly upon St Chad. Turner at first wondered why the dying man was calling upon this particular saint, until he discovered the saint's bones wrapped in buckram on a bedpost and took them into his possession. At Turner's death in 1655 the relics were bequeathed to a Jesuit, John Leveson of Leveson's Moat (see), Willenhall (SR p66) (SCHJ No. 9 p12-13) (VB p24). In the grounds is a spring called St Chad's Well (AMS pp445-446).

Woodsetton Farm Woodsetton. Built at the same time as Woodsetton House. Until after WW1 the house belonged to the Foster family (HC p80).

Woodsetton House Stood close to the Tipton-Sedgley road at Woodsetton. Built in c1800 and is contemporary with Ellowes Hall. It was owned by the families of Hughes and Whitehouse for many years (HC pp62,80). It was also sometime the residence of the Goughs. The house was still standing in 1955. By 1997 a Mormon church was occupying the site (SDSSOP p47p of in 1955).

Woodshutts Suburb of, and 0.5m W of Kidsgrove. Woodshutts housing estate was built by the council before WW2 (KAIW p18).

Wood Side Former hamlet lying at about the S end of Weetman's Bridge on the Stafford-Rugeley road. There are many entries to the Woodside in the C17 in Colwich PR. Settlement and the name occurs on Yates' map, but there is no settlement nor name on the 1834 OS map.

Woodside House 0.75m SW of Dunstall, Tatenhill (1834 OS map).

Woodside House over 1m SW of Ranton (1834 OS map) (Dower's map).

Woodstock House 0.75m SSE of Kidsgrove.

Woodthorne House on the S side of Wergs Road N of Tettenhall Wood. Built in c1867 by Henry Hartley Fowler, 1st Viscount Wolverhampton (1830-1911), MP for Wolverhampton from 1880-1908, and claimed to be the first Wesleyan Methodist to hold government office and to be created a peer. The actual house may have been called Wayside House; Woodthorpe being the estate on which it was built (Wolverhampton Chronicle April 30 1999 p31). Henry's eldest daughter, the novelist, Ellen Thorneycroft Fowler, by his wife Ellen, youngest daughter of George Benjamin Thorneycroft of Tipton (see), was born at Summerfield (see) in 1860. When the house was completed she moved to Woodthorne with her family and lived with her parents at Woodthorne until her marriage to Alfred Lawrence Felkin in 1903. They lived their later

lives at Mershire Lodge (Staffordshire is Mershire in her novels), Westbourne, Bournemouth. Ellen died in June 1929 and is buried in All Saints churchyard, Branksome Park, Bournemouth. These works were written at Woodthorne:- 'Songs and Sonnets (1888), 'Verses: Grave and Gay' (1891), 'Verses Wise or Otherwise' (1895), 'Cupid's Garden' (1897), 'Concerning Isabel Carnaby' (1898), 'A Double Thread' (1899), 'The Farringdons' (1900), perhaps modelled on the Feredays of Ettingshall Park (see), 'Fuel of Fire (1902), set in Tettenhall (see), and 'Place and Power' (1903). She was a contributor to Leisure Hour, Quiver, Cassell's Magazine, Parish Magazine, Silver Link, Speaker, Argosy, and the British Workman (DNB 1922-1930) (PSS pp444- 449 p) (BCSG vol 4 pp40,41) (SLM summer 1955 pp12,13,22) (BCM July 1978 pp44-46. Spring 2000 pp46-49) (VFC p50). Under various guises she refers in her novels to Baggeridge, Compton, Dudley, Ellowes Hall, Sedgley, Tettenhall Towers, Tipton, Weston-under-Lizard, Wodehouse, Wolverhampton, and Wrottesley. In a passage of 'A Double Thread' she describes the main features of St Peter's church, Wolverhampton, and mentions St Michael and All Angels church, Tettenhall, where she married her husband in 1903. In 'Fuel of Fire' she refers to the Royal Hospital as the General Hospital - which her grandfather set up (The Fowler Legacy. Anthony Perry. 1997) (Ellen's Forgotten Mercia. Anthony Perry. 1999) (Wolverhampton Chronicle April 30 1999 p31). The house was taken over by the Ministry of Agriculture and Fisheries in 1946. They demolished it in 1978 and built offices on the site in 1980 (WMAG Sept 1963 p18p) (TCOP p34p) (VCH vol 20 pp5,8) (Wolverhampton Chronicle Sept 19 1997 p12p).

Wood Villa S of Uttoxeter, in Uttoxeter parish. Seat of S Bean but belonging to E Phillips of Barton (W p792). Near Wood Villa are two burial mounds (VCH barrow list). Unlocated by Gunstone (NSJFS 1965 p50).

Woodville House House N of Holyhead Road and to E of Sandwell Lane, Handsworth. The house was built in the later C18 or early C19 and was still standing in 1862 (MNB pp41,47).

Woodwall Green Minute hamlet in high undulating country above and at some distance from the Sow, 0.75m SSW of Croxton. In the Woodland quarter in Eccleshall ancient parish (W p381). Woodwall Green, also referred to as Widow Green, formerly lay on Greatwood Heath (SSE vol 7 1995 p75).

Woodwall Green Manor Elizabethan half-timbered house at Woodwall Green, Croxton. Built in 1609. Belonged to the St Vincent Jervis family of Chatcull. But by the C18 it was being farmed by the Cooper family. Had become a dangerous ruin by 1880 and was pulled down (BOV pp25 il of in 1880, 26 il of only remaining portion in 1949).

Woodwall Well One of two wells in Well Street, on E side of town near Northwood, Hanley. Means 'well in the wood' (H p106) (SHST p214) (HBST p378). (VCH vol 8 p160).

Wooliscroft Over 1m WSW of Hilderstone overlooking Hilderstone Brook. Has appeared as Willanescroft (C12), Wollascroft (1605), Willowescroft (1605), Wylles Croft (1605). The name possibly means Wiglaf's croft (SSE 1997 p91).

Woollaston Fragmented small hamlet on a high pastoral plain near Church Eaton Brook 1.75m SSW of Bradley. In Bradley ancient parish. Has appeared as Ullauestone (DB), Wolaveston (1199), Wollaveston (1206), Wollaston (1334), Wollaston alias Olston (1622) (SPNO p137). The name means 'Wulflaf's tun or town or farmstead' (DUIGNAN) (SPN p112) (SSE 1996 p19). The present (1980) Wollaston Farm was formerly Lower Wollaston (1884. 1963); to the SE that called Wollaston (1980) was formerly Upper Wollaston (1884. 1963) (OS maps 1884, 1963, 1980). At Lower Woollaston a field lying S of the farm was formerly known as Moat Croft. Depressions on both sides of the road at this point may indicate the site of the original manor-house (VCH vol 4 p84) (SSAHST 1982-3 p36). In Windmill Hill Field at SJ 861151 near Upper Wollaston was a windmill (VCH vol 4 p84) (WBJ p15).

Woolley, The House 0.5m SW of Brewood. In Brewood ancient parish (W p447). Has appeared as Wolveley (1199), Wulveley (1273), Wulveley juxta Hyde (1273), Wolveleye (1313), Wolfley (c1680) (SPNO p43) (VCH vol 5 p38). The name means 'the glade or wood of the wolves' (SPNO p43). The N block dates from the late C17 and the S block carries the date 1824. Since the C17 to at least 1956 it was owned by the Giffards (VCH vol 5 p38).

Wootton Small hamlet in undulating country near the head of Gamesley Brook 1.25m S of Eccleshall. Former township in Horsley quarter in Eccleshall ancient parish. The relatively high ground between Wootton and Offley forms the watershed of the Trent and Severn (NSFCT 1910 p201). There was evidence of a Roman road here, known as the Wootton 'Pavement.' ('Britannia' Camden vol 1 p638) (NHS p402). It had vanished by 1910. The field name 'Pavement Crofts' preserves it. Close by are the remains of a moated site, from which it is thought some large sandstone blocks in the lane hedge-bank may have come (NSFCT 1910 pp200-201) (ESH pp55-57) (STM June 1966 p34). Garner noted Roman finds from either this Wootton or Wootton-under-Weaver (GNHS p70). At Wootton Lodge was found some Roman Samian and coarse pottery of the late C1 to early C2 AD in 1924. Is now in WSL (NSFCT vol 59 p192) (NSJFS 1964 p21). Duignan identified this Wootton with DB Wodetone. Eyton identified this Wootton with DB Wodestone, but he is wrong says Duignan; according to Duignan that manor was in Offlow hundred and yet to be discovered (DUIGNAN pp175-176); Eyton identified Wootton-under-Weaver with DB Wodetone. However, it is Eyton's identification for Wootton which has been accepted and this Wootton appears in DB as Wodestone (VCH vol 4 pp41,42) (DB. Phillimore. 1976) (SSE 1996 p19). The name means 'Wuda's town' (DUIGNAN). Or 'settlement near a wood' (NSJFS 1981 p2). There is Danewort, Dane's bane, Dane's blood, or Sambucus Ebulus, a rare species of dwarf elder at Wootton only found elsewhere in the county in the grounds of Tutbury Castle (NSFCT 1885 pp69-70).

Wootton (locally *Woot-tun*). Small village on a shelf of land on the southern slopes of the Weaver Hills 18m NE of Stafford, 1m NW of Ellastone. Former township in Ellastone ancient parish. Became a separate civil parish in 1866 (GLAUE p430). Wootton has three wells; one called Nook Well (see), one in Delbert Lane, and one in Hall Lane (SVB p183-184). The burial mound at SK 09944486, 0.5m WSW of Wootton, 24 paces in diameter and 4.5 feet high (NSJFS 1965 p59) is a listed monument. Garner noted Roman finds from either this Wootton or Wootton-under-Weaver (GNHS p70). Appears in DB as Wodetone (DB. Phillimore. 1976) (see also under Wootton, Eccleshall). Has also appeared as Wotton (1274) (SSE 1996 p19) and Wootton-under-Weaver. The name means 'Wood tun or town' (SVB p183) (SSE 1996 p19). Or 'settlement near a wood' (NSJFS 1981 p2) (SPN p44). Wootton did not have mains water until 1962 (SVB p184). On July 19 1999 Prince Charles visited Wootton Farm Enterprise estate, owned by JCB of Rocester Green, to view the estate's Aberdeen Angus cattle to promote British beef (ES July 20 1999 pp1,8p) (SN July 22 1999 p63p). The local rhyme

> Wootton-under-Weaver,
> Where God comes (or came) never.

alludes to its remoteness (SSC p138 in the intro) (LGS p134) (FOS p149) (SGS p189), or God is a reference to the sun, which never appears in this area (AAD pp249-250), or the godlessness of the place (SCSF p165) (SJC pp2,3). (HWE vol 2 p303) (W p775).

Wootton Dell Possibly from the poem 'Vales of Wever' by Thomas Gisborne

> The Evening bell of distant Ashbourne
> Sounding into Wootton Dell.

or possibly by Tom Moore (NSFCT 1879 p32).

Wootton End Former area of Handsworth ancient parish (HANDR pviii).

Wootton Hall Former low stone mansion 0.5m ESE of Wootton. Different to Wootton Park and Lodge. Built in c1730 by Richard Davenport of Calverly, Ches (NSFCT 1924 pp200-201) (NSJFS 1972 p121) (COPP2 p100p). Italianate in style (Jean-Jacque Rousseau in Staffordshire 1766-1767. JH Broome. 1966). In the C18 it was owned by the Bromley Davenports of Capesthorne Hall, Ches (SVB pp184,185 il). The French writer Jean Jacques Rousseau and his mistress housekeeper, Mlle Therese Le Vasseur, stayed here for 13 months, when it was the property of Richard Davenport. They arrived on March 22 1766 and left on May 1 1767, leaving no clue as to their destination. Rousseau had arrived in England in Jan 1766 (LGS p133) and is said to have chosen Wootton because of its remoteness and to have paid a nominal sum of £30.00 to rent the property. Davenport visited him for three weeks in May 1766, and Malthus visited him in summer 1766 (Rousseau in Staffs. JH Broome. p12). Erasmus Darwin visited him to discuss aspects of botany (NSFCT 1924 p201. 1947 p100) (NSJFS 1972 p121). Whilst at Wootton Rousseau visited Bernard Granville at Calwich Abbey (LGS p133), and made occasional rambles to Dove Dale and is said to have sown the seeds of some curious foreign flowers in the neighbourhood (AAD pp168, 248). Neither Rousseau nor Le Vasseur spoke any English and could only communicate with the servants by signs (LGS p133). Whilst at Wootton he experienced bouts of intense paranoia and believed his friends or the servants were trying to kill him, and Le Vasseur accused the cook of trying to poison him (SSC p26) (AT pp29-35). The weather did not suit him (SVB p184). In July 1766 he quarrelled with his friend and benefactor, David Hume. Whilst at Wootton Rousseau is said to have written some of 'Confessions' (Rousseau in Staffs. JH Broome. 1966. p14) and to have written some of his 'Letters on Botany' in a spot called the Twenty Oaks (see) (LGS p133). After their departure Rousseau and Le Vasseur were remembered by the people of the neighbour-

hood in local dialect as 'Ross Hall' and 'Madam Zell' (HOT pp79-80 notes) (Broughton's Scrapbook p84) (Rousseau in Staffs. JH Broome. 1966. p20) (KES p94) (TFTP pp181-183). The poet John Gisborne rented Wootton Hall from 1792 to 1795 and here in 1793 he wrote the poem 'The Vales of Wever' (1797) (NSFCT 1947 p100) (NSJFS 1966 p58. 1972 p121). Rev Walter Bromley-Davenport was in residence when vicar of Ellastone from 1811 and he much improved and enlarged it in c1837 (W p775) (NSJFS 1972 p121). It was occupied by Rev WD Bromley in 1851 (W p24). Capt Edward Unwin (d1950) has been described as of Wootton Hall (mem in Ellastone church), although the Unwins owned Wootton Lodge. The hall and estate were sold at auction in 1929 (SVB p184). It was demolished in 1931 having become unsafe. The stone from the hall or a lodge went to build Donnithorne Chase (see) (WOY pl 44) (WOY2 p87p) and the retaining walls at the front of a house at Oakamoor called 'The Mount' and in its garden (HAF p399). Also some masonry was used in the renovation of Hanging Bridge, Mayfield. The staircase was purchased by a local gentleman who had it built into his own hall (COPP2 p100). Wootton Hall is perhaps the Donnithorne Chase of George Eliot's novel 'Adam Bede.' Her uncle, Robert Evans, married Harriet Poynton, a domestic servant at Wootton Hall, in May 1801 (LGS p132) (NSFCT 1924 pp200-201). (ESNF p89p).

GROUNDS. The cave grotto in the grounds where Rousseau wrote 'Confessions' went to Consall Hall (Vales of Weever. John Gisborne. 1797) (Visits to Remarkable Places. William Howitt. c1837) (NSJFS 1966 pp47-60. 1967 p81). Situated to 0.25m NE of the house, outside the estate, was an ice-house, shown on OS maps 1882, 1901 and 1924 (IHB p396).

Wootton Lodge Early C17 house 1m SW of Wootton. Reputed to be 'the most beautiful and most beautifully situated house in Staffordshire' (NSFCT 1953 p121). Built for Sir Richard Fleetwood before 1611, the year he became a baronet (SGS p189). Wootton Lodge is one of a group of houses by Robert Smythson or close to him in style. Burton Agnes, East Riding, Yorks, was built by him for Sir Richard's cousin (BOE p328). Others say it was designed by Inigo Jones (W p775) (AAD p253). Sir Richard's emblem of baronetcy, the Red Hand of Ulster, appears at the entrance. He was one of the original baronets created by James I. During the Civil War it was a royalist garrison. It was taken by the parliamentarian John Gell on or slightly before July 8 1643 after a siege of two days and one night during which time the hall was badly damaged; Sir Richard Fleetwood and his two sons and about 70 others were taken prisoner (AAD pp18-19, 253 il facing, 254) (NSFCT 1939 p80) (VB p167) (NSJFS 1972 p127) (BOE p328) (SGS p189). The first entry in Ellastone PR suggests that the Moorlanders could have been skirmishing at Wootton Lodge three weeks before John Gell's attack (HAF pp123-124). The 3rd baronet sold the lodge at the end of the C17 to John Wheeler, a wealthy ironmaster of Stourbridge. The interior was remodelled in c1700. The Wheelers and their descendants, the Unwins, lived at the hall until WW2 (SGS p189). The lodge was restored by James Wheeler Unwin (W p775). At times the hall appears to have been tenanted: In c1800 it was the home of Thomas Wilson Patten owner of Oakamoor copper works (NSJFS 1972 p121), and it was unoccupied in 1851 (W p24). It was the residence of Lady Diana Mosley in 1939 (NSFCT 1939 p80), and her husband, Sir Oswald Mosley (d1980) of Rolleston Hall (see), occasionally stayed here during her residence (My Life. Sir Oswald Mosley. 1968. p363). In 1953 it was the seat of Capt Alan Rook (NSFCT 1953 p121). Rook had a painting by Lely of an ancestor of his, Charles Mordaunt 3rd Earl of Peterborough, in the drawing room (SLM winter 1955 p14). The lodge was the seat of the Bamfords, the excavator manufacturers, by 1974 (BOE p329); the tenth richest family in the United Kingdom in 1996 (TRTC p14). (GNHS p97) (S p87p) (MR pp393,394pc.395). In the Civil War the parliamentarians positioned their guns on Cromwell's Battery, an earthwork 0.25m SW of the house, at SK 093436 (AAD pp18-19, 253 il facing, 254) (OS map 1882) (NSFCT 1939 p80).

Wootton Old Park Medieval deer park enclosed out of forest, held by the de Verduns of Alton Castle (see) (NSFCT 1910 p175). In existence by 1316 (NSJFS 1962 pp73,76).

Wootton Park Park land to NW of Wootton Lodge. Possibly the remains of Wootton Old Park, the medieval deer park. According to Ellastone PR Margaret Leighton was murdered by William Copestake in the park in summer 1634 and a small child Elizabeth Harvey lost her way and starved to death in the park in Oct 1689 and a boy Richard Smith was found hung in the park in 1712 (NSJFS 1972 p127). There was a park stored with deer at Wootton belonging to Mr Wheeler in 1735 (SHOS vol 1 pxxiv) (EDP p178). The house known as Wootton Park was occupied in 1851 by George Walker (W p24) (mem in Ellastone churchyard).

Woottons Fragmented small hamlet on both sides of Croxden Brook on a Roman road, 1.75m SW of Denstone. In Croxden parish (W p771). The Roman road between Derby and Chesterton, Richmilde Street, passed through Woottons. In this area are Roman remains (The Antiquary vol 28 p255). They may be the same as those Redfern noted near Madeley Farm (see) (NSJFS 1964 p21). Woottons Farm to the S of the Roman road was in existence by 1722 (CDS p19).

Wordsley Former village on the W side of Ridge Hill overlooking a tributary of the Stour, now a suburb 1.5m S of Kingswinford. Former liberty in Kingswinford ancient parish (BHOP p5). The **name** has appeared as Wordesley (1834 OS map). It means 'Wulfweard's lea' (DUIGNAN) (SPN p146). There may have been a small village at Wordsley by the C16. The making of **nails** in Kingswinford parish is said to have begun in Wordsley and spread to the rest of the parish (BHOP pp6,7). The Stourbridge Canal was open by 1779 to the S of the village; there was a **food riot** over a barge laden with bags of grain on the canal at Wordsley in 1801. The bargeman had refused to sell to the local people. A troop of the Dudley Yeomanry were called out and one of the rioters, Thomas Pinfold, was killed (TB Nov 1982 p23). The area grew through the manufacture of **fire-bricks**, **iron** and **glass**, the latter was taking place at Wordsley by the later C18 (LGS p260) (SGS p189). On E side of High Street is the church, Holy Trinity. It was consecrated on Dec 9 1831 (WFK p27). The custom of the parishioners bringing lilies and other flowers to the church at Easter was still carried on at Wordsley in 1964 when it was described as a long standing custom (FLJ 1964 p62). A **pseudo Roman bath** is said to have existed at Wordsley, again, like Brindley's Bath, built by a local ironmaster, and perhaps by others of the family of Brindley of Union Hall (TB Sept 1989 p29). For a children's **rhyme** from Wordsley see FSBC p53. For 'Wordsley' as a verb see BCM April 1971 p27. **Natives and visitors**. **Charles II** is said to have taken refreshment at Wordsley as he travelled north escaping from the battle of Worcester (1651) (BCM winter 1989/99 pp51,80). The house in which he is believed to have taken refreshment stood on the corner of High and Kinver Streets until at least the 1950s after which it was demolished and the site used for a modern shop (BHOP p122p). By late 1999 Rose Cottage, a listed C17-looking building in Barnett Lane, was said to be the oldest house in Wordsley (BCM winter 1999/2000 p69p). **'Poor Old Cookey'** allegedly lived to at least the age of 112 (in 1838). He was born in Brierley Hill, and removed from Wordsley (where he had been living for a number of years) to London when in his eighties (Doncaster Chronicle Jan 1838) (Broughton's Scrapbook p425). Webbs Seed Works were established by **William Webb** at Ivy Mills, Wordsley, in 1861 (OS map Sheet 71.06). The mill was situated in the area of, or the firm later moved to, the Brewery Street (later Brierley Hill Road), Plant Street, and Mill Street area. The company name was originally W & E Webb - William and Edward becoming Edward Webb & Sons in 1866 (TB Jan 14 1999 p16ps). The firm produced the 'Wordsley Queen,' a variety of potato; the 'Wordsley Wonder' a variety of pea, the earliest blue wrinkled marrow pea growing 2.5 inch high, exceedingly sweet, produced in pairs at every joint; and the 'Beauty of Wordsley' a variety of melon (BCM July 1971 p8). The site is now given over to new housing and a garden centre (OS map Sheet 71.06). The furthest-travelled balloon by 1971 was the winner of the 1970 Alcan Race, Mrs Jean Bridgens, whose balloon was released from Webbs Garden Centre, Wordsley, on Sept 26 1970 and landed 665 miles away near Starnberg-am-See, West Germany (GBR 1971 p169). In 1874 **John Northwood I** (d1902), born at Wordsley in 1836, and was a glass decorator here, is said to have rediscovered the lost Roman art of cameo glass decoration. In 1874 he exhibited his replica of 'The Portland Vase,' a renowned piece of Roman cameo glass (the original in the BM was smashed and repaired in 1845). By late 1999 a life-size statue of Northwood by Anthony Stones had been, or was to be, erected by Stevens and Williams Glassworks, former employers of Northwood (John Northwood - His contribution to the Stourbridge Flint Glass Industry, 1850-1902. John Northwood II. 1958) (BCM winter 1999/2000 pp70,72-73). **Charles Hatton**, writer and script writer, was born at Wordsley on Sept 4 1905. His works, which include the novels 'Much about Mowbray' (1951), and 'Maiden Over' (1955), sometimes appear under the nom-de-plume Frank Weston. He died on Aug 8 1977 (BCM July 1989 pp16-21). **Don Kenyon** of Wordsley, cricketer, played for England eight times. He was a Test selector and was appointed President of Worcestershire County Cricket Club in 1986 (BHOP2 p124). The actor, **Johnny Briggs**, who plays the part Mike Baldwin in the TV soap opera 'Coronation Street,' was living in Wordsley in 1997 (Daily Telegraph July 10 1997 p3).

Wordsley Brook Rises at Brockmoor and ran through Pensnett Chase and joins the Stour S of Wordsley (KCPC p12) (SNSV vol 1 p359. vol 2 p79). It is fed by a spring to the W of Buckpool, which reputedly had healing properties - especially for sore eyes. The upper reaches of Wordsley Brook have also been called Bedlet Brook, and the brook has also been called Watercress

Brook (SNSV vol 1 p359).

Wordsley Common Lay in the Lawnswood Road area of Wordsley (BCM winter 1999/2000 p69).

Wordsley Green Central point of Wordsley and small street in two parts to W of High Street, Wordsley. Presumably here was Wordsley village green (SNSV vol 1 pp147,382).

Wordsley Hall Wordsley. Benjamin Richardson (d1887) was of Wordsley Hall (mem in Holy Trinity, Wordsley) (BHOP p123p of in c1900).

Wordsley Junction Junction of Dudley Canal Line No. 1 with the Stourbridge Canal.

Wordsley Manor House Lay in large grounds off Kinver Street, and to the W of High Street, Wordsley, the entrance was at one time opposite Plant Street. Built in c1757 (TB Jan 28 1999 p24ps) or in c1800 (SNSV vol 1 p217) and has been added to. Formerly known as Park House (Fowler's map 1822), and Wordsley House (1834 OS map). Early in the C19 it was occupied by Miss Holt. Occupied from the mid 1830s to at least 1851 by William Foster and later (c1860) by the Hodgetts, glass manufacturers at Wordsley. It was eventually occupied by the Firmstone family, iron and coal masters, who came to the house in the 1920s or the 1930s and changed the name of it to Wordsley Manor House (although Wordsley was never a manor). Miss Firmstone was occupying the house in 1987 (W p24) (SNSV vol 1 pp60,218. vol 2 p59) (TB Jan 28 1999 p24) (TB Annual 1999 p35p).

Worfe, River (locally *Wurf*). Rises out of a spring close to Cooper's Coppice near Woodhouse Farm, W of Red Hill, N of Watling Street in Shrops. Some of the up-stream part, known locally as 'the brook,' formed a stretch of the southern Sheriffhales parish (formerly Staffs) boundary. From Timlett Bridge near Tong, Shrops, the river is known as Ruckley Brook. From about Ryton it can be properly called River Worfe. It enters the Severn N of Bridgnorth. Formerly written Wurgh which became Wurf. The name may mean 'active' or 'wandering' or 'erring' (WORF pp7,21). (GNHS p23; River Worf).

Worlds End Worlds End, as in Worlds End Road, on the E side of Handsworth Wood Road, Handsworth Wood, may be from Wyrley's End, being the boundary of the land of the Wyrley family of Hamstead Old and New Halls (HPPE p125).

World's End Cottages N of Ammington Hall on N side of A453 (1834 OS map). Has also appeared as World End Cottages.

Wormhill House 1m NW of Heaton. Formerly in Leek ancient parish. The area of Wormhough and Wormhill was known as Wurnuldehalth in the late 1240s. The present C19 house may stand on the site of New House, in existence in 1702 (VCH vol 7 p186). For a possible meaning of the name see Wormlow.

Wormhough House close to and to W of Wormhill. Formerly in Heaton township in Leek ancient parish (SSE 1993 p4). The area of Wormhough and Wormhill was known as Wurnuldehalth in the late 1240s. There was a house here by the earlier C16 (VCH vol 7 p186).

Worm Low 0.5m ENE of Stile House Farm, 2m NW of Onecote. Formerly in Onecote township in Leek ancient parish. There may have been a burial mound near Wormlow Farm, on account of the fact that the name incorporates the Old English word 'hlaw' meaning burial mound (VCH vol 7 p211). For the cross under 0.25m SW of Wormlow Farm see under Stile House. The name 'Worm' may signify the pagan deities the Earth Spirit, the Wyrm, dragon, or serpent (DPEM pp80,111) (DPMM p116).

Worstead Hall Delves Green 2m S of Walsall. The name is from the Anglo-Saxon personal name, 'Wealhstod' which became the surname of a yeoman family called Walstode, Walstede, or Walstead who lived here in between the C15 and the C17 (DUIGNAN). They gave their name to the hall (SPN p134).

Worston Minute hamlet on the Sow a little down stream from Meece Brook 0.5m NNW of Great Bridgeford. It was considered an extra parochial estate, although it was ecclesiastically annexed to St Mary's parish, Stafford (W p343). Has appeared as Wyverston (1227) (SSE 1996 p19), and Wynreston (SPN p111). The name is from 'Wifel's town' (DUIGNAN). Ekwall gives 'Wigferth's tun' (SSE 1996 p19). Possibly 'Wigfaerd's farmstead' (SPN p111). At SJ 879278, in the vicinity of Worston Hall, there was possibly a village in medieval times, now lost (SSAHST 1970 p36). Wilmot Martin (1875-1963), the 'Staffordshire Harry Lauder,' was born at Worston Mill House, the son of a corn miller. He is buried at Hixon where he spent most of his life (info Hixon Local History Society). The separate civil parish of Worston, created in 1866, was abolished in 1934 when it entered Seighford ancient parish (GLAUE p430).

Worston Hall Worston, Great Bridgeford. Occupied by John Milner (d1838) (mem in Seighford church). J Milner was occupying the hall in 1851 (W p24). Foot-and-mouth disease broke out at Worston Hall Farm in early 1968 (SN Jan 26 1968 p19).

Woundon Dunstall, Wolverhampton. There seems to have been a small settlement at Woundon in the Middle Ages (HOWM p6). The name of the lost settlement was only preserved in Ounehill and the grounds called the Ouen in the late C18 (SHOS vol 2 p175). May be Wermdon (or Oundon), a place now (1919) extinct (SHC 1919 p167).

Wragge Museum Former museum in Stafford. In July 1878 Clement L Wragge FRGS of Oakamoor offered the corporation his collection of ethnographic, zoological, and geological specimens, most of them collected in Egypt, Palestine, Australia, and elsewhere to form the nucleus of a borough museum (SA July 13 1878. Nov 1 1879. Dec 27 1879). In 1879 Stafford adopted the Free Libraries and Museums Act, and in the same year the collection, housed in the borough hall, officially opened as the Wragge Museum. The museum was transferred to a new extension of the borough hall in 1881 (VCH vol 6 p258). To the collection were added the bird collection of F Whitgreave of Burton Hall, the British birds' eggs, Burmese butterflies and moths of Capt Turnor, and fossil collections. The museum contained two human skulls and the skulls of Bos Primigenius and Cervus Elephas all of which were found in the alluvial soil of Stafford (HOSCC pp66,91). The museum was transferred to the new library at The Green when it opened in 1914. It appears to have remained there until at least 1940, but was no longer exhibited by 1976 (VCH vol 6 p258). (SN May 26 1978 p10). The royal coat of arms originally on the old Shire Hall and later on Stafford Windmill at Broad Eye (see) formed a part of the collection.

Wredon Hill Hill in the Weaver Hills 2m NW of Wootton. At SK 08574694 is a burial mound excavated by Carrington in 1848. It is 19 paces in diameter and five feet high. A male skeleton was found (TYD pp122-124) (VCH vol 1 p209. no 10) (Gazetteer of Early Anglo-Saxon Burial Mounds. A Meaney. 1964. p221) (Medieval Archaeology vol 6/7 p43) (NSJFS 1965 p45). It is of Anglian origin (HAF p35). Has appeared as Reedon (1686), and Raydon (1838 OS map) (NHS p404) (SPNO p23). The name is from Anglo-Saxon 'ryge dun' 'the hill where rye grows' (SPNO p23) (SPN p147).

Wren's Nest, The House on N side of Main Road, Little Haywood. Built in the early 1900s. It has been occupied at various times by the Weetman and Copeland families. By 1997 it was known as High Chase (HHHC p63).

'Wren's Nest' Cottage Lodge 0.5m SSE of Tittensor. Has also appeared as Chase Lodge. Originally the entrance lodge to Tittensor Chase (see). The cottage is still occupied (TTOPP p84p).

Wren's Nest Hill Whale-backed dome-shaped outcrop of Silurian limestone in a hill 1.5m SW of Coseley. In Sedgley ancient parish. The name may be from a house or lodge called the Wrennesnest in Le Conigree Park (VCHW vol 3 p100). Another derivation is that a former lord said that he had a 'bit of a wren's nest of much worth' meaning the value of the limestone it contained. Or it may have received its name from it formerly forming a good cover for armed desperadoes. Duignan has suggested that Wren's derived from Wrosne, a family name of the C12. Dr Booker in 'Dudley Castle' noted the hill resembled an inverted bird's nest (AMS p448) (CR p32). The heart of the Wren's Nest Hill is composed of the oldest of the Silurian rocks, the Wenlock Shales. They are followed by a layer of pale grey limestone, the Lower Wenlock Limestone. The Lower Ludlow Shales form the gentle lower slopes of the hills and dip beneath the rocks of the Coal Measures (WMLB pp14,109). Its limestone has been quarried since the Middle Ages. The stone was used for building. By the C18 it was used as flux for iron-smelting and limestone was burnt for use as a fertiliser. Limestone quarrying ceased in 1924 but not before the mine claimed its last victim from a roof fall in Sept of that year (BCM April 1970 pp60-62 il of interior in 1829. Oct 1970 p54) (WMLB p109). Frederick Lester of Netherton, aged 14, fell down a limestone working on Kettle Hill (see) in 1934. Quarrying created marvellous chasms and rock features in the hillside which became tourist attractions. Some of these have been named see: Bottle Cave, Cherry Hole, Devil's Mouth Cave, Ninety-Nine Steps, Peril Hole, and Seven Sisters. The hill is of geological importance, fossil trilobites having been found during quarrying, so numerous the quarrymen called them 'Dudley locusts' (SL p200). For the palaeontology of Wren's Nest see BCM Jan 1971 pp19-23. From 1815 Lord Ward was planting derelict quarries with trees (SL p200). (SVS p415) (BCOPP vol 2 pl 55 of Wren's Nest in 1915) (HC il of from Woodsetton looking S) (VB p45) (MR pp134p,135). The hill was declared a National Nature Reserve in 1956 (the first in the UK for geology) (WNNNR p4).

Wren's Nest Tunnel Canal tunnel built after 1805 and before 1837 by Lord Dudley. It runs for 1,227 yards from Castle Mill Basin to underground limestone quarries in Wren's Nest Hill (info Dudley Canal Trust) (MR p135). (HCMS No. 2).

Wrestlers Farm House nearly 1m NE of Blymhill. Formerly known as Wrestlers Inn. A Wrestler's Barn occurs in 1833 (SPNO p130). The inn was famed

for gaming, cock fighting and wrestling (VB p151) which took place here, apparently, on account of its closeness to Shrops which could be easily entered to evade the Staffs authorities (TB June 1995 p18).

Wright's Rock Rock feature above S of Dimmingsdale, 1.25m SSE of Oakamoor. At SK 058429.

Wrinehill Small village in a low gorge formed by low hills near Checkley Brook 1m S of Betley. The last Ice Age had its southern most extent at Wrinehill (BVC p12). Wrinehill was known as Wrineford or sometimes Wrime throughout the Middle Ages (BVC pp35,45). Has appeared as Wrinehull (1225. 1255) (SSE 1996 p19), Wryme (1299), le Wrimehull (1486) (SPN p148), Wrindford (Erdeswick 1593-1603) (SOS p90), and Wrineford manor of Wrine (M p8). The second element of the name represents hill (or ford where ford appears). The first element may be an unknown (and somewhat corrupted) personal name. Or it may be an earlier name for Checkley Brook (perhaps from Saxon 'wrigian' 'go forward, bend (in the sense meander)', or for the hill itself (SPN p148) (SSE 1996 p23). Or from Old English wri-o-haeme 'dwellers at the river bends or at the twisting river' (BVC p34). (DUIGNAN; Wrim's ford) (M p8). A document of 1293 states that Ralph de Breville held Longton manor by finding military equipment for 40 days at Newcastle and escorting the king in wartime as far as Wrinesford and back (BVC p35). The Newcastle-Nantwich road (here presently called New Road) fording Checkley Brook and passing through Wrinehill served as the boundary between Staffs and Ches. That in Staffs lay in Betley parish, that in Ches (including the former post office and two public houses) lay in Checkley-cum-Wrinehill township in Wybunbury parish (BVC p7). Celia Fiennes, traveller and diarist, passed through Betley in 1698, and noted the village's division (although she implies it is Betley that was divided between two counties); 'one half of the streete in the one (Staffs) and the other in the latter (Ches), so that they often jest on it in travelling one wheele goes in Staffordshire the other wheele in Cheshire' (Illustrated Journeys of Celia Fiennes edited by Chris Morris. 1984. p156). Later the road was turnpiked. The toll board from Wrinehill Upper Gate near the Blue Bell Inn is now (2000) in the inn. Tolls were discontinued in 1877. Wrinehill Lower Gate was next to the Hand and Trumpet (see Inns under Appendix) (BTC p32) (BOPP pl 23) (BVC pl 13 pp163-164). The village was taken wholly into Staffs in 1964 (BVC p7). The well at Wellbank was artesian (BVC p14). For a rhyme containing the name Wrinehill see Betley.

Wrinehill Hall 1.5m S of Betley. Formerly in Madeley parish and manor and is some distance S of Wrinehill village. Stood near Wrinehill Mill and the Mill House. An old hall was the seat of the Hawkestones, lords of Wrinehill, until it passed in the female line to the Egertons in c1400; Sir John Hawkestone was one of the four squires that reputedly accompanied Sir James Audley at the battle of Poitiers (1356) (BOPP pl 27 of the mill). In Elizabeth I's reign the estate was purchased by Sir John Egerton of Egerton and Oulton (d1614). Sir Rowland Egerton (d1646) was an ardent royalist in the Civil War and the hall was ordered to be plundered by parliament. The Egertons disposed of the hall, the Summer House, and the Red Lion Inn in 1815. By the mid C19 the old hall had gone and the new hall was a farmhouse occupied by Thomas Buckley (M p395) (M p8) (BVC pp49-51).

Wrinehill Manor House Wrinehill. A house adjoining the former Wrinehill post office on the W side of New Road, said to have been built in 1750, is referred to in the deeds as The Manor House (SVB p186).

Wrinehill Park There may have been a medieval deer park enclosed out of forest to the E of Wrinehill Hall. The tithe map 1840 shows a number of field names which suggest a former park (NSJFS 1962 p77).

Wrottesley Very fragmented hamlet on a low hill to the W of the Penk, the centre is represented by Wrottesley Hall and its estate buildings which are 14.75m SSW of Stafford. In Tettenhall ancient parish. A palstave, of perhaps Bronze Age origin, found at Wrottesley went to the BM (HOWM p1). For the 'lost city' between Wrottesley and Patshull see Wrottesley Old Park. Has appears as Wrotolei, a manor, in DB, Wrotteslea (1317) (SSE 1996 p19), and Wratesley (c1540) (LI appendix p170). The **name** may mean 'Wrot's leah (woodland clearing)' (HOPTT p139) (SSE 1996 p19). But 'Wrot' may not have been an Anglo-Saxon personal name. In Anglo-Saxon 'Wrot' means a snout, trunk (of Elephant etc) and may have been conferred on a man with a remarkable nose (DUIGNAN) (SPN p145). Wrottesley **manor** is noted for having been held in the male line of the same family for approximately 800 years. In 1164 it was granted to Simon de Wrottesley. His descendants adopted the name Wrottesley and the manor remained with them until the death of the 4th Lord Wrottesley in 1963 (SGS p132) (MR p103). **Deserted village.** By the hall there was a hamlet or tiny village of Wrottesley, probably deserted in the C16 and probably swept away to extend Wrottesley Park (SSAHST 1970 p36) (VCH vol 20 p11) (SL p108). Wrottesley was a **prebend** of Tettenhall

Collegiate Church (HOPTT p67) (VCH vol 3 p320. vol 20 p19) in Tettenhall Clericorum manor (W p205). For Wrottesley **windmill** see WIS pp13p,23. Tobacco pipe clay could be found at Wrottesley in the later C17 (NHS p121). **Robbery**. In 1795 Joel Lunn, a 29 year-old gun-lock filer from Bilston, and his wife Esther were accused of breaking into the house of William Mitton at Wrottesley and stealing some clothes. Lunn was sentenced to death and his wife was transported; their children were placed in Bilston workhouse (TB April 1993 p17). Became a separate **civil parish** in 1894 from the part of Tettenhall ancient parish not in Tettenhall urban district (GLAUE p430). **View**. From Wrottesley Hall John Wrottesley (1798-1867) could see the Malverns through a telescope (drawing of the view in Staffs Views in WSL vol xii).

Wrottesley Hall The lords of Wrottesley manor, the Wrottesleys, had a manor house at Wrottesley in medieval times, which may have been moated (SSAHST 1982-3 p60). The Wrottesleys probably originated as de Verduns, doubtless a junior branch of the baronial house of de Verdun of Alton Castle (see), Staffs. Between 1160 and 1167 Adam de Verdun held Wrottesley manor. He was succeeded by 1199 by his son William de Verdun who assumed the name of Wrottesley (or de Wrottesle). The manor passed in the male line with Sir **Hugh de Wrottesley** KG succeeding in 1320. He fought at Crecy in the division of the Black Prince and was subsequently made one of the Knights of the Garter. On his death in 1381 he was succeeded by his son John de Wrottesley who was succeeded by his son Hugh in 1402. He was succeeded by his son Sir **Walter Wrottesley** in 1464 who was one of the Chamberlains of the Exchequer in Edward IV's reign. His successor, **Richard** (d1521) was high sheriff of Staffs and succeeded by his eldest son **Walter**, high sheriff of Staffs in 1531 and 1546 and died in 1563. He was succeeded by his son **John**, high sheriff of Staffs in 1564; he died in 1578 and was succeeded by his son **Walter**, high sheriff of Staffs in 1597. He was succeeded at his death in 1630 by his son Sir **Hugh** (d1633). He was succeeded by Sir **Walter**, 1st baronet, son by his first marriage to Mary, daughter of Sir Edward Devereux. On Sir Walter's death in 1659 the estate passed to his eldest son Sir **Walter** (c1632-1685), 2nd baronet. He was succeeded by his eldest son Sir **Walter** (1659-1712), 3rd baronet, and he was succeeded by his son Sir **John** (1683-1726), 4th baronet, MP for Staffs in 1708-10. His eldest son Sir **Hugh**, 5th baronet, succeeded and on his death in 1729 he was succeeded by his brother Sir **Walter**, 6th baronet. On his death in 1732 he was succeeded by his brother Rev Sir **Richard**, 7th baronet. On his death in 1769 he was succeeded by his son Sir **John**, 8th baronet. Sir John (b1744), a major general in the army, died in 1787 and was succeeded by his son Sir **John** (1771-1841), 1st Baron Wrottesley and 9th baronet. In 1821 he and the Tankerville family brought a case of libel against the printer and proprietors of John Bull weekly newspaper (Weaver, Arrowsmith and Shackle) and won. The paper had alleged that Caroline Bennet (d1818), daughter of the 4th Earl and Countess of Tankerville, who had married Sir John in 1795, had been 'detected in a criminal intercourse with a menial servant' (Broughton's Scrapbook p175) (Burke's Peerage) (VCH vol 20 p5). The fifth son of Sir John, 8th baronet, was Commander Edward Wrottesley RN (b1785). His son was Rev Edward John Wrottesley (b1814), a minor poet (PSS p474) (Burke's Peerage 1931). Sir John (d1841) was succeeded by his son John (1798-1867), 2nd Baron Wrottesley, who helped found the Royal Astronomical Society in 1820, and was president of the Royal Society from 1854 to 1857 and of the British Association in 1860. He was succeeded by his eldest son **Arthur** (1824-1910), 3rd Baron Wrottesley; his younger brother (third son of 2nd Baron Wrottesley), Major-General George Wrottesley (1827-1909), was a veteran of the Crimean War, genealogist, Staffs historian, founder of the Staffordshire Record Society, and contributor to SHC. Arthur (d1910) was succeeded by his third son **Victor Alexander** (1873-1962), 4th Baron Wrottesley and 12th baronet. He was succeeded by his nephew Sir **Richard John** (b1918), 5th Baron Wrottesley and 13th baronet (Burke's Peerage) (VCH vol 20 p5). Wrottesley continued to be the seat of the family until the end of the C19. The predecessor to the late C17 Palladian house was a Tudor-looking brick building surrounded by a moat (SHC 1903 il facing 301 taken from an old parliamentary map dated 1633). In the Civil War the hall was considered by royalists and parliamentarians as a royalist garrison, although Sir Walter Wrottesley later claimed it had merely been armed for his own protection and he had been neutral. In 1645 he surrendered it to parliament and it became a garrison for parliamentarians (VCH vol 20 pp11,27). The Tudor hall was pulled down and a rectangular brick Palladian house with stone dressings was built by Sir Walter Wrottesley (d1712) by 1693 or in 1698 (HOPTT pp137p facing, 231,233) (TCOP p31 il); others say it was built in 1686 (LGS p233), or 1696 (BOE p329) (SL p66) (VCH vol 20 p27). In the late C18 Shaw noted the Wrottesley coat of arms in the gallery (SHOS vol 2 p205 pl xxvii). The hall was used by Yates as a triangulation point for his map (1775), and by the

surveyors for the first OS map (SHC 4th series vol 12 1984 vii). The hall and its library, containing a first folio Shakespeare and one of the most complete sets of ancient English Chronicles in existence, was destroyed by fire on Dec 15 1897. After the fire the hall remained a burnt-out shell for some time (LGS p233) (ADD p73) (TCOP p32p of the hall in ruins). The fire is the central event of Ellen Thorneycroft Fowler's novel 'Fuel of Fire' (1902) (VCH vol 20 p5). In another novel by Fowler 'The Farringdons' (1900) the hall is Baxendale Hall (BCM July 1978 pp44-46). A smaller hall was built to the designs of FT Beck on the foundations of the old hall in 1923 (TB May 1986 p14p of in C19) (MR p103p) (TCOP p32p) (TPOP p82p of the rear of the hall prior to 1897). The old hall pediment, with garlands and a shield has been incorporated into it (BOE 329). The hall had become a country club by June 1966 (WMAG June 1966 pc front cover). It was converted into three self-contained houses in 1976 (VCH vol 20 p28). The witch of Wrottesley Hall according to folklore is blamed for starting the fires which have burnt down the house. She is reputed to be Vivien of the Glade, a forester's daughter who had bewitched Guy, eldest son of Sir Stephen de Wrottesley, during his convalescence after an hunting accident, perhaps sometime before the Norman Conquest. The figure of a witch has been ceremonially burnt at Halloween parties held at the hall (WMAG Dec 1965 pp22-23).
GROUNDS. The old Holyhead Road which ran through the park and passed in front of the hall had been re-routed by 1894 (HOPTT p233). There is a dovecote in the grounds (KES p205). Five yards W of the Coach House is a C18 ice-house (DoE II). John, Baron Wrottesley, built an astrological observatory under 0.5m NNW of the hall (in Codsall parish) in 1841 (VCH vol 20 p5). A Dutch force, was based at Wrottesley Hall in WW2 (Wolverhampton Chronicle June 26 1998 p10). However, some have erroneously stated that the Dutch force, the Queen Irene Brigade, was based at Perton airfield and were visited there in 1943 by Queen Wilhelmina (TCOP) (Wolverhampton Chronicle June 5 1998 p15p).

Wrottesley Old Park Medieval deer park 1.25m WSW of Wrottesley (NHS p394). There have been Mesolithic, Neolithic, and possibly Bronze Age finds in Wrottesley Old Park (VCH vol 20 p3). Many human bones have been found at Low Hill Field (MR pp104-105). **Ancient British city**. In Wrottesley Old Park are the vestiges of a large encampment of uncertain origin, which some early writers thought to be Roman: Mr Andrews thought it the Roman city of Uxacona. Camden was more inclined to think it an ancient British town (HOPTT p7). Plot, who marks it on his map, believed it to be an ancient British city. Others have believed it to be of Danish construction and to have been occupied when the Danes fought the Saxons at Tettenhall (910) and Wednesfield (911). The remains are marked on the 1886 OS map as 'site of supposed British Town.' By 1980 Plot's interpretation was no longer accepted (VCH vol 20 p3). In the late C17 the encampment was thought to cover parts of Staffs and Shrops; be three or four miles in diameter; comprise the moiety of Wrottesley; the parks of Patshull, Pepperhill and Boningale, and the commons of Kingswood and Westbeech. The most visible traces of the ancient camp in 1894 were in fields lying W of Wrottesley Lodge Farm (HOPTT p7). In the later C17 Plot noted at the malt house at Wrottesley a great stone used as a cistern which he thought might have come from this encampment. Also an ancient dagger and some squared stone have been found in the locality (NHS pp393-395,414) (SD p47) (SHOS vol 2 pp194,205) (HOWW p30) (SC p152). The Wrottesleys had licence to make a park here in 1348 (SOS 2nd ed p360) (EDP p180). It has appeared as le Logge Park (HOPTT p195) and in this form or as the Lodge Park in 1382, and was surrounded by a pale. There was a small moated lodge on the site of the present Wrottesley Lodge Farm (SSAHST 1982-3 p60) (VCH vol 20 pp32-33). NW of the lodge was a conduit head which possibly supplied water to Wrottesley Hall (VCH vol 20 pp32-33). SAH Burne notes the park had the right of deer-leap (ESH p28). Wrottesley Old Park still existed in the 1740s, but by the end of the C18 Wrottesley Park (see) existed (VCH vol 20 p33). Plot noted an oak in Wrottesley Old Park which had been felled in c1660 and which he believed had grown in a triangular form. Sir Walter Wrottesley told him it had had a girth of 15 yards (NHS p210).

Wrottesley Park By the end of the C18 a park to SE of Wrottesley Hall existed (VCH vol 20 p33). An ancient oak called Wrottesley Oak in Wrottesley Park or Old Park has a girth of 45 feet (CCC p64).

Wulfherecester Legendary palace settlement of King Wulfhere and has been identified with Bury Bank (see) hillfort (W p362) (NSFCT 1914 p110). One of the old Stone Priory documents records that 'Robert de Suggenhall and Petronilla of Darlaston (Pirehill hundred), daughter of Engenulf de Gresley, have given to the Prior and Convent of Stone one messuage in the manor of Darlaston (Pirehill hundred), and all that part of the hill which is called Wulfecestre, which belongs to us' (SIS p6). But there is no historical or archaeological proof that Wulfhere occupied Bury Bank. It is perhaps more likely that the site of 'Wulfherecester' remains to be found or that the name refers to the territory or estate of King Wulfhere and in time got identified through folklore with just the hillfort (SPJD p17). Has also appeared as Wulpherecester.

Wulfruna's Well A spring which, according to tradition, Lady Wulfrun of Wolverhampton (see) may have lived near, or at least, she much frequented. The well lies just S of Gorsebrook Road (SLM Feb 1959 p26p) (WMAG Aug 1969 p25p) (TB July 1988 p6p) in Dunstall Park, Wolverhampton (HOWM p4). The well has also appeared as Wulfrun's Well. Drayton implies with these lines which appear at the end of the 12th song of Polyolbion (1613) that Wulfruna's Well is the source of the Smestow

> Thus though th' industrious muse hath been
> imploy'd so long.
> yet is shee loth to doe poore little Smestall wrong.
> That from her Wilfrune's Spring neere Hampton
> plyes to pour
> The wealth shee there receives into her friendly Stour
> Nor shall the little Bourne (Bilston Brook) have
> cause the Muse to blame.
> From these Staffordshire Heathes that strive to
> catch the Tame.

(HOWM p4). The spring was the water supply for Dunstall Hall (SHOS vol 2 p165). It appears to have still been in use by mid C19 (W p76). By 1950 it was overwhelmed by a railway embankment (HOWM p4). (HOWW) (AOW p94) (SCSF p140) (TB July 1988 p6. June 1989 p13p). Close by is Wulfruna's Stone.

Wulfruna's Well To E of Sedgley Beacon at Spring Vale. Gives its name to the Spring Vale area (AOW p92), and has also appeared as Spring Vale Well. According to tradition so called for Lady Wulfrun of Wolverhampton (see) often visited this healing well (SMM p76). The well seems to have been considered 'famous' in about the C16 or C17. Lawley could not locate the site of it. A street in Cann Lane (Hurst Hill), at its northern end is known as Holywell Street (HOBLL pp174-175).

Wybaston Brook The hamlet of Ford Houses grew by a ford across Wybaston Brook (SHOS vol 2 p184).

Wychdon Lodge Large Georgian mansion 1m SW of Hixon at Shirleywich (W p423). Built in 1818 for the owner of Shirleywich salt works, William Moore, described as a banker in 1848. Occupied by the Hughes' family in the early C20 (W p24) (mem in Hixon church). On Sept 10 1943 a Wellington bomber taking off or flying to Hixon airfield hit the chimney of the lodge and crashed; all the crew were killed (info Hixon Local History Society).

Wychnor Minute village on a bank above the Trent Valley 16.5m ESE of Stafford. Former township and chapelry in Tatenhill ancient parish.

EARLY to 1066. Many coins of different **Roman** emperors have been found in Wychnor Park (PT) (SHOS vol 1 p125) (GNHS p70) (W p607). **Anglian.** The pit alignments running NE and SW centring 320 yards N of Wychnor Bridge 0.5m ENE of Wychnor at SK 186164 are a listed monument. The two large enclosures centring 150 metres SE of Baggaley's Wood at SK 175169, 0.5m NNW of Wychnor, are a listed monument. The circular enclosures centring 300 yards W of Wychnor Junction, at SK 192163 are a listed monument. Several inhumation burials, together with iron weapons, pottery and ornaments all of Anglian origin were found in a sandpit on the E of the railway close to Wychnor Junction, at SK 192156, in 1899 (BTNHAST vol 4 p80) (VCH vol 1 p204) (NSJFS 1964 p45) (BTIH p12). A brooch probably of Anglian origin, known as the Wychnor Brooch, was found in 1926 by labourers digging gravel at SK 195156. The site is a known Anglian cemetery; previous finds were made here in 1899, and it lies in close proximity with the Anglo-Saxon settlement at Catholme (A Gazetteer of Early Saxon Burial Sites. Audrey Meaney. 1964 p223) (SSAHST 1977-78 pp5-7p). In 1953 in a gravel pit at SK 192156 Anglo-Saxon spear heads, javelins, knives, shield bosses, ornaments, beads, coloured glass, spindle whorls, urns, deer horn, food vessels, and cups were found. By the 1990s they were in the Bass Museum, Burton upon Trent (info KL Neal). An early Saxon settlement of some size was found by the Trent at Wychnor in 1973 (SL p43) (MR pp397-398). Near the railway at SK 194154 is a rectangular enclosure with irregular ditch lines of uncertain date (MOT p55) (NSJFS 1964 p45).

1066 to PRESENT. Wychnor has appeared as Hwiccenofre (LGS p254), Wicenore, a manor, in DB, Wichenovere (1236), Wichnor (C14 - mid C20), Wichemor (c1540) (LI appendix p172), and Whichnor. **The name means** 'promontory, slope, or bank of the Hwicce' (NSJFS 1981 p3) (SPN p141)

(SSE 1996 p19). The second element is from Anglo-Saxon 'ofre, ofer,' edge, margin, bank (of river) - Wychnor is situated by the Trent (DUIGNAN). The first element is from the Hwicce ('salt people') tribe of the Glous, Worcs, Warws area, who may have had an isolated settlement here. Or Hwicce has been interpreted as a salt pit (LGS p254) or is from the Anglo-Saxon personal name, Hwicce; in Anglo-Saxon it means 'a chest, box, coffer' (HOA p2). Wych has been interpreted as village or a Wych elm (HOPT vol 1 p137). The **church**, St Leonard, in the village centre, as founded in the C12 (LLD). Became a separate ecclesiastical parish in 1792 (GLAUE p430), refounded in 1881 (LGS p254). In 1165 the **manor** became the property of of Sir Walter de Somerville. In Edward III's reign it was held by his descendant, Sir Philip de Somerville, of the Earls of Lancaster, on condition that a flitch of bacon be kept at Wychnor Manor House (see) to reward proven fidelitious and happy male tenants. The manor appears to have passed from the Somervilles to the Griffith family, who were holders of it, or a part, by the early C15. The manor at length came to Sir Francis Boynton of Bramston, Yorks, by his mother who was sister and heir to the last Sir Henry Griffith. In 1661 it was sold to Mary, widow of John Offley, of Madeley, whose grandson, Crewe Offley, sold it in 1765 to John Levett of Lichfield (SHOS vol 1 pp121,124) (SOS (1844) pp321-322). **Deserted village.** Wychnor village was of some size in the Middle Ages but was probably deserted between 1666 and 1775 (SSAHST 1966 p49. 1970 p36) (SL p84). The remaining earthworks representing the village at SK 17821644, SK 17841629, SK 17571618, and SK 17481583 are a listed monument. In 1528 Wychnor's attempt to enclose its **common land** led to violent intervention from the inhabitants of Barton-under-Needwood who consequently had increased pressure on their commons (VCH vol 6 p52). Wychnor became a separate civil parish in 1866 (GLAUE p430). **Natural history.** In the later C17 Plot noted a thorn at Wychnor which grew in a hedgerow W of the church and between there and Wychnor Park, which produced yellow or straw-coloured leaves in the spring but recovers its normal greenness by St James tide. Plot thought this was so because it was affected by a disease or by people cutting it for presents (NHS p208). **Supernatural.** The vision of a young man is often seen at Wychnor (SMM p54).

Wychnor Bridges Tiny settlement which grew up by Wychnor Bridge or Bridges 0.5m E of Wychnor. Near Wychnor Bridges at SK 194154 are two pit alignments (MOT p31) (NSJFS 1964 p45). The name is from there being several bridges within a short stretch one crossing the Trent and one or more crossing marshland often susceptible to being flooded by the Trent. Anne Statham lived with her mother at Wychnor Bridges. By Thomas Webster, a driver of the Birmingham to Sheffield mail coach which took the road about 30 yards from her home, she had a baby boy, which she drowned near a bridge called the Turnover Bridge on the canal between Branston Bridge and the Three Tuns at Barton Turnings sometime between July 23 and July 28 1816. She was convicted of murdering her baby. However, she was probably suffering from post-natal depression and in modern times courts would be more lenient in her case (CCSHO pp87-93).

Wychnor Bridges Bridge Important crossing over the Trent on Ryknild Street. Maintained throughout the Middle Ages. In 1235 Henry III passed along Ryknild Street and ordered there to be a new timber bridge at Wychnor (R&S p9) (SL p48). A member of the Mynors family broke the bridge at Wychnor preventing Edward II crossing the Trent in the revolt of 1322 (NSFCT 1909 p155). From some point in time there were several bridges. One crossed the Trent, with further bridges crossing marshland often susceptible to being flooded by the Trent. Dr Wilkes says 'The meadows are here very flat, without banks on the south side so that several bridges have been built over the river...' The bridge or bridges were not wide enough to allow wheel carriages across them. By 1760 this had been rectified and yet the bridges remained narrow. Wychnor Bridges were demolished by floods in Feb 1795. Hardy says they were replaced by further bridges which were widened in 1823 (HOPT vol 1 p149). Whilst Shaw says a stone bridge of three arches with circular, instead of pointed buttresses, was erected (SHOS vol 1 p125). The common name for the bridge in 1660 was King's Bridge (SHC 1934 p25). (ABMEE pp4-5).

Wychnor Glebe If at cSK 099165, as Gunstone says, then probably is now Glebe Farm 0.75m NE of Handsacre. At Wychnor Glebe was found a Neolithic or Bronze Age axe which went to Lichfield Museum (NSJFS 1964 p26).

Wychnor Hall C18 house 1m WNW of Wychnor. It replaced Wychnor Manor House, SW of the church. It has also appeared as Wychnor Park (OS maps). Built by Crewe Offley (d1739), grandson of Mary Offley, to whom Wychnor manor was sold in 1661. When the seat of the Offleys Gilbert Walmesley is said to have first met with his future wife, Magdalen Aston, here. There is a story that, whilst riding over to see the Offleys, Walmesley slipped the young David Garrick, who was accompanying him, two half-crowns so that he might grandly tip the butler and groom at 'Mr Offleys.' Hon Horace Walpole wrote to Caroline Campbell, Countess Dowager of Ailesbury from Wychnor Park on Aug 23 1760. Crewe Offley's son, John Offley (d1784), sold the manor in 1765 to John Levett of Lichfield (SOS (1844) p322) (HOPT vol 1 pp80,81) (SCSF p69) (EDP p176) (NSFCT 1922 p166; very inaccurate account stating the hall belonged to the Griffiths; from them it was sold to the Levetts in the C17) (HOPT vol 1 p82) (Young Samuel Johnson. James L Clifford. 1955 1962 ed. p219) (SGS p190). The Levetts appear to have been succeeded by the Harrisons in the earlier C20; Lt Col William Edward Harrison OBE of Wychnor Park died in 1937 (mem in Wychnor church). The house is featured in and illustrated in George Griffith's tragedy 'The Two Houses' 1866. The grounds seems to have been the old deer park, Wychnor Park (see), which Horace Walpole described as 'the pretty park, the situation, a brow of a hill commanding sweet meadows, through which the Trent serpentines in numberless windings and branches. The spires of the Lichfield cathedral are in front at a distance, with a variety of other steeples, seats, and farms and the horizon bounded by rich hills covered with blue woods. If you love a prospect, or bacon, you will certainly come hither' (EDP p176). There is an icehouse at SK 159129 (IHB p396).

FLITCH OF BACON CUSTOM. From the old hall came the ancient custom which stipulated a flitch of bacon be preserved at the manor house. The real flitch was replaced, in time, by a wooden replica. It was painted. Shaw noted Pennant had noted it (SHOS vol 1 p125) (LGS p254). That replica may have been the wooden flitch in a display case over the fireplace at the hall in the early C20 (ESNF p16p). In the 1930s Byford Jones met Mr Wassell of Wychnor, an authority on the Flitch, but was prevented from seeing the wooden replica by the Harrisons, then resident at the hall, who wanted to keep it a secret (QML pp113-118). Thorold and Jon Raven noted it here in the 1970s (SGS p190) (FOS p67). It left the hall when sold in c1980 (MR p398p of the hall) (BTOP vol 2 p62).

Wychnor Manor House Formerly situated slightly SW of Wychnor church (SCSF p68). Seat of the Somervilles, lords of Wychnor, from 1165 to Edward III's reign when it passed by marriage to the Griffiths (SHOS vol 1 p121). Has also appeared as Wychnor Old Hall. Leland noted in c1540 that the Trent was liable to flood the hall (SL p85). Henry Griffith, lord of Wychnor, is said to have built or rebuilt Wychnor Manor House in 1584 (SHOS vol 1 p124). James I was entertained at the hall on Aug 21 1621 and Aug 21 1624 (SHOS vol 1 part 1 pp47,51) (W p607). The manor passed to the Offley family in 1661 and they built the new mansion (SCSF p68) - Wychnor Hall (see) - in the C18. The S and E parts of the moat survive. A stream was cut through the site. It was later used as the weir for the Trent and Mersey Canal. It is likely that canal builders had used pieces of masonry to strengthen the wall of the towpath edge (HOA p98) (SSAHST 1982-3 p58).

FLITCH OF BACON CUSTOM. In 1338 or 1347 (FOS p66) (MR p398) the Staffs manors of Wychnor, Ridware, Netherton, Cowley (identified with Cowley Hill see), and Sirescote (or Scirescote) (HOPT vol 1 pp58,60) were held by Sir Philip de Somerville of the Earls of Lancaster on condition that a flitch of bacon be kept at the hall (except at Lent) and could be claimed by any male tenant of the manor of Wychnor (or manors?) if he could prove absolute fidelity and happiness in his marriage for a year and a day. The claimant had to produce two neighbours to swear they had. If successful he was entitled, as a freeman, to half a quarter of wheat and a cheese, and if a villain, to a quarter of rye in addition to the flitch (LGS p254). Sir Philip Somerville held the manor of Birdshall of the Earls of Lancaster by another strange service (NHS p443). (SD pp27,28) (SHOS vol 1 pp120-121) (SSC pp127,131,132 in the intro) (The Spectator Oct 18 1714 No. 607 or 608 or and vol 8 or 608th paper) (The Penny Magazine. Jan 24 1835 pp31-32) (SMC pp109-11, 174) (W p607) (S&W vol 1 p6) (GNHS pp147,148) (NSFCT 1879 p24) (UTR pp74-75) (SCSF pp67-69) (SC pp67-74) (CSL p53) (KES p228) (SJC p11) (FOS pp66,67) (HOA p44; the deed written out in full and original form) (TOS pp59-61). William Wyrley (1565-1618), the antiquarian, whose family originated from Little Wyrley (see), noted the custom (SH p35). There was an inn called The Flitch of Bacon (see) at Wychnor Bridges. For those who noted the flitch or its wooden replica whilst it was at the new hall see Wychnor Hall. The custom at Wychnor is alluded to in George Griffith's tragedy 'The Two Houses' 1866. The custom was revived for the Wedgwood Bicentenary Pageant in Stoke-on-Trent in 1930 (ES Jan 22 1930 p7). There were very similar tenure customs practiced at Dunmow, Essex, and at the Abbey of St Melaine near Rennes, France (MOS pp56-58) (FLJ 1959 p420) (Sunday Times Jan 11 1959) (Strange Story of the Dunmow Flitch. JW Robinson-Scott).

Wychnor Park Medieval deer park enclosed out of forest 1.25m NW of Wychnor (SHOS vol 1 p125). In existence by 1355 (NSJFS 1962 p76). The park was

disparked in the early C19 (EDP p176). In the park are the remains of an encampment (W p607).

Wynbank Wynbank Farm is 0.5m S of Audley. It may have formerly appeared as Wimbank (SGSAS).

Wynbrook 1m NNW of Alsagers Bank, N of Halmer End.

Wyndford Brook There was a Wyndford Mill in Brineton township by Wyndford Brook (VCH vol 4 p70). Has appeared as Waynford (1272), Molendinum de Waynford (c1290), Windford Mill (1583) (SPNO p130). The name means 'the ford suitable for a waggon or cart' from wægen 'cart' and ford with myln 'mill' (SPNO p130).

Wynford Brook Tributary of Dean Brook. Appears in 1817 as Windeford Brook. The name means 'a ford over a winding stream' (SPNO p22).

Wyre Hall Near Haling Dene in Cannock Road, Penkridge. The present (1959) house dates in part from the C17. It was mainly burnt down in 1800 and rebuilt in 1820 on the original foundations using salvaged material. Now modernised (VCH vol 5 p107) (PVH p24).

Wyrley Wyrley without a prefix may relate to Great or Little Wyrley or Norton Canes (see). The Wereleia in DB has been identified with Little Wyrley (DB Phillimore edition 1976). Wyrley means 'the bog myrtle leah or glade' (VB p125) (SPN p148) (SSE 1996 p19). Wyrley without a prefix was used to describe the Station Road area of Great Wyrley on the 1834 OS map; the railway station there opened on Feb 1 1858. The Wyrleys of Hamstead and Perry Barr take their name from one of the Wyrleys. For Wyrley Gang see Great Wyrley.

Wyrley and Essington Canal Built between 1792 and 1798 (WMLB p53). Opened in 1794 (HCMS No. 2), or 1797 (VCH vol 14 p286). Built from Horsley Fields Junction to Landywood (HCMS No. 2), although some say it was built to Lichfield (VCH vol 14 p47). But according to HCMS the line to Lichfield is the Wyrley and Essington Extension Canal. Spurs off from the Birmingham Canal Main Line at Horseley Field Junction. A disaster occurred at a Short Heath mine on July 15 1905 when subsidence caused the canal to sink into the pit and drown three miners (TB Oct 1995 p15). (LAST vol 1 pp20-40). Closure was sanctioned for the section N of Sneyd Junction in 1954 (HCMS No. 2). It is known locally as the 'Curley Wyrley or Wirley' (BTW p104), because of its circuitous nature.

Wyrley and Essington Extension Canal Built from Birchills Junction to Huddlesford Junction on the Coventry Canal and ran S of Lichfield. Opened 1797 (HCMS No. 2). The section between Ogley Junction and Lichfield was abandoned in 1954 and filled in shortly after (VCH vol 14 p47) (SWY p16). Suzanne Peakman, aged 3, drowned in the canal at Norton Road, Pelsall on Aug 15 1997 (ES Aug 16 1997 p1). The Lichfield and Hatherton Canals Restoration Trust, formed in 1988, seek to restore the canal between Ogley Junction and Huddlesford Junction and will rename this section the Lichfield Canal (Trust leaflet)

Wyrley Bank (locally *Worley Bonk* TABC p29). Is now the village Cheslyn Hay (see). It was land near or on Cheslyn Common in Cheslyn Hay extra parochial liberty, which had been from time immemorial in the possession of the freeholders and copyholders of Great Wyrley or overseers of the poor (VCH vol 5 p78) GWY pp25-26). This combination attracted many beggars and 'lawless vagabonds' to squat and build mud huts on the land. The plague of 1665 seems to have affected the squatter community. According to Brewood parish accounts Brewood gave 14s 7d for relief (SCSF p139). From the orders of the Sessions at the end of the C17 one can deduce that the squatters and beggars had become a bit of a nuisance (GWY pp25-26). In 1668 some of Cheslyn Common was enclosed by agreement. In 1701 it was decided to take action concerning the poverty and lawlessness at Wyrley Bank and a sum was raised to remove all migrants to their own parishes and to force the remainder, who had claimed freehold, to pay rents to the overseers of the adjoining parish and manor of Great Wyrley whose ratepayers supported Wyrley Bank poor (GWY pp25-26) (MH 1994 p114). As a further measure to correct poverty at Wyrley Bank and alleviate Great Wyrley ratepayers an act to enclose the common was obtained in 1792 (THS p263) (GLAUE p408) (MH 1994 p114). Wyrley Bank appears on Yates' map as Wirley Bank, and by the late C18 the name was still proverbial for paupers begging about the country - wandering mendicants on being asked where they came from would reply 'From Wyrley Bank God Bless you' - although by that time with the rest of the common enclosed by statute in 1797 and the opening of collieries in the area there was a higher class of person living at Wyrley Bank (SHOS vol 2 p319) (THS p263) (W p455) (S&W p378). The founder of Primitive Methodism, Hugh Bourne (1772-1852), visited the village on July 27 1810 after receiving an invitation by David Buxton of Wyrley (ESSN p67). By 1817 Wyrley Bank had been annexed to Cannock as a township; it obtained civil parish status in 1858 (THS p263) (GLAUE p408) (MH 1994 p114). In the C19 whilst many of the men worked in the collieries in the neighbouring township of Great Wyrley many of the women were occupied in the local craft of ling-besom or broom making using gorse broom collected from Wyrley Common. The brooms were sold round the Black Country towns by the gaily-clothed, loud women of Wyrley Bank on the backs of donkeys. Jon Raven gives a ditty they sang (TABC p29). The original village nucleus, containing cottages erected in an irregular fashion typical of that built by squatters, appears to have been near the junction of High Street (and Pinfold Lane running off it on the S side) and Low Street, in present Cheslyn Hay. There are also some old cottages of C16 origin in Dundalk Lane. Some of the streets have colloquial names Cross Street is 'Townwell,' and Rosemary Road is 'the railroad.' There is 'Bob's Entry' in High Street; 'Hell's Corner' is the corner of Wolverhampton Road and High Street; Park Street is 'The Lot;' 'Bacon Pit's are two ponds which straddle Saredon Road at Middle Hill; there is also a street called 'Jeff's Knob;' a spoil heap from mining, now covered by council houses in the Mitre Road area, was known as 'The Slings' (VCH vol 5 pp100,101) (The Cheslyn Hay Book. Rick Bowring. 1977). The name has appeared as Wirley Bank (Yates' map) and Wyrley Bank (1788) (SPNO p67). Pitt and Jon Raven have inferred that Wyrley Bank is now Great Wyrley (THS p263).

Wyrley Bank Branch of the Wyrley and Essington Canal. Spurred off the Wyrley and Essington Canal at SK 986044 near site of former Norton Cannock Colliery. Ran to Wyrley Bank Wharf, S of Cheslyn Hay. Opened in 1857. Closure sanctioned in 1954 (HCMS No. 2).

Wyrley Common Common 0.5m E of Great Wyrley. During the C18 and even in the C19 it was customary for boon or bonfires to be lit on Wyrley Common on midsummer's eve. Hoops were made and covered with blazing twigs by youths, who bowled them down hill singing this jingle-

> As Ah wor agoin Werley
> Bonk,

> Up Werley Bonk, Up Werley
> Bonk,
> Coomin down,
> The Cart stood still, and the
> Wheel went round,
> Coomin down,
> Agooin up Werley Bonk.

(SSHL) (GWY p26).

Wyrley Hall House 400 yards W of Moat Farm, Great Wyrley. A stucco building dating from the early C19 (VCH vol 5 p78). Moat Farm may be identified with Moat Hall (schools).

Wyrley Hays To S of Wyrley Common (1834 OS map). In Norton Canes ancient parish. Has also appeared as Wyrley Hayes.

Wyrley Town The area surrounding the moat at Moat House, Great Wyrley, has the reputation of being the oldest inhabited part of Wyrley and is known locally as Wyrley Town (GWY p facing p21, p22).

Wysti Area in the vicinity of West Bromwich Manor House at Hall Green, also known as Whisty. In existence by the C13. By at least the mid C16 there was a house at Whisty which was evidently distinct from the manor-house; it was presumably the Whisty House at Hall Green which was stated in 1828 to have been recently demolished. There was a field called Big Whisty on the S side of Hall Green in the mid C19 (VCH vol 17 p6). Ede, who suggested that Wysti, Wisti, or Wistie was a corruption of Mesty (in Wednesbury), placed Wysti Bridge in Crankhall Lane (HOWV) (TMS p103). But Dilworth states that from 1597 an area of ground to the S of the West Bromwich manor, part of the former demesne, was known as the Wisty (Wistie, Wisti). This was about 0.5m from the Hydes Road river crossing, while the Crankhall Lane crossing would be almost a mile from this area. Dilworth assumes that 'Wistibridge' was at Hydes Road than at Crankhall Lane (TMS p104). The word 'wist' is old English for provisions (food) or the ground on which it was grown (TMS p104).

Y and Z

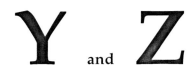

Yarlet Fragmented tiny village on Yarlet Hill at some distance from the Trent 3.75m N of Stafford. Former extra parochial liberty (W p437). A Bronze Age flint scraper was found by Yarlet Hall school tennis courts by a Yarlet Hall schoolboy in 1977 (The Yarlet Story. Nigel Harris. 1993. p1). Between Yarlet and the foot of Pire Hill was found a socketed spearhead thought to have been of Roman origin (NHS p404 tab 33 fig 8) (SD p94) (SMC p174) (GNHS p70) (NSJFS 1964 p44) (The Yarlet Story. Nigel Harris. 1993. p1). Has appeared as Erlide (DB) and Erlida (1167) (SPN p112) and Yarlett. Perhaps from Anglo-Saxon 'geardlyt' (g=y), little yard (or enclosure) (DUIGNAN). Oakden thinks the first element is either 'earn' meaning 'eagle' or 'ear' meaning 'gravel' and the second element is 'hlid' meaning 'slope,' a rare element (SSAHST 1967 p35) (SPN pp111-112) (SSE 1996 p19). Walter Chetwynd deduced it to mean an 'earl's hide,' but he is wrong says Greenslade (SH p45). He may have been right, however, in deducing as early as 1679 that

there had been a deserted C12 village at Yarlet; it was depopulated for a grange of the monks of Combermere, Ches, after Robert de Baskervile granted it to them in Henry II's reign, 1154-1189 (SSAHST 1970 p36) (SL p73). The separate civil parish of Yarlet, created in 1858, was abolished in 1934 when it entered Marston civil parish (GLAUE p430).

Yarlet Hall House at Yarlet, perhaps built by a member of the Tunnicliffe family, was in existence here by at least 1775. In 1851, when it was occupied by George Sidney, it was called Yarlet House (W pp24,437). The present hall was started in c1870 by Henry Tunnicliffe and completed by Rev Walter Earle who established a preparatory school here in 1873 (The Yarlet Story. Nigel Harris. 1993. p2). The school still (2000) continues. It was visited by the celebrated Scottish naturalist, Thomas Edwards, on Dec 1 1878 (NSFCT 1883 p52).

Yarlet Hill Incline leading out of the Trent Valley at Yarlet; is 135 feet high and

Yarlet village is situated on it. The main road from the north to Stafford passed over it. For the people of North Staffs there was an expression to go 'over Yarlet Hill,' which meant to go for trial or imprisonment at Stafford (HOP p88). At the foot of Yarlet Hill by a brook, Thomas Ward, an attorney of Stafford, was robbed and murdered by John Betley of Combermere, Ches, aged 29, John Biddle of London, aged 45, and Richard Ellis of Hanford, Staffs, aged about 27. All three were executed at Stafford on March 20 1793 (Crime broadsheets in the WSL).

Yarnfield Village in low marshy ground on a tributary of Meece Brook 2m SSE of Swynnerton. Former township in Swynnerton ancient parish. Appears in 1266 as Ernefeld (SSE 1996 p19). The name is from perhaps Anglo-Saxon 'gearn' (g=y) or Middle English 'yarn' meaning, originally, thread of any kind spun from natural fibres. Probably, in primitive times, the 'field' or 'fen,' produced a vegetable of which a rude 'yarn' was made (DUIGNAN). Or 'field where eagles are found' or 'clearing where eagles are seen' (SPN p118) (SSE 1996 p19). There was a windmill at SJ 862335 built by Stephen Plant on W edge of the village in the C18. It comprised a windmill plus a separate steam mill. The mill is last recorded in 1861 (WBJ p48) (WIS p25). The reference - SLM spring 1954 p25 - could relate to this or Heamies Mill (see). Yarnfield Green in the centre of the village is still common land (Stone Rural District. The Official Guide. 3rd ed. ND. Late 1940s?). The church, St Barnabas, in the village centre, was built in 1838 (LDD).

Yawning Rock On Gradbach Hill in Quarnford parish (1834 OS map).

Yeatsall House 0.75m WSW of Abbots Bromley. In Abbots Bromley ancient parish. Has appeared as Attesale (1350) (SHC 1908 pp30-31), Yatsall, Yateshall, and Yeatsall Farm (1999). The house at Adsall (see) to the W of Yeatsall was rebuilt as Yeatsall sometime after 1831 (ABMB p53). On July 25 1350 Edelina, former wife of Sir John Bagot Knt (d1349), made a grant to William de Schawe for his life of all the messuages, lands etc which Ralph Bagot formerly held in Yeatsall within the fee of Bromley Bagot, for which he was to render only a rose on St John's Day and a pair of gloves at Christmas (SHC 1908 pp30-31). It has been one of the farms visited by the Abbots Bromley Horn Dancers; they performed here in the morning of Sept 6 1999.

Yeild Hill A house, Yeld Hill, was the seat of the Tunstall family in the C17. Yeld Hill House, 1m WNW of Tunstall, is estimated to be of late C18 or of early C19 date (VCH vol 8 p92).

Yeld Bank House in Knightley quarter in Gnosall ancient parish, 2.5m NNW of Gnosall. Has appeared asle helde (1583), and Yell Bank (1834 OS map). The name is from 'helde' and means 'slope' (SPNO p161).

Yell, The 0.5m NE of Hilton Park, in Shareshill parish. Has also appeared as 'le held' (1562), Yells Farm, and The Yell (1834 OS map) (SPNO p117). Yell is a local dialectal variant of yeld, from helde 'slope or declivity' (SPNO p117).

Yelpersley Tor Wetton. On W side of Manifold Valley in which is a cave like Thors Cave and where there can be found quantities of marble (NHS p172).

Yenbrook Tiny hamlet directly S of Abbots Bromley. In Abbots Bromley parish (W p409). Presumably the brook running E of it is called Yenbrook.

Yeomanry House Originally known as St John's House and stood opposite St John's Hospital, Lichfield. Built in brick before 1732 for Theophilus Levett, town clerk 1721-1746, on the site of Culstrubbe Hall. Still owned by the Levetts in 1847, though then unoccupied. By 1870 was the headquarters of the Lichfield Troop of Staffordshire Yeomanry and the headquarters of the Staffordshire Yeomanry and took the name of Yeomanry House. The Prince of Wales was entertained here in 1894 (VCH vol 14 pp21,29) (info Lt Col German). The building was taken over by the High School for Girls in 1896. Demolished in 1925 (VCH vol 14 p29). Was supposed to be haunted by the ghost of a murdered lady (RSL pp13-14). (Illustrated Guide to Lichfield Cathedral and Ancient and Loyal City of Lichfield. 1897. pl facing p66). The **Staffordshire Yeomanry** (Queen's Own Royal Regiment). Following Parliament's decision in Jan 1794 to establish a volunteer force of cavalry on a county basis for home defence in the event of a French invasion, a committee of Deputy Lieutenants and Staffs magistrates was set up and met at the Swan Inn, Stafford, to launch an appeal for funds to raise and equip a regiment. The new regiment, the Staffordshire Volunteer Cavalry, was embodied on July 4 1794. It was at first commanded by Col E Monckton and divided into five troops, based on Newcastle, Lichfield, Walsall, Stafford and Leek. Later troop formations at Teddesley, Enville, Weston-under-Lizard and Himley were embodied into the regiment, whilst those formed at Bilston, Handsworth, Stone (with Eccleshall), Tamworth, Uttoxeter were at first or entirely independent. The Cavalry chose the Stafford Knot as their badge and 'Pro Aris Et Focis' (For our Altars and our Hearths) as their motto. The first standards were presented by the Countess of Sutherland on Oct 21 1795 (perhaps at the Star Inn, Stafford). It was reorganised in 1798 on a strictly regimental basis. The troop system was then abolished and the title of the force became The

Staffordshire Yeomanry. In 1838 Queen Victoria granted the Yeomanry its secondary title 'The Queen's Own Royal Regiment.' Between 1870 and 1893 the Yeomanry was divided into eight troops. It was then reorganised into four squadrons (Lichfield, Newcastle, Burton-on-Trent, and Himley and Wolverhampton) and brigaded with The 8th Yeomanry Brigade. In 1947 the Yeomanry reformed and continued as a conventional armed regiment in the Territorial Army. In 1958 the Yeomanry became an armoured reconnaissance regiment equipped with armoured cars and latterly Landrovers. With the reduction of the TAVR in 1967, the Yeomanry first became a small cadre attached to 23 SAS and in 1969 merged with other Yeomanry units to become 'A' (Staffs, Warws, and Worcs) Sqn of the Royal Mercian and Lancastrian Yeomanry. From c1898 the Yeomanry headquarters were at the Friary, Lichfield. They are said to have had Tixall Hall as headquarters in WW1. After the war the regiment headquarters were in Bailey Street, Stafford, until reforming after WW2, when they were at Bladon House, Burton upon Trent, until disbandment in 1967. In 1992 the Yeomanry museum formed and opened on an upper floor of the High House (see), Stafford. In the earlier C19 the Yeomanry helped to maintain law and order before the creation of the police force quelling civil unrest at Radford, in the Potteries and in the Black Country, Newcastle, Leek, Stafford, Himley, Tutbury, Longton, and Wolverhampton. Beyond the county they attended disturbances at Oldbury, Dudley, the Lancashire Banketeer riots (1817), the Birmingham Political riots (1817), and the Derby Reform riots (1831). They escorted in Staffs the Earl of Uxbridge from Lichfield to Beaudesert after the battle of Waterloo (1815) and were guard of honour for Queen Victoria's stop at Tamworth in 1853. The Yeomanry served in the Boer War. In WW1 after a spell in Norfolk it served in Egypt and in Palestine from 1916 to 1918, fighting the Turks up to the capture of Damascus. In WW2 after a period with horses in Palestine it saw action in the battle of El Alamein (1942), in Libya and Tunisia. It landed in France on D Day (1944) and crossed the Rhine in 1945 (info Lt Col DJK German and the Yeomanry Museum).

Yerley Hill Hill 0.5m NW of Okeover. A friendly ghost, known as Eli, has been seen wandering up and down Yerley Hill between Mappleton, Derbys, and Blore Hall. The ghost is a tall thin figure dressed in black, like the man on the Sandeman Port bottle but wearing a hat (SBB p190).

Yew Tree Residential suburb 1.75m SSE of Walsall. Does not appear on OS map 1834. Was transferred from Wednesbury borough to West Bromwich county borough in 1931. The council estate here was completed in c1966 (VCH vol 17 pp1,6); the mission church, The Annunciation of Our Lady, on the estate, in Greenside Way, opened in 1958 (VCH vol 17 p60) (LDD).

Yew Tree Yewtree Farm is 1.5m NNE of Whitmore. S of Keele. Marked on Smith's map.

Yew Tree Farm Old Tudor building surrounded by yews at Aston-by-Stone (ES Oct 15 1930 p10p).

Yew Tree Farm Yew Tree was an old estate to SW of Goldenhill. The C19 farmhouse to the S of St John's church, Goldenhill, was part of a scrap-metal yard in 1960 (VCH vol 8 p93).

Yew Tree Farm House at SO 870865, near Prestwood, Stourton, near to the cross roads bordering the Lawnswood estate. One of its mullioned windows is famous for having 365 panes of glass of all conceivable shapes and colours. On one of the kitchen windows is inscribed the name of Price and two daughters. Nancy Price, the famous actress, is the granddaughter, and the names inscribed are those of her two aunts (RKE p19). As part of the Prestwood estate the farm was for sale in 1913 (TB June 1998 p6p). A newspaper boy, Carl Bridgewater, aged 13, was murdered for witnessing a burglary as he delivered newspapers to the farm on Sept 20 1978 (Murder at the Farm. Paul Foot) (MMBC p172). Jimmy Robinson, Vincent and Michael Hickey, and Pat Molloy were convicted of the murder but were freed in Feb 1997 after being found to be innocent: Pat Molloy died in prison in 1981 (Daily Telegraph. Dec 8 1995 p11) (The Guardian July 26 1996 pp1-2) (ES Feb 21 1997 pp1p,3). After the murder the house became derelict and there were calls for it to be demolished because of its association with the murder. However, it was sold in c1997 and has been renamed The Beeches. The new owners hope to restore the building (TB June 1998 p6).

Yew Tree House Has been described as a 'charming little house' built in 1750, and is said to appear on a map of 1794. It stood a little way back from Handsworth Wood Road at the corner of Wood Lane, Handsworth Wood. It was demolished in c1940 when the present nurses home was built, and parts of the stone wall remain (HPPE p128).

Yew Tree House (Dower's map). Is probably the present Yewtree Farm SE of Bromley Green, Whitmore.

Yewtrees 1.5m ENE of Cheddleton. Yews (Dower's map).

Yew Trees House at Yew Trees, Norton-in-the-Moors, was registered for Protestant Dissenters by Hugh Bourne in 1811 (SHC 1960 p22).

Yieldfields Hall Brick house 1.25m N of Bloxwich, on the E side of Stafford Road. The land had belonged to the chantry in Walsall church from 1365 to its sale by the Crown in 1549, when it appears as Yeld feldes. In 1559 it passed into the Cockayne family (VCH vol 17 p179); at the hall is an armorial glass with the arms of the Cokayne (SOB pp97-105p). The hall is a Tudor building built of locally made bricks, and included bunter pebbles (BCM April 1989 p36il). By 1586 Gilbert Wakering had acquired some of the estate which included the hall and by 1593 he was living here. The house was known as Yieldfields by 1596. The hall had passed by marriage from the Wakerings to the St Johns by 1675, and by marriage to the Bernards by 1770. By 1776 the Bernards had sold it to Henry Vernon of Hilton near Featherstone. The Vernons held it until 1936 or 1937 when they sold it to the tenant Mrs ME Yates (VCH vol 17 p179) (SNBP p53p). Some have thought the house may have been occupied by the Purcells (Catholic recusants) at some time. In 1791 it was recognised as a place of Roman Catholic worship. There is no evidence that Henry Purcell, the Musician, was ever at the hall (SOB pp97-105). It was the residence of Frederick Thomas in the late C19 or the early C20 (SOB p178). (SCHJ No. 15 pp1-8). Bloxwich's chapel of St Thomas the Martyr may have been on Church's Lawn next to Yieldfields Hall (SOB p35).

Yieldingtree Small hamlet in Broome parish. Yieldingtree Farm is 0.75m SSW of Broome. Appears as Ildyngtre in the C15 (VCHW vol 3 p33) (SNSV vol 2 p47).

Yockerton Small area on the old road between Barlaston and Trentham by the sewage works.

Youngsgreen House or minute hamlet 1m SSE of Consall.

Yoxall Large village tucked into a hollow on the banks of the Swarbourn (SVB p186) 14m ESE of Stafford.

EARLY. A few years before 1797 40 urns containing cremations were found on a piece of land near Mr Wright's house in Yoxall parish. All were destroyed except for one given to Greene's Museum at Lichfield, which is now lost (GM vol 44 p358 il) (SHOS vol 1 General Intro p35. pp99,331) (Cat of the Lichfield Museum R Green 1782 p27) (GNHS p70) (NSJFS 1964 p45) (MR p399).

900 to PRESENT. Yoxall has appeared as Locheshale, a manor held by the bishop of Chester (Lichfield), in DB, Yoxhal (1222), Iokeshale (1242) (SPN p148), and Yoxwell, as written by Celia Fiennes who passed through on her way to Derby in summer 1698 (Illustrated Journeys of Celia Fiennes edited by Chris Morris. 1984. p149). The name is partly unexplained (NSJFS 1981 p3). Some formerly thought from Jok's or Ioc's hall (HOPT vol 1 p137). The first element is thought to be from Saxon 'geoch' - yoke, a reference to the size of the arable land - 'that which can be ploughed by a yoke of oxen' (SPN p148) (SSE 1996 p23), a 'yokelet' is given in Jacob's Law Dictionary (1748), as 'a little farm, so called from its requiring but a yoke of oxen to till it.' Yoxall lay in Needwood Forest, and probably owes its name to some early squatter who carved out a farm in the forest (DUIGNAN). The second element is thought to be from 'halh' or 'halgh' and represents corner of land, or hollow (SVB p186) (SPN p148) (SSE 1996 p19). **Creation of the parish.** The ancient parish of Yoxall was originally a part of Needwood Forest and as such formed a nominal part of Hanbury parish. It came into being between 1086 and 1291 (SHC 1916 pp197-198). Or the parish boundary between Hamstall and Yoxall strongly suggests that Yoxall was carved out of the 'Ridwara' territory centred on Hamstall Ridware in early Anglo-Saxon times, taking into consideration Yoxall's name (SL p57). The parish **church**, St Peter, on the W side of Main Street between King Street and Savey Lane, has some work of the early C13. The church was mainly rebuilt in 1865-1868 (BOE p330). Parishioners anciently processed to Lichfield cathedral, the mother church, to pay their oblations in 'St Chad Farthings' or other money (SCSF p11). Yoxall **parish feast** was on the first Sunday in July in the C19 (W p612). In the C15 certain Yoxall tenants held their lands on condition that they maintained a 'sluice or floodgate' to drain off floodwaters (SL p71). A **curfew bell** rung nightly at Yoxall between Michaelmas and Lady Day from the C12 to 1938 (YX p13). The Earl of Lancaster was granted a charter on April 1 1300 to hold a **market** here on Saturdays. The market had ceased by 1500 (NSJFS 1971 p51). (SCSF p95). There was no market in 1792 (OWEN), nor in 1888 (LHE p265). Cooke gives Sept 1 as Yoxall's **fair** day (SCSF pp99,104). There was a fair in 1792 (OWEN), but none in 1888 (LHE p265). There was a **windmill** at SK 141190 adjacent to the church, which, due to a dispute between the tenant and the owner, was documented in 1570. There must have been a later mill, probably existing on the same site, since there

are recorded a succession of millers through the C19 (WBJ pp48-49). **Growth and decline.** In Stuart times Yoxall had its own mint. In the C18 Yoxall's population was twice that of the C20 population, with flourishing industries in weaving, tape manufacture, tanning, brick making, brewing and nail making (NSFCT 1954 p93). Yoxall declined because the canal and railway did not come to it (SVB p187). There are or were two **dovecotes** in Yoxall (SLM summer 1958 pp34-35,37). Tom Paget's shop in Hadley Street has been reconstructed at the County Museum at Shugborough (SVB p186). **Floods.** The Swarbourne overflowed and flooded Yoxall in 1935, (1947?), 1955 and 1986. When the Crown Inn becomes flooded the customers continue to use it (TB Feb 1994 p18). **Supernatural.** There is a tradition that a Yoxall blacksmith's apprentice committed suicide whilst his employer was at church because he was so badly treated by his master. He was buried in an unconsecrated grave which no horse will pass (SMM p52). At a tumulus was found the skeleton of a boy who had been speared to death and this, it is said, is the same spot where horses are too scared to pass (SMM p52). Some (for instance SVB p187) have merged the two stories (SMM p52). **Natives and visitors. George Walton**, father of Izaak the angler, lived at Yoxall (YX pp16,17). Birmingham House is said to have been the home of George Walton, grandfather of Izaak Walton (SVB p186). Yoxall is said to have been the home of Izaak's wife (The Way for the Millennium. 2000. p22). In the later C17 a **Mrs Swynbourn** of Yoxall lived to the age of 100 (NHS p319) (SHOS vol 1 p99). Rev **John Riland**, curate of Yoxall, born at Sutton Coldfield, was involved with the early anti-slavery movement (BS p376) (The Way for the Millennium. 2000. p22).

Yoxall Bridge Crosses the Trent 1m SW of Yoxall. The bridge of 'Yoxhall' was mentioned in the Perambulation of Alrewas Hay in 1300. Erdeswick, in the late C16, noted a bridge at King's Bromley over the Trent which was in decay. A bridge with three segmental arches in 1932 seemed to mainly date from the mid C18 (ABMEE pp3-4) (SHC 1934 p25). A WW2 pillbox is situated to the N of Yoxall Bridge at SK 131180 (WMARCH 1993 p36). A new bridge of steel with a single arch, was opened beside the old bridge in 1998 (Staffs County News. Staffs County Council. Oct 1998 p10pc).

Yoxall Grange Former Rectory in Yoxall village. Built in the C17 with timber and brick. Has Dutch gables and a priest hole (KES p244) (BOE p331) (SVB p186) (MR p399).

Yoxall Lodge House over 1.75m NNE of Yoxall by the Lin Brook. Built as a hunting lodge for Needwood Forest and became the lodge of the keepers of Yoxall Ward (ESNF p8). (GNHS p145). Was held by the Hart family who sold the lodge to John Gisborne of Derby in the later C18 (SHOS vol 1 pp67, 104) (UTR p106). John Gisborne was succeeded by his son, Rev Thomas Gisborne (1758-1846), author of the poem 'Walks in a Forest' (1794) (DNB) (NSFCT 1879 pp28,30,31. 1947 p100) (VFC p54); Thomas' brother, John (1770-1851), was author of 'Vales of Wever' (1797) (JAT p70). William Wilberforce was a frequent guest of Thomas Gisborne and wrote from here to James Stephen in 1827 (HOPT vol 1 p164) (NSFCT 1929 p180) (ESNF p90p). Rev Thomas Gisborne was succeeded by his eldest son, Thomas (b1794), MP for Stafford 1830-1832, who died at Yoxall Lodge in 1852 (BS p189). Gisbornes were still in residence at the lodge in the later C18. A later occupant was Henry Walter Featherstone (d1967), founder and first president of the Association of Anaesthetists of Great Britain (mems in Newchurch church). The house bell for Yoxall Lodge had the date 1785. Yoxall Lodge was due for demolition in c1930 (NSFCT 1929 p180). In 1929 the house had no date stones, but in the grounds are two that look like church property, one has the bishop of Lichfield's arms carved on it (NSFCT 1929 p180). The house was rebuilt in 1951 as a farmhouse (SVB p96) (ESNF p8).

Yoxall Park Medieval deer park in the Yoxall area enclosed out of forest. In existence by 1313 (NSJFS 1962 p76).

Yoxall Ward One of the five wards of Needwood Forest. The heirs of the Melbourne family were the hereditary foresters of the ward. Yoxall Ward was bounded on the E side by the Lin Brook and on the N by Aylewardsley Way, the other sides formed the SW edges of the forest (HCT p366) (VCH vol 2 pp349,352). Yoxall Lodge (see) was the residence of the keepers of Yoxall ward.

Zoar Village A plaque on one of four pairs of cottages in Thistleberry Avenue, Newcastle-under-Lyme, built before 1818 on land belonging to Rev T Massey, reads 'Zoar Village.' Who the original inhabitants were and why they built Zoar Village (a tiny cluster of cottages) is unknown (NUL p67p of the plaque)

Appendices

Population of Staffordshire

*Estimated figure by Commander Wedgwood in SHC 1915 pplxxvi, lxxv, lxxvi

YEAR		YEAR		YEAR	
850	10,000*		vol 12 1984 iii p7)		of counties (SL p251)
1086	16,750* (SIS p11) (NSFCT 1952	1801	numbers range from 239,153	1911	1,279,649 (LHSB No. G20)
	p40)		to 254,084* (LGS p13) (KD 1860)	1921	1,348,877 (LGS p13)
1154	15,000*	1811	308,129*	1931	1,433,919 (LHSB No. G20)
1348	40,000*	1821	345,895 (KD 1860)	1951	1,621,013 (Staffs County Council
1361	25,000*	1831	approximately 410,512 (Lewis		Development Plan. 1951)
1377	35,000 (SL p80) or 22,489 (English		Topographical Dictionary of	1961	1,733,887 (HOS p8)
	Historical Documents vol 4)		England 1840) KD 1860)	1971	1,858,000 (SL p251)
1461	45,000*	1841	510,504 (KD 1860)	1981	1,938,289 if figures for the county
1563	70,152* (SL p104)	1851	608,716 (VCH vol 3 p131) or		are added to those for the boroughs
1665	136,146* (SL p104)		630,506 (KD 1860)		of Dudley, Walsall, Warley, West
1701	estimated at 124,000 or 125,000,	1861	746,943 (KD 1912)		Bromwich, Wolverhampton
	similar to Shrops and Cornwall (SL p114)	1871	857,333 (KD 1912)	1991	2,097,475 if same West Midlands
	(SHC 4th series vol 12 1984	1881	981,013 (KD 1912)		boroughs are added to those for the
	iii p7)	1891	1,087,101 (KD 1912)		county.
1781	estimated at 189,000 (SHC 4th series	1901	1,250,000 when it was fourth largest		

Neolithic and Bronze Age activity and burial mounds

See place in main body of encyclopaedia. If * then Neolithic or Bronze Age. If ~ then burial mound assigned to no period, but quite likely to be Bronze Age.
If no * or ~ then of Bronze Age.

Dove basin and Upper Dove
Alton*
Barrowhill~
Birchall~ (Leek)
Bunbury Hill (Alton)
Calwich~
Calwich Common~
Calwich Low~
Caverswall~
Cheadle*
Cheddleton*
Churnet Valley*
Cock Low~ (Leek)
The Dams~ (Caverswall)
Forest Banks*
Harlow~ (Mayfield)
Harplow~ (Upper Tean)
Highwood~ (Uttoxeter)
Hillswood~ (Leek)
Hollington
Leek~
Lower Tean~
Low Fields~ (Stramshall)
Marchington

Mayfield*
Moorhouse Farm~ (Uttoxeter)
Moreton~ (Draycott-in-the-Clay)
Morris House~ (Endon)
Needwood Forest*
Rocester
Roughcote~ (Caverswall)
?Round Knowl (Alton)
Rowleys~ (Church Mayfield)
Rowllow~ (Calwich Common)
St Thomas Trees~ (Dilhorne)
Scounslow Green~
Southlow~ (Wetley Rocks)
Sudden Dale~ (Leek)
Tittesworth Reservoir*
Toot Hill~ (Croxden)
Toot Hill~ (Uttoxeter)
Uttoxeter
?Upper Tean
Wall Grange
The Wentlow~ (Upper Tean)
Werlows~ (Checkley)
?Weston Coney~
Wood Villa~ (Uttoxeter)

Moorlands
Alstonefield*
Arbor Hill~
Arbor Close Low~
Archford Moor*
Astlow Cross~
Beechenhill~ (Castern)
Beelow Hill~ (Cotton)
Beresford Dale*
Beresford Hall*
Big Low~ (Caldon Low)
Bincliff~ (Wetton)
Blackbrook~ (Morridge)
Blakelow (Warslow)
Blazing Star~ (Cotton)
Blore~
Boothlow~
Brownlow (Warslow)
Brownslow~ (Castern)
Brundlow (Sheen)
Bunster Hill~
Burnet's Low
Butterton
Caldon Low~

Calton
Caltonmoor House~
Cart Low (Calton)
Castern
Castlow Cross~
Cheshire Wood Cave*
Cliff Top~ (Swinscoe)
Coatestown
Commonend Farm (Swinscoe)
Crow Low~ (Caldon Low)
Dale Abbey Farm~ (The Dale)
Damgate~
Dan Low~ (Blore)
Deepdale (Grindon)
Ecton Hill~
Ecton Low~
?Eid Low~ (Wootton)
Elderbush Cave*
Falcon Low~ (Wetton)
Far Low (Waterfall)
Gateham~
Gratton Hill~
Green Low~ (Castern)
Greenlow Head~ (Butterton)
Grindon~
Grindon Moor~
Hanging Bank~ (Ecton Hill)
Hazelton Hill~ (Blore)
Hen Cloud
Highfields Mine (Castern)
Hollinsclough~
Hurdlow~ (Upper Hulme)
Hurst Low~ (Grindon)
?Ilam
Ilam Moor
Ilamtops Low
Ipstones*
Izaak Walton Hotel~ (Ilam)
Lady Low (Blore)
Lamber Low~ (Waterhouses)
Latham Hall~ (Calton)
?Lett Low (Warslow)
Lidlow (Warslow)
Little John's Stride~ (Wetton)
Little Low~ (Wetton)
Long Low **significant burial chamber**
The Low~ (Longnor)
Low Bank~ (Fawfieldhead)
Lowend~ (Sheen)
Low Farm*
The Lows~ (Grindon)
Marsden Low~ (Calton)
Marten Hill~ (Okeover)
Mere Hill (Calton)
Merryton Low*
Milestone Edge
Milk Hill~ (Cauldon)
Morridge
Mouse Low
Musden Grange
Musden Low~
Narrowdale Hill
Oldfields Farm~ (Grindon)
Overlow~ (Stanton)
Pea Low~ (Alstonefield)
Pikelow~ (Waterfall)
Ramshorn*
Ribden*
Roaches*
Round Knoll~ (Ribden)
Round Low~ (Grindon)
Rushley~ (Musden)
Rye Low~ (Brund)
St Bertram's Well
Script Low~ (Stanton)
Sevenways Cave* (Manifold)
Sharpcliffe*
Sharpcliffe Hall~
Sheen~
Slip Low~ (Wetton)
Stanshope
Stonesteads~ (Waterhouses)
Swinscoe*
Taylor's Low~ (Wetton)
Thorncliffe~

Thorncliff Low~ (Calton)
Thor's Cave
Thor's Fissure Cave
Thorswood House **gold torc(s?)**
Threelows (Cotton)
Three Lows (Wetton)
?Three Shire Stones~ (Flash)
Throwley~
Throwley Moor
Top Field Low~ (Deepdale)
Top Low **significant grave**
Townend~ (Sheen)
Upper Elkstones
Upper Hulme
Wardlow
Waterfall Low~
Waterhouses
Weaver Hills
Wetton~
Wetton Hill~
Wetton Low~
?Whiston Eaves~
Wootton~
Worm Low~ (Onecote)
Wredon Hill~

Penk basin
Ackbury Heath~
Beacon Hill* (Congreve)
Brewood*
Broomhall Grange
Bushbury Low
Cannock
Codsall*
Congreve*
Dunston
Great Saredon~
Kiddemore Green*
The Laches* (Saredon)
Langley Farm* (Brewood)
Low Hill~ (Bushbury)
Perton
Rowley Hill~ (Stretton)
Shareshill
Standeford*
Stretton
Stretton Mill*

Severn basin
Aqualate
Arley Wood~
Auctioneers Mound
Battlefield~ (Wombourne)
Burnildelow~ (Upper Penn)
Finchfield
Forton*
Greenhill* (Wombourne)
Hawkbatch
Hill Chorlton~
King's Bank~ (Maer Hills)
Loynton Moss~
Maerfield~ (Maer Hills)
?Nanny's Rock~
?The Near Camp~ (Baldwin's Gate)
Norbury~
Oakley Park~
Old Springs
Pattingham **gold torc**
Penn Fields~
Roundabout Tumulus (Norbury)
Sandyford~ (Baldwin's Gate)
Warton
Weston Park*
Wolverhampton*
Wombourne
?Wrottesley

Trent and Tame basin
Alrewas*
Alrewas Hay*
Bangley
Barton-under-Needwood cemetery
Beacon Park* (Lichfield)
Burton*
Callingwood Hall~

Clifton Campville*
Croxall~
Drayton Bassett*
Elford*
Fisherwick
Gaia Lane* (Lichfield)
Hamstall Ridware*
Horninglow
Lichfield
Mytholm~ (Alrewas)
Orgreave*
Robin Hood's Butt~ (Wigginton)
Roddige* (Fradley)
Stretton (Burton)
Syerscote
Tamworth

Upper Tame
Aldridge~
Barr Beacon
Bentley Common~
Bourne Pool
Cats Hill~ (Shire Oak)
?Crow's Castle~ (Hints)
Gainsborough Hill Farm
Great Barr Hall*
Heath Hayes
King's Standing~ (Great Barr)
?Knaves Castle~
Lord Hays Branch (Pelsall Wood)
Newtown* (Great Wyrley)
Owletts Hall*
Pelsall
Round Hill~ (Great Barr)
Rushall Hall~
Sandwell
Sandwell Valley
Shenstone*
Shenstone Hall Farm*
Vigo
Wall
Wednesfield

Upper Trent
Abbey Hulton~
Armitage
Ashley Dale~
Barlaston*
Bignall Hill
Bose's Well
The Brampton* (Newcastle)
Bury Bank
The Bury~ (Milford) **Saucer-barrow**
Camp Hill
Chartley Castle/ Park
Church Leigh*
Cold Norton*
Coneygreave* (Draycott-in-the-Moors)
Copmere End*
Creswell*
?Etching Hill~
Fairoak*
Fairoak House* (Cannock Chase)
?Fenton Low~
Groundslow~
Hanchurch*
Hanchurch Hills*
Henridding
Hilderstone~
Hopton*
King Clump (Swynnerton)
Kings Low (Tixall)
Kings Pool* (Stafford)
Kingstone Hill* (Stafford)
Lane End* (Longton)
Milwich
Mole Cop~ (Fenton)
Monument Hill~ (Tittensor)
?Needwood (parish)
Newcastle*
Norton Farm* (Stone)
Norton-in-the-Moors*
Parkfield* (Barlaston)
Penkhull
Pershall*

Porthill*
Queen's Low~ (Tixall)
Roundilow~ (Meaford)
Rowley* (Stafford)
Saxon's Lowe
Sherbrook Valley~
Shortwood~ (Charnes)
?Shugborough~
Slitting Mill
Smallthorne*
Smart's Buildings
St Stephen's Hill*
Stafford Brook

Stone
Stony Brook
Swilcar Oak
Tittensor*
Tixall
Tixall Heath
Toft~ (Trentham)
Trentham
Trentham Hall*
?Werrington
Wolstanton*
Wychnor Glebe* (Handsacre)
Yarlet

Weaver basin
Betley*
Biddulph*
Bunker's Hill Colliery* (Kidsgrove)
Knight's Low~ (Swythamley)
Madeley~
MadeleyHeath*
Madeley Park Farm~
Madeley Round Barrow~
'Romulus' ~ (Madeley)
Swythamley Park~
Talk

Some County families and their houses

*their arms appear on Dr Plot's map of Staffordshire (1682)

Adderley*	Blake Hall	Edge*	Horton Hall	Lawley*	Canwell Hall; Lords Wenlock
Amphlett*	Clent House	Egerton*	Betley Old Hall	Legge	Sandwell Hall; later Patshull Hall
Anson	Settled at Shugborough Hall in C17 became Earls of Lichfield	Egerton*	Wrinehill Hall	Legh*	Le Leghe, Aldridge
		Eld*	Seighford Hall	Leigh*	Hamstall Hall
Arblaster*	Lysways Hall	Erdeswicke*	Sandon Old Hall	Leigh*	Rushall Hall
Astley*	Patshull Old Hall; later Patshull Hall	Ferrers*	Chartley Castle; Earls of Derby	Leveson*	Great Hall, Wolverhampton, later Trentham Hall
Aston*	Haywood Hall; later Tixall Old Hall	Fitzherbert*	Swynnerton Hall; holders of the Stafford barony from 1913	Leveson-Gower*	Trentham Hall; Earls Gower, Viscounts Trentham; later Marquesses of Stafford, Dukes of Sutherland
Audley	Audley Castle; later Heighley Castle	Fleetwood*	Calwich Priory		
Babbington*	Whittington Hall, Lichfield	Floyer*	Hints Hall		
Bagnall*	Barlaston Manor House	Floyer	Longdon Old Hall	Levett	Wychnor Hall
Bagot*	Bagot's Hall; later Blithfield Hall	Fodon*	Fulford Hall	Littleton*	Pillaton Hall; later Teddesley Hall; later Hatherton Hall
Basset	Blore Hall	Foley*	Longton Hall		
Basset	Drayton Bassett Manor House	Foley*	Prestwood House	Lyttelton*	Arley Castle
Bendy*	Shutt End Hall	Forster	Lysways Hall	Macclesfield*	Chesterton Hall; later? Maer Hall
Beresford	Beresford Hall	Fowke*	Little Wyrley Hall	Mainwaring*	Whitmore Hall
Beresford-Hope	Beresford Hall	Fowler*	St Thomas Becket Priory	Mander	Wightwick Manor
Biddulph*	Biddulph Hall	Fowler*	Pendeford Hall	Mavesyn	Mavesyn Ridward Old Hall
Biddulph*	Elmhurst Hall	Fowler-Butler	Pendeford Hall	Meverell	Throwley Old Hall; later Throwley Hall
Blount*	Blount's Hall	Frith*	Thornes Hall		
Bosville*	Byanna	Fullwood*	Whittington Hall, near Lichfield	Monckton	Somerford Hall; later Stretton Hall
Boughey	Aqualate Hall	Gerrard*	Tittensor Old Manor House, later Gerrard's Bromley Hall	Moreton*	Engleton Hall
Bowes*	Elford Old Manor House			Moseley*	Moseley Hall
Bowyer*	Knypersley Hall	Giffard*	Chillington Hall	Mosley	Rolleston Hall; Bart
Bridgeman	Weston Hall, Weston-under-Lizard; later Earls of Bradford	Goring*	Kingstone Hall and Fradley Hall	Mountfort*	Bescot Manor House
		Gough*	Perry Hall	Mynor (or Minor)*	Hollingbury Hall
Broughton*	Broughton Hall	Grendon	Shenstone Park	Mytton	Weston Hall, Weston-under-Lizard
Browne*	Shredicote Hall Farm	Gresley	Colton Old Hall	Nobel*	Chorley Hall
Caverswall	Caverswall Castle	Grey*	Enville Hall; later Earls of Stamford and of Warrington	Noel*	Ellenhall Old Hall
Chadwick*	Mavesyn Ridward Old Hall			Offley*	Madeley Old Manor
Chetwode*	Oakley Hall	Griffith	Wychnor Manor House	Offley	Wychnor Hall
Chetwynd	Ingestre Hall; later Viscounts Chetwynd	Hanbury*	Norton Old Hall	Okeover*	Okeover Hall; established there since C12
		Harcourt*	Ellenhall Old Hall; later Ranton Priory		
Chetwynd-Talbot	Alton Towers; later Earls of Shrewsbury	Harpur	Rushall Hall	Orme*	Hanch Hall
		Harvey*	Whittington Hall, near Lichfield	Paget*	Beaudesert; Lords Paget; later Earls of Uxbridge, and Marquesses of Anglesey
Collier*	Darlaston Hall	Hawe*	White Hart Inn, Caldmore		
Comberford*	Comberford Hall	Heveningham*	Aston Hall		
Congreve*	Stretton Hall	Hollins*	Mosslee Hall		
Congreve	Ilam Hall	Hollinshead*	Ashenhurst Hall	Parker*	Park Hall (Caverswall)
Cope*	Ranton Priory	Hoo*	Bradley Hall, Bilston	Parker-Jervis	Meaford Hall
Copwood*	Dilhorne Hall	Hope*	Neachells Hall	Parkes	Willingsworth Hall
Corbet	King's Bromley Manor	Howard	Elford Hall; Earls of Berkshire and of Suffolk	Peel	Drayton Manor; Sir Robert was PM in C19
Corbett*	Blakelands				
Cotton*	Beresford Hall	Huntbach*	Featherstone; later of The Showells	Persehouse*	Reynolds Hall
Coyney*	Weston Coyney Hall	Hurt*	Castern Hall	Persehouse*	Turls Hill House? Lower or Upper Gornal?
Crompton*	Stone Park	Hussey	Little Wyrley Hall		
Cumberledge	Cumberledge Park; arms for Cumberledge appear on Plot's map but marked at Stoke-upon-Trent	Inge*	Thorpe Hall	Port*	Ilam Hall
		Jackson*	Stanshope Hall	Pyott*	Streethay Hall
		Jennen*	Shireland Hall	Rode*	Rushton Hall Farm
Curzon	Hagley Hall; Viscounts	Jervis*	Chatcull Old Hall	Rudyard*	Dieulacres Abbey
Degge*	Blythebridge Hall	Jervis	Meaford Hall; later Viscounts St Vincent	Rudyard*	Rudyard Hall
Delves	Delves Halls at Uttoxeter and Apedale			Rugeley	Hawkesyard Hall
		Jodrell*	Moorhouse, Leek	Rugeley*	Marchington Woodlands Manor House
Delves-Broughton	Broughton Hall	Joliffe*	Ashcombe Park		
Devereux	Chartley Hall; Earls of Essex	Joliffe*	Caverswall Castle	Ryder	Dunkirk Hall
De Wasteney	Tixall Old Hall	Kynnersley*	Loxley Hall	Ryder	Sandon Hall; Viscounts Sandon and Earls of Harrowby
Dickens*	Leaton Hall	Lake*	Shenstone Park		
Draycott*	Paynsley Hall	Lane*	Bentley Hall; later King's Bromley Manor	Salt	Baswich House and Standon Hall
Dudley	(alias Sutton) Dudley Castle			Scott*	Great Barr Old Hall; later Great Barr Hall
Dyott*	Freeford Manor				

Shareshall	Shareshill		Viscounts Weymouth	Wells	Hoar Cross Manor House
Shirley	Chartley Hall	Tollet	Betley Hall	Weston*	Hagley Hall
Skeffington*	Fisherwick Hall; later Viscounts	Trafford*	Swythamley Hall	Whitehall*	Lockwood Hall
	Massereene	Trentham	Rocester Abbey	Whitehall*	Pipe Ridware Manor House
Skrymsher*	Aqualate Hall	Trussell	Moat House, Acton Trussell	Whitgreave*	Moseley Old Hall; later Moseley
Skrymsher*	Hill House	Turton*	Oak House, West Bromwich		Court
Skrymsher*	Johnson Hall	Turton*	Orgreave Hall	Whitworth*	Adbaston Manor House; later
Skrymsher*	Norbury Old Manor	Vernon*	Hilton Hall; lords of Hilton held		Adbaston Hall; later Batchacre Hall
Sneyd*	Bradwell Hall; later Keele Hall		Essington by a strange jocular	Whorwood	Sandwell Hall
Sneyd-Kynnersley	Loxley Hall		tenure service involving a small	Wicksted	Betley Hall
Somerford	Somerford Hall		brass figure known as 'Jack'	Wightwick*	Wightwick Hall
Somerville	Wychnor Manor House	Vernon-Yonge	Charnes Hall	Wilbraham*	Weston Hall, Weston-under-Lizard
Stafford*	Stafford Castle; long holders of the	Villiers*	Hanbury Hall	Wilmot*	Eardley Hall
	Stafford barony	Vyse*	Standon Old Hall	Wolferstan*	Statfold Hall
Stamford	Perry Hall	Unwin*	Clough Hall	Wolseley*	Wolseley Hall
Stanley	Elford Old Manor House	Walhouse	Hatherton Hall; Barons Hatherton	Woodhouse*	The Wodehouse
Sutton		Ward*	Dudley Castle; later Himley Hall	Wrottesley*	Wrottesley Hall
(alias Dudley)	Dudley Castle	Ward*	Willingsworth Hall	Wyatt	Thickbroom Hall and Blackbrook
Swinfen*	Swinfen Hall	Wedgwood	Etruria Hall; a branch of these		Farm
Swynnerton	Hilton Hall		successful potters later moved to	Wyrley*	Hamstead Old Hall; later Hamstead
Talbot*	Alton Castle; later Alton Towers; Earls		Maer Hall and Upper House,		New Hall
	of Shrewsbury		Barlaston	Wyrley-Birch	Hamstead New Hall
Thickness*	Balterley Hall	Wedgwood*	Harracles Hall	Yonge*	Charnes Hall
Thynne*	Drayton Bassett Manor House; later				

Some commercial premises

Some named industrial, breweries, business, science park, shopping-centre sites

Albion Brewery Shobnall Road, Burton upon Trent. Built in 1875 for the London-based Mann, Crossman and Paulin (IAS pp153-154).

Albion Mills At SJ 983561, Leek. Leek's best example of an early multi-storey silk factory. Probably completed between 1828 and 1829. The firm of Anthony Ward & Co Ltd had always been and were still the owners in 1976 (IAS pp54p,175).

Alexander Trading Estate Castlefield Street, Shelton, Hanley (Business Directory. City of Stoke-on-Trent. 1997/8).

Allsopp Brewery Burton upon Trent.

Apedale Business Park See Rowhurst Industrial Estate.

Arkwright's Cotton Factory Corn, and at another time a fulling, mill at Rocester at SK 113392. It was bought in 1781 by Richard Arkwright, inventor of the spinning-frame (TSW pp37p of plaque on building, 94). Enlarged 1782; this is now the north-south range. Extended in 1833, and again in 1876, when bought by two brothers, who transferred their business, Tutbury Mill Co Ltd, here, from Tutbury. They renamed it Tutbury Mill (VCH vol 2 p219) (IAS pp185-186), and it has also appeared as Rocester Mill. It was functioning as a 'doubling' mill in the 1960s (NSJFS 1965 p112). The mill closed in 1990 but has now (1995) been bought by JCB Excavators Ltd (ESNF p101p).

Ashford Industrial Estate Dixon Street, Wolverhampton.

Astonfields Industrial Estate 0.75m NNE of Stafford. Built on land once owned by the Aston family of Tixall (SPN p111). Built, from 1970, on the site of Stafford Common saltworks (S&UR p23).

Bague's Amblecote. Here was a glasshouse.

Balliol Business Park Bilbrook, Codsall. In existence by 1998 (SLM Oct 1998 p25).

Bamfords Factory See Rocester Green.

Barnetts Former iron foundry in Lindon Road, Catshill, Brownhills (SNBC p1).

Barton Industrial Estate Mount Pleasant, Bilston.

Bass Breweries See main body of encyclopaedia.

Basset's Mill In the Pattingham area. The foundry is still to be seen (P p60).

Beatty Hall 1.5m SSE of Swynnerton. A hostel built in c1938 for workers, relocated from Woolwich Arsenal, at the new Royal Ordnance factory at Swynnerton. The hall was never used by them, instead they preferred to live in the Potteries. Named after Admiral Beatty. Now a British Telecom training centre.

Beauchamp Industrial Park Belgrave, Amington N of the A5 (Tamworth Business & Industrial Guide 1995/96. A Tamworth Herald Special Publication).

Beldray Industrial Estate Mount Pleasant, Bilston.

Bells Mill On the N side of the Stour 1.5m ENE of Stourton. Formerly Willets Mill, it was known as Bells Mill by 1775 (VCH vol 20 p143) and has also appeared as Bellsmill.

Bell's Mill Shelton, Hanley. It was a working water mill by the early C13; was mentioned in 1296. Henry VII's troops reputedly were fed by the miller here on their way to the battle of Bosworth Field in 1485. For which Henry VII gave the miller, called Bell, freehold tenure (NSFCT 1923 p155) (SHST p537), or the equivalent of about £12 (SOSH p278). However, Greenslade, has found evidence to show that the men of Shelton who ran the mill had fee-farm tenure by the mid C13. The Bell family are recorded owners of it only from the C17. It was known as Bell's Mill by the mid C18 and it was still in existence on the S side of Mill Street (now Etruria Road) in c1837 (VCH vol 8 pp162-163). The mill pool was roughly in the vicinity of Etruria Road (OTP pp130,151) and was filled in the early C20. The freehold estate was in Etruria Road (OTP p202).

Berry Hill Industrial Estate Victoria Road, Fenton (Business Directory. City of Stoke-on-Trent. 1997/8).

Blackham's Mill Caldmore, S of Walsall. Built by John Blackham in c1672. It was probably one of the two windmills in Windmill Field, between Walsall and Caldmore shown on Plot's map, the other was presumably Persehouse's Mill (see). One of the two mills had disappeared between 1732-35. The one that survived still remained at Highgate (see) in 1973 (VCH vol 17 p186). Morteyn's Mill (see) stood in Windmill Field in the C14 (WBJ p41).

Blue Bird Trading Estate, The Park Lane, Park Village, Wolverhampton.

Blythe Vale Business Park Proposed 117 acres development business park at junction of A50 and A521 (ES Feb 9 2000 p10p).

Boundary Industrial Estate Bushbury. To W of A449, N of Ford Houses.

Bridgewood An iron works E of Longton (IANS p42). There is a Bridgewood Street in Longton.

Brindley's Mill Leek. See main body of encyclopaedia.

Britannia Enterprize Park Business park set up in c1980s between Burton Road and the A38, N of Cappers Lane, Lichfield (Lichfield District Economic Development Handbook 1997).

Britannia Park Trading estate on Leek Road, Cobridge (Business Directory. City of Stoke-on-Trent. 1997/8).

Britannia Works Former bar iron works at Lower Bradley, Bilston. In operation between at least 1887 and 1938 (OS maps). The name is preserved in Britannia Road.

Bull Pleck Industrial area in the Black Country in the Willenhall area (BCM April 1987 pp52-53). Could be same as Pleck?

Bunnis Mill 0.75m NW of Whittington.

Burndhurst Mill Former undershot mill on the Blithe at Caverswall, Bramshall. In Uttoxeter parish. There was a mill here by 1775 (TRTC pp121,123p). It had either an overshot (IAS p201) or undershot (TRTC p143) wheel. The house, often flooded when the Blithe rises, was tenanted by the Fisher family in 1882. It was owned by the Rileys to c1939; the Bebbingtons to 1979; and the Broughs to the present (1998) (TRTC pp68p,69,127,143,145). The mill worked until 1945 (Derby Evening Telegraph Aug 24 1979) (TRTC p143) and the wheelhouse of the mill was removed in 1963 (IAS p201). Has also appeared as Burnhurst Mills (W p792). Known locally as Burnthurst, Blunderhurst (MR p163) and Blunders Mill (TRTC p145). In WW2 a British plane made an emergency landing in a field opposite Burndhurst Mill (TRTC p67).

Burslem Enterprize Centre Moorland Road, Burslem (Business Directory. City of Stoke-on-Trent. 1997/8).

Bustleholme Mill In West Bromwich ancient parish. Was situated where the M6 M5 interchange is, 3m S of Walsall. Here was a slitting mill in the C18 (VCH vol 2 p119). Its history goes back 400 years (HOWV p127) (BCM Oct 1968 pp23p-26). It was demolished in c1973 (WBOP p111ps) There is a Bustleholme Lane N of Wigmore. Bustl is a Celtic survival. In Welsh it means 'something bitter, as gall,' and 'bustl y ddaiar' is the common centaury. Centaury seems to include what are popularly known as bachelors' buttons, star thistle, blawort, and loggerheads, which flourish on wet land. Holm is the Norse word for island (DUIGNAN) and is the only 'holme' in S Staffs (NSFCT 1916 p81). In view of the undoubted Norse terminal it seems more rational to derive it from Irish 'bustla,' to bustle or splash about like a fish in water (NSFCT 1916 p81).

Carlton House Estate Copeland Street, Stoke-upon-Trent (Business Directory. City of Stoke-on-Trent. 1997/8).

Central Park A proposed (2000) housing and industrial estate to be built on the former Woolliscroft tile plant site near Etruscan Street, Cliff Vale, Etruria (ES Jan 15 2000 p11).

Central Trading Estate Cable Street, Wolverhampton.

Centrum 100 An industrial or business estate between the Trent and Mersey Canal and Wellington Road, S of Shobnall Road, Burton upon Trent (East Staffordshire Industrial Directory. 1993/94).

Centurion Park Industrial estate to E of Quarry Hill, Tamworth, on S side of A5 (Tamworth Business & Industrial Guide 1995/96. A Tamworth Herald Special Publication).

Chain and Anchor Works At Silver End, Brierley Hill.

Chancel Industrial Estate Hickman Avenue, Wolverhampton.

Chasetown Industrial Estate Between Robins Road and Cannock Road, and to the S of Robins Road, Chasetown (Lichfield District Economic Development Handbook 1997).

Chasewater Heaths Business Park On the S side of Cannock Road, to the E of Chase Park, Chasetown. Developed from 1996 (Lichfield District Economic Development Handbook 1997).

Chatterley Valley Proposed 94 hectares business or industrial development (ES Feb 9 2000 p10p), presumably near the former Whitfield Colliery.

Chillington Ironworks and railway. 1m ESE of Wolverhampton, at SO 928982. In Wolverhampton ancient parish. The Chillington Iron Works (later Tool Co Ltd) lies on the site of moated manor house of Stowheath (see).

Cinderhill Industrial Estate Weston Coyney Road, Longton (Business Directory. City of Stoke-on-Trent. 1997/8).

Cinderhill Mill Longton. It was derelict by 1910 (SHST pp530-532ps). There is a Cinderhill Industrial Estate E of Meir Hay. In Caverswall parish.

Cleveland Works Here the manufacture of locks was carried on, Horseley Field, Wolverhampton.

Cookley Cookley Wharf Industrial Estate and Cookley Works on the S side of the Fens Branch of the Stourbridge Canal, near Brockmoor, take their name from a tin plate works called Cookley set up here by the Baldwin family (of whom Stanley Baldwin PM was one) in the late C19, the firm having moved from Cookley, near Kidderminster, Worcs (info Stan Hill).

Coney Mill A windmill at Boney Hay, Burntwood, at SK 050106, 1m S of Gentleshaw church. Recorded on Yates' map (1775). Following a hurricane in March 1895 the Lichfield Mercury records that the old dilapidated mill had been wrecked (WBJ p25). The Coney Mill or Coney's Mill, by and on the S side of Redmoor Brook at SK 050106, seems to have been a watermill and it was in existence by the C17 (VCH vol 14 pp199, 215).

Coppice Mill Mill in Scotch Brook in the Moddershall Valley in Longton Road, Stone. In the C18 it was a paper mill owned by Henry Fourdrinier, a relation of George Henry Fourdrinier who worked at Ivy House Paper Mill (see) in 1827. By 1853 Coppice Mill had been converted to a flint mill. In 1905 it ground calcined bones. Has also appeared as Shardlow's Mill from the miller Henry Shardlow (SIT) (IAS pp43,195) (SSBOP p61p) (SDOPP p71p) (SPJD p82ps).

Coppice Side Industrial Estate Brownhills.

Cotton Mill Stapenhill. Probably just once a cotton mill. Marked on 1834 OS map.

Crabb's Mill A windmill at Holloway Bank. It has been said Crabb's Mill Farm, which stood on the E side of Holloway Bank in 1742, took its name from a former windmill at approximately SO 994935 (WBJ p45) (Old West Bromwich, a series of articles by WE Jephcott, West Bromwich, Oldbury and Smethwick Midland Chronicle and Free Press, 16 Feb 1945?) (VCH vol 17). Here was John Sheldon's house, where John Wesley formed the first Methodist society in South Staffs on Jan 9 1743. Sheldon lived to the age of 102, although his house was wrecked in the Wednesbury riots of 1743 his grandfather clock survived and was kept by someone as a treasured possession (OWB p90, pl No.17).

Cracker, The Mound of limestone waste from Pelsall Ironworks on the North Common, Pelsall (SNBP p71).

Crossfield Industrial Estate By Crossfield Road on the S side of Burton Road, near its junction with Cappers Lane, Lichfield (Lichfield District Economic Development Handbook 1997).

Crowgutter Mill Consall Forge. In ruins by 1988 (MR p110).

Crown Industrial Estate On W side of Anglesey Road, Burton upon Trent (East Staffordshire Industrial Directory. 1993/94).

Crown Tube Works Former tube factory in central Wednesbury opened in 1823 by James Russell, who in c1813 had discovered a way of making metal tubes longer by joining parallel tubes by means of a small forged-iron socket. In 1824 he patented a tube-making machine, producing 'butt-welded' tubes. However, in 1825 this method was surpassed by another method invented by Cornelius Whitehouse at nearby Wednesbury Forge (see); later Russell bought the patent to this method (WAM p129) (VCH vol 2 pp272-273) (MR p361). In 1919 the works were rebuilt on another site as New Crown Tube Works. This was not a success and in 1929 the firm was bought out and the new owners closed the works (VCH vol 2 pp272-273).

Cupola Mill In the late 1700s the mill was used for grinding frit for Froghall and later lead ore was smelted here. In c1900 the mill closed down because of the unreliable water supply (COPP2 p102p).

Dain's Mill Derelict water mill (HOLF p14) 0.5m N of Upper Hulme. Has also appeared as Dane's Mill. 'Dain' means 'dead' and comes from a burial mound, presumably once here (HOLF p14). Beresford suggested that 'the house of Dodi' a point on the boundary of Dieulacres Abbey was here in medieval times (NSFCT vol 36 p161). 'The house of Dodi' was also a grange of Dieulacres Abbey (NSJFS 1970 p84).

Delph Brewery Brierley Hill.

Dial, The Glassworks at Audnam, at Stourbridge-Wolverhampton road end of Brettell Lane, by the Stourbridge Canal, at SO 893858. The original works was probably founded in 1704 by Joshua Henzey, the younger. The date 1788 appears on a stone above the entrance of the glass-cone, truncated in 1936, is presumably about when Henzey transferred his glassworks to the Dial (IAS p162).

Drake Hall Slindon. See main body of encyclopaedia.

Dresden Mill Hanley (SHST p216).

Eldonwall Trading Estate Lies on the N side of Woden Road West, S of Darlaston (Offlow hundred) (Birmingham A-Z 1995).

Enderley Mills Newcastle-under-Lyme (VCH vol 2 p218).

Eton Park N Burton upon Trent, E of Horninglow. Eton Park Industrial Estate is on the E side of Derby Road, to the W of the railway (East Staffordshire Industrial Directory. 1993/94).

Etruria Valley Proposed 27 acres development business park at Etruria, the third phase of Festival Park (ES Feb 9 2000 p10p).

Far Green Industrial Estate Chell Street, Hanley (Business Directory. City of Stoke-on-Trent. 1997/8).

Federation Road Industrial Estate Federation Road, Burslem (Business Directory. City of Stoke-on-Trent. 1997/8).

Fenpark Industrial Estate and Park. Off King Street, E of Fenton.

Fenton Industrial Estate Off Victoria Road, Fenton (Business Directory. City of Stoke-on-Trent. 1997/8).

Festival Heights Trading estate at Etruria, on high ground to the NE of Festival Park. On a roundabout on the approach road to the park a 12-foot high statue of Lance-sergeant John Baskeyfield VC of Stanfield (see) was unveiled in 1996 (City of Stoke-on-Trent City News. Dec 1996 p1p).

Festival Park See Shelton.

Forest Park Industrial Estate Town Road, Hanley (Business Directory. City of Stoke-on-Trent. 1997/8).

Fradley Park Business Park, developed from the late 1980s, S of Fradley Heath and NW of Icknield Street (Lichfield District Economic Development Handbook 1997).

Freeport Talke. See Jamage.

Furlong Lane Industrial Estate Furlong Lane, Burslem (Business Directory. City of Stoke-on-Trent. 1997/8).

Furnace See Furnace Mill.

Furnace Mill Formerly in Normacot township in Hilderstone quarter in Stone ancient parish (W p371). A furnace was situated to the SW of the intersection of the Stone-Longton and Meir-Blurton roads. It was in operation by 1627 or the mid C17. In c1700 it was in the hands of a partnership which included Lord Foley and Obadiah Lane. It produced pig iron and had ceased production by c1770 or later. By 1820 its site was occupied by a watermill known as Furnace Mill which was in use in 1872. The furnace appears to have given its name to Furnace Brook, and a hamlet called Furnace, which became the Furnace Bank on the 1834 OS map? (SASR 1987 p100) (BNDA p37) (VCH vol 8 p244). Furnace Road N of Upper Belgrave Road, Normacot, preserves the name.

Glass House A restored C17 glass furnace in Bishop's Wood, Fairoak, at SJ 759313 or 759312. (SL p109). It is the only surviving C17 glass furnace in the whole country and the best preserved in Europe. About 1929 some relics of a small glassmaking oven were discovered and reported by T Pape in NSFCT (ROT p8). The glass furnace was discovered by boys of Newcastle Grammar School on Nov 2 1931. The restored glass furnace with a new wooden shed built over it was opened by the Ecclesiastical Commissioners on Aug 11 1933 (NSFCT 1933 pp97-101) (VCH vol 2 p225) (TTTD p253) (IAS p164) (ROT p8,9p). Tom Smith was the discoverer of this or another glass furnace in Bishop's Wood (BOV pp36,37). The furnace is about seven feet square and three feet high. Constructed with sandstone lined with vitreous shards (MR p61ps).

Glass House Stood in the Cedar Road area, N of Chesterton (SVB p55). Name applies to a farm, built perhaps in c1780, on the high ground slightly S of Red Street. The glass works, of C17 date, from which it takes its name has long gone (NSFCT 1930 p46. 1933 pp117-119). The farm had been demolished by 1988 (S&COP pl 37).

Glasshouse Bank It adjoins Glasshouse Meadow see Glasshouse Farm (NSFCT 1933 p77).

Glasshouse Bank Bagot's Bromley (VCH vol 2 p224) (NSFCT vol 68 p77) (SL p109).

Glasshouse Bridge Bradley, Bilston. See Capponfield.

Glasshouse Coppice It adjoins Glasshouse Meadow see Glasshouse Farm (NSFCT 1933 p77).

Glass House Croft Croft belonging to Golden Hill, a farm. The croft is more than a 1m E of another farm called Glass Houses. The croft is so called from there having been a glass house here (NSFCT 1930 pp51-52).

Glasshouse Farm Under 0.25m SE of Gorsty Hill. To the S of it is a hilly field called Glasshouse Meadow (NSFCT 1933 p77).

Glass House Farm Chesterton. See Glass House.

Glass Houses Farm 2m ESE of Hales. The name preserves a C16 glass house site (NSFCT 1919 pp33-35. 1930 pp45,47,49). A glass furnace was discovered here in Oct 1931 and the base was discovered in Jan 1932 (NSFCT 1933 p96). A second site was identified in a field SW of the house in autumn 1932 with the finding of glass relics, but no furnace was found (NSFCT 1933 p103). (SVB p85). The Glass Houses Farm was built between 1775 and 1834. In all probability the squared sandstones used in the retaining wall of the present front garden were part of the building material of the first glass furnace. Numerous glass fragments have been found in the garden of the farmhouse (NSFCT 1933 pp95-96).

Glebe and Glebe Mills. Stoke-upon-Trent (H p20). There were three mills in this area on the Trent which went under the name of Glebe Mills. Two were at Boothen and another at Sideway (demolished in 1925) (SHST p528 plan of their sites).

Globe Tube Works Wednesbury. Set up by Cornelius Whitehouse in 1849 (VCH vol 2 p273).

Gom's Mill Dresden. Here was a quadrangular moat noted by Garner of unknown origin (GNHS p133). By 1632 a corn mill known as this had been erected on Furnace Brook. In the C19 there were Upper Goms Mill and Lower Goms Mill. The mill pools, on SE side of Gom's Mill Road, were dry by the 1870s and gone by the 1950s (VCH vol 8 pp231-232,238). The name is preserved in Goms Mill Road, between Blurton and Edensor.

Gorse Head See Gorstead Mill.

Gorstead Mill House 1.25m SE of Bradnop. Formerly in Bradnop township in Leek ancient parish. Formerly Gorse Head (Yates' map 1775) and Gorsthead Mill (NSFCT 1948 p50). The mill, on Combes Brook, existed for much of the C19 (VCH vol 7 p174).

Great Fenton Haw Business Park Grove Road, Fenton (Business Directory. City of Stoke-on-Trent. 1997/8).

Great Northern Business Park Burton upon Trent. Formerly the Hawkins Lane Industrial Area. So called after being situated on E side of the former Great Northern railway line (info Mr Ludlow) (East Staffordshire Industrial Directory. 1993/94)

Green Birch Green Birch Farm is 1m SW of Tittensor, 3m NW of Stone. In Beech quarter in Stone parish (W p369).

Green Birches Industrial Estate High Street, Tunstall (Business Directory. City of Stoke-on-Trent. 1997/8).

Greenhough Road Industrial Estate On the W side of Beacon Street, near its junction with Wheel Lane, Lichfield (Lichfield District Economic Development Handbook 1997).

Greet Mill May refer to two different watermills on the Tame:

To Sheepwash Mill, at SO 973922 (TMS p149), and 'The Mill' at SO 989905 (VCH vol 17 p24), which has also been called Turton's Mill, and Izon's Mill (TMS p162). The latter was the nucleus of the Mill estate (VCH vol 17 pp24,25).

Greycar Business Park Or Graycar Business Park at Barton-under-Needwood.

Grove Road Industrial Estate Grove Road, Fenton (Business Directory. City of Stoke-on-Trent. 1997/8).

Gulnerdene Mill Betley manor. Mentioned in 1298. It may now (1909) be represented by the place 'Den' on the W side of Betley Mere (SHC 1909 p213 note).

Hailstone Mill See Hawes Hill Mill.

Hawes Hill Mill Post mill situated on Hawes Hill. Recorded on Yates' map (1775), and has appeared as Hailstone Mill. It was probably destroyed by quarrying after 1800 (WBJ p33) by which time another post mill had been built at some distance away, nearer the church, called Rowley Mill (see).

Hazel Mill 1.5m ENE of Penkridge. The site of the mill lies N of Quarry Heath about 200 yards SE of Bangley Park. There may have been a mill here since at least the C13, it being a mill in Pillaton mentioned in c1280. There has been no building in existence since at least 1754. The position of the pool and causeway could still be seen in the 1950s (VCH vol 5 p128).

Heath Mill Industrial Estate On S side of Bridgnorth Road, Wombourne. May take its name from a former mill on the Smestow, near Heath House Drive.

Hyde Park Industrial Estate City Road, Stoke-upon-Trent (Business Directory. City of Stoke-on-Trent. 1997/8).

Imex Business Park On N side of Shobnall Road, Burton upon Trent (East Staffordshire Industrial Directory. 1993/94).

Imex Business Park Ormonde Street, Fenton (Business Directory. City of Stoke-on-Trent. 1997/8).

I-Mex Business Park Upper Villiers Street, Wolverhampton.

Intregrity Industrial Estate Cousins Street, Blakenhall, Wolverhampton.

Ivy House Mill By the Trent S of Bucknall Road, near what is now the junction with Bucknall New Road on the Ivy House estate, Bucknall (VCH vol 8 pp152-153).

Ivy House Paper Mill On the N bank of the Caldon Canal, W of what is now Ivy House Road. Established by the Fourdrinier family, a member of which resided near Stone (see). Ivy House Paper Mill was taken over by Thomas Brittain in 1855 (VCH vol 8 p170) (POTP p99).

Ivy Mill Former mill 1m SSW of Moddershall, at SJ 916354. Built in 1716 as a fulling mill converted to flint grinding in 1756 - was one of the flint-grinding mills of Moddershall Valley (IAS pp43,195) - (COS p51p - perhaps of Mosty Lee Mill?). Has been listed Grade II by DoE. (SPJD p83p) (SIT).

Joan Mill Former ancient mill in Wigmore Lane, 0.75m S of Bustleholme (TMS pp53-57), either on the Tame or on a stream flowing through the Wigmore area and into the Tame. It existed by 1401-2. Owned by Sandwell Priory at its dissolution in 1525 (VCH vol 3 p219. vol 17 p32). The last mill on the site was demolished in 1955 when in a derelict state (TMS p57 pl 4). The name, which has also appeared as Joanne, Jone and Jane Mill, is preserved in Joan Bridge linking Charlemont Road with Ray Hall.

Kems Mill Swindon. See Cockshoot Hill.

Kent's Mill At Hockerhill Farm, Brewood. A windmill which was marked on Yates' map 1775 (and or 1799) at approximately SJ 876084 (WBJ p15). Probably the same mill others mention between Hyde Mill and the Kiddemore Green Road (VCH vol 5 p39) (BDH pp214,215).

Key Business Park Being developed in 2000 on the former Hednesford Brickworks site (SLM April 2000 p49).

King Street Industrial Estate King Street, Fenton (Business Directory. City of Stoke-on-Trent. 1997/8).

Kingswood Lakeside A business park at Churchbridge, near Cannock, close to the forthcoming Birmingham Northern Relief Road (SLM April 2000 p49).

Klondyke Steam Mill A saw mill N of Six Roads End, Draycott-in-the-Clay.

Lichfield Road Industrial Estate Over 1m W of Tamworth. The names of its streets are after astronauts and lunarnauts (VB p33). According to the Birmingham A-Z this district is Staffordshire Moor Industrial Estate, whereas, Lichfield Road Industrial Estate is further to the W.

Lingard Street Industrial Estate Lingard Street, Burslem (Business Directory. City of Stoke-on-Trent. 1997/8).

London Works Cranford Street, Smethwick. Built by Charles Fox (1810-1874), railway engineer, and John Joseph Bramah on part of the Smethwick Grove estate in 1840. The works produced iron work for the Crystal Palace in Hyde Park for the Great Exhibition of 1851, for which Fox was knighted. About this time the works was described as 'the finest and most compact range of (industrial) buildings in South Staffordshire.' The smiths' shop contained 70 forges and was stated to be the largest in the world. As a young man William Siemens (1823-1883), the metallurgist and electrician, worked here (VCH vol 17 pp88,111).

Longus Trading Estate High Street, Tunstall (Business Directory. City of Stoke-on-Trent. 1997/8).

Lord Nelson Industrial Estate Commercial Road, Hanley (Business Directory. City of Stoke-on-Trent. 1997/8).

Malthouse Mill Former tiny hamlet where Salters Lane intersects the Leek Road, 1.75m N of Caverswall, in Caverswall ancient parish. Appears on 1834 OS map. Just opposite cottages at Malthouse Mill is a granite boulder, probably an erratic brought from the Lake District in the Ice Age. There are two others, much smaller, in Green Lane, to the S (WJ pp15,16).

Maltings Industrial Estate S of Ryknild Street, Burton upon Trent (East Staffordshire Industrial Directory. 1993/94).

Mander Centre See Wolverhampton.

Marchington Industrial Estate 0.25m S of Marchington. Formerly Marchington Camp, an army depot. Here is an EEC grain store (MR pp224-225).

Marlborough Industrial Estate Thompson Avenue, Blakenhall, Wolverhampton.

Marcus Industrial Estate Bucknall Road, Bucknall (Business Directory. City of Stoke-on-Trent. 1997/8).

Maullin's Mill Post mill owned by the Maullin family at Roseville, Coseley. Bankruptcy charges declared against James Maullin made him sell the mill in 1813 (WBJ p19). The land on which it stands was anciently copyhold of the manor and was called Stoneacre; it was eventually enfranchised and became freehold in 1871. The mill became a private residence in c1900 (HC p80).

Mayfield Mill By the Dove at Church Mayfield. A mill has stood on this site since 1291, the first being a corn mill. A cotton mill was built in 1793, but it burnt down after 13 years and was left ruinous for another 10 years. After being rebuilt in 1816 it passed through several hands until 1866 when the mill was leased to Joseph Simpson who with his brother George modernised it and considerably enlarged it to its present appearance. The mill closed in 1931 and was not reopened until William Tatton of Leek bought the property and converted it to process silk and man-made fibres (SCSF p112) (MOM p31p). By the early 1970s three (there were formerly four) mill buildings built in the latter C19 survived (BOE p204).

Meir Industrial Estate Whittle Road, Meir (Business Directory. City of Stoke-on-Trent. 1997/8).

Mere Mill A watermill at SO 822886 (MR p147), it was driven by the Philley Brook, N of Enville. Disused by c1935 (IAS p166).

Merry Hill Shopping Centre See Merry Hill.

Milwich Mill (windmill). See Garshall Green.

Morteyn's Mill To S of Walsall. An early post mill, was at approximately SP 013977. In 1304 Sir Thomas Rouse granted to Sir Roger Morteyn a certain road for a horse and cart to the windmill at Walsall. In 1393 it was destroyed in a gale and not rebuilt (WBJ p41). (HOWW p239) (VCH vol 17 p186).

Mosley Business Park On W side of Mosley Street, Burton upon Trent (East Staffordshire Industrial Directory. 1993/94).

Mossfield Industrial Estate Mossfield Road, Mossfield, Longton (Business Directory. City of Stoke-on-Trent. 1997/8).

Mosty Lee Mill Longton Road, 0.75m NE of Oulton. In Kibblestone quarter in Stone ancient parish (W p371). Used to full cloth in the early C18 (SPJD pp78,80pcs,81pcs). Was one of the flint-grinding mills of Moddershall Valley (IAS pp43,195). Has also appeared as Mostelee and Mostylee Mill. The mill ground calcined bones for the bone china industry, stopped working in 1958 (SIT) (SDOPP p73p in 1925). There were plans to turn the mill into a museum after it was restored in 1981 (ES Jan 23 1981 p12p). Kibblestone Manor House may have stood by Mosty Lee Farm (COI p23).

Mount Industrial Estate N side of Mount Road, Stone. Built on former site of Bent's Brewery (closed 1958) by 1980 (SIS 1980 p48).

Mount Road Industrial Estate N of Chase Road, W of New Road and S of Prospect Road, Burntwood (Lichfield District Economic Development Handbook 1997).

Nelson-Linley Industrial Estate The two industrial estates known as Nelson (to the N) and Lindley (to the S) lie N of Linley Road and to W of Congleton Road, Butt Lane (Business Directory Newcastle-under-Lyme Local Authority).

New Albion Works Willenhall. Here was carried on the manufacture of locks and keys.

Newstead Industrial Estate Trentham Road, Trentham (Business Directory. City of Stoke-on-Trent. 1997/8).

Newfield Industrial Estate High Street, Sandyford, Tunstall (Business Directory. City of Stoke-on-Trent. 1997/8).

New Forest Industrial Estate On N side of Town Road, Hanley (Stoke-on-Trent A-Z 1992).

Norton Industrial Estate Bellerton Lane, Norton-in-the-Moors (Business Directory. City of Stoke-on-Trent. 1997/8).

Oak Farm Iron Works Oakfarm, Kingswinford. Founded by Sir Stephen Glynne, Gladstone's brother-in-law in 1836 (SL p195).

Oakley Mill 0.5m S of Croxall. On E side of river Mease. According to 1834 OS map just in Derbys.

Ochre Mill At SJ 920366. Close by to Splashy or Top Mill. Was one of the flint-grinding mills of the Moddershall Valley (IAS p43).

Oldfields Business Park Fenton (Business Directory. City of Stoke-on-Trent. 1997/8).

Old Level Iron Works Most of the works lay N of Level Street, to NE of Brierley Hill. It became part of Round Oak Iron & Steel Works in 1897. Round Oak Steelworks closed in 1982 and the Merry Hill Centre built on the site (OS map Sheet 71.07).

Orbital Retail Park In Leacroft, Cannock (Cannock Chase Past and Present. Britain in Old Photographs. Heritage Independent Photographers. 1996).

Palmbourne Industrial Park or Estate. New estate W of Castletown, Stafford (SN Guide 1999).

Parker Paul Trading Estate Commercial Road, Wolverhampton.

Parkhall Industrial Estate Park Hall Road, Longton (Business Directory. City of Stoke-on-Trent. 1997/8).

Parkhouse Industrial estate 1.75m NNW of Wolstanton. The estate is built on reclaimed land that used to be occupied by clay workings, a colliery, and tileworks. It was started in 1975, at which time it was the largest industrial development in N Staffs. It was an early example of a joint development between the local authority (Newcastle borough council) and a private developer (WA Blackburn Ltd) and was officially opened on Feb 7 1977 (PCCSC pp244p,245). That to the W of the Newcastle-Congleton road is called Parkhouse West Industrial Estate; that to the E of the road is called Parkhouse East Industrial Estate (Business Directory Newcastle-under-Lyme Local Authority).

Park Lane Industrial Estate Park Lane, Fenton (Business Directory. City of Stoke-on-Trent. 1997/8).

Parkside Industrial Estate Hickman Avenue, Wolverhampton.

Pendeford Mill See main body of encyclopaedia.

Pensnett Trading Estate See Becknell Fields Farm.

Perry Trading Estate Bradley, Bilston.

Persehouse's Mill Caldmore, S of Walsall. A windmill at approximately SP 015978 (WBJ p41). Built by John Persehouse between 1612 and 1619. It was probably one of the two windmills in Windmill Field, between Walsall and Caldmore, shown on Plot's map (1682), the other was presumably Blackham's Mill (see). One of the two mills had disappeared between 1732-35. The one that survived still remained at Highgate (see) in 1973 (VCH vol 17 p186). Morteyn's Mill (see) stood in Windmill Field in the C14 (WBJ p41).

Phoenix Industrial Estate Loxdale Street, Bilston.

Phoenix Limeworks Aldridge (VCH vol 2 p196).

Plant Brick Works 0.25m ESE of Kingswinford church.

Pones Mill Water mill at Nether Stowe, Lichfield. A mill here was held by Gilbert Poun, a chamberlain of Bishop Peche, in c1180. In 1242-3 Robert Poun held an estate here called Pones Mill (VCH vol 14 p71). There is a road in Nether Stowe called Pones Green, also a Pones Mill (HOL p510).

Potteries Shopping Centre, The On a site in Hanley bounded by Town and Quadrant Roads, Stafford Street and Market Square, and covering the former River and Empson Streets and Swan Passage. Built by late 1987; Hanley Market in the basement was officially opened on Nov 19 1987 (plaque on wall in market).

Queens Drive Industrial Estate To E of Queen Street, Burntwood (Lichfield District Economic Development Handbook 1997).

Queensway Industrial Estate Longport, Burslem (Business Directory. City of Stoke-on-Trent. 1997/8).

Racecourse Industrial Estate, The Dunstall Lane, Dunstall, Wolverhampton. The name is from the nearby racecourse.

Radial Park Proposed industrial and business park on the E side of the A500 facing the Michelin works, at Sideway, Stoke-upon-Trent (ES May 11 1999 p1).

Railway Enterprise Centre Shelton New Road, Stoke-upon-Trent (Business Directory. City of Stoke-on-Trent. 1997/8).

Raleigh Hall Eccleshall. Hostel built in c1938 for workers at the Royal Ordnance factory at Swynnerton. Now an industrial estate. (SN April 7 1995 p9).

Redhouse Industrial Estate Near Daw End, 1.25m W of Aldridge. Takes its name from Red House (see), Aldridge.

Red House Works Glassworks on a ridge to the E of High Street, Wordsley, by the Stourbridge Canal, at SO 894864. The site was bought by glass maker Richard Bradley in 1788 who built a new works here or developed one already on the site. It is now worked by Stuart & Sons Ltd. The cone or Red Cone, 87 feet high, is the only one intact for some 70 miles since two others at The Dial and the White House Works have been truncated (IAS pp162-163) (MR pp396p,397) (BTBC p37p) (TB Sept 1995 p11p) (WFK p23).

Relay Park Industrial estate to N of the A5 to E of Pennine Way, Glascote Heath, Tamworth (Tamworth Business & Industrial Guide 1995/96. A Tamworth Herald Special Publication).

Rider's Mill Mesty Croft. Stood at approximately SO 997940. It existed on the Rider's estate by 1694 about 0.25m S of their watermill on the Tame. It is shown on a plan of 1767 but not on Yates' map (1775) (WBJ p45) ('Plan of intended Navigation From Birmingham to Canal at Aldersley near Wolverhampton Survey'd 1767. R Whitworth' copy in WSL).

Ringway Industrial Estate On N side of Eastern Avenue, near its junction with Watery Lane, Lichfield. In existence by 1995 (Lichfield District Economic Development Handbook 1997).

Riverside Industrial Estate At Fazeley (Lichfield District Economic Development Handbook 1997).

Rolling Mill Forge or furnace on Cannock Chase near Slitting Mill (SOSH p337).

Round House, The Windmill off Pale Street, Ruiton, at SO 920920. This is Seaby and Smith's tower mill at Lower Gornal. Built in 1830, it was a stone-grinding mill probably to produce the Gornal lily white sand. The sails were removed and it was converted into a house, perhaps in the C19. A photograph shows it as a very short tower built against a bank which must have restricted the air flow through the sails, indeed some of these crushing mills were powered by horses and this may have been one. In time it became uninhabitable and suffered from subsidence. In March 1961 it collapsed (WBJ p35 il xvii in 1950) (WIS p24).

Rowhurst Industrial Estate Rowhurst Close, Apedale Road, Chesterton (Business Directory Newcastle-under-Lyme Local Authority), situated by, or also called, Apedale Business Park (OS Street Atlas: Staffordshire 1995).

Rowley Mill Stood adjacent to Rowley Regis church at SO 969876 and was painted in 1803 by David Parkes (appears

in 'Industrial Archaeology-Molinology' A Dunphy). On the 1834 OS map a windmill is shown here. Has also appeared as Rowley Mill, Iberty Mill and Tipperty Green Mill (BCWJ il facing pp39,72). The mill does not appear in a record of 1887 and the site is now occupied by the graveyard. There was an earlier post mill some distance away which was called Hailstone Mill or Hawes Hill Mill (see), which was destroyed by quarrying after 1800 (WBJ p33).

Royal Albert Works Industrial estate in Parsonage Street, Tunstall (Business Directory. City of Stoke-on-Trent. 1997/8).

Rykn ild Industrial Estate On E side of Derby Road, N of Hawkins Lane, Burton upon Trent (East Staffordshire Industrial Directory. 1993/94).

Sapcote Trading Centre Near Mouse Sweet, Rowley Regis.

Scotia Business Park Scotia Road, Tunstall (Business Directory. City of Stoke-on-Trent. 1997/8).

Scott Lidgett Industrial Estate Scott Lidgett Road, Longport (Business Directory. City of Stoke-on-Trent. 1997/8).

Shardlow's Mill See Coppice Mill, Stone.

Shires Industrial Estate Near the junction of Birmingham Road and Chesterfield Road, Lichfield (Lichfield District Economic Development Handbook 1997).

Smithfield Centre See Leek.

Sneyd Hill Industrial Estate Sneyd Hill, near Hanley (Business Directory. City of Stoke-on-Trent. 1997/8).

Soho Works See Soho Manufactory.

Speedwell Mill See Hammerwich.

Spittlebrook Mill Windmill on the S side of Mill Lane, at SO 845877 on the former Checkhill Common, in Kinver ancient parish. It was built by 1784. Its tower still stands. The remnants of the cap frame still clings to the tower (WBJ pp21,22, il. xv) (IAS p166) (VCH vol 20 p144) (MR p148).

Splashy Mill Mill under 0.5m WSW of Moddershall. SJ 920366. The mill, also known as Top Top, was one of the flint-grinding mills of the Moddershall Valley (IAS p43). There were originally a pair of mills here, believed to have been built by James Brindley. In 1973 one was demolished, the other waterwheel had been restored by 1976 (SIT) (IANS p75p).

Summit Foundry Union Street, West Bromwich. A rival works to Archibald Kenrick & Sons Ltd in Spon Lane. Started in 1822 by Samuel Kenrick. Failed in 1853 (VB p61).

Stag Industrial Estate Oxford Street, Bilston.

Staffordshire Moor Industrial Estate 1m W of Tamworth. The names of its streets are after astronauts and lunarnauts (VB p33). Bird says these streets are on the Lichfield Road Industrial Estate which is further to the W.

Steelpark See Wednesfield.

Stoke Business Park Bowstead Street, off Woodhouse Street, Stoke-upon-Trent (Business Directory. City of Stoke-on-Trent. 1997/8).

Stonewall Industrial Park Stonewall Place, N side of Newcastle Street, Silverdale (Business Directory Newcastle-under-Lyme Local Authority).

Tame Valley Industrial Estate Wilnecote. S of the A5 (Tamworth Business & Industrial Guide 1995/96. A Tamworth Herald Special Publication).

Tamworth Business Park N of Glascote Road and by Mercian Way, S of Amington (Tamworth Business & Industrial Guide 1995/96. A Tamworth Herald Special Publication).

Tilcon Industrial Estate Tilcon Avenue off Baswich Lane, Baswich, Stafford (SN Guide 1999).

Titley's Mill Watermill on the Tean by the Ashbourne Road, N of Uttoxeter. Has also appeared as Uttoxeter Watermill (TRTC p125).

Tollgate Industrial Park An industrial estate in the Beaconside area of N Stafford.

Tollgate Park A business park proposed to be built in 1998 on a 20 acre site beside Tollgate Industrial Park, Stafford (SN July 16 1998 p3).

Tolson's Mill Complex At Fazeley (Lichfield District Economic Development Handbook 1997).

Top Mill At SJ 920366. Could also be called Splashy Mill (see). Formerly one of the flint-grinding mills of the Moddershall Valley. Resembled Cheddleton Mill. The S wheel went in c1915 (IAS pp43,195-196).

Towers Business Park Site being developed in 2000 by Rugeley Power Station (SLM April 2000 p49).

Trentham Lakes Stoke. See Sideway.

Trent Trading Park Botteslow Street, Hanley (Business Directory. City of Stoke-on-Trent. 1997/8).

Tutbury Mill Rocester. See Arkwright's Cotton Factory.

Tutbury Mill Former watermill for cotton spinning, opened in 1781; cotton production moved to Rocester (Arkwright's Cotton Factory) in 1888. Tutbury Mill then became a plaster mill run by Staton & Co of Burton and served the gypsum industry until 1968; the ceiling of the Tower Ballroom in Blackpool, Lancs, is just one example of plaster supplied by Tutbury Mill. The five-storey mill building was demolished in 1972 and the site was then cleared and converted into a picnic area (WTMS p147) (ABTOP p126).

Tutbury (Old) Mill Watermill at SK 287223 to the E of Tutbury on the Mill Fleam of the Dove. The site is perhaps identifiable with a mill in the manor of Rolleston in DB. The present three-storey mill building is of the C18, and may have been known simply as the Old Mill. It ceased work as a corn mill in 1914, and was then adapted to be used as a tannery, which survived until 1986 when part of the associated buildings became a tea-room (IAS p201) (WTMS p147).

Two Woods Trading Estate S of Two Woods Lane, S of Merry Hill Shopping Centre, Brierley Hill (Birmingham A-Z 1995).

Usam Industrial Estate Wood Lane, Bushbury.

Ventura Park Business or industrial estate S of the Tame (Tamworth Business & Industrial Guide 1995/96. A Tamworth Herald Special Publication).

Virage Park New (1999) out-of-town shopping park on the E side of Walsall Road between Bridgtown and Cannock (SLM Oct 1999 'Business Life' xiv).

Waterside Industrial Estate Millfields Road, Ettingshall.

Webner Industrial Estate Ettingshall Road, Ettingshall.

Wednesbury Forge See main body of encyclopaedia.

Westport Lake Industrial Estate Canal Lane, Tunstall (Business Directory. City of Stoke-on-Trent. 1997/8).

Wetmore Mill 0.5m NE of Oulton, at SJ 916359. Was one of the flint-grinding mills of the Moddershall Valley (IAS p43). Closed in 1958. Has also appeared as Whetmore Mill and Kibblestone Mill (SIT).

Whetmore Mill See Wetmore Mill.

Whieldon Road Business Park Whieldon Road, Fenton (Business Directory. City of Stoke-on-Trent. 1997/8).

White House Works On a ridge to E of High Street, Wordsley, by the Stourbridge Canal, at SO 894864. In 1883 it was stated as established in 1812, and is on a map of 1824. The cone, 66 feet diameter at the base, was truncated in 1939 (IAS p163).

Wilson Brewery Burton upon Trent. Probably a reference to the brewery of Benjamin Wilson (d1800) and his son Benjamin (d1812), which became Wilson-Allsopp Brewery.

Winton Works Industrial estate in Newlands Street, Stoke-upon-Trent (Business Directory. City of Stoke-on-Trent. 1997/8).

Wolverhampton Business Park Lies immediately S of the M54, E of the Stafford Road on the approximate side of Lesscroft Farm. Constructed in 1998-9.

Wolverhampton Science Park Lies on the E side of Stafford Road on the site of former gas works, S of Showell Road. Opened in 1996 as a joint venture with Wolverhampton council and partly funded by the University of Wolverhampton (University of Wolverhampton Web Page. 1998).

Wulfrun Trading Estate Stafford Road, Wolverhampton.

Some collieries, mines and quarries

Adderley Green Colliery Longton. At SJ 915451 (IANS p37). Closed in 1939 (TWWW June 1991 p23).

Aldridge Colliery 'No. 1 Pit' or called 'No. 1 Plant' of this colliery was owned by Aldridge Brick Tile and Coal Company and situated near Boatmans Lane, Leighswood, Aldridge. It was nicknamed 'Drybread' as it was said miners working at it were so poor they could only afford to eat dry bread (ALOPPR p38p). Or the same pit was owned by the Aldridge Colliery Company and situated near Coppice Road (ADY p6).

Allen's Rough Colliery Allen's Rough. At SJ 973021. Operated from 1910 to 1932 (SNW p4) (ESSN pp46,47).

Amington Colliery Situated 0.75m SE of Amington at SK 242037. In existence in 1888 (1888 OS map 6 inch).

Anchor Colliery In Anchor Road, Longton. Working in 1859. Seems to have been closed in about the mid 1870s (VCH vol 8 p244).

Apedale Colliery Alsagers Bank. By the 1830s a depth of 2000 feet was attained making it the deepest mine in Britain at the time (IANS p34). There was a disaster here on Sept 23 1878 which killed 23 miners (VCH vol 2 p1) (IANS p38) or it occurred in March (LWF p110). Another disaster occurred on April 2 1881 which killed 10 (LWF p110). Another occurred on June 20 1885, which killed nine miners (IANS p38) (LWF p110). Closed in 1969 (ES Feb 11 1998 p3).

Ashmore Park Colliery Ashmore Park. Operated from 1875 to 1939 (ESSN pp46,47). There was a site at SJ 957018 and another at SJ 960026. Both sites are now built on with housing (OS map 1:25,000).

Ashtree Colliery Old Hill, Rowley Regis appears on 1884 OS map (TB Aug 1982 p11).

Baggeridge Colliery 0.25m S of Gospel End, near Baggeridge Wood Farm, in Sedgley ancient parish. The colliery opened in 1896 (BCM Feb 1968 p21). Some say it opened in 1899 (TEBC). It closed in 1968 and was the last Black Country colliery to close (SL p265). A bronze medallion was made and sold to commemorate its closure (BCM Feb 1968 p21 p of the medallion). In 1910 JJ Shaw, seismologist, embarked on experiments at Jubilee Pit and Baggeridge Colliery to determine whether the moon exerted tidal effects on land masses as well as on sea (BCM spring 1995 p53). The Baggeridge poker, was a free poker given away with every purchase of a ton of coal, and attempted to promote coal sales (TB March 1976 p29p). (AMS pp161-167) (TB June 1998 pp10-11ps) (BCM March 1998 p69).

Balls Hill Colliery On E side of Holloway Bank, Balls Hill. Working by 1812 (VCH vol 17 p40).

Bank Top Colliery Formerly off High Lane, Burslem. Was being worked by 1856. Closed because of flooding in early 1880s (VCH vol 8 p139).

Barcroft Colliery Spring Bank, Willenhall. Operated in the mid C19. The name, from a meadow known as Barr Croft (1841), is preserved in the street named Barcroft (SNW p6).

Bare Bones Colliery Situated near Coppice Road. May be identified with 'No. 2 Pit' of the Aldridge Colliery Company (ADY p6).

Barn Farm Colliery NE of The Lunt, Bilston, at SO 964970. Is shown as working in 1901 (Bilston 1901 OS map 62.16), but disused by 1947 (1947 OS map 1:25,000 sheet 32/99).

Barnfield Colliery See Wednesfield.

Barrs Pit Old Hill, Rowley Regis. The name, which has also appeared as Haden Hall Colliery, is from the owners Messrs Best and Barrs.

Bassiloes Old colliery shaft in the Silverdale area (IANS p128 map).Batchcroft Colliery Lost. Was at Stowlawn, Bilston and appears on OS map 1834; there was also a Batchcroft Colliery NE of Darlaston (Offlow hundred).

Bateswood Colliery Former open cast coalmine to S of Halmer End in existence by 1987 (1987 OS map 1:25,000).

Closed in 1990. In 1997 Staffordshire Wildlife Trust took over the area from British Coal to run it as a nature reserve known as Bateswood Country Park. In Oct 1998 a memorial rock with a plaque was erected in the park to the memory of Bill Parry (d1996) a former ranger of the park (ES Oct 19 1998 p9p. May 10 1999 p3). The name is from a wood called Bates Wood.

Beacon Colliery Formerly to E of New Invention, at SJ 976018. Operated in c1860 (ESSN pp46,47). Beacon Junior and Infant School is now on the site (Birmingham A-Z).

Bedbrook Colliery Slightly S of Woodhead Colliery, NNE of Cheadle (CCT p36 see map).

Belle Isle Colliery Situated SW of Brierley Hill railway station and shown on the 1921 OS map. A school playing field occupies much of the site. The name is preserved in a crescent known as Belle Isle (SNSV vol 1 p35).

Bell's Mill Colliery Shelton. Here human remains were discovered in May 1852 in a pool which itself was of great age. The bones of an infant in one wooden box with bits of cord suggested that the infant in the box had been strangled. In Aug 1868 a boiler exploded. The boiler flew into the air and travelled across Etruria Road and the offices of the Shelton Bar Iron Company and the roof of a rolling mill. Only one man was slightly injured (SHST p630).

Bentley Colliery On the Longton and Adderley Green railway line (NSFCT 1982 p16).

Berry Hill Colliery SW of Berry Hill Farm, Bucknall. At SJ 893460. In operation by 1841, and still operating in 1957 (VCH vol 8 p247). Had a disaster on March 12 1872 which killed six miners (LMV p112). Closed in 1960 (ES Feb 11 1998 p3).

Biddulph Hall Colliery Situated 0.5m WSW of Biddulph Old Hall on the E side of the Congleton Road. The colliery was working in 1853 (BALH p68).

Biddulph Valley Colliery See Victoria Colliery.

Bignall Hill Colliery Bignall Hill, Chesterton. In operation by 1803 when owned by Wedgwood of Bignall Hill (AHJ 1996 p16). There was an explosion here on Dec 24 1874, which killed 17 men (IANS p38) (A p123) (LWF p111). Another disaster here, also caused by an explosion, on Nov 25 1911 took the lives of six men (LWF p111).

Birchenwood Colliery The colliery, also known as Kidsgrove Colliery, was worked from the mid C19. George V and Queen Mary visited the colliery on April 23 1913 (R&S p44) (ES Nov 16 1996 p21). A Zeppelin dropped a bomb on a spoil bank at the colliery in the early hours of Nov 28 1916 (TB July 1994 p19). There was a big explosion and fire at the colliery on Nov 18 1925 which claimed the lives of seven or eight miners, and seriously injured 14. The colliery closed in 1930 or 1931 (TTTD p213) (KNS p160) (LWF p111) (Kidsgrove, Talke and Mow Cop. Postcards from the Past. Roger Simmons 1998 p67).

Black Bat Pit Whiteheath. It was the sound of trapped miners in a tragedy at this pit that many believed found its way onto a tape recorder in 1978 of someone who lived in a house approximately on the old mine site. The mine closed in 1883 (TB Sept 1978 p1).

Blackhills Quarry 1m NW of Smestow.

Black Lake Colliery Black Lake, S of Hill Top, West Bromwich. Had a disaster on Nov 22 1871 which killed eight miners. Thomas Hand, a poet and herbalist of New Cross Street, wrote a poem entitled 'The Dreadful Colliery Accident in the Black Lake Thick Coalpit near Hill Top, West Bromwich' about the tragedy (BCM July 1975 p45) (TB March 1996 p20). The report on a fire at the colliery was a scoop for David Christie Murray (VB p63).

Black Pit Tansey Green. Only a pile of rubble now marks the site of the former engine house (TB June 1985 p17).

Black Wagon Colliery Old Hill, Rowley Regis (TB May 1993 p19). Owned by the New British Iron Co (ORR p100). On Jan 8 1878 the night watchman, Samuel Bowater, was murdered. A burglar killed him and stole his watch which

had been issued by the Earl of Dudley to those involved in the Nine Locks Pit rescue of 1869. The murderer was never found, although in the 1930s the watch turned up with the murderer's name on it, but he had been killed in a mining disaster shortly after the murder (TB June/ July 1972 p10 Oct 1981 p5. March 1982 p5).

Blackwells Colliery Gornal Wood (VCH vol 2 p98).

Bloomfield Colliery Bloomfield. In 1776 a Boulton and Watt pumping engine, the first commercial beam engine in the country, was set up here. It was of unprecedented size and in less than an hour emptied a pit 90 feet deep containing 57 feet of water. It had a 50 inch cylinder and a seven feet stroke. It was the first to embody the separate condenser invented by James Watt and was constructed by the firm of Boulton and Watt. In the grounds of the British Rolling Mills (now Firsteel Cold Rolled Products) a plaque was unveiled by Lord Northesk on behalf of the Newcomen Society in May 27 1959 to commemorate the engine (VCH vol 2 p165) (IAS p87) (TSSOP p8p).

Blue Devils Pit Moxley. Haunted by a pit ghost who followed a thief at the mine near Moxley (BCS pp12-18, 83-86).

Blue Fly Colliery Pelsall. See Lommy Colliery.

Blue Fly Colliery Tipton. Had a disaster in 1849 when 16 men and boys lost their lives (OH p70).

Blue Fly Colliery Wednesbury. In existence in 1897 (WDOP p37).

Boothen Colliery Rushton Grange, Cobridge. To N of the Hanley boundary at Vale Place. In operation by the 1860s Still operated by end of the C19 (VCH vol 8 p140).

Botteslow Colliery Botteslow. Closed in the early 1880s (BUB p37).

Bowmans Harbour Colliery See Wednesfield.

Boyles Hall Colliery Close to Boon Hill. In operation by 1803 when owned by W Burgess (AHJ 1996 pp16,80).

Bradbury's Colliery Biddulph. See Bradley Green Colliery.

Bradley Colliery Bilston. Owned by Capt GB Thorneycroft. A disaster occurred here on May 30 1862. Four men and three boys were lost in No. 7 Pit (TB Dec 1987 p17).

Bradley Green Colliery Bradley Green, Biddulph. Developed after 1838. The colliery was known locally as Bradbury's Colliery. Abandoned in 1894 (BALH p66).

Bradley Hall Colliery See High Hall Colliery.

Bradley Row Colliery To W of Fiery Holes, Moxley. Disused by 1901 (Bilston 1901 OS map 62.16).

Breen Rhydding Colliery Situated to the E of Upper Ettingshall. Operating in 1901 (OS map Sheet 67.03).

Brereton Colliery Brereton. An inrush of water claimed the lives of three miners on Feb 15 1908 (LWF p111).

Brick House Colliery At Cock Green, Rowley Regis (VCH vol 2 p98). It appears to have started up in the 1820s and closed after becoming flooded and unworkable in 1880 (SHC 1950/1 pp245-263) (SL p198) (TB Oct 1988 p16).

Brickhouse Colliery West Bromwich ancient parish. Perhaps in the Brickhouse Lane (Great Bridge) area. In 1873 an attempt was made to drain and reopen the colliery, which had closed c1843 (VCH vol 17 p41).

Brick Kiln Pit Alias Brereton Colliery. It was the last pit in the Brereton area to close (1960) (info Harry Thornton).

Broadfield Colliery Lay to the S of Fenton Park Colliery. In existence by 1832 and closed in the mid 1860s (VCH vol 8 p222).

Broad Lane Colliery N of Dudley Fields, at SJ 990026, on W side of Cannock-Walsall railway. Operated from 1904 to 1918. Also known as the Struggling Monkey (ESSN pp46,47).

Broadwaters Colliery Moxley. A field of the colliery is now the area about Holyhead Road. The battered body of Mrs Esther Baggott, aged 35, was found on the field in Nov 1867. The motive and identity of her murderer has never been discovered. Her husband and father-in-law were not above suspicion, nor her lover, Caudwell; she might have been a witness to a murder some time prior to her murder

(TB Jan 1983 p9). She may be a ghost which haunts in this area (TB Dec 1996 p11).

Brookhouse Colliery NE of Berry Hill, Bucknall. In operation by 1841 (VCH vol 8 p247). Had a disaster on March 2 1864 which killed five miners (LMV p112). It closed in the early 1880s (BUB p37).

Brown End Quarry Waterhouses. Here were a rare variety of rocks to be found (SN 22 May 1987 p2 - but this reference is incorrect). By 1999 Brown End Quarry at SK 090502, of geological interest, was a SSSI nature reserve in the care of the Staffs Wildlife Trust (Staffs Wildlife Trust leaflet).

Brownhills Colliery Brownhills, 1.5m SE of Norton Canes, on S side of Watling Street. Or known as 'Cathedral Pits' (SSE 1994 p47). Brownhills Colliery was opened sometime before 1834 (SNBC p6).

Brownhills Colliery Tunstall. Owned by Robert Heath, was W of Brownhills Road. In operation by the early 1870s. Closed in 1902 (VCH vol 8 p139).

Brown Lees Colliery Brown Lees. In existence by 1866 (BALH p70). Was acquired by Robert Heath from the Williamson family in 1887 (CIOPP p64). A fossilized tree trunk was found in the roof of Holly Lane seam of this colliery, at a depth of 244 yards. It was found on Sept 10 1906 (SMOPP vol 2 p14p). The colliery closed in 1927 (CIOPP p64).

Brymbo Pit See Holditch Colliery.

Bunker's Hill Colliery Bunker's Hill, Kidsgrove. There was an explosion on April 30 1875 at the colliery (ILN May 8 1875 p439il) which killed 42 people. The cause of the explosion remains a mystery (LGS p226) (LWF pp32-35p) (KAIW p17). Some say 43 were killed (VCH vol 2 p93) (IANS p38) (LMV p112). A large stone Neolithic or Bronze Age axe-hammer was found during excavations in 1884 (NSFCT vol 65 p155) (NSJFS 1962 p28. 1964 p38) (KAIW p2). The colliery closed in c1931 (AHJ 1996 p18).

Burley Pit Colliery 0.75m WSW of Chesterton. Had a explosion on June 20 1885 which killed nine men (SA July 18 1885 p6): A chimney with an inscription on the sides of its walls remains as a memorial to a mining disaster (SVB p55). At SJ 820494 (IANS p37). Formerly owned by the Midland Coal, Coke and Iron Company. They also owned Podmore Hall (pit or colliery) and the Minnie Pit (AOPP pl 46).

Butcher Mills Pit Alias Waterfall Lane Colliery, Rowley Regis (TB May 1981 p11).

Bycars Colliery Burslem. In operation by 1816, and was being operated in the 1880s (VCH vol 8 p139). (NSSG p10). Had a disaster on Jan 29 1859 which killed five miners (LMV p112).

Calcroft Colliery To the S of Golden Hill Colliery, Longton. Was working in the mid 1870s (VCH vol 8 p222).

California Colliery Gave its name to California Road, Tividale (TB Jan 1983 p13).

Cannock and Huntington Colliery Opened in 1873 (LHSB 50 p33).

Cannock and Leacroft Colliery Opened in 1871 (LHSB 50 p33).

Cannock and Wimblebury Colliery Opened in 1873 (LHSB 50 p33).

Cannock Chase Colliery Seems to have comprised a number of pits, mainly belonging to the Marquis of Anglesey, situated in the Chase Terrace, Hammerwich and Hednesford areas:- The Marquis (No. 1) (see), The Fly (No. 2) (see), The Preference (No. 3) (see), Hammerwich No. 4 Pit (see), Hammerwich No. 5 Pit (see), No. 6 started in 1866, No. 7 (at SK 035112) started in 1868, No. 8 (at SK 022106) started in 1868, Old Hednesford Colliery (No. 9) (see), and No. 10, which was also situated at Old Hednesford (LHSB 50 p5).

Cannock Lodge Colliery 2m ENE of Essington, at SJ 988044. Operated from 1875 to 1910 (LHSB 50 p33) (ESSN pp46,47).

Cannock Old Coppice Colliery Opened in 1876 (LHSB 50 p33).

Cannock Wood Colliery Cannock Wood. Opened by 1938 and closed in 1973 (CCAP p139).

Castle Bridge Colliery S of Ashmore Park. Between the Wyrley & Essington Canal and Lichfield Road, at SJ 959011, in Wednesfield (see) chapelry. Operated from c1874 to 1885. Was part of Perry Hall Colliery (ESSN pp46,47).

Cathedral, The Hammerwich No. 2 Pit. See The Fly.

Cathedral Pits Brownhills. See Brownhills Colliery.

Cheadle New Colliery 0.25m SE of Cheadle. Established by 1865. Nicknamed the 'Turf field' and was situated off the first corner of Mill Road, opposite what was in 1981 the recreation ground (CCT p109).

Cheadle Park Colliery Cheadle Park. Opened in 1884 or 1886 on a site long known as the Racecourse and used as such for local competition on fair days and holidays, consequently the colliery was known locally as the Racecourse pit. The colliery closed in 1915 (CCT pp131,148,150) (ACOPP p75p).

Cherry Eye Mine A mine which extracted iron ore. It was in the vicinity of Cherry Eye Bridge and was worked until 1921. So called from the ore dust making the miners' eyes red (MR p111).

Churchbridge Colliery Churchbridge, Cannock. Opened in 1874 (LHSB 50 p33).

Church Colliery NE of Priestfield, N of the Wolverhampton Road. In the Green Lanes area. The colliery occurs on the 1885 OS map.

Cinderhill Colliery East Vale, Longton. Working by 1865. Seems to have closed by the mid 1870s (VCH vol 8 p244).

Clanway Colliery Sunk by the Child family in c1800. Closed in 1902 (VCH vol 8 p90).

Clothier Colliery Operating in the mid C19. Takes its name from Clothiers Farm, Willenhall (SNW p18).

Clough Hall Colliery Kidsgrove. Had a disaster March 1 1865 which claimed the lives of five miners (LMV p112). In 1892 a 29-year-old miner was killed when coal tubs ran loose down a sloping tunnel at No. 6 Pit (KAIW pp17-18).

Coal Leasow Colliery By The Leys W of Brockmoor, still operating in 1900 (TB March 1983 p34 see map).

Cobridge Colliery Cobridge. Probably in operation by 1818 and open by 1834. Was working up to c1894 (VCH vol 8 p140).

Cockshead Colliery Norton-in-the-Moors (VCH vol 2 p166). Working in 1778 and in 1817 (ONST 1950 p146).

Cockshutts Colliery Cockshutts, SSE of Wolverhampton. The colliery where Thomas Francis stole a quantity of rope in 1813 and was whipped at the cart's tail (SCSF p129).

Codsall Colliery Stood in the centre of Codsall Coppice, Cradley Heath (SNSV vol 2 p21).

Cole's Farm Colliery In vicinity of Coles Lane, Hill Top. Opened in c1820 by Messrs Botteley and others (OWB p76).

Conduit Colliery Situated 0.75m E of Norton Canes (SSE 1994 p47). Opened in 1873 or 1874 (LHSB 50 p33). Proper name for the colliery is Jeromes' Colliery, after Rev Jerome Clapp Jerome, father of the novelist Jerome K Jerome, who was a prospector in the colliery. Rev Jerome lost everything in the disaster at the colliery on May 2 1860 (CCF pp49-52). A ghost haunted the old cart yard at Jeromes's pit (BCM April 1986 p42). Conduit Colliery had an accident in 1926 when the cage went out of control and fell to the pit bottom. The men received severe injuries but nobody died.

Coneygree Colliery Coneygree. Belonged to Lord Dudley and Ward, sited between the Birmingham Canal and Birmingham New Road and is intersected by the railway line from Dudley to Dudley Port. Lady Meadow (see), land belonging to the colliery, has been identified as the site for Newcomen's steam engine, erected in 1712. The engine is believed to have been the first to be erected in England, and it was employed to drain water out of former coal mines here. An inrush of water claimed the lives of three miners on Feb 10 1865 (LWF p112). Has also appeared as Conygree Colliery. (The Coneygree Story. WKV Gale. 1954).

Conygree Colliery See Coneygree Colliery.

Coppice Colliery Heath Hayes. A disaster occurred here on Feb 6 1861 which claimed the lives of five men and two boys. The colliery flooded on Feb 15 1908 and 30 to 40 men and five pit ponies were drowned (Miners' Memories Council Source Book 1987). Some say the colliery opened in 1893/ 4 and was sunk by Robert Hanbury of Ilam Hall (LHSB 50 p6). Was one of the largest collieries in the Cannock Chase Coalfield in 1954 (VCH vol 5 p62). It was known locally as the Fair Lady Colliery (VB pp124-125) (VCH vol 2 p1. vol 5 p62) after Hanbury's widow who took a benevolent interest in the pit and its workers (LHSB 50 p6).

Coppice Colliery Between Hateley Heath and Black Lake at SO 999930. Appears on 1947 OS map 1:25,000 (sheet 32/99).

Coppice Colliery In the vicinity of Ashmore Park, Wednesfield (WHTOP p76).

Coppy Hall Colliery At Stubbers Green. Working in 1889 (MOA p120). Closed in 1909 (ADY p6).

Corbyn's Hall Colliery Stood near Corbyn's Hall, Kingswinford, near the railway and canal (SNSV vol 1 p82).

Corngreaves Colliery Corngreaves. There was an accident at the colliery on July 3 1852 which caused three deaths (TEBC2 p66).

Corper Colliery Local name for the Cooperative Colliery, Halmer End (IANS p136). It was a small colliery.

Coseley Moor Colliery Coseley Moor. In existence in 1789 (HC p65).

Crablane Colliery To W of Bromley, Kingswinford, S of Bromley Lane, disused by 1900 (TB March 1983 p34 see map).

Crackley Colliery Crackley Gates, Silverdale (IANS pp128 see map, 130).

Crackley Colliery Crackley, Chesterton (IANS p133 see map).

Dale Hall Colliery Middleport. In operation by between the early 1860s and the early 1870s (VCH vol 8 p139).

Dale Mine Between Warslow and Ecton. A lead and copper mine. In operation for about 150 years before closing in 1873 (NSFCT 1979 p23).

Dandy Pit Pensnett. Had a disaster 21 April 1923 which claimed the lives of three miners - William Simmons, Joe Dando, and Tom Jordan. Their graves are in Pensnett parish church churchyard (TB Feb 1978 p7. Jan 1985 p9) (BCOPP vol 2 pl 111). The pit may be the same as Pensnett Pit (see), which had a disaster in 1933.

Deep Ecton Adit See Ecton Deep Adit.

Deepmore Colliery Lay to the N of Bentley Hall. In existence in the later C19 (OS map 6 inch). The name is preserved in Deepmore Avenue (SNWA p36).

Deep Pit Far Green. See Hanley Deep Pit.

Delphouse Colliery To the W of Cheadle and to E of Boundary. First mentioned in 1802. The colliery seems to have reopened in the early C20 and closed in c1917 (CCT pp140-141). Duignan writes of a Delph in N Staffs (DUIGNAN p50). It is another form of the word, delves. (VCH vol 2 p85).

Desseldine Colliery Pensnett Chase (VCH vol 2 p98).

Diglake Colliery At SJ 812499, Bignall End, Audley. Opened in 1818, enlarged and deepened in 1860. It closed in 1895 following a major flooding disaster on Jan 14 1895 at Boyles Hall No. 3 Pit. The numbers killed vary - 77 and only five bodies were recovered (IANS pp38,58p of scenes of the disaster) or 75 and a skeleton was found in c1925 (NSFCT 1984 p16) (LWF p112). It achieved the unusual distinction of recognition in the national press (TSS p35). Paderewski, the great Polish pianist, donated the proceeds of his concert in 1895 at Victoria Hall, Hanley to the victims of the disaster (TSS pp133,135). In 1989 a memorial stone listing the 77 dead (says 78 were killed) was placed over the spot where three unnamed victims of the disaster are buried; their skeletons were found in 1933. 72 bodies still lie buried. (ES March 10 1933 p1. Jan 6 1995 pp10-11p of mem) (STM Sept 1963 p47p of ES Supplement from Jan 14 1895, p of top of the shafts now overgrown) (POTP p156) (TFTP pp100-103) (A pp124-126). The colliery under-manager, William Dodd of Bignall End, at the time of the disaster, was awarded the Albert Medal for bravery by Queen Victoria at Windsor Castle on March 9 1895 (SVB p34).

Dog and Moor Colliery Old mine working. In the Kingsley-Dilhorne area (NSJFS 1965 p112).

Dosthill Colliery Situated to the E of Dosthill, at SK 209000. Formerly in Kingsbury township and ancient parish, Warws. In existence in 1884 (1884 OS map 6 inch).

Drybread Colliery See Aldridge Colliery.

Dumolo's Colliery Colliery N of Wilnecote at SK 228023. Formerly in Bolehall and Glascote township in Tamworth ancient parish. Name is from John Dumolo of Kettlebrook, coal master, living in the early C19 (TDOPP p76). The colliery was disused by 1888 (1888 OS map 6 inch).

Dutchman's Level Lead and copper mine at the foot of Ecton Hill, at SK 098582, Ecton (MR p141). Has also appeared as Dutchman's Mine. Tradition states that a Dutchman riding along Ecton Level suddenly sprang from his horse to examine a stone it had kicked, presumably he noticed it contained copper ore, the result was the mines were reopened and worked. Whether John Rovenzon, was the Dutchman, is not known. He had come over prospecting with the Germans in 1632 (WTCEM p79) (EH pp16-18 -

Dutch Miners, pp5,6,10,11,15,18,20-2,36,40,48,51,81-3,87 - Dutchman Mine). The entrance is now covered by a huge spoil heap (IAS p203) (MR p141).

Ecton Deep Adit Copper mine on the W side of Ecton Hill. It may be identifiable with the Duke of Devonshire's mine, worked to 1825, see under Ecton. Ecton Deep Adit was driven by Robert Shore (IAS p203) or Shaw in 1774 (MR p141) (DMV pp60p,61p). At its close it was believed to be the deepest mine in Great Britain, at 1,650 feet. Although a shaft at Monkwearmouth Colliery in Sutherland was reputed to the deepest at 1600 feet (AAD pp148 -156). The mine was originally called Old Level. The inscription '1774 RS' over the well-constructed entrance, at SK 096581, is not original (IAS p203). A cheese factory had the entrance altered. The entrance is now blocked up (EH pp26il of the entrance prior to alteration, 27,pl 2 p of entrance after alteration c1920, pl 3 p of entrance in early C19, pl 4 inside Ecton Deep Adit, 82).

Eagle Colliery At Cherry Orchard, Old Hill, N of Waterfall Lane Colliery. Opened up by a Welshman, Joshua Morgan, who died in a colliery disaster here. His ghost subsequently haunted the colliery and was responsible, according to miners here, for the murder in c1852 of Archie Cartwright, the colliery foreman with a tyrannical temperament. Cartwright, who was murdered probably by one of the miners in reprisal, is buried in Rowley Regis churchyard (TB April 1983 p5 see map. May 1983 p5).

East Cannock Colliery Hednesford (VCH vol 5 p62). Opened in 1871 (LHSB 50 p33). Closed by May 1957 (CCAP p135).

Eaves Colliery The Eaves, 1m SSE of Cheadle, at SK 011414. Started in 1806 (CCT pp25 see map,61).

Ebenezer Colliery West Bromwich. An explosion of gunpowder in a house of a banksman of the colliery near the colliery on April 30 1826 claimed the lives of four people; the banksman's wife and two of his three children were killed, as well as another child (Broughton's Scrapbook p447).

Elm Tree House Colliery At Kingswinford Cross. May also have been known locally as 'Strip-an'-at-it.' Stood behind Elm Tree House (BCM March 1998 pp23-24).

Empire Colliery Summerhill, Tipton. Appears on 1947 OS map 1:25,000 (sheet 32/99), at SO 959937.

Essington Farm Colliery 1m ESE of Essington, at Sneyd Farm, at SJ 977028. Ran from 1874 to 1904. Hilton Colliery, which continued to 1926, was a part of it (ESSN pp46,47).

Essington Wood Colliery Essington Wood, at SJ 965033. Opened in c1850. Became Holly Bank Colliery in 1895 and closed 1952 (ESSN pp46,47). The site appears to have been built on (OS map 1:25,000).

Fair Lady Colliery See Coppice Colliery.

Fair Lady Pit See Leycett Colliery.

Fair Oak Colliery Cannock Chase (VCH vol 2 p88). Opened in 1871 (LHSB 50 p33).

Fair Oak Colliery Great Wyrley (VB p123). Could be same as above, or could be same as Norton Cannock Colliery (see).

Far Green Colliery Far Green, Hanley. Had a disaster on Nov 5 1859 which killed ten men (IANS p38).

Fenton Park Colliery Mentioned by Ward (HBST p554). Closed in c1879 (VCH vol 8 p222).

Fernley Colliery 0.5m NNE of Froghall. Was operating in 1892 (CCT p31 see map).

Fibbersley Colliery See Longer Moors.

Firestone Pit Bilston. When reopened in 1870 after several decades miners noted the ghost of Abel Hill (d1820), murderer and former collier at Princes End Colliery (TB Dec 3 1998 p5). Princes End Colliery may be the same as this pit.

Fishley Colliery Stood on W side of Fishley Lane, S of Fishley Charity Farm. Fishley Colliery No. 4 plant, at SJ 997044, operated from c1860 to c1905 (ESSN pp46,47). The site S of Fishley Charity Farm was operational in 1887, but disused by 1938 (OS maps 6 inch to 1m). A man from Fishley Colliery told Duignan that Fishley was still (1896) often called 'Thistley,' which supported Duignan's argument on the etymology of Fishley (DUIGNAN). Fishley Plant Colliery only came into full production after the building of the Lord Hay's Branch of the Wyrley & Essington Canal through to Newtown (SOB p124).

Five Ways Colliery At Cradley Heath. It had a disaster on Oct 19 1844 which claimed the lives of 11 men (TB Sept 1981 p17).

Florence Colliery Blurton. Opened by the Duke of Sutherland in 1874 (VCH vol 8 p244). Some say it more properly opened in 1894 (TWWW June 1991 p23). Named after the suburban development Florence. It had the first steam turbine engine in the country, installed by GA Mitcheson (POTP p156). The colliery closed in 1990 (Mining Memories. Fred Leigh). By 1999 the slag mounds of the former colliery had been partly landscaped for public recreation and the area of the former colliery buildings near Lightwood Road was partly built on with two housing estates called Lightwood Park and Lightwood Grange.

Fly, The Nickname for Hammerwich No. 2 Pit of the Cannock Chase Colliery. One of the Marquis of Anglesey's coal mines. Situated at SK 037084, 0.5m WNW of Chasetown. Opened by 1852 and at first known as The Uxbridge. Later known as The Cathedral, and then as The Fly after the speed of winding (BCM vol 9 No. 3 p56). In 1883 electricity was introduced into the pit and The Fly was claimed to be the first pit in the world to be electrically lit. But a pit at Hamilton (Lanarks) claims to have been lit in 1882. Closed in 1940 (VCH vol 14 pp215,216).

Fly Colliery, The Old Hill, Rowley Regis. In existence by 1851 (TB June 1978 p11p. Aug 1982 p11).

Foley Colliery A coal and ironstone colliery, in Heathcote Road, Longton. Had been opened by 1826. From the mid 1860s it was known as the Swingle Hill Colliery. There was a Foley Ash Colliery being worked in conjunction with the Swingle Hill Colliery in 1882 (VCH vol 8 p244 note).

Forest Colliery The Forest, E of Birchills. Was in operation by 1881 (VCH vol 17 p164 note). The name, from The Forest (see) area, is preserved in Forest Lane (SNWA p44) and Forest Comprehensive School on S side of Hawbush Road.

Foxfield Colliery Foxfield, 1m NNE of Dilhorne. Opened in c1880. John Whiterst of Cellarhead was killed by a roof fall in July 1907. Luke Harvey of Godley Lane, aged 72, was killed at the colliery in Oct 1911. Thomas James, a banksman, badly injured his foot at the colliery in 1912 and died shortly after. The colliery closed in 1965 (CCT pp134-138) (ES Feb 11 1998 p3).

Fullwoods End Colliery Fullwoods End, Coseley. In operation in 1901 (OS map Sheet 67.04).

Garratt's Lane Colliery Old Hill in existence by 1851 (TB Aug 1982 p11).

Gatacre Colliery Temple Street, Lower Gornal. It had a disaster on July 7 1923.

Gawn Colliery Rowley Regis (TB Oct 1988 p17 see map).

Gilmour Colliery 0.75m N of Froghall (CCT p31 see map).

Glasshouse Colliery Chesterton. At SJ 826505. So named as it stands near to a C17 glassworks (IANS pp37,133) (VCH vol 2 p86). Closed in 1960 (ES Feb 11 1998 p3) and the area is now Waterhays Village.

Glebe Colliery Fenton. Opened in the 1860s and still operating in the 1950s (VCH vol 8 p222). An explosion on June 15 1963 claimed the lives of three miners (LWF p112). The colliery closed in 1964 (POP pp63,119) (ES Feb 11 1998 p3) and some of its land became Glebedale Park (SOTB p114).

Golden Hill Colliery Longton. Was worked between 1854 until at least 1872 (VCH vol 8 p222).

Golden Hill Colliery Goldenhill. It had a tunnel linking it to the Harecastle Tunnels. A second tunnel which linked this tunnel with the surface was located behind Latebrook House. The connecting tunnel is about 1.5m long (NSFCT 1938 pp61,62).

Golden Orchard Colliery Coombs Wood. Popularly known as 'The New Plant.' Eight miners became trapped and died in the pit on March 18 1929; one man, Jabez Edwards, survived (TB May 1996 p21ps. May 1997 p7p).

Grace Mary Colliery Stood close to the top of Darby's Hill, almost 800 feet above sea level. Its No. 2 shaft at SO 969891 cut through the basalt laccolith to reach the Thick Coal 812 feet below the surface (WMLB p112). The same or another colliery known as Old Grace Mary Pit was on Turners Hill (TB Jan 1983 p13).

Grange Colliery In the Rushton Grange area of Cobridge. Opened by the late 1860s by Robert Heath. Closed by the early 1920s (VCH vol 8 p140).

Great Bridge Colliery Great Bridge. Appears to have been opened between 1812 and 1816 (TB May 1995 p16). In 1873 an attempt was made to drain and reopen the colliery (VCH vol 17 p41).

Great Fenton Colliery Great Fenton. It had a disaster on April 8 1885, which killed eight miners (IANS p38) (LWF p113).

Great Row Colliery WSW of Chesterton (NSFCT 1993-4 New Series vol 19 p32). A small colliery (IANS p131). Was at approximately SJ 822487.

Great Wyrley Colliery Opened in 1875 (LHSB 50 p33).

Grove Colliery Brownhills (near Norton Canes). An explosion at the colliery on Oct 1 1930 claimed 14 lives (ADD p108).

Grove Colliery Knutton. At SJ 828470 (IANS p37).

Grove Pit At Great Wyrley or Norton Canes or Brownhills. An explosion at the pit on Oct 1 1930 killed 14 miners (VB p124) (TB March 1984 p14) (LWF p113) (BWWOPP p5p).

Haden Hill Colliery Haden Hill. No 2 Pit was known locally as the Pretty Pit. By 1901 it was owned by the Barrs family (OS map Sheet 71.08) and during their ownership was known locally as Barrs Pit. During a strike in winter 1858 a miner at the colliery, Alastair McBane, a Scotsman who broke the strike, was murdered by other miners. His ghost is said to haunt the former colliery area (TB July 1982 p5).

Hall End Colliery Church Lane, Hall End, West Bromwich. In existence by the 1830s (VCH vol 17 p39). Had an explosion on Sept 6 1884, which killed seven miners (LWF p113) (TEBC) (TEBC2 p120).'Black' Jack (John) Higginson, a miner at the colliery, murdered with burning coals 'Lame' Joe Marshall, a banksman, in July 1871 (TB April 1976 pp14-15). Leigh lists Hall End as a North Staffs mine (LMV p110).

Hallfields Colliery Hanley. On the high ground at the upper end of Market Street (now Huntbach Street). It was in operation by 1851. Probably closed shortly after 1858 (VCH vol 8 p169).

Hammerwich No. 1 Pit See The Marquis.

Hammerwich No. 2 Pit See The Fly.

Hammerwich No. 3 Pit See The Preference.

Hammerwich No. 4 Pit One of the Marquis of Anglesey's coal mines of the Cannock Chase Colliery. Situated at SK 042084, 0.25m NW of Chasetown. Opened 1854. Disused by 1883 (VCH vol 14 pp215-216).

Hammerwich No. 5 Pit One of the Marquis of Anglesey's coal mines of the Cannock Chase Colliery. Situated at SK 042092, 0.75m N of Chasetown. Was being sunk in 1861 (VCH vol 14 p216) and started in 1862 (LHSB 50 p5). Closed in c1919 (VCH vol 14 p216).

Hamstead Colliery At SP 045928. Hamstead Colliery Co Ltd opened the colliery on the Perry Hall estate in 1875. The colliery has also been called Hamstead Hall Colliery (VH pp1,75-86) (VCH vol 17 p41). Coal was found at 1,836 feet, making this the deepest worked seam in the world at the time (MNB p72). A fall of rock killed miner, Thomas Page, on June 1 1878; he became the colliery's first victim (VH p1). Here was a fire disaster on March 4 1908 which caused the deaths of 23 men and boys (Birmingham Mail 4 March 1908) (TB March 1974 p1. May 1974 p9 postcard. March 1983 p15 postcard) (LWF p113). The colliery ceased production in 1965 (VCH vol 17 p41).

Hanley Deep Pit Pit sunk in 1868 at Far Green, Hanley, or opened in 1854. Formerly part of Shelton Colliery. It was stated in 1869 to be the deepest pit in N Staffs. Was the only colliery working in Hanley from c1937 (VCH vol 8 p169). Closed in 1961 (PCCSC p243) or 1962 (ES Feb 11 1998 p3). Central Forest Park incorporates its grassed-over slag heaps, once known as the 'Three Ugly Sisters;' one had gone by 1972 (VB p190). The old winding wheel is left at the entrance to the Park as a memorial to the Pit (IANS p61p) (MR p177). The colliery has also appeared as Deep Pit (OTP p162). Thompson mentions a Far Green Colliery which may be this (IANS p38). The pit is called Bantock Burden Pit in HG Wells' 'In The Days of the Comet' and 'The New Machiavelli' (ES March 5 1996 p5).

Harden Colliery Harden. Ceased production in 1905 (VCH vol 17 p164 note) (BY p26).

Hardingsfield Colliery Situated S of Daisy Bank, Coseley, at the junction of Barnsley and Skidmore Road and Brierley Lane. Operating between at least 1887 and 1901, but not by 1938 (OS maps).

Harecastle Colliery Stood at the S end of Bath Pool, Harecastle. In operation in the later C19 (Kidsgrove News April May 1998 p9). In 1892 a 17-year-old engine tenter was crushed at the colliery (KAIW p17). Became flooded in 1930; three men drowned (TTTD p213). Closed in c1931 (AHJ 1996 p18).

Harrison's Pit In the S Cannock area (VB p124).
Hatherton Colliery In operation by 1862 (VCH vol 5 p78).
Hawkins' Colliery S of the A5 SW of Cannock (PCC p46) (VB p124). Closed in the early 1960s. The name is from the Hawkins family (The Cheslyn Hay Book. Rick Bowring. 1977).
Hayes Colliery Brereton. Opened by the Marquis of Anglesey in 1817. The colliery attracted many Irish miners to Brereton during the early C19. Closed during the 1950s (AR p52p).
Hayswood Colliery S of Halmerend. Bateswood opencast coalmine covers the site (IANS p135).
Hazlewall Colliery 1.25m WSW of Kingsley, at SJ 993461. Opened in 1874 (CCT p131).
Heath Colliery SE of Heath Town. Opened in 1833 (MH 1984 p65).
Heath Colliery Near Christ Church, West Bromwich. In operation from 1833. Owned by Lord Dartmouth. Coal was becoming exhausted here by the 1860s (VCH vol 17 p40).
Heathcote Hill Colliery See Longton Hall Colliery.
Heath Hayes Pit Heath Hayes. See Coppice Colliery.
Hem Heath Colliery Chesterton. See New Hem Heath Colliery.
Hem Heath Colliery Former colliery at Hem Heath, known as The Big 'A' because of its distinctive A-shaped head gear operating from 1924 (NSJFS 1965 p92 pl VIc); it has also appeared as Trentham Colliery (ES May 12 1993 p1). On Feb 25 1915 there was a disaster here which killed 12 men (IANS p38). The colliery's Moss Seam, at 3,300 feet, was considered the deepest mine workings in the United Kingdom between at least 1969 and 1974 (GBR 1969 p168. 1974 p134). Hem Heath Colliery inspired the musical documentary 'Miner Dig the Coal' which was performed in 1981 (ES May 13 1981 p4p). During the miner's strike of 1984 and 1985 the weighbridge office at Hem Heath was firebombed (LWF p72) (SSE 1987 p229). Three wives of miners, Bridget Bell, Brenda Proctor and Gina Earle, members of the North Staffs Miners' Wives' Action Group, occupied between May 12-15 1993 No. 2 Pit Head to protest against proposed colliery closures by the Government; a play about this protest called 'Nice Girls' has been staged at the New Victoria Theatre at Stoneyfields (see) (ES May 12, 13, 15 1993 p1). (FWNS pp77-80ps). The colliery closed in 1997 and the A-shaped head gear was removed by 1998 (ES March 7 1997 p13). By 1998 an industrial and business park called Trentham Lakes was proposed to be built on the site (ES Aug 1 1998 p6. Feb 9 2000 p10).
Highbridge Colliery Highbridge, Pelsall. Owned by Elias Crapper and was the scene of several accidents. In 1870 two men and a boy were buried alive here (SNBP p81). An inrush of water claimed the lives of three miners on March 31 1871 (MOA p120) (LWF p113). In Nov 1872 a naked candle flame caused an explosion of sulphur in which a man was badly burnt (SNBP p81).
High Carr Colliery High Carr (IANS p134 see map p135).
Highfields Mine See main body of encyclopaedia.
High Hill Colliery S of Essington, at SJ 959027. Operated from 1910 to 1939 (ESSN pp46,47). Has also appeared as Bradley Hall Colliery.
High Lane Open Cast Mine Knutton. Begun by British Coal by 1992 (MIDD vol 1 pp10,11p).
Hill and Waldren Colliery At Caledonia, Amblecote.
Hilton Colliery 1m ESE of Essington. Formerly part of the Essington Farm Colliery which operated from 1874 to 1904. Hilton Colliery closed in 1926 (ESSN pp46,47).
Hilton Main Colliery Under 1.5m WNW of Essington, at SJ 940043 by the Wolverhampton Cannock road. Sunk in 1922 (LHSB 50 p36) to replace Holly Bank Colliery (SNW p36). Officially opened on Sept 30 1924 (BCM spring 1999 p37) and closed on Jan 31 1969 (ESSN pp46,47,87). The colliery site was developed as Hilton Main Industrial Estate in 1980 (info South Staffs Council).
Hobbs Hole Colliery At King's Hill, Wednesbury, at SO 987961. Is shown as disused on 1947 OS map 1:25,000 (sheet 32/99).
Hockley Colliery Situated to W of West Coseley. In operation in 1901 (OS map Sheet 67.07).
Hockley-hall Colliery In existence at SK 219000 to the W of Hockley Hall. Formerly in Kingsbury township and ancient parish. In existence by 1884 (1884 OS map 6 inch).
Holditch Colliery Chesterton. Operating from 1912. An explosion at the colliery's Brymbo pit on July 2 1937 killed 30 miners. When the rescue party were underground there were two massive explosions which killed a further 27 people; a football match at the Victoria Ground, Stoke-upon-Trent, between Stoke City and Glasgow Rangers, on Oct 19 1937, raised money for the relief fund (TSS p114; says 1936) (IANS p38) (LWF p114) (ES Sept 10 1994 p5. Nov 25 1999 p13). What may be a Roman coin of Nerva was found at this colliery (NSJFS 1964 p31). The colliery closed in 1989 and lies in the area to be redeveloped to create Lymedale Park (ES July 3 1997 p3. Feb 11 1998 p3).
Hollins Colliery In Audley parish. In operation by 1803 when owned by RE Heathcote (AHJ 1996 p16).
Holly Bank Colliery Essington Wood, at SJ 965033. Formerly known as Essington Wood Colliery, which had opened in c1850. Became Holly Bank Colliery in 1895 and closed when Hilton Main Colliery opened in 1924. But reopened in WW2 and continued until 1952 (ESSN pp46,47) (SNW pp36,37) (Wolverhampton Chronicle April 28 2000 p22p).
Holly Bush Colliery S of Berry Hill, Fenton. Was operating by at least 1852. Later amalgamated with Berry Hill Colliery (VCH vol 8 p247).
Holly Hurst Kingswinford. An ironstone deposit site (VCH vol 2 p120). Perhaps in the vicinity of Hollyhurst Drive off Stream Road?
Hollywood Old colliery 1m WSW of Silverdale (IANS pp128 see map, 129). (MIDD vol 1 p12).
Homer Hill Colliery Fenton. It had a disaster on Nov 11 1867 in which 12 miners died (IANS p38) (LMV p112).
Hoods Meadow Colliery See Well Street Colliery.
Hope Colliery S of Orchard Farm, 1m NNW of Flash, at SK 01756877. Opened in 1925, and closed in 1932 (VCH vol 7 p52) (SSE 1996 pp70 see map,79,87).
Horton Colliery Close to Ketley Brickworks, Kingswinford. Disused by 1900. (TB March 1983 p34 see map).

Ivy House Colliery The colliery lay between Leek New Road and the Caldon Canal, E of Ivy House Road, Hanley. It was being worked by 1841 and was closed in c1889 (VCH vol 8 p169).

Jackfield Colliery Was being worked by 1832. Closed because of flooding in c1889 (VCH vol 8 p139). Jackfield Pit was part of the Scotia and Pinnox Colliery, Tunstall. It was abandoned in the late C19 (POTP p231).
Jamage Colliery Situated at the foot of Bignall Hill, at SJ 822517. Owned in 1882 by W Rigby & Co on behalf of J Wedgwood (AOPP pl 54) (AHJ 1995 p17). Some pit ponies were rescued out of this colliery on Dec 18 1911 after spending 22 days down the pit (AOPP pl 53). Jamage Pit closed in 1941 (AHJ 1997 p48).
James Bridge Colliery James Bridge. Was working by 1843 and abandoned in 1901 (VCH vol 17 p158).
Jenny Lind Pit See Millpool Colliery.
Jerome's Colliery See Conduit Colliery.
John Wood's Colliery Wednesbury. Here Francis Ward was underground manager; he was John Wesley's host whilst staying at Wednesbury on Jan 5 1743 (SOB p141).
Jubilee Colliery West Bromwich. See Sandwell Park Colliery.
Jubilee Quarry On Darbys Hill (TB Jan 1983 p13. March 1983 p23).

Kemball Colliery Heron Cross, Fenton. Closed in 1963 (ES Feb 11 1998 p3).
Kent's Lane Colliery Former name for Silverdale Colliery (IANS p130) (S&COP pl 23) (MIDD vol 1 p13).
Kettlebrook Colliery Situated 1m ESE of Kettlebrook at SK 226025. In existence in 1888 (1888 OS map 6 inch).
Kevin Quarry Limestone quarry 1.25m NW of Wootton (SVB p137).
Kidsgrove Colliery Kidsgrove. See Birchenwood Colliery.
Kingsley Moor Colliery Old mine working. Situated in the Kingsley Dilhorne area (NSJFS 1965 p112).
Klondyke Colliery Opened in c1900 in the Draycott Cross Harplow area, W of Cheadle. The colliery closed in 1906 and shortly became part of the New Haden Colliery (CCT pp150-151).

Lake Quarry Chief quarry of the Rowley Regis Granite Company (TB March 1983 p23).
Ladymoor Colliery Ladymoor, Sedgley. Operating in 1901. Stood between the canal and Ladymoor Road (OS map Sheet 67.03).
Ladywell Colliery 1.25m N of Cheadle, at SK 003452 (CCT p25 see map).
Lake Quarry Chief quarry of the Rowley Regis Granite Company (TB March 1983 p23).
Lane End Colliery To W of Longton. Probably in operation by 1832. Closed in c1888. Another colliery named this, which may have been a branch, existed in the mid 1860s, in Heathcote Road (VCH vol 8 p244).
Lawn Colliery To SE of Brookhouse Colliery, Bucknall. In existence by the 1870s (VCH vol 8 p247).
Leacroft Colliery Cannock Chase (VCH vol 2 p1). May be the same as Cannock and Leacroft Colliery (see).
Lea Hall Colliery 1m SE of Rugeley. Opened in 1960 (Miners' Memories. Staffs. Council Source Book 1987) (HOS 1998 p103) and was the first completely new mine opened by the National Coal Board after nationalisation (SL p264). Closed in 1990 (E&S Aug 16 1997 p33). The colliery site opened as Towers Business Park in Nov 1998 (ES Nov 21 1998 p9) (VCH vol 2 p89).
Lee Colliery Situated S of Lee House, on the S side of Fold Lane, Biddulph. In existence in 1851 (BALH p68).
Leighswood Colliery Leighswood. An accident occurred here when a hanging scaffold used in a shaft fell 300 yards with two men on it in 1876 (MOA p119). Closed in c1881 (ADY p6).
Leycett Colliery Leycett. Pits like Nelson, Victory and Blucher were first driven in the early C19 (SL p117). The two pits comprising Leycett Colliery appear to have called 'The Fair Lady' and 'Bang Up' (MHSP p56) (LWF p51). A disaster occurred on Jan 3 (IANS p38) or Jan 12 (LWF p51) 1871, and claimed the lives of eight miners (IANS p38). Another disaster on Sept 8 (IANS p38) or Sept 12 (LWF p51) 1879 killed another eight. There was another disaster on Jan 21 1880 killed 62 miners (IANS p38) (LWF p51); according to Kennedy this disaster occurred in 1879 and 31 victims were buried in Madeley churchyard on the same day (MHSP p57). Yet another disaster on Oct 16 1883 killed six miners (LWF p51). Closed in c1957 (AHJ 1997 p48)
Lillydale Colliery Bucknall. It had a disaster on May 3 1881 which killed eight miners (IANS p38). Has also appeared as Lily Dale Colliery (BUB p39-40). Presumably, Lillydale Road, Townend, Bucknall, preserves the name.
Litley Colliery Litley. Opened in 1873 (CCT p131).
Little High Carr Colliery Situated to W of High Carr Farm. Another colliery High Carr Colliery was on the A34 (IANS pp133 see map, 134).
Littleton Colliery At Huntington, operating from 1877 (ES Feb 11 1998 p3). Others say it opened in 1896 (LHSB 50 p33). (VCH vol 2 p1). Closed in 1993 (ES Feb 11 1998 p3). Part of the colliery site was developed as Littleton Business Park in the 1990s (South Staffs Council).
Lodge Hole's Colliery Woods Bank, Darlaston (Offlow hundred). Appears on 1947 OS map 1:25,000 (sheet 32/99), at SO 976962.
Lommy Colliery Lommy or The Lommie was the local name for the Blue Fly Colliery at the end of High Field Road North, Pelsall. It re-opened briefly in the 1920s (SHOP p9) (SNBP p85).
Longhouse Colliery 1m SW of Kingsley. Seems to have opened in the later C19 on the Shawe Hall estate (CCT p122).
Long House Colliery Owned by Lord Hatherton, in the Cannock area (VCH vol 5 p62).
Longton Hall Colliery (coal and ironstone) Longton. Closed in 1895. May have been also called Heathcote Hill Colliery (VCH vol 8 p244 note).
Lyttleton Hall Colliery West Bromwich. There was an explosion at the colliery on Feb 26 1855 (TEBC2 p72).

Madeley and Leycett Colliery Whether two separate collieries - Madeley Colliery, and Leycett Colliery. Had a disaster on Jan 21 1880 which killed 62 miners (IANS p38 - just called Leycett Colliery (see)). Madeley Colliery had some pit head baths designed by WA Woodland, which were of architectural note, but were demolished in c1974 (BOE p200). Madeley Colliery closed in 1957 (ES Feb 11 1998 p3).
Marquis, The Nickname for Hammerwich No. 1 Coal Pit of the Cannock Chase Colliery. At SK 042074, 0.25m SSE of Chasetown. Opened by the Marquis of Anglesey in 1849. The Anglesey Branch Canal, incorporating a feeder from Norton Pool, was cut in 1850 to link the pit with the Wyrley and Essington Canal (VCH vol 14 p215). Closed in 1865 (SVB p86). Has also appeared as The Marquess.
Maryhill Colliery Kidsgrove, presumably in the Maryhill Close area. The colliery closed in 1929 after an inrush of water here on Jan 17 1929 which claimed the lives of three

miners (LWF pp111,115) (KAIW p18).

Meadow Stile Colliery Situated near the junction of Newpool Road and Tower Hill Road, Brown Lees. In existence by 1837 when owned by John Bateman ((BALH p70).

Meir Hay Colliery To SE of The Woodhouse, Longton. In operation by 1791. Closed in 1888. Is possibly the same as Millfield Gate Colliery (VCH vol 8 p244 note) (POTP p157).

Mid-Cannock Colliery Cannock Chase. Started in 1873, was abandoned in 1882. Reopened in 1914 (VCH vol 2 p1. vol 5 p62) (LHSB 50 p33).

Miles Meadow Colliery Ashmore Park, at SJ 962017. Operated from 1889 to c1908. It was part of Pool Hayes Colliery (ESSN pp46,47). The site is now built over with housing (Birmingham A-Z).

Millfield Gate Colliery See Meir Hay Colliery.

Millfields Colliery On W side of Wolverhampton Street, Bilston. Disused by 1901 (Bilston 1901 OS map 62.16).

Mill Hayes Colliery Burslem. Was E of the Sytch Mill. Was being worked by the early 1860s (VCH vol 8 p139).

Millpool Colliery Hateley Heath. Also known as the Jenny Lind Pit after an ale-house of the same name, situated in Allerton Lane (TB Aug 1995 p6).

Minnie Pit See main body of encyclopaedia.

Mitchell's Wood Colliery Red Street (IANS p133 see map).

Moat Colliery Operating in the Summerhill and Tibbington area in the C19 (VCH vol 2 p86). The name is from Old Moat Farm (see), Tipton.

Moat Colliery Wolverhampton. In operation in 1816. Owned by the Marquess of Stafford (MH 1984 p76).

Mobs Bank Colliery N of Bilston. Lost. Is on 1834 OS map. Probably at Mobb's Bank.

Moorland Colliery Blakeley Lane, 2.25m N of Dilhorne on N side of A52. Open cast mine opened in 1955 and seems to have closed in c1965 (CCT pp169-170).

Moor Lane Colliery Withymoor. Lost. In existence 1812. (TB Aug 1984 p14 see map).

Mosey Moor Colliery Moseymoor Wood is 0.5m N of Froghall. A colliery of this name seems to have been worked in 1920s (CCT pp161-162).

Mossfield Colliery Bucknall. Was to the SE of Mossfield. Also known as 'Old Sal' (LWF p58) (WYV p44 - short personal account of a disaster here), perhaps on account of its proximity to Salt's Cottage, which may have been corrupted to 'Sal' (TWWW Jan 1997 p5). It had a disaster Oct 16 1889 in which 64 miners were killed (IANS p38) (LWF pp58-61) (LMV p116) or 66 killed (TWWW Jan 1997 p5). (ES Oct 16 1989). In another disaster on March 21 1940 11 miners died (IANS p38) (LMV p116) (TWWW Jan 1997 p5). Another disaster occurred at the colliery in 1891, or POTP p156 has the wrong date? Longton Cemetery has a memorial to those killed in the 1889 disaster (TFTPM p36 il). The colliery closed in 1963 (ES Feb 11 1998 p3). A rare five-inch tall bee orchid, was discovered by children on a former slag heap of the colliery, described as Berry Hill Fields, in July 1997. Also on Berry Hill Fields was discovered a three feet high block of undercite or glacial erratic in July 1997, transported here in the Ice Age (ES July 9 1997 p1pc. July 10 1997 p1pc).

Mowul Quarry Sandstone quarry at Talke (VCH vol 2 p187).

Nabbs An old colliery shaft N of the Scot Hay road, Silverdale (IANS p128 map).

Nagersfield Colliery Belonged to George King Harrison, firebrick manufacturers, and was situated at the bottom of what is now Harrison Road. In operation in the 1920s (BHOP2 p36p).

Nettle Hill Quarry Mayfield. On the right of Swinscoe Hill. Also known as Nettler Quarry (MOM p73p).

New Grace Mary Pit Colliery on Turner's Hill. Became the Twin Pit (TB Jan 1983 p13).

New Haden Colliery 1.25m W of Cheadle, at approximately SJ 991424. Opened in Oct 1906. At least 25 miners lost their lives during the life of the colliery. The colliery seems to have closed in 1943 (CCT p160) (ACOPP p74p) (COPP2 p31p). It had its own rail line link to the Cheadle railway (IANS p29). The name is from Haden Cross, near Old Hill, Cradley Heath and had been given to the colliery by the owners, the Bassano brothers of Haden Cross, one brother being AH Bassano. The district covered by the colliery has, since the closure of the colliery, adopted the name (CCT p152).

New Hem Heath Colliery To E of Crackley Bank, and S of Parkhouse Road West, Chesterton (IANS p133 see map). There was a fire at the colliery in 1912 (S&COP pl 60).

New Invention Colliery New Invention, at SJ 968018, near Allen's Rough Farm. Operating in c1840 (ESSN pp46,47).

New Plant, The See Golden Orchard Colliery.

Nine Apostles, The A pit at Rowley Regis (TB Sept 1978 p29).

Nine Locks Pit Wallows Colliery, Brierley Hill. Or No. 29 Pit (BCM April 1969 pp29-34). Had a disaster between 17 and 20 March 1869 in which three men were trapped underground for 140 hours, two were saved but one, William Ashmore, died (TB March/ April 1973 p23. Nov 1980 p13. March 1995 p11. April 1995 pp18-19. June 1998 pp1il,18). Other articles in TB say 12 miners were trapped, but all lived (TB March 1986 p15p. Aug 1988 p10). Another account says the Nine Locks Colliery had a disaster in which 13 men and boys were imprisoned for four days and nights by an inlet of water. An epigram, titled the 'Noble band of Volunteers,' was written about the rescue party who managed to save 12 (NEE p14). Stories allege that the trapped men were less noble; choosing, by drawing straws, a 13 year old boy, Tom Sankey to be eaten first if not rescued. Fortunately, the rescuers arrived before such drastic action occurred (TB March/ April 1973 p23p) (MMBCC p94p).

Nook and Wyrley Colliery Cheslyn Hay. Was in operation from 1874 until 1949 (VCH vol 5 p101). Has also appeared as Nook Colliery (The Cheslyn Hay Book. Rick Bowring. 1977).

Northwood Colliery Northwood, Hanley. North of the junction of Bucknall Old and New Roads. Was in operation by the mid 1860s. Closed in c1920 (VCH vol 8 p169). One of its shafts caved in in the middle of the night in Aug 1956 and created holes on a flood-lit training area at Northwood playing fields used by schools and athletic clubs (ES Sept 7 1996 p19p).

Norton Cannock Colliery 2m NE of Essington, at SJ 988050. Otherwise known as The Fair Oak. Operated from 1874 to 1908 (LHSB 50 p33) (ESSN pp46,47).

Norton Colliery Norton-in-the-Moors. The first shaft was sunk in c1860 (ONST 1973 p336). An explosion occurred at the colliery on Feb 12 1912, which was described as the most violent explosion that had happened in any colliery in the country, by mining engineers. No miner was killed but 76 pit ponies died (LMV p40). In 1958 (TFTPM pp90-101) or 1968 (ONST 1973 p336) it became the first pit in N Staffs to operate underground conveyor belts by remote control (TFTPM pp90-101). The colliery closed in 1977 (ONST 1978 p386) (ES Feb 11 1998 p3) and the reclaimed land is now represented by Newford Valley (SOTB p115). (TFTP pp67-70).

Nowell's Bank An old pit mound on King's Hill, Wednesbury (TB Oct 1993 p21).

Nutty Slack Mine at SJ 962027, 0.5m S of Essington. Was part of the Ashmore Park Colliery (ESSN pp46,47).

Oak Farm Colliery (VCH vol 2 p99).

Ocker Hill Colliery The Zeppelin L19 dropped five high explosive bombs on the colliery in its raid over Wednesbury on the night of Jan 31 1916 (BCM autumn 1996 p56).

Old Coppice Colliery Cheslyn Hay. Was in operation by 1851, and still in operation in 1954 (VCH vol 5 p101).

Oldfalls Colliery Cheslyn Hay. Was in operation in 1851, but not by 1880 (VCH vol 5 p101).

Oldfield Colliery Longton. Was operating from c1826. Closed in 1896 (VCH vol 8 p223). Had a disaster on May 25 1855 which killed seven (IANS p38) (LMV p112). Has also appeared as Old Field Colliery. Presumably, was about Oldfield Brick Works and Oldfield Street.

Old Hednesford Colliery or Cannock Chase No. 9 of the Cannock Chase Colliery. Near the Cross Keys Inn. It had a disaster caused by an underground fire in the bottom pit on Dec 14 1911 in which five (or 25) men and 20 pit ponies were killed (CCAP p134) (TB April 1995 p18) (CCAP p134).

Old Lion Colliery Rowley Regis (VCH vol 2 p76). It was the first mine in the area and the name Lion was used for a subsequent iron tube works, a road, and an inn built in the same Cherry Orchard area (OS map Sheet 71.08).

Old Malkins Colliery See Well Street Colliery.

Old Nelson Colliery Kidsgrove. If at SJ 840535 (IANS p37) then was near the N entrance to the Harecastle Tunnel.

Old Sal Nickname for Mossfield Colliery, Longton.

Orchard Common Colliery Main producer of coal in Quarnford parish. Worked in the later C19 (UHAW p46).

Overmoon Open cast mine by Consall village stretching down to Consall New Hall, which had begun by 1956. Is loosely considered to be on the Cheadle coalfield (CCT

p173). Partly in Caverswall and Dilhorne ancient parishes.

'Owd Dan's' Nickname for Pit No. 5 at Biddulph Valley Colliery, Knypersley. Situated on E side of the main Biddulph to Tunstall road. Opened in Sept 1862. Named after Daniel Shufflebotham (BALH p73).

Paddock Colliery Dudley (VCH vol 2 p98). May have been situated at The Paddock, Coseley.

Pagett's Croft Colliery A rope cut in a shaft here on Jan 30 1863 claimed the lives of three miners (LWF p116).

Park Colliery In Castle liberty, Tamworth (W p627). And hence once in Warws.

Parkfield Colliery Parkfield, Sedgley parish. In this colliery have been found 73 fossil trees with roots. These belonged to the fern and club moss type, but were of gigantic proportions (AMS p11).

Parkhall Colliery 1m NW of Cheadle. Opened in 1873 (CCT p133) or in 1876 (ACOPP p74p). In 1920 'Rifter' Coxon of Cheadle was killed at the colliery by runaway tubs and William Oliver of Cheadle was the victim of gas (CCT p133). Had a rail line link to the Cheadle railway (IANS p29). The colliery had closed by 1930 (CCT p134).

Park Hall Colliery 1m E of Longton. At SJ 925435 (IANS p37). Closed in 1962 (ES Feb 11 1998 p3).

Parkhouse Colliery Colliery at SJ 840500 (IANS p37), Chesterton. Tony Walker (b1942) of Goldenhill, cross country running champion, worked as a maintenance fitter at this colliery (TWWW Feb 27 1999 p24). Closed in 1969 (ES Feb 11 1998 p3). Name is probably from Bradwell Old Park (see).

Parklands Colliery Alsagers Bank (NSFCT 1993-4 New Series vol 19 p32).

Park Pits Rushall. Originally the Upper Park Works Limestone Quarry (VCH vol 2 p196).

Pearsons Colliery Old Hill. In operation in 1901 (OS map sheet 71.08). Disused by 1988 (TB Oct 1988 p16) and now covered by housing.

Pear Tree Colliery Situated to the E of Wedgwood Lane, Gillow Heath, Biddulph. In existence in 1842 (BALH p63).

Pelsall Hall Colliery Lay in the Mouse Hill and Hillside Crescent area of Pelsall (SNBP p83). Sister Dora of Walsall (see) came to the aid of those bereaved by the death of 22 men killed in a disaster at the colliery in Nov 1872. Subsequently, she attracted fond attentions from Kenyon Jones, the colliery manager, aged 29 (BCM July 1977 pp44-46) (TOS pp121-124) (ADY p24) (MOA p120). The reporting of the disaster was a scoop for the novelist David Christie Murray (VB p63). The disaster relief fund started for the widows and orphans was still in existence in 1984 (ADY p24).

Pelsall Wood Colliery An accident occurred here when winding machinery was working out of gear in 1859 (MOA p119).

Pendlebury Colliery Between Bentley and Darlaston Green (Offlow hundred). Appears on 1947 OS map 1:25,000 (sheet 32/99), at SO 983983.

Pennant Hill Colliery To NE of Oldhill Iron Works or S of Cock Green. Here was an explosion at the pit bottom in mid Oct 1915 between or around 15 or 22 Oct 1915, which killed four miners and 14 pit ponies (TB May 1976 p1ps. June 1976 p6. July 1976 p16. Oct 1988 p16. Oct 1997 p12).

Penny Hole Colliery S of Orchard Farm, 1m NNW of Flash, at SK 01816872 (SSE 1996 p70 see map). (W p748).

Pensnett Hill Colliery Old Hill. In operation in 1901. Is now covered by housing (OS map Sheet 71.08).

Perry Hall Colliery Perry Hall, at SJ 966011, in Wednesfield (see) chapelry. Operated from 1876 to 1885. Castle Bridge Colliery (see) was a part of it (ESSN pp46,47).

Pensnett Pit Pensnett. Had a disaster in 1933 (TB April 1979 p8). The pit may be the same as Dandy Pit (see).

Perry Sinking Coal mine sunk in 1876 on the Perry Hall estate in the Baltimore Road area of Perry. It was subject to such heavy flooding from alluvium, pebble beds, and sandstone strata as to prove unworkable (MNB p72).

Pinnox Colliery Colliery in operation at Burslem by the late 1820s. Fell into disuse in 1869 and was soon flooded. Taken over by the Chatterley Iron Company by 1888 (VCH vol 8 pp138,139).

Pit Lays Colliery (VCH vol 2 p104).

Pitt Street Colliery Developed by the 4th Earl of Dartmouth, in West Bromwich area (VB p64).

Plant, The Hammerwich No. 3 Pit. See The Preference.

Plant Colliery Pelsall, near the former Pelsall Ironworks (SHOP pp9,11).

Podmore Hall Colliery Situated N of Podmore Hall, Halmer

End. Has also appeared as Podmore Colliery (NSFCT 1993-4 New Series vol 19 p32). Owned by Sir Nigel Gresley in 1803 and in 1882 by Cooper and Craig (AOPP pl 47) (AHJ 1996 p16). Minnie Pit (see) was a part of the Colliery. The colliery had closed by 1983 when there was a local dispute about whether the remaining site should be landscaped (ES July 22 1983).

Pool Dole Colliery Fenton. Was being worked between the early 1850s and at least the late 1860s (VCH vol 8 p222).

Pool Hayes Colliery Pool Hayes, Willenhall. Between the Lichfield Road and Wyrley & Essington Canal, at SJ 968010. Operated from c1870 to c1908. Miles Meadow Colliery (see) was a part of it (ESSN pp46,47).

Preference, The Nickname for Hammerwich No. 3 Pit of the Cannock Chase Colliery. One of the Marquis of Anglesey's coal mines. Situated at SK 036089, 0.75m NW of Chasetown. Also known as The Plant. Was being sunk in 1859. Was the last of the Hammerwich pits to close when closed in 1959 (VCH vol 14 p215,215).

Pretty Pit See Haden Hill Colliery.

Princes End Colliery Princes End. Abel Hill, executed for a double murder in July 1820, was a collier at Princes End Colliery (TB Dec 3 1998 p5). See also Firestone Pit.

Pump House Colliery Near Dudley Port in West Bromwich parish. Had an explosion of foul air in late Oct or early Nov 1835; 24 people were killed, including some women and children (SA Nov 7 1835) (Broughton's Scrapbook p467).

Racecourse Old Colliery Shaft Mine situated between Park Road and High Street, Silverdale. The name, preserved in Racecourse Street (IANS p128 map), appears to be from the old race course on Knutton Heath (see).

Racecourse Pit A mine which commenced in c1870 at the rear of Etruria Hall it had three shafts (OTP p162). The mine ceased in c1937 (VCH vol 8 p169).

Racecourse Pit See Cheadle Park Colliery.

Railway Colliery Duke Street, Fenton. Operating by 1841. Ceased to operate in c1862 (VCH vol 8 p223).

Ramping Old Colliery Shaft S of the Scot Hay Road, Silverdale (IANS p128 map).

Ramrod Hall Colliery By Ramrod Hall. An explosion here on Aug 13 1856 caused by a gas leak killed 11 miners (LWF p117) (TEBC2 p73), two were boys aged 12 (Brierley Hill Advertiser Aug 16 1856. Aug 30 1856) (BCM winter 1989 p67). No. 1 Pit closed in 1903 and No. 2 Pit closed in 1921 (TB Sept 1978 p29. Sept 1986 p27).

Rattlechain Pit In Corngreaves Colliery (TB March/ April 1973 p15. August 1978 p15; is part of Stour Colliery).

Riddings Colliery Old Hill. In operation in 1901 (OS map Sheet 71.08).

Rocket Pit Bradley, Bilston. A section of the pit collapsed on Dec 30 1921 burying some men alive who were later revived (TB Nov 1981 p14). Now the site for a modern housing estate.

Rookery Colliery 0.5m SE of Dunkirk, Audley. Closed in 1947 (AHJ 1997 p48). Owned by the old Bignall End Colliery Co. So called after rooks nesting in the tall trees in the neighbourhood (ES June 14 1965).

Ross Bank Colliery or mine working 0.75m S of Leys, in existence in 1810 (CCT p60). There is a Ross Bridge over the Churnet Valley railway at SK 030458.

Rough Wood Colliery Was in NE corner of Rough Wood Country Park, at SJ 985011. Operated from c1859 to 1897 (ESSN pp46,47). The M6 now passes over the site.

Round Hill Quarry Sedgley Beacon. Operating in the early C20 (SDOP p24p). The site had been declared a SSSI by 1995 (SDOP p124p).

Rowley Hall Colliery Began producing coal in c1870. Abandoned in 1919 (ORR p77p). Presumably stood near Rowley Hall, Rowley Regis.

Royal George Colliery 0.5m NNE of Cheadle at approximately SJ 007442. Was served by an arm of the Woodhead Plateway (CCT p55 see map).

Russian Colliery Darlaston (Offlow hundred). See Woods Bank.

Rusty Mine C19 coal and ironstone mine at Newchapel (SVB p130).

Sandbach Colliery S of Rushton Grange, Cobridge. Opened by 1856. Closed by the early 1920s (VCH vol 8 p140).

Sandwell Park Colliery N of Swan Pool at SP 026924. The first shaft was sunk E of Roebuck Lane in 1870 (VCH vol 17 p41). An explosion at the colliery on Oct 27 1894 injured 13 men; four later died (TEBC) (TEBC2 p137). Has also appeared as Jubilee Colliery. Jubilee Pit at Warstone Fields was opened in 1897 (VCH vol 17 p41) (TEBC). In 1910 JJ Shaw, seismologist, embarked on experiments at Jubilee Pit and Baggeridge Colliery to determine whether the moon exerted tidal effects on land masses as well as on sea (BCM spring 1995 p53). Ceased production in 1960 (VCH vol 17 p41). The site of it was being reclaimed in the 1970s (SL p269).

Scotia Colliery The colliery was probably situated to W of Scotia Road, Tunstall. (POTP p231). In operation by 1818. Fell into disuse in 1869 and was soon flooded. Taken over by the Chatterley Iron Company by 1888 (VCH vol 8 pp138,139). Has also appeared as Scotia and Pinnox Colliery.

Scotwell Colliery Old Hill. In operation in 1901 (OS map Sheet 71.08). Disused by 1988 (TB Oct 1988 p16) and now covered by housing.

Shelton Colliery Hanley. Belonged to the Earl of Granville (VCH vol 2 p99). Was working by at least the 1830s. Deep Pit was a part of it (VCH vol 8 p169).

Short Heath Colliery Between Short Heath and New Invention, at SJ 977012. Operated from c1868 to 1883 (ESSN pp46,47). A disaster occurred at a Short Heath mine on July 15 1905 when subsidence caused the Wyrley and Essington Canal to sink into the pit and drown three miners (TB Oct 1995 p15).

Shutt End Colliery Shutt End. An inrush of water on April 21 1923 caused the deaths of four miners (LWF p118).

Silverdale Colliery Formerly called Kent's Lane Colliery (IANS p130). Sir Joseph Cook PM of Australia worked in the No. 6 Pit (the Big Pit) from the age of nine, in c1869 (TB July 1995 p19). A major disaster occurred at the colliery on July 7 1870 when 19 men were killed in an underground gas explosion (IANS p38) (LMV p112). Another disaster occurred here on April 6 1876 which claimed the lives of five miners (LMV p112). The film, 'The Proud Valley' starring Paul Robeson, about a Welsh mining village made in 1939 was partly shot at the colliery (S&COP pl 28) (ES Aug 21 1995 p8). In 1968 the colliery set the European tunnelling record for a certain type of tunnelling machine (ES Oct 25 1968). The colliery closed due to geological problems on Dec 31 1998. It is planned that the colliery site will become an industrial estate (ES Feb 10 1998 pp1,8-9. Sept 10 1999 p5).

Slater's Hall Colliery W of Bromley, Kingswinford disused by 1900 (TB March 1983 p34 see map).

Sneyd Colliery Sneyd Green. Closed down then reopened by William Heath in the early 1880s and was the only colliery in Burslem area from c1920 (VCH vol 8 p138). An explosion of fire damp on Jan 1 1942 caused the deaths of 57 miners (IANS p38) (TSS p114; 58 miners died) (LWF p118). Closed in 1962 (ES Feb 11 1998 p3).

Sneyd Colliery N of Sneyd Farm, Sneyd, Willenhall. (Birmingham A-Z 1995).

Sneyd Lane Colliery 0.75m WSW of Wallington Heath, at SJ 986024. Operated from c1876 to c1900 (ESSN pp46,47). Has also appeared as Spottlebrook Colliery.

South Cannock Colliery Opened in 1875 (LHSB 50 p33).

Speedwall Colliery To W of The Woodhouse, Longton. In operation in the 1870s (VCH vol 8 p243).

Speedwell Colliery Stood S of the railway line WSW of Aldridge in the present Speedwell Close area. The colliery was known as Victoria Colliery when first sunk in 1849. There was also a Speedwell Lane, probably a section of Dumblederry Lane, in the 1891 census, and in the Electoral register for 1918. Speedwell Farm is noted in the 1930s (SNAR p44).

Spottlebrook Colliery See Sneyd Lane Colliery.

Spring Hill Colliery 1.75m ENE of Essington at SJ 988037. Was part of Essington Farm Colliery (see). There was a second shaft 0.75m to the W (ESSN pp46,47).

Spring Vale Colliery Spring Vale. Operating in 1901 (OS map Sheet 67.03).

Stafford Colliery and Ironworks. At Great Fenton, near Sideway. Opened in the 1860s and still operating in the 1950s (VCH vol 8 p222) (POP p118). It was stated in 1960 to be the deepest in the country at 3,318 feet, with still deeper seams below the existing workings (HOS 1998 p103). Closed in 1969 (ES Feb 11 1998 p3).

Standhills Colliery Colliery to S of Standhills House. Driven from the early C19. Had a disaster on Aug 30 1848 10 miners were killed or injured. It closed after another disaster in the 1870s. The colliery was disused by 1900. It reopened in the late 1920s. Another disaster occurred on Nov 24 1933 which killed four miners (TB March 1983 p34 see map).

Stanfield Colliery Burslem. Was being worked by 1841. Closed because of flooding in c1889 (VCH vol 8 p139).

Steer's Meadow Colliery Small pit which was sunk within 40 yards of Lea Brook, Wednesbury. On the night of Feb 19 1863 the shaft became flooded and William Jones, aged 20, John Pitt aged 50, William Gettings, aged 21, all lost their lives. Job Jones, aged 15, who was with them, managed to squeeze through into a chamber with air and survived (BCM April 1977 pp55-56) (TEBC2 p83).

Stone Row Colliery Colliery in the Potteries area. Described as 'sinking' in 1877. Closed in 1888 or 1889 (VCH vol 8 p244).

Stonetrough Colliery Situated to the ENE of Harriseahead. Here in early 1800 Hugh Bourne undertook some carpentry work. A tramway took coal from it to Congleton (NSJFS 1969 p63. 1971 p122) (BALH p69).

Struggling Monkey Colliery See Broad Lane Colliery.

Sutherland Pit Fenton. Has been described as deepest pit in the country, at 3,318 feet (VCH vol 8 p223) (HOS p46).

Swingle Hill Colliery See Foley Colliery.

Talke Colliery A coal gas explosion on Dec 13 1866 killed 90 miners (KES p201) (KBT vol 2 p23) or 91 miners (LGS p226) (IANS p38) (POTP p199) (A p123) (LWF pp13-22ps - has list of those killed) (LMV p112) (KAIW p17). Queen Victoria ordered a fund be set up for the relatives of the dead in 1866 (ILN Dec 29 1866 p649il) (KBT vol 2 p24). Another disaster on Feb 18 1873 killed 18 miners (ILN March 1 1873 pp205il,206) (VCH vol 2 p93) (IANS p38) (LMV p112) (KBT vol 2 p23). There seems to have been another disaster here in 1875 which killed 22 (LGS p226) or 45 (KBT vol 2 p23). Mee mentions a disaster which occurred in 1785 and killed 42 (KES p201). An explosion at the colliery on May 27 1901 claimed four lives (LWF p118). The colliery, which has also appeared as Talk o' th' Hill Colliery, closed in 1928 (KAIW p18).

Terrace, The A colliery developed by the 4th Earl of Dartmouth in the West Bromwich area (VB p62).

Thistley Field Stone quarry in Castle liberty, Tamworth (W p627), formerly in Warws.

Thors Hole Old quarry at Rowley Regis which had to be closed down because it had claimed the lives of some men (TB Feb 1974 p16).

Three Ugly Sisters Collective name for the slag heaps from Hanley Deep Colliery now grassed-over and a feature of Central Park, Hanley. There were three, but one has now (1978) gone (VB p190).

Tibbington Colliery (VCH vol 2 p86).

Tilehouse Colliery NW of Bromley, Kingswinford. Disused by 1900 (TB March 1983 p34 see map).

Timbertree Colliery Timbertrees. (TB May 1976 p19 engraving from 1872).

Tintam Abbey Colliery It stood in the same area as Caledonia and Mousul cottages (SVS p140).

Top Falls Colliery Situated 0.5m WSW of Falls Colliery. Both collieries were owned by Hugh Henshall Williamson in the mid C19 (BALH p66).

Tower Hill Colliery Towerhill Farm is 1m W of Knypersley, Biddulph. In existence by 1842 and closed probably by 1882 (BALH p70). It may be the cause for the growth of Mow Cop village in the C19.

Trentham Colliery See Hem Heath Colliery.

Twin Pit Colliery off City Road, Rowley Regis. The colliery was originally the Old Grace Mary and the New Grace Mary Pit (TB Jan 1983 p13. July 1984 p5) and has also appeared as Twins Pit and The Twin Pits. Named after newly-born and dead male twins, which were found by a dog on Rowley Hills on March 14 1865. Their post mortems were carried out at the Prince of Wales Inn, Rounds Green. The cause of death was thought to be due to exposure. The mother of the twins was found to be Mary Smith, who was released due to having been seduced and then abandoned and pleaded mercy at her trial (TB Oct 1976 p27p. Feb 1994 p5p).

Union Colliery Green Lane, Birchills (SOB p124).

Union Colliery Albion, West Bromwich. Working by 1812 (VCH vol 17 p40).

Uxbridge, The Hammerwich No. 2 Pit. See The Fly.

Uxbridge Colliery Hednesford. Opened by 1852 (VCH vol 2 p79. vol 5 p71). Was the main reason for Hednesford's expansion.

Valley Colliery Situated 0.5m SSE of Wilnecote at SK

222005. In existence in 1884 (1884 OS map 6 inch).

Victoria Colliery Aldridge. See Speedwell Colliery.

Victoria Colliery Colliery 0.75m S of Knypersley, Biddulph. Opened in c1842 and also known as Biddulph Valley Colliery. On July 1 1872 two men jumped out of the cage at No. 3 Pit as it was being drawn into the headgear by a drunken winding engine man. A third man fell down the shaft to his death. This incident is recorded in Ernald James's 'Unforgettable Countryfolk.' Ernald James himself fired the boilers at the Victoria Colliery in the 1926 coal strike. Closed in July 1982 (ES Feb 11 1998 p3) (CIOPP pp63p,66p) (BALH pp67,73-74). In Jan 1993 the remains of an Aveling and Porter chain engine steamroller, believed to be the first steamroller, was discovered in an 180 feet disused shaft of the colliery. It was last seen during the first test of steam rolling in Hyde Park in Nov 1866 (Daily Telegraph June 1 1993 p10pc).

Waggon Colliery Open cast mine, slightly N of Lower Above Park (CCT p166 see map).

Wallows Colliery Brierley Hill. One of the Earl of Dudley's collieries (BCM April 1969 pp29-34). See Nine Locks Pit.

Walsall Wood Colliery Situated at Paul's Coppice, near the junction of Lindon Road and Brownhills Road, Walsall Wood. Known locally as 'The Coppy' (TB June 1988 p5). Opened in 1875 (LHSB 50 p33). In 1877 it reached 1,677 feet and then became the deepest pit in the Cannock Chase Coalfield (VCH vol 17 p281). Supposedly haunted by a miner ghost called Ode Cloggie (TB June 1988 p5). Closed in 1964 (BWWOPP p36p).

Ward Meadow Colliery Situated to the ENE of Woodcross. Operating in 1901 (OS map Sheet 67.03).

Waterfall Lane Colliery Rowley Regis. Better known as Butcher Mills pit after its owner William Mills (TB May 1981 p11).

Waterloo Colliery By the Walsall Canal, nearly 0.75m WSW of Walsall. Opened by 1868 (VCH vol 17 p158).

Waterloo Colliery Lay off Willenhall Road, Wolverhampton, on 1834 OS map.

Watermills Colliery Under 0.5m NE of Alsagers Bank, at SJ 818488 (IANS p37). Operated until c1900 (IAS p184). All that remains of the colliery is the brick base of the pit chimney. Each side of the base has a plaque with inscriptions; they read 'R.E.H. A.D. 1840;' 'Be Just And Fear Not;' 'Beware the End' (or 'Regard the End' - IAS p184); and 'Live and Let Live.' The initials REH are those of Sir Richard Edensor Heathcote, who owned the Apedale estate in c1840 (IANS pp60p,132). (BOE p61) (SVB pp13,14,55).

Well Street Colliery Well Street, Cheadle. Nicknamed 'Old Malkins' or at other times 'Hoods Colliery' (CCT p101).

West Cannock Colliery Henry Thomas Gaskin, who murdered his wife on Feb 19 1919, was a miner at this colliery (TB April 1993 p22). An explosion here on Nov 16 1933 claimed the lives of six miners (LWF p119). 35 miners of West Cannock Colliery No. 5 ('Tackeroo' Pit at Hednesford - VB p122) claimed a world record in 1981 after digging a 824.8 feet, 12.5 feet wide, 6.5 feet high roadway out of coal at this colliery between March 30 and April 3 1981 (CCAP p158) (GBR 1990 p98).

Whitehall Colliery Near Farley Park, Great Bridge (WBOPP pl 86). Had an explosion in July 1851 which claimed the lives of nine miners (LWF p119).

Whitfield Colliery See main body of encyclopaedia.

Willenhall Colliery NE of Willenhall, on the S side of Bentley Canal. The name occurs on the 1889 OS map. It may be identifiable with Willenhall New Colliery in the Stringes (see) Close area (SNW p68).

Willingsworth Colliery Over 1m WSW of Bilston (WMLB

pp106,107). Lost.

Wilnecote Colliery Situated N of Watling Street, Wilnecote at SK 228015. Disused by 1884 (1888 OS map 6 inch).

Wimblebury Colliery The colliery, still separate by 1961, was later joined underground to West Cannock No. 5 and the Wimblebury shaft was later filled in and the site cleared (CCAP p137).

Wolstanton Colliery To SE of Wolstanton church. In the mid 1960s No. 2 shaft of the colliery was reputed to be the deepest in England at 3,432 feet (GBR 1965 p185. 1966) (POP p171) (NUL p176 at 1045 yards). The colliery closed in Dec 1985 (TWWW June 1991 p23. April 1997 p5p).

Wood Farm Colliery In existence in the later C19 and situated between the Wyrley & Essington Canal and the present M6, at SJ 985014. Formerly in Bentley township in Wolverhampton ancient parish (OS map 6 inch).

Woodhead Colliery 0.75m NNE of Cheadle. Formerly in Farley township in Alton ancient parish (W p768) (HOC p38). Has also appeared as Woodhead Hall Colliery (IANS p158). William Machin, aged 11, was killed in Copper's shaft at the colliery on March 30 1863 (CCT p123).

Woodhouse Colliery At Woodhouse, Biddulph, on the N side of Woodhouse Lane. In existence in 1838 when owned by John Bateman (BALH p66).

Woodshutts Colliery The name of this colliery can be seen on a grave in Talke churchyard. In operation by 1803 when owned by Sir JE Heathcote. Closed in c1931 (AHJ 1996 pp16,18).

Wyrley Colliery Opened in 1872, or earlier (LHSB 50 p33).

Yew Tree Colliery Springhill, Essington, at SJ 973047. Operated from 1947 to 1969 (ESSN pp46,47).

Yew Tree Colliery Situated SW of Daisy Bank, Coseley. Operating in 1901 (OS map Sheet 67.04).

Some potteries

Adams' Factory See Greengates.

Adams' Works Sneyd Street, Cobridge. Was close to Cobridge Hall. Worked by the Daniel family in later C18. Sold to William Adams in 1769. Adams introduced into Staffordshire the manufacture of blue-printed ware and in 1775 the use of copperplate engraving at this pottery. By 1802 it was let out. Sold to Messrs Furnival c1869. Had been pulled down by mid-1920s (VCH vol 8 p137).

Albion Works Hanley (H pp33,34).

Alexander Works Tunstall (OTP p51).

Alexandra Pottery Douglas Street and Arthur Street, behind Furnival's Works, Cobridge. Was one of the works run by William Adams in 1802. From 1903 has been run by Myotts (VCH vol 8 p137).

Alcock's Works, Samuel The facade was built in 1839. Demolished in 1966 (POP p27).

Anchor Pottery Sutherland Road, Anchor Road and Bridgwood Street, Longton, dates from 1859 (VCH vol 8 p242) (NSJFS 1965 pp88,89).

Ashworth's Works Pottery works which stood off Broad Street, Hanley, behind the Mitchell Memorial Theatre. Thomas Astbury, son of John Astbury who allegedly spied on the Elers brothers of Dimsdale Hall (see) and also developed the use of ground flint in ware after seeing flint being burnt whilst on a journey, founded the works on this site in 1725. He was followed by John Baddeley (d1772) who was succeeded by his sons Ralph and John, who rebuilt the works. The new works was held by: J&G Baddeley (c1780 to at least 1806); Hicks & Meigh (1818); Hicks, Meigh and Johnson (1832); William Ridgway, Morley, Wear & Co (c1840); Francis Morley & Co (1851); Morley & Ashworth, and then George L Ashworth & Brothers to at least 1910. After 1848 the firm of Ashworth purchased the moulds and engravings of Charles Mason of Mason's Ironstone Works (see) and adopted the trade name 'Mason's Ironstone;' a huge chimney of the works with a white 'Mason's' mark on Morley Street was very prominent in the late 1970s (POP p69).

Aynsley Works See Portland Works.

Bell House Works See Brickhouse Works.

Bell's Pottery Lower Street, Newcastle-under-Lyme. In the early C18 Samuel Bell of Lower Street is said to have made a certain type of red glazed ware, of which he has been claimed to be the inventor (VCH vol 8 p52). The same or another Samuel Bell was producing high quality ware here from 1724-44. After his death the works were taken over by William Steers of London who produced a high quality porcelain here (POP p170), making it one of the county's oldest china works; Longton Hall also has this claim. Bell's Pottery kiln bases were excavated and taken to Newcastle Museum, The Brampton. A building of the Pottery survives (IANS pp78p,91). (NSFCT 1920 pp46-50).

Big House Pottery Stood close by The Big House, Burslem, on the corner of Wedgwood Street and Moorland Road. Described, in 1976, as long demolished (POP p19). Here Josiah Wedgwood I set up in business (SSW p68). Morland implies it was the pottery of Thomas and John Wedgwood; they became wealthy and built The Big House by it (POP 19).

Big Works Stood on N side of Church Street on E bank of the Newcastle Branch Canal. Up to 1818 it was owned by Thomas Wolfe. Then owned by the Adams family until the present Kingsway was run through the site in the 1870s (VCH vol 8 p203).

Black Bank Near the New Board Schools, High Street, Tunstall (OTP p51).

Bleak Hill Pottery see Bleak Hill.

Boston Pottery Newfield, Tunstall. Formerly Lion Works (NSJFS 1965 pp84,85 plan,87) (VCH vol 8 p99).

Boundary Works S side of King Street, Longton. When built by Josiah Spode in 1819 it was a model pottery factory. It was known as the California Works in the 1860s and 1870s, and by the name of Boundary Works by 1897 (VCH vol 8 p240). The works belonged to Leo Samuels in the 1960s (NSJFS 1965 p88) (IAS p189) (MR pp150p,151) (BOE p260).

Brickhouse Works Burslem. One of the oldest traceable potteries in the Potteries. Founded and brought to prominence by John Adams (d1687) and said to have been the earliest important potworks in Burslem (VCH vol 8 p117) (NSSG p6). It was situated on most of the land S of the

Town Hall, right up to Queen Street; the Wedgwood Memorial Institute is on the site. It was in the hands of the Adams family from C17 to 1762 when its tenant was Josiah Wedgwood I, who developed his 'Egyptian Black' and cream-ware here, and where he erected a bell to bring his workers to work. It was the first works bell erected in the Potteries. Hence the works became known as Bell House Works, or Bell Works (POP pp20,21) (SSW p70) (Chats on Wedgwood Ware. Harry Barnard. Photograph of from an illustration) (POTP p224). Wedgwood left for the Etruria Works in 1769.

Broad Street Works Situated at top of Broad Street (Clementon's Works in c1905), Shelton: On this site were Warner Edwards in c1760; J and G Ridgway in 1792; William Ridgway and Sons in 1840; Joseph Clementon in c1866 (OTP pp175,177 il); probably same as Phoenix Works, Shelton (see).

Brownfields Works See main body of encyclopaedia.

Brownhills Pottery To the N of Burslem, by Brownhills House. First built by John Wood in or soon after 1782, demolished in 1830 when improvements were made to Brownhills House (VCH vol 8 p137).

Brownhills Pottery To the N of Burslem. Had its origins in a pottery of c1805. In the later C19 it was run by the Brownhills Pottery Company. The pottery was known as Brownhills Pottery by the early 1960s (VCH vol 8 p137).

Brownhills Works To the N of Burslem. Its materials went to build the Woodland Works, mid C19 (OTP p44). Perhaps identifiable with a Brownhills Pottery.

Burns Pot Works, William Burslem. Early C18 (POP p27).

Caldon Place Works See Cauldon Place Works.

California Works See Boundary Works.

Caroline Pottery Caroline Street, Longton (BOE p260).

Cauldon Place Works Shelton, Hanley. A pottery of the Ridgeway family (POP p69 - written Caldon). Founded by Job Ridgway in c1802 (OTP p175). John Ridgway (d1860), born in Hanley on Feb 1 1786, poet and author of 'Africa: A Missionary Poem,' became a partner in the firm in 1809. The Rev J Stacey wrote sketches of his life in 'A Prince in Israel' (1862) (PSS p469) (VFC p113). The pottery was demolished and Cauldon College built on the site. Nearby in Stoke Road was a toll house called Cauldon Toll House which had become a newsagents by the 1970s (AGT p134 il).

Central Pottery Burslem (VCH vol 8 p136).

Churchyard Works See main body of encyclopaedia.

Clay Hills Pottery Tunstall area (OTP p51).

Cliff Bank Works See Cliff Bank.

Coalport China London Road, Stoke (IANS p147).

Copeland Pottery See Spode Factory.

Crown Pottery Burslem. Here Charlotte Rhead of Burslem (see) and her father worked (FWNS p60).

Crown Pottery (or Works). Corner of The Strand and Commerce Street, Longton. There was a potworks on this site since the 1790s. By the mid 1850s it was occupied by James Broadhurst. Crown Pottery came into the hands of John Tams Ltd in 1875 (VCH vol 8 p238) (NSJFS 1965 p87 pl Ib) (POP p130) (Churchill China. Rodney Hampson. 1994 p19).

Crown Works Burslem. It was the pottery works of Susie Cooper (1903-1995) of Stanfield (see), and was damaged by fires in 1942 and 1957. The works closed in 1980 and Susie Cooper Ltd, by then part of the Wedgwood group, moved to premises in Furlong Road, Tunstall (FWNS p52).

Cyples Pottery (Cyples) Site now occupied by the Bennett Precinct, Longton (VCH vol 8 p239) (POP p131).

Daisy Bank Pottery Longton (VCH vol 8 p240).

Davenport Works New Bridge Street, Burslem, unlocated. The group of buildings NW of Trubshaw Cross represents part of the Davenport Works. The house remained in c1960 but the factory had been demolished (VCH vol 8 pp135,137).

Dimmocks Pottery Piccadilly/ Cheapside, Hanley. Demolished in 1904 (SHST pp648p, 649p).

Don Pottery and Earthenware Millers, N side of King Street, Longton (IANS p149).

Duchess China Company N side of Uttoxeter Road, Longton (IANS p148).

Eastwood Pottery By the Caldon Canal, Eastwood, Hanley. The pottery or a part of it was demolished in c1960 (VCH vol 8 pl facing p167).

Elder Works Cobridge. Held by the Stevenson family from at least 1775 until 1835 when passed to the Alcocks. Run as the Elder Pottery from at least 1864 until 1910 when it was bought by the Soho Pottery Ltd, it then appears to have become known as Soho Pottery or Potteries. The range that faces Waterloo Road bears the date 1848 and the initials 'J.A.' (John Alcock) (VCH vol 8 pp113,138) (SHST p29). (IAS pp189-190).

Ellgreave Pottery Burslem. Charlotte Rhead was employed here for a time producing her famous red-bodied tableware (FWNS p60p).

Enson Works Chelson Street, Longton; has bottle ovens (ES Aug 18 1999 p8).

Etruria Works See main body of encyclopaedia.

Fenton Low Pottery Fenton. Pottery run by Thomas Whieldon. Believed to have been situated at approximately SJ 884448. S of City Road (IANS pp145-146). Thomas Whieldon had moved from here to a site next to Fenton Manor by 1747 (NSJFS 1968 p118).

Foley China Works The Foley, Fenton. Built by Henry Wileman in 1860. In 1872 James Wileman, son of Henry Wileman, went into partnership with JB Shelley (VCH vol 8 p221).

Foley Potteries See i) Old Foley Pottery, ii) Foley Pottery, iii) Foley Potteries.

Foley Potteries The Foley, Fenton. Built by John Smith in c1820. First occupied by the Elkins, John King Knight and John Bridgwood. Later occupied by the Wisemans (VCH vol 8 p221).

Foley Pottery The Foley, Fenton. Built in c1790 on S side of King Street by Josiah Spode for his second son Samuel (1758-1817), who was believed to be the last salt-glaze potter in Staffs. Later holders of the works were or may have been Charles Bourne, John Hawley, Barkers and Kent, John Knox (VCH vol 8 p219) (FF pp56, 69), and Coalport by 1988 (MR p151). Excavations on the site 1973 and 1974 revealed white salt-glazed stoneware and creamware, all dating from c1760 to 1775 (SASR 1984 pp63-86). May have been later called the Old Foley Pottery.

Fountain Place Pottery Works Situated on Packhorse Lane, Burslem. It covered the sites of four other potteries. Built

by Enoch Wood, son of the modeller Aaron Wood (POP p26) (VCH vol 8 pp135-136 ils from HBST). The three storey block of 1789 was embodying Messrs Alcock's premises by the 1960s (NSJFS 1965 p88). A windmill was erected here for Enoch Wood in the 1780s. Replaced by a stream engine in the early C19 (WBJ p17). Wood gave the name to Fountain Place by erecting a fountain outside his works (POP p31).

Furnivals' Pottery Fronting Elder Road, Cobridge. Dates from the late C18 (VCH vol 8 p113). Was the only works to still have a cupola, apart from the Etruria Works in the 1960s (NSJFS 1965 p87); held by the Blackwells from c1780, the Dillons from 1832 and Furnivals from c1848 (VCH vol 8 p137). Demolished in the 1960s (IAS p39).

George Street Pottery Tunstall? Where William Holdcroft introduced down-draught firing ovens c1865, perhaps, the first in the Potteries (OTP p51), was later Grenville Pottery (NSJFS 1965 pp88-89).

Gladstone Pottery See main body of encyclopaedia.

Globe Pottery By the old High Gate Inn, Brownhills? N of Burslem. Scarratt was told that it was here the Primitive Methodists first met, it was demolished by 1902 (OTP pp15,48).

Globe Pottery Cobridge. Often called 'Warburton's Bank.' Had been turned into a sanitary-ware manufactory by 1902 (OTP p141). Formerly built on the site of part of a works of William Adams in Elder Road. By c1960 it was replaced by Ridgway's Portland Pottery. The Warburton family had two works in Elder Road near the junction with Hot Lane at beginning of the C19, one of these was Villa Pottery (VCH vol 8 p137).

Gordon Pottery Tunstall. Occupied by AG Richardson in the 1930s. Charlotte Rhead was employed here for a time (FWNS p60p).

Goss Works W side of London Road, Stoke, by Kirkham Street. Stood partly on a pottery built by W Kirkham in 1862. In about the 1880s it and adjacent land was purchased by William Henry Goss, pottery manufacturer credited with inventing heraldic porcelain, rebuilt and extended. Most of the factory stood to the 1970s and was then demolished (William Henry Goss. Lynda and Nicholas Pine. 1987 pp162-165ps).

Greendock Works SW side of New Street (present-day Cooke Street), Longton. Peter Hampson, James Broadhurst I and William Broadhurst started in partnership here in 1847 (Churchill China. Rodney Hampson. 1994 p17).

Greenfield Pottery Furlong Road, Tunstall. Lay to the E of the Greengates Pottery. Production ceased in 1956 and then moved to the enlarged Greengates Pottery. The west front, dated 1818, was still standing in the early 1970s (OTP p44) (BOE p266) (VCH vol 8 p100).

Greengates Pottery Furlong Road, Tunstall. Built by William Adams in 1780 (OTP pp13 il in 1850,44). (SOSH p287). The Greengates factory came again into Adams hands in 1896. The pottery was largely rebuilt in 1929 and enlarged to accommodate the production of the Greenfield factory transferred there in 1956 (VCH vol 8 p100). Adams were absorbed into the Wedgwood Group in 1966 (ES Sept 15 1995 p15p). The pottery, or the area in which it lay, appears to have been called Botany Bay from the later C18 to the mid C19 (HBST p103) (OTP p43).

Hawley Pottery Burslem. The boy John Holdcroft worked for this pottery and was making his way here when murdered by Charles Shaw and others in Crabtree Field, Etruria (TOS p93).

Highgate Pottery Brownhills, N of Burslem. Built by George Hood figurine manufacturer in c1820 (OTP p39) and then occupied by Alfred Meakin and then the Johnson Brothers (POTP p125).

Hill Pottery See Royal Pottery.

Hill Top Pottery See Royal Pottery.

Hill Works See Royal Victoria Pottery.

Ivy House Works Residence and potworks to NW of the Big House, Burslem. It probably dated from the later C17 and was little more than a cottage (Life of Josiah Wedgwood. Eliza Meteyard. vol 1 fig 59) (VCH vol 8 p119). In 1759 Josiah Wedgwood I, born at Churchyard House (see), Burslem, rented the Ivy House Works from his cousins John and Thomas Wedgwood of the Big House until he moved to the Brickhouse Works in 1762 (POP p22). The work's site was rediscovered in excavations by the Channel Four Time Team in spring 1998. During the excavations pottery

ware of the C16 was discovered, suggesting that there had been former works on the site (Channel Four. Jan 3 1999). (Chats on Wedgwood Ware. Harry Barnard. Photograph of from a painting) (SOSH p265) (ES Feb 15 1930 p3) (TOS p24).

Keeling's Pottery Tunstall. Here the company, formed in 1781, to work the patent for the manufacture of hard-paste porcelain from Cornish clay and stone, began operations. The company originally consisted of Anthony Keeling, John Turner, Richard Champion, Samuel Hollins, Jacob Warburton, and William Clowes. After a dispute which saw the departure of the first three the company moved to Shelton New Hall, Hanley in 1782 and were known as the New Hall Company by at least 1801 (VCH vol 8 p166).

Kilncroft Works Chapel Lane, Burslem. Dates from at least the early C19. Became part of Royal Doulton Pottery (VCH vol 8 p136).

Kingstone Pottery King Street, Longton (IANS p149).

King Street Works Pottery on N side of King Street, Fenton. To E of Park Lane. Was established by Mr Shelley (probably Thomas Shelley of Lane Delph) towards the end of the C18. Jacob Marsh, the Careys, John Edwards were later occupants (VCH vol 8 p220).

Knowle Works Oldest pottery which can be identified in Burslem. Stood at W end of Hamil Road. Can be traced back to 1651. Operated by the Malkin family to at least 1710. Probably demolished by the end of the C19 (VCH vol 8 p132).

Lion Works See Boston Pottery.

Longton Hall Works See main body of encyclopaedia.

Mason's Ironstone Works Former pottery at the junction of City Road and Victoria Street (which here unite to form King Street) (MR p151) in the area formerly known as Lane Delph (POP p113). The early pottery on the site was bought by Charles and George Mason of the Minerva Works in 1813. The Masons moved in in 1815. Charles had taken out a patent for ironstone china in 1813, a type of china noted for its hardness and durability. The Masons were one of few producers of this type of ware. About the time of their arrival they may have rebuilt or extended the existing works; the new works had the large words 'Patent Iron-Stone China Manufactory' across the front facade. Charles Mason was made bankrupt in 1848 and his moulds and engravings were sold to Francis Morley of the works in Hanley which became known as Ashworth's Works (see) (VCH vol 8 pp220-221) (BOE p259) (MR p151).

May Place Works Burslem. Demolished in the 1960s (IAS p39).

Mersey Pottery Middleport. Built by Anthony Shaw in c1860 (VCH vol 8 p136).

Middleport Pottery By the canal, Middleport. Owned by Burgess and Leigh (AGT pp70,71il) (IANS p77p).

Minerva Works In Park Street, Fenton. In existence by the early 1760s. In 1806 or 1807 it was taken over by Miles Mason (1752-1822) of Liverpool (grandfather of artist, George) (VCH vol 8 p218) (POP p113). He left it to his sons Charles, and George Miles in 1813 (POTP p148). Pratts have also occupied it and most recently have Crown Staffordshire China (POP p113).

Minton Works E side of London Road, Stoke-upon-Trent. Pottery built by Herbert Minton, dating from the mid C19, was extended with Campbell Tile Works in 1876 (VCH vol 8 pp182,204) (IANS p147). For the statue of Colin Minton Campbell see Stoke-upon-Trent.

Moorcroft Pottery Sandbach Road, Burslem.

Newfield Pottery See Newfield Hall.

New Hall Works See Shelton New Hall Works.

New Market Works E of the market, Longton. Named in c1863, probably after the new market. Its front on Chancery Lane is dated 1854 (VCH vol 8 p242).

Newport Pottery Newport, Burslem. Architecturally similar to the Etruria Works (VCH vol 8 p136) (NSJFS 1965 p87). Clarice Cliff (1899-1972), born Tunstall (see), the famous art-deco designer, created her best known work for the Newport Pottery; she also worked briefly for AJ Wilkinson in Newport, Burslem (both companies formed part of the Wedgwood Group by 1970). In 1999 a steel sign with decorative artwork in her style by David Foers was erected to her memory by the canal facing the site of the former Wilkinson factory near Pidduck Street (ES March 18 1999 p15pc).

Old Bank Pottery Situated in Well Street and Cross Street (both now lost, approximate area is now Oldcourt Street?), Tunstall. The pottery faced the Tunstall Manor House (see) and its buildings may have been the manor house's outbuildings (OTP pp63,69 il).

Old Court Pottery (presumably, in Oldcourt Street) Tunstall. There is a notice on the building announcing that here the Potteries begin (MR pp340,342p). Presumably, inferring this is the most northerly pottery works of the Potteries and the beginning of the Potteries for those travelling from the N.

Old Foley Pottery The Foley, Fenton. In the yard of the Old Foley Pottery John Wesley preached one of the last sermons of his life on March 28 1790 (POP p120) (MR p151). Old Pottery may be a later name for the Foley Pottery in the late C19 and early C20 (VCH vol 8 219).

Old Hall Works Hanley. Rebuilt by Job Meigh Snr in 1790 (POTP p150). When a site adjacent to the Albion Hotel was excavated, the kiln from the works was found and removed and exhibited outside the City Museum, Hanley (IANS p90).

Overhouse Manufactory Top of Wedgwood Street, Wedgwood Place, Burslem. Has the longest history of any pottery in Burslem; was in existence by c1700, and was worked by a branch of the Wedgwood family in the C18. The same family sold the works in the early C19 and it was bought by Edward Challinor in 1819. He rebuilt the works in 1869 (VCH vol 8 p133). That building was still standing in the earlier 1970s when it had over the entrance a tablet with this inscription: 'Edward Challinor commenced business here A.D. 1818(9?) and rebuilt the premises A.D. 1869. Over House Manufactory' (AGT pp74,75il).

Paragon Pottery Sutherland Road, Longton (IANS p148).

Park Place Works Adjacent to the Gladstone Pottery, Longton. The site had formed part of a potworks held by the Shelleys before 1789. It then passed to William Ward who split the Shelley site up; a part becoming this works and a part becoming Gladstone Pottery (POP p132) (AGT p166).

Phoenix Pottery Near Phoenix Works at Cliffe Vale, Stoke-upon-Trent (POTP p175).

Phoenix Works King Street, Longton: 1881 (NSJFS 1965 p89 pl IVb).

Phoenix Works High Street, Shelton; held by the Hammersleys in the earlier C19 and by the Clementsons for most of the rest of the C19; the front range of it was still standing in 1960 (VCH vol 8 pp167-168).

Phoenix Works High Street, Tunstall. A pottery works, totally demolished by 1902. Enoch Booth, maker of white ware, had occupied the site in the mid C18 (OTP pp48,49 il). For a period in the earlier C19 it was known as Phoenix Pottery (VCH vol 8 p100). Pinnox Pottery Woodland Street, Tunstall. Built by E Challinor, 1842 (OTP p51).

Price's Teapot Works Longport (NSJFS 1965 p88) (BOE p256).

Portland Pottery Built by John Aynsley by late 1870 between Frederick and Beville Streets, Fenton. It appears to have been named after Wedgwood's famous Portland Vase and there was a replica of the vase on the pediment of the building. Occupied by James Broadhurst (d1897) from 1870 and purchased by him in 1876. The factory closed in 1981 and production moved to Sandyford. James Broadhurst and Sons Ltd, operated by the Roper family from the 1930s, were re-named Churchill Tableware in 1984. The Group was re-named Churchill China PLC in 1992 (Churchill China. Rodney Hampson. 1994 pp28,140,141).

Portland Works Pottery on N side of Sutherland Road, Longton. Built in 1861 by John Aynsley and partners (NSJFS 1965 p88 pl IIIc) (BOE p260) (IANS pp78p,148). Has also appeared as Aynsley's China Works and Aynsley Works (POP p130). Perhaps named after Wedgwood's famous Portland Vase (Churchill China. Rodney Hampson. 1994 p28).

Portmeirion Factory W side of London Road, Stoke.

Queen Anne Works Greendock Street, Longton: Late C19, occupied by Messrs Shaw and Coggins' (NSJFS 1965 p89 pl IVa)).

Rialto Pottery N side of City Road, Fenton. Occupied from 1812 Felix Pratt who had moved here from Lane Delph and became noted for his distinctively coloured ware. Later it was occupied by the firm of F & R Pratt of Fenton who

first perfected the method of multi-colour or polychrome printing in c1840. It was worked as the Rialto Pottery by the British Art Pottery Company between at least 1920 and 1926. Workshops for the blind were built on the site in 1934 (VCH vol 8 p220) (POP p108). The Pratts also occupied the Minerva Works?

Ridgway's Pottery Burslem. Demolished in the 1960s (IAS p39).

Ridgway's Pottery Sutherland Road, Longton, by Park Hall Colliery (NSJFS 1965 p89).

Royal Albert Pottery S side of Uttoxeter Road, Longton (IANS p148).

Royal Albert Pottery N side of King Street, Longton (IANS p149).

Royal Albert and Victoria Potteries Parsonage Street, Tunstall (VCH vol 8 p101). Perhaps identifiable with the Victoria and Albert Works in High Street, Tunstall: Built by Turner and Tomkinson in c1858 (comprised two potteries; the Victoria, and the Albert?) (OTP p47).

Royal Art Pottery See Waterloo Pottery.

Royal Doulton Potteries Nile Street, Burslem. A pottery has existed on the site since the C18. Probably called Hole House Works 1834-51. The works were acquired by Sir Henry Doulton in 1877. After modernisation in the 1950s the works were considered one of the biggest pottery works in the world (VCH vol 8 p136) (IANS p144).

Royal Pottery Westport Road, Burslem. Formerly Hill Pottery, Hill Top Works and Hill Top Pottery. It was operated by Samuel Alcock from 1828-1851 and was demolished in c1968 and another factory built on the site. In 1839 Alcock rebuilt the W elevation in an elaborate classical style which makes it architecturally one of the most ambitious industrial buildings anywhere in the country. It was admired by Arnold Bennett who called it Sytch Pottery in his novel 'Clayhanger' (VCH vol 8 pp134-135) (Arnold Bennett and Stoke-on-Trent. 1966. EJD Warrilow. pp127p,141p,149) (IAS p37) (NSJFS 1965 p88 pls IIb, IIc) (POTP p17). In 1967 workmen discovered at the junction of Westport Road and Greenhead Street a copper-plate on which was engraved 'This stone was laid by Joseph Locker Alcock, eldest son of Samuel Alcock, the founder on the 24th day of April A.D. 1839. Thomas Stanley. Architect. Rainbow, engraver' (NSJFS 1968 p117). The most famous piece of pottery made by the Hill Pottery was a magnificent copy of the Vase of Lecythus discovered by his Royal Highness, the count of Syracuse (SHST pp657il,658,659). (OTP pp92-93).

Royal Venton Pottery Burslem. Occupied site next to Samuel Alcock's Works (POP p27).

Royal Victoria Pottery Burslem. Formerly Hill Works. Opposite side of Westport Road from the Hill Pottery. Held by Enoch and Ralph Wood who produced 'useful and ornamental ware, Egyptian black, cane and various colours, also black figures, seals and syphers' (VCH vol 8 p135). Rebuilt in 1814 by John and Richard Riley. The lower end was completely rebuilt in the 1960s, and no bottle ovens survive (IAS pp191-192).

Ruskin Pottery See Smethwick.

St Gregory Works Sutherland Road area, Longton, close by Sydney Works. It may have been established in 1794, and was demolished by the 1950s (VCH vol 8 pp240-241).

St James' Place Works Situated opposite W end of St James' church, Longton. Demolished by 1960 (VCH vol 8 p242).

St Mary's Works Uttoxeter Road, Longton, existed by 1830: The Wilds, who ran it from 1906, were the first to use mechanical firing commercially in bone china manufacture (VCH vol 8 p243).

Samuels Pottery S side of King Street; oldest dated works in Longton (IANS p149).

Shelton New Hall Works Built as a china works. It was situated by Shelton New Hall (see) and at the junction of Newhall Street and Marsh Street, Hanley (OTP p184). Has also appeared as New Hall Works. The works of the New Hall Company, formed 1781 to work the patent for the manufacture of hard-paste porcelain, moved to Shelton New Hall from Keeling's Pottery (see), Tunstall, in 1782. Some imply the company was first called New Hall Company when formed and their name was given to the hall (POP p51). Others that the company was named after the hall (VCH vol 8 p166 note). It was the first Staffs pottery to use Cornish clay in the manufacture of true 'hard paste' porcelain (IANS p92) (VCH vol 8 p164) (IANS p92). The firm continued to produce hard-paste porcelain until 1810 or 1812 when it changed to bone china despite the patent

expiring in 1796. The premises were later occupied by Ratcliffs, Hackwoods, and Cookson and Harding. John Aynsley of Longton bought the works in 1872. In the C20 it was occupied by the New Hall Pottery Company (VCH vol 8 pp166-167). James Wantling, artist and painter with the New Hall Pottery, is believed to have been the swiftest man in England in the period c1825, having run 100 yards in nine seconds, 200 yards in 19 seconds and 300 yards in 30 seconds; feats never before equalled. He was a Derby man and died at New Brompton, near Chatham (OTP pp164-165).

Soho Pottery See Elder Works.

Spode Factory See main body of encyclopaedia.

Sutherland Pottery S side of Normacot Road, Longton (IANS p147).

Swan Bank Pottery High Street, Burslem. Kept by Aaron Shaw in c1750. Was demolished by 1902 (OTP pp48,139 il). There is now no High Street in Burslem, but, perhaps, it was at the Burslem end of Scotia Road (formerly High Street?).

Sydney Works Sutherland Road, Longton. Built 1879. Textile factory by 1963 (VCH vol 8 p241).

Sylvester Pottery Burslem. In existence by the 1830s; became part of the Royal Doulton Pottery in late C19 (VCH vol 8 p136).

Tams Pottery S side of Uttoxeter Road, Longton (IANS pp77p,148).

Taylor and Kent Pottery N side of Uttoxeter Road, Longton (IANS p148).

Tiger Works China makers factory N of Cherry Orchard, Old Hill (TB April 1983 p5).

Toft Pottery Was probably situated at Tinkersclough, Hanley (NSFCT 1953 pp108-109).

Tuscan China Forrister Street, Longton (IANS p149).

Unicorn Works (later Rathbone), Amicable Street, Burslem. The pottery of William Davenport (OTP pp48,92).

Upper Cliff Bank Works Pottery which stood at Top Square at the junction of Honeywall and what is now Hartshill Road on the site of the C19 St Andrew's Mission Church, Stoke-upon-Trent. It was worked by John and Thomas Alders in the early part of the C18. By the mid C18 Thomas had taken into partnership John Harrison, and from 1751 or 1752 Josiah Wedgwood I, born at Churchyard House (see), Burslem; he having left his brother's Churchyard Works, Burslem, and after having obtained Master Potter status (SSW p67) (POP p21) (NUL p90). Wedgwood left for Thomas Whieldon's works at Fenton Low after one or two years. John Davenport bought the works in 1802, and it was let to William Adams from 1804. It remained in this branch of the Adams family until its demolition in c1840 (VCH vol 8 p202).

Victoria and Albert Works Tunstall. See Royal Albert and Victoria Potteries.

Victoria Pottery To the W of The Strand, Longton. Built by Ralph Shaw in c1828. Victoria Foundry was built on its site in the C20 (VCH vol 8 p242).

Villa Pottery Was one of two works in Elder Road near the junction with Hot Lane, Burslem, at the beginning of the C19 belonging to the Warburton family (VCH vol 8 pp137-138).

Wade and Heath Pottery Westport Road, Burslem: 1814 (NSJFS 1965 p88 pl IIa).

Washington Pottery College Road, Stoke (NSJFS 1965 p90).

Washington Works Waterloo Road, Burslem: 1830s. William Wedgwood may have had a pottery in High Street in the late C17 (NSFCT 1953 p108).

Waterloo Pottery To the W of The Strand, Longton. By 1963 was known as Royal Art Pottery (VCH vol 8 p241).

Wedgwood Pottery Works See Etruria Works and Wedgwood (for the firm post-1938).

Whieldon's Pot-works, Thomas Thomas Whieldon (1719-1795) of Whieldon Grove (see) had a pottery at Fenton Low by 1740 which was extended in 1749. By 1747 he acquired another works adjoining Fenton Hall (see).

Wilds Pottery N side of Uttoxeter Road, Longton (IANS p148).

Woodland Works Woodland Street? Tunstall. Built mid C19 out of materials from Brownhills Works (VCH vol 8 p99) (OTP p44).

Bottle ovens remaining at the end of the 20th Century

Burslem area: Bournes Bank. Has the only remaining examples in the city of downdraught type of potters oven within circular conical hovels (DoE II) (ES Aug 18 1999 p8p). Eastwood Street. Two kilns on Ashdale site (DoE II). Furlong Lane. Two kilns of c1910 at the Furlong Mills Plant (DoE II). Longport. A bottle oven at Price and Kensington by the canal (ES Aug 18 1999 p8p). Moorland Road. c1910 one kiln an experimental four chamber muffle kiln (DoE II). Port Street, Middleport. Built 1889, part of the Middleport Pottery Ltd (DoE II). Sandbach Road.

Moorcroft Pottery had made the chimney of its bottle oven into a display for its museum by 1999 (ES Aug 18 1999 p8). Steventon Place. One kiln (DoE II). Trubshaw Cross. One kiln, mid C19 (DoE II).

Fenton area: Chilton Street, Heron Cross, one kiln of Bencroft Ltd (DoE II).

Hanley and Shelton areas: Cliffe Vale Pottery, Shelton New Road, two calcinating kilns built in 1887 (DoE II). Hanover Street. One kiln on site occupied by Dudson Brothers Ltd (DoE II). By 1999 the oven formed part of the Dudson centre, a museum, here (ES Aug 18 1999 p8). Lichfield Street. One kiln of c1850 on site occupied by Allied Insulators Ltd (DoE II). Town Road. One kiln (DoE II). Warner Street. One kiln attached to a pottery building (DoE II).

Longton area: Chelson Street. Three kilns of the up-draught type on premises occupied by Ashdale Pottery (DoE II) (ES Aug 18 1999 p8p). Commerce Street. Two kilns on Ashdale site (DoE II). King Street. Two kilns at Albion Works (DoE II). Normacot Road. Six kilns (DoE II). Short Street. Could be one, which is part of the six at Normacot Road (DoE I). No. 120 Uttoxeter Road, perhaps part of the one at Normacot Road (DoE II).

Stoke area: Lytton Street at SJ 8845 S/67A, one kiln (DoE II). Sturgess Street. Two kilns examples of down-draught ovens (DoE II). Some were to be saved in 1981 on the site of Portmeirion Potteries (the former Falcon Works and before that the famous WH Goss factory). In 1999 Portmeirion had plans to incorporate its bottle ovens into a new visitor centre under a glass roof (ES May 13 1981 p4p. Aug 18 1999 p8).

Some public houses

Abbey Inn See Burton Abbey (Victorian mansion).

Abbey Inn Inn at Abbey Green, Leekfrith (OL vol 2 p253 il). Is dated 1702 (VCH vol 7 p193). Reputedly haunted (Real Ale In and Around the Potteries. CAMRA. p39).

Abercombie Inn Gaol Square, Stafford. Opened in c1830. In the 1880s it was the original headquarters of the Reformed Order of Old Women, an organisation of about 100 elderly 'sisters' with a partiality for ale. Later the society moved to the Cock Inn and finally to the Three Tuns (SN Feb 21 1959 p12p of in 1905).

Albion Inn Public house. No. 64 Uttoxeter Road, Longton. Certified as one the 12 most haunted pubs in England (Real Ale in and around the Potteries. CAMRA p49) (John Timpson's England. 1987) (HPG pp174,177).

Alexandra Hotel Medieval half-timbered house in Stafford. It was at one period the town house of the Shrewsbury family (OSST 1934 p17). It was due to be demolished in 1959 (NSFCT 1959 p90) and now (1999) no longer exists (info Michael Cockin).

American Hotel Waterloo Road, Burslem. The frontage was similar to The Leopard Inn, Burslem (VCH vol 8 p112).

Anchor Hotel or Inn. Southern end of Dark Lane on W side of the Stour, under 0.25m E of Kinver church. In existence by 1851, prior to which the inn had been a row of four C18 brick cottages (VCH vol 20 p125) (KRH p25).

Anchor Inn The sign from an Anchor Inn hangs in the stables of Shugborough at the County Museum. It may be from Cheadle.

Anchor Inn Brownhills, near Lichfield. Here Mrs Anslow (formerly Mrs Humphries) was murdered by her second husband, Mr Anslow in c1900 (TB Nov 1982 p11).

Anglesey Hotel Situated in the centre of modern Hednesford, 0.5m WNW of St Peter's church. Formerly called Hednesford Lodge or Hedgeford Lodge. Built for Edmund Peel of Fazeley, third son of 1st Sir Robert Peel (CCF pp74-76), in 1831, as summer residence and to provide stabling for racehorses. It was unoccupied in 1851 and became an hotel between 1860 and 1868 (VCH vol 5 p53). It was still being referred to as 'The Hall' by the older inhabitants of the town in the 1930s (CCF p75). Local belief is that it was built as a shooting or hunting lodge by the Pagets (VB p121). (W p452) (MR p180p) (CCAP p28p).

Antelope Inn Stone Road, Stafford. A ghost is said to haunt the cellar of the inn (SN Aug 29 1980 p13. May 8 1987 p3).

Barley Mow Inn See Goscote Manor House.

Barley Mow Inn Pennwood Lane, 0.5m SSE of Penn church, formerly on Penn Common. The inn was in existence by 1840. The name is derived from the fact that malt and barley were grown on Penn Common (PENOP p94p of in the 1920s) (BCP p116p).

Bear Inn The Bear Inn at Bearwood has been described as one of the oldest in Bearwood. There were inns on the site of it since the early 1700s. The present Bear Inn dates from 1907 (BCP pp108-109p). May have also been once called Bear of Smethwick.

Bell Inn Anslow. (ABTOP p119p in c1903).

Bell Inn SE of Clent. Marked on Saxton's map. Probably was used as a marker to help travellers (NSFCT 1919 p60).

Bell Inn, The Quaint narrow inn at Willenhall, said to have

been built in the later C17. A tunnel reputedly ran from it to St Giles' church, Willenhall (BCP p14p).

Bix Iron Pub West Bromwich (SJC p5).

Black Horse Inn Betley. Said to have had a windmill to raise water from a well at the inn (BVC p14). In 1951 here hung a reprint of a proclamation of Betley Fair during Queen Anne's reign (IOM p154).

Black Lion Inn Butterton (Moorlands). Is haunted by the ghost of a ten year old girl (PWPD p32).

Black's Head Inn Warton, Norbury. So called after the Saracen's head appearing in the Skrymsher crest (NSFCT 1888 p65 note).

Blakemere House See main body of encyclopaedia.

Blanketmakers Arms Bilston. Delicensed by 1969 (BEV p49).

Blue Ball Inn Hall End, Wednesbury. See Old Blue Ball Inn.

Blue Ball Inn Quarry Bank, Brierley Hill. Eric Dederfield in 'British Inn Sign and Their Stories' says the Blue Ball was the sign of the fortune teller and a rare name for a pub (BCM April 1983 p33p).

Blue Bell Inn See Lichfield.

Blue Bell Inn Stone. Mentioned in 'Drunken Barnaby's Four Journey's to the North of England' by Barnaby Harrington c1623. It stood on the site of the Town Hall until c1840 (NSFCT 1911 p249. 1921 p51).

Blue Bell Inn See Wrinehill.

Blue Gate Inn Rolfe Street, Smethwick. First mentioned as a licensed house in 1781. It appears to take its name from the tollgates which crossed the turnpike road at this point. The inn was rebuilt in c1850 and again in 1932 (STELE June 29 1956. July 6 1956. July 13 1956. July 20 1956).

Blue Pump Inn Uxbridge Street, Hednesford. Believed to have been frequented by Dick Turpin. According to legend it had a tunnel extending out from its cellars for seven miles to Lichfield cathedral. Wright was able to inspect the cellar and house before its demolition but found no structures suggesting a tunnel entrance save for a small curving of brickwork in one of the walls, but that might have been a drainage hole (CCF pp58-60) (CCAP p30p).

Boar Inn This inn in the centre of Moddershall is reputedly haunted by a soldier who hung himself in one of its outbuildings rather than return to the WW2 (PWNS p57). In the garden grows a yew tree which was topiaried into the shape of a boar's head (SSBOP p64). Close by, across the mill pool was Boar Mill one of the flint-grinding mills of the Moddershall Valley (IAS p43). The mill closed in 1954 and was later demolished (SIT) (SSBOP p64p).

Boar's Head Inn Stood in Aldridge Road, Perry Barr. Built in 1758 and demolished in 1936. Said to have been frequented by soldiers from Birmingham on their way to arrest William Booth at Booth's Farm (see), Perry Barr. The soldiers are said to have stayed too long at the inn and Dorothy Ingley, the wife of one of Booth's men, who was in the inn at the time, was able to warn them of their approach (HPPE pp13,14).

Bottle and Glass Inn Formerly stood in Brierley Hill Road, Brockmoor. It had been moved to the Black Country Museum near Tipton by 1997, where it is said to be haunted by poltergeist activity (GPCE p29p).

Bottom House Inn See main body of encyclopaedia.

Bradford Arms Inn Darlaston (Offlow hundred). Part of the inn dated from the late C18. It was known locally as 'The Frying Pan,' and the Frying Pan Club met here on Sunday evenings. The inn was demolished in the early 1980s (BCP p55p).

Bradford Arms Inn Late Georgian inn on Watling Street at Ivetsey Bank. Built in the neo-Gothick style which has been described as Carpenters' Gothic (NSJFS 1976 fig 9. p45).

Bridge Inn Cheddleton. Has an interesting sign attributed to Isaac Findler. The building is now Flintlock Restaurant (CVH pl 44).

British Oak Inn See main body of encyclopaedia.

British Queen Inn Inn in or near Meadow Lane, Hell Lane, which had a bad reputation (HC p54).

Bromley Arms Inn See Ellastone Old Hall.

Brushmakers Arms Inn Oulton. Unusually named inn (SOK p56). Apparently so called because the first licensee was a brushmaker (SVB p135). Is not listed in HSB.

Buck's Head Farm House on Watling Street (A5) 0.5m E of Weeford. Possibly a former inn.

Bug and Fiddle Inn On Caldon Canal (COS p40).

Bull and Spectacles Inn See main body of encyclopaedia.

Bull Inn See Tamworth Castle.

Bull's Head Inn See Bilston.

Bull's Head Inn Bloxwich Green. By the inn is a tree known as the Wishing Tree. According to tradition a miner called Samuel Moseley would not leave the inn for he enjoyed drinking here so much. In fury Mrs Moseley wished the inn would collapse and bury him. As she uttered the words of condemnation she passed the Wishing Tree (to the left of the photograph in BY p9p) and the roof of the inn did fall in, although no one was hurt. The Bull's Head was demolished in c1938, but the tree was still standing in 1982 (BY p9p).

Bull's Head Inn This inn in Lad Lane, Newcastle-under-Lyme has been known as the Bull's Head since 1734. It is believed to be up to 500 years old and is said to be haunted by the soldier Henry Knight, billeted here in 1842 (ES March 20 1996 p21).

Bull's Head Inn At this inn in Wolverhampton Street, Willenhall, Lavengro in George Borrow's novel 'Lavengro' (1851) reputedly stayed and Borrow himself patronised whilst at Mumper's Dingle between late June and early Aug 1825. It doubled as Willenhall's post office. Its licence was removed in 1908 and the building was demolished in c1920 (LGS p255) (NSFCT 1950 pp18-20 il facing) (AOW p183) (TB March 1998 p10p).

Burnt Gate Inn Anslow. The inn is haunted by a ghost called 'Kit-Mark' a drummer-boy who appeared in the 1960s and 1980s (GLS pp17-18).

Burnsips, The (1834 OS map). On the Cannock-Willenhall road, 0.5m E of Essington. Could be an inn.

Bush Inn See Tipton.

Capesthorne Commercial Hotel Hillchurch Street, Hanley. Accommodated many famous entertainers from the 1920s to the 1940s who appeared at the Theatre Royal, Hanley. The visitors book contains the signatures of GH Elliott, Tommy Trinder, Gracie Fields, Eric Porter and Sophie Tucker. Norman Wisdom and Sid Field have also stayed here (ES June 19 1995 p8). The visitors book also contained the signature of 20-year old Tony Armstrong-Jones (later Lord Snowdon) who stayed one night in 1950, but it was removed by another guest after his engagement to Princess Margaret (ES Oct 1 1995 p25p).

Castle Inn S side of Market Street, Lichfield. Stands on the site of - and in part most probably is - the old Biddulph town house where Lord Brooke lodged before setting off for Dam Street where he was shot dead in the Civil War. George Farquhar, playwright, is said to have written some of the 'Beaux' Stratagem' (1707) here (CL Oct 3 1957 p663).

Castle Inn or Hotel. Silver Street, Tamworth. Here a fire broke out in the night of Nov 2 1838 killing six female servants who became trapped in their lodgings in the attics of the inn. There is a monument to them in St Editha's churchyard, Tamworth (Broughton's Scrapbook p17) (VB p32) (TDOPP p44p).

Castle Inn Walsall. Here the deputy for the county Sheriff held a court in Walsall for the recovery of debts under 40 shillings (SHOS vol 2 p74).

Castle Inn Wood End, Wednesfield. May date back as an inn to 1764 or earlier. The piece of land opposite the inn is called Moat Croft suggesting some kind of fortified building stood in the area (WHTOP p88p); in the vicinity stood a house called Moat House.

Catchems Corner Inn At 161 Uttoxeter Road, Meir. Name originates from a local livestock market. The inn was, or built on the site of, the last chance of catching stray animals from the market, as depicted on the current (1997) inn sign (Real Ale in and around the Potteries. CAMRA. p52). There is a Catchem's Corner on the A50 between Blythe Bridge and Longton, at Q16 p51 on the Geographia Stoke-on-Trent A1 Street Atlas.

Cateham Inn Uttoxeter.

Cat Inn Mount Street, Northwood, Hanley. Inn to which the blind Duke of Devonshire drove to from Chatsworth, Derbys, to see cockfighting in c1780 (NSFCT 1915 p156). It had been rebuilt by 1910 (H p99).

Cat Inn Bloxwich Road South, Willenhall. Formerly the White Swan, but has long been known as the Cat by customers, a name taken probably on account of its proximity to a yard known as Cat Yard (TB Feb 1998 pp18-19).

Cedar Tree, The Inn or hotel in Main Road, Brereton. A C18 brick house. Formerly Cedar Lodge (VCH vol 5 p154).

Clifford Arms Hotel Great Haywood. May have been the gatehouse to Haywood Hall (see). Haywood Hall was the seat of the Astons before they moved to Tixall Old Hall in the C16. Barbara Aston, the last of the Aston family, married Hon Thomas Clifford, and the hotel takes its name from his family (HCMBOPP p3p). The old inn was demolished in c1930 and the present one built (HHHC pp73ps, 97).

Coach and Horses Inn Abbots Bromley. One of the upstairs rooms was formerly a chapel, and the alcove where the altar stood could be plainly seen in 1951. After ceasing to be a chapel, it became a boxing trainer's establishment, and the famous Tiger Smith trained here. In 1951 the inn was the headquarters of the Abbots Bromley Horn Dance (IOM p154).

Coach and Horses Inn Great Haywood. The inn is haunted by the ghost of a former landlord, Reggie Smith, who hung himself in the loft. The ghost is a man who crosses the road in front of the inn making cars swerve (BC) (FOS p19) (GOM p20). There was a sighting of the ghost in 1976 (ES April 1976) (MR p165).

Coalbank Tavern Handsworth. See Thornhill House.

Cock Inn Hanbury. See Fauld Crater.

Cock Inn Stood on the corner of Stockwell Street and Market Place, Leek. According to Plot, in 1660 it was frequented by some men who wagered to go up to Blake Mere on a stormy night. One or more of them went and discovered a lady there about to be murdered (NHS p291) (TOI p165) (TFTPM p109).

Cock Inn See Northwood, Hanley.

Cock Inn Stableford, Chapel Chorlton. Known to have been an inn as early as 1792, and was a coaching stop. Has an oak settle of 1632, once owned by Francis and Catherine, Duke and Duchess of Bedford. Also a genuine drunkards chair, said to be 300 years old (IOI p10).

Court House Inn Former manorial court house for Sedgley manor, by All Saints church, Sedgley. Became an inn in the C19. It obviously continued being used for a dual purpose, for the last court case was heard here as late as 1925 (SDOP p10p). It was an hotel by the early 1960s (TTTD p296).

Cross Guns Inn Cape Hill, Smethwick.

Cross Guns Inn Cradley Heath. See main body of encyclopaedia.

Cross Guns Inn Bromwich Heath. A deserter in the Civil War was shot near it (OWB p73). The area of Heath End seems to have grown up here (VCH vol 17 p4).

Cross Inn Old Hill, Rowley Regis. Cloven-hoof prints, or 'devil marks' were discovered on the outer walls of this inn in 1855 (TB March 1981 p17).

Cross Keys Inn Cradley Heath. See Cross Guns Inn, Cradley Heath.

Cross Keys Inn Old Hednesford. See main body of encyclopaedia.

Cross Keys Inn Former coaching inn High Street, Uttoxeter. Tall brick building dating from the C17 with '1697, Edward Hadley, builder' carved on it. Before the Town Hall was built public meetings and magistrates courts were held here (AUOPP p34p). Recently (1993) the house was Bagshaws Estate Agency (Official Uttoxeter Town Guide. 1993. p32).

Crown Inn See Cannock.

Crown Inn Horton village. It was known as the Court House in 1818, presumably because the manor courts were held here (VCH vol 7 p65).

Crown Inn Rugeley. See Shrewsbury Arms, Rugeley.

Crown Inn Lichfield Road, Queensville, Stafford. Known as the Spittal Brook to 1838 when the name was changed to commemorate Queen Victoria's coronation (SN July 9 1998 p3). Peter, a dog belonging to the licensee William Jones, saved an eight year old boy from drowning in the Sow and was awarded the Daily Mirror Gugnunc Collar for bravery. Peter went on to appear at many shows and in parades (SOPP pl 41p) (ROT p42). The name of the inn reverted to the Spittal Brook in 1998 (SN July 9 1998 p3).

Crown Inn Stone. See main body of encyclopaedia.

Crown, The Uttoxeter. Here the body of the royalist commander the Earl of Northampton was brought after being killed in the battle of Hopton Heath in 1643 (HAF p121).

Crown, The Waterhouses. Ancient inn on the old Earl's Way (later the Leek-Ashbourne turnpike) road (DP pp22, 24p). Until recently there was a board preserved at the inn stating that a certain window was exempt from tax as the room it lit was a dairy, and therefore exempt from window tax (NSFCT 1948 p38).

Dartmouth Hotel Former inn at West Bromwich, opened in 1834. Stands on the site of the Old Bull's Head and previous to that it was called 'The Boot.' The land close by was called 'Boot Meadow' (SHWB 8). The inn served as local courts until 1851. Former licensees included the former West Bromwich Albion footballer Harry Clements and the club chairman at the time of the 1930/31 FA Cup win, William Isaiah Bassett. The inn was demolished after its closure in Feb 1977 (BCP p23p).

Dog and Doublet Inn Sandon. See main body of encyclopaedia.

Dog and Partridge Inn Inn in Tutbury. It was built as the town house of the Curzon family of Kedleston, and dates back to the C15. It was extended in the C18 and C19 and became a coaching inn on the route of the Red Rover stage coach between London and Liverpool (UTR pp143-145p facing p160) (IOM p64-65p facing p68) (PWIS p108p) (LTD p191). The building was restored in 1998 (LTD p191). Has also been called 'Ye Olde Dog and Partridge.' Is reputedly haunted.

Dolphin Inn Stafford. Here Richard Stafford Cooke, titular claimant to the barony of Stafford, stayed in quiet obscurity briefly in Dec 1822. Of his time here it is recorded he rose at seven and consumed two glasses of rum and milk (OSST 1954-56 p33).

Doughty Arms Inn, The Tipton. See Five Ways Inn.

Duke's Head Inn Gnosall. Said to be associated with the betrayal of the Duke of Buckingham by his servant, Humphrey Bannister (NSFCT 1946 p147).

Duncombe Arms Inn Ellastone. Named after Sir Charles Duncombe, once lord of the manor. Dates back to 1640 and was a coaching inn on the Ashbourne-Uttoxeter road. Is the Donnithorne Arms in George Eliot's novel 'Adam Bede' (PWIS p87).

Dyers Arms Inn Leek. Name commemorates Leek's involvement in the dyeing industry (BEV p47).

Earl of Lichfield Inn Lichfield. Has displayed the execution notice (probably a replica) of Charles Shaw who murdered John Oldcroft, aged 9, Richard Tomlinson who murdered Mary Evans, his sweetheart, and Mary Smith who drowned her own child. The notice is dated March 19 1834.

Elm Tree Inn An inn N of Gallowstree Elm, at the S edge o Enville Common. Takes its name from the legendary Gal lows Elm Tree, which stood opposite it. See Gallows Elm Tree.

Endwood Hotel Handsworth. See Church Hill House.

Etruria Inn, The Lord Street, Etruria. On the W side of the Trent and Mersey Canal. The clubroom above the stable became a mission room for St Mark's, Shelton in 1844 the congregation were able to move into their own church St Matthew five years later. Demolished in 1934 (HOI pp161,162,226,269), or since 1976 (AGT pp98,99il).

Falcon Inn Former inn which stood at on the corner of High Street, Stone, and the yard to the Town Mill (now Christchurch Way). Notorious since the landlord William Stafford, aged 24, shot dead his wife Ada Mary, aged 27 here and then committed suicide on Feb 17 1891. The inn was subsequently sometimes known as the 'Blood Tub.' Some foundations of Stone Priory have been found on the site (DMF pp81-89) (info Mark Smith and Mrs JC Beecham). From at least the 1980s the inn has been a night club and is now (1999) Pierre Victoire restaurant.

Fighting Cocks Inn Stood at the junction of Goldthorn Hill and Wolverhampton Road East (formerly Sedgley Road) Parkfield. The inn was so called by 1851 (1851 census). It was rebuilt in the 1930s and this building had been demolished by the early 1990s and a supermarket built on the site.

Five Ways Inn Stood on the corner of Hurst Lane and Sedgley Road West, Tipton. It was demolished and rebuilt in c1923 as The Doughty Arms Inn. By the 1990s the inn was called The Pie Factory, one in the Mad O' Rourke's chain of inns (BCP p29p).

Fleur-de-lis, The Ancient coaching inn on Watling Street on S side, 0.25m S of the church at Norton Canes. Probably opened up in the C17. Known locally as 'The Luce' or 'The Flower de Luce.' It suffered badly from subsidence and had to close in the 1930s and was left derelict. The old inn sign went to Little Wyrley Hall. Three pennies have been found, dated 1779, and a couple of half pennies of 1761, and under one of the floors had been uncovered hundreds of pins of the old fashioned kind (CCF pp189-191) (CCBO pp49,51) (ES Jan 28 1931 p1p).

Flitch of Bacon Inn Stood alongside the turnpike road just in Catholme Lane, Wychnor Bridges. Calvert and Byford-Jones noted this inn. It was demolished when the A38 was widened (UNT p83p). The name is from a flitch of bacon formerly kept at Wychnor Manor House (see), which was a reward for certain tenants of Wychnor manor.

Foaming Quart Inn Brown Edge. It was converted into a restaurant by 1988 (SVB p47).

Foaming Quart Inn Greenhead Street, Burslem (SHST p48p). It was in existence by 1828. The old inn was demolished in c1925.

Fountain Inn Albion Street, Brades Village. The daughter of the publican, Lilian, was shot dead on April 1 1913 by her fiancee, Tom Fletcher (known as The American for he had spent some time in the USA). He was convicted of murder and hung at Worcester in July (TB July 1986 pp4-5).

Fountain Inn Stood SE of Meerbrook. In existence by 1834 (VCH vol 7 p193). But according to tradition it was in existence in 1731 when it is said to have sold out of beer to spectators at John Nadin's hanging on Gun Hill (SVB p123). It was submerged under Tittesworth Reservoir sometime between 1959-1962 (SMOPP vol 2 p28p) (VCH vol 7 p193).

Fountain Inn Corner of Factory Road and Owen Street Tipton. Noted for having had a long association with William Perry, the 'Tipton Slasher.' A plaque commemorating Perry was erected on the inn in c1992 (E&S have a photograph) (MR p332) (TWDOP p13p) (TSSOP p40p) (BCP p13p).

Fountain Inn Holloway Bank, Wednesbury. An old chimney of great age stood beside it (OWB p53). The old inn was replaced in the 1930s (BCP p150p of the old inn).

Fountain Inn New Street, Wolverhampton (BCP p87p of inn c1880).

Four Counties Inn See No Man's Heath.

Four Crosses Inn See Offleybrook

Four Crosses Inn Watling Street. See main body of encyclopaedia.

Freemason's Arms Inn Fairoak. Is a reminder of the stone workers who hewed stone out of a quarry near Fairoak in the Middle Ages (ROT pp11-12p). There is a 'Mason's Rough,' a spinney close to the Bishop's Woods (BPS pp86,171). This was where the inquest which convicted Charles Higginson for the murder of his young son in Bishop's Wood took place in 1843 (EOP p52p). Has an interesting sign. (PWIS p35p).

Freetrade Inn Wood Lane, Pelsall (SJC p5).

French Horn Inn Fountain Square, Hanley. Three coins of the period of George III have been found in its cellars (info Pauline Hicks).

Gardners Arms Inn Liverpool Road, Newcastle-under-Lyme. Was thought to be haunted by the ghost of a former publican's wife, Muriel Humpage (d1983), in 1992, by which time the inn had been renamed the Ale House (ES July 29 1997 p7).

Gate Inn, The See Littleworth, Stafford.

Gate Hangs Well Inn Corner of Tividale Street, Tividale, Tipton. Had an unusual sign made to look like a tiny gate. It no longer exists. There are many inns of this name in the area (BCM Oct 1983 p25p).

George and Dragon Inn Carter Street, Uttoxeter. Reputedly haunted by three ghosts; that of a man in his mid 30s, an elderly woman, and a young boy. The inn has now been converted into flats (GLS p104).

George and Dragon Hotel Stood close to the market place, Wednesbury. Licensed from 1814. Has also been known as 'Loxtons' after the first licensee. Frequented by actors who performed at the local theatre. Demolished in 1965 (BCP p72p).

George and Fox Inn Penkridge. The sign showed the Prince Regent (later George IV) and his friend Charles James Fox, the Whig leader, considering the Royal Marriage Bill aimed at extricating the prince from his matrimonial tangle (SOP p161). The sign at Penkridge was not there for Bird to see in the late 1960s or the early 1970s.

George and Fox Inn Eastgate Street, Stafford (VB p80).

George Hotel Burslem. See main body of encyclopaedia.

George Hotel Lichfield. See main body of encyclopaedia.

George Hotel Junction of Digbeth and Bridge Street, Walsall. Built by Thomas Fletcher in 1781 (VCH vol 17 p167). In 1823 the portico from the recently demolished Fisherwick Hall was erected at the George Hotel (VCH vol 14 p244) (SNWA p19) (WROP p20p). Here Henry Clarson, aged 23, chemist and grocer, poisoned himself on the night of July 16 1866 (THM vol 2 p135). Demolished in 1933 or 1934 (BCP pp52p,70p). Raven says it was Walsall's most famous coaching inn (MR p357). The new hotel built on the site in 1935 was closed in the early 1970s (VCH vol 17 p167) and was demolished in 1979 (BCP p70p).

Gleaners Arms Bilston (BEV p49).

Globe Inn Pleck. The building is said to date from the late C17. Former haunt of dog and cock fights (BCP p118p).

Glynne Arms Himley. See main body of encyclopaedia.

Goats Head Inn Corner of Bagot Street and Market Place, Abbots Bromley. The inn has been the free grammar school and before that, according to tradition, the court house of Abbots Bromley manor (OSST 1935 p28). Dr Wilkes (d1760) mentions the 'Town Hall' in Abbots Bromley in his journal. This may refer to what is now the Goat's Head Inn (The Abbots Bromley Horn Dance. ER Shipman. 1982 p5), or the butter cross (NSFCT 1886 p22). The inn had or has a room named after Dick Turpin, who allegedly stayed here (SLM Nov 1949 vol 3 p35) (AB p194 - refers to Turpin) (STM Aug 1968 p35) (IOI p19) (ABAB p50) (SVB p9).

Gough Arms Inn Stood on the W side of the present Birmingham Road, Great Barr. The inn, latterly called the Old Beacon, was replaced by a palatial roadhouse in the 1930s (MNB p64).

Grange Inn Stood by Rowley church, Rowley Regis. Reputedly haunted (TB June 1975 p15p).

Green Man Inn See Bottom House Inn.

Greyhound Inn Bilston. See main body of encyclopaedia.

Greyhound Inn Penkhull. See main body of encyclopaedia.

Greyhound Inn Lower Penn. Has a datestone '1830 W.B.P.' (William Bradney Persehouse). Formerly called the Persehouse Arms. Was known as the Greyhound by 1901 (PPTP pp67 il facing, 68).

Greyhound Inn Stands N of Warslow church. It was known as the Greyhound and Hare when visited by John Byng, later Viscount Torrington, on June 18 1789. Byng recorded in his diaries that the Greyhound and Hare was 'as miserable an alehouse as could be seen' (NSFCT 1975 p38) (VCH vol 7 p57). Said to be haunted by the ghost of a young serving maid from the C18 (PWPD p72). Has also appeared as Greyhound Hotel.

Haberdashers Arms Inn In Knighton village (BEV p49). The name commemorates William Adams, a native of Knighton and member of the Haberdashers' Company of London, who benefited Knighton (see).

Half Way House Inn, The Three-storey brick inn at Tettenhall (or rather Park Dale or Newbridge?). Said to have stood on the Holyhead road exactly halfway between London and Holyhead (BCP p118p).

Hand and Trumpet Inn, The Main Road, Wrinehill. The name is said to be unique in the country and alludes to the hand of cards, and the look-out's trumpet signal to warn of approaching trouble. It is said the inn was an illegal gambling den (ES May 26 2000 p75). Wrinehill Lower (toll) Gate on the turnpike road stood next to this inn.

Hanging Gate Inn Rushton Spencer. Has or had an unusual sign - that of an actual hanging gate (SMOPP vol 2 p21p in c1910).

Hare and Hounds Inn Mares or Mayer's Green, West Bromwich. Frequented by forger, William Booth, of Booth's Farm (see) prior to 1812. A maid at the inn happened to see some secreted forged notes which gave Booth away and here he was captured (OWB p115) (SOWB pp18-19) (TBS p15). The inn was built in 1797 and rebuilt in 1897 (BCP p22).

Hare and Hounds Inn Inn which formerly formed the nucleus of the old hamlet of Kingstanding, Great Barr, on Kingstanding Road in the area of Rushden Crescent. It was known as the Greyhound by 1884, and may possibly have been called the Fox Tavern (KPP p9).

Hart's Horn Inn Former galleried inn situated in St John's Street, Lichfield, adjacent to St John's Hospital. It was a coaching inn in the C18, but had disappeared in c1790 (CCHCA p21).

Harts Horns Weeford. Lost. Marked on Yates' map (1775). On the site now is Whitehouse Farm near Swinfen. It was probably an inn.

Highwayman Inn Threapwood. Formerly the Green Man Inn. Changed to the Highwayman Inn in the 1960s (SMOPP vol 1 p48p). (HAF p358). Perhaps so called after local highwayman Swift Nick.

Himley House Hotel Formerly the Dower House to Himley Hall. On A449 by Himley church and rectory.

Hit and Miss Inn Former old coaching stop in Manor Close off Short Lane, Barton-under-Needwood (UNT p119). See Barton Old Manor House.

Holly Bush Inn Black and white thatched building at Salt. Reputed to be the second oldest licensed inn in the country. Formerly doubled as the manor court (SVB p147) (Nicholson's Real Ale Guide to the Waterways. p138) (SN Jan 10 1997 p9ps). Many of its customers think it is haunted (SN Oct 29 1993 p8). A Civil War period sword was found in its thatched roof in 1923, see Hopton Heath.

Hop and Barleycorn Inn West Coseley. See main body of encyclopaedia.

Hope and Anchor Inn See Cellarhead.

Hope Inn Inn in the High Street, Cheadle, which only sold non-intoxicating drinks. It lasted only a year in c1878 (SMOPP vol 1 p59p of the notice of Hope Inn in the Cheadle Herald 1878).

Horseshoe Inn Tatenhill. Previously known as the Bulls Head and The Three Horseshoes and has a priest's hole behind the bar to the left (IVNF).

Irish Harp Inn Coaching Inn on Watling Street at Stonnall (CCBO pp48,49). Shaw mentions a traveller who committed suicide at the Welsh Harp at Upper Stonnall (SHOS vol 2 p37). The notorious highwayman, Tom King, is said to have been born at the Irish Harp (ADY p5p). Tom King and Dick Turpin are said to have frequented the Old Irish Harp Inn (see) on the Chester Road, E of Aldridge.

Izaak Walton Hotel 0.75m E of Ilam at foot of Bunster Hill at the entrance to Dove Dale. Tennyson signed the visitors' book, recording his opinion that Dovedale was 'one of the most unique and delicious places in England' (Dovedale Guide. Keith Mantell. 1985). The burial mound 180 metres SE of the hotel at SK 14485064 is a listed monument. Garner noted a burial mound in front of the hotel (GNHSS p6).

Jean Pierre Inn Waterhouses. Uniquely named.

Jovial Potters Inn C16 coaching inn which was situated at the intersection of High Street and Hassell Street, Newcastle-under-Lyme. Here the London to Manchester coaches halted. The inn was replaced with the present building in 1957 (plaque on wall of present building).

Jug, The Hanley. Perhaps, the oldest inn in Hanley. Scarratt noted that the new pub had a plaque, reputedly from the old pub, with the date '1620' on it (OTP p148).

King and Constitution Inn Pelsall (SJC p5).

King Charles in the Oak Inn Stood on N side of Charles Lane, Sandbeds, Willenhall. The name occurs on the 1889 OS map. The name is from Charles II's preservation in the Royal Oak at Boscobel.

King's Arms Inn Lichfield Street, Bilston. Bilston's principal coaching inn and also the court of justice for Bilston and Sedgley. It was here that the murderer Abel Hill was first examined in 1819. It was said that he was placed on the balcony to watch the funeral of his victims, but remained unmoved. At election times the same balcony was used as the hustings. The King's Arms became the Conservative and Unionist Club (BOP p37).

King's Arms Inn Stafford Street, Eccleshall. In an unusual venture the inn, as a 'Learning Pub,' was being used for educational purposes by adult students by April 1999 (You and Yours. BBC Radio 4. April 23 1999).

King's Arms Inn Wallington Heath. See Wallington House.

King's Head Inn Bird Street and St John Street, Lichfield.

Labour In Vain Inn Yarnfield. Its controversial sign, showing a white couple trying in vain to scrub the blackness from a negro boy in a bath tub, was removed and replaced by a sign with less racist connotations in 1994. Some vil lagers complained about the loss of the old sign and it was at length put up in the entrance way (ES Jan 8 1994 p7p. March 16 1994 p9p).

Lamb and Flag Inn Salop Street, Bradley, Bilston. Tommy shop for Banks Bros' Ironworks. Notorious for fights between men, cocks, and dogs. Known as the Hell House. The Lamb and Flag was partly in Bilston and partly in Coseley and consequently it was difficult for parish officers to exercise their authority over the inn (BCP p12p) (BOP p111p) (TB Dec 3 1998 p5).

Lamb Inn High Street, Newcastle-under-Lyme. Its foundations were said, in 1911, to contain red sandstone from Newcastle Castle (SA April 191). It was rebuilt in 1925 (VCH vol 8 p8).

Leopard Inn Market Place, Burslem, S of the old town hall (BOE p255). Here, reputedly, James Brindley met Josiah Wedgwood I to discuss the building of the Trent and Mersey Canal in March 1765. Also present was Earl Gower (POP p41). Referred to as the 'Tiger' in Arnold Bennett's novels (Real Ale in and around The Potteries. CAMRA. 4th ed. p20). The name is probably from an old coin called a leopard, which was worth 1.5 sovereigns (ES Oct 16 1995 p8).

Leopard Inn Lichfield Street, Burton upon Trent. The inn dates from the mid C18. Had a reputation for being haunted in the 1970s. The landlord heard strange noises and a customer felt a tap on the shoulder by a phantom nudger. The hauntings ended in 1979 with the departure of the landlord (HPG p172) (BDMN Jan 15 1980 p6p).

London Apprentice Inn Rushall Street, Walsall. The father-in-law of Mrs Siddons, the famous actress, kept this inn. He lost his life wrestling a man named Denston in 1750. Mrs Siddons, married her husband, some 12 years her senior at Holy Trinity, Coventry in 1773 (TB Sept 1992 p7 il) (SNWA p91).

Mason's Arms Inn See Mayfield.

Mason's Arms Inn Hollington. See Raddle Inn.

Mermaid Inn See Blakemere House.

Mermaid Inn, The Wightwick (BCP p114p).

Mine Borers Arms Darlaston (Offlow hundred). Delicensed by 1969 (BEV p49).

Miner's Rest Inn Chasetown. Reg Morris blew a flame from his mouth to a distance of 31 feet at this inn on Oct 29 1986, setting a world record (GBR 1992 p75).

Mitre Inn Pitt Street, Burslem. Said to be Burslem's oldest inn. In existence as an inn by the C16 when the name was changed to the Crown. It changed back to the Mitre in the C19 (ES Oct 16 1995 p8).

Neptune Inn From the balcony of this public house in Willenhall in 1835 the Rt Hon Charles P Villiers made the first address to the electors of the newly-enfranchised borough of Wolverhampton. It was from here that he made many of his free trade speeches and other public announcements (AOW p182).

New Colliers Inn Cradley Heath. Formerly called Sawbones Inn and the Jolly Collier. The landlord claims the inn is haunted and that he saw a ghost here in March 1995 (TB Jan 1996 p11).

New Inn In the Flash area. Must be one of the highest inns in England for it is situated only slightly lower than the Travellers' Rest Inn, which is considered the third highest (NSFCT 1947 p168).

Noah's Ark Inn Stafford. See main body of encyclopaedia.

Noah's Ark Inn Wood Street, Tipton. Former residence of Tommy Cartwright, legendary local boxing hero, and his wife, Milda. They were haunted by the son of the previous landlord called George (HIE pp176,177) (GOM p22p 4(a) of the pub) (GPCE p47). The inaugural meeting of the Black Country Society was held at the inn in 1967 (TSSOP p41p).

Nag's Head Inn Uttoxeter. The inn Michael Johnson stayed at when selling books, and without, on one occasion, his truculent son, Samuel (later Dr Johnson of Lichfield (see)), for which Samuel returned to atone. Redfern thought Michael Johnson had stayed at the Red Lion (HOU pp107-112,115-119il).

Navigation Inn, The A canal side inn at Etruria, famous in its day (HOE pp161,162,226,269).

Offley Arms Inn Madeley. There is a local tradition that the man who first got drunk at this inn was made the mayor of Madeley (M p29).

Okeover Arms Inn Okeover. Initially a public house but changed to a temperance hotel in the 1920s. It remained dry until 1962 when converted back to a pub (PWNS p90).

Old Barrel Inn Old timber-framed inn which leant to one side. Stood on the corner of Victoria and Bell Streets, Wolverhampton (BCP p86p).

Old Beacon Inn Great Barr. See Gough Arms Inn.

Old Blue Ball Inn Hall End, Wednesbury. It was known locally as Spittles' after Jonah Spittle, its landlord in the 1700s. At that time the inn was popular with local cockfighters and spittle is mentioned in 'A Ballad of Wedgebury Cocking.' It became a Grade II listed building in 1987 (BTBC frontispiece to chapter 2) (BCM winter 1996/7 p41 il).

Old Blue Posts Inn Martin Street, Stafford. Renowned for boarding actors performing at the Lyceum Theatre, Martin Street. Demolished in 1893. A ruby ring given in lieu of payment by an actress who stayed here was in the possession of the descendant of the landlord in the early 1980s (SOPP pl 40).

Old Bush Inn See Hinksford.

Old Cock Inn Cheapside, now Lower High Street, Tutbury (UTR p149)

Old Court House Inn Kingswinford. Brick house built by the Earl of Dudley in the late 1700s, and doubled as a public house and a meeting place for the local manorial court. Later the building was stuccoed or painted white (BCP p135ps).

Old Engine Inn or Brewhouse. Alias Wharwell Farm or Warwell Farm, Wharwell Lane, Great Wyrley. Became a beerhouse in c1800 (GWY p facing p18 pp24-25, 31). The beerhouse became a popular venue for pugilist fights (CCAP p18p). A Plesance is of the opinion a minor skirmish was fought near Wharwell Farm in the Civil War: That the royalists made many sorties, and the manor house of Great Wyrley was destroyed by parliamentarians to prevent its being used for the mounting of artillery against parliamentary positions (GWY p facing p18 pp24-25, 31).

Old Horns Inn, The Queslett. The old inn was built in c1800. It was demolished after 1963. There developed a tradition here of serving free cuts of beef to customers on New Year's eve (BCP p22p).

Old House at Home Inn Lordswood Road, Harborne (HOPP pl 49 p of c1912).

Old House at Home Inn Halfords Lane, Smethwick. One of its licensees was the former West Bromwich Albion full-back footballer and England cap, Billy Williams (BCP p128p).

Old Irish Harp On Chester Road, over 0.5m SSW of Mill Green, 1m E of Aldridge. Dates from the late C17 (BCP p12p). Jack Sheppard (BCP p12), Dick Turpin and Tom King may have been regular visitors here (GATD p102 p of c1895) (ALOPP p8p) (WMVB p11) (SNAR p18p). The inn was still in existence in 1938 (1938 OS map).

Old Jacob's Well A late C18 inn situated at the corner of what became known as Vine Lane and High Street, Wordsley, Kingswinford. In 1832 it became the Spotted Leopard, and by 1838 it had become the Vine (later it became the Duke of Wellington?). Perhaps, named after a well here called Old Jacob's Well. (BCM April 1987 p49).

Old King's Arms Inn Wallington Heath. See Wallington House.

Old Mitre Inn Essington. See main body of encyclopaedia.

Old Red Lion Inn Ipstones. A coaching inn. Built in 1757 (PWIS p83). Here James Brindley, engineer, reputedly slept in a damp bed, whilst surveying the Caldon Canal in 1772. The cold he caught from the damp led to his death (The Caldon Canal. The Caldon Canal Society c1985).

Old Still Hotel, The No. 34 Digbeth, Walsall. Part of the interior was called Doctor Johnson's Corner after Dr Johnson of Lichfield (see), who rested between coaches on his visits back to Lichfield. Demolished in 1959 (BCP pp28p,82p) (WROP p18p).

Old Still Inn King Street, Wolverhampton. Has been a public house since 1836. The father of Maggie Teyte (1886-1976) of Dunstall House (see), opera singer, was an owner of this inn (St Peter's Trail. Wolverhampton Council and Wolverhampton Civic Society), or rather Maggie's mother, Maria, was licensee in 1896, while her father James conducted a wine and spirit business from the premises (BCP p13p).

Old Swan Inn Market Place, Uttoxeter. It existed in Elizabeth I's time when Edward Toyke stayed a night here; he had been in correspondence with Mary, Queen of Scots. He applied to the Queen by letter for one hundred double ducats, on the grounds that his father had some acquaintance with her (perhaps, through negotiations over her proposed marriage with Robert, Earl of Leicester). The letter fell into the hands of spies who suspected some secret matter lurked underneath it. In the inquiry into Toyke's movements he claimed to have spent a night here (HOU p238) (N&Q Sept 1862).

Old Talbot Inn Market Place, Uttoxeter. Oldest domestic building in Uttoxeter, surviving the fires of 1596 and 1672. Restored in the 1980s or the 1990s (Official Uttoxeter Town Guide. 1993. p31). Rev Dr Peter Milne, the first clergyman in England to hold a licence of a public house, was publican of this inn in 1994 and that of The Wellington Inn, Uttoxeter (TB March 1994 p19p) (ES Sept 9 1994 p3).

Old Turf Inn Norton Canes. A coaching inn on or near Watling Street could be between the Fleur-de-Lys and the Irish Harp at Stonnall (CCBO p49).

Old Vine Inn Ludgate Street, Tutbury (UTR pp150-151).

Painters Arms Inn Coseley (BEV p48).

Park Hall Hotel See Sedgley Park.

Park Inn, The Tipton. Is haunted by the ghost of Lady May (HIE p177).

Parson and Clerk Inn, The Streetly. See main body of encyclopaedia.

Pear Tree Inn Lower Gornal. Takes its name from the Tettenhall pear which grows in the garden (SDOP p90p).

Pheasant Inn See Bilston.

Pie Factory Inn Tipton. See Five Ways Inn.

Pig and Whistle Inn Sedgley town. Said to be haunted in the 1830s. It was demolished and rebuilt in 1860 during which workmen discovered a human skeleton (Birmingham Daily Post. Aug 31 1860). The inn no longer survives (PHS p6).

Plough Inn, The Plough Lane, Cheadle Road, Wetley Rocks. Cheddleton township boundary passes through it. Participants in the beating of the bounds used to climb over its roof to follow the boundary (SVB p174).

Plough Inn, The Endon. Is renowned for its sign painted by a customer who could not pay his bill (IOI p28) and for being the venue for meetings of the Endon Friendly Society (E pp164, 165. Facing p177 p of a painting by HW Foster showing the interior in late C19). Busts of Disraeli, an African chieftain, a cobbler and others which were in the inn until the early C20 were taken to Ashes Farm, Endon and now rest against the barn wall there (STM Dec 1968 p52). (ALC p70p).

Poachers Tavern At foot of Whorrocks Bank Road, Rudyard village. Possibly stands on the site of a house described in 1607 as at Whorrocks and then occupied by Thomas Knight: the inn incorporates on its W side a stone with the initials TK and IK and the date 1610. By 1854 the house had been converted into the Railway Inn, named after the Leek-Macclesfield railway line of 1849 which ran along the E side of Rudyard Lake. By 1888 it was called the Railway Hotel and by 1900 the Station Hotel. By 1994 it was called Poachers Tavern (VCH vol 7 p67) (RL pp68p,69p).

Powys Arms Inn Wetley Rocks. Formerly The Arblasters Arms, the Arblasters were of Rownall Hall and held the lordship of Cheddleton between 1620-1787 when it passed by marriage to the Powys family of Shrewsbury (SMOPP vol 2 p72).

Pretty Pigs Inn Amington. Formerly known as the Repington Arms (Around Tamworth in Old Photographs. Richard Sulima. 1994 p149p). The sign was noted for being interesting in the 1950s (SJC p5).

Queen's Head Inn Level Street, Brierley Hill. Has a secret passage (TB Oct 1976 p19p). Allegedly haunted by several ghosts (GOM p15).

Queen's Head Inn Burslem. Childhood home of radio actress Marjorie Westbury who played Steve in the 1950s Paul Temple serial (ES Oct 16 1995 p8).

Queens Hotel North Street, Wolverhampton. Has been haunted by strange unexplained bumping noises from the cellar which have been linked with the spirits of long dead actors from the Queen's Music Hall which used to stand nearby (E&S Dec 1974) (FOS p19) (GOM p20) (FSLBWM p37).

Quiet Woman, The Leek. The sign bears the figure of a headless woman (LGS p162).

Quiet Woman, The Upper Tean. An inn, now a shop. Reputedly the inn was built on the site where a witch called Martha was beheaded - hence the name of the inn? Martha's ghost haunted the inn (GLS pp94-95).

Raddle Inn Hollington. Formerly the Masons Arms and there are compass and square over both fireplaces (PWNS pp68-69).

Railway Inn Corner of Newport Road and Green Lane Eccleshall. So called as it anticipated a railway line though Eccleshall which never came (STM Jan 1964 p43p). By 1998 the inn was called the Badger.

Railway Inn Lower Leigh, in Leigh ancient parish. Is now (1995) a residence. Has a timber facing no longer visible but still displaying S Sherratt's 1751 inscription 'Walk in my friend and drink with me; there's ALE as good as e'er you see...' (ESNF p85p).

Railway Inn or Railway Hotel, Rudyard village. See Poachers Tavern.

Red Cow Inn Cinders, Lower Gornal. At SO 920909. A few years prior to 1970 some bodies were discovered behind the inn, interred in regular rows. Some thought the bodies were victims of the parliamentary attack on Dudley Castle during the Civil War. Or that it was the site of a Quaker burial-ground? (SSAHST 1970 p42).

Red Cow Inn Werrington. Has a fireplace comprising old tombstones. The inn also has a large ship's wheel, taken from the frigate H.M.S. Defiant (IOI p29).

Red Dog Lapley. Is possibly an inn S of the A5.

Red House Inn Caverswall. Has an interesting sign showing a merry go round with the words 'Rum Tum Tardy um' round the top. These words are taken from an old song thought to have started life as a marching song for the Caverswall volunteers during the Napoleonic Wars (VB p103) (SMOPP vol 1 p7p) (SVB p52). The inn had the table napkins formerly used on board Lord Nelson's flagship, the 'Victory,' in 1951 (IOM p67).

Red Lion Hotel Leek. See main body of encyclopaedia.

Red Lion Hotel Wolverhampton. Stood on the site of the Town Hall. It was built in c1697 and was the first brick inn in Wolverhampton (HOWM p130).

Red Lion Inn Green Lane, Bloxwich. Built in the early C19. WC Athersmith, footballer, was some time licensee. He played as a winger for England and for Aston Villa when they won the FA Cup at Crystal Palace in 1894/95 season and when they won the double FA Cup and League Cup in the 1895/6 season (SNBP p30).

Red Lion Inn Bradley. Outside the inn in the later C17 Plot noted a glacial boulder similar to that at Red House Farm High Onn (OSST 1931 p20).

Red Lion Inn Bradnop. See Oxhay Farm and Lane End Farm.

Red Lion Inn On S side of Ruxley Road (formerly High Street), Bucknall. Court leets are said to have been held here (info Alan Adams).

Red Lion Inn Believed to be the oldest house in Burslem (VCH vol 8 p110). Others claim the Mitre (see) is. There is a tile dated 1675 with initials R.D.S. on the front of the building. Here one used to be able to see the coal outcropping in the cellar (POP pp19-20). In the Chartist riots in 1842 a man died outside it, and the rioters probably drunk it dry (ES Oct 16 1995 p8).

Red Lion Inn Boundary, Cheadle. Roman relics are said to have been found in the grounds of the inn (IOI p30).

Red Lion Inn Old coaching inn on Soho Road, Handsworth. The original inn received a license in 1542. During the Civil War, Oliver Cromwell with his army bound for Dudley Castle used the inn, together with Handsworth's Old Town Hall, and Brown's Green, to provide stabling for horses (HPPE p98).

Red Lion Inn Ipstones. See Old Red Lion Inn.

Red Lion Inn Ipstones Edge, on the road to Bottom House. At a spinney near this inn people have felt the presence of, and seen, the ghost of a young woman murdered and buried here. The body was discovered because of the dreams, or nightmares, of her mother. Near the same place four different people have said to have seen what appeared to be three different people standing over a bicycle which, as they approached, all vanished (SMM p49).

Red Lion Inn Talke. Here, Weir, a Government spy, working for the Duke of Cumberland in the 1745 Jacobite Rebellion, was captured by a reconnaissance of Lord George Murray (in the army of Charles Edward Stuart) on the evening of, probably, Dec 2 1745, whilst on his way to dinner (NSFCT 1925 p57).

Red Lion Inn Former inn and hotel, now a shop, on the corner of Market Place, Uttoxeter. Redfern thinks, Michael Johnson, father of Dr Johnson of Lichfield (see), stayed at this former coaching inn when selling books, and without, on one occasion, his truculent son, Samuel, for which Samuel returned to atone. Others have thought it was at the Nag's Head. Mary Allport and Sarah Adams, who climbed Uttoxeter church spire in 1814 to kiss the workmen repairing it, worked here (HOU pp107-112,115-119il, 160-161) (LTD p106). The cellars are said to be haunted by the ghost of a policeman who committed suicide when a barmaid refused his attentions (LTD p106).

Red Lion Inn Formerly stood in the SE corner of St Peter's churchyard, Stoke-upon-Trent. There may have been a beerhouse on this site in medieval times and an inn was probably in existence on this site by 1817 (CAST p43). It belonged to the rector until 1925 when conveyed to Showell's Brewery (VCH vol 8 p191). Demolished in 1973 for the building of the A500. On the roof over the entrance was the figure of a lion. The inn was being re-erected at Crich Transport Museum, Derbys in Sept 1993 (ES Aug 28 1993 p31p. Sept 23 1993 p8. Aug 15 1994 p8p).

Red Lion Inn Ablewell Street, Walsall. Now occupied by Ablewell Street Wesleyan Chapel. Believed by some to be where Queen Henrietta Maria stayed whilst in Walsall in 1642 or 1643. Others believe she stayed at the White Hart, Caldmore (OWB p71).

Red Lion Inn Bridge Street, Wednesbury. Believed to be the hostelry pictured in the C19 painting of the Wednesbury Riots of 1743 by Marshall Claxton RA. The inn was demolished in 1983 (BCP p42p) (WDOP p96p).

Red Lion Inn Wrinehill. See Medicine House.

Red Lion Inn In 1904 this inn was said to have been situated in Red Lion Yard off a winding avenue at the bottom of Salop Street (formerly Barn Street), Wolverhampton. In 1816 the military travelling carriage in which Napoleon fled from the battle of Waterloo was displayed in one of its coach-houses. In 1832 Queen Victoria, when Princess Victoria, took refreshment here whilst in progress round the country with her mother, the Duchess of Kent. The Red Lion closed as an hotel in 1838. In 1845 the property was occupied as a private residence (WJO Jan 1904 p14).

Red, White and Blue Inn Featherstone. So called because it was built of red, white and blue bricks. A fire on June 29-30 1905 destroyed the building. It was not re-opened until May 26 1928 (E&S Aug 16 1997 p8p).

Ring o' Bells Inn See West Bromwich.

Rising Sun Inn Reputed to have been a C18 coaching inn. Located at junction of the Chester Road and Watling Street, Brownhills. Opposite the inn stood a finger post, the original, dated 1777, went to the county museum at Shugborough (BLHT).

Rising Sun Inn, The No. 116 Horseley Road, Horseley Heath, Tipton. The building was derelict up to c1997. The inn was declared the Best Pub in Britain by the Campaign For Real Ale in 2000 (BBC Midlands Today. Jan 26 2000).

Rising Sun Inn Princes End, Tipton. Here fat man Samuel Murfitt died on Jan 21 1887, aged 55. He was six feet one inch tall, 100 inches in girth, and 28 inches round the calf and allegedly 40 stones. Murfitt was buried at Darkhouse Cemetery on Jan 25 1887 (BCM April 1985 p35).

Robin Hood Inn Collis Street, Amblecote (TB Oct 1993 p7).

Robin Hood Inn Lower Road, Ashley. In 1911 WE Vernon Yonge noted there was an inn of this name under Ashley Heath (BPS pp168-169). Still existed in 1998.

Robin Hood Inn See Marchington Cliff.

Robin Hood Inn Pedmore Road, Merry Hill. By 1981 a statue of Robin Hood, which used to stand above the lentil over the door, was re-positioned on the roof (TB Aug 1981 p17p) (MR p56p).

Robin Hood Inn The Crescent, Willenhall (TB March 1997 pp18-19).

Rock Tavern Stourton. See main body of encyclopaedia.

Roebuck Inn Derby Street, Leek. The black and white frontage came from a house built at Hodnet in 1626, removed here in the C19 (OL vol 1 pp76-78 il) (Real Ale in and around the Potteries. CAMRA. p41). The County Planning and Development Department doubt this story (BOE p171). Formerly called The Sun. It has been haunted (DP p75).

Roebuck Inn C18 coaching inn in Newcastle-under-Lyme. Visited by Lord Torrington in 1792. He described it as the largest inn of the town, although one of the most uncouth public houses he had ever entered in the country. There were two inns called the Roebuck in C18, sometimes referred to as the Old Roebuck and the New Roebuck. The Old Roebuck may have been originally the 'Angel' and stood on part of an island site on E side of the High Street (SA April 8 1911) (VCH vol 8 p9).

Rose and Crown Inn Stands opposite the main entrance to Haden Hill Park at Haden Hill. Is reputed to have been the birthplace of Stan Edge who assisted in the design of the Austin Seven motor car (BTBC p19p of the old inn).

Royal Cottage Upper Hulme. See main body of encyclopaedia.

Royal Oak Inn Abbots Bromley. Believed to be haunted (HIE p170).

Royal Oak Inn Market Place, Burton upon Trent. Many landlords have left owing to it being haunted (GLS pp29-30).

Royal Oak Inn C18 coaching inn on S side of High Street, Eccleshall, with arcading onto the street. See Eccleshall and Offleybrook.

Royal Oak Inn Perry Barr. See Parson and Clerk Inn.

Royal Oak Inn Rising Brook, Stafford. Formerly Rising Brook House, which stood on an estate in existence by 1778. The house had become 'The Oak,' a public house by 1860, taking its present name by 1892. Rebuilt in 1928. By the late 1960s it was informally known as 'The Why Not,' allegedly after a nobleman and his friends unexpectedly called in in passing having asked themselves 'Shall we stop for a drink?' (IOI p35p) (SAC p38).

Royal Oak Inn Wetton. There is a tradition that Charles II stayed here (WTCEM p7). Has hosted the World Championship toe wrestling competition (ES April 8 1994 p3).

Saracen's Head Inn Shirleywich. A bottle kept at this inn in the C19 is said to have contained the 'laid' spirit of the father of Preston Moore, a man from Weston-on-Trent (NSFCT 1900 p142).

Saracen's Head Inn Weston-on-Trent. Commemorates the grant of the crest of a Saracen's Head to Lord Ferrers for services to Richard I in the third crusade. On the inn sign the face of the crusader is that of a landlord of the inn (SVB p173).

Scales Inn Market Street, Lichfield. Named after scales used in the weighing-in room of a racecourse, with reference to a racecourse on Whittington Heath. Perhaps a name unique in Britain (VB p14). The cellars are haunted by a headless woman in a black gown with white collar and cuffs (ST p5).

Scott Arms Inn See main body of encyclopaedia.

Seven Stars Inn See Capponfield, Sedgley.

Seven Stars Inn Marked on Smith's map approximately at Wall Heath on current A449, Kingswinford. The inn reputedly had a chained water-otter in the cellar, but it was nothing more than a chained kettle to make the water 'otter ! (TB May 1993 p7).

Shakespeare Inn Stood at foot of Church Hill, Walsall. Here the mayor of Walsall and his brethren met before proceeding in procession to church. Later the inn became a common lodging-house. Later it and houses in adjoining Peal Street were demolished (SNWA p30).

Ship Inn At Danebridge, Rushton Spencer. It contained a relic of the 1745 Jacobite Rebellion - a Highlander's musket and newspaper - which went to a house called The Bagstones, Wincle, Ches (NSFCT 1945 p86). The inn sign shows the 'Nimrod,' Sir E Shackleton's ship on his expedition to the South Pole. Bode implies it is at Wincle consequently in Ches (SMCC p13). (DP pp38-39).

Shoulder of Mutton Inn High Street, Tutbury. Was delicensed by c1946 (UTR pp145-147).

Shrewsbury Arms Rugeley. See main body of encyclopaedia.

Shrewsbury Arms Inn in Eastgate Street, Stafford. The inn was in existence by WW1 (Yesterday's Town: Stafford. Paul Butters. 1984 p88).

Sir Tatton Sykes Inn Former inn on N side of Lichfield Street, Wolverhampton. Named after a horse which won the St Leger in 1846 and in turn named after Sir Tatton Sykes, Bart, of Sledmere, Yorks (1772-1863) who saw 74 St Legers and who rode on horseback each year from his Yorkshire home to Epson to see the Derby. By 1996 the inn had been renamed Lichfields (WOLOP p37p) (BEV p56).

Soho Foundry Tavern Foundry Lane, Smethwick (BCP p125p).

Sow and Pigs Inn Hill Top, West Bromwich, facing Trotters Lane. Considered an old inn in c1875 (BCP p26p).

Spittal Brook Inn Queensville. See Crown Inn.

Spot Gate Inn At Spot Gate (SIS p13), 0.25m SSE of Spot Acre. Adjoining the inn are two 1929 Pullman railway coaches, which have been converted into a restaurant. They are called 'Ursula' and 'Car 75.' One coach is haunted (PWNS p59). One coach, the former Bournemouth Belle Pullman car, was described in 1969 as recently erected (WMAG April 1969).

Spread Eagle Inn Rolleston. This could have been the Eagle and Child mentioned in Parson and Bradshaw Directory (1818), which is the crest of the Stanley family: Henry VII's mother married into the Stanley family; Henry VII was lord of the manor for some time. The inn was re-named the Mosley Arms in the 1840s, but was known as the Spread Eagle by 1851 (UTR p234). Reputedly haunted (local info).

Spring Cottage Inn Bloxwich. Built in the mid C19. The regular drinkers at the inn maintain that it is haunted (SNBP p23).

Staff of Life Inn Old inn in Hill Street, Stoke-upon-Trent. Built in the early 1800s on site of former farm house on ancient crossroads. The farm gave sustenance to travellers, who were mainly travelling to Hulton Abbey. The entry below the inn was, reputedly, part of the old pathway. It was also the custom of the farmer to send a baked wheatsheaf and other farm produce to Stoke church, a custom kept up by the landlord and customers until WW1 (AGT p150il). (N&Q 1904-9 vol vi p487). Popularly known as 'Charlie's' (Real Ale in & around the Potteries. CAMRA. p67). The name the 'Staff of Life' may originate from the old farm (AGT p150). (SOTB p102p).

Stafford Arms Inn Bagnall. Said to have been built in 1400. Reputedly, a room in the inn was used as an armoury for Scottish troops of the Young Pretender in the 1745 Jacobite Rebellion (SMOPP vol 2 p61p). It was known as the King's Arms in 1841 and the Marquis of Stafford Arms in 1879 (B pp117-118ps) (PWNS pp112,118p).

Staffordshire Knot Inn Public house at Lanesfield (BEV p49).

Stags Head Inn Vicarage Road, Penn. Reputedly haunted by the ghost of a lady in a demure Victorian gown. According to local tradition she is the wife of a former vicar who was keen on taking a drink at the inn during her husband's sermons. There was a sighting of this ghost in 1972 (GOT p145).

Star and Garter Inn Formerly Wolverhampton's principal hotel. Stood in Victoria Street (BCP p94p). Charles I may have stayed in a house on or near the hotel in the Civil War (WAIW vol 1 p). It was rebuilt in the early 1800s (BCP p94). In 1905 Henry Irving when in Wolverhampton appearing on the stage was so ill he collapsed in his room at the Star and Garter Inn and a welcome in the Town Hall had to be cancelled (The Book of Wolverhampton. Frank Mason. 1979 p121).

Star Inn Great Wyrley. Here collier, Thomas Farrington, made a drunken boast that he was the Wyrley ripper, for which he received three years penal servitude (TB May 1993 p18).

Star Inn S side of Ironmarket, Newcastle-under-Lyme. Timber-framed. Is known to contain some medieval timbers. It was an inn by at least 1734 (VCH vol 8 p8).

Star Inn Market Place, Stafford. There was a tradition that the standards of the Staffordshire Volunteer Cavalry (later Staffordshire Yeomanry) were passed through a window of the Star Inn whenever the regiment receives their colours. On Oct 21 1795 the Countess of Sutherland presented the first standards for the regiment to Lt Col Monckton through a window of the inn during a parade of the regiment in the Market Place (FSP pp61,62) (info Yeomanry Museum).

Starving Rascal Inn Amblecote. Originally called the Dudley Arms. According to tradition it is now so called after a licensee once turned away a starving beggar, whose frozen body was found the next day close by the inn. The house became known as the Starver. Courage brewery changed it to the Starving Rascal. Its sign shows on one side the beggar turned away and on the other the beggar's ghost being welcomed by a new licensee (BCM Jan 1983 pp55-56p) (GPCE p24).

Station Hotel Rudyard village. See Poacher Tavern.

Stewponey Inn See main body of encyclopaedia.

Swan Bank Tavern Bilston. Known locally as the Blazing Stump, supposedly after a former landlord accidentally set fire to his wooden leg. In 1820 the landlord was Jackie Fellows, the Bilston constable who arrested the murderer, Abel Hill (TB April 1981 p26. Dec 3 1998 p5) (BOP p39p).

Swan Hotel Old coaching inn in Bird Street, Lichfield. Has also appeared as Swan Inn (LAL p42p). The 'Lily White Swan Inn' occupied the site in 1535 (LOPP p17p). Mrs Thrale, friend of Dr Johnson of Lichfield (see), stayed at the Swan when visiting Lichfield in 1774 with her husband and daughter, Queenie Thrale (CCHCA p22). The first meeting of the original SAS was held at the Swan Inn on May 20 1800. For the history of the Society see Bingley Hall.

Swan Hotel Stafford. See main body of encyclopaedia.

Swan Inn There was an inn of this name at Alton by 1818 which closed some time after 1871. Some say it closed immediately after the Earl of Shrewsbury had been successful in a court case over some disputed land with the Duke of Norfolk and in reprisal the earl closed the inn, or he just closed it for his son was spending too much time drinking here (HAF pp353-354). The inn is now (1996) known as Fox House.

Swan Inn The earliest known inn in Leek, in existence by the 1560s. But it may not have stood on the site of the present Swan Inn on the corner of St Edward Street and Mill Street, which was not known as the Swan until 1786 (VCH vol 7 p88).

Swan Inn Lichfield. See Swan Hotel.

Swan Inn Newcastle Road, Trent Vale. Reputedly haunted (Real Ale in and Around the Potteries. CAMRA. p72).

Swan Inn Talke. Here 58 bodies who had died in the Talk o' the' Hill Colliery disaster on Dec 13 1866, were laid out, and here the dead of the Bunkers Hill Colliery disaster were laid out on April 30 1875. The gruesome sight of the dead laid out gained the inn its local name of the 'Chamber of Horrors' (LWF pp13,15p,32).

Swan Inn Old roadside inn at West Bromwich. Probably existed by 1635 and is recorded in 1655 (VCH vol 17 p8). But said to have been built in c1550. The Swan was the badge of Anne of Cleves. It was demolished in 1860 and the present building constructed largely out of the old materials in c1860. It was probably the first inn in West Bromwich. It had extensive gardens and was a pleasure retreat or resort for people from Dudley and Birmingham. In 1770 there was a public library held here (OWB pp49-50) (SHWB 8 p). Gives its name to the Swan Village area (SHWB 8) (SOWB p24).

Swan Inn See Wolverhampton.

Swan with Two Necks Inn Former old coaching inn on the Stafford to Chester road, Croxton. At the turn of the C20 it became 'Meadow's Shop,' a grocery. In the front garden was discovered a stone bearing the date 1645 when the cobble stones were being replaced by concrete (BOV pp18,19,20).

Talbot Arms Inn Rugeley. See Shrewsbury Arms.

Three Crowns 3m E of Walsall off the Sutton Road. Probably the name was from an inn. It persists in Three Crowns Special School.

Three Crowns Inn Lichfield. See main body of encyclopaedia.

Three Loggerheads, The Inn at Loggerheads, Ashley. Vernon-Yonge implies it was formerly just The Loggerheads. The old sign proclaimed 'We Three, Loggerheads be' and showed two clowns or fools. After the onlooker

had wondered why only two fools were represented he was supposed to realise he was the third! But some time ago, wrote Vernon Yonge (1902), another sign was erected which showed three fools so ruining the joke (BPS pp167-168). (NSFCT 1931 pp186-187) (VB pp158-159). In the C19 Ashley was the destination of a day-trip for many from the Potteries. The most famous Loggerheads inn is at Mold, another is in Wiltshire (HSB pp39,458-459).

Three Men in a Boat Inn Stephenson Avenue, Walsall. Named after Jerome K Jerome's popular novel of the same name, published in 1889; JK Jerome was born at Belsize House (see), Walsall. The sign of the inn in the early 1970s depicted JK Jerome with characters out of the book (VB p59).

Tilted Barrel Inn At the junction of Parkes' Lane and High Street, Prince's End. The house, still standing in 1999, leans owing to mining subsidence (CWBT p48p) (SDOP p89p).

Town Hall Vaults Inn See Tamworth Castle.

Travellers Rest Inn Flash. See main body of encyclopaedia.

Trooper Inn, The Harden, Walsall. Licensed to Joseph Lea in the C18 and in 1774 the Amicable Friendly Society had 110 male members at this inn. The old Trooper Inn closed in March 1930 and a new inn of the same name opened the next day (SNBP pp31-32). Shaw noted at Arden (Harden) an inn called the Valiant Trooper in 1800 (SHOS vol 2 p75).

Trooper Inn, The In Wall village. A well in the grounds of the inn was cleared in 1925-26. It proved to be nearly 50 feet deep. Roman bricks and pieces of plaster were recovered from it (NSFCT 1913 p111) (Letocetum. WF Blay. 1925 p25) (NSJFS 1964 p41) (Roman site at Wall. Official Guide. 1979).

Turk's Head Inn Former inn at Hill Top, Burslem. Locally known as Tommy Clew's tumbling down house (MOS pp26,27).

Turk's Head Inn Former public house in Diglake, St Chad's parish, Stafford. Peter Hales (d1643) of Stafford left a rentcharge of 20 shillings a year on this property of which half was to maintain St Chad's church and half to be distributed to the poor of St Chad's parish. By 1786 10 shillings was being distributed in bread, which by the early C19 was given twice yearly to 30 poor; allegedly on Easter and Christmas eves after the collection of the rent on those evenings by St Chad's verger. The other half went to St Chad's churchwardens' fund (VCH vol 6 p268) (FSP p84) (SIOT p75).

Turk's Head Inn Bromford Lane, West Bromwich. Old inn said to date from late Tudor times. Rebuilt in 1924 (SHWB 8).

Turk's Head Inn Sams Lane, West Bromwich. Thinly disguised as 'The Sarcen's Head,' the interior of this inn was vividly described in the novel 'Joseph's Coat' (BCP pp48-49).

Unicorn Inn Stafford. Its sign appeared in an exhibition in London (ES Nov 4 1936 p7p).

Victoria Inn Fletcher Road, Stoke-upon-Trent. Reputed to have been the largest public house in England when built in 1900 ('Real Ale in and Around the Potteries' CAMRA p68).

Victory Cave Inn Bentley Common. The inn had to be evacuated and closed in April 1951 as the building was made unstable by excavations for the proposed railway sidings for the local power station (BCP p119p).

Vine, The Delph Road, Brierley Hill. Famous Black Country inn with the nickname the Bull and Bladder (Nicholson's Real Ale Guide to the Waterways. CAMRA. p22) (BCP p17p).

Vine, The C18 inn on corner of Caldmore Road and Lower Hall Street, Walsall. Rebuilt in 1840s (BCP p149p).

Waggon and Horses Inn Former little old-fashioned low roofed roadside inn on N side of Soho Road, Handsworth. Built in c1700 and demolished in 1870. In 1877 the present Handsworth public offices and free library was built on the site. The inn is said to have been frequented by employees of Boulton and Watt at Soho, and also spies from other parts of the country trying to gather information on new industrial machinery at Soho Foundry and Manufactory (HPPE pp122-123).

Waggon and Horses Inn Inn at junction of Groveland Road and Dudley Road, Tipton. The sign has two illustrations to denote the fact it was owned by two breweries - Banks and

M&B. Also Wagon is spelt Waggon (BCM Jan 1983 p55p).

Wellington Inn, The Uttoxeter. Rev Dr Peter Milne, the first clergyman in England to hold a licence of a public house was publican of this inn in 1994 and that of The Old Talbot Inn, Uttoxeter (TB March 1994 p19p).

Welsh Harp Inn Legendary coaching inn on the old Chester Road, at Stonnall. Haunt of highwaymen and birthplace of highwayman, Tom King (SVB p157). Was a farmhouse by the mid C19 by which time another inn, The Welsh Harp and Swan, had been set up nearby using the same name (SHOS vol 2 p53) (W p584). Is now called Wordsley House. Reputedly has a secret tunnel to the manor house and a hand-print, which mysteriously keeps reappearing on the chimney piece (SVB p157).

Wheatsheaf, The Walsall. See Grove House.

Wheel Inn Situated at the end of High Street, Tutbury. It was formerly the Catherine Wheel, the badge of the Order of the Knights of St Catherine of Mount Sinai, created for the protection of pilgrims. The puritans changed the name to the 'Cat and Wheel' (UTR p149):

White Hart Inn Caldmore Green. See main body of encyclopaedia.

White Hart Inn High Street, Kinver. In existence by 1605 It was used for meetings by the earlier C18 and had become the regular meeting place of the borough and manor courts by the earlier C19. It was known as the White Hart and Angel in the later C18 (VCH vol 20 p121 il facing p128). May have a secret tunnel to Kinver church. In the 1960s a helmet of Civil War origin, belonging to a Roundhead, was discovered in the course of major structural work and placed on show in the bar (PWIS p8).

White Hart Inn S of Gaia Lane, Lichfield. Has also appeared as The White Hall (LPL) and may be same as Whitehale (see). A messuage called the White Hart is referred to in 1531 (SHOS vol 1 p311). Reputedly a hiding place of Dick Turpin (LAL p22p). Has now been demolished.

White Hart Inn Clay Street, Penkridge. There is a tradition that Elizabeth I stayed here for one night (VB p80) (HOP p15) (SVB p136). Or Elizabeth I only dined here, perhaps as the guest of her master of horse, Ambrose Dudley, Earl of Warwick, brother of Robert Dudley, Earl of Lancaster (the white hart is a Lancastrian symbol). Mary Queen o Scots is said to have been refreshed at the White Hart or two occasions during her captivity in Staffs (PVH p20) The present inn is timber-framed and was built in possibly in c1600 (SOP pp93 p of,124,128,129) (VCH vol 5 p107).

White Hart Inn Coaching house on Manchester to London Royal Mail route at Uttoxeter. Built in 1507. In the 1745 Jacobite Rebellion it was the headquarters of the supporters of the Young Pretender, under the command of Sir William Baggatt (IOI p47p). Another account says the Duke of Cumberland, whilst in pursuit of the Young Pretender stayed two nights at the White Hart Inn; however, thereafter, ironically the inn was a meeting place for Jacobite sympathisers (LTD p108). Another account says the Duke stayed at Uttoxeter Manor House (see).

White Lion Inn Darlaston (Offlow hundred). John Wesley and the 'Wednesbury Mob' are said to have stopped outside this inn in 1743 as the mob took Wesley to Bentley Hall. Much later the inn was run by the grandparents of Sue Harmer Nicholls, actress who plays Audrey Roberts in the TV soap opera Coronation Street (BCP p16p).

White Lion Inn House on the Green, Drayton Bassett Former public house. Robert Peel blocked an application for a licence after complaints of rowdiness. For a time it doubled as an inn and a post office with a carpenter working in its outhouse, so that in all, three trades were carried on here (DM pp32,33 il).

White Lion Inn Harlaston. Parts of the inn are about 300 years old. It is supposed to be haunted by a man (who was a cavalier?) at the battle of Bosworth in 1485 (PWIS p125)

White Lion Inn Stafford. See Saint John's Hospital.

White Rose Inn Temple Street, Bilston. The ghost of 'Fagash' Liz Willoughby was said to have been seen at the inn in 1998 (E&S April 15 1998 p13).

White Swan Inn Very popular canalside inn at Fradley Junction. Also known as the 'Dirty Duck.' It was first mentioned as an inn in Sept 1925, but could have been in existence by 1898 (LTM Sept 1972 pp25,26,28p)

Whittington Inn Whittington, Stourton. See main body of encyclopaedia.

Why Not Inn, The Essington (SJC p5). The name first became popular for inns after a horse called Why Not? won the Grand National in 1894 (BEV p56). The Royal Oak

Inn (see), Rising Brook, was formerly called The Why Not.
Windmill Inn Werrington. One of the oldest inns in N Staffs, dates from 1730. It was transferred to new premises (ES May 13 1931 p4).
Windsor Castle By 1780 there was a house called this in Kinver ancient parish. It had probably been an inn, probably in the lane called Windsor Holloway, 0.5m SE of Kinver church (VCH vol 20 p125).
Woodman Inn Inn of late Victorian-origin in Woodman Lane, Clent (1882 OS map). It was probably erected to cater for excursionists to Clent. A life-size statue of a woodman stood for many years in the garden, but it was disposed of after WW2 (SNSV vol 2 p83).

Woolpack Inn Duke Street, Tutbury. It had been divided into a private house by c1946 (UTR p149).
Woolpack Inn Former C15 inn in Walsall. It was rebuilt in the mock Tudor style in 1892 and this building in turn was demolished in 1966 (WROP pp11p,12p).
Wych Elm Inn Burntwood. Name is from a wych elm, a well-known landmark, which grew here (SPN p25).

Ye Old Coach and Horses Inn Abbots Bromley. Has an interesting inn sign hung in a rustic frame made of branches, and the words are made out of sticks in a rustic fashion (SLM Feb 1950 p96p).
Ye Olde Leathern Bottel Inn Vicarage Road, Wednesbury.

Reputed to have been built in 1510 and to have been patronized by Dick Turpin (WDOP p92p of in 1899). The inn was rebuilt in 1913 (BCP p27p).
Yew Tree Inn In Cauldon village (PWNS p107). Is full of antiques collected by the landlord, Alan East, including Pianolas, polyphons, clocks, bicycles, Queen Victoria's stockings and Prince Albert's nightshirt (Real Ale in and around the Potteries. CAMRA. 4th ed. pp21,23p) (ES April 22 2000 p15p).
Yew Tree Inn Enville Road (BHOP2 p99p), Wall Heath, Kingswinford. Could have been a mid C19 coaching inn. The licensee's son was restrained in bed by a supernatural and unknown force at Christmas 1976 (TB March 1981 p4).

Some loose ends

ARGICULTURE. In Staffordshire piecemeal enclosure of land by agreement was occurring from the Middle Ages. And again by agreement, in the C18 and C19, but large whole-field systems were enclosed in the C17 (SL p121); on a few occasions by acts of parliament (SL p121). According to Sir Simon Degge a rule of husbandry in C17 Staffordshire was

Be it wet or be it dry
Spread your muck, and let it dry

(VCH vol 6 p64) (NHS p340 WSL copy with Degge annotations)

ARMS. The arms of Staffordshire county council, granted in 1931, are: A chevron gules charged with a gold Stafford Knot, and on a chief azure a gold lion passant guardant. The crest is - Above a mural crown proper, a gold Stafford Knot. The supporters are: Dexter, a lion regardant gules crowned with a gold ducal coronet; and sinister, a gold griffin, also regardant. The motto is: 'The Knot Unites' (CH p328il). Another motto for the county is: 'Labor Omnia Vincit' (Work Overcomes All Things).

DISHES. The county's special dishes are Beasting's pie, Pikelets, Burton Ale, Collier's Pie, Frumenty, Simnel cake, Oakcakes, and Cheese, made especially for toasting (TE p500). Lumpty Tums, a form of porridge, was popular in the winter in the Moorlands (LTD p13), see

Bradnop.

INDUSTRY. Staffordshire iron production became the largest in England, when Staffs overtook Shrops in the period 1806 to 1823 (SL p117). By the mid C19 Staffordshire had become an industrial county (HOS p46). (NSFCT 1950 p92).

NATURAL HISTORY. The smallest spider found in Britainby 1966 was said to be the Saloca diceros, with a body length of less than one tenth of an inch, found among mosses in Dorset and Staffordshire (GBR 1966 p35). The largest fox ever shot to 1974 was that of one killed on the Staffordshire Worcestershire border on March 11 1956 which weighed 28 lb. 2 oz. and measured 54 inches from nose to tip of brush (GBR 1974 p278). The largest Common Bream ever caught by 1991 was that of one weighing 16 lb. 6 oz caught by Anthony Bromley in private water somewhere in Staffordshire in 1986 (GBR 1991 p227)

RHYMES. This one suggests the county is full of women of low virtue:

Nottingham full of hogs,
Derbyshire full of dogs,
Leicestershire full of beans,
Staffordshire full of queans.

Apparently, Hackwood says, the Staffordshire man only agrees with this rhyme when the last word is spelt 'queens' (SCSF p167) (FOS p150).

Derbyshire for wool and lead,
Staffordshire for beef and bread.

(SL p102).

SPORT. Daniel Defoe, in the early C18, noted the county bred fine runners, especially in the Moorlands and the N of the county (A Tour Through The Whole Island of Great Britain. Daniel Defoe. (Penguin. 1979). p401). The FA Cup came to Staffordshire in 1949 (Staffs County Handbook c1958 p23).

VICTIMS. John H Tunstall, the son of a wealthy Staffs landowner, who emigrated to the USA in the 1860s. By 1870 he had a large cattle range called Rio Feliz. He was murdered by one of his 'hands' William Bonney (d1881), alias 'Billy the Kid' on Feb 18 1878. Bonney then embarked on a series of robberies which made him legendary (TB Oct 1975 pp14-15).

VILLAINS. Judith de Balsham of Staffs was acclaimed in c1264 in Henry III's reign as the woman who could not be hung. She was hung from 9 o' clock on Monday morning to sunrise the following day but survived and was consequently freed and pardoned (BCWJ p108).

Some unlocated places

The exact location of these places has eluded the compiler. Perhaps others already know their whereabouts or can find them by looking at a range of maps, eg: Enclosure Award, Estate, Tithe and large scale Ordnance Survey. Some places are Roman in origin, some Norman: Notable ones, Mediolanium, illustrating the former, and DB Monetvile, illustrating the latter, can be found in the main body of the encyclopaedia.

Adderley House Longton (W p752).
Ad Trivonam Roman settlement situated on the Trent somewhere between Derventio (near Derby) and Letocetum. It has been identified by various writers with Branston, Stretton, Tatenhill and Burton upon Trent (BTIH p10).
Aldersenstone Unlocated.
Aldery Lane Wolstanton ancient parish.
Annesley Burton upon Trent. Old manor in the Burton area, 1m S of Rolleston (SHOS vol 1 pp8, 34).
Ashby Sitch Alrewas.
Aston A place of this name is said to lie under Kinver Edge. From here the Kinver Giant threw the Boltstone (see) (NHS p398).
Aston or **Estone**. Dugdale says a place of this name existed to the E of Wordsbury (Wednesbury), and was a town of some note in Saxon times, but of no importance in the Middle Ages (WAM p52).
Astra Park Estate Stafford. Built on land formerly owned by the MOD and RAF Stafford (SPN p111).
Avis-Hieron Marked on Plot's map near Draycott-in-the-

Clay. Avis is Latin for bird.

Badger's Hills Cannock Chase.
Badger Slade Cannock Chase (CCF p161).
Badger Hole Wetton. About or at Thor's Cave (WTCEM pp128-130).
Ball Bank Burslem. William Clowes, co-founder of the Primitive Methodists and preacher, was born here on March 12 1780 (POTP pp64-65); his maternal grandfather, Aaron Wedgwood had been a leading potter in his day. At the age of 10 William was apprenticed to his uncle Josiah Wedgwood I and trained as a platemaker, later he became a turner (ES March 11 1980). In youth he is said to have won fame as a dancer (LGS p48). In c1800 he moved to Hull where, according to his own account, he lived a dissolute life. Returning to the Potteries he attended a Wesleyan Methodist service in Burslem and was converted, aged 25. He joined the Tunstall Methodist society, and attended the first camp meeting on Mow Cop on May 31 1807 (LGS p48) (POTP p64). He co-founded Primitive Methodism (1812)

with Hugh Bourne of Bemersley Green (see); adherents to Primitive Methodism were formerly known as Clowesites. He was a friend of James Nixon of Goldenhill (see). From 1817 Clowes took his brand of Methodism to various parts of the country and died in Hull in 1851 (ES March 11 1980) (POTP p65). There is a memorial to Clowes in Church Street, unlocated - but there is a Church Street in Mow Cop in Ches - erected by one of Hugh Bourne's associates (OTP p105).
Ball Lane Formerly in Norton-in-the-Moors chapelry in Stoke-upon-Trent ancient parish (SGSAS).
Bank Hay Norton-in-the-Moors ancient parish. Whitfield Brook runs through it (ONST 1978 p386).
Bank House Horsley quarter in Eccleshall ancient parish (W p379).
Barlow Field name in the Wolstanton Schedule. Also there is a White Bar, Bar Croft and Bar Meadow.
Bannister Hollies Needwood Forest in Tatenhill parish (W p604).
Barn Fields Bagnall. At the barn here, according to legend,

a man was murdered by a highwayman and his ghost is said to return. Another story is of gamblers who played in secret in the barn and were visited by the devil (SLM July 1970 pp26,27p).

Barn Meadows Sedgley parish (SGSAS).

Barn Yates Leek.

Bate's Corner Hednesford (PCC p75).

Beacon Bank (Grave in Abbots Bromley churchyard).

Bearmore Farm of 27 acres in the Plants Green area. (TB Nov/Dec 1973 p16).

Bear's Brook Cannock Chase (CCF p223).

Bedley Green Is it the same as Baddeley Green, Milton? (W p401).

Beggar's Well Beneath a low stone arch beside the Green Man Inn (SLM July 1951 p30).

Bellevue Kingswinford parish (SGSAS).

Bellevue Reservoir For the fish in it see English Reservoirs. Bill Howes. 1967 p56.

Belstow An unidentified place near Trysull (HOWM p14 note). Belstow was misprinted as Belstona in HCCW p162 note (but not in the actual text p174) and that form was wrongly taken up by Lawley as the correct Latin form of Bilston (HOBL p4) (WA vol 2 p85) (HOWM p14 note).

Bemersley Farm at Bemersley Green.

Bent Leasow (Gravestone in Church Leigh churchyard).

Berk Hill Maer Hills (could be a misspelling of Berth?) (NSFCT 1891 p41).

Bernertone Appears in DB. It was considered an obsolete place by Eyton. Commander Wedgwood identified it with Barton-in-Bradley (see) (SHC 1916 p169).

Betts Pool An oak is named after it in Bagots Park. Is possibly a variable spelling of Bates' Pool. (CCBO p26).

Birch Dell Cannock Chase (CCF p223).

Birchenfields Armitage parish (W p556).

Birchwood Abbots Bromley ancient parish (SGSAS).

Black Bank Wolstanton ancient parish (SGSAS).

Black Hills Cannock Chase or Beaudesert Old Park (PCC).

Blakeley Bucknall.

Blakemoor Pool Near Woodseaves. Could be same as Blakemere Pool?

Blow o' Ram Waterfall area (W p787).

Boar's Ley Rushton Spencer. (GNHS p13).

Bodly Is it in Staffordshire? mentioned BS p65.

Bog Moor Bednall.

Boote Hall Seat of the Bootes (NSFCT 1932 p33).

Boothen Cobridge. Not Boothen, Stoke-upon-Trent (NSFCT 1910 p176).

Boss Green Cannock Chase (CCBO p103).

Botany Bay Formerly in Stoke-upon-Trent chapelry in Stoke-upon-Trent ancient parish (SGSAS).

Botstone Near the Manifold and 1m W of Butterton (Moorlands). Mayfield parish. A lead mine was worked here in the 1830s (W p784). But to go W of Butterton is to go further from the Manifold?

Bottom Lane Ipstones parish (SGSAS).

Bottom Morredge Ipstones.

Boure, The A small estate and manor in Arley parish, which has also appeared as Le Boure. In the C13 it belonged to Adam de la Bure or Boure. In 1333 it was found to be a member of the manor of Cleobury (VCHW vol 3 p8).

Boundary Pool Castle Church.

Bound Hill Audley parish (SGSAS). Is perhaps the same as Boon Hill.

Bradelie Unidentified DB vill in Pirehill hundred. Eyton and others have thought it an obsolete place (SHC 1908 pp11-13) (SSAHST 1970 p34). It has been identified with Bagot's Bromley; Bramelie being incorrectly spelt Bradelie (SHC 1908 pp11-13). Commander Wedgwood identified it with Bradeley, Burslem (SHC 1916 p169) (DB. Phillimore. 1976) (SSE 1996 p11).

Bradley Moor Bradley, Bilston. The curious phenomena of continuous underground fire feeding on coal seams, commonly known as 'wildfire,' occurred under Bradley Moor (HOBLL p160). Bradley is mentioned in this rhyme:-

> The Devil stood on Bradley Moor
> And heard the forges roar.
> Quoth he: "I've heard a row in Hell
> but none like this before."

(BCSBG) (SCSF pp166-167) (FOS p35) (Wolverhampton AdNews. April 11 1996 p7). The rhyme perhaps formed part of an old ballad. There was a hamlet called Fiery Holes on the W side of Great Bridge Road, Moxley.

Bratches, The Norton Canes. 2m SE of Cannock. The name means 'the new enclosure' (DUIGNAN).

Bremetonacis Roman station. William Harrison's Itinerary says it was at Trentham. Mr Hamps thought the War Stone, Seisdon represented the site of Bremenium (SVS p328 note).

Brereton Hall Biddulph. Seat of the Brereton family (BALH pp37,38).

Brick Hill(s) Walsall parish (SGSAS).

Brickholt A piece of land, which is before Whersted (unlocated), which seems to have been exchanged with a piece of moor called Smalley's Moor (see) on Nov 5 1576 by the custom of livery of seisin (SCSF p121).

Brick Yard Tiny district. Is it in the vicinity of Hurst Hill or anything to do with Mobberley's Brickyard? (TB May 1994 p13).

Brindley's Piece Cannock Chase.

Broad Moor Penkridge area. Here was common land (VCH vol 5 p127).

Broadway, The A modern housing estate in New Invention (Selective Essays on Willenhall. David Potts. 1984. Copy in Willenhall library).

Brocton Brook Brocton.

Brook End Small area of Fazeley (TDOPP p64p of in 1921).

Brookhouse(s) Trentham ancient parish (SGSAS).

Brough Alstone, Brough and Rule extend from 1.25m to 4m NW of Bradley (W p442). In Bradley parish (W p442) or and Gnosall parish (SPNO p155) (SGSAS). May be the same as Brough Hall (see). At Brough is believed to have been a Roman station on the Limes Britannicus known as Veterum alias Veneris of the Notitia (NSFCT 1902 p119). The name means 'fort nook' but Gelling is unsure (NSJFS 1981 p2).

Bryggewatir Field name on the banks of the Trent about Handsacre and Mavesyn Ridware (SHOS vol p179). 'Bubble Spring' Daisy Bank, Bilston (BCM April 1981 p17). Could be present Spring Vale area, S of Bilston.

Bughale Appears in DB as belonging to Haltone, which has been identified with Haughton. Bughale was left unidentified by Eyton (Staffordshire Domesday Studies p98), but Erdeswick, CGO Bridgeman, and Gerald P Mander thought it Burgh Hall or Brough Hall (see) near Ranton and it is this identification which has been accepted by John Morris in the Phillimore edition of DB 1976. But Gen Wrottesley and Col Wedgwood thought it Rownall in Totmonslow hundred (SHC 1916 p167. 1919 pp157,158). JF Moxon, believing Halstone to be Horton near Leek, has identified Bughale with Boot Hall near Horton Hall (HHHL p99).

Bull Bridge Moxley (SCSF p167).

Bullspark Wood Draycott-in-the-Clay.

Bunker's Hill Cannock Chase area? Named after the battle of Bunker's Hill in America (TB June 1992).

Burnildelow In the Upper Penn, Goldenhill area of Wolverhampton. Mentioned in a deed of 1291. Means Brunhild's burial mound (HOWM p8).

Burouestone Appears in DB in Offlow hundred and has appeared as Buroestone. Commander Wedgwood thought it might be Borrowcop Hill (SHC 1916 p170). It was still to be identified in 1951 (NSFCT 1952 p36). PV Bate and DM Palliser think it was either near Swinfen or Longdon. Here was possibly a medieval village (SSAHST 1970 p34). Burston, near Stone, was identified by Duignan and others with Burweston which has been identified with Burouestone (SSE 1996 p11).

Burweston Has been identified with DB Burouestone (DB Phillimore. 1976), a member of Lichfield manor, but not necessarily near Lichfield, or in Offlow hundred. It has thought to have been close to Weeford? Has been identified with Burston (see) near Stone.

Butts Near Thornes Hall, a place where archers practised (SHOS vol 2 p54).

Bycars Farm Fradley (SVB p79). Carr is a Norse word meaning a marsh (SIS p9).

Byrom's Folly Rock feature on the Roaches? (NSFCT 1884 p22).

California Works Stoke-upon-Trent.

Campion Wood Cannock Chase (CCF p223).

Capspelle Here was a settlement before 1086. It was mentioned in DB as waste (ie; lost) because by then it had been incorporated into the Kinver Forest (SL p58) and has appeared as Catspelle. (SVS p577). Erdeswick, Shaw and Eyton believed it was Gospel End. General Wrottesley identified it as Chasepool in SHC vol xi p253 (SHC 1916 p171) (DUIGNAN p36) (DB. Phillimore. 1976) (SNSV vol 2 p33).

Careless Green Place name in the Black Country (BCM autumn 1989 p45).

Castlehill Bank Rolleston parish (SGSAS).

Catune Here was a Benedictine nunnery (OSST 1928 p30)

Causey Hall Haunted by a ghost (TB July 1979 p17). Could be a misspelling or corruption of Causeway, as in Causeway Green?

Cawden Hall The Quaker preacher Frances Dodshon (nee Henshaw) was born at Cawden Hall in 1714, according to Simms (BS p143). Could be in Leek.

Chaveldon In Pirehill hundred. Here was possibly a medieval village, probably deserted after 1539 (SSAHST 1970 p34).

Cherrytree Slade Cannock Chase.

Chetwynd's Coppice To Shaw Chetwynd's Coppice was a charming place on Cannock Chase (SHOS vol 1 p214).

Chotes Here Croxden Abbey was first sited. It is probably now Cotton (VCH vol 3 p226).

Church Hole According to tradition this site, between Bilston and Wednesfield, was fixed upon by a Saxon noble, who had embraced Christianity, for the erection of a church to commemorate his conversion. As the church was being built by day, fairies, who lived there, carried the stones away by night (SCSF p50).

Cinder Hill Brewood parish (SGSAS). Has also appeared as Sinder Hill.

Cinder Pool Stowheath, Wolverhampton. In this pool Harry Park Temple a sailor, Harold Heath and Joey Elmore fell through the ice and drowned in 1927 or 1931 (TB Feb p15. March 1983 p15).

Cippemore A pre-Norman Conquest settlement, now lost. Appears in DB as waste. It probably lay between Enville and Kinver (NSFCT 1952 p36) (DB.Phillimore. John Morris. 1976. Notes) or in Kinver Forest (SSAHST 1970 p34) Some say it was fairly close to Enville. Commander Wedgwood identified it with Comber near Kinver (SHC 1916 p170). Others have identified it with Great Moor (see) in Pattingham parish, for Shipley (sheep lea) adjoins Pattingham parish (SHC 1919 pp164,165) (NSJFS 1968 p46), and with Sheepwalks, SW of Enville (VCH vol 4 p54. vol 20 p93). Cippemore probably means 'sheep moor' or 'shepherd moor' (VCH vol 20 p93).

Clamps-in-the-Wood Close to Castern, Ilam. White says it was a farmhouse in a circular hollow secluded from the rest of the World (W p788).

Clergymen's End Cannock Chase (CCF p223).

Clough Charming ravine traversed by a tributary of the Dane falling in cascades (NSFCT 1888 p69).

Clusterberry Edge Between Clusterberry Edge and Blue Hills, N of Upper Hulme, is a stream coming out of an outlet channel containing salt (or iron) belonging to the coal mine in the Blue Hills which turns the stones and earth a rusty colour and was utilised as a dye for button moulds (NHS p98) (OL vol 2 pp22-23) (NSFCT 1944 p40).

Coal Pitt Way Cannock Chase (CCF p223).

Cobhurst Most of the tiles on Trentham church were made of clay from a field at Cobhurst (TTH p71).

Cobintone Appears in DB. According to Commander Wedgwood, Eyton was wrong to identify it with Kibblestone; he says it is Cubbington near Leamington, Warws (SHC 1916 p169). It may be a lost place in Staffs (DB. Phillimore. John Morris. 1976 notes) (SSAHST 1970 p34).

Colbourne Hall Supposed to be in Staffs. Appears on a memorial to Arthur Lyttelton Annesley in Arley church, his father-in-law John Bradley had a seat of this name. There is a Colbourne Road by the canal by the railway at Dudley Port.

Colmoore A pear tree grew here in the C17 which despite snow and frost blossomed at Christmas (NHS p225).

Combes Eccleshall ancient parish (SGSAS).

Commonside Cheadle parish (SGSAS).

Compton Marked on Gelling's map 3m SSW of Tamworth. Could be a positioning error. The name means 'Coombe settlement' (NSJFS 1981 p3).

Concangii Possible Roman station on the Limes Britannicus, to E of Dieulacres Abbey, Leek (NSFCT 1902 p115).

Coney Greave Farm A worn axe-hammer of local stone, probably of Bronze Age date was found at Coney Greaves Farm near Cheadle (NSFCT 1943 p62).

Cooper's Coppice Cannock Chase (CCBO p69).

Copmere Hamlet in Horsley quarter in Eccleshall ancient parish (W p379). White mentions both hamlets of Copmere and Copmere End.

Coppice, The Kingswinford ancient parish (SGSAS).

Coppice Wood Probably in N Staffs. Arthur Berry (b1925), artist and writer, lived here (ES Feb 12 1981 p10p).

Cote Appears in DB. Eyton says it is 'obsolete, near Penn.' Commander Wedgwood thought it might be connected with Cote Lane in Enville until he agreed with Mr Bridgeman that it was Trescott (SHC 1916 p171).

Cowley's Farm The manor house at Bloxwich (in existence by 1564) was leased to Joan Cowley some time before 1637 and later became known as Cowley's Farm (VCH vol 17 p173).

Cox Bank Uttoxeter area? Seen on a gravestone in Kingstone churchyard.

Cresswell One of the three Cresswells Beresford mentions on The Mark (see) and by the Trent. 'Well' is from 'Wall' (OL vol 2 pp15-16).

Crier's Plain Hamlet near Quarry Bank in Kingswinford ancient parish (W p184).

Criftage Near Ribden in the Weaver Hills, Cauldon (NHS p89).

Cronk Hill Near Butterton (DUIGNAN p46) (NSFCT 1908 p142). Can be neither found near Butterton (Moorlands) nor near Butterton (Newcastle-under-Lyme).

Cronkston Low Near Longnor (DUIGNAN p46) (NSFCT 1908 p142).

Crowley Plain Kingswinford parish (1841 census).

Crowsbridge Sedgley parish (SGSAS). Has also appeared as Croksbridge.

Cubbington Appears in DB under Staffs as Cobintone. Is possibly Cubbington in Warwickshire, near Leamington. It is not however listed in Earl Roger's Warwickshire lands, and the three Warwickshire entries between them constitute two five hide units. It might be a lost place in Staffordshire, although probably not Kibblestone (DB. Phillimore. John Morris. 1976. Notes).

Cuckold Haven On road halfway between Abbots Bromley and Uttoxeter.

Cuckoo Bower Cannock Chase (CCF p223).

Cut-Finger Oak Cannock Chase. Former tree and marker on a parish boundary. Could be on the Pye Green highlands? (CCBO p73 - very little is mentioned).

Cynefares Stane A boundary stone near Kinver mentioned in 964. It has been suggested that Cynefares Stane was at Start's Green on the SW boundary of Kinver; although others have argued that it was Vale's Rock or a vanished hoarstone (BAST vol 53 pp108-109) (VCH vol 20 p119 note).

Daisy Bank Bilston (BCM April 1981 p17). Could be present Spring Vale area, S of Bilston.

Daisy Bank At or near Cheadle (W p757). There is a Daisy Bank in Dilhorne parish (SGSAS).

Dale Close Between Mayfield and Okeover where Roman coins were found in c1740 (AAD p207 note). Plot in the later C17 writes of Roman money being found in the Mayfield area (NHS p404).

Dark Slade Wood Cannock Chase (CCF p161).

Darling's Hayes Cannock Wood (CCF p223). After John Darling of Burton upon Trent (KD 1880) (SPNO p58).

Darlington The name appears on the execution notice of William Wilson as his native home in 1818. Wilson, a young miller, was executed for the murder of his girlfriend, Elizabeth Park (MM pp89,91p). Could be a misspelling of Darlaston.

Darwalls Mentioned in BS around pages 69-74? Is it in Staffordshire?

David's City (SMM p123). Could be just in Ches.

Dead Frenchman's Grave So called as a French Prisoner fought a duel with another French prisoner of the War of 1805 (ROS vol 1 pp127-130). Is perhaps in the Potteries area, if only since most of Henry Wedgwood's stories were from this area.

Deakin's Grave Cannock Chase (CCBO p103)? (CCBO pp113-115). This site relates to the story of John th' Deacon (PCC pp67-68). Has also appeared as Deakin's Grove and Dickins Grave (SPNO p59).

Deansgate Area of Newcastle-under-Lyme.

Deanslow A deserted medieval village is recorded here (SSAHST 1966 p49). Has also appeared as Deaneslow. It may be the duplicate name of Dorueslau (SSAHST 1970 p35).

Deepdene Birthplace of Beresford Hope (BS p55).

Deer Barn Cannock Chase (CCF p223).

Deer Slade Cannock Chase (CCF p223).

Delves Bank Walsall (TB Oct 1983 p4).

Devil's Bridge E Cope implies many bridges are called the Devil's Bridge in the Moorlands. They are said to be so called for the vendors that sold the land for the bridge were considered devils (OL vol 2 p302).

Dickins Lodge Could be Fairoak Lodge? Cannock Chase.

Diglake, The An area of Stafford in which stood Turk's Head Inn from which rent came to support Hales' charity (SIOT p75).

Dimmins Dale Cannock Chase. Appears on a Tithe Award (1840) as Demon's Dale (SPNO p107).

Dovedale Wood Ilam parish (SGSAS).

Dunn's Bank Darlaston (Offlow hundred). Mary Dunn was born here in 1771, she died in 1824 (BS p150).

Dunsmoor Meadows Wells In the Rudyard-Harracles area. Could Dunsmoor be the moor Dunwood is on? Here were or are eight or ten springs which Plot saw in July 1679 in dry weather. They had remained full even though the rivulets near them were nearly dry. None of them run into the river. The biggest was assured to be bottomless by the local inhabitants, but proved to be nine or ten yards deep (NHS p60).

Dunsmore Shaw in the late C18 described Stretton in Cuttlestone hundred as Stretton on Dunsmore (SHOS vol 1 p203).

Dutton In 1270 Nicholas de Colton murdered Adam son of Hereward in a brawl at Dutton. He fled and took sanctuary in Colton church, although the villagers guarded the church to prevent his escape his comrades spirited him away (CWF pp38-39) (his wife Christina was accidentally murdered by John the Priest a year later). Was Dutton in Staffs? Would Nicholas have ridden far to return to Colton?

East Lodge House near Rolleston. Seat of Tonman Mosley (W p575).

Eastwood Vale Stoke-upon-Trent chapelry and ancient parish (SGSAS).

Eaton Park Estate In the Audley area?

Ebon Ash Hamlet in Horsley division in Eccleshall ancient parish (W p379).

Elarenesland Place which occurs in a deed of the C15 relating to Upper Arley (VCHW vol 3 p5).

Elswood End (Yates' map). Could now be under Tittesworth Reservoir.

Estendone A DB Staffs? manor owned by Ormus (c Henry I) (NSFCT 1888 p70). It was identified with Essington by Erdeswick (SOS p552) and Shaw (SHOS vol 1 p*xi) (but Essington appears elsewhere in DB as Eseningtone -SHC 1923 pp24-31). It was left unidentified by Eyton. But was identified with Standon House by Col Wedgwood, a house on 6 inch OS map in Haughton parish a sixth of a mile due W of Four Lanes End and about 0.5m ESE of Haughton. Bridgeman and Mander doubted this but were unable to place it, suggesting it may be near Rodbaston (SHC 1916 p170. 1919 p158). The current accepted identification, made by CGO Bridgeman, is that it is Huntington (SHC 1923 pp24-31) (DB. Phillimore. 1976).

Ettingsfield Wolverhampton.

Far Ley Patshull.

Far Wall A natural spring in Manifold or Hamps Valley (NSFCT 1917).

Feccham West Bromwich (SHOS vol 2 p128).

Finspot Hill S of Wednesbury (Plot's map). Could be Finchpath Hill (Hill Top).

Flash Brook Tributary of the Sow. Has appeared as Fletesbroc (1086), and Flotesbroc (C13). Oakden says this Flash Brook gives its name to Flashbrook hamlet (SPNO p10). However, the Flash Brook which gives its name to Flashbrook is not a tributary of the Sow.

Ford House Occupied by Lewis Clutterbuck and then the Tarratts in the C19 (mems in St Mary's, Bushbury).

Forge SE of Hints (Plot's map). It probably just refers to a forge here.

Forge Farm Old farm house near the Blithe in the Chartley Moss area. Site of an old forge. Has been built on and the new house is called 'Mount Famine' after the barren hill it is on (NSFCT 1886 p38).

Forwel Spring Cannock Chase. A perennial spring (NHS p60).

Foster's Fold Bilston (census returns).

Foulmere Near Cannock Wood (NSFCT 1947 p100). Has also appeared as Foume.

Fowlewell Near Aldershawe (HOL p488). Here was one of the springs which fed a conduit to the Friary in Lichfield.

Fowl Hey Valley (POP p19).

Friar Moor Cheddleton. Perhaps, near Finneylane. Here a hoard of Roman coins was found as reported in GM 1776 p540. The hoard was found and then lost by Fielding Best Fynney (CVH p20) (see Finneylane).

Friar's Hall Bloxwich. In 1851 it was the seat of John S Foster (W pp20,669).

Frodesley Hall Could be Fradley Hall. Fradley appears as Frodeleye in the C12 (SVB p79).

Froggots Farm Abbots Bromley area. In the early 1990s the Abbots Bromley Horn Dance performed here at 13.45pm.

Froghall Tamworth parish (SGSAS).

Frontewell Fountains Near Alreshaw (Alrewas?) (SCSF p140).

Furnace Pool Cannock Chase (CCBO p40). Has appeared as the overfornace and the under fornace poole (1584) (SPNO p108). (SOSH p337).

Gail Hole Between Coseley and Wolverhampton (BCM Oct 1990 p61).

Galacum Is Roman Lichfield in William Harrison's Itinerary. Originally mentioned by Antonine a Glamoventa Mediolano (Milan) (HOL p301 note).

Gallows Tree Newcastle-under-Lyme (SMC p172).

Gallows Tree Croft Stoke-upon-Trent. Preserves the site of the manorial gallows tree (SCSF p123).

Gamston Formerly included in Brewood prebend (SSAHST vol 2 1960-61 p43).

Gap A Staffs place name of Norse origin (NSFCT 1916 p82).

Gaviendhul A place on the boundary of Dieulacres Abbey. It cannot be identified (NSJFS 1970 p85).

Gendall's Wood Uttoxeter area. Gendell is probably a name derived from Grendall which is a myth of Scandinavian and German mythology and bears an analogy to our devil (HOU p267).

Genford A house at Genford, Leek, was registered for Protestant Dissenters by Hugh Bourne and James Bourne in 1806 (SHC 1960 p8).

Glade Hixon.

Glasshouse Coppice Bagot's Bromley (NSFCT 1933 p77) (VCH vol 2 p224) (SL p109).

Glass House Hay A parcel of land in Wolseley Wood (or Park?). A glass furnace here remains unlocated (NSFCT 1933 pp76-77).

Goblin's Green Cannock Chase (CCF p223).

Gospel Place Cannock Chase. Perhaps, close to the Gospel Tree. Very little is mentioned in CCBO p73.

Gospel Tree Cannock Chase. Name for a gospel tree. Very little is mentioned in CCBO p73. It could have been on the Pye Green highlands.

Gospel Trees Hackwood mentions it as a gospel place (SCSF p21).

Gospel Well Cannock Chase. A well, perhaps, close to the Gospel Tree. Very little is mentioned in CCBO p73.

Grange Drayton-in-Hales parish (W p389). Is perhaps a reference to Shifford's Grange.

Grange Normacot quarter in Stone ancient parish (W p371) (SGSAS). Perhaps a reference to Stallington Grange or Normacot Grange.

Great Low Wednesfield. Duignan mentions it (AOW p10).

Great Moor (CCBO p21). The reference suggests it is near or on Cannock Chase.

Green Head Formerly in Grindon township of Grindon parish (W p777).

Green Lane(s) Yoxall parish (SGSAS).

Greensbury Shenstone parish (W p584). Perhaps Gainsborough Hill Farm?

Greensides Waterhouses.

Greenway Bank Baddeley Edge, Milton, Bucknall (W p401).

Goldendale Tunstall. Probably near Goldenhill. A Zeppelin dropped two bombs on Goldendale Iron Works in the early hours of Nov 28 1916 (TB July 1994 p19).

Gorsty Bank Stone parish (SGSAS).

Gorsty Hill Farm Yarnfield. Had some early C17 decorative plaster work. The work is known as Adam and Eve in the garden of Eden (NSFCT 1930 pp158-159).

Gorsty Lea St Michael's parish, Lichfield, possibly in a former out-township of that parish (SGSAS).

Graveyard Sedgley parish (SGSAS).

Greasley Hall Hints.

Green Acres Himley.

Gun Moor In the vicinity of Gun Hill? The army of the Young Pretender came over Gun Moor in the retreat in the 1745 Jacobite Rebellion and two of their swords one being a two-handed claymore were found, also a Lochabar axehead inlaid with brass, a peculiar raised horse shoe, a huge knife, which folds into its handle like a modern razor and a similar fork with two prongs. They all went to Swythamley Hall (NSFCT 1931 pp182-184il,185. 1932 p125).

Gypsy Lane Now City Road, Oakham, Netherton. (TB April 1994 p17). But no City Road can be found at Oakham.

Haddon PV Bate and DM Palliser place it at SJ 801385, which is 1m NW of Chapel Chorlton. Here was possibly a medieval village (SSAHST 1970 p35).

Hagenthorndun The name appears in a charter of 994 concerning a grant given by Lady Wulfrun to the monastery of Wolverhampton (WFW p28).

Hall End Hamlet near Bosty Lane (DUIGNAN). Could Duignan be referring to Heath End or Daw End? (Probably not Daw End because he deals with it, but not Heath End).

Hall End Hall Tamworth. GA Mitcheson, mining engineer, died here in 1934 (POTP p156).

Hallfields Probably in the Thor's Cave, Wetton area. An apparition enveloped in a scarlet cloak has been seen and shot at near Hallfields (WTCEM p93).

Hall Fold Bilston (census return).

Halstone Appears in DB. Has been identified with Haughton (see). Others have identified it with Alton, and Horton near Leek.

Hamsall Hall (SSAHST 1984-85).

Han Clouds, The N of Ashenhurst (Bowen's map).

Hanford Park Trentham.

Harperlee Between Grindon and Wetton. Said to be where the Young Pretender's army camped in the 1745 Jacobite Rebellion (OL vol 1 pp200-201).

Hart's Coppice Cannock Chase (CCF p223).

Hart's Wallowing Place Cannock Chase (CCBO p21).

Haswic Appears in DB. Formerly mistakenly identified by Erdeswick with Hanchurch, and Eyton following him placed it near Newcastle-under-Lyme. Commander Wedgwood identified it with present Ashwood (see) (SHC 1916 p168). Dr Oliver thought it must be in the immediate vicinity of Wolverhampton (HCCW p10 note).

Haunchwood Near Tamworth (DUIGNAN p73).

Hawk's Hill Needwood? Field name derived from an animal name (APB p48). Same as Hawk Hills? (see).

Helfwood Approximately two to three miles W of Longnor (Bleau's map).

Hell Hole Cannock Chase. Finlow does not know why it is so called (RRCC p6).

Hetone Appears in DB. Was left unidentified by Eyton; Commander Wedgwood identified it with Hatton (SHC 1916 p168).

Hewall Grange Grange of Ranton Abbey in Dilhorne parish (VCH vol 3 p253).

Heymeece Chebsey ancient parish (W p389).

High Acres Said to be a smart district of Kingswinford (Daily Express May 11 1996 p7).

High Elms Hamlet in Abbots Bromley parish (W p409).

Highfield Place name in the Black Country (BCM autumn 1989 p45). Is possibly another way of spelling Highfields, in Coseley parish.

High Heath Former common land enclosed under an act passed in 1787 (W p789). Is now called The Heath, and is part of the N suburbs of Uttoxeter?

Highridge On the Limes Britannicus (NSFCT 1902 p116).

Hill Cop Prominent feature of Cannock Heath (S&W p380).

Hills of the Grange Former township which was liable to pay tithes to the incumbents of the Lichfield parishes (HOL p456). Could it be in the Lea Grange, Grange Hill Farm area to the NW of Lichfield?

Hoar Stone Acton Trussell. Also known as the Warstone (William Hamper in Archaeologia p30 1832) (DUIGNAN p74) (FPSB p163).

Hocintune Appears in DB. Appears in Wulfruna's grant of 994. Has been identified with Ogley Hay (see).

Hoe Perhaps a reference to Hoo, Enville. (SPN p63). The name is from Saxon 'hoh' 'spur of hill' or 'ridge of land' (SPN p63).

Holy Bush Burton upon Trent. Edward Kirkpatrick Hall, barrister, was born here in 1844 according to Simms (BS).

Hopshort Gnosall parish (SGSAS).

Hores Clough Near Leek (SSGLST p5). Birthplace of John Nadin who murdered his master, a farmer, at Whitelee (see). Nadin was hang on Gun Hill (see). Has also appeared as Hores Clouth.

Hubbles Wolverhampton County Court District in the mid C19 (W p79).

Hungary Hill Wednesfield parish (1841 census).

Hunger Hill Wolstanton ancient parish (SGSAS).

Hunter's Path Cannock Chase (CCBO p21).

Hurst Low Burial mound. Said to be in Grindon parish (TYD p117) (NSJFS 1965 p39).

Hylbertsholme Mavesyn Ridware. Field name on the banks of the Trent about Handsacre and Mavesyn Ridware (SHOS vol 1 p181). Different to Hildersholme?

Iltone Appears in DB. Was identified by Eyton with Hilton near Featherstone. But others have considered it the Hilton (see) to WNW of Shenstone.

Islington Alstonefield parish (SGSAS).

Kenderdine Farm in Haughton parish; there may have been a hermit's cell here (SPNO p165).

Kenton Mentioned on the memorial to Margaret wife of Sir Walter Devereux, her father Robert Garnish is from here (BAST vols 69-71 part 2 p14). Is it in Staffs?

Kiddlestich Uttoxeter. There was a toll gate here (NSFC B1. 391. F 81/ 21).

Kilne In Staffs? Mentioned on the memorial to Eleanor Mytton in Weston-under-Lizard church, her father Edward Brett is from here.

Kilsall House near Wolverhampton. Was the seat of John Jones in 1851 (W p21).

Kingsley Wood Kingsley parish (SGSAS).

Kirnesford Is mentioned in Lady Wulfrun's charter of 994. In the early C20 Duignan placed this ford 'near Moseley Hole' (WA vol 2 p91). In 1934 Mander considered that it may have been in the Somerford area of Willenhall (WA vol 2 p91). Smallshire, Mander and Tildesley identified it with Moseley Hole Farm, called Kirclesford in 1240, which stood near the site of the old skin and hide factory near the Uplands Estate below Prouds Lane junction with Moseley Road (WFW pp30,45). However, they did not: Mander and Tildesley merely identified it with the Pool Hayes brook crossing near New Invention, and the neighbourhood of Blackhalve (HOWM p29). The name means 'old ford of brook' (HOWM pp28 note,28,29) (WFW p30).

Jackson's Bank Newborough.

John Cooper's Warren Cannock Chase (AFT p190).

John Cope's Warren Cannock Chase (AFT p190).

John O' Clamp's Wood Mentioned by William Howitt or his daughter, Mary, in one of their works; reputed to be inhabited by pixies and ghosts. Is it in the Wetton area since Roberts mentions it in WTCEM p94? Is it a fictional place?

Lady Pool Cannock Chase (CCBO p69).

Ladywood Norbury. Said to be haunted because a suicide has been committed here (COS p54).

Lakeland End North Staffs. Mentioned in Cedric Stoke's novel 'The Staffordshire Assassins.' Since he mentions real places names this may be one.

Lane Head Checkley ancient parish (SGSAS).

Lanehead House 1.5m NNW of Cotton.

Lane Head Rocester ancient parish (SGSAS).

Laund Farm Near Ipstones (NSFCT 1908 p144).

Lavatres Is, perhaps, the name for the castellum at Walton, Stone, of the Notitia (NSFCT 1902 p117).

Lea Hall Eccleshall. Charles Edward Challinor (1862-1911) son of Charles Challinor of Basford Hall, Etruria, was of The Lea (NSF p111). The Challinors or a branch of that family were living at The Lea until at least 1921 (NSF p114). Mrs James Meakin, previously of the Flat, Darlaston Hall, near Stone, lived at Lea Hall, Eccleshall, by 1951 (SHC 1950/ 1 List of Members).

Ledemor Place or area in Abbots Bromley parish. The name occurs in the C13 and means 'leat moor' (ABMB p53).

Lees Here was a cell of Rocester Priory (AAD p298) of the Austin Canons, dedicated to St Michael (OSST 1928 p31). It could be the Lees (Leese House Farm) near Cresswell or Leese Hill at Loxley; also Leys at Whiston was formerly Lees.

Lees Grange Temporal property of St Thomas a Becket Priory (VCH vol 3 p265).

Levens Hall A seat of the Bagots. Haunted by the ghosts of a pink lady and a black dog (E&S Dec 22 1969 p6).

Lichemere Place in or near Tatenhill parish. Means Wet marsh (HOPT vol 1 p137).

Lidlow Burial mound. Warslow parish. Excavated by Sir JH Crewe and Sir G Wilkinson in 1851. A skeleton with a bronze round heeled dagger and two flint spearheads were found (TYD p245) (JBAA vol 18 p42) (ARCH vol 43 p452 pl) (BAP vol 1 p162 fig 0,44) (NSJFS 1965 p51).

Lime Wharf Here the Consall Plateway passed over the Hanley Cheadle road (A52), near Overmoor (NSFCT 1944 p106). Not marked on the 1834 OS map.

Lindore (SPN p79). Name is taken from Saxon 'lind ofer' meaning 'lime trees on a slope' (SPN p79).

Litelbech Appears in DB. Commander Wedgwood thought it an obsolete place-name, but it may be interpreted as Little Beck, a name that would vanish at sometime to make way for something more distinctive (SHC 1916 p170). This DB entry was still unidentified by 1952 (NSFCT 1952 p34). Here was possibly a medieval village, which PV Bate and DM Palliser place near Lichfield (SSAHST 1970 p35). Has also appeared as Littlebeech.

Little Aston Formerly in Great Barr township and chapelry in Aldridge ancient parish (W p552). Perhaps the same as Little Aston in Shenstone ancient parish.

Little Burton Black Country? (BCM July 1985 or Oct 1986).

Little Daisy Bank (CCF p223). Perhaps, Cannock Chase. There is a Daisy Bank 1.5m ESE of Walsall.

Little Haye May have been part of the waste of Bagot's Bromley (SHC 1908 p168).

Little Manchester The suggested site for the Roman station of Mediomanum (see). Perhaps was in the vicinity of Mucklestone, perhaps at Arbour Farm (NSFCT 1908 p115). Perhaps it owed its name to a 'settler' from Manchester who came to live here at the time of Manchester's expansion (NSFCT 1918 p116. 1937 pp117-118,125).

Littleton's Warren Cannock Chase (AFT p190).

Llanty Wood Wolverhampton County Court district in the mid C19 (W p79).

Lodge Yard Oak Bagot's Bromley. (GNHS p409) (CCBO p26).

Lollards, The (NSFCT 1933 p176 - there is another The Lollards in the county, too). Could be a reference to Lud Church.

'Lomfordes' Brook In the Penkridge area. Here was common land (VCH vol 5 p127).

Long Ditch In the Jacobite Rebellion the Young Pretender's army passed by Long Ditch on Dec 4 1745 (BPCSM p7). It is in between Upper Berkhamsytch Farm and Waterfall Cross, on the old Earl's Way.

Longhouse Longford (DUIGNAN p96).

Longscroft 'The park of Longscroft, near Tatenhill, Burton, was purchased by Simon Arden, 1576, on condition that he provide Elizabeth I one light horse, and paid into the royal exchequer £1 6s 8d for his land in Yoxall, then valued at £10' (SCSF p120).

Long Coppice Oak Bagot's Park (CCBO p26).

Longway Former township which paid tithes to the parishes of Lichfield (HOL p456). Perhaps identifiable with Longway House (see)?

Lordly Hill May be in the area of Wednesfield or Willenhall. For the geology of Lordly Hill see WJO June 1908 pp150-151.

Lower End Wombourne parish (SGSAS).

Lower Haddon Miscellaneous earthwork of pre-Norman Conquest origin in Leek Frith parish (SHC 1916 p207).

Lower Shelton Stoke-upon-Trent. Perhaps, that part of Shelton S of Hanley Park?

Lufamesles Appears in Staffs DB. Eyton left it unidentified. Col Wedgwood identified it with Paynsley (Hall) (SHC 1916 p167. 1923 p42) (DB. Phillimore. 1976). It may be represented by Lees House Farm or on earlier maps 'Lees.' It may be that this 'Lees' and Paynsley, 0.5m to the ESE, were in early times both included under and known as Lufamesles. Lufamesles may be of Saxon origin and assuming that the Norman scribe transcribed it with approximate accuracy. Bridgeman supposes the name comes from 'leof-haemes-loesu' that is 'beloved-home's-leasow,' but it may be of Danish origin (SHC 1923 p41).

Madam's Meadow Yoxall Parish (W p613).

Madeley House Croxden. NW of Stramshall, could it be now what is Madeley Farm?

Mansholme In the vicinity of Uttoxeter? Mrs Margery Pyott left a field called Mansholme in her gift 1622. It means a place surrounded by water or to rising ground (HOU pp37, 321).

Meal Ark Clough By the Dane on route from Rushton Spencer to the Dane. Is a sort of second Lud Church by the Dane. Miller notes its farther end blocked with a sheer perpendicular rock, down which a waterfall splashes into a pool below (OL vol 2 p85). Here the Heaton and Swythamley farmers hid their cattle during the 1745 Jacobite Rebellion (NSFCT 1945 p86) (BPCSM p2) (HOLF

p40). Perhaps between Danebridge and Barleighford Bridge.
Meardale Lodge Formerly in Beech quarter in Stone parish (W p369).
Mear Heath Castle Church parish (SGSAS).
'Mersshe' A vill which paid annual rent or custom to the manor of Stafford (VCH vol 5 p88).
Middle Friars Stafford. Here the earthquake of 1904 was felt by a Mr CJ Clay (NSFCT 1905 p134).
Middle Rownall Farm Farm on Westwood Hall estate at Rownall where Capt Powys was taken ill and died whilst overseeing his workmen. Powys had commanded the troops which had opened fire on the Chartist rioters in the Potteries in 1842. The spot in the field where he had last stood curiously went, and remained, bare. No grass would grow in the place where the soles and heels of his boots had rested, but would in the spaces in between. Some suspected the Rownall witch had put a curse on him (CVH pp163-164). There is a Captain's Barn 2.5m S of Rownall at SJ 948455.
Mill Brook Tributary of the Dove about Ellastone.
Millstone Ford Shaw says it is on the Trent a little below Wychnor Forge and suggests the area around Branston had been a famous place for grinding stones, as Erdeswick had said it was (SOS p168), although there is little other evidence (SHOS vol 1 p23).
Moat Street Off Stafford Street, Willenhall (Birmingham A-Z). What moated property does this street name preserve?
Mockbeggar Farm Harborne (RS p122).
'Mora' Village mentioned in a C13 survey. Mander thought 'Mora' could be a reference to Monmore (HOWM pp5,6). Moor Hall (see) near Penkridge appeared as Mora in 1227.
Mossy Lee Cannock Chase (CCF p223).
Mount Zion Denstone (W p770).
Mount Lupin Alrewas parish (SGSAS).
Mousecroft Partly in Wolstanton and Astbury (Ches) parishes (SGSAS).
Murchall Hall Ettingshall.

Near Cotton Alton ancient parish (SGSAS).
Near Hill Hill in the vicinity of Swinscoe. Food vessels of the Beaker people, of the Irish type, have been found on it (NSJFS 1962 p33). Appears in TYD but is not the hill on which Top Low is situated (NSFCT 1929 p90).
Netherwood Alleged site for the original Uttoxeter race meetings. The name means lower wood and Jim Foley suggests it may have been in the vicinity of the present Highwood. A racecourse was seen on an old map of Uttoxeter near Noah's Ark Farm, at the bottom of Redhill, Doveridge (TRTC p19).
New Hall Company (founded in 1781 - POP pp49,51) and New Hall Works - probably Longton (POP p129).
New House Farm Pendeford. William Pitt (1749-1823), author of THS, was a tenant here from 1780 (VCH vol 20 p5; the date 1894, given for his departure from New House Farm, must be wrong).
New Plant Wolverhampton. Name occurs in the PR of St Matthew's, Wolverhampton in the later C19, but not on maps for 1871 and 1884 (TB May 1997 p21).
Nodenhill Sedgley ancient parish (1851 census).
Nook, The In High Offley parish (SGSAS).
Norman's Heath Tamworth. Possibly a reference to Noman's Heath (see No Man's Heath).
Nunmore Here a house belonged to the prioress of Farewell or Fairwell (HOL p359).
Nutt Hall Codsall.

Old Hall Cannock parish. Perhaps at (Old) Hednesford. Seat of the Colemans in the late C16 and C17. Appears in 1703 as 'Le Old Hall' (VCH vol 5 p56) (SPNO p60).
Oldhall Grange A grange in Caverswall parish which belonged to Ranton Priory. It was established by the priory and was a grange by the early C14 (VCH vol 3 p253).
Otley In Sedgley parish (W p200).
Okemere Lost. Has appeared as 'the water of Okemere' (1275) and means 'the pool where oak trees grow' (SPNO p15).
Old Vine Inn (RB vol 3 p76 il by Michael Rothenstein).
Onecote Hall Possibly formerly in Onecote township or in Grindon parish. James Burnett came to live at Onecote Hall in c1747 (OL vol 2 p243). A farmhouse, the property of the Earl of Macclesfield (W p777).
Orberton Former manor and a member of Hopton manor (SHC 1909 p145. 1914 p101 note). It was considered a sizeable village in the Middle Ages, and was deserted for some reason. Richard de Horberton was lord of it sometime in the later C12, after which it passed to St Thomas priory, Basford, and became one of their granges (VCH vol 3 p265). After the Dissolution it passed to the Fowlers (SHC 1909 p145). Under the Whitgreave prebend it was a prebend of Stafford Collegiate Church (SHC 1909 p145). Walter Chetwynd in 1679 noted it as a deserted settlement (SL p82). Rev F Parker thought Orberton may have lain between St Thomas priory and Hopton, not far from Kingston Cover (SHC 1909 p145 note). PV Bate and DM Palliser place it near Stone (SSAHST 1970 p35). Has also appeared as Erberton.
Ordheah's Island Mentioned in the charter of 994 of the bounds of Pelsall. Probably on the boundary somewhere in the Heath End area (PTYV p4).
Oscote Church Eaton parish (SGSAS).
Ougherwall Audley parish (SGSAS).
Out Clough North Staffs (DUIGNAN p42).
Ox Leasowes Said to have been 5m NE of Stone, in Hilderstone chapelry in Stone ancient parish. Occupied in 1851 by James Clewes (W pp22,370).

Pannicroft A possession of the See of Lichfield in the C12. Here was a church (HOL p124).
Pare Tree House Wolstanton.
Park Barn Cotton.
Park Brook Walsall parish and foreign (W p649).
Parkdale Sedgley (TB Nov 1979 p9).
Parkhill Hamlet in the parish and foreign of Walsall (W p649). Could be the Park Hill, Handsworth, or a Park Hall 2m SE of Walsall.
Park Lane Leek parish (SGSAS).
Park Pales Blymhill parish (W p442).
Pastures Farm Flash area. Here counterfeit money or 'Flash Money' was struck under the legitimate guise of a button press; the counterfeiter could quickly flee across the Derbys Ches border to evade the Staffs authorities (VB p210).
Patch Head Flash. Lost.
Peachley Valley Cannock Chase (CCBO p42).
Peacock Green Rowley Regis area (1851 census).
Pear Tree Gorse Cannock Chase (CCF p223).
Peatsmoore Near a Thornes. Is it near Hamstall Ridware? (NHS pp214-215).
Pepperhill Park A deer park which belonged to the Talbots, Earls of Shrewsbury (EDP p180).
Pewit Hill Field name derived from an animal name (APB p48).
Pheasant Pool Needwood? Field name derived from an animal name (APB p48).
Pigginhole The Moorlands (Staffs County Handbook c1958. p89).
Pike Hall Farm at or near Leek.
Pipewell Lichfield. Perhaps by one of the Pipes on W and S side of Lichfield. Simon de Pateshull father of the bishop of Lichfield was buried here (BS).
Porton Lodge In the Longdon area. Perhaps Gorton Lodge? Mrs Robert Landor (nee Mary Noble 2nd daughter of Walter Nobel) died here in 1789. (info from Staffordshire Fashion booklet - costumes from the County Museum).
Portway House Harlaston.
Protector Cottages West Bromwich (W p686). Lost.

Quarry Bank Said to be near Stafford (MCGM pp117-118). Edmund Clarke was murdered by his father-in-law, Joseph Jones, on Dec 1 1906 at his home in Quarry Bank, near Stafford (MCGM pp117-118p of Jones) (TB Aug 1985 p5).
Quateway Place which occurs in a deed of C16 relating to Upper Arley (VCHW vol 3 p5).

Radley A fire stone found near Radley (SM). Is this Rowley, or Radleys?
Radley Moor Ryknild Street passes over it, E of Bosses, Stonnall. Faint traces of the line remained in 1902 (DUIGNAN pp22,123). The name is from Anglo-Saxon 'rad' or Middle English 'rade' - the road lea (DUIGNAN).
Rake's Wood Oak Veteran oak in Bagots Park (GNHS p408) (SG p109) (CCBO p26).
Ranslow St Mary's parish, Stafford (SGSAS).
Ravens House Harborne.
Rawdon Reservoir For the fish in it see English Reservoirs. Bill Howes. 1967 p56.
Raw End Hamlet in Yoxall parish (SHOS vol 1 p98).
Redbaldstone Manor Owned by Ormus about the reign of Henry I (NSFCT 1888 p70). Whether in Staffs?
Redlakefield Lichfield (HOL p500).
Red Row Wolstanton parish (SGSAS).
Rhein Roches Alton Towers. Rock feature in Churnet valley (BATR).
Rise Barn Horsley division, Eccleshall ancient parish (W p379)
Risom Bridge Cannock Chase (VCH vol 2 pp109, 110).
Robin Hood's Wells Vaguely mentioned in TOS p42.
Round Hill A circular site (fort) (STMSM Nov 1972 p41).
Roycroft Near Rushall. Here in the later C17 Dr Plot noted a calf a yard and an inch high with horns on its head at only two days old (NHS p262).
Russells Bank Beaudesert Old Park. In Longdon parish.
Rutunium or Rutunio. Roman camp or settlement listed in the 2nd Antonine Itinerary, or Route ii of the Itinerarium Britannianum, or Iter ii which has long remained unidentified. Camden and the editors of the Monumenta Historica Britannica identified it with Rowton Castle 6m W of Shrewsbury (SHC 1916 p315). Horsley thought it at Wem, Shrops (SHC 1916 p318). Shaw thought it at either Stone, Staffs, or Newport, Shrops, or at Woodcote S of Newport, Shrops, or Wellington, Shrops (SHOS vol 1 p23). It has been placed at Broughton, Staffs (GNHS p118). Rev Thomas Barns thought it at Shawbury-on-the-Roden, Shrops (NSFCT 1908 p114) (SA April 13 1912 p5) or at Harcourt Mill or Moreton Corbet, Shrops (SHC 1916 p318). Others place it at Moston, Shrops (NSFCT 1928 p110). Moston, unlocated, is perhaps Muxton near Lilleshall.
Ryebrook Tributary of the Trent. The name means probably 'the brook by which rye grows' (SPNO p17).
Ryecorn Hill Blymhill parish (SGSAS).
Rylondbrugge Place which occurs in a deed of the C15 relating to Upper Arley (VCHW vol 3 p5).

Sale, The Hanbury ancient parish (SGSAS).
Salter's Bridge 2m NW of Rocester (DUIGNAN) (ESH p16).
Scarlet Lake (Gravestone in Dilhorne churchyard, which states it is in Cheddleton parish).
Scoteslei Appears in DB. Eyton could only identify it as an obsolete place near Colwich, whereas Commander Wedgwood identified it with Coley (see) (SHC 1916 p168).
Seckley Wood Part of Arley parish (SHOS vol 2 p254).
Sedgley Well Sedgley. (SCSF p144).
Seven Stars Hamlet or inn? in the vicinity of Marchington Woodlands (W p563).
Shebdon Manor Bought by Richard Whitworth in 1776 from C Boothby Skrymsher (NSFCT 1927 p30).
Sheepwash Cannock Chase (CCBO p42).
Sirescote Place in or near Tatenhill parish. Means Siric's or Sigeric's cottage (HOPT vol 1 p137).
Skeleton Tree An oak reputed to be where Richard Gordon, a poacher courted Mary Sherwood, on Cannock Chase. They agreed to marry and Gordon agreed to give up poaching. He went out to poach for one last time before his marriage and got caught and was hung. Mary, it is said, drowned herself and the tree lost all its leaves and remained a shell for the next 200 years (TB Jan 1995 p13) (GLS pp51-52).
Slack's Park Field name at or near Yoxall. Its rent or a part of it went to provide coats for two poor men (W p613).
Sladderhill Colliery Apedale. In operation by 1803 when owned by Sir Nigel Bowyer Gresley (AHJ 1996 p16). It had a disaster on April 2 1891; 10 were killed (VCH vol 2 p1; called just Apedale Colliery) (IANS p38).
Small Heath Former common land of the townships of Lutley and Mere. It was enclosed in c1520 (SL p104).
Snapes Wednesfield parish (1841 census).
Snodderswic Shaw, who placed it in Staffs, identified it with the Snodeswic mentioned in the will of Wulfric Spot (c1002), founder of Burton Abbey; others have thought it the DB Esnotrewic (Derbys) which has been identified with Pinxton, near South Normanton, Derbys (SHC 1916 p37).
Spon Well (SCSF p141). Near Spon Lane, West Bromwich?
Springfield Between Beamhurst and Stramshall in Uttoxeter ancient parish (W p792).
Spring Head Wednesbury (SR p107). John Wesley's horse block was moved from High Bullen to Spring Head (OWB pl No. 20 facing p64).
Spring Hill Biddulph. Built in 1872 for William Holt, son of William Henry Holt (Vicar of Biddulph 1831-1873) (CIOPP p26p).
Spring Hill Burntwood.
Spring Vale Wednesbury (SR p107). Possibly same as Wolverhampton Spring Vale.
Spring Vale Farm 0.5m from central Walsall (TB Aug 1988 p21). Site for Walsall Aerodrome. There is an area 0.75m

SE of Walsall called Spring Hill. Amy Johnson came to a display at the aerodrome in 1938 and opened the programme by flying a Kirby Kite (TB Aug 1988 p21).

Starvation Hill Hill about at Knenhall, Moddershall. Has a wide panorama to the W and SW embracing the Wrekin, Caradoc, the Clee Hills and the Long Mynd. So called from its poor agricultural value (NSFCT 1945 p91).

Steeps, The Appears as the Holloway in Rev JR Windsor-Garnett's 'The Village' (1926) (TB Sept 1986 p14). Possibly in Sedgley parish, near Lower Gornal.

Step Hill Cannock Chase (RRCC p10).

Stile's Shaw Cannock Chase (CCF pp221-222).

Stirrups Wood Longton (SHST p529).

Stockbrook Colton (MR p106 see photograph title. This is probably a typing error and Stockwell is meant).

Stockley Ridding In Anslow township of Rolleston ancient parish (W p577).

Stonefield Hall Bilston parish (1841 census).

Strenshall Here was a religious house in medieval times, founded by King Egbert and King Ethelwulph (OSST 1928 p32).

Stretton Hall Stretton (Burton upon Trent). Unlocated, if it ever existed. Shaw wrote, 'The principal family anciently of this place were the ancestors of Okeover of Okeover' (SHOS vol 1 p26).

Swan Gardens Ann Dudley was born here in 1788 (BS p146), is it in Staffs?

Swansmoor Needwood. Field name derived from an animal name (APB p48).

Sweet Bit Cannock Chase (CCF p223).

Sweet Hills (CCT p130).

Swethholme Uttoxeter. Connected with Mary Blount's gift (HOU p318).

Swinsen There was a common of Tatenhill ancient parish at Swinsen (HOPT vol 1 p135).

Stowe Mere Is Stowe Pool?

T.B.B. Well Werrington. (WYV p60 il of).

Tean Hall Woodhouses, Yoxall.

Thew Heath Uttoxeter parish (SGSAS). Is perhaps The Heath.

Thickness A place near Newcastle-under-Lyme. The C14 surname is from this place (AHJ 1995 p44); a Thickness family were living at Balterley Hall in the later C17 and earlier C18.

Thieves Oak Oak in Sherbrook Valley, Cannock Chase. Visited in the Rugeley Perambulation, Madge Oak was another (PCC p13). Could be same as Hangman's Oak?

Thornes It may not be the Thornes near Stonnall. Is it near Hamstall Ridware? (NHS pp214-215).

Thorney Birch Bilston. A field name or estate (W p142).

Thorns Smethwick. An ironstone deposit site (VCH vol 2 p120). Could be Thorn Hill (see).

Three Stones In Waterfall area (W p782).

Thrombelowe Burial mound thrown up over the dead killed in the battle of Tettenhall or Wednesfield 910. By mentioning this as well as Tromelow or Thromelowe Duignan is implying it is different to Thromelowe (see).

Tib Green Here was a forge added in 1702 and 1703 to the 'Staffordshire Works' group (NSFCT 1953 p34).

Tinker Close Land in Colton parish out of which revenue is paid to the poor (W p414).

Tire In the Waterfall area (W p787).

Tofton West Bromwich area (SHOS vol 2 p128).

Tom Hill Pumping station here in Smestow Valley (BCM summer 1994 p24).

Tomkinson Norton Canes.

Top o' th' Trent Knypersley. Central Biddulph?

Tot More Ettingshall (IE p20).

Townhead In Alstonefield parish (SGSAS).

Trimpley Green Kinver (Royal Kinver p1).

Tromwin Name, which is now obsolete, for an area of

Cannock Chase. From the Tromwin family. They were hereditary foresters, the last of the family died in 1357 (PCC p13).

Turkeyshall There was a mill of this name in Rugeley parish. The name has appeared as Turkysall flatt (1570), Turkysall Lane (1671), Turkeysill (1840), Turkeyshall Lane (KD 1880) (SPNO p110).

Turnshill Sedgley parish (SGSAS). Could be same as Turls Hill.

Twiss Grindon township and parish (W p777).

Uriconium Former Roman station or settlement. Camden identified it with Wroxeter, Shrops (SHOS vol 1 p23). SAH Burne identified Uriconium with Uttoxeter (NSFCT 1911 p142).

Ussmore Green In Staffs (CR p34).

Uttoxeter Woodlands Uttoxeter parish (SGSAS).

Uxacona Unidentified Roman settlement which has been identified with several places in Staffs. It has been said to be the Roman name for Uttoxeter. Salmon tried to show that Letocetum was Uxacona (HOWW p19). Most authorities, including Pennant, Mr Dickenson (1796), and Langford, think Uxacona was at Oakengates (or as Langford spells it Ocongate), where a Roman hypocaust has been found (VCH vol 1 p187) (SHC 1916 p319). Horsley thought it was opposite Sheriff Hales (S&W p388). Mr Andrews thought it was the lost city in Wrottesley Old Park (HOPTT p7). CGO Bridgeman prefers Mr Codrington's theory that Uxacona is somewhere near the Red Hill (between Oakengates and Crackley Bank) (Roman Roads in Britain. Codrington. p79) (SHC 1916 p321).

Valentia Mentioned in Staffs DB. Still unidentified by 1952 (NSFCT 1952 p36).

Valley Fields Kingswinford.

Veratinum Roman name for possibly Rocester or Chesterton (NSJFS 1976 p94).

Veterum Possible Roman station on the Limes Britannicus which has been identified with Brough Hall (see), Gnosall.

Vivary Pool The mermaid of Aqualate Mere left this pool when it was cut through to make way for the Shropshire Union Canal in the C18 (Ghosts & Legends. Roy Christian. 1972 p67).

Walk Hill Penkridge area? (TB Dec 1984 p23).

Walk Mill Beech quarter in Stone ancient parish (W p369).

Wall Hill Near Wallbridge, Wall Grange, Leek. (SK p196). See also Hostage Lane. 'Wall' is from an ancient line earthwork called The Mark (see) (OL vol 2 p15).

Walton Grange Church Eaton parish (SGSAS).

War Hill Harvills Hawthorn (TB March 1982 p29).

Waterhouses Fissure Cave (NSJFS 1964 p46).

Watt-hill Trysull. Has also appeared as Oak Hill (SHOS vol 2 p207).

Waycliffe In the W part of Lichfield (HOL p5).

Welshman's Lane Colton area (CWF p179).

Werlows There have been some burial mounds in the vicinity of Checkley called Werlows (HOU p351).

Werrel West Bromwich area (SHOS vol 2 p128).

Werrington Audley ancient parish (SGSAS).

West Cliff Featherstone.

Weston Green Bushbury parish (1841 census).

West Page Hamlet in Patshull ancient parish (SHOS vol 2 p286).

Wet Slade Cannock Chase.

Wheolares, Le Occurs in a deed of the C15 relating to Upper Arley (VCHW vol 3 p5).

Whillocks Pool Audley area. Mentioned in 1733; de Hullokspole was a surname in the later C13 (AHJ 1997 p96).

Whirley Hole A rock in Kinver (SD p34).

Whisper Lane A 'ride' intersecting Swynnerton Old Park.

Suggestive of the medieval superstitions in the days of the woodman (NSFCT 1917 p152).

Whiston Cave Unlocated.

White Gate Stubwood, Denstone. Robin Hood is supposed to have been stationed here when he shot his arrows at Lowfields Low near Combridge, practising his archery (HOU p26).

Whitehouse Hill Hill in the Rowley Hills range (SVS pp432,433 note).

Wichens Near Hen Cloud. Perhaps 'wicken' is a Norse dialect word for the mountain ash (NSFCT 1916 p82).

Wickenstowe (NSFCT 1895 p156). Perhaps a misspelling of Wickenstones. Wichen or wychen is Anglo-Saxon and refers to springs by rocks and stones (NSFCT 1895 p156).

Widow's Hayes Cannock old parish. Appears as Widdoweshay in 1584. The name means widow' enclosure(s) (SPNO p61).

Wilkinson's Bower Cannock Chase (CCF p223).

Willenhall Green Willenhall. Yellow ochre found here was commercially exploited (NHS p124). Perhaps Shepwell Green?

William Cooper's Warren Cannock Chase (AFT p190).

'Williford' Here was common land (VCH vol 5 p127). In the Penkridge area.

Willings Hamlet in Ashley parish (W p384).

Willymore Backs Land in Fulford purchased by the corporation of Stafford. The revenue from its rent went to the poor of Stafford in the mid C19 (W p338).

Windy Harbour E of Betley.

Wishing Oak Old oak in Okeover Park; the oldest of the trees on the Okeover estate. In the 1930s Mee noted it had a girth of 29 feet and a 'crown still green and vigorous' (KES p162). Was hollow inside by 1964 (CL March 1964 p649). The gamekeeper in the 1950s told Elliot Green that it was a tradition to walk backwards six times round its great trunk and silently make a wish (SLM April 1952 p15 il). (MR p250).

Withyford Duignan says it is 0.5m below the bridge at Elford (DUIGNAN p55).

Wobourn Statfold. Fullers earth can be found here (NHS p121).

Wodestone In DB. In Offlow hundred. Eyton (Staffs DB Studies) identifies it with Wootton, Eccleshall, but is wrong (DUIGNAN).

Wolfelowe Possible burial mound on the north-western boundary of Rushton James township (VCH vol 7 p219).

Woodend Ilam ancient parish (SGSAS).

Wood End Lower Gornal. The name appears in the 1861 census.

Woodendale In the vicinity of Berth Hill (NSFCT 1935 p70).

Woodhay In 1567 17 of Lord Paget's tenants complained of encroachments and inclosures in Cannock Chase and the projected inclosure of Woodhay (VCH vol 6 p52).

Woodhouse Codsall parish (SGSAS).

Woodhouse Formerly in Clayton Griffith township in Trentham ancient parish (W p435).

Wood Leasow (Gravestone in Church Leigh churchyard) As opposed to Bent Leasow.

Wood's End Most have thought the Joh' o atte Wodesende who appears in 1327 was of Woodsetton, but Roper thinks he was probably of Wood's End (HC p14).

Wormslee Butterton (Moorlands) (W p785).

Worrall, The Land in Abbots Bromley parish which provided revenue for the poor (W p409).

Wren Clough Near Rushton. Field name derived from an animal name (DUIGNAN p42) (APB p48).

Wudres Occurs in a deed of C15 relating to Upper Arley (VCHW vol 3 p5).

Wylesdale A wood in Colton (CWF p88).

Yew Tree Gate Toll gate at Whiteheath-Blackheath area (TB Nov 1975 p22). In Powke Hillock area.

Some extra-provincial places

This appendix deals with changes to boundaries with neighbouring counties and some places (with the exception of prebends) in neighbouring counties very close to the Staffs border; that either have some Staffs connection, or which have occurred in a source and the source was vague as to its location; suggesting that it may lie in Staffs. Some that have been at some time in Staffs can be found in the main body of encyclopaedia.

CHESHIRE

The W part of Wrinehill and Cracow Moss lay in Ches until 1965 when the boundary was moved further W to run along the railway line. In 1965 a stretch including West Heath NW of Betley protruding to Mere Gutter was removed from Staffs to Ches, whilst the hamlet of Gorstyhill was taken wholly into Staffs, and Balterley Mere, formerly partly in the two counties, was taken wholly into Ches. In 1965 some of Hardings Wood and Red Bull was transferred to Staffs from Ches, whilst Church Lawton ancient parish and Old Rode civil parish took some of Kidsgrove civil parish, Staffs (GLAUE p414).

Bartomley Farm NE of Wincle. Probably formerly Bartonley. Used to belong to the Swythamley estate and near here was found a hoard of Roman relics which went to Swythamley Hall (NSFCT 1931 p183. 1932 p56) (DPEM p141). Near to the farm is a circle of stones (DPEM p141).

Boreham's Hole Over Long Edge (SMM p123), could be just in Ches.

Bosley Cloud Full title of The Cloud (see) (DP p62) (VB p192) (TSW p12) (SGM). Others think not (NSSG p8). Bosley is 1m NE of The Cloud in Cheshire. Derives its name from 'Bosa's lea' (NSFCT 1932 p52).

Catstone, The Tall rock stack about 50 feet high with a flat top, behind Catstones House on SW slopes of the Cloud, NE of Timbersbrook village (SGM p266) at SJ 897636. The name has also appeared as Cat Stones and Cat Tor (SMM p19). 'Cat' or 'Cath' which is Celtic, means either a place of battle, or the site of graves (Scientific Rambles. Dr Sainter. 1878) (SMM p19). Or the name is from the stack resembling the shape of a cat (DPEM pp36,40p), or that it was a sacrificial altar for Bronze Age and Iron Age people worshipping the cat-goddess Hathor, or the goddess Cat Anna, or Catha or Catta (NSFCT 1946 pp148,149) (DPEM pp35,40) (DPTB pp14,15).

Cheshire's Close N of Mow Cop just beyond Staffs.

Cloud, The An irregular mass of Millstone grit, mainly of the Third and Fourth Grits (NSFCT 1946 p148), on the edge of the southern Pennine chain overlooking the Cheshire plain 2m ENE of Rushton Spencer, 21.5m N of Stafford. Its extremely steep W and N escarpments lie in Ches whilst the gentle E and S slopes lie in Staffs. The summit is 1126 feet (VCH vol 7 p223), or 1190 feet high (NSFCT 1874 p8). There is a near **panorama** from the top, which includes hills and mountains in nine Welsh and English counties: Beeston Castle and Jodrell Bank in Ches: Leek in Staffs, from where can be seen the sun setting behind the Cloud twice at midsummer: Axe Edge and Kinder Scout? in Derbys: the Breiddens (55 miles away), Tittestone Clee (1805 feet and 58 miles away), and the Wrekin in Shrops: shipping on the Mersey in Lancs: Barber's Mountain at Llangollen, and the Moel Faman (1845 feet and 48 miles away) in Denbighshire: the Moel-y-Cloddian (1452 feet) and Arthur's Camp (1491 feet) in Flintshire: the Berwyn Mountains in Montgomeryshire and Merionethshire, the highest Cader Berwyn is 2715 feet, 50 miles from the Cloud (SMCC p5) (NSFCT 1882 p21) (DPTB p3). **Prehistoric occupation**. Although it has been claimed the Cloud was occupied by peoples from the Neolithic Age to the Anglo-Saxon period there is little conclusive evidence of occupation from any of these periods, apart from Bridestones burial chamber one mile to the S, which has been assigned to the Neolithic period. The Bronze Age, or more likely Iron Age, hillfort on the SW spur of the Cloud, at a lower level than the summit, noted by Sainter in his Scientific Rambles (1878) p32, has been, since at least 1962, rejected as a hillfort and is instead considered a 'comparatively modern field system' or plantation enclosure. It covers about 3.5 acres. It is rectangular with corners orientated approximately to the points of the compass; the sides are noticeably straight and the single bank and ditch of which they are composed are too slight to be of any military value (LCAST lxxii pp9-46) (History of Congleton. WB Stephens 1970) (DP pp77,79). Claims that the Cloud had early occupation lie in tradition and speculation; that Neolithic people migrated S from the Cloud and settled in isolation on Biddulph Moor (see), their descendants being known in recent times as Biddlemoor Men (Congleton Chronicle 1936. 1939. 1940) (NSFCT 1946 pp148-149) (SMCC p5) (SMM pp110,111); that Bronze Age people made sacrifices to their gods on the rock stack known as The Catstone (see) on the western slopes of the Cloud (NSFCT 1946 pp148-149) (DPTB pp14-15); that a Bronze Age village existed from the evidence of pits 'on the top of the hill' with W-facing entrances believed to have once been dwellings (SMM p112) (DPTB p15); that carvings on rocks on the summit may be the work of, or represent religious symbols of, early people (DP pp76,94p) (DPEM p34) (SMM p114p) (SMCC p5). The **name** has also appeared as Cloud End, Cloud Hill and Bosley Cloud (DP p62) (VB p192) (TSW p12) (PDS&C p119), from Bosley village, 1m to its NE (SGM p265); others think not (NSSG p8). Perhaps Bosley Cloud is a reference to Bosley Minn, 0.75m ENE of Bosley village. Cloud may be a corruption of the Celtic root 'cleith,' a steep hill, from old Celtic 'cletis' (NSFCT 1908 p134). Or from the Celtic 'clawdd' meaning earthwork (NSFCT 1946 p148), or from Anglo-Saxon 'clud' a mass of rock (DUIGNAN) (NSFCT 1932 p53) (VCH vol 7 p223) (SPN p36). Natural or artificial **outcrops** of rock on The Cloud, that have been lost, are: Bully Thrumble, Mareback, Raven Rock, Stepmother Stone and Sugar Rock. Those still existing, are: Drummers Knob, North Quarry, North Buttress, Summit Rocks, The Nose, Secret Slab, and The Catstone. **Aircraft crash**. A Spitfire 1X W 3569 crashed into Bosley Cloud on March 21 1944. The pilot, who was alone, was killed on impact (MD p41). In 1962 the **National Trust** acquired 135 acres of the Cloud, of which 26 acres lie in Staffs (VCH vol 7 p223). The county boundary runs through the summit. The part of the Cloud in Staffs lies in Rushton Spencer in Leek ancient parish. The area was owned by Lord Egerton and in the past there were many disputes regarding **access**. For much of the latter C20 the Cloud has been owned by NT (Congleton and District: A Portrait in Old Picture Postcards. Mary & Colin McLean. 1988 p61); the Staffordshire Way, a footpath running the length of the county, crosses the Cloud.

Cloud End Common name for The Cloud (Congleton Past and Present. R Head. 1887) (DP p77).

Cut-thorn Hill Hill at Three Shires Head. Probably from a thorn used as a marker or boundary point and therefore cut, or it was the court thorn, where the forest or swainmote court met (NSFCT 1932 pp60-61).

Danebridge See main body of encyclopaedia.

Gorsty Hall See main body of encyclopaedia.

Gorstyhill See main body of encyclopaedia.

Knar Farm on the banks of the Dane just below Cutthorn Hill. The name means 'rugged rock.' Occurs in the singular and plural in 'Sir Gawayne and the Green Knight' written in c1360 - 'ruze knokled knarrez (craggy projecting rocks) with knorned stonez (rugged stones)' (NSFCT 1932 p61).

Meresbury A very short lived prebend in Lichfield cathedral, founded in 1241 (VCH vol 3 p143).

Midgeley The name is preserved in Midgeley Farm and Hill SE and E of Allgreave, and Midgleygate N of Gradbach. Dieulacres Abbey claimed the tithes (that should have gone to St Werburg's at Chester) here, and may have claimed 'purlieu' privilege here at one time (NSFCT 1932 p64).

Mousecroft See main body of encyclopaedia.

Nick i' th' Hill Tiny village 1m NW of the church at Biddulph, on the Ches Staffs border, mainly in Cheshire (TSW p14p). Nick i' th' Hill was on a packhorse route taken by carriers taking coal from Biddulph to Congleton until 1789 when an easier route through the Biddulph Valley was made. Here is Girthings Bank, where the girths of the horses were tightened for the descent (BHS June 1968 p15). There are several quarries along the crest of the ridge on which the village is situated (SGM p286). Possibly so named from one of the quarries which made a nick in the hill.

Panniers Pool Bridge Pack-horse bridge over the Dane on the Ches Derbys border at SK 009686. (CDS p1p) (VB p211) (DP p6il). Here four packhorse routes meet (PRT p78). If otherwise Three Shire Heads Bridge then was known as Galleyford Bridge (SSE 1996 p69). In the past the bridge has been widened (PDS&C p63ps). It was once a meeting place for alleged forgers of 'Flash Money' and about here much prize-fighting and cock-fighting took place. The participants could easily avoid the law of Staffs by escaping into either Ches or Derbys (NSFCT 1947 p169) (Real Ale in and around the Potteries. CAMRA. p30).

Pincher's Hole A stretch of the upper Dane Valley, just S of Knar Farm. Some believe this is the place where the boar is trapped in a hole in a water course near a rock, in the medieval epic poem 'Gawain and the Green Knight' (NSJFS 1977 p40) (MR p316).

Red Bull, Aqueduct. See main body of encyclopaedia.

Secret Slab Rock feature on W slopes of The Cloud (SGM p266).

Tarvin Prebend in Lichfield cathedral, founded by Alexander de Stavenby in 1226. In that the prebend of Whittington took over that of Berkswich, this prebend took over that of Burton-in-Wirral (SSAHST vol 2 1960-61 p50). The prebend, which has also appeared as Tervin, was united with Stotfold (Statfold) in the reign of Queen Anne (HOL p251) (SHOS vol 1 p293). But Stotfold and Tarvin are presented separately in the LDD. For a dispute concerning it between the Pope and the king see VCH vol 3 p143. Village 4.75m E of Chester.

Tervin See Tarvin.

West Heath See main body of encyclopaedia.

Whitelee SW of Danebridge just beyond Staffs. Has also appeared as Whitelea. On the farm here John Naden, born at Hores Clough (see), murdered his employer, Robert Bough or Brough, the owner of the farm. Reputedly, he formed a relationship with his employer's wife, who asked him to murder her husband. Nadin was sentenced to hang on Aug 19 1731. The initial hanging took place in late Aug 1731 on a tree by the main door of the farmhouse, where the crime had been committed. Nadin is said to have taken nearly an hour to die. Afterwards his body was hung in chains from the gallows on Gun Hill (see). To witness the execution at Whitelee and the ceremonial hanging on Gun Hill a huge macabre procession including choristers from Leek, Bosley and Winkle who sang psalms as they walked, made a round journey from Leek to Whitelee to Gun Hill and back to Leek; the procession was accompanied by Nadin's body for part of the journey (The Grub Street Journal Sept 16 1731) (OL vol 1 pp17-27) (NSFCT 1945 p86; he is called James Nadin) (ES April 12 1957) (STM April 1969 pp30,31) (TFTPM pp53-62 il) (SVB p123) (DP pp79-80) (HOLF pp8-10) (SMML pp115-116).

DERBYSHIRE

The most north easterly boundary of the county is a very artificial one. Running from a point just N of Orchard Farm it runs in a straight line NE to Cheeks Hill and then almost due S in another straight line to Drystone Edge. Until the C19 this small area of high and remote moorland was the source of controversy between the ancient parishes of Alstonefield (Staffs) and Hartington (Derbys) (SSE 1996 p69). The boundary between Staffs and Derbys thereafter follows the Dove from its head to more or less its confluence with the Trent N of Burton. S of Ashbourne, changes in the river's course over the centuries have meant a boundary heading off to weave across flat meadows seemingly for no particular reason. The boundary ENE of Calwich has actually been moved to follow the Dove, giving a few acres to Staffs. Derbys has lost to Staffs minute stretches along the Dove to W of Abbotsholme School, but gained a patch where the boundary has encroached W of the Dove NE of Brookend, but lost a patch N of Noah's Ark to NE of Uttoxeter. The boundary which followed a loop of the Dove in the C19 N of Marchington now cuts it out (OS maps 1834. 1981), and where it followed the Dove N of Woodhouse it now runs S and N of the river across meadows and even follows the railway line for a few yards at Hatton (Derbys) (OS maps 1834. 1981). A detached portion of Derbys between the Dove and Woodhouse has been removed to Staffs (OS maps 1834. 1981). Likewise a tiny acre-size detached portion of Staffs N of Shotwood Hill has been removed to Derby (OS maps 1834. 1981). N of Rolleston the boundary followed the Fleam or Little Dove in the C19 but has since been moved further N to follow the Dove (OS maps 1834. 1981). Contrary to this change GLAUE p420 says a part of Rolleston ancient parish without population was considered to be in Derbys in the C19 and was transferred to Marston-on-Dove ancient parish (Derbys) in 1903. An island in the Trent on the E side of Catholme,

W of Catton Hall, Derbys, formerly in Staffs has been removed to Derbys (OS maps 1834. 1981). In 1894-5 Stapenhill ancient parish and most of Winshill township were removed from Derbys to Staffs. In 1895 Croxall (including the N part of Edingale village, but excluding Catton township) ancient parish wholly entered Staffs from Derbys.

Axe Edge Former common land (UHAW p11) lying on an edge beyond the most northerly point of the Staffs border. Is the highest table land in England, the Dane rises on it and falls to the Irish Sea, the Dove rises on the other side and falls to the North Sea (NSFCT 1895 p153) (TTTD p93). There is a Trigonometrical station on Axe Edge in Derbys at 1810 feet high (NSFCT 1881 p44). W Adam in 'The Gem of the Peak' (1845) noted that on a clear day the mountains of N Wales can be seen from Axe Edge, and with a telescope the lighthouse beyond Liverpool, 50m to the WNW. In 1842 a party of Royal Sappers and Miners whilst stationed here were able to observe their contemporaries with powerful reflectors stationed on the top of Lincoln cathedral to the E and on the summit of Snowdon, 90m to the W (TTTD p93). Harold Gowdin of St Edward Street, Leek found a Zeppelin bomb on Axe Edge in 1936. The bomb, presumably dropped in WW1, weighed nearly 10 lb. It retained the four fins and was displayed in Mr Godwin's shop in Leek (ES Aug 25 1936 p7). An Oxford HN 429 crashed on Axe Edge on Nov 3 1944. All three of the crew died (MD p46). The name Axe may be of Scandinavian origin (UHAW p75).

Axe Edge End Tiny hamlet just beyond Staffs 1m NNE of Flash. Here was a stone, called the Elliot Stone, marking the county boundary (UHAW p11).

Baley Hill On Derbys side of Dove Dale N of Nibbs Hill. Formerly Bayley Hill (NSFCT 1936 p30).

Blackclough 1.25m NNW of Flash. May have been in Staffs according to some old maps.

Bladon Hill N of Stapenhill, on E side of the Trent. The ancient township of Winshill extended to Bladon Hill prior to 1894. Bladon Castle, a large battlemented and turreted mansion, on the N side of the hill was at first built as a folly in the C18 and finished in 1805. It was built to designs of Sir Jeffry Wyatville for Abraham Hoskins, a local solicitor, and has been called 'Hoskin's Folly' (CBHBT pp15,16) (F p283 pl 139pc) (CL June 24 1999 p136 il by Barbara Jones for her F&G).

Borough Holme Island in the Trent. N of Cat Holme (HOA p18). Has also appeared as Boroughholm.

Bretby Hall and Park. 3m E of Burton upon Trent. In the grounds is a chained cedar tree, which was planted in 1677 and felled in 1953. There was a belief that if a branch fell a death would occur in the family (BTOP vol 2 p51) (GLS p15-16) - these references do not clearly state that Bretby is in Derbys.

Brindley's Tree An ash tree by the birthplace of James Brindley at Tunstead (NSFCT 1938 p66).

Brislington Formerly in Stapenhill parish (W p542).

Brizlincote Hall 1m SSE of Winshill. In 1850 a Saxon brooch and weapons were found at Brizlincote at SK 273220, just to the S of the present county border. By the 1990s the finds were in Cambridge Museum (STMSM Sept 1973 p26) (info KL Neal) (BTIH p11).

Broadfields Farm See main body of encyclopaedia.

Catton Hall House N of Croxall.

Cherry Holme Island in the Dove, lying before Catton Hall.

Chilcote Village 2m E of Clifton Campville in Clifton Campville ancient parish, close to the Staffs border (SHOS vol 1 p403) (W p597). Transferred from Derbys to Leics in 1888.

Chrome Hill (NSFCT 1901 p197). See Packhorse Hill, Staffs.

Clownholme On the border with Staffs, 0.75m ESE of Rocester. Beyond Abbotsholme, to the S, is Monk's Clownholme a house in a curious protrusion of Staffs into Derbys on the E side of the Dove.

Croxall See main body of encyclopaedia.

Dale Brook Rises near Bretby. Ran through Winshill (see) township to the Trent. Later formed the boundary of Burton upon Trent municipal borough. Means 'a brook flowing through a valley' (SPNO p6).

Dove Bridge See main body of encyclopaedia.

Dove Head Small scattered hamlet to E of the up most reaches and source of the Dove. Plot's map places it at about Tenterhill or Colshaw.

Dove Holes Cavern system on Derbys side of Dove Dale. The Stone Circle known as the 'Bull Ring' at Dove Holes and the mound adjoining (DAJ vol 37,27). (PS p122, p on p123) (DDI p16) (AAD p164) (TPC p167).

Dowall Hall NE of Hollinsclough (MR p189).

Dowel Dale N of Dowall Hall (MR p189p).

Dragon's Back, The Local name to describe the neighbouring hills Chrome Hill and Parkhouse Hill (see). It is from the Staffs side that they can be viewed side on and look together like spikes on a dragon's back (MR p189).

Drakelow Former manor and settlement S of Burton upon Trent just in Derbys. In 1962 an Anglo-Saxon urn of C6 origin was found at SK 220185. It went to Derby Museum (BTIH p11il) (info KL Neal). William de Gresley held the manor of Drakelow by a curious custom, that of by gift of a bow, quiver and 12 arrows, yearly. The bow was to be unstrung, but it was stipulated that the quiver should be of 'Tutbury' make and the arrows were to be feathered (UTR p38).

DEVIL OF DRAKELOW. The devil of Drakelow is a story closely connected to Burton Abbey and occurred in the time of Abbot Geffrey de Malaterra, or Evilearth, fourth abbot of Burton (1085-1094). In the early 1090s two serfs belonging to the abbey and tied to land in Stapenhill fled to Roger the Poitevin or Pitcarium, lord of the neighbouring manor of Drakelow. Abbey retainers confiscated seed corn which was to have been sown by the two truants and then raided Stapenhill and stole all the seed corn there. In reprisal Poitevin sent a gang of Drakelow men over the Trent to abbey land at Blakepol or Blackpool (see), where, some say Poitevin's men ruined abbey crops or a a skirmish took place in which abbey servants were defeated. The news of misfortune for the abbey was brought before Abbot Geffrey, who prayed for guidance at St Modwen's shrine. Or some say a humiliation of St Modwen's relics took place in which her shrine was removed from its place of honour on the altar and put on the ground to try to stir her to act for the abbey. These actions proved to have been worth while for in a subsequent battle the abbey was victorious, on account, so they thought, of St Modwen's intervention. The following day the two truant serfs were seized with an illness and died in agony and were buried without delay in Stapenhill graveyard. Soon after, two savage beasts appeared at night time, banging their coffins on house walls of the area and uttering obscene cries and generally terrifying the neighbourhood. It was soon assumed that the serfs' corpses had been transformed into these beasts. Furthermore, a great pestilence struck Drakelow carrying off most of the population. It was thought that this was further punishment for the truants from St Modwen. Drogo, the Drakelow bailiff, and some Stapenhill residents - fearing that the troubles might visit them next - exhumed the serfs' corpses and tore out their hearts and burned them on a hill known as Wodenfreseford. An evil spirit in the form of a large bird, black as a raven, emerged from the flames and disappeared towards heaven. All these misfortunes eventually brought Poitevin to the abbey to beg for pardon (SHOS vol 1 p5) (DAJ vol 17) (Derbys Arch & Nat Hist Soc Journal 1895 p49) (SHC 1898 pp21-23) (SCSF p153) (Burton Daily Mail Nov 18 1980) (Ghosts and Legends of Derbyshire. David Bell. c1992 pp44-45) (SSE 1996 pp32-35).

Drakelow Hall 2m SSW of Burton upon Trent. Demolished in 1932 and Drakelow power station built on the site in 1954 (ABTOP p53).

Eagle and Child Inn N of Gradbach Mill (PDS&C p64 fig 102). The eagle and child is the crest of the Stanley family (UTR p234).

Eaton Banks and Eaton Woods. On E side of the Dove facing Crakemarsh, Derbys. Features in the poems 'Vales of Weaver,'

Ah! Eaton! Soon thy woodlands gay!

and in FNC Mundy's 'Needwood Forest,'

Yes, Eaton banks, in vain I strive.

(HOU p8).

Edingale See main body of encyclopaedia.

Glutton Bridge and Dale. S and W of Earl Sterndale. Close to the Staffs border. Has also appeared as Glutten Dale (LGS p125). The name is thought to be from a personal name, probably a nickname (PNPD).

Grey Mare's Stable Cave See main body of encyclopaedia.

Grit, The See main body of encyclopaedia.

Hanging Bridge See main body of encyclopaedia.

Hanson Grange See Honson Grange.

Hartshorne N of Swadlincote. Here Stebbing Shaw, author of SHOS, was rector, living here from summer 1791 (introduction in SHOS vol 1 1976 edition).

Honson Grange The diarist John Evelyn passed a fine on selling this estate in 1685 to a farmer called Burton. It had come to him as part of his daughter-in-law's portion which was a fourth part of what was divided between the mother and three sisters. The estate is said to be in Staffs (The Diary of John Evelyn. Everyman's Library 1937. vol 2 p214). Perhaps identifiable with Hanson Grange under 0.5m NE of Dove Holes in Dove Dale, a former possession of Burton Abbey (LTD p45).

Iron Tors Mill Dale, Beresford Dale. N of Coldeaton Bridge.

Lin Dale Runs up behind Thorpe Cloud from the Stepping Stones over the Dove.

Lion's Head Rock Rock feature on the Derbys side of Dove Dale, N of Reynards Cave. Is part of the Pickering Tors. Looking at N or S sides of the rock the profile of a lion's face can be made out. (POD p306) (TPC p168) (PS p121p - called the Lion Face Rock) (LGS p123, p facing p126) (TFTPM p66 - called the Lion's Rock) (Dovedale Guide. Keith Mantell. 1985. pp10,11pc) (MR p127) (DMV pp12p,14p).

Lover's Leap A promontory of rock situated on Derbys side of Dove Dale between the Stepping Stones and Tissington Spires approximately opposite the Twelve Apostles (TD p) (PS p120) (DDI p10). So called because a young girl committed suicide by leaping off the rock after being jilted by her lover (NSFCT 1885 p67) (MR p127p) (HLSP p167). Originally called Sharplow Point (TPC pp169,170), called Lover's Leap by 1906 (HLS p28).

Lud Well N of Hartington. Halfway between Pilsbury and Hartington on Staffs Derbys border (Yates' map) (DPEM pp114-121ps). The name is probably from the son or husband of Dana the Celt's Earth Mother who was Lud or Llud or possibly Nudd, a Celtic sky god (DP pp47-48) (DPEM p115).

Lullington Woods Woods, presumably, about Lullington, 1m N of Clifton Campville. Some children from Clifton Campville saw an unidentified flying object over the woods in 1977 (TH 16 Dec 1977) (UFO Study pp126-132) (FSR vol 26 No. 4 p19) (MMSE pp62,287). SH Evershed, early aeroplane builder, died at Lullington Hall (EAS p15).

Midway (on Ashby-Burton road) at Swadlincote, Derbys. A reference to Midway gave the impression it was in Burton upon Trent.

Mill Dale See main body of encyclopaedia.

Monk's Bridge Bridge crossing the Dove at SK 268269. It was, perhaps, on the border of Derbys and Staffs before boundary changes. The old bridge was named after John de Stafford of Stretton, Staffs, Abbot of Burton Abbey, who had it built in the C13. His bridge is said to have replaced a Roman bridge, probably a timber platform laid level upon the present (1923) piers, which had fallen into ruin. He allegedly felt compelled to build it after an inquest found that nobody was liable to repair the old structure. The present three arches on the Derbys side are probably of C13 origin and the piers are either Roman work or Roman work encased in later stonework. The bridge may have been repaired in 1555. The present bridge is now situated between two more recent bridges: Egginton Bridge carrying the A38 slightly farther up stream: Brindley's canal aqueduct carrying the Trent & Mersey Canal slightly farther down stream. The aqueduct is made up of 12 arches. It is far wider than it needs to be, possibly Brindley was allowing for flooding (The Trent & Mersey Canal. Peter Lead. 1980. pl 56 shows the aqueduct). (SHOS vol 1 p6) (NSFCT 1923 pp135-136). (NHS p 400) (SHOS vol 1 part 1 p89 originally called the bridge of Egenton (Egginton)) (Smith's map) (SOSH p125) (APB p16) (LTD p224p).

Nabs, The 1000 feet hill on the Derbys side of Dove Dale, 1m from Milldale, from which one of the finest views in Derbys is to be obtained (NSFCT 1936 p30). At the foot of the Nabs are caverns known as the Dove Holes (LGS p124) (PS p122). Has also appeared as The Nabbs.

Newhall Suburb of Swadlincote.

No Man's Heath See Warwickshire.

Oakley Mill See main body of encyclopaedia.

Panniers Pool Bridge See Cheshire.

Parkhouse Hill Conically-shaped hill just in Derbys. NW of Glutton Bridge. Together with Chrome Hill (to the NNW) Parkhouse Hill is known locally as the 'Dragon's

Back' (MR p189p); the reef limestone running up the edge of the hill has been likened to a dinosaur (LTD pp10p,15). From Crowdecote looking up Dove valley the tops of Parkhouse Hill and Chrome Hill appear majestic and mysterious in a low mist.

Pessall Farm See main body of encyclopaedia.

Pickering Tors A group of rocks in Dove Dale, situated downstream from (or opposite - LGS p123) Ilam Rock and on the Derbys side (DMV pp18-19p). Sometimes called 'the portals of Dovedale' (TPC pp167,168). The right-hand extremity of which (looking down the river) has a profile to a lion's head. One has a cave called Pickering Cave (EF pp73,75). (POD p306) PDS&C p11p) (MR p127).

Pilsbury Castle Hills Hills with motte and baileys 1.75m SE of Longnor, just beyond Staffs (PWPD p84).

Pool Hall Bridge See main body of encyclopaedia.

Reynard's Arch See Reynard's Cave.

Reynard's Cave Limestone cavern on the Derbys side of Dove Dale between Tissington Spires and Lion's Head Rock. The cavern is reached by a steep path. In the foreground is a very impressive natural arch, called Reynard's Arch (PDS&C p10p); the only example in England, that has a pinnacle of rock (Sharplow Point?), nearby (ES April 4 1934 p6ps). There is a narrow crevice in its top and bush growing hardily within it. The enclosure between the arch and the cave is called Reynard's Hall. The cavern entrance or arch is 30 high and 15 feet wide (MR p127) or 40 feet high by 20 feet wide (JAT p2 il). Fragments of pottery from the Neolithic period in the cave went to Buxton Museum. The name probably means 'cave frequented by foxes' (PNPD). After picnicking near here, on July 26 1761, Dr Langton, Dean of Clogher in County Tyrone, (he was staying at Longford Hall, seat of Wenman Coke) tried to climb the steep slope towards Tissington with a young lady, Miss La Roche, riding behind (many like, Raven, suggest she sat behind him). Both fell. Miss La Roche's fall was broken by her hair becoming entangled in a thorn bush, but the Dean died two days later and is buried at Ashbourne (FTP) (LTD p34). Sarah Gould (d1899) of Mill Dale used to place a rope up to the arch every day in the hope of a tip (DMV p15p). (AAD pp166-168) (PS p120p) (NSFCT 1885

p67) (CCOP pp92-93) (TD p) (HLSP p167).

Reynard's Kitchen Cave on the Derbys side of Dove Dale. Situated to the left, and a little above, of Reynard's Cave (Dove Dale Guide. Keith Mantell). According to legend a hermit lived here (PS p121). (NSFCT 1885 p67) (LGS p123) (POD p305) (DDI p14).

Reynard's Hall Is a natural enclosure - open to the sky - in the cliff of Dove Dale on the Derbys side leading to Reynard's Cave (see); a huge natural arch is the entrance to it and forms one side. (DDI p13).

Sandiacre Prebend in Lichfield cathedral founded in c1280 by Roger de Meuland. The name is from a parish and large village 7m E of Derby, on the Derby Notts border (VCH vol 3 p144). The prebendary was exempt from the jurisdiction of the Dean and Chapter and came directly under the archdeacon of Derby. Former holders of the prebend include Walter de Langton and Roger de Northburgh both of whom became bishops of Lichfield (SSAHST vol 2 1960-61 pp48-49).

Sawley Prebend in Lichfield cathedral and village 7m ESE of Derby. The prebend, which has also appeared as Sallow, was founded by Roger de Clinton in the C12 and annexed to the Treasurership. In 1719 it was by Act of Parliament annexed to the new church of St Philip Birmingham (now Birmingham cathedral) (SSAHST vol 2 1960-61 p49). Or and united with Bobenhull (HOL p247). The stall was suspended in 1845 and was still suspended in 1960 (SSAHST vol 2 1960-61 p49) (VCH vol 3 p191), but appears in the list of prebends in the LDD (1992).

Scropton Parish and village on E side of the Dove, 1m NW of Tutbury, 9m WSW of Derby. Between 1656 and 1658 a Commonwealth commission drew up plans to enclose Needwood Forest with half of it going to 22 townships who claimed common rights (VCH vol 2 pp352-353). Scropton is shown to have been allotted a portion (SHOS vol 1 pp62,63). The reason is said to be to reward it for ringing its church bells when parliament destroyed Tutbury Castle in the Civil War (FLJ 1916 pp239-241). There were parts of Scropton parish in Needwood Forest until enclosure in 1801. Scropton's land extended for about three miles in small patches from the New Inn or Five Road Ends, and

about two miles from the Six Road Ends to Yoxall. The rateable properties to Scropton were mostly in large farms and there was very little in small holdings. The roads belonging to Scropton were in varying lengths, from a quarter of a mile to a hundred yards (APB pp45-46). Despite the assertion that Scropton ceased to hold land in the forest after enclosure it seems to have been granted a few hundred acres in Barton and Yoxall wards in May 1811 at the time of the Enclosure Act. The detached portions caused the Scropton overseers much journeying during their twice annual visits. The detached Scropton parish parcels of land were transferred to Staffs for parliamentary purposes in 1832 and transferred to Staffs for all purposes in 1844. The land seems to have remained in Scropton parish, however, until c1880 when Mr Bass of Rangemore, MP for Derby, unwittingly built cottages on land liable to contribute to the upkeep of a school in Scropton parish. This compelled him to deprive Scropton of its Staffs territory and set in operation the Divided Parishes Act which was passed in c1884 (NSFCT 1913 p49 note. 1915 pp182-183) (APB pp45-46) (GLAUE p411).

Sealpey House See main body of encyclopaedia.

Somersal Hall Mrs Maria Elizabeth Jackson, botanical author, lived here (BS p246). Probably at Somersal Herbert.

Stanton And Stanton Manor. 1.5m SE of Stapenhill.

Stapenhill, House, Spring Cottage. Stapenhill.

Tatemanlowe A hundred over the border from Tutbury?

Three Sisters Seems to be a rock feature to S of, and just before, Lion's Head Rock on Derbys side of Dove Dale (NSFCT 1936 p29).

Tissington Spires Group of rocks on Derbys side of Dove Dale. Reynard's Cave is the next rock feature to the N after passing Sharplow Dale (Dovedale Guide. Keith Mantell. 1985 p8) (MR p127). (AAD p168) (TPC p169) (POD p304) (DMV p12p). The name is from Tissington village 1.75m to the E.

Waterloo Clump See main body of encyclopaedia.

Winshill See main body of encyclopaedia.

Witches Pool A pool somewhere not far from Dove Bridge, so possibly in Derbys. It is likely this was a place where witches were drowned (HOU p267).

Wodenfreseford See Drakelow.

LANCASHIRE

Bolton le Moor Former prebend in Lichfield cathedral. Founded by Roger de Clinton in the C12 and annexed to the Archdeaconry of Chester. In 1541 Chester became a separate See and the Prebend went with the Archdeaconry

to the newly-founded Bishopric of Chester (SSAHST vol 2 1960-61 p44).

Flixton Prebend in Lichfield cathedral (SHOS vol 1 p292) (VCH vol 3 p144). On the banks of the Irwell on border

with Cheshire, now Greater Manchester. Founded by Roger de Meuland in c1280 (SSAHST vol 2 1960-61 p46).

'Staffordshire Warehouse' Former 9-storied warehouse to W of central Manchester (LCAST vol 71 pp4,147)

LEICESTERSHIRE

Chilcote See Derbyshire.

Honey Hill Borders with the most easterly tip of Staffs.

No Man's Heath See Warwickshire.

SHROPSHIRE

A large territory E of the Severn comprising the manors of Alveley, Claverley, Kingsnordley, Quatt, Romsley, Rudge, Shipley, and Worfield recorded in DB under Staffs were transferred to Shrops in the C12 (SL p29). The manors of Cheswardine and Chipnall recorded in DB under Staffs had been transferred to Shrops by 1166 (HOS p55). In 1965 the area W of the Shrops Union Canal comprising Tyrley Castle Farm, Pellwall, Salisbury Hill, and Four Alls was removed from Tyrley civil parish in Staffs, to Sutton upon Tern civil parish in Shrops (GLAUE p427). A dispute as to which county Tan House Meadow, an island in the Tern, S of Market Drayton, was settled in Staffs' favour in 1885 (SHC 1945/ 6 p4). From Burlington the county boundary ran a course through the centre of Sheriff Hales ancient parish and village to the N of Chadwell Mill. The whole of Sheriff Hales was transferred to Shrops in 1894-5, save for a part comprising Blymhill Common, Chatwell Park Farm and Brockton Grange which remained in Staffs. In 1895 the Whittimere area was transferred from Shrops to Staffs. Prior to 1895 the county boundary ran eastwards from Halfpenny Green along the Wombourne road, past the War Stone, and N along Abbot's Castle Hill (VCH vol 20 p64). At Whitleyford Bridge there was a conflict of opinion between Staffs and Shrops officials as to the exact course of the boundary in 1927. A tongue of land protruding out for 0.5m to include Islington (a NE suburb of Newport), which included a house called Banshee House, belonged to Staffs prior to 1965 before being removed to Shrops.

Alveley 2.75m WNW of Kinver. In the demesne of Coton, Shrops, Chad, the Saxon missionary and bishop, founded a college of priests at Alveley in the C7. Perhaps this is why this part of Shrops occurs under DB Staffs (KRC p15).

Badger Parish adjoining Patshull parish (SHOS vol 2 p286).

Banshee House See main body of encyclopaedia.

Bearstone Just N of Mucklestone and a former township of Mucklestone ancient parish. The name may be derived from a megalithic chambered tomb here - as at Mucklestone, at the Devil's Ring and Finger, and at the Bradley Stone, Norton-in-Hales (NSFCT 1908 p115).

Beckbury Parish adjoining Patshull parish (SHOS vol 2 p286).

Bloomsbury See main body of encyclopaedia.

Boningale Manor S of Albrighton. Part of the lost city in Wrottesley Old Park (NHS p394).

Boscobel The house is just in Shrops, nearly 1m S of Bish-

op's Wood. It achieved fame by being one of the houses where Charles II took refuge after the battle of Worcester (1651). It is not known exactly when Boscobel was built. The oldest part is the N range. The main part of the house to the S is probably of c1630 and by John Giffard, eldest son of Edward Giffard of Whiteladies, a descendant of the Giffards of Chillington. Blount, writing in 1660, says the house was built 'about 30 years before.' Blount says it derives its name from the remarks of one of John Giffard's friends, Sir Basil Brook (of Madeley), who at a housewarming feast when asked for a name for the new house, suggested 'Boscobel' from the Italian Bosco Bello, 'the house situated in beautiful woods' (Boscobel. English Heritage Guide. 1987) (MR p51). On the death of John Giffard both Whiteladies and Boscobel passed to his daughter, Frances, who in 1633 married John Cotton of Gedding Abbots, Hunts. In 1651 the two houses were still in the

possession of Frances Cotton, by this time a widow. Boscobel was then occupied by William Penderell, caretaker and servant to Frances Cotton, and his wife Jane. CHARLES II AT BOSCOBEL. Charles II arrived at Boscobel after his abortive attempt to cross the Severn at Madeley, Shrops at 3.00am on Saturday Sept 6 1651 (NSFCT 1886 pp46-49). At daybreak after a short time in the house Charles with Major William Careless took refuge in the Royal Oak (see) in nearby woods. At nightfall Charles returned to the house. Some say he left that night for Moseley Old Hall, but most writers, including Thomas Whitgreave the owner of Moseley, say he left for Moseley on the evening of Sunday 7 spending some time in the garden at Boscobel during the day. Charles II left Boscobel accompanied by the five Penderell brothers and their brother-in-law Francis Yates (Boscobel and White Ladies Priory. English Heritage. 1987. p15). They are said to have left him to walk the last stretch to Moseley for it was considered unsafe for them to go with him all the way to the house. Their route to Moseley is uncertain. Some say the Penderells and Yates left him at Pendeford Mill, whilst others say he was left at Featherstone.

(Boscobel, or the Compleat History of His Sacred Majesties Most Miraculous Preservation after the Battle of Worcester 3 Sept 1651. Thomas Blount. 1660; has a part titled 'Ye King's Concealment at Trent' supposed to be written by Anne Wyndham who could be the Old Anna Woman who personally knew of the King's concealment in the Wetton area and in Ratcliffe's Stable, and gave her name to Old Hannah's Cave - WTCEM p88) (NHS pp306-307) (An Account of the Preservation of King Charles II, after the Battle of Worcester by Himself to which are added His Letters to Several Persons. 1766. Glasgow) (SHOS vol 1 part 1 pp73-84 ils facing p79 by Shaw) (The Boscobel Tract: relating to the Escape of Charles the Second after Worcester. J Hughes. 1830) (SM pp375,391) (GNHS pp82-87) (Personal History of Charles the Second 1650-1651. CJ Lyon. 1851) (W pp46-47) (Boscobel Tracts. Count Grammont ed. Sir Walter Scott. 1864) (RVW p13) (Boscobel, a novel. Harrison Ainsworth) (WP p81) (History of Tong and Boscobel. 1894 pp183-193) (The Flight of The King. Allan Fea. 1897) (WTCEM p88) (After Worcester Fight. Allan Fea. 1904) (The King in Exile: The Wanderings of Charles II from June 1646 to 1654. Eva Scott. 1904) (HSS pp61-71) (NSFCT 1918 pp126-127) (WAS 2nd Field Study Trip pp3,4) (Bibliography of Literature relating to the escape of Charles II after the battle of Worcester. WA Horrox. 1924) (SOSH pp211,212p,213-215) (ES Sept 24 1931 p4p) (BAST 1929-30 vol 54 pp53-62) (The Wanderings of Charles II in Staffordshire and Shropshire after the Worcester Fight. HP Kingston. 1933) (KESH pp32-35) (CL Dec 14 1945. Feb 20 1948 p379, 381p of letters patent of Charles II (July 24 1675) for the payment of the pensions to the Penderells, who assisted in the King's escape) (SLM Sept 1951) (Boscobel House and White Ladies Priory. DoE HMSO. 1965. Reprinted 1975) (The Escape of Charles II after the Battle of Worcester. Richard Ollard. 1966) (Charles II's Escape from Worcester: A Collection of Narratives Assembled by Samuel Pepys. William Matthews. 1966) (E p30) (Biography of Charles II. Antonia Fraser. 1979 pp113-114,117,118,119,121) (MR p51).

After 1651 the house passed to Frances' only daughter, Jane Cotton, who in 1648 married Basil Fitzherbert of Norbury (Derbys) and Swynnerton Hall, taking Boscobel to the Fitzherberts (SCHJ No. 9 p13). In the later Stuart period it was customary for the people of the district to make a pilgrimage to one or all of the houses which had sheltered Charles II (SCSF p18). Jon Raven says they made a pilgrimage to all, starting with Bentley and ending with Boscobel (FOS p99). Whiteladies and Boscobel remained in Fitzherbert ownership until 1812, being let to a succession of tenants including descendants of the Penderells. Some relics of St Chad were kept at Boscobel by the later C18. They are believed to have been brought here by Robert Collingwood SJ who may have been entrusted with them by the Jesuit John Leveson of Leveson's Moat (see), Willenhall. Collingwood was living at Boscobel by at least 1715 and died here on Jan 24 1740/1. It may have been him who bequeathed the relics to Thomas Fitzherbert of Swynnerton Hall, the then owner of Boscobel. From Boscobel they were taken to Swynnerton Hall. Collingwood also lived or spent time at Blackladies and some say the relics were kept there (SR p66) (RHPS p258) (SCHJ No. 9 pp13-14) (VB p24). In 1812 the Fitzherberts sold Boscobel to Walter Evans of Darley, Derbys. By 1832 the house was in its present stucco state. In 1918 the estate was bought by the Earl of Bradford who in 1954 placed the house and Royal Oak in the guardianship of the Ministry of Works. Since 1984 it has been administered by English Heritage (Boscobel. English Heritage Guide. 1987). Boscobel has two secret hiding places or priest's holes. One is under the floor of a closet off the Squire's Room. The other is a space, slightly larger than the first, under a trap door in the attic. It is in this second space Charles is reputed to have hid (Boscobel. English Heritage Guide. 1987). (HS pl p255) (BRO pp221-224) (AOW p69) (OHW pl 17) (ES Sept 24 1931 p4p) (SCHJ No. 8 winter 1966-67 pp1-16) (SLM May 1949 pp234,235).

Bradling Stone Large boulder, resting upon a number of smaller stones, situated on the green near Norton-in-Hales church (STELE Feb 29 1952). It is said to have formed part of a megalithic chambered tomb (NSFCT 1908 p115), and possibly was part of the Devil's Ring and Finger, over 0.5m to the SSE in Staffs. The name is from the old custom of 'bradling' or bumping: Anyone found working after noon on Shrove Tuesday was 'bumped' upon this stone by other villagers (STELE Feb 29 1952).

Brockley Moor See main body of encyclopaedia.

Chesterton To SW of Pattingham. The 'Walls of Chesterton' (SVS pp323-324) (OS map 1834) may be a reference to Roman remains. Recorded in DB under Staffs. (SVS pp321-322).

Cheswardine The name means 'Cheese farm' (DUIGNAN p30). Cheswardine was in Staffs at the time of DB and was once a part of Eccleshall ancient parish. The manor appears to have been transferred to Shrops when the l'Estrange family held it in c1166 (SHC 1916 p195). For the castle at Cheswardine see NSFCT 1932 p117.

Chipnall Mentioned in DB under Staffs.

Claverley Recorded in DB under Staffs.

Cosford Albrighton. Here is an airfield and an aerospace museum. It is often loosely said to be near Wolverhampton, consequently misleading some into thinking it is in Staffs. One of the exhibits, a Lincoln bomber, has a ghost (STMSM Aug 1980 pp26,27) (GLS p110) (MGH pp66-67).

Coton Hall and Farm. S of Quatt in Shropshire. Recorded in DB under Staffs: For why it may have been, see Alveley. Coton is believed to be the first Christianised site in West Mercia (KRC pp18,19).

Crackleybank S of Sheriffhales. It has always been in Shrops. Duignan says 'Crack,' perhaps, represents Gaelic 'crioch, criche' or Irish 'crioc, crioch' meaning a boundary, end, limit, frontier (DUIGNAN p116).

Dorrington Just N of Knighton. Formerly in Mucklestone ancient parish.

Gravenhunger Shrops. Formerly in Mucklestone ancient parish. Gravenhunger Moss is to the E of Woore, over 0.75m WSW of Onneley.

Harts Green 3.25m W of Kinver (Royal Kinver p1), just in Shrops. Has also appeared as Hartsgreen.

Hobbal Grange Cottage 1m W of Boscobel. Richard Penderell, one of the Penderell brothers who helped Charles II to escape after the battle of Worcester (1651), lived here. During Charles's attempt to escape to Wales he may have briefly stayed at Hobbal Grange. Charles's account says he got some bread and cheese at one of the Penderells' houses but did not go in (Boscobel House and White Ladies Priory. English Heritage). The cottage or a successor was in a derelict state by the early 1960s and only some ruined walls remained by 1981 (info Bruce Braithwaite, who has photographs of the ruined building).

Horse Collar Oak Oak tree close to Moss Lane Farm, Chipnall, Shrops on the Staffs border 1.75m SW of Fairoak. In fact two oak trees which, Vernon Yonge says, had grown together to form the shape of a gigantic horse collar (BPS p80). (Chipnall and Cheswardine were in Staffs at time of DB (SL p28 fig 1)).

Islington See main body of encyclopaedia.

Kingsnordley Appears under Staffs in DB.

Lizard Hill Shrops. 2m WSW of Weston-under-Lizard. Gives name to Weston-under-Lizard. The word 'lis' is Gaelic from an earthen fort. The 'ard' is Irish 'high' or 'height' (NSFCT 1908 p135).

Madame's Coppice NW of Rudge Hall.

Market Drayton The centre of the town was little more than 0.25m from the former Staffs border. Regarded by Ussher as the Cair Droithan of the British cities in the history of Nennius. The centre of the town was strongly rectangular. Such a British settlement could explain the presence of the Devil's Ring and Finger (see) which is not far away (NSFCT 1922 p170). Market Drayton parish, in the archdeaconry of Salop, contained a piece of territory in Staffs including Tyrley, Hales and Blore (VCH vol 3 p92), which became Drayton-in-Hales parish.

Norton Forge Farm over 1.25m WNW of Mucklestone. The farmhouse, just in Shrops (the farm buildings are in Staffs), stands on the site of cottages for some workers on the Oakley Hall estate (info Mrs Lovatt) (1834 OS map). Occurs as The Forge on Dower's map. The name Norton is from the nearby Shrops village of Norton-in-Hales.

Pepperhill To NE of Patshull. Part of the lost city in Wrottesley Old Park (NHS p394). Pepperhill is mentioned in a letter from L Leveson at Dudley Castle dated 19 Dec 1643 to the Constable of Wrottesley (SHOS vol 1 part 1 p61).

Pipe Gate Hamlet 2.25m NNE of Mucklestone, formerly i Mucklestone ancient parish, Staffs.

Prees Prebend in Lichfield cathedral from soon after 123 (VCH vol 3 p143). Or founded by Roger de Clinton, bisho of Lichfield, in the C12; and the prebendary was patron c Stafford St Chad and of Tipton. The latter living was ex changed with the bishop for that of Prees (SSAHST vol 1960-61 p48). Also known as Pipa Minor (SHOS vol pp292-293) (VCH vol 3 p143). White tried to identify Pree with Prince's End, near Tipton, suggesting Prince's End i a corruption of Prees End, and supported by the fact tha the prebendary held the tithes of the adjoining parish c Tipton (W p200).

Quatt 4m WNW of Enville. Mentioned in DB under Staffs

Renshaw Wood On Staffs Shrops border 1m S of Boscobe where Charles II sheltered from the rain before making fc Boscobel (NHS p307). Although in the later C17 it stretche all about and included the Royal Oak.

Robin Hood Inn On S side of Bishops Wood, at Soudle (BPS pp168-169) (ALW pl 28). There is a Robin Hoo House 0.5m E of Soudley and 0.5m W of the Staffs borde

Romsley Tiny village 1.5m NE of Arley. It was part of th territory E of the Severn in Staffs until the C12 and it i recorded in DB under Staffs. It has been suggested that th Hremesleage mentioned in the will of Wulfric Spot (c1002 founder of Burton Abbey, is this Romsley (SHC 1916 p34

Royal Oak The oak in which Charles II hid after the battl of Worcester (1651) to escape capture by parliamentaria troops and as such the most famous oak tree in the coun try. The present tree is not the oak Charles hid in. It i reputed to be a descendant of it. It lies very close to th Staffs border 0.75m S of Bishop's Wood village, about 15 yards SW of Boscobel house. Occasionally called th Boscobel Oak (NSFCT 1890 p63). Charles II hid in it o Saturday Sept 6 1651 in some discomfort. He is said t have slept for some of the time in it; lying his head in Majo William Careless's lap. According to most writers he sper that evening inside Boscobel house, although Charle claims he went on to Moseley Old Hall. The passion fo souvenirs relating to the old oak was first noted by Tho mas Blount in 1660. No doubt these included chunks o the tree itself. By 1680 the damage to the tree was so grea that the owners of Boscobel, Basil and Jane Fitzherber were forced to crop part of it and protect it with a hig brick wall. Over a door in the wall they placed a ston tablet with an inscription relating its history. In 1706 Joh Evelyn wrote that he had heard that it had nearly been kille by people hacking the boughs and bark. In 1712 Willian Stukeley described the tree as 'almost cut away by travel lers' and he remarks that 'a young thriving plant from on of its acorns' was growing 'close by the side' of it - this i probably the present oak. In 1784 there is an account o the surrounding wall, by this time neglected and ruinous Within its enclosure was just growing the present Roya Oak; the original Royal Oak having been destroyed. In 178 the surrounding wall was rebuilt by Basil and Eliz Fitzherbert descendants of Basil and Jane Fitzherbert, an the original stone tablet, by then damaged or destroye was replaced. The Evans family bought the Boscobel es tate in 1812. In 1817 the second brick wall was replace by iron railings erected by Miss Frances Evans. In 187 Miss Elizabeth Evans placed two large brass plates by th railings whose inscriptions wrongly attribute the oak t being the original Royal Oak. A gardeners' dictionary o 1759 mentions a sapling from an acorn of the Royal Oa in St James's Park. Many snuff boxes and other toys wer made out of the old oak. In early C19 a garden seat is be lieved to have been made out of part of its root (Boscobe Guide. English Heritage. pp28-30). Charles II at his resto ration had intended to institute an order of knighthood called the Knights of the Royal Oak (SHOS vol 1 part p80*). The Earl of Bradford bought Boscobel estate in 191 and in 1951 he planted a sapling oak next to the curren Royal Oak, which is intended to succeed it when it die (SLM Sept 1951 p of. Oct 1951 p14p of the sapling). I 1954 Boscobel and the Royal Oak were placed in th guardianship of the Ministry of Works. Since 1984 the have been administered by English Heritage (Boscobe English Heritage Guide. 1987). (NSFCT 1886 pp48-49 1890 p45 pl facing; in 1889 the current oak was 67 fee high, 16 feet 3 inches in circumference at the ground, 1 feet 10 inches at five feet) (BB pp27,53) (BRO pp199 221) (DD p399) (GM 1809) (GNHS p410) (W p47 note (BCGB pp243-244; the spread of the tree was 40 feet i diameter) (CBD vol 1 pp693-696) (AOW p69) (N & Q vo

171 July 4 1936) (SOSH p214p) (KES p47) (MR p51p) (BDH pp290-293)

Rudge In Staffs in 1086 and is recorded under Staffs in DB. Transferred to Shrops in the C12. Formerly in Pattingham ancient parish in the archdeaconry of Stafford (VCH vol 3 p92). Here is probably the Rudge heath Duignan says is between Wolverhampton and Bridgnorth and the Roman way from Chester to Worcester passed over (DUIGNAN).

Rudge Hall Rudge. It had a tapestry depicting the meeting between Sarra, prioress of St Leonard of Brewood and William-De-Rudge (P p181p facing). Occupied by Thomas Boycott (d1856) and later Capt Cathcart Boycott Wight-Boycott JP (d1891) (mems in Pattingham church).

Sheriffhales See main body of encyclopaedia.

Shipley 2m SSW of Pattingham. It has been suggested that the Sciplea mentioned in the will of Wulfric Spot (c1002), founder of Burton Abbey, is Shipley (SHC 1916 p34). Appears in DB under Staffs as Scipelie. Transferred to Shrops in the C12.

Spring Coppice Wood SE of White Ladies. Charles II hid in it in his escape from the battle of Worcester 1651 after leaving White Ladies and before going on to try and cross the Severn at Madeley and then returning to Boscobel (Boscobel House and White Ladies Priory. English Heritage. 1987 p8).

Saint Cuthred's Tree Ancient tree at Coton Hall, near Quatt, 2.75m W of Enville. In Staffs at the time of DB when this, reputedly, 1000 year old tree was living. It was used for the administration of the Court Leet to hear Forest Pleas. The tree is mentioned in a charter as Cuthredes treow.' Cuthred was king of the West Saxons from 740-756 (KMC p14).

Tuck Hill Small village lining a long steep escarpment high on the W side of the Severn Valley 2m SW of Bobbington, just in Shrops, but the house of Tuckhill Farm is in Staffs; there was settlement at Tuckhill Farm by the 1290s (VCH vol 20 pp65,70). The ecclesiastical parish of Tuck Hill in Shrops, was created out of parts of the parishes of Alveley (Shrops), Claverley (Shrops), Bobbington (Shrops, Staffs), and Enville (Staffs) in 1870 (GLAUE p426).

Wellington Prebend in Lichfield cathedral (SHOS vol 1 p294), founded by Alexander de Stavenby in c1226 or in 1232 (VCH vol 3 p143). One of the famous holders of this prebend was Henry Chicheley who became bishop of St David's and later archbishop of Canterbury (SSAHST vol 2 1960-61 p51).

White Oak Farm S side of Offoxey Road, in Tong parish, 0.5m WSW of Bishop's Wood village. In the garden of White Oak Cottage near here lies a pigsty in the shape of a pyramid adjoining a Tudor-Gothic stable. Both have peculiar inscriptions and both are follies built by George Durant of Tong Castle in the earlier C19 (WORF p60) (F p194; the cottage is said to be at Bishop's Wood).

Woore Formerly in Mucklestone ancient parish in the archdeaconry of Stafford (VCH vol 3 p92).

Worfield Village 4m SW of Pattingham. Recorded in DB under Staffs. Also a parish adjoining Patshull parish (SHOS vol 2 p286).

SHROPSHIRE (HALESOWEN DETACHED)

The manor and ancient parish of Halesowen, some seven miles long and two miles wide, lay in Worcs in 1086 according to DB. Later, Roger de Montgomery, Earl of Shrewsbury, annexed it to Shrops thereafter it formed a detached portion of Shrops, bounded by Staffs and Worcs over 10 miles eastward from the main body of the county. It was removed to the hundred of Upper Halfshire in Worcs in 1844 by an Act of 1839. Some of Oldbury urban district was in Staffs between 1928 to 1966. It was entered into Warley Woods civil parish when created in 1928 which formed a part of Smethwick county borough (STELE Feb 22 1952) (O pp93-94,186) (GLAUE p427).

Barnford Hill Park Park over 1m SSE of Oldbury. The name Barnford Hill appears on the 1834 OS map. In the park in 2000 was a small mass of rock known as the Pudding Rock believed to be haunted by the ghost of a blacksmith (Central News May 1 2000).

Big House, The Church Street, Oldbury. Built in 1705. It formerly belonged to the Palmer family. By 1857 it was used as the offices of Messrs Jones, Son & Vernon, auctioneers and estate agents. The house, empty by 1997, is believed to be haunted by 'Amelia,' the ghost of a young woman who hung herself here after hearing that her fiancee, an officer in the Duke of Cumberland's army, had been killed in the battle of Culloden (1746) (TB Dec 1997 p5p).

Birchley Park Public park over 0.5m SW of Oldbury.

Bleak House 2.25m SSE of Oldbury, formerly in the detached portion of Shrops. A phantom horseman and the 'Grey Lady' ghost were seen by a man in Bleakhouse Lane in the early 1920s (TB Jan 1996 p1).

Blower's Hill Hill in the Rowley Hills range to the WSW of Oldbury (SVS p437). It has also appeared as Timmins Hill.

Blue Ball Inn Oldbury. Is haunted by a ghost wearing C18 costume (TB Dec 1973 pp16-17).

Broadwell Works Very large works 0.25m ENE of Oldbury.

Bury Hill Park Park 0.5m W of Oldbury, at Rounds Green. Opened in 1897 on land given by John W Wilson MP; geologically the park forms part of the Rowley Hills (ORR p26p). The park keeper's cottage was designed by Voysey. It has been brought here from somewhere else (BOEW p91).

Cakemore Formerly in Oldbury. Cakemore Lane runs alongside the M5. A few Roman coins were found here in 1804, one was a denarius of Marcus Aurelius (GM vol 75 part 2 p696) (OWB p13) (NSJFS 1964 p33), suggesting there was a Roman station near the 'Portway' road (O p77). The name means 'Caefea's marshy place' (TB Feb 1974 p29).

Castle Hill Oldbury (JEPS No. 18 pp5-12).

Causeway Green Oldbury.

Church Bridge SW district of Oldbury.

Churchbridge Branch of the Birmingham Canal. Lost canal in the Oldbury area (BCM autumn 1995 p23).

Cockshot Area or field name in Cakemore close to the Staffs border (JEPS No.18 pp5-12).

Coombeswood S of Blackheath. Has also appeared as Coombes Wood.

Coombes Wood Colliery Also known as The Golden Orchard Colliery. It had a disaster on March 18 1929, eight miners died (BCM April 1972 pp22-33) (TB April 1974 p9. Nov 1983 p5).

Crosswell Oldbury. The name is preserved in Crosswells Road at Rood End. So called from a well of healing waters near the holy rood or wayside cross at Rood End (O p19).

Edale Former estate and house at Rounds Green, Oldbury. Situated on the Birmingham New Road (A4123). The entrance was in what is now Florence Road, at the rear of Rounds Green School. In the early C20 it belonged to Lewis Lowe, an edge tool manufacturer (TB Jan 1997 p29).

Flash Brook Brook that runs at Oldbury, through the lowest part which crossed Birmingham Street and ran through Oldbury Green (STELE August 15 1952).

Fountain Well Stood on N side of Oldbury town. It was surrounded by a high wall, and was never known to fail even in the driest seasons (O p192).

Furnace 1.5m S of Rowley Regis near to Staffs border, at junction of Haden Hill, Combes Road and Furnace Hill. Comparatively populous hamlet in 1851 (TB June 1997 p20). The name is preserved in Furnace Hill and Furnace Lane (Birmingham A-Z).

Goodrest Farm 1.5m ENE of St Kenelm's church at Hunnington. Charles II is said to have hid here after the battle of Worcester, 1651 (WMVB p128).

Halesowen (locally *Yells* BCM April 1968 p45). Town, and former manor and ancient parish. Its townships bordering Staffs were Cakemore, Cradley, Hawne, Oldbury, Warley Wigorn, Warley Salop, and Ridgacre (JEPS No.18 pp5-12 with good maps showing boundaries of Halesowen parish). Francis Brett Young (d1954), novelist, was born at The Laurels, Halesowen, on June 29 1884. He is the author of 'The Black Diamond,' 'Dr Bradley Remembers,' 'My Brother Jonathan,' and 'The Iron Age' (1914); Halesowen is Halesby in his novels (BCM April 1968 pp53-56. July 1971 p48. April 1980 pp10-15. July 1986 pp30-31. autumn 1989 p58).

Hawne Former hamlet 1m NW of Halesowen. Former township in Halesowen ancient parish. Now a suburb of Halesowen. Anciently appeared as Halen (STELE Feb 22 1952).

Hawne Colliery Hawne. Is Great Mawne Colliery in the novels of Francis Brett Young (History Around Us. Halesowen. John Billingham).

Hawne House Stood at the end of Fairmile Road, Hawne. The house has been described as 'a rambling mansion at the top of a steep bank overlooking the Stour Valley' (History Around Us: Halesowen. John Billington). It was built by George Attwood (1722-1807). The house was later occupied by George Attwood's son Matthias (1746-1836) (AOBC p53); Matthias's son Thomas Attwood, the celebrated political reformer, was born here on Oct 6 1783 (BCWJ pp54,66,67) (History Around Us: Halesowen. John Billington) (BCM Jan 1984 pp22-24. Oct 1990 p71) (Thomas Attwood, the Biography of a Rebel. David J Moss. 1990). It was built possibly with stones from Corngreaves Castle, and had been demolished by 1972 (TB April 1972 p7p of the foundations).

Hawne Park Another name for the Bellevale area to the W of Hawne (SNSV vol 2 p73).

Holt Colliery At Cakemore, Halesowen (TB May 1984 p13).

Houghton Branch of the Birmingham Canal Old Cut Old Main Line (HCMS No. 2). Ran from S of Oldbury to Old Park Lane (BCM autumn 1995 p23).

Howley Grange Ancient farm at Quinton, 1.5m ENE of Halesowen. Has appeared as Oueley (1270), Oweleye (1271), and Owley Grange. Possibly Howley Grange Farm was originally a grange of Halesowen Abbey. Charles II is said to have hid here after the battle of Worcester (1651) (O) (WMVB p128) (SNSV vol 2 p47). The name is preserved in Howley Grange Road and Middle School.

Hunnington Village 1.5m S of Halesowen.

Illey Hamlet over 1.5m SE of Halesowen.

Kenelmstowe Former settlement in the vicinity of St Kenelm's chapel consisting of 30 houses and an inn called the Red Cow; considered a sizeable village in the Middle Ages. Kenelmstowe lay close to the detached portion of Staffs comprising Clent and Broome parishes; part of St Kenelm's church yard was until the C19 in Clent. The fair or wake in St Kenelm's church yard belonged to the manor and parish of Clent. The village's decline was brought on by the lack of pilgrims visiting St Kenelm's spring after the Reformation. Nash in his 'History of Worcestershire' (1781) wrote 'The name of Kenelmstowe is now sunk in oblivion.' In the early C19 the opening of the Bromsgrove-Dudley turnpike road which by-passed Kenelmstowe, dealt a final blow, and was instrumental in the growth of Romsley, 1m to the SE. (SHOS vol 2 p243) (CR p75) (TB Jan Feb 1973 p17. June 1975 p11p) (St Kenelm's Church Guide. 1976. p6). St Kenelm's church is St Chad's church in Francis Brett Young's novels (BCM autumn 1989 p58). For Margery the Leech, the witch of Kenelmstowe, see TB Feb/ March 1973 p19.

Langley Former town, now a suburb of Birmingham 0.75m S of Oldbury. By 1999 was a ward in Sandwell metropolitan borough. The name is from probably 'lang' Old English 'long,' and 'ley' 'field' 'clearing,' so 'the long clearing' (TB April 1996 p29).

Langley Green District SE of Langley, Oldbury.

Lapal Tunnel Fourth longest canal tunnel in Britain at 3785 yards (BCM summer 1995 pp28,29) or 3795 yards long (over 2m). Opened in 1798. It was low and narrow and never had a towpath. It closed in 1917 due to a roof fall (The Dudley No. 2 Canal Guide. The Lapal Canal Trust) caused by subsidence and has since been largely filled in (SWY p14). It was officially closed in 1953. The Lapal Canal Trust, formed in 1990, were hoping to restore the tunnel in the mid 1990s (BCM summer 1995 pp28,29. winter 1996/7 pp20-23).

Laurels, The See Halesowen.

Leasowes, The House 0.75m ENE of Halesowen. Pronounced Lez-oes (BBC Radio 4 'The Green Detectives' June 27 1999). The house was occupied by Matthias Attwood (1746-1836) from 1806. It was later occupied by Attwood's son-in-law, William Matthews, coal and ironmaster, founder of the Worcestershire Naturalists' Club in 1847; it was at a party at the house on Nov 6 1857 during Matthews' occupation that a group of mountaineering enthusiasts founded a club which became the Alpine Club, the premier British climbing body. Matthews' son, Benjamin St John Matthews, took the name of Attwood-Matthews. The property passed out of the possession of the Attwood family in 1865 when sold (AOBC p53) (SNSV vol 2 p93). The Leasows served as Anstey College of Physical Education in the 1900s (BCM Sept 1998 pp38-42). In one of Francis Brett Young's novels Francis proposed to Jessica at the Leasowes (BCM autumn 1989 p58). GROUNDS. Has been closely associated with Enville, for William Shenstone landscaped both grounds along with Hagley, Worcs. All three were the subject of Joseph Heely's letters published in 1777 - LHEL. The grounds contained all of these designed by Shenstone - **Assignation Seat** situated at the end or near the **Lovers' Walk** (LHEL pp171,172). The **Portico** stood on the verge of a wood (LHEL vol 2 p68). The folly known as the **Priory** was built between 1757 and 1758 possibly using stones from the remains of Halesowen Abbey. It was situated at the foot of a slope overlooking the great pool. It was largely still remaining in the 1930s but had become a pile of stones by the 1950s. In 1998 it was hoped that the Priory would be rebuilt (BCM Sept 1998 pp38-42ps. spring 1999 p67p of in early C20). The **Priory Walk** which was a walk through a gloomy dell alongside a stream approached by a gate and stoned arch proclaiming it the 'Priory Walk,' it contained benches with poems by the contemporary poets on the back of them (LHEL vol 2 pp96-102). **Shepherd's Bush**. View-vantage point (LHEL vol 2 p142). An urn to the memory of poet, William Somerville (1675-1742) (LHEL vol II p115). Virgil's Grove. C18 pleasure ground containing mazes and an obelisk under the shade of old oaks. The obelisk having an inscription to the genius of Virgil (LHEL Vol 2 pp126,197,198,199). During the residence of Matthias Attwood the grounds became somewhat neglected, with the public allowed to roam freely, and a summerhouse was defaced with the graffiti that so shocked Byron (AOBC p53).

Lion Colliery Old Hill, W of Oldbury. It had a disaster on Dec 26 1834 in which seven miners lost their lives (TB March 1986 p15).

Lodgefield 1.25m S of Rowley Regis, close to Staffs border. Comparatively populous hamlet in 1851 (TB June 1997 p20). The name is preserved in Lodgefield Road off Combes Road (Birmingham A-Z).

Londonderry Former hamlet now a district on the Smethwick Oldbury border (BCM Jan 1977 p56). The name occurs as London Derry in 1841 (census return). The ecclesiastical parish of Londonderry was created in 1929 from the ecclesiastical parishes of The Quinton (Worcs), Oldbury (Worcs), and Smethwick (GLAUE p416). The church, St Mark, in Hales Lane, was built in 1935-1936 (VCH vol 17 p129).

Lower Illey To the SW of Illey over 1.5m SSE of Halesowen.

Low Town Oldbury. Here Jack Judge, born in Oldbury (see), writer of the popular song 'It's a long way to Tipperary' (1912), was a fishmonger near the 'Junction,' Low Town. He died in 1938 at Whiteheath Gate (see) (ORR p129p). Others have attributed Jack Yorke of West Bromwich (see) with writing the song.

Murder House, The Stood or stands at Cocksheds Lezzers near Coombeswood. It was said to have been the scene of a terrible murder, where a father, Joseph Harris, an inmate of Powick Lunatic Asylum, killed his wife and two children by throat cutting or with a hatchet on Feb 5 1878. Tradition has it that this made the house haunted. Some have tried to stay a night in the house as a dare but have never succeeded (BCWJ p105) (TB June/ July 1972 p10. Nov 1984 p7).

Oldbury Black Country town by a tributary of the Tame 21.5m SSE of Stafford, 23.5m NNE of Worcester, 34m SE of Shrewsbury. Former township and chapelry in Halesowen ancient parish. Is wrongly shown in Staffs on the maps of Speed and Bowen. The **Roman** forts at Pennocrucium and Metchley were connected by a road which passed through Tipton and Oldbury according to E Chitham in his 'The Black Country' (WFW p32). There was reputedly a Roman fort here. A very old resident informed Hackwood that his father had seen ruins near a pasture called Castle Leasow; and that a castle was said to have stood at the lower end of Castle Leasow near the Well Hill. He added that a causeway still remains in the lands of one Harold directly leading to the Castle Leasow (RS pp37-38). The **name**, according to Erdeswick, may be derived from old borough or old burh (RS pp37-38). The **church**, Christ Church, was built at the expense of the Oldbury People in 1529 (O pp93-94). In 1832 Oldbury wake due to take place on Sunday Sept 2 and two days following was postponed because of the cholera epidemic (TB Feb 1998 p17). The Staffordshire Yeomanry were sent to quell the Oldbury Collier riots of 1833 (info Yeomanry Museum). **Lloyd's Bank** set up its first branch at Oldbury in 1864, apparently for no other reason than to save one of its best industrial customers from having to send a coach to Birmingham to collect money for wages. The premises - 30 Birmingham Street - are still occupied by a bank (Portrait of the Black Country. Harold Parsons. 1986 p113). A fountain with a statue of a woman known locally as **'Polly'** in the centre of Oldbury was knocked down by a Christmas reveller in 1948. It was bequeathed by Mr David Taylor (d1882) and probably erected in c1885/7. The statue of 'Polly' was in the garden of Mr Nightingale in Barnford Crescent until he died in 1950. It was passed on to a number of people in the area until it went to Trowbridge, Wilts. In 1969 it was reclaimed for Oldbury by Mr F Savage (BCM Oct 1969 pp7-8). By 1980 the **smallest tubing** in the world was still that made by Accles & Pollock Ltd of Oldbury. On Sept 9 1963 they announced a pure nickel tube with an outer diameter of 0.0005 inch and an inner diameter of 0.00013 inch (GBR 1980 p155). By 1999 was a ward in Sandwell metropolitan borough. **Persons**. **Jack Judge**, composer, was born in Oldbury in 1872. He became a popular music hall artist and went on tour. It was whilst he was appearing at Stalybridge, Ches, that, he reputedly made a bet that he could write and produce a song in one night. He won his bet by singing that same night, Jan 31 1912, 'It's a long way to Tipperary.' Some say Harry Williams of Balsall Common, Warws, who sometimes worked with Judge, was the originator of the song. Judge was also a fishmonger at Low Town (see). He died in 1938 at Whiteheath Gate (see) and is buried in Rood End Cemetery. In 1953 a memorial tablet commemorating Judge as the originator was erected at Shalybridge (Portrait of the Black Country. Harold Parsons. 1986 p113) (TB Oct 1987 pp12-13. Nov 1987 p13p. Jan 1988 p16) (ORR p129p) (BCM June 1998 pp73-74) (Jack Judge: The Tipperary Man. Verna Hale Gibbons. 1998). Others have attributed Jack Yorke of West Bromwich (see) with writing the song. **Tom Luxton** of Oldbury played an accordion for 84 hours from Aug 4-7 1982 (GBR 1987 p163).

Oldbury Loop Canal Formerly a part of Brindley's Birmingham Old Cut Old Main Line. Was truncated in 1821 (BCM autumn 1995 pp22-23).

Oldbury Old Manor Stood close to Blakeley Hall, Oldbury. Oldbury probably became a separate manor after 1557, after the dissolution of Halesowen Abbey, when Sir Robert Dudley took possession. From Sir Robert Dudley it passed to his wife Amy Robsart. From her it passed to her brother Arthur Robsart, who according to W Ellery Jephcott, took up residence at Blakeley Hall. In the early C17 the manor passed to his grandson, Robert. In the C17 it passed to the Turtons who sold it to Charles Cornwallis. Charles Cornwallis was in residence, according to W Ellery Jephcott, at Blakeley Hall between 1635 and 1640. The manor passed to his heiresses. Later, it had various owners, but none of those was resident (STELE Dec 22 1951). The original manor house was a C14 half-timbered building with a moat and appears to have survived until c1768. It was situated further from the road than Blakeley Hall Farm (TB March 1976 p18p) (ORR p25).

Olive House Occupied in 1851 Thomas Jones (W p22). The Olive Hill on the 1834 OS map lay in the area of Olive Hill Road in Coombeswood, N of Halesowen.

New Hawne Colliery Hawne. New Hawne Colliery is Great Mawne Colliery in Francis Brett Young's novels (BCM autumn 1989 p58).

Perryfields 0.75m WSW of Warley Abbey.

Quinton Former village now a suburb 2.25m S of Oldbury. Former township of Halesowen ancient parish. It has been thought Quinton was on a branch Roman road leading to Ryknild Street, yet no evidence of Roman occupation has been found (SNSV vol 2 p101). Nash thought the **name** derived from the sport known as quintain, brought to Britain by the Romans, and practised in medieval times (Collections for a History of Worcestershire. Rev TR Nash vol 1 p508) (SNSV vol 2 p101). It may derive its name from the meeting of five ways (WMVB p128). Hackwood suggested that Quinton was derived from the Anglo-Saxon word 'cwena,' 'a woman,' so 'the woman's town' (SNSV vol 2 p101). A Mawer and FM Stenton in 'The Place-Names of Worcestershire' (1927) suggested that Quinton was derived from Anglo-Saxon 'Cwenington' meaning 'the farm of Cwena (a personal name)' (SNSV vol 2 p101). Has appeared as Quenton (1221. 1275), Quintain (1658), Queynton (1665), Quintane (1679) (SNSV vol 2 p101) Quinton had a windmill situated at SP 002847, outside Staffs (WBJ p33). Quinton ecclesiastical parish was created in 1841 (STELE May 10 1957). The **church**, Christ Church, Hagley Road, was built in 1840 and restored in 1890 (BOEWA p200). Quinton Road West ecclesiastical parish was created out of The Quinton ecclesiastical parish (Worcs) and Harborne ancient parish (Staffs) in 1958 (GLAUE p420). The church for that parish, St Boniface, Quinton Road West, was built in 1958-1959 (BOEWA p200). Quinton is Tilton in Francis Brett Young's novels (BCM autumn 1989 p58).

Radnall Field Oldbury (JEPS No. 18 pp5-12).

Red Cow Inn Former inn of the lost village of Kenelmstowe. The name commemorated the red cow immortalised in the Kenelm legend (St Kenelm Church Guide. 1976. p6).

Redhall Farm In Ridgacre (JEPS No. 18 pp5-12). Probably at Redall Hill (see).

Ridgacre Former township of Halesowen ancient parish, and tiny hamlet on land rising N from the Bourn Brook that runs through Woodgate Valley, now a large residential district 2.25m ENE of Halesowen. The name means ploughed land on the ridge (WMVB p128) (SNSV vol 2 p102). Has appeared as Ruggacre (1309), Rudgeacre (1311), Ridgeacre (1431) (SNSV vol 2 p102). Ridgacre was intensely developed with housing after WW2 (SNSV vol 2 p102).

Round's Green Former hamlet now a district 0.75m WSW of Oldbury. The name appears on the Plan of the Mines of Lord Dudley 1812. A mine disaster here on Nov 17 1846 claimed the lives of 19 men and boys who died by roasting (TB July 1981 p11).

Saint Kenelms Fragmented tiny hamlet 1.5m NE of Clent on the NE slopes of the Clent Hills, centred on the Saxon church or chapel dedicated to the Saxon saint and prince Kenelm. The church and most of the cemetery was in Halesowen parish, yet the S and W part was supposed to be in Clent (SHOS vol 2 p243). A more compact little hamlet of Kenelmstowe, situated by the church, was deserted long ago.

Saint Kenelm's Well Is near St Kenelm church (NHS pp411-413), at SO 945808. Near the spring, according to tradition, was found the body of St Kenelm (SW pp123-124,192). St Kenelm's church is built upon a pagan well (BCWJ opposite title page; Wilson-Jones, possibly means the church was built by the well, unless there were two wells). There is another St Kenelm's Well at Winchcombe, Glous (SW p124).

Sampson Colliery W of Oldbury.

Tat Bank District over 0.5m SE of Oldbury.

Thimble Mill Small hamlet 2m SE of Oldbury. Now submerged into the residential suburbs of Oldbury and Smethwick. Transferred to Smethwick borough, Staffs, in 1928. The mill from which the hamlet took its name stood on Thimblemill Brook at what is now the junction of Thimblemill Road and Norman Road. The mill was known as Thimble Mill by 1775 (VCH vol 17 p109). It was originally a corn mill but was converted to thimble making in the C18. In the 1830s it was used by WW Blyth for the cutting of files by machinery. It reverted to a corn mill in 1845 when William Summerton took over. The remains of the mill were still standing in the 1890s (ORR p68p of the mill in 1890s).

Thimblemill Pool Pool at Thimble Mill.

Tiger Colliery W of Oldbury.

Timmins Hill Or Blower's Hill.

Titford Canal or Branch of the Birmingham Canal. Diverges from the Birmingham Canal Old Main Line S of Oldbury. Passes through the Titford Locks (Canals of The West Midlands. Charles Hadfield. vol 5 of The Canals of The British Isles. see map p67) or Oldbury Locks (Birmingham A-Z) to end at Whiteheath Gate. Opened in 1837 (HCMS No. 2). Developed around a reservoir in Titford Valley that had been feeding the Birmingham Canal since 1770. Restored between 1972 and 1974. Has branches to Causeway Green and to Portway.

Titford Colliery E of Whiteheath Gate. It had a disaster on July 23 1874 which killed six miners (TB May 1991 p5).

Titford Reservoir Reservoir 0.25m SW of Oldbury.

Tor Abbey See Warley Abbey.

Uffmore Farm, lane and wood lie to the E and N of St Kenelm's chapel (CR p34).

Walloxall Former ancient hamlet in Halesowen ancient parish and gave or derived its name from a family resident here. Other spellings include Walloxhill, Wallokshale, Walloxhale, and Wallokeshale (1309). The prefix is from

Anglo-Saxon masculine personal name Wealuc, and the meaning is Wealuc's meadow land (STELE Dec 8 1951).

Warley Name for the newest of the five Black Country Staffs boroughs. Formed on April 1 1966 by the amalgamation of the county borough of Smethwick and the boroughs of Oldbury and Rowley Regis (BCM April 1968 pp24-26. July 1968 pp66-67). The name is from the manors of Warley, Warley Abbey and Warley Bank, none of which were in Staffs, originally. Warley has appeared as Wernlegh (1292), Wernley (C15), Werneley (C15) (BCM April 1968 p39). A phantom horseman and the 'Grey Lady' ghost were seen by a man in Bleakhouse Lane in the early 1920s (TB Jan 1996 p1). A lady was injured when she touched a ball of lightning which appeared in her kitchen during a thunderstorm in Warley borough on Aug 8 1975 (MMSE pp88,292) (Nature No. 260 1976 p596) (New Scientist No. 1976 p128) (Lightning GLB10X9).

Warley Abbey In the middle of Warley Park, Warley Salop, close to former Staffs border. (BCM April 1968 pp38-39). Built in the Gothic-style by Robert Lugar for Hubert Galton between 1818-1822. Said to have been built on or near the site of a grange of Halesowen Abbey (SHCB p3) (BCM April 1968 p38); a possible moat (lost by 1976) nearby at SP 011862 may represent the site of the grange (STELE 1957) (SSAHST 1982-3 p50). Because of the house's proximity to the supposed grange, the house was called an abbey. It has also appeared as Warley Hall and Tor Abbey, the last name being a reference to a height in the vicinity or the moat of the former grange of Halesowen Abbey (STELE Aug 29 1952) (SSAHST 1982-3 p50). In the late C19 Warley Abbey was thought, wrongly, to date back to medieval times. From at least 1845 the house was leased to John Edwards Piercy (TB Feb 1996 p5). It was some time seat of the Tangye family. By 1888 it was the seat of the newspaper tycoon Hugh Gilzean Reid. During his residency William Gladstone PM and other contemporary notable people were entertained here. The house was in a poor state of repair in 1955 and was demolished in 1957 (ORR p55p) (TB Jan 1996 p5p). The house was reputedly haunted by the 'Grey Lady' ghost, who may be Lady Joan de Somery, a member of the de Somery family of Dudley Castle (see), who willed Warley Wigorn to Halesowen Abbey on condition the monks pray for her soul annually at the abbey gates. When this ceased at the Dissolution it may have awakened her spirit. Others think this unlikely. The last reliable sighting of the 'Grey Lady' was in 1922 (TB Jan 1979 pp19-20ps. Sept 1991 p5. Feb 1996 p5). For the grounds see Warley Park.

Warley Hall Formerly situated not far from Warley Abbey (or Hall) on the site of what is now Warley Hall Road. It was in existence by at least 1576 and was a far older building than Warley Abbey (TB Feb 1996 p5). The name Wartley Hall appears in 1603 (STELE? Sept 29 1951).

Warley Park Former grounds of Warley Abbey. The park is said to have been landscaped by Humphry Repton in the 1790s for Samuel Galton. The Warley Abbey estate was acquired by Birmingham corporation in 1906 and the grounds opened as a public park (ORR p54p). The Grecian Temple, which still stood in the blue bell wood facing Warley Abbey in 1903, was pulled down soon after 1906 (STELE May 3 1957) (ORR p56p). The body of Samuel Whitehouse, murdered on the Halesowen turnpike road at Bearwood (see) in 1822, was found at a spot near the edge of the present park.

Warley Salop Manor anciently forming part of the Dudley Barony. It was the possession of Halesowen Abbey by 1214 (TB Feb 1996 p5). The manor seems to have had many portions dispersed between portions of Warley Wigorn manor (Worcs). Warley Salop was included in Quinton ecclesiastical parish, created in 1841 (STELE May 10 1957).

Warley Tor See Warley Abbey.

Warley Woods Former civil parish in Smethwick county borough, Staffs created in 1928 from Oldbury urban district and civil parish, Worcs. It was abolished in 1966 to enter the county boroughs of West Bromwich (Staffs), Birmingham (Warws), and Warley (Worcs) (GLAUE pp422,427). The church, St Hilda, in Rathbone Road, was built in 1938-1940 (VCH vol 17 p128). Somewhere in the area covered by the later civil parish occurred the murder of Zee Ming Wu, a Chinese national. The man convicted of the murder, Djang Djin Sung, was hung at Worcester in 1919 (TB Oct 1988 p4). Marjorie Vernon (pseudonym Miss M Cottam), romantic novelist, born in Wolverhampton, lived in Harborne Road, Warley Woods.; her first novel was published in 1946 (VFC p136).

Whiteheath Gate Rowley Regis.*

White Horse Colliery Colliery W of Oldbury. SE side of Timmins Hill.

Worlds End To W of Tennal Hall, S of Warley Abbey.

WARWICKSHIRE

The C17 maps of Morden and Bowen show Staffs protruding out to No Man's Heath and it has been suggested that this area was unappropriated common land until the C19. The Warws side of Tamworth town and Tamworth castle were taken into Staffs in 1890 (SL p29) or 1894 (GLAUE p425). The Staffs boundary was further extended in 1932 to take in parts of the civil parishes of Amington and Stoneydelph, Bolehall and Glascote, and Wilnecote and Castle Liberty. In 1965 it was extended still further to take in the rest of Amington and Glascote civil parishes, and parts of the Warws civil parishes of Dordon, and Wilnecote and Castle Liberty as well as parts of the Warws ancient parishes of Kingsbury, Polesworth, and Shuttington (GLAUE p425). A stretch less than 0.5m wide protruding into Staffs up to Little Hay, SE of Shenstone, was taken into Staffs in 1966. A piece of Staffs which extended for 0.25m E of Rosemary Hill Road, Streetly, was removed to Warws in 1966 (OS maps 1834. 1980) (GLAUE p422). Harborne ancient parish (excluding Smethwick county borough) was removed to Birmingham county borough (Warws) in 1891. Handsworth urban district was removed to Birmingham county borough (Warws) in 1911. Much of Perry Barr urban district was transferred to Birmingham county borough (Warws) in 1928 (GLAUE p419). Smethwick county borough entered the new borough of Warley (Worcs) in 1966.

Amington See main body of encyclopaedia.

Ash Hay Probable medieval enclosure within Sutton Coldfield Chase. In 1289 it appears to have been taken into Weeford Park (SHOS vol 2 p23) (SSAHST 1988-89 p50).

Avon Dasset See Dasset Parva.

Bascote 7.5m E of Warwick. The estate of Thomas Moseley. The revenue from it endowed the famous Moseley's Dole in Walsall (W p645).

Belgrave See main body of encyclopaedia.

Birmingham Very large city, lying close to former Staffs border. It is North Bromwich in Francis Brett Young's novels.

Bishop's Itchington Village 7m SE of Warwick. Prebend in Lichfield cathedral, founded by Roger de Clinton. In the Confirmation of Archbishop Boniface (living in 1259) the prebend is called Bishops Itchington and Chadleshunt (Chadshunt) (SSAHST vol 2 1960-61 p43) (VCH vol 3 p141). By the late C20 the prebendary held the office of Precentor in the cathedral (LDD).

Bishop's Tachbrook See Tachbrook.

Bobenhall Prebend in Lichfield cathedral (SHOS vol 1 p291), founded by Roger de Weseham in c1245 (SSAHST vol 2 1960-61 p44). Has also appeared as Bobenhull. Is possibly the village of Bubbenhall 4m SSE of Coventry.

Bole Hall See main body of encyclopaedia.

Bolehall See main body of encyclopaedia.

Castle Liberty See main body of encyclopaedia.

Coleshill Colsale has been identified with Coleshill. The name 'Jhoannes de Colsale' is inscribed on the bell in Milwich church (LGS p188).

Dasset Parva Prebend in Lichfield cathedral (SHOS vol 1 p291). Founded by Roger de Clinton in the C12. In 1706 John Hunter, Dr Johnson's schoolmaster was appointed to this prebendal stall (SSAHST vol 2 1960-61 p45) (VCH vol 3 p143). The prebend has appeared as Little Dassett, and Darset. It is now Avon Dasset, a small village, 10.25m SE of Warwick.

Deritend In the Bordesley area of Birmingham. E of the city centre.

Dernford A prebend in Lichfield cathedral founded by Bishop Clinton (SHOS vol 1 p291). In existence by 1255 (VCH vol 3 p143). Dr Falconer held the prebend in 1784 (SSAHST vol 2 1960-61 p45). It appears to have been confused with Darnford near Lichfield.

Dosthill, Colliery, House, Lodge, Old Manor House. Tamworth.*

Farmer's Bridge Junction Junction of the Birmingham Canal New Cut New Main Line with the Birmingham & Fazeley Canal (SWY p11). S of Newhall Hill, W of Birmingham.

Gib Heath Former common land of Birmingham, on S side of Hockley Brook, adjoining Soho Heath. The area was first settled in the late C18 by workers at the nearby Soho Manufactory; the erection of artisans' dwellings for them in the vicinity of the manufactory had been forbidden by the vestrymen of Handsworth, fearing an influx of men without parish certificates (which made their home parishes responsible for them if they became paupers) (MNB p41).

Gibbett Hill The present Oscott College is situated on this hill. In 1729 a man was hung on Gibbett Hill for murder and highway robbery (DOB p66).

Glascote, Heath. See main body of encyclopaedia.

Harborne Hill Hill in Edgbaston (HOPP pl 63).

Hemlingford NW hundred of Warws which included Birmingham and bordered with Offlow hundred (SHOS vol 1 appendix p22).

Hockley Soho.

Hockley, Brook, Hall, hall-colliery. See main body of encyclopaedia.

Kettlebrook, Colliery. See main body of encyclopaedia.

Lozells Hamlet close to Staffs border, S of Heathfield, 1.25m NNW of Birmingham. In the mid C19 it was implied that it was in Handsworth parish (W p698). The name is said to be a corruption of 'The Louse Hills,' which according to tradition was the old name for this high-situated district (HPPE p68). It is traditionally accepted that Aston Villa Football Club was formed by the young men of Lozells Road Wesleyan Chapel in 1874 and that it took its name from a large house which stood on the corner of the Heathfield and Lozells Roads, which may have been situated in Staffs. The club played their early matches in Aston Park but moved to a site in Wellington Road, Birchfield in Sept 1876 (Aston Villa: A Portrait in Old Picture Postcards. Derrick Spinks. 1991 pvi). By the mid C20 the area was merged into the Birmingham conurbation.

Metchley Just beyond former Staffs border, to ENE of Harborne. There was a Roman camp at Metchley in c48 AD. It covered the area where the Medical School and the University of Birmingham Station now stands. It guarded the crossing of the Bournbrook by the Icknield Street. The Roman roads from Droitwich and Pennocrucium also converge here (HOHE p1) (WFW p32). Others say the camp is either of Celtic, or Roman, or Saxon origin (RS pp9-11).

Metchley Park Near Harborne. Was in Warws (VCHWA vol 7 pp23,50).

Middleton Hall 0.5m S of Drayton Bassett. John Peel, son of Thomas Peel, died here in 1872.

Nineveh A group of cottages near Nineveh Road, close to the Staffs border, S of Soho. It was the site of what was called locally 'The City of Nineveh' (HPPE p88).

New Oscott Residential district 2m ESE of Great Barr. Called New Oscott after the removal to here of Oscott College, or St Mary's College, from Oscott (Old Oscott) 2m to the W. The new college, designed by Joseph Potter of Lichfield, opened in 1838. It was built just outside Staffs in Erdington parish, to the SE of Jordan's Grave on common land (KPP p16) (BOEWA pp196-199) (MNB p72). When aged 24 the architect AWN Pugin was appointed Professor of Ecclesiastical Art and Antiquities at the college at the request of Lord Shrewsbury. Lectures given to students at the college formed the nucleus of Pugin's most original and influential book 'The True Principles of Pointed or Christian Architecture' (1841) (A Vision of Splendour: Gothic Revival in Staffordshire 1840-1890. Michael Fisher. 1995 pp81,103). There is a chair at Oscott College, traditionally believed to belong to Andrew Bromwich, a Catholic recusant of Old Oscott (see) (Maryvale. Beth Penny. 1985 p3p) A highwayman hung and gibbeted by the Chester Road is said to haunt the spot where Oscott College now stands (FSLBWM p42).

No Man's Heath Village 1.75m E of Thorpe Constantine. It developed on part of, or adjoining, wasteland commonly called The Heath (see), or Clifton and Newton Common, over which only Chilcote township in Clifton Campville ancient parish had common rights. This part of the common may never have been appropriated to any township, hence the name (NSFCT 1913 p48). Has also appeared as Nomans Heath. The area began to be settled with squatters in the mid C19 (IOM p153). No Man's Heath was a favourite spot for pugilist combats and cock-fighting on account of its closeness to Derbys, Leics and Warws which could be easily entered to evade the Staffs authorities (TB June 1995 p18). Here was a cross cut into the turf to mark the converging points of Leics, Staffs, Derbys, and Warws (W p597). In 1951 the licensee of The Four Counties Inn, No Man's Heath, paid his water rate to Staffs, general rate to Warws, excise licence to Derbys, and telephone bill to Leics. If there was an accident outside his house, the Leics police intervened. If it occurred on the pavement, that was the affair of Warws. By 1951 the inn reputedly stood half-an-inch over the Warws border; but at one time the four counties met at the fireplace in the parlour (IOM pp153-154).

Oloughton Alias Ufton. Prebend of Lichfield cathedral.

Park Colliery See main body of encyclopaedia.

Perry Common Residential suburb 2.75m ESE of Great Barr. Laid out, and named 'Perry Common,' by Birmingham Corporation on the former Witton Lodge estate in N Witton in Erdington parish, Warwickshire, in the 1920s and 1930s (MNB p75).

Perry Crofts See main body of encyclopaedia.

Perry Well Situated in Witton in Erdington parish. Sunk in the 1870s (MNB p76). Perry Well Pumping Station S of College Road preserves the name.

Pipe Hall Seat of Egerton Bagot who had in his possession the copy of the Lichfield Surrender Articles (HOL p34 note).

Quarry Hill See main body of encyclopaedia.

Rotton Park To E of Three Shire Oak. The name is from a medieval deer park, which extended to Smethwick in Staffs, and comprised the land from Ladywood to the Cape of Good Hope, from Spring Hill south westward to the Holly Bush. The deer park may have had its name from Rounton as in Rowton Well, Sutton Park, or from the Rotton family, or from Rout, a herd of wild beasts. The park, which was enclosed by the lords of Birmingham, may have existed by 1225 and certainly by 1307, when it was known as Parcus de Rotten. The lord of Birmingham held it to c1528. The estate passed to the crown for a time in the C16. It was granted to Thomas Marrow in 1555 and was acquired from the Marrows by Humphrey Perrott of Bell Hall, Belbroughton, Worcs in 1628. The estate broke up later in the C17 with the creation of the Poplar estate and other estates (STELE July 27 1956. Aug 17 1956).

Rowton's Well Sutton Park, close to the Staffs border. Supposed to have been a Roman bathing place (HOWW p24).

Ruiton Prebend in Lichfield cathedral (SHOS vol 1 p293). Founded by Roger de Clinton. It is now called Ryton-under-Dunsmore a small village 3.5m SE of Coventry (SSAHST vol 2 1960-61 p48). By the late C20 the Ryton prebendary held the office of Fourth Canon or Custos in the cathedral (LDD). White identifies Ruiton with Ruiton near Upper Gornal (W p200).

Short Heath Suburb of Birmingham, 4m SE of Great Barr, SE of Perry Common.

Shuttington To E of Shuttington Bridge, Staffs.

Shuttington Bridge See main body of encyclopaedia.

Soho Loop When a winding section of Brindley's Birmingham Canal Old Cut Old Main Line about Winson Green was superseded by the straight New Cut New Main Line in 1827 the old section became the Soho Loop (HCMS No. 2).

Stonydelph See main body of encyclopaedia.

Sutton Park Large public park adoining Great Barr on the E side, so that the W edge formed the boundary with Staffs. The park is believed to be haunted by the ghost of Tom King, a highwayman who was burnt to death for his crimes (FSLBWM p42).

Tachbrook Prebend in Lichfield cathedral (SHOS vol 1 p293), founded by Roger de Clinton (SSAHST vol 2 1960-61 p50). Has also appeared as Tackbrook and is now Bishop's Tachbrook, a village 2.5m SE of Warwick.

Tamworth Colliery Situated by Alvecote, outside Tamworth ancient parish, at SK 247045. In existence in 1888 (1888 OS map 6 inch).

Tardebigge See Worcestershire.

Thistley Field Tamworth.*

Two Gates Tamworth.*

Ufton Parish and small village 5.25m ESE of Warwick Warws. Has also appeared as Ulverton. Here are two prebends in Lichfield cathedral representing roughly two equal divisions of land and buildings in Ufton parish. Ufton Decani or Ulveton alias Oloughton ex parte Decani was founded by Roger de Clinton in the C12; Rev William Buckley (?1520-?1570), poet obituarist and mathematician born at Lichfield, was prebendary of this prebend (VFC p21). The other prebend is known as Ufton Cantoris or Ulveton alias Oloughton ex Parte Cantoris sive Precentoris (SHOS vol 1 pp294-295) (SSAHST vol 2 1960-61 p50) (VCH vol 3 p141). Edmund de Stafford (1344-1419) of Clifton Campville, Staffs, bishop of Exeter, was prebendary of Ufton in 1369.

Ulveton Alias Ufton.

Warwickshire Moor Tamworth.*

White's Hill Tamworth.*

Wilnecote, Colliery, Hall. Tamworth.*

Witton Former village N of Birmingham. Witton Hall is just over 2m ENE of Handsworth parish church. Ecclesiastical parish created in 1926 from Birchfield ecclesiastical parish (Staffs), and Aston juxta Birmingham ancient parish (Warws, in Birmingham diocese) to be in Lichfield diocese (GLAUE p429).

Wolvey Prebend in Lichfield cathedral founded by Bishop Muschamp. It is a small village 7m NE of Coventry (SHOS vol 1 p297) (SSAHST vol 2 1960-61 p51) in c1200 (VCH vol 3 p143).

WORCESTERSHIRE

Clent and Broome ancient parishes, forming an enclave of Staffs surrounded by Worcs from c1016, were returned to Worcs for parliamentary purposes in 1832 and removed to Halfshire hundred for all purposes in 1844. Tongue-like Arley ancient parish was removed to Worcs in 1894-5 (SL p29).

Arley Kings 1m S of Stourport. Could be confused with Arley, Staffs. The C13 poet priest Layamon lived at Arley Kings (Green's History of the English People p121). Has also appeared as Areley Kings and Lower Arley.

Belle Vale Cradley. Former meeting point of Worcs, Staffs and Shrops. The name is still preserved in Bellevale Forge. (TB April 1972 pp6-7ps).

Bewdley Extra-parochial liberty. In Staffs in the C15 although usually considered in Worcs. Its status in Worcs was asserted by statute in 1543 (GLAUE p403).

Bouchall Small hamlet appearing on 1882 OS map S of the Stour, close to the former Staffs border, 0.75m ENE of Stourbridge. The present small area is still called Bouchall (Birmingham A-Z. 1995).

Breadboys Colliery Netherend. Close to the Staffs border.

Broadstone Inn The old inn sign from a pub of this name hangs on a modern inn in Oldnall Road, Cradley. The name is probably from the local stone quarried in the vicinity. A piece of the stone appears, or is incorporated into the inn sign (BCM Oct 1983 p26p).

Carne A hundred of Worcestershire. Oldbury and Warley Wigorn were in it (TB Jan 1979 pp19-20).

Castle Hill Near Kingsford, Worcs (LGS p157). Or called Baron Hill. The royal hunting lodge of Kinver Forest was situated on it.

Colemore Farm of 15 acres near Coleman Hill (formerly Colemore Hill) (BCWJ p74) (TB Nov Dec 1973 p16). The lost hamlet of Colman Hill (1834 OS map) was a mile SE of Cradley. The name is preserved in a road called Colman Hill.

Colley Gate SE of Cradley (SVS p239).

Cradley Black Country town just in Worcs 1m S of Cradley Heath or approximately 20m NNE of Worcester. In 1828 a small coin of Titus Vespasian was found in Cradley Field (SVS p239 note). The name means 'Cridda's ley' (O p22). The present form is pronounced with a long 'a' (BCSG p58). Scott noted to the E of Cradley Park a moated hillock (SVS p240). Cradley Railway Station is just in Staffs at Cradley Forge.

Crow's Rock Rock feature with a cave on Kinver Edge, 1.25m WSW of Kinver church, S of Nanny's Rock. Formerly, and for a long time, known as Vale's Rock. It contained one cave house which was inhabited until the 1960s by a maker of besom brooms. The house had two levels, on each level were many compartments (KRH p19 pls10,11,12) (SVB p107). It has been suggested that Cynefares Stane, a boundary stone mentioned in 964, was Vale's Rock (BAST vol 53 pp108-109) (VCH vol 20 p119 note).

Cuthred's Tree A tree mentioned in a charter of 866 relating to Wolverley, near Kinver. It probably refers to King Cuthred, king of the West Saxons (740-756) (DUIGNAN pp87-88).

Drew's Brook At Cradley. Formed former boundary between Worcs and Shrops ran into the Stour where the three counties of Staffs, Shrops, and Worcs met at Belle Vale.

Gorsty Hill Former small hamlet which existed in the C19. It stood on the edge of a track which led from Halesowen to Rowley Regis. The name is preserved in Gorsty Hill Road SW of Blackheath on Staffs Worcs border. Has appeared as Gosty Hill (W p193), and appears on 1947 OS map 1:25,000 (sheet 32/99). (JEPS No.18 pp5-12). Some say it lies in Rowley Regis parish (SGSAS). However, it can be seen on some maps just in Worcs. The novel 'Ghost in the Water' by Edward Chitham (1973) is set in and around Gosty Hill.

Hagley Hall 2.5m SE of Stourbridge. Part of the park of the hall may have been on Clent Hill and consequently in Staffs (SVS p250). To the ENE is Hagley Wood where there was found in 1941 or 1943 a female skeleton in a rotten and gnarled wych elm. The skeleton has never been identified and has been named 'Bella.' Her identity, and that of her murderer - who presumably put her body in the wych elm - are subjects of much speculation in TB. The lady could have been a Dutch girl called Clara Dronkers, or a victim of a Black Magic execution; a hand was found at some distance from the body (E&S 1943) (TB Feb 1993 pp1,30-31. March 1994 pp30-31p. April 1994 pp20-21) (Black Country Ghosts and Mysteries. Aristotle Tump. 1987) (BBC Radio 4. 'PM' programme. Aug 11 1999).

Harborough Hagley parish. White mentions it under Broome. An ancient mansion it was the seat of William Penn, one of whose daughters was mother of the poet Shenstone, who visited Harborough in his childhood (W p169).

High Town Cradley (TB Jan 1982 p5).

Homer Hill Hill at Cradley (SVS p237).

Hungary Hill S of the Stour in Stourbridge, just in Worcs. Coal mine near Old Swinford (SVS p399).

Kingsford 2m SW of Kinver.

Little Ireland Former local name for the Crown Lane area of Stourbridge because it was the residence of many Irish immigrants in the mid C19 (TB Dec 1997 p10).

Lutley Hamlet 1.75m WSW of Halesowen. It lay in the Wolverhampton (see) Deanery manor (HOWM p26). Lutley Gutter is Lapsley Brook in Francis Brett Young's novels (BCM autumn 1989 p58).

Lyde Green Small hamlet appearing on 1882 OS map S of the Stour, close to the former Staffs border, 0.25m WNW of Cradley. The name is preserved in the street Lyde Green (Birmingham A-Z).

Lye, River (Etymology in BCM April 1971 p26).

Lye Cross Hamlet of Lye. (BCWJ). Here was one of four wayside crosses marking the boundary of Halesowen Abbey lands. The others were at Haden Cross, Holy Cross and Rood End (BCWJ p64).

Lyecross Colliery Known locally as The Big Pit (TB Jan 1983 p13).

Netherend To the W of Cradley (SVS p237).

Overend Cradley (SVS p237). Appears on 1947 OS map 1:25,000 (sheet 32/98), at SO 950850, in Staffs.

Old Swinford Ancient parish which included the township of Amblecote, Staffs, until 1844. Former small village S of Stourbridge. It is now a suburb of that town (VCH vol 2 p227).

Pidock Just S of the Stour by Lye.

Pidock Park N of Stourbridge. Existing in 1812 (TB Aug 1984 p14).

Rednall Hill An eminence in the Clent Hills to E of Ruebury Hill N of Hagley Hall (SVS p295).

Romsley Large village to the N of Romsley Hill, a hill in the Clent Hills, 2m E of Clent. Has never been in Staffs, although, occasionally placed within the Clent detached portion on old maps. It is not in Staffs according to Yates' map. It has been suggested that the Hremesleage mentioned in the will of Wulfric Spot (c1002), founder of Burton Abbey, is this Romsley (SHC 1916 p34). Romsley is Brimsley in Francis Brett Young's novels (BCM autumn 1989 p58).

Saltbrook End Small hamlet appearing on 1882 OS map S of the Stour, close to the former Staffs border, 0.75m WSW of Cradley. The name is preserved in Saltbrook Road (Birmingham A-Z).

Smart's Green Farm just beyond Staffs border. S of Compton Park.

Stakenbridge Tiny hamlet 1m NW of Broom or 2.5m W of Clent.

Stambermill Part of Lye, Stourbridge, close to the Stour (OS map 1:25,000. 1972).

Suicide Bridge Near The Hayes at Netherend. A bridge, perhaps over Salt Brook, reputedly haunted by the ghosts of a courting couple and if seen by a courting couple a misfortune is said to befall one of them (BCWJ p106).

Tardebigge C11 vill ESE of Bromsgrove, formerly Tardebig. It was bought by a courtier called Æthelsige, from the king, who also bought the nearby vill of Clent. Æthelsige intended to grant them to Worcester cathedral but on Æthelsige's death in c1016 the sheriff of Staffordshire seized them and is thought to have transferred them to Staffs for administrative convenience (SL p29). By 1300 it was reckoned that most of the vill had returned to Worcs with a remaining part forming a detached portion of Staffs in Worcs. By the later C18 that part seems to have been in a detached portion of Warws in Worcs (SHOS vol 2 p245).

Top Park Colliery Cradley (TB Jan 21 1999 p1).

Usmere see Ismere. A brook, a rivulet of Wolverley (SVS p375 note). The 'province of Husmere' is first recorded in 736 (Cart Sax 154) (DUIGNAN p122). There was a monastery here, on the border with Kinver Wood (SVS p162). The name is represented by Ismere House, Worcs, 2.25m SE of Kinver (DUIGNAN p122).

Vale's Rock See Crow's Rock.

West Hagley Large village in undulating country to the W of the Clent Hills, 1.5m WNW of Clent.

Windmill Hill Cradley.

Wollaston Former township and hamlet in Old Swinford ancient parish to W of Stourbridge. Ecclesiastically severed in 1845 from Old Swinford to help create Amblecote ecclesiastical parish. Became a separate ecclesiastical parish in 1860 (GLAUE pp401,429). Now a suburb of Stourbridge.

Wollescote Could be in Worcs. For 'Wollescote' as a verb see BCM April 1971 p27.

Wychbury Hill Hill with fort in the Clent Hills to the N of Hagley. In the later C17 Plot found three lows on Clent Heath (NHS p404) probably associated with this hill and hillfort. Various weapons, jars of Roman coins and other antiquities have been found in the vicinity of it. The fort could have been reused by the army of Henry IV in 1405 in pursuit of Owen Glendower (CR p55). (SHOS vol 2 p241). Has also appeared as Wichbury Hill (CR p55).

WORCESTERSHIRE (DUDLEY DETACHED)

Dudley ancient parish formed an enclave of Worcs in Staffs, measuring 11 miles in circumference. Curiously, it was not transferred by an Act of 1844 ordering detached portions of counties to be amalgamated; after 1888 the enclave was the only land detached from its county remaining in England. The area was a county borough from 1889. Some of Coseley urban district on the N side was added to it in 1929 (this was probably Dudley Castle Hill), and in 1954 (addition perhaps included the Mons Hill and Wrens Nest escarpment). Some of Rowley Regis metropolitan borough and Brierley Hill urban district on the S and W sides respectively were added to it in 1954. The enclave was incorporated into Staffs in 1966 but removed to the West Midlands metropolitan county in 1974 (HOS p57 see map) (SL pp29-30,170) (GLAUE pp404,409,420) (OS map Sheet 71.07).

Allport's Pool Pool that lay in an open space by the junction of Shaw Road and Blower's Green Road, Blower's Green. On Nov 25 1923, five boys fell into the pool through ice which had formed on it. They included Albert Edward Parkes, aged 16, Clifford Albert Smith, a chorister at St Thomas' church, Dudley, aged 15, his brother William Thomas Smith, Arthur Rollinson and Arthur Bill. James Horton of Water Street, Kingswinford, a sailor of HMS Hood, aged 19, travelling in a tramcar along Blower's Green Road, saw the disaster and went to their aid. In trying to pull them from the water Horton fell in and drowned. Albert Parkes and Clifford Smith also drowned, but Albert Snow, a father of an on-looker, saved the other boys: For his bravery Snow received a certificate from the Royal Humane Society. There is a memorial to Horton in Kingswinford churchyard. Another pool known as Samson Pool lay near Allport's Pool (mem in churchyard of St Thomas' church, Dudley) (The Dudley Herald Dec 1 1923 p11p) (KES pp120-121) (BCM Autumn 1999 pp32-33).

Baptist End Former hamlet now a suburb of N Netherton, under 1m S of Dudley. Baptist End received its name for it was here Baptists lived. The first Baptist church was built in 1654 near the White Swan Inn. Members of the church were baptised in the 'Warm Hole,' that part where the hot water from the blast furnaces entered the canal (NEE p4). Eventually the Baptists moved to Cinder Bank. Also there was a community of Kilhamites (Methodists), the followers of Alexander Kilham, at Baptist End. They had a meeting place in the 'Wire Yard,' but eventually they moved to Eagle Hill (NEE p27). Oliver Cromwell is said to have passed through Baptist End (NEE p4).

Baths Hill Formerly Stytches Bank, Netherton (NEE p7).

Black Brook Rises near Holly Hall, WSW of Dudley, and runs S of Saltwells SW of Netherton. Joins the Mousesweet Brook at Mushroom Green. Scott in the early 1830s called it Archill Brook. Just W of the Tipsyford Bridge is joined by Knowle Brook. Just S of its confluence with Mousesweet Brook was Cradley Pool, which was fed by these brooks (SNSV vol 1 p87).

Blackbrook Junction Junction of the Dudley Canal Line Two with the Two Lock Line (HCMS No. 2).

Blower's Green Hamlet 1m SW of Dudley. The name appears in the 1841 census. Blower's Green took its name from a local family (OS map Sheet 67.15). Is possibly Bloors' Green between Dudley and Pensnett (SVS p141).

Blue Bell Pit The pit, in operation in 1901, had closed by the outbreak of WW2 by which time it had given its name to Bluebell Road, Mouse Sweet (OS map Sheet 71.08).

Boat Inn St Peter's Road, Netherton. Closed in 1987. It was said to be haunted (GPCE p35).

Bowling Green Hamlet nearly 1m SSE of Netherton. The name appears in the 1841 census.

Brewins Tunnel Tiny tunnel in Dudley Canal Line Two near Highbridge Road, Netherton. Removed by 1994 (HCMS No. 2).

Buffery S of Dudley. Buffery Deeley had blast furnaces at the Buffery End of Bumble Hole Road (NEE p11). The name Buffery's Engine appears on A Plan of the intended Extension of the Dudley Canal into the Birmingham Canal by John Snape 1785. Old Buffery and New Buffery appear as areas for the 'Netherton District' general election in 1835 (NEE p30). The name Bufferies appears in the 1841 census.

Buffery Colliery An underground fire here on Jan 4 1875 killed four (NEE p14).

Buffery Park Dudley. An ironstone deposit site (VCH vol 2 p120), later a public park. Lenny Henry, comedian, grew up in the Buffery Park area and was a pupil at St James Infant and Blue Coat Secondary Modern schools (BCM spring 1996 p74). Has also appeared as Bufferies.

Bumble Hole District E of Netherton (BCM Oct 1986 pp47-50) (WBJ p34). About 1700 the area was the centre of the coal and iron industries; there was a glass house here founded in Queen Anne's reign (IISD p33). The name appears on the Plan of the Mines of Lord Dudley 1812. It is said to be from 'bum-l-ohe' the name for, or local term for the action of, an early steam hammer employed at the works of Bonney Haden (NEE p11). The fanciful cottage folly here known locally as 'Bumble Hole Castle' or 'Siah's Castle' was built over a 23 year period by a Netherton character called Siar (or Siah?). In its garden was a concrete policeman statue (NEE p34) (TB June July 1973 p25p). This became, or here was, an inn called 'The Malt Shovel,' which was frequented by Theophillus Dunn (TB Feb 1977 p10). Theophillus Dunn, alias Dudley Devil, a 'wise man' and cockfighter, allegedly lived in Bumble Hole. He is said to have predicted the 'Tipton Slasher' of Tipton (see). He died on Oct 9 1851, perhaps by suicide (STELE Jan 13 1956. Jan 20 1956) (TB Feb 1977 p10. March 1977 p7. April 1977 p25p of his gravestone. March 1979 p23. July 1982 p16. Nov 1984 p17. May 1986 p13p of his gravestone) (GOM p15) (GPCE p35) (MMBCC p93) (GOD pp22-23).

Bumble Hole Branch of Dudley Canal Line Two. Runs in a small loop from Windmill End Junction back to the Dudley Canal Line Two (HCMS No. 2).

Cabbage Hall The name appears in the Abberley Street area of Dudley in c1861. May appear in the 1841 census as Cabbage Hill.

Caddicks End W side of Dudley, before Russell's Hall. The name appears on A plan of Intended Extension of the Dudley Canal by John Snape surveyed 1785.

California Inn formerly at Kate's Hill, Dudley (TB Jan 1979 p3).

Campbell's Flight A passage off Hall Street, Dudley. So called from the 1834 General Election when Sir John Campbell was ousted by Tory candidate, local nail master, Thomas Hawkins. The defeated candidate was pursued by an incensed mob and only managed to escape down this passage (TB Jan 1981 p10) (BCM June 1997 pp42-48).

Cawney Hill Dixons Green, Dudley. The hill, the highest about Dudley, is 812 feet high (WMAG Feb 1975 p48), or 850 feet high (NSFCT 1876 p9) and has excellent views of the Malverns, Clees and the Wrekin (NSFCT 1876 p9). The name occurs on a Plan of the town of Dudley by J Treasure c1830. Cawney Hill Reservoir was built on the hill by SSWWC in the late 1930s (GHC p22) (BCM winter 1994 p33).

Cinder Bank Former mining hamlet N of Netherton in the C19 and the early C20. Now submerged into suburbs. The name, which appears in the 1841 census as Cinder Banks, is preserved in a road, Cinder Bank, between Blower's Green and Baptist End. It is from a track of cinder heaped up from the works and furnaces in New Road (NEE p7). The Baptists of Baptist End moved to Cinder Bank (NEE p27). The hymn sung in Netherton Market Place at the Netherton Sunday School Union Demonstration on Aug 3 1863 mentions Cinder Bank in the third verse

> May Sweet Turf join with Cinder Bank,
> And Ebenezer swell the rank,
> And may St John's and Primrose Hill,
> With Noah's Art their stations fill.

(NEE p29). There was an explosion at the Hope Tavern here on Aug 24 1899 killing John Devonport, his son James Devonport, and William Ball, all were interred at St Andrew's, Netherton (TB May 1978 p5p).

Constitution Hill Hill and street 0.5m S of Dudley Castle, Dudley (TB March 1977 p9).

Darby End Former hamlet, now submerged into the Black Country conurbation, 0.75m ESE of Netherton. Originally Derby Hand and Darby Hand (BCM Oct 1990 p61), from the horse nail makers who came from Derbyshire to work in Withymoor for Walkers and who resided in Belper Row, so called for they were from Belper (NEE p6). Others say the end of the land owned by the Darby family (TB Feb 1975 p14). Jon Raven has written down an old water cress sellers ballad relating to the place, which ran:

> Water cress, water cress,
> Darby End water cress.
> Every ha'porth makes it less
> Who'll buy me water cress.

(TABC p28). The hymn sung in Netherton Market Place at the Netherton Sunday School Union Demonstration on Aug 3 1863 mentions Darby Hand in the fourth verse

> And may Church Road, and Darby Hand,
> All join in one harmonious band;
> To spread the triumph of our King,

Who did for all salvation bring.

(NEE p29). Samuel Whitehouse (d1953), nicknamed 'Sammy Pigiron,' the 'Darby End Marvel,' born at Darby End, carried 112 lbs of pig iron four miles in 48 minutes 57 seconds during the collieries strike in 1921 (TB April 1972 p2. Feb/ March 1973 p12. March 1977 p9) (MMBCC pp82-89ps).

Devil's Elbow, The Now Doulton's Wharf for loading clay at Sounding Bridge (High Bridge), Highbridge Road, Netherton (NEE p9), on the Dudley Canal Line Two.

Dixon's Green District 0.75m SSE of Dudley. The name occurs on a Plan of the town of Dudley by J Treasure c1830. It is said houses were constructed at Dixon's Green of stones from the old church, some of the gravestones also being used for making ovens so that loaves baked in them bore imprints from epitaphs (VB p48). The Mount Hall of Residence (Dudley College of Education, formerly Dudley Training College) in Dixon's Green Road, demolished in 1982, was haunted by the ghost of a nun who committed suicide on the site when it was occupied by a convent (GOM p17) (GOD p21).

Dock, The Area to the W of Dudley. The name appears on the Plan of the Mines of Lord Dudley 1812. Dock was the local name for an animal pond which was situated here in the late C18 (OS map Sheet 67.15). This may be the former name for Old Dock.

Drakelow 2.5m SSW of Kinver.

Dudley Ancient parish and large Black Country town, known as 'Queen of the Black Country' (MR p131), on a high limestone ridge forming a part of England's main watershed 23.5m NNE of Worcester or 20.75m S of Stafford. EARLY. The Wenlock Limestone about Dudley abound in fossil trilobites 300 million years old (WMAG Sept 1976 p34). The quarrymen who found them in Wren's Nest Hill quarries in the C19 called them **Dudley Locusts** (SL p200) or Dudley Bugs (TTTD p304). The commonest trilobite found was the 'Calymene blumenbachi' and the term Dudley Locust is properly a reference to this type of trilobite. It is included in Dudley's civil armorial bearings (TTTD p304). (NHS pp180-181 tab 11 figs 9,10) (SHOS vol 2 p143) (SVS pp414-416,418-420) (History of Worcs. Nash. vol 1 p360) (SM ils of on preface page, Nos. i - iii) (W p581). The Pitt Rivers and Oxford University Museum, Oxford, has many examples including one huge slab containing 17 types of fauna.

600 to 1500. The **name** is from Dud, Dodo or Dudo, the famous Saxon general, who raised a fortification here (SHOS vol 2 p138). It is of Anglo-Saxon origin, from Dudda, who owned the lea (ley) pasture. Not an Earl Dudley who gave his name to the place (DUIGNAN). Twamley in his History of Dudley Castle says Dudley is derived from an old celtic word 'dodd' a rush or flag, and ley (AMS p1). The parish formed before 1086 (SHC 1916 p193). It is uncertain, which of Dudley's two ancient **churches**, **St Edmund King and Martyr** (Castle Street) (alias 'Bottom Church') and **St Thomas** (High Street) (alias 'Top Church'), was the parish church (E&S Aug 13 1999 p1). It has been suggested that St Edmund's was built for Dudley Castle and its immediate retainers, while St Thomas' was built for the town. Both churches were in existence by the late C12 (The Parish Church of St Thomas, Dudley. AP Shepherd. Revised by JS Roper. 1979. pp6-7). Bishop Sandy's 'Survey' called St Edward's the parish church and St Thomas', a chapel of ease. In 1190 both churches are described as chapels annexed to the mother church of St James' (St James' Priory) - long since disappeared (SPP p167). For **wakes** see Kate's Hill and Netherton. A **market** is recorded at Dudley before 1261, although a market charter may never have been granted (VCHW vol 3 p99) (NSJFS 1971 pp51,52). The town cross is mentioned in a deed of 1338-9 (VCHW vol 3 p90). Habington, writing in the early C17, mentions a **fair** on St James' day (the Great: July 25, or the Younger: May 3). In 1684 Edward Lord Ward received a grant of two new fairs to be held on April 21 and Sept 21. Another fair, held on the first Monday in March, was added after 1792. This fair and the other three fairs, though reduced to pleasure fairs, were still being held in 1913. Their dates were the first Monday in May and Oct and the second Monday in August (VCHW vol 3 p99). The earliest reference to Dudley being a **borough** is in 1261-2. Freedom of the borough was recorded in 1274-5. From at least 1591 a mayor was elected annually and paid by the burgesses. Borough status was probably continuous down to incorporation in 1865 (VCHW vol 3 pp98,99).

(NSJFS 1972 p68). Dudley manor and parish, which at first were co-extensive, were later divided into two districts, the borough and the foreign. But by the beginning of the C19 the borough had spread over the whole parish. In 1868 the borough was widened for parliamentary purposes to include Dudley Castle Hill, Pensnett, Brockmoor, Quarry Bank, Brierley Hill and Reddall Hill (VCHW vol 3 p99). Sometime between March 1153 and his enthronement in 1154 Duke Henry (Henry II) visited Dudley during his campaign to win back the throne of England (SHC vol 1 p19) (HOWM p22 note). Edward III visited Dudley in 1328 and in 1332 but his visits may only have been to Lord Dudley at Dudley Castle (VCHW vol 3 p100). The town was represented in the Parliament of 1295, but not again until the passing of the Reform Act in 1832, which allowed the burgesses to return one member. Dudley was still sending one member by 1913 (VCHW vol 3 p99). For the Dudley barony and honour see Dudley Castle. There was coal and iron-working at Dudley by the late C13 (Worcs Hist Soc vol 1 p195) (VCHW vol 3 pp90,99,100).

1500 to 1800. It has been said that during the C16 and C17 Dudley sunk into great poverty. Sir Amyas Paulet writing in 1585 describes the town as 'one of the poorest townes that I have sene in my life' (VCHW vol 3 p99). When Erdeswick, writing in the late C16, calls it a 'good handsome town' (SOS (1723) p117). VCHW mistakenly assumes Erdeswick was writing in 1723 (VCHW vol 3 p99 note). Habington who made a survey of Worcs in the early C17 approached Dudley 'over hylls resembling with theyre black couller the Moores who are scorched with the sun' (Worcs Hist Soc vol 1 p195) (VCHW vol 3 pp90,99,100). The **Grammar School** was founded in 1562. Alumni: Harry Harrison, dialectic poet and regular contributor to TB (VFC p61); Sir John Chalstrey (b1931), Lord Mayor of London 1995-6 (BCM spring 1997 pp37-42ps). Elizabeth I visited Dudley in 1575 but her visit may have been only to Lord Dudley at Dudley Castle (VCHW vol 3 p100). There was a plague in Dudley and the surrounding environments in 1616 (SCSF pp134-135) or 1617 and the inhabitants, being poor had to petition for aid from the county (VCHW vol 3 p99). Nails were made in Dudley from at least the C15 (VCHW vol 3 p100). **Dudley Muslin** is an obsolete general name for an inferior and coarse type of drapery. The name arose from the fact that Dudley at one time produced large quantities of herben, or bagging, used for packing nails (BCSG vol 4 p69). In the Civil War Dudley Castle (see) was a royalist garrison in 1643 and was besieged in 1644 and 1646. In 1646 St Edmund's was demolished by Col Leveson and later rebuilt mainly at the expense of Richard Bradley and other members of his family (SPP p167). '**Dudley Castle,**' the name for the first steam engine erected in England (reports of two slightly earlier engines erected in Cornwall are inconclusive - SL p207) and Thomas Newcomen's first engine, was erected in 1712 to drain water out of the coal mines of Lord Dudley and Ward. A near-contemporary source placed it 'at Dudley Castle in Staffordshire' and for many years it was believed to have been situated in the grounds of Dudley Castle, or at one of about six sites in the Black Country. The exact site became a matter of some national controversy, but was located to Lady Meadow (see) at Coneygree in 1965. Rioters burnt down Dudley's **dissenter meeting house** on July 18 1715; about 200 were involved (NSFCT 1917 p69). Or the riot occurred on July 17 (LOU p94). **Natives and visitors**. On at least one occasion **John Wesley**, founder of Methodism, visited Dudley (BCM April 1977 pp40-42). Dr Rev **Luke Booker**, master of the free school and minister of St Edmund's church, Dudley was a poet and published 'the Highlander,' 'Malvern' and 'The Hop Garden' at the end of the C18, and two poems relating to Dudley Castle: 'Address to the Ivy Tree' and 'The Ruin' (GM vol 68 p513) (SHOS vol 2 p142). **Thomas Phillips**, artist, was born in Dudley on Oct 18 1770. He was elected a Royal Academician in 1808 and died in London on April 20 1845 (TEBC2 p55). **Sarah Bellany** of Belbroughton, Worcs, born in 1770, was convicted of theft in Dudley and transported with the first fleet to Australia on May 13 1787.

1800 to PRESENT. Dudley received a charter of **incorporation** on April 3 1865 by the title of the mayor, aldermen and burgesses of Dudley (VCHW vol 3 p99). Frederick Smith of The Priory, probably Priory Hall (see), was the first mayor. Dudley borough arms are - Gules a fesse engrailed argent between Dudley Castle in the chief and a salamander in flames proper in the foot with a trilobite between an anchor and a miner's lamp on the fesse. Crest,

a lion's head razed (VCHW vol 3 p99). The motto of Dudley borough is 'Sapiens Qui Prospicit' 'Wise is He who Look Ahead' (WMAG Feb 1975 p48). **Unrest and pestilence** Two canal boats were stopped in an incident of food rioting near Dudley in early May 1800. Troops were involved and a rioter was killed (Aria's Birmingham Gazetteer May 5 1800) (LOU p157). The cholera epidemic of 1832 reached Dudley parish on June 23 and claimed 277 lives in the parish (TB Feb 1998 p17). For the Asiatic Cholera outbreak of 1849 in Dudley see TB March 1994 p20. Riot occurred in Dudley on the Coronation day of William IV on July 19 1821. It was caused mainly by a drunken brawl amongst the men of the Yeomanry (TB Dec 1980 p27). On April 25 1842 the Staffordshire Yeomanry were sent out to suppress the nailers riots in Dudley led by John Chance of Stourbridge (The Black Country Nailer's Riots of 1842 Arthur Willetts. 1995). Riots occurred in the Dudley constituency at the general election on Feb 4 1874. Mobs assembled and outbreaks of violence occurred at Eve Hill, Holly Hall, Queens Cross, Cradley Heath, Brierley Hill, Netherton, Brockmoor and Woodside. A stone was thrown at the Tory headquarters at the Dudley Arms Hotel in the Market Place. The Riot Act was read. A re-run election occurred in May 1874 at which Henry Sheridan, the Liberal candidate won again, this time over a new Conservative candidate, Noah Hingley (BCM summer 1995 pp69-73. autumn 1995 pp42-47). **WW1**. The Zeppelin L19 dropped 17 incendiary bombs on Dudley on its raid over the Black Country on the night of Jan 31 1916: Most of the bombs fell in Dudley Castle grounds (BCM autumn 1994 p56). In the evening of July 10 **1981 rioting** occurred in High Street similar to the riot at Handsworth (see). The manufacture of all kinds of hardware was being carried on in Dudley in the early C20 (VCHW vol 3 p100). **Railways**. The first train ran between Dudley Port and Walsall on May 1 1850 (BCM April 1976 pp53-57) (SSR p11). The first of the two Dudley town railway stations, which were to be situated side by side, was opened in 1852, by the Oxford, Worcester and Wolverhampton Railway which was then part of the West Midland Railway and about to amalgamate with GWR (BCM Oct 1990 p28). The single platform at this station resulted in two passenger train collisions in Oct 1854 and May 1855; the latter causing injury to 40 persons (SSR pp15,22). The second station was opened in 1880 by SSR leased to the LNWR (BCM Oct 1990 p28). The branch line from Dudley Port High Level to the town, or train that ran on it, was known locally as the 'Dudley Dodger' (BCM Jan 1978 p60) (MR p332). Two **forgers** from Dudley were found guilty of forging two Dudley bank notes and executed at Stafford on Aug 30 1800 (TB Jan 1978 p24). **Wife-selling**. Phil Drabble has suggested that the sale of a wife at Dudley in Aug 1859 was perhaps the last occasion of wife selling in the district (BC p140). For the **charities** of Dudley see BCM July 1980 pp52-56. **Dudley Building Society**, founded in June 1858 is still (1998) active (Building Societies Yearbook 1998-99: Official Handbook of the Building Society Association). **Newspapers**. The Stourbridge and Dudley Messenger, printed in Stourbridge, began on May 7 1813. It was shortlived (TEBC2 p17). The Dudley Herald was launched on Dec 22 1866 (TEBC2 p89). The Dudley Chronicle, a liberal newspaper, was founded in 1885. It later amalgamated with the Dudley Herald (TEBC) (TEBC2 p122). The foundation stone of the first **Dudley Opera House** at Castle Hill was laid June 27 1898, and the Opera House opened on Sept 4 1899 (TB May 1996 p11 lil); a fire destroyed the building in Nov 1936 (TB Dec 1979 p5) (BCM winter 1994 p26p). **References to Dudley**. The greatest concentration of people in Britain in 1999 with the surname Hill is in Dudley (Daily Mail July 17 1999 p35). Dudley is Dulston in Francis Brett Young's novels (BCM April 1980 pp10-15. autumn 1989 p58). It is Studley in the novels of Ellen Thorneycroft Fowler (BCM Spring 2000 p47). **Sport**. There was horse racing on a course located between Castle Hill and Tipton Road, Dudley between 1834 and 1848 (TEBC2 p45). The record for a standing jump was set by Joe Darby, born at Windmill End (see) in 1861, when he jumped 12 feet 1.5 inch without weights at Dudley Castle on May 28 1890. He set the record for a standing jump with ankles tied when he cleared six feet at Church Cricket Ground, Dudley on June 11 1892 (GBR 1981 p325). Peter G Dowdeswell of Earls Barton, Northants (b1940) broke the world record for drinking milk when he drank two pints in 3.2 seconds at Dudley Top Rank Club on May 31 1975 (GBR 1987 p178). **Supernatural**. A property, built on the site of an old burial ground, in King Street, is believed to be haunted. The property was, when Solomon was writing, JB's Discotheque with Evan's Garage at the rear. Strange noises and the ghost of a young man dressed in army uniform have been heard and seen (GOM p21 pl 5 (c)) (GOD p10). St Thomas' church may be haunted (GOD pp11-12), and among the ghosts which make St Edmund's churchyard the most haunted in the Midlands is that of Edmund Croaker, executioner, whose body is buried there (TB May/ June 1973 p9). There is a ghost in the cellar in a building in Tower Street (TB Dec 1975 p28p) (GOD pp6-7). Poltergeist activity reputedly haunts the Old Priory At Dudley Inn (see) in New Street. **Natives and visitors**. **Ben Boucher** has been described as 'the Dudley Poet.' One of his poems is titled 'Lines on Dudley Market, 1827' (Dudley Almanac. 1900. E Blocksidge. il) (TB March 1986 p12). The brewery firm of **Julia Hanson** & Son founded in 1847, had the distinction of being the only brewing in the county with a lady's name, before it became a part of a bigger brewery company in 1943: It's trademark was Dudley Castle (Portrait of the Black Country. Harold Parsons. 1986. p50). According to tradition **Robert Baden-Powell**, founder of the Boy Scout movement (1908), whilst staying in Dudley, went to a local shop to buy a pair of braces (John Sparry on BBC Radio 4 April 14 1994 9.45am). The Prince of Wales (later **Edward VIII**) visited Dudley on June 13 1923, opening the Woodside War Memorial and visiting the Guest Hospital (TB Feb 4 1999 p17p). On Jan 29 1929 the body of PC **Harry Stanton** was discovered about 20 yards from the N entrance of the railway tunnel on the GWR near Birmingham Road; his head had been crushed perhaps by a heavy metal instrument. The cause of death remains (1999) a mystery (TB Annual 1999 p81-82). **Dorothy Edith Round** (later Little) (d1982), the outstanding British tennis player of the 1930s, was born in Parkway Road (formerly Park Road), Dudley, on July 13 1909. She was the winner of the women's singles title at Wimbledon in 1934 and 1937. She won the mixed doubles at Wimbledon in 1934, 1935 and 1936; as a Sunday school teacher she refused to play tennis on Sundays, which on one occasion posed difficulties for the authorities at the French Championships (BCM April 1968. Jan 1983 pp38-40) (The Guinness International Who's Who of Sport. Peter Matthews. 1993. p534). **Alan David Keasey** of Wolverhampton Street was murdered by Dennis Howard on April 23 1957 (MMBC pp69-80). **Wally Davis**, pioneer of the hydroglider, was from Dudley (TB May 1974 pp18-19). In football by 1983 England's youngest home international was **Duncan Edwards** (b Dudley Oct 1 1936) who played against Scotland at Wembley on April 2 1955 aged 18 years 183 days. He played for Manchester United as left half and was involved in the Munich air crash on Feb 6 1958 and died from his injuries on Feb 21 1958. On Oct 14 1999 a bronze statue of him to his memory was unveiled in Dudley market place; the artist who designed the statue was James Butler (GBR 1983 p274) (E&S Oct 13 1999 p4p. Oct 15 1999 p7p) (BCM winter 1999/2000 pp32p-33).

Dudley Arms Hotel High Street, Dudley. Built in 1786 on site of The Rose and Crown Inn, which had been built in the 1600s. The hotel was demolished in 1968 to provide a site for a Marks and Spencer store (BCP p149p).

Dudley Foreign See Dudley.

Dudley Wood District between Mushroom Green and Newtown 2.5m S of Dudley. The church, St John, was built in 1931 (BOE p80). The Dudley Wood area was enclosed in the late C18 to be exploited for coal by Lord Dudley. The Saltwell Colliery pits here were exhausted by c1900. The area was developed with housing between WW1 and WW2 (OS map Sheet 71.08).

Dudley Woodside See Woodside.

Eryhytt Place in Dudley parish, occurs in documents of the C16 and C17 (VCHW vol 3 p90). Possibly an early form of a current place name.

Eve Hill District of Dudley, 0.75m W of the town centre. The name may be from a local family (OS map Sheet 67.15). The identity of Eve is pondered upon in Portrait of the Black Country by Harold Parsons (1986) p50. The name appears in the 1841 census. Nearly at New Dock, at SO 935901, was a windmill, possibly originally a postmill, first marked on Plot's map. Replaced by a tower mill by 1808. The mill had disappeared by the 1886 OS map (WBJ p21). The chapel of Thomas Prince ('Tommy Pee' d1884 aged 68) in West Street was said in 1972 to have been closed and forgotten long ago (BCM April 1972 p58). Riots occurred in the Dudley constituency at the general election on Feb 4 1874. Mobs assembled and outbreaks of violence occurred at Eve Hill and other places (BCM summer 1995 pp69-73). The children in the little church school here may have chanted 'Deliver us from eve 'ill,' being the local dialect (Portrait of the Black Country. Harold Parsons. 1986 p50). The prominent tower blocks known as Prince of Wales Court and Millfield Court in Salop Street, built in the mid 1960s, were demolished by being blown up on July 18 1999 (BCM autumn 1999 pp39-40p,41).

Farthing Hall Netherton. See Hill House.

Fens, The Kingswinford.*

Fiery Holes To W of Dudley, NNW of Holly Hall, approximately by Russell's Hall. The name Fire Holes was in existence by 1785 (A Plan of the intended Extension of the Dudley Canal in the Birmingham Canal. John Snape. 1785) (TB July 1974 p18 see map) and is preserved in a modern inn on the E side of Great Bridge Road near Bull Lane. (BOP p106il from ILN Dec 8 1866 p548 of a Black Country Scene about the Fiery Holes area).

Fir Tree Inn At Kate's Hill, Dudley an old inn, which still exists (TB Jan 1979 p3).

Freebodies Former hamlet to E of Dudley in the Kate's Hill area. The name has appeared as Freebody's (1686), Freeberry's (1821), and Freebodies (1841 census). In the later C17 it was the name for land on which was a certain spot with a magnetic force which distorted compasses (NHS p170) (SD pp44,45). Freebodies may have derived its name from an inn or given its name to the inn? (TB Jan 1979 p3. March 1994 p20).

Gadd's Green Tiny district S of Dixon's Green, at SO 952888. Appears on 1947 OS map 1:25,000 (sheet 32/98). Former common land near Dixon's Green later enclosed by a member of the Gadd family. They were from Wales in c1630 and were also known as alias Jones (BCWJ p100).

Gadd's Green Reservoir Created in 1793. Seems to have been drained in 1910 (HCMS No. 2).

Green Man Inn Old inn dating from the C17 at Dudley. Was haunted by a poltergeist who played the piano after the licensee discovered a pair of hidden rooms in 1974 (GOD p10).

Grove Inn On top of Cawney Hill, Dudley. It was situated where the reservoir now stands. According to legend a woman styled Madame Angelo walked 1000 miles in 1000 hours around the grounds of the inn at an average of 24 miles a day for 41.75 days sometime in the period 1860-70? (TB Feb 1985 p25).

'Gypsies Tent, The' Legendary inn in Dudley. Closed in the early 1980s (The Pubs and Breweries of the Old Dudley Borough. John Richards) (Black Country Stories and Sketches. Greg Stokes. 1993 pp104-106).

Hart's Hill An area S of Woodside, 1m NNE of Brierley Hill. Harts Hill first appears in the 1851 census. With Woodside it was a part of Netherton until 1865 (IISD p28). Alfred Meredith, aged 21, of Bond Street, Dudley, who worked as a clerk at Messrs Hall and Smith's Ironworks, Brierley Hill, was murdered by Enoch Whiston somewhere between Parkhead and Woodside in the Hartshill area in 1878. Meredith was returning from collecting his wages from the bank and had been followed by Whiston who shot him for his money. Whiston was tried in Jan 1879 and hung on Feb 10 1879 (MMBC pp97-113) (TB Jan 1979 p17. April 1989 pp10-11).

Hill House Stood in about three acres of ground in Church Road, Netherton. Built by Jas Barker, a draper and general dealer. It was often called 'Farthing Hall' as it was considered to have been built with business farthings. It was later the residence of Mr Skidmore, owner of the Atlas Tube Works at Yew Tree Hills (NEE p5).

Hockley Well Former well for the people of Netherton. Gave its name to Hockley Lane to the S of Netherton (NEE p7).

Holly Hall, The Situated on the Kingswinford Road (SVS p141), Dudley. Seat of George Robinson, mining agent, before he was sent by the Hudson Bay Company to develop a coalfield at Nanaimo, Vancouver Island, British Columbia, Canada in 1854 (TB July 1997 pp16,30. Aug 1997 p25). The hall, apparently, was still standing in 1998 (TB Nov 5 1998 p10). The name was in existence by 1785. It is possibly from a holly tree, a boundary mark; the area is close to the former Staffs border. Has also appeared as Holley Hall. Holly Hall is a place in its own right and has been described as a village. It is now amalgamated into the conurbation known as Low Town, its main street runs at right angles to Pensnett Road and emerges opposite the King William Inn (A Plan of the intended Extension of the Dudley Canal in the Birmingham Canal. John Snape. 1785) (The Villages of Holly Hall, Woodside and Harts Hill. Lavender) (TEBC2 p54) (BCM July 1973 p47) (TB Oct 1989 p13p in c1900. Nov 5 1998 p10). Riots occurred in the Dudley constituency at the general election on Feb 4 1874: Mobs assembled and outbreaks of violence occurred at Holly Hall and other places (BCM summer 1995 pp69-73).

Hope Tavern Netherton. Here on Aug 24 1898 (IISD p43), or 1899 (TB Sept 1981 p17) was an explosion created by a build up of escaping gas. It killed one (IISD p43) or two drinkers (TB Sept 1981 p17), and six others were badly wounded (TB Sept 1981 p17). Has also appeared as Blue Brick Inn.

Ivy House Old inn at Kate's Hill. It still (1979) exists (TB Jan 1979 p3).

Jolly Collier Inn In lower Tower Street, Dudley. It was said to be affected by frequent poltergeist-type activity until its demolition prior to 1990. There have been reports of a young man and a woman occasionally appearing, apparently looking for a doorway that is invisible to human eyes (GOM p19 pl 5(b)) (BCM July 1973 pp47-48). There is another account about a Jolly Collier Inn, at Low Town, Holly Hall, which was haunted by several ghosts; the ghosts were first reported in 1954, exorcised in 1957, and the building was demolished in the 1960s (GOD pp14-16).

Kate's Hill Hill on which grew a hamlet now grown into a suburb of Dudley, 0.75m E of Dudley. The name is said to be from Colonel Cade a Parliamentary commander in the Civil War who camped here during the siege of Dudley Castle. The hill became known as Cade's Hill corrupted to Kate's Hill (TB Jan 1985 p3). Kate's Hill was described as a village in 1855 (MMMR p38). For the murder of Mary Ann Mason in 1855 see under Sailor's Return Inn. Dudley wakes were held annually at Kate's Hill on the Sunday before Oct 21, other Dudley wakes occurred at Netherton (see). They appear to have ceased by 1913 (VCHW vol 3 p99). James Whale (d1957), Hollywood filmmaker, was born at No. 41 Brewery Street, Kate's Hill on July 21 1889. He has directed 'The Invisible Man' (1933), 'Showboat' (1936), 'The Bride of Frankenstein' (1939), and 'The Man in the Iron Mask' (1939) (BCM July 1969 pp30-34) (TB Christmas 1972 p7. March 1981 p10. April 1981 p10. April 1989 p16) (TEBC) (TEBC2 p130).

Knowle Hill Colliery Dudley (VCH vol 2 p98) (TB Aug 1976 p27p).

Lady Wood Small piece of woodland S of Saltwell Clay Field. It was planted in the 1770s under the direction of the then Lady Dudley to hide scars left by some small coalmines. Appears on Yates' map as Lady Dudley's Wood (SNSV vol 1 p87). Has also appeared as Lady Dudley's Plantation. Another account says the main part of the adjacent Saltwells Wood was planted in 1795 by Mary, Lady Dudley, as a way of landscaping former mine workings. In the C19 a part of Lady Wood was destroyed when more small mines were sunk (OS map Sheet 71.07).

Ladywood Spa Or Saltwell.

Leyne, La Place in Dudley parish, occurs in documents of the C14 (VCHW vol 3 p90). Probably an early form of a current place name.

Little Britain Dudley. Thomas Hickman, prize ring fighter, known as the 'Terrible Gas Man,' was born in Ken Lane, Dudley, on Jan 28 1795. His fight with Bill Neat (The Bristol Bull) on Dec 19 1821 was hailed as the bare-knuckle 'fight of the century.' He was killed in a coaching accident on Dec 1822 when returning from the Hudson/ Shelton fight. He was buried in the churchyard at Little Britain, Dudley (BCM July 1968 pp59-65) (TB Nov 1980 p31. Jan 1987 pp12-13il. Feb 1993 pp18-19).

Locomotive Inn Vicar Street, Dudley. Is haunted (GOD pp8-9).

Lodge Farm Old house? 2m SSW of Dudley. To SW of Netherton. At SO 935874 close to the sharp bend in the Dudley Canal was a windmill, shown on a map of 1818. Lodge Farm Reservoir now covers the site (WBJ p21). The name is from probably a medieval hunting lodge established by some distant Earl of Dudley on Pensnett Chase? (TB Aug 1976 pp10-11).

Lodge Farm Reservoir To E of Lodge Farm, Netherton. Covers 14 acres (LHSB No. 6 p26)

Lodge Farm Valley Former burial ground, anciently known as 'The Valley of The Dead' (TB Aug 1976 pp10-11. March 1980 p21). Has also appeared as Lodge Valley.

London Fields Small district and former hamlet 1m W of Dudley Castle. The name appears in the 1861 census. There was a windmill at SO 929905 first shown on Plot's map, but not on maps after 1749 (WBJ p21).

Low Town Old mining settlement to NE of The Holly Hall. Low Town appears in the 1851 census and the place has also appeared as Lowtown. It was known locally as 'down the hole.' The settlement had completely disappeared by the 1980s (OS map Sheet 67.15).

Loyal Washington Inn Primrose Hill, Netherton. Built by William Washington in 1850. His own portrait adorned the sign. So called from him and his branch of the Washington family who had remained loyal to the crown in the war of American Independence (BEV p54).

Malt Shovel, The Bumble Hole (see) (TB Feb 1977 p10).

Mamble In the Minories area of Dudley. The name appears in the 1841 census.

M and M Out Doors An old inn at Kate's Hill. By 1979 had closed and the site lost (TB Jan 1979 p3).

Minories, The Former hamlet in the SW part of central Dudley. The name, which appears in the 1841 census, is preserved in the street called The Minories. Mr Davis, fender maker, lived here. His works had a steam engine, the boiler of which exploded on May 14 1853 and killed four men (TB Oct 1980 p15).

Mouse Sweet Former hamlet 1.75m S of Dudley on the Halesowen Road between Old Hill and Netherton, now merged into Black Country conurbation. Has appears as Mousul (1832) (SVS p140), Mouth Sweet (1841 census), Mousesweet (1881/2 and 1921 OS maps) (SNSV vol 1 p87).

Mushroom Green Former hamlet at the foot of Merry Hill (TB Nov 5 1998 p10), now a suburb, 2m SSW of Dudley. Created on common land on a bank above a stream by squatting nailers and was an inhabited area by 1650. After 1783 the inhabitants turned from nail making to chain making (BCM winter 1994 pp60-62). The hamlet developed in an unplanned fashion - many of the brick cottages are of very curious dimensions - gives the place an untidy charm (SL pp189,190, 271 pl 32). Has appeared as Musham (1834 OS map) (SNSV vol 1 p87) and is pronounced locally Musham Green (TB Oct 1974 p5). The hamlet was designated a Conservation Area by the county borough of Dudley on April 16 1970 (BCM winter 1994 pp60-62) (MR pp114,115p), and in 1975 described as 'the only outstanding conservation area in the West Midlands county' (BCM winter 1994 pp60-62). Shaw wrote that the best sort of iron stone is commonly called Mush (SHOS vol 2 p66). Mush was prevalent in the Rowley Regis area. Or 'mush' is the crumbled, crushed or weathered fragments of shale beds according to a Staffs coal-mining glossary (NSFCT 1915 p56).

Netherton Black Country town on Netherton Hill 1.5m S of Dudley in Dudley ancient parish. Netherton has appeared as Nederton (1420-1573) (NEE p2). Oliver Cromwell is said to have passed through the town on his way to Halesowen (NEE p4). A charter of 1684 granted to it a market on the last week in October for 164 years. The market was held in Market Square (NEE pp3,23). The **church**, St Andrew, crowns the summit of Netherton Hill, 700 feet high, commanding views of the Malverns and the Wrekin (WMLB p118) (WMVB p111). The present church was built in 1827-1830 (BOE p208); the churchyard was haunted in WW2 (TB Jan 1975 p23). Dudley wakes were held annually at Netherton on the last Sunday in Oct, other Dudley wakes occurred at Kate's Hill (see). They appear to have ceased by 1913 (VCHW vol 3 p99). In 1844 Netherton became a separate ecclesiastical parish and remained so until 1865 when it became a ward (NEE p31). **Industry**. The town's main industries have been producing: nails, Hampton Court is said to have Netherton nails (WMVB p111); iron, anchors and cables; and Jews harps, which found a large market in USA in C19 (MR p237). Glazebrooks established their works 'Netherton Iron Works' with blast furnaces in 1800 (NEE p11). Noah Hingley and his firm (founded in 1838) first introduced into the Black Country at Netherton Iron Works the Nasmyth steam hammer (SHC 1950/ 1 p261). The firm was described as 'the world's premier manufacturer of ships' anchors and cables in the period 1890 to 1918.' Their **anchor for the Titanic** made at their Primrose Hill works in 1910 or 1911 was tested by Lloyds British Proving House at Netherton. It weighed 16 tons and took 12 men three weeks to make. The total length was 18 feet 6 inches and 10 feet 9 inches wide and when completed it was described as 'the biggest anchor in the world.' It took 20 horses to draw it on a waggon from the works at Primrose Hill to the London & North Western Station at Dudley (Dudley Herald May 6 1911) (County Express May 6 1911) (TB Aug 1974 p29p) (BCM Jan 1982 p61p. Oct 1983 p33p. autumn 1996 pp19-22. spring 1997 pp9-13ps) (Noah Hingley: The World's Premier Manufacturer of Ships' Anchors and Cables in the period 1890-1918. Kenneth Mallin. 1998). The Dudley Boys Brigade had a replica of it in 1983 (TB Feb 1983 p17). The Prince of Wales visited the works of Noah Hingley on June 13 1923 (BCM Dec 1997 p36). In 1852 occurred a **strike by nailers** of Netherton, Halesowen, Cradley and neighbouring districts. On Feb 18 1852 they drew a waggon of coal from Halesowen district to Bromsgrove (13 miles) to protest against low wages. The waggon of coal was presented to the strikers by T Attwood, and weighed two tons, 13 cwt. It was drawn by about 100 men with chains and ropes. A song 'The Nailmakers' Strike' tells of the march (NEE p17) (TEBC2 p67) (MR p237; says 1862). Riots occurred in the Dudley constituency at the general election on Feb 4 1874. Mobs assembled and outbreaks of violence occurred at Netherton and other places (BCM summer 1995 pp69-73). Netherton **Windmill** was near Lodge Farm (see). There appears to have been a **railway** station on the Oxford, Worcester and Wolverhampton line (opened in 1852-54) to the N of Netherton. In 1878 the Netherton and Halesowen Branch line of the GWR opened spurring off the OW&WR and passing on the E side of Netherton to Old Hill; it closed in the 1960s. In 1879 a goods branch was made off the Netherton and Halesowen Branch line to the Earl of Dudley's canal basin at Withymoor (VCH vol 2 pp310,321,333) (NEE p5). For **Frederick Lester** of Netherton who fell down a limestone working in the Wren's Nest escarpment in 1934 see under Kettle Hill.

Netherton Hall House formerly situated NW of the centre of Netherton, S of Dudley, about 300 yards from the turnpike road; the approach to the hall was by Hall Lane (NEE p5). Sir John Sutton of Dudley Castle (see) died in 1487 seised of a messuage called Netherton (Nederton). In 1586 a house called Netherton, in Pensnett Chase, was among the possessions of Edward Lord Dudley at the time of his death. The house is again mentioned in 1610-11, but after that all trace of it disappears (VCHW vol 3 pp100-101). Miss Mary Folly lived at the hall until 1827 and afterward Henry Guest lived here until 1860. The hall, surrounded by a moat (NEE p5), collapsed due to subsidence in 1860 or 1862 and a farmhouse, Hall Farm, was built on the site, or on land opposite the site and using some of the materials from the old hall (NEE p5). (TB Feb 1974 p5 il. Feb 1983 p16). This too fell into disrepair and was demolished.

Netherton Hill Hill in the Black Country on which stands Netherton church, 620 feet high, above the head of Black Brook.

Netherton Park Public park at Baptist End, Netherton (SNSV vol 2 p60).

Netherton Tunnel Canal tunnel in the Black Country authorised in 1855 (SL p182) (HCMS No. 2). The tunnel opened on Aug 20 1858. Built by Thomas Telford to relieve traffic congestion in Dudley Tunnel. Runs from Bumble Hole in the S to Birmingham Canal New Line in the N (The Dudley No. 2 Canal Guide. The Lapal Canal Trust) (info Dudley Canal Trust). It was the last canal tunnel to be built in England (VCH vol 2 p296) (SL p243) and is reputed to be the widest; a towpath lines both sides (MR p238). It is 3036 yards long and 27 feet wide. (Raven says 5,027 yards long (MR p238), others say it is 3027 yards long (The Dudley No. 2 Canal Guide) (HCMS No. 2)). Nine men were killed in its construction and 18 seriously injured (TB Nov 1979 p5). It had a towpath and was lit by gas (SL p182). It was the third and largest of the tunnels linking the coal mines of the Stour Valley with the more highly developed industrial area N and E of the Rowley Hills (VCH vol 2 pp77,296,297 map) (O p221) (BCM Jan 1969 p6p of the ventilation shaft in Aston Road, Netherton).

Netherton Tunnel Branch of the Dudley Canal. Black Country canal which diverges from the Birmingham Canal New Cut New Main Line at Dudley Port Junction. Soon after running under an aqueduct carrying the Birmingham Canal Old Cut Old Main Line it enters the canal tunnel known as the Netherton Tunnel (see) at the S end of which, at Windmill End Junction, it joins Dudley Canal Line Two.

New Dock To W of Old Dock, Dudley. The name first appears in the 1851 census.

New Park Medieval hunting ground which belonged to Dudley manor and castle. It was made by Roger de Somery of Dudley Castle (see), between the wood of Pensnett and Dudley town, probably in c1247-8 (VCHW vol 3 p100). The names 'The Old Park' and 'Old Park' appear to the W of Dudley in the vicinity of Russell's Hall on the 1834 OS map and Birmingham A-Z and may preserve the name (TB Oct - Nov 1972 p22). Another of Lord Dudley's medieval hunting grounds known as Old Park (see) lay to the E about Dudley Castle. The New Park area is an ironstone deposit site (VCH vol 2 p120).

New Park Colliery Dudley (VCH vol 2 p98).

Old Dock In the Queen's Cross area to SE of Dudley town centre. The name first appears in the 1851 census and appears to have formerly been The Dock (see).

Old Park The names 'The Old Park' and 'Old Park' appear to the W of Dudley on the 1834 OS map. (TB Oct - Nov 1972 p22). 'Old Park' may preserve the name of the medieval hunting ground formerly known as New Park (see), which lay further to the W than Old Park (which lay about Dudley Castle); both belonged to Dudley manor and castle.

Old Priory At Dudley Inn, The New Street, opposite the police station, Dudley. In 1989 the inn was reputedly haunted by poltergeist activity (Birmingham Evening Mail Oct 5 1989) (GOM p15) (MS&S pp37p-39).

Old Soldier Inn Netherton. See Soldier's Hill.

Old Swan Inn Halesowen Road, Netherton. Built in c1900. Said to have been one of the last places in England to brew on the premises (WMVB p111), and the Black Country's last surviving home brew pub. It is universally known as 'Mrs Pardoes' after the lady whose family held the licence from 1932 until 1985. Has also been called the White Swan (BTBC p22p). (WMAG Dec 1979 pp43-44p) (BCP p29p).

Palmer's Green To NW of Netherton (TB July 1974 p1[illegible] see map).

Paradise Suburb 0.5m S of Dudley. The name first appears in the 1851 census. It has its centre at SO 947897.

Parkhead To the ENE of Woodside, Dudley. The name Park Head appears in the 1841 census. The southern entrance of the Dudley Canal Tunnel is called Parkhead portal (V[illegible] p44). It was between Parkhead and Woodside that Alfred Meredith was mugged and murdered (MMBC pp97-113).

Park Head Junction Junction of the Dudley Canal Line No. [illegible] with the Dudley Canal Line No. 2.

Paze Alley Narrow cobbled paved way which stood where New Street, Dudley, now stands. It was here when Elizabeth I visited Dudley (IISD p25).

Pepperfields Former area in the area of the present Weaver Rise, S of Primrose Hill, Netherton (SNSV vol 2 p80).

Pewceter Place in Dudley parish, occurs in documents of the C16 and C17 (VCHW vol 3 p90). Possibly an early form of a current place name.

Primrose Hill Hill and small district over 1.5m S of Dudley, SE of Netherton. The name said to be from the primroses that grew upon its hillside (NEE p7) appears in the 184[illegible] census. A windmill existed to the S of Bumble Hole a[illegible] Greenwood's map records 'Windmill Eng' at approximately SO 948878 (WBJ p34). Noah Hingley (1796-1877), mayor of Dudley in 1869, who lived for a time at Red House, Clent, set up his cable and anchor works at Primrose Hill in c1846. He was succeeded by his son Benjamin Hingley (1830-1905), MP for N Worcs (1885-1895), who was created a baronet in 1893. He was succeeded by his nephew Sir George Benjamin Hingley (1850-1918) (BCSG vol [illegible] p45) (VCH vol 3 p263) (TB Feb 1981 p4) (NEE p32) (BCM spring 1999 pp31-36). For a rhyme about Primrose Hill see Cinder Hill.

Priory, The Dudley. See St James' Priory and Priory Hall.

Priory Hall By St James' Priory, Dudley. Built in 1825 in the neo-Tudor style (WMAG Feb 1976 p31p). Can probably be identified with The Priory, the seat of Frederick Smith, first mayor of Dudley. On Aug 29 1865 he invited every day-scholar and teacher (numbering 4000) from Dudley borough to The Priory to celebrate the incorporation of the borough and partake in tea and plum cake and enjoy games of various kinds (ILN Sept 9 1865 p245il). Priory Hall is now used as offices (BOE p120) (MR p135).

Pupills Hall In the Shaver's End area. The name appears in the 1841 census.

Queen's Cross Former hamlet on high ground 0.5m SW of Dudley, in existence by 1785 (A Plan of the intended Extension of the Dudley Canal in the Birmingham Canal. John Snape. 1785). Rent from it went to endow the Blue Coat School at Walsall (W p645). Riots occurred in the Dudley constituency at the general election on Feb 4 1874. Mobs assembled and outbreaks of violence occurred at Queen's Cross and other places. During the riot here the window of the Wagon and Horses Inn were broken (BCM summer 1995 pp69-73). The name is preserved in a main road.

Russell's Hall District on the western slopes of the watershed at Dudley, 1.25m WSW of Dudley.

Russell's Hall Formerly situated on the site of Kew Drive, London Fields, Dudley. Built in the C16 by Geoffrey or Jeffrey Sutton (alias Dudley), who died at Russell's Hall in 1571. He was a younger son of Edward Lord Dudley KG (SHC 1889 part 2 p10), perhaps Edward, 2nd Lord Dudley (d1531/2) of Dudley Castle (see). The last of the Sutton (alias Dudley) line to reside here was John Dudley, who died intestate in 1723. Here were kept the relics of St Chad until, in fear of the Penal Laws, Bridget and Kathleen Dudley passed them on to Henry Hodshead of Woodsetton (VB p24) (SNSV vol 2 p16); Bowers and Clough say the relics were kept at Russell House, near Worcester (RHPS p258); whilst others say they were kept at Rushall Hall near Walsall (SCHJ No. 9 pp12-15). Russell's Hall was later occupied by the Mallin family (AMS p447). It is described in 1889 as long since taken down (SHC 1889 part 2 p17). Others say it was demolished in 1844 (A History of Russells Hall. Roper) (TEBC2 p54), or in 1884 due to mining (TB Dec 1974 p27il). Some of the stone was reused in garden walls of houses in Himley Road and Dibdale Street, although much of the masonry was taken to 'The Grange,' Halesowen, for its garden (SHC 1889 part 2 p17) (TB Dec 1974 p27il). Two villas known as Sunnyside in Himley Road stood S of the site of the hall by 1901 (AMS p447) (OS map Sheet 67.15).

Russell's Hall Colliery See Windmill End.

Russell's New Hall Formerly situated close to the end of Dibdale Street near the junction of Dibdale Road, London Fields, Dudley. It replaced Russell's Hall and was demolished in 1971 (TB Dec 1974 p27). The name Russell's Hall is preserved in Russell's Hall Estate (TEBC2 p54).

Russell's Old Hall Presumably stood on site of, or near, Russell's Hall (see). Built in the C13? Manor house of the Russell family in the C13. (Johnne de Russell is mentioned in the Lechmore Subsidy Roll 1275). The Russell's tenure was comparatively short: Robert Burnell, Bishop of Bath and Wells took possession in 1293 - 'Russelleshalle' occurs in 1315 when a member of the Burnell family died seised of it (VCHW vol 3 p100). From 1324 it was owned by the Lovell family. By the early C16 Sir Thomas Boleyn, Queen Anne's father was in residence. Geoffrey Sutton (alias Dudley), of the Sutton (or Dudley) family of Dudley Castle (see), followed the Boleyns and he built Russell's Hall (see) in the C16.

Sailor's Return Inn Kate's Hill, Dudley. Here John Meadows, aged 23, deliberately shot his girlfriend, Mary Ann Mason of Woodside, aged 17, whilst she was working at the inn (MMMR pp38-41) on May 11 (MM pp29-33) or May 12 (MMBC pp30-42) (TB Aug 1974 p24) or May 13 1855 (IISD p34). He was hung at Worcester on July 28 1855 (MMMR pp41) (MM pp29-33), or on Aug 4 1855 (IISD p34). Joseph Greensill's pamphlet entitled 'The Restless Shade of Mary Ann Mason' notes the ghost of Mary Ann Mason (TB Sept 1974 p7p of Mason's grave in Kate's Hill churchyard. Nov 1976 p10p of same. Aug 1981 p10p. March 1991 p5) (GOD pp20-21). The inn had disappeared by 1979 (TB Jan 1979 p3).

Saint James' Priory 400 yards W of Dudley Castle, formerly in Worcs, although an engraving made of it by Samuel and Nathaniel Buck, 1731, is titled 'The southwest view of Dudley Priory in the county of Stafford' (VCHW vol 3 p101 note); also it was declared to be in Staffs by papal decree in 1238 (HOS 1998 p20). The priory has also been called the Old Priory, Dudley Priory, and The Priory. It was founded by Gervase Paynel (or Pagnel, Paganel) of Dudley Castle (see) in c1160 (GNHS p179) (MR p134) or c1180 (SL p201) for Cluniac Benedictine monks, and was never very large; there were never more than four resident monks. The priory had a cell at Wenlock, Shrops (GNHS p179). The octagonal turret in the centre of the S wall of the chapel was built in c1400 (BCM Oct 1968 pp42-48. Oct 1989 p39 il of c1800 from an etching showing a small cottage built into the S transept). John de Sutton (or Dudley) (d1487) of Dudley Castle (see) and his widow were buried in St James' Priory (The Complete Peerage). The remains consist of a nave of the early C13, the S transept, the choir, two chancel S chapels, the outline of the cloister, the W wall of the W range and a spiral stair on the E range (WMAG Feb 1976 p31p). In 1913 in the remaining portion of the nave were two C13 stone coffins. The larger one was broken into two, but the smaller one was in a fairly good state of preservation. There were also the remains of the upper part of a stone effigy of a priest dressed in ordinary ecclesiastical vestments (VCHW vol 3 p102). The priory was the property of Dudley Castle from the Dissolution to 1926 when it was bought by Dudley Corporation (WMAG Feb 1976 p31p). Since the Dissolution the buildings have been occupied by a tanner, a thread manufacturer, glass grinders, and polishers of fire irons and fenders (MR p134p of the ruins). F Downing at Dudley Priory had a fossil tree trunk (DC p123) (SVS p461 note). (SMC p171) (WJO Sept 1905 pp237-240ps) (SOSH p108).

Saltwell Saline spring formerly off Saltwell Lane, Saltwells, in Dudley Wood to the S of Saltwells House. Grew from a saline spring with curative properties, called Lady's Well. Said to have been discovered and promoted by a lady of the family of Lord Dudley, probably in the C17 (TB Sept 1995 p17). It was said that there was a shrine at these wells (IISD p25). Rt Hon Edward Lord Ward tried to make salt out of it but found it too weak (NHS p98) (SHOS vol 2 p230). The spa, or called Ladywood Spa after nearby Lady Wood (see) and later called Pensnett Spa (KCPC p26) (SNSV vol 1 p87), was popular in the early C19. Is probably the spa Scott notes where a neat row of buildings had been erected over the spring containing hot and cold baths in 1823 (SVS pp138-140,465-466). The spa was frequented by the Tipton Slasher, Capt Webb, and Jack Price (TB June/ July 1973 p23p. Sept/ Oct 1973 p6p in 1905. Sept 1995 p16). In 1913 the salt springs were described as resembling those at Cheltenham. At the same date there were baths in connection with the springs (VCHW vol 3 p90). The spring waters were sold commercially but the company collapsed in the 1920s. The old buildings were recently investigated by the Black Country Society (BCM Oct 1975 p54p of Geoff Stevens taking a sample of the water) (MR p238).

Saltwells District above a dell by Black Brook nearly 1m SW of Netherton, 3m SW of Dudley. From the saline spa here called Saltwell (see).

Saltwells Clay Field Clay pit to E of Saltwells House. China clay was extracted here between 1870 to 1947, when the pit flooded irretrievably. The pit has also been called Doulton's Claypit and The Marl'ole. It was designated a SSSI in 1981 and is a habitat for rare orchids and some less common birds, notably the redwing (OS map Sheet 71.07).

Saltwells Colliery Netherton. Pit No. 28 lay to the N of Mouse Sweet. Pit No. 18 became covered by Marybent Road (unlocated) (OS map Sheet 71.08). There was an explosion at the colliery on Aug 10 1855 which killed two miners (TEBC2 p72). In the No. 10 Pit 50 tons of coal fell and killed six bandsmen on Feb 9 1864 (NEE p14) or 1865 (TB May 1972 p20. June/ July 1972 p3).

Saltwells House 1m E of Brierley Hill, above a dell by Black Brook. Built by the Earl of Dudley for his mother. She disliked the place, so it was put at the disposal of his mine managers. It is now a special school (OS map Sheet 71.07). To the S of the house was the Saltwell.

Saltwells Inn Ladywood, Netherton. Was on the site of the Saltwell brine baths and wells (IISD p25) (BCP p114p).

Saltwells Wood See Lady Wood.

Saracen's Head and Freemason's Arms Hotel Old coaching inn at Dudley. Named to commemorate the Crusades and still (1991) known by some local inhabitants as the 'Napper.' The additional part of the name is from the fact that the local Freemasons Lodge established its headquarters here (BCP p28p).

Scott's Green Former hamlet on high ground over the Dudley Canal 0.75m SW of Dudley. Now a mainly residential area which straddles the A461 Stourbridge Road (BCTV p32). The name is from a local family (OS map Sheet 67.15) and was in existence by 1785 (A Plan of the intended Extension of the Dudley Canal in the Birmingham Canal. John Snape. 1785).

Seven Stars Inn Kate's Hill (TB Jan 1979 p3).

Shaver's End Very small district of Dudley ancient parish, 0.75m WNW of Dudley, on high ground. The name may be derived from its exposed position. From here to Eve Hill there is said to have been land called 'The Lawyer's Piece.' A house occupied by a lawyer stood here, and he, being a very shrewd man, the land was dubbed 'Shaver's End' (AMS p447). The name of this former small hamlet appears on the Plan of the Mines of Lord Dudley 1812. There was a windmill in Windmill Street, at SO 933908. The mill was first shown on a map of 1800. It was converted into a house by 1900, and appears on a postcard in the 1920s. It was demolished in the 1930s (WBJ p21 il xvi in 1920) (WIS p24). (BCOPP vol 1 pl.78). A long children's rhyme, which appears in BCM April 1970 p67, is thought to have originated at Shaver's End.

Sledmore Sledmore Primary School is 1m SSE of Dudley. Sledmore appears in the 1841 census as Sleadmore.

Smiling Man Inn Dudley (SJC p5).

Soldier's Hill Netherton. So called from The Old Soldier Inn which stood here (NEE p6).

Sot Hole Dudley (IISD p33).

Sounding Bridge Local name for Highbridge (TB July/ Aug 1973 p13ps). One of the most notable and photographed bridges on the Dudley No. 2 Canal, at Netherton. Constructed in 1858 and replaced by a tunnel. It was named after the perfect echoes which were reproduced in the old tunnel (BCOPP vol 1 p85 pl. c1906).

Spring Hill Netherton. From the spring that flowed from Spring Street (NEE p7). In the Marriott Road area.

Springs Mire District 1.5m WSW of Dudley. The name had appeared by 1841 (1841 census) and reflects the wet scrubland from which several streams emerge (BCTV p30).

Springs Mire Reservoir End of Bull Street, Dudley. It was constructed in 1898 by Henry Lovatt of Wolverhampton for water pumped from Smestow Valley. It is rectangular, 200 feet long and 150 feet wide (BCM March 1998 pp19-20p).

Struggling Man Inn Dudley. (SJC p5).

Swan Inn Castle Street, Dudley. The cellar is said to be haunted by the ghost of a C18 executioner (GOM p18 pl 5(a)).

Sweet Turf Area N of the High Street, Netherton (TB Feb 1974 p5. Sept 1974 p18. Feb 1983 p17 see map). The name appears in a song composed for Netherton Sunday School Union Demonstration, see Cinder Bank. The name is from the Sweet Turf Farm here (NEE p7) and appears in the 1841 census.

Tansley Hall There is a memorial to Mary Ann (Cartwright), wife of James Bourne of Tansley Hall, in St Thomas's church, Dudley.

Tansley Hill To the E of Dixons Green, over 0.75m SE of Dudley. The name Tansley occurs on a Plan of the town of Dudley by J Treasure c1830.

Talbott, The Place in Dudley parish, occurs in documents of the C16 and C17 (VCHW vol 3 p90). Possibly an early form of a current place name.

Thornleigh Trading Estate At Blower's Green, Dudley.

Three Swans Inn Dudley. The inn was bombed on the night of Sept 23 1940. It was the only licensed house in Dudley destroyed in either WW1 or WW2 (IISD p34).

Two Lock Line Connected Dudley Canal Line One at Woodside Junction at Pedmore Road with Dudley Canal Line Two at Blackbrook Junction at N of Lodge Farm. Opened in 1858 by Birmingham Canal Navigation. Closed in 1909 (BCM summer 1995 p26). Sanction for closure was given in 1954 (HCMS No. 2).

Watson Green Former hamlet in the Kates Hill area. As Watson's Green the name appears in the 1841 census and is preserved in a street called Watson Green, and Watson's Close (SNSV vol 2 p79).

Watson's Well Well which provided Kates Hill with water until the 1920s (BCM winter 1994 p31).

Withymoor This former area 1m ESE of Netherton has become known as Darby End. The name, which appears in the 1841 census as Wythemore, is preserved in Withymoor Road, and is from the withy trees which grew here. These trees supplied rains, used in the ironworks, and for basket making (NEE pp6-7).

Withymoor Branch of the Dudley Canal Line Two. Spurred off Line Two near Northfield Road. Ran for a short stretch to Darby End. Opened in 1842. Closure sanctioned in 1960 (HCMS No. 2). The purpose of the canal was to serve Withymoor Furnace and Colliery, and it was also known as Withymoor Arm (SNSV vol 1 p374).

Withymoor Colliery Withymoor, Netherton. It had a disaster on Nov 16 1864 at the Counterfield Mine. Some eight miners who were defying a strike at the time lost their lives (NEE p14) (TB Aug 1984 p14).

Withymoor House Soldier's Hill, Withymoor, Netherton. Here lived a Mr Barrs of Withymoor Furnaces. It appears to have been demolished in or by the late 1890s (NEE p6).

Withyries Stretch of land in Netherton which was between the New Road and the Wilderness (NEE p7).

Woodside Former hamlet, now a residential suburb 1.75m SW of Dudley. Has appeared as Dudleywood Side (1785) (A Plan of the intended Extension of the Dudley Canal in the Birmingham Canal. John Snape. 1785), Dudley Woodside (1834 OS map), and Woodside (1841 census). Woodside appears in a rhyme about Satan which may be an appendix to the rhyme about Satan at Brierley Hill:-

He staggered on to Dudley Woodside
And there he laid him down and died.

(KCPC p32) (FOS p35). The last line in local dialect could be 'When he laid him down and very soon doyed' (BCSG vol 5 p64). Or another version is 'At Dudley Woodside the devil laid him down and died;' (SJC pp2,3). It was at Woodside Iron Works that the ironwork was made for the 1851 Exhibition at Hyde Park (IISD p28). For the murder of Mary Ann Mason of Woodside in 1855 see Sailor's Return Inn (see). Woodside along with Hartshill was a part of Netherton until

1865 (IISD p28). Riots occurred in the Dudley constituency at the general election on Feb 4 1874. Mobs assembled and outbreaks of violence occurred at Woodside and other places (BCM summer 1995 pp69-73). For the murder of Alfred Meredith near Woodside in 1878 see Hart's Hill, Brierley Hill. Harold Parsons (1919-1992), editor of BCM (1968-1988), author of MMBC, TEBC and TEBC2, was born at Woodside (BCM July 1992 pp10-13 p). Sue Lawley, broadcaster, was born at Woodside on July 14 1946. She attended Woodside Junior School, and later Dudley Girls' School (BCM Jan 1991 pp10-13 p) (1998 Who's Who).

Woodside Junction Junction of the Dudley Canal Line One with the Two Lock Line (HCMS No. 2).

Woodside Colliery Woodside. Faulty winding gear here caused the death of three men on Feb 8 1893 (NEE p14).

Woodside Park Woodside. Bounded by Stourbridge Road,

Highgate Road, and Avenue Road. Here is a memorial mainly in grey granite, to Job Garrett 'father of Dudley Town Council' (d1908). The memorial, 19 feet high and weighing 12 tons, was erected by CR Davis of Old Hill and unveiled by JA Hillman, Mayor of Dudley, in 191 (BCM Jan 1988 pp16,17).

Woolpack Inn, The Considered Dudley's oldest inn by 193' and said to have had a continuous licence since 1622 (BC p54).

Yewtree Hill Hamlet appearing on 1882 OS map 0.5m SS of Netherton church. The name is from yew trees ancientl planted on top of the hill to provide material for bows (NE p7).

Yorke Park Place in Dudley parish, occurs in documents o the C15 (VCHW vol 3 p90). Possibly an early form of current place name.

WORCESTERSHIRE (WARLEY WIGORN DETACHED)

The fragmented manor of Warley Wigorn had 16 detached portions dispersed between portions of Warley Salop manor (Shrops), itself a fragmented manor on the E side of the detache portion of Shrops. Several portions of Warley Wigorn were less than five acres in extent and so small that they could not be indicated on OS maps. Some abutted Harborne ancient parish Staffs, on their E side (STELE Feb 22 1952). The confusion was alleviated somewhat when the detached portion of Shrops was removed to Worcs in 1844.

Barnford Hill Park Part of this recent public park S of Langley Green lay in a detached portion of Warley Wigorn with Bristnall Hall (1834 OS map).

Brandhall Manor house of Warley Wigorn, 2m S of Oldbury. The name is derived from perhaps the fact that the owner had the right to brand his mark on any cattle found wandering on the road in the vicinity (STELE July 7 1951). The manor house, anciently tenanted by the Fokerhams and at some time known as Brende Hall, is thought to have had a chantry belonging to the Chapel of St Catherine, Halesowen. A grange of Halesowen Abbey may have been here (TB Feb 1996 p5). The old hall, which stood in the vicinity of Cakemore Brickworks, was demolished many years prior to 1951; a small heap of stones which commemorated the site had also disappeared by 1951 (STELE July 7 1951). In 1935 the land was laid out as Oldbury Municipal Golf Course. The house then known as Brandhall Farm, became the club house; it may have formerly been the home farm of the hall (STELE July 7 1951) (ORR p48)

(TB Aug 1986 p15p of the old golf club house and pool). The name is now used for a residential suburb.

Bristnall Fields Residential district nearly 2m SSE of Oldbury. The name means 'Burst or broken hill' (DUIGNAN) (SPN p108). It appears on the 1834 OS map and was a detached portion of Warley Wigorn. Bristnall was a ward of Sandwell metropolitan borough in 1999.

Bristnall Hall A Bristnall Hall appears on the N side of Bristnall Hall Lane S of Londonderry. The name is preserved in Bristnall Hall High School nearby.

Broad Moor Lay in a detached portion of Warley Wigorn with Bristnall Hall (1834 OS map). The name is preserved in Broadmoor Avenue.

Glory Hills Hills about Hilltop, Warley (STELE May 24 1957) (ORR p64p).

Hilltop Former small hamlet (1834 OS map) in the present Hill Top Road area of Bristnall Fields. The area was rural until the 1930s when it was built on with houses (ORR p61).

Rood End Originally a hamlet now a suburb 1m SE o Oldbury. It may have been in a tiny enclave of Worc sandwiched between Staffs and the detached portion o Shrops. Here was one of four wayside crosses, or hol roods, marking the boundary of Halesowen Abbey land (O p19). The others were at Haden Cross, Lye Cross an Holy Cross (BCWJ p64). (TB April 1996 p29). Writte Rude End on 1834 OS map.

Warley Wigorn Former manor in Carne hundred, Worc (SVS p229). The manor house was Brandhall (TB Ja 1979 pp19-20. Feb 1996 p5). The manor ancientl formed part of the Dudley Barony. About 1337 the heir ess of the barony, Lady Joan de Somery, of the Somer family of Dudley Castle (see), willed Warley Wigorn t Halesowen Abbey on condition the monks pray for he soul annually at the abbey gates (TB Jan 1979 pp19 20ps. Sept 1991 p5). Warley Wigorn was included i Quinton ecclesiastical parish, created in 1841 (STEL May 10 1957).

RECENT CHANGES TO STAFFORDSHIRE'S BOUNDARIES

There were proposals in 1948 to change Staffordshire's boundary when the Boundary Commission suggested it be divided into three counties called Stafford North, Stafford Central, an Stafford South but nothing came of the proposal (The Geographical Journal (III, 1948) p187) (NSFCT 1948 p115). The metropolitan county of West Midlands, formed April 1 1974, too in the county boroughs of Dudley, Smethwick, Walsall, West Bromwich, Wolverhampton, and municipal boroughs of Bilston, Tipton, Wednesbury, and urban districts of Amblecote Brierley Hill, Coseley, Darlaston (Offlow hundred), Sedgley, Tettenhall, Wednesfield, and Willenhall. In 1986 the metropolitan county was abolished and the district councils of Dudley Walsall, Sandwell, and Wolverhampton became metropolitan boroughs in West Midlands county.

Cross index

Corrections to the First Edition

These are corrections spotted by the author and others since publication
of the first edition. Please do not hesitate to inform of any more.

Ashcombe Park Sold by the Sneyds in 1926 (not 1936) (info James Hague).

Barr Beacon 3rd line. Longitude = latitude.

Bilston p56 '1830 to PRESENT' should be indented

Blithfield Reservoir Line eight '4,000 gallons' probably incorrect (info Ted Simpson).
'A lady taxi driver driving across the causeway etc' (info Carol Arnall, not Bruce Braithwaite).

Brewood Hall Brook p84 'Brook' should be emboldened

Broughton Hall p94 , 6th line from bottom of entry in col 2 (NSFCT 1922 p131) should read (NSFCT 1923-4 p131). GROUNDS. line 2 (NSFCT 1922 p131) should read (NSFCT 1923-4 p131).

Cannock Chase Supernatural (last paragraph): 'A tall cowled figure has been seen by the roadside near the Commonwealth Cemetery' (info Carol Arnall, not Bruce Braithwaite).

Castle Ring L6 from bottom 'The ghosts of a young monk etc' (info Carol Arnall, not Bruce Braithwaite).

Chapel Ash Houses Should read Chapel Ash House.

Colton Hall p153 This entry is confused with Colton House. Colton Hall (OS 1834), occupied the site of Colton Old Hall at SK 059192, 1m SE of Colton, and is presently called Colton Hall Farm. The information given by LTM Oct 1971 p35 may also be confused with Colton House, for in 1805 (not 1795) a sheriff of Staffs John Heyliger Burt occupied Colton House between 1792-1817. But the old dovecote mentioned in CWF p175 stood at Colton Hall.

Colton House p153. A new entry should be inserted, entitled Colton House. It lies, set back, on S side of Bellamour Way in Colton village and was built in c1730 (BOE p107). Between 1792-1817 it was occupied by John Heyliger Burt, sheriff of Staffs in 1805.

Colton Old Hall p153 last line. Colton Hall was built on the site of Colton Old Hall, but not in c1730.

Dapple Heath in Blithfield not Blithbury

Dodsley p181 House 0.25m WS of Dods Leigh, should be SW

Drayton-in-Hales Drayton-in-Hales was the name for Market Drayton ancient parish, lying in both Staffs and Shrops.

Dunstall (Tatenhill)p191 L4 'appears as _____' (omission)

Fauld Crater p212 L14 insert 'crater' after 100-150 feet deep

Featherstone p213 para 3 after 'Jodie Scrivens, aged 12,' lower case O in on.

Gibridding Wood SK 043447 should read SK 033448.

Halfpenny Green 4th line from bottom - Birmingham Business Airport = Wolverhampton Business Airport?

Hanley p265 col 2 Norman Wright should read Norman Wainwright (info Fred Leigh).

Hill House 0.5m S of Farewell (FAREWELL). The house was known as Hill House or Hill Farm by the later C18. Later as Hill Farm (1834 OS map), later as The Hill Farm (1:25,000 OS map). 'The house dates from the C18 (VCH vol 14 pp210-211)' - Relates to a different property in Pipe Hill?

Leasowes p730 enbolden Virgil's Grove.

Leasows, The In Penkridge ancient parish, not Stretton ancient parish

Lee Lane 2nd line from bottom - insert 'of' between 'loss' and 'an'

Lichfield Cathedral p356 line 12 from top. 1208 should be 1228

Milwich pp395 L8. - There is no known evidence of a salt mill at Milwich (Randle Knight). L 18. Randle Knight is John Shemilt's great, great nephew (not great grandson) (Randle Knight). L 20. Randle Knight is of Brookside (not Brookside House), Milwich. L 21. There is no known evidence that Milwich was ever part of Stone parish (Randle

Knight). Ls 25-31. In SHC xii n.s. p159 it is suggested that the moat at Garshall may be "castellum domini Hervei" (? de Stretton), but nowhere is there a reference to Garshall Castle (Randle Knight). p396 L 6 from bottom - Muggleston is given as an alternative spelling of Muckleston, not Milwich, and no link with the sect is suggested (Randle Knight)

Milwich Hall p396 L10 - The sundial dated 1691 is, and has always been, in the churchyard. However, there was formerly a sundial at the Hall (Randle Knight).

Onecote 7th line up from bottom 'On' should have lower case 'o'

Paradise line 5 should read 'does not appear'

Perry Bridge p455 L5 w18/6/00as should be 'was'.

Perton Hall line 8 - insert after 'may be the 'dark lady' of Shakespeare's sonnets.' The estate was given by Sir Richard Leveson to Richard 3rd Earl of Dorset in 1652 to settle a family dispute. He sold it to Sir Walter Wrottesley in 1664 (SRO D593c/14/4) (History of the Sackville Family. CJ Philips. 1927. vol 1 p407).

Prestwood (Wednesfield) line 9 - insert after 'belonged to the Levesons (HOWM p44)'. Acquired by them on the marriage of Nicholas Leveson to Matilda daughter of John of Prestwood in 1423. It was the main Leveson residence until 1503, and was leased in 1504 (SRO D593 B/1/26/6/ 3517).

Salt Library, William p498 L 12 - There is no known evidence that William Salt intended to sell his collection; he bequeathed it to his wife, saying she could keep it, or dispose of it by gift or sale (Randle Knight. p499 L 2 - Mrs Salt gave the Collection to the County - she did not sell it for £6,000; she stipulated that the money should be raised to set up a fund to pay a librarian and to look after the Collection (Randle Knight). L 5 - The Library moved to Eastgate Street in 1918 (not 1919).

Shugborough Hall Ghosts: 'A certain bedroom is etc' (info Carol Arnall, not Bruce Braithwaite).

Spaw Spring The boundaries of Wolverhampton, Bushbury, and Wednesbury? (Wednesfield) meet at Spa Well (HOWM p2).

Stafford p 539 2nd col L8 from bottom (see above) should be (see below)

Stretton Hall p563 line 3 Stretton Hall perhaps not sold to Conollys in mid C18 - Sunday Telegraph Magazine may be in error (the VCH gives no date). **p563 line 8** Stretton Hall did not pass to the Moncktons in 1845. It was in this year they only moved from Somerford Hall to Stretton Hall (VB p78). Rather the Hon Edward Monckton of Somerford 'seems' to have acquired an interest in the manor (of Stretton) by 1790 and by c1800 he had bought it from the Connolly family (VCH vol 4 p165).

Trentham Gardens Trentham Hall. p599. Insert - There is a picture of the church, hall and pool dated 1599 (SRO D593H/3/339). Then - In the later C17 there was a fountain etc.....(NHS pp90-91,338). For the pool's subsequent history see The Lake, Trentham Park. The layout of the gardens with avenues of trees leading to paths cut through the woods was illustrated in 1723. This formal layout was swept away by Lancelot Brown in 1759-80 (CL Jan 1968) (SHJ vol 35 2002). ... the Perseus and Medusa statue. It is a replica (now insert - by Papi) of a statue sculpted etc.

Trentham Hall line 13 - instead of 'pay a large levy imposed by the Crown' read 'placate the Crown with £5,000' (Sir Richard Leveson - DNB 2004). **p600 lines 8-9 from top** - Instead of 'In 1668 Sir....by his grandnephew.' read:- 'Sir Richard Leveson died in 1661 and was succeeded by his grand nephew, Francis Fowler (d1667), who was succeeded by his infant son, Francis Leveson (d1668). The estate then passed to William Gower (born c1640), 3rd son of Sir Thomas Gower, 2nd Bt of Sittenham, Yorks, by Frances, daughter and coheiress of Sir John Leveson of

Haling, Kent; thus nephew of Sir Richard (d1661) (info Richard Wisker).' **p600 2nd column line 16 from top** Insert, after '(LGS p236)' **Demolition of the hall** The hall had been given up when the library was sold in Nov 1906 it contained several valuable early printed books. The sixday sale total was £8,777. A sale of pictures and sculpture followed in 1907, the BM acquired some Greek works When Staffs CC would not take the hall without an endowment the 4th Duke decided on demolition. The demolition sale began on Sept 22 1911. It took 50 men nine months to do the job. Two semi detached bungalows in Northwood Lane, Trentham, were erected from its stone (ES various dates in Sept and Oct 1911) (info Richard Wisker). 'The West Gates went to etc....'

Trentham Park line 8 - The Lake (revised entry could read:) has its origins in a pool illustrated in 1599 in the Trentham Gardens (see). It was noted by Plot, and in 1695 Rev George Plaxton records it was formed in two sections called canals with a causeway between them. This was removed to form one lake in 1746-47. The lake was extended northwards by Lancelot Brown in 1759-80 (CL Jan 1968) (SHJ vol 35 2002). followed by - The Trent formerly flowed through it etc....

Upper Crowley GNOSALL surely? - Upper Cowley

Wentlow, The Burial mound on the very top of Gorsty Hill Gorsty Hill Road at SJ 1019408, N of Upper Tean (NSFCT 1983 p12). Should read SJ 019408.

Weston Hall (Weston-on-Trent) L6: 'The ghost of a lady in green etc' (info Carol Arnall, not Bruce Braithwaite).

Unlocated places

Birchwood S of B5234 Abbots Bromley to Newborough road, Abbots Bromley ancient parish (info Mrs EA Ford)

Bulls Park Wood Parallel to Forest Road, Draycott in the Clay, Hanbury ancient parish (info Mrs EA Ford).

East Lodge 1m WSW of Anslow Gate, Rolleston township (detached), Rolleston ancient parish (info Mrs EA Ford).

Holy Bush Should read Hollybush (see) (info Mrs EA Ford)

Jacksons Bank W of A515 near Newborough, Newborough township, Hanbury ancient parish (info Mrs EA Ford).

Longscroft Should read Longcroft (see) (info Mrs EA Ford)

Pepperhill Park - on Staffs Shrops border. Pepperhill, a seat in Staffs (Survey Gazetteer of the British Isles Bartholomew. 9th ed). Pepper Hill (house), Patshull, Staff is a view in the Staffordshire Views collection (VII 137b drawing by Cornelius Varley 1820. Font at Pepperel (sic Patshul is another view in the collection (VII 152) (note the well head was moved to Patshull House & re-erected in the garden there).

The Sale May be identified with Sale Farm and Lower Sale House nearly 2m NW of Newborough, formerly in Marchington Woodlands township, Hanbury ancient parish (Over Sale, Yates 1775) (info Mrs EA Ford).

Seven Stars There is a Seven Stars Farm at SK 115293, at the junction of Tinkers, Stock, and Woodroffes Cliff Lanes between Barns Hill and Dambridge Farm (info Mrs EA Ford).

Uttoxeter Woodlands Area roughly between the High Wood in the N to Kingstone in the S, and Wills Lock in the W to Netherland Green/ Scounslow Green in the E, and also covering Quee Lane; Marchington Woodlands is named again an area rather than a wood, and adjoins Uttoxeter Woodlands (Yates' map 1775) (info Mrs EA Ford).

Bibliography

Ede JF Ede, not JR Ede
Rogers MJW Rogers, not MJW Rodgers

Bibliography

by i) Named Author. ii) No Named Author. iii) Many Authors. iv) Newspapers. v) Journals
vi) Archaeological Journals. vii) Magazines. viii) Directories. ix) Maps. x) List of Source Abbreviations

i) NAMED AUTHOR

A

ABERCROMBY, Lord John. BAP
ADAMS, Dave. NAIW. S&COP
ADAMS, Henry. *The education of Henry Adams: an autobiography.* 1918
ADAMS, Percy WL. WWT. NSF
AINSWORTH, William Harrison. BRO
ALBUTT, Michael. ATSH. CPP. ESSN. LSWA
ALDIS, Marion & Pam Inder. JSD
ALLEN, JS. *The Steam Engine of Thomas Newcomen.* 1977
ALLIBONE, S Austin. *Dictionary of Authors.* 1859 volume 1
ALLIES, Jabez. *Antiquities and Folk-lore in Worcestershire.*
AMPHLETT, John. *A Short History of Clent.* 1890 (or 1908?). Reprinted 1991
ANDERSON, Robert. PM
ANDREWS, Alex. *Long Ago: A Journal of Popular Antiquities.* ed 1873
ANDREWS, Anne. *A History of Tixall. volume 1: Tixall's Churches.* 1995
ANDREWS, C Bruyn (editor). TTD
ANSLOW, J. AR. ASOP. SAIW. SOPP. *Stafford in Old Photographs* (Britain in Old Photographs series). 1994. *Around Rugeley* (Archive Photographs series)1996
ANSON, Capt WV. ALV
ARMITAGE, ES. *The Early Norman Castles of the British Isles.* 1912
ARNALL, Carol. MS
ARROWSMITH. AWM
ASTON, JWA. SOWB
ASTON, VG. *History of Penkhull.* ND
ATKINSON, GA. G.H. Darby, *Captain of the Wyrley Gang.* 1914
ATTWATER, SJD. BLS
ATTWATER, Donald. *Penguin Dictionary of Saints.* 1965
AUBREY, John. *Miscellanies.* 1696

B

BADDELEY, Simon. *The Founding of Handsworth Park 1882-1898.* 1997
BAGNALL, JB. HOWBA
BAGOT, Mrs Charles (Sophy Louisa). *Links with the Past.* 1901
BAGOT, Lady Nancy. *Blithfield.* 1979
BAKER, A. *A Battle Atlas of the English Civil War.* 1986
BAKER, Allan C. *The Cheadle Railway.* 1979
BAKER, E. BCSB
BAKER, Margaret. FCRE
BAKERS, Ron. PHS
BALDWIN, AW. *The MacDonald Sisters.* 1960
BALSOM, Bryan. *Guide to Bourne Pool* copy in Walsall Local History Centre.
BAMFORD, Marion. BUBA.
BAND, John. BFS
BARKER, Dudley. Palmer, the Rugeley Poisoner. 1935
BARNARD, Harry. *Chats on Wedgwood Ware.* 1924
BARNETT, Andrew. HLG
BARNS, Thomas. *Mediomanum; a lost Staffordshire station on Watling Street.* 1904
BARTHOLOMEW, John. *Survey Gazetteer of the British Isles.* 9th ed, post 1951
BASS, Elizabeth W. BU. WYV. FWMBS
BATEMAN, Thomas. TYD. VAD
BAUGH, Robert. *Map of Salop.* 1808. Reprinted in 1983 by Shropshire Archaeological Society

BAYLIS, Harry. *The Hospital of St John Baptist without the Barrs of the City of Lichfield: some notes on its history.* 1960
BAYLISS, P. CBL
BEAMAN, Syliva. IHB
BEARDSMORE, CA. *The Story of Bantock House.* 1972
BEARDSMORE, Stephen J. *A Little Bit of Heath Town.* 1989
BEAVER, C. *Normacot and its Church.* 1972
BEBBINGTON, Graham. *From Pit Boy to Prime Minister.* c1986. *Trentham at War.* 1995
BEBINGTON, AN. BSL
BELCHER, Sherry. CCAP
BELL, David. *Ghosts and Legends of Derbyshire.* c1992. GLS. MCS
BEMBROSE, Paul J. NULOP
BENNETT, AJ. HK
BENNETT, Joan. *French Connections.* 1995
BENNETT, Sir Ernest. AAHH
BENNETT, TR. IP
BENTON, Jane. SCSB
BENZ, S. PPP
BERESFORD, Rev William. BOB
BERESFORD, Maurice. HOG. NTMA
BERESFORD, Rev W. MOS
BETT, Henry. *English Legends.* 1950
BIGGS, David. TOPP
BIGLAND, Eileen. *In the Steps of George Borrow.* 1951
BIGNELL, Victor. *Catastrophic Failures.* 1977
BILLINGHAM, John. *History Around Us.* (Halesowen). 2nd ed 1992
BILLINGHAM, Rosalind. *George Heming Mason.* 1982
BILLINGTON, J Somner. AADB
BILLS, DM. KRH. *By Tram to Kinver (1901-1930).*
BINNEY, Marcus. OVH
BIRD, Vivian. BEV. VB
BIRRELL, Dr. *The Honour of Tutbury in the 14th and 15th centuries.* Unpublished thesis
BLACK, JB. *Reign of Elizabeth.*
BLAGG, CJ. *A History of the North Staffordshire Hounds and Country 1825-1902.* 1902
BLAND, James. *The Common Hangman.* 1984.
BLAY, WF. LET. SNWA. SNBP
BLAZIER, Stella M. *The Wolverhampton Chapel Case.* MA Thesis 1985
BLEAU, Johann. *Staffordiensis Comitatus; vulgo Staffordshire* (map of Staffordshire). 1648
BLOCKSIDGE, E. WNH
BLOME, Richard. *A Mapp of Stafford Shire with its hundreds......* (engraved by Wenceslas Hollar). 1671. *A Mapp of Stafford Shire.* (map of Staffordshire). 1673
BLOOR, WA (alias A Scott). BOJ
BLOUNT, Thomas. BB
BOBE, H. SMCC
BODE, H. BPCSM. VBB. VL
BODEN, SE. BNDA
BOLTON, John M. *Canal Town: Stone.* 1981 reprint 1989.
BOOKER, Rev Luke. DC
BORD, Janet & Colin. MMSE. SW
BOSSEN, Winifred M. PHH
BOSWELL, James. *Life of Johnson.* 1860 ed. GB Hill and LF Powell. volume 1
BOTHAN. Bothan's map. 1794
BOTT, Ian M. WDOP
BOULTON, J. PVBC
BOWERS, WH. RHPS
BOWRING, Rick. *The Cheslyn Hay Book.* 1977
BOWYER, G. SMOPP
BOYLAN, Marshall S. MD
BRACKEN, L. *History of the Forest and Chase of Sutton Coldfield.* 1860
BRADFORD, Anne. MGH. MS&S

BRADLEY, JW. SPP
BRAITHWAITE, Bruce. ROT
BRAND, John. PA
BREEZE, Mary. HOLF
BREW, Alec. C&COP. TPOP. WHF
BRIAN, H. *The Faraway Years.*
BRIDDON, Rev WH. HV
BRIDGEMAN, Rev Canon GTO. CE
BRIGGS, JHY. HOLB. NUL
BRIGHT, Hugh. *The Herckenrode Windows in Lichfield Cathedral.* 1962
BRIGHTON, Rev F. TOI. P. OH
BRIMBLE, John. TSSOP
BRITTEN, EDS. *A Dictionary of English Plant-names.* 1965
BROADBENT, RC. BTRA
BROOK, Fred. SIT
BROOKE, Richard Brooke. VBE
BROOKS, John. *The Good Ghost Guide.* 1994
BROOME, JH. *Jean-Jacque Rousseau in Staffordshire 1766-1767.* 1966
BROUGHTON Bt, Sir Delves L. *Records of an Old Cheshire Family.* 1908
BROUGHTON, James. The scrapbook of newspaper cuttings compiled by Broughton covering some of the C18 and the earlier part of the C19 is in WSL. It is referred to as Broughton's Scrapbook in the Encyclopaedia. SM. SMC. SMT
BROWN, Baldwin G. *The Arts in Early England.* volume 4. 1915
BROWN, GN. BTC. TOH
BROWN, Richard S. FSLBWM
BROWNE, Bishop. *An Account of the Three Ancient Cross Shafts, the Font, and St Bertram's Shrine at Ilam.* 1888
BUCHAN, John. Midwinter. *Certain travellers in old England (a novel).* 1923
BUCHANAN, Ian and others. *The Guinness International Who's Who of Sport.* 1993
BUDDEN, D. *History of St Matthew's Hospital.* private print 1989
BULLOCK, WH. IVNF
BURCHCLERE, Lady Winifred. *George Villiers 2nd Duke of Buckingham. 1628-1687.* 2 volumes. 1903
BURKHARDT, F. *The Correspondence of Charles Darwin.* vol I (1821-36) 1985. vol II (1836) 1986?
BURLEIGH, Florence. *Sister Dora: her life and work.*
BURNE, AH. *More Battlefields of England.* 1952.
BURNE, SAH. APB. ESH. OP. OPB. *The Widow of the Wood.* 1964. OPM. *The Staffordshire County Election 1747.* 1967
BURNE, Charlotte Sophia. SFL
BURRITT, Elihu. BCGB
BURROWS, Leslie E. *Little London Baptist Church.* 1997
BUSCOT, Canon Willibrord. *Sedgley Park and Cotton College.* 1940
BUTTERS, Paul. SSTY. *Yesterday's Town: Stafford.* 1984
BYFORD-JONES, W. QBSS. QML. QMMH. QVTM
BYNG, Hon John 5th Viscount Torrington. TTD
BYRNE, Tom. TFTP. TFTPM

C

CALVERT, Charles. HOSCC
CALVERT, Frederick. SSC
CAMDEN, William. *Britannia.* 1st ed 1586
CAMERON, Kenneth. *English Place Names.* 1961
CAMM, Dom Bede. FS
CAMP, John. *One Hundred Years of Medical Murder.* 1982
CAMPBELL, Frances E. KMC. KRC. RKE. SCK
CANTRILL, TC. NFCF

CARTER, Tony. *The Crusade against Crippledom: The Story of Millicent Duchess of Sutherland and the North Staffordshire Cripples Aid Society.* 1991.
CARVEN, Martin. UST
CASON, RA. PBH
CASSON, Sir Hugh. BZ. FZ
CELORIA, FSC. SARCH
CHALLIS, Rev JF. HOTC
CHAMBERS, R. CBD
CHAMBERS, William. DCB
CHANCE, JF. *History of Chance Bros & Co.* 1919
CHAND, RA. *Moseley Old Hall.* National Trust Guide. 1993
CHANDLER, G. D
CHANNER, Nick. PWIS
CHAPMAN, Hester W. *George Villiers; A study of George Villiers 2nd Duke of Buckingham. 1628-1687.* 1949
CHAPMAN, RW. *The Letters of Samuel Johnson.* 1952
CHARLES, Wyndham. *Dora Pattison: the nurse from the Black Country.* 1966
CHARLESWORTH, A. *Atlas of Rural Protest in Britain 1548-1900.*
CHATTOCK, C. *Antiquities.* 1884
CHATWIN, AH. BPP
CHATWIN, Alex. BUOP. *Gailey Crossroads in the 1920s.* c1995
CHATWIN, PB. *The Roman Site at Shenstone, Staffordshire.* 1944
CHEETHAM, J Keith. *Mary Queen of Scots: the Captive Years.* 1982
CHERRY, JL & K. HSS. SIOT
CHESTER, Herbert. *The Iron Valley or Eight Centuries of Iron Making in the Churnet Valley.* 1979. CCT
CHETWYND, W. HPH
CHETWYND-STAPYLTON, HE. COI
CHITHAM, E. HORV
CHITHAM, Edward. *The Black Country.* 1972
CHRISTIAN, Roy. *Ghosts and Legends.* 1972
CHRISTIANSEN, Rex. *A History of the Railways of Great Britain. volume 7 The West Midlands.* 1973
CHURCH, RA. *Kenrick's in Hardware.* 1969
CLANCY, JP. *The earliest Welsh Poetry.* 1970
CLAPHAM, AW. *Romanesque Architecture in England.* 1930
CLARK, CFG. CDBC. COD
CLARK, Howard D. WPP
CLARK, JGD. *The Mesolithic Age in Britain.* 1932
CLARKE, Bob. KEOP
CLARKE, Roy. OHOPP
CLAY, Rotha M. *Hermits and Anchorites of England.* 1914
CLAYTON, Howard. CCHCA. CCHCB. *St John's Hospital, Lichfield.* 1984. MLL
CLIFFORD, Arthur & Sir Thomas. HOT
CLIFFORD, James L. *Young Samuel Johnson.* 1955 1962 ed
CLIFTON, AB. *The Cathedral Church of Lichfield Cathedral: A Description of it fabric and a Brief History of the Episcopal See* (published by George Bell & Sons). 1908.
CLOUGH, JW. RHPS
COBBETT, William. *Rural Rides.* 1853, volumes 1 & 2 Everyman's Library ed 1932
COCKIN, GM. NFCF
CODRINGTON, Thomas. *Roman Roads in Britain.* 1918
COLEMAN, SJ. SJC
COLLINGWOOD, CHD. BRITC
COLLINS, Andrew. *The Circlemakers.* 1992. *The Seventh Sword.* 1991, 2nd ed 1992
COLLINS, Paul. BCFF
COLVIN, Howard. *A Biographical Dictionary of British Architects 1600-1840.* 3rd ed. 1995
CONNER, Patrick. *Oriental Architecture in the West.*
CONWAY, Rev JP. N
COOKE. COOKE
COOKSLEY, MV. GSGH
COPE, Norman A. SIS
CORUM, Tim. *Stoke-on-Trent in Old Photographs* (Britain in Old Photographs series). 1993
COULAM, JT. HONUL
COUNSELL, Michael. HOHE
COX, GA. DOS
COX, Thomas. SD
COX, T. *Magna Britannia.*
COYNE, JJ. *Oscott College, a brief history.*
CRAPPER, JS. ACHRH

CREBER, John. JC
CROSTON, James. FTP
CROWQUILL, A. *The Wanderings of a Pen and Pencil.* 1846
CRYSTAL, David. *The Cambridge Biographical Encyclopedia.* 1994
CULLINGFORD, CHD. *British Caving.* 1962
CUTLER, A. WNNNR

D

DAKEYNE, Miss. LMF
DALE. Antony. *James Wyatt.* 1936
DALE, FW. *A Short History of the Old Windmill which was situated on the site of the present Observatory Inn.* 1912
DANIEL, GE. *Prehistoric Chamber Tombs of England and Wales.* 1950
DARLINGTON, John. SPJD
DAVID, Thomas J. AS
DAVIES, Wendy. *Wales in the early Middle Ages.* 1982
DAVIS, Horace. SNW
DAVISON, C. *A History of British Earthquakes.* 1924
DAWSON, P. DDI
DAY, Brian. *A Chronicle of Folk Customs.* 1998
DAY, Kathleen. *Memories of the Downs Banks.* c1999
DEACON, Rev E. SQCS
DEAN, Richard. HCMS
DEARDEN, John. TTTD
DEAVILLE, Malcolm. PP
DEFOE, Daniel. DD
DENT, R. HS
DENT, Robert K. *Old and New Birmingham.* 1879
DESMOND, Adrian. *Darwin.* 1991
DEVEREAUX, Paul. *The Ley Hunter's Companion.* 1979
DILWORTH, D. *Sandwell Priory.* 1975. TMS
DITCHFIELD, PH. COEA. VED
DODD, AE & EM. PRT
DONNELL O', Elliot. FG. DG
DOUCE, Francis. *Illustrations of Shakespeare.* 1839
DOUGLAS, John. *Abbey Square Sketch Book.* 1872 (-90?)
DOW, George. NSA
DOWER, John. *Map of Staffordshire.* Weekly Dispatch Atlas.
DRABBLE, Margaret. *Arnold Bennett.* 1974
DRABBLE, Phil. PD. BC
DRAKE, Peter. HHHW
DRAYTON, Michael. *Polyolbion.* 1613
DREWETT, John. *Midland Rivers.* 1996
DRINKWATER, Rev Canon FH. AH
DUDLEY, Dud. *Metallum Martis: or, Iron made with Pit-Coale, Sea-Coale, etc.* 1665 (a copy of it appears in Curiosities of Dudley. CFG Clark. 1881)
DUDLEY, Georgina. DIP
DUGDALE, William. *Monasticon Anglicanum.* 1693 (English version). *Antiquities of Warwickshire illustrated etc.* 1656
DUIGNAN, WH. DUIGNAN
DUNICLIFF, Joy. *Mary Howitt: Another Lost Victorian Writer.* 1992
DUNNICLIFF, John. *Uttoxeter Canal and nearby Waterways.* 1987
DUNPHY, Angus. *A Geography of Wombourne and Lower Penn.* 1972. *The Ellowes: Its Owners and Times.* 1983. *Angus Dunphy's Penn.* 1986. PMPD. POAP. PAIP. PONP. PPTP. WMA. *Industrial Archaeology-Molinology.*
DYER, James. *Prehistoric England and Wales.* 1981

E

EASTHAUGH, K. *Havergal Brian, the making of a composer.*
EATON, Susan. HO
EDE, JR. HOWY or HOWV
EDEES, ES. FOSE
EDWARDS. *English Secular Cathedrals.*
EDWARDS. *Old English Customs.* 1842
EDWARDS, Rev FJ. *Notes Illustrative of the History of the Church in Trentham.* 1859
EDWARDS, Jeni. AVH
EDWARDS, Rev N. MT
EKWALL, Eilert. EKWALL. RN

ELLWOOD, J. HOM
ELTON, RF. HR
ELWELL, Charles JL. AOBC. IE
ELWES. *The Trees of Great Britain and Ireland.* volume 6 1913
ENGLAND. *Gazetteer.* 1778
EPSTEIN, J. *The Crisis of 1842: Chartism, the colliers' strike and the outbreak in the Potteries in The Charter Experience.*
ERDESWICK, Sampson. SOS
ESSINGTON, RW. ASE
EVANS, Gareth. *Hoar Cross Hall.* 1986
EVANS, Sir John. ABI. ASI
EVANS, Jim. ESSN
EVELYN, John. *The Diary of John Evelyn.* Everyman's Library. 1936 volumes 1 & 2
EVERITT, Katherine. *Bricks and Flowers.* c1950
EYTON, Rev Robert W. *Domesday Studies: An Analysis and Digest of The Staffordshire Survey.* 1881

FARMAN, Richard. BTOP. ABTOP. ESNF
FARMER, David Hugh. ODS
FARROW, Jan. BWWOPP. ALOPP. ALOPPR
FEA, Allan. *The Flight of The King.* 1897. *After Worcester Fight.* 1904. *Secret Chambers and Hiding Places.* 1901. *Old Midland Manor-houses.*
FERRERS, C. HATC
FERRIS, Anne. BGFB. SBG
FINBERG, HPR. *Lucerna. Studies of some problems in the early history of England.* 1964. *The Early Charters of the West Midlands.* 1961
FINLOW, COL. RRCC
FINNEY, Mrs AJ. CSJA
FISHER, Adrian. *Mazes* (Shire Album Guides)
FISHER, Michael. *St Bertelin of Stafford.* 1977. CSBSS. DA. *A Vision of Splendour: Gothic Revival in Staffordshire 1840-1890.* 1995. *Alton Towers: A Gothic Wonderland.* 1999
FLETCHER, George. *The Life and Career of Dr William Palmer of Rugeley, together with a full account of the murder of John P Cook and a short account of his trial in May 1856.* 1925
FLETCHER, Mark H W. IISD. NEE
FLOYER, Sir John. *History of Cold Bathing.* 1709
FOLEY, Jim. CJF. TRTC
FOOT, Paul. *Murder at the farm, who killed Carl Bridgewater?* 1986, 2nd ed 1988
FORD, David J. LTD
FORD, T. *Caves of Derbyshire.* 1984
FOREMAN, RLE. *Havergal Brian and the performance of his orchestral music.*
FORTESCUE, Mary Teresa. HOCA
FOSTER. FA
FOULKES, Peter. LAWTT
FOX, Betty. SNAR. SNBC
FRASER, Antonia. *Biography of Charles II.* 1979
FREER, Tony. KEOP
FRERE S. *Problems of the Iron Age in Southern Britain.* no date.
FROST, R. VESOP
FULLER. *Church History*
FULLER, Thomas. HWE
FYTTE, Patrick. *One Little Maid: the Memories of Dame Hilda Bracket.* 1980
FYSON, Robert. *The Crisis of 1842: Chartism, the colliers' strike and the outbreak in the Potteries in The Charter Experience.*

G

GALBRAITH, Ann. PTYV. SNBP
GALE, WKY. *Soho Foundry.* 2nd ed. 1948. *The Coneygree Story.* 1954. *The Black Country Iron Industry.* 1966. *Samuel Griffiths' Guide to the Iron Trade of Great Britain.* 1873. New ed 1967. *A History of the Pensnett Railway.* 1975. *A History of Bromford 1780-1880.* 1980
GARDNER, A. *A Handbook of English Medieval Sculpture.* 1951
GARDNER, Steve. UNT
GARNER, Robert. GNHS
GELLING, Margaret. *Signposts to the past, place-names and the history of England.* 1978, 2nd ed 1988. *Place-names in the landscape.* 1984. WMMA

GENGE, Trevor. LAIW. SDOP. SDSSOP
GIBBONS, Gavin. *The Coming of the Space Ships.* 1956.
GIBBONS, Verna Hale. *Jack Judge: The Tipperary Man.* 1998
GIBSON, Gary. SGM
GILBERT, Clive. *The Midlands.* Past-into-Present series. 1978
GILL D. *Caves of Derbyshire.* 1984
GIROUARD, M. *Robert Smythson and the Elizabethan Country House.*
GISBORN, J. *The Vales of Weaver.* 1797
GLEW, EL. HOWG
GODDEN, Geoffrey. *Handbook of British Pottery and Porcelain Marks.* 1986
GODWIN, John. *Lichfield Miscellany.* 1978. JG. EAS. TPP. BPW
GOODE, Harry. *The Natural History of Cannock Chase.* WEA. 1973
GOODMAN, Kevin. GOD
GORDON, JF. SBT
GOUGH, TH. BCSG
GOULD, Jim. MCC. MOA
GRAZEBROOK, Capt RM. SCFK
GREAVES, Richard L. *Deliver us from evil, the radical underground in Britain, 1660-1663.* 1986.
GREEN, Andrew. GOHK. PL. GOT
GREEN, Henry E. *The Limestone Mines of Walsall.* 1977. *The Delves.* 1983
GREEN, John R. *A Short History of the English People.* 1898
GREEN, Richard Lancelyn. *The Uncollected Sherlock Holmes.* 1983
GREENSLADE, MW. HOS. BAH. SH.
GREGORY, S. *First and Last.* 1979
GRESLEY, W. *The Siege of Lichfield: A tale illustrative of the great rebellion.* 1881 2nd ed.
GREYSMITH, Brenda. *The History of Staffordshire Agricultural Society.* c1978
GRICE, Frederick. FTWM
GRIFFITH, Paddy. *The Battle of Hopton Heath 1459.* 1995
GRIFFITHS, WR & E. KRH. *By Tram to Kinver (1901-1930).*
GRIFFITHS, George. TAB
GRIFFITHS, May. WWW. APW
GRIFFITHS, Samuel see GALE, WKV
GRIGSON, Geoffrey. SCA
GRINSELL, Leslie. FPSB
GROSE, F. PG
GUNN, Alexander. *Abbeys, Castles & Ancient Halls of England & Wales. Their Legendary Lore and Popular History.*
GUNSTONE, AJH. *Sylloge of coins of the British Isles.* 17. 1971
GUTCH. *Collectanea Curiosa* vol 3
GUTTERY, DR. *From Broad-glass to Cut Crystal: a history of the Stourbridge Glass Industry.* 1956. FDD. KCPC. KCTJ

H

HACKWOOD, FW. WP. HODW. WW. TFWH. HOWB. RS. SR. OW. RW. WAM. SOBC. CCC. SC. SSHL. AOW. HON. IADC. SWH. O. *Book of Giants.* 1916. OCHW. SGH. SCSF. SG
HADCOCK, R Neville. MRH
HADEN, H Jack. SNSV
HADFIELD, Charles. *The Canals of The West Midlands: Volume 5 of The Canals of The British Isles.*
HADFIELD, John. *The Shell Guide to England.* 1977
HADFIELD, Miles. *History of British Gardening or Gardening in Britain.* 1960.
HAGGAR, Reginald G. M&H. *Staffordshire Chimney Ornaments.* 1955
HAINES, Rev Herbert. BMMB
HAINING, Peter. DOG
HALL, Joseph. *The Iron Question.* 1858
HALL, FTD. *Handsworth: A Summary of Houses, Places, People, Events and Institutions.* 1984. HPPE
HALLAM, Jack. HIE
HAMMOND, Joyce. SHOP
HAMMOND, JL & B. *The Age of The Chartist 1832-1854.*
HANCOCK, H. WMC
HANNAH, IC. D

HARDWICK, WE. HOHH
HARDY, Sir Reginald. HOPT
HARGREAVE. *Hargreave's map.* 1832
HARNAMAN, DG. *A Brief Account of the Life and Writings of Dinah Mullock.*
HARPER, WJ. MC
HARRIS, Nigel. *The Yarlet Story.* 1993
HARRIS, W. CR
HARRIS, William. RDC
HARRISON, Christopher. HOK. *Keele Church.* HOSTK
HARRISS, GL. *Henry V, the practice of kingship.* 1st ed 1985. 1993
HARTILL, Prebendary E. HOPE
HARTLEY, GT. LCWA
HARVEY, Frances A. WOY. WOY2
HARWOOD, Dr. HOL
HAWKES, Harry. *Murder on the A34.* 1970. *The Capture of the Black Panther: Casebook of a killer.* 1978
HAWLEY, JDS. SMASCW
HAY, Douglas. AFT
HAYDEN, Peter. BG
HEADLEY, G. F
HEAP, James. TSS
HEATON, Nell. TRBI
HEATON, Peter. *Shire County Guide.* 1986
HEELY, Joseph. *Description of Hagley, Enville and the Leasows.* ND but earlier than 1777. LHEL. LHEF
HEMER, June. *Handbook for Widows.* 1978
HENRY. *The Trees of Great Britain and Ireland.* volume 6. 1913
HENRY, C. CSL
HEWITT. *Handbook of Lichfield.*
HEYWOOD, Gerald GP. CCR
HIBBERD, Cecil. RBS
HICKES, George (Dean of Worcester). *Linguarum Vett Septentrionalium Thesaurus Grammatico - Criticus et Archaelogicus LP.* 1705
HIGSON, TH. *Stafford Survey.* 1949
HILL. *Treasure Trove in Law and Practice.* 1936
HILL, Stan. BHOP. BHOP2
HILL, J. HS
HILLIER, Caroline. WM. *A Journey to the Heart of England.* 1978
HINCHLIFFE, Rev Edward. BART
HINDE, Alfred. GW
HIPPISLEY, Antony D. HB
HIRONS, RJ. *The Battle of Blore Heath and the Rout at Ludford.* Unpublished BA dissertation. Keele University. 1973
HISCOCK, Ted. GATD
HITCHING, Francis. *The World Atlas of Mysteries.* 1978, 2nd ed 1979
HODGKINS, Keith. TSSOP
HODGKINSON, HR. *The Roman Site at Shenstone, Staffordshire.* 1944
HOLE, Christina. HE. ESS
HOLLAND, Robert. *A Dictionary of English Plant-names.* 1965
HOLLIS, Tony J. SMML
HOLME, Charles. GE
HOLT, Prof JC. RHH
HOLT, DM. SFH
HOMESHAW, J. *Great Wyrley 1051-1951.* 1951
HOMESHAW, James. SOB
HOMESHAW, EJ. WBF
HONE, William. HYB
HOOKE, Della. LASS
HOPE Moncrieff, AR. TPC
HOPKIN, Mary Alden. DJL
HORNE, JS. SCC. CSMS. *History of King Edward VI Grammar School (Stafford).* 1930. SCCC. SOCC
HOROVITZ, David. BDH
HORROX, WA. *Bibliography of Literature relating to the escape of Charles II after the battle of Worcester.* 1924
HORSLEY, John. *Britannia Romana.* 1732
HOTTEN, John Camden. HSB. TEW
HOWES, Bill. *English Reservoirs.* 1967
HOWITT, William. *Visits to Remarkable Places.* C19
HOWSON, Clive. MSM
HOWSON, Gerald. *Thief-Taker General: The Rise and Fall of Jonathan Wild.* 1970
HUCKERBY, E. WSS
HUGHES, John. BT
HUGHES, Mark. SOSH
HUGHES, George Bernard. *The Story of Spode.*

HUMPREYES, George R. *A House in the High Street.* 1973
HUNTBACH, A. H
HUSENBETH, Canon FC. *Sedgley Park.* 1856
HUTCHINGS, FW. *A Map of the County of Stafford.....1832.*
HUTTON, W. *History of Birmingham.* 1783. 2nd ed, and another ed of 1835
HUTTON, William. *History of Derby.* 1st ed 1791. 2nd ed 1817

I

ILLINGWORTH, Rev JA. *A Just Narrative or Account of the Man whose Hands and Legs rotted off: In the parish of Kingswinford in Staffordshire where he died June 21 1677.* 1678
INDER, Pam & Marion Aldis. JSD
INGAMELLS, Jeremiah. *Historical Records and Directory of Newcastle-under-Lyme.* 1871. SSW
INGRAM, John Henry. HHFT
INGRAM, James. *The River Trent.* 1955
INSKIP, KW. SHCB
ISAACSON, Rev S. *Barrow digging by a Barrow-Knight.* 1845

J

JACK, James. HNM
JACKSON, K. *Language and History in Early Britain.* 1953
JACKSON, John. HDCPT. HOLJ
JACKSON, JW. HIL
JACKSON, Robert. *Library of the Unexplained - Great Mysteries.* 1992
JAMIESON, WM. MMM
JENKS, Alfred E. *The Staffordshire and Worcestershire Canal.* 1907
JENNINGS, TS. JHSB
JEKYLL, Gertrude. *Garden Ornament Topiary Work.* 1918. 2nd ed 1982
JEREMIAH, Josephine. *The River Severn: A Pictorial History.* 1998
JERVOISE, E. ABMEE
JEUDA, Basil. RL
JEWITT, LL. *The Wedgwoods.* 1865
JEWITT, LI. *The Ceramic Art of Great Britain.* 1878
JEWITT, Llewellynn FW. JAT. BAT. JGM
JOB, Barry. WBJ
JOHNSON, DA. *Staffordshire and the Great Rebellion.* 1964.
JOHNSON, FJ. VC
JOHNSON, John. *Natural History de Quadruped.*
JOHNSTONE, JD. WJ. WJC
JONES, Barbara. F&G
JONES, Clement. *Aynuk; a collection of over 150 Aynuk Stories.* 1950
JONES, DV. *The Royal Town of Sutton Coldfield: a commemorative history.* 1973
JONES, James P. HM
JONES, James P. HOPTT
JONES, John Morris. MNB
JONES, Mervyn. POT
JONES, P. S&UR
JONES, Pauline. *Milton's Missionary.*
JONES, William Highfield. *History of the Congregational Churches of Wolverhampton; from the years 1662 to 1894.* 1894. *Story of Japan, Tinplate Working, Bicycle and galvanising Trades in Wolverhampton and District.* 1900
JOSTEN, CH. *Elias Ashmole (1617-1692).* 5 vols. 1966

K

KAMP, W Meulen. F
KEATMAN, Martin. GS. EF
KEEN, MH. *England in the Later Middle Ages.* 1973
KELLY, Alison. *The Story of Wedgwood.* 1962. 1975
KEMBLE, John Mitchell. *The Saxons in England. A History of the English Commonwealth till the period of the Northern Conquest.* 1849, 2nd ed 1876
KENDRICK, TD. *Anglo-Saxon Art.* 1938
KENNEDY, Douglas. *English Folk-dancing Today and*

Yesterday. 1964
KENNEDY, Joseph. BALH
KENNEDY, J. MHSP
KENWARD, James. HAS
KERSHAW, E. *History of Orme Boy's School.* 1967
KEYSER, Charles E. NTL
KINGHAM, Diana. *Mazes* (Shire Album Guides)
KINGSTON, HP. *The Wanderings of Charles II in Staffordshire and Shropshire after the Worcester Fight September 3 1651.* 1933
KIP, William. *Staffordiae Comitatus pars olim Cornaviorum* (map of Staffordshire). 1607
KIRK, KE. *The Story of The Woodard Schools.* 1937
KNAPP, WI. *The Life, Writings and Correspondence of George Borrow.* 1899
KNOTT, Cherry Ann. HHH
KNOWLES, David. MRH
KOLBERT, JM. *The Sneyds and Keele Hall.* 1967. *The Sneyds Squires of Keele.* 1976. KH

L

LADELL, Rev AR. *The Abbots Bromley Horn Dance.* 1932
LAFRATI, Joseph P. HPCH
LAITHWAITE, P. *History of St Chad's Church.* 1938
LAMBERT, B. AHH
LAMBERT, Lionel. *St Bertelin of Stafford and the Conversion of the heathen Mercian Folk.* ND. *The Charities of Stafford.* c1931-1955?
LANE, Allen. *Penguin Dictionary of Proverbs.* 1983
LANE, Brian. MCGM
LANGFORD, John Alfred. S&W. *A Century of Birmingham Life: or, a chronicle of local events, from 1741 to 1841.* 1868
LANGFORD, Dr J Ian. S&WC
LANGLEY, Tom. *The Tipton Slasher: His Life and Times.* 1969
LAWLEY, GT. BOW. BSC. HOBL. HOBLL
LAWRENCE, Eric A. *The Life of WF Callaway.* 1890
LAWRENCE-SMITH, Kathleen. TOS
LE STRANGE, Richard. BMB
LEACH, Maria. DFMAL
LEACH, JT. SSR
LEAD, Peter. Historic Waterways Scenes Series '*The Trent and Mersey Canal.*' 1980
LEAH, MD and others. WSS
LEE, Rev JR. HOMD
LEE, Herbert. SHOW
LEE, Thomas Eyre. *Old Meeting House, Wolverhampton.*
LEEDS, ET. *Celtic Ornament.* 1933. *Early Anglo-Saxon Art and Archaeology.* 1936
LEESE, Phillip R. KAIW. KBT
LEIGH. *History of Lancashire, Cheshire and Derbyshire.*
LEIGH, Fred. DMF. LMV. LWF. *The Town That Has Forgot Its Past.* c1998/9
LEIGH, Peter. APW
LELAND, John. LI
LEVIEN, E. ERH
LEWIS, Marilyn. WOPP
LEWIS, Roy. SAIW. SOPP. SDOPP. HCMBOPP. TDOPP. LOPP. S&DOP. AUOPP. *Stafford Past: An Illustrated History.* 1997. *Around Stafford* (Images of England series). 1999
LEWIS, S. *Topographical Dictionary of England.* volume 1
LEWISOHM, Mark. *Radio Times Guide to TV Comedy.* 1998
LEYLAND, John. POD
LLEWELLIN, Frederick G. KNS
LOMAS, AC. LPL
LOMAS, TG. LCPG
LONES, TE. BCC
LONSDALE, Margaret. *Sister Dora.* 1880.
LORD, Peter. *Portrait of the River Trent.* 1972
LOUDON, JC. ECFVA
LOWE, Bernard. TBH
LUDLAM, Harry. *Ghosts Among Us.*1994
LUDLOW, Frederick B. *County Biographies: Staffordshire.* 1901
LUMSDON, Les. *Family Walks in the Staffordshire Peak and Potteries.* 1990. PWPD. PWNS. TSW
LYCETT-SMITH, Roger. *Airfield Focus. No. 34: Stoke-on-Trent (Meir).* 1998

LYON, CJ. *Personal History of Charles the Second 1650-1651.* 1851
LYONS, Amy. BCS
LYONS, Frederick J. *Jonathan Wild: Prince of Robbers.* 1936
LYSONS, Rev Daniel. *Magna Britannia.* Editions 1806-22.

M

MACDONALD, M. *The Symphonies of Havergal Brian* (3 volumes).
MADDISON, John. ORR. SMEOP
MADDOCKS, Robert. *The Good Old Grit: A History of the People of Penkridge 1270-1939.* 1994
MADOX. *Baronia.* 1741
MAJOR, John. *History of Greater Britain.* 1521
MALAM, John P. ALP
MALKIN, Neville. AGT
MALLET, WH. STV
MALLET, Witt. MCSSW
MALLIN, Kenneth. *Noah Hingley: The World's Premier Manufacturer of Ships' Anchors and Cables in the period 1890-1918.* 1998
MALLON, Bill. *The Guinness International Who's Who of Sport.* 1993
MANDER, Charles. *Detail of the Circumstances relative to the Old Meeting House in John Street, Wolverhampton etc.*
MANDER, Gerald P. HOWM. WA. *History of Wolverhampton Grammar School.* 1913
MANKOWITZ, W. M&H
MANTELL, Keith. TD
MANTELL, Keith. *Dovedale Guide.* 1985
MANTLE. Jonathan. GHC
MANTON, Jo. *Sister Dora; The Life of Dorothy Pattison.* 1971
MANVELL, Roger. *Sarah Siddons: Portrait of an Actress.* 1970
MARGARY, ID. *Roman Roads in Britain.* 1957
MARKLAND, R. PSS
MARKS, John. BOOP
MARSHALL. *Planting and Rural Ornaments.* volume 1
MARTIN, Wilmot. *A Minstrel in Staffordshire.* 1923
MARTINEAU, Violet. RSL
MASEFIELD, Charles. LGS
MASON, Sarah. *Found Ready. Memorials of the Rev G Poole.* 1890
MASON, Frank. *The Book of Wolverhampton.* 1979
MASTERS. *Iter Boreale.* 1675
MATTHEWS, Peter and others. *The Guinness International Who's Who of Sport.* 1993
MATTHEWS, Tony. *The Wolves.* 1989. *The Story of Wolverhampton Wanderers.* 1994
MATTHEWS, William. *Charles II's Escape from Worcester: A Collection of Narratives Assembled by Samuel Pepys.* 1966
MATTINGLY, H. *Roman Imperial Coinage.* 1923-51
MAXAM, Andrew. HOPP
MAWER, A. *The Place-Names of Worcestershire.* 1927
MAYO, Rev HR. AOA
MAZZINGHI, Thomas John de. CC
McALDOWIE, Dr AM. SK
McDEVITT, Malcolm. HOPL
McLEAN, Mary & Colin. DVOPP. CDPOPP
McMEEKEN, Louis. PNPD
MEACHEM, Roger Clive. VH
MEANEY, A. *Gazetteer of Early Anglo-Saxon Burial Mounds.* 1964
MEE, A. KES. KESH
MELLOR, GJ. *The Northern Music Hall.*
METEYARD, Eliza. *The Life of Josiah Wedgwood from private correspondence etc.* 1865
MIDDLEFELL, Alfred. BERK. BERK2. SAC
MIDDLETON, Tony & others. *Cannock Chase Past and Present.* (Britain in Old Photographs). 1996
MILES, Susan. *Staffordshire Village Halls Directory.* 1994
MILLER, Matthew. OL
MILLIS, Roger. *City on the Peel.* 1980
MILLS, John. APCC
MILLS, Mary. ACOP. TCOP. WHTOP. APW. BUOP. *Mapping the Past Wolverhampton 1577-1986.* 1993. CCAP. WOLOP. BTW
MILLWARD, L. GMS

MILLWARD, Roy. WMLB
MILNER, Robert. CVH
MITCHELL, HC. TPCM. TTT
MOLYNEUX, William. HOBT. HOTM
MOORE, James. *Darwin.* 1991
MOORE, Lucy. *The Thieves' Opera.* 1997
MORDACQUE, Louis Henry. *History of Names of Men......in their connection with the progress of Civilisation.* 1862.
MORLAND, Bill. POP
MORLEY, WM. *The Staffordshire Bull Terrier.* 1982
MORRIS, Christopher. *The Illustrated Journeys of Celia Fiennes.* 1984
MORRIS, John. DB
MORRIS, Dennis & others. NOPP
MORRIS, Dennis & Barbara. ALW
MOSLEY, Sir Oswald. HCT. NHT
MOSLEY, Sir Oswald. *My Life.* 1968
MOSS, Fletcher. *Old Customs and Tales of My Neighbours.* 1898.
MOULE, Thomas. MECS
MOUNTFORD, Sir James. K
MOXON, JF. HH. HHHL
MOXON, John F. ONS
MURRAY, DC. *Recollections.* 1908
MURRAY, P. VESOP
MURRAY, Peter and Linda. *The Penguin Dictionary of Art & Artists.* 1978. 1st ed 1959
MYERS, Dr Edward D. *A History of Psychiatry in North Staffordshire.* 1997
MYLER, Patrick. *Dan Donnelly, His Life and Legends.*

N

NASH, Rev Dr TR. *Collections for a History of Worcestershire.* volume 1 1781, volume 2 1782
NETTEL, R. *Havergal Brian, the man and his music.*
NIBLETT, Kathy. *Dynamic Design: The British Pottery Industry 1940-1990.* DDBP
NICHOLLS, Robert. HOSC. M. NSSG. SGNS. *History of Stoke-on-Trent.*
NICOLL, ACF. SLS
NICOLL, Jack. UHAW
NIGHTINGALE, Rev Joseph. BEW
NITHSDALE, WH. HLS
NIVEN, W. OSH
NOAKE, John. *Guide to Worcestershire.* 1868.
NOOK, OS. *Historic Railway Disasters.* 1987
NOONAN, Sister Mary Lelia. AE
NORRIS, Rev Henry. TCN
NORTH, Allan (publisher). SHBP
NORWOOD, Rev TW. *An Account of the Ancient Chapel of Rushton.* 1856

O

OAKDEN, JP. OAKDEN. SPNO
OAKES, JC. *St John's Heath Hayes 75th Anniversary.* 1978
OLIVER, Rev Dr G. HCCW
OLIVER, A. IES
OLLARD, Richard. *The Escape of Charles II after the Battle of Worcester.* 1966
ONSLOW, Richard. *One Hundred Years of Racing at Dunstall Park 1887-1987.* 1987?
OSWALD, A. CSBS
OWEN, Colin. BTIH. ANS
OWEN, William. OWEN
OWEN, David E. SWY

P

PACE, A. FSRP
PALLISER, DM. TYS. SL
PALMER, FP. *The Wanderings of a Pen and Pencil.* 1846
PALMER, R. HATC
PALMER, Charles Ferrers. HTCT
PAPE, T. NM. NTS. NRS
PARKE, William. NCB
PARKER, AD. *A Sentimental Journey in and about the Ancient and Loyal City of Lichfield.* 1925.
PARKER, Alfred D. HOLP
PARKER, Rev FP. CWF

PARKES, Geoffrey. *Broome: A Worcestershire Village.* 1978
PARKES, John. HOTIP
PARSONS, Harold. MMBC. TEBC. TEBC2. *Portrait of the Black Country.* 1986
PAYTON, J. CPD
PEARCE. HOWP
PEARSON, George. MOSP
PEARSON, Robert. TWDOP
PEARSON, Robin. BCP. WBOPP. WBOP
PEEL, JHB. *Along the Roman roads of Britain.* 1971. *All over Britain.* 1978
PEGG, Patricia. *A Very Private Heritage.* 1997
PEGGE, Samuel. EMC
PEGLAR, G. OMH
PENN, Cameron. STC
PENNANT, T. *Journey from Chester to London.* 1782. PT
PENNINGTON, R. BBCD
PENNY, Beth. *Maryvale.* 1985
PERRY, Anthony. *The Fowler Legacy.* 1997. *Ellen's Forgotten Mercia.* 1999
PEVSNER, N. BOES. BOEWA. BOEW. BOEC. BOE. BOED.
PHILLIPS, ADM. PCCSC
PHILLIPS, CW. *OS Megalithic Survey.* vol 4. 1934
PHILLIPS, Graham. EF. GS
PHILLIPS, J. *A Map of the County of Stafford.....1832*
PICKERILL, June. *Cannock Chase: The Second Selection.* (Archive Photograph Series). 1997
PICKFORD, Doug. *A Portrait of Macclesfield.* 1995. DP. DPMM. SMM. DPEM. DPTB
PILLING, Patricia. FWNS
PINE, Lynda and Nicholas. *William Henry Goss: The Story of the Staffordshire family of Potters who invented Heraldic Porcelain.* 1987
PIPE, Marian. SSGLST
PITCHFORD, HH. PCBT
PITT, William. AOS. THS
PLANT, R. HOC
PLAYFAIR. *British Family Antiquities.* 1809
PLAYFAIR, Guy Lyon. HPG
PLESANCE, A. GWY
PLOT, Robert. NHS
POINTON, Alan. BEH
POINTON, TJ. LOU
POOLE, Ray. *Yesterday's Town: Leek.* 1988. ALC. *Around Leek in Old Photographs.* (Britain in Old Photographs). 1994. *French Connections.* 1995. HLSP
POOLE, CV. CSL
POOLE, CH. GAS. PSS
POOLE, R. SMOPP
PORTEOUS, Charles. BMWDD. CCOP
PORTER, Lindsey. EH. PDS&C. PSM. *Leek: Thirty Years Ago.* 1991. DMV
POSNER, Michael. MM
POTTS, David. *Selective Essays on Willenhall.* 1984. Copy in Willenhall library
POULTON-SMITH, Anthony. SPN
POWNER, Jonathan R. ADD
PRESTERNE, Tom. HA
PRICE, G. HOLK
PRICE, GLA. *Cobbs Engine House, Windmill End.* 1971
PRICE, Harry. POE
PRICE, John M. SOBP
PRICE, Joseph. BP. *A Brief Narrative of the events relative to the cholera at Bilston in 1832.* 1840
PRICE, Millicent. *In as Much as ....* 1954.
PRICE, Victor J. HANDR
PRIESTLEY, Tony. SSBOP
PRIESTMAN, Vera. *Cheddleton Remembered.* 1978. LR
PRINCE, Henry H. OWB
PRINCE, Rosalind. RPG. RPM. COS. CCSHO

R

RADFORD, GE. *A History of the Burton-upon-Trent Grammar School.* 1973
RADMORE, David. DAIW. DOPP. *Himley Hall and Park: A history.* 1996
RADZINOWICZ, L. *History of English Criminal Law from 1750*
RANDALL, T. AR. ASOP
RANDLES, Jenny. UFO STUDY. UFO REALITY. ABDUCTION

RATHBONE, C. *Dane Valley Story.* 1974
RAVEN, Jon. TABC. FOS. SCS. BTBC. UBCB
RAVEN, Michael & Jon. FSBC
RAVEN, Michael. MR. BCTV. MIDD
RAY, James. *A Complete History of the Rebellion.* 1757
READE, AL. *The Reades of Blackwood Hill etc.* private print 1906. *The Mellards And Their Descendants.* 1915. *Johnsonian Gleanings.* volume 3. 1922
REDFERN, Francis. BATR. HOU
REDGRAVE, Gilbert. *Great Artists.*
REES, Elizabeth. BOP. *Wolverhampton in the 1930s and 1940s.* 1988. PENOP. WHTOP. BUOP
REEVES, Joseph. WB
REILLY, Robin. *Wedgwood.* volumes I & II 1989. *Wedgwood: The New Illustrated Dictionary.* 1995
RHEAD, GW & FA. *Staffordshire Pots and Potters.* 1906
RICE, Marcia Alice. AB
RICHARDS, John. *The Pubs and Breweries of the Old Dudley Borough.*
RICHARDSON, Edward. ECE
RICHARDSON, Eric. WFK
RICHARDSON, John. LHE
RIDGE, WTB. IAANS
RIDLER, Andy. SOTOPP
RILEY, M. CSBSS
RITSON, Joseph. *Robin Hood.* 1972
ROAF, Susan. IHB
ROBERT, HE. *Medieval Monasteries and Minsters.* 1949
ROBERTS, Barrie. *On the Trail of the Walsall Anarchists.* 1992.
ROBERTS, Barrie. MGH. MMMR. MS&S
ROBERTS, Frank. SPCC
ROBERTS, James. WTCEM
ROBERTS, JE. BILP1. BILP2
ROBERTS, John. *Daywalks Cannock Chase with sketches by Liz Johnson.*
ROBERTS, John. *Midland Rivers.*
ROBERTSON, Charles. SLHT
ROBERTSON, James. *Infringement of Religious Liberty exposed etc.* 1819
ROBEY, John. EH
ROBINS, Don. *The Life and Death of a Druid Prince.* 1989
ROBINSON, DH. WORF.
ROBINSON, John Martin. ANE
ROBINSON, John Martin. SNTG. *The Wyatts: An Architectural Dynasty.* 1979
ROBINSON, Adrian. WMLB
ROBINSON-SCOTT, JW. *Strange Story of the Dunmow Flitch.*
ROBY, John & Henry Wood. T
ROCHE, N. KR
RODGERS, F. *Curiosities of the Peak District and Derbyshire.* 1974
RODGERS, MJW. STP
ROGER, Francis. *The Industrial History of Cannock Chase.* 1987
ROGERS, Thorold. *Six Centuries of Work and Wages.* 1894
ROE, Fred. VED
ROLLASON, David. *Saints and Relics in Anglo-Saxon England.* 1989
ROLT, LTC. *Red for danger, a history of railway accidents and railway safety.* 3rd ed 1976, 1978,1982,1986. *The Steam Engine of Thomas Newcomen.* 1977
ROPER, John Stephen. *A History of Russells Hall, Dudley.* Dudley Public Library Transcript No 17. 1973. HC. WAIW
ROSS, Anne. *The Life and Death of a Druid Prince.* 1989
ROWLANDS, H. *Mona Antiqua Restaurata.* 2nd ed. 1766
ROWLEY, NC. FGS
ROXBURGH, ALP. SKYT
ROYDE-SMITH, Naomi. *The private life of Mrs Siddons.* 1933
ROYDS, TF. HRFCP
RUSHTON, Chris. PWNS. TSW
RYAN, Columba. *Guide and History of Hawkesyard Priory and Spode House.* 1962

S

SAINTER, JD. *The Jottings of Some Geological, Archaeological, Botanical, Ornithological and Zoological Rambles Round Macclesfield.* 1878

SALT, Edward. HOPS
SALTER, Mike. CAMS. CHMS. CHMS2
SALWAY, Peter. *Oxford Illustrated History of Roman Britain.* 1993
SAUNDERSON, Tessa. *My Life in Athletics.* 1986
SAUNDERS, Rev Henry. RHS
SAVAGE, HE. *Church Heritage of Lichfield.* 1914
SAWYER, PH. *Medieval settlement, continuity and change.* 1976
SAXTON, Christopher. *Large decorative map of Staffordshire engraved by Francis Scatter.* 1577
SCARRATT, W. OTP
SCHUBERT, HR. *A History of the British Iron and Steel Industry from c450 BC to AD 1775.* 1957.
SCOTT, A (alias WA Bloor). BOJ
SCOTT, Eva. *The King in Exile: The Wanderings of Charles II from June 1646 to 1654.* 1904
SCOTT, Sir Walter. *Boscobel Tracts.* Count Grammont edition. 1864
SCOTT, William. SVS
SCOTT-GILES, C Wilfrid. CH
SCRASE, David. *Drawings and Watercolours. Peter De Wint.* 1979
SCRIVENER, Alex. *Chartley Earthworks and Castle.* 1895
SEABY, WA. WIS
SEEBOHM, F. *The English village community.* 1913 ed
SEECK, O. *Notitia Dignitatum.* 1876
SELBY, Robert J. BBH
SEMBOWER, Charles J. LPCC
SHAW, C. WIWC
SHAW, Simeon. HSP
SHAW, Stebbing. SHOS. SHOSA
SHAW, TY. *A Glossary of Black Country Words and Phrases.* 1930
SHEARS, WS. TE
SHERLOCK, Robert. IAS
SHERRATT, JN. KY
SHERRIN, Ned. *Theatrical Anecdotes.*
SHERWOOD, RE. *Civil Strife in the Midlands 1642-1651.* 1975
SHIPMAN, ER. *The Abbots Bromley Horn Dance.* 1982
SHIRLEY, Evelyn Philip. EDP
SHORT, WG. *Pugin's Gem. Church Guide.* 1981. COPP. SMOPP. ACOPP. COPP2
SHOWELL, William. DOB
SIMMONS, Roger. KTM. *Kidsgrove, Talke and Mow Cop. Postcards from the Past.* 1998
SIMMS, Rupert. BS
SIREN, Oswald. CGE
SKINNER, Father Leonard. SIC
SKIPP, Victor. COE. *A History of Greater Birmingham down to 1830.* 1980
SLEE, Christopher. *The Guinness Book of Lasts.* 1994
SLEIGH, John. HOLS
SMALLSHIRE, John L. WFW
SMILES, Samuel. *Lives of the Engineers.* 1861
SMITH, Alan. *Peak District Monsters.* 1994
SMITH, AC. WIS
SMITH, Christine. DM. DM2
SMITH, Clive. SMASCC
SMITH, David J. *Military airfields of Wales and the North West.* 1990. *Action Stations.* 1981. 2nd ed 1990.
SMITH, James Hicks. BJHS
SMITH, Julia. UTP
SMITH, JF. POA
SMITH, JH. HOB
SMITH, Les. *The Wolves.* 1989. *The Story of Wolverhampton Wanderers.* 1994
SMITH, Pauline V. NI
SMITH, R. *First and Last.* 1979
SMITH, S. *The Correspondence of Charles Darwin.* vol I (1821-36) 1985. vol II (1836) 1986?
SMITH, SM. *A Short History of the Orme Girls' School.* 1961
SMITH, W Bernard. S
SMITH, William. *Staffordia Comitatus (praeter civitatem Lichfield).... (map of Staffordshire).* 1602 (Stent's edition)
SMITH, William Hawkes. VDC
SNELL, S. *Story of Railway Pioneers.* 1921
SOLOMON, Philip. GOM. GOS. GPCE
SOMERS Tracts. *Narrative History of King James.*
SOWERBY, Geoffrey. BTOP. ABTOP. ESNF
SPANTON, WD. ACH

SPEAKE, Robert. A. E. BVC. AOPP. BOPP. FX. B. *Barthomley - The story of an estate village.* 1995. HAF

SPEED, John. *Stafford countie and towne......*(map of Staffordshire). 1608

SPEED, J. *Theatre of Empire of Great Britaine.* 1611

SPINKS, Derrick. *Aston Villa: A Portrait in Old Picture Postcards.* 1991

SPUFFORD, Peter & Margaret. ECC

STAFFORDA. HAH. HAHS

STAMPER, P. WSS

STANWAY, R. FSRP

STANYER, Anne. *Handbook for Widows.* 1978

STEED, June. TTH

STENTON, FM. *The Place-Names of Worcestershire.* 1927

STOCKDALE, John. *Stockdale's map of Staffordshire.* 1794

STOKES, Greg. *Black Country Stories and Sketches.* 1993

STOKES, Whitley. *Glossarial Index to the Martryrology of Oengus.*

STONE, Sir John Benjamin. *Sir Benjamin Stone's Pictures. Records of national life and history etc.* 1906

STRATTON, Michael. BCFF

STRICKLAND, WP. *The Pioneer Bishop: The Life and Times of Francis Asbury.* 1860

STRINGER, Charles Edward. SAL

STUART, DG. HOS

STUART, Denis. CBHBT. YX. CDS. IRB. SSE. IHOBT. POTP

STUBBS, Frank. EFS

STUBBS, Norman. HOA

STUKELEY, W. *Itinerarium Curiosum.*1776

SULIMA, Richard. *Around Tamworth in Old Photographs.* 1994

SUMMERS, Alphonsus J-M, A, M. *History of Witchcraft and Demonology.* 1926

SWIFT, Mabel. HT

SWINNERTON, Rev BT. SAS. *St Peter's Church, Norbury.* Pre 1975

SWINSCOE, David & Martine. SBB

SYDENHAM, EA. *Roman Imperial Coinage.* 1923-51

SYKES, E. *Everymans Dictionary of Non Classical Mythology.* 1952

T

TALBOT, Edward. *Railways In and Around Stafford.* 1994.

TALBOT, Richard. CAST. FF. PRA

TANN, William. MMH

TANNER, Thomas (bishop of Asaph). *Notitia Monastica, or a short history of the Religious Houses in England and Wales.* 1695, 1744, 1787,1821

TATE, WE. SBI

TAYLOR, Isaac (canon of York). *Words and Places.* 1st ed 1864

TAYLOR, Sam. SMSE

THOMAS, Edward. GSP

THOMAS, John. *The Rise of the Staffordshire Potteries.*

THOMAS, K. *Man and the Natural World.*

THOMAS, N. GPE

THOMPSON, D. *The Crisis of 1842: Chartism, the colliers' strike and the outbreak in the Potteries in The Charter Experience.*

THOMPSON, DH. WABH

THOMPSON, WJ. IANS

THOMSON, Ian. *The Ley Hunter's Companion.* 1979

THOROLD, Henry. SGS

THORPE, H. *Birmingham and Its Regional Setting.* 1950

THURSTON, H. BLS

TILDESLEY, JC. HOP

TILDESLEY, NW. HOWI. HOWM

TIMBS, John. *Abbeys, Castles & Ancient Halls of England & Wales; their Legendary lore and popular history.* volume 2 1870

TIMINGS, William. *Guide to the Clent Hills.* 1835

TIMMS. *Garland for the Year.*

TIMMINS, Malcolm. DTT. SNDB

TIMPSON, John. *John Timpson's England.* 1987

TIPTAFT, Norman. IOM

TOEMAN, Rosemary. VFC

TOMKINSON, Albert. PTYV

TORRINGTON. Hon John Byng 5th Viscount. *The Torrington Diaries.* Edited by C Bruyn Andrews. 1936

TRAVIS, Peter. ISS

TRUBSHAW, Miss Susanna. *Old Dick Sleigh's Cave.* 1867

TUMP, Aristotle. MMBCC. *Black Country Ghosts and Mysteries.* 1987.

TURNER, Margaret. ST

TURNER, PM. UOPP

TURNER, Sharon. *The History of the Anglo Saxons from their first appearance etc.* 4 volumes 1799-1805

TURNER, William. *Ancient Remains, near Buxton.* 1899

TWAMLEY, Charles. DCP

TWEMLOW, FR. *The Battle of Blore Heath.* 1912

U

UNDERHILL, CH. HOBTU. UTR

UNDERHILL, Charles. PCBT

UNDERHILL, EA. AMS

UNDERWOOD, Peter. GBG

UPTON, Chris. HOWU

USSHER, Rev Richard. UCC

V

VAISEY, DG. *Staffordshire and the Great Rebellion.* 1964.

VALE, WL. VSSR

VEALL, JR. OHW

VINCENT, David. VE

VODDEN, David F. WROP.

W

WADDY, J Leonard. *The Bitter Sacred Cup* (Wednesbury Riots 1743-44). 1976

WADE, Jean. BCP

WAGNER, AR. *English Genealogy.* 1960

WAIN, John. *Johnson on Johnson.* 1976

WAKEFIELD, Mary E. ABW

WALKER, Alison J. *The Archaeology of Stafford to 1600 AD.* Bradford University MA dissertation. 1976

WALKER, R. *Tour through Northern Countries of England and Borders of Scotland.*

WALL, Canon Arthur G. GAH

WALTERS, G. GDC

WALLACE, Robert (Unitarian minister). *Antitrinitarian Biography: or sketches of the lives and writings of distinguished Antitrinitarians etc.* 1850

WARD, John. HBST

WARNER, Rev RH. LC

WARRENDER, Keith. EL

WARRILLOW, Ernest JD. *Arnold Bennett and Stoke-on-Trent.* 1966. SHST. HOE. LLST. His photographs comprise the Warrillow Collection in Keele University Library.

WARTON, Thomas (Poet Laureate). *The History of English Poetry, from the Close of the eleventh to the commencement of the eighteenth century.* 4 volumes 1774-1781

WATKIN, Edward. EOP

WATKIN, E. TTOPP

WATKIN, W Thompson. *Roman Cheshire.* 1886

WEATE, Mary. LWA

WEATHERILL, Lorna. *The Pottery Trade and North Staffordshire. 1660-1760.* 1971

WEBSTER, G. *The Roman Site at Wall.* 1958. *The Cornovii.* 1975. TC

WEDGWOOD, Barbara & Hensleigh. WCW

WEDGWOOD, Henry Allen. ROS. UDC. PTP

WEDGWOOD, H. UMGH

WEDGWOOD, John. *A Personal Life of the Fifth Josiah Wedgwood 1899-1968.*

WEIGALL, Arthur. TNE

WEIR, Richard. SOTB

WELCH, C see LEAH, MD

WELLS BLADEN, W. NFNS

WELLS, CE see LEAH, MD

WELSH, BJ. *Tutbury Church Guide.*

WENHAM, Peter. WTMS

WESLEY, William. HOBTW

WESTWOOD, Jennifer. *Albion: A Guide to Legendary Britain.* 1985

WHARTON, Henry. *Anglia Sacra etc.* 1691

WHEELER, Sir Charles. *High Relief: the autobiography.* 1968

WHEELHOUSE, Derek J. BIOPP

WHITAKER, Terence. EGH

WHITAKER, Dr Thomas Dunham. HOWWW

WHITE, L. Spode. *A History of the family, factory and wares 1733-1833.*

WHITE, Walter. *All Round the Wrekin.* 1860

WHITE, W. W

WHITEHOUSE, CJ & GP. TFW

WHITELOCK, Dorothy. *English Historical Documents. volume 1 c500-1042.* 1955

WILD, John. MJW

WILDIG, Sue. BAOH

WILKES, C Beryl. CAA. CWBT

WILKES, Dr R. HOSW

WILKES, Robert Charles. SOP

WILKINSON, Roger. LAL

WILKINSON, William & Anne. ACOB.

WILKES, Dr. *Original Collections for History of Staffordshire.* 1832

WILKS, Dudley. FSP

WILLETT, Mary. HOWBW

WILLETTS, Arthur. *The Black Country Nailer's Riots of 1842.* 1995

WILLIAM, Alfred. SLR

WILLIAMS, John K. *A Foxfield Album.* 1978

WILLIAMS, Rev JC. CHPC

WILLIAMS, M. *First and Last.* 1979

WILLIAMS, Moelwyn I. DRBSC

WILLIAMS, Alfred. MCSSW. STV

WILLIAMS, Tracey. WOLOP. BTW

WILLINGTON, FR. *St Editha and Tamworth Church.*

WILLMORE, Frederic W. HOWW. ROR

WILLS, Geoffrey. *Wedgwood.* 1989

WILSON, David M. AASE

WILSON, D. SDW

WILSON, GH. *Cave Hunting Holidays in Peakland.*

WILSON-JONES, J. BCWJ

WILMOT, Frances. The History of Harborne Hall. 1991

WINCHESTER, Angus. *Discovering Parish Boundaries.* 1990

WOLLEY, P. HOM

WOOD, Alison. *A Short History of John Taylor.* 1981

WOOD, Henry. BPT

WOOD, Michael. *In Search of the Dark Ages.* 1981

WOODALL, Richard D. APR. TBS. 1958

WOODHOUSE, Henry. SLC

WOODHOUSE, JC. *A Short Account of the City and Clos of Lichfield.* 1819

WOOLLEY, Eric. BCOPP. WPOPP

WRIGHT, Jenny. BAOH

WRIGHT, Mrs AR. BCC

WRIGHT, Edmund Bealby. BCSBG

WRIGHT, M. CCBO. CCF

WRIGHT, Thomas. *Great Barr and its Haunted Environs.* 1852

WRIGHT, WG. NHOA

WYKES-SNEYD, Roger ES. SNEDE

Y

YONGE, Rev Weston E Vernon. BPS

YOUNG, Frederick A. GLAUE

ii) NO NAMED AUTHOR

About Britain Series No. 5. 1951. ABS
Account of Lichfield. AOL
Aldridge and District Yesterdays.Walsall Archive Service. 1984. ADY
Alton Towers - The Stranger's Guide. 1850. AT
Ashbourne and the Dove. Published by Dawson & Abbson. 1839. AAD
Bloxwich Yesterdays. Walsall Archives Services. 1982. BY
Brownhills History Trail. Millfield Primary School. From 1970. BHT
Brownhills Local History Trail. Walsall Library & Museum Services. BLHT
Cannock Chase Map. Staffordshire County Council. 1984. CCM
The Church of The Holy Evangelist, Normacot. NHE
Dictionary of English Place Names. DEPN
Dictionary of National Biography. DNB
The First £100 Million: A History of the Staffordshire Building Society. 1977.
Get to know The Close of Lichfield Cathedral. Discovery Sheet No. 8. GKCLC
Get to know The Glass in Lichfield Cathedral. Discovery Sheet No. 5. GKGLC
Get to know The Mediaeval Close of Lichfield Cathedral. Discovery Sheet No. 9. GKMCLC
Get to know The Statues, Monuments & Memorials of Lichfield Cathedral. Discovery Sheet No. 4. GKSMCLC
Grammar Schools in Staffordshire 1868. Staffordshire Study Book 14. GSS

Great Barr Park: A Survey of the Landscape. GBP
Guide to Cannock Chase. Friends of Cannock Chase. 1951. GCC
Guinness Book of Records. 1955 - . GBR
Handbook for the City of Lichfield & Neighbourhood. 1884. HCLN
Historical, or New English Dictionary. HED
A Heresy History of The Haywoods and Colwich 1900-1939. The Haywood Society. 1997. HHHC
History of Tutbury Castle. 1843. HTC
Illustrated Map of Staffordshire showing curiosities. limited to 700 copies. Celebrating Sidney Barnes Centenary 1973. ZSB
Inns of Interest. Booklet Sponsored by Express & Star. 1968. IOI
Kingstanding Past and Present. Birmingham Public Libraries. 1968 (1st ed.) 1984. KPP
Lichfield District Official Guide. 1979. LDOG
Lichfield Official Guide. 1927 & 1930. LOG
Letocetum (Wall), Staffordshire. National Trust Guide.1947. LWS
Local History Source Book. LHSB
A Matter of Time. Royal Commission on Historic Monuments. 1960. MOT
Non-Conformist Chapels in Staffordshire and Shropshire. NCSS
Penkridge. A Brief Village History. 1992? PVH
A Photographic History of Newchapel etc. 1989 volumes 1, 2 & 3. ND

Picturesque Staffordshire. North Staffs Railway Company. 1908. PS
Portrait of Cannock Chase. Friends of Cannock Chase. 1957. PCC
Pure & Wholesome Water for One Hundred Years: The Story of the Staffordshire Potteries Water Undertaking. 1849-1949. PWW
Recording Britain. Oxford University Press & Pilgrim Trust. 1943 (3 volumes). RB
Royalty & Staffordshire. Staffordshire County Council. 1977. R&S
Royal Visit to Wolverhampton. 1867. RVW
Short History of West Bromwich. West Bromwich Library. 1964. SHWB
Some Staffordshire Trees. County Planning and Development Dept. 1973. SST
Staffordshire Moorlands in Old Picture Postcards 1. 1991. MOPP
Stone, Eccleshall & District Gazette. April 1987 - Nov 1988. SEDG
Tamworth Castle Guide. 1993. TGT
The Three Decker: History of a 100 years of Brocton, Baswich and Walton-on-the-Hill Churches. 1982
Weston Park Guide. English Life Publications. 1974. WPG
Willenhall and Darlaston Yesterdays. Walsall Library & Museum Services. 1981. WDY
Wolverhampton: 1991 things you wanted to know about Wolverhampton. Partners in Progress. 1991. WF
Wolverhampton Past and Present. 1985. WP&P

iii) MANY AUTHORS

Abbots Bromley: A glimpse into the past. Local History Group. 1982. ABAB
Art and Craft of Garden Making. ACGM
Broughton Hall. A Short History. Franciscan Missionaries of St Joseph. 1972. BH
Book of the Village, Broughton. Women's Institute. 2 editions 1949 & 1986. BOV
The Book of Saints. Compiled by Benedictine Monks of Ramsgate. 1966 5th ed. BSB
Bentilee, Ubberley and Berryhill. Bentilee Scribblers. 1994. BUB

Denstone . Women's Institute. 1949. Unprinted. DH
Great Men of Harborne (Articles from Harborne Parish Church Magazine 1982-83). GMH
History of Wednesbury. 1854. HOW
Medieval Bromley. Local History Group. 1987. ABMB
Barton in the Eighteenth Century. Local History Class. ND. BEC
Meir Remembered. Meir Local History Group. MRM
Memories of Mayfield. Mayfield Heritage Group. 1993. MOM
Places to Visit in Britain. 1988. AA

The Staffordshire Village Book. Staffs Federation of Women's Institutes. 1988. SVB
Story of Berkswich (or Walton-on-the-Hill). Women's Institute. 1950. SOBW
Story of Oulton & Kibblestone. 1977. SOK
Swythamley and its Neighbourhood. 1874. SIN
Victoria County History volumes. VCH
The West Midlands Village Book. Women's Institute. 1989. WMVB
Wheaton Aston: As It Was. Compiled by Local People. 1991. WAAIW

iv) NEWSPAPERS

Agricultural Gazette
Aris's Birmingham Gazette
Birmingham Post
Burton Daily Mail. BDMN
Cannock Chase Courier
Congleton Chronicle
County Express
Daily Mail
Daily Telegraph
Derby Evening Telegraph. DET
Express and Star. E&S
Evening Sentinel. ES
Guardian/ The Manchester Guardian. G
Handsworth Herald

The Independent. I
Kidsgrove News
Leek Times
Lichfield Mercury 1986
Midland Weekly News (S=Supplement). MWN
The News of Wolverhampton
The Observer
Observer Magazine
Shrewsbury Chronicle
Shropshire Star
Smethwick Telephone. STELE
Stafford Post 1989
Staffordshire Advertiser. SA
Staffordshire Chronicle

Staffordshire Newsletter. SN
Staffordshire Sentinel. SS
Sunday People
Sunday Telegraph
Tamworth Herald. TH
Tamworth Herald Michell 'Newspaper Cuttings' Tamworth Library. THM
The Times
Uttoxeter Post and Times
Walsall Chronicle. WC
Walsall Times and South Staffordshire Advertiser
West Bromwich, Oldbury and Smethwick Midland Chronicle and Free Press
Wolverhampton Chronicle

v) JOURNALS

Antiquaries Journal. AJ
Ancient Monument Society Newsletter. AMSN
The Architect
Army Quarterly
Audley Historian. Journal of the Audley and District Family History Society. No. 1 1995 -. AHJ
The Black Countryman Journal. BCM
Biddulph Historical Society Transactions. No. 1 June 1968 - No. 4 Dec 1973. BHS
Birmingham & Midland Society for Genealogy and Heraldry. BMSGH
British Cave Research Association Bulletin

The Bugle (Black Country Bugle). 1972 - . TB
Building News. BN
Chronicles Journal of Leek and District Historical Society. Issue 1 1988 -.
The Countryman
Dancing Times
Ephemeris Epigraphica
Flint History Society Publication
Flying Saucer Review. FSR
Folklore
Folklore Journal 1883-1991. FLJ
Fortean Times

Gentleman's Magazine. GM
International Review of Social History
Journal of English Place-names Society. JEPS
Journal of the English Folk Dance and Song Society
Journal of The Royal Horticultural Society
Lancashire and Cheshire Antiquarian Society Transactions. LCAST
Local Historian
Midland History. volume 1. No. 1 Spring 1971. MH
National Speleological Society Bulletin
Newcomen Society Transactions
Northern UFO News

Notes & Queries Magazine. Nov 1849 - 1988 volume 1 - volume 233. N&Q
Old Nortonian Society Transactions. 1925 - . ONST
Records of Ye Olde Nortonian Society. 1925,1957,1979. YONS
Spotlight.....On the Diocese of Lichfield
Staffordshire Catholic History Journal. No. 1 Autumn

1961, incorporated into Midland Catholic History from No. 1 1991. SCH or SCHJ
Staffordshire Historical Collections. Published by William Salt Archaeological Society from 1880, which became known as the Staffordshire Record Society from 1936. (volume 1, 4th series is SH). SHC

Stafford Historical and Civic Society Transactions. SHCS
Staffordshire History Journal. 1984-. SHJ
Staffordshire Studies. volume 1 1988. SSE
The Way We Were (Sentinel Publication). 1995 - . TWWW
The Wolverhampton Journal. Jan 1902 - Dec 1909. WJO
UFO Study

vi) ARCHAEOLOGICAL JOURNALS

Archaeologia. ARCH
Archaeological Journal. ARCHJ
Birmingham Archeology Society Transactions. BAST
Burton Natural History & Arch Soc Transaction 1889 - 1933. BTNHAST
Chester Archaeology Society Transactions.
County Archaeologist Maps 2.5in to 1 mile. CAM
Current Archaeology Journal. CA
Derbyshire Archaeological Journal. DAJ
Dudley Castle Archaeological Project 1983-85 Report. 1985. DCAP
Journal of the British Archaeological Association. JBAA
Leicestershire Archaeological Society Transactions
Lichfield Archaeological Society Transactions 1960-61. LAST
Medieval Archaeology
Mercian Studies
North Staffordshire Naturalists' Field Club Transactions 1866 to 1960. 1976 -. NSFCT

North Staffordshire Journal of Field Studies (the transactions of the North Staffordshire Field Club between 1960 and 1975). NSJFS
Old Stafford Society Transactions. The society published transactions from 1928 to 1960 OSST. Then SHCST
Peakland Archaeological Society Newsletter. PASN
Post-Medieval Archaeology
Proceedings of the Society of Antiquaries of London
Reliquary. R
Report of the Summer Meeting of RAI at Keele. Reprinted from ARCHJ. 1963. RAIK
Shropshire Archaeological Society Transactions
Stafford Historical and Civic Society Transactions. 1960-. SHCST
Staffordshire Archaeological Studies. volume 1 1984 - . SASR
Stafford Castle Reports. Excavation Report. Circa 1980 onwards. SCR
South Staffordshire Archaeological and Historical Society

Transactions. Became the Staffordshire Archaeologica and Historical Society Transactions in 1994-1995. SSAHST
Stour and Smestow Archaeology Research Group Field Survey Reports
The Shropshire & North Wales Natural History & Antiquarian Society
Transactions of the Lancashire and Cheshire Antiquities Society
Transactions of the Worcestershire Archaeological Society
West Midlands Archaeology. CBA West Midlands. WMARCH
West Midlands Archaeology. WMAT
West Midlands Archaeology News Sheet
Wolverhampton Arch Society. Reports from 1926 to 1936. WAS
Worcestershire Archaeology Newsletter
Worcestershire History Society

vii) MAGAZINES

Antiquity Magazine. 1933
Country Life. 1897 - . CL
Derbyshire Life Magazine. DL
Dublin University Magazine
Geographical Magazine
The Grub Street Journal
Hello Magazine
House and Garden April 1972
Illustrated London News. 1843- . ILN
Leisure Hour Magazine. LHM
Lichfield and Tamworth Life Magazine. Sept 1971 -

March 1973. LTM
The Listener
Lore and Language Magazine. Jan 1980
Lund Studies in English
Melting Pot
Nature
New Scientist
Numismatic Chronicle
Railway Magazine. RM
Reveille. June 30 - July 6 1966

St James Magazine
Sporting Magazine
Staffordshire County Magazine. SCM
Staffordshire Life Magazine. 1947 - 1959, 1983 - . SLM
Six Towns Magazine. STM
Staffordshire Magazine. STMSM
This England Magazine. TEM
Universal Magazine
Wolverhampton Magazine. July 1963 - Sept 1978, Oct 1978 -Dec 1979. WMAG

viii) DIRECTORIES

Birmingham Diocesan Directory. 1998/9
Building Societies Yearbook 1998-99: Official Handbook

of the Building Society Association
Kelly's Directory. KD

Lichfield Diocesan Directory. 1992 and 1999

ix) MAPS

COUNTY MAPS

BLAEU, Johann. Staffordiensis Comitatus; vulgo Staffordshire. 1645
BLOME, Richard. A Mapp of Stafford Shire ... (1671-c1750)
BOWEN, Emanuel. An Improved Map of the County of Stafford..... 1749. Reprint by Staffs Library Services
DOWER, John. Staffordshire. Weekly Dispatch Atlas. 1858 or later
GARNER, Robert. A Geological Map of Staffordshire. 1844
GREENWOOD, Christopher and John Greenwood. A Map of the county of Stafford.... 1820
JEFFERYS, Thomas. A New Map of Staffordshire.... 1747
KIP, William. Staffordiae Comitatus pars olim Cornaviorum. 1607
MOLL, Herman. Stafford Shire... 1724
MORDEN, Robert. Stafford Shire. 1695

PLOT, Robert. ...This Map of Staffordshire newly delineated... 1682
SAXTON, Christopher. Staffordiae Comitatu pfecte et absolute elaboratu.....1577
SMITH, Charles. A New Map of the County of Stafford. 1801
SPEED, John. Stafford countie and towne... 1610
TEESDALE, Henry. Staffordshire. 1830
YATES, William. A Map of the County of Stafford.... 1775

A-Z

Geographers' A-Z Map Co. Ltd series were used Birmingham (1989.1995), Stoke-on-Trent (1987 revised 1989. 1992).

ORDNANCE SURVEY

Sheets 27, 33, 34, 41, 42 of the David & Charles reprints

of the Victorian Old Series editions, dated at 1834 for the Encyclopaedia, although most have additional information.
Most six inch to one mile maps (first series and later series) covering the county in the Staffordshire Record Office, Stafford (often referred to as OS map 6 inch).
The 1:50,000 series used were Sheets 118 (1983); 119 (1979); 127 (1980 and 1981); 128 (1981 and 1991); 138 (1979); 139 (1980); 140 (1980).
Outdoor Leisure Map number 24 'White Peak' scale 1:25,000 was used. 1:25,000 series used were SK 00/ 10 (1976); 01/ 11 (1989); 02/12 (1981); 03/ 13 (1987); 04/ 14 (1985); 20/ 30 (1971); 22/ 32 (1981). SJ 61/ 71 (1994); 62/ 72 (1976); 63/ 73 (1981); 64/ 74 (1987); 80/ 90 (1989); 81/ 91 (1972); 82/ 92 (1977); 83/ 93 (1988); 84/ 94 (1989); 85/ 95 (1979); 86/ 96 (1992). SO 68/ 78 (1982); 87/ 97 (1991); 88/ 98 (1990); 89/ 99 (1988). SP 09/ 19 (1993).

x) LIST OF SOURCE ABBREVIATIONS

A

A. *Audley - An Out of the Way, Quiet Place*. R Speake. 1974

AA. *AA Places to Visit in Britain*. Many Authors. 1988

AAD. *Ashbourne and the Dove*. Published by Dawson & Abbson. 1839

AADB. *About Adbaston*. J Somner Billington. 1982 (private publication. copy in WSL)

AAHH. *Apparitions & Haunted Houses*. Sir Ernest Bennett. 1939

AASE. *Archaeology of Anglo Saxon England*. David M Wilson. 1976

AB. *Abbots Bromley*. Marcia Alice Rice. 1939

ABAB. *Abbots Bromley: A glimpse into the past*. Local History Group. 1982

ABDUCTION. *Abduction*. Jenny Randles. 1988

ABI. *Ancient Bronze Implements etc*. Sir John Evans. 1881

ABMB. *Medieval Bromley*. Local History Group.1987

ABMEE. *Ancient Bridges of Mid and Eastern England*. E Jervoise. 1932

ABTOP. *Around Burton-upon-Trent in Old Photographs*. Geoffrey Sowerby & Richard Farman. 1993.

ABS. *About Britain Series*. No 5. 1951

ABW. *Ancient Brewood*. Mary E Wakefield. 1932

ACGM. *Art & Craft of Garden Making*.

ACH. *The Ancient Corporation of Hanley*. WD Spanton. 1901

ACHRH. *A Revised History of the Ancient Corporation of Hanley*. JS Crapper. 1882

ACOB. *A Chronicle of Bradeley: The Story of an English village from 1000-2000 AD*. William & Anne Wilkinson. 1999

ACOP. *Around Cannock in Old Postcards*. Mary Mills. 1990

ACOPP. *Around Cheadle (The Old Photograph Series)*. W George Short. 1994

ADD. *A Duty Done: The History of Fire-Fighting in Staffordshire*. Jonathan R Powner. 1987

ADY. *Aldridge and District Yesterdays*. Walsall Archive Service. 1984

AE. *History & Ownership of the Alton Estates*. Sister Mary Lelia Noonan. 1986

AFT. *Albion's Fatal Tree*. Douglas Hay. 1975

AGT. *A Grand Tour*. Neville Malkin. 1976

AH. *Aston Hall by Stone*. Rev Canon FH Drinkwater. 1976

AHH. *Ancient High House, Stafford*. B Lambert. 1986

AHJ. *Audley Historian*. 1995 -

AJ. *Antiquaries Journal*.

ALC. *Around Leek in Camera*. Ray Poole. 1990

ALOPP. *Aldridge on Old Picture Postcards*. Jan Farrow. 1993

ALOPPR. *Aldridge Revisited. (Britain in Old Photographs Series)*. Jan Farrow. 1998

ALP. *Archaeological Survey of the Parish of Lower Penn South West Staffordshire*. John P Malam. 1980

ALV. *A Life of Admiral Lord St Vincent*. Capt WV Anson RN. 1913

ALW. *Ashley, Loggerheads and Woore: A Portrait in Old Picture Postcards*. Barbara & Dennis Morris. 1989

AMS. *Story of the Ancient Manor of Sedgley*. EA Underhill. 1941

AMSN. *Ancient Monument Society Newsletter*.

ANE. *Architecture of North England*. John Martin Robinson

ANS. *Anslow*. Colin Owen. 1995

AOA. *Annals of Arley*. Rev HR Mayo. 1914

AOBC. *Aspects of the Black Country*. Charles JL Elwell. 1991

AOL. *Account of Lichfield*.

AOPP. *Audley in Old Picture Postcards*. Robert Speake. 1984

AOS. *Agriculture of Staffordshire*. W Pitt. 1794. 1796

AOW. *Annals of Willenhall*. FW Hackwood. 1908

APB. *Archaeological Papers (reprinted from SA)*. SAH Burne

APCC. *Annals of the Parish Church, Coseley*. John Mills. 1912

APR. *Early Days of Aldridge, Pelsall & Rushall*. Richard D Woodall. ND

APW. *Around Pattingham and Wombourne (Britain in Old Photographs Series)*. May Griffiths, Mary Mills & Peter Leigh. 1992. APW

AR. *Around Rugeley in Old Photographs*. T Randall & J Anslow. 1988

ARCH. *Archaeologia*.

ARCHJ. *Archaeological Journal*.

AS. *Ancient Stafford (reprinted from BAST)*. Thomas J David. 1922?

ASE. *The Annals of Shenstone*. RW Essington. 1899

ASI. *Ancient Stone Implements, Weapons, and Ornaments of Great Britain and Ireland*. Sir John Evans. 1897 2nd edition.

ASOP. *Around Stafford in Old Photographs*. T Randall & J Anslow. 1991

AT. *Alton Towers - The Stranger's Guide*. NA. 1850

ATSH. *Around the Saxon Hill*. Michael Albutt. 1990

AUOPP. *Around Uttoxeter. (Images of England Series)*. Roy Lewis. 1999

AVH. *Alstonefield: A Village History*. Jeni Edwards. 1985

AWM. *Arrowsmith in the West Midlands*. Arrowsmith. 1974

B

B. *Bagnall - on the Fringe of the Moorlands*. R Speake. 1990

BAH. *Barlaston A History*. MW Greenslade. 1966

BALH. *Biddulph A Local History*. Joseph Kennedy. 1980

BAOH. *Birchills: an oral History*. Sue Wildig & Jenny Wright. 1985

BAP. *Bronze Age Pottery*. Lord Abercromby. 1912

BART. *Barthomley: In letters from a former rector to his eldest son*. Rev Edward Hinchliffe. 1856

BAST. *Birmingham Archaeology Society Transactions*. 1870-

BAT. *Black's Guide to Alton Towers*. Llewellynn Jewitt. 1870

BATR. *Brocklehurst's Authentic Excursionists' Guide*. Francis Redfern. 1870

BB. *Boscobel*. Thomas Blount. 1660

BBCD. *Barrows & Bone Caves of Derbyshire*. R Pennington. 1817

BBH. *Burston: A Brief History*. Robert J Selby. 1985 (private thesis)

BC. *Black Country*. Phil Drabble. 1952

BCC. *British Calendar Customs*. Mrs AR Wright & TE Lones. 1938

BCFF. *British Car Factories From 1896 - A complete Historical, Geographical, Architectural & Technological Survey*. Michael Stratton & Paul Collins. 1993.

BCGB. *Walks Black Country and its Green Borderland*. Elihu Burritt. 1868

BCM. *The Black Countryman Journal*. 1968-

BCOPP. *Black Country in Old Picture Postcards*. Eric Woolley. vols 1 and 2 1988. 1990

BCP. *Black Country Pubs (Britain in Old Photographs series)*. Robin Pearson & Jean Wright. 1991

BCS. *Black Country Sketches*. Amy Lyons. 1901

BCSB. *Black Country Stories*. E Baker. 1952

BCSBG. *Black Country Sketchbook Guide*. Edmund Bealby Wright. 1996

BCSG. *Black Country Stories*. TH Gough. 1934 1949 ed.

BCTV. *Black Country Towns and Villages*. Michael Raven. 1991

BCWJ. *The Black Country*. J Wilson-Jones. c1950

BDD. *Birmingham Diocesan Directory*. 1998/9

BDH. *Brewood*. David Horovitz. 1988. 1992

BDMN. *Burton Daily Mail Newspaper*.

BEC. *Barton in the Eighteenth Century*. Local History Class. ND

BEH. *A Brown Edge History*. Alan Pointon. 1998

BERK. *The Story of the Ancient Parish of Berkswich (near Stafford)*. Volume 1. Alfred Middlefell. 1995

BERK2. *The Story of the Ancient Parish of Berkswich (near Stafford)*. Volume 2. Alfred Middlefell. 1996

BEV. *Bird's Eye View: The Midlands*. Vivian Bird. 1969

BEW. *Beauties of England and Wales*. Nightingale. 1813

BFS. *The Battle for Stafford*. John Band. 1985

BG. *Biddulph Grange*. Peter Hayden. 1989

BGFB. *Biddulph Grange written for its league of friends*. Anne Ferris. 1984

BH. *Broughton Hall: A Short History*. Franciscan Missionaries of St Joseph. 1972

BHOP. *Brierley Hill. (Britain in Old Photographs Series)*. Stan Hill. 1995

BHOP2. *Brierley Hill. (Britain in Old Photographs Series)*. Stan Hill. 1996 2nd ed.

BHS. *Biddulph Historical Society (Transactions)*. No. 1 June 1968 - No. 4 Dec 1973

BHT. *Brownhills History Trail*. Millfield Primary School. From 1970

BILP1 *Bilberry Pie*. JE Roberts. 1963

BILP2 *More Bilberry Pie*. JE Roberts. 1966

BIOPP. *Biddulph (The Archive Photographs Series)*. Derek J Wheelhouse. 1997

BJHS. *Brewood (and a Resume 1867)*. James Hicks Smith. 1874

BLHT. *Brownhills Local History Trail*. Walsall Library & Museum Services

BLS. *Butler's Lives of the Saints*. Revised edition H Thurston & SJD Attwater. 1956

BM1923. *British Museum Anglo-Saxon Guide*. 1923

BM1953. *BM Guide to the Later Prehistoric Antiquities*. 1953

BMB. *Guide to British Monumental Brasses*. Richard Le Strange. 1972

BMMB. *A Manuel of Monumental Brasses*. Rev Herbert Haines. 1861 1970 edition

BMQ. *British Museum Quarterly*.

BMSGH. *Birmingham & Midland Society for Genealogy & Heraldry*.

BMWDD. *Beauty & Mystery of Well Dressing, Derbys*. C Porteous. 1949

BN. *Building News*.

BNDA. *Blurton and its Neighbourhood Down the Ages*. SE Boden. 1985

BOB. *Beresford of Beresford*. Rev W Beresford & SB Beresford. 1908

BOE. *Buildings of England: Staffordshire*. N Pevsner. 1974

BOEC. *Buildings of England: Cheshire*. N Pevsner and Edward Hubbard. 1971

BOED. *Buildings of England: Derbyshire*. N Pevsner. 1953 1986 edition

BOES. *Buildings of England: Shropshire*. N Pevsner. 1958

BOEW. *Buildings of England: Worcestershire*. N Pevsner. 1968

BOEWA. *Buildings of England: Warwickshire*. N Pevsner & Alexander Wedgwood. 1966

BOJ. *Book of Jabez*. A Scott (alias WA Bloor). Book 1 1972. Book 2 1973. Book 3 1978

BOOP. *Birmingham on Old Postcards*. John Marks. 1982

BOP. *Bilston in Old Photographs*. Elizabeth A Rees. 1988

BOPP. *Betley in Old Picture Postcards*. Robert Speake. 1984

BOV. *Book of the Village, Broughton*. Women's Institute. 1949 1986 edition

BOW. *Bibliography of Wolverhampton*. GT Lawley. 1890

BP. *An Historical Account of Bilston*. Joseph Price. 1835

BPCSM. *Bonnie Prince Charlie in the Staffordshire Moorlands*. H Bode. 1986

BPP. *Bushbury Parish & People 1550-1950*. AH Chatwin. 1983

BPS. *Bye-Paths of Staffordshire*. Rev Weston E Vernon Yonge. 1911

BPT. *Borough By Prescription: A History of Tamworth*. Henry Wood. 1958

BPW. *Beaudesert, The Pagets and Waterloo*. John Godwin. 1992

BRITC. *British Caving*. CHD Collingwood. 1962

BRO. *Boscobel or The Royal Oak*. William Harrison Ainsworth. ND

BS. *Bibliotheca Staffordiensis*. Rupert Simms. 1894

BSB. *The Book of Saints*. Compiled by Benedictine Monks of Ramsgate. 1966 5th edition

BSC. *Bilston in the Seventeenth Century. (press cuttings)*. GT Lawley. ND

BSL. *History of St Laurence Church*. AN Bebington. ND

BT. *The Boscobel Tract: relating to the Escape of Charles the Second after Worcester*. Edited by John Hughes. 1830

BTBC. *Book of the Black Country*. Jon Raven. 1982

BTC. *Betley Through the Centuries*. GN Brown. 1985

BTIH. *Burton-upon-Trent: The Illustrated History*. Colin Owen. 1994

BTNHAST. *Burton Natural History & Archaeological Society Transactions.* 1889-1933

BTOP. *Burton-upon-Trent on Old Postcards.* Geoffrey Sowerby and Richard Farman. Volumes 1 & 2. 1983. 1984

BTRA. *Burnt Tree Round About.* RC Broadbent. 1983

BTW. *Bilston, Tettenhall and Wednesfield.* (Images of England series). Mary Mills and Tracey Williams. 1998.

BU. *Bucknall.* Elizabeth W Bass. 1989

BUB. *Bentilee, Ubberley and Berryhill.* Bentilee Scribblers. 1994

BUBA. *A Staffordshire Family: Tracing the Bamfords of Uttoxeter.* Marion Bamford. 1978

BUOP. *Bushbury in Old Photographs.* Alex Chatwin, Mary Mills and Elizabeth Rees. 1993

BVC. *Betley A Village of Contrasts.* Robert Speake. 1980

BWWOPP. *Brownhills and Walsall Wood on Old Postcards.* Jan Farrow. 1992

BY. *Bloxwich Yesterdays.* Walsall Archives Services. 1982

BZ. *Bridges - National Benzole Books.* Sir Hugh Casson. 1963

C

CA. *Current Archaeology Journal.*

CAA. *A Walk back in time around Coseley.* C Beryl Wilkes. 1983

C&COP. *Codsall and Claregate.* (Archive Photographs Series). Alec Brew. 1996.

CAM. *County Archaeologist Maps 2.5 inch to 1 mile.*

CAMS. *The Castles and Moated Mansions of Staffordshire and the West Midlands County.* Mike Salter. 1989

CAST. *Church & Ancient Parish of Stoke-upon-Trent.* Richard Talbot. 1969

CBD. *Chambers Book of Days.* Edited by R Chambers. 1888

CBHBT. *County Borough: History of Burton-on-Trent.* Part 1: Edwardian Burton. Denis Stuart. 1975.

CBL. *Collection of Boscobel Literature.* Presented by P Bayliss. 1878 1843 1910

CC or CCME. *Castle Church with some account of its Parish and Manor and of its Escheat Temporary Henry VIII* (Stafford Castle and Manor). TJ de Mazzinghi. ND

CCAP. *Cannock Chase: The Archive Photograph Series.* Sherry Belcher and Mary Mills. 1994

CCBO. *Best of Cannock Chase.* M Wright. 1933

CCC. *Chronicles of Cannock Chase.* FW Hackwood. 1903

CCF. *The Friendship of Cannock Chase.* M Wright. 1935

CCHCA. *Coaching City.* Howard Clayton. 1970

CCHCB. *Cathedral City - A Look at Victorian Lichfield.* Howard Clayton. 1977

CCM. *Cannock Chase Map.* Staffordshire County Council. 1984

CCME see CC

CCOP. *Caves and Caverns of the Peakland.* C Porteous. 1950

CCR. *Charles Cotton and his River.* Gerald GP Heywood. 1928

CCSHO. *Capital Crimes Staffs Hanging Offences.* Ros Prince. 1994

CCT. *Cheadle Coal Town: Eight Centuries of Coal Mining in the The Cheadle District.* Herbert A Chester. 1981

CDBC. *Curiosities of Dudley and the Black Country.* CFG Clark

CDPOPP. *Congleton & District: A Portrait in Old Pictures.* M & C McLean. 1988

CDS. *Croxden.* Denis Stuart. 1984

CE. *Some Account of the Parish of Church Eaton.* Rev Canon GTO Bridgeman. 1884

CGE. *China and the Gardens of Europe in the 18th Century.* Oswald Siren. 1950

CH. *Civic Heraldry of England and Wales.* C Wilfrid Scott-Giles. 1933. 1953

CHMS. *The Old Parish Churches of Staffordshire and the West Midlands County.* Mike Salter. 1989

CHMS2. *The Old Parish Churches of Staffordshire.* Mike Salter. 1996

CHPC. *Cradley Heath Parish Church: St Luke the Evangelist 100 years.* Rev JC Williams. 1947

CIOPP. Could be CDPOPP

CJF. *Checkley.* Jim Foley. c1980

CL. *Country Life.* 1897 -

COD. *Curiosities of Dudley from 1800-1860.* CFG Clark. 1881

COE. *Centre of England.* Victor Skipp.1979

COEA. *The Counties of England: Their Story and Antiquities.* PH Ditchfield. 1912. vol 1

COI. *The Chetwynd's of Ingestre.* HE Chetwynd-Stapylton. 1892

COOKE. *Cooke's Road Book.* 1810

COPP. *Cheadle in Old Picture Postcards.* W George Short. 1985

COPP2. *Cheadle: The Second Selection.* (Images of England series). W George Short. 1999

COS. *Curiosities of Staffordshire.* Ros Prince. 1992

CPD. *Description of the Castle and Priory of Dudley.* J Payton. 1794

CPP. *Codsall: Past and Present.* Michael Albutt. 1989

CR. *Clentine Rambles - Clent Hills Companion.* W Harris. 1895

CSBS. *Church of St Bertelin, Stafford.* A Oswald. 1955

CSBSS. *Church of St Bertelin in Stafford.* M Fisher and M Riley. 1981

CSJA. *Church of St John the Baptist, Ashley.* Mrs AJ Finney. 1988

CSL. *Customs, Superstitions and Legends of Staffordshire.* C Henry and CV Poole. 1875

CSMS. *Church of St Mary, Stafford.* JS Horne. 1920

CVH. *Cheddleton, a Village History.* Robert Milner. 1983

CWBT. *Coseley: A Walk Back In Time.* C Beryl Wilkes. 1994

CWF. *Colton and the De Wasteneys Family.* Rev FP Parker. 1897

D

D. *Dudley as it was and as it is today.* G Chandler and IC Hannah. 1949

DA. *Dieulacres Abbey.* Michael J Fisher. 1984

DAIW. *Dudley As It Was.* David F Radmore. 1977

DAJ. *Derbyshire Archaeological Journal.*

DB. *Domesday Book - Staffordshire.* John Morris. Published by Phillimore. 1976

DC. *Dudley Castle.* Rev Luke Booker. 1825

DCAP. *Dudley Castle Archaeological Project. 1983-85* Report. 1985

DCB. *Designs of Chinese Buildings.* Chambers. 1757

DCP. *Dudley Castle and Priory.* Charles Twamley. 1895

DD. *A Tour Through the Whole Island of Great Britain.* Daniel Defoe. 1724-6

DDI. *Guide to Dovedale and Ilam.* P Dawson. 1854

DDBP. *Dynamic Design: The British Pottery Industry 1940-1990.* Kathy Niblett.

DEPN. *Dictionary of English Place Names.*

DET. *Derby Evening Telegraph.*

DFMAL. *Dictionary of Folklore, Mythology & Legend.* Edited by Maria Leach. 1972

DG. *Dangerous Ghosts.* Elliot O' Donnell. 1954 1962 edition

DH. *Denstone.* Women's Institute. 1949

DIP. *Dudley Illustrated by Photographs.* To Georgina, Countess of Dudley. 1898

DJL. *Dr Johnson's Lichfield.* Mary Alden Hopkin. 1956

DL. *Derbyshire Life Magazine.*

DM. *Drayton Manor and Village.* Christine Smith. 1978

DM2. *Drayton Manor and Village: Home of the Peels.* Christine Smith. 1991

DMF. *Deeds Most Foul.* Fred Leigh. 1997

DMV. *Bygone Days in Dovedale and the Manifold Valley.* Lindsey Porter. 1997

DNB. *Dictionary of National Biography.*

DOB. *Dictionary of Birmingham.* William Showell. 1885 1969 edition

DOG. *A Dictionary of Ghosts.* Peter Haining. 1982

DOPP. *Dudley In Old Picture Postcards.* David F Radmore. 1985

DOS. *Description of Staffordshire.* GA Cox. 1830

DP. *Myths and Legends of East Cheshire and the Moors.* Doug Pickford. 1991

DPEM. *Earth Mysteries of the Three Shires.* Doug Pickford. 1996

DPMM. *Magic Myths and Memories in and around the Peak District.* Doug Pickford. 1993

DPTB. *The Bridestones.* Doug Pickford. 1998

DRBSC. *Directory of Rare Book & Special Collections.* Edited by Moelwyn I Williams. 1985

DTT. *Darlaston Town Trail.* Malcolm Timmins. 1981

DUIGNAN. *Notes on Staffordshire Place Names.* WH Duignan. 1902

DVOPP. *The Dane Valley: A Portrait in Old Picture Postcards.* Mary and Colin McLean. 1991

E

E. *The Old Road to Endon.* Robert Speake. 1974

EAS. *Early Aeronautics in Staffordshire.* John Godwin. 1986

E&S. *Express and Star.*

ECC. *Eccleshall.* Peter & Margaret Spufford. 1964

ECE. *Elford Church Effigies.* Edward Richardson. 1852

ECFVA. *Encyclopedia of Cottage, Farm and Villa.* JC Loudon. 1833

EDP. *Some Account of English Deer Parks.* Evelyn Philip Shirley. 1867

EF. *The Eye of Fire.* Graham Phillips and Martin Keatman. 1986

EFS. *Endon St Luke's Church, The Parochial School, The Well Dressing.* Frank Stubbs. 1994

EGH. *England's Ghostly Heritage.* Terence Whitaker. 198·

EH. *The Copper and Lead Mines of Ecton Hill.* John A Robey & Lindsey Porter. 1972

EKWALL. *The Concise Oxford Dictionary of English Place Names.* E Ekwall. 1947 (3rd ed) 1960 (4th ed)

EL. *Exploring Leek.* Keith Warrender. 1982

EMC. *Eccleshall Manor and Castle.* Samuel Pegge. 1784

EOP. *Eccleshall in Old Picture Postcards.* Edward Watkin. 1989

ERH. *Early Religious Houses in Staffordshire.* E Levien. 1873

ES. *Evening Sentinel.*

ESH. *Excursions into Staffordshire History* (stories first appeared in SA). SAH Burne. 1913

ESNF. *East Staffordshire Needwood Forest to the Weaver Hills* (The Archive Photographs Series). Richard Farman & Geoffrey Sowerby. 1995

ESS. *English Shrines & Sanctuaries.* Christina Hole. 1954

ESSN. *Essington.* Jim Evans and Michael Albutt. 1993

F

F. *Follies.* G Headley and W Meulen Kamp. 1986

F&G. *Follies and Grottoes.* Barbara Jones. 1974

FA. *Foster's Alumni.*

FCRE. *Folklore & Customs of Rural England.* Margaret Baker. 1974

FDD. *From Domesday to Domesday. Some Chapters from the History of Kingswinford.* DR Guttery. 1947

FF. *Fenton - The Town Arnold Bennett Forgot.* Richard Talbot. 1977

FG. *Family Ghosts.* Elliot O' Donnell. 1933

FGS. *Ford Green Story.* NC Rowley. 1983

FLJ. *Folklore Journal.* 1883-1991

FOS. *Folklore of Staffordshire.* Jon Raven. 1978

FOSE. *Flora of Staffordshire: Flowering Plants & Ferns.* ES Edees. 1972

FPSB. *Folklore of Prehistoric Sites in Britain.* Leslie V Grinsell. 1976

FS. *Forgotten Shrines.* Dom Bede Camm. 1910

FSBC. *Folklore and Songs of the Black Country and the West Midlands.* M & J Raven. 1966

FSLBWM. *The Folklore, Superstitions and Legends of Birmingham and the West Midlands.* Richard S Brown. 1992

FSP. *Fragments of Stafford's Past.* Dudley Wilks. c1939

FSR. *Flying Saucer Review.*

FSRP. *Flying Saucer Report.* Roger H Stanway and Anthony Pace. 1968

FTP. *On Foot Through The Peak.* James Croston. 1876

FTWM. *Folk Tales of the West Midlands.* F Grice. 1952

FWMBS. *From Wetley Moor To Bucknall Sands.* Elizabeth W Bass. 1997

FWNS. *Famous Women of North Staffordshire.* Patricia Pilling. 1999

FX. *Foxt.* Robert Speake. 1989

FZ. *Follies - National Benzole Books.* Sir Hugh Casson. 1963

G

G. *Guardian* and *The Manchester Guardian*.
GATD. *Gone Are The Days*. Ted Hiscock. 1986
GAH. *The Glory of Aston Hall*. Canon Arthur G Wall. 1963
GAS. *Glossary of Archaic Words of Staffordshire*. CH Poole. 1880
GBG. *Gazetteer of British Ghosts*. Peter Underwood. 1971
GBP. *Great Barr Park: A Survey of the Landscape*.
GBR. *Guinness Book of Records*. 1955 -
GCC. *Guide to Cannock Chase*. Friends of Cannock Chase. 1951
GDC. *Guide to Dudley Castle*. Published by G Walters. 1840
GE. *The Gardens of England in the Midland & Eastern Counties*. Charles Holme. 1908
GHC. *Good Health to the Customer: The Story of South Staffordshire Water plc*. Jonathan Mantle.1994
GKCLC. *Get to know The Close of Lichfield Cathedral*. Discovery Sheet No. 8
GKGLC. *Get to know The Glass in Lichfield Cathedral*. Discovery Sheet No. 5
GKMCLC. *Get to know The Mediaeval Close of Lichfield Cathedral*. Discovery Sheet No. 9
GKSMCLC. *Get to know The Statues, Monuments & Memorials of Lichfield Cathedral*. Discovery Sheet No. 4
GLAUE. *Guide to the Local Administrative Units of England*. Frederick A Young. vol II. 1991.
GLS. *Ghosts & Legends of Staffordshire & Black Country*. David Bell. 1994
GM. *Gentleman's Magazine*.
GMH. *Great Men of Harborne* (Articles from Harborne Parish Church Magazine 1982-83)
GMS. *Great Men of Staffordshire*. L Millward. 1955
GNHS. *Natural History of Staffordshire*. Robert Garner. 1844
GNHSS. *Natural History of Staffordshire* (Supplement). Robert Garner. 1844
GOD. *Ghosts of Dudley and other weird tales*. Kevin Goodman. 1983
GOHK. *Our Haunted Kingdom*. Andrew Green. 1973
GOM. *Ghosts of the Midlands and How to Detect Them*. Philip Solomon. 1990
GOS. *Ghosts, Legends and Psychic Snippets*. Philip Solomon. 1990
GOT. *Ghosts of Today*. Andrew Green. 1980
GPCE. *Ghosts and Phantoms of Central England*. Philip Solomon. 1997
GPE. *A Guide to Prehistoric England*. Nicholas Thomas. 1960
GS. *The Green Stone*. Graham Phillips and Martin Keatman. 1983
GSGH. *Guide to St Giles' Church, Haughton*. MV Cooksley.1979
GSP. *Guide to Sandon Park*. Edward Thomas
GSS. *Grammar Schools in Staffordshire 1868*. Staffordshire Study Book 14.
GW. *Guide to Wolverhampton*. Alfred Hinde.
GWY. *Great Wyrley 1051-1951*. A Plesance. 1951

H

H. *Hanley, Stoke-on-Trent*. A Huntbach. 1910
HA. *Harborne 'Once upon a time.'* Tom Presterne. 1913
HAF. *A History of Alton and Farley*. Robert Speake. 1996
HAH. *Guide and History of Ancient Haywood*. Stafforda. 1924
HAHS. *Supplement to the History of Haywood*. Staffordia. 1930
HANDR. *Handsworth Remembered*. Victor J Price. 1992
HAS. *Harborne and its Surroundings*. James Kenward. 1885
HATC. *History and Antiquities of Tamworth Castle*. C Ferrers and R Palmer. 1871
HB. *Haunted Britain*. Antony D Hippisley. 1973
HBST. *History of the Borough of Stoke-on-Trent*. John Ward. 1843
HC. *History of Coseley*. JS Roper. 1952
HCCW. *History of the Collegiate Church of Wolverhampton*. Rev Dr G Oliver. 1836
HCLN. *Handbook for the City of Lichfield and its

Neighbourhood*. 1884
HCMBOPP. *The Haywoods, Colwich, Milford and Brocton: A Portrait in Old Picture Postcards*. Roy Lewis. 1993
HCMS. *Historical Canal Maps Series* (No. 2 Canals of Birmingham 1994) (No. 5 Canals of North Staffs 1997). Richard Dean
HCT. *History of the Castle, Priory and Town of Tutbury*. Sir Oswald Mosley. 1832
HDCPT. *Historical Description of the Castle and Priory of Tutbury*. John Jackson. 1796
HE. *Haunted England*. Christina Hole. 1940
HED. *Historical, or New English Dictionary*.
HH. *Horton Hall*. JF Moxon. 1954. (published privately. typescript copy in WSL)
HHFT. *Haunted Homes and Family Traditions*. John Ingram. 1905
HHH. *History of Hilton Hall*. Cherry Ann Knott. 1989
HHHC. *A Heresy History of The Haywoods and Colwich 1900-1939*. The Haywood Society. 1997
HHHL. *The History of Horton Hall*. JF Moxon. 1997
HHHW. *Handsworth, Hockley and Handsworth Wood*. Images of England series. Peter Drake. 1998
HIE. *Haunted Inns of England*. Jack Hallam. 1972
HIL. *Historical Incidents in and around Lichfield*. JW Jackson. 1936
HK. *History of Kinver*. AJ Bennett. 1977 (published privately. typescript copy in WSL)
HLG. *A History of Lower Gornal*. Andrew Barnett. 1975
HLS. *In the Highlands of Staffordshire*. WH Nithsdale. 1906
HLSP. *The Happy Highways 'In the Highlands of Staffordshire'*. Ray Poole. 1998
HM. *The Heart of the Midlands*. James P Jones. 1906
HNM. *History of Norton in the Moors*. James Jack
HO. *St Mary the Virgin, High Offley*. Susan Eaton. 1987
HOA. *History of Alrewas*. Norman Stubbs. 1987
HOB. *History of Brewood*. J Hicks Smith. 1874
HOBL. *History of Bilston*. GT Lawley. 1893. (check also HOBLL)
HOBLL. *History of Bilston*. GT Lawley. 1863. (check also HOBL)
HOBT. *History of Burton-Upon-Trent*. W Molyneux. 1869
HOBTU. *History of Burton-Upon-Trent*. CH Underhill. 1941
HOBTW. *History of Burton-Upon-Trent*. William Wesley. 1848
HOC. *History of Cheadle*. R Plant. 1881
HOCA. *History of Calwich Abbey*. Mary T Fortescue. 1915
HODW. *History of Darlaston*. FW Hackwood. 1887
HOE. *History of Etruria*. E J D Warrillow. 1952
HOG. *History on the Ground*. Maurice Beresford. 1957
HOHE. *A History of Harborne*. Michael Counsell. 1989
HOHH. *Articles on the History of Harborne* (extracted from St Peter's Church Magazine 1935-1941). WE Hardwick
HOK. *History of Keele*. Christopher Harrison. 1986
HOL. *History of Lichfield*. Dr Harwood. 1806
HOLB. *History of Longton*. JHY Briggs. 1982
HOLF. *A History of Leekfrith* (Meerbrook and its Locality). Mary Breeze. 1995
HOLJ. *History of Lichfield*. John Jackson. 1805
HOLK. *History of Locks and Keys*. G Price. 1856
HOLP. *History of Lichfield*. Alfred D Parker. 1925
HOLS. *History of Leek*. John Sleigh. 1862. 1883
HOM. *History of Marchington*. P Wolley & J Ellwood. 1989
HOMD. *History of Market Drayton*. Rev JR Lee. 1861
HON. *Handsworth Old & New*. FW Hackwood. 1908
HONUL. *History of Newcastle-under-Lyme*. JT Coulam. 1908
HOP. *History of Penkridge*. JC Tildesley. 1886
HOPE. *The History of Penn*. Prebendary E Hartill. 1950
HOPL. *A History of Pleck*. Malcolm McDevitt. 1984
HOPP. *Harborne on Old Picture Postcards*. Andrew Maxam. 1996
HOPS. *History of the Parish of Standon*. Edward Salt. 1888
HOPT. *History of the Parish of Tatenhill*. Sir Reginald Hardy. Volumes 1 and 2. 1908
HOPTT. *History of the parish of Tettenhall*. James P Jones. 1894
HORV. *History of Rowley Village*. E Chitham. 1977
HOS. *History of Staffordshire*. MW Greenslade and DG Stuart. 1st ed 1965. 3rd ed 1998

HOSC. *History of Stoke Church*. Robert Nicholls. 1929
HOSCC. *History of Stafford and Guide to the Neighbourhood*. Charles Calvert. 1886
HOSTK. *History of St John the Baptist's, Keele*. CJ Harrison. 1991
HOSW. *History of Staffordshire*. Dr R Wilkes
HOT. *History of Tixall*. Arthur Clifford & Sir Thomas Clifford. 1817
HOTC. *History of Trentham and its Church from 680 AD*. Rev JF Challis. c1958
HOTIP. *History of Tipton*. John Parkes. 1915
HOTM. *History of Trentham*. William Molyneux. 1878
HOU. *History of Uttoxeter*. F Redfern. 1865 1886
HOW. *History of Wednesbury*. Many authors and sources. 1854
HOWB. *History of West Bromwich*. FW Hackwood. 1895
HOWBA. *History of Wednesbury*. JN Bagnall. 1854
HOWBW. *History of West Bromwich*. Mary Willett. 1882
HOWG. *History of Walsall*. EL Glew. 1856
HOWI. *History of Willenhall*. Norman W Tildesley. 1951
HOWM. *History of Wolverhampton*. Gerald P Mander and Norman Tildesley. 1960
HOWP. *History of Walsall*. Pearce. 1813
HOWU. *A History of Wolverhampton*. Chris Upton. 1998
HOWW. *History of Walsall*. Dr Fred W Willmore. 1887
HOWWW. *History of Whalley*. Dr Thomas Dunham Whitaker
HOWY* (or HOWV). *History of Wednesbury*. JR Ede. 1962
HPCH. *History of Canwell Priory and Canwell Hall*. Joseph P Lafrati. 1988
HPG. *The Haunted Pub Guide*. Guy Lyon Playfair. 1985
HPH. *History of the Pirehill Hundred*. W Chetwynd. 1909
HPPE. *Handsworth: A Summary of Houses, Places, People, Events and Institutions*. FTD Hall. 1984.
HR. *Hamstall Ridware*. RF Elton. 1988
HRFCP. *Haughton Rectory or Four Country Parsons*. TF Royds. 1953
HS. *Historic Staffordshire*. R Dent and J Hill. 1896
HSB. *History of Signboards*. John Camden Hotten. 1866
HSP. *History of the Staffordshire Potteries*. Simeon Shaw. 1829
HSS. *Historical Studies, Staffordshire*. JL Cherry and K Cherry. 1908
HT. *Historic Tamworth*. Mabel Swift. 1986
HTC. *History of Tutbury Castle*. NA. 1843
HTCT. *History of the Town and Castle of Tamworth*. Charles Ferrers Palmer. 1845
HV. *Some Aspects of Hixon Village*. Rev WH Briddon. (written 1917) 1992
HYB. *Hone's Year Book*. William Hone. 1832
HWE. *The History of the Worthies of England*. Thomas Fuller. 1662. 1811 ed

I

I. *The Independent*.
IAANS. *In and About North Staffordshire*. WTB Ridge. 1898
IADC. *Inns, Ales, Drinking Customs of Old England*. FW Hackwood. 1909
IANS. *Industrial Archaeology of North Staffordshire*. WJ Thompson. 1976
IAS. *Industrial Archaeology of Staffordshire*. Robert Sherlock. 1976
IE. *The Iron Elwells*. Charles JL Elwell. 1992 2nd ed.
IES. *Incised Effigies of Staffordshire*. A Oliver. 1913
IHB. *Ice-Houses of Britain*. Sylvia P Beaman & Susan Roaf. 1990
IHOBT. *An Illustrated History of Burton-upon-Trent to the 18th Century*. Denis Stuart. ND
IISD. *Inns and Inn Signs of Dudley*. Mark H Washington Fletcher JP. 1952
ILN. *Illustrated London News*. 1843 -
IOI. *Inns of Interest. Booklet Sponsored by Express & Star*. 1968
IOM. *Inns of the Midlands*. Norman Tiptaft. 1951
IP. *Investigating Penn*. TR Bennett. 1st edition 1958. 1975
IRB. *I Remember Burton*. Denis Stuart. 1985
ISS. *In Search of the Supernatural*. Peter Travis. 1975
IVNF. *Inn and Village History of Needwood Forest*. WH Bullock. 1988

J

JAT. *Alton Towers and Dovedale*. Llewellynn Jewitt. 1869

JBAA. *Journal of the British Archaeological Association*.
JC. *North Staffordshire Sketchbook*. John Creber. 1987
JEPS. *Journal of English Place-names Society*.
JG. *Some Staffordshire Characters*. John Godwin. 1982
JGM. *Grave-mounds and their contents*. Llewellynn
  Jewitt. 1870
JHSB. *History of Staffordshire Bells*. TS Jennings. 1968
JSD. *John Sneyd's Diary 1815-1871: Thirty Pieces of
  Silver*. Pam Inder & Marion Aldis. 1998

K

K. *Keele*. Sir James Mountford. 1972
KAIW. *Kidsgrove As It Was*. Philip R Leese. 1984
KBT. *The Best of Kidsgrove Times*. Phillip R Leese.
  Volume 2. 1996
KCPC. *The Story of Pensnett Chase: Chapters from
  Kingswinford History*. DR Guttery. 1950
KCTJ. *The Two Johns Patron & Parson: A C15 Chapter
  from Kingswinford History*. DR Guttery. 1950
KD. *Kelly's Directory*.
KEOP. *Kinver and Enville* (in old photographs). Bob
  Clarke & Tony Freer. 1996
KES. *Kings England Staffordshire*. A Mee. 1937
KESH. *Kings England Shropshire*. A. Mee. 1937
KH. *Keele Hall: A Victorian Country House*. J Kolbert.
  1986
KMC. *Medieval Kinver*. FE Campbell. 1963
KNS. *Kidsgrove and North Staffordshire*. Frederick G
  Llewellin. 1935
KPP. *Kingstanding Past and Present*. Birmingham Public
  Libraries. 1968 1984
KR. *A Short History of Kidsgrove*. N Roche. ND 1965?
KRC. *Royal Kinver*. FE Campbell. 1964
KRH. *Kinver Rock Houses*. DM Bills & E & WR Griffiths.
  1992?
KTM. *Kidsgrove, Talke and Mow Cop in Old Picture
  Postcards*. R Simmons. 1987
KY. *Knypersley, a History for Parish Diamond Jubilee*. JN
  Sherratt. 1982

L

L. *Longnor, St Bartholomew's Church*. 1980
LAIW. *Lanesfield As It Was*. Trevor A Genge. 1993
LAL. *Look at Lichfield*. Roger Wilkinson. 1976
LASS. *Landscape of Anglo-Saxon Staffordshire*. Della
  Hooke. 1983
LAST. *Lichfield Archaeology Society Transactions*. 1960-
  61
LAWTT. *Lichfield A Walk Through Time*. Peter Foulkes.
  1989
LC. *The Life of St Chad*. Rev RH Warner. 1871
LCAST. *Lancashire and Cheshire Antiquarian Society
  Transactions*.
LCPG. *Lichfield Cathedral Painted Glass*. Published by
  TG Lomax. 1823
LCWA. *Some Notes on the Parish of Lapley cum Wheaton
  Aston*. GT Hartley. 1912
LDOG. *Lichfield District Official Guide*. 1979
LDD. *Lichfield Diocesan Directory*. 1992
LET. *Letocetum*. WF Blay. 1925
LGS. *Little Guide to Staffordshire* or '*Staffordshire.*' C
  Masefield. (1910) 1919 (1923) 1930
LHE. *The Local Historian's Encyclopedia*. John
  Richardson. 1974. 1993.
LHEF. *A Companion to the Leasowes, Hagley and Enville
  (and Fisherwick)*. 1789
LHEL. *Letters on the Beauty of Hagley, Enville etc*. Joseph
  Heely. 1777
LHM. *Leisure Hour Magazine*.
LHSB. *Local History Source Books*. Staffs County
  Council. No. 14 (Grammar Schools in Staffordshire.
  1984). No. G.20 (Staffs Population since 1660). L. 6
  (Lichfield in Maps. 1970). No. 38 (Old Chasetown.
  ND but by 1980). No. 50 (Old Heath Hayes).
LI, *Leland's Itinerary in England and Wales*. John Leland.
  1535-43. 1908 edition
LLST. *Lantern Lecture on Stoke-on-Trent*. EJD Warrillow.

1979
LMF. *Legends of the Moorlands and Forest in North
  Staffordshire*. Miss Dakeyne. 1860
LMV. *Most Valiant of Men*. Fred Leigh. 1993
LOG. *Lichfield Official Guide*. 1927 1930
LOPP. *Lichfield in Old Picture Postcards*. Roy Lewis.
  1994?
LOU. *Language of the Unheard: Civil Disorder in
  Staffordshire. 1640-1842*. TJ Pointon. 1991
LPCC. *Life and Poetry of Charles Cotton*. Charles J
  Sembower. 1911
LPL. *Lomax's Pictorial Book of Lichfield*. AC Lomas.
  1968
LR. *Leek Remembered*. Vera Priestman. 1980 (Phd thesis)
LSWA. *The Parish of Lapley: Lapley, Stretton, Wheaton
  Aston*. Michael Albutt. 1991
LTD *The Land of the Dove: The story of an English river,
  visiting: etc*. David J Ford. 1999
LTM. *Lichfield and Tamworth Life Magazine*. Sept 1971 -
  March 1973
LWA. *Lapley with Wheaton Ashton*. Mary Weate. 1982
LWF. *Lest We Forget*. Fred Leigh. 1994
LWS. *Letocetum (Wall), Staffordshire*. National Trust
  Guide. 1947

M

M. *Madeley*. R Nicholls
M &H. *Concise Encyclopaedia of English Pottery*. W
  Mankowitz & R Haggar. 1957
MC. *Short History of Mow Cop*. WJ Harper. 1907
MCC. *The Medieval Cathedral and Close*. Jim Gould.
  1981 (leaflet guide)
MCGM. *Murder Club Guide to the Midlands*. Brian Lane.
  1988
MCS. *Staffordshire & The Black Country Murder
  Casebook*. David Bell. 1996
MCSSW. *Mansions and Country seats of Staffordshire and
  Warwickshire*. Alfred Williams & Witt Mallett. 1899
MD. *A Moorland Dedication*. Marshall S Boylan. 1992
MECS. *Moule's English Counties: Staffordshire* (No. IV).
  Thomas Moule. 1837
MGH. *Midland Ghosts and Hauntings*. Anne Bradford &
  Barrie Roberts. 1994
MH. *Midland History*. Volume 1 No. 1 Spring 1971 -
MHSP. *Madeley, A History of a Staffordshire Parish*. J
  Kennedy. 1970
MIDD. *Midland Digest*. vols 1 - 5. Michael Raven. 1992
MJW. *Maer. A Guide to the Village and Church*. John
  Wild. 1987. 1989
MLL. *Mr Lomax's Lichfield*. Howard Clayton. 1991
MM. *Midland Murders*. Michael Posner. 1973
MMBC. *Murder and Mystery in the Black Country*. Harold
  Parsons. 1989
MMBCC. *A Memorable Medley of Great Black Country
  Characters*. Aristotle Tump. 1986
MMH. *Midlanders Who Made History 1600-1800*.
  William Tann. Volume I 1973
MMM. *Murders, Myths and Monuments of North
  Staffordshire*. WM Jamieson. 1979
MMMR. *Midland Murders & Mysteries*. Barrie Roberts.
  1997
MMSE. *Modern Mysteries of Britain 100 years of Strange
  Events*. Janet & Colin Bord. 1987
MNB. *Manors of North Birmingham*. John Morris Jones.
  1984
MOA. *Men of Aldridge*. Jim Gould. (1957) 1983
MOM. *Memories of Mayfield*. Mayfield Heritage Group.
  1993
MOPP. *Staffordshire Moorlands in Old Picture Postcards*
  I. 1991
MOS. *Memories of Old Staffordshire*. Many authors -
  Forward by Rev W Beresford. 1909
MOSP. *Memories of Stone*. George Pearson. 1981
MOT. *A Matter of Time*. Royal Commission on Historic
  Monuments. 1960
MR. *Staffordshire and the Black Country*. Michael Raven.
  1988
MRH. *Medieval Religious Houses of England and Wales*.
  David Knowles & R Neville Hadcock. 1953
MRM. *Meir Remembered*. Meir Local History Group
MS. *Mystical Staffordshire*. Carol Arnall. 1991
MS&S. *Midland Spirits & Spectres*. Anne Bradford &
  Barrie Roberts. 1998

MSM. *Parish and Church of St Mary, Mucklestone*. Clive
  Howson. 1971
MT. *Medieval Tutbury*. Rev N Edwards. 1949
MWN. *Midland Weekly News* (S=Supplement)

N

N. *Newcastle-under-Lyme*. Rev JP Conway. 1903
N&Q. *Notes & Queries Magazine*. November 1849 - 1988
  Volume 1 - Volume 233
NAIW. *Newcastle-under-Lyme As It Was*. Dave Adams.
  1986
NCB. *Notes and Collections relating to Brewood*. William
  Parke. 1858
NCSS. *Non-Conformist Chapels in Staffordshire and
  Shropshire* (this title is not the proper title).
ND. *A Photographic History of Newchapel and District*. E
  Harding. Volumes 1, 2 and 3 1989
NEE. *Netherton: Edward I - Edward VIII*. Mark H
  Washington Fletcher. (1946) 1969
NFCF. *Neolithic Flints from a Chipping-floor at Cannock
  Wood*. GM Cockin and TC Cantrill. 1917
NFNS. *Notes on the Folklore of North Staffordshire*. W
  Wells Bladen
NHE. *The Church of The Holy Evangelist, Normacot*.
NHOA. *Notes for a History of Armitage*. WG Wright. 195
NHS. *Natural History of Staffordshire*. Robert Plot. 1686
NHT. *Natural History of Tutbury*. Sir Oswald Mosley.
  1863
NI. *Nicholson Institute*. Pauline V Smith. 1984
NM. *Medieval Newcastle-under-Lyme*. T Pape. 1928
NOPP. *The Borough of Newcastle in Old Picture
  Postcards*. Dennis Morris and others. 1987
NSF. *Notes on Some North Staffordshire Families*. Percy
  WL Adams. 1931
NRS. *Newcastle-under-Lyme from the Restoration to 1760*
  Thomas Pape. 1940
NSA. *North Staffordshire Album*. George Dow. 1970
NSFCT. *North Staffordshire Field Club Transactions*. 186!
  - 1959 then incorporated into NSJFS. New series from
  1975
NSJFS. *North Staffordshire Journal of Field Studies*. 1961
  - 1982/5.
NSSG. *North Staffordshire: A Short Guide*. Robert
  Nicholls. 1925?
NTL. *Norman Tymppana and Lintels*. Charles E Keyser.
  1927
NTMA. *New Towns of the Middle Ages*. Maurice
  Beresford. 1967
NTS. *Newcastle-under-Lyme in Tudor and Early Stuart
  Times*. T Pape. 1938
NUL. *Newcastle-under-Lyme 1173 - 1973*. JHY Briggs.
  1973
NULOP. *Newcastle-under-Lyme in Old Picture Postcards*.
  Paul Bembrose. 1983 vol 1. 1990 vol 2.

O

O. *Oldbury and Round About*. FW Hackwood. 1915
OAKDEN. *Lichfield and South Staffordshire Archaeology
  and History Society*. Volume 9 pp31-36
OCHW. *Odd Chapters in the History of Wednesbury*. FW
  Hackwood. 1920
ODS. *Oxford Dictionary of Saints*. David Hugh Farmer.
  1987
OH. *The Venice of the Midlands: Ocker Hill (100 years)*.
  Rev F Brighton. 1949
OHOPP. *Old Harborne (The Old Photographs Series)*. Roy
  Clarke. 1994
OHW. *Old Houses in Wolverhampton and the Neighbour-
  hood*. JR Veall. 1889
OL. *Olde Leek*. Matthew Miller. Volumes 1 and 2. 1891
OMH. *A History of the Old Meeting House, Newcastle-
  under-Lyme*. G Peglar. c1924
ONS. *Old North Staffordshire*. John F Moxon. 1972.
  Volumes 1 and 2
ONST. *Old Nortonian Society Transactions*. 1925 -
OP. *Occasional Papers*. SAH Burne. 1961
OPB. *Occasional Papers*. 2nd Series. SAH Burne. 1963
OPM. *More Occasional Papers*. SAH Burne. 1965

ORR. *Oldbury and Rowley Regis in Old Photographs*.
  John Maddison. 1991

OSH. *Illustrations of Old Staffordshire Houses.* W Niven. 1882

OSST. *Old Stafford Society Transactions.* 1928

OTP. *Old Times in the Potteries.* W Scarratt. 1906 1969

OVH. *Our Vanishing Heritage.* Marcus Binney. 1984

OW. *Olden Wednesbury.* FW Hackwood. 1899

OWB. *Old West Bromwich; or, the story of long ago.* Henry H Prince. 1924

OWEN. *Fairs in England and Wales 'New Book of Fairs.'* Owen. 1792

P

P. *Pattingham.* Rev F Brighton. 1942

PA. *Popular Antiquities.* John Brand. 1777 1905 edition

PAIP. *Penn and Ink.* Angus Dunphy. 1992

PASN. *Peakland Archaeological Society Newsletter* (in Keele University library)

PBH. *Where Numbers Cease to Count: The Parish of Blakenall Heath 1872-1972.* RA Cason. 1972

PCBT. *Parish Church Burton-upon-Trent.* Charles Underhill & HH Pitchford. 1976

PCC. *Portrait of Cannock Chase.* Friends of Cannock Chase. 1957

PCCSC. *The Potteries: Continuity and Change in a Staffordshire Conurbation.* ADM Phillips. 1993

PD. *Staffordshire* (County Book Series). Phil Drabble. 1948

PDS&C. *The Peak District: Its Secrets and Curiosities.* Lindsey Porter. 1988

PENOP. *Penn in Old Photographs.* Elizabeth A Rees. 1990

PG. *Provincial Glossary.* F Grose. 1811

PHH. *A Peep into the History of Hilderstone.* Winifred M Bossen. 1986

PHS. *Pictorial History of Sedgley.* Ron Baker. 1970

PL. *Phantom Ladies.* Andrew Green. 1977

PM. *The Potteries Martyrs.* Robert Anderson. 1992

PMPD. *Memories of Penn and district.* Angus Dunphy. 1988

PNPD. *Place Names of the Peak District.* Louis McMeeken. 1998

POA. *Notes and Collections on Aldridge.* JF Smith. Volumes 1 and 2. 1884 1889

POAP. *Out and About in Penn and district.* Angus Dunphy. 1990

POD. *The Peak of Derbyshire.* John Leyland. 1891

POE. *Poltergeist Over England.* Harry Price. 1945

POP. *Portrait of the Potteries.* Bill Morland. 1978

PONP. *Over and Nether Penn and district.* Angus Dunphy. 1994

POT. *Potbank.* Mervyn Jones. 1961

POTP. *People of the Potteries.* Denis Stuart and others. Volume 1 1985

PP. *Parish of St Philip, Penn Fields.* Malcolm Deaville. 1981

PPP. *Potteries Picture Postcards.* S Benz. Volume 2 1986

PPTP. *Penn to Paper.* Angus Dunphy. 1996

PR. *Parish Register* (followed by parish name)

PRA. *Penkhull Remembered Again.* Richard Talbot. 1987

PRT. *Peakland Roads and Trackway.* AE Dodd & EM Dodd. 1974

PS. *Picturesque Staffordshire.* North Staffordshire Railway Company. 1908

PSM. *Staffordshire Moorlands: Pictures from the Past.* Lindsey Porter. 1983

PSS. *Poets of the Shires: Staffordshire.* CH Poole & R Markland. 1928

PT. *Pennant's Tour.* Thomas Pennant. 1811

PTP. *People of The Potteries.* Henry Allen Wedgwood. 1970

PTYV. *Pelsall: A Thousand years of Village Life.* Ann Galbraith & Albert Tomkinson 1990

PVBC. *Powered Vehicles made in the Black Country (1900 - 1930s).* J Boulton. 1976.

PVH. *Penkridge: a brief Village History and a Selection of Local Walks.* 1992?

PWIS. *Pub Walks in Staffordshire.* Nick Channer. 1995

PWNS. *Pub Walks in North Staffordshire.* Les Lumsdon & Chris Rushton. 1993

PWPD. *Pub Walks in the Peak District.* Les Lumsdon & Martin Smith. 1992

PWW. *Pure & Wholesome Water for One Hundred Years: The Story of the Staffordshire Potteries Water Undertaking. 1849-1949.* NA

Q

QBSS. *Both Sides of the Severn by Quaestor.* W Byford-Jones. 1930s

QML. *Midland Leaves by Quaestor.* W Byford-Jones. 1934

QMMH. *Midlands Murderers, Hauntings by Quaestor.* W Byford-Jones. 1936

QVTM. *Vagabonding Through the Midlands.* W Byford-Jones. 1930s

R

R. *Reliquary.*

R&S. *Royalty and Staffordshire.* Staffordshire County Council. 1977

RAIK. *Report of the Summer Meeting of Royal Archaeology Institute at Keele in 1963.* Reprinted from ARCHJ volume 120.

RB. *Recording Britain.* Oxford University Press & Pilgrim Trust. Volumes 1,2,3 1943

RBS. *Royal Borough of Stafford.* Cecil Hibberd. 1906

RDC. *Rambles about Dudley Castle.* William Harris. 1895

RHH. *Robin Hood.* Professor JC Holt. 1982

RHPS. *Researches into History of Parish of Stone.* WH Bowers & JW Clough. 1929

RHS. *History of Shenstone.* Rev Henry Saunders. 1794

RKE. *Romantic Kinver and Enville with Legends.* Frances E Campbell

RL. *Rudyard Lake. The Bicentenary 1797-1997.* Basil Jeuda. 1997

RM. *Railway Magazine.*

RN. *English River Names.* E Ekwall. 1928

ROR. *Records of Rushall.* Frederic W Willmore. 1892

ROS. *The Romance of Staffordshire.* Henry Allen Wedgwood. Volumes 1,2,3 1877-1879

ROT. *Ripples of Time - following the River Sow.* Bruce Braithwaite. 1987

RPG. *Some Ghosts of Staffordshire.* Rosalind Prince. 1981

RPM. *Some Staffordshire Murders.* Rosalind Price. 1983

RRCC. *Random Rambles on Cannock Chase.* COL Finlow. 1972

RS. *Records of Smethwick.* FW Hackwood. 1896

RSL. *Recollections of Sophie Lonsdale.* Violet Martineau. 1936

RVW. *Royal Visit to Wolverhampton.* Unknown. 1867

RW. *Religious Wednesbury.* FW Hackwood. 1900

S

S. *Staffordshire* (Cambridge County Geographies). W Bernard Smith. 1915

S&COP. *Silverdale and Chesterton in Old Photographs.* Dave Adams. 1988.

S&DOP. *Stafford and District: Postcards from the Past.* Roy Lewis. 1998.

S&UR. *The Stafford & Uttoxeter Railway.* P Jones 1981

S&W. *Stafford and Warwickshire Past and Present.* Langford, John Alfred. 1880

S&WC. *Stafford and Worcestershire Canal.* Dr J Ian Langford. 1974

SA. *Staffordshire Advertiser.* 1795-

SAC. *The Story of the Ancient Parish of Castlechurch.* Alfred Middlefell. 1998

SAIW. *Stafford As It Was.* R Lewis & J Anslow. 1980

SAL. *Short Account of The City of Lichfield.* Charles Edward Stringer. 1819

SARCH. *Staffordshire Archaeology.* Edited by FSC Celoria. 1972 - 1975

SAS. *Swynnerton and the Swynnertons.* Rev BT Swinnerton. 1900 (printed 1971)

SASR. *Staffordshire Archaeological Studies.* Volume 1 1984 -

SBB. *Swinscoe, Blore and the Bassetts.* David & Martine Swinscoe. 1998

SBG. *Story of Biddulph Grange.* A Ferris. 1985 1986

SBI. *Some British Inns* (No. 16). WE Tate

SBT. *Staffordshire Bull Terrier.* JF Gordon. 1971

SC. *Staffordshire Curiosities.* FW Hackwood. 1905

SCA. *Shell County Alphabet.* G Grigson. 1966

SCC. *Story of Clifton Campville.* Presented to WSL by JS Horne. 1892

SCCC. *Stafford Castle and Castle Church.* JS Horne. 1933

SCFK. *Stourton Castle and Forest of Kinver.* Capt RM Grazebrook. 1919

SCH. *Staffordshire Catholic History Journal.* 1961 -

SCHJ. *Staffordshire Catholic Historic Journal.* 1961 -

SCK. *Stewponey Countryside.* Frances E Campbell. 1979

SCM. *Staffordshire County Magazine.*

SCR. *Stafford Castle Reports.* Excavation Report. c1980 onwards

SCS. *Stories, Customs, Superstitions,Tales, Legends and Folklore of the Black Country.* Jon Raven. 1986

SCSB. *St Chad's, Slindon 1894-1944.* Jane Benton. 1993

SCSF. *Staffordshire Customs, Superstitions, Folklore.* FW Hackwood. 1924 1974 edition

SD. *Staffordshire Described.* Thomas Cox. 1728

SDOP. *Sedgley and District* (Britain in Old Photographs Series). Trevor Genge. 1995

SDOPP. *Stone and District: a Portrait in Old Picture Postcards.* Roy Lewis. 1993

SDSSOP. *Sedgley and District: A Second Selection* (Britain in Old Photographs Series). Trevor Genge. 1997

SDW. *Staffordshire Dialect Words: a historical survey.* D Wilson. 1974

SEDG. *Stone, Eccleshall & District Gazette.* April 1987 - Nov 1988

SFH. *Starting From Hartshill.* DM Holt. c1976

SFL. *Shropshire Folklore.* Charlotte Sophia Burne. 1883

SG. *Staffordshire Glimpses* or Glimpses of Bygone. FW Hackwood. 1925

SGH. *Staffordshire Gleanings.* FW Hackwood. 1922

SGM. *Staffordshire Gritstone: Peak District Climbs.* Gary Gibson. 4th Series. Volume 7. 1989

SGNS. *Short Guide to North Staffordshire.* R Nicholls. 1933

SGS. *Shell Guide to Staffordshire.* H Thorold. 1978

SGSAS. *Staffordshire Gazetteer.* Staffordshire Archive Service. Department of Library Arts & Archives. 1994

SH. *The Staffordshire Historians.* MW Greenslade. 1981 (technically part of SHC - 4th series volume 11).

SHBP. *Staffordshire and some Neighbouring Records, Historical, Biographical and Pictorial.* The Mercian Series. Allan North (publisher). ND but shortly after 1910.

SHC. *Staffordshire Historical Collections.*

SHCB. *Smethwick from Hamlet to County Borough: A Brief History.* KW Inskip. 1966

SHCST. *Stafford Historical and Civic Society Transactions.*

SHJ. *Staffordshire History Journal.*

SHOP. *Short History of Pelsall.* Joyce Hammond. 1981

SHOS. *History of Staffordshire.* Stebbing Shaw. Volumes 1, 2 1798 1801

SHOSA. *History of Staffordshire.* Appendix to both Volumes. Stebbing Shaw. 1801

SHOW. *Short History of Walsall.* Herbert Lee. 1927

SHST. *Sociological History of City of Stoke-on-Trent.* Ernest JD Warrilow. 1977

SHWB. *Short History of West Bromwich.* West Bromwich Library. 1964

SIC. *Shelton and its Church.* Father Leonard Skinner. 1985

SIN. *Swythamley and its Neighbourhood.* Various Authors. 1874

SIOT. *Stafford in Olden Times.* JL Cherry. 1890

SIS. *Stone in Staffordshire.* Norman A Cope. 1972

SIT. *Stone: an industrial tour.* Fred Brook. ND, possibly 1975

SJC. *Staffordshire Folklore.* SJ Coleman. 1955

SK. *Staffordshire Knots.* Edited by Dr AM McAldowie. 1895

SKYT. *Stafford: Know Your Town.* ALP Roxburgh. 1948

SL. *Staffordshire Landscape.* DM Palliser. 1976

SLC. *Story of Leek Church.* Henry Woodhouse. 1988

SLHT. *Streetly Local History Trail.* Charles Robertson. ND

SLM. *Staffordshire Life Magazine.* 1947 - 1959, 1983 -

SLR. *Sketches in and around Lichfield and Rugeley.* Alfred William. 1892

SLR. *A Swift Look Round.* Tamworth Herald. 19??

SLS. *St Lukes Church and Parish, Sheen.* ACF Nicoll. 1984

SM. *Staffordshire Miscellanies.* James Broughton. 1831

SMASCC. *St Mary and All Saints Church, Checkley.* Clive

Smith. 1987

SMASCW. *St Mary and All Saints Church, Whitmore*. JDS Hawley. 1984

SMC. *Staffordshire Collections*. James Broughton. 1827

SMCC. *Staffordshire Moorlands and Caldon Canal*. H Bode. 1971

SMEOP. *Smethwick in Old Photographs*. John Maddison. 1989

SMM. *Staffordshire: Its Magic and Mystery*. Doug Pickford. 1994

SMML. *Staffordshire: Murder Myths and Legends*. Tony J Hollis. Late 1990s

SMOPP. *Staffordshire Moorlands in Old Picture Postcards*. WG Short. Volume 1. 1988. G Bowyer & R Poole. Volume 2. 1989

SMSE. *Smallwood Manor: The history of a Staffordshire estate*. Sam Taylor. 1993

SMT. *Staffordshire Tracts*. James Broughton. 1810

SN. *Staffordshire Newsletter* newspapers (starting with the Stafford Newsletter (1906 to Jan 22 1955 when became the Stafford and Mid Staffordshire Newsletter, then became the Stafford Newsletter)). Many of the later references relate to the Staffordshire Newsletter Stone edition, published from 1971.

SNAR. *Street Names of Aldridge, Rushall, Streetly & Pheasey*. Betty Fox. 1996

SNBC. *Street Names of Brownhills, Clayhanger, Shelfield & Walsall Wood*. Betty Fox. 1999

SNBP. *Street Names of Bloxwich & Pelsall*. WF Blay & Ann Galbraith. 1994

SNDB. *Street Names of Darlaston & Bentley*. Malcolm Timmins. 1993

SNEDE. *The Family of Sneyd (Snede)*. Roger ES Wykes-Sneyd. 1986 (copy in Keele University Library)

SNSV. *Street Names of Stourbridge and its Vicinity*. H Jack Haden. vol 1 1988. vol 2 1999

SNTG. *Shugborough*. John Martin Robinson. The National Trust. 1989

SNW. *Street Names of Willenhall*. Horace Davis. 1995

SNWA. *Street Names of Walsall*. WF Blay. 1992

SOB. *Story of Bloxwich*. Ernest James Homeshaw. 1955

SOBC. *Story of the Black Country*. FW Hackwood. 1902

SOBP. *Story of Bilston*. John M Price. 1951

SOBW. *Story of Berkswich (or History of the Walton-on-the-Hill area)*. Women's Institute. 1950

SOCC. *Story of Castle Church*. JS Horne. 1939

SOK. *Story of Oulton and Kibblestone*. Many Authors. 1977

SOP. *The Story of Penkridge*. Robert Charles Wilkes. 1985

SOPP. *Stafford in Old Picture Postcards*. J Anslow & R Lewis. 1984

SOS. *Survey of Staffordshire*. S Erdeswick. 1593-1603

SOSH. *Story of Staffordshire*. M Hughes. 1925

SOTB. *Six of The Best*. Richard Weir. 1988

SOTOPP. *Stoke-on-Trent in Old Picture Postcards*. Andy Ridler. 1987

SOWB. *Story of West Bromwich*. JWA Aston. ND Pre 1973

SPCC. *Sedgley Park and Cotton College*. Frank Roberts. 1985

SPJD. *Stafford Past: A Guide to the Archaeological and Historical Sites of the Stafford Area*. John Darlington. 1994

SPN. *Staffordshire Place Names including the Black Country*. Anthony Poulton-Smith. 1995

SPNO. *Staffordshire Place Names*. JP Oakden. Part 1. 1984

SPP. *Staffordshire Past and Present: An Historical Pictorial and Descriptive Guide*. JW Bradley. 1911

SQCS. *Some Quaint Customs and Superstitions in Staffordshire*. Rev E Deacon

SR. *Sedgley Researches*. FW Hackwood. 1898

SS. *Staffordshire Sentinel*.

SSAHST. *South Staffordshire Archaeology and History Society Transactions*. 1959 -

SSBOP. *Stone, Sandon, Barlaston in Old Picture Postcards*. Tony Priestley. 1988

SSC. *Staffordshire & Shropshire Picturesque Views*. Frederick Calvert. 1830

SSE. *Staffordshire Studies* (Essays presented to Denis Stuart). vol 1 1988

SSGLST. *Secret Staffordshire - Ghosts Legends and Strange Tales*. Marian Pipe. 1994

SSHL. *Staffordshire Stories Historical and Legendary*. FW Hackwood. 1906

SSR. *South Staffordshire Railway*. JT Leach. 1992

SST. *Some Staffordshire Trees*. County Planning & Development Department. 1973

SSTY. *Stafford. The Story of a Thousand Years*. Paul Butters. 1980

SSW. *Some Staffordshire Worthies*. J Ingamells. 1907

ST. *Staffordshire Tales*. Margaret Turner. 1991

STC. *Staffordshire at the opening of the Twentieth Century and Contemporary Biographies*. Edited by WT Pike. Cameron Penn. 1907

STELE. *Smethwick Telephone*.

STM. *Six Towns Magazine*. April 1963 - September 1972

STMSM. *Staffordshire Magazine* (incorporating STM). November 1972 -

STP. *Spirit of The Place* (Caverswall). MJW Rogers. 1979

STV. *Staffordshire Towns and Villages*. Alfred Williams & WH Mallet. 1899

SVB. *The Staffordshire Village Book*. Staffordshire Federation of Women's Institutes. 1988

SVS. *Stourbridge and its Vicinity*. William Scott. 1832

SW. *Sacred Waters*. J and C Bord. 1986

SWH. *Staffordshire Worthies*. FW Hackwood

SWY. *Staffordshire Waterways*. David E Owen. 1986

T

T. *A History of Tamworth*. John & Henry Wood Roby. 1826

TAB. *Tong and Boscobel*. George Griffiths. 1894

TABC. *Tales from Aynuk's Black Country*. Jon Raven. 1978

TB. *The (Black Country) Bugle*. 1972 -

TBH. *Tamworth Building Heritage*. Bernard Lowe

TBS. *The Barr Story*. Richard D Woodall. 1951

TC. *The Cornovii*. G Webster. 1975

TCN. *Tamworth Castle*. Rev Henry Norris. 1899

TCOP. *Around Tettenhall and Codsall in Old Photographs*. Mary Mills. 1990

TD. *This Dovedale - a photographic guide*. Keith Mantell. 1971

TDOPP. *Tamworth and District Portrait in Old Picture Postcards*. Roy Lewis. 1994

TE. *This England*. WS Shears. 1948

TEBC. *A Thousand Events in the 19th Century Black Country*. Harold Parsons. 1981

TEBC2. *A Thousand Events in the C19 Black Country*. Harold Parsons. 1986

TEM. *This England Magazine*.

TEW. *Topography of England and Wales*. JC Hotten. 1863

TFTP. *Tales From The Past*. Tom Byrne. 1977

TFTPM. *More Tales From The Past*. Tom Byrne. 1986

TFW. *A Town for Four Winters* (Military Camps on Cannock Chase). CJ & GP Whitehouse. 1983

TFWH. *Tipton*. FW Hackwood. 1891

TGT. *Tamworth Castle Guide*. 1993

TH. *Tamworth Herald*.

THM. *Tamworth Herald Mitchell 'Newspaper Cuttings'* in Tamworth Library

THS. *Topographic History of Staffordshire*. William Pitt. 1817 (is in two parts: page references usually refer to part one - but if reference does not relate look at part two)

TMS. *The Tame Mills of Staffordshire*. D Dilworth. 1976

TNE. *A Grand Tour of Norman England*. Arthur Weigall. 1927

TOH. *This Old House* (Betley Hall). GN Brown

TOI. *Tale of Ipstones*. Rev F Brighton. 1937

TOPP. *Tamworth in Old Picture Postcards*. David Biggs. 1990

TOS. *Tales of Old Staffordshire*. Kathleen Lawrence-Smith. 1992

TPC. *The Peak Country* - painted by W Biscome Gardner, written by AR Hope Moncrieff. 1908

TPCM. *Tamworth Parish Church*. HC Mitchell. 1935

TPOP. *Tettenhall and Pattingham* (The Archive Photograph Series). Alec Brew. 1997

TPP. *The Pocket Palmer: The story of Rugeley's most infamous character*. John Godwin. 1992

TRBI. *Traditional Recipes of British Isles*. Compiled by Nell Heaton. 1951

TRTC. *The Road to Chartley. Part 1 Uttoxeter to Chartley*. Jim Foley. 1994

TSS. *The Sentinel Story 1873-1973*. Printed by James Heap. 1973

TSSOP. *Tipton: A Second Selection* (Old Photograph Series). John Brimble & Keith Hodgkins. 1997

TSW. *The Staffordshire Way*. Les Lumsdon & Chris Rushton. 1993

TTH. *Trentham: A Church through History*. June Steed. 1994

TTOPP. *Trentham and Tittensor in Old Picture Postcards*. E Watkin and others. 1987

TTT. *Tamworth Tower and Town*. HC Mitchell. 1936

TTTD. *The Tale of the Backbone*. John Dearden. (written 1962) 1986

TWDOP. *Tipton, Wednesbury and Darlaston in Old Photographs*. Robert Pearson. 1989

TWWW. *The Way We Were*. Sentinel Monthly Journal. 1995 -

TYD. *Ten Year's Digging in Celtic & Saxon Grave Hills*. Thomas Bateman. 1861

TYS. *A Thousand Years of Staffordshire*. DM Palliser. 1974

U

UBCB. *The urban and industrial songs of the Black Country and Birmingham*. Jon Raven. 1977

UCC. *An History Sketch of the Parish of Croxall in the County of Derby*. Rev Richard Ussher. 1881

UDC. *Staffordshire up and down the County*. Henry Allen Wedgwood. Volumes 1,2,3. 1881

UFO REALITY. *UFO Reality*. Jenny Randles. 1983

UFO STUDY. *UFO Study*. Jenny Randles. 1981

UHAW. *Up Hill all the Way. St Paul's Quarnford. A History of the Church & Parish 1744-1994*. Jack Nicoll. 1994

UMGH. *Life of Major General Harrison*. Henry Wedgwood. 189?

UNT. *Under the Needwood Tree: A glimpse into the History of Barton-under-Needwood*. Steve Gardner. 1995

UOPP. *Uttoxeter in Old Picture Postcards*. PM Turner. 1994

UST. *Underneath Stafford Town; an archaeological assessment*. Martin Carven. University of Birmingham. 1982

UTP. *Uttoxeter in Times Past*. Julia Smith. 1983

UTR. *History of Tutbury and Rolleston*. Charles Haywood Underhill. ND c1946

V

VAD. *Vestiges of Antiquity in Derbyshire*. Thomas Bateman. 1948

VB. *Staffordshire*. V Bird. 1974

VBB. *Visiting Bradnop*. H Bode. 1973

VBE. *Visits to Fields of Battle in England*. Richard Brooke. 1858

VC. *Victorian Cheadle 1841-81*. FJ Johnson. 1991

VCH. *Victoria County History: Staffordshire*. Volume 1 (Geology, Palaeotology, Botany, Zoology, Natural History, Early Man, Romano-British, Anglo-Saxon, Political History) 1908. Volume II (Industry, Communications, Forests, Sport, Index to volumes I and II) 1967. Volume III (Religion, Religious Houses, Monastic hospitals and colleges) 1970. Volume IV (Staffordshire Domesday, West Cuttlestone hundred) 1958. Volume V (East Cuttlestone hundred) 1959. Volume VI (Agriculture, Schools, Keele University, Stafford) 1979. Volume VII (Leek and the Moorlands) 1995. Volume VIII (Newcastle-under-Lyme, Stoke-on-Trent) 1963. Volume IX (Burton-upon-Trent) in progess in 1999. Volume XIV (Lichfield) 1990. Volume XVII (Smethwick, Walsall, West Bromwich) 1976. Volume XX (South Seisdon hundred) 1984. Other county Victoria County Histories. VCHC: Cheshire. VCHD: Derbyshire. VCHH: Herefordshire. VCHL: Leicestershire. VCHLA: Lancashire. VCHN: Northamptonshire. VCHS: Shropshire. VCHW: Worcestershire. VCHWA: Warwickshire.

VDC. *Views of Dudley Castle and Lime Caverns*. William Hawkes Smith. 1836

VE. *Victorian Eccleshall*. David Vincent. 1982

VED. *Vanishing England*. PH Ditchfield & Fred Roe. 1910

VESOP. *Victorian and Edwardian Staffordshire in Old Photographs*. P Murray & R Frost. 1977

VFC. *Voices of Five Counties: A Guide to writers of Herefordshire, Shropshire, Staffordshire, Warwick-*

shire, Worcestershire. Rosemary Toeman. 1994
VH. *Victorian Hamstead.* Roger Clive Meachem. 1988
VL. *Visiting Leek. Part 1 Town Centre.* H Bode. 1974.
    Part 2 from Ashbourne. H Bode. 1975
VSSR. *History of the South Staffordshire Regiment.* WL
    Vale. 1969

W

W. *History, Gazetteer and Directory of Staffordshire.* W
    White. 1834 1851
WA. *Wolverhampton Antiquary.* GP Mander. Volumes 1, 2.
    1915-1934
WAAIW. *Wheaton Aston: As It Was.* Compiled by Local
    People. 1991
WABH. *Brief History of Wheaton Aston.* DH Thompson.
    1973
WAIW. *Wolverhampton As It Was.* John Roper. Volume 1.
    1974
WAM. *Wednesbury, Ancient and Modern.* FW Hackwood.
    1902
WAS. *Wolverhampton Archaeology Society.* Reports from
    1926 to 1936
WB. *West Bromwich.* Joseph Reeves. 1836
WBF. *The Corporation of the Borough and Foreign of
    Walsall.* EJ Homeshaw. 1960
WBJ. *Staffordshire Windmills.* Barry Job. 1985
WBOP. *West Bromwich in Old Photographs.* Robin
    Pearson. 1989
WBOPP. *West Bromwich in Old Picture Postcards.* Robin
    Pearson. 1988
WC. *Walsall Chronicle.*
WCW. *The Wedgwood Circle 1730-1897.* Barbara &
    Hensleigh Wedgwood. 1980
WDOP. *Wednesbury in Old Photographs.* Ian M Bott.
    1994
WDY. *Willenhall and Darlaston Yesterdays.* Walsall
    Library and Museum Services. 1981
WF. *Wolverhampton: 1991 things you wanted to know

about Wolverhampton.* Partners in Progress. 1991
WFK. *William Fowler's Kingswinford: The man, his maps
    and the people and places of 1822 and 1840.* Eric
    Richardson. 1999
WFW. *Wednesfield:The Field of Woden.* John L
    Smallshire. 1978
WHF. *Willenhall to Horseley Fields.* (Images of England
    Series). Alec Brew. 1998.
WHTOP. *Wednesfield and Heath Town in Old Photo-
    graphs.* Elizabeth A Rees and Mary Mills. 1992
WIS. *Windmills in Staffordshire.* WA Seaby & AC Smith.
    1979
WIWC. *When I was a Child: C Shaw.* C Shaw. 1903 1969
    edition
WJ. *Werrington: Some Notes on its History.* JD Johnstone.
    1946
WJC. *St Peter's Church, Caverswall.* JD Johnstone. 1948
WJO. *The Wolverhampton Journal.* January 1902 -
    December 1909
WM. *West Midlands.* Caroline Hillier. 1976
WMA. *West Midlands Airfields.* Angus Dunphy. Volumes
    1 and 2
WMAG. *Wolverhampton Magazine.* July 1963 -
    September 1978 thereafter West Midlands and
    Wolverhampton Magazine to December 1979
WMARCH. *West Midlands Archaeology.* CBA West
    Midlands
WMAT. *West Midlands Archaeology.* CBA West Midlands
WMC. *Wells of Mow Cop.* H Hancock. 1985
WMLB. *The West Midlands: Landscapes of Britain.* Roy
    Millward & Adrian Robinson. 1971
WMMA. *The West Midlands in the Early Middle Ages.*
    Margaret Gelling. 1992
WMVB. *The West Midlands Village Book.* Women's
    Institute. 1989
WNH. *The Wrens Nest Hill.* E Blocksidge. 1905
WNNNR. *Wren's Nest National Nature Reserve.*
    Geological Handbook and Field Guide. A Cutler. 1990
WOLOP. *Wolverhampton* (The Archive Photographs

Series). Mary Mills & Tracey Williams. 1996
WOPP. *Walsall in Old Picture Postcards.* Marilyn Lewis.
    1982
WORF. *The Wandering Worfe.* DH Robinson. 1980
WOY. *Waterfall of Yesterday.* Frances A Harvey 1977
WOY2. *Waterfall of Yesterday.* Frances A Harvey. 1998
WP. *The Wednesbury Papers.* FW Hackwood. 1884
WP&P. *Wolverhampton Past and Present.* 1985
WPG. *Weston Park Guide.* English Life Publications. 1974
WPOPP. *Wolverhampton: A Portrait in Old Picture
    Postcards.* Eric Woolley. 1989
WPP. *Walsall Past and Present.* Howard D Clark. 1905
WROP. *Walsall Revisited.* (Britain in Old Photographs
    Series). David F Vodden. 1997
WSS. *The Wetlands of Shropshire and Staffordshire.* MD
    Leah, CE Wells, P Stamper, E Huckerby, C Welch.
    1998
WTCEM. *History of Wetton, Thor's Cave and Ecton Mine.*
    James Roberts. 1900
WTMS. *Watermills.* Peter Wenham. 1989
WW. *Wednesbury Workshops.* FW Hackwood.
WWT. *Wolstanton (Wolstan's Town).* Percy WL Adams.
    1908
WWW. *Wombourne What Was.* May Griffiths. 1990
WYV. *Werrington: Yesterday's Voices.* Elizabeth W Bass.
    1983

Y

YONS. *Records of Ye Olde Nortonian Society.*
    1925,1957,1979
YX. *Yoxall: A Walk through History.* Denis Stuart. 1979

Z

ZSB. *Illustrated Map of Staffordshire showing curiosities*
    limited to 700 copies. Celebrating Sidney Barnes
    Centenary 1973.

General Abbreviations

AA	Automobile Association
AAA	Amateur Athletic Association
als	alias
ANZAC	The Australian and New Zealand Army Corps
AONB	Area of Outstanding Natural Beauty
AP	Air-Photograph
APC	armoured personnel carrier
App	Appendix
Apr	April
ARA	Association of the Royal Academy
Arch	Archaeology or Archaeological
ARP	Air Raid Precautions
ASHM	Ashmolean Museum, Oxford
ATV	Associated Television
Aug	August
Ave	Avenue
b	born
BA	Bachelor of Arts
Bart	Baronet
BAS	Birmingham Archaeology Society
Batt	Battalion
BBC	British Broadcasting Corporation
Beds	Bedfordshire
Berks	Berkshire
BHM	Birmingham City Museum
BL	British Library, London
BM	British Museum, London
Brit	British
BRMB	(Birmingham Broadcasting Ltd's radio station for Birmingham)
BSE	bovine spongiform encephalopathy
Bt	Baronet
BTNHAS	Burton-on-Trent Natural History and Archaeological Society
Bucks	Buckinghamshire
BW&DR	Birmingham, Wolverhampton & Dudley

	Railway
BW&SVR	Birmingham, Wolverhampton & Stour Valley Railway
c	about (if before a date)
C	century (if before a number)
Cal Inq	Calendar Inquisitions
Cambs	Cambridgeshire
Capt(s)	Captain(s)
CB	Companion of the Bath
CBE	Commander of the Order of the British Empire
(C)CC	(County) Cricket Club
CC&WR	Cannock Chase & Wolverhampton Railway
CCTV	Close Circuit Television
cf	compare
ch	chapter
Ches	Cheshire
cm(s)	centimetre(s)
Co	Company
col	column
Col	Colonel
CRO	County Record Office
cwt	hundred-weight
d	died
d	Penny, pence
DAPM	Deputy Assistant Provost-Marshal
DB	Domesday Book
DCL	Doctor of Civil Law
DD	Doctor of Divinity
Dec	December
DENS	Denstone College Museum
Dept	Department
Derbys	Derbyshire
dia(s)	diagrams
DoE	Department of the Environment
DSO	Distinguished Service Order

E	East
ed	edition
ES	East West
FA	Football Association
FC	Football Club
Feb	February
fl	person flourished at given date
Flt	Flight
Fri	Friday
FRGS	Fellow of the Royal Geographical Society
FRS	Fellow of the Royal Society
FRSA	Fellow of the Royal Society of Arts
FSA	Fellow of the Royal Society of Antiquaries
FSA	Fellow of the Society of Antiquaries
GCMG	Knight Grand Cross of St Michael and St George
GEC	General Electric Company
Gen	General
GJR	Grand Junction Railway
Glous	Gloucestershire
GNR	Great Northern Railway
GWR	Great Western Railway
Hants	Hampshire
Harl	Harleian Mss
HBMC	Historical Building Monuments Commission
HBRL	Horace Barks Reference Library, City Library, Hanley
Heres	Herefordshire
Herts	Hertfordshire
Hist	History
HMS	His (or Her) Majesty's Ship or Service
Hon	Honourable
HQ	Headquarters
HRH	His (or Her) Royal Highness
ie	for example
il(s)	illustration(s)

ILP	Independent Labour Party
Inc	Incorporated
IRA	Irish Republican Army
ITV	Independent Television
Jan	January
Jnr	Junior
JP(s)	Justice of the Peace(s)
k	kilometre
KB	Knight of the Bath or also Knight Bachelor
KC	King's Counsel
KCB	Knight Commander of the Bath
KG	Knight of the Garter
Knt or knt	Knight
L	Pound(s)/ £
LAH	Licentiate of Apothecaries' Hall, Dublin
Lancs	Lancashire
Lanarks	Lanarkshire
lbs	pounds
Leics	Leicestershire
Lib	Library
Lieut	Lieutenant
Lincs	Lincolnshire
LLB	Bachelor of Laws
LLD	Doctor of Laws
LMSR	London, Midland and Scottish Railway
LNER	London and North Eastern Railway
LNWR	London & North Western Railway
Lt	Lieutenant
m	mile
MA	Master of Arts
Mar	March
MBC	Municipal Borough Council
MBE	Member of the Order of the British Empire
MD	Master of Divinity
MEB	Midlands Electricity Board
mem(s)	memorial(s)
MEP	Member European Parliament
Messrs	Plural of Mr
Mlle	Mademoiselle
MOD	Ministry of Defence
Mon	Monday
MP(s)	Member of Parliament(s)
mph	miles per hour
MR	Midland Railway
Mr	Mister
MRCSE	Member of Royal College of Surgeons of Edinburgh
Mrs	Mistress
Ms	Manuscript
Mss	Manuscripts
Mus	Museum
N	North
ND	No date
NFU	National Farmers' Union
NHS	National Health Service
NMR	National Monuments Record
No.	Number
Northants	Northamptonshire
nos	numbers
Notts	Nottinghamshire
Nov	November
NS	North South
NSFC	North Staffordshire Field Club
NSR	North Staffordshire Railway
NT	National Trust
OBE	Order of the British Empire
Oct	October
OFM	Order of Friars Minor
OFSTED	Office for Standards in Education
OM	Order of Merit
OS	Ordnance Survey
OSAD	Ordnance Survey Archaeology Division
OSB	Order of St Benedict
OSS	Old Stafford Society
OW&WR	Oxford, Worcester & Wolverhampton Railway
Oxon	Oxfordshire
oz	ounces
p	page (if before a number)
p	photograph (if after a page number)
pc	colour photograph (if after a page number)
PC	Police Constable
pcs	colour photographs (if after a page number)
PGA	Professional Golfers Association
pl	plate (if after a page number)
PLC or plc	Public Limited Company
PM	Prime Minister
POW(S) or pow(s)	Prisoner(s) of war
pp	pages
PR	Parish Register
Proc	proceedings
ps	photographs (if after a page number)
PTA	Parent Teacher Association
Pte	Private (soldier)
QC	Queen's Counsel
RA	Royal Academy
RAC	Royal Automobile Association
RAF	Royal Air Force
RAI	Royal Archaeological Institute
RASC	Royal Army Service Corps
RBA	Royal Society of British Artists
RC	Roman Catholic
RCA	Royal College of Arts
Ref(s) or ref(s)	Reference
Regt	Regiment
RFC	Rugby Football Club
RN	Royal Navy
RNAS	Royal Naval Air Service
RNVR	Royal Navy Volunteer Reserve
Rt	Right
RWS	Royal Society of Painters in Watercolours
s	Shilling(s)
S	South
SAS	Staffordshire Agricultural Society
Sat	Saturday
Sc	Scene
Sept	September
Sgt	Sergeant
SHEF	Sheffield Museum
Shrops	Shropshire
SJ	Society of Jesus
SJ	an OS reading
SK	an OS reading
Snr	Senior
Soc	Society
Som	Somersetshire
SP	an OS reading
SPWWC	Staffordshire Potteries Water Works Company
sq	square
Sqn	Squadron
SRO	Staffordshire Record Office at Stafford
SS	Saints
SSAS	South Staffordshire Archaeological Society
SSR	South Staffordshire Railway
SSSI	Site of Special Scientific Interest
SSWWC	South Staffordshire Water Works Company
Staffs	Staffordshire
Sun	Sunday
TAVR	Territorial Army Volunteer Reserve
temp	contemporary with
Thurs	Thursday
Trans	Transactions
TSB	Trustee Savings Bank
TUC	Trade Union Congress
Tues	Tuesday
TV	television
UFO(s)	Unidentified Flying Object(s)
UK	United Kingdom
UOK	University of Keele
USAAF	USA Air Force
V&A	Victoria & Albert Museum, London
VC	Victoria Cross
vol	volume(s)
W	West
WABC	(Beacon radio's sister station)
Warws	Warwickshire
WEA	Workers' Education Association
Wed	Wednesday
Wilts	Wiltshire
WOLV	Wolverhampton Museum and Art Gallery
Worcs	Worcestershire
wpm	words per minute
WRNS	Women's Royal Naval Service
WSAS	William Salt Archaeology Society
WSL	William Salt Library
WW1	World War One
WW2	World War Two
YHA	Youth Hostel Association
Yorks	Yorkshire

* After DoE defines grade of listing; after a page number may identify the second of the same page number for instance in SHOS and GNHS and GNHSS, but was formerly used in the preparation of the book to identify noteworthy references.

Printed in the United Kingdom
by Lightning Source UK Ltd.
132866UK00001BA/14/A

9 780953 901807